# Bowker's Guide To
# CHARACTERS
# IN FICTION

---

# 2004

This edition of
**BOWKER'S GUIDE TO CHARACTERS IN FICTION 2004**
was prepared by R.R. Bowker's Database Publishing Group in
collaboration with the Information Technology Department.

Michael Cairns, President
Gary Aiello, Senior Vice President, Operations
Belinda Tseo, Senior Vice President, Finance
Angela D'Agostino, Vice President, Product Development and Marketing
Boe Horton, Vice President, Worldwide Sales
Roy Crego, Senior Managing Director, Editorial
Andrew Grabois, Senior Director, Publisher Relations and Content Development
Doreen Gravesande, Senior Director, ISBN/SAN/PAD and Data Acquisition
Constance Harbison, Senior Director, BIP Editorial, Quality Assurance, and Subject Guide
Galen Strazza, Creative Director

### International Standard Book Number/Standard Address Number Agency/Publishers Authority Database
Don Riseborough, Senior Managing Editor
Paula Kurdi, Diana Luongo, and James Motley, Senior Editors
Beverly Palacio, Associate Editor
Venus Ayers, David Brassler, Leon Gravesande, Adriana Santiago,
and Heidi Weber, Assistant Editors

### Data Acquisition
Joseph Kalina, Director
Stephanie Halpern, Managing Editor
Patricia McCraney, Public Relations Specialist - Canada
Gladys Osofisan, Data Analyst

### Editorial
Andrew LaCroix, Manager, Editorial Production
Kathleen Cunningham, Lisa Heft, and Eleanor Schubauer, Managing Editors
Adrene Allen, Senior Editor
Misty Harmon, Ila Joseph-Corley, Tom Lucas,
and Dorothy Perry-Gilchrist, Associate Editors
Stacey Volanto, Lynda Williams, and Steve Zaffuto, Assistant Editors

### Subject Guide
Michael Olenick, Database Analyst
Angela Barrett, Senior Associate Editor
Dafina Moore, Assistant Editor

### Data Collection & Processing Group
Valerie Harris, Director of Operations, Tampa
Mervaine Ricks, Editorial Manager
Diane Johnson, Office Manager
John Litzenberger, Network Technician
Cheryl Patrick and Rhonda McKendrick, Editorial Specialists
Janet Foltz and Kathy Griner, Editorial Coordinators
Lori Burnett, Rita Phillips and Sally Snelling, Editorial Assistants
Joyce Bashista and Tasi Peterika, Assistant Editors

### Production
Gordon MacPherson, Director, Electronic and Print Production
Myriam Nunez, Project Manager, Content Integrity
Megan Roxberry, Managing Editor
Kennard McGill, Senior Editor
Jocelyn Kwiatkowski, Associate Editor

### Manufacturing
Delia Tedoff, Director

### Editorial Systems, Information Technology Group
Mark Heinzelman, Director
Frank Morris, Project Manager
Youliang Zhou, Programmer

### Computer Operations Group
John Nesselt, UNIX Administrator
Daniel O'Malley, Manager, Network Administration and Operations

# Bowker's Guide To

# CHARACTERS

# IN FICTION

## 2004 VOLUME 1
## ADULT FICTION

Published by
R.R. Bowker LLC
630 Central Avenue, New Providence
New Jersey 07974

Michael Cairns, President

Telephone: 908-286-1090; Toll-free: 800-521-8110
Fax: 908-219-0098
E-mail address: customerservice@bowker.com
URL: http://www.bowker.com

Readers may send any corrections and/or updates to the information in this work to R.R. Bowker through the corrections option on the Bowker Web site at http://www.bowker.com or may send e-mail directly to the address: Corrections@bowker.com. Publishers may update or add to their listings by accessing the BowkerLink Publisher Access System at http://www.bowkerlink.com. Books In Print is also available via subscription on the web at www.booksinprint.com.

R.R. Bowker has used its best efforts in collecting and preparing material for inclusion in **Bowker's Guide to Characters In Fiction 2004**, but does not warrant that the information herein is complete or accurate, and does not assume, and hereby disclaims, any liability to any persons for any loss or damage caused by errors or omissions in **Bowker's Guide to Characters In Fiction 2004**, whether such omissions result from negligence, accident or any other cause.

**International Standard Book Number**
Set: 0-8352-4608-6
Volume 1: 0-8352-4609-4
Volume 2: 0-8352-4610-8

Printed in the United States of America
Books In Print is a registered trademark of R.R. Bowker LLC, used under license.

ISBN 0-8352-4608-6

9 780835 246088

# CONTENTS

## Volume 1—Adult Fiction

HOW TO USE BOWKER'S GUIDE TO
CHARACTERS IN FICTION 2004 . . . . . . . . . . . . . . . .vii

LIST OF ABBREVIATIONS. . . . . . . . . . . . . . . . . xi

PUBLISHER COUNTRY CODES . . . . . . . . . . . . . . . xiii

LANGUAGE CODES . . . . . . . . . . . . . . . . . . . xv

    LIST OF SUBJECT HEADINGS . . . . . . . . . . . . . 1

    SUBJECT INDEX. . . . . . . . . . . . . . . . . . .31

    PUBLISHER NAME INDEX . . . . . . . . . . . . . .1171

    WHOLESALER & DISTRIBUTOR
    NAME INDEX . . . . . . . . . . . . . . . . . . . .1243

## Volume 2 —Children's Fiction

HOW TO USE BOWKER'S GUIDE TO
CHARACTERS IN FICTION 2004. . . . . . . . . . . . . . . .vii

LIST OF ABBREVIATIONS. . . . . . . . . . . . . . . . . xi

PUBLISHER COUNTRY CODES . . . . . . . . . . . . . . . xiii

LANGUAGE CODES . . . . . . . . . . . . . . . . . . . xv

    LIST OF SUBJECT HEADINGS . . . . . . . . . . . . . 1

    SUBJECT INDEX . . . . . . . . . . . . . . . . . . 9

    PUBLISHER NAME INDEX. . . . . . . . . . . . . . .585

    WHOLESALER & DISTRIBUTOR
    NAME INDEX . . . . . . . . . . . . . . . . . . . .649

# HOW TO USE
# BOWKER'S GUIDE TO
# CHARACTERS IN FICTION
# 2004

This is the introductory edition of **Bowker's Guide to Characters In Fiction**, with Volume 1 devoted to adult fiction and Volume 2 to children's fiction. As the title implies, a large portion of this book is dedicated to fiction featuring a specific character; however, other topics covered in a fictional manner are also addressed (such as ethnic groups and settings). Like most of Bowker's bibliographic directories, it was produced from the Books In Print database. Unlike most of our directories, it brings together books published in three different formats (print, audio, electronic) and includes out-of-print, out-of-stock, and on-demand titles alongside active titles. Virtually none of the items listed in either volume appear in Bowker's **Subject Guide to Books In Print**, making this the perfect companion to our more established publication. Besides the main index, each volume features a List of Subject Headings, a Publisher Index, and a Wholesaler & Distributor Index.

## CLASSIFICATION

**Bowker's Guide to Characters In Fiction** follows the headings assigned by the Library of Congress for cases where LC has established a fiction-related heading. It should be noted that while children's fiction has long been classified by topic, it has been only ten years since LC began classifying children's fiction by fictitious character or imaginary setting, and adult fiction at all. For already established headings, "—FICTION" was merely added as a subdivision (e.g., POLICEWOMEN—FICTION). However, for characters and settings, thousands of new headings had to be created, from BAMBI (FICTITIOUS CHARACTER) to BENNET, ELIZABETH (FICTITIOUS CHARACTER) to BOND, JAMES (FICTITIOUS CHARACTER), before "—FICTION" could be appended. Bowker has always patterned our classification after LC, so we also started to create fiction-related headings in the manner of LC and began applying these to incoming data as well as to titles already in our database (like LC, we had already been classifying children's fiction by topic). As you can imagine, retroactive classification was a massive undertaking. To focus our efforts, we commissioned research to determine under which broad topics readers were most likely to request fiction. The results of this research enabled us to target our efforts, and have also determined the seven topical sections of each main index: Characters, Ethnic Groups, Historical Events, Miscellaneous, Occupations, Relationships, and Settings (each of which is discussed in detail below under ARRANGEMENT AND USAGE OF SUBJECTS). We used classification by the Library of Congress when possible to help determine the headings assigned. However, for areas in which LC is not strong (for example, original paperbacks), other sources were used as well. Several appropriate subjects were assigned, so a book may appear multiple times per section, as well as in several sections.

**Bowker's Guide to Characters In Fiction** Volume 1 (Adult Fiction) contains approximately 142,550 entries appearing 154,000 times under 4,180 populated headings. Volume 2 (Children's Fiction) contains some 64,000 entries appearing 68,000 times under 1,090 subject headings. This first edition includes roughly 88,300 in-print books, 8,700 audiobooks, and 3,270 e-books. We also include 3,065 on-demand titles in addition to titles recently declared out-of stock or out-of-print. No entries appear in both volumes.

For the headings in the Ethnic Groups, Historical Events, Miscellaneous, Occupations, and Relationships sections we based the style of the heading on that of LC. For the Characters and Settings sections, we based any real characters and settings on LC, as well as any fictitious characters or imaginary settings for which LC had authority records. However, we have gone well beyond LC classification in this regard. LC generally only establishes a heading for fictitious characters and imaginary settings if they appear in three or more works - we decided not to set such a limit and have added headings whenever we thought that they would be useful. When this was done, we still adhered to general LC policy for these types of headings (for example, characters are listed under their surnames, when appropriate). LC bibliographic and subject authority information can be found at http://catalog.loc.gov.

In general, **Bowker's Guide to Characters In Fiction** includes any work of adult or children's fiction that has been assigned a Bowker subject ending with "—FICTION" that fits into one of the topical sections (and note that the "—FICTION" subdivision has been retained for each heading). There is no distinction made between novels, single-author short story collections, and multiple author anthologies (although it is less common for anthologies to focus on a specific character, occupation, setting, etc., so the majority of works included are by a single author). That being said, there are several types of related works that it might help to specifically state are excluded:

- Literary criticism dealing with a fictitious character or imaginary setting is not included, but can be found in **Subject Guide to Books In Print** under unsubdivided subjects; (e.g., COMPSON, CADDY (FICTITIOUS CHARACTER); YOKNAPATAWPHA COUNTY (IMAGINARY PLACE).

- Drama and poetry are excluded, even if they feature a character, setting, etc. that has been included.

- Works discussing other aspects of a character are excluded (e.g, no works on Mickey Mouse collectibles or James Bond movies).

Much effort has been put into identifying children's versions of classics and classifying them appropriately. In some cases, this has led to a character appearing in both volumes (e.g., HEATHCLIFF (FICTITIOUS CHARACTER)—FICTION). We tried to limit the definition of "children's version" to mean cases where works generally considered as being for adults were abridged or adapted specifically for younger readers. However, in cases where we were not able to determine this, we went with the publisher's information

- if they told us that their edition of *Wuthering Heights* was a children's edition, then we listed it in the Children's volume, even if it was textually the same as the standard edition.

## GENERAL EDITORIAL POLICIES

Current information was solicited from all publishers in the Books In Print database. These publishers include participants in Bowker's Electronic Data Interchange (EDI) program as well as publishers who regularly submit Advance Book Information (ABI) forms and their current book catalogs. Less active publishers are asked to review their active titles on checklists or online at www.bowker-link.com and every effort was made to get up-to-date, complete information on all titles included in **Bowker's Guide to Characters In Fiction**. All prices and availability are subject to change without notice.

## ARRANGEMENT AND USAGE OF SUBJECTS

The first principle of **Bowker's Guide to Characters In Fiction** was to classify a book using the most specific heading(s) under which someone was likely to look. So if you are interested in a book taking place in a particular city, first look under that city (or even under an area within a city). If nothing is found, then try the next broadest area (such as a state or province) and then continue in this manner through broader terms (such as country, region, or continent). It is possible that a book will be found under both a city and state, or a country and a continent, but it is advised to try the narrowest term first. It should be noted that publishers do not always distinguish between England and Great Britain when conveying information to us, so users are advised to try both place names. Each volume is divided into sections as noted below. Any rules or explanations given apply to both volumes unless stated. Examples may appear in one or both volumes, but a heading will only appear in one section of each volume.

### ■ Characters

This section includes headings for real people (e.g., ROOSEVELT, ELEANOR, 1884-1962—FICTION), as well as fictitious and legendary characters (e.g., BROWN, CHARLIE (FICTITIOUS CHARACTER)—FICTION; MERLIN (LEGENDARY CHARACTER)—FICTION). If a character has a surname, he or she will generally be listed under that name. If someone is known primarily (or only) by a title or rank, then that will be included in the heading, but the person will still be listed under his or her surname (e.g., AHAB, CAPTAIN (FICTITIOUS CHARACTER) —FICTION); COLUMBO, LIEUTENANT (FICTITIOUS CHARACTER —FICTION). Superheroes are generally listed under their assumed identity (e.g., CAPTAIN UNDERPANTS (FICTITIOUS CHARACTER)—FICTION; SPIDER-MAN (FICTITIOUS CHARACTER)—FICTION). Characters with the same name are differentiated by including the author's surname in the heading (e.g., ARTHUR (FICTITIOUS CHARACTER : BROWN)—FICTION; ARTHUR (FICTITIOUS CHARACTER : HOBAN)—FICTION). Besides individual characters, there are headings for combinations of characters, which can take the forms of relatives, families, or other types of groupings (e.g., ARMITAGE SISTERS (FICTITIOUS CHARACTERS)—FICTION; ADDAMS FAMILY (FICTITIOUS CHARACTERS)—FICTION; X-MEN (FICTITIOUS CHARACTERS)—FICTION). Sometimes two characters who always appear together have been combined into one heading (e.g., WALLACE AND GROMIT (FICTITIOUS CHARACTERS)—FICTION).

### ■ Ethnic Groups

This section includes headings for ethnic groups (e.g., CHINESE AMERICANS—FICTION), headings that are usually associated with ethnic groups (e.g., KIBBUTZIM—FICTION; KWANZAA—FICTION), and headings related to a specific religion, whether or not that religion is primarily associated with an ethnic group (e.g., MENNONITES—FICTION).

### ■ Historical Events

The history-related headings in the Adult volume (Volume 1) almost all pertain to a particular war or conflict (e.g., UNITED STATES—HISTORY—WAR OF 1812—FICTION; VIETNAMESE CONFLICT, 1961-1975—FICTION), with an occasional non-military heading (e.g., FRONTIER AND PIONEER LIFE—FICTION). The history-related headings in the Children's volume (Volume 2) include most of what's in the Adult volume plus headings that relate to an event, place, time period, or other aspect of history (e.g., BOSTON TEA PARTY, 1773—FICTION; BRONZE AGE—FICTION; EGYPT—HISTORY—FICTION; MOGUL EMPIRE—FICTION; PONY EXPRESS—FICTION). Note that the Historical Events and Settings sections are both worth checking if you are looking for a book that takes place in a real setting in the past.

### ■ Miscellaneous

For the Adult volume this section represents the handful of headings ending with "—FICTION" that did not fit into any other section. There were about 1,000 children's fiction headings that did not fit into the other sections (remembering that children's fiction classification has been going on much longer than adult fiction classification), so for the Children's volume we decided to offer a selection of headings related to fantasy or the supernatural (e.g., DRAGONS—FICTION; GHOSTS—FICTION; GIANTS—FICTION; MERMAIDS—FICTION; WIZARDS—FICTION). The **Subject Guide to Children's Books In Print** contains all children's fiction (and, of course, nonfiction).

### ■ Occupations

While most headings in this section relate to what one would generally call an occupation (e.g., COLLEGE TEACHERS—FICTION; JOURNALISTS—FICTION), some headings in the Children's volume might be more accurately described as "things people do" (e.g., APPRENTICES—FICTION; EXPLORERS—FICTION).

### ■ Relationships

This section includes headings dealing with family and interpersonal relationships (e.g., DATING (SOCIAL CUSTOMS)—FICTION; FATHERS AND SONS—FICTION; GRANDPARENTS—FICTION; MARRIAGE—FICTION; TWINS—FICTION; WIDOWS—FICTION). It has been extended somewhat to include GAY MEN—FICTION and LESBIANS—FICTION as well. Note that relationships involving recognizable characters may be covered by a heading in the Characters section.

## ■ Settings

Included here are headings for real places (e.g., BEVERLY HILLS (CALIF.)—FICTION; CALIFORNIA—FICTION; WEST (U.S.)—FICTION), as well as imaginary and legendary places (e.g., CAMELOT (LEGENDARY PLACE)—FICTION; TREASURE ISLAND (IMAGINARY PLACE)—FICTION). If an imaginary setting has been identified as existing within a real place, that will be noted (e.g., CABOT COVE (ME : IMAGINARY PLACE)—FICTION). Settings can range from specific schools, streets, hotels, etc. (e.g., FORTY-THREE LIGHT STREET (IMAGINARY PLACE)—FICTION; ROSWELL HIGH (NM : IMAGINARY PLACE)—FICTION) to planets (e.g., DUNE (IMAGINARY PLACE)—FICTION). Note that the Settings and Historical Events sections are both worth checking if you are looking for a book that takes place in a real setting in the past.

Within each section, the presentation of subject headings is alphabetical; however, in accordance with the Library of Congress, the following rules are followed:

- Headings beginning with "Da" and "De" are treated as if there were no space.

- Headings beginning with "Mc" and "Mac" are treated as if they all began with "Mac".

- "Saint" and "St." are treated as alphabetical equals.

- Apostrophes are ignored.

- Hyphens are treated as spaces.

- Real people and fictitious characters are interfiled alphabetically (as are real settings and imaginary ones).

Below are some examples of sequencing. Note that headings may appear between the examples given, and that the examples are all from the Characters section in the Adult volume (although the rules apply to all sections in both volumes).

AUSTEN, CAT (FICTITIOUS CHARACTER)—FICTION

AUSTEN, JANE, 1775-1817—FICTION

AUSTEN, KATE (FICTITIOUS CHARACTER)—FICTION

DASH (FICTITIOUS CHARACTER)—FICTION

DA SILVA, JANE (FICTITIOUS CHARACTER)—FICTION

DATA (FICTITIOUS CHARACTER)—FICTION

MABRY, BUBBA (FICTITIOUS CHARACTER)—FICTION

MCALISTER, HALEY (FICTITIOUS CHARACTER)—FICTION

MACK, RUDYARD (FICTITIOUS CHARACTER)—FICTION

MCVAY, LIZZIE (FICTITIOUS CHARACTER)—FICTION

MADDOCK, JOREY (FICTITIOUS CHARACTER)—FICTION

O'BRIEN, MILES (FICTITIOUS CHARACTER)—FICTION

ODO (FICTITIOUS CHARACTER)—FICTION

O'NEILL, PEGGY (FICTITIOUS CHARACTER)—FICTION

SAINT (FICTITIOUS CHARACTER)—FICTION

SAINT, AUGUST (FICTITIOUS CHARACTER)—FICTION

SAINT-GERMAIN (FICTITIOUS CHARACTER)—FICTION

ST. IVES, PHILIP (FICTITIOUS CHARACTER)—FICTION

SAINT JAMES, QUIN (FICTITIOUS CHARACTER)—FICTION

There are also "see" references provided to lead users from the heading they are looking at to the heading under which books are actually listed, although these are not as extensive as in **Subject Guide to Books In Print**. Subjects with a "see" reference do not have books listed under them. References have generally been added when a person or place is known by more than one name, or when it is not clear if a person is listed under his or her full name or surname. For example:

ADEPT, THE (FICTITIOUS CHARACTER)—FICTION
*see Sinclair, Adam (Fictitious Character)—Fiction*

BEDELIA, AMELIA (FICTITIOUS CHARACTER)—FICTION
*see Amelia-Bedelia (Fictitious Character)—Fiction*

CASTLE AMBER (IMAGINARY PLACE)—FICTION
*see Amber (Imaginary Place)—Fiction*

HANSEN, ANNIKA (FICTITIOUS CHARACTER)—FICTION
*see Seven of Nine (Fictitious Character)—Fiction*

HIGHLANDER (FICTITIOUS CHARACTER)—FICTION
*see MacLeod, Duncan (Fictitious Character)—Fiction*

OBI-WAN KENOBI (FICTITIOUS CHARACTER)—FICTION
*see Kenobi, Obi-Wan (Fictitious Character)—Fiction*

SHIRLEY, ANNE (FICTITIOUS CHARACTER)—FICTION
*see Anne of Green Gables (Fictitious Character)—Fiction*

Note that "see" references will only appear in the volumes and sections in which they are appropriate.

## LIST OF SUBJECT HEADINGS

While in most cases it will be obvious what section a heading will be in (and where it will appear in that section), there are cases where it may not be immediately apparent. To help in the search, we have provided an index at the beginning of each volume that is arranged first by section and then within each section by the sequence in which the headings appear. Furthermore, page references are provided to lead you directly to the heading. Below is an example from the Characters index in Volume 1:

BATMAN (FICTITIOUS CHARACTER) p.49
BATTLE, SUPERINTENDENT (FICTITIOUS CHARACTER) p.50
BAUER, TORY (FICTITIOUS CHARACTER) p.50
BAUER, VICKY (FICTITIOUS CHARACTER) p.50
BAUM, STEVEN (FICTITIOUS CHARACTER) p.51

Note that in this list, the subdivision "—FICTION" has been suppressed from the end of the heading.

## ALPHABETICAL ARRANGEMENT OF ENTRIES WITHIN SUBJECT

After arrangement by section and by subject, entries are arranged alphabetically by author (or other contributor, if no author is given). If no contributor is present, the entry is filed by title within the contributor arrangement. Contributors' names in **Bowker's Guide**

to **Characters In Fiction** have been alphabetized using the following rules:

- Proper names beginning with "Mc" and "Mac" are filed in strict alphabetical order. For example, entries for names such as Mac Adam, MacAvory, and MacCarthy are located prior to entries for names such as McAdam, McCoy, and McDermott.

- Compound names are listed under their first component. For example, Van Holland is listed under Van.

- When contributor names are represented with initials, they are alphabetized before contributor first names. For example, Smith, H. C. appears before Smith, Harold A.

- If more than two contributors performing the same function are responsible for a given title, then only the name of the first is given, followed by "et al".

## INFORMATION INCLUDED IN ENTRIES

Entries include the following bibliographic information (when available): author, co-author, editor, co-editor, translator, co-translator, original language, title, subtitle, title volume number, number of volumes, edition, publication year, series information, original title, current language if other than English, whether or not illustrated, number of pages, whether a book is an original paperback, audience, grade range, binding/format if other than cloth over boards, price, status if other than active or on-demand, ISBN, order number, imprint, and publisher name.

## PUBLISHER NAME INDEX

Indexes to publisher names are found in both volumes (containing more than 2,690 publishers used in the bibliographic entries of Volume 1 and over 2,560 publishers used in the bibliographic entries of Volume 2). Entries in these indexes contain (when available): publisher name, ISBN prefix(es), business affiliation, ordering address(es), SAN (Standard Address Number), telephone number(s), fax and toll-free number(s), editorial address(es) and associated contact numbers, imprints, e-mail and Web site address(es), and the distributors who handle this publisher. Publishers with like or similar names include a "Do not confuse with..." notation within the entry. A dagger (†) preceding a publisher's name and the note "CIP" at the end of an entry indicate that the publisher participates in the Cataloging in Publication Program of the Library of Congress. Full information for distributors, as well as 1,000 book wholesalers, is found in the Wholesaler & Distributor Name Index (in both volumes). Note that publishers who also serve as distributors may be listed both here and in the Publisher Name Index. Foreign publishers with U.S. distributors are listed, followed by their three-character ISO (International Standards Organization) country code ("GBR," "CAN," etc.), ISBN prefix(es), if available, and a cross-reference to their U.S. distributor, as shown below:

**Addison-Wesley Longman, Ltd. (GBR)** (0-582) Dist. by **Trans-Atl Phila**.

In addition, cross-references are provided from imprints to their publisher and from former company name to new name.

## WHOLESALER & DISTRIBUTOR NAME INDEX

The Wholesaler & Distributor Name Index is arranged alphabetically by company name and contains (when available): company name, ISBN prefix(es), business affiliation, full address and ordering information, SAN(s), telephone number(s), fax and toll-free number(s), e-mail and Web site address(es). Wholesalers and distributors with like or similar names include a "Do not confuse with..." notation within the entry.

## ISBN AGENCY

164,700 of the entries included in **Bowker's Guide to Characters In Fiction** have been assigned an International Standard Book Number (ISBN) by the publisher. All ISBNs listed in this volume have been validated by using the check digit control, ensuring accuracy.

Note: The ISBN prefix 0-615 is for decentralized use by the U.S. ISBN Agency and has been assigned to numerous publishers. This prefix is not unique to one exclusive publisher.

ISBNs allow order transmission and bibliographic information updating using the Book Industry Standards and Communications (BISAC) standard format for data transmission. Publishers not currently participating in the ISBN system may request the assignment of an ISBN Publisher Prefix from the ISBN Agency by calling 877-310-7333, fax 908-219-0188, or through the ISBN/SAN Web site at www.isbn.org.

## SAN AGENCY

A feature of the publishers, distributors, and wholesalers entries is the Standard Address Number (SAN). The SAN is a unique identification number assigned to each address of an organization in or served by the publishing industry. It facilitates communications and repetitive transactions with other members of the industry. The SAN functions in its application to activities such as purchasing, billing, shipping, receiving, paying, crediting, and refunding, and can be used for any other communication or transaction between participating organizations. To obtain an application or further information on the SAN system, please contact Diana Luongo, SAN Manager, by calling 908-219-0283, fax 908-219-0188, or visit the ISBN/SAN Web site at www.isbn.org.

## ADDITIONAL RESOURCES

A wealth of current bibliographic data (more than 4.6 million records, including videos) can also be searched by customers on Bowker's Web site: www.booksinprint.com. The Books In Print database is also available on CD-ROM. For further information about subscribing to these services, contact Bowker at 1-888-269-5372. Out-of-print titles are also available on our Web site at www.booksoutofprint.com.

# LIST OF ABBREVIATIONS

| | | | | | |
|---|---|---|---|---|---|
| abr. | abridged | disk | software disk or diskette | i.t.a. | initial teaching alphabet |
| adapt. | adapted | dist. | distributed | J | juvenile audience level |
| addr. | address | Div. | Division | Jr. | Junior |
| affil. | affiliate | doz. | dozen | jt. auth. | joint author |
| aft. | afterword | Dr. | Drive | jt. ed. | joint editor |
| Amer. | American | E | East | k | kindergarten audience level |
| anno. | annotated by | ea. | each | lab | laboratory |
| annot. | annotation(s) | ed. | edited, edition, editor | lang(s). | languages(s) |
| ans. | answer(s) | edit. | editorial | LC | Library of Congress |
| app. | appendix | eds. | editions, editors | lea. | leather |
| Apple II | Apple II disk | educ. | education | lib. | library |
| approx. | approximately | elem. | elementary | lib. bdg. | library binding |
| Apt. | apartment | ency. | encyclopedia | lit. | literature, literary |
| assn. | association | ENG | English | Ln. | Lane |
| assoc(s). | associate | enl. | enlarged | lp | record, album, long playing |
| Ave. | Avenue | epil. | epilogue | LTD | Limited |
| audio | analog audio cassette | exp. | expurgated | ltd. ed. | limited edition |
| auth. | author | expr. | experiments | mac hd | 144M, Mac |
| bd. | bound | fac. | facsimile | mac ld | 800K, Mac |
| bdg. | binding | fasc. | fascicule | mass mkt. | mass market paperbound |
| bds. | boards | fict. | fiction | math. | mathematics |
| bibl(s). | bibliography(ies) | fig(s). | figure(s) | mic. film | microfilm |
| bk(s). | book(s) | flmstrp. | filmstrip | mic. form | microform |
| bklet(s). | booklet(s) | flr. | floor | mod. | modern |
| Bldg. | building | footn. | footnotes | mor. | morocco |
| Blvd. | boulevard | for. | foreign | MS(S) | manuscript(s) |
| boxed | boxed set, slipcase, or caseboard | Ft. | Fort | N | North |
| Bro. | Brother | frwd. | foreword | NE | Northeast |
| C | college audience level | gen. | general | natl. | national |
| c/o | care of | G.P.O. | General Post Office | net | net price (see publisher for specific pricing policies) |
| Cir. | Circle | gr. | grade(s) | | |
| co. | company | hdbk. | handbook | | |
| comm. | commission, committee | hse. | house | NW | Northwest |
| comment. | commentaries | Hwy. | Highway | no(s). | number(s) |
| comp. | compiled | Illus. | illustrated, illustration(s), illustrator(s) | o.p. | out of print |
| cond. | condensed | | | orig. | original text, not a reprint (paperback) |
| contrib. | contributed | in prep. | in preparation | | |
| corp. | corporation | Inc. | Incorporated | o.s.i. | out of stock indefinitely |
| Ct. | Court | incl. | includes, including | | |
| Ctr(s) | Center(s) | | | p. | pages |
| Cty. | county | info. | information | pap. | paper |
| dept. | department | inst. | institute | per. | perfect binding |
| des. | designed | intro. | introduction | photos | photographer, photographs |
| diag(s). | diagram(s) | ISBN | International Standard Book Number | | |
| digital-audio | digital audio cassette | | | Pk. | Park |
| dir. | director | ISO | International Standards Organization | | |

# LIST OF ABBREVIATIONS

| | | | | | |
|---|---|---|---|---|---|
| Pkwy. | Parkway | rpm | revolutions per minute (phono records) | suppl. | supplement |
| Pl. | Place | | | SW | Southwest |
| P.O. | post office | R.R. | Rural Route | tech. | technical |
| pop. ed. | popular edition | Rte. | Route | Terr. | Terrace |
| pr. | press | S | South | text ed. | text edition |
| prep. | preparation | SAN | Standard Address Number | Tpke | Turnpike |
| probs. | problems | | | tr. | translated, translation, translator |
| prog. bk. | programmed books | S&L | Signed and Limited | | |
| ps | preschool audience level | SE | Southeast | trans. | transparencies |
| | | sec. | section | Univ. | University |
| pseud. | pseudonym | sel. | selected | vdisk | videodisk |
| pt(s). | part(s) | ser. | series | VHS | video, VHS format |
| pub. | published, publisher, publishing | Soc. | Society | vol(s). | volume(s) |
| | | sols. | solutions | W | West |
| pubn. | publication | s.p. | school price | wkbk. | workbook |
| R.D. | rural delivery | Sq. | Square | YA | young adult audience level |
| Rd. | Road | Sr. (after given name) | Senior | | |
| ref(s). | reference(s) | | | yrbk. | yearbook |
| reprod(s). | reproduction(s) | Sr. (before given name) | Sister | 3.5 hd | 1.44M, 3.5″ disk, DOS |
| ret. | retold by | | | | |
| rev. | revised | St. | Saint, Street | 3.5 ld | 720, 3.5″ Disk, DOS |
| R.F.D. | rural free delivery | Sta. | Station | 5.25hd | 1.2M, 5.25″ Disk, DOS |
| Rm. | Room | subs. | subsidiary | | |
| | | subscr. | subscription | 5.25 ld | 360 K, 5.25″ Disk, DOS |

# PUBLISHER COUNTRY CODES

Foreign publishers are listed in **Bowker's Guide to Characters In Fiction** with the three-letter International Standards Organization (ISO) code for their country of domicile. This is the complete list of ISO codes, though not all countries may be represented in **Bowker's Guide to Characters In Fiction**. The codes are mnemonic in most cases. The country names listed here may have been shortened to a more common usage form.

| | | | | | |
|---|---|---|---|---|---|
| ABW | Aruba | CMR | Cameroon | GUF | French Guiana |
| AFG | Afghanistan | COD | Congo, Democratic Republic of | GUM | Guam |
| AGO | Angola | | | GUY | Guyana |
| AIA | Anguilla | COG | Congo | HKG | Hong Kong |
| ALB | Albania | COK | Cook Islands | HMD | Heard Island and McDonald Islands |
| AND | Andorra | COL | Colombia | | |
| ANT | Netherland Antilles | COM | Comoros | HND | Honduras |
| ARE | United Arab Emirates | CPV | Cape Verde | HRV | Croatia |
| | | CRI | Costa Rica | HTI | Haiti |
| ARG | Argentina | CSK | Czechoslovakia | HUN | Hungary |
| ARM | Armenia | CUB | Cuba | IDN | Indonesia |
| ASM | American Samoa | CXR | Christmas Island | IND | India |
| ATA | Antarctica | CYN | Cayman Islands | IOT | British Indian Ocean Territory |
| ATF | French Southern Territories | CYP | Cyprus | | |
| | | CZE | Czech Republic | IRL | Ireland |
| ATG | Antigua and Barbuda | DDR | East Germany | IRN | Iran |
| | | DEU | Germany | IRQ | Iraq |
| AUS | Australia | DJI | Djibouti | ISL | Iceland |
| AUT | Austria | DMA | Dominica | ISR | Israel |
| AZE | Azerbaijan | DNK | Denmark | ITA | Italy |
| BDI | Burundi | DOM | Dominican Republic | JAM | Jamaica |
| BEL | Belgium | DZA | Algeria | JOR | Jordan |
| BEN | Benin | ECU | Ecuador | JPN | Japan |
| BFA | Burkina Faso | EGY | Egypt | KAZ | Kazakstan |
| BGD | Bangladesh | ERI | Eritrea | KEN | Kenya |
| BGR | Bulgaria | ESH | Western Sahara | KGZ | Kyrgyzstan |
| BHR | Bahrain | ESP | Spain | KHM | Cambodia |
| BHS | Bahamas | EST | Estonia | KIR | Kiribati |
| BIH | Bosnia and Herzegovina | ETH | Ethiopia | KNA | Saint Kitts and Nevis |
| | | FIN | Finland | | |
| BLR | Belarus | FJI | Fiji | KOR | Korea, Republic of |
| BLZ | Belize | FLK | Falkland Islands | | |
| BMU | Bermuda | FRA | France | KWT | Kuwait |
| BOL | Bolivia | FRO | Faeroe Islands | LAO | Laos |
| BRA | Brazil | FSM | Fed. States of Micronesia | LBN | Lebanon |
| BRB | Barbados | | | LBR | Liberia |
| BUL | Bulgaria | GAB | Gabon | LBY | Libya |
| BRD | West Germany | GBR | United Kingdom | LCA | St. Lucia |
| BRN | Brunei Darussalam | GEO | Georgia | LIE | Liechtenstein |
| BTN | Bhutan | GHA | Ghana | LKA | Sri Lanka |
| BVT | Bouvet Island | GIB | Gibralter | LSO | Lesotho |
| BWA | Botswana | GIN | Guinea | LTU | Lithuania |
| CAF | Central African Republic | GLP | Guadaloupe | LUX | Luxembourg |
| | | GMB | Gambia | LVA | Latvia |
| CAN | Canada | GNB | Guinea-Bissau | MAC | Macau |
| CCK | Cocos (Keeling) Islands | GNQ | Equatorial Guinea | MAR | Morocco |
| | | GRC | Greece | MCO | Monaco |
| CHE | Switzerland | GRD | Grenada | MDA | Moldova |
| CHL | Chile | GRL | Greenland | MDG | Madagascar |
| CHN | China | GTM | Guatemala | MDV | Maldive Islands |
| CIV | Cote D'Ivoire | | | | |

## PUBLISHER COUNTRY CODES

| | | | | | |
|---|---|---|---|---|---|
| MEX | Mexico | PRI | Puerto Rico | TCA | Turks and Caicos Islands |
| MHL | Marshall Islands | PRK | Korea, Democratic People's Rep. of | TCG | Togo |
| MKD | Macedonia | | | THA | Thailand |
| MLI | Mali | PRT | Portugal | TJK | Tajikistan |
| MLT | Malta | PRY | Paraguay | TKL | Tokelau |
| MMR | Myanmar | PSE | Occupied Palestinian Territory | TKM | Turkmenistan |
| MNG | Mongolia | PYF | French Polynesia | TNP | East Timor |
| MNP | Northern Mariana Islands | QAT | Qatar | TON | Tonga |
| MOZ | Mozambique | REU | Reunion | TTO | Trinidad and Tobago |
| MRT | Mauritania | ROM | Romania | | |
| MSR | Montserrat | RUS | Russia | TUN | Tunisia |
| MTQ | Martinique | RWA | Rwanda | TUR | Turkey |
| MUS | Mauritius | SAU | Saudi Arabia | TUV | Tuvalu |
| MWI | Malawi | ADN | Sudan | TWN | Taiwan |
| MYS | Malaysia | SEN | Senegal | TZA | Tanzania |
| MYT | Mayotte | SGP | Singapore | UGA | Uganda |
| NAM | Namibia | SGS | South Georgia and Sandwich Islands | UKR | Ukraine |
| NCL | New Caledonia | | | URY | Uruguay |
| NER | Niger | SHN | Saint Helena | USA | United States |
| NFK | Norfolk Island | SJM | Svalbard and Jan Mayen | UZB | Uzbekistan |
| NGA | Nigeria | | | VAT | Vatican City |
| NIC | Nicauragua | SLB | Solomen Islands | VCT | St. Vincents and Grenadines |
| NIU | Niue | SLE | Sierra Leone | | |
| NLD | Netherlands | SLV | El Salvador | VEN | Venezuela |
| NOR | Norway | SMR | San Marino | VGB | Virgin Islands, British |
| NPL | Nepal | SOM | Somalia | | |
| NRU | Nauru | SPM | Saint Pierre and Miquelon | VIR | Virgin Islands, U.S. |
| NZL | New Zealand | | | VNM | Vietnam |
| OMN | Oman | STP | Sao Tome e Principe | VUT | Vanuatu |
| PAK | Pakistan | | | WLF | Wallis and Futuna |
| PAN | Panama | SUN | U.S.S.R. | | |
| PCN | Pitcairn Islands | SUR | Suriname | WSM | Somoa |
| PER | Peru | SVK | Slovakia | YEM | Yemen |
| PHL | Philippines | SVN | Slovenia | YUG | Yugoslavia |
| PLW | Palau | SWE | Sweden | ZAF | South Africa |
| PNG | Papua New Guinea | SWZ | Swaziland | ZAR | Zaire |
| POL | Poland | SYC | Seychelles | ZMB | Zambia |
| | | SYR | Syrian Arab Republic | ZWE | Zimbabwe |

# LANGUAGE CODES

| | | | | | |
|---|---|---|---|---|---|
| ACE | Acholi | CHV | Chuvash | HAW | Hawaiian |
| AFR | Afrikaans | COP | Coptic | HEB | Hebrew |
| AFA | Afro-Asiatic | COR | Cornish | HER | Hereo |
| AKK | Akkadian | CRE | Cree | HIL | Hiligaynon |
| ALB | Albanian | CRP | Creole | HIN | Hindi |
| ALE | Aleut | | and Pidgin | HUN | Hungarian |
| ALG | Algonquin | CRO | Croatian | HUP | Hupa |
| AMH | Amharic | CUS | Cushitic | IBA | Iban |
| ANG | Anglo-Saxon | CZE | Czech | ICE | Icelandic |
| APA | Apache | DAK | Dakota | IBO | Icelandic |
| ARA | Arabic | DAN | Danish | IBO | Igbo |
| ARC | Aramaic | DEL | Delaware | ILO | Ilocano |
| ARP | Arapaho | DIN | Dinka | INC | Indic |
| ARM | Armenian | DOI | Dogri | INE | Indo-European |
| ASM | Assamese | DRA | Dravidian | IND | Indonesian |
| AVA | Avar | DUA | Duala | INT | Interlingua |
| AVE | Avesta | DUT | Dutch | IKU | Inuktitut |
| AYM | Aymara | EFI | Efik | IRA | Iranian |
| AZE | Azerbaijani | EGY | Egyptian | IRI | Irish |
| BAT | Baltic | ELX | Elamite | IRO | Iroquois |
| BAL | Baluchi | ENG | English | ITA | Italian |
| BAM | Bambara | ENM | English, Middle | JPN | Japanese |
| BAK | Bashkir | ESK | Eskimo | JAV | Javanese |
| BAQ | Basque | ESP | Esperanto | KAC | Kachin |
| BEJ | Beja | EST | Estonian | KAM | Kamba |
| BEL | Belorussian | ETH | Ethiopic | KAN | Kannada |
| BEM | Bemba | EWE | Ewe | KAU | Kanuri |
| BEN | Bengali | FAN | Fang | KAA | Karakalpak |
| BER | Berber Group | FAR | Faroese | KAR | Karen |
| BIH | Bihari | FIJ | Finnish | KAS | Kashmiri |
| BLA | Blackfoot | FIU | Finno-Ugrian | KAZ | Kazakh |
| BRE | Breton | FLE | Flemish | KHA | Khasi |
| BUL | Bulgarian | FON | Fon | KIK | Kikuyu |
| BUR | Burmese | FRE | French | KIN | Kinyarwanda |
| CAD | Caddo | FEM | French, Middle | KIR | Kirghiz |
| CAM | Cambodian | FRO | French, Old | KON | Kongo |
| CAR | Carib | FRI | Frisian | KOK | Konkani |
| CAT | Catalan | GAA | Ga | KOR | Korean |
| CAU | Caucasian | GAE | Gaelic | KPE | Kpelle |
| CEL | Celtic Group | GAL | Galla | KRO | Kru |
| CAI | Central | GAG | Gallegan | KUR | Kurdish |
| | American Indian | GEO | Georgian | KRU | Kurukh |
| CHE | Chechen | GER | German | KUA | Kwanyama |
| CHR | Cherokee | GEH | Germanic | LAD | Ladino |
| CHY | Cheyenne | GON | Gondi | LAH | Lahnda |
| CHB | Chibcha | GOT | Gothic | LAM | Lamba |
| CHI | Chinese | GRE | Greek | LAO | Laotian |
| CHN | Chinook | GEC | Greek, Classical | LAP | Lapp |
| CHO | Choctaw | GUA | Guarani | LAT | Latin |
| CHU | Church Slavic | HAU | Hausa | | |

# LANGUAGE CODES

| | | | | | |
|---|---|---|---|---|---|
| LAV | Latvian | PAA | Papuan-Australian | SUN | Sudanese |
| LIN | Lingala | PER | Persian, Modern | SUS | Susu |
| LIT | Lithuanian | PEO | Persian, Old | SWA | Swahili |
| LOL | Lolo | POL | Polish | SWE | Swedish |
| LUB | Luba | POR | Portuguese | SYR | Syriac |
| LUG | Luganda | PRO | Provencal | TAG | Tagalong |
| LUI | Luiseno | PUS | Pushto | TAJ | Tajik |
| MAC | Macedonian | QUE | Quechua | TAM | Tamil |
| MAI | Maithili | RAJ | Rajasthani | TAR | Tatar |
| MLA | Malagasy | ROA | Romance | TEl | Telugu |
| MAY | Malay | RUM | Romanian | TEM | Temne |
| MAL | Malayalam | ROH | Romansh | TER | Tereno |
| MAP | Malayo-Polynesian | ROM | Romanian | THA | Thai |
| MAN | Mandingo | RUN | Rundi | TIB | Tibetan |
| MNO | Manobo | RUS | Russian | TIG | Tigre |
| Mao | Maori | SAM | Samaritan | TIR | Tigrinya |
| Mar | Marathi | SAO | Sampan | TOG | Tonga, Nyasa |
| MAS | Masai | SAD | Sandawe | TON | Tonga, Tonga Islands |
| MYN | Mayan | SAG | Sango | | |
| MEN | Mende | SAN | Sanskrit | TSI | Tsimshian |
| MIC | Micmac | SRD | Sardinian | TSO | Tsonga |
| MIS | Miscellaneous | SCO | Scots | TSW | Tswana |
| MOL | Moldavian | SEL | Selkup | TUR | Turkish |
| MON | Mongol | SEM | Semitic | TUK | Turkmen |
| MOS | Mossi | SER | Serbian | TUT | Turko-Tataric |
| MUL | Multiple languages | SBC | Serbo-Croatian | TWI | Twi |
| MUS | Muskogee | SRR | Serer | UGA | Ugaritic |
| NAV | Navaho | SHN | Shan | UKR | Ukrainian |
| NDE | Ndebele, Northern | SHO | Shona | UMB | Umbundu |
| NBL | Ndebele, Southern | SID | Sidamo | UND | Undetermined |
| NEP | Nepali | SND | Sindhi | URD | Urdu |
| NEW | Newari | SNH | Singhalese | UZB | Uzbek |
| NIC | Niger-Congo | SIT | Sino-Tibetan | VIE | Vietnamese |
| NAI | North American Indian | SIO | Siouan languages | VOT | Votic |
| | | SLA | Slavik | WAL | Walamo |
| NOR | Norwegian | SLO | Slovak | WAS | Washo |
| NUB | Nubian | SLV | Slovenian | WEL | Welsh |
| NYM | Nyamwezi | SOG | Sogdian | WEN | Wendic |
| NYA | Nyanja | SOM | Somali | WOL | Wolof |
| NYO | Nyoro Group | SON | Songhai | XHO | Xhosa |
| OJI | Ojibwa | NSO | Sotho, Northern | YAO | Yao |
| ORI | Oriya | SOT | Sotho, Southern | YID | Yiddish |
| OSA | Osage | SAI | South American Indian | YOR | Yoruba |
| OES | Ossetic | | | ZAP | Zapotec |
| OTO | Otomi | SPA | Spanish | ZEN | Zenaga |
| PAH | Pahari | SSA | Sub-Saharan African | ZUL | Zulu |
| PAL | Pahlavi | SUK | Sukuma | ZUN | Zuni |
| PLI | Pali | SUX | Sumerian | | |
| PAN | Panjabi | | | | |

# List of Subject Headings
## Adult Fiction

## CHARACTERS

ABAGNARRO, ABBY (FICTITIOUS CHARACTER) p.31

ABBOTT, BEN (FICTITIOUS CHARACTER) p.31

ABBOTT, D. J. (FICTITIOUS CHARACTER) p.31

ABBOTT, LUKE (FICTITIOUS CHARACTER) p.31

ABRAMOWITZ, JOEL (FICTITIOUS CHARACTER) p.31

ACKERLEY, PAUL (FICTITIOUS CHARACTER) p.31

ACKROYD, LAURA (FICTITIOUS CHARACTER) p.31

ACORNA (FICTITIOUS CHARACTER) p.31

ACTIVE, NATHAN (FICTITIOUS CHARACTER) p.31

ADAIR, MADISON (FICTITIOUS CHARACTER) p.31

ADAMS, CLINT (FICTITIOUS CHARACTER) p.31

ADAMS, DOC (FICTITIOUS CHARACTER) p.31

ADAMS, GILLIAN (FICTITIOUS CHARACTER) p.31

ADAMS, HENRY, 1838-1918 p.32

ADAMS, HILDA (FICTITIOUS CHARACTER) p.32

ADAMS, JAGUAR (FICTITIOUS CHARACTER) p.32

ADAMS, KERI (FICTITIOUS CHARACTER) p.32

ADAMS, NICK (FICTITIOUS CHARACTER) p.32

ADAMS, SAMANTHA (FICTITIOUS CHARACTER) p.32

ADARE, PADDY (FICTITIOUS CHARACTER) p.32

ADDAMS, MAX (FICTITIOUS CHARACTER) p.32

ADDAMS FAMILY (FICTITIOUS CHARACTERS) p.32

ADDISON, BEN (FICTITIOUS CHARACTER) p.32

ADDISON, HARRY (FICTITIOUS CHARACTER) p.32

ADEPT, THE (FICTITIOUS CHARACTER) p.32
   see Sinclair, Adam (Fictitious Character)

ADLER, ALEXANDRA (FICTITIOUS CHARACTER) p.32

ADLER, IRENE (FICTITIOUS CHARACTER) p.32

AGNES, SISTER (FICTITIOUS CHARACTER) p.32

AGUIRRE, FRANKIE (FICTITIOUS CHARACTER) p.32

AHAB, CAPTAIN (FICTITIOUS CHARACTER) p.32

AINSLIE, AMBER (FICTITIOUS CHARACTER) p.33

AINSLIE, MALCOLM (FICTITIOUS CHARACTER) p.33

ALARIC, THE MINSTREL (FICTITIOUS CHARACTER) p.33

ALBERG, KARL (FICTITIOUS CHARACTER) p.33

ALBERT, CONSORT OF QUEEN VICTORIA, 1819-1861 p.33

ALBRIGHT, ALEXIS (FICTITIOUS CHARACTER) p.33

ALDINGTON, CLAIRE (FICTITIOUS CHARACTER) p.33

ALETTER, FINNY (FICTITIOUS CHARACTER) p.33

ALEXANDER, RACHEL (FICTITIOUS CHARACTER) p.33

ALICE (FICTITIOUS CHARACTER: CARROLL) p.33

ALLEN, STEVE, 1921-2000 p.34

ALLEYN, RODERICK (FICTITIOUS CHARACTER) p.34

ALLISON, BEN (FICTITIOUS CHARACTER) p.35

ALLISON, OWEN (FICTITIOUS CHARACTER) p.35

ALLON, GABRIEL (FICTITIOUS CHARACTER) p.35

ALTFORD, MILLICENT (FICTITIOUS CHARACTER) p.35

ALTOBELLI, VINNIE (FICTITIOUS CHARACTER) p.35

ALVAREZ, DAVID (FICTITIOUS CHARACTER) p.35

ALVAREZ, ENRIQUE (FICTITIOUS CHARACTER) p.35

AMALFI, ANGIE (FICTITIOUS CHARACTER) p.36

AMISS, ROBERT (FICTITIOUS CHARACTER) p.36

AMNELL, KAHLAN (FICTITIOUS CHARACTER) p.36

ANDERSON, BOBBI (FICTITIOUS CHARACTER) p.36

ANDERSON, JOHN (FICTITIOUS CHARACTER) p.36

ANDERSON, MALI (FICTITIOUS CHARACTER) p.36

ANDERSON, MARION (FICTITIOUS CHARACTER) p.36

ANDERSON, SHIFTY LOU (FICTITIOUS CHARACTER) p.36

ANDERSSON, MARGIT (FICTITIOUS CHARACTER) p.36

ANDREWS, ARCHIE (FICTITIOUS CHARACTER) p.36

ANDREWS, CAMERON (FICTITIOUS CHARACTER) p.36

ANDREWS, JASON (FICTITIOUS CHARACTER) p.36

ANGSTROM, HARRY (FICTITIOUS CHARACTER) p.36

ANHALT, MICI (FICTITIOUS CHARACTER) p.36

ANTERO, AMALRIC (FICTITIOUS CHARACTER) p.36

ANTHEM, JOHNNY (FICTITIOUS CHARACTER) p.36

ANTILLES, WEDGE (FICTITIOUS CHARACTER) p.37

ANTON, ALEC (FICTITIOUS CHARACTER) p.37

ANTONELLI, JOSEPH (FICTITIOUS CHARACTER) p.37

APPLEBAUM, JULIET (FICTITIOUS CHARACTER) p.37

APPLEBY, JOHN, SIR (FICTITIOUS CHARACTER) p.37

APPLEMAN, BELLE (FICTITIOUS CHARACTER) p.38

APPLETON, SUSANNA, LADY (FICTITIOUS CHARACTER) p.38

APPRENTICE ADEPT (FICTITIOUS CHARACTER) p.38

ARAGON, TOM (FICTITIOUS CHARACTER) p.38

ARBATI, CARLO (FICTITIOUS CHARACTER) p.38

ARBOTHNOT, AUBREY (FICTITIOUS CHARACTER) p.38

ARCHER, CAROLYN (FICTITIOUS CHARACTER) p.38

ARCHER, ISABEL (FICTITIOUS CHARACTER) p.38

ARCHER, LEW (FICTITIOUS CHARACTER) p.38

ARCHER, OWEN (FICTITIOUS CHARACTER) p.39

ARDLEIGH, KATHRYN (FICTITIOUS CHARACTER) p.39

ARGYLL, JONATHAN (FICTITIOUS CHARACTER) p.39

ARMITAGE SISTERS (FICTITIOUS CHARACTERS) p.39

ARMSTRONG, EDWARD (FICTITIOUS CHARACTER) p.39

ARNO, HARRY (FICTITIOUS CHARACTER) p.39

ARNOLD, JESSIE (FICTITIOUS CHARACTER) p.39

ARNOLD, LUCY RICHARDS (FICTITIOUS CHARACTER) p.39

ARROWOOD, SPENCER (FICTITIOUS CHARACTER) p.39

ARTHUR, KING p.40

ASCH, JACOB (FICTITIOUS CHARACTER) p.41

AFSAN, THE FAR-SEER (FICTITIOUS CHARACTER) p.41

ASHE, BENNY (FICTITIOUS CHARACTER) p.41

ASHE, GORDON (FICTITIOUS CHARACTER) p.41

ASHER, JAMES (FICTITIOUS CHARACTER) p.41

ASHER, STEVE (FICTITIOUS CHARACTER) p.41

ASHERFELD, AARON (FICTITIOUS CHARACTER) p.41

ASHLEY, BRETT (FICTITIOUS CHARACTER) p.41

ASHTON, CAROL (FICTITIOUS CHARACTER) p.41

ASHTON, PETER (FICTITIOUS CHARACTER) p.42

ASHWORTH, JIM (FICTITIOUS CHARACTER) p.42

ATHAYA (FICTITIOUS CHARACTER) p.42

ATHELSTAN, BROTHER (FICTITIOUS CHARACTER) p.42

ATTLA, RAY (FICTITIOUS CHARACTER) p.42

AUBREY, JACK (FICTITIOUS CHARACTER) p.42

AUDEN, ERIC (FICTITIOUS CHARACTER) p.42

AUDLEY, DAVID (FICTITIOUS CHARACTER) p.42

AURIAN, LADY (FICTITIOUS CHARACTER) p.43

AUSTEN, CAT (FICTITIOUS CHARACTER) p.43

AUSTEN, JANE, 1775-1817 p.43

AUSTEN, KATE (FICTITIOUS CHARACTER) p.43

AUSTIN, AMANDA (FICTITIOUS CHARACTER) p.43

AUSTIN, BETH (FICTITIOUS CHARACTER) p.43

AUSTIN, KURT (FICTITIOUS CHARACTER) p.43

AUSTIN, LYNDA DAWN (FICTITIOUS CHARACTER) p.43

AVERY, BLAINE (FICTITIOUS CHARACTER) p.43

AYERS, SAMMY (FICTITIOUS CHARACTER) p.43

AYESHA (FICTITIOUS CHARACTER: HAGGARD) p.43

AYLA (FICTITIOUS CHARACTER: AUEL) p.43

AZRIEL, SERVANT OF THE BONES (FICTITIOUS CHARACTER) p.44

BABCOCK, ALLIDA (FICTITIOUS CHARACTER) p.44

BACA, SONNY (FICTITIOUS CHARACTER) p.44

BACHELOR BROTHERS (FICTITIOUS CHARACTERS) p.44

BAEIER, KATE (FICTITIOUS CHARACTER) p.44

BAGGINS, BILBO (FICTITIOUS CHARACTER) p.44

BAGGINS, FRODO (FICTITIOUS CHARACTER) p.44

BAGLEY, CALLISTA (FICTITIOUS CHARACTER) p.45

BAILEY, GEOFFREY (FICTITIOUS CHARACTER) p.45

BAILEY, JERUSHA (FICTITIOUS CHARACTER) p.45

BAILEY FAMILY (FICTITIOUS CHARACTERS) p.45

BAIRD, JACK (FICTITIOUS CHARACTER) p.45

BAK, LIEUTENANT (FICTITIOUS CHARACTER) p.45

BAKER, MARY (FICTITIOUS CHARACTER) p.45

BAKER STREET IRREGULARS (FICTITIOUS CHARACTERS) p.45

BALDRIDGE, MASEY (FICTITIOUS CHARACTER) p.45

BALDWIN, SARAH (FICTITIOUS CHARACTER) p.45

BALDWIN, T. T. (FICTITIOUS CHARACTER) p.46

BALEY, ELIJAH (FICTITIOUS CHARACTER) p.46

BALL, HOLLIS (FICTITIOUS CHARACTER) p.46

BALLARD, VIRGIL (FICTITIOUS CHARACTER) p.46

BALLOU, HOSEA, 1771-1852 p.46

BALLOU FAMILY (FICTITIOUS CHARACTERS) p.46

BALLY, MAX (FICTITIOUS CHARACTER) p.46

BALON, SAM, SR. (FICTITIOUS CHARACTER) p.46

BALZIC, MARIO (FICTITIOUS CHARACTER) p.46

BANCROFT, SOPHIA (FICTITIOUS CHARACTER) p.46

BANKS, ALAN (FICTITIOUS CHARACTER) p.46

BANNERMAN, PAUL (FICTITIOUS CHARACTER) p.46

BANNING, KATE (FICTITIOUS CHARACTER) p.46

BANNING, ORIEL (FICTITIOUS CHARACTER) p.47

BANNION, RICK (FICTITIOUS CHARACTER) p.47

BANNON BROTHERS (FICTITIOUS CHARACTERS) p.47

BARBER, NICHOLAS (FICTITIOUS CHARACTER) p.47

BARD, JACK (FICTITIOUS CHARACTER) p.47

BARD, LILY (FICTITIOUS CHARACTER) p.47

BARKER, HOLLY (FICTITIOUS CHARACTER) p.47

BARLEY, JOE (FICTITIOUS CHARACTER) p.47

BARLOW, CHARLIE (FICTITIOUS CHARACTER) p.47

BARLOW, HANNAH (FICTITIOUS CHARACTER) p.47

BARLOW, HONORIA (FICTITIOUS CHARACTER) p.47

BARLOW, MARGARET (FICTITIOUS CHARACTER) p.47

BARLOW, NICHOLAS (FICTITIOUS CHARACTER) p.47

BARNABAS, GEORGE, DOCTOR (FICTITIOUS CHARACTER) p.47

BARNABY, TOM, CHIEF INSPECTOR (FICTITIOUS CHARACTER) p.47

BARNEA, DANIELLE (FICTITIOUS CHARACTER) p.47

BARNES, GINGER (FICTITIOUS CHARACTER) p.47

BARNES, MICHAEL (FICTITIOUS CHARACTER) p.47

BARNES, NIKKI (FICTITIOUS CHARACTER) p.47

BARNETT, HARRY (FICTITIOUS CHARACTER) p.47

BARR, JEREMY (FICTITIOUS CHARACTER) p.48

BARR, TEMPLE (FICTITIOUS CHARACTER) p.48

BARRETT, BEL (FICTITIOUS CHARACTER) p.48

BARRETT, JONATHAN (FICTITIOUS CHARACTER) p.48

BARRETT, SEAN (FICTITIOUS CHARACTER) p.48

BARRINGTON, STONE (FICTITIOUS CHARACTER) p.48

BARRON, PETER (FICTITIOUS CHARACTER) p.48

BARTHOLOMEW, BROTHER (FICTITIOUS CHARACTER) p.48

BARTHOLOMEW, MATTHEW (FICTITIOUS CHARACTER) p.48

BARTHOLOMEW, PETER (FICTITIOUS CHARACTER) p.48

BARTLETT, STEPHEN (FICTITIOUS CHARACTER) p.49

BARWICK, LIZ (FICTITIOUS CHARACTER) p.49

BASCOM, ERNIE (FICTITIOUS CHARACTER) p.49

BASCOME, CARVER (FICTITIOUS CHARACTER) p.49

BASHEARS, ALMA MAE (FICTITIOUS CHARACTER) p.49

BASHIR, JULIAN (FICTITIOUS CHARACTER) p.49

BASILE, BURKE (FICTITIOUS CHARACTER) p.49

BASNETT, ANDREW (FICTITIOUS CHARACTER) p.49

BASS, TITUS (FICTITIOUS CHARACTER) p.49

BASSETT, HENRY (FICTITIOUS CHARACTER) p.49

BAST (FICTITIOUS CHARACTER) p.49

BASTABLE, OSWALD (FICTITIOUS CHARACTER) p.49

BATELLE, JESSIE (FICTITIOUS CHARACTER) p.49

BATEMAN, PAT (FICTITIOUS CHARACTER) p.49

BATES, NORMAN (FICTITIOUS CHARACTER) p.49

BATHORY, DAVID (FICTITIOUS CHARACTER) p.49

BATMAN (FICTITIOUS CHARACTER) p.49

BATTLE, SUPERINTENDENT (FICTITIOUS CHARACTER) p.51

BAUER, TORY (FICTITIOUS CHARACTER) p.51

BAUER, VICKY (FICTITIOUS CHARACTER) p.51

BAUM, STEVEN (FICTITIOUS CHARACTER) p.51

BAUMANN, HENRIK (FICTITIOUS CHARACTER) p.51

BAXTER, JENNIFER (FICTITIOUS CHARACTER) p.51

BAYLES, CHINA (FICTITIOUS CHARACTER) p.51

BAYLOR, RUDY (FICTITIOUS CHARACTER) p.51

BAYNES FAMILY (FICTITIOUS CHARACTERS) p.51

BEACH, TONY (FICTITIOUS CHARACTER) p.51

BEAMON, MARK (FICTITIOUS CHARACTER) p.51

BEAN, MADELINE (FICTITIOUS CHARACTER) p.51

BEAN, QUEENIE (FICTITIOUS CHARACTER) p.51

BEANBLOSSOM, RICK (FICTITIOUS CHARACTER) p.51

BEAR, GOLDY (FICTITIOUS CHARACTER) p.51

BEARPAW, MOLLY (FICTITIOUS CHARACTER) p.52

BEATTY, JIM (FICTITIOUS CHARACTER) p.52

BEAUMONT, INGRID (FICTITIOUS CHARACTER) p.52

BEAUMONT, J. P. (FICTITIOUS CHARACTER) p.52

BEAUMONT, NED (FICTITIOUS CHARACTER) p.52

BEAUMONT, PHIL (FICTITIOUS CHARACTER) p.52

BEAUMONT, THAD (FICTITIOUS CHARACTER) p.52

BEBB, LEO (FICTITIOUS CHARACTER) p.52

BECH, HENRY (FICTITIOUS CHARACTER) p.52

BECK, LIZA (FICTITIOUS CHARACTER) p.52

BECK, MARTIN (FICTITIOUS CHARACTER) p.53

BECKER, JOHN (FICTITIOUS CHARACTER) p.53

BECKER FAMILY (FICTITIOUS CHARACTERS) p.53

BECKETT, SAM (FICTITIOUS CHARACTER) p.53

BECKMAN, GIL (FICTITIOUS CHARACTER) p.53

BECKMANN, GRACE (FICTITIOUS CHARACTER) p.53

BECKWITH, JIM (FICTITIOUS CHARACTER) p.53

BEDWYR, LUTHIEN (FICTITIOUS CHARACTER) p.53
    see Crimson Shadow (Fictitious Character)

BEE, JANE (FICTITIOUS CHARACTER) p.53

BEEF, WILLIAM (FICTITIOUS CHARACTER) p.53

BEHN, APHRA, 1640-1689 p.53

BEHR, DAN (FICTITIOUS CHARACTER) p.53

BEHR, JASON (FICTITIOUS CHARACTER) p.53

BELACQUA, LYRA (FICTITIOUS CHARACTER) p.53

BELANE, NICK (FICTITIOUS CHARACTER) p.53

BELASCOARAN SHAYNE, HECTOR (FICTITIOUS CHARACTER) p.53

BELL, DANIEL (FICTITIOUS CHARACTER) p.53

BELLAMY, ROBERT (FICTITIOUS CHARACTER) p.53

BELOW, DRACHTON (FICTITIOUS CHARACTER) p.53

BELSKI, BECKY (FICTITIOUS CHARACTER) p.53

BENBOW, ANGELA (FICTITIOUS CHARACTER) p.53

BENCOLIN, HENRI (FICTITIOUS CHARACTER) p.54

BENEDETTI, NICCOLO (FICTITIOUS CHARACTER) p.54

BENGAL, ROSALIND (FICTITIOUS CHARACTER) p.54

BENINGTON, PETER (FICTITIOUS CHARACTER) p.54

BENNET, ELIZABETH (FICTITIOUS CHARACTER) p.54

BENNETT, CHASE (FICTITIOUS CHARACTER) p.55

BENNETT, CHRISTINE (FICTITIOUS CHARACTER) p.55

BENNETT, JILL (FICTITIOUS CHARACTER) p.55

BENNETT, LILY (FICTITIOUS CHARACTER) p.55

BENNETT, MILDRED (FICTITIOUS CHARACTER) p.55

BENNETT, REID (FICTITIOUS CHARACTER) p.55

BENNIS, NORMAN (FICTITIOUS CHARACTER) p.55

BENTLEY, WILLIAM (FICTITIOUS CHARACTER) p.55

BENTON, BARBARA (FICTITIOUS CHARACTER) p.55

BENTON, BROOKE (FICTITIOUS CHARACTER) p.55

BERESFORD, TOMMY (FICTITIOUS CHARACTER) p.55

BERESFORD, TUPPENCE (FICTITIOUS CHARACTER) p.55

BERG, MORRIS, 1902-1972 p.56

BERGER, MITCH (FICTITIOUS CHARACTER) p.56

BERGERAC (FICTITIOUS CHARACTER) p.56

BERKELEY BRIGADE (FICTITIOUS CHARACTERS) p.56

BERNARD, ROLF (FICTITIOUS CHARACTER) p.56

BERNHARDT, ALAN (FICTITIOUS CHARACTER) p.56

BERNIER, ALEX (FICTITIOUS CHARACTER) p.56

BERNSTEIN, ELLIE (FICTITIOUS CHARACTER) p.56

BERT THE SHIRT (FICTITIOUS CHARACTER) p.56

BETHANY, TOM (FICTITIOUS CHARACTER) p.56

BEVERLEY SISTERS (FICTITIOUS CHARACTERS) p.56

BIDDLECOMB, ISAAC (FICTITIOUS CHARACTER) p.56

BIERCE, AMBROSE, 1842-1914 p.56

BIG MIKE (FICTITIOUS CHARACTER) p.56

BIGELOW, CARL (FICTITIOUS CHARACTER) p.56

BILBO, CHARLIE (FICTITIOUS CHARACTER) p.56

BILBY, BETTINA (FICTITIOUS CHARACTER) p.56

BILL (FICTITIOUS CHARACTER: HARRISON) p.57

BILLUPS, DARRYL (FICTITIOUS CHARACTER) p.57

BINTON, MARGARET (FICTITIOUS CHARACTER) p.57

BIRCH, JEFFERSON (FICTITIOUS CHARACTER) p.57

BIRDWOOD, VERITY (FICTITIOUS CHARACTER) p.57

BISHOP, JIM (FICTITIOUS CHARACTER) p.57

BISHOP, THOMAS (FICTITIOUS CHARACTER) p.57

BITTERSOHN, MAX (FICTITIOUS CHARACTER) p.57

BIWABAN, ANGIE (FICTITIOUS CHARACTER) p.57

BLACK, HELEN (FICTITIOUS CHARACTER) p.57

BLACK, MORRIS (FICTITIOUS CHARACTER) p.57

BLACK, THOMAS (FICTITIOUS CHARACTER) p.57

BLACK COMPANY (FICTITIOUS CHARACTERS) p.57

BLACK MASK BOYS (FICTITIOUS CHARACTERS) p.58

BLACK SABRES (FICTITIOUS CHARACTERS) p.58

BLACKBIRD SISTERS (FICTITIOUS CHARACTERS) p.58

BLACKBURN, JIMMY (FICTITIOUS CHARACTER) p.58

BLACKE, LOBO (FICTITIOUS CHARACTER) p.58

BLACKWELL, MARK (FICTITIOUS CHARACTER) p.58

BLAINE, JOHN (FICTITIOUS CHARACTER) p.58

BLAIR, JONATHON (FICTITIOUS CHARACTER) p.58

BLAIR, MIKE (FICTITIOUS CHARACTER) p.58

BLAIR, SONORA (FICTITIOUS CHARACTER) p.58

BLAISE, MODESTY (FICTITIOUS CHARACTER) p.58

BLAKE, ANITA (FICTITIOUS CHARACTER) p.58

BLAKE, CATHY (FICTITIOUS CHARACTER) p.58

BLAKE, JULIE (FICTITIOUS CHARACTER) p.58

BLAKE, LELAND (FICTITIOUS CHARACTER) p.58

BLAKE, ROSEMARY (FICTITIOUS CHARACTER) p.58

BLAKE, WILL (FICTITIOUS CHARACTER) p.58

BLAKENEY, PERCY, SIR (FICTITIOUS CHARACTER) p.59

BLALOCK, JOANNE (FICTITIOUS CHARACTER) p.59

BLANCHARD, URSULA (FICTITIOUS CHARACTER) p.59

BLANE, GEORGE (FICTITIOUS CHARACTER) p.59

BLEICHERT, BUCKY (FICTITIOUS CHARACTER) p.59

BLEVINS, HASKELL (FICTITIOUS CHARACTER) p.59

BLISS, LENNY (FICTITIOUS CHARACTER) p.59

BLISS, VICKY (FICTITIOUS CHARACTER) p.59

BLISSBERG, HARVEY (FICTITIOUS CHARACTER) p.59

BLOCK, BELLA (FICTITIOUS CHARACTER) p.59

BLOM, MARTIN (FICTITIOUS CHARACTER) p.59

BLOODWORTH, LEO (FICTITIOUS CHARACTER) p.59

BLOOM, LEOPOLD (FICTITIOUS CHARACTER) p.59

BLOOM, MOLLY (FICTITIOUS CHARACTER) p.60

BLOOMWOOD, BECKY (FICTITIOUS CHARACTER) p.60

BLUENIGHT, LINDA (FICTITIOUS CHARACTER) p.60

BLUME, MOLLY (FICTITIOUS CHARACTER) p.60

BLUMENTHAL, MARISSA (FICTITIOUS CHARACTER) p.60

BOGNAR, T. C. (FICTITIOUS CHARACTER) p.60

BOGNOR, SIMON (FICTITIOUS CHARACTER) p.60

BOLAN, MACK (FICTITIOUS CHARACTER) p.60

BOLDT, LOU (FICTITIOUS CHARACTER) p.62

BOLITAR, MYRON (FICTITIOUS CHARACTER) p.63

BOLITHO, ADAM (FICTITIOUS CHARACTER) p.63

BOLITHO, RICHARD (FICTITIOUS CHARACTER) p.63

BONAPARTE, JUDA (FICTITIOUS CHARACTER) p.63

BONAPARTE, NAPOLEON, INSPECTOR (FICTITIOUS CHARACTER) p.63

BOND, JAMES (FICTITIOUS CHARACTER) p.64

BONE, ROBERT (FICTITIOUS CHARACTER) p.65

BONESTEEL, NORA (FICTITIOUS CHARACTER) p.65

BOOKER, QUINN (FICTITIOUS CHARACTER) p.66

BOOP, BETTY (FICTITIOUS CHARACTER) p.66

BORDEN, LIZZIE, 1860-1927 p.66

BORGIA, GIOVANNI (FICTITIOUS CHARACTER) p.66

BORGIA, LUCREZIA, 1480-1519 p.66

BOSCH, HARRY (FICTITIOUS CHARACTER) p.66

BOUDREAU, PHIL (FICTITIOUS CHARACTER) p.66

BOURNE, JASON (FICTITIOUS CHARACTER) p.66

BOVARY, CHARLES (FICTITIOUS CHARACTER) p.66

BOVARY, EMMA (FICTITIOUS CHARACTER) p.67

BOWDRE, MO (FICTITIOUS CHARACTER) p.67

BOWDRIE, CHICK (FICTITIOUS CHARACTER) p.67

BOWERING, VICTORIA (FICTITIOUS CHARACTER) p.68

BOWLES, SALLY (FICTITIOUS CHARACTER) p.68

BOWMAN FAMILY (FICTITIOUS CHARACTERS) p.68

BOYD, KEMPER (FICTITIOUS CHARACTER) p.68

BOYD, ORIN (FICTITIOUS CHARACTER) p.68

BOYNTON, LEE (FICTITIOUS CHARACTER) p.68

BRACEWELL, NICHOLAS (FICTITIOUS CHARACTER) p.68

BRADDOCK, DUANE (FICTITIOUS CHARACTER) p.68

BRADDOCK, SIMON (FICTITIOUS CHARACTER) p.68

BRADFORD, BEN (FICTITIOUS CHARACTER) p.68

BRADFORD, ELIOT (FICTITIOUS CHARACTER) p.68

BRADFORD, MAGGIE (FICTITIOUS CHARACTER) p.68

BRADLEY, BEATRICE LESTRANGE (FICTITIOUS CHARACTER) p.68

BRADLEY, BO (FICTITIOUS CHARACTER) p.68

BRADLEY, HELEN (FICTITIOUS CHARACTER) p.68

BRADLEY, MARK (FICTITIOUS CHARACTER) p.68

BRADSHAW, CHARLIE (FICTITIOUS CHARACTER) p.68

BRADY, JOANNA (FICTITIOUS CHARACTER) p.69

BRADY, WIN, REVEREND (FICTITIOUS CHARACTER) p.69

BRAGG, JOSEPH (FICTITIOUS CHARACTER) p.69

BRAITHWAITE, THEODORA (FICTITIOUS CHARACTER) p.69

BRAMLETT, GROVER (FICTITIOUS CHARACTER) p.69

BRANDEN, PROFESSOR MICHAEL (FICTITIOUS CHARACTER) p.69

BRANDON, SMOKEY (FICTITIOUS CHARACTER) p.69

BRANDSTETTER, DAVE (FICTITIOUS CHARACTER) p.69

BRANDT, SARAH (FICTITIOUS CHARACTER) p.70

BRANIGAN BROTHERS (FICTITIOUS CHARACTERS) p.70

BRANNIGAN, KATE (FICTITIOUS CHARACTER) p.70

BRANNON, STUART (FICTITIOUS CHARACTER) p.70

BRANSON, JOHN LLOYD (FICTITIOUS CHARACTER) p.70

BRASS, ALEXANDER (FICTITIOUS CHARACTER) p.70

BRASS, COUNT (FICTITIOUS CHARACTER) p.70

BRAUN, CELESTE (FICTITIOUS CHARACTER) p.70

BRAY, NELL (FICTITIOUS CHARACTER) p.70

BRAZIL, NATHAN (FICTITIOUS CHARACTER) p.70

BRENNAN, TEMPERANCE (FICTITIOUS CHARACTER) p.70

BRENNEN, MICHAEL (FICTITIOUS CHARACTER) p.70

BRENNER, JACK (FICTITIOUS CHARACTER) p.71

BRENNER, LUCY TRIMBLE (FICTITIOUS CHARACTER) p.71

BRENNER, PAUL (FICTITIOUS CHARACTER) p.71

BRET, GERVASE (FICTITIOUS CHARACTER) p.71

BREWSTER, LILY (FICTITIOUS CHARACTER) p.71

BREWSTER, MEG (FICTITIOUS CHARACTER) p.71

BREWSTER, ROBERT (FICTITIOUS CHARACTER) p.71

BRICHTER, PETER (FICTITIOUS CHARACTER) p.71

BRIGANCE, JAKE (FICTITIOUS CHARACTER) p.71

BRILL, JANNA (FICTITIOUS CHARACTER) p.71

BRITTEN, ROLAND (FICTITIOUS CHARACTER) p.71

BROCK, DAVID (FICTITIOUS CHARACTER) p.71

BROCKMAN, LISA (FICTITIOUS CHARACTER) p.71

BROD, EMIL (FICTITIOUS CHARACTER) p.71

BROGAN, JERRY (FICTITIOUS CHARACTER) p.71

BROKER, PHIL (FICTITIOUS CHARACTER) p.71

BROKETAIL, BAZIL (FICTITIOUS CHARACTER) p.71

BRONTE, SAM (FICTITIOUS CHARACTER) p.71

BRONWYN (FICTITIOUS CHARACTER: MILLER) p.71

BROOKE, LOVEDAY (FICTITIOUS CHARACTER) p.71

BROOKS, DAN (FICTITIOUS CHARACTER) p.71

BROOKS, JAY (FICTITIOUS CHARACTER) p.71

BROOKS, R. J. (FICTITIOUS CHARACTER) p.71

BROOM, ANDREW (FICTITIOUS CHARACTER) p.71

BROSSARD, PIERRE (FICTITIOUS CHARACTER) p.71

BROTHER CADFAEL (FICTITIOUS CHARACTER) p.71
    see Cadfael, Brother (Fictitious Character)

BROUSSARD, ANDY (FICTITIOUS CHARACTER) p.72

BROUSSARD, ANNIE (FICTITIOUS CHARACTER) p.72

BROWN, CLINTON (FICTITIOUS CHARACTER) p.72

BROWN, FATHER (FICTITIOUS CHARACTER) p.72

BROWN, FRITZ (FICTITIOUS CHARACTER) p.72

BROWN, HERMIONE (FICTITIOUS CHARACTER) p.72

BROWN, JACKIE (FICTITIOUS CHARACTER) p.72

BROWN, MARGO (FICTITIOUS CHARACTER) p.72

BROWNE, AGNES (FICTITIOUS CHARACTER) p.72

BROWNE, CLIO (FICTITIOUS CHARACTER) p.72

BRUNETTI, GUIDO (FICTITIOUS CHARACTER) p.72

BRUNO, ADAM (FICTITIOUS CHARACTER) p.72

BUCHANAN, TOM (FICTITIOUS CHARACTER) p.72

BUCKINGHAM, DARBY (FICTITIOUS CHARACTER) p.73

BUENOROSTRO, RAFE (FICTITIOUS CHARACTER) p.73

BUGLE ANN (FICTITIOUS CHARACTER) p.73

BULMAN, GEORGE (FICTITIOUS CHARACTER) p.73

BUMPPO, NATTY (FICTITIOUS CHARACTER) p.73

BUNKOWSKI, DANIEL "CHAINGANG" (FICTITIOUS CHARACTER) p.74

BURENIN FAMILY (FICTITIOUS CHARACTERS) p.74

BURGOYNE 172 (FICTITIOUS CHARACTER) p.74

BURKE (FICTITIOUS CHARACTER: VACHSS) p.74

BURKE, CALEY (FICTITIOUS CHARACTER) p.74

BURKE, DENISE (FICTITIOUS CHARACTER) p.74

BURKE, EDDIE (FICTITIOUS CHARACTER) p.74

BURKE, TOM (FICTITIOUS CHARACTER) p.74

BURLANE, JAMES (FICTITIOUS CHARACTER) p.74

BURLINGAME, JESSIE (FICTITIOUS CHARACTER) p.75

BURNELL, MAXEY (FICTITIOUS CHARACTER) p.75

BURNS, ANTONIO (FICTITIOUS CHARACTER) p.75

BURNS, CARL (FICTITIOUS CHARACTER) p.75

BURNS, JACOB (FICTITIOUS CHARACTER) p.75

BURNS, MARTY (FICTITIOUS CHARACTER) p.75

BURTON, DENISE (FICTITIOUS CHARACTER) p.75

BURTONALL, CLAIRE, DOCTOR (FICTITIOUS CHARACTER) p.75

BUSCARSELA, FILOMENA (FICTITIOUS CHARACTER) p.75

BUSHYHEAD, MITCHELL (FICTITIOUS CHARACTER) p.75

BYBEE, BRIGHAM (FICTITIOUS CHARACTER) p.75

BYRNE, CHARLIE (FICTITIOUS CHARACTER) p.75

BYRNE, FRANCIS X. (FICTITIOUS CHARACTER) p.75

BYRON, GEORGE GORDON BYRON, BARON, 1788-1824 p.75

CABOT, TARL (FICTITIOUS CHARACTER) p.75

CABOT, WENTWORTH (FICTITIOUS CHARACTER) p.75

CADFAEL, BROTHER (FICTITIOUS CHARACTER) p.75

CADIN, INSPECTOR (FICTITIOUS CHARACTER) p.77

CADOGAN, MARIANNE (FICTITIOUS CHARACTER) p.77

CADY, MAX (FICTITIOUS CHARACTER) p.77

CAFFERY, JACK (FICTITIOUS CHARACTER) p.77

CAGE, ALLEN (FICTITIOUS CHARACTER) p.77

CAHILL, COLETTE (FICTITIOUS CHARACTER) p.77

CAIN, JENNY (FICTITIOUS CHARACTER) p.77

CAINE, JOHN (FICTITIOUS CHARACTER) p.77

CALAVICCI, AL (FICTITIOUS CHARACTER) p.77

CALDER, DEBORAH (FICTITIOUS CHARACTER) p.77

CALDER, KEITH (FICTITIOUS CHARACTER) p.77

CALDER FAMILY (FICTITIOUS CHARACTERS) p.78

CALHOUN, MACKENZIE (FICTITIOUS CHARACTER) p.78

CALHOUN, VINCE (FICTITIOUS CHARACTER) p.78

CALIBAN, CAT (FICTITIOUS CHARACTER) p.78

CALL, WOODROW (FICTITIOUS CHARACTER) p.78

CALLAHAN, BROCK (FICTITIOUS CHARACTER) p.78

CALLAHAN, JAMES (FICTITIOUS CHARACTER) p.78

CALLAHAN, MIKE (FICTITIOUS CHARACTER) p.78

CALLAHAN, ROSE, SISTER (FICTITIOUS CHARACTER) p.78

CALLAHAN, SALLY (FICTITIOUS CHARACTER) p.78

CALLAIS, BERTRAND (FICTITIOUS CHARACTER) p.78

CALLOW, JOHN (FICTITIOUS CHARACTER) p.78

CALRISSIAN, LANDO (FICTITIOUS CHARACTER) p.78

CAMACHO, ELLEN (FICTITIOUS CHARACTER) p.79

CAMBER OF CULDI (FICTITIOUS CHARACTER) p.79

CAMDEN, CLAIRE (FICTITIOUS CHARACTER) p.79

CAMDEN, SHELBY (FICTITIOUS CHARACTER) p.79

CAMERON, BREN (FICTITIOUS CHARACTER) p.79

CAMERON, DONALD (FICTITIOUS CHARACTER) p.79

CAMERON, LUKE (FICTITIOUS CHARACTER) p.79

CAMERON, TROY (FICTITIOUS CHARACTER) p.79

CAMPBELL, CHUCK (FICTITIOUS CHARACTER) p.79

CAMPBELL, JOE (FICTITIOUS CHARACTER) p.79

CAMPBELL, LETTY (FICTITIOUS CHARACTER) p.79

CAMPBELL, LIAM (FICTITIOUS CHARACTER) p.79

CAMPBELL, WAYNE (FICTITIOUS CHARACTER) p.80

CAMPION, ALBERT (FICTITIOUS CHARACTER) p.80

CANCHES, ALEJANDRO (FICTITIOUS CHARACTER) p.80

CANDIDI, BEN (FICTITIOUS CHARACTER) p.80

CANDIOTTI, JANE (FICTITIOUS CHARACTER) p.80

CANFIELD, CAROLINE (FICTITIOUS CHARACTER) p.80

CARD, ROBERT (FICTITIOUS CHARACTER) p.80

CARDENAS, VICTOR (FICTITIOUS CHARACTER) p.80

CARDIGAN (FICTITIOUS CHARACTER: NEBEL) p.80

CARDIGAN, JAKE (FICTITIOUS CHARACTER) p.80

CARDINAL, CAESAR (FICTITIOUS CHARACTER) p.81

CARDOZO, VINCE (FICTITIOUS CHARACTER) p.81

CARELLA, STEVE (FICTITIOUS CHARACTER) p.81

CAREY, NEAL (FICTITIOUS CHARACTER) p.82

CARL, VICTOR (FICTITIOUS CHARACTER) p.82

CARLIN, CARRIE (FICTITIOUS CHARACTER) p.82

CARLOS, THE JACKAL p.82

CARLUCCI, RUGGIERO (FICTITIOUS CHARACTER) p.82

CARLYLE, CARLOTTA (FICTITIOUS CHARACTER) p.83

CARLYLE, KERRY (FICTITIOUS CHARACTER) p.83

CARODINE, CHELSEA (FICTITIOUS CHARACTER) p.83

CAROLINA, MICHAEL (FICTITIOUS CHARACTER) p.83

CARPENTER, ANDY (FICTITIOUS CHARACTER) p.83

CARPENTER, SCOTT (FICTITIOUS CHARACTER) p.83

CARPO, MICHAEL (FICTITIOUS CHARACTER) p.83

CARR, MIKE (FICTITIOUS CHARACTER) p.83

CARR, ROSIE (FICTITIOUS CHARACTER) p.83

CARRADOS, MAX (FICTITIOUS CHARACTER) p.83

CARRICK, JAMES, INSPECTOR (FICTITIOUS CHARACTER) p.83

CARROT (FICTITIOUS CHARACTER: PRATCHETT) p.83

CARSON, JUD (FICTITIOUS CHARACTER) p.83

CARSTAIRS, CHAD (FICTITIOUS CHARACTER) p.83

CARTER, ELWIN (FICTITIOUS CHARACTER) p.83

CARTER, JOHN (FICTITIOUS CHARACTER) p.83

CARTER, TERENCE (FICTITIOUS CHARACTER) p.84

CARTON, LARRY (FICTITIOUS CHARACTER) p.84

CARTWRIGHT, ARNOLD (FICTITIOUS CHARACTER) p.84

CARTWRIGHT, LORD (FICTITIOUS CHARACTER) p.84

CARTWRIGHT FAMILY (FICTITIOUS CHARACTERS) p.84

CARVALHO, PEPE (FICTITIOUS CHARACTER) p.84

CARVER, DAVID (FICTITIOUS CHARACTER) p.84

CARVER, FRANK (FICTITIOUS CHARACTER) p.84

CARVER, FRED (FICTITIOUS CHARACTER) p.84

CARVER, TOMMY (FICTITIOUS CHARACTER) p.84

CASE, CHARLEY (FICTITIOUS CHARACTER) p.84

CASELLA, TONY (FICTITIOUS CHARACTER) p.84

CASEY, SAMANTHA (FICTITIOUS CHARACTER) p.84

CASS, COLIN (FICTITIOUS CHARACTER) p.84

CASSIDY, FAITH (FICTITIOUS CHARACTER) p.84

CASSIDY, HOPALONG (FICTITIOUS CHARACTER) p.84

CASSON, JEAN (FICTITIOUS CHARACTER) p.85

CASTANG, HENRI (FICTITIOUS CHARACTER) p.85

CASTEEL FAMILY (FICTITIOUS CHARACTERS) p.85

CATALONI, STELLA (FICTITIOUS CHARACTER) p.85

CATCHPOLE, HILARY (FICTITIOUS CHARACTER) p.85

CATES, MOLLY (FICTITIOUS CHARACTER) p.85

CATLETT, ANDY (FICTITIOUS CHARACTER) p.85

CATTO, ROB (FICTITIOUS CHARACTER) p.85

CATWOMAN (FICTITIOUS CHARACTER) p.85

CAULDER, RY (FICTITIOUS CHARACTER) p.85

CAULDHAME, FRANK (FICTITIOUS CHARACTER) p.85

CAULFIELD, AM (FICTITIOUS CHARACTER) p.85

CAULFIELD, HOLDEN (FICTITIOUS CHARACTER) p.85

CAUTHORNE, EDWARD (FICTITIOUS CHARACTER) p.86

CAVANAUGH, KATE (FICTITIOUS CHARACTER) p.86

CAVANAUGH, TRACY (FICTITIOUS CHARACTER) p.86

CECILE, SISTER (FICTITIOUS CHARACTER) p.86

CELLARS, COLIN (FICTITIOUS CHARACTER) p.86

CELLINI, EMMANUEL (FICTITIOUS CHARACTER) p.86

CELLUCI, MIKE (FICTITIOUS CHARACTER) p.86

CERVANTES, CHICO (FICTITIOUS CHARACTER) p.86

CHADWICK, GEOFFREY (FICTITIOUS CHARACTER) p.86

CHADWICK SISTERS (FICTITIOUS CHARACTERS) p.86

CHAINEY, MARTHA (FICTITIOUS CHARACTER) p.86

CHAKOTAY (FICTITIOUS CHARACTER) p.86

CHALLENGER, PROFESSOR (FICTITIOUS CHARACTER) p.86

CHAMBERLAIN, JOSHUA LAWRENCE, 1828-1914 p.86

CHAMBERLAIN, LINDSAY (FICTITIOUS CHARACTER) p.86

CHAMBRUN, PIERRE (FICTITIOUS CHARACTER) p.86

CHAN, CHARLIE (FICTITIOUS CHARACTER) p.87

CHAN, DAVID (FICTITIOUS CHARACTER) p.87

CHANCEL, NORA (FICTITIOUS CHARACTER) p.87

CHANDLER, CHUCK (FICTITIOUS CHARACTER) p.87

CHANDLER, JAY (FICTITIOUS CHARACTER) p.87

CHANDLER, LAUREL (FICTITIOUS CHARACTER) p.87

CHANDLER, SHAW (FICTITIOUS CHARACTER) p.87

CHANDLER, SUSAN (FICTITIOUS CHARACTER) p.87

CHANG, MAVRA (FICTITIOUS CHARACTER) p.87

CHANTRY FAMILY (FICTITIOUS CHARACTERS) p.87

CHAPMAN, HARRY (FICTITIOUS CHARACTER) p.87

CHARLES, NICK (FICTITIOUS CHARACTER) p.87

CHARLES, NORA (FICTITIOUS CHARACTER) p.87

CHARTERS, EMILY (FICTITIOUS CHARACTER) p.87

CHASE, ELIZABETH (FICTITIOUS CHARACTER) p.87

CHASE, LINDSAY (FICTITIOUS CHARACTER) p.87

CHASE, NIKKI (FICTITIOUS CHARACTER) p.87

CHASE, SIMON (FICTITIOUS CHARACTER) p.87

CHASTAIN, LAURA (FICTITIOUS CHARACTER) p.87

CHATTO, TOM (FICTITIOUS CHARACTER) p.87

CHAUCER, GEOFFREY, D. 1400 p.87

CHEE, JIM (FICTITIOUS CHARACTER) p.87

CHEKOV, PAVEL (FICTITIOUS CHARACTER) p.88

CHEYSULI (FICTITIOUS CHARACTERS) p.88

CHIA, PAO-YU (FICTITIOUS CHARACTER) p.88

CHILDS, SUNNY (FICTITIOUS CHARACTER) p.88

CHIN, LYDIA (FICTITIOUS CHARACTER) p.88

CHIRKE, NICHOLAS (FICTITIOUS CHARACTER) p.88

CHISHOLM, MARGARET (FICTITIOUS CHARACTER) p.89

CHIUN (FICTITIOUS CHARACTER) p.89

CHIZZIT, EMMA (FICTITIOUS CHARACTER) p.90

CHRESTOMANCI, THE MAGICIAN (FICTITIOUS CHARACTER) p.90

CHRISTENSEN, JIM (FICTITIOUS CHARACTER) p.90

CHRISTOPHER, PAUL (FICTITIOUS CHARACTER) p.90

CIAMPI, MARLENE (FICTITIOUS CHARACTER) p.90

CIMORENE (FICTITIOUS CHARACTER) p.90

CINQ-MARS, EMILE (FICTITIOUS CHARACTER) p.90

CLAH, ELLA (FICTITIOUS CHARACTER) p.90

CLAIBORNE, ADAM (FICTITIOUS CHARACTER) p.90

CLAIBORNE, CLAIRE (FICTITIOUS CHARACTER) p.90

CLAIBORNE, DAN (FICTITIOUS CHARACTER) p.90

CLAIBORNE, DOLORES (FICTITIOUS CHARACTER) p.90

CLANCY, JACK (FICTITIOUS CHARACTER) p.91

CLARK, CAYCE (FICTITIOUS CHARACTER) p.91

CLARK, DESAIX (FICTITIOUS CHARACTER) p.91

CLARK, JOHN (FICTITIOUS CHARACTER) p.91

CLARK, MEGAN (FICTITIOUS CHARACTER) p.91

CLAY, MARCUS (FICTITIOUS CHARACTER) p.91

CLAYBORNE FAMILY (FICTITIOUS CHARACTERS) p.91

CLAYTON, JEFFREY (FICTITIOUS CHARACTER) p.91

CLEEVER, DENISE (FICTITIOUS CHARACTER) p.91

CLEMENS, ATTA OLIVIA (FICTITIOUS CHARACTER) p.91

CLEMENT, JULES (FICTITIOUS CHARACTER) p.91

CLEREMONT, LENORE (FICTITIOUS CHARACTER) p.91

CLEVELAND, DAVID (FICTITIOUS CHARACTER) p.91

CLEY, PHYSIOGNOMIST (FICTITIOUS CHARACTER) p.91

CLIVELY, MIRINDA (FICTITIOUS CHARACTER) p.91

CLUE, NANCY (FICTITIOUS CHARACTER) p.91

COAKLEY, DANA (FICTITIOUS CHARACTER) p.91

COBB, MATT (FICTITIOUS CHARACTER) p.91

COCHRAN, BULL (FICTITIOUS CHARACTER) p.92

COCHRAN, PETER (FICTITIOUS CHARACTER) p.92

COCKRILL, INSPECTOR (FICTITIOUS CHARACTER) p.92

CODY (FICTITIOUS CHARACTER: THOMAS) p.92

COFFEY, JILL (FICTITIOUS CHARACTER) p.92

COFFEY, JOHN (FICTITIOUS CHARACTER) p.92

COFFIN ED JOHNSON (FICTITIOUS CHARACTER) p.92
    see Johnson, Coffin Ed (Fictitious Character)

COFFIN, JOHN (FICTITIOUS CHARACTER) p.92

COHEN, ARTIE (FICTITIOUS CHARACTER) p.92

COHEN, AVRAM (FICTITIOUS CHARACTER) p.92

COHEN, DAVID (FICTITIOUS CHARACTER) p.92

COHEN, MIDGE (FICTITIOUS CHARACTER) p.92

COLDWATER, LAURIE (FICTITIOUS CHARACTER) p.92

COLE, BETH (FICTITIOUS CHARACTER) p.92

COLE, ELVIS (FICTITIOUS CHARACTER) p.92

COLE, HARPER (FICTITIOUS CHARACTER) p.93

COLE, LARRY (FICTITIOUS CHARACTER) p.93

COLE, LEWIS (FICTITIOUS CHARACTER) p.93

COLE, REAGAN (FICTITIOUS CHARACTER) p.93

COLE FAMILY (FICTITIOUS CHARACTERS) p.93

COLEMAN FAMILY (FICTITIOUS CHARACTERS) p.93

COLENE (FICTITIOUS CHARACTER: ANTHONY) p.93

COLFAX, CYRUS CHANDLER (FICTITIOUS CHARACTER) p.93

COLLINS, HAP (FICTITIOUS CHARACTER) p.93

COLLINS, HENRIETTA O'DWYER (FICTITIOUS CHARACTER) p.93
    see Henrie O (Fictitious Character)

COLORADO, KAT (FICTITIOUS CHARACTER) p.93

COLSON, JESSE JAMES (FICTITIOUS CHARACTER) p.93

COLT, CHRIS (FICTITIOUS CHARACTER) p.93

COLTRANE, MITCH (FICTITIOUS CHARACTER) p.93

COLTRANE FAMILY (FICTITIOUS CHARACTERS) p.94

COLUMBO, LIEUTENANT (FICTITIOUS CHARACTER) p.94

COLYER, ROSS (FICTITIOUS CHARACTER) p.94

COMPSON, CADDY (FICTITIOUS CHARACTER) p.94

CONAN (FICTITIOUS CHARACTER) p.94

CONE, TIMOTHY (FICTITIOUS CHARACTER) p.95

CONLAN, KATE (FICTITIOUS CHARACTER) p.95

CONLEY, PATRICIA (FICTITIOUS CHARACTER) p.95

CONNELL, DAN (FICTITIOUS CHARACTER) p.95

CONNOR, GAIL (FICTITIOUS CHARACTER) p.95

CONNOR, LILY (FICTITIOUS CHARACTER) p.95

CONNORS, LIZ (FICTITIOUS CHARACTER) p.95

CONRAD, CLAIRE (FICTITIOUS CHARACTER) p.95

CONSTANTINO, TED (FICTITIOUS CHARACTER) p.95

CONTE, GERRY (FICTITIOUS CHARACTER) p.95

CONTINENTAL OP (FICTITIOUS CHARACTER) p.95

COOK, JEREMY (FICTITIOUS CHARACTER) p.95

COOK, NANCY (FICTITIOUS CHARACTER) p.95

COOKE, CAROLINE (FICTITIOUS CHARACTER) p.95

COOKE, NICHOLAS (FICTITIOUS CHARACTER) p.95

COOPER, ALEXANDRA (FICTITIOUS CHARACTER) p.95

COOPER, IRIS (FICTITIOUS CHARACTER) p.95

COOPER, JOHN (FICTITIOUS CHARACTER) p.95

COOPER, MATT (FICTITIOUS CHARACTER) p.95

COOPERMAN, BENNY (FICTITIOUS CHARACTER) p.95

COPP, JOSEPH (FICTITIOUS CHARACTER) p.96

CORAN, JESSICA (FICTITIOUS CHARACTER) p.96

CORBETT, HARRY (FICTITIOUS CHARACTER) p.96

CORBETT, HUGH (FICTITIOUS CHARACTER) p.96

CORBIE, TOM (FICTITIOUS CHARACTER) p.96

List of Subject Headings - Fiction

COREY, JOHN (FICTITIOUS CHARACTER) p.96
COREY, NICK (FICTITIOUS CHARACTER) p.96
COREY, PATRICK (FICTITIOUS CHARACTER) p.96
CORNELIUS, JERRY (FICTITIOUS CHARACTER) p.96
CORNISH, FRANCIS (FICTITIOUS CHARACTER) p.96
CORUM (FICTITIOUS CHARACTER: MOORCOCK) p.96
CORWIN (FICTITIOUS CHARACTER: ZELAZNY) p.96
COSGROVE, MAE-MAE (FICTITIOUS CHARACTER) p.97
COSINI, ZENO (FICTITIOUS CHARACTER) p.97
COSMO, JASON (FICTITIOUS CHARACTER) p.97
COTTER, KATHLEEN (FICTITIOUS CHARACTER) p.97
COTTER, RALPH (FICTITIOUS CHARACTER) p.97
COTTON, JOHN (FICTITIOUS CHARACTER) p.97
COULTER, JASON (FICTITIOUS CHARACTER) p.97
COURTENEY FAMILY (FICTITIOUS CHARACTERS) p.97
COVENANT, THOMAS (FICTITIOUS CHARACTER) p.97
COYLE, EDDIE (FICTITIOUS CHARACTER) p.97
COYNE, BRADY (FICTITIOUS CHARACTER) p.97
COYNE, DERMOT MICHAEL (FICTITIOUS CHARACTER) p.98
CRABTREE, TEMPE (FICTITIOUS CHARACTER) p.98
CRAIG, MELISSA (FICTITIOUS CHARACTER) p.98
CRAMER, INSPECTOR (FICTITIOUS CHARACTER) p.98
CRANE, RUBY (FICTITIOUS CHARACTER) p.98
CRANMER, TIM (FICTITIOUS CHARACTER) p.98
CRANSTON, SHERRY (FICTITIOUS CHARACTER) p.98
CRAWFORD, FRANCIS (FICTITIOUS CHARACTER) p.98
CRAY, ALI (FICTITIOUS CHARACTER) p.98
CRAY, THE SORCERER (FICTITIOUS CHARACTER) p.98
CREASE, ELLEN (FICTITIOUS CHARACTER) p.98
CREED, LOUIS (FICTITIOUS CHARACTER) p.98
CREEKMORE, BILLY (FICTITIOUS CHARACTER) p.98
CREEVEY, JOHN (FICTITIOUS CHARACTER) p.98
CRIBB, SERGEANT (FICTITIOUS CHARACTER) p.98
CRICHTON, TESSA (FICTITIOUS CHARACTER) p.98
CRIMSON SHADOW (FICTITIOUS CHARACTER) p.99
CRISP, WINSTON (FICTITIOUS CHARACTER) p.99
CROAKER, FEY (FICTITIOUS CHARACTER) p.99
CROFT, FREDDIE (FICTITIOUS CHARACTER) p.99
CROFT, JOSHUA (FICTITIOUS CHARACTER) p.99
CROFT, MIKE (FICTITIOUS CHARACTER) p.99
CROOK, ARTHUR (FICTITIOUS CHARACTER) p.99
CROSS, ALEX (FICTITIOUS CHARACTER) p.99
CROSS, VICTORIA (FICTITIOUS CHARACTER) p.99
CROW, JOE (FICTITIOUS CHARACTER) p.99
CROW, TITUS (FICTITIOUS CHARACTER) p.99
CROWE, JANIE (FICTITIOUS CHARACTER) p.100
CROWELL, FAITH (FICTITIOUS CHARACTER) p.100
CROWNE, RACHEL (FICTITIOUS CHARACTER) p.100
CRUSHER, BEVERLY (FICTITIOUS CHARACTER) p.100
CRUSHER, WESLEY (FICTITIOUS CHARACTER) p.100

CRUSOE, EDWINA (FICTITIOUS CHARACTER) p.100
CRUSOE, ROBINSON (FICTITIOUS CHARACTER) p.100
CSEJTHE, CHRISTOPHER (FICTITIOUS CHARACTER) p.100
CTHULHU (FICTITIOUS CHARACTER) p.100
CUDDY, JOHN (FICTITIOUS CHARACTER) p.101
CULLEN, JOE (FICTITIOUS CHARACTER) p.101
CULLINANE, JASON (FICTITIOUS CHARACTER) p.101
CULLINANE, KARL (FICTITIOUS CHARACTER) p.101
CULVER, HARRY (FICTITIOUS CHARACTER) p.101
CUMMINGS, KRISS (FICTITIOUS CHARACTER) p.101
CUNEEN, MATT (FICTITIOUS CHARACTER) p.101
CUNNINGHAM, JOHN (FICTITIOUS CHARACTER) p.101
CURRAN, GUY (FICTITIOUS CHARACTER) p.101
CURTIS, JOE (FICTITIOUS CHARACTER) p.101
CUTLER FAMILY (FICTITIOUS CHARACTERS) p.101
CYNSTER BROTHERS (FICTITIOUS CHARACTERS) p.101
DAHLQUIST, SERENDIPITY (FICTITIOUS CHARACTER) p.101
DAI, DAVID (FICTITIOUS CHARACTER) p.101
DAIMBERT (FICTITIOUS CHARACTER) p.101
DAIN, EDDIE (FICTITIOUS CHARACTER) p.101
DAKER, JOHN (FICTITIOUS CHARACTER) p.101
DAKOTA, BUSH (FICTITIOUS CHARACTER) p.101
DALGLIESH, ADAM (FICTITIOUS CHARACTER) p.102
DALLAS, EVE (FICTITIOUS CHARACTER) p.102
DALRYMPLE, DAISY (FICTITIOUS CHARACTER) p.102
DALTON, KEVIN (FICTITIOUS CHARACTER) p.103
DALTON, PATRICK (FICTITIOUS CHARACTER) p.103
DALZIEL, ANDREW (FICTITIOUS CHARACTER) p.103
DAMASCO, GLORIA (FICTITIOUS CHARACTER) p.103
DAMEN, BILL (FICTITIOUS CHARACTER) p.103
DAMIANO (FICTITIOUS CHARACTER) p.103
DANDY, JAMES P. (FICTITIOUS CHARACTER) p.103
DANESON, MAUDE (FICTITIOUS CHARACTER) p.103
DANFORTH, ABIGAIL (FICTITIOUS CHARACTER) p.103
DANGER, MIKE (FICTITIOUS CHARACTER) p.103
DANIEL, VICTOR (FICTITIOUS CHARACTER) p.103
DANIEL KEARNY ASSOCIATES (FICTITIOUS CHARACTERS) p.103
DANIELS, AVERY (FICTITIOUS CHARACTER) p.103
DANIELS, CHARMIAN (FICTITIOUS CHARACTER) p.103
DANILOV, DIMITRI (FICTITIOUS CHARACTER) p.104
DANN, PEACHES (FICTITIOUS CHARACTER) p.104
DANTAN, ALPHONSE (FICTITIOUS CHARACTER) p.104
DANTE, JOE (FICTITIOUS CHARACTER) p.104
DARCY, FITZWILLIAM (FICTITIOUS CHARACTER) p.104
DARCY, LORD (FICTITIOUS CHARACTER) p.105
DARCY, MEG (FICTITIOUS CHARACTER) p.105
DARCY, TESS (FICTITIOUS CHARACTER) p.105
DARE, SUSAN (FICTITIOUS CHARACTER) p.105

DARIAN (FICTITIOUS CHARACTER: LACKEY) p.105
DARIUS (FICTITIOUS CHARACTER: ANTHONY) p.105
DARK, NESTOR (FICTITIOUS CHARACTER) p.105
DARK, RUBY (FICTITIOUS CHARACTER) p.105
DARKMAN (FICTITIOUS CHARACTER) p.105
DARLING, ANNIE LAURANCE (FICTITIOUS CHARACTER) p.105
DARLING, MAX (FICTITIOUS CHARACTER) p.105
DARLING, WHIP (FICTITIOUS CHARACTER) p.106
DARNELL, IKE (FICTITIOUS CHARACTER) p.106
DARNELL, JOHN (FICTITIOUS CHARACTER) p.106
DARTELLI, JOE (FICTITIOUS CHARACTER) p.106
DASH (FICTITIOUS CHARACTER) p.106
DA SILVA, JANE (FICTITIOUS CHARACTER) p.106
DATA (FICTITIOUS CHARACTER) p.106
DAVE (FICTITIOUS CHARACTER: YAFFE) p.106
DAVE, THE MONKEY MAN (FICTITIOUS CHARACTER) p.106
    see Enamorado, Dave (Fictitious Character)
DAVENPORT, DEACON (FICTITIOUS CHARACTER) p.106
DAVENPORT, LUCAS (FICTITIOUS CHARACTER) p.106
DAWES, ATHENA (FICTITIOUS CHARACTER) p.107
DAX, EZRI (FICTITIOUS CHARACTER) p.107
DAX, JADZIA (FICTITIOUS CHARACTER) p.107
DAY, JULIAN FAMILY (FICTITIOUS CHARACTERS) p.107
DEAL, JOHN (FICTITIOUS CHARACTER) p.107
DEAN, GEVAN (FICTITIOUS CHARACTER) p.107
DEAN, JEFFREY (FICTITIOUS CHARACTER) p.107
DEAN, SAM (FICTITIOUS CHARACTER) p.107
DEANE, SARAH (FICTITIOUS CHARACTER) p.107
DEATH (FICTITIOUS CHARACTER: PRATCHETT) p.107
DEATHSTALKER, OWEN (FICTITIOUS CHARACTER) p.108
DECKER, HUGH (FICTITIOUS CHARACTER) p.108
DECKER, PETER (FICTITIOUS CHARACTER) p.108
DECKER, RICK (FICTITIOUS CHARACTER) p.108
DECKER, STEVE (FICTITIOUS CHARACTER) p.108
DE CLERQ, ROBERT (FICTITIOUS CHARACTER) p.108
DEDALUS, STEPHEN (FICTITIOUS CHARACTER) p.108
DEE JEN-DJIEH (FICTITIOUS CHARACTER) p.109
DEEMER, ARTIE (FICTITIOUS CHARACTER) p.109
DEENE, CAROLUS (FICTITIOUS CHARACTER) p.109
DE FLEURY, NICHOLAS (FICTITIOUS CHARACTER) p.109
DEFOE, CHASE (FICTITIOUS CHARACTER) p.109
DE GIER, RINUS (FICTITIOUS CHARACTER) p.109
DEKOK, INSPECTOR (FICTITIOUS CHARACTER) p.110
DELACOUR, STEPHANIE (FICTITIOUS CHARACTER) p.110
DELACROIX, MARA (FICTITIOUS CHARACTER) p.110
DELAFIELD, KATE (FICTITIOUS CHARACTER) p.110
DELANCY, RICHARD (FICTITIOUS CHARACTER) p.110
DELANEY, CAT (FICTITIOUS CHARACTER) p.110
DELANEY, EDWARD X. (FICTITIOUS CHARACTER) p.110
DELANEY, PATRICIA (FICTITIOUS CHARACTER) p.110

DELANY, RYKER (FICTITIOUS CHARACTER) p.110

DELAROSA, JOHN (FICTITIOUS CHARACTER) p.110

DELAWARE, ALEX (FICTITIOUS CHARACTER) p.110

DELCHARD, RALPH (FICTITIOUS CHARACTER) p.111

DELEEUW, KIT (FICTITIOUS CHARACTER) p.111

DELL'APPA, HENRY (FICTITIOUS CHARACTER) p.111

DELMARRE, GLADIA (FICTITIOUS CHARACTER) p.111

DELVECCHIO, NICK (FICTITIOUS CHARACTER) p.111

DEMARKIAN, GREGOR (FICTITIOUS CHARACTER) p.111

DEMBO, MAX (FICTITIOUS CHARACTER) p.111

DE MORRISSEY, DAVID (FICTITIOUS CHARACTER) p.111

DENNY, JAMES (FICTITIOUS CHARACTER) p.111
    see Risk, Doctor (Fictitious Character)

DENSON, JOHN (FICTITIOUS CHARACTER) p.111

DENT, ARTHUR (FICTITIOUS CHARACTER) p.111

DENTON, HARRY JAMES (FICTITIOUS CHARACTER) p.112

DE QUINCY, JUSTIN (FICTITIOUS CHARACTER) p.112

DE RATOUR, NORMAN A. (FICTITIOUS CHARACTER) p.112

DEREHAM, JONAH (FICTITIOUS CHARACTER) p.112

DERRY, JONATHAN (FICTITIOUS CHARACTER) p.112

DESALES, FRANK (FICTITIOUS CHARACTER) p.112

DESMOND, TIM (FICTITIOUS CHARACTER) p.112

DE VALIFIERNO, MARQUIS (FICTITIOUS CHARACTER) p.112

DEVEREAUX (FICTITIOUS CHARACTER: GRANGER) p.112

DEVEREAUX, JEFFREY (FICTITIOUS CHARACTER) p.112

DEVITO, ANGIE (FICTITIOUS CHARACTER) p.112

DEVLIN, BROOKE (FICTITIOUS CHARACTER) p.112

DEVLIN, HARRY (FICTITIOUS CHARACTER) p.112

DEVLIN, JACK (FICTITIOUS CHARACTER) p.112

DEVLIN, LIAM (FICTITIOUS CHARACTER) p.112

DEVLIN, MATT (FICTITIOUS CHARACTER) p.113

DEVLIN, MIKE (FICTITIOUS CHARACTER) p.113

DEVLIN, PAUL (FICTITIOUS CHARACTER) p.113

DEVONSHIRE, BETSY (FICTITIOUS CHARACTER) p.113

DEVORE, BURKE (FICTITIOUS CHARACTER) p.113

DEWITT, MOLLY (FICTITIOUS CHARACTER) p.113

DIAMOND, PETER (FICTITIOUS CHARACTER) p.113

DIAMOND, VENUS (FICTITIOUS CHARACTER) p.113

DICHRISTO, NEIL (FICTITIOUS CHARACTER) p.113

DI CILIA, KAREN (FICTITIOUS CHARACTER) p.113

DICKENS, CHARLES, 1812-1870 p.113

DIDIER, AUGUSTE (FICTITIOUS CHARACTER) p.113

DIGRIZ, JAMES BOLIVAR (FICTITIOUS CHARACTER) p.113

DILBERT (FICTITIOUS CHARACTER) p.113

DILGER, JACK (FICTITIOUS CHARACTER) p.114

DILLON, JAMES (FICTITIOUS CHARACTER) p.114

DILLON, RONNY (FICTITIOUS CHARACTER) p.114

DILLON, ROY (FICTITIOUS CHARACTER) p.114

DILLON, SEAN (FICTITIOUS CHARACTER) p.114

DILLWORTH, POPPY (FICTITIOUS CHARACTER) p.114

DILVISH (FICTITIOUS CHARACTER) p.114

DIMAGGIO, TONY (FICTITIOUS CHARACTER) p.114

DIMARCO, JEFF (FICTITIOUS CHARACTER) p.114

DIMITY, AUNT (FICTITIOUS CHARACTER) p.114

DINUNZIO, MARY (FICTITIOUS CHARACTER) p.114

DION (EMBER DION MAMARIN) (FICTITIOUS CHARACTER) p.114

DI PALMA, LAURA (FICTITIOUS CHARACTER) p.114

DISBRO, GIL (FICTITIOUS CHARACTER) p.114

DI STEFANO, FLAVIA (FICTITIOUS CHARACTER) p.114

DOBIE, JOHN (FICTITIOUS CHARACTER) p.115

DOCTOR WHO (FICTITIOUS CHARACTER) p.115

DODGE, HAROLD (FICTITIOUS CHARACTER) p.115

DODGE, LARK (FICTITIOUS CHARACTER) p.115

DOLAN, ABBY (FICTITIOUS CHARACTER) p.115

DOLAN, TRIXIE (FICTITIOUS CHARACTER) p.116

DOLLANGER FAMILY (FICTITIOUS CHARACTERS) p.116

DON QUIXOTE (FICTITIOUS CHARACTER) p.116

DONAHOE, NEAL (FICTITIOUS CHARACTER) p.117

DONAHOO, TOMMY (FICTITIOUS CHARACTER) p.117

DONOVAN, BILL (FICTITIOUS CHARACTER: JAHN) p.117

DONOVAN, BRIGID (FICTITIOUS CHARACTER) p.117

DONOVAN, CAL (FICTITIOUS CHARACTER) p.117

DONOVAN, VICTORIA (FICTITIOUS CHARACTER) p.117

DONOVAN, WILD BILL (FICTITIOUS CHARACTER: GRIFFIN) p.117

DONOVAN FAMILY (FICTITIOUS CHARACTERS) p.117

DOOLITTLE, DELILAH (FICTITIOUS CHARACTER) p.117

DOONE, RONICKY (FICTITIOUS CHARACTER) p.117

DOONESBURY, MIKE (FICTITIOUS CHARACTER) p.118

DORSEY, CARROLL (FICTITIOUS CHARACTER) p.118

DORTMUNDER, JOHN (FICTITIOUS CHARACTER) p.118

DOUGAL, WILLIAM (FICTITIOUS CHARACTER) p.118

DOUGLAS, ANDREW (FICTITIOUS CHARACTER) p.118

DOUGLAS, RAY (FICTITIOUS CHARACTER) p.118

DOVER, WILFRED (FICTITIOUS CHARACTER) p.118

DOWLING, FATHER (FICTITIOUS CHARACTER) p.118

DOWLING, VINCE (FICTITIOUS CHARACTER) p.119

DOYLE, ABBY (FICTITIOUS CHARACTER) p.119

DOYLE, ARTHUR CONAN, SIR, 1859-1930 p.119

DOYLE, TERRY (FICTITIOUS CHARACTER) p.119

DOYLE, TRAVIS (FICTITIOUS CHARACTER) p.119

DRACONIAN, HOB (FICTITIOUS CHARACTER) p.119

DRACUL FAMILY (FICTITIOUS CHARACTERS) p.119

DRACULA, COUNT (FICTITIOUS CHARACTER) p.119

DRAKE, CADENCE (FICTITIOUS CHARACTER) p.120

DRAKE, COTTON (FICTITIOUS CHARACTER) p.120

DRAKE, JESSIE (FICTITIOUS CHARACTER) p.120

DREDD, JUDGE (FICTITIOUS CHARACTER) p.120

DREW, RANDALL (FICTITIOUS CHARACTER) p.120

DRINKWATER, NATHANIEL (FICTITIOUS CHARACTER) p.120

DRISCOLL, KATHERINE (FICTITIOUS CHARACTER) p.120

DRISKILL, BEN (FICTITIOUS CHARACTER) p.120

DRIZZT DO'URDEN (FICTITIOUS CHARACTER) p.120

DROVER, JIMMY (FICTITIOUS CHARACTER) p.121

DUBOIS, AIMEE (FICTITIOUS CHARACTER) p.121

DUBONNET, TUBBY (FICTITIOUS CHARACTER) p.121

DUCKWORTH, MORRIS (FICTITIOUS CHARACTER) p.121

DUFF, MACDOUGAL (FICTITIOUS CHARACTER) p.121

DUGAN (FICTITIOUS CHARACTER) p.121

DUGAN, KIRSTEN (FICTITIOUS CHARACTER) p.121

DUKAT, GUL (FICTITIOUS CHARACTER) p.121

DULCIE (FICTITIOUS CHARACTER: MURPHY) p.121

DULCINEA (FICTITIOUS CHARACTER) p.121

DULUTH, PETER (FICTITIOUS CHARACTER) p.121

DUNCAN, EVE (FICTITIOUS CHARACTER) p.121

DUNCAN, JENNIFER (FICTITIOUS CHARACTER) p.121

DUNCAN, PIERCE (FICTITIOUS CHARACTER) p.121

DUNLOP, LUKE (FICTITIOUS CHARACTER) p.121

DUNN, EMERSON (FICTITIOUS CHARACTER) p.121

DUNN, MICAH (FICTITIOUS CHARACTER) p.121

DUPIN, AUGUSTE (FICTITIOUS CHARACTER) p.121

DU PRE, GABRIEL (FICTITIOUS CHARACTER) p.121

DUPREY, RAE (FICTITIOUS CHARACTER) p.121

DURANT, QUINCY (FICTITIOUS CHARACTER) p.121

DURELL, SAM (FICTITIOUS CHARACTER) p.122

DURSTON, BRIAN (FICTITIOUS CHARACTER) p.122

DUVAKIN, IVAN (FICTITIOUS CHARACTER) p.122

DUVALL, CHENEY (FICTITIOUS CHARACTER) p.122

DYER, MANDY (FICTITIOUS CHARACTER) p.122

DYKE, TOBY (FICTITIOUS CHARACTER) p.122

EASTMAN, WARD (FICTITIOUS CHARACTER) p.122

EASTON, SHARON (FICTITIOUS CHARACTER) p.122

EATON, JAKE (FICTITIOUS CHARACTER) p.122

EBENEZUM (FICTITIOUS CHARACTER) p.122

EBERHARDT, MARSHA (FICTITIOUS CHARACTER) p.122

ECKERT, JAMES (FICTITIOUS CHARACTER) p.122

ECKHART, RALPH (FICTITIOUS CHARACTER) p.122

EDWARDS, COLIN (FICTITIOUS CHARACTER) p.122

EDWARDS, JANE AMANDA (FICTITIOUS CHARACTER) p.122

EISHEID, EARL (FICTITIOUS CHARACTER) p.122

ELDRIDGE, LOUISE (FICTITIOUS CHARACTER) p.122

ELEANOR, OF AQUITAINE, CONSORT OF HENRY II, KING OF ENGLAND, 1122?-1204 p.122

List of Subject Headings - Fiction

List of Subject Headings - Fiction

ELIZABETH I, QUEEN OF ENGLAND, 1533-1603 p.123

ELLER, JACK (FICTITIOUS CHARACTER) p.123

ELLIOT, ELIZABETH (FICTITIOUS CHARACTER) p.123

ELLIOTT, EVE (FICTITIOUS CHARACTER) p.123

ELLIOTT, MAGGIE (FICTITIOUS CHARACTER) p.123

ELLIOTT, SCOTT (FICTITIOUS CHARACTER) p.123

ELLIS, DUSTY (FICTITIOUS CHARACTER) p.123

ELLSWORTH, PETER (FICTITIOUS CHARACTER) p.123

ELM CREEK QUILTERS (FICTITIOUS CHARACTERS) p.123

ELORA DANAN (FICTITIOUS CHARACTER) p.123

ELRIC OF MELNIBONE (FICTITIOUS CHARACTER) p.123

EMERSON, STRETCH (FICTITIOUS CHARACTER) p.123

EMORY, ARIANE (FICTITIOUS CHARACTER) p.123

ENAMORADO, DAVE (FICTITIOUS CHARACTER) p.123

ENDER (FICTITIOUS CHARACTER) p.123

ENDERLY, MARS (FICTITIOUS CHARACTER) p.124

ENDICOTT, BLACKJACK (FICTITIOUS CHARACTER) p.124

ENDICOTT, GABRIEL (FICTITIOUS CHARACTER) p.124

ENGELS, KAY (FICTITIOUS CHARACTER) p.124

ENGLISH, TOM (FICTITIOUS CHARACTER) p.124

EPTON, ROSA (FICTITIOUS CHARACTER) p.124

ERICKSON, REED (FICTITIOUS CHARACTER) p.124

ERNST, WERNER (FICTITIOUS CHARACTER) p.124

ERSKINE, HARRY (FICTITIOUS CHARACTER) p.124

ESPOSITO, JANUARY (FICTITIOUS CHARACTER) p.124

ESSAY, ROGER (FICTITIOUS CHARACTER) p.124

ESTRADA, JOE (FICTITIOUS CHARACTER) p.124

EVANS, EVAN (FICTITIOUS CHARACTER) p.124

EVANS, HOMER (FICTITIOUS CHARACTER) p.124

EVANS, LYNN (FICTITIOUS CHARACTER) p.124

EVANS, TINA (FICTITIOUS CHARACTER) p.124

EVERARD, NICHOLAS (FICTITIOUS CHARACTER) p.124

EVERETT, STEVE (FICTITIOUS CHARACTER) p.124

EVERHARDT, MONIKA (FICTITIOUS CHARACTER) p.125

EVERS, FORREST (FICTITIOUS CHARACTER) p.125

EVESDEN, GODFREY, SIR (FICTITIOUS CHARACTER) p.125

EWING, LUTHER (FICTITIOUS CHARACTER) p.125

EXLEY, ED (FICTITIOUS CHARACTER) p.125

FABIANO (FICTITIOUS CHARACTER) p.125

FABRI, FELIX, 1441 OR 2-1502 p.125

FAFHRD (FICTITIOUS CHARACTER) p.125

FAIRACRE (ENGLAND: IMAGINARY PLACE) p.125

FAIRCHILD, FAITH SIBLEY (FICTITIOUS CHARACTER) p.125

FAIRCHILD, NELSON (FICTITIOUS CHARACTER) p.125

FAIRFAX, PHOEBE (FICTITIOUS CHARACTER) p.125

FAIRWEATHER, DORAN (FICTITIOUS CHARACTER) p.125

FAITH, JOHN (FICTITIOUS CHARACTER) p.126

FALCO, MARCUS DIDIUS (FICTITIOUS CHARACTER) p.126

FALCONER, WILLIAM (FICTITIOUS CHARACTER) p.126

FALKENSTEIN, JESSE (FICTITIOUS CHARACTER) p.126

FALLETTI, FABE (FICTITIOUS CHARACTER) p.126

FALLON, MICHAEL (FICTITIOUS CHARACTER) p.126

FALLS, VIRGINIA (FICTITIOUS CHARACTER) p.126

FALSTAFF, JOHN, SIR (FICTITIOUS CHARACTER) p.126

FANG, YAN (FICTITIOUS CHARACTER) p.126

FANSLER, KATE (FICTITIOUS CHARACTER) p.126

FANTOMAS (FICTITIOUS CHARACTER) p.126

FARADAY, MIKE (FICTITIOUS CHARACTER) p.126

FARGO, SKYE (FICTITIOUS CHARACTER) p.127

FARNHAM, JULIE (FICTITIOUS CHARACTER) p.128

FARO, JEREMY (FICTITIOUS CHARACTER) p.128

FARRAR, BRAT (FICTITIOUS CHARACTER) p.129

FARREL, CASEY (FICTITIOUS CHARACTER) p.129

FARRELL, STEPHANIE (FICTITIOUS CHARACTER) p.129

FARRELL, WESLEY (FICTITIOUS CHARACTER) p.129

FARROW, KAY (FICTITIOUS CHARACTER) p.129

FEARLESS FOSDICK (FICTITIOUS CHARACTER) p.129

FECHTER, RENATA (FICTITIOUS CHARACTER) p.129

FEDORCENKO FAMILY (FICTITIOUS CHARACTERS) p.129

FEEP, LEFTY (FICTITIOUS CHARACTER) p.129

FEIFFER, HARRY (FICTITIOUS CHARACTER) p.129

FEIN, IRVING (FICTITIOUS CHARACTER) p.129

FENIMORE, ANDREW (FICTITIOUS CHARACTER) p.129

FELL, GIDEON (FICTITIOUS CHARACTER) p.129

FELLOWES, IAN (FICTITIOUS CHARACTER) p.129

FELSE, GEORGE (FICTITIOUS CHARACTER) p.129

FELTON, CORA (FICTITIOUS CHARACTER) p.130

FEN, GERVASE (FICTITIOUS CHARACTER) p.130

FENDER, MARTIN (FICTITIOUS CHARACTER) p.130

FENTON, HILARY (FICTITIOUS CHARACTER) p.130

FERGUSON, CHARLES (FICTITIOUS CHARACTER) p.130

FERGUSSON, CLARE (FICTITIOUS CHARACTER) p.130

FERMOYLE, MARIE (FICTITIOUS CHARACTER) p.130

FERRAMI, JEANNIE (FICTITIOUS CHARACTER) p.130

FERRARO, GENE (FICTITIOUS CHARACTER) p.130

FERRIS, NICOLA (FICTITIOUS CHARACTER) p.131

FETT, BOBA (FICTITIOUS CHARACTER) p.131

FIDDLER (FICTITIOUS CHARACTER) p.131

FIDELMA OF KILDAIRE, SISTER (FICTITIOUS CHARACTER) p.131

FIELDING, JOHN, SIR, 1721-1780 p.131

FIELDING, KIT (FICTITIOUS CHARACTER) p.131

FIELDS, TESSA (FICTITIOUS CHARACTER) p.131

FIGUEROA, SUZE (FICTITIOUS CHARACTER) p.131

FINCH, SEPTIMUS (FICTITIOUS CHARACTER) p.131

FINE, MISTY (FICTITIOUS CHARACTER) p.131

FINK, MEL (FICTITIOUS CHARACTER) p.131

FINLEY, PETER (FICTITIOUS CHARACTER) p.131

FINN, HUCKLEBERRY (FICTITIOUS CHARACTER) p.131

FINN, ROB (FICTITIOUS CHARACTER) p.132

FINNEGAN, JACK (FICTITIOUS CHARACTER) p.132

FIORA (FICTITIOUS CHARACTER) p.132

FISCHMAN, NINA (FICTITIOUS CHARACTER) p.132

FISH, SYD (FICTITIOUS CHARACTER) p.132

FISHER (FICTITIOUS CHARACTER: GREEN) p.132

FISHER, PHRYNE (FICTITIOUS CHARACTER) p.132

FITZDUANE, HUGO (FICTITIOUS CHARACTER) p.132

FITZGEOFFREY, CORMAC (FICTITIOUS CHARACTER) p.132

FITZGERALD, COLLEEN (FICTITIOUS CHARACTER) p.132

FITZGERALD, EDWARD (FICTITIOUS CHARACTER) p.132

FITZGERALD, FIONA (FICTITIOUS CHARACTER) p.132

FITZGERALD, STEPHANIE (FICTITIOUS CHARACTER) p.132

FITZGIBBON, ZELDA (FICTITIOUS CHARACTER) p.132

FITZHUGH, ALACRITY (FICTITIOUS CHARACTER) p.132

FITZROY, HENRY (FICTITIOUS CHARACTER) p.133

FLAGG, CONAN (FICTITIOUS CHARACTER) p.133

FLANNERY, JIMMY (FICTITIOUS CHARACTER) p.133

FLANNIGAN, DIXIE (FICTITIOUS CHARACTER) p.133

FLASHMAN, HARRY PAGET (FICTITIOUS CHARACTER) p.133

FLEMING, JACK (FICTITIOUS CHARACTER) p.133

FLEMING, JAMES (FICTITIOUS CHARACTER) p.133

FLEMING, LAURA (FICTITIOUS CHARACTER) p.133

FLETCH (FICTITIOUS CHARACTER) p.133

FLETCHER, JACK (FICTITIOUS CHARACTER) p.134

FLETCHER, JESSICA (FICTITIOUS CHARACTER) p.134

FLETCHER, MARTIN (FICTITIOUS CHARACTER) p.134

FLETCHER, PHILIP (FICTITIOUS CHARACTER) p.134

FLINX OF THE COMMONWEALTH (FICTITIOUS CHARACTER) p.134

FLIPPO, JACK (FICTITIOUS CHARACTER) p.134

FLINT, MIKE (FICTITIOUS CHARACTER) p.134

FLINT, SAM (FICTITIOUS CHARACTER) p.134

FLOYD, C. J. (FICTITIOUS CHARACTER) p.134

FLOYT, HOBART (FICTITIOUS CHARACTER) p.134

FLYNN, FRANCIS XAVIER (FICTITIOUS CHARACTER) p.134

FLYNN, JUDITH MCMONIGLE (FICTITIOUS CHARACTER) p.134

FLYNN, LAURA (FICTITIOUS CHARACTER) p.134

FLYNN, MAGGIE (FICTITIOUS CHARACTER) p.134

FOG, DUSTY (FICTITIOUS CHARACTER) p.135

FOGARTY, LUANNE (FICTITIOUS CHARACTER) p.135

FOLEY, MALACHY (FICTITIOUS CHARACTER) p.135

FOLGER, MERRY (FICTITIOUS CHARACTER) p.135

FOLLOWS, NATHANIEL (FICTITIOUS CHARACTER) p.135

FOLLY, SUPERINTENDENT (FICTITIOUS CHARACTER) p.135

FONTAINE, FELICIA (FICTITIOUS CHARACTER) p.135

FONTANA, MAC (FICTITIOUS CHARACTER) p.135

FORD, ASHTON (FICTITIOUS CHARACTER) p.135

FORD, DOC (FICTITIOUS CHARACTER) p.135

FORD, LOU (FICTITIOUS CHARACTER) p.135

FORESTER, ROBERT (FICTITIOUS CHARACTER) p.135

FORRESTER, LILY (FICTITIOUS CHARACTER)
p.135

FORSYTE FAMILY (FICTITIOUS CHARACTERS)
p.135

FORSYTHE, ROBERT (FICTITIOUS CHARACTER)
p.135

FORTIER, MARGO (FICTITIOUS CHARACTER)
p.136

FORTLOW, SOCRATES (FICTITIOUS CHARACTER)
p.136

FORTUNATO, THERESA (FICTITIOUS CHARACTER)
p.136

FORTUNE, DAN (FICTITIOUS CHARACTER) p.136

FORTUNE, SARAH (FICTITIOUS CHARACTER)
p.136

FOSTER, STICK (FICTITIOUS CHARACTER) p.136

FOUCHEROUX, JEAN-PIERRE (FICTITIOUS
CHARACTER) p.136

FOX, TECUMSEH (FICTITIOUS CHARACTER) p.136

FOX, TRAVIS (FICTITIOUS CHARACTER) p.136

FRADE, CLETUS (FICTITIOUS CHARACTER) p.136

FRALEIGH, OFFICER (FICTITIOUS CHARACTER)
p.136

FRAME, MAX (FICTITIOUS CHARACTER) p.136

FRANCK, CESAR (FICTITIOUS CHARACTER) p.136

FRANK, LANE (FICTITIOUS CHARACTER) p.136

FRANK, LUCAS (FICTITIOUS CHARACTER) p.136

FRANKENSTEIN (FICTITIOUS CHARACTER) p.136

FRANKLIN, ALTON BENJAMIN (FICTITIOUS
CHARACTER) p.137

FRANKLIN, BENJAMIN, 1706-1790 p.137

FRANKLIN, CLYDE WAYNE (FICTITIOUS CHARAC-
TER) p.137

FRANKLIN, DEREK (FICTITIOUS CHARACTER)
p.137

FRANKLYN, KIT (FICTITIOUS CHARACTER) p.137

FRASER, JAMIE (FICTITIOUS CHARACTER) p.137

FRASER, ROBERT (FICTITIOUS CHARACTER) p.138

FRASIER, GEORGE (FICTITIOUS CHARACTER)
p.138

FREDRICKSON, ROBERT, DOCTOR (FICTITIOUS
CHARACTER) p.138
  see Mongo (Fictitious Character)

FREEMAN, GILES (FICTITIOUS CHARACTER) p.138

FREEMAN, LAUREN (FICTITIOUS CHARACTER)
p.138

FREEMAN, MAX (FICTITIOUS CHARACTER) p.138

FREEMARK, NEST (FICTITIOUS CHARACTER)
p.138

FREER, FELIX (FICTITIOUS CHARACTER) p.138

FREER, VIRGINIA (FICTITIOUS CHARACTER) p.138

FREERS, LUCY (FICTITIOUS CHARACTER) p.138

FRENCH, NED (FICTITIOUS CHARACTER) p.138

FRESHOUR, TOM (FICTITIOUS CHARACTER) p.138

FREVISSE, SISTER (FICTITIOUS CHARACTER)
p.138

FREY, NATHAN (FICTITIOUS CHARACTER) p.138

FRIEDMAN, KINKY p.138

FROST, CYNTHIA (FICTITIOUS CHARACTER) p.139

FROST, JACK (FICTITIOUS CHARACTER) p.139

FROST, REUBEN (FICTITIOUS CHARACTER) p.139

FU MANCHU, DOCTOR (FICTITIOUS CHARACTER)
p.139

FULLER, JOSEPHINE (FICTITIOUS CHARACTER)
p.139

FURNESS, JACK (FICTITIOUS CHARACTER) p.139

FURY, NELL (FICTITIOUS CHARACTER) p.139

FURY, NICK (FICTITIOUS CHARACTER) p.139

FYFE, DAVID (FICTITIOUS CHARACTER) p.139

G-8 (FICTITIOUS CHARACTER) p.139

GABLE, CLARK, 1901-1960 p.139

GABRIEL, MATT (FICTITIOUS CHARACTER) p.139

GAIRDEN FAMILY (FICTITIOUS CHARACTERS)
p.139

GALERAN DE LESNEVEN (FICTITIOUS CHARAC-
TER) p.139

GALINDO, DANIEL (FICTITIOUS CHARACTER)
p.139

GALLAGHER, GORDON (FICTITIOUS CHARAC-
TER) p.139

GALLAGHER, MARTIN (FICTITIOUS CHARACTER)
p.139

GALLEGO, GEORGE (FICTITIOUS CHARACTER)
p.139

GALLOWAY, THERESA (FICTITIOUS CHARACTER)
p.139

GALLOWAY, TILLER (FICTITIOUS CHARACTER)
p.139

GALLOWGLASS, MAGNUS (FICTITIOUS CHARAC-
TER) p.140

GALLOWGLASS, ROD (FICTITIOUS CHARACTER)
p.140

GAMADGE, CLARA (FICTITIOUS CHARACTER)
p.140

GAMADGE, HENRY (FICTITIOUS CHARACTER)
p.140

GAMBAR, JIMMY (FICTITIOUS CHARACTER) p.140

GARAK (FICTITIOUS CHARACTER) p.140

GARCIA, LUPE (FICTITIOUS CHARACTER) p.140

GARCIA, RICHARD (FICTITIOUS CHARACTER)
p.140

GARCIA FAMILY (FICTITIOUS CHARACTERS) p.140

GARDNER, ERLE STANLEY, 1889-1970 p.140

GARDNER, NICK (FICTITIOUS CHARACTER) p.140

GARDNER, STEVE (FICTITIOUS CHARACTER)
p.140

GARFIELD (FICTITIOUS CHARACTER) p.140

GARION (FICTITIOUS CHARACTER) p.141

GARLIN, KELRIC (FICTITIOUS CHARACTER) p.141

GARNET, EARL (FICTITIOUS CHARACTER) p.141

GARNISH, HARRY (FICTITIOUS CHARACTER)
p.141

GARON, SETH (FICTITIOUS CHARACTER) p.141

GARRETT (FICTITIOUS CHARACTER: COOK) p.141

GARRETT, AMANDA LEE (FICTITIOUS CHARAC-
TER) p.141

GARRETT, DAVE (FICTITIOUS CHARACTER) p.141

GARRETT, MAGGIE (FICTITIOUS CHARACTER)
p.142

GARRISON, RICHARD (FICTITIOUS CHARACTER)
p.142

GARRITY, JULIA CALLAHAN (FICTITIOUS
CHARACTER) p.142

GASTNER, BILL (FICTITIOUS CHARACTER) p.142

GAUNT, JONATHAN (FICTITIOUS CHARACTER)
p.142

GAUNT, LELAND (FICTITIOUS CHARACTER) p.142

GAUTIER, JEAN-PAUL (FICTITIOUS CHARACTER)
p.142

GED (FICTITIOUS CHARACTER) p.142

GEIGER, ROLF (FICTITIOUS CHARACTER) p.142

GENNARO, ANGELA (FICTITIOUS CHARACTER)
p.142

GENTLY, DIRK (FICTITIOUS CHARACTER) p.142

GENTLY, GEORGE (FICTITIOUS CHARACTER)
p.143

GENTRY, MEG (FICTITIOUS CHARACTER) p.143

GENTRY, MERRY (FICTITIOUS CHARACTER) p.143

GHOTE, GANESH, INSPECTOR (FICTITIOUS
CHARACTER) p.143

GIBBONS, CUTHBERT (FICTITIOUS CHARACTER)
p.143

GIBBS, BOB (FICTITIOUS CHARACTER) p.143

GIBBS, CONOR (FICTITIOUS CHARACTER) p.143

GIBSON, CAROL (FICTITIOUS CHARACTER) p.143

GIBSON, TOM (FICTITIOUS CHARACTER) p.143

GIDEON, GEORGE (FICTITIOUS CHARACTER)
p.143

GILLARD, PATRICK (FICTITIOUS CHARACTER)
p.144

GILLESPIE, CLAIRE (FICTITIOUS CHARACTER)
p.144

GILLIS, MEG (FICTITIOUS CHARACTER) p.144

GIORDANO, TEDDY (FICTITIOUS CHARACTER)
p.144

GIRARD, TERRY (FICTITIOUS CHARACTER) p.144

GIRAUD, JULES (FICTITIOUS CHARACTER) p.144

GIVEN, SUSAN (FICTITIOUS CHARACTER) p.144

GIVENS, RAYLAN (FICTITIOUS CHARACTER)
p.144

GLAUBERMAN, ALEX (FICTITIOUS CHARACTER)
p.144

GLEASON, IZZY (FICTITIOUS CHARACTER) p.144

GLENDOWER, HARRY, LORD (FICTITIOUS
CHARACTER) p.144

GLENDOWER, TOBY (FICTITIOUS CHARACTER)
p.144

GLENNING, PAULA (FICTITIOUS CHARACTER)
p.144

GLICK, MURRAY (FICTITIOUS CHARACTER) p.144

GLITSKY, ABE (FICTITIOUS CHARACTER) p.144

GOD SQUAD (FICTITIOUS CHARACTERS) p.144

GODZILLA (FICTITIOUS CHARACTER) p.144

GOFF, JAMES (FICTITIOUS CHARACTER) p.145

GOICOCHEA, MARTA (FICTITIOUS CHARACTER)
p.145

GOLD, ARIEL (FICTITIOUS CHARACTER) p.145

GOLD, NATALIE (FICTITIOUS CHARACTER) p.145

GOLD, RACHEL (FICTITIOUS CHARACTER) p.145

GOLD, SHELDON (FICTITIOUS CHARACTER) p.145

GOLDMAN, DAVEY (FICTITIOUS CHARACTER)
p.145

GOMEZ, MISS (FICTITIOUS CHARACTER) p.145

GOMEZ, SULLY (FICTITIOUS CHARACTER) p.145

GOOD, SALLY (FICTITIOUS CHARACTER) p.145

GOODMAN, JONATHAN (FICTITIOUS CHARAC-
TER) p.145

GOODMAN, RAYFORD (FICTITIOUS CHARACTER)
p.145

GOODNIGHT, AUGUSTA (FICTITIOUS CHARAC-
TER) p.145

GORDIANUS THE FINDER (FICTITIOUS CHARAC-
TER) p.145

GORDON, LINDSAY (FICTITIOUS CHARACTER)
p.145

GORMENGHAST FAMILY (FICTITIOUS CHARAC-
TER) p.145

GORODISH, SERGE (FICTITIOUS CHARACTER)
p.146

GORZACK, ELEANOR (FICTITIOUS CHARACTER)
p.146

GOSSINGER, HENRY, SIR (FICTITIOUS CHARAC-
TER) p.146

GOULD, JAMES (FICTITIOUS CHARACTER) p.146

GOURMET DETECTIVE (FICTITIOUS CHARACTER)
p.146

GRAFTON, JAKE (FICTITIOUS CHARACTER) p.146

GRAHAM, ALAN (FICTITIOUS CHARACTER) p.146

GRAHAM, CHARLOTTE (FICTITIOUS CHARAC-
TER) p.146

GRAHAM, EMMA (FICTITIOUS CHARACTER) p.146

GRAHAM, LIZ (FICTITIOUS CHARACTER) p.146

GRAHAM, WILL (FICTITIOUS CHARACTER) p.146

GRANNY WEATHERWAX (FICTITIOUS CHARACTER) p.147

GRANT, ALAN, INSPECTOR (FICTITIOUS CHARACTER) p.147

GRANT, CELIA (FICTITIOUS CHARACTER) p.147

GRANT, JOCELYN (FICTITIOUS CHARACTER) p.147

GRANT, MARTIN (FICTITIOUS CHARACTER) p.147

GRANT, PATRICK (FICTITIOUS CHARACTER) p.147

GRANT, SPENCER (FICTITIOUS CHARACTER) p.147

GRAVE DIGGER JONES (FICTITIOUS CHARACTER) p.147
*see* Jones, Grave Digger (Fictitious Character)

GRAVES, BRENT (FICTITIOUS CHARACTER) p.147

GRAY, CORDELIA (FICTITIOUS CHARACTER) p.147

GRAY, HELEN (FICTITIOUS CHARACTER) p.147

GRAY, JENNIFER (FICTITIOUS CHARACTER) p.148

GRAY, P. J. (FICTITIOUS CHARACTER) p.148

GRAYSON, GALE (FICTITIOUS CHARACTER) p.148

GREEN, BEN (FICTITIOUS CHARACTER) p.148

GREEN, DETECTIVE INSPECTOR (FICTITIOUS CHARACTER) p.148

GREENE, CHARLIE (FICTITIOUS CHARACTER) p.148

GREENE, DAVID (FICTITIOUS CHARACTER) p.148

GREENE, TERENCE (FICTITIOUS CHARACTER) p.148

GREENFIELD, C. B. (FICTITIOUS CHARACTER) p.148

GREENWAY, SOPHIE (FICTITIOUS CHARACTER) p.148

GREER, DANIEL (FICTITIOUS CHARACTER) p.148

GREGORY, ALAN (FICTITIOUS CHARACTER) p.148

GREGORY, JOE (FICTITIOUS CHARACTER) p.148

GREY, ANA (FICTITIOUS CHARACTER) p.148

GREY, BRUCE (FICTITIOUS CHARACTER) p.148

GREY, HENRY (FICTITIOUS CHARACTER) p.149

GREY, JOE (FICTITIOUS CHARACTER) p.149

GREY, LAVINIA, MOTHER (FICTITIOUS CHARACTER) p.149

GREY MOUSER (FICTITIOUS CHARACTER) p.149

GRIFFIN (FICTITIOUS CHARACTER: BANTOCK) p.149

GRIFFIN, DEIRDRE (FICTITIOUS CHARACTER) p.149

GRIFFIN, JIMMY (FICTITIOUS CHARACTER) p.149

GRIFFIN, LEW (FICTITIOUS CHARACTER) p.149

GRIFFO, SIMONA (FICTITIOUS CHARACTER) p.149

GRIFFON, NEIL (FICTITIOUS CHARACTER) p.149

GRIJPSTRA, HENK (FICTITIOUS CHARACTER) p.149

GRIST, SIMEON (FICTITIOUS CHARACTER) p.150

GUARNACCIA, MARSHAL (FICTITIOUS CHARACTER) p.150

GUENEVERE, QUEEN (LEGENDARY CHARACTER) p.150

GUIDRY, JUNIOR (FICTITIOUS CHARACTER) p.150

GUIDRY, KARA (FICTITIOUS CHARACTER) p.150

GUILD, LEO (FICTITIOUS CHARACTER) p.150

GUIU, LONIA (FICTITIOUS CHARACTER) p.150

GUMP, FORREST (FICTITIOUS CHARACTER) p.150

GUNNER, AARON (FICTITIOUS CHARACTER) p.150

GUNSMITH (FICTITIOUS CHARACTER) p.150

GUNTHER, BERNHARD (FICTITIOUS CHARACTER) p.151

GUNTHER, JOE (FICTITIOUS CHARACTER) p.151

GUTHRIE, ANSON (FICTITIOUS CHARACTER) p.151

GUTIERREZ, VINCE (FICTITIOUS CHARACTER) p.151

GWEN, LADY (FICTITIOUS CHARACTER) p.151

HAAGEN, ANNEKE (FICTITIOUS CHARACTER) p.151

HACKSHAW, ELIAS (FICTITIOUS CHARACTER) p.151

HAGGERTY, LEO (FICTITIOUS CHARACTER) p.151

HAGGERTY, LINDY (FICTITIOUS CHARACTER) p.151

HAKIM ARIF (FICTITIOUS CHARACTER) p.152

HALE, PETER (FICTITIOUS CHARACTER) p.152

HALE, PRICH (FICTITIOUS CHARACTER) p.152

HALEY, ERIN (FICTITIOUS CHARACTER) p.152

HALFHYDE, ST. VINCENT (FICTITIOUS CHARACTER) p.152

HALL, ADAM (FICTITIOUS CHARACTER) p.152

HALL, MASON (FICTITIOUS CHARACTER) p.152

HALL, SATAN (FICTITIOUS CHARACTER) p.152

HALLAM, LUCAS (FICTITIOUS CHARACTER) p.152

HALLECK, BILLY (FICTITIOUS CHARACTER) p.152

HALLEY, SID (FICTITIOUS CHARACTER) p.152

HALLIGAN, NINA (FICTITIOUS CHARACTER) p.152

HALLORAN, MEG (FICTITIOUS CHARACTER) p.152

HALVORSEN, W. T. (FICTITIOUS CHARACTER) p.152

HAMEL, NEIL (FICTITIOUS CHARACTER) p.152

HAMILTON, ETHAN (FICTITIOUS CHARACTER) p.152

HAMILTON, LISA (FICTITIOUS CHARACTER) p.152

HAMILTON, STEFIE (FICTITIOUS CHARACTER) p.152

HAMLIN, MICHAEL (FICTITIOUS CHARACTER) p.152

HAMMER, JUDY (FICTITIOUS CHARACTER) p.152

HAMMER, MIKE (FICTITIOUS CHARACTER) p.153

HAMPTON, JAKE (FICTITIOUS CHARACTER) p.153

HANKS, ARLY (FICTITIOUS CHARACTER) p.153

HANNAFORD, BENNIS (FICTITIOUS CHARACTER) p.153

HANNAY, RICHARD (FICTITIOUS CHARACTER) p.153

HANRAHAN, MAC (FICTITIOUS CHARACTER) p.153

HANSEN, ANNIKA (FICTITIOUS CHARACTER) p.153
*see* Seven of Nine (Fictitious Character)

HANSEN, EM (FICTITIOUS CHARACTER) p.153

HANSON, BOMBER (FICTITIOUS CHARACTER) p.154

HANSON, WILLY (FICTITIOUS CHARACTER) p.154

HARALD, SIGRID (FICTITIOUS CHARACTER) p.154

HARDAWAY, ANNE (FICTITIOUS CHARACTER) p.154

HARDESTY, WIL (FICTITIOUS CHARACTER) p.154

HARDING (FICTITIOUS CHARACTER) p.154

HARDY, ANNABELLE (FICTITIOUS CHARACTER) p.154

HARDY, CLIFF (FICTITIOUS CHARACTER) p.154

HARDY, DISMAS (FICTITIOUS CHARACTER) p.154

HARISTEEN, HARRY (FICTITIOUS CHARACTER) p.154

HARPER, BENNI (FICTITIOUS CHARACTER) p.155

HARPER, GOODWIN (FICTITIOUS CHARACTER) p.155
*see* Gourmet Detective (Fictitious Character)

HARPER, NANCY (FICTITIOUS CHARACTER) p.155

HARPUR, COLIN (FICTITIOUS CHARACTER) p.155

HARRIGAN, PETER (FICTITIOUS CHARACTER) p.155

HARRINGTON, HONOR (FICTITIOUS CHARACTER) p.155

HARRISON, CATHERINE (FICTITIOUS CHARACTER) p.155

HARRISON, CHIP (FICTITIOUS CHARACTER) p.155

HARRISON, EMALINE (FICTITIOUS CHARACTER) p.155

HARRISON, RICHARD (FICTITIOUS CHARACTER) p.155

HARROD, KATE (FICTITIOUS CHARACTER) p.155

HARTE, EMMA (FICTITIOUS CHARACTER) p.155

HARTRIGHT, WALTER (FICTITIOUS CHARACTER) p.155

HARWICK, EMERALD (FICTITIOUS CHARACTER) p.155

HASKELL, BENTLEY (FICTITIOUS CHARACTER) p.156

HASKELL, ELLIE (FICTITIOUS CHARACTER) p.156
*see* Simons, Ellie (Fictitious Character)

HASKELL, VEJAY (FICTITIOUS CHARACTER) p.156

HASTINGS, ARTHUR, CAPTAIN (FICTITIOUS CHARACTER) p.156

HASTINGS, FRANK (FICTITIOUS CHARACTER) p.156

HASTINGS, STANLEY (FICTITIOUS CHARACTER) p.156

HATCH, JAKE (FICTITIOUS CHARACTER) p.156

HATCHER, CHRISTIAN (FICTITIOUS CHARACTER) p.156

HATFIELD, JIM (FICTITIOUS CHARACTER) p.156

HAVERS, BARBARA (FICTITIOUS CHARACTER) p.156

HAVOC, JOHNNY (FICTITIOUS CHARACTER) p.157

HAWK (FICTITIOUS CHARACTER: GREEN) p.157

HAWK, JASON (FICTITIOUS CHARACTER: PARKER) p.157

HAWKINS, GENE (FICTITIOUS CHARACTER) p.157

HAWKINS, MACKENZIE (FICTITIOUS CHARACTER) p.157

HAWKMOON, DORIAN (FICTITIOUS CHARACTER) p.157

HAWLEY, BILL (FICTITIOUS CHARACTER) p.157

HAWTHORNE, HELEN (FICTITIOUS CHARACTER) p.157

HAWTHORNE, TYRELL (FICTITIOUS CHARACTER) p.157

HAYCASTLE, MATILDA (FICTITIOUS CHARACTER) p.157

HAYDON, STUART (FICTITIOUS CHARACTER) p.157

HAYES, JACK (FICTITIOUS CHARACTER) p.157

HAYES, JESSE (FICTITIOUS CHARACTER) p.157

HAYES, JUDITH (FICTITIOUS CHARACTER) p.157

HAYES, KAREN (FICTITIOUS CHARACTER) p.157

HAYES, LUCINDA (FICTITIOUS CHARACTER) p.157

HAYES, NANETTE (FICTITIOUS CHARACTER) p.157

HAYLE, TAMARA (FICTITIOUS CHARACTER) p.157

HAYS, SHARON (FICTITIOUS CHARACTER) p.157

HAZARD, AMANDA (FICTITIOUS CHARACTER) p.157

HAZARD, PHILLIP HORATIO (FICTITIOUS CHARACTER) p.158

HE WHO HEARS LIKE A COYOTE (FICTITIOUS CHARACTER) p.158

HEARTWOOD, LEANDER (FICTITIOUS CHARACTER) p.158

HEATHCLIFF (FICTITIOUS CHARACTER) p.158

HEENAN, MATTHEW (FICTITIOUS CHARACTER) p.158

HEFFERMAN, HOOKY (FICTITIOUS CHARACTER) p.158

HEHZI OF NHOL, PRINCESS (FICTITIOUS CHARACTER) p.158

HEIMRICH, M. L. (FICTITIOUS CHARACTER) p.158

HELLER, NATHAN (FICTITIOUS CHARACTER) p.158

HELLER, SHERI (FICTITIOUS CHARACTER) p.158

HELM, MATT (FICTITIOUS CHARACTER) p.158

HEMLOCK, JONATHAN (FICTITIOUS CHARACTER) p.159

HENNING, KAREN (FICTITIOUS CHARACTER) p.159

HENRIE O (FICTITIOUS CHARACTER) p.159

HENRY, DALLAS (FICTITIOUS CHARACTER) p.159

HENRY, KATHERINE (FICTITIOUS CHARACTER) p.159

HENRY, VICTOR (FICTITIOUS CHARACTER) p.159

HENSHAW, SUSAN (FICTITIOUS CHARACTER) p.159

HEPBURN, ALAN (FICTITIOUS CHARACTER) p.159

HERCULES (ROMAN MYTHOLOGY) p.159

HERNANDEZ QUINTO, GIMIENDO (FICTITIOUS CHARACTER) p.159

HERRICK, ROBERT (FICTITIOUS CHARACTER) p.159

HERSHEY, CLAUDIA (FICTITIOUS CHARACTER) p.159

HICKOK, WILD BILL, 1837-1876 p.159

HIGGINS, BRETT (FICTITIOUS CHARACTER) p.159

HIGHLANDER (FICTITIOUS CHARACTER) p.159
see MacLeod, Duncan (Fictitious Character)

HIGHTOWER, KAREN (FICTITIOUS CHARACTER) p.159
see Bast (Fictitious Character)

HILDRETH, JANE (FICTITIOUS CHARACTER) p.159

HILL, JUDY (FICTITIOUS CHARACTER) p.159

HILL, MAGGIE (FICTITIOUS CHARACTER) p.160

HILL, TONY (FICTITIOUS CHARACTER) p.160

HILLSDEN, ALEC (FICTITIOUS CHARACTER) p.160

HINES, JAKE (FICTITIOUS CHARACTER) p.160

HIRSCH, MARTI (FICTITIOUS CHARACTER) p.160

HO KUM MENON (FICTITIOUS CHARACTER) p.160

HOAG, STEWART (FICTITIOUS CHARACTER) p.160

HOARE, BARTHOLOMEW (FICTITIOUS CHARACTER) p.160

HOARE, DIDO (FICTITIOUS CHARACTER) p.160

HOBBY, PAT (FICTITIOUS CHARACTER) p.160

HOCKADAY, NEIL (FICTITIOUS CHARACTER) p.160

HOFFMAN, NICK (FICTITIOUS CHARACTER) p.160

HOFFMAN, SAM (FICTITIOUS CHARACTER) p.160

HOITT, JIMMY (FICTITIOUS CHARACTER) p.160

HOLDEN, SIDNEY (FICTITIOUS CHARACTER) p.160

HOLDEN, VICKY (FICTITIOUS CHARACTER) p.160

HOLIDAY, BEN (FICTITIOUS CHARACTER) p.160

HOLLAND, BILLY BOB (FICTITIOUS CHARACTER) p.160

HOLLAND, JAMES (FICTITIOUS CHARACTER) p.160

HOLLAND, PRIMROSE (FICTITIOUS CHARACTER) p.160

HOLLISTER, DEVIN (FICTITIOUS CHARACTER) p.161

HOLLISTER, LAURA (FICTITIOUS CHARACTER) p.161

HOLLOWAY, BARBARA (FICTITIOUS CHARACTER) p.161

HOLLOWAY, SABRINA (FICTITIOUS CHARACTER) p.161

HOLLOWELL, PATRICIA ANNE (FICTITIOUS CHARACTER) p.161
see Patricia Anne (Fictitious Character)

HOLMES, HARRY (FICTITIOUS CHARACTER) p.161

HOLMES, MYCROFT (FICTITIOUS CHARACTER) p.161

HOLMES, SHERLOCK (FICTITIOUS CHARACTER) p.161

HOLOGRAPHIC DOCTOR (FICTITIOUS CHARACTER) p.166

HOLSTROM, CLARK (FICTITIOUS CHARACTER) p.166

HOLT, LUCAS, REVEREND (FICTITIOUS CHARACTER) p.166

HOLT, MITCH (FICTITIOUS CHARACTER) p.166

HOLT, SAMANTHA (FICTITIOUS CHARACTER) p.166

HOLT, WHIP (FICTITIOUS CHARACTER) p.166

HOLT FAMILY (FICTITIOUS CHARACTERS) p.166

HOLYHANDS, DION (FICTITIOUS CHARACTER) p.166

HOOLIHAN, MIKE (FICTITIOUS CHARACTER) p.166

HOPE, ALISON (FICTITIOUS CHARACTER) p.166

HOPE, FRED (FICTITIOUS CHARACTER) p.167

HOPE, MATTHEW (FICTITIOUS CHARACTER) p.167

HOPKINS, LLOYD (FICTITIOUS CHARACTER) p.167

HOPKINS, MARTY (FICTITIOUS CHARACTER) p.167

HOPPER, TURING (FICTITIOUS CHARACTER) p.167

HORN, CORRAN (FICTITIOUS CHARACTER) p.167

HORNBLOWER, HORATIO (FICTITIOUS CHARACTER) p.167

HORNE, EVAN (FICTITIOUS CHARACTER) p.168

HOUSE, DUFFY (FICTITIOUS CHARACTER) p.168

HOUSTON, STEVIE (FICTITIOUS CHARACTER) p.168

HOWARD, ED (FICTITIOUS CHARACTER) p.168

HOWARD, JASON (FICTITIOUS CHARACTER) p.168

HOWARD, JERI (FICTITIOUS CHARACTER) p.168

HOWARD, ROZ (FICTITIOUS CHARACTER) p.168

HOWE, EMMA (FICTITIOUS CHARACTER) p.168

HOWELL, NOAH (FICTITIOUS CHARACTER) p.168

HOWL, THE MAGICIAN (FICTITIOUS CHARACTER) p.168

HOWLAND, EDITH (FICTITIOUS CHARACTER) p.168

HOYLAND, TAMARA (FICTITIOUS CHARACTER) p.168

HUBBERT, T. S. (FICTITIOUS CHARACTER) p.168

HUBBLEY, HARRIET (FICTITIOUS CHARACTER) p.168

HUBER, RACHEL (FICTITIOUS CHARACTER) p.168

HUCKLEBERRY, HONEY (FICTITIOUS CHARACTER) p.168

HUDSON, EMMA (FICTITIOUS CHARACTER) p.168

HUDSON, OLIVIA (FICTITIOUS CHARACTER) p.168

HUDSON, ROBIN (FICTITIOUS CHARACTER) p.168

HUFF, WALTER (FICTITIOUS CHARACTER) p.168

HUGHES, KELLY (FICTITIOUS CHARACTER) p.168

HULL, JAKE (FICTITIOUS CHARACTER) p.168

HUNT, BESSIE (FICTITIOUS CHARACTER) p.168

HUNT, CLAIRE (FICTITIOUS CHARACTER) p.169

HUNT, GIL (FICTITIOUS CHARACTER) p.169

HUNT, MORGAN (FICTITIOUS CHARACTER) p.169

HUNTER, HAWK (FICTITIOUS CHARACTER) p.169

HUNTER, LEAH (FICTITIOUS CHARACTER) p.169

HUNTER, MATT (FICTITIOUS CHARACTER) p.169

HUTCHINSON, SANDY (FICTITIOUS CHARACTER) p.169

HUTTON, CLAIRE (FICTITIOUS CHARACTER) p.169

HYATT, LEXY (FICTITIOUS CHARACTER) p.169

HYDE, PATRICK (FICTITIOUS CHARACTER) p.169

HYLAND, MORN (FICTITIOUS CHARACTER) p.169

ICHIRO, SANO (FICTITIOUS CHARACTER) p.169

IL MORO (FICTITIOUS CHARACTER) p.169

ILES, DESMOND (FICTITIOUS CHARACTER) p.169

IMANISHI EITARO —FICTITIOUS CHARACTER) p.169

INDERMILL, BONNIE (FICTITIOUS CHARACTER) p.169

INGOLD INGLORION (FICTITIOUS CHARACTER) p.169

INNES, RACHEL (FICTITIOUS CHARACTER) p.169

INTERNATIONAL INVESTIGATION-RESCUE COMMITTEE (FICTITIOUS CHARACTERS) p.170

IQBAL, DETECTIVE (FICTITIOUS CHARACTER) p.170

ISAAC OF GIRONA (FICTITIOUS CHARACTER) p.170

ISEN, MARK (FICTITIOUS CHARACTER) p.170

IVES, HANNAH (FICTITIOUS CHARACTER) p.170

IVORY, KATE (FICTITIOUS CHARACTER) p.170

IVORY, MALCOLM (FICTITIOUS CHARACTER) p.170

JACK OF KINROWEN (FICTITIOUS CHARACTER) p.170

JACK, SASSELA (FICTITIOUS CHARACTER) p.170

JACK, THE RIPPER p.170

JACKSON, JACKO (FICTITIOUS CHARACTER) p.170

JACKSON, JEFF (FICTITIOUS CHARACTER) p.170

JACKSON, KEN (FICTITIOUS CHARACTER) p.170

JACOB, MATT (FICTITIOUS CHARACTER) p.170

JACOBS, CALISTA (FICTITIOUS CHARACTER) p.171

JACOBS, CHARLEY (FICTITIOUS CHARACTER) p.171

JACOBS, PETER (FICTITIOUS CHARACTER) p.171

JACOBY, MILES (FICTITIOUS CHARACTER) p.171

JACOBY, PAMELA (FICTITIOUS CHARACTER) p.171

JACOVICH, MILAN (FICTITIOUS CHARACTER) p.171

JACOWICZ, ISADORA 'JAKE' (FICTITIOUS CHARACTER) p.171

JADE, MARA (FICTITIOUS CHARACTER) p.171

JAELLYN (FICTITIOUS CHARACTER: LOGSTON) p.171

JAENELLE (FICTITIOUS CHARACTER) p.171

JAKE (FICTITIOUS CHARACTER: CLEARY) p.171

JAMES, CASSIDY (FICTITIOUS CHARACTER) p.171

JAMES, DEWEY (FICTITIOUS CHARACTER) p.171

JAMES, DUKE (FICTITIOUS CHARACTER) p.171

JAMES, GEMMA (FICTITIOUS CHARACTER) p.171

JAMES, HILTON (FICTITIOUS CHARACTER) p.172

JAMES, JESSE, 1847-1882 p.172

JAMES, JESSE (FICTITIOUS CHARACTER) p.172

JAMES, JESSICA (FICTITIOUS CHARACTER) p.172
see James, Jesse (Fictitious Character)

JAMES, LIZ (FICTITIOUS CHARACTER) p.172
JAMESON, CASS (FICTITIOUS CHARACTER) p.172
JAMESON, MARGARET (FICTITIOUS CHARACTER) p.172
JAMMU, S. (FICTITIOUS CHARACTER) p.172
JANEK, FRANK (FICTITIOUS CHARACTER) p.172
JANEWAY, CLIFF (FICTITIOUS CHARACTER) p.172
JANEWAY, KATHRYN MARGARET (FICTITIOUS CHARACTER) p.172
JANSSON, WILLA (FICTITIOUS CHARACTER) p.172
JANUARY, BENJAMIN (FICTITIOUS CHARACTER) p.172
JARRETT, DAN (FICTITIOUS CHARACTER) p.172
JARVIS, DEREK (FICTITIOUS CHARACTER) p.172
JARVIS, ELENA (FICTITIOUS CHARACTER) p.172
JASPER, ELLEN (FICTITIOUS CHARACTER) p.172
JASPER, JAZZ (FICTITIOUS CHARACTER) p.173
JASPER, KATE (FICTITIOUS CHARACTER) p.173
JAVERT, INSPECTOR (FICTITIOUS CHARACTER) p.173
JAZEN (FICTITIOUS CHARACTER) p.173
JEEVES (FICTITIOUS CHARACTER) p.173
JEFFERS, ANNE (FICTITIOUS CHARACTER) p.174
JEFFERSON, ART (FICTITIOUS CHARACTER) p.174
JEFFRIES, ELISE (FICTITIOUS CHARACTER) p.174
JEFFRIES, HARRIET (FICTITIOUS CHARACTER) p.174
JEFFRIES, MRS. (FICTITIOUS CHARACTER) p.174
JEFFRY, JANE (FICTITIOUS CHARACTER) p.174
JEKYLL, DOCTOR (FICTITIOUS CHARACTER) p.174
JEKYLL, HESTER (FICTITIOUS CHARACTER) p.175
JENNER, JIMMY (FICTITIOUS CHARACTER) p.175
JENNER, VICTOR (FICTITIOUS CHARACTER) p.175
JENNINGS, MARILEE (FICTITIOUS CHARACTER) p.175
JENSEN, ALEX (FICTITIOUS CHARACTER) p.175
JENSEN, POUL (FICTITIOUS CHARACTER) p.175
JENSEN, SMOKE (FICTITIOUS CHARACTER) p.175
JESS, LADY (FICTITIOUS CHARACTER) p.176
JESUS CHRIST p.176
JIN, JOSHUA (FICTITIOUS CHARACTER) p.176
JIREL OF JOIRY (FICTITIOUS CHARACTER) p.176
JOAN, SISTER (FICTITIOUS CHARACTER) p.176
JOEY ONE WAY (FICTITIOUS CHARACTER) p.176
JOHANNSON, HILDA (FICTITIOUS CHARACTER) p.176
JOHNSON, AVA (FICTITIOUS CHARACTER) p.176
JOHNSON, COFFIN ED (FICTITIOUS CHARACTER) p.176
JOHNSON, DAVID (FICTITIOUS CHARACTER) p.176
JOHNSON, MAUREEN (FICTITIOUS CHARACTER) p.176
JOHNSON, TOY (FICTITIOUS CHARACTER) p.176
JOKER (FICTITIOUS CHARACTER) p.177
JONES, ABEL (FICTITIOUS CHARACTER) p.177
JONES, AMELIA (FICTITIOUS CHARACTER) p.177
JONES, BRIDGET (FICTITIOUS CHARACTER) p.177
JONES, CASEY (FICTITIOUS CHARACTER) p.177
JONES, CREIGHTON (FICTITIOUS CHARACTER) p.177
JONES, DAVID (FICTITIOUS CHARACTER) p.177
JONES, DEMARY (FICTITIOUS CHARACTER) p.177
JONES, ELIZABETH (FICTITIOUS CHARACTER) p.177
JONES, FREMONT (FICTITIOUS CHARACTER) p.177

JONES, GENENE (FICTITIOUS CHARACTER) p.177
JONES, GRAVE DIGGER (FICTITIOUS CHARACTER) p.177
JONES, INDIANA (FICTITIOUS CHARACTER) p.177
JONES, JACOB (FICTITIOUS CHARACTER) p.177
JONES, JOY-IN-THE-LORD (FICTITIOUS CHARACTER) p.177
JONES, NEELY (FICTITIOUS CHARACTER) p.177
JONES, NICCOLO (FICTITIOUS CHARACTER) p.177
JONES, SAM (FICTITIOUS CHARACTER) p.177
JONES, TEXANA (FICTITIOUS CHARACTER) p.177
JONES, TYLER (FICTITIOUS CHARACTER) p.178
JORDAN, ALICE (FICTITIOUS CHARACTER) p.178
JORDAN, CAROL (FICTITIOUS CHARACTER) p.178
JORDAN, EMILY (FICTITIOUS CHARACTER) p.178
JORDAN, HARRY (FICTITIOUS CHARACTER) p.178
JORDAN, JOHN (FICTITIOUS CHARACTER) p.178
JORIAN, KING OF XYLAR (FICTITIOUS CHARACTER) p.178
JORY (FICTITIOUS CHARACTER: BASS) p.178
JOSEPH, TREVOR (FICTITIOUS CHARACTER) p.178
JOSHUA (FICTITIOUS CHARACTER: GIRZONE) p.178
JOURDEMAYNE, TRUTH (FICTITIOUS CHARACTER) p.178
JURNET, BENJAMIN (FICTITIOUS CHARACTER) p.178
JURY, RICHARD (FICTITIOUS CHARACTER) p.178
JUSTICE, BENJAMIN (FICTITIOUS CHARACTER) p.179
KACHIGAN, MILO (FICTITIOUS CHARACTER) p.179
KAI LUNG (FICTITIOUS CHARACTER) p.179
KAINE, ALLISON (FICTITIOUS CHARACTER) p.179
KAINE, DANIEL (FICTITIOUS CHARACTER) p.179
KAISER, BILL (FICTITIOUS CHARACTER) p.179
KAMAL, BEN (FICTITIOUS CHARACTER) p.179
KAMIYA FAMILY (FICTITIOUS CHARACTERS) p.179
KANE, GAVIN (FICTITIOUS CHARACTER) p.179
KANTOR, ALEXANDER (FICTITIOUS CHARACTER) p.179
KARDON, DAN (FICTITIOUS CHARACTER) p.179
KARP, BUTCH (FICTITIOUS CHARACTER) p.179
KASDAN, DAN (FICTITIOUS CHARACTER) p.179
KEAN, MAGGIE (FICTITIOUS CHARACTER) p.179
KEANE, OWEN (FICTITIOUS CHARACTER) p.179
KEARNEY, DANIEL (FICTITIOUS CHARACTER) p.179
KEARNY, NEEVE (FICTITIOUS CHARACTER) p.179
KEATE, SARAH (FICTITIOUS CHARACTER) p.180
KEATING, NICKY (FICTITIOUS CHARACTER) p.180
KEBRON, ZAK (FICTITIOUS CHARACTER) p.180
KEDRIGERN (FICTITIOUS CHARACTER) p.180
KEENER, RYDAL (FICTITIOUS CHARACTER) p.180
KELLEHER, BOBBY (FICTITIOUS CHARACTER) p.180
KELLER, LINCOLN (FICTITIOUS CHARACTER) p.180
KELLING, SARAH (FICTITIOUS CHARACTER) p.180
KELLY, ANDRE (FICTITIOUS CHARACTER) p.180
KELLY, HOMER (FICTITIOUS CHARACTER) p.180
KELLY, IRENE (FICTITIOUS CHARACTER) p.180
KELLY, JOHN (FICTITIOUS CHARACTER) p.181
    see Clark, John (Fictitious Character)

KELLY, LUTHER SAGE, 1849-1928 p.181
KELLY, PAUL (FICTITIOUS CHARACTER) p.181
KELLY, VIRGINIA (FICTITIOUS CHARACTER) p.181
KELTNER, JASON (FICTITIOUS CHARACTER) p.181
KELVIN OF RUD (FICTITIOUS CHARACTER) p.181
KEMP, JOHN MASON (FICTITIOUS CHARACTER) p.181
KEMP, LENNOX (FICTITIOUS CHARACTER) p.181
KENDALL, CORAL (FICTITIOUS CHARACTER) p.181
KENDALL, JOHN (FICTITIOUS CHARACTER) p.181
KENDRICK, JONATHAN (FICTITIOUS CHARACTER) p.181
KENDRY, VEIL (FICTITIOUS CHARACTER) p.181
KENNEDY, CHRISTY (FICTITIOUS CHARACTER) p.181
KENNEDY, JERRY (FICTITIOUS CHARACTER) p.181
KENOBI, OBI-WAN (FICTITIOUS CHARACTER) p.181
KENT, CHARLOTTE (FICTITIOUS CHARACTER) p.182
KENWOOD, CHRISTA (FICTITIOUS CHARACTER) p.182
KENZIE, PATRICK (FICTITIOUS CHARACTER) p.182
KEOGH, HARRY (FICTITIOUS CHARACTER) p.182
KEOUGH, JOE (FICTITIOUS CHARACTER) p.182
KEREMOS, HELEN (FICTITIOUS CHARACTER) p.182
KERGULIN, ZOE (FICTITIOUS CHARACTER) p.182
KERN, KAREN (FICTITIOUS CHARACTER) p.182
KERN, LINDSEY (FICTITIOUS CHARACTER) p.182
KERNEY, KEVIN (FICTITIOUS CHARACTER) p.182
KERRIGAN, JOSH (FICTITIOUS CHARACTER) p.182
KES (FICTITIOUS CHARACTER) p.182
KESSINGER, MEG (FICTITIOUS CHARACTER) p.182
KESTREL, JULIAN (FICTITIOUS CHARACTER) p.182
KETTERLING, KATE (FICTITIOUS CHARACTER) p.182
KEYES, BRIAN (FICTITIOUS CHARACTER) p.182
KHAAVREN (FICTITIOUS CHARACTER) p.182
KI (FICTITIOUS CHARACTER) p.182
KICKAHA (FICTITIOUS CHARACTER) p.183
KICKLIGHTER, TRUMAN (FICTITIOUS CHARACTER) p.183
KIDD AND LUELLEN (FICTITIOUS CHARACTERS) p.183
KIET, BAMSAN (FICTITIOUS CHARACTER) p.184
KILBOURN, JOANNE (FICTITIOUS CHARACTER) p.184
KILDARE, DOCTOR (FICTITIOUS CHARACTER) p.184
KILKENNY, NOLAN (FICTITIOUS CHARACTER) p.184
KILLEBREW, COLEY (FICTITIOUS CHARACTER) p.184
KILLIGAN, MICHAEL (FICTITIOUS CHARACTER) p.184
KILMER, JAKE (FICTITIOUS CHARACTER) p.184
KIM, HARRY (FICTITIOUS CHARACTER) p.184
KIM, SISTER (FICTITIOUS CHARACTER) p.184
KIMBERLAIN, JARED (FICTITIOUS CHARACTER) p.184
KINCAID, BEN (FICTITIOUS CHARACTER) p.184
KINCAID, BIFF (FICTITIOUS CHARACTER) p.184
KINCAID, CYNTHIA (FICTITIOUS CHARACTER) p.184
KINCAID, DUNCAN (FICTITIOUS CHARACTER) p.184
KINCAID, LIBBY (FICTITIOUS CHARACTER) p.184

KINCAID FAMILY (FICTITIOUS CHARACTERS) p.185

KING, JESSE (FICTITIOUS CHARACTER) p.185

KING, NATE (FICTITIOUS CHARACTER) p.185

KING, WILLOW (FICTITIOUS CHARACTER) p.185

KING KONG (FICTITIOUS CHARACTER) p.185

KINGSLEY, LUCY (FICTITIOUS CHARACTER) p.185

KINGSLEY, SARA (FICTITIOUS CHARACTER) p.185

KINLEY, JACKSON (FICTITIOUS CHARACTER) p.185

KINLOCH, ALEXANDER (FICTITIOUS CHARACTER) p.185

KINNEY, MICHAEL (FICTITIOUS CHARACTER) p.185

KINSELLA, KATE (FICTITIOUS CHARACTER) p.185

KIRA NERYS (FICTITIOUS CHARACTER) p.185

KIRBY, JACK (FICTITIOUS CHARACTER) p.185

KIRBY, JACQUELINE (FICTITIOUS CHARACTER) p.185

KIRK, DEVLIN (FICTITIOUS CHARACTER) p.185

KIRK, JAMES T. (FICTITIOUS CHARACTER) p.185

KITOLOGITAK, MATTEESIE (FICTITIOUS CHARACTER) p.187

KLEIN, DAVID (FICTITIOUS CHARACTER) p.187

KLEIN, DYLAN (FICTITIOUS CHARACTER) p.187

KLEIN, RAY (FICTITIOUS CHARACTER) p.187

KLICK, CHRIS (FICTITIOUS CHARACTER) p.187

KLINE, HARRY (FICTITIOUS CHARACTER) p.187

KLOTSKY, SONIA 'SONNY' (FICTITIOUS CHARACTER) p.187

KNIGHT, JERRY (FICTITIOUS CHARACTER) p.188

KNIGHT, MICKY (FICTITIOUS CHARACTER) p.188

KNIGHT, PHILIP (FICTITIOUS CHARACTER) p.188

KNIGHT, ROGER (FICTITIOUS CHARACTER) p.188

KNOTT, DEBORAH (FICTITIOUS CHARACTER) p.188

KOCH, ED, 1924- p.188

KODIAK, ATTICUS (FICTITIOUS CHARACTER) p.188

KOERNEY, KATHRYN (FICTITIOUS CHARACTER) p.188

KOESLER, ROBERT, FATHER (FICTITIOUS CHARACTER) p.188

KOHLER, HERMANN (FICTITIOUS CHARACTER) p.189

KOKO (FICTITIOUS CHARACTER) p.189

KOSCUISKO, ANDREJ (FICTITIOUS CHARACTER) p.190

KOSLOW, LEIGH (FICTITIOUS CHARACTER) p.190

KOVAK, MILTON (FICTITIOUS CHARACTER) p.190

KOZAK, THEA (FICTITIOUS CHARACTER) p.190

KOZOL, TONY (FICTITIOUS CHARACTER) p.190

KRAMER, MERRY (FICTITIOUS CHARACTER) p.190

KRAMER, TROMPIE (FICTITIOUS CHARACTER) p.190

KRAYCHIK, STAN (FICTITIOUS CHARACTER) p.190

KREIZLER, LASZLO (FICTITIOUS CHARACTER) p.190

KRISTOS, BROTHER (FICTITIOUS CHARACTER) p.190

KRUEGER, FREDDY (FICTITIOUS CHARACTER) p.190

KRUGER, DAN (FICTITIOUS CHARACTER) p.190

KRUGER, HERBIE (FICTITIOUS CHARACTER) p.190

KRUSE, KIMMY (FICTITIOUS CHARACTER) p.190

LABATARDE, MAGDALENE (FICTITIOUS CHARACTER) p.190

LACEY, MEG (FICTITIOUS CHARACTER) p.190

LA FORGE, GEORDI (FICTITIOUS CHARACTER) p.190

LAIDLAW, JACK (FICTITIOUS CHARACTER) p.191

LAIRD, ANNIE (FICTITIOUS CHARACTER) p.191

LAKE, BARRETT (FICTITIOUS CHARACTER) p.191

LAKE, CONNIE (FICTITIOUS CHARACTER) p.191

LAKEN, DARCY (FICTITIOUS CHARACTER) p.191

LAMAR, KATLIN (FICTITIOUS CHARACTER) p.191

LAMB, ELIZABETH (FICTITIOUS CHARACTER) p.191

LAMB, MATTHEW (FICTITIOUS CHARACTER) p.191

LAMBROS, JULIA (FICTITIOUS CHARACTER) p.191

LAMBROS, NICK (FICTITIOUS CHARACTER) p.191

LAMERINO, GLORIA (FICTITIOUS CHARACTER) p.191

LANDIS, WOODLEY (FICTITIOUS CHARACTER) p.191

LANDON, ARNOLD (FICTITIOUS CHARACTER) p.191

LANDRY FAMILY (FICTITIOUS CHARACTERS) p.191

LANE, MARK (FICTITIOUS CHARACTER) p.191

LANGDON, ROBERT (FICTITIOUS CHARACTER) p.191

LANGDON, SKIP (FICTITIOUS CHARACTER) p.191

LANGE, ELIZABETH (FICTITIOUS CHARACTER) p.192

LANGE, LIZBET (FICTITIOUS CHARACTER) p.192

LANGLEY, INGRID (FICTITIOUS CHARACTER) p.192

LANGSLOW, MEG (FICTITIOUS CHARACTER) p.192

LANGSTON, TOM (FICTITIOUS CHARACTER) p.192

LANNAT, CAPTAIN (FICTITIOUS CHARACTER) p.192

LANNIHAN, WOLF (FICTITIOUS CHARACTER) p.192

LANOIS, ADELE (FICTITIOUS CHARACTER) p.192

LANSING, CLIFF (FICTITIOUS CHARACTER) p.192

LARCH, MARIAN (FICTITIOUS CHARACTER) p.192

LARKIN, ELDON (FICTITIOUS CHARACTER) p.192

LARKIN, POP (FICTITIOUS CHARACTER) p.192

LARKIN FAMILY (FICTITIOUS CHARACTERS) p.192

LAROCHE, RENEE (FICTITIOUS CHARACTER) p.192

LARSON, JACK (FICTITIOUS CHARACTER) p.192

LARUE, CHARLOTTE (FICTITIOUS CHARACTER) p.192

LASH, ERNEST (FICTITIOUS CHARACTER) p.192

LASLOW, DEBRA (FICTITIOUS CHARACTER) p.192

LASSIE (FICTITIOUS CHARACTER) p.192

LASSITER, DANE (FICTITIOUS CHARACTER) p.192

LASSITER, JAKE (FICTITIOUS CHARACTER) p.192

LASTANZA, DINO (FICTITIOUS CHARACTER) p.193

LATHAM, DREW (FICTITIOUS CHARACTER) p.193

LATIMER, CHARLES (FICTITIOUS CHARACTER) p.193

LATIN, MAX (FICTITIOUS CHARACTER) p.193

LATTERLY, HESTER (FICTITIOUS CHARACTER) p.193

LAUGHTON, MITCH (FICTITIOUS CHARACTER) p.193

LAURANO, LAUREN (FICTITIOUS CHARACTER) p.193

LAVINE, ROSIE (FICTITIOUS CHARACTER) p.193

LAVOTINI, SIERRA (FICTITIOUS CHARACTER) p.193

LAWLESS, JANE (FICTITIOUS CHARACTER) p.193

LAWRENCE, MAGGIE (FICTITIOUS CHARACTER) p.193

LAWSON, GARDNER (FICTITIOUS CHARACTER) p.193

LAWSON, LORETTA (FICTITIOUS CHARACTER) p.193

LAZARUS, RINA (FICTITIOUS CHARACTER) p.193

LEAPHORN, JOE, LT. (FICTITIOUS CHARACTER) p.194

LEARY-PARKER, TIMMIE (FICTITIOUS CHARACTER) p.194

LECTER, HANNIBAL (FICTITIOUS CHARACTER) p.194

LEDUC, AIMEE (FICTITIOUS CHARACTER) p.194

LEE, ANNA (FICTITIOUS CHARACTER) p.194

LEE, HEAVEN (FICTITIOUS CHARACTER) p.195

LEE, ROBERT E. (ROBERT EDWARD), 1807-1870 p.195

LEE, WILL (FICTITIOUS CHARACTER) p.195

LEFLER, ROBIN (FICTITIOUS CHARACTER) p.195

LEIA, PRINCESS (FICTITIOUS CHARACTER) p.195

LEIDL, CONSTANCE (FICTITIOUS CHARACTER) p.196

LEIGH, MARTHA (FICTITIOUS CHARACTER) p.196

LEIGH, ROSALIND (FICTITIOUS CHARACTER) p.196

LENAHAN, KIERAN (FICTITIOUS CHARACTER) p.196

LENNOX, BILL (FICTITIOUS CHARACTER) p.196

LENNOX, TORY (FICTITIOUS CHARACTER) p.196

LENSON, DAN (FICTITIOUS CHARACTER) p.196

LEONARDO, DA VINCI, 1452-1519 p.196

LEROY, PETER (FICTITIOUS CHARACTER) p.196

LESTAT (FICTITIOUS CHARACTER) p.197

LESTRADE, INSPECTOR (FICTITIOUS CHARACTER) p.197

LEVENDEUR, CATHERINE (FICTITIOUS CHARACTER) p.197

LEVINE, DANNY (FICTITIOUS CHARACTER) p.197

LEVINE, MICHAEL (FICTITIOUS CHARACTER) p.197

LEWIS, MELDRICK (FICTITIOUS CHARACTER) p.197

LEWIS, MORDECAI (FICTITIOUS CHARACTER) p.197

LEWIS, REBECCA (FICTITIOUS CHARACTER) p.197

LEWIS, SERGEANT (FICTITIOUS CHARACTER) p.197

LEWIS, WYN (FICTITIOUS CHARACTER) p.198

LEWRIE, ALAN (FICTITIOUS CHARACTER) p.198

LIDENBROCK, PROFESSOR (FICTITIOUS CHARACTER) p.198

LIEBERMAN, ABE (FICTITIOUS CHARACTER) p.199

LIFFEY, JACK (FICTITIOUS CHARACTER) p.199

LIGHT, ROBIN (FICTITIOUS CHARACTER) p.199

LIGHTFOOT, MARIE (FICTITIOUS CHARACTER) p.199

LIGHTSTONE, HARRY (FICTITIOUS CHARACTER) p.199

LI'L ABNER (FICTITIOUS CHARACTER) p.199

LIL, AUNTIE (FICTITIOUS CHARACTER) p.199

LINCOLN, EDWARD (FICTITIOUS CHARACTER) p.199

LINDSEY, HOBART (FICTITIOUS CHARACTER) p.199

LINNEAR, NICHOLAS (FICTITIOUS CHARACTER) p.199

LISAN, MAGALIE (FICTITIOUS CHARACTER) p.200

LISLE, DARINA (FICTITIOUS CHARACTER) p.200

List of Subject Headings - Fiction

LITTLE ORPHAN ANNIE (FICTITIOUS CHARACTER) p.200

LITTLEJOHN, ELDON (FICTITIOUS CHARACTER) p.200

LIU, HULAN (FICTITIOUS CHARACTER) p.200

LIVESAY, PETER (FICTITIOUS CHARACTER) p.200

LLOYD, HILARY (FICTITIOUS CHARACTER) p.200

LLOYD, INSPECTOR (FICTITIOUS CHARACTER) p.200

LOCKE, JOHN (FICTITIOUS CHARACTER) p.200

LOCKWOOD, JOHN (FICTITIOUS CHARACTER) p.200

LOGAN (FICTITIOUS CHARACTER: NOLAN) p.200

LOGAN, BRIDGETT (FICTITIOUS CHARACTER) p.200

LOGAN, KATE (FICTITIOUS CHARACTER) p.200

LOGAN, WHITNEY (FICTITIOUS CHARACTER) p.200

LOGAN FAMILY (FICTITIOUS CHARACTERS) p.200

LONDON, ED (FICTITIOUS CHARACTER) p.200

LONDON, TEDDY (FICTITIOUS CHARACTER) p.200

LONG, LAZARUS (FICTITIOUS CHARACTER) p.200

LONG, MAYLAND (FICTITIOUS CHARACTER) p.201

LONGARM (FICTITIOUS CHARACTER) p.201

LONGCHAMP, DAWN (FICTITIOUS CHARACTER) p.203

LONGINUS, CASCA (FICTITIOUS CHARACTER) p.203

LONGMIRE, HARRY (FICTITIOUS CHARACTER) p.203

LONIGAN, STUDS (FICTITIOUS CHARACTER) p.203

LOOMIS, TUCKER (FICTITIOUS CHARACTER) p.203

LORD, EMMA (FICTITIOUS CHARACTER) p.203

LORD WESTFIELD'S MEN (FICTITIOUS CHARACTERS) p.203

LORING, HELEN, LADY (FICTITIOUS CHARACTER) p.203

LOUDERMILK, DOTTIE (FICTITIOUS CHARACTER) p.203

LOUDERMILK, JOE (FICTITIOUS CHARACTER) p.204

LOVE, PHAROAH (FICTITIOUS CHARACTER) p.204

LOVEJOY (FICTITIOUS CHARACTER) p.204

LOVELACE, CLARISSE (FICTITIOUS CHARACTER) p.204

LOWELL, CRAIG (FICTITIOUS CHARACTER) p.204

LOWELL, TONY (FICTITIOUS CHARACTER) p.205

LOWENKOPF, SHELLY (FICTITIOUS CHARACTER) p.205

LOWRY, GIDEON (FICTITIOUS CHARACTER) p.205

LUCIA (FICTITIOUS CHARACTER) p.205

LUCKS, JOLAYNE (FICTITIOUS CHARACTER) p.205

LUFT, BUNNY (FICTITIOUS CHARACTER) p.205

LUGER, DAVID (FICTITIOUS CHARACTER) p.205

LUMSEY, NORA (FICTITIOUS CHARACTER) p.205

LUNT, HENRY (FICTITIOUS CHARACTER) p.205

LUPA, AUGUST (FICTITIOUS CHARACTER) p.205

LUTHER, DOC (FICTITIOUS CHARACTER) p.205

LYNCH, JACK (FICTITIOUS CHARACTER) p.205

LYNDHURST, JOANNA (FICTITIOUS CHARACTER) p.205

LYNLEY, THOMAS (FICTITIOUS CHARACTER) p.205

LYNX, JASON (FICTITIOUS CHARACTER) p.205

LYNX, PHILIP (FICTITIOUS CHARACTER) p.205
    see Flinx of the Commonwealth (Fictitious Character)

LYON, THOMAS (FICTITIOUS CHARACTER) p.205

MABRY, BUBBA (FICTITIOUS CHARACTER) p.205

MCALISTER, HALEY (FICTITIOUS CHARACTER) p.206

MACALISTER, MARTI (FICTITIOUS CHARACTER) p.206

MACALPIN, ALASTAIR (FICTITIOUS CHARACTER) p.206

MCAULIFF, ALEX (FICTITIOUS CHARACTER) p.206

MCAULIFFE, LARRY (FICTITIOUS CHARACTER) p.206

MACBETH, HAMISH (FICTITIOUS CHARACTER) p.206

MCCABE, CASSIDY (FICTITIOUS CHARACTER) p.206

MCCABE, MURDOCK (FICTITIOUS CHARACTER) p.206

MCCADDEN, CARL (FICTITIOUS CHARACTER) p.206

MCCAIN, SAM (FICTITIOUS CHARACTER) p.206

MACCALLISTER FAMILY (FICTITIOUS CHARACTER) p.206

MCCARRON, BLUE (FICTITIOUS CHARACTER) p.206

MCCARTHY, GAIL (FICTITIOUS CHARACTER) p.207

MCCARTHY, JAMES (FICTITIOUS CHARACTER) p.207

MCCAULEY, QUINT (FICTITIOUS CHARACTER) p.207

MCCHANDLER, DOAN (FICTITIOUS CHARACTER) p.207

MCCLEARY, MIKE (FICTITIOUS CHARACTER) p.207

MCCLEARY, WILTON (FICTITIOUS CHARACTER) p.207

MCCLEET, ADAM (FICTITIOUS CHARACTER) p.207

MCCLENDON, ROSE (FICTITIOUS CHARACTER) p.207

MCCLINTOCH, LARA (FICTITIOUS CHARACTER) p.207

MCCLINTOCK, SHIRLEY (FICTITIOUS CHARACTER) p.207

MCCONE, SHARON (FICTITIOUS CHARACTER) p.207

MCCONNELL, JAMES (FICTITIOUS CHARACTER) p.208

MCCORKLE, MAC (FICTITIOUS CHARACTER) p.208

MCCOSKEY, SUNNY (FICTITIOUS CHARACTER) p.208

MCCOY, DOC (FICTITIOUS CHARACTER) p.208

MCCOY, KEN (FICTITIOUS CHARACTER) p.208

MCCOY, LEONARD (FICTITIOUS CHARACTER) p.208

MCCRACKEN, BLAINE (FICTITIOUS CHARACTER) p.209

MCCRAE, AUGUSTUS (FICTITIOUS CHARACTER) p.209

MCCUNN, DICKSON (FICTITIOUS CHARACTER) p.209

MCCUSKER, KATE (FICTITIOUS CHARACTER) p.209

MACDONALD, DEVON (FICTITIOUS CHARACTER) p.209

MCDONALD, PAUL (FICTITIOUS CHARACTER) p.209

MCDOWELL, SCOTT (FICTITIOUS CHARACTER) p.209

MCEVOY, JACK (FICTITIOUS CHARACTER) p.209

MCGAMMON, CLYDE (FICTITIOUS CHARACTER) p.209

MCGARR, PETER (FICTITIOUS CHARACTER) p.209

MCGARVEY, JACK (FICTITIOUS CHARACTER) p.209

MCGARVEY, KIRK (FICTITIOUS CHARACTER) p.209

MCGEE, TRAVIS (FICTITIOUS CHARACTER) p.209

MCGOWAN, JOHN (FICTITIOUS CHARACTER) p.210

MACGOWEN, MAGGIE (FICTITIOUS CHARACTER) p.210

MCGRAIL, NUALA ANNE (FICTITIOUS CHARACTER) p.210

MCGRATH, BILLY (FICTITIOUS CHARACTER) p.210

MCGRATH, KERRY (FICTITIOUS CHARACTER) p.210

MACGREGOR, LAKE (FICTITIOUS CHARACTER) p.210

MACGREGOR FAMILY (FICTITIOUS CHARACTERS) p.210

MCGROGAN, ANNIE (FICTITIOUS CHARACTER) p.210

MCGUFFIN, AMOS (FICTITIOUS CHARACTER) p.210

MCGUIRE, AMY (FICTITIOUS CHARACTER) p.210

MCGUIRE, JOSEPH PETER (FICTITIOUS CHARACTER) p.210

MCGUIRE, MADISON (FICTITIOUS CHARACTER) p.211

MCGUIRE, ROWLAND (FICTITIOUS CHARACTER) p.211

MCHENRY, MARK (FICTITIOUS CHARACTER) p.211

MCILVAIN, BILLY (FICTITIOUS CHARACTER) p.211

MACINTYRE, URBINO (FICTITIOUS CHARACTER) p.211

MACK, RUDYARD (FICTITIOUS CHARACTER) p.211

MACKADE FAMILY (FICTITIOUS CHARACTERS) p.211

MACKAY, KATHERYN (FICTITIOUS CHARACTER) p.211

MCKAY, KEVIN (FICTITIOUS CHARACTER) p.211

MACKENDRICK, ARIELLA (FICTITIOUS CHARACTER) p.211

MCKENNA, BRIAN (FICTITIOUS CHARACTER) p.211

MCKENNA, KATE (FICTITIOUS CHARACTER) p.211

MCKENNA, MICHAEL (FICTITIOUS CHARACTER) p.211

MCKENNA, PATIENCE (FICTITIOUS CHARACTER) p.211

MACKENZIE, AGNES (FICTITIOUS CHARACTER) p.211

MCKENZIE, ALEX (FICTITIOUS CHARACTER) p.211

MCKENZIE, MAC (FICTITIOUS CHARACTER) p.211

MACKENZIE FAMILY (FICTITIOUS CHARACTER) p.211

MCKINNEY, LEE (FICTITIOUS CHARACTER) p.211

MCKINNON, RACHEL (FICTITIOUS CHARACTER) p.211

MCKINNON, SAVANNAH (FICTITIOUS CHARACTER) p.211

MACKLIN, PETER (FICTITIOUS CHARACTER) p.211

MCKNIGHT, ALEX (FICTITIOUS CHARACTER) p.211

MCLAIN, MACE (FICTITIOUS CHARACTER) p.211

MACLANAHAN, PATRICK (FICTITIOUS CHARACTER) p.211

MACLAREN, NEIL (FICTITIOUS CHARACTER) p.212

MACLEAN, KATE, DETECTIVE (FICTITIOUS CHARACTER) p.212

MACLEAN, TOM (FICTITIOUS CHARACTER) p.212

MCLEES, KELLY (FICTITIOUS CHARACTER) p.212

MACLEISH, COOPER (FICTITIOUS CHARACTER) p.212

MCLEISH, JOHN (FICTITIOUS CHARACTER) p.212

MACLEOD, DUNCAN (FICTITIOUS CHARACTER) p.212

MCLEOD, ORLA (FICTITIOUS CHARACTER) p.212

MCMILLEN, BEN (FICTITIOUS CHARACTER) p.212

MCMORROW, JACK (FICTITIOUS CHARACTER) p.212

MCNALLY, ARCHY (FICTITIOUS CHARACTER) p.212

MCNEAL, AARON (FICTITIOUS CHARACTER) p.212

MCNEELY, KATHY (FICTITIOUS CHARACTER) p.213

MCNULTY, ENEAS (FICTITIOUS CHARACTER) p.213

MCPHEE, SUTTON (FICTITIOUS CHARACTER) p.213

MACPHERSON, ANNIE (FICTITIOUS CHARACTER) p.213

MACPHERSON, ELIZABETH (FICTITIOUS CHARACTER) p.213

MACPHERSON, SKY (FICTITIOUS CHARACTER) p.213

MCTAVISH, STONER (FICTITIOUS CHARACTER) p.213

MCVAY, LIZZIE (FICTITIOUS CHARACTER) p.213

MCWHINNY, TISH (FICTITIOUS CHARACTER) p.213

MADDOCK, JOREY (FICTITIOUS CHARACTER) p.213

MADDOCK, YANABA (FICTITIOUS CHARACTER) p.213

MADDOX, JUDY (FICTITIOUS CHARACTER) p.213

MADRIANI, PAUL (FICTITIOUS CHARACTER) p.213

MAGARACZ, NICK (FICTITIOUS CHARACTER) p.213

MAGLIONE, GIANNA (FICTITIOUS CHARACTER) p.213

MAGNUM, CUDDY (FICTITIOUS CHARACTER) p.213

MAGRUDER, TOMBSTONE (FICTITIOUS CHARACTER) p.213

MAGUIRE, MAGGIE (FICTITIOUS CHARACTER) p.213

MAGUIRE, TRISH (FICTITIOUS CHARACTER) p.213

MAGWITCH, ABEL (FICTITIOUS CHARACTER) p.213

MAIGRET, JULES (FICTITIOUS CHARACTER) p.213

MAITLAND, ANTONY (FICTITIOUS CHARACTER) p.216

MAKER, ALVIN (FICTITIOUS CHARACTER) p.216

MALAUSSENE, BENJAMIN (FICTITIOUS CHARACTER) p.216

MALCOLM, IAN (FICTITIOUS CHARACTER) p.216

MALCOLM, TRISH (FICTITIOUS CHARACTER) p.216

MALLARD, TIMOTHY (FICTITIOUS CHARACTER) p.216

MALLEN FAMILY (FICTITIOUS CHARACTER) p.216

MALLETT, DAN (FICTITIOUS CHARACTER) p.216

MALLETT, INSPECTOR (FICTITIOUS CHARACTER) p.216

MALLOREN FAMILY (FICTITIOUS CHARACTER) p.217

MALLORY (FICTITIOUS CHARACTER: COLLINS) p.217

MALLORY, KATHLEEN (FICTITIOUS CHARACTER) p.217

MALLORY, STUART (FICTITIOUS CHARACTER) p.217

MALLORY, WANDA (FICTITIOUS CHARACTER) p.217

MALLOY, CLAIRE (FICTITIOUS CHARACTER) p.217

MALLOY, FRANK (FICTITIOUS CHARACTER) p.217

MALLOY, HANNAH (FICTITIOUS CHARACTER) p.217

MALLOY, KIKI (FICTITIOUS CHARACTER) p.217

MALLOY, MACK (FICTITIOUS CHARACTER) p.217

MALONE, SCOBIE (FICTITIOUS CHARACTER) p.217

MALORY, SHEILA, MRS. (FICTITIOUS CHARACTER) p.217

MALORY, TOM (FICTITIOUS CHARACTER) p.218

MALTRAVERS, AUGUSTUS (FICTITIOUS CHARACTER) p.218

MANCINI, MUNCH (FICTITIOUS CHARACTER) p.218

MANDEL, GREG (FICTITIOUS CHARACTER) p.218

MANDELLA, WILLIAM (FICTITIOUS CHARACTER) p.218

MANION, TERRY (FICTITIOUS CHARACTER) p.218

MANKIND (FICTITIOUS CHARACTER) p.218

MANKOWSKI, CHRIS (FICTITIOUS CHARACTER) p.218

MANLEY, GERARD (FICTITIOUS CHARACTER) p.218

MANN, JACK (FICTITIOUS CHARACTER) p.218

MANNING, MARK (FICTITIOUS CHARACTER) p.218

MANNING, RHODA KATHERINE (FICTITIOUS CHARACTER) p.218

MANNING BROTHERS (FICTITIOUS CHARACTERS) p.218

MANTRELL, MATT (FICTITIOUS CHARACTER) p.218

MAPP, MISS (FICTITIOUS CHARACTER) p.218

MARCH, CARMEL (FICTITIOUS CHARACTER) p.218

MARCH, LAURA (FICTITIOUS CHARACTER) p.218

MARCH FAMILY (FICTITIOUS CHARACTERS) p.218

MARETTO, SUZANNE (FICTITIOUS CHARACTER) p.219

MARIANNE (FICTITIOUS CHARACTER: TEPPER) p.219

MARIE, BETH (FICTITIOUS CHARACTER) p.219

MARK OF TASAVALTA (FICTITIOUS CHARACTER) p.219

MARKBY, ALAN (FICTITIOUS CHARACTER) p.219

MARKHAM, GEORGE (FICTITIOUS CHARACTER) p.219

MARKHAM, ROY (FICTITIOUS CHARACTER) p.219

MARLEY, CAL (FICTITIOUS CHARACTER) p.219

MARLEY, PLATO (FICTITIOUS CHARACTER) p.219

MARLIN, JOE (FICTITIOUS CHARACTER) p.219

MARLOWE, LISA (FICTITIOUS CHARACTER) p.219

MARLOWE, PHILIP (FICTITIOUS CHARACTER) p.219

MAROSI, LIEUTENANT (FICTITIOUS CHARACTER) p.220

MARPLE, JANE (FICTITIOUS CHARACTER) p.220

MARSALA, CAT (FICTITIOUS CHARACTER) p.221

MARSH, EMMA (FICTITIOUS CHARACTER) p.221

MARSH, JENNIFER (FICTITIOUS CHARACTER) p.221

MARSHALL, ANNA (FICTITIOUS CHARACTER) p.221

MARSHALL, JORDAN (FICTITIOUS CHARACTER) p.221

MARSHALL, NEIL (FICTITIOUS CHARACTER) p.221

MARSHALL, SHARON (FICTITIOUS CHARACTER) p.221

MARTELLI, GERRY (FICTITIOUS CHARACTER) p.221

MARTIN, DOROTHY (FICTITIOUS CHARACTER) p.221

MARTIN, JAKE (FICTITIOUS CHARACTER) p.221

MARTIN, KAY (FICTITIOUS CHARACTER) p.221

MARTIN, SAZ (FICTITIOUS CHARACTER) p.222

MARTINDALE, THOMAS (FICTITIOUS CHARACTER) p.222

MARTINELLI, KATE (FICTITIOUS CHARACTER) p.222

MARTINEZ, DOLPH (FICTITIOUS CHARACTER) p.222

MARX, GROUCHO, 1891-1977 p.222

MARY ALICE (FICTITIOUS CHARACTER) p.222

MARY HELEN, SISTER (FICTITIOUS CHARACTER) p.222

MARY TERESA, SISTER (FICTITIOUS CHARACTER) p.222

MASON, MIRIEL (FICTITIOUS CHARACTER) p.222

MASON, PERRY (FICTITIOUS CHARACTER) p.222

MASON, TOM (FICTITIOUS CHARACTER) p.224

MASTERS, CAROLINE (FICTITIOUS CHARACTER) p.224

MASTERS, CHUCK (FICTITIOUS CHARACTER) p.224

MASTERS, GEORGE, DETECTIVE SUPERINTENDENT (FICTITIOUS CHARACTER) p.224

MASTERS, MOLLY (FICTITIOUS CHARACTER) p.224

MASUTO, MASAO (FICTITIOUS CHARACTER) p.224

MATELLI, ANGELA (FICTITIOUS CHARACTER) p.224

MATHIAS, MALCOLM 'MOON' (FICTITIOUS CHARACTER) p.224

MATLOCK, JAMES BARBOUS (FICTITIOUS CHARACTER) p.224

MATSUSHITA, DAIYU (FICTITIOUS CHARACTER) p.225

MATSUYAMA KAZE (FICTITIOUS CHARACTER) p.225

MATTHEWS, CHARLES (FICTITIOUS CHARACTER) p.225

MATTHEWS, DAPHNE (FICTITIOUS CHARACTER) p.225

MATTHEWS, MAREN (FICTITIOUS CHARACTER) p.225

MATTHEWS, NELL (FICTITIOUS CHARACTER) p.225

MATTHEWS, WYATT (FICTITIOUS CHARACTER) p.225

MATTISON, MATT (FICTITIOUS CHARACTER) p.225

MATURIN, STEPHEN (FICTITIOUS CHARACTER) p.225

MAVIN MANYSHAPED (FICTITIOUS CHARACTER) p.226

MAXIMILLIAN THE VAGUELY DISREPUTABLE (FICTITIOUS CHARACTER) p.226

MAXWELL, GEORGIA LEE (FICTITIOUS CHARACTER) p.226

MAXWELL, JACQUES (FICTITIOUS CHARACTER) p.226

MAXWELL, LAUREN (FICTITIOUS CHARACTER) p.226

MAXWELL, MAMA (FICTITIOUS CHARACTER) p.226

MAYFAIR WOMEN (FICTITIOUS CHARACTERS) p.226

MAYHEW, MISS (FICTITIOUS CHARACTER) p.226

MAYNARD, LOIS (FICTITIOUS CHARACTER) p.226

MAYO, ASEY (FICTITIOUS CHARACTER) p.226

MAYO, GIL (FICTITIOUS CHARACTER) p.226

MEADOWS, CHRIS (FICTITIOUS CHARACTER) p.226

MEAGHER, FEARGAL (FICTITIOUS CHARACTER) p.226

MEEHAN, ALVIRAH (FICTITIOUS CHARACTER) p.226

MEIKLEJOHN, CHARLIE (FICTITIOUS CHARACTER) p.226

MELLORS, KRISTIN (FICTITIOUS CHARACTER) p.226

MELVILLE, HERMAN, 1819-1891 p.226

MELVILLE, SUSAN (FICTITIOUS CHARACTER) p.226

MENDOZA, DIANA (FICTITIOUS CHARACTER) p.227

MENDOZA, LUIS (FICTITIOUS CHARACTER) p.227

MENLO, ANNIE (FICTITIOUS CHARACTER) p.227

MENSING, LOREN (FICTITIOUS CHARACTER) p.227

MERCER, PHILIP (FICTITIOUS CHARACTER) p.227

MERCURY, RYAN (FICTITIOUS CHARACTER) p.227

MEREDITH, CALLIOPE (FICTITIOUS CHARACTER) p.227

MEREN, LORD (FICTITIOUS CHARACTER) p.227

MERLIN (LEGENDARY CHARACTER) p.227

MERRICK FAMILY (FICTITIOUS CHARACTERS) p.228

MERRIMAN, MAGNUS (FICTITIOUS CHARACTER) p.228

MERRIVALE, HENRY, SIR (FICTITIOUS CHARACTER) p.228

MERSI, MICK (FICTITIOUS CHARACTER) p.228

MESPIL, LUNZIE (FICTITIOUS CHARACTER) p.228

METCALF, CONRAD (FICTITIOUS CHARACTER) p.228

METELLUS, DECIUS CAECILIUS (FICTITIOUS CHARACTER) p.228

MIATHAN, ARCHMAGE (FICTITIOUS CHARACTER) p.228

MICHAELS, LAURA (FICTITIOUS CHARACTER) p.228

MICHAELSON, RICHARD (FICTITIOUS CHARACTER) p.228

MIDDLETON, MARIS (FICTITIOUS CHARACTER) p.228

MIDDLETON-BROWN, DAVID (FICTITIOUS CHARACTER) p.228

MIDNIGHT, BRENDA (FICTITIOUS CHARACTER) p.228

MIDNIGHT LOUIE (FICTITIOUS CHARACTER) p.228

MILLER, ANNIK (FICTITIOUS CHARACTER) p.229

MILLER, CLAUDIA (FICTITIOUS CHARACTER) p.229

MILLER, LYDIA (FICTITIOUS CHARACTER) p.229

MILLER, PETER, LIEUTENANT (FICTITIOUS CHARACTER) p.229

MILLER, RICHARD MILHOUS 'NIX' (FICTITIOUS CHARACTER) p.229

MILLER, ROBIN (FICTITIOUS CHARACTER) p.229

MILLHOLLAND, KATE (FICTITIOUS CHARACTER) p.229

MILLHONE, KINSEY (FICTITIOUS CHARACTER) p.229

MILLS, TODD (FICTITIOUS CHARACTER) p.230

MILLSAPS, LARRY (FICTITIOUS CHARACTER) p.230

MILODRAGOVITCH, MILO (FICTITIOUS CHARACTER) p.230

MILYUKIN, MIKHAIL (FICTITIOUS CHARACTER) p.230

MINOGUE, MATT (FICTITIOUS CHARACTER) p.230

MIRACLE, TORI (FICTITIOUS CHARACTER) p.230

MITCHELL, CASSANDRA (FICTITIOUS CHARACTER) p.230

MITCHELL, MEREDITH (FICTITIOUS CHARACTER) p.230

MITCHELL, MICHELLE (MITCH) (FICTITIOUS CHARACTER) p.230

MITRY, DESIREE (FICTITIOUS CHARACTER) p.230

MOFFETT, PIERCE (FICTITIOUS CHARACTER) p.230

MOLE, ADRIAN (FICTITIOUS CHARACTER) p.230

MOM (FICTITIOUS CHARACTER: YAFFE) p.231

MONAGHAN, TESS (FICTITIOUS CHARACTER) p.231

MONGO (FICTITIOUS CHARACTER) p.231

MONK, DITTANY HENBIT (FICTITIOUS CHARACTER) p.231

MONK, IVAN (FICTITIOUS CHARACTER) p.231

MONK, JASON (FICTITIOUS CHARACTER) p.231

MONK, OSBERT (FICTITIOUS CHARACTER) p.231

MONK, WILLIAM (FICTITIOUS CHARACTER) p.231

MONMOUTH, ROBERT CAREY, EARL OF, CA. 1560-1639 p.231

MONTANA, KENT (FICTITIOUS CHARACTER) p.231

MONTERO, BRITT (FICTITIOUS CHARACTER) p.231

MONTEZ, LUIS (FICTITIOUS CHARACTER) p.232

MONTGOMERY, INSPECTOR (FICTITIOUS CHARACTER) p.232

MONTGOMERY, KAYLA (FICTITIOUS CHARACTER) p.232

MONTGOMERY, KELLIE (FICTITIOUS CHARACTER) p.232

MONTGOMERY FAMILY (FICTITIOUS CHARACTERS) p.232

MONTONE, JAMES (FICTITIOUS CHARACTER) p.232

MONTROSE, CLAIRE (FICTITIOUS CHARACTER) p.232

MONTROSE, JEAN (FICTITIOUS CHARACTER) p.232

MOODROW, STANLEY (FICTITIOUS CHARACTER) p.232

MOODY, KEITH (FICTITIOUS CHARACTER) p.233

MOODY, SCOTT (FICTITIOUS CHARACTER) p.233

MOON, CHARLIE (FICTITIOUS CHARACTER: DOSS) p.233

MOON, CHARLIE (FICTITIOUS CHARACTER: YARBRO) p.233

MOON, DONOVAN (FICTITIOUS CHARACTER) p.233

MOON, JOHN (FICTITIOUS CHARACTER) p.233

MOON, PHYLLIDA (FICTITIOUS CHARACTER) p.233

MOONDARK, GAN (FICTITIOUS CHARACTER) p.233

MORA, VINCENT (FICTITIOUS CHARACTER) p.233

MORAN, GEORGE (FICTITIOUS CHARACTER) p.233

MORAN, STOKES (FICTITIOUS CHARACTER) p.233

MORELL, CHARLIE (FICTITIOUS CHARACTER) p.233

MORELLI, TEODORA (FICTITIOUS CHARACTER) p.233

MORGAN, AVERY (FICTITIOUS CHARACTER) p.233

MORGAN, CORDELIA (FICTITIOUS CHARACTER) p.233

MORGAN, DANA (FICTITIOUS CHARACTER) p.233

MORGAN, GREG (FICTITIOUS CHARACTER) p.233

MORGAN, JAMES (FICTITIOUS CHARACTER) p.233

MORGAN, SARA (FICTITIOUS CHARACTER) p.233

MORGAN, TAYLOR (FICTITIOUS CHARACTER) p.233

MORIARTY, PROFESSOR (FICTITIOUS CHARACTER) p.233

MORIZIO, SAL (FICTITIOUS CHARACTER) p.233

MORLAND, REBECCA (FICTITIOUS CHARACTER) p.233

MORLEY, IRISH (FICTITIOUS CHARACTER) p.233

MORLEY, SI (FICTITIOUS CHARACTER) p.233

MORRIS, JOHN (FICTITIOUS CHARACTER) p.234

MORRIS, LEE (FICTITIOUS CHARACTER) p.234

MORRIS, RUTHIE KANTOR (FICTITIOUS CHARACTER) p.234

MORRISON, HUGH (FICTITIOUS CHARACTER) p.234

MORRISON, JOE (FICTITIOUS CHARACTER) p.234

MORRISON, MAY (FICTITIOUS CHARACTER) p.234

MORRISSEY, INSPECTOR (FICTITIOUS CHARACTER) p.234

MORRONE, RITA (FICTITIOUS CHARACTER) p.234

MORSE, INSPECTOR (FICTITIOUS CHARACTER) p.234

MORSON, FELIX (FICTITIOUS CHARACTER) p.234

MORTON, GLADYS BABBINGTON (FICTITIOUS CHARACTER) p.235

MORTON, JAMES (FICTITIOUS CHARACTER) p.235

MOSELEY, HOKE (FICTITIOUS CHARACTER) p.235

MOSES, ZEN (FICTITIOUS CHARACTER) p.235

MOSS, GRIFFIN (FICTITIOUS CHARACTER: BANTOCK) p.235
  see Griffin (Fictitious Character: Bantock)

MOSS, WILEY (FICTITIOUS CHARACTER) p.235

MOTO, MR. (FICTITIOUS CHARACTER) p.235

MOTT, ANGUS (FICTITIOUS CHARACTER) p.235

MOUNTAIN MAN (FICTITIOUS CHARACTER) p.235
  see Jensen, Smoke (Fictitious Character)

MOUNTFORD, SUZIE (FICTITIOUS CHARACTER) p.235

MOWGLI (FICTITIOUS CHARACTER) p.235

MOZART, WOLFGANG AMADEUS, 1756-1791 p.235

MUFFIN, CHARLIE (FICTITIOUS CHARACTER) p.235

MULCAHANEY, NORAH (FICTITIOUS CHARACTER) p.235

MULCAY, KATE (FICTITIOUS CHARACTER) p.235

MULDER, FOX (FICTITIOUS CHARACTER) p.235

MULHEISEN, FANG, DETECTIVE SERGEANT (FICTITIOUS CHARACTER) p.235

MULLER, KURT (FICTITIOUS CHARACTER) p.236

MULLIGAN, DOYLE (FICTITIOUS CHARACTER) p.236

MULLINS, BILL (FICTITIOUS CHARACTER) p.236

MULLOY, DENNIS MICHAEL (FICTITIOUS CHARACTER) p.236

MUNN, ALEX (FICTITIOUS CHARACTER) p.236

MUNRO, ANNE (FICTITIOUS CHARACTER) p.236

MUNRO, EWAN (FICTITIOUS CHARACTER) p.236

MURDOCH, ROSS (FICTITIOUS CHARACTER) p.236

MURDOCH, WILLIAM (FICTITIOUS CHARACTER) p.236

MURDOCK, PAGE (FICTITIOUS CHARACTER) p.236

MURPHY, AL (FICTITIOUS CHARACTER) p.236

MURPHY, FRANK (FICTITIOUS CHARACTER) p.236

MURPHY, MRS. (FICTITIOUS CHARACTER) p.236

MURPHY, RUBY (FICTITIOUS CHARACTER) p.236

MURPHY, SEAN (FICTITIOUS CHARACTER) p.236

MUSGRAVE, TOM (FICTITIOUS CHARACTER) p.236

MYER, MELANIE (FICTITIOUS CHARACTER) p.236

MYLES, JORDAN (FICTITIOUS CHARACTER) p.236

MZAR, JEWEL (FICTITIOUS CHARACTER) p.236

NAJARIAN, ERIC (FICTITIOUS CHARACTER) p.236

NAMELESS DETECTIVE (FICTITIOUS CHARACTER) p.236

NARMAN, SABRA (FICTITIOUS CHARACTER) p.237

NASH, DAVID (FICTITIOUS CHARACTER) p.237

NASH, JESTON (FICTITIOUS CHARACTER) p.237

NAUGHTON, TERRY (FICTITIOUS CHARACTER) p.237

NAVARRE, TRES (FICTITIOUS CHARACTER) p.237

NAZHURET (FICTITIOUS CHARACTER) p.237

NEBRASKA (FICTITIOUS CHARACTER) p.237

NEELIX (FICTITIOUS CHARACTER) p.237

NEHMER, KURT (FICTITIOUS CHARACTER) p.237

NELSON, VICKI (FICTITIOUS CHARACTER) p.237

NESS, ELIOT (FICTITIOUS CHARACTER) p.237

NESTLETON, ALICE (FICTITIOUS CHARACTER) p.237

NEVELSON, JACK (FICTITIOUS CHARACTER) p.237

NEWCOMBE, CHLOE (FICTITIOUS CHARACTER) p.237

NEWTON, CASSIE (FICTITIOUS CHARACTER) p.237

NEXT, THURSDAY (FICTITIOUS CHARACTER) p.237

NEZ, LEE (FICTITIOUS CHARACTER) p.238

NICHOLS, JANE (FICTITIOUS CHARACTER) p.238

NICHOLS, NASON (FICTITIOUS CHARACTER) p.238

NICHOLSON, ALIX (FICTITIOUS CHARACTER) p.238

NICKERSON, MARTHA (FICTITIOUS CHARACTER) p.238

NICKLES, EDDIE (FICTITIOUS CHARACTER) p.238

NIFFT THE LEAN (FICTITIOUS CHARACTER) p.238

NIGHTINGALE, DEIRDRE QUINN (FICTITIOUS CHARACTER) p.238

NILSEN, PAM (FICTITIOUS CHARACTER) p.238

NOBLE, KARA (FICTITIOUS CHARACTER) p.238

NOG (FICTITIOUS CHARACTER) p.238

NOLAN, LON (FICTITIOUS CHARACTER) p.238

NOON, FREDDIE URBAN (FICTITIOUS CHARACTER) p.238

NOONAN, MIKE (FICTITIOUS CHARACTER) p.238

NOP (FICTITIOUS CHARACTER) p.238

NORDEJOONG, CHICAGO (FICTITIOUS CHARACTER) p.238

NORE, PHILIP (FICTITIOUS CHARACTER) p.238

NORGREN, CHRIS (FICTITIOUS CHARACTER) p.238

NORSTROM, BRYNNA (FICTITIOUS CHARACTER) p.238

NORTH, HUGH (FICTITIOUS CHARACTER) p.238

NORTH, JERRY (FICTITIOUS CHARACTER) p.238

NORTH, PAM (FICTITIOUS CHARACTER) p.239

NOVA, DAVID (FICTITIOUS CHARACTER) p.239

NOVA, LISA (FICTITIOUS CHARACTER) p.239

NOVAK, JACK (FICTITIOUS CHARACTER) p.239

NOVAK, M. J. (FICTITIOUS CHARACTER) p.239

NOVEMBER MAN (FICTITIOUS CHARACTER) p.239
see Devereaux (Fictitious Character: Granger)

NOWEK, GREGORI (FICTITIOUS CHARACTER) p.239

NUDGER, ALO (FICTITIOUS CHARACTER) p.239

O., OPHELIA (FICTITIOUS CHARACTER) p.239
see Ophelia O. (Fictitious Character)

OAKES, BLACKFORD (FICTITIOUS CHARACTER) p.239

OATLAND, SARAH (FICTITIOUS CHARACTER) p.239

OBI-WAN KENOBI (FICTITIOUS CHARACTER) p.239
see Kenobi, Obi-Wan (Fictitious Character)

O'BRIEN, KALI (FICTITIOUS CHARACTER) p.239

O'BRIEN, MILES (FICTITIOUS CHARACTER) p.239

OCHS, CHARLIE (FICTITIOUS CHARACTER) p.240

O'CLARE, MAIREAD (FICTITIOUS CHARACTER) p.240

O'CONNER, THUNDERBIRD (FICTITIOUS CHARACTER) p.240

O'CONNOR, CORK (FICTITIOUS CHARACTER) p.240

O'CONNOR, DALLAS (FICTITIOUS CHARACTER) p.240

O'CONNOR, KIERAN (FICTITIOUS CHARACTER) p.240

O'CONNOR, RACHEL (FICTITIOUS CHARACTER) p.240

O'DELL, KENDALL (FICTITIOUS CHARACTER) p.240

ODO (FICTITIOUS CHARACTER) p.240

O'DONNELL, DANTE (FICTITIOUS CHARACTER) p.240

O'FLAHERTY, DANNY (FICTITIOUS CHARACTER) p.240

OFSTED, LEE (FICTITIOUS CHARACTER) p.240

OGILVIE, JAMES (FICTITIOUS CHARACTER) p.240

O'GRADY, CANYON (FICTITIOUS CHARACTER) p.240

O'HALLORAN FAMILY (FICTITIOUS CHARACTERS) p.240

O'HARA, FRANK (FICTITIOUS CHARACTER) p.241

OHARA, ISAMU (FICTITIOUS CHARACTER) p.241

O'HARA, NICK (FICTITIOUS CHARACTER) p.241

O'HARA, SCARLETT (FICTITIOUS CHARACTER) p.241

OHAYON, MICHAEL (FICTITIOUS CHARACTER) p.241

O'KEEFE, KATHERINE (FICTITIOUS CHARACTER) p.241

OLIVAW, R. DANEEL (FICTITIOUS CHARACTER) p.241

OLIVER, ARIADNE (FICTITIOUS CHARACTER) p.241

OLIVER, GIDEON (FICTITIOUS CHARACTER) p.241

OLIVEREZ, ELENA (FICTITIOUS CHARACTER) p.241

O'MALLEY, GRACE, 1530?-1600? p.241

O'MALLEY, JAN (FICTITIOUS CHARACTER) p.241

O'MALLEY, JOHN (FICTITIOUS CHARACTER) p.241

O'MALLEY, TOMMY (FICTITIOUS CHARACTER) p.241

O'MALLEY DE MARISCO, SKYE (FICTITIOUS CHARACTER) p.241

OMAR, THE STORYTELLER (FICTITIOUS CHARACTER) p.242

OMEGA, JAY (FICTITIOUS CHARACTER) p.242

ONE-EYED MACK (FICTITIOUS CHARACTER) p.242

O'NEAL, FREDDIE (FICTITIOUS CHARACTER) p.242

O'NEIL, ALLISON (FICTITIOUS CHARACTER) p.242

O'NEILL, CONNOR (FICTITIOUS CHARACTER) p.242

O'NEILL, JIM (FICTITIOUS CHARACTER) p.242

O'NEILL, PEGGY (FICTITIOUS CHARACTER) p.242

OPARA, CHRISTIE (FICTITIOUS CHARACTER) p.242

OPERATOR 5 (FICTITIOUS CHARACTER) p.242

OPHELIA O. (FICTITIOUS CHARACTER) p.242

O'REILLY, PEGGY (FICTITIOUS CHARACTER) p.242

O'RILEY, JOE (FICTITIOUS CHARACTER) p.242

O'ROARKE, JOCELYN (FICTITIOUS CHARACTER) p.242

O'RYAN, JACK (FICTITIOUS CHARACTER) p.242

OSBOURNE, CRAIG (FICTITIOUS CHARACTER) p.242

O'SHAUGHNESSY, KIERNAN (FICTITIOUS CHARACTER) p.242

O'SHEA, VICTORY (FICTITIOUS CHARACTER) p.242

O'SULLIVAN, MICHAEL (FICTITIOUS CHARACTER) p.242

OTANI, TETSUO, SUPERINTENDENT (FICTITIOUS CHARACTER) p.242

OTHMAN, PEREVAL (FICTITIOUS CHARACTER) p.243

O'TOOLE, BRIDGET, SISTER (FICTITIOUS CHARACTER) p.243

OWEN, GARETH CADWALLADER (FICTITIOUS CHARACTER) p.243

OXBY, INSPECTOR JACK (FICTITIOUS CHARACTER) p.243

PACE, STEVE (FICTITIOUS CHARACTER) p.243

PAGAN, FRANK (FICTITIOUS CHARACTER) p.243

PAGE, GIDEON (FICTITIOUS CHARACTER) p.243

PAGE, LORRAINE (FICTITIOUS CHARACTER) p.243

PAGET, CHRISTOPHER (FICTITIOUS CHARACTER) p.243

PAIGE, JENNY (FICTITIOUS CHARACTER) p.243

PAKSENARRION (FICTITIOUS CHARACTER) p.243

PALFREY, PHILIPPA (FICTITIOUS CHARACTER) p.243

PALLARD, FRANK (FICTITIOUS CHARACTER) p.243

PALMA, CARMEN (FICTITIOUS CHARACTER) p.243

PALMER, CHILI (FICTITIOUS CHARACTER) p.243

PALMER, HARRY (FICTITIOUS CHARACTER) p.243

PALMER, JODY (FICTITIOUS CHARACTER) p.243

PALMER-JONES, GEORGE (FICTITIOUS CHARACTER) p.243

PALMER-JONES, MOLLY (FICTITIOUS CHARACTER) p.243

PALMIERI, FELIX (FICTITIOUS CHARACTER) p.244

PAMPLEMOUSSE, ARISTIDE (FICTITIOUS CHARACTER) p.244

PANTALOON (FICTITIOUS CHARACTER) p.244

PARET, IRY (FICTITIOUS CHARACTER) p.244

PARGETER, MRS. (FICTITIOUS CHARACTER) p.244

PARIS, CHARLES (FICTITIOUS CHARACTER) p.244

PARIS, THOMAS (FICTITIOUS CHARACTER) p.245

PARKER (FICTITIOUS CHARACTER: STARK) p.245

PARKER, CHARLIE (FICTITIOUS CHARACTER) p.245

PARKER, CHARLOTTE (FICTITIOUS CHARACTER) p.245

PARKER, CLAIRE (FICTITIOUS CHARACTER) p.245

PARKER, JENNY (FICTITIOUS CHARACTER) p.245

PARKER, QUINN (FICTITIOUS CHARACTER) p.245

PARKMAN, TOBY (FICTITIOUS CHARACTER) p.245

PARNELL, MEGAN (FICTITIOUS CHARACTER) p.245

PARRISH, GEORGE (FICTITIOUS CHARACTER) p.245

PASCALE, LILY (FICTITIOUS CHARACTER) p.245

PASCOE, PETER (FICTITIOUS CHARACTER) p.245

PASMORE, TOM (FICTITIOUS CHARACTER) p.246

PASSAU, LOUIS (FICTITIOUS CHARACTER) p.246

PASTOR, DANNY (FICTITIOUS CHARACTER) p.246

PATRICIA ANNE (FICTITIOUS CHARACTER) p.246

PATRICK, LARA (FICTITIOUS CHARACTER) p.246

PATTERSON, ASHLEY (FICTITIOUS CHARACTER) p.246

PATTERSON, JONELLE (FICTITIOUS CHARACTER) p.246

PATTERSON, MARTHA (FICTITIOUS CHARACTER) p.246

PAULING, ANDI (FICTITIOUS CHARACTER) p.246

PAYNE, MATTHEW (FICTITIOUS CHARACTER) p.246

PAYNE, ROBERT (FICTITIOUS CHARACTER) p.246

PEABODY, AMELIA (FICTITIOUS CHARACTER) p.246

PEACE, CHARLIE (FICTITIOUS CHARACTER) p.247

PEACH, PERCY (FICTITIOUS CHARACTER) p.247

PECKOVER, HENRY (FICTITIOUS CHARACTER) p.247

PECOS, BEN (FICTITIOUS CHARACTER) p.247

PEDERSEN, GUN (FICTITIOUS CHARACTER) p.247

PEEBLES, SAM (FICTITIOUS CHARACTER) p.247

PEL, EVARISTE CLOVIS DESIRE (FICTITIOUS CHARACTER) p.247

PELHAM, ELIZA (FICTITIOUS CHARACTER) p.247

PELLAM, JOHN (FICTITIOUS CHARACTER) p.247

PELLETIER, KAREN (FICTITIOUS CHARACTER) p.247

PELLETIER, LIBBY (FICTITIOUS CHARACTER) p.248

PELMAN THE POWERSHAPER (FICTITIOUS CHARACTER) p.248

PEMBRIDGE, DIANA (FICTITIOUS CHARACTER) p.248

PENDEL, HARRY (FICTITIOUS CHARACTER) p.248

PENETRATOR (FICTITIOUS CHARACTER) p.248

PENN, ALEX (FICTITIOUS CHARACTER) p.248

PENN, SIMON (FICTITIOUS CHARACTER) p.248

PEPPER, AMANDA (FICTITIOUS CHARACTER) p.248

PERCEVAL, LYDIA (FICTITIOUS CHARACTER) p.248

PEREGRINE FAMILY (FICTITIOUS CHARACTERS) p.248

PERKINS, ANDREA (FICTITIOUS CHARACTER) p.248

PERKINS, BEN (FICTITIOUS CHARACTER) p.248

PERKINS, DOUGLAS (FICTITIOUS CHARACTER) p.248

PERRIN, MICHAEL (FICTITIOUS CHARACTER) p.248

PERRIN, REGINALD (FICTITIOUS CHARACTER) p.248

PERROT, DICK (FICTITIOUS CHARACTER) p.248

PERRY, WILL (FICTITIOUS CHARACTER) p.248

PERRY-MONDORI, KAREN (FICTITIOUS CHARACTER) p.248

PETERS, ANNA (FICTITIOUS CHARACTER) p.248

PETERS, TOBY (FICTITIOUS CHARACTER) p.249

PETERSON, MATTHEW (FICTITIOUS CHARACTER) p.249

PETERSON, WESLEY (FICTITIOUS CHARACTER) p.249

PETTIGREW, FRANCIS (FICTITIOUS CHARACTER) p.249

PHANTOM OF THE OPERA (FICTITIOUS CHARACTER) p.249

PHILLIPS, ALEX (FICTITIOUS CHARACTER) p.249

PHILLIPS, BINO (FICTITIOUS CHARACTER) p.250

PHILLIPS, MADDY (FICTITIOUS CHARACTER) p.250

PHULE, WILLARD, CAPTAIN (FICTITIOUS CHARACTER) p.250

PIBBLE, JIMMY (FICTITIOUS CHARACTER) p.250

PICARD, INSPECTOR (FICTITIOUS CHARACTER) p.250

PICARD, JEAN-LUC (FICTITIOUS CHARACTER) p.250

PICKETT, JOE (FICTITIOUS CHARACTER) p.251

PICKETT, MEL (FICTITIOUS CHARACTER) p.251

PIERCE, AMELIA (FICTITIOUS CHARACTER) p.251

PIERCE, TYLER (FICTITIOUS CHARACTER) p.251

PIERCY, JOANNA (FICTITIOUS CHARACTER) p.251

PIGEON, ANNA (FICTITIOUS CHARACTER) p.251

PIGEON, JOSIE (FICTITIOUS CHARACTER) p.252

PIKE, JOE (FICTITIOUS CHARACTER) p.252

PINE, LEONARD (FICTITIOUS CHARACTER) p.252

PINK, MELINDA (FICTITIOUS CHARACTER) p.252

PINKERTON LADY (FICTITIOUS CHARACTER) p.252

PIPER, MOLLY (FICTITIOUS CHARACTER) p.252

PITT, CHARLOTTE (FICTITIOUS CHARACTER) p.252

PITT, DIRK (FICTITIOUS CHARACTER) p.253

PITT, THOMAS, INSPECTOR (FICTITIOUS CHARACTER) p.254

PITTMAN, MRS. (FICTITIOUS CHARACTER) p.254

PITTMORE, DARNELL (FICTITIOUS CHARACTER) p.254

PLANT, MELROSE (FICTITIOUS CHARACTER) p.254

PLANTAINE FAMILY (FICTITIOUS CHARACTERS) p.254

PLATO, CHARLIE (FICTITIOUS CHARACTER) p.255

PLUM, MARVIA (FICTITIOUS CHARACTER) p.255

PLUM, STEPHANIE (FICTITIOUS CHARACTER) p.255

PLUMTREE, ALEX (FICTITIOUS CHARACTER) p.255

PLUNKETT, MARTIN (FICTITIOUS CHARACTER) p.255

POE, JARED (FICTITIOUS CHARACTER) p.255

POE, JOHN CHARLES (FICTITIOUS CHARACTER) p.255

POIROT, HERCULE (FICTITIOUS CHARACTER) p.255

POLDARK, ROSS (FICTITIOUS CHARACTER) p.257

POLLIFAX, EMILY (FICTITIOUS CHARACTER) p.258

POLO, NICK (FICTITIOUS CHARACTER) p.258

POLYCRATES, ROSCO (FICTITIOUS CHARACTER) p.258

POND, MR. (FICTITIOUS CHARACTER) p.258

PONS, SOLAR (FICTITIOUS CHARACTER) p.258

PONTOWSKI, MATT (FICTITIOUS CHARACTER) p.258

POOLE, CHARLIE (FICTITIOUS CHARACTER) p.258

POPEYE (FICTITIOUS CHARACTER) p.258

PORTAL, ELLIS (FICTITIOUS CHARACTER) p.258

PORTER, BEN (FICTITIOUS CHARACTER) p.259

PORTER, RACHEL (FICTITIOUS CHARACTER) p.259

PORTILLO, VICTOR (FICTITIOUS CHARACTER) p.259

PORTUGAL, JOE (FICTITIOUS CHARACTER) p.259

POST, ED (FICTITIOUS CHARACTER) p.259

POTAMOS, JOE (FICTITIOUS CHARACTER) p.259

POTEET, JORDAN (FICTITIOUS CHARACTER) p.259

POTTER, ARTHUR (FICTITIOUS CHARACTER) p.259

POTTER, EUGENIA (FICTITIOUS CHARACTER) p.259

POTTER, FREDERICA (FICTITIOUS CHARACTER) p.259

POWDER, LEROY (FICTITIOUS CHARACTER) p.259

POWELL, ERSKINE (FICTITIOUS CHARACTER) p.259

POWERS, AUSTIN (FICTITIOUS CHARACTER) p.259

POWERS, GEORGINA (FICTITIOUS CHARACTER) p.259

POWERS, VIV (FICTITIOUS CHARACTER) p.259

POWERSCOURT, FRANCIS (FICTITIOUS CHARACTER) p.259

PRATT, TONY (FICTITIOUS CHARACTER) p.259

PREFECT, FORD (FICTITIOUS CHARACTER) p.259

PRENTICE, JOY (FICTITIOUS CHARACTER) p.259

PRESCOTT, AMY (FICTITIOUS CHARACTER) p.259

PRESCOTT, CINDY (FICTITIOUS CHARACTER) p.259

PRESCOTT, JAMIE (FICTITIOUS CHARACTER) p.259

PRESLEY, ELVIS, 1935-1977 p.260

PRESTER, JACK (FICTITIOUS CHARACTER) p.260

PRESTON, KIT (FICTITIOUS CHARACTER) p.260

PRESTON, MARK (FICTITIOUS CHARACTER) p.260

PRIAM, MARGARET (FICTITIOUS CHARACTER) p.260

PRICE, ROBIN (FICTITIOUS CHARACTER) p.260

PRIESTER, SOLOMON (FICTITIOUS CHARACTER) p.260

PRINCIPAL, LAURA (FICTITIOUS CHARACTER) p.260

PRINGLE, G. D. H. (FICTITIOUS CHARACTER) p.260

PRIOR, MATTHEW (FICTITIOUS CHARACTER) p.260

PRIZZI FAMILY (FICTITIOUS CHARACTERS) p.260

PROCTOR, ETHAN (FICTITIOUS CHARACTER) p.260

PROFETT, JOHN (FICTITIOUS CHARACTER) p.260

PROSPERO OF ARGYLLE (FICTITIOUS CHARACTER) p.260

PRY, PAUL (FICTITIOUS CHARACTER) p.261

PRYNNE, HESTER (FICTITIOUS CHARACTER) p.261

PSI-MAN (FICTITIOUS CHARACTER) p.261

PUG (FICTITIOUS CHARACTER) p.261

PUGH, E. J. (FICTITIOUS CHARACTER) p.261

PULASKI, KATHERINE (FICTITIOUS CHARACTER) p.261

PURBRIGHT, WALTER, INSPECTOR (FICTITIOUS CHARACTER) p.261

PURDUE, THOMAS (FICTITIOUS CHARACTER) p.261

PYATNITSKI, MAXIM ARTUROVICH (FICTITIOUS CHARACTER) p.261

PUTTOCK, SIMON (FICTITIOUS CHARACTER) p.262

PYM, HANNAH (FICTITIOUS CHARACTER) p.262

PYNE, PARKER (FICTITIOUS CHARACTER) p.262

Q (FICTITIOUS CHARACTER) p.262

QUANTRILL, DOUGLAS (FICTITIOUS CHARACTER) p.262

QUANTRILL, SNOHOMISH (FICTITIOUS CHARACTER) p.262

QUANTRILL, TED (FICTITIOUS CHARACTER) p.262

QUARK (FICTITIOUS CHARACTER) p.262

QUARRY (FICTITIOUS CHARACTER: COLLINS) p.263

QUASIMODO (FICTITIOUS CHARACTER) p.263

QUATERMAIN, ALLAN (FICTITIOUS CHARACTER) p.263

QUENTIN (FICTITIOUS CHARACTER) p.263

QUI-GON JINN (FICTITIOUS CHARACTER) p.263

QUILLER (FICTITIOUS CHARACTER: HALL) p.263

QUILLIAM, MEG (FICTITIOUS CHARACTER) p.264

QUILLIAM, SARAH (FICTITIOUS CHARACTER) p.264

QUINLAN, TAYLOR (FICTITIOUS CHARACTER) p.264

QUINLIN, JEB (FICTITIOUS CHARACTER) p.264

QUINN, DANIEL (FICTITIOUS CHARACTER) p.264

QUINN, GARNER (FICTITIOUS CHARACTER) p.264

QUINN, GRACE (FICTITIOUS CHARACTER) p.264

QUINN, JASON (FICTITIOUS CHARACTER) p.264

QUINN, JOHN (FICTITIOUS CHARACTER) p.264

QUINN, MARSHALL (FICTITIOUS CHARACTER) p.264

QUINN, RILEY (FICTITIOUS CHARACTER) p.264

QUINN, TERRY (FICTITIOUS CHARACTER) p.264

QUINTAGLIO (FICTITIOUS CHARACTERS) p.264

QUINTANA, ANTHONY (FICTITIOUS CHARACTER) p.264

QUIST, JULIAN (FICTITIOUS CHARACTER) p.264

QUY, IMOGEN (FICTITIOUS CHARACTER) p.264

QWILLERAN, JIM (FICTITIOUS CHARACTER) p.264

RABB, JOSHUA (FICTITIOUS CHARACTER) p.265

RABJOHNS, WILL (FICTITIOUS CHARACTER) p.265

RACE, COLONEL JOHNNY (FICTITIOUS CHARACTER) p.265

RADBURN, ADAM (FICTITIOUS CHARACTER) p.265

RAFFERTY (FICTITIOUS CHARACTER) p.265

RAFFERTY, ALEXANDRA (FICTITIOUS CHARACTER) p.266

RAFFERTY, JOSEPH (FICTITIOUS CHARACTER) p.266

RAFFERTY, NEAL (FICTITIOUS CHARACTER) p.266

RAFFLES (FICTITIOUS CHARACTER) p.266

RAFT, ANNIE (FICTITIOUS CHARACTER) p.266

RAHL, RICHARD (FICTITIOUS CHARACTER) p.266

RAIN, JOHN (FICTITIOUS CHARACTER) p.266

RAINES, BEN (FICTITIOUS CHARACTER) p.266

RAINES, HARRISON (FICTITIOUS CHARACTER) p.266

RAINFINCH, ABE (FICTITIOUS CHARACTER) p.266

RAISIN, AGATHA (FICTITIOUS CHARACTER) p.266

RALSTON, DEB (FICTITIOUS CHARACTER) p.266

RAMADGE, GWENN (FICTITIOUS CHARACTER) p.267

RAMAGE, NICHOLAS (FICTITIOUS CHARACTER) p.267

RAMIREZ, CARMEN (FICTITIOUS CHARACTER) p.267

RAMOS, LUCIA (FICTITIOUS CHARACTER) p.267

RAMOTSWE, PRECIOUS (FICTITIOUS CHARACTER) p.267

RAMSAY, JULIAN (FICTITIOUS CHARACTER) p.267

RAMSAY, STEPHEN (FICTITIOUS CHARACTER) p.267

RAMSEY, CURT (FICTITIOUS CHARACTER) p.267

RAMSEY FAMILY (FICTITIOUS CHARACTERS) p.267

RAMSGILL, JAMIE (FICTITIOUS CHARACTER) p.267

RAND, JOANNA (FICTITIOUS CHARACTER) p.267

RAND AL'THOR (FICTITIOUS CHARACTER) p.267

RANDALL, CLAIRE (FICTITIOUS CHARACTER) p.268

RANDALL, SUNNY (FICTITIOUS CHARACTER) p.268

RANDOLPH, SNOOKY (FICTITIOUS CHARACTER) p.268

RANSOM, ELWIN (FICTITIOUS CHARACTER) p.268

RANSOM, JEREMY (FICTITIOUS CHARACTER) p.268

RAPP, MITCH (FICTITIOUS CHARACTER) p.268

RAVEN, JOHN (FICTITIOUS CHARACTER) p.268

RAWLINGS, CLAIRE (FICTITIOUS CHARACTER) p.268

RAWLINGS, MICKEY (FICTITIOUS CHARACTER) p.268

RAWLINS, EASY (FICTITIOUS CHARACTER) p.268

RAYBURN, JOANN (FICTITIOUS CHARACTER) p.269

REACHER, JACK (FICTITIOUS CHARACTER) p.269

REBUS, INSPECTOR (FICTITIOUS CHARACTER) p.269

RED ORC (FICTITIOUS CHARACTER) p.269

REE, KILLASHANDRA (FICTITIOUS CHARACTER) p.269

REECE, CAITLIN (FICTITIOUS CHARACTER) p.269

REED, ANNABEL (FICTITIOUS CHARACTER) p.269
  *see* Smith, Annabel (Fictitious Character)

REED, EILEEN (FICTITIOUS CHARACTER) p.269

REED, GARR (FICTITIOUS CHARACTER) p.269

REES, CLIO (FICTITIOUS CHARACTER) p.269

REESE, BEN (FICTITIOUS CHARACTER) p.269

REGAN, FRANCIS X. (FICTITIOUS CHARACTER) p.269

REID, SAVANNAH (FICTITIOUS CHARACTER) p.269

REILLY, CASSANDRA (FICTITIOUS CHARACTER) p.270

REILLY, NINA (FICTITIOUS CHARACTER) p.270

REILLY, REGAN (FICTITIOUS CHARACTER) p.270

REITH, ADAM (FICTITIOUS CHARACTER) p.270

RELKIN (FICTITIOUS CHARACTER) p.270

REMO (FICTITIOUS CHARACTER) p.270

REMUS, UNCLE (FICTITIOUS CHARACTER) p.271

RENARD, GIL (FICTITIOUS CHARACTER) p.271

RENKO, ARKADY (FICTITIOUS CHARACTER) p.271

RENNE (FICTITIOUS CHARACTER: PORTER) p.271

RENO, JIM (FICTITIOUS CHARACTER) p.271

RENZLER, MARK (FICTITIOUS CHARACTER) p.271

REPAIRMAN JACK (FICTITIOUS CHARACTER) p.271

RESNICK, CHARLIE (FICTITIOUS CHARACTER) p.272

REUSCHEL, DEENA (FICTITIOUS CHARACTER) p.272

REVILL, NICK (FICTITIOUS CHARACTER) p.272

REYMOND, STEPHANIE (FICTITIOUS CHARACTER) p.272

REYNIER, CLAIRE (FICTITIOUS CHARACTER) p.272

REYNOLDS, ALEX (FICTITIOUS CHARACTER) p.272

REYNOLDS, SAM (FICTITIOUS CHARACTER) p.272

RHENFORD, LIAM (FICTITIOUS CHARACTER) p.272

RHINEHEART, MICHAEL (FICTITIOUS CHARACTER) p.272

RHODENBARR, BERNIE (FICTITIOUS CHARACTER) p.272

RHODES, ANNE (FICTITIOUS CHARACTER) p.273

RHODES, CAROLINE (FICTITIOUS CHARACTER) p.273

RHODES, DAN (FICTITIOUS CHARACTER) p.273

RHODES, DUSTY (FICTITIOUS CHARACTER) p.273

RHODES, EMMA (FICTITIOUS CHARACTER) p.273

RHODES, TRAVIS (FICTITIOUS CHARACTER) p.273

RHOMANDI BROTHERS (FICTITIOUS CHARACTERS) p.273

RHYME, LINCOLN (FICTITIOUS CHARACTER) p.273

RHYS, MADOC (FICTITIOUS CHARACTER) p.273

RICE, DALE (FICTITIOUS CHARACTER) p.273

RICE, HARRY (FICTITIOUS CHARACTER) p.273

RICE, MALINDA (FICTITIOUS CHARACTER) p.273

RICE, PENELOPE "POPPY" (FICTITIOUS CHARACTER) p.273

RICHARDS, NOAH (FICTITIOUS CHARACTER) p.273

RICHARDS, SUZANNE (FICTITIOUS CHARACTER) p.273

RICHARDSON, JESSALEA (FICTITIOUS CHARACTER) p.273

RICHARDSON, RAY (FICTITIOUS CHARACTER) p.273

RICHTER, MARTA (FICTITIOUS CHARACTER) p.273

RICIMER, PIET (FICTITIOUS CHARACTER) p.273

RIDDLE, HARRY (FICTITIOUS CHARACTER) p.273

RIDGWAY, SCHUYLER (FICTITIOUS CHARACTER) p.273

RIDLEY, SAM (FICTITIOUS CHARACTER) p.273

RIKARDON (FICTITIOUS CHARACTER) p.273

RIKER, WILLIAM THOMAS (FICTITIOUS CHARACTER) p.274

RILEY, DAVE (FICTITIOUS CHARACTER) p.274

RINCEWIND THE WIZARD (FICTITIOUS CHARACTER) p.274

RINGWALD, CASSIE (FICTITIOUS CHARACTER) p.274

RIORDAN, MATT (FICTITIOUS CHARACTER) p.274

RIORDANT, PAT (FICTITIOUS CHARACTER) p.274

RIOS, HENRY (FICTITIOUS CHARACTER) p.274

RIPLEY, TOM (FICTITIOUS CHARACTER) p.274

RISK, DOCTOR (FICTITIOUS CHARACTER) p.274

RITTENHOUSE, MEG (FICTITIOUS CHARACTER) p.274

RIVERS, JAMES (FICTITIOUS CHARACTER) p.275

ROBAK, DON (FICTITIOUS CHARACTER) p.275

ROBERTS, AMANDA (FICTITIOUS CHARACTER) p.275

ROBERTS, MITCHELL (FICTITIOUS CHARACTER) p.275

ROBERTS, RALPH (FICTITIOUS CHARACTER) p.275

ROBICHEAUX, DAVE (FICTITIOUS CHARACTER) p.275

ROBINSON, NAN (FICTITIOUS CHARACTER) p.275

ROBINSON, TRISH (FICTITIOUS CHARACTER) p.275

ROCHE, MORGAN (FICTITIOUS CHARACTER) p.275

ROCKFORD, JAMES (FICTITIOUS CHARACTER) p.275

ROCKY MOUNTAIN COMPANY (FICTITIOUS CHARACTERS) p.275

RODE, JIMMY (FICTITIOUS CHARACTER) p.275

RODENSKA, MIKE (FICTITIOUS CHARACTER) p.275

RODRIGUE, JOHN (FICTITIOUS CHARACTER) p.275

ROGER THE CHAPMAN (FICTITIOUS CHARACTER) p.275

ROGERS, BEN (FICTITIOUS CHARACTER) p.276

ROGERS, BUCK (FICTITIOUS CHARACTER) p.276

ROGERS, GEORGE (FICTITIOUS CHARACTER) p.276

ROGERS, TOM (FICTITIOUS CHARACTER) p.276

ROGUE WARRIOR (FICTITIOUS CHARACTER) p.276

ROKE, DANIEL (FICTITIOUS CHARACTER) p.276

ROLAND (FICTITIOUS CHARACTER) p.276

ROLLISON, RICHARD (FICTITIOUS CHARACTER) p.276

ROM (FICTITIOUS CHARACTER) p.276

ROMAN, DAN (FICTITIOUS CHARACTER) p.277

ROME, MAGGIE (FICTITIOUS CHARACTER) p.277

ROMERO, VAL (FICTITIOUS CHARACTER) p.277

ROOSEVELT, ELEANOR, 1884-1962 p.277

ROOSEVELT, THEODORE, 1858-1919 p.277

ROPER, DOUGLAS (FICTITIOUS CHARACTER) p.277

ROPER, IAN (FICTITIOUS CHARACTER) p.277

ROPER, TAGGART (FICTITIOUS CHARACTER) p.277

ROSATO, BENEDETTA (FICTITIOUS CHARACTER) p.277

ROSE, MIKE (FICTITIOUS CHARACTER) p.278

ROSEN, NATE (FICTITIOUS CHARACTER) p.278

ROSS, BARRY (FICTITIOUS CHARACTER) p.278

ROSS, CHIEF INSPECTOR (FICTITIOUS CHARACTER) p.278

ROSS, DANIELLE (FICTITIOUS CHARACTER) p.278

ROSS, JACK (FICTITIOUS CHARACTER) p.278

ROSS, JOHN (FICTITIOUS CHARACTER) p.278

ROSS, WILL (FICTITIOUS CHARACTER) p.278

ROSTNIKOV, PORFIRY PETROVICH (FICTITIOUS CHARACTER) p.278

ROTHMAN, RUBY (FICTITIOUS CHARACTER) p.278

ROUNDTREE, TRUDY (FICTITIOUS CHARACTER) p.278

ROURKE, JOHN THOMAS (FICTITIOUS CHARACTER) p.278

RUBIO, VINCENT (FICTITIOUS CHARACTER) p.278

RULE, KATHERINE (FICTITIOUS CHARACTER) p.278

RUMPOLE, HORACE (FICTITIOUS CHARACTER) p.278

RUNE (FICTITIOUS CHARACTER) p.279

RUSSELL, MARY (FICTITIOUS CHARACTER) p.279

RUTLEDGE, ALEX (FICTITIOUS CHARACTER) p.279

RUTLEDGE, IAN (FICTITIOUS CHARACTER) p.279

RYAN, ANTHONY (FICTITIOUS CHARACTER) p.279

RYAN, BLACKIE (FICTITIOUS CHARACTER) p.279

RYAN, FLIP (FICTITIOUS CHARACTER) p.280

RYAN, JACK (FICTITIOUS CHARACTER) p.280

RYAN, MAGGIE (FICTITIOUS CHARACTER) p.280

RYAN, MICHAEL (FICTITIOUS CHARACTER) p.280

RYAN, PEARL (FICTITIOUS CHARACTER) p.280

RYAN, SAMANTHA (FICTITIOUS CHARACTER) p.280

RYLAND, GARTH (FICTITIOUS CHARACTER) p.280

SAAVIK (FICTITIOUS CHARACTER) p.280

SABICH, RUSTY (FICTITIOUS CHARACTER) p.280

SABINE (FICTITIOUS CHARACTER: BANTOCK) p.280

SACHS, AMELIA (FICTITIOUS CHARACTER) p.281

SACKETT FAMILY (FICTITIOUS CHARACTERS) p.281

SAFFORD, BEN (FICTITIOUS CHARACTER) p.281

SAINT (FICTITIOUS CHARACTER) p.281

SAINT, AUGUST (FICTITIOUS CHARACTER) p.281

SAINT-CYR, JEAN-LOUIS (FICTITIOUS CHARACTER) p.281

SAINT-GERMAIN (FICTITIOUS CHARACTER) p.281

ST. IVES, PHILIP (FICTITIOUS CHARACTER) p.282

SAINT JAMES, QUIN (FICTITIOUS CHARACTER) p.282

ST. JAMES, SIMON (FICTITIOUS CHARACTER) p.282

ST. JOHN, DANNI (FICTITIOUS CHARACTER) p.282

SAINT JOHN, DYLAN (FICTITIOUS CHARACTER) p.282

ST. JOHN, JEREMIAH (FICTITIOUS CHARACTER) p.282

ST. VIRE, NICHOLAS (FICTITIOUS CHARACTER) p.282

SALTER, CHARLIE (FICTITIOUS CHARACTER) p.282

SAM (FICTITIOUS CHARACTER: WOOD) p.282

SAMMS, LANEY (FICTITIOUS CHARACTER) p.282

SAMS, CHARLOTTE (FICTITIOUS CHARACTER) p.282

SAMSON, ALBERT (FICTITIOUS CHARACTER) p.282

SAMSON, BERNARD (FICTITIOUS CHARACTER) p.282

SAMSON, JAKE (FICTITIOUS CHARACTER) p.283

SAMURAI CAT (FICTITIOUS CHARACTER) p.283

SANDBERG FAMILY (FICTITIOUS CHARACTERS) p.283

SANDERS, ALEX (FICTITIOUS CHARACTER) p.283

SANDERS, JOHN, INSPECTOR (FICTITIOUS CHARACTER) p.283

SANDERS, TOM (FICTITIOUS CHARACTER) p.283

SANDILANDS, JOE (FICTITIOUS CHARACTER) p.283

SANDS, INSPECTOR (FICTITIOUS CHARACTER) p.283

SANSI, GEORGE (FICTITIOUS CHARACTER) p.283

SANTANGELO, LUCKY (FICTITIOUS CHARACTER) p.283

SANTOS, VICTORIA (FICTITIOUS CHARACTER) p.283

SASSINAK (FICTITIOUS CHARACTER) p.283

SAVAGE, DOC (FICTITIOUS CHARACTER) p.283

SAVAGE, GILBERT (FICTITIOUS CHARACTER) p.283

SAVAGE, JACK (FICTITIOUS CHARACTER) p.283

SAVICH, DILLON (FICTITIOUS CHARACTER) p.284

SAVILE, JUSTIN (FICTITIOUS CHARACTER) p.284

SAWYER, PETE (FICTITIOUS CHARACTER) p.284

SAWYER, TOM (FICTITIOUS CHARACTER) p.284

SAXON (ROBERTS: FICTITIOUS CHARACTER) p.284

SAXON, ALAN (FICTITIOUS CHARACTER) p.284

SAYLER, CATHERINE (FICTITIOUS CHARACTER) p.284

SCANDAL (FICTITIOUS CHARACTER) p.285

SCARLATTI, ELIZABETH WYCKMAN (FICTITIOUS CHARACTER) p.285

SCARPETTA, KAY (FICTITIOUS CHARACTER) p.285

SCHAFER, WILL (FICTITIOUS CHARACTER) p.285

SCHNEIDER, LENNY (FICTITIOUS CHARACTER) p.285

SCHOFIELD, SHANE (FICTITIOUS CHARACTER) p.285

SCHWARTZ, REBECCA (FICTITIOUS CHARACTER) p.285

SCOTT, LAURA (FICTITIOUS CHARACTER) p.285

SCOTT, LINDA (FICTITIOUS CHARACTER) p.285

SCOTT, MONTGOMERY (FICTITIOUS CHARACTER) p.285

SCOTT, NICKOLETTE (FICTITIOUS CHARACTER) p.286

SCOTT, SHELL (FICTITIOUS CHARACTER) p.286

SCOTT, STEVEN (FICTITIOUS CHARACTER) p.286

SCROOGE, EBENEZER (FICTITIOUS CHARACTER) p.286

SCUDDER, MATT (FICTITIOUS CHARACTER) p.286

SCULLY, DANA (FICTITIOUS CHARACTER) p.287

SCULLY, SHANE (FICTITIOUS CHARACTER) p.287

SCURO, PETER (FICTITIOUS CHARACTER) p.287

SEACOURT, ALEX (FICTITIOUS CHARACTER) p.287

SEAFORT, NICHOLAS (FICTITIOUS CHARACTER) p.287

SEETON, MISS (FICTITIOUS CHARACTER) p.287

SEFERIUS, CLAUDIA (FICTITIOUS CHARACTER) p.287

SEGALLA, NICHOLAS (FICTITIOUS CHARACTER) p.287

SELAR (FICTITIOUS CHARACTER) p.287

SELDON, HARI (FICTITIOUS CHARACTER) p.288

SEREGE, LUJAN (FICTITIOUS CHARACTER) p.288

SEREGIL OF RHIMINEE (FICTITIOUS CHARACTER) p.288

SERRANO, HERIS (FICTITIOUS CHARACTER) p.288

SEVEN OF NINE (FICTITIOUS CHARACTER) p.288

SEWELL, HITCHCOCK (FICTITIOUS CHARACTER) p.288

SHADE, RENE (FICTITIOUS CHARACTER) p.288

SHADER, SUSAN (FICTITIOUS CHARACTER) p.288

SHADOW (FICTITIOUS CHARACTER: LOGSTON) p.288

SHAKESPEARE, WILLIAM, 1564-1616 p.288

SHALLOT, ROGER, SIR (FICTITIOUS CHARACTER) p.288

SHANAHAN, DEETS (FICTITIOUS CHARACTER) p.288

SHAND, RUSSELL (FICTITIOUS CHARACTER) p.288

SHANDY, HELEN (FICTITIOUS CHARACTER) p.288

SHANDY, PETER (FICTITIOUS CHARACTER) p.289

SHANNON, LUCY (FICTITIOUS CHARACTER) p.289

SHAPIRO, DESIREE (FICTITIOUS CHARACTER) p.289

SHAPIRO, FRANK (FICTITIOUS CHARACTER) p.289

SHARKEY, RAY (FICTITIOUS CHARACTER) p.289

SHARPE, RICHARD (FICTITIOUS CHARACTER) p.289

SHARPLES, CLAIRE (FICTITIOUS CHARACTER) p.290

SHARTELLE, CLINTON (FICTITIOUS CHARACTER) p.290

SHAW, HANNAH (FICTITIOUS CHARACTER) p.290

SHAW, MARTHA (FICTITIOUS CHARACTER) p.290

SHAW, SABINA (FICTITIOUS CHARACTER) p.290

SHAW, SIMON (FICTITIOUS CHARACTER) p.290

SHEA, HAROLD (FICTITIOUS CHARACTER) p.290

SHELBY, ELIZABETH PAULA (FICTITIOUS CHARACTER) p.290

SHEPERD, CHYNA (FICTITIOUS CHARACTER) p.290

SHEPHERD, TRACY (FICTITIOUS CHARACTER) p.290

SHERIDAN, ALEXANDER (FICTITIOUS CHARACTER) p.290

SHERIDAN, CHARLES, SIR (FICTITIOUS CHARACTER) p.290

SHERIDAN, DAN (FICTITIOUS CHARACTER) p.290

SHERIDAN, T. S. W. (FICTITIOUS CHARACTER) p.290

SHERLOCK, LACEY (FICTITIOUS CHARACTER) p.290

SHERMAN, WINSTON MARLOWE (FICTITIOUS CHARACTER) p.291

SHIGATA, MARK (FICTITIOUS CHARACTER) p.291

SHILLER, MIKE (FICTITIOUS CHARACTER) p.291

SHILLING, GRACE (FICTITIOUS CHARACTER) p.291

SHIMURA, REI (FICTITIOUS CHARACTER) p.291

SHOCK, BEN (FICTITIOUS CHARACTER) p.291

SHORE, JEMIMA (FICTITIOUS CHARACTER) p.291

SHORE, MARLA (FICTITIOUS CHARACTER) p.291

SHORE, MATT (FICTITIOUS CHARACTER) p.291

SHUGAK, KATE (FICTITIOUS CHARACTER) p.291

SI CWAN (FICTITIOUS CHARACTER) p.291

SIDDEN, JO BETH (FICTITIOUS CHARACTER) p.291

SIDEL, ISAAC (FICTITIOUS CHARACTER) p.291

SIEGEL, ELLIE (FICTITIOUS CHARACTER) p.292

SIEGEL, PHOEBE (FICTITIOUS CHARACTER) p.292

SIGISMONDO (FICTITIOUS CHARACTER) p.292

SILENCE, JOHN (FICTITIOUS CHARACTER) p.292

SILVA, JOE (FICTITIOUS CHARACTER) p.292

SILVER, MAUD (FICTITIOUS CHARACTER) p.292

SILVERHAND (FICTITIOUS CHARACTER) p.292

SIMMONS, RACHEL (FICTITIOUS CHARACTER) p.293

SIMON, MARGO (FICTITIOUS CHARACTER) p.293

SIMONS, BARBARA (FICTITIOUS CHARACTER) p.293

SIMONS, ELLIE (FICTITIOUS CHARACTER) p.293

SIMPLE (FICTITIOUS CHARACTER) p.293

SIMPSON, TIM (FICTITIOUS CHARACTER) p.293

SIMPSON FAMILY (FICTITIOUS CHARACTERS) p.293

SINCLAIR, ADAM (FICTITIOUS CHARACTER) p.293

SINCLAIR, CECILY (FICTITIOUS CHARACTER) p.293

SINCLAIR, EVANGELINE (FICTITIOUS CHARACTER) p.293

SINCLAIR, GAR (FICTITIOUS CHARACTER) p.293

SINCLAIR, JEFFREY (FICTITIOUS CHARACTER) p.293

SINCLAIR, MATTHEW (FICTITIOUS CHARACTER) p.293

SIPOWICZ, ANDY (FICTITIOUS CHARACTER) p.293

SIRA THE SINGER (FICTITIOUS CHARACTER) p.293

SISCO, KAREN (FICTITIOUS CHARACTER) p.293

SISKO, BENJAMIN (FICTITIOUS CHARACTER) p.293

SISKO, JAKE (FICTITIOUS CHARACTER) p.294

SIXSMITH, JOE (FICTITIOUS CHARACTER) p.294

SKEEN (FICTITIOUS CHARACTER) p.294

SKEEVE (FICTITIOUS CHARACTER) p.294

SKINNER, BOB (FICTITIOUS CHARACTER) p.295

SKINNER FAMILY (FICTITIOUS CHARACTERS) p.295

SKINNY (FICTITIOUS CHARACTER: COLBERT) p.295

SKYE, BARNABY (FICTITIOUS CHARACTER) p.295

SKYWALKER, ANAKIN (FICTITIOUS CHARACTER) p.295

SKYWALKER, LUKE (FICTITIOUS CHARACTER) p.295

SLADE, MAGGIE (FICTITIOUS CHARACTER) p.296

SLAIGHT, RY (FICTITIOUS CHARACTER) p.296

SLATE, SUE (FICTITIOUS CHARACTER) p.296

SLATER, JACK (FICTITIOUS CHARACTER) p.296

SLEEPING BEAUTY (FICTITIOUS CHARACTER: ROQUELAURE) p.296

SLIDER, BILL (FICTITIOUS CHARACTER) p.296

SLOAN, C. D. (FICTITIOUS CHARACTER) p.297

SLOAN, CHARLEY (FICTITIOUS CHARACTER) p.297

SLOAN, DUNCAN (FICTITIOUS CHARACTER) p.297

SLOAN, POLLY (FICTITIOUS CHARACTER) p.297

SLOAN, SAM (FICTITIOUS CHARACTER) p.297

SLOAN, VERA (FICTITIOUS CHARACTER) p.297

SLOANE, SYDNEY (FICTITIOUS CHARACTER) p.297

SLOCUM (FICTITIOUS CHARACTER) p.297

SLOCUM, JOHN (FICTITIOUS CHARACTER) p.299
   see Slocum (Fictitious Character)

SLOCUM, NINA (FICTITIOUS CHARACTER) p.299

SMALL, DAVID (FICTITIOUS CHARACTER) p.299

SMILEY, GEORGE (FICTITIOUS CHARACTER) p.299

SMITH, ANNABEL (FICTITIOUS CHARACTER) p.299

SMITH, BILL (FICTITIOUS CHARACTER) p.300

SMITH, BRAD (FICTITIOUS CHARACTER) p.300

SMITH, GRACE (FICTITIOUS CHARACTER) p.300

SMITH, JILL (FICTITIOUS CHARACTER) p.300

SMITH, JOHN (FICTITIOUS CHARACTER) p.300

SMITH, JOHNNY (FICTITIOUS CHARACTER) p.300

SMITH, MAC (FICTITIOUS CHARACTER) p.300

SMITH, TRUMAN (FICTITIOUS CHARACTER) p.300

SMITH, XENIA (FICTITIOUS CHARACTER) p.300

SMITH, ZACHARIAH (FICTITIOUS CHARACTER) p.300

SMOKE, BEN (FICTITIOUS CHARACTER) p.300

SNOPES FAMILY (FICTITIOUS CHARACTERS) p.300

SNOW, CHRISTINE (FICTITIOUS CHARACTER) p.300

SNOW, CHRISTOPHER (FICTITIOUS CHARACTER) p.301

SNOWDEN, REESY (FICTITIOUS CHARACTER) p.301

SNOWMANE, LARISSA (FICTITIOUS CHARACTER) p.301

SOCARIDES, ARISTOTLE PLATO (FICTITIOUS CHARACTER) p.301

SOLANO, LUPE (FICTITIOUS CHARACTER) p.301

SOLETA (FICTITIOUS CHARACTER) p.301

SOLO, ANAKIN (FICTITIOUS CHARACTER) p.301

SOLO, HAN (FICTITIOUS CHARACTER) p.301

SOLO, JACEN (FICTITIOUS CHARACTER) p.302

SOLO, JAINA (FICTITIOUS CHARACTER) p.302

SOLOMON, BRETTA (FICTITIOUS CHARACTER) p.302

SOLOMON, JOHN (FICTITIOUS CHARACTER) p.303

SPACE, SAM (FICTITIOUS CHARACTER) p.303

SPADE, SAM (FICTITIOUS CHARACTER) p.303

SPARHAWK (FICTITIOUS CHARACTER) p.303

SPARROWHAWK (FICTITIOUS CHARACTER) p.303
   see Ged (Fictitious Character)

SPAULDING, DAVID (FICTITIOUS CHARACTER) p.303

SPEARMAN, HENRY (FICTITIOUS CHARACTER) p.303

SPEED, DIANE (FICTITIOUS CHARACTER) p.303

SPEETER, ALEX (FICTITIOUS CHARACTER) p.303

SPENCER, JOAN (FICTITIOUS CHARACTER) p.303

SPENCER, LOU (FICTITIOUS CHARACTER) p.303

SPENSER (FICTITIOUS CHARACTER: PARKER) p.303

SPIDER (FICTITIOUS CHARACTER) p.304

SPIDER-MAN (FICTITIOUS CHARACTER) p.304

SPOCK (FICTITIOUS CHARACTER) p.305

SPRAGGUE, MICHAEL (FICTITIOUS CHARACTER) p.306

SPRING, PENNY (FICTITIOUS CHARACTER) p.306

SPRINGER, JULIA (FICTITIOUS CHARACTER) p.306

SPROWLS, DOLLY MADISON (FICTITIOUS CHARACTER) p.306

SQUIRES, LEE (FICTITIOUS CHARACTER) p.306

STAGNORO, DANTE (FICTITIOUS CHARACTER) p.306

STAINLESS STEEL RAT (FICTITIOUS CHARACTER) p.306
   see Digriz, James Bolivar (Fictitious Character)

STAINTON, ALEC (FICTITIOUS CHARACTER) p.306

STANISLASKI FAMILY (FICTITIOUS CHARACTERS) p.307

STANTON, GREY (FICTITIOUS CHARACTER) p.307

STAPLETON, JACK (FICTITIOUS CHARACTER) p.307

STAPLETON FAMILY (FICTITIOUS CHARACTER) p.307

STAR, JADE (FICTITIOUS CHARACTER) p.307

STARBRANCH, HARRY (FICTITIOUS CHARACTER) p.307

STARBUCK, JESSICA (FICTITIOUS CHARACTER) p.307

STARBUCK, NATHANIEL (FICTITIOUS CHARACTER) p.308

STARBUCK, SHAWN (FICTITIOUS CHARACTER) p.308

STARGARD, CONRAD (FICTITIOUS CHARACTER) p.308

STARHAWK (FICTITIOUS CHARACTER: HAMBLY) p.308

STARK, EARL (FICTITIOUS CHARACTER) p.308

STARK, JOANNA (FICTITIOUS CHARACTER) p.308

STARKEY, CAROL (FICTITIOUS CHARACTER) p.308

STARKEY, DAN (FICTITIOUS CHARACTER) p.308

STEELE, KATHERINE, LADY (FICTITIOUS CHARACTER) p.308

STEELE, KATY (FICTITIOUS CHARACTER) p.308

STEELE, RAYFORD (FICTITIOUS CHARACTER) p.308

STEFANOS, NICK (FICTITIOUS CHARACTER) p.309

STEFANOVICH, JOHN (FICTITIOUS CHARACTER) p.309

STELLA THE STARGAZER (FICTITIOUS CHARACTER) p.309

STEN (FICTITIOUS CHARACTER: COLE) p.309

STERN, ALEJANDRO 'SANDY' (FICTITIOUS CHARACTER) p.309

STEVENS, DELTA 'STORM' (FICTITIOUS CHARACTER) p.309

STEVENS, TED (FICTITIOUS CHARACTER) p.309

STEWART, BLAINE (FICTITIOUS CHARACTER) p.309

STEWART, JOHN (FICTITIOUS CHARACTER) p.309

STEWART, KELLEN (FICTITIOUS CHARACTER) p.309

STEWART, LINDA (FICTITIOUS CHARACTER) p.309

STEWART, TEAL (FICTITIOUS CHARACTER) p.309

STILLWATER, MARTIN (FICTITIOUS CHARACTER) p.309

STOCK, JOAN (FICTITIOUS CHARACTER) p.310

STOCK, MATTHEW (FICTITIOUS CHARACTER) p.310

STONE, DETECTIVE SERGEANT (FICTITIOUS CHARACTER) p.310

STONE, HAZEL (FICTITIOUS CHARACTER) p.310

STONE, JESSE (FICTITIOUS CHARACTER) p.310

STONE, LUCY (FICTITIOUS CHARACTER) p.310

STONE, LUNA (FICTITIOUS CHARACTER) p.310

STONE, MICHAEL (FICTITIOUS CHARACTER) p.310

STONE, NATHAN (FICTITIOUS CHARACTER) p.310

STONE, NICK (FICTITIOUS CHARACTER) p.310

STONER, BELL (FICTITIOUS CHARACTER) p.310

STONER, HARRY (FICTITIOUS CHARACTER) p.310
STORME, WYATT (FICTITIOUS CHARACTER) p.310
STORMS, SERGE (FICTITIOUS CHARACTER) p.310
STORR, NICK (FICTITIOUS CHARACTER) p.311
STOWE, BEECHER (FICTITIOUS CHARACTER) p.311
STRACHEY, DONALD (FICTITIOUS CHARACTER) p.311
STRAIT, JAKE (FICTITIOUS CHARACTER) p.311
STRANAHAN, MICK (FICTITIOUS CHARACTER) p.311
STRANGE, DEREK (FICTITIOUS CHARACTER) p.311
STRANGE, SYLVIA (FICTITIOUS CHARACTER) p.311
STRATTON, JOHN (FICTITIOUS CHARACTER) p.311
STRAUSS, DAVID (FICTITIOUS CHARACTER) p.311
STRAWBERRY SHORTCAKE (FICTITIOUS CHARACTER) p.311
STREET, JASON (FICTITIOUS CHARACTER) p.311
STREET, JIMMY (FICTITIOUS CHARACTER) p.311
STREETER (FICTITIOUS CHARACTER: STONE) p.311
STREUSEL, ROB (FICTITIOUS CHARACTER) p.311
STRICKLAND, DAVE (FICTITIOUS CHARACTER) p.311
STROHEM, SABINE (FICTITIOUS CHARACTER: BANTOCK) p.311
    see Sabine (Fictitious Character: Bantock)
STRUMMAR, SETH (FICTITIOUS CHARACTER) p.311
STRYKER, JACK (FICTITIOUS CHARACTER) p.311
STUART, JANE (FICTITIOUS CHARACTER) p.311
STUART, MATTHEW (FICTITIOUS CHARACTER) p.311
STUBBS, HERMAN 'FATTY' (FICTITIOUS CHARACTER) p.311
STURGIS, MILO (FICTITIOUS CHARACTER) p.311
SUCCORSO, NICK (FICTITIOUS CHARACTER) p.312
SUENO, GEORGE (FICTITIOUS CHARACTER) p.312
SUGHRUE, C. W. (FICTITIOUS CHARACTER) p.312
SULLIVAN, DAVID (FICTITIOUS CHARACTER) p.312
SULLIVAN, LIZ (FICTITIOUS CHARACTER) p.312
SULLIVAN, RITA ANGELA (FICTITIOUS CHARACTER) p.312
SULU, HIKARU (FICTITIOUS CHARACTER) p.312
SUMMER, MAGGIE (FICTITIOUS CHARACTER) p.312
SUN WOLF (FICTITIOUS CHARACTER: HAMBLY) p.312
SUNSET WARRIOR (FICTITIOUS CHARACTER) p.312
SUNDAY, GIDEON (FICTITIOUS CHARACTER) p.312
SUNSTAR, JANDER (FICTITIOUS CHARACTER) p.312
SUPERMAN (FICTITIOUS CHARACTER) p.312
SUSSMAN, ANDY (FICTITIOUS CHARACTER) p.313
SUSSOCK, RAY (FICTITIOUS CHARACTER) p.313
SUTCLIFFE, EVELYN (FICTITIOUS CHARACTER) p.313
SUTCLIFFE, SUPERINTENDENT (FICTITIOUS CHARACTER) p.313
SVENSDOTTER, ESTHER "STAR" (FICTITIOUS CHARACTER) p.313
SVENSON, MIKE (FICTITIOUS CHARACTER) p.313
SWAGGER, BOB LEE (FICTITIOUS CHARACTER) p.313
SWAIN, BERT (FICTITIOUS CHARACTER) p.313
SWANN, CASSANDRA (FICTITIOUS CHARACTER) p.313

SWANN, JACKIE (FICTITIOUS CHARACTER) p.313
SWEENEY, BILL (FICTITIOUS CHARACTER) p.313
SWEENEY, PARIS (FICTITIOUS CHARACTER) p.313
SWEET, DEE (FICTITIOUS CHARACTER) p.313
SWENSEN, HANNAH (FICTITIOUS CHARACTER) p.313
SWIFT, BOBBY (FICTITIOUS CHARACTER) p.313
SWIFT, LOREN (FICTITIOUS CHARACTER) p.313
SWINBROOKE, KATHRYN (FICTITIOUS CHARACTER) p.313
SYLVESTER, BEN (FICTITIOUS CHARACTER) p.314
SYLVESTER, WILLIAM (FICTITIOUS CHARACTER) p.314
TACKETT, DEL (FICTITIOUS CHARACTER) p.314
TAGGERT FAMILY (FICTITIOUS CHARACTERS) p.314
TALLCHIEF FAMILY (FICTITIOUS CHARACTERS) p.314
TALON FAMILY (FICTITIOUS CHARACTERS) p.314
TALTOS, VLAD (FICTITIOUS CHARACTER) p.314
TAMAR, HILARY (FICTITIOUS CHARACTER) p.314
TANAKA, KEN (FICTITIOUS CHARACTER) p.314
TANARI (FICTITIOUS CHARACTER) p.314
TANNER, ALEX (FICTITIOUS CHARACTER) p.314
TANNER, ELI (FICTITIOUS CHARACTER) p.314
TANNER, EVAN (FICTITIOUS CHARACTER) p.314
TANNER, JOHN MARSHALL (FICTITIOUS CHARACTER) p.314
TARZAN (FICTITIOUS CHARACTER) p.315
TATE, GERRY (FICTITIOUS CHARACTER) p.316
TATE, SHELBY KAY (FICTITIOUS CHARACTER) p.316
TATUM TWINS (FICTITIOUS CHARACTERS) p.316
TAVERNER, MILOS (FICTITIOUS CHARACTER) p.316
TAYLOR, DOV (FICTITIOUS CHARACTER) p.316
TAYLOR, EASY (FICTITIOUS CHARACTER) p.316
TAYLOR, FRED (FICTITIOUS CHARACTER) p.316
TAYLOR, HOLLAND (FICTITIOUS CHARACTER) p.316
TAYLOR, JACK (FICTITIOUS CHARACTER) p.316
TAYLOR, MARILYN (FICTITIOUS CHARACTER) p.316
TAYLOR, SANGAMON (FICTITIOUS CHARACTER) p.316
TEAGARDEN, AURORA ROE (FICTITIOUS CHARACTER) p.316
TEAGUE, KATE (FICTITIOUS CHARACTER) p.317
TEAGUE, SYDNEY (FICTITIOUS CHARACTER) p.317
TEMPLAR, SIMON (FICTITIOUS CHARACTER) p.317
    see Saint (Fictitious Character)
TENNISON, JANE (FICTITIOUS CHARACTER) p.317
THACKERAY, CONSTABLE (FICTITIOUS CHARACTER) p.317
THACKERAY, MICHAEL (FICTITIOUS CHARACTER) p.317
THANET, LUKE (FICTITIOUS CHARACTER) p.317
THATCH, KELSEY (FICTITIOUS CHARACTER) p.317
THATCHER, JOHN PUTNAM (FICTITIOUS CHARACTER) p.317
THERMOPYLE, ANGUS (FICTITIOUS CHARACTER) p.317
THOMAS, BIGGER (FICTITIOUS CHARACTER) p.318
THOMAS, HANS (FICTITIOUS CHARACTER) p.318
THOMAS, LENORE (FICTITIOUS CHARACTER) p.318

THOMAS, MAURA (FICTITIOUS CHARACTER) p.318
THOMPSON, DAN, REVEREND (FICTITIOUS CHARACTER) p.318
THONGOR (FICTITIOUS CHARACTER) p.318
THORN (FICTITIOUS CHARACTER) p.318
THORN, PETER (FICTITIOUS CHARACTER) p.318
THORNDYKE, DOCTOR (FICTITIOUS CHARACTER) p.318
THORNE, HOLLY (FICTITIOUS CHARACTER) p.318
THORNE, IRIS (FICTITIOUS CHARACTER) p.318
THORNHILL, RICHARD (FICTITIOUS CHARACTER) p.318
THORNTON, JUDITH (FICTITIOUS CHARACTER) p.318
THORNTON FAMILY (FICTITIOUS CHARACTERS) p.318
THORPE, CALVIN (FICTITIOUS CHARACTER) p.318
THORSSEN, ALIX (FICTITIOUS CHARACTER) p.318
THREE MUSKETEERS (FICTITIOUS CHARACTERS) p.318
TIBALDI, JIMMY (FICTITIOUS CHARACTER) p.319
TIBBETT, EMMY (FICTITIOUS CHARACTER) p.319
TIBBETT, HENRY (FICTITIOUS CHARACTER) p.319
TIBBS, VIRGIL (FICTITIOUS CHARACTER) p.319
TICHY, IJON (FICTITIOUS CHARACTER) p.319
TIDEWATER, JORDAN (FICTITIOUS CHARACTER) p.319
TIMBERLAKE, ABIGAIL (FICTITIOUS CHARACTER) p.319
TINTIN (FICTITIOUS CHARACTER) p.319
TITUS, NICKY (FICTITIOUS CHARACTER) p.319
TITUS, SAM (FICTITIOUS CHARACTER) p.320
TOBIN, MITCH (FICTITIOUS CHARACTER) p.320
TODD, CHARLES (FICTITIOUS CHARACTER) p.320
TOFF, THE (FICTITIOUS CHARACTER) p.320
    see Rollison, Richard (Fictitious Character)
TOLLIVER, BEN (FICTITIOUS CHARACTER) p.320
TONNEMAN, PIETER (FICTITIOUS CHARACTER) p.320
TOOLE, SANTIAGO (FICTITIOUS CHARACTER) p.320
TORRANCE, JACK (FICTITIOUS CHARACTER) p.320
TORRES, B'ELANNA (FICTITIOUS CHARACTER) p.320
TOWNSEND, KEITH (FICTITIOUS CHARACTER) p.320
TOWNSEND, MARK (FICTITIOUS CHARACTER) p.320
TOWNSEND, SUSAN (FICTITIOUS CHARACTER) p.320
TOZZI, MIKE (FICTITIOUS CHARACTER) p.320
TRACY, DICK (FICTITIOUS CHARACTER) p.320
TRAKOS, NIKKI (FICTITIOUS CHARACTER) p.320
TRAMWELL, PRIMROSE (FICTITIOUS CHARACTER) p.320
TRANSFORMERS (FICTITIOUS CHARACTERS) p.320
TRASK, GINNY (FICTITIOUS CHARACTER) p.320
TRAVELER, MORONI (FICTITIOUS CHARACTER) p.320
TRAVERS, FENWICK (FICTITIOUS CHARACTER) p.320
TRAVERS, MOLLY (FICTITIOUS CHARACTER) p.320
TRAVERS, NICK (FICTITIOUS CHARACTER) p.320
TRAVERS, TORY (FICTITIOUS CHARACTER) p.320
TRAVIS, BARRIE (FICTITIOUS CHARACTER) p.320
TRAVIS, MELANIE (FICTITIOUS CHARACTER) p.321

TRAVIS, ROSEMARY (FICTITIOUS CHARACTER) p.321

TRAVIS, SHEILA (FICTITIOUS CHARACTER) p.321

TREASURE, MARK (FICTITIOUS CHARACTER) p.321

TREGALLES, JOHN (FICTITIOUS CHARACTER) p.321

TREGAR, JANE (FICTITIOUS CHARACTER) p.321

TREGARDE, DIANA (FICTITIOUS CHARACTER) p.321

TREGARTH, JESSICA (FICTITIOUS CHARACTER) p.321

TREGARTH, SIMON (FICTITIOUS CHARACTER) p.321

TREHERN, KERARA (FICTITIOUS CHARACTER) p.321

TRELAINE, LUCY MACALPIN (FICTITIOUS CHARACTER) p.321

TRELOAR, GABE (FICTITIOUS CHARACTER) p.321

TRENKA, BETTY (FICTITIOUS CHARACTER) p.321

TRENT, NIGEL (FICTITIOUS CHARACTER) p.321

TRETHEWAY, ALBERT (FICTITIOUS CHARACTER) p.321

TRETHOWAN, PERRY, SUPERINTENDENT (FICTITIOUS CHARACTER) p.321

TREVAYNE, ANDREW (FICTITIOUS CHARACTER) p.321

TREVELLYAN, NICK (FICTITIOUS CHARACTER) p.321

TREVELYAN, ROSE (FICTITIOUS CHARACTER) p.321

TREVOR, HANNAH (FICTITIOUS CHARACTER) p.322

TREWLEY, DETECTIVE SUPERINTENDENT (FICTITIOUS CHARACTER) p.322

TRIBBLE, AMY (FICTITIOUS CHARACTER) p.322

TRIBBLE, EFFY (FICTITIOUS CHARACTER) p.322

TRIPPER, LEE (FICTITIOUS CHARACTER) p.322

TROI, DEANNA (FICTITIOUS CHARACTER) p.322

TROTTER, TILLY (FICTITIOUS CHARACTER) p.322

TROWBRIDGE, DAVID (FICTITIOUS CHARACTER) p.322

TROY, BILL (FICTITIOUS CHARACTER) p.322

TROY, FREDERICK (FICTITIOUS CHARACTER) p.322

TRUE, STARKY (FICTITIOUS CHARACTER) p.322

TRUETT, ELIZABETH (FICTITIOUS CHARACTER) p.322

TRUMBULL, VICTORIA (FICTITIOUS CHARACTER) p.322

TRUMPER, CHARLIE (FICTITIOUS CHARACTER) p.322

TRUMPINGTON, PHILIP (FICTITIOUS CHARACTER) p.322

TRYON, GLYNIS (FICTITIOUS CHARACTER) p.323

TSIA (FICTITIOUS CHARACTER) p.323

TUCKER, FLAP (FICTITIOUS CHARACTER) p.323

TUDOR, BESS (FICTITIOUS CHARACTER) p.323

TULL, RICHARD (FICTITIOUS CHARACTER) p.323

TUNET, TORREY (FICTITIOUS CHARACTER) p.323

TURNBUCKLE, HENRY (FICTITIOUS CHARACTER) p.323

TURNER, NICHOLAS (FICTITIOUS CHARACTER) p.323

TURNER, PAUL (FICTITIOUS CHARACTER) p.323

TURNER, SAM (FICTITIOUS CHARACTER) p.323

TURNER, SAMANTHA (FICTITIOUS CHARACTER) p.323

TUVOK (FICTITIOUS CHARACTER) p.323

TWAIN, MARK, 1835-1910 p.323

TWEETY PIE (FICTITIOUS CHARACTER) p.323

TYGART, MARY 'IKE' (FICTITIOUS CHARACTER) p.323

TYLER, WENDY (FICTITIOUS CHARACTER) p.323

TYRONE, JAMES (FICTITIOUS CHARACTER) p.323

TYSON, BEN (FICTITIOUS CHARACTER) p.323

UBU (FICTITIOUS CHARACTER) p.323

UHURA, NYOTA (FICTITIOUS CHARACTER) p.323

UNDERHILL, FREDDY (FICTITIOUS CHARACTER) p.324

UNDERHILL, TIM (FICTITIOUS CHARACTER) p.324

UNDERWOOD, TONI (FICTITIOUS CHARACTER) p.324

UPSHAW, DANNY (FICTITIOUS CHARACTER) p.324

URSULA, SISTER (FICTITIOUS CHARACTER) p.324

VADER, DARTH (FICTITIOUS CHARACTER) p.324
  see Skywalker, Anakin (Fictitious Character)

VAIL, MARTIN (FICTITIOUS CHARACTER) p.324

VALADAN, WARHORSE OF ESDRAGON (FICTITIOUS CHARACTER) p.324

VALENTINE, AMANDA (FICTITIOUS CHARACTER) p.324

VALENTINE, CLAUDIA (FICTITIOUS CHARACTER) p.324

VALENTINE, DAN (FICTITIOUS CHARACTER) p.324

VALENTINE, TONY (FICTITIOUS CHARACTER) p.324

VALJEAN, JEAN (FICTITIOUS CHARACTER) p.324

VALLANCE, ANTHONY (FICTITIOUS CHARACTER) p.324

VALMONT, EUGENE (FICTITIOUS CHARACTER) p.324

VAN ALSTYNE, RUSS (FICTITIOUS CHARACTER) p.324

VANCE, PHILO (FICTITIOUS CHARACTER) p.324

VANDER, BOBBIE (FICTITIOUS CHARACTER) p.324

VAN DER LYN, DINAH (FICTITIOUS CHARACTER) p.324

VAN DER VALK, ARLETTE (FICTITIOUS CHARACTER) p.324

VAN DER VALK, PIET (FICTITIOUS CHARACTER) p.325

VANE, HARRIET (FICTITIOUS CHARACTER) p.325

VAN VOREEN, LEIGH (FICTITIOUS CHARACTER) p.325

VAN WINKLE, RIP (FICTITIOUS CHARACTER) p.325

VAN ZAND, PETER (FICTITIOUS CHARACTER) p.325

VAN ZANDT, MAGGIE (FICTITIOUS CHARACTER) p.325

VARADAY, FRAN (FICTITIOUS CHARACTER) p.325

VARNEY, HALLY (FICTITIOUS CHARACTER) p.325

VAUGHAN (FICTITIOUS CHARACTER: O'DONOHOE) p.325

VAUGHAN, ROBIN (FICTITIOUS CHARACTER) p.325

VENTANA, RONNIE (FICTITIOUS CHARACTER) p.325

VENTURA, ACE (FICTITIOUS CHARACTER) p.325

VERDEAN, GILLIAN (FICTITIOUS CHARACTER) p.325

VERDI, KATE (FICTITIOUS CHARACTER) p.325

VERGIL MAGUS (FICTITIOUS CHARACTER) p.325

VERINDER, RACHEL (FICTITIOUS CHARACTER) p.325

VERMEILLE, CHARLES (FICTITIOUS CHARACTER) p.326

VERNET, VICTOIRE, MME. (FICTITIOUS CHARACTER) p.326

VERNON, ANNE (FICTITIOUS CHARACTER) p.326

VICENTE, ROSIE (FICTITIOUS CHARACTER) p.326

VICKERS, LISSA (FICTITIOUS CHARACTER) p.326

VICKERY, FRED (FICTITIOUS CHARACTER) p.326

VICTOR, EMMA (FICTITIOUS CHARACTER) p.326

VICTORIA, QUEEN OF GREAT BRITAIN, 1819-1901 p.326

VIERLING, FRANCESCA (FICTITIOUS CHARACTER) p.326

VIRDON, MERCY (FICTITIOUS CHARACTER) p.326

VOLGER, DEENA (FICTITIOUS CHARACTER) p.326

VOINOV, TOLEA (FICTITIOUS CHARACTER) p.326

VON REISDEN, ALEXANDER, BARON (FICTITIOUS CHARACTER) p.326

VOORT, CONRAD (FICTITIOUS CHARACTER) p.326

VORKOSIGAN, MILES (FICTITIOUS CHARACTER) p.326

VOUTE, J. M. (FICTITIOUS CHARACTER) p.326

VRYCE, DAMIEN (FICTITIOUS CHARACTER) p.326

WADE, NYLA (FICTITIOUS CHARACTER) p.326

WAGER, GABRIEL (FICTITIOUS CHARACTER) p.326

WAGNER, LAUREN (FICTITIOUS CHARACTER) p.327

WALES, JOSEY (FICTITIOUS CHARACTER) p.327

WALKER, AMOS (FICTITIOUS CHARACTER) p.327

WALKER, CALICO JACK (FICTITIOUS CHARACTER) p.327

WALKER, CAMELLIA (FICTITIOUS CHARACTER) p.327

WALKER, KIRSTEN (FICTITIOUS CHARACTER) p.327

WALKINSHAW, TOM (FICTITIOUS CHARACTER) p.327

WALLANDER, KURT (FICTITIOUS CHARACTER) p.327

WALSH, JACK (FICTITIOUS CHARACTER) p.327

WALSH, JACKIE (FICTITIOUS CHARACTER: CLEARY) p.327

WALSH, SIDNEY (FICTITIOUS CHARACTER) p.327

WANAWAKE, PENNY (FICTITIOUS CHARACTER) p.327

WARD, EMERSON (FICTITIOUS CHARACTER) p.328

WARD, ERIC (FICTITIOUS CHARACTER) p.328

WARDEN, JESSE (FICTITIOUS CHARACTER) p.328

WAREEN, WYATT (FICTITIOUS CHARACTER) p.328

WAREHAM, LIZ (FICTITIOUS CHARACTER) p.328

WARNER, WILLIAM (FICTITIOUS CHARACTER) p.328

WARREN, PENELOPE (FICTITIOUS CHARACTER) p.328

WARSHAWSKI, V. I. (FICTITIOUS CHARACTER) p.328

WATERMAN, LEO (FICTITIOUS CHARACTER) p.328

WATERS, STANLEY (FICTITIOUS CHARACTER) p.328

WATKINS, MERRILY (FICTITIOUS CHARACTER) p.328

WATSON, EDGAR J. (FICTITIOUS CHARACTER) p.328

WATSON, JOHN H. (FICTITIOUS CHARACTER) p.328

WATSON, LUCIUS (FICTITIOUS CHARACTER) p.329

WAYLES, LUCY (FICTITIOUS CHARACTER) p.330

WAYNEST, JENNY (FICTITIOUS CHARACTER) p.330

WEARIE, EAMON (FICTITIOUS CHARACTER) p.330

WEATHERBY, ARTIE (FICTITIOUS CHARACTER) p.330

WEATHERFORD, BIGGIE (FICTITIOUS CHARACTER) p.330

WEATHERFORD, J. R. (FICTITIOUS CHARACTER) p.330

WEBB, DAVID (FICTITIOUS CHARACTER) p.330

List of Subject Headings - Fiction

List of Subject Headings - Fiction

WEBER, JON (FICTITIOUS CHARACTER) p.330

WEINSTEIN, JOSHUA (FICTITIOUS CHARACTER) p.330

WEISS, SCOTT (FICTITIOUS CHARACTER) p.330

WELFORD, KAREN (FICTITIOUS CHARACTER) p.330

WELLESLEY BROTHERS (FICTITIOUS CHARACTERS) p.330

WELLS, KATHERINE (FICTITIOUS CHARACTER) p.330

WELLS BROTHERS (FICTITIOUS CHARACTERS) p.330

WENTWORTH, BEA (FICTITIOUS CHARACTER) p.330

WENTWORTH, LYON (FICTITIOUS CHARACTER) p.330

WESCOTT SISTERS (FICTITIOUS CHARACTERS) p.330

WEST, DELILAH (FICTITIOUS CHARACTER) p.330

WEST, HELEN (FICTITIOUS CHARACTER) p.330

WEST, MOLLY (FICTITIOUS CHARACTER) p.331

WEST, ROGER, INSPECTOR (FICTITIOUS CHARACTER) p.331

WESTBOROUGH, THEOCRITUS LUCIUS (FICTITIOUS CHARACTER) p.331

WESTCOTT, SAM (FICTITIOUS CHARACTER) p.331

WESTLAKE, PEYTON (FICTITIOUS CHARACTER) p.331
    see Darkman (Fictitious Character)

WESTON, CARLY (FICTITIOUS CHARACTER) p.331

WESTPHAL, CONNER (FICTITIOUS CHARACTER) p.331

WETZON, LESLIE (FICTITIOUS CHARACTER) p.331

WEXFORD, INSPECTOR (FICTITIOUS CHARACTER) p.331

WHALBY, STEPHEN (FICTITIOUS CHARACTER) p.332

WHALE, JAMES (FICTITIOUS CHARACTER) p.332

WHEATLEY, CHAS (FICTITIOUS CHARACTER) p.332

WHEELER, EPHRAIM (FICTITIOUS CHARACTER) p.332

WHELAN, MURRAY (FICTITIOUS CHARACTER) p.332

WHELAN, PAUL (FICTITIOUS CHARACTER) p.332

WHISTLER (FICTITIOUS CHARACTER: CAMPBELL) p.332

WHISTLER, NICHOLAS (FICTITIOUS CHARACTER) p.332

WHITE, BLANCHE (FICTITIOUS CHARACTER) p.332

WHITE, CARRIE (FICTITIOUS CHARACTER) p.332

WHITE, LILY (FICTITIOUS CHARACTER) p.332

WHITEFIELD, JANE (FICTITIOUS CHARACTER) p.332

WHITEHEAD, ANN (FICTITIOUS CHARACTER) p.332

WHITEOAK FAMILY (FICTITIOUS CHARACTERS) p.332

WHITLAW, KAREN (FICTITIOUS CHARACTER) p.332

WIGGIN, ENDER (FICTITIOUS CHARACTER) p.332
    see Ender (Fictitious Character)

WILCOX, CARL (FICTITIOUS CHARACTER) p.332

WILDE, CAT (FICTITIOUS CHARACTER) p.333

WILDER, JOE (FICTITIOUS CHARACTER) p.333

WILDER, JONATHAN (FICTITIOUS CHARACTER) p.333

WILDER, TOM (FICTITIOUS CHARACTER) p.333

WILDER, MARY (FICTITIOUS CHARACTER) p.333

WILL, ELIZABETH (FICTITIOUS CHARACTER) p.333

WILLETT, WOLF (FICTITIOUS CHARACTER) p.333

WILLIAM OF BASKERVILLE (FICTITIOUS CHARACTER) p.333

WILLIAMS, CALEB (FICTITIOUS CHARACTER) p.333

WILLIAMS, CATHERINE (FICTITIOUS CHARACTER) p.333

WILLIAMS, RACE (FICTITIOUS CHARACTER) p.333

WILLIAMS, TERRY (FICTITIOUS CHARACTER) p.333

WILLIAMSON, LUKE (FICTITIOUS CHARACTER) p.333

WILLMARTH, RUTH (FICTITIOUS CHARACTER) p.333

WILLOWS, JACK (FICTITIOUS CHARACTER) p.333

WILLUM, PERSIS (FICTITIOUS CHARACTER) p.333

WILSON, ANGELA (FICTITIOUS CHARACTER) p.333

WILSON, FRANCESCA (FICTITIOUS CHARACTER) p.333

WIMSEY, PETER, LORD (FICTITIOUS CHARACTER) p.333

WINDER, JOE (FICTITIOUS CHARACTER) p.334

WINDROSE, ANTRYG (FICTITIOUS CHARACTER) p.335

WINE, MOSES (FICTITIOUS CHARACTER) p.335

WING, ISADORA (FICTITIOUS CHARACTER) p.335

WING, JAMES (FICTITIOUS CHARACTER) p.335

WINGATE, CALEDONIA (FICTITIOUS CHARACTER) p.335

WINN ADAMI, KAI (FICTITIOUS CHARACTER) p.335

WINSLOW, LAURA (FICTITIOUS CHARACTER) p.335

WINSLOW, LIBBY (FICTITIOUS CHARACTER) p.335

WINSLOW, STEVE (FICTITIOUS CHARACTER) p.335

WINSLOW FAMILY (FICTITIOUS CHARACTERS) p.335

WINSTON, ALEX (FICTITIOUS CHARACTER) p.335

WINSTON, STONEY (FICTITIOUS CHARACTER) p.335

WINTER, DANIEL (FICTITIOUS CHARACTER) p.335

WINTER, HOLLY (FICTITIOUS CHARACTER) p.335

WINTER, PETER (FICTITIOUS CHARACTER) p.336

WINTER, SIMON (FICTITIOUS CHARACTER) p.336

WIRE, BARB (FICTITIOUS CHARACTER) p.336

WITHERALL, LEONIDAS (FICTITIOUS CHARACTER) p.336

WITHERS, HILDEGARDE (FICTITIOUS CHARACTER) p.336

WITHERSPOON, GERALD (FICTITIOUS CHARACTER) p.336

WOHL, PETER (FICTITIOUS CHARACTER) p.336

WOLFE, HANNAH (FICTITIOUS CHARACTER) p.336

WOLFE, NERO (FICTITIOUS CHARACTER) p.336

WOMEN'S MURDER CLUB (FICTITIOUS CHARACTERS) p.337

WONDER WOMAN (FICTITIOUS CHARACTER) p.337

WOO, APRIL (FICTITIOUS CHARACTER) p.338

WOODEND, CHARLIE (FICTITIOUS CHARACTER) p.338

WOODHOUSE, EMMA (FICTITIOUS CHARACTER) p.338

WOODRUFF, BERNARD (FICTITIOUS CHARACTER) p.338

WOOSTER, BERTIE (FICTITIOUS CHARACTER) p.338

WORF (FICTITIOUS CHARACTER) p.339

WORRELL, ERNEST P. (FICTITIOUS CHARACTER) p.339

WORTHING, MATILDA (FICTITIOUS CHARACTER) p.339

WREN, PORTER (FICTITIOUS CHARACTER) p.339

WREN, SUSAN (FICTITIOUS CHARACTER) p.339

WRIGHT, BETH (FICTITIOUS CHARACTER) p.339

WRIGHT, JESSICA (FICTITIOUS CHARACTER) p.339

WU, ARTIE (FICTITIOUS CHARACTER) p.339

WUNTVOR (FICTITIOUS CHARACTER) p.340

WYATT (FICTITIOUS CHARACTER) p.340

WYATT, JOLIE (FICTITIOUS CHARACTER) p.340

WYC, WINSTON (FICTITIOUS CHARACTER) p.340

WYCLIFFE, CHARLES (FICTITIOUS CHARACTER) p.340

WYLIE, EVA (FICTITIOUS CHARACTER) p.340

X, MR. (FICTITIOUS CHARACTER) p.340

X-MEN (FICTITIOUS CHARACTERS) p.340

XENA (FICTITIOUS CHARACTER) p.341

YABLONSKY, ALVIN (FICTITIOUS CHARACTER) p.341

YABLONSKY, BUBBLES (FICTITIOUS CHARACTER) p.341

YAMA (FICTITIOUS CHARACTER) p.341

YANCY, KATE (FICTITIOUS CHARACTER) p.341

YAR, TASHA (FICTITIOUS CHARACTER) p.341

YARBROUGH, MACLAREN (FICTITIOUS CHARACTER) p.341

YATES, GIL (FICTITIOUS CHARACTER) p.341

YEADINGS, MIKE (FICTITIOUS CHARACTER) p.341

YEARMAN, DOLLY (FICTITIOUS CHARACTER) p.342

YODER, MAGDALENA (FICTITIOUS CHARACTER) p.342

YORK, ALAN (FICTITIOUS CHARACTER) p.342

YOUNGER, CECIL (FICTITIOUS CHARACTER) p.342

YUM YUM (FICTITIOUS CHARACTER: BRAUN) p.342

ZARKON, LORD OF THE UNKNOWN (FICTITIOUS CHARACTER) p.343

ZEN, AURELIO (FICTITIOUS CHARACTER) p.343

ZERO, NINA (FICTITIOUS CHARACTER) p.343

ZHONG, FONG, INSPECTOR (FICTITIOUS CHARACTER) p.343

ZIGGY (FICTITIOUS CHARACTER) p.343

ZINDEL, FANNY (FICTITIOUS CHARACTER) p.343

ZONDI, MICKEY (FICTITIOUS CHARACTER) p.343

ZORRO (FICTITIOUS CHARACTER) p.344

ZUCKERMAN, NATHAN (FICTITIOUS CHARACTER) p.344

ZUKAS, HELMA (FICTITIOUS CHARACTER) p.344

# ETHNIC GROUPS

AFRO-AMERICANS p.344

AMISH p.356

ASIAN AMERICANS p.357

BLACKS p.357

CHINESE AMERICANS p.358

CREOLES p.358

CUBAN AMERICANS p.358

DOMINICAN AMERICANS p.358

ESKIMOS p.359

FRENCH-CANADIANS p.359

HISPANIC AMERICANS p.359

INDIAN WOMEN—CANADA p.360

INDIAN WOMEN—NORTH AMERICA p.360

INDIANS OF CENTRAL AMERICA p.360

INDIANS OF MEXICO p.360

INDIANS OF NORTH AMERICA p.360

INDIANS OF SOUTH AMERICA p.372

INUIT p.372

IRISH AMERICANS p.372

ITALIAN AMERICANS p.373

JAPANESE p.374

JAPANESE AMERICANS p.374

JEWS p.375

MENNONITES p.382

MEXICAN AMERICANS p.382

MORMONS p.383

POLISH AMERICANS p.384

## HISTORICAL EVENTS

CHINA—HISTORY—TAIPING REBELLION, 1850-1864 p.384

CRIMEAN WAR, 1853-1856 p.384

CRUSADES p.384

CUBAN MISSILE CRISIS, 1962 p.385

FRANCE—HISTORY—REVOLUTION, 1789-1799 p.385

FRONTIER AND PIONEER LIFE p.385

GREAT BRITAIN—HISTORY—WARS OF THE ROSES, 1455-1485 p.386

GREAT BRITAIN—HISTORY—PURITAN REVOLUTION, 1642-1660 p.386

GREAT BRITAIN—HISTORY—CIVIL WAR, 1642-1649 p.386

HOLOCAUST, JEWISH (1939-1945) p.386

HUNDRED YEARS' WAR, 1339-1453 p.387

INDIA—HISTORY—BRITISH OCCUPATION, 1765-1947 p.387

INDIANS OF NORTH AMERICA—WARS—1866-1895 p.387

IRELAND—HISTORY—EASTER RISING, 1916 p.387

ISRAEL-ARAB WAR, 1948-1949 p.387

ISRAEL-ARAB WAR, 1967 p.388

ISRAEL-ARAB WAR, 1973 p.388

JACOBITE REBELLION, 1745-1746 p.388

KING PHILIP'S WAR, 1675-1676 p.388

KOREAN WAR, 1950-1953 p.388

LEBANON—HISTORY—CIVIL WAR, 1975-1990 p.388

LITTLE BIGHORN, BATTLE OF THE, MONT., 1876 p.388

MEXICAN WAR, 1846-1848 p.388

MEXICO—HISTORY—REVOLUTION, 1910-1920 p.388

NAPOLEONIC WARS, 1800-1815 p.389

NAZIS p.390

PENINSULAR WAR, 1807-1814 p.390

PERSIAN GULF WAR, 1991 p.390

SOUTH AFRICAN WAR, 1899-1902 p.391

SOVIET UNION—HISTORY—REVOLUTION, 1917-1921 p.391

SPAIN—HISTORY—CIVIL WAR, 1936-1939 p.391

SPANISH-AMERICAN WAR, 1898 p.391

TRANSVAAL (SOUTH AFRICA)—HISTORY—WAR OF 1880-1881 p.391

UNITED STATES—HISTORY—FRENCH AND INDIAN WAR, 1755-1763 p.391

UNITED STATES—HISTORY—REVOLUTION, 1775-1783 p.392

UNITED STATES—HISTORY—WAR OF 1812 p.393

UNITED STATES—HISTORY—CIVIL WAR, 1861-1865 p.393

VIETNAMESE CONFLICT, 1961-1975 p.397

WORLD WAR, 1914-1918 p.398

WORLD WAR, 1939-1945 p.399

WORLD WAR III p.406

YUGOSLAV WAR, 1991-1995 p.406

## MISCELLANEOUS

AIDS (DISEASE) p.406

CAT OWNERS p.407

CHRISTIAN LIFE p.408

DOG OWNERS p.409

INTERNET p.410

MISSING PERSONS p.410

PEOPLE WITH DISABILITIES p.413

SERIAL MURDERERS p.413

SLAVES p.414

TERRORISM p.415

TERRORISTS p.415

VAMPIRES p.417

YOUNG WOMEN p.421

## OCCUPATIONS

ACTORS p.424

ACTRESSES p.426

AIR PILOTS p.427

ANTHROPOLOGISTS p.427

ANTIQUE DEALERS p.427

ARCHAEOLOGISTS p.428

ARTISTS p.429

AUTHORS p.434

BASEBALL PLAYERS p.436

BOOKSELLERS AND BOOKSELLING p.436

CATERERS AND CATERING p.438

CATHOLIC CHURCH—CLERGY p.438

CLERGY p.440

COLLEGE TEACHERS p.444

COMPOSERS p.447

COMPUTER INDUSTRY p.447

CRIME AND CRIMINALS p.447

FORENSIC PATHOLOGISTS p.450

FORENSIC PSYCHIATRISTS p.451

GOLFERS p.451

JOCKEYS p.452

JOURNALISTS p.452

LAWYERS p.457

LIBRARIANS p.463

MIDWIVES p.464

MISSIONARIES p.464

MOTION PICTURE INDUSTRY p.465

MUSICIANS p.465

NUNS p.467

PARK RANGERS p.468

PHOTOGRAPHERS p.468

PHYSICIANS p.469

POLICEWOMEN p.473

POLITICIANS p.477

PRESIDENTS p.478

PRESIDENTS—UNITED STATES p.479

PRIVATE INVESTIGATORS p.479

PSYCHOTHERAPISTS p.502

PUBLISHERS AND PUBLISHING p.502

RABBIS p.502

REAL ESTATE AGENTS p.503

SAMURAI p.503

SCIENTISTS p.503

TEACHERS p.504

TEXAS RANGERS p.507

VETERANS p.508

VETERINARIANS p.508

WOMEN ANTHROPOLOGISTS p.508

WOMEN ARCHAEOLOGISTS p.509

WOMEN ARTISTS p.509

WOMEN JOURNALISTS p.510

WOMEN JUDGES p.515

WOMEN LAWYERS p.515

WOMEN PHYSICIANS p.519

WOMEN SCIENTISTS p.520

## RELATIONSHIPS

BROTHERS p.520

BROTHERS AND SISTERS p.523

DATING (SOCIAL CUSTOMS) p.525

FATHERS AND DAUGHTERS p.525

FATHERS AND SONS p.531

FRIENDSHIP p.534

GAY MEN p.539

GRANDPARENTS p.542

LESBIANS p.543

MAN-WOMAN RELATIONSHIPS p.545

MARRIAGE p.558

MARRIED PEOPLE p.562

MOTHER AND CHILD p.567

MOTHERS AND DAUGHTERS p.568

MOTHERS AND SONS p.572

SINGLE WOMEN p.575

SISTERS p.575

TWINS p.580

WIDOWERS p.582

WIDOWS p.583

## SETTINGS

ACAPULCO (MEXICO) p.585

ADIRONDACK MOUNTAINS (N.Y.) p.585

AFGHANISTAN p.585

AFRICA p.585

ALABAMA p.590

ALASKA p.592

ALBANY (N.Y.) p.594

ALBERTA p.594

ALBION (IMAGINARY PLACE) p.594

ALBUQUERQUE (N.M.) p.594

ALEFORD (MASS.: IMAGINARY PLACE) p.595

ALFAR (IMAGINARY PLACE) p.595

ALGERIA p.595

AMBER (IMAGINARY PLACE) p.595

AMHEARST (PA.: IMAGINARY PLACE) p.595

AMSTERDAM (NETHERLANDS) p.595

ANGRIA (IMAGINARY PLACE) p.596
ANTARCTICA p.596
APPALACHIAN MOUNTAINS p.596
ARCTIC REGIONS p.597
ARDEL (IMAGINARY PLACE) p.597
ARGENTINA p.597
ARGYLLE (IMAGINARY PLACE) p.598
ARIZONA p.598
ARKANSAS p.600
ASPEN (COLO.) p.602
ATLANTA (GA.) p.602
ATLANTIC CITY (N.J.) p.603
AUSTIN (TEX.) p.603
AUSTRALIA p.603
AUSTRIA p.608
AVERIDAN (IMAGINARY PLACE) p.609
BADGER'S END (ENGLAND: IMAGINARY PLACE) p.609
BAHAMAS p.609
BAKERHAVEN (CONN.: IMAGINARY PLACE) p.609
BALACLAVA JUNCTION (MASS.: IMAGINARY PLACE) p.609
BALKAN PENINSULA p.609
BALTIMORE (MD.) p.609
BANGLADESH p.610
BARCELONA (SPAIN) p.610
BARNARD'S CROSSING (MASS.: IMAGINARY PLACE) p.610
BARSETSHIRE (ENGLAND: IMAGINARY PLACE) p.611
BARSOOM (IMAGINARY PLACE) p.611
BATON ROUGE (LA.) p.611
BATTLE SCHOOL (IMAGINARY PLACE) p.611
BEARN (IMAGINARY PLACE) p.611
BEIJING (CHINA) p.612
BEKLAN EMPIRE (IMAGINARY PLACE) p.612
BELGIUM p.612
BELIZE p.612
BELLEHAVEN (WASH.: IMAGINARY PLACE) p.612
BENTROCK (MONT.: IMAGINARY PLACE) p.612
BERKELEY (CALIF.) p.612
BERLIN (GERMANY) p.613
BERMUDA ISLANDS p.613
BEVERLY HILLS (CALIF.) p.613
BILOXI (MISS.) p.614
BLACK CAT RIDGE (TEX.: IMAGINARY PLACE) p.614
BLACKSTONE (NEW ENGLAND: IMAGINARY PLACE) p.614
BLISS (SASKATCHEWAN: IMAGINARY PLACE) p.614
BLOSSOM (OREGON: IMAGINARY PLACE) p.614
BLUE DEER (MONT.: IMAGINARY PLACE) p.614
BLUE ISLE (IMAGINARY PLACE) p.614
BLUE RIDGE MOUNTAINS p.614
BOLIVIA p.614
BORDERLANDS (IMAGINARY PLACE) p.614
BORDERVILLE (VA.: IMAGINARY PLACE) p.614
BOSNIA AND HERCEGOVINA p.614
BOSTON (MASS.) p.615
BOTANY (IMAGINARY PLACE) p.620
BOTSWANA p.620
BOULDER (COLO.) p.620
BRANSON (MO.) p.621
BRATTLEBORO (VT.) p.621

BRAZIL p.621
BRITISH COLUMBIA p.621
BROWARD'S ROCK (S.C.: IMAGINARY PLACE) p.622
BUCKSKIN (OKLA.: IMAGINARY PLACE) p.622
BUDAPEST (HUNGARY) p.622
BUENOS AIRES (ARGENTINA) p.622
BUFFALO (N.Y.) p.623
BULGARIA p.623
BURLINGTON (VT.) p.623
CABOT COVE (ME.: IMAGINARY PLACE) p.623
CADWAL (IMAGINARY PLACE) p.623
CAIRO (EGYPT) p.623
CAITHE (IMAGINARY PLACE) p.623
CALEDON (IMAGINARY PLACE) p.623
CALIFORNIA p.623
CALLOWAY CORNERS (IMAGINARY PLACE) p.654
CALUSA (FLA.: IMAGINARY PLACE) p.654
CAMBODIA p.654
CAMBRIDGE (MASS.) p.654
CAMELOT (LEGENDARY PLACE) p.655
CAMULOD (IMAGINARY PLACE) p.655
CANADA p.655
CAPE BRETON ISLAND (N.S.) p.660
CAPE COD (MASS.) p.660
CARIBBEAN AREA p.660
CARLSBAD CAVERNS (N.M.) p.662
CARMEL (CALIF.) p.662
CARROLL (TEX.: IMAGINARY PLACE) p.662
CARTHAGE (EXTINCT CITY) p.662
CASTLE AMBER (IMAGINARY PLACE) p.662
  see Amber (Imaginary Place)
CASTLE PERILOUS (IMAGINARY PLACE) p.663
CASTLE ROCK (ME.: IMAGINARY PLACE) p.663
CATSKILL MOUNTAINS REGION (N.Y.) p.663
CEDAR RAPIDS (IOWA) p.663
CELYDONN (IMAGINARY PLACE) p.663
CENOTAPH ROAD (IMAGINARY PLACE) p.663
CENTRAL AMERICA p.663
CHAMBERLAIN (ME.: IMAGINARY PLACE) p.663
CHARLESTON (S.C.) p.663
CHARLOTTE (N.C.) p.663
CHARLOTTESVILLE (VA.) p.664
CHICAGO (ILL.) p.664
CHILE p.669
CHINA p.669
CHUNG KUO (IMAGINARY PLACE) p.673
CIMMERIA (IMAGINARY PLACE) p.673
CINCINNATI (OHIO) p.674
CLEVELAND (OHIO) p.674
COLOMBIA p.675
COLORADO p.675
CONCORD (MASS.) p.678
CONFLUENCE (IMAGINARY PLACE) p.678
CONNECTICUT p.678
CONTRARY (KY.: IMAGINARY PLACE) p.680
COPENHAGEN (DENMARK) p.680
CORAMONDE (IMAGINARY PLACE) p.680
CORDEN (S.D.: IMAGINARY PLACE) p.680
CORNWALL (ENGLAND: COUNTY) p.681
CORONNAN (IMAGINARY PLACE) p.682
COSTA RICA p.682
COTSWOLD HILLS (ENGLAND) p.682

CRAWFORD COUNTY (TEX.: IMAGINARY PLACE) p.683
CROSSROADS (IMAGINARY PLACE) p.683
CRYSTAL COVE (CALIF.: IMAGINARY PLACE) p.683
CUBA p.683
CUTLER'S COVE (IMAGINARY PLACE) p.684
CYPRUS p.684
CYTEEN (IMAGINARY PLACE) p.684
CZECHOSLOVAKIA p.684
DALLAS (TEX.) p.685
DAMAR (IMAGINARY PLACE) p.685
DARK TOWERS (IMAGINARY PLACE) p.685
DARKOVER (IMAGINARY PLACE) p.685
DARWATH (IMAGINARY PLACE) p.686
DEATH GATE UNIVERSE (IMAGINARY PLACE) p.686
DEATHLANDS (IMAGINARY PLACE) p.686
DELAWARE p.686
DEL MORAY (FLA.: IMAGINARY PLACE) p.687
DENMARK p.687
DENVER (COLO.) p.687
DERRY HILLS (MO.: IMAGINARY PLACE) p.688
DETROIT (MICH.) p.688
DEVELOPING COUNTRIES p.690
DEVERRY (IMAGINARY PLACE) p.690
D'HARAN EMPIRE (IMAGINARY PLACE) p.690
DINOSAUR PLANET (IMAGINARY PLACE) p.690
DISCWORLD (IMAGINARY PLACE) p.690
DOONA (IMAGINARY PLACE) p.691
DORSAI (IMAGINARY PLACE) p.691
DRAGAERA (IMAGINARY PLACE) p.691
DRAGONREALM (IMAGINARY PLACE) p.691
DREAD EMPIRE (IMAGINARY PLACE) p.692
DREAM PARK (IMAGINARY PLACE) p.692
DRYCO (IMAGINARY PLACE) p.692
D'SHAI (IMAGINARY PLACE) p.692
DUBLIN (IRELAND) p.692
DUDLEY (ARIZ.: IMAGINARY PLACE) p.693
DUE EAST (S.C.: IMAGINARY PLACE) p.693
DUNCTON WOOD (IMAGINARY PLACE) p.693
DUNE (IMAGINARY PLACE) p.693
EARTHSEA (IMAGINARY PLACE) p.694
EDINBURGH (SCOTLAND) p.694
EGYPT p.694
EGYPT (ME.: IMAGINARY PLACE) p.697
EIGHTY-SEVENTH PRECINCT (IMAGINARY PLACE) p.697
EL PASO (TEX.) p.698
ELUNDIUM (IMAGINARY PLACE) p.699
EMPTY CREEK (ARIZ.: IMAGINARY PLACE) p.699
ENGLAND p.699
ERDE (IMAGINARY PLACE) p.780
ERIADOR (IMAGINARY PLACE) p.780
ERNA (IMAGINARY PLACE) p.780
ETHIOPIA p.780
EUGENE (OR.) p.780
EUROPE p.780
EUROPE, EASTERN p.782
EVERIEN (IMAGINARY PLACE) p.782
FARBERVILLE (ARK.: IMAGINARY PLACE) p.782
FELICITY GROVE (N.Y.: IMAGINARY PLACE) p.783
FIJI p.783
FINLAND p.783

FIONAVAR (IMAGINARY PLACE) p.783

FISHERSVILLE (N.J.: IMAGINARY PLACE) p.783

FLAT SKUNK (CALIF.: IMAGINARY PLACE) p.783

FLORIDA p.783

FOREST COUNTY (IMAGINARY PLACE) p.791

FOREST KINGDOM (IMAGINARY PLACE: GREEN) p.791

FORGOTTEN REALMS (IMAGINARY PLACE) p.791

FORT LAUDERDALE (FLA.) p.791

FORT WORTH (TEX.) p.792

FORTY-THREE LIGHT STREET (IMAGINARY PLACE) p.792

FRANCE p.792

GAINESVILLE (FLA.) p.808

GALACTIC MILIEU (IMAGINARY PLACE) p.808

GALVESTON (TEX.) p.808

GANDALARA (IMAGINARY PLACE) p.808

GARILLON (IMAGINARY PLACE) p.808

GENEVA (SWITZERLAND) p.808

GEORGIA p.808

GERMANY p.812

GIBBSVILLE (PA.: IMAGINARY PLACE) p.816

GOR (IMAGINARY PLACE) p.816

GORMENGHAST CASTLE (IMAGINARY PLACE) p.816

GRAISTAN (ENGLAND: IMAGINARY PLACE) p.816

GREAT BRITAIN p.816

GREAT BRITAIN—SOCIAL LIFE AND CUSTOMS p.830

GREECE p.831

GREENLAND p.832

GREENWICH (CONN.) p.832

GRENADA p.833

GREYSTONE BAY (IMAGINARY PLACE) p.833

GRYYLTH (IMAGINARY PLACE) p.833

GUATEMALA p.833

GUYANA p.833

HAGERVILLE (MD.: IMAGINARY PLACE) p.833

HAITI p.833

HALRUAA (IMAGINARY PLACE) p.833

HAMPSTEAD (KAN.: IMAGINARY PLACE) p.833

HARDLUCK (ALASKA: IMAGINARY PLACE) p.833

HARPER'S HALL (IMAGINARY PLACE) p.833

HATTERAS, CAPE (N.C.) p.833

HAVANA (CUBA) p.833

HAVEN (IMAGINARY PLACE: GREEN) p.834

HAVEN (ME.: IMAGINARY PLACE) p.834

HAWAII p.834

HELLICONIA (IMAGINARY PLACE) p.835

HEMLOCK FALLS (N.Y.: IMAGINARY PLACE) p.836

HOLLYWOOD (LOS ANGELES, CALIF.) p.836

HONDURAS p.839

HONG KONG (CHINA) p.839

HOUSTON (TEX.) p.839

HUNGARY p.840

ICELAND p.840

IDAHO p.840

ILLINOIS p.841

IMAGINARY PLACES p.845

INDIA p.845

INDIANA p.850

INDIANAPOLIS (IND.) p.851

INDONESIA p.852

IOWA p.852

IRAN p.853

IRELAND p.853

IRIS HOUSE (VICTORIA SPRINGS, MO.: IMAGINARY PLACE) p.861

ISLANDS OF THE INDIAN OCEAN p.861

ISOLA (N.Y.: IMAGINARY PLACE) p.861

ISRAEL p.862

ISTANBUL (TURKEY) p.864

ITALY p.864

JACKSON HOLE (WYO.) p.870

JALNA (CANADA: IMAGINARY PLACE) p.870

JAMAICA p.871

JAMES RIVER (VA.) p.871

JAPAN p.871

JERUSALEM p.874

JESUS CREEK (TENN.: IMAGINARY PLACE) p.875

JOHANNESBURG (SOUTH AFRICA) p.875

JOLIET (ILL.) p.875

JURASSIC PARK (IMAGINARY PLACE) p.875

KANSAS p.875

KANSAS CITY (MO.) p.877

KENTUCKY p.877

KENYA p.879

KEY LARGO (FLA.) p.879

KEY WEST (FLA.) p.879

KINDLE COUNTY (IMAGINARY PLACE) p.880

KOREA p.880

KRONDOR (MIKDEMIA: IMAGINARY PLACE) p.880

KRYNN (IMAGINARY PLACE) p.880

KZIN (IMAGINARY PLACE) p.881

LABORNOK (IMAGINARY PLACE) p.881

LAKE WOBEGON (MINN.: IMAGINARY PLACE) p.881

LAND OF TRUE GAME (IMAGINARY PLACE) p.881

LANDOVER (IMAGINARY PLACE) p.881
    see Magic Kingdom of Landover (Imaginary Place)

LANKHMAR (IMAGINARY PLACE) p.881

LAS VEGAS (NEV.) p.881

LATIN AMERICA p.882

LEBANON p.883

LEMURIA (IMAGINARY PLACE) p.883

LENFELL (IMAGINARY PLACE) p.883

LEXINGTON (KY.) p.883

LIADEN UNIVERSE (IMAGINARY PLACE) p.883

LICKIN CREEK (PA.: IMAGINARY PLACE) p.883

LINCOLN PRAIRIE (ILLINOIS: IMAGINARY PLACE) p.883

LISBON (PORTUGAL) p.883

LITHUANIA p.883

LLANFAIR (WALES: IMAGINARY PLACE) p.883

LOBELIA FALLS (ONT.: IMAGINARY PLACE) p.883

LOCHDUBH (SCOTLAND: IMAGINARY PLACE) p.883

LONDON (ENGLAND) p.884

LONG ISLAND (N.Y.) p.904

LOS ANGELES (CALIF.) p.904

LOS SANTOS (TEX.: IMAGINARY PLACE) p.917

LOUISIANA p.917

LOUISVILLE (KY.) p.922

LUSITANIA (IMAGINARY PLACE) p.922

LYDMOUTH (ENGLAND: IMAGINARY PLACE) p.922

LYRA (IMAGINARY PLACE) p.922

MACONDO (IMAGINARY PLACE) p.922

MADRID (SPAIN) p.923

MAGGODY (ARK.: IMAGINARY PLACE) p.923

MAGIC KINGDOM OF LANDOVER (IMAGINARY PLACE) p.923

MAINE p.923

MAJIPOOR (IMAGINARY PLACE) p.926

MALAYSIA p.927

MALLOREA (IMAGINARY PLACE) p.927

MALTA p.927

MANITOBA p.927

MARIN COUNTY (CALIF.) p.927

MARTHA'S VINEYARD (MASS.) p.927

MARTINIQUE p.927

MARYLAND p.928

MASSACHUSETTS p.929

MATTAGASH (ME.: IMAGINARY PLACE) p.938

MAURITIUS p.938

MEDITERRANEAN REGION p.938

MELNIBONE (IMAGINARY PLACE) p.939

MENSANDOR (IMAGINARY PLACE) p.939

METROPOLIS (IMAGINARY PLACE) p.939

MEXICO p.939

MEXICO CITY (MEXICO) p.942

MIAMI (FLA.) p.942

MICHIGAN p.944

MIDDLE EARTH (IMAGINARY PLACE) p.947

MIDDLE EAST p.948

MIDDLE WEST p.950

MIDKEMIA (IMAGINARY PLACE) p.951

MINNEAPOLIS (MINN.) p.951

MINNESOTA p.952

MIRABEAU (IMAGINARY PLACE: TEX.) p.954

MISSISSIPPI p.954

MISSOURI p.957

MITFORD (N.C.: IMAGINARY PLACE) p.960

MITHGAR (IMAGINARY PLACE) p.960

MONTANA p.960

MONTE CARLO p.964

MONTEREY (CALIF.) p.964

MONTREAL (QUEBEC) p.964

MOONLIGHT BAY (CALIF.: IMAGINARY PLACE) p.964

MOROCCO p.964

MOSCOW (RUSSIA) p.965

MOSPHEIRA (IMAGINARY PLACE) p.965

MURPHY'S HARBOR (ONT.: IMAGINARY PLACE) p.965

MYRIAL (IMAGINARY PLACE) p.966

NANTUCKET ISLAND (MASS.) p.966

NAPA COUNTY (CALIF.) p.966

NASHVILLE (TENN.) p.966

NAVAJO INDIAN RESERVATION p.966

NEBRASKA p.967

NETHERLANDS p.968

NEVADA p.969

NEVYA (IMAGINARY PLACE) p.971

NEW BRUNSWICK (PROVINCE) p.971

NEW ENGLAND p.971

NEW HAMPSHIRE p.974

NEW HAVEN (CONN.) p.975

NEW IBERIA (LA.) p.975

NEW JERSEY p.976

NEW KASSEL (MO.: IMAGINARY PLACE) p.978

NEW MEXICO p.978

NEW ORLEANS (LA.) p.981

List of Subject Headings - Fiction

NEW YORK (N.Y.) p.985

NEW YORK (STATE) p.1011

NEW ZEALAND p.1031

NEWFORD (IMAGINARY PLACE) p.1032

NEWFOUNDLAND AND LABRADOR p.1032

NEWPORT BEACH (CALIF.) p.1032

NEWTON LAUDER (SCOTLAND: IMAGINARY PLACE) p.1032

NEXIS (IMAGINARY PLACE: FUREY) p.1032

NICARAGUA p.1032

NIGERIA p.1032

NODD'S RIDGE (ME.: IMAGINARY PLACE) p.1033

NORTH CAROLINA p.1033

NORTH DAKOTA p.1037

NORTH HOMAGE (KY.: IMAGINARY PLACE) p.1038

NORTHERN IRELAND p.1038

NORTHWEST, PACIFIC p.1038

NORTHWEST TERRITORIES p.1038

NORWAY p.1038

NOVA SCOTIA p.1039

OAKALLA (WISC.: IMAGINARY PLACE) p.1039

OAKLAND (CALIF.) p.1039

OHIO p.1039

OKLAHOMA p.1041

OKLAHOMA CITY (OKLA.) p.1043

OLIVER (IND.: IMAGINARY PLACE) p.1043

OMAHA (NEB.) p.1043

ONTARIO p.1043

OOLSMOUTH (IMAGINARY PLACE) p.1044

ORAN (IMAGINARY PLACE) p.1044

ORANGE COUNTY (CALIF.) p.1044

ORCHARD VALLEY (IMAGINARY PLACE) p.1044

OREGON p.1044

ORISSA (IMAGINARY PLACE) p.1046

OTHERLAND (IMAGINARY PLACE) p.1046

OZ (IMAGINARY PLACE) p.1046

OZARK MOUNTAINS REGION p.1047

PACIFIC AREA p.1047

PAKISTAN p.1047

PALENOC (IMAGINARY PLACE) p.1048

PALESTINE p.1048

PALM SPRINGS (CALIF.) p.1048

PALO ALTO (CALIF.) p.1048

PANAMA p.1048

PAPUA NEW GUINEA p.1048

PARADISE COURT (LONDON, ENGLAND: IMAGINARY PLACE) p.1049

PARADYS (IMAGINARY PLACE) p.1049

PARAGUAY p.1049

PARIS (FRANCE) p.1049

PASADENA (CALIF.) p.1055

PEBBLE BEACH (CALIF.) p.1055

PECAN SPRINGS (TEX.: IMAGINARY PLACE) p.1055

PEGANA (IMAGINARY PLACE) p.1055

PENNSYLVANIA p.1055

PENNYFOOT HOTEL (ENGLAND: IMAGINARY PLACE) p.1058

PERN (IMAGINARY PLACE) p.1058

PETAYBEE (IMAGINARY PLACE) p.1059

PHAZE (IMAGINARY PLACE) p.1059

PHILADELPHIA (PA.) p.1059

PHILIPPINES p.1061

PHOENIX (ARIZ.) p.1061

PICKAX CITY (MICH.: IMAGINARY PLACE) p.1061

PIGEON FORK (KY.: IMAGINARY PLACE) p.1062

PITTSBURGH (PA.) p.1062

POICTESME (IMAGINARY PLACE) p.1062

POLAND p.1062

POLYNESIA p.1063

POMONA (CALIF.) p.1063

POOR RELATION HOTEL (LONDON, ENGLAND: IMAGINARY PLACE) p.1063

PORT SILVA (CALIF.: IMAGINARY PLACE) p.1063

PORT WILLIAM (KY.: IMAGINARY PLACE) p.1063

PORTLAND (OR.) p.1063

PORTUGAL p.1064

POSSILTUM (IMAGINARY PLACE) p.1064

PRAGUE (CZECH REPUBLIC) p.1064

PRAIRIE PROVINCES p.1065

PRIMROSE CREEK (NEV.: IMAGINARY PLACE) p.1065

PROMISE (TEX.: IMAGINARY PLACE) p.1065

PROPHESY COUNTY (OKLA.: IMAGINARY PLACE) p.1065

PROTON (IMAGINARY PLACE) p.1065

PROVINCETOWN (MASS.) p.1065

PUERTO RICO p.1065

QUEBEC (PROVINCE) p.1065

QUIVIRA (LEGENDARY PLACE) p.1066

RAINBOW ROCK (IMAGINARY PLACE) p.1066

RALEIGH (N.C.) p.1066

RAPSTONE VALLEY (ENGLAND: IMAGINARY PLACE) p.1066

RAVENLOFT (IMAGINARY PLACE) p.1066

RECLUCE (IMAGINARY PLACE) p.1066

RELIAN KRU (IMAGINARY PLACE) p.1066

RHODE ISLAND p.1066

RIGANTE (IMAGINARY PLACE) p.1067

RINGWORLD (IMAGINARY PLACE) p.1067

RIO DE JANEIRO (BRAZIL) p.1067

RIVER CITY (MO.: IMAGINARY PLACE) p.1067

RIVERWORLD (IMAGINARY PLACE) p.1067

ROCKSBURG (PA.: IMAGINARY PLACE) p.1067

ROCKY MOUNTAINS p.1067

ROMANIA p.1068

ROME p.1068

ROME (ITALY) p.1070

ROTH (LONDON, ENGLAND: IMAGINARY PLACE) p.1070

RUFFORD (ME.: IMAGINARY PLACE) p.1070

RUSSIA (FEDERATION) p.1070

RUWENDA (IMAGINARY PLACE) p.1072

RYHOPE WOOD (IMAGINARY PLACE) p.1072

SACRAMENTO COUNTY (CALIF.) p.1072

SAINT ANSELM'S EPISCOPAL CHURCH (NEW YORK, N.Y.: IMAGINARY PLACE) p.1072

SAINT BRUNO (LA.: IMAGINARY PLACE) p.1072

SAINT HILAIRE (ME.: IMAGINARY PLACE) p.1072

SAINT LOUIS (MO.) p.1072

SAINT PAUL (MINN.) p.1073

SAINT PETERSBURG (RUSSIA) p.1073

SAINT SIMONS ISLAND (GA.: ISLAND) p.1074

SALEM (MASS.) p.1074

SALT LAKE CITY (UTAH) p.1074

SAMOAN ISLANDS p.1075

SAN ANTONIO (TEX.) p.1075

SAN DIEGO (CALIF.) p.1075

SAN FRANCISCO (CALIF.) p.1075

SANCTUARY (IMAGINARY PLACE) p.1082

SANTA BARBARA (CALIF.) p.1082

SANTA FE (N.M.) p.1082

SANTA TERESA (CALIF.: IMAGINARY PLACE) p.1082

SARANTIUM (IMAGINARY PLACE) p.1083

SARATOGA SPRINGS (N.Y.) p.1083

SASKATCHEWAN p.1083

SAUDI ARABIA p.1084

SAVANNAH (GA.) p.1084

SCOTLAND p.1084

SCOTTSDALE (ARIZ.) p.1091

SEATTLE (WASH.) p.1091

SECTOR GENERAL (IMAGINARY PLACE) p.1093

SEVEN KINGDOMS (IMAGINARY PLACE) p.1093

SHADY HILLS (N.J.: IMAGINARY PLACE) p.1093

SHAKESPEARE (ARK.: IMAGINARY PLACE) p.1093

SHANGHAI (CHINA) p.1094

SHANGRI-LA (IMAGINARY PLACE) p.1094

SHANNARA (IMAGINARY PLACE) p.1094

SHILOH (ARK.: IMAGINARY PLACE) p.1094

SICILY (ITALY) p.1094

SINGAPORE p.1095

SKOLIAN EMPIRE (IMAGINARY PLACE) p.1095

SOUTH AFRICA p.1095

SOUTH AMERICA p.1097

SOUTH CAROLINA p.1098

SOUTH DAKOTA p.1100

SOUTHERN STATES p.1101

SOUTHWEST, NEW p.1104

SOUTHWEST, OLD p.1104

SOUTHWESTERN STATES p.1104

SOVIET UNION p.1104

SPAIN p.1107

SPOKANE (WASH.) p.1109

SPRINGWATER STATION (IMAGINARY PLACE) p.1110

SRI LANKA p.1110

STAGGERFORD (MINN.: IMAGINARY PLACE) p.1110

STOCKHOLM (SWEDEN) p.1110

STONY MAN FARM (VA.: IMAGINARY PLACE) p.1110

SWEDEN p.1110

SWITZERLAND p.1111

SYDNEY (N.S.W.) p.1112

SYRACUSE (N.Y.) p.1112

TAHITI p.1112

TAHOE, LAKE (CALIF. AND NEV.) p.1112

TAIPEI (TAIWAN) p.1112

TAIWAN p.1112

TAVISCOMBE (ENGLAND: IMAGINARY PLACE) p.1112

TEKUMEL (IMAGINARY PLACE) p.1113

TENNESSEE p.1113

TERREILLE (IMAGINARY PLACE) p.1114

TEXAS p.1114

THAILAND p.1125

THALIA (TEX.: IMAGINARY PLACE) p.1126

THRUSH GREEN (IMAGINARY PLACE) p.1126

TIMBERDALE RETIREMENT CENTER (OKLA.: IMAGINARY PLACE) p.1126

TINKER'S COVE (ME.: IMAGINARY PLACE) p.1126

TIR-NAN-OG (IMAGINARY PLACE) p.1126

TOKYO (JAPAN) p.1126

TOMBSTONE (ARIZ.) p.1127

TORONTO (ONT.) p.1127

TRANTORIAN EMPIRE (IMAGINARY PLACE) p.1128

TREASURE ISLAND (IMAGINARY PLACE) p.1128

TRENTON (N.J.) p.1128

TSCHAI (IMAGINARY PLACE) p.1128

TUCSON (ARIZ.) p.1128

TULSA (OKLA.) p.1128

TUNISIA p.1129

TURKEY p.1129

UKRAINE p.1129

UNITED STATES p.1129

UNITED STATES—SOCIAL LIFE AND CUSTOMS p.1131

UTAH p.1133

VALDEMAR (IMAGINARY PLACE) p.1133

VANCOUVER (B.C.) p.1134

VANDAREI (IMAGINARY PLACE) p.1134

VATICAN CITY p.1134

VENEZUELA p.1134

VENICE (ITALY) p.1135

VERMONT p.1135

VICTORIA SPRINGS (MO.: IMAGINARY PLACE) p.1137

VICTORY (WYO.: IMAGINARY PLACE) p.1137

VIDESSOS (IMAGINARY PLACE) p.1137

VIENNA (AUSTRIA) p.1137

VIETNAM p.1137

VIRGIN ISLANDS p.1138

VIRGINIA p.1138

WALES p.1143

WALL STREET p.1144

WALNUT HILLS (CALIF.: IMAGINARY PLACE) p.1144

WARSAW (POLAND) p.1144

WASHINGTON (D.C.) p.1145

WASHINGTON (STATE) p.1150

WATERDEEP (IMAGINARY PLACE) p.1153

WATERSHIP DOWN (IMAGINARY PLACE) p.1153

WELL-BUILT CITY (IMAGINARY PLACE) p.1153

WELL WORLD (IMAGINARY PLACE) p.1153

WENDAR (IMAGINARY PLACE) p.1153

WENTWORTH (OHIO: IMAGINARY PLACE) p.1153

WERNER-BOK LIBRARY (WASHINGTON, D.C.: IMAGINARY PLACE) p.1154

WESSEX (ENGLAND) p.1154

WEST (U.S.) p.1156

WEST INDIES p.1163

WEST VIRGINIA p.1163

WESTLANDS (IMAGINARY PLACE) p.1164

WESTRIA (IMAGINARY PLACE) p.1164

WILDROSE (SASKATCHEWAN: IMAGINARY PLACE) p.1164

WISCONSIN p.1164

WITCH WORLD (IMAGINARY PLACE) p.1165

WORLD OF TIERS (IMAGINARY PLACE) p.1166

WORLD OF TWO MOONS (IMAGINARY PLACE) p.1166

WYOMING p.1166

XANTH (IMAGINARY PLACE) p.1168

XANTIC EMPIRE (IMAGINARY PLACE) p.1168

YOKNAPATAWPHA COUNTY (IMAGINARY PLACE) p.1168

YS (IMAGINARY PLACE) p.1169

YUGOSLAVIA p.1169

YURT (IMAGINARY PLACE) p.1169

ZANZIBAR p.1169

ZENDA (IMAGINARY PLACE) p.1169

List of Subject Headings - Fiction

# Bowker's Guide to Characters In Fiction® 2004

## Volume 1

## Adult Fiction

# CHARACTERS

## A

**ABAGNARRO, ABBY (FICTITIOUS CHARACTER)—FICTION**

Whitney, Polly. Until Death. 1996. per. (0-373-26219-1, 1-26219-5, Worldwide Library) Harlequin Enterprises, Ltd.
—Until Death. 1994. 320p. 21.95 o.p. (0-312-11089-8, Saint Martin's Minotaur) St. Martin's Pr.
—Until It Hurts. 1998. (Worldwide Library Mysteries: Vol. 272). per. (0-373-26272-8, 0-26272-5, Worldwide Library) Harlequin Enterprises, Ltd.
—Until It Hurts: An Ike & Abby Mystery. 1997. 304p. 22.95 o.p. (0-312-15237-X, Saint Martin's Minotaur) St. Martin's Pr.
—Until the End of Time. 1997. per. (0-373-26233-7, 1-26233-6, Worldwide Library) Harlequin Enterprises, Ltd.
—Until the End of Time. 1995. 272p. 21.95 o.p. (0-312-13199-2, Saint Martin's Minotaur) St. Martin's Pr.

**ABBOTT, BEN (FICTITIOUS CHARACTER)—FICTION**

Scott, Justin. FrostLine. 2003. 300p. 24.95 o.s.i (1-59058-062-1) Poisoned Pen Pr.
—HardScape. 1995. (Ben Abbott Mystery Ser.). 288p. pap. 5.95 o.s.i (0-14-023450-0, Penguin Bks.) Penguin Group (USA) Inc.
—HardScape. 2003. 250p. pap. 14.95 o.s.i (1-59058-060-5) Poisoned Pen Pr.
—HardScape. 218p. 3.98 o.p. (0-8317-4999-7) Smithmark Pubs., Inc.
—HardScape. 1994. (Ben Abbott Mystery Ser.). 288p. 19.95 o.p. (0-670-85212-0, Viking) Viking Penguin.
—StoneDust. 1996. (Ben Abbott Mystery Ser.). 304p. pap. 5.95 o.s.i (0-14-023456-X, Viking) Penguin Group (USA) Inc.
—StoneDust. 2003. 250p. pap. 14.95 o.s.i (1-59058-061-3) Poisoned Pen Pr.
—WeakEnd: A Ben Abbott Novel. 1995. (Ben Abbott Mystery Ser.). 304p. 19.95 o.p. (0-670-85213-9, Viking) Viking Penguin.

**ABBOTT, D. J. (FICTITIOUS CHARACTER)—FICTION**

Peters, Elizabeth, pseud. Summer of the Dragon. 1980. 256p. mass mkt. 2.25 o.s.i (0-449-24291-9, Fawcett) Ballantine Bks.
—Summer of the Dragon. unabr. ed. 1998. audio 44.95 (0-7861-1354-5, 2257) Blackstone Audio Bks., Inc.
—Summer of the Dragon. 1989. 256p. mass mkt. 4.99 (0-8125-0754-1, Tor Bks.) Doherty, Tom Assocs., LLC.
—Summer of the Dragon, Set. unabr. ed. 1999. audio 44.95 Highsmith Inc.
—Summer of the Dragon. 2001. 352p. mass mkt. 6.99 (0-380-73122-3, Avon Bks.) Morrow/Avon.
—Summer of the Dragon. l.t. ed. 1981. (Ulverscroft Large Print Ser.). 389p. 29.99 o.p. (0-7089-0624-9, Ulverscroft) Thorpe, F. A. Pubs. GBR. Dist: Ulverscroft Large Print Bks., Ltd., Ulverscroft Large Print Canada, Ltd.

**ABBOTT, LUKE (FICTITIOUS CHARACTER)—FICTION**

Gosling, Paula. Death Penalties. 1991. 297p. 25.00 (0-89296-458-8) Mysterious Pr.
—Death Penalties. 1992. 304p. mass mkt. 4.99 o.s.i (0-446-40189-7) Warner Bks., Inc.
—The Wychford Murders. 1986. (Crime Club Ser.). 192p. 12.95 o.p. (0-385-23551-8) Doubleday Publishing.
—The Wychford Murders. 1988. 224p. reprint ed. mass mkt. (0-373-26009-1, Harlequin Bks.) Harlequin Enterprises, Ltd.
—The Wychford Murders. unabr. ed. 1993. audio 69.95 (1-85089-757-3, 9008X) ISIS Audio Bks. GBR. Dist: Ulverscroft Large Print Bks., Ltd.
—The Wychford Murders. l.t. ed. 1987. (Ulverscroft Large Print Ser.). 528p. o.p. (0-7089-1709-7, Ulverscroft) Thorpe, F. A. Pubs. GBR. Dist: Ulverscroft Large Print Canada, Ltd.

**ABRAMOWITZ, JOEL (FICTITIOUS CHARACTER)—FICTION**

Levin, Donna. California Street. 1992. 336p. mass mkt. 4.50 o.s.i (0-451-40303-7, Onyx) NAL.
—California Street. 1990. 18.95 o.p. (0-671-69300-X, Simon & Schuster) Simon & Schuster.

**ACKERLEY, PAUL (FICTITIOUS CHARACTER)—FICTION**

Dickinson, Peter. The Yellow Room Conspiracy. 1994. 272p. 18.95 o.s.i (0-89296-556-8) Mysterious Pr.
—The Yellow Room Conspiracy. 1995. 256p. mass mkt. 5.99 (0-446-40373-3) Warner Bks., Inc.

**ACKROYD, LAURA (FICTITIOUS CHARACTER)—FICTION**

Hall, Patricia. The Dead of Winter. 1996. (Yorkshire Mystery Ser.). 21.95 o.p. (0-312-15148-9, Saint Martin's Minotaur) St. Martin's Pr.
—Dead on Arrival. l.t. ed. 2000. (Dales Large Print Ser.). 400p. pap. (1-84262-012-6) Dales Large Print Bks. GBR. Dist: Ulverscroft Large Print Canada, Ltd.
—Dead on Arrival. 2001. (Yorkshire Mystery Ser.). 224p. 22.95 o.p. (0-312-26572-7, Saint Martin's Minotaur) St. Martin's Pr.
—Death by Election. l.t. ed. 1994. (Dales Large Print Ser.). 418p. pap. o.p. (1-85389-519-9) Dales Large Print Bks. GBR. Dist: Ulverscroft Large Print Canada, Ltd.
—Death by Election. 1994. (Yorkshire Mystery Ser.). 256p. 20.95 o.p. (0-312-11461-3, Saint Martin's Minotaur) St. Martin's Pr.
—Deep Freeze. l.t. ed. 2002. (Magna Large Print Ser.). 416p. pap. (0-7505-1880-4) Magna Large Print Bks. GBR. Dist: Ulverscroft Large Print Canada, Ltd.
—Deep Freeze. unabr. ed. 2002. (Yorkshire Mystery Ser.). audio 69.95 (1-84283-190-9) Soundings, Ltd. GBR. Dist: Ulverscroft Large Print Bks., Ltd.
—Deep Freeze: A Yorkshire Mystery. 2003. (Yorkshire Mystery Ser.). 272p. 23.95 (0-312-28212-5, Saint Martin's Minotaur) St. Martin's Pr.
—Dying Fall. l.t. ed. 1995. (Dales Large Print Ser.). 432p. pap. o.p. (1-85389-561-X) Dales Large Print Bks. GBR. Dist: Ulverscroft Large Print Canada, Ltd.
—Dying Fall. 1996. 248p. mass mkt. o.s.i (0-7515-1204-4) Little Brown & Co.

—Dying Fall. 1995. (Yorkshire Mystery Ser.). 248p. 21.95 o.p. (0-312-13477-0, Saint Martin's Minotaur) St. Martin's Pr.
—The Italian Girl. 2000. 208p. 21.95 (0-312-26489-5, Saint Martin's Minotaur) St. Martin's Pr.
—Perils of the Night. 1998. (Yorkshire Mystery Ser.). 224p. 22.95 (0-312-19996-1, Saint Martin's Minotaur) St. Martin's Pr.

**ACORNA (FICTITIOUS CHARACTER)—FICTION**

McCaffrey, Anne. Acorna: The Unicorn Girl. 61st ed. 1998. (Acorna Ser.). 416p. mass mkt. 7.50 (0-06-105789-4, Eos) Morrow/Avon.
—Acorna's Quest. Date not set. pap. 12.00 (0-06-105375-9) HarperCollins Pubs.
—Acorna's Search. 2002. 336p. mass mkt. 7.50 (0-380-81846-9) HarperCollins Pubs.
—Acorna's World. 2001. 384p. mass mkt. 6.99 (0-06-105984-6) HarperCollins Pubs.
McCaffrey, Anne & Ball, Margaret. Acorna: The Unicorn Girl. unabr. ed. 1999. audio 56.00 (0-7366-4340-0, 4835) Books on Tape, Inc.
—Acorna: The Unicorn Girl. 1997. 256p. 22.00 o.s.i (0-06-105296-5, Eos) Morrow/Avon.
—Acorna's Quest. (Acorna Ser.). 1999. 416p. mass mkt. 6.99 (0-06-105790-8); 1998. 304p. 23.00 o.s.i (0-06-105297-3) Morrow/Avon. (Eos).
—Acorna's Quest. 1999. 12.55 o.p. (0-606-16537-1) Turtleback Bks.
McCaffrey, Anne & Scarborough, Elizabeth Ann. Acorna's People. 2000. audio 56.00 (0-7366-4847-X); audio compact disk 64.00 (0-7366-5216-7); audio 56.00. (YA). audio compact disk 64.00 Books on Tape, Inc.
—Acorna's People. 2000. 416p. mass mkt. 6.99 (0-06-105983-8) HarperCollins Pubs.
—Acorna's People. Date not set. pap. 15.00 (0-06-107345-8); 1999. 320p. 24.00 (0-06-105094-6) Morrow/Avon. (Eos).
—Acorna's People. 384p. (0-7278-5690-1) Severn Hse. Pubs., Ltd.
—Acorna's People. 2000. 13.04 (0-606-18809-6) Turtleback Bks.
—Acorna's Rebels. 2003. 384p. mass mkt. 7.50 (0-380-81847-7); 320p. mass mkt. 7.50 (0-380-97899-7); 320p. 24.95 (0-380-97899-7) Morrow/Avon. (Eos).
—Acorna's Search. 2001. 304p. 25.00 (0-380-97898-9, Eos) Morrow/Avon.
—Acorna's World. 2000. (Acorna Ser.). 320p. 24.00 (0-06-105095-4, Eos) Morrow/Avon.

**ACTIVE, NATHAN (FICTITIOUS CHARACTER)—FICTION**

Jones, Stan. Shaman Pass: A Nathan Active Mystery. 2003. 288p. 23.00 (1-56947-332-3) Soho Pr., Inc.
—White Sky, Black Ice: An Alaskan Mystery. 1999. 264p. 22.00 (1-56947-152-5) Soho Pr., Inc.

**ADAIR, MADISON (FICTITIOUS CHARACTER)—FICTION**

Pozzessere, Heather G. If Looks Could Kill. 1997. 48p. mass mkt. (1-55166-285-X, 0-66285-8, Mira Bks.) Harlequin Enterprises, Ltd.

**ADAMS, CLINT (FICTITIOUS CHARACTER)—FICTION**

Roberts, J. R. Brothel Inspector, 1Vol. 219. 2000. (Gunsmith Ser.: Vol. 219). 192p. mass mkt. 4.99 o.s.i (0-515-12771-X, Jove) Berkley Publishing Group.

—High Card Dies, 2001. (Gunsmith Ser.: No. 229). 192p. mass mkt. 4.99 o.s.i (0-515-13002-8, Jove) Berkley Publishing Group.
—The Only Law. 2003. (Gunsmith Ser.: No. 261). 192p. mass mkt. 4.99 (0-515-13600-X, Jove) Berkley Publishing Group.
—Pay Dirt. 2001. (Gunsmith Ser.: Vol. 230). 192p. mass mkt. 4.99 o.s.i (0-515-13019-2, Jove) Berkley Publishing Group.
—Treasure Hunt. 2003. (Gunsmith Ser.: No. 255). 192p. mass mkt. 4.99 (0-515-13494-5, Jove) Berkley Publishing Group.

**ADAMS, DOC (FICTITIOUS CHARACTER)—FICTION**

Boyer, Rick. Billingsgate Shoal. 1989. 320p. mass mkt. 5.99 o.s.i (0-8041-0551-0, Ivy Bks.) Ballantine Bks.
—Billingsgate Shoal. unabr. ed. 1997. audio 56.95 Blackstone Audio Bks., Inc.
—Billingsgate Shoal, 001. 1982. 288p. 11.95 o.p. (0-395-32041-0) Houghton Mifflin Co.
—Billingsgate Shoal. 1985. 258p. mass mkt. 3.50 o.s.i (0-446-32739-5) Warner Bks., Inc.
—The Daisy Ducks. 1988. 288p. reprint ed. mass mkt. 3.50 o.s.i (0-8041-0293-7, Ivy Bks.) Ballantine Bks.
—The Daisy Ducks, 001. 1986. 276p. 15.95 o.p. (0-395-35289-4) Houghton Mifflin Co.
—Gone to Earth. 1991. (Boston Mysteries Ser.). mass mkt. 4.99 o.s.i (0-8041-0611-8, Ivy Bks.) Ballantine Bks.
—The Man Who Whispered. 1998. (Doc Adams Mysteries Ser.). 272p. mass mkt. 6.50 o.s.i (0-8041-1044-1, Ivy Bks.) Ballantine Bks.
—Moscow Metal. l.t. ed. 1991. pap. 8.95 o.p. (1-55504-884-6, 182); 1989. 21.95 o.p. (1-55504-883-8, 699) BBC Audiobooks America.
—Moscow Metal. 1988. 288p. reprint ed. mass mkt. 3.95 o.s.i (0-8041-0292-9, Ivy Bks.) Ballantine Bks.
—Moscow Metal: A Doc Adams Suspense Novel. 1987. 15.95 o.p. (0-395-42737-1) Houghton Mifflin Co.
—The Penny Ferry. 1990. 304p. mass mkt. 4.99 o.s.i (0-8041-0550-2, Ivy Bks.) Ballantine Bks.
—The Penny Ferry, 001. 1984. 13.95 o.p. (0-395-35288-6) Houghton Mifflin Co.
—The Penny Ferry. 1986. 272p. mass mkt. 3.50 o.s.i (0-446-32741-7) Warner Bks., Inc.
—Pirate Trade. 1994. (Doc Adams Mysteries Ser.). mass mkt. 4.99 o.s.i (0-8041-0612-6, Ivy Bks.) Ballantine Bks.
—The Whale's Footprints. 1989. 288p. mass mkt. 4.99 o.s.i (0-8041-0450-6, Ivy Bks.) Ballantine Bks.
—The Whale's Footprints. l.t. ed. 1989. (General Ser.). 392p. lib. bdg. 18.95 o.p. (0-8161-4764-7, Macmillan Reference USA) Gale Group.
—The Whale's Footprints. 1988. 288p. 17.95 o.p. (0-395-42738-X) Houghton Mifflin Co.
—Yellow Bird. (Boston Mysteries Ser.). 1992. mass mkt. 4.99 o.s.i (0-8041-1036-0, Ivy Bks.); 1991. 352p. 17.00 o.p. (0-449-90506-3, Fawcett) Ballantine Bks.

**ADAMS, GILLIAN (FICTITIOUS CHARACTER)—FICTION**

Kelly, Nora. Bad Chemistry, Vol. 21. 2000. (Missing Mysteries Ser.: Vol. 21). 240p. pap. 14.95 (1-890208-34-5) Poisoned Pen Pr.

—Bad Chemistry. 1994. 256p. 20.95 o.p. (*0-312-10934-2*, Saint Martin's Minotaur) St. Martin's Pr.
—Hot Pursuit. 2002. 200p. 24.95 o.s.i (*1-59058-014-1*); 325p. pap. (*1-59058-018-4*) Poisoned Pen Pr.
—In the Shadow of Kings. 2000. (Missing Mysteries Ser.: Vol. 12). 189p. pap. 14.95 (*1-890208-22-1*) Poisoned Pen Pr.
—In the Shadow of Kings. 1984. 12.95 o.p. (*0-312-41171-5*) St. Martin's Pr.
—In the Shadow of Kings. l.t. ed. 1995. (Linford Mystery Library). 400p. pap. 17.99 o.p. (*0-7089-7733-2*, Linford) Thorpe, F. A. Pubs. GBR. *Dist:* Ulverscroft Large Print Bks., Ltd., Ulverscroft Large Print Canada, Ltd.
—My Sister's Keeper. 2000. (Missing Mysteries Ser.: Vol. 15). 221p. pap. 14.95 (*1-890208-28-0*) Poisoned Pen Pr.
—My Sister's Keeper. 1992. 224p. 17.95 o.p. (*0-312-08268-1*, Saint Martin's Minotaur) St. Martin's Pr.
—Old Wounds. l.t. ed. 1999. (Magna Large Print Ser.). 464p. (*0-7505-1410-8*) Magna Large Print Bks. GBR. *Dist:* Ulverscroft Large Print Canada, Ltd.
—Old Wounds. 2000. 300p. pap. 12.95 (*1-890208-25-6*) Poisoned Pen Pr.

### ADAMS, HENRY, 1838-1918—FICTION

Zencey, Eric. Panama. 1997. 400p. reprint ed. mass mkt. 6.99 o.s.i (*0-425-15602-8*) Berkley Publishing Group.
—Panama. 1995. 384p. 24.00 o.p. (*0-374-22943-0*) Farrar, Straus & Giroux.
—Panama. unabr. ed. 1995. audio 91.00 (*0-7887-0454-0*, 94646E7) Recorded Bks., LLC.
—Panama. abr. ed. 1995. audio 23.00 (*0-671-54922-7*, 494361, Simon & Schuster Audioworks) Simon & Schuster Audio.
—Panama. l.t. ed. 1996. (Niagara Large Print Ser.). 514p. 29.50 o.p. (*0-7089-5833-8*, Ulverscroft) Thorpe, F. A. Pubs. GBR. *Dist:* Ulverscroft Large Print Bks., Ltd.

### ADAMS, HILDA (FICTITIOUS CHARACTER)—FICTION

Rinehart, Mary Roberts. Miss Pinkerton. reprint ed. lib. bdg. 24.95 (*0-89190-327-5*, Rivercity Pr.) Amereon, Ltd.
—Miss Pinkerton. 1998. 272p. mass mkt. 5.99 o.s.i (*1-57566-255-8*); 1986. 256p. mass mkt. 3.50 o.s.i (*0-8217-1847-9*, Zebra Bks.) Kensington Publishing Corp.

### ADAMS, JAGUAR (FICTITIOUS CHARACTER)—FICTION

Chepaitis, B. A. The Fear of God. 1999. 288p. mass mkt. 5.99 o.s.i (*0-441-00622-1*) Ace Bks.
—The Fear Principle. 1998. 256p. mass mkt. 5.99 o.s.i (*0-441-00497-0*) Ace Bks.
—Learning Fear: A Novel. 2000. 304p. mass mkt. 6.50 o.s.i (*0-441-00696-5*) Ace Bks.

### ADAMS, KERI (FICTITIOUS CHARACTER)—FICTION

Marlowe, Toby. Beyond a Reasonable Doubt. 1997. 352p. mass mkt. 5.99 o.s.i (*0-7860-0429-0*, Pinnacle Bks.) Kensington Publishing Corp.

### ADAMS, NICK (FICTITIOUS CHARACTER)—FICTION

Hemingway, Ernest. In Our Time. Date not set. lib. bdg. 20.95 (*0-8488-1755-9*) Amereon, Ltd.
—In Our Time. 1977. 12.50 o.s.i (*0-89723-002-7*) Bruccoli Clark Layman, Inc.
—In Our Time. 1982. pap. 3.95 o.s.i (*0-684-17470-7*); 1980. 156p. 30.00 (*0-684-16480-9*); 1971. 160p. pap. 10.00 o.s.i (*0-684-71802-2*) Gale Group. (Macmillan Reference USA).
—In Our Time. 2003. E-Book 9.99 (*0-7432-3725-0*); 1996. 160p. pap. 10.00 (*0-684-82276-8*) Simon & Schuster. (Scribner).
—In Our Time, The Torrents of Spring & Men Without Women. unabr. collector's ed. 1989. audio 72.00 (*0-7366-1614-4*, 2473) Books on Tape, Inc.
—Men Without Women. 22.95 (*0-89190-663-0*) Amereon, Ltd.
—Men Without Women. 1983. pap. 4.95 o.s.i (*0-684-18026-X*); 1970. pap. 7.95 o.s.i (*0-684-71803-0*) Gale Group. (Macmillan Reference USA).
—Men Without Women. 2003. E-Book 9.99 (*0-7432-3727-7*); 1997. 160p. reprint ed. pap. 10.00 (*0-684-82586-4*) Simon & Schuster. (Scribner).
—The Nick Adams Stories. 1976. 22.95 (*0-8488-0524-0*) Amereon, Ltd.
—The Nick Adams Stories. 1973. 256p. (gr. 8-12). pap. 3.50 o.p. (*0-553-20072-0*) Bantam Bks.
—The Nick Adams Stories. 1972. 7.95 o.s.i (*0-684-12485-8*, Macmillan Reference USA) Gale Group.
—The Nick Adams Stories. 1981. 272p. pap. 12.00 (*0-684-16940-1*, Scribner) Simon & Schuster.

### ADAMS, SAMANTHA (FICTITIOUS CHARACTER)—FICTION

Shankman, Sarah. Digging up Momma. (Samantha Adams Mystery Ser.). 1998. 288p. 22.00 (*0-671-89753-5*, Atria); 1999. 336p. reprint ed. mass mkt. 6.50 (*0-671-89752-7*, Pocket) Simon & Schuster.
—First Kill All the Lawyers. 1991. mass mkt. 5.99 (*0-671-74893-9*); 1988. 224p. mass mkt. 3.50 (*0-671-64529-3*) Simon & Schuster. (Pocket).
—He Was Her Man. Chelius, Jane, ed. 288p. 1993. 20.00 (*0-671-77553-7*, Atria); 1994. reprint ed. mass mkt. 5.50 (*0-671-77563-4*, Pocket) Simon & Schuster.
—Impersonal Attractions. 1985. 272p. 14.95 o.p. (*0-312-40997-4*) St. Martin's Pr.
—The King Is Dead. Chelius, Jane, ed. 1992. 288p. 20.00 (*0-671-73459-8*, Atria); 1993. 320p. reprint ed. mass mkt. 5.99 (*0-671-73460-1*, Pocket) Simon & Schuster.
—Now Let's Talk of Graves. Chelius, Jane, ed. 1990. 304p. 18.95 o.p. (*0-671-68456-6*, Atria); 1991. 320p. reprint ed. mass mkt. 5.99 (*0-671-68457-4*, Pocket) Simon & Schuster.
—She Walks in Beauty. l.t. ed. 1993. (General Ser.). 484p. 20.95 o.p. (*0-8161-5478-3*, Macmillan Reference USA) Gale Group.
—She Walks in Beauty. 1991. 320p. 20.00 (*0-671-73657-4*, Atria) Simon & Schuster.
—She Walks in Beauty. Chelius, Jane, ed. 1992. 352p. reprint ed. mass mkt. 5.99 (*0-671-73658-2*, Pocket) Simon & Schuster.

### ADARE, PADDY (FICTITIOUS CHARACTER)—FICTION

Kelly, Thomas. Payback. unabr. ed. 1997. audio 78.00 (*0-7887-1594-1*, 95213E7) Recorded Bks., LLC.
—Payback: A Novel. 1997. mass mkt. 6.99 o.s.i (*0-449-00223-3*, Fawcett) Ballantine Bks.
Meltzer, Brad. The Tenth Justice. unabr. ed. 1997. audio 80.00 (*0-7366-4054-1*, 4565) Books on Tape, Inc.
—The Tenth Justice. abr. ed. 1997. audio 18.00 o.s.i (*0-694-51807-7*, CPN 2645, HarperAudio) HarperTrade.

### ADDAMS, MAX (FICTITIOUS CHARACTER)—FICTION

Leitz, David E. Casting in Dead Water. 1996. mass mkt. 5.50 (*0-312-95779-3*, St. Martin's Paperbacks) St. Martin's Pr.
—Dying to Fly Fish: A Max Addams Fly-Fishing Mystery. 1996. (Dead Letter Mysteries Ser.). 292p. mass mkt. 5.99 (*0-312-95983-4*, St. Martin's Paperbacks) St. Martin's Pr.
—Fly-Fishing Can Be Fatal: A Max Addams Mystery. 1997. 260p. (Orig.). mass mkt. 5.99 (*0-312-96162-6*, St. Martin's Paperbacks) St. Martin's Pr.
—The Fly Fishing Corpse. 1994. 160p. 19.95 o.p. (*1-882418-15-8*); pap. 12.95 (*1-882418-13-1*) Centennial Pubns.
—Hooked on Death: A Max Addams Fly Fishing Mystery. 2000. 288p. E-Book 8.00 (*0-7388-8552-5*) Xlibris Corp.

### ADDAMS FAMILY (FICTITIOUS CHARACTERS)—FICTION

Strasser, Todd. Addams Family Values. Todd, Rebecca, ed. 1993. 224p. (Orig.). mass mkt. 4.99 (*0-671-88036-5*, Pocket) Simon & Schuster.

### ADDISON, BEN (FICTITIOUS CHARACTER)—FICTION

Meltzer, Brad. The Tenth Justice. l.t. ed. 1998. (Large Print Book Ser.). 27.95 (*1-56895-518-9*, Wheeler Publishing, Inc.) Gale Group.
—The Tenth Justice. 1997. 400p. 23.00 (*0-688-15089-6*, Morrow, William & Co.) Morrow/Avon.
—The Tenth Justice. 1998. 496p. reprint ed. mass mkt. 7.99 (*0-446-60624-3*) Warner Bks., Inc.

### ADDISON, HARRY (FICTITIOUS CHARACTER)—FICTION

Folsom, Allan. Day of Confession. unabr. ed. 1998. audio 96.00 (*0-7366-4532-2*, 4707) Books on Tape, Inc.
—Day of Confession. l.t. ed. 1999. 27.95 (*1-56895-648-7*, Wheeler Publishing, Inc.) Gale Group.
—Day of Confession. 1998. 576p. (gr. 8). 25.00 (*0-316-28755-5*) Little Brown & Co.
—Day of Confession. 1999. audio (*1-57042-783-6*); 1999. audio (*1-57042-740-2*); 1999. audio (*1-57042-782-8*); 1998. audio 24.98 (*1-57042-578-7*, 695619); 1998. audio 45.98 (*1-57042-579-5*, 136023) Time Warner AudioBooks.
—Day of Confession. 1999. 688p. mass mkt. 7.99 (*0-446-60453-4*) Warner Bks., Inc.

### ADEPT, THE (FICTITIOUS CHARACTER)—FICTION

*see Sinclair, Adam (Fictitious Character)—Fiction*

### ADLER, ALEXANDRA (FICTITIOUS CHARACTER)—FICTION

Saum, Karen. I Never Read Thoreau. 1996. 200p. (Orig.). pap. 10.95 (*0-934678-76-6*) New Victoria Pubs., Inc.

### ADLER, IRENE (FICTITIOUS CHARACTER)—FICTION

Donat, Peter C. & Gould, Barney. Sherlock Holmes & the Shakespeare Solution. 1997. 90p. 24.00 (*1-55246-016-9*); pap. 10.00 (*1-55246-017-7*) Battered Silicon Dispatch Box, The.
Douglas, Carole Nelson. The Adventuress. 2004. 416p. mass mkt. 6.99 (*0-7653-4715-6*, Forge Bks.) Doherty, Tom Assocs., LLC.
—Castle Rouge: A Novel of Suspense Featuring Sherlock Holmes, Irene Adler, & Jack the Ripper. 2002. (Irene Adler Novel Ser.). (Illus.). 544p. 25.95 (*0-312-86941-X*, Forge Bks.) Doherty, Tom Assocs., LLC.
—Chapel Noir. 2001. 480p. 25.95 (*0-312-85493-5*, Forge Bks.) Doherty, Tom Assocs., LLC.
—Femme Fatale. Date not set. mass mkt. (*0-7653-4595-1*); 2003. 554p. 25.95 (*0-7653-0682-4*) Doherty, Tom Assocs., LLC. (Forge Bks.).
—Good Morning, Irene. (Irene Adler Adventure Ser.). 1992. (Illus.). 374p. mass mkt. 4.99 (*0-8125-0949-8*); 1991. 19.95 o.p. (*0-312-93211-1*) Doherty, Tom Assocs., LLC. (Tor Bks.).
—Good Morning, Irene. unabr. ed. 1999. audio 80.00 (*0-7887-2487-8*, 95562E7) Recorded Bks., LLC.
—Good Night, Mr. Holmes. 1991. 408p. mass mkt. 4.99 o.s.i (*0-8125-1430-0*); 1990. 18.95 o.p. (*0-312-93210-3*) Doherty, Tom Assocs., LLC. (Tor Bks.).
—Good Night, Mr. Holmes. unabr. ed. 1998. audio 78.00 (*0-7887-2489-4*, 95564E7) Recorded Bks., LLC.
—Irene at Large. 1993. (Irene Adler Adventure Ser.). 395p. mass mkt. 5.99 (*0-8125-1702-4*, Tor Bks.) Doherty, Tom Assocs., LLC.
—Irene at Large. unabr. ed. 2000. audio 91.00 (*0-7887-2492-4*, 95567E7) Recorded Bks., LLC.
—Irene's Last Waltz. 1994. (Irene Adler Adventure Ser.). 480p. mass mkt. 4.99 (*0-8125-1703-2*); 22.95 o.p. (*0-312-85224-X*) Doherty, Tom Assocs., LLC. (Forge Bks.).
—Irene's Last Waltz. unabr. ed. 2000. audio 97.00 (*0-7887-2493-2*, 95568E7) Recorded Bks., LLC.
Irene & Jack the Ripper. Date not set. (*0-312-87611-4*, Forge Bks.) Doherty, Tom Assocs., LLC.

### AGNES, SISTER (FICTITIOUS CHARACTER)—FICTION

Hough, R. Sister Agnes. 1998. (Illus.). x, 196p. text 45.00 (*0-7195-5561-2*) Murray, John Pubs., Ltd. GBR. *Dist:* Trafalgar Square.
Joseph, Alison. The Hour of Our Death: A Sister Agnes Mystery. 1997. 288p. text 23.95 o.p. (*0-312-15142-X*, Saint Martin's Minotaur) St. Martin's Pr.
—Sacred Hearts: A Mystery Introducing Sister Agnes. 1996. 256p. 22.95 o.p. (*0-312-14405-9*, Saint Martin's Minotaur) St. Martin's Pr.

### AGUIRRE, FRANKIE (FICTITIOUS CHARACTER)—FICTION

Pearson, Ryne Douglas. Capitol Punishment. 1996. 352p. mass mkt. 5.99 (*0-380-72228-3*, Avon Bks.); 1995. 320p. 22.00 o.p. (*0-688-12983-8*, Morrow, William & Co.) Morrow/Avon.
—Cloudburst. 1993. 23.00 o.p. (*0-688-12246-9*, Morrow, William & Co.) Morrow/Avon.
—Cloudburst. unabr. ed. 1993. audio 85.00 (*1-55690-901-2*, 93343E7) Recorded Bks., LLC.
—October's Ghost. 1994. 312p. 23.00 o.p. (*0-688-12984-6*, Morrow, William & Co.); 1995. 464p. reprint ed. mass mkt. 5.99 (*0-380-72227-5*, Avon Bks.) Morrow/Avon.
—October's Ghost. unabr. ed. 1995. audio 91.00 (*0-7887-0101-0*, 94342E7) Recorded Bks., LLC.

### AHAB, CAPTAIN (FICTITIOUS CHARACTER)—FICTION

Gouge, Louise M. Ahab's Bride. 2004. pap. 12.99 (*1-58919-007-6*) RiverOak Publishing.
Melville, Herman. Moby Dick. unabr. ed. 1964. (Classics Ser.). mass mkt. 3.95 (*0-8049-0033-7*, CL-33) Airmont Publishing Co., Inc.
—Moby Dick. Date not set. lib. bdg. 49.95 (*0-8488-0183-0*) Amereon, Ltd.
—Moby Dick. (SPA., Illus.). 11.95 (*84-7281-078-X*, AF1078) Auriga, Ediciones S.A. ESP. *Dist:* Continental Bk. Co., Inc.
—Moby Dick. 1997. (Cyber Classics Ser.). 486p. pap. 14.95 incl. disk (*1-55701-195-8*); 807p. pap. 24.95 (*1-55701-219-9*) BNI Pubns., Inc.
—Moby Dick. 2001. 7.95 (*0-8010-1215-5*) Baker Bks.
—Moby Dick. Walcutt, Charles Child, ed. & intro. by. 1981. 704p. reprint ed. mass mkt. 4.95 (*0-553-21311-3*, Bantam Classics) Bantam Bks.
—Moby Dick. 1977. reprint ed. 2.95 o.p. (*0-460-01179-0*); 9.95 o.p. (*0-460-00179-5*) Biblio Distribution.
—Moby Dick. 2000. audio 69.95 (*0-7861-1865-2*); audio compact disk 160.00 (*0-7861-9813-3*, z2664);Pt. 1. audio 69.95 (*0-7861-0296-9*, 2664A);Pt. 2. audio 49.95 (*0-7861-1934-9*, 2664-B) Blackstone Audio Bks., Inc.
—Moby Dick. 2001. per. 14.00 (*1-58396-098-8*) Blue Unicorn Editions.
—Moby Dick. 2002. audio compact disk 160.00 (*0-7366-8792-0*); 2002. audio 136.00 (*0-7366-8891-9*); Pt. 2. 1984. (J). audio 72.00 (*0-7366-1001-4*, 1934-B); Pt. A. 1984. (J). audio 72.00 (*0-7366-1000-6*, 1934-A) Books on Tape, Inc.
—Moby Dick. 1983. 687p. reprint ed. lib. bdg. 35.95 (*0-89966-478-4*) Buccaneer Bks., Inc.
—Moby Dick. l.t. ed. 1997. 807p. pap. 24.95 (*1-58855-008-7*) Cyber Classics, Inc.
—Moby Dick. 1998. 604p. mass mkt. 5.99 (*0-8125-4156-1*, Tor Classics); 1998. mass mkt. 215.64 (*0-8125-8007-9*); 1996. 608p. mass mkt. 3.99 (*0-8125-4307-6*, Tor Classics) Doherty, Tom Assocs., LLC.
—Moby Dick. 2003. (Dover Thrift Editions Ser.). 432p. pap. 5.00 (*0-486-43215-7*) Dover Pubns., Inc.
—Moby Dick. abr. ed. 1987. audio 16.99 (*0-88646-122-7*, 7122); 1986. (YA). (gr. 7-9). pap. 29.99 incl. audio (*0-88646-815-9*, R 7122) Durkin Hayes Publishing Ltd.
—Moby Dick. E-Book 2.49 (*0-7574-2887-8*) Electric Umbrella Publishing.
—Moby Dick. 1980. Tome I. (FRE.). pap. 11.95 (*0-7859-4134-7*); Tome II. pap. 11.95 (*0-7859-4135-5*) French & European Pubns., Inc.
—Moby Dick. 1998. (SPA.). 426p. (*84-08-02226-1*) GeoPlaneta, Editorial, S. A.
—Moby Dick. 1991. pap. text, stu. ed. 19.95 (*0-8224-9442-6*) Globe Fearon Educational Publishing.
—Moby Dick. unabr. ed. audio 119.95 Halvorson Assocs.
—Moby Dick. abr. ed. 1998. audio 18.00 (*0-694-52018-7*, Caedmon); 1991. audio 17.00 (*1-55994-394-7*, DCN 2077, HarperAudio); 1975. audio 19.95 o.p. (*0-694-50431-9*, SWC 2077, HarperAudio) HarperTrade.
—Moby Dick, Set. abr. ed. 1999. audio 85.95 Highsmith Inc.
—Moby Dick, 001. Kazin, Alfred, ed. 1956. pap. 16.36 (*0-395-05108-8*, Riverside Editions) Houghton Mifflin Co.
—Moby Dick. l.t. ed. 753p. pap. 61.00 (*0-7583-1553-8*); 1690p. pap. 121.00 (*0-7583-1556-2*); 2078p. pap. 143.00 (*0-7583-1557-0*); 2556p. pap. 174.00 (*0-7583-1558-9*); 2965p. pap. 195.00 (*0-7583-1559-7*); 579p. pap. 42.00 (*0-7583-1552-X*); 1031p. pap. 75.00 (*0-7583-1554-6*); 1320p. pap. 93.00 (*0-7583-1555-4*); 2965p. lib. bdg. 219.00 (*0-7583-1551-1*); 2078p. lib. bdg. 161.00 (*0-7583-1549-X*); 1031p. lib. bdg. 87.00 (*0-7583-1546-5*); 1320p. lib. bdg. 105.00 (*0-7583-1547-3*); 1690p. lib. bdg. 139.00 (*0-7583-1548-1*); 753p. lib. bdg. 73.00 (*0-7583-1545-7*); 2556p. lib. bdg. 198.00 (*0-7583-1550-3*); 579p. lib. bdg. 48.00 (*0-7583-1544-9*) Huge Print Pr.
—Moby Dick. 2002. 584p. 100.99 (*1-4043-1862-3*); per. 95.99 (*1-4043-1863-1*) IndyPublish.com.
—Moby Dick. (SPA.). 368p. 14.95 (*84-261-0512-2*, JV0512) Juventud, Editorial ESP. *Dist:* Continental Bk. Co., Inc.
—Moby Dick. 1991. 640p. 20.00 (*0-679-40559-3*, Everyman's Library) Knopf Publishing Group.
—Moby Dick. 1998. (Cloth Bound Pocket Series). 240p. 7.95 (*3-89508-088-8*, 520015) Konemann.
—Moby Dick. 1981. (English As a Second Language Bk.). pap. text 5.95 o.p. (*0-582-53418-6*, 74061) Longman Publishing Group.
—Moby Dick. 1977. (American Classics). 6.12 o.p. (*0-88343-403-2*); pap. 8.92 o.p. (*0-88343-402-4*); audio 111.32 o.p. (*0-88343-420-2*) McDougal Littell Inc.
—Moby Dick. 1950. (C). pap. text 5.00 net. o.p. (*0-07-555614-6*, T26) McGraw-Hill Cos., The.
—Moby Dick. abr. ed. 1999. (Adventure Theatre Ser.). audio 16.95 (*1-56994-505-5*, 331514, Monterey SoundWorks) Monterey Media, Inc.
—Moby Dick. mass mkt. 0.50 o.p. (*0-451-01229-1*, Signet Bks.); 1955. 544p. mass mkt. 4.95 o.s.i (*0-451-52455-1*, Signet Classics); 1955. mass mkt. 2.25 o.p. (*0-451-51404-1*, Signet Classics); 1955. 544p. mass mkt. 2.25 o.p. (*0-451-52021-1*, Signet Classics); 1955. mass mkt. 1.95 o.p. (*0-451-51538-2*, Signet Classics); 1955. mass mkt. 1.95 o.p. (*0-451-51239-1*, Signet Classics); 1955. mass mkt. 1.75 o.p. (*0-451-51118-2*, Signet Classics); 1955. mass mkt. 1.50 o.p. (*0-451-51014-3*, Signet Classics); 1955. mass mkt. 1.25 o.p. (*0-451-50872-6*, Signet Classics); 1955. mass mkt. 0.95 o.p. (*0-451-50730-4*, Signet Classics); 1955. mass mkt. 0.75 o.p. (*0-451-50047-4*, Signet Classics); 150th rev. ed. 1998. 592p. mass mkt. 4.95 (*0-451-52699-6*, Signet Classics) NAL.
—Moby Dick. abr. ed. 1995. (Classic Literature with Classical Music Ser.). audio 22.98 (*962-634-526-8*, NA402614); (J). audio compact disk 26.98 (*962-634-026-6*, NA402612) Naxos of America, Inc. (Naxos AudioBooks).
—Moby Dick. abr. ed. 2001. audio 25.00 (*1-59007-022-4*, New Millennium Audio) New Millennium Entertainment.
—Moby Dick. abr. ed. 1996. audio 19.95 o.p. (*1-55800-812-8*) NewStar Media, Inc.

—Moby Dick. unabr. ed. (Read-along Ser.). 34.95 incl. audio Norton Pubs., Inc., Jeffrey /Audio-Forum.
—Moby Dick. (Critical Editions Ser.). 2001. (C). pap. text 19.50 o.p. (0-393-94677-0); annot. ed. 1967. (Illus.). (C). pap. text o.p. (0-393-09670-X, 9670); 2nd ed. 2001. (Illus.). xv, 726p. pap. 12.00 (0-393-97283-6) Norton, W. W. & Co., Inc.
—Moby Dick. audio 32.95 o.p. Olivia & Hill Pr., The.
—Moby Dick. (Coleccion Clasicos de la Juventud). (SPA., Illus.). 256p. 12.95 (84-7189-052-6, ORT307) Ortells, Alfredo Editorial S.L. ESP. *Dist:* Continental Bk. Co., Inc.
—Moby Dick. 2000. ( World's Classics Ser.). 640p. 18.00 (0-19-210041-6) Oxford Univ. Pr., Inc.
—Moby Dick. Dixson, Robert James, ed. rev. ed. 1987. (American Classics: Bk. 2). (J). (gr. 9 up). audio 65.00 (0-13-024662-X, 58219) Prentice Hall, ESL Dept.
—Moby Dick. 1987. (Radiobook Ser.). audio 4.98 (0-929541-38-3) Radiola Co.
—Moby Dick. 1998. 20.00 o.s.i (0-679-60290-9); 1934. 3.95 o.s.i (0-394-60119-X) Random Hse., Inc.
—Moby Dick, unabr. ed. 1987. audio 120.00 (1-55690-343-X, 87370E7) Recorded Bks., LLC.
—Moby Dick. 1999. mass mkt. 5.99 (0-671-01912-0); 1980. mass mkt. 2.75 (0-671-83670-6); 1975. mass mkt. 0.95 (0-671-47915-6); 1999. (Illus.). 640p. reprint ed. mass mkt. 5.99 (0-671-02835-9) Simon & Schuster. (Pocket).
—Moby Dick. abr. ed. 1984. (Monarch Notes Ser.). audio 7.95 (0-671-54405-5) Simon & Schuster Audio.
—Moby Dick. unabr. ed. audio 10.95 (0-8045-0850-X, SAC 850) Spoken Arts, Inc.
—Moby Dick. (Saddleback Classics). 1999. (Illus.). 13.10 (0-606-21561-1); 1997. lib. bdg. 16.00 (0-606-16017-5); 1955. 11.00 (0-606-01084-X) Turtleback Bks.
—Moby Dick. Lee, A. Robert, ed. 1993. 507p. pap. 3.95 o.p. (0-460-87307-5, Everyman's Classic Library in Paperback) Tuttle Publishing.
—Moby Dick. 1992. 527p. pap. 3.95 o.p. (0-460-87162-5, Everyman's Classic Library in Paperback) Tuttle Publishing.
—Moby Dick. 1992. (Illus.). 564p. reprint ed. lib. bdg. 31.95 o.p. (1-877767-72-7) University Publishing Hse., Inc.
—Moby Dick. Beaver, Harold, ed. 1973. (English Library). 1024p. pap. 5.95 o.p. (0-14-043082-2, Penguin Classics) Viking Penguin.
—Moby Dick. abr. ed. 1996. 4p. audio 23.95 o.s.i (0-14-086172-6, Penguin AudioBooks); 150th annot. ed. 2001. (Illus.). 688p. reprint ed. 14.00 (0-14-200008-6, Penguin Classics) Viking Penguin.
—Moby Dick. 1999. E-Book 4.99 (0-8220-7133-9); E-Book 4.99 (0-8220-7133-9) Wiley, John & Sons, Inc. (Cliff Notes).
—Moby Dick. 496p. 1997. pap. 3.95 (1-85326-574-8); 1995. pap. 3.95 (1-85326-008-8, 0088WW) Wordsworth Editions, Ltd. GBR. *Dist:* Casemate Pubs. & Bk. Distributors, LLC.
—Moby Dick: Or the Whale. Parker, Hershel & Tanselle, Thomas G., eds. 1988. (Northwestern-Newberry Edition of the Writings of Herman Melville: Vol. 6). 1043p. (C). pap. 38.00 (0-8101-0269-2); 113.00 (0-8101-0268-4) Northwestern Univ. Pr.
—Moby Dick: Or the Whale. Hayford, Harrison & Parker, Hershel, eds. 1976. (Illus.). 14.95 o.p. (0-393-04402-5) Norton, W. W. & Co., Inc.
—Moby Dick: Or the Whale. 1992. (Modern Library Ser.). (Illus.). 864p. 21.00 (0-679-60010-8, Modern Library) Random House Adult Trade Publishing Group.
—Moby Dick: Or, the Whale. Tanner, Tony, ed. & intro. by. 1998. (Oxford World's Classics Ser.). 656p. pap. 10.95 (0-19-283385-5) Oxford Univ. Pr., Inc.
—Moby Dick: Or, the Whale. Tanner, Tony, ed. 1988. (Oxford World's Classics Ser.). 666p. pap. 6.95 o.p. (0-19-281780-9) Oxford Univ. Pr., Inc.
—Moby Dick: Or the Whale. Vincent, Howard P. & Mansfield, Luther S., eds. annot. ed. 1962. (Complete Works of Herman Melville Ser.). 909p. 29.95 (0-87532-001-5) Hendricks Hse., Inc.
—Moby Dick: Or the Whale. 150th ed. 2001. xxx, 573p. reprint ed. pap. 17.95 (0-8101-1911-0) Northwestern Univ. Pr.
—Moby Dick: Or the Whale. 1981. (Illus.). 600p. reprint ed. 65.00 (0-520-04354-5); 395.00 o.p. (0-520-04549-1); pap. 29.95 (0-520-04548-3) Univ. of California Pr.
—Moby Dick: Or the Whale. rev. ed. 1992. (Penguin Classics Ser.). (Illus.). 720p. pap. 11.95 o.s.i (0-14-039084-7, Penguin Classics) Viking Penguin.
—Moby Dick: or The Whale. annuals 2000. (Modern Library Classics). (Illus.). 928p. pap. 11.95 (0-679-78327-X, Modern Library) Random House Adult Trade Publishing Group.
Melville, Herman & Library of America Staff. Moby Dick. 1991. 672p. pap. 15.00 o.s.i (0-679-72525-3, Vintage) Knopf Publishing Group.
Melville, Herman & Tanner, Tony. Moby Dick. 1998. E-Book 9.40 (0-585-36170-3) netLibrary, Inc.
Melville, Herman, et al. Moby Dick: Or the Whale. 1988. E-Book 99.95 (0-585-38294-8) netLibrary, Inc.
Moby-Dick: Lifetime Series Classics. 2002. text (0-924967-72-2) JMW Group, Inc.
Naslund, Sena Jeter. Ahab's Wife: Or, the Star Gazer. 2000. (Illus.). 688p. pap. 15.00 (0-688-17785-9, Perennial) HarperTrade.
—Ahab's Wife: Or, the Star Gazer. 1999. (Illus.). 688p. 28.00 (0-688-17187-7, Morrow, William & Co.) Morrow/Avon.
—Ahab's Wife: Or, the Star Gazer. abr. ed. 1999. audio 25.00 o.s.i (0-671-04644-6, Simon & Schuster Audioworks) Simon & Schuster Audio.
Tanselle, Thomas G., et al, eds. Herman Melville: Moby-Dick, Billy Budd & Other Writings. 2000. (Library of America College Editions). 996p. (C). pap. 13.95 (1-883011-89-2) Library of America, The.

**AINSLIE, AMBER (FICTITIOUS CHARACTER)—FICTION**

Stahl, Hilda. Abducted. 1991. (Amber Ainslie Detective Ser.: Bk. 2). 137p. (Orig.). pap. 5.99 o.p. (0-934998-35-3) Evangel Publishing Hse.
—Blackmail. 1990. (Amber Ainslie Detective Ser.: Bk. 4). 174p. pap. 5.99 (0-934998-40-X) Evangel Publishing Hse.
—Deadline. 1989. (Amber Ainslie Detective Ser.: Bk. 1). 154p. (Orig.). pap. 5.99 (0-934998-33-7) Evangel Publishing Hse.
—Undercover. 1990. (Amber Ainslie Detective Ser.: Bk. 3). 172p. pap. 5.99 (0-934998-37-X) Evangel Publishing Hse.

**AINSLIE, MALCOLM (FICTITIOUS CHARACTER)—FICTION**

Hailey, Arthur. Detective. 1998. 608p. reprint ed. mass mkt. 7.99 (0-425-16386-5) Berkley Publishing Group.
—Detective. l.t. ed. 1997. pap. 24.00 o.p. (0-7838-8132-0, Macmillan Reference USA) Gale Group.
—Detective. 1999. (SPA.). (84-08-02910-X) GeoPlaneta, Editorial, S. A.

**ALARIC, THE MINSTREL (FICTITIOUS CHARACTER)—FICTION**

Eisenstein, Phyllis. Born to Exile. 1978. 8.95 o.p. (0-87054-082-3) Arkham Hse. Pubs.
—Born to Exile. 1980. pap. 1.95 o.p. (0-440-10854-3) Dell Publishing.
—Born to Exile. 1989. mass mkt. 3.95 o.p. (0-451-16280-3, 017); mass mkt. 3.95 o.p. (0-451-45093-0, ROC) NAL.
—In the Red Lord's Reach. 1989. (Orig.). mass mkt. 4.50 o.p. (0-451-45105-8, ROC); 272p. mass mkt. 3.95 o.p. (0-451-16073-8, Signet Bks.) NAL.

**ALBERG, KARL (FICTITIOUS CHARACTER)—FICTION**

Wright, Laurali R. Acts of Murder. 1998. 288p. 22.00 (0-684-81381-5, Scribner) Simon & Schuster.
—Acts of Murder. l.t. ed. 1998. (Mystery Ser.). 381p. 27.95 (0-7862-1678-6) Thorndike Pr.
—A Chill Rain in January. 1991. 336p. mass mkt. 7.99 (0-7704-2417-1) Bantam Bks.
—A Chill Rain in January. 1991. (Crime Monthly Ser.). 288p. pap. 4.50 o.p. (0-14-012982-0, Penguin Bks.) Penguin Group (USA) Inc.
—A Chill Rain in January. 1990. 288p. 17.95 o.p. (0-670-83129-8, Viking) Viking Penguin.
—Fall from Grace. l.t. ed. 1992. pap. 17.95 o.p. (0-7927-1270-6); 19.95 o.p. (0-7927-1271-4) BBC Audiobooks America.
—Fall from Grace. 1999. pap. (0-14-099717-2) NAL.
—Fall from Grace. 1992. (Crime Ser.). 256p. reprint ed. pap. 5.95 o.p. (0-14-012981-2, Penguin Bks.) Penguin Group (USA) Inc.
—Fall from Grace. 1991. 256p. 18.95 o.p. (0-670-83130-1, Viking) Viking Penguin.
—Love in the Temperate Zone. 1988. 17.95 o.p. (0-670-81173-4) Viking Penguin.
—Mother Love: A Karl Alberg Mystery with Cassandra Mitchell. 1996. 264p. mass mkt. 7.99 o.s.i (0-7704-2716-2) Bantam Bks.
—Mother Love: A Karl Alberg Mystery with Cassandra Mitchell. 1995. 288p. 26.95 o.p. (0-385-25477-6) Doubleday Publishing.
—Mother Love: A Karl Alberg Mystery with Cassandra Mitchell. 1995. (Illus.). 304p. 21.00 o.p. (0-684-19673-5, Scribner) Simon & Schuster.
—Prized Possessions, No. 5. 1997. 336p. mass mkt. 7.50 (0-7704-2543-7) Bantam Bks.
—Prized Possessions. 1994. (Crime Ser.). 272p. pap. 5.95 o.p. (0-14-017146-0, Penguin Bks.) Penguin Group (USA) Inc.
—Prized Possessions. 1993. 272p. 19.00 o.p. (0-670-84565-5, Viking) Viking Penguin.
—Sleep While I Sing. l.t. ed. 1991. 17.95 o.p. (0-7451-8072-8, AH0107); pap. 15.95 o.p. (0-7927-0555-6, AS0143) BBC Audiobooks America.
—Sleep While I Sing. 1988. 240p. mass mkt. 6.99 (0-7704-2300-0) Bantam Bks.
—Sleep While I Sing. 1988. o.s.i (0-385-25042-8) Doubleday Publishing.
—Sleep While I Sing. 1987. 224p. pap. 3.95 o.p. (0-14-008880-6, Penguin Bks.); 1987. 39.50 o.p. (0-14-778226-0); 1986. 224p. 15.95 o.p. (0-670-81089-4) Viking Penguin.
—Strangers among Us. 1997. 256p. mass mkt. 8.99 (0-7704-2758-8) Bantam Bks.
—Strangers among Us. 1996. 256p. 20.50 o.p. (0-684-81382-3, Scribner) Simon & Schuster.
—Strangers among Us. l.t. ed. 2000. (Mystery Ser.). 360p. 27.95 (0-7862-2557-2) Thorndike Pr.
—The Suspect. 1986. 224p. mass mkt. 7.99 (0-7704-2122-9) Bantam Bks.
—The Suspect. (Crime Ser.). 224p. 1987. pap. 5.95 o.p. (0-14-010477-1, Penguin Bks.); 1985. 15.95 o.p. (0-670-80596-3) Viking Penguin.
—A Touch of Panic: A Karl Alberg Mystery. 1995. 288p. mass mkt. 7.99 o.s.i (0-7704-2620-4) Bantam Bks.
—A Touch of Panic: A Karl Alberg Mystery. 1995. (Crime Ser.). 288p. pap. 5.95 o.s.i (0-14-023300-8, Penguin Bks.) Penguin Group (USA) Inc.
—A Touch of Panic: A Karl Alberg Mystery. 1994. 288p. 20.00 o.s.i (0-684-19672-7, Scribner) Simon & Schuster.

**ALBERT, CONSORT OF QUEEN VICTORIA, 1819-1861—FICTION**

Anthony, Evelyn. Victoria. l.t. ed. 1994. pap. 20.95 o.p. (0-7927-1606-X); 1993. 22.95 o.p. (0-7927-1607-8) BBC Audiobooks America.
Lovesey, Peter. Bertie & the Crime of Passion. 1995. 256p. 19.95 o.s.i (0-89296-550-9) Mysterious Pr.
—Bertie & the Crime of Passion. 1995. 240p. mass mkt. 5.50 o.s.i (0-446-40368-7) Warner Bks., Inc.
—Bertie & the Seven Bodies, Set. unabr. ed. 1993. (Detective Memoirs of King Edward the Eighth Ser.). 54.95 incl. audio (0-7451-6111-1, CAB 623) BBC Audiobooks America.
—Bertie & the Seven Bodies. 1990. 208p. 16.95 o.p. (0-89296-399-9) Mysterious Pr.
—Bertie & the Seven Bodies. 1991. (Audio Books Ser.). audio 53.95 o.p. (0-8161-9247-2) Thorndike Pr.
—Bertie & the Seven Bodies. 1991. mass mkt. 4.95 o.s.i (0-445-40858-8) Warner Bks., Inc.
—Bertie & the Tinman. 1988. 15.95 o.p. (0-89296-196-1) Mysterious Pr.
—Bertie & the Tinman. 1989. mass mkt. 3.95 (0-445-40592-9, Mysterious Pr. Paperback Bks.) Warner Bks., Inc.

**ALBRIGHT, ALEXIS (FICTITIOUS CHARACTER)—FICTION**

Miller, Janice. The Jade Crucible. 1995. 324p. pap. 10.99 o.p. (0-7852-7706-4) Nelson, Thomas Inc.
—Plum Blossoms: Alexis Albright—Private Investigator. 1994. pap. 10.99 o.p. (0-7852-8208-4) Nelson, Thomas Inc.

**ALDINGTON, CLAIRE (FICTITIOUS CHARACTER)—FICTION**

Holland, Isabelle. Darcourt. 1977. pap. 1.75 o.s.i (0-449-23224-7, Fawcett) Ballantine Bks.
—Darcourt. l.t. ed. 1982. 529p. reprint ed. 13.95 o.p. (0-89621-397-8) Thorndike Pr.
—Death at St. Anselm's. 1984. 240p. 13.95 o.p. (0-385-18332-1) Doubleday Publishing.
—A Fatal Advent: A St. Anselm's Mystery. 1990. (St. Anselm's Mystery Ser.). 256p. mass mkt. 3.95 o.s.i (0-449-21879-1, Fawcett) Ballantine Bks.
—Flight of the Archangel. 1986. mass mkt. 2.95 o.s.i (0-449-20977-6, Fawcett) Ballantine Bks.
—The Long Search. 1992. mass mkt. 3.99 o.s.i (0-449-22009-5, Fawcett) Ballantine Bks.
—The Long Search. 1990. 272p. 16.95 o.s.i (0-385-26545-X) Doubleday Publishing.
—The Long Search. l.t. ed. 1993. (Magna Large Print Ser.). 435p. (0-7505-0444-7) Magna Large Print Bks. GBR. *Dist:* Ulverscroft Large Print Canada, Ltd.
—A Lover Scorned. 1987. 256p. mass mkt. 2.95 o.s.i (0-449-21369-2, Fawcett) Ballantine Bks.
—A Lover Scorned. 1986. 240p. 15.95 o.p. (0-385-23169-5) Doubleday Publishing.

**ALETTER, FINNY (FICTITIOUS CHARACTER)—FICTION**

Montgomery, Yvonne. Scavengers. 1990. 256p. pap. 3.50 (0-380-71002-1, Avon Bks.); 1987. 240p. 16.95 o.p. (0-87795-897-1, Morrow, William & Co.) Morrow/Avon.

**ALEXANDER, RACHEL (FICTITIOUS CHARACTER)—FICTION**

Benjamin, Carol Lea. The Dog Who Knew Too Much: A Rachel Alexander & Dash Mystery. 1998. (Rachel Alexander & Dash Mystery Ser.: Vol. 2). 272p. reprint ed. mass mkt. 5.99 o.s.i (0-440-22637-6) Dell Publishing.
—The Dog Who Knew Too Much: A Rachel Alexander & Dash Mystery. 1997. (Rachel Alexander & Dash Mystery Ser.). 256p. 21.95 (0-8027-3312-3) Walker & Co.
—A Hell of a Dog. 1998. (Rachel Alexander & Dash Mystery Ser.). (Illus.). 276p. 22.95 (0-8027-3325-5) Walker & Co.
—A Hell of a Dog: A Rachel Alexander & Dash Mystery. 1999. (Rachel Alexander & Dash Mystery Ser.). 320p. mass mkt. 5.99 (0-440-22548-5) Dell Publishing.
—Lady Vanishes. 1999. (Rachel Alexander & Dash Mystery Ser.). 264p. 23.95 (0-8027-3335-2) Walker & Co.
—The Long Good Boy: A Rachel Alexander & Dash Mystery. 2001. 240p. 23.95 (0-8027-3364-6) Walker & Co.
—This Dog for Hire: A Rachel Alexander & Dash Mystery. 1997. (Rachel Alexander & Dash Mystery Ser.: Vol. 1). 304p. mass mkt. 6.50 (0-440-22520-5) Dell Publishing.
—This Dog for Hire: A Rachel Alexander & Dash Mystery. l.t. ed. 2002. 346p. 28.95 o.p. (0-7862-4191-8) Thorndike Pr.
—This Dog for Hire: A Rachel Alexander & Dash Mystery. 1996. (Rachel Alexander & Dash Mystery Ser.). 224p. 20.95 (0-8027-3292-5) Walker & Co.
—The Wrong Dog: Rachel Alexander & Dash Mystery. 2000. (Rachel Alexander & Dash Mystery Ser.). 231p. 23.95 (0-8027-3348-4) Walker & Co.
Benjamin, Carol Lea & Sallis, James. The Long-Legged Fly: A Lew Griffin Novel. 2001. 200p. pap. 8.95 (0-8027-7620-5) Walker & Co.

**ALICE (FICTITIOUS CHARACTER: CARROLL)—FICTION**

Badger, Gerry & Benton-Harris, John. Through the Looking Glass: Photographic Art in Great Britain, 1945-1989. 1989. (Illus.). 200p. (C). pap. 35.00 o.p. (0-85331-560-4) Brill Academic Pubs., Inc.
Bassett, Jennifer, ed. Through the Looking Glass: And What Alice Found There. 1995. (Illus.). 64p. pap. text 5.95 o.p. (0-19-422749-9) Oxford Univ. Pr., Inc.
Carlson, David & Bryant, Vaughn M., Jr. Through the Looking Glass. 2nd ed. 1994. (C). pap. text 18.00 net. o.p. (0-07-009980-4) McGraw-Hill Cos., The.
Carroll, Lewis, pseud. Alice in Wonderland: Complete Text, Commentary & Glossary. 2001. (CliffsComplete Ser.). (Illus.). 179p. pap. 9.99 (0-7645-8721-8, Cliff Notes) Wiley, John & Sons, Inc.
—Alice in Wonderland: Fairy Tales. Tallarico, Tony, ed. 1987. (Tuffy Story Bks.). 32p. (J). (ps-3). 2.95 o.s.i (0-89828-328-0, 83280, Tuffy Bks.) Putnam Publishing Group, The.
—Alice in Wonderland: Through the Looking Glass. 1998. 188p. reprint ed. lib. bdg. 24.00 (1-58287-012-8) North Bks.
—Alice in Wonderland & Other Favorites. 1983. (Illus.). 288p. (J). (gr. 5 up). mass mkt. 2.95 o.s.i (0-671-46688-7, Pocket) Simon & Schuster.
—Alice in Wonderland & Through the Looking Glass, 2 bks. Incl. Alice's Adventures in Wonderland. Self, Will, intro. 192p. 15.95 (1-58234-174-5); Through the Looking Glass: And What Alice Found There. Smith, Zadie, intro. 224p. 15.95 (1-58234-175-3); (Illus.). 2001. 32.00 (1-58234-222-9) Bloomsbury Publishing.
—Alice in Wonderland & Through the Looking Glass. 1988. (Illus.). 296p. (YA). pap. 7.95 o.p. (0-8092-4488-8) McGraw-Hill/Contemporary.
—Alice in Wonderland & Through the Looking Glass. 1981. (Illustrated Junior Library). (Illus.). 304p. (J). (gr. 4 up). 7.95 o.s.i (0-448-11004-0, Grosset & Dunlap) Penguin Putnam Bks. for Young Readers.
—Alice in Wonderland Coloring Book. 81st ed. 1972. (Illus.). 64p. (J). (gr. k-3). pap. 3.50 (0-486-22853-3) Dover Pubns., Inc.
—Alice in Wonderland Pop-Up Book. 1980. (Illus.). 12p. (J). (gr. k-4). pap. 6.95 o.s.i (0-385-28038-6, Delacorte Pr.) Dell Publishing.
—Alice's Adventures in Wonderland & Through the Looking Glass: And What Alice Found There. 1993. (Everyman Paperback Classics Ser.). 238p. pap. 5.95 (0-460-87359-8, Everyman's Classic Library in Paperback) Tuttle Publishing.
—Alice's Adventures in Wonderland & Through the Looking Glass: And What Alice Found There. Haughton, Hugh, ed. & intro. by. 1998. (Penguin Classics Ser.). (Illus.). 448p. 8.95 o.s.i (0-14-043317-1, Penguin Classics) Viking Penguin.
—Alicia en el Pais de las Maravillas. 2002. (SPA.). 208p. 25.00 (1-4000-0185-4) Random Hse., Inc.
—Carroll Audio Boxed Set. 2015. (Classic, Children's, Audio Ser.). 21.90 o.p. (0-14-086475-X) Penguin Group (USA) Inc.
—Through the Looking Glass. E-Book 2.49 (1-58627-092-3) Electric Umbrella Publishing.
—Through the Looking Glass. l.t. ed. 1997. (Large Print Heritage Ser.). 161p. (YA). (gr. 7-12). lib. bdg. 26.95 (1-58118-007-1, 21495) LRS.

—Through the Looking Glass. E-Book 2.95 (1-57799-889-8) Logos Research Systems, Inc.
—Through the Looking Glass. (Illus.). 176p. 1996. (YA). (gr. 5-9). pap. 4.99 (0-14-036709-8); 1985. (J). (gr. 7 up). pap. 2.99 o.p. (0-14-035039-X) Penguin Putnam Bks. for Young Readers. (Puffin Bks.).
—Through the Looking Glass. 1999. E-Book o.s.i incl. audio compact disk (1-891595-05-9) Quiet Vision Publishing.
—Through the Looking Glass: And What Alice Found There. E-Book 1.00 (1-930161-60-3) Adobe Systems, Inc.
—Through the Looking Glass: And What Alice Found There. 2001. (Illus.). 224p. 15.95 (1-58234-175-3) Bloomsbury Publishing.
—Through the Looking Glass: And What Alice Found There. reprint ed. lib. bdg. 98.00 (0-7426-2274-6); 2001. (Illus.). 244p. pap. text 28.00 (0-7426-7274-3) Classic Bks.
—Through the Looking Glass: And What Alice Found There. 2003. 192p. (J). 4.99 (1-57759-939-X) Dalmatian Pr.
—Through the Looking Glass: And What Alice Found There. unabr. ed. 1994. lib. bdg. 18.95 incl. audio (1-883049-47-4) Sound Room Pubs., Inc.
Chauls. Alice in Wonderland: Vocal Score. 1991. 200p. otabind 35.00 o.p. (0-7935-0412-0, 50488951) Leonard, Hal Corp.
Cliffs Notes Staff. Alice in Wonderland. 1984. (Cliffs-Notes Ser.). 64p. (Orig.). pap. 4.95 o.s.i (0-8220-0140-3, Cliff Notes) Wiley, John & Sons, Inc.
Falco, Maria J., ed. Through the Looking Glass: Epistemology & the Conduct of Inquiry, an Anthology. 1979. pap. text 17.75 o.p. (0-8191-0841-3) Univ. Pr. of America.
Fischer, Kathleen M. Alice in Wonderland. Friedland, J. & Kessler, Rikki, eds. 1996. (Novel-Ties Ser.). (Illus.). 30p. (J). (gr. 6). pap., stu. ed. 15.95 (1-56982-651-X, S0218) Learning Links, Inc.
Glennon, William. Alice in Wonderland. 1985. reprint ed. pap. 5.60 (0-87129-063-4, A44) Dramatic Publishing Co.
Golden Books Staff. Alice in Wonderland. 1997. (J). pap. text o.p. (0-307-08659-3, Golden Bks.) Random Hse. Children's Bks.
—Alice in Wonderland: Follow the White Rabbit. 1998. 48p. (J). (gr. k-3). pap. text o.p. (0-307-09327-1, Golden Bks.) Random Hse. Children's Bks.
Gregory, Andre. Alice in Wonderland. 1972. per. 6.50 (0-8222-0014-7) Dramatists Play Service, Inc.
Howe, D. H., ed. Through the Looking Glass. 2nd ed. 1993. (Illus.). 78p. pap. text 5.95 (0-19-585268-0) Oxford Univ. Pr., Inc.
Hunter, David. Alice in Wonderland: A Masterpiece of Victorian Pornography? 1988. (Illus.). 80p. (Orig.). pap. 9.95 (0-915153-27-0) Gold Star Pr.
Mcgill, Joyce. Through the Looking Glass. 1990. (Silhouette Intimate Moments Ser.: No. 347). pap. (0-373-07347-X, Silhouette) Harlequin Enterprises, Ltd.
Netzel, Sally. Alice in Wonderland - The Musical: In 2 Acts. 1991. (Stage Magic Play Ser.). (Illus.). 56p. pap. 4.50 (0-88680-342-X) Clark, I. E. Pubns.
Nicolson, Sheryl A. & Shipstead, Susan G. Through the Looking Glass: Observations in the Early Childhood Classroom. 1994. 448p. (C). pap. text 36.00 o.p. (0-02-387491-0, Macmillan College) Prentice Hall PTR.
Noble, Marty. Alice in Wonderland Stained Glass Coloring Book. 1998. (Illus.). 8p. (J). pap. 1.00 (0-486-40305-X) Dover Pubns., Inc.
—Alice in Wonderland Sticker Activity Book. 1998. (J). pap. 1.00 (0-486-40314-9) Dover Pubns., Inc.
Noon, Jeff. Automated Alice. (Illus.). 251p. pap. 10.95 (0-552-14478-9); 2001. 256p. pap. 13.00 (0-552-99905-9) Corgi Bks. Ltd. GBR. Dist: Trafalgar Square.
—Automated Alice. ltd. ed. Date not set. (0-517-70721-7, Crown) Crown Publishing Group.
Outlet Book Company Staff. Alice in Wonderland-Sticker Book. 1990. 3.99 o.s.i (0-517-69691-6) Random Hse. Value Publishing.
Seibold, J. Otto. Alice in Wonderland. 2002. 24p. pap. 6.95 (0-634-02404-3); 1985. (Illus.). 36p. pap. 8.95 (0-7935-0034-6, 00359047) Leonard, Hal Corp.
Slater, Teddy. Alice in Wonderland: Junior Novelization. 1995. (Illus.). 64p. (J). (gr. 2-6). pap. 3.50 o.p. (0-7868-4027-7) Disney Pr.
Stephenson, Rex & Cohn, John. Alice in Wonderland: A Musical. 1997. pap. 4.50 (1-57514-291-0, 0028) Encore Performance Publishing.
Through the Looking Glass. (Read-Along Ser.). (YA). pap., stu. ed. 34.95 incl. audio (0-88432-971-2, S23946) Norton Pubs., Inc., Jeffrey /Audio-Forum.
Tierney, Tom. Alice in Wonderland Paper Doll. 1992. (Illus.). (J). (gr. k-3). pap. 1.00 (0-486-27368-7) Dover Pubns., Inc.
Wakeling, Edward. Alice in Wonderland Puzzle & Game Book. 1995. (Illus.). 86p. (J). pap. 7.95 (1-57281-006-8, CBK905, Cove Pr.) U.S. Games Systems, Inc.
—Alice in Wonderland's Deck/Book Set. 1996. (Illus.). 86p. (YA). (gr. 5-9). 19.95 (0-88079-704-5, ALW100) U.S. Games Systems, Inc.
Wilson, Elizabeth & Taylor, Lou. Through the Looking Glass. 1993. (Illus.). 240p. pap. 17.95 o.p. (0-563-21441-4) BBC Bk. Publishing GBR. Dist: Parkwest Pubns., Inc.
Wolfe, Tom. Through the Looking Glass with Tom Wolfe. 1992. (Illus.). 64p. pap. 12.95 (0-88740-380-8) Schiffer Publishing, Ltd.

**ALLEN, STEVE, 1921-2000—FICTION**

Allen, Steve. Die Laughing. 1999. 288p. mass mkt. 5.99 o.s.i (1-57566-380-5); 1998. 304p. 21.00 o.s.i (1-57566-241-8) Kensington Publishing Corp.
—Murder in Manhattan. 1991. 352p. mass mkt. 4.95 o.s.i (0-8217-3440-7, Zebra Bks.) Kensington Publishing Corp.
—Murder on the Atlantic. 1995. 288p. mass mkt. 19.95 o.p. (0-8217-5062-3, Zebra Bks.) Kensington Publishing Corp.
—Murder on the Glitter Box. 1998. 352p. mass mkt. 5.99 o.s.i (1-57566-245-0); 1989. mass mkt. 18.95 o.s.i (0-8217-2752-4, Zebra Bks.) Kensington Publishing Corp.
—Murder on the Glitter Box. abr. ed. 1994. 17.95 o.p. (0-7871-0197-4) NewStar Media, Inc.
—Wake up to Murder. 1997. 384p. mass mkt. 5.99 o.s.i (1-57566-236-1); 1996. 288p. 18.95 o.s.i (1-57566-109-8); 1996. 256p. 19.95 o.s.i (1-57566-090-3, Kensington Bks.) Kensington Publishing Corp.

**ALLEYN, RODERICK (FICTITIOUS CHARACTER)—FICTION**

Marsh, Ngaio. Alleyn & Others: The Collected Short Fiction of Ngaio Marsh. 1995. pap. 6.95 o.s.i (1-55882-133-3); 256p. pap. 10.95 o.p. (1-55882-028-0) International Polygonics, Ltd.
—Artists in Crime. 1976. reprint ed. lib. bdg. 24.95 (0-88411-471-6) Amereon, Ltd.
—Artists in Crime. 1994. 256p. mass mkt. 4.50 o.p. (0-425-14331-7, Prime Crime); 1984. 256p. mass mkt. 3.99 o.p. (0-515-07534-5, Jove); 1982. mass mkt. 2.50 o.s.i (0-515-06341-X, Jove); 1980. mass mkt. 1.95 o.s.i (0-515-05414-3, Jove) Berkley Publishing Group.
—Artists in Crime. unabr. ed. 1994. audio 49.95 (0-7861-0692-1, 1477) Blackstone Audio Bks., Inc.
—Artists in Crime. 1997. (Dead Letter Mysteries Ser.). 256p. mass mkt. 5.99 (0-312-96359-9, St. Martin's Paperbacks) St. Martin's Pr.
—Black As He's Painted. 1976. reprint ed. lib. bdg. 23.95 (0-88411-472-4) Amereon, Ltd.
—Black As He's Painted. (Mystery Ser.). 1984. 224p. mass mkt. 3.99 o.s.i (0-515-07627-9); 1982. mass mkt. 2.50 o.s.i (0-515-06818-7); 1981. mass mkt. 2.25 o.s.i (0-515-05871-8); 1978. mass mkt. 1.50 o.s.i (0-515-04611-6) Berkley Publishing Group. (Jove).
—Black As He's Painted. 1994. reprint ed. lib. bdg. 27.95 (1-56849-307-X) Buccaneer Bks., Inc.
—Black As He's Painted. 1999. 256p. mass mkt. 5.99 (0-312-97279-2, St. Martin's Paperbacks) St. Martin's Pr.
—Clutch of Constables. 1976. reprint ed. lib. bdg. 22.95 (0-88411-473-2) Amereon, Ltd.
—Clutch of Constables. 1986. 224p. mass mkt. 3.99 o.s.i (0-515-08775-0); 1983. mass mkt. 2.50 o.s.i (0-515-07105-6); 1981. mass mkt. 2.25 o.s.i (0-515-06013-5) Berkley Publishing Group. (Jove).
—Clutch of Constables. 1994. reprint ed. lib. bdg. 27.95 (1-56849-308-8) Buccaneer Bks., Inc.
—Clutch of Constables. 1999. 224p. mass mkt. 5.99 (0-312-97084-6, St. Martin's Paperbacks) St. Martin's Pr.
—The Collected Short Fiction of Ngaio Marsh. 1989. 252p. 19.95 o.p. (1-55882-050-7); 1991. 242p. reprint ed. pap. 9.95 o.p. (1-55882-086-8) International Polygonics, Ltd. (Library of Crime Classics).
—Colour Scheme. 1976. reprint ed. lib. bdg. 24.95 (0-88411-474-0) Amereon, Ltd.
—Colour Scheme. 1995. mass mkt. 5.99 o.p. (0-425-14651-0); 1984. 288p. mass mkt. 3.99 o.s.i (0-515-07881-6, Jove); 1982. mass mkt. 2.50 o.s.i (0-515-06014-3, Jove); 1978. mass mkt. 1.75 o.s.i (0-425-03859-9) Berkley Publishing Group.
—Colour Scheme. 1998. (Colour Scheme Ser.: Vol. 1). 288p. mass mkt. 5.99 (0-312-96603-2, St. Martin's Paperbacks) St. Martin's Pr.
—Dead Water. 1976. reprint ed. lib. bdg. 23.95 (0-88411-475-9) Amereon, Ltd.
—Dead Water. 1994. mass mkt. 4.50 o.p. (0-425-14486-0); 1983. 288p. mass mkt. 3.99 o.s.i (0-515-07440-3, Jove); 1982. mass mkt. 2.50 o.s.i (0-515-06017-8, Jove); 1978. mass mkt. 1.75 o.s.i (0-425-03857-2) Berkley Publishing Group.
—Dead Water. unabr. ed. 2000. (Inspector Alleyn Mystery Ser.). audio 49.95 (0-7451-6139-1, CAB 280) Chivers Audio Bks. GBR. Dist: BBC Audiobooks America.
—Dead Water. 1999. 224p. mass mkt. 5.99 (0-312-96990-2, St. Martin's Paperbacks) St. Martin's Pr.
—Dead Water. (G. K. Hall Audio Bks.). 1988. audio 53.95 o.s.i (0-8161-7752-X); 1999. 368p. 26.95 o.p. (0-7862-2050-3) Thorndike Pr.
—Dead Water. l.t. ed. 2000. (Ulverscroft Large Print Ser.). 368p. o.p. (0-7089-4197-4, Ulverscroft) Thorpe, F. A. Pubs. GBR. Dist: Ulverscroft Large Print Bks., Ltd., Ulverscroft Large Print Canada, Ltd.
—Death & the Dancing Footman. 1976. reprint ed. lib. bdg. 27.95 (0-88411-477-5) Amereon, Ltd.
—Death & the Dancing Footman. 320p. 1995. mass mkt. 5.99 o.s.i (0-425-14655-3); 1986. mass mkt. 3.99 o.s.i (0-515-08610-X, Jove) Berkley Publishing Group.
—Death & the Dancing Footman. 1998. (Dead Letter Mysteries Ser.). 320p. mass mkt. 5.99 (0-312-96428-5, St. Martin's Paperbacks) St. Martin's Pr.
—Death at the Bar. 1976. reprint ed. lib. bdg. 25.95 (0-88411-476-7) Amereon, Ltd.
—Death at the Bar. 1995. mass mkt. 4.99 o.s.i (0-425-14654-5); 1984. 272p. mass mkt. 3.99 o.s.i (0-515-07700-3, Jove); 1982. mass mkt. 2.50 o.s.i (0-515-06700-8, Jove); 1981. mass mkt. 2.25 o.s.i (0-515-05998-6, Jove); 1980. mass mkt. 1.95 o.s.i (0-515-05641-3, Jove) Berkley Publishing Group.
—Death at the Bar. unabr. ed. 1997. audio 44.95 (0-7861-1075-9, 1845) Blackstone Audio Bks., Inc.
—Death at the Bar. 1998. (Dead Letter Mysteries Ser.). 272p. mass mkt. 5.99 (0-312-96426-9, St. Martin's Paperbacks) St. Martin's Pr.
—Death at the Bar. l.t. ed. 1975. (Ulverscroft Large Print Ser.). 12.00 o.p. (0-85456-307-5, Ulverscroft) Thorpe, F. A. Pubs. GBR. Dist: Ulverscroft Large Print Bks., Ltd., Ulverscroft Large Print Canada, Ltd.
—Death at the Dolphin. unabr. ed. 2000. (Inspector Alleyn Mystery Ser.). 8p. audio 59.95 (0-7451-6681-4, CAB 1297) Chivers Audio Bks. GBR. Dist: BBC Audiobooks America.
—Death in a White Tie. 1976. reprint ed. lib. bdg. 24.95 (0-88411-479-1) Amereon, Ltd.
—Death in a White Tie. 1994. 352p. mass mkt. 4.50 o.p. (0-425-14408-9); 1986. mass mkt. 3.99 o.s.i (0-515-08591-X, Jove); 1983. mass mkt. 2.50 o.s.i (0-515-06224-3, Jove); 1980. mass mkt. 2.25 o.s.i (0-515-05896-3, Jove); 1980. mass mkt. 1.95 o.s.i (0-515-05628-6, Jove); 1977. mass mkt. 1.50 o.s.i (0-515-04391-5, Jove) Berkley Publishing Group.
—Death in a White Tie. 1997. 352p. mass mkt. 5.99 (0-312-96361-0, St. Martin's Paperbacks) St. Martin's Pr.
—Death in Ecstasy. 1976. reprint ed. lib. bdg. 24.95 (0-88411-478-3) Amereon, Ltd.
—Death in Ecstasy. 1986. 256p. mass mkt. 3.99 o.s.i (0-515-08592-8); 1981. mass mkt. 2.50 o.s.i (0-515-06166-2); 1980. mass mkt. 1.95 o.s.i (0-515-05499-2) Berkley Publishing Group. (Jove).
—Death in Ecstasy. 1997. (Dead Letter Mysteries Ser.). 256p. mass mkt. 5.50 (0-312-96360-2, St. Martin's Paperbacks) St. Martin's Pr.
—Death of a Fool. 1976. reprint ed. lib. bdg. 23.95 (0-88411-480-5) Amereon, Ltd.
—Death of a Fool. 1994. 288p. mass mkt. 4.50 o.p. (0-425-14303-1, Prime Crime); 1983. 288p. mass mkt. 3.50 o.s.i (0-515-07503-5, Jove); 1981. mass mkt. 2.50 o.s.i (0-515-06177-8, Jove); 1981. mass mkt. 1.95 o.s.i (0-515-05762-2, Jove); 1978. mass mkt. 1.75 o.s.i (0-515-05143-8, Jove) Berkley Publishing Group.
—Death of a Fool. 1999. 288p. mass mkt. 5.99 (0-312-96832-9, St. Martin's Paperbacks) St. Martin's Pr.
—Death of a Peer. 1976. reprint ed. lib. bdg. 26.95 (0-88411-481-3) Amereon, Ltd.
—Death of a Peer. 1994. 320p. mass mkt. 4.99 o.p. (0-425-14353-8, Prime Crime); 1986. 320p. mass mkt. 3.99 o.s.i (0-515-08691-6, Jove); 1982. mass mkt. 2.50 o.s.i (0-515-06716-4, Jove); 1981. mass mkt. 2.25 o.s.i (0-515-06091-7, Jove); 1980. mass mkt. 1.95 o.s.i (0-515-05413-5, Jove) Berkley Publishing Group.
—Death of a Peer. 1998. (Dead Letter Mysteries Ser.). 320p. mass mkt. 5.99 (0-312-96427-7, St. Martin's Paperbacks) St. Martin's Pr.
—Died in the Wool. 1976. reprint ed. lib. bdg. 22.95 (0-88411-482-1) Amereon, Ltd.
—Died in the Wool. 1994. 256p. mass mkt. 5.99 o.s.i (0-425-14469-0, Prime Crime); 1983. 256p. mass mkt. 3.99 o.s.i (0-515-07506-X, Jove); 1981. mass mkt. 2.50 o.s.i (0-515-06019-4, Jove); 1981. mass mkt. 2.25 o.s.i (0-425-05050-5); 1978. mass mkt. 1.75 o.s.i (0-425-03860-2) Berkley Publishing Group.
—Died in the Wool. unabr. ed. 1996. audio 44.95 (0-7861-0999-8, 1776) Blackstone Audio Bks., Inc.
—Died in the Wool. 1998. (Inspector Roderick Alleyn Mysteries Ser.). 256p. mass mkt. 5.99 (0-312-96604-0, St. Martin's Paperbacks) St. Martin's Pr.
—Died in the Wool. l.t. ed. 1999. (Mystery Ser.). 437p. 26.95 o.p. (0-7862-1772-3) Thorndike Pr.
—Enter a Murderer. 1976. reprint ed. lib. bdg. 22.95 (0-88411-483-X) Amereon, Ltd.
—Enter a Murderer. 1982. mass mkt. 2.50 o.s.i (0-515-06819-5); 1981. mass mkt. 2.25 o.s.i (0-515-05943-9); 1984. 192p. reprint ed. mass mkt. 3.99 o.s.i (0-515-07447-0); Vol. 2. 1982. pap. Berkley Publishing Group.
—Enter a Murderer. 1998. (Dead Letter Mysteries Ser.). 245p. mass mkt. 5.99 (0-312-96670-9, St. Martin's Paperbacks) St. Martin's Pr.
—False Scent. 1976. reprint ed. lib. bdg. 23.95 (0-88411-484-8) Amereon, Ltd.
—False Scent. (Ngaio Marsh Mystery Ser.). 1984. 224p. mass mkt. 3.99 o.s.i (0-515-08056-X); 1981. mass mkt. 2.50 o.s.i (0-515-06007-0) Berkley Publishing Group. (Jove).
—False Scent. unabr. ed. 2000. (Inspector Alleyn Mystery Ser.). 8p. audio 59.95 (0-7451-6609-1, CAB 1225) Chivers Audio Bks. GBR. Dist: BBC Audiobooks America.
—False Scent. 1999. 224p. mass mkt. 5.99 (0-312-96898-1, St. Martin's Paperbacks) St. Martin's Pr.
—Final Curtain. 1976. reprint ed. lib. bdg. 26.95 (0-88411-485-6) Amereon, Ltd.
—Final Curtain. 1997. (Inspector Roderick Alleyn Mysteries Ser.). audio 34.95 (0-7540-7501-X) BBC Audiobooks America.
—Final Curtain. 1993. mass mkt. 4.99 o.p. (0-425-14320-1); 1983. mass mkt. 2.50 o.s.i (0-515-07074-2, Jove); 1981. mass mkt. 2.25 o.s.i (0-515-06118-2, Jove); 1980. mass mkt. 1.95 o.s.i (0-515-05554-9, Jove) Berkley Publishing Group.
—Final Curtain. unabr. ed. 1994. audio 49.95 (0-7861-0676-X, 1464) Blackstone Audio Bks., Inc.
—Final Curtain. unabr. ed. 2000. (Inspector Alleyn Mystery Ser.). audio 59.95 (0-7451-6484-6, CAB 1100) Chivers Audio Bks. GBR. Dist: BBC Audiobooks America.
—Final Curtain. 1998. (Final Curtain Ser.: Vol. 1). 288p. mass mkt. 5.99 (0-312-96605-9, St. Martin's Paperbacks) St. Martin's Pr.
—Grave Mistake. 1976. 22.95 (0-8488-0577-1) Amereon, Ltd.
—Grave Mistake. unabr. ed. 1993. (Inspector Roderick Alleyn Mysteries Ser.). 69.95 incl. audio (0-7451-6141-3, CAB 144) BBC Audiobooks America.
—Grave Mistake. 1994. mass mkt. 4.50 o.p. (0-425-14243-4); 1987. 256p. mass mkt. 3.50 o.s.i (0-515-08847-1, Jove); 1983. mass mkt. 2.95 o.s.i (0-515-07549-3, Jove); 1981. mass mkt. 2.50 o.s.i (0-515-06178-6, Jove); 1980. mass mkt. 1.95 o.s.i (0-515-05369-4, Jove) Berkley Publishing Group.
—Grave Mistake. 1979. (General Ser.). lib. bdg. 13.95 o.p. (0-8161-6667-6, Macmillan Reference USA) Gale Group.
—Hand in Glove. 1976. reprint ed. lib. bdg. 22.95 (0-88411-486-4) Amereon, Ltd.
—Hand in Glove. 1992. mass mkt. 4.50 o.p. (0-425-14485-2); 1983. 240p. mass mkt. 3.99 o.s.i (0-515-07502-7, Jove); 1982. mass mkt. 2.50 o.s.i (0-515-06309-6, Jove); 1981. mass mkt. 2.25 o.s.i (0-515-06136-0, Jove); 1980. mass mkt. 1.95 o.s.i (0-515-05763-0, Jove); 1979. mass mkt. 1.75 o.s.i (0-515-05202-7, Jove) Berkley Publishing Group.
—Hand in Glove. unabr. ed. 2000. (Inspector Alleyn Mystery Ser.). audio 49.95 (0-7451-6142-1, CAB 196) Chivers Audio Bks. GBR. Dist: BBC Audiobooks America.
—Hand in Glove. 1999. (Dead Letter Mysteries Ser.). 256p. mass mkt. 5.99 (0-312-96908-2, St. Martin's Paperbacks) St. Martin's Pr.
—Hand in Glove. l.t. ed. 1983. (Ulverscroft Large Print Ser.). 368p. 12.50 o.p. (0-7089-1029-7, Ulverscroft) Thorpe, F. A. Pubs. GBR. Dist: Ulverscroft Large Print Bks., Ltd., Ulverscroft Large Print Canada, Ltd.
—Killer Dolphin. 1976. reprint ed. lib. bdg. 25.95 (0-88411-487-2) Amereon, Ltd.
—Killer Dolphin. 1995. mass mkt. 4.99 o.p. (0-425-14657-X); 1986. 256p. mass mkt. 3.99 o.s.i (0-515-08590-1, Jove); 1983. mass mkt. 2.50 o.s.i (0-515-06820-9, Jove); 1981. mass mkt. 2.25 o.s.i (0-515-06071-2, Jove); 1980. mass mkt. 1.95 o.s.i (0-515-05435-6, Jove) Berkley Publishing Group.
—Killer Dolphin. 1999. 288p. mass mkt. 5.99 (0-312-97010-2, St. Martin's Paperbacks) St. Martin's Pr.
—Last Ditch. 1976. 23.95 (0-8488-0578-X) Amereon, Ltd.
—Last Ditch. 1986. 288p. mass mkt. 3.99 o.p. (0-515-08798-X); 1983. mass mkt. 2.50 o.s.i (0-515-06821-7); 1981. mass mkt. 2.25 o.s.i (0-515-05966-8) Berkley Publishing Group. (Jove).
—Last Ditch. l.t. ed. 1977. lib. bdg. 13.50 o.p. (0-8161-6537-8, Macmillan Reference USA) Gale Group.
—Last Ditch. 2000. 288p. mass mkt. 5.99 (0-312-97286-5, St. Martin's Paperbacks) St. Martin's Pr.
—Light Thickens. 1976. 21.95 (0-8488-0579-8) Amereon, Ltd.
—Light Thickens. 240p. 1994. mass mkt. 4.99 o.p. (0-425-14529-8, Prime Crime); 1985. mass mkt. 3.99 o.s.i (0-515-07359-8, Jove) Berkley Publishing Group.

—Light Thickens. 2002. 8p. audio compact disk 79.95 (*0-7540-5528-0*, CCD 219); 1998. audio 59.95 (*0-7540-0231-4*, CAB 1654) Chivers Audio Bks. GBR. *Dist:* BBC Audiobooks America.

—Light Thickens. l.t. ed. 1983. 394p. lib. bdg. 16.95 o.p. (*0-8161-3509-6*, Macmillan Reference USA) Gale Group.

—Light Thickens. 2000. 5.99p. mass mkt. 5.99 (*0-312-97314-4*, St. Martin's Paperbacks) St. Martin's Pr.

—A Man Lay Dead. lib. bdg. 20.95 (*0-8488-2104-1*); 1976. reprint ed. lib. bdg. 21.95 (*0-88411-488-0*) Amereon, Ltd.

—A Man Lay Dead. 1993. mass mkt. 4.50 o.p. (*0-425-14319-8*); 1981. mass mkt. 2.50 o.s.i (*0-515-06496-3*, Jove); 1980. mass mkt. 1.95 o.s.i (*0-515-05729-0*, Jove); 1978. mass mkt. 1.50 o.s.i (*0-515-04529-2*, Jove) Berkley Publishing Group.

—A Man Lay Dead. 1997. (Dead Letter Mysteries Ser.). 192p. mass mkt. 5.99 (*0-312-96358-0*, St. Martin's Paperbacks) St. Martin's Pr.

—New Zealand. 1976. reprint ed. lib. bdg. 24.95 (*0-88411-489-9*) Amereon, Ltd.

—Ngaio Marsh, 5 vols. Incl. Vol. 1. Black As He's Painted. Vol. 2. Enter a Murderer. pap. Vol. 3. Killer Dolphin. pap. Vol. 4. Last Ditch. Vol. 5. Overture to Death. pap. 1982. 12.50 o.s.i (*0-515-06816-0*, Jove) Berkley Publishing Group.

—Ngaio Marsh: Five Complete Novels. 1990. 784p. 11.99 o.s.i (*0-517-41017-6*) Random Hse. Value Publishing.

—Night at the Vulcan. 1976. reprint ed. lib. bdg. 24.95 (*0-88411-490-2*) Amereon, Ltd.

—Night at the Vulcan. 1994. mass mkt. 4.50 o.p. (*0-425-14205-1*); 1983. 256p. mass mkt. 3.50 o.s.i (*0-515-07507-8*, Jove); 1982. mass mkt. 2.50 o.s.i (*0-515-06008-9*, Jove); 1979. mass mkt. 1.75 o.s.i (*0-515-05293-0*, Jove) Berkley Publishing Group.

—Night at the Vulcan. 1998. (Inspector Roderick Alleyn Mysteries Ser.). mass mkt. 5.99 (*0-312-96668-7*, St. Martin's Paperbacks) St. Martin's Pr.

—The Nursing Home Murder. 1976. reprint ed. lib. bdg. 22.95 (*0-88411-491-0*) Amereon, Ltd.

—The Nursing Home Murder. 240p. 1994. mass mkt. 4.50 o.p. (*0-425-14242-6*, Prime Crime); 1984. mass mkt. 3.95 o.s.i (*0-515-07851-4*, Jove) Berkley Publishing Group.

—The Nursing Home Murder. unabr. ed. 1992. (Inspector Alleyn Mystery Ser.). audio 49.95 (*0-7451-6145-6*, CAB 691) Chivers Audio Bks. GBR. *Dist:* BBC Audiobooks America.

—The Nursing Home Murder. 1999. 192p. mass mkt. 5.99 (*0-312-96999-6*, St. Martin's Paperbacks) St. Martin's Pr.

—Opening Night. unabr. ed. 2000. (Inspector Alleyn Mystery Ser.). audio 49.95 (*0-7451-6143-X*, CAB 530) Chivers Audio Bks. GBR. *Dist:* BBC Audiobooks America.

—Opening Night. l.t. ed. 1989. lib. bdg. 21.95 o.p. (*0-7451-7179-6*, Macmillan Reference USA) Gale Group.

—Overture to Death. 1976. reprint ed. lib. bdg. 24.95 (*0-88411-492-9*) Amereon, Ltd.

—Overture to Death. (Ngaio Marsh Mystery Ser.). 1984. 320p. mass mkt. 3.99 o.s.i (*0-515-07606-6*); 1982. mass mkt. 2.50 o.s.i (*0-515-06822-5*); 1981. mass mkt. 2.25 o.s.i (*0-515-06011-9*); 1978. mass mkt. 1.75 o.s.i (*0-515-04531-4*) Berkley Publishing Group. (Jove).

—Overture to Death. 1998. (Dead Letter Mysteries Ser.). 320p. mass mkt. 5.99 (*0-312-96425-0*, St. Martin's Paperbacks) St. Martin's Pr.

—Photo Finish. 1976. 21.95 (*0-8488-0580-1*) Amereon, Ltd.

—Photo Finish. (Ngaio Marsh Mystery Ser.). 1983. 224p. mass mkt. 3.99 o.s.i (*0-515-07505-1*); 1981. mass mkt. 2.50 o.s.i (*0-515-05995-1*) Berkley Publishing Group. (Jove).

—Photo Finish. l.t. ed. 1981. (General Ser.). lib. bdg. 14.95 o.p. (*0-8161-3192-9*, Macmillan Reference USA) Gale Group.

—Photo Finish. 2000. 224p. mass mkt. 5.99 (*0-312-97301-2*, St. Martin's Paperbacks) St. Martin's Pr.

—Scales of Justice. 1976. reprint ed. lib. bdg. 24.95 (*0-88411-493-7*) Amereon, Ltd.

—Scales of Justice. 1994. mass mkt. 4.99 o.p. (*0-425-14487-9*); 1984. 256p. mass mkt. 3.99 o.s.i (*0-515-07917-0*, Jove); 1982. mass mkt. 2.50 o.s.i (*0-515-06497-1*, Jove); 1980. mass mkt. 1.95 o.s.i (*0-515-05436-4*, Jove) Berkley Publishing Group.

—Scales of Justice, unabr. ed. 1996. audio 44.95 (*0-7861-0927-0*, 893480) Blackstone Audio Bks., Inc.

—Scales of Justice. 1999. (Inspector Roderick Alleyn Mysteries Ser.). 256p. mass mkt. 5.99 (*0-312-96671-7*, St. Martin's Paperbacks) St. Martin's Pr.

—Singing in the Shrouds. 1976. reprint ed. lib. bdg. 23.95 (*0-88411-494-5*) Amereon, Ltd.

—Singing in the Shrouds. l.t. ed. 1993. 22.95 o.p. (*0-7927-1780-5*); pap. 20.95 o.p. (*0-7927-1781-3*) BBC Audiobooks America.

—Singing in the Shrouds. 1984. 240p. mass mkt. 3.99 o.s.i (*0-515-07735-6*, Jove) Berkley Publishing Group.

—Spinsters in Jeopardy. 1976. reprint ed. lib. bdg. 23.95 (*0-88411-495-3*) Amereon, Ltd.

—Spinsters in Jeopardy. 1986. 256p. mass mkt. 3.99 o.p. (*0-515-08718-1*); 1981. mass mkt. 2.50 o.s.i (*0-515-06179-4*); 1980. mass mkt. 1.95 o.s.i (*0-515-05716-9*) Berkley Publishing Group. (Jove).

—Spinsters in Jeopardy. 1998. (Inspector Roderick Alleyn Mysteries Ser.). 256p. mass mkt. 5.99 (*0-312-96669-5*, St. Martin's Paperbacks) St. Martin's Pr.

—Surfeit of Lampreys. l.t. ed. 1983. 548p. 15.95 o.p. (*0-7089-0990-6*, Ulverscroft) Thorpe, F. A. Pubs. GBR. *Dist:* Ulverscroft Large Print Bks., Ltd.

—Tied up in Tinsel. 1983. 288p. mass mkt. 3.99 o.s.i (*0-515-07443-8*); 1982. mass mkt. 2.50 o.s.i (*0-515-06015-1*); 1981. mass mkt. 2.25 o.s.i (*0-515-06285-5*); 1978. mass mkt. 1.75 o.s.i (*0-515-04533-0*) Berkley Publishing Group. (Jove).

—Tied up in Tinsel. 1989. audio 53.95 o.s.i (*0-8161-9488-2*) Thorndike Pr.

—Tied Up in Tinsel. 1999. 288p. mass mkt. 5.99 (*0-312-97195-8*, St. Martin's Paperbacks) St. Martin's Pr.

—Tied up in Tinsel. 1976. reprint ed. lib. bdg. 23.95 (*0-88411-496-1*) Amereon, Ltd.

—Tied up in Tinsel. unabr. ed. 1994. audio 44.95 (*0-7861-0683-2*, 1470) Blackstone Audio Bks., Inc.

—Tied up in Tinsel. unabr. ed. 2000. (Inspector Alleyn Mystery Ser.). audio 49.95 (*0-7451-6146-4*, CAB 412) Chivers Audio Bks. GBR. *Dist:* BBC Audiobooks America.

—Vintage Murder. 1976. reprint ed. lib. bdg. 22.95 (*0-88411-497-X*) Amereon, Ltd.

—Vintage Murder. 1985. 272p. mass mkt. 3.99 o.s.i (*0-515-08084-5*); 1982. mass mkt. 2.50 o.s.i (*0-515-06012-7*); 1981. mass mkt. 2.25 o.s.i (*0-515-06164-6*); 1978. mass mkt. 1.75 o.s.i (*0-515-04534-9*) Berkley Publishing Group. (Jove).

—Vintage Murder, Set. unabr. ed. 2000. (Roderick Alleyn Mystery Ser.). audio 69.95 (*0-7540-0412-0*, CAB 1835) Chivers Audio Bks. GBR. *Dist:* BBC Audiobooks America.

—Vintage Murder. 1999. 256p. mass mkt. 5.99 (*0-312-97179-6*, St. Martin's Paperbacks) St. Martin's Pr.

—When in Rome. 1976. lib. bdg. 23.95 (*0-88411-498-8*) Amereon, Ltd.

—When in Rome. 1995. mass mkt. 4.99 o.p. (*0-425-14656-1*); 1983. 224p. mass mkt. 3.99 o.s.i (*0-515-07504-3*, Jove); 1981. mass mkt. 2.50 o.s.i (*0-515-06180-8*, Jove); 1980. mass mkt. 1.95 o.s.i (*0-515-05627-8*, Jove) Berkley Publishing Group.

—When in Rome, unabr. ed. 1998. audio 44.95 Blackstone Audio Bks., Inc.

—When in Rome. unabr. ed. 2000. (Inspector Alleyn Mystery Ser.). audio 49.95 (*0-7451-6147-2*, CAB 466) Chivers Audio Bks. GBR. *Dist:* BBC Audiobooks America.

—When in Rome. 1999. 242p. mass mkt. 5.99 (*0-312-97097-8*, St. Martin's Paperbacks) St. Martin's Pr.

—A Wreath for Rivera. 1994. 336p. mass mkt. 4.50 o.p. (*0-425-14247-7*); 1984. mass mkt. 3.50 o.s.i (*0-515-07501-9*, Jove); 1982. mass mkt. 2.50 o.s.i (*0-515-06016-X*, Jove) Berkley Publishing Group.

—Wreath for Rivera. 1998. (Wreath for Rivera Ser.: Vol. 1). 336p. mass mkt. 5.99 (*0-312-96606-7*, St. Martin's Paperbacks) St. Martin's Pr.

—A Wreath for Rivera. 1976. reprint ed. lib. bdg. 25.95 (*0-88411-499-6*) Amereon, Ltd.

—A Wreath for Rivera. unabr. ed. 1994. 30p. audio 49.95 (*0-7861-0829-0*, 1534) Blackstone Audio Bks., Inc.

—A Wreath for Rivera. 1976. (Crime Fiction Ser.). reprint ed. lib. bdg. 21.00 o.p. (*0-8240-2385-4*) Garland Publishing, Inc.

**ALLISON, BEN (FICTITIOUS CHARACTER)—FICTION**

Ebadi, M., ed. Oxidative Stress in Mitochondria Disorders of Aging: Mitochondria in Disease States. 2001. (Special Issue Ser.: Vol. 10, No. 3-4). (Illus.). 142p. pap. 39.25 (*3-8055-7236-0*) Karger, S. AG.

Fisher, Clay Henry Will. Apache Ransom. 1999. 151p. 19.00 (*0-7540-8067-6*, Gunsmoke) BBC Audiobooks America.

—The Crossing. 1980. 288p. pap. 1.75 o.p. (*0-553-14178-3*) Bantam Bks.

—Outcasts of Canyon Creek. 165p. 17.50 o.p. (*0-7451-4686-4*, Gunsmoke) BBC Audiobooks America.

—Outcasts of Canyon Creek. l.t. ed. 2000. (G. K. Hall Nightingale Ser.). 245p. pap. 20.95 (*0-7838-9175-X*); (*0-7540-4309-6*); (*0-7540-4310-X*) Gale Group. (Macmillan Reference USA).

—Return of the Tall Man. 1989. mass mkt. 2.95 o.s.i (*0-553-27987-4*) Bantam Bks.

—Return of the Tall Man. l.t. ed. 1998. (Paperback Ser.). 309p. pap. 23.95 (*0-7838-0367-2*) Thorndike Pr.

—The Tall Man. 1988. mass mkt. 2.95 o.s.i (*0-553-27644-1*) Bantam Bks.

**ALLISON, OWEN (FICTITIOUS CHARACTER)—FICTION**

Billheimer, John W. The Contrary Blues: An Owen Allison Mystery. 1999. 288p. mass mkt. 5.99 o.s.i (*0-440-23504-9*) Dell Publishing.

—The Contrary Blues: An Owen Allison Mystery. 1998. (Owen Allison Mysteries Ser.). 256p. 21.95 o.p. (*0-312-18565-0*, Saint Martin's Minotaur) St. Martin's Pr.

—Drybone Hollow: An Owen Allison Mystery. 2003. 320p. 24.95 (*0-312-29121-3*, Saint Martin's Minotaur) St. Martin's Pr.

—Highway Robbery. E-Book 5.99 (*0-312-27349-5*) St. Martin's Pr.

—Highway Robbery: An Owen Allison Mystery. 2000. (Owen Allison Mysteries Ser.). 290p. 24.95 (*0-312-25247-1*, Saint Martin's Minotaur) St. Martin's Pr.

—Land Butchers: Dismal Mountain: An Owen Allison Mystery. 2001. (Owen Allison Mysteries Ser.). 304p. 23.95 (*0-312-26981-1*, Saint Martin's Minotaur) St. Martin's Pr.

**ALLON, GABRIEL (FICTITIOUS CHARACTER)—FICTION**

Silva, Daniel. A Death in Vienna. 2004. 416p. 25.95 (*0-399-15143-5*) Putnam Publishing Group, The.

—The English Assassin. unabr. ed. 2002. audio compact disk 72.00 (*0-7366-8558-8*) Books on Tape, Inc.

—The English Assassin. l.t. ed. 2002. (Wheeler Large Print Book Ser.). 29.95 (*1-58724-185-4*, Wheeler Publishing, Inc.) Gale Group.

—The English Assassin. 2003. 416p. reprint ed. mass mkt. 7.99 (*0-451-20818-8*, Signet Bks.) NAL.

—The English Assassin. 2002. 400p. 25.95 o.s.i (*0-399-14851-5*) Putnam Publishing Group, The.

—The English Assassin. abr. ed. 2002. audio compact disk 29.95 (*0-553-71331-0*, RH Audio) Random Hse. Audio Publishing Group.

—The Kill Artist. E-Book 20.95 (*1-58945-641-6*) Adobe Systems, Inc.

—The Kill Artist. 2002. 448p. mass mkt. 6.99 o.s.i (*0-449-00212-8*, Fawcett) Ballantine Bks.

—The Kill Artist. 2004. 448p. mass mkt. 7.99 (*0-451-20933-8*, Signet Bks.) NAL.

—The Kill Artist. 2000. audio 25.95; 2001. audio compact disk 29.95 (*0-375-41668-4*); 2000. audio 25.95 (*0-375-41667-6*) Random Hse. Audio Publishing Group. (RH Audio).

—The Kill Artist. 2001. E-Book 20.95 (*0-375-50672-1*) Random Hse., Inc.

—The Kill Artist. unabr. ed. 2001. audio 71.00 (*0-7887-5983-3*, 96357K8) Recorded Bks., LLC.

**ALTFORD, MILLICENT (FICTITIOUS CHARACTER)—FICTION**

Thomas, Ross. Ah, Treachery! 1994. 288p. 21.95 o.s.i (*0-89296-452-9*) Mysterious Pr.

—Ah, Treachery!, unabr. ed. audio 51.00 (*0-7887-0260-2*, 94469E7) Recorded Bks., LLC.

—Ah, Treachery! 2004. 288p. pap. 13.95 (*0-312-32704-8*, Saint Martin's Griffin) St. Martin's Pr.

—Ah, Treachery! 1995. 272p. mass mkt. 5.99 o.s.i (*0-446-40031-9*) Warner Bks., Inc.

**ALTOBELLI, VINNIE (FICTITIOUS CHARACTER)—FICTION**

Bass, Milton. The Broken-Hearted Detective. Isaacson, Dana, ed. 1994. 256p. (Orig.). mass mkt. 4.99 (*0-671-74243-4*, Pocket) Simon & Schuster.

—The Half-Hearted Detective. Isaacson, Dana, ed. 1993. 256p. (Orig.). mass mkt. 4.99 (*0-671-74242-6*, Pocket) Simon & Schuster.

**ALVAREZ, DAVID (FICTITIOUS CHARACTER)—FICTION**

Schumacher, Aileen. Affirmative Reaction. 2000. (Tory Travers/David Alvarez Mysteries Ser.: Bk. 355). 256p. mass mkt. (*0-373-26355-4*, 1-26355-7, Worldwide Library) Harlequin Enterprises, Ltd.

—Affirmative Reaction. 1999. (Travers/Alvarez Mystery Ser.: No. 4). 310p. 24.95 o.p. (*1-885173-69-5*) Write Way Publishing.

—Engineered for Murder. 1996. 293p. 21.95 o.p. (*1-885173-17-2*); mass mkt. 5.95 o.p. (*1-885173-43-1*) Write Way Publishing.

—Framework for Death. 1998. (Tory Travers/David Alvarez Mysteries Ser.). 360p. 23.95 o.p. (*1-885173-55-5*) Write Way Publishing.

**ALVAREZ, ENRIQUE (FICTITIOUS CHARACTER)—FICTION**

Jeffries, Roderic. Almost Murder. l.t. ed. 1990. (Lythway Ser.). 280p. 20.95 o.p. (*0-7451-1198-X*, Macmillan Reference USA) Gale Group.

—Almost Murder. 1986. 192p. 12.95 o.p. (*0-312-02137-2*) St. Martin's Pr.

—The Ambiguity of Murder: An Inspector Alvarez Novel. 2001. 208p. 22.95 (*0-312-26968-4*, Saint Martin's Minotaur) St. Martin's Pr.

—The Ambiguity of Murder: An Inspector Alvarez Novel. l.t. ed. 2001. 297p. pap. 24.95 (*0-7862-3328-1*); 278p. (*0-7540-4505-6*); 278p. (*0-7540-4506-4*) Thorndike Pr.

—Arcadian Death. 1995. 192p. 19.95 o.p. (*0-312-13922-5*, Saint Martin's Minotaur) St. Martin's Pr.

—An Arcadian Death: An Inspector Alvarez Novel. l.t. ed. 1996. (Nightingale Ser.). 248p. pap. 17.95 o.p. (*0-7838-1698-7*, Macmillan Reference USA) Gale Group.

—An Artful Death: An Inspector Alvarez Mystery. 2000. 211p. (*0-00-232703-1*) HarperCollins Pubs.

—An Artful Death: An Inspector Alvarez Mystery. 2002. 224p. 22.95 (*0-312-30745-4*, Saint Martin's Minotaur) St. Martin's Pr.

—An Artistic Way to Go: An Inspector Alvarez Novel, Vol. 1. 1997. (Artistic Way to Go Ser.: Vol. 1). 192p. 20.95 (*0-312-15472-0*, Saint Martin's Minotaur) St. Martin's Pr.

—An Artistic Way to Go: An Inspector Alvarez Novel. l.t. ed. 1998. (Mystery Ser.). 288p. 26.95 (*0-7862-1545-3*) Thorndike Pr.

—Dead Clever. 1990. 2.99 o.p. (*0-517-05814-6*) Random Hse. Value Publishing.

—Dead Clever. 1989. 14.95 o.p. (*0-312-02899-7*) St. Martin's Pr.

—Deadly Petard. unabr. ed. 2000. audio 44.95 (*1-86042-650-6*, 26506) Soundings, Ltd. GBR. *Dist:* Ulverscroft Large Print Bks., Ltd.

—Deadly Petard. 1983. 160p. 10.95 o.p. (*0-312-18531-6*) St. Martin's Pr.

—Death Takes Time. l.t. ed. 1995. 256p. pap. 18.95 o.p. (*0-7838-1197-7*, Macmillan Reference USA) Gale Group.

—Death Takes Time. 1994. (Inspector Alvarez Mystery Ser.). 208p. 18.95 o.p. (*0-312-11260-2*, Saint Martin's Minotaur) St. Martin's Pr.

—Death Trick. l.t. ed. 1990. 256p. lib. bdg. 20.95 o.p. (*0-7451-1091-6*, Macmillan Reference USA) Gale Group.

—Death Trick. 1988. 192p. 14.95 o.p. (*0-312-02189-5*, Saint Martin's Minotaur) St. Martin's Pr.

—Definitely Deceased: An Inspector Alvarez Novel. 2002. 28.99 (*0-7278-7123-4*); 2001. 250p. 25.99 (*0-7278-5730-4*) Severn Hse. Pubs., Ltd.

—A Fatal Fleece. l.t. ed. 1994. (Dales Large Print Ser.). 340p. pap. 19.99 o.p. (*1-85389-489-3*) Dales Large Print Bks. GBR. *Dist:* Ulverscroft Large Print Bks., Ltd., Ulverscroft Large Print Canada, Ltd.

—A Fatal Fleece. 1992. 208p. 17.95 o.p. (*0-312-08192-8*, Saint Martin's Minotaur) St. Martin's Pr.

—An Intriguing Murder. 2002. 256p. 26.99 (*0-7278-5907-2*) Severn Hse. Pubs., Ltd.

—Layers of Deceit. l.t. ed. 1986. lib. bdg. 17.50 o.p. (*0-7451-0405-3*, Macmillan Reference USA) Gale Group.

—Layers of Deceit: An Inspector Alvarez Novel. 1985. 192p. 12.95 o.p. (*0-312-47571-3*) St. Martin's Pr.

—A Maze of Murders. 1997. (Inspector Alvarez Mystery Ser.). 176p. 19.95 (*0-312-18135-3*, Saint Martin's Minotaur) St. Martin's Pr.

—A Maze of Murders. l.t. ed. 1998. (General Ser.). 240p. pap. 23.95 (*0-7862-1381-7*) Thorndike Pr.

—Murder Begets Murder. 1979. 8.95 o.p. (*0-312-55288-2*) St. Martin's Pr.

—Murder Confounded. l.t. ed. 1994. 279p. lib. bdg. 16.95 (*0-8161-5902-5*, Macmillan Reference USA) Gale Group.

—Murder Confounded. 1993. 176p. 17.95 o.p. (*0-312-09877-4*, Saint Martin's Minotaur) St. Martin's Pr.

—Murder's Long Memory. 1992. 192p. 16.95 o.p. (*0-312-07039-X*, Saint Martin's Minotaur) St. Martin's Pr.

—Relatively Dangerous. l.t. ed. 1988. (Nightingale Ser.). 302p. 12.95 o.p. (*0-8161-4393-5*, Macmillan Reference USA) Gale Group.

—Relatively Dangerous. 1987. 192p. 13.95 o.p. (*0-312-01080-X*, Saint Martin's Minotaur) St. Martin's Pr.

—Seeing is Deceiving. 2002. (Inspector Alvarez Novel Ser.). 256p. 26.99 (*0-7278-5811-4*) Severn Hse. Pubs., Ltd.

—Three & One Make Five: An Inspector Alvarez Novel. 1984. 188p. 11.95 o.p. (*0-312-80240-4*) St. Martin's Pr.

—Too Clever by Half. l.t. ed. 1992. (Lythway Ser.). 272p. 20.50 (*0-7451-1418-0*, Macmillan Reference USA) Gale Group.

—Too Clever by Half. 1992. 1.99 o.p. (*0-517-08492-9*) Random Hse. Value Publishing.

—Too Clever by Half. 1990. 192p. 15.95 o.p. (*0-312-04987-0*, Saint Martin's Minotaur) St. Martin's Pr.

—Troubled Deaths. 1983. 208p. pap. 5.95 o.p. (*0-312-81995-1*, Saint Martin's Griffin); 1978. 7.95 o.p. (*0-312-81994-3*) St. Martin's Pr.

—Two-Faced Death. l.t. ed. 1995. (Dales Large Print Ser.). 332p. pap. o.p. (*1-85389-586-5*) Dales Large Print Bks. GBR. *Dist:* Ulverscroft Large Print Canada, Ltd.

—Unseemly End. 1982. 210p. 9.95 o.p. (*0-312-83372-5*) St. Martin's Pr.

**AMALFI, ANGIE (FICTITIOUS CHARACTER)—FICTION**

Pence, Joanne. Bell, Cook, & Candle: An Angie Amalfi Mystery. 2002. 336p. mass mkt. 6.99 (*0-06-103084-8*, Avon Bks.) Morrow/Avon.
—Cook in Time. 1999. (Angie Amalfi Mysteries Ser.). 352p. mass mkt. 6.99 (*0-06-104454-7*) HarperCollins Pubs.
—Cooking Most Deadly. 1996. (Angie Amalfi Mysteries Ser.). 256p. mass mkt. 6.50 (*0-06-104395-8*, HarperTorch) Morrow/Avon.
—Cooking up Trouble. 1995. (Angie Amalfi Mysteries Ser.). 320p. mass mkt. 6.99 (*0-06-108200-7*, HarperTorch) Morrow/Avon.
—Cook's Night Out. 1998. (Angie Amalfi Mysteries Ser.). 304p. mass mkt. 5.99 (*0-06-104396-6*) HarperCollins Pubs.
—Cooks Overboard. 1998. (Angie Amalfi Mysteries Ser.: Vol. 6). 304p. mass mkt. 5.99 (*0-06-104453-9*, HarperTorch) Morrow/Avon.
—Something's Cooking. 650th ed. 1993. (Angie Amalfi Mysteries Ser.). 336p. mass mkt. 6.50 (*0-06-108096-9*, HarperTorch) Morrow/Avon.
—To Catch a Cook. 2000. (Angie Amalfi Mysteries Ser.). 320p. mass mkt. 5.99 (*0-06-103085-6*, Avon Bks.) Morrow/Avon.
—Too Many Cooks. 1994. (Angie Amalfi Mysteries Ser.). 352p. mass mkt. 6.50 (*0-06-108199-X*, HarperTorch) Morrow/Avon.
—Two Cooks A-Killing. 2003. 352p. mass mkt. 6.99 (*0-06-009216-5*, Avon Bks.) Morrow/Avon.

**AMISS, ROBERT (FICTITIOUS CHARACTER)—FICTION**

Edwards, Ruth Dudley. The Anglo-Irish Murders. l.t. ed. 2001. 288p. pap. 24.95 (*0-7862-3322-2*) Thorndike Pr.
—Clubbed to Death. 1992. 208p. 17.95 o.p. (*0-312-08163-4*, Saint Martin's Minotaur) St. Martin's Pr.
—Corridors of Death. l.t. ed. 2001. 21.95 (*0-7540-8581-3*, Black Dagger); 1983. 335 p. (*0-89340-591-4*); 2000. audio 54.95 (*0-7540-0508-9*, CAB1931) BBC Audiobooks America.
—Corridors of Death. l.t. ed. 2000. (G. K. Hall Nightingale Ser.). 288p. pap. 21.95 (*0-7838-9261-6*); (*0-7540-4301-0*); (*0-7540-4302-9*) Gale Group. (Macmillan Reference USA).
—Corridors of Death. 1982. 196p. 10.95 o.p. (*0-312-17012-2*) St. Martin's Pr.
—The English School of Murder. 1990. 15.95 o.p. (*0-312-04311-2*, Saint Martin's Minotaur) St. Martin's Pr.
—Matricide at St. Martha's. 1995. 192p. 19.95 o.p. (*0-312-13122-4*, Saint Martin's Minotaur) St. Martin's Pr.
—Murder in a Cathedral. 1997. 317 p. (*0-7540-3117-9*) BBC Audiobooks America.
—Murder in a Cathedral. unabr. ed. 1998. audio 49.95 (*0-7540-0067-2*, CAB1490) Chivers Audio Bks. GBR. *Dist:* BBC Audiobooks America.
—Murder in a Cathedral. l.t. ed. 1997. 192p. 20.95 (*0-312-15597-2*, Saint Martin's Minotaur) St. Martin's Pr.
—Murder in a Cathedral. l.t. ed. 1997. (Mystery Ser.). 326p. lib. bdg. 25.95 (*0-7838-8284-X*) Thorndike Pr.
—Publish & Be Murdered. unabr. ed. 1999. audio 54.95 (*0-7540-0238-1*, CAB1661) Chivers Audio Bks. GBR. *Dist:* BBC Audiobooks America.
—Publish & Be Murdered. l.t. unabr. ed. 2000. 282p. 25.95 (*0-7531-5975-9*, 159759); 1999. 304p. pap. 21.99 (*0-7531-5991-0*, 159910) ISIS Large Print Bks. GBR. *Dist:* ISIS Publishing, Ulverscroft Large Print Bks., Ltd., Ulverscroft Large Print Canada, Ltd.
—Publish & Be Murdered. 1999. 217p. pap. 12.95 (*1-890208-13-2*) Poisoned Pen Pr.
—The Saint Valentine's Day Murders. 1985. 192p. 12.95 o.p. (*0-312-69732-5*) St. Martin's Pr.
—The School of English Murder. l.t. ed. 1992. (Mystery Ser.). 432p. 29.99 o.p. (*0-7089-2765-3*, Ulverscroft) Thorpe, F. A. Pubs. GBR. *Dist:* Ulverscroft Large Print Bks., Ltd., Ulverscroft Large Print Canada, Ltd.
—Ten Lords A-Leaping. Wallis, Bill, ed. unabr. ed. 1999. audio 54.95 (*0-7540-0389-2*, CAB1812) Chivers Audio Bks. GBR. *Dist:* BBC Audiobooks America.
—Ten Lords A-Leaping. 1996. 272p. 21.95 o.p. (*0-312-14430-X*, Saint Martin's Minotaur) St. Martin's Pr.
—Ten Lords A-Leaping. l.t. ed. 1997. (Ulverscroft Large Print Ser.). 432p. 29.99 o.p. (*0-7089-3718-7*, Ulverscroft) Thorpe, F. A. Pubs. GBR. *Dist:* Ulverscroft Large Print Bks., Ltd., Ulverscroft Large Print Canada, Ltd.

**AMNELL, KAHLAN (FICTITIOUS CHARACTER)—FICTION**

Goodkind, Terry. Blood of the Fold. unabr. ed. 1999. (Sword of Truth Ser.: Bk. 3). audio 34.95 o.p. (*1-56740-415-4*, 1626, Bookcassette); audio 137.25 (*1-56740-638-6*, 1627, Unabridged Library Editions) Brilliance Audio.
—Blood of the Fold. (Sword of Truth Ser.: Vol. 3). 1997. 623p. mass mkt. 7.99 (*0-8125-5147-8*); 1996. 464p. 29.95 (*0-312-89052-4*) Doherty, Tom Assocs., LLC. (Tor Bks.).
—Blood of the Fold. abr. ed. 1998. (Sword of Truth Ser.: Bk. 3). audio 16.95 (*1-55935-238-8*) Soundelux Audio Publishing.
—Faith of the Fallen. (Sword of Truth Ser.: Bk. 6). 2000. 512p. 27.95 (*0-312-86786-7*, NHC 0167); 2000. 512p. pap. 200.00 (*0-312-87521-5*); 2001. 800p. reprint ed. mass mkt. 7.99 (*0-8125-7639-X*) Doherty, Tom Assocs., LLC. (Tor Bks.).
—Soul of the Fire. unabr. ed. (Sword of Truth Ser.: Bk. 5). 2002. audio 39.95 (*1-59086-297-X*, 3883, Brilliance Audio Unabridged); 1999. 24p. audio 137.25 (*1-56740-632-7*, 1585, Unabridged Library Editions); 1999. audio 34.95 o.p. (*1-56740-403-0*, 1584, Bookcassette) Brilliance Audio.
—Soul of the Fire. (Sword of Truth Ser.: Bk. 5). 2000. 800p. mass mkt. 7.99 (*0-8125-5149-4*); 1999. 528p. 27.95 (*0-312-89054-0*) Doherty, Tom Assocs., LLC. (Tor Bks.).
—Soul of the Fire. unabr. ed. 2003. (Sword of Truth Ser.). audio 29.99 (*1-59335-118-6*, 30214) Soulmate Audio Bks., Inc.
—Stone of Tears. (Sword of Truth Ser.). unabr. ed. 2004. audio 39.95 (*1-59355-555-5*, 5180, Brilliance Audio Unabridged); unabr. ed. 2004. audio 217.25 (*1-59355-556-3*, 5181, Brilliance Audio Unabridged Lib Ed); unabr. ed. 1998. audio 217.25 (*1-56740-556-8*, 1060, Unabridged Library Editions); 2nd unabr. ed. 1998. audio 44.95 (*1-56100-777-3*, 279, Bookcassette) Brilliance Audio.
—Stone of Tears. (Sword of Truth Ser.: Bk. 2). 1996. 982p. mass mkt. 7.99 (*0-8125-4809-4*); 4th ed. 1995. (Illus.). 703p. 27.95 (*0-312-85706-3*, CPHC0706) Doherty, Tom Assocs., LLC. (Tor Bks.).
—The Sword of Truth, 3 vols. 1998. (Sword of Truth Ser.). 23.97 o.s.i (*0-8125-7560-1*, Forge Bks.) Doherty, Tom Assocs., LLC.
—Temple of the Winds. unabr. ed. 1997. (Sword of Truth Ser.: Bk. 4). audio 169.25 (*1-56740-555-X*, 1070, Unabridged Library Editions); audio 35.95 o.p. (*1-56100-776-5*, 287, Bookcassette) Brilliance Audio.
—Temple of the Winds. (Sword of Truth Ser.: Bk. 4). 1999. 0.01 o.p. (*0-312-86406-X*); 1998. 832p. mass mkt. 7.99 (*0-8125-5148-6*); 1997. 416p. 29.95 (*0-312-89053-2*) Doherty, Tom Assocs., LLC. (Tor Bks.).
—Wizard's First Rule. abr. ed. (Sword of Truth Ser.: Bk. 1). 2003. audio compact disk 14.99 (*1-59086-529-4*, 4120, Brilliance Audio Unabridged); 2003. audio compact disk 62.25 (*1-59086-569-3*, 4159, Brilliance Audio Unabridged); 2003. audio 145.25 (*1-59355-498-2*, 5106, Brilliance Audio Unabridged Lib Ed); 2003. audio 39.95 (*1-59355-105-3*, 4711, Brilliance Audio Unabridged); 1994. audio 35.95 (*1-56100-598-3*, 321, Bookcassette); 1994. audio 169.25 (*1-56100-223-2*, 1103, Unabridged Library Editions); Set. 1994. audio 17.00 o.p. (*1-56100-389-1*, 1410, Nova Audio Bks.) Brilliance Audio.
—Wizard's First Rule. (Sword of Truth Ser.: Bk. 1). 2003. 848p. mass mkt. 2.99 o.s.i (*0-7653-4652-4*); 1997. 836p. (J). mass mkt. 7.99 (*0-8125-4805-1*); 1994. (Illus.). 573p. 29.95 (*0-312-85705-5*) Doherty, Tom Assocs., LLC. (Tor Bks.).
—Wizard's First Rule, abr. ed. 2000. (Sword of Truth Ser.: Bk. 1). audio 7.95 (*1-57815-131-7*, 1090, Media Bks. Audio Publishing) Media Bks., L. L. C.
—Wizard's First Rule. unabr. ed. 2003. (Sword of Truth Ser.). audio 29.99 (*1-59335-253-0*, 30351) Soulmate Audio Bks., Inc.

**ANDERSON, BOBBI (FICTITIOUS CHARACTER)—FICTION**

King, Stephen. The Tommyknockers. 752p. 1993. mass mkt. 6.99 o.p. (*0-451-17842-4*, Signet Bks.); 1988. reprint ed. mass mkt. 7.99 (*0-451-15660-9*) NAL.
—The Tommyknockers. 19.95 (*0-399-13699-1*) Penguin Group (USA) Inc.
—The Tommyknockers. 1987. 544p. 19.95 o.p. (*0-399-13314-3*, G. P. Putnam's Sons) Penguin Putnam Bks. for Young Readers.
—The Tommyknockers. 2nd ed. 1999. (Nevedomoe, Neobiasnimoe, Neveroitnoe Ser.: Vol. 102). (SPA., Illus.). 968p. (*84-01-47465-5*) Plaza & Janés Editories, S.A.
—The Tommyknockers. 1992. (SPA.). 704p. 15.50 (*84-01-49998-4*) Plaza & Janés Editories, S.A. ESP. *Dist:* Distribooks, Inc.
—The Tommyknockers. 1987. 14.04 (*0-606-04113-3*) Turtleback Bks.

**ANDERSON, JOHN (FICTITIOUS CHARACTER)—FICTION**

Birch, Peter. To Die For. 1997. (Crime & Passion Ser.). (Illus.). 241p. mass mkt. 5.95 (*0-7535-0034-5*) Virgin Bks. GBR. *Dist:* London Bridge.
Hastings, Juliet. Deadly Affairs. 1997. (Crime & Passion Ser.). 256p. mass mkt. 5.95 (*0-7535-0029-9*) Virgin Bks. GBR. *Dist:* London Bridge.
—Intimate Enemies. 1997. (Crime & Passion Ser.). 243p. mass mkt. 5.95 (*0-7535-0155-4*) Virgin Bks. GBR. *Dist:* London Bridge.
—Waiting Game. 1997. (Crime & Passion Ser.). 255p. mass mkt. 5.95 (*0-7535-0109-0*) Virgin Bks. GBR. *Dist:* London Bridge.

**ANDERSON, MALI (FICTITIOUS CHARACTER)—FICTION**

Edwards, Grace F. Do or Die: A Mali Anderson Mystery. 2000. (Mali Anderson Mystery Ser.). 272p. 22.95 o.s.i (*0-385-49248-0*) Doubleday Publishing.
—If I Should Die. 1998. (Mali Anderson Mystery Ser.). 320p. reprint ed. mass mkt. 6.50 (*0-553-57631-3*) Bantam Bks.
—If I Should Die. 1997. 272p. 21.95 o.s.i (*0-385-48523-9*) Doubleday Publishing.
—No Time to Die. 2000. (Mali Anderson Mystery Ser.). 240p. mass mkt. 5.99 (*0-553-57956-8*) Bantam Bks.
—No Time to Die. 1999. 272p. 22.95 o.s.i (*0-385-49247-2*) Doubleday Publishing.
—A Toast Before Dying. 1999. 304p. mass mkt. 5.99 (*0-553-57953-3*) Bantam Bks.

**ANDERSON, MARION (FICTITIOUS CHARACTER)—FICTION**

Weill, Gus. Flesh. Isaacson, Dana, ed. 1993. 224p. reprint ed. mass mkt. 4.99 (*0-671-70434-6*, Pocket) Simon & Schuster.
—Flesh. 1990. 15.95 o.p. (*0-312-04316-3*) St. Martin's Pr.

**ANDERSON, SHIFTY LOU (FICTITIOUS CHARACTER)—FICTION**

Murray, William. A Fine Italian Hand: A Shifty Lou Anderson Mystery. 1996. 256p. 21.00 o.p. (*0-87131-797-4*) Evans, M. & Co., Inc.
—The Getaway Blues. 1991. 288p. mass mkt. 4.99 o.s.i (*0-553-29103-3*) Bantam Bks.
—The Hard Knocker's Luck. 1985. 276p. 14.95 o.p. (*0-670-80621-8*) Viking Penguin.
—I'm Getting Killed Right Here. 1992. 304p. mass mkt. 4.99 o.s.i (*0-553-29638-8*) Bantam Bks.
—The King of the Nightcap. 1990. 336p. mass mkt. 4.50 o.s.i (*0-553-28426-6*) Bantam Bks.
—Now You See Her, Now You Don't. 1994. 244p. 22.00 o.p. (*0-8050-2971-0*) Holt, Henry & Co.
—Tip on a Dead Crab. (Crime Monthly Ser.). 1985. 230p. pap. 3.95 o.p. (*0-14-007662-X*, Penguin Bks.); 1984. 13.95 o.p. (*0-670-71620-0*) Viking Penguin.
—We're off to See the Killer. 1993. 18.50 o.s.i (*0-385-47035-5*) Doubleday Publishing.
—When the Fat Man Sings. 1990. 56p. mass mkt. 2.25 o.s.i (*0-553-18511-X*); 1988. mass mkt. 3.95 o.s.i (*0-553-27305-1*) Bantam Bks.

**ANDERSSON, MARGIT (FICTITIOUS CHARACTER)—FICTION**

Nunnally, Tiina. Fate of Ravens: A Margit Andersson Mystery. 1998. (Suspense Ser.: Vol. 2). 220p. pap. 12.00 (*0-940242-80-X*) Fjord Pr.
—Runemaker. 1996. (Suspense Ser.: No. 1). 213p. (Orig.). pap. 12.00 (*0-940242-77-X*) Fjord Pr.

**ANDREWS, ARCHIE (FICTITIOUS CHARACTER)—FICTION**

Best of Betty & Veronica. 1985. 16.95 o.p. (*0-399-12667-8*); pap. 12.95 o.p. (*0-399-50557-1*) Putnam Publishing Group, The.
Phillips, Charles. Archie: His First Fifty Years. (Illus.). 128p. 1993. 15.98 (*0-89660-035-1*, Artabras); 1991. 15.98 o.p. (*1-55859-206-7*) Abbeville Pr., Inc.

**ANDREWS, CAMERON (FICTITIOUS CHARACTER)—FICTION**

D'Amuk, Nanisi B. Outside In: A Cameron Andrews Mystery. 1996. 200p. (Orig.). pap. 10.95 (*0-934678-75-8*) New Victoria Pubs., Inc.

**ANDREWS, JASON (FICTITIOUS CHARACTER)—FICTION**

Chase, Jack. Fatal Analysis. 1996. 368p. mass mkt. 5.99 o.s.i (*0-451-18764-4*, Signet Bks.) NAL.

**ANGSTROM, HARRY (FICTITIOUS CHARACTER)—FICTION**

Updike, John. Licks of Love: Short Stories & a Sequel, "Rabbit Remembered" 2001. 368p. reprint ed. pap. 14.00 (*0-345-44201-6*, Ballantine Bks.) Ballantine Bks.
—Licks of Love: Short Stories & a Sequel, "Rabbit Remembered" 2000. 368p. 25.00 (*0-375-41113-5*) Knopf, Alfred A. Inc.
—Rabbit at Rest. 1996. 480p. pap. 13.95 (*0-449-91194-2*, Fawcett); 1991. 448p. mass mkt. 5.99 o.s.i (*0-449-21962-3*, Fawcett); 1991. mass mkt. 5.95 o.s.i (*0-449-22062-1*) Ballantine Bks.
—Rabbit at Rest. unabr. collector's ed. 1990. (Rabbit Quartet). audio 104.00 (*0-7366-1867-8*, 2698) Books on Tape, Inc.
—Rabbit at Rest. 1990. 200.00 o.s.i (*0-394-58952-1*); 512p. 30.00 (*0-394-58815-0*) Knopf, Alfred A. Inc.
—Rabbit at Rest. abr. ed. 1990. audio 15.95 (*0-394-58811-8*, 391434, RH Audio) Random Hse. Audio Publishing Group.
—Rabbit at Rest. 1992. 4.99 o.p. (*0-517-08095-8*); 4.99 o.p. (*0-517-09185-2*) Random Hse. Value Publishing.
—Rabbit Is Rich. 1996. 432p. pap. 14.00 (*0-449-91182-9*, Fawcett); 1992. mass mkt. 5.99 o.p. (*0-449-44945-9*, Fawcett); 1982. 448p. mass mkt. 5.99 o.s.i (*0-449-24548-9*, Fawcett); 1982. mass mkt. 3.25 o.s.i (*0-449-20017-5*) Ballantine Bks.
—Rabbit Is Rich. unabr. collector's ed. 1983. (Rabbit Quartet). audio 96.00 (*0-7366-0738-2*, 1695) Books on Tape, Inc.
—Rabbit Is Rich. 1981. 480p. 30.00 (*0-394-52087-4*); 467p. 40.00 o.p. (*0-394-52047-5*) Knopf, Alfred A. Inc.
—Rabbit Is Rich. 1982. 12.04 (*0-606-16209-7*) Turtleback Bks.
—Rabbit Redux. 1996. 368p. pap. 14.00 (*0-449-91193-4*); 1985. 352p. mass mkt. 5.99 o.s.i (*0-449-20934-2*); 1982. mass mkt. 3.50 o.p. (*0-449-20243-7*); 1982. mass mkt. 3.50 o.p. (*0-449-24087-8*) Ballantine Bks. (Fawcett).
—Rabbit Redux. unabr. collector's ed. 1981. (Rabbit Quartet). audio 80.00 (*0-7366-0293-3*, 1281) Books on Tape, Inc.
—Rabbit Redux. 1971. 416p. 30.00 (*0-394-47273-X*) Knopf, Alfred A. Inc.
—Rabbit, Run. 1996. 272p. pap. 14.95 (*0-449-91165-9*); 1992. mass mkt. 5.99 o.p. (*0-449-44943-2*); 1983. 288p. mass mkt. 5.99 o.s.i (*0-449-20506-1*) Ballantine Bks. (Fawcett).
—Rabbit, Run. unabr. collector's ed. 1980. (Rabbit Quartet). audio 64.00 (*0-7366-0292-5*, 1280) Books on Tape, Inc.
—Rabbit, Run. 1960. 320p. 27.50 (*0-394-44206-7*) Knopf, Alfred A. Inc.
—Rabbit, Run. l.t. ed. 1996. 448p. lib. bdg. 25.95 (*0-7838-1823-8*) Thorndike Pr.
—Rabbit, Run. 1996. 20.05 (*0-606-20873-9*) Turtleback Bks.

**ANHALT, MICI (FICTITIOUS CHARACTER)—FICTION**

O'Donnell, Lillian. Aftershock. 1982. mass mkt. 2.50 o.s.i (*0-449-24479-2*, Fawcett) Ballantine Bks.
—Aftershock. 1977. 7.95 o.p. (*0-399-11951-5*) Putnam Publishing Group, The.
—Falling Star. 1987. 224p. mass mkt. 2.95 o.s.i (*0-449-21395-1*, Fawcett); 1980. mass mkt. 1.95 o.s.i (*0-449-24347-8*) Ballantine Bks.
—Falling Star. 1979. 9.95 o.p. (*0-399-12407-1*) Putnam Publishing Group, The.
—Wicked Designs. 1987. 224p. mass mkt. 2.95 o.s.i (*0-449-21532-6*, Fawcett); 1981. mass mkt. 2.25 o.s.i (*0-449-24437-7*) Ballantine Bks.
—Wicked Designs. 1980. 228p. 9.95 o.p. (*0-399-12523-X*) Putnam Publishing Group, The.

**ANTERO, AMALRIC (FICTITIOUS CHARACTER)—FICTION**

Cole, Alan & Bunch, Chris. The Far Kingdoms: A Mythic Tale. 1994. 448p. mass mkt. 5.99 o.s.i (*0-345-38056-8*) Ballantine Bks.
Cole, Allan. The Warrior Returns: An Epic Fantasy of the Anteros. 1997. (Anteros Ser.). 440p. mass mkt. 6.99 o.s.i (*0-345-41312-1*, Del Rey) Ballantine Bks.
Cole, Allan & Bunch, Chris. The Far Kingdoms: A Mythic Tale. 1993. 432p. 20.00 o.p. (*0-345-38055-X*, Del Rey) Ballantine Bks.
—Kingdoms of the Night. 1996. mass mkt. 5.99 o.s.i (*0-345-38732-5*, Del Rey); 1995. 528p. 23.00 o.s.i (*0-345-38731-7*) Ballantine Bks.
—The Warrior's Tale. 1995. (Wizards of Fantasy Promotion Ser.). mass mkt. 5.99 o.s.i (*0-345-38734-1*, Del Rey) Ballantine Bks.

**ANTHEM, JOHNNY (FICTITIOUS CHARACTER)—FICTION**

Reno, James. Creed's Law. 1988. (Texas Anthem Ser.: No. 5). mass mkt. 3.50 o.p. (*0-451-15664-1*, Signet Bks.) NAL.
—Rogue River. 1988. (Texas Anthem Ser.: No. 4). 224p. mass mkt. 2.95 o.p. (*0-451-15129-1*, Signet Bks.) NAL.
—Shadow Walker. 1987. (Texas Anthem Ser.: No. 3). 224p. mass mkt. 2.95 o.p. (*0-451-14921-1*, Signet Bks.) NAL.
—Texas Anthem. 1986. (Texas Anthem Ser.: No. 1). 352p. mass mkt. 3.50 o.p. (*0-451-14377-9*, Signet Bks.) NAL.
—Texas Born. 1986. (Texas Anthem Ser.: No. 2). 352p. mass mkt. 3.50 o.p. (*0-451-14560-7*, Signet Bks.) NAL.

**ANTILLES, WEDGE (FICTITIOUS CHARACTER)—FICTION**

Allston, Aaron. Iron Fist. 1998. (Star Wars: Bk. 6). 336p. mass mkt. 6.99 (*0-553-57897-9*, Spectra) Bantam Bks.

—Iron Fist. abr. ed. 1998. (Star Wars Ser.: Bk. 6). audio 16.99 (*0-553-52497-6*, RH Audio) Random Hse. Audio Publishing Group.

—Solo Command. 1999. (Star Wars: Bk. 7). 352p. mass mkt. 6.99 (*0-553-57900-2*) Bantam Bks.

—Solo Command, X-Wing 7. abr. ed. 1999. (Star Wars Ser.: Bk. 7). audio 18.00 (*0-553-52539-5*, RH Audio) Random Hse. Audio Publishing Group.

—Starfighters of Adumar. 1999. (Star Wars: Bk. 9). 320p. mass mkt. 6.99 (*0-553-57418-3*) Bantam Bks.

—Wraith Squadron. 1998. (Star Wars: Bk. 5). 432p. mass mkt. 6.99 (*0-553-57894-4*, Spectra) Bantam Bks.

—Wraith Squadron: X-Wings 5. abr. ed. 1998. (Star Wars Ser.: Bk. 5). audio 16.99 (*0-553-47888-5*, RH Audio) Random Hse. Audio Publishing Group.

Dark Horse Comics Staff, et al. Shadows of the Empire. 1997. (Star Wars Ser.). (Illus.). 160p. (YA). (gr. 7 up). pap. 17.95 (*1-56971-183-6*) Dark Horse Comics.

Golden, Christopher. Shadows of the Empire. 1996. (Star Wars Ser.). (Illus.). 176p. (J). (gr. 4-7). pap. text 4.50 o.s.i (*0-440-41303-6*) Dell Publishing.

—Shadows of the Empire: A Junior Novelization. 1996. (Star Wars Ser.). 10.55 (*0-606-11835-7*) Turtleback Bks.

Perry, Steve. Shadows of the Empire. 1997. (Star Wars Ser.). 416p. (gr. 5 up). mass mkt. 6.99 (*0-553-57413-2*, Spectra) Bantam Bks.

—Shadows of the Empire. abr. ed. 1996. (Star Wars Ser.). audio 16.99 (*0-553-47438-3*, 393956, RH Audio) Random Hse. Audio Publishing Group.

—Shadows of the Empire. 1996. (Star Wars Ser.). 12.04 (*0-606-11895-0*) Turtleback Bks.

Perry, Steve, et al. Evolution: Shadows of the Empire. 2000. (Star Wars Ser.). (Illus.). 120p. (YA). (gr. 7 up). pap. 14.95 (*1-56971-441-X*) Dark Horse Comics.

Stackpole, Michael A. The Bacta War. 1997. (Star Wars: Bk. 4). 384p. mass mkt. 6.99 (*0-553-56804-3*, Spectra) Bantam Bks.

—The Bacta War. abr. ed. 1997. (Star Wars Ser.: Bk. 4). audio 16.99 (*0-553-47425-1*, RH Audio) Random Hse. Audio Publishing Group.

—The Bacta War. 1997. (Star Wars: No. 4). (J). (gr. 3-7). 12.04 (*0-606-11900-0*) Turtleback Bks.

—Isard's Revenge. 1999. (Star Wars: Bk. 8). (Illus.). 352p. mass mkt. 6.99 (*0-553-57903-7*) Bantam Bks.

—Isard's Revenge. abr. ed. 1999. (Star Wars Ser.: Bk. 8). audio 18.00 (*0-553-52546-8*, RH Audio) Random Hse. Audio Publishing Group.

—The Kryptos Trap. 1996. (Star Wars: Bk. 3). 384p. mass mkt. 6.99 (*0-553-56803-5*, Spectra) Bantam Bks.

—The Krytos Trap. abr. ed. 1996. (Star Wars Ser.: Bk. 3). audio 16.99 o.s.i (*0-553-47420-0*, 394343, RH Audio) Random Hse. Audio Publishing Group.

—The Krytos Trap. 1996. (Star Wars: Bk. 3). 12.04 (*0-606-11899-3*) Turtleback Bks.

—Rogue Squadron. 1996. (Star Wars: Bk. 1). 416p. mass mkt. 6.99 (*0-553-56801-9*, Spectra) Bantam Bks.

—Rogue Squadron. abr. ed. 1996. (Star Wars Ser.: Bk. 1). audio 16.99 (*0-553-47418-9*, 394341, RH Audio) Random Hse. Audio Publishing Group.

—Rogue Squadron. 1996. (Star Wars: Bk. 1). 12.04 (*0-606-11897-7*) Turtleback Bks.

—Wedge's Gamble. 1996. (Star Wars: Bk. 2). 384p. mass mkt. 6.99 (*0-553-56802-7*, Spectra) Bantam Bks.

—Wedge's Gamble. abr. ed. 1996. (Star Wars Ser.: Bk. 2). audio 16.99 (*0-553-47419-7*, 394342, RH Audio) Random Hse. Audio Publishing Group.

—Wedge's Gamble. 1996. (Star Wars: Bk. 2). 12.04 (*0-606-11898-5*) Turtleback Bks.

Stackpole, Michael A., et al. Battleground: Tatooine X-Wing Rogue Squadron. 1998. (Star Wars Ser.: Bk. 2). (Illus.). 112p. (YA). (gr. 7 up). pap. 12.95 (*1-56971-276-X*) Dark Horse Comics.

—Blood & Honor. 1999. (Star Wars Ser.: Bk. 6). 96p. (YA). (gr. 5 up). pap. 12.95 (*1-56971-387-1*) Dark Horse Comics.

—In the Empire's Service: X-Wing Rogue Squadron. 1999. (Star Wars Ser.: Bk. 5). (Illus.). 96p. (YA). (gr. 7 up). pap. 12.95 (*1-56971-383-9*) Dark Horse Comics.

—Masquerade. 2000. (Star Wars Ser.: Bk. 7). 96p. (YA). (gr. 7 up). pap. 12.95 (*1-56971-487-8*) Dark Horse Comics.

—The Phantom Affair: X-Wing Rogue Squadron. 1997. (Star Wars Ser.: No. 1). 112p. (YA). (gr. 7 up). pap. 12.95 (*1-56971-251-4*) Dark Horse Comics.

—Star Wars X-Wing Rogue Squadron: Requiem for a Rogue. 1999. (Star Wars Ser.: Bk. 4). 112p. (YA). (gr. 5 up). pap. 12.95 (*1-56971-331-6*) Dark Horse Comics.

—Star Wars X-Wing Rogue Squadron: The Warrior Princess. 1998. (Star Wars Ser.: Bk. 3). 96p. (YA). (gr. 5 up). pap. 12.95 (*1-56971-330-8*) Dark Horse Comics.

**ANTON, ALEC (FICTITIOUS CHARACTER)—FICTION**

Henry, Diane & Horrock, Nicholas. Blood Red, Snow White. 1992. 19.95 o.p. (*0-316-35752-9*) Little Brown & Co.

—Blood Red, Snow White. Peters, Sally, ed. 1993. 352p. mass mkt. 5.50 (*0-671-79551-1*, Pocket) Simon & Schuster.

**ANTONELLI, JOSEPH (FICTITIOUS CHARACTER)—FICTION**

Buffa, D. W. The Defense. 1998. 320p. mass mkt. 6.99 (*0-449-00399-X*, Fawcett) Ballantine Bks.

—The Defense. abr. ed. 1998. audio 7.99 o.s.i (*1-56740-262-3*, 1562, Paperback Nova Audio Bks.); 1997. audio 17.95 o.p. (*1-56740-751-X*, 465, Nova Audio Bks.); 1997. audio 23.95 o.p. (*1-56100-772-2*, 88, Bookcassette); 1997. 12p. audio 73.25 o.p. (*1-56740-551-7*, 860, Unabridged Library Editions) Brilliance Audio.

—The Defense. 1997. 320p. 20.00 o.s.i (*0-8050-5307-7*) Holt, Henry & Co.

—The Judgment. l.t. ed. 2001. 658p. 29.95 (*0-7862-3330-3*) Thorndike Pr.

—The Judgment. abr. ed. 2001. audio 24.98 (*1-58621-064-5*); audio 29.98 (*1-58621-102-1*); audio 44.98 (*1-58621-065-3*) Time Warner AudioBooks.

—The Judgment. 2001. 432p. 24.95 o.p. (*0-446-52737-8*); E-Book 14.95 (*0-7595-9364-7*); E-Book 14.95 (*0-7595-8335-8*); E-Book 14.95 (*0-7595-6329-2*); E-Book 14.95 (*0-7595-0330-3*); E-Book 14.95 (*0-7595-4331-3*) Warner Bks., Inc.

—The Prosecution: A Legal Thriller. 2001. 336p. reprint ed. mass mkt. 6.99 (*0-449-00690-5*, Ballantine Bks.) Ballantine Bks.

—The Prosecution: A Legal Thriller. unabr. ed. 1999. audio 29.99 (*0-88646-534-6*, DHA-6534) Durkin Hayes Publishing Ltd.

—The Prosecution: A Legal Thriller. 1999. 274p. 25.00 o.s.i (*0-8050-6107-X*) Holt, Henry & Co.

—The Star Witness: A Joseph Antonelli Novel. abr. ed. 2004. (Joseph Antonelli Ser.). audio 12.99 (*1-59086-795-5*, 4392, Brilliance Audio Paperback Audiobooks); 2003. (Joseph Antonelli Ser.). audio 24.95 (*1-59086-794-7*, 4391); 2003. (The Joseph Antonelli Series: Vol. 5). audio 34.95 (*1-59086-792-0*, 4389, Brilliance Audio Unabridged); 2003. (The Joseph Antonelli Series: Vol. 5). audio 97.25 (*1-59086-793-9*, 4390, Unabridged Library Editions) Brilliance Audio.

—The Star Witness: A Joseph Antonelli Novel. 2004. 432p. mass mkt. 6.99 (*0-451-41133-1*, Onyx) NAL.

—The Star Witness: A Joseph Antonelli Novel. 2003. 400p. 24.95 (*0-399-15034-X*, Putnam & Grosset) Putnam Publishing Group, The.

—The Star Witness: A Joseph Antonelli Novel. unabr. ed. 2003. (Joseph Antonelli Ser.). audio 19.99 (*1-59335-170-4*, 30266) Soulmate Audio Bks., Inc.

**APPLEBAUM, JULIET (FICTITIOUS CHARACTER)—FICTION**

Waldman, Ayelet. The Big Nap: A Mommy Track Mystery. 240p. 2001. 21.95 o.s.i (*0-425-17949-4*); 2002. reprint ed. mass mkt. 6.99 (*0-425-18452-8*) Berkley Publishing Group. (Prime Crime).

—Nursery Crimes: A Mommy Track Mystery. (Mommy-Track Mysteries Ser.). 2000. 215p. 21.95 o.s.i (*0-425-17469-7*); 2001. 240p. reprint ed. mass mkt. 6.99 (*0-425-18000-X*, Prime Crime) Berkley Publishing Group.

—A Playdate with Death: A Mommy Track Mystery. 2002. 240p. 22.95 (*0-425-18473-0*, Prime Crime) Berkley Publishing Group.

**APPLEBY, JOHN, SIR (FICTITIOUS CHARACTER)—FICTION**

Innes, Michael. The Ampersand Papers. 2000. 174p. pap. 9.95 (*1-84232-871-9*) House of Stratus, Inc. GBR. *Dist:* Midpoint Trade Bks., Inc.

—The Ampersand Papers. 1980. (Crime Monthly Ser.). 192p. pap. 3.95 o.p. (*0-14-005163-5*, Penguin Bks.) Viking Penguin.

—Appleby & Honeybath. l.t. ed. 2003. (Dales Large Print Ser.). 304p. pap. 21.99 (*1-84262-221-8*) Dales Large Print Bks. GBR. *Dist:* Ulverscroft Large Print Bks., Ltd., Ulverscroft Large Print Canada, Ltd.

—Appleby & Honeybath. 2000. 176p. pap. 9.95 (*1-84232-718-6*) House of Stratus, Inc. GBR. *Dist:* Midpoint Trade Bks., Inc.

—Appleby & Honeybath. 1984. 160p. pap. 3.95 o.p. (*0-14-007307-8*, Penguin Bks.) Viking Penguin.

—Appleby & the Ospreys. 2001. 170p. pap. 9.95 (*1-84232-719-4*) House of Stratus, Inc. GBR. *Dist:* Midpoint Trade Bks., Inc.

—Appleby & the Ospreys. 1988. 39.50 o.p. (*0-14-778337-2*) Penguin Group (USA) Inc.

—Appleby & the Ospreys. 1988. (Crime Ser.). 192p. pap. 3.95 o.p. (*0-14-011092-5*, Penguin Bks.) Viking Penguin.

—The Appleby File. 2001. 204p. pap. 9.95 (*1-84232-717-8*) House of Stratus, Inc. GBR. *Dist:* Midpoint Trade Bks., Inc.

—The Appleby File. l.t. ed. 1978. (Ulverscroft Large Print Ser.). 29.99 o.p. (*0-7089-0224-3*, Ulverscroft) Thorpe, F. A. Pubs. GBR. *Dist:* Ulverscroft Large Print Bks., Ltd., Ulverscroft Large Print Canada, Ltd.

—Appleby on Ararat: A Sir John Appleby Mystery. 1971. 254p. reprint ed. 69.95 (*0-8371-3377-7*, STAO, Greenwood Pr.) Greenwood Publishing Group, Inc.

—Appleby on Ararat: A Sir John Appleby Mystery. 1983. 288p. reprint ed. pap. 5.95 o.p. (*0-06-080648-6*, Perennial) HarperTrade.

—Appleby on Ararat: A Sir John Appleby Mystery. 2001. 192p. pap. 9.95 (*1-84232-715-1*) House of Stratus, Inc. GBR. *Dist:* Midpoint Trade Bks., Inc.

—Appleby Talks Again. 1977. (Short Story Index Reprint Ser.). 19.95 (*0-8369-3029-0*) Ayer Co. Pubs., Inc.

—Appleby Talks Again. 2001. 185p. pap. 9.95 (*1-84232-723-2*) House of Stratus, Inc. GBR. *Dist:* Midpoint Trade Bks., Inc.

—Appleby's Answer. 2000. 190p. pap. 9.95 (*1-84232-714-3*) House of Stratus, Inc. GBR. *Dist:* Midpoint Trade Bks., Inc.

—Appleby's Answer. 1985. (Crime Monthly Ser.). 160p. pap. 3.95 o.p. (*0-14-003981-3*, Penguin Bks.) Viking Penguin.

—Appleby's End. 1975. 224p. mass mkt. 1.25 o.s.i (*0-345-24409-5*) Ballantine Bks.

—Appleby's End. 1970. 211p. reprint ed. 69.95 (*0-8371-3376-9*, STAE, Greenwood Pr.) Greenwood Publishing Group, Inc.

—Appleby's End. 1983. 224p. pap. 2.95 o.p. (*0-06-080649-4*, P 649, Perennial) HarperTrade.

—Appleby's End. 2001. 218p. pap. 9.95 (*1-84232-716-X*) House of Stratus, Inc. GBR. *Dist:* Midpoint Trade Bks., Inc.

—Appleby's Other Story: A Sir John Appleby Mystery. 1975. 192p. mass mkt. 1.25 o.s.i (*0-345-24505-9*) Ballantine Bks.

—Appleby's Other Story: A Sir John Appleby Mystery. 2001. 179p. pap. 9.95 (*1-84232-720-8*) House of Stratus, Inc. GBR. *Dist:* Midpoint Trade Bks., Inc.

—Appleby's Other Story: A Sir John Appleby Mystery. 1993. (Classic Crime Ser.). 208p. pap. 6.00 o.p. (*0-14-014679-2*, Penguin Bks.) Penguin Group (USA) Inc.

—Appleby's Other Story: A Sir John Appleby Mystery. 1986. (Crime Ser.). 208p. pap. 3.95 o.p. (*0-14-004159-1*, Penguin Bks.) Viking Penguin.

—An Awkward Lie. 2001. 180p. pap. 9.95 (*1-84232-724-0*) House of Stratus, Inc. GBR. *Dist:* Midpoint Trade Bks., Inc.

—An Awkward Lie. 1991. (Classic Crime Ser.). 176p. reprint ed. pap. 4.95 o.p. (*0-14-012785-2*, Penguin Bks.) Penguin Group (USA) Inc.

—An Awkward Lie. 1974. (Crime Ser.). 176p. pap. 3.95 o.p. (*0-14-003664-4*, Penguin Bks.) Viking Penguin.

—The Bloody Wood. 1986. 224p. reprint ed. pap. 4.95 o.p. (*0-06-080811-X*, P 811, Perennial) HarperTrade.

—The Bloody Wood. 2001. 182p. pap. (*1-84232-725-9*) House of Stratus, Inc.

—The Bloody Wood. 1990. 192p. (C). reprint ed. lib. bdg. 19.95 o.p. (*0-8095-9028-X*) Millefleurs.

—Carson's Conspiracy: A Sir John Appleby Mystery Novel. 2001. 174p. pap. 9.95 (*1-84232-726-7*) House of Stratus, Inc. GBR. *Dist:* Midpoint Trade Bks., Inc.

—Carson's Conspiracy: A Sir John Appleby Mystery Novel. 1986. (Crime Monthly Ser.). 192p. pap. 3.95 o.p. (*0-14-008444-4*, Penguin Bks.) Viking Penguin.

—A Comedy of Terrors. 1989. pap. 4.95 o.p. (*0-14-012919-7*); 1987. 256p. mass mkt. 3.95 o.p. (*0-14-010090-3*, Penguin Bks.) Viking Penguin.

—A Connoisseur's Case. 2001. 180p. pap. 9.95 (*1-84232-729-1*) House of Stratus, Inc. GBR. *Dist:* Midpoint Trade Bks., Inc.

—A Connoisseur's Case. l.t. ed. 1980. (Ulverscroft Large Print Ser.). 29.99 o.p. (*0-7089-0421-1*, Ulverscroft) Thorpe, F. A. Pubs. GBR. *Dist:* Ulverscroft Large Print Bks., Ltd., Ulverscroft Large Print Canada, Ltd.

—The Crabtree Affair: A Sir John Appleby Mystery. 1984. 240p. reprint ed. pap. 5.95 o.p. (*0-06-080706-7*, Perennial) HarperTrade.

—The Daffodil Affair. 1976. (Crime Fiction Ser). reprint ed. lib. bdg. 21.00 o.p. (*0-8240-2378-1*) Garland Publishing, Inc.

—The Daffodil Affair. 2001. 230p. pap. 9.95 (*1-84232-730-5*) House of Stratus, Inc. GBR. *Dist:* Midpoint Trade Bks., Inc.

—The Daffodil Affair. (Crime Ser.). 1990. 208p. pap. 5.00 o.p. (*0-14-011498-X*, Penguin Bks.); 1984. 208p. pap. 3.95 o.p. (*0-14-002202-3*, Penguin Bks.); 1983. Viking Penguin.

—Death at the Chase. 2000. 186p. pap. 9.95 (*1-84232-731-3*) House of Stratus, Inc. GBR. *Dist:* Midpoint Trade Bks., Inc.

—Death at the Chase. 1986. (Crime Monthly Ser.). 192p. pap. 3.95 o.p. (*0-14-003243-6*); reprint ed. pap. 6.00 o.p. (*0-14-017242-4*) Viking Penguin. (Penguin Bks.).

—Death at the President's Lodging. 2000. (Illus.). 254p. pap. 9.95 (*1-84232-732-1*) House of Stratus, Inc. GBR. *Dist:* Midpoint Trade Bks., Inc.

—Death at the President's Lodging. 1992. (Penguin Crime Fiction Ser.). 288p. pap. 6.95 o.s.i (*0-14-010555-7*, Penguin Bks.) Penguin Group (USA) Inc.

—Death at the President's Lodging. l.t. ed. 1989. (Ulverscroft Large Print Ser.). 448p. 29.99 o.p. (*0-7089-2012-8*, Ulverscroft) Thorpe, F. A. Pubs. GBR. *Dist:* Ulverscroft Large Print Bks., Ltd., Ulverscroft Large Print Canada, Ltd.

—Death at the President's Lodging. 1983. Viking Penguin.

—Death by Water: A Sir John Appleby Mystery. 1982. 224p. reprint ed. pap. 5.95 o.p. (*0-06-080574-9*, Perennial) HarperTrade.

—Death on a Quiet Day: A Sir John Appleby Mystery. 1983. 224p. pap. o.p. (*0-06-080677-X*, P677) HarperCollins Pubs.

—Death on a Quiet Day: A Sir John Appleby Mystery. 1991. 288p. reprint ed. pap. 8.00 o.p. (*0-06-092137-4*, Perennial) HarperTrade.

—Death on a Quiet Day: A Sir John Appleby Mystery. 1994. 2.99 o.p. (*0-517-12586-2*) Random Hse. Value Publishing.

—The Gay Phoenix. 2001. 184p. pap. 9.95 (*1-84232-735-6*) House of Stratus, Inc. GBR. *Dist:* Midpoint Trade Bks., Inc.

—The Gay Phoenix. l.t. ed. 1992. (Adventure Suspense Ser.). 279p. 29.99 o.p. (*0-7505-0048-4*) Magna Large Print Bks. GBR. *Dist:* Ulverscroft Large Print Bks., Ltd., Ulverscroft Large Print Canada, Ltd.

—The Gay Phoenix. 1981. 192p. pap. 3.50 o.p. (*0-14-004701-8*, Penguin Bks.) Viking Penguin.

—Hamlet, Revenge! 2001. 316p. pap. 9.95 (*1-84232-737-2*) House of Stratus, Inc. GBR. *Dist:* Midpoint Trade Bks., Inc.

—Hamlet, Revenge! l.t. ed. 1994. (Magna Large Print Ser.). 498p. 29.99 o.p. (*0-7505-0493-5*) Magna Large Print Bks. GBR. *Dist:* Ulverscroft Large Print Bks., Ltd., Ulverscroft Large Print Canada, Ltd.

—Hamlet, Revenge! (Classic Crime Ser.). 1990. 288p. pap. 6.00 o.p. (*0-14-011497-1*, Penguin Bks.); 1983.; 1976. 288p. pap. 3.50 o.p. (*0-14-001640-6*, Penguin Bks.) Viking Penguin.

—Hare Sitting Up: A Sir John Appleby Mystery. 1982. 256p. reprint ed. pap. 5.95 o.p. (*0-06-080590-0*, Perennial) HarperTrade.

—Hare Sitting Up: A Sir John Appleby Mystery. 2001. 182p. pap. (*1-84232-738-0*) House of Stratus, Inc.

—Hare Sitting Up: A Sir John Appleby Mystery. l.t. ed. 1992. (Magna Large Print Ser.). 280p. 29.99 (*0-7505-0276-2*) Magna Large Print Bks. GBR. *Dist:* Ulverscroft Large Print Bks., Ltd., Ulverscroft Large Print Canada, Ltd.

—Lament for a Maker: A Sir John Appleby Mystery. 1985. 256p. mass mkt. 9.95 o.p. (*0-553-06514-9*) Bantam Bks.

—Lament for a Maker: A Sir John Appleby Mystery. 1985. 288p. mass mkt. 3.50 o.p. (*0-06-080729-6*, P729); 1990. 272p. reprint ed. pap. 4.95 o.p. (*0-06-081041-6*) HarperTrade. (Perennial).

—Lament for a Maker: A Sir John Appleby Mystery. 2001. 286p. pap. 9.95 (*1-84232-741-0*) House of Stratus, Inc. GBR. *Dist:* Midpoint Trade Bks., Inc.

—Lament for a Maker: A Sir John Appleby Mystery. 1990. 272p. (C). reprint ed. lib. bdg. 19.95 o.p. (*0-8095-9029-8*) Millefleurs.

—The Long Farewell. l.t. ed. 1991. pap. 17.95 o.p. (*0-7927-0142-9*, C0012) BBC Audiobooks America.

—The Long Farewell. 1982. (Sir John Appleby Mystery Ser.). 240p. reprint ed. pap. 5.95 o.p. (*0-06-080575-7*, Perennial) HarperTrade.

—The Long Farewell. 2001. 190p. pap. 9.95 (*1-84232-742-9*) House of Stratus, Inc. GBR. *Dist:* Midpoint Trade Bks., Inc.

—A Night of Errors: A Sir John Appleby Mystery. 1989. 304p. reprint ed. pap. 3.95 o.p. (*0-06-080877-2*, P 877, Perennial) HarperTrade.

—A Night of Errors: A Sir John Appleby Mystery. 2000. 234p. pap. 9.95 (*1-84232-748-8*) House of Stratus, Inc. GBR. *Dist:* Midpoint Trade Bks., Inc.

—One Man Show. Barzun, Jacques & Taylor, W. H., eds. 1983. (Crime Fiction 1950-1975 Ser.). 192p. lib. bdg. 18.00 o.p. (*0-8240-4994-2*) Garland Publishing, Inc.

—One Man Show. 1983. 400p. pap. 5.95 o.p. (*0-06-080672-9*, Perennial) HarperTrade.

—Open House. 1982. pap. 2.95 o.p. (*0-14-003663-6*, Penguin Bks.) Viking Penguin.
—Operation Pax. 2001. 346p. pap. 9.95 (*1-84232-751-8*) House of Stratus, Inc. GBR. *Dist:* Midpoint Trade Bks., Inc.
—The Paper Thunderbolt. 1987. 352p. mass mkt. 3.95 o.p. (*0-14-010089-X*, Penguin Bks.) Viking Penguin.
—Picture of Guilt: A Sir John Appleby Mystery. 1988. 224p. reprint ed. pap. 3.95 o.p. (*0-06-080878-0*, P-878, Perennial) HarperTrade.
—The Secret Vanguard: A Sir John Appleby Mystery. 1982. 288p. reprint ed. pap. 4.95 o.p. (*0-06-080584-6*, Perennial) HarperTrade.
—The Secret Vanguard: A Sir John Appleby Mystery. l.t. ed. 1991. (Magna Large Print Ser.). 284p. o.p. (*1-85057-864-8*) Magna Large Print Bks. GBR. *Dist:* Ulverscroft Large Print Canada, Ltd.
—The Secret Vanguard: A Sir John Appleby Mystery. 2001. 190p. pap. 9.95 (*1-84232-753-4*) Midpoint Trade Bks., Inc.
—Seven Suspects. 1984. (Crime Ser.). 288p. pap. 3.95 o.p. (*0-14-006886-4*, Penguin Bks.) Viking Penguin.
—Sheiks & Adders: A Sir John Appleby Mystery Novel. 1983. 160p. pap. 2.95 o.p. (*0-14-006520-2*, Penguin Bks.) Viking Penguin.
—There Came Both Mist & Snow. 2001. 198p. pap. 9.95 (*1-84232-757-7*) House of Stratus, Inc. GBR. *Dist:* Midpoint Trade Bks., Inc.
—There Came Both Mist & Snow. l.t. ed. 1991. (Magna Large Print Ser.). 302p. o.p. (*1-85057-862-1*) Magna Large Print Bks. GBR. *Dist:* Ulverscroft Large Print Canada, Ltd.
Innes, Michael. Silence Observed. 1975. 160p. mass mkt. 1.25 o.s.i (*0-345-24627-6*) Ballantine Bks.

### APPLEMAN, BELLE (FICTITIOUS CHARACTER)—FICTION

Rosen, Dorothy & Rosen, Sidney. Death & Blintzes. 1998. 180p. reprint ed. pap. 10.95 (*0-89733-450-7*) Academy Chicago Pubs., Ltd.
—Death & Blintzes. 1985. 192p. 14.95 o.p. (*0-8027-5625-5*) Walker & Co.
—Death & Strudel. 1999. 272p. 23.00 (*0-89733-478-7*) Academy Chicago Pubs., Ltd.

### APPLETON, SUSANNA, LADY (FICTITIOUS CHARACTER)—FICTION

Emerson, Kathy Lynn. Face down Across the Western Sea. 2002. 240p. 22.95 (*0-312-28823-9*, Saint Martin's Minotaur) St. Martin's Pr.
—Face down among the Winchester Geese. 1999. (Elizabethan Mysteries Ser.). 256p. (J). 22.95 (*0-312-20542-2*, Saint Martin's Minotaur) St. Martin's Pr.
—Face down Before the Rebel Hooves. 2001. 256p. 23.95 (*0-312-28036-X*, Saint Martin's Minotaur) St. Martin's Pr.
—Face down in the Marrow-Bone Pie: An Elizabethan Mystery. 2000. 256p. mass mkt. 5.99 o.s.i (*1-57566-546-8*) Kensington Publishing Corp.
—Face down in the Marrow-Bone Pie: An Elizabethan Mystery. 1997. (Elizabethan Mysteries Ser.). 208p. 21.95 (*0-312-15123-3*, Saint Martin's Minotaur) St. Martin's Pr.
—Face down upon an Herbal. 2000. 256p. mass mkt. 5.99 (*1-57566-620-0*) Kensington Publishing Corp.
—Face down upon an Herbal. 1998. (Elizabethan Mysteries Ser.). 256p. 21.95 (*0-312-18092-6*, 874707, Saint Martin's Minotaur) St. Martin's Pr.

### APPRENTICE ADEPT (FICTITIOUS CHARACTER)—FICTION

Anthony, Piers. Blue Adept. 1987. (Apprentice Adept Ser.: Vol. 2). 336p. mass mkt. 7.50 (*0-345-35245-9*); 1986. mass mkt. 3.50 o.p. (*0-345-33632-1*); 1983. mass mkt. 2.95 o.p. (*0-345-31424-7*); 1982. mass mkt. 2.75 o.p. (*0-345-28214-0*); 1981. 368p. 10.95 o.s.i (*0-345-29384-3*) Ballantine Bks. (Del Rey).
—Juxtaposition. 1987. (Apprentice Adept Ser.: Vol. 3). 368p. mass mkt. 6.99 (*0-345-34934-2*); 1986. mass mkt. 3.50 o.p. (*0-345-33637-2*); 1983. mass mkt. 2.95 o.p. (*0-345-28215-9*); 1982. 13.50 o.p. (*0-345-30196-X*) Ballantine Bks. (Del Rey).
—Out of Phaze. 1988. (Apprentice Adept Ser.: Vol. 4). 320p. mass mkt. 6.50 o.s.i (*0-441-64465-1*) Ace Bks.
—Out of Phaze. 1987. (Apprentice Adept Ser.: Bk. 4). 288p. 17.95 o.p. (*0-399-13272-4*) Putnam Publishing Group, The.
—Robot Adept. 1989. mass mkt. 5.99 o.s.i (*0-441-73118-X*) Ace Bks.
—Robot Adept. 1988. (Apprentice Adept Ser.: Bk. 5). 288p. 16.95 o.p. (*0-399-13359-3*, G. P. Putnam's Sons) Penguin Putnam Bks. for Young Readers.
—Split Infinity. 1987. (Apprentice Adept Ser.: Vol. 1). 368p. mass mkt. 7.50 (*0-345-35491-5*); 1986. mass mkt. 3.50 o.p. (*0-345-33600-3*); 1982. mass mkt. 2.95 o.p. (*0-345-30761-5*); 1980. mass mkt. 2.50 o.p. (*0-345-28213-2*); 1980. 9.95 o.s.i (*0-345-28645-6*) Ballantine Bks. (Del Rey).
—Unicorn Point. 1990. (Apprentice Adept Ser.: No. 6). 352p. mass mkt. 6.99 o.s.i (*0-441-84563-0*) Ace Bks.
—Unicorn Point. 1989. (Apprentice Adept Ser.). 15.95 o.p. (*0-399-13433-6*, G. P. Putnam's Sons) Penguin Putnam Bks. for Young Readers.

### ARAGON, TOM (FICTITIOUS CHARACTER)—FICTION

Millar, Margaret. Ask for Me Tomorrow. l.t. ed. 1989. (Atlantic Mystery Ser.). 265p. pap. 14.95 o.p. (*1-55504-738-6*, 833) BBC Audiobooks America.
—Ask for Me Tomorrow. (Library of Crime Classics). 1991. 184p. pap. 8.95 o.p. (*1-55882-115-5*); 1985. 179p. reprint ed. pap. 4.95 o.p. (*0-930330-15-3*) International Polygonics, Ltd.
—Ask for Me Tomorrow. 1978. pap. 1.50 o.p. (*0-380-01805-5*, 35618, Avon Bks.) Morrow/Avon.
—Mermaid. 1982. 317p. (*0-89340-543-4*) BBC Audiobooks America.
—Mermaid. 1991. (Library of Crime Classics). 216p. pap. 8.95 (*1-55882-114-7*) International Polygonics, Ltd.
—The Murder of Miranda. 22.95 (*0-89190-156-6*) Amereon, Ltd.
—The Murder of Miranda. l.t. ed. 1980. 459p. lib. bdg. 5.95 o.p. (*0-89340-283-4*, 56) BBC Audiobooks America.
—The Murder of Miranda. 1988. 240p. reprint ed. pap. 4.95 o.p. (*0-930330-95-1*, Library of Crime Classics) International Polygonics, Ltd.
—The Murder of Miranda. 1979. 240p. 8.95 o.p. (*0-394-50509-3*) Random Hse., Inc.

### ARBATI, CARLO (FICTITIOUS CHARACTER)—FICTION

Hill, John Spencer. Ghirlandaio's Daughter. 1998. (WWL Mystery Ser.). per. (*0-373-26279-5*, 1-26279-9, Worldwide Library) Harlequin Enterprises, Ltd.
—Ghirlandaio's Daughter. 1998. 304p. mass mkt. 8.99 (*0-7710-4114-4*); 1997. 320p. 26.99 (*0-7710-4113-6*) McClelland & Stewart/Tundra Bks.
—Ghirlandaio's Daughter: A Detective Carlo Arbati Mystery. 1997. 320p. 22.95 (*0-312-15133-0*, Saint Martin's Minotaur) St. Martin's Pr.
—The Last Castrato. 1997. (WWL Mystery Ser.). per. (*0-373-26229-9*, 1-26229-4, Worldwide Library) Harlequin Enterprises, Ltd.
—The Last Castrato. 1995. 224p. 20.95 (*0-312-13107-0*, Saint Martin's Minotaur) St. Martin's Pr.

### ARBOTHNOT, AUBREY (FICTITIOUS CHARACTER)—FICTION

DeCarlo, Elisa. The Devil You Say. 1993. 192p. (Orig.). mass mkt. 4.50 (*0-380-76993-X*, Avon Bks.) Morrow/Avon.
—Strong Spirits. 1994. 160p. (Orig.). mass mkt. 4.50 (*0-380-77405-4*, Avon Bks.) Morrow/Avon.

### ARCHER, CAROLYN (FICTITIOUS CHARACTER)—FICTION

Ross, Veronica. The Anastasia Connection. 204p. pap. 15.95 (*1-55128-038-8*) Mercury Bks. CAN. *Dist:* LPC/InBook.
—Millicent: A Mystery. 2001. 256p. pap. 7.99 (*1-55128-042-6*) Mercury Bks. CAN. *Dist:* LPC/InBook.

### ARCHER, ISABEL (FICTITIOUS CHARACTER)—FICTION

James, Henry. The Portrait of a Lady. unabr. ed. 1999. audio 53.95; Pt. 1. 1989. audio 53.95 (*1-55685-131-6*) Audio Bk. Contractors, Inc.
—The Portrait of a Lady. 1983. (Bantam Classics Ser.). 560p. mass mkt. 4.95 (*0-553-21127-7*, Bantam Classics) Bantam Bks.
—The Portrait of a Lady. unabr. ed. 1995. audio 99.95 (*0-7861-0899-1*, 1675) Blackstone Audio Bks., Inc.
—The Portrait of a Lady. unabr. ed. 1998. (Bookcassette Classic Collection). 22p. audio 66.25 (*1-56740-622-X*, 1525, Unabridged Library Editions); audio 22.95 (*1-56740-093-0*, 1524, Bookcassette) Brilliance Audio.
—The Portrait of a Lady. 1990. reprint ed. lib. bdg. 21.95 (*0-89966-651-5*) Buccaneer Bks., Inc.
—The Portrait of a Lady. 1998. (Bloom's Notes Ser.). pap. 4.95 (*0-7910-4567-6*) Chelsea Hse. Pubs.
—The Portrait of a Lady. 1908. 495p. (YA). reprint ed. pap. text 28.00 (*1-4047-3379-5*) Classic Textbooks.
—The Portrait of a Lady. abr. ed. 1995. (Classics Ser.). audio 16.95 (*1-56511-126-5*) HighBridge Co.
—The Portrait of a Lady. 1977. (Novels & Tales of Henry James Ser.: Vol. 3). reprint ed. Vol. 1. 437p. lib. bdg. 37.50 (*0-678-02803-6*); Vol. 2. xx, 427p. lib. bdg. 37.50 (*0-678-02804-4*) Kelley, Augustus M. Pubs.
—The Portrait of a Lady. 1992. 640p. pap. 12.50 o.s.i (*0-679-73635-2*, Vintage); 1991. 672p. 18.95 (*0-679-40562-3*, Everyman's Library) Knopf Publishing Group.
—The Portrait of a Lady. 1998. (Cloth Bound Pocket Ser.). 240p. 7.95 (*3-89508-454-9*, 520035) Konemann.
—The Portrait of a Lady. 1966. (Modern Library College Editions Ser.). 591p. (C). pap. 11.25 (*0-07-553637-4*, T47, McGraw-Hill Humanities, Social Sciences & World Languages) McGraw-Hill Higher Education.
—The Portrait of a Lady. 1996. 560p. mass mkt. 5.99 o.s.i (*0-451-19130-7*); 1995. 560p. mass mkt. 5.95 (*0-451-52597-3*); 1963. mass mkt. 0.95 o.p. (*0-451-50358-9*); 1963. mass mkt. 0.75 o.p. (*0-451-50195-0*); 1963. 560p. mass mkt. 4.95 o.p. (*0-451-52288-5*); 1963. mass mkt. 1.25 o.p. (*0-451-50738-X*); 1963. mass mkt. 1.75 o.p. (*0-451-51000-3*); 1963. mass mkt. 3.50 o.p. (*0-451-51605-2*); 1963. mass mkt. 2.25 o.p. (*0-451-51174-3*); 1963. mass mkt. 2.95 o.p. (*0-451-51362-2*) NAL. (Signet Classics).
—The Portrait of a Lady. abr. ed. 1996. audio 22.98 (*962-634-600-0*, NA410014); audio compact disk 26.98 (*962-634-100-9*, NA410012) Naxos of America, Inc. (Naxos AudioBooks).
—The Portrait of a Lady. 1996. 19.95 o.p. (*0-7871-0353-5*, NewStar Pr.) NewStar Media, Inc.
—The Portrait of a Lady. Bamberg, Robert D., ed. 1975. (Critical Editions Ser.). (C). pap. o.p. (*0-393-09259-3*) Norton, W. W. & Co., Inc.
—The Portrait of a Lady. 1999. 704p. 17.00 (*0-19-210038-6*) Oxford Univ. Pr., Inc.
—The Portrait of a Lady. Bradbury, Nicola, ed. & intro. by. 1998. (Oxford World's Classics Ser.). 672p. pap. 8.95 (*0-19-283369-3*) Oxford Univ. Pr., Inc.
—The Portrait of a Lady. 1982. (Oxford World's Classics Ser.). pap. 4.95 o.p. (*0-19-281514-8*) Oxford Univ. Pr., Inc.
—The Portrait of a Lady. Bradbury, Nicola, ed. & intro. by. 2nd rev. ed. 1995. (Oxford World's Classics Ser.). 668p. pap. 6.95 o.p. (*0-19-282362-0*) Oxford Univ. Pr., Inc.
—The Portrait of a Lady. 1975. pap. 3.95 o.p. (*0-14-001921-9*) Penguin Group (USA) Inc.
—The Portrait of a Lady. Dixson, Robert James, ed. rev. ed. 1987. (American Classics: Bk. 7). (gr. 9 up). audio 72.75 o.p. (*0-13-024746-4*, 58229) Prentice Hall, ESL Dept.
—The Portrait of a Lady. 2002. (Modern Library Classics). 640p. pap. 9.95 (*0-375-75919-0*, Modern Library) Random House Adult Trade Publishing Group.
—The Portrait of a Lady. 2nd ed. 1983. 9.95 o.s.i (*0-394-60432-6*) Random Hse., Inc.
—The Portrait of a Lady. 1992. (Notable American Authors Ser.). reprint ed. lib. bdg. 75.00 (*0-7812-3379-8*) Reprint Services Corp.
—The Portrait of a Lady. l.t. ed. 1997. (Perennial Bestsellers Ser.). 465p. lib. bdg. 25.95 (*0-7838-8266-1*);Vol. II. 469p. lib. bdg. 25.95 (*0-7838-8268-8*) Thorndike Pr.
—The Portrait of a Lady. Watson, Priscilla L., ed. 1995. 640p. pap. 4.95 (*0-460-87588-4*, Everyman's Classic Library in Paperback) Tuttle Publishing.
—The Portrait of a Lady. 2003. 656p. pap. 10.00 (*0-14-143963-7*, Penguin Classics); 1996. 610p. 17.95 o.s.i (*0-670-87139-7*) Viking Penguin.
—The Portrait of a Lady. Moore, Geoffrey, ed. & intro. by. 1984. (Penguin Classics Ser.). 688p. 9.95 (*0-14-043223-X*) Viking Penguin.
—The Portrait of a Lady. abr. ed. 1996. audio 23.95 o.s.i (*0-14-086287-0*, Penguin AudioBooks) Viking Penguin.
—The Portrait of a Lady. 1997. (Classics Ser.). 528p. pap. 3.95 (*1-85326-177-7*, 1777WW) Wordsworth Editions, Ltd. GBR. *Dist:* Combined Publishing.
—The Portrait of a Lady. 1998. E-Book 9.40 (*0-585-35135-X*) netLibrary, Inc.
—The Portrait of a Lady: An Authoritative Text, Henry James & the Novel, Reviews & Criticism. Bamberg, Robert D., ed. 2nd ed. 1995. (Critical Editions Ser.). (C). pap. text 13.00 (*0-393-96646-1*) Norton, W. W. & Co., Inc.
—The Portrait of a Lady: Complete Text with Introduction, Historical Contexts. Cohn, Jan, ed. 2001. (New Riverside Editions Ser.). viii, 619p. 12.36 (*0-618-10735-5*) Houghton Mifflin Co.

### ARCHER, LEW (FICTITIOUS CHARACTER)—FICTION

Gale, Robert L. A Ross Macdonald Companion. 2002. 384p. text 74.95 (*0-313-32057-8*, GR2057, Greenwood Pr.) Greenwood Publishing Group, Inc.
MacDonald, Ross, pseud. Archer in Jeopardy, 3 bks., Set. Incl. Zebra-Striped Hearse. 1979. (Lew Archer Mystery Ser.). 1979. 24.95 o.s.i (*0-394-50804-1*) Knopf, Alfred A. Inc.
—The Barbarous Coast. 1975. (Lew Archer Mystery Ser.). 192p. pap. 2.95 o.s.i (*0-553-12249-5*) Bantam Bks.
—The Barbarous Coast. unabr. ed. (Lew Archer Mystery Ser.). 2000. audio compact disk 48.00 (*0-7861-9916-4*, z1819); 1996. audio 39.95 (*0-7861-1047-3*, 1819) Blackstone Audio Bks., Inc.
—The Barbarous Coast. 1990. (Lew Archer Mystery Ser.). 240p. mass mkt. 3.95 o.s.i (*0-446-35882-7*) Warner Bks., Inc.
—Blue City. 1988. 2.99 o.p. (*0-517-68432-2*) Random Hse. Value Publishing.
—Blue City. 1992. (Lew Archer Mystery Ser.). 224p. mass mkt. 4.50 o.s.i (*0-446-35884-3*) Warner Bks., Inc.
—The Blue Hammer. Date not set. (Lew Archer Mystery Ser.). pap. 16.95 (*0-8488-1722-2*); 23.95 (*0-89190-095-0*) Amereon, Ltd.
—The Blue Hammer. 1988. (Lew Archer Mystery Ser.). pap. 3.95 o.s.i (*0-553-27548-8*) Bantam Bks.
—The Blue Hammer. unabr. ed. 1999. (Lew Archer Mystery Ser.). audio 44.95 (*0-7861-1031-7*, 894402) Blackstone Audio Bks., Inc.
—The Blue Hammer. 1976. (Lew Archer Mystery Ser.). reprint ed. lib. bdg. 13.50 o.p. (*0-8161-6431-2*, Macmillan Reference USA) Gale Group.
—The Blue Hammer. 1990. (Lew Archer Mystery Ser.). mass mkt. 3.95 o.s.i (*0-446-35885-1*) Warner Bks., Inc.
—The Chill. 1983. (Lew Archer Mystery Ser.). mass mkt. 2.75 o.s.i (*0-553-24282-2*) Bantam Bks.
—The Chill. unabr. ed. 1996. (Lew Archer Mystery Ser.). audio 44.95 (*0-7861-1066-X*, 894596) Blackstone Audio Bks., Inc.
—The Chill. 2001. 288p. pap. 8.42 (*1-84195-118-8*) Canongate Bks. GBR. *Dist:* Grove/Atlantic, Inc.
—The Chill. 1996. (Lew Archer Mystery Ser.). 288p. pap. 12.00 (*0-679-76807-6*) Random Hse., Inc.
—The Chill. 1990. (Lew Archer Mystery Ser.). mass mkt. 3.95 o.s.i (*0-446-35887-8*) Warner Bks., Inc.
—The Doomsters. 1990. (Lew Archer Mystery Ser.). mass mkt. 3.95 o.s.i (*0-446-35888-6*) Warner Bks., Inc.
—The Drowning Pool. 1975. (Lew Archer Mystery Ser.). 224p. pap. 2.75 o.p. (*0-553-24135-4*) Bantam Bks.
—The Drowning Pool. l.t. ed. 2002. pap. 25.95 (*0-7838-9783-9*) Gale Group.
—The Drowning Pool. Barzun, Jacques & Taylor, Wendell H., eds. 1976. (Lew Archer Mystery Ser.). reprint ed. lib. bdg. 21.00 o.p. (*0-8240-2382-X*) Garland Publishing, Inc.
—The Drowning Pool. 1996. (Lew Archer Mystery Ser.). 256p. pap. 12.00 (*0-679-76806-8*) Random Hse., Inc.
—The Drowning Pool. 1993. (Lew Archer Mystery Ser.). 224p. mass mkt. 4.99 o.s.i (*0-446-35889-4*) Warner Bks., Inc.
—The Far Side of the Dollar. (Lew Archer Mystery Ser.). 2000. audio compact disk 56.00 (*0-7861-9889-3*, ZP1769); 1996. audio 44.95 (*0-7861-0990-4*, 1767) Blackstone Audio Bks., Inc.
—The Far Side of the Dollar. 1990. (Lew Archer Mystery Ser.). mass mkt. 4.99 o.s.i (*0-446-35890-8*) Warner Bks., Inc.
—Find a Victim. unabr. ed. 1999. (Lew Archer Mystery Ser.). audio 39.95 (*0-7861-1493-2*, 758945) Blackstone Audio Bks., Inc.
—Find a Victim. Set. unabr. ed. 1999. (Lew Archer Mystery Ser.). audio 39.95 Highsmith Inc.
—Find a Victim. 2001. (Lew Archer Mystery Ser.). 224p. pap. 12.00 (*0-375-70867-7*, Vintage) Knopf Publishing Group.
—Find a Victim. 1991. (Lew Archer Mystery Ser.). mass mkt. 4.50 o.s.i (*0-446-35892-4*) Warner Bks., Inc.
—The Galton Case. 1980. (Lew Archer Mystery Ser.). pap. 2.75 o.p. (*0-553-22621-5*) Bantam Bks.
—The Galton Case. 1990. (Lew Archer Mystery Ser.). mass mkt. 3.95 o.s.i (*0-446-35893-2*) Warner Bks., Inc.
—The Galton Case: A Lew Archer Novel. 1996. (Lew Archer Mystery Ser.). 256p. pap. 12.00 (*0-679-76864-5*) McKay, David Co., Inc.
—The Goodbye Look. 2000. (Lew Archer Mystery Ser.). 256p. pap. 12.00 (*0-375-70865-0*, Vintage) Knopf Publishing Group.
—The Goodbye Look. 1992. (Lew Archer Mystery Ser.). 224p. mass mkt. 4.50 o.s.i (*0-446-35894-0*) Warner Bks., Inc.
—The Instant Enemy. 1985. (Lew Archer Mystery Ser.). 208p. pap. 2.95 o.p. (*0-553-24738-7*) Bantam Bks.
—The Instant Enemy. 1991. (Lew Archer Mystery Ser.). 224p. mass mkt. 4.50 o.s.i (*0-446-35895-9*) Warner Bks., Inc.
—The Ivory Grin. 1998. (Lew Archer Mystery Ser.). 192p. 19.50 (*0-7540-8519-8*, Black Dagger) BBC Audiobooks America.
—The Ivory Grin. 1992. (Lew Archer Mystery Ser.). 224p. reprint ed. mass mkt. 4.50 o.s.i (*0-446-35896-7*) Warner Bks., Inc.
—Lew Archer Private Investigator. l.t. ed. 1988. (Lew Archer Mystery Ser.). 20.95 o.p. (*1-55504-639-8*); pap. 18.95 o.p. (*1-55504-640-1*) BBC Audiobooks America.
—Lew Archer Private Investigator. 1986. (Lew Archer Mystery Ser.). 10.00 o.p. (*0-89296-033-7*) Mysterious Pr.
—Lew Archer Private Investigator II. l.t. ed. 1988. (Lew Archer Mystery Ser.). pap. 17.95 o.p. (*1-55504-703-3*); lib. bdg. 19.95 o.p. (*1-55504-727-0*) BBC Audiobooks America.

—The Moving Target. l.t. ed. 1991. (Lew Archer Mystery Ser.). pap. 10.95 o.p. (0-89340-171-4, C0096) BBC Audiobooks America.

—The Moving Target. 1979. (Lew Archer Mystery Ser.). lib. bdg. 9.95 o.p. (0-8398-2538-2, Macmillan Reference USA) Gale Group.

—The Moving Target. 1998. (Lew Archer Mystery Ser.). 256p. pap. 11.00 (0-375-70146-X, Vintage) Knopf Publishing Group.

—The Moving Target. 1990. (Lew Archer Mystery Ser.). mass mkt. 4.99 o.s.i (0-446-35898-3) Warner Bks., Inc.

—The Name Is Archer. 1983. (Lew Archer Mystery Ser.). mass mkt. 3.50 o.s.i (0-553-27103-2) Bantam Bks.

—The Name Is Archer. 1991. (Lew Archer Mystery Ser.). 288p. mass mkt. 4.50 o.s.i (0-446-36156-9) Warner Bks., Inc.

—Sleeping Beauty. (Lew Archer Mystery Ser.). 23.95 (0-89190-096-9) Amereon, Ltd.

—Sleeping Beauty. unabr. ed. 1997. (Lew Archer Mystery Ser.). audio 29.95 (1-57270-049-1, N61049u) Audio Partners Publishing Corp.

—Sleeping Beauty. 1984. mass mkt. 3.50 o.s.i (0-553-27101-6) Bantam Bks.

—Sleeping Beauty. unabr. ed. 1998. (Lew Archer Mystery Ser.). audio 44.95 (0-7861-1320-0, 2245) Blackstone Audio Bks., Inc.

—Sleeping Beauty. 2000. (Lew Archer Mystery Ser.). 288p. pap. 12.00 (0-375-70866-9, Vintage) Knopf Publishing Group.

—Sleeping Beauty. 1973. (Lew Archer Mystery Ser). 5.95 o.p. (0-394-48474-6, Knopf Bks. for Young Readers) Random Hse. Children's Bks.

—Sleeping Beauty. 1991. (Lew Archer Mystery Ser.). mass mkt. 4.50 o.s.i (0-446-35899-1) Warner Bks., Inc.

—The Underground Man. 1984. (Lew Archer Mystery Ser.). mass mkt. 3.95 o.s.i (0-553-27183-0) Bantam Bks.

—The Underground Man. 1992. (Lew Archer Mystery Ser.). mass mkt. 4.50 o.s.i (0-446-35901-7) Warner Bks., Inc.

—The Underground Man: A Lew Archer Novel. 1996. (Lew Archer Mystery Ser.). (SPA.). 288p. pap. 12.00 (0-679-76808-4, Vintage) Knopf Publishing Group.

—The Way Some People Die. 1990. (Lew Archer Mystery Ser.). mass mkt. 3.95 o.s.i (0-446-35902-5) Warner Bks., Inc.

—The Wycherly Woman. 1984. (Lew Archer Mystery Ser.). mass mkt. 2.95 o.s.i (0-553-23855-8) Bantam Bks.

—The Wycherly Woman. 1998. (Lew Archer Mystery Ser.). 288p. pap. 12.00 (0-375-70144-3, Vintage) Knopf Publishing Group.

—The Wycherly Woman. 1990. (Lew Archer Mystery Ser.). mass mkt. 3.95 o.s.i (0-446-35903-3) Warner Bks., Inc.

—The Zebra-Striped Hearse. 1998. (Lew Archer Mystery Ser.). 19.50 o.p. (0-7540-8511-2, Black Dagger) BBC Audiobooks America.

—The Zebra-Striped Hearse. 1984. (Lew Archer Mystery Ser.). 224p. mass mkt. 3.95 o.s.i (0-553-27362-0); pap. text 2.95 o.p. (0-553-23996-1) Bantam Bks.

—The Zebra-Striped Hearse. 1998. (Lew Archer Mystery Ser.). 288p. pap. 12.00 (0-375-70145-1, Vintage) Knopf Publishing Group.

—The Zebra-Striped Hearse. 1979. (Lew Archer Mystery Ser.). Knopf, Alfred A. Inc.

—The Zebra-Striped Hearse. 1993. (Lew Archer Mystery Ser.). 272p. mass mkt. 4.99 o.s.i (0-446-35904-1) Warner Bks., Inc.

MacDonald, Ross, pseud, ed. The Ivory Grin. 1988. (Lew Archer Mystery Ser.). 256p. mass mkt. 3.95 o.s.i (0-553-27352-3) Bantam Bks.

McDonald, Ross, photos by. Black Money. 1988. (Lew Archer Mystery Ser.). 208p. pap. 3.95 o.s.i (0-553-27219-5) Bantam Bks.

—Black Money. 1996. (Lew Archer Mystery Ser.). 256p. pap. 11.95 (0-679-76810-6) Random Hse., Inc.

### ARCHER, OWEN (FICTITIOUS CHARACTER)—FICTION

Robb, Candace. The Apothecary Rose. unabr. ed. 1999. audio compact disk 99.95 (0-7531-0706-6, 107066); 1997. (Owen Archer Mystery Ser.: Vol. 1). audio 69.95 ISIS Audio Bks. GBR. Dist: Ulverscroft Large Print Bks., Ltd.

—The Apothecary Rose. 1994. 319p. mass mkt. 6.99 (0-312-95360-7, St. Martin's Paperbacks); 1993. 256p. 19.95 o.p. (0-312-09782-4, Saint Martin's Minotaur) St. Martin's Pr.

—The Cross-Legged Knight. 2003. (An/Owen Archer Mystery Ser.). (Illus.). 336p. 23.95 (0-89296-772-2) Mysterious Pr.

—The Cross-Legged Knight. l.t. ed. 2003. (Owen Archer Mystery Ser.). 517p. 28.95 (0-7862-5611-7) Thorndike Pr.

—The Cross-Legged Knight. 2004. 336p. pap. 12.95 (0-446-69166-6, Mysterious Pr. Paperback Bks.) Warner Bks., Inc.

—A Gift of Sanctuary: An Owen Archer Mystery. 2000. (Owen Archer Mystery Ser.: Vol. 6). 320p. mass mkt. 6.99 (0-312-97477-9, St. Martin's Paperbacks); 1998. 304p. 22.95 o.p. (0-312-19266-5, Saint Martin's Minotaur) St. Martin's Pr.

—A Gift of Sanctuary: An Owen Archer Mystery. l.t. ed. 1999. (Mystery Ser.). 475p. 28.95 (0-7862-1910-6); (0-7540-1302-2); (0-7540-2226-9) Thorndike Pr.

—The King's Bishop. unabr. ed. 1997. audio 69.95 (0-7531-0084-3, 970704) ISIS Audio Bks. GBR. Dist: Ulverscroft Large Print Bks., Ltd.

—The King's Bishop. l.t. unabr. ed. 1999. (Illus.). 416p. 32.50 (0-7531-5951-1, 159511) ISIS Large Print Bks. GBR. Dist: Ulverscroft Large Print Bks., Ltd.

—The King's Bishop. 384p. 1996. 23.95 (0-312-14638-8, Saint Martin's Minotaur); Vol. 1. 1997. mass mkt. 6.99 (0-312-96282-7, St. Martin's Paperbacks) St. Martin's Pr.

—The Lady Chapel. unabr. ed. 1997. audio 84.95 (0-7531-0086-X, 970107) ISIS Audio Bks. GBR. Dist: Ulverscroft Large Print Bks., Ltd.

—The Lady Chapel. 1995. 287p. mass mkt. 6.99 (0-312-95460-3, St. Martin's Paperbacks); 1994. 304p. 20.95 o.p. (0-312-11409-5, Saint Martin's Minotaur) St. Martin's Pr.

—The Nun's Tale. unabr. ed. 1997. audio 69.95 ISIS Audio Bks. GBR. Dist: Ulverscroft Large Print Bks., Ltd.

—The Nun's Tale: An Owen Archer Mystery. 1996. (Nun's Tale Ser.: Vol. 1). 355p. mass mkt. 6.50 (0-312-95982-6, St. Martin's Paperbacks); 1995. 288p. 23.95 o.p. (0-312-13573-4, Saint Martin's Minotaur) St. Martin's Pr.

—The Riddle of St. Leonard's: An Owen Archer Mystery. 1997. 256p. (YA). 21.95 (0-312-16983-3, Saint Martin's Minotaur); Vol. 1. 1998. 304p. mass mkt. 6.99 (0-312-96651-2, St. Martin's Paperbacks) St. Martin's Pr.

—A Spy for the Redeemer. 2002. (Illus.). 320p. 23.95 (0-89296-762-5) Mysterious Pr.

—A Spy for the Redeemer. 2003. 320p. pap. 12.95 (0-446-67965-8, Mysterious Pr. Paperback Bks.) Warner Bks., Inc.

### ARDLEIGH, KATHRYN (FICTITIOUS CHARACTER)—FICTION

Paige, Robin. Death at Bishop's Keep: A Victorian Mystery. 1998. 304p. mass mkt. 6.50 (0-425-16435-7, Prime Crime) Berkley Publishing Group.

—Death at Bishop's Keep: A Victorian Mystery. 1994. pap. 4.99 (0-380-77498-4, Avon Bks.) Morrow/Avon.

—Death at Daisy's Folly. 1997. 288p. mass mkt. 6.50 (0-425-15671-0, Prime Crime) Berkley Publishing Group.

—Death at Devil's Bridge. 1998. (Prime Crime Mysteries Ser.). 288p. mass mkt. 6.50 (0-425-16195-1, Prime Crime) Berkley Publishing Group.

—Death at Gallows Green. 1998. 288p. mass mkt. 6.50 (0-425-16399-7) Berkley Publishing Group.

—Death at Gallows Green. 1995. (Victorian Mystery Ser.). pap. 4.99 (0-380-77499-2, Avon Bks.) Morrow/Avon.

—Death at Rottingdean. 1999. (Victorian Mystery Ser.). 304p. mass mkt. 6.50 (0-425-16782-8, Prime Crime) Berkley Publishing Group.

—Death at Whitechapel. 2000. (Victorian Mystery Ser.: Vol. 6). 288p. mass mkt. 6.50 (0-425-17341-0, Prime Crime) Berkley Publishing Group.

### ARGYLL, JONATHAN (FICTITIOUS CHARACTER)—FICTION

Pears, Iain. Death & Restoration: A Jonathan Argyll Mystery. (Art History Mysteries Ser.). 2000. 288p. mass mkt. 6.50 (0-425-17742-4, Prime Crime); 2000. 223p. mass mkt. 6.50 (0-00-649875-2); 2003. 320p. reprint ed. pap. 13.00 (0-425-19042-0, Prime Crime) Berkley Publishing Group.

—Death & Restoration: A Jonathan Argyll Mystery. 1998. (Jonathan Argyll Mysteries Ser.: Vol. 6). 224p. 22.00 o.s.i (0-684-81461-7, Scribner) Simon & Schuster.

—Giotto's Hand. (Art History Mysteries Ser.). 2000. 288p. mass mkt. 6.50 (0-425-17358-5); 2003. 304p. reprint ed. pap. 13.00 (0-425-18854-X) Berkley Publishing Group. (Prime Crime).

—Giotto's Hand. l.t. ed. 1997. (G. K. Hall Mystery Ser.). 305p. 25.95 o.p. (0-7838-8362-5, Macmillan Reference USA) Gale Group.

—Giotto's Hand. 1997. 224p. 20.50 (0-684-81460-9, Scribner) Simon & Schuster.

—The Immaculate Deception. 2000. 224p. 25.00 o.s.i (0-7432-1257-6, Scribner); 2001. 272p. reprint ed. mass mkt. 7.99 (0-7434-2208-2, Pocket) Simon & Schuster.

—The Immaculate Deception. l.t. ed. 2001. (Thorndike Basic Ser.). 333p. 28.95 (0-7862-3257-9) Thorndike Pr.

—The Last Judgement. 2002. 336p. pap. 13.00 (0-425-18647-4) Berkley Publishing Group.

—The Last Judgement: A Jonathan Argyll Mystery. 1999. (Art History Mysteries Ser.). 288p. mass mkt. 6.50 (0-425-17148-5, Prime Crime) Berkley Publishing Group.

—The Last Judgement: A Jonathan Argyll Mystery. 1996. 224p. 20.50 (0-684-81459-5); 1995. 21.00 (1-57283-001-8) Simon & Schuster. (Scribner).

—The Raphael Affair. 1998. (Prime Crime Mysteries Ser.: Bk. 1). 240p. reprint ed. mass mkt. 6.50 (0-425-16613-9, Prime Crime) Berkley Publishing Group.

—The Raphael Affair. 1992. 191p. 18.95 (0-15-178912-6) Harcourt Trade Pubs.

—The Raphael Affair. l.t. ed. 1991. (Linford Mystery Library). pap. 17.99 o.p. (0-7089-7155-5, Ulverscroft) Thorpe, F. A. Pubs. GBR. Dist: Ulverscroft Large Print Bks., Ltd., Ulverscroft Large Print Canada, Ltd.

—The Titian Committee. 2002. 272p. pap. 12.00 (0-425-18500-1); 1999. 240p. reprint ed. pap. 6.50 (0-425-16895-6, Prime Crime) Berkley Publishing Group.

—The Titian Committee. 1993. 189p. 19.95 (0-15-190472-3) Harcourt Trade Pubs.

### ARMITAGE SISTERS (FICTITIOUS CHARACTERS)—FICTION

Chesney, Marion. Daphne. 1985. (Six Sisters Ser.: Vol. 4). 176p. mass mkt. 2.50 o.s.i (0-449-20583-5, Fawcett) Ballantine Bks.

—Daphne. l.t. ed. 1986. (Six Sisters Ser.: Vol. 4). 280p. 9.95 o.p. (0-8161-3910-5, Macmillan Reference USA) Gale Group.

—Daphne. 1984. (Six Sisters Ser.: Vol. 4). 192p. 10.95 o.p. (0-312-18221-X) St. Martin's Pr.

—Deirdre & Desire. 1985. (Six Sisters Ser.: Vol. 3). 208p. mass mkt. 2.50 o.s.i (0-449-20582-7, Fawcett) Ballantine Bks.

—Deirdre & Desire. l.t. ed. 1985. (Six Sisters Ser.: Vol. 3). 352p. 10.95 o.p. (0-8161-3824-9, Macmillan Reference USA) Gale Group.

—Deirdre & Desire. 1984. (Six Sisters Ser.: Vol. 3). 192p. 10.95 o.p. (0-312-19136-7) St. Martin's Pr.

—Diana the Huntress. 1986. (Six Sisters Ser.: Vol. 5). mass mkt. 2.50 o.s.i (0-449-20584-3, Fawcett) Ballantine Bks.

—Diana the Huntress. l.t. ed. 1986. (Six Sisters Ser.: Vol. 5). 294p. 10.95 o.p. (0-8161-3997-0, Macmillan Reference USA) Gale Group.

—Diana the Huntress. 1985. (Six Sisters Ser.: Vol. 5). 192p. 12.95 o.p. (0-312-19937-6) St. Martin's Pr.

—Frederica in Fashion. 1986. (Six Sisters Ser.: Vol. 6). mass mkt. 2.50 o.s.i (0-449-20585-1, Fawcett) Ballantine Bks.

—Frederica in Fashion. l.t. ed. 1986. (Six Sisters Ser.: Vol. 6). 272p. 10.95 o.p. (0-8161-3996-2, Macmillan Reference USA) Gale Group.

—Frederica in Fashion. 1985. (Six Sisters Ser.: Vol. 6). 176p. 11.95 o.p. (0-312-30363-7) St. Martin's Pr.

—Minerva. 1984. (Six Sisters Ser.: Vol. 1). 192p. mass mkt. 2.25 o.s.i (0-449-20580-0, Fawcett) Ballantine Bks.

—Minerva. l.t. ed. 1985. (Six Sisters Ser.: Vol. 1). 10.95 o.p. (0-8161-3745-5, Macmillan Reference USA) Gale Group.

—Minerva. 1983. (Six Sisters Ser.: Vol. 1). 192p. 10.95 o.p. (0-312-53360-8) St. Martin's Pr.

—The Taming of Annabelle. (Six Sisters Ser.: Vol. 2). 1987. 176p. mass mkt. 2.50 o.s.i (0-449-21457-5); 1984. 192p. mass mkt. 2.25 o.p. (0-449-20581-9) Ballantine Bks. (Fawcett).

—The Taming of Annabelle. l.t. ed. 1985. (Six Sisters Ser.: Vol. 2). 10.95 o.p. (0-8161-3823-0, Macmillan Reference USA) Gale Group.

—The Taming of Annabelle. 1983. (Six Sisters Ser.: Vol. 2). 208p. 10.95 o.p. (0-312-78489-9) St. Martin's Pr.

### ARMSTRONG, EDWARD (FICTITIOUS CHARACTER)—FICTION

Cook, Robin. Acceptable Risk. abr. ed. 1995. audio 22.95 (1-55927-321-6, 692138) Audio Renaissance.

—Acceptable Risk. 1996. 400p. pap. 7.99 (0-425-15186-7) Berkley Publishing Group.

—Acceptable Risk. unabr. ed. 1995. audio 80.00 (0-7366-3038-4, 3720) Books on Tape, Inc.

—Acceptable Risk. l.t. ed. 1995. 26.95 o.p. (1-56895-173-6, Wheeler Publishing, Inc.) Gale Group.

—Acceptable Risk. 2001. 23.95 (0-399-14275-4); 1995. 432p. 23.95 o.s.i (0-399-13971-0, G. P. Putnam's Sons) Penguin Group (USA) Inc.

—Acceptable Risk. 406p. pap. 6.98 o.p. (0-7651-0427-X) Smithmark Pubs., Inc.

### ARNO, HARRY (FICTITIOUS CHARACTER)—FICTION

Leonard, Elmore. Pronto. 1994. 384p. mass mkt. 6.50 o.s.i (0-440-21443-2) Dell Publishing.

—Pronto. 1998. 272p. pap. 9.95 o.s.i (0-385-33290-4) Doubleday Publishing.

—Riding the Rap. 1998. 304p. pap. 10.95 o.s.i (0-385-32417-0, Delta); 1996. 352p. mass mkt. 6.50 o.s.i (0-440-21441-6); 1995. 336p. mass mkt. 6.50 (0-440-29539-4) Dell Publishing.

—Riding the Rap. l.t. ed. 1995. (Large Print Bks.). 27.95 (1-56895-224-4, Wheeler Publishing, Inc.) Gale Group.

—Riding the Rap. 2002. 352p. mass mkt. 7.50 (0-06-008218-6) HarperCollins Pubs.

### ARNOLD, JESSIE (FICTITIOUS CHARACTER)—FICTION

Henry, Sue. Beneath the Ashes. 2001. 336p. mass mkt. 6.99 (0-380-79892-1, Avon Bks.); 2000. 288p. 23.00 (0-380-97662-5, Morrow, William & Co.) Morrow/Avon.

—Cold Company. l.t. ed. 2002. (Large Print Ser.). 27.95 (1-57490-457-4) Beeler, Thomas T. Publisher.

—Cold Company. 2002. (Alaska Mystery Ser.). (Illus.). 304p. 23.95 (0-380-97882-2, Morrow, William & Co.) Morrow/Avon.

—Deadfall: An Alaska Mystery. unabr. ed. 2000. (Alaska Mystery Ser.). audio 29.95 (0-7366-4428-8) Books on Tape, Inc.

—Deadfall: An Alaska Mystery. (Alaska Mysteries Ser.). 1999. 320p. mass mkt. 6.99 (0-380-79891-3); 1998. 304p. 22.00 (0-380-97661-7) Morrow/Avon. (Avon Bks.).

—Death Takes Passage: An Alex Jensen Mystery. (Alaska Mysteries Ser.). 1998. (Illus.). 352p. mass mkt. 6.99 (0-380-78863-2); 1997. 272p. (YA). mass mkt. 22.00 o.p. (0-380-97469-X) Morrow/Avon. (Avon Bks.).

—Death Trap: An Alaska Mystery. 2003. 288p. 23.95 (0-380-97883-0, Morrow, William & Co.) Morrow/Avon.

—Murder on the Yukon Quest. Grader, T. L., ed. 2000. (Alaska Mysteries Ser.). 320p. mass mkt. 6.99 (0-380-78864-0, Avon Bks.) Morrow/Avon.

—Murder on the Yukon Quest. 1959. (Illus.). 304p. 22.00 (0-380-97764-8, Avon Bks.) Morrow/Avon.

### ARNOLD, LUCY RICHARDS (FICTITIOUS CHARACTER)—FICTION

Wood, Jane Roberts. Dance a Little Longer, Vol. 3. unabr. ed. 1995. audio 51.00 (0-7887-0396-X, 94588E7) Recorded Bks., LLC.

—Dance a Little Longer. 3rd ed. 2000. (Lucinda Richards Trilogy Ser.: Vol. 3). iv, 211p. reprint ed. pap. 15.95 (1-57441-080-6) Univ. of North Texas Pr.

—A Place Called Sweet Shrub. 1991. 320p. pap. 10.00 o.s.i (0-440-50305-1, Dell Bks.) Dell Publishing.

—A Place Called Sweet Shrub, Set. unabr. ed. 1996. audio 67.00 Recorded Bks., LLC.

—A Place Called Sweet Shrub. 3rd ed. 2000. (Lucinda Richards Trilogy Ser.: Vol. 2). 286p. reprint ed. pap. 15.95 (1-57441-079-2) Univ. of North Texas Pr.

—The Train to Estelline. 1988. 240p. pap. 11.95 o.s.i (0-385-31289-X, Delta); reprint ed. pap. 10.00 o.s.i (0-440-50033-8, Laurel) Dell Publishing.

—The Train to Estelline. unabr. ed. 1995. audio 44.00 (0-7887-0164-9, 94389E7) Recorded Bks., LLC.

—The Train to Estelline. 1987. 240p. 19.95 (0-936650-05-2) Temple, Ellen C. Publishing, Inc.

—The Train to Estelline. 3rd ed. 2000. (Lucinda Richards Trilogy Ser.: Vol. 1). 209p. reprint ed. pap. 15.95 (1-57441-078-4) Univ. of North Texas Pr.

—The Train to Estelline. 1987. E-Book 19.95 (0-585-16344-8) netLibrary, Inc.

### ARROWOOD, SPENCER (FICTITIOUS CHARACTER)—FICTION

McCrumb, Sharyn. The Ballad of Frankie Silver. unabr. ed. 1998. audio 62.95 (0-7861-1443-6, 2305) Blackstone Audio Bks., Inc.

—The Ballad of Frankie Silver. 1998. 304p. 23.95 o.p. (0-525-93969-5) Dutton/Plume.

—The Ballad of Frankie Silver. l.t. ed. 1998. (Large Print Book Ser.). 27.95 (1-56895-656-8, Wheeler Publishing, Inc.) Gale Group.

—The Ballad of Frankie Silver. 1999. 416p. reprint ed. mass mkt. 7.99 (0-451-19739-9, Signet Bks.) NAL.

—The Ballad of Frankie Silver. abr. ed. 1998. audio 25.00 (0-7871-1713-7, Dove Audio) NewStar Media, Inc.

—The Ballad of Frankie Silver. unabr. ed. 1999. audio compact disk 109.00 (0-7887-3437-7, C1043E7); 1998. audio 94.00 (0-7887-2475-4, 95550E7) Recorded Bks., LLC.

—The Hangman's Beautiful Daughter: A Novel of Suspense. l.t. ed. 1996. lib. bdg. 23.95 (1-57490-069-2, Beeler Large Print Bks.) Beeler, Thomas T. Publisher.

—The Hangman's Beautiful Daughter: A Novel of Suspense. 1992. 288p. 19.00 (0-684-19407-4, Macmillan Reference USA) Gale Group.

—The Hangman's Beautiful Daughter: A Novel of Suspense. 1993. 384p. mass mkt. 7.99 (0-451-40370-3, Onyx) NAL.

—The Hangman's Beautiful Daughter: A Novel of Suspense. unabr. ed. 1993. audio 60.00 (1-55690-786-9, 93104E7) Recorded Bks., LLC.

—The Hangman's Beautiful Daughter: A Novel of Suspense. 1992. 13.55 (0-606-06147-9) Turtleback Bks.

—If Ever I Return, Pretty Peggy-O. 1998. mass mkt. 6.99 (0-345-91352-3); 1995. mass mkt. 5.99 o.p. (0-345-90215-7); 1991. 336p. mass mkt. 6.99 (0-345-36906-8) Ballantine Bks.

—If Ever I Return, Pretty Peggy-O. 1990. 324p. 17.95 o.s.i (0-684-19104-0, Macmillan Reference USA) Gale Group.

—If Ever I Return, Pretty Peggy-O. unabr. ed. 1993. audio 70.00 (1-55690-921-7, 93417E7) Recorded Bks., LLC.

—The Rosewood Casket. 2003. audio compact disk 19.95 (0-7861-9651-3); 1999. audio 49.95 (0-7861-0994-7, 1771); 1996. audio compact disk 72.00 (0-7861-9844-3, 1771) Blackstone Audio Bks., Inc.

—The Rosewood Casket. 1998. 303p. text 24.00 (0-7881-5352-8) DIANE Publishing Co.

—The Rosewood Casket. 1996. (Illus.). 320p. 23.95 o.p. (0-525-94011-1) Dutton/Plume.

—The Rosewood Casket. l.t. ed. 1996. 435p. lib. bdg. 25.95 o.p. (0-7838-1826-2, Macmillan Reference USA) Gale Group.

—The Rosewood Casket. 1997. 432p. mass mkt. 7.99 (0-451-18471-8, Signet Bks.) NAL.

—The Rosewood Casket. unabr. ed. 1996. (Ballad Ser.: Vol. 4). audio 78.00 (0-7887-0522-9, 94717E7) Recorded Bks., LLC.

—The Rosewood Casket. abr. ed. 1996. audio 16.95 o.p. (0-14-086386-9, Penguin AudioBooks) Viking Penguin.

—She Walks These Hills, unabr. ed. 1998. audio 56.95 (0-7861-1351-0, 2254) Blackstone Audio Bks., Inc.

—She Walks These Hills. abr. ed. 1994. audio 16.95 o.p. (1-56100-394-8, 1368, Nova Audio Bks.); audio 73.25 o.p. (1-56100-228-3, 1040, Unabridged Library Editions); audio 23.95 o.p. (1-56100-603-3, 262, Bookcassette) Brilliance Audio.

—She Walks These Hills. l.t. ed. 1996. (Large Print Bks.). 24.95 o.p. (1-56895-357-7, Wheeler Publishing, Inc.) Gale Group.

—She Walks These Hills. abr. ed. 2000. audio 7.95 (1-57815-025-6, 1027, Media Bks. Audio Publishing) Media Bks., L. L. C.

—She Walks These Hills. 1995. 448p. mass mkt. 7.99 (0-451-18472-6, Signet Bks.) NAL.

—She Walks These Hills, unabr. ed. 1999. audio 78.00 (0-7887-0229-7, 94454E7) Recorded Bks., LLC.

—She Walks These Hills. 1994. 320p. 21.00 (0-684-19556-9, Scribner) Simon & Schuster.

## ARTHUR, KING—FICTION

Ashley, Mike, ed. The Pendragon Chronicles: Heroic Fantasy from the Time of King Arthur. 428p. 1991. pap. 9.95 o.p. (0-87226-228-6); 1990. 18.95 o.s.i (0-87226-335-5) McGraw-Hill Children's Publishing. (Bedrick, Peter Bks.).

Attanasio, A. A. The Dragon & the Unicorn. 1996. 512p. pap. 16.00 o.p. (0-06-109297-5) HarperTrade.

—The Dragon & the Unicorn. 1996. 560p. mass mkt. 7.99 (0-06-105779-7, Eos) Morrow/Avon.

—The Eagle & the Sword: An Arthurian Epic. 1999. 448p. mass mkt. 6.50 o.s.i (0-06-105839-4); 1997. 304p. mass mkt. 14.00 o.p. (0-06-109298-3) Morrow/Avon. (Eos).

—The Serpent & the Grail. 1999. 368p. pap. 16.00 o.p. (0-06-107340-7) HarperCollins Pubs.

—The Serpent & the Grail. 2000. 400p. mass mkt. 6.99 (0-06-105973-0, Eos) Morrow/Avon.

—The Wolf & the Crown. 1999. 432p. mass mkt. 5.99 (0-06-105776-2); 1998. 352p. pap. 14.00 o.s.i (0-06-105370-8) Morrow/Avon. (Eos).

Barthelme, Donald. The King. 1990. (Illus.). 176p. 16.95 o.p. (0-06-016195-7) HarperTrade.

—The King. 1992. (Illus.). 160p. pap. 10.00 o.p. (0-14-014992-9, Penguin Bks.) Penguin Group (USA) Inc.

Batt, Catherine. Malory's Morte D'Arthur: Remarking Arthurian Tradition. 2002. (New Middle Ages Ser.). 288p. 55.00 (0-312-22998-4) Palgrave Macmillan.

Berger, Thomas. Arthur Rex. 1979. 512p. pap. 5.95 o.s.i (0-385-28005-X, Delta); 1978. 11.95 o.s.i (0-385-28039-4, Delacorte Pr.) Dell Publishing.

—Arthur Rex. 1990. pap. 10.95 o.p. (0-316-09146-4) Little Brown & Co.

—Arthur Rex. 1985. mass mkt. 4.95 o.p. (0-440-30362-1) Dell Publishing.

Bradley, Marion Zimmer. The Mists of Avalon. 2001. E-Book 15.00 (1-58945-945-8) Adobe Systems, Inc.

—The Mists of Avalon. 2001. E-Book 15.00 (0-345-44816-2, Ballantine Bks.); 2000. 896p. 30.00 (0-345-44118-4, Del Rey); 1985. 396p. pap. 9.95 o.s.i (0-345-33385-3, Del Rey); 1984. pap. 8.95 o.s.i (0-345-31452-2); 1987. 912p. reprint ed. pap. 16.95 (0-345-35049-9, Del Rey) Ballantine Bks.

—The Mists of Avalon. 1982. 16.95 o.p. (0-394-52406-3) Knopf, Alfred A. Inc.

—The Mists of Avalon. unabr. ed. 1993. audio 78.00 (1-55690-938-1, 93434E7); audio 70.00 (1-55690-917-9, 93413E7); audio 78.00 (1-55690-903-9, 93345E7); audio 85.00 (1-55690-868-7, 93310E7) Recorded Bks., LLC.

—The Mists of Avalon. abr. ed. 1995. audio 17.00 (1-57042-205-2, 4-522052) Time Warner AudioBooks.

Bradshaw, Gillian. In Winter's Shadow. 1992. 336p. mass mkt. 4.99 o.s.i (0-553-29899-2, Spectra) Bantam Bks.

—In Winter's Shadow. 1983. mass mkt. 2.95 o.p. (0-451-12276-3, Signet Bks.) NAL.

—In Winter's Shadow. 1982. 15.95 o.p. (0-671-43512-4, Simon & Schuster) Simon & Schuster.

—Kingdom of Summer. 1992. 288p. mass mkt. 4.99 o.s.i (0-553-29964-6, Spectra) Bantam Bks.

—Kingdom of Summer. 1982. mass mkt. 3.50 o.p. (0-451-13553-9, Signet Bks.) NAL.

—Kingdom of Summer. 1981. 12.95 o.p. (0-671-25472-3, Simon & Schuster) Simon & Schuster.

Brown, Thomas Airlie. Celtic Roots. 2001. 276p. pap. (1-55212-585-8) Trafford Publishing.

Canning, Victor. The Circle of the Gods. l.t. ed. 1981. (Ulverscroft Large Print Ser.). 380p. 29.99 o.p. (0-7089-0571-4, Ulverscroft) Thorpe, F. A. Pubs. GBR. Dist: Ulverscroft Large Print Bks., Ltd., Ulverscroft Large Print Canada, Ltd.

—The Crimson Chalice. 1979. 2.50 o.s.i (0-441-12190-X) Ace Bks.

—The Crimson Chalice. l.t. ed. 1980. (Ulverscroft Large Print Ser.). 380p. 29.99 o.p. (0-7089-0543-9, Ulverscroft) Thorpe, F. A. Pubs. GBR. Dist: Ulverscroft Large Print Bks., Ltd., Ulverscroft Large Print Canada, Ltd.

—The Immortal Wound. l.t. ed. 1981. (Ulverscroft Large Print Ser.). 372p. 29.99 o.p. (0-7089-0600-1, Ulverscroft) Thorpe, F. A. Pubs. GBR. Dist: Ulverscroft Large Print Bks., Ltd., Ulverscroft Large Print Canada, Ltd.

Chant, Joy. The High Kings. 1985. mass mkt. 3.50 o.s.i (0-553-24306-3); 1983. 256p. 24.95 o.p. (0-553-05045-1) Bantam Bks. (Spectra).

Chapman, Vera. The Three Damosels. 1996. (Illus.). 383p. (0-575-06340-8) Gollancz, Victor.

Cherryh, C. J. Port Eternity. 1982. (Alliance-Union Universe Ser.). mass mkt. 2.50 o.p. (0-87997-769-8) DAW Bks., Inc.

—Port Eternity. l.t. ed. 2001. (Science Fiction Ser.). 285p. 27.95 (0-7838-9413-9) Thorndike Pr.

Christian, Catherine. The Pendragon. 1979. 10.95 o.p. (0-394-50105-5, Knopf Bks. for Young Readers) Random Hse. Children's Bks.

—The Pendragon. 1984. mass mkt. 3.95 (0-446-32342-X) Warner Bks., Inc.

Cochran, Molly. The Broken Sword. 1997. 384p. 24.95 o.p. (0-312-86283-0, Tor Bks.) Doherty, Tom Assocs., LLC.

Cochran, Molly & Murphy, Warren. The Broken Sword. 1998. 480p. mass mkt. 6.99 (0-8125-4513-3, Tor Bks.) Doherty, Tom Assocs., LLC.

Cornwell, Bernard. Enemy of God: A Novel of Arthur. abr. ed. 1997. (Warlord Chronicles Ser.: Vol. 2). audio 24.95 (1-55927-446-8) Audio Renaissance.

—Enemy of God: A Novel of Arthur. unabr. collector's ed. 1997. audio 96.00 (0-7366-4073-8, 4582) Books on Tape, Inc.

—Enemy of God: A Novel of Arthur. 416p. 1997. (Warlord Chronicles Ser.: Vol. 2). 24.95 (0-312-15523-9); 1998. reprint ed. pap. 15.95 (0-312-18714-9, NPB 0223, Saint Martin's Griffin) St. Martin's Pr.

—Excalibur: A Novel of Arthur. abr. ed. 1998. (Warlord Chronicles Ser.). audio 24.95 (1-55927-499-9) Audio Renaissance.

—Excalibur: A Novel of Arthur, , unabr. collector's ed. 1998. audio 96.00 (0-7366-4276-5, 4774) Books on Tape, Inc.

—Excalibur: A Novel of Arthur. 448p. 1998. (Warlord Chronicles Ser.: Vol. 3). 24.95 o.p. (0-312-18575-8); 1999. reprint ed. pap. 14.95 (0-312-20648-8, NPB 0267, Saint Martin's Griffin) St. Martin's Pr.

—Excalibur: A Novel of Arthur. l.t. ed. 1998. (Basic Ser.). 749p. 29.95 (0-7862-1476-7) Thorndike Pr.

—Excalibur, Enemy of God, the Winter King: Novels of Arthur. 1999. pap. 0.01 (0-312-19070-0, Saint Martin's Griffin) St. Martin's Pr.

—The Winter King: A Novel of Arthur, Set. abr. ed. 1997. (Warlord Chronicles Ser.: Vol. 1). audio 24.95 (1-55927-445-X, 695089) Audio Renaissance.

—The Winter King: A Novel of Arthur. unabr. collector's ed. 1997. audio 104.00 (0-913369-79-9, 4345) Books on Tape, Inc.

—The Winter King: A Novel of Arthur. 1996. 24.95 (0-312-14073-8); 1996. (Warlord Chronicles Ser.: Bk. 1). 448p. text 24.95 o.p. (0-312-14447-4); 3rd ed. 1997. 448p. pap. 14.95 (0-312-15696-0, Saint Martin's Griffin) St. Martin's Pr.

Drake, David. The Dragon Lord. 1998. 320p. pap. 6.99 (0-671-87890-5) Baen Bks.

—The Dragon Lord. 1989. 320p. mass mkt. 4.99 (0-8125-3605-3); 1983. mass mkt. 2.95 (0-523-48552-2) Doherty, Tom Assocs., LLC. (Tor Bks.).

—The Dragon Lord. 1979. 10.95 o.p. (0-399-12380-6) Putnam Publishing Group, The.

Foss, Michael. The World of Camelot: King Arthur & the Knights of the Round Table. (Illus.). 240p. 1998. pap. 17.95 (0-8069-4230-4); 1995. 19.95 o.p. (0-8069-1314-2) Sterling Publishing Co., Inc.

Gilliam, Richard, et al, eds. Excalibur. 1995. 480p. pap. 14.99 o.s.i (0-446-67084-7) Warner Bks., Inc.

Gloag, John. Artorius Rex. 1977. 7.95 o.p. (0-312-05548-X) St. Martin's Pr.

Godwin, Parke. Firelord. 1980. 416p. 13.95 o.p. (0-385-17070-X) Doubleday Publishing.

—Firelord. 1994. pap. 5.50 (0-380-77551-4, Avon Bks.) Morrow/Avon.

Goldstein, Lisa. Strange Devices of the Sun & Moon. 1994. 301p. pap. text 4.99 (0-8125-1951-5); 1993. 304p. 19.95 o.p. (0-312-85460-9) Doherty, Tom Assocs., LLC. (Tor Bks.).

Green, Roger Lancelyn. King Arthur & His Knights of the Round Table. 1980. pap. 2.95 o.p. (0-14-005589-4) Penguin Group (USA) Inc.

—King Arthur & His Knights of the Round Table. 2002. (Perennial Bestsellers Ser.). 28.95 (0-7862-4839-4) Thorndike Pr.

—King Arthur & His Knights of the Round Table. 1980. 11.04 (0-606-01627-9) Turtleback Bks.

Hollick, Helen. The Kingmaking. 1995. (Pendragon's Banner Ser.: Bk. 1). 608p. 24.95 o.p. (0-312-13533-5) St. Martin's Pr.

—Pendragon's Banner. 1996. 560p. 25.95 o.p. (0-312-14699-X) St. Martin's Pr.

—Shadow of the King. 1998. 400p. mass mkt. o.p. (0-7493-2058-3) Random Hse. of Canada, Ltd. CAN. Dist: Random Hse., Inc.

—Shadow of the King. 1997. (Pendragon's Banner Ser.: Vol. 3). 560p. 27.95 o.p. (0-312-17000-9) St. Martin's Pr.

James, Cary. King & Raven. Date not set. (0-312-85889-2); 1997. 533p. mass mkt. 6.99 o.s.i (0-8125-5176-1); 1995. 384p. 23.95 o.p. (0-312-85870-1) Doherty, Tom Assocs., LLC. (Tor Bks.).

—King & Raven. 1995. 384p. per. 19.95 (0-7592-2418-8) ereads.com.

Jones, Courtway. In the Shadow of the Oak King. 1992. 352p. mass mkt. 5.99 (0-671-73404-0, Pocket) Simon & Schuster.

—In the Shadow of the Oak King. Zion, Claire, ed. 1991. 320p. 19.95 (0-671-73403-2, Atria) Simon & Schuster.

Jones, Mary J. Avalon. 1991. 237p. pap. 9.95 o.p. (0-941483-96-7) Naiad Pr., Inc.

Kennealy-Morrison, Patricia. Blackmantle. 1998. (Keltiad Ser.). 640p. mass mkt. 6.99 o.s.i (0-06-105610-3, Eos) Morrow/Avon.

—Blackmantle: A Book of the Keltiad. 1997. 608p. 24.00 o.s.i (0-06-105231-0, Eos) Morrow/Avon.

—The Deer's Cry: A Book of the Keltiad. 1999. 512p. mass mkt. 6.50 o.s.i (0-06-105927-7); 1998. 384p. 24.00 o.s.i (0-06-105059-8) HarperCollins Pubs.

—The Hawk's Gray Feather: A Book of the Keltiad. 1991. (Tales of Arthur Ser.: Vol. 1). 416p. mass mkt. 5.99 o.s.i (0-451-45053-1, ROC); 1990. (Keltiad Ser.). text 18.95 o.p. (0-451-45005-1) NAL.

—The Hedge of Mist. 1996. (Tales of Arthur Ser.: Vol. 3). 528p. mass mkt. 22.00 o.p. (0-06-105230-2) HarperTrade.

—The Oak above the Kings: A Book of the Keltiad. 1995. 432p. mass mkt. 5.99 o.s.i (0-451-45451-0, ROC); 1994. 384p. 17.95 o.p. (0-451-45352-2) NAL.

Lawhead, Stephen R. Arthur. unabr. ed. 1995. (Pendragon Cycle Ser.: Bk. 3). audio 89.95 (0-7861-0766-9, 1615) Blackstone Audio Bks., Inc.

—Arthur. 1989. (Pendragon Cycle Ser.: Bk. 3). 445p. pap. 11.99 o.p. (0-89107-475-9) Crossway Bks.

—Arthur. 1990. (Pendragon Cycle Ser.: Bk. 3). 448p. reprint ed. mass mkt. 7.50 (0-380-70890-6, Eos) Morrow/Avon.

—Arthur. 1996. (Pendragon Cycle Ser.: Bk. 3). 496p. pap. 29.99 (0-310-20507-7) Zondervan.

—Avalon: The Return of King Arthur. 1999. 448p. 25.00 (0-380-97702-8, Eos) Morrow/Avon.

—Grail. 1998. (Pendragon Cycle Ser.: Vol. 5). 400p. mass mkt. 6.99 (0-380-78104-2, Eos); 1997. (Pendragon Cycle Ser.: Bk. 5). 464p. pap. 24.00 (0-380-97526-2, Avon Bks.) Morrow/Avon.

—Pendragon, unabr. ed. 1996. (Pendragon Cycle Ser.: Bk. 4). audio 69.95 (0-7861-0986-6, 1763) Blackstone Audio Bks., Inc.

—Pendragon. (Pendragon Cycle Ser.: Bk. 4). 2000. 23.00 (0-380-97242-5); 1994. 436p. 23.00 o.p. (0-688-13714-8, Avon Bks.); 1995. 448p. reprint ed. mass mkt. 6.99 (0-380-71757-3, Eos) Morrow/Avon.

—The Pendragon Cycle: Taliesin; Merlin; Arthur. 1989. pap. 35.97 o.p. (0-89107-540-2) Crossway Bks.

Malory, Thomas. Le Morte D'Arthur. 432p. 28.95 (0-8488-2616-7) Amereon, Ltd.

—Le Morte D'Arthur. E-Book 2.49 (1-58627-784-7); E-Book 2.49 (1-58627-783-9) Electric Umbrella Publishing.

—Le Morte D'arthur: Complete, Unabridged, New Illustrated Edition. Matthews, John, ed. 2003. (Illus.). 1088p. pap. 24.95 (1-84403-001-6) Cassell P L C GBR. Dist: Sterling Publishing Co., Inc.

Matthews, John. The Romance of Arthur: The Lost Legends of King Arthur & His Knights of the Round Table. 2003. 416p. (1-84333-612-X) Vega Bks.

—Secret Camelot. 1997. (Illus.). 176 p. 29.95 (0-7137-2646-6) Blandford Pr. GBR. Dist: Sterling Publishing Co., Inc.

—The Song of Arthur: Celtic Tales from the High King's Court. 2002. (Illus.). 234p. pap. 19.95 (0-8356-0809-3, Quest Bks.) Theosophical Publishing Hse.

Matthews, John & Stewart, Bob. Tales of Arthur: Stories from the Arthurian Legend. 1989. (Illus.). 128p. (Orig.). pap. 5.95 o.p. (0-7137-2059-X) Blandford Pr. GBR. Dist: Sterling Publishing Co., Inc.

McCaslin, Nellie. The Crowning of Arthur. 1996. 55p. (Orig.). (gr. 1-8). pap. 5.00 (0-88734-450-X) Players Pr., Inc.

Miles, Rosalind. Guenevere, Queen of the Summer Country. (Guenevere Ser.: Bk. 1). 2000. (Illus.). 528p. pap. 11.95 (0-609-80650-5, Crown); 1999. 432p. 24.00 o.s.i (0-609-60362-0) Crown Publishing Group.

—The Knight of the Sacred Lake. 2001. (Guenevere Ser.: Bk. 2). 448p. pap. 11.95 (0-609-80802-8, Three Rivers Pr.) Crown Publishing Group.

Paxson, Diana L. The Book of the Cauldron. 1999. (Hallowed Isle Ser.: Vol. 3). (Illus.). 192p. pap. 10.00 (0-380-80547-2, Eos) Morrow/Avon.

—The Book of the Spear. l.t. ed. 2002. 307p. 27.95 (0-7838-9556-9, Macmillan Reference USA) Gale Group.

—The Book of the Spear. 1999. (Hallowed Isle Ser.: 2). 208p. pap. 10.00 (0-380-80546-4, Eos) Morrow/Avon.

—The Book of the Stone, Bk. 4. 2000. (Hallowed Isle Ser.: Vol. 4 ). (Illus.). 208p. pap. 11.00 (0-380-80548-0, Eos) Morrow/Avon.

—The Book of the Sword. l.t. ed. 2001. (G.K. Hall Large Print Science Fiction Ser.). (Illus.). 263p. 27.95 (0-7838-9558-5, Hall, G. K. & Co.) Gale Group.

—The Book of the Sword & the Book of the Spear. 2000. (Hallowed Isle Ser.). 384p. mass mkt. 6.50 o.s.i (0-380-81367-X, Eos) Morrow/Avon.

—The Hallowed Isle: The Book of the Sword. 1999. (Hallowed Isle Ser.: Vol. 1). (Illus.). 181p. pap. 10.00 (0-380-78870-5, Eos) Morrow/Avon.

Radford, Irene. Guardian of the Trust, Vol. 2. 2001. (Merlin's Descendants Ser.: Vol. 2). 560p. reprint ed. mass mkt. 6.99 (0-88677-995-2) DAW Bks., Inc.

Rice, Robert. The Last Pendragon. 1992. 340p. 19.95 o.p. (0-8027-1180-4) Walker & Co.

Roberson, Jennifer, ed. Out of Avalon: An Anthology of Old Magic & New Myths. 2001. 352p. mass mkt. 5.99 (0-451-45831-1, ROC) NAL.

Steinbeck, John. The Acts of King Arthur & His Noble Knights: From the Winchester Manuscripts of Thomas Malory & Other Sources. 1986. 464p. mass mkt. 5.95 o.s.i (0-345-34512-6); 1980. mass mkt. 2.95 o.p. (0-345-28955-2); 1977. pap. 4.95 o.s.i (0-345-27389-3) Ballantine Bks. (Del Rey).

—The Acts of King Arthur & His Noble Knights: From the Winchester Manuscripts of Thomas Malory & Other Sources. 1993. 364p. pap. 17.00 (0-374-52378-9) Farrar, Straus & Giroux.

—The Acts of King Arthur & His Noble Knights: From the Winchester Manuscripts of Thomas Malory & Other Sources. Horton, Chase, ed. 1976. 364p. 10.00 o.p. (0-374-10085-3) Farrar, Straus & Giroux.

Stewart, Mary. The Crystal Cave. (Book I of the Arthurian Saga Ser.). 1996. 544p. pap. 12.95 o.s.i (0-449-91161-6); 1984. pap. 3.95 o.p. (0-449-44118-0); 1984. 384p. mass mkt. 6.50 o.s.i (0-449-20644-0); 1983. mass mkt. 3.95 o.s.i (0-449-20563-0); 1978. mass mkt. 1.95 o.s.i (0-449-23315-4) Ballantine Bks. (Fawcett).

—The Crystal Cave. unabr. ed. 2000. (Merlin Ser.: Bk. 1). audio 79.95 (0-7451-6305-X, CAB 676) Chivers Audio Bks. GBR. Dist: BBC Audiobooks America.

—The Crystal Cave. l.t. ed. 1982. (Reader's Request Ser.). 19.95 o.p. (0-8161-3338-7, Macmillan Reference USA) Gale Group.

—The Crystal Cave. 2003. (Illus.). 512p. pap. 14.95 (0-06-054825-8, Morrow, William & Co.) Morrow/Avon.

—The Crystal Cave, Set. abr. ed. 1993. audio 16.95 o.p. (1-55800-224-3, Dove Audio) NewStar Media, Inc.

—The Crystal Cave. 1983. 19.00 (0-606-18993-9) Turtleback Bks.

—The Hollow Hills. 1996. (Arthurian Saga Ser.: Vol. 2). 512p. pap. 14.00 o.s.i *(0-449-91173-X)*; 1984. pap. 3.95 o.p. *(0-449-44119-9)*; 1984. mass mkt. 5.95 o.s.i *(0-449-20645-9)*; 1978. mass mkt. 1.95 o.s.i *(0-449-23316-2)* Ballantine Bks. (Fawcett).

—The Hollow Hills. 1991. 400p. reprint ed. lib. bdg. 37.95 *(0-89966-855-0)* Buccaneer Bks., Inc.

—The Hollow Hills. l.t. ed. 1982. 19.95 o.p. *(0-8161-3339-5*, Macmillan Reference USA) Gale Group.

—The Hollow Hills. 2003. (Illus.). 496p. pap. 14.95 *(0-06-054826-6)*; 1973. 512p. 9.95 o.p. *(0-688-00179-3*, Morrow, William & Co.) Morrow/Avon.

—The Hollow Hills. abr. ed. 1993. audio 15.95 o.p. *(1-55800-227-8*, Dove Audio) NewStar Media, Inc.

—The Hollow Hills. 1984. 19.00 *(0-606-18994-7)* Turtleback Bks.

—The Last Enchantment. 1996. (Arthurian Saga Ser.: Vol. 3). 544p. pap. 14.00 o.s.i *(0-449-91176-4)*; 1984. pap. 3.95 o.s.i *(0-449-44120-2)*; 1984. mass mkt. 5.95 o.s.i *(0-449-20646-7)* Ballantine Bks. (Fawcett).

—The Last Enchantment. unabr. ed. 2000. (Merlin Ser.: Bk. 3). audio 79.95 *(0-7451-4128-5*, CAB 811) Chivers Audio Bks. GBR. *Dist:* BBC Audiobooks America.

—The Last Enchantment. l.t. ed. 1982. 19.95 o.p. *(0-8161-3340-9*, Macmillan Reference USA) Gale Group.

—The Last Enchantment. 2003. (Illus.). 528p. pap. 14.95 *(0-06-054827-4*, Morrow, William & Co.) Morrow/Avon.

—The Last Enchantment. abr. ed. 1993. audio 15.95 o.p. *(1-55800-228-6*, Dove Audio) NewStar Media, Inc.

—The Last Enchantment. 1984. 20.05 *(0-606-18995-5)* Turtleback Bks.

—The Prince & the Pilgrim. 1997. (Classics of Arthurian Legend Ser.). 320p. mass mkt. 6.99 *(0-449-22443-0*, Fawcett) Ballantine Bks.

—The Prince & the Pilgrim. 1996. 292p. 23.00 o.p. *(0-688-14538-8*, Morrow, William & Co.) Morrow/Avon.

—The Prince & the Pilgrim, Set. abr. ed. 1996. (J). 17.95 o.p. *(0-7871-0746-8)* NewStar Media, Inc.

—The Prince & the Pilgrim. abr. ed. 1995. audio 16.95 *(1-85998-489-4)* Trafalgar Square.

—The Wicked Day. 1996. (Arthurian Saga Ser.: Vol. 4). 464p. pap. 14.00 o.s.i *(0-449-91185-3)*; 1984. 384p. mass mkt. 5.95 o.s.i *(0-449-20519-3)* Ballantine Bks. (Fawcett).

—The Wicked Day. unabr. ed. 2000. (Merlin Ser.: Bk. 4). audio 69.95 *(0-7451-6689-X*, CAB 1305) Chivers Audio Bks. GBR. *Dist:* BBC Audiobooks America.

—The Wicked Day. l.t. ed. 1984. (General Ser.). 17.95 o.p. *(0-8161-3684-X*, Macmillan Reference USA) Gale Group.

—The Wicked Day. 2003. (Illus.). 432p. pap. 14.95 *(0-06-054828-2)* Morrow/Avon.

—The Wicked Day. abr. ed. 1993. 15.95 o.p. *(1-55800-308-8*, 41350) NewStar Media, Inc.

—The Wicked Day. 1984. 20.05 *(0-606-18996-3)* Turtleback Bks.

Sutcliff, Rosemary. Sword at Sunset. 1987. 512p. mass mkt. 5.99 *(0-8125-8852-5*, Tor Bks.) Doherty, Tom Assocs., LLC.

Twain, Mark. A Connecticut Yankee in King Arthur's Court. 1994. (Illustrated Classics Collection: No. 3). 64p. pap. 3.60 o.p. *(1-56103-525-4)*; pap. 4.95 *(0-7854-0695-6*, 40447) American Guidance Service, Inc.

—A Connecticut Yankee in King Arthur's Court. 1983. 288p. mass mkt. 4.95 *(0-553-21143-9*, Bantam Classics) Bantam Bks.

—A Connecticut Yankee in King Arthur's Court. 2000. (Stratford Festival Ser.). audio 12.92 *(0-660-18178-9)* Canadian Broadcasting Corp./Societe Radio-Canada CAN. *Dist:* Georgetown Terminal Warehouse.

—A Connecticut Yankee in King Arthur's Court. E-Book 2.95 *(1-57799-844-8)* Logos Research Systems, Inc.

—A Connecticut Yankee in King Arthur's Court. E-Book 1.95 *(1-58515-199-8)* MesaView, Inc.

—A Connecticut Yankee in King Arthur's Court. 1963. mass mkt. 1.95 o.p. *(0-451-51874-8)*; 334p. mass mkt. 2.25 o.p. *(0-451-52353-9*, Signet Classics) NAL.

—A Connecticut Yankee in King Arthur's Court. Ensor, Allison E., ed. 1982. (Critical Editions Ser.). (Illus.). (C). 455p. 24.95 o.p. *(0-393-01378-2)*; 450p. pap. text 16.35 *(0-393-95137-5)* Norton, W. W. & Co., Inc.

—A Connecticut Yankee in King Arthur's Court. Inge, M. Thomas, ed. (Oxford World's Classics Ser.). (Illus.). 1999. 400p. pap. 7.95 *(0-19-283902-0)*; 1997. 386p. pap. 5.95 o.p. *(0-19-282721-9)* Oxford Univ. Pr., Inc.

—A Connecticut Yankee in King Arthur's Court. 1987. (Regents Illustrated Classics Ser.). 62p. pap. text 4.65 net. o.p. *(0-13-167701-2*, 20468) Prentice Hall, ESL Dept.

—A Connecticut Yankee in King Arthur's Court. 2000. (Illus.). 260p. pap. 19.99 *(1-57646-258-7)* Quiet Vision Publishing.

—A Connecticut Yankee in King Arthur's Court. 1984. (Illus.). 334p. 12.95 o.p. *(0-89577-185-3)* Reader's Digest Assn., Inc., The.

—A Connecticut Yankee in King Arthur's Court. 1979. 368p. pap. 2.50 *(0-671-41017-2*, Simon Pulse) Simon & Schuster Children's Publishing.

—A Connecticut Yankee in King Arthur's Court. 1960. (Signet Classics Ser.). 11.00 *(0-606-01831-X)* Turtleback Bks.

—A Connecticut Yankee in King Arthur's Court. 1983. (Mark Twain Library: No. 4). (Illus.). 482p. (C). 30.00 o.p. *(0-520-05089-4)*; pap. 14.95 *(0-520-05109-2)* Univ. of California Pr.

—A Connecticut Yankee in King Arthur's Court. Stein, Bernard L., ed. 1979. (Iowa-California Edition of the Works of Mark Twain: No. 9). (Illus.). 847p. text 75.00 *(0-520-03621-2)* Univ. of California Pr.

—A Connecticut Yankee in King Arthur's Court. Kaplan, Justin, ed. & intro. by. 1972. (Classics Ser.). 416p. 7.95 *(0-14-043064-4*, Penguin Classics) Viking Penguin.

—A Connecticut Yankee in King Arthur's Court. Fishkin, Shelley Fisher, ed. 1996. (Oxford Mark Twain Ser.). (Illus.). 656p. 22.00 o.p. *(0-19-510141-3)* Oxford Univ. Pr., Inc.

—A Connecticut Yankee in King Arthur's Court. unabr. ed. 1991. audio 34.95 o.p. *(1-55656-089-3*, DAB015) BBC Audiobooks America.

—A Connecticut Yankee in King Arthur's Court, unabr. ed. 2000. audio 56.95 *(0-7861-1721-4*, 2525) Blackstone Audio Bks., Inc.

—A Connecticut Yankee in King Arthur's Court. 1982. reprint ed. lib. bdg. 19.95 *(0-89966-381-8)* Buccaneer Bks., Inc.

—A Connecticut Yankee in King Arthur's Court. unabr. ed. audio 29.95 o.s.i *(1-55656-034-6)*; 1997. pap. 29.95 incl. audio *(1-55656-200-4)* Dercum Audio.

—A Connecticut Yankee in King Arthur's Court. abr. ed. 1992. audio 16.99 *(0-88646-324-6*, 7324) Durkin Hayes Publishing Ltd.

—A Connecticut Yankee in King Arthur's Court. 1980. (Holiday Editions). (Illus.). reprint ed. 7.95 o.p. *(0-06-014445-9)* HarperCollins Pubs.

—A Connecticut Yankee in King Arthur's Court. abr. ed. 1989. audio 21.00 Jimcin Recordings.

—A Connecticut Yankee in King Arthur's Court. abr. ed. (Ultimate Classics Ser.). 1994. 29.95 o.p. incl. audio compact disk *(0-7871-0059-5)*; 1993. 16.95 o.p. incl. audio *(1-55800-739-3)*; 1993. 16.95 o.p. incl. audio *(1-55800-739-3)* NewStar Media, Inc.

—A Connecticut Yankee in King Arthur's Court. 2000. (Twelve-Point Ser.). 245p. reprint ed. lib. bdg. 25.00 *(1-58287-118-3)* North Bks.

—A Connecticut Yankee in King Arthur's Court. 1988. (Works of Mark Twain). reprint ed. lib. bdg. 79.00 *(0-7812-1121-2)* Reprint Services Corp.

—A Connecticut Yankee in King Arthur's Court: 1889. 1988. mass mkt. 4.95 *(0-938819-79-8*, Aerie) Doherty, Tom Assocs., LLC.

—A Connecticut Yankee in King Arthur's Court: 1889. Fishkin, Shelley Fisher, ed. 1997. (Oxford Mark Twain Ser.). (Illus.). 656p. text 28.00 *(0-19-511410-8)* Oxford Univ. Pr., Inc.

—A Connecticut Yankee in King Arthur's Court Readalong. 1994. (Illustrated Classics Collection: No. 3). 64p. pap. 14.95 incl. audio *(0-7854-0736-7*, 40449) American Guidance Service, Inc.

White, T. H. The Once & Future King. 1996. 688p. pap. 17.95 *(0-441-00383-4)*; 1987. 640p. mass mkt. 7.99 *(0-441-62740-4)* Ace Bks.

—The Once & Future King. 1985. 640p. 4.95 o.s.i *(0-425-09116-3)*; 1985. 4.50 o.s.i *(0-425-08196-6)*; 1983. 3.95 o.s.i *(0-425-06310-0)*; 1982. o.s.i; 1982. 3.50 o.s.i *(0-425-05614-7)*; 1981. 3.25 o.s.i *(0-425-05076-9)*; 1979. 2.95 o.s.i *(0-425-04490-4)*; 1977. 2.75 o.s.i *(0-425-03796-7)*; 1976. 2.25 o.s.i *(0-425-03174-8)*; 1974. 1.95 o.s.i *(0-425-02678-7)*; 1971. 1.25 o.p. *(0-425-02077-0)* Berkley Publishing Group.

—The Once & Future King. 1958. 688p. 25.95 *(0-399-10597-2*, G. P. Putnam's Sons) Penguin Group (USA) Inc.

—The Once & Future King. 1966. (Berkley Medallion Book Ser.). 13.04 *(0-606-01195-1)* Turtleback Bks.

Whyte, Jack. The Eagles' Brood. 1997. (Camulod Chronicles: Bk. 3). 416p. 25.95 *(0-312-85289-4*, Forge Bks.) Doherty, Tom Assocs., LLC.

—The Fort at River's Bend. (Camulod Chronicles: Bk. 5). (Illus.). 2000. 480p. mass mkt. 6.99 *(0-8125-4418-8*, Tor Bks.); 1999. 352p. 24.95 *(0-312-86597-X*, Forge Bks.) Doherty, Tom Assocs., LLC.

—The Saxon Shore. 1998. (Camulod Chronicles: Bk. 4). (Illus.). 496p. 26.95 o.p. *(0-312-86596-1*, Forge Bks.) Doherty, Tom Assocs., LLC.

—The Skystone. (Illus.). 2002. 352p. pap. 14.95 *(0-7653-0372-8*, Forge Bks.); 1996. (Camulod Chronicles: Bk. 1). 498p. mass mkt. 6.99 *(0-8125-5138-9*, Tor Bks.); 1996. (Camulod Chronicles: Bk. 1). 352p. 22.95 o.p. *(0-312-86091-9*, Forge Bks.) Doherty, Tom Assocs., LLC.

—The Sorcerer: Metamorphosis. 1999. (Camulod Chronicles: Bk. 6). (Illus.). 352p. 23.95 *(0-312-86598-8*, Forge Bks.) Doherty, Tom Assocs., LLC.

Wibberley, Leonard. Quest of Excalibur. 1979. (Illus.). 190p. reprint ed. pap. 21.00 *(0-89370-231-5)*; lib. bdg. 31.00 o.p. *(0-89370-131-9)* Millefleurs.

Wolf, Joan. The Road to Avalon. 1989. 432p. mass mkt. 4.50 o.s.i *(0-451-40138-7*, Onyx); 1988. 400p. 18.95 o.p. *(0-453-00607-8)* NAL.

**ASCH, JACOB (FICTITIOUS CHARACTER)—FICTION**

Lyons. Castles Burning. 1981. mass mkt. 2.50 *(0-671-41864-5*, Pocket) Simon & Schuster.

Lyons, Arthur. All God's Children. 1976. mass mkt. 1.50 o.s.i *(0-345-25020-6)* Ballantine Bks.

—All God's Children. 1982. 224p. pap. o.p. *(0-03-060394-3*, Owl Bks.) Holt, Henry & Co.

—At the Hands of Another. 240p. 1986. pap. o.p. *(0-03-008533-0*, Owl Bks.); 1983. o.p. *(0-03-059616-5)* Holt, Henry & Co.

—Castles Burning. 1982. (Rinehart Suspense Novel Ser.). 224p. pap. o.p. *(0-03-062417-7*, Owl Bks.) Holt, Henry & Co.

—The Dead Are Discreet. 1983. 224p. pap. o.p. *(0-03-060393-5*, Owl Bks.) Holt, Henry & Co.

—Dead Ringer. 1983. 240p. pap. o.p. *(0-03-060396-X*, Owl Bks.) Holt, Henry & Co.

—False Pretenses. 1994. 240p. 18.95 o.s.i *(0-89296-220-8)* Mysterious Pr.

—False Pretenses. 1995. 224p. mass mkt. 5.50 o.s.i *(0-446-40422-5)* Warner Bks., Inc.

—Fast Fade: A Jacob Asch Mystery. 1987. 224p. 15.45 *(0-89296-216-X)* Mysterious Pr.

—Fast Fade: A Jacob Asch Mystery. 1988. 208p. mass mkt. 3.95 o.s.i *(0-445-40703-4*, Mysterious Pr. Paperback Bks.) Warner Bks., Inc.

—Hard Trade. 264p. 1983. pap. o.p. *(0-03-063333-8*, Owl Bks.); 1981. o.p. *(0-03-053621-9)* Holt, Henry & Co.

—The Killing Floor. 1982. pap. o.p. *(0-03-060397-8*, Owl Bks.) Holt, Henry & Co.

—Other People's Money. 1989. 213p. 17.95 o.s.i *(0-89296-218-6)* Mysterious Pr.

—Other People's Money. 1990. 224p. mass mkt. 4.95 o.s.i *(0-445-40903-7*, Mysterious Pr. Paperback Bks.) Warner Bks., Inc.

—Three with a Bullet. 240p. 1986. pap. 3.95 o.p. *(0-03-008539-X*, Owl Bks.); 1985. o.p. *(0-03-059617-3)* Holt, Henry & Co.

**AFSAN, THE FAR-SEER (FICTITIOUS CHARACTER)—FICTION**

Sawyer, Robert J. Far-Seer. 1992. mass mkt. 4.99 o.s.i *(0-441-22551-9)* Ace Bks.

—Foreigner. 1994. 304p. (Orig.). mass mkt. 4.99 o.s.i *(0-441-00017-7)* Ace Bks.

—Foreigner. Date not set. (Orig.). pap. *(0-7653-0972-6*, Tor Bks.) Doherty, Tom Assocs., LLC.

—Fossil Hunter. 1993. 304p. (Orig.). mass mkt. 4.99 o.s.i *(0-441-24884-5)* Ace Bks.

—Fossil Hunter. Date not set. (Orig.). pap. *(0-7653-0973-4*, Tor Bks.) Doherty, Tom Assocs., LLC.

**ASHE, BENNY (FICTITIOUS CHARACTER)—FICTION**

West, Richard F. As Crime Goes by. 1998. (Old Gang of Mine Mysteries Ser.). 240p. mass mkt. 5.99 o.s.i *(0-425-16536-1)* Berkley Publishing Group.

—Ghoul of My Dreams. 1999. (Old Gang of Mine Mysteries Ser.). 256p. mass mkt. 5.99 o.s.i *(0-425-16983-9)* Berkley Publishing Group.

—Old Gang of Mine. 1997. 224p. mass mkt. 5.99 o.s.i *(0-425-15964-7*, Prime Crime) Berkley Publishing Group.

**ASHE, GORDON (FICTITIOUS CHARACTER)—FICTION**

Norton, Andre. Echoes in Time. 2000. (Time Traders Adventure Ser.). 320p. mass mkt. 5.99 *(0-8125-5274-1*, Tor Bks.) Doherty, Tom Assocs., LLC.

—The Time Traders. 1987. 224p. mass mkt. 3.99 o.s.i *(0-441-81255-4)*; 1984. mass mkt. 2.50 o.s.i *(0-441-81254-6)*; 1980. mass mkt. 1.95 o.s.i *(0-441-81253-8)* Ace Bks.

—The Time Traders. 2000. 384p. (J). 24.00 *(0-671-31952-3)* Baen Bks.

—The Time Traders. 1979. lib. bdg. 9.95 o.p. *(0-8398-2421-1*, Macmillan Reference USA) Gale Group.

Norton, Andre & Griffin, P. M. Fire Hand. 1995. 288p. mass mkt. 4.99 *(0-8125-1984-1)*; 1994. 224p. 19.95 o.p. *(0-312-85313-0)* Doherty, Tom Assocs., LLC. (Tor Bks.).

Norton, Andre & Smith, Sherwood. Echoes in Time. 1999. (Time Traders Adventure Ser.). 319p. 23.95 *(0-312-85921-X*, Tor Bks.) Doherty, Tom Assocs., LLC.

**ASHER, JAMES (FICTITIOUS CHARACTER)—FICTION**

Hambly, Barbara. Those Who Hunt the Night. 1995. mass mkt. 5.99 o.p. *(0-345-90627-6)*; 1990. 352p. mass mkt. 5.99 o.s.i *(0-345-36132-6)* Ballantine Bks. (Del Rey).

—Traveling with the Dead. 1996. mass mkt. 5.99 o.s.i *(0-345-40740-7*, Del Rey) Ballantine Bks.

**ASHER, STEVE (FICTITIOUS CHARACTER)—FICTION**

Blanchard, Al. Crucial Judgment. 2003. 307p. pap. 19.95 *(0-9741685-3-X)* Koenisha Pubns.

—The Mad Season. 2002. 289p. pap. 19.95 *(0-9718758-1-2)* Koenisha Pubns.

—Murder at Walden Pond: A Steve Asher Mystery. E-Book 7.00 *(1-930486-13-8)*; 2001. 200p. pap. 14.95 *(1-930486-28-6)* Salvo Pr.

**ASHERFELD, AARON (FICTITIOUS CHARACTER)—FICTION**

Berlinski, David. The Body Shop: An Aaron Asherfeld Mystery. 1996. 208p. text 20.95 o.p. *(0-312-13935-7*, Saint Martin's Minotaur) St. Martin's Pr.

—Less than Meets the Eye: An Aaron Asherfield Mystery. 1994. (Aaron Asherfeld Mystery Ser.). 208p. 18.95 o.p. *(0-312-11298-X*, Saint Martin's Minotaur) St. Martin's Pr.

—Less Than Meets the Eye: An Aaron Asherfield Mystery. 1994. 240p. 19.95 *(0-312-10611-4*, Saint Martin's Minotaur) St. Martin's Pr.

**ASHLEY, BRETT (FICTITIOUS CHARACTER)—FICTION**

Hemingway, Ernest. The Sun Also Rises. 256p. 22.95 o.s.i *(0-8488-2455-5)* Amereon, Ltd.

—The Sun Also Rises. 1989. audio compact disk 48.00 *(0-7366-7495-0)*; 2001. audio compact disk 35.95 *(0-7366-5700-2)*; 1999. audio 29.95 *(0-7366-4432-6)* Books on Tape, Inc.

—The Sun Also Rises. 1998. (Bloom's Notes Ser.). pap. 4.95 *(0-7910-4165-4)* Chelsea Hse. Pubs.

—The Sun Also Rises. 2003. E-Book 9.99 *(0-7432-3733-1*, Scribner); 2003. (Illus.). 256p. pap. 13.00 *(0-684-80071-3*, Scribner); 1996. 224p. 25.00 *(0-684-83051-5*, Scribner); 1984. pap. 47.40 o.s.i *(0-684-18261-0*, Scribner Paper Fiction); 1984. pap. 3.95 o.s.i *(0-684-18260-2*, Scribner Paper Fiction); 1982. 256p. pap. 4.95 o.s.i *(0-684-17472-3*, Scribner Paper Fiction); 1977. 248p. 35.00 *(0-684-15327-0*, Scribner); 1920. 256p. 20.00 o.s.i *(0-684-10250-1*, Scribner); 1920. 256p. pap. 10.95 o.s.i *(0-684-71808-1*, Scribner Paper Fiction) Simon & Schuster.

—The Sun Also Rises. l.t. ed. 1994. 310p. lib. bdg. 23.95 *(0-8161-5969-6)* Thorndike Pr.

—The Sun Also Rises. 1995. 18.05 *(0-606-05064-7)* Turtleback Bks.

Hemingway, Ernest & DeFazio, Albert J. Literary Masterpieces: The Sun Also Rises. 2000. (Literary Masterpieces Ser.: Vol. 2). (Illus.). xi, 166p. (YA). (gr. 9 up). 55.00 *(0-7876-3962-1*, GML00502-113768) Gale Group.

**ASHTON, CAROL (FICTITIOUS CHARACTER)—FICTION**

McNab, Claire. Accidental Murder: A Detective Inspector Carol Ashton Mystery. 2002. 208p. pap. 12.95 *(1-931513-16-3)* Bella Bks., Inc.

—Blood Link: A Detective Inspector Carol Ashton Mystery. 2003. 208p. pap. 12.95 *(1-931513-27-9)* Bella Bks., Inc.

—Body Guard. 1994. (Detective Inspector Carol Ashton Mysteries Ser.: Vol. 6). 224p. pap. 11.95 *(1-56280-073-6)* Naiad Pr., Inc.

—Chain Letter: A Carol Ashton Mystery. 1997. (Detective Inspector Carol Ashton Mysteries Ser.: Vol. 9). 224p. (Orig.). pap. 11.95 *(1-56280-181-3)* Naiad Pr., Inc.

—Cop Out. 1991. (Detective Inspector Carol Ashton Mysteries Ser.: Vol. 4). 224p. (Orig.). pap. 10.95 *(0-941483-84-3)* Naiad Pr., Inc.

—Dead Certain. 1992. (Detective Inspector Carol Ashton Mysteries Ser.: No. 5). 224p. pap. 11.95 *(1-56280-027-2)* Naiad Pr., Inc.

—Death Club: A Detective Inspector Carol Ashton Mystery. 2001. 215p. pap. 11.95 *(1-56280-267-4)* Naiad Pr., Inc.

—Death down Under. 1990. (Detective Inspector Carol Ashton Mysteries Ser.: Vol. 3). 240p. pap. 11.95 *(0-941483-39-8)* Naiad Pr., Inc.

—Double Bluff. 1995. (Detective Inspector Carol Ashton Mysteries Ser.: Vol. 7). 192p. pap. 12.95 *(1-56280-096-5)* Naiad Pr., Inc.

—Fatal Reunion. 1989. (Detective Inspector Carol Ashton Mysteries Ser.: Vol. 2). 224p. pap. 11.95 *(0-941483-40-1)* Naiad Pr., Inc.

—Inner Circle: A Carol Ashton Mystery. 1996. (Detective Inspector Carol Ashton Mysteries Ser.: Vol. 8). 256p. pap. 11.95 *(1-56280-135-X)* Naiad Pr., Inc.

—Lessons in Murder. 1988. (Detective Inspector Carol Ashton Mysteries Ser.: Vol. 1). 216p. pap. 11.95 *(0-941483-14-2)* Naiad Pr., Inc.

—Past Due: A Detective Inspector Carol Ashton Mystery. 1998. (Detective Inspector Carol Ashton Mysteries Ser.: No. 10). 224p. pap. 11.95 *(1-56280-217-8)* Naiad Pr., Inc.

—Set Up. 1999. (Detective Inspector Carol Ashton Mysteries Ser.: Vol. 11). 202p. pap. 11.95 *(1-56280-255-0)* Naiad Pr., Inc.

—Under Suspicion. 2000. (Detective Inspector Carol Ashton Mysteries Ser.). 204p. pap. 11.95 (*1-56280-261-5*) Naiad Pr., Inc.

**ASHTON, PETER (FICTITIOUS CHARACTER)—FICTION**

Egleton, Clive. Blood Money. unabr. ed. 1999. audio 94.95 (*1-86042-383-3*, 23833) Soundings, Ltd. GBR. *Dist:* Ulverscroft Large Print Bks., Ltd.

—Blood Money. 1998. 496p. 24.95 (*0-312-18540-5*) St. Martin's Pr.

—Blood Money. l.t. ed. 1998. (Charnwood Large Print Ser.). 528p. 29.99 o.p. (*0-7089-9003-7*, Charnwood) Thorpe, F. A. Pubs. GBR. *Dist:* Ulverscroft Large Print Bks., Ltd., Ulverscroft Large Print Canada, Ltd.

—Cry Havoc: A Peter Ashton Novel. 2003. 352p. 24.95 (*0-312-30943-0*, Saint Martin's Minotaur) St. Martin's Pr.

—Dead Reckoning. unabr. ed. 2000. audio 94.95 (*1-86042-666-2*, 26662) Soundings, Ltd. GBR. *Dist:* Ulverscroft Large Print Bks., Ltd.

—Dead Reckoning. 2nd ed. 1999. 342p. 24.95 (*0-312-24102-X*, Saint Martin's Minotaur) St. Martin's Pr.

—Death Throes. 1995. 361p. 21.95 o.p. (*0-312-11774-4*) St. Martin's Pr.

—Death Throes. l.t. ed. 1996. (Charnwood Large Print Ser.). 544p. 32.99 (*0-7089-8878-4*, Ulverscroft) Thorpe, F. A. Pubs. GBR. *Dist:* Ulverscroft Large Print Bks., Ltd., Ulverscroft Large Print Canada, Ltd.

—The Honey Trap. 12p. 2001. audio 94.95 (*1-86042-897-5*, 28975); 2002. audio compact disk 99.95 (*1-86042-942-4*) Soundings, Ltd. GBR. *Dist:* Ulverscroft Large Print Bks., Ltd.

—Hostile Intent. 1993. 18.95 o.p. (*0-312-08812-4*) St. Martin's Pr.

—Hostile Intent. l.t. ed. 1994. (Charnwood Large Print Ser.). 496p. 29.99 (*0-7089-8799-0*, Ulverscroft) Thorpe, F. A. Pubs. GBR. *Dist:* Ulverscroft Large Print Bks., Ltd., Ulverscroft Large Print Canada, Ltd.

—A Killing in Moscow. 1994. 320p. 21.95 o.p. (*0-312-10487-1*, Saint Martin's Minotaur) St. Martin's Pr.

—A Killing in Moscow. l.t. ed. 1995. (Charnwood Large Print Ser.). 528p. 29.99 (*0-7089-8835-0*, Charnwood) Thorpe, F. A. Pubs. GBR. *Dist:* Ulverscroft Large Print Bks., Ltd., Ulverscroft Large Print Canada, Ltd.

—A Lethal Involvement. 1996. 352p. 23.95 o.p. (*0-312-14313-3*) St. Martin's Pr.

—A Lethal Involvement. l.t. ed. 1997. (Charnwood Large Print Ser.). 528p. 29.99 o.p. (*0-7089-8932-2*, Charnwood) Thorpe, F. A. Pubs. GBR. *Dist:* Ulverscroft Large Print Bks., Ltd., Ulverscroft Large Print Canada, Ltd.

—One Man Running. unabr. ed. 2002. audio 94.95 (*1-84283-153-4*) Soundings, Ltd. GBR. *Dist:* Ulverscroft Large Print Bks., Ltd.

—One Man Running. 2002. 346p. 24.95 (*0-312-28699-6*, Saint Martin's Minotaur) St. Martin's Pr.

—One Man Running. l.t. ed. 2002. (Adventure Ser.). 28.95 (*0-7862-4711-8*) Thorndike Pr.

—Warning Shot. 1997. 410p. 22.95 o.p. (*0-312-15685-5*) St. Martin's Pr.

—Warning Shot. l.t. ed. 1997. (Charnwood Large Print Ser.). 544p. 29.99 o.p. (*0-7089-8966-7*, Ulverscroft) Thorpe, F. A. Pubs. GBR. *Dist:* Ulverscroft Large Print Bks., Ltd., Ulverscroft Large Print Canada, Ltd.

**ASHWORTH, JIM (FICTITIOUS CHARACTER)—FICTION**

Battison, Brian. The Christmas Bow Murder. 2000. (DCI Jim Ashworth Mysteries Ser.). 240p. pap. 12.95 (*0-7490-0475-4*, London Hse.) Allison & Busby, Ltd. GBR. *Dist:* International Publishers Marketing.

—The Christmas Bow Murder. 1994. 224p. 19.95 o.p. (*0-312-11463-X*, Saint Martin's Minotaur) St. Martin's Pr.

—The Christmas Bow Murder. l.t. ed. 1995. (Ulverscroft Large Print Ser.). 480p. 29.99 o.p. (*0-7089-3407-2*, Ulverscroft) Thorpe, F. A. Pubs. GBR. *Dist:* Ulverscroft Large Print Bks., Ltd., Ulverscroft Large Print Canada, Ltd.

—Flying Pigs. 1998. 224p. (*0-09-478550-3*, Constable & Co. Ltd.) Constable & Robinson Ltd.

—Jeopardy's Child: A DCI Jim Ashworth Investigation. 1999. (DCI Jim Ashworth Mysteries Ser.). 352p. mass mkt. 9.95 (*0-7490-0304-9*) Allison & Busby, Ltd. GBR. *Dist:* International Publishers Marketing.

—Jeopardy's Child: A DCI Jim Ashworth Investigation. 1998. 224p. (*0-09-477530-3*, Constable & Co. Ltd.) Constable & Robinson Ltd.

—Jeopardy's Child: A DCI Jim Ashworth Investigation. l.t. ed. 2000. (Ulverscroft Large Print Ser.). 416p. 31.99 (*0-7089-4304-7*, Ulverscroft) Thorpe, F. A. Pubs. GBR. *Dist:* Ulverscroft Large Print Bks., Ltd., Ulverscroft Large Print Canada, Ltd.

—Mirror Image. l.t. ed. 1999. (Ulverscroft Large Print Ser.). 408p. 31.99 (*0-7089-4129-X*, Ulverscroft) Thorpe, F. A. Pubs. GBR. *Dist:* Ulverscroft Large Print Bks., Ltd., Ulverscroft Large Print Canada, Ltd.

—Poetic Justice: A DCI Jim Ashworth Investigation. 267p. pap. 10.95 (*0-7490-0419-3*) Allison & Busby, Ltd. GBR. *Dist:* International Publishers Marketing.

—Truths Not Told. 279p. mass mkt. 9.95 (*0-7490-0366-9*) Sutton Publishing.

—Truths Not Told. l.t. ed. 1998. (Linford Mystery Large Print Ser.). 512p. pap. 17.99 (*0-7089-5293-3*, Linford) Thorpe, F. A. Pubs. GBR. *Dist:* Ulverscroft Large Print Bks., Ltd., Ulverscroft Large Print Canada, Ltd.

—The Witch's Familiar. l.t. ed. 1998. (Linford Mystery Large Print Ser.). 528p. pap. 17.99 (*0-7089-5335-2*, Linford) Thorpe, F. A. Pubs. GBR. *Dist:* Ulverscroft Large Print Bks., Ltd., Ulverscroft Large Print Canada, Ltd.

**ATHAYA (FICTITIOUS CHARACTER)—FICTION**

Smith, Julie D. The Wizard King. 1993. mass mkt. 5.50 o.s.i (*0-345-37153-4*, Del Rey) Ballantine Bks.

Smith, Julie Dean. Call of Madness. 1990. (Caithan Crusade: 1). 320p. mass mkt. 4.95 o.s.i (*0-345-36327-2*, Del Rey) Ballantine Bks.

—Mission of Magic. 1991. (Caithan Crusade: 2). (Orig.). mass mkt. 4.95 o.s.i (*0-345-36627-1*, Del Rey) Ballantine Bks.

—Sage of Sare. 1992. (Caithan Crusade: 3). mass mkt. 4.99 o.s.i (*0-345-37154-2*, Del Rey) Ballantine Bks.

**ATHELSTAN, BROTHER (FICTITIOUS CHARACTER)—FICTION**

Harding, Paul T., pseud. The House of Crows: The Sorrowful Mysteries of Brother Athelstan. 1996. (Illus.). 280p. pap. 13.95 (*0-7472-4918-0*) Headline Bk. Publishing, Ltd. GBR. *Dist:* Trafalgar Square.

—The Nightingale Gallery: Being the First of the Sorrowful Mysteries of Brother Athelstan. 1993. 256p. mass mkt. 4.99 (*0-380-71751-4*, Avon Bks.); 1992. 20.00 o.p. (*0-688-11225-0*, Morrow, William & Co.) Morrow/Avon.

—Red Slayer: Being the Second of the Sorrowful Mysteries of Brother Athelstan. 1995. 288p. mass mkt. 4.99 (*0-380-72106-6*, Avon Bks.); 1994. 283p. 20.00 o.p. (*0-688-12569-7*, Morrow, William & Co.) Morrow/Avon.

**ATTLA, RAY (FICTITIOUS CHARACTER)—FICTION**

Lane, Christopher. The Elements of a Kill. 1998. 416p. mass mkt. 5.99 (*0-380-79870-0*, Avon Bks.) Morrow/Avon.

—The Season of Death: An Inupiat Eskimo Mystery. 1999. 352p. mass mkt. 5.99 (*0-380-79872-7*, Avon Bks.) Morrow/Avon.

—A Shroud of Midnight Sun. 2000. (Inupiat Eskimo Mysteries Ser.). 352p. mass mkt. 5.99 (*0-380-79873-5*, Avon Bks.) Morrow/Avon.

—Silent as the Hunter. 2001. (Inupiat Eskimo Mysteries Ser.). 352p. mass mkt. 6.50 (*0-380-81625-3*, Avon Bks.) Morrow/Avon.

**AUBREY, JACK (FICTITIOUS CHARACTER)—FICTION**

O'Brian, Patrick. Aubrey & Maturin, 18 vols. 1996. 432.00 (*0-393-04117-4*) Norton, W. W. & Co., Inc.

—The Aubrey-Maturin Series, 17 vols. (Aubrey-Maturin Ser.). (C). 1995. 408.00 (*0-393-03975-7*); Set. 1994. 384.00 (*0-393-03749-5*) Norton, W. W. & Co., Inc.

—Blue at the Mizzen. 1999. audio compact disk 64.00 (*0-7366-5201-9*); 2000. audio 29.95 (*0-7366-4686-8*); 2000. audio compact disk 34.95 (*0-7366-4760-0*); 1999. audio 48.00 (*0-7366-4737-6*, 5075) Books on Tape, Inc.

—Blue at the Mizzen. (Aubrey-Maturin Ser.). 1999. (Illus.). 288p. 24.00 (*0-393-04844-6*); 250.00 (*0-393-04874-8*); 2000. (Illus.). 272p. reprint ed. pap. 13.95 (*0-393-32107-X*, Norton Paperbacks) Norton, W. W. & Co., Inc.

—Blue at the Mizzen. abr. ed. 1999. (Aubrey-Maturin Ser.). audio 25.00 (*0-375-40876-2*, RH Audio) Random Hse. Audio Publishing Group.

—Blue at the Mizzen. unabr. ed. (Aubrey-Maturin Ser.). 2000. audio compact disk 81.00 (*0-7887-4204-3*, C1133E7); 1999. audio 60.00 (*0-7887-3769-4*, 95986E7) Recorded Bks., LLC.

—Blue at the Mizzen. l.t. ed. 2000. (Aubrey-Maturin Ser.). 393p. 27.95 (*0-7862-2047-3*); 435p. 30.95 (*0-7862-2046-5*) Thorndike Pr.

—The Commodore. l.t. ed. 1995. (Aubrey-Maturin Ser.). 25.95 (*1-56895-271-6*, Wheeler Publishing, Inc.) Gale Group.

—The Commodore. (Aubrey-Maturin Ser.). 1996. 288p. pap. 13.95 (*0-393-31459-6*, Norton Paperbacks); 1995. 288p. 24.00 (*0-393-03760-6*); 1995. 150.00 o.p. (*0-393-03886-6*) Norton, W. W. & Co., Inc.

—Desolation Island. 1979. (Aubrey-Maturin Ser.). 276p. 9.95 o.s.i (*0-8128-2590-X*); pap. 2.50 o.p. (*0-8128-7066-2*) Madison Bks., Inc. (Scarborough Hse.).

—Desolation Island. (Aubrey-Maturin Ser.). 1994. 24.00 (*0-393-03705-3*); 1991. (Illus.). 325p. pap. 13.95 (*0-393-30812-X*) Norton, W. W. & Co., Inc.

—The Far Side of the World. l.t. ed. 2002. (Aubrey-Maturin Ser.). 538p. 29.95 (*0-7862-1930-0*, Macmillan Reference USA) Gale Group.

—The Far Side of the World. 2003. 366p. pap. 13.95 (*0-393-32476-1*); 1994. 24.00 (*0-393-03710-X*); 1992. 368p. pap. 13.95 (*0-393-30862-6*) Norton, W. W. & Co., Inc.

—The Fortune of War. (Aubrey-Maturin Ser.). 1994. 24.00 (*0-393-03706-1*); 1991. 329p. pap. 13.95 (*0-393-30813-8*) Norton, W. W. & Co., Inc.

—The Fortune of War. l.t. ed. 2001. (Illus.). 311p. (*0-7540-1588-2*); (*0-7540-2449-0*) Thorndike Pr.

—HMS Surprise. (Aubrey-Maturin Ser.). 1994. 24.00 (*0-393-03703-7*); 1991. 379p. pap. 13.95 (*0-393-30761-1*) Norton, W. W. & Co., Inc.

—HMS Surprise. l.t. ed. 2000. (Famous Authors Ser.). 608p. 28.95 (*0-7862-1934-3*, MML06400-170754); (*0-7540-1460-6*); (*0-7540-2350-8*) Thorndike Pr.

—The Hundred Days. (Aubrey-Maturin Ser.). 288p. 1999. pap. 13.95 (*0-393-31979-2*); 1998. 24.00 (*0-393-04674-5*) Norton, W. W. & Co., Inc.

—The Hundred Days. l.t. ed. (Aubrey-Maturin Ser.). 461p. 2000. 26.95 (*0-7862-1749-9*); 1999. 29.95 (*0-7862-1748-0*) Thorndike Pr.

—The Ionian Mission. unabr. ed. 1993. (Aubrey-Maturin Ser.). audio 80.00 (*0-7366-2336-1*, 3115) Books on Tape, Inc.

—The Ionian Mission. (Aubrey-Maturin Ser.). 1994. 24.00 (*0-393-03708-8*); 1992. 368p. pap. 13.95 (*0-393-30821-9*) Norton, W. W. & Co., Inc.

—The Ionian Mission. abr. ed. 2000. (Aubrey-Maturin Ser.). audio 25.00 (*0-375-41577-7*, RH Audio) Random Hse. Audio Publishing Group.

—The Ionian Mission. unabr. ed. 1994. (Aubrey-Maturin Ser.: No. 8). audio 91.00 (*1-55690-985-3*, 94124E7) Recorded Bks., LLC.

—The Ionian Mission. l.t. ed. 2001. (Aubrey-Maturin Ser.). (Illus.). 572p. 28.95 (*0-7862-1928-9*); 576p. (*0-7540-1700-1*); 576p. (*0-7540-9100-7*) Thorndike Pr.

—The Letter of Marque. (Aubrey-Maturin Ser.). 1992. 288p. pap. 13.95 (*0-393-30905-3*); 1990. 284p. 24.00 (*0-393-02874-7*) Norton, W. W. & Co., Inc.

—The Letter of Marque. abr. ed. 2001. (Aubrey-Maturin Ser.: Vol. 12). audio 25.00 (*0-375-41598-X*, RH Audio) Random Hse. Audio Publishing Group.

—The Letter of Marque. l.t. ed. 1999. (Aubrey-Maturin Ser.). 495p. 29.95 (*0-7862-1925-4*) Thorndike Pr.

—Master & Commander. l.t. ed. 1999. (*0-7540-1334-0*); (*0-7540-2248-X*) BBC Audiobooks America.

—Master & Commander. 2003. 412p. pap. 13.95 (*0-393-32517-2*); 1994. 24.00 (*0-393-03701-0*); 1990. (Illus.). 411p. pap. 13.95 (*0-393-30705-0*) Norton, W. W. & Co., Inc.

—Master & Commander. l.t. ed. 1999. (Aubrey-Maturin Ser.). 696p. 28.95 o.p. (*0-7862-1932-7*) Thorndike Pr.

—The Mauritius Command. unabr. ed. 1992. (Aubrey-Maturin Ser.). audio 72.00 (*0-7366-2248-9*, 3037) Books on Tape, Inc.

—The Mauritius Command. l.t. ed. 2000. (Aubrey-Maturin Ser.). (Illus.). 530p. 28.95 (*0-7862-1935-1*, Macmillan Reference USA) Gale Group.

—The Mauritius Command. 1978. (Aubrey-Maturin Ser.). 8.95 o.p. (*0-8128-2476-8*); pap. 2.50 o.p. (*0-8128-7046-8*) Madison Bks., Inc. (Scarborough Hse.).

—The Mauritius Command. (Aubrey-Maturin Ser.). 1994. 24.00 (*0-393-03704-5*); 1991. 348p. pap. 13.95 (*0-393-30762-X*) Norton, W. W. & Co., Inc.

—The Mauritius Command. abr. ed. 1999. (Aubrey-Maturin Ser.). audio 25.00 (*0-375-40875-4*, RH Audio) Random Hse. Audio Publishing Group.

—The Mauritius Command. unabr. ed. 1993. (Aubrey-Maturin Ser.: No. 4). audio 85.00 (*1-55690-804-0*, 93113E7) Recorded Bks., LLC.

—The Mauritius Command. l.t. ed. 2000. (Illus.). 530p. (*0-7540-1519-X*); (*0-7540-2398-2*) Thorndike Pr.

—The Nutmeg of Consolation. (Aubrey-Maturin Ser.). 320p. 1993. pap. 13.95 (*0-393-30906-1*); 1991. 24.00 (*0-393-03032-6*) Norton, W. W. & Co., Inc.

—The Nutmeg of Consolation. l.t. ed. 2002. (Famous Authors Ser.). 516p. 29.95 (*0-7862-1938-6*) Thorndike Pr.

—Post Captain. (Aubrey-Maturin Ser.). 1994. 24.00 (*0-393-03702-9*); 1990. 496p. pap. 13.95 (*0-393-30706-9*) Norton, W. W. & Co., Inc.

—Post Captain. l.t. ed. 2000. (Aubrey-Maturin Ser.). (Illus.). 721p. 27.95 (*0-7862-1933-5*, MML06400-17053); (*0-7540-1423-1*); (*0-7540-2320-6*) Thorndike Pr.

—The Reverse of the Medal. l.t. ed. 2002. (Aubrey-Maturin Ser.). 419p. 29.95 (*0-7862-1931-9*, Macmillan Reference USA) Gale Group.

—The Reverse of the Medal. (Aubrey-Maturin Ser.). 1994. 24.00 (*0-393-03711-8*); 1992. 288p. pap. 13.95 (*0-393-30960-6*) Norton, W. W. & Co., Inc.

—The Surgeon's Mate. l.t. ed. 2001. (Aubrey-Maturin Ser.). (Illus.). 569p. 28.95 (*0-7862-1936-X*, Macmillan Reference USA) Gale Group.

—The Surgeon's Mate. (Aubrey-Maturin Ser.). 1994. 24.00 (*0-393-03707-X*); 1992. 384p. pap. 13.95 (*0-393-30820-0*) Norton, W. W. & Co., Inc.

—The Surgeon's Mate. abr. ed. 2000. (Aubrey-Maturin Ser.). audio 25.00 (*0-375-41020-1*, RH Audio) Random Hse. Audio Publishing Group.

—The Surgeon's Mate. l.t. ed. 2001. (Thorndike Press Large Print Famous Authors Ser.). (Illus.). 624p. (*0-7540-1662-5*); (*0-7540-9076-0*) Thorndike Pr.

—The Thirteen-Gun Salute. (Aubrey-Maturin Ser.). 1992. 336p. pap. 13.95 (*0-393-30907-X*); 1991. 24.00 (*0-393-02974-3*) Norton, W. W. & Co., Inc.

—The Thirteen-Gun Salute. l.t. ed. 2002. (Famous Authors Ser.). 510p. 29.95 (*0-7862-1937-8*) Thorndike Pr.

—Treason's Harbour. (Aubrey-Maturin Ser.). 1994. 24.00 (*0-393-03709-6*); 1992. 334p. pap. 13.95 (*0-393-30863-4*) Norton, W. W. & Co., Inc.

—Treason's Harbour. l.t. ed. 2002. 524p. 29.95 (*0-7862-1929-7*) Thorndike Pr.

—The Truelove. (Aubrey-Maturin Ser.). 1993. 256p. pap. 13.95 (*0-393-31016-7*); 1992. 192p. 24.00 (*0-393-03109-8*) Norton, W. W. & Co., Inc.

—The Wine-Dark Sea. (Aubrey-Maturin Ser.). 1994. 272p. pap. 13.95 (*0-393-31244-5*); 1993. 261p. 24.00 (*0-393-03558-1*) Norton, W. W. & Co., Inc.

—The Yellow Admiral. l.t. ed. 1997. (Aubrey-Maturin Ser.). 27.95 o.p. (*1-56895-430-1*, Wheeler Publishing, Inc.) Gale Group.

—The Yellow Admiral. (Aubrey-Maturin Ser.). 1997. (Illus.). 272p. pap. 13.95 (*0-393-31704-8*); 1996. 262p. 24.00 (*0-393-04044-5*) Norton, W. W. & Co., Inc.

—The Yellow Admiral. 1999. (Aubrey-Maturin Ser.). pap. 12.98 (*0-671-04444-3*, Simon & Schuster Audioworks) Simon & Schuster Audio.

**AUDEN, ERIC (FICTITIOUS CHARACTER)—FICTION**

Gadol, Peter. The Mystery Roast. 1996. 320p. pap. 13.00 o.s.i (*0-312-15176-4*) Picador.

**AUDLEY, DAVID (FICTITIOUS CHARACTER)—FICTION**

Price, Anthony. The Alamut Ambush. l.t. ed. 1988. (Adventure Suspense Ser.). 400p. 29.99 o.p. (*0-7089-1854-9*, Ulverscroft) Thorpe, F. A. Pubs. GBR. *Dist:* Ulverscroft Large Print Bks., Ltd., Ulverscroft Large Print Canada, Ltd.

—The Alamut Ambush. 1986. 224p. reprint ed. mass mkt. 3.95 o.s.i (*0-445-40223-7*, Mysterious Pr. Paperback Bks.) Warner Bks., Inc.

—Colonel Butler's Wolf. 1987. 224p. reprint ed. mass mkt. 3.95 o.s.i (*0-445-40224-5*, Mysterious Pr. Paperback Bks.) Warner Bks., Inc.

—For the Good of the State. 1987. 272p. 16.45 o.p. (*0-89296-224-0*); 45.00 o.p. (*0-89296-230-5*) Mysterious Pr.

—For the Good of the State. 1989. 3.99 o.p. (*0-517-00185-3*) Random Hse. Value Publishing.

—For the Good of the State. 1988. mass mkt. 4.95 o.s.i (*0-445-40701-8*, Mysterious Pr. Paperback Bks.) Warner Bks., Inc.

—The Forty-Four Vintage. 1978. 7.95 o.p. (*0-385-14028-2*) Doubleday Publishing.

—The Forty-Four Vintage. l.t. ed. 1979. (Ulverscroft Large Print Ser.). 29.99 o.p. (*0-7089-0287-1*, Ulverscroft) Thorpe, F. A. Pubs. GBR. *Dist:* Ulverscroft Large Print Bks., Ltd., Ulverscroft Large Print Canada, Ltd.

—The Forty-Four Vintage. 1988. 288p. mass mkt. 4.95 o.s.i (*0-445-40236-9*, Mysterious Pr. Paperback Bks.) Warner Bks., Inc.

—Gunner Kelly. 1984. (Crimee Club Ser.). 192p. 11.95 o.p. (*0-385-19356-4*) Doubleday Publishing.

—Gunner Kelly. unabr. ed. 1999. audio 54.95 (*0-7531-0498-9*, 990113) ISIS Audio Bks. GBR. *Dist:* Ulverscroft Large Print Bks., Ltd.

—Gunner Kelly. l.t. ed. 1988. (Adventure Suspense Ser.). 416p. 29.99 o.p. (*0-7089-1918-9*, Ulverscroft) Thorpe, F. A. Pubs. GBR. *Dist:* Ulverscroft Large Print Bks., Ltd., Ulverscroft Large Print Canada, Ltd.

—Gunner Kelly. 1989. 192p. mass mkt. 4.95 (*0-445-40253-9*, Mysterious Pr. Paperback Bks.) Warner Bks., Inc.

—Here Be Monsters. 1986. 256p. 15.95 (*0-89296-154-6*) Mysterious Pr.

—Here Be Monsters. 1987. mass mkt. 3.95 o.s.i (*0-445-40578-3*, Mysterious Pr. Paperback Bks.) Warner Bks., Inc.

—The Hour of the Donkey. l.t. ed. 1989. (Popular Ser.). lib. bdg. 11.95 o.p. (*1-85057-599-1*, Macmillan Reference USA) Gale Group.

—The Labyrinth Makers. l.t. ed. 1981. (Ulverscroft Large Print Ser.). 369p. 29.99 o.p. (*0-7089-0711-3*, Ulverscroft) Thorpe, F. A. Pubs. GBR. *Dist:* Ulverscroft Large Print Bks., Ltd., Ulverscroft Large Print Canada, Ltd.
—The Labyrinth Makers. 1986. 240p. mass mkt. 3.95 o.s.i (*0-445-40242-3*, Mysterious Pr. Paperback Bks.) Warner Bks., Inc.
—A New Kind of War. 1988. 272p. 17.95 (*0-89296-281-X*); pap. 4.95 o.p. (*0-445-40338-1*) Mysterious Pr.
—October Men. 1987. 256p. reprint ed. mass mkt. 3.95 o.s.i (*0-445-40620-8*, Mysterious Pr. Paperback Bks.) Warner Bks., Inc.
—The Old Vengeful. 1989. 224p. mass mkt. 4.95 (*0-445-40257-1*, Mysterious Pr. Paperback Bks.) Warner Bks., Inc.
—Old Vengeful. 1983. (Crime Club Ser.). 192p. 11.95 o.p. (*0-385-18750-5*) Doubleday Publishing.
—Other Paths to Glory. l.t. ed. 1984. lib. bdg. 15.95 o.p. (*0-89340-780-1*, 665) BBC Audiobooks America.
—Other Paths to Glory. 1987. 256p. mass mkt. 3.95 o.s.i (*0-445-40666-6*, Mysterious Pr. Paperback Bks.) Warner Bks., Inc.
—Sign Crossing. 1987. 45.00 o.p. (*0-89296-111-2*); 1986. 15.95 (*0-89296-114-7*); 1986. pap. 3.95 o.p. (*0-445-40247-4*) Mysterious Pr.
—Sion Crossing. l.t. ed. 1990. (Magna Large Print Ser.). 487p. o.p. (*1-85057-594-0*) Magna Large Print Bks. GBR. *Dist:* Ulverscroft Large Print Canada, Ltd.
—Sion Crossing. 1989. 2.99 o.p. (*0-517-00189-6*) Random Hse. Value Publishing.
—Soldier No More. 1982. (Crime Club Ser.). 240p. 13.95 o.p. (*0-385-18048-9*) Doubleday Publishing.
—Soldier No More. l.t. ed. 1989. 548p. lib. bdg. 11.95 o.p. (*1-85057-589-4*, Macmillan Reference USA) Gale Group.
—Soldier No More. 1989. 336p. mass mkt. 4.95 o.s.i (*0-445-40254-7*, Mysterious Pr. Paperback Bks.) Warner Bks., Inc.
—Tomorrow's Ghost. 1979. (Crime Club Ser.). 9.95 o.p. (*0-385-14029-0*) Doubleday Publishing.
—Tomorrow's Ghost. 1988. 256p. mass mkt. 4.95 o.s.i (*0-445-40237-7*, Mysterious Pr. Paperback Bks.) Warner Bks., Inc.
—War Game. l.t. ed. 1988. (Adventure Suspense Ser.). 512p. 29.99 o.p. (*0-7089-1870-0*, Ulverscroft) Thorpe, F. A. Pubs. GBR. *Dist:* Ulverscroft Large Print Bks., Ltd., Ulverscroft Large Print Canada, Ltd.
—War Game. 1988. 256p. mass mkt. 4.95 o.s.i (*0-445-40238-5*, Mysterious Pr. Paperback Bks.) Warner Bks., Inc.

**AURIAN, LADY (FICTITIOUS CHARACTER)—FICTION**

Furey, Maggie. Aurian. 1994. 608p. mass mkt. 6.99 (*0-553-56525-7*) Bantam Bks.
—Harp of Winds. 1995. 464p. mass mkt. 6.99 (*0-553-56526-5*, Spectra) Bantam Bks.
—Sword of the Flame. 1996. (Bantam Spectra Book Ser.). 464p. mass mkt. 7.50 (*0-553-56527-3*, Spectra) Bantam Bks.

**AUSTEN, CAT (FICTITIOUS CHARACTER)—FICTION**

Iakovou, Takis, et al. Deadly Morsels: Another Curse/ Red or Green?/Cake Job/Sheep in Wolf's Clothing, 4 bks. in 1. 2003. (WWL Mystery Ser.: No. 452). 384p. mass mkt. (*0-373-26452-6*, Worldwide Library) Harlequin Enterprises, Ltd.
Rubino, Jane. Cheat the Devil. 1998. 352p. 24.95 (*1-885173-56-3*) Write Way Publishing.
—Death of a DJ. 1997. 224p. mass mkt. 4.99 o.p. (*0-06-104433-4*, HarperTorch) Morrow/Avon.
—Death of a DJ. 1995. 225p. 20.95 (*1-885173-09-1*) Write Way Publishing.
—Fruitcake. 1997. 384p. 24.95 (*1-885173-29-6*) Write Way Publishing.
—Plot Twist. 2000. 400p. 24.95 (*1-885173-80-6*) Write Way Publishing.

**AUSTEN, JANE, 1775-1817—FICTION**

Barron, Stephanie. Jane & the Genius of the Place. 2000. (Jane Austen Mystery Ser.: Vol. 4). 384p. mass mkt. 6.50 (*0-553-57839-1*) Bantam Bks.
—Jane & the Genius of the Place. l.t. ed. 1999. (Mystery Ser.). 517p. 29.95 (*0-7862-2017-1*) Thorndike Pr.
—Jane & the Ghosts of Netley. 2004. 336p. mass mkt. 6.99 (*0-553-58406-5*); 7th ed. 2003. 304p. 23.95 (*0-553-80222-4*) Bantam Bks.
—Jane & the Man of the Cloth. 1997. (Jane Austen Mystery Ser.: No. 2). 368p. reprint ed. mass mkt. 6.50 (*0-553-57489-2*) Bantam Bks.
—Jane & the Man of the Cloth. unabr. collector's ed. 1997. (Jane Austen Ser.). audio 64.00 (*0-7366-3683-8*, 4362) Books on Tape, Inc.
—Jane & the Prisoner of Wool House. 2002. (Jane Austen Mystery Ser.: Bk. 6). 384p. mass mkt. 6.50 (*0-553-57840-5*, Crimeline) Bantam Bks.
—Jane & the Prisoner of Wool House. unabr. ed. 2001. (Jane Austen Ser.: Bk. 6). audio 56.00 (*0-7366-8483-2*) Books on Tape, Inc.
—Jane & the Stillroom Maid. 2001. (Jane Austen Mystery Ser.: Vol. 5). 336p. reprint ed. mass mkt. 6.50 (*0-553-57837-5*) Bantam Bks.
—Jane & the Unpleasantness at Scargrave Manor. 1996. (Jane Austen Mystery Ser.: No. 1). 352p. mass mkt. 6.50 (*0-553-57593-7*, Crimeline) Bantam Bks.
—Jane & the Unpleasantness at Scargrave Manor. unabr. collector's ed. 1997. (Jane Austen Ser.). audio 64.00 (*0-7366-3569-6*, 4219) Books on Tape, Inc.
—Jane & the Unpleasantness at Scargrave Manor. l.t. ed. 1997. (Jane Austen Mystery Ser.: No. 1). 24.95 o.p. (*1-56895-400-X*, Wheeler Publishing, Inc.) Gale Group.
—Jane & the Wandering Eye. 1998. (Jane Austen Mystery Ser.: No. 3). 272p. (gr. 5 up). 22.95 o.s.i (*0-553-10204-4*); 336p. mass mkt. 6.99 (*0-553-57817-0*) Bantam Bks.
—Jane & the Wandering Eye. unabr. collector's ed. 1998. (Jane Austen Ser.). audio 56.00 (*0-7366-4164-5*, 4667) Books on Tape, Inc.
—Jane & the Wandering Eye. l.t. ed. 1998. (Cloak & Dagger Ser.). 471p. 29.95 (*0-7862-1353-1*) Thorndike Pr.
Cohen, Paula Marantz. Jane Austen in Boca: A Novel. 288p. 2003. pap. 12.95 (*0-312-31975-4*, Saint Martin's Griffin); 2002. 23.95 (*0-312-29088-8*) St. Martin's Pr.
Fowler, Karen Joy. The Jane Austen Book Club. 2004. 256p. 23.95 (*0-399-15161-3*) Putnam Publishing Group, The.
Nathan, Melissa. Pride, Prejudice & Jasmin Field. 2001. 280p. pap. 6.50 (*0-06-107233-8*) HarperCollins Pubs.
Perkins, Wilder. Hoare & the Portsmouth Atrocities. 1998. 224p. 21.95 (*0-312-19283-5*, Saint Martin's Minotaur) St. Martin's Pr.
Wilson, Barbara K. Antipodes Jane. 1985. 330p. 16.95 o.p. (*0-670-80586-6*) Viking Penguin.

**AUSTEN, KATE (FICTITIOUS CHARACTER)—FICTION**

Jacobs, Jonnie. Murder among Friends. 2001. 352p. mass mkt. 5.99 (*0-7582-0098-6*); 1996. 352p. mass mkt. 5.99 o.s.i (*1-57566-089-X*, Kensington Bks.); 1995. 304p. mass mkt. 16.95 o.s.i (*0-8217-5030-5*) Kensington Publishing Corp.
—Murder among Neighbors. 304p. 1995. mass mkt. 5.99 (*1-57566-275-2*); 1995. mass mkt. 4.99 o.s.i (*0-8217-5039-9*); 1994. mass mkt. 16.95 o.p. (*0-8217-4680-4*, Zebra Bks.) Kensington Publishing Corp.
—Murder among Strangers. 2000. (Kate Austen Mystery Ser.). 378p. 20.00 o.s.i (*1-57566-540-9*) Kensington Publishing Corp.
—Murder among Us: A Kate Austen Mystery. 1999. 304p. mass mkt. 5.99 (*1-57566-398-8*); 1998. 336p. 20.00 (*1-57566-276-0*) Kensington Publishing Corp.

**AUSTIN, AMANDA (FICTITIOUS CHARACTER)—FICTION**

Whitney, Phyllis A. The Turquoise Mask. l.t. ed. 1989. 21.95 o.p. (*1-55504-789-0*, 158); 1997. audio 69.95 (*0-7451-6782-9*, CAB 1398) BBC Audiobooks America.
—The Turquoise Mask. 1998. mass mkt. 3.99 o.s.i (*0-449-00511-9*); 1981. mass mkt. 5.99 o.s.i (*0-449-23470-3*) Ballantine Bks. (Fawcett).
—The Turquoise Mask. 1974. 336p. 10.95 o.p. (*0-385-08514-1*) Doubleday Publishing.

**AUSTIN, BETH (FICTITIOUS CHARACTER)—FICTION**

Skom, Edith. The Charles Dickens Murders: A Beth Austin Mystery. (Beth Austin Mysteries Ser.). 304p. 1999. mass mkt. 5.99 (*0-440-21776-8*); 1998. 21.95 o.s.i (*0-385-31230-X*) Dell Publishing.
—The George Eliot Murders: A Beth Austin Mystery. (Beth Austin Mysteries Ser.). 1996. 288p. mass mkt. 5.99 o.s.i (*0-440-21775-X*); 1995. 243p. 19.95 o.s.i (*0-385-31228-8*, Delacorte Pr.) Dell Publishing.
—The Mark Twain Murders: A Beth Austin Mystery. 1989. (Brown Bag Mystery Line Ser.). 277p. 12.95 o.p. (*0-933031-17-3*) Council Oak Bks.
—The Mark Twain Murders: A Beth Austin Mystery. 1990. (Beth Austin Mysteries Ser.). 304p. mass mkt. 5.99 o.s.i (*0-440-20608-1*) Dell Publishing.

**AUSTIN, KURT (FICTITIOUS CHARACTER)—FICTION**

Cussler, Clive. Fire Ice. pap. o.p. (*0-7862-4659-6*) Thorndike Pr.
—Serpent: A Novel from the NUMA Files. abr. ed. 1999. audio 24.00 Highsmith Inc.
—Serpent: A Novel from the NUMA Files. 2001. E-Book 9.99 (*0-7434-2307-0*); 1999. 480p. pap. 16.00 (*0-671-02670-4*) Simon & Schuster. (Pocket).
—Serpent: A Novel from the NUMA Files. abr. ed. 1999. (NUMA Files Ser.: No. 1). audio 24.00 (*0-671-04615-2*, 591144, Simon & Schuster Audioworks) Simon & Schuster Audio.
—Serpent: A Novel from the NUMA Files. 2000. 14.04 (*0-606-19061-9*) Turtleback Bks.
Cussler, Clive & Kemprecos, Paul. Fire Ice. 2004. 448p. pap. 16.00 (*0-425-19602-X*) Berkley Publishing Group.
—Fire Ice. 2002. 384p. 26.95 o.s.i (*0-399-14872-8*); audio compact disk 29.95 o.s.i (*0-399-14906-6*, Putnam Berkley Audio); 12p. audio 44.95 o.s.i (*0-399-14907-4*, Putnam Berkley Audio) Penguin Group (USA) Inc.
—Fire Ice. 2002. (Basic Ser.). 32.95 (*0-7862-4660-X*) Thorndike Pr.
—Serpent: A Novel from the NUMA Files. l.t. ed. 1999. (Wheeler Large Print Book Ser.). 622p. pap. 25.95 (*1-56895-796-3*, Wheeler Publishing, Inc.) Gale Group.
—Serpent: A Novel from the NUMA Files. 2000. (NUMA Files Ser.: Vol. 1). 480p. reprint ed. pap. 7.99 (*0-671-02668-2*, Pocket) Simon & Schuster.
—White Death: A Kurt Austin Adventure. 2003. (Numa Files Ser.). 432p. 26.95 (*0-399-15041-2*) Penguin Group (USA) Inc.

**AUSTIN, LYNDA DAWN (FICTITIOUS CHARACTER)—FICTION**

Bly, Stephen A. The Final Chapter of Chance Mccall. 1996. (Austin-Stoner Files Ser.: Bk. 2). 368p. pap. 11.99 o.p. (*0-89107-903-3*) Crossway Bks.
—The Kill Fee of Cindy Lacoste. 1997. (Austin-Stoner Files Ser.: Bk. 3). 384p. pap. 11.99 (*0-89107-954-8*) Crossway Bks.
—The Lost Manuscript of Martin Taylor Harrison. 1995. (Austin-Stoner Files Ser.: Bk. 1). 352p. pap. 11.99 o.p. (*0-89107-852-5*) Crossway Bks.
—The Lost Manuscript of Martin Taylor Harrison. l.t. ed. 1996. 465p. 21.95 (*0-7838-1596-4*, Macmillan Reference USA) Gale Group.

**AVERY, BLAINE (FICTITIOUS CHARACTER)—FICTION**

Thompson, Carlene. All Fall Down. 1993. pap. 4.99 (*0-380-77021-0*, Avon Bks.) Morrow/Avon.
—All Fall Down. 2002. mass mkt. (*0-312-98462-6*, St. Martin's Paperbacks) St. Martin's Pr.

**AYERS, SAMMY (FICTITIOUS CHARACTER)—FICTION**

Gearino, G. D. What the Deaf-Mute Heard, Set. abr. ed. 1996. audio 16.95 o.p. (*1-55927-380-1*, 393311) Audio Renaissance.
—What the Deaf-Mute Heard. unabr. ed. 1996. audio 42.00 (*0-7366-3366-9*, 4016) Books on Tape, Inc.
—What the Deaf-Mute Heard. 1997. per. 14.00 (*0-671-02073-0*, Pocket); 1996. 224p. 21.00 (*0-684-81337-8*, Simon & Schuster) Simon & Schuster.

**AYESHA (FICTITIOUS CHARACTER: HAGGARD)—FICTION**

Haggard, H. Rider. Ayesha: The Return of She. 1976. reprint ed. lib. bdg. 26.95 (*0-89190-701-7*, Rivercity Pr.) Amereon, Ltd.
—Ayesha: The Return of She. 1990. reprint ed. lib. bdg. 22.95 (*0-89968-512-9*) Buccaneer Bks., Inc.
—Ayesha: The Return of She. 1977. (Forgotten Fantasy Library: Vol. 14). 360p. reprint ed. pap. 5.95 o.p. (*0-87877-113-1*, New Page Bks.) Career Pr., Inc.
—Ayesha: The Return of She. 1978. (Illus.). 189p. reprint ed. pap. 7.95 (*0-486-23649-8*) Dover Pubns., Inc.
—Ayesha: The Return of She. 1971. 359p. reprint ed. spiral bd. 23.60 (*0-7873-1129-4*) Health Research.
—Ayesha: The Return of She. unabr. ed. 2001. audio 69.95 (*1-85695-413-7*, 92103) ISIS Audio Bks. GBR. *Dist:* Ulverscroft Large Print Bks., Ltd.
—Ayesha: The Return of She. Reginald, R. & Menville, Douglas A., eds. 1980. (Newcastle Forgotten Fantasy Library: Vol. 14). 359p. reprint ed. lib. bdg. 19.95 o.p. (*0-89370-513-6*) Millefleurs.
—Ayesha: The Return of She. 1999. 320p. pap. 7.95 (*1-902058-04-6*) Pulp Fictions GBR. *Dist:* 7 Hills Bk. Distributors.
—The Classic Adventures: Sir H. Rider Haggard. 1986. (Illus.). 336p. 7.98 o.p. (*1-85079-043-4*) Sterling Publishing Co., Inc.
—The Legend of She. 1982. pap. 3.95 o.p. (*0-14-005297-6*, Penguin Bks.) Viking Penguin.
—She. 1967. (Airmont Classics Ser.). (gr. 8 up). mass mkt. 1.95 o.p. (*0-8049-0146-5*, CL-146) Airmont Publishing Co., Inc.
—She. 1976. reprint ed. lib. bdg. 23.95 (*0-89190-705-X*, Rivercity Pr.) Amereon, Ltd.
—She. 1978. (Del Rey Bk.). pap. 1.95 o.s.i (*0-345-27453-9*) Ballantine Bks.
—She, unabr. ed. 1996. audio 62.95 (*0-7861-0947-5*, 1696) Blackstone Audio Bks., Inc.
—She. 1990. reprint ed. lib. bdg. 20.95 (*0-89968-514-5*) Buccaneer Bks., Inc.
—She. 1994. 352p. (YA). mass mkt. 5.95 o.s.i (*0-451-52584-1*, Signet Classics) NAL.
—She. 1991. (Oxford World's Classics Ser.). (Illus.). 380p. pap. 7.95 o.p. (*0-19-282767-7*, 6021) Oxford Univ. Pr., Inc.
—She. 1998. xvi, 246p. pap. text 7.95 (*1-902058-03-8*) Pulp Fictions GBR. *Dist:* 7 Hills Bk. Distributors.
—She. 1999. (Gateway Movie Classics Ser.). 382p. pap. 14.95 (*0-89526-328-9*, Gateway Editions) Regnery Publishing, Inc., An Eagle Publishing Co.
—She. 380p. pap. 4.00 o.p. (*1-85326-234-X*) Wordsworth Editions, Ltd. GBR. *Dist:* Casemate Pubs. & Bk. Distributors, LLC.
—She & Allan. reprint ed. lib. bdg. 25.95 (*0-89190-706-8*, Rivercity Pr.) Amereon, Ltd.
—She & Allan. 1978. (Del Rey Bk.). mass mkt. 1.95 o.s.i (*0-345-27449-0*) Ballantine Bks.
—She & Allan. 1975. (Forgotten Fantasy Library: Vol. 6). (Illus.). 302p. pap. 5.95 o.p. (*0-87877-105-0*, F-112, New Page Bks.) Career Pr., Inc.
—She & Allan. Reginald, R. & Menville, Douglas A., eds. 1980. (Forgotten Fantasy Library: Vol. 6). 303p. reprint ed. lib. bdg. 31.00 o.p. (*0-89370-505-5*) Millefleurs.
—She & Allan. 1999. 320p. pap. 7.95 (*1-902058-05-4*) Pulp Fictions GBR. *Dist:* 7 Hills Bk. Distributors.
—She & Allan. 2001. 408p. pap. 19.95 (*1-58715-422-6*) Wildside Pr.
—She, King Solomon's Mines & Allan Quartermain. 1951. 636p. pap. 12.95 (*0-486-20643-2*) Dover Pubns., Inc.
—Wisdom's Daughter: The Life & Love Story of She-Who-Must-Be-Obeyed. 24.95 (*0-89190-714-9*) Amereon, Ltd.
—Wisdom's Daughter: The Life & Love Story of She-Who-Must-Be-Obeyed. Reginald, R. & Melville, Douglas, eds. 1978. (Lost Race & Adult Fantasy Ser.). reprint ed. lib. bdg. 36.95 (*0-405-10983-0*) Ayer Co. Pubs., Inc.
—Wisdom's Daughter: The Life & Love Story of She-Who-Must-Be-Obeyed. 1978. (Del Rey Bk.). mass mkt. 1.95 o.s.i (*0-345-27428-8*) Ballantine Bks.

**AYLA (FICTITIOUS CHARACTER: AUEL)—FICTION**

Auel, Jean M. Los Cazadores de Mamuts. 2002. (ENG & SPA., Illus.). 672p. pap. 13.00 (*0-7432-3604-1*, Fireside) Simon & Schuster.
—El Clan del Oso Cavernario. 2002. (Libros en Espanol Ser.). Orig. Title: Clan of the Cave Bear. 512p. pap. 12.00 (*0-7432-3358-1*, Fireside) Simon & Schuster.
—The Clan of the Cave Bear. 1984. (Earth's Children Ser.: Vol. 1). 528p. mass mkt. 7.99 (*0-553-25042-6*) Bantam Bks.
—The Clan of the Cave Bear, Pt. 2. unabr. collector's ed. 1986. audio 64.00 (*0-7366-0638-6*, 1597-B) Books on Tape, Inc.
—The Clan of the Cave Bear. unabr. ed. (Earth's Children Ser.: Vol. 1). 2002. audio compact disk 155.25 (*1-59086-087-X*, 3636, CD Unabridged Library Edition); 2002. audio compact disk 49.95 (*1-59086-086-1*, 3635, CD Unabridged); 1999. audio 44.95 (*1-56740-471-5*, 1918, Brilliance Audio Unabridged); 1986. audio 26.95 (*0-930435-22-2*, 64, Bookcassette); 1986. audio 105.25 (*1-56100-017-5*, 1142, Unabridged Library Editions) Brilliance Audio.
—The Clan of the Cave Bear. unabr. ed. 2001. audio 99.95 (*0-7451-4001-7*, CAB 698) Chivers Audio Bks. GBR. *Dist:* BBC Audiobooks America.
—The Clan of the Cave Bear. 1980. 480p. 19.95 o.s.i (*0-517-54202-1*, Crown) Crown Publishing Group.
—The Clan of the Cave Bear, Set. unabr. ed. 1999. audio 105.25 Highsmith Inc.
—The Clan of the Cave Bear. audio New Letters on Air.
—The Clan of the Cave Bear. 1998. (Earth's Children Ser.). 480p. 12.99 o.s.i (*0-517-18918-6*) Random Hse. Value Publishing.
—The Clan of the Cave Bear. unabr. ed. 2003. (Earth's Children Ser.). audio 29.99 (*1-59335-105-4*, 30199) Soulmate Audio Bks., Inc.
—The Clan of the Cave Bear. 1980. (Earth's Children Ser.). (J). 14.04 (*0-606-00288-X*) Turtleback Bks.
—The Mammoth Hunters. 1986. 784p. mass mkt. 4.95 o.s.i (*0-553-26096-0*); 1986. mass mkt. o.s.i (*0-553-26592-X*); 1986. (Earth's Children Ser.: No. 3). 752p. mass mkt. 7.99 (*0-553-28094-5*, Bantam Classics); 2002. 656p. pap. 14.95 (*0-553-38164-4*) Bantam Bks.
—The Mammoth Hunters. unabr. collector's ed. 1986. (Earth's Children Ser.). Pt. 1. audio 88.00 (*0-7366-0814-1*, 1764A ); Pt. 2. audio 80.00 (*0-7366-0815-X*, 1764-B) Books on Tape, Inc.
—The Mammoth Hunters. unabr. ed. (Earth's Children Ser.: Vol. 3). 2002. audio compact disk 165.25 (*1-59086-091-8*, 3638, CD Unabridged Library Edition); 1999. audio 49.95 (*1-56740-472-3*, 1919, Brilliance Audio Unabridged); 1986. audio 28.95 o.p. (*0-930435-28-1*, 169, Bookcassette); 1986. audio 162.55 (*1-56100-023-X*, 935, Unabridged Library Editions) Brilliance Audio.

—The Mammoth Hunters. 656p. 2001. 24.95 (*0-609-61099-6*); 1985. 25.00 o.s.i (*0-517-55627-8*) Crown Publishing Group. (Crown).
—The Mammoth Hunters. unabr. ed. 1999. audio 162.55 Highsmith Inc.
—The Mammoth Hunters. l.t. ed. 2002. 1152p. 26.95 (*0-375-43177-2*) Random Hse., Inc.
—The Mammoth Hunters. 1985. (Earth's Children Ser.). (J). 14.04 (*0-606-03115-4*) Turtleback Bks.
—The Plains of Passage. 1991. 880p. mass mkt. 6.99 o.s.i (*0-553-18047-9*); 1991. 896p. mass mkt. 7.99 (*0-553-28941-1*); 2002. 768p. pap. 14.95 (*0-553-38165-2*) Bantam Bks.
—The Plains of Passage, Pt. 1. unabr. collector's ed. 1991. (Earth's Children Ser.). audio 96.00 (*0-7366-1941-0*, 2763-A ) Books on Tape, Inc.
—The Plains of Passage. unabr. ed. (Earth's Children Ser.: Vol. 4). 2002. audio compact disk 184.25 (*1-59086-093-4*, 3642, CD Unabridged Library Edition); 1999. audio 59.95 (*1-56740-474-X*, 1921, Brilliance Audio Unabridged); 1991. 34p. audio 189.55 (*1-56100-074-4*, 986, Unabridged Library Editions); 1991. audio 39.95 (*0-930435-80-X*, 213, Bookcassette) Brilliance Audio.
—The Plains of Passage. 2001. 768p. 24.95 (*0-609-61100-3*, Crown) Crown Publishing Group.
—The Plains of Passage, Set. unabr. ed. 1999. audio 189.55 Highsmith Inc.
—The Plains of Passage. l.t. ed. 2002. 1328p. 26.95 (*0-375-43178-0*) Random Hse., Inc.
—The Plains of Passage. unabr. ed. 1991. Pt. 1. audio 100.00 (*1-55690-416-9*, 91212E7); Pt. 2. audio 82.00 (*1-55690-417-7*, 91213E7) Recorded Bks., LLC.
—Los Refugios de Piedras. 2002. (Libros en Espanol Ser.).Tr. of Shelters of Stone. 832p. pap. 12.00 (*0-7432-3357-3*, Fireside) Simon & Schuster.
—The Shelters of Stone. 2004. 768p. pap. 15.00 (*0-553-38261-6*); 2003. 912p. mass mkt. (*0-553-58662-9*) Bantam Bks.
—The Shelters of Stone, 2 vols. unabr. ed. 2002. (Earth's Children Ser.: Bk. 5). audio 189.25 (*1-58788-990-0*, 3510, Unabridged Library Editions); audio 59.95 (*1-58788-989-7*, 3509, Brilliance Audio Unabridged); audio compact disk 79.95 (*1-58788-991-9*, 3511, CD Unabridged); audio compact disk 209.25 (*1-58788-992-7*, 3512, CD Unabridged Library Edition) Brilliance Audio.
—The Shelters of Stone. (Earth's Children Ser.). (Illus.). 2003. 912p. mass mkt. 7.99 (*0-553-28942-X*, Crown); 2002. 768p. 28.95 (*0-609-61059-7*) Crown Publishing Group.
—The Shelters of Stone. l.t. ed. 2002. 1216p. 28.95 (*0-375-43174-8*) Random Hse., Inc.
—The Shelters of Stone. unabr. ed. 2003. (Earth's Children Ser.). audio 29.99 (*1-59335-106-2*, 30200) Soulmate Audio Bks., Inc.
—The Valley of Horses. 1999. mass mkt. (*0-553-23481-1*); 1999. mass mkt. (*0-553-24561-9*); 1989. 560p. mass mkt. 5.50 o.s.i (*0-553-28092-9*, Bantam Classics); 1984. 576p. mass mkt. 7.99 (*0-553-25053-1*, 2931321) Bantam Bks.
—The Valley of Horses. unabr. collector's ed. 1986. Pt. 1. audio 72.00 (*0-7366-0770-6*, 1726A ); Pt. 2. audio 64.00 (*0-7366-0771-4*, 1726-B) Books on Tape, Inc.
—The Valley of Horses. unabr. ed. (Earth's Children Ser.: Vol. 2). 2002. audio compact disk 49.95 (*1-59086-088-8*, 3639, CD Unabridged); 2002. audio compact disk 155.25 (*1-59086-089-6*, 3640, CD Unabridged Library Edition); 1986. audio 26.95 (*0-930435-27-3*, 306, Bookcassette); 1986. audio 130.55 (*1-56100-022-1*, 1115, Unabridged Library Editions) Brilliance Audio.
—The Valley of Horses. 1982. (Earth's Children Ser.). 512p. 24.95 o.s.i (*0-517-54489-X*, Crown) Crown Publishing Group.
—The Valley of Horses, Set. unabr. ed. 1999. audio 130.55 Highsmith Inc.
—The Valley of Horses. audio New Letters on Air.
—The Valley of Horses. unabr. ed. 2003. (Earth's Children Ser.). audio 29.99 (*1-59335-203-4*, 30300) Soulmate Audio Bks., Inc.
Auel, Jean M. & Burr, Sandra. The Valley of Horses. unabr. ed. 1999. (Earth's Children Ser.: Bk. 2). audio 44.95 (*1-56740-473-1*, 1920, Brilliance Audio Unabridged) Brilliance Audio.

### AZRIEL, SERVANT OF THE BONES (FICTITIOUS CHARACTER)—FICTION

Rice, Anne. Servant of the Bones. 1997. 7.50 (*0-345-41231-1*, Del Rey); 1997. 416p. pap. 15.00 (*0-345-40966-3*); 1996. mass mkt. o.s.i (*0-676-52155-X*) Ballantine Bks.
—Servant of the Bones. 1996. 387p. 26.00 (*0-679-42832-1*) Knopf, Alfred A. Inc.
—Servant of the Bones. l.t. ed. 1996. 640p. 26.00 o.p. (*0-7838-1915-3*); pap. 26.00 (*0-679-75904-2*) Random Hse. Large Print.
—Servant of the Bones. 1996. 400p. 26.00 (*0-679-43301-5*) Random Hse., Inc.
—Servant of the Bones. ltd. ed. 1996. 387p. 150.00 (*0-9631925-6-6*) Trice, B.E. Publishing.

## B

### BABCOCK, ALLIDA (FICTITIOUS CHARACTER)—FICTION

O'Kane, Leslie. Give the Dog a Bone. l.t. ed. 2002. (Mystery Ser.). 378p. 28.95 (*0-7862-4722-3*) Thorndike Pr.
—Play Dead. 1998. (Allie Babcock Mysteries Ser.). 261p. mass mkt. 5.99 o.s.i (*0-449-00159-8*, Fawcett) Ballantine Bks.
—Play Dead. l.t. ed. 2000. (Mystery Ser.). 391p. o.p. (*0-7862-2329-4*) Thorndike Pr.
—Ruff Way to Go. 2000. (Allie Babcock Mysteries Ser.). 240p. mass mkt. 6.50 o.s.i (*0-449-00161-X*, Fawcett) Ballantine Bks.
—Ruff Way to Go. l.t. ed. 2001. (Thorndike Mystery Ser.). 383p. 28.95 (*0-7862-3193-9*) Thorndike Pr.

### BACA, SONNY (FICTITIOUS CHARACTER)—FICTION

Anaya, Rudolfo A. Rio Grande Fall. 1997. 352p. mass mkt. 6.99 (*0-446-60486-0*); 1996. 368p. 23.00 o.p. (*0-446-51844-1*) Warner Bks., Inc.
—Shaman Winter. 2000. 432p. mass mkt. 7.50 (*0-446-60801-7*); 1999. (Illus.). 374p. 30.00 o.p. (*0-446-52374-7*) Warner Bks., Inc.
—Zia Summer. 1996. 13.04 (*0-606-17163-0*) Turtleback Bks.
—Zia Summer. 1996. 368p. mass mkt. 7.50 (*0-446-60316-3*); 1995. 400p. (YA). 21.95 o.p. (*0-446-51843-3*) Warner Bks., Inc.

### BACHELOR BROTHERS (FICTITIOUS CHARACTERS)—FICTION

Richardson, Bill. Bachelor Brothers' Bed & Breakfast. l.t. ed. 1997. 21.95 (*1-57490-131-1*, Beeler Large Print Bks.) Beeler, Thomas T. Publisher.
—Bachelor Brothers' Bed & Breakfast Pillow Book. 1998. 208p. pap. 10.95 (*0-312-19440-4*, Saint Martin's Griffin); 1997. 18.95 (*0-312-16779-2*); 1997. 384p. pap. 11.95 (*0-312-17183-8*, Saint Martin's Griffin); 1996. 160p. 18.95 (*0-312-14546-2*) St. Martin's Pr.

### BAEIER, KATE (FICTITIOUS CHARACTER)—FICTION

Slovo, Gillian. Catnap. 1996. 288p. 23.95 o.p. (*0-312-14561-6*, Saint Martin's Minotaur) St. Martin's Pr.
—Catnap. 1995. 276p. pap. o.s.i (*1-85381-815-1*) Virago Pr., Ltd. GBR. *Dist:* Little Brown & Co.
—Close Call: A Kate Baeier Mystery. 1996. 314p. mass mkt. o.s.i (*1-85381-816-X*) Virago Pr., Ltd. GBR. *Dist:* Little Brown & Co.
—Death Comes Staccato. 1988. 12.95 o.s.i (*0-385-24609-9*) Doubleday Publishing.

### BAGGINS, BILBO (FICTITIOUS CHARACTER)—FICTION

The Hobbit. 1985. incl. 5.25 hd (*0-201-11157-8*); 32.00 incl. disk (*0-201-11158-6*) Addison-Wesley Longman, Inc.
The Hobbit. (J). audio o.p. HarperTrade.
Tolkien, J. R. R. The Fellowship of the Ring: Being the First Part of the Lord of the Rings. unabr. ed. 2002. (Lord of the Rings Ser.: Bk. 1). audio (*0-00-764608-9*) HarperCollins Pubs. Ltd.
—The Hobbit. 1977. 35.00 o.p. (*0-8109-1060-8*) Abrams, Harry N. , Inc.
—The Hobbit. 1989. (Illus.). 14.98 (*0-88365-746-5*, Galahad Bks.) BBS Publishing Corp.
—The Hobbit. 1999. mass mkt. 2.22 o.s.i (*0-345-91742-1*); 1990. (Illus.). pap. 12.95 (*0-345-36858-4*); 1988. mass mkt. 4.95 o.p. (*0-345-00861-8*); 1985. mass mkt. 3.95 o.p. (*0-345-33207-5*); 1984. mass mkt. 2.95 o.p. (*0-345-31858-7*); 1981. mass mkt. 2.50 o.p. (*0-345-29604-4*); 1978. (Illus.). pap. 8.95 o.p. (*0-345-27711-2*); 1977. mass mkt. 2.50 o.p. (*0-345-27257-9*); 1976. mass mkt. 1.95 o.p. (*0-345-25342-6*); 1975. mass mkt. 1.75 o.p. (*0-345-24826-0*); 1973. mass mkt. 1.25 o.p. (*0-345-23512-6*); 1972. mass mkt. 0.95 o.p. (*0-345-21532-X*); 2001. (Illus.). 144p. reprint ed. pap. 15.95 (*0-345-44560-0*, Del Rey) Ballantine Bks.
—The Hobbit. 1992. pap. 5.95 (*0-87129-174-6*, H62) Dramatic Publishing Co.
—The Hobbit. abr. ed. 1994. audio 24.99 (*0-88646-356-4*, LFP 7356) Durkin Hayes Publishing Ltd.
—The Hobbit. abr. ed. 1995. audio 29.95 Filmic Archives.
—The Hobbit. abr. ed. 2001. audio 24.95 (*1-56511-551-1*); 2001. audio compact disk 29.95 (*1-56511-552-X*); 2002. audio compact disk 29.95 (*1-56511-672-0*) HighBridge Co.
—The Hobbit. (Illus.). 1999. 320p. pap. 12.00 (*0-618-00221-9*); 1988. 312p. pap. 11.95 o.p. (*0-395-28265-9*) Houghton Mifflin Co.
—The Hobbit. l.t. ed. 1990. (Illus.). 363p. 24.95 (*1-85089-805-7*) ISIS Large Print Bks. GBR. *Dist:* Transaction Pubs., Ulverscroft Large Print Canada, Ltd.
—The Hobbit. 2001. audio compact disk 39.95 Lodestone Catalog, The.
—The Hobbit. (J). (gr. k up). audio 29.98 Music for Little People, Inc.
—The Hobbit. audio compact disk 39.95. 1992. audio 22.98 o.s.i (*0-553-74505-0*); 1992. audio 18.39 o.s.i (*0-553-70025-1*); 1997. audio 25.95 (*0-553-47107-4*) Random Hse. Audio Publishing Group. (RH Audio).
—The Hobbit. unabr. ed. 2001. audio compact disk 39.99 (*0-7887-8982-1*); 1999. audio compact disk 87.00; 1991. (J). (gr. 6). audio 70.00 (*1-55690-233-6*, 91121E7) Recorded Bks., LLC.
—The Hobbit. 2003. 31.95 (*0-7862-5177-8*); 483p. pap. 13.95 (*1-59413-005-1*, Large Print Pr.) Thorndike Pr.
—The Hobbit. l.t. ed. 1982. (Classics Ser.). 381p. o.p. (*0-7089-8065-1*, Charnwood) Thorpe, F. A. Pubs.
—The Hobbit. 1987. 13.04 (*0-606-00811-X*) Turtleback Bks.
—The Hobbit: BBC Dramatization. abr. ed. 1997. (BBC Radio Presents Ser.). audio compact disk 39.95 (*0-553-45562-1*, RH Audio) Random Hse. Audio Publishing Group.
—The Hobbit: Fiftieth Anniversary Edition. 1987. (Illus.). 320p. 29.95 o.p. (*0-395-45402-6*) Houghton Mifflin Co.
—The Hobbit: The Enchanting Prelude to the Lord of the Rings. rev. ed. 1986. (Lord of the Rings Ser.). 320p. mass mkt. 7.99 (*0-345-33968-1*, Del Rey) Ballantine Bks.
—The Hobbit: 1 Act. 1996. 5.95 (*0-87129-589-X*, H37) Dramatic Publishing Co.
—The Hobbit & The Fellowship of the Ring. unabr. ed. audio 12.00 Blackstone Audio Bks., Inc.
—The Hobbit & The Fellowship of the Ring. abr. ed. audio 9.95 o.p. (*0-89845-222-8*, CPN 1477, Caedmon); 1996. audio 12.00 (*1-55994-631-8*, DCN 1477, HarperAudio) HarperTrade.
—The Hobbit & The Lord of the Rings, 4 vols. 1988. 1540p. 45.95 o.p. (*0-395-48907-5*); 1979. pap. 24.95 o.p. (*0-395-28263-2*) Houghton Mifflin Co.
—The Lord of the Rings, 3 vols. 2001. (Lord of the Rings Ser.). (Illus.). 1216p. 38.00 o.s.i (*0-618-12901-4*) Houghton Mifflin Co.
—The Lord of the Rings. 2001. (Lord of the Rings Ser.). (Illus.). xviii, 1137p. pap. 20.00 o.s.i (*0-618-12902-2*, Mariner Bks.) Houghton Mifflin Co. Trade & Reference Div.
—The Lord of the Rings & The Hobbit Trilogy. 1985. (Lord of the Rings Ser.). 138p. (YA). (gr. 10-12). pap. 3.95 (*0-8120-3523-2*) Barron's Educational Series, Inc.
—The Lord of the Rings & The Hobbit Trilogy. abr. ed. 2002. audio compact disk 89.95 (*1-56511-707-7*) HighBridge Co.
Tolkien, J. R. R. & Gray, Patricia. The Hobbit: A Play. 1967. 5.95 (*0-87129-427-3*, H22) Dramatic Publishing Co.
Tolkien, J. R. R., et al. The Hobbit: A Musical. 1972. 5.95 (*0-87129-393-5*, H03) Dramatic Publishing Co.

### BAGGINS, FRODO (FICTITIOUS CHARACTER)—FICTION

Tolkien, J. R. R. The Fellowship of the Ring: Being the First Part of the Lord of the Rings. 1999. (Lord of the Rings Ser.: Bk. 1). mass mkt. 2.22 o.s.i (*0-345-91743-X*); 1986. (Lord of the Rings Ser.: Bk. 1). 480p. mass mkt. 7.99 (*0-345-33970-3*, Del Rey); 1985. mass mkt. 3.95 o.p. (*0-345-33208-3*); 1972. mass mkt. 0.95 o.p. (*0-345-21533-8*) Ballantine Bks.
—The Fellowship of the Ring: Being the First Part of the Lord of the Rings. 2002. 19.57 (*1-4046-2528-3*) Book Wholesalers, Inc.
—The Fellowship of the Ring: Being the First Part of the Lord of the Rings. unabr. ed. 2002. (Lord of the Rings Ser.: Bk. 1). audio (*0-00-764608-9*) HarperCollins Pubs. Ltd.
—The Fellowship of the Ring: Being the First Part of the Lord of the Rings. abr. unabr. ed. 2002. (Lord of the Rings Ser.: Bk. 1). audio compact disk 19.95 (*1-56511-667-4*, 89123) HighBridge Co.
—The Fellowship of the Ring: Being the First Part of the Lord of the Rings. (Lord of the Rings Ser.). 2003. pap. 12.00 (*0-618-34625-2*); 2002. (Illus.). xx, 1170p. 27.50 (*0-618-26051-X*); 1999. 432p. pap. 12.00 (*0-618-00222-7*); 1992. (Illus.). 440p. 30.00 o.p. (*0-395-64738-X*); 1988. (Illus.). 432p. (gr. 7). 22.00 (*0-395-48931-8*); 2002. 432p. pap. 12.00 o.s.i (*0-618-26026-9*) Houghton Mifflin Co.
—The Fellowship of the Ring: Being the First Part of the Lord of the Rings. l.t. ed. 1996. (Lord of the Rings Ser.: Bk. 1). (Illus.). 513p. 24.95 (*1-85089-414-0*) ISIS Large Print Bks. GBR. *Dist:* Transaction Pubs.
—The Fellowship of the Ring: Being the First Part of the Lord of the Rings. abr. ed. 2001. (Lord of the Rings Ser.: Bk. 1). audio 25.95 (*0-553-71477-5*); audio compact disk 27.50 (*0-553-71478-3*) Random Hse. Audio Publishing Group.
—The Fellowship of the Ring: Being the First Part of the Lord of the Rings. unabr. ed. (Lord of the Rings Ser.: Bk. 1). 2000. audio 120.00 (*1-55690-321-9*, 90014E7); 1999. audio compact disk 158.00 Recorded Bks., LLC.
—The Fellowship of the Ring: Being the First Part of the Lord of the Rings. l.t. ed. 2003. (Lord of the Rings Ser.). 855p. pap. 13.95 (*1-59413-007-8*, Large Print Pr.); 31.95 (*0-7862-5178-6*) Thorndike Pr.
—The Fellowship of the Ring: Being the First Part of the Lord of the Rings. 50th ed. 1982. (Lord of the Rings Ser.: Bk. 1). 13.04 (*0-606-00650-8*) Turtleback Bks.
—The Fellowship of the Ring: Radio Dramatization. 2002. audio 39.95 (*0-563-53054-5*, BBCS 007); audio compact disk 49.95 (*0-563-53055-3*, BBCD 007) BBC Worldwide Americas.
—The Hobbit. 2001. (Illus.). 144p. reprint ed. pap. 15.95 (*0-345-44560-0*, Del Rey) Ballantine Bks.
—The Hobbit & The Fellowship of the Ring. unabr. ed. audio 12.00 Blackstone Audio Bks., Inc.
—The Hobbit & The Fellowship of the Ring. abr. ed. audio 9.95 o.p. (*0-89845-222-8*, CPN 1477, Caedmon); 1996. audio 12.00 (*1-55994-631-8*, DCN 1477, HarperAudio) HarperTrade.
—The Hobbit & The Lord of the Rings, 4 vols. 1988. 1540p. 45.95 o.p. (*0-395-48907-5*); 1979. pap. 24.95 o.p. (*0-395-28263-2*) Houghton Mifflin Co.
—The Lord of the Rings. unabr. ed. (Lord of the Rings Ser.). audio 59.95 Blackstone Audio Bks., Inc.
—The Lord of the Rings. 2003. 35.00 (*0-618-34624-4*); 2003. (Illus.). 1168p. tchr. ed. 38.00 (*0-618-34584-1*); 2003. (Illus.). 1168p. pap. 20.00 (*0-618-34399-7*); 2002. 1168p. 38.00 o.s.i (*0-618-26024-2*); 2002. (Illus.). 1168p. pap. 20.00 o.s.i (*0-618-26025-0*); 2001. (Illus.). 1216p. 38.00 o.s.i (*0-618-12901-4*); 1999. 1216p. pap. 20.00 o.s.i (*0-395-97468-2*); 1992. (Illus.). 90.00 o.p. (*0-395-64741-X*); 1991. (Illus.). 1200p. 251.00 o.p. (*0-395-60423-0*); 1991. (Illus.). 1198p. (gr. 7). 70.00 (*0-395-59511-8*); 1988. (Illus.). 428p. pap. 11.95 o.p. (*0-395-27223-8*); 1988. 65.00 (*0-395-48932-6*); 1978. 1232p. pap. 22.95 o.p. (*0-395-27220-3*); 1976. 45.85 o.p. (*0-395-08257-9*); rev. ed. 1954. 423p. 14.95 o.p. (*0-395-08254-4*); 2nd collector's ed. 1974. (Illus.). 1216p. (gr. 7). 75.00 (*0-395-19395-8*) Houghton Mifflin Co.
—The Lord of the Rings. 2001. (Lord of the Rings Ser.). (Illus.). xviii, 1137p. pap. 20.00 o.s.i (*0-618-12902-2*, Mariner Bks.) Houghton Mifflin Co. Trade & Reference Div.
—The Lord of the Rings. 2nd ed. 1968. (Lord of the Rings Ser.). 1077p. o.p. (*0-04-823087-1*) Independent Pubs. Group.
—The Lord of the Rings. (Lord of the Rings Ser.). (J). (gr. 3 up). audio 59.98 Music for Little People, Inc.
—The Lord of the Rings. (Lord of the Rings Ser.). audio compact disk 64.95. 1993. audio 59.95 (*0-553-47228-3*, RH Audio); 2000. 1216p. (YA). pap. 80.00 incl. audio (*0-8072-8344-4*, LL0187, Listening Library); 1999. 69.95 incl. audio compact disk (*0-553-45653-9*, RH Audio) Random Hse. Audio Publishing Group.
—The Lord of the Rings. unabr. ed. (Lord of the Rings Ser.). audio 49.95 Soundelux Audio Publishing.
—The Lord of the Rings. 1994. 26.05 (*0-606-21597-2*) Turtleback Bks.
—The Lord of the Rings: Millennium Edition, 7 vols. 1999. (Lord of the Rings Ser.). (Illus.). 70.00 o.p. (*0-618-03766-7*) Houghton Mifflin Co.
—The Lord of the Rings: The Fellowship of the Ring; The Two Towers; The Return of the King, 3 bks. 2002. (Lord of the Rings Ser.). (Illus.). 1168p. 80.00 (*0-618-26058-7*); pap. 35.00 o.s.i (*0-618-26029-3*) Houghton Mifflin Co.
—The Lord of the Rings: The Two Towers & The Return of the King. abr. ed. 1998. audio 12.00 (*0-89845-223-6*, CPN 1478, Caedmon) HarperTrade.
—The Lord of the Rings & The Hobbit, 3 vols. 1999. (Lord of the Rings Ser.). (Illus.). pap. 45.00 (*0-618-00225-1*) Houghton Mifflin Co.
—The Lord of the Rings & The Hobbit Trilogy. 1985. (Lord of the Rings Ser.). 138p. (YA). (gr. 10-12). pap. 3.95 (*0-8120-3523-2*) Barron's Educational Series, Inc.
—The Lord of the Rings & The Hobbit Trilogy. abr. ed. 2002. audio compact disk 89.95 (*1-56511-707-7*) HighBridge Co.
—The Return of the King. 1999. (Lord of the Rings Ser.: Bk. 3). mass mkt. 2.22 o.s.i (*0-345-91745-6*); 1986. (Lord of the Rings Ser.: Bk. 3). 512p. mass mkt. 7.99 (*0-345-33973-8*, Del Rey); 1985. mass mkt. 3.95 o.p. (*0-345-33209-1*); 1981. mass mkt. 2.95 o.p. (*0-345-29608-7*); 1977. mass mkt. 2.50 o.p. (*0-345-27260-9*); 1976. mass mkt. 1.95 o.p. (*0-345-25345-0*); 1975. mass mkt. 1.75 o.p. (*0-345-24829-5*); 1974. mass mkt. 1.50 o.p. (*0-345-24034-0*) Ballantine Bks.
—The Return of the King. 2002. (J). 16.60 (*0-7587-5212-1*) Book Wholesalers, Inc.

—The Return of the King. unabr. ed. 2002. (Lord of the Rings Ser.: Bk. 3). audio (0-00-764610-0) HarperCollins Pubs. Ltd.
—The Return of the King. abr. unabr. ed. 2002. (Lord of the Rings Ser.: Bk. 3). audio compact disk 19.95 (1-56511-669-0, 89125) HighBridge Co.
—The Return of the King, 3 vols. (Lord of the Rings Ser.: Bk. 3). 2002. (Illus.). xx, 1170p. 27.50 (0-618-26055-2); 1999. 464p. pap. 12.00 (0-618-00224-3); 1992. (Illus.). 464p. 30.00 o.p. (0-395-64740-1); 1988. (Illus.). 450p. pap. 11.95 o.p. (0-395-27221-1); movie tie-in ed. 2002. 1140p. pap. 12.00 o.s.i (0-618-26028-5); rev. ed. 1967. 14.95 o.p. (0-395-08256-0); 2nd ed. 1988. (Illus.). 448p. (gr. 7). 22.00 (0-395-48930-X) Houghton Mifflin Co.
—The Return of the King. abr. unabr. ed. 2002. (Lord of the Rings Ser.: Bk. 3). (J). audio 25.95 (0-8072-0910-4, Listening Library) Random Hse. Audio Publishing Group.
—The Return of the King. (Lord of the Rings Ser.: Bk. 3). 2001. audio compact disk 49.99 (0-7887-8984-8); 2001. audio 34.99 (0-7887-8955-4); 1997. audio 91.00 (1-55690-320-0, 90016E7) Recorded Bks., LLC.
—The Return of the King. l.t. ed. 2003. (Lord of the Rings Ser.). 864p. pap. 13.95 (1-59413-004-3, Large Print Pr.); 31.95 (0-7862-5176-X) Thorndike Pr.
—The Return of the King. 1983. (Lord of the Rings Ser.: Bk. 3). 13.04 (0-606-01302-4) Turtleback Bks.
—The Return of the King: Being the Third Part of the Lord of the Rings. 2003. (Lord of the Rings Ser.). pap. 12.00 (0-618-34627-9) Houghton Mifflin Co.
—Tolkien Boxed Set, 4 vols. 1986. 29.96 (0-345-34042-6, Del Rey) Ballantine Bks.
—The Two Towers: Being the Second Part of the Lord of the Rings. 1999. (Lord of the Rings Ser.: Bk. 2). mass mkt. 2.22 o.s.i (0-345-91744-8); 1988. (Lord of the Rings Ser.: Bk. 2). mass mkt. 4.95 o.p. (0-345-00863-4); 1986. (Lord of the Rings Ser.: Bk. 2). 416p. mass mkt. 7.99 (0-345-33971-1, Del Rey); 1985. mass mkt. 3.95 o.p. (0-345-33210-5); 1981. mass mkt. 2.95 o.p. (0-345-29606-0); 1977. mass mkt. 2.50 o.p. (0-345-27259-5); 1976. mass mkt. 1.95 o.p. (0-345-25344-2); 1975. mass mkt. 1.75 o.p. (0-345-24828-7); 1974. mass mkt. 1.50 o.p. (0-345-24033-2); 1973. mass mkt. 1.25 o.p. (0-345-23510-X) Ballantine Bks.
—The Two Towers: Being the Second Part of the Lord of the Rings. 2002. 19.57 (1-4046-2531-3) Book Wholesalers, Inc.
—The Two Towers: Being the Second Part of the Lord of the Rings. unabr. ed. 2002. (Lord of the Rings Ser.: Bk. 2). audio (0-00-764609-7) HarperCollins Pubs. Ltd.
—The Two Towers: Being the Second Part of the Lord of the Rings. (Lord of the Rings Ser.). 2003. pap. 12.00 (0-618-34626-0); 2002. (Illus.). xx, 1170p. 27.50 (0-618-26059-5); 1999. 352p. pap. 12.00 (0-618-00223-5); 1992. (Illus.). 368p. 30.00 o.p. (0-395-64739-8); 1988. (Illus.). 356p. pap. 11.95 o.p. (0-395-27222-X); 1967. 14.95 o.p. (0-395-08255-2); movie tie-in ed. 2002. 725p. pap. 12.00 o.s.i (0-618-26027-7); movie tie-in ed. 2001. (Illus.). x, 725p. reprint ed. pap. 12.00 o.s.i (0-618-12908-1); 2nd ed. 1988. (Illus.). 352p. (gr. 7). 22.00 (0-395-48933-4) Houghton Mifflin Co.
—The Two Towers: Being the Second Part of the Lord of the Rings. l.t. ed. 1992. (Lord of the Rings Ser.: Bk. 2). (Illus.). 448p. 24.95 (1-85089-419-1) ISIS Large Print Bks. GBR. Dist: Transaction Pubs.
—The Two Towers: Being the Second Part of the Lord of the Rings. abr. ed. 2002. (Lord of the Rings Ser.: Bk. 2). (J). audio 25.95 (0-8072-0907-4, Listening Library) Random Hse. Audio Publishing Group.
—The Two Towers: Being the Second Part of the Lord of the Rings. unabr. ed. (Lord of the Rings Ser.: Bk. 2). 2001. audio 34.99 (0-7887-8954-6); 1999. audio compact disk 131.00; 1997. (YA). (gr. 8). audio 97.00 (1-55690-322-7, 90015E7) Recorded Bks., LLC.
—The Two Towers: Being the Second Part of the Lord of the Rings. 2003. (Lord of the Rings Ser.: Part II). 746p. 31.95 (0-7862-5175-1); 776p. pap. 13.95 (1-59413-006-X, Large Print Pr.) Thorndike Pr.
—The Two Towers: Being the Second Part of the Lord of the Rings. 50th ed. 1986. (Lord of the Rings Ser.: Bk. 2). 13.04 (0-606-01521-3) Turtleback Bks.
—The Two Towers: Radio Dramatization. 2002. audio 39.95 (0-563-53058-8, BBCS 005); audio compact disk 49.95 (0-563-53059-6, BBCD 005) BBC Worldwide Americas.
—The Two Towers: Reproducible Teaching Unit. 2002. (Lord of the Rings Ser.: Bk. 2). 82p. tchr. ed., ring bd. (1-58049-460-9, TU216) Prestwick Hse., Inc.

**BAGLEY, CALLISTA (FICTITIOUS CHARACTER)—FICTION**

Cameron, Kate. Under the Wolf's Head: The First Callista Bagley Gardening Mystery. 1999. 274p. 24.95 (0-9661879-3-8, SKP98-44) St Kitts Pr.

**BAILEY, GEOFFREY (FICTITIOUS CHARACTER)—FICTION**

Fyfield, Frances. A Clear Conscience. unabr. ed. 1995. audio 69.95 (0-7451-6547-8, CAB 1163) BBC Audiobooks America.
—A Clear Conscience. 1996. (Helen West Mystery Ser.). mass mkt. 5.99 o.s.i (0-345-38508-X) Ballantine Bks.
—A Clear Conscience. unabr. ed. 2000. (West & Bailey Mystery Ser.). audio 59.95 Chivers Audio Bks. GBR. Dist: BBC Audiobooks America.
—A Clear Conscience. deluxe ed. 1995. 20.00 (0-676-50224-5, Pantheon) Knopf Publishing Group.
—A Clear Conscience. 1995. o.p. (0-676-50194-X) Random Hse., Inc.
—Deep Sleep. unabr. ed. 1996. (Prosecutor Helen West Mysteries Ser.). audio 54.95 (0-7451-4144-7, CAB827) BBC Audiobooks America.
—Deep Sleep. Chelius, Jane, ed. 240p. 1993. mass mkt. 4.99 o.p. (0-671-73547-0, Pocket); 1992. 18.00 o.p. (0-671-73546-2, Atria) Simon & Schuster.
—Not That Kind of Place. 1990. 224p. 17.95 o.p. (0-671-67666-0, Atria) Simon & Schuster.
—Not That Kind of Place. Chelius, Jane, ed. 1991. 256p. reprint ed. mass mkt. 5.50 (0-671-73945-X, Pocket) Simon & Schuster.
—A Question of Guilt. unabr. ed. 1993. (Prosecutor Helen West Mysteries Ser.). audio 69.95 (0-7451-5972-9, CAB 602) BBC Audiobooks America.
—A Question of Guilt. unabr. ed. 2000. (West & Bailey Mystery Ser.). audio 59.95 Chivers Audio Bks. GBR. Dist: BBC Audiobooks America.
—A Question of Guilt. 1990. 288p. mass mkt. 4.99 (0-671-67665-2, Pocket); 1989. 16.95 o.p. (0-671-67664-4, Atria) Simon & Schuster.
—A Question of Guilt. 1991. (Audio Books Ser.). audio 69.95 o.p. (0-8161-9227-8) Thorndike Pr.
—Shadow Play. l.t. ed. 1994. 22.95 o.p. (0-7927-1828-3); pap. 20.95 o.p. (0-7927-1827-5); audio 69.95 (0-7451-4232-X, CAB 915) BBC Audiobooks America.
—Shadow Play. 1994. mass mkt. 5.99 o.s.i (0-345-38507-1) Ballantine Bks.
—Shadow Play. unabr. ed. 2000. (West & Bailey Mystery Ser.). audio 59.95 Chivers Audio Bks. GBR. Dist: BBC Audiobooks America.
—Shadow Play. 1999. 288p. pap. 5.99 (0-14-028683-7, Penguin Bks.) Penguin Group (USA) Inc.
—Trial by Fire. l.t. ed. 1992. 18.95 o.p. (0-7927-1200-5); pap. 16.95 o.p. (0-7927-1174-2); 69.95 incl. audio (0-7451-4025-4, CAB 722) BBC Audiobooks America.
—Trial by Fire. unabr. ed. 2000. (West & Bailey Mystery Ser.). audio 59.95 Chivers Audio Bks. GBR. Dist: BBC Audiobooks America.
—Without Consent. unabr. ed. 1997. (West & Bailey Mystery Ser.). audio 59.95 (0-7451-6799-3, CAB 1415) Chivers Audio Bks. GBR. Dist: BBC Audiobooks America.
—Without Consent. 1998. 272p. mass mkt. 5.99 (0-14-027477-4) Penguin Group (USA) Inc.
—Without Consent. l.t. ed. 1998. (Mystery Ser.). 325p. 26.95 (0-7838-8437-0) Thorndike Pr.
—Without Consent. 1997. (Helen West Mystery Ser.). 224p. 21.95 o.p. (0-670-87682-8) Viking Penguin.

**BAILEY, JERUSHA (FICTITIOUS CHARACTER)—FICTION**

Mobley, C. A. Code of Conflict. 1999. 352p. mass mkt. 6.99 o.s.i (0-425-17108-6) Berkley Publishing Group.
—Rites of War. 1998. 352p. mass mkt. 6.99 o.s.i (0-515-12225-4, Jove) Berkley Publishing Group.
—Rules of Command: A Novel of Crisis & Combat at Sea. 1998. 368p. mass mkt. 6.99 o.s.i (0-425-16746-1) Berkley Publishing Group.

**BAILEY FAMILY (FICTITIOUS CHARACTERS)—FICTION**

Marchant, Catherine, pseud. The Bailey Chronicles. l.t. ed. 1990. (General Ser.). 55.95 o.p. (0-8161-4972-0, Macmillan Reference USA) Gale Group.
—The Bailey Chronicles. 1989. 600p. 19.95 o.p. (0-671-62387-7) Summit Bks.
—Bill Bailey. unabr. ed. 1993. audio 54.95 (0-7451-5846-3, CAB 241) BBC Audiobooks America.
—Bill Bailey, Vol. 1. l.t. ed. 1990. (General Ser.). 387p. lib. bdg. 20.95 o.p. (0-8161-4485-0, Macmillan Reference USA) Gale Group.
—Bill Bailey. l.t. ed. 1987. (Ulverscroft Large Print Ser.). 432p. 14.50 o.p. (0-7089-1698-8, Ulverscroft) Thorpe, F. A. Pubs. GBR. Dist: Ulverscroft Large Print Bks., Ltd., Ulverscroft Large Print Canada, Ltd.
—Bill Bailey Omnibus. 2000. 299p. pap. 13.95 (0-552-14624-2) Transworld Publishers Ltd. GBR. Dist: Trafalgar Square.
—Bill Bailey's Daughter. unabr. ed. 1989. audio 54.95 (0-7451-5847-1, CAB 377) BBC Audiobooks America.
—Bill Bailey's Daughter, Vol. 3. l.t. ed. 1990. (General Ser.). 321p. lib. bdg. 20.95 o.p. (0-8161-4768-X, Macmillan Reference USA) Gale Group.
—Bill Bailey's Lot. unabr. ed. 1993. audio 69.95 (0-7451-5848-X, CAB 273) BBC Audiobooks America.
—Bill Bailey's Lot, Vol. 2. l.t. ed. 1990. (General Ser.). 406p. lib. bdg. 21.95 o.p. (0-8161-4767-1, Macmillan Reference USA) Gale Group.

**BAIRD, JACK (FICTITIOUS CHARACTER)—FICTION**

Thornburg, Newton. A Man's Game. 1997. 300p. mass mkt. 6.99 (0-8125-5374-8); 1996. 304p. 22.95 o.p. (0-312-85923-6) Doherty, Tom Assocs., LLC. (Forge Bks.).

**BAK, LIEUTENANT (FICTITIOUS CHARACTER)—FICTION**

Haney, Lauren. A Curse of Silence: A Mystery of Ancient Egypt. 2000. 304p. mass mkt. 6.50 (0-380-81285-1, Avon Bks.) Morrow/Avon.
—A Face Turned Backward. 1999. (Mystery of Ancient Egypt Ser.). 304p. mass mkt. 5.99 (0-380-79267-2, Avon Bks.) Morrow/Avon.
—Path of Shadows. 2003. 320p. mass mkt. 6.99 (0-06-052190-2, Avon Bks.) Morrow/Avon.
—The Right Hand of Amon. 1997. 320p. mass mkt. 6.99 (0-380-79266-4, Avon Bks.) Morrow/Avon.
—A Vile Justice. 1999. 304p. mass mkt. 5.99 (0-380-79265-6, Avon Bks.) Morrow/Avon.

**BAKER, MARY (FICTITIOUS CHARACTER)—FICTION**

Raison, Jennifer & Goldie, Michael. Caraboo: The Servant Girl Princess: The Real Story of the Grand Hoax. 1995. (Illus.). 220p. pap. 13.95 (1-56656-179-5) Interlink Publishing Group, Inc.

**BAKER STREET IRREGULARS (FICTITIOUS CHARACTERS)—FICTION**

Doyle, Arthur Conan. The Crooked Man. 1989. audio 7.95 Jimcin Recordings.
—The Sign of the Four. Date not set. 112p. 16.95 (0-8488-2550-0) Amereon, Ltd.
—The Sign of the Four. unabr. ed. 1991. (Best of Sherlock Holmes Ser.). audio 26.95 o.p. (1-55656-140-7, DAB042) BBC Audiobooks America.
—The Sign of the Four. 2000. (Encore Editions Ser.). 167p. (C). pap. (1-55111-392-9) Broadview Pr.
—The Sign of the Four. unabr. ed. (Best of Sherlock Holmes Ser.). 1998. pap. 21.95 o.s.i incl. audio (1-55656-228-4); 1990. audio 21.95 o.s.i (1-55656-139-3) Dercum Audio.
—The Sign of the Four. 1977. 9.95 o.p. (0-385-12285-3) Doubleday Publishing.
—The Sign of the Four. abr. ed. 1986. (J). (gr. 5-7). audio 29.95 o.p. (0-88646-811-6, R 7094); 1983. audio 15.95 o.p. (0-88646-072-7, TC-LFP 7094) Durkin Hayes Publishing Ltd.
—The Sign of the Four. Goodenough, Simon, ed. 1985. (Illus.). 192p. pap. o.p. (0-316-32009-9) Little Brown & Co.
—The Sign of the Four. Roden, Christopher, ed. 1993. (Oxford Sherlock Holmes Ser.). 192p. (C). 13.95 o.p. (0-19-212316-5, 14614) Oxford Univ. Pr., Inc.
—The Sign of the Four. 1999. 185p. E-Book 3.99 incl. cd-rom (1-57646-181-5) Quiet Vision Publishing.
—The Sign of the Four. unabr. ed. 1986. (Sherlock Holmes Mystery Ser.). audio 26.00 (1-55690-477-0, 86240E7) Recorded Bks., LLC.
—A Study in Scarlet. 1984. 192p. mass mkt. 2.50 o.s.i (0-425-08004-8) Ace Bks.
—A Study in Scarlet. Date not set. 121p. 17.95 (0-8488-2554-3) Amereon, Ltd.
—A Study in Scarlet. unabr. ed. 1998. (C). audio 24.95 (1-55685-608-3) Audio Bk. Contractors, Inc.
—A Study in Scarlet. unabr. ed. 1991. (Best of Sherlock Holmes Ser.: Vol. 4). audio 26.95 o.p. (1-55656-062-1, DAB043) BBC Audiobooks America.
—A Study in Scarlet. 1975. 160p. mass mkt. 1.25 o.p. (0-345-24714-0) Ballantine Bks.
—A Study in Scarlet. Bennett, S. A., ed. 1992. (Adventures of Sherlock Holmes Ser.). (Illus.). 64p. pap. (0-944099-18-1) Bill Barry's Compass Bks.
—A Study in Scarlet. abr. ed. 1999. audio 23.95 (0-7861-1604-8); audio 23.95 Blackstone Audio Bks., Inc.
—A Study in Scarlet. 2001. per. 9.90 (1-891355-68-6); per. 15.50 (1-58396-234-4) Blue Unicorn Editions.
—A Study in Scarlet. unabr. collector's ed. 1982. (J). audio 30.00 (0-7366-3965-9, 9504) Books on Tape, Inc.
—A Study in Scarlet. 1989. lib. bdg. 15.95 (0-89966-231-5) Buccaneer Bks., Inc.
—A Study in Scarlet. (Collected Works of Sir Arthur Conan Doyle). 2001. pap. text 28.00 (0-7426-7676-5); reprint ed. lib. bdg. 98.00 (0-7426-2676-8) Classic Bks.
—A Study in Scarlet. unabr. ed. audio 21.95 o.p. (1-55656-104-0); 1997. (Best of Sherlock Holmes Ser.: Vol. 4). pap. 21.95 o.p. incl. audio (1-55656-229-2) Dercum Audio.
—A Study in Scarlet. 1977. 7.95 o.p. (0-385-12283-7) Doubleday Publishing.
—A Study in Scarlet. abr. ed. 1986. (J). (gr. 5-7). audio 29.95 o.p. (0-88646-784-5, R 7011); 1984. audio 15.95 o.p. (0-88646-087-5, TC-LFP 7011) Durkin Hayes Publishing Ltd.
—A Study in Scarlet. E-Book 2.49 (0-7574-0260-7) Electric Umbrella Publishing.
—A Study in Scarlet. 2001. iv, 156p. pap. 8.95 (0-7551-0638-5) House of Stratus, Inc. GBR. Dist: Midpoint Trade Bks., Inc.
—A Study in Scarlet. 1989. audio 18.00 Jimcin Recordings.
—A Study in Scarlet. E-Book 2.95 (1-57799-808-1) Logos Research Systems, Inc.
—A Study in Scarlet. Edwards, Owen Dudley, ed. 2000. (Oxford World's Classics Ser.). 256p. pap. 6.95 (0-19-283765-6) Oxford Univ. Pr., Inc.
—A Study in Scarlet. Edwards, Owen D., ed. 1993. (Oxford Sherlock Holmes Ser.). 254p. (C). 13.95 o.p. (0-19-212313-0, 14615) Oxford Univ. Pr., Inc.
—A Study in Scarlet. Edwards, Dudley, ed. & intro. by. 1995. (Oxford World's Classics Ser.). 254p. reprint ed. pap. 5.95 o.p. (0-19-282380-9) Oxford Univ. Pr., Inc.
—A Study in Scarlet. 1982. (Classic Crime Ser.). 144p. pap. 6.95 (0-14-005707-2, Penguin Bks.) Penguin Group (USA) Inc.
—A Study in Scarlet. collector's ed. 2002. (Illus.). im. lthr. 38.85 (1-4115-1254-5); pap. 19.95 (1-4115-0521-2); 25.95 (1-4115-0889-0); pap. 17.95 (1-4115-0319-8) Polyglot Pr., Inc.
—A Study in Scarlet. 1999. 191p. E-Book 3.99 incl. cd-rom (1-57646-180-7) Quiet Vision Publishing.
—A Study in Scarlet. 2003. 160p. pap. 6.95 (0-8129-6854-9, Modern Library) Random House Adult Trade Publishing Group.
—A Study in Scarlet. abr. ed. 1999. (Sherlock Holmes Ser.). audio 18.00 o.s.i (0-553-52553-0, RH Audio) Random Hse. Audio Publishing Group.
—A Study in Scarlet. unabr. ed. 1984. (Sherlock Holmes Mystery Ser.). audio 26.00 (1-55690-498-3, 84071E7) Recorded Bks., LLC.
—A Study in Scarlet. E-Book 5.00 (0-7410-1416-5) SoftBook Pr.
—A Study in Scarlet, 1. 1998. pap. text 6.95 (0-9666443-1-X) Thorby Enterprises, Inc.
—A Study in Scarlet. l.t. ed. 2001. (Perennial Bestsellers Ser.). 191p. 27.95 (0-7838-9350-7) Thorndike Pr.
—A Study in Scarlet. E-Book 2.00 (1-58505-984-6) Treeless Pr.
—A Study in Scarlet. 2001. (Classics Ser.). 192p. 7.00 (0-14-043908-0, Penguin Classics) Viking Penguin.
—A Study in Scarlet. 2001. (New Millennium Library). 109p. pap. 9.95 (0-595-01428-3) iUniverse, Inc.
—A Study in Scarlet & The Sign of the Four. l.t. ed. 1969. o.p. (0-7089-0190-5, Ulverscroft) Thorpe, F. A. Pubs.

Doyle, Arthur Conan, as told by. A Study in Scarlet. 2002. E-Book 2.95 (0-9712910-3-9) Twenty Penny Pr., Inc.

Jeffers, H. Paul. Murder Most Irregular. 1983. 160p. 11.95 o.p. (0-312-55313-7) St. Martin's Pr.
—Murder Most Irregular. 2001. 189p. pap. 24.95 (0-7838-9636-0) Thorndike Pr.

**BALDRIDGE, MASEY (FICTITIOUS CHARACTER)—FICTION**

Brewer, James D. No Bottom: A Masey Baldridge/Luke Williamson Mystery. 1994. 256p. 19.95 o.p. (0-8027-3178-3) Walker & Co.
—No Escape. 1998. (Masey Baldridge/Luke Williamson Mystery Ser.). 264p. 22.95 (0-8027-3318-2) Walker & Co.
—No Justice: A Masey Baldridge/Luke Williamson Mystery. 1996. (Masey Baldridge/Luke Williamson Mystery Ser.). 232p. 21.95 (0-8027-3283-6) Walker & Co.
—No Remorse: A Masey Baldridge/Luke Williamson Mystery. 1997. (Luke Williamson/Masey Baldridge Mystery Ser.). 224p. 22.95 (0-8027-3302-6) Walker & Co.
—No Virtue: A Masey Baldridge/Luke Williamson Mystery. 1995. (Masey Baldridge/Luke Williamson Mystery Ser.). 232p. (YA). 20.95 (0-8027-3259-3) Walker & Co.

**BALDWIN, SARAH (FICTITIOUS CHARACTER)—FICTION**

Palmer, Michael. Natural Causes. 1994. 496p. mass mkt. 7.50 (0-553-56876-0) Bantam Bks.
—Natural Causes. abr. ed. 2000. audio 9.99 (0-553-52727-4, RH Audio) Random Hse. Audio Publishing Group.
—Natural Causes. unabr. ed. 1994. audio audio 91.00 (0-7887-0085-5, 94325E7) Recorded Bks., LLC.

Characters

**BALDWIN, T. T. (FICTITIOUS CHARACTER)—FICTION**

O'Cork, Shannon. End of the Line. 1983. (A.T.T. Baldwin Mystery Ser.). mass mkt. 2.95 o.s.i (*0-671-44488-3*, Pocket) Simon & Schuster.
—End of the Line. 1981. 224p. 10.95 o.p. (*0-312-25102-5*) St. Martin's Pr.
—Hell Bent for Heaven. 1983. 224p. 12.95 o.p. (*0-312-36698-1*) St. Martin's Pr.
—Sports Freak. 1980. 8.95 o.p. (*0-312-75331-4*) St. Martin's Pr.

**BALEY, ELIJAH (FICTITIOUS CHARACTER)—FICTION**

Asimov, Isaac. Caves of Steel. 1986. mass mkt. 4.95 o.s.i (*0-345-33820-0*, Del Rey); 1985. mass mkt. 3.50 o.s.i (*0-345-32900-7*, Del Rey); 1982. mass mkt. 2.25 o.s.i (*0-449-20063-9*, Fawcett); 1981. mass mkt. 2.25 o.s.i (*0-449-23782-6*, Fawcett); 1978. mass mkt. 1.50 o.s.i (*0-449-22858-4*, Fawcett) Ballantine Bks.
—Caves of Steel. 1991. 288p. mass mkt. 7.99 (*0-553-29340-0*) Bantam Bks.
—Caves of Steel. 1955. mass mkt. 0.35 o.p. (*0-451-01240-2*, Signet Bks.) NAL.
—Caves of Steel. 1991. 13.04 (*0-606-19272-7*) Turtleback Bks.
—The Naked Sun. 1986. mass mkt. 4.95 o.s.i (*0-345-33821-9*); 1985. mass mkt. 3.50 o.s.i (*0-345-33031-5*, Del Rey); 1983. mass mkt. 2.95 o.s.i (*0-345-31390-9*, Del Rey); 1981. mass mkt. 2.25 o.s.i (*0-449-24243-9*, Fawcett); 1975. mass mkt. 1.50 o.s.i (*0-449-22648-4*) Ballantine Bks.
—The Naked Sun. 1991. 288p. mass mkt. 7.99 (*0-553-29339-7*) Bantam Bks.
—The Naked Sun. 1991. 13.04 (*0-606-19282-4*) Turtleback Bks.
—The Robots of Dawn, Vol. 3. 1984. 416p. mass mkt. 5.95 o.s.i (*0-345-31571-5*, Ballantine Bks.) Ballantine Bks.
—The Robots of Dawn. 1994. 448p. mass mkt. 7.99 (*0-553-29949-2*, Spectra) Bantam Bks.
—The Robots of Dawn. 1983. 432p. 15.95 o.p. (*0-385-18400-X*) Doubleday Publishing.
—The Robots of Dawn. abr. ed. audio 12.95 o.p. (*0-89845-142-6*, SWC 1732, Caedmon) HarperTrade.

**BALL, HOLLIS (FICTITIOUS CHARACTER)—FICTION**

Chappell, Helen. Dead Duck. 1997. (Sam & Hollis Mystery Ser.). mass mkt. 5.50 o.s.i (*0-449-15001-1*, Fawcett) Ballantine Bks.
—Dead Duck. l.t. ed. 2000. (Beeler Large Print Mystery Ser.). 231p. 25.95 (*1-57490-320-9*, Beeler Large Print Bks.) Beeler, Thomas T. Publisher.
—Ghost of a Chance. l.t. ed. 1999. (Beeler Large Print Mystery Ser.). 25.95 (*1-57490-202-4*, Beeler Large Print Bks.) Beeler, Thomas T. Publisher.
—Ghost of a Chance. 1998. (Sam & Hollis Mystery Ser.: No. 3). 256p. mass mkt. 5.99 o.s.i (*0-440-22567-1*) Doubleday Publishing.
—Giving up the Ghost. l.t. ed. 2001. (Beeler Large Print Mystery Ser.). 188p. 25.95 (*1-57490-350-0*, Beeler Large Print Bks.) Beeler, Thomas T. Publisher.
—Giving up the Ghost: A Sam & Hollis Mystery. 1999. (Sam & Hollis Mystery Ser.). 256p. mass mkt. 5.99 o.s.i (*0-440-22575-2*) Dell Publishing.
—Slow Dancing with the Angel of Death. 1996. mass mkt. 5.50 o.s.i (*0-449-14983-8*, Fawcett) Ballantine Bks.

**BALLARD, VIRGIL (FICTITIOUS CHARACTER)—FICTION**

Estleman, Loren D. Red Highway. 1994. 212p. 3.95 o.p. (*0-7867-0178-1*, Carroll & Graf Pubs.) Avalon Publishing Group.
—Red Highway. l.t. ed. 1988. pap. 17.95 o.p. (*1-55504-648-7*); lib. bdg. 19.95 o.p. (*1-55504-647-9*) BBC Audiobooks America.
—Red Highway. 1999. (Mystery Ser.). 195p. 19.95 (*0-7862-2180-1*, Five Star) Gale Group.

**BALLOU, HOSEA, 1771-1852—FICTION**

Cassara, Ernest. Murder on Beacon Hill. 1995. 201p. (Orig.). pap. 10.00 (*0-9625794-6-7*) Miniver, Anne Pr.
—Murder on Boston Common: A Father Ballou & His Dog Spot Mystery. 1998. 174p. pap. 9.95 (*0-9662870-0-2*) Cambridge Cornerstone Pr.

**BALLOU FAMILY (FICTITIOUS CHARACTERS)—FICTION**

McCarthy, Gary. Blue Bullet. unabr. ed. 1994. (Horsemen Ser.: No. 4). audio 39.95 (*1-55686-518-X*) Books in Motion.
—Cherokee Lighthorse. 1992. (Horsemen Ser.: Bk. 2). 192p. 3.99 o.p. (*1-55773-797-5*, Diamond Bks.) Ace Bks.
—Cherokee Lighthorse. unabr. ed. 1994. (Horsemen Ser.: Bk. 2). audio 26.95 (*1-55686-528-7*) Books in Motion.
—The Horsemen, Bk. 1. 1992. 3.99 o.p. (*1-55773-733-9*, Diamond Bks.) Ace Bks.
—The Horsemen. unabr. ed. 1994. (Horsemen Ser.: Bk. 1). audio 26.95 (*1-55686-530-9*) Books in Motion.
—Stallion Valley, Bk. 5. 1994. (Horsemen Ser.). 192p. (Orig.). mass mkt. 3.99 o.s.i (*0-515-11434-0*, Jove) Berkley Publishing Group.
—Texas Mustangers. unabr. ed. 1994. (Horsemen Ser.: Bk. 3). audio 26.95 (*1-55686-534-1*) Books in Motion.

**BALLY, MAX (FICTITIOUS CHARACTER)—FICTION**

Slyke, L. V. Murder on the Rocks. 1995. 256p. (Orig.). mass mkt. 4.99 (*0-380-76798-8*, Avon Bks.) Morrow/Avon.
—Murder with a Twist. 1994. 256p. (Orig.). mass mkt. 4.99 (*0-380-76797-X*, Avon Bks.) Morrow/Avon.

**BALON, SAM, SR. (FICTITIOUS CHARACTER)—FICTION**

Johnstone, William W. The Devil's Cat. 1987. (Horror Ser.). 384p. mass mkt. 3.95 o.s.i (*0-8217-2091-0*, Zebra Bks.) Kensington Publishing Corp.
—The Devil's Heart. 1987. mass mkt. 3.95 o.s.i (*0-8217-2110-0*); 1983. mass mkt. 2.95 o.p. (*0-8217-1156-3*) Kensington Publishing Corp. (Zebra Bks.).
—The Devil's Kiss. 1987. (Orig.). mass mkt. 3.95 o.s.i (*0-8217-2109-7*, Zebra Bks.) Kensington Publishing Corp.
—The Devil's Touch. 1987. (Horror Ser.). mass mkt. 3.95 o.s.i (*0-8217-2111-9*, Zebra Bks.) Kensington Publishing Corp.

**BALZIC, MARIO (FICTITIOUS CHARACTER)—FICTION**

Constantine, K. C. Always a Body to Trade. unabr. ed. 1997. (Mario Balzic Ser.). audio 48.00 (*0-7366-3685-4*, 4364) Books on Tape, Inc.
—Always a Body to Trade: A Mario Balzic Mystery. 1983. 256p. 13.95 o.p. (*0-87923-458-X*); 1993. 248p. reprint ed. pap. 5.95 (*0-87923-952-2*) Godine, David R. Pub.
—Always a Body to Trade: A Mario Balzic Mystery. 1984. (Crime Monthly Ser.). 256p. pap. 3.95 o.p. (*0-14-007059-1*, Penguin Bks.) Viking Penguin.
—Blank Page. 11th ed. 1989. pap. 3.95 o.p. (*0-87923-707-4*) Godine, David R. Pub.
—Blood Mud. 1999. 384p. 23.00 o.s.i (*0-89296-647-5*) Mysterious Pr.
—Blood Mud. l.t. ed. 1999. (Mystery Ser.). 615p. 28.95 (*0-7862-2031-7*) Thorndike Pr.
—Blood Mud. 2000. 384p. pap. 13.95 (*0-446-67640-3*) Warner Bks., Inc.
—Bottom Liner Blues. unabr. ed. 1997. (Mario Balzic Ser.). audio 56.00 (*0-7366-3691-9*, 4370) Books on Tape, Inc.
—Bottom Liner Blues. 1993. 256p. 18.95 (*0-89296-289-5*) Mysterious Pr.
—Bottom Liner Blues. 1994. 272p. mass mkt. 5.99 o.s.i (*0-446-40372-5*) Warner Bks., Inc.
—Brushback. unabr. collector's ed. 1998. (Mario Balzic Ser.). audio 64.00 (*0-7366-4216-1*, 4714) Books on Tape, Inc.
—Brushback. 1998. (Mario Balzic Novel Ser.). 288p. 22.00 (*0-89296-646-7*) Mysterious Pr.
—Brushback. 1999. mass mkt. (*0-446-60675-8*) Warner Bks., Inc.
—Cranks & Shadows. unabr. ed. 1997. (Mario Balzic Ser.). audio 72.00 (*0-7366-3692-7*, 4371) Books on Tape, Inc.
—Cranks & Shadows. 1995. 314p. 19.95 o.p. (*0-89296-543-6*) Mysterious Pr.
—Cranks & Shadows. 1996. 320p. mass mkt. 5.99 o.s.i (*0-446-40353-9*) Warner Bks., Inc.
—Family Values. unabr. ed. 1998. (Mario Balzic Ser.: Vol. 13). audio 48.00 (*0-7366-4035-5*, 4534) Books on Tape, Inc.
—Family Values. l.t. ed. 1997. (G. K. Hall Mystery Ser.). 290p. lib. bdg. 26.95 o.p. (*0-7838-8232-7*, Macmillan Reference USA) Gale Group.
—Family Values. 1998. mass mkt. (*0-446-40355-5*, Mysterious Pr. Paperback Bks.); 1997. 224p. 22.00 o.p. (*0-89296-545-2*); 1998. 256p. mass mkt. 5.99 (*0-446-60594-8*) Warner Bks., Inc.
—A Fix Like This. unabr. ed. 1997. (Mario Balzic Ser.). audio 64.00 (*0-7366-3693-5*, 4372) Books on Tape, Inc.
—A Fix Like This. 1988. 3.95 o.p. (*0-87923-718-X*) Godine, David R. Pub.
—Good Sons. unabr. ed. 1998. (Mario Balzic Ser.). audio 56.00 (*0-7366-4015-0*, 4513) Books on Tape, Inc.
—Good Sons. 1996. 304p. 21.95 o.p. (*0-89296-544-4*) Mysterious Pr.
—Good Sons. 1997. (Rocksburg Novels Ser.). 304p. mass mkt. 5.99 o.s.i (*0-446-40354-7*) Warner Bks., Inc.
—Joey's Case. unabr. ed. 1997. (Mario Balzic Ser.). audio 56.00 (*0-7366-3783-4*, 4455) Books on Tape, Inc.
—Joey's Case. 1989. 224p. mass mkt. 4.50 (*0-445-40786-7*, Mysterious Pr. Paperback Bks.) Warner Bks., Inc.
—Joey's Case: A Mario Balzic Novel. 1988. 15.95 (*0-89296-347-6*) Mysterious Pr.
—The Man Who Liked Slow Tomatoes. 1993. (Mario Balzic Detective Novel Ser.). 192p. pap. 5.95 (*0-87923-953-0*); 1982. (Mario Balzic Mystery Ser.: No. 5). 256p. 13.95 o.p. (*0-87923-407-5*) Godine, David R. Pub.
—The Man Who Liked Slow Tomatoes. 1983. 224p. pap. 2.95 o.p. (*0-14-006621-7*, Penguin Bks.) Viking Penguin.
—The Man Who Liked to Look at Himself. l.t. ed. 1987. (Nightingale Ser.). 249p. 11.95 o.p. (*0-8161-4373-0*, Macmillan Reference USA) Gale Group.
—The Man Who Liked to Look at Himself. Barzun, Jacques & Taylor, W. H., eds. 1983. (Crime Fiction 1950-1975 Ser.). 151p. lib. bdg. 18.00 o.p. (*0-8240-4955-1*) Garland Publishing, Inc.
—The Man Who Liked to Look at Himself. 1987. (Double Detective Ser.: No. 3). 160p. pap. 8.95 o.p. (*0-87923-468-7*); pap. 3.95 o.p. (*0-87923-663-9*) Godine, David R. Pub.
—Man Who Liked to Look at Himself & The Blank Page. unabr. ed. 1997. (Mario Balzic Ser.: Vol. 2 & 3). audio 64.00 (*0-7366-3612-9*, 4271) Books on Tape, Inc.
—Rocksburg Railroad Murder. 1982. 7.95 o.p. (*0-87923-662-0*) Godine, David R. Pub.
—The Rocksburg Railroad Murders. unabr. ed. 1997. (Mario Balzic Ser.: Vol. 1). audio 40.00 (*0-7366-3622-6*, 4281) Books on Tape, Inc.
—Sunshine Enemies. unabr. ed. 1997. (Mario Balzic Ser.). audio 42.00 (*0-7366-3784-2*, 4456) Books on Tape, Inc.
—Sunshine Enemies. 1990. 176p. 18.95 o.p. (*0-89296-288-7*) Mysterious Pr.
—Sunshine Enemies. 1991. mass mkt. 4.95 o.s.i (*0-446-40008-4*, Mysterious Pr. Paperback Bks.) Warner Bks., Inc.
—Upon Some Midnights Clear. 1985. (Mario Balzic Mystery Ser.). 256p. 15.95 o.p. (*0-87923-570-5*) Godine, David R. Pub.
—Upon Some Midnights Clear. 1987. 24p. mass mkt. 3.50 o.p. (*0-14-009404-0*, Penguin Bks.) Viking Penguin.

**BANCROFT, SOPHIA (FICTITIOUS CHARACTER)—FICTION**

Hocker, Karla. The Impertinent Miss Bancroft. 2002. (Zebra Regency Romance Ser.). 256p. mass mkt. 4.99 o.s.i (*0-8217-7360-7*) Kensington Publishing Corp.
—The Impertinent Miss Bancroft. 1991. 224p. 18.95 (*0-8027-1164-2*) Walker & Co.
—The Incorrigible Sophia: A Regency Intrigue. 1992. 208p. 19.95 o.p. (*0-8027-1208-8*) Walker & Co.

**BANKS, ALAN (FICTITIOUS CHARACTER)—FICTION**

Robinson, Peter. Aftermath: An Inspector Banks Novel. 2001. 384p. 25.00 (*0-380-97832-6*, Morrow, William & Co.) Morrow/Avon.
—Blood at the Root. 1998. (Inspector Banks Mystery Ser.: No. 9). 320p. mass mkt. 5.99 (*0-380-79476-4*, Avon Bks.) Morrow/Avon.
—Blood at the Root: An Inspector Banks Mystery. 1997. 352p. mass mkt. 22.00 o.p. (*0-380-97580-7*, Avon Bks.) Morrow/Avon.
—Cold Is the Grave: A Novel of Suspense. 2001. audio (*0-333-90378-1*) Macmillan U.K. GBR. *Dist:* Macmillan Publishing Co., Inc.
—Cold Is the Grave: A Novel of Suspense. 2001. 448p. mass mkt. 6.99 (*0-380-80935-4*, Avon Bks.); 2000. 384p. 24.00 (*0-380-97808-3*, Morrow, William & Co.) Morrow/Avon.
—Dead Right. 320p. mass mkt. (*0-14-026716-6*) Penguin Group (USA) Inc.
—A Dedicated Man. 1991. 272p. 18.95 o.s.i (*0-684-19265-9*, Macmillan Reference USA) Gale Group.
—A Dedicated Man. l.t. ed. 1991. (Magna Large Print Ser.). 396p. o.p. (*1-85057-831-1*) Magna Large Print Bks. GBR. *Dist:* Ulverscroft Large Print Canada, Ltd.
—A Dedicated Man. 1992. (Inspector Banks Mystery Ser.). 352p. mass mkt. 7.50 (*0-380-71645-3*, Avon Bks.) Morrow/Avon.
—A Dedicated Man. 272p. pap. (*0-14-009665-5*) Penguin Group (USA) Inc.
—Final Account: An Inspector Banks Mystery. (Inspector Banks Mystery Ser.). 1995. 320p. 21.95 o.s.i (*0-425-14935-8*, Prime Crime); 1996. 352p. reprint ed. mass mkt. 5.99 o.s.i (*0-425-15382-7*) Berkley Publishing Group.
—Final Account: An Inspector Banks Mystery. 336p. mass mkt. (*0-14-024185-X*) Penguin Group (USA) Inc.
—Final Account: An Inspector Banks Mystery, Set. abr. ed. 1995. (Inspector Banks Mystery Ser.). audio 17.00 (*1-56876-045-0*, 393291) Soundlines Entertainment, Inc.
—Gallows View. 2000. (Inspector Banks Mystery Ser.). 336p. mass mkt. 7.50 (*0-380-71400-0*, Avon Bks.) Morrow/Avon.
—Gallows View: An Inspector Banks Mystery. 1997. 320p. mass mkt. 5.99 o.s.i (*0-425-15672-9*, Prime Crime) Berkley Publishing Group.
—Gallows View: An Inspector Banks Mystery. 1990. 224p. 17.95 o.s.i (*0-684-19266-7*); 1991. 415p. reprint ed. lib. bdg. 11.95 o.p. (*1-85057-940-7*) Gale Group. (Macmillan Reference USA).
—Gallows View: An Inspector Banks Mystery. l.t. ed. 1991. (Magna Large Print Ser.). 415p. o.p. (*1-85057-939-3*) Magna Large Print Bks. GBR. *Dist:* Ulverscroft Large Print Canada, Ltd.
—Gallows View: An Inspector Banks Mystery. 240p. pap. (*0-14-009663-9*) Penguin Group (USA) Inc.
—The Hanging Valley. 1994. (Inspector Banks Mystery Ser.). 272p. mass mkt. 5.99 o.s.i (*0-425-14196-9*) Berkley Publishing Group.
—The Hanging Valley. 1992. (Chief Inspector Banks Ser.: No. 4). 288p. 20.00 o.p. (*0-684-19393-0*, Macmillan Reference USA) Gale Group.
—The Hanging Valley. 288p. pap. (*0-14-011544-7*) Penguin Group (USA) Inc.
—Hanging Valley. 2002. 336p. mass mkt. 6.99 (*0-380-82048-X*) Morrow/Avon.
—The Hanging Valley. l.t. ed. 1992. (Mystery Ser.). 406p. 29.99 o.p. (*0-7505-0345-9*) Magna Large Print Bks. GBR. *Dist:* Ulverscroft Large Print Bks., Ltd., Ulverscroft Large Print Canada, Ltd.
—In a Dry Season. 2000. 480p. mass mkt. 7.50 (*0-380-79477-2*); 1999. 422p. 24.00 (*0-380-97581-5*) Morrow/Avon. (Avon Bks.).
—In a Dry Season. 456p. pap. (*0-330-39201-8*) Pan Bks. Ltd.
—In a Dry Season. 352p. pap. (*0-14-028177-0*) Penguin Bks. Canada, Ltd.
—Innocent Graves: An Inspector Banks Mystery. 400p. 1996. 21.95 o.p. (*0-425-15315-0*); 1997. reprint ed. mass mkt. 5.99 o.s.i (*0-425-15779-2*) Berkley Publishing Group. (Prime Crime).
—Innocent Graves: An Inspector Banks Mystery. 384p. mass mkt. (*0-14-025689-X*) Penguin Group (USA) Inc.
—Innocent Graves: An Inspector Banks Mystery, Set. abr. ed. 1997. (Inspector Banks Mystery Ser.). audio 17.00 (*1-56876-060-4*, 394919) Soundlines Entertainment, Inc.
—Meet Inspector Banks. 800p. pap. (*0-14-100816-4*) Penguin Bks. Canada, Ltd.
—A Necessary End. 1992. 320p. text 19.95 (*0-684-19385-X*, Macmillan Reference USA) Gale Group.
—A Necessary End. l.t. ed. 1992. (Magna Large Print Ser.). 466p. 29.99 (*0-7505-0343-2*) Magna Large Print Bks. GBR. *Dist:* Ulverscroft Large Print Bks., Ltd., Ulverscroft Large Print Canada, Ltd.
—A Necessary End. 1993. (Inspector Banks Mystery Ser.). 352p. mass mkt. 6.99 (*0-380-71946-0*, Avon Bks.) Morrow/Avon.
—A Necessary End. pap. (*0-14-011545-5*) Penguin Group (USA) Inc.
—Past Reason Hated: An Inspector Banks Mystery. 1994. (Inspector Banks Mystery Ser.). 320p. mass mkt. 5.99 o.s.i (*0-425-14489-5*, Prime Crime) Berkley Publishing Group.
—Past Reason Hated: An Inspector Banks Mystery. 1993. 352p. 20.00 o.p. (*0-684-19529-1*, Macmillan Reference USA) Gale Group.
—Past Reason Hated: An Inspector Banks Mystery. 2000. 384p. mass mkt. 6.99 (*0-380-73328-5*, Avon Bks.) Morrow/Avon.
—Past Reason Hated: An Inspector Banks Mystery. 352p. mass mkt. (*0-14-014842-6*) Penguin Group (USA) Inc.
—Playing with Fire. 2004. 368p. 23.95 (*0-06-019877-X*, Morrow, William & Co.) Morrow/Avon.
—Wednesday's Child. 1995. 320p. mass mkt. 5.99 o.s.i (*0-425-14834-3*, Prime Crime) Berkley Publishing Group.
—Wednesday's Child. 2002. 352p. mass mkt. 6.99 (*0-380-82049-8*) Morrow/Avon.
—Wednesday's Child. 2001. (Inspector Banks Mystery Ser.). 357p. pap. (*0-330-48219-X*) Pan Bks. Ltd.
—Wednesday's Child. 352p. mass mkt. (*0-14-017474-5*) Penguin Group (USA) Inc.
—Wednesday's Child. 1994. 352p. 20.00 (*0-684-19644-1*, Scribner) Simon & Schuster.

**BANNERMAN, PAUL (FICTITIOUS CHARACTER)—FICTION**

Maxim, John R. The Bannerman Effect. 1990. 416p. mass mkt. 4.95 o.s.i (*0-553-28559-9*) Bantam Bks.
—The Bannerman Effect. Hershey, J. H., ed. 2000. 400p. mass mkt. 6.99 (*0-380-73009-X*, Avon Bks.) Morrow/Avon.
—Bannerman's Ghosts. 2003. 400p. 24.95 (*0-06-000584-X*) Morrow/Avon.
—A Matter Of Honor. 1993. 544p. mass mkt. 5.99 o.s.i (*0-553-29920-4*) Bantam Bks.

**BANNING, KATE (FICTITIOUS CHARACTER)—FICTION**

Tishy, Cecelia. Cryin' Time. 1998. (Kate Banning Mystery Ser.: No. 2). 336p. 23.95 (*1-891847-01-5*) Dowling Pr., Inc.

—Cryin' Time. 1999. (Kate Banning Mysteries Ser.). 304p. mass mkt. 5.99 o.s.i (0-451-19832-8, Signet Bks.) NAL.
—Fall to Pieces. 1999. (Kate Banning Mystery Ser.). 319p. 24.00 (1-891847-07-4) Dowling Pr., Inc.
—Fall to Pieces. 2000. (Kate Banning Mysteries Ser.). 304p. mass mkt. 5.99 o.s.i (0-451-20094-2, Signet Bks.) NAL.
—Jealous Heart. Sachs, Susan, ed. 1997. 304p. 24.00 o.p. (0-9646452-5-4) Dowling Pr., Inc.
—Jealous Heart. 1999. 272p. mass mkt. 5.99 o.s.i (0-451-19678-3, Signet Bks.) NAL.

**BANNING, ORIEL (FICTITIOUS CHARACTER)—FICTION**

Peart, Jane. A Perilous Bargain. 1997. (Edgecliffe Manor Mysteries Ser.). 240p. (gr. 12). pap. 10.99 o.p. (0-8007-5626-6) Revell, Fleming H. Co.
—A Perilous Bargain. l.t. ed. 2000. (Christian Mystery Ser.). 360p. 24.95 (0-7862-2380-4) Thorndike Pr.

**BANNION, RICK (FICTITIOUS CHARACTER)—FICTION**

Gray, A. W. The Man Offside. 1991. 240p. 18.95 o.p. (0-525-93310-7) Dutton/Plume.
—The Man Offside. 1992. 336p. mass mkt. 4.99 o.s.i (0-451-40318-5, Onyx) NAL.

**BANNON BROTHERS (FICTITIOUS CHARACTERS)—FICTION**

Coyle, Harold. Look Away. 592p. 1997. (Illus.). mass mkt. 3.99 (0-671-00991-5); 1996. mass mkt. 6.99 (0-671-52819-X) Simon & Schuster. (Pocket).
—Look Away: A Novel. unabr. ed. 1995. audio 85.95 (0-7861-0860-6, 1658) Blackstone Audio Bks., Inc.
—Look Away: A Novel. abr. ed. 1995. audio 21.95 (1-55935-171-3); audio 19.95 (1-55935-168-3, 595948) Soundelux Audio Publishing.
—Until the End. 1997. 544p. pap. 6.99 (0-671-89017-4, Pocket); 1996. 464p. 24.50 o.p. (0-684-81140-5, Simon & Schuster) Simon & Schuster.
—Until the End: A Novel of the Civil War. unabr. ed. 1996. audio 76.95 (0-7861-1057-0, 1828) Blackstone Audio Bks., Inc.

**BARBER, NICHOLAS (FICTITIOUS CHARACTER)—FICTION**

Unsworth, Barry. Morality Play. l.t. ed. 1996. 23.95 o.p. (1-56895-297-X, Wheeler Publishing, Inc.) Gale Group.
—Morality Play. 1996. 208p. pap. 13.95 (0-393-31560-6) Norton, W. W. & Co., Inc.

**BARD, JACK (FICTITIOUS CHARACTER)—FICTION**

Downing, Warwick. A Lingering Doubt. Isaacson, Dana, ed. 1993. 320p. (Orig.). mass mkt. 4.99 (0-671-76034-3, Pocket) Simon & Schuster.

**BARD, LILY (FICTITIOUS CHARACTER)—FICTION**

Harris, Charlaine. Shakespeare's Champion. 1998. 274p. pap. 19.00 o.s.i (0-440-61352-3, Delta); 272p. mass mkt. 5.99 (0-440-22421-7) Dell Publishing.
—Shakespeare's Champion. 1997. (Lily Bard Mysteries Ser.). 224p. 20.95 o.p. (0-312-17005-X, Saint Martin's Minotaur) St. Martin's Pr.
—Shakespeare's Champion. l.t. ed. 1998. (Cloak & Dagger Ser.). 327p. 26.95 (0-7862-1454-6) Thorndike Pr.
—Shakespeare's Christmas: A Lily Bard Mystery. 1999. (Lily Bard Mysteries Ser.). 256p. mass mkt. 5.99 (0-440-23499-9) Dell Publishing.
—Shakespeare's Christmas: A Lily Bard Mystery. 1998. 224p. 20.95 (0-312-19330-0, Saint Martin's Minotaur) St. Martin's Pr.
—Shakespeare's Counselor: A Lily Bard Mystery. 2002. E-Book 22.95 (1-59061-729-0) Adobe Systems, Inc.
—Shakespeare's Counselor: A Lily Bard Mystery. E-Book 27.95 (0-312-70340-6); 2001. 240p. 22.95 (0-312-27762-8, Saint Martin's Minotaur) St. Martin's Pr.
—Shakespeare's Counselor: A Lily Bard Mystery. l.t. ed. 2002. 322p. 30.45 (0-7862-4403-8) Thorndike Pr.
—Shakespeare's Landlord. 1997. 256p. pap. 19.00 (0-440-61406-6, Dell Bks.); mass mkt. 5.99 (0-440-22418-7) Dell Publishing.
—Shakespeare's Landlord. 1996. 224p. 20.95 o.p. (0-312-14415-6, Saint Martin's Minotaur) St. Martin's Pr.
—Shakespeare's Trollop. 2004. 208p. mass mkt. 5.99 (0-425-19699-2) Berkley Publishing Group.
—Shakespeare's Trollop. 2000. 227p. 23.95 (0-312-26228-0, Saint Martin's Minotaur) St. Martin's Pr.
—Shakespeare's Trollop. l.t. ed. 2000. (Mystery Ser.). (Illus.). 296p. 28.95 (0-7862-3030-4) Thorndike Pr.

**BARKER, HOLLY (FICTITIOUS CHARACTER)—FICTION**

Woods, Stuart. Blood Orchid. unabr. ed. 2002. (Holly Barker Ser.). audio 29.95 (1-59086-066-7, 3619, Brilliance Audio Unabridged); audio 74.25 (1-59086-068-3, 3620, Unabridged Library Editions); audio compact disk 36.95 (1-59086-067-5, 3621, CD Unabridged); audio compact disk 92.25 (1-59086-069-1, 3622, CD Unabridged Library Edition) Brilliance Audio.
—Blood Orchid. l.t. ed. 2003. 32.95 (1-58724-395-4, Wheeler Publishing, Inc.) Gale Group.
—Blood Orchid. 2003. 368p. reprint ed. mass mkt. 7.99 (0-451-20881-1, Signet Bks.) NAL.
—Blood Orchid. 2002. (Holly Barker Ser.: No. 3). 304p. 25.95 o.s.i (0-399-14929-5); 4p. 24.95 incl. audio (0-399-14953-8, Putnam Berkley Audio) Putnam Publishing Group, The.
—Blood Orchid. unabr. ed. 2003. (Holly Barker Ser.). audio 19.99 (1-59335-059-7, 30144) Soulmate Audio Bks., Inc.
—Orchid Beach. 1999. audio compact disk 56.00 (0-7366-5173-X); 2001. audio compact disk 56.00; 1999. audio 48.00 (0-7366-4503-9, 4938) Books on Tape, Inc.
—Orchid Beach. l.t. ed. 1999. (Wheeler Large Print Book Ser.). 408p. 27.95 o.p. (1-56895-774-2, Wheeler Publishing, Inc.) Gale Group.
—Orchid Beach. 1999. 416p. mass mkt. 7.50 (0-06-101341-2); 1998. 336p. (YA). (gr. 10 up). 25.00 o.s.i (0-06-019181-3) HarperCollins Pubs.
—Orchid Beach. 2003. audio 14.95 (0-06-057746-0); 1998. audio 25.00 (0-694-52058-6, 694524) HarperTrade. (HarperAudio).
—Orchid Beach. unabr. ed. 2000. audio compact disk 78.00 (0-7887-4465-8, C1162E7); 1999. audio 51.00 (0-7887-2915-2, 95505E7) Recorded Bks., LLC.
—Orchid Blues. unabr. ed. 2001. (Holly Barker Ser.). audio 29.95 (1-58788-784-3, 3099, Brilliance Audio Unabridged); audio 69.25 (1-58788-785-1, 3100, Unabridged Library Editions); audio compact disk 87.25 (1-58788-787-8, 3102, CD Unabridged Library Edition); audio compact disk 35.95 (1-58788-786-X, 3101, CD Unabridged) Brilliance Audio.
—Orchid Blues. 2002. 400p. reprint ed. mass mkt. 7.99 (0-451-20671-1, Signet Bks.) NAL.
—Orchid Blues. 2001. 350p. 24.95 o.s.i (0-399-14777-2) Penguin Group (USA) Inc.
—Orchid Blues. abr. ed. 2001. 4p. audio 24.95 o.s.i (0-399-14820-5, Putnam Berkley Audio) Putnam Publishing Group, The.
—Orchid Blues. unabr. ed. 2003. audio 19.99 (1-59335-001-5, 30085) Soulmate Audio Bks., Inc.
—Orchid Blues. l.t. ed. 2003. (Paperback Bestsellers Ser.). pap. 29.95 (0-7838-9747-2) Thorndike Pr.
—Reckless Abandon. 2004. 336p. 25.95 (0-399-15151-6) Putnam Publishing Group, The.

**BARLEY, JOE (FICTITIOUS CHARACTER)—FICTION**

Wright, Eric. The Kidnapping of Rosie Dawn: A Joe Barley Mystery. 2000. 213p. pap. 12.95 (1-880284-40-5, Perseverance Pr.) Daniel, John & Co., Pubs.
—The Kidnapping of Rosie Dawn: A Joe Barley Mystery. l.t. ed. 2001. 306p. 27.95 (0-7862-3478-4); 296p. (0-7540-4673-7); 296p. (0-7540-4674-5) Thorndike Pr.

**BARLOW, CHARLIE (FICTITIOUS CHARACTER)—FICTION**

Jones, Elwyn. Barlow Exposed. 1977. 7.95 o.p. (0-312-06685-6) St. Martin's Pr.

**BARLOW, HANNAH (FICTITIOUS CHARACTER)—FICTION**

Lachnit, Carroll. Akin to Death. 1998. 384p. mass mkt. 6.50 o.s.i (0-425-16409-8) Berkley Publishing Group.
—A Blessed Death. 1996. 336p. mass mkt. 5.99 o.s.i (0-425-15347-9, Prime Crime) Berkley Publishing Group.
—Janie's Law. 1999. (Prime Crime Mysteries Ser.: No. 4). 336p. mass mkt. 6.50 o.s.i (0-425-17150-7, Prime Crime) Berkley Publishing Group.
—Murder in Brief. 1995. 272p. (Orig.). mass mkt. 4.99 o.s.i (0-425-14790-8) Berkley Publishing Group.

**BARLOW, HONORIA (FICTITIOUS CHARACTER)—FICTION**

Allen, Charlotte Vale. Mood Indigo. l.t. ed. 2000. 408p. lib. bdg. 27.95 (1-58547-038-4) Ctr. Point Large Print.
—Mood Indigo. 1997. 288p. 23.95 (0-9657437-1-3) Island Nation Pr., LLC.

**BARLOW, MARGARET (FICTITIOUS CHARACTER)—FICTION**

Osborn, David. Murder in the Napa Valley. unabr. ed. 1993. audio 30.00 (0-7366-2534-8, 3286) Books on Tape, Inc.
—Murder in the Napa Valley. 1995. 224p. mass mkt. 4.99 o.s.i (0-8217-4844-0, Zebra Bks.) Kensington Publishing Corp.
—Murder in the Napa Valley. 2000. 176p. pap. 12.95 (0-7432-1294-0, Simon & Schuster) Simon & Schuster.
—Murder in the Napa Valley: A Margaret Barlow Mystery. 1993. 224p. 19.00 (0-671-70487-7, Simon & Schuster) Simon & Schuster.
—Murder on Martha's Vineyard. unabr. ed. 1992. audio 42.00 (0-7366-2188-1, 2983) Books on Tape, Inc.
—Murder on the Chesapeake. unabr. ed. 1993. audio 36.00 (0-7366-2437-6, 3202) Books on Tape, Inc.
—Murder on the Chesapeake. 2000. 208p. pap. 19.00 (0-7432-1271-1); 1992. 320p. 19.00 o.s.i (0-671-70486-9) Simon & Schuster. (Simon & Schuster).
—Murder on the Chesapeake: A Margaret Barlow Mystery. 1993. 304p. mass mkt. 3.99 o.s.i (0-8217-4165-9, Zebra Bks.) Kensington Publishing Corp.

**BARLOW, NICHOLAS (FICTITIOUS CHARACTER)—FICTION**

Carter, Robert A. Casual Slaughters. 1992. 272p. 17.95 o.p. (0-89296-502-9) Mysterious Pr.
—Casual Slaughters. 1994. 272p. mass mkt. 5.50 (0-446-40302-4, Mysterious Pr. Paperback Bks.) Warner Bks., Inc.
—Final Edit. 1994. 304p. 18.45 o.p. (0-89296-549-5) Mysterious Pr.

**BARNABAS, GEORGE, DOCTOR (FICTITIOUS CHARACTER)—FICTION**

Rayner, Claire. First Blood. l.t. ed. 1995. (Charnwood Large Print Ser.). 480p. 29.99 o.p. (0-7089-8825-3, Charnwood) Thorpe, F. A. Pubs. GBR. Dist: Ulverscroft Large Print Bks., Ltd., Ulverscroft Large Print Canada, Ltd.
—Fourth Attempt. l.t. ed. 1997. (Charnwood Large Print Ser.). 496p. 29.99 o.p. (0-7089-8975-6, Ulverscroft) Thorpe, F. A. Pubs. GBR. Dist: Ulverscroft Large Print Bks., Ltd., Ulverscroft Large Print Canada, Ltd.
—Second Opinion. unabr. ed. 1995. audio 84.95 (0-7451-6539-7, CAB 1155) BBC Audiobooks America.
—Second Opinion. l.t. ed. 1996. (Charnwood Large Print Ser.). 528p. 29.99 o.p. (0-7089-8897-0, Ulverscroft) Thorpe, F. A. Pubs. GBR. Dist: Ulverscroft Large Print Bks., Ltd., Ulverscroft Large Print Canada, Ltd.

**BARNABY, TOM, CHIEF INSPECTOR (FICTITIOUS CHARACTER)—FICTION**

Graham, Caroline. Death in Disguise. 1993. 333p. 22.00 o.p. (0-688-09985-8, Morrow, William & Co.); 1994. 384p. reprint ed. mass mkt. 4.99 (0-380-71296-2, Avon Bks.) Morrow/Avon.
—Death of a Hollow Man: An Inspector Barnaby Mystery. unabr. ed. 1998. audio 69.95 (0-7540-0123-7, CAB1546) BBC Audiobooks America.
—Death of a Hollow Man: An Inspector Barnaby Mystery. 1990. 320p. mass mkt. 4.99 (0-380-70951-1, Avon Bks.); 360p. reprint ed. 17.95 o.p. (0-688-09116-4, Morrow, William & Co.) Morrow/Avon.
—Death of a Hollow Man: An Inspector Barnaby Mystery. l.t. ed. 2002. (General Ser.). 25.95 (0-7862-4509-3) Thorndike Pr.
—Faithful unto Death. 1998. (Chief Inspector Barnaby Mysteries Ser.). 320p. 23.95 o.p. (0-312-18577-4, Saint Martin's Minotaur) St. Martin's Pr.
—Faithful unto Death: A Chief Inspector Barnaby Novel. unabr. ed. 1997. audio 84.95 (0-7540-0015-X, CAB 1438) BBC Audiobooks America.
—Faithful unto Death: A Chief Inspector Barnaby Novel. unabr. ed. 2000. (Inspector Barnaby Mystery Ser.). audio 69.95 Chivers Audio Bks. GBR. Dist: BBC Audiobooks America.
—Faithful unto Death: A Chief Inspector Barnaby Novel. 2000. (Chief Inspector Barnaby Mysteries Ser.). 400p. mass mkt. 6.99 (0-312-97295-4, St. Martin's Paperbacks) St. Martin's Pr.
—The Killings at Badger's Drift. 1988. 264p. 16.95 o.p. (0-917561-41-4) Adler & Adler Pubs., Inc.
—The Killings at Badger's Drift. 2000. audio 34.95 (0-7540-7527-3) BBC Audiobooks America.
—The Killings at Badger's Drift. unabr. ed. 1996. audio 59.95 (0-7451-6621-0, CAB 1237) Chivers Audio Bks. GBR. Dist: BBC Audiobooks America.
—The Killings at Badger's Drift. 1989. 256p. mass mkt. 4.50 (0-380-70563-X, Avon Bks.) Morrow/Avon.
—The Killings at Badger's Drift. l.t. ed. 1999. (Mystery Ser.). 421p. 27.95 (0-7862-2218-2); (0-7540-1376-6); (0-7540-2281-1) Thorndike Pr.
—A Place of Safety: A Chief Inspector Barnaby Mystery. unabr. ed. 2000. 8p. audio 69.95 (0-7540-0452-X, CAB 1875) Chivers Audio Bks. GBR. Dist: BBC Audiobooks America.
—A Place of Safety: A Chief Inspector Barnaby Mystery. l.t. ed. 2000. (G. K. Hall Core Ser.). 434p. 29.95 (0-7838-8968-2, Macmillan Reference USA) Gale Group.
—A Place of Safety: A Chief Inspector Barnaby Mystery. (Chief Inspector Barnaby Mysteries Ser.). 288p. 2001. mass mkt. 6.50 (0-312-97710-7, St. Martin's Paperbacks); 2nd ed. 1999. 23.95 (0-312-24419-3, Saint Martin's Minotaur) St. Martin's Pr.
—Written in Blood: A Detective Barnaby Mystery, Set. unabr. ed. 1999. audio 96.95 (0-7540-0351-5, CAB1774) BBC Audiobooks America.
—Written in Blood: A Detective Barnaby Mystery. l.t. ed. 1995. (Magna Large Print Ser.). 637p. o.p. (0-7505-0848-5) Magna Large Print Bks. GBR. Dist: Ulverscroft Large Print Canada, Ltd.
—Written in Blood: A Detective Barnaby Mystery. 1996. 384p. mass mkt. 5.99 (0-380-71297-0, Avon Bks.); 1995. 288p. 22.00 o.p. (0-688-10024-4, Morrow, William & Co.) Morrow/Avon.

**BARNEA, DANIELLE (FICTITIOUS CHARACTER)—FICTION**

Land, Jon. Blood Diamonds. E-Book 25.95 (0-312-70604-9, Tor Bks.); 2002. 384p. 25.95 (0-7653-0226-8, Forge Bks.); 2003. 416p. reprint ed. mass mkt. 7.99 (0-7653-4148-4, Forge Bks.) Doherty, Tom Assocs., LLC.
—The Blue Widows. Date not set. mass mkt. (0-7653-4526-9); 2003. 384p. 24.95 (0-7653-0599-2) Doherty, Tom Assocs., LLC. (Forge Bks.).
—The Pillars of Solomon. 2000. 438p. mass mkt. 6.99 (0-8125-6672-6); 1999. (Illus.). 352p. 24.95 (0-312-86819-7) Doherty, Tom Assocs., LLC. (Forge Bks.).
—A Walk in the Darkness. 2000. 352p. 25.95 (0-312-87265-8, Forge Bks.) Doherty, Tom Assocs., LLC.
—The Walls of Jericho. 1998. 480p. mass mkt. 6.99 (0-8125-6456-1, Tor Bks.); 1997. 304p. 23.95 (0-312-86267-9, Forge Bks.) Doherty, Tom Assocs., LLC.
—The Walls of Jericho. abr. ed. 1997. audio 17.00 (1-56876-066-3) Soundlines Entertainment, Inc.

**BARNES, GINGER (FICTITIOUS CHARACTER)—FICTION**

Murray, Donna Huston. Farewell Performance: A Ginger Barnes Main Line Mystery. 2000. (Ginger Barnes Main Line Mysteries Ser.). 272p. mass mkt. 5.99 (0-312-97456-6, St. Martin's Paperbacks) St. Martin's Pr.
—Final Arrangements. 1996. (Ginger Barnes Main Line Mysteries Ser.). 290p. pap. text 5.99 (0-312-95765-3, St. Martin's Paperbacks) St. Martin's Pr.
—Lie Like a Rug. 2001. 256p. mass mkt. 6.50 (0-312-97897-9, St. Martin's Paperbacks) St. Martin's Pr.
—The Main Line Is Murder. 1995. (Ginger Barnes Main Line Mysteries Ser.). 294p. mass mkt. 5.99 (0-312-95637-1, St. Martin's Paperbacks) St. Martin's Pr.
—No Bones about It. 1998. (Ginger Barnes Main Line Mysteries Ser.). 227p. mass mkt. 5.99 (0-312-96423-4, St. Martin's Paperbacks) St. Martin's Pr.
—School of Hard Knocks: A Dead Letter Mystery. 1997. (Ginger Barnes Main Line Mysteries Ser.). 288p. mass mkt. 5.99 (0-312-96104-9, St. Martin's Paperbacks) St. Martin's Pr.
—A Score to Settle. 1999. (Ginger Barnes Main Line Mysteries Ser.). 288p. mass mkt. 5.99 (0-312-96951-1, St. Martin's Paperbacks) St. Martin's Pr.

**BARNES, MICHAEL (FICTITIOUS CHARACTER)—FICTION**

McBain, Ed, pseud. Downtown. l.t. ed. 1992. pap. 17.95 o.p. (0-7927-1111-4); 18.95 o.p. (0-7927-1112-2, E0032) BBC Audiobooks America.
—Downtown. unabr. ed. 1992. (Eighty-Seventh Precinct Ser.). audio 48.00 (0-7366-2142-3, 2940) Books on Tape, Inc.
—Downtown. unabr. ed. 1991. audio 22.95 o.p. (0-930435-89-3, 94, Bookcassette); audio 57.25 o.p. (1-56100-083-3, 870, Unabridged Library Editions) Brilliance Audio.
—Downtown. 1991. 302p. 20.00 o.p. (0-688-08736-1, Morrow, William & Co.); 1993. 352p. reprint ed. mass mkt. 5.99 (0-380-70761-6, Avon Bks.) Morrow/Avon.
—Downtown. 1993. 15.95 o.p. (1-55800-454-8) NewStar Media, Inc.
—Downtown. unabr. ed. 1991. audio 70.00 (1-55690-153-4, 91405E7) Recorded Bks., LLC.

**BARNES, NIKKI (FICTITIOUS CHARACTER)—FICTION**

Albarella, Joan. Agenda for Murder: A Nikki Barnes Mystery. 1998. 223p. pap. 11.99 (1-883061-20-2) Rising Tide Pr.
—Called to Kill: A Nikki Barnes Mystery. 2000. 213p. pap. 12.00 (1-883061-28-8) Rising Tide Pr.
—Close to You: A Nikki Barnes Mystery. 2003. 222p. pap. 14.95 (0-595-27303-3, Mystery & Suspense Pr.) iUniverse, Inc.

**BARNETT, HARRY (FICTITIOUS CHARACTER)—FICTION**

Goddard, Robert. Into the Blue. 1999. 541p. mass mkt. (0-552-54593-7); 1997. mass mkt. o.s.i (0-552-13561-5); 1993. mass mkt. o.s.i (0-552-14030-9); 1990. o.s.i (0-593-01808-7) Bantam Bks. (Corgi).
—Into the Blue. unabr. ed. 1995. audio 85.95 (0-7861-0651-4, 1563) Blackstone Audio Bks., Inc.
—Into the Blue. l.t. ed. 1992. (General Ser.). 630p. lib. bdg. 23.95 o.p. (0-8161-5233-0, Macmillan Reference USA) Gale Group.

—Into the Blue. 1991. 416p. 19.95 (*0-671-70482-6*, Simon & Schuster) Simon & Schuster.

—Into the Blue. Rubenstein, Julie, ed. 1992. 528p. reprint ed. mass mkt. 5.99 (*0-671-70483-4*, Pocket) Simon & Schuster.

—Out of the Sun. unabr. ed. 1997. audio 84.95 (*0-7451-6778-0*, CAB 1394) BBC Audiobooks America.

—Out of the Sun. 1997. 410p. mass mkt. (*0-552-14224-7*); 1996. 333p. o.s.i (*0-593-03614-X*) Bantam Bks. (Corgi).

—Out of the Sun. unabr. ed. 2000. audio 69.95 Chivers Audio Bks. GBR. *Dist:* BBC Audiobooks America.

—Out of the Sun. 352p. 1998. pap. 13.00 o.s.i (*0-8050-5836-2*, Owl Bks.); 1997. 25.00 o.s.i (*0-8050-5109-0*) Holt, Henry & Co.

—Out of the Sun. l.t. ed. 1997. (Charnwood Large Print Ser.). 496p. 29.99 o.p. (*0-7089-8967-5*, Ulverscroft) Thorpe, F. A. Pubs. GBR. *Dist:* Ulverscroft Large Print Bks., Ltd., Ulverscroft Large Print Canada, Ltd.

**BARR, JEREMY (FICTITIOUS CHARACTER)—FICTION**

Gibbs, Tony. Dead Run. 1989. mass mkt. 3.50 o.s.i (*0-8041-0420-4*, Ivy Bks.) Ballantine Bks.

—Landfall: A Novel. 1992. 256p. 20.00 o.p. (*0-688-11102-5*, Morrow, William & Co.) Morrow/Avon.

—Running Fix. 1990. 18.95 o.s.i (*0-394-57580-6*) Random Hse., Inc.

**BARR, TEMPLE (FICTITIOUS CHARACTER)—FICTION**

Douglas, Carole Nelson. The Cat & the King of Clubs. 1999. (Mystery Ser.). 227p. 20.95 (*0-7862-1920-3*, Five Star) Gale Group.

—The Cat & the Queen of Hearts. 1999. (Mystery Ser.). 223p. 21.95 (*0-7862-2173-9*, Five Star) Gale Group.

—Cat in a Crimson Haze: A Midnight Louie Mystery. (Midnight Louie Mystery Ser.). 1996. 408p. mass mkt. 6.99 (*0-8125-4414-5*, Forge Bks.); 1996. mass mkt. 219.68 (*0-8125-6330-1*); 1995. 352p. 22.95 o.p. (*0-312-85901-5*, Forge Bks.) Doherty, Tom Assocs., LLC.

—Cat in a Crimson Haze: A Midnight Louie Mystery. l.t. ed. 1995. (Midnight Louie Mystery Ser.). 604p. 24.95 o.p. (*0-7838-1390-2*, Macmillan Reference USA) Gale Group.

—Cat in a Crimson Haze: A Midnight Louie Mystery. 1996. mass mkt. 223.68 (*0-8125-6329-8*) Holtzbrinck Pubs.

—Cat in a Diamond Dazzle: A Midnight Louie Mystery. (Midnight Louie Mystery Ser.). 1997. 411p. mass mkt. 6.99 (*0-8125-5506-6*); 1996. 416p. 24.95 o.p. (*0-312-86085-4*) Doherty, Tom Assocs., LLC. (Forge Bks.).

—Cat in a Flamingo Fedora: A Midnight Louie Mystery. (Midnight Louie Mystery Ser.). 1998. 373p. mass mkt. 6.99 (*0-8125-6535-5*); 1997. 384p. 24.95 o.p. (*0-312-86329-2*) Doherty, Tom Assocs., LLC. (Forge Bks.).

—Cat in a Golden Garland: A Midnight Louie Mystery. (Midnight Louie Mystery Ser.). 1998. 406p. mass mkt. 6.99 (*0-8125-3036-5*); 1997. 352p. 23.95 (*0-312-86386-1*) Doherty, Tom Assocs., LLC. (Forge Bks.).

—Cat in a Golden Garland: A Midnight Louie Mystery. l.t. ed. 1998. (G. K. Hall Core Ser.). 576p. 25.95 o.p. (*0-7838-8419-2*, Macmillan Reference USA) Gale Group.

—Cat in a Jeweled Jumpsuit: A Midnight Louie Mystery. 2000. 432p. mass mkt. 6.99 (*0-8125-6674-2*); 1999. 384p. 24.95 (*0-312-86817-0*) Doherty, Tom Assocs., LLC. (Forge Bks.).

—Cat in a Jeweled Jumpsuit: A Midnight Louie Mystery. abr. ed. 1999. audio 25.00 (*0-7871-2353-6*, Dove Audio) NewStar Media, Inc.

—Cat in a Jeweled Jumpsuit: A Midnight Louie Mystery. l.t. ed. 2000. (Americana Ser.). 599p. 29.95 (*0-7862-2455-X*) Thorndike Pr.

—Cat in a Kiwi Con: A Midnight Louie Mystery. 2000. (Midnight Louie Mystery Ser.). 384p. 24.95 o.p. (*0-312-86955-X*, Forge Bks.) Doherty, Tom Assocs., LLC.

—Cat in a Leopard Spot: A Midnight Louie Mystery. E-Book 24.95 (*0-312-70128-4*, Tor Bks.); 2002. 416p. pap. 6.99 (*0-8125-7022-7*, Forge Bks.); 2001. 384p. 24.95 (*0-312-85370-X*, Forge Bks.) Doherty, Tom Assocs., LLC.

—Cat in a Midnight Choir: A Midnight Louie Mystery. E-Book 24.95 (*0-312-70619-7*, Tor Bks.); 2003. 416p. mass mkt. 24.95 (*0-8125-7021-9*, Forge Bks.); 2002. 336p. 24.95 (*0-312-85797-7*, Forge Bks.) Doherty, Tom Assocs., LLC.

—Cat in a Neon Nightmare. Date not set. mass mkt. (*0-7653-4592-7*, Forge Bks.) Doherty, Tom Assocs., LLC.

—Cat in a Neon Nightmare. l.t. ed. 2003. 582p. 29.95 (*0-7862-5755-5*) Thorndike Pr.

—Cat in a Neon Nightmare: A Midnight Louie Mystery. 2003. (Midnight Louie Mystery Ser.). 384p. 24.95 (*0-7653-0680-8*, Forge Bks.) Doherty, Tom Assocs., LLC.

—Cat in an Indigo Mood: A Midnight Louie Mystery. l.t. ed. 2003. (Large Print Ser.). 29.95 (*1-57490-473-6*, Beeler Large Print Bks.) Beeler, Thomas T. Publisher.

—Cat in an Indigo Mood: A Midnight Louie Mystery. 1999. 384p. mass mkt. 6.99 (*0-8125-6187-2*); (Illus.). 381p. 24.95 (*0-312-86635-6*) Doherty, Tom Assocs., LLC. (Forge Bks.).

—Cat in an Indigo Mood: A Midnight Louie Mystery. abr. ed. 1999. (Midnight Louie Mysteries Ser.). audio 18.00 (*0-7871-1911-3*, Dove Audio) NewStar Media, Inc.

—Cat on a Blue Monday: A Midnight Louie Mystery. l.t. ed. 1994. o.p. (*0-7927-2111-X*); pap. o.p. (*0-7927-2110-1*) BBC Audiobooks America.

—Cat on a Blue Monday: A Midnight Louie Mystery. 1994. (Midnight Louie Mystery Ser.). 374p. mass mkt. 6.99 (*0-8125-3441-7*); 384p. 21.95 o.p. (*0-312-85607-5*) Doherty, Tom Assocs., LLC. (Forge Bks.).

—Cat on a Blue Monday: A Midnight Louie Mystery. l.t. ed. 1994. 540p. pap. 17.95 o.p. (*0-8161-7456-3*, Macmillan Reference USA) Gale Group.

—Cat on a Hyacinth Hunt: A Midnight Louie Mystery. (Midnight Louie Mystery Ser.). 384p. 1999. mass mkt. 6.99 (*0-8125-6186-4*); 1998. 23.95 (*0-312-86634-8*) Doherty, Tom Assocs., LLC. (Forge Bks.).

—Cat on a Hyacinth Hunt: A Midnight Louie Mystery. l.t. ed. 2000. pap. 23.95 (*1-56895-872-2*, Wheeler Publishing, Inc.) Gale Group.

—Cat on a Hyacinth Hunt: A Midnight Louie Mystery. abr. ed. 1998. (Midnight Louie Mysteries Ser.). 3p. audio 19.95 (*0-7871-1749-8*, Dove Audio) NewStar Media, Inc.

—Cat with an Emerald Eye: A Midnight Louie Mystery. (Midnight Louie Mystery Ser.). 384p. 1997. mass mkt. 6.99 (*0-8125-4012-3*); 1996. 24.95 o.p. (*0-312-86228-8*) Doherty, Tom Assocs., LLC. (Forge Bks.).

—Catnap: A Midnight Louie Mystery. l.t. ed. 1993. (Midnight Louie Mystery Ser.). 23.95 o.p. (*0-7927-1644-2*); pap. 21.95 o.p. (*0-7927-1643-4*) BBC Audiobooks America.

—Catnap: A Midnight Louie Mystery. (Midnight Louie Mystery Ser.). 1993. 241p. mass mkt. 6.99 (*0-8125-1682-6*, Forge Bks.); 1992. 256p. 17.95 o.p. (*0-312-85217-7*, Tor Bks.) Doherty, Tom Assocs., LLC.

—Pussyfoot: A Midnight Louie Mystery. l.t. ed. 1994. (Midnight Louie Mystery Ser.). 24.95 o.p. (*0-7927-1846-1*); pap. 22.95 o.p. (*0-7927-1845-3*) BBC Audiobooks America.

—Pussyfoot: A Midnight Louie Mystery. (Midnight Louie Mystery Ser.). 1994. 304p. mass mkt. 5.99 (*0-8125-1683-4*); 1993. 256p. 19.95 o.p. (*0-312-85218-5*) Doherty, Tom Assocs., LLC. (Tor Bks.).

**BARRETT, BEL (FICTITIOUS CHARACTER)—FICTION**

Isenberg, Jane. Death in a Hot Flash: A Bel Barrett Mystery. 2000. (Bel Barrett Mysteries Ser.). 224p. mass mkt. 5.99 (*0-380-80281-3*, Avon Bks.) Morrow/Avon.

—Hot & Bothered. 2003. 288p. mass mkt. 6.99 (*0-380-81888-4*, Avon Bks.) Morrow/Avon.

—The "M" Word: A Bel Barrett Mystery. 1999. 224p. mass mkt. 5.99 (*0-380-80280-5*, Avon Bks.) Morrow/Avon.

—Midlife Can Be Murder. l.t. ed. 2002. 346p. pap. 24.95 (*0-7862-4287-6*) Gale Group.

—Midlife Can Be Murder. 2001. (Bel Barrett Mystery Ser.). 288p. mass mkt. 6.50 (*0-380-81886-8*, Avon Bks.) Morrow/Avon.

—Mood Swings to Murder. 2000. (Bel Barrett Mysteries Ser.). 256p. mass mkt. 6.50 (*0-380-80282-1*, Avon Bks.) Morrow/Avon.

—Mood Swings to Murder: A Bel Barrett Mystery. l.t. ed. 2002. 349p. pap. 25.95 (*0-7862-4007-5*) Gale Group.

**BARRETT, JONATHAN (FICTITIOUS CHARACTER)—FICTION**

Elrod, P. N. Dance of Death. 1996. (Vampire Files Ser.). 352p. (Orig.). mass mkt. 5.99 o.s.i (*0-441-00309-5*) Ace Bks.

—Death & the Maiden. 1994. (Vampire Files Ser.). 256p. (Orig.). mass mkt. 4.99 o.s.i (*0-441-00071-1*) Ace Bks.

—Death Masque. 1995. 272p. (Orig.). mass mkt. 4.99 o.s.i (*0-441-00143-2*) Ace Bks.

—A Red Death. 1993. (Vampire Files Ser.). mass mkt. 4.99 o.s.i (*0-441-71094-8*) Ace Bks.

**BARRETT, SEAN (FICTITIOUS CHARACTER)—FICTION**

Eberhardt, Michael C. Body of a Crime. 1994. 368p. 19.95 o.p. (*0-525-93623-8*, Dutton) Dutton/Plume.

—Body of a Crime. unabr. ed. 1998. audio 103.95 (*1-85903-136-6*) Magna Story Sound GBR. *Dist:* Ulverscroft Large Print Bks., Ltd.

—Body of a Crime. 1995. 448p. mass mkt. 5.99 o.s.i (*0-451-40569-2*, Onyx) NAL.

—Body of a Crime. l.t. ed. 1997. (Niagara Large Print Ser.). 546p. 29.50 o.p. (*0-7089-5803-6*, Ulverscroft) Thorpe, F. A. Pubs. GBR. *Dist:* Ulverscroft Large Print Bks., Ltd., Ulverscroft Large Print Canada, Ltd.

**BARRINGTON, STONE (FICTITIOUS CHARACTER)—FICTION**

Woods, Stuart. Cold Paradise. unabr. ed. 2001. (Stone Barrington Ser.: Vol. 7). audio 69.25 (*1-58788-578-6*, 2851, Unabridged Library Editions); audio 29.95 (*1-58788-577-8*, 2850, Brilliance Audio Unabridged); audio compact disk 35.95 (*1-58788-579-4*, 2852, CD Unabridged); audio compact disk 87.25 (*1-58788-580-8*, 2853, Unabridged Library Editions) Brilliance Audio.

—Cold Paradise. l.t. ed. 2001. 523p. 32.95 (*0-7838-9470-8*, Macmillan Reference USA) Gale Group.

—Cold Paradise. 2002. 432p. reprint ed. mass mkt. 7.99 (*0-451-20562-6*, Signet Bks.) NAL.

—Cold Paradise. 2001. 352p. 24.95 o.p. (*0-399-14736-5*) Penguin Group (USA) Inc.

—Cold Paradise. abr. ed. 2001. audio 24.95 o.p. (*0-399-14759-4*, Putnam Berkley Audio) Putnam Publishing Group, The.

—Cold Paradise. unabr. ed. 2003. (Stone Barrington Ser.). audio 19.99 (*1-59335-070-8*, 30155) Soulmate Audio Bks., Inc.

—Cold Paradise. l.t. ed. 2002. (Paperback Bestsellers Ser.). 440p. pap. 29.95 (*0-7838-9471-6*) Thorndike Pr.

—Dead in the Water. unabr. ed. 1997. audio 56.00 (*0-7366-3753-2*, 4428) Books on Tape, Inc.

—Dead in the Water. l.t. ed. 1997. 26.95 o.p. (*1-56895-508-1*, Wheeler Publishing, Inc.) Gale Group.

—Dead in the Water. 1998. 432p. mass mkt. 7.99 (*0-06-109349-1*) HarperCollins Pubs.

—Dead in the Water. 1997. 336p. 25.00 o.p. (*0-06-018368-3*, HarperCollins);Set. 5p. audio 19.95 (*0-694-51849-2*, 495369, HarperAudio) HarperTrade.

—Dead in the Water. unabr. ed. 1999. audio compact disk 79.00 (*0-7887-3423-7*, C1029E7); 1997. audio 70.00 (*0-7887-1776-6*, 95250E7) Recorded Bks., LLC.

—Dirt. unabr. ed. 1996. audio 48.00 (*0-913369-26-8*, 4177) Books on Tape, Inc.

—Dirt. l.t. ed. 1997. (Large Print Bks.). 26.95 o.p. (*1-56895-398-4*, Wheeler Publishing, Inc.) Gale Group.

—Dirt. 1996. 288p. 24.00 o.p. (*0-06-017666-0*) HarperCollins Pubs.

—Dirt, Set. abr. ed. 1996. audio 18.00 o.s.i (*0-694-51723-2*, 394233, HarperAudio) HarperTrade.

—Dirt. 1997. 448p. mass mkt. 7.99 (*0-06-109423-4*, HarperTorch) Morrow/Avon.

—Dirt, unabr. ed. audio 51.00 (*0-7887-0630-6*, 94805E7) Recorded Bks., LLC.

—Dirty Work. l.t. ed. (Stone Barrington Ser.). 436p. 28.95 (*1-58724-440-3*, Wheeler Publishing, Inc.) Gale Group.

—Dirty Work. 2003. 368p. mass mkt. 7.99 (*0-451-21015-8*, Signet Bks.) NAL.

—Dirty Work. 2003. (Stone Barrington Ser.). 336p. 25.95 (*0-399-14982-1*) Penguin Group (USA) Inc.

—Dirty Work. abr. ed. 2003. (Stone Barrington Ser.). audio 25.95 (*0-399-14994-5*, Putnam Berkley Audio) Putnam Publishing Group, The.

—L. A. Dead. unabr. ed. 2000. (Stone Barrington Ser.). audio 57.25 (*1-58788-074-1*, 2322, Unabridged Library Editions); audio 29.95 (*1-58788-073-3*, 2320, Brilliance Audio Unabridged); audio compact disk 35.95 (*1-58788-169-1*, 2429, CD Unabridged); audio compact disk 73.25 (*1-58788-180-2*, 2453, Unabridged Library Editions) Brilliance Audio.

—L. A. Dead. l.t. ed. 2001. 12.95 (*1-56895-185-X*); 2000. 409p. 29.95 (*1-56895-999-0*) Gale Group. (Wheeler Publishing, Inc.).

—L. A. Dead. 2001. 432p. mass mkt. 7.99 (*0-451-20411-5*, Signet Bks.) NAL.

—L. A. Dead. 2000. (Stone Barrington Ser.). 352p. 24.95 o.s.i (*0-399-14664-4*) Penguin Group (USA) Inc.

—L. A. Dead. abr. ed. 2000. audio 24.95 o.s.i (*0-399-14678-4*, Putnam Berkley Audio) Putnam Publishing Group, The.

—New York Dead. l.t. ed. 1993. pap. 17.95 o.p. (*0-7927-1368-0*); 1992. 19.95 o.p. (*0-7927-1369-9*) BBC Audiobooks America.

—New York Dead. 1991. 320p. 20.00 o.p. (*0-06-017925-2*) HarperTrade.

—New York Dead, abr. ed. 1999. audio 25.00 Highsmith Inc.

—New York Dead. 1995. 79p. mass mkt. 3.99 o.p. (*0-06-109478-1*); 1992. 352p. mass mkt. 7.99 (*0-06-109080-8*) Morrow/Avon. (HarperTorch).

—Reckless Abandon. 2004. 336p. 25.95 (*0-399-15151-6*) Putnam Publishing Group, The.

—The Short Forever. l.t. ed. 2002. (Wheeler Large Print Book Ser.). 29.95 (*1-58724-215-X*, Wheeler Publishing, Inc.) Gale Group.

—The Short Forever. 2003. 368p. reprint ed. mass mkt. 7.99 (*0-451-20808-0*, Signet Bks.) NAL.

—The Short Forever. 2002. 336p. 24.95 o.s.i (*0-399-14868-X*) Putnam Publishing Group, The.

—Swimming to Catalina. unabr. ed. 1998. audio 64.00 (*0-7366-4188-2*, 4686) Books on Tape, Inc.

—Swimming to Catalina. l.t. ed. 1998. (Wheeler Large Print Book Ser.). 27.95 (*1-56895-620-7*, Wheeler Publishing, Inc.) Gale Group.

—Swimming to Catalina. 1998. 320p. 25.00 o.s.i (*0-06-018369-1*) HarperCollins Pubs.

—Swimming to Catalina. abr. ed. 2004. audio 14.95 (*0-06-072533-8*); Set. 1998. audio 25.00 (*0-694-51938-3*, 693583) HarperTrade. (HarperAudio).

—Swimming to Catalina. 1998. 416p. mass mkt. 7.99 (*0-06-109980-5*, HarperTorch) Morrow/Avon.

—Swimming to Catalina, unabr. ed. 1998. audio 60.00 (*0-7887-1973-4*, 95360E7) Recorded Bks., LLC.

—Worst Fears Realized. 1999. audio 48.00 (*0-7366-4743-0*); 1999. audio 48.00; 1999. audio compact disk 56.00 (*0-7366-5203-5*); 2001. audio compact disk 56.00 Books on Tape, Inc.

—Worst Fears Realized. 2000. 416p. mass mkt. 7.99 (*0-06-101342-0*); Set. 1999. 336p. 25.00 o.p. (*0-06-019182-1*) HarperCollins Pubs.

—Worst Fears Realized. abr. ed. 2003. audio 14.95 (*0-06-053574-1*); Set. 1999. audio 25.00 (*0-694-52150-7*) HarperTrade. (HarperAudio).

—Worst Fears Realized, Set. abr. ed. 1999. audio 25.00 Highsmith Inc.

—Worst Fears Realized. unabr. ed. 2000. audio compact disk 75.00 (*0-7887-4205-1*, C1134E7); 1999. (Stone Barrington Ser.: Vol. 5). audio 60.00 (*0-7887-3742-2*, 95868E7) Recorded Bks., LLC.

**BARRON, PETER (FICTITIOUS CHARACTER)—FICTION**

Farris, Michael. Guilt by Association: A Novel. 1997. pap. text 12.99 o.p. (*0-8054-0151-2*); pap. text 12.99 (*0-8054-0155-5*) Broadman & Holman Pubs.

**BARTHOLOMEW, BROTHER (FICTITIOUS CHARACTER)—FICTION**

Manuel, David. A Matter of Diamonds. 2000. (Faith Abbey Mystery Ser.: Vol. 2). xiv, 314p. 23.00 (*1-55725-258-0*, 930-059) Paraclete Pr., Inc.

—A Matter of Diamonds. 2002. 408p. mass mkt. 6.99 (*0-446-60989-7*) Warner Bks., Inc.

—A Matter of Principle: A Faith Abbey Mystery. 2003. 19.95 (*1-55725-346-3*) Paraclete Pr., Inc.

—A Matter of Roses. 1999. (Faith Abbey Mystery Ser.). 330p. 23.00 (*1-55725-234-3*, 930-006) Paraclete Pr., Inc.

—A Matter of Roses. 2001. 480p. mass mkt. 6.99 (*0-446-60988-9*) Warner Bks., Inc.

—A Matter of Time. 2003. (Faith Abbey Mystery Ser.). 304p. mass mkt. 6.99 (*0-446-61255-3*) Warner Bks., Inc.

—A Matter of Time: A Faith Abbey Mystery. 2002. 288p. 23.00 (*1-55725-305-6*) Paraclete Pr., Inc.

**BARTHOLOMEW, MATTHEW (FICTITIOUS CHARACTER)—FICTION**

Gregory, Susanna. A Bone of Contention. 1998. (Illus.). 506p. mass mkt. 7.95 o.s.i (*0-7515-2022-5*) Warner Futura GBR. *Dist:* Trafalgar Square.

—A Bone of Contention: The Second Chronicle of Matthew Bartholomew. 1997. (Illus.). 288p. o.s.i (*0-316-88280-1*) Little Brown & Co.

—A Bone of Contention: The Second Chronicle of Matthew Bartholomew. 1997. (Chronicle of Matthew Bartholomew Ser.: Vol. 2). 288p. 23.95 (*0-312-16792-X*, Saint Martin's Minotaur) St. Martin's Pr.

—A Killer in Winter. 2003. (Illus.). 496p. (*0-316-86011-5*) Time Warner Bks. UK GBR. *Dist:* Trafalgar Square.

—A Plague on Both Your Houses. 1996. (Illus.). 406p. mass mkt. o.s.i (*0-7515-1695-3*) Little Brown & Co.

—A Plague on Both Your Houses. 1998. (Chronicle of Matthew Bartholomew Ser.: Vol. 3). 416p. 24.95 o.p. (*0-312-19318-1*) St. Martin's Pr.

—An Unholy Alliance. 1996. (Illus.). 310p. o.s.i (*0-316-87911-8*) Little Brown & Co.

—An Unholy Alliance. 1998. (Matthew Bartholomew Mysteries Ser.). 336p. mass mkt. 5.99 o.p. (*0-312-96631-8*, St. Martin's Paperbacks); 1996. (Chronicle of Matthew Bartholomew Ser.: Vol. 1). 288p. 23.95 o.p. (*0-312-14752-X*, Saint Martin's Minotaur) St. Martin's Pr.

—A Wicked Deed. 2003. (Illus.). 506p. pap. 7.95 (*0-7515-2544-8*) Warner Bks. GBR. *Dist:* Trafalgar Square.

**BARTHOLOMEW, PETER (FICTITIOUS CHARACTER)—FICTION**

Gunning, Sally. Deep Water. 1996. mass mkt. 5.99 (*0-671-56313-0*, Pocket) Simon & Schuster.

—Dirty Water. 1998. (Peter Bartholomew Mysteries Ser.: Vol. 9). 288p. per. 6.50 o.s.i (*0-671-01736-5*, Pocket) Simon & Schuster.

—Fire Water. 1999. (Peter Bartholomew Mysteries Ser.: Vol. 7). 304p. pap. 6.50 (*0-671-01737-3*, Pocket) Simon & Schuster.
—Hot Water. Chelius, Jane, ed. 1990. 256p. (Orig.). mass mkt. 5.99 (*0-671-72804-0*, Pocket) Simon & Schuster.
—Ice Water. Chelius, Jane, ed. 1993. 256p. (Orig.). mass mkt. 5.50 (*0-671-76005-X*, Pocket) Simon & Schuster.
—Muddy Water. 1997. (Peter Bartholomew Mysteries Ser.). 256p. mass mkt. 6.50 (*0-671-56314-9*, Pocket) Simon & Schuster.
—Rough Water. Chelius, Jane, ed. 1994. 304p. (Orig.). mass mkt. 5.50 (*0-671-87137-4*, Pocket) Simon & Schuster.
—Still Water. 1995. 288p. mass mkt. 5.99 (*0-671-87138-2*, Pocket) Simon & Schuster.
—Troubled Water. Chelius, Jane, ed. 1993. 240p. (Orig.). mass mkt. 5.50 (*0-671-76006-8*, Pocket) Simon & Schuster.
—Under Water. Chelius, Jane, ed. 1992. 224p. (Orig.). mass mkt. 5.99 (*0-671-72805-9*, Pocket) Simon & Schuster.

**BARTLETT, STEPHEN (FICTITIOUS CHARACTER)—FICTION**

Elwood, Roger. Code Name Bloody Winter. 1996. mass mkt. 5.99 o.p. (*0-8499-3883-X*); 1993. pap. 8.99 o.p. (*0-8499-3388-9*) W Publishing Group.
—Deadly Sanction. 1995. mass mkt. 5.99 o.p. (*0-8499-3885-6*); 1993. pap. 8.99 o.p. (*0-8499-3387-0*) W Publishing Group.
—Wolf's Lair. 1995. mass mkt. 5.99 o.p. (*0-8499-3884-8*); 1993. 224p. pap. 8.99 o.p. (*0-8499-3386-2*) W Publishing Group.

**BARWICK, LIZ (FICTITIOUS CHARACTER)—FICTION**

Woods, Stuart. Palindrome. l.t. ed. 1998. pap. 24.95 (*1-56895-688-6*, Wheeler Publishing, Inc.) Gale Group.
—Palindrome. 1991. 352p. 239.40 o.p. (*0-06-017913-9*) HarperCollins Pubs.
—Palindrome. 1991. (Illus.). 368p. 19.95 o.p. (*0-06-017911-2*) HarperTrade.
—Palindrome. 1995. 79p. mass mkt. 3.99 o.p. (*0-06-109482-X*); 1991. 464p. mass mkt. 7.99 (*0-06-109936-8*) Morrow/Avon. (HarperTorch).
—Palindrome. abr. ed. 2000. audio 25.00 (*0-7871-2165-7*, Dove Audio) NewStar Media, Inc.

**BASCOM, ERNIE (FICTITIOUS CHARACTER)—FICTION**

Limon, Martin. Buddha's Money. 1999. 416p. mass mkt. 5.99 o.s.i (*0-553-57610-0*) Bantam Bks.
—Jade Lady Burning. 1994. 224p. pap. 13.00 (*1-56947-020-0*); 1992. 226p. 19.95 (*0-939149-71-0*) Soho Pr., Inc.

**BASCOME, CARVER (FICTITIOUS CHARACTER)—FICTION**

Davis, Kenn. Acts of Homicide. 1989. 224p. mass mkt. 3.50 o.s.i (*0-449-13351-6*, Fawcett) Ballantine Bks.
—As October Dies. 1987. 240p. mass mkt. 2.95 o.s.i (*0-449-13097-5*, Fawcett) Ballantine Bks.
—Blood of Poets. 1990. 208p. (Orig.). mass mkt. 3.95 o.s.i (*0-449-13352-4*, Fawcett) Ballantine Bks.
—Melting Point. 1986. 256p. (Orig.). mass mkt. 2.95 o.s.i (*0-449-12901-2*, Fawcett) Ballantine Bks.
—Nijinsky Is Dead. 1987. 240p. mass mkt. 2.95 o.s.i (*0-449-13096-7*, Fawcett) Ballantine Bks.
—Words Can Kill. 1984. (Orig.). mass mkt. 2.50 o.s.i (*0-449-12667-6*, Fawcett) Ballantine Bks.

**BASHEARS, ALMA MAE (FICTITIOUS CHARACTER)—FICTION**

Collins, Tess. The Law of Revenge. 9999. mass mkt. o.p. (*0-345-41484-5*); 1997. (*0-449-91075-X*, Fawcett); 1997. mass mkt. 6.99 (*0-449-22534-8*, Fawcett); 1997. mass mkt. 5.99 o.s.i (*0-8041-1684-9*, Ivy Bks.) Ballantine Bks.
—The Law of Revenge. l.t. ed. 1997. (Niagara Large Print Ser.). 416p. 29.50 o.p. (*0-7089-5888-5*, Ulverscroft) Thorpe, F. A. Pubs. GBR. *Dist:* Ulverscroft Large Print Bks., Ltd.
—The Law of the Dead. 1999. mass mkt. 6.99 o.s.i (*0-8041-1795-0*, Ivy Bks.) Ballantine Bks.

**BASHIR, JULIAN (FICTITIOUS CHARACTER)—FICTION**

Betancourt, John. Devil in the Sky. (Star Trek Deep Space Nine Ser.: No. 11). E-Book 6.95 (*0-7434-2042-X*, Star Trek) Simon & Schuster.
Cox, Greg. Devil in the Sky. 1995. (Star Trek Deep Space Nine Ser.: No. 11). (Illus.). 288p. (J). mass mkt. 5.50 (*0-671-88114-0*, Star Trek) Simon & Schuster.
David, Peter, et al. Wrath of the Prophets. 1997. (Star Trek Deep Space Nine Ser.: No. 20). 304p. pap. 5.99 (*0-671-53817-9*, Star Trek) Simon & Schuster.
Dillard, J. M. Dark Victory. 1993. (Star Trek Deep Space Nine Ser.: No. 1). per. 5.50 (*0-671-78958-9*, Star Trek) Simon & Schuster.
—Dark Victory. Stern, Dave, ed. 1993. (Star Trek Deep Space Nine Ser.). 288p. mass mkt. 5.50 (*0-671-79858-8*, Star Trek) Simon & Schuster.
—Dark Victory. (Star Trek Deep Space Nine Ser.: No. 1). 1989. audio 17.00 (*0-671-79102-8*); 1999. audio 18.00 (*0-671-04385-4*) Simon & Schuster Audio. (Simon & Schuster Audioworks).
—Emissary. 1993. (Star Trek Deep Space Nine Ser.: No. 1). E-Book 6.99 (*0-7434-1220-6*, Star Trek) Simon & Schuster.
Dillard, J. M., et al. Emissary; The Siege; Bloodletter; The Big Game; Betrayal, 5 bks. 1997. (Star Trek). pap. text 0.95 o.p. (*0-8359-1492-5*) Globe Fearon Educational Publishing.
Friesner, Esther M. Warchild. (Star Trek Deep Space Nine Ser.: No. 7). E-Book 6.99 (*0-7434-2038-1*, Star Trek) Simon & Schuster.
—Warchild. Ordover, John, ed. 1994. (Star Trek Deep Space Nine Ser.: No. 7). 288p. mass mkt. 5.50 (*0-671-88116-7*, Star Trek) Simon & Schuster.
Graf, L. A. Armageddon Sky: Day of Honor. Keenan, Randall, ed. 1997. (Star Trek, The Next Generation: Vol. 2). 304p. pap. 5.99 o.s.i (*0-671-00675-4*, Star Trek) Simon & Schuster.
Hugh, Dafydd ab. The Courageous. (Star Trek Deep Space Nine Ser.: No. 25). E-Book 6.99 (*0-7434-2056-X*, Star Trek) Simon & Schuster.
—Fallen Heroes. (Star Trek Deep Space Nine Ser.: No. 5). 1999. E-Book 6.50 (*0-671-04114-2*); 1994. E-Book 6.99 (*0-7434-1224-9*) Simon & Schuster. (Star Trek).
—Fallen Heroes. Ordover, John, ed. 1994. (Star Trek Deep Space Nine Ser.: No. 5). 288p. mass mkt. 5.50 (*0-671-88459-X*, Star Trek) Simon & Schuster.
—Fallen Heroes. abr. ed. 1994. (Star Trek Deep Space Nine Ser.: No. 5). audio 16.00 (*0-671-89182-0*, Simon & Schuster Audioworks) Simon & Schuster Audio.
—Fallen Heroes Star Trek Continuity. 1999. 12.99 (*0-671-02166-4*, Star Trek) Simon & Schuster.
—The Liberated. (Star Trek Deep Space Nine Ser.: No. 26). E-Book 6.99 (*0-7434-2057-8*, Star Trek) Simon & Schuster.
—Vengeance. 1998. (Star Trek Deep Space Nine Ser.: No. 22). 304p. pap. 6.50 (*0-671-00468-9*, Star Trek) Simon & Schuster.
Jeter, K. W. Bloodletter. 1993. (Star Trek Deep Space Nine Ser.: No. 3). 288p. mass mkt. 5.50 (*0-671-87275-3*, Star Trek) Simon & Schuster.
—The Bloodletter. 1993. (Star Trek Deep Space Nine Ser.: No. 3). E-Book 6.99 (*0-7434-1222-2*, Star Trek) Simon & Schuster.
Martin, Michael A. & Mangels, Andy. Mission Gamma: Cathedral. 2002. (Star Trek Deep Space Nine Ser.: Bk. 3). 432p. mass mkt. 6.99 (*0-7434-4564-3*, Star Trek) Simon & Schuster.
Robinson, Andrew J. A Stitch in Time. (Star Trek Deep Space Nine Ser.: No. 27). E-Book 6.95 (*0-7434-2058-6*); 2000. (Illus.). 432p. pap. 6.50 (*0-671-03885-0*) Simon & Schuster. (Star Trek).
Sheckley, Robert. Laertian Gamble. 1995. (Star Trek Deep Space Nine Ser.: No. 12). 288p. mass mkt. 5.99 (*0-671-88690-8*, Star Trek) Simon & Schuster.
Shimerman, Armin. The Merchant Prince. 2001. E-Book 23.95 (*1-58945-288-7*) Adobe Systems, Inc.
—The Merchant Prince. 2001. (Illus.). 368p. reprint ed. mass mkt. 6.99 (*0-671-03613-0*, Star Trek); Bk. 2. 2001. 320p. reprint ed. E-Book 6.99 (*0-7434-1748-8*, Star Trek); Bk. 3. 2003. 368p. mass mkt. 7.99 (*0-671-03594-0*, Pocket Star) Simon & Schuster.
Shimerman, Armin & Scott, Michael. The Merchant Prince. 2000. 320p. 23.95 o.s.i (*0-671-03592-4*, Atria); Book 3. 2003. E-Book (*0-7434-8044-9*, Pocket) Simon & Schuster.
Smith, Dean Wesley. The Core. 2003. 256p. mass mkt. 6.99 (*0-7434-6398-6*, Pocket) Simon & Schuster.
Smith, Dean Wesley & Rusch, Kristine K. The Long Night. (Star Trek Deep Space Nine Ser.: No. 14). E-Book 6.99 (*0-7434-2045-4*, Star Trek) Simon & Schuster.
A Stitch in Time. 2000. per. 6.50 (*0-7434-1111-0*, Pocket) Simon & Schuster.
Sutcliffe, Katherine. Fever. 2001. 416p. pap. 6.99 (*0-7434-1197-8*); E-Book 6.99 (*0-7434-1774-7*) Simon & Schuster. (Pocket).

**BASILE, BURKE (FICTITIOUS CHARACTER)—FICTION**

Brown, Sandra. Fat Tuesday. l.t. ed. 1997. (Wheeler Large Print Book Ser.). 27.95 (*1-56895-465-4*, Wheeler Publishing, Inc.) Gale Group.
—Fat Tuesday. abr. ed. 1997. audio 24.00 (*0-553-47825-7*, 695225); audio compact disk 29.95 o.s.i (*0-553-45557-5*) Random Hse. Audio Publishing Group. (RH Audio).
—Fat Tuesday. 1997. 464p. 23.50 o.p. (*0-446-51632-5*); 1998. 480p. reprint ed. mass mkt. 7.99 (*0-446-60558-1*) Warner Bks., Inc.

**BASNETT, ANDREW (FICTITIOUS CHARACTER)—FICTION**

Ferrars, E. X. A Choice of Evils. unabr. ed. 1996. audio 49.95 (*1-85695-223-1*, 951209) ISIS Audio Bks. GBR. *Dist:* Ulverscroft Large Print Bks., Ltd.
—The Crime & the Crystal. 1985. (Crime Club Ser.). 192p. 12.95 o.p. (*0-385-19996-1*) Doubleday Publishing.
—The Crime & the Crystal. l.t. ed. 1999. (Ulverscroft Large Print Ser.). 320p. 12.50 o.p. (*0-7089-1485-3*, Ulverscroft) Thorpe, F. A. Pubs. GBR. *Dist:* Ulverscroft Large Print Bks., Ltd., Ulverscroft Large Print Canada, Ltd.
—A Hobby of Murder: An Andrew Basnett Mystery. unabr. ed. 2000. audio 49.95 (*0-7451-4359-8*, CAB 1042) Chivers Audio Bks. GBR. *Dist:* BBC Audiobooks America.
—A Hobby of Murder: An Andrew Basnett Mystery. l.t. ed. 1995. (Magna Large Print Ser.). 301p. o.p. (*0-7505-0753-5*) Magna Large Print Bks. GBR. *Dist:* Ulverscroft Large Print Canada, Ltd.
—A Murder Too Many. unabr. ed. 2001. audio 54.95 (*1-85089-773-5*, 90103) ISIS Audio Bks. GBR. *Dist:* Ulverscroft Large Print Bks., Ltd.
—A Murder Too Many. l.t. ed. 1990. (Ulverscroft Large Print Ser.). 29.99 o.p. (*0-7089-2302-X*, Ulverscroft) Thorpe, F. A. Pubs. GBR. *Dist:* Ulverscroft Large Print Bks., Ltd., Ulverscroft Large Print Canada, Ltd.
—The Other Devil's Name. 1987. (Crime Club Ser.). 192p. 12.95 o.s.i (*0-385-23553-4*) Doubleday Publishing.
—The Other Devil's Name. l.t. ed. 1988. (Ulverscroft Large Print Ser.). 336p. 29.99 o.p. (*0-7089-1833-6*, Ulverscroft) Thorpe, F. A. Pubs. GBR. *Dist:* Ulverscroft Large Print Bks., Ltd., Ulverscroft Large Print Canada, Ltd.
—Root of All Evil. 1984. (Crime Club Ser.). 192p. 11.95 o.p. (*0-385-19580-X*) Doubleday Publishing.
—Root of All Evil. l.t. ed. 1985. (General Ser.). 312p. 14.95 o.p. (*0-8161-3879-6*, Macmillan Reference USA) Gale Group.
—Root of All Evil. 1993. (Audio Books Ser.). 46.95 o.p. incl. audio (*0-7838-8019-7*) Thorndike Pr.
—Smoke Without Fire. unabr. ed. 2001. audio 54.95 (*1-85089-878-2*, 92085) ISIS Audio Bks. GBR. *Dist:* Ulverscroft Large Print Bks., Ltd.
—Something Wicked. unabr. ed. 1991. (Audio Ser.). audio 54.95 (*0-7451-5923-0*, CAT 4069) BBC Audiobooks America.
—Something Wicked. 1984. (Crime Club Ser.). 192p. 11.95 o.p. (*0-385-19254-1*) Doubleday Publishing.
—Something Wicked. l.t. ed. 1985. (Nightingale Ser.). 253p. pap. 9.95 o.p. (*0-8161-3763-3*, Macmillan Reference USA) Gale Group.

**BASS, TITUS (FICTITIOUS CHARACTER)—FICTION**

Johnston, Terry C. Borderlords. 1986. 528p. mass mkt. 6.99 (*0-553-26224-6*) Bantam Bks.
—Borderlords. 1985. (Frontier Library). 500p. 19.95 (*0-915463-11-3*, Frontier Library, The) Jameson Bks., Inc.
—Buffalo Palace. 1997. 576p. mass mkt. 7.50 (*0-553-57283-0*) Bantam Bks.
—Carry the Wind. 1997. (Illus.). 704p. mass mkt. 7.50 (*0-553-25572-X*) Bantam Bks.
—Carry the Wind. 1982. 571p. 18.95 o.s.i (*0-89803-106-0*, Frontier Library, The) Jameson Bks., Inc.
—Carry the Wind. abr. ed. 1994. audio 9.98 (*1-57042-075-0*, 4-520750) Time Warner AudioBooks.
—A Crack in the Sky. 1997. 496p. 23.95 o.s.i (*0-553-09078-X*); 1998. 672p. reprint ed. mass mkt. 7.50 (*0-553-57284-9*) Bantam Bks.
—Dance on the Wind. 1996. 640p. mass mkt. 7.50 (*0-553-57281-4*); 1995. 528p. 21.95 o.s.i (*0-553-09071-2*) Bantam Bks.
—Death Rattle. 2000. 592p. mass mkt. 6.99 (*0-553-57286-5*) Bantam Bks.
—One-Eyed Dream. 1994. 592p. mass mkt. 7.50 (*0-553-28139-9*) Bantam Bks.
—One-Eyed Dream. 1988. (Frontier Library). 450p. 19.95 (*0-915463-38-5*, Frontier Library, The) Jameson Bks., Inc.
—Ride the Moon Down: The Plainsmen. 1999. 592p. mass mkt. 6.99 (*0-553-57282-2*) Bantam Bks.

**BASSETT, HENRY (FICTITIOUS CHARACTER)—FICTION**

Burden, Pat. Bury Him Kindly. 1992. 192p. 16.50 o.s.i (*0-385-42234-2*) Doubleday Publishing.
—Bury Him Kindly. l.t. ed. 1992. (Magna Large Print Ser.). 296p. 29.99 o.p. (*0-7505-0368-8*) Magna Large Print Bks. GBR. *Dist:* Ulverscroft Large Print Bks., Ltd., Ulverscroft Large Print Canada, Ltd.
—Screaming Bones. 1992. 224p. mass mkt. 4.50 o.s.i (*0-553-29936-0*) Bantam Bks.
—Screaming Bones. 1990. 192p. 14.95 o.s.i (*0-385-41522-2*) Doubleday Publishing.
—Wreath of Honesty. 1991. 192p. 15.00 o.s.i (*0-385-41863-9*) Doubleday Publishing.
—Wreath of Honesty. l.t. ed. 1992. 368p. 29.99 (*0-7089-2583-9*, Ulverscroft) Thorpe, F. A. Pubs. GBR. *Dist:* Ulverscroft Large Print Bks., Ltd.

**BAST (FICTITIOUS CHARACTER)—FICTION**

Edghill, Rosemary. Bell, Book & Murder. 3rd ed. 1998. (Bast Novels). 448p. pap. 17.95 (*0-312-86768-9*, CPB1211, Forge Bks.) Doherty, Tom Assocs., LLC.
—Book of Moons. 1996. mass mkt. 5.99 (*0-8125-3439-5*, Tor Bks.); 1995. 224p. 20.95 o.p. (*0-312-85605-9*, Forge Bks.) Doherty, Tom Assocs., LLC.
—Bowl of Night. 1997. mass mkt. 5.99 (*0-8125-3440-9*, Tor Bks.) Doherty, Tom Assocs., LLC.
—Speak Daggers to Her. 1995. 222p. mass mkt. 5.99 (*0-8125-3438-7*, Tor Bks.); 1994. 224p. 19.95 o.p. (*0-312-85604-0*, Forge Bks.) Doherty, Tom Assocs., LLC.

**BASTABLE, OSWALD (FICTITIOUS CHARACTER)—FICTION**

Moorcock, Michael. The Land Leviathan. 19.95 (*0-89190-153-1*) Amereon, Ltd.
—The Land Leviathan. (Science Fiction Ser.). 1982. mass mkt. 2.25 o.p. (*0-87997-774-4*, UE1774); 1976. mass mkt. 1.50 o.p. (*0-87997-448-6*); 1976. mass mkt. 1.25 o.p. (*0-87997-214-9*) DAW Bks., Inc.
—The Steel Tsar. 1982. 160p. mass mkt. 2.25 o.p. (*0-87997-773-6*) DAW Bks., Inc.
—The Warlord of the Air. (Science Fiction Ser.). (Orig.). 1982. mass mkt. 2.25 o.p. (*0-87997-775-2*); 1978. mass mkt. 1.50 o.p. (*0-87997-380-3*) DAW Bks., Inc.

**BATELLE, JESSIE (FICTITIOUS CHARACTER)—FICTION**

Van Dyke, Annette. Hooded Murder: A Jessie Batelle Mystery. 1996. 208p. pap. 10.95 o.p. (*1-56280-134-1*) Naiad Pr., Inc.

**BATEMAN, PAT (FICTITIOUS CHARACTER)—FICTION**

Ellis, Bret Easton. American Psycho. 1991. (Vintage Contemporaries Ser.). 416p. pap. 14.00 (*0-679-73577-1*, Vintage) Knopf Publishing Group.
—American Psycho. 1991. 400p. 19.95 (*0-671-66397-6*, Simon & Schuster) Simon & Schuster.

**BATES, NORMAN (FICTITIOUS CHARACTER)—FICTION**

Bloch, Robert. Psycho. reprint ed. lib. bdg. 21.95 (*0-88411-077-X*) Amereon, Ltd.
—Psycho. 2001. E-Book 4.95 (*1-4014-0090-6*); E-Book 4.95 (*1-4014-0092-2*) Barnes & Noble Digital.
—Psycho. 1993. reprint ed. lib. bdg. 18.95 (*0-89968-420-3*, Lightyear Pr.) Buccaneer Bks., Inc.
—Psycho. 1991. 223p. mass mkt. 5.99 (*0-8125-1932-9*, Tor Bks.) Doherty, Tom Assocs., LLC.
—Psycho. abr. ed. 1999. 3p. audio 16.99 (*0-88646-492-7*); Set. audio 16.99 (*0-88646-165-0*, 7166) Durkin Hayes Publishing Ltd.
—Psycho. l.t. ed. 1985. 11.95 o.p. (*0-8166-0114-3*, Macmillan Reference USA) Gale Group.
—Psycho. ltd. ed. 1994. (Classics Revisited Ser.). 60.00 o.p. (*0-9629659-9-5*) Gauntlet, Inc.
—Psycho. 1982. 224p. pap. 2.75 o.s.i (*0-446-90803-7*) Warner Bks., Inc.
—Psycho. 2003. 224p. mass mkt. 6.99 (*0-7434-5907-5*) ibooks, Inc.
—Psycho II. 1989. pap. 3.95 o.p. (*0-8125-0033-4*, Tor Bks.) Doherty, Tom Assocs., LLC.
—Psycho II. 1982. 320p. mass mkt. 3.50 (*0-446-90804-5*) Warner Bks., Inc.
—Psycho II. 1982. 224p. 16.00 (*0-918372-09-7*); 36.00 (*0-918372-08-9*) Whispers Pr.
—Psycho II. 2003. 320p. pap. 6.99 (*0-7434-7472-4*) ibooks, Inc.

**BATHORY, DAVID (FICTITIOUS CHARACTER)—FICTION**

Baker, Scott. Ancestral Hungers. 320p. 1996. pap. 14.95 (*0-312-86305-5*); 1996. mass mkt. 5.99 (*0-8125-0259-0*); 1995. 21.95 o.p. (*0-312-85868-X*) Doherty, Tom Assocs., LLC. (Tor Bks.).

**BATMAN (FICTITIOUS CHARACTER)—FICTION**

Abnett, Dan & Lanning, Andy. Batman: Two Faces. O'Neil, Dennis, ed. 1998. (Illus.). 64p. pap. 4.95 (*1-56389-395-9*) DC Comics.
Adams, Neal, illus. Batman, Vol. 1. Date not set. 240p. 49.95 (*1-4012-0041-9*) DC Comics.
Adams, Neil. Greatest Batman Stories Ever Told. 1997. (DC Comics Ser.). 352p. pap. 15.95 (*0-930289-66-8*) DC Comics.
Augustyn, Brian. Batman: Master of the Future. O'Neil, Dennis, ed. 1991. 64p. pap. 5.95 (*1-56389-015-1*) DC Comics.
Bader, Hilary J. Batman Adventures: The Lost Years. 1999. (Batman Adventures Ser.). (Illus.). 128p. pap. 9.95 o.p. (*1-56389-483-1*) DC Comics.
Barr, Mike W. Batman: Dark Knight Dynasty. 1999. (Batman Ser.). (Illus.). 128p. pap. 14.95 (*1-56389-390-8*); 24.95 o.p. (*1-56389-384-3*) DC Comics.

—Batman: Son of the Demon. Giordano, Dick, ed. 1991. (Illus.). 80p. pap. 9.95 (*0-930289-25-0*) DC Comics.

—Batman: Year Two. Bruning, Richard, ed. 1990. (Illus.). 104p. pap. 9.95 o.p. (*0-930289-49-8*) DC Comics.

—Batman: Year Two. 1990. pap. 9.95 o.s.i (*0-446-39191-3*) Warner Bks., Inc.

Barretto. Batman: Scar of the Bat. O'Neil, Dennis, ed. 1996. (Prestige Bk.). (Illus.). 48p. pap. 4.95 (*1-56389-231-6*) DC Comics.

Batman: The Animated Series - Almost Got'Im. 1993. (Golden Book Ser.). (Illus.). 32p. (J). (ps-3). o.p. incl. audio (*0-307-14376-7*, 14376, Golden Bks.) Random Hse. Children's Bks.

Batman: The Animated Series - Plants of Peril. 1993. (Golden Book Ser.). (Illus.). 32p. (J). (ps-3). o.p. incl. audio (*0-307-14375-9*, 14375, Golden Bks.) Random Hse. Children's Bks.

Batman in the 50's. 2002. 192p. pap. 19.95 (*1-56389-810-1*) DC Comics.

Beatty, Ty. Gotham Adventures. 2000. (Batman Ser.). (Illus.). 155p. pap. 9.95 (*1-56389-616-8*) DC Comics.

Bisley, Simon & Kane, Bob, contrib. by. Batman: Black & White. 1999. (Illus.). 240p. pap. 19.95 (*1-56389-439-4*) DC Comics.

Bolland, Brian. Batman: Black & White. 1997. 240p. pap. 39.95 (*1-56389-332-0*) DC Comics.

Bruce Wayne: Murderer? A Graphic Novel. 2002. (Batman Ser.). (Illus.). 264p. pap. 19.95 (*1-56389-913-2*) DC Comics.

Canwell, Bruce. Batman: The Gauntlet. Peterson, Scott, ed. 1997. (Illus.). 48p. pap. 4.95 (*1-56389-364-9*) DC Comics.

Chaykin, Howard. Batman: Dark Allegiances. O'Neil, Dennis, ed. 1995. (Illus.). 64p. pap. 5.95 o.p. (*1-56389-233-2*) DC Comics.

Chaykin, Howard & Moore, J. F. Batman & Houdini: The Devil's Workshop. O'Neil, Dennis, ed. 1993. (Prestige Bk.). (Illus.). 64p. pap. 5.95 (*1-56389-113-1*) DC Comics.

Chichester, D. G. Daredevil & Batman: An Eye for an Eye. 1997. pap. 5.99 (*0-7851-0552-2*) Marvel Enterprises.

David, Peter. Batman Forever. 1995. 17.00 (*1-57042-273-7*); 256p. mass mkt. 5.99 o.p. (*0-446-60217-5*, Warner Vision) Warner Bks., Inc.

DC Comics Staff. Batman. 1995. 8.98 (*1-57042-296-6*) Warner Bks., Inc.

—Batman: Contagion. Kahan, Bob, ed. 1996. (Illus.). 264p. pap. 12.95 o.p. (*1-56389-293-6*) DC Comics.

—The Greatest Batman Stories Ever Told: Catwoman & the Penguin. 1992. (Illus.). (Orig.). pap. 14.99 o.s.i (*0-446-39427-0*) Warner Bks., Inc.

DC Comics Staff, et al. Batman: Dark Legends. 1996. (Batman Ser.). (Illus.). 176p. pap. 14.95 (*1-56389-266-9*) DC Comics.

Delano, Jamie. Batman: Man Bat. 1997. (Batman Ser.). (Illus.). 160p. pap. 14.95 (*1-56389-320-7*) DC Comics.

DeLisa, Jeannette, ed. Batman & Robin. 1997. 52p. (C). 16.95 (*0-7692-0163-6*, PF9725) Warner Bros. Pubns.

DeMatteis, J. M. Batman: Two-Face - Crime & Punishment. Peterson, Scott, ed. 1995. (Illus.). 48p. pap. 4.95 (*1-56389-197-2*) DC Comics.

Demetteis, J. M. & Ashmore, Brian. Batman: Absolution. 2002. (Illus.). 96p. 24.95 (*1-56389-934-5*) DC Comics.

Desris, Joe, intro. Batman in Detective Comics: Featuring the Complete Covers of the First 25 Years. 1993. (Tiny Folios Ser.). (Illus.). 320p. pap. 11.95 (*1-55859-643-7*) Abbeville Pr., Inc.

Dini, Paul. Batman: Mr. Freeze. 1997. (Illus.). 48p. (Orig.). pap. 4.95 o.p. (*1-56389-302-9*) DC Comics.

—Batman: War on Crime. 1999. (Illus.). 64p. pap. 9.95 (*1-56389-576-5*) DC Comics.

—Batman & Superman Adventures: World's Finest. 1997. (Illus.). 64p. pap. 6.95 (*1-56389-386-X*) DC Comics.

Dini, Paul & Timm, Bruce. The Batman Adventures: Mad Love. 1995. (Batman Adventures Ser.). (Illus.). 64p. pap. 5.95 (*1-56389-244-8*) DC Comics.

Dixon, C., et al. Batman: Knightfall: Broken Bat. Kahan, Bob, ed. 1993. (Batman Ser.: Vol. 1). (Illus.). 272p. pap. 14.95 (*1-56389-142-5*) DC Comics.

—Batman: Knightfall: Who Rules the Night, Vol.2. Kahan, Bob, ed. 1993. (Batman Ser.). (Illus.). 280p. pap. 14.95 (*1-56389-148-4*) DC Comics.

Dixon, Chuck. Batman: Bane. 1997. (Illus.). 48p. (Orig.). pap. 4.95 (*1-56389-303-7*) DC Comics.

—Batman: The Chalice. 1999. (Batman Ser.). (Illus.). 95p. pap. 24.95 o.p. (*1-56389-592-7*) DC Comics.

—Batman: The Joker's Apprentice. 1996. (Illus.). 32p. (J). (gr. k-3). 13.95 o.p. (*0-316-17798-9*) Little Brown & Co.

—Batman vs. Predator III: Blood Ties. 1998. (Illus.). 136p. pap. 7.95 o.p. (*1-56389-418-1*) DC Comics.

—The Joker: Devil's Advocate. 1995. (Illus.). 96p. 24.95 o.p. (*1-56389-240-5*) DC Comics.

Dixon, Chuck & Nolan, Graham. The Joker: Devil's Advocate. 1996. (Illus.). 96p. pap. 12.95 (*1-56389-280-4*, Vertigo) DC Comics.

Dixon, Chuck, et al. Batman: Legacy. 1997. (Illus.). 280p. pap. 17.95 o.p. (*1-56389-337-1*) DC Comics.

—Batman Pt. 3: Knightsend. 1995. (Batman Ser.). (Illus.). 320p. pap. 14.95 (*1-56389-191-3*) DC Comics.

Edginton, Ian & Johnson, Staz Hodgkins. Batman: Aliens Two. 2003. (Illus.). 160p. pap. 14.95 (*1-4012-0081-8*) DC Comics.

Englehart, Steve. Batman: Strange Apparitions. 1999. (Batman Ser.). (Illus.). 175p. pap. 12.95 (*1-56389-500-5*) DC Comics.

Finger, Bill. Batman: The Dark Knight Archives, Vol. 2. Kahan, Bob, ed. 1995. (Illus.). 244p. 59.95 (*1-56389-183-2*) DC Comics.

Finger, Bill & Cameron, Don. Batman Archives, Vol. 4. 1998. (Batman Archives Ser.: Vol. 4). (Illus.). 224p. pap. 49.95 (*1-56389-414-9*) DC Comics.

Finger, Bill, et al. The Dark Knight Archives. 2000. (Batman Ser.: Vol. 3). (Illus.). 224p. 49.95 (*1-56389-615-X*) DC Comics.

Friedman, Michael Jan. Batman & Robin. 1997. 224p. mass mkt. 5.99 (*0-446-60458-5*) Warner Bks., Inc.

Gale, Bob & Grayson, Devin K. Batman: No Man's Land. 1999. (Batman Ser.: Vol. 1). (Illus.). 200p. pap. 12.95 (*1-56389-564-1*) DC Comics.

Gale, Bob & Rucka, Greg. Batman: No Man's Land. 2000. (Batman Ser.: Vol. 2). (Illus.). 208p. pap. 12.95 (*1-56389-599-4*) DC Comics.

Gardner, Craig S. Batman. 1989. 224p. (Orig.). mass mkt. 4.95 o.s.i (*0-446-35487-2*) Warner Bks., Inc.

—Batman Returns. 1992. 256p. (Orig.). mass mkt. 4.99 o.s.i (*0-446-36303-0*) Warner Bks., Inc.

Gibbons, Dave. Batman Versus Predator: The Collected Edition. Kahan, Bob, ed. 1993. (Batman Ser.). (Illus.). 128p. pap. 7.95 o.s.i (*1-56389-092-5*) DC Comics.

—Batman Versus Predator: The Collected Edition. 1993. (Batman Ser.). (Illus.). (J). 14.00 (*0-606-22043-7*) Turtleback Bks.

Gold, Mike & Kahan, Bob, eds. Batman Archives, Vol. 1. 1990. (Batman Archives Ser.: Vol. 1). (Illus.). 306p. 39.95 (*0-930289-60-9*) DC Comics.

Goodwin, A. & Hampton, S. Batman: Night Cries. Goodwin, Archie, ed. 1998. (Illus.). 96p. pap. 12.95 (*1-56389-066-6*) DC Comics.

Grant, Alan. Batman: Anarky. 1999. (Illus.). 208p. pap. 12.95 (*1-56389-437-8*) DC Comics.

—Batman: Knightfall & Beyond. 1994. 176p. pap. 3.99 o.s.i (*0-553-48187-8*) Bantam Bks.

—Batman: No Man's Land. 2000. (Illus.). 160p. (J). (gr. 4-7). pap. 3.99 (*0-671-03829-X*, Aladdin) Simon & Schuster Children's Publishing.

—Batman: Scottish Connection. 1998. (Illus.). 64p. pap. 5.95 (*1-56389-372-X*) DC Comics.

—Batman: Shadow the Last Arkham. Kahan, Bob, ed. 1995. (Illus.). 112p. pap. 12.95 o.p. (*1-56389-190-5*) DC Comics.

—Batman Forever. 1995. (Illus.). 160p. (J). (gr. 3-7). pap. 2.95 o.p. (*0-316-32418-3*) Little Brown & Co.

—Batman Forever, Vol. 1. 1995. 8.98 (*1-57042-266-4*) Warner Bks., Inc.

Grant, Alan, et al. Batman: Four of a Kind. 1998. (Illus.). 208p. pap. 14.95 (*1-56389-413-0*) DC Comics.

Grant Staff & Wagner. Batman - Judge Dredd: The Ultimate Riddle. Peterson, ed. 1995. (Illus.). 48p. pap. 4.95 (*1-56389-206-5*) DC Comics.

Greenberg, Martin H., ed. Adventures of the Batman. 1995. 556p. 10.98 (*1-56731-077-X*, MJF Bks.) Fine Communications.

—Legends of the Batman. 1997. 528p. 10.98 o.s.i (*1-56731-219-5*, MJF Bks.) Fine Communications.

—Tales of the Batman. 1995. 554p. 10.98 (*1-56731-076-1*, MJF Bks.) Fine Communications.

Grell, Mike. Batman: Masque. Peterson, Scott, ed. 1997. (Illus.). 64p. pap. 6.95 (*1-56389-309-6*) DC Comics.

Hall, Bob. Batman: I Joker. 1998. (Illus.). 48p. pap. 4.95 o.p. (*1-56389-400-9*) DC Comics.

Hamm, Sam, frwd. Batman: Tales of the Demon. 1992. (Illus.). 208p. reprint ed. pap. 14.99 o.s.i (*0-446-39364-9*) Warner Bks., Inc.

Hill, M. & Kahan, Bob, eds. Batman: The Dark Knight Archives, Vol. 1. 1992. (Batman: The Dark Knight Archives Ser.: Vol. 1). (Illus.). 224p. 49.95 (*1-56389-050-X*) DC Comics.

Jones, Gerard. Fortunate Son. Goodwin, Archie & Gorfinkel, Jordan, eds. 1999. (Batman Ser.). (Illus.). 89p. 24.95 (*1-56389-578-1*) DC Comics.

Kahan, Bob, ed. Batman: Collected Legends of the Dark Knight. 1994. (Illus.). 160p. pap. 12.95 o.p. (*1-56389-147-6*) DC Comics.

—Batman: Featuring Two-Face & the Riddler. 1995. (Illus.). 192p. pap. 12.95 (*1-56389-198-0*) DC Comics.

Kane, Bob. Batman: Knightflight. 1994. 17.00 (*1-57042-081-5*) Warner Bks., Inc.

—Batman: The Dailies 1944-1945, Vol. 2. Poplaski, Peter, ed. 1990. (Batman Ser.). (Illus.). 192p. pap. 12.95 (*0-87816-130-9*) Kitchen Sink Pr., Inc.

—Batman Vol. 1: The Dailies, 1943-1944. Poplaski, Peter, ed. 1990. (Batman Ser.). (Illus.). 192p. pap. 12.95 (*0-87816-119-8*) Kitchen Sink Pr., Inc.

—Batman Vol. 3: 1945-1946. Poplaski, Peter, ed. 1991. (Illus.). 192p. pap. 12.95 (*0-87816-147-3*) Kitchen Sink Pr., Inc.

—Batman in the 60's. 1999. (Illus.). 224p. pap. 19.95 (*1-56389-491-2*) DC Comics.

Kane, Bob & Finger, Bill. Batman Archives. Kahan, Bob et al, eds. 1993. (Batman Archives Ser.: Vol. 3). (Illus.). 224p. 39.95 (*1-56389-099-2*) DC Comics.

Kane, Bob, et al. Batman: The Dailies, 1943-46. Schreiner, Dave, ed. deluxe ed. 1991. (Illus.). 550p. 60.00 (*0-87816-149-X*) Kitchen Sink Pr., Inc.

—Batman: The Sunday Classics, 1943-46. Schreiner, Dave, ed. 1992. (Illus.). 208p. pap. 19.95 (*0-87816-148-1*); bds. 75.00 (*0-87816-163-5*) Kitchen Sink Pr., Inc.

—Batman Archives, Vol. 2. Gold, Mike & Kahan, Bob, eds. 1991. (Batman Archives Ser.: Vol. 2). (Illus.). 288p. 49.95 (*1-56389-000-3*) DC Comics.

Loeb, Jeph. Batman: Haunted Knight. Kahan, Bob, ed. 1996. (Batman Ser.). (Illus.). 192p. pap. 14.95 (*1-56389-273-1*) DC Comics.

—Batman: Hush. 2004. 128p. pap. 12.95 (*1-4012-0060-5*) DC Comics.

—Batman: Long Halloween. 1998. (Illus.). 368p. 29.95 o.p. (*1-56389-427-0*) DC Comics.

—Batman: The Long Halloween. 1999. (Illus.). 368p. pap. 19.95 (*1-56389-469-6*) DC Comics.

—Batman Vol. 2: Hush. 2004. 176p. 19.95 (*1-4012-0084-2*) DC Comics.

Loeb, Jeph & Lee, Jim. Batman: Hush. 2003. (Illus.). 128p. 19.95 (*1-4012-0061-3*) DC Comics.

Maggin, Elliot S. Batman. 1983. (Super Powers Which Way Bks.). (YA). (gr. 8-12). pap. o.p. (*0-671-47565-7*, Simon Pulse) Simon & Schuster Children's Publishing.

Marz, Ron. Aliens. 1998. (Batman Ser.). (Illus.). 128p. (YA). (gr. 9-12). pap. 14.95 o.p. (*1-56971-305-7*) Dark Horse Comics.

Miller, Frank. Batman: Dark Knight. 1999. 12.95 o.s.i (*0-446-38672-3*) Warner Bks., Inc.

—Batman: The Dark Knight Strikes Again. Date not set. 256p. 19.95 (*1-56389-929-9*) DC Comics.

—Batman: Year One. Bruning, Richard, ed. 1988. 208p. 12.95 o.s.i (*0-930289-32-3*) DC Comics.

—Batman Year One. Bruning, Richard, ed. 1997. (Batman Ser.). (Illus.). 96p. mass mkt. 9.95 (*0-930289-33-1*) DC Comics.

—Spawn & Batman. 1994. (Illus.). 52p. pap. 4.95 (*1-58240-019-9*) Image Comics.

Miller, Frank & Mazzucchelli, David. Batman: Year One. 1988. pap. 10.95 o.s.i (*0-446-38923-4*) Warner Bks., Inc.

Miller, Frank & Varley, Lynn. Batman: The Dark Knight Strikes Again. 2002. (Illus.). 256p. 29.95 (*1-56389-844-6*) DC Comics.

—The Dark Knight Strikes Again. 80p. 2001. pap. 7.95 (*1-56389-870-5*); Vol. 2. 2002. pap. 7.95 (*1-56389-871-3*); Vol. 3. 2002. pap. 7.95 (*1-56389-872-1*) DC Comics.

Miller, Frank, et al. Batman: The Dark Knight Returns. 2002. (Illus.). 224p. 24.95 (*1-56389-341-X*) DC Comics.

—Batman: The Dark Knight Returns. 10th anniv. ed. 1997. (Batman Ser.). (Illus.). 224p. pap. 14.95 (*1-56389-342-8*) DC Comics.

Moench, Doug. Batman: Bloodstorm. O'Neil, Dennis, ed. 1995. (Illus.). 96p. pap. 12.95 (*1-56389-185-9*) DC Comics.

—Batman: Crimson Mist. 1998. (Batman Ser.). (Illus.). 96p. 24.95 (*1-56389-477-7*) DC Comics.

—Batman & Dracula: Red Rain. O'Neil, Dennis, ed. 1997. (DC Comics Ser.). (Illus.). 96p. pap. 12.95 (*1-56389-036-4*) DC Comics.

Moench, Doug, et al. Batman: Prey. 1993. 136p. pap. 12.99 o.s.i (*0-446-39521-8*) Warner Bks., Inc.

—Batman: Prodigal. 1998. (Batman Ser.). (Illus.). 288p. pap. 14.95 (*1-56389-334-7*) DC Comics.

—Batman - Spawn: War Devil. O'Neil, Dennis, ed. 1994. (Batman Ser.). (Illus.). 48p. pap. 4.95 (*1-56389-144-1*) DC Comics.

—Batman & Dracula: Red Rain. 1992. 96p. pap. 9.99 o.s.i (*0-446-39465-3*) Warner Bks., Inc.

—Batman vs. Predator II: Bloodmatch. 1995. (Batman Ser.). (Illus.). 144p. pap. 7.95 (*1-56389-221-9*) DC Comics.

Moore, Alan. Batman: The Killing Joke. O'Neil, Dennis, ed. 1995. (Batman Ser.). 48p. mass mkt. 4.95 (*0-930289-45-5*) DC Comics.

Moore, John F. Batman: Poison Ivy. 1997. (Illus.). 48p. (Orig.). pap. 4.95 o.p. (*1-56389-304-5*) DC Comics.

Morrison, Grant. Batman: Arkham Asylum. Berger, Karen, ed. 1997. (DC Comics Ser.). (Illus.). 128p. pap. 14.95 (*0-930289-56-0*) DC Comics.

—Batman: Gothic. Hill, Michael, ed. 1998. 128p. pap. 12.95 (*1-56389-028-3*) DC Comics.

—JLA: American Dreams. 1998. (Illus.). 112p. pap. 7.95 (*1-56389-394-0*) DC Comics.

—JLA: New World Order. 1997. (Illus.). 96p. pap. 5.95 (*1-56389-369-X*) DC Comics.

Morrison, Grant & Janson, Klaus. Batman Gothic. 1992. (Illus.). (Orig.). pap. 12.99 o.s.i (*0-446-39428-9*) Warner Bks., Inc.

Morrison, Grant & McKeon, David. Batman: Arkham Asylum. 1990. pap. 14.95 o.s.i (*0-446-39189-1*) Warner Bks., Inc.

Motter, Dean. Batman: Nine Lives. 2003. 128p. pap. 17.95 (*1-56389-979-5*) DC Comics.

O'Neil, Dennis. Batman: Birth of the Demon. Goodwin, Archie, ed. 1993. (Illus.). 112p. pap. 12.95 o.p. (*1-56389-081-X*) DC Comics.

—Batman: Forever Movie Adaptation. Peterson, ed. 1995. (Illus.). 64p. pap. 5.95 (*1-56389-199-9*) DC Comics.

—Batman: Knightfall. 1995. 416p. mass mkt. 5.99 o.s.i (*0-553-57260-1*, Spectra) Bantam Bks.

—Batman: Shaman. Kahan, Bob, ed. 1998. (Illus.). 136p. pap. 12.95 (*1-56389-083-6*) DC Comics.

—Batman: Sword of Azrael. Kahan, Bob, ed. 1993. (Batman Ser.). (Illus.). 112p. pap. 9.95 (*1-56389-100-X*) DC Comics.

—Batman: Tales of the Demon. O'Neil, Dennis et al, eds. 1998. (Batman Ser.). (Illus.). 208p. pap. 17.95 (*0-930289-94-3*) DC Comics.

—Batman: Venom. Kahan, Bob, ed. 1993. (Illus.). 136p. pap. 9.95 (*1-56389-101-8*) DC Comics.

—Batman - Green Arrow: The Poison Tomorrow. Goodwin, Archie, ed. 1992. (Illus.). 64p. pap. 5.95 (*0-930289-15-3*) DC Comics.

—Batman - Punisher: Lake of Fire. Goodwin, A., ed. 1994. (Illus.). 48p. pap. 4.95 o.p. (*1-56389-161-1*) DC Comics.

—Batman & Robin Movie Adaptation. 1997. (Illus.). 64p. pap. 5.95 o.p. (*1-56389-306-1*) DC Comics.

—Batman in the 70's. 2000. (Illus.). 192p. pap. 19.95 (*1-56389-565-X*) DC Comics.

O'Neil, Dennis, et al. Batman: Shaman. 1993. 136p. pap. 12.99 o.s.i (*0-446-39522-6*) Warner Bks., Inc.

—Batman: The Movies. 1997. (Batman Ser.). (Illus.). 280p. pap. 19.95 (*1-56389-326-6*) DC Comics.

Puckett, Kelley. The Batman: Adventures. Kahan, Bob, ed. 1993. (Illus.). 144p. pap. 7.95 (*1-56389-098-4*) DC Comics.

—Batman: Batgirl. 1997. (Illus.). 48p. (Orig.). pap. 4.95 o.p. (*1-56389-305-3*) DC Comics.

—Batman: Dark Knight Adventure, Vol. 2. Kahan, Bob, ed. 1994. (Batman Adventures Ser.). (Illus.). 144p. mass mkt. 7.95 (*1-56389-124-7*) DC Comics.

—Batman's Dark Secret. 2000. (Hello Reader! Ser.). (Illus.). 32p. (J). (gr. 1-3). mass mkt. 3.99 (*0-439-09551-4*) Scholastic, Inc.

Rucka, Greg. Batman: Evolution. 2001. (Batman Ser.). (Illus.). 224p. pap. 12.95 (*1-56389-726-1*) DC Comics.

—Batman: No Man's Land. 2000. (Illus.). 448p. 23.95 o.s.i (*0-671-03828-1*, Atria); 2001. 480p. reprint ed. mass mkt. 6.99 (*0-671-77455-7*, Pocket Star) Simon & Schuster.

—Batman: No Man's Land. 2000. (Illus.). (J). 10.04 (*0-606-18364-7*) Turtleback Bks.

—Batman Vol. 3: No Man's Land. 2000. (Batman Ser.: Vol. 3). (Illus.). 208p. pap. 12.95 (*1-56389-634-6*) DC Comics.

Rucka, Greg & Brubaker, Ed. New Gotham 2: Officer Down. 2001. (Batman Ser.). 168p. pap. text 12.95 (*1-56389-787-3*) DC Comics.

Rucka, Greg, et al. Batman: Bruce Wayne Fugitive, Vol. 2. 2003. 176p. pap. 12.95 (*1-56389-947-7*) DC Comics.

Starlin, Jim. Batman: Death in the Family. O'Neil, Dennis, ed. 1988. (Batman Ser.). (Illus.). 144p. pap. 12.95 (*0-930289-44-7*) DC Comics.

Taylor, Dave, illus. Batman: Cataclysm. 1999. (Batman Ser.). 317p. pap. 19.95 (*1-56389-527-7*) DC Comics.

Vachss, Andrew. Batman: The Ultimate Evil. abr. ed. 1995. audio 17.00 (*1-57042-275-3*) Time Warner AudioBooks.

—Batman: The Ultimate Evil. 196p. 1996. mass mkt. 5.99 (*0-446-60336-8*); 1995. 19.95 o.s.i (*0-446-51912-X*) Warner Bks., Inc. (Aspect).

Vachss, Andrew & Hechler, David. Batman: The Ultimate Evil. 2001. 196p. reprint ed. 20.00 (*0-7881-9977-3*) DIANE Publishing Co.

Wagner, John & Grant, Alan. Batman - Judge Dredd: Judgement on Gotham. O'Neil, Dennis, ed. 1991. (Illus.). 64p. pap. 5.95 (*1-56389-022-4*) DC Comics.

Wagner, Matt. Batman: Faces. Kahan, Bob, ed. 1995. (Illus.). 96p. pap. 9.95 (*1-56389-126-3*) DC Comics.

—Batman: Riddler-The Riddle Factory. O'Neil, Dennis, ed. 1995. (Illus.). 48p. pap. 4.95 (*1-56389-196-4*) DC Comics.

Wein, Len. The Untold Legend of the Batman. 1992. 128p. mass mkt. 3.50 (*0-8125-2042-4*, Tor Bks.) Doherty, Tom Assocs., LLC.
Wolfman, Marv. Batman: A Lonely Place of Dying. Carlson, K. C., ed. 1998. (Illus.). 128p. pap. 5.95 (*0-930289-63-3*) DC Comics.

**BATTLE, SUPERINTENDENT (FICTITIOUS CHARACTER)—FICTION**

Christie, Agatha. Cards on the Table. mass mkt. 3.50 o.s.i (*0-425-12577-7*); 2001. E-Book 5.99 (*0-425-17790-4*); 1998. mass mkt. 3.99 o.s.i (*0-425-16924-3*); 1986. mass mkt. 2.95 o.s.i (*0-425-09317-4*); 1984. mass mkt. 2.95 o.s.i (*0-425-06778-5*) Berkley Publishing Group.
—Cards on the Table. 1980. pap. 2.95 o.p. (*0-440-11052-1*) Dell Publishing.
—Cards on the Table. 1987. (Agatha Christie Ser.). 14.95 (*0-396-09010-9*, G. P. Putnam's Sons) Penguin Putnam Bks. for Young Readers.
—Cards on the Table. 1984. (Hercule Poirot Mystery Ser.). 12.04 (*0-606-12211-7*) Turtleback Bks.
—The Cards on the Table. 1987. (Hercule Poirot Mystery Ser.). 224p. mass mkt. 5.99 (*0-425-10567-9*) Berkley Publishing Group.
—Cards on the Table. l.t. ed. 1983. 352p. 12.50 o.p. (*0-7089-1151-X*, Ulverscroft) Thorpe, F. A. Pubs. GBR. *Dist:* Ulverscroft Large Print Bks., Ltd.

**BAUER, TORY (FICTITIOUS CHARACTER)—FICTION**

Taylor, Kathleen. Cold Front. 2000. (Tory Bauer Mystery Ser.). 352p. mass mkt. 5.99 (*0-380-81204-5*, Avon Bks.) Morrow/Avon.
—Funeral Food. 1998. (Tory Bauer Mystery Ser.). 256p. mass mkt. 5.99 (*0-380-79380-6*, Avon Bks.) Morrow/Avon.
—Hotel South Dakota. 1997. (Tory Bauer Mystery Ser.). 304p. mass mkt. 6.50 (*0-380-78356-8*, Avon Bks.) Morrow/Avon.
—Mourning Shift. 1998. (Tory Bauer Mystery Ser.: No. 4). 288p. mass mkt. 5.99 (*0-380-79943-X*, Avon Bks.) Morrow/Avon.
—Sex & Salmonella. 1996. 288p. (Orig.). mass mkt. 5.50 (*0-380-78355-X*, Avon Bks.) Morrow/Avon.

**BAUER, VICKY (FICTITIOUS CHARACTER)—FICTION**

Gom, Leona. After-Image: A Vicky Bauer Mystery. 310p. pap. 14.95 (*0-929005-91-0*) Second Story Pr. CAN. *Dist:* Orca Bk. Pubs.
—After-Image: A Vicky Bauer Mystery. 1996. 256p. 22.95 o.p. (*0-312-14537-3*, Saint Martin's Minotaur) St. Martin's Pr.
—Double Negative: A Vicky Bauer Mystery. 1998. 476p. pap. 12.95 (*1-896764-07-X*) Second Story Pr. CAN. *Dist:* LPC/InBook.

**BAUM, STEVEN (FICTITIOUS CHARACTER)—FICTION**

Blauner, Peter. Slow Motion Riot. 1992. 384p. pap. 6.99 (*0-380-71306-3*, Avon Bks.); 1991. 352p. 20.00 o.p. (*0-688-10068-6*, Morrow, William & Co.) Morrow/Avon.

**BAUMANN, HENRIK (FICTITIOUS CHARACTER)—FICTION**

Finder, Joseph. The Zero Hour. abr. ed. 1996. audio 16.95 o.p. (*1-56100-888-5*, 1119, Nova Audio Bks.); 1996. audio 25.95 o.p. (*1-56100-687-4*, 326, Bookcassette); 1996. audio 89.25 o.p. (*1-56100-312-3*, 1118, Unabridged Library Editions); Set. 1997. audio 7.99 o.p. (*1-56740-165-1*, 721, Nova Audio Bks.) Brilliance Audio.
—The Zero Hour. l.t. ed. 1996. (G. K. Hall Core Ser.). 630p. lib. bdg. 25.95 (*0-7838-1825-4*, Macmillan Reference USA) Gale Group.
—The Zero Hour. 1997. pap. 6.99 (*0-380-72665-3*, Avon Bks.); 1996. 432p. 25.00 o.p. (*0-688-14450-0*, Morrow, William & Co.) Morrow/Avon.

**BAXTER, JENNIFER (FICTITIOUS CHARACTER)—FICTION**

Coffman, Elaine. Escape Not My Love. 1997. mass mkt. 5.99 o.s.i (*0-449-15057-7*, Fawcett) Ballantine Bks.
—Escape Not My Love. 1990. 468p. reprint ed. mass mkt. 4.50 o.s.i (*0-440-20529-8*, Dell Bks.) Dell Publishing.
—Escape Not My Love. l.t. ed. 1997. (Large Print Book Ser.). 26.95 (*1-56895-509-X*, Wheeler Publishing, Inc.) Gale Group.

**BAYLES, CHINA (FICTITIOUS CHARACTER)—FICTION**

Albert, Susan Wittig. Bloodroot. 2003. 320p. reprint ed. mass mkt. 6.99 (*0-425-18814-0*) Berkley Publishing Group.
—Bloodroot. l.t. ed. 2002. (Mystery Ser.). 427p. 30.95 o.p. (*0-7862-3841-0*) Gale Group.
—Bloodroot: A China Bayles Mystery. 2001. 320p. 22.95 (*0-425-18190-1*, Prime Crime) Berkley Publishing Group.
—Chile Death. 1999. (West Coast Crime Ser.: No. 7). 320p. reprint ed. mass mkt. 6.99 (*0-425-17147-7*, Prime Crime) Berkley Publishing Group.
—Chile Death. abr. ed. 1999. (China Bayles Mystery Ser.). audio 17.95 (*1-56511-323-3*) HighBridge Co.
—Chile Death: A China Bayles Mystery. 1998. (China Bayles Mystery Ser.). 320p. 21.95 o.s.i (*0-425-16539-6*, Prime Crime) Berkley Publishing Group.
—Chile Death: A China Bayles Mystery. l.t. ed. 2001. 435p. 29.95 (*0-7862-3161-0*) Thorndike Pr.
—Hangman's Root: A China Bayles Mystery. 1995. 272p. mass mkt. 6.99 (*0-425-14898-X*) Berkley Publishing Group.
—Hangman's Root: A China Bayles Mystery. 1994. 256p. 20.00 (*0-684-19677-8*); 1995. 319p. pap. 19.95 (*0-7838-1246-9*) Gale Group. (Macmillan Reference USA).
—Indigo Dying. 2004. 288p. mass mkt. 6.99 (*0-425-19377-2*); 2003. 320p. 22.95 (*0-425-18828-0*) Berkley Publishing Group.
—Lavender Lies. 2000. (Prime Crime Mysteries Ser.). 320p. reprint ed. mass mkt. 6.99 (*0-425-17700-9*) Berkley Publishing Group.
—Lavender Lies. abr. ed. 1999. (China Bayles Mystery Ser.). audio 17.95 (*1-56511-332-2*) HighBridge Co.
—Lavender Lies: A China Bayles Mystery. 1999. (China Bayles Mystery Ser.: No. 8). 320p. 21.95 o.s.i (*0-425-17032-2*, Prime Crime) Berkley Publishing Group.
—Lavender Lies: A China Bayles Mystery. l.t. ed. 2001. 437p. o.p. (*0-7862-3162-9*) Thorndike Pr.
—Love Lies Bleeding: A China Bayles Mystery. (China Bayles Mystery Ser.). 1997. 320p. 21.95 o.s.i (*0-425-15969-8*); 1998. 336p. reprint ed. mass mkt. 6.99 (*0-425-16611-2*) Berkley Publishing Group. (Prime Crime).
—Mistletoe Man: A China Bayles Mystery. 2000. (China Bayles Ser.). 304p. 21.95 o.s.i (*0-425-17673-8*) Berkley Publishing Group.
—Mistletoe Man: A China Bayles Mystery. l.t. ed. 2001. (Thorndike Mystery Ser.). 408p. 29.95 (*0-7862-3163-7*) Thorndike Pr.
—The Mistletoe Man: A China Bayles Mystery. 2001. 320p. reprint ed. mass mkt. 6.99 (*0-425-18201-0*, Prime Crime) Berkley Publishing Group.
—Rosemary Remembered: A China Bayles Mystery. 304p. 1996. mass mkt. 6.99 (*0-425-15405-X*); 1995. 19.95 o.p. (*0-425-14937-4*, Prime Crime) Berkley Publishing Group.
—Rueful Death: A China Bayles Mystery. 1996. 320p. 21.95 o.p. (*0-425-15469-6*); 1997. 304p. reprint ed. mass mkt. 6.99 (*0-425-15941-8*, Prime Crime) Berkley Publishing Group.
—Thyme of Death: A Mystery Introducing China Bayles. 1994. (West Coast Crime Ser.). 320p. mass mkt. 6.99 (*0-425-14098-9*) Berkley Publishing Group.
—Thyme of Death: A Mystery Introducing China Bayles. 1992. 256p. bds. 20.00 o.s.i (*0-684-19522-4*, Scribner) Simon & Schuster.
—Unthymely Death: And Other Garden Mysteries. 2003. 272p. pap. 14.00 (*0-425-19002-1*) Berkley Publishing Group.
—Witches' Bane: A China Bayles Mystery. 1994. 272p. reprint ed. mass mkt. 6.99 (*0-425-14406-2*, Prime Crime) Berkley Publishing Group.
—Witches' Bane: A China Bayles Mystery. 1993. 256p. bds. 20.00 o.p. (*0-684-19636-0*, Scribner) Simon & Schuster.

**BAYLOR, RUDY (FICTITIOUS CHARACTER)—FICTION**

Grisham, John. The Rainmaker. abr. ed. audio 22.95 Books on Tape, Inc.
—The Rainmaker. 1996. 608p. mass mkt. 7.99 (*0-440-22165-X*); 1995. (YA). mass mkt. 9.99 o.s.i (*0-440-91092-7*) Dell Publishing.
—The Rainmaker. 1995. (YA). mass mkt. 7.50 (*0-440-29542-4*); 448p. 27.95 (*0-385-42473-6*); 784p. 29.95 o.s.i (*0-385-47512-8*); (YA). 250.00 o.s.i (*0-385-47513-6*) Doubleday Publishing.
—The Rainmaker. unabr. ed. 1999. audio 49.95 Highsmith Inc.
—The Rainmaker, Level 5. 2000. (Penguin Reader Ser.). pap. 7.93 (*0-582-36412-4*) Longman Publishing Group.
—The Rainmaker. abr. ed. 1995. audio 27.95 (*0-553-47305-0*, 692837, RH Audio) Random Hse. Audio Publishing Group.

**BAYNES FAMILY (FICTITIOUS CHARACTERS)—FICTION**

McCord, John S. The California Eagles. 1995. (Baynes Clan Ser.: No. 4). 256p. mass mkt. 4.99 o.s.i (*0-515-11725-0*, Jove) Berkley Publishing Group.
—Kansas Gambler. 1997. (Baynes Clan Ser.). 224p. mass mkt. 4.99 o.s.i (*0-425-15719-9*) Berkley Publishing Group.
—Montana Horseman, Vol. 1. 1995. (Baynes Clan Ser.). 256p. mass mkt. 4.99 o.s.i (*0-515-11532-0*, Jove) Berkley Publishing Group.
—Montana Horsemen. 1990. (Baynes Clan Ser.). 192p. 14.95 o.s.i (*0-385-41102-2*) Doubleday Publishing.
—Nevada Tough. 1996. mass mkt. 4.99 o.s.i (*0-425-14982-X*) Berkley Publishing Group.
—Texas Comebacker. 1991. 192p. 15.00 o.s.i (*0-385-41497-8*) Doubleday Publishing.
—Texas Comebacker No. 2. 1995. 256p. (Orig.). mass mkt. 4.99 o.s.i (*0-515-11585-1*, Jove) Berkley Publishing Group.
—Wyoming Giant No. 3. 1995. 256p. mass mkt. 4.99 o.s.i (*0-515-11651-3*, Jove) Berkley Publishing Group.

**BEACH, TONY (FICTITIOUS CHARACTER)—FICTION**

Francis, Dick. Proof. 1999. audio 34.95 (*0-7540-7529-X*); 1993. audio 69.95 (*0-7451-4114-5*, CAB 797) BBC Audiobooks America.
—Proof. l.t. ed. 1986. 352p. mass mkt. 5.95 o.s.i (*0-449-20754-4*, Fawcett) Ballantine Bks.
—Proof. 1997. 368p. mass mkt. 6.99 (*0-515-12120-7*, Jove) Berkley Publishing Group.
—Proof. unabr. ed. 2000. audio 59.95 Chivers Audio Bks. GBR. *Dist:* BBC Audiobooks America.
—Proof. abr. ed. 1985. audio 16.99 (*0-88646-133-2*, 7134) Durkin Hayes Publishing Ltd.
—Proof. l.t. ed. 1985. (General Ser.). 465p. 17.95 o.p. (*0-8161-3927-X*); 10.95 o.p. (*0-8161-3944-X*) Gale Group. (Macmillan Reference USA).
—Proof. 1985. 324p. 16.95 o.p. (*0-399-13036-5*, G. P. Putnam's Sons) Penguin Putnam Bks. for Young Readers.
—Proof. 1993. audio 15.99 o.s.i (*0-553-47144-9*, RH Audio) Random Hse. Audio Publishing Group.
—Proof. unabr. ed. 1985. audio 60.00 (*0-7887-3485-7*, 95768E7) Recorded Bks., LLC.
—Proof. l.t. ed. 1993. 39.95 (*0-7066-1001-6*) Remploy Pr. CAN. *Dist:* State Mutual Bk. & Periodical Service, Ltd.

**BEAMON, MARK (FICTITIOUS CHARACTER)—FICTION**

Mills, Kyle. Free Fall. 2000. audio compact disk 96.00 (*0-7366-6071-2*); 2001. audio 80.00 (*0-7366-5449-6*); 2001. audio compact disk 96.00 Books on Tape, Inc.
—Free Fall. 2000. 400p. 25.00 (*0-06-019333-6*); 640p. pap. 25.00 (*0-06-095575-9*) HarperCollins Pubs.
—Free Fall. abr. ed. 2000. audio 25.00 (*0-694-52171-X*, HarperAudio) HarperTrade.
—Free Fall. 2001. 496p. mass mkt. 7.50 (*0-06-109802-7*, Avon Bks.) Morrow/Avon.
—Rising Phoenix. 1998. audio compact disk 88.00 (*0-7366-8535-9*); audio 72.00 (*0-7366-4119-X*, 4623) Books on Tape, Inc.
—Rising Phoenix. 1997. 384p. 24.00 o.p. (*0-06-101248-3*) HarperCollins Pubs.
—Rising Phoenix. abr. ed. 2000. audio 9.99 (*0-694-52327-5*); 1997. audio 18.00 o.s.i (*0-694-51890-5*, CPN 2696) HarperTrade. (HarperAudio).
—Rising Phoenix. 1998. 528p. mass mkt. 7.99 (*0-06-101249-1*, HarperTorch) Morrow/Avon.
—Storming Heaven. 1998. audio compact disk 80.00 (*0-7366-8286-4*); 1999. audio 64.00 (*0-7366-4278-1*, 4776) Books on Tape, Inc.
—Storming Heaven. 2000. 528p. mass mkt. 6.99 (*0-06-101251-3*); 1998. 400p. 25.00 o.s.i (*0-06-101250-5*) HarperCollins Pubs.
—Storming Heaven, Set. abr. ed. 1998. audio 18.00 o.s.i (*0-694-51971-5*, HarperAudio) HarperTrade.

**BEAN, MADELINE (FICTITIOUS CHARACTER)—FICTION**

Farmer, Jerrilyn. Immaculate Reception. l.t. ed. 2002. (Mystery Ser.). 396p. 28.95 (*0-7862-4755-X*) Gale Group.
—Immaculate Reception. 1999. (Madeline Bean Catering Mysteries Ser.). 256p. mass mkt. 6.50 (*0-380-79597-3*, Avon Bks.) Morrow/Avon.
—Killer Wedding. 2000. (Madeline Bean Catering Mysteries Ser.). 256p. mass mkt. 6.50 (*0-380-79598-1*, Avon Bks.) Morrow/Avon.
—Mumbo Gumbo: A Madeline Bean Novel. 2004. 368p. mass mkt. 6.99 (*0-380-81719-5*, Avon Bks.); 2003. 272p. 19.95 (*0-380-97889-X*, Morrow, William & Co.) Morrow/Avon.
—Perfect Sax: A Madeline Bean Novel. 2004. 304p. 22.95 (*0-380-97890-3*, Morrow, William & Co.) Morrow/Avon.
—Sympathy for the Devil. 1998. (Madeline Bean Mystery Ser.). 256p. mass mkt. 5.99 (*0-380-79596-5*, Avon Bks.) Morrow/Avon.
—Sympathy for the Devil. l.t. ed. 2002. (Mystery Ser.). 404p. 28.95 (*0-7862-4743-6*) Thorndike Pr.

**BEAN, QUEENIE (FICTITIOUS CHARACTER)—FICTION**

Dallas, Sandra. The Persian Pickle Club, Set. abr. ed. 1995. audio 22.95 (*1-56876-047-7*, 693294) Soundlines Entertainment, Inc.
—The Persian Pickle Club. 208p. 1995. 20.95 o.p. (*0-312-13586-6*); 1996. reprint ed. pap. 12.95 (*0-312-14701-5*, NPB 0319, Saint Martin's Griffin) St. Martin's Pr.
—The Persian Pickle Club. l.t. ed. 1998. (Niagara Large Print Ser.). 270p. 29.50 o.p. (*0-7089-5856-7*, Linford) Thorpe, F. A. Pubs. GBR. *Dist:* Ulverscroft Large Print Bks., Ltd., Ulverscroft Large Print Canada, Ltd.

**BEANBLOSSOM, RICK (FICTITIOUS CHARACTER)—FICTION**

Thayer, Steve. Silent Snow. 2000. 416p. reprint ed. mass mkt. 6.99 (*0-451-18664-8*, Signet Bks.) NAL.
—Silent Snow. abr. ed. 2000. audio 18.00 (*0-7871-1980-6*); 1999. audio 30.00 (*0-7871-1979-2*) NewStar Media, Inc. (Dove Audio).
—Silent Snow, unabr. ed. 1999. audio 66.00 (*0-7887-3767-8*, 95984E7) Recorded Bks., LLC.
—Silent Snow. 1999. 416p. 24.95 o.s.i (*0-670-86572-9*, Viking) Viking Penguin.
—The Weatherman. 1996. 416p. mass mkt. 7.99 (*0-451-18438-6*, Signet Bks.) NAL.
—The Weatherman, Set. abr. ed. 1995. audio 16.95 (*1-879371-88-X*, 391877) Publishing Mills, Inc., The.
—The Weatherman. unabr. ed. 1995. audio 91.00 (*0-7887-0267-X*, 94476E7) Recorded Bks., LLC.
—The Weatherman. 1995. 22.95 (*0-670-77309-3*); 464p. 21.95 o.s.i (*0-670-84958-8*, Viking) Viking Penguin.

**BEAR, GOLDY (FICTITIOUS CHARACTER)—FICTION**

Davidson, Diane Mott. Catering to Nobody. 1998. pap. 5.99 (*0-449-45882-2*); 1998. pap. 5.99 (*0-449-45833-4*); 1992. 320p. reprint ed. mass mkt. 5.99 o.s.i (*0-449-22046-X*) Ballantine Bks. (Fawcett).
—Catering to Nobody. l.t. ed. 1999. (Beeler Large Print Mystery Ser.). 25.95 (*1-57490-204-0*, Beeler Large Print Bks.) Beeler, Thomas T. Publisher.
—Catering to Nobody. abr. ed. 2001. (Culinary Mysteries Ser.). audio 7.95 (*1-57815-191-0*, Media Bks. Audio Publishing) Media Bks., L. L. C.
—Catering to Nobody. unabr. ed. 2003. audio compact disk 49.95 (*1-59007-436-X*) New Millennium Entertainment.
—Catering to Nobody, abr. ed. 1996. audio 16.95 (*1-57511-020-2*) Publishing Mills, Inc., The.
—Catering to Nobody. unabr. ed. 2001. audio compact disk 78.00 (*0-7887-7163-9*, C1416); 1999. (Catering Mystery Ser.: Vol. 1). audio 51.00 (*0-7887-0647-0*, 94824E7) Recorded Bks., LLC.
—Catering to Nobody. 1990. 17.95 (*0-312-04277-9*, Saint Martin's Minotaur) St. Martin's Pr.
—The Cereal Murders. 1994. 368p. mass mkt. 6.99 (*0-553-56773-X*) Bantam Bks.
—The Cereal Murders. l.t. ed. 1999. pap. 23.95 o.p. (*1-56895-743-2*, Wheeler Publishing, Inc.) Gale Group.
—The Cereal Murders. abr. ed. 2001. (Culinary Mysteries Ser.). audio 7.95 (*1-57815-192-9*, Media Bks. Audio Publishing) Media Bks., L. L. C.
—The Cereal Murders. unabr. ed. 2003. audio compact disk 49.95 (*1-59007-437-8*) New Millennium Entertainment.
—The Cereal Murders. abr. ed. 1994. (Goldy Bear Mystery Ser.). audio 16.95 Publishing Mills, Inc., The.
—The Cereal Murders. unabr. ed. 1997. (Catering Mystery Ser.: Vol. 4). audio 60.00 (*0-7887-0721-3*, 94898E7) Recorded Bks., LLC.
—Chopping Spree. 2003. 368p. mass mkt. 6.99 (*0-553-57835-9*); 2002. 320p. 23.95 (*0-553-10730-5*) Bantam Bks.
—Chopping Spree. l.t. ed. pap. o.p. (*0-7862-4677-4*); 2003. 484p. 13.95 (*1-4104-0085-9*); 2002. 484p. 32.95 (*0-7862-4676-6*) Thorndike Pr.
—Dying for Chocolate. 1993. (Culinary Mysteries Ser.). (Illus.). 352p. mass mkt. 6.99 (*0-553-56024-7*) Bantam Bks.
—Dying for Chocolate. l.t. ed. 2000. pap. 22.95 o.p. (*1-56895-821-8*, Wheeler Publishing, Inc.) Gale Group.
—Dying for Chocolate, abr. ed. 2000. (Culinary Mysteries Ser.). audio 7.95 (*1-57815-142-2*, 1101, Media Bks. Audio Publishing) Media Bks., L. L. C.
—Dying for Chocolate. unabr. ed. 2003. audio compact disk 55.00 (*1-59007-438-6*) New Millennium Entertainment.
—Dying for Chocolate. abr. ed. 1995. (Culinary Mysteries Ser.). audio 16.95 (*1-879371-78-2*, 393464) Publishing Mills, Inc., The.
—Dying for Chocolate. unabr. ed. 1996. audio 60.00 (*0-7887-0576-8*, 94754E7) Recorded Bks., LLC.
—The Grilling Season. 1998. 432p. reprint ed. mass mkt. 6.99 (*0-553-57466-3*) Bantam Bks.
—The Grilling Season. abr. ed. 1997. (Culinary Mysteries Ser.). audio 22.95 (*0-553-47912-1*, 695429, RH Audio) Random Hse. Audio Publishing Group.
—Killer Pancake. 1996. 368p. mass mkt. 6.99 (*0-553-57204-0*) Bantam Bks.
—Killer Pancake. abr. ed. 2001. (Culinary Mysteries Ser.). audio 7.95 (*1-57815-193-7*, Media Bks. Audio Publishing) Media Bks., L. L. C.
—Killer Pancake. unabr. ed. 2003. audio compact disk 59.95 (*1-59007-439-4*) New Millennium Entertainment.

—Killer Pancake, Set. abr. ed. 1995. (Cordon Bleu Ser.). audio 16.95 (*1-57511-005-9*, 393521) Publishing Mills, Inc., The.

—Killer Pancake. unabr. ed. 1997. (Catering Mystery Ser.: Vol. 6). audio 70.00 (*0-7887-0837-6*, 94982E7) Recorded Bks., LLC.

—The Last Suppers. 1995. 304p. mass mkt. 6.99 (*0-553-57258-X*, Crimeline) Bantam Bks.

—The Last Suppers. l.t. ed. 1999. pap. 24.95 o.p. (*1-56895-640-1*, Wheeler Publishing, Inc.) Gale Group.

—The Last Suppers. abr. ed. 2001. (Culinary Mysteries Ser.). audio 7.95 (*1-57815-194-5*, Media Bks. Audio Publishing) Media Bks., L. L. C.

—The Last Suppers. abr. ed. 1994. audio 16.95 (*1-879371-75-8*, 40290);Set. 3p. audio 16.95 o.p. (*1-879371-77-4*) Publishing Mills, Inc., The.

—The Last Suppers. unabr. ed. 1997. (Catering Mystery Ser.: Vol. 5). audio 60.00 (*0-7887-0666-7*, 94843E7) Recorded Bks., LLC.

—The Main Corpse. 1997. (Culinary Mysteries Ser.). 384p. reprint ed. mass mkt. 6.99 (*0-553-57463-9*, Crimeline) Bantam Bks.

—The Main Corpse. l.t. ed. 1997. (Large Print Bks.). 25.95 o.p. (*1-56895-409-3*, Wheeler Publishing, Inc.) Gale Group.

—The Main Corpse. abr. ed. (Culinary Mysteries Ser.). 1996. audio 12.99 (*1-57815-209-7*); 2002. audio compact disk 14.99 (*1-57815-547-9*, 4423CD5) Media Bks., L. L. C. (Media Bks. Audio Publishing).

—The Main Corpse. abr. ed. 1996. (Cordon Bleu Ser.). audio 24.95 (*1-57511-019-9*, 694404) Publishing Mills, Inc., The.

—The Main Corpse. unabr. ed. 1996. (Catering Mystery Ser.: Vol. 3). audio. audio 60.00 (*0-7887-0788-4*, 94931E7) Recorded Bks., LLC.

—Prime Cut. 2000. (Illus.). 384p. reprint ed. mass mkt. 6.99 (*0-553-57467-1*) Bantam Bks.

—Prime Cut. l.t. ed. 1999. 27.95 o.p. (*1-56895-588-X*, Wheeler Publishing, Inc.) Gale Group.

—Prime Cut. abr. ed. 1998. (Culinary Mysteries Ser.). audio 25.00 (*0-553-52535-2*, 693716, RH Audio) Random Hse. Audio Publishing Group.

—Prime Cut. unabr. ed. 1999. (Catering Mystery Ser.). audio 72.00 (*0-7887-2922-5*, 95647E7); audio compact disk 83.00 (*0-7887-3432-6*, C1038E7) Recorded Bks., LLC.

—Sticks & Scones. l.t. ed. 2001. (Large Print Book Ser.). 410p. 29.95 (*1-58724-027-0*, Wheeler Publishing, Inc.) Gale Group.

—Sticks & Scones. abr. ed. 2001. audio 25.00 (*0-553-52767-3*, RH Audio) Random Hse. Audio Publishing Group.

—Sticks & Scones. unabr. ed. 2001. audio 78.00 (*0-7887-5316-9*) Recorded Bks., LLC.

—Tough Cookie. 2001. 336p. reprint ed. mass mkt. 6.99 (*0-553-57830-8*, Fanfare) Bantam Bks.

—Tough Cookie. l.t. ed. 2001. pap. 12.95 o.p. (*1-56895-149-3*); 2000. 31.95 (*1-56895-892-7*) Gale Group. (Wheeler Publishing, Inc.).

—Tough Cookie. abr. ed. 2000. (Culinary Mysteries Ser.). audio 25.00 (*0-553-52687-1*, RH Audio) Random Hse. Audio Publishing Group.

—Tough Cookie. unabr. ed. 2001. (Catering Mystery Ser.: Vol. 9). audio 37.95 (*0-7887-4352-X*, 96268 ) Recorded Bks., LLC.

## BEARPAW, MOLLY (FICTITIOUS CHARACTER)—FICTION

Hager, Jean. Ravenmocker. 1992. 272p. 17.95 (*0-89296-493-6*) Mysterious Pr.

—Ravenmocker. 1994. 256p. reprint ed. mass mkt. 5.99 o.s.i (*0-446-40107-2*) Warner Bks., Inc.

—The Redbird's Cry. l.t. ed. 1994. 357p. pap. 18.95 (*0-8161-7402-4*, Macmillan Reference USA) Gale Group.

—The Redbird's Cry. 1994. 288p. 18.95 (*0-89296-494-4*) Mysterious Pr.

—The Redbird's Cry. 1995. 256p. reprint ed. mass mkt. 5.50 (*0-446-40106-4*) Warner Bks., Inc.

—Seven Black Stones. 1995. (Molly Bearpaw Ser.). 304p. 18.95 o.s.i (*0-89296-565-7*) Mysterious Pr.

—Seven Black Stones. 1996. 256p. reprint ed. mass mkt. 5.99 (*0-446-40386-5*) Warner Bks., Inc.

—The Spirit Caller. 1997. 272p. 21.50 o.p. (*0-89296-640-8*) Mysterious Pr.

—The Spirit Caller. 1998. mass mkt. (*0-446-40488-8*, Mysterious Pr. Paperback Bks.); 320p. mass mkt. 6.99 (*0-446-60595-6*) Warner Bks., Inc.

## BEATTY, JIM (FICTITIOUS CHARACTER)—FICTION

Cummings, Jack. Dead Man's Medal. 1992. 256p. reprint ed. mass mkt. 3.50 o.p. (*1-55817-664-0*, Pinnacle Bks.) Kensington Publishing Corp.

—Dead Man's Medal. 1984. (Western Ser.). 192p. 12.95 o.s.i (*0-8027-4028-6*) Walker & Co.

## BEAUMONT, INGRID (FICTITIOUS CHARACTER)—FICTION

Dietz, Denise. Footprints in the Butter: An Ingrid Beaumont Mystery Co-Starring Hitchcock the Dog. 1999. 224p. 21.95 (*0-9663397-2-X*, 16579330) Delphi Bks.

## BEAUMONT, J. P. (FICTITIOUS CHARACTER)—FICTION

Jance, J. A. Birds of Prey: A Novel of Suspense. unabr. ed. 2001. (J. P. Beaumont Mystery Ser.: Bk. 15). audio 64.95 (*1-58116-149-2*); audio compact disk 71.50 (*1-58116-150-6*) Books in Motion.

—Birds of Prey: A Novel of Suspense. abr. ed. 2001. audio 25.95 (*0-694-52499-9*, HarperAudio); 464p. pap. 24.00 (*0-06-018562-7*, HarperLargePrint) HarperTrade.

—Birds of Prey: A Novel of Suspense. 2002. 416p. mass mkt. 7.99 (*0-380-71654-2*); 2001. 390p. 24.00 (*0-380-97407-X*, Morrow, William & Co.) Morrow/Avon.

—Birds of Prey: A Novel of Suspense. unabr. ed. audio 37.95 (*0-7887-9033-1*, RF326) Recorded Bks., LLC.

—Breach of Duty. unabr. ed. 1999. (J. P. Beaumont Mystery Ser.: Bk. 14). audio 49.95 (*1-55686-897-9*) Books in Motion.

—Breach of Duty. 1999. (J. P. Beaumont Mystery Ser.). 384p. mass mkt. 7.50 (*0-380-71843-X*); 352p. 23.00 (*0-380-97406-1*) Morrow/Avon. (Avon Bks.).

—Breach of Duty. 2002. (Famous Authors Ser.). 29.95 (*0-7862-4758-4*) Thorndike Pr.

—Dismissed with Prejudice. unabr. ed. 1993. (J. P. Beaumont Mystery Ser.: Bk. 7). audio 39.95 (*1-55686-474-4*, 752465) Books in Motion.

—Dismissed with Prejudice. 1989. (J. P. Beaumont Mystery Ser.). 384p. mass mkt. 7.50 (*0-380-75547-5*, Avon Bks.) Morrow/Avon.

—Dismissed with Prejudice. 2003. (J. P. Beaumont Mystery Ser.). 384p. 26.99 (*0-7278-5981-1*) Severn Hse. Pubs., Ltd.

—Failure to Appear. unabr. ed. 1995. (J. P. Beaumont Mystery Ser.: Bk. 11). audio 49.95 (*1-55686-562-7*, 892559) Books in Motion.

—Failure to Appear. unabr. collector's ed. 1998. (J. P. Beaumont Ser.: Vol. 11). audio 56.00 (*0-7366-4042-8*, 4541) Books on Tape, Inc.

—Failure to Appear. (J. P. Beaumont Mystery Ser.). 1994. 384p. mass mkt. 7.50 (*0-380-75839-3*, Avon Bks.); 1993. 269p. 20.00 o.p. (*0-688-12674-X*, Morrow, William & Co.) Morrow/Avon.

—Failure to Appear. 2003. (Famous Authors Ser.). 29.95 (*0-7862-4760-6*) Thorndike Pr.

—Hour of the Hunter. unabr. ed. 1994. (Joanna Brady Mystery Ser.). audio 64.95 (*1-55686-470-1*, 112714) Books in Motion.

—Hour of the Hunter. (J. P. Beaumont Mystery Ser.). 1992. 416p. mass mkt. 7.99 (*0-380-71107-9*, Avon Bks.); 1991. 356p. 20.00 o.p. (*0-688-09630-1*, Morrow, William & Co.) Morrow/Avon.

—Hour of the Hunter. l.t. ed. 2003. 669p. 29.95 (*0-7862-5321-5*) Thorndike Pr.

—Improbable Cause. unabr. ed. 1993. (J. P. Beaumont Mystery Ser.: Bk. 5). audio 39.95 (*1-55686-462-0*, 752414) Books in Motion.

—Improbable Cause. unabr. collector's ed. 1997. (J. P. Beaumont Ser.). audio 48.00 (*0-7366-3609-9*, 4266) Books on Tape, Inc.

—Improbable Cause. 2003. (J. P. Beaumont Mystery Ser.). 352p. mass mkt. 7.50 (*0-380-75412-6*, Avon Bks.) Morrow/Avon.

—Improbable Cause. 1992. 224p. reprint ed. 19.00 o.p. (*0-7278-4314-1*) Severn Hse. Pubs., Ltd.

—Injustice for All. unabr. ed. 1992. (J. P. Beaumont Mystery Ser.: Bk. 2). audio 39.95 (*1-55686-415-9*, 415) Books in Motion.

—Injustice for All. unabr. collector's ed. 1997. (J. P. Beaumont Ser.: Vol. 2). audio 56.00 (*0-7366-3568-8*, 4217) Books on Tape, Inc.

—Injustice for All. 1986. (J. P. Beaumont Mystery Ser.). 384p. mass mkt. 7.50 (*0-380-89641-9*, Avon Bks.) Morrow/Avon.

—Injustice for All. 1993. 19.00 o.p. (*0-7278-4431-8*) Severn Hse. Pubs., Ltd.

—Lying in Wait. unabr. ed. 1994. (J. P. Beaumont Mystery Ser.: Bk. 12). audio 49.95 (*1-55686-563-5*, 102592) Books in Motion.

—Lying in Wait. (J. P. Beaumont Mystery Ser.). 1996. 400p. mass mkt. 7.99 (*0-380-71841-3*, Avon Bks.); 1994. 303p. 17.95 o.p. (*0-688-02013-5*, Morrow, William & Co.) Morrow/Avon.

—Lying in Wait. l.t. ed. 2003. (J. P. Beaumont Mystery Ser.). 447p. 29.95 (*0-7862-4762-2*) Thorndike Pr.

—Minor in Possession. unabr. ed. 1993. (J. P. Beaumont Mystery Ser.). audio 49.95 (*1-55686-475-2*, 892536) Books in Motion.

—Minor in Possession. unabr. collector's ed. 1997. (J. P. Beaumont Ser.). audio 56.00 (*0-7366-3824-5*, 4492) Books on Tape, Inc.

—Minor in Possession. 1990. (J. P. Beaumont Mystery Ser.). 384p. mass mkt. 7.50 (*0-380-75546-7*, Avon Bks.) Morrow/Avon.

—A More Perfect Union. unabr. ed. 1993. (J. P. Beaumont Mystery Ser.: Bk. 6). audio 39.95 (*1-55686-466-3*, 752467) Books in Motion.

—A More Perfect Union. unabr. collector's ed. 1997. (J. P. Beaumont Ser.). audio 48.00 (*0-7366-3822-9*, 4490) Books on Tape, Inc.

—A More Perfect Union. 2003. (J. P. Beaumont Mystery Ser.). 352p. mass mkt. 7.50 (*0-380-75413-4*, Avon Bks.) Morrow/Avon.

—A More Perfect Union. 1992. 224p. reprint ed. 19.00 o.p. (*0-7278-4361-3*) Severn Hse. Pubs., Ltd.

—Name Withheld. l.t. ed. 2001. 320p. 28.95 (*1-57490-357-8*, Beeler Large Print Bks.) Beeler, Thomas T. Publisher.

—Name Withheld. unabr. ed. 1996. (J. P. Beaumont Mystery Ser.: Bk. 13). audio 46.95 (*1-55686-651-8*, 893938) Books in Motion.

—Name Withheld. (J. P. Beaumont Mystery Ser.). 1997. 400p. mass mkt. 6.99 (*0-380-71842-1*, Avon Bks.); 1996. 293p. 22.00 o.p. (*0-688-11460-1*, Morrow, William & Co.) Morrow/Avon.

—Partner in Crime. 2002. E-Book 19.95 (*0-06-009827-9*); E-Book 19.95 (*0-06-009826-0*); E-Book 19.95 (*0-06-009825-2*); E-Book 19.95 (*0-06-009828-7*) HarperCollins General Bks. Group. (Perfect-Bound).

—Partner in Crime. l.t. ed. 2002. 512p. pap. 24.95 (*0-06-009393-5*, HarperLargePrint) HarperTrade.

—Partner in Crime. 2003. 400p. mass mkt. 7.99 (*0-380-80470-0*); 2002. 384p. 24.95 (*0-380-97730-3*); 2002. 384p. 24.95 (*0-380-97730-3*); 2002. audio 25.95 (*0-06-009260-2*); 2002. audio compact disk 29.95 (*0-06-050164-2*) Morrow/Avon. (Morrow, William & Co.).

—Payment in Kind. unabr. ed. 1992. (J. P. Beaumont Mystery Ser.: Bk. 9). audio 49.95 (*1-55686-410-8*, 892515) Books in Motion.

—Payment in Kind. unabr. collector's ed. 1997. audio 56.00 (*0-7366-3825-3*, 4493) Books on Tape, Inc.

—Payment in Kind, Bk. 9. 1991. (J. P. Beaumont Mystery Ser.). 384p. mass mkt. 7.50 (*0-380-75836-9*, Avon Bks.) Morrow/Avon.

—Taking the Fifth. unabr. ed. 1993. (J. P. Beaumont Mystery Ser.: Bk. 4). audio 39.95 (*1-55686-458-2*, 752411) Books in Motion.

—Taking the Fifth. unabr. collector's ed. 1997. (J. P. Beaumont Ser.: Vol. 4). audio 48.00 (*0-7366-3626-9*, 4286) Books on Tape, Inc.

—Taking the Fifth. 1987. (J. P. Beaumont Mystery Ser.). 320p. mass mkt. 7.99 (*0-380-75139-9*, Avon Bks.) Morrow/Avon.

—Taking the Fifth. 320p. 25.99 (*0-7278-5944-7*) Severn Hse. Pubs., Ltd.

—Trial by Fury. unabr. ed. 1993. (J. P. Beaumont Mystery Ser.: Bk. 3). audio 39.95 (*1-55686-456-6*, 752468) Books in Motion.

—Trial by Fury. unabr. collector's ed. 1997. (J. P. Beaumont Ser.: Vol. 3). audio 48.00 (*0-7366-3582-3*, 4236) Books on Tape, Inc.

—Trial by Fury. 1986. (J. P. Beaumont Mystery Ser.). 384p. mass mkt. 7.99 (*0-380-75138-0*, Avon Bks.) Morrow/Avon.

—Trial by Fury. 384p. 26.00 (*0-7278-5609-X*) Severn Hse. Pubs., Ltd.

—Until Proven Guilty. l.t. ed. 1991. 21.95 o.p. (*0-7927-0825-3*, CH080); pap. 19.95 o.p. (*0-7927-0826-1*, CS0176) BBC Audiobooks America.

—Until Proven Guilty. unabr. ed. 1992. (J. P. Beaumont Mystery Ser.: Bk. 1). audio 39.95 (*1-55686-414-0*, 752460) Books in Motion.

—Until Proven Guilty. unabr. collector's ed. 1997. (J. P. Beaumont Ser.: Vol. 1). audio 48.00 (*0-7366-3584-X*, 4238) Books on Tape, Inc.

—Until Proven Guilty. 1985. (J. P. Beaumont Mystery Ser.). 352p. mass mkt. 7.99 (*0-380-89638-9*, Avon Bks.) Morrow/Avon.

—Without Due Process. unabr. ed. 1993. (J. P. Beaumont Mystery Ser.: Bk. 10). audio 49.95 (*1-55686-476-0*, 892538) Books in Motion.

—Without Due Process. unabr. collector's ed. 1998. (J. P. Beaumont Ser.). audio 56.00 (*0-7366-4041-X*, 4540) Books on Tape, Inc.

—Without Due Process. (J. P. Beaumont Mystery Ser.). 1993. 384p. mass mkt. 7.50 (*0-380-75837-7*, Avon Bks.); 1992. 302p. 20.00 o.p. (*0-688-11459-8*, Morrow, William & Co.) Morrow/Avon.

—Without Due Process. 4.98 o.p. (*0-8317-8577-2*) Smithmark Pubs., Inc.

## BEAUMONT, NED (FICTITIOUS CHARACTER)—FICTION

Hammett, Dashiell. The Glass Key. Date not set. 148p. 18.95 (*0-8488-2437-7*) Amereon, Ltd.

—The Glass Key. unabr. ed. 1998. audio 48.00 (*0-7366-4039-8*, 4538) Books on Tape, Inc.

—The Glass Key. unabr. ed. 2000. audio compact disk 64.95 (*0-7531-0901-8*, 109018); 1996. audio 54.95 (*1-85695-712-8*, 940413) ISIS Audio Bks. GBR. *Dist:* Ulverscroft Large Print Bks., Ltd.

—The Glass Key. 1989. (Vintage Crime Ser.). 224p. pap. 11.00 (*0-679-72262-9*, Vintage) Knopf Publishing Group.

—The Glass Key. 1972. pap. 4.95 o.p. (*0-394-71773-2*) Random Hse., Inc.

## BEAUMONT, PHIL (FICTITIOUS CHARACTER)—FICTION

Satterthwait, Walter. Escapade. 1996. 355p. mass mkt. 5.99 (*0-312-95920-6*, St. Martin's Paperbacks); 1995. 336p. 22.95 o.p. (*0-312-13068-6*, Saint Martin's Minotaur) St. Martin's Pr.

—Masquerade. 1999. 336p. mass mkt. 5.99 (*0-312-96989-9*, St. Martin's Paperbacks); Vol. 1. 1998. (Masquerade Ser.: Vol. 1). 272p. 22.95 (*0-312-18629-0*, Saint Martin's Minotaur) St. Martin's Pr.

## BEAUMONT, THAD (FICTITIOUS CHARACTER)—FICTION

King, Stephen. The Dark Half. l.t. ed. 1991. (General Ser.). 623p. 14.95 o.p. (*0-8161-5123-7*); xxiii, 608p. lib. bdg. 22.95 o.p. (*0-8161-5109-1*) Gale Group. (Macmillan Reference USA).

—The Dark Half. 496p. 1993. mass mkt. 5.99 o.p. (*0-451-17181-0*); 1990. reprint ed. mass mkt. 7.99 (*0-451-16731-7*) NAL. (Signet Bks.).

—The Dark Half. 1990. 14.04 (*0-606-04648-8*) Turtleback Bks.

—The Dark Half. 1989. 448p. text 27.95 (*0-670-82982-X*) Viking Penguin.

## BEBB, LEO (FICTITIOUS CHARACTER)—FICTION

Buechner, Frederick. The Book of Bebb. 544p. 2001. pap. 20.00 (*0-06-251769-4*); 1990. reprint ed. pap. 16.95 o.p. (*0-00-001210-6*) HarperSanFrancisco.

—The Book of Bebb. 1979. 512p. 19.95 o.s.i (*0-689-10986-5*, Scribner) Simon & Schuster.

—Lion Country: A Novel. 1984. (Books of Bebb). 240p. pap. 3.95 o.p. (*0-06-061164-2*) HarperSanFrancisco.

—Lion Country: A Novel. 1971. 5.95 o.p. (*0-689-10382-4*) Simon & Schuster.

—Love Feast. 1984. (Books of Bebb). 380p. mass mkt. 3.95 o.p. (*0-06-061167-7*, P-5009) HarperSanFrancisco.

—Love Feast. 1974. 7.95 o.p. (*0-689-10612-2*, Atheneum) Simon & Schuster Children's Publishing.

—Open Heart. 1984. (Books of Bebb). mass mkt. 3.95 o.p. (*0-06-061166-9*, P-5008) HarperSanFrancisco.

—Open Heart. 1972. 5.95 o.p. (*0-689-10498-7*, Atheneum) Simon & Schuster Children's Publishing.

—Treasure Hunt. 1984. (Books of Bebb). mass mkt. 3.95 o.p. (*0-06-061168-5*, P-5010) HarperSanFrancisco.

—Treasure Hunt. 1977. 7.95 o.p. (*0-689-10800-1*, Atheneum) Simon & Schuster Children's Publishing.

## BECH, HENRY (FICTITIOUS CHARACTER)—FICTION

Updike, John. Bech: A Book. 1999. pap. 12.00 (*0-449-45933-0*); 1998. 224p. pap. 12.95 (*0-449-00452-X*) Ballantine Bks. (Fawcett).

—Bech: A Book. 1980. 206p. pap. 5.95 o.p. (*0-394-74509-4*, Vintage) Knopf Publishing Group.

—Bech: A Book. 1970. 13.95 o.s.i (*0-394-41638-4*) Knopf, Alfred A. Inc.

—Bech at Bay: A Quasi-Novel. mass mkt. 7.50 (*0-449-00565-8*); 1999. 256p. pap. 12.00 (*0-449-00404-X*) Ballantine Bks. (Fawcett).

—Bech at Bay: A Quasi-Novel. l.t. ed. pap. 23.00 o.p. (*0-7838-0264-1*, Macmillan Reference USA) Gale Group.

—Bech at Bay: A Quasi-Novel. 1998. 240p. 23.00 (*0-375-40368-X*) Knopf, Alfred A. Inc.

—Bech Is Back. 1999. pap. 12.00 (*0-449-45934-9*); 1998. 208p. pap. 12.00 (*0-449-00453-8*); 1983. 192p. mass mkt. 5.99 o.s.i (*0-449-20277-1*) Ballantine Bks. (Fawcett).

—Bech Is Back. 1982. (Illus.). 224p. 50.00 o.p. (*0-394-52849-2*); 195p. 25.00 o.s.i (*0-394-52806-9*) Knopf, Alfred A. Inc.

—The Complete Henry Bech. 2001. (Everyman's Library). 544p. 23.00 (*0-375-41176-3*) Knopf, Alfred A. Inc.

## BECK, LIZA (FICTITIOUS CHARACTER)—FICTION

Rendell, Ruth. The Crocodile Bird, Set. abr. ed. 1993. audio 16.95 (*1-55927-258-9*, 390580) Audio Renaissance.

—The Crocodile Bird. 1997. 368p. mass mkt. 7.99 (*0-7704-2598-4*) Bantam Bks.

—The Crocodile Bird. unabr. collector's ed. 1994. audio 56.00 (*0-7366-2670-0*, 3407) Books on Tape, Inc.

—The Crocodile Bird. 1994. 384p. mass mkt. 6.99 (*0-440-21865-9*) Dell Publishing.

—The Crocodile Bird. 1993. 368p. 25.95 o.s.i (*0-385-25429-6*) Doubleday Publishing.

—The Crocodile Bird. unabr. ed. 1994. audio 78.00 (*1-55690-944-6*, 93440E7) Recorded Bks., LLC.

Characters

**BECK, MARTIN (FICTITIOUS CHARACTER)—FICTION**

Sjowall, Maj & Wahloo, Per. The Abominable Man. 21.95 (*0-89190-378-X*) Amereon, Ltd.
—The Abominable Man. 1993. reprint ed. lib. bdg. 17.95 o.p. (*1-56849-222-7*) Buccaneer Bks., Inc.
—The Abominable Man. 1980. (Martin Beck Detective Ser.). pap. 3.95 o.s.i (*0-394-74273-7*, Vintage) Knopf Publishing Group.
—Cop Killer. 1978. pap. 3.95 o.s.i (*0-394-72444-5*, Vintage) Knopf Publishing Group.
—Cop Killer: The Story of a Crime. 23.95 (*0-89190-377-1*) Amereon, Ltd.
—The Fire Engine That Disappeared. 1977. pap. 4.95 o.s.i (*0-394-72340-6*, Vintage) Knopf Publishing Group.
—The Laughing Policeman. Blair, Alan, tr. from SWE. l.t. ed. 1993. (Nightingale Ser.). 378p. lib. bdg. 16.95 o.p. (*0-8161-5767-7*, Macmillan Reference USA) Gale Group.
—The Laughing Policeman. 1992. 224p. pap. 12.00 (*0-679-74223-9*); 1977. pap. 4.95 o.p. (*0-394-72341-4*) Knopf Publishing Group. (Vintage).
—The Locked Room. 1980. pap. 4.95 o.p. (*0-394-74274-5*, Vintage) Knopf Publishing Group.
—The Locked Room: The Story of a Crime. Austin, Paul B., tr. from SWE. 1992. (Crime - Black Lizard Ser.). 320p. pap. 12.95 (*0-679-74222-0*, Vintage) Knopf Publishing Group.
—The Man on the Balcony. Date not set. lib. bdg. 18.95 (*0-8488-2163-7*) Amereon, Ltd.
—The Man on the Balcony. 1976. pap. 4.50 o.p. (*0-394-71777-5*, Vintage) Knopf Publishing Group.
—The Man on the Balcony: The Story of a Crime. Blair, Alan, tr. 1993. (Vintage Crime/Black Lizard Ser.). 192p. pap. 11.95 (*0-679-74596-3*, Vintage) Knopf Publishing Group.
—The Man Who Went up in Smoke. Date not set. lib. bdg. 18.95 (*0-8488-2164-5*) Amereon, Ltd.
—The Man Who Went up in Smoke. Tate, Joan, tr. from SWE. 1993. (Vintage Crime/Black Lizard Ser.). 192p. pap. 11.00 (*0-679-74597-1*, Vintage) Knopf Publishing Group.
—The Man Who Went up in Smoke. 1976. pap. 3.95 o.p. (*0-394-71778-3*, Vintage) Knopf Publishing Group.
—Murder at the Savoy. 1977. pap. 5.95 o.s.i (*0-394-72342-2*, Vintage) Knopf Publishing Group.
—Roseanna. Roth, Lois, tr. from SWE. 1993. (Vintage Crime/Black Lizard Ser.). 224p. pap. 12.95 (*0-679-74598-X*, Vintage) Knopf Publishing Group.
—Roseanna. 1976. pap. 4.95 o.p. (*0-394-71779-1*, Vintage) Knopf Publishing Group.
—The Terrorists. 1977. pap. 4.95 o.s.i (*0-394-72452-6*, Vintage); 1976. 320p. 7.95 o.p. (*0-394-48532-7*, Pantheon) Knopf Publishing Group.

**BECKER, JOHN (FICTITIOUS CHARACTER)—FICTION**

Wiltse, David. Blown Away. l.t. ed. 1997. 368p. mass mkt. 6.50 o.s.i (*0-425-15971-X*) Berkley Publishing Group.
—Blown Away. l.t. ed. 1997. (G. K. Hall Core Ser.). 469p. lib. bdg. 26.95 (*0-7838-2009-7*, Macmillan Reference USA) Gale Group.
—Blown Away. 1996. 352p. 24.95 o.s.i (*0-399-14208-8*, G. P. Putnam's Sons) Penguin Group (USA) Inc.
—Blown Away: A John Becker Thriller. abr. ed. 1997. audio 17.00 (*1-56876-063-9*) Soundlines Entertainment, Inc.
—Bone Deep. 1996. 400p. reprint ed. mass mkt. 6.99 o.s.i (*0-425-15340-1*) Berkley Publishing Group.
—Bone Deep. 1995. 320p. 23.95 o.p. (*0-399-14093-X*, G. P. Putnam's Sons) Penguin Group (USA) Inc.
—Bone Deep. abr. ed. 1996. audio 17.00 (*1-56876-052-3*) Soundlines Entertainment, Inc.
—Close to the Bone. 1993. 352p. mass mkt. 6.50 o.s.i (*0-425-13976-X*) Berkley Publishing Group.
—Close to the Bone. 1992. 304p. 21.95 o.p. (*0-399-13718-1*, G. P. Putnam's Sons) Penguin Group (USA) Inc.
—The Edge of Sleep. 1994. 368p. reprint ed. mass mkt. 5.99 o.s.i (*0-425-14333-3*) Berkley Publishing Group.
—The Edge of Sleep. 1993. 320p. 22.95 o.p. (*0-399-13880-3*, G. P. Putnam's Sons) Penguin Group (USA) Inc.
—Into the Fire. 1995. 384p. mass mkt. 6.99 o.s.i (*0-425-15012-7*) Berkley Publishing Group.
—Into the Fire. 1994. 320p. 22.95 o.p. (*0-399-13969-9*, G. P. Putnam's Sons) Penguin Group (USA) Inc.
—Prayer for the Dead. 1992. 352p. mass mkt. 6.50 o.s.i (*0-425-13398-2*) Berkley Publishing Group.
—Prayer for the Dead. 1991. 320p. 19.95 o.p. (*0-399-13607-X*, G. P. Putnam's Sons) Penguin Group (USA) Inc.

**BECKER FAMILY (FICTITIOUS CHARACTERS)—FICTION**

Schaeffer, Frank. Portofino. 304p. 1999. pap. 14.00 o.s.i (*0-425-16694-5*); 1996. mass mkt. 6.99 o.s.i (*0-425-14981-1*) Berkley Publishing Group.
—Portofino. unabr. ed. 1994. audio 39.95 (*0-7861-0474-0*, 1426) Blackstone Audio Bks., Inc.
—Portofino. 2002. 256p. pap. 17.95 (*0-7432-4687-X*, Scribner) Simon & Schuster.
—Saving Grandma. 1997. 368p. pap. 14.00 o.s.i (*0-425-15776-8*) Berkley Publishing Group.

**BECKETT, SAM (FICTITIOUS CHARACTER)—FICTION**

Barrett, Julie. Quantum Leap: A to Z. 1995. 288p. (Orig.). mass mkt. 5.99 o.s.i (*1-57297-044-8*) Boulevard Bks.
Crandall, Melissa. Quantum Leap: Search & Rescue, No. 5. 1994. 240p. (Orig.). mass mkt. 4.99 o.s.i (*0-441-00122-X*) Ace Bks.
—Search & Rescue. 1994. (Quantum Leap Ser.: Vol. 5). mass mkt. 5.99 o.s.i (*1-57297-178-9*) Boulevard Bks.
Davis, Carol & Reese, Esther D. Mirror's Edge: Quantum Leap. 2000. (Quantum Leap Ser.: No. XVIII). 304p. mass mkt. 6.99 o.s.i (*0-425-17351-8*) Berkley Publishing Group.
Defilippis, Christopher. Quantam Leap: Foreknowledge. 1998. (Quantum Leap Ser.). 256p. mass mkt. 6.99 o.s.i (*0-425-16487-X*) Berkley Publishing Group.
—Quantum Leap Foreknowledge. 1998. (Quantum Leap Ser.). mass mkt. 5.99 (*1-57297-343-9*) Boulevard Bks.
Henderson, C. J. Quantum Leap: Double or Nothing, No. IX. 1995. 240p. (Orig.). mass mkt. 5.99 o.s.i (*1-57297-055-3*) Boulevard Bks.
Kent, Melanie. Heat Wave. 1997. (Quantum Leap Ser.: No. XV). 240p. mass mkt. 5.99 o.s.i (*1-57297-312-9*) Boulevard Bks.
McConnell, Ashley. The Novel. 1992. (Quantum Leap Ser.). mass mkt. 5.99 o.s.i (*1-57297-094-4*) Boulevard Bks.
—Prelude. 1994. (Quantum Leap Ser.). mass mkt. 5.99 o.s.i (*1-57297-134-7*) Boulevard Bks.
—Quantum Leap: Random Measures. 1995. 240p. (Orig.). mass mkt. 4.99 o.s.i (*0-441-00182-3*) Ace Bks.
—Quantum Leap: The Novel. 1992. 304p. mass mkt. 4.99 o.s.i (*0-441-69322-9*) Ace Bks.
—Quantum Leap: The Wall. 1994. 256p. mass mkt. 4.99 o.s.i (*0-441-00015-0*) Ace Bks.
—Quantum Leap: Too Close for Comfort. 1993. 272p. (Orig.). mass mkt. 4.99 o.s.i (*0-441-69323-7*) Ace Bks.
—Quantum Leap No. 4: Prelude. 1994. 256p. (Orig.). mass mkt. 4.99 o.s.i (*0-441-00076-2*) Ace Bks.
—Too Close for Comfort. 1994. (Quantum Leap Ser.: No. 2). mass mkt. 5.99 o.s.i (*1-57297-157-6*) Boulevard Bks.
—The Wall. 1994. (Quantum Leap Ser.). mass mkt. 5.99 o.s.i (*1-57297-216-5*) Boulevard Bks.
Peel, John. Independence, No. 11. 1996. (Quantum Leap Ser.). mass mkt. 5.99 o.s.i (*1-57297-150-9*) Boulevard Bks.
Peterman, Mindy. Quantum Leap: Song & Dance. 1998. (Quantum Leap Ser.: Vol. 17). 256p. mass mkt. 6.99 o.s.i (*0-425-16577-9*) Berkley Publishing Group.
Rawn, Melanie. The Knights of the Morningstar. 1996. (Quantum Leap Ser.: No. 4). mass mkt. 5.99 o.s.i (*1-57297-171-1*) Boulevard Bks.
—Quantum Leap: Knights of the Morningstar. 1994. 224p. (Orig.). mass mkt. 4.99 o.s.i (*0-441-00092-4*) Ace Bks.
Schofield, Sandy. Loch Ness Leap, No. 14. 1997. (Quantum Leap Ser.: No. XIV). 256p. mass mkt. 5.99 o.s.i (*1-57297-231-9*) Boulevard Bks.
Storm, L. Elizabeth. Angels Unaware, No. 12. 1997. (Quantum Leap Ser.). 320p. mass mkt. 5.99 o.s.i (*1-57297-206-8*) Boulevard Bks.
—Pulitzer, No. VIII. 1995. (Quantum Leap Ser.). 352p. mass mkt. 5.99 o.s.i (*1-57297-022-7*) Boulevard Bks.

**BECKMAN, GIL (FICTITIOUS CHARACTER)—FICTION**

Davis, W. E. Black Dragon. l.t. ed. 1995. (Gil Beckman Mystery Ser.: Bk. 3). 192p. pap. 8.99 o.p. (*0-89107-870-3*) Crossway Bks.
—Drastic Park: A Gil Beckman Mystery. 1997. (Gil Beckman Mystery Ser.). 208p. pap. 8.99 (*0-89107-962-9*) Crossway Bks.
—Drastic Park: A Gil Beckman Mystery. l.t. ed. 1998. (Christian Fiction Ser.). 315p. 24.95 (*0-7862-1403-1*) Thorndike Pr.
—Suspended Animation, No. 1. 1994. (Gil Beckman Mystery Ser.: Bk. 1). 192p. pap. 8.99 o.p. (*0-89107-802-9*) Crossway Bks.
—Victim of Circumstance. 1995. (Gil Beckman Mystery Ser.: Vol. 2). 208p. pap. 8.99 o.p. (*0-89107-843-6*) Crossway Bks.
—Victim of Circumstance, No. 2. l.t. ed. 1996. 320p. 21.95 o.p. (*0-7838-1701-0*, Macmillan Reference USA) Gale Group.

**BECKMANN, GRACE (FICTITIOUS CHARACTER)—FICTION**

Lewin, Jackie. Death Flies on Final. 1999. 192p. lib. bdg. 18.95 (*0-8034-9338-X*, Avalon Bks.) Bouregy, Thomas & Co., Inc.
—Death Flies on Final. 2000. (WWL Mystery Ser.: Vol. 367). mass mkt. (*0-373-26367-8*, 1-26367-2, Worldwide Library) Harlequin Enterprises, Ltd.
—Murder Flies Left Seat. 1998. 192p. 18.95 (*0-8034-9288-X*, Avalon Bks.) Bouregy, Thomas & Co., Inc.
—Murder Flies Left Seat. 2000. (WWL Mystery Ser.: Vol. 357). 256p. mass mkt. (*0-373-26357-0*, Worldwide Library) Harlequin Enterprises, Ltd.

**BECKWITH, JIM (FICTITIOUS CHARACTER)—FICTION**

Braun, Matt. Bloody Hand. 1985. 384p. pap. 3.50 o.p. (*0-523-42381-0*, Pinnacle Bks.) Kensington Publishing Corp.
—Bloody Hand. 1996. 378p. reprint ed. mass mkt. 5.99 (*0-312-95839-0*, St. Martin's Paperbacks) St. Martin's Pr.

**BEDWYR, LUTHIEN (FICTITIOUS CHARACTER)—FICTION**

*see Crimson Shadow (Fictitious Character)—Fiction*

**BEE, JANE (FICTITIOUS CHARACTER)—FICTION**

Benison, C. C. Death at Buckingham Palace: Her Majesty Investigates. 1996. (Her Majesty Investigates Ser.). 288p. mass mkt. 6.99 (*0-553-57476-0*, Crimeline) Bantam Bks.
—The Death at Sandringham House. 1996. (Her Majesty Investigates Ser.). 384p. mass mkt. 6.50 (*0-553-57477-9*, Crimeline) Bantam Bks.
—Death at Windsor Castle: Her Majesty Investigates. 1998. (Her Majesty Investigates Ser.). 400p. mass mkt. 6.99 (*0-553-57478-7*, Crimeline) Bantam Bks.

**BEEF, WILLIAM (FICTITIOUS CHARACTER)—FICTION**

Bruce, Leo. Case for Sergeant Beef. 1985. (Sergeant Beef Mystery Ser.). 14.95 o.s.i (*0-89733-037-4*); pap. 4.95 o.s.i (*0-89733-036-6*) Academy Chicago Pubs., Ltd.
—Case for Sergeant Beef. l.t. ed. 1982. (Ulverscroft Large Print Ser.). 320p. 29.99 o.p. (*0-7089-0842-X*, Ulverscroft) Thorpe, F. A. Pubs. GBR. *Dist:* Ulverscroft Large Print Bks., Ltd., Ulverscroft Large Print Canada, Ltd.
—Case for Three Detectives. 1985. (Sgt. Beef Mystery Ser.). 240p. pap. 10.95 (*0-89733-033-1*) Academy Chicago Pubs., Ltd.
—Case for Three Detectives. 1995. 248p. 19.50 (*0-7451-8661-0*, Black Dagger) BBC Audiobooks America.
—Case with No Conclusion. (Sergeant Beef Mystery Ser.). 288p. pap. 5.95 o.s.i (*0-89733-118-4*); 1984. 15.00 o.s.i (*0-89733-117-6*) Academy Chicago Pubs., Ltd.
—Case with Ropes & Rings. 1990. pap. 4.95 o.s.i (*0-89733-329-2*); 192p. reprint ed. 14.95 o.s.i (*0-89733-034-X*); 192p. reprint ed. pap. 4.95 o.s.i (*0-89733-035-8*) Academy Chicago Pubs., Ltd.
—Case Without a Corpse. 1990. (Sergeant Beef Mystery Ser.). 284p. reprint ed. 14.95 o.p. (*0-89733-052-8*); pap. 4.95 o.p. (*0-89733-051-X*) Academy Chicago Pubs., Ltd.
—Neck & Neck. 1980. (Sergeant Beef Mystery Ser.). 224p. reprint ed. 15.00 o.s.i (*0-89733-041-2*); pap. 5.95 o.s.i (*0-89733-040-4*) Academy Chicago Pubs., Ltd.
—Neck & Neck. l.t. ed. 1983. (Ulverscroft Large Print Ser.). 368p. 29.99 o.p. (*0-7089-0898-5*, Ulverscroft) Thorpe, F. A. Pubs. GBR. *Dist:* Ulverscroft Large Print Bks., Ltd., Ulverscroft Large Print Canada, Ltd.

**BEHN, APHRA, 1640-1689—FICTION**

Brown, Molly. Invitation to a Funeral: A Tale of Restoration Intrigue. 288p. 1999. mass mkt. 5.99 (*0-312-97094-3*, St. Martin's Paperbacks); 1998. (YA). 22.95 o.p. (*0-312-18598-7*, Saint Martin's Minotaur) St. Martin's Pr.

**BEHR, DAN (FICTITIOUS CHARACTER)—FICTION**

North, Darian. Thief of Souls. 1997. 368p. 23.95 o.p. (*0-525-94200-9*) Dutton/Plume.
—Thief of Souls. 1998. 432p. mass mkt. 6.99 o.s.i (*0-451-18896-9*, Signet Bks.) NAL.

**BEHR, JASON (FICTITIOUS CHARACTER)—FICTION**

Grayson, George. The Revolutionary's Confession. 2000. 331p. 24.95 (*1-890768-21-9*, Intrigue Pr.) Corvus Publishing.

**BELACQUA, LYRA (FICTITIOUS CHARACTER)—FICTION**

Pullman, Philip. The Golden Compass. unabr. ed. 1999. (His Dark Materials Ser.: Bk. 1). (YA). (gr. 7-12). audio Random Hse. Audio Publishing Group.

**BELANE, NICK (FICTITIOUS CHARACTER)—FICTION**

Bukowski, Charles. Pulp. deluxe ed. 1994. 200p. 40.00 o.p. (*0-87685-928-7*, Black Sparrow Pr.) Godine, David R. Pub.
—Pulp. 1998. reprint ed. 202p. 25.00 (*0-87685-927-9*); 208p. pap. 15.00 (*0-87685-926-0*) HarperCollins Pubs.

**BELASCOARAN SHAYNE, HECTOR (FICTITIOUS CHARACTER)—FICTION**

Taibo, Paco Ignacio, II. An Easy Thing. 2002. (Missing Mystery Ser.: Vol. 49). 240p. pap. 14.95 o.s.i (*1-59058-006-0*) Poisoned Pen Pr.
—An Easy Thing. Neuman, William I., tr. 1990. 240p. 16.95 o.p. (*0-670-82462-3*, Viking) Viking Penguin.
—An Easy Thing. 1990. (Crime Ser.). 240p. reprint ed. pap. 4.50 o.p. (*0-14-011523-4*, Penguin Bks.) Viking Penguin.
—No Happy Ending. Neuman, William I., tr. 1993. 192p. 17.95 (*0-89296-517-7*) Mysterious Pr.
—No Happy Ending. 2003. 254p. pap. 14.95 o.s.i (*1-59058-038-9*) Poisoned Pen Pr.
—No Happy Ending. Neuman, William I., tr. 1994. 192p. mass mkt. 5.50 (*0-446-40329-6*, Mysterious Pr. Paperback Bks.) Warner Bks., Inc.
—Return to the Same City. Dail, Laura, tr. from SPA. 1996. Tr. of Regreso a la Misma Ciudad y Bajo la Lluvia. 192p. 25.00 (*0-89296-590-8*) Mysterious Pr.
—Return to the Same City. Dail, Laura, tr. 1997. Tr. of Regreso a la Misma Ciudad y Bajo la Lluvia. 176p. mass mkt. 5.99 (*0-446-40520-5*) Warner Bks., Inc.
—Some Clouds. Neuman, William I., tr. 1993. (Crime Ser.). 176p. pap. 9.00 o.p. (*0-14-014896-5*, Penguin Bks.) Penguin Group (USA) Inc.
—Some Clouds. 2002. 250p. pap. 14.95 o.s.i (*1-59058-032-X*) Poisoned Pen Pr.
—Some Clouds. Neuman, William I., tr. from SPA. 1992. 176p. 19.00 o.p. (*0-670-83825-X*, Viking) Viking Penguin.

**BELL, DANIEL (FICTITIOUS CHARACTER)—FICTION**

Komarnicki, Todd. Famine. 1997. 256p. 22.95 (*1-55970-365-2*) Arcade Publishing, Inc.
—Famine. 1998. 288p. pap. 12.95 o.s.i (*0-452-27932-1*, Plume) Dutton/Plume.

**BELLAMY, ROBERT (FICTITIOUS CHARACTER)—FICTION**

Sheldon, Sidney. The Doomsday Conspiracy. 1991. 22.00 (*0-688-08489-3*); 25.00 o.p. (*0-688-10444-4*) Morrow/Avon. (Morrow, William & Co.).
—The Doomsday Conspiracy. Set. abr. ed. 1993. 15.95 o.p. (*1-55800-382-7*, 390674); 39.95 o.p. (*1-55800-432-7*) NewStar Media, Inc.
—The Doomsday Conspiracy. 1991. pap. 4.98 o.p. (*0-8317-0937-5*) Smithmark Pubs., Inc.
—The Doomsday Conspiracy. 1992. 416p. reprint ed. mass mkt. 7.99 (*0-446-36366-9*) Warner Bks., Inc.

**BELOW, DRACHTON (FICTITIOUS CHARACTER)—FICTION**

Ford, Jeffrey. The Beyond. 304p. 2002. pap. 12.95 (*0-380-81288-6*); 2001. 24.00 (*0-380-97897-0*) Morrow/Avon. (Eos).
—Memoranda. 1999. 240p. pap. 12.00 (*0-380-80262-7*); 2000. 256p. reprint ed. mass mkt. 5.99 (*0-380-81368-8*) Morrow/Avon. (Eos).
—Memoranda. l.t. ed. 2003. 392p. 27.95 (*0-7862-5777-6*) Thorndike Pr.
—The Physiognomy. 1998. 256p. mass mkt. 5.99 (*0-380-79332-6*, Eos); 1997. 218p. pap. 12.00 (*0-380-79331-8*, Avon Bks.) Morrow/Avon.
—The Physiognomy. 2002. (Science Fiction Ser.). 27.95 (*0-7862-4907-2*) Thorndike Pr.

**BELSKI, BECKY (FICTITIOUS CHARACTER)—FICTION**

Haddad, C. A. Caught in the Shadows: A Mystery. 1994. (WWL Mystery Ser.). per. (*0-373-26138-1*, 1-26138-7, Harlequin Bks.) Harlequin Enterprises, Ltd.
—Caught in the Shadows: A Mystery. 1992. 272p. 17.95 o.p. (*0-312-07666-5*, Saint Martin's Minotaur) St. Martin's Pr.

**BENBOW, ANGELA (FICTITIOUS CHARACTER)—FICTION**

Sawyer, Corinne Holt. The Geezer Factory Murders. 1997. 263p. mass mkt. 5.99 o.s.i (*0-449-22532-1*, Fawcett) Ballantine Bks.
—The Geezer Factory Murders. 1996. (Benbow/Wingate Mystery Ser.). 240p. 21.95 o.s.i (*1-55611-497-4*, Dutton) Fine, Donald I. Bks.
—Ho-Ho Homicide. 1996. mass mkt. 5.99 o.s.i (*0-449-22409-0*, Fawcett) Ballantine Bks.
—Ho-Ho Homicide. 1995. (Benbow/Wingate Mystery Ser.). 256p. 20.95 o.s.i (*1-55611-459-1*) Fine, Donald I. Bks.

—The J. Alfred Prufrock Murders. 1989. 256p. mass mkt. 4.99 o.s.i (*0-449-21743-4*, Fawcett) Ballantine Bks.

—The J. Alfred Prufrock Murders. 1988. (Benbow/Wingate Mystery Ser.). 17.95 o.s.i (*1-55611-081-2*) Fine, Donald I. Bks.

—Murder by Owl Light. 1994. mass mkt. 4.99 o.s.i (*0-449-22171-7*) Ballantine Bks.

—Murder by Owl Light. 1992. (Benbow/Wingate Mystery Ser.). 240p. 19.00 o.p. (*1-55611-332-3*) Fine, Donald I. Bks.

—Murder Has No Calories. 1995. mass mkt. 5.99 o.s.i (*0-449-22338-8*, Fawcett) Ballantine Bks.

—Murder Has No Calories. 1994. (Benbow/Wingate Mystery Ser.). 224p. 19.95 o.p. (*1-55611-412-5*) Fine, Donald I. Bks.

—Murder in Gray & White. 1989. (Benbow/Wingate Mystery Ser.). 17.95 o.p. (*1-55611-153-3*) Fine, Donald I. Bks.

—Murder in Grey & White. 1991. 272p. mass mkt. 3.95 o.s.i (*0-449-21965-8*, Fawcett) Ballantine Bks.

—Murder Ole! 1998. 260p. mass mkt. 5.99 o.s.i (*0-449-00034-6*, Fawcett) Ballantine Bks.

—Murder Ole! 1997. (Benbow/Wingate Mystery Ser.). 272p. 22.95 (*1-55611-514-8*) Fine, Donald I. Bks.

—The Peanut Butter Murders. 1994. mass mkt. 4.99 o.s.i (*0-449-22172-5*) Ballantine Bks.

—The Peanut Butter Murders. 1993. (Benbow/Wingate Mystery Ser.). 233p. 18.95 o.p. (*1-55611-350-1*) Fine, Donald I. Bks.

**BENCOLIN, HENRI (FICTITIOUS CHARACTER)—FICTION**

Carr, John Dickson. Castle Skull. 1987. 240p. mass mkt. 3.50 o.p. (*0-8217-1974-2*, Zebra Bks.) Kensington Publishing Corp.

—The Corpse in the Waxworks: A Monsieur Bencolin Mystery. 1990. 192p. reprint ed. mass mkt. 4.95 o.p. (*0-06-081039-4*, Perennial) HarperTrade.

—The Corpse in the Waxworks: A Monsieur Bencolin Mystery. 1990. 192p. (C). reprint ed. lib. bdg. 20.00 o.p. (*0-8095-9026-3*) Millefleurs.

—The Door to Doom & Other Detections. Greene, Douglas G., ed. 1992. 352p. pap. 10.95 o.p. (*1-55882-102-3*) International Polygonics, Ltd.

—The Four False Weapons: A Monsieur Bencolin Mystery. 1989. 256p. reprint ed. mass mkt. 4.95 o.p. (*0-06-081017-3*, Perennial) HarperTrade.

—It Walks by Night. 1997. 19.50 o.p. (*0-7451-8698-X*, Black Dagger) BBC Audiobooks America.

—It Walks by Night. 1986. 256p. mass mkt. 3.50 o.p. (*0-8217-1931-9*, Zebra Bks.) Kensington Publishing Corp.

—The Lost Gallows. 1986. 344p. pap. 3.50 o.p. (*0-88184-202-8*, Carroll & Graf Pubs.) Avalon Publishing Group.

**BENEDETTI, NICCOLO (FICTITIOUS CHARACTER)—FICTION**

DeAndrea, William L. The Hog Murders. 1999. (*0-7862-1942-4*, Five Star) Gale Group.

—The Hog Murders. 1999. 210p. pap. 8.95 o.p. (*1-55882-030-2*, Library of Crime Classics) International Polygonics, Ltd.

—The Hog Murders. 1985. pap. 1.95 o.p. (*0-380-47548-0*, 47548-0, Avon Bks.) Morrow/Avon.

—The Manx Murders: A Professor Niccolo Benedetti Mystery. 1994. 17.00 o.s.i (*0-385-42500-7*) Doubleday Publishing.

—The Manx Murders: A Professor Niccolo Benedetti Mystery. 1994. 256p. 20.00 (*1-883402-66-2*, Scribner) Simon & Schuster.

—The Werewolf Murders. 1992. 240p. 16.50 o.s.i (*0-385-42089-7*) Doubleday Publishing.

**BENGAL, ROSALIND (FICTITIOUS CHARACTER)—FICTION**

Forbes, Leslie. Bombay Ice. 1999. 416p. reprint ed. pap. 13.95 (*0-553-38047-8*) Bantam Bks.

—Bombay Ice. unabr. ed. 1998. audio 76.95 (*0-7861-1430-4*, 2316) Blackstone Audio Bks., Inc.

—Bombay Ice. 1998. (*0-374-90777-3*); 400p. 24.00 o.p. (*0-374-11530-3*) Farrar, Straus & Giroux.

—Bombay Ice. abr. ed. 1998. 3p. audio 17.95 (*1-55935-277-9*) Soundelux Audio Publishing.

—Bombay Ice. (GER.). pap. (*3-548-24703-2*) Ullstein-Taschenbuch-Verlag DEU. *Dist:* International Bk. Import Service, Inc.

**BENINGTON, PETER (FICTITIOUS CHARACTER)—FICTION**

West, Richard F. As Crime Goes by. 1998. (Old Gang of Mine Mysteries Ser.). 240p. mass mkt. 5.99 o.s.i (*0-425-16536-1*) Berkley Publishing Group.

—Ghoul of My Dreams. 1999. (Old Gang of Mine Mysteries Ser.). 256p. mass mkt. 5.99 o.s.i (*0-425-16983-9*) Berkley Publishing Group.

—Old Gang of Mine. 1997. 224p. mass mkt. 5.99 o.s.i (*0-425-15964-7*, Prime Crime) Berkley Publishing Group.

**BENNET, ELIZABETH (FICTITIOUS CHARACTER)—FICTION**

Aiken, Joan & Austen, Jane. Eliza's Daughter. 1994. 384p. 20.95 o.p. (*0-312-10972-5*) St. Martin's Pr.

Aston, Elizabeth. Mr. Darcy's Daughters: A Novel. 2003. 368p. pap. 14.00 (*0-7432-4397-8*, Touchstone) Simon & Schuster.

Austen, Jane. Pride & Prejudice. 2000. 252p. E-Book 9.95 (*0-594-05313-7*) 1873 Pr.

—Pride & Prejudice. 1998. pap. 4.99 o.p. (*1-57840-200-X*) Acclaim Bks.

—Pride & Prejudice. 1997. pap. text o.p. (*0-17-556586-4*) Addison-Wesley Longman, Inc.

—Pride & Prejudice. unabr. ed. 1962. (Classics Ser.). mass mkt. 4.95 (*0-8049-0001-9*, CL-1) Airmont Publishing Co., Inc.

—Pride & Prejudice. Date not set. lib. bdg. 25.95 (*0-8488-0420-1*) Amereon, Ltd.

—Pride & Prejudice, Set. unabr. ed. 1986. audio 53.95 (*1-55685-025-5*) Audio Bk. Contractors, Inc.

—Pride & Prejudice. unabr. ed. 1997. audio 34.95 (*1-57270-055-6*, F81055u, Cover to Cover Classics) Audio Partners Publishing Corp.

—Pride & Prejudice. unabr. ed. audio 84.95 o.p. (*1-85549-911-8*, CTC 001); 1998. audio 84.95 (*0-7540-0149-0*, CAB 1572, Sterling Audio Bks.) BBC Audiobooks America.

—Pride & Prejudice. abr. ed. 1999. audio 16.85 (*0-563-55816-4*) BBC Bk. Publishing GBR. *Dist:* Ulverscroft Large Print Bks., Ltd.

—Pride & Prejudice. 2001. 7.95 (*0-8010-1211-2*) Baker Bks.

—Pride & Prejudice. 1991. mass mkt. 4.95 (*0-553-54088-2*); 1983. mass mkt. 1.95 o.s.i (*0-553-21215-X*); 1983. 352p. reprint ed. mass mkt. 4.95 (*0-553-21310-5*, Bantam Classics) Bantam Bks.

—Pride & Prejudice. 1999. (Classic Novels ). 392p. pap. 8.95 (*0-7641-1147-7*) Barron's Educational Series, Inc.

—Pride & Prejudice. Kendrick, Walter, ed. 1980. (Mcdonald Classics Ser.). 410p. 19.95 (*0-8464-1071-0*) Beekman Pubs., Inc.

—Pride & Prejudice. unabr. ed. 2000. audio compact disk 88.00 (*0-7861-9894-X*, z1054); 1989. audio 56.95 (*0-7861-0057-5*, 1054) Blackstone Audio Bks., Inc.

—Pride & Prejudice. unabr. collector's ed. audio compact disk 80.00 (*0-7366-6054-2*); 1996. audio 72.00 (*0-7366-3370-7*, 4020) Books on Tape, Inc.

—Pride & Prejudice. 2000. 6.98 (*0-681-99449-5*, 50885514) Borders Pr.

—Pride & Prejudice. unabr. ed. 2002. audio 29.95 (*1-59086-151-5*, 3711, Brilliance Audio Unabridged); 1993. audio 59.25 (*1-56100-118-X*, 992, Unabridged Library Editions); 1993. audio 19.95 o.p. (*1-56100-484-7*, 219, Bookcassette) Brilliance Audio.

—Pride & Prejudice. Irvine, Robert P., ed. 2002. (Broadview Literary Texts Ser.). (Illus.). 493p. pap. (*1-55111-028-8*) Broadview Pr.

—Pride & Prejudice. 1988. lib. bdg. 19.95 (*0-89966-243-9*) Buccaneer Bks., Inc.

—Pride & Prejudice. 1997. (Cambridge Literature Ser.). audio 16.95 o.p. (*0-521-59792-7*); audio compact disk 22.95 o.p. (*0-521-59791-9*) Cambridge Univ. Pr.

—Pride & Prejudice. Bain, Richard, ed. 1996. (Literature Ser.). (Illus.). 384p. pap. text 11.95 o.p. (*0-521-57654-7*) Cambridge Univ. Pr.

—Pride & Prejudice. unabr. ed. 2001. audio 69.95; 2000. 10p. audio compact disk 94.95 (*0-7540-5338-5*, CCD 029) Chivers Audio Bks. GBR. *Dist:* BBC Audiobooks America.

—Pride & Prejudice, 3 Vols. reprint ed. lib. bdg. 294.00 (*0-7426-2071-9*); 2001. pap. text 84.00 (*0-7426-7071-6*) Classic Bks.

—Pride & Prejudice. audio 59.95 Cover to Cover Cassettes, Ltd.

—Pride & Prejudice. 1994. 332p. mass mkt. 3.99 (*0-8125-2336-9*, Tor Classics) Doherty, Tom Assocs., LLC.

—Pride & Prejudice. l.t. unabr. ed. (Large Print Classics). 2001. 476p. pap. 14.95 (*0-486-41775-1*); 1995. 272p. pap. 2.50 (*0-486-28473-5*) Dover Pubns., Inc.

—Pride & Prejudice. 1942. 107p. pap. 5.60 (*0-87129-686-1*, P36) Dramatic Publishing Co.

—Pride & Prejudice. abr. ed. audio 15.95 o.p. (*0-88646-029-8*, 7042); 1986. audio 29.95 o.p. (*0-88646-795-0*, R 7042);Set. 1992. audio 16.99 (*0-88646-278-9*, 7278) Durkin Hayes Publishing Ltd.

—Pride & Prejudice. 1985. (Illus.). 352p. 20.00 o.p. (*0-525-18381-7*, Dutton) Dutton/Plume.

—Pride & Prejudice. 2003. (Barnes & Noble Classics Ser.). 400p. pap. 4.95 (*1-59308-020-4*) Fine Communications.

—Pride & Prejudice. 1980. (Reader's Request Ser.). lib. bdg. 13.95 o.p. (*0-8161-3076-0*, Macmillan Reference USA) Gale Group.

—Pride & Prejudice. l.t. ed. 1999. 480p. pap. 20.00 (*0-06-093325-9*) HarperCollins Pubs.

—Pride & Prejudice. abr. ed. 1984. audio 8.98; 1978. audio 12.95 o.p. (*0-694-50321-5*, SWC 1595, HarperAudio) HarperTrade.

—Pride & Prejudice. Clay, N. L., ed. 1986. (Guide Novel Ser.). pap. text 4.50 o.p. (*0-435-16041-9*) Heinemann.

—Pride & Prejudice, Set. unabr. ed. 1999. audio 56.95 Highsmith Inc.

—Pride & Prejudice. 2002. audio 15.95 (*1-84032-728-6*); 2000. audio 13.95 (*1-84032-471-6*); 1999. audio 16.95 (*1-85998-013-9*); 1999. audio 11.95 (*1-85998-486-X*) Hodder Headline Audiobooks GBR. *Dist:* Trafalgar Square.

—Pride & Prejudice. 1997. pap. 8.25 (*0-03-051487-8*) Holt, Rinehart & Winston.

—Pride & Prejudice. Schorer, Mark, ed. 1956. pap. 16.36 (*0-395-05101-0*, Riverside Editions) Houghton Mifflin Co.

—Pride & Prejudice. l.t. ed. 1444p. pap. 95.94 (*0-7583-1943-6*); 484p. pap. 36.91 (*0-7583-1938-X*); 623p. pap. 45.49 (*0-7583-1939-8*); 349p. pap. 29.76 (*0-7583-1937-1*); 995p. pap. 74.61 (*0-7583-1941-X*); 276p. pap. 24.62 (*0-7583-1936-3*); 806p. pap. 63.79 (*0-7583-1940-1*); 1224p. pap. 85.50 (*0-7583-1942-8*); 995p. lib. bdg. 86.61 (*0-7583-1933-9*); 349p. lib. bdg. 35.76 (*0-7583-1929-0*); 1444p. lib. bdg. 107.94 (*0-7583-1935-5*); 276p. lib. bdg. 30.62 (*0-7583-1928-2*); 484p. lib. bdg. 42.91 (*0-7583-1930-4*); 623p. lib. bdg. 51.49 (*0-7583-1931-2*); 806p. lib. bdg. 75.79 (*0-7583-1932-0*); 1224p. lib. bdg. 97.50 (*0-7583-1934-7*) Huge Print Pr.

—Pride & Prejudice. 2002. (Lifetime Series Classics). text (*0-924967-69-2*) JMW Group, Inc.

—Pride & Prejudice. 1991. 327p. (*1-85715-001-5*, Everyman's Library) Knopf Publishing Group.

—Pride & Prejudice. 1991. 416p. 17.00 (*0-679-40542-9*) Knopf, Alfred A. Inc.

—Pride & Prejudice. 1998. (Cloth Bound Pocket Ser.). 240p. 7.95 (*3-89508-207-4*, 521305) Konemann.

—Pride & Prejudice. l.t. ed. 1997. (Large Print Heritage Ser.). 560p. lib. bdg. 36.95 (*1-58118-009-8*, 21967) LRS.

—Pride & Prejudice. 1993. audio 50.60 (*1-56544-019-6*, 350003); audio Literate Ear, Inc.

—Pride & Prejudice. (Longman Fiction Ser.). 1997. pap. 9.07 (*0-582-27508-3*); 1993. pap. text 6.50 o.p. (*0-582-09674-X*, 79823) Longman Publishing Group.

—Pride & Prejudice. Adams, Richard, ed. 1983. (Study Texts Ser.). pap. text 5.95 (*0-582-33086-6*, 72039) Longman Publishing Group.

—Pride & Prejudice, Level 5. 2000. (Penqui Reading Lab Ser.). pap. 7.66 (*0-582-41935-2*) Longman Publishing Group.

—Pride & Prejudice. abr. ed. 2000. audio 7.95 (*1-57815-123-6*, 1085, Media Bks. Audio Publishing) Media Bks., L. L. C.

—Pride & Prejudice. 9999. o.p.; 1996. 336p. mass mkt. 4.95 (*0-451-52588-4*, Signet Classics); 1961. mass mkt. 0.75 o.p. (*0-451-50843-2*, Signet Classics); 1961. mass mkt. 1.95 o.p. (*0-451-51491-2*, Signet Classics); 1961. mass mkt. 1.50 o.p. (*0-451-51662-1*, Signet Classics); 1961. mass mkt. 1.75 o.p. (*0-451-51916-7*, Signet Classics); 1961. mass mkt. 1.50 o.p. (*0-451-51253-7*, Signet Classics); 1961. mass mkt. 1.75 o.p. (*0-451-51396-7*, Signet Classics); 1961. mass mkt. 1.25 o.p. (*0-451-51111-5*, Signet Classics); 1961. mass mkt. 0.50 o.p. (*0-451-50082-2*, Signet Classics); 1961. mass mkt. 0.60 o.p. (*0-451-50721-5*, Signet Classics); 1961. mass mkt. 0.95 o.p. (*0-451-50977-3*, Signet Classics); 1950. 336p. mass mkt. 3.95 o.p. (*0-451-52365-2*); 1950. mass mkt. 2.25 o.p. (*0-451-52226-5*, Signet Classics); 1950. mass mkt. 1.95 o.p. (*0-451-52075-0*, Signet Classics) NAL.

—Pride & Prejudice. audio 7.95 National Recording Co.

—Pride & Prejudice. abr. ed. 1996. (Works of Jane Austen). audio 17.98 (*962-634-604-3*, NA310414); audio compact disk 19.98 (*962-634-104-1*, NA310412) Naxos of America, Inc. (Naxos AudioBooks).

—Pride & Prejudice. Worrall, Andrew, ed. 1997. (Thornes Classic Novels Ser.). (Illus.). 376p. pap. 16.95 (*0-7487-2977-1*) Nelson Thornes GBR. *Dist:* Trans-Atlantic Pubns., Inc.

—Pride & Prejudice. abr. ed. 2002. audio 25.00 (*1-59007-132-8*, New Millennium Audio) New Millennium Entertainment.

—Pride & Prejudice. abr. ed. 1996. 19.95 o.p. (*0-7871-0306-3*) NewStar Media, Inc.

—Pride & Prejudice. l.t. ed. 1998. 480p. lib. bdg. 26.00 (*0-939495-50-3*); 355p. reprint ed. lib. bdg. 25.00 (*1-58287-058-6*) North Bks.

—Pride & Prejudice. (C). pap. text (*0-393-99771-5*) Norton, W. W. & Co., Inc.

—Pride & Prejudice. Gray, Donald J., ed. 1966. (Critical Editions Ser.). 450p. (C). pap. o.p. (*0-393-09668-8*) Norton, W. W. & Co., Inc.

—Pride & Prejudice. 3rd ed. 2000. (Critical Editions Ser.). viii, 413p. (C). pap. 7.25 (*0-393-97604-1*, Norton Paperbacks) Norton, W. W. & Co., Inc.

—Pride & Prejudice. 1999. 9.95 (*1-56137-766-X*) Novel Units, Inc.

—Pride & Prejudice. 1999. (Oxford World's Classics Ser.). 366p. 12.50 o.p. (*0-19-210026-2*) Oxford Univ. Pr., Inc.

—Pride & Prejudice. Kinsley, James, ed. 1998. (Oxford World's Classics Ser.). 410p. pap. 6.95 (*0-19-283355-3*) Oxford Univ. Pr., Inc.

—Pride & Prejudice. Hedge, Tricia, ed. 1995. (Illus.). 112p. pap. text 5.95 o.p. (*0-19-422710-3*) Oxford Univ. Pr., Inc.

—Pride & Prejudice. Kinsley, James, ed. 1990. (Oxford World's Classics Ser.). 390p. pap. 5.95 o.p. (*0-19-282760-X*) Oxford Univ. Pr., Inc.

—Pride & Prejudice. Kinsley, James & Bradbrook, F. W., eds. 1980. (Oxford World's Classics Ser.). pap. 2.25 o.p. (*0-19-281503-2*) Oxford Univ. Pr., Inc.

—Pride & Prejudice. 2nd ed. 1993. (Illus.). 126p. pap. text 5.95 (*0-19-585472-1*) Oxford Univ. Pr., Inc.

—Pride & Prejudice, Vol. II. Chapman, R. W., ed. 3rd ed. 1988. (Illus.). 432p. reprint ed. 21.50 (*0-19-254702-X*) Oxford Univ. Pr., Inc.

—Pride & Prejudice. 2000. 384p. pap. 2.99 o.s.i (*0-14-130930-X*) Penguin Putnam Bks. for Young Readers.

—Pride & Prejudice. 1996. 144p. pap. 20.00 (*81-209-0025-1*) Pitambar Publishing IND. *Dist:* State Mutual Bk. & Periodical Service, Ltd.

—Pride & Prejudice. collector's ed. 2002. (Illus.). im. lthr. 38.85 (*1-931927-42-1*); pap. 19.95 (*1-931927-43-X*); 25.95 (*1-931927-41-3*); pap. 17.95 (*1-931927-01-4*) Polyglot Pr., Inc.

—Pride & Prejudice. text (*0-13-981465-5*) Prentice Hall (Schl. Div.).

—Pride & Prejudice. (Jane Austen Works: Vol. 7). 2000. 280p. lib. bdg. 36.99 (*1-57646-350-8*); 2000. 280p. pap. 19.99 o.p. (*1-57646-267-6*); 1999. 200p. E-Book 3.99 incl. audio compact disk (*1-57646-150-5*); 2000. 518p. lib. bdg. 42.99 (*1-57646-352-4*); 2000. 518p. pap. 34.99 (*1-57646-351-6*) Quiet Vision Publishing.

—Pride & Prejudice. 1987. (Radiobook Ser.). audio 4.98 (*0-929541-27-8*) Radiola Co.

—Pride & Prejudice. (Modern Library Ser.). 2000. E-Book 4.95 (*0-679-64112-2*); 2000. 320p. pap. 7.95 (*0-679-78326-1*); 1995. (Illus.). 304p. 14.95 (*0-679-60168-6*) Random House Adult Trade Publishing Group. (Modern Library).

—Pride & Prejudice. 1987. audio 14.95 o.p. (*0-394-56408-1*); 1995. audio 24.00 o.s.i (*0-553-47396-4*) Random Hse. Audio Publishing Group. (RH Audio).

—Pride & Prejudice. 1988. 3.99 o.s.i (*0-517-38589-9*) Random Hse. Value Publishing.

—Pride & Prejudice. 1988. (Zodiac Press Ser.). 248p. o.p. (*0-7011-1236-0*) Random Hse. of Canada, Ltd. CAN. *Dist:* Random Hse., Inc.

—Pride & Prejudice. 1996. o.s.i (*0-679-60252-6*); 1989. o.s.i (*1-85381-097-5*); 1986. pap. 16.00 o.s.i incl. audio (*0-394-55731-X*); 1986. pap. 16.00 o.s.i incl. audio (*0-394-55731-X*) Random Hse., Inc.

—Pride & Prejudice. 1984. (Illus.). 368p. 25.00 o.p. (*0-89577-198-5*) Reader's Digest Assn., Inc., The.

—Pride & Prejudice. 2000. audio compact disk 97.00 (*0-7887-4914-5*, C1295E7); 1980. audio 70.00 (*1-55690-424-X*, 80020E7) Recorded Bks., LLC.

—Pride & Prejudice. (Literary Classics Ser.). 368p. 2002. 9.00 o.p. (*0-7624-0550-3*); 1992. text 5.98 o.p. (*1-56138-171-3*, Courage Bks.) Running Pr. Bk. Pubs.

—Pride & Prejudice. 2000. 416p. mass mkt. 4.99 (*0-439-10135-2*) Scholastic, Inc.

—Pride & Prejudice. 2000. E-Book 2.95 (*1-58853-022-1*) Sensory Publishing, Inc.

—Pride & Prejudice. 400p. 2005. (Illus.). mass mkt. 4.99 (*0-7434-6748-5*); 2004. mass mkt. 4.95 (*0-7434-8759-1*) Simon & Schuster. (Pocket).

—Pride & Prejudice. Shefter, Harry, ed. 1985. (Enriched Classics Ser.). mass mkt. 2.50 o.p. (*0-671-41678-2*, Pocket) Simon & Schuster.

—Pride & Prejudice. 1982. 464p. mass mkt. 2.95 o.s.i (*0-671-44389-5*, Pocket) Simon & Schuster.

—Pride & Prejudice. 1996. (Classic Library). 12.98 o.p. (*0-7651-9980-7*) Smithmark Pubs., Inc.

—Pride & Prejudice. unabr. ed. 2003. audio 19.99 (*1-59335-191-7*, 30287) Soulmate Audio Bks., Inc.

—Pride & Prejudice. unabr. ed. 2002. audio compact disk 18.95 (*1-58472-394-7*, In Audio) Sound Room Pubs., Inc.

—Pride & Prejudice. abr. ed. audio 14.95 o.p. (*0-88142-378-5*) Soundelux Audio Publishing.

—Pride & Prejudice. 2003. (Perennial Bestsellers Ser.). 28.95 (*0-7862-4964-1*) Thorndike Pr.

—Pride & Prejudice. l.t. ed. 1984. (Charnwood Large Print Ser.). 532p. 29.99 (*0-7089-8228-X*, Charnwood) Thorpe, F. A. Pubs. GBR. *Dist:* Ulverscroft Large Print Bks., Ltd., Ulverscroft Large Print Canada, Ltd.

—Pride & Prejudice. Daleski, H. M., ed. 2003. 456p. 9.95 (*1-59264-001-X*); pap. 7.95 (*1-59264-000-1*) Toby Pr.

—Pride & Prejudice. 1986. (Illus.). 352p. 25.95 o.p. (*0-7126-1011-1*) Trafalgar Square.

—Pride & Prejudice. 1999. (Signature Classics Ser.). (Illus.). 352p. 24.95 (*1-58279-032-9*); 29.95 (*1-58279-044-2*) Trident Pr. International.

—Pride & Prejudice. 1950. 11.00 (*0-606-01933-2*) Turtleback Bks.

—Pride & Prejudice. Norris, Pamela, ed. 1993. 384p. pap. 3.95 (*0-460-87212-5*, Everyman's Classic Library in Paperback) Tuttle Publishing.

—Pride & Prejudice. 1906. 352p. pap. 4.95 o.p. (*0-460-11022-5*, Everyman's Classic Library in Paperback) Tuttle Publishing.

—Pride & Prejudice. (Penguin Classics Ser.). 2002. 480p. pap. 8.00 (*0-14-143951-3*, Penguin Classics); 1997. 384p. pap. 7.95 o.s.i (*0-14-043426-7*, Penguin Classics); 1996. 400p. pap. 9.95 o.p. (*0-14-043596-4*) Viking Penguin.

—Pride & Prejudice. Tanner, Tony, ed. 1980. pap. 1.95 o.p. (*0-14-005774-9*) Viking Penguin.

—Pride & Prejudice. 1976. 2.95 o.p. (*0-460-01022-0*) Viking Penguin.

—Pride & Prejudice. Tanner, Tony, ed. 1972. (English Library). 400p. pap. 7.95 o.s.i (*0-14-043072-5*, Penguin Classics) Viking Penguin.

—Pride & Prejudice. abr. ed. 2003. (Classics on Audio Ser.). 4p. audio 16.95 (*0-14-086060-6*, 693102, Penguin Classics) Viking Penguin.

—Pride & Prejudice. 2000. text 6.00 (*0-8220-7172-X*, Cliff Notes) Wiley, John & Sons, Inc.

—Pride & Prejudice. 1997. (Classics Library). 288p. pap. 3.95 (*1-85326-000-2*, 0002WW) Wordsworth Editions, Ltd. GBR. *Dist:* Casemate Pubs. & Bk. Distributors, LLC.

—Pride & Prejudice. 1992. E-Book 8.98 (*0-585-25816-3*) netLibrary, Inc.

Austen, Jane & Hemmant, Lynette. Pride & Prejudice. 1980. 14.95 o.p. (*0-437-24575-6*) Trafalgar Square.

Austen, Jane & Kinsley, James. Pride & Prejudice. 1990. E-Book 13.13 (*0-585-37761-8*) netLibrary, Inc.

Bader, Ted, et al. Desire & Duty: A Sequel to Jane Austen's Pride & Prejudice. 1997. (Illus.). 286p. 19.95 (*0-9654299-0-3*, 97-1) Revive Publishing.

Barrett, Julia, pseud. Presumption. 238p. pap. 11.95 (*1-85479-993-2*) O'Mara, Michael Bks., Ltd. GBR. *Dist:* Andrews McMeel Publishing.

—Presumption: An Entertainment Sequel to Jane Austen's Pride & Prejudice. unabr. collector's ed. 1995. audio 48.00 (*0-7366-2954-8*, 3648) Books on Tape, Inc.

Barrett, Julia, pseud & Austen, Jane. Presumption: An Entertainment: A Sequel to Pride & Prejudice. 1993. 240p. 19.95 o.p. (*0-87131-736-2*) Evans, M. & Co., Inc.

—Presumption: An Entertainment: A Sequel to Pride & Prejudice. 1995. 238p. reprint ed. pap. 12.00 (*0-226-03813-0*) Univ. of Chicago Pr.

Bebris, Carrie. Pride & Prescience. 2004. 288p. 21.95 (*0-7653-0508-9*, Forge Bks.) Doherty, Tom Assocs., LLC.

Berdoll, Linda. The Bar Sinister: Pride & Prejudice Continues. 1999. 468p. pap. 18.50 (*0-9674817-0-8*) Well There It Is Pubs.

Calvit, Christina. Pride & Prejudice. unabr. ed. 1997. audio 22.95 (*1-58081-052-7*, CTA55) L. A. Theatre Works.

Dawkins, Jane. Letters from Pemberley: The First Year. 1999. 200p. pap. 12.00 (*1-893337-00-6*) Chicken Soup Pr., Inc.

Fasman, Marjorie. The Diary of Henry Fitzwilliam Darcy. 1997. 262p. 29.95 (*0-9660778-5-7*); 1997. 262p. lthr. 100.00 (*0-9660778-3-0*); 1998. 252p. pap. 16.00 (*0-9660778-1-4*) New Leaf Pr.

Newark, Elizabeth. Consequence: Or, Whatever Became of Charlotte Lucas. 1997. (Illus.). 135p. pap. 12.50 (*0-9659147-0-4*) New Ark Productions.

Prentice-Hall Staff. Pride & Prejudice. 2nd ed. text, stu. ed. (*0-13-716978-7*) Prentice Hall (Schl. Div.).

Robinson, Pamela. Pride & Prejudice: Dramatic Reading. 1968. audio 11.95 Norton Pubs., Inc., Jeffrey /Audio-Forum.

Tennant, Emma. Pemberley: Or Pride & Prejudice Continued, Set. unabr. ed. 1996. audio 54.95 (*0-7451-2729-0*, SAB 095, Sterling Audio Bks.) BBC Audiobooks America.

—Pemberley: Or Pride & Prejudice Continued. l.t. ed. 1995. (Charnwood Large Print Ser.). 272p. 29.99 o.p. (*0-7089-8826-1*, Charnwood) Thorpe, F. A. Pubs. GBR. *Dist:* Ulverscroft Large Print Bks., Ltd., Ulverscroft Large Print Canada, Ltd.

—An Unequal Marriage: Or Pride & Prejudice Twenty Years Later. unabr. ed. 1996. audio 39.95 (*0-7451-2748-7*, SAB114, Sterling Audio Bks.) BBC Audiobooks America.

Tennant, Emma & Austen, Jane. Pemberley: Or Pride & Prejudice Continued. 1993. 184p. pap. 18.95 (*0-312-10793-5*) St. Martin's Pr.

—An Unequal Marriage: Or Pride & Prejudice Twenty Years Later. 1994. 224p. 18.95 o.p. (*0-312-11533-4*) St. Martin's Pr.

**BENNETT, CHASE (FICTITIOUS CHARACTER)—FICTION**

Locke, Thomas. The Omega Network. 1995. (Thomas Locke Ser.: Bk. 2). 256p. pap. 8.99 o.p. (*1-55661-502-7*) Bethany Hse. Pubs.

—The Omega Network. l.t. ed. 2001. (Christian Mystery Ser.). 363p. 24.95 (*0-7862-3579-9*) Thorndike Pr.

**BENNETT, CHRISTINE (FICTITIOUS CHARACTER)—FICTION**

Harris, Lee. The April Fool's Day Murder. l.t. ed. 2001. 355p. 27.95 (*0-7862-3714-7*) Thorndike Pr.

—The Christening Day Murder. 1993. (Christine Bennett Mysteries Ser.: Vol. 3). 224p. mass mkt. 6.99 (*0-449-14871-8*, Fawcett) Ballantine Bks.

—The Christmas Night Murder. 1994. (Christine Bennett Mysteries Ser.: Vol. 5). 224p. mass mkt. 6.99 (*0-449-14922-6*, Fawcett) Ballantine Bks.

—The Christmas Night Murder. unabr. ed. 1999. audio 39.95 (*0-7861-1672-2*, 2500) Blackstone Audio Bks., Inc.

—The Father's Day Murder. 1999. (Christine Bennett Mysteries Ser.: Vol. 11). 272p. mass mkt. 6.99 (*0-449-00441-4*, Fawcett) Ballantine Bks.

—The Good Friday Murder. 1992. (Christine Bennett Mysteries Ser.: Vol. 1). 208p. mass mkt. 6.99 (*0-449-14762-2*, Fawcett) Ballantine Bks.

—The Good Friday Murder. abr. ed. 1997. audio 19.95 (*0-9658148-0-7*, SA111) Scheherazade AudioVisions, Inc.

—The Labor Day Murder. 1998. 272p. (Christine Bennett Mysteries Ser.: Vol. 10). mass mkt. 5.99 (*0-449-15017-8*); pap. 19.00 (*0-345-46760-4*) Ballantine Bks. (Fawcett).

—The Mother's Day Murder. 2000. (Christine Bennett Mysteries Ser.: Vol. 12). 272p. mass mkt. 6.50 (*0-449-00442-2*, Fawcett) Ballantine Bks.

—The New Year's Eve Murder. 1997. (Christine Bennett Mysteries Ser.: Vol. 9). 272p. mass mkt. 6.99 (*0-449-15018-6*, Fawcett) Ballantine Bks.

—The Passover Murder. 1996. (Christine Bennett Mysteries Ser.: Vol. 7). 288p. mass mkt. 6.99 (*0-449-14963-3*, Fawcett) Ballantine Bks.

—The St. Patrick's Day Murder. 1994. (Christine Bennett Mysteries Ser.: Vol. 4). 224p. (Orig.). mass mkt. 6.99 (*0-449-14872-6*, Fawcett) Ballantine Bks.

—The Thanksgiving Day Murder. 1995. (Christine Bennett Mysteries Ser.: Vol. 6). 256p. mass mkt. 6.50 (*0-449-14923-4*, Fawcett) Ballantine Bks.

—The Thanksgiving Day Murder. unabr. ed. 1999. (Christine Bennett Mysteries Ser.). audio 39.95 (*0-7861-1645-5*, 2473) Blackstone Audio Bks., Inc.

—The Valentine's Day Murder. 1996. (Christine Bennett Mysteries Ser.: Vol. 8). 272p. mass mkt. 6.99 (*0-449-14964-1*, Fawcett) Ballantine Bks.

—The Yom Kippur Murder. 1992. (Christine Bennett Mysteries Ser.: Vol. 2). 224p. (Orig.). mass mkt. 6.99 (*0-449-14763-0*, Fawcett) Ballantine Bks.

**BENNETT, JILL (FICTITIOUS CHARACTER)—FICTION**

Heggan, Christiane. Deception. abr. ed. 1998. audio 7.99 (*1-55204-155-7*) Durkin Hayes Publishing Ltd.

—Deception. 1998. (Mira Bks.). mass mkt. (*1-55166-466-6*, 1-66466-3, Mira Bks.) Harlequin Enterprises, Ltd.

**BENNETT, LILY (FICTITIOUS CHARACTER)—FICTION**

Kellogg, Marne Davis. Bad Manners. 1998. 270p. reprint ed. lib. bdg. 29.95 (*0-7351-0056-X*) Replica Bks.

—Bad Manners. 1996. (Illus.). 288p. mass mkt. 5.99 o.s.i (*0-446-60357-0*); 1995. 272p. 21.45 o.p. (*0-446-51836-0*) Warner Bks., Inc.

—Birthday Party: A Lilly Bennett Mystery. 2000. 272p. mass mkt. 5.99 o.s.i (*0-553-58049-3*) Bantam Bks.

—Birthday Party: A Lilly Bennett Mystery. 1999. (Lilly Bennett Mysteries Ser.). 272p. 21.95 o.s.i (*0-385-49333-9*) Doubleday Publishing.

—Curtsey. 1996. 272p. 21.95 o.p. (*0-446-51837-9*) Warner Bks., Inc.

—Tramp. 1998. (Lilly Bennett Mysteries Ser.). 352p. mass mkt. 5.99 o.s.i (*0-553-57992-4*) Bantam Bks.

**BENNETT, MILDRED (FICTITIOUS CHARACTER)—FICTION**

McShea, Susanna H. Hometown Heroes. 1992. (Hometown Heroes Ser.). 320p. mass mkt. 4.99 (*0-380-71675-5*, Avon Bks.) Morrow/Avon.

—Hometown Heroes. 1990. (Hometown Heroes Ser.). 18.95 o.p. (*0-312-04681-2*, Saint Martin's Minotaur) St. Martin's Pr.

—Ladybug, Ladybug. 1995. (Hometown Heroes Ser.). 352p. reprint ed. mass mkt. 5.50 (*0-380-71981-9*, Avon Bks.) Morrow/Avon.

—Ladybug, Ladybug. 1994. (Hometown Heroes Ser.). 3352p. (J). (ps-k). 21.95 o.p. (*0-312-11017-0*, Saint Martin's Minotaur) St. Martin's Pr.

—The Pumpkin-Shell Wife. 1993. (Hometown Heroes Ser.). 352p. mass mkt. 4.99 (*0-380-71980-0*, Avon Bks.) Morrow/Avon.

—The Pumpkin-Shell Wife. 1992. (Hometown Heroes Ser.). 352p. 19.95 o.p. (*0-312-07768-8*, Saint Martin's Minotaur) St. Martin's Pr.

**BENNETT, REID (FICTITIOUS CHARACTER)—FICTION**

Wood, Ted. Corkscrew. 1987. (Reid Bennett Mystery Ser.). 240p. 14.95 o.p. (*0-684-18853-8*, Macmillan Reference USA) Gale Group.

—Corkscrew. 1989. 224p. reprint ed. mass mkt. (*0-373-26024-5*, Harlequin Bks.) Harlequin Enterprises, Ltd.

—Corkscrew. 2001. E-Book 6.99 (*0-7592-1043-8*); 1999. 188p. per. 19.95 (*1-58586-863-9*) eread-s.com.

—Dead in the Water. 1984. 160p. mass mkt. 2.95 o.s.i (*0-7704-2006-0*) Bantam Bks.

—Flashback. l.t. ed. 1994. 21.95 o.p. (*0-7927-1819-4*); pap. 19.95 o.p. (*0-7927-1818-6*) BBC Audiobooks America.

—Flashback. 1992. 256p. text 20.00 (*0-684-19414-7*, Macmillan Reference USA) Gale Group.

—Flashback. 1994. (WWL Mystery Ser.). per. (*0-373-26137-3*, 1-26137-9, Harlequin Bks.) Harlequin Enterprises, Ltd.

—Fool's Gold. 1986. 192p. 13.95 o.s.i (*0-684-18568-7*, Macmillan Reference USA) Gale Group.

—Fool's Gold. 1988. 224p. reprint ed. mass mkt. (*0-373-26019-9*, Harlequin Bks.) Harlequin Enterprises, Ltd.

—Live Bait. 1986. (Mystery Ser.). 208p. mass mkt. 2.95 o.s.i (*0-553-25558-4*) Bantam Bks.

—Live Bait. 1985. 192p. 12.95 o.s.i (*0-684-18330-7*, Macmillan Reference USA) Gale Group.

—Live Bait. 2002. 174p. pap. 6.99 (*1-58586-855-8*); E-Book 6.99 (*1-58586-852-3*); E-Book 6.99 (*0-7592-1039-X*); E-Book 6.99 (*0-7592-0395-4*) ereads.com.

—Murder on Ice. 1985. 176p. mass mkt. 2.95 o.s.i (*0-7704-2049-4*) Bantam Bks.

—Murder on Ice. 1984. 160p. 12.95 o.s.i (*0-684-18134-7*, Macmillan Reference USA) Gale Group.

—On the Inside: A Reid Bennett Mystery. 1990. 256p. 18.95 o.s.i (*0-684-19090-7*, Macmillan Reference USA) Gale Group.

—On the Inside: A Reid Bennett Mystery. 1991. 224p. reprint ed. pap. (*0-373-26076-8*, Harlequin Bks.) Harlequin Enterprises, Ltd.

—Snowjob. 1995. (Mystery Ser.). 251p. per. (*0-373-26182-9*, 1-26182-5, Worldwide Library) Harlequin Enterprises, Ltd.

—Snowjob. 1993. 256p. 20.00 o.p. (*0-684-19563-1*, Scribner) Simon & Schuster.

—When the Killing Starts. 1990. mass mkt. (*0-373-26043-1*, Harlequin Bks.) Harlequin Enterprises, Ltd.

—When the Killing Starts. 1989. 224p. 16.95 o.s.i (*0-684-18331-5*, Scribner) Simon & Schuster.

**BENNIS, NORMAN (FICTITIOUS CHARACTER)—FICTION**

D'Amato, Barbara. Killer.app. 350p. 1997. mass mkt. 5.99 (*0-8125-5391-8*); 1996. 22.95 o.p. (*0-312-85991-0*) Doherty, Tom Assocs., LLC. (Forge Bks.).

**BENTLEY, WILLIAM (FICTITIOUS CHARACTER)—FICTION**

Needle, Jan. A Fine Boy for Killing. 1983. 256p. (gr. 9 up). 10.95 o.p. (*0-233-97106-8*) Blackwell Publishing.

—A Fine Boy for Killing. 2000. (Sea Officer William Bentley Ser.: Vol. 1). 320p. pap. 15.95 (*0-935526-86-2*) McBooks Pr., Inc.

—The Wicked Trade. 2001. (Sea Officer William Bentley Ser.: Vol. 2). 382p. pap. 16.95 (*0-935526-95-1*) McBooks Pr., Inc.

**BENTON, BARBARA (FICTITIOUS CHARACTER)—FICTION**

Stuart, Dee. Deadly Legacy. 1996. 352p. mass mkt. 4.99 o.s.i (*0-8217-5316-9*) Kensington Publishing Corp.

**BENTON, BROOKE (FICTITIOUS CHARACTER)—FICTION**

Harper, Karen. The Dark Road Home. l.t. ed. 1998. 26.95 (*1-57490-135-4*, Beeler Large Print Bks.) Beeler, Thomas T. Publisher.

—The Dark Road Home. 1996. 448p. mass mkt. 5.99 o.s.i (*0-451-18725-3*) NAL.

**BERESFORD, TOMMY (FICTITIOUS CHARACTER)—FICTION**

Christie, Agatha. Affair of the Pink Pearl. unabr. ed. 1992. audio 5.99 (*0-88646-602-4*, PAC-7602) Durkin Hayes Publishing Ltd.

—By the Pricking of My Thumbs. abr. ed. 2003. (Agatha Christie Audio Mystery Ser.). (Illus.). audio 12.95 (*1-55927-904-4*) Audio Renaissance.

—By the Pricking of My Thumbs. unabr. ed. 1995. audio 69.95 o.p. (*0-7451-4197-8*, CAB 880) BBC Audiobooks America.

—By the Pricking of My Thumbs. 2000. (Tommy & Tuppence Mysteries Ser.). 224p. mass mkt. 5.99 (*0-451-20052-7*, Signet Bks.) NAL.

—By the Pricking of My Thumbs. 1986. (Agatha Christie Ser.). 14.95 o.s.i (*0-396-08863-5*, G. P. Putnam's Sons) Penguin Putnam Bks. for Young Readers.

—By the Pricking of My Thumbs. 1990. mass mkt. 4.99 o.p. (*0-671-70609-8*); 1983. mass mkt. 2.95 o.s.i (*0-671-46807-3*) Simon & Schuster. (Pocket).

—By the Pricking of My Thumbs. l.t. ed. 1987. (Ulverscroft Large Print Ser.). 432p. o.p. (*0-7089-1571-X*, Ulverscroft) Thorpe, F. A. Pubs. GBR. *Dist:* Ulverscroft Large Print Canada, Ltd.

—By the Pricking of My Thumbs. 1992. 12.04 (*0-606-12207-9*) Turtleback Bks.

—The Mysterious Affair at Styles & The Secret Adversary: An Agatha Christie Omnibus. 1998. 464p. pap. 12.95 (*0-7867-0434-9*, Carroll & Graf Pubs.) Avalon Publishing Group.

—N or M? unabr. ed. 1997. (Tuppence & Tommy Beresford Mysteries Ser.). audio 54.95 o.p. (*0-7451-5832-3*, CAB 653) BBC Audiobooks America.

—N or M? (Agatha Christie Ser.). 1998. mass mkt. 3.99 o.s.i (*0-425-16929-4*); 1986. 240p. mass mkt. 5.99 o.s.i (*0-425-09845-1*); 1986. mass mkt. 2.95 o.s.i (*0-425-09329-8*); 1984. mass mkt. 2.95 o.s.i (*0-425-06796-3*) Berkley Publishing Group.

—N or M? 1974. 192p. pap. 2.50 o.s.i (*0-440-16254-8*) Dell Publishing.

—N or M? 2000. (Tommy & Tuppence Mysteries Ser.). 224p. mass mkt. 5.99 (*0-451-20113-2*, Signet Bks.) NAL.

—N or M? 1987. (Agatha Christie Ser.). 14.95 o.s.i (*0-396-09163-6*, G. P. Putnam's Sons) Penguin Putnam Bks. for Young Readers.

—N or M? l.t. ed. 1984. (Ulverscroft Large Print Ser.). 336p. 32.50 (*0-7089-1156-0*, Ulverscroft) Thorpe, F. A. Pubs. GBR. *Dist:* Ulverscroft Large Print Bks., Ltd., Ulverscroft Large Print Canada, Ltd.

—Partners in Crime. 224p. 21.95 o.s.i (*0-8488-2448-2*) Amereon, Ltd.

—Partners in Crime. 1987. (Agatha Christie Ser.). 240p. mass mkt. 5.99 o.s.i (*0-425-10352-8*) Berkley Publishing Group.

—Partners in Crime. 1971. 224p. pap. 2.50 o.s.i (*0-440-16848-1*) Dell Publishing.

—Partners in Crime. unabr. ed. audio 42.25 o.p. 1989. audio 15.95 o.p. Durkin Hayes Publishing Ltd.

—Partners in Crime. l.t. ed. 1986. 416p. (*0-7089-1540-X*, Ulverscroft) Thorpe, F. A. Pubs.

—Postern of Fate. 1974. (HC Collection). 288p. reprint ed. mass mkt. 3.50 o.s.i (*0-553-25493-6*) Bantam Bks.

—Postern of Fate. l.t. ed. (General Ser.). 1992. 376p. lib. bdg. 19.95 o.p. (*0-8161-4593-8*); 1985. 488p. 10.95 o.p. (*0-8161-3123-6*); 1974. 492p. reprint ed. lib. bdg. 11.95 o.p. (*0-8161-6197-6*) Gale Group. (Macmillan Reference USA).

—Postern of Fate. 2000. (Tommy & Tuppence Mysteries Ser.). 240p. mass mkt. 5.99 (*0-451-20053-5*, Signet Bks.) NAL.

—Postern of Fate. 1991. (General Ser.). 12.04 (*0-606-12483-7*) Turtleback Bks.

—Postern of Fate. l.t. ed. 2001. (Ulverscroft Large Print Ser.). 480p. 32.50 (*0-7089-2708-4*) Ulverscroft Large Print Bks., Ltd.

—The Secret Adversary. unabr. ed. 1996. audio 35.95 (*1-55685-450-1*) Audio Bk. Contractors, Inc.

—The Secret Adversary. unabr. ed. audio 69.95 o.p. BBC Audiobooks America.

—The Secret Adversary. 1983. 224p. mass mkt. 3.50 o.s.i (*0-553-26477-X*) Bantam Bks.

—The Secret Adversary. 1991. (Agatha Christie Ser.). 240p. mass mkt. 5.99 o.s.i (*0-425-13027-4*) Berkley Publishing Group.

—The Secret Adversary. unabr. ed. 1998. audio 44.95 (*0-7861-1336-7*, 2230) Blackstone Audio Bks., Inc.

—The Secret Adversary. unabr. collector's ed. 1998. audio 56.00 (*0-7366-4213-7*, 4711) Books on Tape, Inc.

—The Secret Adversary. 1988. lib. bdg. 19.95 o.p. (*0-8161-4464-8*); 1989. 363p. 13.95 o.p. (*0-8161-4503-2*) Gale Group. (Macmillan Reference USA).

—The Secret Adversary. unabr. ed. 1999. audio 44.95 Highsmith Inc.

—The Secret Adversary. E-Book 1.95 (*1-58515-018-5*) MesaView, Inc.

—The Secret Adversary. 1999. E-Book 8.99 incl. cd-rom (*1-891595-61-X*) Quiet Vision Publishing.

—The Secret Adversary. l.t. ed. 2001. (Ulverscroft Large Print Ser.). 32.50 (*0-7089-2441-7*) Ulverscroft Large Print Bks., Ltd.

**BERESFORD, TUPPENCE (FICTITIOUS CHARACTER)—FICTION**

Christie, Agatha. Affair of the Pink Pearl. unabr. ed. 1992. audio 5.99 (*0-88646-602-4*, PAC-7602) Durkin Hayes Publishing Ltd.

—By the Pricking of My Thumbs. abr. ed. 2003. (Agatha Christie Audio Mystery Ser.). (Illus.). audio 12.95 (*1-55927-904-4*) Audio Renaissance.

—By the Pricking of My Thumbs. unabr. ed. 1995. audio 69.95 o.p. (*0-7451-4197-8*, CAB 880) BBC Audiobooks America.

—By the Pricking of My Thumbs. 2000. (Tommy & Tuppence Mysteries Ser.). 224p. mass mkt. 5.99 (*0-451-20052-7*, Signet Bks.) NAL.

—By the Pricking of My Thumbs. 1986. (Agatha Christie Ser.). 14.95 o.s.i (*0-396-08863-5*, G. P. Putnam's Sons) Penguin Putnam Bks. for Young Readers.

—By the Pricking of My Thumbs. 1990. mass mkt. 4.99 o.p. (*0-671-70609-8*); 1983. mass mkt. 2.95 o.s.i (*0-671-46807-3*) Simon & Schuster. (Pocket).

—By the Pricking of My Thumbs. l.t. ed. 1987. (Ulverscroft Large Print Ser.). 432p. o.p. (*0-7089-1571-X*, Ulverscroft) Thorpe, F. A. Pubs. GBR. *Dist:* Ulverscroft Large Print Canada, Ltd.

—By the Pricking of My Thumbs. 1992. 12.04 (*0-606-12207-9*) Turtleback Bks.

—The Mysterious Affair at Styles & The Secret Adversary: An Agatha Christie Omnibus. 1998. 464p. pap. 12.95 (*0-7867-0434-9*, Carroll & Graf Pubs.) Avalon Publishing Group.

—N or M? unabr. ed. 1997. (Tuppence & Tommy Beresford Mysteries Ser.). audio 54.95 o.p. (*0-7451-5832-3*, CAB 653) BBC Audiobooks America.

—N or M? (Agatha Christie Ser.). 1998. mass mkt. 3.99 o.s.i (*0-425-16929-4*); 1986. 240p. mass mkt. 5.99 o.s.i (*0-425-09845-1*); 1986. mass mkt. 2.95 o.s.i (*0-425-09329-8*); 1984. mass mkt. 2.95 o.s.i (*0-425-06796-3*) Berkley Publishing Group.

—N or M? 1974. 192p. pap. 2.50 o.s.i (*0-440-16254-8*) Dell Publishing.

—N or M? 2000. (Tommy & Tuppence Mysteries Ser.). 224p. mass mkt. 5.99 (*0-451-20113-2*, Signet Bks.) NAL.

—N or M? 1987. (Agatha Christie Ser.). 14.95 o.s.i (*0-396-09163-6*, G. P. Putnam's Sons) Penguin Putnam Bks. for Young Readers.

—N or M? l.t. ed. 1984. (Ulverscroft Large Print Ser.). 336p. 32.50 (*0-7089-1156-0*, Ulverscroft) Thorpe, F. A. Pubs. GBR. *Dist:* Ulverscroft Large Print Bks., Ltd., Ulverscroft Large Print Canada, Ltd.

—Partners in Crime. 224p. 21.95 o.s.i (*0-8488-2448-2*) Amereon, Ltd.

—Partners in Crime. 1987. (Agatha Christie Ser.). 240p. mass mkt. 5.99 o.s.i (*0-425-10352-8*) Berkley Publishing Group.

—Partners in Crime. 1971. 224p. pap. 2.50 o.s.i (*0-440-16848-1*) Dell Publishing.

—Partners in Crime. unabr. ed. audio 42.25 o.p. 1989. audio 15.95 o.p. Durkin Hayes Publishing Ltd.

—Partners in Crime. l.t. ed. 1986. 416p. (*0-7089-1540-X*, Ulverscroft) Thorpe, F. A. Pubs.

—Postern of Fate. 1974. (HC Collection). 288p. reprint ed. mass mkt. 3.50 o.s.i (*0-553-25493-6*) Bantam Bks.

—Postern of Fate. l.t. ed. (General Ser.). 1992. 376p. lib. bdg. 19.95 o.p. (*0-8161-4593-8*); 1985. 488p. 10.95 o.p. (*0-8161-3123-6*); 1974. 492p. reprint ed. lib. bdg. 11.95 o.p. (*0-8161-6197-6*) Gale Group. (Macmillan Reference USA).

—Postern of Fate. 2000. (Tommy & Tuppence Mysteries Ser.). 240p. mass mkt. 5.99 (*0-451-20053-5*, Signet Bks.) NAL.

—Postern of Fate. 1991. (General Ser.). 12.04 (*0-606-12483-7*) Turtleback Bks.

—Postern of Fate. l.t. ed. 2001. (Ulverscroft Large Print Ser.). 480p. 32.50 (*0-7089-2708-4*) Ulverscroft Large Print Bks., Ltd.

—The Secret Adversary. unabr. ed. 1996. audio 35.95 (*1-55685-450-1*) Audio Bk. Contractors, Inc.

—The Secret Adversary. unabr. ed. audio 69.95 o.p. BBC Audiobooks America.

—The Secret Adversary. 1983. 224p. mass mkt. 3.50 o.s.i (*0-553-26477-X*) Bantam Bks.

—The Secret Adversary. 1991. (Agatha Christie Ser.). 240p. mass mkt. 5.99 o.s.i (*0-425-13027-4*) Berkley Publishing Group.

—The Secret Adversary, unabr. ed. 1998. audio 44.95 (*0-7861-1336-7*, 2230) Blackstone Audio Bks., Inc.

—The Secret Adversary. unabr. collector's ed. 1998. audio 56.00 (*0-7366-4213-7*, 4711) Books on Tape, Inc.

—The Secret Adversary. 1988. lib. bdg. 19.95 o.p. (*0-8161-4464-8*); 1989. 363p. 13.95 o.p. (*0-8161-4503-2*) Gale Group. (Macmillan Reference USA).

—The Secret Adversary, unabr. ed. 1999. audio 44.95 Highsmith Inc.

—The Secret Adversary. E-Book 1.95 (*1-58515-018-5*) MesaView, Inc.

—The Secret Adversary. 1999. E-Book 8.99 incl. cd-rom (*1-891595-61-X*) Quiet Vision Publishing.

—The Secret Adversary. l.t. ed. 2001. (Ulverscroft Large Print Ser.). 32.50 (*0-7089-2441-7*) Ulverscroft Large Print Bks., Ltd.

**BERG, MORRIS, 1902-1972—FICTION**

Willinger, Kurt. The Spy in a Catcher's Mask. 1995. 282p. 19.95 (*1-879094-45-2*); pap. 12.95 (*1-879094-44-4*) Momentum Bks., LLC. (Sabre Pr.).

**BERGER, MITCH (FICTITIOUS CHARACTER)—FICTION**

Handler, David. The Bright Silver Star. Date not set. pap. (*0-312-30715-2*, Saint Martin's Griffin); Date not set. mass mkt. (*0-312-99461-3*, St. Martin's Paperbacks); Date not set. mass mkt. (*0-312-99620-9*, St. Martin's Paperbacks); mass mkt. (*0-312-98578-9*, St. Martin's Paperbacks); E-Book (*0-312-70566-2*); 2003. 320p. 24.95 (*0-312-30714-4*, Saint Martin's Minotaur) St. Martin's Pr.

—The Cold Blue Blood. 2002. 320p. mass mkt. 6.50 (*0-312-98610-6*, St. Martin's Paperbacks); 2001. 304p. 23.95 (*0-312-28003-3*, Saint Martin's Minotaur) St. Martin's Pr.

—The Hot Pink Farmhouse. Date not set. mass mkt. (*0-312-98579-7*, St. Martin's Paperbacks); E-Book 17.95 (*0-312-70893-9*); 2002. 336p. 23.95 (*0-312-28015-7*, Saint Martin's Minotaur) St. Martin's Pr.

**BERGERAC (FICTITIOUS CHARACTER)—FICTION**

Saville, Andrew. Bergerac & the Fatal Weakness. unabr. ed. 1993. audio 39.95 (*0-7451-6254-1*) BBC Audiobooks America.

—Bergerac & the Fatal Weakness. 1990. audio 39.95 o.p. (*0-8161-9514-5*) Thorndike Pr.

—Bergerac & the Jersey Rose. unabr. ed. audio 54.95 (*0-7451-4020-3*) BBC Audiobooks America.

—Bergerac & the Moving Fever. unabr. ed. 1991. (Audio Ser.). audio 54.95 (*0-7451-6255-X*) BBC Audiobooks America.

—Bergerac & the Traitor's Child. unabr. ed. 1993. audio 39.95 (*0-7451-6256-8*) BBC Audiobooks America.

**BERKELEY BRIGADE (FICTITIOUS CHARACTERS)—FICTION**

Smith, Joan. Murder & Misdeeds. 1997. mass mkt. 4.50 o.s.i (*0-449-28791-2*, Fawcett) Ballantine Bks.

—Murder Comes to Mind. 1998. mass mkt. 4.99 o.s.i (*0-449-00287-X*, Fawcett) Ballantine Bks.

—Murder While I Smile. 1997. mass mkt. 4.99 o.s.i (*0-449-22494-5*, Fawcett) Ballantine Bks.

—Murder Will Speak. 1997. mass mkt. 4.50 o.s.i (*0-449-22465-1*, Fawcett) Ballantine Bks.

—Murder Will Speak. 1996. 208p. 21.95 o.p. (*0-312-14378-8*, Saint Martin's Minotaur) St. Martin's Pr.

**BERNARD, ROLF (FICTITIOUS CHARACTER)—FICTION**

Graham, Daniel, Jr. The Gatekeepers. 464p. 1996. mass mkt. 5.99 o.s.i (*0-671-87716-X*); 1995. 22.00 o.s.i (*0-671-87684-8*) Baen Bks.

**BERNHARDT, ALAN (FICTITIOUS CHARACTER)—FICTION**

Wilcox, Collin. Bernhardt's Edge. 1991. pap. 3.95 o.p. (*0-8125-1148-4*); 1988. 320p. 17.95 o.p. (*0-312-93076-3*) Doherty, Tom Assocs., LLC. (Tor Bks.).

—Except for the Bones. 1991. 288p. 18.95 o.p. (*0-312-93162-X*, Tor Bks.) Doherty, Tom Assocs., LLC.

—Find Her a Grave. 1993. 288p. 19.95 o.p. (*0-312-85244-4*, Forge Bks.) Doherty, Tom Assocs., LLC.

—Silent Witness. 1992. mass mkt. 3.99 (*0-8125-1149-2*); 1990. 17.95 o.p. (*0-312-93161-1*) Doherty, Tom Assocs., LLC. (Tor Bks.).

**BERNIER, ALEX (FICTITIOUS CHARACTER)—FICTION**

Saulnier, Beth. Bad Seed. 2002. 384p. 23.95 (*0-89296-749-8*) Mysterious Pr.

—Bad Seed. 2003. (Alex Bernier Mysteries Ser.). 432p. mass mkt. 6.99 (*0-446-61206-5*) Warner Bks., Inc.

—Distemper. unabr. ed. 2000. audio 54.95 (*0-7927-2417-8*, CSL 306, Chivers Sound Library) BBC Audiobooks America.

—Distemper. 2000. (Alex Bernier Mysteries Ser.). 400p. reprint ed. mass mkt. 6.50 (*0-446-60861-0*) Warner Bks., Inc.

—Ecstasy. 2003. (Alex Bernier Mystery Ser.). 352p. 23.95 (*0-89296-750-1*) Mysterious Pr.

—Ecstasy. 2004. (Illus.). 752p. mass mkt. 7.99 (*0-446-61370-3*) Warner Bks., Inc.

—The Fourth Wall. 2001. 432p. reprint ed. mass mkt. 6.99 (*0-446-60998-6*) Warner Bks., Inc.

—Reliable Sources. 1999. 352p. reprint ed. mass mkt. 6.50 (*0-446-60781-9*) Warner Bks., Inc.

**BERNSTEIN, ELLIE (FICTITIOUS CHARACTER)—FICTION**

Dietz, Denise. Beat up a Cookie: An Ellie Bernstein Mystery. 2000. per. (*0-373-26340-6*, Harlequin Bks.) Harlequin Enterprises, Ltd.

—Beat up a Cookie: An Ellie Bernstein Mystery. 1994. 216p. 19.95 o.p. (*0-8027-3186-4*) Walker & Co.

—Throw Darts at a Cheesecake. 1999. per. (*0-373-26334-1*, Harlequin Bks.) Harlequin Enterprises, Ltd.

—Throw Darts at a Cheesecake. 1992. 211p. 19.95 o.p. (*0-8027-1237-1*) Walker & Co.

**BERT THE SHIRT (FICTITIOUS CHARACTER)—FICTION**

Shames, Laurence. Florida Straits. unabr. collector's ed. 1998. audio 48.00 (*0-7366-4079-7*, 4588) Books on Tape, Inc.

—Florida Straits. 1993. 368p. mass mkt. 6.50 (*0-440-21511-0*) Dell Publishing.

—Florida Straits, unabr. ed. 1997. audio 60.00 (*0-7887-1751-0*, 95229E7) Recorded Bks., LLC.

—Florida Straits. 1992. 256p. 20.00 o.p. (*0-671-74933-1*, Simon & Schuster) Simon & Schuster.

—Mangrove Squeeze. abr. ed. 1998. audio 16.95 (*1-55927-485-9*) Audio Renaissance.

—Mangrove Squeeze. 1999. 352p. mass mkt. 6.99 (*0-345-43306-8*) Ballantine Bks.

—Mangrove Squeeze. unabr. collector's ed. 1998. audio 56.00 (*0-7366-4261-7*, 4760) Books on Tape, Inc.

—Mangrove Squeeze. 1998. 320p. 22.95 o.p. (*0-7868-6301-3*); mass mkt. 5.99 (*0-7868-8945-4*) Hyperion Pr.

—Mangrove Squeeze, unabr. ed. 1998. audio 60.00 (*0-7887-2037-6*, 95401E7) Recorded Bks., LLC.

—Sunburn. unabr. collector's ed. 1998. audio 48.00 (*0-7366-4167-X*, 4669) Books on Tape, Inc.

—Sunburn. 1996. 384p. mass mkt. 4.99 (*0-7868-8903-9*); 1995. 288p. 21.95 (*0-7868-6068-5*) Hyperion Pr.

—Sunburn, unabr. ed. 1998. audio 60.00 (*0-7887-1882-7*, 95304E7) Recorded Bks., LLC.

**BETHANY, TOM (FICTITIOUS CHARACTER)—FICTION**

Doolittle, Jerome. Bear Hug. Grose, Bill, ed. 240p. 1993. mass mkt. 4.99 (*0-671-74569-7*, Pocket); 1992. 20.00 (*0-671-74568-9*, Atria) Simon & Schuster.

—Body Scissors. Grose, Bill, ed. 240p. 1990. 17.95 o.p. (*0-671-70752-3*, Atria); 1991. reprint ed. mass mkt. 5.50 (*0-671-70753-1*, Pocket) Simon & Schuster.

—Half Nelson. Grose, Bill, ed. 1994. 288p. 20.00 o.p. (*0-671-50289-1*, Atria) Simon & Schuster.

—Half Nelson: A Tom Bethany Mystery. 1995. 288p. mass mkt. 5.50 (*0-671-79979-7*, Pocket) Simon & Schuster.

—Head Lock. Grose, Bill, ed. 1993. 272p. 20.00 (*0-671-79978-9*, Atria) Simon & Schuster.

—Head Lock. 1900. per. 4.99 (*0-671-50288-3*, Pocket) Simon & Schuster.

—Head Lock. 262p. 3.98 o.p. (*0-8317-2353-X*) Smithmark Pubs., Inc.

—Kill Story. 304p. 1996. mass mkt. 5.99 (*0-671-79981-9*, Pocket); 1995. 22.00 o.p. (*0-671-79980-0*, Atria) Simon & Schuster.

—Strangle Hold. Grose, Bill, ed. 1992. 304p. reprint ed. mass mkt. 4.99 (*0-671-74571-9*, Pocket) Simon & Schuster.

—Stranglehold: A Tom Bethany Mystery. 1991. 304p. 20.00 (*0-671-70754-X*, Atria) Simon & Schuster.

**BEVERLEY SISTERS (FICTITIOUS CHARACTERS)—FICTION**

Chesney, Marion. The Banishment. 1996. (Daughters of Mannerling Ser.: Vol. 1). mass mkt. 4.50 o.s.i (*0-449-22419-8*, Fawcett) Ballantine Bks.

—The Banishment. l.t. ed. 1996. (Daughters of Mannerling Ser.: Vol. 1). 221p. pap. 17.95 o.p. (*0-7838-1519-0*, Macmillan Reference USA) Gale Group.

—The Banishment. 1995. (Daughters of Mannerling Ser.: Vol. 1). 17.95 o.p. (*0-312-11749-3*) St. Martin's Pr.

—The Deception. 1997. (Daughters of Mannerling Ser.: Vol. 3). mass mkt. 4.50 o.s.i (*0-449-22559-3*, Fawcett) Ballantine Bks.

—The Deception. 1996. (Daughters of Mannerling Ser.: Vol. 3). 160p. 18.95 o.p. (*0-312-13465-7*) St. Martin's Pr.

—The Folly. 1997. (Daughters of Mannerling Ser.: Vol. 4). mass mkt. 4.50 o.s.i (*0-449-28775-0*, Fawcett) Ballantine Bks.

—The Folly. 1996. (Daughters of Mannerling Ser.: Vol. 4). 192p. 16.00 (*0-312-14338-9*) St. Martin's Pr.

—The Folly. l.t. ed. 1998. (Nightingale Ser.). 255p. pap. 21.95 (*0-7838-8288-2*) Thorndike Pr.

—The Homecoming. 1998. (Daughters of Mannerling Ser.: Vol. 6). mass mkt. 4.99 o.s.i (*0-449-28777-7*, Fawcett) Ballantine Bks.

—The Homecoming. l.t. ed. 2000. (G. K. Hall Nightingale Ser.). 226p. pap. 21.95 (*0-7838-8982-8*, Macmillan Reference USA) Gale Group.

—The Homecoming. 1997. (Daughters of Mannerling Ser.: Vol. 6). 144p. 18.95 o.p. (*0-312-16865-9*) St. Martin's Pr.

—The Intrigue. 1996. (Daughters of Mannerling Ser.: Vol. 2). mass mkt. 4.50 o.p. (*0-449-22420-1*, Fawcett) Ballantine Bks.

—The Intrigue. l.t. ed. 1997. (Daughters of Mannerling Ser.: Vol. 2). pap. 18.95 o.p. (*0-7838-8034-0*, Macmillan Reference USA) Gale Group.

—The Intrigue. 1995. (Daughters of Mannerling Ser.: Vol. 2). 160p. 18.95 o.p. (*0-312-13096-1*) St. Martin's Pr.

—The Romance. 1998. (Daughters of Mannerling Ser.: Vol. 5). mass mkt. 4.99 o.s.i (*0-449-28776-9*, Fawcett) Ballantine Bks.

—The Romance. 1997. (Daughters of Mannerling Ser.: Vol. 5). 192p. 20.95 (*0-312-15202-7*) St. Martin's Pr.

—The Romance. l.t. ed. 1998. (Nightingale Ser.). 238p. pap. 21.95 (*0-7838-8385-4*) Thorndike Pr.

**BIDDLECOMB, ISAAC (FICTITIOUS CHARACTER)—FICTION**

Nelson, James L. By Force of Arms. Wolverton, Peter, ed. 1996. (Revolution at Sea Trilogy Ser.: Vol. 1). 336p. pap. 14.00 (*0-671-51924-7*, Pocket) Simon & Schuster.

—By Force of Arms. l.t. ed. 1999. (Sea Trilogy Ser.: Vol. 1). 469p. 28.95 (*0-7838-8526-1*) Thorndike Pr.

—The Continental Risque. 1998. (Revolution at Sea Saga Ser.: Vol. 3). 384p. pap. 14.00 (*0-671-01381-5*, Atria) Simon & Schuster.

—Lords of the Ocean. 368p. 1999. (Revolution at Sea Saga Ser.: Vol. 4). (Illus.). 23.00 o.s.i (*0-671-03490-1*); 2000. reprint ed. pap. 13.95 (*0-671-01383-1*) Simon & Schuster. (Atria).

—The Maddest Idea. 1997. (Revolution at Sea Trilogy Ser.: Vol. 2). 432p. pap. 14.00 (*0-671-51925-5*, Atria) Simon & Schuster.

**BIERCE, AMBROSE, 1842-1914—FICTION**

Fuentes, Carlos. El Gringo Viejo. 1991. (Coleccion Tierra Firme Ser.).Tr. of Old Gringo. (SPA.). 191p. pap. 14.95 (*968-16-1782-7*, FC1105) Fondo de Cultura Economica MEX. *Dist:* Continental Bk. Co., Inc.

—The Old Gringo. 1997. Tr. of Grinjo Viejo. 208p. pap. 13.00 (*0-374-52522-6*) Farrar, Straus & Giroux.

—The Old Gringo. Peden, Margaret Sayers, tr. from SPA. 1985. Tr. of Grinjo Viejo. 180p. 14.95 o.s.i (*0-374-22578-8*) Farrar, Straus & Giroux.

—The Old Gringo.Tr. of Grinjo Viejo. 208p. reprint ed. 1991. pap. 12.00 o.p. (*0-06-097063-4*, PL/7063); 1989. pap. 7.95 o.p. (*0-06-097258-0*) HarperTrade. (Perennial).

—The Old Gringo. 1994. Tr. of Grinjo Viejo. 200p. lib. bdg. 33.00 o.p. (*0-8095-9136-7*) Millefleurs.

Hall, Oakley M. Ambrose Bierce & the Death of Kings. 2002. 288p. 6.99 (*0-14-200133-3*) Viking Penguin.

—Ambrose Bierce & the Queen of Spades: A Novel. 2000. 288p. pap. 5.99 (*0-14-028860-0*, Penguin Bks.) Penguin Group (USA) Inc.

—Ambrose Bierce & the Queen of Spades: A Novel. 1998. 321p. text 22.95 (*0-520-21555-9*) Univ. of California Pr.

—Ambrose Bierce & the Trey of Pearls. 2004. 224p. 24.95 (*0-670-03270-0*, Viking) Viking Penguin.

**BIG MIKE (FICTITIOUS CHARACTER)—FICTION**

Allen, Garrison. Desert Cat. 1994. 304p. mass mkt. 3.99 o.s.i (*0-8217-4503-4*, Zebra Bks.) Kensington Publishing Corp.

—Movie Cat. 1999. (Big Mike Mystery Ser.). 304p. 20.00 o.s.i (*1-57566-413-5*) Kensington Publishing Corp.

**BIGELOW, CARL (FICTITIOUS CHARACTER)—FICTION**

Thompson, Jim. Savage Night. 1985. 176p. reprint ed. pap. 4.95 o.p. (*0-916870-97-9*, Black Mask) Creative Arts Bk. Co.

—Savage Night. 1991. (Vintage Crime/Black Lizard Ser.). 160p. pap. 10.00 (*0-679-73310-8*, Vintage) Knopf Publishing Group.

**BILBO, CHARLIE (FICTITIOUS CHARACTER)—FICTION**

Thrasher, L. L. Charlie's Bones. l.t. ed. 2000. (Dales Large Print Ser.). 304p. pap. (*1-84137-000-2*) Magna Large Print Bks. GBR. *Dist:* Ulverscroft Large Print Bks., Ltd., Ulverscroft Large Print Canada, Ltd.

—Charlie's Bones. 1998. 224p. 21.95 (*1-885173-47-4*) Write Way Publishing.

—Charlie's Web. 2000. 225p. 23.95 (*1-885173-66-0*) Write Way Publishing.

**BILBY, BETTINA (FICTITIOUS CHARACTER)—FICTION**

Babson, Marian. The Diamond Cat. l.t. ed. 1995. 256p. pap. 17.95 o.p. (*0-7838-1456-9*, Macmillan Reference USA) Gale Group.

—The Diamond Cat. unabr. ed. 2000. audio 46.00 (*1-84197-067-0*, H1064E7, Clipper Audio) Recorded Bks., LLC.

—The Diamond Cat. 1996. mass mkt. 5.99 (*0-312-95660-6*, St. Martin's Paperbacks); 1995. 224p. 20.95 o.p. (*0-312-13049-X*, Saint Martin's Minotaur) St. Martin's Pr.

**BILL (FICTITIOUS CHARACTER: HARRISON)—FICTION**

Harrison, Harry. Bill, the Galactic Hero. 1979. 192p. mass mkt. 4.50 (0-380-00395-3, Avon Bks.) Morrow/Avon.

—Bill, the Galactic Hero on the Planet of the Robot Slaves. 1989. (Bill, the Galactic Hero Ser.: No. 1). pap. 4.50 (0-380-75661-7, Avon Bks.) Morrow/Avon.

—Galactic Dreams. 1995. 222p. pap. text 4.99 (0-8125-5058-7); 1994. 224p. 19.95 o.p. (0-312-85246-0) Doherty, Tom Assocs., LLC. (Tor Bks.).

Harrison, Harry & Bischoff, David. Bill, the Galactic Hero on the Planet of Tasteless Pleasure, 1991. (Bill, the Galactic Hero Ser.: No. 3). (Orig.). pap. 3.95 (0-380-75664-1, Avon Bks.) Morrow/Avon.

—Bill, the Galactic Hero on the Planet of Ten Thousand Bars, 1991. (Bill, the Galactic Hero Ser.: No. 5). 208p. (Orig.). mass mkt. 3.99 (0-380-75666-8, Avon Bks.) Morrow/Avon.

Harrison, Harry & Haldeman, Jack C., II. Bill, the Galactic Hero on the Planet of Zombie Vampires, 1991. (Bill, the Galactic Hero Ser.: No. 4). (Illus.). pap. 3.95 (0-380-75665-X, Avon Bks.) Morrow/Avon.

Harrison, Harry & Harris, David. Bill, the Galactic Hero: The Final Incoherent Adventure, 1992. (Bill, the Galactic Hero Ser.: No. 6). (J). pap. 4.50 (0-380-75667-6, Avon Bks.) Morrow/Avon.

Harrison, Harry & Sheckley, Robert. Bill, the Galactic Hero on the Planet of Bottled Brains. 1990. (Bill, the Galactic Hero Ser.: No. 2). pap. 3.95 (0-380-75662-5, Avon Bks.) Morrow/Avon.

**BILLUPS, DARRYL (FICTITIOUS CHARACTER)—FICTION**

Walker, Blair S. Don't Believe Your Lying Eyes: A Darryl Billups Mystery. 2002. 240p. 22.95 (0-345-44682-8) Ballantine Bks.

—Hidden in Plain View. abr. ed. 2001. audio 12.99 (1-57815-207-0, Media Bks. Audio Publishing) Media Bks., L. L. C.

—Hidden in Plain View. 1999. (Easy Rawlins Mystery Ser.). 240p. 22.00 o.s.i (0-380-97421-5, Avon Bks.) Morrow/Avon.

—Hidden in Plain View, abr. ed. 1999. audio 24.95 (1-57511-061-X) Publishing Mills, Inc., The.

—Hidden in Plain View: A Darryl Billups Mystery. 2000. (Darryl Billups Ser.). 240p. mass mkt. 5.99 o.s.i (0-380-79026-2, Avon Bks.) Morrow/Avon.

—Up Jumped the Devil. abr. ed. 2001. audio 12.99 (1-57815-210-0, Media Bks. Audio Publishing) Media Bks., L. L. C.

—Up Jumped the Devil. 1999. 272p. mass mkt. 5.99 o.s.i (0-380-79025-4, Avon Bks.) Morrow/Avon.

—Up Jumped the Devil, Set. abr. ed. 1997. audio 24.95 (1-57511-027-X) Publishing Mills, Inc., The.

**BINTON, MARGARET (FICTITIOUS CHARACTER)—FICTION**

Barth, Richard. Blood Doesn't Tell. 1990. (Margaret Binton Mystery Ser.). 192p. mass mkt. 3.95 o.s.i (0-449-21797-3, Fawcett) Ballantine Bks.

—Blood Doesn't Tell. 1989. 192p. 15.95 o.p. (0-312-02547-5, Saint Martin's Minotaur) St. Martin's Pr.

—The Condo Kill. 1991. (Margaret Binton Mystery Ser.). 160p. mass mkt. 3.95 o.s.i (0-449-21812-0, Fawcett) Ballantine Bks.

—The Condo Kill. 1985. (Margaret Binton Mystery Ser.). 192p. 13.95 o.s.i (0-684-18474-5, Macmillan Reference USA) Gale Group.

—Deadly Climate. 1989. mass mkt. 3.50 o.s.i (0-449-21723-X, Fawcett) Ballantine Bks.

—Deadly Climate. unabr. ed. 2000. (Margaret Binton Mysteries Ser.). audio 44.00 (1-55690-844-X, 93211E7) Recorded Bks., LLC.

—Deadly Climate. 1988. 208p. 14.95 o.p. (0-312-01756-1, Saint Martin's Minotaur) St. Martin's Pr.

—Deathics: A Margaret Binton Mystery. 1993. 212p. 18.95 o.p. (0-312-08764-0, Saint Martin's Minotaur) St. Martin's Pr.

—One Dollar Death. 1991. 176p. mass mkt. 3.95 o.s.i (0-449-21813-9, Fawcett) Ballantine Bks.

—One Dollar Death. 1982. 228p. 14.95 o.p. (0-385-27633-8) Doubleday Publishing.

—One Dollar Death. l.t. ed. 1993. 313p. reprint ed. 11.95 o.p. (0-89621-419-2) Thorndike Pr.

—The Rag Bag Clan. 1989. mass mkt. 3.50 o.s.i (0-449-21814-7, Fawcett) Ballantine Bks.

—A Ragged Plot. 1990. mass mkt. 3.95 o.s.i (0-449-21815-5, Fawcett) Ballantine Bks.

—A Ragged Plot. 1981. 224p. 10.95 o.p. (0-385-27165-4) Doubleday Publishing.

—A Ragged Plot. 1982. 176p. pap. 2.25 o.p. (0-380-59162-6, 59162-6, Avon Bks.) Morrow/Avon.

—A Ragged Plot. unabr. ed. 1992. (Margaret Binton Mysteries Ser.). audio 44.00 (1-55690-721-4, 92417E7) Recorded Bks., LLC.

**BIRCH, JEFFERSON (FICTITIOUS CHARACTER)—FICTION**

Lee, Wendi. Cannon's Revenge. l.t. ed. 1996. 20.00 (0-7838-1628-6); pap. 17.95 o.p. (0-7838-1619-7) Gale Group. (Macmillan Reference USA).

—Cannon's Revenge. 1995. 171p. 19.95 o.s.i (0-8027-4147-9) Walker & Co.

—Outlaw's Fortune. 1993. 154p. 19.95 (0-8027-1270-3) Walker & Co.

—Rancher's Blood. l.t. ed. 1994. (Linford Western Large Print Ser.). 288p. pap. 17.99 (0-7089-7579-8, Linford) Thorpe, F. A. Pubs. GBR. Dist: Ulverscroft Large Print Bks., Ltd., Ulverscroft Large Print Canada, Ltd.

—Rancher's Blood. 1991. 192p. 18.95 o.p. (0-8027-4120-7) Walker & Co.

—Robber's Trail. 1992. 150p. 18.95 o.p. (0-8027-4133-9) Walker & Co.

—Rogue's Gold. 1989. 192p. 17.95 (0-8027-4096-0) Walker & Co.

—Rustler's Venom. l.t. ed. 1994. (Linford Western Large Print Ser.). 336p. pap. 17.99 (0-7089-7491-0, Linford) Thorpe, F. A. Pubs. GBR. Dist: Ulverscroft Large Print Bks., Ltd., Ulverscroft Large Print Canada, Ltd.

—Rustler's Venom. 1990. 192p. 18.95 o.p. (0-8027-4112-6) Walker & Co.

**BIRDWOOD, VERITY (FICTITIOUS CHARACTER)—FICTION**

Rowe, Jennifer. Death in Store. 1994. 208p. mass mkt. 4.99 o.s.i (0-553-56875-2) Bantam Bks.

—Death in Store. 1992. 192p. 17.00 o.s.i (0-385-42598-8) Doubleday Publishing.

—Grim Pickings. l.t. ed. 1991. 11.95 o.p. (0-947072-39-X, 152); pap. 9.95 o.p. (1-86340-083-4, C1135) BBC Audiobooks America.

—Grim Pickings. 1991. 416p. mass mkt. 4.99 o.s.i (0-553-29122-X) Bantam Bks.

—Grim Pickings. unabr. ed. 1998. audio (1-86340-605-0, 551105) Bolinda Publishing Pty, Ltd.

—Lamb to the Slaughter. 1996. 288p. mass mkt. 4.99 o.s.i (0-553-56820-5, Crimeline) Bantam Bks.

—The Makeover Murders. 1994. 304p. mass mkt. 4.99 o.s.i (0-553-29740-6) Bantam Bks.

—The Makeover Murders. unabr. ed. 1998. audio (1-86340-569-0, 571230) Bolinda Publishing Pty, Ltd.

—The Makeover Murders: Moonrider. 1994. 352p. mass mkt. 5.50 o.s.i (0-553-29693-0) Bantam Bks.

—Murder by the Book. 1991. 304p. mass mkt. 4.50 o.s.i (0-553-29373-7) Bantam Bks.

—Murder by the Book, unabr. ed. 1998. audio (1-86340-604-2, 560309) Bolinda Publishing Pty, Ltd.

—Stranglehold. 1995. 256p. mass mkt. 4.99 o.s.i (0-553-56819-1) Bantam Bks.

—Stranglehold. l.t. ed. 1995. 338p. lib. bdg. 19.95 (0-7838-1247-7, Macmillan Reference USA) Gale Group.

**BISHOP, JIM (FICTITIOUS CHARACTER)—FICTION**

Klavan, Andrew. Dynamite Road. Date not set. mass mkt. (0-7653-4694-X); 2003. 320p. 25.95 (0-7653-0785-5) Doherty, Tom Assocs., LLC. (Forge Bks.).

**BISHOP, THOMAS (FICTITIOUS CHARACTER)—FICTION**

Stevens, Shane. By Reason of Insanity. 1990. 540p. mass mkt. 5.95 o.p. (0-88184-609-0); 2nd ed. 1997. 576p. pap. 13.95 (0-7867-0463-2) Avalon Publishing Group. (Carroll & Graf Pubs.).

—By Reason of Insanity. 1980. pap. 2.75 o.p. (0-440-11028-9) Dell Publishing.

—By Reason of Insanity. 1979. 11.95 o.s.i (0-671-24058-7, Simon & Schuster) Simon & Schuster.

**BITTERSOHN, MAX (FICTITIOUS CHARACTER)—FICTION**

MacLeod, Charlotte. The Balloon Man. 1998. (Sarah Kelling & Max Bittersohn Mysteries Ser.). 240p. 23.00 o.s.i (0-89296-657-2) Mysterious Pr.

—The Balloon Man. 2000. 288p. mass mkt. 6.50 (0-446-60835-1) Warner Bks., Inc.

—The Bilbao Looking Glass. 1983. (Crime Club Ser.). 192p. 11.95 o.p. (0-385-18336-4) Doubleday Publishing.

—The Bilbao Looking Glass. 1984. 208p. pap. 3.50 (0-380-67454-8, Avon Bks.) Morrow/Avon.

—The Bilbao Looking Glass. 2003. 192p. pap. 6.99 (0-7434-7492-9) ibooks, Inc.

—The Convivial Codfish. 1984. (Crime Club Ser.). 192p. 11.95 o.p. (0-385-19333-5) Doubleday Publishing.

—The Convivial Codfish. 1985. 224p. pap. 3.50 (0-380-69865-X, Avon Bks.) Morrow/Avon.

—The Convivial Codfish. 2003. 208p. mass mkt. 6.99 (0-7434-7493-7) ibooks, Inc.

—The Family Vault. 1979. 10.95 o.p. (0-385-14871-2) Doubleday Publishing.

—The Family Vault. 1980. 240p. mass mkt. 4.50 (0-380-49080-3, Avon Bks.) Morrow/Avon.

—The Gladstone Bag: A Sarah Kelling Mystery. 1990. 16.95 o.p. (0-89296-370-0) Mysterious Pr.

—The Gladstone Bag: A Sarah Kelling Mystery. 1992. 3.99 o.p. (0-517-08076-1) Random Hse. Value Publishing.

—The Gladstone Bag: A Sarah Kelling Mystery. 1991. mass mkt. 5.99 o.p. (0-446-40002-5, Mysterious Pr. Paperback Bks.) Warner Bks., Inc.

—The Odd Job. l.t. ed. 1995. 352p. reprint ed. 21.95 o.p. (0-7838-1374-0, Macmillan Reference USA) Gale Group.

—The Odd Job. 1995. 288p. 18.95 o.s.i (0-89296-571-1) Mysterious Pr.

—The Odd Job. 1996. 272p. mass mkt. 5.99 o.p. (0-446-40397-0) Warner Bks., Inc.

—The Palace Guard. 1981. 192p. 10.95 o.p. (0-385-17533-7) Doubleday Publishing.

—The Palace Guard. 1982. 176p. mass mkt. 3.99 (0-380-59857-4, Avon Bks.) Morrow/Avon.

—The Palace Guard. l.t. ed. 1982. 325p. reprint ed. 11.95 o.p. (0-89621-345-5) Thorndike Pr.

—The Palace Guard. 2003. 192p. mass mkt. 6.99 (0-7434-5912-1) ibooks, Inc.

—The Plain Old Man. 1985. (Crime Club Ser.). 192p. 12.95 o.p. (0-385-23003-6) Doubleday Publishing.

—The Plain Old Man. l.t. ed. 1986. (Nightingale Ser.). 336p. 10.95 o.p. (0-8161-4025-1, Macmillan Reference USA) Gale Group.

—The Plain Old Man. 1986. 224p. mass mkt. 3.99 (0-380-70148-0, Avon Bks.) Morrow/Avon.

—The Plain Old Man. 2003. 224p. mass mkt. 6.99 (0-7434-7479-1) ibooks, Inc.

—The Recycled Citizen. l.t. ed. 1989. (General Ser.). 352p. lib. bdg. 19.95 o.p. (0-8161-4777-9, Macmillan Reference USA) Gale Group.

—The Recycled Citizen. 1988. 208p. 15.45 o.p. (0-89296-187-2) Mysterious Pr.

—The Recycled Citizen. 1992. 4.50 (0-446-77518-5); 1989. 272p. mass mkt. 4.99 o.p. (0-445-40689-5, Mysterious Pr. Paperback Bks.) Warner Bks., Inc.

—The Resurrection Man: A Sarah Kelling & Max Bittersohn Mystery. l.t. ed. 1993. (Magna Large Print Ser.). 381p. o.p. (0-7505-0496-X) Magna Large Print Bks. GBR. Dist: Ulverscroft Large Print Canada, Ltd.

—The Resurrection Man: A Sarah Kelling & Max Bittersohn Mystery. 1992. 256p. 17.95 o.p. (0-89296-443-X) Mysterious Pr.

—The Resurrection Man: A Sarah Kelling & Max Bittersohn Mystery. 1993. 256p. mass mkt. 5.99 o.p. (0-446-40332-6, Mysterious Pr. Paperback Bks.) Warner Bks., Inc.

—The Resurrection Man: A Sarah Kelling & Max Bittersohn Mystery. 2001. 256p. mass mkt. 6.99 (0-7434-2377-1) ibooks, Inc.

—The Silver Ghost: A Sarah Kelling Mystery. l.t. ed. 1990. (Magna Large Print Ser.). 339p. 29.99 o.p. (1-85057-592-4) Magna Large Print Bks. GBR. Dist: Ulverscroft Large Print Bks., Ltd., Ulverscroft Large Print Canada, Ltd.

—The Silver Ghost: A Sarah Kelling Mystery. 1988. (Sarah Kelling Mystery Ser.). 224p. 15.95 (0-89296-189-9) Mysterious Pr.

—The Silver Ghost: A Sarah Kelling Mystery. 1989. 224p. reprint ed. mass mkt. 4.99 o.p. (0-445-40828-6, Mysterious Pr. Paperback Bks.) Warner Bks., Inc.

—The Withdrawing Room. 1980. (Crime Club Ser.). 192p. 8.95 o.p. (0-385-17181-1) Doubleday Publishing.

—The Withdrawing Room. 1982. 192p. mass mkt. 3.99 (0-380-56473-4, Avon Bks.) Morrow/Avon.

—The Withdrawing Room. 2002. 192p. pap. 6.99 (0-7434-5258-5) ibooks, Inc.

**BIWABAN, ANGIE (FICTITIOUS CHARACTER)—FICTION**

Trainor, J. F. Corona Blue. 1995. mass mkt. 4.99 o.s.i (0-8217-5134-4); 1994. 357p. mass mkt. 16.95 o.s.i (0-8217-4739-8, Zebra Bks.) Kensington Publishing Corp.

—Dynamite Pass. 1993. 384p. mass mkt. 3.99 o.s.i (0-8217-4227-2, Zebra Bks.) Kensington Publishing Corp.

—High Country Murder: An Angela Biwaban Mystery. 1996. 400p. mass mkt. 4.99 o.s.i (1-57566-107-1); 1995. 390p. mass mkt. 18.95 o.p. (0-8217-5124-7, Kensington Bks.) Kensington Publishing Corp.

—Target for Murder. 1993. 288p. mass mkt. 3.99 o.s.i (0-8217-4069-5, Zebra Bks.) Kensington Publishing Corp.

—Whiskey Jack. 1994. 384p. mass mkt. 3.99 o.s.i (0-8217-4439-9, Zebra Bks.) Kensington Publishing Corp.

**BLACK, HELEN (FICTITIOUS CHARACTER)—FICTION**

Welch, Pat. A Day Too Long: A Helen Black Mystery. 2003. 240p. pap. 12.95 (1-931513-22-8) Bella Bks., Inc.

—Fallen from Grace. 1998. (Helen Black Mysteries Ser.: No. 6). 224p. pap. 11.95 (1-56280-209-7) Naiad Pr., Inc.

—Murder by the Book. 1990. 256p. pap. 9.95 o.p. (0-941483-59-2) Naiad Pr., Inc.

—Open House. 1995. (Helen Black Mysteries Ser.). 224p. pap. 10.95 (1-56280-102-3) Naiad Pr., Inc.

—A Proper Burial. 1993. (Helen Black Mysteries Ser.). 176p. pap. 9.95 (1-56280-033-7) Naiad Pr., Inc.

—Smoke & Mirrors: A Helen Black Mystery. 1996. (Helen Black Mysteries Ser.). 224p. (Orig.). pap. 10.95 (1-56280-143-0) Naiad Pr., Inc.

—Snake Eyes. 1999. (Helen Black Mysteries Ser.: No. 7). 249p. pap. 11.95 (1-56280-242-9) Naiad Pr., Inc.

—Still Waters. 1991. (Helen Black Mysteries Ser.). 176p. pap. 9.95 o.p. (0-941483-97-5) Naiad Pr., Inc.

**BLACK, MORRIS (FICTITIOUS CHARACTER)—FICTION**

Hyde, Christopher. A Gathering of Saints. abr. ed. 1997. audio 7.99 o.p. (1-56740-174-0, 654, Paperback Nova Audio Bks.); 1996. audio 16.95 o.p. (1-56100-906-7, 878, Nova Audio Bks.); 1996. audio 25.95 o.p. (1-56100-697-1, 119, Bookcassette); 1996. audio 89.25 o.p. (1-56100-322-0, 1208, Unabridged Library Editions) Brilliance Audio.

—A Gathering of Saints. 1997. 438p. per. 6.99 (0-671-87581-7, Pocket); 1996. 432p. 24.00 (0-671-87580-9, Atria) Simon & Schuster.

**BLACK, THOMAS (FICTITIOUS CHARACTER)—FICTION**

Emerson, Earl. Catfish Cafe. 1999. 304p. mass mkt. 6.99 (0-345-42212-0); 1998. 272p. 22.00 o.p. (0-345-42202-3) Ballantine Bks.

—Deception Pass. 1998. (Thomas Black Mysteries Ser.). 304p. mass mkt. 6.99 (0-345-40069-0) Ballantine Bks.

—Deviant Behavior. 1990. (Thomas Black Mysteries Ser.). 224p. mass mkt. 6.50 (0-345-36028-1) Ballantine Bks.

—Deviant Behavior. 1988. 256p. 17.95 o.p. (0-688-08335-8, Morrow, William & Co.) Morrow/Avon.

—Fat Tuesday. 1988. (Thomas Black Mysteries Ser.). 288p. mass mkt. 6.99 (0-345-35223-8) Ballantine Bks.

—Fat Tuesday. 1987. 288p. 16.95 o.p. (0-688-06770-0, Morrow, William & Co.) Morrow/Avon.

—The Million-Dollar Tattoo. 1997. (Thomas Black Mysteries Ser.). 304p. mass mkt. 5.99 (0-345-40067-4) Ballantine Bks.

—The Million-Dollar Tattoo. unabr. ed. 1997. (Thomas Black Mystery Ser.: Vol. 9). audio 51.00 (0-7887-0813-9, 94963E7) Recorded Bks., LLC.

—Nervous Laughter. 1998. mass mkt. 3.99 o.s.i (0-345-42945-1); 1997. 288p. mass mkt. 6.50 (0-345-41407-1) Ballantine Bks.

—Nervous Laughter. 1986. mass mkt. 4.99 (0-380-89906-X, Avon Bks.) Morrow/Avon.

—The Portland Laugher. 1995. (Thomas Black Mysteries Ser.). 352p. mass mkt. 6.50 (0-345-39782-7) Ballantine Bks.

—Poverty Bay. 1998. mass mkt. 3.99 o.s.i (0-345-42944-3); 1997. 320p. mass mkt. 6.99 (0-345-41406-3) Ballantine Bks.

—Poverty Bay. 1985. 256p. mass mkt. 4.99 (0-380-89647-8, Avon Bks.) Morrow/Avon.

—Poverty Bay. unabr. ed. 1994. (Thomas Black Mystery Ser.: Vol. 2). audio 51.00 (1-55690-980-2, 94119E7) Recorded Bks., LLC.

—The Rainy City. 1998. mass mkt. 3.99 o.s.i (0-345-42943-5); 1997. 288p. mass mkt. 6.99 (0-345-41405-5) Ballantine Bks.

—The Rainy City. 1985. (Thomas Black Ser.). 240p. mass mkt. 4.99 (0-380-89517-X, Avon Bks.) Morrow/Avon.

—The Rainy City. unabr. ed. 1992. (Thomas Black Mystery Ser.: Vol. 1). audio 51.00 (1-55690-723-0, 92218E7) Recorded Bks., LLC.

—The Vanishing Smile. (Thomas Black Mysteries Ser.). 1996. 320p. mass mkt. 6.99 (0-345-40453-X); 1995. 272p. 21.00 o.s.i (0-345-38486-5) Ballantine Bks.

—Yellow Dog Party: A Thomas Black Mystery. 1992. (Thomas Black Mysteries Ser.). 256p. mass mkt. 6.99 (0-345-37716-8) Ballantine Bks.

—Yellow Dog Party: A Thomas Black Mystery. 1991. 288p. 19.00 o.p. (0-688-09635-2, Morrow, William & Co.) Morrow/Avon.

**BLACK COMPANY (FICTITIOUS CHARACTERS)—FICTION**

Cook, Glen. The Black Company. (Orig.). 1992. (Chronicle of the Black Company Ser.: No. 1). 319p. mass mkt. 6.99 (0-8125-2139-0); 1989. pap. 3.95 o.s.i (0-8125-0389-9); 1984. mass mkt. 2.95 o.s.i (0-8125-3370-4) Doherty, Tom Assocs., LLC. (Tor Bks.).

—Bleak Seasons. (Glittering Stone Ser.: 1). 1997. 316p. pap. text 5.99 (0-8125-5532-5); 1996. 320p. 22.95 o.p. (0-312-86105-2) Doherty, Tom Assocs., LLC. (Tor Bks.).

—Dreams of Steel: The Fifth Chronicle of the Black Company, Vol. 5. 1990. 346p. mass mkt. 5.99 (0-8125-0210-8, Tor Bks.) Doherty, Tom Assocs., LLC.

—Shadow Games. 1989. (Shadow Games Ser.: Vol. 4). 311p. mass mkt. 7.99 (0-8125-3382-8, Tor Bks.) Doherty, Tom Assocs., LLC.

—Shadows Linger. 1984. 320p. mass mkt. 2.95 (*0-8125-3372-0*); Vol. 2. 1990. 319p. mass mkt. 6.99 (*0-8125-0842-4*) Doherty, Tom Assocs., LLC. (Tor Bks.).

—She Is the Darkness. 1997. (Glittering Stone Ser.: 2). 384p. 23.95 (*0-312-85907-4*, Tor Bks.) Doherty, Tom Assocs., LLC.

—Soldiers Live. 2001. (Glittering Stone Ser.: Vol. 4). 576p. mass mkt. 6.99 (*0-8125-6655-6*, Tor Bks.) Doherty, Tom Assocs., LLC.

—Soldiers Live: The Ninth Chronicle of the Black Company. 2000. (Glittering Stone Ser.: Vol. 4). 496p. 25.95 (*0-312-89057-5*, Tor Bks.) Doherty, Tom Assocs., LLC.

—Water Sleeps. 2000. (Book of Glittering Stone Ser.: Vol. 3). 480p. mass mkt. 6.99 (*0-8125-5534-1*); No. 3. 1999. (Glittering Stone Ser.: 3). (Illus.). 412p. 24.95 (*0-312-85909-0*) Doherty, Tom Assocs., LLC. (Tor Bks.).

—The White Rose. (White Rose Ser.: Vol. 3). 1990. 317p. pap. 6.99 (*0-8125-0844-0*); 1985. 320p. mass mkt. 2.95 (*0-8125-3374-7*) Doherty, Tom Assocs., LLC. (Tor Bks.).

**BLACK MASK BOYS (FICTITIOUS CHARACTERS)—FICTION**

Nolan, William F. Marble Orchard. 1995. 224p. 20.95 o.p. (*0-312-14011-8*, Saint Martin's Minotaur) St. Martin's Pr.

—Sharks Never Sleep, unabr. ed. 1999. audio 44.95 (*0-7861-1629-3*, 2457) Blackstone Audio Bks., Inc.

—Sharks Never Sleep. 1998. 288p. 22.95 o.p. (*0-312-19331-9*, Saint Martin's Minotaur) St. Martin's Pr.

Nolan, William F., ed. The Black Mask Boys: Masters in the Hard-Boiled School of Detective Fiction. 1984. 288p. 16.95 o.p. (*0-688-03966-9*, Morrow, William & Co.) Morrow/Avon.

—The Black Mask Boys: Masters in the Hard-Boiled School of Detective Fiction. 1987. 272p. reprint ed. 8.95 o.p. (*0-89296-931-8*) Mysterious Pr.

—The Black Mask Murders. 1994. 224p. 19.95 o.p. (*0-312-10942-3*, Saint Martin's Minotaur) St. Martin's Pr.

**BLACK SABRES (FICTITIOUS CHARACTERS)—FICTION**

Willard, Tom. Buffalo Soldiers: A Novel. unabr. collector's ed. 1997. (Black Sabre Chronicles). audio 48.00 (*0-7366-3555-6*, 4200) Books on Tape, Inc.

—Buffalo Soldiers: A Novel. 1996. (Black Sabre Chronicles Ser.: Bk. 1). 336p. 22.95 o.p. (*0-312-86041-2*, Forge Bks.) Doherty, Tom Assocs., LLC.

—Buffalo Soldiers: A Novel. l.t. ed. 1997. (West-Hall Ser.). 441p. lib. bdg. 21.95 (*0-7838-1943-9*, Macmillan Reference USA) Gale Group.

—Buffalo Soldiers: A Novel. 1997. 12.04 (*0-606-20473-3*) Turtleback Bks.

—Sable Doughboys. 1996. (Black Sabre Chronicles: Bk. 2). 319p. 22.95 o.p. (*0-312-86040-4*, Forge Bks.) Doherty, Tom Assocs., LLC.

—Sable Doughboys. 1998. 12.04 (*0-606-19669-2*) Turtleback Bks.

—The Sable Doughboys. unabr. collector's ed. 1997. audio 48.00 (*0-7366-3672-2*, 4349) Books on Tape, Inc.

—Wings of Honor. 1998. (Black Sabre Chronicles Ser.: Vol. 3). (Illus.). 320p. 23.95 (*0-312-86967-3*, Forge Bks.); 1997. 299.40 o.s.i (*0-312-86053-6*, Tor Bks.); Bk. 3. 2000. (Black Sabre Chronicles Ser.: Vol. 3). 352p. mass mkt. 6.99 (*0-8125-6477-4*, Forge Bks.) Doherty, Tom Assocs., LLC.

**BLACKBIRD SISTERS (FICTITIOUS CHARACTERS)—FICTION**

Martin, Nancy. Dead Girls Don't Wear Diamonds: A Blackbird Sisters Mystery. 2003. 272p. mass mkt. 6.50 (*0-451-20886-2*, Signet Bks.) NAL.

—How to Murder a Millionaire. 2002. 272p. mass mkt. 6.50 (*0-451-20724-6*, Signet Bks.) NAL.

—How to Murder a Millionaire. 2003. (Mystery Ser.). 359p. 28.95 (*0-7862-5391-6*) Thorndike Pr.

—Some Like It Lethal. 2004. 320p. mass mkt. 6.99 (*0-451-21174-X*, Signet Bks.) NAL.

**BLACKBURN, JIMMY (FICTITIOUS CHARACTER)—FICTION**

Denton, Bradley. Blackburn: A Novel. 1995. 304p. pap. 12.00 (*0-312-13029-5*) Picador.

—Blackburn: A Novel. 1993. 19.95 o.p. (*0-312-08705-5*) St. Martin's Pr.

**BLACKE, LOBO (FICTITIOUS CHARACTER)—FICTION**

DeAndrea, William L. The Fatal Elixir: A Lobo Blacke-Quinn Booker Mystery. 1997. (Lobo Black/Quinn Booker Mystery Ser.). 208p. 22.95 (*0-8027-3289-5*) Walker & Co.

—Written in Fire: A Lobo Blacke-Quinn Booker Mystery. 1995. 168p. 19.95 (*0-8027-3270-4*) Walker & Co.

**BLACKWELL, MARK (FICTITIOUS CHARACTER)—FICTION**

Brandon, Jay. Fade the Heat. 1991. 368p. mass mkt. 6.99 (*0-671-70261-0*, Pocket) Simon & Schuster.

—Fade the Heat. Gross, Bill, ed. 1990. 352p. 18.95 o.p. (*0-671-70260-2*, Atria) Simon & Schuster.

—Fade the Heat. abr. ed. 1990. audio 14.95 (*0-671-70893-7*, Simon & Schuster Audioworks) Simon & Schuster Audio.

—Loose among the Lambs. Grose, Bill, ed. 1993. 384p. 22.00 (*0-671-76032-7*, Atria); 1994. 400p. reprint ed. mass mkt. 5.99 (*0-671-76033-5*, Pocket); 1994. reprint ed. pap. 6.50 (*0-671-88315-1*, Pocket) Simon & Schuster.

**BLAINE, JOHN (FICTITIOUS CHARACTER)—FICTION**

Banville, Vincent. Cannon Law. 2002. 300p. pap. 14.95 (*1-902602-61-7*) New Island Bks. IRL. *Dist:* Dufour Editions, Inc.

**BLAIR, JONATHON (FICTITIOUS CHARACTER)—FICTION**

Smith, Martin Cruz. Rose. 2000. 416p. mass mkt. 7.99 (*0-345-42252-X*); 1997. 384p. pap. 14.00 (*0-345-39044-X*); 1997. mass mkt. 7.99 o.s.i (*0-345-41232-X*) Ballantine Bks.

—Rose. unabr. collector's ed. 1997. audio 64.00 (*0-913369-68-3*, 4319) Books on Tape, Inc.

—Rose. l.t. ed. 1996. 588p. 25.00 o.p. (*0-7838-1681-2*, Macmillan Reference USA) Gale Group.

—Rose. 1998. (Coleccion Bestseller Mundial). (SPA., Illus.). 410p. (*84-08-02445-0*) GeoPlaneta, Editorial, S. A.

—Rose, unabr. ed. 1997. audio 85.00 (*0-7887-0918-6*, 95058E7) Recorded Bks., LLC.

**BLAIR, MIKE (FICTITIOUS CHARACTER)—FICTION**

Searls, Hank. The Adventures of Mike Blair. 1988. (Dime Detective Bk.). 224p. 8.95 o.p. (*0-89296-918-0*) Mysterious Pr.

**BLAIR, SONORA (FICTITIOUS CHARACTER)—FICTION**

Hightower, Lynn S. Eyeshot. 1996. 368p. 23.00 o.p. (*0-06-017649-0*) HarperCollins Pubs.

—Eyeshot. 1997. 368p. mass mkt. 6.50 o.p. (*0-06-109609-1*, HarperTorch) Morrow/Avon.

—Flashpoint. 1995. 352p. 22.00 o.p. (*0-06-017648-2*) HarperTrade.

—Flashpoint. 1996. 448p. mass mkt. 6.50 o.s.i (*0-06-109456-0*, HarperTorch) Morrow/Avon.

—No Good Deed. unabr. ed. 1998. audio 44.95 (*0-7861-1438-X*, 2324) Blackstone Audio Bks., Inc.

—No Good Deed. 1998. (Sonora Blair Mysteries Ser.). 400p. mass mkt. 6.50 (*0-440-22531-0*); 336p. 22.95 o.s.i (*0-385-32359-X*, Delacorte Pr.) Dell Publishing.

**BLAISE, MODESTY (FICTITIOUS CHARACTER)—FICTION**

O'Donnell, Peter. Cobra Trap. 2001. (Modesty Blaise Series Ser.). 272p. 24.95 (*0-285-63332-5*) Souvenir Pr. Ltd. GBR. *Dist:* Independent Pubs. Group.

—Dead Man's Handle. (Modesty Blaise Adventure Ser.). 1987. 45.00 o.p. (*0-89296-155-4*); 1986. 15.95 (*0-89296-245-3*); 1986. pap. 3.95 (*0-445-40587-2*) Mysterious Pr.

—Dragon's Claw. 1987. 288p. mass mkt. 3.95 (*0-8125-8654-9*, Tor Bks.) Doherty, Tom Assocs., LLC.

—Dragon's Claw. (Modesty Blaise Ser.). 1987. 45.00 o.p. (*0-89296-106-6*); 1986. 15.95 o.p. (*0-89296-105-8*) Mysterious Pr.

—I, Lucifer. 1984. (Modesty Blaise Ser.). reprint ed. pap. 3.95 o.p. (*0-89296-096-5*) Mysterious Pr.

—The Impossible Virgin. 1985. (Modesty Blaise Ser.). 256p. reprint ed. pap. 3.95 o.p. (*0-89296-100-7*) Mysterious Pr.

—Last Day in Limbo. 2003. (Modesty Blaise Series Ser.). 256p. pap. 14.95 (*0-285-63675-8*) Souvenir Pr. Ltd. GBR. *Dist:* Independent Pubs. Group.

—Last Day in Limbo: A Modesty Blaise Novel. 1988. 288p. mass mkt. 3.50 (*0-8125-8655-7*, Tor Bks.) Doherty, Tom Assocs., LLC.

—Last Day in Limbo: A Modesty Blaise Novel. 1986. 45.00 (*0-89296-104-X*); 1985. 14.95 o.p. (*0-89296-103-1*) Mysterious Pr.

—Modesty Blaise. 1984. reprint ed. pap. 3.95 o.p. (*0-89296-090-6*) Mysterious Pr.

—Modesty Blaise: Death in Slow Motion; The Alternative Man; Sweet Caroline. Yronwode, Catherine, ed. 1986. (Comic Strip Ser.). (Illus.). 72p. (Orig.). pap. 5.95 (*0-912277-30-0*) Pierce, Ken Bks.

—Modesty Blaise: Live Bait. 2002. (Illus.). 100p. (C). pap. 19.95 (*0-936414-11-1*) Manuscript Pr.

—Modesty Blaise: The Head Girls; The Black Pearl; The Magnified Man. Yronwode, Catherine, ed. & intro. by. 1983. (Comic Strip Ser.). (Illus.). 64p. (Orig.). pap. 5.95 o.p. (*0-912277-10-6*) Pierce, Ken Bks.

—Modesty Blaise: The Jericho Caper; The Killing Ground; Bad Suki. Yronwode, Catherine, ed. 1982. (Comic Strip Ser.). (Illus.). 56p. (Orig.). pap. 5.95 o.p. (*0-912277-09-2*) Pierce, Ken Bks.

—Modesty Blaise: The Lady Killer; Garvin's Travels; The Scarlet Maiden. Yronwode, Catherine, ed. & intro. by. 1984. (Comic Strip Ser.). (Illus.). 72p. pap. 5.95 (*0-912277-25-4*) Pierce, Ken Bks.

—Modesty Blaise: The Mind of Mrs. Drake; Uncle Happy. Yronwode, Catherine, ed. 1981. (Comic Strip Ser.). (Illus.). 64p. (Orig.). pap. 5.95 (*0-912277-08-4*) Pierce, Ken Bks.

—Modesty Blaise: The Moon Man; A Few Flowers for the Colonel; The Balloonatic. Yronwode, Catherine, ed. 1985. (Comic Strip Ser.). (Illus.). 72p. (Orig.). pap. 5.95 (*0-912277-28-9*) Pierce, Ken Bks.

—Modesty Blaise: The Return of the Mammoth; Plato's Republic; The Sword of the Bruce. Yronwode, Catherine, ed. 1986. (Comic Strip Ser.). (Illus.). 72p. (Orig.). pap. 5.95 (*0-912277-33-5*) Pierce, Ken Bks.

—Modesty Blaise: Top Traitor; The Vikings. Yronwode, Catherine, ed. & intro. by. 1981. (Comic Strip Ser.). (Illus.). 64p. (Orig.). pap. 5.95 o.p. (*0-912277-07-6*) Pierce, Ken Bks.

—The Night of Morningstar. 1988. 288p. mass mkt. 3.95 (*0-8125-0730-4*, Tor Bks.) Doherty, Tom Assocs., LLC.

—The Night of Morningstar. 1987. 272p. reprint ed. 15.45 o.p. (*0-89296-222-4*); 45.00 o.s.i (*0-89296-236-4*) Mysterious Pr.

—The Night of Morningstar. l.t. ed. 1996. (Ulverscroft Large Print Ser.). 560p. 29.99 o.p. (*0-7089-3543-5*, Ulverscroft) Thorpe, F. A. Pubs. GBR. *Dist:* Ulverscroft Large Print Bks., Ltd., Ulverscroft Large Print Canada, Ltd.

—Pieces of Modesty. 1990. mass mkt. (*0-8125-0732-0*, Tor Bks.) Doherty, Tom Assocs., LLC.

—Pieces of Modesty. 1986. 192p. reprint ed. 15.95 (*0-89296-172-4*); 45.00 o.s.i (*0-89296-267-4*) Mysterious Pr.

—Sabre Tooth. 1984. pap. 3.95 o.p. (*0-89296-092-2*) Mysterious Pr.

—Sabre-Tooth. 2003. (Modesty Blaise Series Ser.). 288p. pap. 14.95 (*0-285-63676-6*) Souvenir Pr. Ltd. GBR. *Dist:* Independent Pubs. Group.

—The Silver Mistress. 1986. 288p. reprint ed. pap. 3.50 o.p. (*0-8125-8650-6*, Tor Bks.) Doherty, Tom Assocs., LLC.

—The Silver Mistress. (Modesty Blaise Ser.). 256p. reprint ed. 1999. 14.95 (*0-89296-101-5*); 1987. 45.00 o.p. (*0-89296-102-3*) Mysterious Pr.

—The Silver Mistress. 2002. (Modesty Blaise Ser.). reprint ed. 290p. pap. 14.95 o.p. (*0-285-62112-2*); 256p. pap. 14.95 (*0-285-63644-8*) Souvenir Pr. Ltd. GBR. *Dist:* Independent Pubs. Group.

—A Taste for Death. 1984. (Modesty Blaise Ser.). 256p. reprint ed. pap. 3.95 o.p. (*0-89296-094-9*) Mysterious Pr.

—A Taste for Death. l.t. ed. 1997. (Ulverscroft Large Print Ser.). 528p. 29.99 o.p. (*0-7089-3672-5*, Ulverscroft) Thorpe, F. A. Pubs. GBR. *Dist:* Ulverscroft Large Print Bks., Ltd., Ulverscroft Large Print Canada, Ltd.

—The Xanadu Talisman. 1987. 288p. reprint ed. pap. 3.50 o.p. (*0-8125-8653-0*, Tor Bks.) Doherty, Tom Assocs., LLC.

—The Xanadu Talisman. reprint ed. 1999. 14.95 (*0-89296-107-4*); 1987. 45.00 (*0-89296-108-2*) Mysterious Pr.

—The Xanadu Talisman. 2002. 288p. pap. 15.00 (*0-285-63643-X*); 290p. reprint ed. pap. 14.95 o.p. (*0-285-62412-1*) Souvenir Pr. Ltd. GBR. *Dist:* Independent Pubs. Group.

**BLAKE, ANITA (FICTITIOUS CHARACTER)—FICTION**

Hamilton, Laurell K. Bloody Bones. 1996. (Anita Blake Vampire Hunter Ser.). 384p. mass mkt. 6.99 o.s.i (*0-441-00374-5*) Ace Bks.

—Bloody Bones. 2002. 384p. mass mkt. 6.99 (*0-515-13446-5*) Berkley Publishing Group.

—Blue Moon. 1998. (Anita Blake Vampire Hunter Ser.: Bk. 8). 432p. mass mkt. 6.99 o.s.i (*0-441-00574-8*) Ace Bks.

—Burnt Offerings. 1998. (Anita Blake Vampire Hunter Ser.). 400p. mass mkt. 6.99 o.s.i (*0-441-00524-1*) Ace Bks.

—Burnt Offerings. 2002. 400p. mass mkt. 7.50 (*0-515-13447-3*) Berkley Publishing Group.

—Cerulean Sins. 2003. (Anita Blake Vampire Hunter Ser.). 416p. 23.95 (*0-425-18836-1*) Berkley Publishing Group.

—Circus of the Damned. 1995. (Anita Blake Vampire Hunter Ser.). 336p. (Orig.). mass mkt. 6.99 o.s.i (*0-441-00197-1*) Ace Bks.

—Circus of the Damned. (Orig.). 2004. 320p. 22.95 (*0-425-19427-2*); 2002. 336p. mass mkt. 6.99 (*0-515-13448-1*) Berkley Publishing Group.

—Guilty Pleasures. 1993. (Anita Blake Vampire Hunter Ser.). 272p. mass mkt. 6.99 o.s.i (*0-441-30483-4*) Ace Bks.

—Guilty Pleasures. 2004. 368p. pap. 13.00 (*0-425-19754-9*); 2002. 272p. mass mkt. 6.99 (*0-515-13449-X*); 2002. 320p. reprint ed. 21.95 (*0-425-18756-X*) Berkley Publishing Group.

—Guilty Pleasures. 2002. (Anita Blake Vampire Hunter Ser.). E-Book 6.99 (*0-7865-2898-2*) Penguin Putnam, Inc E-Books.

—The Killing Dance. 1997. (Anita Blake Vampire Hunter Ser.). 400p. mass mkt. 6.99 o.s.i (*0-441-00452-0*) Ace Bks.

—The Killing Dance. 2002. 400p. mass mkt. 7.99 (*0-515-13451-1*) Berkley Publishing Group.

—The Laughing Corpse. 1994. (Anita Blake Vampire Hunter Ser.). 304p. mass mkt. 6.99 o.s.i (*0-441-00091-6*) Ace Bks.

—The Laughing Corpse. 2003. 320p. 22.95 (*0-425-19200-8*); 2002. 304p. mass mkt. 7.50 (*0-515-13444-9*) Berkley Publishing Group.

—The Lunatic Cafe. 1996. (Anita Blake Vampire Hunter Ser.). 384p. mass mkt. 6.99 o.s.i (*0-441-00293-5*) Ace Bks.

—The Lunatic Cafe. 2002. 384p. mass mkt. 6.99 (*0-515-13452-X*) Berkley Publishing Group.

—Narcissus in Chains. 2001. 432p. 22.95 (*0-425-18168-5*); 2002. 656p. reprint ed. mass mkt. 7.99 (*0-515-13387-6*, Jove) Berkley Publishing Group.

—Obsidian Butterfly: An Anita Blake Vampire Hunter Novel. 2000. (Anita Blake Ser.). 400p. 21.95 (*0-441-00684-1*); 608p. reprint ed. mass mkt. 7.50 o.s.i (*0-441-00781-3*) Ace Bks.

—Obsidian Butterfly: An Anita Blake Vampire Hunter Novel. 2002. 608p. mass mkt. 7.99 (*0-515-13450-3*) Berkley Publishing Group.

**BLAKE, CATHY (FICTITIOUS CHARACTER)—FICTION**

Ross, Dana Fuller, pseud. Colorado! 1984. mass mkt. 3.95 o.s.i (*0-553-24694-1*); 368p. mass mkt. 4.95 o.s.i (*0-553-26546-6*) Bantam Bks.

—Colorado! 1982. (Reader's Request Ser.). lib. bdg. 16.95 o.p. (*0-8161-3320-4*, Macmillan Reference USA) Gale Group.

—Nevada! abr. ed. 2003. (Wagon West Ser.: No. 8). audio 25.00 (*1-58807-013-1*) Americana Publishing, Inc.

—Nevada! l.t. ed. 1982. 15.95 o.p. (*0-8161-3396-4*, Macmillan Reference USA) Gale Group.

—Texas! 1984. mass mkt. 3.99 o.s.i (*0-553-80005-1*); 368p. mass mkt. 4.99 o.s.i (*0-553-26070-7*) Bantam Bks.

—Texas! 1982. (Reader's Request Ser.). lib. bdg. 16.95 o.p. (*0-8161-3318-2*, Macmillan Reference USA) Gale Group.

**BLAKE, JULIE (FICTITIOUS CHARACTER)—FICTION**

Chapman, Sally. Cyberkiss. 1997. (WWL Mystery Ser.: No. 242). 252p. per. (*0-373-26242-6*, 1-26242-7, Worldwide Library) Harlequin Enterprises, Ltd.

—Cyberkiss. 1996. 272p. 21.95 o.p. (*0-312-13952-7*, Saint Martin's Minotaur) St. Martin's Pr.

—Hardwired. 1998. (WWL Mystery Ser.: Vol. 288). per. (*0-373-26288-4*, 1-26288-0, Worldwide Library) Harlequin Enterprises, Ltd.

—Hardwired. 1997. 272p. 22.95 (*0-312-15542-5*, Saint Martin's Minotaur) St. Martin's Pr.

—Raw Data. 1991. 17.95 o.p. (*0-312-05953-1*, Saint Martin's Minotaur) St. Martin's Pr.

**BLAKE, LELAND (FICTITIOUS CHARACTER)—FICTION**

Ross, Dana Fuller, pseud. Colorado! 1984. mass mkt. 3.95 o.s.i (*0-553-24694-1*); 368p. mass mkt. 4.95 o.s.i (*0-553-26546-6*) Bantam Bks.

—Colorado! 1982. (Reader's Request Ser.). lib. bdg. 16.95 o.p. (*0-8161-3320-4*, Macmillan Reference USA) Gale Group.

—Nevada! abr. ed. 2003. (Wagon West Ser.: No. 8). audio 25.00 (*1-58807-013-1*) Americana Publishing, Inc.

—Nevada! l.t. ed. 1982. 15.95 o.p. (*0-8161-3396-4*, Macmillan Reference USA) Gale Group.

—Texas! 1984. mass mkt. 3.99 o.s.i (*0-553-80005-1*); 368p. mass mkt. 4.99 o.s.i (*0-553-26070-7*) Bantam Bks.

—Texas! 1982. (Reader's Request Ser.). lib. bdg. 16.95 o.p. (*0-8161-3318-2*, Macmillan Reference USA) Gale Group.

**BLAKE, ROSEMARY (FICTITIOUS CHARACTER)—FICTION**

Babson, Marian. Whiskers & Smoke. 1997. (Dead Letter Mysteries Ser.). 214p. mass mkt. 5.99 (*0-312-96181-2*, St. Martin's Paperbacks) St. Martin's Pr.

—Whiskers & Smoke. abr. ed. 1997. audio 16.96 o.p. (*1-56431-214-3*) Sunset Products.

**BLAKE, WILL (FICTITIOUS CHARACTER)—FICTION**

Smith, Charlie. Chimney Rock: A Novel. 1997. 352p. pap. 14.00 o.p. (*0-8050-5592-4*, Owl Bks.); 1993. 400p. 22.50 o.p. (*0-8050-2244-9*) Holt, Henry & Co.

**BLAKENEY, PERCY, SIR (FICTITIOUS CHARACTER)—FICTION**

Orczy, Baroness Emmuska. Adventures of the Scarlet Pimpernel. 1983. 321p. reprint ed. lib. bdg. 35.95 (*0-89966-459-8*) Buccaneer Bks., Inc.

—Eldorado. lib. bdg. 22.95 (*0-8488-2010-X*) Amereon, Ltd.

—Eldorado. 1980. 435p. reprint ed. lib. bdg. 35.95 (*0-89968-195-6*, Lightyear Pr.) Buccaneer Bks., Inc.

—The Elusive Pimpernel. 288p. 23.95 (*0-8488-2521-7*) Amereon, Ltd.

—The Elusive Pimpernel. unabr. ed. 1998. audio 49.95 (*0-7861-1279-4*, 2169) Blackstone Audio Bks., Inc.

—The Elusive Pimpernel. 1984. 419p. lib. bdg. 35.95 (*0-89966-488-1*); 1976. lib. bdg. 31.95 o.p. (*0-89968-073-9*, Lightyear Pr.) Buccaneer Bks., Inc.

—The First Sir Percy. 2000. 320p. reprint ed. 37.95 (*1-56849-734-2*) Buccaneer Bks., Inc.

—I Will Repay. unabr. ed. 1994. audio 44.95 (*0-7861-0778-2*, 1506) Blackstone Audio Bks., Inc.

—I Will Repay. 2000. 192p. reprint ed. 29.95 (*1-56849-732-6*) Buccaneer Bks., Inc.

—The League of the Scarlet Pimpernel. Date not set. 282p. 23.95 (*0-8488-2377-X*) Amereon, Ltd.

—The League of the Scarlet Pimpernel. 1981. 238p. reprint ed. lib. bdg. 35.95 (*0-89966-286-2*) Buccaneer Bks., Inc.

—Lord Tony's Wife. 1986. (gr. 4-7). reprint ed. lib. bdg. 37.95 (*0-89966-553-5*) Buccaneer Bks., Inc.

—Pimpernel & Rosemary. 312p. 24.95 (*0-8488-2543-8*) Amereon, Ltd.

—Pimpernel & Rosemary. 1996. 37.95 (*0-89966-462-8*) Buccaneer Bks., Inc.

—The Scarlet Pimpernel. 1964. (Airmont Classics Ser.). (J). (gr. 7 up). mass mkt. 2.95 o.p. (*0-8049-0028-0*, CL-28) Airmont Publishing Co., Inc.

—The Scarlet Pimpernel. 20.95 (*0-8488-0601-8*) Amereon, Ltd.

—The Scarlet Pimpernel. 1994. (Illustrated Classics Collection). 64p. pap. 3.60 o.p. (*1-56103-606-4*); pap. 4.95 (*0-7854-0755-3*, 40518) American Guidance Service, Inc.

—The Scarlet Pimpernel. 1987. audio 41.95 (*1-55685-110-3*) Audio Bk. Contractors, Inc.

—The Scarlet Pimpernel. 1992. (Bantam Classics Ser.). 272p. mass mkt. 4.95 (*0-553-21402-0*, Bantam Classics) Bantam Bks.

—The Scarlet Pimpernel. unabr. ed. 1982. audio 49.95 (*0-7861-0524-0*, 2023) Blackstone Audio Bks., Inc.

—The Scarlet Pimpernel. unabr. ed. 1983. (J). audio 56.00 (*0-7366-3882-2*, 9106) Books on Tape, Inc.

—The Scarlet Pimpernel. unabr. ed. 1999. (Bookcassette Classic Collection). audio 17.95 (*1-56740-452-9*, 1806, Bookcassette); audio 57.25 (*1-56740-678-5*, 1807, Unabridged Library Editions) Brilliance Audio.

—The Scarlet Pimpernel. 1976. lib. bdg. 21.95 o.p. (*0-89968-072-0*, Lightyear Pr.); 1984. 256p. reprint ed. lib. bdg. 21.95 (*0-89966-508-X*) Buccaneer Bks., Inc.

—The Scarlet Pimpernel. 2002. (Dover Thrift Editions Ser.). 176p. pap. 2.50 (*0-486-42122-8*) Dover Pubns., Inc.

—The Scarlet Pimpernel. abr. ed. (Read-Along Ser.). 1994. pap. 29.99 incl. audio (*0-88646-844-2*, LSR 7268); 1990. audio 16.99 (*0-88646-268-1*, 7268) Durkin Hayes Publishing Ltd.

—The Scarlet Pimpernel. E-Book 2.49 (*1-58627-775-8*) Electric Umbrella Publishing.

—The Scarlet Pimpernel. (Reader's Request Ser.). 1984. lib. bdg. 12.95 o.p. (*0-8161-3077-9*, Macmillan Reference USA); 2002. 437p. 28.95 (*0-7862-4012-1*) Gale Group.

—The Scarlet Pimpernel. abr. ed. audio 12.95 o.p. (*0-694-50950-7*, SWC 1647, Caedmon) HarperTrade.

—The Scarlet Pimpernel. l.t. ed. 1104p. pap. 79.99 (*0-7583-2158-9*); 445p. pap. 34.00 (*0-7583-2154-6*); 325p. pap. 27.00 (*0-7583-2153-8*); 729p. pap. 51.00 (*0-7583-2156-2*); 250p. pap. 23.00 (*0-7583-2152-X*); 570p. pap. 42.00 (*0-7583-2155-4*); 897p. pap. 69.00 (*0-7583-2157-0*); 1280p. pap. 89.00 (*0-7583-2159-7*); 897p. lib. bdg. 81.00 (*0-7583-2149-X*); 1280p. lib. bdg. 101.00 (*0-7583-2151-1*); 445p. lib. bdg. 40.00 (*0-7583-2146-5*); 729p. lib. bdg. 57.00 (*0-7583-2148-1*); 570p. lib. bdg. 48.00 (*0-7583-2147-3*); 325p. lib. bdg. 33.40 (*0-7583-2145-7*); 1104p. lib. bdg. 91.99 (*0-7583-2150-3*); 250p. lib. bdg. 29.00 (*0-7583-2144-9*) Huge Print Pr.

—The Scarlet Pimpernel. unabr. ed. 1984. audio 56.00 Jimcin Recordings.

—The Scarlet Pimpernel. 1999. 320p. (gr. 8-12). 14.95 (*0-375-40658-1*) Knopf, Alfred A. Inc.

—The Scarlet Pimpernel. l.t. ed. 2002. (LRS Large Print Heritage Ser.). lib. bdg. 34.95 (*1-58118-093-4*) LRS.

—The Scarlet Pimpernel. E-Book 1.95 (*1-58515-047-9*) MesaView, Inc.

—The Scarlet Pimpernel. (Signet Classics). 2000. 288p. mass mkt. 4.95 (*0-451-52762-3*, Signet Bks.); 1974. mass mkt. 1.95 o.p. (*0-451-51699-0*, Signet Classics); 1974. mass mkt. 1.50 o.p. (*0-451-51029-1*, Signet Classics); 1974. mass mkt. 1.25 o.p. (*0-451-50725-8*, Signet Classics); 1974. mass mkt. 1.75 o.p. (*0-451-51376-2*, Signet Classics); 1974. mass mkt. 2.50 o.p. (*0-451-51762-8*, Signet Classics) NAL.

—The Scarlet Pimpernel. abr. ed. 1995. (Classic, Ultimate, Dove Ser.). (gr. 4-7). audio 19.95 o.p. (*1-55800-924-8*, 692917, Dove Audio) NewStar Media, Inc.

—The Scarlet Pimpernel. 2000. (Twelve-Point Ser.). 245p. reprint ed. lib. bdg. 24.00 o.p. (*1-58287-122-1*) North Bks.

—The Scarlet Pimpernel. 1985. 11.95 (*0-396-08690-X*, G. P. Putnam's Sons) Penguin Putnam Bks. for Young Readers.

—The Scarlet Pimpernel. 2000. (YA). pap., stu. ed. 73.20 incl. audio (*0-7887-3191-2*, 40926X4) Recorded Bks., LLC.

—The Scarlet Pimpernel. 1998. 304p. pap. 12.95 (*0-89526-365-3*, Gateway Editions) Regnery Publishing, Inc., An Eagle Publishing Co.

—The Scarlet Pimpernel. abr. ed. 1982. (Radio Ser.). audio 7.95 o.p. (*0-88142-412-9*) Soundelux Audio Publishing.

—The Scarlet Pimpernel. abr. ed. 1998. mass mkt. 16.95 incl. audio (*1-85998-958-6*) Trafalgar Square.

—The Scarlet Pimpernel. 1974. 11.00 (*0-606-00955-8*) Turtleback Bks.

—The Scarlet Pimpernel & Other Tales. Wellborn, Sandra, ed. 2000. cd-rom 9.95 (*1-930430-02-7*) Waltsan Publishing, LLC.

—Sir Percy Hits Back. 2000. 320p. reprint ed. 37.95 (*1-56849-733-4*) Buccaneer Bks., Inc.

—Sir Percy Leads the Band. 2002. reprint ed. lib. bdg. 35.95 (*1-56849-737-7*) Buccaneer Bks., Inc.

—The Triumph of the Scarlet Pimpernel. 320p. 24.95 (*0-8488-2557-8*) Amereon, Ltd.

—The Triumph of the Scarlet Pimpernel. 1983. 321p. reprint ed. lib. bdg. 35.95 (*0-89966-460-1*) Buccaneer Bks., Inc.

—The Triumph of the Scarlet Pimpernel. abr. ed. pap. incl. audio (*1-85998-959-4*) Hodder Children's Audio.

—The Triumph of the Scarlet Pimpernel. abr. ed. 1999. audio 16.85 (*1-84032-118-0*) Hodder Headline Audiobooks GBR. *Dist:* Ulverscroft Large Print Bks., Ltd.

—The Way of the Scarlet Pimpernel. 24.95 (*0-8488-1442-8*) Amereon, Ltd.

—The Way of the Scarlet Pimpernel. 1983. 318p. reprint ed. lib. bdg. 37.95 (*0-89966-461-X*) Buccaneer Bks., Inc.

**BLALOCK, JOANNE (FICTITIOUS CHARACTER)—FICTION**

Goldberg, Leonard S. Deadly Care. 1996. 336p. 23.95 o.s.i (*0-525-94092-8*, Dutton) Dutton/Plume.

—Deadly Care. 1997. 416p. mass mkt. 6.99 o.s.i (*0-451-18742-3*, Signet Bks.) NAL.

—Deadly Exposure. 1998. 336p. 23.95 o.p. (*0-525-94427-3*) Dutton/Plume.

—Deadly Exposure. 2000. 416p. reprint ed. mass mkt. 6.99 (*0-451-40872-1*, Signet Bks.) NAL.

—Deadly Harvest. 1997. 320p. 23.95 o.s.i (*0-525-94093-6*) Dutton/Plume.

—Deadly Harvest. 1998. 416p. mass mkt. 6.99 o.s.i (*0-451-18743-1*, Signet Bks.) NAL.

—Deadly Medicine. 1992. 352p. (Orig.). mass mkt. 6.99 (*0-451-17439-9*, Signet Bks.) NAL.

—Deadly Practice. 1994. 320p. (Orig.). mass mkt. 6.99 (*0-451-17945-5*) NAL.

—Lethal Measures: A Novel of Medical Suspense. 2000. (Illus.). 304p. 24.95 o.s.i (*0-525-94528-8*, Dutton) Dutton/Plume.

—Lethal Measures: A Novel of Medical Suspense. 2000. 416p. mass mkt. 6.99 o.s.i (*0-451-20156-6*, Onyx) NAL.

**BLANCHARD, URSULA (FICTITIOUS CHARACTER)—FICTION**

Buckley, Fiona. The Doublet Affair. unabr. ed. 2000. audio 49.95 (*0-7861-1725-7*, 2530) Blackstone Audio Bks., Inc.

—The Doublet Affair. 1999. (Illus.). 416p. mass mkt. 6.99 (*0-671-01532-X*, Pocket) Simon & Schuster.

—The Doublet Affair. l.t. ed. 2000. (Ulverscroft Large Print Ser.). 408p. 31.99 o.p. (*0-7089-4180-X*, Ulverscroft) Thorpe, F. A. Pubs. GBR. *Dist:* Ulverscroft Large Print Bks., Ltd., Ulverscroft Large Print Canada, Ltd.

—The Doublet Affair: An Ursula Blanchard Mystery at Queen Elizabeth I's Court. 1998. 304p. 21.00 o.s.i (*0-684-83842-7*, Scribner) Simon & Schuster.

—The Fugitive Queen: An Ursula Blanchard Mystery at Queen Elizabeth I's Court. 2003. 288p. 24.00 (*0-7432-3751-X*, Scribner) Simon & Schuster.

—A Pawn for a Queen: An Ursula Blanchard Mystery at Queen Elizabeth I's Court. 2002. 288p. 24.00 (*0-7432-0265-1*, Scribner) Simon & Schuster.

—The Queen of Ambition. 2003. (Illus.). 384p. pap. 6.99 (*0-7434-1030-0*, Pocket) Simon & Schuster.

—Queen's Ransom. 2003. 336p. reprint ed. mass mkt. 6.99 (*0-671-03293-3*, Pocket) Simon & Schuster.

—Queen's Ransom: A Mystery at Queen Elizabeth I's Court Featuring Ursula Blanchard. 2000. E-Book 23.00 (*0-7432-1362-9*); 352p. 23.00 o.s.i (*0-684-86267-0*) Simon & Schuster. (Scribner).

—The Robsart Mystery. l.t. ed. 1998. (Ulverscroft Large Print Ser.). 480p. 29.99 o.p. (*0-7089-4009-9*, Ulverscroft) Thorpe, F. A. Pubs. GBR. *Dist:* Ulverscroft Large Print Bks., Ltd., Ulverscroft Large Print Canada, Ltd.

—To Ruin a Queen: An Ursula Blanchard Mystery at Queen Elizabeth I's Court. 2000. E-Book 23.00 (*0-7432-1365-3*); (Illus.). 288p. 23.00 o.s.i (*0-684-86268-9*) Simon & Schuster. (Scribner).

—To Shield the Queen. unabr. ed. 1999. audio 49.95 (*0-7861-1532-7*, 2382) Blackstone Audio Bks., Inc.

—To Shield the Queen: A Mystery at Queen Elizabeth I's Court. 1997. (Mystery at Queen Elizabeth I's Court Ser.). (Illus.). 288p. 21.00 (*0-684-83841-9*, Scribner) Simon & Schuster.

Powers, Anne. Queen's Ransom. 1986. 400p. reprint ed. mass mkt. 3.95 o.s.i (*0-8439-2352-0*) Dorchester Publishing Co., Inc.

**BLANE, GEORGE (FICTITIOUS CHARACTER)—FICTION**

Daniel, Mark. Unbridled. 1990. 224p. 17.95 o.p. (*0-89919-922-4*) Houghton Mifflin Co.

—Unbridled. 1992. 256p. mass mkt. 4.99 (*0-380-71443-4*, Avon Bks.) Morrow/Avon.

**BLEICHERT, BUCKY (FICTITIOUS CHARACTER)—FICTION**

Ellroy, James. The Black Dahlia. unabr. collector's ed. 1990. (L. A. Quartet). audio 88.00 (*0-7366-1816-3*, 2652) Books on Tape, Inc.

—The Black Dahlia. 1987. 336p. 16.95 (*0-89296-206-2*) Mysterious Pr.

—The Black Dahlia. 1998. 336p. pap. 13.99 (*0-446-67436-2*); 1988. 384p. mass mkt. 5.99 (*0-445-40525-2*) Warner Bks., Inc.

**BLEVINS, HASKELL (FICTITIOUS CHARACTER)—FICTION**

McCafferty, Taylor. Bed Bugs. Chelius, Jane, ed. 1993. 256p. (Orig.). mass mkt. 5.50 (*0-671-75468-8*, Pocket) Simon & Schuster.

—Hanky Panky. 1995. 256p. mass mkt. 5.50 (*0-671-51049-5*, Pocket) Simon & Schuster.

—Pet Peeves. Chelius, Jane, ed. 1990. 224p. (Orig.). mass mkt. 4.99 (*0-671-72802-4*, Pocket) Simon & Schuster.

—Ruffled Feathers. Chelius, Jane, ed. 1992. 224p. (Orig.). mass mkt. 4.50 (*0-671-72803-2*, Pocket) Simon & Schuster.

—Thin Skins. 1994. 256p. mass mkt. 4.99 (*0-671-79977-0*, Pocket) Simon & Schuster.

**BLISS, LENNY (FICTITIOUS CHARACTER)—FICTION**

Sloan, Bob. Bliss. 1996. 192p. 21.00 (*0-684-82250-4*, Scribner) Simon & Schuster.

—Bliss Jumps the Gun: A Lenny Bliss Mystery. (Lenny Bliss Mysteries Ser.). 2000. 288p. pap. 7.95 (*0-393-32114-2*, Norton Paperbacks); 1999. 224p. text 22.95 o.p. (*0-393-04750-4*) Norton, W. W. & Co., Inc.

—The Middle of Nowhere: A Lenny Bliss Mystery. 2003. 224p. 23.00 (*0-87113-872-7*, Atlantic Monthly Pr.) Grove/Atlantic, Inc.

**BLISS, VICKY (FICTITIOUS CHARACTER)—FICTION**

Peters, Elizabeth, pseud. Borrower of the Night. l.t. ed. 1992. 15.95 o.p. (*0-7927-0652-8*); 1991. 17.95 o.p. (*0-7927-0651-X*, E0008) BBC Audiobooks America.

—Borrower of the Night. 1992. mass mkt. 4.99 (*0-8125-2355-5*); 1990. pap. 3.95 o.s.i (*0-8125-0752-5*) Doherty, Tom Assocs., LLC. (Tor Bks.).

—Borrower of the Night. 2000. (Vicky Bliss Mysteries Ser.). 336p. mass mkt. 6.99 (*0-380-73339-0*, Avon Bks.) Morrow/Avon.

—Borrower of the Night. 1994. reprint ed. lib. bdg. 20.00 o.p. (*0-7278-4664-7*) Severn Hse. Pubs., Ltd.

—Night Train to Memphis. unabr. ed. 1997. (Vicky Bliss Mysteries Ser.). audio 28.00 (*1-885608-26-8*) Airplay.

—Night Train to Memphis. unabr. ed. 1996. audio 62.95 (*0-7861-1065-1*, 1836) Blackstone Audio Bks., Inc.

—Night Train to Memphis. unabr. ed. 1995. (Vicky Bliss Mystery Ser.: Vol. 5). audio 85.00 (*0-7887-0109-6*, 94372E7) Recorded Bks., LLC.

—Night Train to Memphis. 354p. pap. 5.98 o.p. (*0-7651-0300-1*) Smithmark Pubs., Inc.

—Night Train to Memphis. 368p. 1995. mass mkt. 7.50 (*0-446-60248-5*); 1994. 21.95 o.s.i (*0-446-51586-8*) Warner Bks., Inc.

—Silhouette in Scarlet. 1990. mass mkt. 4.50 (*0-8125-0940-4*, Tor Bks.) Doherty, Tom Assocs., LLC.

—Silhouette in Scarlet. l.t. ed. 1986. 10.00 o.p. (*0-8161-3592-4*, Macmillan Reference USA) Gale Group.

—Silhouette in Scarlet. unabr. ed. (Vicky Bliss Mystery Ser.: Vol. 3). audio 44.00 (*0-7887-0160-6*, 94385E7) Recorded Bks., LLC.

—Silhouette in Scarlet. l.t. ed. 1985. (Ulverscroft Large Print Ser.). 29.99 o.p. (*0-7089-1315-6*, Ulverscroft) Thorpe, F. A. Pubs. GBR. *Dist:* Ulverscroft Large Print Bks., Ltd., Ulverscroft Large Print Canada, Ltd.

—Silhouette in Scarlet. 1994. 224p. mass mkt. 5.50 o.p. (*0-446-36482-7*) Warner Bks., Inc.

—Street of the Five Moons. 1979. pap. 1.95 o.s.i (*0-449-23897-0*, Fawcett) Ballantine Bks.

—Street of the Five Moons. 1990. 256p. mass mkt. 5.99 (*0-8125-1244-8*); 1988. pap. 3.95 o.s.i (*0-8125-0795-9*); 1987. 256p. pap. 3.50 o.s.i (*0-8125-0766-5*) Doherty, Tom Assocs., LLC. (Tor Bks.).

—Street of the Five Moons. l.t. ed. 1991. (General Ser.). 350p. pap. 18.95 o.p. (*0-8161-4906-2*, Macmillan Reference USA) Gale Group.

—Street of the Five Moons. 2000. (Vicky Bliss Mysteries Ser.). 384p. mass mkt. 6.99 (*0-380-73121-5*, Avon Bks.) Morrow/Avon.

—Street of the Five Moons. unabr. ed. 1994. (Vicky Bliss Mystery Ser.: Vol. 2). audio 51.00 (*0-7887-0040-5*, 94239E7) Recorded Bks., LLC.

—Trojan Gold. unabr. ed. 1998. (Vicky Bliss Ser.). audio 28.00 (*1-885608-32-2*) Airplay.

—Trojan Gold. 1992. mass mkt. 5.99 o.p. (*0-8125-2357-1*); 1988. 416p. pap. 3.95 o.s.i (*0-8125-0758-4*) Doherty, Tom Assocs., LLC. (Tor Bks.).

—Trojan Gold. 2000. (Vicky Bliss Mysteries Ser.). 368p. mass mkt. 6.99 (*0-380-73123-1*, Avon Bks.) Morrow/Avon.

—Trojan Gold. unabr. ed. 1992. (Vicky Bliss Mystery Ser.: Vol. 4). audio 70.00 (*1-55690-735-4*, 92229E7) Recorded Bks., LLC.

—Trojan Gold. 1987. 288p. 15.95 o.p. (*0-689-11621-7*, Scribner) Simon & Schuster.

**BLISSBERG, HARVEY (FICTITIOUS CHARACTER)—FICTION**

Rosen, Richard D. Dead Ball: A Harvey Blissberg Mystery. 2001. 252p. 23.95 (*0-8027-3366-2*) Walker & Co.

—Fadeaway. 1986. 256p. 15.95 o.p. (*0-06-015599-X*) HarperTrade.

—Fadeaway. 1987. 288p. mass mkt. 3.95 o.p. (*0-451-40148-4*); mass mkt. 3.95 o.p. (*0-451-40046-1*) NAL. (Onyx).

—Saturday Night Dead. 1989. mass mkt. 3.95 o.p. (*0-451-40134-4*, Onyx) NAL.

—Saturday Night Dead. 1988. 28p. 16.95 o.p. (*0-670-81977-8*) Viking Penguin.

—Strike Three, You're Dead. l.t. ed. 1986. 19.95 o.p. (*1-55504-143-4*) BBC Audiobooks America.

—Strike Three, You're Dead. 1986. mass mkt. 2.95 o.p. (*0-451-14233-0*, Signet Bks.); 256p. mass mkt. 3.95 o.p. (*0-451-40142-5*, Onyx) NAL.

—Strike Three, You're Dead. 1984. 192p. 12.95 o.s.i (*0-8027-5587-9*); 2001. 225p. reprint ed. pap. 8.95 (*0-8027-7608-6*) Walker & Co.

—World of Hurt. 1994. 264p. 20.95 (*0-8027-3251-8*) Walker & Co.

**BLOCK, BELLA (FICTITIOUS CHARACTER)—FICTION**

Gercke, Doris. How Many Miles to Babylon. Hamilton, Anna, tr. from GER. 1991. 100p. (Orig.). pap. 8.95 o.p. (*1-879679-02-7*) Women In Translation.

**BLOM, MARTIN (FICTITIOUS CHARACTER)—FICTION**

Thomson, Rupert. The Insult. 1997. pap. 14.00 (*0-679-78150-1*, Vintage) Knopf Publishing Group.

**BLOODWORTH, LEO (FICTITIOUS CHARACTER)—FICTION**

Lochte, Dick. Laughing Dog. 1988. (Leo Bloodworth-Serendipity Dahlquist Mystery Ser.: Bk. 2). 272p. 17.95 o.p. (*0-87795-941-2*, Morrow, William & Co.) Morrow/Avon.

—Laughing Dog. 2001. 240p. pap. 13.95 (*1-890208-79-5*) Poisoned Pen Pr.

—Laughing Dog. 1989. 400p. reprint ed. mass mkt. 3.95 o.s.i (*0-446-35724-3*) Warner Bks., Inc.

—Lucky Dog & Other Tales of Murder. 2000. (Five Star Mystery Ser.). 207p. 20.95 (*0-7862-2688-9*, Five Star) Gale Group.

—Sleeping Dog. 1985. 288p. 15.95 o.p. (*0-87795-738-X*, Morrow, William & Co.) Morrow/Avon.

—Sleeping Dog. 2001. (Missing Mystery Ser.: Vol. 29). 292p. pap. 14.95 (*1-890208-51-5*) Poisoned Pen Pr.

—Sleeping Dog. 1986. 288p. mass mkt. 3.95 o.s.i (*0-446-32661-5*) Warner Bks., Inc.

**BLOOM, LEOPOLD (FICTITIOUS CHARACTER)—FICTION**

Costello, Peter. The Life of Leopold Bloom: A Novel. 1993. 197p. (Orig.). pap. 9.95 (*1-879373-34-3*) Rinehart, Roberts Pubs.

Joyce, James. Ulysses. 799p. 38.95 (*0-8488-2569-1*) Amereon, Ltd.
—Ulysses. 1992. reprint ed. lib. bdg. 27.95 (*0-89968-284-7*, Lightyear Pr.) Buccaneer Bks., Inc.
—Ulysses, 3 vols. Gabler, Hans W. & Melchior, Claus, eds. 1984. 1954p. text 202.00 o.p. (*0-8240-4375-8*) Garland Publishing, Inc.
—Ulysses. abr. ed. 1972. audio 12.95 o.s.i (*0-694-50050-X*, SWC 1063, Caedmon); Set. 1984. audio 19.95 (*0-694-50866-7*, SWC 328, Caedmon); Set. 1992. audio 18.00 o.s.i (*1-55994-633-4*, DCN 328, HarperAudio) HarperTrade.
—Ulysses. 1990. 816p. pap. 17.00 (*0-679-72276-9*, Vintage) Knopf Publishing Group.
—Ulysses. 1997. 1136p. 25.00 (*0-679-45513-2*) Knopf, Alfred A. Inc.
—Ulysses. 2015. 880p. mass mkt. 7.95 o.s.i (*0-451-52674-0*, Signet Classics) NAL.
—Ulysses. abr. ed. (Works of James Joyce). 1996. audio 22.98 (*962-634-511-X*, NA401114); 1994. audio compact disk 26.98 (*962-634-011-8*, NA401112) Naxos of America, Inc. (Naxos AudioBooks).
—Ulysses. Date not set. 35.00 (*0-393-03390-2*) Norton, W. W. & Co., Inc.
—Ulysses. 1998. 732p. 75.00 (*0-914061-70-4*) Orchises Pr.
—Ulysses. Johnson, Jeri, ed. & intro. by. unexpurg. ed. 1993. (Oxford World's Classics Ser.). (Illus.). 1056p. pap. 15.95 o.p. (*0-19-282866-5*) Oxford Univ. Pr., Inc.
—Ulysses. 1993. audio 22.00 o.s.i (*0-553-47163-5*, RH Audio) Random Hse. Audio Publishing Group.
—Ulysses. (Modern Library of the World's Best Bks.). 1992. 816p. 22.95 (*0-679-60011-6*); 1967. 20.00 o.p. (*0-394-45005-1*); 1967. pap. 10.95 o.p. (*0-394-70380-4*); 1940. 5.95 o.s.i (*0-394-60752-X*) Random Hse., Inc.
—Ulysses. 2004. audio compact disk 79.99 (*1-4025-7203-4*); Pt. 2, set. audio o.s.i; Set. 1999. audio 186.00 (*0-7887-0225-4*, 94502); Vols. 1 & 2. 1996. audio 186.00 (*0-7887-0309-9*, 94502E7) Recorded Bks., LLC.
—Ulysses. 1040p. 1999. pap. 14.95 (*0-14-118086-2*); 1998. pap. 14.95 (*0-14-018558-5*, Penguin Classics) Viking Penguin.
—Ulysses: A Facsimile of the Manuscript & the Manuscript & First Printings Compared, 3 vols. 1975. 100.00 o.p. (*0-374-94440-7*) Univ. Pr. of Virginia.
—Ulysses: A Reader's Edition. Rose, Danis, ed. 1998. 826p. pap. 19.95 (*0-330-35230-X*); 1997. 824p. 47.50 o.p. (*0-330-35229-6*) Picador GBR. *Dist:* Trans-Atlantic Pubns., Inc.
—Ulysses: The Corrected Text. 1986. 608p. 29.95 o.s.i (*0-394-55373-X*); 680p. pap. 19.00 (*0-394-74312-1*) Knopf Publishing Group. (Vintage).
—Ulysses: The Corrected Text. rev. ed. 1986. 16.95 (*0-07-544944-7*) McGraw-Hill Cos., The.
Joyce, James, contrib. by. Ulysses. 1997. (*1-874675-98-8*); (*1-874675-99-6*) Dufour Editions, Inc.

**BLOOM, MOLLY (FICTITIOUS CHARACTER)—FICTION**

Joyce, James. Ulysses. 799p. 38.95 (*0-8488-2569-1*) Amereon, Ltd.
—Ulysses. 1992. reprint ed. lib. bdg. 27.95 (*0-89968-284-7*, Lightyear Pr.) Buccaneer Bks., Inc.
—Ulysses, 3 vols. Gabler, Hans W. & Melchior, Claus, eds. 1984. 1954p. text 202.00 o.p. (*0-8240-4375-8*) Garland Publishing, Inc.
—Ulysses. abr. ed. 1972. audio 12.95 o.s.i (*0-694-50050-X*, SWC 1063, Caedmon); Set. 1984. audio 19.95 (*0-694-50866-7*, SWC 328, Caedmon); Set. 1992. audio 18.00 o.s.i (*1-55994-633-4*, DCN 328, HarperAudio) HarperTrade.
—Ulysses. 1990. 816p. pap. 17.00 (*0-679-72276-9*, Vintage) Knopf Publishing Group.
—Ulysses. 1997. 1136p. 25.00 (*0-679-45513-2*) Knopf, Alfred A. Inc.
—Ulysses. 2015. 880p. mass mkt. 7.95 o.s.i (*0-451-52674-0*, Signet Classics) NAL.
—Ulysses. abr. ed. (Works of James Joyce). 1996. audio 22.98 (*962-634-511-X*, NA401114); 1994. audio compact disk 26.98 (*962-634-011-8*, NA401112) Naxos of America, Inc. (Naxos AudioBooks).
—Ulysses. Date not set. 35.00 (*0-393-03390-2*) Norton, W. W. & Co., Inc.
—Ulysses. 1998. 732p. 75.00 (*0-914061-70-4*) Orchises Pr.
—Ulysses. Johnson, Jeri, ed. & intro. by. unexpurg. ed. 1993. (Oxford World's Classics Ser.). (Illus.). 1056p. pap. 15.95 o.p. (*0-19-282866-5*) Oxford Univ. Pr., Inc.
—Ulysses. 1993. audio 22.00 o.s.i (*0-553-47163-5*, RH Audio) Random Hse. Audio Publishing Group.
—Ulysses. (Modern Library of the World's Best Bks.). 1992. 816p. 22.95 (*0-679-60011-6*); 1967. 20.00 o.p. (*0-394-45005-1*); 1967. pap. 10.95 o.p. (*0-394-70380-4*); 1940. 5.95 o.s.i (*0-394-60752-X*) Random Hse., Inc.
—Ulysses. 2004. audio compact disk 79.99 (*1-4025-7203-4*); Pt. 2, set. audio o.s.i; Set. 1999. audio 186.00 (*0-7887-0225-4*, 94502); Vols. 1 & 2. 1996. audio 186.00 (*0-7887-0309-9*, 94502E7) Recorded Bks., LLC.
—Ulysses. 1040p. 1999. pap. 14.95 (*0-14-118086-2*); 1998. pap. 14.95 (*0-14-018558-5*, Penguin Classics) Viking Penguin.
—Ulysses: A Facsimile of the Manuscript & the Manuscript & First Printings Compared, 3 vols. 1975. 100.00 o.p. (*0-374-94440-7*) Univ. Pr. of Virginia.
—Ulysses: A Reader's Edition. Rose, Danis, ed. 1998. 826p. pap. 19.95 (*0-330-35230-X*); 1997. 824p. 47.50 o.p. (*0-330-35229-6*) Picador GBR. *Dist:* Trans-Atlantic Pubns., Inc.
—Ulysses: The Corrected Text. 1986. 608p. 29.95 o.s.i (*0-394-55373-X*); 680p. pap. 19.00 (*0-394-74312-1*) Knopf Publishing Group. (Vintage).
—Ulysses: The Corrected Text. rev. ed. 1986. 16.95 (*0-07-544944-7*) McGraw-Hill Cos., The.
Joyce, James, contrib. by. Ulysses. 1997. (*1-874675-98-8*); (*1-874675-99-6*) Dufour Editions, Inc.

**BLOOMWOOD, BECKY (FICTITIOUS CHARACTER)—FICTION**

Kinsella, Sophie. Confessions of a Shopaholic. 2003. 384p. mass mkt. 6.99 (*0-440-24141-3*, Dell Bks.); 2001. (Illus.). 320p. pap. 11.95 (*0-385-33548-2*, Delta) Dell Publishing.
—Confessions of a Shopaholic. audio 29.99 (*1-4025-3603-8*) Recorded Bks., LLC.
—Shopaholic Takes Manhattan. Orig. Title: Shopaholic Abroad. 2004. 416p. mass mkt. 6.99 (*0-440-24181-2*); 2002. 336p. pap. 11.95 (*0-385-33588-1*, Delta) Dell Publishing.
—Shopaholic Takes Manhattan. Orig. Title: Shopaholic Abroad. audio 29.99 (*1-4025-3624-0*) Recorded Bks., LLC.
—Shopaholic Ties the Knot. 2003. 352p. pap. 10.95 (*0-385-33617-9*, Delta) Dell Publishing.
—Shopaholic Ties the Knot. audio 29.99 (*1-4025-3625-9*) Recorded Bks., LLC.

**BLUENIGHT, LINDA (FICTITIOUS CHARACTER)—FICTION**

Cramer, Rebecca. Mission to Sonora. 1998. 298p. pap. 10.95 (*1-881542-50-5*) Book World, Inc.
—View from Frog Mountain. Date not set. 10.95 (*1-881542-63-7*) Book World, Inc.

**BLUME, MOLLY (FICTITIOUS CHARACTER)—FICTION**

Krich, Rochelle Majer. Blues in the Night. 352p. 2003. mass mkt. 6.99 (*0-449-00726-X*); 2002. 23.95 (*0-345-44971-1*, Ballantine Bks.) Ballantine Bks.
—Blues in the Night. unabr. ed. 2002. (Molly Blume Ser.). audio 74.25 (*1-59086-425-5*, 4017, Unabridged Library Editions) Brilliance Audio.
—Blues in the Night. 2003. (Women's Fiction Ser.). 29.95 (*0-7862-5188-3*) Thorndike Pr.

**BLUMENTHAL, MARISSA (FICTITIOUS CHARACTER)—FICTION**

Cook, Robin. Outbreak. 1988. 352p. mass mkt. 7.99 (*0-425-10687-X*) Berkley Publishing Group.
—Outbreak. unabr. ed. 1993. audio 48.00 (*0-7366-2348-5*, 3126) Books on Tape, Inc.
—Outbreak. l.t. ed. 1987. (General Ser.). 383p. 19.95 o.p. (*0-8161-4316-1*, Macmillan Reference USA) Gale Group.
—Outbreak. 1987. 368p. 17.95 o.p. (*0-399-13187-6*) Putnam Publishing Group, The.
—Outbreak. 1988. 14.04 (*0-606-00934-5*) Turtleback Bks.
—Vital Signs. 1992. 352p. pap. 7.99 (*0-425-13176-9*) Berkley Publishing Group.
—Vital Signs. unabr. ed. 1991. audio 72.00 (*0-7366-1964-X*, 2785) Books on Tape, Inc.
—Vital Signs. 1994. reprint ed. lib. bdg. 32.95 (*1-56849-267-7*) Buccaneer Bks., Inc.
—Vital Signs. l.t. ed. 1991. 560p. pap. 16.95 o.p. (*0-8161-5304-3*); lib. bdg. 22.95 o.p. (*0-8161-5303-5*) Gale Group. (Macmillan Reference USA).
—Vital Signs. 1991. 400p. 21.95 o.p. (*0-399-13575-8*, G. P. Putnam's Sons) Penguin Group (USA) Inc.
—Vital Signs. abr. ed. 1991. audio 15.95 (*0-671-72972-1*, Simon & Schuster Audioworks) Simon & Schuster Audio.
—Vital Signs. 1992. 14.04 (*0-606-00935-3*) Turtleback Bks.

**BOGNAR, T. C. (FICTITIOUS CHARACTER)—FICTION**

Largent, R. Karl. Red Ice. 448p. (Orig.). 1995. pap. 5.99 (*0-8439-3774-2*); 1999. reprint ed. mass mkt. 6.99 (*0-8439-4604-0*, Leisure Bks.) Dorchester Publishing Co., Inc.
—Red Sand. 1997. 400p. (Orig.). mass mkt. 6.99 (*0-8439-4301-7*, Leisure Bks.) Dorchester Publishing Co., Inc.
—Red Skies. 1996. 400p. mass mkt. 6.99 (*0-8439-4117-0*) Dorchester Publishing Co., Inc.
—Red Skies. 1996. E-Book 9.95 (*0-585-28852-6*) netLibrary, Inc.
—Red Tide. 448p. (Orig.). 1992. pap. 4.99 (*0-8439-3366-6*); 1999. reprint ed. mass mkt. 6.99 (*0-8439-4602-4*, Leisure Bks.) Dorchester Publishing Co., Inc.
—Red Wind. 368p. 1998. pap. 5.99 (*0-8439-4361-0*); 1999. reprint ed. mass mkt. 5.99 (*0-8439-4603-2*) Dorchester Publishing Co., Inc. (Leisure Bks.).
—Red Wing. 1999. E-Book 9.95 (*0-585-30984-1*) netLibrary, Inc.

**BOGNOR, SIMON (FICTITIOUS CHARACTER)—FICTION**

Heald, Tim. Blue Blood Will Out. 1980. 192p. mass mkt. 2.25 o.s.i (*0-345-28904-8*) Ballantine Bks.
—Blue Blood Will Out. 1974. 192p. 15.95 o.p. (*0-8128-1688-9*, Scarborough Hse.) Madison Bks., Inc.
—Business Unusual. 1990. 14.95 o.s.i (*0-385-41337-8*) Doubleday Publishing.
—Business Unusual, Set. unabr. ed. 1998. audio 63.95 o.p. (*1-872672-99-X*) Magna Story Sound GBR. *Dist:* Ulverscroft Large Print Bks., Ltd.
—Deadline. 1980. mass mkt. 2.25 o.s.i (*0-345-28905-6*) Ballantine Bks.
—Deadline. 1975. 192p. 6.95 o.p. (*0-8128-1757-5*, Scarborough Hse.) Madison Bks., Inc.
—Just Desserts. 1980. mass mkt. 1.95 o.s.i (*0-345-28683-9*) Ballantine Bks.
—Just Desserts. 1990. 296p. lib. bdg. 20.95 o.p. (*0-7451-1142-4*, Macmillan Reference USA) Gale Group.
—Let Sleeping Dogs Die. 1981. 192p. mass mkt. 2.25 o.p. (*0-345-28903-X*) Ballantine Bks.
—Murder at Moosejaw. 1981. (Crime Club Ser.). 192p. 10.95 o.p. (*0-385-17754-2*) Doubleday Publishing.
—Red Herrings. 1986. (Crime Club Ser.). 192p. 12.95 o.p. (*0-385-23354-X*) Doubleday Publishing.
—Red Herrings. l.t. ed. 1987. lib. bdg. 18.50 o.p. (*0-7451-0581-5*, Macmillan Reference USA) Gale Group.
—A Small Masterpiece. 1982. (Crime Club Ser.). 192p. 10.95 o.p. (*0-385-17942-1*) Doubleday Publishing.
—Unbecoming Habits. 1980. 192p. mass mkt. 1.95 o.s.i (*0-345-28902-1*) Ballantine Bks.

**BOLAN, MACK (FICTITIOUS CHARACTER)—FICTION**

Donnelly, Jane. Flash Point. 1982. (SuperBolan Ser.: No. 12). 352p. pap. o.p. (*0-373-02456-8*, Harlequin Bks.) Harlequin Enterprises, Ltd.
Little, Denise, ed. Vengeance. 2002. 336p. mass mkt. 6.99 (*0-7564-0084-8*) DAW Bks., Inc.
Pendleton, Don. Acapulco Rampage. 1989. (Executioner Ser.: No. 26). mass mkt. 3.50 o.s.i (*1-55817-284-X*, Pinnacle Bks.) Kensington Publishing Corp.
—Age of War. 2003. (SuperBolan Ser.: No. 90). 352p. mass mkt. (*0-373-61490-X*, Gold Eagle) Harlequin Enterprises, Ltd.
—Ambush. 1994. mass mkt. (*0-373-61438-1*, 1-61438-7, Harlequin Bks.) Harlequin Enterprises, Ltd.
—Ambush on Blood River. 1983. (Executioner Ser.: No. 58). 192p. mass mkt. o.s.i (*0-373-61058-0*, Harlequin Bks.) Harlequin Enterprises, Ltd.
—Arizona Ambush. 1990. (Executioner Ser.: No. 31). mass mkt. 3.50 o.s.i (*1-55817-342-0*, Pinnacle Bks.) Kensington Publishing Corp.
—Armageddon Exit. 2002. (Executioner Ser.: No. 286). 224p. mass mkt. (*0-373-64286-5*, Worldwide Library) Harlequin Enterprises, Ltd.
—Armed Force. 1995. (Executioner Ser.: No. 197). per. (*0-373-61197-8*, 1-61197-9, Harlequin Bks.) Harlequin Enterprises, Ltd.
—Asian Crucible. 1996. (Executioner Ser.: No. 209). per. (*0-373-64209-1*, 1-64209-9, Worldwide Library) Harlequin Enterprises, Ltd.
—Assassin's Creed. 1992. (Executioner Ser.: No. 166). mass mkt. (*0-373-61166-8*, 1-61166-4, Harlequin Bks.) Harlequin Enterprises, Ltd.
—Assault. 1990. (SuperBolan Ser.: No. 19). mass mkt. (*0-373-61419-5*, Harlequin Bks.) Harlequin Enterprises, Ltd.
—Assault Reflex. 1999. (Executioner Ser.: No. 243). (Orig.). per. (*0-373-64243-1*, 1-64243-8, Worldwide Library) Harlequin Enterprises, Ltd.
—Backlash. 1990. (SuperBolan Ser.: No. 420). mass mkt. (*0-373-61420-9*, Harlequin Bks.) Harlequin Enterprises, Ltd.
—Baja Blitz. 1993. (Executioner Ser.: No. 170). per. (*0-373-61170-6*, 1-61170-6, Harlequin Bks.) Harlequin Enterprises, Ltd.
—La Batalla del Caribe. Blanco, Osvaldo J., tr. from ENG. 1974. (Compadre Collection, el Verdugo Ser.: No. 10). Tr. of Caribbean Kill. (SPA.). 160p. pap. 0.75 o.p. (*0-88473-310-6*) Fiesta Bk. Co.
—Battle Force. 1993. (SuperBolan Ser.). mass mkt. (*0-373-61432-2*, 1-61432-0, Harlequin Bks.) Harlequin Enterprises, Ltd.
—Battle Ground: 176. 1993. (Executioner Ser.: No. 175). mass mkt. (*0-373-61175-7*, 1-61175-5, Harlequin Bks.) Harlequin Enterprises, Ltd.
—Battle Lines. 1990. (Executioner Ser.: No. 137). pap. (*0-373-61137-4*, Harlequin Bks.) Harlequin Enterprises, Ltd.
—Battle Mask. (Executioner Ser.: No. 3). 1988. mass mkt. 3.50 o.p. (*1-55817-026-X*); 1986. 192p. pap. 2.50 o.p. (*0-523-42344-6*) Kensington Publishing Corp. (Pinnacle Bks.).
—Battle Plan 174. 1993. (Executioner Ser.: No. 174). mass mkt. (*0-373-61174-9*, 1-61174-8, Harlequin Bks.) Harlequin Enterprises, Ltd.
—The Big Kill. 1989. (Executioner Ser.: No. 13). pap. (*0-373-61132-3*, Harlequin Bks.) Harlequin Enterprises, Ltd.
—Bird of Prey. 1996. (StonyMan Ser.: No. 24). per. (*0-373-61908-1*, Worldwide Library) Harlequin Enterprises, Ltd.
—Black Dawn Rising. 1999. (Executioner Ser.: No. 247). 224p. per. (*0-373-64247-4*, 1-64247-9, Worldwide Library) Harlequin Enterprises, Ltd.
—Black Hand. 1993. (Executioner Ser.: No. 178). mass mkt. (*0-373-61178-1*, 1-61178-9, Harlequin Bks.) Harlequin Enterprises, Ltd.
—Blast Radius. 2003. (Executioner Ser.: No. 301). 224p. mass mkt. (*0-373-64301-2*, Gold Eagle) Harlequin Enterprises, Ltd.
—Blind Eagle. 1994. (StonyMan Ser.). mass mkt. (*0-373-61896-4*, 1-61896-6, Harlequin Bks.) Harlequin Enterprises, Ltd.
—Blood & Fire. abr. ed. 1999. (Executioner Ser.: Vol. 221). audio 7.99 (*1-55204-421-1*, GOL-3421) Durkin Hayes Publishing Ltd.
—Blood & Sand. 2002. (SuperBolan Ser.: No. 86). 352p. mass mkt. (*0-373-61486-1*, Worldwide Library) Harlequin Enterprises, Ltd.
—Blood & Thunder. 1986. (Executioner Ser.: No. 95). mass mkt. o.s.i (*0-373-61095-5*, Harlequin Bks.) Harlequin Enterprises, Ltd.
—Blood Circle. 1997. (Executioner Ser.: No. 227). per. (*0-373-64227-X*, 1-64227-1, Worldwide Library) Harlequin Enterprises, Ltd.
—Blood Debt. 1995. (StonyMan Ser.). mass mkt. (*0-373-61899-9*, 1-61899-0, Harlequin Bks.) Harlequin Enterprises, Ltd.
—Blood Fever. 1989. (SuperBolan Ser.: No. 17). mass mkt. (*0-373-61417-9*, Harlequin Bks.) Harlequin Enterprises, Ltd.
—Blood Harvest. abr. ed. 1999. (Executioner Ser.: Vol. 213). audio 7.99 (*1-55204-397-5*, GOL-3397) Durkin Hayes Publishing Ltd.
—Blood Harvest. 1996. (Executioner Ser.: No. 213). per. (*0-373-64213-X*, Worldwide Library) Harlequin Enterprises, Ltd.
—Blood of the Earth. 1999. (Executioner Ser.: No. 246). per. (*0-373-64246-6*, 1-64246-1, Worldwide Library) Harlequin Enterprises, Ltd.
—Blood of the Lion. 1988. (Executioner Ser.: No. 112). pap. o.s.i (*0-373-61112-9*, Harlequin Bks.) Harlequin Enterprises, Ltd.
—Blood Price. 1992. (Executioner Ser.: No. 168). mass mkt. (*0-373-61168-4*, 1-61168-0, Harlequin Bks.) Harlequin Enterprises, Ltd.
—Blood Rules. 1991. (Executioner Ser.: No. 149). mass mkt. (*0-373-61149-8*, Worldwide Library) Harlequin Enterprises, Ltd.
—Blood Run. 1989. (Executioner Ser.: No. 133). pap. (*0-373-61133-1*, Harlequin Bks.) Harlequin Enterprises, Ltd.
—Blood Strike. 1994. (SuperBolan Ser.). per. (*0-373-61439-X*, 1-61439-5, Harlequin Bks.) Harlequin Enterprises, Ltd.
—Bloodsport. 1982. (Executioner Ser.: No. 46). 192p. mass mkt. o.s.i (*0-373-61046-7*, Harlequin Bks.) Harlequin Enterprises, Ltd.
—Border Sweep. 1988. (Executioner Ser.: No. 120). pap. (*0-373-61120-X*, Harlequin Bks.) Harlequin Enterprises, Ltd.
—Boston Blitz. 1988. (Executioner Ser.: No. 12). mass mkt. 3.50 o.s.i (*1-55817-071-5*, Pinnacle Bks.) Kensington Publishing Corp.
—Breach of Trust. 1999. (StonyMan Ser.: No. 39). per. (*0-373-61923-5*, 1-61923-8, Worldwide Library) Harlequin Enterprises, Ltd.
—Breached. 2003. (SuperBolan Ser.: No. 92). 352p. mass mkt. (*0-373-61492-6*, Gold Eagle) Harlequin Enterprises, Ltd.
—Breakaway. 2002. (SuperBolan Ser.). 352p. mass mkt. (*0-373-61485-3*, Worldwide Library) Harlequin Enterprises, Ltd.
—California Hit. 1988. (Executioner Ser.: No. 11). mass mkt. 3.50 o.s.i (*1-55817-070-7*, Pinnacle Bks.) Kensington Publishing Corp.
—Canadian Crisis. 1989. (Executioner Ser.: No. 24). mass mkt. 3.50 o.s.i (*1-55817-267-X*, Pinnacle Bks.) Kensington Publishing Corp.
—Capitol Hit. 1993. (Executioner Ser.: No. 173). per. (*0-373-61173-0*, 1-61173-0, Harlequin Bks.) Harlequin Enterprises, Ltd.
—Caribbean Kill. 1988. (Executioner Ser.: No. 10). mass mkt. 3.50 o.s.i (*1-55817-069-3*, Pinnacle Bks.) Kensington Publishing Corp.
—Cayman Strike. 1991. (Executioner Ser.: No. 157). mass mkt. (*0-373-61157-9*, Harlequin Bks.) Harlequin Enterprises, Ltd.

—Chicago Payoff. 1990. (Executioner Ser.: No. 145). pap. (*0-373-61145-5*, Worldwide Library) Harlequin Enterprises, Ltd.
—Chicago Wipeout. 1988. (Executioner Ser.: No. 8). mass mkt. 3.50 o.s.i (*1-55817-067-7*, Pinnacle Bks.) Kensington Publishing Corp.
—Chill Effect. (Executioner Ser.: No. 254). Date not set. E-Book (*0-373-86006-4*, Gold Eagle); 2000. per. (*0-373-64254-7*, 1-64254-5, Worldwide Library) Harlequin Enterprises, Ltd.
—Circle of Steel. 1988. (Executioner Ser.: No. 115). pap. o.s.i (*0-373-61115-3*, Harlequin Bks.) Harlequin Enterprises, Ltd.
—Clean Sweep. 1994. (Executioner Ser.: No. 183). mass mkt. (*0-373-61183-8*, 1-61183-9, Harlequin Bks.) Harlequin Enterprises, Ltd.
—Cleansing Flame. 1994. (Executioner Ser.: No. 187). mass mkt. (*0-373-61187-0*, 1-61187-0, Harlequin Bks.) Harlequin Enterprises, Ltd.
—Cleveland Pipeline. 1990. (Executioner Ser.: No. 30). mass mkt. 3.50 o.s.i (*1-55817-327-7*, Pinnacle Bks.) Kensington Publishing Corp.
—Code of Conflict. 1999. (SuperBolan Ser.: Vol. 68). 352p. per. (*0-373-61468-3*, Worldwide Library) Harlequin Enterprises, Ltd.
—Cold Judgment. 1988. (Executioner Ser.: No. 114). pap. o.s.i (*0-373-61114-5*, Harlequin Bks.) Harlequin Enterprises, Ltd.
—Colorado Kill Zone. 1989. (Executioner Ser.: No. 25). (Orig.). mass mkt. 3.50 o.s.i (*1-55817-275-0*, Pinnacle Bks.) Kensington Publishing Corp.
—Colors of Hell. 1992. (Executioner Ser.: No. 162). mass mkt. (*0-373-61162-5*, 1-61162-3, Harlequin Bks.) Harlequin Enterprises, Ltd.
—Combat Stretch. 1991. (Executioner Ser.: No. 152). mass mkt. (*0-373-61152-8*, Harlequin Bks.) Harlequin Enterprises, Ltd.
—Combat Zone. abr. ed. 1998. (Executioner Ser.: Vol. 202). audio 7.99 (*1-55204-373-8*) Durkin Hayes Publishing Ltd.
—Combat Zone. 1995. (Executioner Ser.: No. 202). 219p. per. (*0-373-64202-4*, 1-64202-4, Harlequin Bks.) Harlequin Enterprises, Ltd.
—Command Strike. 1990. (Executioner Ser.: No. 29). mass mkt. 3.50 o.s.i (*1-55817-318-8*, Pinnacle Bks.) Kensington Publishing Corp.
—Conflagration. 2000. (SuperBolan Ser.: No. 72). 352p. per. (*0-373-61472-1*, Gold Eagle) Harlequin Enterprises, Ltd.
—Conflict Imperative. 2000. (StonyMan Ser.: Vol. 48). 352p. mass mkt. (*0-373-61932-4*, 1-61932-9, Worldwide Library) Harlequin Enterprises, Ltd.
—Continental Contract. 1988. (Executioner Ser.: No. 5). mass mkt. 3.50 o.p. (*1-55817-028-6*, Pinnacle Bks.) Kensington Publishing Corp.
—Crimson Tide. 1998. (Executioner Ser.: No. 238). per. (*0-373-64238-5*, 1-64238-8, Worldwide Library) Harlequin Enterprises, Ltd.
—Crisis Point. abr. ed. 1998. (Executioner Ser.: Vol. 200). audio 7.99 (*1-55204-370-3*) Durkin Hayes Publishing Ltd.
—Crisis Point. 1995. (Executioner Ser.: No. 200). 220p. per. (*0-373-61200-1*, 1-61200-1, Harlequin Bks.) Harlequin Enterprises, Ltd.
—Crude Kill. 1983. (Executioner Ser.: No. 59). 192p. mass mkt. o.s.i (*0-373-61059-9*, Harlequin Bks.) Harlequin Enterprises, Ltd.
—Cutting Edge. 1990. (Executioner Ser.: No. 139). pap. (*0-373-61139-0*, Harlequin Bks.) Harlequin Enterprises, Ltd.
—Day of Mourning. 1984. (Executioner Ser.: No. 62). 192p. mass mkt. o.s.i (*0-373-61062-9*, Harlequin Bks.) Harlequin Enterprises, Ltd.
—Dayhunt. 2000. (Executioner Ser.: No. 260). 224p. per. (*0-373-64260-1*, 1-64260-2, Worldwide Library) Harlequin Enterprises, Ltd.
—Dead Easy. 1986. (SuperBolan Ser.: No. 6). 384p. mass mkt. o.s.i (*0-373-61406-3*, Harlequin Bks.) Harlequin Enterprises, Ltd.
—Dead Line. 1989. (Executioner Ser.: No. 130). pap. (*0-373-61130-7*, Harlequin Bks.) Harlequin Enterprises, Ltd.
—Dead Man's Tale. 1989. (Executioner Ser.: No. 125). pap. (*0-373-61125-0*, Harlequin Bks.) Harlequin Enterprises, Ltd.
—Deadly Contest. 1995. (Executioner Ser.: No. 194). mass mkt. (*0-373-61194-3*, 1-61194-6, Harlequin Bks.) Harlequin Enterprises, Ltd.
—Deadly Force: Mack Bolan. 1993. (Executioner Ser.: No. 171). mass mkt. (*0-373-61171-4*, 1-61171-4, Harlequin Bks.) Harlequin Enterprises, Ltd.
—Deadly Pursuit. 2003. (Executioner Ser.: No. 297). 224p. mass mkt. (*0-373-64297-0*, Gold Eagle) Harlequin Enterprises, Ltd.
—Deadly Tactics. 1991. (Executioner Ser.: No. 146). mass mkt. (*0-373-61146-3*, Worldwide Library) Harlequin Enterprises, Ltd.
—Death Force. unabr. ed. 1999. (Executioner Ser.: Vol. 216). audio 7.99 (*1-55204-406-8*, GOL-3406) Durkin Hayes Publishing Ltd.
—Death Force. 1996. (Executioner Ser.: No. 216). per. (*0-373-64216-4*, 1-64216-4, Worldwide Library) Harlequin Enterprises, Ltd.
—Death Has a Name. 1986. (Executioner Ser.: No. 96). mass mkt. o.s.i (*0-373-61096-3*, Harlequin Bks.) Harlequin Enterprises, Ltd.
—Death Load. 1991. (Executioner Ser.: No. 150). mass mkt. (*0-373-61150-1*, Worldwide Library) Harlequin Enterprises, Ltd.
—Death Merchants. 2003. (Executioner Ser.: No. 293). 224p. mass mkt. (*0-373-64293-8*, Gold Eagle) Harlequin Enterprises, Ltd.
—Death Trail. 1992. (Executioner Ser.: No. 164). mass mkt. (*0-373-61164-1*, Harlequin Bks.) Harlequin Enterprises, Ltd.
—Death Warrant. 1994. (Executioner Ser.: No. 184). mass mkt. (*0-373-61184-6*, 1-61184-7, Harlequin Bks.) Harlequin Enterprises, Ltd.
—Death Whisper. 1996. (Executioner Ser.: No. 208). per. (*0-373-64208-3*, 1-64208-1, Worldwide Library) Harlequin Enterprises, Ltd.
—Death Wind. 1989. (Executioner Ser.: No. 1 126). pap. (*0-373-61126-9*, Harlequin Bks.) Harlequin Enterprises, Ltd.
—Death's Head. 1994. (SuperBolan Ser.). mass mkt. (*0-373-61435-7*, 1-61435-3, Harlequin Bks.) Harlequin Enterprises, Ltd.
—Deep Alert. 1995. (StonyMan Ser.). mass mkt. (*0-373-61900-6*, 1-61900-6, Harlequin Bks.) Harlequin Enterprises, Ltd.
—Deep & Swift. 1991. (Executioner Ser.: No. 148). mass mkt. (*0-373-61148-X*, Harlequin Bks.) Harlequin Enterprises, Ltd.
—Deep Attack. 1998. (Executioner Ser.: No. 230). per. (*0-373-64230-X*, 1-64230-5, Worldwide Library) Harlequin Enterprises, Ltd.
—Desert Strike. 1989. (Executioner Ser.: No. 122). pap. (*0-373-61122-6*, Harlequin Bks.) Harlequin Enterprises, Ltd.
—Destiny's Hour. 2001. (SuperBolan Ser.: No. 78). 349p. mass mkt. (*0-373-61478-0*, 1-61478-3, Worldwide Library) Harlequin Enterprises, Ltd.
—Detroit Deathwatch. 1989. (Executioner Ser.: No. 19). mass mkt. 3.50 o.s.i (*1-55817-218-1*, Pinnacle Bks.) Kensington Publishing Corp.
—Devil Force. 1990. (Executioner Ser.: No. 135). pap. (*0-373-61135-8*, Harlequin Bks.) Harlequin Enterprises, Ltd.
—Devil's Army. 2002. (Executioner Ser.: Vol. 284). 224p. mass mkt. (*0-373-64284-9*, Worldwide Library) Harlequin Enterprises, Ltd.
—Devil's Guard. 1998. (Executioner Ser.: No. 240). per. (*0-373-64240-7*, 1-64240-4, Worldwide Library) Harlequin Enterprises, Ltd.
—Direct Hit. 1990. (Executioner Ser.: No. 141). pap. (*0-373-61141-2*, Worldwide Library) Harlequin Enterprises, Ltd.
—Dirty War. 1985. (SuperBolan Ser.: No. 5). 384p. mass mkt. o.s.i (*0-373-61404-7*, Harlequin Bks.) Harlequin Enterprises, Ltd.
—Dixie Convoy. 1989. (Executioner Ser.: No. 27). mass mkt. 3.50 o.s.i (*1-55817-294-7*, Pinnacle Bks.) Kensington Publishing Corp.
—Don Pendleton's Mack Bolan: Anvil of Hell. 1988. (Gold Eagle Ser.). 352p. pap. o.s.i (*0-373-61411-X*, Harlequin Bks.) Harlequin Enterprises, Ltd.
—Doomsday Conspiracy. 1999. (Executioner Ser.: No. 242). per. (*0-373-64242-3*, Harlequin Bks.) Harlequin Enterprises, Ltd.
—Doomsday Disciples. 1982. (Executioner Ser.: No. 49). 192p. mass mkt. o.s.i (*0-373-61049-1*, Harlequin Bks.) Harlequin Enterprises, Ltd.
—Double Action. 1992. (Executioner Ser.: No. 167). per. (*0-373-61167-6*, 1-61167-2, Harlequin Bks.) Harlequin Enterprises, Ltd.
—Double Crossfire. 1982. (Executioner Ser.: No. 40). 192p. pap. o.s.i (*0-373-61040-8*, Harlequin Bks.) Harlequin Enterprises, Ltd.
—Down & Dirty. 1990. (Executioner Ser.: No. 136). pap. (*0-373-61136-6*, Harlequin Bks.) Harlequin Enterprises, Ltd.
—Edge of Night. 1999. (StonyMan Ser.: No. 42). mass mkt. (*0-373-61926-X*, 1-61926-1, Worldwide Library) Harlequin Enterprises, Ltd.
—End Game. unabr. ed. 1999. (Executioner Ser.). audio 7.99 (*1-55204-412-2*, GOL-3412) Durkin Hayes Publishing Ltd.
—End Game. 1997. (Executioner Ser.: No. 218). per. (*0-373-64218-0*, 1-64218-0, Worldwide Library) Harlequin Enterprises, Ltd.
—Evil Alliance. 2000. (SuperBolan Ser.: Vol. 75). mass mkt. (*0-373-61475-6*, 1-61475-9, Worldwide Library) Harlequin Enterprises, Ltd.
—Evil Code: No.177. 1993. (Executioner Ser.: No. 177). mass mkt. (*0-373-61177-3*, 1-61177-1, Harlequin Bks.) Harlequin Enterprises, Ltd.
—The Executioner. 2000. audio 21.00 (*1-55204-936-1*) Durkin Hayes Publishing Ltd.
—The Executioner, 12 vols. (Executioner Ser.). 1998. per. (*0-373-91954-9*); 1997. per. (*0-373-91376-1*); 1997. per. (*0-373-90285-9*) Harlequin Enterprises, Ltd. (Gold Eagle).
—Executive Action. 2000. (SuperBolan Ser.: No. 70). mass mkt. (*0-373-61470-5*, 1-61470-0, Worldwide Library) Harlequin Enterprises, Ltd.
—Eye of the Storm. 1992. (Executioner Ser.: No. 161). mass mkt. (*0-373-61161-7*, 1-61161-5, Harlequin Bks.) Harlequin Enterprises, Ltd.
—Fast Strike 172. 1993. (Executioner Ser.: No. 172). mass mkt. (*0-373-61172-2*, 1-61172-2, Harlequin Bks.) Harlequin Enterprises, Ltd.
—Fatal Error. 1990. (Executioner Ser.: No. 142). pap. (*0-373-61142-0*, Worldwide Library) Harlequin Enterprises, Ltd.
—The Fiery Cross. 1988. (Executioner Ser.: No. 111). pap. o.s.i (*0-373-61111-0*, Harlequin Bks.) Harlequin Enterprises, Ltd.
—Fight or Die. unabr. ed. 1999. (Executioner Ser.: Vol. 217). audio 7.99 (*1-55204-409-2*, GOL-3409) Durkin Hayes Publishing Ltd.
—Fight or Die. 1996. (Executioner Ser.: No. 217). mass mkt. (*0-373-64217-2*, 1-64217-2, Worldwide Library) Harlequin Enterprises, Ltd.
—Final Play. 2003. (Executioner Ser.: No. 298). 224p. mass mkt. (*0-373-64298-9*, Gold Eagle) Harlequin Enterprises, Ltd.
—Fire Burst. 1994. (Executioner Ser.: No. 186). mass mkt. (*0-373-61186-2*, 1-61186-2, Harlequin Bks.) Harlequin Enterprises, Ltd.
—The Fire Eaters. 1986. (Executioner Ser.: No. 93). mass mkt. o.s.i (*0-373-61093-9*, Harlequin Bks.) Harlequin Enterprises, Ltd.
—Fire Hammer. abr. ed. 1999. (Executioner Ser.: Vol. 215). audio 7.99 (*1-55204-403-3*, GOL-3403) Durkin Hayes Publishing Ltd.
—Fire Lash. abr. ed. 1999. (Executioner Ser.). audio 7.99 (*1-55204-389-4*, GOL-3389) Durkin Hayes Publishing Ltd.
—Fire Lash. 1996. (Executioner Ser.: No. 210). per. (*0-373-64210-5*, 1-64210-7, Worldwide Library) Harlequin Enterprises, Ltd.
—Fire Sweep. 1992. (Executioner Ser.: No. 165). mass mkt. (*0-373-61165-X*, 1-61165-6, Harlequin Bks.) Harlequin Enterprises, Ltd.
—Firebase Florida. 1991. (Executioner Ser.: No. 153). per. (*0-373-61153-6*, Harlequin Bks.) Harlequin Enterprises, Ltd.
—Firebase Seattle. 1989. (Executioner Ser.: No. 21). mass mkt. 3.50 o.s.i (*1-55817-236-X*, Pinnacle Bks.) Kensington Publishing Corp.
—Firing Line. 1992. (Executioner Ser.: No. 158). mass mkt. (*0-373-61158-7*, 1-61158-1, Harlequin Bks.) Harlequin Enterprises, Ltd.
—Fission Fury. 1996. (Executioner Ser.: No. 214). per. (*0-373-64214-8*, 1-64214-9, Worldwide Library) Harlequin Enterprises, Ltd.
—Flames of Wrath. 1997. per. (*0-373-61453-5*, 1-61453-6, Worldwide Library) Harlequin Enterprises, Ltd.
—Flesh Wounds. 1983. (Executioner Ser.: No. 57). 192p. mass mkt. o.s.i (*0-373-61057-2*, Harlequin Bks.) Harlequin Enterprises, Ltd.
—Flight Seven Four One. 1986. (SuperBolan Ser.). 384p. pap. o.s.i (*0-373-61405-5*, Harlequin Bks.) Harlequin Enterprises, Ltd.
—Force Down. 1993. (Executioner Ser.: No. 180). mass mkt. (*0-373-61180-3*, 1-61180-5, Harlequin Bks.) Harlequin Enterprises, Ltd.
—Freedom Strike. 1996. (Executioner Ser.: No. 207). 221p. per. (*0-373-64207-5*, 1-64207-3, Worldwide Library) Harlequin Enterprises, Ltd.
—Friday's Feast. 1990. (Executioner Ser.: No. 37). (Orig.). mass mkt. 3.50 o.s.i (*1-55817-420-6*, Pinnacle Bks.) Kensington Publishing Corp.
—Haitian Hit. 1989. (Executioner Ser.: No. 129). pap. (*0-373-61129-3*, Harlequin Bks.) Harlequin Enterprises, Ltd.
—Hard Contact. 1995. (Executioner Ser.: No. 203). 221p. per. (*0-373-64203-2*, 1-64203-2, Worldwide Library) Harlequin Enterprises, Ltd.
—Hardline. 1991. (SuperBolan Ser.: No. 25). mass mkt. (*0-373-61425-X*, Harlequin Bks.) Harlequin Enterprises, Ltd.
—Hawaiian Heat. 1991. (Executioner Ser.: No. 155). mass mkt. (*0-373-61155-2*, Harlequin Bks.) Harlequin Enterprises, Ltd.
—Hawaiian Hellground. 1989. (Executioner Ser.: No. 22). (Orig.). mass mkt. 3.50 o.p. (*1-55817-246-7*, Pinnacle Bks.) Kensington Publishing Corp.
—Hell Road. 1995. (Executioner Ser.: No. 205). 218p. per. (*0-373-64205-9*, 1-64205-7, Worldwide Library) Harlequin Enterprises, Ltd.
—Helldust Cruise. 1990. (Executioner Ser.: No. 143). pap. (*0-373-61143-9*, Worldwide Library) Harlequin Enterprises, Ltd.
—Hellfire Trigger. 1998. (Executioner Ser.: No. 237). per. (*0-373-64237-7*, 1-64237-0, Worldwide Library) Harlequin Enterprises, Ltd.
—Hellground. 1994. mass mkt. (*0-373-61436-5*, 1-61436-1, Harlequin Bks.) Harlequin Enterprises, Ltd.
—Hong Kong Hit List. 1987. (Executioner Ser.: No. 109). mass mkt. o.s.i (*0-373-61109-9*, Gold Eagle) Harlequin Enterprises, Ltd.
—Hostile Action. 1994. (Executioner Ser.: No. 193). mass mkt. (*0-373-61193-5*, 1-61193-8, Harlequin Bks.) Harlequin Enterprises, Ltd.
—Hostile Instinct: Stony Man. 2000. (StonyMan Ser.: Vol. 46). per. (*0-373-61930-8*, Harlequin Bks.) Harlequin Enterprises, Ltd.
—Hour of Conflict. 1997. (Executioner Ser.: No. 223). per. (*0-373-64223-7*, 1-64223-0, Worldwide Library) Harlequin Enterprises, Ltd.
—Hunting Cry. 1996. (Executioner Ser.: No. 206). 219p. per. (*0-373-64206-7*, 1-64206-5, Worldwide Library) Harlequin Enterprises, Ltd.
—Ice Wolf. 1989. (Executioner Ser.: No. 131). pap. (*0-373-61131-5*, Harlequin Bks.) Harlequin Enterprises, Ltd.
—Inferno. 1994. (SuperBolan Ser.). mass mkt. (*0-373-61437-3*, 1-61437-9, Harlequin Bks.) Harlequin Enterprises, Ltd.
—Invisible Assassins. 1983. (Executioner Ser.: No. 53). 192p. mass mkt. o.s.i (*0-373-61053-X*, Harlequin Bks.) Harlequin Enterprises, Ltd.
—The Iranian Hit. 1982. (Executioner Ser.: No. 42). 192p. mass mkt. o.s.i (*0-373-61042-4*, Harlequin Bks.) Harlequin Enterprises, Ltd.
—Island Deathtrap. 1983. (Executioner Ser.: No. 56). 192p. mass mkt. o.s.i (*0-373-61056-4*, Harlequin Bks.) Harlequin Enterprises, Ltd.
—Jackal Hunt. 1998. (Executioner Ser.: No. 232). per. (*0-373-64232-6*, 1-64232-1, Worldwide Library) Harlequin Enterprises, Ltd.
—Jersey Guns. 1988. (Executioner Ser.: No. 17). mass mkt. 3.50 o.s.i (*1-55817-176-2*, Pinnacle Bks.) Kensington Publishing Corp.
—Kill Radius. (Executioner Ser.: No. 251). Date not set. E-Book (*0-373-86024-2*, Gold Eagle); 1999. per. (*0-373-64251-2*, 1-64251-1, Worldwide Library) Harlequin Enterprises, Ltd.
—Kill Trap. 1990. (Executioner Ser.: No. 138). pap. (*0-373-61138-2*, Harlequin Bks.) Harlequin Enterprises, Ltd.
—Kill Zone. 1989. (Executioner Ser.: No. 127). pap. (*0-373-61127-7*, Harlequin Bks.) Harlequin Enterprises, Ltd.
—Killing Range. 1994. (Executioner Ser.: No. 190). mass mkt. (*0-373-61190-0*, 1-61190-4, Harlequin Bks.) Harlequin Enterprises, Ltd.
—The Killing Urge. 1988. (Executioner Ser.: No. 116). pap. o.s.i (*0-373-61116-1*, Harlequin Bks.) Harlequin Enterprises, Ltd.
—Killpoint. 1995. (SuperBolan Ser.). mass mkt. (*0-373-61440-3*, 1-61440-3, Harlequin Bks.) Harlequin Enterprises, Ltd.
—Killsport. 2000. (SuperBolan Ser.: 71). 352p. per. (*0-373-61471-3*, Worldwide Library) Harlequin Enterprises, Ltd.
—Lethal Agent: No.182. 1994. (Executioner Ser.: No. 182). per. (*0-373-61182-X*, 1-61182-1, Harlequin Bks.) Harlequin Enterprises, Ltd.
—Lethal Impact. 1992. per. (*0-373-61429-2*, 1-61429-6, Harlequin Bks.) Harlequin Enterprises, Ltd.
—Line of Fire. 1988. (Executioner Ser.: No. 119). pap. (*0-373-61119-6*, Harlequin Bks.) Harlequin Enterprises, Ltd.
—Mack Bolan: Stony Man Doctrine. abr. ed. audio 16.99 (*0-88646-173-1*, 7174) Durkin Hayes Publishing Ltd.
—Mack Bolan: Terminal Velocity. 1984. (Gold Eagle Ser.: No. 2). 384p. mass mkt. o.s.i (*0-373-61402-0*, Harlequin Bks.) Harlequin Enterprises, Ltd.
—Mack Bolan: The Executioner. 1998. (*0-373-96225-8*, Harlequin Bks.) Harlequin Enterprises, Ltd.
—Maximum Impact. 1994. (Executioner Ser.: No. 192). mass mkt. (*0-373-61192-7*, 1-61192-0, Harlequin Bks.) Harlequin Enterprises, Ltd.
—Meltdown. 1986. (Executioner Ser.: No. 97). mass mkt. o.s.i (*0-373-61097-1*, Harlequin Bks.) Harlequin Enterprises, Ltd.
—Message to Medellin. 1991. (Executioner Ser.: No. 151). mass mkt. (*0-373-61151-X*, Harlequin Bks.) Harlequin Enterprises, Ltd.
—Miami Massacre. 1982. (Executioner Ser.: No. 4). pap. 2.25 o.p. (*0-523-41823-X*, Pinnacle Bks.) Kensington Publishing Corp.
—Monday's Mob. (Executioner Ser.: No. 33). 1990. mass mkt. 3.50 o.s.i (*1-55817-371-4*); 1981. pap. 2.25 o.p. (*0-523-41815-9*) Kensington Publishing Corp. (Pinnacle Bks.).
—Mountain Rampage. 1983. (Executioner Ser.: No. 54). 192p. mass mkt. o.s.i (*0-373-61054-8*, Harlequin Bks.) Harlequin Enterprises, Ltd.
—New Orleans Knockout. 1989. (Executioner Ser.: No. 20). mass mkt. 3.50 o.s.i (*1-55817-219-X*, Pinnacle Bks.) Kensington Publishing Corp.
—The New War. (Executioner Ser.: No. 39). 1989. per. (*0-373-15128-4*); 1981. 192p. pap. o.s.i (*0-373-61039-4*) Harlequin Enterprises, Ltd. (Harlequin Bks.).
—Night Hit. 1991. (Executioner Ser.: No. 154). mass mkt. (*0-373-61154-4*, Harlequin Bks.) Harlequin Enterprises, Ltd.
—Night Kill. 1989. (Executioner Ser.: No. 124). pap. (*0-373-61124-2*, Harlequin Bks.) Harlequin Enterprises, Ltd.

—Nightfire. 2000. (Executioner Ser.: No. 259). per. (*0-373-64259-8*, 1-64259-4, Worldwide Library) Harlequin Enterprises, Ltd.

—Nightmare in New York. 1988. (Executioner Ser.: No. 7). mass mkt. 3.50 o.s.i (*1-55817-066-9*, Pinnacle Bks.) Kensington Publishing Corp.

—Panic in Philly. 1988. (Executioner Ser.: No. 15). mass mkt. 3.50 o.s.i (*1-55817-174-6*, Pinnacle Bks.) Kensington Publishing Corp.

—Paradine's Gauntlet. 1983. (Executioner Ser.: No. 55). 192p. mass mkt. o.s.i (*0-373-61055-6*, Harlequin Bks.) Harlequin Enterprises, Ltd.

—Paramilitary Plot. 1982. (Executioner Ser.: No. 45). 192p. pap. o.s.i (*0-373-61045-9*, Harlequin Bks.) Harlequin Enterprises, Ltd.

—Patriot Gambit. 1997. (Executioner Ser.: No. 222). per. (*0-373-64222-9*, 1-64222-2, Worldwide Library) Harlequin Enterprises, Ltd.

—Payback Game. 1991. (Executioner Ser.: No. 147). mass mkt. (*0-373-61147-1*, Worldwide Library) Harlequin Enterprises, Ltd.

—Phantom Force. 1991. (Executioner Ser.: No. 156). mass mkt. (*0-373-61156-0*, Harlequin Bks.) Harlequin Enterprises, Ltd.

—Plague Wind. 1998. (Executioner Ser.: No. 235). per. (*0-373-64235-0*, 1-64235-4, Worldwide Library) Harlequin Enterprises, Ltd.

—Point of Impact. (Executioner Ser.: No. 256). Date not set. E-Book (*0-373-86001-3*, Gold Eagle); 2000. 224p. per. (*0-373-64256-3*, Harlequin Bks.) Harlequin Enterprises, Ltd.

—Point Position. 2004. (Executioner Ser.: No. 305). 224p. mass mkt. (*0-373-64305-5*, Gold Eagle) Harlequin Enterprises, Ltd.

—Precision Kill. 1996. (SuperBolan Ser.: Vol. 46). 349p. per. (*0-373-61446-2*, 1-61446-0, Worldwide Library) Harlequin Enterprises, Ltd.

—Precision Play. 2000. (Executioner Ser.: No. 257). 221p. per. (*0-373-64257-1*, Harlequin Bks.) Harlequin Enterprises, Ltd.

—The Prime Target. 1995. (Executioner Ser.: No. 201). per. (*0-373-64201-6*, Harlequin Bks.) Harlequin Enterprises, Ltd.

—Rampage. 1993. (SuperBolan Ser.). mass mkt. (*0-373-61433-0*, 1-61433-8, Harlequin Bks.) Harlequin Enterprises, Ltd.

—Ransom Run. 1993. (Executioner Ser.: No. 176). per. (*0-373-61176-5*, 1-61176-3, Harlequin Bks.) Harlequin Enterprises, Ltd.

—Renegade Agent. 1982. (Executioner Ser.: No. 47). 192p. mass mkt. o.s.i (*0-373-61047-5*, Harlequin Bks.) Harlequin Enterprises, Ltd.

—Resurrection Day. 1985. (SuperBolan Ser.: No. 3). 384p. mass mkt. o.s.i (*0-373-61403-9*, Harlequin Bks.) Harlequin Enterprises, Ltd.

—Retribution. 1998. (SuperBolan Ser.: No. 63). mass mkt. (*0-373-61463-2*, 0-61463-6, Worldwide Library) Harlequin Enterprises, Ltd.

—Return to Vietnam. 1982. (Executioner Ser.: No. 43). 192p. pap. o.p. (*0-373-61043-2*, Harlequin Bks.) Harlequin Enterprises, Ltd.

—Ride the Beast. abr. ed. 1999. (Executioner Ser.: Vol. 212). audio 7.99 (*1-55204-394-0*, GOL-3394) Durkin Hayes Publishing Ltd.

—Ride the Beast. 1996. (Executioner Ser.: No. 212). per. (*0-373-64212-1*, 1-64212-3, Worldwide Library) Harlequin Enterprises, Ltd.

—Risk Factor. (Executioner Ser.: No. 253). Date not set. E-Book (*0-373-86005-6*, Gold Eagle); 1999. 221p. per. (*0-373-64253-9*, Harlequin Bks.) Harlequin Enterprises, Ltd.

—Rogue Agent. 1995. (Executioner Ser.: No. 199). per. (*0-373-61199-4*, 1-61199-5, Harlequin Bks.) Harlequin Enterprises, Ltd.

—San Diego Siege. 1988. (Executioner Ser.: No. 14). mass mkt. 3.50 o.s.i (*1-55817-173-8*, Pinnacle Bks.) Kensington Publishing Corp.

—Satan's Sabbath. (Executioner Ser.: No. 38). 1990. mass mkt. 3.50 o.s.i (*1-55817-444-3*); 1980. pap. 2.25 o.p. (*0-523-41796-9*) Kensington Publishing Corp. (Pinnacle Bks.).

—Savage Fire. 1990. (Executioner Ser.: No. 28). mass mkt. 3.50 o.p. (*1-55817-309-9*, Pinnacle Bks.) Kensington Publishing Corp.

—Save the Children. 1986. (Executioner Ser.: No. 94). mass mkt. o.s.i (*0-373-61094-7*, Harlequin Bks.) Harlequin Enterprises, Ltd.

—Scorpion Rising. 2003. (Executioner Ser.: No. 294). 224p. mass mkt. (*0-373-64294-6*, Gold Eagle) Harlequin Enterprises, Ltd.

—Sea of Terror. 2004. (Executioner Ser.: No. 303). 224p. mass mkt. (*0-373-64303-9*, Gold Eagle) Harlequin Enterprises, Ltd.

—Secret Arsenal. 1994. mass mkt. (*0-373-61894-8*, Harlequin Bks.) Harlequin Enterprises, Ltd.

—Select Fire. 1995. (Executioner Ser.: No. 195). mass mkt. (*0-373-61195-1*, 1-61195-3, Harlequin Bks.) Harlequin Enterprises, Ltd.

—Shadow Search. 2004. (Executioner Ser.: No. 302). 224p. mass mkt. (*0-373-64302-0*, Gold Eagle) Harlequin Enterprises, Ltd.

—Shadow Target. 1999. (Executioner Ser.: No. 249). mass mkt. (*0-373-64249-0*, 1-64249-5, Worldwide Library) Harlequin Enterprises, Ltd.

—Shifting Target. 1993. (Executioner Ser.: No. 181). per. (*0-373-61181-1*, 1-61181-3, Harlequin Bks.) Harlequin Enterprises, Ltd.

—Shoot Down. 1995. (Executioner Ser.: No. 198). per. (*0-373-61198-6*, 1-61198-7, Harlequin Bks.) Harlequin Enterprises, Ltd.

—Showdown. 1995. 348p. per. (*0-373-61445-4*, 1-61445-2, Worldwide Library) Harlequin Enterprises, Ltd.

—Sicilian Slaughter. (Executioner Ser.: No. 16). 1988. mass mkt. 3.50 o.s.i (*1-55817-175-4*); 1980. pap. 1.95 o.p. (*0-523-41080-8*) Kensington Publishing Corp. (Pinnacle Bks.).

—Slaughter Squad. 1998. (Executioner Ser.: No. 231). per. (*0-373-64231-8*, 1-64231-3, Worldwide Library) Harlequin Enterprises, Ltd.

—Sold for Slaughter. 1983. (Executioner Ser.: No. 60). 192p. mass mkt. o.s.i (*0-373-61060-2*, Harlequin Bks.) Harlequin Enterprises, Ltd.

—St. Louis. 1989. (Executioner Ser.: No. 23). mass mkt. 3.50 o.s.i (*1-55817-257-2*) Kensington Publishing Corp.

—St. Louis Showdown. 1982. (Executioner Ser.: No. 23). 192p. pap. 2.25 o.p. (*0-523-42036-6*, Pinnacle Bks.) Kensington Publishing Corp.

—Stalk Line. 1995. per. (*0-373-61442-X*, 1-61442-9, Harlequin Bks.) Harlequin Enterprises, Ltd.

—Steel & Flame. 1992. (Executioner Ser.: No. 159). mass mkt. (*0-373-61159-5*, 1-61159-9, Harlequin Bks.) Harlequin Enterprises, Ltd.

—Steel Claws. abr. ed. 1999. (Executioner Ser.: Vol. 211). audio 7.99 (*1-55204-391-6*, GOL-3391) Durkin Hayes Publishing Ltd.

—Steel Claws. 1996. (Executioner Ser.: No. 211). per. (*0-373-64211-3*, 1-64211-5, Worldwide Library) Harlequin Enterprises, Ltd.

—Stony Man Doctrine. 1983. (Executioner Ser.: No. 1). 384p. mass mkt. o.s.i (*0-373-61401-2*, Harlequin Bks.) Harlequin Enterprises, Ltd.

—Stony Man II. 1991. (StonyMan Ser.: Vol. 2). per. (*0-373-61886-7*, Harlequin Bks.) Harlequin Enterprises, Ltd.

—Stony Man IV. 1992. (StonyMan Ser.: No. 888). per. (*0-373-61888-3*, 1-61888-3, Harlequin Bks.) Harlequin Enterprises, Ltd.

—Stony Man V. 1992. (StonyMan Ser.). mass mkt. o.s.i (*0-373-61889-1*, 1-61889-1, Harlequin Bks.) Harlequin Enterprises, Ltd.

—Stony Man VI. 1993. mass mkt. (*0-373-61890-5*, 1-61890-9, Harlequin Bks.) Harlequin Enterprises, Ltd.

—Stony Man VII. 1993. mass mkt. (*0-373-61891-3*, 1-61891-7, Harlequin Bks.) Harlequin Enterprises, Ltd.

—Stony Man VIII. 1993. mass mkt. (*0-373-61892-1*, 1-61892-5, Harlequin Bks.) Harlequin Enterprises, Ltd.

—Storm Front. 2000. (SuperBolan Ser.: Bk. 73). 352p. per. (*0-373-61473-X*, 1-61473-4, Worldwide Library) Harlequin Enterprises, Ltd.

—Storm Warning. 1992. (Executioner Ser.: No. 160). mass mkt. (*0-373-61160-9*, 1-61160-7, Harlequin Bks.) Harlequin Enterprises, Ltd.

—Sudan Slaughter. 1989. (Executioner Ser.: No. 128). pap. (*0-373-61128-5*, Harlequin Bks.) Harlequin Enterprises, Ltd.

—Sudden Death. 1987. (SuperBolan Ser.: No. 7). 384p. mass mkt. o.s.i (*0-373-61407-1*, Harlequin Bks.) Harlequin Enterprises, Ltd.

—Takedown. 1994. (SuperBolan Ser.). mass mkt. (*0-373-61434-9*, 1-61434-6, Harlequin Bks.) Harlequin Enterprises, Ltd.

—Target Command. 1998. (Executioner Ser.: No. 234). per. (*0-373-64234-2*, 1-64234-7, Worldwide Library) Harlequin Enterprises, Ltd.

—Target Lock. 2000. (Executioner Ser.: No. 258). per. (*0-373-64258-X*, Worldwide Library) Harlequin Enterprises, Ltd.

—Tennessee Smash. (Executioner Ser.: No. 32). 1990. mass mkt. 3.50 o.s.i (*1-55817-354-4*); 1980. pap. 1.95 o.p. (*0-523-41096-4*) Kensington Publishing Corp. (Pinnacle Bks.).

—Terminal Option. 1997. per. (*0-373-64228-8*, 1-64228-9, Worldwide Library) Harlequin Enterprises, Ltd.

—Termination Point: Four Horsemen Trilogy. 1999. (SuperBolan Ser.: No. 66). per. (*0-373-61466-7*, 1-61466-8, Worldwide Library) Harlequin Enterprises, Ltd.

—Terrible Tuesday. (Executioner Ser.: No. 34). 1990. mass mkt. 3.50 o.s.i (*1-55817-382-X*, Pinnacle Bks.); 1981. pap. 2.25 o.p. (*0-523-41765-9*) Kensington Publishing Corp.

—Terror Intent. unabr. ed. 1999. (Executioner Ser.: Vol. 219). audio 7.99 (*1-55204-415-7*, GOL-3415) Durkin Hayes Publishing Ltd.

—Terror Intent. 1997. (Executioner Ser.: No. 219). per. (*0-373-64219-9*, 1-64219-8, Worldwide Library) Harlequin Enterprises, Ltd.

—Terror Spin. 1997. per. (*0-373-61456-X*, 1-61456-9, Worldwide Library) Harlequin Enterprises, Ltd.

—Terrorist Summit. 1982. (Executioner Ser.: No. 44). 192p. pap. o.p. (*0-373-61044-0*, Harlequin Bks.) Harlequin Enterprises, Ltd.

—Texas Storm. 1988. (Executioner Ser.: No. 18). mass mkt. 3.50 o.s.i (*1-55817-177-0*, Pinnacle Bks.) Kensington Publishing Corp.

—Thermal Thursday. (Executioner Ser.: No. 36). 1990. mass mkt. 3.50 o.s.i (*1-55817-407-9*); 1982. pap. 2.25 o.p. (*0-523-41854-X*) Kensington Publishing Corp. (Pinnacle Bks.).

—Tiger Stalk. unabr. ed. 1999. (Executioner Ser.). audio 7.99 (*1-55204-418-1*, GOL-3418) Durkin Hayes Publishing Ltd.

—Tiger Stalk. 1997. (Executioner Ser.: No. 220). per. (*0-373-64220-2*, 1-64220-6, Worldwide Library) Harlequin Enterprises, Ltd.

—Tiger War. 1983. (Executioner Ser.: No. 61). 192p. mass mkt. o.s.i (*0-373-61061-0*, Harlequin Bks.) Harlequin Enterprises, Ltd.

—Tough Justice. 1998. (Executioner Ser.: No. 233). per. (*0-373-64233-4*, 0-64233-0, Worldwide Library) Harlequin Enterprises, Ltd.

—Triburst. 1995. (Executioner Ser.: No. 196). per. (*0-373-61196-X*, 1-61196-1, Harlequin Bks.) Harlequin Enterprises, Ltd.

—Triple Strike. 1998. (StonyMan Ser.: Vol. 37). 352p. per. (*0-373-61921-9*, 1-61921-2, Worldwide Library) Harlequin Enterprises, Ltd.

—Trojan Horse. 1988. (Executioner Ser.: No. 110). mass mkt. o.s.i (*0-373-61110-2*, Harlequin Bks.) Harlequin Enterprises, Ltd.

—Tropic Heat. 1987. (SuperBolan Ser.: No. 9). 384p. mass mkt. o.s.i (*0-373-61409-8*, Harlequin Bks.) Harlequin Enterprises, Ltd.

—Tuscany Terror. 1983. (Executioner Ser.: No. 52). 192p. mass mkt. o.s.i (*0-373-61052-1*, Harlequin Bks.) Harlequin Enterprises, Ltd.

—Twisted Path. 1988. (Executioner Ser.: No. 121). pap. (*0-373-61121-8*, Harlequin Bks.) Harlequin Enterprises, Ltd.

—Vegas Vendetta. 1988. (Executioner Ser.: No. 9). mass mkt. 3.50 o.s.i (*1-55817-068-5*) Kensington Publishing Corp.

—Vendetta. 1995. (SuperBolan Ser.). per. (*0-373-61441-1*, 1-61441-1, Harlequin Bks.) Harlequin Enterprises, Ltd.

—Vendetta in Venice. 1988. (Executioner Ser.: No. 117). pap. o.s.i (*0-373-61117-X*, Harlequin Bks.) Harlequin Enterprises, Ltd.

—Vengeance. 1999. (SuperBolan Ser.: Vol. 69). mass mkt. (*0-373-61469-1*, Worldwide Library) Harlequin Enterprises, Ltd.

—Vengeance Rising. 1998. (Executioner Ser.: No. 236 ). per. (*0-373-64236-9*, 1-64236-2, Worldwide Library) Harlequin Enterprises, Ltd.

—Vietnam Fallout. 1988. (Executioner Ser.: No. 113). pap. o.s.i (*0-373-61113-7*, Harlequin Bks.) Harlequin Enterprises, Ltd.

—The Violent Streets. 1982. (Executioner Ser.: No. 41). 192p. mass mkt. o.s.i (*0-373-61041-6*, Harlequin Bks.) Harlequin Enterprises, Ltd.

—Virtual Destruction. 1999. (Executioner Ser.: No. 245). per. (*0-373-64245-8*, 1-64245-3, Harlequin Bks.) Harlequin Enterprises, Ltd.

—Vulture's Vengeance. 1983. (Executioner Ser.: No. 51). 192p. mass mkt. o.s.i (*0-373-61051-3*, Harlequin Bks.) Harlequin Enterprises, Ltd.

—War Against the Mafia. 1981. (Executioner Ser.: No. 1). 192p. pap. 2.25 o.p. (*0-523-41065-4*, Pinnacle Bks.) Kensington Publishing Corp.

—War Born. 1989. (Executioner Ser.: No. 123). pap. (*0-373-61123-4*, Harlequin Bks.) Harlequin Enterprises, Ltd.

—War Hammer. 1993. (Executioner Ser.: No. 179). mass mkt. (*0-373-61179-X*, 1-61179-7, Harlequin Bks.) Harlequin Enterprises, Ltd.

—War Paint. 1994. (Executioner Ser.: No. 188). per. (*0-373-61188-9*, 1-61188-8, Harlequin Bks.) Harlequin Enterprises, Ltd.

—Warhead. 1994. mass mkt. (*0-373-61897-2*, 1-61897-4, Harlequin Bks.) Harlequin Enterprises, Ltd.

—Warning Shot. 1999. (Executioner Ser.: No. 250). 221p. mass mkt. (*0-373-64250-4*, 1-64250-3, Worldwide Library) Harlequin Enterprises, Ltd.

—Warrior's Edge. 1992. (Executioner Ser.: No. 163). mass mkt. (*0-373-61163-3*, Harlequin Bks.) Harlequin Enterprises, Ltd.

—Warrior's Requiem. 2003. (Executioner Ser.: No. 300). 224p. mass mkt. (*0-373-64300-4*, Gold Eagle) Harlequin Enterprises, Ltd.

—Washington I. O. U. 1988. (Executioner Ser.: No. 13). mass mkt. 3.50 o.s.i (*1-55817-172-X*, Pinnacle Bks.) Kensington Publishing Corp.

—Wednesday's Wrath. (Executioner Ser.: No. 35). 1990. mass mkt. 3.50 o.s.i (*1-55817-425-7*); 1981. pap. 2.25 o.p. (*0-523-41801-9*) Kensington Publishing Corp. (Pinnacle Bks.).

—Wellfire. 1994. (Executioner Ser.: No. 189). per. (*0-373-61189-7*, 1-61189-6, Harlequin Bks.) Harlequin Enterprises, Ltd.

—Whipsaw. 1990. (Executioner Ser.: No. 144). pap. (*0-373-61144-7*, Worldwide Library) Harlequin Enterprises, Ltd.

—White Heat. 1992. (Executioner Ser.: No. 169). mass mkt. (*0-373-61169-2*, 1-61169-8, Harlequin Bks.) Harlequin Enterprises, Ltd.

—Wild Card. 1990. (Executioner Ser.: No. 140). pap. (*0-373-61140-4*, Harlequin Bks.) Harlequin Enterprises, Ltd.

—Zero Hour. 1999. (StonyMan Ser.: No. 43). per. (*0-373-61927-8*, 1-61927-9, Worldwide Library) Harlequin Enterprises, Ltd.

—Zero Tolerance. 1997. (Executioner Ser.: No. 229). per. (*0-373-64229-6*, 1-64229-7, Worldwide Library) Harlequin Enterprises, Ltd.

Pendleton, Don & Wilson, Gar. Argentine Deadline. 1982. (Phoenix Force Ser.). 192p. mass mkt. o.s.i (*0-373-61301-6*, Harlequin Bks.) Harlequin Enterprises, Ltd.

—Atlantic Scramble. 1982. (Phoenix Force Ser.: No. 3). 192p. mass mkt. o.s.i (*0-373-61303-2*, Harlequin Bks.) Harlequin Enterprises, Ltd.

—Guerilla Games. 1982. (Phoenix Force Ser.: No. 2). 192p. mass mkt. o.s.i (*0-373-61302-4*, Harlequin Bks.) Harlequin Enterprises, Ltd.

Pendleton, Laura & Pendleton, Don. Night of the Jaguar. 1997. (StonyMan Ser.: No. 31). per. (*0-373-61915-4*, 1-61915-4, Worldwide Library) Harlequin Enterprises, Ltd.

**BOLDT, LOU (FICTITIOUS CHARACTER)—FICTION**

Pearson, Ridley. The Angel Maker. 1994. 464p. mass mkt. 7.50 o.s.i (*0-440-21632-X*) Dell Publishing.

—The Angel Maker. 2003. (Illus.). 368p. reprint ed. mass mkt. 6.99 (*0-7868-9008-8*) Hyperion Pr.

—The Angel Maker. abr. ed. 1999. audio 9.99 o.s.i (*0-553-70195-9*, RH Audio) Random Hse. Audio Publishing Group.

—The Art of Deception. abr. ed. 2003. (Lou Boldt/Daphne Matthews Ser.). audio 12.99 (*1-59086-077-2*, 3630, Brilliance Audio Paperback Audiobooks); 2002. (Lou Boldt & Daphne Matthews Mystery Ser.: Vol. 8). audio 24.95 o.p. (*1-59086-076-4*, 3629, Nova Audio Bks.); 2002. (Lou Boldt & Daphne Matthews Mystery Ser.: Vol. 8). audio 87.25 (*1-59086-075-6*, 3628, Unabridged Library Editions); 2002. (Lou Boldt & Daphne Matthews Mystery Ser.: Vol. 8). audio 32.95 (*1-59086-074-8*, 3627, Brilliance Audio Unabridged); 2002. (Lou Boldt & Daphne Matthews Mystery Ser.: Vol. 8). audio compact disk 40.95 (*1-59086-226-0*, 3798, CD Unabridged); 2002. (Lou Boldt & Daphne Matthews Mystery Ser.: Vol. 8). audio compact disk 102.25 (*1-59086-227-9*, 3799, CD Unabridged Library Edition) Brilliance Audio.

—The Art of Deception. 2003. 464p. mass mkt. 7.99 (*0-7868-9000-2*); 2003. E-Book (*1-4013-9841-3*); 2003. E-Book 5.99 (*1-4013-9838-3*); 2003. E-Book 5.99 (*1-4013-9837-5*); 2003. E-Book 5.99 (*1-4013-9840-5*); 2003. E-Book 5.99 (*1-4013-9839-1*); 2002. 384p. 23.95 (*0-7868-6724-8*) Hyperion Pr.

—The Art of Deception. unabr. ed. 2003. (Lou Boldt/Daphne Matthews Ser.). audio 19.99 (*1-59335-200-X*, 30297) Soulmate Audio Bks., Inc.

—The Art of Deception. 2003. (Basic Ser.). 31.95 (*0-7862-4967-6*) Thorndike Pr.

—Beyond Recognition. unabr. ed. 1998. audio 96.00 (*0-7366-4092-4*, 4599) Books on Tape, Inc.

—Beyond Recognition. abr. ed. 1997. (Lou Boldt & Daphne Matthews Mystery Ser.). 3p. audio 7.99 (*1-56740-228-3*, 627, Paperback Nova Audio Bks.); audio 16.95 o.p. (*1-56100-970-9*, 1134, Nova Audio Bks.); audio 27.95 (*1-56100-733-1*, 45, Bookcassette); audio 105.25 (*1-56100-807-9*, 809) Brilliance Audio.

—Beyond Recognition. 1997. 496p. 22.95 o.p. (*0-7868-6240-8*); 2003. 656p. reprint ed. mass mkt. 7.99 (*0-7868-8928-4*) Hyperion Pr.

—The Body of David Hayes. 2003. 23.95 (*0-7868-6725-6*) Hyperion Pr.

—The First Victim. abr. ed. (Lou Boldt/Daphne Matthews Ser.). 2000. audio 7.99 (*1-56740-980-6*, 2116, Paperback Nova Audio Bks.); 1999. audio 17.95 o.p. (*1-56740-836-2*, 1676, Nova Audio Bks.); 1999. audio 35.95 (*1-56740-423-5*, 1674, Brilliance Audio Unabridged); 1999. 9p. audio 57.25 (*1-56740-649-1*, 1675, Unabridged Library Editions) Brilliance Audio.

—The First Victim. aut. ltd. ed. 1999. 400p. 23.95 (*0-7868-6558-X*) Disney Pr.

—The First Victim. l.t. ed. 2001. (Large Print Bks.). 475p. pap. 23.95 (*1-58724-099-8*, Wheeler Publishing, Inc.) Gale Group.

—The First Victim, Set. abr. ed. 1999. audio 17.95 Highsmith Inc.

—The First Victim. 2001. 400p. E-Book 5.95 (*0-7868-7143-1*); 2001. 400p. E-Book 5.95 (*0-7868-7146-6*); 2001. 400p. E-Book 5.95 (*0-7868-7144-X*); 2001. 400p. E-Book 5.95 (*0-7868-7145-8*); 2001. 400p. E-Book 5.95 (*0-7868-7142-3*); 1999. 381p. 23.95 (*0-7868-6440-0*); 2003. 416p. reprint ed. mass mkt. 7.99 (*0-7868-8966-7*) Hyperion Pr.

—Middle of Nowhere. abr. ed. (Lou Boldt & Daphne Matthews Mystery Ser.). 2001. audio 12.99 (*1-58788-296-5*, 2657, Paperback Nova Audio Bks.); 2000. audio 24.95 o.p. (*1-56740-893-1*, 2053, Nova Audio Bks.); 2000. audio 73.25 (*1-56740-716-1*, 2052, Unabridged Library Editions); 2000. audio 32.95 (*1-56740-498-7*, 2051, Brilliance Audio Unabridged) Brilliance Audio.
—Middle of Nowhere. l.t. ed. 2001. (Large Print Book Ser.). 516p. 29.95 (*1-58724-013-0*, Wheeler Publishing, Inc.) Gale Group.
—Middle of Nowhere. 2001. 384p. E-Book 5.95 (*0-7868-7197-0*); 2001. 384p. E-Book 5.95 (*0-7868-7149-0*); 2001. 384p. E-Book 5.95 (*0-7868-7198-9*); 2000. 375p. 23.95 (*0-7868-6563-6*); 2003. 384p. reprint ed. mass mkt. 7.99 (*0-7868-8960-8*) Hyperion Pr.
—No Witnesses. unabr. ed. 1995. (Lou Boldt & Daphne Matthews Mystery Ser.). audio 72.00 (*0-7366-2950-5*, 3644) Books on Tape, Inc.
—No Witnesses. 1996. 480p. mass mkt. 7.50 o.s.i (*0-440-22142-0*) Dell Publishing.
—No Witnesses. 1994. 384p. 22.95 (*0-7868-6066-9*); 2003. 480p. reprint ed. mass mkt. 6.99 (*0-7868-9006-1*) Hyperion Pr.
—No Witnesses. abr. ed. 1999. audio 9.99 o.s.i (*0-553-70215-7*, RH Audio) Random Hse. Audio Publishing Group.
—The Pied Piper. unabr. ed. 1999. audio 88.00 Books on Tape, Inc.
—The Pied Piper. abr. ed. (Lou Boldt & Daphne Matthews Mystery Ser.). 1999. audio 7.99 o.s.i (*1-56740-302-6*, 1864, Paperback Nova Audio Bks.); 1998. 10p. audio 89.25 (*1-56740-569-X*, 983); 1998. audio 28.95 (*1-56100-790-0*, 19, Bookcassette); Set. 1998. audio 17.95 o.p. (*1-56740-765-X*, 451, Nova Audio Bks.) Brilliance Audio.
—The Pied Piper. l.t. ed. 2000. pap. 23.95 (*1-56895-834-X*, Wheeler Publishing, Inc.) Gale Group.
—The Pied Piper. 1998. 497p. 23.95 (*0-7868-6300-5*); 2003. 528p. reprint ed. mass mkt. 7.99 (*0-7868-8955-1*) Hyperion Pr.
—The Pied Piper & Beyond Recognition. 1998. (*0-7868-6433-8*) Disney Pr.
—Undercurrents. 2000. E-Book 4.99 (*1-58910-004-2*) PreviewPort.com.
—Undercurrents. 1992. mass mkt. 6.99 (*0-312-92958-7*, St. Martin's Paperbacks); 1989. mass mkt. 4.95 o.s.i (*0-312-91485-7*, St. Martin's Paperbacks); 1988. 416p. 18.95 o.p. (*0-312-01841-X*) St. Martin's Pr.

**BOLITAR, MYRON (FICTITIOUS CHARACTER)—FICTION**

Coben, Harlan. Back Spin. 1997. (Myron Bolitar Mystery Ser.). 368p. mass mkt. 6.99 (*0-440-22270-2*) Dell Publishing.
—Deal Breaker: A Myron Bolitar Mystery. 1995. (Myron Bolitar Mystery Ser.). 368p. mass mkt. 6.99 (*0-440-22044-0*) Dell Publishing.
—Dropshot. 1996. (Myron Bolitar Mystery Ser.). 368p. mass mkt. 6.99 (*0-440-22045-9*) Dell Publishing.
—Fade Away. 1996. (Myron Bolitar Mystery Ser.). 368p. mass mkt. 6.99 (*0-440-22268-0*) Dell Publishing.
—The Final Detail. 2000. 384p. mass mkt. 6.99 (*0-440-22545-0*) Dell Publishing.
—One False Move. unabr. ed. 2000. audio 48.00 (*0-7366-4828-3*, 5174) Books on Tape, Inc.
—One False Move: A Myron Bolitar Novel. 1999. (Myron Bolitar Mystery Ser.). 400p. mass mkt. 7.50 (*0-440-22544-2*) Dell Publishing.
Coben, Harlan. Fade Away. unabr. ed. 2001. (Myron Bolitar Mystery Ser.). audio 29.95 (*0-7366-4951-4*) Books on Tape, Inc.

**BOLITHO, ADAM (FICTITIOUS CHARACTER)—FICTION**

Kent, Alexander. Man of War. 2003. 320p. (*0-434-01008-1*) Heinemann, William Ltd. GBR. *Dist:* Random Hse. of Canada, Ltd.
—Man of War. 2003. (Richard Bolitho Novels Ser.: Vol. 26). 320p. 24.95 (*1-59013-066-9*) McBooks Pr., Inc.
—Relentless Pursuit. (Richard Bolitho Novels Ser.: No. 25). 2002. 368p. pap. 16.95 (*1-59013-026-X*); 2001. 320p. 24.95 (*1-59013-000-6*) McBooks Pr., Inc.
—Relentless Pursuit. unabr. ed. 2003. audio 85.00 (*1-4025-1806-4*) Recorded Bks., LLC.
—Second to None. unabr. ed. 2000. audio 84.95 (*0-7540-0526-7*, CAB 1949) Chivers Audio Bks. GBR. *Dist:* BBC Audiobooks America.
—Second to None. 2001. (Richard Bolitho Novels Ser.: Vol. 24). 350p. pap. 16.95 (*0-935526-94-3*) McBooks Pr., Inc.
—Sword of Honour. Set unabr. ed. 1999. audio 69.95 (*0-7540-0298-5*, CAB 1721) BBC Audiobooks America.
—Sword of Honour. 2001. (Richard Bolitho Ser.: Vol. 23). 320p. pap. 15.95 (*0-935526-93-5*) McBooks Pr., Inc.

**BOLITHO, RICHARD (FICTITIOUS CHARACTER)—FICTION**

Kent, Alexander. Beyond the Reef. unabr. ed. 2000. (Richard Bolitho Adventure Ser.). audio 59.95 (*0-7451-4146-3*, CAB 829) Chivers Audio Bks. GBR. *Dist:* BBC Audiobooks America.
—Beyond the Reef. 2000. (Richard Bolitho Ser.: Vol. 19). 349p. pap. 14.95 (*0-935526-82-X*) McBooks Pr., Inc.
—Colors Aloft! 1987. mass mkt. 3.50 o.s.i (*0-425-10264-5*) Berkley Publishing Group.
—Colors Aloft! 1999. 288p. reprint ed. 31.95 (*1-56849-728-8*) Buccaneer Bks., Inc.
—Colors Aloft! 1986. 16.95 o.p. (*0-399-12988-X*) Putnam Publishing Group, The.
—Colours Aloft. 2000. (Richard Bolitho Ser.: Vol. 16). 300p. reprint ed. pap. 14.95 (*0-935526-72-2*) McBooks Pr., Inc.
—Colours Aloft. l.t. ed. 1987. (Charnwood Large Print Ser.). 432p. 29.99 o.p. (*0-7089-8380-4*, Charnwood) Thorpe, F. A. Pubs. GBR. *Dist:* Ulverscroft Large Print Bks., Ltd., Ulverscroft Large Print Canada, Ltd.
—Command a King's Ship. 1984. 320p. mass mkt. 3.50 o.s.i (*0-515-07866-2*, Jove); 1979. 1.95 o.p. (*0-425-04083-6*) Berkley Publishing Group.
—Command a King's Ship. 1993. reprint ed. lib. bdg. 25.95 (*1-56849-028-3*) Buccaneer Bks., Inc.
—Command a King's Ship. 1998. (Richard Bolitho Ser.: Vol. 6). 352p. pap. 14.95 (*0-935526-50-1*) McBooks Pr., Inc.
—Command a King's Ship. l.t. ed. 1987. (Charnwood Large Print Ser.). 528p. 29.99 o.p. (*0-7089-8440-1*, Ulverscroft) Thorpe, F. A. Pubs. GBR. *Dist:* Ulverscroft Large Print Bks., Ltd., Ulverscroft Large Print Canada, Ltd.
—Cross of St. George. 2001. (Richard Bolitho Ser.: Vol. 22). 320p. pap. 16.95 (*0-935526-92-7*) McBooks Pr., Inc.
—Cross of St. George: A Richard Bolitho Adventure. unabr. ed. 1997. audio 69.95 (*0-7451-8781-1*, CAB 1416) BBC Audiobooks America.
—The Darkening Sea. unabr. ed. 1998. audio 84.95 (*0-7540-0222-5*, CAB 1645) BBC Audiobooks America.
—The Darkening Sea. 2000. (Richard Bolitho Ser.: Vol. 20). 351p. pap. 14.95 (*0-935526-83-8*) McBooks Pr., Inc.
—Enemy in Sight! 1976. 25.95 (*0-8488-0550-X*) Amereon, Ltd.
—Enemy in Sight! 1985. mass mkt. 3.50 o.s.i (*0-515-08177-9*, Z2609, Jove) Berkley Publishing Group.
—Enemy in Sight! 1999. (Richard Bolitho Ser.: Vol. 10). 352p. reprint ed. pap. 14.95 (*0-935526-60-9*) McBooks Pr., Inc.
—The Flag Captain. 1984. 352p. mass mkt. 3.50 o.s.i (*0-515-07749-6*, Jove) Berkley Publishing Group.
—The Flag Captain. 1999. (Richard Bolitho Ser.: Vol. 11). 384p. reprint ed. pap. 15.95 (*0-935526-66-8*) McBooks Pr., Inc.
—For My Country's Freedom. unabr. ed. 2000. (Richard Bolitho Adventure Ser.). audio 59.95 (*0-7451-6700-4*, CAB 1316) Chivers Audio Bks. GBR. *Dist:* BBC Audiobooks America.
—For My Country's Freedom. 2000. (Richard Bolitho Ser.: Vol. 21). 300p. pap. 15.95 (*0-935526-84-6*) McBooks Pr., Inc.
—Form Line of Battle. 1985. mass mkt. 3.50 o.s.i (*0-515-07699-6*, Jove); 1984. mass mkt. 3.50 o.s.i (*0-515-07500-0*, Jove); 1983. mass mkt. 2.95 o.s.i (*0-515-06804-7*, Jove); 1979. mass mkt. 1.95 o.s.i (*0-425-04113-1*); 1977. mass mkt. 1.75 o.s.i (*0-425-03645-6*); 1975. mass mkt. 1.50 o.s.i (*0-425-03100-4*) Berkley Publishing Group.
—Form Line of Battle. 1993. reprint ed. lib. bdg. 37.95 (*1-56849-027-5*) Buccaneer Bks., Inc.
—Form Line of Battle. 1999. (Richard Bolitho Ser.: Vol. 9). 416p. pap. 14.95 (*0-935526-59-5*) McBooks Pr., Inc.
—Honour This Day. unabr. ed. 1993. audio 69.95 (*0-7451-6093-X*, CAB 529) BBC Audiobooks America.
—Honour This Day. 1987. 287 p. (*0-434-38834-3*, Butterworth-Heinemann) Elsevier Science & Technology Bks.
—Honour This Day. 2000. (Richard Bolitho Ser.: Vol. 17). 316p. reprint ed. pap. 15.95 (*0-935526-73-0*) McBooks Pr., Inc.
—Honour This Day. l.t. ed. 1988. (Ulverscroft Large Print Ser.). 560p. 29.99 o.p. (*0-7089-1880-8*, Ulverscroft) Thorpe, F. A. Pubs. GBR. *Dist:* Ulverscroft Large Print Bks., Ltd., Ulverscroft Large Print Canada, Ltd.
—In Gallant Company. 1984. mass mkt. 3.50 o.s.i (*0-515-07856-5*, Jove); 1983. mass mkt. 2.95 o.s.i (*0-515-07064-5*, Jove); 1978. mass mkt. 1.95 o.s.i (*0-425-03987-0*) Berkley Publishing Group.
—In Gallant Company. 1992. reprint ed. lib. bdg. 21.95 (*0-89966-973-5*) Buccaneer Bks., Inc.
—In Gallant Company. 1977. 287 p. (*0-09-128830-4*) Hutchinson.
—In Gallant Company. 1998. (Richard Bolitho Ser.: Vol. 3). 320p. pap. 13.95 (*0-935526-43-9*) McBooks Pr., Inc.
—In Gallant Company. 1977. 8.95 o.p. (*0-399-11987-6*) Putnam Publishing Group, The.
—In Gallant Company. unabr. ed. 1998. audio 70.00 (*0-7887-2607-2*, 95618E7) Recorded Bks., LLC.
—The Inshore Squadron. 1984. 256p. mass mkt. 3.50 o.s.i (*0-515-07984-7*, Jove) Berkley Publishing Group.
—The Inshore Squadron. 1999. (Richard Bolitho Ser.: Vol. 13). 288p. pap. 13.95 (*0-935526-68-4*) McBooks Pr., Inc.
—The Inshore Squadron. l.t. ed. 1983. (Ulverscroft Large Print Ser.). 480p. 29.99 o.p. (*0-7089-0905-1*, Ulverscroft) Thorpe, F. A. Pubs. GBR. *Dist:* Ulverscroft Large Print Bks., Ltd., Ulverscroft Large Print Canada, Ltd.
—Midshipman Bolitho. unabr. ed. 1993. audio 54.95 (*0-7451-4006-8*, CAB 703) BBC Audiobooks America.
—Midshipman Bolitho. 1998. (Richard Bolitho Ser.: Vol. 1). 240p. pap. 11.95 (*0-935526-41-2*) McBooks Pr., Inc.
—Midshipman Bolitho & the Avenger. 1976. 19.95 (*0-8488-1398-7*) Amereon, Ltd.
—Midshipman Bolitho & the Avenger. 1990. 144p. reprint ed. lib. bdg. 25.95 (*0-89966-732-5*) Buccaneer Bks., Inc.
—Midshipman Bolitho & the Avenger. 1978. (J). (gr. 6-8). 6.95 o.p. (*0-399-20652-3*) Putnam Publishing Group, The.
—The Only Victor. unabr. ed. 1991. audio 84.95 (*0-7451-6092-1*, CAB 586) BBC Audiobooks America.
—The Only Victor. 2000. (Richard Bolitho Ser.: Vol. 18). 384p. reprint ed. pap. 15.95 (*0-935526-74-9*) McBooks Pr., Inc.
—Passage to Mutiny. 1985. mass mkt. 3.50 o.s.i (*0-515-08261-9*); 1984. mass mkt. 3.50 o.s.i (*0-515-07445-4*); 1983. mass mkt. 2.95 o.s.i (*0-515-06746-6*); 1980. mass mkt. 1.95 o.s.i (*0-515-05437-2*) Berkley Publishing Group. (Jove).
—Passage to Mutiny. 1993. reprint ed. lib. bdg. 37.95 (*1-56849-029-1*) Buccaneer Bks., Inc.
—Passage to Mutiny. 1999. (Richard Bolitho Ser.: Vol. 7). 352p. reprint ed. pap. 14.95 (*0-935526-58-7*) McBooks Pr., Inc.
—Signal-Close Action. 1984. 352p. mass mkt. 3.50 o.s.i (*0-515-07437-3*); 1983. mass mkt. 2.95 o.s.i (*0-515-06883-7*) Berkley Publishing Group. (Jove).
—Signal-Close Action. 1999. (Richard Bolitho Ser.: Vol. 12). 368p. reprint ed. pap. 15.95 (*0-935526-67-6*) McBooks Pr., Inc.
—Sloop of War. 1984. mass mkt. 3.50 o.s.i (*0-515-07975-8*); 1982. mass mkt. 2.95 o.s.i (*0-515-06726-1*); 1979. mass mkt. 1.95 o.s.i (*0-515-05370-8*) Berkley Publishing Group. (Jove).
—Sloop of War. 1992. reprint ed. lib. bdg. 37.95 (*0-89966-974-3*) Buccaneer Bks., Inc.
—Sloop of War. 1998. (Richard Bolitho Ser.: Vol. 4). 352p. pap. 15.95 (*0-935526-48-X*) McBooks Pr., Inc.
—Sloop of War. l.t. ed. 1987. (Charnwood Large Print Ser.). 512p. 29.99 o.p. (*0-7089-8405-3*, Charnwood) Thorpe, F. A. Pubs. GBR. *Dist:* Ulverscroft Large Print Bks., Ltd., Ulverscroft Large Print Canada, Ltd.
—Stand into Danger. 1984. mass mkt. 3.50 o.s.i (*0-515-07641-4*); 1983. mass mkt. 2.95 o.s.i (*0-515-06888-8*) Berkley Publishing Group. (Jove).
—Stand into Danger. 1992. reprint ed. lib. bdg. 37.95 (*0-89966-972-7*) Buccaneer Bks., Inc.
—Stand into Danger. 1998. (Richard Bolitho Ser.: Vol. 2). 288p. pap. 13.95 (*0-935526-42-0*) McBooks Pr., Inc.
—Stand into Danger. 1981. 300p. 10.95 o.p. (*0-399-12539-6*) Putnam Publishing Group, The.
—Stand into Danger. l.t. ed. 1982. 481p. 15.95 o.p. (*0-7089-0753-9*, Ulverscroft) Thorpe, F. A. Pubs. GBR. *Dist:* Ulverscroft Large Print Bks., Ltd.
—Success to the Brave. 1984. mass mkt. 3.50 o.s.i (*0-515-08052-7*, Jove) Berkley Publishing Group.
—Success to the Brave. 2000. (Richard Bolitho Ser.: Vol. 15). 287p. reprint ed. pap. 13.95 (*0-935526-71-4*) McBooks Pr., Inc.
—Success to the Brave. 1983. 284p. 13.95 o.p. (*0-399-12878-6*, G. P. Putnam's Sons) Penguin Putnam Bks. for Young Readers.
—Success to the Brave. l.t. ed. 1985. (Ulverscroft Large Print Ser.). 512p. 29.99 o.p. (*0-7089-1255-9*, Ulverscroft) Thorpe, F. A. Pubs. GBR. *Dist:* Ulverscroft Large Print Bks., Ltd., Ulverscroft Large Print Canada, Ltd.
—To Glory We Steer. 1976. 23.95 (*0-8488-0551-8*) Amereon, Ltd.
—To Glory We Steer. 1984. mass mkt. 3.50 o.s.i (*0-515-07636-8*, Jove); 1983. mass mkt. 2.95 o.s.i (*0-515-06892-6*, Jove); 1980. mass mkt. 2.25 o.s.i (*0-515-05732-0*, Jove); 1976. mass mkt. 1.75 o.s.i (*0-425-03371-6*) Berkley Publishing Group.
—To Glory We Steer. 1993. reprint ed. lib. bdg. 32.95 (*1-56849-026-7*) Buccaneer Bks., Inc.
—To Glory We Steer. Set. unabr. ed. 2000. audio 84.95 (*0-7540-0399-X*, CAB 1822) Chivers Audio Bks. GBR. *Dist:* BBC Audiobooks America.
—To Glory We Steer. 1998. (Richard Bolitho Ser.: Vol. 5). 352p. pap. 15.95 (*0-935526-49-8*) McBooks Pr., Inc.
—To Glory We Steer. l.t. ed. 1987. (Charnwood Large Print Ser.). 528p. 29.99 o.p. (*0-7089-8423-1*, Charnwood) Thorpe, F. A. Pubs. GBR. *Dist:* Ulverscroft Large Print Bks., Ltd., Ulverscroft Large Print Canada, Ltd.
—A Tradition of Victory. 296p. mass mkt. (*0-09-928370-0*) Arrow Bks., Ltd.
—A Tradition of Victory. 1984. 304p. mass mkt. 3.50 o.s.i (*0-515-07871-9*, Jove) Berkley Publishing Group.
—A Tradition of Victory. 1982. 304p. 12.95 o.p. (*0-399-12706-2*) Putnam Publishing Group, The.
—Tradition of Victory. 1983. mass mkt. 2.95 o.s.i (*0-515-07116-1*, Jove) Berkley Publishing Group.
—A Tradition of Victory. l.t. ed. 1985. (Ulverscroft Large Print Ser.). 528p. 29.99 o.p. (*0-7089-1367-9*, Ulverscroft) Thorpe, F. A. Pubs. GBR. *Dist:* Ulverscroft Large Print Bks., Ltd., Ulverscroft Large Print Canada, Ltd.
—Tradition of Victory. 2000. (Richard Bolitho Ser.: Vol. 14). 302p. reprint ed. pap. 14.95 (*0-935526-70-6*) McBooks Pr., Inc.
—With All Despatch. 1990. mass mkt. 4.50 o.s.i (*0-515-10330-6*, Jove) Berkley Publishing Group.
—With All Despatch. 1993. (Illus.). reprint ed. lib. bdg. 37.95 (*1-56849-030-5*) Buccaneer Bks., Inc.
—With All Despatch. 1988. 272 p. (*0-434-38836-X*, Butterworth-Heinemann) Elsevier Science & Technology Bks.
—With All Despatch. 1999. (Richard Bolitho Ser.: Vol. 8). 352p. reprint ed. pap. 14.95 (*0-935526-61-7*) McBooks Pr., Inc.
—With All Despatch. 1989. 288p. 18.95 o.p. (*0-399-13430-1*, G. P. Putnam's Sons) Penguin Putnam Bks. for Young Readers.
—With All Despatch. l.t. ed. 1989. (Charnwood Large Print Ser.). 29.99 o.p. (*0-7089-8530-0*, Ulverscroft) Thorpe, F. A. Pubs. GBR. *Dist:* Ulverscroft Large Print Bks., Ltd., Ulverscroft Large Print Canada, Ltd.

**BONAPARTE, JUDA (FICTITIOUS CHARACTER)—FICTION**

Nassr, Donald. In the Shadows of the Cross. 1994. 410p. 24.95 (*0-9642463-0-9*) ICAM Publishing Co.
—The Scroll. 368p. 1997. 24.95 (*0-9642463-2-5*); Date not set. pap. 24.95 (*0-9642463-3-3*) ICAM Publishing Co.

**BONAPARTE, NAPOLEON, INSPECTOR (FICTITIOUS CHARACTER)—FICTION**

Upfield, Arthur W. An Author Bites the Dust. (Napoleon Bonaparte Mysteries Ser.). 21.95 (*0-89190-566-9*) Amereon, Ltd.
—The Bachelors of Broken Hill. 1998. (Inspector Napoleon Bonaparte Mystery Ser.). 256p. pap. 11.00 (*0-684-85058-3*, Touchstone) Simon & Schuster.
—The Bachelors of Broken Hill. l.t. ed. 1974. (Ulverscroft Large Print Ser.). 29.99 o.p. (*0-85456-296-6*, Ulverscroft) Thorpe, F. A. Pubs. GBR. *Dist:* Ulverscroft Large Print Bks., Ltd., Ulverscroft Large Print Canada, Ltd.
—The Bachelors of Broken Hill: An Inspector Napoleon Bonaparte Mystery. 1984. 256p. pap. 6.00 (*0-684-18246-7*, Macmillan Reference USA) Gale Group.
—The Battling Prophet. (Napoleon Bonaparte Mysteries Ser.). reprint ed. lib. bdg. 21.95 (*0-89190-551-0*, Rivercity Pr.) Amereon, Ltd.
—The Battling Prophet. 1994. reprint ed. lib. bdg. 29.95 (*1-56849-352-5*) Buccaneer Bks., Inc.
—The Body at Madmen's Bend. (Napoleon Bonaparte Mysteries Ser.). reprint ed. lib. bdg. 23.95 (*0-89190-552-9*) Amereon, Ltd.
—The Bone Is Pointed. (Napoleon Bonaparte Mysteries Ser.). 23.95 (*0-89190-568-5*) Amereon, Ltd.
—The Bone Is Pointed. 1976. (Crime Fiction Ser.). reprint ed. lib. bdg. 21.00 o.p. (*0-8240-2395-1*) Garland Publishing, Inc.
—The Bone Is Pointed. 2nd l.t. ed. 1993. 385p. 21.95 (*1-85695-335-1*) ISIS Large Print Bks. GBR. *Dist:* Transaction Pubs.
—The Bone Is Pointed. 1998. (Inspector Napoleon Bonaparte Mystery Ser.). 304p. pap. 11.00 (*0-684-85057-5*, Touchstone) Simon & Schuster.
—The Bone Is Pointed: An Inspector Napoleon Bonaparte Mystery. 1984. 288p. pap. 6.00 o.p. (*0-684-18247-5*, Macmillan Reference USA) Gale Group.
—The Bone Is Pointed: An Inspector Napoleon Bonaparte Mystery. unabr. ed. 1994. audio 58.00 (*0-7887-0030-8*, 94229) Recorded Bks., LLC.
—Bony & the Black Virgin. (Napoleon Bonaparte Mysteries Ser.). reprint ed. lib. bdg. 20.95 (*0-89190-553-7*, Rivercity Pr.) Amereon, Ltd.

—Bony & the Kelly Gang. (Napoleon Bonaparte Mysteries Ser.). 21.95 (*0-89190-554-5*) Amereon, Ltd.
—Bony & the Mouse. (Napoleon Bonaparte Mysteries Ser.). 22.95 (*0-89190-561-8*) Amereon, Ltd.
—Bony & the Mouse. l.t. ed. 1973. 12.00 o.p. (*0-85456-186-2*, Ulverscroft) Thorpe, F. A. Pubs. GBR. *Dist:* Ulverscroft Large Print Bks., Ltd.
—Bony & the White Savage. l.t. ed. 1976. (Ulverscroft Large Print Ser.). 29.99 o.p. (*0-85456-407-1*, Ulverscroft) Thorpe, F. A. Pubs. GBR. *Dist:* Ulverscroft Large Print Bks., Ltd., Ulverscroft Large Print Canada, Ltd.
—Bony Buys a Woman. 1984. 21.95 (*0-89190-555-3*) Amereon, Ltd.
—Breakaway House. l.t. ed. 1991. 11.95 o.p. (*0-947072-72-1*, 1033); pap. 9.95 o.p. (*1-86340-102-4*, AUS027) BBC Audiobooks America.
—Bushranger of the Skies. unabr. ed. 1999. audio (*1-86442-387-0*, 590378) Bolinda Publishing Pty, Ltd.
—Bushranger of the Skies. l.t. ed. 1978. (Ulverscroft Large Print Ser.). 29.99 o.p. (*0-7089-0132-8*, Ulverscroft) Thorpe, F. A. Pubs. GBR. *Dist:* Ulverscroft Large Print Bks., Ltd., Ulverscroft Large Print Canada, Ltd.
—Cake in the Hat Box. (Napoleon Bonaparte Mysteries Ser.). 20.95 (*0-89190-567-7*) Amereon, Ltd.
—Cake in the Hat Box. l.t. ed. 1979. 12.00 o.p. (*0-7089-0335-5*, Ulverscroft) Thorpe, F. A. Pubs. GBR. *Dist:* Ulverscroft Large Print Bks., Ltd.
—The Clue of the New Shoe. l.t. ed. 1974. (Ulverscroft Large Print Ser.). 29.99 o.p. (*0-85456-258-3*, Ulverscroft) Thorpe, F. A. Pubs. GBR. *Dist:* Ulverscroft Large Print Bks., Ltd., Ulverscroft Large Print Canada, Ltd.
—Death of a Lake. 1983. 192p. pap. 6.00 o.s.i (*0-684-17886-9*, Macmillan Reference USA) Gale Group.
—Death of a Swagman. unabr. ed. 1999. audio (*1-86442-385-4*, 590372) Bolinda Publishing Pty, Ltd.
—Death of a Swagman. 1982. 224p. pap. 6.00 o.s.i (*0-684-17482-0*, Macmillan Reference USA) Gale Group.
—Death of a Swagman. l.t. ed. 1975. 12.00 o.p. (*0-85456-374-1*, Ulverscroft) Thorpe, F. A. Pubs. GBR. *Dist:* Ulverscroft Large Print Bks., Ltd.
—The Devil's Steps. (Napoleon Bonaparte Mysteries Ser.). reprint ed. lib. bdg. 22.95 (*0-89190-556-1*) Amereon, Ltd.
—The Devil's Steps. unabr. ed. 1999. audio (*1-876584-28-9*, 590788) Bolinda Publishing Pty, Ltd.
—The Devil's Steps: An Inspector Napoleon Bonaparte Mystery. 1982. 288p. pap. 6.00 o.s.i (*0-684-17668-8*, Macmillan Reference USA) Gale Group.
—Gripped by Drought. 1990. 288p. reprint ed. 30.00 o.p. (*0-939767-19-8*) McMillan, Dennis Pubns.
—The House of Cain. 1983. (Illus.). 296p. reprint ed. 20.00 o.p. (*0-9609986-0-8*) McMillan, Dennis Pubns.
—The Lake Frome Monster. (Napoleon Bonaparte Mysteries Ser.). reprint ed. lib. bdg. 18.95 (*0-89190-557-X*) Amereon, Ltd.
—The Lake Frome Monster. 2nd l.t. ed. 1993. 273p. 21.95 (*1-85695-340-8*) ISIS Large Print Bks. GBR. *Dist:* Transaction Pubs.
—The Lake Frome Monster: An Inspector Napoleon Bonaparte Mystery, Set. unabr. ed. 1994. audio 34.00 (*1-85695-505-2*, 94370) Recorded Bks., LLC.
—The Lure of the Bush. (Napoleon Bonaparte Mysteries Ser.). 21.95 (*0-89190-569-3*) Amereon, Ltd.
—Madman's Bend. l.t. ed. 1977. (Ulverscroft Large Print Ser.). 29.99 o.p. (*0-7089-0032-1*, Ulverscroft) Thorpe, F. A. Pubs. GBR. *Dist:* Ulverscroft Large Print Bks., Ltd., Ulverscroft Large Print Canada, Ltd.
—Man of Two Tribes. Date not set. (Napoleon Bonaparte Mysteries Ser.). lib. bdg. 20.95 (*0-8488-2170-X*) Amereon, Ltd.
—The Mountains Have a Secret. 20.95 (*0-8488-0653-0*) Amereon, Ltd.
—The Mountains Have a Secret. 1985. 192p. pap. 4.95 o.s.i (*0-684-18501-6*, Macmillan Reference USA) Gale Group.
—The Mountains Have a Secret. l.t. ed. 1975. (Ulverscroft Large Print Ser.). 29.99 o.p. (*0-85456-341-5*, Ulverscroft) Thorpe, F. A. Pubs. GBR. *Dist:* Ulverscroft Large Print Bks., Ltd., Ulverscroft Large Print Canada, Ltd.
—Mr. Jelly's Business: Murder down Under. (Napoleon Bonaparte Mysteries Ser.). reprint ed. lib. bdg. 24.95 (*0-89190-558-8*, Rivercity Pr.) Amereon, Ltd.
—The Murchison Murders. ltd. ed. 1987. 96p. reprint ed. 15.00 o.p. (*0-9609986-9-1*) McMillan, Dennis Pubns.
—Murder down Under. 1983. 304p. pap. 6.00 (*0-684-17887-7*, Macmillan Reference USA) Gale Group.
—Murder down Under. 1998. (Inspector Napoleon Bonaparte Mystery Ser.). 304p. pap. 12.00 (*0-684-85059-1*, Touchstone) Simon & Schuster.
—Murder Must Wait. (Napoleon Bonaparte Mysteries Ser.). reprint ed. lib. bdg. 21.95 (*0-89190-559-6*, Rivercity Pr.) Amereon, Ltd.
—The Mystery of Swordfish Reef. (Napoleon Bonaparte Mysteries Ser.). 20.95 (*0-89190-562-6*) Amereon, Ltd.
—The Mystery of Swordfish Reef. 1994. reprint ed. lib. bdg. 32.95 (*1-56849-351-7*) Buccaneer Bks., Inc.
—The Mystery of Swordfish Reef. 1998. (Inspector Napoleon Bonaparte Mystery Ser.). 272p. pap. 12.00 (*0-684-85060-5*, Touchstone) Simon & Schuster.
—The Mystery of Swordfish Reef: An Inspector Napoleon Bonaparte Mystery. 1985. 272p. pap. 5.95 o.s.i (*0-684-18412-5*, Macmillan Reference USA) Gale Group.
—The New Shoe. 1983. 192p. pap. 4.95 (*0-684-18020-0*, Macmillan Reference USA) Gale Group.
—No Footprints in the Bush. 20.95 (*0-89190-560-X*) Amereon, Ltd.
—The Sands of Windee. (Napoleon Bonaparte Mysteries Ser.). 21.95 (*0-89190-570-7*) Amereon, Ltd.
—The Sands of Windee. 2nd l.t. ed. 1993. 282p. 22.95 (*1-85695-345-9*) ISIS Large Print Bks. GBR. *Dist:* Transaction Pubs.
—The Sands of Windee. 1985. 224p. pap. 4.95 o.s.i (*0-684-18502-4*, Scribner Paper Fiction) Simon & Schuster.
—The Sands of Windee: A Napoleon Bonaparte Mystery. unabr. ed. 1994. audio 58.00 (*1-55690-983-7*, 94122) Recorded Bks., LLC.
—Sinister Stones. (Napoleon Bonaparte Mysteries Ser.). 19.95 (*0-8488-1211-5*) Amereon, Ltd.
—Sinister Stones. 1983. 192p. pap. 6.00 o.s.i (*0-684-18021-9*, Scribner Paper Fiction) Simon & Schuster.
—The Torn Branch. Date not set. (Napoleon Bonaparte Mysteries Ser.). lib. bdg. 18.95 (*0-8488-2171-8*) Amereon, Ltd.
—The Torn Branch. 1986. 160p. pap. 5.95 o.s.i (*0-02-025930-1*, Scribner Paper Fiction) Simon & Schuster.
—Venom House. (Napoleon Bonaparte Mysteries Ser.). 22.95 (*0-8488-1212-3*) Amereon, Ltd.
—Venom House. unabr. ed. 1998. audio (*1-86442-318-8*, 581157) Bolinda Publishing Pty, Ltd.
—Venom House. 1989. 268p. pap. 6.00 o.s.i (*0-02-025901-8*, Scribner Paper Fiction) Simon & Schuster.
—The Widows of Broome. l.t. ed. 1980. (Ulverscroft Large Print Ser.). 354p. 29.99 o.p. (*0-7089-0490-4*, Ulverscroft) Thorpe, F. A. Pubs. GBR. *Dist:* Ulverscroft Large Print Bks., Ltd., Ulverscroft Large Print Canada, Ltd.
—The Widows of Broome: An Inspector Napoleon Bonaparte Mystery. 1985. 256p. pap. 5.95 (*0-684-18389-7*, Scribner Paper Fiction) Simon & Schuster.
—The Will of the Tribe. (Napoleon Bonaparte Mysteries Ser.). 20.95 (*0-8488-1213-1*) Amereon, Ltd.
—The Will of the Tribe. 1984. 216p. pap. 5.95 o.s.i (*0-684-18141-X*, Scribner Paper Fiction) Simon & Schuster.
—Winds of Evil. (Napoleon Bonaparte Mysteries Ser.). 20.95 (*0-89190-563-4*) Amereon, Ltd.
—Winds of Evil. 1987. 256p. pap. 4.95 o.s.i (*0-02-025910-7*, Scribner Paper Fiction) Simon & Schuster.
—Winds of Evil. l.t. ed. 1977. (Ulverscroft Large Print Ser.). 29.99 o.p. (*0-7089-0054-2*, Ulverscroft) Thorpe, F. A. Pubs. GBR. *Dist:* Ulverscroft Large Print Bks., Ltd., Ulverscroft Large Print Canada, Ltd.
—Wings above the Diamantina. Date not set. (Napoleon Bonaparte Mysteries Ser.). lib. bdg. 23.95 (*0-8488-2172-6*) Amereon, Ltd.
—Wings above the Diamantina. l.t. ed. 1977. (Ulverscroft Large Print Ser.). 29.99 o.p. (*0-7089-0009-7*, Ulverscroft) Thorpe, F. A. Pubs. GBR. *Dist:* Ulverscroft Large Print Bks., Ltd., Ulverscroft Large Print Canada, Ltd.

## BOND, JAMES (FICTITIOUS CHARACTER)—FICTION

Alexander, Judy. James Bond Story Book. 1985. (Illus.). 64p. (J). (gr. 3 up). 6.95 o.p. (*0-448-18972-0*, Grosset & Dunlap) Penguin Putnam Bks. for Young Readers.
Benson, Raymond. Die Another Day. novel ed. 2002. 224p. mass mkt. 6.99 (*0-425-18963-5*) Berkley Publishing Group.
—Die Another Day. 2002. audio 17.95 (*0-7861-2371-0*); audio compact disk 19.95 (*0-7861-9381-6*); audio 23.95 (*0-7861-2359-1*); audio compact disk 24.00 (*0-7861-9392-1*) Blackstone Audio Bks., Inc.
—Die Another Day. unabr. ed. 2002. (James Bond Ser.). audio 24.95 (*1-59086-512-X*, 4103, Brilliance Audio Unabridged); audio 62.25 (*1-59086-513-8*, 4104, Unabridged Library Editions); audio compact disk 29.95 (*1-59086-514-6*, 4105, CD Unabridged); audio compact disk 74.25 (*1-59086-515-4*, 4106, CD Unabridged Library Edition) Brilliance Audio.
—Die Another Day. 2003. (Adventure Ser.). 28.95 (*0-7862-5117-4*) Thorndike Pr.
—Double Shot. l.t. ed. 2000. (Basic Ser.). 427p. 27.95 (*0-7862-2870-9*) Thorndike Pr.
—Doubleshot. 2001. 304p. reprint ed. mass mkt. 7.50 (*0-515-13061-3*, Jove) Berkley Publishing Group.
—Doubleshot. 2000. (James Bond Ser.). 272p. 23.95 o.s.i (*0-399-14614-8*) Penguin Group (USA) Inc.
—The Facts of Death. 1999. 304p. reprint ed. mass mkt. 6.99 o.s.i (*0-515-12550-4*, Jove) Berkley Publishing Group.
—The Facts of Death: The New James Bond Adventure. 1998. 288p. 23.95 o.p. (*0-399-14405-6*, G. P. Putnam's Sons) Penguin Group (USA) Inc.
—High Time to Kill. 2000. (James Bond Ser.). 304p. mass mkt. 6.99 o.s.i (*0-515-12833-3*, Jove) Berkley Publishing Group.
—High Time to Kill. 1999. (James Bond Adventure Ser.). 272p. 23.95 o.p. (*0-399-14500-1*, G. P. Putnam's Sons) Penguin Group (USA) Inc.
—High Time to Kill. l.t. ed. 2000. 496p. (*0-7540-1389-8*); 28.95 (*0-7862-2338-3*); (*0-7540-2293-5*) Thorndike Pr.
—The Man with the Red Tattoo. 2003. (James Bond Ser.). 320p. mass mkt. 7.99 (*0-515-13563-1*, Jove) Berkley Publishing Group.
—The Man with the Red Tattoo. unabr. ed. 2002. audio compact disk 19.95 (*0-7861-9111-2*) Blackstone Audio Bks., Inc.
—The Man with the Red Tattoo. 2002. 272p. 23.95 o.s.i (*0-399-14884-1*) Penguin Group (USA) Inc.
—Never Dream of Dying. 2002. 320p. reprint ed. mass mkt. 7.50 (*0-515-13307-8*, Jove) Berkley Publishing Group.
—Never Dream of Dying. l.t. ed. 2001. 407p. 28.95 (*0-7838-9624-7*, Hall, G. K. & Co.) Gale Group.
—Never Dream of Dying. 2001. 272p. 23.95 o.p. (*0-399-14746-2*) Penguin Group (USA) Inc.
—Tomorrow Never Dies. 1997. (James Bond Ser.). 256p. mass mkt. 6.99 o.s.i (*1-57297-345-5*) Boulevard Bks.
—The World Is Not Enough. 1999. (James Bond Ser.). 256p. mass mkt. 6.99 o.s.i (*0-425-17350-X*) Boulevard Bks.
—Zero Minus Ten. 1998. (007 Ser.). 304p. reprint ed. mass mkt. 6.99 o.s.i (*0-515-12336-6*, Jove) Berkley Publishing Group.
—Zero Minus Ten. 1997. 288p. 22.95 o.p. (*0-399-14257-6*, G. P. Putnam's Sons) Penguin Group (USA) Inc.
Dorling Kindersley Publishing Staff. The Secret World of 007. l.t. ed. 2000. (Illus.). 144p. 21.45 o.p. (*0-7513-2860-X*) Thorpe, F. A. Pubs. GBR. *Dist:* Ulverscroft Large Print Bks., Ltd., Ulverscroft Large Print Canada, Ltd.
Favors, Jean M. James Bond in Programmed For Danger. 1985. (Find Your Fate Adventure Ser.: No. 13). 128p. mass mkt. 1.95 o.s.i (*0-345-32456-0*) Ballantine Bks.
Fleming, Ian. Bonded Fleming. 1965. 5.75 o.p. (*0-670-17825-X*) Viking Penguin.
—Casino Royale. 1987. 3.50 o.s.i (*0-441-09400-7*) Ace Bks.
—Casino Royale. 1985. (James Bond Ser.). mass mkt. 4.50 o.s.i (*0-425-08162-1*) Berkley Publishing Group.
—Casino Royale. 2003. audio compact disk 19.95 (*0-7861-9667-X*) Blackstone Audio Bks., Inc.
—Casino Royale. 2002. audio (*0-14-180287-1*) Penguin Bks., Ltd.
—Casino Royale. 1983. mass mkt. 2.95 o.s.i (*0-425-06392-5*); 1982. mass mkt. 2.75 o.s.i (*0-425-05363-6*) Berkley Publishing Group.
—Casino Royale. 1994. (James Bond Ser.). 9.98 o.s.i (*1-56731-056-7*, MJF Bks.) Fine Communications.
—Casino Royale. 1962. (James Bond Ser.). mass mkt. 0.60 o.p. (*0-451-02724-8*); mass mkt. 0.50 o.p. (*0-451-01997-0*); mass mkt. 0.35 o.p. (*0-451-01762-5*) NAL. (Signet Bks.).
—Casino Royale. unabr. ed. 1993. audio 54.95 (*0-7451-5927-3*, CAB 345) BBC Audiobooks America.
—Casino Royale. unabr. ed. 2001. audio compact disk 19.95; 2001. audio 24.95 (*0-7861-1910-1*); 2000. audio 32.95 (*0-7861-1817-2*, 2616); 2000. audio compact disk 32.00 (*0-7861-9854-0*, z2616) Blackstone Audio Bks., Inc.
—Casino Royale. 1995. reprint ed. lib. bdg. 24.95 (*1-56849-655-9*) Buccaneer Bks., Inc.
—Casino Royale. 2002. 192p. reprint ed. 13.00 (*0-14-200202-X*) Viking Penguin.
—Diamonds Are Forever. 1976. 21.95 (*0-8488-1005-8*) Amereon, Ltd.
—Diamonds Are Forever. 1985. (James Bond Ser.). 224p. mass mkt. 4.50 o.s.i (*0-425-08986-X*) Berkley Publishing Group.
—Diamonds Are Forever. 1993. (BookCard Ser.). 4.95 o.p. (*0-8118-0735-5*); 29.70 o.p. (*0-8118-0305-8*) Chronicle Bks. LLC.
—Diamonds Are Forever. 2002. 192p. 13.00 (*0-14-200205-4*); audio (*0-14-180289-8*) Viking Penguin.
—Diamonds Are Forever. (James Bond Ser.). 1983. mass mkt. 2.95 o.s.i (*0-425-06393-3*); 1982. mass mkt. 2.75 o.s.i (*0-425-05364-4*) Berkley Publishing Group.
—Diamonds Are Forever. 1961. (James Bond Ser.). mass mkt. 0.50 o.p. (*0-451-02029-4*); mass mkt. 0.60 o.p. (*0-451-02725-6*) NAL. (Signet Bks.).
—Diamonds Are Forever. abr. ed. audio 15.95 o.p. (*0-88646-109-X*, TC-LFP 7089) Durkin Hayes Publishing Ltd.
—Diamonds Are Forever. 1995. (James Bond Ser.). 216p. reprint ed. 9.98 o.s.i (*1-56731-050-8*, MJF Bks.) Fine Communications.
—Diamonds Are Forever. unabr. ed. 1990. audio 54.95 (*0-7451-5928-1*, CAB 511) BBC Audiobooks America.
—Diamonds Are Forever. unabr. ed. 2001. audio 39.95 (*0-7861-1941-1*, 2712); audio compact disk 48.00 (*0-7861-9779-X*, z2712) Blackstone Audio Bks., Inc.
—Diamonds Are Forever. unabr. ed. 2002. 3p. audio compact disk (*0-14-180414-9*) Viking Penguin.
—Doctor No. 1983. mass mkt. 2.95 o.s.i (*0-425-06394-1*); 1982. mass mkt. 2.75 o.s.i (*0-425-05365-2*) Berkley Publishing Group.
—Doctor No. 1994. (James Bond Ser.). 256p. 9.98 o.s.i (*1-56731-054-0*, MJF Bks.) Fine Communications.
—Doctor No. 1959. (James Bond Ser.). mass mkt. 1.25 o.p. (*0-451-07202-2*); mass mkt. 0.50 o.p. (*0-451-02036-7*); mass mkt. 0.60 o.p. (*0-451-02726-4*); mass mkt. 0.35 o.p. (*0-451-01670-X*) NAL. (Signet Bks.).
—Dr. No. 1985. (James Bond Ser.). 240p. mass mkt. 4.50 o.s.i (*0-425-08679-8*) Berkley Publishing Group.
—Dr. No. abr. ed. 1997. (James Bond Ser.). audio 16.95 o.p. (*1-56100-936-9*, 466, Nova Audio Bks.) Brilliance Audio.
—Dr. No. unabr. ed. 2000. (James Bond Ser.: Bk. 6). audio 49.95 Chivers Audio Bks. GBR. *Dist:* BBC Audiobooks America.
—Dr. No. 1959. (James Bond Ser.). mass mkt. 1.50 o.p. (*0-451-08195-1*, W8195, Signet Bks.) NAL.
—Dr. No. 2002. audio (*0-14-180290-1*) Penguin Bks., Ltd.
—Dr. No. 1987. (James Bond Ser.). audio 8.95 o.p. (*0-671-63140-3*, Simon & Schuster Audioworks) Simon & Schuster Audio.
—Dr. No. 2002. 192p. reprint ed. 13.00 (*0-14-200203-8*) Viking Penguin.
—For Your Eyes Only. 1985. 192p. 3.50 o.s.i (*1-55773-123-3*, Diamond Bks.) Ace Bks.
—For Your Eyes Only. 1985. (James Bond Ser.). 192p. mass mkt. 3.50 o.s.i (*0-425-08167-2*, Jove) Berkley Publishing Group.
—For Your Eyes Only. 2002. audio (*0-14-180293-6*) Viking Penguin.
—For Your Eyes Only. 1983. mass mkt. 2.95 o.s.i (*0-425-06395-X*); 1982. mass mkt. 2.75 o.s.i (*0-425-05366-0*) Berkley Publishing Group.
—For Your Eyes Only. 1995. (James Bond Ser.). reprint ed. 9.98 o.s.i (*1-56731-049-4*, MJF Bks.) Fine Communications.
—For Your Eyes Only. (James Bond Ser.). mass mkt. 0.35 o.p. (*0-451-01948-2*); mass mkt. 0.60 o.p. (*0-451-02727-2*); mass mkt. 0.50 o.p. (*0-451-02054-5*) NAL. (Signet Bks.).
—For Your Eyes Only. 2003. 192p. pap. 13.00 (*0-14-200322-0*) Penguin Group (USA) Inc.
—For Your Eyes Only. 1960. (James Bond Ser.). 3.50 o.p. (*0-670-32474-4*) Viking Penguin.
—For Your Eyes Only. unabr. ed. 2000. (James Bond Ser.: Bk. 8). audio 49.95 (*0-7451-6776-4*, CAB 1392) Chivers Audio Bks. GBR. *Dist:* BBC Audiobooks America.
—From Russia with Love. Date not set. lib. bdg. 22.95 (*0-8488-2142-4*) Amereon, Ltd.
—From Russia with Love. 1985. (James Bond Ser.). 256p. mass mkt. 3.95 o.s.i (*0-425-08620-8*) Berkley Publishing Group.
—From Russia with Love. 2002. audio (*0-14-180291-X*) Penguin Bks., Ltd.
—From Russia with Love. 2002. 192p. 13.00 (*0-14-200207-0*) Viking Penguin.
—From Russia with Love. mass mkt. 3.50 o.s.i (*0-425-08164-8*); 1983. mass mkt. 2.95 o.s.i (*0-425-06589-8*); 1982. mass mkt. 2.75 o.s.i (*0-425-05367-9*) Berkley Publishing Group.
—From Russia with Love. 1994. (James Bond Ser.). 252p. 9.98 o.s.i (*1-56731-053-2*, MJF Bks.) Fine Communications.
—From Russia with Love. (James Bond Ser.). mass mkt. 0.60 o.p. (*0-451-02728-0*); mass mkt. 0.35 o.p. (*0-451-01563-0*); mass mkt. 0.50 o.p. (*0-451-02030-8*) NAL. (Signet Bks.).
—From Russia with Love. l.t. ed. 1992. pap. 15.95 o.p. (*0-7927-1268-4*); 18.95 o.p. (*0-7927-1269-2*) BBC Audiobooks America.
—From Russia with Love. abr. ed. 1985. audio 15.95 o.p. (*0-88646-136-7*, TC-LFP 7137) Durkin Hayes Publishing Ltd.

—Goldfinger. 1985. (James Bond Ser.). 272p. mass mkt. 4.50 o.s.i (*0-425-08165-6*) Berkley Publishing Group.

—Goldfinger. 2002. 2p. audio (*0-14-180288-X*) Viking Penguin.

—Goldfinger. 1983. mass mkt. 2.95 o.s.i (*0-425-06396-8*); 1982. mass mkt. 2.75 o.s.i (*0-425-05368-7*) Berkley Publishing Group.

—Goldfinger. 1994. (James Bond Ser.). 318p. 9.98 o.s.i (*1-56731-051-6*, MJF Bks.) Fine Communications.

—Goldfinger. (James Bond Ser.). mass mkt. 0.35 o.p. (*0-451-01822-2*); mass mkt. 0.50 o.p. (*0-451-02052-9*); mass mkt. 0.60 o.p. (*0-451-02729-9*) NAL. (Signet Bks.).

—Goldfinger. l.t. ed. 1993. pap. 17.95 o.p. (*0-7927-1472-5*); 1993. pap. 17.95 o.p. (*0-7927-1319-2*); 1992. 19.95 o.p. (*0-7927-1320-6*) BBC Audiobooks America.

—Goldfinger. abr. ed. 1985. audio 15.95 o.p. (*0-88646-143-X*, 7144) Durkin Hayes Publishing Ltd.

—Goldfinger. 2002. 224p. reprint ed. 13.00 (*0-14-200204-6*) Viking Penguin.

—James Bond in You Only Live Twice, abr. ed. 1997. (James Bond Ser.). audio 16.95 o.p. (*1-56100-941-5*, 518, Nova Audio Bks.) Brilliance Audio.

—James Bond Omnibus: From Russia, with Love, Doctor No, Goldfinger. 1997. 832p. 12.98 o.s.i (*1-56731-160-1*, MJF Bks.) Fine Communications.

—James Bond Omnibus Vol. 2: Thunderball, on Her Majesty's Secret Service, You Only Live Twice. 1997. 800p. 12.98 o.s.i (*1-56731-161-X*, MJF Bks.) Fine Communications.

—James Bond 007: Five Complete Novels. 1988. 2.00 o.s.i (*0-517-65352-4*) Random Hse. Value Publishing.

—Live & Let Die. 1989. (James Bond Ser.). 3.95 (*1-55773-263-9*, Diamond Bks.) Berkley Publishing Group.

—Live & Let Die. mass mkt. 3.50 o.s.i (*0-425-08163-X*); 1985. mass mkt. 3.50 o.s.i (*0-425-08759-X*); 1983. mass mkt. 2.95 o.s.i (*0-425-06398-4*); 1982. mass mkt. 2.75 o.s.i (*0-425-05369-5*) Berkley Publishing Group.

—Live & Let Die. (James Bond Ser.). mass mkt. 0.35 o.p. (*0-451-01723-4*); mass mkt. 0.50 o.p. (*0-451-02051-0*); mass mkt. 0.60 o.p. (*0-451-02730-2*) NAL. (Signet Bks.).

—Live & Let Die. 2003. 240p. pap. 13.00 (*0-14-200323-9*) Penguin Group (USA) Inc.

—Live & Let Die. 1995. reprint ed. lib. bdg. 24.95 (*1-56849-656-7*) Buccaneer Bks., Inc.

—Live & Let Die. abr. ed. audio 15.95 o.p. (*0-88646-108-1*, TC-LFP 7088) Durkin Hayes Publishing Ltd.

—Live & Let Die. abr. ed. 2002. 2p. audio (*0-14-180299-5*, Penguin AudioBooks) Viking Penguin.

—Live & Let Die. 1995. (James Bond Ser.). 218p. reprint ed. 9.98 o.s.i (*1-56731-057-5*, MJF Bks.) Fine Communications.

—Live & Let Die. unabr. ed. 2000. (James Bond Ser.: Bk. 2). audio 49.95 Chivers Audio Bks. GBR. *Dist:* BBC Audiobooks America.

—The Living Daylights. abr. ed. 1994. (James Bond Ser.). audio 5.99 (*0-88646-701-2*, Pac-7701) Durkin Hayes Publishing Ltd.

—The Man with the Golden Gun. 1966. (James Bond Ser.). mass mkt. 2.95 o.p. (*0-451-13705-1*); 160p. mass mkt. 4.50 o.p. (*0-451-15855-5*) NAL. (Signet Bks.).

—The Man with the Golden Gun. 2002. audio (*0-14-180292-8*) Penguin Bks., Ltd.

—The Man with the Golden Gun. 1987. audio 8.95 o.p. (*0-671-63142-X*); audio 8.95 o.p. (*0-671-63142-X*) Simon & Schuster Audio. (Simon & Schuster Audioworks).

—The Man with the Golden Gun. 1999. 190p. pap. text 24.95 (*0-7658-0654-1*) Transaction Pubs.

—The Man with the Golden Gun. (James Bond Ser.). 4.50 o.p. (*0-453-00042-8*); 1974. 3.50 o.p. (*0-453-00366-4*) Dutton/Plume. (Dutton).

—The Man with the Golden Gun. (James Bond Ser.). 1974. mass mkt. 0.60 o.p. (*0-451-02735-3*); 1974. mass mkt. 1.25 o.p. (*0-451-06208-6*); 1966. mass mkt. 1.50 o.p. (*0-451-08187-0*); 1966. mass mkt. 2.50 o.p. (*0-451-12106-6*); 1966. mass mkt. 1.75 o.p. (*0-451-09330-5*) NAL. (Signet Bks.).

—The Man with the Golden Gun. 2004. 192p. pap. 13.00 (*0-14-200328-X*) Penguin Group (USA) Inc.

—The Man with the Golden Gun, unabr. ed. 1993. 39.95 incl. audio (*0-7451-5933-8*, CAB 266) BBC Audiobooks America.

—Moonraker. 1988. 3.95 (*1-55773-185-3*, Diamond Bks.); 1987. 240p. mass mkt. 4.50 o.s.i (*0-425-13493-8*) Berkley Publishing Group.

—Moonraker. 2002. 192p. 13.00 (*0-14-200206-2*); audio (*0-14-180296-0*) Viking Penguin.

—Moonraker. 1984. mass mkt. 2.95 o.s.i (*0-425-07656-3*) Berkley Publishing Group.

—Moonraker. 1994. (James Bond Ser.). 224p. 9.98 o.s.i (*1-56731-055-9*, MJF Bks.) Fine Communications.

—Moonraker. (James Bond Ser.). mass mkt. 0.35 o.p. (*0-451-01850-8*); mass mkt. 0.50 o.p. (*0-451-02053-7*); mass mkt. 0.60 o.p. (*0-451-02731-0*) NAL. (Signet Bks.).

—Moonraker. abr. ed. 1987. (James Bond Ser.). audio 8.95 o.p. (*0-671-63141-1*, Simon & Schuster Audioworks) Simon & Schuster Audio.

—Moonraker. l.t. ed. 1975. 12.00 o.p. (*0-85456-308-3*, Ulverscroft) Thorpe, F. A. Pubs. GBR. *Dist:* Ulverscroft Large Print Bks., Ltd.

—Octopussy. 1976. 17.95 (*0-8488-1006-6*) Amereon, Ltd.

—Octopussy. 1967. (James Bond Ser.). 128p. mass mkt. 4.50 o.s.i (*0-451-15624-2*); mass mkt. 2.50 o.p. (*0-451-11878-2*) NAL. (Signet Bks.).

—Octopussy; The Living Daylights. 2002. audio (*0-14-180301-0*) Penguin Bks., Ltd.

—Octopussy, The Living Daylights & The Property of a Lady: Featuring James Bond. unabr. ed. 1996. audio 24.95 (*0-7451-6717-9*, CAB 1333) BBC Audiobooks America.

—On Her Majesty's Secret Service. 1964. (James Bond Ser.). 192p. mass mkt. 4.50 o.p. (*0-451-15432-0*); mass mkt. 2.95 o.p. (*0-451-13707-8*) NAL. (Signet Bks.).

—On Her Majesty's Secret Service. 2002. audio (*0-14-180295-2*) Viking Penguin.

—On Her Majesty's Secret Service. 1995. (James Bond Ser.). 288p. 9.98 o.s.i (*1-56731-079-6*, MJF Bks.) Fine Communications.

—On Her Majesty's Secret Service, unabr. ed. 1993. 54.95 incl. audio (*0-7451-5932-X*, CAB 291) BBC Audiobooks America.

—On Her Majesty's Secret Service. abr. ed. 1997. (James Bond Ser.). audio 16.95 o.p. (*1-56100-940-7*, 499, Nova Audio Bks.) Brilliance Audio.

—The Spy Who Loved Me. 1987. 192p. 3.50 o.s.i (*0-441-77870-4*) Ace Bks.

—The Spy Who Loved Me. 1989. 3.95 (*1-55773-300-7*, Diamond Bks.); 1986. mass mkt. 4.50 o.s.i (*0-425-08681-X*) Berkley Publishing Group.

—The Spy Who Loved Me. 2002. audio (*0-14-180298-7*) Viking Penguin.

—The Spy Who Loved Me. 1995. (James Bond Ser.). 9.98 o.s.i (*1-56731-052-4*, MJF Bks.) Fine Communications.

—The Spy Who Loved Me. (James Bond Ser.). mass mkt. 0.50 o.p. (*0-451-02280-7*); mass mkt. 0.60 o.p. (*0-451-02733-7*) NAL. (Signet Bks.).

—The Spy Who Loved Me. 2003. 176p. pap. 13.00 (*0-14-200326-3*) Penguin Group (USA) Inc.

—The Spy Who Loved Me. 1962. (James Bond Ser.). 3.95 o.p. (*0-670-66593-2*) Viking Penguin.

—Thunderball. 1985. (James Bond Ser.). mass mkt. 3.95 o.s.i (*0-425-08634-8*) Berkley Publishing Group.

—Thunderball. 2002. audio (*0-14-180297-9*) Viking Penguin.

—Thunderball. 1983. mass mkt. 2.95 o.s.i (*0-425-06428-X*); 1982. mass mkt. 2.75 o.s.i (*0-425-05344-X*) Berkley Publishing Group.

—Thunderball. 1994. (James Bond Ser.). 9.98 o.s.i (*1-56731-048-6*, MJF Bks.) Fine Communications.

—Thunderball. 1962. (James Bond Ser.). mass mkt. 0.50 o.p. (*0-451-02126-6*); mass mkt. 0.60 o.p. (*0-451-02734-5*); mass mkt. 0.75 o.p. (*0-451-05569-1*) NAL. (Signet Bks.).

—Thunderball. 2003. 272p. pap. 13.00 (*0-14-200324-7*) Penguin Group (USA) Inc.

—Thunderball. 1961. (James Bond Ser.). 3.95 o.p. (*0-670-71146-2*) Viking Penguin.

—You Only Live Twice. 1995. (James Bond Ser.). 256p. 9.98 (*1-56731-080-X*, MJF Bks.) Fine Communications.

—You Only Live Twice. 1965. (James Bond Ser.). mass mkt. 2.95 o.p. (*0-451-13708-6*, AE2108, Signet Bks.); 160p. mass mkt. 4.50 o.p. (*0-451-15348-0*) NAL.

—You Only Live Twice. 2002. audio (*0-14-180294-4*) Viking Penguin.

—You Only Live Twice. (James Bond Ser.). 4.50 o.p. (*0-453-00018-5*, Dutton) Dutton/Plume.

—You Only Live Twice. (James Behind Ser.). 1967. mass mkt. 0.60 o.p. (*0-451-02712-4*); 1965. mass mkt. 2.50 o.p. (*0-451-12108-2*); 1965. mass mkt. 1.50 o.p. (*0-451-08503-5*); 1965. mass mkt. 2.50 o.p. (*0-451-11439-6*); 1965. mass mkt. 1.75 o.p. (*0-451-09382-8*) NAL. (Signet Bks.).

—You Only Live Twice. 2003. 224p. pap. 13.00 (*0-14-200327-1*) Penguin Group (USA) Inc.

Fleming, Ian, et al. The Man with the Golden Gun. 2004. (James Bond 007 Ser.). (Illus.). 80p. pap. 16.95 (*1-84023-690-6*) Titan Bks. Ltd. GBR. *Dist:* Client Distribution Services.

Gardner, John E. Brokenclaw. l.t. ed. 1991. 22.95 o.p. (*0-7927-0935-7*, CH0146); pap. 20.95 o.p. (*0-7927-0936-5*, CS0243) BBC Audiobooks America.

—Brokenclaw. 1991. mass mkt. 5.50 o.p. (*0-425-12721-4*) Berkley Publishing Group.

—Brokenclaw. 1990. 320p. 14.95 o.p. (*0-399-13541-3*, G. P. Putnam's Sons) Penguin Putnam Bks. for Young Readers.

—Death Is Forever. l.t. ed. 1994. 19.95 o.p. (*0-7927-1751-1*); pap. 17.95 o.p. (*0-7927-1750-3*) BBC Audiobooks America.

—Death Is Forever. 1993. 352p. mass mkt. 5.99 o.s.i (*0-425-13700-7*) Berkley Publishing Group.

—Death Is Forever. 1992. (James Bond Adventure Ser.). 304p. 15.95 o.p. (*0-399-13716-5*, G. P. Putnam's Sons) Penguin Group (USA) Inc.

—Death Is Forever. abr. ed. 1992. audio 14.00 o.p. (*0-679-41049-X*, RH Audio) Random Hse. Audio Publishing Group.

—Ian Fleming's James Bond: Three Complete Novels. 1988. 592p. 11.99 o.s.i (*0-517-67250-2*); 1987. 672p. 7.99 o.s.i (*0-517-64293-X*) Random Hse. Value Publishing.

—License to Kill. unabr. ed. 1992. (James Bond Ser.). audio 54.95 (*0-7451-5973-7*, CAB 669) BBC Audiobooks America.

—License to Kill. 1989. (James Bond Ser.). 4.50 (*1-55773-192-6*, Diamond Bks.) Berkley Publishing Group.

—The Man from Barbarossa. l.t. ed. 1993. pap. 17.95 o.p. (*0-7927-1350-8*); 1992. 19.95 o.p. (*0-7927-1351-6*) BBC Audiobooks America.

—The Man from Barbarossa. 1992. mass mkt. 5.50 o.s.i (*0-425-13234-X*) Berkley Publishing Group.

—The Man from Barbarossa. 1991. (James Bond Adventure Ser.). 304p. 14.95 o.p. (*0-399-13625-8*, G. P. Putnam's Sons) Penguin Group (USA) Inc.

—Never Send Flowers. 1994. pap. 19.95 o.p. (*0-7927-1924-7*); 21.95 o.p. (*0-7927-1950-6*) BBC Audiobooks America.

—Never Send Flowers. 1994. 336p. reprint ed. mass mkt. 5.99 o.s.i (*0-425-14250-7*) Berkley Publishing Group.

—Never Send Flowers. 1993. (James Bond Adventure Ser.). 304p. 18.95 o.p. (*0-399-13809-9*) Penguin Group (USA) Inc.

—Nobody Lives Forever. unabr. ed. 1992. (James Bond Ser.). audio 54.95 (*0-7451-4048-3*, CAB 745) BBC Audiobooks America.

—Nobody Lives Forever. 1990. (James Bond Ser.). mass mkt. 4.99 o.s.i (*0-425-12320-0*) Berkley Publishing Group.

—Nobody Lives Forever. 1986. 13.95 o.p. (*0-399-13151-5*) Putnam Publishing Group, The.

—Role of Honor. 1987. 4.50 o.s.i (*0-441-73437-5*) Ace Bks.

—Role of Honor. 1988. 4.50 (*1-55773-125-X*, Diamond Bks.); 1986. 304p. pap. 3.95 o.s.i (*0-425-09497-9*); 1985. mass mkt. 4.95 o.s.i (*0-425-07671-7*) Berkley Publishing Group.

—Role of Honor. l.t. ed. 1985. (General Ser.). 15.95 o.p. (*0-8161-3850-8*, Macmillan Reference USA) Gale Group.

—Role of Honor. 1984. (James Bond Adventure Ser.). 304p. 11.95 o.p. (*0-399-12912-X*, G. P. Putnam's Sons) Penguin Putnam Bks. for Young Readers.

—Scorpius. 1991. mass mkt. 4.99 o.p. (*0-425-13140-8*) Berkley Publishing Group.

—Scorpius. 1988. (James Bond Adventure Ser.). 320p. 12.95 o.p. (*0-399-13347-X*, G. P. Putnam's Sons) Penguin Putnam Bks. for Young Readers.

—Seafire. 1995. 304p. mass mkt. 6.99 o.s.i (*0-425-14775-4*) Berkley Publishing Group.

—Seafire. 1994. 288p. 18.95 o.p. (*0-399-13938-9*, G. P. Putnam's Sons) Penguin Group (USA) Inc.

—Seafire. 286p. 5.98 o.p. (*0-7651-0182-3*) Smithmark Pubs., Inc.

—Win, Lose or Die. 1990. mass mkt. 4.95 o.s.i (*0-425-12261-1*) Berkley Publishing Group.

—Win, Lose or Die. l.t. ed. 1990. (Large Print Bks.). 393p. lib. bdg. 19.95 o.p. (*0-8161-4996-8*, Macmillan Reference USA) Gale Group.

—Win, Lose or Die. 1989. (James Bond Adventure Ser.). 320p. 13.95 o.p. (*0-399-13436-0*, G. P. Putnam's Sons) Penguin Putnam Bks. for Young Readers.

Hyatt, Angela C. N. The James Bond Internet Guide. 2000. 40p. pap. 10.00 o.p. (*1-883573-41-6*, Lightning Rod Limited) Windstorm Creative Ltd.

Lycett, Andrew. Ian Fleming: The Man Behind James Bond. 1999. (Illus.). 486p. reprint ed. text 25.00 (*0-7881-6656-5*) DIANE Publishing Co.

McReynolds, B.S. The 007 Dossier. 1999. (Illus.). 188p. 23.95 (*0-9667203-7-7*) BS Bk. Publishing.

Moench, Doug. James Bond 007 Bk. 1: Serpent's Tooth. 1995. (Illus.). 160p. pap. 15.95 (*1-878574-78-7*) Dark Horse Comics.

Moench, Doug & Gulacy, Paul. James Bond 007: Serpent's Tooth. Prosser, Jerry, ed. 1992. (Illus.). 48p. (Orig.). Vol. 2. pap. 4.95 o.p. (*1-878574-39-6*); Vol. 3. pap. 4.95 o.p. (*1-878574-40-X*) Dark Horse Comics.

—James Bond 007 Bk. 1: Serpent's Tooth. Prosser, Jerry, ed. 1992. (Illus.). 48p. pap. 4.95 o.p. (*1-878574-38-8*) Dark Horse Comics.

Otfinoski, Steven. James Bond in Barracuda Run. 1985. (Find Your Fate Adventure Ser.: No. 14). mass mkt. 1.95 o.s.i (*0-345-32468-4*) Ballantine Bks.

Siegel, Barbara & Siegel, Scott. James Bond in Win, Place or Die. 1985. (Find Your Fate Adventure Ser.: No. 11). mass mkt. 1.95 o.s.i (*0-345-32404-8*) Ballantine Bks.

Siegel, Scott. James Bond in Strike It Deadly. 1985. (Find Your Fate Adventure Ser.: No. 12). mass mkt. 2.50 o.s.i (*0-345-32405-6*) Ballantine Bks.

Snelling, O. James Bond, A Report: 007. 1964. 160p. 10.00 o.p. (*0-87556-700-2*) Saifer, Albert Pub.

Snelling, O. F. 007 James Bond, a Report. Date not set. 128p. 17.95 (*0-8488-2605-1*) Amereon, Ltd.

## BONE, ROBERT (FICTITIOUS CHARACTER)—FICTION

Stacey, Susannah. Body of Opinion. 1990. mass mkt. o.s.i (*0-552-13470-8*, Corgi) Bantam Bks.

—Body of Opinion. 1990. 17.95 o.p. (*0-671-69170-8*, Simon & Schuster) Simon & Schuster.

—Body of Opinion. Chelius, Jane, ed. 1991. 224p. reprint ed. mass mkt. 4.99 (*0-671-73427-X*, Pocket) Simon & Schuster.

—Bone Idle. 320p. 1996. mass mkt. 5.99 (*0-671-51062-2*, Pocket); 1995. 21.00 o.p. (*0-671-73531-4*, Atria) Simon & Schuster.

—Dead Serious. 1997. (Superintendent Bone Mystery Ser.). 320p. per. 5.99 (*0-671-00118-3*, Pocket) Simon & Schuster.

—Goodbye, Nanny Gray. 1989. mass mkt. 4.50 (*0-671-65779-8*, Pocket) Simon & Schuster.

—Goodbye, Nanny Gray. 1988. 16.95 o.p. (*0-671-65778-X*) Summit Bks.

—Grave Responsibility: A Superintendent Bone Mystery. l.t. ed. 1992. 20.95 o.p. (*0-7927-1054-1*); pap. 18.95 o.p. (*0-7927-1055-X*) BBC Audiobooks America.

—Grave Responsibility: A Superintendent Bone Mystery. Chelius, Jane, ed. 1992. 224p. reprint ed. mass mkt. 4.50 (*0-671-77827-7*, Pocket) Simon & Schuster.

—Grave Responsibility: A Superintendent Bone Mystery. 1991. 160p. 17.95 o.p. (*0-671-69171-6*) Summit Bks.

—Hunters Quarry. 1998. 352p. mass mkt. 6.50 (*0-671-00119-1*, Pocket) Simon & Schuster.

—A Knife at the Opera: An Inspector Bone Mystery. 1990. 224p. mass mkt. 4.99 (*0-671-70508-3*, Pocket) Simon & Schuster.

—A Knife at the Opera: An Inspector Bone Mystery. 1989. 17.95 o.p. (*0-671-65780-1*) Summit Bks.

—The Late Lady. l.t. ed. 1993. 23.95 o.p. (*0-7927-1692-2*); pap. 21.95 o.p. (*0-7927-1691-4*) BBC Audiobooks America.

—The Late Lady. 1994. 256p. mass mkt. 4.99 (*0-671-73895-X*, Pocket) Simon & Schuster.

—The Late Lady. Chelius, Jane, ed. 1993. 256p. 20.00 (*0-671-73530-6*, Atria) Simon & Schuster.

Staynes, Jill. Goodbye, Nanny Gray. l.t. ed. 1990. (Ulverscroft Large Print Ser.). 29.99 o.p. (*0-7089-2261-9*, Ulverscroft) Thorpe, F. A. Pubs. GBR. *Dist:* Ulverscroft Large Print Bks., Ltd., Ulverscroft Large Print Canada, Ltd.

## BONESTEEL, NORA (FICTITIOUS CHARACTER)—FICTION

McCrumb, Sharyn. The Ballad of Frankie Silver, unabr. ed. 1998. audio 62.95 (*0-7861-1443-6*, 2305) Blackstone Audio Bks., Inc.

—The Ballad of Frankie Silver. 1998. 304p. 23.95 o.p. (*0-525-93969-5*) Dutton/Plume.

—The Ballad of Frankie Silver. l.t. ed. 1998. (Large Print Book Ser.). 27.95 (*1-56895-656-8*, Wheeler Publishing, Inc.) Gale Group.

—The Ballad of Frankie Silver. 1999. 416p. reprint ed. mass mkt. 7.99 (*0-451-19739-9*, Signet Bks.) NAL.

—The Ballad of Frankie Silver. abr. ed. 1998. audio 25.00 (*0-7871-1713-7*, Dove Audio) NewStar Media, Inc.

—The Ballad of Frankie Silver. unabr. ed. 1999. audio compact disk 109.00 (*0-7887-3437-7*, C1043E7); 1998. audio 94.00 (*0-7887-2475-4*, 95550E7) Recorded Bks., LLC.

—The Hangman's Beautiful Daughter: A Novel of Suspense. l.t. ed. 1996. lib. bdg. 23.95 (*1-57490-069-2*, Beeler Large Print Bks.) Beeler, Thomas T. Publisher.

—The Hangman's Beautiful Daughter: A Novel of Suspense. 1992. 288p. 19.00 (*0-684-19407-4*, Macmillan Reference USA) Gale Group.

—The Hangman's Beautiful Daughter: A Novel of Suspense. 1993. 384p. mass mkt. 7.99 (*0-451-40370-3*, Onyx) NAL.

—The Hangman's Beautiful Daughter: A Novel of Suspense. unabr. ed. 1993. audio 60.00 (*1-55690-786-9*, 93104E7) Recorded Bks., LLC.

—The Hangman's Beautiful Daughter: A Novel of Suspense. 1992. 13.55 (*0-606-06147-9*) Turtleback Bks.

—If Ever I Return, Pretty Peggy-O. 1998. mass mkt. 6.99 (*0-345-91352-3*); 1995. mass mkt. 5.99 o.p. (*0-345-90215-7*); 1991. 336p. mass mkt. 6.99 (*0-345-36906-8*) Ballantine Bks.

—If Ever I Return, Pretty Peggy-O. 1990. 324p. 17.95 o.s.i (*0-684-19104-0*, Macmillan Reference USA) Gale Group.

—If Ever I Return, Pretty Peggy-O. unabr. ed. 1993. audio 70.00 (*1-55690-921-7*, 93417E7) Recorded Bks., LLC.

—The Rosewood Casket. 2003. audio compact disk 19.95 (*0-7861-9651-3*); 1999. audio 49.95 (*0-7861-0994-7*, 1771); 1996. audio compact disk 72.00 (*0-7861-9844-3*, 1771) Blackstone Audio Bks., Inc.

—The Rosewood Casket. 1998. 303p. text 24.00 (*0-7881-5352-8*) DIANE Publishing Co.

—The Rosewood Casket. 1996. (Illus.). 320p. 23.95 o.p. (*0-525-94011-1*) Dutton/Plume.

—The Rosewood Casket. l.t. ed. 1996. 435p. lib. bdg. 25.95 o.p. (*0-7838-1826-2*, Macmillan Reference USA) Gale Group.

—The Rosewood Casket. 1997. 432p. mass mkt. 7.99 (*0-451-18471-8*, Signet Bks.) NAL.

—The Rosewood Casket. unabr. ed. 1996. (Ballad Ser.: Vol. 4). audio 78.00 (*0-7887-0522-9*, 94717E7) Recorded Bks., LLC.

—The Rosewood Casket. abr. ed. 1996. audio 16.95 o.p. (*0-14-086386-9*, Penguin AudioBooks) Viking Penguin.

—She Walks These Hills, unabr. ed. 1998. audio 56.95 (*0-7861-1351-0*, 2254) Blackstone Audio Bks., Inc.

—She Walks These Hills. abr. ed. 1994. audio 16.95 o.p. (*1-56100-394-8*, 1368, Nova Audio Bks.); audio 73.25 o.p. (*1-56100-228-3*, 1040, Unabridged Library Editions); audio 23.95 o.p. (*1-56100-603-3*, 262, Bookcassette) Brilliance Audio.

—She Walks These Hills. l.t. ed. 1996. (Large Print Bks.). 24.95 o.p. (*1-56895-357-7*, Wheeler Publishing, Inc.) Gale Group.

—She Walks These Hills. abr. ed. 2000. audio 7.95 (*1-57815-025-6*, 1027, Media Bks. Audio Publishing) Media Bks., L. L. C.

—She Walks These Hills. 1995. 448p. mass mkt. 7.99 (*0-451-18472-6*, Signet Bks.) NAL.

—She Walks These Hills, unabr. ed. 1999. audio 78.00 (*0-7887-0229-7*, 94454E7) Recorded Bks., LLC.

—She Walks These Hills. 1994. 320p. 21.00 (*0-684-19556-9*, Scribner) Simon & Schuster.

### BOOKER, QUINN (FICTITIOUS CHARACTER)—FICTION

DeAndrea, William L. The Fatal Elixir: A Lobo Blacke-Quinn Booker Mystery. 1997. (Lobo Black/Quinn Booker Mystery Ser.). 208p. 22.95 (*0-8027-3289-5*) Walker & Co.

—Written in Fire: A Lobo Blacke-Quinn Booker Mystery. 1995. 168p. 19.95 (*0-8027-3270-4*) Walker & Co.

### BOOP, BETTY (FICTITIOUS CHARACTER)—FICTION

Fleischer, Max. Betty Boop. 1975. pap. 3.45 o.p. (*0-380-00294-9*, Avon Bks.) Morrow/Avon.

—Betty Boop's Sunday Best. (Illus.). 112p. 1995. 34.95 (*0-87816-365-4*); 1998. reprint ed. pap. 19.95 (*0-87816-363-8*) Kitchen Sink Pr., Inc.

Fleischer, Max, illus. Betty Boop's Hollywood Chronicles. 1990. mass mkt. 5.95 (*0-380-76072-X*, Avon Bks.) Morrow/Avon.

Hackney, Rick. Starring Betty Boop. 1984. (Illus.). 3.95 (*0-915696-85-1*) Determined Productions, Inc.

King Features Staff. Boop-Oop-a-Doop Means I Love You. 2003. 80p. 9.95 (*0-7407-3844-5*) Andrews McMeel Publishing.

### BORDEN, LIZZIE, 1860-1927—FICTION

Engstrom, Elizabeth. Lizzie Borden. 1997. 352p. pap. 14.95 (*0-312-86154-0*, Forge Bks.); 1992. 352p. mass mkt. 4.99 (*0-8125-0591-3*, Tor Bks.); 1990. 18.95 o.p. (*0-312-93204-9*, Tor Bks.) Doherty, Tom Assocs., LLC.

Geary, Rick. A Treasury of Victorian Murder: The Borden Tragedy. 1997. (Treasury of Victorian Murder Ser.). (Illus.). 64p. pap. 8.95 (*1-56163-189-2*) NBM Publishing Co.

### BORGIA, GIOVANNI (FICTITIOUS CHARACTER)—FICTION

Haasse, Hella S. The Scarlet City: A Novel of Sixteenth-Century Italy. Miller, Anita, tr. from DUT. & intro. by. 1990. 594p. 22.95 o.p. (*0-89733-349-7*) Academy Chicago Pubs., Ltd.

—The Scarlet City: A Novel of Sixteenth-Century Italy. Miller, Anita, tr. from DUT. 2nd ed. 1997. 368p. reprint ed. pap. 18.95 (*0-89733-372-1*) Academy Chicago Pubs., Ltd.

### BORGIA, LUCREZIA, 1480-1519—FICTION

Davis, Genevieve. A Passion in the Blood. 1980. pap. 1.95 o.p. (*0-523-40255-4*, Pinnacle Bks.) Kensington Publishing Corp.

—A Passion in the Blood. 1977. 9.95 o.s.i (*0-671-02249-0*) Simon & Schuster.

Kenyon, F. W. The Naked Sword. 1979. reprint ed. pap. 1.95 o.s.i (*0-505-51341-2*) Dorchester Publishing Co., Inc.

Plaidy, Jean. Light on Lucrezia. 1977. 240p. mass mkt. 1.75 o.s.i (*0-449-23108-9*, Fawcett) Ballantine Bks.

—Light on Lucrezia. 1976. 8.95 o.p. (*0-399-11723-7*) Putnam Publishing Group, The.

—Madonna of the Seven Hills. 1976. 288p. mass mkt. 1.75 o.s.i (*0-449-23026-0*, Fawcett) Ballantine Bks.

Seymour, Miranda. Daughter of Shadows. 1977. 8.95 o.p. (*0-698-10784-5*) Putnam Publishing Group, The.

### BOSCH, HARRY (FICTITIOUS CHARACTER)—FICTION

Connelly, Michael. Angels Flight. 1999. (*0-7540-2211-0*) BBC Audiobooks America.

—Angels Flight. unabr. ed. 1999. (Harry Bosch Novel Ser.). audio 39.95 (*1-56740-410-3*, 1512, Brilliance Audio Unabridged) Brilliance Audio.

—Angels Flight, unabr. ed. 1999. audio 73.25 Highsmith Inc.

—Angels Flight. 1999. (Detective Harry Bosch Mysteries Ser.). 400p. (YA). (gr. 8 up). 25.00 o.p. (*0-316-15219-6*) Little Brown & Co.

—Angels Flight. l.t. ed. (Thorndike/G. K. Hall Paperback Bestsellers Ser.). 595p. 2000. pap. 27.95 (*0-7862-1865-7*); 1999. 30.95 (*0-7862-1864-9*) Thorndike Pr.

—Angels Flight. abr. ed. 1999. (Detective Harry Bosch Mysteries Ser.). (gr. 8 up). audio 24.00 (*1-57042-645-7*) Time Warner AudioBooks.

—Angels Flight. 2000. 480p. reprint ed. mass mkt. 7.99 (*0-446-60727-4*) Warner Bks., Inc.

—The Black Echo. abr. ed. 2001. (Harry Bosch Novel Ser.: Vol. 1). audio 12.99 (*1-58788-310-4*, 2848, Paperback Nova Audio Bks.); 2000. (Harry Bosch Ser.). audio 24.95 o.p. (*1-58788-076-8*, 2323, Nova Audio Bks.); 2003. (Harry Bosch Ser.). audio 29.95 (*1-59355-417-6*, 5038, Bookcassette); 1998. (Harry Bosch Ser.). 11p. audio 89.25 (*1-56740-623-8*, 1478, Unabridged Library Editions); 1998. (Harry Bosch Ser.). audio 28.95 (*1-56740-094-9*, 1476, Bookcassette) Brilliance Audio.

—The Black Echo. unabr. ed. 2000. (Detective Harry Bosch Mystery Ser.). audio Chivers Audio Bks. GBR. *Dist:* BBC Audiobooks America.

—The Black Echo. 1992. 19.95 o.p. (*0-316-15361-3*) Little Brown & Co.

—The Black Echo. unabr. ed. 2003. (Harry Bosch Ser.). audio 19.99 (*1-59335-254-9*, 30352) Soulmate Audio Bks., Inc.

—The Black Echo. 10th ed. 1993. 418p. mass mkt. 7.99 (*0-312-95048-9*, St. Martin's Paperbacks) St. Martin's Pr.

—The Black Echo. l.t. ed. 2001. 647p. 30.95 (*0-7862-3309-5*); 2001. 584p. (*0-7540-9073-6*); 2001. 584p. (*0-7540-1659-5*); Set. 1994. audio 89.95 o.p. (*0-7862-9984-3*) Thorndike Pr.

—The Black Echo. 2002. 496p. reprint ed. mass mkt. 7.99 (*0-446-61273-1*) Warner Bks., Inc.

—The Black Ice. abr. ed. 2001. (Harry Bosch Novel Ser.: Vol. 2). audio 12.99 (*1-58788-340-6*, 2951, Paperback Nova Audio Bks.); 2000. (Harry Bosch Ser.). audio 24.95 o.s.i (*1-58788-075-X*, 2324, Nova Audio Bks.); 2003. (Harry Bosch Ser.). audio 29.95 (*1-59355-416-8*, 5037, Brilliance Audio Unabridged); 1998. (Harry Bosch Ser.). 11p. audio 73.25 (*1-56740-624-6*, 1480, Unabridged Library Editions); 1998. (Harry Bosch Ser.). audio 26.95 (*1-56740-095-7*, 1479, Bookcassette) Brilliance Audio.

—The Black Ice. unabr. ed. 2000. (Detective Harry Bosch Mystery Ser.). audio Chivers Audio Bks. GBR. *Dist:* BBC Audiobooks America.

—The Black Ice. l.t. ed. 1994. 90.95 o.p. (*0-7862-9985-1*, Macmillan Reference USA) Gale Group.

—The Black Ice. 1993. 322p. 19.95 o.p. (*0-316-15382-6*) Little Brown & Co.

—The Black Ice. 1994. 374p. mass mkt. 7.99 o.s.i (*0-312-95281-3*, St. Martin's Paperbacks) St. Martin's Pr.

—The Black Ice. 2003. 448p. mass mkt. 7.99 (*0-446-61344-4*, Warner Vision) Warner Bks., Inc.

—Chasing the Dime. 2002. 384p. 25.95 (*0-316-15391-5*); E-Book 14.95 (*0-7595-4710-6*); (Illus.). 544p. 25.95 (*0-316-16046-6*) Little Brown & Co.

—Chasing the Dime. 2003. 448p. mass mkt. 7.99 (*0-446-61162-X*, Warner Vision) Warner Bks., Inc.

—City of Bones. 2002. 400p. 25.95 (*0-316-15405-9*); E-Book 14.95 (*0-7595-8691-8*); 528p. 25.95 (*0-316-15431-8*) Little Brown & Co.

—City of Bones. abr. ed. 2002. audio 31.98 (*1-58621-202-8*); audio 26.98 (*1-58621-201-X*); audio 39.98 (*1-58621-203-6*, 2C362) Time Warner AudioBooks.

—City of Bones. 2003. 448p. mass mkt. 7.99 (*0-446-61161-1*, Warner Vision) Warner Bks., Inc.

—City of Bones. 2002. E-Book 14.95 (*0-7595-6682-8*) ereads.com.

—The Concrete Blonde. abr. ed. 1994. (Harry Bosch Ser.). audio 16.95 o.p. (*1-56100-375-1*, 1642, Nova Audio Bks.); 13p. audio 89.25 (*1-56100-198-8*, 1160, Unabridged Library Editions); 13p. audio 25.95 (*1-56100-572-X*, 67, Bookcassette) Brilliance Audio.

—The Concrete Blonde. 1994. 382p. 21.95 o.p. (*0-316-15383-4*) Little Brown & Co.

—The Concrete Blonde. abr. ed. 2000. audio 7.95 (*1-57815-004-3*, 1031, Media Bks. Audio Publishing) Media Bks., L. L. C.

—The Concrete Blonde. 1995. 397p. mass mkt. 7.99 (*0-312-95500-6*, St. Martin's Paperbacks) St. Martin's Pr.

—A Darkness More Than Night. unabr. collector's ed. 2000. audio 35.95 (*0-7366-5932-3*) Books on Tape, Inc.

—A Darkness More Than Night. 2001. 432p. 25.95 o.p. (*0-316-15407-5*); 400p. E-Book 14.95 (*0-7595-0067-3*); 400p. E-Book 14.95 (*0-7595-4069-1*); 400p. E-Book 14.95 (*0-7595-9076-1*) Little Brown & Co.

—A Darkness More Than Night. l.t. ed. 608p. 2002. 30.95 (*0-7862-2821-0*); 2001. 31.95 (*0-7862-2820-2*) Thorndike Pr.

—A Darkness More Than Night. abr. ed. 2002. audio 25.98 (*1-58621-105-6*); 2001. audio 25.98 (*1-57042-971-5*); 2001. audio 29.98 (*1-57042-985-5*); 2002. audio 25.98 (*1-58621-106-4*); 2001. audio 39.98 (*1-57042-972-3*) Time Warner AudioBooks.

—A Darkness More Than Night. deluxe ltd. ed. 2000. 150.00 (*1-890885-10-X*) Trice, B.E. Publishing.

—A Darkness More Than Night. 2002. 488p. reprint ed. mass mkt. 7.99 (*0-446-66790-0*) Warner Bks., Inc.

—The Harry Bosch Novels: The Black Echo; The Black Ice; The Concrete Blonde. 2001. 800p. 16.95 (*0-316-15497-0*) Little Brown & Co.

—The Harry Bosch Novels: The Black Echo; The Black Ice; The Concrete Blonde, 3 vols. 2001. 800p. E-Book 9.95 (*0-7595-4598-7*) Time Warner Bks. UK GBR. *Dist:* Little Brown & Co.

—The Harry Bosch Novels: The Black Echo, The Black Ice, The Concrete Blonde. 2001. 800p. E-Book 9.95 (*0-7595-8604-7*); E-Book 9.95 (*0-7595-9666-2*) Little Brown & Co.

—The Harry Bosch Novels: The Black Echo, The Black Ice, The Concrete Blonde. 2001. 800p. E-Book (*0-7595-0595-0*) Time Warner Bks. UK.

—The Last Coyote. abr. ed. (Harry Bosch Novel Ser.). 1996. audio 7.99 o.s.i (*1-56740-118-X*, 671, Paperback Nova Audio Bks.); 1995. audio 16.95 o.p. (*1-56100-409-X*, 1270, Nova Audio Bks.); 1995. 13p. audio 89.25 (*1-56100-241-0*, 922, Unabridged Library Editions); 1995. audio 25.95 (*1-56100-616-5*, 157, Bookcassette) Brilliance Audio.

—The Last Coyote. l.t. ed. 1995. (Large Print Bks.). pap. 24.95 (*1-56895-272-4*, Wheeler Publishing, Inc.) Gale Group.

—The Last Coyote. l.t. ed. 1995. 383p. 22.95 o.p. (*0-316-15390-7*) Little Brown & Co.

—The Last Coyote. 5th ed. 1996. 416p. reprint ed. mass mkt. 7.99 (*0-312-95845-5*, St. Martin's Paperbacks) St. Martin's Pr.

—Lost Light. 2003. 368p. 25.95 (*0-316-15460-1*); 496p. 25.95 (*0-316-71117-9*) Little Brown & Co.

—Lost Light. unabr. ed. 2003. audio 36.98 (*1-58621-488-8*); audio 46.98 (*1-58621-489-6*) Time Warner AudioBooks.

—Lost Light. 2003. E-Book 15.95 (*0-7595-8757-4*); E-Book 15.95 (*0-7595-4750-5*) Time Warner Bk. Group.

—Lost Light. aut. ltd. num. ed. 2003. 150.00 (*1-890885-16-9*) Trice, B.E. Publishing.

—Lost Light. 2004. mass mkt. 7.99 (*0-446-61163-8*, Warner Vision) Warner Bks., Inc.

—The Narrows. 2004. 352p. 25.95 (*0-316-00073-6*) Little Brown & Co.

—The Narrows. unabr. ed. 2004. audio 36.98 (*1-58621-636-8*); audio compact disk 46.98 (*1-58621-635-X*) Time Warner AudioBooks.

—Trunk Music. abr. ed. 1997. (Harry Bosch Novel Ser.). audio 7.99 o.s.i (*1-56740-201-1*, 713, Paperback Nova Audio Bks.); audio 25.95 o.s.i (*1-56100-724-2*, 301, Bookcassette); 15p. audio 89.25 (*1-56100-801-X*, 1110, Unabridged Library Editions) Brilliance Audio.

—Trunk Music. l.t. ed. 1997. 27.95 (*1-56895-440-9*, Wheeler Publishing, Inc.) Gale Group.

—Trunk Music. 1997. 400p. 23.45 o.p. (*0-316-15244-7*) Little Brown & Co.

—Trunk Music. 1998. 438p. mass mkt. 7.99 (*0-312-96329-7*, St. Martin's Paperbacks) St. Martin's Pr.

Connelly, Michael, contrib. by. Angels Flight. 1999. (*0-7540-1281-6*) BBC Audiobooks America.

### BOUDREAU, PHIL (FICTITIOUS CHARACTER)—FICTION

Thorp, Roderick. River: A Novel of the Green River Killings. 1996. mass mkt. o.p. (*0-8041-0985-0*, Ivy Bks.); mass mkt. 5.99 o.p. (*0-449-22514-3*, Fawcett); mass mkt. 5.99 o.s.i (*0-8041-1535-4*, Ivy Bks.) Ballantine Bks.

### BOURNE, JASON (FICTITIOUS CHARACTER)—FICTION

Ludlum, Robert. The Bourne Identity. 1984. 544p. mass mkt. 7.99 (*0-553-26011-1*); mass mkt. 3.99 o.s.i (*0-553-19941-2*) Bantam Bks.

—The Bourne Identity. 1983. Pt. I. audio 64.00; Pt. II. audio 48.00 Books on Tape, Inc.

—The Bourne Identity. 1980. 12.95 o.s.i (*0-399-90070-5*) Putnam Publishing Group, The.

—The Bourne Identity. abr. ed. 1987. audio 18.00 (*0-553-45053-0*, RH Audio) Random Hse. Audio Publishing Group.

—The Bourne Identity, Pts. 1 & 2. unabr. collector's ed. Incl. Pt. I. audio 64.00 Pt. II. audio 48.00 1983. 1983. Set audio 104.00 (*0-7366-0809-5*, 1760) Books on Tape, Inc.

—The Bourne Supremacy. 1989. 656p. mass mkt. 7.99 (*0-553-26322-6*); 1987. mass mkt. o.s.i (*0-553-26651-9*); 1987. 656p. mass mkt. 3.99 o.s.i (*0-553-19942-0*) Bantam Bks.

—The Bourne Supremacy. unabr. collector's ed. 1986. Pt. 1. audio 72.00 (*0-7366-0867-2*, 1818-A); Pt. 2. audio 64.00 (*0-7366-0868-0*, 1818-B) Books on Tape, Inc.

—The Bourne Supremacy. l.t. ed. 1987. 21.95 o.p. (*0-8161-4224-6*, Macmillan Reference USA) Gale Group.

—The Bourne Supremacy. abr. ed. 1989. audio 18.00 (*0-553-45159-6*, RH Audio) Random Hse. Audio Publishing Group.

—The Bourne Supremacy. 1986. 608p. 19.95 o.s.i (*0-394-54396-3*) Random Hse., Inc.

—The Bourne Ultimatum. 672p. 1991. mass mkt. 7.95 o.s.i (*0-553-29194-7*); 1991. mass mkt. 7.99 (*0-553-28773-7*); 1991. mass mkt. 3.99 o.s.i (*0-553-19943-9*); 1990. mass mkt. 5.50 o.s.i (*0-553-17342-1*) Bantam Bks.

—The Bourne Ultimatum. unabr. collector's ed. 1990. Pt. 1. audio 64.00 (*0-7366-1702-7*, 2547A); Pt. 2. audio 64.00 (*0-7366-1703-5*, 2547B) Books on Tape, Inc.

—The Bourne Ultimatum. 1990. audio 14.39 o.s.i (*0-553-70028-6*); audio 18.99 o.s.i (*0-553-45206-1*) Random Hse. Audio Publishing Group. (RH Audio).

—The Bourne Ultimatum. 1992. 6.99 o.p. (*0-517-08090-7*) Random Hse. Value Publishing.

### BOVARY, CHARLES (FICTITIOUS CHARACTER)—FICTION

Ch, Weir. Madame Bovary. 1948. (C). pap. text 4.50 o.p. (*0-03-009895-5*) Harcourt College Pubs.

Flaubert, Gustave. Madame Bovary. 2000. 252p. E-Book 9.95 (*0-594-03963-0*) 1873 Pr.

—Madame Bovary. 1965. (Airmont Classics Ser.). (YA). (gr. 11 up). mass mkt. 2.50 o.p. (*0-8049-0089-2*, CL-89) Airmont Publishing Co., Inc.

—Madame Bovary. unabr. ed. 1988. (Classic Books on Cassettes Ser.). audio 53.95 (*1-55685-099-9*) Audio Bk. Contractors, Inc.

—Madame Bovary. unabr. ed. 1997. (Illus.). audio 39.95 (*1-57270-056-4*, F91056u, Cover to Cover Classics) Audio Partners Publishing Corp.

—Madame Bovary. unabr. ed. audio 94.95 o.p. (*1-85549-946-0*, CTC 120) BBC Audiobooks America.

—Madame Bovary. Bair, Lowell, tr. 1982. (Bantam Classics Ser.). 448p. mass mkt. 5.95 (*0-553-21341-5*); (gr. 9-12). mass mkt. 2.50 o.s.i (*0-553-21101-3*) Bantam Bks. (Bantam Classics).

—Madame Bovary. 1985. (Barron's Book Notes Ser.). (Illus.). 122p. (YA). (gr. 10-12). pap. 3.95 (*0-8120-3524-0*) Barron's Educational Series, Inc.

—Madame Bovary. unabr. ed. 1983. audio 62.95 (*0-7861-0569-0*, 2059) Blackstone Audio Bks., Inc.

—Madame Bovary. unabr. ed. (FRE.). pap. 7.95 (*2-87714-130-6*) Bookking International FRA. *Dist:* Distribooks, Inc.

—Madame Bovary. 1983. (Illus.). 320p. reprint ed. lib. bdg. 27.95 (*0-89966-324-9*) Buccaneer Bks., Inc.

—Madame Bovary. (Early Best Sellers Ser.). reprint ed. lib. bdg. 48.00 (*0-7426-1025-X*); 2001. (Illus.). pap. text 28.00 (*0-7426-6025-7*) Classic Bks.

—Madame Bovary. Marmur, Mildred, tr. 1997. (New York Public Library Collector's Edition Ser.). (Illus.). 384p. 18.50 (*0-385-48719-3*) Doubleday Publishing.

—Madame Bovary. unabr. ed. 1996. (Thrift Editions Ser.). 256p. reprint ed. pap. 2.50 (*0-486-29257-6*) Dover Pubns., Inc.

—Madame Bovary. Aveling, Eleanor Marx, tr. 2004. (Barnes & Noble Classics Ser.). 400p. pap. 5.95 (*1-59308-052-2*) Fine Communications.

—Madame Bovary. (FRE.). 11.25 (*2-08-070464-8*, GF0086E) Flammarion et Cie FRA. *Dist:* Continental Bk. Co., Inc.

—Madame Bovary. Gothot-Mesch, ed. 1961. (FRE.). pap. 11.95 (*0-8288-9748-4*, 2266033581) French & European Pubns., Inc.

—Madame Bovary. Steegmuller, Francis, tr. l.t. ed. 1993. 499p. lib. bdg. 20.95 o.p. (*0-8161-5680-8*, Macmillan Reference USA) Gale Group.

—Madame Bovary. l.t. ed. 1999. (SPA.). 512p. 32.50 (*84-397-0569-7*) Grijalbo Mondadori, S.A.-Junior ESP. *Dist:* Continental Bk. Co., Inc.

—Madame Bovary. l.t. ed. 2000. 544p. pap. 22.00 (*0-06-095695-X*, HarperCollins) HarperTrade.

—Madame Bovary. 001. Bree, Germaine, ed. Lawrence, Merloyd, tr. 1969. (C). pap. 15.16 o.p. (*0-395-05210-6*, Riverside Editions) Houghton Mifflin Co.
—Madame Bovary. 2002. 336p. 26.99 (*1-4043-1578-0*); per. 21.99 (*1-4043-1579-9*) IndyPublish.com.
—Madame Bovary. 1989. audio 59.00 Jimcin Recordings.
—Madame Bovary. Steegmuller, Francis, tr. 1991. (Vintage Bks.). (Illus.). 432p. pap. 12.00 (*0-679-73636-0*, Vintage) Knopf Publishing Group.
—Madame Bovary. Steegmuller, Francis, tr. 1993. (Everyman's Library). (Illus.). 368p. 17.00 (*0-679-42031-2*) Knopf, Alfred A. Inc.
—Madame Bovary. 2000. 7.95 (*3-89508-252-X*, 520219) Konemann.
—Madame Bovary. Hardy, Thomas, ed. 1999. (Cloth Bound Pocket Ser.). (Illus.). 7.95 (*3-8290-3006-1*) Konemann.
—Madame Bovary. (FRE.). pap. 8.95 (*2-253-00486-3*, LP0088E) Librairie Generale Francaise, LGF FRA. *Dist:* Continental Bk. Co., Inc.
—Madame Bovary. 1982. 396p. (C). pap. 11.25 (*0-07-554378-8*, McGraw-Hill Humanities, Social Sciences & World Languages) McGraw-Hill Higher Education.
—Madame Bovary. 1972. (FRE.). (C). pap. 13.95 (*0-8442-1758-1*, VF1758-1) McGraw-Hill/ Contemporary.
—Madame Bovary. Marmur, Mildred, tr. from FRE. 2001. 408p. mass mkt. 5.95 (*0-451-52820-4*, Signet Classics) NAL.
—Madame Bovary. 1970. mass mkt. 0.50 o.p. (*0-451-50234-5*, Signet Classics); 1970. mass mkt. 0.60 o.p. (*0-451-50511-5*, Signet Classics); 1964. mass mkt. 1.50 o.p. (*0-451-51008-9*, Signet Classics); 1964. mass mkt. 2.25 o.p. (*0-451-51805-5*, Signet Classics); 1964. mass mkt. 2.50 o.p. (*0-451-51914-0*, Signet Classics); 1964. mass mkt. 2.75 o.p. (*0-451-52240-0*); 1964. mass mkt. 1.95 o.p. (*0-451-51681-8*, Signet Classics); 1964. mass mkt. 2.75 o.p. (*0-451-51487-4*, Signet Classics); 1964. mass mkt. 0.95 o.p. (*0-451-50692-8*, Signet Classics); 1964. mass mkt. 0.75 o.p. (*0-451-50592-1*, Signet Classics); 1964. mass mkt. 1.75 o.p. (*0-451-51214-6*, Signet Classics); 1964. mass mkt. 2.25 o.p. (*0-451-51365-7*, Signet Classics) NAL.
—Madame Bovary. Marmur, Mildred, tr. 1964. (Illus.). 400p. mass mkt. 5.95 o.s.i (*0-451-52387-3*, Signet Classics) NAL.
—Madame Bovary. abr. ed. 1999. (Classic Fiction Ser.). audio 22.98 (*962-634-678-7*, NA216814); audio compact disk 26.98 (*962-634-178-5*, NA417814) Naxos of America, Inc. (Naxos AudioBooks).
—Madame Bovary. abr. ed. 1994. (Classic, Ultimate, Dove Ser.). audio 19.95 o.p. (*1-55800-946-9*, 693105, Dove Audio) NewStar Media, Inc.
—Madame Bovary. 2001. (Twelve-Point Ser.). 318p. lib. bdg. 25.00 (*1-58287-151-5*); 519p. 26.00 (*1-58287-634-7*) North Bks.
—Madame Bovary. (C). pap. 15.75 (*0-393-94860-9*); 1965. (Illus.). xvi, 462p. pap. text 10.50 (*0-393-09608-4*, 9608) Norton, W. W. & Co., Inc.
—Madame Bovary. De Man, Paul, ed. & tr. by. 2nd ed. 2004. pap. (*0-393-97917-2*) Norton, W. W. & Co., Inc.
—Madame Bovary. audio 89.95 o.p. 1991. audio 59.95Pts. 1 & 2. audio 34.95Pts. 1 & 2. audio 34.95 Olivia & Hill Pr., The.
—Madame Bovary. Mauldon, Margaret, tr. 2004. (Oxford World's Classics Hardcovers Ser.). 384p. 26.00 (*0-19-280549-5*) Oxford Univ. Pr., Inc.
—Madame Bovary. 1999. (Oxford World's Classics Ser.). 400p. 15.00 (*0-19-210025-4*) Oxford Univ. Pr., Inc.
—Madame Bovary. Cave, Terence, ed. 1989. (Oxford World's Classics Ser.). 390p. pap. 6.95 o.p. (*0-19-281564-4*) Oxford Univ. Pr., Inc.
—Madame Bovary. abr. ed. 1992. (Classics on Cassette). audio 15.95 (*0-453-00784-8*) Penguin/ HighBridge.
—Madame Bovary. (FRE.). pap. 11.95 (*2-266-08314-7*) Presses Pocket FRA. *Dist:* Distribooks, Inc.
—Madame Bovary. Steegmuller, Francis, tr. 1992. 476p. 16.95 o.s.i (*0-679-60013-2*) Random Hse., Inc.
—Madame Bovary. Steegmuller, Francis, tr. & intro. by. 1952. 396p. 3.95 o.s.i (*0-394-60028-2*, T17) Random Hse., Inc.
—Madame Bovary, unabr. ed. 1989. audio 78.00 (*1-55690-328-6*, 89393E7) Recorded Bks., LLC.
—Madame Bovary. Brombert, Victor, ed. 1985. (ENG & FRE.). 440p. 6.95 (*0-88332-467-9*) Schoenhof's Foreign Bks., Inc.
—Madame Bovary. 1976. (Folio Ser.: No. 804). (FRE.). pap. 10.95 (*2-07-036804-1*) Schoenhof's Foreign Bks., Inc.
—Madame Bovary. audio Spoken Arts, Inc.
—Madame Bovary. 2003. 28.95 (*0-7862-5602-8*) Thorndike Pr.
—Madame Bovary. 1964. 12.00 (*0-606-00911-6*) Turtleback Bks.
—Madame Bovary. 2001. 185p. pap. 9.95 (*1-57002-154-6*) University Publishing Hse., Inc.
—Madame Bovary. 2002. 384p. pap. 10.00 (*0-14-044912-4*, Penguin Classics) Viking Penguin.
—Madame Bovary. Wall, Geoffrey, tr. & intro. by. 1993. (Penguin Classics Ser.). (Illus.). 320p. pap. 10.00 o.s.i (*0-14-044526-9*, Penguin Classics) Viking Penguin.
—Madame Bovary. Russell, Alan, tr. 1951. (Penguin Classics Ser.). 368p. pap. 3.95 o.p. (*0-14-044015-1*, Penguin Classics) Viking Penguin.
—Madame Bovary. 1998. (Classics Library). (Illus.). 288p. pap. 3.95 (*1-85326-078-9*, 0789WW) Wordsworth Editions, Ltd. GBR. *Dist:* Casemate Pubs. & Bk. Distributors, LLC.
—Madame Bovary. 2000. (SPA.). 420p. pap. 18.95 (*1-58348-813-8*) iUniverse, Inc.
—Madame Bovary Level 4. (FRE.). 7.25 (*2-09-031993-3*, CL9933E) Cle International FRA. *Dist:* Continental Bk. Co., Inc.
—Madame Bovary Level 4. 1998. (Oxford World's Classics Ser.). 400p. pap. 8.95 (*0-19-283399-5*) Oxford Univ. Pr., Inc.
Flaubert, Gustave, et al. Madame Bovary. 1998. E-Book 8.35 (*0-585-36395-1*) netLibrary, Inc.

## BOVARY, EMMA (FICTITIOUS CHARACTER)—FICTION

Ch, Weir. Madame Bovary. 1948. (C). pap. text 4.50 o.p. (*0-03-009895-5*) Harcourt College Pubs.
Flaubert, Gustave. Madame Bovary. 2000. 252p. E-Book 9.95 (*0-594-03963-0*) 1873 Pr.
—Madame Bovary. 1965. (Airmont Classics Ser.). (YA). (gr. 11 up). mass mkt. 2.50 o.p. (*0-8049-0089-2*, CL-89) Airmont Publishing Co., Inc.
—Madame Bovary. unabr. ed. 1988. (Classic Books on Cassettes Ser.). audio 53.95 (*1-55685-099-9*) Audio Bk. Contractors, Inc.
—Madame Bovary. unabr. ed. 1997. (Illus.). audio 39.95 (*1-57270-056-4*, F91056u, Cover to Cover Classics) Audio Partners Publishing Corp.
—Madame Bovary. unabr. ed. audio 94.95 o.p. (*1-85549-946-0*, CTC 120) BBC Audiobooks America.
—Madame Bovary. Bair, Lowell, tr. 1982. (Bantam Classics Ser.). 448p. mass mkt. 5.95 (*0-553-21341-5*); (gr. 9-12). mass mkt. 2.50 o.s.i (*0-553-21101-3*) Bantam Bks. (Bantam Classics).
—Madame Bovary. 1985. (Barron's Book Notes Ser.). (Illus.). 122p. (YA). (gr. 10-12). pap. 3.95 (*0-8120-3524-0*) Barron's Educational Series, Inc.
—Madame Bovary. unabr. ed. 1983. audio 62.95 (*0-7861-0569-0*, 2059) Blackstone Audio Bks., Inc.
—Madame Bovary. unabr. ed. (FRE.). pap. 7.95 (*2-87714-130-6*) Bookking International FRA. *Dist:* Distribooks, Inc.
—Madame Bovary. 1983. (Illus.). 320p. reprint ed. lib. bdg. 27.95 (*0-89966-324-9*) Buccaneer Bks., Inc.
—Madame Bovary. (Early Best Sellers Ser.). reprint ed. lib. bdg. 48.00 (*0-7426-1025-X*); 2001. (Illus.). pap. text 28.00 (*0-7426-6025-7*) Classic Bks.
—Madame Bovary. Marmur, Mildred, tr. 1997. (New York Public Library Collector's Edition Ser.). (Illus.). 384p. 18.50 (*0-385-48719-3*) Doubleday Publishing.
—Madame Bovary. unabr. ed. 1996. (Thrift Editions Ser.). 256p. reprint ed. pap. 2.50 (*0-486-29257-6*) Dover Pubns., Inc.
—Madame Bovary. Aveling, Eleanor Marx, tr. 2004. (Barnes & Noble Classics Ser.). 400p. pap. 5.95 (*1-59308-052-2*) Fine Communications.
—Madame Bovary. (FRE.). 11.25 (*2-08-070464-8*, GF0086E) Flammarion et Cie FRA. *Dist:* Continental Bk. Co., Inc.
—Madame Bovary. Gothot-Mesch, ed. 1961. (FRE.). pap. 11.95 (*0-8288-9748-4*, 2266033581) French & European Pubns., Inc.
—Madame Bovary. Steegmuller, Francis, tr. l.t. ed. 1993. 499p. lib. bdg. 20.95 o.p. (*0-8161-5680-8*, Macmillan Reference USA) Gale Group.
—Madame Bovary. l.t. ed. 1999. (SPA.). 512p. 32.50 (*84-397-0569-7*) Grijalbo Mondadori, S.A.-Junior ESP. *Dist:* Continental Bk. Co., Inc.
—Madame Bovary. l.t. ed. 2000. 544p. pap. 22.00 (*0-06-095695-X*, HarperCollins) HarperTrade.
—Madame Bovary, 001. Bree, Germaine, ed. Lawrence, Merloyd, tr. 1969. (C). pap. 15.16 o.p. (*0-395-05210-6*, Riverside Editions) Houghton Mifflin Co.
—Madame Bovary. 2002. 336p. 26.99 (*1-4043-1578-0*); per. 21.99 (*1-4043-1579-9*) IndyPublish.com.
—Madame Bovary. 1989. audio 59.00 Jimcin Recordings.
—Madame Bovary. Steegmuller, Francis, tr. 1991. (Vintage Bks.). (Illus.). 432p. pap. 12.00 (*0-679-73636-0*, Vintage) Knopf Publishing Group.
—Madame Bovary. Steegmuller, Francis, tr. 1993. (Everyman's Library). (Illus.). 368p. 17.00 (*0-679-42031-2*) Knopf, Alfred A. Inc.
—Madame Bovary. 2000. 7.95 (*3-89508-252-X*, 520219) Konemann.
—Madame Bovary. Hardy, Thomas, ed. 1999. (Cloth Bound Pocket Ser.). (Illus.). 7.95 (*3-8290-3006-1*) Konemann.
—Madame Bovary. (FRE.). pap. 8.95 (*2-253-00486-3*, LP0088E) Librairie Generale Francaise, LGF FRA. *Dist:* Continental Bk. Co., Inc.
—Madame Bovary. 1982. 396p. (C). pap. 11.25 (*0-07-554378-8*, McGraw-Hill Humanities, Social Sciences & World Languages) McGraw-Hill Higher Education.
—Madame Bovary. 1972. (FRE.). (C). pap. 13.95 (*0-8442-1758-1*, VF1758-1) McGraw-Hill/ Contemporary.
—Madame Bovary. Marmur, Mildred, tr. from FRE. 2001. 408p. mass mkt. 5.95 (*0-451-52820-4*, Signet Classics) NAL.
—Madame Bovary. 1970. mass mkt. 0.60 o.p. (*0-451-50511-5*, Signet Classics); 1970. mass mkt. 0.50 o.p. (*0-451-50234-5*, Signet Classics); 1964. mass mkt. 1.75 o.p. (*0-451-51214-6*, Signet Classics); 1964. mass mkt. 1.50 o.p. (*0-451-51008-9*, Signet Classics); 1964. mass mkt. 0.95 o.p. (*0-451-50692-8*, Signet Classics); 1964. mass mkt. 0.75 o.p. (*0-451-50592-1*, Signet Classics); 1964. mass mkt. 2.25 o.p. (*0-451-51365-7*, Signet Classics); 1964. mass mkt. 2.50 o.p. (*0-451-51914-0*, Signet Classics); 1964. mass mkt. 2.25 o.p. (*0-451-51805-5*, Signet Classics); 1964. mass mkt. 2.75 o.p. (*0-451-52240-0*); 1964. mass mkt. 1.95 o.p. (*0-451-51681-8*, Signet Classics); 1964. mass mkt. 2.75 o.p. (*0-451-51487-4*, Signet Classics) NAL.
—Madame Bovary. Marmur, Mildred, tr. 1964. (Illus.). 400p. mass mkt. 5.95 o.s.i (*0-451-52387-3*, Signet Classics) NAL.
—Madame Bovary. abr. ed. 1999. (Classic Fiction Ser.). audio 22.98 (*962-634-678-7*, NA216814); audio compact disk 26.98 (*962-634-178-5*, NA417814) Naxos of America, Inc. (Naxos AudioBooks).
—Madame Bovary. abr. ed. 1994. (Classic, Ultimate, Dove Ser.). audio 19.95 o.p. (*1-55800-946-9*, 693105, Dove Audio) NewStar Media, Inc.
—Madame Bovary. 2001. (Twelve-Point Ser.). 318p. lib. bdg. 25.00 (*1-58287-151-5*); 519p. 26.00 (*1-58287-634-7*) North Bks.
—Madame Bovary. (C). pap. 15.75 (*0-393-94860-9*); 1965. (Illus.). xvi, 462p. pap. text 10.50 (*0-393-09608-4*, 9608) Norton, W. W. & Co., Inc.
—Madame Bovary. De Man, Paul, ed. & tr. by. 2nd ed. 2004. pap. (*0-393-97917-2*) Norton, W. W. & Co., Inc.
—Madame Bovary. audio 89.95 o.p. 1991. audio 59.95Pts. 1 & 2. audio 34.95Pts. 1 & 2. audio 34.95 Olivia & Hill Pr., The.
—Madame Bovary. Mauldon, Margaret, tr. 2004. (Oxford World's Classics Hardcovers Ser.). 384p. 26.00 (*0-19-280549-5*) Oxford Univ. Pr., Inc.
—Madame Bovary. 1999. (Oxford World's Classics Ser.). 400p. 15.00 (*0-19-210025-4*) Oxford Univ. Pr., Inc.
—Madame Bovary. Cave, Terence, ed. 1989. (Oxford World's Classics Ser.). 390p. pap. 6.95 o.p. (*0-19-281564-4*) Oxford Univ. Pr., Inc.
—Madame Bovary. abr. ed. 1992. (Classics on Cassette). audio 15.95 (*0-453-00784-8*) Penguin/ HighBridge.
—Madame Bovary. (FRE.). pap. 11.95 (*2-266-08314-7*) Presses Pocket FRA. *Dist:* Distribooks, Inc.
—Madame Bovary. Steegmuller, Francis, tr. 1992. 476p. 16.95 o.s.i (*0-679-60013-2*) Random Hse., Inc.
—Madame Bovary. Steegmuller, Francis, tr. & intro. by. 1952. 396p. 3.95 o.s.i (*0-394-60028-2*, T17) Random Hse., Inc.
—Madame Bovary, unabr. ed. 1989. audio 78.00 (*1-55690-328-6*, 89393E7) Recorded Bks., LLC.
—Madame Bovary. Brombert, Victor, ed. 1985. (ENG & FRE.). 440p. 6.95 (*0-88332-467-9*) Schoenhof's Foreign Bks., Inc.
—Madame Bovary. 1976. (Folio Ser.: No. 804). (FRE.). pap. 10.95 (*2-07-036804-1*) Schoenhof's Foreign Bks., Inc.
—Madame Bovary. audio Spoken Arts, Inc.
—Madame Bovary. 2003. 28.95 (*0-7862-5602-8*) Thorndike Pr.
—Madame Bovary. 1964. 12.00 (*0-606-00911-6*) Turtleback Bks.
—Madame Bovary. 2001. 185p. pap. 9.95 (*1-57002-154-6*) University Publishing Hse., Inc.
—Madame Bovary. 2002. 384p. pap. 10.00 (*0-14-044912-4*, Penguin Classics) Viking Penguin.
—Madame Bovary. Wall, Geoffrey, tr. & intro. by. 1993. (Penguin Classics Ser.). (Illus.). 320p. pap. 10.00 o.s.i (*0-14-044526-9*, Penguin Classics) Viking Penguin.
—Madame Bovary. Russell, Alan, tr. 1951. (Penguin Classics Ser.). 368p. pap. 3.95 o.p. (*0-14-044015-1*, Penguin Classics) Viking Penguin.
—Madame Bovary. 1998. (Classics Library). (Illus.). 288p. pap. 3.95 (*1-85326-078-9*, 0789WW) Wordsworth Editions, Ltd. GBR. *Dist:* Casemate Pubs. & Bk. Distributors, LLC.
—Madame Bovary. 2000. (SPA.). 420p. pap. 18.95 (*1-58348-813-8*) iUniverse, Inc.
—Madame Bovary Level 4. (FRE.). 7.25 (*2-09-031993-3*, CL9933E) Cle International FRA. *Dist:* Continental Bk. Co., Inc.
—Madame Bovary Level 4. 1998. (Oxford World's Classics Ser.). 400p. pap. 8.95 (*0-19-283399-5*) Oxford Univ. Pr., Inc.
Flaubert, Gustave, et al. Madame Bovary. 1998. E-Book 8.35 (*0-585-36395-1*) netLibrary, Inc.

## BOWDRE, MO (FICTITIOUS CHARACTER)—FICTION

Page, Jake. A Certain Malice. 1997. mass mkt. 6.99 (*0-345-40539-0*) Ballantine Bks.
—The Deadly Canyon. 1994. 240p. 20.00 o.s.i (*0-345-37930-6*) Ballantine Bks.
—The Deadly Canyon. unabr. ed. 1994. audio 57.25 o.p. (*1-56100-168-6*, 859, Unabridged Library Editions); audio 21.95 o.p. (*1-56100-540-1*, 86, Bookcassette) Brilliance Audio.
—The Deadly Canyon. 1995. 272p. mass mkt. 4.99 o.s.i (*0-345-37931-4*, House of Collectibles) Random Hse. Information Group.
—The Deadly Canyon. 2002. (Illus.). 228p. pap. 13.95 (*0-8263-2861-X*) Univ. of New Mexico Pr.
—The Knotted Strings. 1995. mass mkt. 5.99 o.s.i (*0-345-38783-X*); 256p. 20.00 o.s.i (*0-345-38782-1*) Ballantine Bks.
—The Knotted Strings. abr. ed. 1995. audio 16.95 o.p. (*1-56100-406-5*, 1318, Nova Audio Bks.); audio 57.25 o.p. (*1-56100-238-0*, 921, Unabridged Library Editions); audio 23.95 o.p. (*1-56100-613-0*, 156, Bookcassette) Brilliance Audio.
—The Knotted Strings. abr. ed. 2000. audio 7.95 (*1-57815-016-7*, 1040, Media Bks. Audio Publishing) Media Bks., L. L. C.
—The Knotted Strings. 2003. 256p. pap. 13.95 (*0-8263-2862-8*) Univ. of New Mexico Pr.
—The Lethal Partner. 1996. 293p. mass mkt. 5.99 o.s.i (*0-345-38785-6*); 240p. 21.00 o.s.i (*0-345-38784-8*) Ballantine Bks.
—The Lethal Partner. unabr. ed. 1997. audio 48.00 (*0-913369-64-0*, 4305) Books on Tape, Inc.
—The Lethal Partner. 2003. 246p. pap. 13.95 (*0-8263-2863-6*) Univ. of New Mexico Pr.
—The Stolen Gods. (Southwest Mysteries Ser.). 1994. 272p. mass mkt. 4.99 o.s.i (*0-345-37929-2*); 1993. 256p. 19.00 o.s.i (*0-345-37928-4*) Ballantine Bks.
—The Stolen Gods. 2002. 260p. pap. 13.95 (*0-8263-2860-1*) Univ. of New Mexico Pr.

## BOWDRIE, CHICK (FICTITIOUS CHARACTER)—FICTION

L'Amour, Louis. Bowdrie. 1990. 192p. mass mkt. 4.50 (*0-553-28106-2*); 1983. mass mkt. 2.95 o.s.i (*0-553-23368-8*) Bantam Bks.
—Bowdrie. l.t. ed. 1984. (General Ser.). lib. bdg. 12.95 o.p. (*0-8161-3660-2*, Macmillan Reference USA) Gale Group.
—Bowdrie Follows a Cold Trail. 1992. audio 7.99 o.s.i (*0-553-70001-4*); 2003. audio 9.99 (*0-553-47053-1*) Random Hse. Audio Publishing Group. (RH Audio).
—Bowdrie Passes Through. 1988. audio 7.99 o.s.i (*0-553-70002-2*); audio 9.99 o.s.i (*0-553-45124-3*) Random Hse. Audio Publishing Group. (RH Audio).
—Bowdrie's Law. 1984. 224p. mass mkt. 4.50 (*0-553-24550-3*) Bantam Bks.
—Bowdrie's Law. l.t. ed. 1985. 13.95 o.p. (*0-8161-3878-8*, Macmillan Reference USA) Gale Group.
—Case Closed - No Prisoners. abr. ed. 1987. audio 9.99 o.s.i (*0-553-45060-3*, RH Audio) Random Hse. Audio Publishing Group.
—Chick Bowdrie. abr. ed. 1990. 21.99 o.s.i incl. audio (*0-553-45193-6*, RH Audio) Random Hse. Audio Publishing Group.
—Down Sonora Way. abr. ed. 1994. audio 9.99 o.s.i (*0-553-47286-0*); audio 9.98 o.s.i (*0-553-74621-9*) Random Hse. Audio Publishing Group. (RH Audio).
—More Brains Than Bullets. abr. ed. 1996. audio 9.99 o.s.i (*0-553-47186-4*, RH Audio) Random Hse. Audio Publishing Group.
—The Outlaws of Poplar Creek. 1993. audio 7.99 o.s.i (*0-553-70052-9*); audio 9.99 o.s.i (*0-553-47184-8*) Random Hse. Audio Publishing Group. (RH Audio).
—Rain on the Mountain Fork. 1993. audio 7.99 o.s.i (*0-553-70051-0*); 2001. audio 9.99 (*0-553-47149-X*) Random Hse. Audio Publishing Group. (RH Audio).
—A Ranger Rides for Justice. abr. ed. 1993. 23.99 o.s.i incl. audio (*0-553-47168-6*, RH Audio) Random Hse. Audio Publishing Group.
—A Ranger Rides to Town. abr. ed. 2004. audio 7.99 (*0-553-45219-3*, RH Audio) Random Hse. Audio Publishing Group.
—The Road to Casa Piedras. abr. ed. 1990. (Bowdrie's Law Collection). audio 9.99 (*0-553-45239-8*, RH Audio) Random Hse. Audio Publishing Group.

Characters

—South of Deadwood. abr. ed. 1986. audio 9.99 (*0-553-45021-2*, 395502, RH Audio) Random Hse. Audio Publishing Group.
—Strawhouse Trail. abr. ed. 1997. audio 9.99 o.s.i (*0-553-47869-9*, 394643, RH Audio) Random Hse. Audio Publishing Group.
—Too Tough to Brand. 1989. audio 7.99 o.s.i (*0-553-70015-4*); 1999. audio 9.99 (*0-553-45161-8*) Random Hse. Audio Publishing Group. (RH Audio).
—A Trail to the West. abr. ed. 1986. audio 9.99 o.s.i (*0-553-45009-3*, RH Audio) Random Hse. Audio Publishing Group.
—Where Buzzards Fly: A Chick Bowdrie Story. abr. ed. 1986. audio 9.99 o.s.i (*0-553-45015-8*, RH Audio) Random Hse. Audio Publishing Group.

**BOWERING, VICTORIA (FICTITIOUS CHARACTER)—FICTION**

Yeager, Dorian. Cancellation by Death. 1994. (WWL Mystery Ser.). per. (*0-373-26159-4*, 1-26159-3, Harlequin Bks.) Harlequin Enterprises, Ltd.
—Cancellation by Death. 1992. 240p. 17.95 o.p. (*0-312-08152-9*, Saint Martin's Minotaur) St. Martin's Pr.
—Eviction by Death. 1995. per. (*0-373-26176-4*, Harlequin Bks.) Harlequin Enterprises, Ltd.
—Eviction by Death: A Victoria Bowering Mystery. 1993. 192p. 17.95 o.p. (*0-312-09803-0*, Saint Martin's Minotaur) St. Martin's Pr.
—Libation by Death. 1998. (Vic Bowering Mystery Ser.). 240p. 21.95 (*0-312-18128-0*, 874692, Saint Martin's Minotaur) St. Martin's Pr.
—Ovation by Death. 1996. 208p. 20.95 o.p. (*0-312-14022-3*, Saint Martin's Minotaur) St. Martin's Pr.

**BOWLES, SALLY (FICTITIOUS CHARACTER)—FICTION**

Isherwood, Christopher. The Berlin of Sally Bowles. 1975. 583 p. (*0-7012-0407-9*) Hogarth Pr., The.

**BOWMAN FAMILY (FICTITIOUS CHARACTERS)—FICTION**

Eastlake, William. The Bronc People. 1991. 254p. pap. 11.00 o.p. (*0-9627387-5-1*) Bamberger Bks.
—The Bronc People. 1975. (Zia Bks.). 263p. reprint ed. pap. 8.95 o.p. (*0-8263-0379-X*) Univ. of New Mexico Pr.
—Go in Beauty. 1991. 279p. pap. 11.00 o.p. (*0-9627387-3-5*) Bamberger Bks.
—Go in Beauty. 1980. (Zia Bks.). 286p. pap. 8.95 o.p. (*0-8263-0538-5*) Univ. of New Mexico Pr.
—Lyric of the Circle Heart: The Bowman Family Trilogy. rev. ed. 1996. 518p. pap. 14.95 (*1-56478-136-4*) Dalkey Archive Pr.
—Portrait of an Artist with Twenty-Six Horses. 1991. 221p. pap. 11.00 o.p. (*0-9627387-4-3*) Bamberger Bks.
—Portrait of an Artist with Twenty-Six Horses. 1980. (Zia Bks.). 230p. reprint ed. pap. 8.95 o.p. (*0-8263-0558-X*) Univ. of New Mexico Pr.

**BOYD, KEMPER (FICTITIOUS CHARACTER)—FICTION**

Ellroy, James. American Tabloid: A Novel. 1997. 592p. pap. 12.00 o.s.i (*0-449-00090-7*, Fawcett); 1996. mass mkt. o.p. (*0-449-22454-6*, Fawcett); 1995. 544p. mass mkt. 6.99 o.s.i (*0-8041-1449-8*, Ivy Bks.) Ballantine Bks.
—American Tabloid: A Novel. unabr. collector's ed. 1996. audio 112.00 (*0-7366-3279-4*, 3935) Books on Tape, Inc.

**BOYD, ORIN (FICTITIOUS CHARACTER)—FICTION**

Westermann, John. Exit Wounds. McCarthy, Paul, ed. 1991. 320p. reprint ed. mass mkt. 5.99 (*0-671-72935-7*, Pocket) Simon & Schuster.
—Exit Wounds. 2000. 304p. pap. 12.00 (*1-56947-223-8*); 1989. 273p. 18.95 o.p. (*0-939149-27-3*) Soho Pr., Inc.
—The Honor Farm. 2000. 320p. pap. 6.99 (*0-671-87126-9*, Pocket Star); 1997. (Illus.). 368p. pap. 6.99 (*0-671-87123-4*, Pocket); 1996. 320p. 22.00 o.p. (*0-671-87122-6*, Atria) Simon & Schuster.

**BOYNTON, LEE (FICTITIOUS CHARACTER)—FICTION**

Thomas, Michael M. Black Money. abr. ed. 1994. audio 16.95 o.p. (*1-55927-285-6*) Audio Renaissance.
—Black Money. 1994. 309p. 22.00 o.s.i (*0-517-59523-0*) Crown Publishing Group.
—Black Money. 1995. 343p. pap. text 6.50 o.p. (*0-312-95680-0*, St. Martin's Paperbacks) St. Martin's Pr.

**BRACEWELL, NICHOLAS (FICTITIOUS CHARACTER)—FICTION**

Marston, Edward. The Bawdy Basket. 2002. (An Elizabethan Theater Mystery Featuring Nicholas Bracewell Ser.). 288p. 23.95 (*0-312-28501-9*, Saint Martin's Minotaur) St. Martin's Pr.
—The Devil's Apprentice: An Elizabethan Theater Mystery Featuring Nicholas Bracewell. 2001. 288p. 23.95 (*0-312-26574-3*, Saint Martin's Minotaur) St. Martin's Pr.
—The Fair Maid of Bohemia: A Novel. 2002. 271p. pap. 14.95 o.s.i (*1-59058-005-2*) Poisoned Pen Pr.
—The Fair Maid of Bohemia: A Novel. 1997. 229p. 21.95 o.p. (*0-312-15606-5*, Saint Martin's Minotaur) St. Martin's Pr.
—The Laughing Hangman. 2002. (Missing Mystery Ser.: Vol. 50). 200p. pap. 14.95 o.s.i (*1-59058-023-0*) Poisoned Pen Pr.
—The Laughing Hangman. 1996. 320p. 21.95 o.p. (*0-312-14305-2*, Saint Martin's Minotaur) St. Martin's Pr.
—The Mad Courtesan. 1994. reprint ed. mass mkt. 4.99 o.s.i (*0-449-22246-2*, Fawcett) Ballantine Bks.
—The Mad Courtesan. 1992. 240p. 18.95 o.p. (*0-312-08259-2*, Saint Martin's Minotaur) St. Martin's Pr.
—The Merry Devils. 1991. (Elizabethan Mystery Ser.). 240p. mass mkt. 3.95 o.s.i (*0-449-21880-5*, Fawcett) Ballantine Bks.
—The Merry Devils. 1990. mass mkt. o.s.i (*0-552-13293-4*, Corgi) Bantam Bks.
—The Merry Devils. 2001. (Missing Mystery Ser.: Vol. 30). 200p. pap. 14.95 o.s.i (*1-890208-55-8*) Poisoned Pen Pr.
—The Merry Devils. 1989. 240p. 16.95 o.p. (*0-312-03863-1*, Saint Martin's Minotaur) St. Martin's Pr.
—The Nine Giants. 1993. mass mkt. 4.50 o.s.i (*0-449-22128-8*, Fawcett) Ballantine Bks.
—The Nine Giants. 1991. 224p. 17.95 o.p. (*0-312-06426-8*, Saint Martin's Minotaur) St. Martin's Pr.
—The Queen's Head. 1990. 224p. mass mkt. 3.95 o.s.i (*0-449-21791-4*, Fawcett) Ballantine Bks.
—The Queen's Head. 1989. mass mkt. o.s.i (*0-552-13292-6*, Corgi) Bantam Bks.
—The Queen's Head. 2000. (Missing Mysteries Ser.: No. 19). 300p. pap. 14.95 (*1-890208-45-0*) Poisoned Pen Pr.
—The Queen's Head. 1989. 16.95 o.p. (*0-312-02970-5*, Saint Martin's Minotaur) St. Martin's Pr.
—The Roaring Boy. 1996. 296p. mass mkt. 5.99 o.s.i (*0-449-22431-7*, Fawcett) Ballantine Bks.
—The Roaring Boy. 2002. 250p. pap. 14.95 o.s.i (*1-59058-001-X*) Poisoned Pen Pr.
—The Roaring Boy. 1995. 272p. 14.99 o.p. (*0-312-13155-0*, Saint Martin's Minotaur) St. Martin's Pr.
—The Silent Woman. 1995. mass mkt. 5.99 o.s.i (*0-449-22375-2*, Fawcett) Ballantine Bks.
—The Silent Woman. 2002. 240p. pap. 14.95 o.s.i (*1-59058-000-1*) Poisoned Pen Pr.
—The Silent Woman. 1994. 320p. 21.95 o.p. (*0-312-11115-0*, Saint Martin's Minotaur) St. Martin's Pr.
—The Trip to Jerusalem: An Elizabethan Whodunit. 1991. 240p. mass mkt. 3.99 o.s.i (*0-449-21987-9*, Fawcett) Ballantine Bks.
—The Trip to Jerusalem: An Elizabethan Whodunit. 1991. mass mkt. o.s.i (*0-552-13294-2*, Corgi) Bantam Bks.
—The Trip to Jerusalem: An Elizabethan Whodunit. 2001. (Missing Mystery Ser.: Vol. 32). 200p. pap. 14.95 o.s.i (*1-890208-60-4*) Poisoned Pen Pr.
—The Trip to Jerusalem: An Elizabethan Whodunit. 1990. 224p. 15.95 o.p. (*0-312-05174-3*, Saint Martin's Minotaur) St. Martin's Pr.
—The Vagabond Clown: An Elizabethan Theater Mystery Featuring Nicholas Bracewell. Date not set. pap. (*0-312-30790-X*, Saint Martin's Griffin); mass mkt. (*0-312-98612-2*, St. Martin's Paperbacks); E-Book (*0-312-70591-3*); 2003. 352p. 24.95 (*0-312-30789-6*, Saint Martin's Minotaur) St. Martin's Pr.
—The Wanton Angel. 2nd ed. 1999. 288p. 23.95 (*0-312-20391-8*, Saint Martin's Minotaur) St. Martin's Pr.

**BRADDOCK, DUANE (FICTITIOUS CHARACTER)—FICTION**

Bodine, Jack. Apache Moon. 1993. (Pecos Kid Ser.: No. 3). 304p. mass mkt. 3.50 o.p. (*0-06-100620-3*, HarperTorch) Morrow/Avon.
—Apache Moon. l.t. ed. 2002. (Pecos Kid Ser.). 25.95 (*0-7862-3832-1*) Thorndike Pr.
—Bad to the Bone. 1994. (Pecos Kid Ser.: No. 6). 256p. mass mkt. 3.50 o.p. (*0-06-100657-2*, HarperTorch) Morrow/Avon.
—Bad to the Bone: Western Series. l.t. ed. 2003. (Pecos Kid Ser.). 25.95 (*0-7862-3860-7*) Thorndike Pr.
—Beginner's Luck. 1992. (Pecos Kid Ser.: No. 1). 272p. mass mkt. 3.50 o.p. (*0-06-100508-8*, HarperTorch) Morrow/Avon.
—Beginner's Luck: Pecos Kid. l.t. ed. 2002. (Thorndike Western Ser.). 342p. 25.95 (*0-7862-3831-3*) Gale Group.
—Devil's Creek Massacre. l.t. ed. 2003. 312p. 25.95 (*0-7862-3830-5*) Thorndike Pr.
—Outlaw Hell. l.t. ed. 2002. (Pecos Kid Ser.). 24.95 (*0-7862-3829-1*) Thorndike Pr.
—The Reckoning. 1993. (Pecos Kid Ser.: No. 02). 288p. mass mkt. 3.50 o.p. (*0-06-100586-X*, HarperTorch) Morrow/Avon.
—The Reckoning: The Pecos Kid. l.t. ed. 2002. (Western Ser.). 335p. 25.95 (*0-7862-3828-3*) Thorndike Pr.

**BRADDOCK, SIMON (FICTITIOUS CHARACTER)—FICTION**

Doster, Paul. Mind Set. 1997. 416p. mass mkt. 5.99 o.s.i (*0-451-19042-4*, Signet Bks.) NAL.

**BRADFORD, BEN (FICTITIOUS CHARACTER)—FICTION**

Kennedy, Douglas. The Big Picture. unabr. collector's ed. 1998. audio 72.00 (*0-7366-4078-9*, 4587) Books on Tape, Inc.
—The Big Picture. l.t. ed. 1997. (Wheeler Large Print Book Ser.). 491p. 27.95 (*1-56895-459-X*, Wheeler Publishing, Inc.) Gale Group.
—The Big Picture. 1998. 496p. mass mkt. 6.99 o.p. (*0-7868-8937-3*); 1997. 374p. 23.95 o.p. (*0-7868-6298-X*) Hyperion Pr.
—The Big Picture. abr. ed. 1990. audio 24.00 (*0-671-57564-3*, 495078, Simon & Schuster Audioworks) Simon & Schuster Audio.

**BRADFORD, ELIOT (FICTITIOUS CHARACTER)—FICTION**

Washburn, James. The Piedmont Conspiracy. 1996. 19.95 (*1-56833-075-8*) Madison Bks., Inc.

**BRADFORD, MAGGIE (FICTITIOUS CHARACTER)—FICTION**

Patterson, James. Hide & Seek. unabr. ed. 1996. audio 48.00 (*0-7366-3379-0*, 4029) Books on Tape, Inc.
—Hide & Seek. l.t. ed. 1996. 26.95 o.p. (*1-56895-345-3*, Wheeler Publishing, Inc.) Gale Group.
—Hide & Seek. 1995. 368p. 23.95 (*0-316-69386-3*) Little Brown & Co.
—Hide & Seek. unabr. ed. 1996. audio 51.00 (*0-7887-0518-0*, 94713E7) Recorded Bks., LLC.
—Hide & Seek. abr. ed. 1996. (gr. 8 up). audio 17.00 (*1-57042-383-0*, 393394) Time Warner AudioBooks.
—Hide & Seek. 1996. 464p. reprint ed. mass mkt. 7.99 (*0-446-60371-6*) Warner Bks., Inc.

**BRADLEY, BEATRICE LESTRANGE (FICTITIOUS CHARACTER)—FICTION**

Mitchell, Gladys. Cold, Lone & Still. l.t. ed. 1987. (Nightingale Paperbacks Ser.). 304p. 11.95 o.p. (*0-8161-4374-9*, Macmillan Reference USA) Gale Group.
—The Dancing Druids. 1986. 239p. 14.95 o.p. (*0-312-18207-4*) St. Martin's Pr.
—Death at the Opera. 1992. 248p. reprint ed. 14.95 o.p. (*0-86220-835-1*, Black Dagger) BBC Audiobooks America.
—The Death-Cap Dancers. (Fingerprint Mysteries Ser.). 192p. 1983. pap. 5.95 o.p. (*0-312-18609-6*, Saint Martin's Griffin); 1981. 9.95 o.p. (*0-312-18608-8*) St. Martin's Pr.
—Faintley Speaking. 1986. 224p. 14.95 o.p. (*0-312-27957-4*) St. Martin's Pr.
—Here Lies Gloria Mundy. 1983. 192p. 9.95 o.p. (*0-312-36986-7*) St. Martin's Pr.
—Late, Late in the Evening. 1995. 192p. reprint ed. 19.00 o.p. (*0-7278-4793-7*) Severn Hse. Pubs., Ltd.
—Late, Late in the Evening. l.t. ed. 1996. (Linford Mystery Library). 400p. pap. 17.99 o.p. (*0-7089-7941-6*, Ulverscroft) Thorpe, F. A. Pubs. GBR. *Dist:* Ulverscroft Large Print Bks., Ltd., Ulverscroft Large Print Canada, Ltd.
—No Winding-Sheet. l.t. ed. 1989. (Popular Ser.). lib. bdg. 11.95 o.p. (*1-85057-319-0*, Macmillan Reference USA) Gale Group.
—The Rising of the Moon. 1984. 11.95 o.p. (*0-312-68442-8*) St. Martin's Pr.
—Speedy Death. 1999. 21.95 (*0-7540-8547-3*, Black Dagger) BBC Audiobooks America.
—Spotted Hemlock: A Murder Mystery. 1985. 240p. 14.95 o.p. (*0-312-75350-0*) St. Martin's Pr.
—St. Peter's Finger. 1986. 352p. 15.95 (*0-312-00192-4*) St. Martin's Pr.
—Three Quick & Five Dead, Set. unabr. ed. 1999. audio 47.95 (*1-86015-418-2*) Beeler, Thomas T. Publisher.
—Uncoffin'd Clay. 1982. 189p. 9.95 o.p. (*0-312-82857-8*) St. Martin's Pr.
—Watson's Choice. 1976. 6.95 o.p. (*0-679-50658-6*) McKay, David Co., Inc.
—Winking at the Brim. 1977. (McKay-Washburn Mystery Ser.). 6.95 o.p. (*0-679-50732-9*) McKay, David Co., Inc.

**BRADLEY, BO (FICTITIOUS CHARACTER)—FICTION**

Padgett, Abigail. Child of Silence. 1993. 208p. 17.95 (*0-89296-488-X*) Mysterious Pr.
—Child of Silence. 1994. 208p. mass mkt. 5.99 o.p. (*0-446-40184-6*, Mysterious Pr. Paperback Bks.) Warner Bks., Inc.
—The Dollmaker's Daughters. (Bo Bradley Mystery Ser.). 1998. 320p. mass mkt. 6.50 (*0-446-40536-1*); 1997. 288p. 22.00 o.p. (*0-89296-614-9*) Warner Bks., Inc.
—Moonbird Boy. 1996. 82p. 21.95 o.s.i (*0-89296-613-0*) Mysterious Pr.
—Moonbird Boy. 1997. 256p. mass mkt. 5.99 o.p. (*0-446-40513-2*, Mysterious Pr. Paperback Bks.) Warner Bks., Inc.
—Strawgirl. 1994. 256p. 18.95 o.s.i (*0-89296-489-8*) Mysterious Pr.
—Strawgirl. 1995. 240p. mass mkt. 5.50 o.p. (*0-446-40199-4*, Mysterious Pr. Paperback Bks.) Warner Bks., Inc.
—Turtle Baby. 1995. 288p. 19.95 o.s.i (*0-89296-580-0*) Mysterious Pr.
—Turtle Baby. l.t. ed. 1996. (Large Print Ser.). 496p. 29.99 o.p. (*0-7089-3560-5*, Ulverscroft) Thorpe, F. A. Pubs. GBR. *Dist:* Ulverscroft Large Print Bks., Ltd., Ulverscroft Large Print Canada, Ltd.
—Turtle Baby. 1996. 256p. mass mkt. 5.99 o.p. (*0-446-40478-0*, Mysterious Pr. Paperback Bks.) Warner Bks., Inc.

**BRADLEY, HELEN (FICTITIOUS CHARACTER)—FICTION**

Rushford, Patricia H. Haunting Refrain. 1998. (Helen Bradley Mysteries Ser.: Vol. 3). 256p. pap. 9.99 o.p. (*1-55661-732-1*) Bethany Hse. Pubs.
—Haunting Refrain. l.t. ed. 1999. (Christian Mystery Ser.). 413p. 24.95 (*0-7862-1799-5*) Thorndike Pr.
—Now I Lay Me down to Sleep. 1997. (Helen Bradley Mysteries Ser.: No. 1). 240p. pap. 9.99 o.p. (*1-55661-730-5*) Bethany Hse. Pubs.
—Now I Lay Me down to Sleep. unabr. ed. 2001. audio 42.95 NorthStar Audio Bks.
—Now I Lay Me down to Sleep. unabr. ed. 2001. audio 58.00 (*0-7887-5113-1*, K0027E7) Recorded Bks., LLC.
—Red Sky in Mourning. 1997. (Helen Bradley Mysteries Ser.: Vol. 2). 240p. pap. 9.99 o.p. (*1-55661-731-3*) Bethany Hse. Pubs.
—Red Sky in Mourning. unabr. ed. 2001. audio 38.95 NorthStar Audio Bks.
—Red Sky in Mourning. l.t. ed. 1999. (Christian Mystery Ser.). 360p. 23.95 o.p. (*0-7862-1693-X*) Thorndike Pr.
—When Shadows Fall. (Helen Bradley Mysteries Ser.: Vol. 4). 2000. 240p. pap. 9.99 o.p. (*1-55661-733-X*); 1999. pap. 9.99 (*0-7642-1733-X*) Bethany Hse. Pubs.

**BRADLEY, MARK (FICTITIOUS CHARACTER)—FICTION**

Cutler, Stan. Best Performance by a Patsy. 1991. (Goodman-Bradley Mystery Ser.). 352p. 18.95 o.p. (*0-525-93317-4*) Dutton/Plume.
—Best Performance by a Patsy. 1993. (Goodman-Bradley Mystery Ser.). 336p. mass mkt. 4.50 o.p. (*0-451-40359-2*, Onyx) NAL.
—The Face on the Cutting Room Floor. 1991. 320p. 18.95 o.p. (*0-525-93381-6*, Dutton) Dutton/Plume.
—The Face on the Cutting Room Floor. 1993. (Goodman-Bradley Mystery Ser.). 272p. mass mkt. 4.50 o.s.i (*0-451-40394-0*, Signet Bks.) NAL.
—Rough Cut. 1994. 336p. (Orig.). mass mkt. 4.99 o.s.i (*0-451-18253-7*) NAL.
—Shot on Location. 1993. (Goodman-Bradley Mystery Ser.). 352p. 19.00 o.p. (*0-525-93576-2*) Dutton/Plume.
—Shot on Location. 1994. (Goodman-Bradley Mystery Ser.). 336p. mass mkt. 4.99 o.p. (*0-451-40391-6*, Signet Bks.) NAL.

**BRADSHAW, CHARLIE (FICTITIOUS CHARACTER)—FICTION**

Dobyns, Stephen. Saratoga Backtalk. unabr. collector's ed. 1995. audio 36.00 (*0-7366-2969-6*, 3660) Books on Tape, Inc.
—Saratoga Backtalk. l.t. ed. 1995. (Large Print Bks.). pap. 21.95 o.p. (*1-56895-089-6*, Wheeler Publishing, Inc.) Gale Group.
—Saratoga Backtalk. 1994. 221p. 19.95 o.p. (*0-393-03659-6*) Norton, W. W. & Co., Inc.
—Saratoga Backtalk. 1995. (Charlie Bradshaw Mystery Ser.). 224p. pap. 5.99 o.s.i (*0-14-024708-4*, Penguin Bks.) Penguin Group (USA) Inc.
—Saratoga Bestiary. unabr. collector's ed. 1994. audio 42.00 (*0-7366-2792-8*, 3507) Books on Tape, Inc.
—Saratoga Bestiary. (Charlie Bradshaw Mystery Ser.). 1990. 304p. pap. 4.50 o.p. (*0-14-010613-8*, Penguin Bks.); 1988. 272p. 16.95 o.p. (*0-670-82024-5*) Viking Penguin.
—Saratoga Fleshpot. unabr. collector's ed. 1996. audio 36.00 (*0-7366-3356-1*, 4007) Books on Tape, Inc.
—Saratoga Fleshpot. 1995. 220p. 21.00 (*0-393-03805-X*) Norton, W. W. & Co., Inc.
—Saratoga Fleshpot. 1996. (Charlie Bradshaw Mystery Ser.). 224p. pap. 5.95 o.p. (*0-14-025535-4*, Penguin Bks.) Penguin Group (USA) Inc.
—Saratoga Haunting. unabr. collector's ed. 1994. audio 36.00 (*0-7366-2836-3*, 3544) Books on Tape, Inc.
—Saratoga Haunting. 1994. (Charlie Bradshaw Mystery Ser.). 224p. pap. 6.95 o.p. (*0-14-017162-2*, Penguin Bks.) Penguin Group (USA) Inc.

—Saratoga Haunting. 1993. (Charlie Bradshaw Mystery Ser.). 224p. 19.00 o.p. (*0-670-84581-7*, Viking) Viking Penguin.
—Saratoga Headhunter. unabr. collector's ed. 1994. audio 36.00 (*0-7366-2754-5*, 3477) Books on Tape, Inc.
—Saratoga Headhunter. 1991. (Charlie Bradshaw Mystery Ser.). 224p. pap. 4.95 o.p. (*0-14-015606-2*, Penguin Bks.) Penguin Group (USA) Inc.
—Saratoga Headhunter. (Crime Monthly Ser.). 1986. pap. 3.50 o.p. (*0-14-007772-3*, Penguin Bks.); 1985. 13.95 o.p. (*0-670-80488-6*) Viking Penguin.
—Saratoga Hexameter. unabr. collector's ed. 1994. audio 48.00 (*0-7366-2890-8*, 3590) Books on Tape, Inc.
—Saratoga Hexameter. l.t. ed. 1991. (General Ser.). 391p. lib. bdg. 20.95 (*0-8161-5133-4*, Macmillan Reference USA) Gale Group.
—Saratoga Hexameter. 1991. (Crime Monthly Ser.). 256p. pap. 4.95 o.p. (*0-14-011691-5*, Penguin Bks.) Penguin Group (USA) Inc.
—Saratoga Hexameter. 1990. (Charlie Bradshaw Mystery Ser.). 256p. 16.95 o.p. (*0-670-82568-9*, Viking) Viking Penguin.
—Saratoga Longshot. unabr. collector's ed. 1994. audio 36.00 (*0-7366-2698-0*, 3432) Books on Tape, Inc.
—Saratoga Longshot. 1987. (Charlie Bradshaw Mystery Ser.). 256p. pap. 3.95 o.p. (*0-14-009627-2*, Penguin Bks.) Viking Penguin.
—Saratoga Snapper. unabr. collector's ed. 1994. audio 42.00 (*0-7366-2793-6*, 3508) Books on Tape, Inc.
—Saratoga Snapper. l.t. ed. 1988. 329p. 17.95 o.p. (*0-8161-4348-X*, Macmillan Reference USA) Gale Group.
—Saratoga Snapper. (Charlie Bradshaw Mystery Ser.). 1987. 272p. pap. 3.95 o.p. (*0-14-008812-1*, Penguin Bks.); 1986. 288p. 15.95 o.p. (*0-670-81059-2*) Viking Penguin.
—Saratoga Strongbox, , unabr. collector's ed. 1999. audio 32.00 (*0-7366-4295-1*, 4788) Books on Tape, Inc.
—Saratoga Strongbox. l.t. ed. 2000. pap. 23.95 (*1-56895-848-X*, Wheeler Publishing, Inc.) Gale Group.
—Saratoga Strongbox. 1999. (Charlie Bradshaw Mysteries Ser.). 224p. pap. 5.99 o.s.i (*0-14-028012-X*) Penguin Group (USA) Inc.
—Saratoga Strongbox. 1998. (Charlie Bradshaw Mysteries Ser.). 208p. 21.95 o.p. (*0-670-87692-5*) Viking Penguin.
—Saratoga Swimmer. unabr. collector's ed. 1994. audio 36.00 (*0-7366-2753-7*, 3476) Books on Tape, Inc.
—Saratoga Swimmer. 1981. 12.95 o.p. (*0-689-11193-2*, Scribner) Simon & Schuster.
—Saratoga Swimmer. 1983. (Charlie Bradshaw Mystery Ser.). 224p. pap. 5.95 o.p. (*0-14-006357-9*, Penguin Bks.) Viking Penguin.
—Saratoga Trifecta. 1995. (Charlie Bradshaw Mystery Ser.). 544p. pap. 24.00 o.s.i (*0-14-025196-0*, Penguin Bks.) Penguin Group (USA) Inc.

**BRADY, JOANNA (FICTITIOUS CHARACTER)—FICTION**

Jance, J. A. Dead to Rights. unabr. ed. 1999. (Joanna Brady Mystery Ser.: Bk. 4). audio 49.95 (*1-55686-831-6*) Books in Motion.
—Dead to Rights. abr. ed. (Joanna Brady Mystery Ser.). 1997. audio 7.99 o.p. (*1-56740-189-9*, 641, Paperback Nova Audio Bks.); 1996. audio 16.95 o.p. (*1-56100-958-X*, 1174, Nova Audio Bks.); 1996. 9p. audio 23.95 o.p. (*1-56100-719-6*, 85, Bookcassette); 1996. 9p. audio 57.25 o.p. (*1-56100-344-1*, 857, Unabridged Library Editions) Brilliance Audio.
—Dead to Rights. (Joanna Brady Mystery Ser.). 2003. 384p. mass mkt. 7.50 (*0-380-72432-4*); 1996. 373p. mass mkt. 22.00 o.p. (*0-380-97394-4*) Morrow/Avon. (Avon Bks.).
—Desert Heat. l.t. ed. 2001. 269p. 26.95 (*1-57490-371-3*, Beeler Large Print Bks.) Beeler, Thomas T. Publisher.
—Desert Heat. unabr. ed. (Joanna Brady Mystery Ser.: Bk. 1). 1994. audio 36.95 (*1-55686-490-6*, 752470); Bk. 1. 1995. audio 39.95 (*1-55686-637-2*) Books in Motion.
—Desert Heat. 1993. (Joanna Brady Mystery Ser.). 384p. mass mkt. 7.50 (*0-380-76545-4*, Avon Bks.) Morrow/Avon.
—Devil's Claw. l.t. ed. 2000. (Wheeler Softcover Ser.). 449p. 25.95 (*1-56895-140-X*, Wheeler Publishing, Inc.) Gale Group.
—Devil's Claw. 2001. (Joanna Brady Mystery Ser.). 416p. mass mkt. 7.50 (*0-380-79249-4*) HarperCollins Pubs.
—Devil's Claw. 2000. (Joanna Brady Mystery Ser.). 384p. 24.00 (*0-380-97501-7*, Morrow, William & Co.) Morrow/Avon.
—Exit Wounds: A Novel of Suspense. l.t. ed. 2003. 480p. pap. 24.95 (*0-06-054549-6*, HarperLargePrint) HarperTrade.
—Exit Wounds: A Novel of Suspense. 2003. 384p. 24.95 (*0-380-97731-1*, Morrow, William & Co.) Morrow/Avon.
—Outlaw Mountain, Set. abr. ed. 1999. audio 25.00. audio 36.00 Highsmith Inc.
—Outlaw Mountain. (Joanna Brady Mystery Ser.). 384p. 2000. mass mkt. 6.99 (*0-380-79248-6*); 1999. 24.00 (*0-380-97500-9*) Morrow/Avon. (Avon Bks.).
—Outlaw Mountain. abr. ed. 1999. (Joanna Brady Mystery Ser.). audio 25.00 (*0-7871-1970-9*); audio 36.00 (*0-7871-1973-3*) NewStar Media, Inc. (Dove Audio).
—Paradise Lost. 2001. E-Book 7.99 (*0-06-001044-4*) HarperCollins Pubs.
—Paradise Lost. abr. ed. 2001. audio 25.95 (*0-694-52573-1*, HarperAudio); 448p. pap. 25.00 (*0-06-621403-3*) HarperTrade.
—Paradise Lost. (Joanna Brady Mystery Ser.). 2002. 432p. mass mkt. 7.99 (*0-380-80469-7*, Avon Bks.); 2001. 384p. 25.00 (*0-380-97729-X*, Morrow, William & Co.) Morrow/Avon.
—Partner in Crime. 2002. E-Book 19.95 (*0-06-009826-0*); E-Book 19.95 (*0-06-009825-2*); E-Book 19.95 (*0-06-009828-7*); E-Book 19.95 (*0-06-009827-9*) HarperCollins General Bks. Group. (Perfect-Bound).
—Partner in Crime. l.t. ed. 2002. 512p. pap. 24.95 (*0-06-009393-5*, HarperLargePrint) HarperTrade.
—Partner in Crime. 2003. 400p. mass mkt. 7.99 (*0-380-80470-0*); 2002. 384p. 24.95 (*0-380-97730-3*); 2002. 384p. 24.95 (*0-380-97730-3*); 2002. audio 25.95 (*0-06-009260-2*); 2002. audio compact disk 29.95 (*0-06-050164-2*) Morrow/Avon. (Morrow, William & Co.).
—Rattlesnake Crossing. unabr. ed. 1999. (Joanna Brady Mystery Ser.: Bk. 6). audio 49.95 (*1-55686-888-X*) Books in Motion.
—Rattlesnake Crossing. unabr. ed. 1998. (Joanna Brady Mystery Ser.). audio 24.95 (*1-56740-071-X*, 21, Bookcassette); 9p. audio 57.25 (*1-56740-600-9*, 999, Unabridged Library Editions) Brilliance Audio.
—Rattlesnake Crossing. l.t. ed. 2000. (Large Print Book Ser.). 408p. pap. 25.95 (*1-56895-938-9*, Wheeler Publishing, Inc.) Gale Group.
—Rattlesnake Crossing. abr. ed. 1999. (Joanna Brady Mystery Ser.). audio 25.00. audio 57.25 Highsmith Inc.
—Rattlesnake Crossing. (Joanna Brady Mystery Ser.). 2003. 384p. mass mkt. 6.99 (*0-380-79247-8*); 1998. 371p. 23.00 o.p. (*0-380-97499-1*) Morrow/Avon. (Avon Bks.).
—Rattlesnake Crossing. abr. ed. 1998. (Joanna Brady Mystery Ser.). audio 26.95 (*0-7871-1732-3*, 696020) NewStar Media, Inc.
—Sheriff Brady, Vol. 5. 1924. o.s.i (*0-688-13822-5*, Morrow, William & Co.) Morrow/Avon.
—Shoot, Don't Shoot. unabr. ed. 1996. (Joanna Brady Mystery Ser.: Bk. 3). audio 49.95 (*1-55686-656-9*) Books in Motion.
—Shoot, Don't Shoot. l.t. ed. 1998. (Large Print Book Ser.). 25.95 (*1-56895-517-0*, Wheeler Publishing, Inc.) Gale Group.
—Shoot, Don't Shoot. (Joanna Brady Mystery Ser.). 1996. 384p. mass mkt. 7.99 (*0-380-76548-9*, Avon Bks.); 1995. 320p. (YA). 21.00 o.p. (*0-688-13821-7*, Morrow, William & Co.) Morrow/Avon.
—Shoot, Don't Shoot. unabr. ed. 1996. audio 70.00 (*0-7887-0477-X*, 94670E7) Recorded Bks., LLC.
—Skeleton Canyon. unabr. ed. 1999. (Joanna Brady Mystery Ser.: Bk. 5). audio 49.95 (*1-55686-883-9*) Books in Motion.
—Skeleton Canyon. abr. ed. (Joanna Brady Mystery Ser.). 1998. audio 7.99 o.p. (*1-56740-206-2*, 1370, Paperback Nova Audio Bks.); 1997. 9p. audio 57.25 o.p. (*1-56100-836-2*, 1047, Unabridged Library Editions); 1997. audio 23.95 (*1-56100-761-7*, 266, Bookcassette) Brilliance Audio.
—Skeleton Canyon. (Joanna Brady Mystery Ser.). 1998. 400p. mass mkt. 7.50 (*0-380-72433-2*); 1997. 384p. mass mkt. 23.00 o.p. (*0-380-97395-2*) Morrow/Avon. (Avon Bks.).
—Skeleton Canyon. l.t. ed. 1998. (Mystery Ser.). 437p. 28.95 (*0-7838-8356-0*) Thorndike Pr.
—Tombstone Courage. unabr. ed. 1998. (Joanna Brady Mystery Ser.: Bk. 2). audio 49.95 (*1-55686-817-0*) Books in Motion.
—Tombstone Courage. abr. ed. 1994. audio 16.95 o.p. (*1-56100-373-5*, 1391, Nova Audio Bks.); audio 57.25 o.p. (*1-56100-196-1*, 1080, Unabridged Library Editions); audio 21.95 o.p. (*1-56100-570-3*, 292, Bookcassette) Brilliance Audio.
—Tombstone Courage, Set. unabr. ed. 1999. audio 57.25 Highsmith Inc.
—Tombstone Courage. abr. ed. 2000. (Joanna Brady Mystery Ser.). audio 7.95 (*1-57815-031-0*, 1047, Media Bks. Audio Publishing) Media Bks., L. L. C.
—Tombstone Courage. (Joanna Brady Mystery Ser.). 1995. 416p. mass mkt. 7.99 (*0-380-76546-2*, Avon Bks.); 1994. 300p. 20.00 o.p. (*0-688-13247-2*, Morrow, William & Co.) Morrow/Avon.
—Tombstone Courage. l.t. ed. 2001. (Joanna Brady Mystery Ser.). 496p. 28.95 (*0-7862-3115-7*) Thorndike Pr.

**BRADY, WIN, REVEREND (FICTITIOUS CHARACTER)—FICTION**

Kritlow, William. Blood Money: A Novel. 1997. (Lake Champlain Mysteries Ser.). 288p. 10.99 (*0-7852-8027-8*) Nelson, Thomas Inc.
—Crimson Snow: A Novel. 1995. 10.99 o.p. (*0-7852-8098-7*) Nelson, Thomas Inc.
—Fire on the Lake: A Novel. 1996. (Lake Champlain Mysteries Ser.: Bk. 2). 288p. pap. 11.99 (*0-7852-8099-5*) Nelson, Thomas Inc.

**BRAGG, JOSEPH (FICTITIOUS CHARACTER)—FICTION**

Harrison, Ray. Akin to Murder. l.t. ed. 1995. (Magna Large Print Ser.). 468p. (*0-7505-0873-6*) Magna Large Print Bks. GBR. *Dist:* Ulverscroft Large Print Canada, Ltd.
—Counterfeit of Murder. 1989. mass mkt. 3.95 o.p. (*0-425-11645-X*) Berkley Publishing Group.
—Counterfeit of Murder. 1987. 320p. 15.95 o.p. (*0-312-00585-7*) St. Martin's Pr.
—Death of a Dancing Lady. 1988. mass mkt. 2.95 o.s.i (*0-425-11047-8*) Berkley Publishing Group.
—Death of a Dancing Lady: A Sargent Bragg-Constable Morton Mystery. 1986. 256p. 13.95 o.p. (*0-684-18581-4*, Macmillan Reference USA) Gale Group.
—Death of an Honourable Member. 1988. mass mkt. 3.50 o.p. (*0-425-11189-X*) Berkley Publishing Group.
—Death of an Honourable Member. 1985. 160p. 11.95 o.p. (*0-684-18245-9*, Macmillan Reference USA) Gale Group.
—Deathwatch. 1989. mass mkt. 3.50 o.p. (*0-425-11392-2*) Berkley Publishing Group.
—Deathwatch. 1986. 176p. 13.95 o.p. (*0-684-18425-7*, Macmillan Reference USA) Gale Group.
—Draught of Death. l.t. ed. 2000. (Dales Large Print Ser.). 352p. pap. (*1-84137-009-6*) Magna Large Print Bks. GBR. *Dist:* Ulverscroft Large Print Bks., Ltd., Ulverscroft Large Print Canada, Ltd.
—Facets of Murder. l.t. ed. 1998. (Ulverscroft Large Print Ser.). 368p. 29.99 (*0-7089-3952-X*, Ulverscroft) Thorpe, F. A. Pubs. GBR. *Dist:* Ulverscroft Large Print Bks., Ltd., Ulverscroft Large Print Canada, Ltd.
—Hallmark of Murder. l.t. ed. 1996. (Dales Large Print Ser.). (Illus.). 403p. pap. 19.99 (*1-85389-663-2*) Dales Large Print Bks. GBR. *Dist:* Ulverscroft Large Print Bks., Ltd.
—Harvest of Death. 1990. mass mkt. 3.95 o.s.i (*0-425-11979-3*) Berkley Publishing Group.
—Harvest of Death. 1988. 288p. 16.95 o.p. (*0-312-02218-2*, Saint Martin's Minotaur) St. Martin's Pr.
—Murder by Design. l.t. ed. 1997. (Linford Mystery Library). 416p. pap. 17.99 o.p. (*0-7089-5071-X*, Linford) Thorpe, F. A. Pubs. GBR. *Dist:* Ulverscroft Large Print Bks., Ltd., Ulverscroft Large Print Canada, Ltd.
—Patently Murder. l.t. ed. 1996. (Magna Large Print Ser.). 492p. 29.99 (*0-7505-0922-8*) Magna Large Print Bks. GBR. *Dist:* Ulverscroft Large Print Bks., Ltd.
—Patently Murder: A Sergeant Bragg & Constable Morton Mystery. 1991. 256p. 18.95 o.p. (*0-312-07058-6*, Saint Martin's Minotaur) St. Martin's Pr.
—A Season for Death. 1988. 288p. 15.95 o.p. (*0-312-01815-0*, Saint Martin's Minotaur) St. Martin's Pr.
—Season of Death. 1989. mass mkt. 3.95 o.p. (*0-425-11639-5*) Berkley Publishing Group.
—Sphere of Death. 1990. 17.95 o.p. (*0-312-05161-1*, Saint Martin's Minotaur) St. Martin's Pr.
—Tincture of Death. 1991. mass mkt. 3.95 o.p. (*0-425-12550-5*) Berkley Publishing Group.
—Tincture of Death. 1989. 240p. 15.95 o.p. (*0-312-03442-3*, Saint Martin's Minotaur) St. Martin's Pr.
—Why Kill Arthur Potter? 1984. 160p. 11.95 o.s.i (*0-684-18131-2*, Scribner) Simon & Schuster.
—Why Kill Arthur Potter? 1985. mass mkt. 2.95 o.s.i (*0-445-20053-7*) Warner Bks., Inc.

**BRAITHWAITE, THEODORA (FICTITIOUS CHARACTER)—FICTION**

Greenwood, D. M. Clerical Errors. 1991. 224p. 17.95 o.p. (*0-312-06931-6*, Saint Martin's Minotaur) St. Martin's Pr.
—Every Deadly Sin. l.t. ed. 2003. lib. bdg. 24.45 (*0-7862-5166-2*) Thorndike Pr.
—Idol Bones. 1993. 224p. 18.95 o.p. (*0-312-09829-4*, Saint Martin's Minotaur) St. Martin's Pr.
—Unholy Ghosts. 1992. 224p. 17.95 o.p. (*0-312-08515-X*, Saint Martin's Minotaur) St. Martin's Pr.
—Unholy Ghosts. l.t. ed. 2001. 288p. pap. 23.95 (*0-7838-9596-8*) Thorndike Pr.

**BRAMLETT, GROVER (FICTITIOUS CHARACTER)—FICTION**

Armistead, John. Cruel as the Grave: A Sheriff Bramlett Mystery. 1998. (Sheriff Bramlett Mystery Ser.). 368p. mass mkt. 5.99 o.s.i (*0-440-22437-3*) Doubleday Publishing.
—Cruel as the Grave: A Sheriff Bramlett Mystery. unabr. ed. 1966. (Sheriff Bramlett Mystery Ser.). audio 78.00 (*0-7887-4053-9*, 96004E7) Recorded Bks., LLC.
—Cruel the Grave: A Sheriff Bramlett Mystery. 1996. 256p. 21.00 (*0-7867-0303-2*, Carroll & Graf Pubs.) Avalon Publishing Group.
—A Homecoming for Murder: A Sheriff Bramlett Mystery. 1995. 272p. 19.95 (*0-7867-0197-8*, Carroll & Graf Pubs.) Avalon Publishing Group.
—A Homecoming for Murder: A Sheriff Bramlett Mystery. 1997. (Sheriff Bramlett Mystery Ser.). 368p. mass mkt. 5.99 o.s.i (*0-440-22435-7*) Dell Publishing.
—A Homecoming for Murder: A Sheriff Bramlett Mystery. unabr. ed. 1999. (Sheriff Bramlett Mystery Ser.). audio 70.00 (*0-7887-3777-5*, 95994E7) Recorded Bks., LLC.
—A Legacy of Vengeance. 1994. 256p. 8.95 (*0-7867-0059-9*, Carroll & Graf Pubs.) Avalon Publishing Group.
—A Legacy of Vengeance. 1997. (Sheriff Brimley Mystery Ser.). 304p. mass mkt. 5.50 o.s.i (*0-440-22384-9*) Dell Publishing.
—A Legacy of Vengeance. unabr. ed. 1994. (Sheriff Bramlett Mystery Ser.). audio 60.00 (*0-7887-3489-X*, 95896E7) Recorded Bks., LLC.

**BRANDEN, PROFESSOR MICHAEL (FICTITIOUS CHARACTER)—FICTION**

Gaus, P. L. Blood of the Prodigal: An Ohio Amish Mystery. 1999. (Ohio Amish Mysteries Ser.). 230p. pap. 12.95 (*0-8214-1277-9*); 24.95 (*0-8214-1276-0*) Ohio Univ. Pr.
—Broken English: An Ohio Amish Mystery. 2000. (Ohio Amish Mysteries Ser.). 205p. 24.95 (*0-8214-1325-2*); pap. 12.95 (*0-8214-1326-0*) Ohio Univ. Pr. (Ohio Univ. Ctr. for International Studies).
—Cast a Blue Shadow: An Ohio Amish Mystery. 2003. (Ohio Amish Mysteries Ser.). 24.95 (*0-8214-1529-8*); pap. 12.95 (*0-8214-1530-1*) Ohio Univ. Pr.
—Clouds Without Rain: An Ohio Amish Mystery. 2001. (Ohio Amish Mysteries Ser.). vii, 196p. 24.95 (*0-8214-1379-1*); pap. 12.95 (*0-8214-1380-5*) Ohio Univ. Pr.

**BRANDON, SMOKEY (FICTITIOUS CHARACTER)—FICTION**

Ayres, Noreen. Carcass Trade. unabr. ed. 1995. audio 56.00 (*0-7366-2934-3*, 3630) Books on Tape, Inc.
—Carcass Trade. 1994. 285p. 20.00 o.p. (*0-688-10875-X*, Morrow, William & Co.); 1995. 352p. reprint ed. mass mkt. 4.99 o.p. (*0-380-71572-4*, Avon Bks.) Morrow/Avon.
—The Juan Doe Murders: A Smokey Brandon Mystery. 2000. (Five Star Mystery Ser.). 204p. 20.95 (*0-7862-2897-0*, Five Star) Gale Group.
—A World the Color of Salt. unabr. ed. 1992. audio 32.00 (*0-7366-2321-3*, 3101) Books on Tape, Inc.
—A World the Color of Salt. 1993. 304p. mass mkt. 4.99 (*0-380-71571-6*, Avon Bks.); 1992. 352p. 19.00 o.p. (*0-688-10824-5*, Morrow, William & Co.) Morrow/Avon.

**BRANDSTETTER, DAVE (FICTITIOUS CHARACTER)—FICTION**

Hansen, Joseph. The Boy Who Was Buried This Morning. 1991. 192p. reprint ed. pap. 5.95 o.p. (*0-452-26617-3*, Plume) Dutton/Plume.
—The Boy Who Was Buried This Morning. 1990. 176p. 16.95 o.p. (*0-670-83324-X*) Viking Penguin.
—Country of Old Men: The Last Dave Brandstetter Mystery. 1992. 192p. pap. 7.00 o.p. (*0-452-26805-2*, Plume) Dutton/Plume.
—Country of Old Men: The Last Dave Brandstetter Mystery. 1991. 192p. 17.95 o.p. (*0-670-83826-8*) Viking Penguin.
—Death Claims. 2001. (Dave Brandstetter Mystery Ser.: Vol. 2). 176p. pap. 11.95 o.p. (*1-55583-551-1*) Alyson Pubns.
—Death Claims. 1980. pap. 3.95 o.p. (*0-03-057484-6*); 88p. pap. 5.95 o.p. (*0-8050-0622-2*) Holt, Henry & Co. (Owl Bks.).
—Death Claims. 192p. pap. 9.95 o.p. (*1-874061-62-9*) Oldcastle Bks., Ltd. GBR. *Dist:* Trafalgar Square.
—Early Graves. 1987. 208p. 15.95 o.p. (*0-89296-249-6*) Mysterious Pr.
—Early Graves. 1988. 208p. mass mkt. 3.95 o.s.i (*0-445-40735-2*, Mysterious Pr. Paperback Bks.) Warner Bks., Inc.
—Fadeout. 2000. (Dave Brandstetter Mysteries Ser.). 256p. reprint ed. pap. 11.95 o.p. (*1-55583-552-X*, Alyson Bks.) Alyson Pubns.
—Fadeout. unabr. ed. 1995. (Dave Brandstetter Mystery Ser.: No. 1). audio 24.95 (*1-888348-01-1*, HCB201) Hall Closet Bk. Co.

Characters

—Fadeout. 1980. 88p. pap. 5.95 o.p. (*0-8050-1054-8*);Vol. 1. pap. 3.95 o.p. (*0-03-057486-2*) Holt, Henry & Co. (Owl Bks.).
—Gravedigger. 1985. pap. o.p. (*0-03-003682-8*, Owl Bks.); 1985. 192p. pap. 5.95 o.p. (*0-8050-0196-4*, Owl Bks.); 1982. o.p. (*0-03-056063-2*) Holt, Henry & Co.
—The Little Dog Laughed: A Dave Brandstetter Mystery. 1987. 192p. pap. 5.95 o.p. (*0-8050-0627-3*, Owl Bks.); 1986. 15.95 o.p. (*0-8050-0083-6*) Holt, Henry & Co.
—The Man Everybody Was Afraid Of. 1981. pap. o.p. (*0-03-059894-X*, Owl Bks.); 1981. 192p. pap. 5.95 o.p. (*0-8050-0723-7*, Owl Bks.); 1978. 192p. o.p. (*0-03-042376-7*) Holt, Henry & Co.
—The Man Everybody Was Afraid Of. 192p. pap. 9.95 o.p. (*1-874061-66-1*) Oldcastle Bks., Ltd. GBR. *Dist:* Trafalgar Square.
—Nightwork. 1985. (Dave Brandsetter Mystery Ser.). 88p. pap. 5.95 o.p. (*0-8050-1055-6*); pap. 3.95 o.p. (*0-03-003679-8*) Holt, Henry & Co. (Owl Bks.).
—Obedience. 1988. 208p. 16.95 (*0-89296-296-8*) Mysterious Pr.
—Obedience. 1989. mass mkt. 4.95 (*0-445-40844-8*, Mysterious Pr. Paperback Bks.) Warner Bks., Inc.
—Skinflick. 1980. 192p. pap. o.p. (*0-03-057641-5*, Owl Bks.); 1980. 89p. pap. 5.95 o.p. (*0-8050-0197-2*, Owl Bks.); 1979. 192p. o.p. (*0-03-048931-8*) Holt, Henry & Co.
—Troublemaker: A Dave Brandstetter Mystery. 2002. 176p. pap. 12.95 (*1-55583-710-7*) Alyson Pubns.
—Troublemaker: A Dave Brandstetter Mystery. 1981. pap. 3.95 o.p. (*0-03-057487-0*); 1988. 89p. reprint ed. pap. 5.95 o.p. (*0-8050-0812-8*) Holt, Henry & Co. (Owl Bks.).

**BRANDT, SARAH (FICTITIOUS CHARACTER)—FICTION**

Thompson, Victoria. Murder on Astor Place. 1999. (Gaslight Mysteries Ser.). 288p. mass mkt. 6.99 (*0-425-16896-4*, Prime Crime) Berkley Publishing Group.
—Murder on Gramercy Park. 2001. 336p. mass mkt. 6.99 (*0-425-17886-2*) Berkley Publishing Group.
—Murder on St. Mark's Place. 2000. (Gaslight Mysteries Ser.). 288p. mass mkt. 6.99 (*0-425-17361-5*, Prime Crime) Berkley Publishing Group.

**BRANIGAN BROTHERS (FICTITIOUS CHARACTERS)—FICTION**

Guccione, Leslie D. Branigan's Break. 1994. (Silhouette Desire Ser.). (Illus.). 185p. per. (*0-373-05902-7*, 1-05902-1, Silhouette) Harlequin Enterprises, Ltd.
—Private Practice. 1990. (Silhouette Desire Ser.: No. 554). pap. (*0-373-05554-4*, Silhouette) Harlequin Enterprises, Ltd.

**BRANNIGAN, KATE (FICTITIOUS CHARACTER)—FICTION**

McDermid, Val. Blue Genes: A Kate Brannigan Mystery. l.t. ed. 1997. (G. K. Hall Mystery Ser.). 358p. lib. bdg. 24.95 o.p. (*0-7838-8141-X*, Macmillan Reference USA) Gale Group.
—Blue Genes: A Kate Brannigan Mystery. 1997. 304p. 21.50 (*0-684-83398-0*, Scribner) Simon & Schuster.
—Blue Genes: A Kate Brannigan Mystery. unabr. ed. 2000. audio 54.95 (*0-7531-0620-5*, 990703); 8p. audio compact disk 64.95 (*0-7531-0899-2*, 108992) Ulverscroft Large Print Bks., Ltd.
—Clean Break. 2002. 12.95 (*1-883523-51-6*) Spinsters Ink Bks.
—Clean Break: A Kate Brannigan Mystery. 1996. 288p. mass mkt. 4.99 o.p. (*0-06-104393-1*, HarperTorch) Morrow/Avon.
—Clean Break: A Kate Brannigan Mystery. 1995. 288p. 20.00 o.s.i (*0-684-80461-1*, Scribner) Simon & Schuster.
—Crack Down. 1994. 288p. 20.00 (*0-684-19756-1*, Macmillan Reference USA) Gale Group.
—Crack Down. 1996. 256p. mass mkt. 4.99 o.s.i (*0-06-104394-X*) HarperCollins Pubs.
—Crack Down. 2002. 12.95 (*1-883523-50-8*) Spinsters Ink Bks.
—Dead Beat. 1993. 207p. 16.95 o.p. (*0-312-08754-3*, Saint Martin's Minotaur) St. Martin's Pr.
—Dead Beat. l.t. ed. 1997. pap. 20.95 o.p. (*0-7862-0929-1*) Thorndike Pr.
—Kickback. 1993. 192p. 17.95 o.p. (*0-312-09836-7*, Saint Martin's Minotaur) St. Martin's Pr.

**BRANNON, STUART (FICTITIOUS CHARACTER)—FICTION**

Bly, Stephen A. False Claims at the Little Stephen Mine. 1992. (Stuart Brannon Western Adventure Ser.: No. 2). 192p. pap. 7.99 o.p. (*0-89107-642-5*) Crossway Bks.
—False Claims at the Little Stephen Mine. l.t. ed. 1994. 269p. lib. bdg. 18.95 (*0-8161-7405-9*, Macmillan Reference USA) Gale Group.
—Final Justice at Adobe Wells. 1993. (Stuart Brannon Western Adventure Ser.: No. 5). 192p. pap. 8.99 (*0-89107-744-8*) Crossway Bks.
—Hard Winter at Broken Arrow Crossing. 1991. (Stuart Brannon Western Ser.: No. 1). 192p. pap. 8.99 o.p. (*0-89107-620-4*) Crossway Bks.
—Hard Winter at Broken Arrow Crossing. l.t. ed. 1993. 234p. lib. bdg. 18.95 (*0-8161-5822-3*, Macmillan Reference USA) Gale Group.
—Last Hanging at Paradise Meadow. 1992. (Stuart Brannon Western Adventure Ser.: Vol. 3). 192p. pap. 8.99 o.p. (*0-89107-672-7*) Crossway Bks.
—Last Hanging at Paradise Meadow. l.t. ed. 1995. 254p. lib. bdg. 19.95 o.p. (*0-7838-1249-3*, Macmillan Reference USA) Gale Group.
—Son of an Arizona Legend. 1994. (Stuart Brannon Western Ser.: Vol. 6). 192p. pap. 8.99 (*0-89107-770-7*) Crossway Bks.
—Son of an Arizona Legend. l.t. ed. 1996. (Western Ser.). 242p. 19.95 o.p. (*0-7838-1783-5*, Macmillan Reference USA) Gale Group.
—Standoff at Sunrise Creek. 1993. (Stuart Brannon Western Ser.: Vol. 4). 192p. pap. 8.99 (*0-89107-695-6*) Crossway Bks.
—Standoff at Sunrise Creek. l.t. ed. 1995. 270p. 20.95 o.p. (*0-7838-1275-2*, Macmillan Reference USA) Gale Group.

**BRANSON, JOHN LLOYD (FICTITIOUS CHARACTER)—FICTION**

Meredith, Doris R. Murder by Deception. 1989. mass mkt. 4.99 o.s.i (*0-345-35243-2*) Ballantine Bks.
—Murder by Deception. 2004. 288p. mass mkt. 6.99 (*0-7434-7999-8*) ibooks, Inc.
—Murder by Impulse. 1987. 288p. mass mkt. 4.99 o.s.i (*0-345-34671-8*) Ballantine Bks.
—Murder by Impulse. Holland, Steve, ed. abr. ed. 1993. audio 24.95 (*1-883268-05-2*) Spellbinders, Inc.
—Murder by Impulse. 2003. 288p. mass mkt. 6.99 (*0-7434-7968-8*) ibooks, Inc.
—Murder by Masquerade. 1990. (John Lloyd Branson Ser.). 256p. mass mkt. 4.99 o.s.i (*0-345-35986-0*) Ballantine Bks.
—Murder by Masquerade. Holland, Stephen, ed. abr. ed. 1994. audio 24.95 (*1-883268-11-7*) Spellbinders, Inc.
—Murder by Reference. 1991. 272p. mass mkt. 4.99 o.s.i (*0-345-36861-4*) Ballantine Bks.
—Murder by Reference. abr. ed. 1997. audio 25.00 (*1-883268-28-1*) Spellbinders, Inc.
—Murder by Sacrilege. 1993. mass mkt. 4.99 o.s.i (*0-345-37693-5*) Ballantine Bks.

**BRASS, ALEXANDER (FICTITIOUS CHARACTER)—FICTION**

Kurland, Michael. Girls in High Heeled Shoes. 1998. (Alexander Brass Mysteries Ser.). 256p. 22.95 (*0-312-18104-3*, 874694, Saint Martin's Minotaur) St. Martin's Pr.
—Too Soon Dead. 1997. 288p. 22.95 o.p. (*0-312-15228-0*, Saint Martin's Minotaur) St. Martin's Pr.

**BRASS, COUNT (FICTITIOUS CHARACTER)—FICTION**

Moorcock, Michael. The Champion of Garathorm. 1986. (Chronicles of Castle Brass Ser.: No. 2). 160p. 2.95 o.s.i (*0-425-09042-6*); 1985. 2.75 o.s.i (*0-425-07646-6*) Berkley Publishing Group.
—The Champion of Garathorm. 1981. pap. 2.25 o.p. (*0-440-11173-0*) Dell Publishing.
—Count Brass, No. 1. 1988. (Chronicles of Castle Brass Ser.). mass mkt. 2.95 o.s.i (*0-441-11775-9*) Ace Bks.
—Count Brass. 1985. (Chronicles of Castle Brass Ser.: No. 1). 160p. 2.75 o.s.i (*0-425-07514-1*) Berkley Publishing Group.
—Count Brass. 1981. pap. 2.25 o.p. (*0-440-11541-8*) Dell Publishing.
—Count Brass. 2000. (Eternal Champion Ser.: Vol. 15). (Illus.). 339p. 24.99 (*1-56504-987-X*) White Wolf Publishing, Inc.
—Jewel in the Skull. 1977. mass mkt. 1.25 o.p. (*0-87997-276-9*); mass mkt. 1.95 o.p. (*0-87997-712-4*); mass mkt. 2.50 o.p. (*0-87997-841-4*); mass mkt. 2.75 o.p. (*0-88677-043-2*); mass mkt. 1.50 o.p. (*0-87997-419-2*); mass mkt. 1.75 o.p. (*0-87997-547-4*); (Runestaff Ser.: Bk. 1). 224p. mass mkt. 2.95 o.p. (*0-88677-175-7*) DAW Bks., Inc.
—The Mad God's Amulet. 1977. mass mkt. 1.25 o.p. (*0-87997-289-0*); 1977. mass mkt. 2.75 o.p. (*0-88677-044-0*); 1977. mass mkt. 1.95 o.p. (*0-87997-688-8*); 1977. mass mkt. 1.50 o.p. (*0-87997-391-9*); Bk. 2. 1985. mass mkt. 2.95 o.p. (*0-88677-216-8*, UJ2216) DAW Bks., Inc.
—The Quest for Tanelorn, No. 3. 1987. (Chronicles of Castle Brass Ser.). mass mkt. 2.95 o.s.i (*0-441-69712-7*) Ace Bks.
—The Quest for Tanelorn. 1985. (Chronicles of Castle Brass Ser.: No. 3). 160p. 2.75 o.s.i (*0-425-07707-1*) Berkley Publishing Group.
—The Quest for Tanelorn. 1981. pap. 2.25 o.p. (*0-440-17193-8*) Dell Publishing.
—The Runestaff. 1991. mass mkt. 4.50 o.s.i (*0-441-31848-7*) Ace Bks.
—The Runestaff. 1977. mass mkt. 1.75 o.p. (*0-87997-616-0*); 1977. mass mkt. 2.75 o.p. (*0-88677-046-7*); 1977. mass mkt. 1.50 o.p. (*0-87997-422-2*); 1977. mass mkt. 1.25 o.p. (*0-87997-324-2*); Bk. 4. 1985. mass mkt. 2.95 o.p. (*0-88677-218-4*, UE2218) DAW Bks., Inc.
—The Runestaff No. 1: Jewel in the Skull. 1990. mass mkt. 3.50 o.s.i (*0-441-31847-9*) Ace Bks.
—The Runestaff No. 2: Mad God's Amulet. 1990. mass mkt. 3.95 o.s.i (*0-441-51388-3*) Ace Bks.
—The Sword of the Dawn. 1977. (Science Fiction Ser.: No. 3). 224p. mass mkt. 2.95 o.p. (*0-88677-173-0*) DAW Bks., Inc.

**BRAUN, CELESTE (FICTITIOUS CHARACTER)—FICTION**

Jordan, B. B. Principal Investigation. 1997. (Scientific Mysteries Ser.). 320p. mass mkt. 5.99 o.s.i (*0-425-16090-4*, Prime Crime) Berkley Publishing Group.
—Secondary Immunization: A Scientific Mystery. 1999. (Scientific Mysteries Ser.). 272p. (YA). mass mkt. 5.99 o.s.i (*0-425-17118-3*, Prime Crime) Berkley Publishing Group.
—Triplet Code. 2001. (Illus.). 224p. mass mkt. 5.99 o.s.i (*0-425-17920-6*, Prime Crime) Berkley Publishing Group.

**BRAY, NELL (FICTITIOUS CHARACTER)—FICTION**

Linscott, Gillian. Absent Friends. l.t. ed. 2000. (Magna Large Print Ser.). 368p. (*0-7505-1488-4*) Magna Large Print Bks. GBR. *Dist:* Ulverscroft Large Print Bks., Ltd., Ulverscroft Large Print Canada, Ltd.
—Absent Friends. 1999. 288p. 22.95 (*0-312-20765-4*, Saint Martin's Minotaur) St. Martin's Pr.
—Crown Witness. l.t. ed. 1997. (Dales Large Print Ser.). 383p. pap. 19.99 (*1-85389-712-4*) Dales Large Print Bks. GBR. *Dist:* Ulverscroft Large Print Bks., Ltd.
—Crown Witness. 1996. 218p. mass mkt. o.s.i (*0-7515-1657-0*); 1995. 256p. o.s.i (*0-316-91419-3*) Little Brown & Co.
—Crown Witness. 1995. 224p. 20.95 o.p. (*0-312-13456-8*, Saint Martin's Minotaur) St. Martin's Pr.
—Dance on Blood. l.t. ed. 1999. (Magna Large Print Ser.). 384p. (*0-7505-1385-3*) Magna Large Print Bks. GBR. *Dist:* Ulverscroft Large Print Canada, Ltd.
—Dance on Blood. 1998. (Nell Bray Mystery Ser.). 256p. 22.95 o.p. (*0-312-18075-6*, 853567, Saint Martin's Minotaur) St. Martin's Pr.
—Dance on Blood. 1998. 250p. pap. o.s.i (*1-86049-312-2*) Virago Pr., Ltd. GBR. *Dist:* Little Brown & Co.
—Dead Man's Sweetheart. 1996. 272p. 21.95 o.p. (*0-312-14579-9*, Saint Martin's Minotaur) St. Martin's Pr.
—An Easy Day for a Lady. 1995. 210p. 19.95 o.p. (*0-312-11811-2*, Saint Martin's Minotaur) St. Martin's Pr.
—Hanging on the Wire. 1992. 215p. 17.95 o.p. (*0-312-08806-X*, Saint Martin's Minotaur) St. Martin's Pr.
—The Perfect Daughter. 2001. (Nell Bray Mystery Ser.). 256p. 23.95 (*0-312-27296-0*, Saint Martin's Minotaur) St. Martin's Pr.
—Sister Beneath the Sheet. l.t. ed. 1992. 18.95 o.p. (*0-7451-8355-7*); pap. 16.95 o.p. (*0-7927-1103-3*) BBC Audiobooks America.
—Sister Beneath the Sheet. 1991. 224p. 17.95 o.p. (*0-312-06464-0*, Saint Martin's Minotaur) St. Martin's Pr.
—Stage Fright. l.t. ed. 1994. 20.95 o.p. (*0-7927-2044-X*); pap. 19.95 o.p. (*0-7927-2043-1*) BBC Audiobooks America.
—Stage Fright. 1993. 192p. 17.95 o.p. (*0-312-09812-X*, Saint Martin's Minotaur) St. Martin's Pr.

**BRAZIL, NATHAN (FICTITIOUS CHARACTER)—FICTION**

Chalker, Jack L. Echoes of the Well of Souls. 1993. (Watchers at the Well Ser.: Bk. 1). 320p. mass mkt. 5.99 o.s.i (*0-345-38686-8*); 352p. pap. 19.00 (*0-345-36201-2*) Ballantine Bks. (Del Rey).
—Exiles at the Well of Souls. 1984. (Saga of the Well World Ser.: Bk. 2). mass mkt. 5.99 o.s.i (*0-345-32437-4*); 1983. mass mkt. 2.50 o.p. (*0-345-31239-2*) Ballantine Bks. (Del Rey).
—Gods of the Well of Souls. (Watchers at the Well Ser.: Bk. 3). 1995. mass mkt. 5.99 o.s.i (*0-345-38850-X*); 1994. 448p. pap. 10.00 o.p. (*0-345-36203-9*) Ballantine Bks. (Del Rey).
—Midnight at the Well of Souls. 1985. (Saga of the Well World Ser.: Bk. 1). mass mkt. 5.99 o.s.i (*0-345-32445-5*, Del Rey) Ballantine Bks.
—Quest for the Well of Souls. Baen, James P., ed. 2003. 352p. mass mkt. 7.99 (*0-7434-7153-9*) Baen Bks.
—Quest for the Well of Souls. 1985. (Saga of the Well World Ser.: Bk. 3). mass mkt. 5.99 o.s.i (*0-345-32450-1*); 1983. mass mkt. 2.50 o.p. (*0-345-31120-5*) Ballantine Bks. (Del Rey).
—The Return of Nathan Brazil. 1986. (Return of Nathan Brazil Ser.: Bk. 4). mass mkt. 5.99 o.s.i (*0-345-34105-8*, Del Rey) Ballantine Bks.
—Shadow of the Well of Souls. 1994. (Watchers at the Well Ser.: Bk. 2). (Orig.). 368p. mass mkt. 5.99 o.s.i (*0-345-38846-1*); 345p. pap. 10.00 o.s.i (*0-345-36202-0*, Del Rey) Ballantine Bks.
—Twilight at the Well of Souls: The Legacy of Nathan Brazil. 1986. (Saga of the Well World Ser.: Bk. 5). 320p. mass mkt. 5.99 o.s.i (*0-345-34408-1*, Del Rey) Ballantine Bks.

**BRENNAN, TEMPERANCE (FICTITIOUS CHARACTER)—FICTION**

Reichs, Kathy. Bare Bones. 2003. (Illus.). 320p. 25.00 (*0-7432-3346-8*); E-Book 19.99 (*0-7432-6008-2*); 448p. 25.00 o.s.i (*0-7432-4675-6*) Simon & Schuster. (Scribner).
—Deadly Decisions. 2001. E-Book 25.00 (*1-58945-163-5*) Adobe Systems, Inc.
—Deadly Decisions. 2000. 336p. 25.00 (*0-684-85971-8*, Scribner); 2000. E-Book 25.00 (*0-7432-1077-8*, Scribner); 2000. 464p. 25.00 o.s.i (*0-7432-0429-8*, Scribner); 2001. 384p. reprint ed. mass mkt. 7.99 (*0-671-02836-7*, Pocket) Simon & Schuster.
—Deadly Decisions. abr. ed. 2000. audio 25.00 (*0-7435-0054-7*, Simon & Schuster Audioworks) Simon & Schuster Audio.
—Death du Jour. unabr. ed. 2002. audio compact disk 110.95; 2000. audio 96.95 (*0-7927-2346-5*, CSL235, Chivers Sound Library) BBC Audiobooks America.
—Death du Jour. unabr. ed. 2000. 12p. audio compact disk 110.95 (*0-7540-5330-X*, CCD 021) Chivers Audio Bks. GBR. *Dist:* BBC Audiobooks America.
—Death du Jour. 1999. 384p. mass mkt. 7.99 (*0-671-03472-3*, Pocket); 1999. E-Book 25.00 (*0-7432-0080-2*, Scribner); 1999. 384p. 25.00 (*0-684-84118-5*, Scribner); 1999. 384p. 25.00 (*0-684-86906-3*, Scribner); 2000. (Illus.). 480p. reprint ed. mass mkt. 7.99 (*0-671-01137-5*, Pocket) Simon & Schuster.
—Death du Jour, Set. abr. ed. 1999. audio 24.00 (*0-671-04370-6*, 599126, Simon & Schuster Audioworks) Simon & Schuster Audio.
—Death du Jour. l.t. ed. (Thorndike/G. K. Hall Paperback Bestsellers Ser.). 632p. 2000. (FRE.). pap. 27.95 (*0-7862-1997-1*); 1999. 30.95 (*0-7862-1996-3*) Thorndike Pr.
—Death du Jour. abr. ed. 1999. audio 24.35 (*1-85686-522-3*) Ulverscroft Audio (U.S.A.).
—Deja Dead. 2001. E-Book 9.99 (*1-58945-168-6*) Adobe Systems, Inc.
—Deja Dead. 1998. (Illus.). 411p. (J). o.p. (*0-434-00427-8*) Random Hse. of Canada, Ltd. CAN. *Dist:* Random Hse., Inc.
—Deja Dead. unabr. ed. 1998. audio 96.00 (*0-7887-1750-2*, 95228E7) Recorded Bks., LLC.
—Deja Dead. 2000. E-Book 9.99 (*0-684-83906-7*, Scribner); 1998. (Illus.). 560p. mass mkt. 7.99 (*0-671-01136-7*, Pocket); 1997. 282.00 (*0-684-00611-1*, Scribner); 1997. (Illus.). 416p. 24.00 (*0-684-84117-7*, Scribner) Simon & Schuster.
—Deja Dead. abr. ed. 1997. 5p. audio 24.00 (*0-671-57706-9*, 495419, Simon & Schuster Audioworks) Simon & Schuster Audio.
—Deja Dead. l.t. ed. 1998. (Basic Ser.). 664p. 30.95 (*0-7862-1265-9*) Thorndike Pr.
—Fatal Voyage. 2001. 368p. 25.00 (*0-684-85972-6*); E-Book (*0-7432-1822-1*); 368p. 25.00 o.s.i (*0-7432-2281-4*); 528p. 25.00 (*0-7432-1662-8*) Simon & Schuster. (Scribner).
—Fatal Voyage. abr. ed. 2001. audio 26.00 (*0-7435-0462-3*); audio compact disk 30.00 (*0-7435-0463-1*) Simon & Schuster Audio. (Simon & Schuster Audioworks).
—Grave Secrets. unabr. ed. 2002. 8p. audio compact disk 79.95 (*0-7927-2647-2*, SLD 481, Chivers Sound Library) BBC Audiobooks America.
—Grave Secrets. 2003. 400p. mass mkt. 7.99 (*0-671-02838-3*, Pocket Star); 2003. mass mkt. (*0-7434-5738-2*, Pocket Star); 2002. 336p. 25.00 o.s.i (*0-7432-4414-1*, Scribner); 2002. (Illus.). 336p. 25.00 (*0-684-85973-4*, Scribner); 2002. 624p. 25.00 (*0-7432-3364-6*, Scribner) Simon & Schuster.
—Grave Secrets. unabr. ed. 2002. audio 35.00 (*0-7435-2627-9*, Simon & Schuster Audioworks) Simon & Schuster Audio.
—Grave Secrets. l.t. ed. 2002. (Core Collection). 516p. 32.95 (*0-7862-4664-2*) Thorndike Pr.

**BRENNEN, MICHAEL (FICTITIOUS CHARACTER)—FICTION**

Zackel, Fred. Cinderella After Midnight. 1980. 11.95 o.p. (*0-698-10990-2*) Putnam Publishing Group, The.
—Cocaine & Blue Eyes. 1983. 320p. mass mkt. 2.95 o.p. (*0-425-06241-4*) Berkley Publishing Group.
—Cocaine & Blue Eyes. 1978. 8.95 o.p. (*0-698-10934-1*) Putnam Publishing Group, The.

**BRENNER, JACK (FICTITIOUS CHARACTER)—FICTION**

Latreille, Stan. Perjury. 1999. 384p. reprint ed. mass mkt. 6.99 o.s.i (*0-451-19687-2*, Onyx) NAL.

**BRENNER, LUCY TRIMBLE (FICTITIOUS CHARACTER)—FICTION**

Wright, Eric. Death of a Sunday Writer. 1996. 224p. text 21.00 (*0-88150-377-0*) Norton, W. W. & Co., Inc.

—Death on the Rocks: A Lucy Trimble Mystery. 1999. 240p. 15.95 (*0-312-20525-2*, Saint Martin's Minotaur) St. Martin's Pr.

—Death on the Rocks: A Lucy Trimble Mystery. l.t. ed. 1999. (Mystery Ser.). 343p. 27.95 (*0-7862-2205-0*) Thorndike Pr.

**BRENNER, PAUL (FICTITIOUS CHARACTER)—FICTION**

DeMille, Nelson. The General's Daughter. unabr. collector's ed. 1999. audio 80.00 (*0-7366-2573-9*, 3322) Books on Tape, Inc.

—The General's Daughter. abr. ed. 2002. audio 9.99 (*0-553-75603-6*); 1997. audio 8.99 o.s.i (*0-679-46024-1*) Random Hse. Audio Publishing Group. (RH Audio).

—Up Country. abr. ed. 2002. audio 29.98 (*1-58621-134-X*); audio 42.98 (*1-58621-135-8*); audio 69.98 (*1-58621-136-6*) Time Warner AudioBooks.

—Up Country. 2002. (Illus.). 720p. 26.95 o.p. (*0-446-51657-0*); 1184p. 26.95 o.p. (*0-446-52993-1*) Warner Bks., Inc.

**BRET, GERVASE (FICTITIOUS CHARACTER)—FICTION**

Marston, Edward. The Dragons of Archenfield. 1996. mass mkt. 5.99 o.s.i (*0-449-22545-3*, Fawcett) Ballantine Bks.

—The Dragons of Archenfield. 1995. 256p. 14.30 o.p. (*0-312-13472-X*, Saint Martin's Minotaur) St. Martin's Pr.

—The Hawks of Delamere. 2000. (Domesday Bks.: Vol. 7). (Illus.). 246p. 22.95 (*0-312-20948-7*, Saint Martin's Minotaur) St. Martin's Pr.

—The Lions of the North. 1996. 227p. 21.95 (*0-312-14671-X*, Saint Martin's Minotaur) St. Martin's Pr.

—The Ravens of Blackwater. 1996. mass mkt. 5.99 o.s.i (*0-449-22410-4*, Fawcett) Ballantine Bks.

—The Ravens of Blackwater. 1994. 20.95 o.p. (*0-312-11330-7*, Saint Martin's Minotaur) St. Martin's Pr.

—The Serpents of Harbledown: A Novel. 1998. (Domesday Bks.: Vol. 5). 288p. 22.95 (*0-312-18021-7*, Saint Martin's Minotaur) St. Martin's Pr.

—The Stallions of Woodstock. 1998. (Domesday Bks.: Vol. 6). 288p. 22.95 (*0-312-20021-8*, Saint Martin's Minotaur) St. Martin's Pr.

—The Wolves of Savernake. 1995. mass mkt. 5.99 o.s.i (*0-449-22310-8*, Fawcett) Ballantine Bks.

—The Wolves of Savernake. 1993. 256p. 19.95 o.p. (*0-312-09942-8*, Saint Martin's Minotaur) St. Martin's Pr.

**BREWSTER, LILY (FICTITIOUS CHARACTER)—FICTION**

Churchill, Jill. Anything Goes: A Grace & Favor Mystery. 1999. 272p. mass mkt. 6.99 (*0-380-80244-9*, Avon Bks.) Morrow/Avon.

—In the Still of the Night: A Grace & Favor Mystery. 2000. 272p. mass mkt. 6.99 (*0-380-80245-7*, Avon Bks.) Morrow/Avon.

—It Had to Be You: A Grace & Favor Mystery. 2004. 224p. 23.95 (*0-06-052843-5*, Morrow, William & Co.) Morrow/Avon.

—Love for Sale: A Grace & Favor Mystery. l.t. ed. 2003. 280p. 29.95 (*0-7862-5919-1*) Gale Group.

—Love for Sale: A Grace & Favor Mystery. 2004. 272p. mass mkt. 6.99 (*0-06-103122-4*, Avon Bks.); 2003. 224p. 23.95 (*0-06-019942-3*, Morrow, William & Co.) Morrow/Avon.

—Someone to Watch over Me: A Grace & Favor Mystery. l.t. ed. 2002. 309p. 28.95 (*0-7862-4356-2*) Gale Group.

—Someone to Watch over Me: A Grace & Favor Mystery. 2002. 272p. mass mkt. 6.99 (*0-06-103123-2*, Avon Bks.); 2001. 240p. 24.00 (*0-06-019941-5*, Morrow, William & Co.) Morrow/Avon.

**BREWSTER, MEG (FICTITIOUS CHARACTER)—FICTION**

Eulo, Ken & Mauck, Joe. Claw. 1994. 22.00 o.s.i (*0-671-79963-0*, Simon & Schuster) Simon & Schuster.

—Claw. 320p. 3.98 o.p. (*0-7651-0133-5*) Smithmark Pubs., Inc.

—Claw. 1995. 319p. pap. text 5.50 (*0-312-95595-2*, St. Martin's Paperbacks) St. Martin's Pr.

**BREWSTER, ROBERT (FICTITIOUS CHARACTER)—FICTION**

Churchill, Jill. Anything Goes: A Grace & Favor Mystery. 1999. 272p. mass mkt. 6.99 (*0-380-80244-9*, Avon Bks.) Morrow/Avon.

—In the Still of the Night: A Grace & Favor Mystery. 2000. 272p. mass mkt. 6.99 (*0-380-80245-7*, Avon Bks.) Morrow/Avon.

—It Had to Be You: A Grace & Favor Mystery. 2004. 224p. 23.95 (*0-06-052843-5*, Morrow, William & Co.) Morrow/Avon.

—Love for Sale: A Grace & Favor Mystery. l.t. ed. 2003. 280p. 29.95 (*0-7862-5919-1*) Gale Group.

—Love for Sale: A Grace & Favor Mystery. 2004. 272p. mass mkt. 6.99 (*0-06-103122-4*, Avon Bks.); 2003. 224p. 23.95 (*0-06-019942-3*, Morrow, William & Co.) Morrow/Avon.

—Someone to Watch over Me: A Grace & Favor Mystery. l.t. ed. 2002. 309p. 28.95 (*0-7862-4356-2*) Gale Group.

—Someone to Watch over Me: A Grace & Favor Mystery. 2002. 272p. mass mkt. 6.99 (*0-06-103123-2*, Avon Bks.); 2001. 240p. 24.00 (*0-06-019941-5*, Morrow, William & Co.) Morrow/Avon.

**BRICHTER, PETER (FICTITIOUS CHARACTER)—FICTION**

Pulver, Mary M. Ashes to Ashes. 1992. 256p. 4.50 o.p. (*1-55773-768-1*, Diamond Bks.) Ace Bks.

—Ashes to Ashes. 1988. 288p. 16.95 o.p. (*0-312-02164-X*, Saint Martin's Minotaur) St. Martin's Pr.

—Knight Fall. 1992. 4.50 o.p. (*1-55773-648-0*, Diamond Bks.) Ace Bks.

—Murder at the War: A Modern-Day Mystery with a Medieval Setting. 1987. 228p. 16.95 o.p. (*0-312-00622-5*) St. Martin's Pr.

—Original Sin. 1993. 256p. 4.50 o.p. (*1-55773-846-7*, Diamond Bks.) Ace Bks.

—Original Sin. 1991. 192p. 18.95 o.s.i (*0-8027-5770-7*) Walker & Co.

—Show Stopper: A Kori & Peter Brichter Mystery. 1993. 240p. 4.50 o.s.i (*1-55773-925-0*, Diamond Bks.) Ace Bks.

—Show Stopper: A Kori & Peter Brichter Mystery. 1993. mass mkt. 4.50 o.p. (*0-425-15828-4*) Berkley Publishing Group.

—Show Stopper: A Kori & Peter Brichter Mystery. 1992. 204p. 19.95 (*0-8027-3210-0*) Walker & Co.

—The Unforgiving Minutes. 1992. 4.50 o.p. (*1-55773-686-3*, Diamond Bks.) Ace Bks.

—The Unforgiving Minutes. 1988. 336p. 17.95 o.p. (*0-312-01528-3*, Saint Martin's Minotaur) St. Martin's Pr.

**BRIGANCE, JAKE (FICTITIOUS CHARACTER)—FICTION**

Grisham, John. A Time to Kill. 1993. audio compact disk 112.00 (*0-7366-8912-5*); audio 88.00 (*0-7366-2362-0*, 3136) Books on Tape, Inc.

—A Time to Kill. 1992. 528p. mass mkt. 7.99 (*0-440-21172-7*) Dell Publishing.

—A Time to Kill. 1993. 496p. 30.00 (*0-385-47081-9*); 800p. 27.00 o.s.i (*0-385-47078-9*); 496p. 200.00 o.s.i (*0-385-47112-2*) Doubleday Publishing.

—A Time to Kill. l.t. ed. 1993. (*0-8161-5590-9*, Macmillan Reference USA) Gale Group.

—A Time to Kill, Set. unabr. ed. 1999. audio 49.95 Highsmith Inc.

—A Time to Kill, Level 5. 2000. pap. 7.93 (*0-582-36410-8*) Longman Publishing Group.

—A Time to Kill. 1992. audio 15.95 o.s.i (*0-553-74519-0*); 1992. audio 12.79 o.s.i (*0-553-70018-9*); 2001. audio 9.99 (*0-553-70220-3*); 2001. audio compact disk 23.95 (*0-553-71264-0*); 1992. audio 16.99 (*0-553-47069-8*, 391785); 1991. audio 13.59 o.s.i (*0-553-70067-7*); 1998. audio 49.95 (*0-553-50222-0*, 133760) Random Hse. Audio Publishing Group. (RH Audio).

—A Time to Kill. 1993. 415p. o.s.i (*0-7126-5906-4*) Random Hse. of Canada, Ltd. CAN. *Dist:* Random Hse., Inc.

—A Time to Kill. 1992. 14.04 (*0-606-14351-3*) Turtleback Bks.

—A Time to Kill. 1991. 416p. pap. 9.95 o.p. (*0-922066-72-8*); 1989. 384p. 18.95 o.p. (*0-922066-03-5*) Wynwood.

**BRILL, JANNA (FICTITIOUS CHARACTER)—FICTION**

Killough, Lee. Bridling Chaos. rev. ed. 1998. 624p. pap. 19.00 (*0-9658345-3-0*) Meisha Merlin Publishing, Inc.

—The Doppelganger Gambit. 1979. mass mkt. 1.95 o.s.i (*0-345-28267-1*) Ballantine Bks.

—Dragon's Teeth. 1990. mass mkt. 4.95 o.s.i (*0-445-20906-2*) Warner Bks., Inc.

—Spider Play. 1986. pap. 3.50 o.s.i (*0-445-20273-4*) Warner Bks., Inc.

**BRITTEN, ROLAND (FICTITIOUS CHARACTER)—FICTION**

Francis, Dick. Risk. 1993. 288p. mass mkt. 6.99 (*0-449-22239-X*, Fawcett) Ballantine Bks.

—Risk. unabr. ed. 1999. audio 39.95 (*0-7861-1482-7*, 2334) Blackstone Audio Bks., Inc.

—Risk. unabr. ed. 1994. audio 48.00 (*0-7366-2834-7*, 3542) Books on Tape, Inc.

—Risk. 1994. reprint ed. lib. bdg. 37.95 (*1-56849-281-2*) Buccaneer Bks., Inc.

—Risk. unabr. ed. 2000. audio 49.95 (*0-7451-5955-9*, CAB 660) Chivers Audio Bks. GBR. *Dist:* BBC Audiobooks America.

—Risk. l.t. ed. 1994. 329p. lib. bdg. 21.95 o.p. (*0-8161-5782-0*, Macmillan Reference USA) Gale Group.

—Risk. 1978. o.p. (*0-06-011302-2*) HarperCollins Pubs.

—Risk. 1990. audio 15.95; audio 17.00 o.p. (*1-55994-131-6*, CPN 2131) HarperTrade. (HarperAudio).

—Risk, Set. unabr. ed. 1999. audio 39.95 Highsmith Inc.

—Risk. abr. ed. 2000. audio 7.95 (*1-57815-048-5*, 1020, Media Bks. Audio Publishing) Media Bks., L. L. C.

—Risk. unabr. ed. 2000. audio 51.00 (*0-7887-0356-0*, 94548E7) Recorded Bks., LLC.

—Risk. 1990. mass mkt. 4.95 (*0-671-70469-9*); 1988. mass mkt. 3.95 (*0-671-68078-1*); 1984. mass mkt. 3.50 (*0-671-50755-9*); 1982. mass mkt. 2.95 o.s.i (*0-671-45074-3*) Simon & Schuster. (Pocket).

—Risk. l.t. ed. 1979. o.p. (*0-7089-0309-6*, Ulverscroft) Thorpe, F. A. Pubs.

**BROCK, DAVID (FICTITIOUS CHARACTER)—FICTION**

Maitland, Barry. Babel. 2003. (Illus.). 288p. 24.95 (*1-55970-668-6*) Arcade Publishing, Inc.

**BROCKMAN, LISA (FICTITIOUS CHARACTER)—FICTION**

Krich, Rochelle Majer. Fertile Ground: A Mystery. 1999. mass mkt. 6.99 (*0-380-78953-1*); 1998. 352p. mass mkt. 22.00 (*0-380-97378-2*) Morrow/Avon. (Avon Bks.).

**BROD, EMIL (FICTITIOUS CHARACTER)—FICTION**

Steinhauer, Olen. The Bridge of Sighs: A Novel. 288p. 2004. pap. 13.95 (*0-312-32601-7*, Saint Martin's Griffin); 2003. 23.95 (*0-312-30245-2*, Saint Martin's Minotaur) St. Martin's Pr.

**BROGAN, JERRY (FICTITIOUS CHARACTER)—FICTION**

Breen, Jon L. Hot Air: A Jerry Brogan Mystery. 1991. 208p. 19.00 o.p. (*0-671-68105-2*, Simon & Schuster) Simon & Schuster.

—Listen for the Click. 1983. 192p. 12.95 o.p. (*0-8027-5492-9*) Walker & Co.

—Loose Lips. 1992. 2.99 o.p. (*0-517-08070-2*) Random Hse. Value Publishing.

—Loose Lips. 1990. 17.95 o.p. (*0-671-68104-4*, Simon & Schuster) Simon & Schuster.

—Triple Crown. 1986. 192p. 13.95 o.p. (*0-8027-5627-1*) Walker & Co.

**BROKER, PHIL (FICTITIOUS CHARACTER)—FICTION**

Logan, Chuck. The Big Law. 1999. 448p. mass mkt. 7.50 (*0-06-109687-3*); 1998. 368p. 24.00 o.s.i (*0-06-019133-3*) HarperCollins Pubs.

—The Big Law. unabr. ed. 1998. audio 87.00 (*0-7887-3244-7*, 95848E7) Recorded Bks., LLC.

—The Price of Blood. 1997. 400p. 24.00 o.p. (*0-06-017492-7*) HarperCollins Pubs.

—The Price of Blood. 1998. 496p. mass mkt. 7.50 (*0-06-109622-9*, HarperTorch) Morrow/Avon.

**BROKETAIL, BAZIL (FICTITIOUS CHARACTER)—FICTION**

Rowley, Christopher B. Battle Dragon. 1995. (Basil Broketail Ser.). 416p. mass mkt. 5.99 o.s.i (*0-451-45343-3*, ROC) NAL.

—Bazil Broketail. 1992. (Bazil Broketail Ser.). 480p. mass mkt. 6.99 (*0-451-45206-2*, ROC) NAL.

—A Dragon at World's End. 1997. (Bazil Broketail Ser.). 416p. mass mkt. 6.99 o.s.i (*0-451-45546-0*, ROC) NAL.

—Dragon Ultimate. 1999. (Bazil Broketail Ser.). 384p. mass mkt. 6.99 o.s.i (*0-451-45548-7*, ROC) NAL.

—Dragons of Argonath. 1998. (Bazil Broketail Ser.: Vol. 6). 432p. mass mkt. 6.99 o.s.i (*0-451-45547-9*, ROC) NAL.

—Dragons of War. 1994. (Bazil Broketail Ser.). 496p. (Orig.). mass mkt. 6.99 o.s.i (*0-451-45342-5*, ROC) NAL.

—A Sword for a Dragon. 1993. (Bazil Broketail Ser.). 480p. (Orig.). mass mkt. 6.99 o.s.i (*0-451-45235-6*, ROC) NAL.

**BRONTE, SAM (FICTITIOUS CHARACTER)—FICTION**

Morris, Alan & Morris, Gilbert. Imperial Intrigue. 1996. (Katy Steele Adventures Ser.: Vol. 2). 275p. pap. 8.99 o.p. (*0-8423-2040-7*) Tyndale Hse. Pubs.

—Tracks of Deceit. l.t. ed. 1998. (Christian Fiction Ser.). 357p. 24.95 (*0-7862-1412-0*) Thorndike Pr.

—Tracks of Deceit. 1996. (Katy Steele Adventures Ser.: No. 1). 256p. pap. 8.99 o.p. (*0-8423-2039-3*) Tyndale Hse. Pubs.

**BRONWYN (FICTITIOUS CHARACTER: MILLER)—FICTION**

Miller, Ron. Hearts & Armor. 1992. (Bronwyn Trilogy Ser.: No. 3). 240p. (Orig.). mass mkt. 4.50 o.s.i (*0-441-32119-4*) Ace Bks.

—Silk & Steel. 1992. (Bronwyn Trilogy Ser.: Bk. 2). mass mkt. 3.99 o.s.i (*0-441-76489-4*) Ace Bks.

**BROOKE, LOVEDAY (FICTITIOUS CHARACTER)—FICTION**

Pirkis, Catherine L. The Experiences of Loveday Brooke, Lady Detective. 1986. 112p. reprint ed. pap. 4.95 o.p. (*0-486-25164-0*) Dover Pubns., Inc.

—The Murder at Troyte's Hill. 1981. audio Jimcin Recordings.

**BROOKS, DAN (FICTITIOUS CHARACTER)—FICTION**

Nathanson, E. M. & Bank, Aaron. Knight's Cross. unabr. collector's ed. 1995. audio 60.00 (*0-7366-2943-2*, 3638) Books on Tape, Inc.

—Knight's Cross: A Novel. 1995. 448p. mass mkt. 5.99 (*0-8439-3724-6*) Dorchester Publishing Co., Inc.

**BROOKS, JAY (FICTITIOUS CHARACTER)—FICTION**

Hoag, Tami. Guilty As Sin. 1997. 624p. mass mkt. 7.99 (*0-553-56452-8*) Bantam Bks.

—Guilty As Sin. l.t. ed. 1996. 825p. 25.95 o.p. (*0-7838-1821-1*, Macmillan Reference USA) Gale Group.

—Guilty As Sin. abr. ed. 1996. 6p. audio 23.00 (*1-56876-057-4*) Soundlines Entertainment, Inc.

—Night Sins. 1995. 576p. mass mkt. 7.99 (*0-553-56451-X*, Fanfare) Bantam Bks.

—Night Sins. l.t. ed. 1995. 821p. 25.95 o.p. (*0-7838-1348-1*, Macmillan Reference USA) Gale Group.

—Night Sins, abr. ed. 1996. audio 17.00 (*1-56876-058-2*, 394501) Soundlines Entertainment, Inc.

**BROOKS, R. J. (FICTITIOUS CHARACTER)—FICTION**

Bogart, Stephen Humphrey. Play It Again. 1996. 246p. pap. text 5.99 (*0-8125-5162-1*); 1995. 240p. 19.95 o.p. (*0-312-85665-2*) Doherty, Tom Assocs., LLC. (Forge Bks.).

—The Remake: As Time Goes By. 288p. 1997. 22.95 o.p. (*0-312-85666-0*); Vol. 1. 1998. (Remake Ser.: Vol. 1). mass mkt. 6.99 (*0-8125-5164-8*) Doherty, Tom Assocs., LLC. (Forge Bks.).

**BROOM, ANDREW (FICTITIOUS CHARACTER)—FICTION**

McInerny, Ralph. Body & Soil: An Andrew Broom Mystery. 1990. mass mkt. (*0-373-26063-6*, Harlequin Bks.) Harlequin Enterprises, Ltd.

—Body & Soil: An Andrew Broom Mystery. 1989. 224p. 17.95 o.p. (*0-689-12036-2*, Scribner) Simon & Schuster.

—Cause & Effect: An Andrew Broom Mystery. 1990. mass mkt. (*0-373-26046-6*, Harlequin Bks.) Harlequin Enterprises, Ltd.

—Cause & Effect: An Andrew Broom Mystery. 1987. 224p. 15.95 o.p. (*0-689-11894-5*, Scribner) Simon & Schuster.

—Frigor Mortis. l.t. ed. 1991. 19.95 o.p. (*0-7927-0733-8*, CH017); pap. 17.95 o.p. (*0-7927-0734-6*, CS0121) BBC Audiobooks America.

—Frigor Mortis. 1991. reprint ed. mass mkt. (*0-373-26080-6*, Harlequin Bks.) Harlequin Enterprises, Ltd.

—Frigor Mortis. 1989. 288p. 18.95 o.s.i (*0-689-12081-8*, Scribner) Simon & Schuster.

—Heirs & Parents: An Andrew Broom Mystery. 2000. (Andrew Broom Mysteries Ser.). 240p. 23.95 (*0-312-20311-X*, Saint Martin's Minotaur) St. Martin's Pr.

—Law & Ardor: An Andrew Broom Mystery. l.t. ed. 2001. (Beeler Large Print Mystery Ser.). 202p. 25.95 (*1-57490-410-8*, Beeler Large Print Bks.) Beeler, Thomas T. Publisher.

—Law & Ardor: An Andrew Broom Mystery. 1995. 256p. 21.00 (*0-684-80462-X*, Scribner) Simon & Schuster.

—Mom & Dead: An Andrew Broom Mystery. 256p. 2002. pap. 15.95 (*0-7432-3644-0*); 1994. 20.00 o.p. (*0-689-12181-4*) Simon & Schuster. (Scribner).

—Savings & Loam: An Andrew Broom Mystery. 1992. (WWL Mystery Ser.: No. 91). mass mkt. (*0-373-26091-1*, 1-26091-8, Harlequin Bks.) Harlequin Enterprises, Ltd.

—Savings & Loam: An Andrew Broom Mystery. 1993. 2.99 o.p. (*0-517-09633-1*) Random Hse. Value Publishing.

—Savings & Loam: An Andrew Broom Mystery. 1990. 224p. 17.95 o.s.i (*0-689-12037-0*, Scribner) Simon & Schuster.

**BROSSARD, PIERRE (FICTITIOUS CHARACTER)—FICTION**

Moore, Brian. The Statement. 2003. 224p. pap. 19.95 (*0-394-28199-3*, Plume); 1997. 256p. pap. 13.00 (*0-452-27632-2*, Plume); 1996. 256p. 22.95 o.p. (*0-525-94128-2*, Dutton) Dutton/Plume.

—The Statement. unabr. ed. 1998. audio 44.00 (*0-7887-1311-6*, 95085E7) Recorded Bks., LLC.

**BROTHER CADFAEL (FICTITIOUS CHARACTER)—FICTION**

*see Cadfael, Brother (Fictitious Character)—Fiction*

**BROUSSARD, ANDY (FICTITIOUS CHARACTER)—FICTION**

Donaldson, D. J. Blood on the Bayou. 1991. 16.95 o.p. (*0-312-05387-8*, Saint Martin's Minotaur) St. Martin's Pr.

—Cajun Nights. 1989. pap. 3.95 o.p. (*0-312-91610-8*, St. Martin's Paperbacks); 1988. 256p. 16.95 o.p. (*0-312-02175-5*, Saint Martin's Minotaur) St. Martin's Pr.

—Louisiana Fever. (Andy Broussard/Kit Franklyn Mysteries Ser.). 288p. 1997. mass mkt. 5.99 o.p. (*0-312-96257-6*, St. Martin's Paperbacks); 1996. 21.95 o.p. (*0-312-14362-1*, Saint Martin's Minotaur) St. Martin's Pr.

—New Orleans Requiem. 1995. (Mystery Ser.). 250p. per. (*0-373-26188-8*, 1-26188-2, Worldwide Library) Harlequin Enterprises, Ltd.

—New Orleans Requiem. 1994. 240p. 19.95 o.p. (*0-312-10495-2*, Saint Martin's Minotaur) St. Martin's Pr.

—No Mardi Gras for the Dead. 1995. (WWL Mystery Ser.). mass mkt. (*0-373-26163-2*, 1-26163-5, Harlequin Bks.) Harlequin Enterprises, Ltd.

—No Mardi Gras for the Dead. 1992. (Andy Broussard - Kit Franklyn Mystery Ser.). 216p. 17.95 o.p. (*0-312-08271-1*) St. Martin's Pr.

—Sleeping with the Crawfish: An Andy Broussard & Kit Franklyn Mystery. (Andy Broussard/Kit Franklyn Mysteries Ser.). 272p. 1998. mass mkt. 5.99 (*0-312-96681-4*, St. Martin's Paperbacks); 1997. 21.95 o.p. (*0-312-17025-4*, Saint Martin's Minotaur) St. Martin's Pr.

**BROUSSARD, ANNIE (FICTITIOUS CHARACTER)—FICTION**

Hoag, Tami. A Thin Dark Line. 1998. 608p. reprint ed. mass mkt. 7.99 (*0-553-57188-5*) Bantam Bks.

—A Thin Dark Line. 2002. pap. incl. audio (*0-7435-2754-2*) Encore Performance Publishing.

—A Thin Dark Line. l.t. ed. 1997. (Large Print Book Ser.). 26.95 o.p. (*1-56895-450-6*, Wheeler Publishing, Inc.) Gale Group.

—A Thin Dark Line, unabr. ed. 1997. audio 117.00 (*0-7887-1766-9*, 95244E7) Recorded Bks., LLC.

—A Thin Dark Line. abr. ed. 1997. audio 23.00 (*0-671-57477-9*, 495077, Simon & Schuster Audioworks) Simon & Schuster Audio.

**BROWN, CLINTON (FICTITIOUS CHARACTER)—FICTION**

Thompson, Jim. The Nothing Man. 1997. 224p. pap. 11.00 (*0-375-70031-5*, Vintage) Knopf Publishing Group.

—The Nothing Man. 1988. 208p. mass mkt. 4.50 o.s.i (*0-445-40570-8*, Mysterious Pr. Paperback Bks.) Warner Bks., Inc.

**BROWN, FATHER (FICTITIOUS CHARACTER)—FICTION**

Chesterton, G. K. The Annotated Innocence of Father Brown. 1998. (Illus.). 336p. pap. 12.95 (*0-486-29859-0*) Dover Pubns., Inc.

—The Annotated Innocence of Father Brown. Gardner, Martin, ed. 1988. 288p. pap. 7.95 o.p. (*0-19-282164-4*); 1987. (Illus.). 256p. 18.95 o.p. (*0-19-217748-6*) Oxford Univ. Pr., Inc.

—The Astonishing Father Brown. 1998. (Father Brown Mystery Ser.). audio 21.95 o.s.i (*1-55656-301-9*); audio 16.95 o.p. (*1-55656-300-0*) Dercum Audio.

—The Best of Father Brown. 1991. (Father Brown Mystery Ser.). 282p. pap. 7.95 o.p. (*0-460-87073-4*, Everyman's Classic Library in Paperback) Tuttle Publishing.

—The Best of Father Brown. Keating, H. R. F., ed. abr. ed. 1993. (Father Brown Mystery Ser.). 310p. pap. 9.95 (*0-460-87395-4*, Everyman's Classic Library in Paperback) Tuttle Publishing.

—The Blue Cross - A Father Brown Mystery. abr. ed. 1997. (Father Brown Mysteries Ser.). 3p. audio 16.99 (*0-88646-447-1*, 7447) Durkin Hayes Publishing Ltd.

—The Book of Father Brown. (Father Brown Mystery Ser.). reprint ed. lib. bdg. 19.95 (*0-89190-576-6*, Rivercity Pr.) Amereon, Ltd.

—The Book of Father Brown. 1990. (Father Brown Mystery Ser.). reprint ed. lib. bdg. 16.95 (*0-89968-494-7*) Buccaneer Bks., Inc.

—The Complete Father Brown. 1987. (Father Brown Mystery Ser.). 720p. pap. 16.95 (*0-14-009766-X*, Penguin Bks.) Penguin Group (USA) Inc.

—Father Brown: Selected Stories. 1995. (Father Brown Mystery Ser.). 582p. pap. (*0-19-282309-4*) Oxford Univ. Pr., Inc.

—Father Brown: Selected Stories. 1998. (Father Brown Mystery Ser.). pap. 3.95 (*1-85326-003-7*, 0037WW) Wordsworth Editions, Ltd. GBR. *Dist:* Casemate Pubs. & Bk. Distributors, LLC.

—Father Brown & the Church of Rome. 270p. 2002. pap. 13.95 (*0-89870-953-9*); 1996. 17.95 (*0-89870-590-8*) Ignatius Pr.

—Father Brown Crime Stories. 1990. (Father Brown Mystery Ser.). 12.99 o.s.i (*0-517-00182-9*) Random Hse. Value Publishing.

—The Father Brown Stories, Set. 1992. (Father Brown Mystery Ser.). audio 65.95 (*1-55685-269-X*) Audio Bk. Contractors, Inc.

—Favorite Father Brown Stories. 1993. (Father Brown Mystery Ser.). (Illus.). 96p. reprint ed. pap. 1.00 (*0-486-27545-0*) Dover Pubns., Inc.

—Following Father Brown. unabr. ed. (Father Brown Mystery Ser.). audio 21.95 o.p. (*1-55656-013-3*, DAB 038) BBC Audiobooks America.

—The Incredulity of Father Brown. (Father Brown Mystery Ser.). 20.95 (*0-89190-339-9*) Amereon, Ltd.

—The Incredulity of Father Brown. unabr. ed. 1992. (Father Brown Ser.). audio 44.95 (*0-7861-0126-1*, 1112) Blackstone Audio Bks., Inc.

—The Incredulity of Father Brown. unabr. collector's ed. 1986. (Father Brown Mystery Ser.). audio 48.00 (*0-7366-0893-1*, 1837) Books on Tape, Inc.

—The Incredulity of Father Brown. l.t. ed. 1984. (Father Brown Mystery Ser.). 9.95 o.p. (*0-8161-3680-7*); lib. bdg. 11.95 o.p. (*0-8161-3732-3*) Gale Group. (Macmillan Reference USA).

—The Incredulity of Father Brown. audio 38.95 NorthStar Audio Bks.

—The Incredulity of Father Brown. 1975. (Father Brown Mystery Ser.). pap. 3.95 o.p. (*0-14-001069-6*) Penguin Group (USA) Inc.

—The Incredulity of Father Brown. 1987. (Father Brown Mystery Ser.). 192p. pap. 4.95 o.p. (*0-14-008258-1*, Penguin Bks.) Viking Penguin.

—The Innocence of Father Brown. (Father Brown Mystery Ser.). 22.95 (*0-89190-338-0*) Amereon, Ltd.

—The Innocence of Father Brown. l.t. ed. 1991. (Father Brown Mystery Ser.). pap. 16.95 o.p. (*0-7927-0373-1*, CS042) BBC Audiobooks America.

—The Innocence of Father Brown. unabr. ed. 1992. (Father Brown Ser.). audio 44.95 (*0-7861-0124-5*, 1110) Blackstone Audio Bks., Inc.

—The Innocence of Father Brown. unabr. collector's ed. 1984. (Father Brown Mystery Ser.). audio 48.00 (*0-7366-0812-5*, 1762) Books on Tape, Inc.

—The Innocence of Father Brown. 1976. (Father Brown Mystery Ser.). reprint ed. lib. bdg. 21.00 o.p. (*0-8240-2359-5*) Garland Publishing, Inc.

—The Innocence of Father Brown. audio 42.95 NorthStar Audio Bks.

—The Innocence of Father Brown. 1975. (Father Brown Mystery Ser.). pap. 3.95 o.p. (*0-14-000765-2*) Penguin Group (USA) Inc.

—The Innocence of Father Brown. unabr. ed. 1989. (Father Brown Mystery Ser.). audio 51.00 (*1-55690-255-7*, 89930E7) Recorded Bks., LLC.

—The Innocence of Father Brown. 1987. (Father Brown Mystery Ser.). 256p. pap. 4.95 o.p. (*0-14-008257-3*, Penguin Bks.) Viking Penguin.

—The Invisible Man - A Father Brown Mystery. unabr. ed. 1998. (Father Brown Mysteries Ser.). audio 16.99 (*0-88646-455-2*, 7455) Durkin Hayes Publishing Ltd.

—The Scandal of Father Brown, unabr. ed. 1993. (Father Brown Mystery Ser.). audio 39.95 (*0-7451-5828-5*, CAT 4027) BBC Audiobooks America.

—The Scandal of Father Brown. unabr. ed. 1988. (Father Brown Ser.). audio 32.95 (*0-7861-0058-3*, 1055) Blackstone Audio Bks., Inc.

—The Scandal of Father Brown. unabr. collector's ed. 1994. (Father Brown Mystery Ser.). audio 36.00 (*0-7366-2756-1*, 3479) Books on Tape, Inc.

—The Scandal of Father Brown. l.t. ed. 1986. (Father Brown Mystery Ser.). 292p. 10.95 o.p. (*0-8161-3930-X*, Macmillan Reference USA) Gale Group.

—The Scandal of Father Brown. 2000. 182p. pap. 9.95 (*0-7551-0026-3*) House of Stratus, Inc. GBR. *Dist:* Midpoint Trade Bks., Inc.

—The Scandal of Father Brown. 1988. (Father Brown Mystery Ser.). audio 35.95 o.s.i (*0-8161-7782-1*) Thorndike Pr.

—The Scandal of Father Brown. (Father Brown Mystery Ser.). 1988. 176p. pap. 4.95 o.p. (*0-14-008256-5*); 1982. pap. 3.50 o.p. (*0-14-004739-5*) Viking Penguin. (Penguin Bks.).

—The Secret of Father Brown. (Father Brown Mystery Ser.). 20.95 (*0-89190-337-2*) Amereon, Ltd.

—The Secret of Father Brown. unabr. ed. 1999. (Father Brown Mystery Ser.). audio 39.95 (*0-7861-0016-8*, 1016) Blackstone Audio Bks., Inc.

—The Secret of Father Brown. unabr. collector's ed. 1994. (Father Brown Mystery Ser.). audio 42.00 (*0-7366-2755-3*, 3478) Books on Tape, Inc.

—The Secret of Father Brown. unabr. ed. 2000. (Father Brown Mystery Ser). audio 49.95 (*0-7451-5829-3*, CAB 428) Chivers Audio Bks. GBR. *Dist:* BBC Audiobooks America.

—The Secret of Father Brown. l.t. ed. 1985. (Father Brown Mystery Ser.). 312p. 9.95 o.p. (*0-8161-3929-6*, Macmillan Reference USA) Gale Group.

—The Secret of Father Brown. 2000. 204p. pap. 9.95 (*0-7551-0027-1*) House of Stratus, Inc. GBR. *Dist:* Midpoint Trade Bks., Inc.

—The Secret of Father Brown. unabr. ed. 2001. audio 38.95 NorthStar Audio Bks.

—The Secret of Father Brown. 1975. (Father Brown Mystery Ser.). pap. 3.50 o.p. (*0-14-003807-8*) Penguin Group (USA) Inc.

—The Secret of Father Brown. 1989. (Father Brown Mystery Ser.). audio 53.95 o.s.i (*0-8161-7726-0*) Thorndike Pr.

—The Secret of Father Brown. 1987. (Father Brown Mystery Ser.). 176p. pap. 4.95 o.p. (*0-14-008255-7*, Penguin Bks.) Viking Penguin.

—The Wisdom of Father Brown. (Father Brown Mystery Ser.). 21.95 (*0-89190-336-4*) Amereon, Ltd.

—The Wisdom of Father Brown. unabr. ed. 1992. (Father Brown Mystery Ser.). audio 44.95 (*0-7861-0125-3*, 1111) Blackstone Audio Bks., Inc.

—The Wisdom of Father Brown. unabr. collector's ed. 1986. (Father Brown Mystery Ser.). audio 48.00 (*0-7366-0813-3*, 1763) Books on Tape, Inc.

—The Wisdom of Father Brown. 2001. audio 42.95 NorthStar Audio Bks.

—The Wisdom of Father Brown. 1975. (Father Brown Mystery Ser.). pap. 3.50 o.p. (*0-14-003118-9*) Penguin Group (USA) Inc.

—The Wisdom of Father Brown. l.t. ed. 2000. (Father Brown Mystery Ser.). 280p. pap. 18.95 (*1-888725-27-3*, MacroPrintBooks) Science & Humanities Pr.

—The Wisdom of Father Brown. 1987. (Father Brown Mystery Ser.). 208p. pap. 4.95 o.p. (*0-14-008159-3*, Penguin Bks.) Viking Penguin.

Following Father Brown. unabr. ed. Incl. Absence of Mr. Glass. audio o.p. Blast of the Book. audio o.p. Man in the Passage. audio o.p. Oracle of the Dog. audio o.p. 1986. (Father Brown Mystery Ser.). 1986. Set audio 16.95 o.p. (*1-55656-008-7*) Dercum Audio.

Kendrick, Stephen. Night Watch. 2003. 272p. pap. 13.00 (*0-425-19167-2*, Prime Crime) Berkley Publishing Group.

—Night Watch: A Long-Lost Adventure in Which Sherlock Holmes Meets Father Brown. 2001. (Illus.). 272p. 23.00 (*0-375-40367-1*, Pantheon) Knopf Publishing Group.

**BROWN, FRITZ (FICTITIOUS CHARACTER)—FICTION**

Ellroy, James. Brown's Requiem. 1998. 256p. pap. 13.00 (*0-380-73177-0*); 1981. pap. 4.99 (*0-380-78741-5*) Morrow/Avon. (Avon Bks.).

**BROWN, HERMIONE (FICTITIOUS CHARACTER)—FICTION**

Yorke, Margaret. Dangerous to Know. 1994. 272p. 17.95 o.p. (*0-89296-500-2*); 1995. pap. 21.95 o.p. (*0-7927-2055-5*); 1994. 23.95 o.p. (*0-7927-2056-3*) BBC Audiobooks America.

—Dangerous to Know. 1995. 256p. mass mkt. 5.50 o.s.i (*0-446-40198-6*) Warner Bks., Inc.

**BROWN, JACKIE (FICTITIOUS CHARACTER)—FICTION**

Leonard, Elmore. Jackie Brown. 1997. 352p. mass mkt. 6.50 o.s.i (*0-440-22606-6*) Dell Publishing.

—Rum Punch. 1998. 304p. pap. 9.95 o.s.i (*0-385-33280-7*, Dell Bks.) Dell Publishing.

Tarantino, Quentin & Leonard, Elmore. Jackie Brown: A Screenplay. 1997. (Illus.). 144p. pap. 10.95 (*0-7868-8349-9*) Hyperion Pr.

**BROWN, MARGO (FICTITIOUS CHARACTER)—FICTION**

Day, Marlis. Death of a Hoosier Schoolmaster. 2002. 192p. pap. 11.95 (*1-56315-288-6*) SterlingHouse Pubs., Inc.

—Why Johnny Died. 1999. 192p. pap. 11.95 (*1-56315-184-7*); 1998. 200p. pap. 11.95 (*1-56315-114-6*) SterlingHouse Pubs., Inc.

**BROWNE, AGNES (FICTITIOUS CHARACTER)—FICTION**

Huxley, Aldous. Brave New World & Brave New World Revisited. unabr. ed. 2002. audio compact disk 37.95 (*1-57270-302-4*) Audio Partners Publishing Corp.

O'Carroll, Brendan. Agnes Browne - The Mammy: MTV. 2000. 176p. pap. 10.95 o.s.i (*0-452-28169-5*, Plume) Dutton/Plume.

—The Chisellers. unabr. collector's ed. 2000. audio 24.95 (*0-7366-4948-4*) Books on Tape, Inc.

—The Chisellers. 2000. 192p. pap. 11.95 (*0-452-28122-9*, Plume) Dutton/Plume.

—The Chisellers. l.t. ed. 2000. (G. K. Hall Core Ser.). 230p. 28.95 (*0-7838-9259-4*, Macmillan Reference USA) Gale Group.

—The Granny. l.t. ed. 2000. (G. K. Hall Core Ser.). 229p. 29.95 (*0-7838-9260-8*, Macmillan Reference USA) Gale Group.

—The Granny: A Novel. 2000. 192p. pap. 11.95 (*0-452-28184-9*, Plume) Dutton/Plume.

—The Mammy. 2000. audio 24.95 (*0-7366-4691-4*); 1999. audio compact disk 40.00 (*0-7366-5196-9*); 2000. audio 29.95 (*0-7366-4696-5*); 1999. audio 32.00 (*0-7366-4657-4*, 5039) Books on Tape, Inc.

—The Mammy. l.t. ed. 2000. 262p. lib. bdg. 26.95 (*1-58547-037-6*) Ctr. Point Large Print.

—The Mammy. 1999. 176p. pap. 11.95 (*0-452-28103-2*, Plume) Dutton/Plume.

—The Mammy. 1994. 174 p. (*0-86278-372-0*) O'Brien Pr., Ltd., The.

—The Mammy. abr. ed. 1999. audio 18.95 (*0-14-180079-8*, Penguin AudioBooks) Viking Penguin.

—The Young Wan: An Agnes Browne Novel. 2003. 224p. 23.95 (*0-670-03114-3*, Viking) Viking Penguin.

**BROWNE, CLIO (FICTITIOUS CHARACTER)—FICTION**

Komo, Dolores. Clio Browne: Private Investigator. 1988. (WomanSleuth Mystery Ser.). 200p. pap. 6.95 o.p. (*0-89594-320-4*); lib. bdg. 22.95 o.p. (*0-89594-321-2*) Crossing Pr., Inc., The.

**BRUNETTI, GUIDO (FICTITIOUS CHARACTER)—FICTION**

Leon, Donna. Acqua Alta, unabr. collector's ed. 1998. audio 48.00 (*0-7366-4294-3*, 4787) Books on Tape, Inc.

—Acqua Alta. 1996. 288p. 22.50 o.p. (*0-06-018651-8*) HarperCollins Pubs.

—Death & Judgement. unabr. ed. 1998. audio 44.95 Blackstone Audio Bks., Inc.

—Death & Judgement. 1995. 304p. 20.00 o.p. (*0-06-017796-9*) HarperCollins Pubs.

—Death & Judgment. 1996. 304p. mass mkt. 4.99 o.p. (*0-06-109523-0*, HarperTorch) Morrow/Avon.

—Death at la Fenice. 1995. 288p. mass mkt. 6.99 (*0-06-104337-0*, HarperTorch) Morrow/Avon.

—Death at la Fenice. l.t. ed. 2003. (General Ser.). (FRE.). lib. bdg. 24.95 (*0-7862-5107-7*) Thorndike Pr.

—Death at La Fenice. unabr. ed. 1999. audio 27.95 (*0-7861-1538-6*); 1997. audio 44.95 (*0-7861-1193-3*, 1951) Blackstone Audio Bks., Inc.

—Death at La Fenice. unabr. collector's ed. 1998. (Guido Brunetti Mystery Ser.). audio 48.00 (*0-7366-4217-X*, 4715) Books on Tape, Inc.

—Death at La Fenice: A Novel of Suspense. 1992. 224p. 19.00 o.p. (*0-06-016871-4*) HarperTrade.

—Death in a Strange Country: A Guido Brunetti Mystery, unabr. ed. 1997. audio 44.95 (*0-7861-1228-X*, 1971) Blackstone Audio Bks., Inc.

—Death in a Strange Country: A Guido Brunetti Mystery. unabr. collector's ed. 1998. (Guido Brunetti Mystery Ser.). audio 48.00 (*0-7366-4218-8*, 4716) Books on Tape, Inc.

—Death in a Strange Country: A Guido Brunetti Mystery. 1993. 304p. 20.00 o.p. (*0-06-017008-5*) HarperTrade.

—Death in a Strange Country: A Guido Brunetti Mystery. 1995. 288p. mass mkt. 4.50 o.p. (*0-06-109406-4*, HarperTorch) Morrow/Avon.

—Dressed for Death, unabr. ed. 1997. audio 44.95 (*0-7861-1194-1*, 1953) Blackstone Audio Bks., Inc.

—Dressed for Death, , unabr. collector's ed. 1999. (Guido Brunetti Mystery Ser.). audio 48.00 (*0-7366-4317-6*, 4785) Books on Tape, Inc.

—Dressed for Death. 1994. 288p. 20.00 o.p. (*0-06-017795-0*) HarperTrade.

—Dressed for Death. 1995. 304p. mass mkt. 4.99 o.p. (*0-06-109418-8*, HarperTorch) Morrow/Avon.

—Uniform Justice. 2003. 280p. 19.95 (*0-87113-903-0*, Atlantic Monthly Pr.) Grove/Atlantic, Inc.

—Uniform Justice. 2004. 320p. mass mkt. 7.99 (*0-14-200422-7*) Penguin Group (USA) Inc.

**BRUNO, ADAM (FICTITIOUS CHARACTER)—FICTION**

Topor, Tom. The Codicil. abr. ed. 1996. audio 7.99 o.p. (*1-56740-106-6*, 826, Paperback Nova Audio Bks.); 1995. audio 16.95 o.p. (*1-56100-429-4*, 1146, Nova Audio Bks.); 1995. audio 89.25 o.p. (*1-56100-262-3*, 827, Unabridged Library Editions); 1995. audio 25.95 o.p. (*1-56100-637-8*, 66, Bookcassette) Brilliance Audio.

—The Codicil. 1995. 352p. 21.95 (*0-7868-6153-3*); 1996. 576p. reprint ed. mass mkt. 5.99 (*0-7868-8906-3*) Hyperion Pr.

—The Codicil. l.t. ed. 1995. 600p. 24.95 o.p. (*0-7838-1375-9*) Thorndike Pr.

**BUCHANAN, TOM (FICTITIOUS CHARACTER)—FICTION**

Holms, Joyce. Hot Potato. 2003. 240p. 24.95 (*0-7490-0605-6*) Allison & Busby, Ltd. GBR. *Dist:* International Publishers Marketing.

Ward, Jonas. Buchanan Calls the Shots. (Buchanan Ser.). 1981. 144p. mass mkt. 1.95 o.s.i (*0-449-14210-8*, Fawcett); 1978. mass mkt. 1.25 o.s.i (*0-449-13760-0*) Ballantine Bks.

—Buchanan Calls the Shots. l.t. ed. 1990. (Linford Western Large Print Ser.). pap. 17.99 (*0-7089-6943-7*, Linford) Thorpe, F. A. Pubs. GBR. *Dist:* Ulverscroft Large Print Bks., Ltd., Ulverscroft Large Print Canada, Ltd.

—Buchanan Gets Mad. 1981. (Buchanan Ser.). mass mkt. 1.95 o.s.i (*0-449-14209-4*, Fawcett) Ballantine Bks.

—Buchanan Gets Mad. l.t. ed. 1996. (Western Ser.). 199p. 23.95 (*0-7838-1661-8*) Thorndike Pr.

—Buchanan on the Prod. (Buchanan Ser.). 1981. 144p. mass mkt. 1.95 o.s.i (*0-449-14107-1*, Fawcett); 1975. mass mkt. 1.25 o.s.i (*0-449-13472-5*) Ballantine Bks.

—Buchanan on the Prod. l.t. ed. 1985. (Linford Western Library). 304p. pap. 17.99 (*0-7089-6144-4*, Linford) Thorpe, F. A. Pubs. GBR. *Dist:* Ulverscroft Large Print Bks., Ltd., Ulverscroft Large Print Canada, Ltd.

—Buchanan on the Run. (Buchanan Ser.). 1981. mass mkt. 1.75 o.s.i (*0-449-14208-6*, Fawcett); 1975. mass mkt. 1.25 o.s.i (*0-449-13474-1*) Ballantine Bks.

—Buchanan Says No. (Buchanan Ser.). 1981. mass mkt. 1.95 o.s.i (*0-449-14164-0*, Fawcett); 1978. mass mkt. 1.25 o.s.i (*0-449-13862-3*); 1974. mass mkt. 0.95 o.s.i (*0-449-13022-3*) Ballantine Bks.

—Buchanan Says No. l.t. ed. 1985. (Linford Western Library). 256p. pap. 17.99 (*0-7089-6140-1*, Linford) Thorpe, F. A. Pubs. GBR. *Dist:* Ulverscroft Large Print Bks., Ltd., Ulverscroft Large Print Canada, Ltd.

—Buchanan Takes Over. 1981. mass mkt. 1.95 o.s.i (*0-449-14063-6*, Fawcett) Ballantine Bks.

—Buchanan Takes Over. l.t. ed. 1989. (Linford Western Large Print Ser.). pap. 17.99 (*0-7089-6772-8*, Linford) Thorpe, F. A. Pubs. GBR. *Dist:* Ulverscroft Large Print Bks., Ltd., Ulverscroft Large Print Canada, Ltd.

—Buchanan's Big Fight. 1981. mass mkt. 1.95 o.s.i (*0-449-14406-2*, Fawcett) Ballantine Bks.

—Buchanan's Big Fight. l.t. ed. 1990. (Linford Western Large Print Ser.). pap. 17.99 (*0-7089-6868-6*, Linford) Thorpe, F. A. Pubs. GBR. *Dist:* Ulverscroft Large Print Bks., Ltd., Ulverscroft Large Print Canada, Ltd.

—Buchanan's Big Showdown. 1981. (Buchanan Ser.). 176p. mass mkt. 1.95 o.s.i (*0-449-14109-8*, Fawcett) Ballantine Bks.

—Buchanan's Black Sheep. 1984. (Buchanan Ser.). 176p. mass mkt. 2.50 o.s.i (*0-449-12412-6*, Fawcett) Ballantine Bks.

—Buchanan's Black Sheep. l.t. ed. 1990. (Linford Western Large Print Ser.). pap. 17.99 (*0-7089-6938-0*, Linford) Thorpe, F. A. Pubs. GBR. *Dist:* Ulverscroft Large Print Bks., Ltd., Ulverscroft Large Print Canada, Ltd.

—Buchanan's Gamble. (Buchanan Ser.). 1981. mass mkt. 1.95 o.s.i (*0-449-14177-2*, Fawcett); 1975. mass mkt. 1.25 o.s.i (*0-449-13473-3*) Ballantine Bks.

—Buchanan's Gamble. l.t. ed. 1989. (Linford Western Library). 305p. pap. 17.99 (*0-7089-6683-7*, Linford) Thorpe, F. A. Pubs. GBR. *Dist:* Ulverscroft Large Print Bks., Ltd., Ulverscroft Large Print Canada, Ltd.

—Buchanan's Gun. 1982. (Buchanan Ser.). 160p. mass mkt. 1.95 o.s.i (*0-449-14211-6*, Fawcett) Ballantine Bks.

—Buchanan's Gun. l.t. ed. 1976. (Ulverscroft Large Print Ser.). 29.99 o.p. (*0-85456-437-3*, Ulverscroft) Thorpe, F. A. Pubs. GBR. *Dist:* Ulverscroft Large Print Bks., Ltd., Ulverscroft Large Print Canada, Ltd.

—Buchanan's Manhunt. 1981. mass mkt. 1.75 o.s.i (*0-449-14119-5*, Fawcett) Ballantine Bks.

—Buchanan's Manhunt. l.t. ed. 1989. (Linford Western Library). pap. 17.99 (*0-7089-6760-4*, Linford) Thorpe, F. A. Pubs. GBR. *Dist:* Ulverscroft Large Print Bks., Ltd., Ulverscroft Large Print Canada, Ltd.

—Buchanan's Range War. 1980. (Buchanan Ser.). 224p. mass mkt. 1.75 o.s.i (*0-449-14357-0*, Fawcett) Ballantine Bks.

—Buchanan's Range War. l.t. ed. 1987. (Linford Western Library). 240p. pap. 17.99 o.p. (*0-7089-6351-X*, Linford) Thorpe, F. A. Pubs. GBR. *Dist:* Ulverscroft Large Print Bks., Ltd., Ulverscroft Large Print Canada, Ltd.

—Buchanan's Revenge. 1982. (Buchanan Ser.). 144p. mass mkt. 2.25 o.s.i (*0-449-12361-8*, Fawcett) Ballantine Bks.

—Buchanan's Revenge. l.t. ed. 1996. (G. K. Hall Western Ser.). 227p. 21.95 (*0-7838-1877-7*) Thorndike Pr.

—Buchanan's Revenge. l.t. ed. 1985. (Ulverscroft Large Print Ser.). 496p. 29.99 o.p. (*0-7089-1291-5*, Ulverscroft) Thorpe, F. A. Pubs. GBR. *Dist:* Ulverscroft Large Print Bks., Ltd., Ulverscroft Large Print Canada, Ltd.

—Buchanan's Showdown. 1976. mass mkt. 1.25 o.s.i (*0-449-13553-5*) Ballantine Bks.

—Buchanan's Siege. 1982. 160p. mass mkt. 2.25 o.s.i (*0-449-14086-5*, Fawcett) Ballantine Bks.

—Buchanan's Siege. l.t. ed. 1990. (Linford Western Library). pap. 17.99 (*0-7089-6804-X*, Linford) Thorpe, F. A. Pubs. GBR. *Dist:* Ulverscroft Large Print Bks., Ltd., Ulverscroft Large Print Canada, Ltd.

—Buchanan's Stage Line. 1986. (Buchanan Ser.). 176p. mass mkt. 2.50 o.s.i (*0-449-12847-4*, Fawcett) Ballantine Bks.

—Buchanan's Stage Line. l.t. ed. 1987. (Linford Western Library). 272p. pap. 17.99 o.p. (*0-7089-6427-3*, Linford) Thorpe, F. A. Pubs. GBR. *Dist:* Ulverscroft Large Print Bks., Ltd., Ulverscroft Large Print Canada, Ltd.

—Buchanan's Stolen Railway. 1979. (Buchanan Ser.). mass mkt. 1.75 o.s.i (*0-449-13977-8*, Fawcett) Ballantine Bks.

—Buchanan's Texas Treasure. 1982. (Buchanan Ser.). 160p. mass mkt. 2.25 o.s.i (*0-449-14175-6*, Fawcett) Ballantine Bks.

—Buchanan's Texas Treasure. l.t. ed. 1991. (Linford Western Large Print Ser.). pap. 17.99 (*0-7089-6960-7*, Ulverscroft) Thorpe, F. A. Pubs. GBR. *Dist:* Ulverscroft Large Print Bks., Ltd., Ulverscroft Large Print Canada, Ltd.

—Buchanan's War. (Buchanan Ser.). 1981. mass mkt. 1.95 o.s.i (*0-449-14137-3*, Fawcett); 1974. mass mkt. 0.95 o.s.i (*0-449-13025-8*) Ballantine Bks.

—Buchanan's War. l.t. ed. 1997. (G. K. Hall Western Ser.). 233p. lib. bdg. 20.95 (*0-7838-1878-5*) Thorndike Pr.

—Get Buchanan! 1979. (Buchanan Ser.). mass mkt. 1.50 o.s.i (*0-449-14062-8*, Fawcett) Ballantine Bks.

—Get Buchanan! l.t. ed. 1990. (Linford Western Library). pap. 17.99 o.p. (*0-7089-6811-2*, Ulverscroft) Thorpe, F. A. Pubs. GBR. *Dist:* Ulverscroft Large Print Bks., Ltd., Ulverscroft Large Print Canada, Ltd.

—The Name's Buchanan. (Buchanan Ser.). 1980. 128p. mass mkt. 1.75 o.s.i (*0-449-14135-7*, Fawcett); 1977. mass mkt. 1.25 o.s.i (*0-449-13858-5*) Ballantine Bks.

—The Name's Buchanan. l.t. ed. 1995. 204p. 18.95 (*0-7838-1471-2*, Macmillan Reference USA) Gale Group.

—Trap for Buchanan. 1979. (Buchanan Ser.). 144p. mass mkt. 1.50 o.s.i (*0-449-14082-2*, Fawcett) Ballantine Bks.

—Trap for Buchanan. l.t. ed. 1989. (Linford Western Library). 256p. pap. 17.99 (*0-7089-6715-9*, Linford) Thorpe, F. A. Pubs. GBR. *Dist:* Ulverscroft Large Print Bks., Ltd., Ulverscroft Large Print Canada, Ltd.

### BUCKINGHAM, DARBY (FICTITIOUS CHARACTER)—FICTION

McCarthy, Gary. The Comstock Camels. unabr. ed. 1995. (Derby Man Ser.: Bk. 11). audio 39.95 (*1-55686-620-8*) Books in Motion.

—Mustang Fever. unabr. ed. 1994. (Derby Man Ser.: Bk. 3). audio 39.95 (*1-55686-551-1*) Books in Motion.

—Mustang Fever. 1981. pap. 1.95 o.p. (*0-440-15308-5*) Dell Publishing.

—Mustang Fever. 1980. (Double D Western Ser.). 10.95 o.p. (*0-385-15472-0*) Doubleday Publishing.

—Whiskey Creek. unabr. ed. 1995. (Derby Man Ser.: Bk. 10). audio 39.95 (*1-55686-617-8*) Books in Motion.

—Whiskey Creek. 1992. 192p. 15.00 o.s.i (*0-385-41989-9*) Doubleday Publishing.

### BUENOROSTRO, RAFE (FICTITIOUS CHARACTER)—FICTION

Hinojosa, Rolando. Los Amigos de Becky. 1991. (Klail City Death Trip Ser.). (SPA.). 128p. pap. 9.50 o.p. (*1-55885-021-X*) Arte Publico Pr.

—Ask a Policeman: A Rafe Buenrostro Mystery. 1998. (Rafe Buenrostro Mysteries Ser.). 256p. pap. text 12.95 (*1-55885-226-3*) Arte Publico Pr.

—Becky & Her Friends. 1990. (Klail City Death Trip Ser.). 160p. pap. 9.50 (*1-55885-006-6*) Arte Publico Pr.

—Claros Varones de Belken: Fair Gentlemen of Belken County, Bilingual Edition. Cruz, Julia, tr. 1986. (United States Hispanic Creative Literature Ser.).Tr. of Fair Gentlemen of Belken County. (ENG & SPA.). 224p. pap. text 16.00 (*0-916950-65-4*); 223p. lib. bdg. 26.00 (*0-916950-64-6*) Bilingual Pr./Editorial Bilingue.

—El Condado de Belken-Klail City. 1994. (Clasicos Chicanos - Chicano Classics Ser.: No. 8). 168p. 25.00 (*0-927534-33-9*); pap. 15.00 (*0-927534-34-7*) Bilingual Pr./Editorial Bilingue.

—Dear Rafe. 1985. 136p. pap. 8.50 (*0-934770-38-7*) Arte Publico Pr.

—Estampas del Valle. 1994. (Clasicos Chicanos - Chicano Classics Ser.: No. 7). (SPA.). 144p. 24.00 (*0-927534-24-X*); pap. 13.00 (*0-927534-25-8*) Bilingual Pr./Editorial Bilingue.

—Klail City. 1987. (Klail City Death Trip Ser.). 144p. pap. 9.00 (*0-934770-54-9*) Arte Publico Pr.

—Mi Querido Rafa. 1981. (Klail City Death Trip Ser.). (SPA.). 112p. (C). pap. 8.50 o.p. (*0-934770-10-7*) Arte Publico Pr.

—Partners in Crime. 1985. 248p. (C). pap. 10.00 (*0-934770-37-9*) Arte Publico Pr.

—Rites & Witnesses. 1982. (Klail City Death Trip Ser.). 112p. pap. 8.50 o.p. (*0-934770-19-0*) Arte Publico Pr.

—The Useless Servants. 1993. 192p. (C). 8.95 (*1-55885-068-6*) Arte Publico Pr.

—The Valley. 1983. (Klail City Death Trip Ser.). 112p. 18.00 (*0-916950-37-9*); pap. 10.00 (*0-916950-38-7*) Bilingual Pr./Editorial Bilingue.

### BUGLE ANN (FICTITIOUS CHARACTER)—FICTION

Kantor, MacKinlay. The Voice of Bugle Ann & the Daughter of Bugle Ann. 1980. 192p. 1.95 o.s.i (*0-515-05458-5*, Jove) Berkley Publishing Group.

—The Voice of Bugle Ann & the Romance of Rosy Ridge. 1994. lib. bdg. 21.95 (*1-56849-379-7*) Buccaneer Bks., Inc.

### BULMAN, GEORGE (FICTITIOUS CHARACTER)—FICTION

Royce, Kenneth. Shadows. 1996. 288p. 22.00 (*0-7278-4878-X*); 384p. 26.00 o.p. (*0-7278-7006-8*) Severn Hse. Pubs., Ltd.

### BUMPPO, NATTY (FICTITIOUS CHARACTER)—FICTION

Cooper, James Fenimore. The Deerslayer. 1964. (YA). (gr. 6 up). pap. 2.95 o.p. (*0-8049-0031-0*, CL31) Airmont Publishing Co., Inc.

—The Deerslayer. Date not set. 410p. 27.95 (*0-8488-2517-9*) Amereon, Ltd.

—The Deerslayer. 1991. (States & Their Symbols Ser.). 528p. (gr. 9-12). mass mkt. 5.95 (*0-553-21085-8*, Bantam Classics) Bantam Bks.

—The Deerslayer. unabr. collector's ed. 1983. Pt. A. (J). audio 64.00 (*0-7366-3981-0*, 9529A); Pt. B. audio 64.00 (*0-7366-3982-9*, 9529-B) Books on Tape, Inc.

—The Deerslayer. 1984. 517p. lib. bdg. 27.95 o.p. (*0-89966-490-3*); 1976. lib. bdg. 21.95 (*0-89968-162-X*, Lightyear Pr.) Buccaneer Bks., Inc.

—The Deerslayer. 1841. 572p. (YA). reprint ed. pap. text 34.00 (*1-4047-2387-0*) Classic Textbooks.

—The Deerslayer. l.t. ed. 298p. lib. bdg. 32.00 (*0-7583-3384-6*) Huge Print Pr.

—The Deerslayer. 1963. 544p. (J). (gr. 7). mass mkt. 2.95 o.p. (*0-451-51645-1*); mass mkt. 5.95 (*0-451-52484-5*, CE1645) NAL. (Signet Classics).

—The Deerslayer. Peck, Daniel H., ed. 2000. (Oxford World's Classics Ser.). (Illus.). 592p. pap. 10.95 (*0-19-283725-7*) Oxford Univ. Pr., Inc.

—The Deerslayer. 1993. (Oxford World's Classics Ser.). (Illus.). 588p. pap. 7.95 o.p. (*0-19-282811-8*) Oxford Univ. Pr., Inc.

—The Deerslayer. 1990. (Works of James Fenimore Cooper). reprint ed. lib. bdg. 79.00 (*0-7812-2387-3*) Reprint Services Corp.

—The Deerslayer. Pease, Donald, ed. & intro. by. 1996. (Classics Ser.). 576p. pap. 10.95 (*0-14-039061-8*, Penguin Classics) Viking Penguin.

—The Deerslayer. 1998. (Classics Library). pap. 3.95 (*1-85326-552-7*, 5527WW) Wordsworth Editions, Ltd. GBR. *Dist:* Combined Publishing.

—The Deerslayer, or the First Warpath. 1990. (Scribner Illustrated Classics Ser.). (Illus.). 480p. (YA). (gr. 7 up). 27.00 (*0-684-19224-1*, Atheneum) Simon & Schuster Children's Publishing.

—The Deerslayer, or the First Warpath. 1987. 12.00 (*0-606-00553-6*) Turtleback Bks.

—The Deerslayer or the First Warpath. Schachterle, Lance, ed. & intro. by. 1987. (Writings of James Fenimore Cooper Ser.). 682p. (C). pap. text 19.95 (*0-87395-790-3*); text 59.50 (*0-87395-361-4*) State Univ. of New York Pr.

—The Deerslayer, or the First Warpath. deluxe ed. 1990. (Illustrated Classics Ser.). (Illus.). 480p. (YA). 75.00 o.s.i (*0-684-19234-9*, Atheneum) Simon & Schuster Children's Publishing.

—The Last of the Mohicans. 1997. (Classics Illustrated Study Guides). (Illus.). mass mkt. 4.99 (*1-57840-053-8*) Acclaim Bks.

—The Last of the Mohicans. 27.95 (*0-89190-895-1*) Amereon, Ltd.

—The Last of the Mohicans. 1994. (Illustrated Classics Collection). 64p. pap. 4.95 (*0-7854-0699-9*, 40459); pap. 3.60 o.p. (*1-56103-537-8*) American Guidance Service, Inc.

—The Last of the Mohicans, Set. audio 65.95 (*1-55685-399-8*) Audio Bk. Contractors, Inc.

—The Last of the Mohicans. 1982. (Bantam Classics Ser.). (Illus.). 400p. mass mkt. 4.95 (*0-553-21329-6*, Bantam Classics) Bantam Bks.

—The Last of the Mohicans. 1991. mass mkt. 3.95 (*0-425-12674-9*) Berkley Publishing Group.

—The Last of the Mohicans. unabr. ed. 1993. audio 85.95 (*0-7861-0453-8*, 1405) Blackstone Audio Bks., Inc.

—The Last of the Mohicans. unabr. collector's ed. 1994. (YA). audio 88.00 (*0-7366-2687-5*, 3422) Books on Tape, Inc.

—The Last of the Mohicans. unabr. ed. 1993. (Bookcassette Classic Collection). audio 59.25 (*1-56100-121-X*, 924); (Illus.). audio 19.95 o.p. (*1-56100-487-1*, 159, Bookcassette) Brilliance Audio.

—The Last of the Mohicans. 1983. 450p. reprint ed. lib. bdg. 26.95 o.p. (*0-89966-312-5*) Buccaneer Bks., Inc.

—The Last of the Mohicans. 2001. (Early Best Sellers Ser.). (Illus.). reprint ed. pap. text 28.00 (*0-7426-6013-3*) Classic Bks.

—The Last of the Mohicans. 1992. (Illus.). 434p. pap. text 3.99 (*0-8125-2297-4*, Tor Classics) Doherty, Tom Assocs., LLC.

—The Last of the Mohicans. 2003. (Dover Thrift Editions Ser.). 288p. 3.00 (*0-486-42678-5*) Dover Pubns., Inc.

—The Last of the Mohicans. abr. ed. (Read-Along Ser.). 1994. pap. 29.99 incl. audio (*0-88646-841-8*, LSR 7332); Set. 1992. (Illus.). audio 16.99 (*0-88646-332-7*, 7332) Durkin Hayes Publishing Ltd.

—The Last of the Mohicans. 2003. (Barnes & Noble Classics Ser.). 480p. mass mkt. 4.95 (*1-59308-065-4*) Fine Communications.

—The Last of the Mohicans. l.t. ed. 1993. 21.95 o.p. (*1-56895-002-0*, Wheeler Publishing, Inc.) Gale Group.

—The Last of the Mohicans, Set. unabr. ed. 1999. audio 85.95 Highsmith Inc.

—The Last of the Mohicans. l.t. ed. 683p. pap. 45.77 (*0-7583-1338-1*); 877p. pap. 64.12 (*0-7583-1339-X*); 398p. pap. 31.50 (*0-7583-1336-5*); 497p. pap. 37.14 (*0-7583-1337-3*); 1998p. pap. 123.32 (*0-7583-1343-8*); 1129p. pap. 76.55 (*0-7583-1340-3*); 1389p. pap. 89.59 (*0-7583-1341-1*); 1708p. pap. 110.73 (*0-7583-1342-X*); 497p. lib. bdg. 43.14 (*0-7583-1329-2*); 683p. lib. bdg. 51.77 (*0-7583-1330-6*); 398p. lib. bdg. 37.50 (*0-7583-1328-4*); 877p. lib. bdg. 76.12 (*0-7583-1331-4*); 1389p. lib. bdg. 101.59 (*0-7583-1333-0*); 1998p. lib. bdg. 143.86 (*0-7583-1335-7*); 1129p. lib. bdg. 88.55 (*0-7583-1332-2*); 1708p. lib. bdg. 128.92 (*0-7583-1334-9*) Huge Print Pr.

—The Last of the Mohicans. 2002. 372p. 26.99 (*1-4043-1560-8*); per. 22.99 (*1-4043-1561-6*) IndyPublish.com.

—The Last of the Mohicans. unabr. ed. 1984. audio 69.00 Jimcin Recordings.

—The Last of the Mohicans. E-Book 1.95 (*1-57799-933-9*) Logos Research Systems, Inc.

—The Last of the Mohicans, Level 2. 2000. (C). pap. 11.33 (*0-582-34279-1*) Longman Publishing Group.

—The Last of the Mohicans. E-Book 1.95 (*1-58515-169-6*) MesaView, Inc.

—The Last of the Mohicans. (Signet Classics). 2000. (Illus.). 432p. mass mkt. 4.95 (*0-451-52765-8*, Signet Bks.); 1970. mass mkt. 0.75 o.p. (*0-451-50521-2*, Signet Classics); 1970. mass mkt. 0.60 o.p. (*0-451-50320-1*, Signet Classics); 1970. mass mkt. 0.50 o.p. (*0-451-50148-9*, Signet Classics); 1962. mass mkt. 0.95 o.p. (*0-451-50707-X*, Signet Classics); 1962. mass mkt. 1.50 o.p. (*0-451-51054-2*, Signet Classics); 1962. mass mkt. 2.50 o.p. (*0-451-51495-5*); 1962. mass mkt. 1.25 o.p. (*0-451-50866-1*, Signet Classics); 1962. mass mkt. 1.95 o.p. (*0-451-51282-0*, Signet Classics) NAL.

—The Last of the Mohicans. abr. ed. 1996. audio 17.98 (*962-634-587-X*, NA308714); audio compact disk 19.98 (*962-634-087-8*, NA308712) Naxos of America, Inc. (Naxos AudioBooks).

—The Last of the Mohicans. abr. ed. (Ultimate Classics Ser.). 1994. audio 29.95 o.p. (*0-7871-0061-7*); 1993. (Illus.). audio 16.95 o.p. (*1-55800-579-X*) NewStar Media, Inc. (Dove Audio).

—The Last of the Mohicans. l.t. ed. 2003. 476p. E-Book 2.99 (*1-932681-32-9*) NuVision Pubns.

—The Last of the Mohicans. McWilliams, John, ed. & intro. by. 1998. (Oxford World's Classics Ser.). (Illus.). 464p. pap. 9.95 (*0-19-283505-X*) Oxford Univ. Pr., Inc.

—The Last of the Mohicans. McWilliams, John P., Jr., ed. 1990. (Oxford World's Classics Ser.). (Illus.). 408p. pap. 7.95 o.p. (*0-19-282638-7*) Oxford Univ. Pr., Inc.

—The Last of the Mohicans. 1984. 12.95 o.p. (*0-396-08260-2*) Putnam Publishing Group, The.

—The Last of the Mohicans. 1999. (Illus.). E-Book 3.99 incl. cd-rom (*1-57646-016-9*) Quiet Vision Publishing.

—The Last of the Mohicans. 2001. (Modern Library Classics). 400p. pap. 9.95 (*0-375-75764-3*, Modern Library) Random House Adult Trade Publishing Group.

—The Last of the Mohicans. 1986. 3.99 o.s.i (*0-517-62630-6*) Random Hse. Value Publishing.

—The Last of the Mohicans. 1984. (Illus.). 432p. 12.95 o.p. (*0-89577-199-3*) Reader's Digest Assn., Inc., The.

—The Last of the Mohicans, unabr. ed. 2001. audio 91.00 (*1-55690-298-0*, 89630E7) Recorded Bks., LLC.

—The Last of the Mohicans. 1990. (Works of James Fenimore Cooper). reprint ed. lib. bdg. 79.00 (*0-7812-2374-1*) Reprint Services Corp.

—The Last of the Mohicans. Peters, Sally, ed. 1992. 432p. mass mkt. 5.99 (*0-671-75931-0*, Pocket) Simon & Schuster.

—The Last of the Mohicans. Shefter, Harry, ed. 1985. pap. 0.95 o.s.i (*0-671-47962-8*, Washington Square Pr.) Simon & Schuster.

—The Last of the Mohicans. Beard, James F., ed. & intro. by. 1983. (Writings of James Fenimore Cooper Ser.). 418p. (C). pap. text 19.95 (*0-87395-470-X*) State Univ. of New York Pr.

—The Last of the Mohicans. 1983. (Writings of James Fenimore Cooper Ser.). (Illus.). 418p. (C). text 20.50 (*0-87395-362-2*) State Univ. of New York Pr.

—The Last of the Mohicans. l.t. ed. 2003. 630p. 29.95 (*0-7862-5790-3*) Thorndike Pr.

—The Last of the Mohicans. 2000. (Signature Classics Ser.). 376p. 24.95 (*1-58279-089-2*); lib. bdg. 29.95 (*1-58279-085-X*) Trident Pr. International.

—The Last of the Mohicans. 1980. 11.00 (*0-606-02760-2*) Turtleback Bks.

—The Last of the Mohicans. 1970. 410p. pap. 3.95 o.p. (*0-460-87137-4*); 1994. 432p. pap. 5.95 (*0-460-87545-0*) Tuttle Publishing. (Everyman's Classic Library in Paperback).

—The Last of the Mohicans. 1992. (Illus.). 391p. reprint ed. 29.95 o.p. (*1-877767-70-0*) University Publishing Hse., Inc.

—The Last of the Mohicans. Slotkin, Richard, ed. & intro. by. 1986. (Penguin Classics Ser.). (Illus.). 384p. pap. 9.95 (*0-14-039024-3*, Penguin Classics) Viking Penguin.

—The Last of the Mohicans. 1997. (Classics Ser.). (Illus.). 336p. pap. 3.95 (*1-85326-049-5*, 0495WW) Wordsworth Editions, Ltd. GBR. *Dist:* Casemate Pubs. & Bk. Distributors, LLC.

—The Last of the Mohicans Read-Along. 1994. (Illustrated Classics Collection). 64p. pap. 14.95 incl. audio (*0-7854-0740-5*, 40461); pap. 13.50 o.p. incl. audio (*1-56103-539-4*) American Guidance Service, Inc.

—The Leatherstocking Tales: The Pioneers; The Last of the Mohicans; The Prairie. Nevius, Blake, ed. 1985. (Library of America: Vol. 1). 1347p. 40.00 (*0-940450-20-8*, C10461) Library of America, The.

—The Leatherstocking Tales Vol. 2: The Pathfinder; The Deerslayer. Nevius, Blake, ed. 1985. (Library of America: Vol. 2). 1051p. 35.00 (*0-940450-21-6*, C12048) Library of America, The.

—The Pathfinder. 1998. pap. 4.99 o.p. (*1-57840-198-4*) Acclaim Bks.

—The Pathfinder. 1964. (Airmont Classics Ser.). (YA). (gr. 6 up). mass mkt. 2.95 (*0-8049-0035-3*, CL-35) Airmont Publishing Co., Inc.

—The Pathfinder. 1976. lib. bdg. 26.95 (*0-89968-159-X*, Lightyear Pr.); 1984. 419p. reprint ed. lib. bdg. 26.95 o.p. (*0-89966-491-1*) Buccaneer Bks., Inc.

—The Pathfinder. 1840. 502p. (YA). reprint ed. pap. text 34.00 (*1-4047-2386-2*) Classic Textbooks.

—The Pathfinder. 1961. (Leatherstocking Tale Ser.). (Illus.). 448p. (J). (gr. k-10). mass mkt. 5.95 (*0-451-52257-5*, Signet Classics) NAL.

—The Pathfinder. 1990. (Works of James Fenimore Cooper). reprint ed. lib. bdg. 79.00 (*0-7812-2386-5*) Reprint Services Corp.

—The Pathfinder. 1961. 12.00 (*0-606-02759-9*) Turtleback Bks.

—The Pathfinder. House, Kay S., ed. & intro. by. 1989. (Classics Ser.). 512p. pap. 12.00 (*0-14-039071-5*, Penguin Classics) Viking Penguin.

—The Pathfinder: Or, the Inland Sea. Date not set. 351p. 25.95 (*0-8488-2541-1*) Amereon, Ltd.

—The Pathfinder: Or, the Inland Sea. Kelly, William P., ed. (Oxford World's Classics Ser.). 2000. 528p. pap. 11.95 (*0-19-283989-6*); 1993. 522p. pap. 7.95 o.p. (*0-19-282956-4*) Oxford Univ. Pr., Inc.

—The Pathfinder: Or, the Inland Sea. 1980. (Writings of James Fenimore Cooper Ser.). 569p. (C). text 59.50 o.p. (*0-87395-360-6*); pap. text 19.95 (*0-87395-477-7*) State Univ. of New York Pr.

—The Pathfinder: Or, the Inland Sea. 1992. (Illus.). 417p. reprint ed. lib. bdg. 31.95 o.p. (*1-877767-65-4*) University Publishing Hse., Inc.

—The Pioneers. Date not set. 346p. 25.95 (*0-8488-2544-6*) Amereon, Ltd.

—The Pioneers. 1993. 608p. mass mkt. 4.50 o.s.i (*0-553-21417-9*, Bantam Classics) Bantam Bks.

—The Pioneers. 1976. lib. bdg. 26.95 (*0-89968-157-3*, Lightyear Pr.); 1984. 493p. reprint ed. lib. bdg. 26.95 o.p. (*0-89966-492-X*) Buccaneer Bks., Inc.

—The Pioneers, Set. unabr. ed. 1999. audio 85.95 Highsmith Inc.

—The Pioneers. 1969. mass mkt. 0.75 o.p. (*0-451-50480-1*, Signet Classics); 1969. mass mkt. 0.60 o.p. (*0-451-50214-0*, Signet Classics); 1964. mass mkt. 1.50 o.p. (*0-451-50921-8*, Signet Classics); 1964. mass mkt. 2.50 o.p. (*0-451-51416-5*, Signet Classics); 1964. mass mkt. 3.95 o.p. (*0-451-52145-5*); 1964. mass mkt. 3.50 o.p. (*0-451-51621-4*, Signet Classics); 1964. mass mkt. 1.25 o.p. (*0-451-50746-0*, Signet Classics); 1964. mass mkt. 1.95 o.p. (*0-451-51156-5*, Signet Classics) NAL.

—The Pioneers. unabr. ed. 2001. audio 68.95 NorthStar Audio Bks.

—The Pioneers. Wallace, James D., ed. & intro. by. 2000. (Oxford World's Classics Ser.). (Illus.). 496p. pap. 10.95 (*0-19-283667-6*) Oxford Univ. Pr., Inc.

—The Pioneers. Wallace, James D., ed. 1992. (Oxford World's Classics Ser.). (Illus.). 484p. pap. 7.95 o.p. (*0-19-282802-9*, 4581) Oxford Univ. Pr., Inc.

—The Pioneers. 1990. (Works of James Fenimore Cooper). reprint ed. lib. bdg. 79.00 (*0-7812-2371-7*) Reprint Services Corp.

—The Pioneers. Clark, Robert, ed. 1993. (Illus.). 444p. pap. 6.95 o.p. (*0-460-87187-0*, Everyman's Classic Library in Paperback) Tuttle Publishing.

—The Pioneers. Ringe, Donald A., ed. & intro. by. 1988. (Classics Ser.). 480p. pap. 11.00 (*0-14-039007-3*, Penguin Classics) Viking Penguin.

—The Pioneers or the Sources of the Susquehanna: A Descriptive Tale. 1980. (Writings of James Fenimore Cooper Ser.). 460p. (C). pap. text 31.95 (*0-87395-423-8*) State Univ. of New York Pr.

—The Pioneers or the Susquehanna: A Descriptive Tale. 1980. (Writings of James Fenimore Cooper Ser.). 460p. (C). text 18.50 o.p. (*0-87395-359-2*) State Univ. of New York Pr.

—Prairie. Date not set. 411p. 27.95 (*0-8488-2546-2*) Amereon, Ltd.

—The Prairie. unabr. ed. 1995. audio 76.95 (*0-7861-0911-4*, 1705) Blackstone Audio Bks., Inc.

—The Prairie. 1976. lib. bdg. 28.95 (*0-89968-160-3*, Lightyear Pr.) Buccaneer Bks., Inc.

—The Prairie, Set. unabr. ed. 1999. audio 76.95 Highsmith Inc.

—The Prairie. 1970. mass mkt. 0.75 o.p. (*0-451-50519-0*); 1970. mass mkt. 0.60 o.p. (*0-451-50223-X*); 1964. mass mkt. 1.25 o.p. (*0-451-50794-0*); 1964. mass mkt. 3.95 o.p. (*0-451-51780-6*); 1964. mass mkt. 2.95 o.p. (*0-451-51511-0*); 1964. mass mkt. 1.75 o.p. (*0-451-51202-2*); 1964. mass mkt. 1.50 o.p. (*0-451-50987-0*); 1964. mass mkt. 0.95 o.p. (*0-451-50623-5*) NAL. (Signet Classics).

—The Prairie. Ringe, Donald A., ed. (Oxford World's Classics Ser.). 2000. 432p. pap. 11.95 (*0-19-283766-4*); 1992. 418p. pap. 8.95 o.p. (*0-19-282824-X*) Oxford Univ. Pr., Inc.

—The Prairie. 1990. (Works of James Fenimore Cooper). reprint ed. lib. bdg. 79.00 (*0-7812-2375-X*) Reprint Services Corp.

—The Prairie. Elliott, James P., ed. 1985. 566p. (C). pap. text 19.95 (*0-87395-672-9*) State Univ. of New York Pr.

—The Prairie. Elliott, James P., ed. & intro. by. 1985. 566p. (C). text 21.50 (*0-87395-363-0*) State Univ. of New York Pr.

—The Prairie. Nevius, Blake, ed. & intro. by. 1987. (Classics Ser.). 416p. pap. 13.00 (*0-14-039026-X*, Penguin Classics) Viking Penguin.

### BUNKOWSKI, DANIEL "CHAINGANG" (FICTITIOUS CHARACTER)—FICTION

Miller, Rex. Butcher. Grad, Doug, ed. 1994. 320p. mass mkt. 5.50 (*0-671-86882-9*, Pocket) Simon & Schuster.

—Butcher. 2002. 273p. pap. 6.99 (*1-58586-076-X*); 2000. E-Book 6.99 (*1-58586-235-5*); 2000. E-Book 6.99 (*1-58586-075-1*); 2000. 273p. E-Book 6.99 (*1-58586-074-3*) ereads.com.

—Chaingang. Grad, Doug, ed. 1992. 320p. mass mkt. 4.99 (*0-671-74847-5*, Pocket) Simon & Schuster.

—Chaingang. 2002. 217p. pap. 6.99 (*1-58586-079-4*); 2000. 6.99 (*1-58586-236-3*); 2000. E-Book 6.99 (*1-58586-078-6*); 2000. 217p. E-Book 6.99 (*1-58586-077-8*) ereads.com.

—Savant. Grad, Doug, ed. 1994. 288p. mass mkt. 5.99 (*0-671-74848-3*, Pocket) Simon & Schuster.

—Savant. E-Book 6.99 (*0-7592-0788-7*); 2000. pap. 19.95 (*1-58586-150-2*); 2000. E-Book 6.99 (*1-58586-148-0*); 2000. E-Book 6.99 (*1-58586-271-1*); 2000. E-Book 6.99 (*1-58586-149-9*) ereads.com.

—Slob. 1988. mass mkt. 4.95 o.p. (*0-451-40065-8*, Onyx); 1987. 304p. mass mkt. 3.95 o.p. (*0-451-15005-8*, Signet Bks.) NAL.

—Slob. 2002. 168p. pap. 6.99 (*1-58586-155-3*); 2000. E-Book 6.99 (*1-58586-154-5*); 2000. E-Book 6.99 (*1-58586-273-8*); 1987. 168p. E-Book 6.99 (*1-58586-153-7*) ereads.com.

—Stone Shadow. 1989. mass mkt. 3.95 o.p. (*0-451-40164-6*, 036, Onyx) NAL.

—Stone Shadow. E-Book 6.99 (*0-7592-0797-6*); 2000. pap. 19.95 (*1-58586-164-2*); 2000. E-Book 6.99 (*1-58586-162-6*); 2000. E-Book 6.99 (*1-58586-163-4*); 2000. E-Book 6.99 (*1-58586-280-0*) ereads.com.

### BURENIN FAMILY (FICTITIOUS CHARACTERS)—FICTION

Pella, Judith. Dawning of Deliverance. 1995. (Russians Ser.: Bk. 5). 432p. pap. 12.99 (*1-55661-359-8*) Bethany Hse. Pubs.

—Heirs of the Motherland. 1993. (Russians Ser.: Vol. 4). 384p. pap. 12.99 (*1-55661-358-X*) Bethany Hse. Pubs.

—Passage into Light. 1998. (Russians Ser.: Vol. 7). 304p. pap. 11.99 (*1-55661-869-7*) Bethany Hse. Pubs.

—Russians, 5 vols., Vol. 1-5, set. 1995. (Russians Ser.: Vol. 1-5). pap. 64.99 (*1-55661-795-X*) Bethany Hse. Pubs.

—White Nights, Red Morning. 1996. (Russians Ser.: Bk. 6). 416p. pap. 12.99 (*1-55661-360-1*) Bethany Hse. Pubs.

Phillips, Michael & Pella, Judith. The Crown & the Crucible. 1991. (Russians Ser.: Bk. 1). 416p. pap. 12.99 (*1-55661-172-2*) Bethany Hse. Pubs.

—A House Divided. 1992. (Russians Ser.: Vol. 2). 352p. pap. 12.99 (*1-55661-173-0*) Bethany Hse. Pubs.

—The Russians Series, Vols. 1-3. 1992. (Russians Ser.). pap. 32.99 o.p. (*1-55661-770-4*, 252770) Bethany Hse. Pubs.

—Travail & Triumph Vol. 3: The Russians. 1992. (Russians Ser.: Vol. 3). 400p. pap. 12.99 (*1-55661-174-9*) Bethany Hse. Pubs.

### BURGOYNE 172 (FICTITIOUS CHARACTER)—FICTION

David, Peter. Double or Nothing. 1999. (Star Trek, The Next Generation Ser.: Vol. 5). 277p. pap. 6.50 o.s.i (*0-671-03478-2*, Star Trek) Simon & Schuster.

—End Game. 1997. (Star Trek Ser.: No. 4). (Illus.). 208p. pap. 3.99 (*0-671-01398-X*, Star Trek) Simon & Schuster.

—Excalibur: Renaissance. 2000. (Star Trek Ser.: No. 10). 288p. pap. 6.99 (*0-671-04239-4*, Star Trek) Simon & Schuster.

—House of Cards; Into the Void; The Two-Front War; End Game. abr. ed. 1997. (Star Trek Ser.: Nos. 1-4). audio 22.00 (*0-671-57625-9*, Simon & Schuster Audioworks) Simon & Schuster Audio.

—Into the Void. 1997. (Star Trek Ser.: No. 2). (Illus.). 176p. pap. 3.99 (*0-671-01396-3*, Star Trek) Simon & Schuster.

—Martyr. 1998. (Star Trek Ser.: No. 5). (Illus.). 288p. pap. 6.50 (*0-671-02036-6*, Star Trek) Simon & Schuster.

### BURKE (FICTITIOUS CHARACTER: VACHSS)—FICTION

Vachss, Andrew. Blossom. 2001. E-Book 11.50 (*1-59061-234-5*) Adobe Systems, Inc.

—Blossom. 1991. 320p. mass mkt. 5.95 o.s.i (*0-8041-0751-3*, Ivy Bks.) Ballantine Bks.

—Blossom. 1996. 272p. pap. 13.00 (*0-679-77261-8*) McKay, David Co., Inc.

—Blue Belle. 2001. E-Book 11.00 (*1-59061-228-0*) Adobe Systems, Inc.

—Blue Belle. 1994. lib. bdg. 24.95 o.p. (*1-56849-463-7*) Buccaneer Bks., Inc.

—Blue Belle. 1990. 336p. mass mkt. 4.95 o.p. (*0-451-16290-0*, Signet Bks.) NAL.

—Blue Belle. 1995. 352p. pap. 13.00 (*0-679-76168-3*) Random Hse., Inc.

—Choice of Evil: A Burke Novel. 2001. E-Book 11.50 (*1-59061-222-1*) Adobe Systems, Inc.

—Choice of Evil: A Burke Novel. 2000. (Crime - Black Lizard Ser.). 336p. pap. 13.00 (*0-375-70662-3*, Vintage) Knopf Publishing Group.

—Choice of Evil: A Burke Novel. 1999. (Burke Novels Ser.). 305p. 23.00 o.s.i (*0-375-40647-6*) Knopf, Alfred A. Inc.

—Choice of Evil: A Burke Novel. 2001. E-Book 7.99 (*0-375-71913-X*) Random Hse., Inc.

—Dead & Gone. 2001. E-Book 11.50 (*1-59061-224-8*) Adobe Systems, Inc.

—Dead & Gone. 2001. 352p. pap. 13.00 (*0-375-72526-1*, Vintage) Knopf Publishing Group.

—Dead & Gone. 2001. E-Book 7.99 (*0-375-41361-8*) Random Hse., Inc.

—Down in the Zero. 2001. E-Book 11.00 (*1-59061-229-9*) Adobe Systems, Inc.

—Down in the Zero. 1995. pap. 7.00 o.s.i (*0-679-76087-3*); 272p. pap. 12.00 (*0-679-76066-0*) Random Hse., Inc.

—False Allegations: A Burke Novel. 2001. E-Book 11.00 (*1-59061-235-3*) Adobe Systems, Inc.

—False Allegations: A Burke Novel. 1997. 240p. pap. 12.00 (*0-679-77293-6*, Vintage) Knopf Publishing Group.

—False Allegations: A Burke Novel. 1996. 229p. 23.00 (*0-679-45109-9*) Knopf, Alfred A. Inc.

—Flood: A Burke Novel. 2002. E-Book 11.50 (*1-59061-886-6*) Adobe Systems, Inc.

—Flood: A Burke Novel. 1994. lib. bdg. 24.95 o.p. (*1-56849-465-3*) Buccaneer Bks., Inc.

—Flood: A Burke Novel. 1985. 341p. 17.95 o.s.i (*0-917657-43-8*) Fine, Donald I. Bks.

—Flood: A Burke Novel. 1986. mass mkt. 5.99 (*0-671-61905-5*, Pocket) Simon & Schuster.

—Footsteps of the Hawk. 2001. E-Book 11.00 (*1-59061-233-7*) Adobe Systems, Inc.

—Footsteps of the Hawk. 1996. 256p. pap. 12.00 (*0-679-76663-4*) Random Hse., Inc.

—Hard Candy. 2001. E-Book 11.00 (*1-59061-230-2*) Adobe Systems, Inc.

—Hard Candy. 1994. lib. bdg. 24.95 o.p. (*1-56849-464-5*) Buccaneer Bks., Inc.

—Hard Candy. 1990. mass mkt. 4.95 o.p. (*0-451-16690-6*, Signet Bks.) NAL.

—Hard Candy. 1990. 4.99 o.p. (*0-517-05629-1*) Random Hse. Value Publishing.

—Hard Candy. 1995. 256p. pap. 12.00 (*0-679-76169-1*) Random Hse., Inc.

—Only Child: A Burke Novel. 2002. 288p. 24.00 (*0-375-41487-8*) Knopf, Alfred A. Inc.

—Pain Management: A Burke Novel. 2001. E-Book 19.00 (*1-59061-376-7*) Adobe Systems, Inc.

—Pain Management: A Burke Novel. 2002. 336p. pap. 13.00 (*0-375-72647-0*) Random Hse., Inc.

—Sacrifice. 2001. E-Book 11.00 (*1-59061-231-0*) Adobe Systems, Inc.

—Sacrifice. 1992. mass mkt. 5.99 o.s.i (*0-8041-0919-2*, Ivy Bks.) Ballantine Bks.

—Sacrifice. 1992. 4.99 o.p. (*0-517-09513-0*) Random Hse. Value Publishing.

—Sacrifice. 1996. 288p. pap. 12.00 (*0-679-76410-0*) Random Hse., Inc.

—Safe House: A Burke Novel. 2001. E-Book 11.00 (*1-59061-225-6*) Adobe Systems, Inc.

—Safe House: A Burke Novel. 1999. 320p. pap. 12.00 (*0-375-70074-9*, Vintage) Knopf Publishing Group.

—Safe House: A Burke Novel. 2001. E-Book 7.99 (*0-375-71912-1*) Random Hse., Inc.

—Strega. 2001. E-Book 11.00 (*1-59061-232-9*) Adobe Systems, Inc.

—Strega. 1991. mass mkt. 5.99 o.s.i (*0-8041-0925-7*, Ivy Bks.) Ballantine Bks.

—Strega. 1987. 293p. 18.95 o.s.i (*0-394-55937-1*) Knopf, Alfred A. Inc.

—Strega. 1988. mass mkt. 4.50 o.p. (*0-451-15179-8*, Signet Bks.) NAL.

—Strega. 1988. 3.99 o.p. (*0-517-68183-8*) Random Hse. Value Publishing.

—Strega. 1996. 304p. pap. 12.00 (*0-679-76409-7*) Random Hse., Inc.

### BURKE, CALEY (FICTITIOUS CHARACTER)—FICTION

McKenna, Bridget. Caught Dead. 1995. 240p. (Orig.). mass mkt. 4.99 o.s.i (*0-425-14493-3*, Prime Crime) Berkley Publishing Group.

—Dead Ahead. 1994. 208p. (Orig.). mass mkt. 4.50 o.s.i (*0-425-14300-7*, Prime Crime) Berkley Publishing Group.

—Murder Beach. 1993. 208p. (Orig.). 4.50 o.p. (*1-55773-967-6*, Diamond Bks.) Ace Bks.

### BURKE, DENISE (FICTITIOUS CHARACTER)—FICTION

Smith, Mary-Ann Tirone. An American Killing. 1999. 352p. mass mkt. 6.99 (*0-449-00579-8*, Fawcett) Ballantine Bks.

—An American Killing. abr. ed. 1998. audio 17.95 o.p. (*1-56740-801-X*, 1447, Nova Audio Bks.); audio 26.95 o.s.i (*1-56740-077-9*, 1446, Bookcassette); audio 73.25 (*1-56740-606-8*, 1448, Unabridged Library Editions) Brilliance Audio.

—An American Killing. 1999. E-Book 6.99 (*0-8050-6250-5*); 1998. 368p. 23.00 o.s.i (*0-8050-5702-1*) Holt, Henry & Co.

### BURKE, EDDIE (FICTITIOUS CHARACTER)—FICTION

Lance, Peter. First Degree Burn. 1997. 384p. mass mkt. 5.99 o.s.i (*0-425-15698-2*, Prime Crime) Berkley Publishing Group.

### BURKE, TOM (FICTITIOUS CHARACTER)—FICTION

Hunt, E. Howard. Body Count. 1993. mass mkt. (*0-312-92945-5*, St. Martin's Paperbacks); 1991. 336p. 19.95 o.p. (*0-312-06911-1*) St. Martin's Pr.

### BURLANE, JAMES (FICTITIOUS CHARACTER)—FICTION

Abercrombie, Neil & Hoyt, Richard. Blood of Patriots. 1997. 317p. pap. 6.99 (*0-8125-6795-1*); 1996. 352p. 24.95 o.p. (*0-312-86166-4*) Doherty, Tom Assocs., LLC. (Forge Bks.).

Hoyt, Richard. The Dragon Portfolio. 352p. 1988. pap. 4.99 o.p. (*0-8125-0496-8*); 1986. 15.95 o.p. (*0-312-93168-9*) Doherty, Tom Assocs., LLC. (Tor Bks.).

—Japanese Game. 1996. 308p. mass mkt. 5.99 (*0-8125-3107-8*); 1995. 288p. 13.99 o.p. (*0-312-85553-2*) Doherty, Tom Assocs., LLC. (Forge Bks.).

—Marimba. 1993. 352p. mass mkt. 4.99 o.p. (*0-8125-1563-3*); 1992. 288p. 18.95 o.p. (*0-312-85193-6*) Doherty, Tom Assocs., LLC. (Tor Bks.).

—Red Card. 1995. 275p. pap. 4.99 o.p. (*0-8125-3096-9*); 1994. 256p. 19.95 o.p. (*0-312-85554-0*) Doherty, Tom Assocs., LLC. (Forge Bks.).

—Tyger! Tyger! 1999. 253p. pap. 5.99 (*0-8125-5071-4*); 1996. 256p. 21.95 o.p. (*0-312-85804-3*) Doherty, Tom Assocs., LLC. (Forge Bks.).

**BURLINGAME, JESSIE (FICTITIOUS CHARACTER)—FICTION**

King, Stephen. Gerald's Game. 1993. 448p. mass mkt. 7.99 (0-451-17646-4); pap. 6.99 (0-451-17811-4) NAL. (Signet Bks.).

—Gerald's Game. abr. unabr. ed. 1992. audio 34.95 (0-453-00800-3) Penguin/HighBridge.

—Gerald's Game. 1992. pap. 6.98 o.p. (0-8317-2752-7) Smithmark Pubs., Inc.

—Gerald's Game. 1992. 14.04 (0-606-05310-7) Turtleback Bks.

—Gerald's Game. 1992. 352p. 23.50 o.s.i (0-670-84650-3) Viking Penguin.

—El Juego de Gerald. unabr. ed. 1995. Tr. of Gerald's Game. (SPA.). audio 49.95 o.p. (0-7871-0601-1, 113236) NewStar Media, Inc.

**BURNELL, MAXEY (FICTITIOUS CHARACTER)—FICTION**

Cail, Carol. If Two of Them Are Dead. 1997. 272p. mass mkt. 5.50 o.s.i (0-440-22299-0) Dell Publishing.

—If Two of Them Are Dead. pap. 15.95 (0-312-30032-8, Saint Martin's Griffin); pap. 15.95 (0-312-30101-4, Saint Martin's Griffin); 1996. 224p. 15.95 (0-312-14361-3, Saint Martin's Minotaur) St. Martin's Pr.

—Private Lies. 1993. 256p. mass mkt. 4.50 o.p. (0-06-108057-8, HarperTorch) Morrow/Avon.

—Unsafe Keeping. 1996. 304p. mass mkt. 5.50 o.s.i (0-440-22298-2) Dell Publishing.

—Unsafe Keeping. pap. (0-312-30031-X, Saint Martin's Griffin); pap. 15.95 (0-312-29194-9, Saint Martin's Griffin); 1995. 218p. 15.95 (0-312-13198-4, Saint Martin's Minotaur) St. Martin's Pr.

—Who Was Sylvia? 1999. (Maxey Burnell Mystery Ser.). 180p. pap. text 16.99 (1-886199-04-3, Madison Publishing Co.) Deadly Alibi Pr., Ltd.

**BURNS, ANTONIO (FICTITIOUS CHARACTER)—FICTION**

McKinzie, Clinton. The Edge of Justice. unabr. ed. 2002. audio 64.00 (0-7366-8660-6); audio compact disk 80.00 (0-7366-8663-0) Books on Tape, Inc.

—The Edge of Justice. 2003. 448p. mass mkt. 6.99 (0-440-23723-8); 2002. 336p. 21.95 (0-385-33625-X, Delacorte Pr.) Dell Publishing.

—The Edge of Justice. 2002. audio 25.00 (0-553-71343-4); audio compact disk 29.95 (0-553-71344-2) Random Hse. Audio Publishing Group. (RH Audio).

—Point of Law. 2003. 448p. mass mkt. 6.99 (0-440-24080-8) Dell Publishing.

**BURNS, CARL (FICTITIOUS CHARACTER)—FICTION**

Crider, Bill. A Dangerous Thing. 1996. per. (0-373-26216-7, 1-26216-1, Worldwide Library) Harlequin Enterprises, Ltd.

—A Dangerous Thing. 1994. 200p. 19.95 (0-8027-3187-2) Walker & Co.

—Dying Voices. 1989. 192p. 14.95 o.p. (0-312-03328-1, Saint Martin's Minotaur) St. Martin's Pr.

—One Dead Dean. 1988. 208p. 17.95 (0-8027-5711-1) Walker & Co.

**BURNS, JACOB (FICTITIOUS CHARACTER)—FICTION**

Witten, Matt. Breakfast at Madeline's. 1999. (Signet Book Ser.). 256p. mass mkt. 5.99 o.s.i (0-451-19681-3) NAL.

—Grand Illusion. 2000. (Jacob Burns Mysteries Ser.). 256p. mass mkt. 5.99 o.s.i (0-451-19897-2, Signet Bks.) NAL.

—Strange Bedfellows: A Jacob Burns Mystery. 2000. (Jacob Burns Mysteries Ser.). 240p. mass mkt. 6.50 o.s.i (0-451-20159-0) NAL.

—Strange Bedfellows: A Jacob Burns Mystery. l.t. ed. 2001. (Thorndike Mystery Ser.). 352p. 27.95 (0-7862-3214-5) Thorndike Pr.

**BURNS, MARTY (FICTITIOUS CHARACTER)—FICTION**

Russell, Jay S. Burning Bright. 1998. 288p. 23.95 o.p. (0-312-18545-6) St. Martin's Pr.

—Celestial Dogs. 1997. 272p. 22.95 o.p. (0-312-15076-8, Saint Martin's Minotaur) St. Martin's Pr.

**BURTON, DENISE (FICTITIOUS CHARACTER)—FICTION**

Schiller, Gerald A. Deadly Dreams. unabr. ed. 1996. 228p. pap. 9.95 (1-881164-81-0) Intercontinental Publishing, Inc.

**BURTONALL, CLAIRE, DOCTOR (FICTITIOUS CHARACTER)—FICTION**

Gash, Jonathan. Different Women Dancing. l.t. ed. 1997. (Large Print Book Ser.). pap. 23.95 o.p. (1-56895-512-X, Wheeler Publishing, Inc.) Gale Group.

—Different Women Dancing. 1998. 304p. pap. 5.99 o.s.i (0-14-026411-6) Penguin Group (USA) Inc.

—Different Women Dancing. 1997. 320p. 21.95 o.s.i (0-670-87369-1) Viking Penguin.

—Prey Dancing. l.t. ed. 1999. (Dr. Clare Burtonall Mysteries Ser.). pap. 24.95 (1-56895-626-6, Wheeler Publishing, Inc.) Gale Group.

—Prey Dancing. 1999. (Dr. Clare Burtonall Mysteries Ser.). 288p. pap. 5.99 o.s.i (0-14-028016-2, Penguin Bks.) Penguin Group (USA) Inc.

—Prey Dancing. 1998. (Dr. Clare Burtonall Mysteries Ser.). 288p. 21.95 o.p. (0-670-87764-6) Viking Penguin.

**BUSCARSELA, FILOMENA (FICTITIOUS CHARACTER)—FICTION**

Wishnia, K. J. A. Blood Lake: A Filomena Buscarsela Mystery. 2002. (Illus.). 272p. 24.95 (0-312-28186-2, Saint Martin's Minotaur) St. Martin's Pr.

—Flat Rate & Other Tales. 1997. vi, 106p. (Orig.). pap. 4.95 (0-9656814-0-8) Imaginary Pr., The.

—The Glass Factory: A Filomena Buscarsela Mystery. 2000. (Filomena Buscarsela Mysteries Ser.). 224p. 23.95 o.s.i (0-525-94545-8, Dutton) Dutton/Plume.

—The Glass Factory: A Filomena Buscarsela Mystery. 2001. 256p. reprint ed. mass mkt. 5.99 o.s.i (0-451-19751-8, Signet Bks.) NAL.

—The Glass Factory: A Filomena Buscarsela Mystery. l.t. ed. 2000. (Mystery Ser.). 375p. 27.95 (0-7862-2841-5) Thorndike Pr.

—Red House. 2002. E-Book 23.95 (1-59061-727-4) Adobe Systems, Inc.

—Red House. 2002. 288p. mass mkt. 6.50 (0-312-98500-2, St. Martin's Paperbacks) St. Martin's Pr.

—Red House: A Filomena Buscarsela Mystery. 2001. 288p. 23.95 (0-312-28182-X, Saint Martin's Minotaur) St. Martin's Pr.

—Soft Money. 1999. (Filomena Se La Busca Misteriosamente Ser.). 226p. 23.95 o.p. (0-525-94501-6) Dutton/Plume.

—23 Shades of Black. 1997. pap. text 7.95 o.p. (0-9656814-1-6) Imaginary Pr., The.

—23 Shades of Black. 1998. (Filomena Buscarsela Mysteries Ser.). 304p. mass mkt. 6.99 o.s.i (0-451-19748-8, Signet Bks.) NAL.

—23 Shades of Black. 1998. 13.04 (0-606-15828-6) Turtleback Bks.

**BUSHYHEAD, MITCHELL (FICTITIOUS CHARACTER)—FICTION**

Hager, Jean. The Fire Carrier. 1996. 82p. 21.95 o.s.i (0-89296-566-5) Mysterious Pr.

—The Fire Carrier. 1997. 224p. reprint ed. mass mkt. 5.99 o.s.i (0-446-40387-3) Warner Bks., Inc.

—Ghostland. 1993. mass mkt. (0-373-26117-9, 1-26117-1, Harlequin Bks.) Harlequin Enterprises, Ltd.

—Ghostland. 1991. 272p. 18.95 o.p. (0-312-06982-0, Saint Martin's Minotaur) St. Martin's Pr.

—The Grandfather Medicine. 1993. per. (0-373-83303-2, 1-83303-7); 1990. 224p. mass mkt. (0-373-26059-8) Harlequin Enterprises, Ltd. (Harlequin Bks.).

—The Grandfather Medicine. 1998. 248p. pap. 11.95 (0-9662145-2-8) Southmont Publishing.

—The Grandfather Medicine. 1989. 16.95 o.p. (0-312-02923-3, Saint Martin's Minotaur) St. Martin's Pr.

—Masked Dancers. 1998. 288p. 23.00 o.p. (0-89296-641-6) Mysterious Pr.

—Masked Dancers. l.t. ed. 1998. (Cloak & Dagger Ser.). 376p. 25.95 (0-7862-1485-6) Thorndike Pr.

—Night Walker. 1991. reprint ed. mass mkt. (0-373-26085-7, Harlequin Bks.) Harlequin Enterprises, Ltd.

—Night Walker. 1990. 15.95 o.p. (0-312-05138-7, Saint Martin's Minotaur) St. Martin's Pr.

**BYBEE, BRIGHAM (FICTITIOUS CHARACTER)—FICTION**

Gates, John. Brigham's Day. 2000. 187p. 23.95 (0-8027-3344-1) Walker & Co.

—Sister Wife: A Brigham Bybee Novel. 2001. 228p. 23.95 (0-8027-3363-8) Walker & Co.

**BYRNE, CHARLIE (FICTITIOUS CHARACTER)—FICTION**

Adams, George. Insider's Price. Chelius, Jane, ed. 1993. 384p. (Orig.). mass mkt. 4.99 (0-671-70171-1, Pocket) Simon & Schuster.

**BYRNE, FRANCIS X. (FICTITIOUS CHARACTER)—FICTION**

Walsh, Michael. Exchange Alley. abr. ed. 1997. audio 19.00 o.p. Beeler, Thomas T. Publisher.

—Exchange Alley. abr. ed. 1997. audio 17.98 (1-57042-529-9, 390019) Time Warner AudioBooks.

—Exchange Alley. 1998. 480p. mass mkt. 6.99 (0-446-60563-8); 1997. 400p. 23.50 o.p. (0-446-52069-1) Warner Bks., Inc.

**BYRON, GEORGE GORDON BYRON, BARON, 1788-1824—FICTION**

Holland, Tom. The Lord of the Dead. 1998. 336p. pap. 14.00 (0-671-02411-6, Pocket) Simon & Schuster.

—The Lord of the Dead: Slave of My Thirst. 1997. 368p. per. 6.99 (0-671-53426-2, Pocket) Simon & Schuster.

—Lord of the Dead: The Secret History of Byron. Chernoff, Dona, ed. 1996. 336p. 23.00 o.p. (0-671-53425-4, Atria) Simon & Schuster.

# C

**CABOT, TARL (FICTITIOUS CHARACTER)—FICTION**

Norman, John. Assassin of Gor. 1986. mass mkt. 4.95 o.s.i (0-345-34502-9); 1984. mass mkt. 2.95 o.s.i (0-345-31922-2, Del Rey); 1981. mass mkt. 2.75 o.s.i (0-345-30282-6, Del Rey); 1980. mass mkt. 2.50 o.s.i (0-345-29417-3, Del Rey); 1978. mass mkt. 1.95 o.s.i (0-345-28133-0, Del Rey); 1975. mass mkt. 1.50 o.s.i (0-345-24686-1); 1973. mass mkt. 0.95 o.s.i (0-345-22489-2) Ballantine Bks.

—Beasts of Gor. 1978. (Gor Ser.). mass mkt. 2.25 o.p. (0-87997-471-0); mass mkt. 2.95 o.p. (0-87997-677-2); mass mkt. 3.50 o.p. (0-87997-903-8); mass mkt. 1.95 o.p. (0-87997-363-3); mass mkt. 3.95 o.p. (0-88677-028-9, UE2028) DAW Bks., Inc.

—Blood Brothers of Gor. 1982. (Gor Ser.: No. 18). mass mkt. 3.95 o.p. (0-88677-157-9); mass mkt. 3.50 o.p. (0-87997-777-9) DAW Bks., Inc.

—Captive of Gor. 1981. mass mkt. 2.75 o.s.i (0-345-30281-8, Del Rey); 1980. mass mkt. 2.50 o.s.i (0-345-29414-9, Del Rey); No. 7. 1986. (Gor Ser.: No. 7). mass mkt. 4.95 o.s.i (0-345-34199-6) Ballantine Bks.

—Captive of Gor. 1997. (Gor Ser.: No. 7). 408p. mass mkt. 6.95 (1-56333-581-6) Masquerade Bks., Inc.

—Dancer of Gor. 1985. (Gor Ser.). mass mkt. 3.95 o.p. (0-88677-100-5); mass mkt. 4.50 o.p. (0-88677-301-6) DAW Bks., Inc.

—Explorers of Gor. 1979. (Gor Ser.). mass mkt. 2.25 o.p. (0-87997-449-4); mass mkt. 2.50 o.p. (0-87997-607-1); mass mkt. 2.95 o.p. (0-87997-685-3); mass mkt. 3.50 o.p. (0-87997-905-4, UE1905) DAW Bks., Inc.

—Fighting Slave of Gor. 1980. (Gor Ser.). mass mkt. 2.25 o.p. (0-87997-522-9); mass mkt. 2.95 o.p. (0-87997-681-0); mass mkt. 3.50 o.p. (0-87997-882-1) DAW Bks., Inc.

—Guardsman of Gor. 1981. (Gor Ser.). mass mkt. 2.95 o.p. (0-87997-664-0); mass mkt. 3.50 o.p. (0-87997-890-2, UE 1890) DAW Bks., Inc.

—Hunters of Gor. 1974. (Gor Ser.). mass mkt. 2.25 o.p. (0-87997-472-9); mass mkt. 2.75 o.p. (0-87997-678-0); mass mkt. 1.95 o.p. (0-87997-368-4); mass mkt. 1.50 o.p. (0-87997-102-9); mass mkt. 1.75 o.p. (0-87997-294-7); mass mkt. 2.95 o.p. (0-88677-010-6); mass mkt. 3.95 o.p. (0-88677-205-2) DAW Bks., Inc.

—Hunters of Gor. 1998. (Gor Ser.: No. 8). 352p. reprint ed. mass mkt. 6.95 (1-56333-592-1) Masquerade Bks., Inc.

—Hunters of Gor. E-Book 6.99 (1-58586-495-1) ereads.com.

—Kajira of Gor. 1983. (Gor Ser.: No. 19). 448p. mass mkt. 3.50 o.p. (0-87997-807-4) DAW Bks., Inc.

—Magicians of Gor. 1988. (Gor Ser.: No. 25). mass mkt. 4.95 o.p. (0-88677-279-6) DAW Bks., Inc.

—Marauders of Gor. 1975. (Gor Ser.). mass mkt. 2.95 o.p. (0-87997-901-1); mass mkt. 1.75 o.p. (0-87997-295-5); mass mkt. 1.95 o.p. (0-87997-369-2); mass mkt. 2.75 o.p. (0-87997-676-4); mass mkt. 2.25 o.p. (0-87997-465-6); mass mkt. 1.50 o.p. (0-87997-160-6); mass mkt. 3.50 o.p. (0-88677-025-4, UE2025) DAW Bks., Inc.

—Marauders of Gor. 1998. (Gor Ser.: No. 9). reprint ed. mass mkt. 6.95 (1-56333-662-6, Masquerade SF) Masquerade Bks., Inc.

—Mercenaries of Gor. 1985. (Gor Ser.). mass mkt. 3.95 o.p. (0-88677-018-1); mass mkt. 4.95 o.p. (0-88677-369-5) DAW Bks., Inc.

—Nomads of Gor. 1981. mass mkt. 2.50 o.s.i (0-345-29722-9, Del Rey); 1978. mass mkt. 1.95 o.s.i (0-345-27795-3, Del Rey); 1975. mass mkt. 1.50 o.s.i (0-345-24784-1); 1969. mass mkt. 0.75 o.s.i (0-345-21765-9) Ballantine Bks.

—Nomads of Gor. 1997. (Gor Ser.: No. 4). mass mkt. 6.95 (1-56333-527-1, Masquerade SF) Masquerade Bks., Inc.

—Nomads of Gor. 2002. 482p. mass mkt. 9.95 (1-58586-200-2) ereads.com.

—The Nomads of Gor, No. 4. 1985. (Gor Ser.: No. 4). mass mkt. 3.95 o.s.i (0-345-33421-3) Ballantine Bks.

—Outlaw of Gor. (Gor Ser.: No. 2). E-Book 6.99 (1-58586-498-6) ereads.com.

—The Outlaw of Gor. 1984. (Gor Ser.: No. 2). mass mkt. 3.95 o.s.i (0-345-32394-7) Ballantine Bks.

—Outlaw of Gor. 1997. (Gor Ser.: No. 2). reprint ed. mass mkt. 6.95 (1-56333-487-9, Masquerade SF) Masquerade Bks., Inc.

—Priest Kings of Gor. 1980. (Gor Ser.: No. 3). mass mkt. 3.95 o.s.i (0-345-29539-0); 1978. mass mkt. 1.95 o.s.i (0-345-28132-2, Del Rey); 1977. mass mkt. 1.75 o.s.i (0-345-27199-8, Del Rey); 1976. mass mkt. 1.50 o.s.i (0-345-25181-4); 1975. mass mkt. 1.50 o.s.i (0-345-24783-3); 1973. mass mkt. 0.95 o.s.i (0-345-22487-6); 1969. mass mkt. 0.75 o.s.i (0-345-21832-9); 1968. mass mkt. 0.75 o.s.i (0-345-21096-4) Ballantine Bks.

—Priest Kings of Gor. 1996. (Gor Ser.: No. 3). mass mkt. 6.95 (1-56333-488-7) Masquerade Bks., Inc.

—Priest Kings of Gor. 2002. 419p. mass mkt. 9.95 (0-7592-0036-X); 2000. (Gor Ser.: No. 3). E-Book 6.99 (1-58586-134-0); 2000. (Gor Ser.: No. 3). E-Book 6.99 (1-58586-266-5); 2000. (Gor Ser.: No. 3). E-Book 6.99 (1-58586-133-2) ereads.com.

—Raiders of Gor. 1985. (Gor Ser.: No. 6). mass mkt. 3.95 o.s.i (0-345-33109-5); 1980. mass mkt. 2.50 o.s.i (0-345-29538-2, Del Rey); 1978. mass mkt. 1.95 o.s.i (0-345-28134-9, Del Rey); 1975. mass mkt. 1.50 o.s.i (0-345-24701-9) Ballantine Bks.

—Raiders of Gor. 1997. (Gor Ser.: No. 6). mass mkt. 6.95 (1-56333-558-1) Masquerade Bks., Inc.

—Renegades of Gor. 1986. (Gor Ser.). mass mkt. 3.95 o.p. (0-88677-112-9); mass mkt. 4.95 o.p. (0-88677-382-2) DAW Bks., Inc.

—Rogue of Gor. 1981. (Gor Ser.). mass mkt. 2.95 o.p. (0-87997-710-8); mass mkt. 2.50 o.p. (0-87997-602-0); mass mkt. 3.50 o.p. (0-87997-892-9) DAW Bks., Inc.

—Savages of Gor. 1982. (Gor Ser.: No. 17). mass mkt. 3.95 o.p. (0-88677-191-9); mass mkt. 3.50 o.p. (0-87997-715-9) DAW Bks., Inc.

—Slave Girl of Gor. 1977. (Gor Ser.). mass mkt. 1.95 o.p. (0-87997-285-8); mass mkt. 2.25 o.p. (0-87997-474-5); mass mkt. 3.95 o.p. (0-88677-027-0); mass mkt. 2.95 o.p. (0-87997-679-9); mass mkt. 3.50 o.p. (0-87997-904-6); mass mkt. 4.95 o.p. (0-88677-370-9) DAW Bks., Inc.

—Tarnsman of Gor. 1981. (Gor Ser.: No. 1). mass mkt. 2.75 o.s.i (0-345-30284-2) Ballantine Bks.

—Tarnsman of Gor. 1997. (Gor Ser.: No. 1). mass mkt. 6.95 (1-56333-486-0, Masquerade SF) Masquerade Bks., Inc.

—Tarnsmen of Gor. E-Book 6.99 (1-58586-224-X) ereads.com.

—Tribesmen of Gor. 1976. (Gor Ser.). mass mkt. 2.95 o.p. (0-87997-720-5); mass mkt. 3.50 o.p. (0-87997-893-7); mass mkt. 2.25 o.p. (0-87997-473-7); mass mkt. 1.50 o.p. (0-87997-223-8); mass mkt. 1.95 o.p. (0-87997-370-6); mass mkt. 1.75 o.p. (0-87997-296-3) DAW Bks., Inc.

—Tribesmen of Gor. annuals 1998. (Gor Ser.: No. 10). mass mkt. 6.95 (1-56333-677-4, Masquerade SF) Masquerade Bks., Inc.

—Vagabonds of Gor. 1987. (Gor Ser.: No. 24). mass mkt. 3.95 o.p. (0-88677-188-9) DAW Bks., Inc.

**CABOT, WENTWORTH (FICTITIOUS CHARACTER)—FICTION**

Heck, Peter J. A Connecticut Yankee in Criminal Court. 1997. (Mark Twain Mystery Ser.). 320p. mass mkt. 5.99 o.s.i (0-425-16034-3, Prime Crime) Berkley Publishing Group.

—A Connecticut Yankee in Criminal Court: A Mark Twain Mystery. 1996. (Mark Twain Mystery Ser.). 320p. 21.95 o.p. (0-425-15470-X); viii, 311p. pap. o.p. (0-425-15474-2) Berkley Publishing Group. (Prime Crime).

—Death on the Mississippi. 1996. (Mark Twain Mystery Ser.). (Illus.). x, 290p. mass mkt. 5.99 o.s.i (0-425-15512-9) Berkley Publishing Group.

—Death on the Mississippi: A Mark Twain Mystery. 1995. (Mark Twain Mystery Ser.). 304p. 21.95 o.p. (0-425-14938-2); pap. 10.00 o.p. (0-425-14939-0) Berkley Publishing Group. (Prime Crime).

—Guilty Abroad. 1999. (Mark Twain Mystery Ser.). 320p. mass mkt. 6.50 o.s.i (0-425-17122-1) Berkley Publishing Group.

—The Prince & the Prosecutor. (Mark Twain Mystery Ser.: No. 3). 336p. 1998. mass mkt. 5.99 o.s.i (0-425-16567-1); 1997. 21.95 o.s.i (0-425-15970-1) Berkley Publishing Group. (Prime Crime).

**CADFAEL, BROTHER (FICTITIOUS CHARACTER)—FICTION**

Peters, Ellis, pseud. The Benediction of Brother Cadfael. 1992. (Chronicles of Brother Cadfael Ser.). 364p. 35.00 o.p. (0-89296-449-9) Mysterious Pr.

—Brother Cadfael's Penance. l.t. ed. 1995. (Chronicles of Brother Cadfael Ser.: Vol. 20). 352p. 21.95 o.p. (0-7838-1175-6, Macmillan Reference USA) Gale Group.

—Brother Cadfael's Penance. 1994. (Chronicles of Brother Cadfael Ser.: Vol. 20). 292p. 18.95 (0-89296-599-1) Mysterious Pr.

—Brother Cadfael's Penance. abr. ed. 1994. (Chronicles of Brother Cadfael Ser.: Vol. 20). audio 17.95 o.p. (0-7871-0376-4, 393552) NewStar Media, Inc.

—Brother Cadfael's Penance. 1996. (Chronicles of Brother Cadfael Ser.: Vol. 20). 272p. mass mkt. 6.99 (0-446-40453-5) Warner Bks., Inc.

—The Confession of Brother Haluin. unabr. ed. 1995. (Chronicles of Brother Cadfael Ser.: Vol. 15). audio 54.95 (0-7451-4380-6, CAB 1064) BBC Audiobooks America.

—The Confession of Brother Haluin. l.t. ed. 1990. (Chronicles of Brother Cadfael Ser.: Vol. 15). 282p. lib. bdg. 20.95 (*0-8161-4859-7*, Macmillan Reference USA) Gale Group.

—The Confession of Brother Haluin. 1990. (Chronicles of Brother Cadfael Ser.: Vol. 15). 15.95 o.p. (*0-89296-349-2*) Mysterious Pr.

—The Confession of Brother Haluin. unabr. ed. (Chronicles of Brother Cadfael Ser.: Vol. 15). audio 51.00 (*0-7887-0322-6*, 94514E7) Recorded Bks., LLC.

—The Confession of Brother Haluin. l.t. ed. 1989. (Ulverscroft Large Print Ser.). 336p. 17.95 o.p. (*0-7089-2032-2*, Ulverscroft) Thorpe, F. A. Pubs. GBR. *Dist:* Ulverscroft Large Print Bks., Ltd., Ulverscroft Large Print Canada, Ltd.

—The Confession of Brother Haluin. 1989. (Chronicles of Brother Cadfael Ser.: Vol. 15). 208p. mass mkt. 6.99 (*0-445-40855-3*) Warner Bks., Inc.

—Dead Man's Ransom. 1986. (Chronicles of Brother Cadfael Ser.: Vol. 9). mass mkt. 4.95 o.s.i (*0-449-20819-2*, Fawcett) Ballantine Bks.

—Dead Man's Ransom. 2003. audio compact disk 19.95 (*0-7861-9657-2*); 2001. (Chronicles of Brother Cadfael Ser.: Vol. 9). audio compact disk 19.95; 2000. (Chronicles of Brother Cadfael Ser.: Vol. 9). audio 44.95 (*0-7861-1825-3*, 2624); 2000. (Chronicles of Brother Cadfael Ser.: Vol. 9). audio compact disk 56.00 (*0-7861-9848-6*, z2624) Blackstone Audio Bks., Inc.

—Dead Man's Ransom. unabr. ed. 2000. (Chronicles of Brother Cadfael Ser.: Vol. 9). audio 49.95 (*0-7451-4039-4*, CAB 736) Chivers Audio Bks. GBR. *Dist:* BBC Audiobooks America.

—Dead Man's Ransom. abr. ed. 1998. (Chronicles of Brother Cadfael Ser.: Vol. 9). audio 16.85 (*1-84032-155-5*) Hodder Headline Audiobooks GBR. *Dist:* Ulverscroft Large Print Bks., Ltd.

—Dead Man's Ransom. 1995. (Chronicles of Brother Cadfael Ser.: Vol. 9). 271p. mass mkt. o.s.i (*0-7515-1109-9*) Little Brown & Co.

—Dead Man's Ransom. Williams, Jennifer, ed. 1985. (Chronicles of Brother Cadfael Ser.: Vol. p). 224p. reprint ed. 13.95 o.p. (*0-688-04194-9*, Morrow, William & Co.) Morrow/Avon.

—Dead Man's Ransom. unabr. ed. 1993. (Chronicles of Brother Cadfael Ser.: Vol. 9). audio 51.00 (*1-55690-931-4*, 93427E7) Recorded Bks., LLC.

—Dead Man's Ransom. l.t. ed. 1999. (Chronicles of Brother Cadfael Ser.: Vol. 9). 304p. pap. 24.95 (*0-7862-1829-0*) Thorndike Pr.

—Dead Man's Ransom. l.t. ed. 1986. (Chronicles of Brother Cadfael Ser.: Vol. 9). 384p. 12.50 o.p. (*0-7089-1407-1*, Ulverscroft) Thorpe, F. A. Pubs. GBR. *Dist:* Ulverscroft Large Print Bks., Ltd.

—Dead Man's Ransom. 1997. (Chronicles of Brother Cadfael Ser.: Vol. 9). 288p. mass mkt. 6.99 (*0-446-40516-7*) Warner Bks., Inc.

—The Devil's Novice. 1985. (Chronicles of Brother Cadfael Ser.: Vol. 8). 224p. mass mkt. 3.95 o.s.i (*0-449-20701-3*, Fawcett) Ballantine Bks.

—The Devil's Novice. unabr. ed. 1999. (Chronicles of Brother Cadfael Ser.: Vol. 8). audio 44.95 Blackstone Audio Bks., Inc.

—The Devil's Novice. unabr. ed. 2000. (Chronicles of Brother Cadfael Ser.: Vol. 8). audio 49.95 (*0-7451-4104-8*, CAB 787) Chivers Audio Bks. GBR. *Dist:* BBC Audiobooks America.

—The Devil's Novice. 1995. (Chronicles of Brother Cadfael Ser.: Vol. 8). (Illus.). 286p. mass mkt. o.s.i (*0-7515-1399-7*) Little Brown & Co.

—The Devil's Novice. Williams, Jennifer, ed. 1984. (Chronicles of Brother Cadfael Ser.: Vol. 8). 192p. 13.95 o.p. (*0-688-03247-8*, Morrow, William & Co.) Morrow/Avon.

—The Devil's Novice. unabr. ed. 1993. (Chronicles of Brother Cadfael Ser.: Vol. 8). audio 51.00 (*1-55690-885-7*, 93327E7) Recorded Bks., LLC.

—The Devil's Novice. l.t. ed. 1999. (Chronicles of Brother Cadfael Ser.: Vol. 8). 304p. pap. 24.95 (*0-7862-1668-9*) Thorndike Pr.

—The Devil's Novice. l.t. ed. 1985. (Chronicles of Brother Cadfael Ser.: Vol. 8). 368p. 12.50 o.p. (*0-7089-1342-3*, Ulverscroft) Thorpe, F. A. Pubs. GBR. *Dist:* Ulverscroft Large Print Bks., Ltd.

—The Devil's Novice. 1997. (Chronicles of Brother Cadfael Ser.: Vol. 8). 288p. mass mkt. 6.99 (*0-446-40515-9*) Warner Bks., Inc.

—An Excellent Mystery. unabr. ed. 2000. (Chronicles of Brother Cadfael Ser.: Vol. 11). audio 29.95 (*1-57270-140-4*, N61140u, Audio Editions Mystery Masters) Audio Partners Publishing Corp.

—An Excellent Mystery. 1987. mass mkt. 4.95 o.s.i (*0-449-21224-6*, Fawcett) Ballantine Bks.

—An Excellent Mystery. unabr. ed. 2000. (Chronicles of Brother Cadfael Ser.: Bk. 11 ). audio 49.95 (*0-7451-4184-6*, CAB 867) Chivers Audio Bks. GBR. *Dist:* BBC Audiobooks America.

—An Excellent Mystery. 1995. (Chronicles of Brother Cadfael Ser.). 253p. pap. text o.s.i (*0-7515-1111-0*) Little Brown & Co.

—An Excellent Mystery. Williams, Jennifer, ed. 1986. (Chronicles of Brother Cadfael Ser.: Vol. 11). 224p. reprint ed. 15.95 o.p. (*0-688-06250-4*, Morrow, William & Co.) Morrow/Avon.

—An Excellent Mystery. unabr. ed. 1994. (Chronicles of Brother Cadfael Ser.: Vol. 11). audio 51.00 (*0-7887-0112-6*, 94353E7) Recorded Bks., LLC.

—An Excellent Mystery. l.t. ed. 2000. (General Ser.). 299p. pap. 24.95 (*0-7862-2269-7*) Thorndike Pr.

—An Excellent Mystery. l.t. ed. 1987. 384p. 14.50 o.p. (*0-7089-1660-0*, Ulverscroft) Thorpe, F. A. Pubs. GBR. *Dist:* Ulverscroft Large Print Bks., Ltd.

—An Excellent Mystery. 1997. (Chronicles of Brother Cadfael Ser.: Vol. 11). 224p. mass mkt. 6.99 (*0-446-40532-9*) Warner Bks., Inc.

—The Heretic's Apprentice. l.t. ed. 2001. (Chronicles of Brother Cadfael Ser.: Vol. 16). 342p. lib. bdg. 25.95 (*1-58547-138-0*) Ctr. Point Large Print.

—The Heretic's Apprentice. 1990. (Chronicles of Brother Cadfael Ser.: Vol. 16). 16.95 o.p. (*0-89296-381-6*) Mysterious Pr.

—The Heretic's Apprentice. abr. ed. 1995. (Chronicles of Brother Cadfael Ser.: Vol. 16). audio 17.95 o.p. (*0-7871-0373-X*) NewStar Media, Inc.

—The Heretic's Apprentice. unabr. ed. 1997. (Chronicles of Brother Cadfael Ser.: Vol. 16). audio 51.00 (*0-7887-1074-5*, 95087E7) Recorded Bks., LLC.

—The Heretic's Apprentice. 1991. (Chronicles of Brother Cadfael Ser.: Vol. 16). 256p. mass mkt. 6.99 (*0-446-40000-9*) Warner Bks., Inc.

—The Hermit of Eyton Forest. 1998. (Chronicles of Brother Cadfael Ser.: Vol. 14). audio 29.95 (*0-7540-7521-4*) BBC Audiobooks America.

—The Hermit of Eyton Forest. l.t. ed. 1989. (Chronicles of Brother Cadfael Ser.: Vol. 14). 329p. lib. bdg. 19.95 o.p. (*0-8161-4677-2*, Macmillan Reference USA) Gale Group.

—The Hermit of Eyton Forest. 1987. (Chronicles of Brother Cadfael Ser.: Vol. 14). 224p. (*0-7472-0037-8*) Headline Bk. Publishing, Ltd.

—The Hermit of Eyton Forest. 1988. (Chronicles of Brother Cadfael Ser.: Vol. 14). 15.45 o.p. (*0-89296-290-9*) Mysterious Pr.

—The Hermit of Eyton Forest. unabr. ed. (Chronicles of Brother Cadfael Ser.: Vol. 14). audio 51.00 (*0-7887-0308-0*, 94501E7) Recorded Bks., LLC.

—The Hermit of Eyton Forest. 1989. (Chronicles of Brother Cadfael Ser.: Vol. 14). 240p. mass mkt. 6.50 (*0-445-40347-0*) Warner Bks., Inc.

—The Holy Thief. l.t. ed. 1994. (Chronicles of Brother Cadfael Ser.: Vol. 19). 19.95 o.p. (*0-7927-1744-9*); pap. 18.95 o.p. (*0-7927-1743-0*) BBC Audiobooks America.

—The Holy Thief, Set. abr. ed. 1993. (Chronicles of Brother Cadfael Ser.: Vol. 19). 58p. audio 16.99 (*0-88646-357-2*, 390926) Durkin Hayes Publishing Ltd.

—The Holy Thief. 1993. (Chronicles of Brother Cadfael Ser.: Vol. 19). 256p. 17.95 (*0-89296-524-X*) Mysterious Pr.

—The Holy Thief. 1994. (Chronicles of Brother Cadfael Ser.: Vol. 19). 256p. mass mkt. 6.99 (*0-446-40363-6*) Warner Bks., Inc.

—The Leper of St. Giles. 1999. (Chronicles of Brother Cadfael Ser.: Vol. 5). audio 9.95 (*1-56938-267-0*, AMP-2670) Acorn Media Publishing, Inc.

—The Leper of St. Giles. unabr. ed. 1996. (Chronicles of Brother Cadfael Ser.: Vol. 5). audio 20.97 o.p. (*0-7451-2843-2*) BBC Audiobooks America.

—The Leper of St. Giles. 1985. (Chronicles of Brother Cadfael Ser.: Vol. 5). 208p. mass mkt. 4.95 o.s.i (*0-449-20541-X*, Fawcett) Ballantine Bks.

—The Leper of St. Giles. unabr. ed. 1999. (Chronicles of Brother Cadfael Ser.: Vol. 5). audio 39.95 (*0-7861-1260-3*, 2181) Blackstone Audio Bks., Inc.

—The Leper of St. Giles. 1995. (Chronicles of Brother Cadfael Ser.: Vol. 5). (Illus.). 223p. mass mkt. o.s.i (*0-7515-1105-6*) Little Brown & Co.

—The Leper of St. Giles. 1982. (Chronicles of Brother Cadfael Ser.: Vol. 5). 224p. 11.50 o.p. (*0-688-01097-0*, Morrow, William & Co.) Morrow/Avon.

—The Leper of St. Giles. unabr. ed. 1992. (Chronicles of Brother Cadfael Ser.: Vol. 5). audio 60.00 (*1-55690-686-2*, 92339E7) Recorded Bks., LLC.

—The Leper of St. Giles. l.t. ed. 1983. (Chronicles of Brother Cadfael Ser.: Vol. 5). 352p. 29.99 o.p. (*0-7089-1020-3*, Ulverscroft) Thorpe, F. A. Pubs. GBR. *Dist:* Ulverscroft Large Print Bks., Ltd.

—The Leper of St. Giles. 1995. (Chronicles of Brother Cadfael Ser.: Vol. 5). 208p. mass mkt. 6.99 (*0-446-40437-3*) Warner Bks., Inc.

—Monk's Hood. 1999. (Chronicles of Brother Cadfael Ser.: Vol. 3). audio 9.95 (*1-56938-266-2*, AMP-2662) Acorn Media Publishing, Inc.

—Monk's Hood. (Chronicles of Brother Cadfael Ser.: Vol. 3). 1999. audio 29.95 (*0-7451-2828-9*); 1990. audio 54.95 (*0-7451-6189-8*, CAB 524) BBC Audiobooks America.

—Monk's Hood. 1986. (Chronicles of Brother Cadfael Ser.: Vol. 3). 224p. mass mkt. 4.95 o.s.i (*0-449-20699-8*, Fawcett) Ballantine Bks.

—Monk's Hood. unabr. ed. 1999. (Chronicles of Brother Cadfael Ser.: Vol. 3). audio 44.95 Blackstone Audio Bks., Inc.

—Monk's Hood. unabr. ed. 2000. (Chronicles of Brother Cadfael Ser.: Vol. 3). audio 49.95 Chivers Audio Bks. GBR. *Dist:* BBC Audiobooks America.

—Monk's Hood. 1995. (Chronicles of Brother Cadfael Ser.: Vol. 3). (Illus.). 268p. mass mkt. o.s.i (*0-7515-1103-X*) Little Brown & Co.

—Monk's Hood. abr. ed. 1995. (Chronicles of Brother Cadfael Ser.: Vol. 3). 17.95 o.p. (*0-7871-0254-7*, 391199) NewStar Media, Inc.

—Monk's Hood. unabr. ed. 1991. (Chronicles of Brother Cadfael Ser.: Vol. 3). audio 60.00 (*1-55690-630-7*, 91409E7) Recorded Bks., LLC.

—Monk's Hood. l.t. ed. 1982. (Chronicles of Brother Cadfael Ser.: Vol. 3). 368p. 12.50 o.p. (*0-7089-0829-2*, Ulverscroft) Thorpe, F. A. Pubs. GBR. *Dist:* Ulverscroft Large Print Bks., Ltd.

—Monk's Hood. 1992. (Chronicles of Brother Cadfael Ser.: Vol. 3). 224p. mass mkt. 6.99 (*0-446-40300-8*) Warner Bks., Inc.

—A Morbid Taste for Bones. 1985. (Chronicles of Brother Cadfael Ser.: Vol. 1). 224p. mass mkt. 4.95 o.s.i (*0-449-20700-5*, Fawcett) Ballantine Bks.

—A Morbid Taste for Bones. unabr. ed. 1997. (Chronicles of Brother Cadfael Ser.: Vol. 1). audio 39.95 (*0-7861-1099-6*, 1863) Blackstone Audio Bks., Inc.

—A Morbid Taste for Bones. unabr. ed. 1991. (Chronicles of Brother Cadfael Ser.: Vol. 1). audio 16.99 (*0-88646-275-4*, 391202) Durkin Hayes Publishing Ltd.

—A Morbid Taste for Bones. 1995. (Chronicles of Brother Cadfael Ser.: Vol. 1). pap. o.s.i (*0-7515-1101-3*) Little Brown & Co.

—A Morbid Taste for Bones. unabr. ed. 1991. (Chronicles of Brother Cadfael Ser.: Vol. 1). audio 51.00 (*1-55690-349-9*, 91206E7) Recorded Bks., LLC.

—A Morbid Taste for Bones. l.t. ed. 1981. (Chronicles of Brother Cadfael Ser.: Vol. 1). 344p. 12.00 o.p. (*0-7089-0659-1*, Ulverscroft) Thorpe, F. A. Pubs. GBR. *Dist:* Ulverscroft Large Print Bks., Ltd.

—A Morbid Taste for Bones. 1994. (Chronicles of Brother Cadfael Ser.: Vol. 1). 208p. mass mkt. 6.99 (*0-446-40015-7*) Warner Bks., Inc.

—One Corpse Too Many. 1999. (Chronicles of Brother Cadfael Ser.: Vol. 2). audio 9.95 (*1-56938-265-4*, AMP-2654) Acorn Media Publishing, Inc.

—One Corpse Too Many. 1985. (Chronicles of Brother Cadfael Ser.: Vol. 2). 224p. mass mkt. 4.95 o.s.i (*0-449-20702-1*, Fawcett) Ballantine Bks.

—One Corpse Too Many. unabr. ed. 1997. (Chronicles of Brother Cadfael Ser.: Vol. 2). audio 44.95 Blackstone Audio Bks., Inc.

—One Corpse Too Many. abr. ed. 1994. (Chronicles of Brother Cadfael Ser.: Vol. 2). audio 16.99 (*0-88646-350-5*, 391312) Durkin Hayes Publishing Ltd.

—One Corpse Too Many. 1998. (Chronicles of Brother Cadfael Ser.: Vol. 2). audio 16.85 (*1-84032-150-4*) Hodder Headline Audiobooks GBR. *Dist:* Ulverscroft Large Print Bks., Ltd.

—One Corpse Too Many. 1995. (Chronicles of Brother Cadfael Ser.: Vol. 2). (Illus.). 254p. mass mkt. o.s.i (*0-7515-1102-1*) Little Brown & Co.

—One Corpse Too Many. unabr. ed. 1991. (Chronicles of Brother Cadfael Ser.: Vol. 2). audio 60.00 (*1-55690-392-8*, 91302E7) Recorded Bks., LLC.

—One Corpse Too Many. 1994. (Chronicles of Brother Cadfael Ser.: Vol. 2). 224p. mass mkt. 6.99 (*0-446-40051-3*) Warner Bks., Inc.

—The Pilgrim of Hate. unabr. ed. 2000. (Chronicles of Brother Cadfael Ser.: Vol. 10). audio 29.95 (*1-57270-127-7*, N61127u, Audio Editions Bks. on Cassette) Audio Partners Publishing Corp.

—The Pilgrim of Hate. 1986. (Chronicles of Brother Cadfael Ser.: Vol. 10). mass mkt. 4.95 o.s.i (*0-449-21223-8*, Fawcett) Ballantine Bks.

—The Pilgrim of Hate. (Chronicles of Brother Cadfael Ser.: Vol. 10). 1999. mass mkt. o.s.i (*0-7515-0220-0*); 1995. 271p. mass mkt. o.s.i (*0-7515-1110-2*) Little Brown & Co.

—The Pilgrim of Hate. Williams, Jennifer, ed. 1985. (Chronicles of Brother Cadfael Ser.: Vol. 10). 190p. reprint ed. 14.95 o.p. (*0-688-04964-8*, Morrow, William & Co.) Morrow/Avon.

—The Pilgrim of Hate. unabr. ed. 1994. (Chronicles of Brother Cadfael Ser.: No. 10). audio 51.00 (*0-7887-0005-7*, 94144E7) Recorded Bks., LLC.

—The Pilgrim of Hate. l.t. ed. 1999. (General Ser.). 288p. pap. 24.95 (*0-7862-1945-9*) Thorndike Pr.

—The Pilgrim of Hate. l.t. ed. 1986. (Chronicles of Brother Cadfael Ser.: Vol. 10). 368p. o.p. (*0-7089-1535-3*, Ulverscroft) Thorpe, F. A. Pubs.

—The Pilgrim of Hate. 1997. (Chronicles of Brother Cadfael Ser.: Vol. 10). 256p. mass mkt. 6.99 (*0-446-40531-0*) Warner Bks., Inc.

—The Potter's Field. unabr. ed. 2003. audio 29.95 (*1-57270-298-2*) Audio Partners Publishing Corp.

—The Potter's Field. unabr. ed. 2000. (Chronicles of Brother Cadfael Ser.: Vol. 17). audio 49.95 (*0-7451-6513-3*, CAB 1129) Chivers Audio Bks. GBR. *Dist:* BBC Audiobooks America.

—The Potter's Field. l.t. ed. 1991. (Chronicles of Brother Cadfael Ser.: Vol. 17). 303p. lib. bdg. 19.95 o.p. (*0-8161-5194-6*, Macmillan Reference USA) Gale Group.

—The Potter's Field. 1990. (Chronicles of Brother Cadfael Ser.: Vol. 17). 240p. 16.95 o.p. (*0-89296-419-7*) Mysterious Pr.

—The Potter's Field. abr. ed. 1996. (Chronicles of Brother Cadfael Ser.: Vol. 17). 17.95 o.p. (*0-7871-0375-6*) NewStar Media, Inc.

—The Potter's Field. unabr. ed. 1997. (Chronicles of Brother Cadfael Ser.: Vol. 17). audio 51.00 (*0-7887-1089-3*, 95092E7) Recorded Bks., LLC.

—The Potter's Field. 1991. (Chronicles of Brother Cadfael Ser.: Vol. 17). 224p. mass mkt. 6.99 (*0-446-40058-0*) Warner Bks., Inc.

—A Rare Benedictine: The Advent of Brother Cadfael. 1991. mass mkt. 6.99 (*0-446-40088-2*) Warner Bks., Inc.

—The Raven in the Foregate. 1987. (Chronicles of Brother Cadfael Ser.: Vol. 12). 208p. mass mkt. 4.95 o.s.i (*0-449-21225-4*, Fawcett) Ballantine Bks.

—The Raven in the Foregate. unabr. ed. 1998. (Chronicles of Brother Cadfael Ser.: Vol. 12). audio 39.95 Blackstone Audio Bks., Inc.

—The Raven in the Foregate. unabr. ed. 2000. (Chronicles of Brother Cadfael Ser.: Vol. 12). audio 49.95 (*0-7451-4229-X*, CAB 912) Chivers Audio Bks. GBR. *Dist:* BBC Audiobooks America.

—The Raven in the Foregate, Bk 12. 1995. (Chronicles of Brother Cadfael Ser.: Vol. 12). (Illus.). 252p. mass mkt. o.s.i (*0-7515-1740-2*) Little Brown & Co.

—The Raven in the Foregate. Williams, Jennifer, ed. 1986. (Chronicles of Brother Cadfael Ser.: Vol 12). 204p. reprint ed. 15.95 o.p. (*0-688-06558-9*, Morrow, William & Co.) Morrow/Avon.

—The Raven in the Foregate. unabr. ed. 1995. (Chronicles of Brother Cadfael Ser.: Vol. 12). audio 51.00 (*0-7887-0163-0*, 94388E7) Recorded Bks., LLC.

—The Raven in the Foregate. l.t. ed. 1987. (Chronicles of Brother Cadfael Ser.: Vol. 12). 368p. 16.95 o.p. (*0-7089-1731-3*, Ulverscroft) Thorpe, F. A. Pubs. GBR. *Dist:* Ulverscroft Large Print Bks., Ltd.

—The Raven in the Foregate. 1997. (Chronicles of Brother Cadfael Ser.: Vol. 12). 240p. mass mkt. 6.99 (*0-446-40534-5*) Warner Bks., Inc.

—The Rose Rent. 1998. (Chronicles of Brother Cadfael Ser.: Vol. 13). 18p. audio 29.95 (*0-7540-7515-X*) BBC Audiobooks America.

—The Rose Rent. 1988. (Chronicles of Brother Cadfael Ser.: Vol. 13). mass mkt. 4.95 o.s.i (*0-449-21495-8*, Fawcett) Ballantine Bks.

—The Rose Rent, unabr. ed. 1990. (Chronicles of Brother Cadfael Ser.: Vol. 13). audio 39.95 (*0-7861-0100-8*, 752403) Blackstone Audio Bks., Inc.

—The Rose Rent. unabr. ed. 1994. (Chronicles of Brother Cadfael Ser.: Vol. 13). audio 49.95 (*0-7451-4290-7*, CAB 973) Chivers Audio Bks. GBR. *Dist:* BBC Audiobooks America.

—The Rose Rent. 1995. (Chronicles of Brother Cadfael Ser.: Vol. 13). mass mkt. o.s.i (*0-7515-1113-7*); (Illus.). 270p. mass mkt. o.s.i (*0-7515-1741-0*) Little Brown & Co.

—The Rose Rent. Williams, Jennifer, ed. 1987. (Chronicles of Brother Cadfael Ser.: Vol. 13). 201p. 15.95 o.p. (*0-688-06982-7*, Morrow, William & Co.) Morrow/Avon.

—The Rose Rent. 1990. (Chronicles of Brother Cadfael Ser.: Vol. 13). 2.99 o.p. (*0-517-05798-0*) Random Hse. Value Publishing.

—The Rose Rent. unabr. ed. 1995. (Chronicles of Brother Cadfael Ser.: Vol. 13). audio 51.00 (*0-7887-0223-8*, 94448E7) Recorded Bks., LLC.

—The Rose Rent. l.t. ed. 2000. (Chronicles of Brother Cadfael Ser.: Vol. 13). (Illus.). 289p. pap. 24.95 (*0-7862-2569-6*); (*0-7540-4168-9*); (*0-7540-4169-7*) Thorndike Pr.

—The Rose Rent. l.t. ed. 1988. (Chronicles of Brother Cadfael Ser.: Vol. 13). 368p. 15.95 o.p. (*0-7089-1776-3*, Ulverscroft) Thorpe, F. A. Pubs. GBR. *Dist:* Ulverscroft Large Print Bks., Ltd.

—The Rose Rent. 1997. (Chronicles of Brother Cadfael Ser.: Vol. 13). 240p. mass mkt. 6.99 (*0-446-40533-7*) Warner Bks., Inc.

—The Sanctuary Sparrow. 1984. (Chronicles of Brother Cadfael Ser.: Vol. 7). 224p. mass mkt. 3.95 o.s.i (*0-449-20613-0*, Fawcett) Ballantine Bks.

—The Sanctuary Sparrow. (Chronicles of Brother Cadfael Ser.: Vol. 7). 1999. mass mkt. o.s.i (*0-7515-0217-0*); 1995. 271p. mass mkt. o.s.i (*0-7515-1107-2*) Little Brown & Co.

—The Sanctuary Sparrow. 1983. (Chronicles of Brother Cadfael Ser.: Vol. 7). 12.50 o.p. (*0-688-02252-9*, Morrow, William & Co.) Morrow/Avon.

—The Sanctuary Sparrow. l.t. ed. 1999. (Chronicles of Brother Cadfael Ser.: Vol. 7). 312p. pap. 24.95 (*0-7862-1599-2*) Thorndike Pr.
—The Sanctuary Sparrow. l.t. ed. 1985. (Chronicles of Brother Cadfael Ser.: Vol. 7). 384p. o.p. (*0-7089-1288-5*, Ulverscroft) Thorpe, F. A. Pubs.
—The Sanctuary Sparrow. 1995. (Chronicles of Brother Cadfael Ser.: Vol. 7). 224p. mass mkt. 6.99 (*0-446-40429-2*) Warner Bks., Inc.
—St. Peter's Fair. (Chronicles of Brother Cadfael Ser.: Vol. 4). 1986. mass mkt. 3.95 o.s.i (*0-449-21354-4*); 1984. 224p. mass mkt. 2.50 o.s.i (*0-449-20540-1*) Ballantine Bks. (Fawcett).
—St. Peter's Fair. 1981. (Chronicles of Brother Cadfael Ser.: Vol. 4). 220p. 19.95 (*0-333-31050-0*) Macmillan U.K. GBR. *Dist:* Trans-Atlantic Pubns., Inc.
—St. Peter's Fair. l.t. ed. 1998. (Chronicles of Brother Cadfael Ser.: Vol. 4). 302p. pap. 24.95 (*0-7862-1074-5*) Thorndike Pr.
—St. Peter's Fair. l.t. ed. 1983. (Chronicles of Brother Cadfael Ser.: Vol. 4). 416p. 15.95 o.p. (*0-7089-0933-7*, Ulverscroft) Thorpe, F. A. Pubs. GBR. *Dist:* Ulverscroft Large Print Bks., Ltd.
—St. Peter's Fair. 1992. (Chronicles of Brother Cadfael Ser.: Vol. 4). 224p. mass mkt. 6.99 (*0-446-40301-6*) Warner Bks., Inc.
—The Summer of the Danes. 1991. (Chronicles of Brother Cadfael Ser.: Vol. 18). 256p. 16.95 o.p. (*0-89296-448-0*) Mysterious Pr.
—The Summer of the Danes. abr. ed. 1996. (Chronicles of Brother Cadfael Ser.: Vol. 18). 17.95 o.p. (*0-7871-0278-4*, 394020) NewStar Media, Inc.
—The Summer of the Danes. l.t. ed. 1993. (Ulverscroft Large Print Ser.). 480p. 29.99 o.p. (*0-7089-2941-9*, Ulverscroft) Thorpe, F. A. Pubs. GBR. *Dist:* Ulverscroft Large Print Bks., Ltd., Ulverscroft Large Print Canada, Ltd.
—The Summer of the Danes. 1992. (Chronicles of Brother Cadfael Ser.: Vol. 18). 256p. mass mkt. 6.99 (*0-446-40018-1*) Warner Bks., Inc.
—The Virgin in the Ice. 1986. (Chronicles of Brother Cadfael Ser.: Vol. 6). mass mkt. 4.95 o.s.i (*0-449-21121-5*); 1984. mass mkt. 2.50 o.s.i (*0-449-20537-1*) Ballantine Bks. (Fawcett).
—The Virgin in the Ice. 1995. (Chronicles of Brother Cadfael Ser.: Vol. 6). (Illus.). 271p. mass mkt. o.s.i (*0-7515-1401-2*) Little Brown & Co.
—The Virgin in the Ice. l.t. ed. 1998. (General Ser.). 320p. pap. 24.95 (*0-7862-1479-1*) Thorndike Pr.
—The Virgin in the Ice. l.t. ed. 1985. (Chronicles of Brother Cadfael Ser.: Vol. 6). 400p. o.p. (*0-7089-1258-3*, Ulverscroft) Thorpe, F. A. Pubs.
—The Virgin in the Ice. 1995. (Chronicles of Brother Cadfael Ser.: Vol. 6). 208p. mass mkt. 6.99 (*0-446-40428-4*) Warner Bks., Inc.

**CADIN, INSPECTOR (FICTITIOUS CHARACTER)—FICTION**

Daeninckx, Didier. Meurtres pour Memoire. 1988. Tr. of Murder in Memoriam. (FRE.). 215p. pap. 10.95 (*0-7859-2094-3*, 2070380491) French & European Pubns., Inc.
—Murder in Memoriam. Heron, Liz, tr. from FRE. 1992. (Mask Noir Ser.). Orig. Title: Meurtres pour Memoire. 176p. (Orig.). pap. (*1-85242-206-8*) Serpent's Tail Ltd.

**CADOGAN, MARIANNE (FICTITIOUS CHARACTER)—FICTION**

Gallagher, Stephen. Nightmare, with Angel. 9999. pap. o.p. (*0-449-90866-6*, Fawcett); 1995. reprint ed. mass mkt. 5.99 o.s.i (*0-345-38966-2*, Ivy Bks.) Ballantine Bks.
—Nightmare, with Angel. audio HarperTrade.

**CADY, MAX (FICTITIOUS CHARACTER)—FICTION**

MacDonald, John D. Cape Fear. 1986. mass mkt. 5.99 o.s.i (*0-449-13190-4*, Fawcett) Ballantine Bks.
—Cape Fear. 1994. reprint ed. lib. bdg. 27.95 o.p. (*1-56849-304-5*) Buccaneer Bks., Inc.

**CAFFERY, JACK (FICTITIOUS CHARACTER)—FICTION**

Hayder, Mo. Birdman. 2000. 448p. mass mkt. 6.99 (*0-440-23616-9*) Dell Publishing.
—The Treatment: A Novel. 2002. 416p. mass mkt. 7.50 (*0-440-23617-7*, Delta) Dell Publishing.
—The Treatment: A Novel. 2002. 368p. 23.95 (*0-385-49695-8*, Image) Doubleday Publishing.

**CAGE, ALLEN (FICTITIOUS CHARACTER)—FICTION**

Jones, Edward R. Stoneface. 1991. 256p. 18.95 o.p. (*1-55611-311-0*) Fine, Donald I. Bks.

**CAHILL, COLETTE (FICTITIOUS CHARACTER)—FICTION**

Truman, Margaret. Murder in the CIA. 1999. 6.99 (*0-449-45925-X*); 1988. 320p. reprint ed. mass mkt. 6.99 (*0-449-21275-0*) Ballantine Bks. (Fawcett).
—Murder in the CIA. l.t. ed. 1988. (General Ser.). 412p. 19.95 o.p. (*0-8161-4406-0*); 11.95 o.p. (*0-8161-4407-9*) Gale Group. (Macmillan Reference USA).
—Murder in the CIA. 1993. audio. audio 49.00 (*1-56544-013-7*, 250030) Literate Ear, Inc.
—Murder in the CIA. abr. ed. 1988. audio 16.00 o.s.i (*0-394-57184-3*); Set. 1996. audio 8.99 o.s.i (*0-679-45597-3*, 391229) Random Hse. Audio Publishing Group. (RH Audio).
—Murder in the CIA, unabr. ed. 1991. audio 70.00 (*1-55690-364-2*, 91219E7) Recorded Bks., LLC.

**CAIN, JENNY (FICTITIOUS CHARACTER)—FICTION**

Pickard, Nancy. Bum Steer. unabr. ed. 2000. (Jenny Cain Mystery Ser.). audio 49.95 (*0-7927-2238-8*, CSL 127) Chivers Audio Bks. GBR. *Dist:* BBC Audiobooks America.
—Bum Steer. 1990. (Jenny Cain Mystery Ser.). 256p. 16.95 o.p. (*0-671-68040-4*, Atria) Simon & Schuster.
—Bum Steer. Marrow, Linda, ed. 1991. (Jenny Cain Mystery Ser.). 288p. reprint ed. mass mkt. 5.99 (*0-671-68042-0*, Pocket) Simon & Schuster.
—But I Wouldn't Want to Die There. 1993. (Jenny Cain Mystery Ser.). 256p. 20.00 (*0-671-72330-8*, Atria) Simon & Schuster.
—But I Wouldn't Want to Die There. Marrow, Linda, ed. 1994. (Jenny Cain Mystery Ser.). 272p. reprint ed. mass mkt. 5.50 (*0-671-72331-6*, Pocket) Simon & Schuster.
—Confession. (Jenny Cain Mystery Ser.). 1995. 336p. mass mkt. 5.99 (*0-671-78262-2*, Pocket); 1994. 320p. 20.00 o.p. (*0-671-78261-4*, Atria) Simon & Schuster.
—Dead Crazy. 1988. (Jenny Cain Mystery Ser.). 256p. 16.95 o.s.i (*0-684-18761-2*, Macmillan Reference USA) Gale Group.
—Dead Crazy. (Jenny Cain Mystery Ser.). 1990. mass mkt. 3.95 (*0-671-70267-X*); 1989. mass mkt. 3.50 (*0-671-64337-1*) Simon & Schuster. (Pocket).
—Dead Crazy. Marrow, Linda, ed. 1989. 320p. mass mkt. 6.50 (*0-671-73430-X*, Pocket) Simon & Schuster.
—Generous Death. l.t. ed. 1999. (Beeler Large Print Mystery Ser.). 26.95 (*1-57490-207-5*, Beeler Large Print Bks.) Beeler, Thomas T. Publisher.
—Generous Death. 1986. (Jenny Cain Mystery Ser.). 240p. pap. 2.50 o.p. (*0-380-85993-9*, 85993-9, Avon Bks.) Morrow/Avon.
—Generous Death. (Jenny Cain Mystery Ser.). 1990. mass mkt. 3.95 (*0-671-70268-8*); 1987. 320p. mass mkt. 3.50 (*0-671-64614-1*); 1987. mass mkt. 5.50 (*0-671-73264-1*) Simon & Schuster. (Pocket).
—I. O. U. 1993. (Jenny Cain Mystery Ser.). 3.99 o.p. (*0-517-09728-1*) Random Hse. Value Publishing.
—I. O. U. Marrow, Linda, ed. (Jenny Cain Mystery Ser.). 1992. 240p. mass mkt. 4.99 (*0-671-68043-9*, Pocket); 1991. 17.95 o.p. (*0-671-68041-2*, Atria) Simon & Schuster.
—Marriage Is Murder. Marrow, Linda, ed. 1988. (Jenny Cain Mystery Ser.). mass mkt. 5.50 (*0-671-73428-8*, Pocket) Simon & Schuster.
—No Body. 1986. (Jenny Cain Mystery Ser.). 224p. 13.95 o.p. (*0-684-18593-8*, Macmillan Reference USA) Gale Group.
—No Body. (Jenny Cain Mystery Ser.). 1989. mass mkt. 3.95 (*0-671-69179-1*); 1987. mass mkt. 5.99 (*0-671-73429-6*); 1987. mass mkt. (*0-671-64335-5*) Simon & Schuster. (Pocket).
—Say No to Murder. 1999. (Jenny Cain Mystery Ser.). 242p. 20.95 (*0-7862-1703-0*, Five Star) Gale Group.
—Say No to Murder. 1985. (Jenny Cain Mystery Ser.). 192p. pap. 2.95 o.p. (*0-380-89642-7*, Avon Bks.) Morrow/Avon.
—Say No to Murder. (Jenny Cain Mystery Ser.). 1990. mass mkt. 3.95 (*0-671-70269-6*); 1988. mass mkt. 3.50 (*0-671-66396-8*) Simon & Schuster. (Pocket).
—Say No to Murder. Marrow, Linda, ed. 1988. (Jenny Cain Mystery Ser.). mass mkt. 5.50 (*0-671-73431-8*, Pocket) Simon & Schuster.
—Twilight. Set. unabr. ed. 1999. (Jenny Cain Mystery Ser.). audio 96.95 (*0-7927-2302-3*, CSL191, Chivers Sound Library) BBC Audiobooks America.
—Twilight. 1996. (Jenny Cain Mystery Ser.). 320p. pap. 6.99 (*0-671-78290-8*, Pocket) Simon & Schuster.
—Twilight. Marrow, Linda, ed. 1995. (Jenny Cain Mystery Ser.). 320p. 22.00 o.p. (*0-671-78271-1*, Atria) Simon & Schuster.

**CAINE, JOHN (FICTITIOUS CHARACTER)—FICTION**

Knief, Charles. Diamond Head. (John Caine Mysteries Ser.). 1998. 240p. mass mkt. 6.50 (*0-312-96547-8*, St. Martin's Paperbacks); 1996. 256p. 21.95 o.p. (*0-312-14558-6*, Saint Martin's Minotaur) St. Martin's Pr.
—Emerald Flash. (John Caine Mysteries Ser.). 2000. 304p. mass mkt. 5.99 (*0-312-97058-7*, St. Martin's Paperbacks); 1999. 292p. 23.95 (*0-312-19866-3*, Saint Martin's Minotaur) St. Martin's Pr.
—Sand Dollars. (John Caine Mysteries Ser.). 1999. 304p. mass mkt. 5.99 (*0-312-96682-2*, St. Martin's Paperbacks); 1998. 336p. 23.95 (*0-312-18170-1*, 874700, Saint Martin's Minotaur) St. Martin's Pr.
—Silversword. mass mkt. (*0-312-98025-6*, St. Martin's Paperbacks); 2001. 400p. 24.95 (*0-312-27302-9*, Saint Martin's Minotaur) St. Martin's Pr.

**CALAVICCI, AL (FICTITIOUS CHARACTER)—FICTION**

Barrett, Julie. Quantum Leap: A to Z. 1995. 288p. (Orig.). mass mkt. 5.99 o.s.i (*1-57297-044-8*) Boulevard Bks.
Crandall, Melissa. Quantum Leap: Search & Rescue, No. 5. 1994. 240p. (Orig.). mass mkt. 4.99 o.s.i (*0-441-00122-X*) Ace Bks.
—Search & Rescue. 1994. (Quantum Leap Ser.: Vol. 5). mass mkt. 5.99 o.s.i (*1-57297-178-9*) Boulevard Bks.
Davis, Carol & Reese, Esther D. Mirror's Edge: Quantum Leap. 2000. (Quantum Leap Ser.: No. XVIII). 304p. mass mkt. 6.99 o.s.i (*0-425-17351-8*) Berkley Publishing Group.
Defilippis, Christopher. Quantam Leap: Foreknowledge. 1998. (Quantum Leap Ser.). 256p. mass mkt. 6.99 o.s.i (*0-425-16487-X*) Berkley Publishing Group.
—Quantum Leap Foreknowledge. 1998. (Quantum Leap Ser.). mass mkt. 5.99 (*1-57297-343-9*) Boulevard Bks.
Henderson, C. J. Quantum Leap: Double or Nothing, No. IX. 1995. 240p. (Orig.). mass mkt. 5.99 o.s.i (*1-57297-055-3*) Boulevard Bks.
Kent, Melanie. Heat Wave. 1997. (Quantum Leap Ser.: No. XV). 240p. mass mkt. 5.99 o.s.i (*1-57297-312-9*) Boulevard Bks.
McConnell, Ashley. The Novel. 1992. (Quantum Leap Ser.). mass mkt. 5.99 o.s.i (*1-57297-094-4*) Boulevard Bks.
—Prelude. 1994. (Quantum Leap Ser.). mass mkt. 5.99 o.s.i (*1-57297-134-7*) Boulevard Bks.
—Quantum Leap: Random Measures. 1995. 240p. (Orig.). mass mkt. 4.99 o.s.i (*0-441-00182-3*) Ace Bks.
—Quantum Leap: The Novel. 1992. 304p. mass mkt. 4.99 o.s.i (*0-441-69322-9*) Ace Bks.
—Quantum Leap: The Wall. 1994. 256p. mass mkt. 4.99 o.s.i (*0-441-00015-0*) Ace Bks.
—Quantum Leap: Too Close for Comfort. 1993. 272p. (Orig.). mass mkt. 4.99 o.s.i (*0-441-69323-7*) Ace Bks.
—Quantum Leap No. 4: Prelude. 1994. 256p. (Orig.). mass mkt. 4.99 o.s.i (*0-441-00076-2*) Ace Bks.
—Too Close for Comfort. 1994. (Quantum Leap Ser.: No. 2). mass mkt. 5.99 o.s.i (*1-57297-157-6*) Boulevard Bks.
—The Wall. 1994. (Quantum Leap Ser.). mass mkt. 5.99 o.s.i (*1-57297-216-5*) Boulevard Bks.
Peel, John. Independence, No. 11. 1996. (Quantum Leap Ser.). mass mkt. 5.99 o.s.i (*1-57297-150-9*) Boulevard Bks.
Peterman, Mindy. Quantum Leap: Song & Dance. 1998. (Quantum Leap Ser.: Vol. 17). 256p. mass mkt. 6.99 o.s.i (*0-425-16577-9*) Berkley Publishing Group.
Rawn, Melanie. The Knights of the Morningstar. 1996. (Quantum Leap Ser.: No. 4). mass mkt. 5.99 o.s.i (*1-57297-171-1*) Boulevard Bks.
—Quantum Leap: Knights of the Morningstar. 1994. 224p. (Orig.). mass mkt. 4.99 o.s.i (*0-441-00092-4*) Ace Bks.
Schofield, Sandy. Loch Ness Leap, No. 14. 1997. (Quantum Leap Ser.: No. XIV). 256p. mass mkt. 5.99 o.s.i (*1-57297-231-9*) Boulevard Bks.
Storm, L. Elizabeth. Angels Unaware, No. 12. 1997. (Quantum Leap Ser.). 320p. mass mkt. 5.99 o.s.i (*1-57297-206-8*) Boulevard Bks.
—Pulitzer, No. VIII. 1995. (Quantum Leap Ser.). 352p. mass mkt. 5.99 o.s.i (*1-57297-022-7*) Boulevard Bks.

**CALDER, DEBORAH (FICTITIOUS CHARACTER)—FICTION**

Hammond, Gerald. The Executor. 1987. 176p. 12.95 o.p. (*0-312-00593-8*) St. Martin's Pr.
—The Executor. l.t. ed. 1997. (Linford Mystery Library). 320p. pap. 17.99 o.p. (*0-7089-5155-4*, Ulverscroft) Thorpe, F. A. Pubs. GBR. *Dist:* Ulverscroft Large Print Bks., Ltd., Ulverscroft Large Print Canada, Ltd.
—Home to Roost. 1991. 160p. 16.95 o.p. (*0-312-06369-5*, Saint Martin's Minotaur) St. Martin's Pr.
—In Camera. l.t. ed. 1993. (Dales Large Print Ser.). 247p. pap. 19.99 o.p. (*1-85389-390-0*) Dales Large Print Bks. GBR. *Dist:* Ulverscroft Large Print Bks., Ltd., Ulverscroft Large Print Canada, Ltd.
—In Camera. 1992. 192p. 16.95 o.p. (*0-312-06997-9*, Saint Martin's Minotaur) St. Martin's Pr.
—Snatch Crop. l.t. ed. 1993. (Mystery Ser.). 224p. pap. 19.99 o.p. (*1-85389-389-7*) Dales Large Print Bks. GBR. *Dist:* Ulverscroft Large Print Bks., Ltd., Ulverscroft Large Print Canada, Ltd.
—Snatch Crop. 1993. 154p. 16.95 o.p. (*0-312-08891-4*, Saint Martin's Minotaur) St. Martin's Pr.

**CALDER, KEITH (FICTITIOUS CHARACTER)—FICTION**

Hammond, Gerald. Adverse Report. 1990. 2.99 o.p. (*0-517-05806-5*) Random Hse. Value Publishing.
—Adverse Report. 1989. 14.95 o.p. (*0-312-02858-X*, Saint Martin's Minotaur) St. Martin's Pr.
—Adverse Report. l.t. ed. 1990. (Ulverscroft Large Print Ser.). 29.99 o.p. (*0-7089-2119-1*, Ulverscroft) Thorpe, F. A. Pubs. GBR. *Dist:* Ulverscroft Large Print Bks., Ltd., Ulverscroft Large Print Canada, Ltd.
—A Brace of Skeet. 1990. 192p. 15.95 o.p. (*0-312-04688-X*, Saint Martin's Minotaur) St. Martin's Pr.
—A Brace of Skeet. l.t. ed. 1991. (Ulverscroft Large Print Ser.). 29.99 o.p. (*0-7089-2480-8*, Ulverscroft) Thorpe, F. A. Pubs. GBR. *Dist:* Ulverscroft Large Print Bks., Ltd., Ulverscroft Large Print Canada, Ltd.
—Carriage of Justice. l.t. ed. 1996. 221p. pap. 20.95 (*0-7838-1633-2*, Macmillan Reference USA) Gale Group.
—Carriage of Justice. 1995. 192p. 19.95 o.p. (*0-312-13941-1*, Saint Martin's Minotaur) St. Martin's Pr.
—Cousin Once Removed. 1984. 192p. 10.95 o.p. (*0-312-17055-6*) St. Martin's Pr.
—Cousin Once Removed. l.t. ed. 1988. (Linford Mystery Library). 256p. pap. 17.99 o.p. (*0-7089-6616-0*, Linford) Thorpe, F. A. Pubs. GBR. *Dist:* Ulverscroft Large Print Bks., Ltd., Ulverscroft Large Print Canada, Ltd.
—The Executor. 1987. 176p. 12.95 o.p. (*0-312-00593-8*) St. Martin's Pr.
—The Executor. l.t. ed. 1997. (Linford Mystery Library). 320p. pap. 17.99 o.p. (*0-7089-5155-4*, Ulverscroft) Thorpe, F. A. Pubs. GBR. *Dist:* Ulverscroft Large Print Bks., Ltd., Ulverscroft Large Print Canada, Ltd.
—Fair Game. 1982. 224p. 9.95 o.p. (*0-312-27961-2*) St. Martin's Pr.
—Fair Game. l.t. ed. 1983. (Ulverscroft Large Print Ser.). 336p. 29.99 o.p. (*0-7089-1014-9*, Ulverscroft) Thorpe, F. A. Pubs. GBR. *Dist:* Ulverscroft Large Print Bks., Ltd., Ulverscroft Large Print Canada, Ltd.
—The Game. 1982. 176p. 10.95 o.p. (*0-312-31590-2*) St. Martin's Pr.
—Home to Roost. 1991. 160p. 16.95 o.p. (*0-312-06369-5*, Saint Martin's Minotaur) St. Martin's Pr.
—Hook or Crook. l.t. ed. 1995. 209p. pap. 19.95 o.p. (*0-7838-1174-8*, Macmillan Reference USA) Gale Group.
—Hook or Crook. 1995. 154p. 17.95 o.p. (*0-312-11825-2*, Saint Martin's Minotaur) St. Martin's Pr.
—In Camera. l.t. ed. 1993. (Dales Large Print Ser.). 247p. pap. 19.99 o.p. (*1-85389-390-0*) Dales Large Print Bks. GBR. *Dist:* Ulverscroft Large Print Bks., Ltd., Ulverscroft Large Print Canada, Ltd.
—In Camera. 1992. 192p. 16.95 o.p. (*0-312-06997-9*, Saint Martin's Minotaur) St. Martin's Pr.
—Let Us Prey. 1991. 15.95 o.p. (*0-312-05891-8*, Saint Martin's Minotaur) St. Martin's Pr.
—Let Us Prey. l.t. ed. 1993. (Mystery Ser.). 256p. 29.99 o.p. (*0-7089-2893-5*, Ulverscroft) Thorpe, F. A. Pubs. GBR. *Dist:* Ulverscroft Large Print Bks., Ltd., Ulverscroft Large Print Canada, Ltd.
—Pursuit of Arms. 1985. 192p. 12.95 o.p. (*0-312-65697-1*) St. Martin's Pr.
—Pursuit of Arms. l.t. ed. 1998. (Linford Mystery Library). 320p. pap. 17.99 (*0-7089-5215-1*, Linford) Thorpe, F. A. Pubs. GBR. *Dist:* Ulverscroft Large Print Bks., Ltd., Ulverscroft Large Print Canada, Ltd.
—The Revenge Game. 1981. 192p. 9.95 o.p. (*0-312-67930-0*) St. Martin's Pr.
—The Reward Game. 1980. 224p. 9.95 o.p. (*0-312-68078-3*) St. Martin's Pr.
—The Reward Game. l.t. ed. 1981. (Ulverscroft Large Print Ser.). 326p. 29.99 o.p. (*0-7089-0717-2*, Ulverscroft) Thorpe, F. A. Pubs. GBR. *Dist:* Ulverscroft Large Print Bks., Ltd., Ulverscroft Large Print Canada, Ltd.
—Sauce for the Pigeon. 1985. 192p. 12.95 o.p. (*0-312-69977-8*) St. Martin's Pr.
—Sauce for the Pigeon. l.t. ed. 1989. (Linford Mystery Library). 305p. pap. 17.99 o.p. (*0-7089-6631-4*, Linford) Thorpe, F. A. Pubs. GBR. *Dist:* Ulverscroft Large Print Bks., Ltd., Ulverscroft Large Print Canada, Ltd.
—Silver City Scandal. 1986. 12.95 o.p. (*0-312-72588-4*) St. Martin's Pr.
—Silver City Scandal. l.t. ed. 1987. (Ulverscroft Large Print Ser.). 272p. 29.99 o.p. (*0-7089-1639-2*, Ulverscroft) Thorpe, F. A. Pubs. GBR. *Dist:* Ulverscroft Large Print Bks., Ltd., Ulverscroft Large Print Canada, Ltd.

—Sink or Swim. 1997. 176p. 19.95 o.p. (*0-312-15657-X*, Saint Martin's Minotaur) St. Martin's Pr.

—Sink or Swim. l.t. ed. 1997. (General Ser.). 224p. pap. 24.95 (*0-7862-1071-0*) Thorndike Pr.

—Stray Shot. 1989. 192p. 14.95 o.p. (*0-312-03435-0*, Saint Martin's Minotaur) St. Martin's Pr.

—Stray Shot. l.t. ed. 1990. (Ulverscroft Large Print Ser.). 29.99 o.p. (*0-7089-2211-2*, Ulverscroft) Thorpe, F. A. Pubs. GBR. *Dist:* Ulverscroft Large Print Bks., Ltd., Ulverscroft Large Print Canada, Ltd.

—Thin Air. 1994. 144p. 17.95 o.p. (*0-312-11339-0*, Saint Martin's Minotaur) St. Martin's Pr.

## CALDER FAMILY (FICTITIOUS CHARACTERS)—FICTION

Dailey, Janet. Calder Born, Calder Bred. 2000. 412p. pap. 26.00 (*0-7278-5469-0*) Severn Hse. Pubs., Ltd.

—Calder Born, Calder Bred. 1993. mass mkt. 6.99 (*0-671-87500-0*); 1990. 416p. mass mkt. 5.99 (*0-671-73479-2*); 1989. mass mkt. (*0-671-70072-3*); 1987. mass mkt. (*0-671-63786-X*); 1984. mass mkt. 3.95 (*0-671-50250-6*); Vol. 4. 1999. 416p. reprint ed. mass mkt. 6.99 (*0-671-04049-9*) Simon & Schuster. (Pocket).

—Calder Pride. 1999. 368p. 23.95 (*0-06-017699-7*); 560p. pap. 23.95 (*0-06-093302-X*) HarperCollins Pubs.

—Calder Pride, abr. ed. 1999. audio 25.00 (*0-694-51925-1*, HarperAudio) HarperTrade.

—Calder Pride, abr. ed. 1999. audio 25.00 Highsmith Inc.

—Calder Pride. 2000. 464p. reprint ed. mass mkt. 7.50 (*0-06-109459-5*, HarperTorch) Morrow/Avon.

—Shifting Calder Wind. 2004. 384p. mass mkt. 7.99 (*0-8217-7223-6*); 2003. 304p. 24.00 (*0-7582-0067-6*) Kensington Publishing Corp.

—Shifting Calder Wind. l.t. ed. 2004. 495p. pap. 13.95 (*1-59413-019-1*, Large Print Pr.); 2003. 447p. 32.95 (*0-7862-5652-4*) Thorndike Pr.

—Stands a Calder Man. 1998. (Calder Saga Ser.: Vol. 2). 432p. 25.00 (*0-7278-5383-X*) Severn Hse. Pubs., Ltd.

—Stands a Calder Man. 1993. mass mkt. 6.99 (*0-671-87516-7*); 1991. mass mkt. 5.99 (*0-671-74287-6*); Vol. 2. 1999. 432p. pap. 6.99 (*0-671-04050-2*) Simon & Schuster. (Pocket).

—Stands a Calder Man. 15.80 o.s.i (*0-671-90082-X*, Simon Pulse) Simon & Schuster Children's Publishing.

—This Calder Range. 1998. 448p. pap. 25.00 (*0-7278-5291-4*) Severn Hse. Pubs., Ltd.

—This Calder Range. 1993. mass mkt. 6.99 (*0-671-87517-5*); 1990. mass mkt. 5.99 (*0-671-73210-2*); 1989. mass mkt. 4.95 (*0-671-68586-4*); 1987. mass mkt. 4.50 (*0-671-63385-6*); 1983. mass mkt. 3.95 (*0-671-83608-0*); Vol. 1. 1999. 448p. pap. 7.99 (*0-671-04048-0*) Simon & Schuster. (Pocket).

—This Calder Range & Stands a Calder Man. abr. ed. 1993. 19.95 o.p. (*1-55800-642-7*) NewStar Media, Inc.

—This Calder Sky. l.t. ed. 1999. (Magna Large Print Ser.). 560p. 31.99 (*0-7505-1327-6*) Magna Large Print Bks. GBR. *Dist:* Ulverscroft Large Print Bks., Ltd., Ulverscroft Large Print Canada, Ltd.

—This Calder Sky. Pocket Bks.

—This Calder Sky. 1999. 496p. 26.00 (*0-7278-5401-1*) Severn Hse. Pubs., Ltd.

—This Calder Sky. 1993. mass mkt. 6.99 (*0-671-87518-3*); 1991. mass mkt. 5.99 (*0-671-73969-7*); 1990. mass mkt. 5.50 (*0-671-70881-3*); 1988. mass mkt. (*0-671-68081-1*); 1987. mass mkt. 4.50 (*0-671-63442-9*); 1982. mass mkt. 3.95 o.s.i (*0-671-46478-7*); Vol. 3. 1999. 496p. pap. 7.99 (*0-671-04051-0*) Simon & Schuster. (Pocket).

—This Calder Sky & Calder Born, Calder Bred. abr. ed. 1993. 19.95 o.p. (*1-55800-644-3*) NewStar Media, Inc.

## CALHOUN, MACKENZIE (FICTITIOUS CHARACTER)—FICTION

David, Peter. Dark Allies. 1999. (Star Trek Ser.: No. 8). (Illus.). 288p. pap. 6.50 (*0-671-02080-3*, Star Trek) Simon & Schuster.

—Double or Nothing. 1999. (Star Trek, The Next Generation Ser.: Vol. 5). 277p. pap. 6.50 o.s.i (*0-671-03478-2*, Star Trek) Simon & Schuster.

—End Game. 1997. (Star Trek Ser.: No. 4). (Illus.). 208p. pap. 3.99 (*0-671-01398-X*, Star Trek) Simon & Schuster.

—Fire on High. 1998. (Star Trek Ser.: No. 6). 288p. pap. 6.50 (*0-671-02037-4*, Star Trek) Simon & Schuster.

—House of Cards. 1997. (Star Trek Ser.: No. 1). 168p. per. 3.99 o.s.i (*0-671-01395-5*, Star Trek) Simon & Schuster.

—House of Cards; Into the Void; The Two-Front War; End Game. 1998. (Star Trek Ser.: Nos. 1-4). 704p. 15.00 (*0-671-01978-3*, Star Trek) Simon & Schuster.

—House of Cards; Into the Void; The Two-Front War; End Game. abr. ed. 1997. (Star Trek Ser.: Nos. 1-4). audio 22.00 (*0-671-57625-9*, Simon & Schuster Audioworks) Simon & Schuster Audio.

—Into the Void. 1997. (Star Trek Ser.: No. 2). (Illus.). 176p. pap. 3.99 (*0-671-01396-3*, Star Trek) Simon & Schuster.

—Martyr. 1998. (Star Trek Ser.: No. 5). (Illus.). 288p. pap. 6.50 (*0-671-02036-6*, Star Trek) Simon & Schuster.

—The Quiet Place. (Star Trek Ser.: No. 7). 288p. 2002. E-Book 6.99 (*0-7434-5574-6*); 1999. pap. 6.50 (*0-671-02079-X*) Simon & Schuster. (Star Trek).

—The Two-Front War. 1997. (Star Trek Ser.: No. 3). 304p. per. 3.99 (*0-671-01397-1*, Star Trek) Simon & Schuster.

David, Peter, told to. Once Burned. 1998. (Star Trek: Bk. 5). 288p. pap. 6.50 (*0-671-02078-1*, Star Trek) Simon & Schuster.

## CALHOUN, VINCE (FICTITIOUS CHARACTER)—FICTION

Harrington, Kent. Dia de los Muertos. 1997. Tr. of Day of the Dead. (SPA.). 244p. 30.00 (*0-939767-30-9*) McMillan, Dennis Pubns.

## CALIBAN, CAT (FICTITIOUS CHARACTER)—FICTION

Borton, D. B. Five Alarm Fire. 1996. 240p. mass mkt. 5.99 o.s.i (*0-425-15338-X*, Prime Crime) Berkley Publishing Group.

—Four Elements of Murder. 1995. 256p. (Orig.). mass mkt. 5.99 o.s.i (*0-425-14722-3*, Prime Crime) Berkley Publishing Group.

—One for the Money. 1993. 208p. 4.50 o.s.i (*1-55773-869-6*) Ace Bks.

—One for the Money. 1993. 208p. mass mkt. 4.99 o.s.i (*0-425-15328-2*) Berkley Publishing Group.

—Six Feet Under. 1997. 240p. mass mkt. 5.99 o.s.i (*0-425-15700-8*, Prime Crime) Berkley Publishing Group.

—Three Is a Crowd. 1994. 240p. (Orig.). mass mkt. 4.99 o.s.i (*0-425-14327-9*, Prime Crime) Berkley Publishing Group.

—Two Points for Murder. 1993. mass mkt. 4.99 o.s.i (*0-425-13947-6*) Berkley Publishing Group.

## CALL, WOODROW (FICTITIOUS CHARACTER)—FICTION

McMurtry, Larry. Comanche Moon. unabr. ed. 1999. Pt. 1. audio 72.00; Pt. 2. (Lonesome Dove Ser.: No. 2). audio 64.00 Books on Tape, Inc.

—Comanche Moon, Set. unabr. ed. 1999. (Lonesome Dove Ser.: No. 2). audio 45.00 Highsmith Inc.

—Comanche Moon. 2000. (Lonesome Dove Ser.: No. 2). 720p. pap. 16.00 (*0-684-85755-3*, Simon & Schuster); 1998. (Lonesome Dove Ser.: No. 2). 816p. pap. 7.99 (*0-671-02064-1*, Pocket); 1998. mass mkt. 6.99 (*0-671-02049-8*, Pocket); 1997. (Lonesome Dove Ser.: No. 2). 752p. 28.50 (*0-684-80754-8*, Simon & Schuster) Simon & Schuster.

—Comanche Moon. unabr. ed. 1997. (Lonesome Dove Ser.: No. 2). 24p. audio 60.00 (*0-671-57730-1*, 135489, Simon & Schuster Audioworks) Simon & Schuster Audio.

—Comanche Moon. l.t. ed. 1999. (Paperback Bestsellers Ser.: No. 2). 921p. pap. 28.95 (*0-7862-1392-2*) Thorndike Pr.

—Comanche Moon. 1998. 14.04 (*0-606-16182-1*) Turtleback Bks.

—Dead Man's Walk. unabr. ed. 1996. audio 80.00 (*0-7366-3211-5*, 3874) Books on Tape, Inc.

—Dead Man's Walk. l.t. ed. (Lonesome Dove Ser.: No. 1). 1999. 800p. 27.95 o.p. (*0-7838-1510-7*); 1996. pap. 25.95 o.p. (*0-7838-1511-5*) Gale Group. (Macmillan Reference USA).

—Dead Man's Walk. (Lonesome Dove Ser.: No. 1). 2000. 464p. pap. 15.00 (*0-684-85754-5*, Simon & Schuster); 1995. 480p. 26.00 (*0-684-80753-X*, Simon & Schuster); 1996. 528p. pap. 7.99 (*0-671-00116-7*, Pocket) Simon & Schuster.

—Dead Man's Walk. unabr. ed. 1995. (Lonesome Dove Ser.: No. 1). audio 45.00 (*0-671-55169-8*, 113285, Simon & Schuster Audioworks) Simon & Schuster Audio.

—Dead Man's Walk. l.t. ed. 1998. (Lonesome Dove Ser.: No. 1). 5.98 o.p. (*0-7651-0771-6*) Smithmark Pubs., Inc.

—Dead Man's Walk. 2000. 21.05 (*0-606-20274-9*) Turtleback Bks.

—Lonesome Dove, Pt. 1. unabr. collector's ed. 1986. audio 56.00 (*0-7366-0582-7*, 1552-A) Books on Tape, Inc.

—Lonesome Dove. unabr. ed. 1993. (Lonesome Dove Ser.: No. 3). Vol. 1. 49.95 o.p. (*1-55800-481-5*); Vol. 2. 49.95 o.p. (*1-55800-622-2*); Vols. 1 & 2. audio 69.95 o.p. (*1-55800-719-9*) NewStar Media, Inc.

—Lonesome Dove. Grose, Bill, ed. 2000. (Lonesome Dove Ser.: No. 3). 960p. mass mkt. 7.99 (*0-671-79589-9*, Pocket) Simon & Schuster.

—Lonesome Dove. 2000. (Simon & Schuster Classic Editions: No. 3). (Illus.). 864p. 30.00 (*0-684-87122-X*, Simon & Schuster); 2000. (Lonesome Dove Ser.: No. 3). 864p. pap. 16.00 (*0-684-85752-9*, Simon & Schuster); 1993. (Lonesome Dove Ser.: No. 3). mass mkt. 6.99 (*0-671-74471-2*, Pocket); 1985. (Lonesome Dove Ser.: No. 3). 848p. 28.00 (*0-671-50420-7*, Simon & Schuster); No. 3. 1988. 960p. mass mkt. 7.99 (*0-671-68390-X*, Pocket) Simon & Schuster.

—Streets of Laredo. l.t. ed. 1994. (Lonesome Dove Ser.: No. 4). 795p. lib. bdg. 19.95 (*0-8161-5956-4*); lib. bdg. 25.95 o.p. (*0-8161-5955-6*) Gale Group. (Macmillan Reference USA).

—Streets of Laredo. (Lonesome Dove Ser.: No. 4). 2000. 544p. pap. 15.00 (*0-684-85753-7*, Simon & Schuster); 1995. 560p. mass mkt. 7.99 (*0-671-53746-6*, Pocket); 1994. 560p. mass mkt. 6.99 o.s.i (*0-671-79282-2*, Pocket); 1993. 589p. pap. 25.00 o.p. (*0-671-79281-4*, Simon & Schuster) Simon & Schuster.

—Streets of Laredo. unabr. ed. (Lonesome Dove Ser.: No. 4). 1995. audio 50.00 (*0-671-86998-1*, Simon & Schuster Audioworks); 1995. audio 45.00 (*0-671-56871-X*, Simon & Schuster Audioworks); 1993. audio 45.00 Simon & Schuster Audio.

—Streets of Laredo. 1993. (Lonesome Dove Ser.: No. 4). 14.04 (*0-606-06771-X*) Turtleback Bks.

## CALLAHAN, BROCK (FICTITIOUS CHARACTER)—FICTION

Gault, William C. Cat & Mouse. 1988. 176p. 12.95 o.p. (*0-312-01398-1*, Saint Martin's Minotaur) St. Martin's Pr.

—The Chicano War. 1986. 192p. 14.95 o.p. (*0-8027-5640-9*) Walker & Co.

—Come Die with Me. 1987. 188p. 2.95 o.s.i (*0-441-11539-X*, Diamond Bks.) Berkley Publishing Group.

—County Kill. 1988. 2.95 (*1-55773-017-2*, Diamond Bks.) Berkley Publishing Group.

—Day of the Ram. 1988. 2.95 (*1-55773-091-1*, Diamond Bks.) Berkley Publishing Group.

—Dead Hero. 1988. 2.95 (*1-55773-037-7*, Diamond Bks.) Berkley Publishing Group.

—Dead Pigeon. 1992. (Mystery Scene Bk.). 160p. pap. 3.95 o.p. (*0-88184-839-5*, Carroll & Graf Pubs.) Avalon Publishing Group.

—Dead Seed. l.t. ed. 1987. pap. 13.95 o.p. (*1-55504-039-X*) BBC Audiobooks America.

—Dead Seed. 1985. 12.95 o.p. (*0-8027-5604-2*) Walker & Co.

—Death in Donegal Bay. 1984. 192p. 12.95 o.p. (*0-8027-5591-7*) Walker & Co.

—Murder in the Raw. 1988. 2.95 (*1-55773-061-X*, Diamond Bks.) Berkley Publishing Group.

## CALLAHAN, JAMES (FICTITIOUS CHARACTER)—FICTION

Blanchard, Al. The Disappearance of Jenna Drago. 2002. 306p. pap. 19.95 (*0-9718758-8-X*) Koenisha Pubns.

—The Iscariot Conspiracy. 2001. (Leiutenant James Callahan Mystery: Vol. 1). 278p. pap. 19.95 (*0-9700458-6-7*) Koenisha Pubns.

## CALLAHAN, MIKE (FICTITIOUS CHARACTER)—FICTION

Robinson, Spider. Callahan Chronicals. 1997. (Callahan Ser.). 399p. pap. 10.99 (*0-8125-3937-0*, Tor Bks.) Doherty, Tom Assocs., LLC.

—The Callahan Touch. 1995. 240p. mass mkt. 5.99 o.s.i (*0-441-00133-5*); 1993. 228p. 18.95 o.p. (*0-441-09075-3*) Ace Bks.

—Callahan's Crosstime Saloon. 1987. 192p. mass mkt. 4.50 o.s.i (*0-441-09043-5*); 1984. mass mkt. 2.50 o.s.i (*0-441-09069-9*); 1983. mass mkt. 2.50 o.s.i (*0-441-09068-0*); 1982. mass mkt. 2.25 o.s.i (*0-441-09037-0*); 1977. xix, 170p. 1.50 o.s.i (*0-441-09034-6*) Ace Bks.

—Callahan's Crosstime Saloon. 1987. 192p. 2.95 o.s.i (*0-425-09586-X*); 1985. xix, 170p. 2.75 o.s.i (*0-425-09155-4*) Berkley Publishing Group.

—Callahan's Crosstime Saloon. 1999. 205p. mass mkt. 6.99 (*0-8125-7227-0*, Tor Bks.) Doherty, Tom Assocs., LLC.

—Callahan's Crosstime Saloon. 1978. reprint ed. 13.95 o.p. (*0-89490-014-5*) Enslow Pubs., Inc.

—Callahan's Lady. 1990. mass mkt. 4.99 o.s.i (*0-441-09072-9*); 11th ed. 1989. 16.95 o.p. (*0-441-09073-7*) Ace Bks.

—Callahan's Lady. 2001. 320p. pap. 6.99 (*0-671-31831-4*) Baen Bks.

—Callahan's Legacy. (Callahan Ser.). 1997. 214p. pap. text 5.99 (*0-8125-5035-8*); 1996. 224p. 20.95 o.p. (*0-312-85776-4*) Doherty, Tom Assocs., LLC. (Tor Bks.).

—Callahan's Secret. 1988. mass mkt. 4.50 o.s.i (*0-441-09074-5*) Ace Bks.

—Callahan's Secret. 1986. 192p. 2.95 o.s.i (*0-425-10059-6*); 2.95 o.s.i (*0-425-09082-5*) Berkley Publishing Group.

—Lady Slings the Booze. 272p. 1993. mass mkt. 5.99 o.s.i (*0-441-46929-9*); 1992. 18.95 o.p. (*0-441-46928-0*) Ace Bks.

—Time Traveler's Strictly Cash. 1987. 208p. mass mkt. 4.99 o.s.i (*0-441-80713-5*) Ace Bks.

## CALLAHAN, ROSE, SISTER (FICTITIOUS CHARACTER)—FICTION

Woodworth, Deborah. Deadly Shaker Spring. 1998. (Sister Rose Callahan Mystery Ser.). 304p. mass mkt. 5.99 (*0-380-79203-6*, Avon Bks.) Morrow/Avon.

—The Death of a Winter Shaker. 1997. (Sister Rose Callahan Mystery Ser.). 224p. mass mkt. 5.50 (*0-380-79201-X*, Avon Bks.) Morrow/Avon.

—A Simple Shaker Murder. 2000. (Sister Rose Callahan Mystery Ser.). 256p. mass mkt. 5.99 (*0-380-80425-5*, Avon Bks.) Morrow/Avon.

—The Sins of a Shaker Summer: A Sister Rose Callahan Mystery. 1999. 272p. mass mkt. 5.99 (*0-380-79204-4*, Avon Bks.) Morrow/Avon.

## CALLAHAN, SALLY (FICTITIOUS CHARACTER)—FICTION

Robinson, Spider. Callahan's Lady. 1990. mass mkt. 4.99 o.s.i (*0-441-09072-9*); 11th ed. 1989. 16.95 o.p. (*0-441-09073-7*) Ace Bks.

—Callahan's Lady. 2001. 320p. pap. 6.99 (*0-671-31831-4*) Baen Bks.

—Lady Slings the Booze. 272p. 1993. mass mkt. 5.99 o.s.i (*0-441-46929-9*); 1992. 18.95 o.p. (*0-441-46928-0*) Ace Bks.

## CALLAIS, BERTRAND (FICTITIOUS CHARACTER)—FICTION

Endore, Guy. The Werewolf of Paris. 1993. reprint ed. lib. bdg. 18.95 (*0-89968-425-4*, Lightyear Pr.) Buccaneer Bks., Inc.

—The Werewolf of Paris. 1976. pap. 1.95 o.s.i (*0-671-80584-3*, Pocket) Simon & Schuster.

## CALLOW, JOHN (FICTITIOUS CHARACTER)—FICTION

Taylor, Bernard. Evil Intent. 1996. 352p. reprint ed. mass mkt. 4.99 (*0-8439-3904-4*, Leisure Bks.) Dorchester Publishing Co., Inc.

—Evil Intent, Set. unabr. ed. 1998. audio 83.95 o.p. (*1-85903-096-3*) Magna Story Sound GBR. *Dist:* Ulverscroft Large Print Bks., Ltd.

## CALRISSIAN, LANDO (FICTITIOUS CHARACTER)—FICTION

Anderson, Kevin J. The Jedi Academy Trilogy Omnibus. abr. ed. 1997. (Star Wars Ser.). (gr. 5 up). 29.95 incl. audio (*0-553-47848-6*, RH Audio) Random Hse. Audio Publishing Group.

—Jedi Search. 1994. (Star Wars: Vol. 1). 384p. mass mkt. 6.99 (*0-553-29798-8*) Bantam Bks.

—Jedi Search. abr. ed. 1994. (star wars: Vol. 1). audio 16.98 o.s.i (*0-553-74512-3*); audio 16.99 (*0-553-47199-6*) Random Hse. Audio Publishing Group. (RH Audio).

—Jedi Search. 1994. (Star Wars: Vol. 1). 12.04 (*0-606-08202-6*) Turtleback Bks.

—Jedi Trilogy: Jedi Search; Dark Apprentice; Champions of the Force, 3 vols. 1997. (Star Wars). (YA). (gr. 5). 20.97 (*0-553-64839-X*) Bantam Bks.

Baron, Mike, et al. Dark Force Rising. 1998. (Star Wars Ser.). (Illus.). 160p. (YA). (gr. 7 up). pap. 17.95 (*1-56971-269-7*) Dark Horse Comics.

Crispin, A. C. The Hans Solo Omnibus. abr. ed. 2000. (Star Wars Ser.). (gr. 5 up). 29.95 incl. audio (*0-553-52700-2*, RH Audio) Random Hse. Audio Publishing Group.

—Rebel Dawn. 1998. (Star Wars: Vol. 3). 400p. mass mkt. 6.99 (*0-553-57417-5*) Bantam Bks.

—Rebel Dawn. abr. ed. 1998. (Star Wars: Vol. 3). (gr. 5). audio 16.99 (*0-553-47746-3*, 395670, RH Audio) Random Hse. Audio Publishing Group.

Daley, Brian. The Empire Strikes Back: The National Public Radio Dramatization. 1995. (Star Wars Ser.). (Illus.). 320p. pap. 19.00 o.s.i (*0-345-39605-7*, Del Rey) Ballantine Bks.

—Return of the Jedi: The National Public Radio Dramatization. 1996. 208p. pap. 15.00 o.s.i (*0-345-40782-2*) Ballantine Bks.

—Star Wars: The National Public Radio Dramatization. 1994. (Star Wars Ser.). (Illus.). 352p. pap. 19.00 o.s.i (*0-345-39109-8*, Del Rey) Ballantine Bks.

Dark Horse Comics Staff, et al. Shadows of the Empire. 1997. (Star Wars Ser.). (Illus.). 160p. (YA). (gr. 7 up). pap. 17.95 (*1-56971-183-6*) Dark Horse Comics.

Davids, Paul. The Queen of the Empire. 1993. (Star Wars: Bk. 5). 128p. (YA). (gr. 4-7). pap. 4.50 o.s.i (*0-553-15891-0*) Bantam Bks.

Gardner, J. J. The Empire Strikes Back. 1997. (Star Wars Ser.). (Illus.). (J). (gr. 5-7). mass mkt. 5.99 (*0-590-06656-0*) Scholastic, Inc.

Glut, Donald F. The Empire Strikes Back. 1997. (Star Wars Ser.). pap. 5.99 (*0-345-91183-0*); 1995. (Star Wars Ser.). 224p. 16.00 o.s.i (*0-345-40078-X*); 1985. (Star Wars Ser.: Vol. 2). 224p. mass mkt. 5.99 (*0-345-32022-0*); 1980. mass mkt. 2.25 o.p. (*0-345-28392-9*) Ballantine Bks. (Del Rey).

Golden, Christopher. Shadows of the Empire. 1996. (Star Wars Ser.). (Illus.). 176p. (J). (gr. 4-7). pap. text 4.50 o.s.i (*0-440-41303-6*) Dell Publishing.

—Shadows of the Empire: A Junior Novelization. 1996. (Star Wars Ser.). 10.55 (*0-606-11835-7*) Turtleback Bks.

Goodwin, Archie. The Empire Strikes Back: Classic Star Wars. 1995. (Star Wars Ser.). (Illus.). 104p. pap. 9.95 o.p. (*1-56971-088-0*) Dark Horse Comics.

Goodwin, Archie, et al. The Empire Strikes Back: Special Edition. 1997. (Star Wars Ser.). 104p. (J). (gr. 3 up). pap. 9.95 (*1-56971-234-4*) Dark Horse Comics.

—Return of the Jedi: Special Edition. 1997. (Star Wars Ser.). 104p. (YA). (gr. 3 up). pap. 9.95 (*1-56971-235-2*) Dark Horse Comics.

Hambly, Barbara. Planet of Twilight. 1998. (Star Wars Ser.). 416p. reprint ed. mass mkt. 6.99 (*0-553-57517-1*) Bantam Bks.

—Planet of Twilight. abr. ed. 1997. (Star Wars Ser.). audio 16.99 (*0-553-47196-1*, RH Audio) Random Hse. Audio Publishing Group.

Hamill, Mark, et al. Star Wars: The Original Radio Drama. abr. unabr. ed. 1993. (Star Wars Ser.). audio 39.95 (*0-942110-99-4*, 692313); audio compact disk 64.95 (*1-56511-005-6*) HighBridge Co.

Jones, Bruce, et al. Star Wars Trilogy: A New Hope, Empire Strikes Back, Return of the Jedi. 2nd ed. 1997. (Star Wars Ser.). (Illus.). (J). (gr. 3 up). pap. 29.85 o.p. (*1-56971-257-3*) Dark Horse Comics.

Kahn, James. Return of the Jedi. (Star Wars Ser.). 1997. mass mkt. 5.99 (*0-345-91184-9*, Del Rey); 1995. 240p. 16.00 (*0-345-40079-8*, Del Rey); 1983. (Illus.). 224p. mass mkt. 5.95 o.p. (*0-345-30960-X*); 1983. 192p. mass mkt. 5.99 (*0-345-30767-4*, Del Rey) Ballantine Bks.

Kube-McDowell, Michael P. Before the Storm. 1996. (Star Wars: Bk. 1). 336p. mass mkt. 6.99 (*0-553-57273-3*, Spectra) Bantam Bks.

—Before the Storm. abr. ed. 1996. (Star Wars: Bk. 1). audio 16.99 (*0-553-47422-7*, 394259, RH Audio) Random Hse. Audio Publishing Group.

—Before the Storm. 1996. (Star Wars: Bk. 1). 12.04 (*0-606-11884-5*) Turtleback Bks.

—Shield of Lies. 1996. (Star Wars: Bk. 2). pap. 10.95 o.s.i (*0-553-84010-X*); 368p. mass mkt. 6.99 (*0-553-57277-6*, Spectra) Bantam Bks.

—Shield of Lies. abr. ed. 1996. (Star Wars: Bk. 2). audio 16.99 o.s.i (*0-553-47424-3*, 394260, RH Audio) Random Hse. Audio Publishing Group.

—Shield of Lies. 1996. (Star Wars: Bk. 2). 12.04 (*0-606-11885-3*) Turtleback Bks.

—Tyrant's Test. 1996. (Star Wars: Bk. 3). (Illus.). 400p. (gr. 5 up). mass mkt. 6.99 (*0-553-57275-X*, Spectra) Bantam Bks.

—Tyrant's Test. abr. ed. 1996. (Star Wars: Bk. 3). audio 16.99 (*0-553-47421-9*, 394598, RH Audio) Random Hse. Audio Publishing Group.

—Tyrant's Test. 1997. (Star Wars: Bk. 3). 12.04 (*0-606-11886-1*) Turtleback Bks.

Levy, Elizabeth, adapted by. Return of the Jedi. 1995. (Illus.). 64p. (J). (gr. 4-7). pap. 3.99 (*0-679-87205-1*) Random Hse., Inc.

Lucas, George. The Empire Strikes Back. 1994. 8.98 (*1-57042-172-2*) Warner Bks., Inc.

—The Empire Strikes Back: The Original Radio Drama. abr. unabr. ed. 1993. (Star Wars Ser.). audio 39.95 (*1-56511-000-5*, 492026); audio compact disk 59.95 (*1-56511-007-2*) HighBridge Co.

—Return of the Jedi. 1997. mass mkt. 5.99 o.s.i (*0-345-41356-3*, Del Rey) Ballantine Bks.

—Return of the Jedi. 1995. 8.98 (*1-57042-208-7*) Warner Bks., Inc.

—Return of the Jedi: The Original Radio Drama. abr. unabr. ed. 1996. (Star Wars Ser.). audio 25.95 (*1-56511-157-5*); audio compact disk 34.95 (*1-56511-158-3*) HighBridge Co.

Lucas, George. Star Wars Trilogy: Star Wars; The Empire Strikes Back; Return of the Jedi. unabr. ed. 1994. (Star Wars Ser.). audio 50.00 o.p. (*1-57042-157-9*, 4-521579); audio 75.00 o.p. (*1-57042-169-2*, 2-521579) Time Warner AudioBooks.

Lucas, George & Kasdan, Lawrence. Return of the Jedi. deluxe ed. 1998. (Star Wars Ser.). (Illus.). 144p. pap. 18.95 (*0-345-42082-9*, Ballantine Bks.) Ballantine Bks.

—Return of the Jedi: The Illustrated Screenplay. 1998. (Illus.). 208p. pap. 12.00 (*0-345-42079-9*, Del Rey) Ballantine Bks.

Lucas, George, et al. The Empire Strikes Back. deluxe ed. 1998. (Star Wars Ser.). (Illus.). 160p. pap. 18.95 o.s.i (*0-345-42081-0*, Del Rey) Ballantine Bks.

—Star Wars Trilogy: Star Wars; The Empire Strikes Back; Return of the Jedi. (Star Wars Ser.). 1997. mass mkt. 6.99 (*0-345-91126-1*); 1993. 480p. mass mkt. 7.99 (*0-345-38438-5*, Del Rey); 1987. 480p. pap. 12.95 (*0-345-34806-0*, Del Rey) Ballantine Bks.

—Star Wars Trilogy: Star Wars; The Empire Strikes Back; Return of the Jedi. 1987. (J). (gr. 3-7). 16.05 (*0-606-01231-1*) Turtleback Bks.

Lucasfilm Ltd. The Complete Trilogy Cassette Gift-Pack: Star Wars, The Empire Strikes Back, & Return of the Jedi. abr. ed. 1996. (Star Wars Ser.). audio 105.85 o.p. (*1-56511-173-7*) HighBridge Co.

Lucasfilm Ltd. Staff. The Last Command. unabr. ed. 1996. (Star Wars: Bk. 3). audio 104.00. audio Books on Tape, Inc.

Perry, Steve. Shadows of the Empire. 1997. (Star Wars Ser.). 416p. (gr. 5 up). mass mkt. 6.99 (*0-553-57413-2*, Spectra) Bantam Bks.

—Shadows of the Empire. abr. ed. 1996. (Star Wars Ser.). audio 16.99 (*0-553-47438-3*, 393956, RH Audio) Random Hse. Audio Publishing Group.

—Shadows of the Empire. 1996. (Star Wars Ser.). 12.04 (*0-606-11895-0*) Turtleback Bks.

Perry, Steve, et al. Evolution: Shadows of the Empire. 2000. (Star Wars Ser.). (Illus.). 120p. (YA). (gr. 7 up). pap. 14.95 (*1-56971-441-X*) Dark Horse Comics.

Rusch, Kristine K. The New Rebellion. 1997. (Star Wars Ser.). 560p. mass mkt. 6.99 (*0-553-57414-0*, Spectra) Bantam Bks.

—The New Rebellion. 1997. (Star Wars Ser.). 12.04 (*0-606-11894-2*) Turtleback Bks.

—New Rebellion. abr. ed. 1996. (Star Wars Ser.). audio 16.99 (*0-553-47743-9*, RH Audio) Random Hse. Audio Publishing Group.

Smith, L. Neil. The Adventures of Lando Calrissian: Lando Calrissian & the Mindharp of Sharu; Lando Calrissian & the Flamewind of Oseon; Lando Calrissian & the Starcave of Thonboka. 1994. (Star Wars). 416p. (gr. 5 up). mass mkt. 6.99 (*0-345-39110-1*, Del Rey) Ballantine Bks.

—Lando Calrissian & the Flamewind of Oseon. 1983. (Star Wars: Bk. 2). 192p. (YA). (gr. 5 up). mass mkt. 2.50 o.s.i (*0-345-31163-9*, Del Rey) Ballantine Bks.

—Lando Calrissian & the Mindharp of Sharu. 1983. (Star Wars: Bk. 1). (YA). (gr. 5 up). mass mkt. 2.50 o.s.i (*0-345-31158-2*, Del Rey) Ballantine Bks.

—Lando Calrissian & the Starcave of Thonboka. 1983. (Star Wars: Bk. 3). 192p. (YA). (gr. 5 up). mass mkt. 2.50 o.s.i (*0-345-31164-7*, Del Rey) Ballantine Bks.

—Star Wars: The Adventures of Lando Calrissian, 3 bks. in 1. 1994. (Star Wars). (Illus.). 410p. (YA). (gr. 5 up). mass mkt. 10.00 o.s.i (*0-345-39443-7*, Del Rey) Ballantine Bks.

Star Wars Trilogy: Star Wars; The Empire Strikes Back; Return of the Jedi, 3 vols. 1987. (Star Wars Ser.). pap. 8.65 o.p. (*0-345-32964-3*, Del Rey) Ballantine Bks.

Weinberg, Larry. The Empire Strikes Back: Classic Star Wars. 1995. (Star Wars Ser.). (Illus.). 54p. (J). (gr. 4-7). pap. 3.99 o.s.i (*0-679-87204-3*) Random Hse., Inc.

Zahn, Timothy. Dark Force Rising. (Star Wars: Bk. 2). 1993. 448p. mass mkt. 6.99 (*0-553-56071-9*); 1992. 368p. 18.50 o.s.i (*0-553-08574-3*); Vol. 2. 1992. 384p. 125.00 o.s.i (*0-553-08907-2*, Spectra) Bantam Bks.

—Dark Force Rising. unabr. ed. 1995. (Star Wars: Bk. 2). audio 96.00 Books on Tape, Inc.

—Dark Force Rising. abr. ed. 1992. (Star Wars: Bk. 2). audio 16.99 (*0-553-47055-8*, RH Audio) Random Hse. Audio Publishing Group.

—Heir to the Empire. (Star Wars: Bk. 1). 9999. pap. 9.90 o.s.i (*0-593-02481-8*); 1992. 432p. mass mkt. 6.99 (*0-553-29612-4*); 1991. 368p. 22.95 o.s.i (*0-553-07327-3*); 1991. 368p. 125.00 o.s.i (*0-553-07340-0*, Spectra) Bantam Bks.

—Heir to the Empire. unabr. ed. 1995. (Star Wars: Bk. 1). audio 88.00 Books on Tape, Inc.

—Heir to the Empire. abr. ed. 1991. (Star Wars: Bk. 1). audio 16.99 (*0-553-45296-7*, 391663, RH Audio) Random Hse. Audio Publishing Group.

—Heir to the Empire. 1993. (Star Wars: Bk. 1). 64.95 o.p. incl. audio (*0-7838-1100-4*) Thorndike Pr.

—Heir to the Empire. 1991. (Star Wars: Bk. 1). 12.04 (*0-606-00751-2*) Turtleback Bks.

—The Last Command. (Star Wars: Bk. 3). 1994. 496p. mass mkt. 6.99 (*0-553-56492-7*, Spectra); 1993. 416p. 125.00 o.s.i (*0-553-09500-5*) Bantam Bks.

—The Last Command. abr. ed. 1993. (Star Wars: Bk. 3). audio 16.99 (*0-553-47157-0*, RH Audio) Random Hse. Audio Publishing Group.

—The Last Command. 1994. (Star Wars: Bk. 3). 12.04 (*0-606-08205-0*) Turtleback Bks.

—Specter of the Past. 1998. (Star Wars Hand of Thrawn Ser.: No. 1). 416p. (gr. 5 up). mass mkt. 6.99 (*0-553-29804-6*) Bantam Bks.

—Specter of the Past. abr. ed. 1997. (Star Wars Ser.: Vol. 1). (gr. 5 up). audio 16.99 (*0-553-47893-1*, RH Audio) Random Hse. Audio Publishing Group.

—Specter of the Past. l.t. ed. 1998. (Star Wars). 512p. 25.95 (*0-7838-8434-6*) Thorndike Pr.

—The Thrawn Trilogy. abr. ed. 2000. (Star Wars: Bk. 1,2,3). 29.95 incl. audio (*0-553-52699-5*);Set. (YA). 29.95 incl. audio Random Hse. Audio Publishing Group.

—Vision of the Future. 1999. (Star Wars Hand of Thrawn Ser.: No. 2). 720p. (gr. 5 up). mass mkt. 6.99 (*0-553-57879-0*) Bantam Bks.

—Vision of the Future. abr. ed. 1998. (Star Wars Ser.: Vol. 2). (gr. 5 up). audio 16.99 (*0-553-47921-0*, 392221, RH Audio) Random Hse. Audio Publishing Group.

Zahn, Timothy, et al. Heir to the Empire. 1996. (Star Wars Ser.). (Illus.). 160p. (YA). (gr. 7 up). pap. 19.95 (*1-56971-202-6*) Dark Horse Comics.

**CAMACHO, ELLEN (FICTITIOUS CHARACTER)—FICTION**

Fox, Zachary Alan. All Fall Down. 1997. 480p. mass mkt. 5.99 o.s.i (*0-7860-0450-9*, Pinnacle Bks.); 384p. 22.00 o.p. (*1-57566-139-X*, Kensington Bks.) Kensington Publishing Corp.

**CAMBER OF CULDI (FICTITIOUS CHARACTER)—FICTION**

Kurtz, Katherine. Camber of Culdi. 1985. mass mkt. 3.50 o.p. (*0-345-33594-5*, Del Rey); 1983. mass mkt. 2.95 o.p. (*0-345-31296-1*, Del Rey); 1982. mass mkt. 2.75 o.p. (*0-345-30855-7*, Del Rey); 1979. mass mkt. 2.25 o.p. (*0-345-28559-X*, Del Rey); 1976. mass mkt. 1.95 o.p. (*0-345-24590-3*); Vol. 1. 1987. (Legends of Camber of Culdi Ser.: Bk. 1). 376p. mass mkt. 4.95 o.s.i (*0-345-34767-6*, Del Rey); Vol. 1. 1979. (Legends of Culdi Ser.). 8.95 o.p. (*0-345-28031-8*, Del Rey) Ballantine Bks.

—Camber the Heretic. 1985. mass mkt. 3.50 o.p. (*0-345-33142-7*); 1981. mass mkt. 2.95 o.p. (*0-345-27784-8*); Vol. 3. 1987. (Legends of Camber of Culdi Ser.: Bk. 3). 512p. mass mkt. 5.99 o.s.i (*0-345-34754-4*) Ballantine Bks. (Del Rey).

—Saint Camber. 1982. mass mkt. 2.95 o.p. (*0-345-30862-X*); 1979. mass mkt. 2.25 o.p. (*0-345-25952-1*) Ballantine Bks. (Del Rey).

—Saint Camber. 1992. o.p. (*0-7126-9549-4*) Random Hse. UK, Ltd. GBR. *Dist:* Random Hse. of Canada, Ltd.

**CAMDEN, CLAIRE (FICTITIOUS CHARACTER)—FICTION**

Peterson, Audrey. Dartmoor Burial. Isaacson, Dana, ed. 1992. 256p. (Orig.). mass mkt. 5.50 o.s.i (*0-671-72970-5*, Pocket) Simon & Schuster.

—Death Too Soon. Isaacson, Dana, ed. 1994. 288p. (Orig.). mass mkt. 4.99 o.s.i (*0-671-79509-0*, Pocket) Simon & Schuster.

—Shroud for a Scholar. 1995. 272p. mass mkt. 5.50 o.s.i (*0-671-79510-4*, Pocket) Simon & Schuster.

**CAMDEN, SHELBY (FICTITIOUS CHARACTER)—FICTION**

Dreher, Sarah. Solitaire & Brahms. 1997. 292p. pap. 12.95 (*0-934678-85-5*) New Victoria Pubs., Inc.

**CAMERON, BREN (FICTITIOUS CHARACTER)—FICTION**

Cherryh, C. J. Defender. 2001. (Foreigner Ser.: No. 5). 448p. 23.95 (*0-88677-911-1*); Vol. 2. 2002. 464p. reprint ed. mass mkt. 6.99 (*0-7564-0020-1*) DAW Bks., Inc.

—Foreigner. 1994. (Daw Book Collectors Ser.: Bk. 1). 432p. mass mkt. 6.99 (*0-88677-637-6*); 320p. 20.00 o.p. (*0-88677-590-6*) DAW Bks., Inc.

—Inheritor. (Foreigner Ser.: Bk. 3). 1997. 464p. mass mkt. 6.99 (*0-88677-728-3*); 1996. 432p. 21.95 o.p. (*0-88677-689-9*) DAW Bks., Inc.

—Invader. (Foreigner Trilogy Ser.: Bk. 2). 1995. 384p. 19.95 o.p. (*0-88677-638-4*); Vol. 2. 1996. 432p. mass mkt. 6.99 (*0-88677-687-2*) DAW Bks., Inc.

—Precursor. (Foreigner Ser.). 1999. (Illus.). 416p. 23.95 o.s.i (*0-88677-836-0*, D A W Fiction); 2000. 464p. reprint ed. mass mkt. 6.99 (*0-88677-910-3*) DAW Bks., Inc.

—Precursor. 2000. 13.04 (*0-606-19369-3*) Turtleback Bks.

**CAMERON, DONALD (FICTITIOUS CHARACTER)—FICTION**

McCutchan, Philip. Cameron & the Kaiserhof. 1984. 192p. 10.95 o.p. (*0-312-11443-5*) St. Martin's Pr.

—Cameron Comes Through. 1986. 160p. 12.95 o.p. (*0-312-11444-3*) St. Martin's Pr.

—Cameron in Command. 1986. pap. 3.50 o.p. (*0-312-90468-1*, St. Martin's Paperbacks); 1984. 176p. 10.95 o.p. (*0-312-11446-X*) St. Martin's Pr.

—Cameron in the Gap. 1999. audio 44.95 Soundings, Ltd. GBR. *Dist:* Ulverscroft Large Print Bks., Ltd.

—Cameron in the Gap. 1983. 160p. 9.95 o.p. (*0-312-11448-6*) St. Martin's Pr.

—Cameron in the Gap. l.t. ed. 1999. (General Ser.). 232p. pap. 23.95 (*0-7862-1964-5*); (*0-7540-3810-6*); (*0-7540-3809-2*) Thorndike Pr.

—Cameron of the Castle Bay. unabr. ed. 2001. audio 44.95 (*1-85496-708-8*, 67088) Soundings, Ltd. GBR. *Dist:* Ulverscroft Large Print Bks., Ltd.

—Cameron's Chase. unabr. ed. 1997. audio 49.95 (*1-85496-934-X*, 6934X) Soundings, Ltd. GBR. *Dist:* Ulverscroft Large Print Bks., Ltd.

—Cameron's Chase. 1987. pap. 3.50 o.p. (*0-312-90703-6*, St. Martin's Paperbacks); 1986. 182p. 12.95 o.p. (*0-312-11450-8*) St. Martin's Pr.

—Cameron's Commitment. 1989. 192p. 14.95 o.p. (*0-312-02532-7*) St. Martin's Pr.

—Cameron's Convoy. 156p. 14.99 o.p. (*0-7278-4771-6*) Severn Hse. Pubs., Ltd.

—Cameron's Convoy. 2001. audio 44.95 (*1-85496-138-1*, 61381) Soundings, Ltd. GBR. *Dist:* Ulverscroft Large Print Bks., Ltd.

—Cameron's Convoy. l.t. ed. 1999. (General Ser.). 240p. pap. 23.95 (*0-7862-1821-5*) Thorndike Pr.

—Cameron's Crossing. 1993. 176p. 17.95 o.p. (*0-312-09762-X*) St. Martin's Pr.

—Cameron's Raid, unabr. ed. 1999. audio 54.95 (*1-86042-388-4*, 23884) Soundings, Ltd. GBR. *Dist:* Ulverscroft Large Print Bks., Ltd.

—Cameron's Raid. 1986. pap. 3.50 o.p. (*0-312-90081-3*, St. Martin's Paperbacks); 1985. 11.95 o.p. (*0-312-11452-4*) St. Martin's Pr.

—Cameron's Troop Lift. 1987. 208p. 13.95 o.p. (*0-312-01008-7*) St. Martin's Pr.

—Lieutenant Cameron RNVR. unabr. ed. 1998. audio 63.95 (*1-85903-068-8*) Magna Story Sound GBR. *Dist:* Ulverscroft Large Print Bks., Ltd.

—Lieutenant Cameron RNVR. 1987. pap. 3.50 o.p. (*0-312-90691-9*, St. Martin's Paperbacks); 1985. 160p. 11.95 o.p. (*0-312-48373-2*) St. Martin's Pr.

—Orders for Cameron. l.t. ed. 1985. lib. bdg. 14.50 o.p. (*0-7451-0246-8*); 13.50 o.p. (*0-8166-0246-8*) Gale Group. (Macmillan Reference USA).

—Orders for Cameron. unabr. ed. 1996. audio 49.95 (*1-86042-123-7*, 21237) Soundings, Ltd. GBR. *Dist:* Ulverscroft Large Print Bks., Ltd.

—Orders for Cameron. 1983. 160p. 10.95 o.p. (*0-312-58722-8*) St. Martin's Pr.

**CAMERON, LUKE (FICTITIOUS CHARACTER)—FICTION**

Anderson, Jack. Zero Time. 1993. 512p. mass mkt. 4.99 o.s.i (*0-8217-4087-3*); 1990. mass mkt. 19.95 o.s.i (*0-8217-3176-9*) Kensington Publishing Corp. (Zebra Bks.).

**CAMERON, TROY (FICTITIOUS CHARACTER)—FICTION**

Bunker, Edward. Dog Eat Dog. 240p. 1997. pap. 13.95 (*0-312-16818-7*, Saint Martin's Griffin); 1996. 22.95 o.p. (*0-312-14314-1*) St. Martin's Pr.

**CAMPBELL, CHUCK (FICTITIOUS CHARACTER)—FICTION**

Monson, J. Bruce. Crimson Ice, Sugar & Spice: A Novel of Suspense. 1994. 224p. (Orig.). pap. 10.95 (*1-56474-083-8*) Fithian Pr.

**CAMPBELL, JOE (FICTITIOUS CHARACTER)—FICTION**

Dershowitz, Alan M. The Advocate's Devil. abr. ed. 1994. audio 17.95 o.p. (*0-7871-0408-6*, Dove Audio) NewStar Media, Inc.

—The Advocate's Devil. 1999. 352p. reprint ed. lib. bdg. 35.95 (*0-7351-0066-7*) Replica Bks.

—The Advocate's Devil. 384p. 2001. pap. 4.95 (*0-446-51759-3*); 1995. mass mkt. 6.50 (*0-446-60291-4*) Warner Bks., Inc.

**CAMPBELL, LETTY (FICTITIOUS CHARACTER)—FICTION**

Fritchley, Alma. Chicken Feed. 138p. pap. 11.95 (*0-7043-4692-3*); 1999. 222p. pap. 13.95 (*0-7043-4570-6*) Women's Pr., Ltd., The GBR. *Dist:* Trafalgar Square.

—Chicken Out. 2000. (Letty Campbell Mystery Ser.: No. 3). 164p. pap. 13.95 (*0-7043-4619-2*) Women's Pr., Ltd., The GBR. *Dist:* Trafalgar Square.

—Chicken Run: A Letty Campbell Mystery. 1998. 136p. pap. 13.95 (*0-7043-4515-3*) Women's Pr., Ltd., The GBR. *Dist:* Trafalgar Square.

**CAMPBELL, LIAM (FICTITIOUS CHARACTER)—FICTION**

Stabenow, Dana. Better to Rest. 2002. 29.95 (*1-58724-352-0*, Wheeler Publishing, Inc.) Gale Group.

—Better to Rest. 2003. 304p. mass mkt. 6.99 (*0-451-20960-5*, Signet Bks.); 2002. 272p. 23.95 (*0-451-20702-5*) NAL.

—Fire & Ice: A Liam Campbell Mystery. unabr. collector's ed. 1999. audio 56.00 (*0-7366-4860-7*, 5187) Books on Tape, Inc.

—Fire & Ice: A Liam Campbell Mystery. 1998. 272p. 23.95 o.p. (*0-525-94438-9*) Dutton/Plume.

—Fire & Ice: A Liam Campbell Mystery. 1999. (Liam Campbell Mysteries Ser.). 304p. mass mkt. 6.99 (*0-451-19770-4*, Signet Bks.) NAL.

—Fire & Ice: A Liam Campbell Mystery. l.t. ed. 1999. (Mystery Ser.). 463p. 29.95 (*0-7862-1903-3*) Thorndike Pr.

—Nothing Gold Can Stay: A Liam Campbell Mystery. 2000. (Liam Campbell Mysteries Ser.). 288p. 23.95 o.s.i (*0-525-94559-8*, Dutton) Dutton/Plume.

—So Sure of Death: A Liam Campbell Mystery. 1999. (Liam Campbell Mysteries Ser.). 288p. 23.95 o.s.i (*0-525-94519-9*) Dutton/Plume.

Characters

—So Sure of Death: A Liam Campbell Mystery. l.t. ed. 2000. (Mystery Ser.). 477p. 29.95 (0-7862-2478-9) Thorndike Pr.

**CAMPBELL, WAYNE (FICTITIOUS CHARACTER)—FICTION**

Myers, Mike. Wayne's World: Extreme Close-Up. 1992. 96p. pap. 7.95 o.p. (1-56282-979-3) Hyperion Bks. for Children.

**CAMPION, ALBERT (FICTITIOUS CHARACTER)—FICTION**

Allingham, Margery. The Allingham Case-Book. 18.95 o.p. (0-89190-915-X) Amereon, Ltd.

—The Allingham Case-Book. 2nd ed. 1992. 240p. mass mkt. 3.95 (0-88184-889-1, Carroll & Graf Pubs.) Avalon Publishing Group.

—The Allingham Case-Book. 1998. 224p. lib. bdg. 21.95 (1-56723-000-8) Yestermorrow, Inc.

—The Black Dudley Murder. 176p. reprint ed. lib. bdg. 19.95 o.p. (0-89190-188-4, Rivercity Pr.) Amereon, Ltd.

—The Black Dudley Murder. 2000. 224p. mass mkt. 5.95 (0-7867-0754-2, Carroll & Graf Pubs.) Avalon Publishing Group.

—The Black Dudley Murder. 1994. reprint ed. lib. bdg. 27.95 (1-56849-252-9) Buccaneer Bks., Inc.

—The Black Dudley Murder. 1988. 224p. mass mkt. 3.99 (0-380-70575-3, Avon Bks.) Morrow/Avon.

—The Black Dudley Murder. 1998. 227p. lib. bdg. 22.95 (1-56723-001-6) Yestermorrow, Inc.

—Black Plumes. 1993. 276p. reprint ed. 19.95 o.p. (0-89190-191-4) Amereon, Ltd.

—Black Plumes. 1995. 192p. mass mkt. 3.95 (0-7867-0290-7, Carroll & Graf Pubs.) Avalon Publishing Group.

—Black Plumes. 1985. mass mkt. 2.95 o.s.i (0-553-25214-3) Bantam Bks.

—Black Plumes. 1994. lib. bdg. 18.95 (1-56849-458-0) Buccaneer Bks., Inc.

—Black Plumes. 1944. mass mkt. 0.25 o.p. (0-451-00534-1, Signet Bks.) NAL.

—Black Plumes. 1998. lib. bdg. 23.95 (1-56723-002-4) Yestermorrow, Inc.

—Cargo of Eagles. 1989. pap. (0-7012-0612-8) Chatto & Windus GBR. *Dist:* Random Hse. of Canada, Ltd.

—Cargo of Eagles. 1990. 224p. reprint ed. mass mkt. 3.99 (0-380-70576-1, Avon Bks.) Morrow/Avon.

—Cargo of Eagles. 1998. 206p. lib. bdg. 21.95 (1-56723-003-2) Yestermorrow, Inc.

—The Case of the Late Pig. (0-7540-3642-1); 1999. 165 p. (0-7540-3641-3) BBC Audiobooks America.

—The Case of the Late Pig. abr. ed. 1990. audio 16.99 (0-88646-264-9, 7264) Durkin Hayes Publishing Ltd.

—The Case of the Late Pig. 1989. 160p. mass mkt. 3.50 (0-380-70577-X, Avon Bks.) Morrow/Avon.

—The Case of the Late Pig. l.t. ed. 1999. (G. K. Hall Nightingale Ser.). 176p. pap. 19.95 (0-7838-8507-5) Thorndike Pr.

—The China Governess. 1990. 272p. mass mkt. 4.50 (0-380-70578-8, Avon Bks.) Morrow/Avon.

—The China Governess. l.t. ed. 1979. (Ulverscroft Large Print Ser.). 463p. 12.50 o.p. (0-7089-0353-3, Ulverscroft) Thorpe, F. A. Pubs. GBR. *Dist:* Ulverscroft Large Print Bks., Ltd., Ulverscroft Large Print Canada, Ltd.

—The China Governess. 1998. 224p. lib. bdg. 21.95 (1-56723-004-0) Yestermorrow, Inc.

—Coroner's Pidgin. 1993. 243p. 19.95 o.p. (0-89190-177-9) Amereon, Ltd.

—Coroner's Pidgin. unabr. ed. 1996. (Albert Campion Mysteries Ser.). audio 54.95 (0-7451-5734-3, CAB182) BBC Audiobooks America.

—Coroner's Pidgin. l.t. ed. 1979. 418p. 12.00 o.p. (0-7089-0269-3, Ulverscroft) Thorpe, F. A. Pubs. GBR. *Dist:* Ulverscroft Large Print Bks., Ltd.

—Coroner's Pidgin. 1998. lib. bdg. 22.95 (1-56723-005-9) Yestermorrow, Inc.

—The Crime at Black Dudley. l.t. ed. 1978. 388p. 12.00 o.p. (0-7089-0130-1, Ulverscroft) Thorpe, F. A. Pubs. GBR. *Dist:* Ulverscroft Large Print Bks., Ltd.

—The Crime at Black Dudley. 1983.; 1950. pap. 2.50 o.p. (0-14-000770-9, Penguin Bks.) Viking Penguin.

—Dancers in Mourning. 1993. 240p. reprint ed. lib. bdg. 19.95 o.p. (0-89190-189-2) Amereon, Ltd.

—Dancers in Mourning. 1996. (Albert Campion Mysteries Ser.). 272p. mass mkt. 4.95 (0-7867-0384-9, Carroll & Graf Pubs.) Avalon Publishing Group.

—Dancers in Mourning. 1984. 256p. pap. text 2.95 o.p. (0-553-24852-9); 1983. 272p. mass mkt. 3.95 o.s.i (0-553-23880-9) Bantam Bks.

—Dancers in Mourning. 1976. (Crime Fiction Ser). reprint ed. lib. bdg. 21.00 o.p. (0-8240-2351-X) Garland Publishing, Inc.

—Dancers in Mourning. l.t. ed. 1978. 548p. 12.00 o.p. (0-7089-0213-8, Ulverscroft) Thorpe, F. A. Pubs. GBR. *Dist:* Ulverscroft Large Print Bks., Ltd.

—Dancers in Mourning. 1998. lib. bdg. 22.95 (1-56723-006-7) Yestermorrow, Inc.

—Deadly Duo. 1993. 167p. 16.95 o.p. (0-89190-193-0) Amereon, Ltd.

—Deadly Duo. 1985. 208p. mass mkt. 2.95 o.s.i (0-553-25411-1) Bantam Bks.

—Deadly Duo. 1993. reprint ed. lib. bdg. 15.95 (0-89968-452-1) Buccaneer Bks., Inc.

—Deadly Duo. 1998. lib. bdg. 19.95 (1-56723-007-5) Yestermorrow, Inc.

—Death of a Ghost. 1993. 175p. reprint ed. 16.95 (0-89190-195-7) Amereon, Ltd.

—Death of a Ghost. 1997. 192p. mass mkt. 4.95 (0-7867-0441-1, Carroll & Graf Pubs.) Avalon Publishing Group.

—Death of a Ghost. 1985. 224p. mass mkt. 4.50 o.s.i (0-553-24958-4) Bantam Bks.

—Death of a Ghost. 1993. reprint ed. lib. bdg. 15.95 (0-89968-453-X) Buccaneer Bks., Inc.

—Death of a Ghost. unabr. ed. 2001. (Albert Campion Mystery Ser.: Bk. 6). audio 59.95 (0-7451-5724-6, CAB 228) Chivers Audio Bks. GBR. *Dist:* BBC Audiobooks America.

—Death of a Ghost. 1987. audio 69.95 o.s.i (0-8161-7680-9) Thorndike Pr.

—Death of a Ghost. 1998. 175p. lib. bdg. 19.95 (1-56723-008-3) Yestermorrow, Inc.

—The Estate of the Beckoning Lady. 1990. 256p. mass mkt. 3.99 (0-380-70574-5, Avon Bks.) Morrow/Avon.

—The Estate of the Beckoning Lady. 1998. lib. bdg. 22.95 (1-56723-009-1) Yestermorrow, Inc.

—Fashion in Shrouds. 1993. 255p. reprint ed. 19.95 o.p. (0-89190-194-9) Amereon, Ltd.

—Fashion in Shrouds. 1995. 280p. mass mkt. 4.95 (0-7867-0224-9, Carroll & Graf Pubs.) Avalon Publishing Group.

—Fashion in Shrouds. 1985. 288p. mass mkt. 2.95 o.s.i (0-553-25412-X) Bantam Bks.

—Fashion in Shrouds. 1993. reprint ed. lib. bdg. 18.95 (0-89968-454-8) Buccaneer Bks., Inc.

—Fashion in Shrouds. 2002. 10p. 94.95 (0-7540-5536-1, CCD 227); Set. 2000. (Albert Campion Mystery Ser.: No. 10). audio 84.95 (0-7540-0418-X, CAB 1841) Chivers Audio Bks. GBR. *Dist:* BBC Audiobooks America.

—Fashion in Shrouds. 1986. o.p. (0-434-01875-9) David & Charles Pubs.

—Fashion in Shrouds. l.t. ed. 432p. 2001. pap. 21.99 o.p. (0-7531-6208-3); 2000. 32.50 (0-7531-6102-8) ISIS Large Print Bks. GBR. *Dist:* Ulverscroft Large Print Bks., Ltd., Ulverscroft Large Print Canada, Ltd.

—Fashion in Shrouds. l.t. ed. 1978. 579p. 12.00 o.p. (0-7089-0152-2, Ulverscroft) Thorpe, F. A. Pubs. GBR. *Dist:* Ulverscroft Large Print Bks., Ltd.

—Fashion in Shrouds. 1998. lib. bdg. 22.95 (1-56723-010-5) Yestermorrow, Inc.

—The Fear Sign. 192p. reprint ed. lib. bdg. 17.95 o.p. (0-89190-190-6, Rivercity Pr.) Amereon, Ltd.

—The Fear Sign. 2000. 240p. mass mkt. 5.95 (0-7867-0755-0, Carroll & Graf Pubs.) Avalon Publishing Group.

—The Fear Sign. 1989. 240p. pap. 3.95 (0-380-70571-0, Avon Bks.) Morrow/Avon.

—The Fear Sign. 1998. lib. bdg. 20.95 (1-56723-011-3) Yestermorrow, Inc.

—Flowers for the Judge. 1995. (Illus.). 248p. mass mkt. 4.50 (0-7867-0291-5, Carroll & Graf Pubs.) Avalon Publishing Group.

—Flowers for the Judge. 1984. 256p. mass mkt. 3.95 o.s.i (0-553-24190-7) Bantam Bks.

—The Gyrth Chalice Mystery. 1989. 256p. mass mkt. 3.99 (0-380-70572-9, Avon Bks.) Morrow/Avon.

—Hide My Eyes. unabr. ed. 1995. audio 54.95 (0-7451-5725-4, CAB 111) BBC Audiobooks America.

—Look to the Lady. unabr. ed. 1989. audio 54.95 (0-7451-5726-2, CAB 365) BBC Audiobooks America.

—Look to the Lady. l.t. unabr. ed. 2000. 320p. o.p. (0-7531-6101-X, 16101X) ISIS Large Print Bks. GBR. *Dist:* Ulverscroft Large Print Canada, Ltd.

—Look to the Lady. l.t. ed. 1979. 414p. 12.00 o.p. (0-7089-0293-6, Ulverscroft) Thorpe, F. A. Pubs. GBR. *Dist:* Ulverscroft Large Print Bks., Ltd.

—Look to the Lady. 1983. Viking Penguin.

—The Margery Allingham Omnibus. Incl. Crime at Black Dudley. Look to the Lady. Mystery Mile. Matthews, Francis, reader. 29.95 592p. 1983. Set pap. 7.95 o.p. (0-14-006058-8, Penguin Bks.) Viking Penguin.

—The Mind Readers. 20.95 o.p. (0-89190-179-5) Amereon, Ltd.

—The Mind Readers. 1990. 272p. pap. 3.95 (0-380-70570-2, Avon Bks.) Morrow/Avon.

—The Mind Readers. 1998. 286p. lib. bdg. 23.95 (1-56723-012-1) Yestermorrow, Inc.

—More Work for the Undertaker. 19.95 o.p. (0-89190-180-9) Amereon, Ltd.

—More Work for the Undertaker. 1989. 272p. mass mkt. 3.95 (0-380-70573-7, Avon Bks.) Morrow/Avon.

—More Work for the Undertaker. 1952. pap. 3.50 o.p. (0-14-000864-0) Penguin Group (USA) Inc.

—More Work for the Undertaker. 1988. audio 49.95 o.p. (0-8161-9448-3) Thorndike Pr.

—More Work for the Undertaker. l.t. ed. 1978. (Ulverscroft Large Print Ser.). 470p. 29.99 o.p. (0-7089-0233-2, Ulverscroft) Thorpe, F. A. Pubs. GBR. *Dist:* Ulverscroft Large Print Bks., Ltd., Ulverscroft Large Print Canada, Ltd.

—More Work for the Undertaker. 1998. 253p. lib. bdg. 22.95 (1-56723-013-X) Yestermorrow, Inc.

—Mr. Campion & Others. 1991. 272p. mass mkt. 3.95 (0-380-70579-6, Avon Bks.) Morrow/Avon.

—Mr. Campion & Others. 1950. pap. 1.95 o.p. (0-14-000762-8, Penguin Bks.) Viking Penguin.

—Mr. Campion's Lucky Day & Other Stories. 1992. 240p. mass mkt. 3.95 (0-88184-890-5, Carroll & Graf Pubs.) Avalon Publishing Group.

—Mystery Mile. 22.95 o.p. (0-89190-178-7) Amereon, Ltd.

—Mystery Mile. unabr. ed. 2000. (Albert Campion Mysteries Ser.). audio 29.95 (1-57270-137-4, N61137u, Audio Editions Bks. on Cassette) Audio Partners Publishing Corp.

—Mystery Mile. 1994. 250p. mass mkt. 4.50 (0-7867-0168-4, Carroll & Graf Pubs.) Avalon Publishing Group.

—Mystery Mile. 1990. 256p. mass mkt. 3.95 o.s.i (0-553-29013-4) Bantam Bks.

—Mystery Mile. unabr. ed. (Albert Campion Mystery Ser.). 2000. 8p. audio compact disk 79.95 (0-7540-5336-9, CCD 027); 1992. audio 59.95 (0-7451-5728-9, CAB 651) Chivers Audio Bks. GBR. *Dist:* BBC Audiobooks America.

—Mystery Mile. l.t. ed. 1975. 388p. 12.00 o.p. (0-85456-358-X, Ulverscroft) Thorpe, F. A. Pubs. GBR. *Dist:* Ulverscroft Large Print Bks., Ltd.

—Mystery Mile. 1983. 29.95; 1950. pap. 2.50 o.p. (0-14-000761-X, Penguin Bks.) Viking Penguin.

—Mystery Mile. 1998. 264p. lib. bdg. 25.95 (1-56723-014-8) Yestermorrow, Inc.

—Pearls Before Swine. 192p. reprint ed. lib. bdg. 18.95 (0-89190-196-5, Rivercity Pr.) Amereon, Ltd.

—Pearls Before Swine. 1996. 224p. mass mkt. 4.95 (0-7867-0338-5, Carroll & Graf Pubs.) Avalon Publishing Group.

—Pearls Before Swine. 1984. 224p. mass mkt. 2.95 o.s.i (0-553-24548-1) Bantam Bks.

—Pearls Before Swine. 1998. 240p. lib. bdg. 21.95 (1-56723-016-4) Yestermorrow, Inc.

—Police at the Funeral. 1994. 232p. mass mkt. 3.95 (0-7867-0169-2, Carroll & Graf Pubs.) Avalon Publishing Group.

—Police at the Funeral. 1989. 240p. mass mkt. 3.95 o.s.i (0-553-28506-8) Bantam Bks.

—Police at the Funeral. 1949. pap. 3.50 o.p. (0-14-000219-7, Penguin Bks.) Viking Penguin.

—Police at the Funeral. 1998. lib. bdg. 21.95 (1-56723-017-2) Yestermorrow, Inc.

—The Return of Mr. Campion: Uncollected Stories. Morpurgo, J. E., ed. & intro. by. 1991. 192p. pap. 3.95 (0-380-71448-5, Avon Bks.) Morrow/Avon.

—The Return of Mr. Campion: Uncollected Stories. Morpurgo, J. E., ed. & intro. by. 1990. 15.95 o.p. (0-312-04413-5, Saint Martin's Minotaur) St. Martin's Pr.

—Sweet Danger. l.t. ed. 1981. (Ulverscroft Large Print Ser.). o.p. (0-7089-0589-7, Ulverscroft) Thorpe, F. A. Pubs. GBR. *Dist:* Ulverscroft Large Print Canada, Ltd.

—Sweet Danger. 1988. 256p. mass mkt. 5.95 (0-14-008779-6, Penguin Bks.); 1950. pap. 3.50 o.p. (0-14-000769-5) Viking Penguin.

—Take Two at Bedtime. Date not set. lib. bdg. 20.95 (0-8488-1951-9) Amereon, Ltd.

—Tether's End. 176p. reprint ed. lib. bdg. 16.95 (0-89190-197-3, Rivercity Pr.) Amereon, Ltd.

—Tether's End. 1996. 208p. mass mkt. 4.95 (0-7867-0383-0, Carroll & Graf Pubs.) Avalon Publishing Group.

—Tether's End. 1984. 208p. mass mkt. 3.95 o.s.i (0-553-25102-3); 1983. mass mkt. 3.95 o.s.i (0-553-23605-9) Bantam Bks.

—Tether's End. 1998. 216p. lib. bdg. 20.95 (1-56723-018-0) Yestermorrow, Inc.

—The Tiger in the Smoke. 21.95 (0-89190-198-1) Amereon, Ltd.

—The Tiger in the Smoke. 232p. 2000. mass mkt. 5.95 (0-7867-0719-4); 1995. mass mkt. 4.95 o.p. (0-7867-0225-7) Avalon Publishing Group. (Carroll & Graf Pubs.).

—The Tiger in the Smoke, Set. unabr. ed. 1990. audio 69.95 (0-7451-5737-8, CAB 482) BBC Audiobooks America.

—The Tiger in the Smoke. 1985. 240p. pap. 2.95 o.p. (0-553-24814-6) Bantam Bks.

—The Tiger in the Smoke. 1994. lib. bdg. 17.95 (1-56849-459-9) Buccaneer Bks., Inc.

—Traitor's Purse. 176p. reprint ed. lib. bdg. 16.95 (0-89190-199-X, Rivercity Pr.) Amereon, Ltd.

—Traitor's Purse. unabr. ed. 2002. audio (1-57270-159-5) Audio Partners Publishing Corp.

—Traitor's Purse. 1997. 224p. mass mkt. 4.95 (0-7867-0447-0, Carroll & Graf Pubs.) Avalon Publishing Group.

—Traitor's Purse. unabr. ed. 1998. audio 54.95 (0-7451-5733-5, CAB259) BBC Audiobooks America.

—Traitor's Purse. 1990. 192p. mass mkt. 4.50 o.s.i (0-553-23822-1) Bantam Bks.

—Traitor's Purse. 1994. reprint ed. lib. bdg. 24.95 (1-56849-251-0) Buccaneer Bks., Inc.

—Traitor's Purse. 1998. 176p. lib. bdg. 19.95 (1-56723-019-9) Yestermorrow, Inc.

Allingham, Margery & Carter, Youngman. Mr. Campion's Farthing. 1990. 191p. mass mkt. 3.95 (0-88184-667-8, Carroll & Graf Pubs.) Avalon Publishing Group.

—Mr. Campion's Quarry. 1991. 240p. mass mkt. 3.95 (0-88184-724-0, Carroll & Graf Pubs.) Avalon Publishing Group.

**CANCHES, ALEJANDRO (FICTITIOUS CHARACTER)—FICTION**

Benson, Ann. The Burning Road. 2000. 720p. mass mkt. 6.50 (0-440-22591-4) Dell Publishing.

—The Plague Tales. 1998. 688p. mass mkt. 6.99 (0-440-22510-8) Dell Publishing.

Conord, Bruce. Hunter Adventure Guide to the Yucatan: Cancun & Cozumel. E-Book 9.95 (1-58843-125-8) Hunter Publishing, Inc.

**CANDIDI, BEN (FICTITIOUS CHARACTER)—FICTION**

Wyle, Dirk. Amazon Gold: A Ben Candidi Mystery. 2003. (The Ben Candidi Mystery Series: 4). 336p. pap. 14.95 (1-56825-095-9, 095-9) Rainbow Bks., Inc.

—Biotechnology Is Murder: A Ben Candidi Mystery. 2000. 271p. pap. 14.95 (1-56825-045-2, 045-2) Rainbow Bks., Inc.

—Medical School Is Murder: A Ben Candidi Mystery. 2001. (The Ben Candidi Mystery Series). 286p. (C). pap. 14.95 (1-56825-084-3) Rainbow Bks., Inc.

—Pharmacology Is Murder: A Novel. 1998. 388p. pap. 16.95 (1-56825-038-X, 038X) Rainbow Bks., Inc.

**CANDIOTTI, JANE (FICTITIOUS CHARACTER)—FICTION**

Phillips, Clyde. Blindsided: A Mystery. 2000. 320p. 24.00 (0-688-17154-0, Morrow, William & Co.) Morrow/Avon.

—Fall from Grace: A Noir Thriller. 1998. 320p. 24.00 o.p. (0-688-15744-0, Morrow, William & Co.) Morrow/Avon.

—Fall from Grace: A Noir Thriller. 1999. 448p. reprint ed. pap. 6.50 (0-671-03428-6, Pocket) Simon & Schuster.

—Sacrifice. 2003. 320p. 24.95 (0-06-621237-5, Morrow, William & Co.) Morrow/Avon.

**CANFIELD, CAROLINE (FICTITIOUS CHARACTER)—FICTION**

Fiedler, Jacqueline. Sketches with Wolves. 2001. 384p. pap. 6.99 (0-671-01560-5, Pocket) Simon & Schuster.

—Tiger's Palette. 1998. (Caroline Canfield Mystery Ser.). pap. 5.99 (0-671-01559-1, Pocket) Simon & Schuster.

**CARD, ROBERT (FICTITIOUS CHARACTER)—FICTION**

Harper, Brian. Shudder. 1994. 416p. mass mkt. 4.99 o.s.i (0-451-17693-6, Signet Bks.) NAL.

**CARDENAS, VICTOR (FICTITIOUS CHARACTER)—FICTION**

Rubino, Jane. Cheat the Devil. 1998. 352p. 24.95 (1-885173-56-3) Write Way Publishing.

—Death of a DJ. 1997. 224p. mass mkt. 4.99 o.p. (0-06-104433-4, HarperTorch) Morrow/Avon.

—Death of a DJ. 1995. 225p. 20.95 (1-885173-09-1) Write Way Publishing.

—Fruitcake. 1997. 384p. 24.95 (1-885173-29-6) Write Way Publishing.

—Plot Twist. 2000. 400p. 24.95 (1-885173-80-6) Write Way Publishing.

**CARDIGAN (FICTITIOUS CHARACTER: NEBEL)—FICTION**

Nebel, Frederick. The Adventures of Cardigan. 1988. (Dime Detective Bk.). 208p. 9.95 o.p. (0-89296-950-4) Mysterious Pr.

**CARDIGAN, JAKE (FICTITIOUS CHARACTER)—FICTION**

Shatner, William. Tek Kill. 1997. 288p. mass mkt. 6.99 o.s.i (0-441-00489-X) Ace Bks.

—Tek Kill. 1996. 304p. 22.95 o.p. (0-399-14202-9, Ace/Putnam) Penguin Group (USA) Inc.

—Tek Lab. 1993. 320p. mass mkt. 5.99 o.s.i (0-441-80011-4) Ace Bks.

—Tek Lab. 1991. 19.95 o.p. (*0-399-13736-X*, G. P. Putnam's Sons) Penguin Group (USA) Inc.
—Tek Lords. 1992. 304p. mass mkt. 5.99 o.s.i (*0-441-80010-6*) Ace Bks.
—Tek Lords. 1991. (Jake Cardigan Ser.). 224p. 19.95 o.p. (*0-399-13616-9*, G. P. Putnam's Sons) Penguin Group (USA) Inc.
—Tek Lords. abr. ed. 1991. audio 15.95 (*0-671-73951-4*, Simon & Schuster Audioworks) Simon & Schuster Audio.
—Tek Money. 1996. 320p. mass mkt. 6.99 o.s.i (*0-441-00390-7*) Ace Bks.
—Tek Money. 1995. 288p. 21.95 o.p. (*0-399-14109-X*, Ace/Putnam) Penguin Group (USA) Inc.
—Tek Net. 1999. 272p. reprint ed. mass mkt. 6.99 o.s.i (*0-441-00604-3*) Ace Bks.
—Tek Net. 1997. 256p. 22.95 o.p. (*0-399-14339-4*, Ace/Putnam) Penguin Group (USA) Inc.
—Tek Power. 1995. 304p. mass mkt. 5.99 o.s.i (*0-441-00289-7*) Ace Bks.
—Tek Power. 1994. 224p. 19.95 o.p. (*0-399-13997-4*) Penguin Group (USA) Inc.
—Tek Secret. 1994. 304p. (Orig.). mass mkt. 5.99 o.s.i (*0-441-00119-X*) Ace Bks.
—Tek Secret. 1993. 224p. (Orig.). 19.95 o.p. (*0-399-13892-7*) Penguin Group (USA) Inc.
—Tek Vengeance. 1993. 304p. mass mkt. 5.99 o.s.i (*0-441-80012-2*) Ace Bks.
—Tek Vengeance. 1993. 224p. 19.95 o.p. (*0-399-13788-2*, Ace/Putnam) Penguin Group (USA) Inc.
—Tek War, 3 vols. 1993. 16.50 o.s.i (*0-441-00003-7*); 1990. mass mkt. 5.99 o.s.i (*0-441-80208-7*) Ace Bks.
—Tek War. 1989. 17.95 o.p. (*0-399-13495-6*, G. P. Putnam's Sons) Penguin Putnam Bks. for Young Readers.
—Tek War. deluxe ed. 1989. 75.00 (*0-932096-50-6*) Phantasia Pr.
—Tek War. 1991. 3.99 o.p. (*0-517-07428-1*) Random Hse. Value Publishing.

**CARDINAL, CAESAR (FICTITIOUS CHARACTER)—FICTION**

Robbins, Harold. Stiletto. 1992. mass mkt. 4.95 o.s.i (*0-440-18289-1*); 1978. 256p. mass mkt. 0.50 o.s.i (*0-440-18284-0*) Dell Publishing.
—Stiletto. 1997. 240p. 21.95 o.p. (*1-55611-516-4*) Fine, Donald I. Bks.
—Stiletto. 1999. 320p. mass mkt. 6.99 o.s.i (*0-451-19743-7*, Signet Bks.) NAL.
—Stiletto. l.t. ed. 1983. (Charnwood Large Print Ser.). 272p. 29.99 o.p. (*0-7089-8101-1*, Ulverscroft) Thorpe, F. A. Pubs. GBR. *Dist:* Ulverscroft Large Print Bks., Ltd., Ulverscroft Large Print Canada, Ltd.

**CARDOZO, VINCE (FICTITIOUS CHARACTER)—FICTION**

Stewart, Edward. Deadly Rich. 1992. 640p. mass mkt. 5.99 o.s.i (*0-440-21288-X*) Dell Publishing.
—Jury Double. 1996. 512p. mass mkt. 6.50 o.s.i (*0-440-22278-8*) Dell Publishing.
—Mortal Grace. 1995. 560p. mass mkt. 6.50 o.s.i (*0-440-21697-4*) Dell Publishing.
—Privileged Lives. 1989. 528p. mass mkt. 6.99 o.s.i (*0-440-20230-2*) Dell Publishing.

**CARELLA, STEVE (FICTITIOUS CHARACTER)—FICTION**

McBain, Ed, pseud. And All Through the House. 1994. 48p. 12.45 o.p. (*0-446-51845-X*) Warner Bks., Inc.
—Ax. unabr. ed. 1996. (Eighty-Seventh Precinct Ser.). audio 30.00 (*0-7366-3506-8*, 4145) Books on Tape, Inc.
—Ax. 1977. (87th Precinct Mystery Ser.). mass mkt. 2.95 o.p. (*0-451-14599-2*); mass mkt. 1.25 o.p. (*0-451-07654-0*, Signet Bks.); 160p. mass mkt. 4.50 o.s.i (*0-451-16407-5*, Signet Bks.) NAL.
—Ax. 1964. 3.50 o.p. (*0-671-06283-2*) Simon & Schuster.
—The Big Bad City. abr. ed. 1998. (Eighty Seventh Precinct Ser.). audio 24.95 (*1-55927-536-7*, 696064) Audio Renaissance.
—The Big Bad City. unabr. ed. 1999. (Eighty-Seventh Precinct Ser.). audio 40.00 (*0-7366-4460-1*, 4905) Books on Tape, Inc.
—The Big Bad City. l.t. ed. 1999. 27.95 (*1-56895-714-9*, Wheeler Publishing, Inc.) Gale Group.
—The Big Bad City. 1999. 272p. mass mkt. 7.99 (*0-671-03473-1*, Pocket); 25.00 (*0-684-85512-7*, Simon & Schuster) Simon & Schuster.
—Blood Relatives. 1977. pap. 1.50 o.p. (*0-394-25462-7*) Ballantine Bks.
—Blood Relatives. 1978. (Eighty-Seventh Precinct Ser). pap. 1.75 o.p. (*0-553-11759-9*) Bantam Bks.
—Blood Relatives. unabr. ed. 1987. (Eighty-Seventh Precinct Ser.). audio 36.00 (*0-7366-1147-9*, 2071) Books on Tape, Inc.
—Blood Relatives. 1987. mass mkt. 3.50 o.p. (*0-451-15084-8*, Signet Bks.) NAL.
—Bread. unabr. ed. 1987. (Eighty-Seventh Precinct Ser.). audio 42.00 (*0-7366-1198-3*, 2116) Books on Tape, Inc.
—Bread. 1987. 176p. mass mkt. 4.50 (*0-380-70368-8*, Avon Bks.) Morrow/Avon.
—Bread. 1982. mass mkt. 2.25 o.p. (*0-451-11279-2*, AE1279); 1975. mass mkt. 1.25 o.p. (*0-451-06754-1*) NAL. (Signet Bks.).
—Bread. 1974. 213p. (J). o.p. (*0-394-48580-7*) Random Hse., Inc.
—Bread. 1997. (Eighty Seventh Precinct Ser.). 224p. reprint ed. mass mkt. 6.50 (*0-446-60425-9*) Warner Bks., Inc.
—Calypso. 1980. 208p. pap. 1.95 o.s.i (*0-553-13399-3*) Bantam Bks.
—Calypso. unabr. ed. 1998. (Eighty-Seventh Precinct Ser.). audio 42.00 (*0-7366-3775-3*, 4448) Books on Tape, Inc.
—Calypso. 1988. 208p. mass mkt. 4.99 (*0-380-70591-5*, Avon Bks.) Morrow/Avon.
—Calypso. 1979. 10.95 o.p. (*0-670-20030-1*) Viking Penguin.
—The Con Man. unabr. ed. 1993. audio 54.95 (*0-7451-4157-9*, CAB 840) BBC Audiobooks America.
—The Con Man. unabr. ed. 1990. (Eighty-Seventh Precinct Ser.). audio 36.00 (*0-7366-1787-6*, 2624) Books on Tape, Inc.
—The Con Man. l.t. ed. 1986. (Nightingale Ser.). 296p. 10.95 o.p. (*0-8161-3982-2*, Macmillan Reference USA) Gale Group.
—The Con Man. (Eighty-Seventh Precinct Mysteries Ser.). 1987. 160p. mass mkt. 3.99 o.s.i (*0-451-15085-6*); 1980. mass mkt. 1.75 o.p. (*0-451-09351-8*); 1974. mass mkt. 0.95 o.p. (*0-451-05863-1*) NAL. (Signet Bks.).
—Cop Hater. unabr. ed. 1992. (Eighty-Seventh Precinct Novels Ser.). audio 54.95 (*0-7451-6153-7*, CAB 674) BBC Audiobooks America.
—Cop Hater. unabr. ed. 1990. (Eighty-Seventh Precinct Ser.). audio 36.00 (*0-7366-1710-8*, 2552) Books on Tape, Inc.
—Cop Hater. l.t. ed. 1989. (Nightingale Ser.). 316p. 13.95 o.p. (*0-8161-4517-2*, Macmillan Reference USA) Gale Group.
—Cop Hater. (Eighty-Seventh Precinct Mysteries Ser.). 9999. 160p. mass mkt. 3.95 o.p. (*0-451-16441-5*); 1987. 160p. mass mkt. 3.99 o.p. (*0-451-15079-1*); 1980. mass mkt. 1.75 o.p. (*0-451-09170-1*); 1973. mass mkt. 0.95 o.p. (*0-451-05617-5*) NAL. (Signet Bks.).
—Cop Hater. 1999. (Eighty-Seventh Precinct Ser.). (Illus.). 272p. pap. 7.99 (*0-671-77547-2*, Pocket) Simon & Schuster.
—Doll. 1981. mass mkt. 2.25 o.s.i (*0-345-29289-8*) Ballantine Bks.
—Doll. unabr. ed. 1996. (Eighty-Seventh Precinct Ser.). audio 30.00 (*0-7366-3512-2*, 4151) Books on Tape, Inc.
—Doll. 1986. (Eighty-Seventh Precinct Novel Ser.). 160p. mass mkt. 4.50 (*0-380-70082-4*, Avon Bks.) Morrow/Avon.
—Doll. 1997. (Eighty Seventh Precinct Ser.). 208p. reprint ed. mass mkt. 5.99 (*0-446-60146-2*) Warner Bks., Inc.
—Ed McBain: Three Complete Novels: Wings Suspense. 1992. (Illus.). 528p. 13.99 o.s.i (*0-517-06499-5*) Random Hse. Value Publishing.
—Eight Black Horses. l.t. ed. 1986. (General Ser.). 350p. 15.95 o.p. (*0-8161-4022-7*, Macmillan Reference USA) Gale Group.
—Eight Black Horses. (Eighty-Seventh Precinct Novel Ser.). 1986. 256p. mass mkt. 4.99 (*0-380-70029-8*, Avon Bks.); 1985. 15.95 o.p. (*0-87795-681-2*, Morrow, William & Co.) Morrow/Avon.
—Eight Black Horses. 2003. (Illus.). 336p. pap. 7.99 (*0-7434-6308-0*, Pocket) Simon & Schuster.
—Eighty Million Eyes. 1983. 192p. mass mkt. 2.25 o.s.i (*0-345-29292-8*); 1975. mass mkt. 1.25 o.s.i (*0-345-24604-7*) Ballantine Bks.
—Eighty Million Eyes. unabr. ed. 1997. (Eighty-Seventh Precinct Ser.). audio 30.00 (*0-7366-3565-3*, 4209) Books on Tape, Inc.
—Eighty Million Eyes. l.t. ed. 2000. 229p. lib. bdg. 25.95 (*1-58547-011-2*) Ctr. Point Large Print.
—Eighty Million Eyes. 1987. 176p. mass mkt. 4.50 (*0-380-70367-X*, Avon Bks.) Morrow/Avon.
—Eighty Million Eyes. 1997. (Eighty Seventh Precinct Ser.). 208p. reprint ed. mass mkt. 5.99 (*0-446-60386-4*) Warner Bks., Inc.
—The Eighty-Seventh Precinct Companion. 1995. (Orig.). pap. (*0-89296-989-X*, Mysterious Pr. Paperback Bks.) Warner Bks., Inc.
—The Empty Hours. unabr. ed. 1996. (Eighty-Seventh Precinct Ser.). audio 36.00 (*0-7366-3409-6*, 4056) Books on Tape, Inc.
—The Empty Hours. (87th Precinct Mystery Ser.). 1982. mass mkt. 2.25 o.p. (*0-451-11835-9*); 1982. 256p. mass mkt. 4.50 o.p. (*0-451-14601-8*); 1977. mass mkt. 1.25 o.p. (*0-451-07287-1*) NAL. (Signet Bks.).
—Fuzz. unabr. ed. 1995. (87th Precinct Mystery Ser.). audio 54.95 (*0-7451-6157-X*, CAB 133) BBC Audiobooks America.
—Fuzz. unabr. ed. 1997. (Eighty-Seventh Precinct Ser.). audio 42.00 (*0-7366-3637-4*, 4298) Books on Tape, Inc.
—Fuzz. (Eighty-Seventh Precinct Mysteries Ser.). 1978. 192p. mass mkt. 3.99 o.p. (*0-451-15554-8*, E8399); 1978. mass mkt. 1.75 o.p. (*0-451-08399-7*); 1972. mass mkt. 0.75 o.p. (*0-451-05151-3*); 1969. mass mkt. 0.60 o.p. (*0-451-04001-5*) NAL. (Signet Bks.).
—Fuzz. E-Book 6.99 (*0-7953-0322-X*); E-Book 6.99 (*0-7953-0320-3*) RosettaBooks.
—Fuzz. 2000. (Eighty Seventh Precinct Ser.). 288p. mass mkt. 6.50 o.s.i (*0-446-60971-4*) Warner Bks., Inc.
—Ghosts. 1981. 176p. pap. 2.50 o.p. (*0-553-23240-1*) Bantam Bks.
—Ghosts. unabr. ed. 1998. (Eighty-Seventh Precinct Ser.). audio 36.00 (*0-7366-4109-2*, 4614) Books on Tape, Inc.
—Ghosts. 1980. 212p. 9.95 o.p. (*0-670-33806-0*) Viking Penguin.
—Give the Boys a Great Big Hand. unabr. ed. 1992. (Eighty-Seventh Precinct Ser.). audio 36.00 (*0-7366-2251-9*, 3040) Books on Tape, Inc.
—Give the Boys a Great Big Hand. l.t. ed. 1988. (Nightingale Ser.). 307p. 12.95 o.p. (*0-8161-4516-4*, Macmillan Reference USA) Gale Group.
—Give the Boys a Great Big Hand. (87th Precinct Mystery Ser.). 1981. 240p. mass mkt. 4.50 o.p. (*0-451-15921-7*); 1981. mass mkt. 2.25 o.p. (*0-451-11081-1*); 1981. mass mkt. 2.95 o.p. (*0-451-13900-3*); 1975. mass mkt. 1.25 o.p. (*0-451-06683-9*) NAL. (Signet Bks.).
—Hail, Hail, the Gang's All Here. unabr. ed. 1997. (Eighty-Seventh Precinct Ser.). audio 36.00 (*0-7366-3752-4*, 4427) Books on Tape, Inc.
—Hail, Hail, the Gang's All Here. 1972. 307p. (J). (*0-8161-6025-2*, Macmillan Reference USA) Gale Group.
—Hail, Hail, the Gang's All Here. 1972. 160p. mass mkt. 3.99 o.s.i (*0-451-15609-9*, Signet Bks.) NAL.
—Hail to the Chief. unabr. ed. 1995. audio o.p. audio 36.00 o.p. audio 30.00 (*0-7366-3199-2*, 3863) Books on Tape, Inc.
—Hail to the Chief. l.t. ed. 2003. lib. bdg. 28.95 (*1-58547-307-3*, Premier) Ctr. Point Large Print.
—Hail to the Chief. 1987. (Eighty-Seventh Precinct Novel Ser.). 160p. mass mkt. 4.50 o.p. (*0-380-70370-X*, Avon Bks.) Morrow/Avon.
—Hail to the Chief. 1981. mass mkt. 2.25 o.p. (*0-451-11214-8*); 1975. mass mkt. 1.25 o.p. (*0-451-06548-4*) NAL. (Signet Bks.).
—Hail to the Chief. 1973. 182p. o.p. (*0-394-48581-5*) Random Hse., Inc.
—Hail to the Chief. 1997. 192p. reprint ed. mass mkt. 5.99 (*0-446-60405-4*) Warner Bks., Inc.
—He Who Hesitates. 1981. 160p. mass mkt. 2.25 o.s.i (*0-345-29291-X*); 1975. mass mkt. 1.25 o.s.i (*0-345-24757-4*) Ballantine Bks.
—He Who Hesitates. l.t. ed. 1990. (Nightingale Ser.). 248p. 13.95 o.p. (*0-8161-4769-8*, Macmillan Reference USA) Gale Group.
—He Who Hesitates. 2000. mass mkt. 3.50 (*0-380-64198-4*); 1986. 160p. mass mkt. 4.50 (*0-380-70084-0*, Avon Bks.) Morrow/Avon.
—He Who Hesitates. 1996. 160p. reprint ed. mass mkt. 5.99 (*0-446-60147-0*) Warner Bks., Inc.
—Heat. 1987. 208p. mass mkt. 3.95 o.s.i (*0-345-34597-5*); 1983. mass mkt. 2.95 o.s.i (*0-345-30673-2*) Ballantine Bks.
—Heat. unabr. ed. 1998. (Eighty-Seventh Precinct Ser.). audio 42.00 (*0-7366-4110-6*, 4615) Books on Tape, Inc.
—Heat. 1992. (Eighty-Seventh Precinct Mysteries Ser.). 208p. mass mkt. 4.99 o.s.i (*0-451-17078-4*, Signet Bks.) NAL.
—Heat. 1981. 288p. 12.95 o.p. (*0-670-36479-7*) Viking Penguin.
—The Heckler. unabr. ed. 1996. (Eighty-Seventh Precinct Ser.). audio 36.00 (*0-7366-3254-9*, 3911) Books on Tape, Inc.
—The Heckler. 1982. mass mkt. 2.25 o.p. (*0-451-11421-3*); 1982. 176p. mass mkt. 4.50 o.p. (*0-451-15970-5*); 1982. mass mkt. 2.95 o.p. (*0-451-13901-1*); 1976. mass mkt. 1.25 o.p. (*0-451-06839-4*) NAL. (Signet Bks.).
—The Heckler. 2003. (Illus.). 288p. pap. 7.99 (*0-7434-6307-2*, Pocket) Simon & Schuster.
—Ice. unabr. ed. 1995. (Eighty-Seventh Precinct Ser.). audio 56.00 (*0-7366-3180-1*, 3849) Books on Tape, Inc.
—Ice. l.t. ed. 1983. 510p. lib. bdg. 17.95 o.p. (*0-8161-3568-1*, Macmillan Reference USA) Gale Group.
—Ice. 1984. 320p. pap. 5.99 (*0-380-67108-5*, Avon Bks.); 1983. 305p. 15.50 o.p. (*0-87795-468-2*, Morrow, William & Co.) Morrow/Avon.
—Ice. 2003. (Best Mysteries of All Time Ser.). 360p. (*0-7621-8889-8*, Impress) Scriptorium Pr., The.
—Ice. 1996. 336p. reprint ed. mass mkt. 5.99 o.p. (*0-446-60390-2*) Warner Bks., Inc.
—Jigsaw. unabr. ed. 1997. (Eighty-Seventh Precinct Ser.). audio 30.00 (*0-7366-3641-2*, 4303) Books on Tape, Inc.
—Jigsaw. 1970. (Eighty-Seventh Precinct Mysteries Ser.). 160p. mass mkt. 4.50 o.p. (*0-451-15480-0*, Signet Bks.) NAL.
—Killer's Choice. 1981. mass mkt. 2.25 o.s.i (*0-345-29288-X*) Ballantine Bks.
—Killer's Choice. unabr. ed. 1991. (Eighty-Seventh Precinct Ser.). audio 36.00 (*0-7366-2064-8*, 2872) Books on Tape, Inc.
—Killer's Choice. 1986. (Eighty-Seventh Precinct Novel Ser.). pap. 4.50 (*0-380-70083-2*, Avon Bks.) Morrow/Avon.
—Killer's Choice. 1996. 160p. mass mkt. 5.99 o.s.i (*0-446-60144-6*) Warner Bks., Inc.
—Killer's Payoff. unabr. ed. 1991. (Eighty-Seventh Precinct Ser.). audio 36.00 (*0-7366-2065-6*, 2873) Books on Tape, Inc.
—Killer's Payoff. l.t. ed. 1987. (Nightingale Ser.). 295p. 11.95 o.p. (*0-8161-4257-2*, Macmillan Reference USA) Gale Group.
—Killer's Payoff. (Eighty-Seventh Precinct Mysteries Ser.). 1987. 160p. mass mkt. 3.99 o.p. (*0-451-15081-3*); 1980. mass mkt. 1.75 o.p. (*0-451-09464-6*); 1974. mass mkt. 0.95 o.p. (*0-451-05939-5*) NAL. (Signet Bks.).
—Killer's Payoff. 2003. (Illus.). 272p. pap. 6.99 (*0-7434-6306-4*, Pocket) Simon & Schuster.
—Killer's Wedge. unabr. ed. 1992. (Eighty-Seventh Precinct Ser.). audio 36.00 (*0-7366-2105-9*, 2909) Books on Tape, Inc.
—Killer's Wedge. l.t. ed. 2000. 198p. lib. bdg. 27.95 o.p. (*1-58547-032-5*) Ctr. Point Large Print.
—Killer's Wedge. 1981. mass mkt. 1.75 o.p. (*0-451-09614-2*); 1981. 160p. mass mkt. 3.99 o.p. (*0-451-16336-2*); 1981. mass mkt. 2.95 o.p. (*0-451-14597-6*); 1974. mass mkt. 0.95 o.p. (*0-451-06219-1*) NAL. (Signet Bks.).
—King's Ransom. unabr. ed. 1991. (Eighty-Seventh Precinct Ser.). audio 42.00 (*0-7366-1894-5*, 2721) Books on Tape, Inc.
—King's Ransom. l.t. ed. 1986. (Nightingale Ser.). 327p. 11.95 o.p. (*0-8161-4127-4*, Macmillan Reference USA) Gale Group.
—King's Ransom. (87th Precinct Mystery Ser.). 1981. 176p. mass mkt. 4.50 o.p. (*0-451-15933-0*); 1981. mass mkt. 2.25 o.p. (*0-451-09815-3*, Signet Bks.); 1981. mass mkt. 2.95 o.p. (*0-451-13898-8*, Signet Bks.); 1975. mass mkt. 1.25 o.p. (*0-451-06467-4*, Signet Bks.) NAL.
—Kiss. unabr. ed. 1992. (Eighty-Seventh Precinct Ser.). audio 64.00 (*0-7366-2286-1*, 3072) Books on Tape, Inc.
—Kiss. unabr. ed. 1992. audio 22.95 o.p. (*1-56100-461-8*, 155, Bookcassette); audio 57.25 o.p. (*1-56100-095-7*, 543, Unabridged Library Editions) Brilliance Audio.
—Kiss. l.t. ed. 1993. (General Ser.). 458p. 16.95 o.p. (*0-8161-5589-5*); 21.95 o.p. (*0-8161-5588-7*) Gale Group. (Macmillan Reference USA).
—Kiss. 2002. 400p. audio 9.99 (*0-06-008392-1*); 2002. 400p. audio 9.99 (*0-06-008392-1*); 1992. audio 16.00 o.p. (*1-55994-461-7*) HarperTrade. (Harper-Audio).
—Kiss. abr. ed. 2000. (Eighty Seventh Precinct Novels Ser.). audio 7.95 (*1-57815-052-3*, 1013, Media Bks. Audio Publishing) Media Bks., L. L. C.
—Kiss. 1992. 384p. pap. 5.99 (*0-380-71382-9*, Avon Bks.); 330p. 17.00 o.p. (*0-688-10220-4*, Morrow, William & Co.) Morrow/Avon.
—Kiss. 1993. 4.99 o.p. (*0-517-11033-4*) Random Hse. Value Publishing.
—Lady Killer. unabr. ed. 1995. (Eighty-Seventh Precinct Novels Ser.). audio 39.95 BBC Audiobooks America.
—Lady Killer. unabr. ed. 1996. (Eighty-Seventh Precinct Ser.). audio 30.00 (*0-7366-3219-0*, 3882) Books on Tape, Inc.
—Lady Killer. l.t. ed. 1984. (General Ser.). lib. bdg. 12.95 o.p. (*0-8161-3665-3*, Macmillan Reference USA) Gale Group.
—Lady Killer. (Eighty-Seventh Precinct Mysteries Ser.). 1987. 160p. mass mkt. 4.50 o.s.i (*0-451-15082-1*); 1980. mass mkt. 1.75 o.p. (*0-451-09532-4*); 1974. mass mkt. 0.95 o.p. (*0-451-06067-9*) NAL. (Signet Bks.).
—Lady, Lady, I Did It! unabr. ed. 1996. (Eighty-Seventh Precinct Ser.). audio 30.00 (*0-7366-3495-9*, 4135) Books on Tape, Inc.
—Lady, Lady, I Did It! (87th Precinct Mystery Ser.). 1982. 256p. mass mkt. 4.50 o.p. (*0-451-15841-5*); 1982. mass mkt. 2.25 o.p. (*0-451-11779-4*); 1982. mass mkt. 2.95 o.p. (*0-451-13899-6*); 1976. mass mkt. 1.25 o.p. (*0-451-07151-4*) NAL. (Signet Bks.).
—Lady, Lady, I Did It! 1961. 3.50 o.p. (*0-671-40555-1*) Simon & Schuster.
—The Last Dance. l.t. ed. 2000. (Wheeler Large Print Book Ser.). 27.95 (*1-56895-814-5*, Wheeler Publishing, Inc.) Gale Group.
—The Last Dance. 2000. (Illus.). 272p. 25.00 o.s.i (*0-684-85513-5*, Simon & Schuster); 1999. E-Book 25.00 (*0-7432-0047-0*, Simon & Schuster); 2000. (Illus.). 336p. reprint ed. mass mkt. 7.99 (*0-671-02570-8*, Pocket) Simon & Schuster.
—The Last Dance. abr. ed. 2000. audio 25.00 (*0-671-78479-X*, Simon & Schuster Audioworks) Simon & Schuster Audio.

—Let's Hear It for the Deaf Man. unabr. ed. 1998. (Eighty-Seventh Precinct Ser.). audio 36.00 (*0-7366-3776-1*, 4449) Books on Tape, Inc.
—Let's Hear It for the Deaf Man. 1973. 231p. (J). o.p. (*0-385-01600-X*) Doubleday Publishing.
—Let's Hear It for the Deaf Man. 1974. (87th Precinct Mystery Ser.). 160p. mass mkt. 3.99 o.p. (*0-451-15403-7*, Signet Bks.) NAL.
—Lightning. 1999. (Eighty-Seventh Precinct Ser.). audio 56.00 (*0-7366-4624-8*, 5009) Books on Tape, Inc.
—Lightning. abr. ed. audio 17.00 o.p. (*0-694-51547-7*, CPN 2489, HarperAudio) HarperTrade.
—Lightning. (Eighty-Seventh Precinct Novel Ser.). 1985. 304p. mass mkt. 4.95 (*0-380-69974-5*, Avon Bks.); 1984. 15.95 o.p. (*0-87795-581-6*, Morrow, William & Co.) Morrow/Avon.
—Like Love. unabr. ed. 1996. (Eighty-Seventh Precinct Ser.). audio 36.00 (*0-7366-3496-7*, 4136) Books on Tape, Inc.
—Like Love. l.t. ed. 1993. (Nightingale Ser.). 304p. lib. bdg. 15.95 o.p. (*0-8161-5705-7*, Macmillan Reference USA) Gale Group.
—Like Love. (87th Precinct Mystery Ser.). 1982. 176p. mass mkt. 2.95 o.p. (*0-451-13903-8*); 1982. 160p. mass mkt. 4.50 o.s.i (*0-451-16383-4*); 1982. mass mkt. 2.25 o.p. (*0-451-11628-3*); 1976. mass mkt. 1.25 o.p. (*0-451-07221-9*) NAL. (Signet Bks.).
—Long Time No See. 1982. pap. 2.50 o.p. (*0-553-23130-8*) Bantam Bks.
—Long Time No See. unabr. ed. 1986. (Eighty-Seventh Precinct Ser.). audio 40.00 (*0-7366-0823-0*, 1773) Books on Tape, Inc.
—Long Time No See. abr. ed. audio 17.00 o.p. (*0-694-51546-9*, CPN 2488, HarperAudio) HarperTrade.
—Long Time No See. 1987. 272p. mass mkt. 4.99 (*0-380-70369-6*, Avon Bks.) Morrow/Avon.
—Long Time No See. 1997. 304p. mass mkt. 5.99 (*0-446-60449-6*) Warner Bks., Inc.
—Lullaby. unabr. ed. 1992. (Audio Bks.). audio 69.95 (*0-7451-6154-5*, CAB 549) BBC Audiobooks America.
—Lullaby. 1999. audio 48.00 (*0-7366-4872-0*); 1989. audio 48.00 Books on Tape, Inc.
—Lullaby. l.t. ed. 1990. (General Ser.). 437p. 20.95 o.p. (*0-8161-4923-2*, Macmillan Reference USA) Gale Group.
—Lullaby. abr. ed. audio 16.00 o.p. (*1-55994-819-1*, CPN 2392, HarperAudio) HarperTrade.
—Lullaby. abr. ed. 2000. (Eighty Seventh Precinct Novels Ser.). audio 7.95 (*1-57815-050-7*, 1014, Media Bks. Audio Publishing) Media Bks., L. L. C.
—Lullaby. 1990. 352p. mass mkt. 5.99 (*0-380-70384-X*, Avon Bks.); 1989. 17.95 o.p. (*0-87795-994-3*, Morrow, William & Co.) Morrow/Avon.
—Mischief. l.t. ed. 1995. pap. 23.95 o.p. (*0-7927-2014-8*); 1994. 25.95 o.p. (*0-7927-2015-6*) BBC Audiobooks America.
—Mischief. unabr. ed. 1993. (Eighty-Seventh Precinct Ser.). audio 64.00 (*0-7366-2591-7*, 3336) Books on Tape, Inc.
—Mischief. unabr. ed. 1993. 57.25 o.p. incl. audio (*1-56100-147-3*, 942, Unabridged Library Editions); audio 21.95 o.p. (*1-56100-514-2*, 176, Bookcassette) Brilliance Audio.
—Mischief. abr. ed. 2000. audio 9.99 (*0-694-52329-1*, HarperAudio) HarperTrade.
—Mischief. abr. ed. 2000. (Eighty Seventh Precinct Novels Ser.). audio 7.95 (*1-57815-051-5*, 1043, Media Bks. Audio Publishing) Media Bks., L. L. C.
—Mischief. 1994. 352p. pap. 5.99 o.p. (*0-380-71384-5*, Avon Bks.); 1993. 346p. 20.00 o.p. (*0-688-10221-2*, Morrow, William & Co.) Morrow/Avon.
—The Mugger. unabr. ed. 1995. (Eighty-Seventh Precinct Novels Ser.). audio 39.95 (*0-7451-6855-8*, CAB 321) BBC Audiobooks America.
—The Mugger. 1981. 160p. mass mkt. 2.25 o.s.i (*0-345-29290-1*) Ballantine Bks.
—The Mugger. unabr. ed. 1990. (Eighty-Seventh Precinct Ser.). audio 36.00 (*0-7366-1721-3*, 2562) Books on Tape, Inc.
—The Mugger. 1986. (Eighty-Seventh Precinct Novel Ser.). 160p. mass mkt. 3.50 (*0-380-70081-6*, Avon Bks.) Morrow/Avon.
—The Mugger. 1996. 192p. mass mkt. 5.99 (*0-446-60143-8*) Warner Bks., Inc.
—Nocturne. abr. ed. 1997. (Eighty Seventh Precinct Ser.). audio 24.95 (*1-55927-439-5*, 695087) Audio Renaissance.
—Nocturne. unabr. ed. 1997. (Eighty-Seventh Precinct Ser.). audio 48.00 (*0-7366-3777-X*, 4450) Books on Tape, Inc.
—Nocturne. (Eighty Seventh Precinct Ser.). 1998. mass mkt. 188.73 (*0-446-16558-1*); 1997. 320p. 23.50 o.p. (*0-446-51805-0*); 1998. 352p. reprint ed. mass mkt. 6.99 (*0-446-60538-7*) Warner Bks., Inc.
—Poison. 2001. audio 64.00 (*0-7366-5935-8*) Books on Tape, Inc.
—Poison. l.t. ed. 1988. 352p. 19.95 o.p. (*0-8161-4299-8*, Macmillan Reference USA) Gale Group.
—Poison. 1988. 256p. mass mkt. 4.99 (*0-380-70030-1*, Avon Bks.); 1987. 242p. 16.95 o.p. (*0-87795-787-8*, Morrow, William & Co.) Morrow/Avon.
—Poison. abr. ed. 1987. audio 14.95 (*0-671-64160-3*, Simon & Schuster Audioworks) Simon & Schuster Audio.
—The Pusher. unabr. ed. 1994. (Eighty-Seventh Precinct Novels Ser.). audio 54.95 (*0-7451-4228-1*, CAB 911) BBC Audiobooks America.
—The Pusher. unabr. ed. 1992. (Eighty-Seventh Precinct Ser.). audio 36.00 (*0-7366-2155-5*, 2954) Books on Tape, Inc.
—The Pusher. l.t. ed. 1987. (Large Print Books, Nightingale Ser.). 266p. 11.95 o.p. (*0-8161-4258-0*, Macmillan Reference USA) Gale Group.
—The Pusher. 9999. pap. 3.95 o.p. (*0-451-16480-6*); 1987. 160p. mass mkt. 3.99 o.p. (*0-451-15080-5*, Signet Bks.); 1980. mass mkt. 1.75 o.p. (*0-451-09256-2*, Signet Bks.); 1973. mass mkt. 0.95 o.p. (*0-451-05705-8*, Signet Bks.) NAL.
—The Pusher. 2002. 256p. pap. 6.99 (*0-7434-6305-6*, Pocket) Simon & Schuster.
—Romance. unabr. ed. 1995. (Eighty-Seventh Precinct Ser.). audio 48.00 (*0-7366-3122-4*, 3798) Books on Tape, Inc.
—Romance. abr. ed. audio 17.00 o.p. (*1-55994-995-3*, CPN 2484, HarperAudio) HarperTrade.
—Romance. 338p. pap. 5.98 o.p. (*0-7651-0365-6*) Smithmark Pubs., Inc.
—Romance. 1995. 336p. 22.95 o.s.i (*0-446-51804-2*); 1996. 352p. reprint ed. mass mkt. 6.50 o.s.i (*0-446-60280-9*) Warner Bks., Inc.
—Sadie When She Died. unabr. ed. 1998. (Eighty-Seventh Precinct Ser.). audio 30.00 (*0-7366-3993-4*, 4356) Books on Tape, Inc.
—Sadie When She Died. 1973. (87th Precinct Mystery Ser.). 160p. mass mkt. 3.99 o.s.i (*0-451-15366-9*, Signet Bks.) NAL.
—See Them Die. unabr. ed. 1996. (Eighty-Seventh Precinct Ser.). audio 36.00 (*0-7366-3359-6*, 4009) Books on Tape, Inc.
—See Them Die. (87th Precinct Mystery Ser.). 1982. mass mkt. 2.95 o.p. (*0-451-14596-8*); 1982. mass mkt. 2.25 o.p. (*0-451-11561-9*, Signet Bks.); 1976. mass mkt. 1.25 o.p. (*0-451-07030-5*, Signet Bks.); 1982. 160p. reprint ed. mass mkt. 4.50 o.p. (*0-451-16426-1*, Signet Bks.) NAL.
—Shotgun. unabr. ed. 1997. (Eighty-Seventh Precinct Ser.). audio 30.00 (*0-7366-3578-5*, 4230) Books on Tape, Inc.
—Shotgun. 1970. (87th Precinct Mystery Ser.). 176p. mass mkt. 4.50 o.p. (*0-451-15674-9*); mass mkt. 2.50 o.p. (*0-451-11971-1*) NAL. (Signet Bks.).
—So Long As You Both Shall Live. unabr. ed. 1998. (Eighty-Seventh Precinct Ser.). audio 30.00 (*0-7366-3778-8*, 4451) Books on Tape, Inc.
—So Long As You Both Shall Live. 1977. mass mkt. 3.50 o.p. (*0-451-15718-4*); mass mkt. 1.50 o.p. (*0-451-07749-0*) NAL. (Signet Bks.).
—Ten Plus One. unabr. ed. 1997. (Eighty-Seventh Precinct Ser.). audio 36.00 (*0-7366-3532-7*, 4171) Books on Tape, Inc.
—Ten Plus One. (87th Precinct Mystery Ser.). 1982. mass mkt. 2.95 o.p. (*0-451-14598-4*); 1982. mass mkt. 2.25 o.p. (*0-451-11923-1*, Signet Bks.); 1982. 176p. mass mkt. 4.50 o.s.i (*0-451-16367-2*, Signet Bks.); 1977. mass mkt. 1.25 o.p. (*0-451-07463-7*, Signet Bks.) NAL.
—'Til Death. unabr. ed. 1992. (Eighty-Seventh Precinct Ser.). audio 36.00 (*0-7366-2123-7*, 2925) Books on Tape, Inc.
—'Til Death. (Eighty-Seventh Precinct Mysteries Ser.). 1989. 176p. mass mkt. 4.50 o.s.i (*0-451-15891-1*); 1981. mass mkt. 2.25 o.p. (*0-451-09734-3*); 1981. mass mkt. 2.95 o.p. (*0-451-13896-1*) NAL. (Signet Bks.).
—Till Death Us Do Part. 1975. mass mkt. 1.25 o.p. (*0-451-06320-1*, Signet Bks.) NAL.
—Tricks. unabr. ed. 1992. (Eighty-Seventh Precinct Novels Ser.). audio 54.95 (*0-7451-6156-1*, CAB 616) BBC Audiobooks America.
—Tricks. 2001. audio 56.00 (*0-7366-6021-6*) Books on Tape, Inc.
—Tricks. 256p. 1987. 16.95 o.p. (*0-87795-927-7*, Morrow, William & Co.); 1989. reprint ed. mass mkt. 5.99 (*0-380-70383-1*, Avon Bks.) Morrow/Avon.
—Tricks. 1989. 3.99 o.p. (*0-517-69431-X*) Random Hse. Value Publishing.
—Tricks. abr. ed. 1988. audio 14.95 Simon & Schuster Audio.
—Vespers. unabr. ed. 1990. (Eighty-Seventh Precinct Ser.). audio 64.00 (*0-7366-1807-4*, 2644) Books on Tape, Inc.
—Vespers. l.t. ed. 1991. 470p. 24.95 o.p. (*1-85089-498-1*) ISIS Large Print Bks. GBR. *Dist:* Transaction Pubs.
—Vespers. 1991. 352p. mass mkt. 5.99 (*0-380-70385-8*, Avon Bks.); 1990. 350p. 18.95 o.p. (*0-87795-987-0*, Morrow, William & Co.) Morrow/Avon.
—Widows. unabr. ed. 1991. (Eighty-Seventh Precinct Ser.). audio 64.00 (*0-7366-1965-8*, 2786) Books on Tape, Inc.
—Widows. l.t. ed. 1992. (General Ser.). 454p. lib. bdg. 21.95 o.p. (*0-8161-5311-6*, Macmillan Reference USA) Gale Group.
—Widows. abr. ed. 2000. (Eighty Seventh Precinct Novels Ser.). audio 7.95 (*1-57815-056-6*, 1054, Media Bks. Audio Publishing) Media Bks., L. L. C.
—Widows. 1991. 330p. 19.00 o.p. (*0-688-10219-0*, Morrow, William & Co.); 1992. 336p. reprint ed. mass mkt. 6.50 (*0-380-71383-7*, Avon Bks.) Morrow/Avon.

## CAREY, NEAL (FICTITIOUS CHARACTER)—FICTION

Winslow, Don. Cool Breeze on the Underground. 1991. 17.95 o.p. (*0-312-05407-6*, Saint Martin's Minotaur) St. Martin's Pr.
—A Long Walk up the Water Slide. (Neal Carey Mysteries Ser.). 1998. 277p. mass mkt. 5.99 (*0-312-96617-2*, St. Martin's Paperbacks); 1994. 256p. 20.95 o.p. (*0-312-11389-7*, Saint Martin's Minotaur) St. Martin's Pr.
—The Trail to Buddha's Mirror. 384p. 1992. 21.95 o.p. (*0-312-07099-3*, Saint Martin's Minotaur); Vol. 1. 1997. mass mkt. 5.99 (*0-312-96309-2*, St. Martin's Paperbacks) St. Martin's Pr.
—Way down on the High Lonely. 1998. (Dead Letter Mysteries Ser.). 288p. mass mkt. 5.99 (*0-312-96422-6*, St. Martin's Paperbacks) St. Martin's Pr.
—Way down on the High Lonely: A Neal Carey Mystery. 1993. 288p. 19.95 o.p. (*0-312-09934-7*, Saint Martin's Minotaur) St. Martin's Pr.
—While Drowning in the Desert. 1998. (Neal Carey Mysteries Ser.). 224p. mass mkt. 5.99 (*0-312-96118-9*, St. Martin's Paperbacks) St. Martin's Pr.
—While Drowning in the Desert: A Neal Carey Mystery. 1996. 192p. 20.95 o.p. (*0-312-14446-6*, Saint Martin's Minotaur) St. Martin's Pr.

## CARL, VICTOR (FICTITIOUS CHARACTER)—FICTION

Lashner, William. Hostile Witness. l.t. ed. 1995. (Large Print Bks.). 25.95 o.p. (*1-56895-248-1*, Wheeler Publishing, Inc.) Gale Group.
—Hostile Witness. 1995. 501p. 23.00 o.p. (*0-06-039146-4*) HarperCollins Pubs.
—Hostile Witness. 1996. 608p. mass mkt. 7.50 (*0-06-100988-1*, ReganBooks); 1995. audio 17.00 o.p. (*0-694-51559-0*, HarperAudio) HarperTrade.
—Hostile Witness. unabr. ed. 1998. audio 112.00 (*0-7887-1954-8*, 95352E7) Recorded Bks., LLC.
—Veritas. 1997. 464p. 25.00 o.p. (*0-06-039147-2*, ReganBooks);Set. audio 18.00 (*0-694-51789-5*, 392878, HarperAudio) HarperTrade.
—Veritas. 1997. 592p. mass mkt. 6.50 o.s.i (*0-06-101023-5*, HarperTorch) Morrow/Avon.
—Veritas. unabr. ed. 1997. audio 112.00 (*0-7887-1768-5*, 95246E5) Recorded Bks., LLC.

## CARLIN, CARRIE (FICTITIOUS CHARACTER)—FICTION

Tesler, Nancy. Golden Eggs & Other Deadly Things. 2000. (Carrie Carlin Mystery Ser.). 256p. mass mkt. 5.99 o.s.i (*0-440-22615-5*) Dell Publishing.
—Pink Balloons & Other Deadly Things. 1997. (Carrie Carlin Mystery Ser.). 224p. (Orig.). mass mkt. 5.50 o.s.i (*0-440-22406-3*) Dell Publishing.
—Sharks, Jellyfish & Other Deadly Things. 1998. (Carrie Carlin Mystery Ser.). 224p. mass mkt. 5.99 o.s.i (*0-440-22409-8*, Dell Bks.) Dell Publishing.
—Shooting Stars & Other Deadly Things. 1999. (Carrie Carlin Mystery Ser.). 256p. mass mkt. 5.99 o.s.i (*0-440-22614-7*) Dell Publishing.

## CARLOS, THE JACKAL—FICTION

Aline, Countess of Romanones. The Well-Mannered Assassin. 1995. 368p. mass mkt. 5.99 o.s.i (*0-515-11533-9*, Jove) Berkley Publishing Group.
—The Well-Mannered Assassin. unabr. ed. 1999. audio 76.95 (*0-7861-1663-3*, 2491) Blackstone Audio Bks., Inc.
—The Well-Mannered Assassin. l.t. ed. 1994. 584p. lib. bdg. 24.95 (*0-8161-7447-4*, Macmillan Reference USA) Gale Group.
—The Well-Mannered Assassin. 1994. 320p. 22.95 o.p. (*0-399-13863-3*, G. P. Putnam's Sons) Penguin Group (USA) Inc.
Ludlum, Robert. The Bourne Identity. 1984. 544p. mass mkt. 7.99 (*0-553-26011-1*); mass mkt. 3.99 o.s.i (*0-553-19941-2*) Bantam Bks.
—The Bourne Identity. 1980. 12.95 o.s.i (*0-399-90070-5*) Putnam Publishing Group, The.
—The Bourne Supremacy. 1989. 656p. mass mkt. 7.99 (*0-553-26322-6*); 1987. mass mkt. o.s.i (*0-553-26651-9*); 1987. 656p. mass mkt. 3.99 o.s.i (*0-553-19942-0*) Bantam Bks.
—The Bourne Supremacy. unabr. collector's ed. 1986. Pt. 1. audio 72.00 (*0-7366-0867-2*, 1818-A); Pt. 2. audio 64.00 (*0-7366-0868-0*, 1818-B) Books on Tape, Inc.
—The Bourne Supremacy. l.t. ed. 1987. 21.95 o.p. (*0-8161-4224-6*, Macmillan Reference USA) Gale Group.
—The Bourne Supremacy. abr. ed. 1989. audio 18.00 (*0-553-45159-6*, RH Audio) Random Hse. Audio Publishing Group.
—The Bourne Supremacy. 1986. 608p. 19.95 o.s.i (*0-394-54396-3*) Random Hse., Inc.
—The Bourne Ultimatum. 672p. 1991. mass mkt. 7.95 o.s.i (*0-553-29194-7*); 1991. mass mkt. 7.99 (*0-553-28773-7*); 1991. mass mkt. 3.99 o.s.i (*0-553-19943-9*); 1990. mass mkt. 5.50 o.s.i (*0-553-17342-1*) Bantam Bks.
—The Bourne Ultimatum. 1990. audio 14.39 o.s.i (*0-553-70028-6*, RH Audio) Random Hse. Audio Publishing Group.
—The Bourne Ultimatum. 1992. 6.99 o.p. (*0-517-08090-7*) Random Hse. Value Publishing.

## CARLUCCI, RUGGIERO (FICTITIOUS CHARACTER)—FICTION

Constantine, K. C. Always a Body to Trade. unabr. ed. 1997. (Mario Balzic Ser.). audio 48.00 (*0-7366-3685-4*, 4364) Books on Tape, Inc.
—Always a Body to Trade: A Mario Balzic Mystery. 1983. 256p. 13.95 o.p. (*0-87923-458-X*); 1993. 248p. reprint ed. pap. 5.95 (*0-87923-952-2*) Godine, David R. Pub.
—Always a Body to Trade: A Mario Balzic Mystery. 1984. (Crime Monthly Ser.). 256p. pap. 3.95 o.p. (*0-14-007059-1*, Penguin Bks.) Viking Penguin.
—Blank Page. 11th ed. 1989. pap. 3.95 o.p. (*0-87923-707-4*) Godine, David R. Pub.
—Bottom Liner Blues. unabr. ed. 1997. (Mario Balzic Ser.). audio 56.00 (*0-7366-3691-9*, 4370) Books on Tape, Inc.
—Bottom Liner Blues. 1993. 256p. 18.95 (*0-89296-289-5*) Mysterious Pr.
—Bottom Liner Blues. 1994. 272p. mass mkt. 5.99 o.s.i (*0-446-40372-5*) Warner Bks., Inc.
—Brushback. unabr. collector's ed. 1998. (Mario Balzic Ser.). audio 64.00 (*0-7366-4216-1*, 4714) Books on Tape, Inc.
—Brushback. 1998. (Mario Balzic Novel Ser.). 288p. 22.00 (*0-89296-646-7*) Mysterious Pr.
—Brushback. 1999. mass mkt. (*0-446-60675-8*) Warner Bks., Inc.
—Cranks & Shadows. unabr. ed. 1997. (Mario Balzic Ser.). audio 72.00 (*0-7366-3692-7*, 4371) Books on Tape, Inc.
—Cranks & Shadows. 1995. 314p. 19.95 o.p. (*0-89296-543-6*) Mysterious Pr.
—Cranks & Shadows. 1996. 320p. mass mkt. 5.99 o.s.i (*0-446-40353-9*) Warner Bks., Inc.
—Family Values. unabr. ed. 1998. (Mario Balzic Ser.: Vol. 13). audio 48.00 (*0-7366-4035-5*, 4534) Books on Tape, Inc.
—Family Values. l.t. ed. 1997. (G. K. Hall Mystery Ser.). 290p. lib. bdg. 26.95 o.p. (*0-7838-8232-7*, Macmillan Reference USA) Gale Group.
—Family Values. 1998. mass mkt. (*0-446-40355-5*, Mysterious Pr. Paperback Bks.); 1997. 224p. 22.00 o.p. (*0-89296-545-2*); 1998. 256p. mass mkt. 5.99 (*0-446-60594-8*) Warner Bks., Inc.
—A Fix Like This. unabr. ed. 1997. (Mario Balzic Ser.). audio 64.00 (*0-7366-3693-5*, 4372) Books on Tape, Inc.
—A Fix Like This. 1988. 3.95 o.p. (*0-87923-718-X*) Godine, David R. Pub.
—Good Sons. unabr. ed. 1998. (Mario Balzic Ser.). audio 56.00 (*0-7366-4015-0*, 4513) Books on Tape, Inc.
—Good Sons. 1996. 304p. 21.95 o.p. (*0-89296-544-4*) Mysterious Pr.
—Good Sons. 1997. (Rocksburg Novels Ser.). 304p. mass mkt. 5.99 o.s.i (*0-446-40354-7*) Warner Bks., Inc.
—Grievance. l.t. ed. 2001. (Large Print Bks.). 399p. pap. 23.95 o.p. (*1-56895-946-X*, Wheeler Publishing, Inc.) Gale Group.
—Grievance: A Rugs Carlucci Novel. unabr. ed. 2000. audio 69.95 (*0-7927-2407-0*, CSL 296, Chivers Sound Library) BBC Audiobooks America.
—Grievance: A Rugs Carlucci Novel. 2000. 288p. 23.95 o.p. (*0-89296-648-3*) Mysterious Pr.
—Joey's Case. unabr. ed. 1997. (Mario Balzic Ser.). audio 56.00 (*0-7366-3783-4*, 4455) Books on Tape, Inc.
—Joey's Case. 1989. 224p. mass mkt. 4.50 (*0-445-40786-7*, Mysterious Pr. Paperback Bks.) Warner Bks., Inc.
—Joey's Case: A Mario Balzic Novel. 1988. 15.95 (*0-89296-347-6*) Mysterious Pr.
—The Man Who Liked Slow Tomatoes. 1993. (Mario Balzic Detective Novel Ser.). 192p. pap. 5.95 (*0-87923-953-0*); 1982. (Mario Balzic Mystery Ser.: No. 5). 256p. 13.95 o.p. (*0-87923-407-5*) Godine, David R. Pub.
—The Man Who Liked Slow Tomatoes. 1983. 224p. pap. 2.95 o.p. (*0-14-006621-7*, Penguin Bks.) Viking Penguin.

—The Man Who Liked to Look at Himself. l.t. ed. 1987. (Nightingale Ser.). 249p. 11.95 o.p. (*0-8161-4373-0*, Macmillan Reference USA) Gale Group.
—The Man Who Liked to Look at Himself. Barzun, Jacques & Taylor, W. H., eds. 1983. (Crime Fiction 1950-1975 Ser.). 151p. lib. bdg. 18.00 o.p. (*0-8240-4955-1*) Garland Publishing, Inc.
—The Man Who Liked to Look at Himself. 1987. (Double Detective Ser.: No. 3). 160p. pap. 3.95 o.p. (*0-87923-663-9*); pap. 8.95 o.p. (*0-87923-468-7*) Godine, David R. Pub.
—Man Who Liked to Look at Himself & The Blank Page. unabr. ed. 1997. (Mario Balzic Ser.: Vol. 2 & 3). audio 64.00 (*0-7366-3612-9*, 4271) Books on Tape, Inc.
—The Rocksburg Railroad Murders. unabr. ed. 1997. (Mario Balzic Ser.: Vol. 1). audio 40.00 (*0-7366-3622-6*, 4281) Books on Tape, Inc.
—Sunshine Enemies. unabr. ed. 1997. (Mario Balzic Ser.). audio 42.00 (*0-7366-3784-2*, 4456) Books on Tape, Inc.
—Sunshine Enemies. 1990. 176p. 18.95 o.p. (*0-89296-288-7*) Mysterious Pr.
—Sunshine Enemies. 1991. mass mkt. 4.95 o.s.i (*0-446-40008-4*, Mysterious Pr. Paperback Bks.) Warner Bks., Inc.
—Upon Some Midnights Clear. unabr. ed. 1997. (Mario Balzic Ser.). audio 48.00 (*0-7366-3694-3*, 4373) Books on Tape, Inc.
—Upon Some Midnights Clear. 1985. (Mario Balzic Mystery Ser.). 256p. 15.95 o.p. (*0-87923-570-5*) Godine, David R. Pub.
—Upon Some Midnights Clear. 1987. 24p. mass mkt. 3.50 o.p. (*0-14-009404-0*, Penguin Bks.) Viking Penguin.

### CARLYLE, CARLOTTA (FICTITIOUS CHARACTER)—FICTION

Barnes, Linda. The Big Dig. l.t. ed. 2003. lib. bdg. 29.95 (*1-58547-264-6*, Platinum) Ctr. Point Large Print.
—The Big Dig. 2003. 352p. mass mkt. 6.99 (*0-312-98969-5*, St. Martin's Paperbacks); 2002. 288p. 23.95 (*0-312-28270-2*, Saint Martin's Minotaur) St. Martin's Pr.
—Cold Case. 1998. 496p. mass mkt. 5.99 o.s.i (*0-440-21226-X*, Dell Bks.) Dell Publishing.
—Cold Case. l.t. ed. 1997. (Large Print Book Ser.). 27.95 (*1-56895-427-1*, Wheeler Publishing, Inc.) Gale Group.
—Cold Case. unabr. ed. 1997. (Carlotta Carlyle Mysteries Ser. : NO. 7). audio 90.00 (*0-7887-1316-7*, 95174E7) Recorded Bks., LLC.
—Coyote. 1991. 304p. mass mkt. 5.99 o.s.i (*0-440-21089-5*) Dell Publishing.
—Coyote. l.t. ed. 1991. (General Ser.). 332p. lib. bdg. 20.95 (*0-8161-5197-0*, Macmillan Reference USA) Gale Group.
—Coyote. unabr. ed. 1994. audio. (Carlotta Carlyle Mysteries Ser. : No. 3). audio 44.00 (*0-7887-0036-7*, 94235E7) Recorded Bks., LLC.
—Flashpoint. l.t. ed. 2000. (Wheeler Large Print Book Ser.). 354p. 26.95 (*1-56895-856-0*, Wheeler Publishing, Inc.) Gale Group.
—Flashpoint. 2001. 432p. mass mkt. 6.99 (*0-7868-8948-9*); 1999. 288p. 22.95 (*0-7868-6317-X*) Hyperion Pr.
—Hardware. 1996. 400p. mass mkt. 5.99 o.s.i (*0-440-21223-5*) Dell Publishing.
—The Snake Tattoo. 1990. 208p. mass mkt. 5.99 o.s.i (*0-449-21759-0*, Fawcett) Ballantine Bks.
—The Snake Tattoo. l.t. ed. 1990. (General Ser.). 350p. lib. bdg. 19.95 o.p. (*0-8161-4866-X*, Macmillan Reference USA) Gale Group.
—The Snake Tattoo. unabr. ed. 1993. (Carlotta Carlyle Mysteries Ser. : No. 2). audio 44.00 (*1-55690-923-3*, 93419E7) Recorded Bks., LLC.
—The Snake Tattoo. 2004. 320p. mass mkt. 6.99 (*0-312-99355-2*, St. Martin's Paperbacks); 1989. 288p. 17.95 o.p. (*0-312-02643-9*) St. Martin's Pr.
—Snapshot. 1994. 400p. mass mkt. 5.99 o.s.i (*0-440-21220-0*) Dell Publishing.
—Snapshot. l.t. ed. 1994. (Magna Large Print Ser.). 530p. (*0-7505-0706-3*) Magna Large Print Bks. GBR. *Dist:* Ulverscroft Large Print Canada, Ltd.
—Snapshot. unabr. ed. 1994. (Carlotta Carlyle Mysteries Ser. : No. 5). audio 70.00 (*1-55690-969-1*, 94112E7) Recorded Bks., LLC.
—Steel Guitar. 1992. 272p. pap. 19.00 o.s.i (*0-440-61399-X*); mass mkt. 5.99 o.s.i (*0-440-21268-5*) Dell Publishing.
—Steel Guitar. unabr. ed. 1993. (Carlotta Carlyle Mysteries Ser. : No. 4). audio 44.00 (*1-55690-787-7*, 93102E7) Recorded Bks., LLC.
—A Trouble of Fools. 1988. mass mkt. 5.99 o.s.i (*0-449-21640-3*, Fawcett) Ballantine Bks.
—A Trouble of Fools. l.t. ed. 1989. (General Ser.). 370p. lib. bdg. 19.95 o.p. (*0-8161-4714-0*, Macmillan Reference USA) Gale Group.
—A Trouble of Fools. 2001. 224p. mass mkt. 4.50 (*0-7868-8953-5*) Hyperion Pr.
—A Trouble of Fools. unabr. ed. 2000. (Carlotta Carlyle Mysteries Ser. : No. 1). audio 51.00 (*1-55690-834-2*, 93202E7) Recorded Bks., LLC.
—A Trouble of Fools. 1987. 228p. 15.95 o.p. (*0-312-01100-8*) St. Martin's Pr.

### CARLYLE, KERRY (FICTITIOUS CHARACTER)—FICTION

Frake, Anne Gustafson. The Emerald Elephant. 1997. 224p. pap. 4.00 (*1-56722-198-X*) Word Aflame Pr.
—The Golden Bee. 1998. (Kerry Carlyle Ser.: Vol. 2). 248p. pap. 7.00 (*1-56722-216-1*) Word Aflame Pr.

### CARODINE, CHELSEA (FICTITIOUS CHARACTER)—FICTION

Tarvin, Al. Chelsea & Sally. Haycox, Bobbi & Wordsmiths Unlimited Staff, eds. 1997. (Chelsea Ser.: No. 4). 280p. pap. 12.95 (*0-9643250-4-7*) CJH Enterprises.
—Chelsea & the Lords. 1999. (Chelsea Ser.: No. 5). 300p. pap. 12.95 (*0-9643250-5-5*) CJH Enterprises.
—Chelsea, Chelsea. Ausley, Lisa, ed. rev. ed. (Chelsea Ser.: No. 1). 233p. 1996. reprint ed. pap. 12.95 (*0-9643250-6-3*); Vol. 1. 1994. (Illus.). pap. 12.95 o.p. (*0-9643250-0-4*) CJH Enterprises.
—Chelsea, the Final Chapter. 2nd rev. ed. 1997. (Chelsea Ser.: No. 5). 305p. reprint ed. pap. 12.95 o.p. (*0-9643250-7-1*); (Illus.). pap. 12.95 (*0-9643250-1-2*) CJH Enterprises.
—Run, Chelsea, Run, Vol. 3. Haycox, Bobbi & CJH Enterprises Staff, eds. 1996. (Chelsea Ser.: Vol. 5). 260p. pap. 12.95 (*0-9643250-3-9*) CJH Enterprises.

### CAROLINA, MICHAEL (FICTITIOUS CHARACTER)—FICTION

Briody, Thomas G. Rogue's Isles. 1995. 273p. 21.95 o.p. (*0-312-13157-7*, Saint Martin's Minotaur) St. Martin's Pr.
—Rogue's Justice: A Michael Carolina Mystery. 1996. 288p. 22.95 o.p. (*0-312-14402-4*, Saint Martin's Minotaur) St. Martin's Pr.
—Rogues Regatta. 1999. 272p. 23.95 (*0-312-24235-2*, Saint Martin's Minotaur) St. Martin's Pr.
—Rogue's Wager: A Michael Carolina Mystery. 1997. (Michael Carolina Mystery Ser.). 160p. 21.95 (*0-312-16990-6*, Saint Martin's Minotaur) St. Martin's Pr.

### CARPENTER, ANDY (FICTITIOUS CHARACTER)—FICTION

Rosenfelt, David. First Degree. 2003. 240p. 23.95 (*0-89296-754-4*) Mysterious Pr.
—First Degree. l.t. ed. 2003. 342p. 28.95 (*0-7862-5859-4*, Large Print Pr.) Thorndike Pr.
—First Degree. 2004. mass mkt. (*0-446-61386-X*) Warner Bks., Inc.
—Open & Shut. 2002. 256p. 23.95 (*0-89296-748-X*) Mysterious Pr.
—Open & Shut. l.t. ed. 2002. (Americana Ser.). 442p. 29.95 (*0-7862-4494-1*) Thorndike Pr.
—Open & Shut. 2003. 320p. reprint ed. mass mkt. 6.99 (*0-446-61253-7*) Warner Bks., Inc.

### CARPENTER, SCOTT (FICTITIOUS CHARACTER)—FICTION

Zubro, Mark Richard. Are You Nuts? (Tom & Scott Mystery Ser.). 256p. 1999. pap. 12.95 (*0-312-20634-8*, Saint Martin's Griffin); 1998. 21.95 (*0-312-18528-6*, Saint Martin's Minotaur) St. Martin's Pr.
—An Echo of Death: A Tom & Scott Mystery. (Tom & Scott Mystery Ser.). 1995. 208p. pap. 11.95 (*0-312-13480-0*, Saint Martin's Griffin); 1994. 192p. 18.95 o.p. (*0-312-11268-8*, Saint Martin's Minotaur) St. Martin's Pr.
—Here Comes the Corpse. 2002. (Tom & Scott Mystery Ser.: No. 9). 256p. 23.95 (*0-312-28098-X*, Saint Martin's Minotaur) St. Martin's Pr.
—One Dead Drag Queen. E-Book 22.95 (*0-312-27586-2*); 2001. 256p. pap. 12.95 (*0-312-27702-4*, Saint Martin's Griffin); 2000. 256p. 22.95 o.s.i (*0-312-20937-1*, Saint Martin's Minotaur) St. Martin's Pr.
—The Only Good Priest. (Tom & Scott Mystery Ser.). 1992. 192p. pap. 10.95 (*0-312-07054-3*, Saint Martin's Griffin); 1991. 8.99 o.p. (*0-312-05486-6*, Saint Martin's Minotaur) St. Martin's Pr.
—The Principal Cause of Death. (Tom & Scott Mystery Ser.). 1993. 192p. pap. 11.95 (*0-312-09896-0*, Saint Martin's Griffin); 1992. 208p. 11.99 o.p. (*0-312-07767-X*, Saint Martin's Minotaur) St. Martin's Pr.
—Rust on the Razor. (Tom & Scott Mystery Ser.). 224p. 1997. pap. 11.95 (*0-312-15644-8*, Saint Martin's Griffin); 1996. text 20.95 o.p. (*0-312-14404-0*, Saint Martin's Minotaur) St. Martin's Pr.
—A Simple Suburban Murder. (Stonewall Inn Editions Ser.). 1990. 6.50 o.p. (*0-312-03887-9*, Saint Martin's Minotaur); 1990. 224p. pap. 8.95 (*0-312-03933-6*, Saint Martin's Griffin); 1989. 224p. 15.95 o.p. (*0-312-02640-4*, Saint Martin's Minotaur) St. Martin's Pr.
—Why Isn't Becky Twitchell Dead? 1970. 208p. 15.00 o.p. (*0-312-03955-7*) Palgrave Macmillan.
—Why Isn't Becky Twitchell Dead? 1991. (Stonewall Inn Editions Ser.). 189p. pap. 12.95 (*0-312-05996-5*, Saint Martin's Griffin) St. Martin's Pr.

### CARPO, MICHAEL (FICTITIOUS CHARACTER)—FICTION

Miano, Mark. Dead of Summer. 224p. 2002. mass mkt. 5.99 o.s.i (*1-57566-717-7*, Kensington Bks.); 1999. 20.00 o.s.i (*1-57566-404-6*) Kensington Publishing Corp.
—Flesh & Stone: A Michael Carpo Mystery. (Michael Carpo Mystery Ser.). 288p. 1998. mass mkt. 5.99 o.s.i (*1-57566-273-6*); 1997. 18.95 o.p. (*1-57566-128-4*, Kensington Bks.) Kensington Publishing Corp.
—The Street Where She Lived: A Michael Carpo Mystery. 1998. (Michael Carpo Mystery Ser.). 320p. 20.00 o.s.i (*1-57566-270-1*, Kensington Bks.) Kensington Publishing Corp.

### CARR, MIKE (FICTITIOUS CHARACTER)—FICTION

Ashford, Jeffrey. The Price of Failure. 1997. 195p. 20.95 o.p. (*0-312-18156-6*, Saint Martin's Minotaur) St. Martin's Pr.
—The Price of Failure. l.t. ed. 1998. (Nightingale Ser.). 278p. pap. 20.95 (*0-7838-8111-8*) Thorndike Pr.

### CARR, ROSIE (FICTITIOUS CHARACTER)—FICTION

Willis, Ted. The Bells of Autumn. 1993. 2.99 o.p. (*0-517-09906-3*) Random Hse. Value Publishing.
—The Bells of Autumn. 1991. 256p. 18.95 o.p. (*0-312-06303-2*) St. Martin's Pr.
—The Bells of Autumn. l.t. ed. 1993. (General Ser.). 464p. 29.99 o.p. (*0-7089-2888-9*, Ulverscroft) Thorpe, F. A. Pubs. GBR. *Dist:* Ulverscroft Large Print Bks., Ltd., Ulverscroft Large Print Canada, Ltd.
—The Green Leaves of Summer: The Second Season of Rosie Carr. 1989. 17.95 o.p. (*0-312-03354-0*) St. Martin's Pr.
—The Green Leaves of Summer: The Second Season of Rosie Carr. l.t. ed. 1989. (Ulverscroft Large Print Ser.). 29.99 o.p. (*0-7089-2113-2*, Ulverscroft) Thorpe, F. A. Pubs. GBR. *Dist:* Ulverscroft Large Print Bks., Ltd., Ulverscroft Large Print Canada, Ltd.
—Spring at The Winged Horse: The First Season of Rosie Carr. 1983. 288p. 12.95 o.p. (*0-688-02135-2*, Morrow, William & Co.) Morrow/Avon.

### CARRADOS, MAX (FICTITIOUS CHARACTER)—FICTION

Bramah, Ernest. Best Max Carrados Detective Stories. Bleiler, Everett F., ed. 1972. 245p. pap. 5.95 o.p. (*0-486-20064-7*) Dover Pubns., Inc.
—Best Max Carrados Detective Stories. 1983. 7.50 o.p. (*0-8446-4517-6*) Smith, Peter Pub., Inc.
—Max Carrados. 1976. (Crime Fiction Ser.). reprint ed. lib. bdg. 21.00 o.p. (*0-8240-2355-2*) Garland Publishing, Inc.

### CARRICK, JAMES, INSPECTOR (FICTITIOUS CHARACTER)—FICTION

Duffy, Margaret. Dressed To Kill. 1994. 240p. 19.95 o.p. (*0-312-11295-5*, Saint Martin's Minotaur) St. Martin's Pr.
—Dressed to Kill. l.t. ed. 1995. (Dales Large Print Ser.). 355p. pap. 19.99 o.p. (*1-85389-520-2*) Dales Large Print Bks. GBR. *Dist:* Ulverscroft Large Print Bks., Ltd., Ulverscroft Large Print Canada, Ltd.
—Prospect of Death. 1996. 224p. 20.95 o.p. (*0-312-14396-6*, Saint Martin's Minotaur) St. Martin's Pr.

### CARROT (FICTITIOUS CHARACTER: PRATCHETT)—FICTION

Pratchett, Terry. Feet of Clay. 1997. (Discworld Ser.). (Illus.). 414p. mass mkt. 7.99 (*0-552-14237-9*) Bantam Bks.
—Feet of Clay. unabr. ed. (Discworld Ser.). 2000. audio 69.95 (*0-7531-0519-5*, 990903); 1999. 8p. audio compact disk 79.95 (*0-7531-0744-9*, 107449) ISIS Audio Bks. GBR. *Dist:* Ulverscroft Large Print Bks., Ltd.
—Feet of Clay. (Discworld Ser.). pap. o.s.i (*0-06-105339-2*, Eos); 1997. 384p. mass mkt. 6.99 (*0-06-105764-9*, HarperTorch); 1996. 256p. 20.00 o.p. (*0-06-105250-7*, Eos) Morrow/Avon.
—The Fifth Elephant. 2001. 464p. mass mkt. (*0-552-14616-1*, Corgi) Bantam Bks.
—The Fifth Elephant. l.t. ed. 2000. (Discworld Ser.: Vol. 24). 494p. 27.95 (*0-7838-9307-8*, Macmillan Reference USA) Gale Group.
—The Fifth Elephant. 2001. (Discworld Ser.: Vol. 24). 400p. mass mkt. 6.99 (*0-06-102040-0*) HarperCollins Pubs.
—The Fifth Elephant. 2001. audio compact disk 89.95 (*0-7531-1132-2*, 111322); 10p. audio 84.95 (*0-7531-0839-9*, 001205) ISIS Audio Bks. GBR. *Dist:* Ulverscroft Large Print Bks., Ltd.
—The Fifth Elephant. 2002. 108p. pap. 12.95 (*0-413-77115-6*) Methuen Publishing Ltd. GBR. *Dist:* Consortium Bk. Sales & Distribution.
—The Fifth Elephant. 2000. (Discworld Ser.: Vol. 24). 336p. 24.00 (*0-06-105157-8*, Eos) Morrow/Avon.
—The Fifth Elephant. 1999. audio 16.95 (*0-552-14720-6*) Trafalgar Square.
—Guards! Guards! 1998. 411p. mass mkt. (*0-552-13462-7*, Corgi) Bantam Bks.
—Guards! Guards! unabr. ed. (Discworld Ser.). 2000. audio compact disk 99.95 (*0-7531-0697-3*, 106973); 1998. audio 69.95 (*0-7531-0016-9*, 951202) ISIS Audio Bks. GBR. *Dist:* Ulverscroft Large Print Bks., Ltd.
—Guards! Guards! 1991. (Discworld Ser.). (Illus.). 352p. mass mkt. 4.99 o.p. (*0-451-45089-2*, ROC) NAL.
—Jingo. 1999. 413p. mass mkt. (*0-552-14598-X*, Corgi) Bantam Bks.
—Jingo. 1998. (Discworld Ser.). 336p. (YA). 24.00 o.s.i (*0-06-105047-4*) HarperCollins Pubs.
—Jingo. 2000. (Discworld Ser.). audio 69.95 (*0-7531-0521-7*, 000203); 10p. audio compact disk 89.95 (*0-7531-0884-4*, 108844) ISIS Audio Bks. GBR. *Dist:* Ulverscroft Large Print Bks., Ltd.
—Jingo. 1999. (Discworld Ser.). 464p. mass mkt. 6.99 (*0-06-105906-4*, HarperTorch) Morrow/Avon.
—Jingo. abr. ed. 1998. (Discworld Ser.). audio 18.70 (*0-552-14684-6*) Ulverscroft Audio (U.S.A.).
—Men at Arms. 1995. (Discworld Ser.). mass mkt. 6.99 (*0-552-14028-7*) Bantam Bks.
—Men at Arms. 1996. (Discworld Ser.). 384p. 20.00 o.s.i (*0-06-109218-5*) HarperTrade.
—Men at Arms, unabr. ed. 1998. (Discworld Ser.). audio 69.95 (*0-7531-0017-7*, 960403) ISIS Audio Bks. GBR. *Dist:* ISIS Publishing.
—Men at Arms. 1997. (Discworld Ser.). 400p. mass mkt. 6.99 (*0-06-109219-3*, Eos) Morrow/Avon.
—Men at Arms. 2000. (Discworld Ser.). xviii, 182p. pap. 12.95 (*0-552-14432-0*) Transworld Publishers Ltd. GBR. *Dist:* Trafalgar Square.

### CARSON, JUD (FICTITIOUS CHARACTER)—FICTION

Montgomery, Ian A. Dead Duck: A Jud Carson Mystery. Spafford, Jacalyn A., ed. 1993. 120p. (Orig.). pap. 9.95 (*1-890538-15-9*) Rhiannon Pubns.

### CARSTAIRS, CHAD (FICTITIOUS CHARACTER)—FICTION

Follett, Ken. The Big Needle. 1996. mass mkt. 5.99 o.s.i (*0-8217-5675-3*); 1993. 176p. mass mkt. 3.99 o.s.i (*0-8217-4516-6*, Zebra Bks.); 1989. 176p. mass mkt. 3.50 o.p. (*0-8217-2776-1*); 1982. mass mkt. 2.50 o.p. (*0-8217-1076-1*); 1901. mass mkt. 2.25 o.p. (*0-89083-787-2*) Kensington Publishing Corp.

### CARTER, ELWIN (FICTITIOUS CHARACTER)—FICTION

Jefferson, Roland S. The School on 103rd Street. 1997. (Old School Bks.). 192p. pap. 11.00 (*0-393-31662-9*) Norton, W. W. & Co., Inc.

### CARTER, JOHN (FICTITIOUS CHARACTER)—FICTION

Burroughs, Edgar Rice. The Chessmen of Mars. E-Book 3.95 (*0-594-03498-1*) 1873 Pr.
—The Chessmen of Mars. rev. ed. 2001. 250p. per. 9.90 (*1-58396-014-7*) Blue Unicorn Editions.
—The Chessmen of Mars. E-Book 3.49 (*1-929120-16-8*) Electric Umbrella Publishing.
—The Chessmen of Mars. E-Book 1.95 (*1-58515-085-1*) MesaView, Inc.
—The Chessmen of Mars. (John Carter of Mars Ser.: Vol. 5). 2000. 172p. pap. 9.99 (*1-57646-234-X*); 2000. 172p. lib. bdg. 16.99 (*1-57646-459-8*); 1999. 437p. E-Book 3.99 o.p. incl. cd-rom (*1-891595-52-0*); 2000. 358p. pap. 17.99 (*1-57646-460-1*); 2000. 358p. lib. bdg. 34.99 (*1-57646-461-X*) Quiet Vision Publishing.
—A Fighting Man of Mars. 1986. 192p. mass mkt. 4.99 o.s.i (*0-345-34511-8*); 1984. mass mkt. 2.25 o.p. (*0-345-32052-2*, Del Rey); 1979. mass mkt. 1.95 o.s.i (*0-345-27840-2*); 1973. mass mkt. 1.25 o.p. (*0-345-23584-3*) Ballantine Bks.
—A Fighting Man of Mars. 1975. (Illus.). reprint ed. 30.00 o.p. (*0-940724-02-2*) Hunt, Paul.
—The Gods of Mars. 2000. 252p. pap. 9.95 (*0-594-04715-3*); E-Book 3.95 (*0-594-04718-8*) 1873 Pr.
—The Gods of Mars. Date not set. 190p. 20.95 (*0-8488-2222-6*) Amereon, Ltd.
—The Gods of Mars, abr. ed. 1999. (Mars Ser.). audio 16.95 (*1-882071-77-8*, 394313) B&B Audio, Inc.
—The Gods of Mars. rev. ed. 2001. 250p. per. 9.90 (*1-58396-015-5*) Blue Unicorn Editions.
—The Gods of Mars. E-Book 3.49 (*1-929120-17-6*) Electric Umbrella Publishing.
—The Gods of Mars. 1975. (Illus.). reprint ed. 35.00 o.p. (*0-940724-03-0*) Hunt, Paul.
—The Gods of Mars. E-Book 1.95 (*1-58515-078-9*) MesaView, Inc.
—The Gods of Mars. (John Carter of Mars Ser.: Vol. 2). 2000. 164p. pap. 9.99 (*1-57646-227-7*); 2000. 164p. lib. bdg. 16.99 (*1-57646-447-4*); 1999. 418p.

E-Book 3.99 o.p. incl. cd-rom (*1-891595-34-2*); 2000. 338p. pap. 17.99 (*1-57646-448-2*); 2000. 338p. lib. bdg. 33.99 (*1-57646-449-0*) Quiet Vision Publishing.

—John Carter of Mars. 1985. 158p. mass mkt. 4.99 o.s.i (*0-345-32955-4*, Del Rey); 1979. mass mkt. 1.95 o.p. (*0-345-27844-5*, Del Rey); 1973. mass mkt. 1.25 o.p. (*0-345-23588-6*) Ballantine Bks.

—John Carter of Mars. 1982. (Illus.). 12.50 o.p. (*0-940724-04-9*) Hunt, Paul.

—The John Carter of Mars Collection. 1999. E-Book 8.99 incl. cd-rom (*1-57646-062-2*) Quiet Vision Publishing.

—Llana of Gathol. 1985. 192p. mass mkt. 4.99 o.s.i (*0-345-32443-9*, Del Rey); 1979. mass mkt. 1.95 o.p. (*0-345-27843-7*, Del Rey); 1977. mass mkt. 1.50 o.p. (*0-345-25829-0*, Del Rey); 1973. mass mkt. 1.25 o.p. (*0-345-23587-8*) Ballantine Bks.

—The Martian Tales, 4 vols. 1982. pap. 7.80 o.s.i (*0-345-26213-1*, Del Rey) Ballantine Bks.

—A Princess of Mars. 2000. 252p. pap. 9.95 (*0-594-04525-8*); E-Book 3.95 (*0-594-04528-2*) 1873 Pr.

—A Princess of Mars. Date not set. 159p. 18.95 (*0-8488-2221-8*) Amereon, Ltd.

—A Princess of Mars. unabr. ed. 2000. audio 35.95 Audio Bk. Contractors, Inc.

—A Princess of Mars. abr. ed. 1999. (Mars Ser.). (YA). (gr. 8-12). audio 16.95 (*1-882071-51-4*, 393368) B&B Audio, Inc.

—A Princess of Mars. 1985. (Mars Ser.: Vol. 1). 160p. mass mkt. 6.50 (*0-345-33138-9*, Del Rey) Ballantine Bks.

—A Princess of Mars. 2001. per. 12.50 (*1-891355-72-4*); per. 15.50 (*1-58396-238-7*) Blue Unicorn Editions.

—A Princess of Mars, Bk. 1. unabr. ed. 1993. (Mars Ser.: Bk. 1). audio 39.95 (*1-55686-482-5*, 482) Books in Motion.

—A Princess of Mars. unabr. collector's ed. 1988. audio 48.00 (*0-7366-3945-4*, 9191) Books on Tape, Inc.

—A Princess of Mars. E-Book 3.50 (*1-929120-14-1*) Electric Umbrella Publishing.

—A Princess of Mars. unabr. ed. 1989. audio 36.00 Jimcin Recordings.

—A Princess of Mars. E-Book 1.95 (*1-58515-076-2*) MesaView, Inc.

—A Princess of Mars. (John Carter of Mars Ser.). 2000. 156p. lib. bdg. 16.99 (*1-57646-444-X*); 2000. 156p. pap. 9.99 (*1-57646-226-9*); 1999. 301p. E-Book 3.99 o.p. incl. cd-rom (*1-891595-33-4*); 2000. 272p. pap. 17.99 (*1-57646-445-8*); 2000. 272p. lib. bdg. 29.99 (*1-57646-446-6*) Quiet Vision Publishing.

—A Princess of Mars. E-Book 5.00 (*0-7410-0764-9*) SoftBook Pr.

—A Princess of Mars. l.t. ed. 2001. (Science Fiction Ser.). 288p. 26.95 (*0-7838-9347-7*) Thorndike Pr.

—Swords of Mars. 1985. 190p. mass mkt. 4.99 o.s.i (*0-345-32956-2*, Del Rey); 1979. mass mkt. 1.95 o.p. (*0-345-27841-0*, Del Rey); 1977. mass mkt. 1.50 o.p. (*0-345-27546-2*) Ballantine Bks.

—Thuvia, Maid of Mars. 2000. 252p. pap. 9.95 (*0-594-04545-2*); E-Book 3.95 (*0-594-04548-7*) 1873 Pr.

—Thuvia, Maid of Mars. abr. ed. 2000. (Martian Tales of Edgar Rice Burroughs: No. 4). audio 16.95 (*1-882071-96-4*) B&B Audio, Inc.

—Thuvia, Maid of Mars, No. 4. 1986. 160p. mass mkt. 4.99 o.s.i (*0-345-33993-2*, Del Rey) Ballantine Bks.

—Thuvia, Maid of Mars. unabr. ed. 2002. audio 39.95 (*0-7861-2124-6*); audio compact disk 40.00 (*0-7861-9632-7*); audio compact disk 19.95 (*0-7861-9151-1*) Blackstone Audio Bks., Inc.

—Thuvia, Maid of Mars. E-Book 1.49 (*1-929120-38-9*) Electric Umbrella Publishing.

—Thuvia, Maid of Mars. E-Book 1.95 (*1-58515-088-6*) MesaView, Inc.

—Thuvia, Maid of Mars. (John Carter of Mars Ser.: Vol. 4). 2000. 122p. pap. 9.99 (*1-57646-229-3*); 2000. 122p. lib. bdg. 16.99 (*1-57646-453-9*); 1999. 268p. E-Book 3.99 o.p. incl. cd-rom (*1-891595-51-2*); 2000. 210p. pap. 17.99 (*1-57646-454-7*); 2000. 210p. lib. bdg. 26.99 (*1-57646-455-5*) Quiet Vision Publishing.

—Thuvia, Maid of Mars. unabr. ed. 2001. (Mars Ser.: Vol. 4). audio compact disk 20.00 (*1-4001-5019-1*); audio compact disk 33.00 (*1-4001-0019-4*) Tantor Media, Inc.

—The Warlord of Mars. 2000. 252p. pap. 9.95 (*0-594-04540-1*); (Martian Tales Ser.: No. 3). E-Book 3.95 (*0-594-04543-6*) 1873 Pr.

—The Warlord of Mars. Date not set. 158p. 18.95 (*0-8488-2224-2*) Amereon, Ltd.

—The Warlord of Mars. abr. ed. 2000. (Martian Tales of Edgar Rice Burroughs). audio 16.95 (*1-882071-91-3*) B&B Audio, Inc.

—The Warlord of Mars. 1985. (Mars Ser.: Vol. 3). 160p. mass mkt. 5.99 (*0-345-32453-6*, Del Rey) Ballantine Bks.

—The Warlord of Mars. 1976. reprint ed. lib. bdg. 21.95 (*0-89966-045-2*) Buccaneer Bks., Inc.

—The Warlord of Mars. (John Carter of Mars Ser.: Vol. 3). 2000. 138p. pap. 9.99 (*1-57646-228-5*); 2000. 138p. lib. bdg. 16.99 (*1-57646-450-4*); 1999. 291p. E-Book 3.99 o.p. incl. cd-rom (*1-891595-50-4*); 2000. 240p. pap. 17.99 (*1-57646-451-2*); 2000. 240p. lib. bdg. 28.99 (*1-57646-452-0*) Quiet Vision Publishing.

**CARTER, TERENCE (FICTITIOUS CHARACTER)—FICTION**

Price, John-Allen. Siege of Ocean Valkyrie. 1992. mass mkt. 4.50 o.s.i (*0-8217-3662-0*, Zebra Bks.) Kensington Publishing Corp.

**CARTON, LARRY (FICTITIOUS CHARACTER)—FICTION**

Moore, Robin. The Sparrowhook Curse. 1996. 424p. (Orig.). pap. 12.95 (*0-924771-70-4*, Covered Bridge Pr.) Douglas Charles, Ltd.

**CARTWRIGHT, ARNOLD (FICTITIOUS CHARACTER)—FICTION**

Rathbone, Julian. Sand Blind. 1994. (Mask Noir Ser.). 304p. pap. (*1-85242-281-5*) Serpent's Tail Ltd.

—Sand Blind. 288p. (*0-7278-5565-4*) Severn Hse. Pubs., Ltd.

**CARTWRIGHT, LORD (FICTITIOUS CHARACTER)—FICTION**

Martin, Michelle. The Queen of Hearts. 1994. mass mkt. 3.99 o.s.i (*0-449-22203-9*, Fawcett) Ballantine Bks.

**CARTWRIGHT FAMILY (FICTITIOUS CHARACTERS)—FICTION**

Hewitt, Edward. Emma: The Cartwright Saga. l.t. ed. 2000. (Cartwright Saga Ser.: Vol. 4). 384p. 31.99 (*0-7089-4254-7*, Ulverscroft) Thorpe, F. A. Pubs. GBR. *Dist:* Ulverscroft Large Print Bks., Ltd., Ulverscroft Large Print Canada, Ltd.

—The Harbinger of Doom. l.t. ed. 2000. (Cartwright Saga Ser.: 2). 312p. 31.99 (*0-7089-4168-0*, Ulverscroft) Thorpe, F. A. Pubs. GBR. *Dist:* Ulverscroft Large Print Bks., Ltd., Ulverscroft Large Print Canada, Ltd.

—The Miller's Daughters. l.t. ed. 2000. (Cartwright Saga Ser.: 3). 248p. 31.99 (*0-7089-4205-9*, Ulverscroft) Thorpe, F. A. Pubs. GBR. *Dist:* Ulverscroft Large Print Bks., Ltd., Ulverscroft Large Print Canada, Ltd.

—Where Waters Meet. l.t. ed. 1999. (Cartwright Saga Ser.: Vol. 1). 368p. 31.99 (*0-7089-4148-6*, Ulverscroft) Thorpe, F. A. Pubs. GBR. *Dist:* Ulverscroft Large Print Bks., Ltd., Ulverscroft Large Print Canada, Ltd.

**CARVALHO, PEPE (FICTITIOUS CHARACTER)—FICTION**

Montalban, Manuel Vazquez. The Angst-Ridden Executive. Emery, Ed, tr. from SPA. 1990. (Masks Noir Ser.). 240p. pap. o.p. (*1-85242-159-2*) Serpent's Tail Ltd.

—The Angst-Ridden Executive. 5th ed. 2002. 229p. pap. 13.00 (*1-85242-740-X*) Serpent's Tail Ltd. GBR. *Dist:* Consortium Bk. Sales & Distribution.

—The Buenos Aires Quintet. 2003. 252p. pap. 15.00 (*1-85242-640-3*) Serpent's Tail Ltd. GBR. *Dist:* Consortium Bk. Sales & Distribution.

—Murder in the Central Committee. 1985. 203p. 13.95 o.p. (*0-89733-125-7*) Academy Chicago Pubs., Ltd.

—Murder in the Central Committee. Camiller, Patrick, tr. from SPA. 1999. 203p. (*1-85242-731-0*) Gallery Pr.

—Murder in the Central Committee. 1997. (Mask Noir Ser.). 224p. pap. text (*1-85242-131-2*) Serpent's Tail Ltd.

—Off Side. 2001. 278p. (Orig.). pap. 13.00 (*1-85242-742-6*) Serpent's Tail Ltd. GBR. *Dist:* Consortium Bk. Sales & Distribution.

—Olympic Death. 2000. (Mask Noir Ser.). 207p. pap. o.p. (*1-85242-257-2*) Serpent's Tail Ltd.

—Southern Seas. 2000. 214p. pap. (*1-85242-700-0*) Serpent's Tail Ltd.

—Southern Seas. Camiller, Patrick, tr. from SPA. 1990. 224p. pap. o.p. (*1-85242-132-0*) Serpent's Tail Ltd.

—Southern Seas. 1990. pap. 9.95 o.p. (*0-7453-0204-1*) Westview Pr.

**CARVER, DAVID (FICTITIOUS CHARACTER)—FICTION**

King, Stephen. Desperation. 1999. 690p. reprint ed. text 28.00 (*0-7881-6597-6*) DIANE Publishing Co.

—Desperation. l.t. ed. 1997. 761p. 28.95 (*1-56895-420-4*, Wheeler Publishing, Inc.) Gale Group.

—Desperation. 1997. 560p. mass mkt. 7.99 (*0-451-18846-2*, Signet Bks.) NAL.

—Desperation. unabr. ed. 1997. audio 125.00 (*0-7887-0950-X*, 95010E7) Recorded Bks., LLC.

—Desperation. 1996. 704p. 27.95 o.s.i (*0-670-86836-1*); audio 29.95 o.p. (*0-14-086318-4*, Penguin AudioBooks) Viking Penguin.

**CARVER, FRANK (FICTITIOUS CHARACTER)—FICTION**

Wallingford, Lee. Clear-Cut Murder: A Frank Carver - Ginny Trask Mystery. 1995. (WWL Mystery Ser.). mass mkt. (*0-373-26165-9*, 1-26165-0, Harlequin Bks.) Harlequin Enterprises, Ltd.

—Clear-Cut Murder: A Frank Carver - Ginny Trask Mystery. 1993. 212p. 19.95 o.s.i (*0-8027-3231-3*) Walker & Co.

—Cold Tracks. 1993. (Mystery Ser.). mass mkt. (*0-373-26114-4*, 1-26114-8, Harlequin Bks.) Harlequin Enterprises, Ltd.

—Cold Tracks. 1991. 192p. 18.95 (*0-8027-5783-9*) Walker & Co.

**CARVER, FRED (FICTITIOUS CHARACTER)—FICTION**

Lutz, John. Blood Fire. 1991. 17.95 o.p. (*0-8050-0969-8*) Holt, Henry & Co.

—Blood Fire. 1992. (Fred Carver Mystery Ser.). 224p. reprint ed. mass mkt. 3.99 (*0-380-71446-9*, Avon Bks.) Morrow/Avon.

—Burn: A Fred Carver Mystery. 1995. (Henry Holt Mystery Ser.). 278p. 22.50 o.p. (*0-8050-3480-3*) Holt, Henry & Co.

—Flame. unabr. ed. 1990. audio 57.25 o.p. (*1-56100-050-7*, 1197, Unabridged Library Editions); Set. audio 19.95 o.p. (*0-930435-56-7*, 344, Bookcassette) Brilliance Audio.

—Flame. 1996. 88p. pap. 5.95 o.p. (*0-8050-4567-8*, Owl Bks.) Holt, Henry & Co.

—Flame. 1991. 272p. pap. 3.95 (*0-380-71070-6*, Avon Bks.) Morrow/Avon.

—Hot: A Fred Carver Mystery. 1992. 288p. 18.95 o.p. (*0-8050-1584-1*) Holt, Henry & Co.

—Hot: A Fred Carver Mystery. 1993. 256p. mass mkt. 4.99 (*0-380-71447-7*, Avon Bks.) Morrow/Avon.

—Kiss. unabr. ed. 1990. audio 57.25 o.p. (*1-56100-056-6*, 920, Unabridged Library Editions); audio 19.95 o.p. (*0-930435-62-1*, 2030, Bookcassette) Brilliance Audio.

—Kiss. (Fred Carver Mystery Ser.). 1996. 88p. pap. 5.95 o.p. (*0-8050-4566-X*, Owl Bks.); 1988. 17.95 o.p. (*0-8050-0412-2*) Holt, Henry & Co.

—Kiss. 1990. 272p. pap. 3.95 (*0-380-70934-1*, Avon Bks.) Morrow/Avon.

—Lightning: A Fred Carver Mystery. unabr. ed. 1996. (P. I. Fred Carver Mystery Ser.). audio 48.00 (*0-7366-3519-X*, 4156) Books on Tape, Inc.

—Lightning: A Fred Carver Mystery. 1996. 88p. 22.50 o.p. (*0-8050-4379-9*) Holt, Henry & Co.

—Scorcher. unabr. ed. 1990. audio 57.25 o.p. (*1-56100-060-4*, 1030, Unabridged Library Editions); audio 19.95 o.p. (*0-930435-66-4*, 252, Bookcassette) Brilliance Audio.

—Scorcher. 272p. 1995. pap. 5.95 o.p. (*0-8050-3829-9*, Owl Bks.); 1987. 16.95 o.p. (*0-8050-0411-4*) Holt, Henry & Co.

—Scorcher. 1988. 256p. pap. 3.95 (*0-380-70526-5*, Avon Bks.) Morrow/Avon.

—Spark: A Fred Carver Mystery. 1993. 288p. 19.95 o.p. (*0-8050-1993-6*) Holt, Henry & Co.

—Torch. 1994. (Henry Holt Mystery Ser.). 290p. 22.00 o.p. (*0-8050-2610-X*) Holt, Henry & Co.

—Tropical Heat. l.t. ed. 1991. 21.95 o.p. (*1-55504-579-0*); pap. 6.95 o.p. (*1-55504-550-2*, 456) BBC Audiobooks America.

—Tropical Heat. unabr. ed. 1989. (P. I. Fred Carver Mystery Ser.). audio 19.95 o.p. (*0-930435-53-2*, 359, Bookcassette); audio 57.25 o.p. (*1-56100-047-7*, 1107, Unabridged Library Editions) Brilliance Audio.

—Tropical Heat. 1995. 252p. pap. 5.95 o.p. (*0-8050-3828-0*, Owl Bks.); 1986. 224p. o.p. (*0-03-006958-0*) Holt, Henry & Co.

—Tropical Heat. 1987. 256p. pap. 3.95 (*0-380-70309-2*, Avon Bks.) Morrow/Avon.

**CARVER, TOMMY (FICTITIOUS CHARACTER)—FICTION**

Thompson, Jim. Cropper's Cabin. 1992. 160p. pap. 15.00 (*0-679-73315-9*, Vintage) Knopf Publishing Group.

**CASE, CHARLEY (FICTITIOUS CHARACTER)—FICTION**

Spencer, John B. Quake City. 1997. 158p. pap. 12.95 (*1-899344-02-0*) Dufour Editions, Inc.

**CASELLA, TONY (FICTITIOUS CHARACTER)—FICTION**

Beinhart, Larry. Foreign Exchange. 1992. mass mkt. 5.99 o.s.i (*0-345-36665-4*) Ballantine Bks.

—No One Rides for Free. 1993. mass mkt. 4.99 o.s.i (*0-345-37294-8*) Ballantine Bks.

—No One Rides for Free. 1987. 240p. pap. 3.95 (*0-380-70283-5*, Avon Bks.); 1986. 256p. 16.95 o.p. (*0-688-06057-9*, Morrow, William & Co.) Morrow/Avon.

—You Get What You Pay For. 1989. 368p. mass mkt. 4.95 o.s.i (*0-345-36406-6*) Ballantine Bks.

—You Get What You Pay For. 1988. 356p. 18.95 o.p. (*0-688-06613-5*, Morrow, William & Co.) Morrow/Avon.

**CASEY, SAMANTHA (FICTITIOUS CHARACTER)—FICTION**

Tooley, S. D. Nothing Else Matters. 2000. (Sam Casey Mystery Ser.). 288p. 22.95 (*0-9666021-2-9*) Full Moon Publishing.

—When the Dead Speak. 2000. (Sam Casey Mystery Ser.). 304p. pap. 6.50 (*0-9666021-3-7*) Full Moon Publishing.

—When the Dead Speak. Roerden, Chris, ed. 1999. (Sam Casey Mystery Ser.). 304p. 21.95 (*0-9666021-0-2*) Full Moon Publishing.

**CASS, COLIN (FICTITIOUS CHARACTER)—FICTION**

Livingston, Nancy. Quiet Murder. l.t. ed. 1993. 23.95 o.p. (*0-7927-1797-X*); pap. 21.95 o.p. (*0-7927-1796-1*) BBC Audiobooks America.

—Quiet Murder. 1995. 253p. per. (*0-373-26186-1*, 1-26186-6, Worldwide Library) Harlequin Enterprises, Ltd.

—Quiet Murder. l.t. ed. 1993. (Magna Large Print Ser.). 388p. o.p. (*0-7505-0582-6*) Magna Large Print Bks. GBR. *Dist:* Ulverscroft Large Print Canada, Ltd.

—Quiet Murder. 1993. 17.95 o.p. (*0-312-08878-7*, Saint Martin's Minotaur) St. Martin's Pr.

**CASSIDY, FAITH (FICTITIOUS CHARACTER)—FICTION**

Dain, Catherine. Death of the Party: A Faith Cassidy Mystery. 2000. (Five Star Mystery Ser.). 238p. 21.95 (*0-7862-2538-6*, Five Star) Gale Group.

—Follow the Murder. 2003. 256p. mass mkt. (*0-373-26468-2*) Harlequin Enterprises, Ltd.

—Follow the Murder: A Faith Cassidy Mystery. 2002. (Five Star First Edition Mystery Ser.). 222p. 25.95 (*0-7862-4316-3*, Five Star) Gale Group.

**CASSIDY, HOPALONG (FICTITIOUS CHARACTER)—FICTION**

L'Amour, Louis. The Riders of High Rock. 1994. 224p. mass mkt. 4.99 o.s.i (*0-553-56829-9*); 272p. mass mkt. 4.99 (*0-553-56782-9*) Bantam Bks.

—The Riders of High Rock. l.t. ed. 1993. 352p. 24.95 o.s.i (*0-385-47040-1*, Bantam Large Type) Bantam Doubleday Dell Large Print Group, Inc.

—The Riders of High Rock. 5.98 o.p. (*0-8317-4692-0*) Smithmark Pubs., Inc.

—The Riders of High Rock. l.t. ed. 1998. (Western Ser.). 261p. 27.95 o.p. (*0-7838-1955-2*) Thorndike Pr.

—The Rustlers of West Fork: A Hopalong Cassidy Novel. 1992. 288p. mass mkt. 4.99 (*0-553-29539-X*) Bantam Bks.

—The Rustlers of West Fork: A Hopalong Cassidy Novel. l.t. ed. 1991. 368p. 22.00 o.s.i (*0-385-41996-1*, Bantam Large Type) Bantam Doubleday Dell Large Print Group, Inc.

—The Rustlers of West Fork: A Hopalong Cassidy Novel. l.t. ed. 1994. 353p. pap. 19.95 o.p. (*0-8161-5798-7*, Macmillan Reference USA) Gale Group.

—The Trail to Seven Pines: A Hopalong Cassidy Novel. 1993. 256p. mass mkt. 4.99 (*0-553-56178-2*) Bantam Bks.

—The Trail to Seven Pines: A Hopalong Cassidy Novel. l.t. ed. 1994. 269p. pap. 19.95 o.p. (*0-8161-5799-5*, Macmillan Reference USA) Gale Group.

—Trouble Shooter: A Hopalong Cassidy Novel. 1995. 240p. mass mkt. 4.99 (*0-553-57187-7*) Bantam Bks.

—Trouble Shooter: A Hopalong Cassidy Novel. l.t. ed. 1999. (Western Ser.). 309p. 26.95 (*0-7862-0896-1*) Thorndike Pr.

Mulford, Clarence E. Bar Twenty. 1974. (Hopalong Cassidy Ser.). 382p. reprint ed. lib. bdg. 27.95 (*0-88411-213-6*) Amereon, Ltd.

—Bar-20. 1992. 288p. mass mkt. 4.99 (*0-8125-2290-7*, Tor Bks.) Doherty, Tom Assocs., LLC.

—Bar-20: Hopalong Cassidy's Rustler Roundup. Banis, Robert, ed. 2000. 225p. per. 12.95 (*1-888725-34-6*, BeachHouse Bks.) Science & Humanities Pr.

—Bar-20: Hopalong Cassidy's Rustler Roundup. l.t. ed. 2000. 393p. per. 18.95 (*1-888725-42-7*, MacroPrintBooks) Science & Humanities Pr.

—Bar-20 Rides Again. Date not set. lib. bdg. 25.95 (*0-88411-215-2*, Aeonian Pr.) Amereon, Ltd.

—Buck Peters, Ranchman. 1973. reprint ed. lib. bdg. 26.95 (*0-88411-202-0*) Amereon, Ltd.

—Buck Peters, Ranchman. 1993. 320p. mass mkt. 5.99 (*0-8125-2499-3*, Tor Bks.) Doherty, Tom Assocs., LLC.

—H. C. Serves Writ. 1976. 23.95 (*0-88411-220-9*) Amereon, Ltd.

—Hopalong Cassidy. 1976. reprint ed. lib. bdg. 27.95 (*0-88411-217-9*) Amereon, Ltd.

—Hopalong Cassidy. Kaye, Jocelyn, ed. abr. ed. 1995. audio 12.95 (*1-882071-38-7*) B&B Audio, Inc.

—Hopalong Cassidy. 1992. (Illus.). 320p. mass mkt. 5.99 (*0-8125-2242-7*, Tor Bks.) Doherty, Tom Assocs., LLC.

—Hopalong Cassidy & the Eagle's Brood. 1976. reprint ed. 24.95 (*0-88411-206-3*) Amereon, Ltd.

—Johnny Nelson. 1976. 26.95 (*0-88411-222-5*) Amereon, Ltd.

—Johnny Nelson. 1997. 304p. mass mkt. 5.99 (*0-8125-6766-8*, Forge Bks.) Doherty, Tom Assocs., LLC.
—Mesquite Jenkins. l.t. ed. 1976. 24.95 (*0-88411-236-5*); reprint ed. 24.95 (*0-88411-208-X*) Amereon, Ltd.
—Mesquite Jenkins, Tumbleweed. 1976. 24.95 (*0-88411-224-1*) Amereon, Ltd.
—Tex. 1976. (Hopalong Cassidy Ser.). reprint ed. lib. bdg. 24.95 (*0-88411-226-8*) Amereon, Ltd.
—Tex. l.t. ed. 1992. 19.95 o.p. (*0-7927-1331-1*); pap. 17.95 o.p. (*0-7927-1330-3*) BBC Audiobooks America.
—Tex. 1999. 288p. mass mkt. 5.99 (*0-8125-6687-4*, Forge Bks.) Doherty, Tom Assocs., LLC.
—Trail Dust. l.t. ed. Date not set. lib. bdg. 24.95 (*0-88411-240-3*, Aeonian Pr.); 1976. reprint ed. 24.95 (*0-88411-212-8*) Amereon, Ltd.
Nevins, Francis M. Bar-20: The Life of Clarence E. Mulford, Creator of Hopalong Cassidy, with Seven Original Stories Reprinted. 1993. (Illus.). 264p. lib. bdg. 37.50 o.p. (*0-89950-870-7*) McFarland & Co., Inc. Pubs.

**CASSON, JEAN (FICTITIOUS CHARACTER)—FICTION**

Furst, Alan. Red Gold. 2000. 283p. reprint ed. pap. 13.00 (*0-00-649903-1*) HarperCollins Pubs. Ltd. GBR. *Dist:* Trafalgar Square.
—Red Gold. l.t. ed. 2000. (Ulverscroft Large Print Ser.). 432p. 31.99 (*0-7089-4253-9*, Ulverscroft) Thorpe, F. A. Pubs. GBR. *Dist:* Ulverscroft Large Print Bks., Ltd., Ulverscroft Large Print Canada, Ltd.
—Red Gold: A Novel. 1999. (Illus.). 288p. 23.95 o.s.i (*0-679-45186-2*) Random Hse., Inc.
—The World at Night. 2000. 320p. pap. 13.00 (*0-00-651097-3*) HarperCollins Pubs. Ltd. GBR. *Dist:* Trafalgar Square.
—The World at Night, abr. ed. 2000. audio compact disk 79.95 (*0-7531-0704-X*, 10704X); 1998. audio 69.95 (*0-7531-0383-4*, 980508) ISIS Audio Bks. GBR. *Dist:* Ulverscroft Large Print Bks., Ltd.
—The World at Night. l.t. ed. 1999. (Ulverscroft Large Print Ser.). 448p. 31.99 o.p. (*0-7089-4024-2*, Ulverscroft) Thorpe, F. A. Pubs. GBR. *Dist:* Ulverscroft Large Print Bks., Ltd., Ulverscroft Large Print Canada, Ltd.

**CASTANG, HENRI (FICTITIOUS CHARACTER)—FICTION**

Freeling, Nicolas. The Back of the North Wind. (Crime Monthly Ser.). 1984. 224p. pap. 3.95 o.p. (*0-14-006953-4*, Penguin Bks.); 1983. 192p. 13.95 o.p. (*0-670-14398-7*) Viking Penguin.
—The Bugles Blowing. 1980. (Henri Castang Mystery Ser.). pap. 1.95 o.p. (*0-394-74551-5*) Random Hse., Inc.
—Castang's City. 2001. 284p. pap. 9.95 (*1-84232-855-7*) House of Stratus, Inc. GBR. *Dist:* Midpoint Trade Bks., Inc.
—Castang's City. 1980. 9.95 o.p. (*0-394-50895-5*, Pantheon) Knopf Publishing Group.
—Castang's City. 1981. (Henri Castang Mystery Ser.). 304p. pap. 3.95 o.p. (*0-394-74747-X*) Random Hse., Inc.
—Cold Iron. 2001. 260p. pap. (*1-84232-861-1*) House of Stratus, Inc.
—Cold Iron. 1990. 24p. pap. 4.50 o.p. (*0-14-009984-0*); 1988. 240p. pap. 3.95 o.p. (*0-14-009252-8*, Penguin Bks.); 1986. 15.95 o.p. (*0-670-81180-7*) Viking Penguin.
—A Dressing of Diamond. 1974. (Harper Novel of Suspense Ser.). 256p. 7.95 o.p. (*0-06-011352-9*) HarperCollins Pubs.
—A Dressing of Diamond. 1976. (Crime Ser.). 232p. pap. 3.95 o.p. (*0-14-004131-1*, Penguin Bks.) Viking Penguin.
—A Dwarf Kingdom. l.t. ed. 1996. 325p. pap. 20.95 o.p. (*0-7838-1867-X*, Macmillan Reference USA) Gale Group.
—A Dwarf Kingdom. 2001. 210p. pap. 9.95 (*1-84232-869-7*) House of Stratus, Inc. GBR. *Dist:* Midpoint Trade Bks., Inc.
—A Dwarf Kingdom. 214p. 1997. mass mkt. o.s.i (*0-7515-1867-0*); 1996. o.s.i (*0-316-87892-8*) Little Brown & Co.
—A Dwarf Kingdom. 1996. 256p. 21.95 o.s.i (*0-89296-615-7*) Mysterious Pr.
—A Dwarf Kingdom. 1997. 208p. mass mkt. 5.99 (*0-446-40518-3*) Warner Bks., Inc.
—Flanders Sky. 1992. 224p. 25.00 (*0-89296-492-8*) Mysterious Pr.
—Flanders Sky. 1993. 224p. mass mkt. 5.50 o.s.i (*0-446-40352-0*) Warner Bks., Inc.
—Lady Macbeth. 2001. 276p. pap. (*1-84232-862-X*) House of Stratus, Inc.
—The Night Lords. 2001. 290p. pap. 9.95 (*1-84232-854-9*) House of Stratus, Inc. GBR. *Dist:* Midpoint Trade Bks., Inc.
—The Night Lords. 1978. 7.95 o.p. (*0-394-50281-7*, Pantheon) Knopf Publishing Group.
—The Night Lords. 1980. (Henri Castang Mystery Ser.). pap. 1.95 o.s.i (*0-394-74552-3*) Random Hse., Inc.
—No Part in Your Death. 2001. 254p. pap. 9.95 (*1-84232-859-X*) House of Stratus, Inc. GBR. *Dist:* Midpoint Trade Bks., Inc.
—No Part in Your Death. (Crime Monthly Ser.). 240p. 1986. pap. 3.95 o.p. (*0-14-007450-3*, Penguin Bks.); 1984. 13.95 o.p. (*0-670-51441-1*) Viking Penguin.
—Not As Far As Velma. 2001. 246p. pap. 9.95 (*1-84232-863-8*) House of Stratus, Inc. GBR. *Dist:* Midpoint Trade Bks., Inc.
—Not as Far as Velma. 1989. 17.95 o.s.i (*0-89296-380-8*) Mysterious Pr.
—Not as Far as Velma. 1990. 240p. mass mkt. 4.95 o.s.i (*0-445-40811-1*, Mysterious Pr. Paperback Bks.) Warner Bks., Inc.
—Sabine. 1978. (Harper Novel of Suspense Ser.). 7.95 o.p. (*0-06-011356-1*) HarperCollins Pubs.
—Sabine. 1980. (Henri Castang Mystery Ser.). pap. 1.95 o.p. (*0-394-74553-1*) Random Hse., Inc.
—The Seacoast of Bohemia: A Henri Castang Mystery. l.t. ed. 1995. 312p. pap. 20.95 o.p. (*0-7838-1567-0*, Macmillan Reference USA) Gale Group.
—The Seacoast of Bohemia: A Henri Castang Mystery. 1996. 213p. mass mkt. o.s.i (*0-7515-1494-2*) Little Brown & Co.
—The Seacoast of Bohemia: A Henri Castang Mystery. 1995. 213p. 18.95 o.s.i (*0-89296-555-X*) Mysterious Pr.
—The Seacoast of Bohemia: A Henri Castang Mystery. 1996. 208p. mass mkt. 5.99 o.s.i (*0-446-40371-7*) Warner Bks., Inc.
—Those in Peril. l.t. ed. 1991. 17.95 o.p. (*0-7451-8172-4*, AH0226); pap. 15.95 o.p. (*0-7927-0707-9*, AS0262) BBC Audiobooks America.
—Those in Peril. 2001. 218p. pap. 9.95 (*1-84232-865-4*) House of Stratus, Inc. GBR. *Dist:* Midpoint Trade Bks., Inc.
—Those in Peril. 1991. 18.95 o.p. (*0-89296-412-X*) Mysterious Pr.
—Those in Peril. 1992. mass mkt. 4.99 o.s.i (*0-446-40089-0*) Warner Bks., Inc.
—Wolfnight. 2001. 242p. pap. 9.95 (*1-84232-857-3*) House of Stratus, Inc. GBR. *Dist:* Midpoint Trade Bks., Inc.
—Wolfnight. (Henri Castang Mystery Ser.). 1983. 288p. pap. 2.95 o.p. (*0-394-71381-8*, Vintage); 1982. 12.00 o.p. (*0-394-52266-4*, Pantheon) Knopf Publishing Group.
—You Know Who. l.t. ed. 1995. 279p. 21.95 (*0-7838-1182-9*, Macmillan Reference USA) Gale Group.
—You Know Who. 1995. 250p. mass mkt. o.s.i (*0-7515-1028-9*) Little Brown & Co.
—You Know Who. 1994. 192p. 18.95 o.s.i (*0-89296-554-1*) Mysterious Pr.
—You Know Who. 1995. 208p. mass mkt. 5.50 o.s.i (*0-446-40370-9*) Warner Bks., Inc.

**CASTEEL FAMILY (FICTITIOUS CHARACTERS)—FICTION**

Andrews, V. C. Dark Angel. unabr. ed. 1990. (Casteel Ser.). audio 72.00 (*0-7366-1762-0*, 2601) Books on Tape, Inc.
—Dark Angel. l.t. unabr. ed. 1987. (General Ser.). 524p. 19.95 o.p. (*0-8161-4336-6*, Macmillan Reference USA) Gale Group.
—Dark Angel. unabr. ed. 1995. audio 84.95 (*1-85695-643-1*, 931201) ISIS Audio Bks. GBR. *Dist:* Ulverscroft Large Print Bks., Ltd.
—Dark Angel. Marrow, Linda, ed. 1990. (Casteel Ser.). 488p. mass mkt. 7.99 (*0-671-72939-X*, Pocket) Simon & Schuster.
—Dark Angel. 1987. mass mkt. (*0-671-65659-7*, Pocket); 1986. 440p. 17.45 (*0-671-63370-8*, Simon & Schuster) Simon & Schuster.
—Dark Angel. 1986. (J). 12.60 o.p. (*0-606-02624-X*) Turtleback Bks.
—Fallen Hearts. unabr. ed. 1990. audio 64.00 (*0-7366-1763-9*, 2602) Books on Tape, Inc.
—Fallen Hearts. l.t. ed. 1989. (General Ser.). 466p. 19.95 o.p. (*0-8161-4765-5*, Macmillan Reference USA) Gale Group.
—Fallen Hearts. unabr. ed. 1995. 45p. audio 84.95 (*1-85695-870-1*, 941108) ISIS Audio Bks. GBR. *Dist:* Ulverscroft Large Print Bks., Ltd.
—Fallen Hearts. Marrow, Linda, ed. 1990. (Casteel Ser.). 416p. mass mkt. 7.99 (*0-671-72940-3*, Pocket) Simon & Schuster.
—Fallen Hearts. 1988. 352p. 19.45 o.p. (*0-671-64258-8*, Simon & Schuster) Simon & Schuster.
—Fallen Hearts. 1988. 14.04 (*0-606-03782-9*) Turtleback Bks.
—Gates of Paradise. unabr. ed. 1991. audio 72.00 (*0-7366-1888-0*, 2716) Books on Tape, Inc.
—Gates of Paradise. l.t. ed. 1990. (Large Print Bks.). 492p. lib. bdg. 20.95 o.p. (*0-8161-4916-X*, Macmillan Reference USA) Gale Group.
—Gates of Paradise. unabr. ed. 1996. audio 94.95 (*1-85695-731-4*, 940206) ISIS Audio Bks. GBR. *Dist:* Ulverscroft Large Print Bks., Ltd.
—Gates of Paradise. Marrow, Linda, ed. 1990. (Casteel Ser.). 488p. mass mkt. 7.99 (*0-671-72943-8*, Pocket) Simon & Schuster.
—Gates of Paradise. 1989. 19.95 o.p. (*0-671-67063-8*, Simon & Schuster) Simon & Schuster.
—Gates of Paradise. 1989. (J). 14.04 (*0-606-04227-X*) Turtleback Bks.
—Heaven. unabr. ed. 1990. (Casteel Ser.). audio 80.00 (*0-7366-1736-1*, 2576) Books on Tape, Inc.
—Heaven. l.t. ed. 1986. (General Ser.). 588p. 19.95 o.p. (*0-8161-4078-2*); 10.95 o.p. (*0-8161-4079-0*) Gale Group. (Macmillan Reference USA).
—Heaven. unabr. ed. 1995. audio 84.95 (*1-85695-865-5*, 940904) ISIS Audio Bks. GBR. *Dist:* Ulverscroft Large Print Bks., Ltd.
—Heaven. 1997. 464p. mass mkt. 3.99 (*0-671-01005-0*, Pocket) Simon & Schuster.
—Heaven. Marrow, Linda, ed. 1990. (Casteel Ser.). 448p. mass mkt. 7.99 (*0-671-72944-6*, Pocket) Simon & Schuster.
—Heaven. 1985. 16.45 o.s.i (*0-671-60536-4*, Simon & Schuster) Simon & Schuster.
—Heaven. 1985. 14.04 (*0-606-00660-5*) Turtleback Bks.
—Web of Dreams. unabr. ed. 1991. audio 80.00 (*0-7366-1908-9*, 2734) Books on Tape, Inc.
—Web of Dreams. l.t. ed. 1991. (General Ser.). 581p. pap. 17.95 (*0-8161-5039-7*); lib. bdg. 20.95 o.p. (*0-8161-5038-9*) Gale Group. (Macmillan Reference USA).
—Web of Dreams. Marrow, Linda, ed. 1990. (Casteel Saga Ser.). 432p. mass mkt. 7.99 (*0-671-72949-7*, Pocket) Simon & Schuster.
—Web of Dreams. 1990. 19.95 o.p. (*0-671-70057-X*, Atria) Simon & Schuster.
—Web of Dreams. 1990. (Casteel Saga Ser.). (J). 14.04 (*0-606-04418-3*) Turtleback Bks.

**CATALONI, STELLA (FICTITIOUS CHARACTER)—FICTION**

Rosenberg, Nancy Taylor. Trial by Fire. unabr. ed. 1996. audio 64.00 (*0-7366-3433-9*, 4077) Books on Tape, Inc.
—Trial by Fire. 1996. 352p. 22.95 o.p. (*0-525-93767-6*) Dutton/Plume.
—Trial by Fire. l.t. ed. 1996. (Large Print Bks.). 27.95 (*1-56895-305-4*, Wheeler Publishing, Inc.) Gale Group.
—Trial by Fire. 1996. 448p. mass mkt. 7.99 (*0-451-18005-4*, Signet Bks.) NAL.
—Trial by Fire, unabr. ed. audio 78.00 (*0-7887-0521-0*, 94716E7) Recorded Bks., LLC.
—Trial by Fire. abr. ed. 1996. audio 16.95 o.s.i (*0-14-086200-5*, Penguin AudioBooks) Viking Penguin.

**CATCHPOLE, HILARY (FICTITIOUS CHARACTER)—FICTION**

Symons, Julian. Playing Happy Families. unabr. ed. 1996. audio 69.95 (*0-7451-2747-9*, SAB 113, Sterling Audio Bks.) BBC Audiobooks America.
—Playing Happy Families. 1995. 320p. 28.00 (*0-89296-578-9*) Mysterious Pr.
—Playing Happy Families. 1995. 288p. mass mkt. 5.50 (*0-446-40412-8*, Mysterious Pr. Paperback Bks.) Warner Bks., Inc.

**CATES, MOLLY (FICTITIOUS CHARACTER)—FICTION**

Walker, Mary Willis. All the Dead Lie Down. unabr. ed. 1998. audio 64.00 (*0-7366-4220-X*, 4718) Books on Tape, Inc.
—All the Dead Lie Down. l.t. ed. 1998. (Large Print Bks.). 26.95 (*1-56895-669-X*, Wheeler Publishing, Inc.) Gale Group.
—All the Dead Lie Down, unabr. ed. 1998. audio 78.00 (*0-7887-2166-6*, 95462E7) Recorded Bks., LLC.
—The Red Scream. 1995. 416p. mass mkt. 6.99 (*0-553-57172-9*, Crimeline) Bantam Bks.
—The Red Scream. unabr. ed. 1996. audio 64.00 (*0-7366-3381-2*, 4031) Books on Tape, Inc.
—The Red Scream. 1994. 19.95 o.s.i (*0-385-46858-X*) Doubleday Publishing.
—The Red Scream, unabr. ed. 1996. audio 85.00 (*0-7887-0468-0*, 94661E7) Recorded Bks., LLC.
—The Red Scream. l.t. ed. 1997. (Niagara Large Print Ser.). 524p. 29.50 o.p. (*0-7089-5814-1*, Ulverscroft) Thorpe, F. A. Pubs. GBR. *Dist:* Ulverscroft Large Print Bks., Ltd., Ulverscroft Large Print Canada, Ltd.
—Under the Beetle's Cellar. 1996. 368p. reprint ed. mass mkt. 6.50 (*0-553-57173-7*, Crimeline) Bantam Bks.
—Under the Beetle's Cellar. unabr. ed. 1996. audio 64.00 (*0-7366-3382-0*, 4032) Books on Tape, Inc.
—Under the Beetle's Cellar. l.t. ed. 1996. pap. 22.95 o.p. (*1-56895-313-5*, Wheeler Publishing, Inc.) Gale Group.
—Under the Beetle's Cellar. unabr. ed. audio 75.00 (*0-7887-0515-6*, 94709E7); 1999. audio compact disk 99.00 (*0-7887-3410-5*, C1016E7) Recorded Bks., LLC.

**CATLETT, ANDY (FICTITIOUS CHARACTER)—FICTION**

Berry, Wendell. Remembering. 1990. 124p. pap. 11.00 o.p. (*0-86547-331-5*); 1988. 144p. 14.95 o.p. (*0-86547-330-7*) Farrar, Straus & Giroux. (North Point Pr.).
—A World Lost. 160p. 1997. pap. text 12.50 (*1-887178-54-6*); 1996. text 20.00 o.p. (*1-887178-22-8*) Basic Bks. (Counterpoint Pr.).

**CATTO, ROB (FICTITIOUS CHARACTER)—FICTION**

McLean, Duncan. Bunker Man. 1997. 297p. 13.00 (*0-393-31616-5*); 25.00 (*0-393-04121-2*) Norton, W. W. & Co., Inc.

**CATWOMAN (FICTITIOUS CHARACTER)—FICTION**

Abbey, Lynn & Asprin, Robert L. Catwoman. 1992. 208p. mass mkt. 4.99 (*0-446-36043-0*) Warner Bks., Inc.
DC Comics Staff. The Greatest Batman Stories Ever Told: Catwoman & the Penguin. 1992. (Illus.). (Orig.). pap. 14.99 o.s.i (*0-446-39427-0*) Warner Bks., Inc.
Dixon, Chuck, et al. Catwoman: The Catfile. 1996. (Illus.). 128p. pap. 9.95 (*1-56389-262-6*) DC Comics.
Gardner, Craig S. Batman Returns. 1992. 256p. (Orig.). mass mkt. 4.99 o.s.i (*0-446-36303-0*) Warner Bks., Inc.
Newell, Mindy. The Catwoman: Her Sister's Keeper. O'Neil, Dennis, ed. 1991. (Illus.). 104p. pap. 9.95 (*0-930289-97-8*) DC Comics.
Newell, Mindy, et al. The Catwoman: Her Sister's Keeper. 1992. (Illus.). 87p. reprint ed. pap. 9.99 o.s.i (*0-446-39366-5*) Warner Bks., Inc.

**CAULDER, RY (FICTITIOUS CHARACTER)—FICTION**

Lankford, Terrill. Angry Moon, unabr. ed. 1998. audio 49.95 (*0-7861-1347-2*, 2250) Blackstone Audio Bks., Inc.
—Angry Moon. 317p. 1999. mass mkt. 5.99 (*0-8125-4834-5*, Tor Bks.); 1997. 22.95 (*0-312-85726-8*, Forge Bks.) Doherty, Tom Assocs., LLC.

**CAULDHAME, FRANK (FICTITIOUS CHARACTER)—FICTION**

Banks, Iain M. The Wasp Factory, 001. 1984. 184p. 13.95 o.p. (*0-395-36296-2*) Houghton Mifflin Co.
—The Wasp Factory. 1998. 192p. pap. 13.00 (*0-684-85315-9*, Simon & Schuster) Simon & Schuster.
—The Wasp Factory. 1986. 192p. mass mkt. 3.95 o.s.i (*0-446-34087-1*) Warner Bks., Inc.

**CAULFIELD, AM (FICTITIOUS CHARACTER)—FICTION**

Russell, Alan. The Fat Innkeeper. 1995. 352p. 19.95 (*0-89296-539-8*) Mysterious Pr.
—The Fat Innkeeper. 1996. 304p. mass mkt. 5.99 (*0-446-40349-0*, Mysterious Pr. Paperback Bks.) Warner Bks., Inc.
—The Hotel Detective. 1994. 352p. 18.95 o.s.i (*0-89296-538-X*) Mysterious Pr.
—The Hotel Detective. 1995. 304p. mass mkt. 5.50 (*0-446-40348-2*) Warner Bks., Inc.

**CAULFIELD, HOLDEN (FICTITIOUS CHARACTER)—FICTION**

Salinger, J. D. The Catcher in the Rye. l.t. ed. 1993. pap. 19.95 o.p. (*0-7927-1516-0*) BBC Audiobooks America.
—The Catcher in the Rye. 1984. 224p. mass mkt. 3.95 o.s.i (*0-553-25025-6*) Bantam Bks.
—The Catcher in the Rye. 2002. 13.19 (*0-7587-7857-0*) Book Wholesalers, Inc.
—The Catcher in the Rye. 1991. 300p. reprint ed. lib. bdg. 23.95 o.p. (*0-89966-782-1*) Buccaneer Bks., Inc.
—The Catcher in the Rye. 2000. (RUS.). pap. 12.95 (*966-03-0586-9*) Folio, Editions UKR. *Dist:* Distribooks, Inc.
—The Catcher in the Rye. 2001. (Illus.). 288p. pap. 13.95 (*0-316-76917-7*, Back Bay); 1951. 277p. 25.95 (*0-316-76953-3*); 1991. 224p. reprint ed. mass mkt. 5.99 (*0-316-76948-7*) Little Brown & Co.
—The Catcher in the Rye. 1959. mass mkt. 0.50 o.p. (*0-451-01667-X*); mass mkt. 0.50 o.p. (*0-451-01001-9*) NAL. (Signet Bks.).
—The Catcher in the Rye, 2 vols., Set. l.t. ed. reprint ed. 10.00 (*0-89064-019-X*) National Assn. for Visually Handicapped.
—The Catcher in the Rye. 1991. 12.04 (*0-606-04887-1*) Turtleback Bks.
—The Catcher in the Rye. 2000. text 6.00 (*0-8220-7038-3*, Cliff Notes) Wiley, John & Sons, Inc.
—El Guardian Entre el Centeno.Tr. of Catcher in the Rye. (SPA.). 232p. 11.95 (*84-206-1689-3*); 2001. (Illus.). 236p. 11.95 (*84-206-3409-3*, AZ9200) Alianza Editorial, S. A. ESP. *Dist:* AIMS International Bks., Inc., Distribooks, Inc., AIMS International Bks., Inc., Lectorum Pubns., Inc.

—El Guardian Entre el Centeno. 1978. Tr. of Catcher in the Rye. 16.00 (*0-606-13453-0*) Turtleback Bks.

**CAUTHORNE, EDWARD (FICTITIOUS CHARACTER)—FICTION**

Thomas, Ross. The Singapore Wink. 1986. 224p. pap. 2.25 o.p. (*0-380-58537-5*, 58537-5, Avon Bks.) Morrow/Avon.

—The Singapore Wink. 1990. mass mkt. 4.95 (*0-445-77299-9*); 1987. mass mkt. 3.95 (*0-445-40558-9*); 1988. 224p. reprint ed. mass mkt. 5.99 (*0-445-40134-6*) Warner Bks., Inc.

**CAVANAUGH, KATE (FICTITIOUS CHARACTER)—FICTION**

John, Cathie, et al. Add One Dead Critic: Journals of Kate Cavanaugh. 1997. 249p. pap. 12.95 (*0-9634183-4-3*, Journey Bk. Pr.) C C Publishing.

—Beat a Rotten Egg to the Punch: Journals of Kate Cavanaugh. 1998. (Journals of Kate Cavanaugh Ser.). 287p. pap. 12.95 (*0-9634183-5-1*) C C Publishing.

—Carve a Witness to Shreds: A Kate Cavanaugh Mystery. 1999. (Journals of Kate Cavanaugh Ser.). 260p. (Orig.). pap. 12.95 (*0-9634183-6-X*, Journey Bk. Pr.) C C Publishing.

**CAVANAUGH, TRACY (FICTITIOUS CHARACTER)—FICTION**

Margolin, Phillip. After Dark. 1996. 384p. mass mkt. 7.99 (*0-553-56908-2*) Bantam Bks.

—After Dark. unabr. ed. 1996. audio 64.00 (*0-7366-3200-X*, 3864) Books on Tape, Inc.

—After Dark. l.t. ed. 1995. (Large Print Bks.). 24.95 o.p. (*1-56895-240-6*, Wheeler Publishing, Inc.) Gale Group.

—After Dark. 1995. audio 23.98 o.s.i (*0-553-74587-5*, RH Audio) Random Hse. Audio Publishing Group.

**CECILE, SISTER (FICTITIOUS CHARACTER)—FICTION**

Sullivan, Winona. Dead South: A Sister Cecile Mystery. 1997. (Sister Cecile Mystery Ser.). 275p. mass mkt. 5.99 o.s.i (*0-8041-1513-3*, Ivy Bks.) Ballantine Bks.

—Dead South: A Sister Cecile Mystery. 1996. 288p. 21.95 o.p. (*0-312-13959-4*, Saint Martin's Minotaur) St. Martin's Pr.

—Death's a Beach: A Sister Cecile Mystery. 1997. (Sister Cecile Mystery Ser.). 276p. mass mkt. 5.99 o.s.i (*0-8041-1568-0*, Ivy Bks.) Ballantine Bks.

—Saving Death: A Sister Cecile Mystery. 2000. 256p. mass mkt. 6.50 (*0-8041-1899-X*, Ivy Bks.) Ballantine Bks.

—A Sudden Death at the Norfolk Cafe: A Sister Cecile Mystery. 1995. (Sister Cecile Mystery Ser.). mass mkt. 5.99 o.s.i (*0-8041-1213-4*, Ivy Bks.) Ballantine Bks.

—A Sudden Death at the Norfolk Cafe: A Sister Cecile Mystery. 1993. 214p. 17.95 o.p. (*0-312-08899-X*, Saint Martin's Minotaur) St. Martin's Pr.

**CELLARS, COLIN (FICTITIOUS CHARACTER)—FICTION**

Goddard, Ken. First Evidence. 2000. (Illus.). 464p. reprint ed. mass mkt. 7.50 (*0-553-57913-4*) Bantam Bks.

—Outer Perimeter. 2001. 496p. mass mkt. 6.99 (*0-553-57916-9*) Bantam Bks.

**CELLINI, EMMANUEL (FICTITIOUS CHARACTER)—FICTION**

Hunt, Kyle, pseud. As Merry as Hell. 1974. 192p. 13.95 o.p. (*0-8128-1662-5*, Scarborough Hse.) Madison Bks., Inc.

—This Man Did I Kill? 1985. 256p. pap. 2.95 o.p. (*0-8128-8133-8*, Scarborough Hse.) Madison Bks., Inc.

**CELLUCI, MIKE (FICTITIOUS CHARACTER)—FICTION**

Huff, Tanya. Blood Debt. 1997. (Victory Nelson Ser.). 336p. mass mkt. 6.99 (*0-88677-739-9*) DAW Bks., Inc.

—Blood Lines, Bk. 3. 1993. (Daw Book Collectors Ser.: Vol. 901). 272p. (Orig.). mass mkt. 5.99 o.s.i (*0-88677-530-2*) DAW Bks., Inc.

—Blood Pact. 1993. (Daw Book Collectors Ser.: Vol. 931). 336p. mass mkt. 5.99 o.s.i (*0-88677-582-5*) DAW Bks., Inc.

—Blood Price. 1991. (Daw Book Collectors Ser.: Vol. 850). 272p. (Orig.). mass mkt. 6.99 (*0-88677-471-3*) DAW Bks., Inc.

—Blood Trail. 1992. (Victor Nelson Investigator Ser.: Vol. 3). 304p. (Orig.). mass mkt. 6.99 (*0-88677-502-7*) DAW Bks., Inc.

**CERVANTES, CHICO (FICTITIOUS CHARACTER)—FICTION**

Cook, Bruce. Death As a Career Move. 1992. 272p. 18.95 o.p. (*0-312-06946-4*, Saint Martin's Minotaur) St. Martin's Pr.

—Mexican Standoff. 1988. 256p. 16.95 o.p. (*0-531-15089-5*, Watts, Franklin) Scholastic Library Publishing.

—Mexican Standoff. 1990. mass mkt. 3.95 (*0-312-92114-4*, St. Martin's Paperbacks) St. Martin's Pr.

—Rough Cut. 1992. 2.99 o.p. (*0-517-09052-X*) Random Hse. Value Publishing.

—Rough Cut. 1990. 240p. 16.95 o.p. (*0-312-05149-2*, Saint Martin's Minotaur) St. Martin's Pr.

—The Sidewalk Hilton. 1994. 320p. 21.95 o.p. (*0-312-11062-6*, Saint Martin's Minotaur) St. Martin's Pr.

**CHADWICK, GEOFFREY (FICTITIOUS CHARACTER)—FICTION**

Phillips, Edward O. Buried on Sunday: A Geoffrey Chadwick Novel. 2000. 240p. pap. 11.99 (*1-896332-12-9*) Riverbank, Pr., The CAN. *Dist:* General Distribution Services, Inc.

—Buried on Sunday: A Geoffrey Chadwick Novel. 1988. 192p. 13.95 o.p. (*0-312-01742-1*, Saint Martin's Minotaur) St. Martin's Pr.

—Sunday's Child: A Geoffry Chadwick Novel. 2000. 280p. pap. 11.99 (*1-896332-07-2*) Riverbank, Pr., The CAN. *Dist:* General Distribution Services, Inc.

—Sunday's Child: A Geoffry Chadwick Novel. (Stonewall Inn Editions Ser.). 240p. 1988. pap. 7.95 o.p. (*0-312-02294-8*, Saint Martin's Griffin); 1987. 15.95 o.p. (*0-312-01097-4*) St. Martin's Pr.

**CHADWICK SISTERS (FICTITIOUS CHARACTERS)—FICTION**

Rogers, Evelyn. Angel. 1995. mass mkt. 4.99 o.s.i (*0-8217-5163-8*) Kensington Publishing Corp.

—Flame. 1994. 448p. mass mkt. 4.50 o.s.i (*0-8217-4491-7*, Zebra Bks.) Kensington Publishing Corp.

—Raven. 1995. 384p. mass mkt. 4.99 o.s.i (*0-8217-4800-9*, Zebra Bks.) Kensington Publishing Corp.

**CHAINEY, MARTHA (FICTITIOUS CHARACTER)—FICTION**

Phillips, Gary. High Hand. 2000. 32p. reprint ed. 22.00 o.s.i (*1-57566-616-2*, Dafina) Kensington Publishing Corp.

—High Hand: A Martha Chainey Mystery. 2001. 34p. mass mkt. 5.99 o.s.i (*1-57566-684-7*) Kensington Publishing Corp.

—Shooter's Point. 2002. 34p. mass mkt. 5.99 (*1-57566-745-2*); 2001. 24p. 22.00 (*1-57566-682-0*) Kensington Publishing Corp.

**CHAKOTAY (FICTITIOUS CHARACTER)—FICTION**

Carey, Diane L. Equinox. 1999. (Star Trek Voyager Ser.). 272p. (J). pap. 6.99 (*0-671-04295-5*, Star Trek) Simon & Schuster.

Cox, Greg. The Black Shore. 1997. (Star Trek Voyager Ser.: No. 13). (Illus.). 288p. mass mkt. 5.99 (*0-671-56061-1*, Star Trek) Simon & Schuster.

Galanter, Dave & Brodeur, Greg. Battle Lines. 1999. (Star Trek Voyager Ser.: No. 18). 264p. mass mkt. 6.50 o.s.i (*0-671-00259-7*, Star Trek) Simon & Schuster.

Garland, Mark A. & McGraw, Charles G. Ghost of a Chance. 1996. (Star Trek Voyager Ser.: No. 7). 288p. pap. 5.99 (*0-671-56798-5*, Star Trek) Simon & Schuster.

Golden, Christie. Ghost Dance Vol. 2: Dark Matters Trilogy. 2000. (Star Trek Voyager Ser.: No. 20). 288p. pap. 6.99 (*0-671-03583-5*, Star Trek) Simon & Schuster.

—Homecoming. 2003. (Star Trek Voyager Ser.). 288p. mass mkt. 6.99 (*0-7434-6754-X*);Bk. 1. E-Book 5.99 (*0-7434-7563-1*) Simon & Schuster. (Star Trek).

—Marooned. 1997. (Star Trek Voyager Ser.: No. 14). (Illus.). 304p. pap. 5.99 (*0-671-01423-4*, Star Trek) Simon & Schuster.

—The Murdered Sun. 1996. (Star Trek Voyager Ser.: No. 6). 288p. mass mkt. 5.99 o.s.i (*0-671-53783-0*, Star Trek) Simon & Schuster.

Graf, L. A. Caretaker. abr. ed. 1995. (Star Trek Voyager Ser.: No. 1). 17.00 o.s.i incl. audio (*0-671-52142-X*) Baen Bks.

—Caretaker. Ordover, John, ed. 1995. (Star Trek Voyager Ser.: No. 1). 288p. mass mkt. 5.99 Simon & Schuster.

Haber, Karen. Bless the Beasts. 1996. (Star Trek Voyager Ser.: No. 10). 288p. pap. 5.99 (*0-671-56780-2*, Star Trek) Simon & Schuster.

Lewitt, S. N. Cybersong. 1996. (Star Trek Voyager Ser.: No. 8). 288p. mass mkt. 5.99 (*0-671-56783-7*, Star Trek) Simon & Schuster.

Taylor, Jeri. Pathways. 1999. (Star Trek Voyager Ser.: Vol. 2). 528p. pap. 6.50 o.s.i (*0-671-02626-7*, Star Trek) Simon & Schuster.

—Pathways. abr. ed. 1998. (Star Trek Voyager Ser.: Vol. 2). 24.00 incl. audio (*0-671-58230-5*, Simon & Schuster Audioworks) Simon & Schuster Audio.

—Pathways. 1999. (Star Trek Voyager Ser.). 12.55 (*0-606-19503-3*) Turtleback Bks.

—Star Trek Voyager: Pathways. abr. ed. 1999. (Star Trek Voyager Ser.). audio 24.35 (*0-671-01115-4*) Ulverscroft Audio (U.S.A.).

Vornholt, John. Double Helix: Quarantine. 1999. (Star Trek, The Next Generation Ser.: No. 54). (Illus.). 304p. pap. 6.99 (*0-671-03477-4*, Star Trek) Simon & Schuster.

Wright, Susan. Violations. 1995. (Star Trek Voyager Ser.: No. 4). 288p. mass mkt. 5.99 (*0-671-52046-6*, Star Trek) Simon & Schuster.

**CHALLENGER, PROFESSOR (FICTITIOUS CHARACTER)—FICTION**

Doyle, Arthur Conan. The Lost World. 1989. 320p. pap. 12.00 (*0-89733-331-4*) Academy Chicago Pubs., Ltd.

—The Lost World. 1992. pap. text (*0-17-556535-X*) Addison-Wesley Longman, Inc.

—The Lost World. 1976. 21.95 (*0-8488-0990-4*) Amereon, Ltd.

—The Lost World. unabr. ed. 1998. audio 35.95 (*1-55685-583-4*) Audio Bk. Contractors, Inc.

—The Lost World. 1977. (J). (gr. 10 up). 0.95 o.s.i (*0-425-03514-X*) Berkley Publishing Group.

—The Lost World. unabr. ed. 1994. audio 44.95 (*0-7861-0844-4*, 1524) Blackstone Audio Bks., Inc.

—The Lost World. unabr. ed. 1989. audio 39.95 (*1-55686-294-6*, 294) Books in Motion.

—The Lost World. unabr. collector's ed. 1992. (J). audio 48.00 (*0-7366-2287-X*, 3073) Books on Tape, Inc.

—The Lost World. 1988. lib. bdg. 18.95 (*0-89966-233-1*) Buccaneer Bks., Inc.

—The Lost World. 248p. 1997. mass mkt. 4.99 (*0-8125-6483-9*, Tor Classics); 1993. mass mkt. 4.99 o.s.i (*0-8125-3468-9*, Tor Bks.) Doherty, Tom Assocs., LLC.

—The Lost World. 1998. (Thrift Editions Ser.). 176p. pap. 2.00 (*0-486-40060-3*) Dover Pubns., Inc.

—The Lost World. abr. ed. 1986. audio 29.95 o.p. (*0-88646-802-7*, R 7070) Durkin Hayes Publishing Ltd.

—The Lost World. l.t. ed. 1998. (Large Print Heritage Ser.). 340p. lib. bdg. 31.95 (*1-58118-034-9*, 22017) LRS.

—The Lost World. Matthews, Sarah, ed. 1996. (Thornes Classic Novels Ser.). (Illus.). 243p. pap. 16.95 (*0-7487-2481-8*) Nelson Thornes GBR. *Dist:* Trans-Atlantic Pubns., Inc.

—The Lost World. 1999. (Twelve-Point Ser.). lib. bdg. 25.00 (*1-58287-112-4*) North Bks.

—The Lost World. Duncan, Ian, ed. 1998. (Oxford World's Classics Ser.). 768p. pap. 9.95 (*0-19-283352-9*) Oxford Univ. Pr., Inc.

—The Lost World. Duncan, Ian & Trotter, David, eds. 1995. (Oxford Popular Fiction Ser.). 216p. pap. 7.95 o.p. (*0-19-283186-0*) Oxford Univ. Pr., Inc.

—The Lost World. 2003. (Illus.). 272p. pap. 8.95 (*0-8129-6725-9*, Modern Library) Random House Adult Trade Publishing Group.

—The Lost World. unabr. ed. 1999. audio 51.00 (*0-7887-0474-5*, 94667E7) Recorded Bks., LLC.

—The Lost World. abr. ed. audio 10.95 Spoken Arts, Inc.

—The Lost World. adapted ed. 1998. audio 15.00 (*0-9661287-1-0*) Star Quest Entertainment.

—The Lost World. unabr. ed. 2003. audio compact disk 39.00 (*1-4001-0086-0*); (YA). audio compact disk 20.00 (*1-4001-5086-8*) Tantor Media, Inc.

—The Lost World. 1998. (Classics Library). 480p. pap. 3.95 (*1-85326-245-5*, 2455WW) Wordsworth Editions, Ltd. GBR. *Dist:* Casemate Pubs. & Bk. Distributors, LLC.

—The Lost World, 2 Cass. 1996. audio 18.00 (*1-884214-02-9*) Ziggurat Productions.

Doyle, Arthur Conan, et al. The Annotated Lost World. 1996. (Illus.). 288p. 34.95 (*0-938501-23-2*) Wessex Pr.

**CHAMBERLAIN, JOSHUA LAWRENCE, 1828-1914—FICTION**

Shaara, Jeff. The Last Full Measure. 1998. 576p. 27.95 (*0-345-40491-2*) Ballantine Bks.

—The Last Full Measure: A Novel. l.t. ed. 1998. pap. 25.00 o.s.i (*0-375-70291-1*) Random Hse. Large Print.

Shaara, Jeff, ed. The Last Full Measure. 2000. 640p. mass mkt. 7.99 (*0-345-43481-1*, Ballantine Bks.); 1999. (Illus.). 576p. pap. 14.95 (*0-345-42548-0*); 1998. 25.95 o.s.i (*0-345-43003-4*) Ballantine Bks.

—The Last Full Measure. l.t. ed. 1998. pap. 25.00 o.p. (*0-7838-0155-6*, Macmillan Reference USA) Gale Group.

—The Last Full Measure. 2000. E-Book 12.50 (*0-345-43850-7*) Random Hse., Inc.

Shaara, Michael. The Killer Angels. unabr. ed. 1997. audio 39.95 (*1-57270-058-0*, M91058u, Audio Editions Bks. on Cassette) Audio Partners Publishing Corp.

—The Killer Angels. 1996. 400p. pap. 13.95 (*0-345-40727-X*); 1993. mass mkt. 5.99 o.p. (*0-345-01999-7*); 1987. (Illus.). 384p. mass mkt. 7.99 (*0-345-34810-9*); 1983. mass mkt. 2.95 o.p. (*0-345-31640-1*); 1980. mass mkt. 2.75 o.p. (*0-345-29535-8*); 1980. mass mkt. 2.50 o.p. (*0-345-28605-7*); 1978. mass mkt. 1.95 o.p. (*0-345-27652-3*); 1976. mass mkt. 1.95 o.p. (*0-345-25487-2*); 1975. mass mkt. 1.95 o.p. (*0-345-24528-8*) Ballantine Bks.

—The Killer Angels. unabr. ed. 1994. audio 62.95 (*1-886175-00-4*, C137) Blackstone Audio Bks., Inc.

—The Killer Angels. unabr. collector's ed. 1986. audio 72.00 (*0-7366-1031-6*, 1961) Books on Tape, Inc.

—The Killer Angels. abr. ed. 1995. audio 24.95 o.p. (*1-886175-02-0*); 1994. audio 49.95 (*1-886175-01-2*); Set. 1994. 49.95 incl. audio Cathedral Audio Bks., Inc.

—The Killer Angels. 1974. 19.95 o.s.i (*0-679-50466-4*) McKay, David Co., Inc.

—The Killer Angels. l.t. ed. 2004. 592p. 27.95 (*0-375-43310-4*) Random Hse. Large Print.

—The Killer Angels. 1993. (Illus.). 400p. 25.00 o.s.i (*0-679-42541-1*) Random Hse., Inc.

—The Killer Angels. unabr. ed. 1991. audio 109.00 (*1-55690-282-4*, 91118E7) Recorded Bks., LLC.

—The Killer Angels. 1975. 14.04 (*0-606-01203-6*) Turtleback Bks.

**CHAMBERLAIN, LINDSAY (FICTITIOUS CHARACTER)—FICTION**

Connor, Beverly. Airtight Case. (Lindsay Chamberlain Novel Ser.). (Illus.). 2002. 480p. mass mkt. 7.99 (*1-58182-295-2*); 2000. 423p. 22.95 (*1-58182-123-9*) Cumberland Hse. Publishing.

—Dressed to Die: A Lindsay Chamberlain Novel. 1998. (Lindsay Chamberlain Mysteries Ser.). 320p. 20.95 (*1-888952-89-X*) Cumberland Hse. Publishing.

—Questionable Remains. 1997. (Lindsay Chamberlain Mysteries Ser.). 288p. 20.95 (*1-888952-53-9*) Cumberland Hse. Publishing.

—Questionable Remains. 2001. (WWL Mystery Ser.: No. 385). 248p. mass mkt. (*0-373-26385-6*, 1-26385-4, Worldwide Library) Harlequin Enterprises, Ltd.

—A Rumor of Bones. 1996. (Lindsay Chamberlain Mysteries Ser.: Vol. 1). (Illus.). 254p. 20.95 o.p. (*1-888952-08-3*) Cumberland Hse. Publishing.

—Skeleton Crew. 1999. (Lindsay Chamberlain Mysteries Ser.: Vol. 3). (Illus.). 352p. 20.95 (*1-58182-042-9*, Cumberland Hearthside) Cumberland Hse. Publishing.

—Skeleton Crew: A Lindsay Chamberlain Novel. 2002. (Illus.). 432p. reprint ed. mass mkt. 7.99 (*1-58182-287-1*) Cumberland Hse. Publishing.

**CHAMBRUN, PIERRE (FICTITIOUS CHARACTER)—FICTION**

Pentecost, Hugh. Bargain with Death. 1989. 224p. reprint ed. mass mkt. (*0-373-26018-0*, Harlequin Bks.) Harlequin Enterprises, Ltd.

—Beware Young Lovers. 1982. (Nightingale Ser.). pap. 9.95 o.p. (*0-8161-3458-8*, Macmillan Reference USA) Gale Group.

—Beware Young Lovers. 1990. 224p. mass mkt. (*0-373-26057-1*, Harlequin Bks.) Harlequin Enterprises, Ltd.

—The Cannibal Who Overate. 1990. 191p. mass mkt. 3.95 (*0-88184-614-7*, Carroll & Graf Pubs.) Avalon Publishing Group.

—The Cannibal Who Overate. l.t. ed. 1986. (Nightingale Ser.). 283p. 10.95 o.p. (*0-8161-3998-9*, Macmillan Reference USA) Gale Group.

—The Copycat Killers. l.t. ed. 1984. (Nightingale Ser.). pap. 9.95 o.p. (*0-8161-3662-9*, Macmillan Reference USA) Gale Group.

—Death After Breakfast. 1980. pap. 2.25 o.p. (*0-440-11687-2*) Dell Publishing.

—Fourteen Dilemma. 1990. mass mkt. (*0-373-26045-8*, Harlequin Bks.) Harlequin Enterprises, Ltd.

—Murder As Usual. l.t. ed. 1997. (Linford Mystery Library). 368p. pap. 17.99 o.p. (*0-7089-5103-1*, Linford) Thorpe, F. A. Pubs. GBR. *Dist:* Ulverscroft Large Print Bks., Ltd., Ulverscroft Large Print Canada, Ltd.

—Murder Goes Round & Round. l.t. ed. 1998. (Linford Mystery Library). 272p. pap. 17.99 o.p. (*0-7089-5218-6*, Linford) Thorpe, F. A. Pubs. GBR. *Dist:* Ulverscroft Large Print Bks., Ltd., Ulverscroft Large Print Canada, Ltd.

—Murder in High Places. 1992. (WWL Mystery Ser.: No. 94). mass mkt. (*0-373-26094-6*, 1-26094-2, Harlequin Bks.) Harlequin Enterprises, Ltd.

—Murder in Luxury. 1991. 224p. mass mkt. (*0-373-26069-5*, Harlequin Bks.) Harlequin Enterprises, Ltd.

—Nightmare Time: A Pierre Chambrun Mystery Novel. 1988. 224p. mass mkt. (*0-373-26001-6*, Harlequin Bks.) Harlequin Enterprises, Ltd.

—Nightmare Time: A Pierre Chambrun Mystery Novel. l.t. ed. 1988. (Linford Mystery Library). 304p. pap. 17.99 o.p. (*0-7089-6563-6*, Linford) Thorpe, F. A. Pubs. GBR. *Dist:* Ulverscroft Large Print Bks., Ltd., Ulverscroft Large Print Canada, Ltd.

—Pattern for Terror. 1990. 15.95 o.p. (*0-88184-519-1*, Carroll & Graf Pubs.) Avalon Publishing Group.

—Pattern for Terror. l.t. ed. 1993. (Nightingale Ser.). 208p. pap. 14.95 o.p. (*0-8161-5637-9*, Macmillan Reference USA) Gale Group.

—Random Killer. 1981. pap. 2.25 o.p. (*0-440-17210-1*) Dell Publishing.

—Remember to Kill Me. l.t. ed. 1985. (Nightingale Ser.). 299p. 10.95 o.p. (*0-8161-3848-6*, Macmillan Reference USA) Gale Group.
—Remember to Kill Me. 1988. 224p. reprint ed. pap. (*0-373-26010-5*, Harlequin Bks.) Harlequin Enterprises, Ltd.
—Time of Terror. 1989. mass mkt. (*0-373-26033-4*, Harlequin Bks.) Harlequin Enterprises, Ltd.
—Walking Dead Man. l.t. ed. 1997. (Linford Mystery Library). 368p. pap. 17.99 o.p. (*0-7089-5158-9*, Ulverscroft) Thorpe, F. A. Pubs. GBR. *Dist:* Ulverscroft Large Print Bks., Ltd., Ulverscroft Large Print Canada, Ltd.
—With Intent to Kill: A Pierre Chambrun Mystery Movel. 1991. reprint ed. mass mkt. (*0-373-26081-4*, Harlequin Bks.) Harlequin Enterprises, Ltd.

**CHAN, CHARLIE (FICTITIOUS CHARACTER)—FICTION**

Biggers, Earl Derr. Behind that Curtain. 1987. 240p. reprint ed. mass mkt. 3.95 o.s.i (*0-445-40214-8*, Mysterious Pr. Paperback Bks.) Warner Bks., Inc.
—The Black Camel. Date not set. 224p. 21.95 (*0-8488-2211-0*) Amereon, Ltd.
—The Black Camel. 1978. reprint ed. lib. bdg. 27.95 (*0-89966-077-0*) Buccaneer Bks., Inc.
—The Black Camel. 1987. 224p. reprint ed. mass mkt. 3.95 o.s.i (*0-445-40215-6*, Mysterious Pr. Paperback Bks.) Warner Bks., Inc.
—Charlie Chan Carries On. 1976. (Charlie Chan Mysteries Ser.). reprint ed. lib. bdg. 23.95 o.p. (*0-89966-073-8*) Buccaneer Bks., Inc.
—Charlie Chan Carries On. 1987. 224p. mass mkt. 3.95 o.s.i (*0-445-40221-0*, Mysterious Pr. Paperback Bks.) Warner Bks., Inc.
—The Chinese Parrot. 1990. mass mkt. 3.95 o.p. (*0-445-40212-1*); 1987. 224p. reprint ed. mass mkt. 3.95 o.s.i (*0-445-40211-3*, Mysterious Pr. Paperback Bks.) Warner Bks., Inc.
—The House Without a Key. Date not set. lib. bdg. 24.95 (*0-8488-1956-X*) Amereon, Ltd.
—The House Without a Key. 1979. reprint ed. lib. bdg. 35.95 (*0-89966-081-9*) Buccaneer Bks., Inc.
—The House Without a Key. 2003. 316p. pap. 14.95 (*1-891936-65-4*, D'Asia Vu Reprint Library) EastBridge.
—The House Without a Key. 1994. 316p. 35.00 (*1-883402-23-9*, Scribner) Simon & Schuster.
—The House Without a Key. 1986. 240p. mass mkt. 3.95 o.s.i (*0-445-40219-9*, Mysterious Pr. Paperback Bks.) Warner Bks., Inc.
—Keeper of the Keys. 1988. 224p. mass mkt. 3.95 o.s.i (*0-445-40217-2*, Mysterious Pr. Paperback Bks.) Warner Bks., Inc.
Mitchell, Charles P. A Guide to Charlie Chan Films. 1999. (Bibliographies & Indexes in the Performing Arts Ser.: Vol. 23). 312p. text 76.95 (*0-313-30985-X*) Greenwood Publishing Group, Inc.

**CHAN, DAVID (FICTITIOUS CHARACTER)—FICTION**

Hurst, Jim. Fatal Image. 1998. 200p. (Orig.). pap. 14.50 (*0-88739-120-6*) Creative Arts Bk. Co.

**CHANCEL, NORA (FICTITIOUS CHARACTER)—FICTION**

Straub, Peter. Circulo Diabolico. 1998. (SPA.). 466p. (*84-08-02053-6*) GeoPlaneta, Editorial, S. A.
—The Hellfire Club. 1997. (ACE.). 544p. mass mkt. 7.99 (*0-345-41500-0*); mass mkt. 6.99 o.s.i (*0-345-41505-1*) Ballantine Bks.
—The Hellfire Club. l.t. ed. 1996. (Large Print Bks.). 25.95 o.p. (*1-56895-337-2*, Wheeler Publishing, Inc.) Gale Group.
—The Hellfire Club. abr. ed. 1996. 6p. audio 25.00 (*0-671-73860-7*, Simon & Schuster Audioworks) Simon & Schuster Audio.

**CHANDLER, CHUCK (FICTITIOUS CHARACTER)—FICTION**

Woods, Stuart. Choke. unabr. ed. 1995. audio 56.00 (*0-7366-3192-5*, 3858) Books on Tape, Inc.
—Choke. l.t. ed. 1995. (Large Print Bks.). 25.95 o.p. (*1-56895-265-1*, Wheeler Publishing, Inc.) Gale Group.
—Choke. 1995. 320p. 23.00 o.p. (*0-06-017667-9*, Perennial); audio 17.00 o.p. (*0-694-51603-1*, HarperAudio) HarperTrade.
—Choke. 1996. 352p. mass mkt. 7.99 (*0-06-109422-6*, HarperTorch) Morrow/Avon.
—Choke, unabr. ed. audio 60.00 (*0-7887-0446-X*, 94642E7) Recorded Bks., LLC.

**CHANDLER, JAY (FICTITIOUS CHARACTER)—FICTION**

Faust, Ron. Lord of the Dark Lake. 2000. 320p. pap. 13.95 (*0-312-87510-X*, Forge Bks.); 1998. mass mkt. 6.99 (*0-8125-3023-3*, Tor Bks.); 1996. 320p. 22.95 o.p. (*0-312-85535-4*, Forge Bks.) Doherty, Tom Assocs., LLC.

**CHANDLER, LAUREL (FICTITIOUS CHARACTER)—FICTION**

Hoag, Tami. Cry Wolf. 1997. 560p. mass mkt. 7.99 (*0-553-56160-X*) Bantam Bks.

**CHANDLER, SHAW (FICTITIOUS CHARACTER)—FICTION**

Hall, James W. Bones of Coral. 1993. 400p. mass mkt. 7.50 (*0-440-21453-X*) Dell Publishing.
—Bones of Coral. 1992. 3.99 o.p. (*0-517-08828-2*) Random Hse. Value Publishing.
—Bones of Coral, unabr. ed. audio 85.00 (*1-55690-668-4*, 92316E7) Recorded Bks., LLC.

**CHANDLER, SUSAN (FICTITIOUS CHARACTER)—FICTION**

Clark, Mary Higgins. You Belong to Me. unabr. ed. 1998. audio 56.00 (*0-7366-4189-0*, 4687) Books on Tape, Inc.
—You Belong to Me. 2000. E-Book 9.95 (*0-7432-0629-0*, Simon & Schuster); 1999. 384p. mass mkt. 7.99 (*0-671-00454-9*, Pocket); 1998. 320p. 25.00 (*0-684-83595-9*, Simon & Schuster); 1998. 496p. 25.00 (*0-684-84330-7*, Simon & Schuster) Simon & Schuster.
—You Belong to Me. abr. ed. 1998. audio compact disk 22.50 (*0-671-58196-1*); audio 18.00 (*0-671-58066-3*, 393596) Simon & Schuster Audio. (Simon & Schuster Audioworks).

**CHANG, MAVRA (FICTITIOUS CHARACTER)—FICTION**

Chalker, Jack L. Echoes of the Well of Souls. 1993. (Watchers at the Well Ser.: Bk. 1). 320p. mass mkt. 5.99 o.s.i (*0-345-38686-8*); 352p. pap. 19.00 (*0-345-36201-2*) Ballantine Bks. (Del Rey).
—Gods of the Well of Souls. (Watchers at the Well Ser.: Bk. 3). 1995. mass mkt. 5.99 o.s.i (*0-345-38850-X*); 1994. 448p. pap. 10.00 o.p. (*0-345-36203-9*) Ballantine Bks. (Del Rey).
—Shadow of the Well of Souls. 1994. (Watchers at the Well Ser.: Bk. 2). (Orig.). 368p. mass mkt. 5.99 o.s.i (*0-345-38846-1*); 345p. pap. 10.00 o.s.i (*0-345-36202-0*, Del Rey) Ballantine Bks.

**CHANTRY FAMILY (FICTITIOUS CHARACTERS)—FICTION**

L'Amour, Louis. Borden Chantry. 1999. mass mkt. (*0-553-22814-5*); 1995. 176p. mass mkt. 4.50 (*0-553-27863-0*); 1988. mass mkt. 3.50 o.s.i (*0-553-28030-9*); 1984. mass mkt. 2.95 o.s.i (*0-553-25030-2*) Bantam Bks.
—Borden Chantry. l.t. ed. 1979. 12.50 o.p. (*0-7089-0312-6*, Ulverscroft) Thorpe, F. A. Pubs. GBR. *Dist:* Ulverscroft Large Print Bks., Ltd.
—Fair Blows the Wind. 1999. mass mkt. (*0-553-20865-9*); 1981. mass mkt. 2.95 o.s.i (*0-553-25612-2*); 1981. 288p. mass mkt. 4.50 (*0-553-27629-8*) Bantam Bks.
—Fair Blows the Wind. 1978. 7.95 o.p. (*0-525-10260-4*, Dutton) Dutton/Plume.
—Fair Blows the Wind. 1979. (gr. 7-12). lib. bdg. 14.95 o.p. (*0-8161-6719-2*, Macmillan Reference USA) Gale Group.
—The Ferguson Rifle. 1985. 192p. mass mkt. 4.50 (*0-553-25303-4*) Bantam Bks.
—The Ferguson Rifle. l.t. ed. 1983. (Ulverscroft Large Print Ser.). 288p. o.p. (*0-7089-0977-9*, Ulverscroft) Thorpe, F. A. Pubs. GBR. *Dist:* Ulverscroft Large Print Canada, Ltd.
—North to the Rails. 1987. 192p. mass mkt. 4.50 (*0-553-28086-4*); 1982. 176p. mass mkt. 2.95 o.s.i (*0-553-25973-3*) Bantam Bks.
—North to the Rails. l.t. ed. 1975. o.p. (*0-85456-312-1*, Ulverscroft) Thorpe, F. A. Pubs.
—Over on the Dry Side. 1999. mass mkt. (*0-553-20795-4*); 1985. 192p. reprint ed. mass mkt. 4.50 (*0-553-25321-2*) Bantam Bks.
—Over on the Dry Side. 1975. 224p. 6.95 o.p. (*0-8415-0389-3*, Dutton) Dutton/Plume.
—Over on the Dry Side. l.t. ed. 1976. (Winter Adult Ser.). reprint ed. lib. bdg. 9.95 o.p. (*0-8161-6410-X*, Macmillan Reference USA) Gale Group.

**CHAPMAN, HARRY (FICTITIOUS CHARACTER)—FICTION**

Allbeury, Ted. A Time Without Shadows. 1991. 19.95 o.p. (*0-89296-432-4*) Mysterious Pr.
—A Time Without Shadows, unabr. ed. 1991. audio 60.00 (*1-55690-515-7*, 91324E7) Recorded Bks., LLC.
—A Time Without Shadows. 1992. 304p. mass mkt. 4.99 (*0-446-40090-4*, Mysterious Pr. Paperback Bks.) Warner Bks., Inc.

**CHARLES, NICK (FICTITIOUS CHARACTER)—FICTION**

Hammett, Dashiell. The Thin Man. Date not set. (Thin Man Ser.). 137p. 18.95 (*0-8488-2438-5*) Amereon, Ltd.
—The Thin Man. unabr. ed. 1998. audio 42.00 (*0-7366-4002-9*, 4501) Books on Tape, Inc.
—The Thin Man, , abr. ed. 1987. (Thin Man Ser.). audio 17.00 o.s.i (*0-89845-591-X*, CPN2106, Caedmon) HarperTrade.
—The Thin Man. (Thin Man Ser.). 1992. pap. 9.00 (*0-394-23905-9*); 1989. 208p. pap. 11.00 (*0-679-72263-7*) Knopf Publishing Group. (Vintage).
—The Thin Man. (Thin Man Ser.). 1992. pap. 9.00 (*0-679-74092-9*); 1972. pap. 2.95 o.p. (*0-394-71774-0*) Random Hse., Inc.
—The Thin Man. 1994. (Thin Man Ser.). 272p. 35.00 (*1-883402-70-0*, Scribner) Simon & Schuster.
—The Thin Man. l.t. ed. 2001. (Perennial Bestsellers Ser.). 269p. 28.95 (*0-7838-9460-0*) Thorndike Pr.

**CHARLES, NORA (FICTITIOUS CHARACTER)—FICTION**

Hammett, Dashiell. The Thin Man. Date not set. (Thin Man Ser.). 137p. 18.95 (*0-8488-2438-5*) Amereon, Ltd.
—The Thin Man. unabr. ed. 1998. audio 42.00 (*0-7366-4002-9*, 4501) Books on Tape, Inc.
—The Thin Man, , abr. ed. 1987. (Thin Man Ser.). audio 17.00 o.s.i (*0-89845-591-X*, CPN2106, Caedmon) HarperTrade.
—The Thin Man. (Thin Man Ser.). 1992. pap. 9.00 (*0-394-23905-9*); 1989. 208p. pap. 11.00 (*0-679-72263-7*) Knopf Publishing Group. (Vintage).
—The Thin Man. (Thin Man Ser.). 1992. pap. 9.00 (*0-679-74092-9*); 1972. pap. 2.95 o.p. (*0-394-71774-0*) Random Hse., Inc.
—The Thin Man. 1994. (Thin Man Ser.). 272p. 35.00 (*1-883402-70-0*, Scribner) Simon & Schuster.
—The Thin Man. l.t. ed. 2001. (Perennial Bestsellers Ser.). 269p. 28.95 (*0-7838-9460-0*) Thorndike Pr.

**CHARTERS, EMILY (FICTITIOUS CHARACTER)—FICTION**

Hunter, Fred. Presence of Mind. 1998. (WWL Mystery Ser.). per. (*0-373-26282-5*, 1-26282-3, Worldwide Library) Harlequin Enterprises, Ltd.
—Presence of Mind. 1994. 19.95 (*0-8027-3245-3*) Walker & Co.
—Ransom at Sea. 2003. 272p. 23.95 (*0-312-30066-2*, Saint Martin's Minotaur) St. Martin's Pr.
—Ransom at the Opera. E-Book 22.95 (*0-312-27643-5*); 2000. 244p. 22.95 (*0-312-26257-4*, Saint Martin's Minotaur) St. Martin's Pr.
—Ransom for a Holiday. 1997. (Jeremy Ransom/Emily Charters Mysteries Ser.). 240p. 20.95 (*0-312-16976-0*, Saint Martin's Minotaur) St. Martin's Pr.
—Ransom for a Killing, 329. 1999. (WWL Mystery Ser.: Vol. 329). mass mkt. (*0-373-26329-5*, Worldwide Library) Harlequin Enterprises, Ltd.
—Ransom for a Killing. 1998. (Jeremy Ransom/Emily Charters Mysteries Ser.). 240p. 21.95 o.p. (*0-312-19323-8*, Saint Martin's Minotaur) St. Martin's Pr.
—Ransom for an Angel. 1996. mass mkt. (*0-373-26224-8*, 1-26224-5, Worldwide Library) Harlequin Enterprises, Ltd.
—Ransom for an Angel. 1995. 246p. 19.95 (*0-8027-3253-4*) Walker & Co.
—Ransom for Our Sins. 1997. per. (*0-373-26249-3*, 1-26249-2, Worldwide Library) Harlequin Enterprises, Ltd.
—Ransom for Our Sins. 1996. 238p. 22.95 (*0-8027-3284-4*) Walker & Co.
—Ransom Unpaid. 2000. (WWL Mystery Ser.: Vol. 365). mass mkt. (*0-373-26365-1*, 1-26365-6, Worldwide Library) Harlequin Enterprises, Ltd.
—Ransom Unpaid. 1999. 216p. 22.95 (*0-312-24233-6*, Saint Martin's Minotaur) St. Martin's Pr.
Smith, Barbara B., et al. 'Tis the Season for Murder: Christmas Crimes. 1998. mass mkt. (*0-373-26290-6*, 1-26290-6, Worldwide Library) Harlequin Enterprises, Ltd.

**CHASE, ELIZABETH (FICTITIOUS CHARACTER)—FICTION**

Lawrence, Martha C. Aquarius Descending. (Elizabeth Chase Mysteries Ser.). 2000. 320p. mass mkt. 5.99 (*0-312-97284-9*, St. Martin's Paperbacks); 1998. 304p. 23.95 o.p. (*0-312-19829-9*, Saint Martin's Minotaur) St. Martin's Pr.
—Aquarius Descending Newsletter Kit. Date not set. pap. (*0-312-20695-X*, Saint Martin's Griffin) St. Martin's Pr.
—Aries Raging. 2002. 288p. mass mkt. 6.99 (*0-312-98041-8*, St. Martin's Paperbacks) St. Martin's Pr.
—Ashes of Aries. 2001. 256p. 23.95 (*0-312-20299-7*, Saint Martin's Minotaur) St. Martin's Pr.
—The Cold Heart of Capricorn. 240p. 1996. text 21.95 o.p. (*0-312-14569-1*, Saint Martin's Minotaur); Vol. 1. 1998. mass mkt. 5.99 o.s.i (*0-312-96294-0*, St. Martin's Paperbacks) St. Martin's Pr.
—Murder in Scorpio. 1996. 227p. mass mkt. 5.50 (*0-312-95984-2*, St. Martin's Paperbacks); 1995. 256p. 21.95 (*0-312-13567-X*, Saint Martin's Minotaur) St. Martin's Pr.
—Pisces Rising. 2000. 254p. 23.95 o.p. (*0-312-20298-9*, Saint Martin's Minotaur); 2001. 272p. reprint ed. mass mkt. 6.50 (*0-312-97447-7*, St. Martin's Paperbacks) St. Martin's Pr.

**CHASE, LINDSAY (FICTITIOUS CHARACTER)—FICTION**

Rossi, Mitchell S. The Hong Kong Sanction. 1997. 384p. mass mkt. 5.99 o.s.i (*0-7860-0400-2*, Pinnacle Bks.) Kensington Publishing Corp.

**CHASE, NIKKI (FICTITIOUS CHARACTER)—FICTION**

Thomas-Graham, Pamela. Blue Blood. (Ivy League Mysteries Ser.). 1999. 288p. 23.00 (*0-684-84527-X*, Simon & Schuster); 2000. 320p. reprint ed. pap. 6.99 (*0-671-01671-7*, Pocket) Simon & Schuster.
—A Darker Shade of Crimson: An Ivy League Mystery. (Ivy League Mysteries Ser.). 1999. (Illus.). 416p. pap. 6.99 (*0-671-01670-9*, Pocket); 1998. 288p. 23.00 (*0-684-84526-1*, Simon & Schuster) Simon & Schuster.

**CHASE, SIMON (FICTITIOUS CHARACTER)—FICTION**

Benchley, Peter. Peter Benchley's Creature. 1998. 352p. mass mkt. 6.99 (*0-312-96573-7*, St. Martin's Paperbacks) St. Martin's Pr.
—White Shark. l.t. ed. 1995. (Magna Large Print Ser.). (Illus.). 497p. o.p. (*0-7505-0860-4*) Magna Large Print Bks. GBR. *Dist:* Ulverscroft Large Print Canada, Ltd.
—White Shark. 1995. 340p. mass mkt. 6.50 (*0-312-95573-1*, St. Martin's Paperbacks) St. Martin's Pr.

**CHASTAIN, LAURA (FICTITIOUS CHARACTER)—FICTION**

Kelly, Lelia. False Witness. 2000. 416p. mass mkt. 6.99 o.s.i (*0-7860-1193-9*); 312p. 23.00 o.s.i (*1-57566-490-9*, Kensington Bks.) Kensington Publishing Corp.
—Presumption of Guilt. 1998. 352p. mass mkt. 5.99 (*0-7860-0584-X*, Pinnacle Bks.); 224p. 22.95 o.s.i (*1-57566-249-3*) Kensington Publishing Corp.

**CHATTO, TOM (FICTITIOUS CHARACTER)—FICTION**

McCutchan, Philip. The New Lieutenant. 1997. 192p. 20.95 (*0-312-15604-9*) St. Martin's Pr.
—The New Lieutenant. l.t. ed. 1997. (General Ser.). 266p. pap. 22.95 (*0-7862-1127-X*) Thorndike Pr.

**CHAUCER, GEOFFREY, D. 1400—FICTION**

Darby, Catherine. Love Knot. 1991. 16.95 o.p. (*0-312-04996-X*) St. Martin's Pr.
Devlin, Mary. Murder on the Canterbury Pilgrimage: A Geoffrey Chaucer Murder Mystery. 2000. 252p. pap. 13.95 (*0-595-09878-9*, Writers Club Pr.) iUniverse, Inc.
Grace, C. L. The Merchant of Death. 1995. 182p. (YA). 19.95 (*0-312-13124-0*, Saint Martin's Minotaur) St. Martin's Pr.
Robb, Candace. A Gift of Sanctuary: An Owen Archer Mystery. 2000. (Owen Archer Mystery Ser.: Vol. 6). 320p. mass mkt. 6.99 (*0-312-97477-9*, St. Martin's Paperbacks); 1998. 304p. 22.95 o.p. (*0-312-19266-5*, Saint Martin's Minotaur) St. Martin's Pr.
—A Gift of Sanctuary: An Owen Archer Mystery. l.t. ed. 1999. (Mystery Ser.). 475p. 28.95 (*0-7862-1910-6*); (*0-7540-1302-2*); (*0-7540-2226-9*) Thorndike Pr.

**CHEE, JIM (FICTITIOUS CHARACTER)—FICTION**

Hillerman, Tony. Coyote Waits. unabr. ed. 1990. audio 42.00 (*0-7366-1788-4*, 2625) Books on Tape, Inc.
—Coyote Waits. 1990. 292p. 75.00 o.p. (*0-06-016422-0*); 1990. 292p. 19.95 o.p. (*0-06-016370-4*); 1995. 3p. audio 18.00 o.s.i (*1-55994-198-7*, 390569, HarperAudio); 1990. pap. 19.95 o.p. (*0-06-016423-9*) HarperTrade.
—Coyote Waits. 1992. 368p. mass mkt. 6.99 (*0-06-109932-5*, HarperTorch) Morrow/Avon.
—Coyote Waits. 1990. audio 10.00 New Letters on Air.
—Coyote Waits. 1990. (J). 13.04 (*0-606-01125-0*) Turtleback Bks.
—The Dark Wind. unabr. ed. 1994. audio 42.00 (*0-7366-2689-1*, 3424) Books on Tape, Inc.
—The Dark Wind. 1982. 224p. o.p. (*0-06-014936-1*) HarperCollins Pubs.
—The Dark Wind. 1990. 320p. reprint ed. mass mkt. 6.99 (*0-06-100003-5*, Perennial); Set. 1993. audio 18.00 (*1-55994-774-8*, CPN 4032, HarperAudio) HarperTrade.
—The Dark Wind. 1993. audio 39.80. audio Literate Ear, Inc.
—The Dark Wind. 1992. 79p. mass mkt. 5.99 o.p. (*0-06-100491-X*, HarperTorch); 1983. 224p. pap. 3.50 o.p. (*0-380-63321-3*, Avon Bks.) Morrow/Avon.
—The Dark Wind. unabr. ed. 1990. (Jim Chee Mystery Ser.: Vol. 2). (YA). (gr. 10 up). audio 51.00 (*1-55690-136-4*, 91101E7) Recorded Bks., LLC.
—The Fallen Man. unabr. ed. 1997. audio 42.00 (*0-913369-37-3*, 4211) Books on Tape, Inc.
—The Fallen Man. 1996. 304p. 24.00 o.p. (*0-06-017773-X*) HarperCollins Pubs.

—The Fallen Man, Set. abr. ed. 1996. (Joe Leaphorn Mystery Ser.). audio 25.00 (*1-55994-978-3*, 694496, HarperAudio) HarperTrade.
—The Fallen Man. 1997. 320p. mass mkt. 6.99 (*0-06-109288-6*, HarperTorch) Morrow/Avon.
—The Fallen Man. unabr. ed. 1997. (Jim Chee Mystery Ser.: Vol. 9). audio 51.00 (*0-7887-0907-0*, 94961E7) Recorded Bks., LLC.
—The Fallen Man. 1998. 5.98 o.p. (*0-7651-0823-2*) Smithmark Pubs., Inc.
—The First Eagle. 1998. 224p. 25.00 (*0-00-224569-8*); 288p. 25.00 o.s.i (*0-06-017581-8*); 25.00 o.s.i (*0-06-099536-X*) HarperCollins Pubs.
—The First Eagle. unabr. ed. 1998. audio 34.95 (*0-694-52051-9*, 896038);Set. audio 25.00 (*0-694-52011-X*, 696034) HarperTrade. (HarperAudio).
—The First Eagle. 1999. 336p. mass mkt. 6.99 (*0-06-109785-3*, HarperTorch) Morrow/Avon.
—The First Eagle. unabr. ed. (Joe Leaphorn Mystery Ser.). 1999. audio compact disk 58.00 (*0-7887-3445-8*, C1051E7); 1998. audio 56.00 (*0-7887-2160-7*, 95456E7) Recorded Bks., LLC.
—The First Eagle. l.t. ed. (Paperback Bestsellers Ser.). 360p. 1999. pap. 28.95 o.p. (*0-7862-1625-5*); 1998. 30.95 (*0-7862-1624-7*) Thorndike Pr.
—The First Eagle. 1999. 13.04 (*0-606-16536-3*) Turtleback Bks.
—The Ghostway. unabr. ed. 1994. audio 42.00 (*0-7366-2748-0*, 3473) Books on Tape, Inc.
—The Ghostway. 1985. 224p. 13.95 o.p. (*0-06-015396-2*); 1992. 3p. audio 18.00 (*1-55994-606-7*, CPN 2301, HarperAudio) HarperTrade.
—The Ghostway. 1993. audio. audio 47.20 (*1-56544-040-4*, 250033) Literate Ear, Inc.
—The Ghostway. 1992. 320p. mass mkt. 6.99 (*0-06-100345-X*, HarperTorch); 1986. 208p. mass mkt. 4.95 (*0-380-70024-7*, Avon Bks.) Morrow/Avon.
—The Ghostway. unabr. ed. 1990. (Jim Chee Mystery Ser.: Vol. 3). audio 44.00 (*1-55690-194-1*, 90098E7) Recorded Bks., LLC.
—The Ghostway. 1984. (J). 12.55 (*0-606-01124-2*) Turtleback Bks.
—Hunting Badger. 1999. 288p. 26.00 (*0-06-019289-5*); 26.00 (*0-00-224550-7*) HarperCollins Pubs.
—Hunting Badger. l.t. ed. 1999. 256p. pap. 26.00 (*0-06-095564-3*, HarperLargePrint); 2000. audio compact disk 29.95 (*0-694-52287-2*, HarperAudio); Set. 2000. 30p. audio 25.00 (*0-694-52057-8*, HarperAudio) HarperTrade.
—Hunting Badger. 2001. 352p. mass mkt. 7.50 (*0-06-109786-1*, HarperTorch) Morrow/Avon.
—Hunting Badger. unabr. ed. 1999. (Joe Leaphorn Mystery Ser.). audio 29.95 (*0-7887-3894-1*, 96076 ) Recorded Bks., LLC.
—The Jim Chee Mysteries: Three Classic Hillerman Mysteries Featuring Officer Jim Chee: The Dark Wind, People of Darkness & The Ghostway. 1990. 576p. 26.00 (*0-06-016478-6*) HarperTrade.
—The Jim Chee Mysteries: Three Classic Hillerman Mysteries Featuring Officer Jim Chee: The Dark Wind, People of Darkness & The Ghostway. 1993. 576p. 13.99 o.s.i (*0-517-09281-6*) Random Hse. Value Publishing.
—Leaphorn & Chee: Three Classic Mysteries Featuring Lt. Joe Leaphorn & Officer Jim Chee. 1992. 512p. 19.00 o.p. (*0-06-016909-5*) HarperTrade.
—People of Darkness. unabr. ed. 1994. audio 36.00 (*0-7366-2725-1*, 3455) Books on Tape, Inc.
—People of Darkness. 1988. 196p. reprint ed. mass mkt. 4.95 o.p. (*0-06-080950-7*, P 950, Perennial) HarperTrade.
—People of Darkness. 1993. audio. audio 44.20 (*1-56544-037-4*, 250034) Literate Ear, Inc.
—People of Darkness. 1991. 304p. mass mkt. 6.99 (*0-06-109915-5*, HarperTorch); 1983. 192p. pap. 2.95 o.p. (*0-380-57778-X*, Avon Bks.) Morrow/ Avon.
—People of Darkness. unabr. ed. 1990. (Jim Chee Mystery Ser.: Vol. 1). audio 44.00 (*1-55690-405-3*, 90087E7) Recorded Bks., LLC.
—Sacred Clowns. unabr. ed. 1994. audio 48.00 (*0-7366-2645-X*, 3382) Books on Tape, Inc.
—Sacred Clowns. 1994. 368p. mass mkt. 6.99 (*0-06-109260-6*) HarperCollins Pubs.
—Sacred Clowns. 1993. 304p. 100.00 o.p. (*0-06-016830-7*); 304p. 23.00 o.p. (*0-06-016767-X*); audio 17.00 (*1-55994-549-4*, 391505, HarperAudio) HarperTrade.
—Sacred Clowns. unabr. ed. 1993. (Jim Chee Mystery Ser.: Vol. 8). audio 51.00 (*1-55690-910-1*, 93406E7) Recorded Bks., LLC.
—Sacred Clowns. 1994. 13.04 (*0-606-16175-9*) Turtleback Bks.
—Sacred Clowns: A Novel. 2003. 320p. pap. 11.95 (*0-06-053805-8*, Perennial) HarperTrade.
—The Sinister Pig. 2003. (*0-06-601944-3*) HarperCollins Pubs.
—The Sinister Pig. 2003. 240p. 25.95 (*0-06-019443-X*, HarperCollins); E-Book 19.95 (*0-06-055860-1*, HarperCollins); 320p. pap. 25.95 (*0-06-054543-7*, HarperLargePrint) HarperTrade.
—The Sinister Pig. 2004. mass mkt. (*0-06-109878-7*, HarperTorch) Morrow/Avon.
—Skinwalkers. unabr. ed. 1994. audio 36.00 (*0-7366-2795-2*, 3510) Books on Tape, Inc.
—Skinwalkers. 1990. 320p. mass mkt. 6.99 (*0-06-100017-5*); 1987. mass mkt. 4.95 o.p. (*0-06-080893-4*, P/893) HarperCollins Pubs.
—Skinwalkers. 1990. audio 15.95; 1987. 224p. 19.95 o.p. (*0-06-015695-3*); 1991. audio 18.00 (*1-55994-166-9*, CPN 2152, HarperAudio) HarperTrade.
—Skinwalkers. 1993. audio 39.80 (*1-56544-007-2*, 250032); audio Literate Ear, Inc.
—Skinwalkers. unabr. ed. 1990. (Jim Chee Mystery Ser.: Vol. 4). audio 44.00 (*1-55690-480-0*, 90074E7) Recorded Bks., LLC.
—Skinwalkers. 1987. 13.04 (*0-606-03655-5*) Turtleback Bks.
—Talking God. unabr. ed. 1989. audio 42.00 (*0-7366-1656-X*, 2507) Books on Tape, Inc.
—Talking God. 2003. E-Book 6.99 (*0-06-054725-1*) HarperCollins Pubs.
—Talking God. 1991. 368p. mass mkt. 6.99 (*0-06-109918-X*, Perennial); 1989. 17.95 o.p. (*0-06-016118-3*) HarperTrade.
—Talking God. 1989. 13.04 (*0-606-04823-5*) Turtleback Bks.
—A Thief of Time. unabr. ed. 1994. audio 36.00 (*0-7366-2841-X*, 3549) Books on Tape, Inc.
—A Thief of Time. l.t. ed. 1990. 14.95 o.p. (*0-8161-5061-3*); 1989. 344p. 18.95 o.p. (*0-8161-4699-3*) Gale Group. (Macmillan Reference USA).
—A Thief of Time. 2002. E-Book 6.99 (*0-06-054713-8*); E-Book (*0-06-054720-0*) HarperCollins Pubs.
—A Thief of Time. 1988. 224p. 15.45 o.p. (*0-06-015938-3*); 2002. 176p. audio 9.99 (*0-06-008296-8*, HarperAudio); 2002. 176p. audio 9.99 (*0-06-008296-8*, HarperAudio); Set. 1995. audio 18.00 (*0-89845-794-7*, 391761, HarperAudio) HarperTrade.
—A Thief of Time. 1990. 352p. reprint ed. mass mkt. 6.99 (*0-06-100004-3*, HarperTorch) Morrow/Avon.
—A Thief of Time. 1989. 13.04 (*0-606-04346-2*) Turtleback Bks.
—The Wailing Wind. 2002. (Illus.). 240p. 25.95 (*0-06-019444-8*); E-Book (*0-06-054708-1*); E-Book 19.95 (*0-06-054703-0*) HarperCollins Pubs.
—The Wailing Wind. l.t. ed. 2002. 320p. pap. 25.95 (*0-06-009388-9*, HarperLargePrint); 384p. 29.95 (*0-06-009258-0*, Caedmon); audio 26.95 (*0-694-52348-8*, HarperAudio) HarperTrade.
—The Wailing Wind. 2003. 368p. mass mkt. 7.99 (*0-06-109879-5*, HarperTorch) Morrow/Avon.
—The Wailing Wind. unabr. ed. 2002. audio 29.95 (*1-4025-2394-7*, RG087); audio compact disk 66.00 (*1-4025-2904-X*, C1816); audio 48.00 (*1-4025-2393-9*) Recorded Bks., LLC.

Hillerman, Tony, reader. Talking God, , abr. ed. 1995. audio 18.00 (*0-89845-956-7*, CPN 2122, HarperAudio) HarperTrade.

### CHEKOV, PAVEL (FICTITIOUS CHARACTER)—FICTION

David, Peter. The Captain's Daughter. (Star Trek: No. 76). 2000. E-Book 6.99 (*0-7434-2027-6*); 1995. 288p. mass mkt. 5.99 o.s.i (*0-671-52047-4*) Simon & Schuster. (Star Trek).

Duane, Diane. Doctor's Orders. (Star Trek: No. 50). 2000. E-Book 6.99 (*0-7434-2001-2*); 1990. 288p. mass mkt. 5.50 (*0-671-66189-2*) Simon & Schuster. (Star Trek).

Ecklar, Julia. The Kobayashi Maru. 1989. (Star Trek: No. 47). mass mkt. 5.50 (*0-671-65817-4*, Star Trek) Simon & Schuster.
—The Kobayashi Maru. (Star Trek Ser.: No. 47). 1999. audio 5.98 (*0-671-04486-9*); 1990. audio 11.00 (*0-671-70895-3*) Simon & Schuster Audio. (Simon & Schuster Audioworks).

Friedman, Michael Jan. Faces of Fire. 2000. (Star Trek: No. 58). E-Book 6.99 (*0-7434-2009-8*, Star Trek) Simon & Schuster.
—Faces of Fire. Stern, Dave, ed. 1992. (Star Trek: No. 58). 320p. mass mkt. 5.50 (*0-671-74992-7*, Star Trek) Simon & Schuster.
—Faces of Fire. 1992. (Star Trek Ser.: No. 58). audio 16.00 o.s.i (*0-671-77802-1*, Simon & Schuster Audioworks) Simon & Schuster Audio.

Graf, L. A. Death Count. Stern, Dave, ed. 1992. (Star Trek Ser.: No. 62). 288p. mass mkt. 4.99 (*0-671-79322-5*, Star Trek) Simon & Schuster.
—Firestorm. (Star Trek: No. 68). 2000. E-Book 6.99 (*0-7434-2019-5*); 1994. 288p. mass mkt. 5.50 (*0-671-86588-9*) Simon & Schuster. (Star Trek).
—Ice Trap. 2000. (Star Trek: No. 60). E-Book 6.99 (*0-7434-2011-X*, Star Trek) Simon & Schuster.
—New Earth No. 3: Rough Trails. 2000. (Star Trek: No. 91). reprint ed. E-Book 6.50 (*0-7434-1117-X*, Star Trek) Simon & Schuster.
—New Earth No. 33: Rough Trails. 2000. (Star Trek: No. 91). 400p. pap. 6.50 (*0-671-03600-9*, Star Trek) Simon & Schuster.
—Traitor Winds. 2000. (Star Trek: No. 70). E-Book 6.99 (*0-7434-2021-7*, Star Trek) Simon & Schuster.
—Traitor Winds. Ryan, Kevin, ed. 1994. (Star Trek Ser.: No. 70). 288p. mass mkt. 5.50 (*0-671-86913-2*, Star Trek) Simon & Schuster.

Graf, L. A. & Ecklar, Julia. Ice Trap. Stern, Dave, ed. 1992. (Star Trek: No. 60). 288p. mass mkt. 4.99 (*0-671-78068-9*, Star Trek) Simon & Schuster.

Kagan, Janet. Uhura's Song. (Star Trek: No. 21). 384p. 1987. mass mkt. 5.50 (*0-671-65227-3*); 1985. mass mkt. 3.50 o.s.i (*0-671-54730-5*); 2000. pap. 3.99 (*0-7434-0373-8*) Simon & Schuster. (Star Trek).
—Uhura's Song. 1985. (Star Trek Ser.: No. 21). 373p. 20.00 o.p. (*0-89366-169-4*) Ultramarine Publishing Co., Inc.

Kramer-Rolls, Dana. Home Is the Hunter. Stern, David, ed. 1990. (Star Trek: No. 52). 288p. mass mkt. 4.99 (*0-671-66662-2*, Star Trek) Simon & Schuster.

Mangels, Andy & Martin, Michael A. Lost Era: Sundered. 2003. (Star Trek Ser.). 416p. mass mkt. 6.99 (*0-7434-6401-X*, Star Trek) Simon & Schuster.

Mitchell, V. E. Enemy Unseen. Stern, David, ed. 1990. (Star Trek: No. 51). 288p. mass mkt. 4.99 (*0-671-68403-5*, Star Trek) Simon & Schuster.

Vardeman, Robert E. The Klingon Gambit. (Star Trek: No. 3). 1990. mass mkt. 4.50 (*0-671-70767-1*); 1987. mass mkt. 3.95 o.s.i (*0-671-66342-9*); 1986. per. 3.50 (*0-671-62744-9*); 1985. mass mkt. 3.50 o.s.i (*0-671-62231-5*); 1983. mass mkt. 2.95 o.s.i (*0-671-47720-X*) Simon & Schuster. (Star Trek).

Weinstein, Howard. Deep Domain. (Star Trek: No. 33). 2000. E-Book 6.99 (*0-7434-1984-7*); 1989. mass mkt. 5.50 (*0-671-70549-0*); 1988. 288p. mass mkt. 3.95 o.s.i (*0-671-67077-8*) Simon & Schuster. (Star Trek).

### CHEYSULI (FICTITIOUS CHARACTERS)—FICTION

Roberson, Jennifer. Daughter of the Lion. 1989. (Chronicles of the Cheysuli Ser.: Bk. 6). 384p. (Orig.). mass mkt. 6.99 o.s.i (*0-88677-324-5*) DAW Bks., Inc.
—Flight of the Raven. 1990. (Chronicles of the Cheysuli Ser.: Bk. 7). 384p. mass mkt. 5.99 o.s.i (*0-88677-422-5*) DAW Bks., Inc.
—Legacy of the Sword. 1986. (Orig.). (Cheysuli Ser.). mass mkt. 3.50 o.p. (*0-88677-124-2*); (Chronicles of the Cheysuli Ser.: Bk. III). 384p. mass mkt. 4.99 o.s.i (*0-88677-316-4*) DAW Bks., Inc.
—The Legacy of the Wolf, Vol. 2. 2001. (Cheysuli Ser.). (Illus.). 752p. mass mkt. 7.99 (*0-88677-997-9*) DAW Bks., Inc.
—The Pride of Princes, No. 5. 1988. (Chronicles of the Cheysuli Ser.: Bk. 5). 464p. (Orig.). mass mkt. 6.99 o.s.i (*0-88677-261-3*) DAW Bks., Inc.
—Shapechangers. 1984. (Orig.). (Cheysuli Ser.). mass mkt. 2.95 o.p. (*0-87997-907-0*); (Chronicles of the Cheysuli Ser.: Bk. 1). 224p. mass mkt. 5.99 o.s.i (*0-88677-140-4*) DAW Bks., Inc.
—Shapechanger's Song, Vol. 1. 2001. (Cheysuli Ser.). (Illus.). 624p. mass mkt. 7.99 (*0-88677-976-6*) DAW Bks., Inc.
—Song of Homana. 1985. (Cheysuli Ser.). mass mkt. 3.50 o.p. (*0-88677-057-2*); (Cheysuli Ser.). mass mkt. 3.50 o.p. (*0-88677-195-1*); (Cheysuli Ser.). mass mkt. 3.95 o.p. (*0-88677-317-2*); (Chronicles of the Cheysuli Ser.: Bk. 2). 352p. mass mkt. 5.99 o.s.i (*0-88677-434-9*) DAW Bks., Inc.
—A Tapestry of Lions, Vol. 8. 1992. (Chronciles of the Cheysuli Ser.: Bk. 8). 544p. (Orig.). mass mkt. 7.50 o.s.i (*0-88677-524-8*) DAW Bks., Inc.
—Track of the White Wolf. 1987. (Chronicles of the Cheysuli Ser.: Bk. 4). 384p. mass mkt. 5.99 o.s.i (*0-88677-193-5*) DAW Bks., Inc.

### CHIA, PAO-YU (FICTITIOUS CHARACTER)—FICTION

Cao Xue Qin. A Dream of Red Mansions. 1978. 19.95 (*0-8351-0485-0*); 1978. 46.95 o.p. (*0-8351-0874-0*); Pt. II. 24.95 (*0-8351-0583-0*); Pt. III. 24.95 (*0-8351-0803-1*) China Bks. & Periodicals, Inc.
—A Dream of Red Mansions. Yang, Hsien-yi et al, trs. from CHI. (Illus.). Vol. 1. 1978. 599p. o.s.i (*0-917056-66-3*); Vol. 3. 1980. 586p. (C). o.s.i (*0-917056-68-X*) Foreign Languages Teaching & Research Pr.
—The Dream of the Red Chamber. McHugh, Florence & McHugh, Isabel, trs. from GER. 1975. (Illus.). 604p. reprint ed. 65.95 (*0-8371-8113-5*, TSDR, Greenwood Pr.) Greenwood Publishing Group, Inc.
—The Dream of the Red Chamber. 1996. (Classic Ser.). 96p. pap. 0.95 o.p. (*0-14-600176-1*) Penguin Group (USA) Inc.
—The Dream of the Red Chamber. 1998. lib. bdg. 22.95 (*1-56723-060-1*) Yestermorrow, Inc.

Cao Xue Qin & Gao, E. A Dream of Red Mansions. Xianyi, Yang & Yang, Gladys, trs. deluxe ed. 2001. (Library of Chinese Classics). 3577p. 179.95 (*7-119-02411-6*) Beijing Foreign Languages Pr. CHN. *Dist:* China Bks. & Periodicals, Inc.
—A Dream of Red Mansions. Xinqu, Huang, tr. from CHI. abr. ed. 1995. 298p. pap. 14.95 (*0-8351-2529-7*) China Bks. & Periodicals, Inc.

Cao Xue Qin & Kao, Ngo. A Dream of Red Mansions. Yang, Hsien-yi & Yang, Gladys, trs. from CHI. abr. ed. 1996. 503p. (C). pap. 24.95 (*0-88727-178-2*) Cheng & Tsui Co.

Cao Xue Qin, et al. A Dream of Red Mansions, Vol. 2. Yang, Hsien-yi & Yang, Gladys, trs. from CHI. 1978. (Illus.). 701p. o.s.i (*0-917056-67-1*) Foreign Languages Teaching & Research Pr.

Hsueh-Chin, Tsao, et al. The Dream of the Red Chamber. 1958. 352p. pap. 13.95 (*0-385-09379-9*) Doubleday Publishing.

Xiugui, Zhang. CliffsNotes TM Dream of the Red Chamber. 1999. E-Book 3.95 (*0-8220-7060-X*, Cliff Notes) Wiley, John & Sons, Inc.

### CHILDS, SUNNY (FICTITIOUS CHARACTER)—FICTION

Birmingham, Ruth. Atlanta Graves. 1998. (Sunny Childs Mysteries Ser.). 288p. mass mkt. 5.99 o.s.i (*0-425-16267-2*) Berkley Publishing Group.
—Fulton County Blues. 1999. (Fulton County Blues Ser.: Vol. 2). 288p. mass mkt. 5.99 o.s.i (*0-425-16697-X*, Prime Crime) Berkley Publishing Group.
—Fulton County Blues. 2000. 12.04 (*0-606-19296-4*) Turtleback Bks.
—Sweet Georgia. 2000. (Sunny Childs Mysteries Ser.). 320p. mass mkt. 5.99 o.s.i (*0-425-17671-1*, Prime Crime) Berkley Publishing Group.

### CHIN, LYDIA (FICTITIOUS CHARACTER)—FICTION

Rozan, S. J. A Bitter Feast. 1998. 320p. 23.95 o.p. (*0-312-19259-2*, Saint Martin's Minotaur); 1999. 336p. reprint ed. mass mkt. 5.99 (*0-312-97011-0*, St. Martin's Paperbacks) St. Martin's Pr.
—A Bitter Feast. l.t. ed. 1999. (Mystery Ser.). 519p. 27.95 (*0-7862-1773-1*) Thorndike Pr.
—A Bitter Feast: A Bill Smith-Lydia Chin Mystery. unabr. ed. 1999. audio 69.95 (*0-7927-2280-9*, CSL169, Chivers Sound Library) BBC Audiobooks America.
—China Trade. 1994. 263 p. 20.95 o.p. (*0-312-11254-8*, Saint Martin's Minotaur); 1995. (Lydia Chin, Bill Smith Mystery Ser.: Vol. 1). 275p. reprint ed. mass mkt. 6.50 (*0-312-95590-1*, St. Martin's Paperbacks) St. Martin's Pr.
—Concourse: A Bill Smith-Lydia Chin Mystery. unabr. ed. 1998. audio 69.95 (*0-7927-2245-0*, CSL134, Chivers Sound Library) BBC Audiobooks America.
—Concourse: A Bill Smith-Lydia Chin Mystery. 1995. 288p. 21.95 o.p. (*0-312-13453-3*, Saint Martin's Minotaur); 3rd ed. 1996. (Lydia Chin, Bill Smith Mystery Ser.: Vol. 2). 291p. mass mkt. 6.50 (*0-312-95944-3*, St. Martin's Paperbacks) St. Martin's Pr.
—Mandarin Plaid. (Lydia Chin, Bill Smith Mystery Ser.: Vol. 3). 288p. 1996. 22.95 o.p. (*0-312-14674-4*, Saint Martin's Minotaur); Vol. 1. 1997. mass mkt. 6.50 (*0-312-96283-5*, St. Martin's Paperbacks) St. Martin's Pr.
—No Colder Place. 1998. (No Colder Place Ser.: Vol. 1). 304p. pap. 6.99 (*0-312-96664-4*, St. Martin's Paperbacks); 1997. (Lydia Chin, Bill Smith Mystery Ser.). 288p. 23.95 (*0-312-16811-X*, Saint Martin's Minotaur) St. Martin's Pr.
—No Colder Place. l.t. ed. 1997. (Cloak & Dagger Ser.). 473p. lib. bdg. 28.95 (*0-7862-1251-9*) Thorndike Pr.
—Reflecting the Sky. 2001. 312p. 24.95 (*0-312-24427-4*, Saint Martin's Minotaur); 2002. 384p. reprint ed. mass mkt. 6.50 (*0-312-98134-1*, St. Martin's Paperbacks) St. Martin's Pr.
—Stone Quarry. l.t. ed. 2003. 29.95 (*1-57490-532-5*) Beeler, Thomas T. Publisher.
—Stone Quarry. 2001. 336p. mass mkt. 6.50 (*0-312-97703-4*, St. Martin's Paperbacks); 1999. 288p. 23.95 o.p. (*0-312-20912-6*, Saint Martin's Minotaur) St. Martin's Pr.
—Winter & Night. E-Book 18.95 (*0-312-70434-8*); 2003. 400p. mass mkt. 6.99 (*0-312-98668-8*, St. Martin's Paperbacks); 2002. 304p. 24.95 (*0-312-24555-6*, Saint Martin's Minotaur) St. Martin's Pr.

### CHIRKE, NICHOLAS (FICTITIOUS CHARACTER)—FICTION

Doherty, P. C. An Ancient Evil: The Knight's Tale of Mystery & Murder as He Goes on Pilgrimage from London to Canterbury. unabr. ed. 1998. audio 69.95 (*1-85903-149-8*) Magna Story Sound GBR. *Dist:* Ulverscroft Large Print Bks., Ltd.
—An Ancient Evil: The Knight's Tale of Mystery & Murder as He Goes on Pilgrimage from London to Canterbury. 1995. 248p. 21.00 o.p. (*0-312-11740-X*, Saint Martin's Minotaur) St. Martin's Pr.
—An Ancient Evil: The Knight's Tale of Mystery & Murder as He Goes on Pilgrimage from London to Canterbury. l.t. ed. 1995. (Ulverscroft Large Print Ser.). 432p. 29.99 o.p. (*0-7089-3409-9*, Ulverscroft) Thorpe, F. A. Pubs. GBR. *Dist:* Ulverscroft Large Print Bks., Ltd., Ulverscroft Large Print Canada, Ltd.

—Ghostly Murders: The Priest's Tale of Mystery & Murder as He Goes on Pilgrimage from London to Canterbury. 1998. 256p. 21.95 (*0-312-19418-8*, Saint Martin's Minotaur) St. Martin's Pr.

—Ghostly Murders: The Priest's Tale of Mystery & Murder as He Goes on Pilgrimage from London to Canterbury. l.t. ed. 1999. (Ulverscroft Large Print Ser.). 368p. 31.99 o.p. (*0-7089-4059-5*, Ulverscroft) Thorpe, F. A. Pubs. GBR. *Dist:* Ulverscroft Large Print Bks., Ltd., Ulverscroft Large Print Canada, Ltd.

—A Tapestry of Murders: The Lawyer's Tale of Mystery & Murder as He Goes on a Pilgrimage from London to Canterbury. unabr. ed. 1998. audio 69.95 (*1-85903-165-X*) Magna Story Sound GBR. *Dist:* Ulverscroft Large Print Bks., Ltd.

—A Tapestry of Murders: The Lawyer's Tale of Mystery & Murder as He Goes on a Pilgrimage from London to Canterbury. 1996. 256p. 21.95 (*0-312-14052-5*, Saint Martin's Minotaur) St. Martin's Pr.

—A Tapestry of Murders: The Lawyer's Tale of Mystery & Murder as He Goes on a Pilgrimage from London to Canterbury. l.t. ed. 1996. (Ulverscroft Large Print Ser.). 416p. 29.99 o.p. (*0-7089-3446-3*, Ulverscroft) Thorpe, F. A. Pubs. GBR. *Dist:* Ulverscroft Large Print Bks., Ltd., Ulverscroft Large Print Canada, Ltd.

—A Tournament of Murders: The Franklin's Tale of Mystery & Murder As He Goes on Pilgrimage from London to Canterbury. 1997. 256p. 21.95 (*0-312-17048-3*, Saint Martin's Minotaur) St. Martin's Pr.

—A Tournament of Murders: The Franklin's Tale of Mystery & Murder As He Goes on Pilgrimage from London to Canterbury. l.t. ed. 1998. (Ulverscroft Large Print Ser.). 384p. 29.99 o.p. (*0-7089-3938-4*, Ulverscroft) Thorpe, F. A. Pubs. GBR. *Dist:* Ulverscroft Large Print Bks., Ltd., Ulverscroft Large Print Canada, Ltd.

**CHISHOLM, MARGARET (FICTITIOUS CHARACTER)—FICTION**

Lira, Gonzalo. Counterparts. 1999. 400p. reprint ed. mass mkt. 6.99 o.s.i (*0-515-12429-X*, Jove) Berkley Publishing Group.

—Counterparts. 1997. 343p. 24.95 o.p. (*0-399-14312-2*, G. P. Putnam's Sons) Penguin Group (USA) Inc.

—Counterparts. 1998. o.p. (*0-399-14361-0*) Putnam Publishing Group, The.

**CHIUN (FICTITIOUS CHARACTER)—FICTION**

Murphy, Warren. Acid Rock. 1989. (Destroyer Ser.: No. 13). mass mkt. 3.50 o.s.i (*1-55817-195-9*, Pinnacle Bks.) Kensington Publishing Corp.

—American Obsession. 1997. (Destroyer Ser.: No. 109). per. (*0-373-63224-X*, 1-63224-9, Worldwide Library) Harlequin Enterprises, Ltd.

—Assassin's Play-Off. 1989. (Destroyer Ser.: No. 20). mass mkt. 3.50 o.s.i (*1-55817-211-4*, Pinnacle Bks.) Kensington Publishing Corp.

—Bamboo Dragon. 1997. (Destroyer Ser.: No. 108). per. (*0-373-63223-1*, 1-63223-1, Worldwide Library) Harlequin Enterprises, Ltd.

—Bay City Blast. 1990. (Destroyer Ser.: No. 38). mass mkt. 3.50 o.s.i (*1-55817-443-5*, Pinnacle Bks.) Kensington Publishing Corp.

—Blue Smoke. 1989. (Destroyer Ser.: No. 78). mass mkt. 4.50 o.p. (*0-451-16219-6*, Signet Bks.) NAL.

—Bottom Line. 1990. (Destroyer Ser.: No. 37). mass mkt. 3.50 o.s.i (*1-55817-419-2*, Pinnacle Bks.) Kensington Publishing Corp.

—Brain Drain. 1989. (Destroyer Ser.: No. 22). (Orig.). mass mkt. 3.50 o.p. (*1-55817-247-5*, Pinnacle Bks.) Kensington Publishing Corp.

—Chained Reaction. 1990. (Destroyer Ser.: No. 34). mass mkt. 3.50 o.s.i (*1-55817-383-8*, Pinnacle Bks.) Kensington Publishing Corp.

—Child's Play. 1989. (Destroyer Ser.: No. 23). mass mkt. 3.50 o.s.i (*1-55817-258-0*, Pinnacle Bks.) Kensington Publishing Corp.

—Chinese Puzzle. (Destroyer Ser.: No. 3). (Orig.). 1988. mass mkt. 3.50 o.s.i (*1-55817-038-3*); 1984. 192p. pap. 2.95 o.p. (*0-523-42414-0*) Kensington Publishing Corp. (Pinnacle Bks.).

—The Color of Fear. 1995. (Destroyer Ser.: No. 99). per. (*0-373-63214-2*, 1-63214-0, Harlequin Bks.) Harlequin Enterprises, Ltd.

—Created, the Destroyer. 1988. (Destroyer Ser.: No. 1). mass mkt. 3.50 o.p. (*1-55817-036-7*, Pinnacle Bks.) Kensington Publishing Corp.

—Created, the Destroyer. 1986. (Destroyer Ser.: No. 1). pap. 2.50 o.p. (*0-380-70195-2*, Avon Bks.) Morrow/Avon.

—Dangerous Games. 1991. (Destroyer Ser.: No. 40). 192p. (Orig.). mass mkt. 3.50 o.s.i (*1-55817-468-0*, Pinnacle Bks.) Kensington Publishing Corp.

—Date with Death. 1984. (Destroyer Ser.: No. 57). 192p. pap. 2.50 o.p. (*0-523-41567-2*, Pinnacle Bks.) Kensington Publishing Corp.

—Deadly Seeds. 1989. (Destroyer Ser.: No. 21). (Orig.). mass mkt. 3.50 o.s.i (*1-55817-237-8*, Pinnacle Bks.) Kensington Publishing Corp.

—Death Check. 1988. (Destroyer Ser.: No. 2). mass mkt. 3.50 o.s.i (*1-55817-037-5*, Pinnacle Bks.) Kensington Publishing Corp.

—Death Sentence. 1990. (Destroyer Ser.: No. 80). mass mkt. 3.95 o.p. (*0-451-16471-7*, Signet Bks.) NAL.

—Death Therapy. 1988. (Destroyer Ser.: No. 6). mass mkt. 3.50 o.s.i (*1-55817-041-3*, Pinnacle Bks.) Kensington Publishing Corp.

—Dr. Quake. 1988. (Destroyer Ser.: No. 5). mass mkt. 3.50 o.s.i (*1-55817-040-5*, Pinnacle Bks.) Kensington Publishing Corp.

—Encounter Group. 1984. (Destroyer Ser.: No. 56). 192p. pap. 2.50 o.p. (*0-523-41566-4*, Pinnacle Bks.) Kensington Publishing Corp.

—Feast or Famine. 1997. (Destroyer Ser.: No. 107). per. (*0-373-63222-3*, 1-63222-3, Worldwide Library) Harlequin Enterprises, Ltd.

—The Final Death. 1990. (Destroyer Ser.: No. 29). mass mkt. 3.50 o.s.i (*1-55817-319-6*, Pinnacle Bks.) Kensington Publishing Corp.

—Firing Line. 1991. (Destroyer Ser.: No. 41). 192p. (Orig.). mass mkt. 3.50 o.s.i (*1-55817-483-4*, Pinnacle Bks.) Kensington Publishing Corp.

—Funny Money. 1989. (Destroyer Ser.: No. 18). mass mkt. 3.50 o.s.i (*1-55817-200-9*, Pinnacle Bks.) Kensington Publishing Corp.

—The Head Men. 1990. (Destroyer Ser.: No. 31). mass mkt. 3.50 o.s.i (*1-55817-343-9*, Pinnacle Bks.) Kensington Publishing Corp.

—High Priestess. 1999. (Destroyer Ser.: No. 95). pap. 4.50 (*0-451-17771-1*, Signet Bks.) NAL.

—Holy Terror. 1989. (Destroyer Ser.: No. 19). mass mkt. 3.50 o.s.i (*1-55817-210-6*, Pinnacle Bks.) Kensington Publishing Corp.

—In Enemy Hands. (Destroyer Ser.: No. 26). 1989. mass mkt. 3.50 o.s.i (*1-55817-285-8*); 1979. pap. 1.75 o.p. (*0-523-40902-8*) Kensington Publishing Corp. (Pinnacle Bks.).

—Infernal Revenue. 1994. (Destroyer Ser.: No. 96). mass mkt. (*0-373-63211-8*, 1-63211-6, Harlequin Bks.) Harlequin Enterprises, Ltd.

—Judgement Day. 1989. (Destroyer Ser.: No. 14). mass mkt. 3.50 o.s.i (*1-55817-196-7*) Kensington Publishing Corp.

—Killer Chromosomes. (Destroyer Ser.: No. 32). 1990. mass mkt. 3.50 o.s.i (*1-55817-355-2*); 1979. pap. 1.75 o.p. (*0-523-40908-7*) Kensington Publishing Corp. (Pinnacle Bks.).

—Killing Time. 1982. (Destroyer Ser.: No. 50). 208p. pap. 2.25 o.p. (*0-523-41560-5*, Pinnacle Bks.) Kensington Publishing Corp.

—King's Curse. (Destroyer Ser.: No. 24). 1989. mass mkt. 3.50 o.s.i (*1-55817-268-8*); 1980. pap. 1.95 o.p. (*0-523-41239-8*) Kensington Publishing Corp. (Pinnacle Bks.).

—Last Call. (Destroyer Ser.: No. 35). 1990. mass mkt. 3.50 o.p. (*1-55817-395-1*); 1980. pap. 1.95 o.p. (*0-523-41250-9*) Kensington Publishing Corp. (Pinnacle Bks.).

—Last Drop. 1983. (Destroyer Ser.: No. 54). 208p. pap. 2.50 o.p. (*0-523-41564-8*, Pinnacle Bks.) Kensington Publishing Corp.

—The Last Temple. 1989. (Destroyer Ser.: No. 27). mass mkt. 3.50 o.s.i (*1-55817-295-5*, Pinnacle Bks.) Kensington Publishing Corp.

—Last War Dance. 1989. (Destroyer Ser.: No. 17). mass mkt. 3.50 o.s.i (*1-55817-199-1*, Pinnacle Bks.) Kensington Publishing Corp.

—Mafia Fix. (Destroyer Ser.: No. 4). 1988. mass mkt. 3.50 o.s.i (*1-55817-039-1*); 1982. 192p. pap. 2.25 o.p. (*0-523-41758-6*) Kensington Publishing Corp. (Pinnacle Bks.).

—Missing Link. (Destroyer Ser.: No. 39). 1990. mass mkt. 3.50 o.s.i (*1-55817-457-5*); 1980. pap. 1.95 o.p. (*0-523-41254-1*) Kensington Publishing Corp. (Pinnacle Bks.).

—Mugger Blood. 1990. (Destroyer Ser.: No. 30). mass mkt. 3.50 o.s.i (*1-55817-328-5*, Pinnacle Bks.) Kensington Publishing Corp.

—Murder Ward. (Destroyer Ser.: No. 15). 1989. mass mkt. 3.50 o.s.i (*1-55817-197-5*); 1981. pap. 2.25 o.p. (*0-523-41768-3*) Kensington Publishing Corp. (Pinnacle Bks.).

—Never Say Die. 1998. (Destroyer Ser.: No. 110). per. (*0-373-63225-8*, 1-63225-6, Worldwide Library) Harlequin Enterprises, Ltd.

—Next of Kin. 1981. (Destroyer Ser.: No. 46). 192p. pap. 1.95 o.p. (*0-523-40720-3*, Pinnacle Bks.) Kensington Publishing Corp.

—Oil Slick. 1989. (Destroyer Ser.: No. 16). mass mkt. 3.50 o.s.i (*1-55817-198-3*, Pinnacle Bks.) Kensington Publishing Corp.

—Power Play. (Destroyer Ser.: No. 36). 1990. mass mkt. 3.50 o.s.i (*1-55817-406-0*); 1981. pap. 1.95 o.p. (*0-523-41251-7*) Kensington Publishing Corp. (Pinnacle Bks.).

—Profit Motive. 1982. (Destroyer Ser.: No. 48). 256p. pap. 2.75 o.p. (*0-523-41558-3*, Pinnacle Bks.) Kensington Publishing Corp.

—Prophet of Doom. 1998. (Destroyer Ser.: No. 111). per. (*0-373-63226-6*, 1-63226-4, Worldwide Library) Harlequin Enterprises, Ltd.

—Scorched Earth. 1996. (Destroyer Ser.: No. 105). per. (*0-373-63220-7*, 1-63220-7, Worldwide Library) Harlequin Enterprises, Ltd.

—Ship of Death. 1990. (Destroyer Ser.: No. 28). mass mkt. 3.50 o.s.i (*1-55817-310-2*, Pinnacle Bks.) Kensington Publishing Corp.

—Shock Value. 1983. (Destroyer Ser.: No. 51). 208p. pap. text 2.25 o.p. (*0-523-41561-3*, Pinnacle Bks.) Kensington Publishing Corp.

—Spoils of War. 1981. (Destroyer Ser.: No. 45). 192p. pap. 1.95 o.p. (*0-523-40719-X*, Pinnacle Bks.) Kensington Publishing Corp.

—Survival Course. 1990. (Destroyer Ser.: No. 82). mass mkt. 4.50 o.p. (*0-451-16736-8*, Signet Bks.) NAL.

—Sweet Dreams. (Destroyer Ser.: No. 25). 1989. mass mkt. 3.50 o.s.i (*1-55817-276-9*); 1979. pap. 1.75 o.p. (*0-523-40901-X*) Kensington Publishing Corp. (Pinnacle Bks.).

—Terror Squad. 1985. (Destroyer Ser.: No. 10). 192p. pap. 2.95 o.p. (*0-523-42415-9*, Pinnacle Bks.) Kensington Publishing Corp.

—Timber Lane. 1981. (Destroyer Ser.: No. 42). 192p. pap. 2.25 o.p. (*0-523-41767-5*, Pinnacle Bks.) Kensington Publishing Corp.

—Time Trial. 1983. (Destroyer Ser.: No. 53). 208p. pap. 2.50 o.p. (*0-523-41563-X*, Pinnacle Bks.) Kensington Publishing Corp.

—Voodoo Die. (Destroyer Ser.: No. 33). 1990. mass mkt. 3.50 o.s.i (*1-55817-370-6*); 1979. pap. 1.75 o.p. (*0-523-40909-5*) Kensington Publishing Corp. (Pinnacle Bks.).

—White Water. 1997. (Destroyer Ser.: No. 106). 352p. per. (*0-373-63221-5*, 1-63221-5, Worldwide Library) Harlequin Enterprises, Ltd.

Murphy, Warren & Sapir. Angry White Mailmen. 1996. (Destroyer Ser.: No. 104). per. (*0-373-63219-3*, 1-63219-9, Worldwide Library) Harlequin Enterprises, Ltd.

Murphy, Warren & Sapir, Richard. Angry White Mailmen. abr. ed. 2000. (Destroyer Ser.: No. 104). audio 7.99 (*1-55204-441-6*, GOL-3441) Durkin Hayes Publishing Ltd.

—Arms of Kali. 1984. (Destroyer Ser.: No. 59). mass mkt. 3.95 o.p. (*0-451-15569-6*, Signet Bks.) NAL.

—Bidding War. abr. ed. 2000. (Destroyer Ser.: Vol. 101). audio 7.99 (*1-55204-426-2*, GOL-3426) Durkin Hayes Publishing Ltd.

—Blood Ties. 1987. (Destroyer Ser.). mass mkt. 4.50 o.p. (*0-451-16813-5*); (Destroyer Ser.: No. 69). mass mkt. 3.95 o.p. (*0-451-14879-7*) NAL. (Signet Bks.).

—Brain Drain. 1985. (Destroyer Ser.: No. 22). 192p. (Orig.). pap. 2.95 o.p. (*0-523-42418-3*, Pinnacle Bks.) Kensington Publishing Corp.

—Coin of the Realm. 1989. (Destroyer Ser.: No. 77). 256p. (Orig.). mass mkt. 3.95 o.p. (*0-451-16057-6*, Signet Bks.) NAL.

—The Color of Fear. unabr. ed. 1999. (Destroyer Ser.: No. 99). audio 7.99 (*1-55204-417-3*, GOL-3417) Durkin Hayes Publishing Ltd.

—Deadly Genes. 1999. (Destroyer Ser.: No. 117). per. (*0-373-63232-0*, 1-63232-2, Worldwide Library) Harlequin Enterprises, Ltd.

—The Destroyer Collector's Edition. collector's ed. 2000. No. 2. audio 21.99 (*1-55204-923-X*, CGS-9923); No. 3. audio 21.99 (*1-55204-931-0*, CGS-9931) Durkin Hayes Publishing Ltd.

—Eleventh Hour. 1987. (Destroyer Ser.: No. 70). 224p. mass mkt. 3.50 o.p. (*0-451-15001-5*, Signet Bks.) NAL.

—The Empire Dreams. 1998. (Destroyer Ser.: No. 113). 352p. per. (*0-373-63228-2*, 1-63228-0, Worldwide Library) Harlequin Enterprises, Ltd.

—The End of the Game. 1985. (Destroyer Ser.: No. 60). mass mkt. 3.50 o.p. (*0-451-15265-4*, Signet Bks.) NAL.

—Engines of Destruction. 1996. (Destroyer Ser.: No. 103). per. (*0-373-63218-5*, 1-63218-1, Worldwide Library) Harlequin Enterprises, Ltd.

—Fade to Black. 2000. (Destroyer Ser.: No. 119). 348p. per. (*0-373-63234-7*, Harlequin Bks.) Harlequin Enterprises, Ltd.

—Failing Marks. 1999. (Destroyer Ser.: No. 114). per. (*0-373-63229-0*, Harlequin Bks.) Harlequin Enterprises, Ltd.

—Final Crusade. 1989. (Destroyer Ser.: No. 76). 224p. mass mkt. 4.50 o.p. (*0-451-15913-6*, Signet Bks.) NAL.

—The Final Reel. 1999. (Destroyer Ser.: No. 116). per. (*0-373-63231-2*, Worldwide Library) Harlequin Enterprises, Ltd.

—Fool's Gold. 1983. (Destroyer Ser.: No. 52). 256p. pap. 2.95 o.p. (*0-523-41562-1*, Pinnacle Bks.) Kensington Publishing Corp.

—High Priestess. abr. ed. 1999. (Destroyer Ser.: No. 95). audio 7.99 (*1-55204-393-2*, GOL-3393) Durkin Hayes Publishing Ltd.

—High Priestess. 1994. (Destroyer Ser.: No. 95). per. (*0-373-63210-X*, Harlequin Bks.) Harlequin Enterprises, Ltd.

—Identity Crisis. abr. ed. 1999. (Destroyer Ser.: No. 97). audio 7.99 (*1-55204-405-X*, GOL-3405) Durkin Hayes Publishing Ltd.

—Identity Crisis. 1994. (Destroyer Ser.: No. 97). per. (*0-373-63212-6*, 1-63212-4, Harlequin Bks.) Harlequin Enterprises, Ltd.

—Infernal Revenue. abr. ed. 1999. (Destroyer Ser.: No. 96). audio 7.99 (*1-55204-399-1*, GOL-3399) Durkin Hayes Publishing Ltd.

—Kill or Cure. 1988. (Destroyer Ser.: No. 11). (Orig.). mass mkt. 3.50 o.s.i (*1-55817-148-7*, Pinnacle Bks.) Kensington Publishing Corp.

—Killer Watts. 2000. (Destroyer Ser.: No. 118). mass mkt. (*0-373-63233-9*, 1-63233-0, Worldwide Library) Harlequin Enterprises, Ltd.

—The Last Alchemist. 1986. (Destroyer Ser.). mass mkt. 2.95 o.p. (*0-451-14221-7*); (Destroyer Ser.: No. 64). mass mkt. 3.50 o.p. (*0-451-15274-3*) NAL. (Signet Bks.).

—The Last Monarch. 2000. (Destroyer Ser.: No. 120). 352p. per. (*0-373-63235-5*, 1-63235-5, Worldwide Library) Harlequin Enterprises, Ltd.

—Last Rites. unabr. ed. 1999. (Destroyer Ser.: No. 100). audio 7.99 (*1-55204-423-8*, GOL-3423) Durkin Hayes Publishing Ltd.

—Line of Succession. 1988. (Destroyer Ser.: No. 73). 256p. mass mkt. 3.95 o.p. (*0-451-15396-0*, Signet Bks.) NAL.

—Look into My Eyes. 1987. (Destroyer Ser.: No. 67). mass mkt. 4.50 o.p. (*0-451-14646-8*, Signet Bks.) NAL.

—Lords of the Earth. 1985. (Destroyer Ser.: No. 61). mass mkt. 3.50 o.p. (*0-451-13560-1*, Signet Bks.) NAL.

—Lost Yesterday. 1986. (Destroyer Ser.: No. 65). 256p. mass mkt. 3.95 o.p. (*0-451-15735-4*, Signet Bks.) NAL.

—Master's Challenge. 1984. (Destroyer Ser.: No. 55). 256p. pap. 2.95 o.p. (*0-523-41565-6*, Pinnacle Bks.) Kensington Publishing Corp.

—Misfortune Teller. 1999. (Destroyer Ser.: No. 115). per. (*0-373-63230-4*, 1-63230-6, Harlequin Bks.) Harlequin Enterprises, Ltd.

—Mugger Blood. 1985. (Destroyer Ser.: No. 30). 192p. pap. 2.95 o.p. (*0-523-42419-1*, Pinnacle Bks.) Kensington Publishing Corp.

—Murder's Shield. 1988. (Destroyer Ser.: No. 9). (Orig.). mass mkt. 3.50 o.s.i (*1-55817-146-0*, Pinnacle Bks.) Kensington Publishing Corp.

—An Old-Fashioned War. 1987. (Destroyer Ser.: No. 68). mass mkt. 4.50 o.p. (*0-451-14776-6*, Signet Bks.) NAL.

—Rain of Terror. 1989. (Destroyer Ser.: No. 75). mass mkt. 3.95 o.p. (*0-451-15752-4*, Signet Bks.) NAL.

—Return Engagement. 1988. (Destroyer Ser.: No. 71). 256p. mass mkt. 3.95 o.p. (*0-451-15244-1*, Signet Bks.) NAL.

—Scorched Earth. abr. ed. 2000. (Destroyer Ser.: No. 105). audio 7.99 (*1-55204-446-7*, GOL-3446) Durkin Hayes Publishing Ltd.

—The Seventh Stone. 1985. (Destroyer Ser.). mass mkt. 2.95 o.p. (*0-451-13756-6*); (Destroyer Ser.: No. 62). mass mkt. 3.50 o.p. (*0-451-15571-8*) NAL. (Signet Bks.).

—Skull Duggery. 1991. (Destroyer Ser.: No. 83). 256p. mass mkt. 4.50 o.p. (*0-451-16905-0*, Signet Bks.) NAL.

—The Sky Is Falling. 1986. (Destroyer Ser.: No. 63). mass mkt. 3.95 o.p. (*0-451-15279-4*, Signet Bks.) NAL.

—Slave Safari. 1988. (Destroyer Ser.: No. 12). mass mkt. 3.50 o.s.i (*1-55817-149-5*, Pinnacle Bks.) Kensington Publishing Corp.

—Sole Survivor. 1988. (Destroyer Ser.: No. 72). mass mkt. 3.50 o.p. (*0-451-15359-6*, Signet Bks.) NAL.

—Sue Me. 1986. (Destroyer Ser.). mass mkt. 2.95 o.p. (*0-451-14556-9*); (Destroyer Ser.: No. 66). mass mkt. 3.50 o.p. (*0-451-15278-6*) NAL. (Signet Bks.).

—Summit Chase. 1988. (Destroyer Ser.: No. 8). (Orig.). mass mkt. 3.50 o.p. (*1-55817-145-2*, Pinnacle Bks.) Kensington Publishing Corp.

—Target of Opportunity. unabr. ed. 1999. (Destroyer Ser.: No. 98). audio 7.99 (*1-55204-411-4*, GOL-3411) Durkin Hayes Publishing Ltd.

—Target of Opportunity. 1994. (Destroyer Ser.: No. 98). mass mkt. (*0-373-63213-4*, 1-63213-2, Harlequin Bks.) Harlequin Enterprises, Ltd.

—Terror Squad. 1988. (Destroyer Ser.: No. 10). mass mkt. 3.50 o.s.i (*1-55817-147-9*, Pinnacle Bks.) Kensington Publishing Corp.

—Total Recall. 1984. (Destroyer Ser.: No. 58). pap. 2.50 o.p. (*0-523-41568-0*, Pinnacle Bks.) Kensington Publishing Corp.

—The Ultimate Death. 1992. (Destroyer Ser.: No. 88). 256p. (Orig.). mass mkt. 4.50 o.s.i (*0-451-17115-2*, Signet Bks.) NAL.

—Union Bust. 1988. (Destroyer Ser.: No. 7). (Orig.). mass mkt. 3.50 o.s.i (*1-55817-144-4*, Pinnacle Bks.) Kensington Publishing Corp.

—Unite & Conquer. 1996. (Destroyer Ser.: No. 102). 346p. per. (*0-373-63217-7*, 1-63217-3, Worldwide Library) Harlequin Enterprises, Ltd.

—Walking Wounded. 1988. (Destroyer Ser.: No. 74). mass mkt. 3.50 o.p. (*0-451-15600-5*, Signet Bks.) NAL.

—White Water. abr. ed. 2000. (Destroyer Ser.: No. 106). audio 7.99 (*1-55204-451-3*, GOL-3451) Durkin Hayes Publishing Ltd.

Murphy, Warren & Sapir, Richard, creators. Arabian Nightmare. 1991. (Destroyer Ser.: No. 86). 256p. mass mkt. 4.50 o.p. (*0-451-17060-1*, Signet Bks.) NAL.

—Bidding War. 1995. (Destroyer Ser.: No. 101). 347p. per. (*0-373-63216-9*, 1-63216-5, Worldwide Library) Harlequin Enterprises, Ltd.

—Blood Lust. 1991. (Destroyer Ser.: No. 85). (Illus.). 256p. mass mkt. 4.50 o.p. (*0-451-16990-5*, Signet Bks.) NAL.

—Last Rites. 1995. (Destroyer Ser.: No. 100). 349p. per. (*0-373-63215-0*, 1-63215-7, Harlequin Bks.) Harlequin Enterprises, Ltd.

Murphy, Warren & Sapir, Richard, eds. Hostile Takeover. 1990. (Destroyer Ser.: No. 81). 256p. mass mkt. 4.50 o.p. (*0-451-16601-9*, Signet Bks.) NAL.

Sapir, Richard. Mob Psychology. 1992. (Destroyer Ser.: No. 87). 256p. mass mkt. 4.50 o.p. (*0-451-17114-4*, Signet Bks.) NAL.

Sapir, Richard, ed. Cold Warrior. 1993. (Destroyer Ser.: No. 91). 256p. (Orig.). mass mkt. 4.50 o.p. (*0-451-17484-4*, Signet Bks.) NAL.

—Dark Horse. 1992. (Destroyer Ser.: No. 89). 256p. (Orig.). mass mkt. 4.50 o.s.i (*0-451-17116-0*, Signet Bks.) NAL.

—Feeding Frenzy. 1993. (Destroyer Ser.: No. 94). 256p. (Orig.). mass mkt. 4.50 o.p. (*0-451-17700-2*, Signet Bks.) NAL.

—Ghost in the Machine. 1992. (Destroyer Ser.: No. 90). 256p. mass mkt. 4.50 o.p. (*0-451-17326-0*, Signet Bks.) NAL.

—Ground Zero. 1991. (Destroyer Ser.: No. 84). 256p. (Orig.). mass mkt. 4.50 o.p. (*0-451-16934-4*, Signet Bks.) NAL.

—The Last Dragon. 1993. (Destroyer Ser.: No. 92). 256p. (Orig.). mass mkt. 4.50 o.s.i (*0-451-17558-1*, Signet Bks.) NAL.

—Shooting Schedule. 1990. (Destroyer Ser.: No. 79). 256p. mass mkt. 4.50 o.p. (*0-451-16358-3*, Signet Bks.) NAL.

—Terminal Transmission. 1993. (Destroyer Ser.: No. 93). 256p. (Orig.). mass mkt. 4.50 o.p. (*0-451-17668-5*, Signet Bks.) NAL.

Sapir, Richard & Murphy, Warren. Political Pressure. 2004. (Destroyer Ser.: No. 135). 352p. mass mkt. (*0-373-63250-9*, Gold Eagle) Harlequin Enterprises, Ltd.

**CHIZZIT, EMMA (FICTITIOUS CHARACTER)—FICTION**

Hall, Mary B. Emma Chizzit & the Mother Lode Marauder. 1995. per. (*0-373-26178-0*, Harlequin Bks.) Harlequin Enterprises, Ltd.

—Emma Chizzit & the Mother Lode Marauder. 1993. 19.95 (*0-8027-3225-9*) Walker & Co.

—Emma Chizzit & the Napa Nemesis. 1992. 202p. 19.95 (*0-8027-3211-9*) Walker & Co.

—Emma Chizzit & the Queen Anne Killer. 1989. 224p. 17.95 o.s.i (*0-8027-5751-0*) Walker & Co.

—Emma Chizzit & the Sacramento Stalker. 1995. (WWL Mystery Ser.). pap. (*0-373-28023-8*, 1-28023-9, Harlequin Bks.) Harlequin Enterprises, Ltd.

—Emma Chizzit & the Sacramento Stalker. 1991. 192p. 17.95 o.s.i (*0-8027-5777-4*) Walker & Co.

**CHRESTOMANCI, THE MAGICIAN (FICTITIOUS CHARACTER)—FICTION**

Jones, Diana Wynne. Charmed Life. unabr. ed. 1992. (J). audio 32.95 (*0-7451-4432-2*, CCA 3198, Chivers Children's Audio Bks.) BBC Audiobooks America.

—The Lives of Christopher Chant. (Chrestomanci Quartet Ser.). (J). (gr. 5 up). 2001. 336p. 15.95 (*0-06-029877-4*, Greenwillow Bks.); 1998. (Illus.). 240p. reprint ed. pap. 5.99 (*0-688-16365-3*, Harper Trophy) HarperCollins Children's Bk. Group.

—The Lives of Christopher Chant. 2000. (J). (gr. 4-8). 20.00 o.p. (*0-8446-7145-2*) Smith, Peter Pub., Inc.

—The Magicians of Caprona. (MagicQuest Ser.: No. 12). (YA). pap. 2.25 o.s.i (*0-441-51556-8*) Ace Bks.

—The Magicians of Caprona. 1999. (Chrestomanci Quartet Ser.). (Illus.). 224p. (J). (gr. 5 up). pap. 5.99 (*0-688-16613-X*, Harper Trophy) HarperCollins Children's Bk. Group.

—The Magicians of Caprona. 1999. 12.00 (*0-606-22058-5*) Turtleback Bks.

—Witch Week. (Chrestomanci Quartet Ser.). 2001. 288p. (J). (gr. 5 up). 15.95 (*0-06-029879-0*, Greenwillow Bks.); 1997. (Illus.). 224p. (J). (gr. 5-9). pap. 5.99 (*0-688-15545-6*, Harper Trophy); 1993. 224p. (YA). (gr. 7 up). 14.00 o.p. (*0-688-12374-0*, Greenwillow Bks.); 1982. 224p. (YA). (gr. 7 up). 12.95 o.p. (*0-688-01534-4*, Greenwillow Bks.) HarperCollins Children's Bk. Group.

—Witch Week. 1988. 256p. (J). (gr. 3-7). reprint ed. pap. 3.50 o.p. (*0-394-80600-X*, Knopf Bks. for Young Readers) Random Hse. Children's Bks.

—Witch Week. 1997. (Chrestomanci Quartet Ser.). (J). 12.00 (*0-606-12106-4*) Turtleback Bks.

**CHRISTENSEN, JIM (FICTITIOUS CHARACTER)—FICTION**

Smith, Martin J. Shadow Image. 1998. 384p. mass mkt. 5.99 o.s.i (*0-515-12286-6*, Jove) Berkley Publishing Group.

—Straw Men. 2001. 336p. mass mkt. 6.99 o.s.i (*0-515-12950-X*, Jove) Berkley Publishing Group.

—Time Release. 1997. 352p. mass mkt. 5.99 o.s.i (*0-515-12028-6*, Jove) Berkley Publishing Group.

**CHRISTOPHER, PAUL (FICTITIOUS CHARACTER)—FICTION**

McCarry, Charles. The Bride of the Wilderness. 1989. mass mkt. 5.99 o.p. (*0-451-15958-6*, Signet Bks.); 1988. 420p. text 18.95 o.p. (*0-453-00592-6*) NAL.

—The Last Supper. 1983. 384p. 15.95 o.p. (*0-525-24173-6*, 01549-460, Dutton) Dutton/Plume.

—The Last Supper. 1984. 448p. mass mkt. 4.95 o.p. (*0-451-16047-9*); mass mkt. 3.50 o.p. (*0-451-12857-5*); mass mkt. 3.95 o.p. (*0-451-15124-0*) NAL. (Signet Bks.).

—The Last Supper. l.t. ed. 1986. (Charnwood Large Print Ser.). 656p. 29.99 o.p. (*0-7089-8322-7*, Charnwood) Thorpe, F. A. Pubs. GBR. *Dist:* Ulverscroft Large Print Bks., Ltd., Ulverscroft Large Print Canada, Ltd.

—The Miernik Dossier. 1976. mass mkt. 1.95 o.s.i (*0-345-25640-9*) Ballantine Bks.

—The Miernik Dossier. 1985. 320p. mass mkt. 4.50 o.p. (*0-451-16064-9*); mass mkt. 3.95 o.p. (*0-451-13652-7*) NAL. (Signet Bks.).

—Second Sight: The Last Paul Christopher Thriller. 1991. 480p. 19.95 o.p. (*0-525-24985-0*) Dutton/Plume.

—Second Sight: The Last Paul Christopher Thriller. 1992. 496p. mass mkt. 5.99 o.p. (*0-451-17251-5*) NAL.

—The Secret Lovers. 1978. mass mkt. 1.95 o.s.i (*0-449-23549-1*, Fawcett) Ballantine Bks.

—The Secret Lovers. 1977. 8.95 o.p. (*0-525-19934-9*, Dutton) Dutton/Plume.

—The Secret Lovers. 1984. mass mkt. 3.95 o.p. (*0-451-13243-2*); 320p. mass mkt. 4.50 o.p. (*0-451-16005-3*) NAL. (Signet Bks.).

—Shelley's Heart. 1997. mass mkt. 6.99 o.s.i (*0-8041-1474-9*, Ivy Bks.); 1996. mass mkt. 6.99 o.s.i (*0-449-22168-7*, Fawcett) Ballantine Bks.

—The Tears of Autumn. 1975. 320p. mass mkt. 1.95 o.s.i (*0-449-22649-2*, C2649, Fawcett) Ballantine Bks.

—The Tears of Autumn. 1984. mass mkt. 3.95 o.p. (*0-451-13128-2*); 320p. mass mkt. 4.50 o.p. (*0-451-16039-8*) NAL. (Signet Bks.).

**CIAMPI, MARLENE (FICTITIOUS CHARACTER)—FICTION**

Tanenbaum, Robert K. Absolute Rage. 2003. (Illus.). 480p. mass mkt. 7.99 (*0-7434-0345-2*, Pocket) Simon & Schuster.

—Act of Revenge. unabr. ed. 1999. (Butch Karp Mystery Ser.). audio 88.00 (*0-7366-4742-2*, 5080) Books on Tape, Inc.

—Act of Revenge. l.t. ed. 2001. (Large Print Book Ser.). 575p. 28.95 (*1-58724-025-4*, Wheeler Publishing, Inc.) Gale Group.

—Act of Revenge. 1999. 416p. o.p. (*0-06-019218-6*, HarperFlamingo) HarperCollins Pubs. Canada, Ltd.

—Act of Revenge. 2000. 544p. mass mkt. 7.50 (*0-06-109730-6*, HarperTorch) Morrow/Avon.

—Corruption of Blood. unabr. ed. 1998. (Butch Karp Mystery Ser.). audio 80.00 (*0-7366-4045-2*, 4544) Books on Tape, Inc.

—Corruption of Blood. 1995. 368p. 22.95 o.p. (*0-525-93870-2*, Dutton) Dutton/Plume.

—Corruption of Blood. 1996. 416p. mass mkt. 7.99 (*0-451-18196-4*, Signet Bks.) NAL.

—Depraved Indifference. 1989. 18.95 o.p. (*0-453-00679-5*); 1990. 400p. reprint ed. mass mkt. 7.99 (*0-451-16842-9*, Signet Bks.) NAL.

—Falsely Accused. unabr. ed. 1998. (Butch Karp Mystery Ser.). audio 56.00 (*0-7366-4026-6*, 452511.95) Books on Tape, Inc.

—Falsely Accused. 1996. 320p. 23.95 o.s.i (*0-525-94168-1*) Dutton/Plume.

—Falsely Accused. 1997. 448p. mass mkt. 7.99 (*0-451-19000-9*, Signet Bks.) NAL.

—Immoral Certainty. unabr. ed. 1997. (Butch Karp Mystery Ser.). audio 64.00 (*0-7366-3689-7*, 4368) Books on Tape, Inc.

—Immoral Certainty. 1991. 304p. 18.95 o.p. (*0-525-24941-9*, Dutton) Dutton/Plume.

—Immoral Certainty. 1992. 400p. reprint ed. mass mkt. 7.99 (*0-451-17186-1*, Signet Bks.) NAL.

—Irresistible Impulse. unabr. ed. 1998. (Butch Karp Mystery Ser.). audio 64.00 (*0-7366-4134-3*, 4639) Books on Tape, Inc.

—Irresistible Impulse. 1997. 352p. 24.95 o.p. (*0-525-94310-2*) Dutton/Plume.

—Irresistible Impulse. 1998. 445p. mass mkt. 6.99 (*0-451-19261-3*, Signet Bks.) NAL.

—Justice Denied. unabr. ed. 1997. (Butch Karp Mystery Ser.). audio 64.00 (*0-7366-3688-9*, 4367) Books on Tape, Inc.

—Justice Denied. 1994. 320p. 18.95 o.p. (*0-525-93814-1*) Dutton/Plume.

—Justice Denied. abr. ed. 1994. pap. 16.00 o.p. incl. audio (*0-453-00903-4*, 25024-33894) Penguin/HighBridge.

—Material Witness. unabr. ed. 1997. (Butch Karp Mystery Ser.). audio 64.00 (*0-7366-3687-0*, 4366) Books on Tape, Inc.

—Material Witness. 1993. 320p. 20.00 o.p. (*0-525-93579-7*, Dutton) Dutton/Plume.

—Material Witness. 1994. 416p. mass mkt. 7.99 (*0-451-18020-8*, Signet Bks.) NAL.

—No Lesser Plea. 1988. 368p. reprint ed. mass mkt. 7.99 (*0-451-15496-7*, Signet Bks.) NAL.

—Reckless Endangerment. unabr. ed. 1999. (Butch Karp Mystery Ser.). audio 88.00 (*0-7366-4351-6*, 4828) Books on Tape, Inc.

—Reckless Endangerment. abr. ed. 1998. audio 17.95 o.p. (*1-56740-784-6*, 443, Nova Audio Bks.); audio 26.95 (*1-56740-059-0*, 10, Bookcassette); audio 73.25 o.p. (*1-56740-588-6*, 1001) Brilliance Audio.

—Reckless Endangerment. 1998. 352p. 23.95 o.p. (*0-525-94347-1*) Dutton/Plume.

—Reckless Endangerment. 1999. 448p. reprint ed. mass mkt. 7.99 (*0-451-19328-8*, Signet Bks.) NAL.

—Reversible Error. unabr. ed. 1997. (Butch Karp Mystery Ser.). audio 56.00 (*0-7366-3686-2*, 4365) Books on Tape, Inc.

—Reversible Error. 1992. 288p. 20.00 o.p. (*0-525-93423-5*, Dutton) Dutton/Plume.

—Reversible Error. 1993. 448p. reprint ed. mass mkt. 7.99 (*0-451-17519-0*, Signet Bks.) NAL.

—True Justice. unabr. ed. 2001. 10p. audio 84.95 (*0-7927-2397-X*, CSL 286); audio compact disk 115.95 (*0-7927-9984-4*, SLD 035) BBC Audiobooks America. (Chivers Sound Library).

—True Justice. 2000. 384p. 24.95 o.s.i (*0-7434-0589-7*, Atria); 2001. (Illus.). 464p. reprint ed. mass mkt. 7.99 (*0-7434-0590-0*, Pocket) Simon & Schuster.

—True Justice. 2002. audio 14.95 (*0-7435-2759-3*, Encore); 2000. audio 25.00 (*0-7435-0553-0*, Simon & Schuster Audioworks) Simon & Schuster Audio.

—True Justice. l.t. ed. 2001. (Thorndike Mystery Ser.). 681p. 30.95 (*0-7862-3032-0*) Thorndike Pr.

**CIMORENE (FICTITIOUS CHARACTER)—FICTION**

Wrede, Patricia C. Dealing with Dragons. unabr. ed. 1996. (Enchanted Forest Ser.: Bk. 1). (J). (gr. 7-12). audio 32.00 (*0-8072-7634-0*, YA906CX, Listening Library) Random Hse. Audio Publishing Group.

—Dealing with Dragons. unabr. ed. 1996. (Enchanted Forest Ser.: Bk. 1). 212p. (J). (gr. 3-6). pap. 37.00 incl. audio (*0-8072-7635-9*, YA906SP, Listening Library) Random Hse. Audio Publishing Group.

—Dealing with Dragons, Set. unabr. ed. 1999. (YA). audio 29.98 Highsmith Inc.

**CINQ-MARS, EMILE (FICTITIOUS CHARACTER)—FICTION**

Farrow, John. City of Ice: A Novel. 1999. 403p. 25.95 o.s.i (*0-375-50140-1*) Random Hse., Inc.

—Ice Lake: A Novel. 2001. 368p. pap. 19.00 (*0-8129-9264-4*) Random House Adult Trade Publishing Group.

—Ice Lake: A Novel. 2001. E-Book 19.95 (*1-58836-016-4*) Random Hse., Inc.

**CLAH, ELLA (FICTITIOUS CHARACTER)—FICTION**

Thurlo, Aimee & Thurlo, David. Bad Medicine. 384p. 1998. mass mkt. 6.99 (*0-8125-6458-8*); 1997. 23.95 (*0-312-86328-4*) Doherty, Tom Assocs., LLC. (Forge Bks.).

—Blackening Song. (Ella Clah Novel Ser.). 1997. 429p. mass mkt. 5.99 (*0-8125-6756-0*); 1995. 384p. 14.99 o.p. (*0-312-85652-0*); 2001. 384p. reprint ed. pap. 14.95 (*0-7653-0256-X*) Doherty, Tom Assocs., LLC. (Forge Bks.).

—Changing Woman. E-Book 24.95 (*0-312-70549-2*, Tor Bks.); 2nd ed. 2002. 384p. 24.95 (*0-312-87059-0*, CPHC0654, Forge Bks.) Doherty, Tom Assocs., LLC.

—Death Walker: An Ella Clah Novel. (Ella Clah Novel Ser.). 1997. 338p. mass mkt. 6.99 (*0-8125-6758-7*); 1996. 352p. 23.95 o.p. (*0-312-85651-2*); 2003. 384p. reprint ed. pap. 14.95 (*0-7653-0651-4*) Doherty, Tom Assocs., LLC. (Forge Bks.).

—Enemy Way. (Ella Clah Novel Ser.: No. 4). 1999. 352p. mass mkt. 6.99 (*0-8125-6459-6*); 1998. 350p. 23.95 (*0-312-85520-6*) Doherty, Tom Assocs., LLC. (Forge Bks.).

—Plant Them Deep. mass mkt. (*0-7653-4398-3*); 2003. 336p. 24.95 (*0-7653-0478-3*) Doherty, Tom Assocs., LLC. (Forge Bks.).

—Shooting Chant: An Ella Clah Novel. 2000. 349p. 23.95 (*0-312-87061-2*, Forge Bks.) Doherty, Tom Assocs., LLC.

—Tracking Bear. E-Book 24.95 (*0-312-71003-8*, Tor Bks.); 2003. (Ella Clah Novel Ser.: No. 8). 384p. 24.95 (*0-7653-0476-7*, Forge Bks.) Doherty, Tom Assocs., LLC.

—Tracking Bear: An Ella Clah Novel. 2004. (Ella Clah Ser.). 384p. mass mkt. 6.99 (*0-7653-4396-7*, Forge Bks.) Doherty, Tom Assocs., LLC.

**CLAIBORNE, ADAM (FICTITIOUS CHARACTER)—FICTION**

Schilling, Vivian. Sacred Prey. 1996. 279p. pap. 5.50 (*0-312-95693-2*, St. Martin's Paperbacks) St. Martin's Pr.

—Sacred Prey. Lovendahl, Shari, ed. 2nd ed. 1994. 245p. 9.95 (*0-9637846-0-9*, 784605) Truman Pr., Inc.

**CLAIBORNE, CLAIRE (FICTITIOUS CHARACTER)—FICTION**

Dunbar, Sophie. A Bad Hair Day: An Eclaire Mystery. 295th ed. 1998. (Eclaire Mysteries Ser.: No. 3). 296p. reprint ed. mass mkt. 5.95 (*1-890768-08-1*, Intrigue Pr.) Corvus Publishing.

—A Bad Hair Day: An Eclaire Mystery. 1996. 272p. 22.95 o.p. (*0-312-13926-8*, Saint Martin's Minotaur) St. Martin's Pr.

—Behind Eclaire's Doors. unabr. ed. 1998. (Claire & Dan Claiborne Eclaire Mystery Ser.: Bk. 1). audio 39.95 (*1-55686-804-9*) Books in Motion.

—Behind Eclaire's Doors. 1994. mass mkt. 4.99 o.p. (*0-312-95259-7*, St. Martin's Paperbacks) St. Martin's Pr.

—Behind Eclaire's Doors: A Tale of Murder & Mayhem in New Orleans. 1993. 224p. 17.95 o.p. (*0-312-09280-6*, Saint Martin's Minotaur) St. Martin's Pr.

—Behind Eclaire's Doors: An Eclaire Mystery. 1998. (Eclaire Mysteries Ser.: No. 1). 296p. reprint ed. mass mkt. 5.95 (*1-890768-10-3*, Intrigue Pr.) Corvus Publishing.

—Redneck Riviera: An Eclaire Mystery. 1998. (Eclaire Mysteries Ser.: Vol. 2). 290p. mass mkt. 5.50 (*1-890768-06-5*, Intrigue Pr.) Corvus Publishing.

—Shiveree. (Eclaire Mysteries Ser.: 4). 416p. 2000. mass mkt. 5.95 (*1-890768-24-3*); 1999. 22.95 (*1-890768-11-1*) Corvus Publishing. (Intrigue Pr.).

**CLAIBORNE, DAN (FICTITIOUS CHARACTER)—FICTION**

Dunbar, Sophie. A Bad Hair Day: An Eclaire Mystery. 295th ed. 1998. (Eclaire Mysteries Ser.: No. 3). 296p. reprint ed. mass mkt. 5.95 (*1-890768-08-1*, Intrigue Pr.) Corvus Publishing.

—A Bad Hair Day: An Eclaire Mystery. 1996. 272p. 22.95 o.p. (*0-312-13926-8*, Saint Martin's Minotaur) St. Martin's Pr.

—Behind Eclaire's Doors. unabr. ed. 1998. (Claire & Dan Claiborne Eclaire Mystery Ser.: Bk. 1). audio 39.95 (*1-55686-804-9*) Books in Motion.

—Behind Eclaire's Doors. 1994. mass mkt. 4.99 o.p. (*0-312-95259-7*, St. Martin's Paperbacks) St. Martin's Pr.

—Behind Eclaire's Doors: A Tale of Murder & Mayhem in New Orleans. 1993. 224p. 17.95 o.p. (*0-312-09280-6*, Saint Martin's Minotaur) St. Martin's Pr.

—Behind Eclaire's Doors: An Eclaire Mystery. 1998. (Eclaire Mysteries Ser.: No. 1). 296p. reprint ed. mass mkt. 5.95 (*1-890768-10-3*, Intrigue Pr.) Corvus Publishing.

—Redneck Riviera: An Eclaire Mystery. 1998. (Eclaire Mysteries Ser.: Vol. 2). 290p. mass mkt. 5.50 (*1-890768-06-5*, Intrigue Pr.) Corvus Publishing.

—Shiveree. (Eclaire Mysteries Ser.: 4). 416p. 2000. mass mkt. 5.95 (*1-890768-24-3*); 1999. 22.95 (*1-890768-11-1*) Corvus Publishing. (Intrigue Pr.).

**CLAIBORNE, DOLORES (FICTITIOUS CHARACTER)—FICTION**

King, Stephen. Dolores Claiborne. (FRE.). pap. 12.95 (*2-277-04742-2*) 84, Editions FRA. *Dist:* Distribooks, Inc.

—Dolores Claiborne. l.t. ed. (General Ser.). 355p. 1993. pap. 17.95 (*0-8161-5641-7*); 1992. lib. bdg. 25.00 o.p. (*0-8161-5640-9*) Gale Group. (Macmillan Reference USA).

—Dolores Claiborne. 384p. 1995. mass mkt. 6.99 o.p. (*0-451-18411-4*); 1993. reprint ed. mass mkt. 7.99 (*0-451-17709-6*) NAL. (Signet Bks.).

—Dolores Claiborne. unabr. ed. 1995. (SPA.). 29.95 o.p. (*0-7871-0643-7*, 893235) NewStar Media, Inc.

—Dolores Claiborne. abr. unabr. ed. 1995. pap. 30.00 o.p. incl. audio (*0-453-00957-3*); Set. 1993. 30.00 o.p. incl. audio (*0-453-00803-8*, 892486) Penguin/HighBridge.

—Dolores Claiborne. 6.98 o.p. (*0-8317-1186-8*) Smithmark Pubs., Inc.

—Dolores Claiborne. 1993. 14.04 (*0-606-05811-7*) Turtleback Bks.

—Dolores Claiborne. 1993. 320p. 23.50 o.s.i (*0-670-84452-7*); 352p. 25.00 o.p. (*0-670-84936-7*) Viking Penguin. (Viking).

**CLANCY, JACK (FICTITIOUS CHARACTER)—FICTION**

Beck, K. K. Death in a Deck Chair. 1987. 176p. mass mkt. 4.99 o.s.i (*0-8041-0118-3*, Ivy Bks.) Ballantine Bks.
—Death in a Deck Chair. 1984. 12.95 (*0-8027-5601-8*) Walker & Co.
—Murder in a Mummy Case. l.t. ed. 1989. pap. 8.95 o.p. (*1-55504-841-2*) BBC Audiobooks America.
—Murder in a Mummy Case. 1987. 176p. mass mkt. 3.95 o.s.i (*0-8041-0117-5*, Ivy Bks.) Ballantine Bks.
—Murder in a Mummy Case. 1986. 176p. 15.95 o.s.i (*0-8027-5655-7*) Walker & Co.
—Peril under the Palms. 1990. 176p. mass mkt. 4.99 o.s.i (*0-8041-0594-4*, Ivy Bks.) Ballantine Bks.
—Peril under the Palms. 1989. 208p. 18.95 (*0-8027-5715-4*) Walker & Co.

**CLARK, CAYCE (FICTITIOUS CHARACTER)—FICTION**

Eberhart, Mignon G. Another Man's Murder. 19.95 (*0-89190-539-1*) Amereon, Ltd.
—Another Man's Murder. 1988. 160p. mass mkt. 5.50 o.s.i (*0-446-34930-5*) Warner Bks., Inc.

**CLARK, DESAIX (FICTITIOUS CHARACTER)—FICTION**

Pieczenik, Steve. Maximum Vigilance. 1993. 576p. mass mkt. 5.99 o.p. (*0-446-36468-1*); 1992. 448p. 19.95 o.p. (*0-446-51556-6*) Warner Bks., Inc.
—Pax Pacifica. 1995. 352p. mass mkt. 5.99 o.p. (*0-446-60250-7*); (*0-446-51818-2*); 336p. 22.95 o.s.i (*0-446-51557-4*) Warner Bks., Inc.

**CLARK, JOHN (FICTITIOUS CHARACTER)—FICTION**

Clancy, Tom. The Bear & the Dragon. 2000. 752p. 28.95 (*0-399-14563-X*) Penguin Group (USA) Inc.
—The Bear & the Dragon. abr. ed. 2000. audio 27.95 (*0-375-41582-3*); audio compact disk 31.95 (*0-375-41583-1*) Random Hse. Audio Publishing Group. (RH Audio).
—The Bear & the Dragon. l.t. ed. 1504p. 2001. pap. 15.95 (*0-375-72810-4*); 2000. 28.95 (*0-375-43069-5*) Random Hse. Large Print.
—The Cardinal of the Kremlin. 1989. 560p. mass mkt. 7.99 (*0-425-11684-0*) Berkley Publishing Group.
—The Cardinal of the Kremlin. unabr. ed. 1988. audio 112.00 (*0-7366-1408-7*, 2297-A) Books on Tape, Inc.
—The Cardinal of the Kremlin. 1988. 544p. 27.95 (*0-399-13345-3*, G. P. Putnam's Sons) Penguin Group (USA) Inc.
—The Cardinal of the Kremlin. abr. ed. 1988. audio 17.00 (*0-671-66074-8*, Simon & Schuster Audioworks) Simon & Schuster Audio.
—The Cardinal of the Kremlin. l.t. ed. 1991. 871p. lib. bdg. 25.95 (*0-89621-232-7*) Thorndike Pr.
—The Cardinal of the Kremlin. 1989. 13.09 o.p. (*0-606-00979-5*) Turtleback Bks.
—Clear & Present Danger. 704p. 1994. mass mkt. 7.50 o.s.i (*0-425-14437-2*); 1990. mass mkt. 7.99 (*0-425-12212-3*) Berkley Publishing Group.
—Clear & Present Danger, Pt. 1. unabr. ed. 1989. audio 80.00 (*0-7366-1630-6*, 2488-A) Books on Tape, Inc.
—Clear & Present Danger. unabr. ed. 1990. audio 162.55 (*1-56100-055-8*, 1144, Unabridged Library Editions); audio 38.95 (*0-930435-61-3*, 65, Bookcassette) Brilliance Audio.
—Clear & Present Danger. l.t. ed. 1990. (Magna Large Print Ser.). 1140p. o.p. (*1-85057-853-2*) Magna Large Print Bks. GBR. *Dist:* Ulverscroft Large Print Canada, Ltd.
—Clear & Present Danger. 1989. 544p. 27.95 (*0-399-13440-9*, G. P. Putnam's Sons) Penguin Putnam Bks. for Young Readers.
—Clear & Present Danger, Set. abr. ed. 1994. (Jack Ryan Adventure Ser.). 180p. audio 17.00 (*0-671-89800-0*, 390531, Simon & Schuster Audioworks) Simon & Schuster Audio.
—Clear & Present Danger. 1990. 13.09 o.p. (*0-606-00980-9*) Turtleback Bks.
—Executive Orders. 1997. 1376p. mass mkt. 7.99 (*0-425-15863-2*); (YA). 7.50 (*0-425-16057-2*) Berkley Publishing Group.
—Executive Orders. unabr. ed. 1996. Pt. 1. audio 104.00 (*0-7366-3513-0*, 4152-A); Pt. 2. audio 104.00 (*0-7366-3514-9*, 4152-B); Pt. 3. audio 80.00 (*0-7366-3515-7*, 4152-C) Books on Tape, Inc.
—Executive Orders. 1996. 896p. 27.95 (*0-399-14218-5*); 752p. 150.00 (*0-399-14219-3*) Penguin Group (USA) Inc. (G. P. Putnam's Sons).
—Executive Orders, Set. abr. ed. 2000. audio 25.95 (*0-375-43696-0*); 1996. audio 26.95 (*0-679-43696-0*, 694152); 1996. audio compact disk 29.95 (*0-679-45789-5*) Random Hse. Audio Publishing Group. (RH Audio).
—Executive Orders. 1998. (YA). 7.98 o.p. (*0-7651-0899-2*) Smithmark Pubs., Inc.
—Executive Orders. l.t. ed. 1996. (Basic Ser.). 1437p. 30.95 (*0-7862-0855-4*) Thorndike Pr.
—Executive Orders. 1996. 14.04 (*0-606-17126-6*) Turtleback Bks.
—Ordenes Ejecutivas I. 3rd ed. 1998. (SPA., Illus.). 348p. (*84-08-02448-5*) GeoPlaneta, Editorial, S. A.
—Ordenes Ejecutivas II. 1998. (SPA., Illus.). 468p. (*84-08-02449-3*) GeoPlaneta, Editorial, S. A.
—Peligro Imminente. 6th ed. 1998. (Jet de Plaza & Janes Ser.: Vol. 150). Orig. Title: Clear & Present Danger. (SPA., Illus.). 617p. pap. 8.50 (*84-01-49525-3*) Plaza & Janés Editories, S.A. ESP. *Dist:* Lectorum Pubns., Inc.
—Rainbow Six. 1999. 7.99 (*0-425-17005-5*); 912p. reprint ed. mass mkt. 8.50 (*0-425-17034-9*) Berkley Publishing Group.
—Rainbow Six, Pt. 2. unabr. ed. 1998. audio 96.00 (*0-7366-4531-4*, 4703-B) Books on Tape, Inc.
—Rainbow Six. l.t. ed. 1999. pap. 27.95 o.p. (*0-7838-0160-2*, Macmillan Reference USA) Gale Group.
—Rainbow Six. abr. ed. 1999. audio 25.95 Highsmith Inc.
—Rainbow Six. 1998. 752p. 27.95 (*0-399-14390-4*); 800p. 150.00 (*0-399-14413-7*) Penguin Group (USA) Inc. (G. P. Putnam's Sons).
—Rainbow Six. abr. ed. 1998. audio 26.95 (*0-375-40267-5*, 696023); audio compact disk 31.95 (*0-375-40347-7*) Random Hse. Audio Publishing Group. (RH Audio).
—Rainbow Six. l.t. ed. 1998. 800p. pap. 27.95 (*0-375-70324-1*) Random Hse. Large Print.
—Rainbow Six. 1998. 14.55 (*0-606-17207-6*) Turtleback Bks.
—The Sum of All Fears. 1992. 928p. mass mkt. 7.99 o.s.i (*0-425-13354-0*) Berkley Publishing Group.
—The Sum of All Fears, Pt. 1. unabr. ed. 1991. audio 112.00 (*0-7366-2026-5*, 2841-A) Books on Tape, Inc.
—The Sum of All Fears. 1991. 100.00 o.p. (*0-399-13631-2*); 640p. 27.95 (*0-399-13615-0*) Penguin Group (USA) Inc.
—The Sum of All Fears. abr. ed. 1991. (Jack Ryan Adventure Ser.). audio 24.00 (*0-671-73806-2*, 692319, Simon & Schuster Audioworks) Simon & Schuster Audio.
—The Sum of All Fears. l.t. ed. 1992. (Paperback Bestsellers Ser.). 1507p. pap. 20.95 (*1-56054-947-5*) Thorndike Pr.
—The Sum of All Fears. 1992. 14.04 (*0-606-00978-7*) Turtleback Bks.
—Without Remorse. 1993. 640p. 25.95 (*0-399-13825-0*); 150.00 o.s.i (*0-399-13840-4*) Penguin Group (USA) Inc. (G. P. Putnam's Sons).

**CLARK, MEGAN (FICTITIOUS CHARACTER)—FICTION**

Meredith, Doris R. By Hook or by Book. 2000. (Prime Crime Mysteries Ser.). 272p. mass mkt. 5.99 (*0-425-17465-4*, Prime Crime) Berkley Publishing Group.
—Murder in Volume. 2000. (Prime Crime Mysteries Ser.). 256p. mass mkt. 6.50 (*0-425-17309-7*, Prime Crime) Berkley Publishing Group.
—Murder Past Due. 2001. 240p. mass mkt. 5.99 (*0-425-17800-5*, Prime Crime) Berkley Publishing Group.

**CLAY, MARCUS (FICTITIOUS CHARACTER)—FICTION**

Pelecanos, George P. King Suckerman. 1998. 336p. mass mkt. 6.99 (*0-440-22595-7*) Dell Publishing.
—King Suckerman. 1997. 288p. (gr. 8). 28.00 o.p. (*0-316-69590-4*) Little Brown & Co.
—The Sweet Forever. 1999. 384p. mass mkt. 6.99 (*0-440-23493-X*) Dell Publishing.
—The Sweet Forever. 1998. 304p. (gr. 8). 23.95 (*0-316-69109-7*) Little Brown & Co.

**CLAYBORNE FAMILY (FICTITIOUS CHARACTERS)—FICTION**

Garwood, Julie. The Clayborne Brides: One Pink Rose, One White Rose, One Red Rose. 1998. (Clayborne Brides Ser.). 464p. pap. 7.99 (*0-671-02177-X*, Pocket) Simon & Schuster.
—The Clayborne Brides: The Rose Trilogy. l.t. ed. 1998. (Large Print Bks.). 26.95 o.p. (*1-56895-515-4*, Wheeler Publishing, Inc.) Gale Group.
—Come the Spring. l.t. ed. 1999. 28.95 (*1-56895-630-4*, Wheeler Publishing, Inc.) Gale Group.
—Come the Spring. unabr. ed. 1998. audio 66.00 (*0-7887-1969-6*, 95356E7) Recorded Bks., LLC.
—Come the Spring. 2003. 384p. mass mkt. 5.99 (*0-7434-6712-4*, Pocket); 1998. 384p. per. 6.99 (*0-671-01741-1*, Pocket); 1997. 368p. 24.00 o.s.i (*0-671-00333-X*, Atria); 1998. 384p. reprint ed. pap. 7.99 (*0-671-00334-8*, Pocket) Simon & Schuster.
—Come the Spring. 2003. audio 9.95 (*0-7435-3300-3*, Encore); 2003. audio compact disk 9.95 (*0-7435-3302-X*, Encore); 1999. audio 9.98 (*0-671-04685-3*, Simon & Schuster Audioworks); 1997. audio 18.00 o.s.i (*0-671-57684-4*, 395487, Simon & Schuster Audioworks) Simon & Schuster Audio.
—For the Roses. 2001. pap. 6.99 (*0-671-00992-3*, Pocket); 1999. per. 3.99 (*0-671-02183-4*, Pocket); 1997. mass mkt. 6.99 (*0-671-01498-6*, Pocket); 1996. 576p. mass mkt. 7.99 (*0-671-87098-X*, Pocket); 1995. 512p. 23.00 o.p. (*0-671-87097-1*, Atria) Simon & Schuster.
—For the Roses, Set. abr. ed. 1995. audio 17.00 o.s.i (*0-671-53447-5*, Simon & Schuster Audioworks) Simon & Schuster Audio.
—For the Roses. l.t. ed. 1996. (Romance Ser.). 808p. lib. bdg. 27.95 (*0-7838-1639-1*) Thorndike Pr.
—One Pink, One White & One Red Rose. abr. ed. 1997. audio 18.00 (*0-671-57690-9*, Simon & Schuster Audioworks) Simon & Schuster Audio.
—One Pink Rose. 1997. per. 2.66 (*0-671-02019-6*); 128p. pap. 2.99 (*0-671-01008-5*) Simon & Schuster. (Pocket).
—One Red Rose. 1997. per. 2.66 (*0-671-02024-2*); 160p. mass mkt. 2.99 o.s.i (*0-671-01010-7*) Simon & Schuster. (Pocket).
—One White Rose. 1997. per. 2.66 (*0-671-02020-X*); 128p. mass mkt. 2.99 o.s.i (*0-671-01009-3*) Simon & Schuster. (Pocket).

**CLAYTON, JEFFREY (FICTITIOUS CHARACTER)—FICTION**

Katzenbach, John. State of Mind. 1998. 544p. mass mkt. 6.99 (*0-345-42253-8*); 1997. 409p. 24.00 o.s.i (*0-345-38631-0*, Ballantine Bks.) Ballantine Bks.
—State of Mind. l.t. ed. 1998. (Large Print Book Ser.). 26.95 o.p. (*1-56895-528-6*, Wheeler Publishing, Inc.) Gale Group.

**CLEEVER, DENISE (FICTITIOUS CHARACTER)—FICTION**

McNab, Claire. Death by Death: A Denise Cleever Thriller. 2003. 216p. pap. 12.95 (*1-931513-34-1*) Bella Bks., Inc.
—Death Understood: A Denise Cleever Thriller. 2000. 222p. pap. 11.95 (*1-56280-264-X*) Naiad Pr., Inc.
—Murder Undercover: A Denise Cleever Thriller. 1999. (Denise Cleever Thrillers Ser.). 240p. pap. 12.95 (*1-56280-259-3*) Naiad Pr., Inc.
—Recognition Factor: A Denise Cleever Thriller. 2002. 208p. pap. 12.95 (*1-931513-24-4*) Bella Bks., Inc.

**CLEMENS, ATTA OLIVIA (FICTITIOUS CHARACTER)—FICTION**

Yarbro, Chelsea Quinn. A Candle for d'Artagnan. 1994. 485p. pap. 15.95 (*0-312-89019-2*, Orb Bks.); 1989. (Illus.). ix,485p. pap. 22.95 o.p. (*0-312-93202-2*, Tor Bks.) Doherty, Tom Assocs., LLC.
—Crusader's Torch. 1989. mass mkt. 4.95 (*0-8125-0178-0*); 1988. xiii,459p. 18.95 o.p. (*0-312-93088-7*) Doherty, Tom Assocs., LLC. (Tor Bks.).
—A Flame in Byzantium. 1988. 480p. mass mkt. 4.50 (*0-8125-2804-2*); 1987. ix, 470p. 17.95 o.p. (*0-312-93026-7*) Doherty, Tom Assocs., LLC. (Tor Bks.).

**CLEMENT, JULES (FICTITIOUS CHARACTER)—FICTION**

Harrison, Jamie. Blue Deer Thaw: A Mystery. l.t. ed. 2001. (Softcover Ser.). 376p. pap. 23.95 (*1-58724-082-3*, Wheeler Publishing, Inc.) Gale Group.
—Blue Deer Thaw: A Mystery. 2000. 271p. 22.95 (*0-7868-6422-2*) Hyperion Pr.
—Blue Deer Thaw: A Mystery. 2001. 288p. mass mkt. 6.50 (*0-312-97885-5*, St. Martin's Paperbacks) St. Martin's Pr.
—The Edge of the Crazies. 1995. 384p. 20.95 (*0-7868-6085-5*) Hyperion Pr.
—The Edge of the Crazies. 1996. 324p. mass mkt. 6.99 (*0-312-95942-7*, St. Martin's Paperbacks) St. Martin's Pr.
—Going Local. 1996. (Sheriff Jules Clement Ser.: Bk. 2). 323p. 21.95 o.p. (*0-7868-6108-8*) Hyperion Pr.
—Going Local. (Dead Letter Mysteries Ser.). 1998. 336p. mass mkt. 5.99 (*0-312-96484-6*, St. Martin's Paperbacks); Vol. 1. 1997. mass mkt. (*0-312-96271-1*) St. Martin's Pr.
—An Unfortunate Prairie Occurrence. 1998. 304p. 22.95 o.p. (*0-7868-6260-2*) Hyperion Pr.
—An Unfortunate Prairie Occurrence. 1999. (Dead Letter Mysteries Ser.). 400p. mass mkt. 5.99 (*0-312-96829-9*, St. Martin's Paperbacks) St. Martin's Pr.
—An Unfortunate Prairie Occurrence. l.t. ed. 1998. (Americana Ser.). 624p. 28.95 (*0-7862-1459-7*) Thorndike Pr.

**CLEREMONT, LENORE (FICTITIOUS CHARACTER)—FICTION**

Holt, Victoria. The Silk Vendetta. unabr. ed. 1993. 84.95 incl. audio (*0-7451-4063-7*, CAB 760) BBC Audiobooks America.
—The Silk Vendetta. 1997. mass mkt. 3.50 (*0-449-00054-0*); 1988. mass mkt. 5.99 o.s.i (*0-449-21548-2*) Ballantine Bks. (Fawcett).
—The Silk Vendetta. l.t. ed. (General Ser.). 507p. 1988. 20.95 o.p. (*0-8161-4638-1*); 1989. 13.95 o.p. (*0-8161-4639-X*) Gale Group. (Macmillan Reference USA).

**CLEVELAND, DAVID (FICTITIOUS CHARACTER)—FICTION**

Francis, Dick. Slay Ride. l.t. ed. 1993. 19.95 o.p. (*0-7927-1431-8*); pap. o.p. (*0-7927-1430-X*); 54.95 incl. audio (*0-7451-5956-7*) BBC Audiobooks America.
—Slay Ride. 1987. 272p. reprint ed. mass mkt. 5.95 o.s.i (*0-449-21271-8*, Fawcett) Ballantine Bks.
—Slay Ride. 288p. 2004. mass mkt. 6.99 (*0-425-19673-9*); 2000. mass mkt. 6.99 (*0-515-12926-7*, Jove) Berkley Publishing Group.
—Slay Ride. unabr. ed. 1991. audio 42.00 (*0-7366-2081-8*, 2886) Books on Tape, Inc.
—Slay Ride. 1984. mass mkt. 3.50 (*0-671-50731-1*); 1983. mass mkt. 2.95 (*0-671-47021-3*) Simon & Schuster. (Pocket).
—Slay Ride. l.t. ed. 1975. o.p. (*0-85456-337-7*, Ulverscroft) Thorpe, F. A. Pubs.

**CLEY, PHYSIOGNOMIST (FICTITIOUS CHARACTER)—FICTION**

Ford, Jeffrey. The Beyond. 304p. 2002. pap. 12.95 (*0-380-81288-6*); 2001. 24.00 (*0-380-97897-0*) Morrow/Avon. (Eos).
—Memoranda. 1999. 240p. pap. 12.00 (*0-380-80262-7*); 2000. 256p. reprint ed. mass mkt. 5.99 (*0-380-81368-8*) Morrow/Avon. (Eos).
—Memoranda. l.t. ed. 2003. 392p. 27.95 (*0-7862-5777-6*) Thorndike Pr.
—The Physiognomy. 1998. 256p. mass mkt. 5.99 (*0-380-79332-6*, Eos); 1997. 218p. pap. 12.00 (*0-380-79331-8*, Avon Bks.) Morrow/Avon.
—The Physiognomy. 2002. (Science Fiction Ser.). 27.95 (*0-7862-4907-2*) Thorndike Pr.

**CLIVELY, MIRINDA (FICTITIOUS CHARACTER)—FICTION**

Crowleigh, Ann. Dead As Dead Can Be. 1993. 256p. mass mkt. 3.99 o.s.i (*0-8217-4099-7*, Zebra Bks.) Kensington Publishing Corp.

**CLUE, NANCY (FICTITIOUS CHARACTER)—FICTION**

Maney, Mabel. The Case of the Good-for-Nothing Girlfriend. (Nancy Clue Mystery Ser.). 1994. (Illus.). 180p. pap. 10.95 o.p. (*0-939416-91-3*); 1994. (Illus.). 180p. lib. bdg. 24.95 o.p. (*0-939416-90-5*); 2nd ed. 1998. 300p. pap. 14.95 (*1-57344-075-2*) Cleis Pr.
—The Case of the Not-So-Nice Nurse. 160p. 1993. 24.95 o.p. (*0-939416-75-1*); 1993. pap. 9.95 (*0-939416-76-X*); 2nd ed. 2003. (Illus.). 14.95 (*1-57344-165-1*) Cleis Pr.
—A Ghost in the Closet. 1995. (Nancy Clue & the Hardly Boys Ser.: No. 3). 180p. 24.95 o.p. (*1-57344-013-2*); pap. 10.95 o.p. (*1-57344-012-4*) Cleis Pr.

**COAKLEY, DANA (FICTITIOUS CHARACTER)—FICTION**

White, Ellen E. All Emergencies, Ring Super. (Dead Letter Mysteries Ser.). 300p. 1998. pap. 5.99 (*0-312-96601-6*, St. Martin's Paperbacks); 1997. 22.95 o.p. (*0-312-15651-0*, Saint Martin's Minotaur) St. Martin's Pr.

**COBB, MATT (FICTITIOUS CHARACTER)—FICTION**

DeAndrea, William L. Killed in Fringe Time: A Matt Cobb Mystery. 1995. 208p. 21.00 o.p. (*0-684-81498-6*, Simon & Schuster); 21.00 (*1-883402-26-3*, Scribner) Simon & Schuster.
—Killed in Paradise. 1988. (Matt Cobb Mystery Ser.). 176p. 15.95 o.p. (*0-89296-346-8*) Mysterious Pr.
—Killed in Paradise. 1989. 192p. mass mkt. 3.95 o.s.i (*0-445-40818-9*, Mysterious Pr. Paperback Bks.) Warner Bks., Inc.
—Killed in the Act. 1981. (Crime Club Ser.). 240p. 12.95 o.p. (*0-385-17824-7*) Doubleday Publishing.
—Killed in the Act. 1987. 288p. reprint ed. pap. 3.50 o.s.i (*0-445-40603-8*, Mysterious Pr. Paperback Bks.) Warner Bks., Inc.
—Killed in the Fog. l.t. ed. 1997. (Large Print Book Ser.). pap. 23.95 (*1-56895-434-4*, Wheeler Publishing, Inc.) Gale Group.
—Killed in the Fog. 1996. 222p. 20.50 (*0-684-83054-X*, Simon & Schuster); 20.00 (*1-883402-30-1*, Scribner) Simon & Schuster.
—Killed in the Ratings. 1986. 252p. pap. 4.95 o.p. (*0-15-647050-0*, Harvest Bks.) Harcourt Trade Pubs.
—Killed in the Ratings. 1986. pap. 1.95 o.p. (*0-380-43612-4*, 43612-4, Avon Bks.) Morrow/Avon.
—Killed on the Ice. 1984. (Crime Club Ser.). 192p. 11.95 o.p. (*0-385-18276-7*) Doubleday Publishing.
—Killed on the Ice. 1987. 224p. reprint ed. pap. 3.50 o.s.i (*0-445-40606-2*, Mysterious Pr. Paperback Bks.) Warner Bks., Inc.
—Killed on the Rocks. 1990. 240p. 17.95 o.p. (*0-89296-210-0*) Mysterious Pr.
—Killed on the Rocks. 1992. 2.99 o.p. (*0-517-08869-X*) Random Hse. Value Publishing.
—Killed on the Rocks. 1991. 240p. mass mkt. 4.99 (*0-446-40060-2*, Mysterious Pr. Paperback Bks.) Warner Bks., Inc.

—Killed with a Passion. 1983. (Crime Club Ser.). 192p. 11.95 o.p. (*0-385-18275-9*) Doubleday Publishing.

—Killed with a Passion. 1987. 224p. reprint ed. pap. 3.50 o.s.i (*0-445-40604-6*, Mysterious Pr. Paperback Bks.) Warner Bks., Inc.

**COCHRAN, BULL (FICTITIOUS CHARACTER)—FICTION**

Nighbert, David F. Shutout. 1995. 307p. 21.95 o.p. (*0-312-11890-2*, Saint Martin's Minotaur) St. Martin's Pr.

—Squeezeplay: A Mystery. 1992. 272p. 18.95 o.p. (*0-312-07847-1*, Saint Martin's Minotaur) St. Martin's Pr.

—Strikezone. 1989. 14.95 o.p. (*0-312-02987-X*, Saint Martin's Minotaur) St. Martin's Pr.

**COCHRAN, PETER (FICTITIOUS CHARACTER)—FICTION**

Billings, Andrew. Tainted Blood. 1997. 544p. mass mkt. 6.99 o.s.i (*0-515-12046-4*, Jove) Berkley Publishing Group.

**COCKRILL, INSPECTOR (FICTITIOUS CHARACTER)—FICTION**

Brand, Christianna. Death in High Heels. unabr. ed. 1993. audio 54.95 (*0-7451-5798-X*, CAT 4037) BBC Audiobooks America.

—Death of Jezebel. unabr. ed. 1994. audio 54.95 (*0-7451-5800-5*, CAB 4050) BBC Audiobooks America.

—Fog of Doubt. 272p. 1995. mass mkt. 4.95 (*0-7867-0219-2*); 1984. pap. 3.50 o.p. (*0-88184-065-3*) Avalon Publishing Group. (Carroll & Graf Pubs.).

—Fog of Doubt. 1979. lib. bdg. 9.95 o.p. (*0-8398-2535-8*, Macmillan Reference USA) Gale Group.

—Green for Danger. 1997. 256p. mass mkt. 4.95 (*0-7867-0386-5*); 1990. 254p. pap. 3.95 o.p. (*0-88184-612-0*); 1989. 254p. pap. 7.95 o.p. (*0-88184-483-7*) Avalon Publishing Group. (Carroll & Graf Pubs.).

—Green for Danger. l.t. ed. 1990. pap. 16.95 o.p. (*0-7927-0442-8*, C0400); 1993. audio 54.95 (*0-7451-2418-6*, CDA 019, Chivers Children's Audio Bks.) BBC Audiobooks America.

—Green for Danger. 1986. (Mystery Ser.). mass mkt. 9.95 o.p. (*0-553-06517-3*) Bantam Bks.

—Green for Danger. 1978. (Illus.). 271p. reprint ed. 18.95 o.p. (*0-89163-046-5*) Boulevard Bks.

—Green for Danger. 1981. 256p. pap. 2.50 o.p. (*0-06-080551-X*, P 551) HarperCollins Pubs.

—The Spotted Cat & Other Mysteries from Inspector Cockrill's Casebook. Medawar, Tony, ed. 2002. (Lost Classics Ser.). 224p. 29.00 (*1-932009-00-0*); pap. 19.00 (*1-932009-01-9*) Crippen & Landru, Pubs.

—Suddenly at His Residence. (Black Dagger Crime Ser.). 1990. 18.50 o.p. (*0-86220-791-6*, C1031, Black Dagger); 1992. audio 54.95 (*0-7451-2404-6*, CD 005) BBC Audiobooks America.

—Suddenly at His Residence. 1988. 176p. mass mkt. 3.50 o.s.i (*0-553-25465-0*) Bantam Bks.

—Suddenly at His Residence. l.t. ed. 1997. (Linford Mystery Library). 416p. pap. 17.99 o.p. (*0-7089-5107-4*, Linford) Thorpe, F. A. Pubs. GBR. *Dist:* Ulverscroft Large Print Bks., Ltd., Ulverscroft Large Print Canada, Ltd.

—Tour de Force. 1996. 272p. mass mkt. 4.95 (*0-7867-0340-7*, Carroll & Graf Pubs.) Avalon Publishing Group.

—Tour de Force. 1997. 21.50 (*0-7540-8502-3*, Black Dagger) BBC Audiobooks America.

—Tour de Force. 1982. 192p. pap. o.p. (*0-06-080572-2*, P 572, Perennial) HarperTrade.

Brand, Christianna & Boyd, Carole. Death in High Heels. unabr. ed. 1989. audio 53.95 o.s.i (*0-8161-9375-4*) BBC Audiobooks America.

Brand, Christianna & Melling, John K. Death of Jezebel. 1990. (Black Dagger Crime Ser.). 208p. reprint ed. text 12.95 o.p. (*0-86220-774-6*) Chivers Pr. GBR. *Dist:* BBC Audiobooks America.

**CODY (FICTITIOUS CHARACTER: THOMAS)—FICTION**

Thomas. A Day at a Time. 1998. pap. 12.95 (*1-57558-026-8*) Hearthstone Publishing, Ltd.

**COFFEY, JILL (FICTITIOUS CHARACTER)—FICTION**

Gorman, Ed. Cold Blue Midnight. 1998. 352p. reprint ed. mass mkt. 4.99 (*0-8439-4417-X*, Leisure Bks.) Dorchester Publishing Co., Inc.

—Cold Blue Midnight. 1996. 352p. 23.95 o.p. (*0-312-14568-3*, Saint Martin's Minotaur) St. Martin's Pr.

—Cold Blue Midnight. 1998. E-Book 9.95 (*0-585-28972-7*) netLibrary, Inc.

**COFFEY, JOHN (FICTITIOUS CHARACTER)—FICTION**

King, Stephen. The Bad Death of Eduard Delacroix. 1996. (Green Mile Ser.: Vol. 4). 96p. mass mkt. 2.99 o.s.i (*0-451-19055-6*, Signet Bks.) NAL.

—The Bad Death of Eduard Delacroix. 1996. 8.09 (*0-606-09366-4*) Turtleback Bks.

—Coffey on the Mile. 1996. (Green Mile Ser.: Vol. 6). 144p. mass mkt. 3.99 o.s.i (*0-451-19057-2*, Signet Bks.) NAL.

—Coffey on the Mile. 1996. 10.04 (*0-606-09368-0*) Turtleback Bks.

—Coffey on the Mile. abr. ed. 1996. (Green Mile Ser.). audio 7.95 o.p. (*0-14-086382-6*, Penguin AudioBooks) Viking Penguin.

—Coffey's Hands. 1996. (Green Mile Ser.: Vol. 3). 96p. mass mkt. 2.99 o.s.i (*0-451-19054-8*, Signet Bks.) NAL.

—The Green Mile. unabr. ed. 1999. audio 39.95 (*0-671-04721-3*); audio compact disk 49.95 (*0-671-04725-6*) Simon & Schuster Audio. (Simon & Schuster Audioworks).

—The Green Mile. unabr. ed. 1996. (Green Mile Ser.). 39.95 o.p. (*0-14-771135-5*); 39.95 o.p. (*0-14-771135-5*) Viking Penguin. (Penguin AudioBooks).

—The Green Mile: The Complete Serial Novel. 1997. (Illus.). 480p. pap. 14.95 o.p. (*0-452-27890-2*, Plume) Dutton/Plume.

—The Green Mile: The Complete Serial Novel. 1996. 18.94 o.s.i (*0-451-93302-8*, Signet Bks.) NAL.

—The Green Mile: The Complete Serial Novel. (Illus.). 2000. 400p. 25.00 (*0-7432-1089-1*, Scribner); 1999. 544p. pap. 7.99 (*0-671-04178-9*, Pocket); 1999. 536p. reprint ed. mass mkt. 7.99 (*0-671-03265-8*, Pocket) Simon & Schuster.

—The Green Mile: The Complete Serial Novel. 1999. 14.04 (*0-606-17409-5*) Turtleback Bks.

—Der Grune Meile. 1999. Tr. of Green Mile. (GER.). pap. 22.95 (*3-404-13958-5*) Lubbe, Gustav Verlag GmbH DEU. *Dist:* Distribooks, Inc.

—The Mouse on the Mile. 1996. (Green Mile Ser.: Vol. 2). 96p. mass mkt. 2.99 o.s.i (*0-451-19052-1*, Signet Bks.) NAL.

—The Mouse on the Mile. 1996. 8.09 (*0-606-09364-8*) Turtleback Bks.

—The Night Journey. 1996. (Green Mile Ser.: Vol. 5). 96p. mass mkt. 2.99 o.s.i (*0-451-19056-4*, Signet Bks.) NAL.

—The Night Journey. 1996. 9.04 (*0-606-09367-2*) Turtleback Bks.

—The Two Dead Girls. 1996. (Green Mile Ser.: Vol. 1). (Illus.). 96p. mass mkt. 2.99 o.s.i (*0-451-19049-1*, Signet Bks.) NAL.

—The Two Dead Girls. 1996. 8.09 o.p. (*0-606-09363-X*) Turtleback Bks.

—The Two Dead Girls. abr. ed. 1996. (Green Mile Ser.: Vol. 1). audio 7.95 o.p. (*0-14-086377-X*, Penguin AudioBooks) Viking Penguin.

**COFFIN ED JOHNSON (FICTITIOUS CHARACTER)—FICTION**

*see Johnson, Coffin Ed (Fictitious Character)—Fiction*

**COFFIN, JOHN (FICTITIOUS CHARACTER)—FICTION**

Butler, Gwendoline. Coffin & the Paper Man. 1993. (WWL Mystery Ser.). mass mkt. o.s.i (*0-373-26133-0*, 1-26133-8, Harlequin Bks.) Harlequin Enterprises, Ltd.

—Coffin & the Paper Man. pap. 15.95 (*0-312-29192-2*, Saint Martin's Griffin); 1991. 16.95 (*0-312-05835-7*, Saint Martin's Minotaur) St. Martin's Pr.

—Coffin for Baby. (Black Dagger Crime Ser.). 1993. 192p. 16.50 o.p. (*0-7451-8606-8*, Black Dagger); 1994. 18.95 o.p. (*0-7451-6458-7*) BBC Audiobooks America.

—A Coffin for Charley. 1996. (WWL Mystery Ser.). mass mkt. o.s.i (*0-373-26200-0*, 1-26200-5, Worldwide Library) Harlequin Enterprises, Ltd.

—A Coffin for Charley. l.t. ed. 1994. (Magna Large Print Ser.). 358p. o.p. (*0-7505-0705-5*) Magna Large Print Bks. GBR. *Dist:* Ulverscroft Large Print Canada, Ltd.

—A Coffin for Charley. 1994. 256p. 20.95 o.p. (*0-312-11466-4*, Saint Martin's Minotaur) St. Martin's Pr.

—A Coffin from the Past. l.t. ed. 1993. pap. 16.95 o.p. (*0-7451-6419-6*); 1992. 18.95 o.p. (*0-7451-6413-7*); 1993. audio 39.95 (*0-7451-5814-5*, CSL 075) BBC Audiobooks America.

—A Coffin from the Past. (Black Dagger Crime Ser.). 224p. 12.95 o.p. (*0-86220-706-1*) Chivers Pr. GBR. *Dist:* BBC Audiobooks America.

—Coffin in Fashion. 1992. mass mkt. o.s.i (*0-373-26100-4*, Harlequin Bks.) Harlequin Enterprises, Ltd.

—Coffin in Fashion. pap. 15.95 (*0-312-29177-9*, Saint Martin's Griffin); 1989. 176p. 16.95 (*0-312-03802-X*, Saint Martin's Minotaur) St. Martin's Pr.

—Coffin in Malta. unabr. ed. 1989. audio 39.95 (*0-7451-5815-3*, CAT 4038) BBC Audiobooks America.

—Coffin in Malta. 1989. (Black Dagger Crime Ser.). 224p. reprint ed. text 12.95 o.p. (*0-86220-752-5*) Chivers Pr. GBR. *Dist:* BBC Audiobooks America.

—Coffin in Malta. 1985. (Walker's British Paperback Mysteries Ser.). 192p. reprint ed. pap. 2.95 o.s.i (*0-8027-3111-2*) Walker & Co.

—Coffin in the Black Museum. unabr. ed. 1991. (Audio Ser.). audio 54.95 (*0-7451-5816-1*, CAT 4068) BBC Audiobooks America.

—Coffin in the Museum of Crime. 1993. (Mystery Ser.). mass mkt. o.s.i (*0-373-26121-7*, 1-26121-3, Harlequin Bks.) Harlequin Enterprises, Ltd.

—Coffin in the Museum of Crime. 1990. 16.95 (*0-312-04282-5*, Saint Martin's Minotaur) St. Martin's Pr.

—Coffin on Murder Street. 1994. (Mystery Ser.). mass mkt. o.s.i (*0-373-26147-0*, 1-26147-8, Harlequin Bks.) Harlequin Enterprises, Ltd.

—Coffin on Murder Street. 1992. 224p. 16.95 (*0-312-07673-8*, Saint Martin's Minotaur) St. Martin's Pr.

—Coffin on the Water. 1992. (WWL Mystery Ser.: No. 90). mass mkt. o.s.i (*0-373-26090-3*, 1-26090-0, Harlequin Bks.) Harlequin Enterprises, Ltd.

—Coffin on the Water. 1990. 2.99 o.p. (*0-517-05811-1*) Random Hse. Value Publishing.

—Coffin on the Water. 1989. 192p. 14.95 (*0-312-02561-0*, Saint Martin's Minotaur) St. Martin's Pr.

—The Coffin Tree. 1997. mass mkt. o.s.i (*0-373-26250-7*, 1-26250-0, Worldwide Library) Harlequin Enterprises, Ltd.

—The Coffin Tree. pap. 15.95 (*0-312-29189-2*, Saint Martin's Griffin); 1995. 240p. 21.95 (*0-312-13946-2*, Saint Martin's Minotaur) St. Martin's Pr.

—Coffin Underground. l.t. ed. 1989. 336p. lib. bdg. 11.95 o.p. (*1-85057-722-6*, Macmillan Reference USA) Gale Group.

—Coffin Underground. 1992. per. (*0-373-26110-1*, 1-26110-6, Harlequin Bks.) Harlequin Enterprises, Ltd.

—Coffin Underground. pap. 14.95 (*0-312-31071-4*, Saint Martin's Griffin); 1989. 16.95 (*0-312-02886-5*, Saint Martin's Minotaur) St. Martin's Pr.

—Coffin Waiting. unabr. ed. 1992. (Crimson Dagger Audio Bks.). audio 39.95 (*0-7451-2406-2*, CDA 007) BBC Audiobooks America.

—Coffin's Game. l.t. ed. 1999. (Thorndike General Ser.). 307p. pap. 22.95 o.p. (*0-7862-1946-7*, Macmillan Reference USA) Gale Group.

—Coffin's Game. 2000. (Commander John Coffin Mysteries Ser.: Bk. 353). 256p. mass mkt. o.s.i (*0-373-26353-8*, 1-26353-2, Worldwide Library) Harlequin Enterprises, Ltd.

—Coffin's Game. 1999. (Commander John Coffin Mysteries Ser.). 240p. 21.95 (*0-312-20512-0*, Saint Martin's Minotaur) St. Martin's Pr.

—Coffin's Ghost. 2001. 224p. 22.95 (*0-312-27997-3*, Saint Martin's Minotaur) St. Martin's Pr.

—Coffin's Ghost. l.t. ed. 2000. (General Ser.). 318p. 22.95 (*0-7862-2803-2*); (*0-7540-4245-6*); (*0-7540-4246-4*) Thorndike Pr.

—Cold Coffin. l.t. ed. 2002. (Magna Large Print Ser.). 352p. (*0-7505-1832-4*) Magna Large Print Bks. GBR. *Dist:* Ulverscroft Large Print Canada, Ltd.

—Cold Coffin. unabr. ed. 2002. audio compact disk 71.95 (*1-84283-304-9*); 2001. audio 54.95 (*1-86042-985-8*, 2-985-8) Soundings, Ltd. GBR. *Dist:* Ulverscroft Large Print Bks., Ltd.

—Cracking Open a Coffin. 1995. (WWL Mystery Ser.). 250p. mass mkt. o.s.i (*0-373-26171-3*, 1-29171-8, Harlequin Bks.) Harlequin Enterprises, Ltd.

—Cracking Open a Coffin. 1993. 240p. 16.95 (*0-312-09777-8*, Saint Martin's Minotaur) St. Martin's Pr.

—A Dark Coffin. 1998. (WWL Mystery Ser.). mass mkt. o.s.i (*0-373-26265-5*, 1-26265-8, Worldwide Library) Harlequin Enterprises, Ltd.

—A Dark Coffin. unabr. ed. 2001. audio 54.95 ISIS Audio Bks. GBR. *Dist:* Ulverscroft Large Print Bks., Ltd.

—A Dark Coffin. l.t. ed. 1996. (Magna Large Print Ser.). 325p. o.p. (*0-7505-1049-8*) Magna Large Print Bks. GBR. *Dist:* Ulverscroft Large Print Canada, Ltd.

—A Dark Coffin. 1996. 240p. 21.95 (*0-312-14577-2*, Saint Martin's Minotaur) St. Martin's Pr.

—Death Lives Next Door. 1992. (John Coffin Ser.). 192p. 16.95 o.p. (*0-312-08175-8*, Saint Martin's Minotaur) St. Martin's Pr.

—A Double Coffin. 1999. (WWL Mystery Ser.: No. 313). per. (*0-373-26313-9*, 1-26313-6, Worldwide Library) Harlequin Enterprises, Ltd.

—A Double Coffin. 1998. 240p. 21.95 o.p. (*0-312-18569-3*, Saint Martin's Minotaur) St. Martin's Pr.

—A Double Coffin. l.t. ed. 1998. (General Ser.). 336p. pap. 24.95 (*0-7862-1481-3*) Thorndike Pr.

—A Double Coffin: A Detective Coffin Mystery. unabr. ed. 2000. (Inspector John Coffin Mystery Ser.). audio 69.95 (*0-7540-0002-8*, CAB 142559.95) Chivers Audio Bks. GBR. *Dist:* BBC Audiobooks America.

—A Grave Coffin. 2000. 256p. 22.95 (*0-312-26167-5*, Saint Martin's Minotaur) St. Martin's Pr.

—A Nameless Coffin. l.t. ed. 2000. (General Ser.). 335p. pap. 23.95 (*0-7862-2302-2*); (*0-7540-3993-5*); (*0-7540-3994-3*) Thorndike Pr.

—A Nameless Coffin. 1985. pap. 2.95 o.s.i (*0-8027-3081-7*) Walker & Co.

Butler, Gwendoline & Melling, John K. Coffin Waiting. 1990. (Black Dagger Crime Ser.). 200p. reprint ed. text 12.95 o.p. (*0-86220-767-3*) Chivers Pr. GBR. *Dist:* BBC Audiobooks America.

**COHEN, ARTIE (FICTITIOUS CHARACTER)—FICTION**

Nadelson, Reggie. Hot Poppies. l.t. ed. 1999. (Ulverscroft Large Print Ser.). 384p. 31.99 (*0-7089-4077-3*, Ulverscroft) Thorpe, F. A. Pubs. GBR. *Dist:* Ulverscroft Large Print Bks., Ltd., Ulverscroft Large Print Canada, Ltd.

—Hot Poppies: An Artie Cohen Mystery. 1998. 256p. 22.95 o.p. (*0-312-19986-4*, Saint Martin's Minotaur) St. Martin's Pr.

—Red Hot Blues. 1998. Orig. Title: Red Mercury Blues. 272p. 22.95 (*0-312-18166-3*, Saint Martin's Minotaur) St. Martin's Pr.

**COHEN, AVRAM (FICTITIOUS CHARACTER)—FICTION**

Rosenberg, Robert. An Accidental Murder. 1999. (Avram Cohen Mysteries Ser.). 288p. 22.00 o.s.i (*0-684-85032-X*, Scribner) Simon & Schuster.

—Crimes of the City. 1992. (Crime Ser.). 288p. pap. 5.95 o.p. (*0-14-016686-6*, Penguin Bks.) Penguin Group (USA) Inc.

—Crimes of the City. 1997. (Missing Mysteries Ser.: Vol. 3). mass mkt. 7.95 (*1-890208-03-5*) Poisoned Pen Pr.

—Crimes of the City. 1991. 272p. 18.95 o.p. (*0-671-70222-X*, Simon & Schuster) Simon & Schuster.

—The Cutting Room: An Avram Cohen Mystery. 1993. (Crime Ser.). 304p. reprint ed. pap. 5.95 o.p. (*0-14-023112-9*, Penguin Bks.) Penguin Group (USA) Inc.

—The Cutting Room: An Avram Cohen Mystery. 1993. 320p. 20.00 (*0-671-74344-9*, Simon & Schuster) Simon & Schuster.

—House of Guilt: An Avram Cohen Mystery. 1996. 368p. 21.50 o.p. (*0-684-82654-2*, Scribner) Simon & Schuster.

**COHEN, DAVID (FICTITIOUS CHARACTER)—FICTION**

Berman, Richard. Hostile Witness. 1996. 304p. (Orig.). mass mkt. 5.99 (*0-380-77813-0*, Avon Bks.) Morrow/Avon.

—Unjust Death. 1995. 352p. (Orig.). mass mkt. 5.50 (*0-380-77812-2*, Avon Bks.) Morrow/Avon.

**COHEN, MIDGE (FICTITIOUS CHARACTER)—FICTION**

Brill, Toni. Date with a Dead Doctor. 1992. per. (*0-373-26109-8*, 1-26109-8, Harlequin Bks.) Harlequin Enterprises, Ltd.

—Date with a Dead Doctor. 1991. 17.95 o.p. (*0-312-05409-2*, Saint Martin's Minotaur) St. Martin's Pr.

—Date with a Plummeting Publisher. 1995. (WWL Mystery Ser.). per. (*0-373-26161-6*, 1-26161-9, Harlequin Bks.) Harlequin Enterprises, Ltd.

—Date with a Plummeting Publisher. 1993. 240p. 17.95 o.p. (*0-312-08753-5*, Saint Martin's Minotaur) St. Martin's Pr.

**COLDWATER, LAURIE (FICTITIOUS CHARACTER)—FICTION**

Webb, Cynthia. No Daughter of the South. 1997. 200p. (Orig.). pap. 10.95 (*0-934678-82-0*) New Victoria Pubs., Inc.

**COLE, BETH (FICTITIOUS CHARACTER)—FICTION**

Stewart, Ed. Doomsday Flight. 1995. 475p. pap. 11.99 (*1-56476-482-6*, 6-3482) Cook Communications Ministries.

—Millennium's Dawn. 1994. 480p. pap. 11.99 o.p. (*1-56476-345-5*, 6-3345) Cook Communications Ministries.

—Millennium's Eve. 1993. 448p. pap. 12.99 (*1-56476-133-9*, 6-3133) Cook Communications Ministries.

**COLE, ELVIS (FICTITIOUS CHARACTER)—FICTION**

Crais, Robert. The Devil's Cantina. 1999. 288p. 22.95 (*0-7868-6355-2*) Hyperion Pr.

—The Forgotten Man: A Novel. 2004. 400p. 24.95 (*0-385-50428-4*) Doubleday Publishing.

—Free Fall. 1994. (Elvis Cole Mystery Ser.). mass mkt. 4.99 o.s.i (*0-553-56831-0*, Crimeline); 304p. mass mkt. 6.99 (*0-553-56509-5*) Bantam Bks.

—Indigo Slam. 2003. (Elvis Cole Mystery Ser.). 320p. mass mkt. 7.99 (*0-345-43564-8*, Ballantine Bks.) Ballantine Bks.

—Indigo Slam. unabr. ed. 1997. (Elvis Cole Mystery Ser.). audio 48.00 (*0-7366-3833-4*, 4553) Books on Tape, Inc.

—Indigo Slam. abr. ed. (Elvis Cole Mystery Ser.). 2000. audio 7.99 o.s.i (*1-58788-097-0*, 2352, Paperback Nova Audio Bks.); 1998. audio 7.99 o.s.i (*1-56740-252-6*, 2379, Nova Audio Bks.); 1997. audio 16.95 o.p. (*1-56100-977-6*, 1236, Nova Audio Bks.); 1997. audio 16.95 o.p.; 1997. audio 23.95 (*1-56100-752-8*, 144, Bookcassette); 1997. audio 57.25 (*1-56100-827-3*, 907, Unabridged Library Editions) Brilliance Audio.

—Indigo Slam. (Elvis Cole Mystery Ser.). 1999. 384p. mass mkt. 5.99 (*0-7868-8929-2*); 1997. 304p. 22.95 (*0-7868-6261-0*) Hyperion Pr.

—L. A. Requiem. 2000. (Elvis Cole Mystery Ser.). 416p. mass mkt. 6.99 (*0-345-43447-1*, Ballantine Bks.) Ballantine Bks.

—L. A. Requiem. l.t. ed. 2000. (Elvis Cole Mystery Ser.). 538p. 27.95 (*1-56895-881-1*, Wheeler Publishing, Inc.) Gale Group.

—L. A. Requiem, Set. abr. ed. 1999. (Elvis Cole Mystery Ser.). audio 25.00 Highsmith Inc.

—L. A. Requiem. abr. ed. 1999. (Elvis Cole Mystery Ser.). audio 25.00 (*0-553-52648-0*, RH Audio) Random Hse. Audio Publishing Group.

—The Last Detective. 2004. 352p. mass mkt. 7.99 (*0-345-45190-2*) Ballantine Bks.

—The Last Detective. abr. ed. 2004. (Elvis Cole Ser.). audio 9.99 (*1-58788-523-9*, 2755, Brilliance Audio Paperback Audiobooks); 2003. (Elvis Cole Mystery Ser.: Vol. 9). audio 19.95 (*1-58788-520-4*, 2752, Nova Audio Bks.); 2003. (Elvis Cole Mystery Ser.: Vol. 9). audio 29.95 (*1-58788-518-2*, 2750, Brilliance Audio Unabridged); 2003. (Elvis Cole Mystery Ser.: Vol. 9). audio 74.25 (*1-58788-519-0*, 2751); 2003. (Elvis Cole Mystery Ser.: Vol. 9). audio compact disk 87.25 (*1-58788-522-0*, 2754); 2003. (Elvis Cole Mystery Ser.: Vol. 9). audio compact disk 38.95 (*1-58788-521-2*, 2753, Brilliance Audio Unabridged) Brilliance Audio.

—The Last Detective. 2003. 320p. 24.95 (*0-385-50426-8*) Doubleday Publishing.

—The Last Detective. unabr. ed. 2003. (Elvis Cole Ser.). audio 19.99 (*1-59335-096-1*, 30188) Soulmate Audio Bks., Inc.

—The Last Detective. l.t. ed. 2003. (Basic Ser.). 30.95 (*0-7862-5229-4*) Thorndike Pr.

—The Last Detective. aut. ltd. num. ed. 2003. 150.00 (*1-890885-14-2*) Trice, B.E. Publishing.

—Lullaby Town. (Elvis Cole Mystery Ser.). 1993. 352p. mass mkt. 6.99 (*0-553-29951-4*); 1992. 304p. 20.00 o.s.i (*0-553-08197-7*) Bantam Bks.

—The Monkey's Raincoat. (Elvis Cole Mystery Ser.). 1987. 208p. mass mkt. 2.95 o.s.i (*0-553-26336-6*); 1992. 224p. reprint ed. mass mkt. 7.50 (*0-553-27585-2*) Bantam Bks.

—Stalking the Angel. 1992. (Elvis Cole Mystery Ser.). 288p. mass mkt. 7.50 (*0-553-28644-7*) Bantam Bks.

—Sunset Express. unabr. ed. 1997. (Elvis Cole Mystery Ser.). audio 56.00 (*0-913369-89-6*, 4389) Books on Tape, Inc.

—Sunset Express. abr. ed. (Elvis Cole Mystery Ser.). 1997. audio 7.99 o.p. (*1-56740-166-X*, 707, Nova Audio Bks.); 1996. audio 16.95 o.p. (*1-56100-905-9*, 1066, Nova Audio Bks.); 1996. audio 57.25 o.p. (*1-56100-320-4*, 1065, Unabridged Library Editions); 1996. audio 23.95 o.p. (*1-56100-695-5*, 284, Bookcassette) Brilliance Audio.

—Sunset Express. (Elvis Cole Mystery Ser.). 1996. 288p. 21.95 o.p. (*0-7868-6096-0*); 2002. 416p. reprint ed. mass mkt. 6.99 (*0-7868-8915-2*) Hyperion Pr.

—Sunset Express. l.t. ed. 2001. (Elvis Cole Mystery Ser.). 288p. 28.95 (*0-7862-3401-6*); 485p. (*0-7540-2496-2*); 485p. (*0-7540-1644-7*) Thorndike Pr.

—Voodoo River. l.t. ed. 2002. (Elvis Cole Mystery Ser.). 499p. 29.95 (*0-7862-3404-0*) Gale Group.

—Voodoo River. (Elvis Cole Mystery Ser.). 1995. 304p. 21.95 (*0-7868-6076-6*); 2003. 416p. reprint ed. mass mkt. 7.99 (*0-7868-8905-5*) Hyperion Pr.

—Voodoo River. abr. ed. 1995. (Elvis Cole Mystery Ser.). audio 17.00 (*1-56876-040-X*, 393047) Soundlines Entertainment, Inc.

**COLE, HARPER (FICTITIOUS CHARACTER)—FICTION**

Iles, Greg. Mortal Fear. 1997. 576p. 24.95 o.s.i (*0-525-93792-7*) Dutton/Plume.

—Mortal Fear. 1998. 624p. mass mkt. 7.99 (*0-451-18041-0*, Signet Bks.) NAL.

—Mortal Fear. unabr. ed. 1997. audio 125.00 (*0-7887-0911-9*, 95051E7) Recorded Bks., LLC.

—Mortal Fear. 1997. audio 23.95Set. pap. 23.95 o.s.i incl. audio (*0-14-086315-X*, 694609, Penguin AudioBooks) Viking Penguin.

**COLE, LARRY (FICTITIOUS CHARACTER)—FICTION**

Holton, Hugh. Chicago Blues. 1997. 373p. mass mkt. 5.99 (*0-8125-4464-1*); 1996. 384p. 23.95 o.p. (*0-312-85984-8*) Doherty, Tom Assocs., LLC. (Forge Bks.).

—The Left Hand of God. 2000. 416p. mass mkt. 6.99 (*0-8125-7084-7*); 1998. (Illus.). 384p. 24.95 (*0-312-86763-8*) Doherty, Tom Assocs., LLC. (Forge Bks.).

—Presumed Dead. 1995. 351p. pap. 5.99 (*0-8125-4813-2*); 1994. 320p. 21.95 o.p. (*0-312-85710-1*) Doherty, Tom Assocs., LLC. (Forge Bks.).

—Presumed Dead. 318p. 3.98 o.p. (*0-8317-5214-9*) Smithmark Pubs., Inc.

—Red Lightning. 320p. 1999. mass mkt. 6.99 (*0-8125-8912-2*); 1998. 23.95 o.p. (*0-312-86687-9*) Doherty, Tom Assocs., LLC. (Forge Bks.).

—Red Lightning. 1998. 6.99 (*0-312-87125-2*) St. Martin's Pr.

—Time of the Assassins. 2000. 383p. 24.95 (*0-312-87333-6*, Forge Bks.) Doherty, Tom Assocs., LLC.

—Violent Crimes. 1998. (Illus.). 512p. mass mkt. 6.99 (*0-8125-7187-8*); 1996. 384p. text 23.95 o.p. (*0-312-86281-4*) Doherty, Tom Assocs., LLC. (Forge Bks.).

—Violent Crimes. 1999. 6.99 (*0-312-87126-0*) St. Martin's Pr.

—Windy City. 1996. 310p. mass mkt. 5.99 (*0-8125-6714-5*, Tor Bks.); 1996. mass mkt. 5.99 (*0-8125-3695-9*, Forge Bks.); 1995. 352p. 22.95 o.p. (*0-312-85711-X*, Forge Bks.) Doherty, Tom Assocs., LLC.

**COLE, LEWIS (FICTITIOUS CHARACTER)—FICTION**

DuBois, Brendan. Black Tide: A Lewis Cole Mystery. 1996. 400p. mass mkt. 5.99 (*0-671-89999-6*, Pocket); 1995. 398p. 21.50 (*1-883402-58-1*, Scribner) Simon & Schuster.

—Dead Sand: A Lewis Cole Mystery. 1996. 320p. mass mkt. 5.99 (*0-671-54521-3*, Pocket) Simon & Schuster.

—Dead Sand: A Lewis Cole Mystery. Grose, Bill, ed. 1995. 336p. mass mkt. 5.50 (*0-671-89998-8*, Pocket) Simon & Schuster.

—Dead Sand: A Lewis Cole Mystery. 1994. 304p. 21.00 (*1-883402-45-X*, Scribner) Simon & Schuster.

—The Killer Waves: A Lewis Cole Mystery. 2002. 352p. 24.95 (*0-312-28487-X*, Saint Martin's Minotaur) St. Martin's Pr.

—Shattered Shell. 2nd ed. 1999. 368p. 24.95 (*0-312-19332-7*, Saint Martin's Minotaur) St. Martin's Pr.

**COLE, REAGAN (FICTITIOUS CHARACTER)—FICTION**

Stewart, Ed. Doomsday Flight. 1995. 475p. pap. 11.99 (*1-56476-482-6*, 6-3482) Cook Communications Ministries.

—Millennium's Dawn. 1994. 480p. pap. 11.99 o.p. (*1-56476-345-5*, 6-3345) Cook Communications Ministries.

—Millennium's Eve. 1993. 448p. pap. 12.99 (*1-56476-133-9*, 6-3133) Cook Communications Ministries.

**COLE FAMILY (FICTITIOUS CHARACTERS)—FICTION**

Gordon, Noah. Matters of Choice. 1996. 368p. 24.95 o.p. (*0-525-94080-4*, Dutton) Dutton/Plume.

—Matters of Choice. 1997. 448p. mass mkt. 6.99 o.s.i (*0-451-18726-1*, Signet Bks.); 1996. pap. 12.95 (*0-452-27635-7*) NAL.

—The Physician. 1987. 640p. mass mkt. 6.99 o.s.i (*0-449-21426-5*, Fawcett) Ballantine Bks.

—The Physician. 1986. 624p. 18.45 o.p. (*0-671-47748-X*, Simon & Schuster) Simon & Schuster.

—The Physician. 2002. 720p. pap. 8.95 (*0-7515-0389-4*) Warner Bks. GBR. *Dist:* Trafalgar Square.

—Shaman. 1992. 528p. 23.00 o.p. (*0-525-93554-1*, Dutton) Dutton/Plume.

—Shaman. 1993. pap. o.p. (*0-451-17929-3*); 576p. mass mkt. 6.99 o.s.i (*0-451-17701-0*) NAL. (Signet Bks.).

—Shaman. 2002. 652p. pap. 8.95 (*0-7515-0082-8*) Warner Bks. GBR. *Dist:* Trafalgar Square.

**COLEMAN FAMILY (FICTITIOUS CHARACTERS)—FICTION**

Michaels, Fern. Kentucky Rich. abr. ed. (Kentucky Ser.: Vol. 1). 2002. audio 9.99 (*1-58788-486-0*, 2781, Paperback Nova Audio Bks.); 2001. audio 19.95 o.p. (*1-58788-238-8*, 2499, Nova Audio Bks.); 2001. audio 32.95 (*1-58788-236-1*, 2497, Brilliance Audio Unabridged) Brilliance Audio.

—Kentucky Rich. l.t. ed. 2002. 13.95 (*1-56895-195-7*); 2001. 425p. 31.95 (*1-58724-105-6*) Gale Group. (Wheeler Publishing, Inc.).

—Kentucky Rich. 2002. 48p. mass mkt. 7.99 (*0-8217-7234-1*); 2001. 336p. 24.00 o.s.i (*1-57566-761-4*, Kensington Bks.) Kensington Publishing Corp.

—Kentucky Rich. unabr. ed. 2003. (Kentucky Ser.). audio 19.99 (*1-59335-019-8*, 30101) Soulmate Audio Bks., Inc.

—Texas Fury. 1996. pap. 8.95 o.s.i (*0-345-40569-2*); 1989. 512p. mass mkt. 6.99 (*0-345-31375-5*, Ballantine Bks.) Ballantine Bks.

—Texas Fury. 1991. reprint ed. 21.95 o.p. (*0-7278-4269-2*) Severn Hse. Pubs., Ltd.

—Texas Heat. 1989. mass mkt. 4.95 o.p. (*0-345-01028-0*); 1986. 512p. mass mkt. 6.99 (*0-345-33100-1*) Ballantine Bks.

—Texas Heat. 1989. reprint ed. 20.00 o.p. (*0-7278-4007-X*) Severn Hse. Pubs., Ltd.

—Texas Rich. 1995. pap. 8.95 o.p. (*0-345-40114-X*); 1987. 576p. mass mkt. 6.99 (*0-345-33540-6*, Ivy Bks.); 1985. mass mkt. 3.95 o.p. (*0-345-31374-7*) Ballantine Bks.

—Texas Rich. 1989. reprint ed. 19.95 o.p. (*0-7278-1758-2*) Severn Hse. Pubs., Ltd.

—Texas Sunrise. 1994. 384p. mass mkt. 7.50 (*0-345-36593-3*) Ballantine Bks.

—Texas Trilogy. 1989. pap. 17.93 o.p. (*0-345-36424-4*) Ballantine Bks.

—Vegas Heat. abr. ed. 1997. (Vegas Ser.). audio 7.99 o.p. (*1-56740-236-4*, 715, Paperback Nova Audio Bks.); audio 16.95 o.p. (*1-56100-973-3*, 1399, Nova Audio Bks.); 15p. audio 89.25 o.p. (*1-56100-810-9*, 1086, Unabridged Library Editions); audio 29.95 o.p. (*1-56100-735-8*, 308, Bookcassette) Brilliance Audio.

—Vegas Heat. 1997. 480p. mass mkt. 6.99 o.s.i (*0-8217-5758-X*); 400p. 25.00 o.s.i (*1-57566-138-1*) Kensington Publishing Corp.

—Vegas Rich. abr. ed. (Vegas Ser.). 1997. audio 7.99 o.p. (*1-56740-183-X*, 714, Paperback Nova Audio Bks.); 1996. audio 16.95 o.p. (*1-56100-914-8*, 1400, Nova Audio Bks.); 1996. audio 29.95 o.p. (*1-56100-706-4*, 307, Bookcassette); 1996. audio 121.25 o.p. (*1-56100-331-X*, 1087, Unabridged Library Editions) Brilliance Audio.

—Vegas Rich, Vol. 1. l.t. ed. 1996. 26.95 o.p. (*1-56895-370-4*, Wheeler Publishing, Inc.) Gale Group.

—Vegas Rich. 1997. 544p. mass mkt. 6.99 o.s.i (*0-8217-5594-3*); 1996. 512p. 25.00 o.s.i (*1-57566-057-1*) Kensington Publishing Corp.

—Vegas Sunrise. abr. ed. (Vegas Ser.). 1998. audio 7.99 o.s.i (*1-56740-259-3*, 1402, Paperback Nova Audio Bks.); 1997. audio 16.95 o.p. (*1-56100-995-4*, 514, Nova Audio Bks.); 1999. audio 17.95 o.p. (*1-56740-844-3*, 1727, Bookcassette); 1997. audio 89.25 (*1-56100-844-3*, 1088, Unabridged Library Editions); 1997. audio 25.95 (*1-56100-769-2*, 309, Bookcassette) Brilliance Audio.

—Vegas Sunrise. l.t. ed. 1998. 28.95 (*1-56895-571-5*, Wheeler Publishing, Inc.) Gale Group.

—Vegas Sunrise. 1998. 48p. mass mkt. 7.50 o.s.i (*0-8217-7208-2*); 1998. 480p. mass mkt. 6.99 o.s.i (*0-8217-5983-3*); 1997. 384p. 25.00 o.s.i (*1-57566-214-0*) Kensington Publishing Corp.

**COLENE (FICTITIOUS CHARACTER: ANTHONY)—FICTION**

Anthony, Piers. Chaos Mode. 1995. (Virtual Mode Ser.). 368p. mass mkt. 7.50 (*0-441-00132-7*) Ace Bks.

—Chaos Mode. unabr. ed. 1994. (Mode Ser.). audio 23.95 o.p. (*1-56100-538-X*, 423, Bookcassette); audio 73.25 o.p. (*1-56100-166-X*, 606, Unabridged Library Editions);Set. audio 17.00 o.p. (*1-56100-357-3*, 824, Nova Audio Bks.) Brilliance Audio.

—Chaos Mode. abr. ed. 2000. (Mode Ser.). audio 7.95 (*1-57815-005-1*, 1011, Media Bks. Audio Publishing) Media Bks., L. L. C.

—Chaos Mode. 1994. 304p. 19.95 o.p. (*0-399-13893-5*) Penguin Group (USA) Inc.

—Dooon Mode. 2001. 448p. 25.95 (*0-312-87463-4*); 2002. reprint ed. mass mkt. 6.99 (*0-8125-7542-3*) Doherty, Tom Assocs., LLC. (Tor Bks.).

—Fractal Mode. 1992. (Mode Ser.). 336p. mass mkt. 6.99 o.s.i (*0-441-25126-9*) Ace Bks.

—Fractal Mode. unabr. ed. 1992. (Mode Ser.). audio 23.95 o.p. (*1-56100-454-5*, 430, Bookcassette); audio 73.25 o.p. (*1-56100-084-1*, 612, Unabridged Library Editions) Brilliance Audio.

—Fractal Mode. 1992. 304p. 18.95 o.p. (*0-399-13649-5*, Ace/Putnam) Penguin Group (USA) Inc.

—Virtual Mode. 1991. (Mode Ser.). mass mkt. 6.99 (*0-441-86503-8*) Ace Bks.

—Virtual Mode. unabr. ed. 1991. (Mode Ser.). audio 23.95 o.p. (*0-930435-86-9*, 434, Bookcassette); audio 73.25 o.p. (*1-56100-080-9*, 616, Unabridged Library Editions) Brilliance Audio.

—Virtual Mode. 1991. 304p. 16.95 o.p. (*0-399-13661-4*, Ace/Putnam) Penguin Group (USA) Inc.

**COLFAX, CYRUS CHANDLER (FICTITIOUS CHARACTER)—FICTION**

Krentz, Jayne Ann. Sharp Edges. l.t. ed. 1998. 26.95 (*1-56895-549-9*, Wheeler Publishing, Inc.) Gale Group.

—Sharp Edges. 1998. (Illus.). 400p. mass mkt. 7.50 (*0-671-52409-7*, Pocket Star); 320p. 24.00 (*0-671-52310-4*, Atria) Simon & Schuster.

—Sharp Edges. abr. ed. 1998. audio 18.00 o.s.i (*0-671-57613-5*, 395615, Simon & Schuster Audioworks) Simon & Schuster Audio.

**COLLINS, HAP (FICTITIOUS CHARACTER)—FICTION**

Lansdale, Joe R. Bad Chili. 1997. 288p. 22.00 o.p. (*0-89296-619-X*) Mysterious Pr.

—Bad Chili. 1998. 272p. mass mkt. 6.99 (*0-446-60602-2*); 1997. mass mkt. (*0-446-60421-6*) Warner Bks., Inc.

—Captains Outrageous. 2001. 336p. 24.45 o.p. (*0-89296-728-5*) Mysterious Pr.

—Captains Outrageous. 2003. 336p. pap. 12.95 (*0-446-67963-1*, Mysterious Pr. Paperback Bks.) Warner Bks., Inc.

—Mucho Mojo. 1994. 320p. 19.95 o.s.i (*0-89296-490-1*) Mysterious Pr.

—Mucho Mojo. 1995. 304p. mass mkt. 5.99 (*0-446-40187-0*) Warner Bks., Inc.

—Rumble Tumble. 1998. 244p. 22.00 o.p. (*0-89296-620-3*) Mysterious Pr.

—Rumble Tumble. 1999. 272p. mass mkt. 6.50 o.s.i (*0-446-60757-6*) Warner Bks., Inc.

—Savage Season. 1990. mass mkt. 4.50 o.s.i (*0-553-28563-7*) Bantam Bks.

—Savage Season. 1995. 192p. mass mkt. 5.50 o.p. (*0-446-40431-4*) Warner Bks., Inc.

—Savage Season. 1990. 200p. 25.00 o.p. (*0-929480-23-6*) Ziesing, Mark V.

—The Two-Bear Mambo. 1995. 273p. 19.95 o.s.i (*0-89296-491-X*) Mysterious Pr.

—The Two-Bear Mambo. 1996. 288p. mass mkt. 5.99 (*0-446-40188-9*) Warner Bks., Inc.

**COLLINS, HENRIETTA O'DWYER (FICTITIOUS CHARACTER)—FICTION**

*see Henrie O (Fictitious Character)—Fiction*

**COLORADO, KAT (FICTITIOUS CHARACTER)—FICTION**

Kijewski, Karen. Alley Kat Blues. 1996. (Kat Colorado Mysteries Ser.). 384p. mass mkt. 6.99 (*0-553-57315-2*, Crimeline) Bantam Bks.

—Alley Kat Blues. 1995. 22.95 o.s.i (*0-385-46852-0*) Doubleday Publishing.

—Copy Kat. 1990. (Kat Colorado Mysteries Ser.). 400p. mass mkt. 6.99 (*0-553-29883-6*) Bantam Bks.

—Honky Tonk Kat. 1997. (Kat Colorado Mysteries Ser.). 368p. mass mkt. 6.99 o.s.i (*0-425-15860-8*) Berkley Publishing Group.

—Honky Tonk Kat. 1996. viii, 323p. 22.95 o.s.i (*0-399-14133-2*, G. P. Putnam's Sons) Penguin Group (USA) Inc.

—Honky Tonk Kat. 22.95 o.s.i (*0-399-14424-2*) Putnam Publishing Group, The.

—Honky Tonk Kat. abr. ed. 1996. (Kat Colorado Mysteries Ser.). 5p. audio 23.00 (*1-56876-059-0*) Soundlines Entertainment, Inc.

—Kat Scratch Fever. 1998. (Kat Colorado Mysteries Ser.). 368p. mass mkt. 6.99 o.s.i (*0-425-16339-3*) Berkley Publishing Group.

—Kat Scratch Fever. 1997. 323p. 22.95 o.p. (*0-399-14245-2*) Penguin Group (USA) Inc.

—Katapult. 1992. (Kat Colorado Mysteries Ser.). 288p. reprint ed. mass mkt. 6.99 (*0-380-71486-8*, Avon Bks.) Morrow/Avon.

—Katapult. 1990. 244p. 16.95 o.p. (*0-312-04679-0*, Saint Martin's Minotaur) St. Martin's Pr.

—Kat's Cradle. 1997. (Kat Colorado Mysteries Ser.). 320p. mass mkt. 6.99 (*0-553-29391-5*) Bantam Bks.

—Katwalk. 1990. (Kat Colorado Mysteries Ser.). 240p. reprint ed. mass mkt. 6.99 (*0-380-71187-7*, Avon Bks.) Morrow/Avon.

—Katwalk. 1989. 232p. 16.95 o.p. (*0-312-02969-1*, Saint Martin's Minotaur) St. Martin's Pr.

—Stray Kat Waltz. 1999. (Kat Colorado Mysteries Ser.). 352p. reprint ed. pap. 6.99 o.s.i (*0-425-16988-X*) Berkley Publishing Group.

—Stray Kat Waltz. 1998. (Kat Colorado Mysteries Ser. ). 311p. 22.95 o.s.i (*0-399-14368-8*, G. P. Putnam's Sons) Penguin Group (USA) Inc.

—Wild Kat. 1994. (Kat Colorado Mysteries Ser.). 400p. mass mkt. 6.99 (*0-553-56877-9*) Bantam Bks.

**COLSON, JESSE JAMES (FICTITIOUS CHARACTER)—FICTION**

Cooke, John Peyton. The Chimney Sweeper. 1995. 320p. 21.95 o.s.i (*0-89296-523-1*) Mysterious Pr.

—The Chimney Sweeper. 1996. 288p. mass mkt. 5.99 (*0-446-40388-1*) Warner Bks., Inc.

**COLT, CHRIS (FICTITIOUS CHARACTER)—FICTION**

Bendell, Don. Blazing Colts. 1999. 320p. mass mkt. 5.99 o.s.i (*0-451-19570-1*, Signet Bks.) NAL.

—Chief of Scouts. 1993. (Chief of Scouts Ser.). 288p. mass mkt. 4.50 o.s.i (*0-451-17690-1*, Signet Bks.) NAL.

—Colt: Chief of Scouts, Vol. 3. 1994. (Chief of Scouts Ser.). 352p. (Orig.). mass mkt. 4.50 o.s.i (*0-451-17830-0*, Signet Bks.) NAL.

—Eagle. 1996. 352p. mass mkt. 5.99 o.s.i (*0-451-18535-8*, Signet Bks.) NAL.

—Horse Soldiers. 1993. (Chief of Scouts Ser.: Vol. II). 288p. (Orig.). mass mkt. 4.50 o.s.i (*0-451-17720-7*, Signet Bks.) NAL.

—Matched Colts. 1997. 320p. mass mkt. 5.99 o.s.i (*0-451-19128-5*, Signet Bks.) NAL.

—War Bonnet. 2000. (Signet Historical Fiction Ser.). 320p. mass mkt. 5.99 o.s.i (*0-451-19812-3*, Signet Bks.) NAL.

—Warrior. 1995. 320p. (Orig.). mass mkt. 4.50 o.s.i (*0-451-18241-3*, Signet Bks.) NAL.

**COLTRANE, MITCH (FICTITIOUS CHARACTER)—FICTION**

Morrell, David. Double Image. audio 12.99 (*1-57815-292-5*, 4438); 2002. audio compact disk 14.99 (*1-57815-549-5*, 4438CD5) Media Bks., L. L. C. (Media Bks. Audio Publishing).

—Double Image, Set. abr. ed. 1998. audio 25.00 (*0-7871-1701-3*, Dove Audio) NewStar Media, Inc.

—Double Image. l.t. ed. 1998. (Core Ser.). 599p. 28.95 (*0-7838-0144-0*) Thorndike Pr.

—Double Image. 1998. 448p. 25.00 o.p. (*0-446-51963-4*) Warner Bks., Inc.

—Double Image. Warner, ed. 1999. 528p. reprint ed. mass mkt. 7.50 (*0-446-60696-0*) Warner Bks., Inc.

**COLTRANE FAMILY (FICTITIOUS CHARACTERS)—FICTION**

Hagan, Patricia. Love & Dreams. 1988. 352p. pap. 3.95 (*0-380-75159-3*, Avon Bks.) Morrow/Avon.

—Love & Fury. 1986. 384p. pap. 3.95 (*0-380-89614-1*, Avon Bks.) Morrow/Avon.

—Love & Glory. 1982. (Trilogy Bks.: No. 3). 384p. pap. 3.95 (*0-380-79665-1*, Avon Bks.) Morrow/Avon.

—Love & Honor. 1989. 336p. (Orig.). pap. 3.95 (*0-380-75557-2*, Avon Bks.) Morrow/Avon.

—Love & Splendor. 1987. 352p. pap. 3.95 (*0-380-75158-5*, Avon Bks.) Morrow/Avon.

—Love & Triumph. 1991. 320p. (Orig.). mass mkt. 4.95 (*0-380-75558-0*, Avon Bks.) Morrow/Avon.

—Love & War. 1994. 560p. mass mkt. 5.50 o.p. (*0-06-108218-X*) HarperCollins Pubs.

—Love & War. 1978. (Trilogy Bks.: No. 1). 544p. pap. 3.95 (*0-380-01947-0*, Avon Bks.) Morrow/Avon.

—Love & War. 1990. 18.95 o.p. (*0-7278-4025-8*) Severn Hse. Pubs., Ltd.

—Raging Hearts. 1997. 464p. mass mkt. 5.50 o.p. (*0-06-108477-8*, HarperTorch); 1979. (Trilogy Bks.: No. 2). 480p. pap. 3.95 o.p. (*0-380-46201-X*, 60028-5, Avon Bks.) Morrow/Avon.

—Raging Hearts. 1991. 19.95 o.p. (*0-7278-4115-7*) Severn Hse. Pubs., Ltd.

**COLUMBO, LIEUTENANT (FICTITIOUS CHARACTER)—FICTION**

Grenville, Hilary. Past Imperfect. l.t. ed. 2001. (Nightingale Ser.). 332p. pap. 23.95 (*0-7838-9325-6*) Thorndike Pr.

Harrington, William. Columbo: The Game Show Killer. 1996. 224p. 21.95 o.p. (*0-312-86178-8*, Forge Bks.) Doherty, Tom Assocs., LLC.

—Columbo: The Game Show Killer. l.t. ed. 1999. (Nightingale Ser.). 256p. pap. 20.95 (*0-7838-8595-4*) Thorndike Pr.

—Columbo: The Glitter Murder. (Columbo Ser.). 1997. 240p. 21.95 o.p. (*0-312-86161-3*); Vol. 5. 1998. 192p. mass mkt. 5.99 (*0-8125-6273-9*) Doherty, Tom Assocs., LLC. (Forge Bks.).

—Columbo: The Glitter Murder. l.t. ed. 1998. (Nightingale Ser.). 256p. pap. 21.95 (*0-7838-0134-3*) Thorndike Pr.

—Columbo: The Grassy Knoll. l.t. ed. 1994. 22.95 o.p. (*0-7927-2032-6*); pap. 21.95 o.p. (*0-7927-2031-8*) BBC Audiobooks America.

—Columbo: The Grassy Knoll. 1994. 320p. mass mkt. 4.99 (*0-8125-3024-1*, Tor Bks.); 1993. 288p. 18.95 o.p. (*0-312-85536-2*, Forge Bks.) Doherty, Tom Assocs., LLC.

—Columbo: The Helter Skelter Murders. (Columbo Ser.). 1995. 303p. mass mkt. 5.99 (*0-8125-3026-8*); 1994. 288p. 19.95 o.p. (*0-312-85537-0*) Doherty, Tom Assocs., LLC. (Forge Bks.).

—Columbo: The Hoffa Connection. 1995. 288p. 21.95 o.p. (*0-312-85816-7*, Forge Bks.) Doherty, Tom Assocs., LLC.

—Columbo: The Hoover Files. (Columbo Ser.). 224p. 1999. mass mkt. 5.99 (*0-8125-6274-7*); 1997. 21.95 o.p. (*0-312-86027-7*) Doherty, Tom Assocs., LLC. (Forge Bks.).

—Columbo: The Hoover Files. l.t. ed. 2000. (G. K. Hall Nightingale Ser.). 272p. pap. 21.95 (*0-7838-8925-9*, Macmillan Reference USA) Gale Group.

—The Game Show Killer. 1997. (Columbo Ser.: Vol. 4). 211p. pap. 5.99 (*0-8125-5080-3*, Forge Bks.) Doherty, Tom Assocs., LLC.

—Hoffa Connection. 1996. (Columbo Ser.). 245p. mass mkt. 5.99 (*0-8125-5078-1*, Forge Bks.) Doherty, Tom Assocs., LLC.

**COLYER, ROSS (FICTITIOUS CHARACTER)—FICTION**

Rosenbaum, Ray. Condors: A Novel. 1995. 340p. 21.95 o.p. (*0-89141-478-9*, Presidio Pr.) Ballantine Bks.

—Eagles: Book Four of the Wings of War. 1997. 368p. 22.95 o.p. (*0-89141-557-2*, Presidio Pr.) Ballantine Bks.

—Falcons: A Novel. 1993. 362p. 21.95 o.p. (*0-89141-476-2*, Presidio Pr.) Ballantine Bks.

—Falcons Bk. 1: Wings of War. 1995. 416p. (Orig.). pap. 9.95 o.p. (*0-89141-559-9*, Presidio Pr.) Ballantine Bks.

—Hawks: A Novel. 1994. 314p. 21.95 o.p. (*0-89141-477-0*, Presidio Pr.) Ballantine Bks.

**COMPSON, CADDY (FICTITIOUS CHARACTER)—FICTION**

Faulkner, William. The Sound & the Fury. 1985. (Barron's Book Notes Ser.). 119p. (gr. 10-12). pap. 2.95 (*0-8120-3541-0*) Barron's Educational Series, Inc.

—The Sound & the Fury. Polk, Noel, ed. 1987. (William Faulkner Manuscripts). 464p. text 55.00 (*0-8240-6806-8*); 192p. text 40.00 o.p. (*0-8240-6805-X*) Garland Publishing, Inc.

—The Sound & the Fury. l.t. ed. 1987. (Mainstream Ser.). 377p. reprint ed. 15.95 o.p. (*1-85089-143-5*) ISIS Large Print Bks. GBR. *Dist:* Transaction Pubs.

—The Sound & the Fury. 1991. (Vintage International Ser.). 336p. pap. 10.95 (*0-679-73224-1*, Vintage) Knopf Publishing Group.

—The Sound & the Fury. Polk, Noel, ed. 1987. (Illus.). 448p. pap. 7.95 o.p. (*0-394-74774-7*, Vintage) Knopf Publishing Group.

—The Sound & the Fury. 1967. (Modern Library College Editions Ser.). 427p. (C). pap. 11.25 (*0-07-553666-8*, T94, McGraw-Hill Humanities, Social Sciences & World Languages) McGraw-Hill Higher Education.

—The Sound & the Fury. mass mkt. 0.50 o.p. (*0-451-01628-9*, Signet Bks.) NAL.

—The Sound & the Fury. Minter, David, ed. 2nd ed. 1993. (Critical Editions Ser.). xv, 446p. (C). pap. text 7.50 (*0-393-96481-7*) Norton, W. W. & Co., Inc.

—The Sound & the Fury. (Modern Library of the World's Best Bks.). 1992. 368p. 15.95 (*0-679-60017-5*); 1984. 25.00 o.s.i (*0-394-53241-4*); 1966. 3.95 o.s.i (*0-394-60187-4*); 1966. 14.00 o.s.i (*0-394-44640-2*) Random Hse., Inc.

—The Sound & the Fury. Polk, Noel, ed. rev. ed. 1954. 384p. pap. 3.95 o.p. (*0-394-70005-8*) Random Hse., Inc.

—The Sound & the Fury. 2003. (SparkNotes Literature Study Guides). 72p. pap. 4.95 (*1-58663-436-4*) Spark Publishing Group.

—The Sound & the Fury. 1954. 16.05 (*0-606-04951-7*) Turtleback Bks.

**CONAN (FICTITIOUS CHARACTER)—FICTION**

Anderson, Poul. Conan the Rebel. 1988. mass mkt. 3.95 o.s.i (*0-441-11642-6*) Ace Bks.

—Conan the Rebel. 1980. 224p. pap. 2.50 o.p. (*0-553-22731-9*) Bantam Bks.

Buscema, John & Thomas, Roy. Conan the Rogue. 1991. 64p. 9.95 o.p. (*0-87135-842-5*) Marvel Enterprises.

Carpenter, Leonard. Conan Lord of the Black River. 1996. 274p. mass mkt. 5.99 o.s.i (*0-8125-5266-0*, Tor Bks.) Doherty, Tom Assocs., LLC.

—Conan of the Red Brotherhood. 1993. (Conan the Barbarian Ser.). 288p. (Orig.). mass mkt. 5.99 o.s.i (*0-8125-1413-0*, Tor Bks.) Doherty, Tom Assocs., LLC.

—Conan, Scourge of the Bloody Coast. 1994. 256p. (Orig.). mass mkt. 4.99 (*0-8125-2488-8*, Tor Bks.) Doherty, Tom Assocs., LLC.

—Conan the Gladiator. 1995. (Tor Fantasy Ser.). 288p. mass mkt. 5.99 (*0-8125-2492-6*, Tor Bks.) Doherty, Tom Assocs., LLC.

—Conan the Great. 1990. 277p. mass mkt. 5.99 (*0-8125-0714-2*, Tor Bks.) Doherty, Tom Assocs., LLC.

—Conan the Hero. 1989. mass mkt. 3.50 (*0-8125-3318-6*); 1991. 278p. reprint ed. mass mkt. 5.99 o.s.i (*0-8125-1907-8*) Doherty, Tom Assocs., LLC. (Tor Bks.).

—Conan the Outcast. 1991. mass mkt. 5.99 (*0-8125-0928-5*, Tor Bks.) Doherty, Tom Assocs., LLC.

—Conan the Raider. 288p. 1986. pap. 6.95 o.s.i (*0-8125-4256-8*); 1987. reprint ed. mass mkt. 3.50 (*0-8125-4262-2*) Doherty, Tom Assocs., LLC. (Tor Bks.).

—Conan the Renegade. 1986. 288p. (Orig.). mass mkt. 2.95 (*0-8125-4250-9*, Tor Bks.) Doherty, Tom Assocs., LLC.

—Conan the Savage. 1993. 320p. mass mkt. 5.99 (*0-8125-1412-2*); 1992. 288p. pap. 7.99 o.p. (*0-8125-2238-9*) Doherty, Tom Assocs., LLC. (Tor Bks.).

—Conan the Warlord. 1988. 273p. reprint ed. mass mkt. 5.99 (*0-8125-4268-1*, Tor Bks.) Doherty, Tom Assocs., LLC.

Conan. 2nd ed. 1985. 11.80 (*0-8125-9707-9*, Tor Bks.) Doherty, Tom Assocs., LLC.

de Camp, L. Sprague. Conan & the Spider God. 1989. (Conan the Barbarian Ser.: No. 18). mass mkt. 3.95 o.s.i (*0-441-11609-4*) Ace Bks.

—Conan & the Spider God. 1982. 192p. mass mkt. 2.50 o.s.i (*0-553-22730-0*) Bantam Bks.

—Conan & the Spider God. Date not set. pap. (*0-7653-0076-1*); Date not set. pap. (*0-7653-0074-5*); E-Book 23.95 (*0-312-70541-7*); 2002. 256p. 23.95 (*0-7653-0071-0*) Doherty, Tom Assocs., LLC. (Tor Bks.).

—Conan the Liberator: Road of Kings. 2002. (Illus.). 256p. 24.95 (*0-7653-0070-2*, Tor Bks.) Doherty, Tom Assocs., LLC.

de Camp, L. Sprague & Carter, Lin. The Buccaneer. 1986. (Conan the Barbarian Ser.: No. 6). 192p. mass mkt. 4.50 o.s.i (*0-441-11585-3*) Ace Bks.

—Conan of Aquilonia. 1987. 192p. mass mkt. 4.50 o.s.i (*0-441-11484-9*) Ace Bks.

—Conan the Barbarian. 1982. pap. 2.50 o.p. (*0-553-22544-8*) Bantam Bks.

—Conan the Liberator. 1987. (Conan the Barbarian Ser.: No. 14). mass mkt. 3.95 o.s.i (*0-441-11617-5*) Ace Bks.

—Conan the Liberator, No. 2. 1979. pap. 1.95 o.p. (*0-553-12706-3*) Bantam Bks.

—Conan the Swordsman, No. 1. 1978. pap. 1.95 o.p. (*0-553-12018-2*) Bantam Bks.

de Camp, L. Sprague, et al. Conan the Swordsman. 2002. (Conan Ser.). (Illus.). 256p. 23.95 (*0-7653-0069-9*, Tor Bks.) Doherty, Tom Assocs., LLC.

—The Swordsman. 1987. (Conan the Barbarian Ser.: No. 13). 224p. mass mkt. 3.95 o.s.i (*0-441-11479-2*) Ace Bks.

The Further Chronicles of Conan. 2005. pap. (*0-7653-0301-9*, Tor Bks.) Doherty, Tom Assocs., LLC.

Green, Roland. Conan & the Gods of the Mountain. 1993. 276p. mass mkt. 5.99 o.s.i (*0-8125-1414-9*, Tor Bks.) Doherty, Tom Assocs., LLC.

—Conan & the Mists of Doom. 1995. mass mkt. 4.99 (*0-8125-2494-2*, Tor Bks.) Doherty, Tom Assocs., LLC.

—Conan at the Demon's Gate. 1996. mass mkt. 5.99 (*0-8125-6355-7*); 1994. 278p. pap. text 7.99 (*0-8125-2491-8*) Doherty, Tom Assocs., LLC. (Tor Bks.).

—Conan the Valiant. 1989. 280p. mass mkt. 5.99 o.s.i (*0-8125-0082-2*); 1988. 288p. pap. 6.95 o.p. (*0-8125-4270-3*) Doherty, Tom Assocs., LLC. (Tor Bks.).

Green, Roland J. Conan & the Death Lord of Thanza. 1997. 272p. mass mkt. 5.99 (*0-8125-5268-7*, Tor Bks.) Doherty, Tom Assocs., LLC.

—Conan the Guardian. 1991. 280p. mass mkt. 5.99 (*0-8125-0961-7*, Tor Bks.) Doherty, Tom Assocs., LLC.

—Conan the Relentless. 1992. mass mkt. 5.99 (*0-8125-0962-5*, Tor Bks.) Doherty, Tom Assocs., LLC.

Hocking, John C. Conan & the Emerald Lotus. (Conan Ser.). 1999. 288p. mass mkt. 5.99 (*0-8125-9061-9*); 1995. pap. 9.99 o.p. (*0-8125-4499-4*) Doherty, Tom Assocs., LLC. (Tor Bks.).

Howard, Robert E. Conan, Nos. 10, 11, 12, 13, 14. 1988. 14.75 o.s.i (*0-441-11606-X*) Ace Bks.

—Conan: The Devil in Iron. 1978. 6.95 o.p. (*0-448-14580-4*) Putnam Publishing Group, The.

—Conan: The Treasure of Tranicos. 1985. 192p. mass mkt. 2.95 o.s.i (*0-441-82246-0*) Ace Bks.

—Conan of Cimmeria, No. 2. 1984. 2.75 o.s.i (*0-441-11455-5*) Ace Bks.

—Conan of the Isles. 1986. (Conan Ser.: No. 12). 192p. reprint ed. mass mkt. 4.50 o.s.i (*0-441-11623-X*) Ace Bks.

—Conan the Warrior. 1986. (Conan Ser.: No. 7). (Illus.). 224p. mass mkt. 4.50 o.s.i (*0-441-11586-1*) Ace Bks.

—Conan the Warrior. de Camp, L. Sprague, ed. 1985. (Conan Ser.: No. 7). 192p. mass mkt. 2.95 o.s.i (*0-441-11704-X*) Ace Bks.

—The Usurper. (Conan Ser.: No. 8). (Orig.). 1986. mass mkt. 3.50 o.s.i (*0-441-11589-6*); 1983. mass mkt. 2.50 o.s.i (*0-441-11602-7*) Ace Bks.

Howard, Robert E. & de Camp, L. Sprague. The Adventurer. 1986. (Conan the Barbarian Ser.: No. 5). 224p. mass mkt. 4.50 o.s.i (*0-441-11858-5*) Ace Bks.

—Conan, No. 1. 1985. mass mkt. 2.95 o.s.i (*0-441-11452-0*) Ace Bks.

—Conan! The Flame Knife. 1986. (Conan Ser.). 160p. mass mkt. 2.95 o.s.i (*0-441-11716-3*) Ace Bks.

—Conan the Conqueror. 1986. 224p. mass mkt. 4.50 o.s.i (*0-441-11590-X*) Ace Bks.

—Conan, the Freebooter. 1986. (Conan Ser.: No. 3). 224p. mass mkt. 4.50 o.s.i (*0-441-11863-1*) Ace Bks.

—The Usurper. 1990. (Conan the Barbarian Ser.: No. 8). 256p. (Orig.). mass mkt. 4.50 o.s.i (*0-441-11591-8*) Ace Bks.

Howard, Robert E., et al. Conan, No. 1. 1987. 224p. mass mkt. 4.50 o.s.i (*0-441-11481-4*) Ace Bks.

—Conan of Cimmeria. 1990. 192p. mass mkt. 4.50 o.s.i (*0-441-11453-9*) Ace Bks.

—Conan the Avenger, No. 10. 1987. 192p. mass mkt. 4.50 o.s.i (*0-441-11483-0*) Ace Bks.

—Conan the Wanderer. 1985. 224p. mass mkt. 4.50 o.s.i (*0-441-11597-7*) Ace Bks.

Jackson, Steve, Games Staff. GURPS Conan. 1995. (Illus.). (Orig.). pap. 16.95 o.p. (*1-55634-148-2*) Jackson, Steve Games, Inc.

Jones Staff. Conan Doyle & the Spirits. 1983. 14.95 (*0-85030-837-2*) Aquarian Pr. GBR. *Dist:* Harper-SanFrancisco.

Jordan, Robert. Conan, Set. 1986. mass mkt. 11.80 (*0-8125-9852-0*); 1984. mass mkt. 11.80 (*0-8125-9608-0*) Doherty, Tom Assocs., LLC. (Tor Bks.).

—The Conan Chronicles. 1995. 510p. 19.95 (*0-312-85929-5*, Tor Bks.) Doherty, Tom Assocs., LLC.

—Conan the Defender. 1991. mass mkt. 3.95 (*0-8125-1394-0*); 1983. 298p. mass mkt. 2.95 (*0-8125-4228-2*); 1982. 298p. mass mkt. 5.95 (*0-523-48063-6*) Doherty, Tom Assocs., LLC. (Tor Bks.).

—Conan the Destroyer. 2004. (*0-7653-0290-X*); 2004. pap. (*0-7653-0291-8*); 1993. 271p. pap. text 4.50 (*0-8125-3136-1*); 1991. 288p. mass mkt. 3.99 o.s.i (*0-8125-1401-7*); 1984. mass mkt. 2.95 (*0-8125-4238-X*) Doherty, Tom Assocs., LLC. (Tor Bks.).

—Conan the Invincible. 1990. mass mkt. 3.95 (*0-8125-0997-8*); 1985. 288p. pap. 2.95 o.s.i (*0-8125-4225-8*); 1982. 288p. mass mkt. 2.95 o.p. (*0-523-48050-4*) Doherty, Tom Assocs., LLC. (Tor Bks.).

—Conan the Magnificent. (Orig.). 1991. 288p. mass mkt. 3.99 o.s.i (*0-8125-1593-5*); 1989. mass mkt. 3.95 (*0-8125-0099-7*); Vol. 5. 1984. mass mkt. 2.95 o.s.i (*0-8125-4236-3*) Doherty, Tom Assocs., LLC. (Tor Bks.).

—Conan the Triumphant. 1991. mass mkt. 3.95 (*0-8125-1398-3*); 1988. mass mkt. 3.50 (*0-8125-4279-7*); 1983. (Illus.). 280p. pap. 6.95 o.s.i (*0-8125-4234-7*) Doherty, Tom Assocs., LLC. (Tor Bks.).

—Conan the Unconquered. 1991. 286p. mass mkt. 3.99 (*0-8125-1400-9*); 1988. 3.50 o.s.i (*0-8125-4277-0*); 1983. (Tor Conan Ser.: Bk. 3). 288p. mass mkt. 2.95 (*0-523-48053-9*) Doherty, Tom Assocs., LLC. (Tor Bks.).

—Conan the Victorious. 1991. 280p. mass mkt. 3.95 (*0-8125-1399-1*); 1984. (Illus.). pap. 6.95 o.s.i (*0-8125-4240-1*) Doherty, Tom Assocs., LLC. (Tor Bks.).

—The Further Chronicles of Conan. 1999. (Illus.). 509p. 24.95 (*0-312-87195-3*, Tor Bks.) Doherty, Tom Assocs., LLC.

—The Further Chronicles of Conan. abr. ed. 2001. audio 22.95 o.p. (*1-56511-588-0*) HighBridge Co.

—The Further Chronicles of Conan. abr. ed. 1999. audio 22.95 (*1-55935-328-7*) Soundelux Audio Publishing.

Kraar, et al. Conan: Witch Queen of Acheron. 1985. 64p. 6.50 o.p. (*0-87135-085-8*) Marvel Enterprises.

Kraar, Don & Severin. Conan the Reaver. 1987. 64p. 9.95 o.p. (*0-87135-289-3*) Marvel Enterprises.

Moench, et al. Conan: Skull of Set. 1989. 64p. 8.95 o.p. (*0-87135-579-5*) Marvel Enterprises.

Moore, Roger E. Conan & the Prophecy. Charette, Beverly, ed. 1985. (Endless Quest Bks.). (Illus.). 160p. (J). (gr. 4 up). pap. text 2.25 o.p. (*0-88038-121-3*) TSR, Inc.

—Conan the Outlaw. 1985. (Endless Quest Bks.). (Illus.). 160p. (J). (gr. 4-7). pap. 2.25 o.p. (*0-394-73974-4*, Random Hse. Bks. for Young Readers) Random Hse. Children's Bks.

—Conan the Outlaw. Larson, William, ed. 1985. (Endless Quest Bks.). (Illus.). 160p. (J). (gr. 4 up). pap. text 2.25 o.p. (*0-88038-222-8*) TSR, Inc.

Moore, Sean A. Conan & the Grim Grey God. (Conan Ser.). 1996. 224p. pap. 9.99 o.s.i (*0-8125-5267-9*); Vol. 1. 1997. 204p. pap. text 5.99 (*0-8125-9062-7*) Doherty, Tom Assocs., LLC. (Tor Bks.).

—Conan & the Shaman's Curse. 1996. mass mkt. 4.99 (*0-8125-5265-2*, Tor Bks.) Doherty, Tom Assocs., LLC.

—Conan the Hunter. 1994. 245p. mass mkt. 4.99 (*0-8125-3531-6*, Tor Bks.) Doherty, Tom Assocs., LLC.

Offutt, Andrew J. Conan, the Mercenary. 1987. (Conan Ser.). 192p. (Orig.). mass mkt. 2.95 o.s.i (*0-441-11482-2*) Ace Bks.

—The Sword of Skelos. 1987. (Conan the Barbarian Ser.: No. 15). mass mkt. 3.95 o.s.i (*0-441-11480-6*) Ace Bks.

—The Sword of Skelos. 1979. (Conan Ser.: No. 3). pap. 2.50 o.p. (*0-553-22729-7*) Bantam Bks.

Perry, Steve. Conan the Defiant. 1988. mass mkt. 3.50 (*0-8125-4273-8*); 1987. 256p. pap. 6.95 o.p. (*0-8125-4264-9*) Doherty, Tom Assocs., LLC. (Tor Bks.).

—Conan the Fearless. (Orig.). 1989. mass mkt. 3.95 (*0-8125-0096-2*); 1987. 288p. pap. 2.95 o.s.i (*0-8125-4258-4*); 1986. mass mkt. 6.95 (*0-8125-4248-7*) Doherty, Tom Assocs., LLC. (Tor Bks.).

—Conan the Formidable. 1991. 288p. mass mkt. 5.99 (*0-8125-1377-0*); 1990. pap. text 7.95 o.p. (*0-8125-0998-6*) Doherty, Tom Assocs., LLC. (Tor Bks.).

—Conan the Freelance. 1990. 279p. mass mkt. 5.99 (*0-8125-0690-1*, Tor Bks.) Doherty, Tom Assocs., LLC.

—Conan the Indomitable. 1990. mass mkt. 3.95 (*0-8125-0860-2*); 1989. pap. 7.95 o.p. (*0-8125-0295-7*) Doherty, Tom Assocs., LLC. (Tor Bks.).

Roberts, John M. Conan & the Amazon. 1995. 288p. mass mkt. 5.99 (*0-8125-2493-4*, Tor Bks.) Doherty, Tom Assocs., LLC.

—Conan & the Manhunters. 1994. (Conan Ser.). 320p. mass mkt. 5.99 (*0-8125-2489-6*, Tor Bks.) Doherty, Tom Assocs., LLC.

—Conan & the Treasure of Python. (Orig.). 1994. 288p. mass mkt. 4.99 (*0-8125-5000-5*); 1993. mass mkt. 7.99 (*0-8125-1415-7*) Doherty, Tom Assocs., LLC. (Tor Bks.).

—Conan the Bold. 1989. 282p. mass mkt. 5.99 o.s.i (*0-8125-5210-5*, Tor Bks.) Doherty, Tom Assocs., LLC.

—Conan the Champion. 1989. mass mkt. 3.95 (*0-8125-0094-6*); 1987. pap. 3.50 o.s.i (*0-8125-4260-6*) Doherty, Tom Assocs., LLC. (Tor Bks.).
—Conan the Marauder. 1992. 277p. mass mkt. 4.50 (*0-8125-3149-3*); 1988. pap. 3.50 o.s.i (*0-8125-4266-5*) Doherty, Tom Assocs., LLC. (Tor Bks.).
—Conan the Rogue. (Orig.). 1992. 304p. mass mkt. 5.99 o.s.i (*0-8125-2141-2*); 1991. mass mkt. 7.99 (*0-8125-1411-4*) Doherty, Tom Assocs., LLC. (Tor Bks.).
—Conan the Valorous. (Orig.). 1992. mass mkt. 3.99 (*0-8125-1809-8*); 1986. 288p. pap. 2.95 o.s.i (*0-8125-4252-5*); 1985. 320p. mass mkt. 6.95 (*0-8125-4244-4*) Doherty, Tom Assocs., LLC. (Tor Bks.).
Thomas, Roy, et al. Conan: Ravagers of Time. 1992. 64p. 9.95 o.p. (*0-87135-911-1*) Marvel Enterprises.
—Conan: The Horn of Azoth. 1990. 64p. 8.95 o.p. (*0-87135-639-2*) Marvel Enterprises.
—Conan of the Isles. 1988. (Illus.). 96p. 8.95 o.p. (*0-87135-483-7*) Marvel Enterprises.
Turtledove, Harry. Conan of Venarium. Date not set. mass mkt. (*0-7653-4388-6*); 2003. (Illus.). 272p. 24.95 (*0-7653-0466-X*) Doherty, Tom Assocs., LLC. (Tor Bks.).
Wagner, Karl Edward. Conan: The Road of Kings. 2001. (Conan Ser.). 224p. mass mkt. 5.99 (*0-7653-4020-8*, Tor Bks.) Doherty, Tom Assocs., LLC.
—Road of Kings. 1987. (Conan the Barbarian Ser.: No. 16). 224p. mass mkt. 3.95 o.s.i (*0-441-11618-3*) Ace Bks.

**CONE, TIMOTHY (FICTITIOUS CHARACTER)—FICTION**

Sanders, Lawrence. Three Complete Novels: The Timothy Files, Timothy's Game, Sullivan's Sting. 1999. 784p. 12.98 o.s.i (*0-399-14531-1*) Penguin Group (USA) Inc.
—The Timothy Files. 1988. mass mkt. 7.50 (*0-425-10924-0*) Berkley Publishing Group.
—The Timothy Files. l.t. ed. 1988. (General Ser.). 508p. 19.95 o.p. (*0-8161-4479-6*, Macmillan Reference USA) Gale Group.
—The Timothy Files. 1987. 384p. 18.95 o.p. (*0-399-13261-9*, G. P. Putnam's Sons) Penguin Putnam Bks. for Young Readers.
—Timothy's Game. 1989. 352p. mass mkt. 7.50 (*0-425-11641-7*) Berkley Publishing Group.
—Timothy's Game. l.t. ed. 1989. (General Ser.). 468p. lib. bdg. 19.95 o.p. (*0-8161-4757-4*, Macmillan Reference USA) Gale Group.
—Timothy's Game. 1988. 384p. 18.95 o.p. (*0-399-13368-2*, G. P. Putnam's Sons) Penguin Putnam Bks. for Young Readers.
—Timothy's Game. abr. ed. 1988. audio 14.95 (*0-671-67015-8*, Simon & Schuster Audioworks) Simon & Schuster Audio.

**CONLAN, KATE (FICTITIOUS CHARACTER)—FICTION**

Hoag, Tami. Ashes to Ashes. unabr. ed. 2001. audio compact disk 119.95 (*0-7927-9992-5*, SLD 043); 2000. 12p. audio 96.95 (*0-7927-2365-1*, CSL 254) BBC Audiobooks America. (Chivers Sound Library).
—Ashes to Ashes. 1999. 496p. 24.95 o.s.i (*0-553-10633-3*); 2000. 592p. reprint ed. mass mkt. 7.99 (*0-553-57960-6*) Bantam Bks.
—Ashes to Ashes. l.t. ed. 2000. 12.95 (*1-56895-983-4*); 1999. 26.95 o.p. (*1-56895-713-0*) Gale Group. (Wheeler Publishing, Inc.).
—Ashes to Ashes. abr. ed. 1999. audio 25.00 Highsmith Inc.
—Ashes to Ashes. abr. ed. 2003. audio 14.95 (*0-7435-3294-5*, Encore); 2003. audio compact disk 14.95 (*0-7435-3295-3*, Encore); 1999. audio 25.00 (*0-671-58232-1*, 594124, Simon & Schuster Audioworks) Simon & Schuster Audio.

**CONLEY, PATRICIA (FICTITIOUS CHARACTER)—FICTION**

Coleman, Evelyn. What a Woman's Gotta Do. 1999. 400p. mass mkt. 6.99 (*0-440-23500-6*) Dell Publishing.
—What a Woman's Gotta Do. 1998. 320p. 23.00 (*0-684-83175-9*, Simon & Schuster) Simon & Schuster.

**CONNELL, DAN (FICTITIOUS CHARACTER)—FICTION**

Pronzini, Bill. Dead Run. 1992. (Mystery Scene Bk.). 194p. pap. 3.95 o.p. (*0-88184-838-7*, Carroll & Graf Pubs.) Avalon Publishing Group.
—The Jade Figurine. 1991. 208p. pap. 3.95 (*0-88184-773-9*, Carroll & Graf Pubs.) Avalon Publishing Group.

**CONNOR, GAIL (FICTITIOUS CHARACTER)—FICTION**

Parker, Barbara. Suspicion of Betrayal. 1999. 352p. 23.95 o.s.i (*0-525-94468-0*, Dutton Studio) Dutton/Plume.
—Suspicion of Betrayal. 2000. 432p. mass mkt. 6.99 (*0-451-19838-7*, Signet Bks.) NAL.
—Suspicion of Betrayal. l.t. ed. 1999. (Mystery Ser.). 568p. 29.95 (*0-7862-2000-7*) Thorndike Pr.
—Suspicion of Deceit. 1998. 368p. 23.95 o.p. (*0-525-94401-X*) Dutton/Plume.
—Suspicion of Deceit. 1999. 432p. reprint ed. mass mkt. 6.99 (*0-451-19549-3*, Signet Bks.) NAL.
—Suspicion of Deceit. unabr. ed. 1998. audio 78.00 (*0-7887-3572-1*, 95937E7) Recorded Bks., LLC.
—Suspicion of Deceit. l.t. ed. 1998. (Cloak & Dagger Ser.). 615p. 26.95 o.p. (*0-7862-1460-0*) Thorndike Pr.
—Suspicion of Guilt. 1995. 400p. 22.95 o.p. (*0-525-93769-2*, Dutton) Dutton/Plume.
—Suspicion of Guilt. l.t. ed. 1995. 26.95 (*1-56895-232-5*, Wheeler Publishing, Inc.) Gale Group.
—Suspicion of Guilt. 1996. 432p. mass mkt. 6.99 (*0-451-17703-7*, Signet Bks.) NAL.
—Suspicion of Guilt. unabr. ed. 1995. audio 91.00 (*0-7887-0353-6*, 94545E7) Recorded Bks., LLC.
—Suspicion of Innocence. 1994. 20.95 (*0-525-93747-1*); 352p. 20.95 o.p. (*0-525-93744-7*) Dutton/Plume. (Dutton).
—Suspicion of Innocence. 1994. 448p. mass mkt. 6.99 (*0-451-17340-6*, Signet Bks.) NAL.
—Suspicion of Innocence, unabr. ed. 1994. audio 85.00 (*0-7887-0024-3*, 94223E7) Recorded Bks., LLC.
—Suspicion of Innocence. 344p. 4.98 o.p. (*0-8317-4569-X*) Smithmark Pubs., Inc.
—Suspicion of Madness. 2003. (Illus.). 368p. 24.95 (*0-525-94681-0*) Dutton/Plume.
—Suspicion of Madness. 2003. 416p. mass mkt. 7.99 (*0-451-21089-1*, Signet Bks.) NAL.
—Suspicion of Madness. 2003. (Gail Connor & Anthony Quintana Novel Ser.). 597p. 30.95 (*0-7862-5422-X*) Thorndike Pr.
—Suspicion of Malice. 2000. 352p. 22.95 o.s.i (*0-525-94542-3*) Dutton/Plume.
—Suspicion of Malice. 2001. 432p. reprint ed. mass mkt. 6.99 (*0-451-20125-6*, Signet Bks.) NAL.
—Suspicion of Malice. l.t. ed. 2000. (Mystery Ser.). 565p. 29.95 (*0-7862-2655-2*) Thorndike Pr.
—Suspicion of Vengeance. 2001. 368p. 23.95 o.s.i (*0-525-94601-2*, Dutton) Dutton/Plume.
—Suspicion of Vengeance. l.t. ed. 2002. 30.95 (*0-7862-3751-1*) Gale Group.
—Suspicion of Vengeance. 2003. 448p. reprint ed. mass mkt. 7.50 (*0-451-20451-4*, Signet Bks.) NAL.

**CONNOR, LILY (FICTITIOUS CHARACTER)—FICTION**

Blake, Michelle. The Book of Light: A Lilly Connor Mystery. 2003. 224p. 24.95 (*0-399-15046-3*) Putnam Publishing Group, The.

**CONNORS, LIZ (FICTITIOUS CHARACTER)—FICTION**

Kelly, Susan. The Gemini Man. 1986. 304p. mass mkt. 2.95 o.s.i (*0-345-33113-3*) Ballantine Bks.
—The Gemini Man. 1985. 221p. 14.95 o.s.i (*0-8027-5613-1*) Walker & Co.
—Out of the Darkness. unabr. ed. 1992. audio 21.95 o.p. (*1-56100-478-2*, 204, Bookcassette); audio 57.25 o.p. (*1-56100-112-0*, 974, Unabridged Library Editions) Brilliance Audio.
—Out of the Darkness. 1994. 352p. mass mkt. 4.50 o.s.i (*0-8217-4620-0*) Kensington Publishing Corp.
—Out of the Darkness. 1992. 278p. 18.00 o.s.i (*0-679-41131-3*, Villard Bks.) Random House Adult Trade Publishing Group.
—The Summertime Soldiers. 1986. 192p. 14.95 o.p. (*0-8027-5646-8*) Walker & Co.
—Trail of the Dragon. 1990. 256p. mass mkt. 3.95 o.s.i (*0-345-35749-3*) Ballantine Bks.
—Trail of the Dragon. 1988. 282p. 17.95 (*0-8027-5696-4*) Walker & Co.
—Until Proven Innocent. unabr. ed. 1991. audio 57.25 o.p. (*1-56100-067-1*, 593); audio 21.95 o.p. (*0-930435-73-7*, 411) Brilliance Audio.
—Until Proven Innocent. 1990. 288p. 16.95 o.s.i (*0-394-58414-7*, Villard Bks.) Random House Adult Trade Publishing Group.

**CONRAD, CLAIRE (FICTITIOUS CHARACTER)—FICTION**

Howe, Melodie J. Beauty Dies. 1996. (Crime Ser.). 272p. pap. 5.95 o.s.i (*0-14-023565-5*) Penguin Group (USA) Inc.
—Beauty Dies: A Claire Conrad - Maggie Hill Mystery. 1994. 272p. 19.95 o.p. (*0-670-85449-2*, Viking) Viking Penguin.

**CONSTANTINO, TED (FICTITIOUS CHARACTER)—FICTION**

Beck, K. K. The Body in the Cornflakes. 1994. (Northwest Mysteries Ser.). mass mkt. 4.99 o.s.i (*0-8041-1175-8*, Ivy Bks.) Ballantine Bks.
—The Body in the Cornflakes. pap. 15.95 (*0-312-29184-1*, Saint Martin's Griffin); 1992. 224p. 17.95 (*0-312-08146-4*, Saint Martin's Minotaur) St. Martin's Pr.

**CONTE, GERRY (FICTITIOUS CHARACTER)—FICTION**

Amato, Angela & Sharkey, Joe. Lady Gold. 1999. 384p. mass mkt. 6.99 (*0-312-96765-9*, St. Martin's Paperbacks); 1999. E-Book 23.95 (*0-312-20726-3*); 1998. 354p. 23.95 (*0-312-18541-3*) St. Martin's Pr.

**CONTINENTAL OP (FICTITIOUS CHARACTER)—FICTION**

Hammett, Dashiell. The Continental Op. Marcus, Steven, ed. 1992. pap. 10.00 (*0-394-23902-4*); 1989. 352p. pap. 13.00 (*0-679-72258-0*) Knopf Publishing Group. (Vintage).
—The Continental Op. Marcus, Steven, ed. 1992. pap. 10.00 (*0-679-74095-3*) Random Hse., Inc.
—The Dain Curse. Date not set. 150p. 18.95 (*0-8488-2429-6*); 1976. 21.95 (*0-8488-1039-2*) Amereon, Ltd.
—The Dain Curse. unabr. ed. 1980. audio 42.00 (*0-7366-0264-X*, 1259) Books on Tape, Inc.
—The Dain Curse. unabr. ed. 1996. audio 54.95 (*1-85695-717-9*, 941101) ISIS Audio Bks. GBR. *Dist:* Ulverscroft Large Print Bks., Ltd.
—The Dain Curse. 1989. 240p. pap. 12.00 (*0-679-72260-2*); 1978. pap. 1.50 o.p. (*0-394-72624-3*) Knopf Publishing Group. (Vintage).
—The Dain Curse. 1972. pap. 3.95 o.p. (*0-394-71827-5*) Random Hse., Inc.
—Red Harvest. Date not set. 143p. 18.95 (*0-8488-2348-6*) Amereon, Ltd.
—Red Harvest. unabr. ed. 1996. audio 42.00 (*0-7366-3442-8*, 4086) Books on Tape, Inc.
—Red Harvest. unabr. ed. 2000. audio compact disk 64.95 (*0-7531-0705-8*, 107058); 1996. audio 54.95 (*1-85695-707-1*, 940903) ISIS Audio Bks. GBR. *Dist:* Ulverscroft Large Print Bks., Ltd.
—Red Harvest. 1992. pap. 9.00 (*0-394-23904-0*); 1989. 224p. pap. 11.00 (*0-679-72261-0*) Knopf Publishing Group. (Vintage).
—Red Harvest. 1992. pap. 9.00 (*0-679-74093-7*); 1972. pap. 3.95 o.p. (*0-394-71828-3*) Random Hse., Inc.
—Red Harvest. 1994. 209p. 35.00 (*1-883402-95-6*, Scribner) Simon & Schuster.

**COOK, JEREMY (FICTITIOUS CHARACTER)—FICTION**

Carkeet, David. Double Negative. 1980. 256p. 11.95 o.p. (*0-385-27140-9*) Doubleday Publishing.
—Double Negative. Rosenman, Jane, ed. 1991. 252p. reprint ed. pap. (*0-671-73690-6*, Washington Square Pr.) Simon & Schuster.
—Double Negative. 1982. 246p. pap. 3.95 o.p. (*0-14-006070-7*, Penguin Bks.) Viking Penguin.
—The Error of Our Ways: A Novel. 288p. 1998. pap. 13.00 o.s.i (*0-8050-5604-1*, Owl Bks.); 1997. per. 15.00 (*0-8050-7114-8*); 1997. 25.00 o.s.i (*0-8050-4502-3*) Holt, Henry & Co.
—The Error of Our Ways: A Novel. l.t. ed. 1997. (Niagara Large Print Ser.). 352p. 29.50 o.p. (*0-7089-5865-6*, Ulverscroft) Thorpe, F. A. Pubs. GBR. *Dist:* Ulverscroft Large Print Bks., Ltd.
—The Full Catastrophe. 1990. 18.95 o.p. (*0-671-64319-3*, Simon & Schuster) Simon & Schuster.
—The Full Catastrophe. Rosenman, Jane, ed. 1991. 324p. reprint ed. pap. (*0-671-73245-5*, Washington Square Pr.) Simon & Schuster.

**COOK, NANCY (FICTITIOUS CHARACTER)—FICTION**

Jones, D. J. H. Murder in the New Age. 192p. 2000. pap. 13.95 (*0-8263-2236-0*); 1997. 19.95 (*0-8263-1813-4*) Univ. of New Mexico Pr.

**COOKE, CAROLINE (FICTITIOUS CHARACTER)—FICTION**

Rovin, Jeff. Return of the Wolfman. 1998. 352p. mass mkt. 6.99 o.s.i (*0-425-16576-0*) Berkley Publishing Group.

**COOKE, NICHOLAS (FICTITIOUS CHARACTER)—FICTION**

Cowell, Stephanie. Nicholas Cooke: Actor, Soldier, Physician, Priest. 1994. 448p. reprint ed. pap. 12.00 o.s.i (*0-345-39016-4*) Ballantine Bks.
—Nicholas Cooke: Actor, Soldier, Physician, Priest. 1993. 442p. 24.00 o.p. (*0-393-03543-3*) Norton, W. W. & Co., Inc.
—The Physician of London: The 2nd Part of the Seventeenth-Century Trilogy of Nicholas Cooke. 1995. 416p. 23.00 o.p. (*0-393-03873-4*) Norton, W. W. & Co., Inc.

**COOPER, ALEXANDRA (FICTITIOUS CHARACTER)—FICTION**

Fairstein, Linda. The Bone Vault: A Novel. 2004. 528p. mass mkt. 7.99 (*0-7434-3667-9*, Pocket Star); 2003. 400p. 25.00 (*0-7432-2354-3*, Scribner); 2003. mass mkt. (*0-7434-6273-4*, Pocket Star); 2003. 592p. 27.00 (*0-7432-4091-X*, Scribner) Simon & Schuster.
—The Bone Vault: A Novel. abr. ed. 2003. audio 26.00 (*0-7435-2481-0*); audio compact disk 30.00 (*0-7435-2494-2*) Simon & Schuster Audio. (Simon & Schuster Audioworks).
—Cold Hit. l.t. ed. 2000. (Wheeler Large Print Book Ser.). 469p. 27.95 (*1-56895-816-1*, Wheeler Publishing, Inc.) Gale Group.
—Cold Hit. (Alexandra Cooper Mysteries Ser.). 2003. (Illus.). 464p. pap. 7.99 (*0-671-01955-4*, Pocket); 2002. 416p. E-Book (*0-7432-3006-X*, Scribner); 1999. 416p. 25.00 o.s.i (*0-684-84846-5*, Scribner); 2000. 416p. reprint ed. 7.99 (*0-671-04212-2*, Pocket) Simon & Schuster.
—Cold Hit. abr. ed. 1999. (Alexandra Cooper Ser.). audio 24.00 (*0-671-04550-4*, Simon & Schuster Audioworks) Simon & Schuster Audio.
—The Dead-House. 2001. E-Book 25.00 (*1-59061-256-6*) Adobe Systems, Inc.
—The Dead-House. 2003. 528p. mass mkt. 7.99 (*0-671-01954-6*, Pocket); 2001. (Illus.). 416p. 25.00 (*0-684-84904-6*, Scribner); 2001. 416p. E-Book 25.00 (*0-7432-3007-8*, Scribner); 2001. 560p. 25.00 (*0-7432-2403-5*, Scribner) Simon & Schuster.
—The Dead-House. abr. ed. 2001. audio 26.00 (*0-7435-0902-1*); audio compact disk 30.00 (*0-7435-0903-X*) Simon & Schuster Audio. (Simon & Schuster Audioworks).
—Final Jeopardy. unabr. ed. 1998. audio 64.00 (*0-7366-4203-X*, 4699) Books on Tape, Inc.
—Final Jeopardy. 1998. 336p. mass mkt. 3.99 (*0-671-02487-6*, Pocket); 1997. (Illus.). 336p. pap. 7.99 (*0-671-01012-3*, Pocket); 1996. 23.00 o.p. (*0-684-00314-7*, Scribner); 1996. 400p. 22.50 o.p. (*0-684-81489-7*, Scribner) Simon & Schuster.
—Final Jeopardy. 2003. audio 9.95 (*0-7435-3249-X*, Encore); 2003. audio compact disk 9.98 (*0-7435-3267-8*, Encore); 1996. audio 18.00 (*0-671-57340-3*, 647494, Simon & Schuster Audioworks) Simon & Schuster Audio.
—The Kills. 2004. 400p. 25.00 (*0-7432-2355-1*); 2003. 624p. 25.00 (*0-7432-5380-9*) Simon & Schuster. (Scribner).
—Likely to Die. unabr. ed. 1999. audio 64.00 (*0-7366-4888-7*, 5110) Books on Tape, Inc.
—Likely to Die. (Alexandra Cooper Mysteries Ser.). 1998. (Illus.). 448p. mass mkt. 7.99 (*0-671-01493-5*, Pocket); 1997. 400p. 24.00 (*0-684-81488-9*, Scribner) Simon & Schuster.
—Likely to Die. 2003. audio 9.95 (*0-7435-3250-3*, Encore); 2003. audio compact disk 9.95 (*0-7435-3277-5*, Encore); 1997. audio 18.00 o.s.i (*0-671-52134-9*, Simon & Schuster Audioworks) Simon & Schuster Audio.

**COOPER, IRIS (FICTITIOUS CHARACTER)—FICTION**

Beck, K. K. Death in a Deck Chair. 1987. 176p. mass mkt. 4.99 o.s.i (*0-8041-0118-3*, Ivy Bks.) Ballantine Bks.
—Death in a Deck Chair. 1984. 12.95 (*0-8027-5601-8*) Walker & Co.
—Murder in a Mummy Case. l.t. ed. 1989. 8.95 o.p. (*0-7451-9460-5*, 352); pap. 8.95 o.p. (*1-55504-841-2*) BBC Audiobooks America.
—Murder in a Mummy Case. 1987. 176p. mass mkt. 3.95 o.s.i (*0-8041-0117-5*, Ivy Bks.) Ballantine Bks.
—Murder in a Mummy Case. 1986. 176p. 15.95 o.s.i (*0-8027-5655-7*) Walker & Co.
—Peril under the Palms. 1990. 176p. mass mkt. 4.99 o.s.i (*0-8041-0594-4*, Ivy Bks.) Ballantine Bks.
—Peril under the Palms. 1989. 208p. 18.95 (*0-8027-5715-4*) Walker & Co.

**COOPER, JOHN (FICTITIOUS CHARACTER)—FICTION**

Gifford, Thomas. The First Sacrifice. 1995. 560p. mass mkt. 6.50 o.s.i (*0-553-57217-2*) Bantam Bks.
—The First Sacrifice. l.t. ed. 1995. (Large Print Bks.). pap. 22.95 o.p. (*1-56895-097-7*, Wheeler Publishing, Inc.) Gale Group.
—The Wind Chill Factor. 1985. 384p. mass mkt. 5.99 o.s.i (*0-345-32336-X*) Ballantine Bks.
—The Wind Chill Factor. 464p. 1998. pap. 23.00 (*0-553-76268-0*); 1992. mass mkt. 6.99 o.s.i (*0-553-29752-X*) Bantam Bks.
—The Wind Chill Factor. 1975. 350p. 8.95 o.p. (*0-399-11439-4*) Putnam Publishing Group, The.
—Wind Chill Factor. 1994. mass mkt. 1.99 o.s.i (*0-553-56920-1*) Bantam Bks.

**COOPER, MATT (FICTITIOUS CHARACTER)—FICTION**

Hunter, Jack D. Slingshot. unabr. ed. 1995. 5p. audio 62.95 (*0-7861-0872-X*, 113377) Blackstone Audio Bks., Inc.
—Slingshot. 1996. 432p. pap. text 6.99 o.p. (*0-8125-2457-8*); 1994. 384p. 22.95 o.p. (*0-312-85500-1*) Doherty, Tom Assocs., LLC. (Forge Bks.).
—Slingshot. 2000. 29.95 (*0-7351-0450-6*) Replica Bks.

**COOPERMAN, BENNY (FICTITIOUS CHARACTER)—FICTION**

Engel, Howard. A City Called July. 1988. 39.50 o.p. (*0-14-778233-3*) Penguin Group (USA) Inc.
—A City Called July. 1986. 256p. 15.95 o.p. (*0-312-13986-1*) St. Martin's Pr.

—A City Called July. l.t. ed. 1989. (Ulverscroft Large Print Ser.). 481p. 29.99 o.p. (0-7089-1957-X, Ulverscroft) Thorpe, F. A. Pubs. GBR. Dist: Ulverscroft Large Print Bks., Ltd., Ulverscroft Large Print Canada, Ltd.

—A City Called July. 1988. 228p. pap. 3.95 o.p. (0-14-010454-2, Penguin Bks.) Viking Penguin.

—Dead & Buried. 290p. 2003. pap. 14.95 (1-58567-281-5); 2001. 24.95 (1-58567-155-X) Overlook Pr., The.

—Dead & Buried. l.t. ed. 2001. (Core Ser.). 394p. 28.95 (0-7838-9659-X) Thorndike Pr.

—Getting Away with Murder. 1998. (Benny Cooperman Mystery Ser.). 248p. 22.95 (0-87951-829-4) Overlook Pr., The.

—Murder on Location. 1986. 35.00 o.p. (0-14-779206-1) Penguin Group (USA) Inc.

—Murder on Location. 1985. 222p. 12.95 o.p. (0-312-55314-5) St. Martin's Pr.

—Murder on Location. 1986. (Crime Monthly Ser.). 222p. pap. 3.50 o.p. (0-14-007742-1, Penguin Bks.) Viking Penguin.

—Murder Sees the Light: A Benny Cooperman Mystery. 1985. 256p. 13.95 o.p. (0-312-55324-2) St. Martin's Pr.

—Murder Sees the Light: A Benny Cooperman Mystery. l.t. ed. 1988. (Ulverscroft Large Print Ser.). 432p. 29.99 o.p. (0-7089-1911-1, Ulverscroft) Thorpe, F. A. Pubs. GBR. Dist: Ulverscroft Large Print Bks., Ltd., Ulverscroft Large Print Canada, Ltd.

—Murder Sees the Light: A Benny Cooperman Mystery. 1986. 240p. pap. 3.50 o.p. (0-14-008975-6, Penguin Bks.) Viking Penguin.

—The Ransom Game. 1984. 218p. 11.95 o.p. (0-312-66383-8) St. Martin's Pr.

—The Ransom Game. l.t. ed. 1989. (Ulverscroft Large Print Ser.). 29.99 o.p. (0-7089-2052-7, Ulverscroft) Thorpe, F. A. Pubs. GBR. Dist: Ulverscroft Large Print Bks., Ltd., Ulverscroft Large Print Canada, Ltd.

—The Ransom Game. 1986. (Crime Monthly Ser.). 224p. pap. 3.95 o.p. (0-14-007741-3, Penguin Bks.) Viking Penguin.

—The Suicide Murders. l.t. ed. 1987. pap. 13.95 o.p. (1-55504-257-0) BBC Audiobooks America.

—The Suicide Murders. 1984. 200p. 11.95 o.p. (0-312-77527-X) St. Martin's Pr.

—The Suicide Murders. 1985. (Crime Ser.). 208p. pap. 3.95 o.p. (0-14-007740-5, Penguin Bks.) Viking Penguin.

—There Was an Old Woman. 2000. (Benny Cooperman Mystery Ser.). 262p. 24.95 (1-58567-044-8) Overlook Pr., The.

—A Victim Must Be Found: A Benny Cooperman Mystery. l.t. ed. 1989. 383p. lib. bdg. 17.95 o.p. (1-85057-734-X, Macmillan Reference USA) Gale Group.

—A Victim Must Be Found: A Benny Cooperman Mystery. 1988. 288p. 16.95 o.p. (0-312-02315-4, Saint Martin's Minotaur) St. Martin's Pr.

—A Victim Must Be Found: A Benny Cooperman Mystery. 1990. 288p. pap. 3.95 o.p. (0-14-011205-7, Penguin Bks.) Viking Penguin.

**COPP, JOSEPH (FICTITIOUS CHARACTER)—FICTION**

Pendleton, Don. Copp for Hire. 1987. 272p. 16.95 o.p. (1-55611-064-2) Fine, Donald I. Bks.

—Copp in Deep. 1989. 252p. 17.95 o.p. (1-55611-141-X) Fine, Donald I. Bks.

—Copp in Deep. 1991. 256p. mass mkt. 4.50 o.p. (0-06-100248-8, HarperTorch) Morrow/Avon.

—Copp in Shock. 1992. 256p. 19.95 o.p. (1-55611-287-4) Fine, Donald I. Bks.

—Copp in Shock. 1993. 256p. mass mkt. 4.99 o.p. (0-06-100459-6, HarperTorch) Morrow/Avon.

—Copp in the Dark. l.t. ed. 1991. 19.95 o.p. (0-7927-0982-9, CH0157); pap. 17.95 o.p. (0-7927-0983-7, CS0256) BBC Audiobooks America.

—Copp in the Dark. 1990. (Joe Copp Ser.: No. 4). 18.95 o.p. (1-55611-210-6) Fine, Donald I. Bks.

—Copp in the Dark. 1992. 256p. mass mkt. 4.99 o.p. (0-06-100347-6, HarperTorch) Morrow/Avon.

—Copp on Fire. 1988. 16.95 o.p. (1-55611-088-X) Fine, Donald I. Bks.

—Copp on Fire. 1990. 256p. mass mkt. 4.50 o.p. (0-06-100036-1, HarperTorch) Morrow/Avon.

—Copp on Ice. 1991. 18.95 o.p. (1-55611-235-1) Fine, Donald I. Bks.

—Copp on Ice. 1992. 240p. mass mkt. 4.99 o.p. (0-06-100458-8, HarperTorch) Morrow/Avon.

**CORAN, JESSICA (FICTITIOUS CHARACTER)—FICTION**

Walker, Robert W. Blind Instinct: A Jessica Coren Novel. 2000. 369p. 21.95 o.s.i (0-425-17234-1) Berkley Publishing Group.

—Darkest Instinct. 1996. 464p. mass mkt. 6.99 o.s.i (0-515-11856-7, Jove) Berkley Publishing Group.

—Extreme Instinct. 1998. 400p. mass mkt. 6.99 o.s.i (0-515-12195-9, Jove) Berkley Publishing Group.

—Fatal Instinct. 1993. 5.99 o.s.i (1-55773-950-1, Diamond Bks.) Ace Bks.

—Fatal Instinct. 1995. 320p. mass mkt. 6.99 o.s.i (0-515-11913-X, Jove) Berkley Publishing Group.

—Grave Instinct. 2003. 400p. 23.95 (0-425-19170-2) Berkley Publishing Group.

—Killer Instinct. 1992. 336p. 5.99 o.s.i (1-55773-743-6, Diamond Bks.) Ace Bks.

—Killer Instinct. 1995. 336p. mass mkt. 6.99 o.s.i (0-515-11790-0, Jove) Berkley Publishing Group.

—Primal Instinct. 1994. 368p. (Orig.). pap. 5.99 o.s.i (0-7865-0055-7, Diamond Bks.) Ace Bks.

—Primal Instinct. 1995. 368p. (Orig.). mass mkt. 6.99 o.s.i (0-515-11949-0, Jove) Berkley Publishing Group.

—Pure Instinct. 1995. 432p. (Orig.). mass mkt. 6.99 (0-515-11755-2, Jove) Berkley Publishing Group.

—Unnatural Instinct: A Jessica Coran Novel. 2003. 304p. mass mkt. 7.99 (0-515-13529-1, Jove); 2002. 320p. 22.95 (0-425-18492-7) Berkley Publishing Group.

**CORBETT, HARRY (FICTITIOUS CHARACTER)—FICTION**

Palmer, Michael. Silent Treatment. 1996. 480p. reprint ed. mass mkt. 7.50 (0-553-57221-0) Bantam Bks.

—Silent Treatment. l.t. ed. (Core Collection). 632p. 1996. 23.95 (0-7838-1405-4); 1995. 26.95 o.p. (0-7838-1406-2) Gale Group. (Macmillan Reference USA).

—Silent Treatment. abr. ed. 1995. audio 16.99 o.s.i (0-553-47345-X, RH Audio) Random Hse. Audio Publishing Group.

—Silent Treatment. unabr. ed. audio 85.00 (0-7887-0268-8, 94477E7) Recorded Bks., LLC.

**CORBETT, HUGH (FICTITIOUS CHARACTER)—FICTION**

Doherty, P. C. Angel of Death. 1990. 176p. 14.95 o.p. (0-312-03791-0, Saint Martin's Minotaur) St. Martin's Pr.

—The Assassin in the Greenwood: A Medieval Mystery Featuring Hugh Corbett. unabr. ed. 1998. audio 69.95 (1-85903-123-4) Magna Story Sound GBR. Dist: Ulverscroft Large Print Bks., Ltd.

—The Assassin in the Greenwood: A Medieval Mystery Featuring Hugh Corbett. 1994. 224p. 19.95 o.p. (0-312-11554-7, Saint Martin's Minotaur) St. Martin's Pr.

—The Assassin in the Greenwood: A Medieval Mystery Featuring Hugh Corbett. l.t. ed. 1996. (Ulverscroft Large Print Ser.). 384p. 29.99 o.p. (0-7089-3535-4, Ulverscroft) Thorpe, F. A. Pubs. GBR. Dist: Ulverscroft Large Print Bks., Ltd., Ulverscroft Large Print Canada, Ltd.

—Corpse Candle: A Medieval Mystery Featuring Hugh Corbett. 2002. 320p. 24.95 (0-312-30087-5, Saint Martin's Minotaur) St. Martin's Pr.

—The Crown in Darkness. l.t. ed. 1999. (Linford Mystery Large Print Ser.). 304p. pap. 18.99 o.p. (0-7089-5601-7, Linford) Thorpe, F. A. Pubs. GBR. Dist: Ulverscroft Large Print Bks., Ltd., Ulverscroft Large Print Canada, Ltd.

—The Devil's Hunt. 1998. 256p. 21.95 o.p. (0-312-18084-5, Saint Martin's Minotaur) St. Martin's Pr.

—The Devil's Hunt. l.t. ed. 1998. (Ulverscroft Large Print Ser.). 368p. 29.99 o.p. (0-7089-3988-0, Ulverscroft) Thorpe, F. A. Pubs. GBR. Dist: Ulverscroft Large Print Bks., Ltd., Ulverscroft Large Print Canada, Ltd.

—Murder Wears a Cowl: A Medieval Mystery Featuring Hugh Corbett. unabr. ed. 1998. audio 69.95 (1-85903-142-0) Magna Story Sound GBR. Dist: Ulverscroft Large Print Bks., Ltd.

—Murder Wears a Cowl: A Medieval Mystery Featuring Hugh Corbett. 1993. 256p. 20.95 o.p. (0-312-10506-1, Saint Martin's Minotaur) St. Martin's Pr.

—Murder Wears a Cowl: A Medieval Mystery Featuring Hugh Corbett. l.t. ed. 1996. (Ulverscroft Large Print Ser.). 400p. 29.99 o.p. (0-7089-3495-1, Ulverscroft) Thorpe, F. A. Pubs. GBR. Dist: Ulverscroft Large Print Bks., Ltd., Ulverscroft Large Print Canada, Ltd.

—The Prince of Darkness. 1995. (WWL Mystery Ser.). per. (0-373-26164-0, 1-26164-3, Harlequin Bks.) Harlequin Enterprises, Ltd.

—The Prince of Darkness. 1993. 247p. 18.95 o.p. (0-312-08876-0, Saint Martin's Minotaur) St. Martin's Pr.

—The Prince of Darkness. l.t. ed. 1996. (Ulverscroft Large Print Ser.). 400p. 29.99 o.p. (0-7089-3482-X, Ulverscroft) Thorpe, F. A. Pubs. GBR. Dist: Ulverscroft Large Print Bks., Ltd., Ulverscroft Large Print Canada, Ltd.

—Satan in St. Mary's. 1988. mass mkt. 3.50 (0-312-91357-5, St. Martin's Paperbacks); 1987. 176p. 12.95 o.p. (0-312-00059-6) St. Martin's Pr.

—Satan in St. Mary's. l.t. ed. 1999. (Linford Mystery Large Print Ser.). 320p. pap. 18.99 o.p. (0-7089-5594-0, Linford) Thorpe, F. A. Pubs. GBR. Dist: Ulverscroft Large Print Bks., Ltd., Ulverscroft Large Print Canada, Ltd.

—Satan's Fire: A Medieval Mystery Featuring Hugh Corbett. 1996. 256p. 21.95 (0-312-14728-7, Saint Martin's Minotaur) St. Martin's Pr.

—The Song of a Dark Angel: A Medieval Mystery Featuring Hugh Corbett. unabr. ed. 1998. audio 69.95 (1-85903-104-8) Magna Story Sound GBR. Dist: Ulverscroft Large Print Bks., Ltd.

—The Song of a Dark Angel: A Medieval Mystery Featuring Hugh Corbett. 1995. 249p. 21.95 o.p. (0-312-13605-6, Saint Martin's Minotaur) St. Martin's Pr.

—The Song of a Dark Angel: A Medieval Mystery Featuring Hugh Corbett. l.t. ed. 1996. (Large Print Ser.). 400p. 29.99 o.p. (0-7089-3611-3, Ulverscroft) Thorpe, F. A. Pubs. GBR. Dist: Ulverscroft Large Print Bks., Ltd., Ulverscroft Large Print Canada, Ltd.

—Spy in Chancery. 1989. 14.95 o.p. (0-312-02984-5, Saint Martin's Minotaur) St. Martin's Pr.

—Spy in Chancery. l.t. ed. 2000. (Linford Mystery Large Print Ser.). 304p. pap. 18.99 o.p. (0-7089-5653-X, Linford) Thorpe, F. A. Pubs. GBR. Dist: Ulverscroft Large Print Bks., Ltd., Ulverscroft Large Print Canada, Ltd.

**CORBIE, TOM (FICTITIOUS CHARACTER)—FICTION**

Farmer, Philip Jose. Nothing Burns in Hell. 1999. 287p. mass mkt. 6.99 (0-8125-6495-2, Tor Bks.); 1998. 288p. 22.95 o.p. (0-312-86470-1, Forge Bks.) Doherty, Tom Assocs., LLC.

**COREY, JOHN (FICTITIOUS CHARACTER)—FICTION**

DeMille, Nelson. The Lion's Game. unabr. ed. 2000. audio 48.00. audio 54.00 Books on Tape, Inc.

—The Lion's Game. unabr. ed. 1999. audio 44.98 Highsmith Inc.

—The Lion's Game. l.t. ed. (Thorndike General Ser.). 2001. 1049p. pap. 29.95 (0-7862-2020-1); 2000. 1037p. 31.95 (0-7862-2019-8) Thorndike Pr.

—The Lion's Game. abr. ed. 2002. audio (1-57042-992-8); 2000. audio 29.98 (1-57042-660-0); 2000. audio compact disk 29.98 (1-57042-701-1); 2002. audio (1-57042-993-6); 2000. audio 69.98 (1-57042-661-9) Time Warner AudioBooks.

—The Lion's Game. 2000. E-Book 6.95 (0-446-92370-2) Time Warner Bk. Group.

—The Lion's Game. 2000. 944p. E-Book 6.95 (0-446-91357-X); 2000. 944p. E-Book 6.95 (0-446-96090-X); 2000. 944p. E-Book 6.95 (0-446-92862-3); 2000. E-Book 6.95 (0-446-93138-1); 2000. 944p. E-Book 6.95 (0-446-92265-X); 2000. 688p. 26.95 (0-446-52065-9); 2002. 720p. reprint ed. pap. 15.95 (0-446-67909-7); 2000. 944p. reprint ed. mass mkt. 7.99 (0-446-60826-2) Warner Bks., Inc.

—Plum Island. abr. ed. 1997. audio 24.00 o.s.i (0-394-58389-2, 495350, RH Audio) Random Hse. Audio Publishing Group.

—Plum Island. l.t. ed. 1998. (Paperback Bestsellers Ser.). 821p. pap. 28.95 (0-7862-0980-1) Thorndike Pr.

—Plum Island. 2001. 576p. E-Book 6.95 (0-7595-8263-7); 2001. 576p. E-Book 6.95 (0-7595-0257-9); 2001. 576p. E-Book 6.95 (0-7595-6257-1); 2001. 576p. E-Book 6.95 (0-7595-9290-X); 2001. 576p. E-Book 6.95 (0-7595-4260-0); 1998. mass mkt. 287.64 (0-446-16544-1); 1997. 528p. 24.50 o.p. (0-446-51506-X); 2002. 592p. reprint ed. pap. 15.95 (0-446-67908-9); 1998. 592p. reprint ed. mass mkt. 7.99 (0-446-60540-9) Warner Bks., Inc.

**COREY, NICK (FICTITIOUS CHARACTER)—FICTION**

Thompson, Jim. Pop. 1280. 1984. 224p. reprint ed. pap. 4.95 o.p. (0-916870-76-6, Black Mask) Creative Arts Bk. Co.

—Pop. 1280. 1990. (Vintage Crime Ser.). 224p. pap. 11.00 (0-679-73249-7, Vintage) Knopf Publishing Group.

**COREY, PATRICK (FICTITIOUS CHARACTER)—FICTION**

Siodmak, Curt. Donovan's Brain. 1985. 234p. pap. 3.50 o.p. (0-88184-154-4, Carroll & Graf Pubs.) Avalon Publishing Group.

—Donovan's Brain. 1993. reprint ed. lib. bdg. 18.95 (0-89968-369-X, Lightyear Pr.) Buccaneer Bks., Inc.

—Donovan's Brain. abr. ed. 1986. audio 16.99 (0-88646-141-3, 7142) Durkin Hayes Publishing Ltd.

—Donovan's Brain. 1942. (Illus.). 182p. pap. 19.95 (1-58445-078-9) Pulpless.com, Inc.

—Donovan's Brain: Hauser's Memory, 2 vols. in 1, Set. 1992. 448p. pap. 4.99 (0-8439-3355-0) Dorchester Publishing Co., Inc.

—Forrest J. Ackerman Presents Hauser's Memory. 1999. 233p. pap. 19.95 (1-58445-117-3) Pulpless.com, Inc.

—Gabriel's Body. 1992. 368p. (Orig.). pap. 4.99 (0-8439-3346-1) Dorchester Publishing Co., Inc.

Welles, Orson. Donovan's Brain. (Old Time Radio Classic Singles Ser.). audio 4.95 (1-57816-095-2, DB135) Audio File, The.

—Donovan's Brain. 1944. audio 7.95 National Recording Co.

—Donovan's Brain. 1944. (Suspense Ser.). audio 6.00 Once Upon A Radio.

**CORNELIUS, JERRY (FICTITIOUS CHARACTER)—FICTION**

Moorcock, Michael. The Cornelius Chronicles. Vol. 1. 1977. 992p. mass mkt. 4.95 (0-380-00878-5); Vol. II. 1986. pap. 3.50 (0-380-75003-1); Vol. III. 1987. 352p. pap. 3.50 (0-380-70255-X) Morrow/Avon. (Avon Bks.).

—The Lives & Times of Jerry Cornelius: Stories of the Comic Apocalypse. 2003. pap. 16.00 (1-56858-273-0) Four Walls Eight Windows.

**CORNISH, FRANCIS (FICTITIOUS CHARACTER)—FICTION**

Davies, Robertson. The Cornish Trilogy: The Rebel Angels; What's Bred in the Bone; The Lyre of Orpheus. 1992. 1200p. 22.95 (0-14-015850-2) Viking Penguin.

—The Lyre of Orpheus. l.t. ed. 1990. (General Ser.). 586p. 21.95 o.p. (0-8161-4839-2, Macmillan Reference USA) Gale Group.

—The Lyre of Orpheus. 1990. (Cornish Trilogy Ser.). 480p. pap. 15.00 (0-14-011433-5, Penguin Bks.) Penguin Group (USA) Inc.

—The Lyre of Orpheus. 1989. (Cornish Trilogy Ser.). 480p. 19.95 o.p. (0-670-82416-X) Viking Penguin.

—The Rebel Angels. 1983. (Cornish Trilogy Ser.). 336p. pap. 13.95 (0-14-006271-8, Penguin Bks.) Penguin Group (USA) Inc.

—What's Bred in the Bone. l.t. ed. 1987. 641p. 20.95 o.p. (0-8161-4133-9, Macmillan Reference USA) Gale Group.

—What's Bred in the Bone. 1986. (Cornish Trilogy Ser.). 448p. pap. 15.00 (0-14-009711-2, Penguin Bks.) Penguin Group (USA) Inc.

—What's Bred in the Bone. 1985. (Cornish Trilogy Ser.). 17.95 o.p. (0-670-80916-0, Viking) Viking Penguin.

**CORUM (FICTITIOUS CHARACTER: MOORCOCK)—FICTION**

Moorcock, Michael. The Bull & the Spear. 1986. (Books of Corum: Bk. 4). 100p. 2.95 o.s.i (0-425-09359-X); 1974. 0.75 o.p. (0-425-02508-X) Berkley Publishing Group.

—The Chronicles of Corum, Vol. II. 1987. mass mkt. 4.99 o.s.i (0-441-10483-5) Ace Bks.

—The Chronicles of Corum. 1986. 3.95 o.s.i (0-425-09533-9); 1985. 3.50 o.s.i (0-425-08221-0); 1984. 3.25 o.s.i (0-425-07477-3); 1983. 2.95 o.s.i (0-425-05849-2); 1978. 1.95 o.s.i (0-425-03855-6) Berkley Publishing Group.

—Corum: The Coming of Chaos. (Eternal Champion Ser.: Vol. 7). (Illus.). 1999. 400p. pap. 16.99 (1-56504-196-8, 12522); 1997. 21.99 (1-56504-182-8, 12508) White Wolf Publishing, Inc.

—The Eternal Champion: Prince with the Silver Hand. 1999. (Eternal Champion Ser.: No. 8). (Illus.). reprint ed. 24.99 (1-56504-188-7, 12514) White Wolf Publishing, Inc.

—The King of the Swords, Bk. 3. 1986. (Book of Corum: 3). 160p. 2.95 o.s.i (0-425-09201-1) Berkley Publishing Group.

—The Knight of the Swords. 1987. mass mkt. 2.95 o.s.i (0-441-45131-4) Ace Bks.

—The Knight of the Swords. 1986. 160p. 2.95 o.s.i (0-425-08533-3) Berkley Publishing Group.

—The Oak & the Ram. 1986. (Books of Corum: Bk. 5). 100p. 2.95 o.p. (0-425-09052-3); 1974. 0.75 o.p. (0-425-02534-9) Berkley Publishing Group.

—The Queen of the Swords. 1986. 2.95 o.s.i (0-425-10130-4); 160p. 2.95 o.s.i (0-425-08737-9) Berkley Publishing Group.

—The Sword & the Stallion. 1974. 0.75 o.p. (0-425-02548-9); Bk. 6. 1986. 160p. 2.95 o.s.i (0-425-09391-3) Berkley Publishing Group.

**CORWIN (FICTITIOUS CHARACTER: ZELAZNY)—FICTION**

Zelazny, Roger. The Courts of Chaos. 2003. audio compact disk 25.00 (1-58807-257-6); 2003. audio compact disk (1-58807-688-1); 2002. audio (1-58807-518-4); 2002. (Amber Ser.: No. 5). audio 18.00 (1-58807-130-8) Americana Publishing, Inc.

—The Courts of Chaos. 1978. 183p. 9.95 o.p. (0-385-13685-4) Doubleday Publishing.

—The Courts of Chaos. 1979. (Chronicles of Amber Ser.: Bk. 5). 144p. (YA). (gr. 9 up). reprint ed. pap. 4.99 (0-380-47175-2, Avon Bks.) Morrow/Avon.

—The Courts of Chaos. l.t. ed. 2000. (Science Fiction Ser.). 208p. 25.95 (0-7838-9064-8) Thorndike Pr.

—The Guns of Avalon. 1976. 224p. reprint ed. mass mkt. 5.99 (0-380-00083-0, Avon Bks.) Morrow/Avon.

—The Guns of Avalon. l.t. ed. 1999. (Science Fiction Ser.). 287p. 24.95 (0-7838-8504-0) Thorndike Pr.

—The Hand of Oberon. 1977. 192p. (YA). (gr. 7 up). reprint ed. pap. 5.99 (0-380-01664-8, Avon Bks.) Morrow/Avon.

—The Hand of Oberon. l.t. ed. 2000. (Science Fiction Ser.). 261p. 25.95 (*0-7838-8985-2*) Thorndike Pr.
—Nine Princes in Amber. 2003. audio compact disk (*1-58807-684-9*); 2002. audio (*1-58807-502-8*); 2003. (Amber Ser.: No. 1). audio compact disk 25.00 (*1-58807-253-3*); 2002. (Amber Ser.). audio 18.00 (*1-58807-126-X*) Americana Publishing, Inc.
—Nine Princes in Amber. 1977. 176p. (YA). (gr. 9 up). reprint ed. pap. 5.99 (*0-380-01430-0*, Avon Bks.) Morrow/Avon.
—Nine Princes in Amber. l.t. ed. 1998. (Science Fiction Ser.). 255p. 23.95 (*0-7838-8425-7*) Thorndike Pr.
—Sign of the Unicorn. 2003. audio compact disk 25.00 (*1-58807-255-X*); 2003. audio compact disk (*1-58807-686-5*); 2002. audio (*1-58807-510-9*); 2002. (Amber Ser.: No. 3). audio 18.00 (*1-58807-128-6*) Americana Publishing, Inc.
—Sign of the Unicorn. 1986. 192p. reprint ed. pap. 5.99 o.p. (*0-380-00831-9*, Avon Bks.) Morrow/Avon.
—Sign of the Unicorn. l.t. ed. 1999. (Science Fiction Ser.). 243p. 24.95 (*0-7838-8505-9*) Thorndike Pr.

**COSGROVE, MAE-MAE (FICTITIOUS CHARACTER)—FICTION**

Sorrells, Walter. Will to Murder. 1996. 304p. (Orig.). mass mkt. 5.50 (*0-380-78020-8*, Avon Bks.) Morrow/Avon.

**COSINI, ZENO (FICTITIOUS CHARACTER)—FICTION**

Schmitz, Ettore. Confessions of Zeno. DeZoete, Beryl, tr. 1973. 412p. reprint ed. lib. bdg. 22.50 o.p. (*0-8371-5537-1*, SCCZ) Greenwood Publishing Group, Inc.
Svevo, Italo. Confessions of Zeno. de Zoete, Beryl, tr. 1989. (Vintage International Ser.). 432p. pap. 14.00 o.s.i (*0-679-72234-3*, Vintage) Knopf Publishing Group.
—Further Confessions of Zeno. Johnson, Ben & Furbank, P. N., trs. 1969. pap. 7.95 o.p. (*0-520-01753-6*) Univ. of California Pr.

**COSMO, JASON (FICTITIOUS CHARACTER)—FICTION**

McGirt, Dan. Dirty Work. 1993. (Jason Cosmo Ser.). 288p. (Orig.). mass mkt. 4.50 o.s.i (*0-451-45215-1*, ROC) NAL.
—Jason Cosmo. 1989. 240p. mass mkt. 3.95 o.s.i (*0-451-16288-9*, Signet Bks.) NAL.
—Royal Chaos. 1990. 240p. mass mkt. 3.95 o.s.i (*0-451-45014-0*) NAL.

**COTTER, KATHLEEN (FICTITIOUS CHARACTER)—FICTION**

Forster, R. A. Character Witness. 1997. 304p. mass mkt. 5.99 o.s.i (*0-7860-0378-2*, Pinnacle Bks.) Kensington Publishing Corp.

**COTTER, RALPH (FICTITIOUS CHARACTER)—FICTION**

McCoy, Horace. Kiss Tomorrow Goodbye. 1997. 250p. (Orig.). (C). reprint ed. pap. text (*1-85242-433-8*) Serpent's Tail Ltd.

**COTTON, JOHN (FICTITIOUS CHARACTER)—FICTION**

Hillerman, Tony. The Fly on the Wall. unabr. ed. 1993. audio 42.00 (*0-7366-2571-2*, 3320) Books on Tape, Inc.
—The Fly on the Wall. l.t. ed. 1992. (General Ser.). 308p. 20.95 o.p. (*0-8161-5381-7*); 15.95 o.p. (*0-8161-5382-5*) Gale Group. (Macmillan Reference USA).
—The Fly on the Wall. Barzun, Jacques & Taylor, W. H., eds. 1983. (Crime Fiction 1950-1975 Ser.). 212p. lib. bdg. 18.00 o.p. (*0-8240-4993-4*) Garland Publishing, Inc.
—The Fly on the Wall. 1990. audio 15.95; 2000. audio 9.99 (*0-694-52326-7*); 1995. 3p. audio 15.95 o.s.i (*1-55994-196-0*, 390794) HarperTrade. (HarperAudio).
—The Fly on the Wall. 1990. 368p. mass mkt. 6.99 (*0-06-100028-0*, HarperTorch); 1979. 224p. pap. 3.95 (*0-380-44156-X*, Avon Bks.) Morrow/Avon.
—The Fly on the Wall. 1990. 13.04 (*0-606-16168-6*) Turtleback Bks.

**COULTER, JASON (FICTITIOUS CHARACTER)—FICTION**

Levitt, J. R. Carnivores. 1990. 256p. mass mkt. 3.95 o.p. (*0-451-16845-3*, Signet Bks.) NAL.
—Carnivores. 1989. 208p. 15.95 o.p. (*0-312-02553-X*, Saint Martin's Minotaur) St. Martin's Pr.
—Ten of Swords. 1991. 15.95 o.p. (*0-312-05386-X*, Saint Martin's Minotaur) St. Martin's Pr.

**COURTENEY FAMILY (FICTITIOUS CHARACTERS)—FICTION**

Frister, Roman. The Cap: The Price of a Life. Halkin, Hillel, tr. from HEB. 2000. 380p. 25.00 o.p. (*0-8021-1659-0*, Grove Pr.) Grove/Atlantic, Inc.
Smith, Wilbur. Birds of Prey, Pt. 1. unabr. ed. 1997. (Courtney Novels). audio 72.00 (*0-7366-3740-0*, 4417-A) Books on Tape, Inc.
—Birds of Prey, 2 cass. 2001. audio 16.95 (*0-333-69866-5*) Macmillan U.K. GBR. *Dist:* Trafalgar Square.
—Birds of Prey. abr. ed. 1997. 25.00 o.p. (*0-7871-1468-5*) NewStar Media, Inc.
—Birds of Prey. 1997. 554p. 25.95 (*0-312-15791-6*); Vol. 1. 1998. 664p. mass mkt. 7.50 (*0-312-96381-5*, St. Martin's Paperbacks) St. Martin's Pr.
—Birds of Prey. l.t. ed. 1997. (Basic Ser.). 968p. lib. bdg. 29.95 (*0-7862-1190-3*) Thorndike Pr.
—The Burning Shore. 1987. 512p. mass mkt. 7.50 (*0-449-21189-4*, Fawcett); 1986. mass mkt. 3.50 o.s.i (*0-449-21198-3*) Ballantine Bks.
—The Burning Shore, Pt. 1. unabr. collector's ed. 1988. (Courtney Novels). audio 64.00 (*0-7366-1256-4*, 2170-A) Books on Tape, Inc.
—The Burning Shore. 1985. 432p. 17.95 o.p. (*0-385-18738-6*) Doubleday Publishing.
—Golden Fox. 1993. 480p. mass mkt. 6.99 (*0-449-14906-4*, Fawcett) Ballantine Bks.
—Golden Fox. unabr. ed. 1993. (Courtney Novels). audio 120.00 (*0-7366-2524-0*, 3277) Books on Tape, Inc.
—Golden Fox. unabr. ed. 2000. (Sean Courtney Adventure Ser.). audio 89.95 (*0-7451-4160-9*, CAB 843) Chivers Audio Bks. GBR. *Dist:* BBC Audiobooks America.
—Golden Fox. 1993. 4.99 o.p. (*0-517-09806-7*) Random Hse. Value Publishing.
—Golden Fox. l.t. ed. 1991. (Charnwood Library). 29.99 o.p. (*0-7089-8584-X*, Ulverscroft) Thorpe, F. A. Pubs. GBR. *Dist:* Ulverscroft Large Print Bks., Ltd., Ulverscroft Large Print Canada, Ltd.
—Power of the Sword. Date not set. 671p. 36.95 (*0-8488-2394-X*) Amereon, Ltd.
—Power of the Sword. 1987. 672p. mass mkt. 6.99 o.s.i (*0-449-21414-1*, Fawcett); mass mkt. 3.95 o.s.i (*0-449-21427-3*) Ballantine Bks.
—Power of the Sword, Pt. 1. unabr. collector's ed. 1988. (Courtney Novels). audio 88.00 (*0-7366-1378-1*, 2272-A) Books on Tape, Inc.
—Power of the Sword. 1986. 19.95 (*0-316-80171-2*) Little Brown & Co.
—Rage. 1989. 672p. mass mkt. 6.99 o.s.i (*0-449-21613-6*, Fawcett) Ballantine Bks.
—Rage, Pt. 1. unabr. collector's ed. 1988. (Courtney Novels). audio 88.00 (*0-7366-1294-7*, 2202-A) Books on Tape, Inc.
—Rage. 1987. 640p. 19.95 (*0-316-80179-8*) Little Brown & Co.
—The Sound of Thunder. 1991. 416p. mass mkt. 6.99 (*0-449-14819-X*, Fawcett) Ballantine Bks.
—The Sound of Thunder. unabr. ed. 1998. audio 110.95 o.p. Brilliance Audio.
—The Sound of Thunder. unabr. ed. 1998. (Sean Courtney Adventure Ser.). audio 89.95 (*0-7540-0189-X*, CAB 1612) Chivers Audio Bks. GBR. *Dist:* BBC Audiobooks America.
—The Sound of Thunder. abr. ed. 2001. audio 16.95 (*0-333-90276-9*) Macmillan U.K. GBR. *Dist:* Trafalgar Square.
—A Sparrow Falls, Pt. 2. unabr. collector's ed. 1989. (Courtney Novels). audio 64.00 (*0-7366-1476-1*, 2353-B) Books on Tape, Inc.
—A Sparrow Falls. 1991. 608p. reprint ed. lib. bdg. 49.95 (*0-89966-779-1*) Buccaneer Bks., Inc.
—A Sparrow Falls. 1978. 10.95 o.p. (*0-385-13603-X*) Doubleday Publishing.
—A Sparrow Falls. 1995. mass mkt. 6.99 o.p. (*0-7493-2192-X*) Heinemann.
—A Sparrow Falls. abr. ed. 2001. audio 16.95 (*0-333-90277-7*) Macmillan U.K. GBR. *Dist:* Trafalgar Square.
—A Time to Die. 1991. 496p. mass mkt. 6.99 (*0-449-14761-4*, Fawcett) Ballantine Bks.
—A Time to Die. unabr. ed. 1993. (Courtney Novels). Pt. 1. audio 72.00 (*0-7366-2360-4*, 3135A); Pt. 2. audio 64.00 Books on Tape, Inc.
—A Time to Die. abr. ed. 2001. audio 16.95 (*0-333-78269-0*) Macmillan U.K. GBR. *Dist:* Trafalgar Square.
—A Time to Die. 1992. 5.99 o.p. (*0-517-08097-4*) Random Hse. Value Publishing.
—A Time to Die. l.t. ed. 1990. (Charnwood Large Print Ser.). 29.99 o.p. (*0-7089-8537-8*, Ulverscroft) Thorpe, F. A. Pubs. GBR. *Dist:* Ulverscroft Large Print Bks., Ltd., Ulverscroft Large Print Canada, Ltd.
—When the Lion Feeds. 1989. mass mkt. 5.95 o.s.i (*0-449-21553-9*, Ballantine Bks.) Ballantine Bks.
—When the Lion Feeds. unabr. collector's ed. 1989. (Courtney Novels). audio 104.00 (*0-7366-1477-X*, 2354) Books on Tape, Inc.
—When the Lion Feeds. unabr. ed. 2000. (Sean Courtney Adventure Ser.). audio 89.95 (*0-7540-0073-7*, CAB 1496) Chivers Audio Bks. GBR. *Dist:* BBC Audiobooks America.
—When the Lion Feeds. 1989. mass mkt. 6.99 (*0-7493-2292-6*) Heinemann.
—When the Lion Feeds. abr. ed. 2001. audio 16.95 (*0-333-90275-0*) Macmillan U.K. GBR. *Dist:* Trafalgar Square.
—When the Lion Feeds. 1964. 5.95 o.p. (*0-670-75974-0*) Viking Penguin.
—When the Lion Feeds. 1999. lib. bdg. 27.95 (*1-56723-133-0*, 144) Yestermorrow, Inc.

**COVENANT, THOMAS (FICTITIOUS CHARACTER)—FICTION**

Donaldson, Stephen R. The Illearth War. 1997. (Chronicles of Thomas Covenant the Unbeliever Ser.: Vol. 2). 407p. pap. 19.00 (*0-345-41844-1*, Del Rey); 1984. mass mkt. 3.95 o.p. (*0-345-32601-6*, Del Rey); 1982. mass mkt. 3.50 o.p. (*0-345-31029-2*, Del Rey); Vol. 2. 1987. (Chronicles of Thomas Covenant the Unbeliever Ser.). 544p. mass mkt. 7.50 (*0-345-34866-4*) Ballantine Bks.
—The Illearth War. 1977. 14.95 o.p. (*0-03-022776-3*) Holt, Henry & Co.
—Lord Foul's Bane. 1997. (Chronicles of Thomas Covenant the Unbeliever Ser.). pap. 25.00 (*0-345-41843-3*, Del Rey); 1987. (Lord Foul's Bane Ser.: Vol. 1). 496p. mass mkt. 7.50 (*0-345-34865-6*); 1985. mass mkt. 3.95 o.p. (*0-345-32603-2*, Del Rey); 1982. mass mkt. 3.50 o.p. (*0-345-31011-X*, Del Rey) Ballantine Bks.
—Lord Foul's Bane, Vol. 1. 1977. 14.95 o.p. (*0-03-022771-2*) Holt, Henry & Co.
—The One Tree. 1997. pap. 12.00 o.p. (*0-345-41847-6*); 1987. (Second Chronicles of Thomas Covenant Ser.: Bk. 2). 496p. mass mkt. 7.50 (*0-345-34869-9*); 1982. (Second Chronicles of Thomas Covenant Ser.: Bk. 2). 14.50 o.s.i (*0-345-29898-5*) Ballantine Bks. (Del Rey).
—The Power That Preserves. (Chronicles of Thomas Covenant the Unbeliever Ser.). 1997. pap. 12.00 o.s.i (*0-345-41845-X*); 1987. 512p. mass mkt. 7.50 (*0-345-34867-2*) Ballantine Bks. (Del Rey).
—The Power That Preserves, Vol. 1. 1977. 14.95 o.p. (*0-03-022781-X*) Holt, Henry & Co.
—The Second Chronicles of Thomas Covenant, 3 vols. 1985. pap. 11.85 o.p. (*0-345-32963-5*); 1984. pap. 10.95 o.p. (*0-345-32088-3*) Ballantine Bks. (Del Rey).
—White Gold Wielder. 1997. pap. 12.00 o.p. (*0-345-41848-4*); 1987. (Second Chronicles of Thomas Covenant Ser.: Vol. 3). 512p. mass mkt. 7.50 (*0-345-34870-2*, Del Rey); 1983. mass mkt. 3.50 o.p. (*0-345-30308-3*, Del Rey); 1983. (Second Chronicles of Thomas Covenant Ser.: Bk. 3). 480p. 14.95 o.s.i (*0-345-30307-5*, Del Rey) Ballantine Bks.
—White Gold Wielder. abr. ed. 1984. audio 8.98 HarperTrade.
—The Wounded Land. 1982. mass mkt. 3.50 o.p. (*0-345-31042-X*, Del Rey); Bk. 1. 1997. (Second Chronicles of Thomas Covenant Ser.: Bk. 1). pap. 12.00 o.s.i (*0-345-41846-8*, Del Rey); Bk. 1. 1987. (Second Chronicles of Thomas Covenant Ser.: Bk.1). 512p. mass mkt. 7.50 (*0-345-34868-0*, Del Rey); Bk. 1. 1981. (Second Chronicles of Thomas Covenant Ser.: Bk. 1). mass mkt. 2.95 o.p. (*0-345-27831-3*, Del Rey); Bk. 1. 1980. (Second Chronicles of Thomas Covenant Ser.: Bk. 1). 512p. 12.95 o.p. (*0-345-28647-2*) Ballantine Bks.

**COYLE, EDDIE (FICTITIOUS CHARACTER)—FICTION**

Higgins, George V. The Friends of Eddie Coyle. 1980. 176p. mass mkt. 2.50 o.s.i (*0-345-28635-9*) Ballantine Bks.
—The Friends of Eddie Coyle. unabr. collector's ed. 1990. audio 36.00 (*0-7366-1859-7*, 2690) Books on Tape, Inc.
—The Friends of Eddie Coyle. (John MacRae Bks.). 192p. 2000. pap. 13.00 (*0-8050-6598-9*); 1995. pap. 13.00 o.s.i (*0-8050-4152-4*) Holt, Henry & Co. (Owl Bks.).
—The Friends of Eddie Coyle. 1972. 15.95 o.s.i (*0-394-47327-2*) Knopf, Alfred A. Inc.
—The Friends of Eddie Coyle. unabr. ed. 1996. audio. audio 35.00 (*0-7887-0643-8*, 94820E7) Recorded Bks., LLC.
—The Friends of Eddie Coyle. 1987. 192p. mass mkt. 3.95 o.p. (*0-14-010232-9*, Penguin Bks.) Viking Penguin.

**COYNE, BRADY (FICTITIOUS CHARACTER)—FICTION**

Craig, Philip R. & Tapply, William G. First Light. l.t. ed. 2002. 443p. 29.95 (*0-7862-4185-3*) Gale Group.
—First Light: The First Ever Brady Coyne/J. W. Jackson Novel. 2002. 352p. E-Book 24.00 (*0-7432-3484-7*); 24.00 (*0-7432-2208-3*) Simon & Schuster. (Scribner).
Tapply, William G. Client Privilege. l.t. ed. 1991. 23.95 o.p. (*0-7927-0888-1*, CH099); pap. 21.95 o.p. (*0-7927-0889-X*, CS0199) BBC Audiobooks America.
—Client Privilege. 1991. 288p. mass mkt. 4.50 o.s.i (*0-440-20866-1*) Dell Publishing.
—Close to the Bone. 1999. E-Book (*0-312-20712-3*); 1996. 224p. 20.95 o.p. (*0-312-14567-5*, Saint Martin's Minotaur) St. Martin's Pr.
—Close to the Bone: A Brady Coyne Mystery. unabr. ed. 2000. audio 49.95 (*0-7927-2212-4*, CSL 101) Chivers Audio Bks. GBR. *Dist:* BBC Audiobooks America.
—Cutter's Run. unabr. ed. 1999. audio 69.95 (*0-7927-2317-1*, CSL206, Chivers Sound Library) BBC Audiobooks America.
—Cutter's Run. l.t. ed. 1999. pap. 24.95 (*1-56895-706-8*, Wheeler Publishing, Inc.) Gale Group.
—Cutter's Run. 1998. (Brady Coyne Mysteries Ser.). 274p. 23.95 (*0-312-18561-8*, Saint Martin's Minotaur) St. Martin's Pr.
—Dead Meat. l.t. ed. 1991. pap. 8.95 o.p. (*1-55504-857-9*, 162); 1989. 15.95 o.p. (*0-7451-9473-7*, 546) BBC Audiobooks America.
—Dead Meat. 1988. 240p. mass mkt. 3.50 o.s.i (*0-345-34730-7*) Ballantine Bks.
—Dead Meat: A Brady Coyne Mystery. 1987. 14.95 o.p. (*0-684-18682-9*, Macmillan Reference USA) Gale Group.
—Dead Winter. 1990. 240p. mass mkt. 3.95 o.s.i (*0-440-20566-2*); 1989. 16.95 o.s.i (*0-440-50171-7*, Delacorte Pr.) Dell Publishing.
—Dead Winter. l.t. ed. 1991. (General Ser.). 350p. lib. bdg. 18.95 o.p. (*0-8161-5003-6*, Macmillan Reference USA) Gale Group.
—Dead Winter. l.t. ed. 1991. (Magna Large Print Ser.). 318p. o.p. (*0-7505-0126-X*) Magna Large Print Bks. GBR. *Dist:* Ulverscroft Large Print Canada, Ltd.
—Death at Charity's Point. l.t. ed. 1991. pap. 10.95 o.p. (*0-7927-0109-7*, C0136) BBC Audiobooks America.
—Death at Charity's Point. 1985. 240p. mass mkt. 2.95 o.s.i (*0-345-32014-X*) Ballantine Bks.
—Death at Charity's Point. 1984. 224p. 12.95 o.p. (*0-684-18056-1*, Macmillan Reference USA) Gale Group.
—Death at Charity's Point. 1997. (Missing Mysteries Ser.: Vol. 2). 244p. reprint ed. pap. 7.95 (*1-890208-02-7*) Poisoned Pen Pr.
—The Dutch Blue Error. 1985. 224p. mass mkt. 2.95 o.s.i (*0-345-32341-6*) Ballantine Bks.
—The Dutch Blue Error. 1984. 240p. 12.95 o.s.i (*0-684-18213-0*, Macmillan Reference USA) Gale Group.
—Dutch Blue Error. l.t. ed. 1986. 321p. 16.95 o.p. (*0-89340-937-5*) BBC Audiobooks America.
—A Fine Line. 2004. mass mkt. (*0-312-98978-4*, St. Martin's Paperbacks) St. Martin's Pr.
—A Fine Line: A Brady Coyne Novel. 2002. 320p. 24.95 (*0-312-30352-1*, Saint Martin's Minotaur) St. Martin's Pr.
—A Fine Line: A Brady Coyne Novel. l.t. ed. 2003. (Mystery Ser.). 30.95 (*0-7862-5208-1*) Thorndike Pr.
—Follow the Sharks. 1985. (Brady Coyne Mystery Ser.). 224p. 13.95 o.p. (*0-684-18446-X*, Macmillan Reference USA) Gale Group.
—Follow the Sharks! 1986. mass mkt. 4.99 o.s.i (*0-345-32906-6*) Ballantine Bks.
—Follow the Sharks. l.t. ed. 1988. pap. 8.95 o.p. (*1-55504-346-1*) BBC Audiobooks America.
—The Marine Corpse. 1987. 240p. mass mkt. 3.95 o.s.i (*0-345-34057-4*) Ballantine Bks.
—The Marine Corpse: A Brady Coyne Mystery. 1986. 240p. 13.95 o.s.i (*0-684-18681-0*, Macmillan Reference USA) Gale Group.
—Past Tense. 2004. mass mkt. 6.99 (*0-312-99551-2*, St. Martin's Paperbacks) St. Martin's Pr.
—Past Tense. l.t. ed. 2002. (Core Collection). 382p. 28.95 (*0-7862-4678-2*) Thorndike Pr.
—Past Tense: A Brady Coyne Mystery. 2001. E-Book 34.95 (*1-59061-424-0*) Adobe Systems, Inc.
—Past Tense: A Brady Coyne Mystery. 2001. 304p. 24.95 (*0-312-28442-X*, Saint Martin's Minotaur) St. Martin's Pr.
—Scar Tissue. 2000. 276p. 24.95 (*0-312-26679-0*, Saint Martin's Minotaur) St. Martin's Pr.
—Seventh Enemy: A Brady Coyne Mystery. 1995. 234p. 21.00 (*1-883402-99-9*, Scribner) Simon & Schuster.
—Shadow of Death: A Brady Coyne Novel. 2003. 320p. 24.95 (*0-312-30377-7*, Saint Martin's Minotaur) St. Martin's Pr.
—The Snake Eater. 1993. 273p. 20.00 o.p. (*1-883402-04-2*, Scribner) Simon & Schuster.
—The Spotted Cats: A Brady Coyne Mystery. 1992. 256p. mass mkt. 4.50 o.s.i (*0-440-21191-3*) Dell Publishing.
—Tight Lines. l.t. ed. 1995. (Magna Large Print Ser.). 421p. (*0-7505-0796-9*) Magna Large Print Bks. GBR. *Dist:* Ulverscroft Large Print Canada, Ltd.
—Tight Lines: A Brady Coyne Mystery. 1993. 288p. mass mkt. 4.99 o.s.i (*0-440-21410-6*) Dell Publishing.
—A Void in Hearts. 1990. 192p. mass mkt. 3.95 o.s.i (*0-345-35868-6*) Ballantine Bks.
—A Void in Hearts. l.t. ed. 1990. (General Ser.). 427p. lib. bdg. 18.95 o.p. (*0-8161-4822-8*, Macmillan Reference USA) Gale Group.

—A Void in Hearts. 1988. (Brady Coyne Mystery Ser.: No. 7). 224p. 16.95 o.s.i (*0-684-18793-0*, Scribner) Simon & Schuster.

—The Vulgar Boatman. l.t. ed. 1991. 8.95 o.p. (*0-7451-9583-0*, 5054); pap. 10.95 o.p. (*0-7927-0011-2*, 618) BBC Audiobooks America.

—The Vulgar Boatman. 1989. 256p. mass mkt. 3.95 o.s.i (*0-345-35577-6*) Ballantine Bks.

—The Vulgar Boatman. l.t. ed. 1989. viii, 315 p. pap. (*0-7451-9595-4*) Chivers Pr.

—The Vulgar Boatman. 1988. (Brady Coyne Mystery Ser.). 240p. 14.95 o.s.i (*0-684-18792-2*, Scribner) Simon & Schuster.

**COYNE, DERMOT MICHAEL (FICTITIOUS CHARACTER)—FICTION**

Greeley, Andrew M. Irish Eyes: A Nuala Anne McGrail Novel. 2000. 320p. 24.95 (*0-312-86570-8*); 2001. 352p. reprint ed. mass mkt. 6.99 (*0-8125-9024-4*) Doherty, Tom Assocs., LLC. (Forge Bks.).

—Irish Eyes: A Nuala Anne McGrail Novel. l.t. ed. 2001. 525p. 29.95 (*0-7862-3091-6*); (*0-7540-1621-8*) Thorndike Pr.

—Irish Gold: A Nuala Anne McGrail Novel. (Nuala Anne McGrail Novel Ser.). 1995. 493p. pap. 7.99 (*0-8125-5076-5*); 1994. 336p. 14.29 o.p. (*0-312-85813-2*) Doherty, Tom Assocs., LLC. (Forge Bks.).

—Irish Gold: A Nuala Anne McGrail Novel. abr. ed. 1994. 17.95 o.p. (*0-7871-0332-2*, 390987) NewStar Media, Inc.

—Irish Lace: A Nuala Anne McGrail Novel. (Nuala Anne McGrail Novel Ser.). 1997. 345p. pap. 6.99 (*0-8125-5077-3*, Tor Bks.); 1996. 304p. 23.95 o.p. (*0-312-86234-2*, Forge Bks.) Doherty, Tom Assocs., LLC.

—Irish Lace: A Nuala Anne McGrail Novel. abr. ed. 1996. 17.95 o.p. (*0-7871-1022-1*, 394462) NewStar Media, Inc.

—Irish Lace: A Nuala Anne McGrail Novel. 1998. 4.98 o.p. (*0-7651-1156-X*) Smithmark Pubs., Inc.

—Irish Mist: A Nuala Anne McGrail Novel. (Nuala Anne McGrail Novel Ser.). 2000. 384p. mass mkt. 6.99 (*0-8125-9023-6*); 1999. (Illus.). 319p. 23.95 (*0-312-86569-4*) Doherty, Tom Assocs., LLC. (Forge Bks.).

—Irish Mist: A Nuala Anne McGrail Novel. abr. ed. 1999. audio 16.99 (*0-88646-491-9*); audio 39.99 (*0-88646-530-3*, DHA-6530) Durkin Hayes Publishing Ltd.

—Irish Mist: A Nuala Anne McGrail Novel. l.t. ed. 2001. (Basic Ser.). 517p. 28.95 (*0-7862-3085-1*) Thorndike Pr.

—Irish Stew: A Nuala Anne McGrail Novel. 2002. 304p. 25.95 (*0-312-87188-0*, Forge Bks.) Doherty, Tom Assocs., LLC.

—Irish Stew: A Nuala Anne McGrail Novel. l.t. ed. 2003. 25.95 (*1-58724-413-6*, Wheeler Publishing, Inc.) Gale Group.

—Irish Whiskey: A Nuala Anne McGrail Novel. 1998. (Nuala Anne McGrail Novel Ser.). 309p. pap. 6.99 (*0-8125-7770-1*, Tor Bks.); 304p. 23.95 o.p. (*0-312-85596-6*, Forge Bks.) Doherty, Tom Assocs., LLC.

—Irish Whiskey: A Nuala Anne McGrail Novel, Set. abr. ed. 1998. audio 18.00 (*0-7871-1684-X*, Dove Audio) NewStar Media, Inc.

—Irish Whiskey: A Nuala Anne McGrail Novel. l.t. ed. 2000. (Basic Ser.). 549p. 28.95 (*0-7862-2930-6*) Thorndike Pr.

**CRABTREE, TEMPE (FICTITIOUS CHARACTER)—FICTION**

Meredith, Marilyn. Deadly Omen. 1999. (Tempe Crabtree Mystery Ser.). 230p. pap. 7.95 (*1-891940-03-1*) Golden Eagle Pr.

—Deadly Omen. 2001. E-Book 5.50 (*0-7599-0296-8*) Hard Shell Word Factory.

—Deadly Trail. 2002. 144p. pap. 10.95 (*0-7599-0461-8*); 2001. E-Book 5.50 (*0-7599-0370-0*) Hard Shell Word Factory.

—Intervention. 2002. (Tempe Crabtree Mystery Ser.: No. 3). mass mkt. 7.95 (*1-891940-07-4*) Golden Eagle Pr.

—Unequally Yoked. 2000. (Tempe Crabtree Mystery Ser.: Vol. 2). 164p. mass mkt. 7.95 (*1-891940-05-8*) Golden Eagle Pr.

**CRAIG, MELISSA (FICTITIOUS CHARACTER)—FICTION**

Rowlands, Betty. Exhaustive Enquiries: A Melissa Craig Mystery. 1995. 240p. mass mkt. 4.99 o.p. (*0-425-14689-8*, Prime Crime) Berkley Publishing Group.

—Exhaustive Enquiries: A Melissa Craig Mystery. 1994. 252p. 19.95 o.p. (*0-8027-3180-5*) Walker & Co.

—Finishing Touch: A Melissa Craig Mystery. 1993. 256p. mass mkt. 4.50 o.s.i (*0-515-11059-0*, Jove) Berkley Publishing Group.

—Finishing Touch: A Melissa Craig Mystery. 1992. 253p. 19.95 (*0-8027-3209-7*) Walker & Co.

—A Little Gentle Sleuthing. 1992. 240p. mass mkt. 3.99 o.s.i (*0-515-10878-2*, Jove) Berkley Publishing Group.

—A Little Gentle Sleuthing. l.t. ed. 1992. (Mystery Ser.). 512p. 29.99 o.p. (*0-7089-2736-X*, Ulverscroft) Thorpe, F. A. Pubs. GBR. *Dist:* Ulverscroft Large Print Bks., Ltd., Ulverscroft Large Print Canada, Ltd.

—A Little Gentle Sleuthing. 1991. 272p. 18.95 o.s.i (*0-8027-5781-2*) Walker & Co.

—The Man at the Window. 2001. audio 54.95 (*1-84283-012-0*) Soundings, Ltd. GBR. *Dist:* Ulverscroft Large Print Bks., Ltd.

—Over the Edge: A Melissa Craig Mystery. 1994. 240p. reprint ed. mass mkt. 4.50 o.p. (*0-425-14329-5*, Prime Crime) Berkley Publishing Group.

—Over the Edge: A Melissa Craig Mystery. 1993. 252p. 19.95 (*0-8027-3228-3*) Walker & Co.

**CRAMER, INSPECTOR (FICTITIOUS CHARACTER)—FICTION**

Stout, Rex. Red Threads. 1995. 272p. pap. 19.00 (*0-553-76299-0*); mass mkt. 4.99 (*0-553-22530-8*, Crimeline) Bantam Bks.

**CRANE, RUBY (FICTITIOUS CHARACTER)—FICTION**

Dereske, Jo. Cut & Dry. 1997. (Ruby Crane Mystery Ser.). 352p. mass mkt. 5.99 o.s.i (*0-440-22222-2*) Dell Publishing.

—Savage Cut. 1996. (Ruby Crane Mystery Ser.). 320p. mass mkt. 5.50 o.s.i (*0-440-22221-4*) Dell Publishing.

—Short Cut: A Ruby Crane Mystery. 1998. 336p. mass mkt. 5.99 o.s.i (*0-440-22223-0*) Dell Publishing.

**CRANMER, TIM (FICTITIOUS CHARACTER)—FICTION**

Le Carré, John. Our Game. (George Smiley Ser.). 1997. 320p. pap. 19.00 (*0-345-41831-X*); 1996. 352p. mass mkt. 7.99 (*0-345-40000-3*) Ballantine Bks.

—Our Game. unabr. ed. 1996. (George Smiley Ser.). audio 56.95 (*0-7861-1085-6*, 1853) Blackstone Audio Bks., Inc.

—Our Game. unabr. ed. 2000. (George Smiley Novels Ser.). audio 84.95 (*0-7451-6592-3*, CAB 1208) Chivers Audio Bks. GBR. *Dist:* BBC Audiobooks America.

—Our Game, unabr. ed. 1997. (George Smiley Novels Ser.). audio 42.95 (*0-7887-0809-0*, RD802) Recorded Bks., LLC.

**CRANSTON, SHERRY (FICTITIOUS CHARACTER)—FICTION**

Blackstock, Terri. Blind Trust. 1997. (Second Chances Ser.: Vol. 3). 256p. pap. 10.99 (*0-310-20710-X*) Zondervan.

**CRAWFORD, FRANCIS (FICTITIOUS CHARACTER)—FICTION**

Dunnett, Dorothy. Checkmate. 1976. 34.95 (*0-8488-1292-1*) Amereon, Ltd.

—Checkmate. 1983. 425p. lib. bdg. 39.95 (*0-89966-319-2*) Buccaneer Bks., Inc.

—Checkmate. 1997. (Legendary Lymond Chronicles: Vol. 6). (Illus.). 608p. pap. 15.95 (*0-679-77748-2*, Vintage) Knopf Publishing Group.

—Checkmate. 1984. 736p. mass mkt. 4.95 o.s.i (*0-446-31301-7*) Warner Bks., Inc.

—The Disorderly Knights. 1976. 31.95 (*0-8488-1297-2*) Amereon, Ltd.

—The Disorderly Knights. 1981. 334p. reprint ed. lib. bdg. 47.95 (*0-89966-295-1*) Buccaneer Bks., Inc.

—The Disorderly Knights. 1997. (Legendary Lymond Chronicles: Vol. 3). 528p. pap. 15.00 (*0-679-77745-8*, Vintage) Knopf Publishing Group.

—The Disorderly Knights. 1984. 576p. mass mkt. 3.95 o.s.i (*0-446-31290-8*) Warner Bks., Inc.

—The Game of Kings. 1976. 22.95 o.p. (*0-8488-1298-0*) Amereon, Ltd.

—The Game of Kings. 1983. 425p. lib. bdg. 39.95 (*0-89966-318-4*) Buccaneer Bks., Inc.

—The Game of Kings. 1997. (Legendary Lymond Chronicles: Vol. 1). 560p. pap. 15.00 (*0-679-77743-1*, Vintage) Knopf Publishing Group.

—Pawn in Frankincense. 1976. 33.95 (*0-8488-1300-6*) Amereon, Ltd.

—Pawn in Frankincense. 1983. 425p. reprint ed. lib. bdg. 39.95 (*0-89966-321-4*) Buccaneer Bks., Inc.

—Pawn in Frankincense. 1997. (Legendary Lymond Chronicles: Vol. 4). 512p. pap. 15.00 (*0-679-77746-6*, Vintage) Knopf Publishing Group.

—Pawn in Frankincense. 1984. 576p. mass mkt. 3.95 o.s.i (*0-446-31294-0*) Warner Bks., Inc.

—Queen's Play. 1976. 21.95 (*0-8488-1301-4*) Amereon, Ltd.

—Queen's Play. 1983. 425p. reprint ed. lib. bdg. 39.95 (*0-89966-320-6*) Buccaneer Bks., Inc.

—Queen's Play. 1997. (Legendary Lymond Chronicles: Vol. 2). 448p. pap. 15.00 (*0-679-77744-X*, Vintage) Knopf Publishing Group.

—Queen's Play. 1984. 512p. mass mkt. 3.95 o.s.i (*0-446-31288-6*) Warner Bks., Inc.

—The Ringed Castle. 1976. 32.95 (*0-8488-1302-2*) Amereon, Ltd.

—The Ringed Castle. 1983. 425p. reprint ed. lib. bdg. 39.95 (*0-89966-322-2*) Buccaneer Bks., Inc.

—The Ringed Castle. 1997. (Legendary Lymond Chronicles: Vol. 5). 544p. pap. 15.00 (*0-679-77747-4*, Vintage) Knopf Publishing Group.

—The Ringed Castle. 1984. 640p. mass mkt. 4.95 o.s.i (*0-446-31296-7*) Warner Bks., Inc.

**CRAY, ALI (FICTITIOUS CHARACTER)—FICTION**

O'Connell, Carol. Judas Child. 1999. 432p. reprint ed. mass mkt. 7.99 (*0-515-12549-0*, Jove) Berkley Publishing Group.

—Judas Child. abr. ed. 1999. audio 7.99 o.s.i (*1-56740-294-1*, 1863, Paperback Nova Audio Bks.); 1998. audio 28.95 (*1-56100-797-8*, 16, Bookcassette); 1998. audio 89.25 (*1-56740-576-2*, 913, Unabridged Library Editions); Set. 1998. audio 17.95 o.p. (*1-56740-771-4*, 447, Nova Audio Bks.) Brilliance Audio.

—Judas Child. 1998. 340p. 24.95 o.p. (*0-399-14380-7*, G. P. Putnam's Sons) Penguin Group (USA) Inc.

**CRAY, THE SORCERER (FICTITIOUS CHARACTER)—FICTION**

Eisenstein, Phyllis. The Crystal Palace. 1988. mass mkt. 3.95 o.p. (*0-451-15678-1*, Signet Bks.) NAL.

—Sorcerer's Son. 1981. mass mkt. 2.50 o.s.i (*0-345-29766-0*); 1979. mass mkt. 1.95 o.p. (*0-345-27642-6*) Ballantine Bks. (Del Rey).

—Sorcerer's Son. 1989. 384p. mass mkt. 3.95 o.p. (*0-451-15683-8*, Signet Bks.) NAL.

**CREASE, ELLEN (FICTITIOUS CHARACTER)—FICTION**

Margolin, Phillip. The Undertaker's Widow. 1999. 336p. reprint ed. mass mkt. 7.99 (*0-553-58088-4*) Bantam Bks.

—The Undertaker's Widow. unabr. ed. 1998. audio 48.00 (*0-7366-4219-6*, 4717) Books on Tape, Inc.

—The Undertaker's Widow. abr. ed. 1998. audio 29.95 o.s.i (*0-553-50218-2*, 751090, RH Audio) Random Hse. Audio Publishing Group.

—The Undertaker's Widow. l.t. ed. 2000. (Charnwood Large Print Ser.). 392p. (*0-7089-9146-7*, Ulverscroft) Thorpe, F. A. Pubs. GBR. *Dist:* Ulverscroft Large Print Bks., Ltd., Ulverscroft Large Print Canada, Ltd.

**CREED, LOUIS (FICTITIOUS CHARACTER)—FICTION**

King, Stephen. Pet Sematary. 1994. reprint ed. lib. bdg. 29.95 (*1-56849-545-5*) Buccaneer Bks., Inc.

—Pet Sematary. 1983. 384p. 30.00 o.s.i (*0-385-18244-9*) Doubleday Publishing.

—Pet Sematary. l.t. ed. (General Ser.). x, 634p. 1985. 9.95 o.p. (*0-8161-3756-0*); 1984. 18.95 o.p. (*0-8161-3691-2*) Gale Group. (Macmillan Reference USA).

—Pet Sematary. 1984. (J). mass mkt. 4.50 o.p. (*0-451-15024-4*); (J). mass mkt. 4.50 o.p. (*0-451-13975-5*); (J). mass mkt. 4.50 o.p. (*0-451-13237-8*); 416p. (YA). mass mkt. 4.95 o.p. (*0-451-15775-3*); 416p. reprint ed. mass mkt. 7.99 o.s.i (*0-451-16207-2*) NAL. (Signet Bks.).

—Pet Sematary. abr. ed. 1998. audio 18.00 (*0-671-58227-5*, 393645, Simon & Schuster Audioworks) Simon & Schuster Audio.

—Pet Sematary. 1984. 14.04 (*0-606-01108-0*) Turtleback Bks.

**CREEKMORE, BILLY (FICTITIOUS CHARACTER)—FICTION**

McCammon, Robert R. Mystery Walk. 1991. mass mkt. 5.99 o.s.i (*0-345-31514-6*, Ballantine Bks.) Ballantine Bks.

—Mystery Walk. 1983. 396p. o.p. (*0-03-061832-0*) Holt, Henry & Co.

—Mystery Walk. Peters, Sally, ed. rev. ed. 1992. (Illus.). 432p. mass mkt. 7.99 (*0-671-76991-X*, Pocket) Simon & Schuster.

**CREEVEY, JOHN (FICTITIOUS CHARACTER)—FICTION**

Rendell, Ruth. Talking to Strange Men. 1988. 328p. mass mkt. 5.99 o.s.i (*0-345-35174-6*) Ballantine Bks.

—Talking to Strange Men. unabr. ed. 2000. audio 59.95 (*0-7451-6236-3*, CAB 439) Chivers Audio Bks. GBR. *Dist:* BBC Audiobooks America.

—Talking to Strange Men. 1987. 280p. 16.95 o.s.i (*0-394-56324-7*, Pantheon) Knopf Publishing Group.

—Talking to Strange Men. 1990. audio 69.95 o.s.i (*0-8161-9141-7*) Thorndike Pr.

**CRIBB, SERGEANT (FICTITIOUS CHARACTER)—FICTION**

Hitt, Jack, et al. Perfect Murder: Five Great Mystery Writers Create the Perfect Crime, Set. abr. ed. 1992. audio 16.99 (*0-88646-317-3*, 7317) Durkin Hayes Publishing Ltd.

Lovesey, Peter. Abracadaver. 1994. 224p. 16.95 o.p. (*0-7451-8645-9*, Black Dagger); 1996. audio 54.95 (*0-7451-6110-3*, CAB294) BBC Audiobooks America.

—Abracadaver. 1989. 256p. reprint ed. pap. 4.50 o.p. (*0-06-081000-9*, Perennial) HarperTrade.

—Abracadaver. l.t. ed. 2000. (General Ser.). 284p. 24.95 (*0-7862-2802-4*) Thorndike Pr.

—Abracadaver. 1981. 224p. pap. 3.95 o.p. (*0-14-005803-6*, Penguin Bks.) Viking Penguin.

—Bertie & the Seven Bodies, Set. unabr. ed. 1993. (Detective Memoirs of King Edward the Eighth Ser.). 54.95 incl. audio (*0-7451-6111-1*, CAB 623) BBC Audiobooks America.

—Bertie & the Seven Bodies. 1991. (Audio Books Ser.). audio 53.95 o.p. (*0-8161-9247-2*) Thorndike Pr.

—Bertie & the Tin Man, from the Detective Memoirs of King Edward the Seventh. unabr. ed. 1990. audio 54.95 (*0-7451-6113-8*) BBC Audiobooks America.

—The Bloodhounds. unabr. ed. 1999. audio 84.95 (*1-86042-283-7*, 22837) Soundings, Ltd. GBR. *Dist:* Ulverscroft Large Print Bks., Ltd.

—A Case of Spirits. l.t. ed. 2002. (General Ser.). 280p. pap. 24.95 (*0-7862-4224-8*) Thorndike Pr.

—A Case of Spirits. 1977. (Crime Ser.). 192p. pap. 3.95 o.p. (*0-14-004333-0*, Penguin Bks.) Viking Penguin.

—The Detective Wore Silk Drawers. 1988. audio 35.95 o.p. (*0-8161-9452-1*) Thorndike Pr.

—The Detective Wore Silk Drawers. 1980. (Crime Monthly Ser.). pap. 3.95 o.p. (*0-14-005558-4*, Penguin Bks.) Viking Penguin.

—The Detective Wore Silk Drawers: A Sergeant Cribb Adventure. unabr. ed. 1995. audio 39.95 (*0-7451-6112-X*, CAB 338) BBC Audiobooks America.

—The Detective Wore Silk Drawers: A Sergeant Cribb Mystery. 1989. 208p. reprint ed. pap. 4.50 o.p. (*0-06-080999-X*, Perennial) HarperTrade.

—The Detective Wore Silk Drawers: A Sergeant Cribb Mystery. l.t. ed. 2000. (General Ser.). 268p. pap. 23.95 (*0-7862-2426-6*) Thorndike Pr.

—Invitation to a Dynamite Party. 1981. 176p. pap. 3.95 o.p. (*0-14-004029-3*, Penguin Bks.) Viking Penguin.

—Invitation to a Dynamite Party: A Sergeant Cribb Mystery. l.t. ed. 2003. (General Ser.). lib. bdg. 24.95 (*0-7862-5133-6*) Thorndike Pr.

—Mad Hatter's Holiday. 1990. 256p. reprint ed. pap. 4.50 o.p. (*0-06-081022-X*, Perennial) HarperTrade.

—Mad Hatter's Holiday. 1990. 256p. (C). reprint ed. lib. bdg. 20.00 o.p. (*0-8095-9022-0*) Millefleurs.

—Mad Hatter's Holiday. l.t. ed. 2001. 246p. pap. 25.95 (*0-7862-3498-9*); 259p. (*0-7540-4593-5*); 259p. (*0-7540-4594-3*) Thorndike Pr.

—Mad Hatter's Holiday. 1981. 192p. pap. 3.95 o.p. (*0-14-005804-4*, Penguin Bks.) Viking Penguin.

—Rough Cider. unabr. ed. 2001. audio 54.95 (*1-85089-785-9*, 88022) ISIS Audio Bks. GBR. *Dist:* Ulverscroft Large Print Bks., Ltd.

—Rough Cider. l.t. ed. 1987. (Mainstream Ser.). 242p. reprint ed. 15.95 o.p. (*1-85089-149-4*) ISIS Large Print Bks. GBR. *Dist:* Transaction Pubs.

—Rough Cider. 1987. 224p. 15.95 (*0-89296-194-5*) Mysterious Pr.

—Rough Cider. 2001. 206p. pap. 13.00 (*1-56947-228-9*) Soho Pr., Inc.

—Rough Cider. 1988. mass mkt. 3.95 (*0-445-40545-7*, Mysterious Pr. Paperback Bks.) Warner Bks., Inc.

—Swing, Swing Together. 1976. 21.95 (*0-89190-093-4*) Amereon, Ltd.

—Swing, Swing Together. 1990. 352p. (C). reprint ed. lib. bdg. 20.00 o.p. (*0-8095-9023-9*) Millefleurs.

—Swing, Swing Together. 1978. (Crime Ser.). pap. 3.95 o.p. (*0-14-004618-6*, Penguin Bks.) Viking Penguin.

—Swing, Swing Together: A Sergeant Cribb Mystery. 1990. 352p. reprint ed. pap. 4.50 o.p. (*0-06-081023-8*, Perennial) HarperTrade.

—Swing, Swing Together: A Sergeant Cribb Mystery. 2002. (General Ser.). 24.95 (*0-7862-4408-9*) Thorndike Pr.

—Waxwork. l.t. ed. 1978. 12.95 o.p. (*0-8161-6651-X*, Macmillan Reference USA) Gale Group.

—Waxwork. 1978. 7.95 o.p. (*0-394-50066-0*, Pantheon) Knopf Publishing Group.

—Waxwork. 1980. (Crime Monthly Ser.). pap. 3.95 o.p. (*0-14-004887-1*, Penguin Bks.) Viking Penguin.

—Wobble to Death. l.t. ed. 1999. (General Ser.). 272p. pap. 23.95 (*0-7862-1868-1*) Thorndike Pr.

—Wobble to Death. 1980. pap. 3.95 o.p. (*0-14-005557-6*, Penguin Bks.) Viking Penguin.

**CRICHTON, TESSA (FICTITIOUS CHARACTER)—FICTION**

Morice, Anne. Dead on Cue. l.t. ed. 1986. (Nightingale Ser.). 291p. 11.95 o.p. (*0-8161-4118-5*, Macmillan Reference USA) Gale Group.

—Dead on Cue. 1985. 208p. 12.95 o.p. (*0-312-18519-7*) St. Martin's Pr.

—Death & the Dutiful Daughter. l.t. ed. 1986. (Nightingale Ser.). 288p. 10.95 o.p. (*0-8161-3866-4*, Macmillan Reference USA) Gale Group.
—Death in the Round. 1980. 192p. 8.95 o.p. (*0-312-18616-9*) St. Martin's Pr.
—Death in the Round. 1981. (Crime Monthly Ser.). 192p. pap. 2.95 o.p. (*0-14-005997-0*, Penguin Bks.) Viking Penguin.
—Death of a Wedding Guest. 1976. 7.95 o.p. (*0-312-18830-7*) St. Martin's Pr.
—Design for Dying. unabr. ed. 1991. (Audio Ser.). audio 39.95 (*0-7451-6174-X*, CAT 4070) BBC Audiobooks America.
—Design for Dying. 1988. 192p. 14.95 o.p. (*0-312-01759-6*, Saint Martin's Minotaur) St. Martin's Pr.
—Fatal Charm. l.t. ed. 1990. (Nightingale Ser.). 276p. pap. 13.95 o.p. (*0-8161-4925-9*, Macmillan Reference USA) Gale Group.
—Fatal Charm. 1989. 192p. 14.95 o.p. (*0-312-03338-9*, Saint Martin's Minotaur) St. Martin's Pr.
—Getting Away with Murder? l.t. ed. 1985. (Nightingale Ser.). 304p. 10.95 o.p. (*0-8161-3865-6*, Macmillan Reference USA) Gale Group.
—Getting Away with Murder? 1984. 11.95 o.p. (*0-312-32633-5*) St. Martin's Pr.
—Hollow Vengeance. 1982. 196p. 10.95 o.p. (*0-312-38834-9*) St. Martin's Pr.
—The Men in Her Death. 1981. 224p. 9.95 o.p. (*0-312-52939-2*) St. Martin's Pr.
—Murder by Proxy. 1978. 7.95 o.p. (*0-312-55292-0*) St. Martin's Pr.
—Murder in Outline. 1986. 176p. mass mkt. 2.95 o.s.i (*0-553-25647-5*) Bantam Bks.
—Murder in Outline. 1979. 8.95 o.p. (*0-312-55303-X*) St. Martin's Pr.
—Murder Post-Dated. 1986. 208p. mass mkt. 2.95 o.s.i (*0-553-25652-1*) Bantam Bks.
—Murder Post-Dated. l.t. ed. 1985. (Nightingale Ser.). 396p. pap. 11.95 o.p. (*0-8161-3769-2*, Macmillan Reference USA) Gale Group.
—Murder Post-Dated. 1984. 192p. 10.95 o.p. (*0-312-55321-8*) St. Martin's Pr.
—Nursery Tea & Poison, Vol. 1. 1975. 6.95 o.p. (*0-312-58030-4*) St. Martin's Pr.
—Planning for Murder. l.t. ed. 1991. (Nightingale Ser.). 267p. pap. 14.95 o.p. (*0-8161-5246-2*, Macmillan Reference USA) Gale Group.
—Planning for Murder. 1991. 15.95 o.p. (*0-312-04869-6*, Saint Martin's Minotaur) St. Martin's Pr.
—Publish & Be Killed. l.t. ed. 1988. (Nightingale Ser.). 294p. 12.95 o.p. (*0-8161-4394-3*, Macmillan Reference USA) Gale Group.
—Publish & Be Killed. 1986. 192p. 12.95 o.p. (*0-312-00178-9*) St. Martin's Pr.
—Scared to Death. 1986. mass mkt. 2.95 o.s.i (*0-553-25628-9*) Bantam Bks.
—Scared to Death. 1978. (General Ser.). lib. bdg. 10.95 o.p. (*0-8161-6584-X*, Macmillan Reference USA) Gale Group.
—Scared to Death. (Mystery Bookshelf Selection Ser.). 1978. pap. 2.95 o.p. (*0-312-70044-X*, Saint Martin's Griffin); 1977. 7.95 o.p. (*0-312-70043-1*) St. Martin's Pr.
—Sleep of Death. 1986. mass mkt. 2.95 o.s.i (*0-553-25877-X*) Bantam Bks.
—Sleep of Death. 1982. 176p. 10.95 o.p. (*0-312-72863-8*) St. Martin's Pr.
—Treble Exposure. l.t. ed. 1988. (Nightingale Ser.). 312p. 12.95 o.p. (*0-8161-4622-5*, Macmillan Reference USA) Gale Group.
—Treble Exposure. 1988. 192p. 13.95 o.p. (*0-312-01525-9*, Saint Martin's Minotaur) St. Martin's Pr.

**CRIMSON SHADOW (FICTITIOUS CHARACTER)—FICTION**

Salvatore, R. A. The Dragon King. 1996. 352p. 19.95 o.p. (*0-446-51728-3*); 1997. 384p. reprint ed. mass mkt. 6.99 (*0-446-60485-2*, Aspect) Warner Bks., Inc.
—Luthien's Gamble. 1996. (Crimson Shadow Ser.: Bk. 2). 82p. 18.95 o.s.i (*0-446-51727-5*); 336p. reprint ed. mass mkt. 6.99 (*0-446-60361-9*) Warner Bks., Inc. (Aspect).
—The Sword of Bedwyr. 1995. (Crimson Shadow Ser.: Bk. 1). 256p. 18.95 o.s.i (*0-446-51726-7*); 1996. 320p. reprint ed. mass mkt. 6.99 (*0-446-60272-8*) Warner Bks., Inc. (Aspect).

**CRISP, WINSTON (FICTITIOUS CHARACTER)—FICTION**

Crossman, David A. Dead of Winter: A Winston Crisp Maine Island Mystery. 1999. 349p. 22.95 (*0-89272-445-5*) Down East Bks.
—A Show of Hands. 288p. 1998. pap. 14.95 (*0-89272-398-X*); 1997. 22.95 o.p. (*0-89272-412-9*) Down East Bks.

**CROAKER, FEY (FICTITIOUS CHARACTER)—FICTION**

Bishop, Paul. Chalk Whispers. 2000. 368p. 25.00 (*0-684-87157-2*, Scribner) Simon & Schuster.
—Chalk Whispers: A Fey Croaker LAPD Crime Novel. 2000. (Fey Croaker Novels Ser.). 368p. 25.00 o.s.i (*0-684-83010-8*, Scribner) Simon & Schuster.
—Kill Me Again. unabr. ed. 1996. (Fey Croaker Mystery Ser.: Bk. 1). audio 49.95 (*1-55686-614-3*) Books in Motion.
—Kill Me Again. 1994. 288p. mass mkt. 4.99 (*0-380-76890-9*, Avon Bks.) Morrow/Avon.
—Tequila Mockingbird. 1998. (Fey Croaker Novels Ser.). 400p. pap. 6.99 (*0-671-02531-7*, Pocket) Simon & Schuster.
—Tequila Mockingbird: A Fey Croaker Novel. 1997. (Fey Croaker Novels Ser.). 400p. 23.00 o.s.i (*0-684-83009-4*, Scribner) Simon & Schuster.
—Twice Dead. unabr. ed. 1996. (Fey Croaker Mystery Ser.: Bk. 2). audio 64.95 (*1-55686-710-7*) Books in Motion.
—Twice Dead. 1996. 336p. mass mkt. 5.50 (*0-380-77862-9*, Avon Bks.) Morrow/Avon.

**CROFT, FREDDIE (FICTITIOUS CHARACTER)—FICTION**

Francis, Dick. Driving Force. 1993. 384p. mass mkt. 6.99 (*0-449-22139-3*, Fawcett) Ballantine Bks.
—Driving Force. unabr. ed. 1994. audio 64.00 (*0-7366-2613-1*, 3355) Books on Tape, Inc.
—Driving Force. abr. ed. 1992. audio 17.00 o.p. (*1-55994-537-0*, HarperAudio) HarperTrade.
—Driving Force. 1992. 320p. 21.95 o.p. (*0-399-13776-9*, G. P. Putnam's Sons) Penguin Group (USA) Inc.
—Driving Force. unabr. ed. 1993. audio 60.00 (*1-55690-788-5*, 93107E7) Recorded Bks., LLC.

**CROFT, JOSHUA (FICTITIOUS CHARACTER)—FICTION**

Satterthwait, Walter. Accustomed to the Dark. 1998. (WWL Mystery Ser.). per. (*0-373-26263-9*, 1-26263-3, Worldwide Library) Harlequin Enterprises, Ltd.
—Accustomed to the Dark. 1996. 256p. 21.95 o.p. (*0-312-14535-7*, Saint Martin's Minotaur) St. Martin's Pr.
—At Ease with the Dead. 1993. per. (*0-373-83266-4*, 1-83266-6); 1991. mass mkt. (*0-373-26072-5*) Harlequin Enterprises, Ltd. (Harlequin Bks.).
—At Ease with the Dead. 1990. 16.95 o.p. (*0-312-04260-4*, Saint Martin's Minotaur) St. Martin's Pr.
—At Ease with the Dead: A Joshua Croft Mystery. 2002. 256p. pap. 13.95 (*0-8263-2970-5*) Univ. of New Mexico Pr.
—A Flower in the Desert. 1993. (WWL Mystery Ser.). per. (*0-373-26134-9*, 1-26134-6, Harlequin Bks.) Harlequin Enterprises, Ltd.
—A Flower in the Desert. 1992. 240p. 17.95 o.p. (*0-312-07751-3*, Saint Martin's Minotaur) St. Martin's Pr.
—A Flower in the Desert: A Joshua Croft Mystery. 2003. 256p. pap. 13.95 (*0-8263-3203-X*); pap. 13.95 (*0-8263-2914-4*) Univ. of New Mexico Pr.
—The Hanged Man: A Joshua Croft Mystery. 1995. (WWL Mystery Ser.). 250p. per. (*0-373-26173-X*, 1-26173-4, Harlequin Bks.) Harlequin Enterprises, Ltd.
—The Hanged Man: A Joshua Croft Mystery. 1993. 256p. 19.95 o.p. (*0-312-09827-8*, Saint Martin's Minotaur) St. Martin's Pr.
—The Hanged Man: A Joshua Croft Mystery. 2003. 258p. pap. 13.95 (*0-8263-3365-6*) Univ. of New Mexico Pr.
—Wall of Glass. 1993. per. (*0-373-83265-6*, 1-83265-8); 1989. mass mkt. (*0-373-26032-6*) Harlequin Enterprises, Ltd. (Harlequin Bks.).
—Wall of Glass. 1988. 256p. 16.95 o.p. (*0-312-01530-5*, Saint Martin's Minotaur) St. Martin's Pr.
—Wall of Glass: A Joshua Croft Mystery. 2002. 250p. pap. 13.95 (*0-8263-2887-3*) Univ. of New Mexico Pr.

Smith, Barbara B., et al. 'Tis the Season for Murder: Christmas Crimes. 1998. mass mkt. (*0-373-26290-6*, 1-26290-6, Worldwide Library) Harlequin Enterprises, Ltd.

**CROFT, MIKE (FICTITIOUS CHARACTER)—FICTION**

Adams, Jane. Fade to Grey. 2003. 270p. pap. o.p. (*0-330-37487-7*) Macmillan Children's Bks.
—Fade to Grey. l.t. ed. 1999. (Ulverscroft Large Print Ser.). 328p. 31.99 (*0-7089-4153-2*, Ulverscroft) Thorpe, F. A. Pubs. GBR. *Dist:* Ulverscroft Large Print Bks., Ltd., Ulverscroft Large Print Canada, Ltd.
—The Greenway. 1997. 264p. mass mkt. 5.99 o.s.i (*0-449-22543-7*, Fawcett) Ballantine Bks.
—The Greenway. unabr. ed. 1998. audio 63.95 (*1-85903-119-6*) Magna Story Sound GBR. *Dist:* Ulverscroft Large Print Bks., Ltd.
—The Greenway. l.t. ed. 1997. (Ulverscroft Large Print Ser.). 384p. 31.50 (*0-7089-3659-8*, Ulverscroft) Thorpe, F. A. Pubs. GBR. *Dist:* Ulverscroft Large Print Bks., Ltd., Ulverscroft Large Print Canada, Ltd.

**CROOK, ARTHUR (FICTITIOUS CHARACTER)—FICTION**

Gilbert, Anthony. The Black Stage. unabr. ed. 1989. (C). audio 54.95 (*0-7451-5982-6*) BBC Audiobooks America.
—The Black Stage. (Black Dagger Crime Ser.). 232p. 12.95 o.p. (*0-86220-727-4*) Chivers Pr. GBR. *Dist:* BBC Audiobooks America.
—Death Takes a Wife. l.t. ed. 1991. pap. 16.95 o.p. (*0-7927-0515-7*, CS0114) BBC Audiobooks America.
—The Mouse Who Wouldn't Play Ball. l.t. ed. 1991. pap. 16.95 o.p. (*0-7927-0711-7*, CS0247) BBC Audiobooks America.
—Murder Comes Home. l.t. ed. 1992. pap. 14.95 o.p. (*0-7927-1067-3*) BBC Audiobooks America.
—A Nice Little Killing. l.t. ed. 1991. pap. 10.95 o.p. (*0-7927-0146-1*, C0102) BBC Audiobooks America.
—Passenger to Nowhere. l.t. ed. 1990. pap. 16.95 o.p. (*0-7927-0161-5*, C0253) BBC Audiobooks America.
—Snake in the Grass. (Black Dagger Crime Ser.). 1993. 192p. 16.50 o.p. (*0-7451-8616-5*, Black Dagger); 1994. 18.95 o.p. (*0-7451-6459-5*) BBC Audiobooks America.

**CROSS, ALEX (FICTITIOUS CHARACTER)—FICTION**

Patterson, James. Along Came a Spider. l.t. ed. (General Ser.). 486p. 1994. pap. 18.95 o.s.i (*0-8161-5753-7*); 1993. 22.95 o.p. (*0-8161-5752-9*) Gale Group. (Macmillan Reference USA).
—Along Came a Spider. abr. ed. 1993. audio 18.00 o.p. (*1-55994-751-9*, 390336, HarperAudio) HarperTrade.
—Along Came a Spider. 2001. 528p. E-Book 6.95 (*0-7595-9172-5*); 2001. 528p. E-Book 6.95 (*0-7595-6150-8*); 2001. 528p. E-Book 6.95 (*0-7595-4152-3*); 1993. 435p. 19.95 (*0-316-69364-2*) Little Brown & Co.
—Along Came a Spider. 2002. E-Book 4.99 (*0-7953-0895-7*) RosettaBooks.
—Along Came a Spider. 2003. 464p. pap. 13.95 (*0-446-69263-8*); 1993. 528p. reprint ed. mass mkt. 7.99 (*0-446-36419-3*) Warner Bks., Inc.
—The Big Bad Wolf. 2003. 400p. 27.95 (*0-316-60290-6*) Little Brown & Co.
—The Big Bad Wolf. 2003. 400p. pap. 16.00 (*0-446-69257-3*) Warner Bks., Inc.
—Cat & Mouse. unabr. ed. 1998. audio 56.00 (*0-7366-4138-6*, 4643) Books on Tape, Inc.
—Cat & Mouse. 1997. 400p. 24.95 o.p. (*0-316-69329-4*) Little Brown & Co.
—Cat & Mouse. unabr. ed. 1999. audio compact disk 69.00 (*0-7887-3411-3*, C1017E7); 1998. audio 70.00 (*0-7887-2022-8*, 95395E7) Recorded Bks., LLC.
—Cat & Mouse. l.t. ed. (Paperback Bestsellers Ser.). 472p. 1999. pap. 27.95 (*0-7838-8345-5*); 1998. 30.95 (*0-7838-8344-7*) Thorndike Pr.
—Cat & Mouse. abr. ed. 1999. audio (*1-57042-737-2*); 1997. audio 24.00 (*1-57042-577-9*, 695410) Time Warner AudioBooks.
—Cat & Mouse. 2003. E-Book 5.95 (*0-7595-4742-4*) Time Warner Bk. Group.
—Cat & Mouse. 2003. 432p. pap. 13.95 (*0-446-69264-6*); 1998. 480p. reprint ed. mass mkt. 7.99 (*0-446-60618-9*) Warner Bks., Inc.
—Four Blind Mice. 2002. 400p. 27.95 (*0-316-69300-6*); 432p. 27.95 (*0-316-14786-9*) Little Brown & Co.
—Four Blind Mice. unabr. ed. 2002. audio 29.98 (*1-58621-404-7*) Time Warner AudioBooks.
—Four Blind Mice. 2003. 416p. mass mkt. 7.99 (*0-446-61326-6*, Warner Vision); 2002. 400p. pap. 16.00 (*0-446-69052-X*) Warner Bks., Inc.
—Jack & Jill. 1997. audio compact disk 80.00 (*0-7366-8519-7*); audio 64.00 (*0-913369-41-1*, 4218) Books on Tape, Inc.
—Jack & Jill. 1996. 448p. 24.95 (*0-316-69371-5*) Little Brown & Co.
—Jack & Jill. unabr. ed. 1999. audio compact disk 99.00 (*0-7887-3415-6*, C1021E7); 1997. audio 85.00 (*0-7887-0804-X*, 94953E7) Recorded Bks., LLC.
—Jack & Jill. l.t. ed. 1998. (Paperback Bestsellers Ser.). 537p. pap. 27.95 (*0-7862-0939-9*) Thorndike Pr.
—Jack & Jill. abr. ed. 1996. (Alex Cross Mystery Ser.). (gr. 8 up). audio 17.00 (*1-57042-437-3*, 394457) Time Warner AudioBooks.
—Jack & Jill. 2003. E-Book 5.95 (*0-7595-4743-2*) Time Warner Bk. Group.
—Jack & Jill. 480p. 2003. pap. 13.95 (*0-446-69265-4*); 1997. reprint ed. mass mkt. 7.99 (*0-446-60480-1*) Warner Bks., Inc.
—Kiss the Girls. unabr. ed. 1995. audio 64.00 (*0-7366-3082-1*, 3762) Books on Tape, Inc.
—Kiss the Girls. l.t. ed. 2001. 432p. 31.95 o.p. (*0-7838-9437-6*, Macmillan Reference USA) Gale Group.
—Kiss the Girls. 1995. 451p. 22.95 (*0-316-69370-7*) Little Brown & Co.
—Kiss the Girls. unabr. ed. audio audio 78.00 (*0-7887-0340-4*, 94532E7) Recorded Bks., LLC.
—Kiss the Girls. abr. ed. 1995. (Alex Cross Mystery Ser.). (gr. 8 up). audio 17.00 (*1-57042-029-7*, 391029) Time Warner AudioBooks.
—Kiss the Girls. 2002. E-Book 4.95 (*0-7595-4718-1*) Time Warner Bk. Group.
—Kiss the Girls. 496p. reprint ed. 2000. pap. 13.95 (*0-446-67738-8*); 1995. mass mkt. 7.99 (*0-446-60124-1*) Warner Bks., Inc.
—Pop! Goes the Weasel. 1999. 432p. (YA). (gr. 8). 26.95 o.p. (*0-316-69328-6*) Little Brown & Co.
—Pop! Goes the Weasel. l.t. ed. 496p. 2000. pap. 13.95 (*0-375-72793-0*); 1999. 26.95 (*0-375-40854-1*) Random Hse. Large Print.
—Pop! Goes the Weasel. 2003. E-Book 5.95 (*0-7595-4739-4*) Time Warner Bk. Group.
—Pop! Goes the Weasel. 2000. 480p. reprint ed. mass mkt. 7.99 (*0-446-60881-5*) Warner Bks., Inc.
—Roses Are Red. 2000. 400p. 26.95 o.p. (*0-316-69325-1*); pap. 16.00 (*0-316-66620-3*) Little Brown & Co.
—Roses Are Red. l.t. ed. 2000. 448p. 26.95 (*0-375-43090-3*) Random Hse. Large Print.
—Roses Are Red. abr. ed. 2000. audio 29.98 (*1-57042-922-7*); audio 24.98 (*1-57042-920-0*); audio 32.98 (*1-57042-921-9*) Time Warner AudioBooks.
—Roses Are Red. 2001. 400p. reprint ed. mass mkt. 7.99 (*0-446-60548-4*) Warner Bks., Inc.
—Violets Are Blue. 2001. 400p. 27.95 o.p. (*0-316-69323-5*); 432p. 27.95 o.p. (*0-316-68656-5*) Little Brown & Co.
—Violets Are Blue. abr. ed. 2001. audio 25.98 (*1-58621-195-1*); audio 29.98 (*1-58621-196-X*); audio 32.98 (*1-58621-197-8*); audio 39.98 (*1-58621-198-6*) Time Warner AudioBooks.
—Violets Are Blue. 2001. pap. 16.00 o.s.i (*0-446-67860-0*) Warner Bks., Inc.

**CROSS, VICTORIA (FICTITIOUS CHARACTER)—FICTION**

Sumner, Penny. Crosswords: The 2nd Victoria Cross Mystery. 1994. 256p. pap. 9.95 (*1-56280-064-7*) Naiad Pr., Inc.
—The End of April. 1992. (Victoria Cross Mystery Ser.). 256p. pap. 8.95 o.p. (*1-56280-007-8*) Naiad Pr., Inc.

**CROW, JOE (FICTITIOUS CHARACTER)—FICTION**

Hautman, Pete. Drawing Dead. 1997. 320p. pap. 5.99 (*0-671-00302-X*, Pocket); 1993. 285p. 20.50 (*0-671-79374-8*, Simon & Schuster) Simon & Schuster.
—Ring Game. 1998. 480p. pap. 6.50 (*0-671-02145-1*, Pocket); 1997. 320p. 21.50 (*0-684-83242-9*, Simon & Schuster); 1997. 320p. 22.00 (*0-684-84718-3*, Simon & Schuster) Simon & Schuster.
—Short Money. 1997. 336p. pap. 5.99 (*0-671-00303-8*, Pocket); 1995. 287p. 20.50 o.p. (*0-684-80211-2*, Simon & Schuster) Simon & Schuster.

**CROW, TITUS (FICTITIOUS CHARACTER)—FICTION**

Lumley, Brian. The Burrowers Beneath. ltd. ed. 1988. (Titus Crow Ser.: Vol. 1). (Illus.). 192p. reprint ed. 22.50 (*0-932445-30-6*); 37.50 o.p. (*0-932445-31-4*) Ganley Pub.
—The Clock of Dreams. deluxe ltd. ed. 1994. (Titus Crow Ser.: Vol. 3). (Illus.). reprint ed. 42.50 (*0-932445-52-7*); 26.50 (*0-932445-51-9*) Ganley Pub.
—The Compleat Crow. 1987. (Illus.). 192p. 21.00 (*0-932445-22-5*); 35.00 o.p. (*0-932445-23-3*); pap. 7.50 o.p. (*0-932445-21-7*) Ganley Pub.
—Harry Keogh: Necroscope & Other Heroes! 2003. 320p. 25.95 (*0-7653-0847-9*, Tor Bks.) Doherty, Tom Assocs., LLC.
—In the Moons of Borea. 1979. (Titus Crow Ser.: Vol. 5). 1.75 o.s.i (*0-515-05125-X*, Jove) Berkley Publishing Group.
—In the Moons of Borea. 2000. (Titus Crow Ser.: Vol. 5). 380p. pap. 15.95 (*0-312-86866-9*, Tor Bks.) Doherty, Tom Assocs., LLC.
—In the Moons of Borea. 1995. (Titus Crow Ser.: Vol. 5). (Illus.). 192p. 27.50 (*0-932445-61-6*); reprint ed. 45.00 (*0-932445-62-4*) Ganley Pub.
—Spawn of the Winds. deluxe ed. 1995. (Titus Crow Ser.: Vol. 4). (Illus.). 42.50 (*0-932445-60-8*); reprint ed. 26.50 (*0-932445-59-4*) Ganley Pub.
—Titus Crow. 1996. 352p. 24.95 o.p. (*0-312-86299-7*); 2nd ed. 1999. (Titus Crow Omnibus Ser.: Vol. 1). 347p. reprint ed. pap. 15.95 (*0-312-86867-7*, NPB 0259); Vol. 2. 1997. (Titus Crow Ser.: Vol. 2). 384p. 24.95 o.p. (*0-312-86347-0*); Vol. 3. 1997. (Titus Crow Ser.: Vol. 3). 384p. 24.95 o.p. (*0-312-86365-9*) Doherty, Tom Assocs., LLC. (Tor Bks.).
—Titus Crow Vol. 2: The Clock of Dreams & Spawn of the Winds, Vol. 2. 1999. (Titus Crow Ser.: Vol. 2). 318p. pap. 14.95 (*0-312-86868-5*, Tor Bks.) Doherty, Tom Assocs., LLC.
—The Transition of Titus Crow. 1975. (Titus Crow Ser.: Vol. 2). mass mkt. 1.50 o.p. (*0-87997-173-8*, UW1173) DAW Bks., Inc.

Characters

—The Transition of Titus Crow. rev. ed. 1992. (Titus Crow Ser.: Vol. 2). (Illus.). 192p. reprint ed. 25.00 (*0-932445-45-4*); 40.00 (*0-932445-46-2*) Ganley Pub.

**CROWE, JANIE (FICTITIOUS CHARACTER)—FICTION**

Benson, Ann. The Burning Road. 2000. 720p. mass mkt. 6.50 (*0-440-22591-4*) Dell Publishing.

—The Plague Tales. 1998. 688p. mass mkt. 6.99 (*0-440-22510-8*) Dell Publishing.

**CROWELL, FAITH (FICTITIOUS CHARACTER)—FICTION**

Hitchcock, Jane S. Trick of the Eye. l.t. ed. 1993. 23.95 o.p. (*0-7927-1482-2*); pap. 21.95 o.p. (*0-7927-1481-4*) BBC Audiobooks America.

—Trick of the Eye. 1992. 288p. 19.00 o.p. (*0-525-93529-0*, Dutton) Dutton/Plume.

—Trick of the Eye. 1993. 256p. pap. o.p. (*0-451-17480-1*); 368p. mass mkt. 5.50 o.s.i (*0-451-17673-1*) NAL. (Signet Bks.).

**CROWNE, RACHEL (FICTITIOUS CHARACTER)—FICTION**

Rawlings, Ellen. Deadly Harvest. 1997. mass mkt. 5.99 o.s.i (*0-449-14987-0*, Fawcett) Ballantine Bks.

—The Murder Lover. 1996. mass mkt. 5.99 o.s.i (*0-449-14988-9*, Fawcett) Ballantine Bks.

**CRUSHER, BEVERLY (FICTITIOUS CHARACTER)—FICTION**

Betancourt, John Gregory. Infection Vol. 1: Double Helix. 1999. (Star Trek, The Next Generation Ser.: No. 51). (Illus.). 256p. pap. 6.50 (*0-671-03255-0*, Star Trek) Simon & Schuster.

Carey, Diane L. Double Helix No. 3: Red Sector. 1999. (Star Trek, The Next Generation Ser.: No. 53). (Illus.). 336p. mass mkt. 6.50 (*0-671-03257-7*, Star Trek) Simon & Schuster.

Carter, Carmen. The Children of Hamlin. Stern, Dave, ed. 1990. (Star Trek, The Next Generation Ser.: No. 3). mass mkt. 5.50 o.s.i (*0-671-73555-1*, Star Trek) Simon & Schuster.

—The Children of Hamlin. 1989. (Star Trek, The Next Generation Ser.: No. 3). E-Book 6.99 (*0-7434-1215-X*, Star Trek) Simon & Schuster.

Dillard, J. M. First Contact. abr. ed. 1996. (Star Trek Ser.: No. 8). audio 18.00 (*0-671-57391-8*, Simon & Schuster Audioworks) Simon & Schuster Audio.

Johnson, Kij & Cox, Greg. Dragon's Honor. Ordover, John, ed. 1996. (Star Trek, The Next Generation Ser.: No. 38). 288p. mass mkt. 5.99 (*0-671-50107-0*, Star Trek) Simon & Schuster.

Mitchell, V. E. Imbalance. (Star Trek, The Next Generation Ser.: No. 22). E-Book 6.99 (*0-7434-2102-7*, Star Trek) Simon & Schuster.

—Imbalance. Stern, Dave, ed. 1992. (Star Trek, The Next Generation Ser.: No. 22). 288p. mass mkt. 5.50 (*0-671-77571-5*, Star Trek) Simon & Schuster.

Peel, John. Death of Princes. 1996. (Star Trek, The Next Generation Ser.: No. 44). 304p. pap. 5.99 (*0-671-56808-6*, Star Trek) Simon & Schuster.

**CRUSHER, WESLEY (FICTITIOUS CHARACTER)—FICTION**

Carter, Carmen. The Children of Hamlin. Stern, Dave, ed. 1990. (Star Trek, The Next Generation Ser.: No. 3). mass mkt. 5.50 o.s.i (*0-671-73555-1*, Star Trek) Simon & Schuster.

—The Children of Hamlin. 1989. (Star Trek, The Next Generation Ser.: No. 3). E-Book 6.99 (*0-7434-1215-X*, Star Trek) Simon & Schuster.

David, Peter. Strike Zone. (Star Trek, The Next Generation Ser.: No. 5). 1991. mass mkt. 5.99 (*0-671-74647-2*); 1990. mass mkt. 4.50 o.s.i (*0-671-73516-0*) Simon & Schuster. (Star Trek).

—The Strike Zone. 1989. (Star Trek, The Next Generation Ser.: No. 5). E-Book 6.99 (*0-7434-1217-6*, Star Trek) Simon & Schuster.

Gilden, Mel. Boogeymen. (Star Trek, The Next Generation Ser.: No. 17). E-Book 6.99 (*0-7434-2097-7*, Star Trek) Simon & Schuster.

—Boogeymen. Stern, Dave, ed. 1991. (Star Trek, The Next Generation Ser.: No. 17). 288p. mass mkt. 5.50 (*0-671-70970-4*, Star Trek) Simon & Schuster.

Hugh, Dafydd ab. Balance of Power. Ryan, Kevin, ed. 1994. (Star Trek, The Next Generation Ser.: No. 33). 304p. mass mkt. 5.50 (*0-671-52003-2*, Star Trek) Simon & Schuster.

Thompson, W. R. Debtor's Planet. Ordover, John, ed. 1994. (Star Trek, The Next Generation Ser.: No. 30). 288p. (Orig.). mass mkt. 5.99 o.s.i (*0-671-88341-0*, Star Trek) Simon & Schuster.

Weinstein, Howard. Perchance to Dream. Stern, David, ed. 1991. (Star Trek, The Next Generation Ser.: No. 19). 288p. (Orig.). mass mkt. 5.50 (*0-671-70837-6*, Star Trek) Simon & Schuster.

**CRUSOE, EDWINA (FICTITIOUS CHARACTER)—FICTION**

Kittredge, Mary. Cadaver. 1993. 250p. mass mkt. 3.99 o.p. (*0-312-95002-0*, St. Martin's Paperbacks) St. Martin's Pr.

—Cadaver: An Edwina Crusoe Medical Mystery. 1992. 208p. 17.95 o.p. (*0-312-06920-0*, Saint Martin's Minotaur) St. Martin's Pr.

—Fatal Diagnosis. 1997. 208p. mass mkt. 5.50 o.s.i (*0-553-57590-2*, Crimeline) Bantam Bks.

—Fatal Diagnosis. 1990. pap. 15.95 o.p. (*0-312-04315-5*, Saint Martin's Minotaur) St. Martin's Pr.

—Kill or Cure. 1996. 288p. mass mkt. 5.50 o.s.i (*0-553-57585-6*, Crimeline) Bantam Bks.

—Kill or Cure: An Edwina Crusoe Medical Mystery. 1995. 216p. 19.95 o.p. (*0-312-13103-8*, Saint Martin's Minotaur) St. Martin's Pr.

—Rigor Mortis. 1991. 14.95 o.p. (*0-312-05504-8*, Saint Martin's Minotaur); 1992. 201p. reprint ed. mass mkt. 3.99 o.p. (*0-312-92865-3*, St. Martin's Paperbacks) St. Martin's Pr.

—Walking Dead Man. 1993. mass mkt. 3.99 o.p. (*0-312-95157-4*, St. Martin's Paperbacks); 1992. 208p. 17.95 o.p. (*0-312-08333-5*, Saint Martin's Minotaur) St. Martin's Pr.

**CRUSOE, ROBINSON (FICTITIOUS CHARACTER)—FICTION**

Defoe, Daniel. The Adventures of Robinson Crusoe. 1999. (Shakespeare Head Edition of the Writings of Daniel Defoe Ser.: Vol. 11). reprint ed. Pt. 1. 250p. lib. bdg. 88.00 (*1-58201-063-3*); Pt. 2. 222p. lib. bdg. 88.00 (*1-58201-064-1*); Pt. 3. 88.00 (*1-58201-065-X*) Classic Bks.

—The Farther Adventures of Robinson Crusoe, Being the Second & Last Part of His Life. 1999. (Focus on the Family Great Stories Ser.). (Illus.). 352p. pap. 9.99 o.p. (*1-56179-764-2*) Focus on the Family Publishing.

—The Life & Strange, Surprising Adventures of Robinson Crusoe of York, Mariner. (Illus.). reprint ed. (*0-404-07911-3*) AMS Pr., Inc.

—The Life & Strange, Surprising Adventures of Robinson Crusoe of York, Mariner. Crowley, Joseph Donald, ed. & intro. by. 1998. (Oxford World's Classics Ser.). (Illus.). 352p. pap. 7.95 (*0-19-283382-0*) Oxford Univ. Pr., Inc.

—The Life & Strange, Surprising Adventures of Robinson Crusoe of York, Mariner. Crowley, Joseph Donald, ed. 1982. (Oxford World's Classics Ser.). (Illus.). 346p. pap. 4.95 o.p. (*0-19-281555-5*) Oxford Univ. Pr., Inc.

—Robinson Crusoe. 1997. (Classics Illustrated Study Guides). (Illus.). mass mkt. 4.99 (*1-57840-043-0*) Acclaim Bks.

—Robinson Crusoe. 1992. (York Notes Ser.). pap. text 9.95 (*0-582-78111-6*) Addison-Wesley Longman, Ltd. GBR. *Dist:* Trans-Atlantic Pubns., Inc.

—Robinson Crusoe. 24.95 (*0-88411-594-1*) Amereon, Ltd.

—Robinson Crusoe. abr. ed. audio. audio 5.95 (*0-89926-195-7*, 1005) Audio Bk. Co.

—Robinson Crusoe. 1982. mass mkt. 1.95 o.s.i (*0-553-21105-6*, Bantam Classics) Bantam Bks.

—Robinson Crusoe. 2003. (Barnes & Noble Classics Ser.). 352p. pap. 4.95 (*1-59308-011-5*) Barnes & Noble, Inc.

—Robinson Crusoe. 1991. (Illus.). 3.95 (*0-425-12664-1*) Berkley Publishing Group.

—Robinson Crusoe. abr. ed. 1996. audio 26.95 (*1-885546-12-2*) Big Ben Audio, Inc.

—Robinson Crusoe. unabr. ed. 1989. audio 56.95 (*0-7861-0056-7*, 1053) Blackstone Audio Bks., Inc.

—Robinson Crusoe. 1996. (FRE.). Vol. I. pap. 7.95 (*2-87714-319-8*); Vol. II. pap. 7.95 (*2-87714-320-1*) Bookking International FRA. *Dist:* Distribooks, Inc.

—Robinson Crusoe. unabr. ed. audio 39.95 (*1-55686-107-9*, 107) Books in Motion.

—Robinson Crusoe. unabr. ed. 2002. audio 29.95 (*1-59086-280-5*, 3866, Brilliance Audio Unabridged); 1995. 11p. audio 59.25 (*1-56100-259-3*, 1013, Unabridged Library Editions); 1995. audio 19.95 o.p. (*1-56100-634-3*, 235, Bookcassette) Brilliance Audio.

—Robinson Crusoe. 1982. reprint ed. lib. bdg. 25.95 (*0-89966-403-2*) Buccaneer Bks., Inc.

—Robinson Crusoe. (Early Best Sellers Ser.). reprint ed. lib. bdg. 48.00 (*0-7426-1016-0*); 2001. (Illus.). pap. text 28.00 (*0-7426-6016-8*) Classic Bks.

—Robinson Crusoe, Level 4. 1988. mass mkt. 4.95 (*0-938819-94-1*, Aerie) Doherty, Tom Assocs., LLC.

—Robinson Crusoe. unabr. ed. 1998. (Thrift Editions Ser.). 288p. pap. 2.50 (*0-486-40427-7*) Dover Pubns., Inc.

—Robinson Crusoe. 1972. 2.95 o.p. (*0-460-01059-X*); 1956. 11.50 o.p. (*0-460-00059-4*) Dutton/Plume. (Dutton).

—Robinson Crusoe. 1997. (Classic Collection). 14.99 o.p. (*1-56179-557-7*) Focus on the Family Publishing.

—Robinson Crusoe. 1998. (SPA.). 352p. (*84-320-4866-6*) GeoPlaneta, Editorial, S. A.

—Robinson Crusoe. unabr. ed. audio 35.95 Halvorson Assocs.

—Robinson Crusoe. unabr. ed. 1999. audio 56.95 Highsmith Inc.

—Robinson Crusoe. l.t. ed. 1992. (Isis Large Print Bks.). 358p. 24.95 (*1-85089-459-0*) ISIS Large Print Bks. GBR. *Dist:* Transaction Pubs., Ulverscroft Large Print Canada, Ltd.

—Robinson Crusoe, l.t. ed. 2001. 467p. lib. bdg. 35.95 net. (*1-58118-082-9*) LRS.

—Robinson Crusoe. 2002. (SPA.). 14.95 (*84-392-0909-6*, EV30592) Lectorum Pubns., Inc.

—Robinson Crusoe. (ACE.). E-Book 1.95 (*1-57799-935-5*) Logos Research Systems, Inc.

—Robinson Crusoe, Level 2. 2001. pap. 7.66 (*0-582-42696-0*) Longman Publishing Group.

—Robinson Crusoe. abr. ed. 2000. audio 7.95 (*1-57815-124-4*, 1086, Media Bks. Audio Publishing) Media Bks., L. L. C.

—Robinson Crusoe. 1999. E-Book 1.95 (*1-58515-063-0*) MesaView, Inc.

—Robinson Crusoe. 1961. mass mkt. 1.95 o.p. (*0-451-51606-0*); 1961. mass mkt. 0.50 o.p. (*0-451-50055-5*); 1961. mass mkt. 1.75 o.p. (*0-451-51389-4*); 1961. mass mkt. 1.50 o.p. (*0-451-51052-6*); 1961. mass mkt. 0.60 o.p. (*0-451-50542-5*); 1961. mass mkt. 0.95 o.p. (*0-451-50862-9*); 1961. mass mkt. 0.75 o.p. (*0-451-50627-8*); 1998. 320p. mass mkt. 5.95 (*0-451-52701-1*) NAL. (Signet Classics).

—Robinson Crusoe. abr. ed. 1995. audio 17.98 (*962-634-565-9*, NA306514); audio compact disk 19.98 (*962-634-065-7*, NA306512) Naxos of America, Inc. (Naxos AudioBooks).

—Robinson Crusoe. 2000. (Twelve-Point Ser.). reprint ed. 370p. lib. bdg. 25.00 (*1-58287-119-1*); 465p. lib. bdg. 26.00 (*0-939495-98-8*) North Bks.

—Robinson Crusoe. unabr. ed. 2001. audio 50.95 NorthStar Audio Bks.

—Robinson Crusoe. Shinagel, Michael, ed. 1975. (Critical Editions Ser.). 399p. (C). pap. o.p. (*0-393-09231-3*) Norton, W. W. & Co., Inc.

—Robinson Crusoe. audio 26.95 o.p. Olivia & Hill Pr., The.

—Robinson Crusoe. 1999. 320p. 13.50 o.p. (*0-19-210033-5*); 2nd ed. 1993. (Illus.). 94p. pap. text 5.95 (*0-19-585336-9*) Oxford Univ. Pr., Inc.

—Robinson Crusoe. abr. ed. 2015. audio 16.95 (*0-14-086281-1*) Penguin Group (USA) Inc.

—Robinson Crusoe. 1987. (Classics for Young Readers Ser.). 240p. pap. 3.50 o.p. (*0-14-035072-1*, Puffin Bks.) Penguin Putnam Bks. for Young Readers.

—Robinson Crusoe. 1999. (Prentice-Hall Literature). text (*0-13-981432-9*) Prentice Hall PTR.

—Robinson Crusoe. 1999. (Illus.). E-Book 3.99 incl. cd-rom (*1-891595-93-8*) Quiet Vision Publishing.

—Robinson Crusoe. 1987. audio 14.95 o.p. (*0-394-56407-3*); 1986. audio 16.00 o.s.i (*0-394-55727-1*) Random Hse. Audio Publishing Group. (RH Audio).

—Robinson Crusoe. Ross, Angus, ed. & intro. by. 1988. (A - Z Activity Bks.). 3.99 o.s.i (*0-517-38590-2*) Random Hse. Value Publishing.

—Robinson Crusoe, unabr. ed. 1991. audio 78.00 (*1-55690-447-9*, 91407E) Recorded Bks., LLC.

—Robinson Crusoe. (Literary Classics Ser.). 1995. 288p. text 5.98 o.p. (*1-56138-652-9*); 1991. (Illus.). 370p. text 12.98 o.p. (*0-89471-997-1*) Running Pr. Bk. Pubs. (Courage Bks.).

—Robinson Crusoe. E-Book 5.00 (*0-7410-0473-9*) SoftBook Pr.

—Robinson Crusoe. unabr. ed. 2003. audio 19.99 (*1-59335-195-X*, 30291) Soulmate Audio Bks., Inc.

—Robinson Crusoe. 1986. audio; audio 10.95 Spoken Arts, Inc.

—Robinson Crusoe. l.t. ed. 2002. (Perennial Bestsellers Ser.). 482p. 28.95 (*0-7862-4564-6*) Thorndike Pr.

—Robinson Crusoe. 1999. (Signature Classics Ser.). (Illus.). xv, 492p. 24.95 (*1-58279-034-5*); 29.95 (*1-58279-046-9*) Trident Pr. International.

—Robinson Crusoe. 1981. 12.00 (*0-606-08465-7*) Turtleback Bks.

—Robinson Crusoe. Man, John, ed. 1994. 336p. pap. 4.50 o.p. (*0-460-87439-X*, Everyman's Classic Library in Paperback) Tuttle Publishing.

—Robinson Crusoe. 2001. 300p. pap. 14.95 (*1-57002-147-3*) University Publishing Hse., Inc.

—Robinson Crusoe. (ACE.). pap. 9.95 (*0-14-043597-2*); 1996. audio 10.95 o.s.i (*0-14-086179-3*, Penguin AudioBooks) Viking Penguin.

—Robinson Crusoe. 1997. (Classics Library). 272p. pap. 3.95 (*1-85326-045-2*, 0452WW) Wordsworth Editions, Ltd. GBR. *Dist:* Combined Publishing.

—Robinson Crusoe: An Authoritative Text, Backgrounds & Sources, Criticism. Shinagel, Michael, ed. 2nd ed. 1993. (Critical Editions Ser.). (C). pap. text (*0-393-96452-3*) Norton, W. W. & Co., Inc.

—Robinson Crusoe: Extracts from His Journal. abr. ed. 1989. (gr. 4-6). audio 9.95 o.p. (*1-55994-061-1*, CPN 1461, Caedmon) HarperTrade.

—Robinson Crusoe: Illustrated Christian Classics. 1996. 160p. pap. text 1.99 o.p. (*1-55748-902-5*) Barbour Publishing, Inc.

—Robinson Crusoe: Movie Tie-In Art. 1996. mass mkt. 4.99 (*0-8125-5763-8*, Tor Bks.) Doherty, Tom Assocs., LLC.

—Robinson Crusoe: Tie-In Art. 1996. mass mkt. 4.99 (*0-8125-5736-0*, Tor Bks.) Doherty, Tom Assocs., LLC.

—Robinson Crusoe Level 4. 1999. (Focus on the Family Great Stories Ser.).Tr. of Robinson Crusoe. 360p. pap. 8.99 o.p. (*1-56179-743-X*) Focus on the Family Publishing.

—Robinson Crusoe Level 4. 2001. Tr. of Robinson Crusoe. (SPA.). (*84-305-2198-4*) Lectorum Pubns., Inc.

—Robinson Crusoe & Other Writings. Sutherland, James, ed. 1977. (Gotham Library Ser.). 416p. pap. 12.50 o.p. (*0-8147-7785-6*) New York Univ. Pr.

—Robinson Crusoe & The Further Adventures of Robinson Crusoe. 1968. 320p. mass mkt. 2.95 o.s.i (*0-671-47227-5*, Pocket) Simon & Schuster.

—Robinson Crusoe Readalong. 1994. (Illustrated Classics Collection). 64p. pap. 13.50 o.p. incl. audio (*1-56103-605-6*); pap. 14.95 incl. audio (*0-7854-0770-7*, 40517) American Guidance Service, Inc.

—Serious Reflections During the Life & Surprising Adventures of Robinson Crusoe, with His Vision of the Angelic World. (Illus.). reprint ed. 32.50 (*0-404-07913-X*) AMS Pr., Inc.

Defoe, Daniel & Conrad, Joseph. Robinson Crusoe. 1982. (Bantam Classics Ser.). 288p. mass mkt. 5.95 (*0-553-21373-3*, Bantam Classics) Bantam Bks.

Defoe, Daniel & Richetti, John J. Robinson Crusoe. 2003. 288p. pap. 8.00 (*0-14-143982-3*, Penguin Classics) Viking Penguin.

Odell, Eric. Robinson Crusoe's Return. Reginald, R. & Menville, Douglas A., eds. 1976. (Supernatural & Occult Fiction Ser.). reprint ed. lib. bdg. 18.95 (*0-405-08158-8*) Ayer Co. Pubs., Inc.

**CSEJTHE, CHRISTOPHER (FICTITIOUS CHARACTER)—FICTION**

Simmons, William Mark. One Foot in the Grave. 1996. 352p. pap. 5.99 (*0-671-87721-6*) Baen Bks.

**CTHULHU (FICTITIOUS CHARACTER)—FICTION**

Bond, Jonathan. Shadowrun Vol. 34: Terminus Report, 34. 1999. (Shadowrun Ser.: Vol. 34). 272p. mass mkt. 5.99 o.s.i (*0-451-45704-8*, ROC) NAL.

Derleth, August. The Quest for Cthulhu. 2000. 448p. pap. 12.95 (*0-7867-0752-6*, Carroll & Graf Pubs.) Avalon Publishing Group.

FASA Corporation Staff. Corporate Download. 1999. (Shadowrun Ser.). 144p. pap. 18.00 (*1-55560-362-9*, 03629F) FASA Corp.

Kenson, Stephen. Crossroads. 1999. (Shadowrun Ser.: Vol. 36). 288p. mass mkt. 5.99 o.s.i (*0-451-45740-4*) NAL.

—Ragnarock. 2000. (Shadowrun Ser.: Vol. 38). 288p. mass mkt. 5.99 o.s.i (*0-451-45774-9*, ROC) NAL.

—Technobabel, Vol. 31. 1998. (Shadowrun Ser.). mass mkt. 5.99 o.s.i (*0-451-45699-8*, ROC) NAL.

Lovecraft, H. P. Call of Cthulhu & Other Weird Stories. Joshi, S. T., ed. 1999. (Twentieth Century Classics Ser.). 304p. 12.95 (*0-14-118234-2*, Penguin Classics) Viking Penguin.

—Tales of the Cthulhu Mythos. 1975. Vol. 1. mass mkt. 1.50 o.s.i (*0-345-24687-X*); Vol. 2. o.p. (*0-345-24688-8*) Ballantine Bks.

Lovecraft, H. P., et al. Innsmouth Cycle: The Taint of the Deep Ones in 13 Tales. Price, Robert M., ed. 1998. (Maverick Guide Ser.). 240p. pap. 12.95 o.p. (*1-56882-113-1*, Chaosium Fiction Series) Chaosium, Inc.

—Tales of the Cthulhu Mythos. 1990. (Illus.). 525p. 26.95 (*0-87054-159-5*) Arkham Hse. Pubs.

—Tales of the Cthulhu Mythos. 1998. 480p. pap. 13.95 (*0-345-42204-X*, Del Rey) Ballantine Bks.

Price, Robert. Tsathoggua Cycle. 2004. (Cthulhu Cycle Bks.). pap. text 14.95 (*1-56882-131-X*) Chaosium, Inc.

Pulver, Joseph S., Sr. Nightmare's Disciple: The Stars Are Right... For Murder! 1999. (Call of Cthulhu Fiction Ser.). 396p. pap. 14.95 (*1-56882-118-2*, Chaosium Fiction Series) Chaosium, Inc.

Smedman, Lisa. Blood Sport. 1998. (Shadowrun Ser.: No. 29). 288p. mass mkt. 5.99 o.s.i (*0-451-45625-4*, ROC) NAL.

—Psychotrope. 1998. (Shadowrun Ser.: Vol. 33). 288p. mass mkt. 5.99 o.s.i (*0-451-45708-0*, ROC) NAL.

Stackpole, Michael A. The Wolf & the Raven. 1998. (Shadowrun Ser.: Vol. 32). 288p. mass mkt. 5.99 o.s.i (*0-451-45995-4*, ROC) NAL.

Tierney, Richard L. Scroll of Thoth: Tales of Simon Magus & the Great Old Ones. Price, Robert M., ed. 1997. (Maverick Guide Ser.). 400p. pap. 12.95 o.p. (*1-56882-105-0*, Chaosium Fiction Series) Chaosium, Inc.

Turner, Jim, ed. Cthulhu 2000. 1999. 416p. pap. 13.95 (*0-345-42203-1*) Ballantine Bks.

CUDDY, JOHN (FICTITIOUS CHARACTER)—FICTION

Healy, Jeremiah. Act of God. Chelius, Jane, ed. 1995. 336p. mass mkt. 5.50 (*0-671-79559-7*, Pocket); 1994. 352p. 20.00 (*0-671-79558-9*, Atria) Simon & Schuster.
—Blunt Darts. l.t. ed. 1985. lib. bdg. 16.95 o.p. (*0-89340-918-9*, 482) BBC Audiobooks America.
—Blunt Darts. Chelius, Jane, ed. 1991. 192p. reprint ed. mass mkt. 5.50 (*0-671-73742-2*, Pocket) Simon & Schuster.
—Blunt Darts. 1984. 192p. 12.95 o.s.i (*0-8027-5570-4*) Walker & Co.
—Blunt Darts. 1986. 192p. mass mkt. 3.50 o.s.i (*0-445-20210-6*) Warner Bks., Inc.
—Foursome. 1993. 352p. 20.00 (*0-671-79556-2*, Atria) Simon & Schuster.
—Foursome. Chelius, Jane, ed. 1994. 352p. reprint ed. mass mkt. 5.99 (*0-671-79557-0*, Pocket) Simon & Schuster.
—Invasion of Privacy. l.t. ed. 1997. (Large Print Book Ser.). pap. 23.95 (*1-56895-484-0*, Wheeler Publishing, Inc.) Gale Group.
—Invasion of Privacy. (John Francis Cuddy Mystery Ser.). 1997. 320p. pap. 5.99 (*0-671-89874-4*, Pocket); 1996. 352p. 21.00 o.p. (*0-671-89876-0*, Atria) Simon & Schuster.
—The Only Good Lawyer. (John Francis Cuddy Mystery Ser.). 1998. 304p. 23.00 o.s.i (*0-671-00953-2*, Atria); 1999. (Illus.). 400p. reprint ed. pap. 6.99 (*0-671-00954-0*, Pocket) Simon & Schuster.
—Rescue. 1996. 384p. pap. 5.99 (*0-671-89875-2*, Pocket) Simon & Schuster.
—Rescue. Chelius, Jane, ed. 1995. 368p. 20.00 o.p. (*0-671-89877-9*, Atria) Simon & Schuster.
—Right to Die. Chelius, Jane, ed. 1991. 256p. 18.95 o.p. (*0-671-70809-0*, Atria); 1992. 288p. reprint ed. mass mkt. 5.99 (*0-671-70810-4*, Pocket) Simon & Schuster.
—Shallow Graves. Chelius, Jane, ed. 1992. 288p. 19.00 (*0-671-70811-2*, Atria) Simon & Schuster.
—Shallow Graves. 1993. 288p. reprint ed. mass mkt. 5.99 (*0-671-70812-0*, Pocket) Simon & Schuster.
—So Like Sleep. 1987. 256p. 15.95 o.p. (*0-06-015693-7*) HarperTrade.
—So Like Sleep. 1991. mass mkt. 4.50 (*0-671-74328-7*, Pocket) Simon & Schuster.
—Spiral: A John Frances Cuddy Mystery. (John Francis Cuddy Mystery Ser.). 1999. 368p. 23.00 o.s.i (*0-671-00955-9*, Atria); 2000. 400p. reprint ed. pap. 6.99 (*0-671-00956-7*, Pocket) Simon & Schuster.
—The Staked Goat. 1986. 224p. 14.95 o.p. (*0-06-015515-9*) HarperTrade.
—The Staked Goat. 1991. 320p. mass mkt. 5.99 (*0-671-74284-1*, Pocket) Simon & Schuster.
—Swan Dive. 1991. mass mkt. 5.99 (*0-671-74329-5*); 1989. mass mkt. 3.95 (*0-671-67185-5*) Simon & Schuster. (Pocket).
—Swan Dive: A Novel of Suspense. 1988. 224p. 16.95 o.p. (*0-06-015921-9*) HarperTrade.
—Yesterday's News: A Novel of Suspense. l.t. ed. 1990. 19.95 o.p. (*0-7927-0586-6*, C0581); pap. 17.95 o.p. (*0-7927-0587-4*) BBC Audiobooks America.
—Yesterday's News: A Novel of Suspense. 1989. 16.95 o.p. (*0-06-015922-7*) HarperTrade.
—Yesterday's News: A Novel of Suspense. Chelius, Jane, ed. 1990. 256p. reprint ed. mass mkt. 5.50 (*0-671-69584-3*, Pocket) Simon & Schuster.

CULLEN, JOE (FICTITIOUS CHARACTER)—FICTION

Oster, Jerry. Fixin' to Die. 1992. 320p. mass mkt. 4.99 o.s.i (*0-553-29908-5*) Bantam Bks.
—Internal Affairs. 1990. 320p. reprint ed. mass mkt. 4.50 o.s.i (*0-553-28676-5*) Bantam Bks.

CULLINANE, JASON (FICTITIOUS CHARACTER)—FICTION

Rosenberg, Joel. The Heir Apparent. 1987. (Guardians of the Flame Ser.: No. 4). 256p. mass mkt. 3.50 o.p. (*0-451-14820-7*, Signet Bks.); 320p. mass mkt. 4.99 o.s.i (*0-451-16212-9*, ROC) NAL.
—The Warrior Lives: A Guardians of the Flame Novel. (Guardians of the Flame Ser.: No. 5). 1990. 272p. mass mkt. 4.99 o.s.i (*0-451-45001-9*, ROC); 1988. 288p. 17.95 o.p. (*0-453-00628-0*) NAL.
—The Warrior Lives: A Guardians of the Flame Novel. 1992. 1.99 o.p. (*0-517-08010-9*) Random Hse. Value Publishing.

CULLINANE, KARL (FICTITIOUS CHARACTER)—FICTION

Rosenberg, Joel. The Silver Crown. 1985. (Guardians of the Flame Ser.). mass mkt. 3.50 o.p. (*0-451-14947-5*); (Guardians of the Flame Ser.). mass mkt. 2.95 o.p. (*0-451-13531-8*); (Book of Guardians of the Flame Ser.: No. 3). 304p. mass mkt. 4.99 o.s.i (*0-451-15983-7*) NAL. (ROC).
—The Sleeping Dragon. (Guardians of the Flame Ser.). 1993. 256p. mass mkt. 4.99 o.s.i (*0-451-45350-6*, ROC); 1986. 256p. mass mkt. 3.50 o.p. (*0-451-14833-9*, Signet Bks.); 1986. 256p. mass mkt. 3.95 o.p. (*0-451-16213-7*, ROC); 1983. mass mkt. 2.95 o.p. (*0-451-12574-6*, ROC) NAL.
—The Sword & the Chain. (Guardians of the Flame Ser.). 1987. mass mkt. 3.50 o.p. (*0-451-14946-7*); 1987. 256p. mass mkt. 3.95 o.p. (*0-451-15982-9*); 1984. mass mkt. 2.95 o.p. (*0-451-12883-4*); 1984. 256p. mass mkt. 4.99 o.s.i (*0-451-45351-4*) NAL. (ROC).

CULVER, HARRY (FICTITIOUS CHARACTER)—FICTION

Goddard, Kenneth M. Cheater. 1997. 542p. mass mkt. 6.99 (*0-8125-5388-8*, Tor Bks.); 1996. 416p. 24.95 o.p. (*0-312-85945-7*, Forge Bks.) Doherty, Tom Assocs., LLC.
—Digger. 1991. 448p. mass mkt. 4.95 o.s.i (*0-553-28982-9*) Bantam Bks.

CUMMINGS, KRISS (FICTITIOUS CHARACTER)—FICTION

Himes, Chester B. End of a Primitive. 1997. 220p. pap. 12.00 (*0-393-31540-1*) Norton, W. W. & Co., Inc.

CUNEEN, MATT (FICTITIOUS CHARACTER)—FICTION

Armstrong, Charlotte. Dream of Fair Woman. 1992. 256p. mass mkt. 3.99 o.s.i (*0-8217-3964-6*, Zebra Bks.) Kensington Publishing Corp.

CUNNINGHAM, JOHN (FICTITIOUS CHARACTER)—FICTION

Hammond, Gerald. Bloodlines. 1997. 224p. 20.95 o.p. (*0-312-18052-7*, Saint Martin's Minotaur) St. Martin's Pr.
—Bloodlines. l.t. ed. 1998. (General Ser.). 256p. pap. 23.95 (*0-7862-1497-X*) Thorndike Pr.
—The Curse of the Cockers. unabr. ed. 1999. audio 44.95 (*0-7531-0479-2*, 981009) ISIS Audio Bks. GBR. *Dist:* Ulverscroft Large Print Bks., Ltd.
—The Curse of the Cockers. 1994. 192p. 18.95 o.p. (*0-312-10446-4*, Saint Martin's Minotaur) St. Martin's Pr.
—Dog in the Dark. 1992. 1.99 o.p. (*0-517-08390-6*) Random Hse. Value Publishing.
—Dog in the Dark. 1990. 192p. 14.95 o.p. (*0-312-03819-4*, Saint Martin's Minotaur) St. Martin's Pr.
—Dog in the Dark. l.t. ed. 1990. (Ulverscroft Large Print Ser.). 29.99 o.p. (*0-7089-2285-6*, Ulverscroft) Thorpe, F. A. Pubs. GBR. *Dist:* Ulverscroft Large Print Bks., Ltd., Ulverscroft Large Print Canada, Ltd.
—Doghouse. 1992. 192p. 16.95 o.p. (*0-312-07733-5*, Saint Martin's Minotaur) St. Martin's Pr.
—Give a Dog a Name. 1993. 144p. 16.95 o.p. (*0-312-09297-0*, Saint Martin's Minotaur) St. Martin's Pr.
—Mad Dogs & Scotsmen. l.t. ed. 1996. 20.95 (*0-7838-1890-4*, Macmillan Reference USA) Gale Group.
—Mad Dogs & Scotsmen. 1996. 192p. 20.95 (*0-312-14818-6*, Saint Martin's Minotaur) St. Martin's Pr.
—Sting in the Tail. 1995. 160p. 19.95 o.p. (*0-312-13189-5*, Saint Martin's Minotaur) St. Martin's Pr.
—Sting in the Tail. l.t. ed. 1996. (Ulverscroft Large Print Ser.). 368p. 29.99 o.p. (*0-7089-3517-6*, Ulverscroft) Thorpe, F. A. Pubs. GBR. *Dist:* Ulverscroft Large Print Bks., Ltd., Ulverscroft Large Print Canada, Ltd.
—Twice Bitten. 1999. 230p. 22.95 (*0-312-24256-5*, Saint Martin's Minotaur) St. Martin's Pr.
—Whose Dog Are You? 1991. 15.95 o.p. (*0-312-05536-6*, Saint Martin's Minotaur) St. Martin's Pr.
—Whose Dog Are You? l.t. ed. 1992. (Ulverscroft Large Print Ser.). 288p. 29.99 o.p. (*0-7089-2575-8*, Ulverscroft) Thorpe, F. A. Pubs. GBR. *Dist:* Ulverscroft Large Print Bks., Ltd., Ulverscroft Large Print Canada, Ltd.

CURRAN, GUY (FICTITIOUS CHARACTER)—FICTION

Rendell, Ruth. Going Wrong. l.t. ed. 1992. pap. 15.95 o.p. (*0-7927-0822-9*); 302p. 19.95 o.p. (*0-7927-0821-0*, E0016) BBC Audiobooks America.
—Going Wrong. 1991. 272p. mass mkt. 6.99 (*0-7704-2435-X*) Bantam Bks.
—Going Wrong. unabr. collector's ed. 1991. audio 48.00 (*0-7366-1920-8*, 2744) Books on Tape, Inc.
—Going Wrong. 1990. 256p. 24.95 o.p. (*0-385-25281-1*) Doubleday Publishing.
—Going Wrong. 1990. 304p. 18.95 o.p. (*0-89296-389-1*) Mysterious Pr.
—Going Wrong. 1993. 3.99 o.p. (*0-517-09872-5*) Random Hse. Value Publishing.
—Going Wrong. 1991. mass mkt. 4.99 o.s.i (*0-446-40028-9*) Warner Bks., Inc.

CURTIS, JOE (FICTITIOUS CHARACTER)—FICTION

Holden, Craig. The Last Sanctuary. abr. ed. 1996. pap. 16.95 incl. audio (*1-55927-383-6*) Audio Renaissance.
—The Last Sanctuary. 1997. 448p. mass mkt. 6.50 o.s.i (*0-440-21733-4*) Dell Publishing.
—The Last Sanctuary, unabr. ed. audio 85.00 (*0-7887-0525-3*, 94720E7) Recorded Bks., LLC.

CUTLER FAMILY (FICTITIOUS CHARACTERS)—FICTION

Andrews, V. C. Darkest Hour. l.t. ed. 471p. 1994. lib. bdg. 18.95 (*0-8161-5876-2*); 1993. lib. bdg. 23.95 (*0-8161-5875-4*) Gale Group. (Macmillan Reference USA).
—Darkest Hour, Vol. 4. Marrow, Linda, ed. 1993. 400p. 22.00 (*0-671-75933-7*, Atria); mass mkt. 7.99 (*0-671-75932-9*, Pocket) Simon & Schuster.
—Darkest Hour. 1993. 14.04 (*0-606-05225-9*) Turtleback Bks.
—Dawn. unabr. ed. 1991. (Cutler Ser.). audio 64.00 (*0-7366-1944-5*, 2765) Books on Tape, Inc.
—Dawn. l.t. ed. 1991. (General Ser.). 472p. pap. 17.95 (*0-8161-5186-5*); lib. bdg. 20.95 (*0-8161-5184-9*) Gale Group. (Macmillan Reference USA).
—Dawn. 2003. audio 76.95 (*0-7531-1772-X*); audio compact disk 89.95 (*0-7531-2231-6*) ISIS Audio Bks. GBR. *Dist:* Ulverscroft Large Print Bks., Ltd.
—Dawn. 1990. 19.95 (*0-671-67067-0*, Atria) Simon & Schuster.
—Dawn. Marrow, Linda, ed. 1990. (Cutler Ser.). 416p. mass mkt. 7.99 (*0-671-67068-9*, Pocket) Simon & Schuster.
—Dawn. 1990. 14.04 (*0-606-04649-6*) Turtleback Bks.
—Midnight Whispers. unabr. ed. 1993. audio 72.00 (*0-7366-2532-1*, 3284) Books on Tape, Inc.
—Midnight Whispers. l.t. ed. 1993. (G. K. Hall Large Print Book Ser.). 515p. 19.95 o.p. (*0-8161-5656-5*); lib. bdg. 23.95 (*0-8161-5655-7*) Gale Group. (Macmillan Reference USA).
—Midnight Whispers. Marrow, Linda, ed. 1992. 448p. (Midnight Whispers Ser.: Vol. 5). mass mkt. 7.99 (*0-671-69516-9*, Pocket);Vol. 5. 22.00 (*0-671-69517-7*, Atria) Simon & Schuster.
—Midnight Whispers. 1992. 14.04 (*0-606-02201-5*) Turtleback Bks.
—Secrets of the Morning. unabr. ed. 1993. (Cutler Ser.). audio 64.00 (*0-7366-2356-6*, 3131) Books on Tape, Inc.
—Secrets of the Morning. l.t. ed. 1992. (General Ser.). 487p. pap. 17.95 (*0-8161-5386-8*); lib. bdg. 20.95 (*0-8161-5385-X*) Gale Group. (Macmillan Reference USA).
—Secrets of the Morning. unabr. ed. 2003. audio 84.95 (*0-7531-1773-8*) ISIS Audio Bks. GBR. *Dist:* Ulverscroft Large Print Bks., Ltd.
—Secrets of the Morning. Marrow, Linda, ed. 1991. (Cutler Ser.). 416p. mass mkt. 7.99 (*0-671-69512-6*, Pocket);Vol. 2. 384p. 21.95 (*0-671-69513-4*, Atria) Simon & Schuster.
—Secrets of the Morning. 1991. 14.04 (*0-606-05012-4*) Turtleback Bks.
—Twilight's Child. unabr. ed. 1993. (Dawn Ser.: Vol. 3). audio 72.00 (*0-7366-2406-6*, 3175) Books on Tape, Inc.
—Twilight's Child. l.t. ed. 1993. (General Ser.). 555p. pap. 17.95 (*0-8161-5525-9*); lib. bdg. 20.95 (*0-8161-5524-0*) Gale Group. (Macmillan Reference USA).
—Twilight's Child. Marrow, Linda, ed. 1992. 416p. (Twilight's Child Ser.: Vol. 3). mass mkt. 7.99 (*0-671-69514-2*, Pocket);Vol. 3. 22.00 o.p. (*0-671-69515-0*, Atria) Simon & Schuster.
—Twilight's Child. 1992. 14.04 (*0-606-00810-1*) Turtleback Bks.

CYNSTER BROTHERS (FICTITIOUS CHARACTERS)—FICTION

Laurens, Stephanie. All about Love. l.t. ed. 2001. (G. K. Hall Romance Ser.). 407p. 29.95 (*0-7838-9497-X*, Macmillan Reference USA) Gale Group.
—All about Love. 2001. E-Book 6.99 (*0-06-050190-1*); E-Book 6.99 (*0-06-050189-8*); E-Book 6.99 (*0-06-050187-1*); E-Book 6.99 (*0-06-050188-X*) HarperCollins General Bks. Group. (PerfectBound).
—All about Love. 2001. 416p. mass mkt. 7.50 (*0-380-81201-0*, Avon Bks.) Morrow/Avon.
—Devil's Bride. 2001. E-Book 6.99 (*0-06-009514-8*); E-Book 6.99 (*0-06-009515-6*) HarperCollins General Bks. Group. (PerfectBound).
—The Devil's Bride. 1998. (Avon Romantic Treasure Ser.). 400p. mass mkt. 7.50 (*0-380-79456-X*, Avon Bks.) Morrow/Avon.
—The Perfect Lover. 2003. 368p. 22.95 (*0-06-050571-0*) Morrow/Avon.
—The Promise in a Kiss. 2001. E-Book 13.95 (*0-06-008695-5*); E-Book 13.95 (*0-06-008697-1*) HarperCollins General Bks. Group. (PerfectBound).
—The Promise in a Kiss. 2002. 400p. mass mkt. 7.50 (*0-06-103175-5*); E-Book 13.95 (*0-06-009511-3*) HarperCollins Pubs.
—The Promise in a Kiss. 2001. (Illus.). 304p. 18.00 (*0-06-018888-X*, Morrow, William & Co.) Morrow/Avon.
—A Rake's Vow. 2001. E-Book 6.99 (*0-06-009508-3*); E-Book 6.99 (*0-06-009510-5*) HarperCollins General Bks. Group. (PerfectBound).
—A Rake's Vow. 1998. (Avon Romantic Treasure Ser.). 384p. mass mkt. 7.50 (*0-380-79457-8*, Avon Bks.) Morrow/Avon.
—A Rogue's Proposal. 2001. E-Book 6.99 (*0-06-009507-5*); E-Book 6.99 (*0-06-009505-9*); E-Book 6.99 (*0-06-009520-2*) HarperCollins General Bks. Group. (PerfectBound).
—A Rogue's Proposal. 1999. (Avon Romance Ser.). 416p. mass mkt. 7.50 (*0-380-80569-3*, Avon Bks.) Morrow/Avon.
—Scandal's Bride. 2001. E-Book 6.99 (*0-06-009504-0*); E-Book 6.99 (*0-06-009501-6*); E-Book 6.99 (*0-06-009503-2*) HarperCollins General Bks. Group. (PerfectBound).
—Scandal's Bride. 1999. (Avon Historical Romance Ser.). 416p. mass mkt. 7.50 (*0-380-80568-5*, Avon Bks.) Morrow/Avon.
—A Secret Love. 2001. E-Book 6.99 (*0-06-009499-0*, PerfectBound) HarperCollins General Bks. Group.
—A Secret Love. 2001. E-Book 6.99 (*0-06-009497-4*) HarperCollins Pubs.
—A Secret Love. 2000. (Illus.). 384p. mass mkt. 7.50 (*0-380-80570-7*) Morrow/Avon.

## D

DAHLQUIST, SERENDIPITY (FICTITIOUS CHARACTER)—FICTION

Lochte, Dick. Laughing Dog. 1988. (Leo Bloodworth-Serendipity Dahlquist Mystery Ser.: Bk. 2). 272p. 17.95 o.p. (*0-87795-941-2*, Morrow, William & Co.) Morrow/Avon.
—Laughing Dog. 2001. 240p. pap. 13.95 (*1-890208-79-5*) Poisoned Pen Pr.
—Laughing Dog. 1989. 400p. reprint ed. mass mkt. 3.95 o.s.i (*0-446-35724-3*) Warner Bks., Inc.
—Lucky Dog & Other Tales of Murder. 2000. (Five Star Mystery Ser.). 207p. 20.95 (*0-7862-2688-9*, Five Star) Gale Group.
—Sleeping Dog. 1985. 288p. 15.95 o.p. (*0-87795-738-X*, Morrow, William & Co.) Morrow/Avon.
—Sleeping Dog. 2001. (Missing Mystery Ser.: Vol. 29). 292p. pap. 14.95 (*1-890208-51-5*) Poisoned Pen Pr.
—Sleeping Dog. 1986. 288p. mass mkt. 3.95 o.s.i (*0-446-32661-5*) Warner Bks., Inc.

DAI, DAVID (FICTITIOUS CHARACTER)—FICTION

McHugh, Maureen F. Half the Day Is Night. 1994. 320p. 21.95 o.p. (*0-312-85479-X*, Tor Bks.) Doherty, Tom Assocs., LLC.
—Half the Day is Night. 1996. 320p. mass mkt. 5.99 o.p. (*0-8125-2410-1*, Tor Bks.) Doherty, Tom Assocs., LLC.

DAIMBERT (FICTITIOUS CHARACTER)—FICTION

Brittain, C. Dale. A Bad Spell in Yurt. 1991. 320p. pap. 5.99 (*0-671-72075-9*) Baen Bks.
—Daughter of Magic. 1996. 352p. pap. 5.99 (*0-671-87720-8*) Baen Bks.
—Mage Quest. 1993. 368p. (Orig.). mass mkt. 4.99 o.s.i (*0-671-72169-0*) Baen Bks.
—The Witch & the Cathedral. 1995. 352p. (Orig.). mass mkt. 5.99 o.s.i (*0-671-87661-9*) Baen Bks.
—The Wood Nymph & the Cranky Saint. 1993. 320p. pap. 4.99 (*0-671-72156-9*) Baen Bks.

DAIN, EDDIE (FICTITIOUS CHARACTER)—FICTION

Gores, Joe. Dead Man, set. unabr. ed. 1995. audio 69.95 (*0-7862-9974-6*, CSL 083) BBC Audiobooks America.
—Dead Man. 1993. 272p. 18.95 (*0-89296-541-X*) Mysterious Pr.
—Dead Man. 1994. 272p. mass mkt. 5.50 o.s.i (*0-446-40391-1*) Warner Bks., Inc.

DAKER, JOHN (FICTITIOUS CHARACTER)—FICTION

Moorcock, Michael. The Dragon in the Sword, No. 3. 1987. 272p. mass mkt. 3.50 o.s.i (*0-441-16610-5*) Ace Bks.
—The Dragon in the Sword. 1986. 304p. 16.95 o.p. (*0-441-16609-1*, Diamond Bks.) Berkley Publishing Group.
—The Eternal Champion. 1979. pap. 1.95 o.p. (*0-440-12383-6*) Dell Publishing.
—The Eternal Champion. 1996. (Eternal Champion Ser.: Vol. 1). (Illus.). pap. text 14.99 (*1-56504-191-7*); reprint ed. 19.99 o.p. (*1-56504-176-3*, 12516) White Wolf Publishing, Inc.
—The Silver Warriors. 1986. 2.95 o.s.i (*0-425-09456-1*); 1985. 2.95 o.s.i (*0-425-08078-1*); No. 2. 1986. 224p. 2.95 o.p. (*0-425-10146-0*) Berkley Publishing Group.
—The Silver Warriors. 1977. pap. 1.75 o.p. (*0-440-17994-7*) Dell Publishing.

DAKOTA, BUSH (FICTITIOUS CHARACTER)—FICTION

Dana, Mitchell. Beware the Smiling Stranger. 1977. pap. 1.25 o.p. (*0-380-00830-0*, 30965, Avon Bks.) Morrow/Avon.

**DALGLIESH, ADAM (FICTITIOUS CHARACTER)—FICTION**

James, P. D. The Black Tower. unabr. ed. 1993. audio 72.00 (*0-7366-2509-7*, 3265) Books on Tape, Inc.

—The Black Tower. (Paperback Ser.). 1990. 464p. 13.95 o.p. (*0-8161-4983-6*); 1981. 14.95 o.p. (*0-8161-6789-3*) Gale Group. (Macmillan Reference USA).

—The Black Tower. 2001. 352p. pap. 12.00 (*0-7432-1961-9*, Touchstone) Simon & Schuster.

—The Black Tower. 1990. audio 69.95 o.p. (*0-8161-9622-2*) Thorndike Pr.

—The Black Tower. 1988. 288p. mass mkt. 6.99 o.p. (*0-446-31502-8*) Warner Bks., Inc.

—A Certain Justice: An Adam Dalgliesh Mystery. 2003. 448p. pap. 13.95 (*0-345-42532-4*); 1999. 7.99 (*0-345-91605-0*); 1998. mass mkt. 5.99 (*0-345-42533-2*); 1998. 448p. mass mkt. 7.99 (*0-345-43057-3*); 1998. mass mkt. 6.99 (*0-345-42564-2*, Del Rey) Ballantine Bks.

—A Certain Justice: An Adam Dalgliesh Mystery. unabr. ed. 1998. audio 104.00 (*0-7366-4067-3*, 4578) Books on Tape, Inc.

—A Certain Justice: An Adam Dalgliesh Mystery. unabr. ed. 2000. audio 79.95 (*0-7540-0079-6*, CAB 1502) Chivers Audio Bks. GBR. *Dist:* BBC Audiobooks America.

—A Certain Justice: An Adam Dalgliesh Mystery. 1997. 390p. (*0-571-19164-9*) Faber & Faber, Inc.

—A Certain Justice: An Adam Dalgliesh Mystery. l.t. ed. pap. 25.00 o.p. (*0-7838-8251-3*, Macmillan Reference USA) Gale Group.

—A Certain Justice: An Adam Dalgliesh Mystery. 1997. 364p. 25.00 o.s.i (*0-375-40109-1*) Knopf, Alfred A. Inc.

—A Certain Justice: An Adam Dalgliesh Mystery. unabr. ed. 1997. audio 44.95 (*0-679-46085-3*, 115588, RH Audio) Random Hse. Audio Publishing Group.

—A Certain Justice: An Adam Dalgliesh Mystery. l.t. ed. 1997. 640p. pap. 25.00 (*0-679-77452-1*) Random Hse. Large Print.

—A Certain Justice: An Adam Dalgliesh Mystery. 1999. (Remainder Ser.). 5.99 o.s.i (*0-517-46309-1*) Random Hse. Value Publishing.

—A Certain Justice: An Adam Dalgliesh Mystery. unabr. ed. 1998. (Inspector Dalgliesh Mystery Ser.: Vol. 10). audio 97.00 (*0-7887-1966-1*, 95354E7) Recorded Bks., LLC.

—A Certain Justice: An Adam Dalgliesh Mystery. 2003. E-Book 8.99 (*0-7953-2798-6*) RosettaBooks.

—Cover Her Face. unabr. ed. 1993. audio 56.00 (*0-7366-2330-2*, 3110) Books on Tape, Inc.

—Cover Her Face. unabr. ed. 2000. audio 49.95 (*0-7451-6065-4*, CAB 138) Chivers Audio Bks. GBR. *Dist:* BBC Audiobooks America.

—Cover Her Face. 1979. (General Ser.). lib. bdg. 12.95 o.p. (*0-8161-6793-1*, Macmillan Reference USA) Gale Group.

—Cover Her Face. Barzun, Jacques & Taylor, W. H., eds. 1982. (Crime Fiction 1950-1975 Ser.). 254p. lib. bdg. 18.00 o.p. (*0-8240-4983-7*) Garland Publishing, Inc.

—Cover Her Face. unabr. ed. 1992. (Inspector Dalgliesh Mystery Ser.: Vol. 1). audio 51.00 (*1-55690-676-5*, 92329E7) Recorded Bks., LLC.

—Cover Her Face. 2001. 256p. pap. 12.00 (*0-7432-1957-0*, Touchstone) Simon & Schuster.

—Cover Her Face. 1990. 18.05 (*0-606-22453-X*) Turtleback Bks.

—Cover Her Face. 1989. 256p. mass mkt. 6.99 o.p. (*0-446-31221-5*); 1987. mass mkt. 3.50 (*0-446-31437-4*) Warner Bks., Inc.

—Crime Times Three. 1981. 4.95 o.p. (*0-684-16065-X*); pap. 9.95 o.p. (*0-684-16738-7*) Gale Group. (Macmillan Reference USA).

—Death in Holy Orders. unabr. ed. 2001. audio 49.95 (*0-375-41882-2*, 822, RH Audio) Random Hse. Audio Publishing Group.

—Death in Holy Orders. l.t. ed. 2001. 640p. 25.00 (*0-375-43117-9*) Random Hse. Large Print.

—Death of An Expert Witness. 1978. lib. bdg. 13.95 o.p. (*0-8161-6600-5*, Macmillan Reference USA) Gale Group.

—Death of An Expert Witness. 2003. 496p. mass mkt. (*0-7704-2915-7*) Seal Bks. CAN. *Dist:* Random Hse. of Canada, Ltd.

—Death of An Expert Witness. 2001. 368p. pap. 12.00 (*0-7432-1962-7*, Touchstone) Simon & Schuster.

—Death of An Expert Witness. 1988. 352p. mass mkt. 6.99 o.p. (*0-446-31472-2*) Warner Bks., Inc.

—Death of an Expert Witness. l.t. ed. 1992. (General Ser.). 443p. pap. 18.95 (*0-8161-5575-5*, Macmillan Reference USA) Gale Group.

—Death of An Expert Witness. unabr. ed. 1993. audio 72.00 (*0-7366-2569-0*, 3318) Books on Tape, Inc.

—Death of An Expert Witness. unabr. ed. 2000. audio 59.95 (*0-7451-6066-2*, CAB 311) Chivers Audio Bks. GBR. *Dist:* BBC Audiobooks America.

—Death of An Expert Witness. unabr. ed. 1993. (Inspector Dalgliesh Mystery Ser.: Vol. 6). audio 70.00 (*1-55690-884-9*, 93326E7) Recorded Bks., LLC.

—Devices & Desires. unabr. collector's ed. 1990. audio 96.00 (*0-7366-1819-8*, 2655) Books on Tape, Inc.

—Devices & Desires. l.t. ed. 1990. (General Ser.). 608p. pap. 15.95 o.p. (*0-8161-5045-1*); lib. bdg. 14.95 o.p. (*0-8161-5044-3*) Gale Group. (Macmillan Reference USA).

—Devices & Desires. 2004. 480p. pap. 12.95 (*1-4000-7624-2*, Vintage) Knopf Publishing Group.

—Devices & Desires. 1992. 5.99 o.p. (*0-517-08846-0*); 1991. 4.99 o.p. (*0-517-07898-8*) Random Hse. Value Publishing.

—Devices & Desires. unabr. ed. 1990. (Inspector Dalgliesh Mystery Ser.: Vol. 8). audio 97.00 (*1-55690-141-0*, 90089E7) Recorded Bks., LLC.

—Devices & Desires. 1992. audio 96.95 o.p. (*0-8161-3212-7*, 90089) Thorndike Pr.

—Devices & Desires. 480p. 1991. mass mkt. 7.99 (*0-446-35975-0*); 2002. reprint ed. pap. 13.95 (*0-446-67919-4*) Warner Bks., Inc.

—A Mind to Murder. unabr. ed. 1993. audio 56.00 (*0-7366-2396-5*, 3165) Books on Tape, Inc.

—A Mind to Murder. (General Ser.). 1980. lib. bdg. 12.95 o.p. (*0-8161-3057-4*); 1994. 304p. pap. 17.95 (*0-8161-5645-X*) Gale Group. (Macmillan Reference USA).

—A Mind to Murder. 2001. 256p. pap. 12.00 (*0-7432-1958-9*, Touchstone) Simon & Schuster.

—A Mind to Murder. 1986. audio 49.95 o.s.i (*0-8161-9903-5*) Thorndike Pr.

—A Mind to Murder. 1991. 18.05 (*0-606-22454-8*) Turtleback Bks.

—A Mind to Murder. 1988. 256p. mass mkt. 6.99 o.p. (*0-446-31480-3*); 1987. mass mkt. 3.95 (*0-446-34828-7*); 1985. mass mkt. 3.50 (*0-446-31395-5*) Warner Bks., Inc.

—Murder in Triplicate. 1982. 720p. pap. 12.95 o.p. (*0-684-17646-7*); 1980. 4.95 o.p. (*0-684-16748-4*) Gale Group. (Macmillan Reference USA).

—The Murder Room. unabr. ed. 2003. audio 72.00 (*0-7366-9445-5*); audio compact disk (*0-7366-9606-7*) Books on Tape, Inc.

—The Murder Room. 2003. 432p. 25.95 (*1-4000-4141-4*, Everyman's Library) Knopf Publishing Group.

—The Murder Room. unabr. ed. 2003. audio 39.95 (*0-7393-0670-7*); audio compact disk 44.95 (*0-7393-0756-8*) Random Hse. Audio Publishing Group. (Listening Library).

—The Murder Room. l.t. ed. 2003. 691p. 27.95 (*0-375-43223-X*) Random Hse. Large Print.

—Original Sin. unabr. ed. 1995. audio 120.00 (*0-7366-3044-9*, 3726) Books on Tape, Inc.

—Original Sin. unabr. ed. 2000. 14p. audio compact disk 115.95 (*0-7540-5357-1*, CCD 048) Chivers Audio Bks. GBR. *Dist:* BBC Audiobooks America.

—Original Sin. l.t. ed. 1995. 23.00 o.s.i (*0-679-76033-4*) Random Hse., Inc.

—Original Sin. unabr. ed. audio. 2000. (Inspector Dalgliesh Mystery Ser.: Vol. 9). audio 97.00 (*0-7887-0273-4*, 94484E7) Recorded Bks., LLC.

—Original Sin. 1996. 560p. mass mkt. 7.99 (*0-446-60234-5*); 2002. 512p. reprint ed. pap. 13.95 (*0-446-67922-4*) Warner Bks., Inc.

—P. D. James: Three Complete Novels. 1988. 9.99 o.s.i (*0-517-64111-9*) Random Hse. Value Publishing.

—P. D. James in Murderous Company: Unnatural Causes, An Unsuitable Job for a Woman, The Black Tower. 1988. 9.99 o.s.i (*0-517-65994-8*); 1992. 688p. reprint ed. 13.99 o.s.i (*0-517-07228-9*) Random Hse. Value Publishing.

—Shroud for a Nightingale. unabr. ed. 1993. audio 72.00 (*0-7366-2443-0*, 3208) Books on Tape, Inc.

—Shroud for a Nightingale. unabr. ed. 2000. audio 59.95 (*0-7451-6069-7*, CAB 388) Chivers Audio Bks. GBR. *Dist:* BBC Audiobooks America.

—Shroud for a Nightingale. (Paperback Ser.). 1991. 448p. pap. 15.95 o.p. (*0-8161-5032-X*); 1982. lib. bdg. 14.95 o.p. (*0-8161-6791-5*) Gale Group. (Macmillan Reference USA).

—Shroud for a Nightingale. 2002. (Best Mysteries of All Time Ser.). 310p. (*0-7621-8879-0*, Impress) Scriptorium Pr., The.

—Shroud for a Nightingale. 2001. 368p. pap. 13.00 (*0-7432-1960-0*, Touchstone) Simon & Schuster.

—Shroud for a Nightingale. 1988. 288p. mass mkt. 6.99 o.p. (*0-446-31303-3*) Warner Bks., Inc.

—A Taste for Death. audio 8.95 American Audio Prose Library, Inc.

—A Taste for Death. 2003. 480p. pap. 13.95 (*0-345-46938-0*); 1999. mass mkt. 6.99 (*0-345-42916-8*); 1998. 480p. mass mkt. 7.99 (*0-345-43058-1*) Ballantine Bks.

—A Taste for Death. 1994. audio 64.00 (*0-7366-2704-9*);Pt. 1. audio 64.00 (*0-7366-2703-0*, 3437-A);Pt. 2. audio 64.00 Books on Tape, Inc.

—A Taste for Death. unabr. ed. 2000. audio 79.95 (*0-7451-6063-8*, CAB 547) Chivers Audio Bks. GBR. *Dist:* BBC Audiobooks America.

—A Taste for Death. l.t. ed. 1987. 713p. 20.95 o.p. (*0-8161-4265-3*); 12.95 o.p. (*0-8161-4266-1*) Gale Group. (Macmillan Reference USA).

—A Taste for Death. 1987. 512p. mass mkt. 6.50 (*0-446-32352-7*) Warner Bks., Inc.

—Trilogy of Death. 1984. 976p. 19.95 o.s.i (*0-684-18243-2*, Scribner) Simon & Schuster.

—Unnatural Causes. unabr. ed. 1993. 54.95 incl. audio (*0-7451-6071-9*, CAB 072); 54.95 incl. audio (*0-7451-6071-9*, CAB 072) BBC Audiobooks America.

—Unnatural Causes. unabr. ed. 1992. audio 56.00 (*0-7366-2318-3*, 3098) Books on Tape, Inc.

—Unnatural Causes. l.t. ed. 1993. 340p. pap. 16.95 o.p. (*0-8161-5646-8*, Macmillan Reference USA) Gale Group.

—Unnatural Causes. unabr. ed. 1993. (Inspector Dalgliesh Mystery Ser.: Vol. 3). audio 51.00 (*1-55690-832-6*, 93128E7) Recorded Bks., LLC.

—Unnatural Causes. 2003. 352p. mass mkt. (*0-7704-2912-2*) Seal Bks. CAN. *Dist:* Random Hse. of Canada, Ltd.

—Unnatural Causes. 2001. 272p. pap. 12.00 (*0-7432-1959-7*, Touchstone) Simon & Schuster.

—Unnatural Causes. 2001. 18.05 (*0-606-22455-6*) Turtleback Bks.

—Unnatural Causes. 1988. 256p. mass mkt. 7.50 o.p. (*0-446-31219-3*) Warner Bks., Inc.

**DALLAS, EVE (FICTITIOUS CHARACTER)—FICTION**

Robb, J. D., pseud. Betrayal in Death. 2001. 368p. mass mkt. 7.99 (*0-425-17857-9*) Berkley Publishing Group.

—Betrayal in Death. l.t. ed. 2001. 536p. (*0-7862-3397-4*) Thorndike Pr.

—Ceremony in Death. 1997. 336p. mass mkt. 7.99 (*0-425-15762-8*) Berkley Publishing Group.

—Conspiracy in Death. 1999. 400p. mass mkt. 7.99 (*0-425-16813-1*) Berkley Publishing Group.

—Divided in Death. 2004. 448p. 23.95 (*0-399-15154-0*, Putnam & Grosset) Putnam Publishing Group, The.

—Glory in Death. 1995. 320p. mass mkt. 7.99 (*0-425-15098-4*) Berkley Publishing Group.

—Glory in Death. abr. ed. (In Death Ser.). 2001. audio 53.25 (*1-58788-197-7*, 2444, Library Edition); 2004. audio 29.95 (*1-59355-829-5*, 5452, Brilliance Audio Unabridged); 2004. audio compact disk 33.95 (*1-59355-831-7*, 5454, Brilliance Audio on CD Unabridged) Brilliance Audio.

—Glory in Death. 2004. 320p. reprint ed. 19.95 (*0-399-15158-3*) Putnam Publishing Group, The.

—Glory in Death. 2001. audio compact disk 89.00 (*0-7887-5168-9*, C1330) Recorded Bks., LLC.

—Holiday in Death. 1998. 336p. mass mkt. 7.99 (*0-425-16371-7*) Berkley Publishing Group.

—Imitation in Death. 2003. 352p. mass mkt. 7.99 (*0-425-19158-3*) Berkley Publishing Group.

—Imitation in Death. abr. ed. 2005. (In Death Ser.). audio 12.99 (*1-59086-726-2*, 4317, Brilliance Audio Paperback Audiobooks); 2003. (In Death Series: Vol. 17). audio 24.95 (*1-59086-725-4*, 4316); 2003. (In Death Series: Vol. 17). audio 30.95 (*1-59086-723-8*, 4314, Brilliance Audio Unabridged); 2003. (In Death Series: Vol. 17). audio 87.25 (*1-59086-724-6*, 4315) Brilliance Audio.

—Immortal in Death. 1996. 320p. mass mkt. 7.99 (*0-425-15378-9*) Berkley Publishing Group.

—Immortal in Death. 2004. 288p. reprint ed. 19.95 (*0-399-15159-1*) Putnam Publishing Group, The.

—Immortal in Death. 1996. audio 39.95 (*0-7887-5447-5*, 96126) Recorded Bks., LLC.

—Judgment in Death. 2000. 368p. mass mkt. 7.99 (*0-425-17630-4*) Berkley Publishing Group.

—Judgment in Death. abr. ed. (In Death Ser.). 2005. audio 12.99 (*1-58788-323-6*, 2902, Brilliance Audio Paperback Audiobooks); 2000. audio 24.95 (*1-58788-079-2*, 2327, Nova Audio Bks.); 2000. audio 44.25 (*1-58788-174-8*, 2447, Unabridged Library Editions) Brilliance Audio.

—Judgment in Death. l.t. ed. 2002. (Core Ser.). 472p. pap. 30.95 (*0-7838-9335-3*) Gale Group.

—Judgment in Death. l.t. ed. 2001. (Core Ser.). 472p. 32.95 (*0-7838-9334-5*) Thorndike Pr.

—Loyalty in Death. 1999. 368p. mass mkt. 7.99 (*0-425-17140-X*) Berkley Publishing Group.

—Loyalty in Death. l.t. ed. 2000. (Americana Ser.). 539p. 30.95 (*0-7862-2443-6*) Thorndike Pr.

—Una Muerte Desnuda. 1999. (SPA.). 368p. 19.95 (*84-01-46800-0*) Lectorum Pubns., Inc.

—Naked in Death. 1995. 320p. mass mkt. 7.99 (*0-425-14829-7*) Berkley Publishing Group.

—Naked in Death. abr. ed. (In Death Ser.). 2005. audio 12.99 (*1-58788-350-3*, 2847, Brilliance Audio Paperback Audiobooks); 2000. audio 24.95 (*1-58788-080-6*, 2328, Nova Audio Bks.); 2000. audio 44.25 (*1-58788-195-0*, 2442, Unabridged Library Editions) Brilliance Audio.

—Naked in Death. 2004. 304p. reprint ed. 19.95 (*0-399-15157-5*) Putnam Publishing Group, The.

—Naked in Death. unabr. ed. 2000. audio 70.00 (*0-7887-4049-0*, 96125E7) Recorded Bks., LLC.

—Naked in Death. l.t. ed. 2000. (Americana Ser.). 445p. 29.95 (*0-7862-2415-0*) Thorndike Pr.

—Rapture in Death. 1996. 320p. mass mkt. 7.99 (*0-425-15518-8*) Berkley Publishing Group.

—Reunion in Death. 2002. 384p. mass mkt. 7.99 (*0-425-18397-1*) Berkley Publishing Group.

—Reunion in Death. abr. ed. (In Death Ser.). 2005. audio 12.99 (*1-58788-688-X*, 2983, Brilliance Audio Paperback Audiobooks); 2002. audio 24.95 (*1-58788-687-1*, 2982, Nova Audio Bks.); 2002. audio 78.25 (*1-58788-686-3*, 2981, Unabridged Library Editions); 2002. audio 30.95 (*1-58788-685-5*, 2980, Brilliance Audio Unabridged) Brilliance Audio.

—Reunion in Death. unabr. ed. 2003. (In Death Ser.). audio 19.99 (*1-59335-140-2*, 30236) Soulmate Audio Bks., Inc.

—Vengeance in Death. 1997. 384p. mass mkt. 7.99 (*0-425-16039-4*) Berkley Publishing Group.

—Vengeance in Death. abr. ed. (In Death Ser.). 2005. audio 12.99 (*1-58788-438-0*, 2707, Brilliance Audio Paperback Audiobooks); 2002. audio 62.25 (*1-58788-437-2*, 2706, Library Edition); 2002. audio 24.95 (*1-58788-436-4*, 2705, Nova Audio Bks.) Brilliance Audio.

—Witness in Death. 2000. 368p. mass mkt. 7.99 (*0-425-17363-1*) Berkley Publishing Group.

—Witness in Death. l.t. ed. 2001. 28.95 (*0-7862-2716-8*); 2000. 547p. 30.95 (*0-7862-2715-X*) Thorndike Pr.

Robb, J. D., pseud, et al. Silent Night. 1998. 352p. mass mkt. 7.50 (*0-515-12385-4*, Jove) Berkley Publishing Group.

Roberts, Nora. Remember When. 2004. 512p. mass mkt. 7.99 (*0-425-19547-3*) Berkley Publishing Group.

—Remember When. abr. ed. 2004. audio 12.99 (*1-59355-189-4*, 4799, Brilliance Audio Paperback Audiobooks); 2003. audio 24.95 (*1-59355-186-X*, 4796); 2003. audio 97.25 (*1-59355-185-1*, 4795, Brilliance Audio Unabridged Lib Ed); 2003. audio compact disk 39.95 (*1-59355-187-8*, 4797, Brilliance Audio on CD Unabridged); 2003. audio compact disk 112.25 (*1-59355-188-6*, 4798, Brilliance Audio on CD Unabridged Lib Ed) Brilliance Audio.

Roberts, Nora & Robb, J. D. Remember When. unabr. ed. 2003. audio 36.95 (*1-59355-184-3*, 4794, Brilliance Audio Unabridged) Brilliance Audio.

—Remember When. 2003. 448p. 25.95 (*0-399-15106-0*, Putnam & Grosset) Putnam Publishing Group, The.

—Remember When. l.t. ed. 2004. 544p. pap. 14.95 (*1-59413-022-1*); 2003. 729p. 32.95 (*0-7862-5695-8*) Thorndike Pr. (Large Print Pr.).

**DALRYMPLE, DAISY (FICTITIOUS CHARACTER)—FICTION**

Dunn, Carola. Damsel in Distress: A Daisy Dalrymple Mystery. 2002. (Daisy Dalrymple Mystery Ser.). 256p. mass mkt. 5.99 (*1-57566-754-1*, Kensington Bks.) Kensington Publishing Corp.

—Damsel in Distress: A Daisy Dalrymple Mystery. 1997. (Daisy Dalrymple Mysteries Ser.). 234p. 21.95 o.p. (*0-312-16806-3*, Saint Martin's Minotaur) St. Martin's Pr.

—Dead in the Water. 2002. 256p. mass mkt. 5.99 (*1-57566-756-8*, Kensington Bks.) Kensington Publishing Corp.

—Dead in the Water. 1998. (Daisy Dalrymple Mysteries Ser.). 256p. 22.95 o.p. (*0-312-19181-2*, Saint Martin's Minotaur) St. Martin's Pr.

—Death at Wentwater Court. 2000. (Daisy Dalrymple Mysteries Ser.). (Illus.). 256p. (J). mass mkt. 5.99 (*1-57566-750-9*) Kensington Publishing Corp.

—Death at Wentwater Court. 1994. 240p. 19.95 o.p. (*0-312-11030-8*, Saint Martin's Minotaur) St. Martin's Pr.

—Misletoe & Murder: A Daisy Dalrymple Mystery. 2002. 256p. 23.95 (*0-312-28775-5*, Saint Martin's Minotaur) St. Martin's Pr.

—Murder on the Flying Scotsman. 1996. (Daisy Dalrymple Mysteries Ser.). 240p. 21.95 (*0-312-15175-6*, Saint Martin's Minotaur) St. Martin's Pr.

—Rattle His Bones: A Daisy Dalrymple Mystery. 2003. 256p. mass mkt. 5.99 (*0-7582-0168-0*) Kensington Publishing Corp.

—Rattle His Bones: A Daisy Dalrymple Mystery. 2000. (Daisy Dalrymple Mysteries Ser.). (Illus.). 243p. 22.95 (*0-312-20572-4*, Saint Martin's Minotaur) St. Martin's Pr.

—Rattle His Bones: A Daisy Dalrymple Mystery. l.t. ed. 2000. (Mystery Ser.). (Illus.). 355p. 26.95 (*0-7862-2913-6*) Thorndike Pr.

—Requiem for a Mezzo: A Daisy Dalrymple Mystery. 1996. (Daisy Dalrymple Mysteries Ser.). 240p. 20.95 (*0-312-14036-3*, Saint Martin's Minotaur) St. Martin's Pr.

—Requiem for a Mezzo: A Daisy Dalrymple Mystery. l.t. ed. 1996. 285p. pap. 23.95 (*0-7838-1857-2*) Thorndike Pr.

—Styx & Stones: A Daisy Dalrymple Mystery. 2nd ed. 1999. (Daisy Dalrymple Mysteries Ser.). 240p. 22.95 *(0-312-20592-9*, Saint Martin's Minotaur) St. Martin's Pr.

—To Davy Jones Below: A Daisy Dalrymple Mystery. 2003. mass mkt. 5.99 *(0-7582-0169-9)* Kensington Publishing Corp.

—To Davy Jones Below: A Daisy Dalrymple Mystery. 2001. (Daisy Dalrymple Mysteries Ser.). 256p. 22.95 *(0-312-26669-3*, Saint Martin's Minotaur) St. Martin's Pr.

—The Winter Garden Mystery. l.t. ed. 1995. 326p. 23.95 o.p. *(0-7838-1487-9*, Macmillan Reference USA) Gale Group.

—The Winter Garden Mystery. 2001. (Daisy Dalrymple Mysteries Ser.). 256p. mass mkt. 5.99 *(1-57566-751-7*, Kensington Bks.) Kensington Publishing Corp.

—The Winter Garden Mystery. 1995. (Daisy Dalrymple Mysteries Ser.). 224p. 21.95 o.p. *(0-312-13217-4*, Saint Martin's Minotaur) St. Martin's Pr.

**DALTON, KEVIN (FICTITIOUS CHARACTER)—FICTION**

Pineiro, R. J. Retribution. unabr. ed. 1995. audio 85.95 *(0-7861-0901-7*, 1709) Blackstone Audio Bks., Inc.

—Retribution. 1995. 384p. 23.95 o.p. *(0-312-85940-6*, Forge Bks.); Vol. 1. 1996. (Retribution Ser.: Vol. 1). 530p. mass mkt. 6.99 o.p. *(0-8125-4463-3*, Tor Bks.) Doherty, Tom Assocs., LLC.

**DALTON, PATRICK (FICTITIOUS CHARACTER)—FICTION**

Parkinson, Dan. The Fox & the Faith. 1998. 352p. mass mkt. 4.99 o.s.i *(0-7860-0555-6)*; 1989. 350p. mass mkt. 3.95 o.s.i *(1-55817-204-1)* Kensington Publishing Corp. (Pinnacle Bks.).

—The Fox & the Faith. 1999. (Illus.). 352p. 25.00 *(0-7278-2284-5)* Severn Hse. Pubs., Ltd.

—The Fox & the Faith. l.t. ed. 2000. (Ulverscroft Large Print Ser.). 408p. 31.99 *(0-7089-4185-0*, Ulverscroft) Thorpe, F. A. Pubs. GBR. *Dist:* Ulverscroft Large Print Bks., Ltd., Ulverscroft Large Print Canada, Ltd.

—The Fox & the Flag. 1990. mass mkt. 3.95 o.s.i *(1-55817-349-8*, Pinnacle Bks.) Kensington Publishing Corp.

—The Fox & the Flag. l.t. ed. 2001. (Ulverscroft Large Print Ser.). 512p. 31.99 *(0-7089-4338-1*, Ulverscroft) Thorpe, F. A. Pubs. GBR. *Dist:* Ulverscroft Large Print Bks., Ltd., Ulverscroft Large Print Canada, Ltd.

—The Fox & the Fortune. 1992. mass mkt. 3.99 o.s.i *(1-55817-600-4*, Pinnacle Bks.) Kensington Publishing Corp.

—The Fox & the Fortune. 256p. 26.00 *(0-7278-5628-6)* Severn Hse. Pubs., Ltd.

—The Fox & the Fortune. l.t. ed. 2001. (Ulverscroft Large Print Ser.). 416p. 32.50 *(0-7089-4394-2*, Ulverscroft) Thorpe, F. A. Pubs. GBR. *Dist:* Ulverscroft Large Print Bks., Ltd., Ulverscroft Large Print Canada, Ltd.

—The Fox & the Fury. 1989. mass mkt. 3.95 o.s.i *(1-55817-291-2*, Pinnacle Bks.) Kensington Publishing Corp.

**DALZIEL, ANDREW (FICTITIOUS CHARACTER)—FICTION**

Hill, Reginald. An Advancement of Learning. unabr. ed. 2000. (Dalziel & Pascoe Mystery Ser.). audio 59.95 *(0-7451-6688-1*, CAB 1304) Chivers Audio Bks. GBR. *Dist:* BBC Audiobooks America.

—An Advancement of Learning. 1985. 254p. 14.95 o.s.i *(0-88150-053-4)* Countryman Pr.

—An Advancement of Learning. 1987. 256p. mass mkt. 4.50 o.p. *(0-451-14656-5*, Signet Bks.) NAL.

—An April Shroud. 1986. 256p. 15.95 o.p. *(0-88150-065-8)* Countryman Pr.

—An April Shroud. 1987. mass mkt. 3.50 o.p. *(0-451-14783-9*, Signet Bks.) NAL.

—An April Shroud. l.t. ed. 1999. (Charnwood Large Print Ser.). 320p. 31.99 o.p. *(0-7089-9084-3*, Ulverscroft) Thorpe, F. A. Pubs. GBR. *Dist:* Ulverscroft Large Print Bks., Ltd., Ulverscroft Large Print Canada, Ltd.

—Arms & the Women. (Dalziel & Pascoe Mystery Ser.). 2000. 512p. mass mkt. 6.99 *(0-440-22594-9)*; 1999. 416p. 23.95 o.s.i *(0-385-33279-3*, Delacorte Pr.) Dell Publishing.

—Asking for the Moon. 1998. (Dalziel & Pascoe Mystery Ser.). 336p. reprint ed. mass mkt. 6.50 *(0-440-22583-3)* Doubleday Publishing.

—Asking for the Moon. l.t. ed. 1997. (Charnwood Large Print Ser.). 384p. 29.99 o.p. *(0-7089-8974-8*, Ulverscroft) Thorpe, F. A. Pubs. GBR. *Dist:* Ulverscroft Large Print Bks., Ltd., Ulverscroft Large Print Canada, Ltd.

—Bones & Silence. 1991. (Dalziel & Pascoe Mystery Ser.). 448p. mass mkt. 6.99 *(0-440-20935-8)* Dell Publishing.

—Bones & Silence. l.t. ed. 1992. (Mystery Ser.). 528p. 29.99 o.p. *(0-7089-8673-0*, Ulverscroft) Thorpe, F. A. Pubs. GBR. *Dist:* Ulverscroft Large Print Bks., Ltd., Ulverscroft Large Print Canada, Ltd.

—Child's Play. l.t. ed. 1988. (Ulverscroft Large Print Ser.). 560p. 29.99 o.p. *(0-7089-1912-X*, Ulverscroft) Thorpe, F. A. Pubs. GBR. *Dist:* Ulverscroft Large Print Bks., Ltd., Ulverscroft Large Print Canada, Ltd.

—Child's Play. 1988. mass mkt. 3.95 *(0-446-34533-4)* Warner Bks., Inc.

—A Clubbable Woman. unabr. ed. 2000. (Dalziel & Pascoe Mystery Ser.). audio 59.95 *(0-7451-6613-X*, CAB 1230) Chivers Audio Bks. GBR. *Dist:* BBC Audiobooks America.

—A Clubbable Woman. 1984. 256p. reprint ed. 12.95 o.p. *(0-88150-032-1)* Countryman Pr.

—A Clubbable Woman. 1985. mass mkt. 3.50 o.p. *(0-451-15516-5)*; mass mkt. 2.95 o.p. *(0-451-13810-4)* NAL. (Signet Bks.).

—Deadheads, Set unabr. ed. 1999. (Superintendent Daiziel & Sergeant Pascoe Mysteries Ser.). audio 69.95 BBC Audiobooks America.

—Deadheads. 1985. mass mkt. 3.95 o.p. *(0-451-15895-4*, Signet Bks.); mass mkt. 3.50 o.p. *(0-451-13559-8*, ROC) NAL.

—Deadheads. l.t. ed. 1985. 512p. o.p. *(0-7089-1312-1*, Ulverscroft) Thorpe, F. A. Pubs.

—Deadheads: A Dalziel & Pascoe Mystery, Set unabr. ed. 1999. audio 69.95 *(0-7540-0286-1*, CAB 1709) BBC Audiobooks America.

—Death's Jest-Book. 2003. 512p. *(0-385-65963-6)* Doubleday Canada, Ltd. CAN. *Dist:* Random Hse., Inc.

—Death's Jest-Book. 2004. 704p. mass mkt. *(0-7704-2924-6)* Seal Bks. CAN. *Dist:* Random Hse. of Canada, Ltd.

—Death's Jest Book. 2003. 576p. 25.95 *(0-06-052805-2)* HarperCollins Pubs.

—Dialogues of the Dead. 2002. mass mkt. 6.99 *(0-440-23728-9)* Dell Publishing.

—Dialogues of the Dead. 2003. 528p. mass mkt. 7.50 *(0-06-052809-5)* HarperCollins Pubs.

—Dialogues of the Dead. 2003. 624p. mass mkt. *(0-7704-2892-4)* Seal Bks. CAN. *Dist:* Random Hse. of Canada, Ltd.

—Exit Lines. 1986. mass mkt. 3.50 o.p. *(0-451-14252-7*, Signet Bks.); 256p. mass mkt. 3.99 o.s.i *(0-451-16166-1)* NAL.

—Exit Lines. l.t. ed. 1985. (Charnwood Large Print Ser.). 400p. 29.99 o.p. *(0-7089-8266-2*, Ulverscroft) Thorpe, F. A. Pubs. GBR. *Dist:* Ulverscroft Large Print Bks., Ltd., Ulverscroft Large Print Canada, Ltd.

—A Killing Kindness. 1989. 269p. reprint ed. pap. 5.95 o.s.i *(1-55882-003-5*, Library of Crime Classics) International Polygonics, Ltd.

—A Killing Kindness. 1981. 10.95 o.p. *(0-394-51910-8*, Pantheon) Knopf Publishing Group.

—A Killing Kindness: A Dalziel & Pascoe Mystery, Set. unabr. ed. 1999. audio 69.95 *(0-7540-0382-5*, CAB1805) BBC Audiobooks America.

—On Beulah Height. 1999. (Dalziel & Pascoe Mystery Ser.). 560p. mass mkt. 6.99 *(0-440-22590-6)* Dell Publishing.

—On Beulah Height. 1998. 384p. o.s.i *(0-385-25734-1)* Doubleday Canada, Ltd. CAN. *Dist:* Random Hse., Inc.

—On Beulah Height. l.t. ed. 1999. (Charnwood Large Print Ser.). 624p. 31.99 o.p. *(0-7089-9056-8*, Charnwood) Thorpe, F. A. Pubs. GBR. *Dist:* Ulverscroft Large Print Bks., Ltd., Ulverscroft Large Print Canada, Ltd.

—On Beulah Height: A Dalziel-Pascoe Murder Mystery. 1998. 384p. 22.95 o.s.i *(0-385-33278-5)* Doubleday Publishing.

—Pictures of Perfection. 1995. (Dalziel & Pascoe Mystery Ser.). 352p. mass mkt. 6.99 *(0-440-21800-4)* Dell Publishing.

—Pictures of Perfection. l.t. ed. 1995. (Charnwood Large Print Ser.). 432p. 29.99 o.p. *(0-7089-8845-8*, Charnwood) Thorpe, F. A. Pubs. GBR. *Dist:* Ulverscroft Large Print Bks., Ltd., Ulverscroft Large Print Canada, Ltd.

—A Pinch of Snuff. 1990. 336p. mass mkt. 6.99 *(0-440-16912-7)* Dell Publishing.

—A Pinch of Snuff. 1978. (Harper Novel of Suspense Ser.). 9.95 o.p. *(0-06-011876-8)* HarperCollins Pubs.

—Recalled to Life. 1993. (Dalziel & Pascoe Mystery Ser.). 400p. mass mkt. 6.99 *(0-440-21573-0)* Dell Publishing.

—Ruling Passion. unabr. ed. 2000. (Dalziel & Pascoe Mystery Ser.). audio 69.95 *(0-7540-0042-7*, CAB 1465) Chivers Audio Bks. GBR. *Dist:* BBC Audiobooks America.

—Ruling Passion. 1990. 336p. mass mkt. 6.99 *(0-440-16889-9)* Dell Publishing.

—Ruling Passion. l.t. ed. 2001. (Charnwood Large Print Ser.). 376p. 31.99 o.p. *(0-7089-9230-7*, Ulverscroft) Thorpe, F. A. Pubs. GBR. *Dist:* Ulverscroft Large Print Bks., Ltd., Ulverscroft Large Print Canada, Ltd.

—Underworld. 1989. 288p. mass mkt. 4.50 *(0-446-34534-2)* Warner Bks., Inc.

—Underworld: A New Dalziel-Pascoe Murder Mystery. 1988. 288p. 14.95 o.s.i *(0-684-18931-3*, Scribner) Simon & Schuster.

—The Wood Beyond. 1997. (Dalziel & Pascoe Mystery Ser.). 448p. mass mkt. 6.99 *(0-440-21803-9)* Dell Publishing.

—The Wood Beyond, Set. unabr. ed. 1997. audio 94.95 Eye in the Ear Inc.

—The Wood Beyond. l.t. ed. 1996. 25.95 o.p. *(0-7838-1864-5*, Macmillan Reference USA) Gale Group.

**DAMASCO, GLORIA (FICTITIOUS CHARACTER)—FICTION**

Corpi, Lucha. Black Widow's Wardrobe. 1999. (Gloria Damasco Detective Ser.). 193p. pap. 12.95 o.p. *(1-55885-288-3)* Arte Publico Pr.

—Cactus Blood: A Mystery Novel. 1995. 249p. 9.50 o.p. *(1-55885-134-8)* Arte Publico Pr.

—Eulogy for a Brown Angel: A Mystery Novel. 2002. 208p. pap. 12.95 *(1-55885-356-1)*; 1992. 200p. 9.00 *(1-55885-050-3)* Arte Publico Pr.

**DAMEN, BILL (FICTITIOUS CHARACTER)—FICTION**

Calder, James. Knockout Mouse: A Silicon Valley Mystery. 2002. 224p. pap. 11.95 *(0-8118-3499-9)* Chronicle Bks. LLC.

Seelig, Tina L. Games for Your Brain: Bug Cards. 2003. (Illus.). 224p. (J). 9.95 *(0-8118-3474-3)* Chronicle Bks. LLC.

**DAMIANO (FICTITIOUS CHARACTER)—FICTION**

MacAvoy, R. A. Damiano. 1984. 243p. mass mkt. 2.95 o.s.i *(0-553-25347-6*, Spectra) Bantam Bks.

—Damiano's Lute. 1984. mass mkt. 2.75 o.s.i *(0-553-24102-8)*; 272p. mass mkt. 2.95 o.s.i *(0-553-25977-6*, Spectra) Bantam Bks.

—Raphael. 1984. 240p. mass mkt. 2.95 o.s.i *(0-553-25978-4)* Bantam Bks.

—Trio for Lute. 1988. mass mkt. 4.95 o.s.i *(0-553-27480-5*, Spectra) Bantam Bks.

**DANDY, JAMES P. (FICTITIOUS CHARACTER)—FICTION**

Abresch, Peter. Bloody Bonsai. 1999. (WWL Mystery Ser.: No. 321). per. *(0-373-26321-X*, 1-26321-9, Worldwide Library) Harlequin Enterprises, Ltd.

—Bloody Bonsai. l.t. ed. 1999. (Thorndike Senior Lifestyle Ser.). 360p. 27.95 *(0-7862-1787-1)* Thorndike Pr.

—Bloody Bonsai. 1998. 240p. 21.95 *(1-885173-34-2)* Write Way Publishing.

—Killing Thyme. l.t. ed. 2002. 386p. pap. 25.95 *(0-7862-4336-8)* Gale Group.

—Killing Thyme. 2000. (James P. Dandy Elderhostel Mysteries Ser.). 256p. mass mkt. *(0-373-26356-2*, 1-26356-5, Harlequin Bks.) Harlequin Enterprises, Ltd.

—Killing Thyme. 1999. (Jim Dandy Elderhostel Mystery Ser.: No. 2). 279p. 23.95 *(1-885173-68-7)* Write Way Publishing.

—Painted Lady. 2004. (WWL Mystery Ser.: No. 488). 256p. mass mkt. *(0-373-26488-7*, Worldwide Library) Harlequin Enterprises, Ltd.

Iakovou, Takis, et al. Deadly Morsels: Another Curse/ Red or Green?/Cake Job/Sheep in Wolf's Clothing, 4 bks. in 1. 2003. (WWL Mystery Ser.: No. 452). 384p. mass mkt. *(0-373-26452-6*, Worldwide Library) Harlequin Enterprises, Ltd.

**DANESON, MAUDE (FICTITIOUS CHARACTER)—FICTION**

Babson, Marian. The Twelve Deaths of Christmas. 1981. 192p. mass mkt. 2.25 o.s.i *(0-440-19183-1)* Dell Publishing.

—The Twelve Deaths of Christmas. l.t. ed. 1993. 11.50 o.p. *(0-8161-3183-X*, Macmillan Reference USA) Gale Group.

—The Twelve Deaths of Christmas, Vol. 1. 1996. (Twelve Deaths of Christmas Ser.: Vol. 1). 170p. mass mkt. 4.99 *(0-312-96039-5*, St. Martin's Paperbacks) St. Martin's Pr.

—The Twelve Deaths of Christmas. 1980. 180p. 10.95 o.p. *(0-8027-5426-0)* Walker & Co.

**DANFORTH, ABIGAIL (FICTITIOUS CHARACTER)—FICTION**

Jackson, Marian J. A. Diamond Head: A Miss Danforth Mystery. 1994. 2.99 o.p. *(0-517-12526-9)* Random Hse. Value Publishing.

—Diamond Head: A Miss Danforth Mystery. 1992. 167p. 18.95 *(0-8027-1247-9)* Walker & Co.

—Diamond Head: A Miss Danforth Mystery. 2001. 236p. pap. 15.95 *(0-595-19440-0*, Mystery Writers of America Presents) iUniverse, Inc.

—Miss Danforth Mystery: The Arabian Pearl. 1990. mass mkt. 3.50 o.p. *(1-55817-401-X*, Pinnacle Bks.) Kensington Publishing Corp.

—The Punjat's Ruby: A Miss Danforth Mystery. 1990. (Miss Danforth Mystery Ser.: No. 1). mass mkt. 3.50 o.s.i *(1-55817-338-2*, Pinnacle Bks.) Kensington Publishing Corp.

—The Sunken Treasure: A Miss Danforth Mystery. 1994. (Miss Danforth Mystery Ser.). 224p. 19.95 *(0-8027-3191-0)* Walker & Co.

**DANGER, MIKE (FICTITIOUS CHARACTER)—FICTION**

Spillane, Mickey. Mickey Spilane's Mike Danger Collection, Vol. 1. 1996. (Mike Danger Collection). (Illus.). 160p. (Orig.). reprint ed. pap. 15.95 *(1-57780-001-X)* Big Entertainment, Inc.

**DANIEL, VICTOR (FICTITIOUS CHARACTER)—FICTION**

Pierce, David M. Angels in Heaven. 1992. 240p. 17.95 o.p. *(0-89296-483-9)* Mysterious Pr.

—Angels in Heaven. 1993. 208p. mass mkt. 4.99 *(0-446-40163-3*, Mysterious Pr. Paperback Bks.) Warner Bks., Inc.

—As She Rides By. 1996. 224p. 20.95 o.p. *(0-312-13924-1*, Saint Martin's Minotaur) St. Martin's Pr.

—Down in the Valley. 1990. 224p. pap. 4.95 o.p. *(0-14-011411-4*, Penguin Bks.) Viking Penguin.

—Hear the Wind Blow, Dear. 1990. 192p. pap. 4.95 o.p. *(0-14-011413-0*, Penguin Bks.) Viking Penguin.

—Roses Love Sunshine. 1990. 240p. pap. 4.95 o.p. *(0-14-011414-9*, Penguin Bks.) Viking Penguin.

—Write Me a Letter. 1993. 272p. 18.95 *(0-89296-484-7)* Mysterious Pr.

**DANIEL KEARNY ASSOCIATES (FICTITIOUS CHARACTERS)—FICTION**

Gores, Joe. Contract Null & Void. 1996. 82p. 21.95 o.s.i *(0-89296-592-4)* Mysterious Pr.

—Contract Null & Void. 1997. (Dka File Novel Ser.). 336p. mass mkt. 6.50 o.s.i *(0-446-40447-0)* Warner Bks., Inc.

—Dead Skip. 1981. mass mkt. 2.25 o.s.i *(0-345-29206-5)*; 1974. mass mkt. 1.25 o.p. *(0-345-24129-0)* Ballantine Bks.

—Dead Skip. 1992. 208p. reprint ed. mass mkt. 4.99 o.s.i *(0-446-40312-1*, Mysterious Pr. Paperback Bks.) Warner Bks., Inc.

—Final Notice. 1992. 208p. reprint ed. mass mkt. 4.99 *(0-446-40314-8*, Mysterious Pr. Paperback Bks.) Warner Bks., Inc.

—Gone, No Forwarding. 1981. mass mkt. 2.25 o.s.i *(0-345-29208-1)* Ballantine Bks.

—Gone, No Forwarding. 1993. 224p. mass mkt. 5.50 o.s.i *(0-446-40315-6)* Warner Bks., Inc.

—32 Cadillacs. 1992. 352p. 18.95 *(0-89296-298-4)* Mysterious Pr.

—32 Cadillacs. 1993. 352p. mass mkt. 5.99 o.s.i *(0-446-40360-1)* Warner Bks., Inc.

**DANIELS, AVERY (FICTITIOUS CHARACTER)—FICTION**

Brown, Sandra. Mirror Image. 1991. reprint ed. 21.95 o.p. *(0-7278-4192-0)* Severn Hse. Pubs., Ltd.

—Mirror Image. 1990. 448p. reprint ed. mass mkt. 6.99 *(0-446-35395-7)* Warner Bks., Inc.

**DANIELS, CHARMIAN (FICTITIOUS CHARACTER)—FICTION**

Melville, Jennie. Dead Again: A Charmian Daniels Mystery. l.t. ed. 2000. 281p. *(0-7540-4212-X)*; *(0-7540-4213-8)* Gale Group. (Macmillan Reference USA).

—Dead Again: A Charmian Daniels Mystery. l.t. ed. 2000. (Nightingale Ser.). 281p. pap. 20.95 *(0-7838-9099-0)* Thorndike Pr.

—Dead Set: A Charmian Daniels Mystery. 1995. (WWL Mystery Ser.). 252p. per. *(0-373-26174-8*, 1-26174-2, Harlequin Bks.) Harlequin Enterprises, Ltd.

—Dead Set: A Charmian Daniels Mystery. 1992. 17.95 *(0-312-08757-8*, Saint Martin's Minotaur) St. Martin's Pr.

—Death in the Family. 1995. 277p. 21.00 *(0-312-11772-8*, Saint Martin's Minotaur) St. Martin's Pr.

—A Different Kind of Summer. l.t. ed. 1993. 18.95 o.p. *(0-7451-6437-4)*; 1992. audio 39.95 *(0-7451-2401-1*, CD 002) BBC Audiobooks America.

—A Different Kind of Summer. (Black Dagger Crime Ser.). 12.95 o.p. *(0-86220-800-9*, BD005) Chivers Pr. GBR. *Dist:* BBC Audiobooks America.

—Footsteps in the Blood. pap. 15.95 *(0-312-29187-6*, Saint Martin's Griffin); 1993. 192p. 17.95 *(0-312-09813-8*, Saint Martin's Minotaur) St. Martin's Pr.

—Making Good Blood. 1990. 15.95 o.p. *(0-312-04344-9*, Saint Martin's Minotaur) St. Martin's Pr.

—The Morbid Kitchen. 208p. 1996. 20.95 *(0-312-14681-7*, Saint Martin's Minotaur); 1995. per. 15.95 *(0-312-29172-8*, Saint Martin's Griffin) St. Martin's Pr.

—Murder Has a Pretty Face. 1991. reprint ed. per. *(0-373-26079-2*, Harlequin Bks.) Harlequin Enterprises, Ltd.

—Murder Has a Pretty Face. l.t. ed. 1996. (Magna Large Print Ser.). 400p. 29.99 *(0-7505-1047-1)* Magna Large Print Bks. GBR. *Dist:* Ulverscroft Large Print Bks., Ltd., Ulverscroft Large Print Canada, Ltd.

—Murder Has a Pretty Face. 1989. 256p. 16.95 o.p. (*0-312-03405-9*, Saint Martin's Minotaur) St. Martin's Pr.

—Murder in the Garden. 1991. 2.99 o.p. (*0-517-07814-7*) Random Hse. Value Publishing.

—Murder in the Garden. pap. 15.95 (*0-312-29185-X*, Saint Martin's Griffin); 1990. 224p. 15.95 (*0-312-03895-X*, Saint Martin's Minotaur) St. Martin's Pr.

—Revengeful Death. l.t. ed. 1998. (Magna Large Print Ser.). 272p. (*0-7505-1232-6*) Magna Large Print Bks. GBR. *Dist:* Ulverscroft Large Print Canada, Ltd.

—Tarot's Tower. 1979. mass mkt. 1.75 o.s.i (*0-449-24001-0*, Fawcett) Ballantine Bks.

—Tarot's Tower. 1978. 8.95 o.s.i (*0-671-22905-2*, Simon & Schuster) Simon & Schuster.

—Whoever Has the Heart. 218p. 3.95 o.p. (*0-8317-5152-5*) Smithmark Pubs., Inc.

—Whoever Has the Heart. pap. 15.95 (*0-312-29175-2*, Saint Martin's Griffin); 1994. 224p. 19.95 (*0-312-11099-5*, Saint Martin's Minotaur) St. Martin's Pr.

—Windsor Red. pap. 9.95 (*1-902002-01-6*) CT Publishing GBR. *Dist:* Trafalgar Square.

—Windsor Red. 1990. mass mkt. (*0-373-26051-2*, Harlequin Bks.) Harlequin Enterprises, Ltd.

—Windsor Red. 1988. 256p. 16.95 o.p. (*0-312-01846-0*, Saint Martin's Minotaur) St. Martin's Pr.

—Witching Murder. 1991. (Lythway Adult Ser.). 280p. 20.50 o.p. (*0-7451-1374-5*) Chivers Pr. GBR. *Dist:* BBC Audiobooks America.

—Witching Murder. pap. 15.95 (*0-312-29186-8*, Saint Martin's Griffin); 1991. 15.95 (*0-312-05999-X*, Saint Martin's Minotaur) St. Martin's Pr.

### DANILOV, DIMITRI (FICTITIOUS CHARACTER)—FICTION

Freemantle, Brian. No Time for Heroes. l.t. ed. 1995. 648p. lib. bdg. 24.95 o.p. (*0-7838-1276-0*, Macmillan Reference USA) Gale Group.

—No Time for Heroes. 1996. 472p. mass mkt. 6.99 (*0-312-95927-3*, St. Martin's Paperbacks); 1995. 23.95 o.p. (*0-312-11866-X*) St. Martin's Pr.

### DANN, PEACHES (FICTITIOUS CHARACTER)—FICTION

Squire, Elizabeth Daniels. Forget about Murder. 2000. (Peaches Dan Mysteries Ser.). 268p. mass mkt. 5.99 o.s.i (*0-425-17343-7*, Prime Crime) Berkley Publishing Group.

—Is There a Dead Man in the House? 1998. 256p. mass mkt. 5.99 o.s.i (*0-425-16142-0*, Prime Crime) Berkley Publishing Group.

—Is There a Dead Man in the House? l.t. ed. 2004. 333p. pap. 23.95 (*1-58724-606-6*, Wheeler Publishing, Inc.) Gale Group.

—Is There a Dead Man in the House? 1998. 12.04 (*0-606-19297-2*) Turtleback Bks.

—Kill the Messenger. l.t. ed. 2000. (G. K. Hall Paperback Ser.). 313p. pap. 23.95 (*0-7838-8856-2*, Macmillan Reference USA) Gale Group.

—Kill the Messenger. 1991. mass mkt. 3.95 (*0-312-92436-4*, St. Martin's Paperbacks); 1989. 240p. 16.95 o.p. (*0-312-03854-2*, Saint Martin's Minotaur) St. Martin's Pr.

—Memory Can Be Murder. 1995. 256p. mass mkt. 5.99 o.s.i (*0-425-14772-X*) Berkley Publishing Group.

—Memory Can Be Murder. l.t. ed. 2001. (G. K. Hall Paperback Ser.). 335p. pap. 24.95 (*0-7838-9408-2*, Macmillan Reference USA) Gale Group.

—Remember the Alibi. 1994. 272p. mass mkt. 4.99 o.s.i (*0-425-14351-1*, Prime Crime) Berkley Publishing Group.

—Remember the Alibi. l.t. ed. 2000. (G. K. Hall Paperback Ser.). 397p. pap. 23.95 o.p. (*0-7838-8858-9*, Macmillan Reference USA) Gale Group.

—Where There's a Will. 1999. (Peaches Dan Mysteries Ser.). 256p. mass mkt. 5.99 o.s.i (*0-425-16984-7*, Prime Crime) Berkley Publishing Group.

—Where There's a Will. 2003. (Paperback Ser.). lib. bdg. 25.95 (*0-7862-5246-4*) Thorndike Pr.

—Who Killed What's-Her-Name? 1994. mass mkt. 4.99 o.s.i (*0-425-14208-6*) Berkley Publishing Group.

—Who Killed What's-Her-Name? l.t. ed. 1999. (Paperback Ser.). 429p. pap. 23.95 (*0-7838-8497-4*) Thorndike Pr.

—Who Killed What's-Her-Name? A Peaches Dann Mystery. 2000. 240p. pap. 14.95 (*1-57090-092-2*) aBOOKS Distributing.

—Whose Death Is It, Anyway? 1997. 256p. mass mkt. 5.99 o.s.i (*0-425-15627-3*, Prime Crime) Berkley Publishing Group.

—Whose Death Is It, Anyway? 2001. pap. 13.95 (*1-57072-193-9*, Silver Dagger Mysteries) Overmountain Pr.

### DANTAN, ALPHONSE (FICTITIOUS CHARACTER)—FICTION

Blank, Hannah. Brave Man Dead: An Alphonse Dantan. 2000. (Alphonse Dantan Mystery Ser.: No. 2). 300p. (*0-9652778-3-6*, Hightrees Bks.) Prism Corp.

—A Murder of Convenience. 1999. 24.95 (*0-9652778-1-X*, Hightrees Bks.) Prism Corp.

—A Short Life on a Sunny Isle: An Alphonse Dantan Mystery. 2002. 260p. 24.95 (*0-9652778-5-2*) Prism Corp.

### DANTE, JOE (FICTITIOUS CHARACTER)—FICTION

Newman, Christopher. Dead End Game. 1995. 320p. mass mkt. 5.99 o.s.i (*0-425-14564-6*) Berkley Publishing Group.

—Dead End Game. 1994. 256p. 21.95 o.p. (*0-399-13952-4*, G. P. Putnam's Sons) Penguin Group (USA) Inc.

—Hit & Run. 1997. (Lt. Joe Dante Novels Ser.). 352p. mass mkt. 5.99 o.s.i (*0-440-22263-X*) Dell Publishing.

—Killer. 1996. (Lt. Joe Dante Novels Ser.). 320p. mass mkt. 5.99 o.s.i (*0-440-22262-1*) Dell Publishing.

—Killer. 1997. 21.95 (*0-399-14044-1*, G. P. Putnam's Sons) Penguin Putnam Bks. for Young Readers.

—Knock-Off. 1989. mass mkt. 5.99 o.s.i (*0-449-13294-3*, Fawcett) Ballantine Bks.

—Midtown North. 1991. mass mkt. 5.95 o.s.i (*0-449-14689-8*, Fawcett) Ballantine Bks.

—Midtown South. 1986. mass mkt. 5.99 o.s.i (*0-449-13064-9*, Fawcett) Ballantine Bks.

—Nineteenth Precinct. 1992. mass mkt. 5.99 o.s.i (*0-449-14732-0*, Fawcett) Ballantine Bks.

—Precinct Command. 1993. mass mkt. 5.99 o.s.i (*0-449-14795-9*, Fawcett) Ballantine Bks.

—Sixth Precinct. 1987. 320p. mass mkt. 5.99 o.s.i (*0-449-13174-2*, Fawcett) Ballantine Bks.

### DARCY, FITZWILLIAM (FICTITIOUS CHARACTER)—FICTION

Aston, Elizabeth. Mr. Darcy's Daughters: A Novel. 2003. 368p. pap. 14.00 (*0-7432-4397-8*, Touchstone) Simon & Schuster.

Austen, Jane. Pride & Prejudice. 2000. 252p. E-Book 9.95 (*0-594-05313-7*) 1873 Pr.

—Pride & Prejudice. 1998. pap. 4.99 o.p. (*1-57840-200-X*) Acclaim Bks.

—Pride & Prejudice. 1997. pap. text o.p. (*0-17-556586-4*) Addison-Wesley Longman, Inc.

—Pride & Prejudice. unabr. ed. 1962. (Classics Ser.). mass mkt. 4.95 (*0-8049-0001-9*, CL-1) Airmont Publishing Co., Inc.

—Pride & Prejudice. Date not set. lib. bdg. 25.95 (*0-8488-0420-1*) Amereon, Ltd.

—Pride & Prejudice, Set. unabr. ed. 1986. audio 53.95 (*1-55685-025-5*) Audio Bk. Contractors, Inc.

—Pride & Prejudice. unabr. ed. 1997. audio 34.95 (*1-57270-055-6*, F81055u, Cover to Cover Classics) Audio Partners Publishing Corp.

—Pride & Prejudice. unabr. ed. audio 84.95 o.p. (*1-85549-911-8*, CTC 001); 1998. audio 84.95 (*0-7540-0149-0*, CAB 1572, Sterling Audio Bks.) BBC Audiobooks America.

—Pride & Prejudice. abr. ed. 1999. audio 16.85 (*0-563-55816-4*) BBC Bk. Publishing GBR. *Dist:* Ulverscroft Large Print Bks., Ltd.

—Pride & Prejudice. 2001. 7.95 (*0-8010-1211-2*) Baker Bks.

—Pride & Prejudice. 1991. mass mkt. 4.95 (*0-553-54088-2*); 1983. mass mkt. 1.95 o.s.i (*0-553-21215-X*); 1983. 352p. reprint ed. mass mkt. 4.95 (*0-553-21310-5*, Bantam Classics) Bantam Bks.

—Pride & Prejudice. 1999. (Classic Novels ). 392p. pap. 8.95 (*0-7641-1147-7*) Barron's Educational Series, Inc.

—Pride & Prejudice. Kendrick, Walter, ed. 1980. (Mcdonald Classics Ser.). 410p. 19.95 (*0-8464-1071-0*) Beekman Pubs., Inc.

—Pride & Prejudice. unabr. ed. 2000. audio compact disk 88.00 (*0-7861-9894-X*, z1054); 1989. audio 56.95 (*0-7861-0057-5*, 1054) Blackstone Audio Bks., Inc.

—Pride & Prejudice. unabr. collector's ed. 1996. audio 72.00 (*0-7366-3370-7*, 4020) Books on Tape, Inc.

—Pride & Prejudice. unabr. ed. 1993. (For Antoinette Ser.). audio 19.95 o.p. (*1-56100-484-7*, 219, Bookcassette); audio 59.25 (*1-56100-118-X*, 992, Unabridged Library Editions) Brilliance Audio.

—Pride & Prejudice. 1988. lib. bdg. 19.95 (*0-89966-243-9*) Buccaneer Bks., Inc.

—Pride & Prejudice. Bain, Richard, ed. 1996. (Literature Ser.). (Illus.). 384p. pap. text 11.95 o.p. (*0-521-57654-7*) Cambridge Univ. Pr.

—Pride & Prejudice. unabr. ed. 2000. 10p. audio compact disk 94.95 (*0-7540-5338-5*, CCD 029) Chivers Audio Bks. GBR. *Dist:* BBC Audiobooks America.

—Pride & Prejudice, 3 Vols. reprint ed. lib. bdg. 294.00 (*0-7426-2071-9*); 2001. pap. text 84.00 (*0-7426-7071-6*) Classic Bks.

—Pride & Prejudice. audio 59.95 Cover to Cover Cassettes, Ltd.

—Pride & Prejudice. 1994. 332p. mass mkt. 3.99 (*0-8125-2336-9*, Tor Classics) Doherty, Tom Assocs., LLC.

—Pride & Prejudice. unabr. ed. 1995. (Thrift Editions Ser.). 272p. pap. 2.50 (*0-486-28473-5*) Dover Pubns., Inc.

—Pride & Prejudice. 1942. 107p. pap. 5.60 (*0-87129-686-1*, P36) Dramatic Publishing Co.

—Pride & Prejudice. abr. ed. audio 15.95 o.p. (*0-88646-029-8*, 7042); 1986. audio 29.95 o.p. (*0-88646-795-0*, R 7042);Set. 1992. audio 16.99 (*0-88646-278-9*, 7278) Durkin Hayes Publishing Ltd.

—Pride & Prejudice. 1985. (Illus.). 352p. 20.00 o.p. (*0-525-18381-7*, Dutton) Dutton/Plume.

—Pride & Prejudice. 1980. (Reader's Request Ser.). lib. bdg. 13.95 o.p. (*0-8161-3076-0*, Macmillan Reference USA) Gale Group.

—Pride & Prejudice. abr. ed. 1984. audio 8.98; 1978. audio 12.95 o.p. (*0-694-50321-5*, SWC 1595, HarperAudio) HarperTrade.

—Pride & Prejudice. Clay, N. L., ed. 1986. (Guide Novel Ser.). pap. text 4.50 o.p. (*0-435-16041-9*) Heinemann.

—Pride & Prejudice, Set. unabr. ed. 1999. audio 56.95 Highsmith Inc.

—Pride & Prejudice. abr. ed. 1999. audio 16.95 (*1-85998-013-9*) Hodder Headline Audiobooks GBR. *Dist:* Trafalgar Square.

—Pride & Prejudice. 1997. pap. 8.25 (*0-03-051487-8*) Holt, Rinehart & Winston.

—Pride & Prejudice. Schorer, Mark, ed. 1956. pap. 16.36 (*0-395-05101-0*, Riverside Editions) Houghton Mifflin Co.

—Pride & Prejudice. l.t. ed. 623p. pap. 45.49 (*0-7583-1939-8*); 995p. pap. 74.61 (*0-7583-1941-X*); 1444p. pap. 95.94 (*0-7583-1943-6*); 1224p. pap. 85.50 (*0-7583-1942-8*); 806p. pap. 63.79 (*0-7583-1940-1*); 349p. pap. 29.76 (*0-7583-1937-1*); 484p. pap. 36.91 (*0-7583-1938-X*); 276p. pap. 24.62 (*0-7583-1936-3*); 276p. lib. bdg. 30.62 (*0-7583-1928-2*); 623p. lib. bdg. 51.49 (*0-7583-1931-2*); 995p. lib. bdg. 86.61 (*0-7583-1933-9*); 1224p. lib. bdg. 97.50 (*0-7583-1934-7*); 1444p. lib. bdg. 107.94 (*0-7583-1935-5*); 349p. lib. bdg. 35.76 (*0-7583-1929-0*); 806p. lib. bdg. 75.79 (*0-7583-1932-0*); 484p. lib. bdg. 42.91 (*0-7583-1930-4*) Huge Print Pr.

—Pride & Prejudice. 1991. 327p. (*1-85715-001-5*, Everyman's Library) Knopf Publishing Group.

—Pride & Prejudice. 1991. 416p. 17.00 (*0-679-40542-9*) Knopf, Alfred A. Inc.

—Pride & Prejudice. 1998. (Cloth Bound Pocket Ser.). 240p. 7.95 (*3-89508-207-4*, 521305) Konemann.

—Pride & Prejudice. l.t. ed. 1997. (Large Print Heritage Ser.). 560p. lib. bdg. 36.95 (*1-58118-009-8*, 21967) LRS.

—Pride & Prejudice. 1993. audio. audio 50.60 (*1-56544-019-6*, 350003) Literate Ear, Inc.

—Pride & Prejudice. (Longman Fiction Ser.). 1997. pap. 9.07 (*0-582-27508-3*); 1993. pap. text 6.50 o.p. (*0-582-09674-X*, 79823) Longman Publishing Group.

—Pride & Prejudice. Adams, Richard, ed. 1983. (Study Texts Ser.). pap. text 5.95 (*0-582-33086-6*, 72039) Longman Publishing Group.

—Pride & Prejudice. abr. ed. 2000. audio 7.95 (*1-57815-123-6*, 1085, Media Bks. Audio Publishing) Media Bks., L. L. C.

—Pride & Prejudice. 9999. o.p.; 1996. 336p. mass mkt. 4.95 (*0-451-52588-4*, Signet Classics); 1950. 336p. mass mkt. 3.95 o.p. (*0-451-52365-2*); 1950. mass mkt. 2.25 o.p. (*0-451-52226-5*, Signet Classics) NAL.

—Pride & Prejudice. audio 7.95 National Recording Co.

—Pride & Prejudice. abr. ed. 1996. (Works of Jane Austen). audio 17.98 (*962-634-604-3*, NA310414); audio compact disk 19.98 (*962-634-104-1*, NA310412) Naxos of America, Inc. (Naxos AudioBooks).

—Pride & Prejudice. Worrall, Andrew, ed. 1997. (Thornes Classic Novels Ser.). (Illus.). 376p. pap. 16.95 (*0-7487-2977-1*) Nelson Thornes GBR. *Dist:* Trans-Atlantic Pubns., Inc.

—Pride & Prejudice. abr. ed. 1996. 19.95 o.p. (*0-7871-0306-3*) NewStar Media, Inc.

—Pride & Prejudice. l.t. ed. 1998. 480p. lib. bdg. 26.00 (*0-939495-50-3*); 355p. reprint ed. lib. bdg. 25.00 (*1-58287-058-6*) North Bks.

—Pride & Prejudice. (C). pap. text (*0-393-99771-5*) Norton, W. W. & Co., Inc.

—Pride & Prejudice. Gray, Donald J., ed. 1966. (Critical Editions Ser.). 450p. (C). pap. o.p. (*0-393-09668-8*) Norton, W. W. & Co., Inc.

—Pride & Prejudice. 3rd ed. 2000. (Critical Editions Ser.). viii, 413p. (C). pap. 7.25 (*0-393-97604-1*, Norton Paperbacks) Norton, W. W. & Co., Inc.

—Pride & Prejudice. 1999. (Oxford World's Classics Ser.). 366p. 12.50 o.p. (*0-19-210026-2*) Oxford Univ. Pr., Inc.

—Pride & Prejudice. Kinsley, James, ed. 1998. (Oxford World's Classics Ser.). 410p. pap. 6.95 (*0-19-283355-3*) Oxford Univ. Pr., Inc.

—Pride & Prejudice. Hedge, Tricia, ed. 1995. (Illus.). 112p. pap. text 5.95 o.p. (*0-19-422710-3*) Oxford Univ. Pr., Inc.

—Pride & Prejudice. Kinsley, James, ed. 1990. (Oxford World's Classics Ser.). 390p. pap. 5.95 o.p. (*0-19-282760-X*) Oxford Univ. Pr., Inc.

—Pride & Prejudice. Kinsley, James & Bradbrook, F. W., eds. 1980. (Oxford World's Classics Ser.). pap. 2.25 o.p. (*0-19-281503-2*) Oxford Univ. Pr., Inc.

—Pride & Prejudice. 2nd ed. 1993. (Illus.). 126p. pap. text 5.95 (*0-19-585472-1*) Oxford Univ. Pr., Inc.

—Pride & Prejudice, Vol. II. Chapman, R. W., ed. 3rd ed. 1988. (Illus.). 432p. reprint ed. 21.50 (*0-19-254702-X*) Oxford Univ. Pr., Inc.

—Pride & Prejudice. 1996. 144p. pap. 20.00 (*81-209-0025-1*) Pitambar Publishing IND. *Dist:* State Mutual Bk. & Periodical Service, Ltd.

—Pride & Prejudice. text (*0-13-981465-5*) Prentice Hall (Schl. Div.).

—Pride & Prejudice. (Jane Austen Works: Vol. 7). 2000. 280p. lib. bdg. 36.99 (*1-57646-350-8*); 2000. 280p. pap. 19.99 o.p. (*1-57646-267-6*); 1999. 200p. E-Book 3.99 incl. audio compact disk (*1-57646-150-5*); 2000. 518p. pap. 34.99 (*1-57646-351-6*) Quiet Vision Publishing.

—Pride & Prejudice. 1987. (Radiobook Ser.). audio 4.98 (*0-929541-27-8*) Radiola Co.

—Pride & Prejudice. (Modern Library Ser.). 2000. E-Book 4.95 (*0-679-64112-2*); 2000. 320p. pap. 7.95 (*0-679-78326-1*); 1995. (Illus.). 304p. 14.95 (*0-679-60168-6*) Random House Adult Trade Publishing Group. (Modern Library).

—Pride & Prejudice. abr. unabr. ed. 1995. (BBC Radio Presents Ser.). audio 24.00 o.s.i (*0-553-47396-4*, RH Audio) Random Hse. Audio Publishing Group.

—Pride & Prejudice. 1988. (Zodiac Press Ser.). 248p. o.p. (*0-7011-1236-0*) Random Hse. of Canada, Ltd. CAN. *Dist:* Random Hse., Inc.

—Pride & Prejudice. 1996. o.s.i (*0-679-60252-6*); 1989. o.s.i (*1-85381-097-5*); 1986. pap. 16.00 o.s.i incl. audio (*0-394-55731-X*); 1986. pap. 16.00 o.s.i incl. audio (*0-394-55731-X*) Random Hse., Inc.

—Pride & Prejudice. 1984. (Illus.). 368p. 25.00 o.p. (*0-89577-198-5*) Reader's Digest Assn., Inc., The.

—Pride & Prejudice, unabr. ed. 1980. audio 70.00 (*1-55690-424-X*, 80020E7) Recorded Bks., LLC.

—Pride & Prejudice. (Literary Classics Ser.). 368p. 2002. 9.00 o.p. (*0-7624-0550-3*); 1992. text 5.98 o.p. (*1-56138-171-3*, Courage Bks.) Running Pr. Bk. Pubs.

—Pride & Prejudice. 2000. 416p. mass mkt. 4.99 (*0-439-10135-2*) Scholastic, Inc.

—Pride & Prejudice. 2000. E-Book 2.95 (*1-58853-022-1*) Sensory Publishing, Inc.

—Pride & Prejudice. 2004. 400p. mass mkt. 4.95 (*0-7434-8759-1*, Pocket) Simon & Schuster.

—Pride & Prejudice. Shefter, Harry, ed. 1985. (Enriched Classics Ser.). mass mkt. 2.50 o.p. (*0-671-41678-2*, Pocket) Simon & Schuster.

—Pride & Prejudice. 1982. 464p. mass mkt. 2.95 o.s.i (*0-671-44389-5*, Pocket) Simon & Schuster.

—Pride & Prejudice. 1996. (Classic Library). 12.98 o.p. (*0-7651-9980-7*) Smithmark Pubs., Inc.

—Pride & Prejudice. abr. ed. audio 14.95 o.p. (*0-88142-378-5*) Soundelux Audio Publishing.

—Pride & Prejudice. l.t. ed. 1984. (Charnwood Large Print Ser.). 532p. 29.99 (*0-7089-8228-X*, Charnwood) Thorpe, F. A. Pubs. GBR. *Dist:* Ulverscroft Large Print Bks., Ltd., Ulverscroft Large Print Canada, Ltd.

—Pride & Prejudice. 1986. (Illus.). 352p. 25.95 o.p. (*0-7126-1011-1*) Trafalgar Square.

—Pride & Prejudice. 1999. (Signature Classics Ser.). (Illus.). 352p. 24.95 (*1-58279-032-9*); 29.95 (*1-58279-044-2*) Trident Pr. International.

—Pride & Prejudice. Norris, Pamela, ed. 1993. 384p. pap. 3.95 (*0-460-87212-5*, Everyman's Classic Library in Paperback) Tuttle Publishing.

—Pride & Prejudice. 1906. 352p. pap. 4.95 o.p. (*0-460-11022-5*, Everyman's Classic Library in Paperback) Tuttle Publishing.

—Pride & Prejudice. (Penguin Classics Ser.). 1997. 384p. pap. 7.95 o.s.i (*0-14-043426-7*, Penguin Classics); 1996. 400p. pap. 9.95 o.p. (*0-14-043596-4*) Viking Penguin.

—Pride & Prejudice. Tanner, Tony, ed. 1980. pap. 1.95 o.p. (*0-14-005774-9*) Viking Penguin.

—Pride & Prejudice. 1976. 2.95 o.p. (*0-460-01022-0*) Viking Penguin.

—Pride & Prejudice. Tanner, Tony, ed. 1972. (English Library). 400p. pap. 7.95 o.s.i (*0-14-043072-5*, Penguin Classics) Viking Penguin.

—Pride & Prejudice. abr. ed. 2003. (Classics on Audio Ser.). 4p. audio 16.95 (*0-14-086060-6*, 693102, Penguin Classics) Viking Penguin.

—Pride & Prejudice. 2000. text 6.00 (*0-8220-7172-X*, Cliff Notes) Wiley, John & Sons, Inc.

—Pride & Prejudice. 1997. (Classics Library). 288p. pap. 3.95 (*1-85326-000-2*, 0002WW) Wordsworth Editions, Ltd. GBR. *Dist:* Casemate Pubs. & Bk. Distributors, LLC.

—Pride & Prejudice. 1992. E-Book 8.98 (*0-585-25816-3*) netLibrary, Inc.

Austen, Jane & Hemmant, Lynette. Pride & Prejudice. 1980. 14.95 o.p. (*0-437-24575-6*) Trafalgar Square.
Austen, Jane & Kinsley, James. Pride & Prejudice. 1990. E-Book 13.13 (*0-585-37761-8*) netLibrary, Inc.
Bader, Ted, et al. Desire & Duty: A Sequel to Jane Austen's Pride & Prejudice. 1997. (Illus.). 286p. 19.95 (*0-9654299-0-3*, 97-1) Revive Publishing.
Barrett, Julia, pseud. Presumption. 238p. pap. 11.95 (*1-85479-993-2*) O'Mara, Michael Bks., Ltd. GBR. *Dist:* Andrews McMeel Publishing.
—Presumption: An Entertainment Sequel to Jane Austen's Pride & Prejudice. unabr. collector's ed. 1995. audio 48.00 (*0-7366-2954-8*, 3648) Books on Tape, Inc.
Barrett, Julia, pseud & Austen, Jane. Presumption: An Entertainment: A Sequel to Pride & Prejudice. 1993. 240p. 19.95 o.p. (*0-87131-736-2*) Evans, M. & Co., Inc.
—Presumption: An Entertainment: A Sequel to Pride & Prejudice. 1995. 238p. reprint ed. pap. 12.00 (*0-226-03813-0*) Univ. of Chicago Pr.
Bebris, Carrie. Pride & Prescience. 2004. 288p. 21.95 (*0-7653-0508-9*, Forge Bks.) Doherty, Tom Assocs., LLC.
Calvit, Christina. Pride & Prejudice. unabr. ed. 1997. audio 22.95 (*1-58081-052-7*, CTA55) L. A. Theatre Works.
Dawkins, Jane. Letters from Pemberley: The First Year. 1999. 200p. pap. 12.00 (*1-893337-00-6*) Chicken Soup Pr., Inc.
Prentice-Hall Staff. Pride & Prejudice. 2nd ed. text, stu. ed. (*0-13-716978-7*) Prentice Hall (Schl. Div.).
Robinson, Pamela. Pride & Prejudice: Dramatic Reading. 1968. audio 11.95 Norton Pubs., Inc., Jeffrey /Audio-Forum.
Tennant, Emma. Pemberley: Or Pride & Prejudice Continued, Set. unabr. ed. 1996. audio 54.95 (*0-7451-2729-0*, SAB 095, Sterling Audio Bks.) BBC Audiobooks America.
—Pemberley: Or Pride & Prejudice Continued. l.t. ed. 1995. (Charnwood Large Print Ser.). 272p. 29.99 o.p. (*0-7089-8826-1*, Charnwood) Thorpe, F. A. Pubs. GBR. *Dist:* Ulverscroft Large Print Bks., Ltd., Ulverscroft Large Print Canada, Ltd.
—An Unequal Marriage: Or Pride & Prejudice Twenty Years Later. unabr. ed. 1996. audio 39.95 (*0-7451-2748-7*, SAB114, Sterling Audio Bks.) BBC Audiobooks America.
Tennant, Emma & Austen, Jane. Pemberley: Or Pride & Prejudice Continued. 1993. 184p. pap. 18.95 (*0-312-10793-5*) St. Martin's Pr.
—An Unequal Marriage: Or Pride & Prejudice Twenty Years Later. 1994. 224p. 18.95 o.p. (*0-312-11533-4*) St. Martin's Pr.

**DARCY, LORD (FICTITIOUS CHARACTER)—FICTION**

Garrett, Randall. Lord Darcy Investigates. 1983. 192p. (Orig.). mass mkt. 2.75 o.s.i (*0-441-49142-1*) Ace Bks.
—Murder & Magic. 1984. mass mkt. 2.75 o.s.i (*0-441-54543-2*); 1982. 272p. mass mkt. 2.75 o.s.i (*0-441-54542-4*); 1981. mass mkt. 2.50 o.s.i (*0-441-54541-6*) Ace Bks.
—Too Many Magicians. 1983. 352p. mass mkt. 2.95 o.s.i (*0-441-81698-3*) Ace Bks.
Kurland, Michael. A Study in Sorcery. 1989. mass mkt. 3.50 o.s.i (*0-441-79092-5*) Ace Bks.
—Ten Little Wizards. 1988. mass mkt. 2.95 o.s.i (*0-441-80057-2*) Ace Bks.

**DARCY, MEG (FICTITIOUS CHARACTER)—FICTION**

Marcy, Jean. Cemetery Murders: A Meg Darcy Mystery. 1997. 200p. pap. 10.95 (*0-934678-83-9*) New Victoria Pubs., Inc.
—Dead & Blonde: A Meg Darcy Mystery. 1998. (Meg Darcy Mysteries Ser.: No. 2). 227p. pap. 10.95 (*0-934678-98-7*) New Victoria Pubs., Inc.
—Mommy Deadest: A Meg Darcy Mystery. 2000. (Meg Darcy Mysteries Ser.). 224p. pap. 11.95 (*1-892281-12-0*) New Victoria Pubs., Inc.

**DARCY, TESS (FICTITIOUS CHARACTER)—FICTION**

Hager, Jean. Blooming Murder. 1994. (Iris House Mystery Ser.). pap. 5.50 (*0-380-77209-4*, Avon Bks.) Morrow/Avon.
—Blooming Murder. l.t. ed. 2001. (Illus.). 339p. (*0-7862-3215-3*) Thorndike Pr.
—Bride & Doom. l.t. ed. 2001. (Beeler Large Print Mystery Ser.). 230p. 25.95 (*1-57490-408-6*, Beeler Large Print Bks.) Beeler, Thomas T. Publisher.
—Bride & Doom. 2000. (Iris House Mystery Ser.: No. 2). 224p. mass mkt. 5.99 (*0-380-80376-3*, Avon Bks.) Morrow/Avon.
—Dead & Buried. 1995. (Iris House Mystery Ser.). mass mkt. 5.50 (*0-380-77210-8*, Avon Bks.) Morrow/Avon.
—Dead & Buried. l.t. ed. 2000. (Mystery Ser.). (Illus.). 339p. 27.95 (*0-7862-2928-4*) Thorndike Pr.
—Death on the Drunkard's Path. 1996. (Iris House Mystery Ser.: No. 3). pap. 5.50 (*0-380-77211-6*, Avon Bks.) Morrow/Avon.
—Death on the Drunkard's Path. l.t. ed. 2000. (Mystery Ser.). 328p. 26.95 (*0-7862-2353-7*) Thorndike Pr.
—The Last Noel. 1997. (Iris House Mystery Ser.). 224p. mass mkt. 5.99 (*0-380-78637-0*, Avon Bks.) Morrow/Avon.
—Sew Deadly. l.t. ed. 2001. 303p. (*0-7838-9498-8*); (*0-7540-4587-0*); (*0-7540-4588-9*) Gale Group. (Macmillan Reference USA).
—Sew Deadly. 1998. (Iris House Mystery Ser.). 224p. mass mkt. 5.99 (*0-380-78638-9*, Avon Bks.) Morrow/Avon.
—Weigh Dead. 2003. (Mystery Ser.). 27.95 (*1-57490-468-X*) Beeler, Thomas T. Publisher.
—Weigh Dead. 1999. (Iris House Mystery Ser.: Vol. 6). 224p. mass mkt. 5.99 (*0-380-80375-5*, Avon Bks.) Morrow/Avon.

**DARE, SUSAN (FICTITIOUS CHARACTER)—FICTION**

Eberhart, Mignon G. The Cases of Susan Dare. 1975. 303p. reprint ed. lib. bdg. 20.95 (*0-88411-751-0*) Amereon, Ltd.

**DARIAN (FICTITIOUS CHARACTER: LACKEY)—FICTION**

Lackey, Mercedes. Owlflight. 1998. 13.04 (*0-606-18981-5*) Turtleback Bks.
Lackey, Mercedes & Dixon, Larry. Owlflight. (Darian's Tale Ser.: Vol. 1). 1998. (Illus.). 352p. mass mkt. 6.99 (*0-88677-804-2*); 1997. 304p. 21.95 o.s.i (*0-88677-754-2*) DAW Bks., Inc.
—Owlknight. 1999. (Darian's Tale Ser.: Vol. 3). (Illus.). 336p. 24.95 o.s.i (*0-88677-851-4*, D A W Fiction); Vol. 3. 2000. 464p. reprint ed. mass mkt. 6.99 (*0-88677-916-2*) DAW Bks., Inc.
—Owlsight. (Darian's Tale Ser.: Vol. 2). 1999. 464p. mass mkt. 6.99 (*0-88677-803-4*, D A W Fiction); 1998. (Illus.). 304p. 24.95 o.s.i (*0-88677-802-6*) DAW Bks., Inc.

**DARIUS (FICTITIOUS CHARACTER: ANTHONY)—FICTION**

Anthony, Piers. Chaos Mode. 1995. (Virtual Mode Ser.). 368p. mass mkt. 7.50 (*0-441-00132-7*) Ace Bks.
—Chaos Mode. unabr. ed. 1994. (Mode Ser.). audio 23.95 o.p. (*1-56100-538-X*, 423, Bookcassette); audio 73.25 o.p. (*1-56100-166-X*, 606, Unabridged Library Editions);Set. audio 17.00 o.p. (*1-56100-357-3*, 824, Nova Audio Bks.) Brilliance Audio.
—Chaos Mode. abr. ed. 2000. (Mode Ser.). audio 7.95 (*1-57815-005-1*, 1011, Media Bks. Audio Publishing) Media Bks., L. L. C.
—Chaos Mode. 1994. 304p. 19.95 o.p. (*0-399-13893-5*) Penguin Group (USA) Inc.
—Dooon Mode. 2001. 448p. 25.95 (*0-312-87463-4*); 2002. reprint ed. mass mkt. 6.99 (*0-8125-7542-3*) Doherty, Tom Assocs., LLC. (Tor Bks.).
—Fractal Mode. 1992. (Mode Ser.). 336p. mass mkt. 6.99 o.s.i (*0-441-25126-9*) Ace Bks.
—Fractal Mode. unabr. ed. 1992. (Mode Ser.). audio 23.95 o.p. (*1-56100-454-5*, 430, Bookcassette); audio 73.25 o.p. (*1-56100-084-1*, 612, Unabridged Library Editions) Brilliance Audio.
—Fractal Mode. 1992. 304p. 18.95 o.p. (*0-399-13649-5*, Ace/Putnam) Penguin Group (USA) Inc.
—Virtual Mode. 1991. (Mode Ser.). mass mkt. 6.99 (*0-441-86503-8*) Ace Bks.
—Virtual Mode. unabr. ed. 1991. (Mode Ser.). audio 23.95 o.p. (*0-930435-86-9*, 434, Bookcassette); audio 73.25 o.p. (*1-56100-080-9*, 616, Unabridged Library Editions) Brilliance Audio.
—Virtual Mode. 1991. 304p. 16.95 o.p. (*0-399-13661-4*, Ace/Putnam) Penguin Group (USA) Inc.

**DARK, NESTOR (FICTITIOUS CHARACTER)—FICTION**

Rosenfeld, Arthur. Dark Money. 1992. 256p. (Orig.). mass mkt. 4.99 (*0-380-76486-5*, Avon Bks.) Morrow/Avon.
—Dark Tracks. 1992. 224p. (Orig.). mass mkt. 4.99 (*0-380-76487-3*, Avon Bks.) Morrow/Avon.

**DARK, RUBY (FICTITIOUS CHARACTER)—FICTION**

Most, Bruce W. Bonded for Murder: A Ruby Dark Mystery. 1996. (Dead Letter Mysteries Ser.). 279p. mass mkt. 5.99 (*0-312-96051-4*, St. Martin's Paperbacks) St. Martin's Pr.
—Missing Bonds, Vol. 1. 1997. (Ruby Dark Ser.). 288p. mass mkt. 5.99 (*0-312-96273-8*, St. Martin's Paperbacks) St. Martin's Pr.

**DARKMAN (FICTITIOUS CHARACTER)—FICTION**

Boyll, Randall. Darkman. 1990. mass mkt. 3.95 o.s.i (*0-515-10378-0*, Jove) Berkley Publishing Group.
—Darkman. Ryan, Kevin, ed. 1994. 224p. mass mkt. 4.99 (*0-671-78764-0*, Pocket) Simon & Schuster.
—The Gods of Hell. Shannon, Scott, ed. 1994. (Darkman Ser.: No. 3). 224p. (Orig.). mass mkt. 5.50 (*0-671-79435-3*, Pocket) Simon & Schuster.
—In the Face of Death. 1995. (Illus.). 224p. mass mkt. 5.50 (*0-671-79436-1*, Pocket) Simon & Schuster.
—The Price of Fear. Shannon, Scott, ed. 1994. (Darkman Ser.: No. 2). 224p. (Orig.). mass mkt. 5.50 (*0-671-79434-5*, Pocket) Simon & Schuster.

**DARLING, ANNIE LAURANCE (FICTITIOUS CHARACTER)—FICTION**

Hart, Carolyn. Murder Walks the Plank. 2004. 304p. 23.95 (*0-06-000474-6*, Morrow, William & Co.) Morrow/Avon.
Hart, Carolyn G. April Fool Dead. 2002. 304p. 23.95 (*0-380-97774-5*) Morrow/Avon.
—The Christie Caper. 1992. (Annie Darling Ser.). 400p. mass mkt. 6.99 (*0-553-29569-1*) Bantam Bks.
—The Christie Caper. unabr. ed. 1996. (Annie Laurance Darling Ser.). audio 64.00 (*0-7366-3457-6*, 4101) Books on Tape, Inc.
—Crime on Her Mind: A Collection of Short Stories. 1999. (Mystery Ser.). 268p. 21.95 (*0-7862-1735-9*, Five Star) Gale Group.
—Deadly Valentine. 1991. (Death on Demand Ser.). 272p. mass mkt. 6.99 incl. audio (*0-553-28847-4*) Bantam Bks.
—Deadly Valentine. l.t. ed. 1998. (Beeler Large Print Mystery Ser.). 25.95 (*1-57490-189-3*, Beeler Large Print Bks.) Beeler, Thomas T. Publisher.
—Deadly Valentine. unabr. ed. 1996. (Annie Laurance Darling Ser.). audio 48.00 (*0-7366-3407-X*, 4053) Books on Tape, Inc.
—Deadly Valentine. 1990. 192p. 14.95 o.s.i (*0-385-26518-2*) Doubleday Publishing.
—Death on Demand. 1989. 208p. mass mkt. 1.95 o.s.i (*0-553-18502-0*); 1987. 224p. mass mkt. 6.99 (*0-553-26351-X*) Bantam Bks.
—Death on Demand. l.t. ed. 2000. (Mystery Ser.). (Illus.). 227p. 26.95 (*1-57490-276-8*, Beeler Large Print Bks.) Beeler, Thomas T. Publisher.
—Death on Demand. 2000. audio 40.00 (*0-7366-4838-0*); audio compact disk 48.00 (*0-7366-7500-0*); (Books on Demand Ser.: 1). audio 30.00 Books on Tape, Inc.
—Death on Demand. l.t. ed. 2000. (Wheeler Softcover Ser.). 280p. pap. 24.95 (*1-56895-914-1*, Wheeler Publishing, Inc.) Gale Group.
—Design for Murder. 1988. 320p. mass mkt. 6.99 (*0-553-26562-8*) Bantam Bks.
—Design for Murder. l.t. ed. 2000. (Beeler Large Print Mystery Ser.). 208p. (*1-57490-291-1*, Beeler Large Print Bks.) Beeler, Thomas T. Publisher.
—Design for Murder. unabr. ed. 1999. (Annie Laurance Darling Ser.). audio 48.00 (*0-7366-4457-1*, 4902) Books on Tape, Inc.
—Design for Murder. l.t. ed. 2001. (Large Print Bks.). (Illus.). 345p. pap. 23.95 o.p. (*1-58724-112-9*, Wheeler Publishing, Inc.) Gale Group.
—Engaged to Die. 2003. 320p. 23.95 (*0-06-000469-X*, Morrow, William & Co.) Morrow/Avon.
—Engaged to Die: A Death on Demand Mystery. l.t. ed. 2003. (Core Ser.). 31.95 (*0-7862-5553-6*) Thorndike Pr.
—Honeymoon for Murder. 1994. 20.00 o.p. (*0-7278-4590-X*) Severn Hse. Pubs., Ltd.
—Honeymoon with Murder. 1988. 256p. mass mkt. 6.99 (*0-553-27608-5*) Bantam Bks.
—A Little Class on Murder. l.t. ed. 1992. pap. 21.95 o.p. (*0-7927-1140-8*, CS0306); 1991. 23.95 o.p. (*0-7927-1139-4*, CH0234) BBC Audiobooks America.
—A Little Class on Murder. 1989. 272p. mass mkt. 6.99 (*0-553-28208-5*) Bantam Bks.
—A Little Class on Murder. unabr. collector's ed. 1996. (Annie Laurance Darling Ser.). audio 48.00 (*0-7366-3419-3*, 894409) Books on Tape, Inc.
—A Little Class on Murder. 1989. 12.95 o.s.i (*0-385-26452-6*) Doubleday Publishing.
—Mint Julep Murder. 1996. 256p. mass mkt. 6.99 (*0-553-57202-4*); 1995. 288p. 19.95 o.s.i (*0-553-09463-7*) Bantam Bks.
—Mint Julep Murder. unabr. ed. 1996. (Annie Laurance Darling Ser.). audio 48.00 (*0-7366-3498-3*, 4138) Books on Tape, Inc.
—Mint Julep Murder. l.t. ed. 1996. 362p. 23.95 o.p. (*0-7838-1496-8*, Macmillan Reference USA) Gale Group.
—Something Wicked. 1988. 256p. mass mkt. 6.99 (*0-553-27222-5*) Bantam Bks.
—Something Wicked. 1994. 20.00 (*0-7278-4656-6*) Severn Hse. Pubs., Ltd.
—Southern Ghost. 1993. (Annie Darling Ser.). 320p. mass mkt. 6.99 (*0-553-56275-4*) Bantam Bks.
—Southern Ghost. unabr. ed. 1996. (Annie Laurance Darling Ser.). audio 56.00 (*0-7366-3501-7*, 4141) Books on Tape, Inc.
—Sugarplum Dead. l.t. ed. 2001. (G. K. Hall Core Ser.). 472p. 30.95 (*0-7838-9377-9*, Macmillan Reference USA) Gale Group.
—Sugarplum Dead. (Death on Demand Mysteries Ser.). 2001. 416p. mass mkt. 6.99 (*0-380-80719-X*, Avon Bks.); 2000. 352p. 24.00 (*0-380-97772-9*, Morrow, William & Co.) Morrow/Avon.
—White Elephant Dead. (Death on Demand Mysteries Ser.). 2000. 304p. mass mkt. 6.99 (*0-380-79325-3*); 1999. 277p. 23.00 (*0-380-97530-0*) Morrow/Avon. (Avon Bks.).
—White Elephant Dead. l.t. ed. 2000. (Mystery Ser.). 431p. 29.95 o.p. (*0-7862-2341-3*) Thorndike Pr.
—Yankee Doodle Dead. l.t. ed. 1999. pap. 24.95 (*1-56895-718-1*, Wheeler Publishing, Inc.) Gale Group.
—Yankee Doodle Dead. 1999. 304p. mass mkt. 6.99 (*0-380-79326-1*); 1998. 288p. 21.00 (*0-380-97529-7*) Morrow/Avon. (Avon Bks.).

**DARLING, MAX (FICTITIOUS CHARACTER)—FICTION**

Hart, Carolyn G. April Fool Dead. 2002. 304p. 23.95 (*0-380-97774-5*) Morrow/Avon.
—The Christie Caper. unabr. ed. 1996. (Annie Laurance Darling Ser.). audio 64.00 (*0-7366-3457-6*, 4101) Books on Tape, Inc.
—Deadly Valentine. 1991. (Death on Demand Ser.). 272p. mass mkt. 6.99 incl. audio (*0-553-28847-4*) Bantam Bks.
—Deadly Valentine. l.t. ed. 1998. (Beeler Large Print Mystery Ser.). 25.95 (*1-57490-189-3*, Beeler Large Print Bks.) Beeler, Thomas T. Publisher.
—Deadly Valentine. unabr. ed. 1996. (Annie Laurance Darling Ser.). audio 48.00 (*0-7366-3407-X*, 4053) Books on Tape, Inc.
—Deadly Valentine. 1990. 192p. 14.95 o.s.i (*0-385-26518-2*) Doubleday Publishing.
—Death on Demand. 1989. 208p. mass mkt. 1.95 o.s.i (*0-553-18502-0*); 1987. 224p. mass mkt. 6.99 (*0-553-26351-X*) Bantam Bks.
—Death on Demand. l.t. ed. 2000. (Mystery Ser.). (Illus.). 227p. 26.95 (*1-57490-276-8*, Beeler Large Print Bks.) Beeler, Thomas T. Publisher.
—Death on Demand. 2000. audio 40.00 (*0-7366-4838-0*); audio compact disk 48.00 (*0-7366-7500-0*); (Books on Demand Ser.: 1). audio 30.00 Books on Tape, Inc.
—Death on Demand. l.t. ed. 2000. (Wheeler Softcover Ser.). 280p. pap. 24.95 (*1-56895-914-1*, Wheeler Publishing, Inc.) Gale Group.
—Design for Murder. 1988. 320p. mass mkt. 6.99 (*0-553-26562-8*) Bantam Bks.
—Design for Murder. l.t. ed. 2000. (Beeler Large Print Mystery Ser.). 208p. (*1-57490-291-1*, Beeler Large Print Bks.) Beeler, Thomas T. Publisher.
—Design for Murder. unabr. ed. 1999. (Annie Laurance Darling Ser.). audio 48.00 (*0-7366-4457-1*, 4902) Books on Tape, Inc.
—Design for Murder. l.t. ed. 2001. (Large Print Bks.). (Illus.). 345p. pap. 23.95 o.p. (*1-58724-112-9*, Wheeler Publishing, Inc.) Gale Group.
—Engaged to Die. 2003. 320p. 23.95 (*0-06-000469-X*, Morrow, William & Co.) Morrow/Avon.
—Engaged to Die: A Death on Demand Mystery. l.t. ed. 2003. (Core Ser.). 31.95 (*0-7862-5553-6*) Thorndike Pr.
—A Little Class on Murder. l.t. ed. 1992. pap. 21.95 o.p. (*0-7927-1140-8*, CS0306); 1991. 23.95 o.p. (*0-7927-1139-4*, CH0234) BBC Audiobooks America.
—A Little Class on Murder. 1989. 272p. mass mkt. 6.99 (*0-553-28208-5*) Bantam Bks.
—A Little Class on Murder. unabr. collector's ed. 1996. (Annie Laurance Darling Ser.). audio 48.00 (*0-7366-3419-3*, 894409) Books on Tape, Inc.
—A Little Class on Murder. 1989. 12.95 o.s.i (*0-385-26452-6*) Doubleday Publishing.
—Mint Julep Murder. 1996. 256p. mass mkt. 6.99 (*0-553-57202-4*); 1995. 288p. 19.95 o.s.i (*0-553-09463-7*) Bantam Bks.
—Mint Julep Murder. unabr. ed. 1996. (Annie Laurance Darling Ser.). audio 48.00 (*0-7366-3498-3*, 4138) Books on Tape, Inc.
—Mint Julep Murder. l.t. ed. 1996. 362p. 23.95 o.p. (*0-7838-1496-8*, Macmillan Reference USA) Gale Group.
—Southern Ghost. 1993. (Annie Darling Ser.). 320p. mass mkt. 6.99 (*0-553-56275-4*) Bantam Bks.
—Southern Ghost. unabr. ed. 1996. (Annie Laurance Darling Ser.). audio 56.00 (*0-7366-3501-7*, 4141) Books on Tape, Inc.
—Sugarplum Dead. 2001. (Death on Demand Mysteries Ser.). 416p. mass mkt. 6.99 (*0-380-80719-X*, Avon Bks.) Morrow/Avon.
—White Elephant Dead. (Death on Demand Mysteries Ser.). 2000. 304p. mass mkt. 6.99 (*0-380-79325-3*); 1999. 277p. 23.00 (*0-380-97530-0*) Morrow/Avon. (Avon Bks.).
—White Elephant Dead. l.t. ed. 2000. (Mystery Ser.). 431p. 29.95 o.p. (*0-7862-2341-3*) Thorndike Pr.
—Yankee Doodle Dead. l.t. ed. 1999. pap. 24.95 (*1-56895-718-1*, Wheeler Publishing, Inc.) Gale Group.


Characters

—Yankee Doodle Dead. 1999. 304p. mass mkt. 6.99 (*0-380-79326-1*); 1998. 288p. 21.00 (*0-380-97529-7*) Morrow/Avon. (Avon Bks.).

**DARLING, WHIP (FICTITIOUS CHARACTER)—FICTION**

Benchley, Peter. Beast. 1992. 336p. mass mkt. 5.99 o.s.i (*0-449-22089-3*, Fawcett) Ballantine Bks.
—Beast. l.t. ed. (General Ser.). 1993. 432p. 16.95 (*0-8161-5447-3*); 1992. 389p. lib. bdg. 20.95 o.p. (*0-8161-5422-8*) Gale Group. (Macmillan Reference USA).
—Beast. 1993. audio 8.99 o.s.i (*0-679-42336-2*, RH Audio) Random Hse. Audio Publishing Group.

**DARNELL, IKE (FICTITIOUS CHARACTER)—FICTION**

Litman, Robert B. Allergy Shots. 1993. 254p. (Orig.). pap. text 9.95 (*0-918921-04-X*) Ivy League Pr., Inc.

**DARNELL, JOHN (FICTITIOUS CHARACTER)—FICTION**

McCarver, Sam. The Case of Cabin 13. 1999. (John Darnell Mysteries Ser.). 256p. mass mkt. 5.99 o.s.i (*0-451-19690-2*) NAL.
—The Case of Cabin 13: A John Darnell Mystery. l.t. ed. 2000. (Mystery Ser.). 344p. 26.95 (*0-7862-2487-8*) Thorndike Pr.
—Case of Compartment 7. 2000. (John Darnell Mysteries Ser.). 256p. mass mkt. 5.99 o.s.i (*0-451-19959-6*, Signet Bks.) NAL.
—The Case of the 2nd Seance: A John Darnell Mystery. l.t. ed. 2001. 344p. 27.95 (*0-7862-3331-1*) Thorndike Pr.
—To Die, or Not to Die- A John Darnell Mystery. l.t. ed. 2003. (Five Star First Edition Mystery Ser.). 215p. 25.95 (*0-7862-5444-0*, Five Star) Gale Group.

**DARTELLI, JOE (FICTITIOUS CHARACTER)—FICTION**

Pearson, Ridley. Chain of Evidence. 1997. audio 15.99 o.p. (*1-57375-356-4*) Audioscope.
—Chain of Evidence. unabr. ed. 1996. audio 72.00 (*0-7366-3377-4*, 4027) Books on Tape, Inc.
—Chain of Evidence. l.t. ed. 1995. 25.95 o.p. (*1-56895-268-6*, Wheeler Publishing, Inc.) Gale Group.
—Chain of Evidence. 1995. 368p. 22.95 (*0-7868-6172-X*); 2003. 512p. reprint ed. mass mkt. 7.99 (*0-7868-8908-X*) Hyperion Pr.

**DASH (FICTITIOUS CHARACTER)—FICTION**

Benjamin, Carol Lea. The Dog Who Knew Too Much: A Rachel Alexander & Dash Mystery. 1998. (Rachel Alexander & Dash Mystery Ser.: Vol. 2). 272p. reprint ed. mass mkt. 5.99 o.s.i (*0-440-22637-6*) Dell Publishing.
—The Dog Who Knew Too Much: A Rachel Alexander & Dash Mystery. 1997. (Rachel Alexander & Dash Mystery Ser.). 256p. 21.95 (*0-8027-3312-3*) Walker & Co.
—A Hell of a Dog. 1998. (Rachel Alexander & Dash Mystery Ser.). (Illus.). 276p. 22.95 (*0-8027-3325-5*) Walker & Co.
—A Hell of a Dog: A Rachel Alexander & Dash Mystery. 1999. (Rachel Alexander & Dash Mystery Ser.). 320p. mass mkt. 5.99 (*0-440-22548-5*) Dell Publishing.
—Lady Vanishes. 1999. (Rachel Alexander & Dash Mystery Ser.). 264p. 23.95 (*0-8027-3335-2*) Walker & Co.
—The Long Good Boy: A Rachel Alexander & Dash Mystery. 2001. 240p. 23.95 (*0-8027-3364-6*) Walker & Co.
—This Dog for Hire: A Rachel Alexander & Dash Mystery. 1997. (Rachel Alexander & Dash Mystery Ser.: Vol. 1). 304p. mass mkt. 6.50 (*0-440-22520-5*) Dell Publishing.
—This Dog for Hire: A Rachel Alexander & Dash Mystery. l.t. ed. 2002. 346p. 28.95 o.p. (*0-7862-4191-8*) Thorndike Pr.
—This Dog for Hire: A Rachel Alexander & Dash Mystery. 1996. (Rachel Alexander & Dash Mystery Ser.). 224p. 20.95 (*0-8027-3292-5*) Walker & Co.
—The Wrong Dog: Rachel Alexander & Dash Mystery. 2000. (Rachel Alexander & Dash Mystery Ser.). 231p. 23.95 (*0-8027-3348-4*) Walker & Co.
Benjamin, Carol Lea & Sallis, James. The Long-Legged Fly: A Lew Griffin Novel. 2001. 200p. pap. 8.95 (*0-8027-7620-5*) Walker & Co.

**DA SILVA, JANE (FICTITIOUS CHARACTER)—FICTION**

Beck, K. K. Amateur Night: A Jane Da Silva mystery. 2001. 256p. E-Book 4.95 (*0-7595-8412-5*) Warner Bks., Inc.
—Amateur Night: A Jane Da Silva Mystery. 1993. 288p. 18.95 (*0-89296-480-4*) Mysterious Pr.
—Amateur Night: A Jane Da Silva Mystery. 256p. 2001. E-Book 4.95 (*0-7595-6406-X*); 2001. E-Book 4.95 (*0-7595-4408-5*); 1994. mass mkt. 5.50 o.s.i (*0-446-40145-5*) Warner Bks., Inc.
—Cold Smoked: A Jane Da Silva Mystery. 2001. 240p. E-Book 4.95 (*0-7595-4405-0*); 2001. 240p. E-Book 4.95 (*0-7595-9445-7*); 2001. 240p. E-Book 4.95 (*0-7595-8409-5*); 1995. 320p. 18.95 o.s.i (*0-89296-537-1*) Mysterious Pr.
—Cold Smoked: A Jane Da Silva Mystery. 1996. (Jane da Silva Mystery Ser.). 240p. mass mkt. 5.99 (*0-446-40351-2*) Warner Bks., Inc.
—Electric City: A Jane Da Silva Mystery. 1994. 304p. 18.95 o.s.i (*0-89296-536-3*) Mysterious Pr.
—Electric City: A Jane Da Silva Mystery. 2001. 288p. E-Book 4.95 (*0-7595-4407-7*); 2001. 288p. E-Book 4.95 (*0-7595-6405-1*); 2001. 288p. E-Book 4.95 (*0-7595-9468-6*); 2001. 288p. E-Book 4.95 (*0-7595-8411-7*); 1995. 224p. mass mkt. 5.50 (*0-446-40350-4*) Warner Bks., Inc.
—A Hopeless Case. 1992. 18.95 o.p. (*0-89296-479-0*) Mysterious Pr.
—A Hopeless Case. 1993. 272p. mass mkt. 4.99 o.s.i (*0-446-40144-7*) Warner Bks., Inc.

**DATA (FICTITIOUS CHARACTER)—FICTION**

Betancourt, John Gregory. Infection Vol. 1: Double Helix. 1999. (Star Trek, The Next Generation Ser.: No. 51). (Illus.). 256p. pap. 6.50 (*0-671-03255-0*, Star Trek) Simon & Schuster.
Bischoff, David. Grounded. Stern, David, ed. 1993. (Star Trek, The Next Generation Ser.: No. 25). 288p. mass mkt. 5.50 (*0-671-79747-6*, Star Trek) Simon & Schuster.
Carey, Diane L. Day of Honor No. 1: Ancient Blood. 1997. (Star Trek, The Next Generation: Vol. 1). (Illus.). 304p. pap. 5.99 (*0-671-00238-4*, Star Trek) Simon & Schuster.
—Descent. 1993. (Star Trek, The Next Generation Ser.). 288p. mass mkt. 5.99 (*0-671-88267-8*, Star Trek) Simon & Schuster.
—Double Helix No. 3: Red Sector. 1999. (Star Trek, The Next Generation Ser.: No. 53). (Illus.). 336p. mass mkt. 6.50 (*0-671-03257-7*, Star Trek) Simon & Schuster.
—Ghost Ship. (Star Trek, The Next Generation Ser.: No. 1). 1991. mass mkt. 5.50 (*0-671-74608-1*); 1990. mass mkt. 4.50 o.s.i (*0-671-73515-2*); 1988. E-Book 6.99 (*0-7434-1213-3*) Simon & Schuster. (Star Trek).
Crispin, A. C. The Eyes of the Beholders. (Star Trek, The Next Generation Ser.: No. 13). E-Book 6.99 (*0-7434-2093-4*, Star Trek) Simon & Schuster.
—The Eyes of the Beholders. Stern, David, ed. 1990. (Star Trek, The Next Generation Ser.: No. 13). 256p. mass mkt. 5.50 (*0-671-70010-3*, Star Trek) Simon & Schuster.
David, Peter. Strike Zone. (Star Trek, The Next Generation Ser.: No. 5). 1991. mass mkt. 5.99 (*0-671-74647-2*); 1990. mass mkt. 4.50 o.s.i (*0-671-73516-0*) Simon & Schuster. (Star Trek).
—The Strike Zone. 1989. (Star Trek, The Next Generation Ser.: No. 5). E-Book 6.99 (*0-7434-1217-6*, Star Trek) Simon & Schuster.
—Vendetta. 1991. (Star Trek, The Next Generation Ser.). mass mkt. 5.99 (*0-671-74145-4*, Star Trek) Simon & Schuster.
—Vendetta. Stern, Dave, ed. 1991. (Star Trek, The Next Generation Ser.). 416p. mass mkt. 5.99 (*0-671-73305-2*, Star Trek) Simon & Schuster.
De Lancie, John. I, Q. 2003. (Star Trek Ser.). audio 9.95 (*0-7435-3256-2*); audio compact disk 9.95 (*0-7435-3275-9*) Simon & Schuster Audio. (Encore).
De Lancie, John & David, Peter. I, Q. (Star Trek Ser.). 2000. 256p. pap. 6.99 (*0-671-02444-2*); 1999. E-Book 23.00 (*0-7434-0079-8*); 1999. 256p. 22.95 o.s.i (*0-671-02443-4*); 1900. 252p. mass mkt. (*0-671-03581-9*) Simon & Schuster. (Star Trek).
—I, Q. abr. ed. 1999. (Star Trek Ser.). audio 18.00 (*0-671-04378-1*, Simon & Schuster Audioworks) Simon & Schuster Audio.
DeWeese, Gene. Into the Nebula. (Star Trek, The Next Generation Ser.: No. 36). E-Book 6.99 (*0-7434-2137-X*); 1995. 288p. mass mkt. 5.99 (*0-671-89453-6*) Simon & Schuster. (Star Trek).
—The Peacekeepers. (Star Trek, The Next Generation Ser.: No. 2). 1990. mass mkt. 5.50 (*0-671-73653-1*); 1988. E-Book 6.99 (*0-7434-1214-1*); 1988. mass mkt. 3.95 o.s.i (*0-671-66929-X*) Simon & Schuster. (Star Trek).
Dillard, J. M. First Contact. abr. ed. 1996. (Star Trek Ser.: No. 8). audio 18.00 (*0-671-57391-8*, Simon & Schuster Audioworks) Simon & Schuster Audio.
—Generations. (Star Trek Ser.: No. 7). 1995. (Illus.). 304p. mass mkt. 5.99 (*0-671-53753-9*); 1994. 288p. 20.00 o.p. (*0-671-51742-2*) Simon & Schuster. (Star Trek).
—Generations. 1994. (Star Trek Ser.: No. 7). pap. 17.00 incl. audio (*0-671-51996-4*, Simon & Schuster Audioworks) Simon & Schuster Audio.
—Insurrection. abr. ed. (Star Trek Ser.: No. 9). 1998. audio 18.00 o.s.i (*0-671-58259-3*, 396208, Simon & Schuster Audioworks); 2003. audio 9.95 (*0-7435-3254-6*, Encore) Simon & Schuster Audio.
Dillard, J. M. & Berman, Rick. Insurrection. 1998. (Star Trek Ser.: No. 9). 304p. 22.00 o.s.i (*0-671-02447-7*, Star Trek) Simon & Schuster.
Dillard, J. M. & O'Malley, Kathleen. Possession. 1996. (Star Trek, The Next Generation Ser.: No. 40). 288p. mass mkt. 5.99 (*0-671-86485-8*, Star Trek) Simon & Schuster.
Duane, Diane. Intellivore. 1997. (Star Trek, The Next Generation Ser.: No. 45). 272p. mass mkt. 6.50 o.s.i (*0-671-56832-9*, Star Trek) Simon & Schuster.
Friedman, Michael Jan. Stargazer: Three, Bk. 3. 2003. (Star Trek, The Next Generation Ser.). 288p. mass mkt. 6.99 (*0-7434-4852-9*, Star Trek) Simon & Schuster.
Gilden, Mel. Boogeymen. (Star Trek, The Next Generation Ser.: No. 17). E-Book 6.99 (*0-7434-2097-7*, Star Trek) Simon & Schuster.
—Boogeymen. Stern, Dave, ed. 1991. (Star Trek, The Next Generation Ser.: No. 17). 288p. mass mkt. 5.50 (*0-671-70970-4*, Star Trek) Simon & Schuster.
Greenberger, Robert. The Romulan Stratagem. 1995. (Star Trek, The Next Generation Ser.: No. 35). 288p. mass mkt. 5.99 (*0-671-87997-9*, Star Trek) Simon & Schuster.
Johnson, Kij & Cox, Greg. Dragon's Honor. Ordover, John, ed. 1996. (Star Trek, The Next Generation Ser.: No. 38). 288p. mass mkt. 5.99 (*0-671-50107-0*, Star Trek) Simon & Schuster.
Lorrah, Jean. Metamorphosis. 1990. (Star Trek, The Next Generation Ser.). 416p. mass mkt. 5.99 (*0-671-68402-7*, Star Trek) Simon & Schuster.
—Survivors. Stern, Dave, ed. 1991. (Star Trek, The Next Generation Ser.: No. 4). 256p. mass mkt. 5.50 (*0-671-74290-6*, Star Trek) Simon & Schuster.
—Survivors. 1989. (Star Trek, The Next Generation Ser.: No. 4). E-Book 6.99 (*0-7434-1216-8*, Star Trek) Simon & Schuster.
Mancour, T. L. Spartacus. (Star Trek, The Next Generation Ser.: No. 20). E-Book 6.99 (*0-7434-2100-0*, Star Trek) Simon & Schuster.
—Spartacus. Stern, Dave, ed. 1992. (Star Trek, The Next Generation Ser.: No. 20). 288p. mass mkt. 5.50 (*0-671-76051-3*, Star Trek) Simon & Schuster.
Neason, Rebecca. Guises of the Mind. Ryan, Kevin, ed. 1993. (Star Trek, The Next Generation Ser.: No. 27). 288p. (Orig.). mass mkt. 5.50 (*0-671-79831-6*, Star Trek) Simon & Schuster.
Peel, John. Here There Be Dragons. Ryan, Kevin, ed. 1993. (Star Trek, The Next Generation Ser.: No. 28). 288p. (Orig.). mass mkt. 5.99 (*0-671-86571-4*, Star Trek) Simon & Schuster.
Sargent, Pamela & Zebrowski, George. A Fury Scorned. 1996. (Star Trek, The Next Generation Ser.: No. 43). 288p. pap. 5.99 (*0-671-52703-7*, Star Trek) Simon & Schuster.
Shatner, William, et al. The Return. (Star Trek Ser.). 1997. 400p. mass mkt. 6.99 (*0-671-52609-X*, Star Trek); 1996. 384p. 22.00 o.p. (*0-671-52610-3*, Atria) Simon & Schuster.
—The Return. abr. ed. 1996. (Star Trek Ser.). audio 18.00 o.s.i (*0-671-56848-5*, 393928, Simon & Schuster Audioworks) Simon & Schuster Audio.
—Star Trek: The Return. l.t. ed. 1996. (Star Trek Ser.). 456p. 24.95 (*1-56895-359-3*, Wheeler Publishing, Inc.) Gale Group.
Smith, Dean Wesley. Invasion! No. 2: The Soldiers of Fear. (Star Trek, The Next Generation Ser.: No. 41). E-Book 6.99 (*0-7434-2119-1*, Star Trek) Simon & Schuster.
Smith, Dean Wesley, et al. The Soldiers of Fear No. 2: Invasion! 1996. (Star Trek, The Next Generation Ser.: No. 41). 288p. (J). pap. 6.50 (*0-671-54174-9*, Star Trek) Simon & Schuster.
Somtow, S. P. Do Comets Dream? 2003. (Star Trek, The Next Generation Ser.). 288p. pap. 6.99 (*0-7434-1130-7*, Star Trek) Simon & Schuster.
Taylor, Jeri. Unification. (Star Trek, The Next Generation Ser.). E-Book 6.99 (*0-7434-2073-X*); 1991. 256p. mass mkt. 5.50 o.s.i (*0-671-77056-X*) Simon & Schuster. (Star Trek).
Vornholt, John. Gemworld. (Star Trek, The Next Generation Ser.). E-Book 6.99 (*0-7434-2142-6*);No. 1. 2000. E-Book 6.99 (*0-7434-0677-X*);No. 1. 2000. (Illus.). 288p. pap. 6.99 (*0-671-04270-X*) Simon & Schuster. (Star Trek).
—Rogue Saucer. 1996. (Star Trek, The Next Generation Ser.: No. 39). 288p. mass mkt. 5.99 (*0-671-54917-0*, Star Trek) Simon & Schuster.
—War Drums. (Star Trek, The Next Generation Ser.). E-Book 6.99 (*0-7434-2103-5*, Star Trek) Simon & Schuster.
—War Drums. Stern, Dave, ed. 1992. (Star Trek, The Next Generation Ser.: No. 23). 288p. mass mkt. 5.50 (*0-671-79236-9*, Star Trek) Simon & Schuster.
Wright, Susan. Badlands. 1999. (Star Trek Ser.: Bk. 1). (Illus.). 304p. pap. 6.50 (*0-671-03957-1*, Star Trek) Simon & Schuster.
—The Badlands, No. 1. 2000. (Star Trek Ser.). E-Book 6.99 (*0-7434-0674-5*, Star Trek) Simon & Schuster.

**DAVE (FICTITIOUS CHARACTER: YAFFE)—FICTION**

Yaffe, James. Mom among the Liars. 1994. (WWL Mystery Ser.). mass mkt. (*0-373-26142-X*, 1-26142-9, Harlequin Bks.) Harlequin Enterprises, Ltd.
—Mom among the Liars. 1992. 224p. 17.95 o.p. (*0-312-08264-9*, Saint Martin's Minotaur) St. Martin's Pr.
—Mom Doth Murder Sleep. 1992. (WWL Mystery Ser.: No. 98). mass mkt. (*0-373-26098-9*, 1-26098-3, Harlequin Bks.) Harlequin Enterprises, Ltd.
—Mom Doth Murder Sleep. 1991. 16.95 o.p. (*0-312-05898-5*, Saint Martin's Minotaur) St. Martin's Pr.
—Mom Meets Her Maker. 1991. 224p. mass mkt. (*0-373-26067-9*, Harlequin Bks.) Harlequin Enterprises, Ltd.
—Mom Meets Her Maker. 1990. 256p. 16.95 o.p. (*0-312-03893-3*, Saint Martin's Minotaur) St. Martin's Pr.
—My Mother, the Detective: The Complete "Mom" Short Stories. 1996. 175p. pap. 15.00 (*1-885941-11-0*); 40.00 o.p. (*1-885941-10-2*) Crippen & Landru, Pubs.
—A Nice Murder for Mom. 1990. mass mkt. (*0-373-26044-X*, Harlequin Bks.) Harlequin Enterprises, Ltd.
—A Nice Murder for Mom. 1988. 208p. 15.95 o.p. (*0-312-02260-3*, Saint Martin's Minotaur) St. Martin's Pr.

**DAVE, THE MONKEY MAN (FICTITIOUS CHARACTER)—FICTION**

*see Enamorado, Dave (Fictitious Character)—Fiction*

**DAVENPORT, DEACON (FICTITIOUS CHARACTER)—FICTION**

Dovell, Michael. The Dahlia Connection: A Deacon Davenport Mystery. Dunn, Brian, ed. 1995. (Illus.). 212p. 24.95 (*1-877882-19-4*); pap. 11.95 (*1-877882-18-6*) SCW Pubns.

**DAVENPORT, LUCAS (FICTITIOUS CHARACTER)—FICTION**

Sandford, John, pseud. Certain Prey. 7.99 (*0-425-17521-9*); 2000. 384p. mass mkt. 7.99 (*0-425-17427-1*) Berkley Publishing Group.
—Certain Prey. abr. ed. 1999. audio 24.95 Highsmith Inc.
—Certain Prey. 1999. 384p. 24.95 o.s.i (*0-399-14496-X*, G. P. Putnam's Sons); 24.95 (*0-399-14520-6*, 690326, Putnam Berkley Audio) Penguin Group (USA) Inc.
—Certain Prey. unabr. ed. 1999. (Prey Ser.: No. 10). audio compact disk 83.00 (*0-7887-3974-3*, C1093E7); audio 75.00 (*0-7887-3096-7*, 95807E7) Recorded Bks., LLC.
—Certain Prey. l.t. ed. (Thorndike/G. K. Hall Paperback Bestsellers Ser.). 2000. 518p. pap. 27.95 (*0-7862-2007-4*); 1999. 512p. 30.95 (*0-7862-2006-6*) Thorndike Pr.
—Chosen Prey. 2002. 400p. mass mkt. 7.99 (*0-425-18287-8*) Berkley Publishing Group.
—Chosen Prey. l.t. ed. 2002. 477p. pap. 13.95 (*0-7838-9589-5*, Wheeler Publishing, Inc.) Gale Group.
—Chosen Prey. 2001. 416p. 26.95 o.s.i (*0-399-14728-4*) Penguin Group (USA) Inc.
—Chosen Prey. abr. ed. 2001. 4p. audio 24.95 o.s.i (*0-399-14758-6*); audio compact disk 29.95 (*0-399-14767-5*); audio 39.95 o.p. (*0-399-14766-7*) Putnam Publishing Group, The. (Putnam Berkley Audio).
—Chosen Prey. unabr. ed. 2001. (Prey Ser.: No. 12). audio 71.00 (*0-7887-5984-1*, 96260K8) Recorded Bks., LLC.
—Chosen Prey. l.t. ed. 2001. 480p. 32.95 (*0-7838-9588-7*) Thorndike Pr.
—Easy Prey. 2001. 400p. reprint ed. mass mkt. 7.99 (*0-425-17876-5*) Berkley Publishing Group.
—Easy Prey. 2000. (Prey Ser.). 384p. 25.95 o.s.i (*0-399-14613-X*) Penguin Group (USA) Inc.
—Easy Prey. abr. ed. 2000. 6p. audio 24.95 o.s.i (*0-399-14633-4*, Putnam Berkley Audio) Putnam Publishing Group, The.
—Easy Prey. unabr. ed. 2000. (Prey Ser.: No. 11). audio 83.00 (*0-7887-4359-7*, 96311E7) Recorded Bks., LLC.
—Easy Prey. l.t. ed. (Core Ser.). 519p. 2001. pap. 29.95 (*0-7838-9073-7*); 2000. 31.95 (*0-7838-9074-5*) Thorndike Pr.
—Eyes of Prey. 1992. 368p. mass mkt. 7.99 (*0-425-13204-8*) Berkley Publishing Group.
—Eyes of Prey. abr. ed. audio 15.95 o.p. (*1-55994-420-X*, 326336, HarperAudio) HarperTrade.
—Eyes of Prey. 1991. 320p. 19.95 o.s.i (*0-399-13629-0*, G. P. Putnam's Sons) Penguin Group (USA) Inc.
—Eyes of Prey. 19.95 o.s.i (*0-399-13846-3*) Putnam Publishing Group, The.
—Eyes of Prey, unabr. ed. 1993. (Prey Ser.: No. 3). audio 85.00 (*1-55690-826-1*, 93141K8) Recorded Bks., LLC.

—John Sandford - Three Complete Novels: Mind Prey; Sudden Prey; Secret Prey. 2000. 752p. 14.98 *(0-399-14651-2)* Penguin Group (USA) Inc.
—John Sandford - Three Complete Novels: Rules of Prey, Shadows of Prey, Eyes of Prey. 1995. 752p. 11.98 o.p. *(0-399-14007-7*, G. P. Putnam's Sons) Penguin Group (USA) Inc.
—John Sandford - Three Complete Novels: Silent Prey; Winter Prey; Night Prey. 1996. 752p. 12.98 o.p. *(0-399-14191-X*, G. P. Putnam's Sons) Penguin Group (USA) Inc.
—Mind Prey. 1996. 368p. mass mkt. 7.99 *(0-425-15289-8)* Berkley Publishing Group.
—Mind Prey. l.t. ed. 1995. 25.95 o.p. *(1-56895-233-3*, Wheeler Publishing, Inc.) Gale Group.
—Mind Prey. 1995. 323p. 23.95 o.p. *(0-399-14009-3*, G. P. Putnam's Sons); o.p. *(0-399-19275-1)* Penguin Group (USA) Inc.
—Mind Prey. 23.95 o.s.i *(0-399-14291-6)* Putnam Publishing Group, The.
—Mind Prey, unabr. ed. 1995. (Prey Ser.: No. 7). audio 78.00 *(0-7887-0387-0*, 94578K8) Recorded Bks., LLC.
—Mind Prey, abr. ed. 1995. audio 18.00 o.s.i *(0-671-52290-6*, 392984, Simon & Schuster Audioworks) Simon & Schuster Audio.
—Mortal Prey. 2002. 416p. 26.95 o.s.i *(0-399-14863-9)*; audio 24.95 o.s.i *(0-399-14894-9*, Putnam Berkley Audio) Penguin Group (USA) Inc.
—Mortal Prey. l.t. ed. 2002. (Basic Ser.). 559p. 32.95 *(0-7862-4368-6)* Thorndike Pr.
—Naked Prey. 2003. 368p. 26.95 *(0-399-15043-9)* Penguin Group (USA) Inc.
—Naked Prey. abr. ed. 2003. 360p. audio 25.95 *(0-399-15066-8)*; 360p. audio compact disk 29.95 *(0-399-15067-6)*; 690p. audio 39.95 *(0-399-15068-4)* Putnam Publishing Group, The. (Putnam Berkley Audio).
—Naked Prey. l.t. ed. 2003. 460p. 32.95 *(0-7862-5569-2)* Thorndike Pr.
—Night Prey. 1995. 416p. mass mkt. 7.99 *(0-425-14641-3)* Berkley Publishing Group.
—Night Prey. l.t. ed. 1994. pap. 21.95 o.p. *(1-56895-075-6*, Wheeler Publishing, Inc.) Gale Group.
—Night Prey. 1994. 320p. 22.95 o.p. *(0-399-13914-1*, G. P. Putnam's Sons) Penguin Group (USA) Inc.
—Night Prey. 22.95 o.s.i *(0-399-14176-6)* Putnam Publishing Group, The.
—Night Prey. unabr. ed. 1995. (Prey Ser.: No. 6). audio 70.00 *(0-7887-0192-4*, 94416E7) Recorded Bks., LLC.
—Night Prey, abr. ed. 1999. audio 17.00 *(0-671-51174-2*, 391266, Simon & Schuster Audioworks) Simon & Schuster Audio.
—Rules of Prey. 368p. 2003. pap. 10.00 *(0-425-19519-8)*; 1990. mass mkt. 7.99 *(0-425-12163-1)* Berkley Publishing Group.
—Rules of Prey. 16.95 *(0-399-13635-5)* Penguin Group (USA) Inc.
—Rules of Prey. 1989. 320p. 16.95 o.s.i *(0-399-13465-4*, G. P. Putnam's Sons) Penguin Putnam Bks. for Young Readers.
—Rules of Prey. 2002. E-Book 7.99 *(0-7865-2677-7)* Penguin Putnam, Inc E-Books.
—Secret Prey. 1999. 400p. reprint ed. mass mkt. 7.99 *(0-425-16829-8)* Berkley Publishing Group.
—Secret Prey. l.t. ed. 1998. 27.95 *(1-56895-673-8*, Wheeler Publishing, Inc.) Gale Group.
—Secret Prey. 1998. 384p. 24.95 o.p. *(0-399-14382-3*, G. P. Putnam's Sons); 24.95 o.p. *(0-399-14402-1*, 692929) Penguin Group (USA) Inc.
—Secret Prey, unabr. ed. 1998. (Prey Ser.: No. 9). audio 80.00 *(0-7887-2161-5*, 95457E7) Recorded Bks., LLC.
—Shadow Prey. 1991. 368p. mass mkt. 7.99 *(0-425-12606-4)* Berkley Publishing Group.
—Shadow Prey. abr. ed. audio 15.95 o.p. *(1-55994-419-6*, 326323, HarperAudio) HarperTrade.
—Shadow Prey. abr. ed. 2000. 3p. audio 7.95 *(1-57815-054-X*, 1036, Media Bks. Audio Publishing) Media Bks., L. L. C.
—Shadow Prey. 1990. 352p. 18.95 o.p. *(0-399-13543-X*, G. P. Putnam's Sons) Penguin Putnam Bks. for Young Readers.
—Shadow Prey. 18.95 o.s.i *(0-399-13750-5)* Putnam Publishing Group, The.
—Silent Prey. 1993. 384p. mass mkt. 7.99 *(0-425-13756-2)* Berkley Publishing Group.
—Silent Prey. 1992. 320p. 21.95 o.p. *(0-399-13742-4*, G. P. Putnam's Sons) Penguin Group (USA) Inc.
—Silent Prey. 21.95 o.s.i *(0-399-13905-2)* Putnam Publishing Group, The.
—Silent Prey, unabr. ed. 1993. (Prey Ser.: No. 4). audio 67.00 *(1-55690-918-7*, 93414K8) Recorded Bks., LLC.
—Sudden Prey. 1997. 400p. mass mkt. 7.99 *(0-425-15753-9)* Berkley Publishing Group.
—Sudden Prey. 23.95 *(0-399-14428-5)*; 1996. 320p. 23.95 o.s.i *(0-399-14138-3*, G. P. Putnam's Sons) Penguin Group (USA) Inc.
—Sudden Prey, unabr. ed. 1997. (Prey Ser.: No. 8). audio 80.00 Recorded Bks., LLC.
—Sudden Prey. abr. ed. 1996. audio 18.00 *(0-671-57421-3*, 394521, Simon & Schuster Audioworks) Simon & Schuster Audio.
—Sudden Prey. l.t. ed. 1996. (Core Ser.). 516p. 28.95 *(0-7838-1832-7)* Thorndike Pr.
—Winter Prey. 1994. 352p. mass mkt. 7.99 *(0-425-14123-3)* Berkley Publishing Group.
—Winter Prey. 1994. lib. bdg. 18.95 o.p. *(0-8161-5833-9)*; 1993. 464p. lib. bdg. 24.95 *(0-8161-5832-0)* Gale Group. (Macmillan Reference USA).
—Winter Prey. abr. ed. 2000. audio 9.99 *(0-694-52325-9*, HarperAudio) HarperTrade.
—Winter Prey. 1993. 320p. 21.95 o.p. *(0-399-13815-3*, G. P. Putnam's Sons) Penguin Group (USA) Inc.
—Winter Prey. 21.95 o.s.i *(0-399-14071-9)* Putnam Publishing Group, The.
—Winter Prey, unabr. ed. 1995. (Prey Ser.: No. 5). audio 78.00 *(0-7887-0255-6*, 94464E7) Recorded Bks., LLC.

**DAWES, ATHENA (FICTITIOUS CHARACTER)—FICTION**

Gentry, Anita. Night Summons. 1998. (WWL Mystery Ser.). per. *(0-373-26276-0*, 1-26276-5, Worldwide Library) Harlequin Enterprises, Ltd.
—Night Summons. 1996. 256p. 22.95 o.p. *(0-312-14691-4*, Saint Martin's Minotaur) St. Martin's Pr.

**DAX, EZRI (FICTITIOUS CHARACTER)—FICTION**

Palmieri, Marco, ed. The Lives of Dax. (Star Trek Ser.). 1999. xii, 347p. (J). pap. 14.00 *(0-671-02840-5)*; 1999. E-Book 14.00 *(0-7434-0081-X)*; 2003. 400p. reprint ed. pap. 6.99 *(0-7434-5682-3)* Simon & Schuster. (Star Trek).

**DAX, JADZIA (FICTITIOUS CHARACTER)—FICTION**

Dillard, J. M. Dark Victory. 1993. (Star Trek Deep Space Nine Ser.: No. 1). per. 5.50 *(0-671-78958-9*, Star Trek) Simon & Schuster.
—Dark Victory. Stern, Dave, ed. 1993. (Star Trek Deep Space Nine Ser.). 288p. mass mkt. 5.50 *(0-671-79858-8*, Star Trek) Simon & Schuster.
—Dark Victory. (Star Trek Deep Space Nine Ser.: No. 1). 1989. audio 17.00 *(0-671-79102-8)*; 1999. audio 18.00 *(0-671-04385-4)* Simon & Schuster Audio. (Simon & Schuster Audioworks).
—Emissary. 1993. (Star Trek Deep Space Nine Ser.: No. 1). E-Book 6.99 *(0-7434-1220-6*, Star Trek) Simon & Schuster.
Friedman, Michael Jan. Saratoga. 1996. (Star Trek Deep Space Nine Ser.: No. 18). 288p. mass mkt. 5.99 *(0-671-56897-3*, Star Trek) Simon & Schuster.
Friesner, Esther M. Warchild. (Star Trek Deep Space Nine Ser.: No. 7). E-Book 6.99 *(0-7434-2038-1*, Star Trek) Simon & Schuster.
—Warchild. Ordover, John, ed. 1994. (Star Trek Deep Space Nine Ser.: No. 7). 288p. mass mkt. 5.50 *(0-671-88116-7*, Star Trek) Simon & Schuster.
Graf, L. A. Invasion! No. 3: Time's Enemy. 1999. (Star Trek Deep Space Nine Ser.: No. 16). E-Book 6.99 *(0-671-04097-9*, Star Trek) Simon & Schuster.
—Time's Enemy: Invasion! 1996. (Star Trek Deep Space Nine Ser.: No. 16). 352p. (J). pap. 5.99 *(0-671-54150-1*, Star Trek) Simon & Schuster.
Hugh, Dafydd ab. The Liberated No. 3: Rebels. 1999. (Resistance Trilogy Ser.: No. 26). 256p. mass mkt. 6.50 o.s.i *(0-671-01142-1*, Star Trek) Simon & Schuster.
—Rebels: The Conquered. (Star Trek Deep Space Nine Ser.: No. 24). E-Book 6.99 *(0-7434-2055-1*, Star Trek) Simon & Schuster.
Palmieri, Marco, ed. The Lives of Dax. (Star Trek Ser.). 1999. xii, 347p. (J). pap. 14.00 *(0-671-02840-5)*; 1999. E-Book 14.00 *(0-7434-0081-X)*; 2003. 400p. reprint ed. pap. 6.99 *(0-7434-5682-3)* Simon & Schuster. (Star Trek).
Scott, Melissa. Proud Helios. Ordover, John, ed. 1995. (Star Trek Deep Space Nine Ser.: No. 9). 288p. mass mkt. 5.50 *(0-671-88390-9*, Star Trek) Simon & Schuster.
Sheckley, Robert. Laertian Gamble. 1995. (Star Trek Deep Space Nine Ser.: No. 12). 288p. mass mkt. 5.99 *(0-671-88690-8*, Star Trek) Simon & Schuster.
Vornholt, John. Antimatter. (Star Trek Deep Space Nine Ser.: No. 8). (Orig.). E-Book 6.95 *(0-7434-2039-X*, Star Trek) Simon & Schuster.
—Antimatter. Ordover, John, ed. 1994. (Star Trek Deep Space Nine Ser.: No. 8). 288p. (Orig.). mass mkt. 5.50 o.s.i *(0-671-88560-X*, Star Trek) Simon & Schuster.
Wright, Susan. The Tempest. 1997. (Star Trek Deep Space Nine Ser.: No. 19). (Illus.). 304p. pap. 5.99 *(0-671-00227-9*, Star Trek) Simon & Schuster.

**DAY, JULIAN FAMILY (FICTITIOUS CHARACTERS)—FICTION**

Thane, Elswyth. Dawn's Early Light. reprint ed. lib. bdg. 26.95 *(0-88411-974-2)* Amereon, Ltd.
—Dawn's Early Light. 1982. 352p. pap. 2.95 o.p. *(0-553-22581-2)* Bantam Bks.
—Dawn's Early Light. 1996. lib. bdg. 28.95 *(1-56849-475-0)* Buccaneer Bks., Inc.
—Dawn's Early Light. 1943. 10.00 o.p. *(0-8015-1957-8*, Dutton) Dutton/Plume.
—Dawn's Early Light. 1981. (Reader's Request Ser.). lib. bdg. 16.95 o.p. *(0-8161-3167-8*, Macmillan Reference USA) Gale Group.
—Ever After. 1976. reprint ed. lib. bdg. 26.95 *(0-88411-958-0)* Amereon, Ltd.
—Ever After. 1983. mass mkt. 3.50 o.s.i *(0-553-22933-8)* Bantam Bks.
—Ever After. 1993. reprint ed. lib. bdg. 31.95 *(1-56849-230-8)* Buccaneer Bks., Inc.
—Ever After. 1981. (Reader's Request Ser.). lib. bdg. 17.95 o.p. *(0-8161-3165-1*, Macmillan Reference USA) Gale Group.
—Homing. 272p. reprint ed. lib. bdg. 23.95 *(0-88411-969-6)* Amereon, Ltd.
—Homing. 1994. lib. bdg. 29.95 *(1-56849-479-3)* Buccaneer Bks., Inc.
—Homing. l.t. ed. 1981. lib. bdg. 15.95 o.p. *(0-8161-3164-3*, Macmillan Reference USA) Gale Group.
—Kissing Kin. 374p. reprint ed. lib. bdg. 27.95 *(0-88411-970-X)* Amereon, Ltd.
—Kissing Kin. 1994. lib. bdg. 29.95 *(1-56849-477-7)* Buccaneer Bks., Inc.
—Kissing Kin. 1981. (Reader's Request Ser.: No. 5). lib. bdg. 16.95 o.p. *(0-8161-3162-7*, Macmillan Reference USA) Gale Group.
—The Light Heart. 1974. reprint ed. lib. bdg. 26.95 *(0-88411-951-3)* Amereon, Ltd.
—The Light Heart. 1996. lib. bdg. 29.95 *(1-56849-476-9)* Buccaneer Bks., Inc.
—The Light Heart. 1977. 10.00 o.p. *(0-8015-4543-9*, Dutton) Dutton/Plume.
—The Light Heart. 1981. (Williamsburg Ser.: No. 4). lib. bdg. 17.95 o.p. *(0-8161-3163-5*, Macmillan Reference USA) Gale Group.
—This Was Tomorrow. 1976. reprint ed. lib. bdg. 24.95 *(0-88411-962-9)* Amereon, Ltd.
—This Was Tomorrow. 1994. lib. bdg. 29.95 *(1-56849-478-5)* Buccaneer Bks., Inc.
—This Was Tomorrow. 1981. (Williamsburg Ser.: No. 6). lib. bdg. 14.95 o.p. *(0-8161-3161-9*, Macmillan Reference USA) Gale Group.
—Yankee Stranger. 1976. reprint ed. lib. bdg. 25.95 *(0-88411-963-7)* Amereon, Ltd.
—Yankee Stranger. 1993. reprint ed. lib. bdg. 31.95 *(1-56849-229-4)* Buccaneer Bks., Inc.
—Yankee Stranger. 1981. (Williamsburg Ser.: No. 2). lib. bdg. 16.95 o.p. *(0-8161-3166-X*, Macmillan Reference USA) Gale Group.
—Yankee Stranger. unabr. ed. 2001. audio 84.95 *(1-85089-622-4*, 91014) ISIS Audio Bks. GBR. *Dist:* Ulverscroft Large Print Bks., Ltd.

**DEAL, JOHN (FICTITIOUS CHARACTER)—FICTION**

Standiford, Les. Bone Key: A John Deal Novel. 2002. 320p. 24.95 *(0-399-14874-4)* Putnam Publishing Group, The.
—Deal on Ice. 1997. 256p. 23.00 o.p. *(0-06-017620-2)* HarperCollins Pubs.
—Deal on Ice. 1998. 400p. mass mkt. 6.50 o.s.i *(0-06-109338-6*, HarperTorch) Morrow/Avon.
—Deal to Die For. 1995. 352p. 22.00 o.p. *(0-06-017621-0)* HarperTrade.
—Deal to Die For. 1996. 352p. mass mkt. 5.99 o.p. *(0-06-109337-8*, HarperTorch) Morrow/Avon.
—Deal with the Dead. 2001. 336p. 24.95 o.s.i *(0-399-14704-7)* Penguin Group (USA) Inc.
—Done Deal. 1993. 288p. 20.00 o.p. *(0-06-017731-4)* HarperTrade.
—Done Deal. 1994. 336p. mass mkt. 5.50 o.s.i *(0-06-109143-X*, HarperTorch) Morrow/Avon.
—Done Deal. 2002. 299p. pap. 14.95 o.s.i *(1-59058-002-8)* Poisoned Pen Pr.
—Done Deal, unabr. ed. 1998. audio 60.00 *(0-7887-1887-8*, 95309E7) Recorded Bks., LLC.
—Havana Run. 2004. 288p. mass mkt. 7.99 *(0-425-19717-4)* Berkley Publishing Group.
—Havana Run. l.t. ed. 2003. (John Deal Novel Ser.). 422p. 29.95 *(0-7862-5565-X)* Thorndike Pr.
—The Havana Run: A John Deal Novel. 2003. 320p. 24.95 *(0-399-15059-5*, Putnam & Grosset) Putnam Publishing Group, The.
—Presidential Deal. 1998. 304p. 24.00 o.s.i *(0-06-018655-0)* HarperCollins Pubs.
—Presidential Deal. 1999. 432p. mass mkt. 6.50 o.s.i *(0-06-109553-2*, HarperTorch) Morrow/Avon.
—Presidential Deal, 1998. audio 80.00 *(0-7887-2503-3*, 95575E7) Recorded Bks., LLC.
—Raw Deal. 1994. 288p. 22.00 o.p. *(0-06-017732-2)* HarperCollins Pubs.
—Raw Deal. 1995. 384p. mass mkt. 5.50 o.s.i *(0-06-109144-8*, HarperTorch) Morrow/Avon.
—Raw Deal. 2003. 320p. pap. 14.95 o.s.i *(1-59058-106-7)* Poisoned Pen Pr.
—Raw Deal, unabr. ed. 1998. audio 70.00 *(0-7887-1318-3*, 95176E7) Recorded Bks., LLC.

**DEAN, GEVAN (FICTITIOUS CHARACTER)—FICTION**

MacDonald, John D. Area of Suspicion. 1986. (Travis McGee Novel Ser.). 208p. mass mkt. 5.99 o.s.i *(0-449-13099-1*, Fawcett) Ballantine Bks.

**DEAN, JEFFREY (FICTITIOUS CHARACTER)—FICTION**

Warga, Wayne. Fatal Impressions. 1989. 224p. 16.95 o.p. *(0-87795-990-0*, Morrow, William & Co.) Morrow/Avon.
—Fatal Impressions. 1990. 224p. pap. 3.95 o.p. *(0-14-012431-4*, Penguin Bks.) Viking Penguin.
—Hardcover. 1985. 256p. 15.95 o.p. *(0-87795-749-5*, Morrow, William & Co.) Morrow/Avon.
—Hardcover. 1987. (Illus.). 288p. pap. o.s.i *(0-14-012875-1)*; pap. 3.95 o.p. *(0-14-009703-1)* Viking Penguin. (Penguin Bks.).
—Singapore Transfer: A Jeffrey Dean Mystery. 1992. (Jeffrey Dean Ser.). 160p. reprint ed. pap. 4.95 o.p. *(0-14-014383-1*, Penguin Bks.) Penguin Group (USA) Inc.
—Singapore Transfer: A Jeffrey Dean Mystery. 1991. (Jeffrey Dean Ser.). 224p. 17.95 o.p. *(0-670-83569-2)* Viking Penguin.

**DEAN, SAM (FICTITIOUS CHARACTER)—FICTION**

Phillips, Mike. Blood Rights. 1990. 208p. reprint ed. mass mkt. 3.95 o.s.i *(0-440-20702-9)* Dell Publishing.
—Blood Rights. 1989. 15.95 o.p. *(0-312-02874-1*, Saint Martin's Minotaur) St. Martin's Pr.
—Image to Die For: A Sam Dean Mystery. 1997. 239p. 22.95 o.p. *(0-312-15147-0*, Saint Martin's Minotaur) St. Martin's Pr.
—The Late Candidate. 1991. 320p. mass mkt. 3.99 o.s.i *(0-440-20942-0)* Dell Publishing.
—The Late Candidate. 1990. 256p. 17.95 o.p. *(0-312-04866-1*, Saint Martin's Minotaur) St. Martin's Pr.
—Point of Darkness: A Sam Dean Mystery. 1995. 310p. 21.95 o.p. *(0-312-11875-9*, Saint Martin's Minotaur) St. Martin's Pr.

**DEANE, SARAH (FICTITIOUS CHARACTER)—FICTION**

Borthwick, J. S. Bodies of Water. 1991. 287p. mass mkt. 5.99 *(0-312-92603-0*, St. Martin's Paperbacks); 1990. 17.95 o.p. *(0-312-04269-8*, Saint Martin's Minotaur) St. Martin's Pr.
—The Bridled Groom: A Dead Letter Mystery. 1995. 336p. mass mkt. 6.50 *(0-312-95505-7*, St. Martin's Paperbacks) St. Martin's Pr.
—The Bridled Groom: A Mystery. 1994. 304p. 20.95 o.p. *(0-312-10435-9*, Saint Martin's Minotaur) St. Martin's Pr.
—The Case of the Hook-Billed Kites. (Dead Letter Mysteries Ser.). 256p. 1991. (Illus.). mass mkt. 5.99 *(0-312-92604-9*, St. Martin's Paperbacks); 1982. 12.95 o.p. *(0-312-12335-3)* St. Martin's Pr.
—The Case of the Hook-Billed Kites. 1983. 256p. pap. 3.95 o.p. *(0-14-006785-X*, Penguin Bks.) Viking Penguin.
—Coup de Grace. 2000. (Illus.). x, 335p. 24.95 *(0-312-25313-3*, Saint Martin's Minotaur) St. Martin's Pr.
—The Down-East Murders. 1991. 296p. mass mkt. 6.50 *(0-312-92606-5*, St. Martin's Paperbacks) St. Martin's Pr.
—The Down-East Murders: A Mystery Set on the Coast of Maine. 1985. 288p. 14.95 o.p. *(0-312-21855-9)* St. Martin's Pr.
—Dude on Arrival: A Christmas Mystery. 1992. 306p. mass mkt. 6.50 *(0-312-92955-2*, St. Martin's Paperbacks); 1991. 320p. 19.95 o.p. *(0-312-06341-5*, Saint Martin's Minotaur) St. Martin's Pr.
—The Garden Plot. (Dead Letter Mysteries Ser.). 1998. 336p. pap. 6.50 *(0-312-96291-6*, St. Martin's Paperbacks); 1997. 352p. 23.95 *(0-312-15131-4*, Saint Martin's Minotaur) St. Martin's Pr.
—Murder in the Rough. 2003. 352p. mass mkt. 6.50 *(0-312-98453-7*, St. Martin's Paperbacks); 2002. (Illus.). 336p. 24.95 *(0-312-28829-8*, Saint Martin's Minotaur) St. Martin's Pr.
—My Body Lies over the Ocean. (Sarah Deane Mysteries Ser.). 304p. 2000. mass mkt. 6.50 *(0-312-97040-4*, St. Martin's Paperbacks); 1998. 22.95 o.p. *(0-312-19991-0*, Saint Martin's Minotaur) St. Martin's Pr.
—The Student Body. 1991. 293p. mass mkt. 6.50 *(0-312-92605-7*, St. Martin's Paperbacks); 1987. mass mkt. 3.50 o.s.i *(0-312-90738-9*, St. Martin's Paperbacks); 1986. 320p. 16.95 o.p. *(0-312-76934-2)* St. Martin's Pr.

**DEATH (FICTITIOUS CHARACTER: PRATCHETT)—FICTION**

Pratchett, Terry. Hogfather. 1998. (Discworld Ser.). 352p. mass mkt. 8.99 *(0-552-14542-4)* Bantam Bks.
—Hogfather. unabr. ed. 2000. (Discworld Ser.). audio compact disk 69.95 *(0-7531-0759-7*, 107597); audio 69.95 *(0-7531-0520-9*, 991202) ISIS Audio Bks. GBR. *Dist:* Ulverscroft Large Print Bks., Ltd.

—Hogfather. 1998. (Discworld Ser.). 304p. 24.00 o.s.i (*0-06-105046-6*, Eos) Morrow/Avon.
—Mort. 1989. (Discworld Ser.). 272p. mass mkt. 6.99 (*0-552-13106-7*) Bantam Bks.
—Mort. 2001. (Discworld Ser.). 272p. mass mkt. 6.99 (*0-06-102068-0*) HarperCollins Pubs.
—Mort, unabr. ed. 1998. (Discworld Ser.). audio 54.95 (*1-85695-845-0*, 950901) ISIS Audio Bks. GBR. *Dist:* Ulverscroft Large Print Bks., Ltd.
—Mort. 1989. (Discworld Ser.). mass mkt. 3.95 o.p. (*0-451-15923-3*); 240p. mass mkt. 5.99 o.p. (*0-451-45113-9*) NAL. (ROC).
—Mort. 2000. audio 16.95 (*0-552-14015-5*) Trafalgar Square.
—Mort. 2000. (Discworld Ser.). xix, 167p. pap. 8.95 (*0-552-14429-0*) Transworld Publishers Ltd. GBR. *Dist:* Trafalgar Square.
—Reaper Man. 1992. (Discworld Ser.). 352p. mass mkt. 5.99 o.p. (*0-451-45168-6*, ROC) NAL.
—The Reaper Man. 1998. 286p. mass mkt. (*0-552-13464-3*, Corgi) Bantam Bks.
—Reaper Man, unabr. ed. 1998. (Discworld Ser.). audio 54.95 (*0-7531-0019-3*, 951103) ISIS Audio Bks. GBR. *Dist:* Ulverscroft Large Print Bks., Ltd.
—Reaper Man. unabr. ed. 2000. audio 16.95 (*0-552-14009-0*) Trafalgar Square.
—Soul Music. 1995. (Discworld Ser.). 377p. mass mkt. 6.99 (*0-552-14029-5*) Bantam Bks.
—Soul Music. 1995. (Discworld Ser.). 400p. mass mkt. 6.99 (*0-06-105489-5*) HarperCollins Pubs.
—Soul Music, unabr. ed. 1998. (Discworld Ser.). audio 69.95 (*0-7531-0120-3*, 961204) ISIS Audio Bks. GBR. *Dist:* Ulverscroft Large Print Bks., Ltd.
—Soul Music. l.t. unabr. ed. 1998. (Discworld Ser.). 24.95 (*0-7531-5157-X*, 15157X) ISIS Large Print Bks. GBR. *Dist:* ISIS Publishing.
—Soul Music. 1994. (Discworld Ser.). 80p. 20.00 o.p. (*0-06-105203-5*) Prentice Hall PTR.
—Soul Music. abr. ed. 2000. audio (*0-552-14424-X*) Transworld Publishers Ltd.
Pratchett, Terry, abr. Hogfather. 1999. (Discworld Ser.). 384p. mass mkt. 6.99 (*0-06-105905-6*, Eos) Morrow/Avon.

**DEATHSTALKER, OWEN (FICTITIOUS CHARACTER)—FICTION**

Green, Simon R. Deathstalker. 1995. (Owen Deathstalker Ser.: 1). 528p. mass mkt. 7.99 (*0-451-45435-9*, ROC) NAL.
—Deathstalker Destiny. 1999. (Owen Deathstalker Ser.: Vol. 5). 432p. mass mkt. 6.99 (*0-451-45756-0*, ROC) NAL.
—Deathstalker Honor. 1998. (Owen Deathstalker Ser.: 5). 528p. mass mkt. 7.50 (*0-451-45648-3*, ROC) NAL.
—Deathstalker Legacy. 2003. 480p. mass mkt. 7.50 (*0-451-45954-7*); 23.95 (*0-451-45907-5*) NAL. (ROC).
—Deathstalker Rebellion. 1996. (Owen Deathstalker Ser.: 2). 512p. mass mkt. 6.99 (*0-451-45552-5*, ROC) NAL.
—Deathstalker Return. 2004. 480p. 23.95 (*0-451-42821-8*, ROC) NAL.
—Deathstalker War. 1997. (Owen Deathstalker Ser.: 3). 528p. mass mkt. 7.50 (*0-451-45608-4*, ROC) NAL.

**DECKER, HUGH (FICTITIOUS CHARACTER)—FICTION**

Kenrick, Tony. Neon Tough. 1989. mass mkt. 4.50 o.s.i (*0-440-20475-5*) Dell Publishing.
—Neon Tough. 1988. 320p. 19.95 o.p. (*0-399-13392-5*, G. P. Putnam's Sons) Penguin Putnam Bks. for Young Readers.

**DECKER, PETER (FICTITIOUS CHARACTER)—FICTION**

Kellerman, Faye. Day of Atonement: A Peter Decker & Rina Lazarus Novel. 1998. 368p. mass mkt. 6.99 o.s.i (*0-449-00323-X*); 1992. mass mkt. 6.99 o.s.i (*0-449-14824-6*) Ballantine Bks. (Fawcett).
—Day of Atonement: A Peter Decker & Rina Lazarus Novel. l.t. ed. 1992. (Large Print Bks.). 401p. lib. bdg. 21.95 (*0-8161-5351-5*, Macmillan Reference USA) Gale Group.
—Day of Atonement: A Peter Decker & Rina Lazarus Novel. 2004. 400p. mass mkt. 7.99 (*0-06-055489-4*, HarperTorch); 1991. 359p. 20.00 o.p. (*0-688-08604-7*, Morrow, William & Co.) Morrow/Avon.
—False Prophet: A Peter Decker & Rina Lazarus Novel. 1998. 416p. mass mkt. 7.99 (*0-449-00329-9*); 1994. mass mkt. 5.99 o.p. (*0-449-45337-5*); 1993. mass mkt. 5.99 o.s.i (*0-449-14840-8*); 1993. mass mkt. 5.99 o.s.i (*0-449-14898-X*) Ballantine Bks. (Fawcett).
—False Prophet: A Peter Decker & Rina Lazarus Novel. l.t. ed. 1994. (Large Print Bks.). 554p. lib. bdg. 23.95 (*0-8161-7458-X*, Macmillan Reference USA) Gale Group.
—False Prophet: A Peter Decker & Rina Lazarus Novel. 1992. 367p. 20.00 o.p. (*0-688-10553-X*, Morrow, William & Co.) Morrow/Avon.
—The Forgotten: A Peter Decker & Rina Lazarus Novel. l.t. ed. 2001. 592p. pap. 25.00 (*0-06-620958-7*) HarperCollins Pubs.
—The Forgotten: A Peter Decker & Rina Lazarus Novel. 2001. 384p. 26.00 (*0-688-15614-2*, Morrow, William & Co.) Morrow/Avon.
—The Forgotten: A Peter Decker & Rina Lazarus Novel. abr. ed. 2001. audio 25.00 (*0-671-58271-2*); audio compact disk 30.00 o.s.i (*0-7435-0761-4*) Simon & Schuster Audio. (Simon & Schuster Audioworks).
—Grievous Sin. unabr. ed. 2003. audio 19.99 (*1-59335-087-2*, 30179) Soulmate Audio Bks., Inc.
—Grievous Sin: A Peter Decker & Rina Lazarus Novel. 1998. 400p. mass mkt. 7.99 (*0-449-00330-2*); 1994. mass mkt. 6.99 o.s.i (*0-449-14839-4*) Ballantine Bks. (Fawcett).
—Grievous Sin: A Peter Decker & Rina Lazarus Novel. unabr. ed. 1996. audio 72.00 (*0-7366-3321-9*, 3973) Books on Tape, Inc.
—Grievous Sin: A Peter Decker & Rina Lazarus Novel. unabr. ed. 1993. audio 23.95 o.p. (*1-56100-518-5*, 129, Bookcassette); audio 73.25 (*1-56100-150-3*, 885, Unabridged Library Editions) Brilliance Audio.
—Grievous Sin: A Peter Decker & Rina Lazarus Novel. l.t. ed. 1994. (Large Print Bks.). 552p. lib. bdg. 24.95 (*0-8161-7460-1*, Macmillan Reference USA) Gale Group.
—Grievous Sin: A Peter Decker & Rina Lazarus Novel. 1993. 368p. 20.00 o.p. (*0-688-10554-8*, Morrow, William & Co.) Morrow/Avon.
—Jupiter's Bones: A Peter Decker & Rina Lazarus Novel. l.t. ed. 552p. 2000. pap. 28.95 (*0-7838-8783-3*); 1999. 31.95 (*0-7838-8782-5*) Gale Group. (Macmillan Reference USA).
—Jupiter's Bones: A Peter Decker & Rina Lazarus Novel. Feron, C. F., ed. 2000. 448p. mass mkt. 7.50 (*0-380-73082-0*, Avon Bks.) Morrow/Avon.
—Jupiter's Bones: A Peter Decker & Rina Lazarus Novel. 1999. 375p. 25.00 o.p. (*0-688-15612-6*, Morrow, William & Co.) Morrow/Avon.
—Jupiter's Bones: A Peter Decker & Rina Lazarus Novel. abr. ed. 1999. audio 25.00 (*0-671-57759-X*, Simon & Schuster Audioworks) Simon & Schuster Audio.
—Justice: A Peter Decker & Rina Lazarus Novel. unabr. ed. 1996. audio 80.00 (*0-7366-3275-1*, 3931) Books on Tape, Inc.
—Justice: A Peter Decker & Rina Lazarus Novel. abr. ed. 1996. audio 7.99 o.p. (*1-56740-129-5*, 665, Paperback Nova Audio Bks.); 1995. audio 16.95 o.p. (*1-56100-850-8*, 1258, Nova Audio Bks.); 1995. audio 89.25 o.p. (*1-56100-283-6*, 914, Unabridged Library Editions); 1995. audio 25.95 o.p. (*1-56100-658-0*, 150, Bookcassette) Brilliance Audio.
—Justice: A Peter Decker & Rina Lazarus Novel. l.t. ed. 1995. 563p. 26.95 (*0-7838-1494-1*, Macmillan Reference USA) Gale Group.
—Justice: A Peter Decker & Rina Lazarus Novel. abr. ed. 2000. audio 7.95 (*1-57815-172-4*, 1115, Media Bks. Audio Publishing) Media Bks., L. L. C.
—Justice: A Peter Decker & Rina Lazarus Novel. 1996. 465p. mass mkt. 7.99 (*0-380-72498-7*); 1995. 388p. 23.00 o.p. (*0-688-04613-4*, Morrow, William & Co.) Morrow/Avon.
—Milk & Honey: A Peter Decker & Rina Lazarus Novel. 384p. 1998. mass mkt. 6.99 o.s.i (*0-449-00313-2*); 1991. mass mkt. 5.99 o.s.i (*0-449-14728-2*) Ballantine Bks. (Fawcett).
—Milk & Honey: A Peter Decker & Rina Lazarus Novel. 2003. 432p. mass mkt. 7.99 (*0-380-73268-8*, Avon Bks.); 1990. 384p. 18.95 o.p. (*0-688-08603-9*, Morrow, William & Co.) Morrow/Avon.
—Prayers for the Dead: A Peter Decker & Rina Lazarus Novel. unabr. ed. 1997. audio 80.00 Books on Tape, Inc.
—Prayers for the Dead: A Peter Decker & Rina Lazarus Novel. abr. ed. 1997. audio 7.99 o.p. (*1-56740-181-3*, 689, Nova Audio Bks.); 1996. audio 16.95 o.p. (*1-56100-919-9*, 1349, Nova Audio Bks.); 1996. audio 25.95 o.p. (*1-56100-709-9*, 218, Bookcassette); 1996. audio 89.25 o.p. (*1-56100-334-4*, 991, Unabridged Library Editions) Brilliance Audio.
—Prayers for the Dead: A Peter Decker & Rina Lazarus Novel. l.t. ed. 1996. (Large Print Bks.). 586p. 26.95 (*0-7838-1910-2*, Macmillan Reference USA) Gale Group.
—Prayers for the Dead: A Peter Decker & Rina Lazarus Novel. 1997. 424p. mass mkt. 7.99 (*0-380-72624-6*); 1996. 406p. 24.00 o.p. (*0-688-14367-9*, Morrow, William & Co.) Morrow/Avon.
—The Quality of Mercy. 1990. 544p. mass mkt. 6.99 o.s.i (*0-449-21892-9*, Fawcett) Ballantine Bks.
—The Quality of Mercy. 1989. 607p. 19.95 o.p. (*1-55710-027-6*, Morrow, William & Co.) Morrow/Avon.
—The Ritual Bath: A Peter Decker & Rina Lazarus Novel. 1998. mass mkt. 6.99 (*0-449-45814-8*); 1987. 288p. mass mkt. 6.99 o.s.i (*0-449-21373-0*) Ballantine Bks. (Fawcett).
—The Ritual Bath: A Peter Decker & Rina Lazarus Novel. l.t. ed. 2000. (G. K. Hall Core Ser.). 368p. 30.95 (*0-7838-9046-X*, Macmillan Reference USA) Gale Group.
—The Ritual Bath: A Peter Decker & Rina Lazarus Novel. 2004. 352p. pap. 12.95 (*0-06-056375-3*, Perennial) HarperTrade.
—The Ritual Bath: A Peter Decker & Rina Lazarus Novel. 1999. 384p. mass mkt. 6.99 (*0-380-73266-1*) Morrow/Avon.
—Sacred & Profane: A Peter Decker & Rina Lazarus Novel. 1998. mass mkt. 6.99 (*0-449-45815-6*); 1988. mass mkt. 6.99 o.s.i (*0-449-21502-4*, Fawcett) Ballantine Bks.
—Sacred & Profane: A Peter Decker & Rina Lazarus Novel. l.t. ed. 2001. (Magna Large Print Ser.). 400p. (*0-7505-1667-4*) Magna Large Print Bks. GBR. *Dist:* Ulverscroft Large Print Canada, Ltd.
—Sacred & Profane: A Peter Decker & Rina Lazarus Novel. 1999. 384p. mass mkt. 6.99 (*0-380-73267-X*, Avon Bks.); 1987. 311p. 16.95 o.p. (*0-87795-887-4*, Morrow, William & Co.) Morrow/Avon.
—Sacred & Profane: A Peter Decker & Rina Lazarus Novel. 1990. 3.99 o.p. (*0-517-05799-9*) Random Hse. Value Publishing.
—Sanctuary: A Peter Decker & Rina Lazarus Novel. unabr. ed. 1996. audio 72.00 (*0-7366-3355-3*, 4006) Books on Tape, Inc.
—Sanctuary: A Peter Decker & Rina Lazarus Novel. abr. ed. 1994. audio 16.95 o.p. (*1-56100-386-7*, 1359, Nova Audio Bks.); audio 89.25 o.p. (*1-56100-221-6*, 1023, Unabridged Library Editions); audio 25.95 o.p. (*1-56100-596-7*, 246, Bookcassette) Brilliance Audio.
—Sanctuary: A Peter Decker & Rina Lazarus Novel. l.t. ed. 1995. 509p. pap. 23.95 o.p. (*1-56895-090-X*, Wheeler Publishing, Inc.) Gale Group.
—Sanctuary: A Peter Decker & Rina Lazarus Novel. abr. ed. 2000. audio 7.95 (*1-57815-022-1*, 1006, Media Bks. Audio Publishing) Media Bks., L. L. C.
—Sanctuary: A Peter Decker & Rina Lazarus Novel. 1994. 396p. 22.00 o.p. (*0-688-04612-6*, Morrow, William & Co.); 1995. 428p. reprint ed. pap. 6.99 (*0-380-72497-9*, Avon Bks.) Morrow/Avon.
—Serpent's Tooth: A Peter Decker & Rina Lazarus Novel. unabr. ed. 1997. audio 72.00 (*0-7366-4049-5*, 4548) Books on Tape, Inc.
—Serpent's Tooth: A Peter Decker & Rina Lazarus Novel. l.t. ed. 539p. 2001. pap. 30.00 (*0-7838-8323-4*); 1997. lib. bdg. 28.95 o.p. (*0-7838-8322-6*) Gale Group. (Macmillan Reference USA).
—Serpent's Tooth: A Peter Decker & Rina Lazarus Novel. 1998. 432p. mass mkt. 6.99 (*0-380-72625-4*, Avon Bks.); 1997. 416p. 24.50 (*0-688-14368-7*, Morrow, William & Co.); 1997. 416p. 294.00 (*0-688-15649-5*, Morrow, William & Co.) Morrow/Avon.
—Serpent's Tooth: A Peter Decker & Rina Lazarus Novel. abr. ed. 1997. audio 24.00 (*0-671-57757-3*, 495448, Simon & Schuster Audioworks) Simon & Schuster Audio.
—Stalker: A Peter Decker & Rina Lazarus Novel. unabr. ed. 2001. audio compact disk 115.95 (*0-7927-9987-9*, SLD 038, Chivers Sound Library) BBC Audiobooks America.
—Stalker: A Peter Decker & Rina Lazarus Novel. l.t. ed. 2000. 624p. pap. 25.00 (*0-06-019729-3*, HarperLargePrint) HarperTrade.
—Stalker: A Peter Decker & Rina Lazarus Novel. 2001. 448p. mass mkt. 7.99 (*0-380-81769-1*, Avon Bks.); 2001. 448p. mass mkt. 7.99 (*0-380-81854-X*, Avon Bks.); 2000. 416p. 25.00 (*0-688-15613-4*, Morrow, William & Co.) Morrow/Avon.
—Stalker: A Peter Decker & Rina Lazarus Novel. abr. ed. 2000. audio 25.00 (*0-671-57760-3*, Simon & Schuster Audioworks) Simon & Schuster Audio.
—Stone Kiss. 2003. 528p. mass mkt. 7.99 (*0-446-61147-6*, Warner Vision); 2002. 400p. 25.95 (*0-446-53038-7*); 2002. 668p. 25.95 (*0-446-53078-6*) Warner Bks., Inc.

**DECKER, RICK (FICTITIOUS CHARACTER)—FICTION**

DeBrosse, Jim. Hidden City: A Rick Decker Mystery. 1991. 304p. 18.95 o.p. (*0-312-06368-7*, Saint Martin's Minotaur) St. Martin's Pr.
—The Serpentine Wall. 1988. 336p. 17.95 o.p. (*0-312-02278-6*, Saint Martin's Minotaur) St. Martin's Pr.
—Southern Cross. 1994. 240p. 19.95 o.p. (*0-312-11070-7*, Saint Martin's Minotaur) St. Martin's Pr.

**DECKER, STEVE (FICTITIOUS CHARACTER)—FICTION**

Morrell, David. Extreme Denial. abr. ed. 1996. audio 24.95 o.p. (*0-7871-0582-1*) NewStar Media, Inc.
—Extreme Denial. 480p. 1996. 32.00 (*0-446-51962-6*); 1997. reprint ed. mass mkt. 7.50 (*0-446-60396-1*) Warner Bks., Inc.

**DE CLERQ, ROBERT (FICTITIOUS CHARACTER)—FICTION**

Slade, Michael. Cutthroat. 1992. 400p. (Orig.). mass mkt. 5.99 o.s.i (*0-451-17452-6*, Signet Bks.) NAL.
—Evil Eye. 1997. 432p. mass mkt. 6.99 o.s.i (*0-451-40695-8*, Onyx) NAL.
—Ghoul. 1988. 416p. 18.95 o.p. (*0-688-07550-9*, Morrow, William & Co.) Morrow/Avon.
—Ghoul. 1989. 400p. mass mkt. 6.99 o.s.i (*0-451-15959-4*, Signet Bks.) NAL.
—Headhunter. 1985. (Illus.). 480p. 17.95 o.p. (*0-688-04710-6*, Morrow, William & Co.) Morrow/Avon.
—Headhunter. 1986. mass mkt. 4.50 o.p. (*0-451-40137-9*); 424p. mass mkt. 6.99 o.s.i (*0-451-40172-7*, Onyx); mass mkt. 3.95 o.p. (*0-451-40005-4*) NAL.
—Primal Scream: Scream If You Want, Live If You Can. 1998. 432p. mass mkt. 6.99 o.s.i (*0-451-19566-3*, Signet Bks.) NAL.
—Ripper. 1994. 416p. (Orig.). mass mkt. 4.99 o.s.i (*0-451-17702-9*, Signet Bks.) NAL.

**DEDALUS, STEPHEN (FICTITIOUS CHARACTER)—FICTION**

Joyce, James. A Portrait of an Artist As a Young Man. 1992. 256p. mass mkt. 4.95 (*0-553-21404-7*, Bantam Classics) Bantam Bks.
—A Portrait of the Artist As a Young Man. 22.95 (*0-89190-725-4*) Amereon, Ltd.
—A Portrait of the Artist As a Young Man, Set. unabr. ed. 1994. audio 41.95 (*1-55685-317-3*) Audio Bk. Contractors, Inc.
—A Portrait of the Artist As a Young Man. unabr. ed. 1995. audio 49.95 (*0-7861-0655-7*, 1559) Blackstone Audio Bks., Inc.
—A Portrait of the Artist As a Young Man. unabr. collector's ed. 1992. (J). audio 56.00 (*0-7366-2301-9*, 3085) Books on Tape, Inc.
—A Portrait of the Artist As a Young Man. 1992. 350p. reprint ed. lib. bdg. 26.95 (*0-89966-899-2*) Buccaneer Bks., Inc.
—A Portrait of the Artist As a Young Man. reprint ed. lib. bdg. 98.00 (*0-7426-3127-3*) Classic Bks.
—A Portrait of the Artist As a Young Man. 1994. (Thrift Editions Ser.). 192p. reprint ed. pap. 2.00 (*0-486-28050-0*) Dover Pubns., Inc.
—A Portrait of the Artist As a Young Man. abr. ed. 1993. audio 16.99 (*0-88646-343-2*) Durkin Hayes Publishing Ltd.
—A Portrait of the Artist As a Young Man. abr. ed. audio 12.95 o.p. (*0-694-50084-4*, SWC 1110, Caedmon) HarperTrade.
—A Portrait of the Artist As a Young Man. unabr. ed. 1993. (YA). (gr. 11-12). audio 28.00 Jimcin Recordings.
—A Portrait of the Artist As a Young Man. 1993. 288p. pap. 10.00 (*0-679-73989-0*, Vintage) Knopf Publishing Group.
—A Portrait of the Artist As a Young Man. 1991. (Everyman's Library: Vol. 9). 368p. 17.00 (*0-679-40575-5*) Knopf, Alfred A. Inc.
—A Portrait of the Artist As a Young Man. 1991. 256p. mass mkt. 4.95 (*0-451-52544-2*, Signet Classics) NAL.
—A Portrait of the Artist As a Young Man. l.t. ed. 1995. 410p. lib. bdg. 26.00 (*0-939495-86-4*); 1998. 255p. reprint ed. lib. bdg. 25.00 (*1-58287-057-8*) North Bks.
—A Portrait of the Artist As a Young Man. Kershner, R. B., ed. 1993. (Case Studies in Contemporary Criticism). 416p. (C). text 35.00 o.p. (*0-312-08987-2*) Palgrave Macmillan.
—A Portrait of the Artist As a Young Man. 1999. (Penguin Great Books of the 20th Century Ser.). 240p. pap. 10.95 (*0-14-028328-5*) Penguin Group (USA) Inc.
—A Portrait of the Artist As a Young Man. 1996. (Modern Library Ser.). 368p. 17.95 (*0-679-60232-1*) Random Hse., Inc.
—A Portrait of the Artist As a Young Man, unabr. ed. 1999. audio 70.00 (*1-55690-421-5*, 91106E7) Recorded Bks., LLC.
—A Portrait of the Artist As a Young Man. 1998. (Enriched Classics Ser.). (Illus.). 288p. reprint ed. mass mkt. 5.99 (*0-671-01538-9*, Pocket) Simon & Schuster.
—A Portrait of the Artist As a Young Man. 1995. pap. 13.95 o.p. (*0-312-13845-8*) St. Martin's Pr.
—A Portrait of the Artist As a Young Man. 1916. 15.00 (*0-606-02826-9*) Turtleback Bks.
—A Portrait of the Artist As a Young Man. 1993. (Penguin Twentieth-Century Classics Ser.). 384p. pap. 8.95 o.s.i (*0-14-018683-2*, Penguin Classics) Viking Penguin.
—A Portrait of the Artist As a Young Man. Ellmann, Richard, ed. 1982. 17.50 o.p. (*0-670-56683-7*) Viking Penguin.
—A Portrait of the Artist As a Young Man. 1964. 256p. pap. 7.00 o.p. (*0-14-004221-0*, Penguin Bks.) Viking Penguin.

—A Portrait of the Artist As a Young Man. 1997. (Classics Ser.). 208p. pap. 3.95 (*1-85326-006-1*, 0061WW) Wordsworth Editions, Ltd. GBR. *Dist:* Casemate Pubs. & Bk. Distributors, LLC.
—A Portrait of the Artist As a Young Man: Text & Criticism. Anderson, Chester G., ed. (Critical Studies). 1977. 576p. 15.95 (*0-14-015503-1*); 1964. (J). (gr. 9 up). pap. 8.95 o.p. (*0-670-56648-9*) Viking Penguin.
—Ulysses. 799p. 38.95 (*0-8488-2569-1*) Amereon, Ltd.
—Ulysses. 1992. reprint ed. lib. bdg. 27.95 (*0-89968-284-7*, Lightyear Pr.) Buccaneer Bks., Inc.
—Ulysses, 3 vols. Gabler, Hans W. & Melchior, Claus, eds. 1984. 1954p. text 202.00 o.p. (*0-8240-4375-8*) Garland Publishing, Inc.
—Ulysses. abr. ed. 1972. audio 12.95 o.s.i (*0-694-50050-X*, SWC 1063, Caedmon); Set. 1984. audio 19.95 (*0-694-50866-7*, SWC 328, Caedmon); Set. 1992. audio 18.00 o.s.i (*1-55994-633-4*, DCN 328, HarperAudio) HarperTrade.
—Ulysses. 1990. 816p. pap. 17.00 (*0-679-72276-9*, Vintage) Knopf Publishing Group.
—Ulysses. 1997. 1136p. 25.00 (*0-679-45513-2*) Knopf, Alfred A. Inc.
—Ulysses. 2015. 880p. mass mkt. 7.95 o.s.i (*0-451-52674-0*, Signet Classics) NAL.
—Ulysses. abr. ed. (Works of James Joyce). 1996. audio 22.98 (*962-634-511-X*, NA401114); 1994. audio compact disk 26.98 (*962-634-011-8*, NA401112) Naxos of America, Inc. (Naxos AudioBooks).
—Ulysses. Date not set. 35.00 (*0-393-03390-2*) Norton, W. W. & Co., Inc.
—Ulysses. 1993. audio 22.00 o.s.i (*0-553-47163-5*, RH Audio) Random Hse. Audio Publishing Group.
—Ulysses. (Modern Library of the World's Best Bks.). 1992. 816p. 22.95 (*0-679-60011-6*); 1967. 20.00 o.p. (*0-394-45005-1*); 1967. pap. 10.95 o.p. (*0-394-70380-4*); 1940. 5.95 o.s.i (*0-394-60752-X*) Random Hse., Inc.
—Ulysses. 2004. audio compact disk 79.99 (*1-4025-7203-4*); Pt. 2, set. audio o.s.i; Set. 1999. audio 186.00 (*0-7887-0225-4*, 94502); Vols. 1 & 2. 1996. audio 186.00 (*0-7887-0309-9*, 94502E7) Recorded Bks., LLC.
—Ulysses. 1040p. 1999. pap. 14.95 (*0-14-118086-2*); 1998. pap. 14.95 (*0-14-018558-5*, Penguin Classics) Viking Penguin.
—Ulysses: A Facsimile of the Manuscript & the Manuscript & First Printings Compared, 3 vols. 1975. 100.00 o.p. (*0-374-94440-7*) Univ. Pr. of Virginia.
—Ulysses: A Reader's Edition. Rose, Danis, ed. 1998. 826p. pap. 19.95 (*0-330-35230-X*); 1997. 824p. 47.50 o.p. (*0-330-35229-6*) Picador GBR. *Dist:* Trans-Atlantic Pubns., Inc.
—Ulysses: The Corrected Text. 1986. 608p. 29.95 o.s.i (*0-394-55373-X*); 680p. pap. 19.00 (*0-394-74312-1*) Knopf Publishing Group. (Vintage).
—Ulysses: The Corrected Text. rev. ed. 1986. 16.95 (*0-07-544944-7*) McGraw-Hill Cos., The.
Joyce, James, contrib. by. Ulysses. 1997. (*1-874675-98-8*); (*1-874675-99-6*) Dufour Editions, Inc.
Joyce, James, et al. A Portrait of the Artist As a Young Man. 1999. (Literature Made Easy Ser.). 85p. pap. 4.95 (*0-7641-0825-5*) Barron's Educational Series, Inc.

**DEE JEN-DJIEH (FICTITIOUS CHARACTER)—FICTION**

Van Gulik, Robert H. Celebrated Cases of Judge Dee: An Authentic Eighteenth Century Chinese Detective Novel. 1976. (Illus.). 237p. reprint ed. pap. 6.95 (*0-486-23337-5*) Dover Pubns., Inc.
—The Chinese Bell Murders. 288p. 2004. pap. 12.95 (*0-06-072888-4*, Perennial); 1983. (Illus.). 10.95 o.p. (*0-06-015205-2*) HarperTrade.
—The Chinese Bell Murders. 1977. (Illus.). x, 298p. pap. 10.00 (*0-226-84862-0*) Univ. of Chicago Pr.
—The Chinese Gold Murders. 224p. 2004. pap. 12.95 (*0-06-072867-1*, Perennial); 1983. (Illus.). 10.95 o.p. (*0-06-015206-0*) HarperTrade.
—The Chinese Gold Murders. 1979. (Illus.). x, 214p. pap. 8.50 (*0-226-84864-7*) Univ. of Chicago Pr.
—The Chinese Lake Murders. 1979. (Illus.). viii, 215p. pap. 10.00 (*0-226-84865-5*) Univ. of Chicago Pr.
—Chinese Maze Murders. 1997. (Judge Dee Mysteries Ser.). (Illus.). 321p. pap. 11.00 (*0-226-84878-7*) Univ. of Chicago Pr.
—The Chinese Nail Murders. 1977. 220p. pap. 9.00 (*0-226-84863-9*) Univ. of Chicago Pr.
—The Emperor's Pearl: A Judge Dee Mystery. 1982. o.p. (*0-434-82559-X*) David & Charles Pubs.
—The Emperor's Pearl: A Judge Dee Mystery. 1994. (Judge Dee Mysteries Ser.). (Illus.). vi, 186p. pap. 8.50 (*0-226-84872-8*) Univ. of Chicago Pr.
—The Haunted Monastery: A Judge Dee Mystery. 1983. 168p. pap. 2.95 o.p. (*0-684-17975-X*, Macmillan Reference USA) Gale Group.
—The Haunted Monastery: A Judge Dee Mystery, unabr. ed. 1986. (Judge Dee Mysteries Ser.). audio 26.00 (*1-55690-218-2*, 86530E7) Recorded Bks., LLC.
—The Haunted Monastery: A Judge Dee Mystery. 1997. (Judge Dee Mysteries Ser.). (Illus.). 198p. pap. 9.00 (*0-226-84879-5*) Univ. of Chicago Pr.
—The Haunted Monastery & the Chinese Maze Murders: A Judge Dee Mystery. 1978. (Illus.). 328p. 8.95 (*0-486-23502-5*) Dover Pubns., Inc.
—Judge Dee at Work. unabr. ed. 1986. (Judge Dee Mysteries Ser.). audio 26.00 (*1-55690-274-3*, 86560E7) Recorded Bks., LLC.
—Judge Dee at Work: Eight Chinese Detective Stories. 1979. (Judge Dee Mysteries Ser.). pap. 4.95 o.p. (*0-684-16179-6*, SL858, Macmillan Reference USA) Gale Group.
—Judge Dee at Work: Eight Chinese Detective Stories. 1992. (Judge Dee Mysteries Ser.). (Illus.). vi, 174p. pap. 8.00 (*0-226-84866-3*) Univ. of Chicago Pr.
—The Lacquer Screen: A Chinese Detective Story. 1982. o.p. (*0-434-82560-3*) David & Charles Pubs.
—The Lacquer Screen: A Chinese Detective Story. 1982. 192p. pap. 4.95 o.s.i (*0-684-17633-5*, Macmillan Reference USA) Gale Group.
—The Lacquer Screen: A Chinese Detective Story. Barzun, Jacques & Taylor, W. H., eds. 1983. (Crime Fiction 1950-1975 Ser.). (Illus.). 182p. lib. bdg. 5.00 o.p. (*0-8240-4951-9*) Garland Publishing, Inc.
—The Lacquer Screen: A Chinese Detective Story, unabr. ed. 1988. (Judge Dee Mysteries Ser.). audio 35.00 (*1-55690-290-5*, 88080E7) Recorded Bks., LLC.
—The Lacquer Screen: A Chinese Detective Story. 1992. (Judge Dee Mysteries Ser.). (Illus.). x, 180p. pap. 12.00 (*0-226-84867-1*) Univ. of Chicago Pr.
—Monkey & the Tiger. 1980. (J). pap. 2.95 (*0-684-16737-9*, Macmillan Reference USA) Gale Group.
—The Monkey & the Tiger: Two Chinese Detective Stories. 1992. (Judge Dee Mysteries Ser.). (Illus.). vii, 143p. pap. 8.00 (*0-226-84869-8*) Univ. of Chicago Pr.
—Murder in Canton: A Judge Dee Mystery. 1993. (Judge Dee Mysteries Ser.). (Illus.). viii, 207p. pap. 7.95 (*0-226-84874-4*) Univ. of Chicago Pr.
—Necklace & Calabash: A Chinese Detective Story. 1979. (Judge Dee Mysteries Ser.). pap. 3.95 o.p. (*0-684-16329-2*, Macmillan Reference USA) Gale Group.
—Necklace & Calabash: A Chinese Detective Story. 1992. (Illus.). viii, 143p. pap. 8.00 (*0-226-84870-1*) Univ. of Chicago Pr.
—The Phantom of the Temple, unabr. ed. 1986. (Judge Dee Mysteries Ser.). audio 35.00 (*1-55690-411-8*, 86880E7) Recorded Bks., LLC.
—The Phantom of the Temple. 1979. (Judge Dee Mysteries Ser.). pap. 4.95 o.p. (*0-684-16178-8*, Scribner Paper Fiction) Simon & Schuster.
—The Phantom of the Temple. 1995. (Judge Dee Mysteries Ser.). (Illus.). 205p. pap. 9.00 (*0-226-84877-9*) Univ. of Chicago Pr.
—Poets & Murder: A Judge Dee Mystery. 1979. (Judge Dee Mysteries Ser.). 192p. pap. 4.95 o.s.i (*0-684-16180-X*, Scribner Paper Fiction) Simon & Schuster.
—Poets & Murder: A Judge Dee Mystery. 1996. (Judge Dee Mysteries Ser.). (Illus.). vi, 176p. pap. 8.00 (*0-226-84876-0*) Univ. of Chicago Pr.
—The Red Pavilion, unabr. ed. 1986. (Judge Dee Mysteries Ser.). audio 35.00 (*1-55690-438-X*, 86550E7) Recorded Bks., LLC.
—The Red Pavilion. 1984. (Illus.). 184p. pap. 3.50 o.p. (*0-684-18142-8*, Scribner Paper Fiction) Simon & Schuster.
—The Red Pavilion. 1994. (Judge Dee Mysteries Ser.). (Illus.). 173p. (C). pap. 8.00 (*0-226-84873-6*) Univ. of Chicago Pr.
—The Red Tape Murder & Other Stories, unabr. ed. 1986. (Judge Dee Mysteries Ser.). audio 18.00 (*1-55690-440-1*, 86160E7) Recorded Bks., LLC.
—The Willow Pattern: A Judge Dee Mystery, unabr. ed. 1987. (Judge Dee Mysteries Ser.). audio 26.00 (*1-55690-565-3*, 87840E7) Recorded Bks., LLC.
—The Willow Pattern: A Judge Dee Mystery. 1993. (Judge Dee Mysteries Ser.). (Illus.). viii, 183p. pap. 10.00 (*0-226-84875-2*) Univ. of Chicago Pr.

**DEEMER, ARTIE (FICTITIOUS CHARACTER)—FICTION**

Murphy, Dallas. Don't Explain. 1997. 288p. mass mkt. 5.99 (*0-671-86688-5*, Pocket) Simon & Schuster.
—Don't Explain. Grose, Bill, ed. 1996. 304p. 22.00 o.p. (*0-671-86687-7*, Atria) Simon & Schuster.
—Lover Man. 1988. mass mkt. 5.50 (*0-671-66188-4*, Pocket) Simon & Schuster.
—Lover Man: A Mystery Introducing Artie Deemer. 1987. 14.95 o.p. (*0-684-18757-4*, Macmillan Reference USA) Gale Group.
—Lush Life. 1993. 288p. (Orig.). mass mkt. 4.99 (*0-671-68556-2*, Pocket) Simon & Schuster.
—Lush Life. Chelius, Jane, ed. 1992. 288p. (Orig.). pap. 20.00 (*0-671-68555-4*, Atria) Simon & Schuster.

**DEENE, CAROLUS (FICTITIOUS CHARACTER)—FICTION**

Bruce, Leo. A Bone & a Hank of Hair. 1985. (Carolus Deene Mystery Ser.). 192p. reprint ed. 20.00 o.p. (*0-89733-176-1*); pap. 5.95 o.s.i (*0-89733-175-3*) Academy Chicago Pubs., Ltd.
—Dead Man's Shoes. 1987. (Carolus Deene Mystery Ser.). 216p. pap. 7.95 (*0-89733-271-7*) Academy Chicago Pubs., Ltd.
—Death at Hallows End. 2003. 221p. 22.50 (*0-89733-516-3*) Academy Chicago Pubs., Ltd.
—Death at St Asprey's School. 1984. (Carolus Deene Mystery Ser.). 221p. 14.95 o.p. (*0-89733-095-1*); pap. 7.95 (*0-89733-094-3*) Academy Chicago Pubs., Ltd.
—Death in Albert Park. 1983. (Carolus Deene Mystery Ser.). 239p. reprint ed. pap. 7.95 (*0-89733-073-0*) Academy Chicago Pubs., Ltd.
—Death of a Commuter. 1988. (Carolus Deene Mystery Ser.). 192p. pap. 7.95 (*0-89733-326-8*) Academy Chicago Pubs., Ltd.
—Death on All Hallowe'en. 1988. (Carolus Deene Mystery Ser.). 176p. pap. 7.95 (*0-89733-292-X*) Academy Chicago Pubs., Ltd.
—Death with Blue Ribbon. 1994. (Carolus Deene Mystery Ser.). 176p. pap. 7.95 (*0-89733-345-4*) Academy Chicago Pubs., Ltd.
—Die All, Die Merrily. 1987. (Carolus Deene Mystery Ser.). 192p. pap. 7.95 (*0-89733-253-9*) Academy Chicago Pubs., Ltd.
—Furious Old Women. 1983. (Carolus Deene Mystery Ser.). 191p. reprint ed. pap. 7.95 (*0-89733-084-6*) Academy Chicago Pubs., Ltd.
—Furious Old Women. Barzun, Jacques & Taylor, W. H., eds. 1983. (Crime Fiction 1950-1975 Ser.). 191p. lib. bdg. 5.00 o.p. (*0-8240-4976-4*) Garland Publishing, Inc.
—Jack on the Gallows Tree. 1983. (Carolus Deene Mystery Ser.). 189p. 15.00 (*0-89733-071-4*); pap. 7.95 (*0-89733-072-2*) Academy Chicago Pubs., Ltd.
—Nothing Like Blood. 1986. 4.95 o.p. (*0-89733-127-3*); 1985. 192p. 15.00 (*0-89733-128-1*) Academy Chicago Pubs., Ltd.
—Our Jubilee Is Death. 1986. (Carolus Deene Mystery Ser.). 189p. pap. 7.95 (*0-89733-229-6*) Academy Chicago Pubs., Ltd.
—Such Is Death. (Carolus Deene Mystery Ser.). 192p. 1986. 15.00 (*0-89733-159-1*); 1985. pap. 7.95 (*0-89733-160-5*) Academy Chicago Pubs., Ltd.

**DE FLEURY, NICHOLAS (FICTITIOUS CHARACTER)—FICTION**

Dunnett, Dorothy. Caprice & Rondo: The Seventh Book of the House of Niccolo. 1999. (House of Niccolo Ser.). (Illus.). 576p. pap. 15.00 (*0-375-70612-7*) Knopf, Alfred A. Inc.
—Gemini: The Eighth Book of the House of Niccolo. 2001. (House of Niccolo Ser.: Vol. 8). (Illus.). 720p. reprint ed. pap. 15.00 (*0-375-70856-1*, Vintage) Knopf Publishing Group.
—Gemini: The Eighth Book of the House of Niccolo. 2000. (Illus.). 720p. 27.50 (*0-375-41083-X*) Knopf, Alfred A. Inc.
—Niccolo Rising: The First Book of the House of Niccolo. 1992. reprint ed. lib. bdg. 33.95 (*0-89966-963-8*) Buccaneer Bks., Inc.
—Niccolo Rising: The First Book of the House of Niccolo. unabr. ed. 2000. audio 99.95 (*0-7451-6478-1*, CAB 1094) Chivers Audio Bks. GBR. *Dist:* BBC Audiobooks America.
—Niccolo Rising: The First Book of the House of Niccolo. 1988. reprint ed. mass mkt. 4.95 o.s.i (*0-440-20072-5*) Dell Publishing.
—Niccolo Rising: The First Book of the House of Niccolo. 1999. (House of Niccolo Ser.: Vol. I). (Illus.). 496p. pap. 15.00 (*0-375-70477-9*, Vintage) Knopf Publishing Group.
—Scales of Gold: Fourth Book of the House of Niccolo. 1999. (House of Niccolo Ser.: Vol. 4). (Illus.). 544p. pap. 15.00 (*0-375-70480-9*) Knopf, Alfred A. Inc.
—The Spring of the Ram: Second Book of the House of Niccolo. 1992. reprint ed. lib. bdg. 33.95 (*0-89966-964-6*) Buccaneer Bks., Inc.
—The Spring of the Ram: Second Book of the House of Niccolo. 1989. mass mkt. 4.95 o.s.i (*0-440-20355-4*) Dell Publishing.
—The Spring of the Ram: Second Book of the House of Niccolo. 1999. (House of Niccolo Ser.: Vol. II). (Illus.). 496p. pap. 15.00 (*0-375-70478-7*, Vintage) Knopf Publishing Group.
—To Lie with Lions: The Sixth Book of the House of Niccolo. 1999. (House of Niccolo Ser.). (Illus.). 672p. pap. 15.00 (*0-375-70482-5*, Vintage) Knopf Publishing Group.
—To Lie with Lions: The Sixth Book of the House of Niccolo. 1996. 640p. 27.00 o.s.i (*0-394-58629-8*) Random Hse., Inc.
—The Unicorn Hunt: The Fifth Book of the House of Niccolo. 1999. (House of Niccolo Ser.: Vol. 5). (Illus.). 688p. pap. 15.00 (*0-375-70481-7*, Vintage) Knopf Publishing Group.

**DEFOE, CHASE (FICTITIOUS CHARACTER)—FICTION**

Day, DeForest. August Ice. 1991. 2.99 o.p. (*0-517-07663-2*) Random Hse. Value Publishing.
—August Ice. 1990. 288p. 17.95 o.p. (*0-312-03793-7*, Saint Martin's Minotaur) St. Martin's Pr.
—A Cold Killing. 1990. 208p. 17.95 o.p. (*0-88184-577-9*, Carroll & Graf Pubs.) Avalon Publishing Group.
—Fatal Recall. 1991. 272p. 18.95 o.p. (*0-88184-681-3*, Carroll & Graf Pubs.) Avalon Publishing Group.

**DE GIER, RINUS (FICTITIOUS CHARACTER)—FICTION**

Van de Wetering, Janwillem. The Amsterdam Cops: Collected Stories. 2000. 240p. pap. 12.00 (*1-56947-210-6*); 1999. 254p. 22.00 (*1-56947-171-1*) Soho Pr., Inc.
—The Blond Baboon. 1987. 224p. mass mkt. 2.95 o.s.i (*0-345-34497-9*) Ballantine Bks.
—The Blond Baboon. l.t. ed. 1993. 12.50 o.p. (*0-8161-6646-3*, Macmillan Reference USA) Gale Group.
—The Blond Baboon, 001. 1978. 7.95 o.p. (*0-395-26307-7*) Houghton Mifflin Co.
—The Blond Baboon. 1979. (gr. 12). pap. 1.95 o.s.i (*0-671-82318-3*, Pocket) Simon & Schuster.
—The Blond Baboon. 1996. 218p. pap. 12.00 (*1-56947-063-4*) Soho Pr., Inc.
—The Corpse on the Dike. 1987. 224p. mass mkt. 3.50 o.s.i (*0-345-33130-3*) Ballantine Bks.
—The Corpse on the Dike, 001. 1976. 6.95 o.p. (*0-395-24675-X*) Houghton Mifflin Co.
—The Corpse on the Dike. 1982. mass mkt. 2.95 o.s.i (*0-671-43527-2*, Pocket) Simon & Schuster.
—The Corpse on the Dike. 1995. 232p. pap. 12.00 (*1-56947-049-9*) Soho Pr., Inc.
—Death of a Hawker. 1987. 256p. mass mkt. 3.50 o.s.i (*0-345-33131-1*) Ballantine Bks.
—Death of a Hawker. 1977. 6.95 o.p. (*0-395-25171-0*) Houghton Mifflin Co.
—Death of a Hawker. 1980. (gr. 12). pap. 2.25 o.s.i (*0-671-83557-2*, Pocket) Simon & Schuster.
—Hard Rain. 1987. pap. o.s.i (*0-345-00732-8*); mass mkt. 3.95 o.s.i (*0-345-33964-9*) Ballantine Bks.
—Hard Rain. 1986. 288p. 15.95 o.s.i (*0-394-54924-4*, Pantheon) Knopf Publishing Group.
—Hard Rain. 1997. 313p. pap. 12.00 (*1-56947-104-5*) Soho Pr., Inc.
—The Hollow-Eyed Angel. 282p. 1997. pap. 13.00 (*1-56947-091-X*); 1996. 22.00 (*1-56947-056-1*) Soho Pr., Inc.
—The Japanese Corpse. 1987. mass mkt. 3.50 o.s.i (*0-345-33128-1*) Ballantine Bks.
—The Japanese Corpse, 001. 1977. 7.95 o.p. (*0-395-25777-8*) Houghton Mifflin Co.
—The Japanese Corpse. 1982. mass mkt. 2.95 o.s.i (*0-671-43528-0*, Pocket) Simon & Schuster.
—The Japanese Corpse. 1996. 296p. pap. 12.00 (*1-56947-057-X*) Soho Pr., Inc.
—Just a Corpse at Twilight, unabr. ed. 1998. (Grijpstra & De Gier Mystery Ser.). audio 44.00 (*0-7887-2181-X*, 95477E7) Recorded Bks., LLC.
—Just a Corpse at Twilight. 1995. 266p. pap. 12.00 (*1-56947-075-8*); 1994. 265p. 20.00 (*1-56947-016-2*) Soho Pr., Inc.
—The Maine Massacre. 1988. 240p. reprint ed. mass mkt. 3.95 o.s.i (*0-345-34496-0*) Ballantine Bks.
—The Maine Massacre, 001. 1978. 8.95 o.p. (*0-395-27395-1*) Houghton Mifflin Co.
—The Maine Massacre, unabr. ed. 1998. (Grijpstra & De Gier Mystery Ser.). audio 51.00 (*0-7887-2025-2*, 95400E7) Recorded Bks., LLC.
—The Maine Massacre. 1980. pap. 2.50 o.s.i (*0-671-82865-7*, Pocket) Simon & Schuster.
—The Maine Massacre. 1996. 231p. pap. 12.00 (*1-56947-064-2*) Soho Pr., Inc.
—The Mind-Murders. 1988. 208p. mass mkt. 3.95 o.s.i (*0-345-34495-2*) Ballantine Bks.
—The Mind-Murders, 001. 1981. 9.95 o.p. (*0-395-30544-6*) Houghton Mifflin Co.
—The Mind-Murders. 1984. mass mkt. 3.95 o.s.i (*0-671-54065-3*, Pocket) Simon & Schuster.
—The Mind-Murders. 1997. 224p. pap. 12.00 (*1-56947-092-8*) Soho Pr., Inc.
—Outsider in Amsterdam. 1986. mass mkt. 3.50 o.s.i (*0-345-33126-5*) Ballantine Bks.
—Outsider in Amsterdam. 1976. ix, 245p. (*0-434-85920-6*, Butterworth-Heinemann) Elsevier Science & Technology Bks.
—Outsider in Amsterdam, 001. 1975. 256p. 6.95 o.p. (*0-395-20705-3*) Houghton Mifflin Co.
—Outsider in Amsterdam. 1978. pap. 2.50 o.s.i (*0-671-43471-3*, Pocket) Simon & Schuster.
—Outsider in Amsterdam. 1994. 304p. pap. 12.00 (*1-56947-017-0*) Soho Pr., Inc.
—The Perfidious Parrot. 280p. 1998. (Amsterdam Cops Ser.: No. 14). pap. 12.00 (*1-56947-130-4*); 1997. 22.00 (*1-56947-102-9*) Soho Pr., Inc.
—The Rattle-Rat. 1986. mass mkt. 3.50 o.s.i (*0-345-32872-8*) Ballantine Bks.

Characters

—The Rattle-Rat. l.t. ed. 1986. 392p. 17.95 o.p. (*0-8161-4121-5*, Macmillan Reference USA) Gale Group.

—The Rattle-Rat. 1985. 14.95 o.s.i (*0-394-54710-1*, Pantheon) Knopf Publishing Group.

—The Rattle-Rat. 1997. 294p. pap. 12.00 (*1-56947-103-7*) Soho Pr., Inc.

—The Sergeant's Cat. l.t. ed. 1991. 8.95 o.p. (*0-7451-9503-2*, 78) BBC Audiobooks America.

—The Streetbird. 1983. 288p. 13.95 o.p. (*0-399-12808-5*, G. P. Putnam's Sons) Penguin Putnam Bks. for Young Readers.

—The Streetbird. 1985. mass mkt. 3.50 o.s.i (*0-671-47521-5*, Pocket) Simon & Schuster.

—The Streetbird. 1997. 288p. pap. 12.00 (*1-56947-093-6*) Soho Pr., Inc.

—Tumbleweed. 1987. mass mkt. 3.50 o.s.i (*0-345-33127-3*) Ballantine Bks.

—Tumbleweed. l.t. ed. 1978. lib. bdg. 11.50 o.p. (*0-8161-6569-6*, Macmillan Reference USA) Gale Group.

—Tumbleweed, 001. 1976. 6.95 o.p. (*0-395-24352-1*) Houghton Mifflin Co.

—Tumbleweed. 1994. (Crime Ser.). 224p. pap. 12.00 (*1-56947-018-9*) Soho Pr., Inc.

### DEKOK, INSPECTOR (FICTITIOUS CHARACTER)—FICTION

Baantjer, Albert C. Dekok & Death of a Clown. Smittenaar, H. G., tr. from DUT. 1997. 240p. pap. 8.95 o.p. (*1-881164-20-9*) Intercontinental Publishing, Inc.

—Dekok & Murder by Melody. Smittenaar, H. G., tr. from DUT. 1997. 240p. pap. 8.95 o.p. (*1-881164-19-5*) Intercontinental Publishing, Inc.

—Dekok & Murder in Ecstacy. Smittenaar, H. G., tr. from DUT. 1998. (Dekok Ser.: Vol. 16). Tr. of Decock en de Moord in Extase. 196p. pap. 9.95 (*1-881164-16-0*) Intercontinental Publishing, Inc.

—Dekok & Murder in Seance. Smittenaar, H. G., tr. from DUT. 1996. 205p. pap. 8.95 (*1-881164-15-2*) Intercontinental Publishing, Inc.

—DeKok & Murder on the Menu. Smittenaar, H. G., tr. from DUT. 1992. (Dekok Ser.: Vol. 31). 180p. pap. 7.95 (*1-881164-31-4*) Intercontinental Publishing, Inc.

—Dekok & the Begging Death. Smittenaar, H. G., tr. from DUT. 1999. (Dekok Ser.: Vol. 17). 200p. pap. 9.95 (*1-881164-17-9*) Intercontinental Publishing, Inc.

—DeKok & the Brothers of the Easy Death. Smittenaar, H. G., tr. from DUT. 1995. 196p. pap. 7.95 (*1-881164-13-6*) Intercontinental Publishing, Inc.

—DeKok & the Careful Killer. Smittenaar, H. G., tr. from DUT. 1993. 245p. pap. 7.95 (*1-881164-07-1*) Intercontinental Publishing, Inc.

—DeKok & the Corpse at the Church Wall. Smittenaar, H. G., tr. from DUT. 1994. 202p. pap. 7.95 (*1-881164-10-1*) Intercontinental Publishing, Inc.

—DeKok & the Dancing Death. Smittenaar, H. G., tr. from DUT. 1994. 217p. (Orig.). pap. 7.95 (*1-881164-11-X*) Intercontinental Publishing, Inc.

—DeKok & the Dead Harlequin. Smittenaar, H. G., tr. from DUT. 1993. 226p. pap. 7.95 (*1-881164-04-7*) Intercontinental Publishing, Inc.

—Dekok & the Deadly Accord. Smittenaar, H. G., tr. from DUT. 1996. 205p. pap. 8.95 (*1-881164-14-4*) Intercontinental Publishing, Inc.

—DeKok & the Disillusioned Corpse. Smittenaar, H. G., tr. from DUT. 1993. 246p. (Orig.). pap. 7.95 (*1-881164-06-3*) Intercontinental Publishing, Inc.

—DeKok & the Dying Stroller. Smittenaar, H. G., tr. from DUT. 1994. 199p. pap. 7.95 (*1-881164-09-8*) Intercontinental Publishing, Inc.

—Dekok & the Geese of Death. Smittenaar, H. G., tr. from DUT. 2001. 200p. pap. 9.95 (*1-881164-18-7*) Intercontinental Publishing, Inc.

—DeKok & the Naked Lady. Smittenaar, H. G., tr. from DUT. 1994. (Dekok Ser.: Vol. 12). 205p. pap. 7.95 (*1-881164-12-8*) Intercontinental Publishing, Inc.

—DeKok & the Romantic Murder. Smittenaar, H. G., tr. from DUT. 1994. 199p. (Orig.). pap. 7.95 (*1-881164-08-X*) Intercontinental Publishing, Inc.

—DeKok & the Somber Nude. Smittenaar, H. G., tr. from DUT. 1992. 232p. (Orig.). pap. 7.95 (*1-881164-01-2*) Intercontinental Publishing, Inc.

—DeKok & the Sorrowing Tomcat. Smittenaar, H. G., tr. from DUT. 1993. 240p. pap. 13.95 (*1-881164-61-6*); pap. 7.95 (*1-881164-05-5*) Intercontinental Publishing, Inc.

—DeKok & the Sorrowing Tomcat: Mystery. 2001. 256p. 23.95 (*0-312-24191-7*, Saint Martin's Minotaur) St. Martin's Pr.

—Dekok & Variations on Murder. Smittenaar, H. G., tr. from DUT. 1997. 240p. pap. 8.95 o.p. (*1-881164-21-7*) Intercontinental Publishing, Inc.

—Murder in Amsterdam: Two "Dekok" Adventures: "Dekok & the Sunday Strangler" & "Dekok & the Corpse on Christmas Eve" Smittenaar, H. G., tr. from DUT. 1996. (Dekok Ser.: Vol. 1). 215p. reprint ed. pap. 9.95 (*1-881164-00-4*) Intercontinental Publishing, Inc.

### DELACOUR, STEPHANIE (FICTITIOUS CHARACTER)—FICTION

Kristeva, Julia. Possessions. Bray, Barbara, tr. from FRE. 1998. 256p. 33.50 (*0-231-10998-9*) Columbia Univ. Pr.

### DELACROIX, MARA (FICTITIOUS CHARACTER)—FICTION

Blake, Jennifer. Royal Passion. 384p. 1991. mass mkt. 5.99 o.s.i (*0-449-14790-8*); 1986. pap. 8.95 o.p. (*0-449-90101-7*) Ballantine Bks. (Fawcett).

—Royal Passion. 1993. 20.00 o.p. (*0-7278-4419-9*) Severn Hse. Pubs., Ltd.

### DELAFIELD, KATE (FICTITIOUS CHARACTER)—FICTION

Forrest, Katherine V. Amateur City. 1984. (Kate Delafield Mystery Ser.: Vol. 1). 224p. pap. 11.95 (*0-930044-55-X*) Naiad Pr., Inc.

—Amateur City: A Kate Delafield Mystery. 2003. (Kate Delafield Mystery Ser.). 216p. pap. 12.95 (*1-55583-718-2*) Alyson Pubns.

—Apparition Alley. (Kate Delafield Mystery Ser.). 256p. 1997. 21.95 o.s.i (*0-425-15966-3*); 1998. reprint ed. mass mkt. 5.99 o.s.i (*0-425-16632-5*) Berkley Publishing Group. (Prime Crime).

—The Beverly Malibu. (Kate Delafield Mystery Ser.). 1989. 16.95 o.p. (*0-941483-47-9*); 1991. 288p. reprint ed. pap. 11.95 (*0-941483-48-7*) Naiad Pr., Inc.

—The Beverly Malibu: A Kate Delafield Mystery. 2003. (Kate Delafield Mystery Ser.). 280p. pap. 12.95 (*1-55583-716-6*, Alyson Bks.) Alyson Pubns.

—Flashpoint. 256p. 1995. pap. 10.95 o.p. (*1-56280-079-5*); 1994. 22.95 (*1-56280-043-4*) Naiad Pr., Inc.

—Liberty Square: A Kate Delafield Mystery. (Kate Delafield Mystery Ser.). 256p. 2000. pap. 13.00 o.s.i (*0-425-17675-4*); 1997. mass mkt. 5.99 o.s.i (*0-425-15899-3*); 1996. 21.95 o.s.i (*0-425-15467-X*) Berkley Publishing Group. (Prime Crime).

—Murder at the Nightwood Bar. 1987. (Kate Delafield Mystery Ser.: Vol. 2). 240p. pap. 11.95 o.p. (*0-930044-92-4*) Naiad Pr., Inc.

—Murder at the Nightwood Bar: A Kate Delafield Mystery. 2003. (Kate Delafield Mystery Ser.). 216p. pap. 12.95 (*1-55583-717-4*) Alyson Pubns.

—Murder by Tradition. 288p. 1991. text 18.95 o.p. (*0-941483-89-4*); 1993. (Kate Delafield Mystery Ser.: Vol. 4). reprint ed. pap. 11.95 (*1-56280-002-7*) Naiad Pr., Inc.

—Murder by Tradition: A Kate Delafield Mystery. 2003. (Kate Delafield Mystery Ser.). 280p. pap. 12.95 (*1-55583-719-0*, Alyson Bks.) Alyson Pubns.

—Sleeping Bones: A Kate Delafield Mystery. (Kate Delafield Mystery Ser.). 272p. 1999. 21.95 o.s.i (*0-425-17029-2*); 2000. reprint ed. pap. 13.00 (*0-425-17484-0*, Prime Crime) Berkley Publishing Group.

### DELANCY, RICHARD (FICTITIOUS CHARACTER)—FICTION

Parkinson, C. Northcote. Dead Reckoning, 001. 1978. 10.95 o.p. (*0-395-27115-0*) Houghton Mifflin Co.

—Dead Reckoning. 1978. 276p. (J). (*0-7195-3484-4*) Murray, John Pubs., Ltd. GBR. *Dist:* Trafalgar Square.

—Devil to Pay. 1973. 278p. text (*0-7195-2838-0*) Murray, John Pubs., Ltd. GBR. *Dist:* Trafalgar Square.

—The Fireship. 1980. (Parkinson Hist Sea Adventure Ser.: No. 2). 208p. 2.25 (*0-87216-685-6*, Jove) Berkley Publishing Group.

—The Fireship, 001. 1975. 192p. 6.95 o.p. (*0-395-20428-3*) Houghton Mifflin Co.

—The Fireship. 1975. 187p. (J). (*0-7195-3175-6*) Murray, John Pubs., Ltd. GBR. *Dist:* Trafalgar Square.

—Touch & Go. 1980. 272p. 2.25 (*0-87216-713-5*, Jove) Berkley Publishing Group.

—Touch & Go. 1978. (General Ser.). lib. bdg. 13.50 o.p. (*0-8161-6592-0*, Macmillan Reference USA) Gale Group.

—Touch & Go, 001. 1977. (Illus.). 230p. 8.95 o.p. (*0-395-25592-9*) Houghton Mifflin Co.

—Touch & Go. 1977. 230p. (J). (*0-7195-3371-6*) Murray, John Pubs., Ltd. GBR. *Dist:* Trafalgar Square.

### DELANEY, CAT (FICTITIOUS CHARACTER)—FICTION

Brown, Sandra. Charade. abr. ed. 1993. audio 16.95 o.p. (*0-7871-0015-3*, 390507, Dove Audio); 1994. 39.95 o.p. (*0-7871-0101-X*, 112717) NewStar Media, Inc.

—Charade. 1994. 416p. 21.95 o.s.i (*0-446-51656-2*); 1995. 496p. reprint ed. mass mkt. 7.99 (*0-446-60185-3*) Warner Bks., Inc.

### DELANEY, EDWARD X. (FICTITIOUS CHARACTER)—FICTION

Sanders, Lawrence. The Anderson Tapes. 22.95 (*0-89190-854-4*) Amereon, Ltd.

—The Anderson Tapes. unabr. ed. 1986. audio 41.65 Audio Bk. Co.

—The Anderson Tapes. 1987. 336p. mass mkt. 7.50 (*0-425-10364-1*) Berkley Publishing Group.

—The Anderson Tapes. 1994. reprint ed. lib. bdg. 32.95 o.p. (*1-56849-331-2*) Buccaneer Bks., Inc.

—The Anderson Tapes. l.t. ed. 2000. 319p. lib. bdg. 25.95 (*1-58547-023-6*) Ctr. Point Large Print.

—The Anderson Tapes. 1971. pap. 2.50 o.p. (*0-440-10217-0*) Dell Publishing.

—Lawrence Sanders - Three Complete Novels: The Anderson Tapes; The Tenth Commandment; The Fourth Deadly Sin. 1996. 752p. 12.98 o.p. (*0-399-14182-0*) Penguin Group (USA) Inc.

—Three Complete Novels: The First Deadly Sin; The Secondly Deadly Sin, The Third Deadly Sin. 1993. 896p. 11.98 o.p. (*0-399-13877-3*, G. P. Putnam's Sons) Penguin Group (USA) Inc.

—The 1st Deadly Sin. audio 95.20 Audio Bk. Co.

—The 1st Deadly Sin. 1987. 640p. mass mkt. 7.99 (*0-425-10427-3*); 1986. mass mkt. 4.50 o.s.i (*0-425-10061-8*); 1986. mass mkt. 4.50 o.s.i (*0-425-09310-7*); 1985. mass mkt. 4.50 o.s.i (*0-425-08169-9*); 1983. mass mkt. 3.95 o.s.i (*0-425-07154-5*); 1983. mass mkt. 4.95 o.s.i (*0-425-07039-5*); 1983. mass mkt. 3.95 o.s.i (*0-425-06299-6*); 1982. mass mkt. 3.75 o.s.i (*0-425-05604-X*); 1980. mass mkt. 2.95 o.s.i (*0-425-04692-3*); 1978. mass mkt. 2.50 o.s.i (*0-425-03904-8*); 1976. mass mkt. 2.25 o.s.i (*0-425-03424-0*); 1974. mass mkt. 1.95 o.s.i (*0-425-02506-3*) Berkley Publishing Group.

—The 1st Deadly Sin, Pt. 2. unabr. collector's ed. 1999. audio 64.00 (*0-7366-4365-6*, 4818-B) Books on Tape, Inc.

—The 1st Deadly Sin. 1994. reprint ed. lib. bdg. 35.95 o.p. (*1-56849-330-4*) Buccaneer Bks., Inc.

—The 1st Deadly Sin. 1989. audio 16.00 o.s.i (*0-394-29961-2*, RH Audio) Random Hse. Audio Publishing Group.

—The 2nd Deadly Sin. abr. ed. audio 59.50 Audio Bk. Co.

—The 2nd Deadly Sin. mass mkt. 4.50 o.s.i (*0-425-08170-2*); 1990. 448p. mass mkt. 7.99 (*0-425-12519-X*); 1987. mass mkt. 4.95 o.s.i (*0-425-10428-1*); 1985. mass mkt. 4.50 o.s.i (*0-425-08801-4*); 1983. mass mkt. 3.95 o.s.i (*0-425-07155-3*); 1983. mass mkt. 4.95 o.s.i (*0-425-06993-1*); 1983. mass mkt. 3.95 o.s.i (*0-425-06300-3*); 1982. mass mkt. 3.75 o.s.i (*0-425-05992-8*); 1982. mass mkt. 3.50 o.s.i (*0-425-05545-0*); 1981. mass mkt. 2.95 o.s.i (*0-425-04806-3*); 1978. mass mkt. 2.50 o.s.i (*0-425-03923-4*); 1978. mass mkt. 2.25 o.s.i (*0-425-03802-5*) Berkley Publishing Group.

—The 2nd Deadly Sin. unabr. collector's ed. 1999. audio 80.00 (*0-7366-4492-X*, 4930) Books on Tape, Inc.

—The 2nd Deadly Sin. 1977. 9.95 o.s.i (*0-399-12023-8*) Putnam Publishing Group, The.

—The 3rd Deadly Sin. 1985. mass mkt. 4.50 o.s.i (*0-425-09151-1*); 1985. mass mkt. 4.50 o.s.i (*0-425-08171-0*); 1984. mass mkt. 3.95 o.s.i (*0-425-07172-3*); 1982. mass mkt. 3.95 o.s.i (*0-425-05465-9*); 1982. mass mkt. 4.50 o.s.i (*0-425-05507-8*); 1987. 416p. mass mkt. 7.99 (*0-425-10429-X*) Berkley Publishing Group.

—The 3rd Deadly Sin. unabr. collector's ed. 1999. audio 88.00 (*0-7366-4513-6*, 4944) Books on Tape, Inc.

—The 3rd Deadly Sin. l.t. ed. 1982. 17.95 o.p. (*0-8161-3405-7*, Macmillan Reference USA) Gale Group.

—The 3rd Deadly Sin. 1981. 480p. 13.95 o.s.i (*0-399-12614-7*) Putnam Publishing Group, The.

—The 4th Deadly Sin. 1986. 352p. mass mkt. 7.99 (*0-425-09078-7*) Berkley Publishing Group.

—The 4th Deadly Sin. l.t. ed. 1986. (Special Editions Ser.). 512p. 18.95 o.p. (*0-8161-3989-X*); 10.95 o.p. (*0-8161-3990-3*) Gale Group. (Macmillan Reference USA).

—The 4th Deadly Sin. 1985. 384p. 17.95 o.p. (*0-399-13062-4*, G. P. Putnam's Sons) Penguin Putnam Bks. for Young Readers.

### DELANEY, PATRICIA (FICTITIOUS CHARACTER)—FICTION

Short, Sharon G. The Death We Share. 1995. mass mkt. 5.99 o.s.i (*0-449-14916-1*, Fawcett) Ballantine Bks.

—Past Pretense. 1994. (Orig.). mass mkt. 4.99 o.s.i (*0-449-14915-3*, Fawcett) Ballantine Bks.

Short, Sharon Gwyn. Angel's Bidding. 1993. (Midwest Mysteries Ser.). mass mkt. 4.99 o.s.i (*0-449-14873-4*, Fawcett) Ballantine Bks.

### DELANY, RYKER (FICTITIOUS CHARACTER)—FICTION

Baxter, Mary L. Hard Candy. 1998. 376p. mass mkt. (*1-55166-440-2*, Harlequin Bks.) Harlequin Enterprises, Ltd.

### DELAROSA, JOHN (FICTITIOUS CHARACTER)—FICTION

Scott, Barbara & Younce, Carrie. Secrets of the Gathering Darkness. 1996. 288p. pap. 11.99 o.p. (*0-7852-7776-5*) Nelson, Thomas Inc.

—Sedona Storm. 1993. 10.99 o.p. (*0-7852-8266-1*) Nelson, Thomas Inc.

### DELAWARE, ALEX (FICTITIOUS CHARACTER)—FICTION

Kellerman, Jonathan. Bad Love. 2003. 512p. mass mkt. 7.99 (*0-345-46072-3*, Ballantine Bks.) Ballantine Bks.

—Bad Love. 1994. (Alex Delaware Novel Ser.). 512p. mass mkt. 7.99 o.s.i (*0-553-56870-1*); 496p. mass mkt. 6.99 o.s.i (*0-553-18118-1*); 27.50 o.s.i (*0-553-09636-2*) Bantam Bks.

—Bad Love. unabr. ed. 1994. audio 64.00 Books on Tape, Inc.

—Bad Love. l.t. ed. 2001. 386p. 31.95 (*0-7838-9456-2*, Macmillan Reference USA) Gale Group.

—Bad Love. 1994. audio 13.59 o.s.i (*0-553-70076-6*, RH Audio) Random Hse. Audio Publishing Group.

—Billy Straight. 1999. 448p. mass mkt. 7.99 (*0-345-41386-5*) Ballantine Bks.

—Billy Straight. 1998. pap. 25.95 o.p. (*0-7838-0268-4*, Macmillan Reference USA) Gale Group.

—Billy Straight: A Novel. l.t. ed. 1998. 663p. pap. 25.95 (*0-375-70422-1*) Random Hse. Large Print.

—Billy Straight: A Novel. 1998. 467p. 25.95 o.s.i (*0-679-45959-6*) Random Hse., Inc.

—Blood Test. 2003. 320p. mass mkt. 7.99 (*0-345-46661-6*, Ballantine Bks.) Ballantine Bks.

—Blood Test. 1995. (Alex Delaware Novel Ser.). 320p. mass mkt. 7.99 o.s.i (*0-553-56963-5*) Bantam Bks.

—Blood Test. 2000. audio compact disk 64.00 (*0-7366-8058-6*); 2000. audio 56.00 (*0-7366-5642-1*); 2001. audio 29.95 (*0-7366-5718-5*) Books on Tape, Inc.

—Blood Test. l.t. ed. 2002. (Famous Authors Ser.). 405p. 29.95 (*0-7862-3753-8*) Gale Group.

—Blood Test. 1987. mass mkt. 4.50 o.p. (*0-451-15434-7*, Signet Bks.); mass mkt. 4.50 o.p. (*0-451-14737-5*, Signet Bks.); 352p. mass mkt. 5.99 o.p. (*0-451-15929-2*, Signet Bks.); mass mkt. 5.99 o.s.i (*0-451-17802-5*) NAL.

—Blood Test. abr. ed. 2002. audio 9.99 o.s.i (*0-553-75609-5*, RH Audio) Random Hse. Audio Publishing Group.

—Blood Test. 1986. 258p. bds. 14.95 o.s.i (*0-689-11634-9*, Scribner) Simon & Schuster.

—The Clinic. 2003. 496p. mass mkt. 7.99 (*0-345-46074-X*, Ballantine Bks.) Ballantine Bks.

—The Clinic. 1997. (Alex Delaware Novel Ser.). 496p. mass mkt. 7.99 o.s.i (*0-553-57230-X*); mass mkt. 6.99 (*0-553-84009-6*) Bantam Bks.

—The Clinic. unabr. ed. 1997. (Alex Delaware Mystery Ser.). audio 64.00 (*0-913369-47-0*, 4251) Books on Tape, Inc.

—The Clinic. abr. ed. 1997. (Alex Delaware Mystery Ser.). audio compact disk 29.95 (*0-553-45552-4*, RH Audio) Random Hse. Audio Publishing Group.

—The Clinic. l.t. ed. 1998. (Thorndike/G. K. Hall Paperback Bestsellers Ser.). 600p. pap. 28.95 (*0-7862-0983-6*) Thorndike Pr.

—A Cold Heart. 2003. 432p. mass mkt. 7.99 (*0-345-45256-9*); 400p. 26.95 (*0-345-45255-0*, Ballantine Bks.); E-Book 18.85 (*0-345-46365-X*, Ballantine Bks.) Ballantine Bks.

—Devil's Waltz. 2003. 528p. mass mkt. 7.99 (*0-345-46071-5*, Ballantine Bks.) Ballantine Bks.

—Devil's Waltz. 1993. (Alex Delaware Novel Ser.). 528p. mass mkt. 7.99 (*0-553-56352-1*); 512p. mass mkt. 6.50 o.s.i (*0-553-18101-7*) Bantam Bks.

—Devil's Waltz. unabr. ed. 1993. audio 72.00 (*0-7366-2424-4*, 3189) Books on Tape, Inc.

—Devil's Waltz. 1993. audio 15.95 o.s.i (*0-553-74528-X*); 1993. audio 12.79 o.s.i (*0-553-70060-X*); 1999. audio 9.99 o.s.i (*0-553-70211-4*) Random Hse. Audio Publishing Group. (RH Audio).

—Devil's Waltz. 6.98 o.p. (*0-8317-4339-5*) Smithmark Pubs., Inc.

—Dr. Death. l.t. ed. 2000. 592p. 26.95 (*0-375-43079-2*) Random Hse. Large Print.

—Flesh & Blood. abr. ed. 2001. audio 25.95 (*0-375-41940-3*); audio compact disk 29.95 (*0-375-41941-1*); audio 39.95 (*0-375-41942-X*) Random Hse. Audio Publishing Group. (RH Audio).

—Flesh & Blood. l.t. ed. 2001. 592p. 26.95 (*0-375-43129-2*) Random Hse. Large Print.

—Flesh & Blood. 2001. E-Book 21.95 (*1-58836-141-1*) Random Hse., Inc.

—Monster. 2000. 416p. mass mkt. (*0-345-44172-9*); mass mkt. 7.99 (*0-345-41387-3*, Ballantine Bks.) Ballantine Bks.

—Monster. l.t. ed. 512p. 2000. pap. 14.95 (*0-375-72794-9*); 1999. 25.95 (*0-375-40868-1*) Random Hse. Large Print.
—The Murder Book. 2003. 544p. mass mkt. 7.99 (*0-345-41390-3*); 2002. 416p. 26.95 (*0-345-45253-4*); 2002. E-Book 18.95 (*0-345-45864-8*) Ballantine Bks. (Ballantine Bks.).
—The Murder Book. l.t. ed. 2002. 672p. 28.95 (*0-375-43173-X*) Random Hse. Large Print.
—Over the Edge. 2000. audio compact disk 112.00 (*0-7366-7135-8*); audio 88.00 (*0-7366-5643-X*) Books on Tape, Inc.
—Over the Edge. 1988. 448p. mass mkt. 5.99 o.p. (*0-451-15219-0*); mass mkt. 7.99 o.s.i (*0-451-17801-7*) NAL. (Signet Bks.).
—Over the Edge. abr. ed. 2000. (Alex Delaware Novel Ser.). audio 9.99 (*0-375-40967-X*, RH Audio) Random Hse. Audio Publishing Group.
—Over the Edge. 1987. 384p. bds. 17.95 o.s.i (*0-689-11635-7*, Scribner) Simon & Schuster.
—Private Eyes. 2003. 560p. mass mkt. 7.99 (*0-345-46070-7*, Ballantine Bks.) Ballantine Bks.
—Private Eyes. audio 15.99. 1992. 560p. mass mkt. 7.99 o.s.i (*0-553-29950-6*); 1992. pap. 5.50 (*0-553-18085-1*) Bantam Bks.
—Private Eyes. l.t. ed. 1992. 720p. 25.00 o.s.i (*0-385-42283-0*, Bantam Large Type) Bantam Doubleday Dell Large Print Group, Inc.
—Private Eyes. unabr. ed. 1993. audio 88.00 (*0-7366-2351-5*, 3128) Books on Tape, Inc.
—Private Eyes. 1992. audio 12.79 o.s.i (*0-553-70022-7*, RH Audio); 2004. audio compact disk 14.99 (*0-7393-1223-5*, RH Audio Price-Less); 1999. audio 9.99 o.s.i (*0-553-70201-7*, RH Audio) Random Hse. Audio Publishing Group.
—Self-Defense. 1995. 528p. mass mkt. 6.99 o.s.i (*0-553-84002-9*); (Illus.). reprint ed. mass mkt. 7.99 o.s.i (*0-553-57220-2*) Bantam Bks.
—Self-Defense. unabr. ed. 1995. audio 64.00 (*0-7366-2958-0*, 3651) Books on Tape, Inc.
—Self-Defense. l.t. ed. 1995. (Large Print Bks.). 556p. 26.95 o.p. (*1-56895-206-6*, Wheeler Publishing, Inc.) Gale Group.
—Self-Defense. abr. ed. 1995. audio 16.98 o.s.i (*0-553-74598-0*, RH Audio) Random Hse. Audio Publishing Group.
—Self-Defense. 2002. (Illus.). 528p. mass mkt. 7.99 (*0-345-45883-4*) Random Hse., Inc.
—Silent Partner. 2003. 512p. mass mkt. 7.99 (*0-345-46068-5*, Ballantine Bks.) Ballantine Bks.
—Silent Partner. 1990. 512p. mass mkt. 5.50 o.s.i (*0-553-17339-1*); mass mkt. 7.99 o.s.i (*0-553-28592-0*) Bantam Bks.
—Silent Partner. unabr. ed. 1992. (Alex Delaware Mystery Ser.). audio 88.00 (*0-7366-2266-7*, 3054) Books on Tape, Inc.
—Silent Partner. l.t. ed. 1996. (Large Print Bks.). 585p. pap. 23.95 o.p. (*1-56895-362-3*, Wheeler Publishing, Inc.) Gale Group.
—Silent Partner. 1989. audio 15.95 o.s.i (*0-553-74579-4*, RH Audio); 2003. audio compact disk 14.99 (*0-7393-0376-7*, RH Audio Price-Less); 1999. audio 9.99 o.s.i (*0-553-70196-7*, RH Audio); 1989. audio 16.99 o.s.i (*0-553-45191-X*, RH Audio) Random Hse. Audio Publishing Group.
—Survival of the Fittest. l.t. ed. 1998. 621p. (*0-7540-2083-5*) BBC Audiobooks America.
—Survival of the Fittest. 1998. (Alex Delaware Novel Ser.). 544p. mass mkt. 7.99 o.s.i (*0-553-57232-6*) Bantam Bks.
—Survival of the Fittest. unabr. ed. 1998. audio 72.00 (*0-7366-3995-0*, 4461) Books on Tape, Inc.
—Survival of the Fittest. abr. ed. 1997. (Alex Delaware Mystery Ser.). audio compact disk 29.95 o.s.i (*0-553-45569-9*, , RH Audio) Random Hse. Audio Publishing Group.
—Survival of the Fittest. 2002. (Illus.). 544p. mass mkt. 7.99 (*0-345-45884-2*) Random Hse., Inc.
—Survival of the Fittest. l.t. ed. (Paperback Bestsellers Ser.). 667p. 1999. 27.95 o.p. (*0-7862-1283-7*); 1998. 30.95 (*0-7862-1282-9*) Thorndike Pr.
—Time Bomb. 2003. 496p. mass mkt. 7.99 (*0-345-46069-3*, Ballantine Bks.) Ballantine Bks.
—Time Bomb. 1991. (Alex Delaware Novel Ser.). 496p. mass mkt. 7.99 o.s.i (*0-553-29170-X*); 480p. mass mkt. 5.95 o.s.i (*0-553-18041-X*) Bantam Bks.
—Time Bomb. unabr. ed. 1992. audio 88.00 (*0-7366-2267-5*, 3055) Books on Tape, Inc.
—Time Bomb. abr. ed. 1990. audio 16.99 o.s.i (*0-553-45237-1*, RH Audio) Random Hse. Audio Publishing Group.
—The Web. 2003. 448p. mass mkt. 7.99 (*0-345-46073-1*, Ballantine Bks.) Ballantine Bks.
—The Web. 1996. 448p. mass mkt. 7.99 o.s.i (*0-553-57227-X*) Bantam Bks.
—The Web. unabr. ed. 1996. (Alex Delaware Mystery Ser.). audio 64.00 (*0-7366-3277-8*, 3933) Books on Tape, Inc.
—The Web. l.t. ed. 1996. (Alex Delaware Ser.). 454p. 26.95 o.p. (*1-56895-311-9*, Wheeler Publishing, Inc.) Gale Group.
—The Web. abr. ed. 1996. (Alex Delaware Mystery Ser.). audio 23.95 o.s.i (*0-553-47430-8*, 693452, RH Audio) Random Hse. Audio Publishing Group.
—When the Bough Breaks. 2003. 448p. mass mkt. 7.99 (*0-345-46660-8*, Ballantine Bks.) Ballantine Bks.
—When the Bough Breaks. 1994. (Alex Delaware Novel Ser.). 448p. mass mkt. 7.99 o.s.i (*0-553-56961-9*) Bantam Bks.
—When the Bough Breaks. 2000. audio compact disk 88.00 (*0-7366-8057-8*); audio 72.00 (*0-7366-5588-3*) Books on Tape, Inc.
—When the Bough Breaks. 1986. mass mkt. 4.50 o.p. (*0-451-14870-3*); mass mkt. 3.95 o.p. (*0-451-14249-7*); mass mkt. 5.99 o.s.i (*0-451-17803-3*); 352p. mass mkt. 5.99 o.p. (*0-451-16862-3*); mass mkt. 4.95 o.p. (*0-451-15874-1*) NAL. (Signet Bks.).
—When the Bough Breaks. 1988. audio 16.98 o.s.i (*0-553-74595-6*); Set. 2000. audio 9.99 (*0-375-40968-8*) Random Hse. Audio Publishing Group. (RH Audio).
—When the Bough Breaks. 1985. 304p. bds. 15.95 o.s.i (*0-689-11519-9*, Scribner) Simon & Schuster.
—When the Bough Breaks. l.t. ed. 2001. 608p. 28.95 o.p. (*0-7862-3752-X*); (*0-7540-1721-4*); (*0-7540-9118-X*) Thorndike Pr.

**DELCHARD, RALPH (FICTITIOUS CHARACTER)—FICTION**

Marston, Edward. The Dragons of Archenfield. 1996. mass mkt. 5.99 o.s.i (*0-449-22545-3*, Fawcett) Ballantine Bks.
—The Dragons of Archenfield. 1995. 256p. 14.30 o.p. (*0-312-13472-X*, Saint Martin's Minotaur) St. Martin's Pr.
—The Hawks of Delamere. 2000. (Domesday Bks.: Vol. 7). (Illus.). 246p. 22.95 (*0-312-20948-7*, Saint Martin's Minotaur) St. Martin's Pr.
—The Lions of the North. 1996. 227p. 21.95 (*0-312-14671-X*, Saint Martin's Minotaur) St. Martin's Pr.
—The Ravens of Blackwater. 1996. mass mkt. 5.99 o.s.i (*0-449-22410-4*, Fawcett) Ballantine Bks.
—The Ravens of Blackwater. 1994. 20.95 o.p. (*0-312-11330-7*, Saint Martin's Minotaur) St. Martin's Pr.
—The Serpents of Harbledown: A Novel. 1998. (Domesday Bks.: Vol. 5). 288p. 22.95 (*0-312-18021-7*, Saint Martin's Minotaur) St. Martin's Pr.
—The Stallions of Woodstock. 1998. (Domesday Bks.: Vol. 6). 288p. 22.95 (*0-312-20021-8*, Saint Martin's Minotaur) St. Martin's Pr.
—The Wolves of Savernake. 1995. mass mkt. 5.99 o.s.i (*0-449-22310-8*, Fawcett) Ballantine Bks.
—The Wolves of Savernake. 1993. 256p. 19.95 o.p. (*0-312-09942-8*, Saint Martin's Minotaur) St. Martin's Pr.

**DELEEUW, KIT (FICTITIOUS CHARACTER)—FICTION**

Katz, Jon. Death by Station Wagon. 1994. (Suburban Detective Mysteries Ser.). 336p. mass mkt. 5.99 o.s.i (*0-553-29881-X*) Bantam Bks.
—Death Row: A Suburban Detective Mystery. 1999. 288p. mass mkt. 5.99 o.s.i (*0-553-57816-2*) Bantam Bks.
—The Family Stalker. 1995. 336p. mass mkt. 5.50 o.s.i (*0-553-56954-6*) Bantam Bks.
—The Family Stalker: A Suburban Detective Mystery. 1994. 320p. 18.95 o.s.i (*0-385-46903-9*) Doubleday Publishing.
—The Fathers' Club. 1997. (Suburban Detective Mysteries Ser.). 272p. mass mkt. 5.99 o.s.i (*0-553-57536-8*) Bantam Bks.
—The Fathers' Club. l.t. ed. 1997. (Large Print Bks.). 24.95 (*1-56895-406-9*, Wheeler Publishing, Inc.) Gale Group.
—The Last Housewife. 1996. 384p. mass mkt. 5.99 o.s.i (*0-553-56793-4*) Bantam Bks.
—The Last Housewife. 1995. 19.95 (*0-385-47743-0*) Doubleday Publishing.
—The Last Housewife. l.t. ed. 1995. (Niagara Large Print Ser.). 467p. 29.50 o.p. (*0-7089-5811-7*, Ulverscroft) Thorpe, F. A. Pubs. GBR. *Dist:* Ulverscroft Large Print Bks., Ltd.

**DELL'APPA, HENRY (FICTITIOUS CHARACTER)—FICTION**

Higgins, George V. Bomber's Law. unabr. ed. 1994. audio 72.00 (*0-7366-2805-3*, 3519) Books on Tape, Inc.
—Bomber's Law. unabr. ed. 1997. audio 85.00 (*0-7887-0668-3*, 94845E7) Recorded Bks., LLC.
—Bomber's Law: A Novel. 304p. 1994. pap. 11.00 o.s.i (*0-8050-3566-4*, Owl Bks.); 1993. 22.50 o.p. (*0-8050-2329-1*) Holt, Henry & Co.

**DELMARRE, GLADIA (FICTITIOUS CHARACTER)—FICTION**

Asimov, Isaac. Robots & Empire. 1986. 512p. mass mkt. 5.99 o.s.i (*0-345-32894-9*, Del Rey); mass mkt. 3.95 o.s.i (*0-345-33769-7*) Ballantine Bks.
—The Robots of Dawn, Vol. 3. 1984. 416p. mass mkt. 5.95 o.s.i (*0-345-31571-5*, Ballantine Bks.) Ballantine Bks.
—The Robots of Dawn. 1994. 448p. mass mkt. 7.99 (*0-553-29949-2*, Spectra) Bantam Bks.
—The Robots of Dawn. 1983. 432p. 15.95 o.p. (*0-385-18400-X*) Doubleday Publishing.
—The Robots of Dawn. abr. ed. audio 12.95 o.p. (*0-89845-142-6*, SWC 1732, Caedmon) HarperTrade.

**DELVECCHIO, NICK (FICTITIOUS CHARACTER)—FICTION**

Randisi, Robert J. The Dead of Brooklyn: A Nick Delvecchio Mystery. pap. 12.95 (*1-931755-19-1*) Mystery Vault, Inc.
—The Dead of Brooklyn: A Nick Delvecchio Mystery. 1991. 272p. 18.95 o.p. (*0-312-06330-X*, Saint Martin's Minotaur) St. Martin's Pr.
—The Dead of Brooklyn: A Nick Delvecchio Mystery. l.t. ed. 2002. (Mystery Ser.). 341p. 28.95 (*0-7862-4399-6*) Thorndike Pr.
—Delvecchio's Brooklyn: A Short Story Collection. l.t. ed. 2001. 207p. 23.95 (*0-7862-3044-4*, Five Star) Gale Group.
—No Exit from Brooklyn: A Nick Delvecchio Mystery. 1989. mass mkt. 3.95 (*0-8125-0825-4*, Tor Bks.) Doherty, Tom Assocs., LLC.
—No Exit from Brooklyn: A Nick Delvecchio Mystery. l.t. ed. 2002. (Mystery Ser.). 408p. 28.95 o.p. (*0-7862-3886-0*) Gale Group.
—No Exit from Brooklyn: A Nick Delvecchio Mystery. 2001. 277p. reprint ed. pap. 12.95 (*1-931755-13-2*) Mystery Vault, Inc.
—No Exit from Brooklyn: A Nick Delvecchio Mystery. 1987. 288p. 16.95 o.p. (*0-312-00169-X*) St. Martin's Pr.

**DEMARKIAN, GREGOR (FICTITIOUS CHARACTER)—FICTION**

Haddam, Jane. Act of Darkness. 1991. 288p. mass mkt. 4.50 o.s.i (*0-553-29086-X*) Bantam Bks.
—And One to Die On: A Birthday Mystery. 1997. 304p. mass mkt. 5.99 o.s.i (*0-553-56448-X*) Bantam Bks.
—Baptism in Blood. 1996. 352p. mass mkt. 5.99 o.s.i (*0-553-57464-7*, Crimeline) Bantam Bks.
—Bleeding Hearts. 1995. 368p. mass mkt. 5.50 o.s.i (*0-553-56936-8*) Bantam Bks.
—Conspiracy Theory: A Gregor Demarkian Novel. 2003. 288p. 24.95 (*0-312-27188-3*) St. Martin's Pr.
—Deadly Beloved. 1998. 336p. mass mkt. 5.99 o.s.i (*0-553-57200-8*) Bantam Bks.
—Dear Old Dead. 1994. 352p. mass mkt. 5.50 o.s.i (*0-553-56447-1*) Bantam Bks.
—Feast of Murder. 1992. 336p. mass mkt. 5.50 o.s.i (*0-553-29389-3*) Bantam Bks.
—A Festival of Deaths. 1994. 384p. mass mkt. 5.99 o.s.i (*0-553-56085-9*) Bantam Bks.
—The Fountain of Death. 1995. 352p. (Orig.). mass mkt. 5.50 o.s.i (*0-553-56449-8*, Crimeline) Bantam Bks.
—A Great Day for the Deadly. 1992. 288p. mass mkt. 5.50 o.s.i (*0-553-29388-5*) Bantam Bks.
—Headmaster's Wife. Date not set. mass mkt. (*0-312-98911-3*, St. Martin's Paperbacks) St. Martin's Pr.
—Murder Superior. 1993. 304p. mass mkt. 5.99 o.s.i (*0-553-56084-0*) Bantam Bks.
—Not a Creature Was Stirring: A Gregor Demarkian Holiday Mystery. 1990. 320p. mass mkt. 5.99 o.s.i (*0-553-28792-3*) Bantam Bks.
—Precious Blood. 1991. 336p. mass mkt. 5.99 o.s.i (*0-553-28913-6*) Bantam Bks.
—Quoth the Raven. 1991. 288p. mass mkt. 5.99 o.s.i (*0-553-29255-2*) Bantam Bks.
—Skeleton Key. 2000. 276p. 23.95 o.p. (*0-312-20909-6*, Saint Martin's Minotaur) St. Martin's Pr.
—Somebody Else's Music: A Gregor Demarkian Mystery. 2003. 496p. mass mkt. 6.99 (*0-312-98306-9*, St. Martin's Paperbacks); 2002. 336p. 24.95 (*0-312-27186-7*, Saint Martin's Minotaur) St. Martin's Pr.
—A Stillness in Bethlehem. 1993. (Gregor Demarkian Holiday Mystery Ser.). 368p. mass mkt. 5.50 o.s.i (*0-553-29390-7*) Bantam Bks.
—True Believers. 2002. 432p. mass mkt. 6.99 (*0-312-98286-0*, St. Martin's Paperbacks) St. Martin's Pr.
—True Believers: A Gregor Demarkian Mystery. 2001. (Gregor Demarkian Mystery Ser.). 328p. 24.95 (*0-312-20929-0*, Saint Martin's Minotaur) St. Martin's Pr.
—Untitled Gregor Demarkian, No. 2. Date not set. mass mkt. (*0-312-98912-1*, St. Martin's Paperbacks) St. Martin's Pr.

**DEMBO, MAX (FICTITIOUS CHARACTER)—FICTION**

Bunker, Edward. No Beast So Fierce: A Novel. 1993. (Vintage Crime/Black Lizard Ser.). pap. 10.00 o.s.i (*0-679-74155-0*, Vintage) Knopf Publishing Group.

**DE MORRISSEY, DAVID (FICTITIOUS CHARACTER)—FICTION**

Herter, Lori. Confession. 1992. 288p. (Orig.). mass mkt. 4.99 o.p. (*0-425-13358-3*) Berkley Publishing Group.
—Eternity. 1993. 288p. (Orig.). mass mkt. 4.99 o.s.i (*0-425-13978-6*) Berkley Publishing Group.
—Obsession. 1991. mass mkt. 4.50 o.p. (*0-425-12817-2*) Berkley Publishing Group.
—Possession. 1992. mass mkt. 4.99 o.p. (*0-425-13133-5*) Berkley Publishing Group.

**DENNY, JAMES (FICTITIOUS CHARACTER)—FICTION**

*see* Risk, Doctor (Fictitious Character)—Fiction

**DENSON, JOHN (FICTITIOUS CHARACTER)—FICTION**

Hoyt, Richard. Bigfoot. 1995. 246p. pap. text 4.99 (*0-8125-1948-5*, Forge Bks.); 1992. 224p. 17.95 o.p. (*0-312-85278-9*, Tor Bks.) Doherty, Tom Assocs., LLC.
—Decoys: A John Denson Mystery. 1980. 204p. 8.95 o.p. (*0-87131-330-8*) Evans, M. & Co., Inc.
—Decoys: A John Denson Mystery. 1984. (Crime Ser.). 208p. pap. 3.95 o.p. (*0-14-007217-9*, Penguin Bks.) Viking Penguin.
—Fish Story. 1987. 288p. reprint ed. pap. 3.95 o.p. (*0-8125-0491-7*, Tor Bks.) Doherty, Tom Assocs., LLC.
—Fish Story. 1985. (Mystery Ser.). 224p. 13.95 o.p. (*0-670-31672-5*) Viking Penguin.
—Siskiyou. 1984. 304p. (Orig.). pap. 3.50 o.p. (*0-8125-0487-9*, Tor Bks.) Doherty, Tom Assocs., LLC.
—Snake Eyes. (John Denson Mystery Ser.). 1996. 250p. mass mkt. 5.99 (*0-8125-5072-2*); 1995. 256p. 27.95 o.p. (*0-312-85805-1*) Doherty, Tom Assocs., LLC. (Forge Bks.).
—Thirty for a Harry: A John Denson Mystery. l.t. ed. 1991. 8.95 o.p. (*0-7451-9624-1*, 5043); pap. 10.95 o.p. (*0-7927-0024-4*, 647) BBC Audiobooks America.
—Thirty for a Harry: A John Denson Mystery. 1981. 192p. 8.95 o.p. (*0-87131-357-X*) Evans, M. & Co., Inc.
—Thirty for a Harry: A John Denson Mystery. 1984. (Crime Monthly Ser.). 192p. pap. 3.95 o.p. (*0-14-007216-0*, Penguin Bks.) Viking Penguin.
—Whoo? 2000. 224p. mass mkt. 5.99 (*0-8125-1276-6*, Forge Bks.); 1991. 17.95 o.p. (*0-312-85149-9*, Tor Bks.) Doherty, Tom Assocs., LLC.

**DENT, ARTHUR (FICTITIOUS CHARACTER)—FICTION**

Adams, Douglas. The Hitchhiker's Guide to the Galaxy. (Hitchhiker's Guide Ser.: No. 1). 224p. 1997. pap. 13.95 (*0-345-41891-3*); 1995. mass mkt. 7.50 (*0-345-39180-2*) Ballantine Bks.
—The Hitchhiker's Guide to the Galaxy. unabr. ed. 1994. (Hitchhiker's Guide Ser.). audio 30.00 (*0-7366-2681-6*, 3417) Books on Tape, Inc.
—The Hitchhiker's Guide to the Galaxy. 10th anniv. ed. 1989. (Hitchhiker's Guide Ser.: No. 1). 224p. reprint ed. 18.00 (*0-517-54209-9*) Crown Publishing Group.
—The Hitchhiker's Guide to the Galaxy. unabr. ed. 1993. (Hitchhiker's Guide Ser.). 24.95 o.p. (*1-55800-273-1*, 692228);Set. audio 99.95 o.p. (*1-55800-758-X*) NewStar Media, Inc.
—The Hitchhiker's Guide to the Galaxy. (Hitchhiker's Guide Ser.: No. 1). 1991. mass mkt. 5.99 (*0-671-74606-5*); 1990. mass mkt. 4.95 (*0-671-70159-2*); 1988. 224p. mass mkt. 4.50 (*0-671-66496-4*); 1983. mass mkt. 3.50 o.s.i (*0-671-47709-9*) Simon & Schuster. (Pocket).
—The Hitchhiker's Guide to the Galaxy. abr. ed. 1986. (Hitchhiker's Guide Ser.). audio 11.95 (*0-671-62964-6*, Simon & Schuster Audioworks) Simon & Schuster Audio.
—The Hitchhiker's Guide to the Galaxy. unabr. ed. 1994. (Hitchhiker's Guide Ser.). audio 65.00 o.p. (*1-57042-126-9*, 4-521269); audio compact disk 65.00 o.p. (*1-57042-155-2*) Time Warner AudioBooks.
—The Hitchhiker's Guide to the Galaxy. 1997. (Hitchhiker's Guide Ser.: No. 1). 19.00 (*0-606-12336-9*) Turtleback Bks.
—The Hitchhiker's Guide to the Galaxy: Live at the Almeida. Set. abr. ed. 1996. (Hitchhiker's Guide Ser.). 17.95 o.p. (*0-7871-0896-0*) NewStar Media, Inc.
—Life, the Universe & Everything. (Hitchhiker's Guide Ser.). 1997. pap. 11.00 o.s.i (*0-345-41890-5*); 1995. 240p. mass mkt. 7.50 (*0-345-39182-9*) Ballantine Bks.
—Life, the Universe & Everything. unabr. ed. 1993. (Hitchhiker's Guide Ser.). 24.95 o.p. (*1-55800-292-8*, 70180) NewStar Media, Inc.
—Life, the Universe & Everything. 1982. (Hitchhiker's Guide Ser.: No. 3). 3.99 o.p. (*0-517-54874-7*) Random Hse. Value Publishing.
—Life, the Universe & Everything. 1991. (Hitchhiker's Guide Ser.: No. 3). 240p. mass mkt. 5.99 (*0-671-73967-0*, Pocket) Simon & Schuster.
—Life, the Universe & Everything. 1982. (Hitchhiker's Guide Ser.: No. 3). (J). 12.04 (*0-606-03137-5*) Turtleback Bks.

—Life, the Universe & Everything. 1996. Bk. 2. E-Book (*1-59019-736-4*); Bk. 3. E-Book (*1-59019-737-2*) ipicturebooks, LLC.

—The More Than Complete Hitchhiker's Guide: Complete & Unabridged, 5 bks. in 1. deluxe unabr. ed. 1987. (Hitchhiker's Guide Ser.). 624p. 19.95 o.p. (*0-681-40322-5*) Borders Pr.

—The More Than Complete Hitchhiker's Guide: Complete & Unabridged. 1989. (Hitchhiker's Guide Ser.). 13.99 o.s.i (*0-517-69311-9*) Random Hse. Value Publishing.

—Mostly Harmless. (Hitchhiker's Guide Ser.: No. 5). 2000. 240p. mass mkt. 7.50 (*0-345-41877-8*); 1993. 288p. pap. 12.95 (*0-345-37933-0*) Ballantine Bks.

—Mostly Harmless. l.t. ed. 1996. (Isis Large Print Bks.). 272p. 24.95 o.p. (*1-85695-333-5*) ISIS Large Print Bks. GBR. *Dist:* Transaction Pubs.

—Mostly Harmless. unabr. ed. 1994. (Hitchhiker's Guide Ser.: Vol. 5). audio 24.95 o.p. (*1-55800-568-4*, Dove Audio) NewStar Media, Inc.

—The Original Hitchhiker Radio Scripts: 10th Anniversary Edition. Perkins, Geoffrey, ed. & intro. by. 1995. pap. 15.00 o.s.i (*0-517-88384-8*, Harmony) Crown Publishing Group.

—The Restaurant at the End of the Universe. (Hitchhiker's Guide Ser.: No. 2). 1997. pap. 11.00 o.s.i (*0-345-41892-1*); 1995. 256p. mass mkt. 7.50 (*0-345-39181-0*) Ballantine Bks.

—The Restaurant at the End of the Universe. 1982. (Hitchhiker's Guide Ser.: No. 2). 256p. 12.95 o.s.i (*0-517-54535-7*, Harmony) Crown Publishing Group.

—The Restaurant at the End of the Universe. abr. ed. (Hitchhiker's Guide Ser.). audio 15.95 o.p. (*0-88646-102-2*, 7115) Durkin Hayes Publishing Ltd.

—The Restaurant at the End of the Universe. unabr. ed. 1993. (Hitchhiker's Guide Ser.). 24.95 o.p. (*1-55800-294-4*, 692297) NewStar Media, Inc.

—The Restaurant at the End of the Universe. (Hitchhiker's Guide Ser.: No. 2). 1990. mass mkt. 5.99 (*0-671-70160-6*); 1988. 256p. mass mkt. 4.50 (*0-671-66494-8*); 1983. mass mkt. 3.50 o.s.i (*0-671-49304-3*) Simon & Schuster. (Pocket).

—So Long & Thanks for All the Fish. (Hitchhiker's Guide Ser.: No. 4). 1991. mass mkt. 6.99 (*0-671-74553-0*); 1988. 224p. mass mkt. 4.50 (*0-671-66493-X*) Simon & Schuster. (Pocket).

—So Long & Thanks for All the Fish. 1985. (Hitchhiker's Guide Ser.: No. 4). 12.09 o.p. (*0-606-00985-X*) Turtleback Bks.

—So Long, & Thanks for All the Fish. 1999. (Hitchhiker's Guide Ser.: No. 4). 224p. mass mkt. 6.99 (*0-345-39183-7*) Ballantine Bks.

—So Long & Thanks for All the Fish. abr. ed. 1985. (Hitchhiker's Guide Ser.). audio 15.95 o.p. (*0-88646-144-8*, 7145) Durkin Hayes Publishing Ltd.

—So Long & Thanks for All the Fish. unabr. ed. 1994. (Hitchhiker's Guide Ser.). 24.95 o.p. (*1-55800-293-6*) NewStar Media, Inc.

—The Ultimate Hitchhiker's Guide. (Hitchhiker's Guide Ser.). 1996. (Illus.). 832p. 14.99 (*0-517-14925-7*); 1999. 816p. 6.75 (*0-517-12485-8*) Random Hse. Value Publishing.

Adams, Douglas, et al. The Hitchhiker's Guide to the Galaxy. Kahan, Bob, ed. 1997. (Hitchhiker's Guide Ser.: No. 1). (Illus.). 144p. pap. 14.95 (*1-56389-271-5*) DC Comics.

### DENTON, HARRY JAMES (FICTITIOUS CHARACTER)—FICTION

Womack, Steven. Chain of Fools. (Harry James Denton Mysteries Ser.). 320p. 1996. mass mkt. 6.50 (*0-345-39687-1*); 1995. pap. 19.00 (*0-345-46187-8*, Ballantine Bks.) Ballantine Bks.

—Chain of Fools. l.t. ed. 1997. (Ulverscroft Large Print Ser.). 544p. 29.99 (*0-7089-3730-6*, Ulverscroft) Thorpe, F. A. Pubs. GBR. *Dist:* Ulverscroft Large Print Bks., Ltd., Ulverscroft Large Print Canada, Ltd.

—Dead Folks' Blues. 272p. 1995. pap. 19.00 (*0-345-46186-X*, Ballantine Bks.); 1992. mass mkt. 5.99 o.s.i (*0-345-37674-9*) Ballantine Bks.

—Dead Folks' Blues. Haywood, Richard, ed. abr. ed. 1995. (Harry Denton Trilogy Ser.). audio 17.00 (*1-883268-25-7*) Spellbinders, Inc.

—Dirty Money. 2000. 320p. pap. 19.00 (*0-345-46190-8*, Ballantine Bks.); mass mkt. 6.50 (*0-345-41448-9*, Fawcett) Ballantine Bks.

—Murder Manual. 1998. (Harry James Denton Mysteries Ser.). 336p. mass mkt. 5.99 (*0-345-41447-0*); pap. 19.00 (*0-345-46189-4*, Ballantine Bks.) Ballantine Bks.

—Torch Town Boogie. 288p. 1995. pap. 19.00 (*0-345-46317-X*); 1993. mass mkt. 6.50 o.s.i (*0-345-38010-X*) Ballantine Bks.

—Torch Town Boogie. abr. ed. 1997. audio 17.00 (*1-883268-32-X*) Spellbinders, Inc.

—Torch Town Boogie. l.t. ed. 1996. (Ulverscroft Large Print Ser.). 480p. 29.99 o.p. (*0-7089-3600-8*, Ulverscroft) Thorpe, F. A. Pubs. GBR. *Dist:* Ulverscroft Large Print Bks., Ltd., Ulverscroft Large Print Canada, Ltd.

—Way Past Dead. 1995. 352p. pap. 19.00 (*0-345-46188-6*, Ballantine Bks.); 272p. mass mkt. 6.50 (*0-345-39043-1*) Ballantine Bks.

—Way Past Dead. abr. ed. 1997. audio 17.00 (*1-883268-30-3*) Spellbinders, Inc.

### DE QUINCY, JUSTIN (FICTITIOUS CHARACTER)—FICTION

Penman, Sharon Kay. Cruel As the Grave: A Medieval Mystery. (Reader's Circle Ser.). 272p. 1999. pap. 12.00 (*0-345-43422-6*, Ballantine Bks.); 2001. reprint ed. mass mkt. 6.99 (*0-345-44144-3*, Fawcett) Ballantine Bks.

—Cruel As the Grave: A Medieval Mystery. 1998. 304p. (YA). (gr. 6 up). 22.00 o.s.i (*0-8050-5608-4*) Holt, Henry & Co.

—Dragon's Lair: A Medieval Mystery. 2003. 336p. 23.95 (*0-399-15077-3*, Putnam & Grosset) Putnam Publishing Group, The.

—The Queen's Man: A Medieval Mystery. (Medieval Mysteries Ser.). 2000. 288p. mass mkt. 6.50 (*0-345-42316-X*, Fawcett); 1998. 320p. pap. 12.00 (*0-345-41718-6*) Ballantine Bks.

—The Queen's Man: A Medieval Mystery. 1996. 304p. 20.00 o.s.i (*0-8050-3885-X*) Holt, Henry & Co.

### DE RATOUR, NORMAN A. (FICTITIOUS CHARACTER)—FICTION

Alcorn, Alfred. Murder in the Museum of Man. 1998. 273p. pap. 13.00 o.p. (*0-944072-78-X*); 1997. 320p. 23.95 o.p. (*0-944072-77-1*) Steerforth Pr. (Zoland Bks., Inc.).

### DEREHAM, JONAH (FICTITIOUS CHARACTER)—FICTION

Francis, Dick. Knockdown. l.t. ed. 1995. pap. 18.95 o.p. (*0-7927-1879-8*); 1994. 19.95 o.p. (*0-7927-1880-1*); 1995. audio 54.95 (*0-7451-6830-2*, CAB 613) BBC Audiobooks America.

—Knockdown. 1993. 256p. mass mkt. 6.99 (*0-449-22113-X*, Fawcett) Ballantine Bks.

—Knockdown. unabr. ed. 1994. audio 36.00 (*0-7366-2780-4*, 3499) Books on Tape, Inc.

—Knockdown. unabr. ed. 2000. audio 49.95 Chivers Audio Bks. GBR. *Dist:* BBC Audiobooks America.

—Knockdown. abr. ed. audio 15.95 o.p. (*1-55994-143-X*, CPN 2140, HarperAudio) HarperTrade.

—Knockdown. unabr. ed. 1994. audio 44.00 (*0-7887-0106-1*, 94347E7) Recorded Bks., LLC.

—Knockdown. 1989. mass mkt. 4.95 (*0-671-68768-9*); 1984. 208p. mass mkt. 3.50 (*0-671-50760-5*) Simon & Schuster. (Pocket).

—Knockdown. l.t. ed. 1979. 12.50 o.p. (*0-7089-0288-X*, Ulverscroft) Thorpe, F. A. Pubs. GBR. *Dist:* Ulverscroft Large Print Bks., Ltd.

### DERRY, JONATHAN (FICTITIOUS CHARACTER)—FICTION

Francis, Dick. Twice Shy. unabr. ed. 1993. 69.95 o.p. incl. audio (*0-7451-5958-3*); 69.95 o.p. incl. audio (*0-7451-5958-3*) BBC Audiobooks America.

—Twice Shy. 1997. mass mkt. 5.99 (*0-449-45728-1*, Fawcett); 1986. 352p. mass mkt. 5.99 o.s.i (*0-449-21314-5*, Fawcett); 1986. mass mkt. 4.50 o.p. (*0-449-21035-9*, Fawcett); 1985. mass mkt. o.s.i (*0-449-20756-0*); 1983. mass mkt. 3.50 o.p. (*0-449-20053-1*, Fawcett) Ballantine Bks.

—Twice Shy. 2003. 304p. mass mkt. 6.99 (*0-515-13488-0*, Jove) Berkley Publishing Group.

—Twice Shy. l.t. ed. 1982. 458p. lib. bdg. 14.95 o.p. (*0-8161-3445-6*, Macmillan Reference USA) Gale Group.

—Twice Shy. 1982. 13.95 o.s.i (*0-399-12707-0*) Putnam Publishing Group, The.

—Twice Shy. unabr. ed. 1998. audio 61.00 (*0-7887-2510-6*, 95582E7) Recorded Bks., LLC.

### DESALES, FRANK (FICTITIOUS CHARACTER)—FICTION

Boyle, Thomas. Brooklyn Three. 1992. (Crime Ser.). 256p. pap. 4.95 o.p. (*0-14-012706-2*, Penguin Bks.) Penguin Group (USA) Inc.

—Brooklyn Three. 1991. 256p. 18.95 o.p. (*0-670-83019-4*) Viking Penguin.

—Only the Dead Know Brooklyn. l.t. ed. 1989. 412p. lib. bdg. 11.95 o.p. (*1-85057-479-0*, Macmillan Reference USA) Gale Group.

—Only the Dead Know Brooklyn. 1985. 288p. 15.95 o.p. (*0-87923-565-9*) Godine, David R. Pub.

—Only the Dead Know Brooklyn. mass mkt. 0.25 o.p. (*0-451-00950-9*, Signet Bks.) NAL.

—Only the Dead Know Brooklyn. 1986. (Crime Ser.). pap. 4.95 o.p. (*0-14-017155-X*); 288p. mass mkt. 3.50 o.p. (*0-14-009257-9*) Viking Penguin. (Penguin Bks.).

—Post-Mortem Effects. 1988. 39.50 o.p. (*0-14-778385-2*) Penguin Group (USA) Inc.

—Post-Mortem Effects. (Crime Ser.). 1988. 288p. pap. 3.95 o.p. (*0-14-009753-8*, Penguin Bks.); 1987. 15.95 o.p. (*0-670-81325-7*) Viking Penguin.

### DESMOND, TIM (FICTITIOUS CHARACTER)—FICTION

Friesner, Esther M. Gnome Man's Land. 1991. mass mkt. 4.50 o.s.i (*0-441-08122-3*) Ace Bks.

—Harpy High. 1991. mass mkt. 4.50 o.s.i (*0-441-31762-6*) Ace Bks.

—Unicorn U. 1992. mass mkt. 4.50 o.s.i (*0-441-37844-7*) Ace Bks.

—Yesterday We Saw Mermaids. 1993. 157p. mass mkt. 3.99 (*0-8125-1345-2*); 1992. 160p. 16.95 o.p. (*0-312-85352-1*) Doherty, Tom Assocs., LLC. (Tor Bks.).

### DE VALIFIERNO, MARQUIS (FICTITIOUS CHARACTER)—FICTION

Noah, Robert. The Man Who Stole the Mona Lisa. 1998. 256p. 22.95 o.p. (*0-312-16916-7*) St. Martin's Pr.

### DEVEREAUX (FICTITIOUS CHARACTER: GRANGER)—FICTION

Granger, Bill. The British Cross. 1984. mass mkt. 3.50 o.s.i (*0-671-52361-9*, Pocket) Simon & Schuster.

—Burning the Apostle. 1993. 368p. mass mkt. 5.99 (*0-446-36499-1*); 341p. 19.95 o.p. (*0-446-51693-7*) Warner Bks., Inc.

—Hemingway's Notebook. 1986. 2.99 o.p. (*0-517-55937-4*) Random Hse. Value Publishing.

—Hemingway's Notebook. 1986. 384p. mass mkt. 4.50 (*0-446-30284-8*) Warner Bks., Inc.

—Henry McGee Is Not Dead. 1989. 384p. 18.45 o.s.i (*0-446-51286-9*); mass mkt. 4.95 (*0-446-35621-2*) Warner Bks., Inc.

—The Infant of Prague. l.t. ed. 1988. (General Ser.). 392p. 18.95 o.p. (*0-8161-4521-0*, Macmillan Reference USA) Gale Group.

—The Infant of Prague. 1988. 352p. 16.45 o.s.i (*0-446-51285-0*); mass mkt. 4.95 (*0-446-34780-9*) Warner Bks., Inc.

—The Last Good German. 1992. 288p. mass mkt. 5.99 o.s.i (*0-446-36364-8*); 1991. 320p. 18.95 o.p. (*0-446-51552-3*) Warner Bks., Inc.

—League of Terror. l.t. ed. 2001. 376p. lib. bdg. 27.95 (*1-58547-139-9*) Ctr. Point Large Print.

—League of Terror. 1991. mass mkt. 5.99 (*0-446-36126-7*); 1990. 19.95 o.p. (*0-446-51551-5*) Warner Bks., Inc.

—The Man Who Heard Too Much. 1990. mass mkt. 4.95 o.s.i (*0-446-36086-4*); 1989. 18.45 o.s.i (*0-446-51503-5*) Warner Bks., Inc.

—The November Man. 1979. mass mkt. 1.95 o.p. (*0-449-14245-0*, Fawcett) Ballantine Bks.

—The November Man. 1988. mass mkt. 3.95 (*0-446-73751-8*); 352p. mass mkt. 5.99 (*0-446-32473-6*) Warner Bks., Inc.

—Schism. 1982. mass mkt. 3.50 o.s.i (*0-671-45274-6*, Pocket) Simon & Schuster.

—The Shattered Eye. 1984. 320p. mass mkt. 3.95 (*0-671-47756-0*, Pocket) Simon & Schuster.

—There Are No Spies. 1987. 384p. 16.45 o.s.i (*0-446-51283-4*); mass mkt. 3.95 (*0-446-34705-1*) Warner Bks., Inc.

—The Zurich Numbers. 1984. 256p. 3.99 o.p. (*0-517-55446-1*) Random Hse. Value Publishing.

—The Zurich Numbers. 1986. mass mkt. 3.95 o.s.i (*0-671-55399-2*, Pocket) Simon & Schuster.

### DEVEREAUX, JEFFREY (FICTITIOUS CHARACTER)—FICTION

Dandola, John. Wicked Is the Wind: A Jeffrey Devereaux—Kirsten Eriksson Novel. 2001. (Illus.). 222p. pap. 11.95 (*1-878452-28-2*, Compass Point Mysteries) Quincannon Publishing Group.

—Wind of Time. 1995. (Illus.). 200p. pap. 9.95 o.p. (*1-878452-22-3*, Rune-Tales) Quincannon Publishing Group.

—Wind of Time: A Jeffrey Devereaux - Kirsten Eriksson Novel. 2001. (Illus.). 190p. pap. 11.95 (*1-878452-27-4*, Compass Point Mysteries) Quincannon Publishing Group.

### DEVITO, ANGIE (FICTITIOUS CHARACTER)—FICTION

Shaffer, Louise. All My Suspects: A Daytime Crime Mystery. 1995. 224p. mass mkt. 4.99 o.s.i (*0-425-14770-3*, Prime Crime) Berkley Publishing Group.

—All My Suspects: A Daytime Crime Mystery. 1994. 224p. 19.95 o.p. (*0-399-13965-6*, G. P. Putnam's Sons) Penguin Group (USA) Inc.

—Talked to Death. 1996. mass mkt. 5.99 o.s.i (*0-425-15407-6*) Berkley Publishing Group.

—Talked to Death. 1995. 256p. 22.95 o.p. (*0-399-14095-6*, G. P. Putnam's Sons) Penguin Group (USA) Inc.

### DEVLIN, BROOKE (FICTITIOUS CHARACTER)—FICTION

Kruger, Mary. Death on the Cliff Walk. 1995. mass mkt. 4.99 o.s.i (*0-8217-5164-6*); 1994. mass mkt. 16.95 o.s.i (*0-8217-4769-X*, Zebra Bks.) Kensington Publishing Corp.

—Masterpiece of Murder: A Gilded Age Mystery. 1997. (Gilded Age Mystery Ser.). 272p. mass mkt. 5.50 o.s.i (*1-57566-229-9*) Kensington Publishing Corp.

—No Honeymoon for Death: A Gilded Age Mystery. 1996. 304p. mass mkt. 5.50 o.s.i (*1-57566-110-1*); 1995. 288p. mass mkt. 18.95 o.s.i (*0-8217-5159-X*) Kensington Publishing Corp.

### DEVLIN, HARRY (FICTITIOUS CHARACTER)—FICTION

Edwards, Martin. All the Lonely People. 2003. (Five Star First Edition Titles Ser.). 278p. 25.95 (*1-59414-069-3*, Five Star) Gale Group.

—Eve of Destruction: A Harry Devlin Mystery. 1998. 208p. 22.95 (*0-393-04635-4*) Norton, W. W. & Co., Inc.

—Suspicious Minds. l.t. ed. 1995. (Magna Large Print Ser.). 365p. o.p. (*0-7505-0865-5*) Magna Large Print Bks. GBR. *Dist:* Ulverscroft Large Print Canada, Ltd.

—Yesterday's Papers. l.t. ed. 1996. (Magna Large Print Ser.). 380p. (*0-7505-0867-1*) Magna Large Print Bks. GBR. *Dist:* Ulverscroft Large Print Canada, Ltd.

### DEVLIN, JACK (FICTITIOUS CHARACTER)—FICTION

Clarkson, John. And Justice for One. 1993. 368p. mass mkt. 5.99 o.s.i (*0-515-11055-8*, Jove) Berkley Publishing Group.

—And Justice for One. 1994. 4.99 o.p. (*0-517-12688-5*) Random Hse. Value Publishing.

—One Man's Law. 1994. 368p. (Orig.). mass mkt. 5.99 o.s.i (*0-425-14249-3*) Berkley Publishing Group.

—One Way Out. 1996. 400p. (Orig.). mass mkt. 5.99 o.s.i (*0-515-11802-8*, Jove) Berkley Publishing Group.

### DEVLIN, LIAM (FICTITIOUS CHARACTER)—FICTION

Higgins, Jack. Confessional. l.t. ed. 1986. (General Ser.). 352p. 17.95 o.p. (*0-8161-3945-8*, Macmillan Reference USA) Gale Group.

—Confessional. 1989. 15.95 o.p. (*0-8128-3025-3*, Scarborough Hse.) Madison Bks., Inc.

—Confessional. 1986. 352p. pap. 4.95 (*0-451-16536-5*); mass mkt. 5.99 o.s.i (*0-451-14375-2*) NAL. (Signet Bks.).

—Confessional. 1997. 304p. mass mkt. 6.99 (*0-671-00033-0*, Pocket) Simon & Schuster.

—The Eagle Has Flown. l.t. ed. 1992. (General Ser.). 373p. lib. bdg. 22.95 (*0-8161-5363-9*, Macmillan Reference USA) Gale Group.

—The Eagle Has Flown. 2002. 336p. mass mkt. 7.99 (*0-7434-5650-5*, Pocket); 1991. 336p. mass mkt. 7.99 (*0-671-74669-3*, Pocket); 1991. 352p. 21.95 o.p. (*0-671-72458-4*, Simon & Schuster) Simon & Schuster.

—The Eagle Has Flown. abr. ed. 1991. audio 15.95 (*0-671-72465-7*, 296620, Simon & Schuster Audioworks) Simon & Schuster Audio.

—The Eagle Has Flown. l.t. ed. 1992. (G. K. Hall Large Print Book Ser.). 373p. pap. 19.95 (*0-8161-5364-7*) Thorndike Pr.

—The Eagle Has Landed. 1946. pap. text o.p. (*0-17-556767-0*) Addison-Wesley Longman, Inc.

—The Eagle Has Landed. 1982. 368p. mass mkt. 3.95 o.s.i (*0-553-23345-9*); mass mkt. 4.50 o.s.i (*0-553-27042-7*) Bantam Bks.

—The Eagle Has Landed. 2000. 368p. mass mkt. 7.99 (*0-425-17718-1*) Berkley Publishing Group.

—The Eagle Has Landed. 1995. reprint ed. lib. bdg. 26.95 (*1-56849-593-5*) Buccaneer Bks., Inc.

—The Eagle Has Landed. abr. ed. audio 15.95 o.p. (*0-88646-027-1*, 7040) Durkin Hayes Publishing Ltd.

—The Eagle Has Landed. l.t. ed. 1992. 17.95 o.p. (*0-8161-5474-0*); 1975. reprint ed. lib. bdg. 14.95 o.p. (*0-8161-6330-8*) Gale Group. (Macmillan Reference USA).

—The Eagle Has Landed. 1975. o.p. (*0-03-013746-2*) Holt, Henry & Co.

—The Eagle Has Landed. abr. ed. 1996. 24.95 o.p. (*0-7871-0960-6*); 39.95 o.p. (*0-7871-0959-2*, 103449) NewStar Media, Inc.

—The Eagle Has Landed. 1993. audio 15.99 o.s.i (*0-553-47143-0*, RH Audio) Random Hse. Audio Publishing Group.

—The Eagle Has Landed. 1997. 400p. pap. 19.95 o.p. (*0-671-01934-1*); 1989. bds. 4.95 (*0-671-66529-4*) Simon & Schuster. (Pocket).

—The Eagle Has Landed. Rubenstein, Julie, ed. 1990. 336p. reprint ed. mass mkt. 7.99 (*0-671-72773-7*, Pocket) Simon & Schuster.

—The Eagle Has Landed. rev. ed. 1991. 368p. 21.95 o.p. (*0-671-73310-9*, Simon & Schuster) Simon & Schuster.

—The Eagle Has Landed. l.t. ed. 1983. 528p. 12.50 o.p. (*0-7089-0973-6*, Ulverscroft) Thorpe, F. A. Pubs. GBR. *Dist:* Ulverscroft Large Print Bks., Ltd.

—Eye of the Storm. 1993. 352p. mass mkt. 7.99 (*0-425-13823-2*) Berkley Publishing Group.

—Eye of the Storm. abr. ed. 1994. 16.95 o.p. (*1-55800-635-4*) NewStar Media, Inc.

—Eye of the Storm. 1992. 320p. 22.95 o.p. (*0-399-13758-0*, G. P. Putnam's Sons) Penguin Group (USA) Inc.
—Touch the Devil, Set. abr. ed. audio 16.99 (*0-88646-117-0*, 391797) Durkin Hayes Publishing Ltd.
—Touch the Devil. 1983. (General Ser.). lib. bdg. 16.95 o.p. (*0-8161-3484-7*, Macmillan Reference USA) Gale Group.
—Touch the Devil. Madison Bks., Inc.
—Touch the Devil. 1983. 352p. mass mkt. 6.99 o.s.i (*0-451-16677-9*); 352p. mass mkt. 4.50 o.p. (*0-451-15688-9*); mass mkt. 3.95 o.p. (*0-451-12468-5*) NAL. (Signet Bks.).
—Touch the Devil. Grose, Bill, ed. 1993. 352p. mass mkt. 6.50 (*0-671-67620-2*, Pocket) Simon & Schuster.

**DEVLIN, MATT (FICTITIOUS CHARACTER)—FICTION**

Kruger, Mary. Death on the Cliff Walk. 1995. mass mkt. 4.99 o.s.i (*0-8217-5164-6*); 1994. mass mkt. 16.95 o.s.i (*0-8217-4769-X*, Zebra Bks.) Kensington Publishing Corp.
—Masterpiece of Murder: A Gilded Age Mystery. 1997. (Gilded Age Mystery Ser.). 272p. mass mkt. 5.50 o.s.i (*1-57566-229-9*) Kensington Publishing Corp.
—No Honeymoon for Death: A Gilded Age Mystery. 1996. 304p. mass mkt. 5.50 o.s.i (*1-57566-110-1*); 1995. 288p. mass mkt. 18.95 o.s.i (*0-8217-5159-X*) Kensington Publishing Corp.

**DEVLIN, MIKE (FICTITIOUS CHARACTER)—FICTION**

Lindsay, Paul. Code Name: Gentkill. 1996. mass mkt. 5.99 o.s.i (*0-449-14902-1*, Fawcett) Ballantine Bks.
—Code Name: Gentkill. l.t. ed. 1996. (Niagara Large Print Ser.). 401p. 29.50 o.p. (*0-7089-5839-7*, Ulverscroft) Thorpe, F. A. Pubs. GBR. *Dist:* Ulverscroft Large Print Bks., Ltd.
—Freedom to Kill: A Novel of the FBI. 1998. mass mkt. 6.99 o.s.i (*0-449-14994-3*, Fawcett) Ballantine Bks.
—Witness to the Truth. unabr. ed. 1993. audio 21.95 o.p. (*1-56100-491-X*, 320, Bookcassette); audio 57.25 o.p. (*1-56100-125-2*, 1102, Unabridged Library Editions) Brilliance Audio.

**DEVLIN, PAUL (FICTITIOUS CHARACTER)—FICTION**

Heffernan, William. Blood Rose. 1991. 320p. 18.95 o.p. (*0-525-24962-1*, Dutton) Dutton/Plume.
—Blood Rose. 1992. 448p. mass mkt. 6.99 o.s.i (*0-451-17163-2*, Signet Bks.) NAL.
—Red Angel: A Paul Devlin Mystery. 2001. 320p. mass mkt. 6.99 (*0-380-81881-7*, Avon Bks.); 2000. 273p. 24.00 (*0-688-16563-X*, Morrow, William & Co.) Morrow/Avon.
—Ritual. 1990. 352p. mass mkt. 5.99 o.s.i (*0-451-16397-4*, Signet Bks.); 1989. 284p. 18.95 o.p. (*0-453-00618-3*) NAL.
—Scarred. 1993. 384p. (Orig.). mass mkt. 5.99 o.s.i (*0-451-17863-7*, Signet Bks.) NAL.
—Tarnished Blue. 1995. 384p. (Orig.). mass mkt. 5.99 o.s.i (*0-451-18295-2*, Onyx) NAL.
—Unholy Order: A Paul Devlin Mystery. 2002. 272p. mass mkt. 6.99 (*0-380-81882-5*, Avon Bks.); (Illus.). 288p. 24.95 (*0-688-16564-8*, Morrow, William & Co.) Morrow/Avon.
—Winter's Gold. 1997. 400p. mass mkt. 6.50 o.s.i (*0-451-18865-9*, Signet Bks.) NAL.

**DEVONSHIRE, BETSY (FICTITIOUS CHARACTER)—FICTION**

Ferris, Monica. Cutwork. 2004. 272p. mass mkt. 6.99 (*0-425-19389-6*) Berkley Publishing Group.
—Framed in Lace. 1999. (Needlecraft Mystery Ser.). 256p. mass mkt. 5.99 (*0-425-17149-3*) Berkley Publishing Group.
—A Murderous Yarn. 2002. 256p. mass mkt. 5.99 (*0-425-18403-X*) Berkley Publishing Group.
—A Stitch in Time. 2000. (Needlecraft Mysteries Ser.). 256p. mass mkt. 5.99 (*0-425-17511-1*, Prime Crime) Berkley Publishing Group.
—Unraveled Sleeve. 2001. (Needlecraft Mysteries Ser.). (Illus.). 256p. mass mkt. 5.99 (*0-425-18045-X*, Prime Crime) Berkley Publishing Group.
Ferris, Monica & Bookman, Terry. Crewel World. 1999. (Needlecraft Mysteries Ser.). 256p. (Orig.). mass mkt. 5.99 (*0-425-16780-1*, Prime Crime) Berkley Publishing Group.

**DEVORE, BURKE (FICTITIOUS CHARACTER)—FICTION**

Westlake, Donald E. The Ax. unabr. collector's ed. 1997. (Dortmunder Ser.). audio 56.00 (*0-7366-3774-5*, 4447) Books on Tape, Inc.
—The Ax. 1997. 288p. 22.50 o.p. (*0-89296-587-8*) Mysterious Pr.
—The Ax. 1998. mass mkt. (*0-446-40434-9*, Mysterious Pr. Paperback Bks.); mass mkt. 188.73 (*0-446-16658-8*); 352p. reprint ed. mass mkt. 6.99 (*0-446-60608-1*) Warner Bks., Inc.

**DEWITT, MOLLY (FICTITIOUS CHARACTER)—FICTION**

Woods, Sherryl. Hot Money. 1993. 288p. mass mkt. 4.99 o.s.i (*0-440-21485-8*) Dell Publishing.
—Hot Money. l.t. ed. 1995. 231p. pap. 19.95 o.p. (*0-7838-1192-6*, Macmillan Reference USA) Gale Group.
—Hot Property. 1992. 272p. mass mkt. 4.50 o.s.i (*0-440-21003-8*) Dell Publishing.
—Hot Schemes. 1994. 288p. mass mkt. 4.99 o.s.i (*0-440-21486-6*) Dell Publishing.
—Hot Schemes. l.t. ed. 1995. 248p. pap. 19.95 (*0-7838-1193-4*, Macmillan Reference USA) Gale Group.
—Hot Secret. 1992. 256p. mass mkt. 4.99 o.s.i (*0-440-21004-6*) Dell Publishing.

**DIAMOND, PETER (FICTITIOUS CHARACTER)—FICTION**

Lovesey, Peter. Bloodhounds. l.t. ed. 1997. (G. K. Hall Mystery Ser.). 509p. 26.95 o.p. (*0-7838-8097-9*, Macmillan Reference USA) Gale Group.
—Bloodhounds. (Peter Diamond Mystery Ser.). 368p. 1997. mass mkt. 5.99 o.p. (*0-446-40535-3*); 1996. 22.00 o.p. (*0-89296-645-9*) Warner Bks., Inc.
—The Bloodhounds. unabr. ed. 1999. audio 84.95 (*1-86042-283-7*, 22837) Soundings, Ltd. GBR. *Dist:* Ulverscroft Large Print Bks., Ltd.
—Diamond Dust. unabr. ed. 2002. 10p. audio 84.95 (*0-7540-0877-0*) Chivers Audio Bks. GBR. *Dist:* BBC Audiobooks America.
—Diamond Dust. 2003. 356p. pap. 13.00 (*1-56947-322-6*); 2002. 296p. 24.00 (*1-56947-291-2*); 2002. 304p. 23.00 (*1-56947-300-5*) Soho Pr., Inc.
—Diamond Dust. 2002. (Basic Ser.). 27.95 (*0-7862-4894-7*) Thorndike Pr.
—Diamond Solitaire. 2002. 327p. pap. 13.00 (*1-56947-292-0*) Soho Pr., Inc.
—Diamond Solitaire. 1994. 336p. mass mkt. 5.50 o.p. (*0-446-40347-4*, Mysterious Pr. Paperback Bks.) Warner Bks., Inc.
—The Last Detective. 1992. 416p. mass mkt. 4.99 o.s.i (*0-553-29619-1*) Bantam Bks.
—The Last Detective. 2000. 368p. pap. 13.00 (*1-56947-209-2*) Soho Pr., Inc.
—The Summons. 1995. (Peter Diamond Mystery Ser.). 352p. 21.95 o.p. (*0-89296-551-7*) Mysterious Pr.
—The Summons. 1996. 352p. mass mkt. 5.99 o.s.i (*0-446-40369-5*) Warner Bks., Inc.
—Upon a Dark Night. 1998. 384p. 23.00 o.p. (*0-89296-669-6*) Mysterious Pr.
—Upon a Dark Night. l.t. ed. 1998. (Mystery Ser.). 583p. 27.95 (*0-7862-1530-5*) Thorndike Pr.
—The Vault. 2000. 331p. 23.00 (*1-56947-208-4*); 2001. 332p. reprint ed. pap. 13.00 (*1-56947-256-4*) Soho Pr., Inc.
—The Vault. l.t. ed. 2001. (Basic Ser.). 496p. 28.95 (*0-7862-3063-0*) Thorndike Pr.

**DIAMOND, VENUS (FICTITIOUS CHARACTER)—FICTION**

Moody, Skye Kathleen. Blue Poppy. 1998. (WWL Mystery Ser.: No. 293). per. (*0-373-26293-0*, 0-26293-1, Worldwide Library) Harlequin Enterprises, Ltd.
—Blue Poppy. 1997. (Pacific Northwest Mysteries Ser.). 256p. 23.95 (*0-312-15479-8*, Saint Martin's Minotaur) St. Martin's Pr.
—Habitat. 1999. (Illus.). 274p. 24.95 (*0-312-20390-X*, Saint Martin's Minotaur) St. Martin's Pr.
—K Falls. 2001. E-Book 23.95 (*1-59061-040-7*) Adobe Systems, Inc.
—K Falls. 2002. (WWL Mystery Ser.). 256p. mass mkt. (*0-373-26426-7*, Worldwide Library) Harlequin Enterprises, Ltd.
—Rain Dance. 1998. (WWL Mystery Ser.). per. (*0-373-26278-7*, 1-26278-1, Worldwide Library) Harlequin Enterprises, Ltd.
—Rain Dance. 1996. 256p. 21.95 (*0-312-14713-9*, Saint Martin's Minotaur) St. Martin's Pr.
—Wildcrafters. 1999. (WWL Mystery Ser.: Vol. 332). 272p. per. (*0-373-26332-5*, Harlequin Bks.) Harlequin Enterprises, Ltd.
—Wildcrafters. 1998. (Pacific Northwest Mysteries Ser.). 320p. 23.95 o.p. (*0-312-19364-5*, Saint Martin's Minotaur) St. Martin's Pr.

**DICHRISTO, NEIL (FICTITIOUS CHARACTER)—FICTION**

Girard, Sonny. Snake Eyes. 1900. 416p. pap. 6.50 (*0-671-78500-1*, Pocket) Simon & Schuster.

**DI CILIA, KAREN (FICTITIOUS CHARACTER)—FICTION**

Leonard, Elmore. Gold Coast. 1985. mass mkt. 3.95 o.s.i (*0-553-27627-1*); 224p. mass mkt. 3.50 o.s.i (*0-553-26267-X*) Bantam Bks.
—Gold Coast. 1999. mass mkt. (*0-553-13321-7*) Bantam Dell Publishing Group.
—Gold Coast. unabr. collector's ed. 1995. audio 42.00 (*0-7366-3160-7*, 3831) Books on Tape, Inc.
—Gold Coast. 1999. mass mkt. (*0-553-25006-X*); 1990. 224p. mass mkt. 7.50 o.s.i (*0-440-20832-7*) Dell Publishing.
—Gold Coast. 2002. 352p. mass mkt. 7.50 (*0-06-008405-7*) Morrow/Avon.
—Gold Coast, unabr. ed. 1995. audio 44.00 (*0-7887-0257-2*, 94466E7) Recorded Bks., LLC.

**DICKENS, CHARLES, 1812-1870—FICTION**

Barlow, Eleanor Poe. The Master's Cat: The Story of Charles Dickens as Told by His Cat. 1998. (Illus.). 132p. (YA). (gr. 7 up). 24.00 (*0-9518525-3-1*) Dickens Publishing GBR. *Dist:* Hood, Alan C. & Co., Inc.
—The Master's Cat: The Story of Charles Dickens as Told by His Cat. 1999. 132p. (YA). pap. 16.50 (*1-880158-22-1*) Townsend, J.N. Publishing.
Busch, Frederick. The Mutual Friend. 1983. (Nonpareil Bk.). 224p. reprint ed. pap. 8.95 o.p. (*0-87923-482-2*) Godine, David R. Pub.
—The Mutual Friend. 1978. 8.95 o.p. (*0-06-010527-5*) HarperCollins Pubs.
—The Mutual Friend. 1994. (Paperbook Ser.: Vol. 774). 240p. reprint ed. pap. 9.95 (*0-8112-1258-0*, NDP774) New Directions Publishing Corp.
Davis, Patricia K. A Midnight Carol: A Novel of How Charles Dickens Saved Christmas. 1999. 192p. 16.95 o.p. (*0-312-24523-8*); 2000. 208p. reprint ed. mass mkt. 4.99 (*0-312-97698-4*, St. Martin's Paperbacks) St. Martin's Pr.
Dickens, Charles. The Mystery of Edwin Drood. Cox, Arthur J., ed. 1986. pap. 3.95 o.p. (*0-14-009258-7*, Penguin Bks.) Viking Penguin.
McHugh, Stuart D. Knock on the Nursery Door: Tales of the Dickens Children. 1973. 9.95 o.p. (*0-7181-1031-5*) Transatlantic Arts, Inc.
Meckier, Jerome. Dickens's Great Expectations: Misnar's Pavilion versus Cinderella. 2002. 296p. 38.00 (*0-8131-2228-7*) Univ. Pr. of Kentucky.
Palmer, William J. The Detective & Mr. Dickens: A Secret Victorian Journal. 1992. reprint ed. mass mkt. 3.99 o.s.i (*0-345-37471-1*) Ballantine Bks.
—The Highwayman & Mr. Dickens: A Secret Victorian Journal, Attributed to Wilkie Collins. 1993. reprint ed. mass mkt. 4.99 o.s.i (*0-345-38252-8*) Ballantine Bks.
—The Hoydens & Mr. Dickens. 1996. 256p. 21.95 o.p. (*0-312-15145-4*) St. Martin's Pr.
Palmer, William J., ed. The Detective & Mr. Dickens: A Secret Victorian Journal. 1990. 320p. 17.95 o.p. (*0-312-05073-9*) St. Martin's Pr.
—The Highwayman & Mr. Dickens: A Secret Victorian Journal, Attributed to Wilkie Collins. 1992. 288p. text 18.95 o.p. (*0-312-08207-X*, Saint Martin's Minotaur) St. Martin's Pr.
Rackham, Jeff. The Rag & Bone Shop. 2001. 320p. 25.00 o.p. (*1-58195-105-1*, Zoland Bks., Inc.) Steerforth Pr.
—The Rag & Bone Shop. 2002. 320p. 14.00 (*0-14-200225-9*) Viking Penguin.
Watts, Alan S. The Confessions of Charles Dickens: A Very Factual Fiction. 1992. (Dickens' Universe Ser.: Vol. 1). 179p. (C). text 24.00 o.p. (*0-8204-1533-2*) Lang, Peter Publishing, Inc.

**DIDIER, AUGUSTE (FICTITIOUS CHARACTER)—FICTION**

Myers, Amy. Murder at Plum's. pap. 9.95 (*0-7472-3397-7*) Headline Bk. Publishing, Ltd. GBR. *Dist:* Trafalgar Square.
—Murder at Plum's. 1993. 224p. mass mkt. 4.50 (*0-380-76586-1*, Avon Bks.) Morrow/Avon.
—Murder at Plum's. l.t. ed. 1993. (General Ser.). 432p. 29.99 o.p. (*0-7089-2847-1*, Ulverscroft) Thorpe, F. A. Pubs. GBR. *Dist:* Ulverscroft Large Print Bks., Ltd., Ulverscroft Large Print Canada, Ltd.
—Murder at the Masque. 1993. 256p. mass mkt. 4.99 (*0-380-76584-5*, Avon Bks.) Morrow/Avon.
—Murder at the Music Hall. 1999. 345p. pap. 11.00 (*0-7472-4843-5*) Headline Bk. Publishing, Ltd. GBR. *Dist:* Trafalgar Square.
—Murder in Pug's Parlour. 1992. 256p. mass mkt. 4.50 (*0-380-76587-X*, Avon Bks.) Morrow/Avon.
—Murder in Pug's Parlour. l.t. ed. 1992. (Ulverscroft Large Print Ser.). 432p. 29.99 o.p. (*0-7089-2732-7*, Ulverscroft) Thorpe, F. A. Pubs. GBR. *Dist:* Ulverscroft Large Print Bks., Ltd., Ulverscroft Large Print Canada, Ltd.
—Murder in the Limelight. 1992. 224p. mass mkt. 4.50 (*0-380-76585-3*, Avon Bks.) Morrow/Avon.
—Murder in the Limelight. l.t. ed. 1991. (General Ser.). 29.99 o.p. (*0-7089-2435-2*, Ulverscroft) Thorpe, F. A. Pubs. GBR. *Dist:* Ulverscroft Large Print Bks., Ltd., Ulverscroft Large Print Canada, Ltd.
—Murder in the Motor Stable. 1999. 311p. pap. 11.00 (*0-7472-4844-3*) Headline Bk. Publishing, Ltd. GBR. *Dist:* Trafalgar Square.
—Murder in the Queen's Boudoir. l.t. ed. 28.99 (*0-7278-7159-5*); 2000. 256p. 26.00 (*0-7278-5561-1*) Severn Hse. Pubs., Ltd.
—Murder in the Smokehouse: An Auguste Didier Whodunit. 1997. 312p. 23.95 o.p. (*0-312-15598-0*, Saint Martin's Minotaur) St. Martin's Pr.
—Murder Makes an Entree. 1996. 288p. 21.95 o.p. (*0-312-14376-1*, Saint Martin's Minotaur) St. Martin's Pr.
—Murder with Majesty. 1999. 288p. 25.00 (*0-7278-5415-1*) Severn Hse. Pubs., Ltd.

**DIGRIZ, JAMES BOLIVAR (FICTITIOUS CHARACTER)—FICTION**

Harrison, Harry. The Adventures of the Stainless Steel Rat. 1987. mass mkt. 6.99 o.s.i (*0-441-00422-9*) Ace Bks.
—The Adventures of the Stainless Steel Rat. 1986. 3.95 o.p. (*0-425-10141-X*); 1986. 3.95 o.s.i (*0-425-09531-2*); 1984. 3.50 o.s.i (*0-425-08111-7*); 1984. 3.25 o.s.i (*0-425-07479-X*); 1983. 2.95 o.s.i (*0-425-06170-1*); 1981. 2.50 o.s.i (*0-425-04378-9*); 1978. 2.25 o.s.i (*0-425-03819-X*) Berkley Publishing Group.
—The Stainless Steel Rat. 1986. 192p. mass mkt. 3.50 o.s.i (*0-441-77924-7*) Ace Bks.
—The Stainless Steel Rat. 1987. 0.75 o.p. (*0-425-02015-0*) Berkley Publishing Group.
—The Stainless Steel Rat for President. (Stainless Steel Rat Bks.). 1988. 192p. mass mkt. 4.99 o.s.i (*0-553-27612-3*, Spectra); 1982. mass mkt. 3.50 o.s.i (*0-553-27252-7*); 1982. 192p. mass mkt. 2.95 o.s.i (*0-553-25661-0*, Spectra) Bantam Bks.
—The Stainless Steel Rat Gets Drafted. 1988. (Stainless Steel Rat Bks.). 288p. mass mkt. 4.99 o.s.i (*0-553-27307-8*, Spectra) Bantam Bks.
—The Stainless Steel Rat Goes to Hell. (Stainless Steel Rat Bks.). 1998. 253p. mass mkt. 5.99 (*0-8125-5107-9*); Vol. 1. 1996. 256p. 21.95 (*0-312-86063-3*) Doherty, Tom Assocs., LLC. (Tor Bks.).
—A Stainless Steel Rat Is Born. 1985. (Orig.). mass mkt. 3.50 o.s.i (*0-553-27244-6*); mass mkt. 2.95 o.s.i (*0-553-24708-5*); 224p. mass mkt. 4.99 o.s.i (*0-553-27942-4*) Bantam Bks. (Spectra).
—The Stainless Steel Rat Joins the Circus. 2000. 269p. mass mkt. 6.99 (*0-8125-7535-0*); 1999. 272p. 23.95 (*0-312-86934-7*) Doherty, Tom Assocs., LLC. (Tor Bks.).
—The Stainless Steel Rat Saves the World. 1987. 192p. mass mkt. 3.50 o.s.i (*0-441-77913-1*) Ace Bks.
—The Stainless Steel Rat Saves the World. 1971. 0.75 o.p. (*0-425-02475-X*) Berkley Publishing Group.
—The Stainless Steel Rat Sings the Blues. 1995. 256p. mass mkt. 5.99 o.s.i (*0-553-56939-2*) Bantam Bks.
—The Stainless Steel Rat Wants You! 1988. 160p. mass mkt. 4.99 o.s.i (*0-553-27611-5*, Spectra); 1982. mass mkt. 2.95 o.s.i (*0-553-25395-6*) Bantam Bks.
—The Stainless Steel Rat's Revenge. 1986. 192p. mass mkt. 2.95 o.s.i (*0-441-77912-3*) Ace Bks.
—The Stainless Steel Rat's Revenge. 1989. mass mkt. 4.95 o.s.i (*0-553-17395-2*, Spectra) Bantam Bks.
—The Stainless Steel Rat's Revenge. 1973. 0.75 o.p. (*0-425-02304-4*) Berkley Publishing Group.
—You Can Be the Stainless Steel Rat: An Interactive Game Book. 1988. mass mkt. 3.50 o.s.i (*0-441-94978-9*) Ace Bks.

**DILBERT (FICTITIOUS CHARACTER)—FICTION**

Adams, Scott. Access Denied: Dilbert's Quest for Love in the Nineties. 1996. (Cartoon Bks.). (Illus.). 80p. 4.95 (*0-8362-2191-5*) Andrews McMeel Publishing.
—Always Postpone Meetings with Time-Wasting Morons. 1994. (Dilbert Bks.). (Illus.). 112p. 10.95 (*0-8362-1758-6*) Andrews McMeel Publishing.
—Always Postpone Meetings with Time-Wasting Morons. 1992. (Dilbert Collection Ser.). (Illus.). 112p. pap. 7.95 o.p. (*0-88687-688-5*) World Almanac Bks.
—Build a Better Life by Stealing Office Supplies: Dogbert's Big Book of Business. 1994. (Dilbert Bks.). (Illus.). 112p. (Orig.). pap. 10.95 (*0-8362-1757-8*) Andrews McMeel Publishing.
—Build a Better Life by Stealing Office Supplies: Dogbert's Big Book of Business. 1991. (Illus.). 112p. (Orig.). pap. 7.95 o.p. (*0-88687-637-0*) World Almanac Bks.
—The Dilbert Audio Collection. unabr. ed. 1997. 250p. audio 29.95 (*0-694-51893-X*, HarperAudio) HarperTrade.
—Dilbert Book of Days: Trapped in a Dilbert World. 1998. (Illus.). 136p. spiral bd. 17.95 o.p. (*0-7683-2030-5*) CEDCO Publishing.
—The Dilbert Future: Thriving on Stupidity in the 21st Century. abr. ed. 1997. audio 12.00 (*0-694-51842-5*, CPN 10109, HarperAudio) HarperTrade.
—The Dilbert Future: Thriving on Stupidity in the 21st Century. abr. ed. 2001. audio (*0-333-73220-0*) Macmillan U.K. GBR. *Dist:* Macmillan Publishing Co., Inc.
—Dilbert Meeting Book: Exceeding Tech Limits, Large. 1998. (Illus.). 112p. spiral bd. 19.95 o.p. (*0-7683-2028-3*) CEDCO Publishing.
—Dilbert Meeting Book: Exceeding Tech Limits, Small. 1998. (Illus.). 112p. spiral bd. 12.95 o.p. (*0-7683-2029-1*) CEDCO Publishing.
—Dilbert Postcard Book. 1996. (Illus.). 30p. pap. 8.95 (*0-8362-1331-9*) Andrews McMeel Publishing.

—The Dilbert Principle: A Cubicle's-Eye View of Bosses, Meetings, Management Fads & Other Workplace Afflictions. abr. ed. audio 9.95 Books on Tape, Inc.
—The Dilbert Principle: A Cubicle's-Eye View of Bosses, Meetings, Management Fads & Other Workplace Afflictions. abr. ed. 1996. audio 12.00 (*0-694-51692-9*, CPN 10079, HarperAudio) HarperTrade.
—The Dilbert Principle: A Cubicle's-Eye View of Bosses, Meetings, Management Fads & Other Workplace Afflictions. 2001. audio (*0-333-72218-3*) Macmillan U.K. GBR. *Dist:* Macmillan Publishing Co., Inc.
—The Dilbert Principle: A Cubicle's-Eye View of Bosses, Meetings, Management Fads & Other Workplace Afflictions. unabr. ed. 1999. audio compact disk 49.00 (*0-7887-3419-9*, C1025E7); 1997. audio 49.00 (*0-7887-1162-8*, 95047E7) Recorded Bks., LLC.
—Dogbert's Top Secret Management Handbook. (Illus.). 1997. 192p. pap. 14.95 (*0-88730-881-3*); 1996. 176p. 16.00 o.s.i (*0-88730-788-4*) HarperInformation. (HarperBusiness).
—Dogbert's Top Secret Management Handbook. abr. ed. 1996. 90p. audio 12.00 (*0-694-51772-0*, CPN 10097, HarperAudio) HarperTrade.
—The Joy of Work: Dilbert's Guide to Finding Happiness at the Expense of Your Co-Workers. abr. ed. 1998. audio 12.00 (*0-694-51987-1*, HarperAudio) HarperTrade.
—No... You'd Better Watch Out! 1997. (Cartoon Bks.). (Illus.). 80p. 4.95 (*0-8362-3739-0*) Andrews McMeel Publishing.
—Please Don't Feed the Egos: And Other Tips for Corporate Survival. 1997. (Main Street Editions Ser.). (Illus.). 48p. 6.95 (*0-8362-3224-0*) Andrews McMeel Publishing.
—Seven Years of Highly Defective People: Scott Adams' Guided Tour of the Evolution of Dilbert. 1997. (Dilbert Bks.). 256p. 19.95 (*0-8362-5129-6*); (Illus.). pap. 12.95 (*0-8362-3668-8*) Andrews McMeel Publishing.
—Shave the Whales. 1994. (Dilbert Bks.). (Illus.). 128p. pap. 10.95 (*0-8362-1740-3*) Andrews McMeel Publishing.
—Telling It Like It Isn't: A Tiptoe Approach to Communications - A Dilbert Little Book. 1996. (Cartoon Bks.). (Illus.). 80p. 4.95 (*0-8362-1324-6*) Andrews McMeel Publishing.
—Words You Don't Want to Hear During Your Annual Review. 2003. 128p. pap. 10.95 (*0-7407-3805-4*) Andrews McMeel Publishing.

**DILGER, JACK (FICTITIOUS CHARACTER)—FICTION**

Daley, Robert. Nowhere to Run. abr. ed. 1997. audio 7.99 o.p. (*1-56740-191-0*, 685, Paperback Nova Audio Bks.); 1996. audio 16.95 o.p. (*1-56100-920-2*, 1309, Nova Audio Bks.); 1996. audio 25.95 o.p. (*1-56100-710-2*, 200, Bookcassette); 1996. audio 89.25 o.p. (*1-56100-335-2*, 968, Unabridged Library Editions) Brilliance Audio.
—Nowhere to Run. l.t. ed. 1997. (G. K. Hall Mystery Ser.). 631p. lib. bdg. 26.95 o.p. (*0-7838-2012-7*, Macmillan Reference USA) Gale Group.
—Nowhere to Run. 1997. 480p. mass mkt. 6.99 o.p. (*0-446-60470-4*); 1997. mass mkt. 188.73 (*0-446-16416-X*); 1996. 464p. 24.00 o.p. (*0-446-52063-2*) Warner Bks., Inc.

**DILLON, JAMES (FICTITIOUS CHARACTER)—FICTION**

Thompson, Jim. Now & on Earth. 1994. 320p. pap. 12.00 (*0-679-74013-9*) Random Hse., Inc.

**DILLON, RONNY (FICTITIOUS CHARACTER)—FICTION**

Deitz, Tom. Dreambuilder. 1992. 432p. (Orig.). mass mkt. 4.99 (*0-380-76290-0*, Avon Bks.) Morrow/Avon.
—Soulsmith. 1991. 464p. (Orig.). mass mkt. 4.99 (*0-380-76289-7*, Avon Bks.) Morrow/Avon.
—Wordwright. 1993. 400p. (Orig.). mass mkt. 4.99 (*0-380-76291-9*, Avon Bks.) Morrow/Avon.

**DILLON, ROY (FICTITIOUS CHARACTER)—FICTION**

Thompson, Jim. The Grifters. 1985. 196p. reprint ed. pap. 3.95 o.p. (*0-916870-90-1*, Black Mask) Creative Arts Bk. Co.
—The Grifters. 1990. (Vintage Crime/Black Lizard Ser.). 208p. pap. 11.00 (*0-679-73248-9*, Vintage) Knopf Publishing Group.

**DILLON, SEAN (FICTITIOUS CHARACTER)—FICTION**

Higgins, Jack. Angel of Death. 1996. 352p. mass mkt. 7.99 (*0-425-15223-5*) Berkley Publishing Group.
—Angel of Death. unabr. ed. 1995. 24.95 o.p. (*0-7871-0391-8*, 692879) NewStar Media, Inc.
—Angel of Death. 2001. 23.95 (*0-399-14274-6*); 1995. 311p. 23.95 (*0-399-14042-5*, G. P. Putnam's Sons) Penguin Group (USA) Inc.
—Angel of Death. l.t. ed. 1996. (Paperback Bestsellers Ser.). 402p. lib. bdg. 24.95 (*0-7862-0465-6*) Thorndike Pr.
—Day of Reckoning. 2001. 304p. mass mkt. 7.99 (*0-425-17877-3*) Berkley Publishing Group.
—Day of Reckoning. l.t. ed. 2000. (Wheeler Large Print Book Ser.). 293p. 28.95 (*1-56895-852-8*, Wheeler Publishing, Inc.) Gale Group.
—Day of Reckoning. 2000. 304p. 25.95 o.s.i (*0-399-14585-0*) Penguin Group (USA) Inc.
—Day of Reckoning. abr. ed. 2000. audio 24.95 (*0-399-14610-5*, Putnam Berkley Audio) Putnam Publishing Group, The.
—Drink with the Devil. 1997. 336p. mass mkt. 7.99 (*0-425-15754-7*); mass mkt. 6.99 o.s.i (*0-425-16049-1*) Berkley Publishing Group.
—Drink with the Devil, Set. unabr. ed. 1999. audio 29.95 Highsmith Inc.
—Drink with the Devil. abr. ed. 1996. 2 cass. audio 17.95 o.p. (*0-7871-0966-5*); Set. 29.95 o.p. (*0-7871-0872-3*, 893923) NewStar Media, Inc.
—Drink with the Devil. 1996. 320p. 24.95 o.p. (*0-399-14154-5*, G. P. Putnam's Sons) Penguin Group (USA) Inc.
—Drink with the Devil. 1998. 5.98 o.p. (*0-7651-0898-4*) Smithmark Pubs., Inc.
—Drink with the Devil. l.t. ed. 1999. 430p. pap. 26.95 (*0-7862-0797-3*) Thorndike Pr.
—Edge of Danger. 2001. 304p. 25.95 o.s.i (*0-399-14701-2*) Penguin Group (USA) Inc.
—Edge of Danger. abr. unabr. ed. 2001. audio 24.95 o.s.i (*0-399-14721-7*, Putnam Berkley Audio) Putnam Publishing Group, The.
—Edge of Danger. unabr. ed. 2001. audio 48.00 (*0-7887-5259-6*) Recorded Bks., LLC.
—Edge of Danger. l.t. ed. 2001. 341p. 29.95 (*0-7862-3171-8*); 32.95 (*0-7862-3170-X*); (*0-7540-2464-4*); (*0-7540-1608-0*) Thorndike Pr.
—Eye of the Storm. 1993. 352p. mass mkt. 7.99 (*0-425-13823-2*) Berkley Publishing Group.
—Eye of the Storm. unabr. ed. 2001. 7p. audio (*0-7531-0889-5*) ISIS Audio Bks. GBR. *Dist:* Ulverscroft Large Print Bks., Ltd.
—Eye of the Storm. abr. ed. 1994. 16.95 o.p. (*1-55800-635-4*) NewStar Media, Inc.
—Eye of the Storm. 1992. 320p. 22.95 o.p. (*0-399-13758-0*, G. P. Putnam's Sons) Penguin Group (USA) Inc.
—Midnight Runner. 2003. 304p. mass mkt. 7.99 (*0-425-18941-4*) Berkley Publishing Group.
—Midnight Runner. 2002. 288p. 25.95 o.s.i (*0-399-14833-7*, Riverhead Bks. (Hardcovers)) Penguin Group (USA) Inc.
—Midnight Runner. abr. ed. 2002. 6p. audio compact disk 29.95 (*0-399-14855-8*, Putnam & Grosset); 4p. audio 24.95 (*0-399-14856-6*, Putnam Berkley Audio) Putnam Publishing Group, The.
—Midnight Runner. l.t. ed. 13.95 (*1-4104-0090-5*, Large Print Pr.); 2003. 449p. 13.95 (*0-7862-4107-1*); 2002. 449p. 32.95 (*0-7862-4106-3*) Thorndike Pr.
—On Dangerous Ground. 1995. 336p. mass mkt. 7.99 (*0-425-14828-9*) Berkley Publishing Group.
—On Dangerous Ground. 1995. reprint ed. lib. bdg. 26.95 (*1-56849-595-1*) Buccaneer Bks., Inc.
—On Dangerous Ground. unabr. ed. 1999. audio 29.95 Highsmith Inc.
—On Dangerous Ground. abr. ed. 1993. 17.95 o.p. (*0-7871-0026-9*); 29.95 o.p. (*0-7871-0043-9*) NewStar Media, Inc.
—On Dangerous Ground. 1994. 320p. 22.95 o.p. (*0-399-13933-8*, G. P. Putnam's Sons) Penguin Group (USA) Inc.
—The President's Daughter. 2003. 320p. pap. 14.95 (*0-425-19294-6*); 1998. 320p. mass mkt. 7.99 (*0-425-16341-5*); 1998. mass mkt. 6.99 (*0-425-16542-6*) Berkley Publishing Group.
—The President's Daughter. l.t. ed. 1997. (Large Print Book Ser.). 26.95 o.p. (*1-56895-495-6*, Wheeler Publishing, Inc.) Gale Group.
—The President's Daughter. unabr. ed. 1999. audio 35.00 Highsmith Inc.
—The President's Daughter. abr. ed. 1997. 25.00 o.p. (*0-7871-1358-1*, 695116); 35.00 o.p. (*0-7871-1458-8*, 895269) NewStar Media, Inc.
—The President's Daughter. 1997. 320p. 23.95 o.s.i (*0-399-14239-8*, G. P. Putnam's Sons) Penguin Group (USA) Inc.
—Thunder Point. 1994. 368p. reprint ed. mass mkt. 7.99 (*0-425-14357-0*) Berkley Publishing Group.
—Thunder Point. unabr. ed. 1994. audio 72.00 (*0-7366-2651-4*, 3388) Books on Tape, Inc.
—Thunder Point. 1995. reprint ed. lib. bdg. 26.95 (*1-56849-594-3*) Buccaneer Bks., Inc.
—Thunder Point. l.t. ed. 1993. 26.95 o.p. (*1-56895-037-3*, Wheeler Publishing, Inc.) Gale Group.
—Thunder Point. abr. ed. 2003. audio 34.95 (*1-59007-378-9*, New Millennium Audio) New Millennium Entertainment.
—Thunder Point. abr. ed. 1993. audio 16.95 o.p. (*1-55800-786-5*) NewStar Media, Inc.
—Thunder Point. 1993. 320p. 22.95 o.p. (*0-399-13835-8*, G. P. Putnam's Sons) Penguin Group (USA) Inc.
—Thunder Point. 5.98 o.s.i (*0-8317-6524-0*) Smithmark Pubs., Inc.
—The White House Connection. 2000. 304p. mass mkt. 7.99 (*0-425-17541-3*) Berkley Publishing Group.
—The White House Connection. unabr. ed. 1999. 7p. audio 57.25 (*1-56740-676-9*, 1797, Unabridged Library Editions); audio 35.95 (*1-56740-450-2*, 1796, Brilliance Audio Unabridged) Brilliance Audio.
—The White House Connection. unabr. ed. 1999. audio 57.25 Highsmith Inc.
—The White House Connection. 1999. 323p. 25.95 o.p. (*0-399-14489-7*, G. P. Putnam's Sons); 24.95 (*0-399-14528-1*, Putnam Berkley Audio) Penguin Group (USA) Inc.
—The White House Connection. l.t. ed. (Thorndike/G. K. Hall Paperback Bestsellers Ser.). 2000. 377p. 27.95 (*0-7862-2023-6*); 1999. 413p. 30.95 (*0-7862-2022-8*); 1999. (*0-7540-1328-6*); 1999. (*0-7540-2244-7*) Thorndike Pr.

**DILLWORTH, POPPY (FICTITIOUS CHARACTER)—FICTION**

Tell, Dorothy. The Hallelujah Murders. 1991. (Poppy Dillworth Mystery Ser.). 176p. pap. 8.95 (*0-941483-88-6*) Naiad Pr., Inc.
—Murder at Red Rook Ranch. 1990. 224p. pap. 8.95 (*0-941483-80-0*) Naiad Pr., Inc.
—Wilderness Trek. 1990. 160p. pap. 8.95 o.p. (*0-941483-60-6*) Naiad Pr., Inc.

**DILVISH (FICTITIOUS CHARACTER)—FICTION**

Zelazny, Roger. The Changing Land. 1986. mass mkt. 4.99 o.s.i (*0-345-34441-3*, Ballantine Bks.); 1986. 224p. mass mkt. 4.99 o.s.i (*0-345-90174-6*, Del Rey); 1981. mass mkt. 2.50 o.p. (*0-345-25389-2*, Del Rey) Ballantine Bks.
—Dilvish the Damned. 1985. mass mkt. 4.99 o.s.i (*0-345-90175-4*, Del Rey) Ballantine Bks.
—Dilvish, the Damned. 1985. mass mkt. 4.99 o.s.i (*0-345-33417-5*, Del Rey) Ballantine Bks.

**DIMAGGIO, TONY (FICTITIOUS CHARACTER)—FICTION**

Lupica, Mike. Jump. 384p. 2002. mass mkt. 6.99 (*0-7860-1522-5*); 1996. mass mkt. 5.99 o.s.i (*1-57566-112-8*); 1996. mass mkt. 5.99 o.s.i (*0-7860-0303-0*) Kensington Publishing Corp.

**DIMARCO, JEFF (FICTITIOUS CHARACTER)—FICTION**

Disney, Doris M. Chandler Policy. 1971. 4.95 o.p. (*0-399-10127-6*) Putnam Publishing Group, The.

**DIMITY, AUNT (FICTITIOUS CHARACTER)—FICTION**

Atherton, Nancy. Aunt Dimity: Detective. l.t. ed. 2002. (Mystery Ser.). 274p. 30.45 (*0-7862-3843-7*) Gale Group.
—Aunt Dimity & the Duke. 1995. (Crime Fiction Ser.). 304p. pap. 6.99 (*0-14-017841-4*, Penguin Bks.) Penguin Group (USA) Inc.
—Aunt Dimity & the Duke. 1994. (Aunt Dimity Mystery Ser.). 304p. 19.95 o.p. (*0-670-84964-2*, Viking) Viking Penguin.
—Aunt Dimity Beats the Devil. l.t. ed. 2001. (Thorndike Mystery Ser.). 309p. 29.95 (*0-7862-2935-7*) Thorndike Pr.
—Aunt Dimity Beats the Devil. 2000. (Illus.). 224p. (J). 22.95 o.s.i (*0-670-89179-7*, Viking) Viking Penguin.
—Aunt Dimity, Detective. 2003. 240p. mass mkt. 6.99 (*0-14-200154-6*) Penguin Group (USA) Inc.
—Aunt Dimity, Detective. 2001. 256p. 22.95 o.s.i (*0-670-03021-X*, Viking) Viking Penguin.
—Aunt Dimity Digs In. 1999. 288p. pap. 6.99 (*0-14-027569-X*) Penguin Group (USA) Inc.
—Aunt Dimity Digs In. 1998. (Aunt Dimity Mystery Ser.). 288p. 21.95 o.p. (*0-670-87061-7*) Viking Penguin.
—Aunt Dimity Snowbound. 2004. (Aunt Dimity Mystery Ser.). 240p. 22.95 (*0-670-03278-6*) Viking Penguin.
—Aunt Dimity Takes a Holiday. 2004. 224p. mass mkt. 6.99 (*0-14-200393-X*) Penguin Group (USA) Inc.
—Aunt Dimity Takes a Holiday. 2003. (Mystery Ser.). 30.45 (*0-7862-5119-0*) Thorndike Pr.
—Aunt Dimity Takes a Holiday. 2003. 208p. 22.95 (*0-670-03200-X*, Viking) Viking Penguin.
—Aunt Dimity's Christmas. l.t. ed. 2000. (Beeler Large Print Mystery Ser.). 25.95 (*1-57490-260-1*, Beeler Large Print Bks.) Beeler, Thomas T. Publisher.
—Aunt Dimity's Christmas. 2000. (Illus.). 224p. pap. 6.99 (*0-14-029630-1*) Penguin Group (USA) Inc.
—Aunt Dimity's Christmas. 1999. 224p. text 22.95 (*0-670-88453-7*, Viking) Viking Penguin.
—Aunt Dimity's Death. 1993. (Special Study of the Kennan Institute for Advanced Russian S Ser.). 256p. reprint ed. pap. 6.99 (*0-14-017840-6*) Penguin Group (USA) Inc.
—Aunt Dimity's Death. 1992. (Aunt Dimity Mystery Ser.). 256p. 19.00 o.p. (*0-670-84449-7*, Viking) Viking Penguin.
—Aunt Dimity's Good Deed. 1998. (Aunt Dimity Mystery Ser.). 288p. pap. 6.99 (*0-14-025881-7*) Penguin Group (USA) Inc.
—Aunt Dimity's Good Deed. 1996. (Aunt Dimity Mystery Ser.). 288p. 20.95 o.s.i (*0-670-86715-2*, Viking) Viking Penguin.

**DINUNZIO, MARY (FICTITIOUS CHARACTER)—FICTION**

Scottoline, Lisa. Everywhere That Mary Went. l.t. ed. 2000. (Wheeler Large Print Book Ser.). 350p. 25.95 o.p. (*1-56895-854-4*, Wheeler Publishing, Inc.) Gale Group.
—Everywhere That Mary Went. 2003. 352p. pap. 11.95 (*0-06-054047-8*, Perennial) HarperTrade.
—Everywhere That Mary Went. 1993. 368p. mass mkt. 7.99 (*0-06-104293-5*, HarperTorch) Morrow/Avon.
—Moment of Truth. 2000. 358p. 25.00 (*0-06-019609-2*); 544p. pap. 25.00 (*0-06-095611-9*) HarperCollins Pubs.
—Moment of Truth. abr. ed. 2000. audio 25.00 (*0-694-52310-0*); audio 39.95 (*0-694-52305-4*) HarperTrade. (HarperAudio).
—Moment of Truth. 2001. 448p. mass mkt. 7.50 (*0-06-103059-7*, HarperTorch) Morrow/Avon.
—Moment of Truth. unabr. ed. 1999. audio 75.00 (*0-7887-4152-7*, 96182E7) Recorded Bks., LLC.

**DION (EMBER DION MAMARIN) (FICTITIOUS CHARACTER)—FICTION**

Harper, Tara K. Grayheart. 1996. 352p. mass mkt. 6.99 (*0-345-38053-3*, Del Rey) Ballantine Bks.
—Shadow Leader. 1991. 336p. mass mkt. 6.99 (*0-345-37163-1*, Ballantine Bks.) Ballantine Bks.
—Storm Runner. 1993. (Tales of the Wolves Ser.: Bk. 3). 320p. mass mkt. 6.99 (*0-345-37162-3*, Ballantine Bks.) Ballantine Bks.
—Wolf's Bane. 1997. 352p. mass mkt. 6.99 (*0-345-40634-6*, Del Rey) Ballantine Bks.
—Wolfwalker. 1990. 320p. (Orig.). mass mkt. 6.99 (*0-345-36539-9*, Del Rey) Ballantine Bks.

**DI PALMA, LAURA (FICTITIOUS CHARACTER)—FICTION**

Matera, Lia. Designer Crimes: A Laura Di Palma Mystery. (Laura Di Palma Mystery Ser.). 1996. 288p. pap. 6.50 (*0-671-00196-5*, Pocket); 1995. 240p. 21.00 o.s.i (*0-684-80312-7*, Simon & Schuster) Simon & Schuster.
—Face Value: A Laura Di Palma Mystery. (Laura Di Palma Ser.). 1995. o.s.i (*0-684-88840-8*, Pocket); 1995. (Illus.). 272p. mass mkt. 5.99 (*0-671-88840-4*, Pocket); 1994. 221p. 20.00 (*0-671-74197-7*, Simon & Schuster) Simon & Schuster.
—The Good Fight. 1991. (Laura Di Palma Ser.). mass mkt. 5.99 o.s.i (*0-345-37107-0*, Ballantine Bks.) Ballantine Bks.
—The Good Fight. 1990. 17.95 o.p. (*0-671-68561-9*, Simon & Schuster) Simon & Schuster.
—A Hard Bargain. 1993. (Laura Di Palma Ser.). mass mkt. 5.99 o.s.i (*0-345-38059-2*) Ballantine Bks.
—A Hard Bargain. 1992. 224p. 19.00 o.p. (*0-671-74196-9*, Simon & Schuster) Simon & Schuster.
—Radical Departure. 1991. (Laura Di Palma Ser.). 224p. (Orig.). mass mkt. 5.99 o.s.i (*0-345-37126-7*) Ballantine Bks.
—The Smart Money. 1991. 192p. (Orig.). mass mkt. 5.99 o.s.i (*0-345-37127-5*) Ballantine Bks.
—The Smart Money. 1988. 208p. (Orig.). mass mkt. 3.50 o.s.i (*0-553-27268-3*) Bantam Bks.

**DISBRO, GIL (FICTITIOUS CHARACTER)—FICTION**

Martin, James E. And Then You Die: A Novel. 1993. 224p. mass mkt. 4.99 (*0-380-71696-8*, Avon Bks.); 1992. 18.00 o.p. (*0-688-11198-X*, Morrow, William & Co.) Morrow/Avon.
—A Fine & Private Place. 1995. 256p. mass mkt. 4.99 (*0-380-71697-6*, Avon Bks.) Morrow/Avon.
—A Fine & Private Place: A Gil Disbro Mystery. 1994. 23.00 o.p. (*0-688-11211-0*, Morrow, William & Co.) Morrow/Avon.
—The Flip Side of Life. 1991. 256p. mass mkt. 3.99 (*0-380-71407-8*, Avon Bks.) Morrow/Avon.
—The Flip Side of Life. 1990. 256p. 21.95 o.p. (*0-399-13523-5*, G. P. Putnam's Sons) Penguin Putnam Bks. for Young Readers.
—The Mercy Trap. 1990. 256p. pap. 3.95 (*0-380-71041-2*, Avon Bks.) Morrow/Avon.
—The Mercy Trap. 1989. 256p. 18.95 o.p. (*0-399-13441-7*, G. P. Putnam's Sons) Penguin Putnam Bks. for Young Readers.

**DI STEFANO, FLAVIA (FICTITIOUS CHARACTER)—FICTION**

Pears, Iain. The Bernini Bust. 1994. 192p. 19.95 o.s.i (*0-15-111830-2*) Harcourt Trade Pubs.

—Death & Restoration: A Jonathan Argyll Mystery. (Art History Mysteries Ser.). 2000. 288p. mass mkt. 6.50 (*0-425-17742-4*, Prime Crime); 2000. 223p. mass mkt. 6.50 (*0-00-649875-2*); 2003. 320p. reprint ed. pap. 13.00 (*0-425-19042-0*, Prime Crime) Berkley Publishing Group.

—Death & Restoration: A Jonathan Argyll Mystery. 1998. (Jonathan Argyll Mysteries Ser.: Vol. 6). 224p. 22.00 o.s.i (*0-684-81461-7*, Scribner) Simon & Schuster.

—Giotto's Hand. (Art History Mysteries Ser.). 2000. 288p. mass mkt. 6.50 (*0-425-17358-5*); 2003. 304p. reprint ed. pap. 13.00 (*0-425-18854-X*) Berkley Publishing Group. (Prime Crime).

—Giotto's Hand. l.t. ed. 1997. (G. K. Hall Mystery Ser.). 305p. 25.95 o.p. (*0-7838-8362-5*, Macmillan Reference USA) Gale Group.

—Giotto's Hand. 1997. 224p. 20.50 (*0-684-81460-9*, Scribner) Simon & Schuster.

—The Immaculate Deception. 2000. 224p. 25.00 o.s.i (*0-7432-1257-6*, Scribner); 2001. 272p. reprint ed. mass mkt. 7.99 (*0-7434-2208-2*, Pocket) Simon & Schuster.

—The Immaculate Deception. l.t. ed. 2001. (Thorndike Basic Ser.). 333p. 28.95 (*0-7862-3257-9*) Thorndike Pr.

—The Last Judgement. 2002. 336p. pap. 13.00 (*0-425-18647-4*) Berkley Publishing Group.

—The Last Judgement: A Jonathan Argyll Mystery. 1999. (Art History Mysteries Ser.). 288p. mass mkt. 6.50 (*0-425-17148-5*, Prime Crime) Berkley Publishing Group.

—The Last Judgement: A Jonathan Argyll Mystery. 1996. 224p. 20.50 (*0-684-81459-5*); 1995. 21.00 (*1-57283-001-8*) Simon & Schuster. (Scribner).

—The Raphael Affair. 1998. (Prime Crime Mysteries Ser.: Bk. 1). 240p. reprint ed. mass mkt. 6.50 (*0-425-16613-9*, Prime Crime) Berkley Publishing Group.

—The Raphael Affair. 1992. 191p. 18.95 (*0-15-178912-6*) Harcourt Trade Pubs.

—The Raphael Affair. l.t. ed. 1991. (Linford Mystery Library). pap. 17.99 o.p. (*0-7089-7155-5*, Ulverscroft) Thorpe, F. A. Pubs. GBR. *Dist:* Ulverscroft Large Print Bks., Ltd., Ulverscroft Large Print Canada, Ltd.

—The Titian Committee. 2002. 272p. pap. 12.00 (*0-425-18500-1*); 1999. 240p. reprint ed. pap. 6.50 (*0-425-16895-6*, Prime Crime) Berkley Publishing Group.

—The Titian Committee. 1993. 189p. 19.95 (*0-15-190472-3*) Harcourt Trade Pubs.

**DOBIE, JOHN (FICTITIOUS CHARACTER)—FICTION**

Cory, Desmond. The Catalyst. 1991. 15.95 o.p. (*0-312-05832-2*, Saint Martin's Minotaur) St. Martin's Pr.

—The Dobie Paradox. 1994. 240p. 19.95 o.p. (*0-312-10969-5*, Saint Martin's Minotaur) St. Martin's Pr.

—The Mask of Zeus. 1993. 256p. 19.95 o.p. (*0-312-09873-1*, Saint Martin's Minotaur) St. Martin's Pr.

**DOCTOR WHO (FICTITIOUS CHARACTER)—FICTION**

Anghelides, Peter. Frontier Worlds. 2000. (Doctor Who Ser.). 288p. pap. text 6.95 (*0-563-55589-0*) BBC Bk. Publishing GBR. *Dist:* General Distribution Services, Inc.

—Kursaal. 1998. (Doctor Who Ser.). 282p. (J). pap. text 5.95 (*0-563-40578-3*) BBC Worldwide Americas.

Baker, Bob & Martin, David C. Garden of Evil. 1986. (Doctor Who Ser.: No. 3). mass mkt. 2.50 o.s.i (*0-345-33226-1*) Ballantine Bks.

Baker, Pip & Baker, Jane. Mission to Venus. 1986. (Doctor Who Ser.: No. 4). mass mkt. 2.95 o.s.i (*0-345-33229-6*) Ballantine Bks.

Baxendale, Trevor. Coldheart. 2000. (Doctor Who Ser.). 288p. pap. text 6.95 (*0-563-55595-5*) BBC Bk. Publishing GBR. *Dist:* General Distribution Services, Inc.

BBC Worldwide Publishing Staff. Short Trips: A Collection of Short Stories. 1998. (Doctor Who Ser.). viii, 336p. pap. 5.95 (*0-563-40560-0*) BBC Worldwide Americas.

Blum, Jonathan. Vampire Science. 1998. (Doctor Who Ser.). (Illus.). 283p. pap. o.p. (*0-563-40566-X*) BBC Bk. Publishing.

Blum, Jonathan & Orman, Kate. Seeing I. 1998. (Doctor Who Ser.). 288p. (J). pap. text 5.95 (*0-563-40586-4*) BBC Worldwide Americas.

Boucher, Chris. Last Man Running. 1998. (Doctor Who Ser.). (Illus.). 251p. pap. text 5.95 (*0-563-40594-5*) BBC Worldwide Americas.

—Psi-ence Fiction. 2001. (Doctor Who Ser.: No. 4). 283p. pap. text 6.95 (*0-563-53814-7*) BBC Worldwide Americas.

Bucher-Jones, Simon & Clapham, Mark. The Taking of Planet 5. 2000. (Doctor Who Ser.). 288p. pap. 6.95 (*0-563-55585-8*) BBC Bk. Publishing GBR. *Dist:* General Distribution Services, Inc.

Bucher-Jones, Simon & Haley, Kelly. Grimm Reality. 2001. (Doctor Who Ser.: No. 8 ). 276p. pap. text 6.95 (*0-563-53841-4*) BBC Worldwide Americas.

Bulis, Christopher. The Imperial Moon: A Fifth Doctor & Turlough Novel. 2000. (Doctor Who Ser.). 288p. pap. text 6.95 (*0-563-53801-5*) BBC Bk. Publishing GBR. *Dist:* General Distribution Services, Inc.

—Palace of the Red Sun. 2002. (Doctor Who Ser.: No. 6). 284p. pap. text 6.95 (*0-563-53849-X*) BBC Worldwide Americas.

—Ultimate Treasure. 1998. (Doctor Who Ser.). 281p. pap. o.p. (*0-563-40571-6*) BBC Bk. Publishing.

—Vanderdeken's Children. 1998. (Doctor Who Ser.). (Illus.). 288p. pap. text 5.95 (*0-563-40590-2*) BBC Worldwide Americas.

Clapham, Mark. Hope. 2002. (Doctor Who Ser.: No. 8). 249p. (Orig.). pap. text 6.95 (*0-563-53846-5*) BBC Worldwide Americas.

Cole, Stephen. The Vanishing Point. 2001. (Doctor Who Ser.). (Illus.). 288p. pap. 6.95 (*0-563-53829-5*) BBC Worldwide Americas.

Cole, Stephen & Rayner, Jacqueline, eds. Short Trips & Side Steps. 2000. (Doctor Who Ser.). 288p. pap. text 6.95 (*0-563-55599-8*) BBC Bk. Publishing GBR. *Dist:* General Distribution Services, Inc.

Collier, Michael. The Longest Day. 1998. (Doctor Who Ser.). x, 276p. (J). pap. text 5.95 (*0-563-40581-3*) BBC Worldwide Americas.

Cornell, Paul. The Storming of Avalon. 2000. (Doctor Who Ser.). 288p. pap. text 6.95 (*0-563-55588-2*) BBC Bk. Publishing GBR. *Dist:* General Distribution Services, Inc.

Dallaire, Natalie & Cole, Stephen. Parallel 59. 2000. (Doctor Who Ser.). 288p. pap. text 6.95 (*0-563-55590-4*) BBC Bk. Publishing GBR. *Dist:* General Distribution Services, Inc.

Day, Martin. Bunker Soldiers. 2001. (Doctor Who Ser.). 282p. pap. (*0-563-53819-8*) Doctor Who Bks.

Dicks, Terrance. Catastrophea. 1998. (Doctor Who Ser.). 248p. pap. text 5.95 (*0-563-40584-8*) BBC Worldwide Americas.

—Doctor Who & the Android Invasion. 17.95 (*0-8488-0150-4*) Amereon, Ltd.

—Doctor Who & the Day of the Daleks. 18.95 (*0-8488-0151-2*) Amereon, Ltd.

—Doctor Who & the Genesis of the Daleks. 17.95 (*0-8488-0152-0*) Amereon, Ltd.

—Doctor Who & the Giant Robot. 17.95 (*0-8488-0153-9*) Amereon, Ltd.

—Doctor Who & the Image of the Fendall. 17.95 (*0-8488-0154-7*) Amereon, Ltd.

—Doctor Who & the Loch Ness Monster. 17.95 (*0-8488-0155-5*) Amereon, Ltd.

—Doctor Who & the Revenge of the Cybermen. 17.95 (*0-8488-0156-3*) Amereon, Ltd.

—Dr. Who & the Day of the Daleks. 1979. (Dr. Who Ser.: No. 1). pap. 1.95 o.p. (*0-523-42496-5*, Pinnacle Bks.) Kensington Publishing Corp.

—The Eight Doctors. 1998. (Doctor Who Ser.). 280p. mass mkt. 5.95 o.s.i (*0-563-40563-5*) BBC Worldwide Americas.

Doctor Who: The Audio Scripts. 2003. 192p. 22.95 (*1-84435-005-3*) Reynolds & Hearn GBR. *Dist:* Trafalgar Square.

Doctor Who: Timewyrm: Exodus. 1992. pap. 5.95 o.p. (*0-426-20357-7*) Doctor Who.

Doctor Who & the Rebel's Gamble. 1986. pap. 3.95 o.p. (*0-931787-68-8*) FASA Corp.

Doctor Who & the Vortex Crystal. 1986. pap. 3.95 o.p. (*0-931787-67-X*) FASA Corp.

Emms, William. Race Against Time. 1986. (Doctor Who Ser.: No. 6). mass mkt. 2.50 o.s.i (*0-345-33228-8*) Ballantine Bks.

Fantasimulations Associates Staff. The Daleks, 2 bks., Set. 1986. (Doctor Who Ser.). 62p. pap. 11.00 o.p. (*0-931787-93-9*) FASA Corp.

Forward, Simon A. Drift. 2002. (Doctor Who Ser.: No. 4). 283p. pap. text 6.95 (*0-563-53843-0*) BBC Worldwide Americas.

Gatiss, Mark. Last of the Gaderene. 2000. (Doctor Who Ser.). 288p. pap. text 6.95 (*0-563-55587-4*) BBC Bk. Publishing GBR. *Dist:* General Distribution Services, Inc.

—Roundheads. 1998. (Doctor Who Ser.). 282p. (J). pap. text (*0-563-40576-7*) BBC Bk. Publishing.

Haining, Peter. Doctor Who: A Celebration. 1995. (Illus.). 240p. pap. 19.95 (*0-86369-932-4*) Virgin Bks. GBR. *Dist:* London Bridge.

Holt, Michael. Dr. Who: Find Your Fate, No. 2. 1986. 128p. mass mkt. 2.50 o.s.i (*0-345-33225-3*, Del Rey) Ballantine Bks.

Howe, David J. & Stammers, Mark. Companions. 1996. (Illus.). 128p. pap. 19.95 (*0-86369-921-9*); 24.95 o.p. (*1-85227-582-0*) Virgin Bks. GBR. *Dist:* London Bridge.

Howe, David J., et al. The 80s. 1997. (Illus.). 192p. pap. 19.95 (*0-7535-0128-7*) Virgin Bks. GBR. *Dist:* London Bridge.

Keith, J. Andrew. The Master, 2 bks. 1986. (Doctor Who Ser.). 78p. (Orig.). pap. 11.00 o.p. (*0-931787-94-7*) FASA Corp.

Lane, Andy. Original Sin. 1995. (Dr. Who New Adventures Ser.). mass mkt. 5.95 o.p. (*0-426-20444-1*) Virgin Bks. GBR. *Dist:* London Bridge.

Leonard, Paul. Dream Stone Moon. 1998. (Doctor Who Ser.). 250p. pap. text 5.95 (*0-563-40585-6*) BBC Worldwide Americas.

—Genocide. 1998. (Doctor Who Ser.). 281p. pap. text 5.95 (*0-563-40572-4*) BBC Worldwide Americas.

—The Turing Test: An Eighth Doctor Novel. 2000. (Doctor Who Ser.). 242p. pap. 6.95 (*0-563-53806-6*) Piatkus Bks. GBR. *Dist:* London Bridge.

Lewis, Mick. Rags. 2001. (Doctor Who Ser.). 288p. pap. 6.95 (*0-563-53826-0*) BBC Worldwide Americas.

Lofficier, Jean-Marc. Doctor Who Handbook: The Ninth Doctor. 1997. (Doctor Who Ser.). 256p. mass mkt. 5.95 o.p. (*0-426-20499-9*) Virgin Bks. GBR. *Dist:* London Bridge.

Lyons, Steve. The Final Sanction. 2000. (Doctor Who Ser.). 288p. pap. text 6.95 (*0-563-55584-X*) BBC Bk. Publishing GBR. *Dist:* General Distribution Services, Inc.

—Murder Game. 1998. (Doctor Who Ser.). (Illus.). 288p. pap. (*0-563-40565-1*) BBC Bk. Publishing.

—Space Age. 2000. (Doctor Who Ser.). (Illus.). 288p. (J). pap. text 6.95 (*0-563-53800-7*) BBC Worldwide Americas.

—Witch Hunters. 1998. (Doctor Who Ser.). 282p. pap. 5.95 o.p. (*0-563-40579-1*) BBC Worldwide Americas.

Magrs, Paul. Mad Dogs & Englishmen. 2002. (Doctor Who Ser.: No. 8). 249p. pap. text 6.95 (*0-563-53845-7*) BBC Worldwide Americas.

—The Scarlet Empress. 1998. (Doctor Who Ser.). (Illus.). 283p. pap. text 5.95 (*0-563-40595-3*) BBC Worldwide Americas.

—Verdigris. 2000. (Doctor Who Ser.). 288p. pap. text (*0-563-55592-0*) BBC Bk. Publishing.

Martin, David C. Search for the Doctor. 1986. (Doctor Who Ser.: No. 1). mass mkt. 2.50 o.s.i (*0-345-33224-5*) Ballantine Bks.

McIntee, David A. Face of the Enemy. 1998. (Doctor Who Ser.). 281p. pap. text 5.95 (*0-563-40580-5*) BBC Worldwide Americas.

—Mission Impractical. 1998. (Doctor Who Ser.). 280p. pap. text 5.95 (*0-563-40592-9*) BBC Worldwide Americas.

Messingham, Simon. The Face Eater. 1999. (Doctor Who Ser.). 279p. pap. text 5.95 (*0-563-55569-6*) BBC Worldwide Americas.

—The Tomb of Valdemar. 2000. (Doctor Who Ser.). 288p. pap. text 6.95 (*0-563-55591-2*) BBC Bk. Publishing GBR. *Dist:* General Distribution Services, Inc.

—Zeta Major. 1998. (Doctor Who Ser.). 282p. pap. text 5.95 (*0-563-40597-X*) BBC Worldwide Americas.

Miles, Lawrence. Alien Bodies. 8th ed. 1998. (Doctor Who Ser.). 313p. pap. text 5.95 (*0-563-40577-5*) BBC Worldwide Americas.

—Christmas on a Rational Planet. 1996. (Dr. Who New Adventures Ser.). 280p. mass mkt. 5.95 (*0-426-20476-X*) Virgin Bks. GBR. *Dist:* London Bridge.

Miller, Jon De Burgh. Dying in the Sun. 2001. (Doctor Who Ser.: No. 2). 281p. pap. text 6.95 (*0-563-53840-6*) BBC Worldwide Americas.

Morris, Jonathan. Anachrophobia. 2002. (Doctor Who Ser.: No. 8). 277p. pap. text 6.95 (*0-563-53847-3*) BBC Worldwide Americas.

—Festival of Death: A Fourth Doctor & Romana Novel. 2000. (Doctor Who Ser.). 280p. pap. 6.95 (*0-563-53803-1*) Piatkus Bks. GBR. *Dist:* London Bridge.

Morris, Mark. Bodysnatchers. 1998. (Doctor Who Ser.). 280p. pap. o.p. (*0-563-40568-6*) BBC Bk. Publishing.

Mortimore, Jim. Campaign. 2000. (Doctor Who Ser.). 288p. mass mkt. (*0-563-55593-9*) BBC Bk. Publishing.

—Eye of Heaven. 1998. (Doctor Who Ser.). 277p. pap. text 5.95 (*0-563-40567-8*) BBC Worldwide Americas.

Muir, John K. A Critical History of Doctor Who on Television. 1999. (Illus.). 504p. lib. bdg. 65.00 (*0-7864-0442-6*) McFarland & Co., Inc. Pubs.

Parkhouse, Steve & Ridgeway. Doctor Who: Voyager. 1989. (Illus.). 100p. 8.95 o.p. (*1-85400-045-4*) Marvel Enterprises.

Parkin, Lance. A History of the Universe. 1996. (Illus.). 256p. (Orig.). mass mkt. 10.95 o.p. (*0-426-20471-9*) Virgin Bks. GBR. *Dist:* London Bridge.

—Just War. 1996. (Dr. Who New Adventures Ser.). 288p. (Orig.). mass mkt. 5.95 (*0-426-20463-8*) Virgin Bks. GBR. *Dist:* London Bridge.

Peel, John. Legacy of the Daleks. 1998. (Doctor Who Ser.). 245p. pap. text o.p. (*0-563-40574-0*) BBC Bk. Publishing.

—War of the Daleks. 1998. (Doctor Who Ser.). 277p. pap. text 5.95 o.p. (*0-563-40573-2*) BBC Worldwide Americas.

Perry, Robert & Tucker, Mike. The Matrix. 1998. (Doctor Who Ser.). (Illus.). 280p. text 5.95 (*0-563-40596-1*) BBC Worldwide Americas.

Raynor, J. Earthworld. 2001. (Doctor Who Ser.). 288p. pap. 6.95 (*0-563-53827-9*) BBC Worldwide Americas.

Richards, Justin. Dreams of Empire. 1998. (Doctor Who Ser.). (Illus.). 288p. pap. text 5.95 (*0-563-40598-8*) BBC Worldwide Americas.

—Grave Matter. 2000. (Doctor Who Ser.). (Illus.). 288p. (J). pap. text (*0-563-55598-X*) BBC Bk. Publishing.

—Option Lock. 1998. (Doctor Who Ser.). 280p. (J). pap. text 5.95 (*0-563-40583-X*) BBC Worldwide Americas.

Richards, Justin & Cole, Stephen. The Shadow in the Glass. 2001. (Doctor Who Ser.: No. 6). 286p. pap. text 6.95 (*0-563-53838-4*) BBC Worldwide Americas.

Rose, Lloyd. The City of the Dead. 2001. (Doctor Who Ser.: No. 8). 278p. pap. text 6.95 (*0-563-53839-2*) BBC Worldwide Americas.

Russell, Gary. Business Unusual. 1998. (Doctor Who Ser.). 277p. pap. (*0-563-40575-9*) BBC Bk. Publishing.

—Placebo Effect. 1998. (Doctor Who Ser.). (Illus.). 279p. (J). text 5.95 (*0-563-40587-2*) BBC Worldwide Americas.

Segal, Philip. Doctor Who: Regeneration. 2001. (Illus.). 186p. 22.95 (*0-00-712025-7*) Trafalgar Square.

Segal, Philip & Russell, Gary. Doctor Who: Regeneration. 2001. (Illus.). 168p. 29.95 (*0-00-710591-6*) HarperCollins Pubs. Ltd. GBR. *Dist:* Trafalgar Square.

Stone, Dave. Heart of Tardis. 2001. (Doctor Who Ser.: Vol. 4). 288p. pap. text 6.95 (*0-563-55596-3*) BBC Worldwide Americas.

Topping, Keith & Day, Martin. The Devil Goblins from Neptune. 1998. (Doctor Who Ser.). 283p. pap. text 5.95 (*0-563-40564-3*) BBC Worldwide Americas.

—The Hollow Men. 1998. (Doctor Who Ser.). 284p. (J). pap. text 5.95 (*0-563-40582-1*) BBC Worldwide Americas.

Tucker, Mike. Illegal Alien. 1998. (Doctor Who Ser.). 288p. pap. (*0-563-40570-8*) BBC Bk. Publishing.

Tulloch, John & Alvarado, Manuel. Doctor Who: The Unfolding Text. 1984. 342p. pap. 9.95 o.p. (*0-312-21488-X*); 356p. text 30.00 o.p. (*0-312-21485-5*) Palgrave Macmillan.

Walters, Nick. The Fall of Yquatine. 2000. (Doctor Who Ser.). 288p. pap. text 6.95 (*0-563-55594-7*) BBC Bk. Publishing GBR. *Dist:* General Distribution Services, Inc.

Winninger, Ray. The Cybermen, 2 bks. 1986. (Doctor Who Ser.). 64p. (Orig.). pap. 11.00 o.p. (*0-931787-73-4*) FASA Corp.

**DODGE, HAROLD (FICTITIOUS CHARACTER)—FICTION**

Reed, Philip. Bird Dog. (Car Noir Thrillers Ser.). 1998. 336p. pap. 6.50 (*0-671-00165-5*, Pocket Star); 1997. 304p. 22.00 (*0-671-00163-9*, Atria) Simon & Schuster.

—Low Rider. 1999. 320p. pap. 6.50 (*0-671-00167-1*, Pocket); 1998. 336p. 23.00 (*0-671-00166-3*, Atria) Simon & Schuster.

—Low Rider. l.t. ed. 1999. (Americana Ser.). 456p. 27.95 (*0-7862-1758-8*) Thorndike Pr.

**DODGE, LARK (FICTITIOUS CHARACTER)—FICTION**

Simonson, Sheila. Larkspur. 1991. 224p. reprint ed. mass mkt. (*0-373-26074-1*, Harlequin Bks.) Harlequin Enterprises, Ltd.

—Larkspur: A Mystery. 1990. 16.95 o.p. (*0-312-04338-4*, Saint Martin's Minotaur) St. Martin's Pr.

—Malarkey. 1998. (WWL Mystery Ser.). per. (*0-373-26275-2*, 1-26275-7, Worldwide Library) Harlequin Enterprises, Ltd.

—Malarkey. 1996. 288p. 23.95 o.p. (*0-312-15168-3*, Saint Martin's Minotaur) St. Martin's Pr.

—Meadowlark. 1997. (WWL Mystery Ser.: No. 240). per. (*0-373-26240-X*, 1-26240-1, Worldwide Library) Harlequin Enterprises, Ltd.

—Meadowlark. 1996. 256p. 21.95 o.p. (*0-312-14013-4*, Saint Martin's Minotaur) St. Martin's Pr.

—Skylark. 1994. per. (*0-373-26145-4*, 1-26145-2, Harlequin Bks.) Harlequin Enterprises, Ltd.

—Skylark. 1992. 272p. 17.95 o.p. (*0-312-08294-0*, Saint Martin's Minotaur) St. Martin's Pr.

**DOLAN, ABBY (FICTITIOUS CHARACTER)—FICTION**

Palmer, Michael. Critical Judgment. 1997. 464p. mass mkt. 6.99 o.s.i (*0-553-84015-0*); 1998. 480p. reprint ed. mass mkt. 7.50 (*0-553-57408-6*) Bantam Bks.

—Critical Judgment. unabr. ed. 1997. audio 80.00 (*0-913369-35-7*, 4206) Books on Tape, Inc.

—Critical Judgment. l.t. ed. 1996. (Core Collection). 605p. 27.95 (*0-7838-1940-4*) Thorndike Pr.

**DOLAN, TRIXIE (FICTITIOUS CHARACTER)—FICTION**

Babson, Marian. Break a Leg, Darlings. l.t. ed. 1997. (G. K. Hall Nightingale Ser.). 300p. lib. bdg. 18.95 o.p. (*0-7838-8036-7*, Macmillan Reference USA) Gale Group.

—Break a Leg, Darlings. 1997. 183p. 20.95 o.p. (*0-312-15285-X*, Saint Martin's Minotaur) St. Martin's Pr.

—Encore Murder. l.t. ed. 1991. (Nightingale Ser.). 275p. pap. 14.95 o.p. (*0-8161-5139-3*, Macmillan Reference USA) Gale Group.

—Encore Murder. 1990. 15.95 o.p. (*0-312-04964-1*, Saint Martin's Minotaur) St. Martin's Pr.

—Reel Murder, unabr. ed. 1993. audio 39.95 (*0-7451-5753-X*, CAT 4025) BBC Audiobooks America.

—Reel Murder. 1988. mass mkt. 3.50 o.s.i (*0-553-27361-2*) Bantam Bks.

—Reel Murder. l.t. ed. 1988. (Nightingale Ser.). 307p. 12.95 o.p. (*0-8161-4492-3*, Macmillan Reference USA) Gale Group.

—Reel Murder. 1987. 192p. 12.95 o.p. (*0-312-00227-0*) St. Martin's Pr.

—Reel Murder. 1988. audio 35.95 o.p. (*0-8161-7780-5*) Thorndike Pr.

—Shadows in Their Blood. l.t. ed. 1994. 322p. lib. bdg. 16.95 (*0-8161-5952-1*, Macmillan Reference USA) Gale Group.

—Shadows in Their Blood. 1993. 192p. 16.95 o.p. (*0-312-09383-7*, Saint Martin's Minotaur) St. Martin's Pr.

**DOLLANGER FAMILY (FICTITIOUS CHARACTERS)—FICTION**

Andrews, V. C. Flowers in the Attic. unabr. ed. 1988. audio 70.00 (*0-7366-1326-9*, 2230) Books on Tape, Inc.

—Flowers in the Attic. l.t. ed. 1993. 69.95 o.p. incl. audio compact disk (*0-7838-1108-X*); 1983. 584p. 18.95 o.p. (*0-8161-3428-6*) Gale Group. (Macmillan Reference USA).

—Flowers in the Attic. unabr. ed. 2001. audio compact disk 142.00; 1996. audio 97.00 (*0-7887-0473-7*, 94666E7) Recorded Bks., LLC.

—Flowers in the Attic. (Dollanganger Ser.). 2003. 416p. mass mkt. 5.99 (*0-7434-6716-7*); 1997. (Illus.). 432p. mass mkt. 3.99 (*0-671-01944-9*) Simon & Schuster. (Pocket).

—Flowers in the Attic. Marrow, Linda, ed. 1990. (Dollanganger Ser.). 416p. mass mkt. 7.99 (*0-671-72941-1*, Pocket) Simon & Schuster.

—Flowers in the Attic. 1980. 12.95 o.s.i (*0-671-41124-1*, Simon & Schuster) Simon & Schuster.

—Flowers in the Attic. abr. ed. 1986. audio 13.95 (*0-671-62850-X*, Simon & Schuster Audioworks) Simon & Schuster Audio.

—Flowers in the Attic. 1979. 14.04 (*0-606-00295-2*) Turtleback Bks.

—Flowers in the Attic, Set. Incl. If There Be Thorns. 1984. 1984. 15.80 (*0-671-90083-8*, Pocket) Simon & Schuster.

—Flowers in the Attic - If There Be Thorns - Petals on the Wind - Seeds of Yesterday. 1996. (Dollanger Saga Ser.). pap. 27.96 (*0-671-85156-X*, Pocket) Simon & Schuster.

—Garden of Shadows. unabr. ed. 1990. audio 64.00 (*0-7366-1717-5*, 2558) Books on Tape, Inc.

—Garden of Shadows. l.t. ed. 1988. (General Ser.). 401p. 19.95 o.p. (*0-8161-4683-7*, Macmillan Reference USA) Gale Group.

—Garden of Shadows, unabr. ed. 1996. audio 78.00 (*0-7887-0491-5*, 94683E7) Recorded Bks., LLC.

—Garden of Shadows. 1987. 448p. 18.45 o.p. (*0-671-64259-6*, Simon & Schuster); mass mkt. (*0-671-64257-X*, Pocket) Simon & Schuster.

—Garden of Shadows, Vol. 1. Marrow, Linda, ed. 1990. (Garden of Shadows Ser.: Vol. 1). 384p. mass mkt. 7.99 (*0-671-72942-X*, Pocket) Simon & Schuster.

—Garden of Shadows. 1990. 14.04 (*0-606-03582-6*) Turtleback Bks.

—If There Be Thorns. unabr. ed. 1989. (Dollanganger Ser.). audio 72.00 (*0-7366-1483-4*, 2359) Books on Tape, Inc.

—If There Be Thorns. 1983. (Reader's Request Ser.). lib. bdg. 18.95 o.p. (*0-8161-3429-4*, Macmillan Reference USA) Gale Group.

—If There Be Thorns. 1984. Pocket Bks.

—If There Be Thorns. 2003. (Dollanganger Ser.). 384p. mass mkt. 5.99 (*0-7434-6724-8*, Pocket) Simon & Schuster.

—If There Be Thorns. Marrow, Linda, ed. 1990. (Dollanganger Ser.). 384p. mass mkt. 7.99 (*0-671-72945-4*, Pocket) Simon & Schuster.

—If There Be Thorns. 1989. mass mkt. 5.50 (*0-671-68289-X*, Pocket); 1987. 384p. mass mkt. (*0-671-64814-4*, Pocket); 1981. 14.95 o.s.i (*0-671-43122-6*, Simon & Schuster) Simon & Schuster.

—If There Be Thorns. 1981. 14.04 (*0-606-00256-1*) Turtleback Bks.

—Petals on the Wind. unabr. ed. 1988. audio 96.00 (*0-7366-1361-7*, 2260) Books on Tape, Inc.

—Petals on the Wind. 1983. (Reader's Request Ser.). lib. bdg. 19.95 o.p. (*0-8161-3427-8*, Macmillan Reference USA) Gale Group.

—Petals on the Wind, unabr. ed. 1996. audio 112.00 (*0-7887-0578-4*, 94756E7) Recorded Bks., LLC.

—Petals on the Wind. 2003. (Dollanganger Ser.). 448p. mass mkt. 5.99 (*0-7434-6708-6*, Pocket) Simon & Schuster.

—Petals on the Wind. Marrow, Linda, ed. 1990. (Dollanganger Ser.). 448p. mass mkt. 7.99 (*0-671-72947-0*, Pocket) Simon & Schuster.

—Petals on the Wind. 1985. mass mkt. 4.50 (*0-671-60638-7*, Pocket); 1980. 14.95 o.s.i (*0-671-41125-X*, Simon & Schuster); 1980. mass mkt. (*0-671-82977-7*, Pocket) Simon & Schuster.

—Petals on the Wind. abr. ed. 1989. audio 12.95 (*0-671-68353-5*, Simon & Schuster Audioworks) Simon & Schuster Audio.

—Petals on the Wind. 1980. 14.04 (*0-606-00253-7*) Turtleback Bks.

—Seeds of Yesterday. unabr. ed. 1989. audio 88.00 (*0-7366-1602-0*, 2463) Books on Tape, Inc.

—Seeds of Yesterday. (Dollanganger Ser.). 2003. 416p. mass mkt. 5.99 (*0-7434-6733-7*); 1989. mass mkt. (*0-671-68290-3*); 1987. mass mkt. (*0-671-64815-2*); 1985. mass mkt. 4.50 (*0-671-60687-5*); 1984. mass mkt. 3.95 (*0-671-44328-3*) Simon & Schuster. (Pocket).

—Seeds of Yesterday, Vol. 5. Marrow, Linda, ed. 1990. (Dollanganger Ser.). 416p. mass mkt. 7.99 (*0-671-72948-9*, Pocket) Simon & Schuster.

—Seeds of Yesterday. 1984. 14.04 (*0-606-03235-5*) Turtleback Bks.

**DON QUIXOTE (FICTITIOUS CHARACTER)—FICTION**

Avellaneda, Alonso F. Don Quixote de la Mancha (Avellaneda's Continuation) Being the Spurious Continuation of Miguel de Cervantes's Part I. Server, Alberta Wilson & Keller, John Esten, trs. 1980. (Documentacion Cervantina Ser.: Vol. 2). (Illus.). xiv, 350p. (C). 18.95 (*0-936388-01-3*) Juan de la Cuesta-Hispanic Monographs.

Brack, O. M., ed. The History & Adventures of the Renowned Don Quixote. Cervantes Saavedra, Miguel de & Smollett, Tobias George, trs. from SPA. 2003. (Illus.). 1056p. 100.00 (*0-8203-2430-2*) Univ. of Georgia Pr.

Cervantes Saavedra, Miguel de. The Adventures of Don Quixote de la Mancha. Smollett, Tobias George, tr. from SPA. 1986. 845p. 24.50 o.p. (*0-374-14232-7*); pap. 18.00 o.s.i (*0-374-51943-9*) Farrar, Straus & Giroux.

—The Adventures of Don Quixote de la Mancha. Jones, Olive, ed. Cohen, J. M., tr. from SPA. 1980. (Illus.). 10.95 o.p. (*0-416-87910-1*, NO.0189) Routledge.

—The Adventures of Don Quixote de la Mancha. 1950. (J). 15.00 (*0-606-03005-0*) Turtleback Bks.

—The Adventures of Don Quixote de la Mancha. Cohen, John M., tr. from SPA. 1951. (Penguin Classics Ser.). 944p. pap. 8.95 o.s.i (*0-14-044010-0*, PE0100, Penguin Classics) Viking Penguin.

—Don Quijote de la Mancha. (SPA., Illus.). 160p. 11.95 (*84-7281-097-6*, AF1097) Auriga, Ediciones S.A. ESP. *Dist:* Continental Bk. Co., Inc.

—Don Quijote de la Mancha. 2000. (SPA.). per. 14.00 (*1-891355-12-0*) Blue Unicorn Editions.

—Don Quijote de la Mancha. unabr. ed. (SPA.). Vol. I. pap. 7.95 (*84-410-0004-2*); Vol. II. pap. 7.95 (*84-410-0005-0*) Bookking International FRA. *Dist:* Distribooks, Inc.

—Don Quijote de la Mancha. 2000. (SPA.). 720p. 10.95 (*84-8403-030-X*) Edimat Libros, S. A. ESP. *Dist:* Independent Pubs. Group.

—Don Quijote de la Mancha. 1990. (SPA.). pap. (*968-15-0812-2*) Editores Mexicanos Unidos.

—Don Quijote de la Mancha. (SPA.). stu. ed. 11.98 (*968-15-0087-3*) Editores Mexicanos Unidos MEX. *Dist:* Lectorum Pubns., Inc.

—Don Quijote de la Mancha. annot. ed. (Coleccion Centro Literario). (SPA.). Vol. I. pap., stu. ed. 7.95 (*958-02-0485-3*, CAR012); Vol. II. pap., stu. ed. 7.95 (*958-02-0539-6*, CAR013) Editorial Voluntad S.A. COL. *Dist:* Continental Bk. Co., Inc.

—Don Quijote de la Mancha. Blecua, Alberto, ed. (SPA.). 272p. (*84-239-1950-1*) Elliot's Bks.

—Don Quijote de la Mancha, 2 vols., Set. deluxe ed. 1989. (SPA., Illus.). 952p. 850.00 (*84-239-4133-7*) Elliot's Bks.

—Don Quijote de la Mancha. 1998. (Coleccion Austral Ser.: Vol. 150). (SPA., Illus.). 1152p. (*84-239-9599-2*) Espasa Calpe, S.A.

—Don Quijote de la Mancha. (SPA.). 19.95 (*84-239-0150-5*, ECS150) Espasa Calpe, S.A. ESP. *Dist:* Continental Bk. Co., Inc.

—Don Quijote de la Mancha. (SPA.). 848p. 31.95 (*84-241-2608-4*, EV9173); 2003. (Illus.). 336p. (*84-241-5930-6*, EV6500) Everest de Ediciones y Distribucion, S.L. ESP. *Dist:* Lectorum Pubns., Inc.

—Don Quijote de la Mancha. 1989. 1184p. pap. (*0-7859-5151-2*); Set. 1989. (SPA.). 22.95 o.p. (*0-8288-2562-9*, S50624); Set. 1984. (SPA.). 1096p. 29.95 o.p. (*0-8288-7040-3*, S37320); Vol. 2. 1990. 592p. pap. 15.95 (*0-7859-5999-8*, 8437601185) French & European Pubns., Inc.

—Don Quijote de la Mancha. Tardy, William T., ed. 2001. audio 15.00 (*0-8442-7071-7*) Glencoe/ McGraw-Hill.

—Don Quijote de la Mancha. (SPA.). 19.50 o.p. incl. audio Interlingua Foreign Language AudioBooks.

—Don Quijote de la Mancha, Part I. Lathrop, Tom, ed. 1997. (Illus.). 423p. 12.00 o.p. (*0-936388-80-3*) Juan de la Cuesta-Hispanic Monographs.

—Don Quijote de la Mancha, 2 vols., Set. (SPA.). 1100p. 21.95 (*84-261-0513-0*, JV0513) Juventud, Editorial ESP. *Dist:* AIMS International Bks., Inc., Continental Bk. Co., Inc., Distribooks, Inc.

—Don Quijote de la Mancha. 2001. (SPA.). audio 16.95 Norton Pubs., Inc., Jeffrey /Audio-Forum.

—Don Quijote de la Mancha. Raffel, Burton, tr. from SPA. 1996. 752p. pap. 19.95 (*0-393-31509-6*) Norton, W. W. & Co., Inc.

—Don Quijote de la Mancha. deluxe gif. ed. (SPA.). 248p. 19.95 (*84-7189-285-5*, ORT002) Ortells, Alfredo Editorial S.L. ESP. *Dist:* Continental Bk. Co., Inc.

—Don Quijote de la Mancha. Parr, James A. & Fajardo, Salvador, eds. 1998. (Spanish Classical Texts Ser.: Vol. 3). (SPA.). 900p. (C). text 29.95 (*1-889818-11-9*) Pegasus Pr.

—Don Quijote de la Mancha. 1997. (Clasicos Ser.). (SPA.). 860p. pap. (*0-929441-91-5*) Publicaciones Puertorriquenas, Inc.

—Don Quijote de la Mancha. (SPA.). 160p. 14.95 (*84-321-2482-6*, ORT839) Rialp, Ediciones, S.A. ESP. *Dist:* Continental Bk. Co., Inc.

—Don Quijote de la Mancha. 1998. (Clasicos Esenciales Ser.). (SPA., Illus.). 232p. (YA). (gr. 9-12). 11.95 (*84-294-4559-5*) Santillana USA Publishing Co., Inc.

—Don Quijote de la Mancha. (Coleccion Estrella). (SPA., Illus.). 64p. 14.95 (*950-11-0004-9*, SGM004) Sigmar ARG. *Dist:* Continental Bk. Co., Inc.

—Don Quijote de la Mancha. (SPA.). 270p. 36.98 (*84-305-8682-2*) Susaeta Ediciones, S.A. ESP. *Dist:* AIMS International Bks., Inc.

—Don Quijote de la Mancha: A New Translation, Backgrounds & Contexts, Criticism. Raffel, Burton, tr. from SPA. 1999. (Critical Editions Ser.). pap. 12.50 (*0-393-97281-X*, WW81X) Norton, W. W. & Co., Inc.

—Don Quijote de la Mancha: Primera Parte, Level D. (Spanish Easy Reader Library: Level D). (SPA., Illus.). pap. 9.50 (*0-88436-056-3*, 70275) EMC/Paradigm Publishing.

—Don Quijote de la Mancha: Segunda Parte. 2000. (SPA.). per. 14.00 (*1-891355-15-5*) Blue Unicorn Editions.

—Don Quijote de la Mancha: Segunda Parte, Level D. 1989. (Spanish Easy Reader Library: Level D). (SPA., Illus.). pap. 9.50 (*0-88436-887-4*, 70276) EMC/Paradigm Publishing.

—Don Quijote de la Mancha I. (Clasicos Castalia). (SPA., Illus.). 640p. 18.50 (*84-7039-285-9*, CC512) Castalia, Editorial S.A. ESP. *Dist:* Continental Bk. Co., Inc.

—Don Quijote de la Mancha I. 19th ed. (SPA., Illus.). 592p. 16.95 (*84-376-0117-7*, CT1100) Ediciones Cátedra ESP. *Dist:* AIMS International Bks., Inc., Continental Bk. Co., Inc.

—Don Quijote de la Mancha I. annot. ed. (SPA., Illus.). 21.95 (*84-207-2888-8*, ANY024) Grupo Anaya, S.A. ESP. *Dist:* Continental Bk. Co., Inc.

—Don Quijote de la Mancha II. (Clasicos Castalia). (SPA., Illus.). 624p. 18.50 (*84-7039-286-7*, CC513) Castalia, Editorial S.A. ESP. *Dist:* Continental Bk. Co., Inc.

—Don Quijote de la Mancha II. 20th ed. (SPA., Illus.). 592p. 16.95 (*84-376-0118-5*, CT1101) Ediciones Cátedra ESP. *Dist:* AIMS International Bks., Inc., Continental Bk. Co., Inc.

—Don Quijote de la Mancha II. (SPA.). (*84-89163-45-6*) Grafalco, S.A.

—Don Quijote de la Mancha II, 2 vols. annot. ed. (SPA., Illus.). 21.95 (*84-207-2796-2*, ANY025) Grupo Anaya, S.A. ESP. *Dist:* Continental Bk. Co., Inc.

—Don Quixote. 1967. (Airmont Classics Ser.). mass mkt. 4.95 o.p. (*0-8049-0153-8*, CL-153) Airmont Publishing Co., Inc.

—Don Quixote. 1994. (Illustrated Classics Collection). 64p. pap. 4.95 (*0-7854-0776-6*, 40547) American Guidance Service, Inc.

—Don Quixote. unabr. collector's ed. 1990. Pt. 1. audio 104.00 (*0-7366-1658-6*, 2509A); Pt. 2. audio 112.00 (*0-7366-1659-4*, 2509B) Books on Tape, Inc.

—Don Quixote. 1981. reprint ed. lib. bdg. 37.95 o.s.i (*0-89966-383-4*) Buccaneer Bks., Inc.

—Don Quixote. E-Book 2.49 (*1-58744-084-9*) Electric Umbrella Publishing.

—Don Quixote, Pt. I, set. unabr. ed. audio 84.95 Halvorson Assocs.

—Don Quixote. Grossman, Edith & Bloom, Harold, trs. from SPA. 2003. 976p. 29.95 (*0-06-018870-7*, Ecco) HarperTrade.

—Don Quixote. abr. ed. 1997. (Classics Ser.). audio 16.95 (*1-56511-180-X*) HighBridge Co.

—Don Quixote. l.t. ed. 3017p. pap. 195.31 (*0-7583-0764-0*); 3711p. pap. 227.38 (*0-7583-0765-9*); 4564p. pap. 275.69 (*0-7583-0766-7*); 5294p. pap. 314.65 (*0-7583-0767-5*); 2357p. pap. 156.76 (*0-7583-0763-2*); 1841p. pap. 123.30 (*0-7583-0762-4*); 1075p. pap. 78.86 (*0-7583-0760-8*); 1344p. pap. 94.08 (*0-7583-0761-6*); 3017p. lib. bdg. 225.31 (*0-7583-0756-X*); 3711p. lib. bdg. 259.37 (*0-7583-0757-8*); 2357p. lib. bdg. 180.76 (*0-7583-0755-1*); 1075p. lib. bdg. 90.86 (*0-7583-0752-7*); 4564p. lib. bdg. 330.63 (*0-7583-0758-6*); 5294p. lib. bdg. 381.89 (*0-7583-0759-4*); 1344p. lib. bdg. 106.08 (*0-7583-0753-5*); 1841p. lib. bdg. 141.30 (*0-7583-0754-3*) Huge Print Pr.

—Don Quixote. abr. ed. 2000. audio 7.95 (*1-57815-116-3*, 1078, Media Bks. Audio Publishing) Media Bks., L. L. C.

—Don Quixote. 1999. E-Book 1.95 (*1-58515-213-7*) MesaView, Inc.

—Don Quixote. 2001. 1056p. mass mkt. 7.95 (*0-451-52786-0*); 1970. mass mkt. 1.25 o.p. (*0-451-50273-6*, Signet Classics); 1970. mass mkt. 1.65 o.p. (*0-451-50510-7*, Signet Classics) NAL.

—Don Quixote. Starkie, Walter, tr. 1968. mass mkt. 0.60 o.p. (*0-451-60407-5*); mass mkt. 0.95 o.p. (*0-451-60814-3*); mass mkt. 0.50 o.p. (*0-451-60207-2*) NAL. (Signet Bks.).

—Don Quixote. 1965. 1056p. mass mkt. 7.95 o.s.i (*0-451-52507-8*, Signet Bks.); 1965. mass mkt. 2.25 o.p. (*0-451-50777-0*, Signet Classics); 1965. mass mkt. 1.95 o.p. (*0-451-50622-7*, Signet Classics); 1965. mass mkt. 2.50 o.p. (*0-451-50945-5*, Signet Classics); 1965. mass mkt. 2.95 o.p. (*0-451-51210-3*, Signet Classics); 1965. mass mkt. 3.50 o.p. (*0-451-51364-9*, Signet Classics); 1965. mass mkt. 3.95 o.p. (*0-451-51521-8*, Signet Classics); 1965. mass mkt. 4.50 o.p. (*0-451-51682-6*, Signet Classics); 1957. mass mkt. 1.75 o.p. (*0-451-61528-X*, Signet Bks.) NAL.

—Don Quixote. Starkie, Walter, tr. 1957. mass mkt. 3.50 o.p. (*0-451-62512-9*); mass mkt. 1.25 o.p. (*0-451-61163-2*); mass mkt. 1.50 o.p. (*0-451-61378-3*); mass mkt. 1.95 o.p. (*0-451-61775-4*); mass mkt. 2.95 o.p. (*0-451-61987-0*) NAL. (Signet Bks.).

—Don Quixote. abr. ed. 1957. mass mkt. 3.95 o.p. (*0-451-62611-7*) NAL.

—Don Quixote. Starkie, Walter, tr. abr. ed. 1957. 432p. mass mkt. 6.99 (*0-451-62684-2*, Mentor) NAL.

—Don Quixote. unabr. ed. 1965. mass mkt. 4.95 o.p. (*0-451-51821-7*) NAL.

—Don Quixote. Starkie, Walter, tr. unabr. ed. 1965. mass mkt. 5.95 o.p. (*0-451-52371-7*, CE1821, Signet Classics) NAL.

—Don Quixote. abr. ed. (Classic Fiction Ser.). 1996. audio 17.98 (*962-634-522-5*, NA302214); 1995. audio compact disk 19.98 (*962-634-022-3*, NA302212) Naxos of America, Inc. (Naxos AudioBooks).

—Don Quixote, Set. abr. ed. 1997. audio 20.00 o.p. (*0-7871-1206-2*, 695117) NewStar Media, Inc.

—Don Quixote. 1975. (Oxford Progressive English Readers Ser.). (Illus.). pap. text 3.50 o.p. (*0-19-638224-6*) Oxford Univ. Pr., Inc.

—Don Quixote. annuals 1998. (Modern Library Ser.). 1280p. 25.95 (*0-679-60286-0*) Random Hse., Inc.

—Don Quixote. Motteux, Peter A., tr. from SPA. 1991. (Everyman's Library Pocket Poets Ser.). 1104p. 23.00 (*0-679-40758-8*, RH7588) Random Hse., Inc.

—Don Quixote. Putnam, Samuel, tr. & intro. by. 1978. 1043p. 17.95 o.s.i (*0-394-60438-5*) Random Hse., Inc.

—Don Quixote. Rutherford, John, tr. from SPA. 2001. (Classics Ser.). 1072p. pap. 13.00 o.s.i (*0-14-044804-7*, Penguin Classics) Viking Penguin.

—Don Quixote. 992p. pap. 5.95 (*1-85326-795-3*); 1997. 784p. pap. 3.95 (*1-85326-036-3*, 0363WW) Wordsworth Editions, Ltd. GBR. *Dist:* Combined Publishing, Casemate Pubs. & Bk. Distributors, LLC.

—Don Quixote: A Landmark New Translation. Rutherford, J., tr. from SPA. 2001. 1056p. pap. 10.00 o.s.i (*0-14-044561-7*, Penguin Classics) Viking Penguin.

—Don Quixote: The Ormsby Translation, Revised, Backgrounds & Sources, Criticism. Jones, Joseph R. & Douglas, Kenneth, eds. 1981. (Critical Editions Ser.). (C). pap. text o.p. (*0-393-09018-3*); 29.95 o.p. (*0-393-04514-5*) Norton, W. W. & Co., Inc.

—Don Quixote de la Mancha. 1976. 21.95 (*0-8488-0438-4*) Amereon, Ltd.

—Don Quixote de la Mancha. 1954. 9.95 o.p. (*0-460-00386-0*); Vol. 1. 1975. reprint ed. 9.95 o.p. (*0-460-00385-2*) Biblio Distribution.

—Don Quixote de la Mancha. unabr. ed. 1997. Pt. 1. audio 85.95 (0-7861-1242-5, 2150A); Pt. 2. audio 89.95 (0-7861-1250-6, 2150B) Blackstone Audio Bks., Inc.
—Don Quixote de la Mancha. Jarvis, Charles, tr. from SPA. 1999. (Oxford World's Classics Ser.: Vol. 8). 1126p. 20.00 o.p. (0-19-210032-7) Oxford Univ. Pr., Inc.
—Don Quixote de la Mancha. Riley, E. C., ed. & tr. by. 1998. (Oxford World's Classics Ser.). 1120p. pap. 7.95 (0-19-283483-5) Oxford Univ. Pr., Inc.
—Don Quixote de la Mancha. Riley, E. C., ed. Jarvis, Charles, tr. 1992. (Oxford World's Classics Ser.). 1,110p. pap. 7.95 o.p. (0-19-282726-X) Oxford Univ. Pr., Inc.
—Don Quixote de la Mancha. 2001. (Modern Library Classics). (Illus.). 1168p. pap. 11.95 (0-375-75699-X, Modern Library) Random House Adult Trade Publishing Group.
—Don Quixote de la Mancha. Pt. 1. 1985. 29.95 o.p. incl. audio (0-295-75537-7); Pt. 2. 1986. audio 29.95 o.p. (0-295-75538-5) Univ. of Washington Pr.
—Don Quixote de la Mancha: An Old Spelling Control Edition Based on the First Editions of Parts 1 & 2, 2 vols. Flores, R. M., ed. 1988. Set. 700p. (0-7748-0301-0); Vol. 2. 635p. (0-7748-0314-2) Univ. of British Columbia Pr.
—Don Quixote Readalong. 1994. (Illustrated Classics Collection). 64p. pap. 14.95 incl. audio (0-7854-0792-8, 40549) American Guidance Service, Inc.
—El Ingenioso Hidalgo Don Quijote de la Mancha. 1989. (SPA.). 7.95 (0-8288-2561-0) French & European Pubns., Inc.
—El Ingenioso Hidalgo Don Quijote de la Mancha, Pts. I & II. Lathrop, Tom, ed. unabr. ed. 2000. (Documentacion Cervantina Ser.: Vol. 16). xlviii, 871p. pap. 16.00 o.p. (0-936388-87-0) Juan de la Cuesta-Hispanic Monographs.
Cervantes Saavedra, Miguel de & De Riquer, Martin. Don Quijote de la Mancha. 17th ed. 1997. (Clasicos Universales Ser.). (SPA., Illus.). 1224p. (84-08-01882-5) GeoPlaneta, Editorial, S. A.
Cervantes Saavedra, Miguel de, et al. Don Quixote. 1949. 12.50 o.p. (0-670-27880-7) Viking Penguin.
Darion, Joe & Wasserman, Dale. Man of La Mancha. 1966. 112p. pap. 9.95 (0-394-40619-2); 9.95 o.s.i (0-394-40621-4) Random Hse., Inc.
Greene, Graham. Monsignor Quixote. unabr. ed. 1993. 54.95 incl. audio (0-7451-5991-5, CSL 027) BBC Audiobooks America.
—Monsignor Quixote. unabr. ed. 1988. audio 48.00 (0-7366-1273-4, 2182) Books on Tape, Inc.
—Monsignor Quixote. unabr. ed. 2000. audio 49.95 Chivers Audio Bks. GBR. *Dist:* BBC Audiobooks America.
—Monsignor Quixote. l.t. ed. 1983. (General Ser.). lib. bdg. 14.95 o.p. (0-8161-3535-5, Macmillan Reference USA) Gale Group.
—Monsignor Quixote. 1990. 221p. mass mkt. 5.50 (0-671-72223-9, Pocket); 1983. pap. 3.95 (0-671-47470-7, Pocket); 1982. 75.00 o.p. (0-671-45984-8, Simon & Schuster); 1982. 12.50 o.s.i (0-671-45818-3, Simon & Schuster) Simon & Schuster.
Leigh, Mitch & Darion, Joe. Man of La Mancha: Complete Vocal Score. (Illus.). 150p. pap. 40.00 (0-89524-265-6, 3709) Cherry Lane Music Co.
—Man of La Mancha: Vocal Score. Flato, Ludwig, ed. 1990. (Illus.). 150p. (Orig.). pap. 50.00 (0-89524-558-2) Cherry Lane Music Co.

## DONAHOE, NEAL (FICTITIOUS CHARACTER)—FICTION

Gibbs, Tony. Fade to Black. 1997. 256p. 22.50 o.p. (0-89296-602-5); 1996. 328p. 21.95 o.p. (0-89296-603-3) Mysterious Pr.
—Shot in the Dark. 1997. 320p. mass mkt. 5.99 (0-446-40519-1) Warner Bks., Inc.

## DONAHOO, TOMMY (FICTITIOUS CHARACTER)—FICTION

Trolley, Jack. Balboa Firefly. 1994. 272p. 3.95 (0-7867-0117-X, Carroll & Graf Pubs.) Avalon Publishing Group.
—Juarez Justice. 1996. 272p. 22.00 o.p. (0-7867-0356-3, Carroll & Graf Pubs.) Avalon Publishing Group.
— La Jolla Spindrift. 1998. 208p. 22.00 o.p. (0-7867-0513-2, Carroll & Graf Pubs.) Avalon Publishing Group.
—Manila Time: A Novel. 1995. 304p. 21.00 o.p. (0-7867-0255-9, Carroll & Graf Pubs.) Avalon Publishing Group.

## DONOVAN, BILL (FICTITIOUS CHARACTER: JAHN)—FICTION

Jahn, Michael. City of God. 1992. 352p. 21.95 o.p. (0-312-06927-8, Saint Martin's Minotaur) St. Martin's Pr.
—Death Games. 1989. mass mkt. 3.95 o.p. (0-425-11305-1) Berkley Publishing Group.
—Death Games: A Novel. 1987. 15.95 o.p. (0-393-02465-2) Norton, W. W. & Co., Inc.
—Murder at the Museum of Natural History. 2000. (Mystery Ser.: No. 337). per. (0-373-26337-6, 1-26337-5, Worldwide Library) Harlequin Enterprises, Ltd.
—Murder at the Museum of Natural History. 1994. (Lt. Bill Donovan Mystery Ser.). 304p. 20.95 o.p. (0-312-11453-2, Saint Martin's Minotaur) St. Martin's Pr.
—Murder in Central Park. 2001. (WWL Mystery Ser.: No. 383). 251p. mass mkt. (0-373-26383-X, 1-26383-9, Worldwide Library) Harlequin Enterprises, Ltd.
—Murder in Central Park. 2000. (Bill Donovan Mysteries Ser.). 343p. 24.95 (0-312-24222-0, Saint Martin's Minotaur) St. Martin's Pr.
—Murder on Coney Island: A Bill Donovan Mystery. 2003. 320p. 24.95 (0-312-30801-9, Saint Martin's Minotaur) St. Martin's Pr.
—Murder on Fifth Avenue, Vol. 1. 1998. (Murder on Fifth Avenue Ser.: Vol. 1). 320p. 23.95 (0-312-18632-0, Saint Martin's Minotaur) St. Martin's Pr.
—Murder on the Waterfront: A Bill Donovan Mystery. 2001. 304p. 23.95 (0-312-27857-8, Saint Martin's Minotaur) St. Martin's Pr.
—Murder on Theater Row. 1997. 304p. text 23.95 o.p. (0-312-14685-X, Saint Martin's Minotaur) St. Martin's Pr.
—Murder on Theatre Row. 2000. (Bill Donovan Mysteries Ser.). per. (0-373-26346-5, Harlequin Bks.) Harlequin Enterprises, Ltd.
—Night Rituals: A Novel. 1982. 224p. 12.95 o.p. (0-393-01630-7) Norton, W. W. & Co., Inc.

## DONOVAN, BRIGID (FICTITIOUS CHARACTER)—FICTION

Saum, Karen. Murder Is Germane. 1991. (Brigid Donovan Mystery Ser.). 288p. (Orig.). pap. 8.95 o.p. (0-941483-98-3) Naiad Pr., Inc.
—Murder Is Germane. 1991. (Brigid Donovan Mystery Ser.). 224p. (Orig.). pap. 8.95 (0-934678-56-1) New Victoria Pubs., Inc.
—Murder Is Material. 1994. (Brigid Donovan Mystery Ser.). 192p. (Orig.). pap. 9.95 (0-934678-57-X) New Victoria Pubs., Inc.
—Murder Is Relative. 1990. 256p. pap. 8.95 o.p. (0-941483-70-3) Naiad Pr., Inc.
—Murder Is Relative. 1990. (Brigid Donovan Mystery Ser.). 256p. pap. 8.95 (0-934678-55-3) New Victoria Pubs., Inc.

## DONOVAN, CAL (FICTITIOUS CHARACTER)—FICTION

Bannister, Jo. A Bleeding of Innocents. 1999. 304p. (0-7540-3481-X); pap. (0-7540-3482-8) BBC Audiobooks America.
—A Bleeding of Innocents. 1997. (WWL Mystery Ser.: No. 241). per. (0-373-26241-8, 1-26241-9, Worldwide Library) Harlequin Enterprises, Ltd.
—A Bleeding of Innocents. unabr. ed. 1998. audio 69.95 (1-872672-97-3) Magna Story Sound GBR. *Dist:* Ulverscroft Large Print Bks., Ltd.
—A Bleeding of Innocents. 1993. 224p. 18.95 o.p. (0-312-09750-6, Saint Martin's Minotaur) St. Martin's Pr.
—A Bleeding of Innocents. l.t. ed. 1998. (General Ser.). 304p. pap. 24.95 (0-7862-1610-7) Thorndike Pr.
—Broken Lines. 2000. (Castlemere Mystery Ser.). 272p. per. (0-373-26338-4, Harlequin Bks.) Harlequin Enterprises, Ltd.
—Broken Lines. 1999. 304p. 22.95 (0-312-19842-6, Saint Martin's Minotaur) St. Martin's Pr.
—Broken Lines. l.t. ed. 1999. (General Ser.). 336p. pap. 23.95 (0-7862-1682-4) Thorndike Pr.
—Changelings. 2002. (WWL Mystery Ser.: No. 410). mass mkt. (0-373-26410-0, 1-26410-0, Worldwide Library) Harlequin Enterprises, Ltd.
—Changelings. 2000. 374p. (0-333-90189-4) Macmillan Pr.
—Changelings. l.t. ed. 2001. (Magna Large Print Ser.). 368p. (0-7505-1761-1) Magna Large Print Bks. GBR. *Dist:* Ulverscroft Large Print Canada, Ltd.
—Changelings. 2000. 384p. 23.95 (0-312-26567-0, Saint Martin's Minotaur) St. Martin's Pr.
—Charisma. 1997. per. (0-373-26253-1, 1-26253-4, Worldwide Library) Harlequin Enterprises, Ltd.
—Charisma. 1994. 208p. 18.95 o.p. (0-312-11252-1, Saint Martin's Minotaur) St. Martin's Pr.
—The Hireling's Tale. 1999. 316p. 23.95 (0-312-24400-2, Saint Martin's Minotaur) St. Martin's Pr.
—The Hireling's Tale. l.t. ed. 1999. (General Ser.). 352p. pap. 22.95 (0-7862-2163-1) Thorndike Pr.
—No Birds Sing. 1998. (WWL Mystery Ser.). per. (0-373-26283-3, 1-26283-1, Worldwide Library) Harlequin Enterprises, Ltd.
—No Birds Sing. 1996. 240p. 21.95 (0-312-14382-6, Saint Martin's Minotaur) St. Martin's Pr.
—No Birds Sing. l.t. ed. 1997. (Ulverscroft Large Print Ser.). 464p. 29.99 o.p. (0-7089-3732-2, Ulverscroft) Thorpe, F. A. Pubs. GBR. *Dist:* Ulverscroft Large Print Bks., Ltd., Ulverscroft Large Print Canada, Ltd.
—A Taste for Burning. 1997. (Castlemere Mystery Ser.). per. (0-373-26259-0, 1-26259-1, Worldwide Library) Harlequin Enterprises, Ltd.
—A Taste for Burning. 1995. 208p. 19.95 o.p. (0-312-13191-7, Saint Martin's Minotaur) St. Martin's Pr.

## DONOVAN, VICTORIA (FICTITIOUS CHARACTER)—FICTION

Franks, Georgina. Damaged Goods. 1997. (Crime & Passion Ser.). 254p. mass mkt. 5.95 (0-7535-0124-4) Virgin Bks. GBR. *Dist:* London Bridge.

## DONOVAN, WILD BILL (FICTITIOUS CHARACTER: GRIFFIN)—FICTION

Griffin, W. E. B. The Fighting Agents. 2001. (Men at War Ser.: Vol. 4). 448p. reprint ed. mass mkt. 7.99 (0-515-13052-4, Jove) Berkley Publishing Group.
—The Fighting Agents. 2000. audio compact disk 88.00 (0-7366-8006-3); audio 72.00 (0-7366-5509-3, 5349) Books on Tape, Inc.
—The Fighting Agents. 2000. (Men at War Ser.: Vol. 4). 311p. 25.95 o.s.i (0-399-14612-1) Penguin Group (USA) Inc.
—The Fighting Agents. abr. ed. 2000. (Men at War Ser.: Vol. 4). audio 24.95 o.s.i (0-399-14635-0, Putnam Berkley Audio) Putnam Publishing Group, The.
—The Fighting Agents. 1990. (Men at War Ser.: Vol. 4). mass mkt. 4.95 (0-671-73280-3, Pocket) Simon & Schuster.
—The Fighting Agents. l.t. ed. 2001. pap. 29.95 (0-7862-2830-X); 2000. 674p. 31.95 (0-7862-2829-6) Thorndike Pr.
—The Last Heroes. 1998. (Men at War Ser.: No. 1). 400p. mass mkt. 7.99 (0-515-12329-3, Jove) Berkley Publishing Group.
—The Last Heroes. unabr. ed. 1998. (Men at War Ser.: No. 1). audio 64.00 (0-7366-4097-5, 4602) Books on Tape, Inc.
—The Last Heroes. l.t. ed. 1998. (Men at War Ser.: No. 1). pap. 24.95 o.p. (1-56895-654-1, Wheeler Publishing, Inc.) Gale Group.
—The Last Heroes. 1997. (Men at War Ser.: No. 1). 352p. 24.95 o.p. (0-399-14289-4, G. P. Putnam's Sons); 4p. 24.95 o.p. (0-399-14296-7, 695053) Penguin Group (USA) Inc.
—The Last Heroes. (Men at War Ser.: No. 1). 1988. mass mkt. 5.99 (0-671-67822-1); 1985. mass mkt. 3.50 (0-671-49778-2) Simon & Schuster. (Pocket).
—The Last Heroes. 1998. (Men at War Ser.). 13.55 (0-606-15608-9) Turtleback Bks.
—The Secret Warriors. 1999. (Men at War Ser.: No. 2). 416p. reprint ed. mass mkt. 7.99 (0-515-12490-7, Jove) Berkley Publishing Group.
—The Secret Warriors, unabr. ed. 1999. (Men at War Ser.: No. 2). audio 72.00 (0-7366-4394-X, 4856) Books on Tape, Inc.
—The Secret Warriors, abr. ed. 1999. (Men at War Ser.: No. 2). (J). audio 24.95 Highsmith Inc.
—The Secret Warriors. 1998. (Men at War Ser.: No. 2). 336p. 24.95 o.p. (0-399-14381-5, G. P. Putnam's Sons); 24.95 o.s.i (0-399-14403-X, 692928, Putnam Berkley Audio) Penguin Group (USA) Inc.
—The Secret Warriors. (Men at War Ser.: No. 2). 1989. mass mkt. 4.50 (0-671-68443-4); 1985. mass mkt. 3.50 (0-671-49779-0) Simon & Schuster. (Pocket).
—The Secret Warriors. l.t. ed. 1998. (Men at War Ser.: No. 2). 607p. 30.95 (0-7862-1555-0) Thorndike Pr.
—The Soldier Spies. l.t. ed. 2000. (Men at War Ser.: No. 3). 12.95 (1-56895-978-8); 562p. 27.95 (1-56895-815-3) Gale Group. (Wheeler Publishing, Inc.).
—The Soldier Spies. 1999. (Men at War Ser.: No. 3). 352p. 25.95 o.p. (0-399-14494-3, G. P. Putnam's Sons) Penguin Group (USA) Inc.
—The Soldier Spies. (Men at War Ser.: No. 3). 1989. mass mkt. 4.50 (0-671-68444-2); 1986. mass mkt. 3.95 (0-671-60757-X) Simon & Schuster. (Pocket).

## DONOVAN FAMILY (FICTITIOUS CHARACTERS)—FICTION

Lowell, Elizabeth. Amber Beach. abr. ed. 1997. audio 17.95 o.p. (1-56100-993-8, 456, Nova Audio Bks.); audio 23.95 o.p. (1-56100-767-6, 33, Bookcassette); 11p. audio 73.25 o.p. (1-56100-842-7, 796, Unabridged Library Editions) Brilliance Audio.
—Jade Island. abr. ed. 1999. audio 7.99 o.s.i (1-56740-311-5, 1856, Paperback Nova Audio Bks.); 1998. audio 17.95 o.p. (1-56740-798-6, 1458, Nova Audio Bks.); 1998. 11p. audio 73.25 (1-56740-603-3, 1459, Unabridged Library Editions); 1998. audio 26.95 (1-56740-074-4, 1456, Bookcassette) Brilliance Audio.
—Jade Island. l.t. ed. 1998. 26.95 o.p. (1-56895-691-6, Wheeler Publishing, Inc.) Gale Group.
—Jade Island. 2002. E-Book 7.50 (0-06-050380-7); E-Book 7.50 (0-06-050379-3); E-Book 7.50 (0-06-050381-5); E-Book 7.50 (0-06-050378-5) HarperCollins General Bks. Group. (PerfectBound).
—Jade Island. unabr. ed. 1999. audio 73.25 Highsmith Inc.
—Jade Island. 1999. 372p. mass mkt. 7.50 (0-380-78987-6); 1998. 375p. 23.00 (0-380-97403-7) Morrow/Avon. (Avon Bks.).
—Midnight in Ruby Bayou. abr. ed. (Donovan Ser.). 2001. audio 12.99 (1-58788-304-X, 2680, Paperback Nova Audio Bks.); 2000. audio 24.95 o.p. (1-56740-902-4, 2084, Nova Audio Bks.); 2000. 11p. audio 73.25 (1-56740-724-2, 2085, Unabridged Library Editions); 2000. audio 35.95 (1-56740-357-3, 2083, Brilliance Audio Unabridged) Brilliance Audio.
—Midnight in Ruby Bayou. 2002. E-Book 7.50 (0-06-050519-2); E-Book 7.50 (0-06-050517-6); E-Book 7.50 (0-06-050518-4); E-Book 7.50 (0-06-050520-6) HarperCollins General Bks. Group. (PerfectBound).
—Midnight in Ruby Bayou. l.t. ed. 2000. 592p. pap. 24.00 (0-06-019740-4) HarperCollins Pubs.
—Midnight in Ruby Bayou. 2001. 448p. mass mkt. 7.50 (0-380-78989-2); 2000. 386p. 24.00 (0-380-97405-3, Morrow, William & Co.) Morrow/Avon.
—Pearl Cove. abr. ed. 2000. audio 7.99 o.s.i (1-56740-348-4, 2109, Paperback Nova Audio Bks.); 1999. audio 17.95 o.p. (1-56740-835-4, 1670, Nova Audio Bks.); 1999. audio 39.95 (1-56740-422-7, 1668, Brilliance Audio Unabridged); 1999. audio 73.25 (1-56740-648-3, 1669, Unabridged Library Editions) Brilliance Audio.
—Pearl Cove. l.t. ed. 1999. (Wheeler Press Paperback Ser.). pap. 11.95 (1-56895-964-8); 28.95 o.p. (1-56895-746-7) Gale Group. (Wheeler Publishing, Inc.).
—Pearl Cove. 2002. E-Book 7.50 (0-06-050385-8); E-Book 7.50 (0-06-050384-X); E-Book 7.50 (0-06-050383-1); E-Book 7.50 (0-06-050382-3) HarperCollins General Bks. Group. (PerfectBound).
—Pearl Cove. 2000. 432p. mass mkt. 7.50 (0-380-78988-4); 1999. 376p. 24.00 (0-380-97404-5) Morrow/Avon. (Avon Bks.).
Roberts, Nora. Captivated. 2004. 304p. mass mkt. (0-373-28500-0); 1992. mass mkt. (0-373-09768-9, 5-09768-8) Harlequin Enterprises, Ltd. (Silhouette).
—Charmed. 1992. mass mkt. (0-373-09780-8, 09780-3, Silhouette) Harlequin Enterprises, Ltd.
—The Donovan Legacy. 1999. 581p. pap. (0-373-48397-X, Harlequin Bks.) Harlequin Enterprises, Ltd.
—Enchanted: The Donovan Legacy. 1999. (Silhouette Intimate Moments Ser.: Vol. 961). 256p. mass mkt. (0-373-07961-3, 1-07961-5, Harlequin Bks.) Harlequin Enterprises, Ltd.
—Enchanted: The Donovan Legacy. l.t. ed. 2000. (Americana Ser.). 301p. 30.95 o.p. (0-7862-2599-8) Thorndike Pr.
—Entranced. 1992. mass mkt. (0-373-09774-3, 5-09774-6, Silhouette) Harlequin Enterprises, Ltd.

## DOOLITTLE, DELILAH (FICTITIOUS CHARACTER)—FICTION

Guiver, Patricia. The Beastly Bloodline: A Delilah Doolittle Pet Detective Mystery. 2003. (Perseverance Press Mystery Ser.). 192p. pap. 13.95 (1-880284-69-3, Perseverance Pr.) Daniel, John & Co., Pubs.
—Delilah Doolittle & the Canine Chorus. 2001. (Delilah Doolittle, Pet Detective Ser.: No. 5). 192p. 5.99 o.s.i (0-425-17801-3, Prime Crime) Berkley Publishing Group.
—Delilah Doolittle & the Careless Coyote. 1998. (Pet Detective Mystery Ser.: Bk. 3). 208p. mass mkt. 5.99 o.s.i (0-425-16612-0, Prime Crime) Berkley Publishing Group.
—Delilah Doolittle & the Missing Macaw. 2000. (Pet Detective Mystery Ser.). 192p. mass mkt. 5.99 o.s.i (0-425-17342-9, Prime Crime) Berkley Publishing Group.
—Delilah Doolittle & the Motley Mutts. 1998. (Pet Detective Mystery Ser.: Vol. 2). 208p. mass mkt. 5.99 o.s.i (0-425-16266-4, Prime Crime) Berkley Publishing Group.
—Delilah Doolittle & the Purloined Pooch. 1997. (Pet Detective Mystery Ser.: Vol. 1). 208p. mass mkt. 5.99 o.s.i (0-425-15963-9, Prime Crime) Berkley Publishing Group.

## DOONE, RONICKY (FICTITIOUS CHARACTER)—FICTION

Brand, Max. Ronicky Doone. unabr. ed. 1994. (Doone Ser.). 57.25 o.p. incl. audio (1-56100-158-9, 1015, Unabridged Library Editions); audio 19.95 o.p. (1-56100-530-4, 237, Bookcassette) Brilliance Audio.
—Ronicky Doone. 1995. 256p. mass mkt. 5.50 (0-8439-3738-6) Dorchester Publishing Co., Inc.
—Ronicky Doone. 1995. E-Book 9.95 (0-585-29880-7) netLibrary, Inc.
—Ronicky Doone's Reward. unabr. ed. 1996. (Doone Ser.). audio 59.25 o.p. (1-56100-300-X, 1016, Unabridged Library Editions); audio 19.95 o.p. (1-56100-675-0, 238, Bookcassette) Brilliance Audio.

—Ronicky Doone's Reward. 1995. 224p. mass mkt. 5.50 (*0-8439-3779-3*) Dorchester Publishing Co., Inc.

—Ronicky Doone's Reward. l.t. ed. 1995. 326p. lib. bdg. 20.95 o.p. (*0-8161-5999-8*, Macmillan Reference USA) Gale Group.

—Ronicky Doone's Treasure. unabr. ed. 1995. (Doone Ser.). audio 57.25 o.p. (*1-56100-288-7*, 1017, Unabridged Library Editions); audio 19.95 o.p. (*1-56100-663-7*, 239, Bookcassette) Brilliance Audio.

—Ronicky Doone's Treasure. 1995. 256p. mass mkt. 5.50 (*0-8439-3748-3*) Dorchester Publishing Co., Inc.

—Ronicky Doone's Treasure. l.t. ed. 1994. 261p. lib. bdg. 20.95 (*0-8161-5998-X*, Macmillan Reference USA) Gale Group.

—Ronicky Doone's Treasure. 1995. E-Book 9.95 (*0-585-28201-3*) netLibrary, Inc.

**DOONESBURY, MIKE (FICTITIOUS CHARACTER)—FICTION**

Hubley, John & Hubley, Faith. A Doonesbury Special. 1978. pap. 5.95 o.p. (*0-8362-1103-0*) Andrews McMeel Publishing.

O'Hare, Jeffrey A. Doonesbury Trivia: An Unofficial Final Exam. 1984. 224p. (Orig.). pap. 2.95 o.p. (*0-446-32441-8*) Warner Bks., Inc.

Satin, Allan D. A Doonesbury Index: An Index to the Syndicated Daily Newspaper Strip "Doonesbury" by G. B. Trudeau Nineteen Seventy to Nineteen Eighty-Three. 1985. 281p. 24.00 o.p. (*0-8108-1800-0*) Scarecrow Pr., Inc.

Trudeau, G. B. Action Figure! The Life & Times of Doonesbury's Uncle Duke. 1992. (Illus.). 224p. (Orig.). pap. 19.95 (*0-8362-1702-0*) Andrews McMeel Publishing.

—Buck Wild Doonesbury. 1999. (Doonesbury Bks.). (Illus.). 152p. pap. 14.95 (*0-7407-0015-4*) Andrews McMeel Publishing.

—The Bundled Doonesbury: A Pre-Millennial Anthology. 1998. (Doonesbury Ser.). (Illus.). 256p. pap. 22.95 incl. cd-rom (*0-8362-6752-4*) Andrews McMeel Publishing.

—But the Pension Fund Was Just Sitting There. 1980. pap. 1.75 o.p. (*0-553-13464-7*) Bantam Bks.

—But the Pension Fund Was Just Sitting There. 1979. (Doonesbury Ser.). pap. o.p. (*0-03-049176-2*, Owl Bks.) Holt, Henry & Co.

—Calling Dr. Whoopee. 1987. (Illus.). 128p. pap. 5.95 o.p. (*0-8050-0642-7*, Owl Bks.) Holt, Henry & Co.

—Doonesbury. 1971. text 7.95 o.p. (*0-07-065294-5*) McGraw-Hill Cos., The.

—Doonesbury: The Original Yale Cartoons. 1979. (Alligator Bks.). (Illus.). 96p. (Orig.). pap. 4.95 (*0-8362-0550-2*) Andrews McMeel Publishing.

—The Doonesbury Chronicles. 1975. 224p. o.p. (*0-03-014906-1*); 224p. pap. 16.95 o.p. (*0-8050-1062-9*, Owl Bks.); pap. 12.95 o.p. (*0-03-015256-9*, Owl Bks.) Holt, Henry & Co.

—Doonesbury Deluxe: Selected Glances Askance. 1987. (Illus.). 224p. 22.95 o.p. (*0-8050-0595-1*); 88p. pap. 16.95 o.p. (*0-8050-0596-X*, Owl Bks.) Holt, Henry & Co.

—Doonesbury Dossier: The Reagan Years. 1984. 224p. o.p. (*0-03-061729-4*); pap. 12.95 o.p. (*0-03-000072-6*, Owl Bks.) Holt, Henry & Co.

—Doonesbury Nation. 1995. (Doonesbury Ser.). (Illus.). 96p. pap. 7.95 (*0-8362-1784-5*) Andrews McMeel Publishing.

—Doonesbury Television. 1978. o.p. (*0-03-042571-9*) Holt, Henry & Co.

—Doonesbury's Greatest Hits. 1978. pap. 12.95 o.p. (*0-03-044856-5*, Owl Bks.); (Illus.). 224p. o.p. (*0-03-044851-4*); (Illus.). 224p. pap. 16.95 o.s.i (*0-8050-0883-7*, Owl Bks.) Holt, Henry & Co.

—An Especially Tricky People. 1979. pap. 1.75 o.p. (*0-553-14007-8*) Bantam Bks.

—An Especially Tricky People. 1977. (Doonesbury Ser.). pap. o.p. (*0-03-020681-2*, Owl Bks.) Holt, Henry & Co.

—An Especially Tricky People. 1990. 2.99 o.p. (*0-517-05484-1*) Random Hse. Value Publishing.

—Flashbacks: Twenty-Five Years of Doonesbury. 1995. (Doonesbury Ser.). (Illus.). 336p. 24.95 (*0-8362-0437-9*) Andrews McMeel Publishing.

—Give Those Nymphs Some Hooters! A Doonesbury Book. 1989. (Illus.). 96p. (Orig.). pap. 6.95 (*0-8362-1858-2*) Andrews McMeel Publishing.

—Got War? 2003. 152p. pap. 16.95 (*0-7407-3817-8*) Andrews McMeel Publishing.

—In Search of Cigarette Holder Man. 1994. (Doonesbury Bks.). (Illus.). 96p. pap. 7.95 (*0-8362-1767-5*) Andrews McMeel Publishing.

—Peoples Doonesbury. 1981. pap. 18.95 o.p. (*0-8050-1074-2*, Owl Bks.) Holt, Henry & Co.

—The People's Doonesbury: Notes from Underfoot. 1981. (Illus.). 224p. o.p. (*0-03-049166-5*); pap. 12.95 o.p. (*0-03-049171-1*, Owl Bks.) Holt, Henry & Co.

—Planet Doonesbury. 1997. (Doonesbury Ser.). (Illus.). 152p. (Orig.). pap. 12.95 (*0-8362-3686-6*) Andrews McMeel Publishing.

—The Portable Doonesbury. 1993. (Doonesbury Ser.). (Illus.). 256p. (Orig.). pap. 12.95 (*0-8362-1734-9*) Andrews McMeel Publishing.

—Quality Time on Highway 1. 1993. (Doonesbury Bks.). (Illus.). 96p. pap. 7.95 (*0-8362-1712-8*) Andrews McMeel Publishing.

—Recycled Doonesbury: 2nd Thoughts on a Gilded Age. 1990. (Doonesbury Ser.). (Illus.). 256p. (Orig.). pap. 12.95 (*0-8362-1824-8*) Andrews McMeel Publishing.

—Virtual Doonesbury. 1996. (Doonesbury Bks.). (Illus.). 152p. pap. 12.95 (*0-8362-1032-8*) Andrews McMeel Publishing.

—Washed Out Bridges & Other Disasters. 1994. (Doonesbury Ser.). (Illus.). 96p. pap. 7.95 (*0-8362-1747-0*) Andrews McMeel Publishing.

—We're Not Out of the Woods Yet. 1980. 128p. pap. 1.75 o.p. (*0-553-13804-9*) Bantam Bks.

—We're Not Out of the Woods Yet. 1979. (Doonesbury Ser.). (Illus.). pap. o.p. (*0-03-049181-9*, Owl Bks.) Holt, Henry & Co.

—We're Not Out of the Woods Yet. 1990. 2.99 o.p. (*0-517-05503-1*) Random Hse. Value Publishing.

—What Is It, Tink, Is Pan in Trouble? 1992. (Doonesbury Bks.). (Illus.). 96p. pap. 7.95 (*0-8362-1886-8*) Andrews McMeel Publishing.

Trudeau, G. B., illus. Flashbacks: Twenty-Five Years of Doonesbury. 1995. (Doonesbury Ser.). 336p. pap. 18.95 (*0-8362-0436-0*) Andrews McMeel Publishing.

**DORSEY, CARROLL (FICTITIOUS CHARACTER)—FICTION**

Lipinski, Thomas. Death in the Steel City. 2000. (Carroll Dorsey Mystery Ser.: Vol. 4). 224p. mass mkt. 5.99 (*0-380-79432-2*, Avon Bks.) Morrow/Avon.

—The Fall-Down Artist. 1994. (Carroll Dorsey Mystery Ser.). 304p. 20.95 o.p. (*0-312-10461-8*, Saint Martin's Minotaur) St. Martin's Pr.

—Picture of Her Tombstone. 1998. (Carroll Dorsey Mystery Ser.: 2). mass mkt. 5.99 (*0-380-73024-3*, Avon Bks.) Morrow/Avon.

—Picture of Her Tombstone. 1996. 240p. 21.95 (*0-312-14390-7*, Saint Martin's Minotaur) St. Martin's Pr.

—Steel City Confessions. 1999. (Carroll Dorsey Mystery Ser.: Vol. 3). 224p. mass mkt. 5.99 (*0-380-79431-4*, Avon Bks.) Morrow/Avon.

**DORTMUNDER, JOHN (FICTITIOUS CHARACTER)—FICTION**

Westlake, Donald E. Bad News. l.t. ed. 2001. 344p. lib. bdg. 28.95 (*1-58547-123-2*) Ctr. Point Large Print.

—Bad News. 2002. 384p. mass mkt. 7.50 (*0-446-61084-4*) Warner Bks., Inc.

—Bank Shot. unabr. collector's ed. 1996. (Dortmunder Ser.). audio 36.00 (*0-7366-3455-X*, 4099) Books on Tape, Inc.

—Bank Shot. 1987. mass mkt. 3.95 o.s.i (*0-445-40610-0*); 1989. 192p. reprint ed. mass mkt. 5.50 o.s.i (*0-445-40883-9*) Warner Bks., Inc.

—Don't Ask. unabr. collector's ed. 1997. (Dortmunder Ser.). audio 64.00 (*0-7366-3491-6*, 4131) Books on Tape, Inc.

—Don't Ask. 1993. 336p. 18.95 (*0-89296-469-3*) Mysterious Pr.

—Don't Ask. 1994. (Dortmunder Novel Ser.). 352p. reprint ed. mass mkt. 7.50 (*0-446-40095-5*) Warner Bks., Inc.

—Drowned Hopes. unabr. collector's ed. 1997. (Dortmunder Ser.). audio 88.00 (*0-7366-3677-3*, 4357) Books on Tape, Inc.

—Drowned Hopes. 1990. 75.00 (*0-89296-421-9*); 18.95 o.p. (*0-89296-178-3*) Mysterious Pr.

—Drowned Hopes. abr. ed. 1993. 15.95 o.p. (*1-55800-316-9*) NewStar Media, Inc.

—Drowned Hopes. 1991. 464p. mass mkt. 5.99 o.s.i (*0-446-40006-8*) Warner Bks., Inc.

—Good Behavior. unabr. collector's ed. 1997. (Dortmunder Ser.). audio 48.00 (*0-7366-3673-0*, 4350) Books on Tape, Inc.

—Good Behavior. 1988. mass mkt. 3.95 (*0-8125-1060-7*, Tor Bks.) Doherty, Tom Assocs., LLC.

—Good Behavior. l.t. ed. 1987. (General Ser.). 383p. 17.95 o.p. (*0-8161-4275-0*, Macmillan Reference USA) Gale Group.

—Good Behavior. 1986. 256p. 15.45 o.p. (*0-89296-240-2*) Mysterious Pr.

—Good Behavior. 1990. 2.99 o.p. (*0-517-68035-1*) Random Hse. Value Publishing.

—The Hot Rock. unabr. collector's ed. 1996. (Dortmunder Ser.). audio 42.00 (*0-7366-3417-7*, 4063) Books on Tape, Inc.

—The Hot Rock. 1987. 256p. reprint ed. mass mkt. 5.50 o.s.i (*0-445-40608-9*) Warner Bks., Inc.

—Jimmy the Kid. 1975. mass mkt. 1.50 o.p. (*0-345-24650-0*) Ballantine Bks.

—Jimmy the Kid. unabr. collector's ed. 1996. audio 36.00 (*0-7366-3517-3*, 4154) Books on Tape, Inc.

—Jimmy the Kid. 1974. 192p. 6.95 o.p. (*0-87131-157-7*) Holt, Henry & Co.

—Jimmy the Kid. 192p. 1994. mass mkt. 5.50 (*0-446-40409-8*, Mysterious Pr. Paperback Bks.); 1989. mass mkt. 5.50 o.s.i (*0-445-40747-6*) Warner Bks., Inc.

—Nobody's Perfect. 1979. mass mkt. 1.95 o.s.i (*0-449-23909-8*, Fawcett) Ballantine Bks.

—Nobody's Perfect. unabr. collector's ed. 1996. (Dortmunder Ser.: Vol. 4). audio 42.00 (*0-7366-3542-4*, 4189) Books on Tape, Inc.

—Nobody's Perfect. 1977. 228p. 7.95 o.p. (*0-87131-249-2*) Holt, Henry & Co.

—Nobody's Perfect. 1994. pap. (*0-446-40715-1*, Mysterious Pr. Paperback Bks.); 1989. 240p. mass mkt. 5.50 o.s.i (*0-445-40715-8*) Warner Bks., Inc.

—What's the Worst That Could Happen? unabr. collector's ed. 1997. (Dortmunder Ser.). audio 56.00 (*0-7366-3773-7*, 4446) Books on Tape, Inc.

—What's the Worst That Could Happen? 1996. 384p. 22.00 o.p. (*0-89296-586-X*) Mysterious Pr.

—What's the Worst That Could Happen? movie tie-in ed. 1997. (Dortmunder Novel Ser.). 336p. reprint ed. mass mkt. 6.50 (*0-446-60471-2*) Warner Bks., Inc.

—Why Me? unabr. collector's ed. 1997. (Dortmunder Ser.). audio 42.00 (*0-7366-3653-6*, 4318) Books on Tape, Inc.

—Why Me? 1985. 288p. reprint ed. mass mkt. 3.50 (*0-8125-1052-6*, Tor Bks.) Doherty, Tom Assocs., LLC.

—Why Me? 1983. 204p. 13.50 o.p. (*0-670-76569-4*) Viking Penguin.

—Why Me? 1994. 240p. mass mkt. 5.50 (*0-446-40346-6*) Warner Bks., Inc.

**DOUGAL, WILLIAM (FICTITIOUS CHARACTER)—FICTION**

Taylor, Andrew. Blood Relation. 1991. 192p. 14.95 o.s.i (*0-385-41761-6*) Doubleday Publishing.

—Caroline Minuscule. l.t. ed. 2002. 289p. pap. 24.95 (*0-7862-4008-3*) Gale Group.

—Caroline Minuscule. 2001. 200p. pap. 13.95 (*1-890208-71-X*) Poisoned Pen Pr.

—An Old School Tie. 1987. 224p. pap. 3.50 o.p. (*0-14-010087-3*, Penguin Bks.) Viking Penguin.

—Our Fathers Lies. 1986. 240p. pap. 3.50 o.p. (*0-14-008838-5*, Penguin Bks.) Viking Penguin.

—Our Father's Lies. 1986. 35.00 o.p. (*0-14-778054-3*) Penguin Group (USA) Inc.

**DOUGLAS, ANDREW (FICTITIOUS CHARACTER)—FICTION**

Francis, Dick. Banker. 1986. 352p. mass mkt. 6.99 (*0-449-21199-1*, Fawcett) Ballantine Bks.

—The Danger. unabr. ed. 2000. audio 34.95 (*1-57270-128-5*, N81128u, Audio Editions Mystery Masters) Audio Partners Publishing Corp.

—The Danger. 1999. mass mkt. 6.99 (*0-449-45824-5*); 1986. 384p. mass mkt. 6.99 (*0-449-21037-5*); 1985. mass mkt. 3.95 o.p. (*0-449-20263-1*) Ballantine Bks. (Fawcett).

—The Danger. Set. abr. ed. 1985. 5p. audio 16.99 (*0-88646-113-8*, 390606) Durkin Hayes Publishing Ltd.

—The Danger. l.t. ed. 1984. (General Ser.). 17.95 o.p. (*0-8161-3724-2*); 9.95 o.p. (*0-8161-3767-6*) Gale Group. (Macmillan Reference USA).

—The Danger. 1984. 15.95 o.p. (*0-399-12890-5*, G. P. Putnam's Sons) Penguin Putnam Bks. for Young Readers.

—The Danger. 1988. audio 64.95 o.p. (*0-8161-9437-8*) Thorndike Pr.

**DOUGLAS, RAY (FICTITIOUS CHARACTER)—FICTION**

Daley, Robert. A Faint Cold Fear. abr. ed. 1991. audio 15.95 o.p. (*1-55927-142-6*) Audio Renaissance.

—A Faint Cold Fear. 1990. 19.95 o.p. (*0-316-17184-0*) Little Brown & Co.

—A Faint Cold Fear. abr. ed. 1991. audio 7.95 (*1-57815-038-8*, 1010) Media Bks., L. L. C.

—A Faint Cold Fear. 1992. 480p. mass mkt. 5.99 o.s.i (*0-446-36219-0*) Warner Bks., Inc.

**DOVER, WILFRED (FICTITIOUS CHARACTER)—FICTION**

Porter, Joyce. Dead Easy for Dover. 1991. (Inspector Dover of Scotland Yard Ser.). 176p. reprint ed. pap. 6.50 (*0-88150-212-X*, Foul Play) Norton, W. W. & Co., Inc.

—Dead Easy for Dover. 1978. 7.95 o.p. (*0-312-18492-1*) St. Martin's Pr.

—Dover: The Collected Short Stories. 1995. (Inspector Dover of Scotland Yard Ser.). 304p. 20.00 (*0-88150-342-8*, Foul Play) Norton, W. W. & Co., Inc.

—Dover & the Claret Tappers. 1989. (Inspector Dover of Scotland Yard Ser.). 203p. 16.95 o.s.i (*0-88150-148-4*) Countryman Pr.

—Dover & the Claret Tappers. 1989. (Chief Inspector Dover Mysteries Ser.). 208p. pap. 6.00 (*0-88150-245-6*, Foul Play) Norton, W. W. & Co., Inc.

—Dover & the Unkindest Cut of All. 1990. (Inspector Dover of Scotland Yard Ser.). 188p. reprint ed. pap. 5.95 (*0-88150-174-3*, Foul Play) Norton, W. W. & Co., Inc.

—Dover Beats the Band. 1991. 169p. 17.95 o.p. (*0-88150-195-6*) Countryman Pr.

—Dover Beats the Band. 1993. (Inspector Dover of Scotland Yard Ser.). 170p. pap. 6.00 (*0-88150-268-5*, Foul Play) Norton, W. W. & Co., Inc.

—Dover Goes to Pott. 1990. (Inspector Dover of Scotland Yard Ser.). 192p. reprint ed. pap. 5.95 (*0-88150-173-5*, Foul Play) Norton, W. W. & Co., Inc.

—Dover One. 1989. (Inspector Dover of Scotland Yard Ser.). 176p. reprint ed. pap. 6.95 (*0-88150-134-4*, Foul Play) Norton, W. W. & Co., Inc.

—Dover Strikes Again. 1991. (Inspector Dover of Scotland Yard Ser.). 202p. reprint ed. pap. 5.95 (*0-88150-211-1*, Foul Play) Norton, W. W. & Co., Inc.

—Dover Three. 1989. (Inspector Dover of Scotland Yard Ser.). 188p. reprint ed. pap. 6.50 (*0-88150-147-6*, Foul Play) Norton, W. W. & Co., Inc.

—Dover Two. 1989. (Inspector Dover of Scotland Yard Ser.). 192p. reprint ed. pap. 7.95 (*0-88150-135-2*, Foul Play) Norton, W. W. & Co., Inc.

—It's Murder with Dover. 2002. (Crime ser.). 192p. 21.95 (*0-7540-8625-9*, Black Dagger) BBC Audiobooks America.

—It's Murder with Dover. 1992. (Inspector Dover of Scotland Yard Ser.). 192p. pap. 6.00 (*0-88150-233-2*, Foul Play) Norton, W. W. & Co., Inc.

**DOWLING, FATHER (FICTITIOUS CHARACTER)—FICTION**

McInerny, Ralph. Abracadaver. l.t. ed. 1990. (Nightingale Ser.). pap. 12.95 o.p. (*0-8161-4904-6*, Macmillan Reference USA) Gale Group.

—Abracadaver. 1994. (WWL Mystery Ser.). per. (*0-373-26152-7*, 1-26152-8, Harlequin Bks.) Harlequin Enterprises, Ltd.

—Abracadaver. 1989. 176p. 14.95 o.p. (*0-312-02533-5*, Saint Martin's Minotaur) St. Martin's Pr.

—The Basket Case. l.t. ed. 1992. (Nightingale Ser.). 280p. pap. 14.95 o.p. (*0-8161-5569-0*, Macmillan Reference USA) Gale Group.

—The Basket Case. 1988. mass mkt. 3.50 (*0-312-91157-2*, St. Martin's Paperbacks); 1987. 208p. 14.95 o.p. (*0-312-00997-6*, Saint Martin's Minotaur) St. Martin's Pr.

—A Cardinal Offense. 1994. 384p. 21.95 o.p. (*0-312-11283-1*, Saint Martin's Minotaur) St. Martin's Pr.

—Desert Sinner. 1994. (WWL Mystery Ser.). per. (*0-373-26158-6*, 1-26158-5, Harlequin Bks.) Harlequin Enterprises, Ltd.

—Desert Sinner. 1992. (Father Dowling Mysteries Ser.). 192p. 16.95 o.p. (*0-312-08177-4*, Saint Martin's Minotaur) St. Martin's Pr.

—Easeful Death. 1994. 3.99 o.p. (*0-517-11437-2*) Random Hse. Value Publishing.

—Easeful Death. 1991. 256p. 19.95 o.s.i (*0-689-12131-8*, Scribner) Simon & Schuster.

—Four on the Floor. 1994. pap. (*0-373-26154-3*, Harlequin Bks.) Harlequin Enterprises, Ltd.

—Four on the Floor. 1989. 192p. 15.95 o.p. (*0-312-03345-1*, Saint Martin's Minotaur) St. Martin's Pr.

—Getting a Way with Murder. l.t. ed. 1985. (Nightingale Ser.). 256p. 9.95 o.p. (*0-8161-3924-5*, Macmillan Reference USA) Gale Group.

—Grave Undertakings: A Father Dowling Mystery. 2000. (Father Dowling Mysteries Ser.). 374p. 24.95 (*0-312-20309-8*, Saint Martin's Minotaur) St. Martin's Pr.

—Grave Undertakings: A Father Dowling Mystery. l.t. ed. 2000. (Basic Ser.). 448p. 29.95 (*0-7862-2925-X*) Thorndike Pr.

—Her Death of Cold. 1979. (Father Dowling Mysteries Ser.). 224p. 1.95 o.s.i (*0-441-32780-X*) Ace Bks.

—Infra Dig. l.t. ed. 1993. 21.95 o.p. (*0-7927-1461-X*); pap. 19.95 o.p. (*0-7927-1460-1*) BBC Audiobooks America.

—Infra Dig. 1992. 218p. 19.00 o.s.i (*0-689-12132-6*) Central Bureau voor Schimmelcultures NLD. *Dist:* Lubrecht & Cramer, Ltd.

—Judas Priest: A Father Dowling Mystery. 1994. per. (*0-373-26156-X*, 1-26156-9, Harlequin Bks.) Harlequin Enterprises, Ltd.

—Judas Priest: A Father Dowling Mystery. 1991. 208p. 17.95 o.p. (*0-312-06375-X*, Saint Martin's Minotaur) St. Martin's Pr.

—Last Things. Date not set. pap. (*0-312-30900-7*, Saint Martin's Griffin); mass mkt. (*0-312-98690-4*, St. Martin's Paperbacks); 2003. 352p. 24.95 (*0-312-30899-X*, Saint Martin's Minotaur) St. Martin's Pr.

—Last Things. l.t. ed. 2003. (Father Dowling Mystery Ser.). 460p. 29.95 (*0-7862-5735-0*) Thorndike Pr.

—Lying Three. 1980. 256p. 2.25 o.s.i (*0-441-50515-5*) Ace Bks.

—Lying Three. l.t. ed. 1981. 374p. reprint ed. 11.95 o.p. (*0-89621-304-8*) Thorndike Pr.

—Prodigal Father. l.t. ed. 2003. (Mystery Ser.). 28.95 (*1-57490-487-6*, Beeler Large Print Bks.) Beeler, Thomas T. Publisher.
—Prodigal Father. E-Book 24.95 (*0-312-70741-X*); 2002. 384p. 24.95 (*0-312-29129-9*, Saint Martin's Minotaur) St. Martin's Pr.
—Rest in Pieces. l.t. ed. 1991. (Nightingale Ser.). 280p. lib. bdg. 13.95 o.p. (*0-8161-5107-5*, Macmillan Reference USA) Gale Group.
—Second Vespers. 1981. (Father Dowling Mysteries Ser.). 2.50 o.s.i (*0-441-75724-3*) Ace Bks.
—Second Vespers. l.t. ed. 1981. reprint ed. 10.95 o.p. (*0-89621-272-6*) Thorndike Pr.
—Seed of Doubt. 1993. 352p. 19.95 o.p. (*0-312-09381-0*) St. Martin's Pr.
—The Seventh Station. 1979. (Father McDowling Ser.). 224p. 1.95 o.s.i (*0-441-75947-5*) Ace Bks.
—The Tears of Things. 1996. o.p. (*0-03-214746-5*); 368p. text 24.95 o.p. (*0-312-14746-5*, Saint Martin's Minotaur) St. Martin's Pr.
—Triple Pursuit: A Father Dowling Mystery. 2002. E-Book 24.95 (*1-59061-754-1*) Adobe Systems, Inc.
—Triple Pursuit: A Father Dowling Mystery. E-Book 24.95 (*0-312-70145-4*); 2001. 371p. 24.95 (*0-312-26948-X*, Saint Martin's Minotaur) St. Martin's Pr.
—Triple Pursuit: A Father Dowling Mystery. l.t. ed. 2001. 547p. (*0-7862-3295-1*) Thorndike Pr.

**DOWLING, VINCE (FICTITIOUS CHARACTER)—FICTION**

Mullen, Jack. Behind the Shield. 1996. 352p. (Orig.). mass mkt. 5.99 (*0-380-78236-7*, Avon Bks.) Morrow/Avon.
—In the Line of Duty. 1995. 320p. (Orig.). mass mkt. 5.50 o.p. (*0-380-77614-6*, Avon Bks.) Morrow/Avon.

**DOYLE, ABBY (FICTITIOUS CHARACTER)—FICTION**

Ashwood-Collins, Anna. Red Roses for a Dead Trucker. E-Book 5.95 (*0-9712538-2-X*); 2002. 210p. pap. 16.95 (*0-9712538-4-6*) Pendulum Pr.

**DOYLE, ARTHUR CONAN, SIR, 1859-1930—FICTION**

Frost, Mark. The List of Seven. 1993. 368p. 20.00 o.p. (*0-688-12245-0*, Morrow, William & Co.) Morrow/Avon.
—The List of Seven. abr. ed. 1993. audio 16.95 o.p. (*1-55800-840-3*) NewStar Media, Inc.
—The List of Seven. 1994. (Super Sound Buy, Dove Ser.). 8.99 o.p. (*0-7871-0238-5*) Penguin Group (USA) Inc.
—The List of 7. 1994. 416p. mass mkt. 5.99 (*0-380-72019-1*, Avon Bks.) Morrow/Avon.
—The Six Messiahs. 1996. pap. 6.99 (*0-380-72229-1*, Avon Bks.); 1995. 448p. 23.00 o.p. (*0-688-13092-5*, Morrow, William & Co.) Morrow/Avon.
—The Six Messiahs. abr. ed. 1995. 24.95 o.p. (*0-7871-0399-3*) NewStar Media, Inc.
McCarver, Sam. The Case of the 2nd Seance: A John Darnell Mystery. l.t. ed. 2001. 344p. 27.95 (*0-7862-3331-1*) Thorndike Pr.
O'Connor, J Regis. The Sacred Seal. 1998. (New Adventures of Sherlock Holmes Ser.). 24.00 (*1-55246-110-6*) Battered Silicon Dispatch Box, The.
Pirie, David. The Patient's Eyes Murder Rooms: The Dark Beginnings of Sherlock Holmes. unabr. ed. 2001. audio 40.00 (*0-7366-8482-4*) Books on Tape, Inc.
—The Patient's Eyes Murder Rooms: The Dark Beginnings of Sherlock Holmes. 2002. (Illus.). 252p. 23.95 (*0-312-29095-0*, Saint Martin's Minotaur) St. Martin's Pr.
Rogow, Roberta. The Problem of the Evil Editor: A Charles Dodgson/Arthur Conan Doyle Mystery. 2000. (Charles Dodgson/Arthur Conan Doyle Mysteries Ser.). 298p. 23.95 (*0-312-20903-7*, Saint Martin's Minotaur) St. Martin's Pr.
—Problem of the Spiteful Spiritualist. 1999. (Charles Dodgson/Arthur Conan Doyle Mysteries Ser.). 282p. 23.95 (*0-312-20570-8*, Saint Martin's Minotaur) St. Martin's Pr.
—The Problem of the Surly Servant. 2001. (Charles Dodgson/Arthur Conan Doyle Mysteries Ser.). 288p. 24.95 (*0-312-26638-3*, Saint Martin's Minotaur) St. Martin's Pr.
Satterthwait, Walter. Escapade. 1996. 355p. mass mkt. 5.99 (*0-312-95920-6*, St. Martin's Paperbacks); 1995. 336p. 22.95 o.p. (*0-312-13068-6*, Saint Martin's Minotaur) St. Martin's Pr.
Rogow, Roberta. Problem of the Missing Miss. 1998. 272p. 22.95 (*0-312-18553-7*, Saint Martin's Minotaur) St. Martin's Pr.

**DOYLE, TERRY (FICTITIOUS CHARACTER)—FICTION**

Carroll, James. The City Below. 1996. 432p. pap. 14.00 (*0-395-82522-9*); 1994. 422p. 22.95 o.s.i (*0-395-59070-1*) Houghton Mifflin Co.

**DOYLE, TRAVIS (FICTITIOUS CHARACTER)—FICTION**

Houston, James D. Continental Drift. 1987. 336p. pap. text 4.95 o.p. (*0-07-030488-2*) McGraw-Hill Cos., The.
—Continental Drift. 1978. 8.95 o.p. (*0-394-50124-1*, Knopf Bks. for Young Readers) Random Hse. Children's Bks.
—Continental Drift. 1996. (California Fiction Ser.). 337p. (C). pap. 15.95 (*0-520-20713-0*) Univ. of California Pr.
—The Last Paradise. (Literature of the American West Ser.). 384p. 2000. pap. 17.95 (*0-8061-3290-6*); 1998. 24.95 (*0-8061-3033-4*) Univ. of Oklahoma Pr.

**DRACONIAN, HOB (FICTITIOUS CHARACTER)—FICTION**

Sheckley, Robert. The Alternative Detective. 256p. 1997. pap. 13.95 o.p. (*0-312-85381-5*); 1993. 19.95 o.p. (*0-312-85023-9*) Doherty, Tom Assocs., LLC. (Forge Bks.).
—Draconian New York. 224p. 1997. pap. 12.95 (*0-312-86359-4*); 1996. 20.95 o.p. (*0-312-85130-8*) Doherty, Tom Assocs., LLC. (Forge Bks.).
—Soma Blues. 224p. 1998. pap. 13.95 (*0-312-86579-1*); 1997. 20.95 o.p. (*0-312-86273-3*) Doherty, Tom Assocs., LLC. (Forge Bks.).

**DRACUL FAMILY (FICTITIOUS CHARACTERS)—FICTION**

Kalogridis, Jeanne. Children of the Vampire. abr. ed. 1996. audio 7.99 o.p. (*1-56740-135-X*, 633, Paperback Nova Audio Bks.); 1995. audio 17.95 o.p. (*1-56100-444-8*, 1637, Nova Audio Bks.); 1995. audio 57.25 o.p. (*1-56100-276-3*, 1150, Unabridged Library Editions); 1995. audio 23.95 o.p. (*1-56100-651-3*, 62, Bookcassette) Brilliance Audio.
—Children of the Vampire. 1996. (Diaries of the Family Dracula: Vol. 2). 368p. mass mkt. 6.99 (*0-440-22269-9*) Dell Publishing.
—Covenant with the Vampire: The Diaries of the Family Dracula. abr. ed. 1994. audio 16.95 o.p. (*1-56100-393-X*, 1552, Nova Audio Bks.); audio 73.25 o.p. (*1-56100-227-5*, 849, Unabridged Library Editions); audio 23.95 o.p. (*1-56100-602-5*, 71, Bookcassette) Brilliance Audio.
—Covenant with the Vampire: The Diaries of the Family Dracula. 1995. (Diaries of the Family Dracula: Vol. 1). 384p. mass mkt. 6.99 (*0-440-21543-9*) Dell Publishing.
—Covenant with the Vampire: The Diaries of the Family Dracula. l.t. ed. 1995. (Charnwood Large Print Ser.). 448p. 29.99 o.p. (*0-7089-8872-5*, Charnwood) Thorpe, F. A. Pubs. GBR. *Dist:* Ulverscroft Large Print Bks., Ltd., Ulverscroft Large Print Canada, Ltd.
—Lord of the Vampires: The Diaries of the Family Dracul. 1997. (Diaries of the Family Dracula: Vol. 3). 384p. mass mkt. 6.50 (*0-440-22442-X*); 1996. 336p. 22.95 o.s.i (*0-385-31414-0*, Delacorte Pr.) Dell Publishing.

**DRACULA, COUNT (FICTITIOUS CHARACTER)—FICTION**

Anscombe, Roderick. The Secret Life of Laszlo, Count Dracula. 1994. 416p. 22.95 (*0-7868-6040-5*) Hyperion Pr.
—The Secret Life of Laszlo, Count Dracula. 1995. 480p. mass mkt. 6.50 o.p. (*0-06-100943-1*, HarperTorch) Morrow/Avon.
Deane, Hamilton & Balderston, John L. Dracula: The Ultimate, Illustrated Edition of the World-Famous Vampire Play. 1993. (Illus.). 176p. pap. 14.95 o.p. (*0-312-09279-2*, Saint Martin's Griffin) St. Martin's Pr.
Elrod, P. N., ed. Dracula in London. 2001. 272p. pap. 14.95 (*0-441-00858-5*) Ace Bks.
Estleman, Loren D. Sherlock Holmes vs. Dracula or, The Adventure of the Sanguinary Count. 2000. 224p. pap. 14.00 (*0-7434-0714-8*) ibooks, Inc.
Estleman, Loren D. & Watson, John H. Sherlock Holmes vs. Dracula or, The Adventure of the Sanguinary Count. 1978. 7.95 o.p. (*0-385-14051-7*) Doubleday Publishing.
—Sherlock Holmes vs. Dracula or, The Adventure of the Sanguinary Count. 1979. 224p. pap. 3.95 o.p. (*0-14-005262-3*, Penguin Bks.) Viking Penguin.
Florescu, Radu & McNally, Raymond T. The Complete Dracula, 001, Vol. 1. 1992. pap. 19.95 o.p. (*0-87411-595-7*) Copley Publishing Group, Inc.
Greenberg, Martin H., ed. Dracula: Prince of Darkness. 1992. (Daw Book Collectors Ser.: Vol. 889). 320p. (Orig.). mass mkt. 4.99 o.s.i (*0-88677-531-0*) DAW Bks., Inc.
Jones, Stephen, ed. The Mammoth Book of Dracula. 1997. (Mammoth Bks.). 512p. pap. 10.95 (*0-7867-0428-4*, Carroll & Graf Pubs.) Avalon Publishing Group.
—The Mammoth Book of Vampires. 1992. (Mammoth Bks.). 512p. pap. 9.95 (*0-88184-796-8*, Carroll & Graf Pubs.) Avalon Publishing Group.
Kellecher, Victor. Into the Dark. 1999. 393p. pap. (*0-670-88464-2*, Viking) Viking Penguin.
Knight, Amarantha. The Darker Passions: Dracula. 1995. (Darker Passions Ser.). mass mkt. 5.95 o.s.i (*1-56333-326-0*) Masquerade Bks., Inc.
Lee, Earl. Drakulya: The Lost Journal of Mircea Drakulya, Lord of the Undead. 1994. 224p. pap. 10.95 o.p. (*1-884365-02-7*) See Sharp Pr.
Marrero, Robert G. Dracula: The Vampire Legend on Film. 1992. (Illus.). 128p. pap. 12.95 (*0-9634982-0-7*) Fantasma Bks.
Muth, Jon J. Dracula: A Symphony in Moonlight & Nightmares. 1986. (Illus.). 80p. 7.95 o.p. (*0-87135-171-4*) Marvel Enterprises.
—Dracula: A Symphony in Moonlight & Nightmares. 1993. 80p. 45.00 o.p. (*1-56163-060-8*); 2nd ed. pap. 7.99 o.p. (*1-56163-059-4*) NBM Publishing Co.
Newman, Kim. Judgement of Tears: Anno Dracula 1959. 1998. 240p. 22.95 o.p. (*0-7867-0558-2*, Carroll & Graf Pubs.) Avalon Publishing Group.
Preiss, Byron, ed. The Ultimate Dracula. 2003. 368p. mass mkt. 7.99 (*0-7434-5820-6*) ibooks, Inc.
Saberhagen, Fred. Dominion. (Orig.). 1992. 320p. mass mkt. 5.99 (*0-8125-2386-5*); 1990. pap. 3.95 o.s.i (*0-8125-0855-6*) Doherty, Tom Assocs., LLC. (Tor Bks.).
—The Dominion. 1982. 320p. (Orig.). mass mkt. 2.95 o.s.i (*0-523-48536-0*, Tor Bks.) Doherty, Tom Assocs., LLC.
—The Dracula Tape. 1985. 288p. mass mkt. 2.95 o.s.i (*0-441-16601-6*) Ace Bks.
—The Dracula Tape. 1999. 288p. mass mkt. 5.99 (*0-671-57839-1*) Baen Bks.
—The Dracula Tape. 1992. 280p. mass mkt. 5.99 (*0-8125-2383-0*); 1989. pap. 3.95 o.s.i (*0-8125-2581-7*) Doherty, Tom Assocs., LLC. (Tor Bks.).
—Holmes-Dracula File. 1982. mass mkt. 2.50 o.s.i (*0-441-34247-7*); 1981. mass mkt. 2.25 o.s.i (*0-441-34246-9*) Ace Bks.
—Holmes-Dracula File. 1992. 249p. mass mkt. 4.99 (*0-8125-2384-9*); 1989. pap. 3.95 o.s.i (*0-8125-0255-8*) Doherty, Tom Assocs., LLC. (Tor Bks.).
—A Matter of Taste. 1992. 288p. mass mkt. 3.99 (*0-8125-2575-2*); 1990. 16.95 o.p. (*0-312-85046-8*) Doherty, Tom Assocs., LLC. (Tor Bks.).
—An Old Friend of the Family. 1981. 256p. mass mkt. 2.50 o.s.i (*0-441-62161-9*) Ace Bks.
—An Old Friend of the Family. 1992. 247p. mass mkt. 4.99 (*0-8125-2385-7*); 1987. 256p. reprint ed. pap. 3.50 o.s.i (*0-8125-2550-7*) Doherty, Tom Assocs., LLC. (Tor Bks.).
—A Question of Time. 1993. 278p. pap. text 5.99 (*0-8125-2577-9*); 1992. 272p. 19.95 o.p. (*0-312-85129-4*) Doherty, Tom Assocs., LLC. (Tor Bks.).
—Seance for a Vampire. 1994. 288p. 21.95 o.p. (*0-312-85562-1*); Vol. 1. 1997. 310p. pap. 5.99 o.s.i (*0-8125-3348-8*) Doherty, Tom Assocs., LLC. (Tor Bks.).
—Sharpness on the Neck. 1996. 352p. 23.95 o.p. (*0-312-85799-3*, Tor Bks.) Doherty, Tom Assocs., LLC.
—Thorn. 1980. mass mkt. 2.75 o.s.i (*0-441-80744-5*) Ace Bks.
—Thorn. 1990. mass mkt. 4.95 (*0-8125-0316-3*, Tor Bks.) Doherty, Tom Assocs., LLC.
Saberhagen, Fred & Hart, James V. Bram Stoker's Dracula. 1992. 304p. mass mkt. 4.99 o.p. (*0-451-17575-1*, Signet Bks.) NAL.
Stoker, Bram. Dracula. 2000. 252p. E-Book 9.95 (*0-594-05212-2*) 1873 Pr.
—Dracula. Date not set. pap. text (*0-17-557040-X*) Addison-Wesley Longman, Inc.
—Dracula. Date not set. reprint ed. lib. bdg. 27.95 (*0-88411-131-8*, Aeonian Pr.) Amereon, Ltd.
—Dracula, Set. 1995. audio 77.95 (*1-55685-359-9*) Audio Bk. Contractors, Inc.
—Dracula. 2000. (SPA.). 496p. 10.95 (*84-406-5500-2*) B Ediciones S.A. ESP. *Dist:* Distribooks, Inc.
—Dracula. abr. ed. 1995. audio 19.95 (*1-882071-36-0*) B&B Audio, Inc.
—Dracula. unabr. ed. 1996. audio 39.95 (*1-888928-00-X*) BIG RADIO Productions, Inc.
—Dracula. 1983. mass mkt. 1.95 o.s.i (*0-553-21148-X*, Bantam Classics) Bantam Bks.
—Dracula. E-Book 5.00 (*0-7607-1358-8*) Barnes & Noble, Inc.
—Dracula. Bennett, S. A., ed. 1992. (Illus.). 64p. pap. (*0-944099-20-3*) Bill Barry's Compass Bks.
—Dracula. unabr. ed. 1998. audio 76.95 (*0-7861-1322-7*, 2247) Blackstone Audio Bks., Inc.
—Dracula. unabr. collector's ed. 1983. audio 80.00 (*0-7366-0419-7*, 1391) Books on Tape, Inc.
—Dracula. 2002. pap. 4.50 (*1-59109-321-X*) Booksurge, LLC.
—Dracula. 1992. 320p. reprint ed. pap. 9.95 (*0-86322-143-2*) Brandon Bk. Pubs., Ltd. IRL. *Dist:* Irish Bks. & Media, Inc.
—Dracula. unabr. ed. 2002. audio 29.95 (*1-59086-287-2*, 3873, Brilliance Audio Unabridged); 1994. audio 59.25 (*1-56100-218-6*, 871, Unabridged Library Editions); 1994. audio 19.95 o.p. (*1-56100-593-2*, 95, Bookcassette) Brilliance Audio.
—Dracula. Byron, Glennis, ed. 1997. (Literary Texts Ser.). 400p. (C). pap. (*1-55111-136-5*) Broadview Pr.
—Dracula. 1990. reprint ed. lib. bdg. 26.95 (*0-89966-692-2*) Buccaneer Bks., Inc.
—Dracula. ed. 1999. (J). (gr. 2). spiral bd. (*0-616-01788-X*) Canadian National Institute for the Blind/Institut National Canadien pour les Aveugles.
—Dracula. 2002. 16p. audio compact disk 119.95 (*0-7540-5547-7*, CCD 238); 14p. audio 110.95 (*0-7540-0891-6*, CAB 2313) Chivers Audio Bks. GBR. *Dist:* BBC Audiobooks America.
—Dracula. reprint ed. lib. bdg. 98.00 (*0-7426-2890-6*); 2001. pap. text 28.00 (*0-7426-7890-3*) Classic Bks.
—Dracula. 1997. 384p. 21.95 (*0-312-86358-6*, Tor Bks.); 1992. 384p. mass mkt. 4.99 (*0-8125-2301-6*, Tor Classics); 1988. mass mkt. 4.95 (*1-55902-006-7*, Aerie) Doherty, Tom Assocs., LLC.
—Dracula. 1959. 7.95 o.p. (*0-385-00383-8*) Doubleday Publishing.
—Dracula. 2000. 320p. pap. 2.00 (*0-486-41109-5*) Dover Pubns., Inc.
—Dracula. 1980. 82p. (YA). (gr. 7 up). pap. 5.60 (*0-87129-308-0*, D35) Dramatic Publishing Co.
—Dracula. unabr. ed. 1992. audio 5.99 (*0-88646-621-0*, PAC-7621) Durkin Hayes Publishing Ltd.
—Dracula. E-Book 3.49 (*1-58627-516-X*) Electric Umbrella Publishing.
—Dracula. 2000. lib. bdg. 21.89 (*0-06-029212-1*) HarperCollins Pubs.
—Dracula. abr. ed. 1984. audio 8.98 (*0-89845-215-5*, CP 1468, Caedmon) HarperTrade.
—Dracula, Set. abr. ed. 1999. audio 16.95 Highsmith Inc.
—Dracula. l.t. ed. 1792p. pap. 110.00 (*0-7583-3190-8*); 1185p. pap. 76.00 (*0-7583-3188-6*); 528p. pap. 37.00 (*0-7583-3185-1*); 2079p. pap. 123.00 (*0-7583-3191-6*); 926p. pap. 64.00 (*0-7583-3187-8*); 723p. pap. 45.00 (*0-7583-3186-X*); 406p. pap. 32.00 (*0-7583-3184-3*); 926p. lib. bdg. 76.00 (*0-7583-3179-7*); 1457p. lib. bdg. 102.00 (*0-7583-3181-9*); 2079p. lib. bdg. 148.00 (*0-7583-3183-5*); 723p. lib. bdg. 51.00 (*0-7583-3178-9*); 406p. lib. bdg. 38.00 (*0-7583-3176-2*); 1792p. lib. bdg. 133.00 (*0-7583-3182-7*); 1185p. lib. bdg. 88.00 (*0-7583-3180-0*); 528p. lib. bdg. 43.00 (*0-7583-3177-0*) Huge Print Pr.
—Dracula. abr. ed. 1980. audio 7.95. audio 56.00 Jimcin Recordings.
—Dracula. 1998. (Cloth Bound Pocket Ser.). 240p. 7.95 (*3-89508-096-9*, 520018) Konemann.
—Dracula. 2002. (Classics for Young Readers Ser.). (SPA.). (YA). 14.95 (*84-392-0934-7*, EV30652) Lectorum Pubns., Inc.
—Dracula. 1996. Bk. 1, Episodes 1-16. audio 49.95 (*1-57677-059-1*, BIGR001); Bk. 2, Episodes 9-16. audio 24.95 (*1-57677-060-5*) Lodestone Catalog, The.
—Dracula. 2000. (English As a Second Language Bk.). pap. text 5.95 o.p. (*0-582-53523-9*) Longman Publishing Group.
—Dracula. 1989. 368p. 19.95 o.p. (*0-87226-189-1*, Bedrick, Peter Bks.) McGraw-Hill Children's Publishing.
—Dracula. 1995. 2p. audio (*0-14-086007-X*); 1992. 392p. mass mkt. 3.99 o.p. (*0-451-17581-6*, Signet Classics); 1986. mass mkt. 2.50 o.p. (*0-451-52097-1*); 1973. mass mkt. 0.60 o.p. (*0-451-02793-0*, Signet Bks.); 1973. mass mkt. 0.95 o.p. (*0-451-05438-5*, Signet Bks.); 1965. mass mkt. 1.95 o.p. (*0-451-51889-6*, Signet Classics); 1965. mass mkt. 2.50 o.p. (*0-451-51670-2*, Signet Classics); 1965. mass mkt. 1.75 o.p. (*0-451-51129-8*, Signet Classics); 1965. mass mkt. 1.50 o.p. (*0-451-51030-5*, Signet Classics); 1965. mass mkt. 1.25 o.p. (*0-451-50717-7*, Signet Classics) NAL.
—Dracula. 1938. audio 7.95 National Recording Co.
—Dracula. abr. ed. 1997. audio 17.98 (*962-634-615-9*, NA311514); audio compact disk 19.98 (*962-634-115-7*, NA311512) Naxos of America, Inc. (Naxos AudioBooks).
—Dracula. abr. ed. 2001. (Ultimate Classics Ser.). audio 18.00 (*1-931056-84-6*, New Millennium Audio) New Millennium Entertainment.
—Dracula. abr. ed. 1993. (Ultimate Classics Ser.). audio 16.95 o.p. (*1-55800-578-1*, Dove Audio) NewStar Media, Inc.
—Dracula. l.t. ed. (Large Print Ser.). 1993. 558p. lib. bdg. 26.00 (*0-939495-43-0*); 1998. 435p. reprint ed. lib. bdg. 25.00 (*1-58287-024-1*) North Bks.
—Dracula. l.t. ed. 2003. 448p. E-Book 2.99 (*1-932681-17-5*) NuVision Pubns.
—Dracula. 1995. (FRE.). Pt. 1, set. audio 36.95; Pt. 2, set. audio 36.95; Pt. 3, set. audio 34.95; Pts. 1-3, set. audio 98.95 Olivia & Hill Pr., The.

—Dracula. Ellmann, Maud, ed. & intro. by. 1998. (Oxford World's Classics Ser.). 432p. pap. 9.95 (*0-19-283386-3*) Oxford Univ. Pr., Inc.

—Dracula. 1995. (Illus.). 126p. pap. text 5.95 (*0-19-586322-4*); 1984. 408p. pap. 4.95 o.p. (*0-19-281598-9*) Oxford Univ. Pr., Inc.

—Dracula. Ellman, Maud, ed. & intro. by. 2nd ed. 1996. (Oxford World's Classics Ser.). 428p. pap. 6.95 o.p. (*0-19-282462-7*) Oxford Univ. Pr., Inc.

—Dracula. Teresa Agnes, ed. Heller, Rudolf, tr. 1979. (SPA., Illus.). 64p. stu. ed. 1.50 (*0-88301-566-8*); pap. text 3.95 (*0-88301-446-7*) Pendulum Pr., Inc.

—Dracula. abr. ed. 1992. (Classics on Cassette). 15.95 o.p. incl. audio (*0-453-00786-4*) Penguin/ HighBridge.

—Dracula. 1993. (SPA.). 464p. (*84-01-49200-9*) Plaza & Janés Editories, S.A.

—Dracula. unabr. ed. 2001. audio 39.95 (*1-57511-094-6*) Publishing Mills, Inc., The.

—Dracula. (Paperback Classics Ser.). 2001. 432p. pap. 10.95 (*0-375-75670-1*); 2000. E-Book 4.95 (*0-679-64197-1*) Random House Adult Trade Publishing Group. (Modern Library).

—Dracula. (Modern Library Ser.). 1996. 448p. 17.95 o.s.i (*0-679-60229-1*); 1978. 6.95 o.s.i (*0-394-60447-4*) Random Hse., Inc.

—Dracula. unabr. ed. 1980. audio 97.00 (*1-55690-156-9*, 80090E7) Recorded Bks., LLC.

—Dracula. 2002. E-Book 4.95 (*0-9712207-1-9*) Riverdale Electronic Bks.

—Dracula. unabr. ed. 1995. 528p. text 8.98 o.p. (*1-56138-515-8*, Courage Bks.) Running Pr. Bk. Pubs.

—Dracula. abr. ed. 2001. audio compact disk (*1-894003-24-1*) Scenario Productions.

—Dracula. 2003. 528p. mass mkt. 5.99 (*0-7434-7736-7*, Pocket) Simon & Schuster.

—Dracula. unabr. ed. 2003. audio 19.99 (*1-59335-044-9*, 30129) Soulmate Audio Bks., Inc.

—Dracula. unabr. ed. 2002. audio compact disk 18.95 (*1-58472-385-8*, In Audio) Sound Room Pubs., Inc.

—Dracula. abr. ed. 1983. audio 9.98 o.p. (*0-88142-360-2*); Set. 1995. audio 13.95 o.p. (*1-55935-189-6*, 394105) Soundelux Audio Publishing.

—Dracula. abr. ed. audio 10.95 (*0-8045-1087-3*, SAC 1087) Spoken Arts, Inc.

—Dracula. l.t. ed. 1993. 592p. lib. bdg. 22.95 (*0-8161-5692-1*) Thorndike Pr.

—Dracula. audio Thorsons.

—Dracula. Johnson, Beth, ed. & afterword by by. 2003. 428p. mass mkt. 2.00 (*1-59194-003-6*) Townsend Pr.

—Dracula. 2001. (Classics of Mystery & Suspense Ser.). 334p. (*1-58279-187-2*) Trident Pr. International.

—Dracula. 1965. (Signet Classics Ser.). 11.00 (*0-606-00578-1*) Turtleback Bks.

—Dracula. 1993. 432p. pap. 5.95 o.p. (*0-460-87189-7*, Everyman's Classic Library in Paperback) Tuttle Publishing.

—Dracula. Howes, Marjorie, ed. rev. ed. 1995. 400p. pap. 5.95 (*0-460-87598-1*, Everyman's Classic Library in Paperback) Tuttle Publishing.

—Dracula. (Penguin Classics Ser.). 560p. 2003. pap. 11.00 (*0-14-143984-X*, Penguin Classics); 1999. pap. (*0-14-043381-3*) Viking Penguin.

—Dracula. annuals Hindle, Maurice, ed. & intro. by. 1993. (Classics Ser.). 560p. 10.95 (*0-14-043406-2*, Penguin Classics) Viking Penguin.

—Dracula. 1979. 448p. pap. 4.95 o.p. (*0-14-005280-1*, Penguin Bks.) Viking Penguin.

—Dracula. 2002. 324p. pap. 18.95 (*1-58715-588-5*); lib. bdg. 29.95 (*1-58715-589-3*) Wildside Pr.

—Dracula. 1999. E-Book 5.99 (*0-8220-7059-6*, Cliff Notes) Wiley, John & Sons, Inc.

—Dracula. 1997. (Classics Library). 336p. pap. 3.95 (*1-85326-086-X*, 086XWW) Wordsworth Editions, Ltd. GBR. *Dist:* Casemate Pubs. & Bk. Distributors, LLC.

—Dracula. l.t. ed. 1994. 592p. pap. 14.95 o.p. (*0-8161-5817-7*) World Pubns., Inc.

—Dracula. abr. ed. 2000. audio 8.95 o.p. (*1-889974-04-8*) Ziplow Productions.

—Dracula: Authoritative Text, Contexts, Reviews & Reactions, Criticism, Dramatic & Film Variations. Auerbach, Nina & Skal, David J., eds. 1996. (Critical Editions Ser.). (C). pap. text 14.20 (*0-393-97012-4*) Norton, W. W. & Co., Inc.

—Dracula's Guest. 1990. 160p. reprint ed. pap. 9.95 o.p. (*0-86322-120-3*) Brandon Bk. Pubs., Ltd. IRL. *Dist:* Irish Bks. & Media, Inc.

Stoker, Bram & Byron, Glennis. Dracula. 1998. E-Book 9.95 (*0-585-29380-5*) netLibrary, Inc.

Stoker, Bram & Outlet Book Company Staff. Dracula. 1992. 9.99 o.s.i (*0-517-06973-3*) Random Hse. Value Publishing.

Stoker, Bram & Riquelme, John P. Dracula. 2001. (Illus.). xv, 622p. pap. text 10.00 (*0-312-24170-4*) Bedford/Saint Martin's.

Stoker, Bram & Shelley, Mary Wollstonecraft. Dracula - Frankenstein. 1973. xiii, 655p. o.p. (*0-385-09580-5*) Doubleday Publishing.

—Dracula - Frankenstein. l.t. ed. 1999. (Illus.). E-Book 24.95 incl. cd-rom (*1-929077-39-4*, Books OnScreen) PageFree Publishing, Inc.

—Frankenstein, Dracula, Dr. Jekyll & Mr. Hyde. 1978. mass mkt. 4.50 o.p. (*0-451-52170-6*, Signet Classics) NAL.

Wolf, Leonard & Preiss, Byron. The Ultimate Dracula. 1991. 358p. pap. 13.95 o.s.i (*0-440-50353-1*, Dell Bks.) Dell Publishing.

Wolf, Leonard & Stoker, Bram. The Essential Dracula. 1993. (Essentials Ser.). (Illus.). 512p. pap. 16.95 o.p. (*0-452-26943-1*, Plume) Dutton/Plume.

### DRAKE, CADENCE (FICTITIOUS CHARACTER)—FICTION

Lisle, Holly. Hunting the Corrigan's Blood. 1997. 320p. mass mkt. 5.99 (*0-671-87768-2*) Baen Bks.

### DRAKE, COTTON (FICTITIOUS CHARACTER)—FICTION

Deford, Frank. Love & Infamy. 1995. 576p. mass mkt. 5.99 (*0-8217-0122-3*, Zebra Bks.); mass mkt. 5.99 o.s.i (*0-7860-0122-4*, Pinnacle Bks.) Kensington Publishing Corp.

—Love & Infamy. 1993. 576p. 24.00 o.p. (*0-670-82995-1*) Viking Penguin.

### DRAKE, JESSIE (FICTITIOUS CHARACTER)—FICTION

Krich, Rochelle Majer. Angel of Death. 1994. 384p. 27.00 (*0-89296-508-8*) Mysterious Pr.

—Angel of Death. 372p. pap. 4.98 o.p. (*0-7651-0305-2*) Smithmark Pubs., Inc.

—Angel of Death. 1996. 368p. mass mkt. 5.99 o.s.i (*0-446-40311-3*) Warner Bks., Inc.

—Blood Money: A Mystery. 2000. 352p. mass mkt. 6.99 (*0-380-78954-X*); 1999. 341p. 23.00 (*0-380-97379-0*) Morrow/Avon. (Avon Bks.).

—Dead Air: A Jessie Drake Mystery. 2001. 416p. mass mkt. 6.99 (*0-380-80701-7*); 2000. 304p. 23.00 (*0-380-97769-9*) Morrow/Avon. (Avon Bks.).

—Fair Game. 1994. 320p. mass mkt. 5.50 o.s.i (*0-446-40310-5*) Warner Bks., Inc.

### DREDD, JUDGE (FICTITIOUS CHARACTER)—FICTION

Barrett. Judge Dredd. 1995. mass mkt. 4.99 (*0-312-95628-2*, St. Martin's Paperbacks) St. Martin's Pr.

Bishop, David. Cursed Earth Asylum. 1995. (Judge Dredd Ser.). mass mkt. 5.95 (*0-352-32893-2*) Virgin Bks. GBR. *Dist:* London Bridge.

Ennis, Garth. Judge Dredd: Goodnight Kiss. 2003. (2000 AD Presents Ser.). (Illus.). 96p. pap. 14.95 (*1-84023-346-X*) Titan Bks. Ltd. GBR. *Dist:* Client Distribution Services.

—Judge Dredd: Helter Skelter. 2003. (2000 AD Presents Ser.). (Illus.). 80p. pap. 14.95 (*1-84023-348-6*) Titan Bks. Ltd. GBR. *Dist:* Client Distribution Services.

Ennis, Garth & Doherty, Peter. Judge Dredd: Death Aid. 2002. (2000 AD Presents Ser.). (Illus.). 80p. pap. 14.95 (*1-84023-344-3*) Titan Bks. Ltd. GBR. *Dist:* Client Distribution Services.

Grant, Alan. Lobo - Judge Dredd: Psycho Bikers vs. Mutants from Hell. Raspler, Dan, ed. 1995. (Illus.). 48p. pap. 4.95 o.p. (*1-56389-239-1*) DC Comics.

Grant Staff & Wagner. Batman - Judge Dredd: The Ultimate Riddle. Peterson, ed. 1995. (Illus.). 48p. pap. 4.95 (*1-56389-206-5*) DC Comics.

Helfer, A. Judge Dredd-The Official Movie Adaptation. Kupperberg, Paul, ed. 1995. (Illus.). 64p. pap. 5.95 o.p. (*1-56389-245-6*) DC Comics.

Marley, Stephen. Dread Dominion. 1995. (Judge Dredd Ser.). mass mkt. 5.95 (*0-352-32929-7*) Virgin Bks. GBR. *Dist:* London Bridge.

Stone, Dave. Judge Dredd: Deathmasques. 1995. (Judge Dredd Ser.). mass mkt. 5.95 (*0-352-32873-8*) Virgin Bks. GBR. *Dist:* London Bridge.

—Wetworks. 1995. (Judge Dredd Ser.). mass mkt. 5.95 (*0-352-32975-0*) Virgin Bks. GBR. *Dist:* London Bridge.

Wagner, John & Alcatena, Enrique. Predator vs. Judge Dredd. 1998. (Predator Ser.). (Illus.). 80p. (YA). (gr. 9 up). pap. 9.95 (*1-56971-345-6*) Dark Horse Comics.

Wagner, John & Ezquerra, Carlos. Necropolis. 2003. (2000 Ad Presents Ser.). (Illus.). 144p. pap. 19.95 (*1-84023-635-3*); 19.95 (*1-84023-601-9*) Titan Bks. Ltd. GBR. *Dist:* Client Distribution Services.

Wagner, John & Grant, Alan. The Apocalypse War. 2004. (2000 Ad Collector's Edition Hardback Ser.). (Illus.). 224p. 29.95 (*1-84023-634-5*) Titan Bks. Ltd. GBR. *Dist:* Client Distribution Services.

—Batman - Judge Dredd: Judgement on Gotham. O'Neil, Dennis, ed. 1991. (Illus.). 64p. pap. 5.95 (*1-56389-022-4*) DC Comics.

Wagner, John & MacNeil, Colin. The Complete America. 2003. (2000 Ad Presents Ser.). (Illus.). 120p. pap. 18.95 (*1-84023-615-9*) Titan Bks. Ltd. GBR. *Dist:* Client Distribution Services.

Wagner, John, et al. The Day the Law Died. (2000 Ad Presents Ser.). (Illus.). 144p. 2004. pap. 19.95 (*1-84023-776-7*); 2003. 24.95 (*1-84023-480-6*) Titan Bks. Ltd. GBR. *Dist:* Client Distribution Services.

### DREW, RANDALL (FICTITIOUS CHARACTER)—FICTION

Francis, Dick. Trial Run. l.t. ed. 1994. 19.95 o.p. (*0-7927-2170-5*); 1994. pap. 18.95 o.p. (*0-7927-2169-1*); 1993. 54.95 incl. audio (*0-7451-5957-5*) BBC Audiobooks America.

—Trial Run. 1987. mass mkt. 5.95 o.s.i (*0-449-21273-4*, Fawcett) Ballantine Bks.

—Trial Run. 2001. 272p. mass mkt. 6.99 (*0-515-12997-6*, Jove) Berkley Publishing Group.

—Trial Run. unabr. ed. 1991. audio 48.00 (*0-7366-2029-X*, 2843) Books on Tape, Inc.

—Trial Run. 1983. mass mkt. 3.50 o.s.i (*0-671-50732-X*); mass mkt. 2.95 (*0-671-47022-1*) Simon & Schuster. (Pocket).

—Trial Run. l.t. ed. 1980. 404p. 12.00 o.p. (*0-7089-0456-4*, Ulverscroft) Thorpe, F. A. Pubs. GBR. *Dist:* Ulverscroft Large Print Bks., Ltd.

### DRINKWATER, NATHANIEL (FICTITIOUS CHARACTER)—FICTION

Woodman, Richard. Baltic Mission. 1996. 320p. mass mkt. o.s.i (*0-7515-1495-0*) Little Brown & Co.

—Baltic Mission. l.t. ed. 2001. (Magna Large Print Ser.). 384p. (*0-7505-1735-2*) Magna Large Print Bks. GBR. *Dist:* Ulverscroft Large Print Canada, Ltd.

—Baltic Mission. 2000. (Mariner's Library Fiction Classics). 211p. pap. 14.95 (*1-57409-097-6*) Sheridan Hse., Inc.

—Beneath the Aurora. 1996. 312p. mass mkt. o.s.i (*0-7515-1142-0*) Little Brown & Co.

—Beneath the Aurora: A Nathaniel Drinkwater Novel. 2001. (Mariner's Library Fiction Classics: Vol. 12). 256p. pap. 14.95 (*1-57409-102-6*) Sheridan Hse., Inc.

—The Bomb Vessel. 1995. mass mkt. o.s.i (*0-7515-1018-1*) Little Brown & Co.

—The Bomb Vessel, Set. unabr. ed. 1994. (Nathaniel Drinkwater Ser.: No. 4). audio 42.00 (*0-7887-0002-2*, 94141) Recorded Bks., LLC.

—The Bomb Vessel. 2000. (Nathaniel Drinkwater Ser.). (Illus.). 215p. reprint ed. pap. 14.95 (*1-57409-099-2*) Sheridan Hse., Inc.

—The Bomb Vessel. 1986. 215p. 15.95 o.p. (*0-8027-0886-2*) Walker & Co.

—A Brig of War. 1984. 224p. pap. 2.95 o.p. (*0-523-41978-3*, Pinnacle Bks.) Kensington Publishing Corp.

—A Brig of War. 1995. mass mkt. o.s.i (*0-7515-1304-0*) Little Brown & Co.

—A Brig of War. 1998. 320p. mass mkt. 5.99 o.p. (*0-446-60463-1*) Warner Bks., Inc.

—A Brig of War: A Nathaniel Drinkwater Novel. 2001. (Mariner's Library Fiction Classics). (Illus.). 240p. reprint ed. pap. 14.95 (*1-57409-125-5*) Sheridan Hse., Inc.

—The Corvette. 1996. (Illus.). 310p. mass mkt. o.s.i (*0-7515-1303-2*) Little Brown & Co.

—The Corvette, Set. unabr. ed. 1992. audio 49.00 (*1-55690-679-X*, 92331) Recorded Bks., LLC.

—Decision at Trafalgar. 1987. 16.95 o.p. (*0-8027-0993-1*) Walker & Co.

—Ebb Tide. l.t. ed. 1999. (Magna Large Print Ser.). 448p. (*0-7505-1441-8*) Magna Large Print Bks. GBR. *Dist:* Ulverscroft Large Print Canada, Ltd.

—Ebb Tide Bk. 14: A Nathaniel Drinkwater Novel. 2002. (Mariner's Library Fiction Classics: Vol. 14). 240p. pap. 14.95 (*1-57409-104-2*) Sheridan Hse., Inc.

—An Eye of the Fleet. 1997. 288p. mass mkt. 5.99 o.p. (*0-446-60461-5*) Warner Bks., Inc.

—An Eye of the Fleet: A Nathaniel Drinkwater Novel. 2001. (Mariner's Library Fiction Classics: Bk. 1). 192p. reprint ed. pap. 14.95 (*1-57409-123-9*) Sheridan Hse., Inc.

—The Flying Squadron. l.t. ed. 1994. (Magna Large Print Ser.). 424p. (*0-7505-0691-1*) Magna Large Print Bks. GBR. *Dist:* Ulverscroft Large Print Canada, Ltd.

—The Flying Squadron: A Nathaniel Drinkwater Novel. 1999. (Illus.). 256p. pap. 14.95 (*1-57409-077-1*) Sheridan Hse., Inc.

—In Distant Waters. 1996. 320p. mass mkt. o.s.i (*0-7515-1491-8*) Little Brown & Co.

—In Distant Waters. l.t. ed. 2002. (Magna Large Print Ser.). 400p. (*0-7505-1736-0*) Magna Large Print Bks. GBR. *Dist:* Ulverscroft Large Print Canada, Ltd.

—In Distant Waters. 1988. 256p. 16.95 o.p. (*0-312-02586-6*) St. Martin's Pr.

—In Distant Waters: A Nathaniel Drinkwater Novel. 2000. (Mariner's Library Fiction Classics). (Illus.). 256p. pap. 14.95 (*1-57409-098-4*) Sheridan Hse., Inc.

—A King's Cutter. 1984. 224p. pap. 2.50 o.p. (*0-523-41977-5*, Pinnacle Bks.) Kensington Publishing Corp.

—A King's Cutter. 1995. (Illus.). 273p. mass mkt. o.s.i (*0-7515-0895-0*) Little Brown & Co.

—A King's Cutter. 1997. (Nathan DrinkWater Ser.: Bk. 2). 224p. mass mkt. 5.99 o.p. (*0-446-60462-3*) Warner Bks., Inc.

—A King's Cutter: A Nathaniel Drinkwater Novel. 2001. (Captain Drinkwater Ser.: Bk. 2). (Illus.). 176p. reprint ed. pap. 14.95 (*1-57409-124-7*) Sheridan Hse., Inc.

—A Private Revenge. 1996. (Illus.). 247p. mass mkt. o.s.i (*0-7515-0724-5*) Little Brown & Co.

—A Private Revenge. l.t. ed. 2002. (Magna Large Print Ser.). 384p. (*0-7505-1737-9*) Magna Large Print Bks. GBR. *Dist:* Ulverscroft Large Print Canada, Ltd.

—A Private Revenge. 1990. 16.95 o.p. (*0-312-04405-4*) St. Martin's Pr.

—A Private Revenge: A Nathaniel Drinkwater Novel. 1999. (Mariner's Library). 256p. pap. 14.95 (*1-57409-078-X*) Sheridan Hse., Inc.

—The Shadow of the Eagle. unabr. ed. 2000. audio 59.95 (*0-7540-0108-3*, CAB 1531) Chivers Audio Bks. GBR. *Dist:* BBC Audiobooks America.

—The Shadow of the Eagle Bk. 13: A Nathaniel Drinkwater Novel. 2002. (Mariner's Library Fiction Classics: Vol. 13). (Illus.). 272p. pap. 14.95 (*1-57409-103-4*) Sheridan Hse., Inc.

—The Shadow of the Eagle Bk. 13: A Nathaniel Drinkwater Novel. 1997. (Illus.). 372p. pap. o.s.i (*0-7515-2051-9*) Warner Futura GBR. *Dist:* Little Brown & Co.

—Under False Colours: A Nathaniel Drinkwater Novel. 1999. (Illus.). 256p. pap. 14.95 (*1-57409-079-8*) Sheridan Hse., Inc.

—1805. 1996. (Illus.). 306p. mass mkt. o.s.i (*0-7515-1479-9*) Little Brown & Co.

—1805. unabr. ed. 1993. (Nathaniel Drinkwater Ser.: No. 6). audio 49.00 (*1-55690-946-2*, 93428) Recorded Bks., LLC.

—1805: A Nathaniel Drinkwater Novel. 2001. (Mariner's Library Fiction Classics). (Illus.). 224p. pap. 14.95 (*1-57409-101-8*) Sheridan Hse., Inc.

### DRISCOLL, KATHERINE (FICTITIOUS CHARACTER)—FICTION

Walker, Mary Willis. Zero at the Bone. 1997. 336p. mass mkt. 6.50 (*0-553-57505-8*) Bantam Bks.

—Zero at the Bone. unabr. ed. 1998. audio 56.00 (*0-7366-4131-9*, 4634) Books on Tape, Inc.

—Zero at the Bone. 1993. (Mystery Ser.). mass mkt. (*0-373-26122-5*, 1-26122-1, Harlequin Bks.) Harlequin Enterprises, Ltd.

—Zero at the Bone. 1991. 336p. 18.95 (*0-312-06495-0*, Saint Martin's Minotaur) St. Martin's Pr.

—Zero at the Bone. l.t. ed. 1998. (Niagara Large Print Ser.). 392p. 29.50 o.p. (*0-7089-5830-3*, Ulverscroft) Thorpe, F. A. Pubs. GBR. *Dist:* Ulverscroft Large Print Bks., Ltd., Ulverscroft Large Print Canada, Ltd.

### DRISKILL, BEN (FICTITIOUS CHARACTER)—FICTION

Gifford, Thomas. The Assassini. 1991. 688p. mass mkt. 6.99 o.s.i (*0-553-28740-0*); 1990. (*0-593-02172-X*); 1990. 688p. pap. 29.00 (*0-553-76236-2*) Bantam Bks.

—The Assassini. 1924. o.s.i (*0-688-04723-8*, Morrow, William & Co.) Morrow/Avon.

—The Assassini. 1991. audio 12.79 o.s.i (*0-553-70023-5*); 1999. audio 9.99 o.s.i (*0-553-70203-3*) Random Hse. Audio Publishing Group. (RH Audio).

—Saints Rest. 1997. 448p. mass mkt. 6.99 o.s.i (*0-553-57226-1*) Bantam Bks.

—Saint's Rest. 1997. 448p. pap. 23.00 (*0-553-76269-9*, Crimeline) Bantam Bks.

### DRIZZT DO'URDEN (FICTITIOUS CHARACTER)—FICTION

Salvatore, R. A. The Crystal Shard. 1988. (Forgotten Realms Ser.: Bk. 1). (Illus.). 333p. pap. 7.99 (*0-88038-535-9*, TSR08411) Wizards of the Coast.

—The Dark Elf Trilogy. (Illus.). 1998. 805p. 24.99 o.p. (*0-7869-1176-X*); 2000. 808p. pap. 19.95 (*0-7869-1588-9*) Wizards of the Coast.

—The Dark Elf Trilogy Gift Set: Homeland; Exile; Sojourn, 3 bks., Set. gif. ed. 2001. (Forgotten Realms Ser.). 960p. reprint ed. mass mkt. 23.97 (*0-7869-2683-X*) Wizards of the Coast.

—Exile. rev. ed. 1990. (Forgotten Realms Dark Elf Trilogy Bks.: Vol. 2). (Illus.). 306p. mass mkt. 7.99 (*0-88038-920-6*) Wizards of the Coast.

—The Halfling's Gem. 1990. (Forgotten Realms Ser.: Bk. 3). (Illus.). 314p. mass mkt. 7.99 (*0-88038-901-X*) Wizards of the Coast.

—Homeland. (Illus.). (Orig.). 2004. 352p. 25.95 (*0-7869-3123-X*); 1990. (Forgotten Realms Dark Elf Trilogy Bks.: Bk. 1). 314p. pap. 7.99 (*0-88038-905-2*) Wizards of the Coast.

—The Icewind Dale Trilogy. collector's ed. 2000. (Forgotten Realms Ser.). (Illus.). 1040p. 27.95 (*0-7869-1557-9*) Wizards of the Coast.

—Sojourn. 1991. (Forgotten Realms Dark Elf Trilogy Bks.: Bk. 3). (Illus.). 309p. mass mkt. 7.99 (*1-56076-047-8*) Wizards of the Coast.

—Streams of Silver. 1989. (Forgotten Realms Ser.: Bk. 2). 342p. mass mkt. 7.99 (0-88038-672-X) Wizards of the Coast.

DROVER, JIMMY (FICTITIOUS CHARACTER)—FICTION

Granger, Bill. Drover. 1992. 272p. mass mkt. 4.99 (0-380-71210-5, Avon Bks.) Morrow/Avon.
—Drover & the Designated Hitter. 1995. 240p. mass mkt. 4.99 o.p. (0-380-71909-6, Avon Bks.); 1994. 223p. 20.00 o.p. (0-688-11884-4, Morrow, William & Co.) Morrow/Avon.
—Drover & the Zebras. 1993. 240p. mass mkt. 4.99 (0-380-71211-3, Avon Bks.); 1992. 20.00 o.p. (0-688-09857-6, Morrow, William & Co.) Morrow/Avon.

DUBOIS, AIMEE (FICTITIOUS CHARACTER)—FICTION

Edwards, Louis. N: A Romantic Mystery. 240p. 1998. pap. 12.95 o.s.i (0-452-27788-4, Plume); 1997. 22.95 o.p. (0-525-94182-7) Dutton/Plume.

DUBONNET, TUBBY (FICTITIOUS CHARACTER)—FICTION

Dunbar, Tony. City of Beads. 1996. 256p. mass mkt. 5.99 o.s.i (0-425-15578-1, Prime Crime) Berkley Publishing Group.
—City of Beads. 1996. 256p. 21.95 o.p. (0-399-14081-6, G. P. Putnam's Sons) Penguin Group (USA) Inc.
—The Crime Czar: A Tubby Dubonnet Mystery. 1998. (Tubby Dubonnet Mysteries Ser.). 240p. mass mkt. 5.99 o.s.i (0-440-22658-9) Dell Publishing.
—Crooked Man. 1996. 208p. mass mkt. 4.99 o.s.i (0-425-15138-7) Berkley Publishing Group.
—Crooked Man. 1994. 240p. 21.95 o.p. (0-399-13973-7, G. P. Putnam's Sons) Penguin Group (USA) Inc.
—Lucky Man. 1999. (Tubby Dubonnet Mysteries Ser.). 240p. mass mkt. 5.99 o.s.i (0-440-22662-7) Dell Publishing.
—Shelter from the Storm. 1998. 224p. mass mkt. 5.99 o.s.i (0-425-16644-9) Berkley Publishing Group.
—Shelter from the Storm. l.t. ed. 1998. (Large Print Book Ser.). pap. 23.95 (1-56895-607-X, Wheeler Publishing, Inc.) Gale Group.
—Shelter from the Storm. 1997. 256p. 24.95 o.p. (0-399-14301-7, G. P. Putnam's Sons) Penguin Group (USA) Inc.
—Trick Question. l.t. ed. 1997. (Tubby Dubonnet Mysteries Ser.). 224p. mass mkt. 5.99 o.s.i (0-425-16092-0, Prime Crime) Berkley Publishing Group.
—Trick Question. 1997. 256p. 22.95 o.p. (0-399-14184-7, G. P. Putnam's Sons) Penguin Group (USA) Inc.

DUCKWORTH, MORRIS (FICTITIOUS CHARACTER)—FICTION

Parks, Tim. Juggling the Stars. 2001. 224p. pap. 12.95 (1-55970-551-5) Arcade Publishing, Inc.
—Juggling the Stars. l.t. ed. 1993. 21.95 o.p. (0-7927-1642-6); pap. 19.95 o.p. (0-7927-1641-8) BBC Audiobooks America.
—Juggling the Stars. 1993. 218p. 19.95 o.p. (0-8021-1501-2) Grove/Atlantic, Inc.
—Mimi's Ghost: A Novel. (Illus.). 2001. 313p. 24.95 (1-55970-556-6); 2002. 320p. reprint ed. pap. 12.95 (1-55970-602-3) Arcade Publishing, Inc.

DUFF, MACDOUGAL (FICTITIOUS CHARACTER)—FICTION

Armstrong, Charlotte. The Case of the Weird Sisters. 1992. 256p. mass mkt. 3.99 o.s.i (0-8217-3803-8, Zebra Bks.) Kensington Publishing Corp.
—Innocent Flower. 1990. mass mkt. 3.50 o.s.i (0-8217-2897-0, Zebra Bks.) Kensington Publishing Corp.
—Lay on, MacDuff! 1993. 224p. mass mkt. 3.99 o.s.i (0-8217-4037-7, Zebra Bks.) Kensington Publishing Corp.

DUGAN (FICTITIOUS CHARACTER)—FICTION

Walker, David J. A Beer at a Bawdy House. E-Book 23.95 o.p. (0-312-27340-1); 2000. 307p. 23.95 (0-312-25242-0, Saint Martin's Minotaur) St. Martin's Pr.
—Ticket to Die For. 1998. (Wild Onion Ltd. Mysteries Ser.). 272p. 22.95 (0-312-19345-9, Saint Martin's Minotaur) St. Martin's Pr.

DUGAN, KIRSTEN (FICTITIOUS CHARACTER)—FICTION

Walker, David J. A Beer at a Bawdy House. E-Book 23.95 o.p. (0-312-27340-1); 2000. 307p. 23.95 (0-312-25242-0, Saint Martin's Minotaur) St. Martin's Pr.
—Ticket to Die For. 1998. (Wild Onion Ltd. Mysteries Ser.). 272p. 22.95 (0-312-19345-9, Saint Martin's Minotaur) St. Martin's Pr.

DUKAT, GUL (FICTITIOUS CHARACTER)—FICTION

Smith, Dean Wesley & Rusch, Kristine K. Vectors No. 2: Double Helix. 1999. (Star Trek, The Next Generation: No. 52). (Illus.). 304p. pap. 6.50 (0-671-03256-9, Star Trek) Simon & Schuster.

DULCIE (FICTITIOUS CHARACTER: MURPHY)—FICTION

Murphy, Shirley Rousseau. Cat in the Dark. 1999. 272p. 22.00 o.s.i (0-06-105096-2) HarperCollins Pubs.
—Cat in the Dark. 1999. (Joe Grey Mysteries Ser.). 320p. mass mkt. 6.99 (0-06-105947-1, Eos) Morrow/Avon.
—Cat Laughing Last. 2002. (Joe Grey Mysteries Ser.). 368p. mass mkt. 6.99 (0-06-101562-8, Avon Bks.) Morrow/Avon.
—Cat Laughing Last: A Joe Grey Mystery. 2002. 288p. 23.95 (0-06-620951-X) HarperCollins Pubs.
—Cat on the Edge. 1996. 288p. mass mkt. 6.99 (0-06-105600-6, Eos) Morrow/Avon.
—Cat Raise the Dead. 1997. 304p. mass mkt. 6.99 (0-06-105602-2, Eos) Morrow/Avon.
—Cat Spitting Mad. l.t. ed. 2002. (Wheeler Large Print Book Ser.). 281p. pap. 23.95 o.p. (1-58724-158-7, Wheeler Publishing, Inc.) Gale Group.
—Cat Spitting Mad. 2000. (Joe Grey Mysteries Ser.). 240p. 23.00 (0-06-105098-9) HarperCollins Pubs.
—Cat Spitting Mad. 2001. 304p. mass mkt. 6.99 (0-06-105989-7, Avon Bks.) Morrow/Avon.
—Cat to the Dogs: A Joe Grey Mystery. l.t. ed. 2000. 243p. 24.95 (1-57490-264-4, Beeler Large Print Bks.) Beeler, Thomas T. Publisher.
—Cat to the Dogs: A Joe Grey Mystery. 1999. (Joe Grey Mysteries Ser.). 256p. 23.00 (0-06-105097-0) HarperCollins Pubs.
—Cat to the Dogs: A Joe Grey Mystery. 2000. (Joe Grey Mysteries Ser.). 304p. mass mkt. 6.99 (0-06-105988-9, Avon Bks.) Morrow/Avon.
—Cat under Fire. 1997. 256p. mass mkt. 6.99 (0-06-105601-4, Eos) Morrow/Avon.

DULCINEA (FICTITIOUS CHARACTER)—FICTION

Brack, O. M., ed. The History & Adventures of the Renowned Don Quixote. Cervantes Saavedra, Miguel de & Smollett, Tobias George, trs. from SPA. 2003. (Illus.). 1056p. 100.00 (0-8203-2430-2) Univ. of Georgia Pr.

DULUTH, PETER (FICTITIOUS CHARACTER)—FICTION

Quentin, Patrick. Black Widow. 1992. 218p. pap. 8.95 o.p. (1-55882-111-2) International Polygonics, Ltd.
—Puzzle for Fiends. 1979. pap. 2.25 o.p. (0-380-45518-8, 45518-8, Avon Bks.) Morrow/Avon.
—Puzzle for Fiends. 1987. (Classic Crime Ser.). 224p. pap. 5.95 o.p. (0-14-008082-1, Penguin Bks.) Viking Penguin.
—Puzzle for Fools. 1985. 208p. pap. 2.25 o.p. (0-380-50294-1, 50294-1, Avon Bks.) Morrow/Avon.
—Puzzle for Fools. 1987. (Classic Crime Ser.). 224p. pap. 5.95 o.p. (0-14-008081-3, Penguin Bks.) Viking Penguin.
—Puzzle for Pilgrims. 1985. pap. 2.25 o.p. (0-380-47209-0, 47209-0, Avon Bks.) Morrow/Avon.
—Puzzle for Pilgrims. 1987. (Classic Crime Ser.). 224p. pap. 5.95 o.p. (0-14-008083-X, Penguin Bks.) Viking Penguin.
—Puzzle for Players. 1989. 250p. reprint ed. pap. 5.95 o.p. (1-55882-008-6, Library of Crime Classics) International Polygonics, Ltd.
—Puzzle for Players. 1985. pap. 2.25 o.p. (0-380-48025-5, 48025-5, Avon Bks.) Morrow/Avon.
—Puzzle for Puppets. 1989. 206p. pap. 7.95 o.p. (1-55882-020-5, Library of Crime Classics) International Polygonics, Ltd.
—Puzzle for Puppets. 1985. pap. 2.25 o.p. (0-380-48579-6, 48579-6, Avon Bks.) Morrow/Avon.
—Puzzle for Wantons. 1990. 229p. reprint ed. pap. 7.95 o.p. (1-55882-063-9) International Polygonics, Ltd.
—Puzzle for Wantons. 1985. 208p. pap. 2.25 o.p. (0-380-49643-7, 49643, Avon Bks.) Morrow/Avon.
—Run to Death. 1991. 192p. reprint ed. pap. 5.95 o.p. (1-55882-095-7, Library of Crime Classics) International Polygonics, Ltd.

DUNCAN, EVE (FICTITIOUS CHARACTER)—FICTION

Johansen, Iris. Body of Lies: A Novel. 2003. 400p. mass mkt. 7.50 (0-553-58214-3); 2002. 352p. 24.95 (0-553-80097-3) Bantam Bks.
—Body of Lies: A Novel. abr. ed. 2002. audio 25.95 (0-553-71496-1); audio compact disk 29.95 (0-553-71497-X) Random Hse. Audio Publishing Group.
—Body of Lies: A Novel. l.t. ed. 2002. 480p. 24.95 (0-375-43158-6) Random Hse. Large Print.
—The Face of Deception, Set. unabr. ed. 1999. (Eve Duncan Mystery Ser.: Vol. 1). audio 69.95 (0-7927-2329-5, CSL 218, Chivers Sound Library) BBC Audiobooks America.
—The Face of Deception. 1999. 480p. mass mkt. 7.50 (0-553-57802-2) Broadway Bks.
—The Face of Deception. l.t. ed. 1999. 454p. 27.95 (1-56895-633-9, Wheeler Publishing, Inc.) Gale Group.
—The Face of Deception. abr. ed. 1998. audio 25.00 (0-553-52542-5, 696036); audio compact disk 29.95 o.s.i (0-553-45617-2) Random Hse. Audio Publishing Group. (RH Audio).
—The Killing Game, unabr. ed. 2000. (Eve Duncan Mystery Ser.: Vol. 2). audio 69.95 (0-7927-2338-4, CSL 227, Chivers Sound Library) BBC Audiobooks America.
—The Killing Game. 2000. 384p. mass mkt. 7.50 (0-553-58155-4) Bantam Bks.
—The Killing Game. l.t. ed. 2000. (Thorndike/G. K. Hall Paperback Bestsellers Ser.). 443p. pap. 29.95 (0-7838-8852-X); 463p. 31.95 (0-7838-8851-1) Gale Group. (Macmillan Reference USA).
—The Killing Game. abr. ed. 1999. audio 25.00 Highsmith Inc.

DUNCAN, JENNIFER (FICTITIOUS CHARACTER)—FICTION

Denton, Anne. Heart of Stone. Smith, James C., Jr., ed. 1994. 196p. pap. 12.95 o.p. (0-86534-224-5) Sunstone Pr.

DUNCAN, PIERCE (FICTITIOUS CHARACTER)—FICTION

Gores, Joe. Cases. 1999. 354p. 23.00 (0-89296-593-2) Mysterious Pr.
—Cases. l.t. ed. 1999. (Mystery Ser.). 555p. 27.95 (0-7862-1882-7) Thorndike Pr.
—Cases. 1999. mass mkt. (0-446-60703-7) Warner Bks., Inc.

DUNLOP, LUKE (FICTITIOUS CHARACTER)—FICTION

Ebisch, Glen. Lou Dunlop: Private Eye. E-Book (1-55316-974-3) LTDBooks.
—Lou Dunlop: Private Eye. (YA). 2002. E-Book 5.00 (1-55316-029-0); 2001. pap. 17.99 (1-55316-536-5) LTDBooks CAN. Dist: Lightning Source, Inc., Baker & Taylor Bks.

DUNN, EMERSON (FICTITIOUS CHARACTER)—FICTION

Maynard, Roy. The Old Man. 1994. (Emerson Dunn Mystery Ser.). 192p. pap. 7.99 o.p. (0-89107-772-3) Crossway Bks.
—A Quick Thirty Seconds. 1993. (Emerson Dunn Mystery Ser.). 192p. (YA). pap. 7.99 o.p. (0-89107-745-6) Crossway Bks.
—Thirty-Eight Caliber. 1992. (Emerson Dunn Mystery Ser.). 192p. (Orig.). pap. 7.99 o.p. (0-89107-674-3) Crossway Bks.
—Twenty-Two Automatic. 1993. (Emerson Dunn Mystery Ser.). 192p. pap. 7.99 o.p. (0-89107-696-4) Crossway Bks.

DUNN, MICAH (FICTITIOUS CHARACTER)—FICTION

Shuman, M. K. Caesar Clue. 1990. 16.95 o.p. (0-312-04275-2, Saint Martin's Minotaur) St. Martin's Pr.
—Deep Kill. 1993. 2.99 o.p. (0-517-09907-1) Random Hse. Value Publishing.
—Deep Kill. 1991. 16.95 o.p. (0-312-05854-3, Saint Martin's Minotaur) St. Martin's Pr.
—The Last Man to Die: A Micah Dunn Mystery. 1992. 240p. 17.95 o.p. (0-312-07858-7, Saint Martin's Minotaur) St. Martin's Pr.
—The Maya Stone Murders. 1989. 256p. 16.95 o.p. (0-312-02608-0, Saint Martin's Minotaur) St. Martin's Pr.

DUPIN, AUGUSTE (FICTITIOUS CHARACTER)—FICTION

Poe, Edgar Allan. The Murders in the Rue Morgue. 1985. audio Dercum Audio.
—The Murders in the Rue Morgue. 1984. audio; 1977. audio 7.95 Jimcin Recordings.
—The Murders in the Rue Morgue. 1998. (Cloth Bound Pocket Ser.). 240p. 7.95 (3-89508-090-X, 520019) Konemann.
—The Murders in the Rue Morgue. 1977. (American Classics). (gr. 9-12). pap. 9.08 o.p. (0-88343-404-0) McDougal Littell Inc.
—The Murders in the Rue Morgue. 1996. (Classic Ser.). 64p. pap. 0.95 o.p. (0-14-600191-5) Penguin Group (USA) Inc.
—The Murders in the Rue Morgue. 1981. audio Recorded Bks., LLC.
—The Murders in the Rue Morgue. (Radio Ser.). audio 7.95 o.p. (0-88142-430-7, 126) Soundelux Audio Publishing.
—The Murders in the Rue Morgue & Other Stories. unabr. collector's ed. 1992. audio 30.00 (0-7366-2189-X, 2984) Books on Tape, Inc.
—The Murders in the Rue Morgue & Other Stories. 1999. 322p. pap. 7.95 (1-902058-02-X) Pulp Fictions GBR. Dist: 7 Hills Bk. Distributors.
—The Murders in the Rue Morgue & Other Tales. l.t. ed. 1997. (Murders in the Rue Morgue & Other Tales Ser.: Vol. 2). 240p. text 22.95 (1-56000-535-1) Transaction Pubs.
—The Purloined Letter. 1985. audio Dercum Audio.
—The Purloined Letter. 1984. audio; 1977. audio Jimcin Recordings.
—The Purloined Letter. 1980. audio Random Hse. Audio Publishing Group.
The Purloined Letter & Other Works. abr. ed. Incl. Dream Within a Dream. audio Ulalume. audio Valley of Unrest. audio 1984. Set audio 9.95 (1-55994-101-4, CPN 1288, Caedmon) HarperTrade.

DU PRE, GABRIEL (FICTITIOUS CHARACTER)—FICTION

Bowen, Peter. Ash Child: A Montana Mystery Featuring Gabriel Du Pre. 2002. 256p. 23.95 (0-312-28850-6, Saint Martin's Minotaur) St. Martin's Pr.
—Badlands: A Montana Mystery Featuring Gabriel Du Pre. 2003. 272p. 23.95 (0-312-26252-3, Saint Martin's Minotaur) St. Martin's Pr.
—Coyote Wind. 1994. 160p. 18.95 o.p. (0-312-10957-1, Saint Martin's Minotaur) St. Martin's Pr.
—Coyote Wind & Specimen Song: Two Montana Mysteries Featuring Gabriel du Pre. 2000. 368p. pap. 14.95 (0-312-26514-X, Saint Martin's Griffin) St. Martin's Pr.
—Cruzatte & Maria: A Montana Mystery Featuring Gabriel Du Pre. 2001. (Montana Mystery Ser.). 256p. 22.95 (0-312-26253-1, Saint Martin's Minotaur) St. Martin's Pr.
—Gabriel du Pre. 2004. 224p. 22.95 (0-312-27733-4); 12th ed. Date not set. (0-312-27730-X) St. Martin's Pr. (Saint Martin's Minotaur).
—Long Son. 1999. (Gabriel Du Pre Mystery Ser.: Vol. 6). 272p. 22.95 o.p. (0-312-19917-1, Saint Martin's Minotaur) St. Martin's Pr.
—Long Son: A Montana Mystery Featuring. 2nd ed. 2000. 272p. pap. 13.95 (0-312-25398-2, CPB1132, Saint Martin's Griffin) St. Martin's Pr.
—Notches: A Gabriel Du Pre Mystery. (Montana Mystery Ser.). 1998. 224p. mass mkt. 5.50 (0-312-96492-7, St. Martin's Paperbacks); 1996. 208p. text 20.95 o.p. (0-312-15181-0, Saint Martin's Minotaur) St. Martin's Pr.
—Specimen Song. (Montana Mystery Ser.). 1996. mass mkt. 5.50 (0-312-95763-7, St. Martin's Paperbacks); 1995. 201p. 18.95 o.p. (0-312-11896-1, Saint Martin's Minotaur) St. Martin's Pr.
—Stick Game: A Montana Mystery Featuring Gabriel Du Pre. 2000. (Montana Mystery Ser.). 282p. 23.95 (0-312-20297-0, Saint Martin's Minotaur) St. Martin's Pr.
—The Stick Game: A Montana Mystery Featuring Gabriel Du Pre. 2004. 272p. pap. 13.95 (0-312-32614-9, Saint Martin's Griffin) St. Martin's Pr.
—Thunder Horse. (Montana Mystery Ser.). 1999. 256p. mass mkt. 5.99 (0-312-96887-6, St. Martin's Paperbacks); 1998. 304p. 22.95 o.p. (0-312-18303-8, Saint Martin's Minotaur) St. Martin's Pr.
—Thunder Horse: A Montana Mystery Featuring Gabriel Du Pre. 2003. 256p. pap. 13.95 (0-312-31771-9, Saint Martin's Griffin) St. Martin's Pr.
—Wolf, No Wolf. l.t. ed. 1997. (Core Ser.). 286p. lib. bdg. 25.95 (0-7838-8215-7, Macmillan Reference USA) Gale Group.
—Wolf, No Wolf. 1996. 224p. 20.95 o.p. (0-312-14078-9, Saint Martin's Minotaur); 1997. 226p. mass mkt. 5.99 (0-312-96103-0, St. Martin's Paperbacks) St. Martin's Pr.
—Wolf, No Wolf & Notches: The Third & Fourth Montana Mysteries Featuring Gabriel Du Pre. 2002. 384p. pap. 15.95 (0-312-28963-4, Saint Martin's Griffin) St. Martin's Pr.

DUPREY, RAE (FICTITIOUS CHARACTER)—FICTION

Cuthbert, Margaret. The Silent Cradle. 1999. 496p. mass mkt. 6.99 (0-671-01514-1, Pocket); 1998. 368p. 23.00 o.s.i (0-671-01513-3, Atria) Simon & Schuster.
—The Silent Cradle. abr. ed. 1998. audio 18.00 (0-671-58064-7, 393598, Simon & Schuster Audioworks) Simon & Schuster Audio.
—The Silent Cradle. abr. ed. 1999. audio 16.85 (0-671-01116-2) Ulverscroft Audio (U.S.A.).

DURANT, QUINCY (FICTITIOUS CHARACTER)—FICTION

Thomas, Ross. Chinaman's Chance. 1979. pap. 2.25 o.p. (0-380-41517-8, 41517-8, Avon Bks.) Morrow/Avon.
—Chinaman's Chance, unabr. ed. 1985. (Durant & Wu Ser.). audio 60.00 (1-55690-100-3, 85450E7) Recorded Bks., LLC.
—Chinaman's Chance. 1978. 9.95 o.p. (0-671-24070-6, Simon & Schuster) Simon & Schuster.
—Chinaman's Chance. 1988. 352p. mass mkt. 5.99 o.s.i (0-445-40725-5) Warner Bks., Inc.
—Out on the Rim. E-Book 13.95 (0-312-70961-7) Holtzbrinck Pubs.
—Out on the Rim. 1987. 320p. 17.95 o.p. (0-89296-212-7) Mysterious Pr.
—Out on the Rim, unabr. ed. 1988. (Durant & Wu Ser.). audio 70.00 (1-55690-399-5, 88883E7) Recorded Bks., LLC.
—Out on the Rim. 2003. 336p. reprint ed. pap. 13.95 (0-312-29059-4, Saint Martin's Griffin) St. Martin's Pr.

—Out on the Rim. 1988. 336p. mass mkt. 5.99 o.s.i (*0-445-40693-3*) Warner Bks., Inc.

—Voodoo, Ltd. l.t. ed. 1993. (General Ser.). 367p. lib. bdg. 21.95 (*0-8161-5679-4*, Macmillan Reference USA) Gale Group.

—Voodoo, Ltd. 1992. 288p. 19.95 (*0-89296-451-0*) Mysterious Pr.

—Voodoo, Ltd., unabr. ed. 1993. (Durant & Wu Ser.). audio 51.00 (*1-55690-785-0*, 93105E7) Recorded Bks., LLC.

—Voodoo, Ltd. 1993. 320p. mass mkt. 5.99 (*0-446-40030-0*, Mysterious Pr. Paperback Bks.) Warner Bks., Inc.

### DURELL, SAM (FICTITIOUS CHARACTER)—FICTION

Aarons, Edward S. Assignment—Afghan Dragon. 1982. (Assignment Ser.). mass mkt. 2.25 o.s.i (*0-449-14085-7*, Fawcett) Ballantine Bks.

—Assignment—Amazon Queen. 1976. (Assignment Ser.). mass mkt. 1.25 o.s.i (*0-449-13544-6*, Fawcett) Ballantine Bks.

—Assignment—Angelina. 1986. mass mkt. 2.25 o.s.i (*0-449-12989-6*, M2989, Fawcett) Ballantine Bks.

—Assignment—Ankara. 1975. 176p. pap. 1.25 o.p. (*0-449-13377-X*, P3377, Fawcett) Ballantine Bks.

—Assignment—Black Viking. 1978. (Assignment Ser.). mass mkt. 1.75 o.s.i (*0-449-14017-2*, Fawcett) Ballantine Bks.

—Assignment—Budapest. 1977. mass mkt. 1.25 o.s.i (*0-449-13785-6*, Fawcett) Ballantine Bks.

—Assignment—Ceylon. 1981. (Assignment Ser.). 208p. mass mkt. 1.95 o.s.i (*0-449-13583-7*, Fawcett) Ballantine Bks.

—Assignment—Helene. 1978. (Sam Durrell Ser.). mass mkt. 1.50 o.s.i (*0-449-13955-7*, Fawcett) Ballantine Bks.

—Assignment—Lili Lamaris. 1978. (Assignment Ser.). mass mkt. 1.50 o.s.i (*0-449-13934-4*, Fawcett) Ballantine Bks.

—Assignment—Mermaid. 1979. (Assignment Ser.). mass mkt. 1.75 o.s.i (*0-449-14203-5*, Fawcett) Ballantine Bks.

—Assignment—Moon Girl. 1977. pap. 1.50 o.s.i (*0-449-13856-9*, Fawcett) Ballantine Bks.

—Assignment—Nuclear Nude. 1984. 192p. mass mkt. 2.95 o.s.i (*0-449-12815-6*, Fawcett) Ballantine Bks.

—Assignment—Quayle Question. 1979. pap. 1.75 o.s.i (*0-449-14226-4*, Fawcett); 1977. mass mkt. 1.50 o.s.i (*0-449-13823-2*) Ballantine Bks.

—Assignment—Star Stealers. 1977. mass mkt. 1.50 o.s.i (*0-449-13944-1*, Fawcett) Ballantine Bks.

—Assignment—the Girl in the Gondola. (Assignment Ser.). 1979. mass mkt. 1.75 (*0-449-14165-9*, Fawcett); 1977. mass mkt. 1.50 o.s.i (*0-449-13897-6*) Ballantine Bks.

—Assignment—Unicorn. 1978. mass mkt. 1.50 o.s.i (*0-449-13998-0*, Fawcett) Ballantine Bks.

—Assignment—Zoraya. 1981. (Assignment Ser.). mass mkt. 1.95 o.s.i (*0-449-14184-5*, Fawcett) Ballantine Bks.

—Assignment Bangkok. l.t. ed. 1988. 20.95 o.p. (*1-55504-622-3*); pap. 18.95 o.p. (*1-55504-623-1*) BBC Audiobooks America.

—Assignment Bangkok. 1988. 192p. mass mkt. 3.95 o.s.i (*0-449-13343-5*, P3343-125, Fawcett) Ballantine Bks.

—Assignment Black Gold. l.t. ed. 1988. 20.95 o.p. (*1-55504-537-5*); pap. 18.95 o.p. (*1-55504-514-6*) BBC Audiobooks America.

—Assignment Black Gold. 1980. (Assignment Ser.). 92p. mass mkt. 1.95 o.s.i (*0-449-13354-0*, Fawcett) Ballantine Bks.

—Assignment Golden Girl. (Assignment Ser.). 1981. mass mkt. 2.25 o.s.i (*0-449-14140-3*, Fawcett); 1977. mass mkt. 1.50 o.s.i (*0-449-13801-1*) Ballantine Bks.

—Assignment Maltese Maiden. l.t. ed. 1992. (Adventure Travel Guide Ser.). 368p. 29.99 o.p. (*0-7089-2618-5*, Ulverscroft) Thorpe, F. A. Pubs. GBR. *Dist:* Ulverscroft Large Print Bks., Ltd., Ulverscroft Large Print Canada, Ltd.

—Assignment Manchurian Doll. l.t. ed. 1990. 12.95 o.p. (*0-7927-0225-5*); pap. 16.95 o.p. (*0-7927-0226-3*, C0246) BBC Audiobooks America.

—Assignment Manchurian Doll. 1979. (Assignment Ser.). mass mkt. 1.75 o.s.i (*0-449-13449-0*, Fawcett) Ballantine Bks.

—Assignment Palermo. l.t. ed. 1989. (Linford Mystery Large Print Ser.). pap. 17.99 o.p. (*0-7089-6741-8*, Linford) Thorpe, F. A. Pubs. GBR. *Dist:* Ulverscroft Large Print Bks., Ltd., Ulverscroft Large Print Canada, Ltd.

—Assignment Peking. l.t. ed. 1989. 19.95 o.p. (*1-55504-837-4*, 311) BBC Audiobooks America.

—Assignment Silver Scorpion. l.t. ed. 1991. 12.95 o.p. (*1-55504-914-1*, 37); pap. 10.95 o.p. (*1-55504-915-X*, 235) BBC Audiobooks America.

—Assignment Silver Scorpion. 1979. mass mkt. 1.95 o.s.i (*0-449-14294-9*, Fawcett); 1976. mass mkt. 1.50 o.s.i (*0-449-13615-9*) Ballantine Bks.

—Assignment Sulu Sea. l.t. ed. 1990. pap. 16.95 o.p. (*0-7927-0426-6*, C0485); 18.95 o.p. (*0-7927-0425-8*, C0257) BBC Audiobooks America.

—Assignment Sulu Sea. 1981. (Assignment Ser.). 160p. mass mkt. 1.95 o.s.i (*0-449-13875-5*, Fawcett) Ballantine Bks.

—Assignment to Disaster. l.t. ed. 1993. (Linford Mystery Library). 368p. pap. 17.99 o.p. (*0-7089-7429-5*, Linford) Thorpe, F. A. Pubs. GBR. *Dist:* Ulverscroft Large Print Bks., Ltd., Ulverscroft Large Print Canada, Ltd.

—Assignment Treason. l.t. ed. 1991. 12.95 o.p. (*0-7927-0029-5*, 454); pap. 10.95 o.p. (*0-7927-0030-9*, 518) BBC Audiobooks America.

—Assignment Treason. 1977. mass mkt. 1.50 o.s.i (*0-449-13913-1*, Fawcett) Ballantine Bks.

—Sam Durell: Assignment Suicide. l.t. ed. 1988. pap. 17.95 o.p. (*1-55504-708-4*); lib. bdg. 19.95 o.p. (*1-55504-732-7*) BBC Audiobooks America.

### DURSTON, BRIAN (FICTITIOUS CHARACTER)—FICTION

Martin, Stephen H. Death in Advertising: A Whodunit. 1997. 256p. pap. 14.95 (*0-9646601-1-3*) Oaklea Pr., The.

### DUVAKIN, IVAN (FICTITIOUS CHARACTER)—FICTION

Olcott, Anthony. Rough Beast. 1992. 320p. text 20.00 (*0-684-19406-6*, Scribner) Simon & Schuster.

### DUVALL, CHENEY (FICTITIOUS CHARACTER)—FICTION

Morris, Lynn & Morris, Gilbert. Cheney Duvall, M. D. Series, Vols. 1-3. 1995. (Cheney Duvall, M. D. Ser.). pap. 29.99 o.p. (*1-55661-798-4*, 252798) Bethany Hse. Pubs.

—A City Not Forsaken. 1995. (Cheney Duvall, M. D. Ser.: Bk. 3). 336p. pap. 11.99 (*1-55661-424-1*) Bethany Hse. Pubs.

—A City Not Forsaken. 2000. (Christian Fiction Ser.: Bk. 3). 312p. 23.95 (*0-7862-2227-1*, Five Star); 1997. (Inspirational Ser.). 498p. lib. bdg. 23.95 (*0-7838-2025-9*, Macmillan Reference USA) Gale Group.

—Driven with the Wind. 2000. (Cheney Duvall, M. D. Ser.: 8). (Illus.). 320p. pap. 11.99 (*1-55661-699-6*) Bethany Hse. Pubs.

—Driven with the Wind. 2002. (Five Star Christian Fiction Ser.). 376p. 24.95 (*0-7862-4790-8*, Five Star) Gale Group.

—In the Twilight, in the Evening, 6. 1997. (Cheney Duvall, M. D. Ser.: Vol. 6). 320p. pap. 11.99 (*1-55661-427-6*) Bethany Hse. Pubs.

—In the Twilight, in the Evening. 1998. 23.95 (*0-7862-1365-5*, Five Star) Gale Group.

—Island of the Innocent. 1998. (Cheney Duvall, M. D. Ser.: Bk. 7). 320p. pap. 11.99 (*1-55661-698-8*) Bethany Hse. Pubs.

—The Secret Place of Thunder. 1996. (Cheney Duvall, M. D. Ser.: No. 5). 336p. pap. 11.99 (*1-55661-426-8*) Bethany Hse. Pubs.

—The Secret Place of Thunder. l.t. ed. 1998. (Cheney Duvall, M. D. Ser.: Vol. 5). 393p. 24.95 (*0-7862-1514-3*) Thorndike Pr.

—Shadow of the Mountains. 1994. (Cheney Duvall, M. D. Ser.: No. 2). 336p. pap. 11.99 (*1-55661-423-3*) Bethany Hse. Pubs.

—Shadow of the Mountains. (Christian Fiction Ser.). 1999. 23.95 (*0-7862-2089-9*, Five Star); 1995. 481p. 21.95 (*0-7838-1489-5*, Macmillan Reference USA) Gale Group.

—The Stars for a Light. 1994. (Cheney Duvall, M. D. Ser.: Bk. 1). 320p. pap. 11.99 (*1-55661-422-5*) Bethany Hse. Pubs.

—The Stars for a Light. 1999. (Christian Fiction Ser.: Vol. 1). (Illus.). 344p. 23.95 (*0-7862-1828-2*, Five Star); 1995. 355p. 21.95 o.p. (*0-7838-1376-7*, Macmillan Reference USA) Gale Group.

—Toward the Sunrising. 1996. (Cheney Duvall, M. D. Ser.: Vol. 4). 368p. pap. 11.99 (*1-55661-425-X*) Bethany Hse. Pubs.

—Toward the Sunrising. 1998. (Cheney Duvall, M. D. Ser.: Vol. 4). 362p. 23.95 (*0-7862-1436-8*, Five Star) Gale Group.

### DYER, MANDY (FICTITIOUS CHARACTER)—FICTION

Johnson, Dolores. A Dress to Die For: A Mandy Dyer Mystery. 1998. (Mandy Dyer Mystery Ser.: Vol. 3). 272p. mass mkt. 5.99 (*0-440-22355-5*) Dell Publishing.

—Homicide & Old Lace. 2000. (Mandy Dyer Mystery Ser.). 288p. mass mkt. 5.99 o.s.i (*0-440-23524-3*, Dell Bks.) Dell Publishing.

—Hung up to Die. 1997. (Mandy Dyer Mystery Ser.: Vol. 2). 256p. mass mkt. 5.99 o.s.i (*0-440-22353-9*) Dell Publishing.

—Taken to the Cleaners. 1997. (Mandy Dyer Mystery Ser.: Vol. 1). 272p. mass mkt. 5.50 o.s.i (*0-440-22370-9*) Dell Publishing.

—Wash, Fold & Die: A Mandy Dyer Mystery. 1999. (Mandy Dyer Mystery Ser.). 288p. mass mkt. 5.99 o.s.i (*0-440-23523-5*) Dell Publishing.

### DYKE, TOBY (FICTITIOUS CHARACTER)—FICTION

Ferrars, E. X. Death in Botanists Bay. l.t. ed. 1989. 17.95 o.p. (*0-7089-2070-5*, Ulverscroft) Thorpe, F. A. Pubs. GBR. *Dist:* Ulverscroft Large Print Bks., Ltd.

—Murder of a Suicide. unabr. ed. 2001. audio 54.95 ISIS Audio Bks. GBR. *Dist:* Ulverscroft Large Print Bks., Ltd.

—Murder of a Suicide. l.t. ed. 1997. (Magna Large Print Ser.). 363p. 29.99 o.p. (*0-7505-1202-4*) Magna Large Print Bks. GBR. *Dist:* Ulverscroft Large Print Bks., Ltd.

—Neck in a Noose. l.t. ed. 1995. 288p. pap. 17.95 (*0-7838-1170-5*, Macmillan Reference USA) Gale Group.

—Remove the Bodies. unabr. ed. 1993. audio 54.95 (*0-7451-5922-2*, CAT 4046) BBC Audiobooks America.

—Remove the Bodies. l.t. ed. 1989. (Ulverscroft Large Print Ser.). 390p. 29.99 o.p. (*0-7089-1943-X*, Ulverscroft) Thorpe, F. A. Pubs. GBR. *Dist:* Ulverscroft Large Print Bks., Ltd., Ulverscroft Large Print Canada, Ltd.

## E

### EASTMAN, WARD (FICTITIOUS CHARACTER)—FICTION

Van Valkenburgh, Norman J. Mayhem in the Catskills. 1994. 158p. 25.00 o.p. (*0-935796-60-6*); 2nd ed. pap. 12.50 (*0-935796-59-2*) Purple Mountain Pr., Ltd.

—Mischief in the Catskills: A Ward Eastman Mystery with Five Short Stories. 2001. 159p. pap. 12.50 (*0-935796-94-0*, 94) Purple Mountain Pr., Ltd.

### EASTON, SHARON (FICTITIOUS CHARACTER)—FICTION

Blair, Clifford. The Guns of Sacred Heart. 1991. 192p. 18.95 (*0-8027-4123-1*) Walker & Co.

—Storm over the Lightning L. 1993. 192p. 19.95 (*0-8027-1236-3*) Walker & Co.

### EATON, JAKE (FICTITIOUS CHARACTER)—FICTION

Maness, Larry. Nantucket Revenge: A Jake Eaton Mystery. 1995. 208p. 19.95 o.s.i (*0-89141-566-1*, Presidio Pr.) Ballantine Bks.

—A Once Perfect Place: A Jake Eaton Mystery. 1996. 208p. 19.95 o.s.i (*0-89141-567-X*, Presidio Pr.) Ballantine Bks.

—Strangler: A Jake Eaton Mystery. 1998. 192p. 19.95 o.p. (*0-89141-568-8*, Presidio Pr.) Ballantine Bks.

### EBENEZUM (FICTITIOUS CHARACTER)—FICTION

Gardner, Craig S. A Difficulty with Dwarves. 1987. 192p. (Orig.). mass mkt. 5.99 (*0-441-14779-8*) Ace Bks.

—A Disagreement with Death. 1989. 192p. mass mkt. 5.99 (*0-441-14924-3*) Ace Bks.

—An Excess of Enchantments. 1988. 192p. mass mkt. 5.99 (*0-441-22363-X*) Ace Bks.

—A Malady of Magicks. 1986. 240p. mass mkt. 5.99 o.s.i (*0-441-51662-9*) Ace Bks.

—A Multitude of Monsters. 1986. 208p. mass mkt. 5.99 o.s.i (*0-441-54523-8*) Ace Bks.

—A Night in the Netherhells. 1987. 192p. mass mkt. 5.99 o.s.i (*0-441-02314-2*) Ace Bks.

### EBERHARDT, MARSHA (FICTITIOUS CHARACTER)—FICTION

Berne, Suzanne. A Crime in the Neighborhood. 1997. 294p. tchr. ed. 17.95 (*1-56512-165-1*, 72165) Algonquin Bks. of Chapel Hill.

—A Crime in the Neighborhood. 1998. pap. (*0-8050-5852-4*); 304p. pap. 13.00 (*0-8050-5580-0*) Holt, Henry & Co. (Owl Bks.).

—A Crime in the Neighborhood. unabr. ed. 2000. audio 58.00 (*0-7887-4456-9*, 96277E7) Recorded Bks., LLC.

### ECKERT, JAMES (FICTITIOUS CHARACTER)—FICTION

Dickson, Gordon R. The Dragon & the Djinn. 400p. 1998. mass mkt. 6.99 o.s.i (*0-441-00495-4*); 1996. 21.95 o.p. (*0-441-00297-8*) Ace Bks.

—The Dragon & the Fair Maid of Kent. 2000. 416p. 26.95 (*0-312-86160-5*, Tor Bks.) Doherty, Tom Assocs., LLC.

—The Dragon & the George. 1987. 288p. mass mkt. 6.99 (*0-345-35050-2*, Del Rey); 1978. mass mkt. 1.95 o.p. (*0-345-27201-3*, Del Rey); 1976. mass mkt. 1.95 o.p. (*0-345-25361-2*) Ballantine Bks.

—The Dragon & the Gnarly King. 1998. 480p. mass mkt. 6.99 o.s.i (*0-8125-6270-4*); 1997. 384p. 24.95 o.p. (*0-312-86157-5*) Doherty, Tom Assocs., LLC. (Tor Bks.).

—The Dragon at War. 1993. mass mkt. 5.99 o.s.i (*0-441-16611-3*); 1992. 18.95 o.p. (*0-441-75698-0*) Ace Bks.

—The Dragon in Lyonesse. (Tor Fantasy Ser.). 1999. 608p. mass mkt. 6.99 (*0-8125-6271-2*); 1998. 381p. 25.95 (*0-312-86159-1*) Doherty, Tom Assocs., LLC. (Tor Bks.).

—The Dragon in Lyonesse. 1999. 13.04 (*0-606-17028-6*) Turtleback Bks.

—The Dragon Knight. 1991. 512p. mass mkt. 6.99 o.s.i (*0-8125-0943-9*); Vol. 1. 1990. 19.95 o.p. (*0-312-93129-8*) Doherty, Tom Assocs., LLC. (Tor Bks.).

—The Dragon on the Border. 1993. 400p. mass mkt. 6.99 o.s.i (*0-441-16657-1*); 1992. 18.95 o.p. (*0-441-34233-7*) Ace Bks.

—The Dragon, the Earl & the Troll. 448p. (Orig.). 1996. mass mkt. 6.99 o.s.i (*0-441-00282-X*); 1994. 21.95 o.p. (*0-441-00098-3*) Ace Bks.

### ECKHART, RALPH (FICTITIOUS CHARACTER)—FICTION

Bram, Christopher. Gossip. 352p. 1998. pap. 13.95 o.s.i (*0-452-27338-2*, Plume); 1997. 23.95 o.p. (*0-525-93914-8*) Dutton/Plume.

### EDWARDS, COLIN (FICTITIOUS CHARACTER)—FICTION

Willey, Gordon R. Selena. 1995. (Mystery Ser.). 250p. per. (*0-373-26190-X*, 1-26190-8, Harlequin Bks.) Harlequin Enterprises, Ltd.

—Selena. 1993. 208p. 19.95 (*0-8027-3227-5*) Walker & Co.

### EDWARDS, JANE AMANDA (FICTITIOUS CHARACTER)—FICTION

Russell, Charlotte M. Cook up a Crime. Schantz, Tom & Schantz, Enid, eds. 1998. 160p. reprint ed. pap. 13.00 (*0-915230-18-6*) Rue Morgue Pr.

### EISHEID, EARL (FICTITIOUS CHARACTER)—FICTION

Daley, Robert. To Kill a Cop. 1978. mass mkt. 2.25 o.s.i (*0-345-27644-2*); 1977. mass mkt. 2.25 o.s.i (*0-345-25945-9*) Ballantine Bks.

—To Kill a Cop. 1996. 400p. mass mkt. 6.50 o.s.i (*0-446-36571-8*) Warner Bks., Inc.

### ELDRIDGE, LOUISE (FICTITIOUS CHARACTER)—FICTION

Ripley, Ann. The Christmas Garden Affair. 2003. 304p. mass mkt. 5.99 (*1-57566-778-9*, Kensington Bks.) Kensington Publishing Corp.

—The Christmas Garden Affair: A Gardening Mystery. 2002. 304p. 22.00 (*1-57566-777-0*) Kensington Publishing Corp.

—Death of a Garden Pest. 1996. (Louise Eldridge Mystery Ser.). 288p. 22.95 (*0-312-14311-7*, Saint Martin's Minotaur) St. Martin's Pr.

—Death of a Garden Pest: A Gardening Mystery. 1997. (Gardening Mysteries Ser.). 304p. mass mkt. 5.99 o.s.i (*0-553-57730-1*, Crimeline) Bantam Bks.

—Death of a Political Plant: A Gardening Mystery. 1998. (Gardening Mysteries Ser.). 336p. mass mkt. 5.99 o.s.i (*0-553-57735-2*) Bantam Bks.

—Death of a Political Plant: A Gardening Mystery. unabr. ed. 2001. (Garden Mystery Ser.). audio 39.95 (*1-55686-875-8*) Books in Motion.

—The Garden Tour Affair: A Gardening Mystery. 1999. (Gardening Mysteries Ser.). 320p. mass mkt. 5.99 o.s.i (*0-553-57736-0*); 22.95 o.s.i (*0-553-10693-7*) Bantam Bks.

—Harvest of Murder: A Gardening Mystery. l.t. ed. 2002. 412p. 29.95 (*0-7862-3924-7*) Gale Group.

—Harvest of Murder: A Gardening Mystery. 34p. 2002. mass mkt. 5.99 (*1-57566-776-2*); 2001. 22.00 o.s.i (*1-57566-775-4*) Kensington Publishing Corp.

—Mulch. 1998. (Gardening Mysteries Ser.). (Illus.). 304p. reprint ed. mass mkt. 5.99 (*0-553-57734-4*) Bantam Bks.

—Mulch. 1994. 224p. 19.95 o.p. (*0-312-11029-4*, Saint Martin's Minotaur) St. Martin's Pr.

—The Perennial Killer: A Gardening Mystery. 2000. (Gardening Mysteries Ser.). 352p. mass mkt. 5.99 o.s.i (*0-553-57737-9*); 20.01 (*0-553-10694-5*) Bantam Bks.

### ELEANOR, OF AQUITAINE, CONSORT OF HENRY II, KING OF ENGLAND, 1122?-1204—FICTION

Gregory, Kristiana. Eleanor: Crown Jewel of Aquitaine. 2002. (Royal Diaries Ser.). 112p. (YA). (gr. 4-9). 10.95 (*0-439-16484-2*, Scholastic Pr.) Scholastic, Inc.

Jones, Ellen. Beloved Enemy: A Novel. 1994. 570p. 23.00 (*0-671-87279-6*, Simon & Schuster) Simon & Schuster.

Penman, Sharon Kay. Dragon's Lair: A Medieval Mystery. 2003. 336p. 23.95 (*0-399-15077-3*, Putnam & Grosset) Putnam Publishing Group, The.

—Time & Chance. 2003. 544p. pap. 15.95 (*0-345-39672-3*) Ballantine Bks.

—Time & Chance. 2002. (Illus.). 512p. 27.95 o.s.i (*0-399-14785-3*, Wood, Marian Bks.) Putnam Publishing Group, The.

—When Christ & His Saints Slept. 1996. (Eleanor of Aquitaine Trilogy Ser.: Bk. 1). 768p. pap. 15.95 (*0-345-39668-5*) Ballantine Bks.

**ELIZABETH I, QUEEN OF ENGLAND, 1533-1603—FICTION**

Buckley, Fiona. The Fugitive Queen: An Ursula Blanchard Mystery at Queen Elizabeth I's Court. 2003. 288p. 24.00 (*0-7432-3751-X*, Scribner) Simon & Schuster.

—A Pawn for a Queen: An Ursula Blanchard Mystery at Queen Elizabeth I's Court. 2002. 288p. 24.00 (*0-7432-0265-1*, Scribner) Simon & Schuster.

—Queen of Ambition: An Ursula Blanchard Mystery at Queen Elizabeth I's Court. 2002. 288p. 23.00 (*0-7432-0264-3*, Scribner) Simon & Schuster.

—Queen's Ransom. 2003. 336p. reprint ed. mass mkt. 6.99 (*0-671-03293-3*, Pocket) Simon & Schuster.

—Queen's Ransom: A Mystery at Queen Elizabeth I's Court Featuring Ursula Blanchard. 2000. E-Book 23.00 (*0-7432-1362-9*); 352p. 23.00 o.s.i (*0-684-86267-0*) Simon & Schuster. (Scribner).

—To Ruin a Queen: An Ursula Blanchard Mystery at Queen Elizabeth I's Court. 2000. E-Book 23.00 (*0-7432-1365-3*); (Illus.). 288p. 23.00 o.s.i (*0-684-86268-9*) Simon & Schuster. (Scribner).

Harper, Karen. The Thorne Maze: An Elizabeth I Mystery. 2003. (Elizabeth I Mystery Ser.). 320p. mass mkt. 6.99 (*0-312-99349-8*, St. Martin's Paperbacks); (Illus.). 288p. 23.95 (*0-312-30176-6*, Saint Martin's Minotaur) St. Martin's Pr.

—The Tidal Poole: An Elizabeth I Mystery. (Elizabeth I Mysteries Ser.). 2001. 336p. mass mkt. 6.50 (*0-440-22593-0*); 2000. (Illus.). 304p. 22.95 o.s.i (*0-385-33284-X*, Delacorte Pr.) Dell Publishing.

—The Tidal Poole: An Elizabeth I Mystery. l.t. ed. 2000. (Wheeler Large Print Book Ser.). 306p. 28.95 (*1-56895-894-3*, Wheeler Publishing, Inc.) Gale Group.

Letton, Jennette F. & Letton, Francis. The Robsart Affair. reprint ed. lib. bdg. 22.95 (*0-89190-237-6*, Rivercity Pr.); 1976. 268p. lib. bdg. 22.95 (*0-89244-015-5*, Queens Hse., Inc.) Amereon, Ltd.

Maxwell, Robin. The Wild Irish: A Novel. 2003. 400p. 24.95 (*0-06-009142-8*, Morrow, William & Co.) Morrow/Avon.

Parry, Edward Abbott. England's Elizabeth. E-Book 3.95 (*0-594-02713-6*) 1873 Pr.

Powers, Anne. Queen's Ransom. 1986. 400p. reprint ed. mass mkt. 3.95 o.s.i (*0-8439-2352-0*) Dorchester Publishing Co., Inc.

**ELLER, JACK (FICTITIOUS CHARACTER)—FICTION**

Haymon, S. T. A Beautiful Death. 1993. 19.95 o.p. (*0-312-10420-0*, Saint Martin's Minotaur) St. Martin's Pr.

—Death & the Pregnant Virgin. 208p. 1991. mass mkt. 2.50 o.s.i (*0-553-18513-6*); 1984. pap. text 2.95 o.p. (*0-553-23703-9*) Bantam Bks.

—Death & the Pregnant Virgin. unabr. ed. 1993. audio 61.95 (*1-85089-848-0*, 40791) ISIS Audio Bks. GBR. *Dist:* Ulverscroft Large Print Bks., Ltd.

—Death & the Pregnant Virgin. 1980. 224p. 9.95 o.p. (*0-312-18592-8*) St. Martin's Pr.

—Death of a God. 1990. 256p. mass mkt. 3.95 o.s.i (*0-553-27266-7*) Bantam Bks.

—Death of a God. 1992. 1.99 o.p. (*0-517-08388-4*) Random Hse. Value Publishing.

—Death of a God. 1987. 224p. 14.95 o.p. (*0-312-00119-3*) St. Martin's Pr.

—Death of a Hero. l.t. ed. 2000. pap. 21.99 (*0-7531-6225-3*) ISIS Large Print Bks. GBR. *Dist:* Ulverscroft Large Print Bks., Ltd., Ulverscroft Large Print Canada, Ltd.

—Death of a Hero. 1996. 256p. 21.95 o.p. (*0-312-14582-9*, Saint Martin's Minotaur) St. Martin's Pr.

—Death of a Warrior Queen. l.t. ed. 1996. 352p. 24.95 (*1-85695-334-3*) ISIS Large Print Bks. GBR. *Dist:* Transaction Pubs.

—Death of a Warrior Queen. 1991. 224p. 17.95 o.p. (*0-312-06950-2*, Saint Martin's Minotaur) St. Martin's Pr.

—Ritual Murder. 1991. 256p. mass mkt. 4.50 o.s.i (*0-553-29385-0*) Bantam Bks.

—Ritual Murder. 1984. 256p. pap. 2.50 o.p. (*0-523-42175-3*, Pinnacle Bks.) Kensington Publishing Corp.

—Ritual Murder. 1982. 224p. 11.95 o.p. (*0-312-68478-9*) St. Martin's Pr.

—Stately Homicide. 1984. 11.95 o.p. (*0-312-75708-5*) St. Martin's Pr.

—Stately Homicide. 1985. 256p. mass mkt. 3.50 o.s.i (*0-445-20161-4*) Warner Bks., Inc.

—A Very Particular Murder. 1991. 288p. mass mkt. 4.50 o.s.i (*0-553-28880-6*) Bantam Bks.

—A Very Particular Murder. 1992. 2.99 o.p. (*0-517-09061-9*) Random Hse. Value Publishing.

—A Very Particular Murder. 1989. 16.95 o.p. (*0-312-02998-5*) St. Martin's Pr.

**ELLIOT, ELIZABETH (FICTITIOUS CHARACTER)—FICTION**

Allen, Irene. Quaker Indictment: An Elizabeth Elliot Mystery. 256p. 1999. (Quaker Sojourn Ser.: 4). (Illus.). mass mkt. 5.99 (*0-312-96684-9*, St. Martin's Paperbacks); 1997. (Elizabeth Elliot Mystery Ser.). 21.95 o.p. (*0-312-16970-1*, Saint Martin's Minotaur) St. Martin's Pr.

—Quaker Silence: An Elizabeth Elliot Mystery. 1992. 210p. 17.00 o.s.i (*0-679-41414-2*, Villard Bks.) Random House Adult Trade Publishing Group.

—Quaker Testimony. 272p. 1996. text 21.95 o.p. (*0-312-14709-0*, Saint Martin's Minotaur); Vol. 1. 1998. (Quaker Testimony Ser.: Vol. 1). (Illus.). mass mkt. 5.99 (*0-312-96424-2*, St. Martin's Paperbacks) St. Martin's Pr.

—Quaker Witness. 1993. 254p. 18.00 o.s.i (*0-679-41415-0*, Villard Bks.) Random House Adult Trade Publishing Group.

—Quaker Witness. 2001. 272p. mass mkt. 5.99 (*0-312-97285-7*, St. Martin's Paperbacks) St. Martin's Pr.

**ELLIOTT, EVE (FICTITIOUS CHARACTER)—FICTION**

Lee, Barbara. Dead Man's Fingers. 1999. (Chesapeake Bay Mysteries Ser.). 276p. 22.95 o.p. (*0-312-20524-4*, Saint Martin's Minotaur) St. Martin's Pr.

—Death in Still Waters: A Chesapeake Bay Mystery. 1996. 226p. pap. text 5.50 (*0-312-95780-7*, St. Martin's Paperbacks); 1995. 240p. 20.95 o.p. (*0-312-13048-1*, Saint Martin's Minotaur) St. Martin's Pr.

—Final Closing. 1999. (WWL Mystery Ser.: No. 304). per. (*0-373-26304-X*, 1-26304-5, Worldwide Library) Harlequin Enterprises, Ltd.

—Final Closing: An Eve Elliot Mystery. 1997. (Eve Elliot Mystery Ser.). 304p. 22.95 o.p. (*0-312-16762-8*, Saint Martin's Minotaur) St. Martin's Pr.

**ELLIOTT, MAGGIE (FICTITIOUS CHARACTER)—FICTION**

Armbruster, Ann & Taylor, Elizabeth Atwood. Astronaut Training. 1990. (First Bks.). (Illus.). 64p. (J). (gr. 5-8). mass mkt. 12.90 o.p. (*0-531-10862-7*, Watts, Franklin) Scholastic Library Publishing.

Taylor, Elizabeth Atwood. The Cable Car Murder. 1988. 240p. reprint ed. mass mkt. 4.99 o.s.i (*0-8041-0281-3*, Ivy Bks.) Ballantine Bks.

—The Cable Car Murder. (Fingerprint Mysteries Ser.). 224p. 1983. pap. 5.95 o.p. (*0-312-11312-9*, Saint Martin's Griffin); 1981. 11.95 o.p. (*0-312-11311-0*) St. Martin's Pr.

—The Cable Car Murders. l.t. ed. 1982. 412p. reprint ed. 12.95 o.p. (*0-89621-360-9*) Thorndike Pr.

—Murder at Vassar. 1988. mass mkt. 4.95 o.s.i (*0-8041-0212-0*, Ivy Bks.) Ballantine Bks.

—Murder at Vassar. 1987. 256p. 15.95 o.p. (*0-312-00160-6*) St. Martin's Pr.

—The Northwest Murders. 1992. 288p. 18.95 o.p. (*0-312-07753-X*, Saint Martin's Minotaur) St. Martin's Pr.

**ELLIOTT, SCOTT (FICTITIOUS CHARACTER)—FICTION**

Faherty, Terence. Come Back Dead. 1997. 336p. 22.00 o.p. (*0-684-83084-1*, Simon & Schuster) Simon & Schuster.

—Kill Me Again: A Scott Elliott Mystery. 1996. 304p. 22.00 o.p. (*0-684-82688-7*, Simon & Schuster) Simon & Schuster.

—Raise the Devil. 2000. (Scott Elliott Mysteries Ser.). 264p. 23.95 (*0-312-26640-5*, Saint Martin's Minotaur) St. Martin's Pr.

**ELLIS, DUSTY (FICTITIOUS CHARACTER)—FICTION**

Harrell, Janice. The Murder Game. Ashby, Ruth, ed. 1993. 160p. (Orig.). (J). mass mkt. 2.99 (*0-671-78541-9*, Simon Pulse) Simon & Schuster Children's Publishing.

**ELLSWORTH, PETER (FICTITIOUS CHARACTER)—FICTION**

Schiele, Paul. Chasing the Wild Geese: Another Peter Ellsworth Mystery. Ewing, Jeanne B., ed. 1996. 200p. (Orig.). pap. 20.95 (*1-884690-12-2*) Owl Pr., The.

—Under Cover of Night: A Peter Ellsworth Mystery. 1995. 235p. (Orig.). pap. 19.95 (*1-884690-16-5*) Owl Pr., The.

**ELM CREEK QUILTERS (FICTITIOUS CHARACTERS)—FICTION**

Chiaverini, Jennifer. The Cross-Country Quilters: An Elm Creek Quilts Novel. 2002. 368p. pap. 13.00 (*0-452-28308-6*, Plume) Dutton/Plume.

—The Cross-Country Quilters: An Elm Creek Quilts Novel. l.t. ed. 2001. 495p. 29.95 (*0-7838-9559-3*, Macmillan Reference USA) Gale Group.

—The Cross-Country Quilters: An Elm Creek Quilts Novel. 2001. 368p. 21.00 (*0-7432-0257-0*, Simon & Schuster) Simon & Schuster.

—The Master Quilter: An Elm Creek Quilts Novel. 2004. (Illus.). 256p. 22.00 (*0-7432-3615-7*, Simon & Schuster) Simon & Schuster.

—The Quilter's Apprentice. l.t. ed. 2003. 426p. 28.95 (*0-7862-5740-7*) Thorndike Pr.

—The Quilter's Apprentice: A Novel. 2000. 272p. pap. 13.00 (*0-452-28172-5*, Plume) Dutton/Plume.

—The Quilter's Apprentice: A Novel. 1999. 272p. 18.00 (*0-684-84972-0*, Simon & Schuster) Simon & Schuster.

—Quilter's Legacy. 2004. 320p. pap. 13.00 (*0-452-28467-8*, Plume) Dutton/Plume.

—The Quilter's Legacy. l.t. ed. 2003. 438p. 30.95 (*0-7862-5568-4*) Thorndike Pr.

—The Quilter's Legacy: An Elm Creek Quilts Novel. 2003. (Illus.). 320p. 22.00 (*0-7432-3613-0*, Simon & Schuster) Simon & Schuster.

—Round Robin: An Elm Creek Quilts Novel. 2001. 304p. pap. 13.00 (*0-452-28227-6*, Plume) Dutton/ Plume.

—Round Robin: An Elm Creek Quilts Novel. l.t. ed. 2000. (Large Print Bks.). 420p. pap. 24.95 (*1-56895-952-4*, Wheeler Publishing, Inc.) Gale Group.

—Round Robin: An Elm Creek Quilts Novel. 2000. 336p. 20.00 (*0-684-86892-X*, Simon & Schuster) Simon & Schuster.

—The Runaway Quilt: An Elm Creek Quilts Novel. 2003. 336p. reprint ed. pap. 13.00 (*0-452-28398-1*, Plume) Dutton/Plume.

—The Runaway Quilt: An Elm Creek Quilts Novel. 2002. (Illus.). 336p. 21.00 (*0-7432-2226-1*, Simon & Schuster) Simon & Schuster.

—The Runaway Quilt: An Elm Creek Quilts Novel. l.t. ed. 2002. (Core Ser.). 29.95 (*0-7862-4472-0*) Thorndike Pr.

**ELORA DANAN (FICTITIOUS CHARACTER)—FICTION**

Claremont, Chris & Lucas, George. Shadow Dawn: Second in the Chronicles of the Shadow War. 1998. (Shadow Wars Ser.). 544p. reprint ed. mass mkt. 6.99 (*0-553-57289-X*) Bantam Bks.

—Shadow Moon. 1995. 464p. pap. 12.99 o.s.i (*0-593-03926-2*) Bantam Bks.

—Shadow Moon: First in the Chronicles of the Shadow War. 1996. 464p. mass mkt. 7.50 (*0-553-57285-7*) Bantam Bks.

—Shadow Star. 2000. (Shadow Wars Ser.). 544p. mass mkt. 6.50 (*0-553-57288-1*) Bantam Bks.

**ELRIC OF MELNIBONE (FICTITIOUS CHARACTER)—FICTION**

Moorcock, Michael. The Bane of the Black Sword. 1987. (Elric Saga). 160p. mass mkt. 5.99 o.s.i (*0-441-04885-4*) Ace Bks.

—The Bane of the Black Sword. 1986. 160p. 2.95 o.s.i (*0-425-10132-0*); 1986. 2.95 o.s.i (*0-425-09281-X*); 1985. 2.95 o.s.i (*0-425-08503-1*); 1984. 2.75 o.s.i (*0-425-07636-9*); 1984. 2.50 o.s.i (*0-425-06537-5*) Berkley Publishing Group.

—The Bane of the Black Sword. 1977. mass mkt. 1.50 o.p. (*0-87997-421-4*); mass mkt. 1.95 o.p. (*0-87997-628-4*); mass mkt. 1.75 o.p. (*0-87997-515-6*); mass mkt. 1.25 o.p. (*0-87997-316-1*);No. 5. mass mkt. 2.25 o.p. (*0-87997-805-8*, UE1805) DAW Bks., Inc.

—Elric at the End of Time. 1985. (Elric Saga). mass mkt. 2.95 o.p. (*0-88677-040-8*); 224p. mass mkt. 4.50 o.p. (*0-88677-228-1*) DAW Bks., Inc.

—Elric at the End of Time. 1985. (Elric Saga). 224p. mass mkt. 4.50 o.s.i (*0-88677-410-1*, Abrahams, William Bks.) Dutton/Plume.

—Elric of Melnibone. 1987. (Elric Saga: Bk. 1). 192p. mass mkt. 5.99 o.s.i (*0-441-20398-1*) Ace Bks.

—Elric of Melnibone. (Elric Saga). 1986. 192p. 2.95 o.s.i (*0-425-09957-1*); 1985. 2.95 o.s.i (*0-425-08843-X*); 1985. 2.95 o.s.i (*0-425-08195-8*); 1984. 2.75 o.s.i (*0-425-07634-2*); 1983. 2.50 o.s.i (*0-425-06044-6*) Berkley Publishing Group.

—Elric of Melnibone. 1976. (Elric Saga). mass mkt. 1.95 o.p. (*0-87997-644-6*); mass mkt. 1.50 o.p. (*0-87997-356-0*, UW1356); mass mkt. 2.25 o.p. (*0-87997-734-5*); mass mkt. 1.25 o.p. (*0-87997-259-9*) DAW Bks., Inc.

—The Fortress of the Pearl. (Elric Saga: Bk. 7). 1990. mass mkt. 4.99 o.s.i (*0-441-24866-7*); 1989. 16.95 o.p. (*0-441-19123-1*) Ace Bks.

—The Revenge of the Rose. 1994. 256p. mass mkt. 5.99 o.s.i (*0-441-00106-8*); 1991. 17.95 o.p. (*0-441-71844-2*) Ace Bks.

—The Sailor on the Seas of Fate. 1987. (Elric Saga: Bk. 2). 160p. mass mkt. 5.99 o.s.i (*0-441-74863-5*) Ace Bks.

—The Sailor on the Seas of Fate. 1987. 160p. 2.95 o.s.i (*0-425-10329-3*) Berkley Publishing Group.

—The Skrayling Tree: The Albino in America. (Elric Noel Book Ser.: No. 2). 2004. mass mkt. (*0-446-61340-1*); 2003. 336p. 24.95 (*0-446-53104-9*) Warner Bks., Inc. (Aspect).

—Stormbringer. 1987. (Elric Saga: Vol. 6). mass mkt. 5.50 o.s.i (*0-441-78754-1*) Ace Bks.

—Stormbringer. (Elric Saga: No. 6). 1986. 224p. 2.95 o.s.i (*0-425-10249-1*); 1986. 2.95 o.s.i (*0-425-09280-1*); 1984. 2.50 o.s.i (*0-425-06559-6*) Berkley Publishing Group.

—Stormbringer. 1977. (Elric Saga). mass mkt. 2.50 o.p. (*0-87997-755-8*); mass mkt. 1.50 o.p. (*0-87997-335-8*); mass mkt. 2.75 o.p. (*0-87997-842-2*); mass mkt. 2.25 o.p. (*0-87997-691-8*); mass mkt. 1.75 o.p. (*0-87997-574-1*) DAW Bks., Inc.

—The Vanishing Tower. 1987. (Elric Saga: Vol. 4). 176p. mass mkt. 5.99 o.s.i (*0-441-86039-7*) Ace Bks.

—The Vanishing Tower. 1986. 2.95 o.s.i (*0-425-10171-1*); 1986. 2.95 o.s.i (*0-425-09535-5*); 1984. 2.75 o.s.i (*0-425-07762-4*); 1983. 2.50 o.s.i (*0-425-06406-9*) Berkley Publishing Group.

—The Vanishing Tower. 1977. mass mkt. 1.75 o.p. (*0-87997-553-9*); mass mkt. 2.50 o.p. (*0-87997-796-5*); mass mkt. 2.25 o.p. (*0-87997-693-4*); mass mkt. 1.50 o.p. (*0-87997-406-0*); mass mkt. 1.25 o.p. (*0-87997-304-8*) DAW Bks., Inc.

—The Weird of the White Wolf, Vol. 3. 1988. (Elric Saga: Bk. 3). 160p. mass mkt. 5.99 o.s.i (*0-441-88805-4*) Ace Bks.

—The Weird of the White Wolf. 1985. 2.95 o.s.i (*0-425-08904-5*); 1985. 2.95 o.s.i (*0-425-08267-9*); 1984. 2.50 o.s.i (*0-425-07176-6*); 1983. 2.50 o.s.i (*0-425-06289-9*) Berkley Publishing Group.

—The Weird of the White Wolf. 1977. mass mkt. 1.25 o.p. (*0-87997-286-6*); mass mkt. 1.50 o.p. (*0-87997-390-0*); mass mkt. 1.75 o.p. (*0-87997-528-8*) DAW Bks., Inc.

Moorcock, Michael & Matthews, Rodney. Elric at the End of Time. 9999. (Illus.). 128p. pap. 17.95 o.p. (*1-85028-032-0*) Penguin Group (USA) Inc.

**EMERSON, STRETCH (FICTITIOUS CHARACTER)—FICTION**

Grover, Marshall. Emerson's Hex: Larry & Stretch. l.t. ed. 1994. (Linford Western Library). 272p. pap. 17.99 (*0-7089-7490-2*, Ulverscroft) Thorpe, F. A. Pubs. GBR. *Dist:* Ulverscroft Large Print Bks., Ltd., Ulverscroft Large Print Canada, Ltd.

—Turn the Key on Emerson: Larry & Stretch. l.t. ed. 1991. (Linford Western Library). pap. 17.99 (*0-7089-6966-6*, Linford) Thorpe, F. A. Pubs. GBR. *Dist:* Ulverscroft Large Print Bks., Ltd., Ulverscroft Large Print Canada, Ltd.

**EMORY, ARIANE (FICTITIOUS CHARACTER)—FICTION**

Cherryh, C. J. Cyteen. 1988. 18.45 o.s.i (*0-446-51428-4*); 1995. 696p. reprint ed. pap. 14.99 (*0-446-67127-4*) Warner Bks., Inc.

—Cyteen Pt. 1: The Betrayal. 1989. 368p. mass mkt. 5.50 (*0-445-20452-4*, Aspect) Warner Bks., Inc.

—Cyteen Pt. 2: The Rebirth. 1989. 256p. mass mkt. 4.99 o.s.i (*0-445-20454-0*) Warner Bks., Inc.

—Cyteen Pt. 3: The Vindication. 1989. 320p. mass mkt. 5.50 o.s.i (*0-445-20430-3*) Warner Bks., Inc.

**ENAMORADO, DAVE (FICTITIOUS CHARACTER)—FICTION**

Jackson, Hialeah. The Alligator's Farewell. 1998. (Annabelle Hardy Mystery Ser.: No. 1). 368p. mass mkt. 5.99 o.s.i (*0-440-22660-0*) Dell Publishing.

**ENDER (FICTITIOUS CHARACTER)—FICTION**

Card, Orson Scott. Children of the Mind. 1997. (Ender Ser.: Bk. 4). 370p. mass mkt. 7.99 (*0-8125-2239-7*); 1996. (Ender Ser.: Bk. 4). 352p. 23.95 o.p. (*0-312-85395-5*); 1996. (Ender Ser.: Bk. 4). 200.00 (*0-312-86191-5*); 2002. 352p. reprint ed. pap. 15.95 (*0-7653-0474-0*) Doherty, Tom Assocs., LLC. (Tor Bks.).

—Children of the Mind. 1997. (Ender Wiggin Ser.). 13.04 (*0-606-17120-7*) Turtleback Bks.

—The Ender Wiggin Saga. abr. ed. 1999. audio 44.95 (*1-55927-575-8*); Set. 1993. audio 29.95 (*1-55927-249-X*) Audio Renaissance.

—Ender's Game. abr. ed. 1991. audio 15.95 o.p. (*1-55927-162-0*) Audio Renaissance.

—Ender's Game. Date not set. mass mkt. (*0-7655-5070-9*, Tor Bks.); 2000. (Ender Ser.: Bk. 1). 349p. mass mkt. 3.99 o.p. (*0-8125-8904-1*, Tor Bks.); 1994. (Ender Ser.: Bk. 1). 384p. mass mkt. 6.99 (*0-8125-2358-X*, Tor Bks.); 1992. (Ender Ser.: Bk. 1). 256p. pap. 13.95 (*0-312-85323-8*, Tor Bks.); 1991. (Ender Ser.: Bk. 1). mass mkt. 4.95 o.s.i (*0-8125-1349-5*, Tor Bks.); 1987. (Ender Ser.: Bk. 1). pap. 3.95 o.s.i (*0-8125-3355-0*, Tor Bks.); ltd. ed. 1992. (Ender Ser.: Bk. 1). 256p. 200.00 (*0-312-85402-1*, Tor Bks.); 2002. 324p. (J). reprint ed. mass mkt. 5.99 (*0-7653-4229-4*, Starscape); 1991. (Ender Ser.: Bk. 1). 368p. reprint ed. mass mkt. 4.99 o.s.i (*0-8125-1911-6*, Tor Bks.); rev. ed. 1994. (Ender Ser.: Bk. 1). 384p. pap. 6.99 (*0-8125-5070-6*, Tor Bks.); 4th rev. ed. 1985. (Ender Ser.: Bk. 1). 226p. 24.95 (*0-312-93208-1*, Tor Bks.) Doherty, Tom Assocs., LLC.

—Ender's Game. 1993. audio 55.00 (*1-56544-043-9*, 550001); audio Literate Ear, Inc.

—Ender's Game. 1985. (Ender Ser.: Bk. 1). 13.04 (*0-606-04043-9*) Turtleback Bks.

—Ender's Shadow. Date not set. E-Book (*0-312-70367-8*, Tor Bks.); (Ender Ser.: Bk. 5). mass mkt., tchr. ed. (*0-7653-4061-5*, Tor Bks.); (Ender Ser.: Bk. 5). E-Book 47.80 (*0-312-27772-5*, Tor

Characters

Bks.); 2002. (YA). (gr. 5 up). mass mkt. 5.99 (*0-7653-4240-5*, Starscape); 2000. (Ender Ser.: Bk. 5). 469p. mass mkt. 7.99 (*0-8125-7571-7*, Tor Bks.); 2000. (Ender Ser.: Bk. 5). 24.95 (*0-312-85758-6*, Tor Bks.); deluxe ed. 2000. (Ender Ser.: Bk. 5). 384p. lib. bdg. 200.00 (*0-312-87297-6*, Tor Bks.); 5th ed. 1999. (Ender Ser.: Bk. 5). 379p. 24.95 (*0-312-86860-X*, Tor Bks.) Doherty, Tom Assocs., LLC.

—Ender's Shadow. abr. ed. 1999. audio 25.00 (*0-7871-1997-0*) NewStar Media, Inc.

—Ender's Shadow. (Ender Ser.: Bk. 5). E-Book 24.95 (*0-312-87922-9*) St. Martin's Pr.

—Ender's Shadow. 2000. 13.04 (*0-606-20510-1*) Turtleback Bks.

—Shadow of the Hegemon. 2001. (Ender Ser.: Bk. 6). 365p. trans. 25.95 (*0-312-87651-3*); 464p. reprint ed. mass mkt. 7.99 (*0-8125-6595-9*) Doherty, Tom Assocs., LLC. (Tor Bks.).

—Shadow Puppets. E-Book 25.95 (*0-312-70713-4*); 2002. 352p. 200.00 o.s.i (*0-7653-0475-9*); 2002. 352p. 25.95 (*0-7653-0017-6*) Doherty, Tom Assocs., LLC. (Tor Bks.).

—Speaker for the Dead. abr. ed. audio 15.95 o.p. (*1-55927-160-4*) Audio Renaissance.

—Speaker for the Dead. (Ender Ser.: Bk. 2). 1994. 382p. mass mkt. 7.99 (*0-8125-5075-7*); 1992. 280p. pap. 13.95 (*0-312-85325-4*); 1991. 432p. mass mkt. 4.95 o.s.i (*0-8125-1350-9*); 1987. mass mkt. 3.95 o.s.i (*0-8125-3257-0*); rev. ed. 1991. 416p. mass mkt. 5.99 o.s.i (*0-8125-2015-7*); 2nd ed. 1986. 280p. 24.95 (*0-312-93738-5*) Doherty, Tom Assocs., LLC. (Tor Bks.).

—Speaker for the Dead. 1993. audio. audio 63.40 (*1-56544-044-7*, 550002) Literate Ear, Inc.

—Speaker for the Dead. 1994. (Ender Ser.: Bk. 2). 14.04 (*0-606-11866-7*) Turtleback Bks.

—Xenocide. abr. ed. 1991. audio 15.95 o.p. (*1-55927-161-2*) Audio Renaissance.

—Xenocide. (Ender Ser.: Bk. 3). 1992. 592p. mass mkt. 7.99 (*0-8125-0925-0*); 1991. 21.95 o.p. (*0-312-85056-5*); 2nd ed. 1996. 394p. pap. 14.95 (*0-312-86187-7*) Doherty, Tom Assocs., LLC. (Tor Bks.).

—Xenocide. 2002. 16.15 (*0-7857-1634-3*) Econo-Clad Bks.

—Xenocide. 1993. audio. audio 78.60 (*1-56544-045-5*, 550006) Literate Ear, Inc.

—Xenocide. 1992. (Ender Ser.: Bk. 3). 14.04 (*0-606-12119-6*) Turtleback Bks.

### ENDERLY, MARS (FICTITIOUS CHARACTER)—FICTION

Simon, Frank. Veiled Threats. 1996. 356p. pap. 12.99 o.p. (*0-89107-880-0*) Crossway Bks.

—Walls of Terror. 1997. 368p. pap. 12.99 o.p. (*0-89107-952-1*) Crossway Bks.

### ENDICOTT, BLACKJACK (FICTITIOUS CHARACTER)—FICTION

Roosevelt, Elliott. New Deal for Death. l.t. ed. 2001. 264p. lib. bdg. 25.95 o.p. (*1-58547-062-7*) Ctr. Point Large Print.

—New Deal for Death. 1994. (Blackjack Endicott Ser.: No. 2). 288p. mass mkt. 4.99 (*0-312-95238-4*, St. Martin's Paperbacks); 1993. (Blackjack Endicott Novel Ser.). 256p. 18.95 o.p. (*0-312-09267-9*, Saint Martin's Minotaur) St. Martin's Pr.

—The President's Man: A "Blackjack" Endicott Novel. l.t. ed. 1992. (General Ser.). 354p. 20.95 o.p. (*0-8161-5396-5*); lib. bdg. 16.95 o.p. (*0-8161-5397-3*) Gale Group. (Macmillan Reference USA).

—The President's Man: A "Blackjack" Endicott Novel. 1992. 290p. mass mkt. 4.99 (*0-312-92828-9*, St. Martin's Paperbacks); 1991. 256p. 18.95 o.p. (*0-312-06443-8*) St. Martin's Pr.

### ENDICOTT, GABRIEL (FICTITIOUS CHARACTER)—FICTION

Carlon, Patricia. The Running Woman. 1998. 189p. pap. 12.00 (*1-56947-132-0*); 196p. 21.00 (*1-56947-110-X*) Soho Pr., Inc.

—The Running Woman. l.t. ed. 1998. (Mystery Ser.). 320p. 26.95 (*0-7862-1671-9*) Thorndike Pr.

### ENGELS, KAY (FICTITIOUS CHARACTER)—FICTION

Stein, Triss. Digging up Death: A Kay Engles Mystery. 1999. (WWL Mystery Ser.: Bk. 310). per. (*0-373-26310-4*, 1-26310-2, Harlequin Bks.) Harlequin Enterprises, Ltd.

—Digging up Death: A Kay Engles Mystery. 1998. (Kay Engles Mystery Ser.). 204p. 22.95 (*0-8027-3319-0*) Walker & Co.

—Murder at the Class Reunion. 1995. 253p. per. (*0-373-26181-0*, 1-26181-7, Harlequin Bks.) Harlequin Enterprises, Ltd.

—Murder at the Class Reunion. 1993. 205p. 19.95 (*0-8027-3232-1*) Walker & Co.

### ENGLISH, TOM (FICTITIOUS CHARACTER)—FICTION

Dark Winter. 1991. 208p. 15.00 o.s.i (*0-385-26568-9*) Doubleday Publishing.

### EPTON, ROSA (FICTITIOUS CHARACTER)—FICTION

Underwood, Michael. A Compelling Case. 1994. audio 49.95 (*1-85496-592-1*, 65921); Set. 1999. audio 39.95 Soundings, Ltd. GBR. *Dist:* Ulverscroft Large Print Bks., Ltd., ISIS Publishing.

—A Compelling Case. 1989. 14.95 o.p. (*0-312-02887-3*, Saint Martin's Minotaur) St. Martin's Pr.

—A Compelling Case. l.t. ed. 1991. (Ulverscroft Large Print Ser.). 29.99 (*0-7089-2381-X*, Ulverscroft) Thorpe, F. A. Pubs. GBR. *Dist:* Ulverscroft Large Print Bks., Ltd., Ulverscroft Large Print Canada, Ltd.

—Crime upon Crime. 1980. 224p. 9.95 o.p. (*0-312-17204-4*) St. Martin's Pr.

—A Dangerous Business. 1991. 15.95 o.p. (*0-312-05842-X*, Saint Martin's Minotaur) St. Martin's Pr.

—A Dangerous Business. l.t. ed. 1993. (Mystery Ser.). 368p. 29.99 o.p. (*0-7089-2923-0*, Ulverscroft) Thorpe, F. A. Pubs. GBR. *Dist:* Ulverscroft Large Print Bks., Ltd., Ulverscroft Large Print Canada, Ltd.

—Death at Deepwood Grange. 1986. 192p. 12.95 o.p. (*0-312-18604-5*) St. Martin's Pr.

—Death at Deepwood Grange. 1993. (Audio Books Ser.). 39.95 o.p. incl. audio (*0-7838-8012-X*) Thorndike Pr.

—Death at Deepwood Grange. l.t. ed. 1987. (Ulverscroft Large Print Ser.). 336p. 29.99 o.p. (*0-7089-1673-2*, Ulverscroft) Thorpe, F. A. Pubs. GBR. *Dist:* Ulverscroft Large Print Bks., Ltd., Ulverscroft Large Print Canada, Ltd.

—Death in Camera. l.t. ed. 1985. (Nightingale Ser.). 288p. 10.95 o.p. (*0-8161-3811-7*, Macmillan Reference USA) Gale Group.

—Death in Camera. 1984. 192p. 11.95 o.p. (*0-312-18612-6*) St. Martin's Pr.

—Double Jeopardy. 1981. 224p. 9.95 o.p. (*0-312-21814-1*) St. Martin's Pr.

—Double Jeopardy. l.t. ed. 1982. (Ulverscroft Large Print Ser.). 336p. 29.99 o.p. (*0-7089-0885-3*, Ulverscroft) Thorpe, F. A. Pubs. GBR. *Dist:* Ulverscroft Large Print Bks., Ltd., Ulverscroft Large Print Canada, Ltd.

—Dual Enigma. 1988. 192p. 15.95 o.p. (*0-312-02197-6*, Saint Martin's Minotaur) St. Martin's Pr.

—Dual Enigma. l.t. ed. 1990. (Ulverscroft Large Print Ser.). 29.99 o.p. (*0-7089-2263-5*, Ulverscroft) Thorpe, F. A. Pubs. GBR. *Dist:* Ulverscroft Large Print Bks., Ltd., Ulverscroft Large Print Canada, Ltd.

—Goddess of Death. 1982. 224p. 10.95 o.p. (*0-312-33056-1*) St. Martin's Pr.

—Guilty Conscience. 1999. audio 54.95 Soundings, Ltd. GBR. *Dist:* Ulverscroft Large Print Bks., Ltd.

—Guilty Conscience. 1993. 208p. 18.95 o.p. (*0-312-09824-3*, Saint Martin's Minotaur) St. Martin's Pr.

—Guilty Conscience. l.t. ed. 1994. (Ulverscroft Large Print Ser.). 432p. 29.99 o.p. (*0-7089-3103-0*, Ulverscroft) Thorpe, F. A. Pubs. GBR. *Dist:* Ulverscroft Large Print Bks., Ltd., Ulverscroft Large Print Canada, Ltd.

—The Hidden Man. 1999. audio 49.95 Soundings, Ltd. GBR. *Dist:* Ulverscroft Large Print Bks., Ltd.

—The Hidden Man. 1985. 196p. 10.95 o.p. (*0-312-37196-9*) St. Martin's Pr.

—The Hidden Man. l.t. ed. 1986. (Ulverscroft Large Print Ser.). 352p. 29.99 o.p. (*0-7089-1536-1*, Ulverscroft) Thorpe, F. A. Pubs. GBR. *Dist:* Ulverscroft Large Print Bks., Ltd., Ulverscroft Large Print Canada, Ltd.

—The Injudicious Judge. unabr. ed. 1993. audio 49.95 (*1-85496-682-0*, 66820) Soundings, Ltd. GBR. *Dist:* Ulverscroft Large Print Bks., Ltd.

—The Injudicious Judge. 1988. 224p. 15.95 o.p. (*0-312-01447-3*, Saint Martin's Minotaur) St. Martin's Pr.

—The Injudicious Judge. l.t. ed. 1989. (Ulverscroft Large Print Ser.). 29.99 o.p. (*0-7089-2083-7*, Ulverscroft) Thorpe, F. A. Pubs. GBR. *Dist:* Ulverscroft Large Print Bks., Ltd., Ulverscroft Large Print Canada, Ltd.

—A Party to Murder. unabr. ed. 1993. audio 49.95 (*1-85496-667-7*, 66677) Soundings, Ltd. GBR. *Dist:* Ulverscroft Large Print Bks., Ltd.

—A Party to Murder. 1984. 200p. 10.95 o.p. (*0-312-59768-1*) St. Martin's Pr.

—A Party to Murder. l.t. ed. 1985. (Ulverscroft Large Print Ser.). 320p. 12.50 o.p. (*0-7089-1246-X*, Ulverscroft) Thorpe, F. A. Pubs. GBR. *Dist:* Ulverscroft Large Print Bks., Ltd., Ulverscroft Large Print Canada, Ltd.

—Rosa's Dilemma. 1992. 1.99 o.p. (*0-517-08491-0*) Random Hse. Value Publishing.

—Rosa's Dilemma. 1990. 15.95 o.p. (*0-312-04416-X*, Saint Martin's Minotaur) St. Martin's Pr.

—Rosa's Dilemma. l.t. ed. 1992. (Romance Ser.). 368p. 29.99 o.p. (*0-7089-2780-7*, Ulverscroft) Thorpe, F. A. Pubs. GBR. *Dist:* Ulverscroft Large Print Bks., Ltd., Ulverscroft Large Print Canada, Ltd.

—The Seeds of Murder. 1992. 224p. 17.95 o.p. (*0-312-07800-5*, Saint Martin's Minotaur) St. Martin's Pr.

—The Seeds of Murder. l.t. ed. 1993. (Mystery Ser.). 416p. 29.99 o.p. (*0-7089-2979-6*, Ulverscroft) Thorpe, F. A. Pubs. GBR. *Dist:* Ulverscroft Large Print Bks., Ltd., Ulverscroft Large Print Canada, Ltd.

—The Uninvited Corpse. unabr. ed. 1993. 49.95 incl. audio (*1-85496-712-6*, 67126) Soundings, Ltd. GBR. *Dist:* Ulverscroft Large Print Bks., Ltd.

—The Uninvited Corpse. 1987. 224p. 15.95 o.p. (*0-312-00023-5*) St. Martin's Pr.

—The Uninvited Corpse. l.t. ed. 1988. 336p. 17.95 o.p. (*0-7089-1889-1*, Ulverscroft) Thorpe, F. A. Pubs. GBR. *Dist:* Ulverscroft Large Print Bks., Ltd.

### ERICKSON, REED (FICTITIOUS CHARACTER)—FICTION

Landers, Gunnard. The Deer Killers. 1990. 209p. 21.95 (*0-8027-1134-0*) Walker & Co.

—Eskimo Money. 1999. (Wilderness Badge Ser.: Vol. 1). 206p. pap. 14.95 (*1-57223-149-1*, 1491) Willow Creek Pr., Inc.

—The Violators. 1991. 250p. 19.95 o.p. (*0-8027-1179-0*) Walker & Co.

### ERNST, WERNER (FICTITIOUS CHARACTER)—FICTION

Dooling, Richard. Critical Care. 288p. 1993. mass mkt. 4.99 (*0-380-71759-X*, Avon Bks.); 1992. 20.00 o.p. (*0-688-10926-8*, Morrow, William & Co.) Morrow/Avon.

—Critical Care. 1996. 256p. pap. 12.00 (*0-312-14304-4*) Picador.

—Critical Care. unabr. ed. 1994. audio 70.00 (*1-55690-665-X*, 92135E7) Recorded Bks., LLC.

—Critical Care Movieed. 1996. pap. 12.00 o.s.i (*0-312-17943-X*) Picador.

### ERSKINE, HARRY (FICTITIOUS CHARACTER)—FICTION

Masterton, Graham. Burial. 1996. 480p. mass mkt. 5.99 (*0-8125-3629-0*); 1994. 384p. 22.95 o.p. (*0-312-85681-4*) Doherty, Tom Assocs., LLC. (Tor Bks.).

—The Manitou. 1987. 224p. pap. 3.95 o.p. (*0-8125-2183-8*); 1982. pap. 2.95 o.p. (*0-523-48070-9*) Doherty, Tom Assocs., LLC. (Tor Bks.).

—Revenge of the Manitou. 1987. 272p. pap. 3.95 o.p. (*0-8125-2181-1*); 1982. pap. 2.95 o.p. (*0-523-48071-7*) Doherty, Tom Assocs., LLC. (Tor Bks.).

### ESPOSITO, JANUARY (FICTITIOUS CHARACTER)—FICTION

Dowling, Gregory. Every Picture Tells a Story. 1991. 22.95 o.p. (*0-312-05815-2*, Saint Martin's Minotaur) St. Martin's Pr.

—A Nice Steady Job. 1994. 296p. 20.95 o.p. (*0-312-11035-9*, Saint Martin's Minotaur) St. Martin's Pr.

—See Naples & Kill. 1988. 256p. 15.95 o.p. (*0-312-02277-8*, Saint Martin's Minotaur) St. Martin's Pr.

### ESSAY, ROGER (FICTITIOUS CHARACTER)—FICTION

Ackerman, Morris. Multiplex Man: And the One Penny Orange Mystery. 1997. 324p. (Orig.). pap. 9.95 (*0-9657743-0-9*) Chevy Chase Publishing Co.

### ESTRADA, JOE (FICTITIOUS CHARACTER)—FICTION

Friedman, Philip. Inadmissible Evidence. 1993. 640p. mass mkt. 7.99 (*0-8041-0852-8*, Ivy Bks.) Ballantine Bks.

—Inadmissible Evidence. unabr. ed. 1993. Pt. 1. audio 64.00; Pt. 2. audio 64.00 Books on Tape, Inc.

—Inadmissible Evidence. 1992. 480p. 23.00 o.p. (*1-55611-330-7*) Fine, Donald I. Bks.

—Inadmissible Evidence. abr. ed. 1993. audio 25.00 (*0-671-86568-4*, Simon & Schuster Audioworks) Simon & Schuster Audio.

### EVANS, EVAN (FICTITIOUS CHARACTER)—FICTION

Bowen, Rhys. Evan & Elle. l.t. ed. 2000. (Beeler Large Print Mystery Ser.). 236p. 26.95 (*1-57490-319-5*, Beeler Large Print Bks.) Beeler, Thomas T. Publisher.

—Evan & Elle: A Constable Evans Mystery. 2001. 224p. reprint ed. mass mkt. 5.99 (*0-425-17888-9*, Prime Crime) Berkley Publishing Group.

—Evan & Elle: A Constable Evans Mystery. 2000. 274p. 22.95 (*0-312-25244-7*, Saint Martin's Minotaur) St. Martin's Pr.

—Evan Can Wait: A Constable Evans Mystery. l.t. ed. 2001. (G. K. Hall Core Ser.). 365p. 29.95 (*0-7838-9451-1*, Macmillan Reference USA) Gale Group.

—Evan Can Wait: A Constable Evans Mystery. 2001. 259p. 22.95 (*0-312-26587-5*, Saint Martin's Minotaur) St. Martin's Pr.

—Evan Help Us. l.t. ed. 1999. (Beeler Large Print Mystery Ser.). 25.95 (*1-57490-213-X*, Beeler Large Print Bks.) Beeler, Thomas T. Publisher.

—Evan Help Us. 1999. (Constable Evan Evans Mysteries Ser.). 224p. reprint ed. mass mkt. 5.99 (*0-425-17261-9*, Prime Crime) Berkley Publishing Group.

—Evan Help Us. 1998. (Constable Evans Mysteries Ser.). 224p. 21.95 (*0-312-19411-0*, Saint Martin's Minotaur) St. Martin's Pr.

—Evan Only Knows: A Constable Evans Mystery. 2004. 272p. mass mkt. 6.50 (*0-425-19607-0*) Berkley Publishing Group.

—Evan Only Knows: A Constable Evans Mystery. 2003. 256p. 23.95 (*0-312-30113-8*, Saint Martin's Minotaur) St. Martin's Pr.

—Evan Only Knows: A Constable Evans Mystery. l.t. ed. 2003. 29.95 (*0-7862-5445-9*) Thorndike Pr.

—Evanly Choirs. l.t. ed. 1999. (Beeler Large Print Mystery Ser.). 249p. 25.95 (*1-57490-241-5*, Beeler Large Print Bks.) Beeler, Thomas T. Publisher.

—Evanly Choirs. 2000. (Constable Evan Evans Mysteries Ser.). 256p. mass mkt. 5.99 (*0-425-17613-4*) Berkley Publishing Group.

—Evanly Choirs. 1999. (Constable Evans Mysteries Ser.). x, 256p. 22.95 (*0-312-20539-2*, Saint Martin's Minotaur) St. Martin's Pr.

—Evans Above. l.t. ed. 1999. (Beeler Large Print Mystery Ser.). 218p. 25.95 (*1-57490-208-3*, Beeler Large Print Bks.) Beeler, Thomas T. Publisher.

—Evans Above. 1998. (Constable Evan Evans Mysteries Ser.). 224p. reprint ed. mass mkt. 5.99 (*0-425-16642-2*, Prime Crime) Berkley Publishing Group.

Bowen, Rhys & Bowen, J. Evans Above. 1997. (Evan Evans Ser.). 236p. 21.95 (*0-312-16828-4*, Saint Martin's Minotaur) St. Martin's Pr.

### EVANS, HOMER (FICTITIOUS CHARACTER)—FICTION

Paul, Elliot. Hugger-Mugger in the Louvre: A Homer Evans Murder Mystery. 1986. viii, 328p. reprint ed. pap. 5.95 o.p. (*0-486-25185-3*) Dover Pubns., Inc.

—Mayhem in B-Flat: A Homer Evans Murder Mystery. 1988. 320p. reprint ed. pap. 6.95 (*0-486-25621-9*) Dover Pubns., Inc.

—The Mysterious Mickey Finn. 1984. 256p. reprint ed. pap. 5.95 o.p. (*0-486-24751-1*) Dover Pubns., Inc.

### EVANS, LYNN (FICTITIOUS CHARACTER)—FICTION

McKay, Claudia. The Kali Connection. 1994. 190p. (Orig.). pap. 9.95 (*0-934678-54-5*) New Victoria Pubs., Inc.

—Twist of Lime: A Lynn Evans Mystery. 1997. (Lynn Evans Mystery Ser.). 166p. pap. 10.95 (*0-934678-88-X*) New Victoria Pubs., Inc.

### EVANS, TINA (FICTITIOUS CHARACTER)—FICTION

Koontz, Dean. The Eyes of Darkness. 1996. 384p. reprint ed. mass mkt. 7.99 (*0-425-15397-5*) Berkley Publishing Group.

—The Eyes of Darkness. l.t. ed. 1995. (Magna Large Print Ser.). 500p. o.p. (*0-7505-0840-X*) Magna Large Print Bks. GBR. *Dist:* Ulverscroft Large Print Canada, Ltd.

### EVERARD, NICHOLAS (FICTITIOUS CHARACTER)—FICTION

Fullerton, Alexander. All the Drowning Seas. unabr. ed. 2002. audio compact disk 99.95 (*1-84283-109-7*); 2000. audio 84.95 (*1-86042-631-X*, 2631X) Soundings, Ltd. GBR. *Dist:* Ulverscroft Large Print Bks., Ltd.

—All the Drowning Seas. l.t. ed. 1984. (Ulverscroft Large Print Ser.). 560p. 29.99 o.p. (*0-7089-1159-5*, Ulverscroft) Thorpe, F. A. Pubs. GBR. *Dist:* Ulverscroft Large Print Bks., Ltd., Ulverscroft Large Print Canada, Ltd.

—The Blooding of the Guns. 1998. 286p. pap. text o.s.i (*0-7515-1620-1*) Little Brown & Co.

—The Blooding of the Guns. (Everard Naval Ser.: Vol. 1). 286p. 2002. pap. 13.00 (*1-56947-313-7*); 2001. 24.00 (*1-56947-259-9*) Soho Pr., Inc.

—The Blooding of the Guns. l.t. ed. 1987. (Ulverscroft Large Print Ser.). 512p. 29.99 o.p. (*0-7089-1726-7*, Ulverscroft) Thorpe, F. A. Pubs. GBR. *Dist:* Ulverscroft Large Print Bks., Ltd., Ulverscroft Large Print Canada, Ltd.

—The Blooding of the Guns. 1984. 192p. 12.95 o.s.i (*0-8027-0780-7*) Walker & Co.

—Sixty Minutes for St. George. 2003. 320p. pap. 13.00 (*1-56947-321-8*); 2002. 308p. 24.00 (*1-56947-293-9*) Soho Pr., Inc.

—Sixty Minutes for St. George. l.t. ed. 1988. (Ulverscroft Large Print Ser.). 480p. 29.99 o.p. (*0-7089-1761-5*, Ulverscroft) Thorpe, F. A. Pubs. GBR. *Dist:* Ulverscroft Large Print Bks., Ltd., Ulverscroft Large Print Canada, Ltd.

### EVERETT, STEVE (FICTITIOUS CHARACTER)—FICTION

Klavan, Andrew. True Crime. 1996. mass mkt. 6.99 (*0-449-22512-7*, Fawcett) Ballantine Bks.

—True Crime. 1997. 400p. mass mkt. 6.99 (*0-440-22403-9*) Dell Publishing.

—True Crime. l.t. ed. 1995. 522p. 24.95 o.p. (*0-7838-1438-0*, Macmillan Reference USA) Gale Group.

—True Crime. abr. ed. 1996. audio 8.99 o.s.i (*0-679-45596-5*, 391811); 1995. audio 17.00 o.s.i (*0-679-44455-6*) Random Hse. Audio Publishing Group. (RH Audio).

**EVERHARDT, MONIKA (FICTITIOUS CHARACTER)—FICTION**

Sullivan, Eleanor. Twice Dead. 2002. 300p. pap. 14.95 (*1-59133-005-X*); 254p. (*1-59133-004-1*) Hilliard & Harris.

**EVERS, FORREST (FICTITIOUS CHARACTER)—FICTION**

Judd, Bob. Burn. 1993. 290p. mass mkt. 4.99 o.p. (*0-425-13946-8*) Berkley Publishing Group.
—Curve. 1994. 288p. mass mkt. 4.99 o.p. (*0-425-14466-6*, Prime Crime) Berkley Publishing Group.
—Formula One. 1991. 384p. pap. 3.95 (*0-380-71014-5*, Avon Bks.); 1990. 330p. reprint ed. 19.95 o.p. (*0-688-09398-1*, Morrow, William & Co.) Morrow/Avon.
—Monza. l.t. ed. 1993. (Magna Large Print Ser.). 400p. 29.99 (*0-7505-0533-8*) Magna Large Print Bks. GBR. *Dist:* Ulverscroft Large Print Bks., Ltd.
—Monza. 1992. 20.00 o.p. (*0-688-11320-6*, Morrow, William & Co.) Morrow/Avon.
—The Race. 1992. 272p. mass mkt. 4.99 (*0-380-71556-2*, Avon Bks.); 1991. 302p. 18.00 o.p. (*0-688-10463-0*, Morrow, William & Co.) Morrow/Avon.
—Spin. 1994. 277p. mass mkt. 4.99 o.p. (*0-425-14179-9*) Berkley Publishing Group.

**EVESDEN, GODFREY, SIR (FICTITIOUS CHARACTER)—FICTION**

Doherty, P. C. An Ancient Evil: The Knight's Tale of Mystery & Murder as He Goes on Pilgrimage from London to Canterbury. unabr. ed. 1998. audio 69.95 (*1-85903-149-8*) Magna Story Sound GBR. *Dist:* Ulverscroft Large Print Bks., Ltd.
—An Ancient Evil: The Knight's Tale of Mystery & Murder as He Goes on Pilgrimage from London to Canterbury. 1995. 248p. 21.00 o.p. (*0-312-11740-X*, Saint Martin's Minotaur) St. Martin's Pr.
—An Ancient Evil: The Knight's Tale of Mystery & Murder as He Goes on Pilgrimage from London to Canterbury. l.t. ed. 1995. (Ulverscroft Large Print Ser.). 432p. 29.99 o.p. (*0-7089-3409-9*, Ulverscroft) Thorpe, F. A. Pubs. GBR. *Dist:* Ulverscroft Large Print Bks., Ltd., Ulverscroft Large Print Canada, Ltd.
—Ghostly Murders: The Priest's Tale of Mystery & Murder as He Goes on Pilgrimage from London to Canterbury. 1998. 256p. 21.95 (*0-312-19418-8*, Saint Martin's Minotaur) St. Martin's Pr.
—Ghostly Murders: The Priest's Tale of Mystery & Murder as He Goes on Pilgrimage from London to Canterbury. l.t. ed. 1999. (Ulverscroft Large Print Ser.). 368p. 31.99 o.p. (*0-7089-4059-5*, Ulverscroft) Thorpe, F. A. Pubs. GBR. *Dist:* Ulverscroft Large Print Bks., Ltd., Ulverscroft Large Print Canada, Ltd.
—A Tapestry of Murders: The Lawyer's Tale of Mystery & Murder as He Goes on a Pilgrimage from London to Canterbury. unabr. ed. 1998. audio 69.95 (*1-85903-165-X*) Magna Story Sound GBR. *Dist:* Ulverscroft Large Print Bks., Ltd.
—A Tapestry of Murders: The Lawyer's Tale of Mystery & Murder as He Goes on a Pilgrimage from London to Canterbury. 1996. 256p. 21.95 (*0-312-14052-5*, Saint Martin's Minotaur) St. Martin's Pr.
—A Tapestry of Murders: The Lawyer's Tale of Mystery & Murder as He Goes on a Pilgrimage from London to Canterbury. l.t. ed. 1996. (Ulverscroft Large Print Ser.). 416p. 29.99 o.p. (*0-7089-3446-3*, Ulverscroft) Thorpe, F. A. Pubs. GBR. *Dist:* Ulverscroft Large Print Bks., Ltd., Ulverscroft Large Print Canada, Ltd.
—A Tournament of Murders: The Franklin's Tale of Mystery & Murder As He Goes on Pilgrimage from London to Canterbury. 1997. 256p. 21.95 (*0-312-17048-3*, Saint Martin's Minotaur) St. Martin's Pr.
—A Tournament of Murders: The Franklin's Tale of Mystery & Murder As He Goes on Pilgrimage from London to Canterbury. l.t. ed. 1998. (Ulverscroft Large Print Ser.). 384p. 29.99 o.p. (*0-7089-3938-4*, Ulverscroft) Thorpe, F. A. Pubs. GBR. *Dist:* Ulverscroft Large Print Bks., Ltd., Ulverscroft Large Print Canada, Ltd.

**EWING, LUTHER (FICTITIOUS CHARACTER)—FICTION**

Crow, Michael. The Bite: A Luther Ewing Thriller. 2003. 304p. text 24.95 (*0-670-03222-0*, Viking) Viking Penguin.
—Red Rain. 2003. 304p. reprint ed. mass mkt. 6.99 (*0-451-41086-6*, Onyx) NAL.
—Red Rain. 2002. 368p. 25.95 o.s.i (*0-670-03090-2*, Viking) Viking Penguin.

**EXLEY, ED (FICTITIOUS CHARACTER)—FICTION**

Ellroy, James. L. A. Confidential. unabr. collector's ed. 1991. (L. A. Quartet). audio 80.00 (*0-7366-2012-5*, 116014) Books on Tape, Inc.
—L. A. Confidential. 1990. 19.95 (*0-89296-293-3*); 75.00 o.p. (*0-89296-424-3*) Mysterious Pr.
—L. A. Confidential. abr. ed. 2001. audio 9.99 (*0-553-70244-0*); Set. 1997. audio 18.00 o.s.i (*0-375-40213-6*, 390277) Random Hse. Audio Publishing Group. (RH Audio).
—L. A. Confidential. 1997. 480p. pap. text 9.23 (*0-09-925508-1*) Random Hse. Value Publishing.
—L. A. Confidential. 1997. (*0-446-60605-7*); 1997. 512p. pap. 14.95 (*0-446-67424-9*); 1991. mass mkt. 5.99 (*0-446-40010-6*) Warner Bks., Inc.
—White Jazz. 1997. 368p. pap. 13.00 o.s.i (*0-449-00088-5*, Fawcett) Ballantine Bks.
—White Jazz. unabr. collector's ed. 1992. (L. A. Quartet). audio 64.00 (*0-7366-2323-X*, 3103) Books on Tape, Inc.
—White Jazz. 2001. 368p. pap. 13.00 (*0-375-72736-1*, Vintage) Knopf Publishing Group.
—White Jazz: A Novel. 1993. (Los Angeles Mysteries Ser.). 368p. mass mkt. 5.99 o.s.i (*0-449-14841-6*, Fawcett) Ballantine Bks.

## F

**FABIANO (FICTITIOUS CHARACTER)—FICTION**

Ramos, Graciliano. Barren Lives. Dimmick, Ralph E., tr. from SPA. (Texas Pan American Ser.). (Illus.). 165p. 1971. pap. 12.95 (*0-292-70133-0*); 1965. 12.95 o.p. (*0-292-73172-8*) Univ. of Texas Pr.

**FABRI, FELIX, 1441 OR 2-1502—FICTION**

Holman, Sheri. A Stolen Tongue. 1998. 352p. pap. 13.00 (*0-385-49124-7*, Delacorte Pr.) Dell Publishing.
—A Stolen Tongue. 1997. 320p. 23.00 o.p. (*0-87113-669-4*, Atlantic Monthly Pr.) Grove/Atlantic, Inc.

**FAFHRD (FICTITIOUS CHARACTER)—FICTION**

Leiber, Fritz. The Knight & Knave of Swords. 1990. mass mkt. 3.95 o.s.i (*0-441-45125-X*) Ace Bks.
—Swords Against Death. (Fafhrd & Grey Mouser Ser.). 1986. mass mkt. 3.95 o.p. (*0-441-79193-X*); 1984. mass mkt. 2.75 o.s.i (*0-441-79190-5*); 1983. mass mkt. 2.75 o.s.i (*0-441-79158-1*); 1982. mass mkt. 2.50 o.s.i (*0-441-79157-3*); 1981. mass mkt. 2.25 o.s.i (*0-441-79156-5*) Ace Bks.
—Swords Against Death. 1977. (Science Fiction Ser.). lib. bdg. 9.95 o.p. (*0-8398-2399-1*, Macmillan Reference USA) Gale Group.
—Swords Against Death. 2003. 304p. mass mkt. 6.99 (*0-7434-5828-1*) ibooks, Inc.
—Swords Against Wizardry. 1986. (Fafhrd & Grey Mouser Ser.). mass mkt. 3.95 o.s.i (*0-441-79194-8*) Ace Bks.
—Swords Against Wizardry. 1977. (Science Fiction Ser.). lib. bdg. 9.95 o.p. (*0-8398-2401-7*, Macmillan Reference USA) Gale Group.
—Swords Against Wizardry. E-Book 6.99 (*1-58586-363-7*); 2001. E-Book 6.99 (*0-7592-0913-8*) ereads.com.
—Swords Against Wizardry. 2003. 240p. mass mkt. 6.99 (*0-7434-7537-2*) ibooks, Inc.
—Swords & Deviltry. 1986. (Fafhrd & Grey Mouser Ser.: No. 1). 256p. mass mkt. 2.95 o.s.i (*0-441-79198-0*); 1985. mass mkt. 2.95 o.s.i (*0-441-79197-2*); 1985. mass mkt. 2.95 o.s.i (*0-441-79191-3*); 1983. mass mkt. 2.75 o.s.i (*0-441-79179-4*); 1982. mass mkt. 2.50 o.s.i (*0-441-79177-8*); 1981. mass mkt. 2.25 o.s.i (*0-441-79176-X*) Ace Bks.
—Swords & Deviltry. 1977. (Fafhrd & Grey Mouser Ser.). lib. bdg. 9.95 o.p. (*0-8398-2398-3*, Macmillan Reference USA) Gale Group.
—Swords & Deviltry. 2003. 224p. mass mkt. 6.99 (*0-7434-4558-9*) ibooks, Inc.
—Swords & Ice Magic. 1986. mass mkt. 3.95 o.s.i (*0-441-79196-4*); 1984. mass mkt. 2.75 o.s.i (*0-441-79189-1*); 1983. mass mkt. 2.50 o.s.i (*0-441-79178-6*); 1981. mass mkt. 2.25 o.s.i (*0-441-79169-7*) Ace Bks.
—Swords & Ice Magic. 1977. lib. bdg. 9.95 o.p. (*0-8398-2403-3*, Macmillan Reference USA) Gale Group.
—Swords in the Mist. mass mkt. 3.95 o.s.i (*0-441-79129-8*); 1985. mass mkt. 3.95 o.s.i (*0-441-79192-1*); 1983. mass mkt. 2.50 o.s.i (*0-441-79186-7*); 1981. mass mkt. 2.25 o.s.i (*0-441-79185-9*) Ace Bks.
—Swords in the Mist. 1977. (Science Fiction Ser.). lib. bdg. 9.95 o.p. (*0-8398-2400-9*, Macmillan Reference USA) Gale Group.
—Swords in the Mist. E-Book 6.99 (*1-58586-366-1*); E-Book 6.99 (*0-7592-0914-6*) ereads.com.
—Swords in the Mist. 2003. pap. 6.99 (*0-7434-7465-1*) ibooks, Inc.
—The Swords of Lankhmar. 1986. (Fafhrd & Grey Mouser Ser.: No. 4). 320p. mass mkt. 3.95 o.s.i (*0-441-79195-6*) Ace Bks.
—The Swords of Lankhmar. Date not set. 224p. 21.95 (*0-8488-2352-4*) Amereon, Ltd.

**FAIRACRE (ENGLAND: IMAGINARY PLACE)—FICTION**

Read, Miss. Tiggy & the Fairacre Festival. l.t. ed. 2000. (General Ser.). 200p. pap. 24.95 (*0-7862-2314-6*) Thorndike Pr.
Read, Miss. Changes at Fairacre. l.t. ed. 1993. 20.95 o.p. (*0-7927-1593-4*) BBC Audiobooks America.
—Changes at Fairacre. 2001. 252p. pap. 12.00 (*0-618-15457-4*); 1992. (Illus.). 256p. 19.95 o.p. (*0-395-63126-2*) Houghton Mifflin Co.
—Changes at Fairacre. unabr. ed. 1994. audio 49.95 o.p. (*1-85903-010-6*) Magna Story Sound GBR. *Dist:* Ulverscroft Large Print Bks., Ltd.
—Chronicles of Fairacre, 3 vols. 1977. 10.95 o.p. (*0-395-25181-8*) Houghton Mifflin Co.
—The Fairacre Festival. 1990. (Illus.). 104p. reprint ed. pap. 12.00 (*0-89733-333-0*) Academy Chicago Pubs., Ltd.
—The Fairacre Festival. Date not set. lib. bdg. 21.95 (*0-8488-1698-6*) Amereon, Ltd.
—The Fairacre Festival. 2002. lib. bdg. 27.95 (*1-58547-235-2*, Premier) Ctr. Point Large Print.
—The Fairacre Festival: And Tiggy. l.t. ed. 2000. (*0-7540-3996-X*); (*0-7540-3997-8*) Thorndike Pr.
—Farewell to Fairacre. unabr. ed. 1995. (Fairacre Chronicles). audio 54.95 (*0-7451-4331-8*, CAB 1014) BBC Audiobooks America.
—Farewell to Fairacre. 2001. 224p. pap. 12.00 (*0-618-15456-6*); 1994. 192p. 19.95 o.p. (*0-395-68994-5*) Houghton Mifflin Co.
—Mrs. Pringle of Fairacre. 2001. 176p. pap. 12.00 (*0-618-15588-0*) Houghton Mifflin Co.
—Storm in the Village. 1987. (Illus.). 247p. pap. 9.00 o.p. (*0-89733-244-X*) Academy Chicago Pubs., Ltd.
—Storm in the Village. Date not set. lib. bdg. 22.95 (*0-8488-1691-9*) Amereon, Ltd.
—Storm in the Village, Set. unabr. ed. 1998. audio 69.95 o.p. (*1-872672-14-0*) Magna Story Sound GBR. *Dist:* Ulverscroft Large Print Bks., Ltd.
—Storm in the Village. (G. K. Hall Audio Bks.). 1992. audio 53.95 o.p. (*0-8161-7608-6*); 1996. (Illus.). 305p. 27.95 (*0-7838-1655-3*) Thorndike Pr.
—Summer at Fairacre. unabr. ed. 2000. (Fairacre Chronicles). audio 49.95 (*0-7451-6220-7*, CAB 139) Chivers Audio Bks. GBR. *Dist:* BBC Audiobooks America.
—Summer at Fairacre, 001. 1985. (Illus.). 256p. 14.95 o.p. (*0-395-38016-2*) Houghton Mifflin Co.
—Village Diary. 1986. (Illus.). 255p. pap. 9.00 o.p. (*0-89733-212-1*) Academy Chicago Pubs., Ltd.
—Village Diary. Date not set. lib. bdg. 22.95 (*0-8488-1690-0*) Amereon, Ltd.
—Village Diary. l.t. ed. 1993. 19.95 o.p. (*0-7927-1536-5*); 1993. pap. o.p. (*0-7927-1535-7*); 1991. audio 54.95 (*0-7451-6223-1*, CAB 558) BBC Audiobooks America.
—Village School. 1986. (Illus.). 239p. pap. 9.00 o.p. (*0-89733-211-3*) Academy Chicago Pubs., Ltd.
—Village School. Date not set. lib. bdg. 21.95 (*0-8488-1689-7*) Amereon, Ltd.
—Village School. l.t. ed. 1994. 18.95 o.p. (*0-7927-1763-5*); 1994. pap. 17.95 o.p. (*0-7927-1762-7*); 1993. 54.95 incl. audio (*0-7451-6224-X*, CSL 057) BBC Audiobooks America.

**FAIRCHILD, FAITH SIBLEY (FICTITIOUS CHARACTER)—FICTION**

Page, Katherine Hall. The Body in the Basement. l.t. ed. 1999. (Beeler Large Print Mystery Ser.). 25.95 (*1-57490-206-7*, Beeler Large Print Bks.) Beeler, Thomas T. Publisher.
—The Body in the Basement. 1995. (Faith Fairchild Mystery Ser.). 368p. reprint ed. mass mkt. 6.99 (*0-380-72339-5*, Avon Bks.) Morrow/Avon.
—The Body in the Basement. 1994. 272p. 20.95 o.p. (*0-312-11470-2*, Saint Martin's Minotaur) St. Martin's Pr.
—The Body in the Belfry. 1991. 320p. reprint ed. mass mkt. 6.99 (*0-380-71328-4*, Avon Bks.) Morrow/Avon.
—The Body in the Belfry. 1990. 272p. 16.95 (*0-312-03798-8*, Saint Martin's Minotaur) St. Martin's Pr.
—The Body in the Big Apple. l.t. ed. 2001. (Beeler Large Print Mystery Ser.). 272p. 26.95 (*1-57490-367-5*, Beeler Large Print Bks.) Beeler, Thomas T. Publisher.
—The Body in the Big Apple. 1999. 239p. 22.00 (*0-688-15748-3*, Morrow, William & Co.) Morrow/Avon.
—The Body in the Bog. l.t. ed. 1997. 299p. lib. bdg. 23.95 (*1-57490-087-0*, Beeler Large Print Bks.) Beeler, Thomas T. Publisher.
—The Body in the Bog. 1997. 384p. mass mkt. 6.99 (*0-380-72712-9*, Avon Bks.); 1996. 256p. 22.00 o.p. (*0-688-14573-6*, Morrow, William & Co.) Morrow/Avon.
—The Body in the Bonfire. 2002. 256p. 23.95 (*0-380-97843-1*, Morrow, William & Co.) Morrow/Avon.
—The Body in the Bookcase. l.t. ed. 2001. (Wheeler Large Print Book Ser.). 333p. pap. 22.95 (*1-58724-018-1*, Wheeler Publishing, Inc.) Gale Group.
—The Body in the Bookcase. (Faith Fairchild Mysteries Ser.). 1999. 384p. mass mkt. 6.99 (*0-380-73237-8*, Avon Bks.); 1998. 272p. 22.00 (*0-688-15747-5*, Morrow, William & Co.) Morrow/Avon.
—The Body in the Bouillon. 1992. 304p. mass mkt. 6.99 (*0-380-71896-0*, Avon Bks.) Morrow/Avon.
—The Body in the Bouillon. 1991. 224p. text 17.95 o.p. (*0-312-06309-1*, Saint Martin's Minotaur) St. Martin's Pr.
—The Body in the Cast. l.t. ed. 1999. (Beeler Large Print Mystery Ser.). 24.95 (*1-57490-239-3*, Beeler Large Print Bks.) Beeler, Thomas T. Publisher.
—The Body in the Cast. 1994. 368p. mass mkt. 6.99 (*0-380-72338-7*, Avon Bks.) Morrow/Avon.
—The Body in the Cast. 1993. 224p. 19.95 o.p. (*0-312-09755-7*, Saint Martin's Minotaur) St. Martin's Pr.
—The Body in the Fjord. l.t. ed. 1998. pap. 24.95 (*1-56895-562-6*, Wheeler Publishing, Inc.) Gale Group.
—The Body in the Fjord. 1998. 304p. mass mkt. 6.99 (*0-380-73129-0*, Avon Bks.); 1997. 272p. 22.00 (*0-688-14574-4*, Morrow, William & Co.) Morrow/Avon.
—The Body in the Kelp. l.t. ed. 1998. (Beeler Large Print Mystery Ser.). (Illus.). 246p. 25.95 (*1-57490-188-5*, Beeler Large Print Bks.) Beeler, Thomas T. Publisher.
—The Body in the Kelp. 1992. 304p. mass mkt. 6.99 (*0-380-71329-2*, Avon Bks.) Morrow/Avon.
—The Body in the Kelp. 1990. 16.95 o.p. (*0-312-05392-4*, Saint Martin's Minotaur) St. Martin's Pr.
—The Body in the Lighthouse. l.t. ed. 2003. (Mystery Ser.). 28.95 (*1-57490-508-2*) Beeler, Thomas T. Publisher.
—The Body in the Lighthouse. 2004. 352p. mass mkt. 6.99 (*0-380-81386-6*, Avon Bks.); 2003. 256p. 23.95 (*0-380-97844-X*, Morrow, William & Co.) Morrow/Avon.
—The Body in the Moonlight. 2002. 352p. mass mkt. 6.99 (*0-380-81384-X*, Avon Bks.); 2001. 256p. 23.00 (*0-380-97842-3*, Morrow, William & Co.) Morrow/Avon.
—The Body in the Vestibule. l.t. ed. 2000. (Beeler Large Print Mystery Ser.). 223p. 26.95 (*1-57490-318-7*, Beeler Large Print Bks.) Beeler, Thomas T. Publisher.
—The Body in the Vestibule. 1993. 352p. mass mkt. 6.99 (*0-380-72079-5*, Avon Bks.) Morrow/Avon.
—The Body in the Vestibule. 1992. 234p. 17.95 o.p. (*0-312-08148-0*, Saint Martin's Minotaur) St. Martin's Pr.

**FAIRCHILD, NELSON (FICTITIOUS CHARACTER)—FICTION**

Johnson, Denis. Already Dead: A California Gothic. 1997. 448p. 25.00 o.p. (*0-06-018737-9*) HarperCollins Pubs.
—Already Dead: A California Gothic. 1998. 448p. pap. 13.95 (*0-06-092909-X*, Perennial) HarperTrade.

**FAIRFAX, PHOEBE (FICTITIOUS CHARACTER)—FICTION**

North, Suzanne. Healthy, Wealthy & Dead: A Phoebe Fairfax Mystery. 1994. pap. 6.95 (*0-920897-55-X*) NeWest Pubs., Ltd. CAN. *Dist:* General Distribution Services, Inc.
—Seeing Is Deceiving. 1997. (Phoebe Fairfax Mystery Ser.). 336p. mass mkt. 6.99 (*0-7710-6806-9*) McClelland & Stewart/Tundra Bks.
—Seeing Is Deceiving: A Phoebe Fairfax Mystery. 1996. 288p. 25.99 o.p. (*0-7710-6805-0*) McClelland & Stewart/Tundra Bks.

**FAIRWEATHER, DORAN (FICTITIOUS CHARACTER)—FICTION**

Hardwick, Mollie. The Bandersnatch. 1994. mass mkt. 4.50 o.s.i (*0-449-22029-X*, Fawcett) Ballantine Bks.
—The Bandersnatch. 1989. 15.95 o.p. (*0-312-02865-2*, Saint Martin's Minotaur) St. Martin's Pr.
—The Bandersnatch. l.t. ed. 1991. (Ulverscroft Large Print Ser.). 29.99 o.p. (*0-7089-2534-0*, Ulverscroft) Thorpe, F. A. Pubs. GBR. *Dist:* Ulverscroft Large Print Bks., Ltd., Ulverscroft Large Print Canada, Ltd.
—Come Away, Death. 1997. 214p. mass mkt. 5.50 (*0-449-22421-X*, Fawcett) Ballantine Bks.
—The Dreaming Damozel. 1995. mass mkt. 4.99 o.s.i (*0-449-22073-7*, Fawcett) Ballantine Bks.
—The Dreaming Damozel. l.t. ed. 1992. (Nightingale Series Large Print Bks.). 337p. pap. 14.95 o.p. (*0-8161-5323-X*, Macmillan Reference USA) Gale Group.
—The Dreaming Damozel. 1991. 15.95 o.p. (*0-312-05421-1*, Saint Martin's Minotaur) St. Martin's Pr.
—Malice Domestic. 1992. mass mkt. 4.50 o.s.i (*0-449-22032-X*, Fawcett) Ballantine Bks.
—Malice Domestic. 1989. mass mkt. o.s.i (*0-552-13235-7*, Corgi) Bantam Bks.
—Malice Domestic. 1986. 208p. 13.95 o.p. (*0-312-50940-5*) St. Martin's Pr.
—Malice Domestic. l.t. ed. 1988. 400p. o.p. (*0-7089-1835-2*, Ulverscroft) Thorpe, F. A. Pubs.

—Parson's Pleasure. 1992. mass mkt. 4.50 o.s.i (*0-449-22031-1*, Fawcett) Ballantine Bks.
—Parson's Pleasure. 1989. mass mkt. o.s.i (*0-552-13236-5*, Corgi) Bantam Bks.
—Parson's Pleasure. 1987. 208p. 14.95 o.p. (*0-312-00642-X*) St. Martin's Pr.
—Parson's Pleasure. l.t. ed. 1989. 332p. 17.95 o.p. (*0-7089-1932-4*, Ulverscroft) Thorpe, F. A. Pubs. GBR. *Dist:* Ulverscroft Large Print Bks., Ltd.
—Perish in July. 1994. mass mkt. 4.99 o.s.i (*0-449-22028-1*, Fawcett) Ballantine Bks.
—Perish in July. 1991. mass mkt. o.s.i (*0-552-13664-6*, Corgi) Bantam Bks.
—Perish in July. 1990. 15.95 o.p. (*0-312-04402-X*, Saint Martin's Minotaur) St. Martin's Pr.
—Uneaseful Death. 1993. mass mkt. 5.99 o.s.i (*0-449-22030-3*, Fawcett) Ballantine Bks.
—Uneaseful Death. 1989. mass mkt. o.s.i (*0-552-13411-2*, Corgi) Bantam Bks.
—Uneaseful Death. 1988. 192p. 14.95 o.p. (*0-312-01842-8*, Saint Martin's Minotaur) St. Martin's Pr.
—Uneaseful Death. l.t. ed. 1990. (Ulverscroft Large Print Ser.). 29.99 o.p. (*0-7089-2252-X*, Ulverscroft) Thorpe, F. A. Pubs. GBR. *Dist:* Ulverscroft Large Print Bks., Ltd., Ulverscroft Large Print Canada, Ltd.

**FAITH, JOHN (FICTITIOUS CHARACTER)—FICTION**

Pronzini, Bill. A Wasteland of Strangers. 1997. 256p. 21.95 (*0-8027-3301-8*); 1999. 264p. reprint ed. pap. 8.95 (*0-8027-7560-8*) Walker & Co.

**FALCO, MARCUS DIDIUS (FICTITIOUS CHARACTER)—FICTION**

Davis, Lindsey. The Accusers. 2004. (*0-89296-811-7*) Mysterious Pr.
—A Body in the Bath House. 2003. 368p. pap. 12.95 (*0-446-69170-4*, Mysterious Pr. Paperback Bks.) Warner Bks., Inc.
—A Dying Light in Corduba. l.t. ed. 1997. (G. K. Hall Mystery Ser.). 589p. 26.95 o.p. (*0-7838-8347-1*, Macmillan Reference USA) Gale Group.
—A Dying Light in Corduba. 1998. 400p. 23.00 o.p. (*0-89296-664-5*) Mysterious Pr.
—A Dying Light in Corduba. unabr. ed. 1996. audio 97.00 (*0-7887-3108-4*, 95819E7) Recorded Bks., LLC.
—A Dying Light in Corduba. 1999. (Marcus Didius Falco Mystery Ser.). 464p. mass mkt. 6.99 (*0-446-60680-4*) Warner Bks., Inc.
—The Iron Hand of Mars. 1994. 320p. mass mkt. 6.50 o.s.i (*0-345-38024-X*) Ballantine Bks.
—The Iron Hand of Mars. unabr. ed. 2000. (Marcus Didius Falco Ser.: Vol. 4). audio 85.00 (*0-7887-0226-2*, 94451E7) Recorded Bks., LLC.
—The Jupiter Myth. 2003. (Illus.). 336p. 24.95 (*0-89296-777-3*) Mysterious Pr.
—Last Act in Palmyra. l.t. ed. 1995. (Magna Large Print Ser.). 693p. o.p. (*0-7505-0839-6*) Magna Large Print Bks. GBR. *Dist:* Ulverscroft Large Print Canada, Ltd.
—Last Act in Palmyra. 1996. 82p. 22.95 o.p. (*0-89296-625-4*) Mysterious Pr.
—Last Act in Palmyra. unabr. ed. 1997. (Marcus Didius Falco Ser.: Vol. 6). audio 104.00 (*0-7887-1306-X*, 95144E7) Recorded Bks., LLC.
—Last Act in Palmyra. 1997. 432p. reprint ed. mass mkt. 6.99 (*0-446-40474-8*) Warner Bks., Inc.
—Ode to a Banker. 2001. (Marcus Didius Falco Mystery Ser.). (Illus.). 368p. 23.45 o.p. (*0-89296-740-4*) Mysterious Pr.
—Ode to a Banker. 2002. 384p. pap. 12.95 (*0-446-67906-2*, Mysterious Pr. Paperback Bks.) Warner Bks., Inc.
—One Virgin Too Many. 2000. E-Book 14.95 (*0-7595-6032-3*); 368p. E-Book 14.95 (*0-7595-9037-0*); E-Book 14.95 (*0-7595-4032-2*); 368p. E-Book 14.95 (*0-7595-8033-2*); 368p. E-Book 14.95 (*0-7595-0032-0*); (Illus.). 356p. 23.95 (*0-89296-716-1*) Mysterious Pr.
—One Virgin Too Many. 2001. 368p. reprint ed. pap. 12.95 (*0-446-67769-8*) Warner Bks., Inc.
—Poseidon's Gold. 1995. 352p. mass mkt. 5.99 o.s.i (*0-345-38025-8*) Ballantine Bks.
—Poseidon's Gold. 1994. 288p. 22.00 o.s.i (*0-517-59241-X*, Crown) Crown Publishing Group.
—Poseidon's Gold. l.t. ed. 1994. (Magna Large Print Ser.). 560p. (*0-7505-0733-0*) Magna Large Print Bks. GBR. *Dist:* Ulverscroft Large Print Canada, Ltd.
—Poseidon's Gold. unabr. ed. 1995. (Marcus Didius Falco Ser.: Vol. 5). audio 97.00 (*0-7887-0391-9*, 94583E7) Recorded Bks., LLC.
—Shadows in Bronze. 1992. 384p. mass mkt. 6.50 o.s.i (*0-345-37426-6*) Ballantine Bks.
—Shadows in Bronze. 1993. 3.99 o.p. (*0-517-09846-6*) Random Hse. Value Publishing.
—Shadows in Bronze. unabr. ed. 1992. (Marcus Didius Falco Ser.: Vol. 2). audio 97.00 (*1-55690-728-1*, 92223E7) Recorded Bks., LLC.
—Silver Pigs. 1991. 256p. mass mkt. 5.99 o.s.i (*0-345-36907-6*) Ballantine Bks.
—Silver Pigs. 1989. 18.95 o.s.i (*0-517-57363-6*, Crown) Crown Publishing Group.
—Silver Pigs. unabr. ed. 1992. (Marcus Didius Falco Ser.: Vol. 1). audio 70.00 (*1-55690-635-8*, 92103E7) Recorded Bks., LLC.
—Three Hands in the Fountain. 1999. (Marcus Didius Falco Mystery Ser.). 368p. 30.00 o.p. (*0-89296-691-2*) Mysterious Pr.
—Three Hands in the Fountain. 2000. 432p. mass mkt. 6.99 (*0-446-60774-6*) Warner Bks., Inc.
—Time to Depart. unabr. ed. 1998. (Marcus Didius Falco Ser.: Vol. 7). audio 97.00 (*0-7887-1922-X*, 95343E7) Recorded Bks., LLC.
—Time to Depart. l.t. ed. 1998. (Marcus Didius Falco Mystery Ser.). 432p. mass mkt. 6.99 (*0-446-60591-3*) Warner Bks., Inc.
—Time to Depart: A Marcus Didius Falco Mystery Novel. 1998. 432p. pap. 6.50 (*0-446-40528-0*, Mysterious Pr. Paperback Bks.); 1997. 416p. 22.50 o.p. (*0-89296-626-2*) Warner Bks., Inc.
—Two for the Lions. 2000. 464p. 23.95 (*0-89296-693-9*); E-Book 4.95 (*0-7595-6030-7*); 464p. E-Book 4.95 (*0-7595-0030-4*); 464p. E-Book 4.95 (*0-7595-4030-6*); 464p. E-Book 4.95 (*0-7595-9035-4*) Mysterious Pr.
—Two for the Lions. 2000. (Marcus Didius Falco Mystery Ser.). 464p. mass mkt. 6.99 (*0-446-60902-1*); E-Book 4.95 (*0-7595-8031-6*) Warner Bks., Inc.
—Venus in Copper. 1993. 288p. mass mkt. 5.99 o.s.i (*0-345-37390-1*) Ballantine Bks.
—Venus in Copper. unabr. ed. 1992. (Marcus Didius Falco Ser.: Vol. 3). audio 78.00 (*1-55690-738-9*, 92334E7) Recorded Bks., LLC.

**FALCONER, WILLIAM (FICTITIOUS CHARACTER)—FICTION**

Morson, Ian. Falconer & the Face of God. 1997. 208p. mass mkt. 5.99 (*0-312-96410-2*, St. Martin's Paperbacks) St. Martin's Pr.
—Falconer & the Face of God: A William Falconer Medieval Mystery. 1997. 192p. text 21.95 o.p. (*0-312-15124-1*, Saint Martin's Minotaur) St. Martin's Pr.
—Falconer & the Great Beast. l.t. unabr. ed. 1998. (Illus.). 272p. 32.50 (*0-7531-5938-4*, 159384) ISIS Large Print Bks. GBR. *Dist:* Ulverscroft Large Print Bks., Ltd., Ulverscroft Large Print Canada, Ltd.
—Falconer & the Great Beast: A Medieval Oxford Mystery. 1999. (Medieval Oxford Mysteries Ser.). (Illus.). 220p. (YA). 21.95 (*0-312-20543-0*, Saint Martin's Minotaur) St. Martin's Pr.
—Falconer's Crusade. 1996. mass mkt. 4.99 (*0-312-95697-5*, St. Martin's Paperbacks); 1995. 190p. 18.95 o.p. (*0-312-11784-1*, Saint Martin's Minotaur) St. Martin's Pr.
—Falconer's Judgement. (Dead Letter Mysteries Ser.). 1997. 224p. mass mkt. 5.99 (*0-312-96151-0*, St. Martin's Paperbacks); 1996. 192p. 20.95 o.p. (*0-312-13971-3*, Saint Martin's Minotaur) St. Martin's Pr.
—A Psalm for Falconer, Vol. 1. Date not set. mass mkt. (*0-312-96534-6*, St. Martin's Paperbacks) St. Martin's Pr.
—A Psalm for Falconer: A William Falconer Medieval Mystery. 1997. 220p. 21.95 o.p. (*0-312-16833-0*, Saint Martin's Minotaur) St. Martin's Pr.

**FALKENSTEIN, JESSE (FICTITIOUS CHARACTER)—FICTION**

Egan, Lesley. Chain of Violence. 1985. (Crime Club Ser.). 192p. 12.95 o.p. (*0-385-19807-8*) Doubleday Publishing.
—Little Boy Lost. 1983. (Crime Club Ser.). (Illus.). 192p. 11.95 o.p. (*0-385-18840-4*) Doubleday Publishing.
—Little Boy Lost. l.t. ed. 1986. (Ulverscroft Large Print Ser.). 384p. 29.99 o.p. (*0-7089-1417-9*, Ulverscroft) Thorpe, F. A. Pubs. GBR. *Dist:* Ulverscroft Large Print Bks., Ltd., Ulverscroft Large Print Canada, Ltd.
—Look Back on Death. 1978. 7.95 o.p. (*0-385-14303-6*) Doubleday Publishing.
—Look Back on Death. l.t. ed. 1981. reprint ed. 9.95 o.p. (*0-89621-267-X*) Thorndike Pr.
—The Miser. 1981. (Crime Club Ser.). 192p. 9.95 o.p. (*0-385-17626-0*) Doubleday Publishing.
—The Miser. l.t. ed. 1984. 368p. o.p. (*0-7089-1069-6*, Ulverscroft) Thorpe, F. A. Pubs.
—Motive in Shadow. 1980. (Crime Club Ser.). 10.95 o.p. (*0-385-15605-7*) Doubleday Publishing.
—Motive in Shadow. l.t. ed. 1986. (Ulverscroft Large Print Ser.). 384p. 29.99 o.p. (*0-7089-1471-3*, Ulverscroft) Thorpe, F. A. Pubs. GBR. *Dist:* Ulverscroft Large Print Bks., Ltd., Ulverscroft Large Print Canada, Ltd.

**FALLETTI, FABE (FICTITIOUS CHARACTER)—FICTION**

Izzi, Eugene. The Take. 1988. mass mkt. 3.50 (*0-312-91120-3*, St. Martin's Paperbacks); 1987. 256p. 16.95 o.p. (*0-312-01038-9*) St. Martin's Pr.

**FALLON, MICHAEL (FICTITIOUS CHARACTER)—FICTION**

Maxim, John R. The Shadow Box. 1997. mass mkt. 6.99 (*0-380-78668-0*); 1996. 384p. mass mkt. 23.00 o.p. (*0-380-97300-6*) Morrow/Avon. (Avon Bks.).

**FALLS, VIRGINIA (FICTITIOUS CHARACTER)—FICTION**

Carter, Betty Smartt. The Tower, the Mask, & the Grave: A Mystery. 2000. 304p. pap. 12.99 (*0-87788-559-1*, Shaw) WaterBrook Pr.

**FALSTAFF, JOHN, SIR (FICTITIOUS CHARACTER)—FICTION**

Nye, Robert. Falstaff: A Novel. 464p. 2001. pap. 25.95 (*1-55970-591-4*); 2003. reprint ed. pap. 14.95 (*1-55970-649-X*) Arcade Publishing, Inc.
—Falstaff: A Novel. 1976. 8.95 o.p. (*0-316-61738-5*) Little Brown & Co.
—Falstaff: A Novel. 1976. 450p. o.p. (*0-241-89429-8*, Hamilton, Hamish) Viking Penguin.
Wray, David. A Fool's Pilgrimage. E-Book (*1-84045-042-8*) Online Originals.

**FANG, YAN (FICTITIOUS CHARACTER)—FICTION**

Shuo, Wang. Playing for Thrills: A Mystery. Goldblatt, Howard, tr. from CHI. 1997. 256p. 23.00 (*0-688-13046-1*, Morrow, William & Co.) Morrow/Avon.
—Playing for Thrills: A Mystery. Goldblatt, Howard, tr. 1998. 336p. 12.95 (*0-14-026971-1*) Viking Penguin.

**FANSLER, KATE (FICTITIOUS CHARACTER)—FICTION**

Cross, Amanda. Amanda Cross: The Collected Stories. l.t. ed. 1997. (Wheeler Large Print Book Ser.). pap. 24.95 (*1-56895-453-0*, Wheeler Publishing, Inc.) Gale Group.
—Collected Stories of Amanda Cross. 1998. 192p. pap. 12.00 (*0-345-42113-2*) Ballantine Bks.
—Death in a Tenured Position. (Kate Fansler Novels Ser.). 1986. 208p. mass mkt. 6.99 (*0-345-34041-8*); 1982. mass mkt. 2.50 o.p. (*0-345-30215-X*) Ballantine Bks.
—Death in a Tenured Position. 1981. 10.50 o.p. (*0-525-08935-7*, 01019-310, Dutton) Dutton/Plume.
—Death in a Tenured Position. l.t. ed. 1981. reprint ed. 11.95 o.p. (*0-89621-321-8*) Thorndike Pr.
—The Edge of Doom. 2003. 240p. mass mkt. 6.99 (*0-345-45237-2*); 2002. 272p. 22.95 (*0-345-45236-4*) Ballantine Bks.
—The Edge of Doom. 2003. (Basic Ser.). 29.95 (*0-7862-4968-4*) Thorndike Pr.
—Honest Doubt. 2001. 256p. reprint ed. mass mkt. 6.99 (*0-449-00704-9*, Ballantine Bks.) Ballantine Bks.
—Honest Doubt. l.t. ed. 2001. 299p. 29.95 (*0-7862-3317-6*) Thorndike Pr.
—An Imperfect Spy. 1995. (Kate Fansler Novels Ser.). 224p. mass mkt. 6.99 (*0-345-39005-9*); 240p. 20.00 o.p. (*0-345-38917-4*); 224p. pap. 15.00 (*0-345-46493-1*) Ballantine Bks.
—An Imperfect Spy. l.t. ed. 1995. 232p. pap. 18.95 o.p. (*0-7838-1299-X*, Macmillan Reference USA) Gale Group.
—An Imperfect Spy. unabr. ed. 1996. audio 49.95 o.p. (*1-85903-093-9*, 30939) Magna Story Sound GBR. *Dist:* Ulverscroft Large Print Bks., Ltd.
—In the Last Analysis. 2001. (Kate Fansler Novels Ser.: Vol. 1). 224p. mass mkt. 6.50 (*0-449-00711-1*, Fawcett) Ballantine Bks.
—In the Last Analysis. Barzun, Jacques & Taylor, W. H., eds. 1983. (Crime Fiction 1950-1975 Ser.). 187p. lib. bdg. 18.00 o.p. (*0-8240-4960-8*) Garland Publishing, Inc.
—In the Last Analysis. 1981. 176p. mass mkt. 5.50 (*0-380-54510-1*, Avon Bks.) Morrow/Avon.
—In the Last Analysis. l.t. ed. 1982. 305p. reprint ed. 10.95 o.p. (*0-89621-335-8*) Thorndike Pr.
—James Joyce Murder. 1985. mass mkt. 2.95 o.p. (*0-345-33141-9*) Ballantine Bks.
—The James Joyce Murders. 1987. (Kate Fansler Novels Ser.). 208p. mass mkt. 6.50 (*0-345-34686-6*) Ballantine Bks.
—The James Joyce Murders. 1982. 176p. 9.95 o.p. (*0-525-24101-9*, 0995-300, Dutton) Dutton/Plume.
—The James Joyce Murders. l.t. ed. 1993. (Nightingale Ser.). 282p. pap. 16.95 o.p. (*0-8161-5779-0*, Macmillan Reference USA) Gale Group.
—The James Joyce Murders. l.t. ed. 1982. 275p. reprint ed. 9.95 o.p. (*0-89621-373-0*) Thorndike Pr.
—No Word from Winifred. 1988. pap. 3.95 o.p. (*0-345-00728-X*); 1987. 272p. mass mkt. 6.99 (*0-345-33381-0*) Ballantine Bks.
—No Word from Winifred. 1986. 14.95 o.p. (*0-525-24432-8*, Dutton) Dutton/Plume.
—The Players Come Again. 1991. (Kate Fansler Novels Ser.). 240p. mass mkt. 6.99 (*0-345-36998-X*, Ballantine Bks.) Ballantine Bks.
—The Players Come Again. l.t. ed. 1994. 300p. lib. bdg. 15.95 o.p. (*0-8161-5990-4*, Macmillan Reference USA) Gale Group.
—The Players Come Again. 1992. 3.99 o.p. (*0-517-09455-X*) Random Hse. Value Publishing.
—The Players Come Again. l.t. ed. 1991. (Charnwood Large Print Ser.). 29.99 o.p. (*0-7089-8615-3*, Charnwood) Thorpe, F. A. Pubs. GBR. *Dist:* Ulverscroft Large Print Bks., Ltd., Ulverscroft Large Print Canada, Ltd.
—Poetic Justice. 2001. (Kate Fansler Novels Ser.). 224p. mass mkt. 6.50 (*0-449-00703-0*, Fawcett) Ballantine Bks.
—Poetic Justice. 1979. 176p. mass mkt. 4.99 (*0-380-44222-1*, Avon Bks.) Morrow/Avon.
—Poetic Justice. l.t. ed. 1981. 286p. reprint ed. 9.95 o.p. (*0-89621-291-2*) Thorndike Pr.
—The Puzzled Heart. 1998. (Kate Fansler Novels Ser.). 256p. mass mkt. 6.99 (*0-345-41884-0*) Ballantine Bks.
—The Puzzled Heart. l.t. ed. 1998. (*0-7540-3401-1*); (*0-7540-3402-X*) Thorndike Pr.
—The Question of Max. 1987. (Kate Fansler Novels Ser.). 224p. mass mkt. 6.50 (*0-345-35489-3*) Ballantine Bks.
—The Question of Max. 1977. lib. bdg. 10.95 o.p. (*0-8161-6451-7*, Macmillan Reference USA) Gale Group.
—The Question of Max. 1984. 7.95 o.p. (*0-394-48223-9*); mass mkt. 2.50 o.p. (*0-345-31385-2*) Knopf, Alfred A. Inc.
—Sweet Death, Kind Death. 1995. 224p. pap. 15.00 (*0-345-46763-9*); 1987. 244p. mass mkt. 5.99 (*0-345-35254-8*); 1985. mass mkt. 2.95 o.s.i (*0-345-31177-9*) Ballantine Bks.
—Sweet Death, Kind Death. 1984. 192p. 13.95 o.p. (*0-525-24241-4*, 01354-410, Dutton) Dutton/Plume.
—Sweet Death, Kind Death. l.t. ed. 1987. (Nightingale Ser.). 279p. pap. 11.95 o.p. (*0-8161-4222-X*, Macmillan Reference USA) Gale Group.
—The Theban Mysteries. 2001. (Kate Fansler Novels Ser.). 224p. mass mkt. 6.50 (*0-449-00706-5*, Fawcett) Ballantine Bks.
—The Theban Mysteries. 1979. 192p. pap. 4.99 (*0-380-45021-6*, Avon Bks.) Morrow/Avon.
—The Theban Mysteries. l.t. ed. 1982. 275p. reprint ed. 11.95 o.p. (*0-89621-362-5*) Thorndike Pr.
—A Trap for Fools. l.t. ed. 1990. pap. 5.00 (*0-7451-1286-2*) BBC Audiobooks America.
—A Trap for Fools. 1990. (Kate Fansler Novels Ser.). 224p. mass mkt. 5.99 (*0-345-35947-X*) Ballantine Bks.
—A Trap for Fools. 1989. 160p. 16.95 o.p. (*0-525-24754-8*, Dutton) Dutton/Plume.
—A Trap for Fools. l.t. ed. 1990. (Nightingale Ser.). 263p. 14.95 o.p. (*0-8161-4935-6*, Macmillan Reference USA) Gale Group.

**FANTOMAS (FICTITIOUS CHARACTER)—FICTION**

Allain, Marcel. Fantomas, le Paravent Chinois, Set. 1996. (FRE.). audio 28.95 Olivia & Hill Pr., The.
—The Silent Executioner: Being the Second in the Series of Fantomas Adventures. 1987. (Fantomas Ser.: No. 2). (Illus.). 288p. 15.95 o.p. (*0-688-07265-8*, Morrow, William & Co.) Morrow/Avon.
—La Vengeance de Fantomas, Set. adapted ed. 1996. (FRE.). audio 28.95 Olivia & Hill Pr., The.
Allain, Marcel & Souvestre, Pierre. Fantomas: The Legendary French Thriller. Ashbery, John, tr. 1987. mass mkt. 3.95 o.s.i (*0-345-34421-9*) Ballantine Bks.
—Fantomas: The Legendary French Thriller. Ashbery, John, tr. 1986. 320p. 17.95 o.p. (*0-688-04360-7*, Morrow, William & Co.) Morrow/Avon.
Souvestre, Pierre. Silent Executioner. 1989. mass mkt. 3.95 o.s.i (*0-345-35297-1*) Ballantine Bks.

**FARADAY, MIKE (FICTITIOUS CHARACTER)—FICTION**

Copper, Basil. Bad Scene. l.t. ed. 2000. (G. K. Hall Nightingale Ser.). 217p. pap. 20.95 (*0-7838-8997-6*, Macmillan Reference USA) Gale Group.
—Bad Scene. l.t. ed. 1991. (Linford Mystery Large Print Ser.). pap. 17.99 o.p. (*0-7089-7021-4*, Ulverscroft) Thorpe, F. A. Pubs. GBR. *Dist:* Ulverscroft Large Print Bks., Ltd., Ulverscroft Large Print Canada, Ltd.
—The Breaking Point. l.t. ed. 1995. (Linford Mystery Large Print Ser.). 320p. pap. 17.99 o.p. (*0-7089-7805-3*, Linford) Thorpe, F. A. Pubs. GBR. *Dist:* Ulverscroft Large Print Bks., Ltd., Ulverscroft Large Print Canada, Ltd.
—The Caligari Complex. l.t. ed. 1999. (Linford Mystery Large Print Ser.). 304p. pap. 18.99 (*0-7089-5504-5*, Linford) Thorpe, F. A. Pubs. GBR. *Dist:* Ulverscroft Large Print Bks., Ltd., Ulverscroft Large Print Canada, Ltd.
—Crack in the Sidewalk. l.t. ed. 1997. (Linford Mystery Library). 320p. pap. 17.99 o.p. (*0-7089-5065-5*, Linford) Thorpe, F. A. Pubs. GBR. *Dist:* Ulverscroft Large Print Bks., Ltd., Ulverscroft Large Print Canada, Ltd.

—The Dark Mirror. (Black Dagger Crime Ser.). 16.50 o.p. (*0-86220-796-7*, BD001, Black Dagger) BBC Audiobooks America.
—The Dark Mirror. l.t. ed. 1997. (Linford Mystery Library). 416p. pap. 17.99 o.p. (*0-7089-5101-5*, Linford) Thorpe, F. A. Pubs. GBR. *Dist:* Ulverscroft Large Print Bks., Ltd., Ulverscroft Large Print Canada, Ltd.
—Dead File. l.t. ed. 1991. (Linford Mystery Large Print Ser.). pap. 17.99 o.p. (*0-7089-7001-X*, Ulverscroft) Thorpe, F. A. Pubs. GBR. *Dist:* Ulverscroft Large Print Bks., Ltd., Ulverscroft Large Print Canada, Ltd.
—Death Squad. l.t. ed. 1999. (Linford Mystery Large Print Ser.). 304p. pap. 18.99 (*0-7089-5460-X*, Linford) Thorpe, F. A. Pubs. GBR. *Dist:* Ulverscroft Large Print Bks., Ltd., Ulverscroft Large Print Canada, Ltd.
—Die Now, Live Later. l.t. ed. 1993. (Linford Mystery Library). 336p. pap. 17.99 o.p. (*0-7089-7341-8*, Ulverscroft) Thorpe, F. A. Pubs. GBR. *Dist:* Ulverscroft Large Print Bks., Ltd., Ulverscroft Large Print Canada, Ltd.
—Don't Bleed on Me. l.t. ed. 1991. (Linford Mystery Library). pap. 17.99 o.p. (*0-7089-7081-8*, Ulverscroft) Thorpe, F. A. Pubs. GBR. *Dist:* Ulverscroft Large Print Bks., Ltd., Ulverscroft Large Print Canada, Ltd.
—The Far Horizon. 2001. 219p. (*0-7540-4399-1*); (*0-7540-4400-9*) Gale Group. (Macmillan Reference USA).
—The Far Horizon. l.t. ed. 2001. (G. K. Hall Nightingale Ser.). 219p. pap. 23.95 (*0-7838-9327-2*) Thorndike Pr.
—The Far Horizon. l.t. ed. 1993. (Linford Mystery Library). 336p. pap. 17.99 o.p. (*0-7089-7378-7*, Ulverscroft) Thorpe, F. A. Pubs. GBR. *Dist:* Ulverscroft Large Print Bks., Ltd., Ulverscroft Large Print Canada, Ltd.
—Feedback. l.t. ed. 2001. 225p. pap. 23.95 (*0-7838-9592-5*) Thorndike Pr.
—Feedback. l.t. ed. 1991. (Linford Mystery Library). pap. 17.99 o.p. (*0-7089-7129-6*, Ulverscroft) Thorpe, F. A. Pubs. GBR. *Dist:* Ulverscroft Large Print Bks., Ltd., Ulverscroft Large Print Canada, Ltd.
—A Good Place to Die. l.t. ed. 1989. (Linford Mystery Library). pap. 17.99 o.p. (*0-7089-6742-6*, Ulverscroft) Thorpe, F. A. Pubs. GBR. *Dist:* Ulverscroft Large Print Bks., Ltd., Ulverscroft Large Print Canada, Ltd.
—A Great Year for Dying. l.t. ed. 1993. (Linford Mystery Library). 352p. pap. 17.99 o.p. (*0-7089-7349-3*, Ulverscroft) Thorpe, F. A. Pubs. GBR. *Dist:* Ulverscroft Large Print Bks., Ltd., Ulverscroft Large Print Canada, Ltd.
—The High Wall. l.t. ed. 1987. (Linford Mystery Library). 304p. pap. 17.99 o.p. (*0-7089-6455-9*, Linford) Thorpe, F. A. Pubs. GBR. *Dist:* Ulverscroft Large Print Bks., Ltd., Ulverscroft Large Print Canada, Ltd.
—Impact. l.t. ed. 1997. (Linford Mystery Library). 320p. pap. 17.99 o.p. (*0-7089-5070-1*, Linford) Thorpe, F. A. Pubs. GBR. *Dist:* Ulverscroft Large Print Bks., Ltd., Ulverscroft Large Print Canada, Ltd.
—The Lonely Place. l.t. ed. 1997. (Linford Mystery Library). 304p. pap. 17.99 o.p. (*0-7089-5060-4*, Ulverscroft) Thorpe, F. A. Pubs. GBR. *Dist:* Ulverscroft Large Print Bks., Ltd., Ulverscroft Large Print Canada, Ltd.
—The Long Rest. l.t. ed. 1994. 221p. lib. bdg. 16.95 (*0-8161-7421-0*, Macmillan Reference USA) Gale Group.
—The Marble Orchard. l.t. ed. 1998. (Linford Mystery Large Print Ser.). 256p. pap. 17.99 (*0-7089-5265-8*, Linford) Thorpe, F. A. Pubs. GBR. *Dist:* Ulverscroft Large Print Bks., Ltd., Ulverscroft Large Print Canada, Ltd.
—Night Frost. 2000. 21.95 (*0-7540-8574-0*, Black Dagger) BBC Audiobooks America.
—Night Frost. l.t. ed. 1996. (Linford Mystery Library). 368p. pap. 17.99 o.p. (*0-7089-7868-1*, Linford) Thorpe, F. A. Pubs. GBR. *Dist:* Ulverscroft Large Print Bks., Ltd., Ulverscroft Large Print Canada, Ltd.
—No Flowers for the General. l.t. ed. 2000. (Linford Mystery Large Print Ser.). 304p. pap. 18.99 (*0-7089-5774-9*, Linford) Thorpe, F. A. Pubs. GBR. *Dist:* Ulverscroft Large Print Bks., Ltd., Ulverscroft Large Print Canada, Ltd.
—No Letters from the Grave. l.t. ed. 1998. (Linford Mystery Library). 240p. pap. 17.99 (*0-7089-5223-2*, Linford) Thorpe, F. A. Pubs. GBR. *Dist:* Ulverscroft Large Print Bks., Ltd., Ulverscroft Large Print Canada, Ltd.
—Print-Out. l.t. ed. 1993. (Dales Mystery Ser.). 246p. pap. 19.99 o.p. (*1-85389-380-3*) Dales Large Print Bks. GBR. *Dist:* Ulverscroft Large Print Bks., Ltd., Ulverscroft Large Print Canada, Ltd.
—Print-Out. l.t. ed. 1996. (Linford Mystery Library). 304p. pap. 17.99 o.p. (*0-7089-7861-4*, Linford) Thorpe, F. A. Pubs. GBR. *Dist:* Ulverscroft Large Print Bks., Ltd., Ulverscroft Large Print Canada, Ltd.
—A Quiet Room in Hell. l.t. ed. 1998. (Linford Mystery Large Print Ser.). 288p. pap. 17.99 (*0-7089-5294-1*, Linford) Thorpe, F. A. Pubs. GBR. *Dist:* Ulverscroft Large Print Bks., Ltd., Ulverscroft Large Print Canada, Ltd.
—Ricochet. l.t. ed. 1993. (Linford Mystery Library). 304p. pap. 17.99 o.p. (*0-7089-7382-5*, Linford) Thorpe, F. A. Pubs. GBR. *Dist:* Ulverscroft Large Print Bks., Ltd., Ulverscroft Large Print Canada, Ltd.
—Scratch on the Dark. 2002. 192p. 21.95 (*0-7540-8610-0*, Black Dagger) BBC Audiobooks America.
—Scratch on the Dark. l.t. ed. 2000. (Linford Mystery Large Print Ser.). 264p. pap. 18.99 (*0-7089-5767-6*, Ulverscroft) Thorpe, F. A. Pubs. GBR. *Dist:* Ulverscroft Large Print Bks., Ltd., Ulverscroft Large Print Canada, Ltd.
—Shock-Wave. l.t. ed. 1994. (Linford Mystery Library). 320p. pap. 17.99 o.p. (*0-7089-7629-8*, Linford) Thorpe, F. A. Pubs. GBR. *Dist:* Ulverscroft Large Print Bks., Ltd., Ulverscroft Large Print Canada, Ltd.
—Strong-Arm. l.t. ed. 1989. (Linford Mystery Library). 319p. pap. 17.99 o.p. (*0-7089-6629-2*, Linford) Thorpe, F. A. Pubs. GBR. *Dist:* Ulverscroft Large Print Bks., Ltd., Ulverscroft Large Print Canada, Ltd.
—Tight Corner. l.t. ed. 1994. (Linford Mystery Library). 304p. pap. 17.99 o.p. (*0-7089-7564-X*, Linford) Thorpe, F. A. Pubs. GBR. *Dist:* Ulverscroft Large Print Bks., Ltd., Ulverscroft Large Print Canada, Ltd.
—Trigger-Man. l.t. ed. 1994. (Linford Mystery Library). 320p. pap. 17.99 o.p. (*0-7089-7561-5*, Linford) Thorpe, F. A. Pubs. GBR. *Dist:* Ulverscroft Large Print Bks., Ltd., Ulverscroft Large Print Canada, Ltd.
—A Voice from the Dead. l.t. ed. 1998. (Linford Mystery Large Print Ser.). 304p. pap. 17.99 (*0-7089-5287-9*, Linford) Thorpe, F. A. Pubs. GBR. *Dist:* Ulverscroft Large Print Bks., Ltd., Ulverscroft Large Print Canada, Ltd.
—The Year of the Dragon. l.t. ed. 1991. (Linford Mystery Library). pap. 17.99 o.p. (*0-7089-7077-X*, Linford) Thorpe, F. A. Pubs. GBR. *Dist:* Ulverscroft Large Print Bks., Ltd., Ulverscroft Large Print Canada, Ltd.

**FARGO, SKYE (FICTITIOUS CHARACTER)—FICTION**

Sharpe, Jon. Ambush at Skull Pass. 1994. (Trailsman Ser.: No. 154). 176p. (Orig.). mass mkt. 3.99 o.s.i (*0-451-17890-4*, Signet Bks.) NAL.
—Apache Arrows. 1996. (Trailsman Ser.: No. 178). 176p. mass mkt. 4.99 o.s.i (*0-451-18668-0*, Signet Bks.) NAL.
—Apache Gold. 1984. (Trailsman Ser.: No. 32). mass mkt. 2.50 o.p. (*0-451-13116-9*, Signet Bks.) NAL.
—Apache Wells. 1999. (Trailsman Ser.: Vol. 213). 176p. mass mkt. 4.99 o.s.i (*0-451-19822-0*) NAL.
—Arizona Renegades. 1999. (Trailsman Ser.: Vol. 208). 176p. mass mkt. 4.99 o.s.i (*0-451-19756-9*, Signet Bks.) NAL.
—Arizona Silver Strike. 2000. (Trailsman Ser.: Vol. 219). 176p. mass mkt. 4.99 o.s.i (*0-451-19932-4*) NAL.
—Arizona Slaughter. 1991. (Trailsman Ser.: No. 118). 176p. (Orig.). mass mkt. 3.50 o.p. (*0-451-17067-9*, Signet Bks.) NAL.
—Arkansas Assault. 2003. (Trailsman Ser.: No. 263). 176p. mass mkt. 4.99 (*0-451-20966-4*, Signet Bks.) NAL.
—Arrowhead Territory. 1983. (Trailsman Ser.: No. 14). 176p. mass mkt. 2.50 o.p. (*0-451-12080-9*, Signet Bks.) NAL.
—Aztec Gold. (Trailsman Ser.). 2000. 272p. mass mkt. 5.99 o.s.i (*0-451-19890-5*, Signet Bks.); 1999. 176p. mass mkt. 4.99 o.s.i (*0-451-19891-3*) NAL.
—The Badge. 1984. (Trailsman Ser.: No. 36). mass mkt. 2.50 o.p. (*0-451-13280-7*, Signet Bks.) NAL.
—Badlands Bloodbath. 1999. (Trailsman Ser.: Vol. 211). 176p. mass mkt. 4.99 o.s.i (*0-451-19694-5*) NAL.
—Beartown Bloodshed. 1992. (Trailsman Ser.: No. 131). 176p. (Orig.). mass mkt. 3.50 o.p. (*0-451-17372-4*, Signet Bks.) NAL.
—Betrayal at El Diablo. 1996. (Trailsman Ser.: No. 175). 176p. mass mkt. 4.99 o.s.i (*0-451-18667-2*, Signet Bks.) NAL.
—Black Hills Blood. 1990. (Trailsman Ser.: No. 105). 176p. mass mkt. 3.50 o.p. (*0-451-16726-0*, Signet Bks.) NAL.
—Black Mesa Treachery. 1995. (Trailsman Ser.: No. 167). 176p. mass mkt. 4.50 o.s.i (*0-451-18224-3*, Signet Bks.) NAL.
—Blackgulch Gamble. 1998. (Trailsman Ser.: Vol. 198). 176p. mass mkt. 4.99 o.s.i (*0-451-19248-6*, Signet Bks.) NAL.
—Blood Canyon. 1991. (Trailsman Ser.: No. 111). 176p. mass mkt. 3.50 o.p. (*0-451-16920-4*, Signet Bks.) NAL.
—Blood Oath. 1986. (Trailsman Ser.: No. 50). mass mkt. 2.75 o.p. (*0-451-14124-5*, Signet Bks.) NAL.
—Blood Pass. 1988. (Trailsman Ser.: No. 80). 176p. (Orig.). mass mkt. 2.95 o.p. (*0-451-15482-7*, Signet Bks.) NAL.
—Blood Prairie. 1992. (Trailsman Ser.: No. 125). 176p. (Orig.). mass mkt. 3.50 o.s.i (*0-451-17238-8*, Signet Bks.) NAL.
—Border Arrows. 1983. (Trailsman Ser.: No. 22). mass mkt. 2.50 o.p. (*0-451-12520-7*, Signet Bks.) NAL.
—Brothel Bullets. 1989. (Trailsman Ser.: No. 87). 176p. (Orig.). mass mkt. 2.95 o.p. (*0-451-15842-3*, Signet Bks.) NAL.
—Buffalo Guns. 1993. (Trailsman Ser.: No. 139). 176p. (Orig.). mass mkt. 3.50 o.p. (*0-451-17666-9*, Signet Bks.) NAL.
—Bullet Caravan. 1987. (Trailsman Ser.: No. 61). mass mkt. 2.75 o.p. (*0-451-14657-3*, Signet Bks.) NAL.
—Bullets & Brides. 1998. (Trailsman Ser.: No. 193). 176p. mass mkt. 4.99 o.s.i (*0-451-19284-2*, Signet Bks.) NAL.
—Buzzard's Gap. 1989. (Trailsman Ser.: No. 96). 176p. mass mkt. 3.50 o.p. (*0-451-16338-9*, Signet Bks.) NAL.
—Calico Kill. 1987. (Trailsman Ser.: No. 72). 176p. mass mkt. 2.75 o.p. (*0-451-15107-0*, Signet Bks.) NAL.
—California Crusader. 2000. (Trailsman Ser.: Vol. 221). 176p. mass mkt. 4.99 o.s.i (*0-451-19977-4*, Signet Bks.) NAL.
—California Quarry. 1994. (Trailsman Ser.: No. 148). 176p. (Orig.). mass mkt. 3.50 o.s.i (*0-451-17883-1*, Signet Bks.) NAL.
—Camp St. Lucifer. 1990. (Trailsman Ser.: No. 99). 176p. mass mkt. 3.50 o.p. (*0-451-16443-1*) NAL.
—Cave of Death. 1989. (Trailsman Ser.: No. 91). 176p. (Orig.). mass mkt. 2.95 o.p. (*0-451-16071-1*, Signet Bks.) NAL.
—Cheyenne Crossfire. 1994. (Trailsman Ser.: No. 145). 176p. mass mkt. 3.50 o.p. (*0-451-17757-6*, Signet Bks.) NAL.
—Chimney Rock Burial: Genocide at Coyote. 1999. (Trailsman Ser.: Vol. 207). 176p. mass mkt. 4.99 o.s.i (*0-451-19386-5*) NAL.
—Colorado Carnage. 1995. (Trailsman Ser.: No. 166). 176p. mass mkt. 4.50 o.s.i (*0-451-18223-5*, Signet Bks.) NAL.
—Colorado Cutthroats, Vol. 257. 2003. 176p. mass mkt. 4.99 (*0-451-20827-7*) NAL.
—Colorado Diamond Dupe. 2000. (Trailsman Ser.: Vol. 222). 176p. mass mkt. 4.99 o.s.i (*0-451-20007-1*, Signet Bks.) NAL.
—Colorado Quarry. 1992. (Trailsman Ser.: No. 124). 176p. (Orig.). mass mkt. 3.50 o.s.i (*0-451-17213-2*, Signet Bks.) NAL.
—Colorado Wolfpack. 1996. (Trailsman Ser.: No. 177). 176p. mass mkt. 4.99 o.s.i (*0-451-18759-8*, Signet Bks.) NAL.
—Comanche Crossing. 1990. (Trailsman Ser.: No. 104). 176p. mass mkt. 3.50 o.p. (*0-451-16705-8*, Signet Bks.) NAL.
—The Comstock Killers. 1983. (Trailsman Ser.: No. 23). 192p. mass mkt. 2.50 o.p. (*0-451-12568-1*, Signet Bks.) NAL.
—Confederate Challenge. 1987. (Trailsman Ser.: No. 69). 176p. mass mkt. 2.75 o.p. (*0-451-14964-5*, Signet Bks.) NAL.
—The Coronado Killers. 1990. (Trailsman Ser.: No. 102). 176p. mass mkt. 3.50 o.p. (*0-451-16583-7*, Signet Bks.) NAL.
—Cougar Dawn. 1993. (Trailsman Ser.: No. 134). 176p. (Orig.). mass mkt. 3.50 o.s.i (*0-451-17503-4*, Signet Bks.) NAL.
—Counterfeit Cargo. 1991. (Trailsman Ser.: No. 110). 176p. mass mkt. 3.50 o.p. (*0-451-16894-1*, Signet Bks.) NAL.
—Crowheart's Revenge. 1994. (Trailsman Ser.: No. 151). 176p. (Orig.). mass mkt. 3.50 o.s.i (*0-451-17887-4*) NAL.
—Cry Revenge. 1989. (Trailsman Ser.: No. 95). 176p. mass mkt. 3.50 o.p. (*0-451-16275-7*, 013) NAL.
—Cry the Cheyenne. 1983. (Trailsman Ser.: No. 18). mass mkt. 2.50 o.p. (*0-451-12343-3*, Signet Bks.) NAL.
—Curse of the Grizzly. 1996. (Trailsman Ser.: No. 176). 176p. mass mkt. 4.99 o.s.i (*0-451-18689-3*, Signet Bks.) NAL.
—Dakota Death House. 1995. (Trailsman Ser.: No. 165). 176p. mass mkt. 4.50 o.s.i (*0-451-18222-7*, Signet Bks.) NAL.
—Dakota Death Rattle. 2003. 176p. mass mkt. 4.99 (*0-451-21000-X*, Signet Bks.) NAL.
—Dakota Deception. 1999. (Trailsman Ser.: Vol. 217). 176p. mass mkt. 4.99 o.s.i (*0-451-19759-3*, Signet Classics) NAL.
—Dakota Wild. 1981. (Trailsman Ser.: No. 6). (Orig.). mass mkt. 2.50 o.p. (*0-451-11988-6*, AE1988, Signet Bks.) NAL.
—Dead Mans Forest. 1988. (Trailsman Ser.: No. 83). mass mkt. 2.95 o.p. (*0-451-15676-5*, Signet Bks.) NAL.
—Death Ranch. 1991. (Canyon O'Grady Ser.: No. 15). 176p. (Orig.). mass mkt. 3.50 o.p. (*0-451-17049-0*, Signet Bks.) NAL.
—Death Trails. 1994. (Trailsman Ser.: No. 147). 176p. (Orig.). mass mkt. 3.50 o.p. (*0-451-17882-3*, Signet Bks.) NAL.
—Deathblow Trail. 1993. (Trailsman Ser.: No. 143). 176p. mass mkt. 3.50 o.s.i (*0-451-17754-1*, Signet Bks.) NAL.
—Death's Caravan. 1989. (Trailsman Ser.: No. 92). 176p. mass mkt. 2.95 o.p. (*0-451-16111-4*, Signet Bks.) NAL.
—Desert Desperados. 1990. (Trailsman Ser.: No. 98). 176p. mass mkt. 3.50 o.p. (*0-451-16408-3*) NAL.
—Devil's Den. 1988. (Trailsman Ser.: No. 77). mass mkt. 2.75 o.p. (*0-451-15321-9*, Signet Bks.) NAL.
—The Doomsday Wagons. 1991. (Trailsman Ser.: No. 112). 176p. (Orig.). mass mkt. 3.50 o.p. (*0-451-16942-5*, Signet Bks.) NAL.
—Duet for Six-Guns. 1999. (Trailsman Ser.: Vol. 215). 176p. mass mkt. 4.99 o.s.i (*0-451-19866-2*, Signet Bks.) NAL.
—Fargo's Woman. 1987. (Trailsman Ser.: No. 64). mass mkt. 2.75 o.p. (*0-451-14785-5*, Signet Bks.) NAL.
—Ghost Ranch Massacre. 1995. (Trailsman Ser.: No. 157). 176p. mass mkt. 3.99 o.s.i (*0-451-18161-1*, Signet Bks.) NAL.
—Gold Fever. 1992. (Trailsman Ser.: No. 122). 176p. mass mkt. 3.50 o.p. (*0-451-17175-6*, Signet Bks.) NAL.
—Gold Mine Madness. 1991. (Trailsman Ser.: No. 115). (Illus.). 176p. mass mkt. 3.50 o.p. (*0-451-16996-4*, Signet Bks.) NAL.
—Golden Bullets. 1993. (Trailsman Ser.: No. 142). 176p. (Orig.). mass mkt. 3.50 o.s.i (*0-451-17753-3*, Signet Bks.) NAL.
—The Grizzly Man. 1985. (Trailsman Ser.: No. 40). mass mkt. 2.75 o.p. (*0-451-13526-1*, Signet Bks.) NAL.
—Gun Valley. 1991. (Trailsman Ser.: No. 117). 176p. (Orig.). mass mkt. 3.50 o.p. (*0-451-17048-2*, Signet Bks.) NAL.
—Guns of Hungry Horse. 1986. (Trailsman Ser.: No. 56). 192p. mass mkt. 2.75 o.p. (*0-451-14443-0*, Signet Bks.) NAL.
—Gunsmoke Gulch. 1990. (Trailsman Ser.: No. 107). 176p. (Orig.). mass mkt. 3.50 o.p. (*0-451-16803-8*, Signet Bks.) NAL.
—The Hanging Trail. 1980. (Trailsman Ser.: No. 2). (Orig.). mass mkt. 2.50 o.p. (*0-451-13293-9*, AE3293, Signet Bks.) NAL.
—Hell Town. 1985. (Trailsman Ser.: No. 46). mass mkt. 2.75 o.p. (*0-451-13862-7*, Signet Bks.) NAL.
—High Sierra Horror. 1999. (Trailsman Ser.: Vol. 216). 176p. mass mkt. 4.99 o.s.i (*0-451-19860-3*, Signet Bks.) NAL.
—Horsethief Crossing. 1987. (Trailsman Ser.: No. 62). 192p. mass mkt. 2.75 o.p. (*0-451-14714-6*, Signet Bks.) NAL.
—Hostage Arrows. 1987. (Trailsman Ser.: No. 70). 176p. mass mkt. 2.75 o.p. (*0-451-15012-0*, Signet Bks.) NAL.
—Hostage Trail. 1984. (Trailsman Ser.: No. 28). mass mkt. 2.50 o.p. (*0-451-12876-1*, Signet Bks.) NAL.
—Idaho Ghost Town. 2000. (Trailsman Ser.: Vol. 223). 176p. mass mkt. 4.99 o.s.i (*0-451-20024-1*, Signet Bks.) NAL.
—The Judas Killer. 1983. (Trailsman Ser.: No. 20). mass mkt. 2.50 o.p. (*0-451-12454-5*, Signet Bks.) NAL.
—Kansas Carnage. 1998. (Trailsman Ser.: Vol. 196). 176p. mass mkt. 4.99 o.s.i (*0-451-19385-7*, Signet Bks.) NAL.
—Kansas Kill. 1991. (Trailsman Ser.: No. 116). 176p. (Orig.). mass mkt. 3.50 o.p. (*0-451-17023-7*, Signet Bks.) NAL.
—Kentucky Colts. 1992. (Trailsman Ser.: No. 132). 176p. (Orig.). mass mkt. 3.50 o.p. (*0-451-17374-0*, Signet Bks.) NAL.
—Killer Caravan. 1985. (Trailsman Ser.: No. 45). mass mkt. 2.75 o.p. (*0-451-13811-2*, Signet Bks.) NAL.
—Killer Clan. 1986. (Trailsman Ser.: No. 54). mass mkt. 2.75 o.p. (*0-451-14308-6*, Signet Bks.) NAL.
—The Killing Corridor. 1993. (Trailsman Ser.: No. 140). 176p. (Orig.). mass mkt. 3.50 o.p. (*0-451-17751-7*, Signet Bks.) NAL.
—Kiowa Command. 1995. (Trailsman Ser.: Vol. 168). 176p. mass mkt. 4.50 o.s.i (*0-451-18515-3*, Signet Bks.) NAL.
—Kiowa Kill. 1984. (Trailsman Ser.: No. 36). mass mkt. 2.50 o.p. (*0-451-13251-3*, Signet Bks.) NAL.
—Leavenworth Express. 1998. (Trailsman Ser.: Vol. 204). 176p. mass mkt. 4.99 o.s.i (*0-451-19580-9*, Signet Bks.) NAL.
—Longhorn Guns. 1986. (Trailsman Ser.: No. 53). mass mkt. 2.75 o.p. (*0-451-14264-0*, Signet Bks.) NAL.

—The Lost Patrol. 1985. (Trailsman Ser.: No. 38). mass mkt. 2.75 o.p. (*0-451-13411-7*, Signet Bks.) NAL.

—Manitoba Mauraders. 2000. (Trailsman Ser.: Vol. 229). 176p. mass mkt. 4.99 o.s.i (*0-451-20164-7*) NAL.

—Maverick Maiden. 1984. (Trailsman Ser.: No. 25). 192p. mass mkt. 2.50 o.p. (*0-451-12685-8*, Signet Bks.) NAL.

—Mercy Manhunt. 1997. (Trailsman Ser.: No. 188). 176p. mass mkt. 4.99 o.s.i (*0-451-19138-2*, Signet Bks.) NAL.

—Mesabi Huntdown. 1989. (Trailsman Ser.: No. 90). mass mkt. 2.95 o.p. (*0-451-16011-8*, Signet Bks.) NAL.

—Mesquite Manhunt. 1985. (Trailsman Ser.: No. 43). 192p. mass mkt. 2.75 o.p. (*0-451-13664-0*, Signet Bks.) NAL.

—Mexican Massacre. 1989. (Trailsman Ser.: No. 88). mass mkt. 2.95 o.p. (*0-451-15922-5*, Signet Bks.) NAL.

—Minnesota Missionary. 1988. (Trailsman Ser.: No. 78). mass mkt. 2.75 o.p. (*0-451-15367-7*, Signet Bks.) NAL.

—Montana Fire Smoke. 1992. (Trailsman Ser.: No. 130). 176p. (Orig.). mass mkt. 3.50 o.p. (*0-451-17371-6*, Signet Bks.) NAL.

—Montana Gun Sharps. 2000. (Trailsman Ser.: Vol. 220). 176p. mass mkt. 4.99 o.s.i (*0-451-19964-2*, Signet Bks.) NAL.

—Montana Maiden. 1982. (Trailsman Ser.: No. 11). mass mkt. 2.50 o.p. (*0-451-11632-1*, AE1632, Signet Bks.) NAL.

—Montana Mayhem. 1993. (Trailsman Ser.: No. 135). 176p. (Orig.). mass mkt. 3.50 o.s.i (*0-451-17527-1*, Signet Bks.) NAL.

—Moon Lake Massacre. 1993. (Trailsman Ser.: No. 137). 176p. (Orig.). mass mkt. 3.50 o.s.i (*0-451-17594-8*, Signet Bks.) NAL.

—Mountain Man Kill. 1980. (Trailsman Ser.: No. 3). (Orig.). mass mkt. 2.50 o.p. (*0-451-12100-7*, AE2100, Signet Bks.) NAL.

—Mountain Mankillers. 1998. (Trailsman Ser.: Vol. 205). 176p. mass mkt. 4.99 o.s.i (*0-451-19504-3*, Signet Bks.) NAL.

—Navajo Revenge. 2000. (Trailsman Ser.: Vol. 227). 176p. mass mkt. 4.99 o.s.i (*0-451-20133-7*, Signet Bks.) NAL.

—Nebraska Nightmare. 1994. (Trailsman Ser.: No. 146). 176p. (Orig.). mass mkt. 3.50 o.s.i (*0-451-17876-9*, Signet Bks.) NAL.

—Nebraska Slaying Ground. 2000. (Trailsman Ser.: Vol. 226). 176p. mass mkt. 4.99 o.s.i (*0-451-20097-7*, Signet Bks.) NAL.

—Nevada Warpath. 1992. (Trailsman Ser.: No. 127). 176p. (Orig.). mass mkt. 3.50 o.p. (*0-451-17303-1*, Signet Bks.) NAL.

—Nez Perce Nightmare: The Trailsman. 1995. (Trailsman Ser.: No. 164). 176p. (Orig.). mass mkt. 3.99 o.s.i (*0-451-18221-9*, Signet Bks.) NAL.

—Oklahoma Ordeal. 1994. (Trailsman Ser.: No. 155). 176p. (Orig.). mass mkt. 3.99 o.s.i (*0-451-17891-2*) NAL.

—Oregon Outrider, 206. 1999. (Trailsman Ser.: Vol. 206). 176p. mass mkt. 4.99 o.s.i (*0-451-19581-7*, Signet Bks.) NAL.

—Pawnee Bargain. 1990. (Trailsman Ser.: No. 108). 176p. (Orig.). mass mkt. 3.50 o.p. (*0-451-16857-7*, Signet Bks.) NAL.

—Posse from Hell. 1986. (Trailsman Ser.: No. 52). mass mkt. 2.75 o.p. (*0-451-14234-9*, Signet Bks.) NAL.

—Prairie Fire. 1994. (Trailsman Ser.: No. 152). 176p. (Orig.). mass mkt. 3.99 o.s.i (*0-451-17888-2*, Signet Bks.) NAL.

—Prairie Firestorm, No. 225. 2000. (Trailsman Ser.: Vol. 225). 176p. mass mkt. 4.99 o.s.i (*0-451-20072-1*, Signet Bks.) NAL.

—Queen's High Bid. 1990. (Trailsman Ser.: No. 97). 176p. mass mkt. 3.50 o.p. (*0-451-16369-9*) NAL.

—The Range Killers. 1985. (Trailsman Ser.: No. 41). mass mkt. 2.75 o.p. (*0-451-13572-5*, Signet Bks.) NAL.

—Red River Revenge. 1984. (Trailsman Ser.: No. 33). mass mkt. 2.50 o.p. (*0-451-13164-9*, Signet Bks.) NAL.

—Redwood Revenge. 1992. (Trailsman Ser.: No. 121). 176p. mass mkt. 3.50 o.p. (*0-451-17130-6*, Signet Bks.) NAL.

—The Renegade Command. 1985. (Trailsman Ser.: No. 42). 192p. mass mkt. 2.75 o.p. (*0-451-13622-5*, Signet Bks.) NAL.

—Renegade Rebellion. 1987. (Trailsman Ser.: No. 71). 176p. mass mkt. 2.75 o.p. (*0-451-15051-1*, Signet Bks.) NAL.

—Renegade Rifles. 1991. (Trailsman Ser.: No. 119). 176p. mass mkt. 3.50 o.s.i (*0-451-17093-8*, Signet Bks.) NAL.

—Renegade Rifles. l.t. ed. 2000. (Western Ser.). 210p. 20.95 (*0-7862-2588-2*) Thorndike Pr.

—Revenge at Lost Creek. 1995. (Trailsman Ser.: No. 162). 176p. (Orig.). mass mkt. 3.99 o.s.i (*0-451-18219-7*, Signet Bks.) NAL.

—Ride the Wild Shadow. 1983. (Trailsman Ser.: No. 17). mass mkt. 2.50 o.p. (*0-451-12280-1*, Signet Bks.) NAL.

—River Kill. 1987. (Trailsman Ser.: No. 65). 176p. mass mkt. 2.75 o.p. (*0-451-14818-5*, Signet Bks.) NAL.

—The River Raiders. 1981. (Trailsman Ser.: No. 5). mass mkt. 2.25 o.p. (*0-451-11199-0*, AE1199) NAL.

—Riverboat Gold. 1990. (Trailsman Ser.: No. 100). mass mkt. 3.95 o.p. (*0-451-16481-4*) NAL.

—Rogue River Feud. 1995. (Trailsman Ser.: No. 161). 176p. (Orig.). mass mkt. 3.99 o.s.i (*0-451-18218-9*, Signet Bks.) NAL.

—Sagebrush Skeletons. 1996. (Trailsman Ser.: No. 179). 176p. mass mkt. 4.99 o.s.i (*0-451-18693-1*) NAL.

—Saguaro Showdown. 1994. (Trailsman Ser.: No. 153). 176p. (Orig.). mass mkt. 3.99 o.p. (*0-451-17889-0*, Signet Bks.) NAL.

—Salmon River Rage. 1998. (Trailsman Ser.: Vol. 201). 176p. mass mkt. 4.99 o.s.i (*0-451-19249-4*, Signet Bks.) NAL.

—Salt Lake Siren. 2001. (Trailsman Ser.: Vol. 231). 176p. mass mkt. 4.99 o.s.i (*0-451-20222-8*) NAL.

—Santa Fe Slaughter. 1988. (Trailsman Ser.: No. 73). 176p. mass mkt. 2.75 o.p. (*0-451-15139-9*, Signet Bks.) NAL.

—Savage Guns. 1994. (Trailsman Ser.: No. 150). 176p. (Orig.). mass mkt. 3.50 o.s.i (*0-451-17886-6*) NAL.

—The Sawdust Trail. 1994. (Trailsman Ser.: No. 156). 176p. mass mkt. 3.99 o.s.i (*0-451-18160-3*, Signet Bks.) NAL.

—Scorpion Trail. 1985. (Trailsman Ser.: No. 44). mass mkt. 2.75 o.p. (*0-451-13774-4*, Signet Bks.) NAL.

—Secret Sixguns. 1990. (Trailsman Ser.: No. 103). 176p. mass mkt. 3.50 o.p. (*0-451-16611-6*, Signet Bks.) NAL.

—Seven Wagons West. 1980. (Trailsman Ser.: No. 1). 192p. (Orig.). mass mkt. 4.99 o.s.i (*0-451-12729-3*, AE2729, Signet Bks.) NAL.

—Sharps Justice. 1984. (Trailsman Ser.: No. 34). mass mkt. 2.50 o.p. (*0-451-13199-1*, Signet Bks.) NAL.

—Shoshoni Spirit. 1990. (Trailsman Ser.: No. 101). 176p. mass mkt. 3.50 o.p. (*0-451-16548-9*, Signet Bks.) NAL.

—Sierra Shootout. 1990. (Trailsman Ser.: No. 106). 176p. mass mkt. 3.50 o.p. (*0-451-16746-5*, Signet Bks.) NAL.

—Silver City Slayer. 2002. (Trailsman Ser.: Vol. 249). 192p. mass mkt. 4.99 o.s.i (*0-451-20660-6*, Signet Bks.) NAL.

—Silver Fury. 1993. (Trailsman Ser.: No. 138). 176p. (Orig.). mass mkt. 3.50 o.s.i (*0-451-17615-4*, Signet Bks.) NAL.

—Silver Hooves, No. 203. 1998. (Trailsman Ser.). mass mkt. 4.99 o.s.i (*0-451-19579-5*, Signet Bks.) NAL.

—The Silver Maria. 1992. (Trailsman Ser.: No. 129). 176p. (Orig.). mass mkt. 3.50 o.p. (*0-451-17369-4*, Signet Bks.) NAL.

—Sioux Captive. 1986. (Trailsman Ser.: No. 51). mass mkt. 2.75 o.p. (*0-451-14166-0*, Signet Bks.) NAL.

—Sioux Stampede. 1999. (Trailsman Ser.: Vol. 212). 176p. mass mkt. 4.99 o.s.i (*0-451-19757-7*) NAL.

—Six-Gun Drive. 1981. (Trailsman Ser.: No. 8). (Orig.). mass mkt. 2.50 o.p. (*0-451-12172-4*, AE2172, Signet Bks.) NAL.

—Six-Gun Salvation. 1985. (Trailsman Ser.: No. 47). mass mkt. 2.75 o.p. (*0-451-13919-4*, Signet Bks.) NAL.

—Six Gun Scholar. 2003. 176p. mass mkt. 4.99 (*0-451-21001-8*, Signet Bks.) NAL.

—Six-Gun Sombreros. 1984. (Trailsman Ser.: No. 31). mass mkt. 2.50 o.p. (*0-451-13059-6*, Signet Bks.) NAL.

—Sixguns by the Sea. anniv. ed. 1998. (Trailsman Ser.: Vol. 200). 256p. mass mkt. 5.99 o.s.i (*0-451-19709-7*, Signet Bks.) NAL.

—Slaughter Express. 1986. (Trailsman Ser.: No. 58). 192p. mass mkt. 2.75 o.p. (*0-451-14524-0*, Signet Bks.) NAL.

—Snake River Butcher. 1992. (Trailsman Ser.: No. 128). 176p. mass mkt. 3.50 o.p. (*0-451-17368-6*, Signet Bks.) NAL.

—Snake River Ruins. 2003. 176p. mass mkt. 4.99 (*0-451-20999-0*, Signet Bks.) NAL.

—Socorro Slaughter. 1996. (Trailsman Ser.: No. 169). 176p. mass mkt. 4.99 o.s.i (*0-451-18523-4*, Signet Bks.) NAL.

—Southern Belles. 1991. (Trailsman Ser.: No. 113). 176p. mass mkt. 3.50 o.p. (*0-451-16963-8*, Signet Bks.) NAL.

—Spoon River Stud. 1983. (Trailsman Ser.: No. 19). mass mkt. 2.50 o.p. (*0-451-12387-5*, AE2389, Signet Bks.) NAL.

—Springfield Sharpshooters. 1994. (Trailsman Ser.: No. 149). 176p. (Orig.). mass mkt. 3.50 o.s.i (*0-451-17885-8*, Signet Bks.) NAL.

—Stagecoach to Hell. 1987. (Trailsman Ser.: No. 63). mass mkt. 2.75 o.p. (*0-451-14751-0*, Signet Bks.) NAL.

—The Stalking Horse. 1983. (Trailsman Ser.: No. 15). 176p. mass mkt. 2.50 o.p. (*0-451-12143-0*, Signet Bks.) NAL.

—Stallion Search. 1998. (Trailsman Ser.: Vol. 202). 176p. mass mkt. 4.99 o.s.i (*0-451-19503-5*, Signet Bks.) NAL.

—The Sundown Searchers. 1980. (Trailsman Ser.: No. 4). (Orig.). mass mkt. 2.50 o.p. (*0-451-12200-3*, AE2200, Signet Bks.) NAL.

—Sutter's Secret. 1996. (Trailsman Ser.: Vol. 172). 176p. mass mkt. 4.99 o.s.i (*0-451-18540-4*, Signet Bks.) NAL.

—The Swamp Slayers. 1986. (Trailsman Ser.: No. 49). mass mkt. 2.75 o.p. (*0-451-14051-6*, Signet Bks.) NAL.

—Tamarind Trail. 1991. (Trailsman Ser.: No. 14). 176p. mass mkt. 3.50 o.p. (*0-451-16979-4*, Signet Bks.) NAL.

—Target Conestoga. 1989. (Trailsman Ser.: No. 89). mass mkt. 2.95 o.p. (*0-451-15971-3*, Signet Bks.) NAL.

—Texas Hell Country. 1989. (Trailsman Ser.: No. 86). 176p. mass mkt. 2.95 o.p. (*0-451-15812-1*, Signet Bks.) NAL.

—Texas Hellion. 1999. (Trailsman Ser.: Vol. 214). 176p. mass mkt. 4.99 o.s.i (*0-451-19758-5*) NAL.

—Texas Tinhorns. 2000. (Trailsman Ser.: Vol. 224). 176p. mass mkt. 4.99 o.s.i (*0-451-20041-1*, Signet Bks.) NAL.

—The Texas Train. 1989. (Trailsman Ser.: No. 93). mass mkt. 3.50 o.p. (*0-451-16154-8*, Signet Bks.) NAL.

—Texas Triggers. 1993. (Trailsman Ser.: No. 136). 176p. (Orig.). mass mkt. 3.50 o.s.i (*0-451-17565-4*, Signet Bks.) NAL.

—Thief River Showdown. 1986. (Trailsman Ser.: No. 55). mass mkt. 2.75 o.p. (*0-451-14390-6*, Signet Bks.) NAL.

—Thunderhawk. 1986. (Trailsman Ser.: No. 59). 192p. mass mkt. 2.75 o.p. (*0-451-14573-9*, Signet Bks.) NAL.

—Timber Terror. 1999. (Trailsman Ser.: No. 209). 176p. mass mkt. 4.99 o.s.i (*0-451-19791-7*) NAL.

—Tornado Trail. 1995. (Trailsman Ser.: No. 160). 176p. mass mkt. 3.99 o.s.i (*0-451-18217-0*, Signet Bks.) NAL.

—Trailsman. (Trailsman Ser.: Vol. 195). 1998. 176p. mass mkt. 4.99 o.s.i (*0-451-19247-8*); 1998. 176p. mass mkt. 4.99 o.s.i (*0-451-19384-9*); 1997. 176p. mass mkt. 4.99 o.s.i (*0-451-19235-4*); 1997. 176p. mass mkt. 4.99 o.s.i (*0-451-19163-3*); 1997. mass mkt. 4.99 o.s.i (*0-451-19162-5*); 1997. 176p. mass mkt. 4.99 o.s.i (*0-451-18763-6*); 1997. 128p. mass mkt. 4.99 o.s.i (*0-451-19137-4*); 1997. 176p. mass mkt. 4.99 o.s.i (*0-451-18740-7*); 1982. mass mkt. 2.25 o.p. (*0-451-11465-5*); 1982. mass mkt. 2.25 o.p. (*0-451-11280-6*); 1981. mass mkt. 2.25 o.p. (*0-451-11084-6*); 1981. mass mkt. 2.25 o.p. (*0-451-09905-2*); 1981. mass mkt. 2.25 o.p. (*0-451-09777-7*); 1981. mass mkt. 1.95 o.p. (*0-451-09615-0*); 1981. mass mkt. 2.50 o.p. (*0-451-12718-8*); 1980. mass mkt. 1.75 o.p. (*0-451-09533-2*); 1980. mass mkt. 2.25 o.p. (*0-451-11158-3*); 1980. mass mkt. 1.95 o.p. (*0-451-09839-0*); 1980. mass mkt. 2.25 o.p. (*0-451-11130-3*); 1980. mass mkt. 1.75 o.p. (*0-451-09353-4*); 1980. mass mkt. 1.75 o.p. (*0-451-09307-0*); 1980. mass mkt. 1.75 o.p. (*0-451-09308-9*); 1980. mass mkt. 2.25 o.p. (*0-451-11053-6*); 1980. mass mkt. 2.25 o.s.i (*0-451-11052-8*) NAL. (Signet Bks.).

—The Trailsman. 176p. 2004. mass mkt. 4.99 (*0-451-21190-1*); 2002. (Trailsman Ser.: Vol. 253). mass mkt. 4.99 (*0-451-20744-0*); 1996. (Trailsman Ser.: No. 180). mass mkt. 4.99 o.s.i (*0-451-18760-1*) NAL. (Signet Bks.).

—Trailsman, No. 94. 1989. (Trailsman Ser.). mass mkt. 3.50 o.p. (*0-451-16231-5*, Signet Bks.) NAL.

—The Trailsman. 1996. (Trailsman Ser.: Vol. 171). 176p. No. 171. mass mkt. 4.99 o.s.i (*0-451-18539-0*); No. 173. mass mkt. 4.99 o.s.i (*0-451-18541-2*); No. 174. mass mkt. 4.99 o.s.i (*0-451-18542-0*) NAL. (Signet Bks.).

—Trailsman. 1997. (Trailsman Ser.: Vol. 183). No. 183. 176p. mass mkt. 4.99 o.s.i (*0-451-18762-8*); No. 184. 176p. mass mkt. 4.99 o.s.i (*0-451-19160-9*); No. 187. 176p. mass mkt. 4.99 o.s.i (*0-451-19161-7*); No. 191. 128p. mass mkt. 4.99 o.s.i (*0-451-19146-3*) NAL. (Signet Bks.).

—The Trailsman: Colorado Diamond Dupe. l.t. ed. 2000. (Wheeler Large Print Book Ser.). 201p. pap. 24.95 o.p. (*1-56895-888-9*, Wheeler Publishing, Inc.) Gale Group.

—Trailsman: The Bush League. 1999. (Trailsman Ser.: Vol. 210). 176p. mass mkt. 4.99 o.s.i (*0-451-19684-8*) NAL.

—The Trailsman: Tomahawk Justice, No. 141. 1993. (Trailsman Ser.). 176p. mass mkt. 3.50 o.s.i (*0-451-17752-5*, Signet Bks.) NAL.

—The Trailsman No. 10: Slave Hunter. 1982. (Trailsman Ser.). mass mkt. 2.50 o.p. (*0-451-12498-7*, Signet Bks.) NAL.

—The Trailsman No. 12: Condor Pass. 1982. (Trailsman Ser.). 176p. mass mkt. 2.50 o.p. (*0-451-11837-5*, AE1837, Signet Bks.) NAL.

—The Trailsman No. 13: Blood Chase. 1982. (Trailsman Ser.). mass mkt. 2.50 o.p. (*0-451-11927-4*, AE1927, Signet Bks.) NAL.

—The Trailsman No. 21: The Whiskey Guns. 1983. (Trailsman Ser.). 192p. mass mkt. 2.50 o.p. (*0-451-12487-1*, Signet Bks.) NAL.

—The Trailsman No. 26: Warpaint Rifles. 1984. (Trailsman Ser.). 192p. mass mkt. 2.50 o.p. (*0-451-12775-7*, Signet Bks.) NAL.

—The Trailsman No. 29: High Mountain Guns. 1984. (Trailsman Ser.). 192p. mass mkt. 2.50 o.p. (*0-451-12917-2*, Signet Bks.) NAL.

—The Trailsman No. 67: Manitoba Murders. 1987. (Trailsman Ser.). 192p. mass mkt. 2.75 o.p. (*0-451-14890-8*, Signet Bks.) NAL.

—The Trailsman No. 75: Colorado Robber. 1988. (Trailsman Ser.). 176p. mass mkt. 2.75 o.p. (*0-451-15226-3*, Signet Bks.) NAL.

—The Trailsman No. 76: Wildcat Wagons. 1988. (Trailsman Ser.). 176p. mass mkt. 2.75 o.p. (*0-451-15294-8*, Signet Bks.) NAL.

—The Trailsman No. 126: Coins of Death. 1992. (Trailsman Ser.). 176p. mass mkt. 3.50 o.p. (*0-451-17260-4*) NAL.

—The Trailsman No. 158: Texas Terror. 1995. (Trailsman Ser.). 176p. (Orig.). mass mkt. 3.99 o.s.i (*0-451-18215-4*, Signet Bks.) NAL.

—The Trailsman No. 159: North Country Guns. 1995. (Trailsman Ser.). 176p. (Orig.). mass mkt. 3.99 o.s.i (*0-451-18216-2*, Signet Bks.) NAL.

—The Trailsman No. 160: The Tornado Trail. 1995. 176p. (Orig.). mass mkt. 3.99 (*0-451-18271-5*) NAL.

—Trapper Rampage. 1987. (Trailsman Ser.: No. 68). 176p. mass mkt. 2.75 o.p. (*0-451-14931-9*, Signet Bks.) NAL.

—Treachery Pass. 1987. (Trailsman Ser.: No. 66). mass mkt. 2.75 o.p. (*0-451-14862-2*, Signet Bks.) NAL.

—Twisted Noose. 1983. (Trailsman Ser.: No. 24). 192p. (Orig.). mass mkt. 2.50 o.p. (*0-451-12620-3*, Signet Bks.) NAL.

—Twisted Trails. 1988. (Trailsman Ser.: No. 81). 176p. mass mkt. 2.95 o.p. (*0-451-15555-6*, Signet Bks.) NAL.

—Utah Slaughter. 1988. (Trailsman Ser.: No. 84). mass mkt. 2.95 o.p. (*0-451-15719-2*, Signet Bks.) NAL.

—Utah Trackdown. 1996. (Trailsman Ser.: No. 170). 176p. mass mkt. 4.99 o.s.i (*0-451-18538-2*, Signet Bks.) NAL.

—Utah Uprising. 1998. (Trailsman Ser.: Vol. 19). 176p. mass mkt. 4.99 o.s.i (*0-451-19501-9*, Signet Bks.) NAL.

—Utah Uproar, Vol. 251. 2002. 176p. mass mkt. 4.99 o.s.i (*0-451-20697-5*) NAL.

—Valley of Death. 1985. (Trailsman Ser.: No. 37). mass mkt. 2.75 o.p. (*0-451-13337-4*, Signet Bks.) NAL.

—Vengeance at Dead Man Rapids. 1997. (Trailsman Ser.: No. 181). 176p. mass mkt. 4.99 o.s.i (*0-451-18669-9*, Signet Bks.) NAL.

—Wayward Lassie. 1986. (Trailsman Ser.: No. 60). 192p. mass mkt. 2.75 o.p. (*0-451-14617-4*, Signet Bks.) NAL.

—White Hell. 1988. (Trailsman Ser.: No. 74). 176p. mass mkt. 2.75 o.p. (*0-451-15193-3*, Signet Bks.) NAL.

—The White Hell Trail. 1985. (Trailsman Ser.: No. 48). mass mkt. 2.75 o.p. (*0-451-14012-5*, Signet Bks.) NAL.

—White Savage. 1984. (Trailsman Ser.: No. 30). mass mkt. 2.50 o.p. (*0-451-12972-5*, Signet Bks.) NAL.

—Wyoming Manhunt. 1991. (Trailsman Ser.: No. 120). 176p. mass mkt. 3.50 o.p. (*0-451-17106-3*, Signet Bks.) NAL.

—Wyoming War Cry. 2000. (Trailsman Ser.: Vol. 228). 176p. mass mkt. 4.99 o.s.i (*0-451-20148-5*, Signet Bks.) NAL.

—Wyoming Wildcats. 1998. (Trailsman Ser.: Vol. 199). 176p. mass mkt. 4.99 o.s.i (*0-451-19502-7*, Signet Bks.) NAL.

—Yukon Massacre. 1995. (Trailsman Ser.: No. 163). 176p. (Orig.). mass mkt. 3.99 o.s.i (*0-451-18220-0*, Signet Bks.) NAL.

**FARNHAM, JULIE (FICTITIOUS CHARACTER)—FICTION**

Eberhart, Mignon G. A Fighting Chance. 1987. 256p. mass mkt. 5.50 o.s.i (*0-446-32350-0*) Warner Bks., Inc.

**FARO, JEREMY (FICTITIOUS CHARACTER)—FICTION**

Knight, Alanna. Blood Line: An Inspector Faro Mystery. 1989. 224p. 15.95 o.p. (*0-312-03295-1*, Saint Martin's Minotaur) St. Martin's Pr.

—The Bull Slayers: An Inspector Faro Mystery. l.t. ed. 1997. 290p. 21.95 (*0-7838-8045-6*, Macmillan Reference USA) Gale Group.

—The Coffin Lane Murders. 2001. 218p. pap. 11.95 (*1-902927-23-0*) B & W Publishing GBR. *Dist:* Interlink Publishing Group, Inc.

—Deadly Beloved. l.t. ed. 1992. (Mystery Ser.). 336p. 29.99 o.p. (*0-7089-2646-0*, Ulverscroft) Thorpe, F. A. Pubs. GBR. *Dist:* Ulverscroft Large Print Bks., Ltd., Ulverscroft Large Print Canada, Ltd.
—Enter Second Murderer. 1989. 14.95 o.p. (*0-312-03021-5*) St. Martin's Pr.
—Enter Second Murderer. l.t. ed. 1998. (General Ser.). 269p. pap. 23.95 (*0-7862-1308-6*) Thorndike Pr.
—Enter Second Murderer. l.t. ed. 1990. (Ulverscroft Large Print Ser.). 29.99 o.p. (*0-7089-2236-8*, Ulverscroft) Thorpe, F. A. Pubs. GBR. *Dist:* Ulverscroft Large Print Bks., Ltd., Ulverscroft Large Print Canada, Ltd.
—Enter Second Murderer: An Inspector Faro Mystery. Set. unabr. ed. 1999. audio 54.95 (*0-7540-0352-3*, CAB1775) BBC Audiobooks America.
—The Evil That Men Do. l.t. ed. 1996. 281p. pap. 20.95 o.p. (*0-7838-1649-9*, Macmillan Reference USA) Gale Group.
—Killing Cousins: An Inspector Faro Mystery. l.t. ed. 1992. (Lythway Ser.). 248p. lib. bdg. 20.50 o.p. (*0-7451-1419-9*, Macmillan Reference USA) Gale Group.
—Killing Cousins: An Inspector Faro Mystery. 1991. 256p. 17.95 o.p. (*0-312-07008-X*, Saint Martin's Minotaur) St. Martin's Pr.
—The Missing Duchess. l.t. ed. 1996. pap. 20.95 (*0-7838-1650-2*, Macmillan Reference USA) Gale Group.
—Murder by Appointment: An Inspector Faro Mystery. l.t. ed. 1997. pap. 20.95 o.p. (*0-7838-8044-8*, Macmillan Reference USA) Gale Group.
Knight, Alanna & Lawhead, Stephen R. Deadly Beloved. 1990. 192p. 15.95 o.p. (*0-312-05069-0*, Saint Martin's Minotaur) St. Martin's Pr.

**FARRAR, BRAT (FICTITIOUS CHARACTER)—FICTION**

Tey, Josephine. Brat Farrar. 1981. reprint ed. lib. bdg. 16.00 (*0-8376-0445-1*) Bentley Pubs.
—Brat Farrar. unabr. ed. 2000. audio 59.95 (*0-7451-6320-3*, CAB 499) Chivers Audio Bks. GBR. *Dist:* BBC Audiobooks America.
—Brat Farrar. 1997. 288p. pap. 12.00 (*0-684-80385-2*, Touchstone); 1982. mass mkt. 2.95 o.s.i (*0-671-44190-6*, Pocket) Simon & Schuster.
—Brat Farrar. l.t. ed. 2000. (Mystery Ser.). 437p. 27.95 o.p. (*0-7862-2554-8*) Thorndike Pr.

**FARREL, CASEY (FICTITIOUS CHARACTER)—FICTION**

Matthews, Patricia & Matthews, Clayton. The Scent of Fear. 1992. 320p. 18.95 o.p. (*0-7278-4350-8*) Severn Hse. Pubs., Ltd.
—The Sound of Murder. 1994. 20.00 o.p. (*0-7278-4594-2*) Severn Hse. Pubs., Ltd.
—Taste of Evil. 1993. 256p. lib. bdg. 20.00 o.p. (*0-7278-4505-5*) Severn Hse. Pubs., Ltd.
—Touch of Terror. 1995. 256p. 20.00 (*0-7278-4746-5*) Severn Hse. Pubs., Ltd.
—Vision of Death. 1993. 256p. lib. bdg. 19.00 (*0-7278-4397-4*) Severn Hse. Pubs., Ltd.

**FARRELL, STEPHANIE (FICTITIOUS CHARACTER)—FICTION**

Heggan, Christiane. Betrayals. 1994. 416p. (Orig.). mass mkt. 4.99 o.s.i (*0-451-40508-0*, Onyx) NAL.

**FARRELL, WESLEY (FICTITIOUS CHARACTER)—FICTION**

Skinner, Robert E. Blood to Drink: A Wesley Farrell Novel. 251p. 2001. pap. 14.95 o.s.i (*1-890208-67-1*); 2000. 23.95 (*1-890208-33-7*) Poisoned Pen Pr.
—Cat-Eyed Trouble. 1999. 256p. mass mkt. 5.99 o.s.i (*1-57566-381-3*); 1998. 288p. 19.95 o.s.i (*1-57566-250-7*) Kensington Publishing Corp.
—Daddy's Gone A-Hunting: A Wesley Farrell Novel. 1999. 256p. 22.00 o.s.i (*1-57566-376-7*) Kensington Publishing Corp.
—Daddy's Gone A-Hunting: A Wesley Farrell Novel. 2000. (Illus.). 306p. 23.95 (*1-890208-17-5*) Poisoned Pen Pr.
—Pale Shadow: A Wesley Farrell Novel. 2003. 226p. pap. 14.95 o.s.i (*1-890208-87-6*); 2001. 300p. 23.95 (*1-890208-66-3*) Poisoned Pen Pr.
—The Righteous Cut: A Wesley Farrell Novel. 2002. 275p. 24.95 o.s.i (*1-59058-029-X*); 253p. pap. (*1-59058-044-3*) Poisoned Pen Pr.
—Skin Deep, Blood Red. 1998. 256p. mass mkt. 5.99 o.s.i (*1-57566-254-X*); 1997. 288p. 19.95 o.s.i (*1-57566-092-X*, Kensington Bks.) Kensington Publishing Corp.

**FARROW, KAY (FICTITIOUS CHARACTER)—FICTION**

Hunt, David, pseud. The Magician's Tale. 1998. 416p. reprint ed. mass mkt. 7.50 o.s.i (*0-425-16482-9*) Berkley Publishing Group.
—The Magician's Tale. 1997. 416p. 24.95 o.s.i (*0-399-14260-6*, G. P. Putnam's Sons) Penguin Group (USA) Inc.
—Trick of Light. 1999. 416p. reprint ed. mass mkt. 7.50 o.s.i (*0-425-17035-7*) Berkley Publishing Group.
—Trick of Light. 1998. 400p. 24.95 o.p. (*0-399-14393-9*, G. P. Putnam's Sons) Penguin Group (USA) Inc.

**FEARLESS FOSDICK (FICTITIOUS CHARACTER)—FICTION**

Capp, Al. Fearless Fosdick. Schreiner, Dave & Collins, Max Allan, eds. 1991. (Illus.). 112p. (Orig.). reprint ed. pap. 11.95 (*0-87816-108-2*) Kitchen Sink Pr., Inc.
—Fearless Fosdick: The Hole Story! Schreiner, Dave, ed. 1992. (Illus.). 128p. (Orig.). pap. 11.95 (*0-87816-164-3*) Kitchen Sink Pr., Inc.

**FECHTER, RENATA (FICTITIOUS CHARACTER)—FICTION**

Rathbone, Julian. Accidents Will Happen. 1997. (Mask Noir Ser.). 256p. pap. text (*1-85242-312-9*) Serpent's Tail Ltd.
—Accidents Will Happen. 296p. 26.00 (*0-7278-5619-7*) Severn Hse. Pubs., Ltd.
—The Brandenburg Concerto. 1998. (Mask Noir Ser.). 224p. pap. (*1-85242-525-3*) Serpent's Tail Ltd.
—The Brandenburg Concerto. 256p. 25.99 (*0-7278-5716-9*) Severn Hse. Pubs., Ltd.

**FEDORCENKO FAMILY (FICTITIOUS CHARACTERS)—FICTION**

Pella, Judith. Dawning of Deliverance. 1995. (Russians Ser.: Bk. 5). 432p. pap. 12.99 (*1-55661-359-8*) Bethany Hse. Pubs.
—Heirs of the Motherland. 1993. (Russians Ser.: Vol. 4). 384p. pap. 12.99 (*1-55661-358-X*) Bethany Hse. Pubs.
—Passage into Light. 1998. (Russians Ser.: Vol. 7). 304p. pap. 11.99 (*1-55661-869-7*) Bethany Hse. Pubs.
—Russians, 5 vols., Vol. 1-5, set. 1995. (Russians Ser.: Vol. 1-5). pap. 64.99 (*1-55661-795-X*) Bethany Hse. Pubs.
—White Nights, Red Morning. 1996. (Russians Ser.: Bk. 6). 416p. pap. 12.99 (*1-55661-360-1*) Bethany Hse. Pubs.
Phillips, Michael & Pella, Judith. The Crown & the Crucible. 1991. (Russians Ser.: Bk. 1). 416p. pap. 12.99 (*1-55661-172-2*) Bethany Hse. Pubs.
—A House Divided. 1992. (Russians Ser.: Vol. 2). 352p. pap. 12.99 (*1-55661-173-0*) Bethany Hse. Pubs.
—The Russians Series, Vols. 1-3. 1992. (Russians Ser.). pap. 32.99 o.p. (*1-55661-770-4*, 252770) Bethany Hse. Pubs.
—Travail & Triumph Vol. 3: The Russians. 1992. (Russians Ser.: Vol. 3). 400p. pap. 12.99 (*1-55661-174-9*) Bethany Hse. Pubs.

**FEEP, LEFTY (FICTITIOUS CHARACTER)—FICTION**

Bloch, Robert. Lost in Time & Space with Lefty Feep. Stanley, John, ed. 1987. (Lefty Feep Ser.: Vol. 1). (Illus.). 276p. 40.00 o.p. (*0-940064-02-2*); pap. 12.95 (*0-940064-01-4*) Creatures at Large.
Bloch, Robert & Stanley, John. Lost in Time & Space with Lefty Feep. 1987. (*0-940064-03-0*) Creatures at Large.

**FEIFFER, HARRY (FICTITIOUS CHARACTER)—FICTION**

Marshall, William. The Far-Away Man: A Yellowthread Street Mystery. 1985. o.p. (*0-03-070527-4*) Holt, Henry & Co.
—The Far-Away Man: A Yellowthread Street Mystery. 1988. 208p. mass mkt. 3.95 o.s.i (*0-445-40662-3*, Mysterious Pr. Paperback Bks.) Warner Bks., Inc.
—Frogmouth. 1987. 192p. 15.45 o.p. (*0-89296-197-X*) Mysterious Pr.
—Frogmouth. 1988. mass mkt. 3.50 o.s.i (*0-445-40705-0*, Mysterious Pr. Paperback Bks.) Warner Bks., Inc.
—Gelignite. l.t. ed. 1911. 12.95 o.p. (*1-55504-976-1*, 31); pap. 10.95 o.p. (*1-55504-975-3*, 448) BBC Audiobooks America.
—Gelignite. 1977. o.p. (*0-03-016906-2*) Holt, Henry & Co.
—Gelignite. 1988. (Yellowthread Street Mystery Ser.). 208p. pap. 3.50 o.s.i (*0-445-40660-7*, Mysterious Pr. Paperback Bks.) Warner Bks., Inc.
—The Hatchet Man: A Yellowthread Street Mystery. l.t. ed. 1989. 8.95 o.p. (*1-55504-887-0*, 549); pap. 8.95 o.p. (*1-55504-888-9*) BBC Audiobooks America.
—The Hatchet Man: A Yellowthread Street Mystery. 1977. o.p. (*0-03-016901-1*) Holt, Henry & Co.
—The Hatchet Man: A Yellowthread Street Mystery. 1988. (Yellowthread Street Mystery Ser.). 208p. 3.50 o.s.i (*0-445-40659-3*, Mysterious Pr. Paperback Bks.) Warner Bks., Inc.
—Head First: A Yellowthread Street Mystery. l.t. ed. 1988. (Yellowthread Street Mystery Ser.). 18.95 o.p. (*1-55504-348-8*); pap. 16.95 o.p. (*1-55504-473-5*) BBC Audiobooks America.
—Head First: A Yellowthread Street Mystery. 1986. (Rinehart Suspense Novel Ser.). 192p. 14.95 o.p. (*0-8050-0061-5*) Holt, Henry & Co.
—Head First: A Yellowthread Street Mystery. 1988. 208p. pap. 3.50 o.s.i (*0-445-40665-8*, Mysterious Pr. Paperback Bks.) Warner Bks., Inc.
—Inches. 1994. 304p. 19.95 o.s.i (*0-89296-368-9*) Mysterious Pr.
—Inches. 1995. 256p. mass mkt. 5.99 (*0-446-40455-1*, Mysterious Pr. Paperback Bks.) Warner Bks., Inc.
—Nightmare Syndrome. 1997. 256p. 21.50 o.p. (*0-89296-574-6*) Warner Bks., Inc.
—Out of Nowhere. 1988. 224p. 15.45 o.p. (*0-89296-199-6*) Mysterious Pr.
—Out of Nowhere. 1989. mass mkt. 3.95 (*0-445-40842-1*, Mysterious Pr. Paperback Bks.) Warner Bks., Inc.
—Perfect End. 1984. pap. o.p. (*0-03-071062-6*, Owl Bks.); 1983. 204p. 13.00 o.p. (*0-03-047481-7*) Holt, Henry & Co.
—Roadshow. l.t. ed. 1987. (Yellowthread Street Mystery Ser.). 19.95 o.p. (*1-55504-326-7*); pap. 17.95 o.p. (*1-55504-467-0*) BBC Audiobooks America.
—Roadshow. 1985. 192p. 14.95 o.p. (*0-03-001744-0*) Holt, Henry & Co.
—Sci-Fi. 1984. pap. o.p. (*0-03-071063-4*, Owl Bks.); 1981. 192p. o.p. (*0-03-047486-8*) Holt, Henry & Co.
—Skulduggery. 1984. pap. o.p. (*0-03-071064-2*, Owl Bks.); 1980. 192p. o.p. (*0-03-047491-4*) Holt, Henry & Co.
—Thin Air: A Yellowthread Street Mystery. 1978. o.p. (*0-03-021071-2*) Holt, Henry & Co.
—Thin Air: A Yellowthread Street Mystery. 1982. (Crime Monthly Ser.). 192p. pap. 2.95 o.p. (*0-14-006137-1*, Penguin Bks.) Viking Penguin.
—To the End. 1998. (Yellowthread Street Mysteries Ser.). 240p. 23.00 (*0-89296-575-4*) Mysterious Pr.
—War Machine. 1988. 15.45 o.p. (*0-89296-198-8*) Mysterious Pr.
—War Machine. 1989. (Yellowthread Street Mystery Ser.). mass mkt. 3.95 (*0-445-40595-3*, Mysterious Pr. Paperback Bks.) Warner Bks., Inc.
—Yellowthread Street. 1976. o.p. (*0-03-016836-8*) Holt, Henry & Co.
—Yellowthread Street. 1988. 144p. pap. 3.50 o.s.i (*0-445-40548-1*, Mysterious Pr. Paperback Bks.) Warner Bks., Inc.

**FEIN, IRVING (FICTITIOUS CHARACTER)—FICTION**

Safire, William. Sleeper Spy. 2nd ed. 1997. 416p. mass mkt. 6.99 (*0-312-96156-1*, St. Martin's Paperbacks) St. Martin's Pr.

**FENIMORE, ANDREW (FICTITIOUS CHARACTER)—FICTION**

Hathaway, Robin. The Doctor & the Dead Man's Chest. 2001. (Illus.). 352p. 24.95 (*0-312-26956-0*) St. Martin's Pr.
—The Doctor Digs a Grave. 272p. 1998. 22.95 (*0-312-18568-5*, Saint Martin's Minotaur); Vol. 1. 2nd ed. 1999. mass mkt. 5.99 (*0-312-96703-9*, St. Martin's Paperbacks) St. Martin's Pr.
—The Doctor Makes a Dollhouse Call: A Doctor Fenimore Mystery. E-Book 5.99 (*0-312-27341-X*) St. Martin's Pr.
—Doctor Makes a Dollhouse Call: Doctor Fenimore Mystery. 2000. (Doctor Fenimore Mysteries Ser.). 272p. 23.95 (*0-312-24192-5*, Saint Martin's Minotaur) St. Martin's Pr.

**FELL, GIDEON (FICTITIOUS CHARACTER)—FICTION**

Carr, John Dickson. The Arabian Nights Murder: A Dr. Gideon Fell Mystery. 1989. 320p. reprint ed. pap. 4.95 o.p. (*0-06-080981-7*, P 981, Perennial) HarperTrade.
—Below Suspicion. 1986. (Library of Crime Classics). 186p. pap. 4.95 o.p. (*0-930330-50-1*) International Polygonics, Ltd.
—The Blind Barber: A Dr. Gideon Fell Mystery. l.t. ed. 1992. pap. 14.95 o.p. (*0-7927-1064-9*) BBC Audiobooks America.
—The Blind Barber: A Dr. Gideon Fell Mystery. 1990. 256p. reprint ed. mass mkt. 4.95 o.p. (*0-06-081038-6*, Perennial) HarperTrade.
—The Blind Barber: A Dr. Gideon Fell Mystery. 1990. 256p. (C). reprint ed. lib. bdg. 20.00 o.p. (*0-8095-9027-1*) Millefleurs.
—The Case of the Constant Suicides. 2002. 168p. 21.95 (*0-7540-8615-1*, Black Dagger) BBC Audiobooks America.
—The Crooked Hinge: A Dr. Gideon Fell Mystery. 1976. 283p. 18.95 o.p. (*0-89163-026-0*) Boulevard Bks.
—The Crooked Hinge: A Dr. Gideon Fell Mystery. 1989. 256p. reprint ed. mass mkt. 3.95 o.p. (*0-06-080980-9*, P 980, Perennial) HarperTrade.
—Dark of the Moon. 1987. pap. 3.50 o.p. (*0-88184-304-0*); 2nd ed. 1995. 256p. mass mkt. 4.95 (*0-7867-0222-2*) Avalon Publishing Group. (Carroll & Graf Pubs.).
—Dark of the Moon. l.t. ed. 2001. (Ulverscroft Large Print Ser.). 448p. 32.50 (*0-7089-4441-8*) Ulverscroft Large Print Bks., Ltd.
—The Dead Man's Knock. 1987. 272p. mass mkt. 3.50 o.p. (*0-8217-2099-6*, Zebra Bks.) Kensington Publishing Corp.
—Death Turns the Tables. 1985. 200p. pap. 4.95 o.p. (*0-930330-22-6*) International Polygonics, Ltd.
—Death-Watch: A Dr. Gideon Fell Mystery. 1990. 256p. reprint ed. mass mkt. 4.95 o.p. (*0-06-081040-8*, Perennial) HarperTrade.
—The Eight of Swords. 1986. 256p. mass mkt. 3.50 o.p. (*0-8217-1881-9*); mass mkt. 3.99 o.s.i (*0-8217-3649-3*) Kensington Publishing Corp. (Zebra Bks.).
—Hag's Nook. 1976. 291p. lib. bdg. 25.95 (*0-89966-047-9*) Buccaneer Bks., Inc.
—Hag's Nook. 1985. 1985p. pap. 5.95 o.p. (*0-930330-28-5*) International Polygonics, Ltd.
—He Who Whispers. 1986. (Ipl Library of Crime Classics). 190p. pap. 5.95 o.p. (*0-930330-38-2*) International Polygonics, Ltd.
—The Hollow Man. 1994. 264p. 16.95 o.p. (*0-7451-8637-8*, Black Dagger) BBC Audiobooks America.
—The House at Satan's Elbow. 1980. 1.95 o.s.i (*0-441-34372-4*) Ace Bks.
—The House at Satan's Elbow. 1987. (Library of Crime Classics). 200p. pap. 4.95 o.p. (*0-930330-61-7*) International Polygonics, Ltd.
—In Spite of Thunder. 1987. 224p. 3.50 o.p. (*0-88184-287-7*, Carroll & Graf Pubs.) Avalon Publishing Group.
—The Mad Hatter Mystery: A Dr. Gideon Fell Mystery. 1989. 288p. reprint ed. mass mkt. 4.95 o.p. (*0-06-080997-3*, Perennial) HarperTrade.
—Man Who Could Not Shudder. 1986. mass mkt. 3.50 o.s.i (*0-8217-1703-0*, Zebra Bks.) Kensington Publishing Corp.
—Panic in Box C. 1987. 272p. mass mkt. 3.50 o.p. (*0-88184-288-5*, Carroll & Graf Pubs.) Avalon Publishing Group.
—The Problem of the Green Capsule. 1986. (Library of Crime Classics). 256p. pap. 5.95 o.p. (*0-930330-51-X*) International Polygonics, Ltd.
—The Problem of the Wire Cage. 1986. mass mkt. 3.95 o.s.i (*0-8217-3384-2*, Zebra Bks.) Kensington Publishing Corp.
—The Problem of the Wire Cage. 1982. 224p. 20.00 o.p. (*0-7278-0249-6*) State Mutual Bk. & Periodical Service, Ltd.
—The Sleeping Sphinx. 1985. (Dr. Fell Detective Ser.). 199p. pap. 4.95 (*0-930330-24-2*) International Polygonics, Ltd.
—The Three Coffins. 1989. lib. bdg. 25.95 (*0-89966-048-7*) Buccaneer Bks., Inc.
—The Three Coffins. 1986. 160p. pap. 6.95 o.s.i (*0-930330-39-0*) International Polygonics, Ltd.
—The Three Coffins. 1979. 306p. reprint ed. 25.00 (*0-89366-259-3*) Ultramarine Publishing Co., Inc.
—Till Death Do Us Part. 1985. 200p. pap. 4.95 o.p. (*0-930330-21-8*); 1989. 224p. reprint ed. pap. 5.95 (*1-55882-017-5*, Library of Crime Classics) International Polygonics, Ltd.
—To Wake the Dead: A Dr. Gideon Fell Mystery. 1989. 256p. reprint ed. mass mkt. 4.50 o.p. (*0-06-080998-1*, Perennial) HarperTrade.

**FELLOWES, IAN (FICTITIOUS CHARACTER)—FICTION**

Hammond, Gerald. Home to Roost. 1991. 160p. 16.95 o.p. (*0-312-06369-5*, Saint Martin's Minotaur) St. Martin's Pr.

**FELSE, GEORGE (FICTITIOUS CHARACTER)—FICTION**

Peters, Ellis, pseud. Black is the Colour of My True Love's Heart. 2002. (Inspector George Felse Mystery Ser.: Vol. 6). 220p. mass mkt. 7.95 (*0-7515-1233-8*) Warner Bks. GBR. *Dist:* Trafalgar Square.
—Black is the Colour of My True Love's Heart. 1992. (Inspector George Felse Mystery Ser.: Vol. 6). 208p. mass mkt. 5.99 o.p. (*0-446-40072-6*) Warner Bks., Inc.
—Black Is the Colour of My True Love's Heart. unabr. ed. 1993. (Inspector George Felse Mystery Ser.: Vol. 6 ). audio 41.00 (*1-55690-894-6*, 93336E7) Recorded Bks., LLC.
—City of Gold & Shadows. unabr. ed. 1991. (Inspector George Felse Mystery Ser.: Vol. 12). audio 51.00 (*1-55690-104-6*, 91207E7) Recorded Bks., LLC.
—City of Gold & Shadows. l.t. ed. 1979. (Inspector George Felse Mystery Ser.: Vol. 12). 12.00 o.p. (*0-7089-0354-1*, Ulverscroft) Thorpe, F. A. Pubs. GBR. *Dist:* Ulverscroft Large Print Bks., Ltd.
—Death & the Joyful Woman. l.t. ed. (Insoector George Felse Mystery Ser.: Vol. 2). 1993. pap. 16.95 o.p. (*0-7927-1403-2*); 1992. 18.95 o.p. (*0-7927-1404-0*) BBC Audiobooks America.
—Death & the Joyful Woman. unabr. ed. 1992. (Inspector George Felse Mystery Ser.: Vol. 2). audio 44.00 (*1-55690-657-9*, 92227E7) Recorded Bks., LLC.
—Death & the Joyful Woman. 1995. (Inspector George Felse Mystery Ser.: Vol. 2). 224p. mass mkt. 5.50 (*0-446-40068-8*) Warner Bks., Inc.

—Death to the Landlords! l.t. ed. 1992. (Inspector George Felse Mystery Ser.: Vol. 11). 256p. lib. bdg. 20.95 o.p. (*0-7451-7324-1*, Macmillan Reference USA) Gale Group.
—Death to the Landlords! unabr. ed. (Inspector George Felse Mystery Ser.: Vol. 11). 2000. audio compact disk 64.95 (*0-7531-0905-0*, 109050); 1996. audio 54.95 (*1-85695-994-5*, 960309) ISIS Audio Bks. GBR. *Dist:* Ulverscroft Large Print Bks., Ltd.
—Death to the Landlords! l.t. ed. 1979. (Inspector George Felse Mystery Ser.: Vol. 11). 12.00 o.p. (*0-7089-0304-5*, Ulverscroft) Thorpe, F. A. Pubs. GBR. *Dist:* Ulverscroft Large Print Bks., Ltd.
—Fallen into the Pit. l.t. ed. 1994. (Inspector George Felse Mystery Ser.: Vol. 1). 24.95 (*1-56895-116-7*, Wheeler Publishing, Inc.) Gale Group.
—Fallen into the Pit. 1994. (Inspector George Felse Mystery Ser.: Vol. 1). 336p. 17.95 o.s.i (*0-89296-519-3*) Mysterious Pr.
—Fallen into the Pit. unabr. ed. 1991. (Inspector George Felse Mystery Ser.: Vol. 1). audio 70.00 (*1-55690-623-4*, 91419E7) Recorded Bks., LLC.
—Fallen into the Pit. 1996. (Inspector George Felse Mystery Ser.: Vol. 1). 336p. mass mkt. 6.99 (*0-446-40318-0*) Warner Bks., Inc.
—Flight of a Witch. l.t. ed. 1992. (Inspector George Felse Mystery Ser.: Vol. 3). 320p. lib. bdg. 19.95 o.p. (*0-8161-5315-9*, Macmillan Reference USA) Gale Group.
—Flight of a Witch. unabr. ed. 1997. (Inspector George Felse Mystery Ser.: Vol. 3). audio 54.95 (*1-85695-993-7*, 960509) ISIS Audio Bks. GBR. *Dist:* Ulverscroft Large Print Bks., Ltd.
—Flight of a Witch. 1991. (Inspector George Felse Mystery Ser.: Vol. 3). 16.95 o.p. (*0-89296-404-9*) Mysterious Pr.
—Flight of a Witch. 1992. (Inspector George Felse Mystery Ser.: Vol. 3). 240p. mass mkt. 5.99 o.s.i (*0-446-40146-3*) Warner Bks., Inc.
—The Grass Widow's Tale. unabr. ed. (Inspector George Felse Mystery Ser.: Vol. 7). 2000. audio compact disk 64.95 (*0-7531-0707-4*, 107074); 1995. audio 54.95 (*1-85695-989-9*, 950709) ISIS Audio Bks. GBR. *Dist:* Ulverscroft Large Print Bks., Ltd.
—The House of Green Turf. l.t. ed. 1993. (Inspector George Felse Mystery Ser.: Vol. 8). pap. 16.95 o.p. (*0-7927-1582-9*); 18.95 o.p. (*0-7927-1583-7*) BBC Audiobooks America.
—The House of Green Turf. unabr. ed. 1993. (Inspector George Felse Mystery Ser.: Vol. 8). audio 44.00 (*1-55690-922-5*, 93418E7) Recorded Bks., LLC.
—The Knocker on Death's Door. unabr. ed. 1994. (Inspector George Felse Mystery Ser.: Vol. 10). audio 44.00 (*1-55690-991-8*, 94130E7) Recorded Bks., LLC.
—The Knocker on Death's Door. 2003. (Inspector George Felse Mystery Ser.: Vol. 10). lib. bdg. 25.95 (*0-7862-4744-4*) Thorndike Pr.
—The Knocker on Death's Door. l.t. ed. 1981. (Inspector George Felse Mystery Ser.: Vol. 10). 331p. 12.00 o.p. (*0-7089-0633-8*, Ulverscroft) Thorpe, F. A. Pubs. GBR. *Dist:* Ulverscroft Large Print Bks., Ltd.
—The Knocker on Death's Door. 1992. (Inspector George Felse Mystery Ser.: Vol. 10). 208p. mass mkt. 5.99 o.p. (*0-446-40016-5*) Warner Bks., Inc.
—The Knocker on Death's Door. 1997. (Inspector George Felse Mystery Ser.: Vol. 10). 221p. mass mkt. o.s.i (*0-7515-2079-9*) Warner Futura GBR. *Dist:* Little Brown & Co.
—Mourning Raga. unabr. ed. 1996. (Inspector George Felse Mystery Ser.: Vol. 9). audio 54.95 (*1-85695-992-9*, 951210) ISIS Audio Bks. GBR. *Dist:* Ulverscroft Large Print Bks., Ltd.
—Mourning Raga. l.t. ed. 1981. (Inspector George Felse Mystery Ser.: Vol. 9). o.p. (*0-7089-0576-5*, Ulverscroft) Thorpe, F. A. Pubs.
—A Nice Derangement of Epitaphs. 2003. (Inspector George Felse Mystery Ser.: Vol. 4). 192p. 21.95 (*0-7540-8632-1*, Black Dagger) BBC Audiobooks America.
—A Nice Derangement of Epitaphs. l.t. ed. 1992. (Inspector George Felse Mystery Ser.: Vol. 4). 316p. 18.95 (*0-7505-0311-4*) Magna Large Print Bks. GBR. *Dist:* Ulverscroft Large Print Bks., Ltd.
—A Nice Derangement of Epitaphs. unabr. ed. 1991. (Inspector George Felse Mystery Ser.: Vol. 4). audio 44.00 (*1-55690-374-X*, 91226E7) Recorded Bks., LLC.
—A Nice Derangement of Epitaphs. 1992. (Inspector George Felse Mystery Ser.: Vol. 4). 208p. mass mkt. 6.00 o.p. (*0-446-40069-6*) Warner Bks., Inc.
—The Piper on the Mountain. l.t. ed. 1993. (Magna Large Print Ser.). 342p. 29.99 o.p. (*0-7505-0584-2*) Magna Large Print Bks. GBR. *Dist:* Ulverscroft Large Print Bks., Ltd., Ulverscroft Large Print Canada, Ltd.
—The Piper on the Mountain. unabr. ed. (Inspector George Felse Mystery Ser.: Vol. 5). audio 44.00 (*1-55690-716-8*, 92344E7) Recorded Bks., LLC.
—The Piper on the Mountain. 1996. (Inspector George Felse Mystery Ser.: Vol. 5). 208p. mass mkt. 5.99 (*0-446-40071-8*) Warner Bks., Inc.
—Rainbow's End. unabr. ed. 1991. (Inspector George Felse Mystery Ser.: Vol. 13). audio 44.00 (*1-55690-433-9*, 91232E7) Recorded Bks., LLC.
—Rainbow's End. l.t. ed. 1992. (Inspector George Felse Mystery Ser.: Vol. 13). 368p. 29.99 o.p. (*0-7089-2733-5*, Ulverscroft) Thorpe, F. A. Pubs. GBR. *Dist:* Ulverscroft Large Print Bks., Ltd., Ulverscroft Large Print Canada, Ltd.
—Rainbow's End. 1992. (Inspector George Felse Mystery Ser.: Vol. 13). 208p. mass mkt. 5.99 o.p. (*0-446-40017-3*) Warner Bks., Inc.

**FELTON, CORA (FICTITIOUS CHARACTER)—FICTION**

Hall, Parnell. A Clue for the Puzzle Lady. 2000. 336p. mass mkt. 6.50 (*0-553-58140-6*); 1999. 304p. 23.95 o.s.i (*0-553-80096-5*) Bantam Bks.
—A Clue for the Puzzle Lady. l.t. ed. 2000. (Thorndike Senior Lifestyle Ser.). 456p. 28.95 o.p. (*0-7862-2542-4*) Thorndike Pr.
—The Last Puzzle & Testament. 2001. (Illus.). 400p. mass mkt. 6.50 (*0-553-58143-0*, Spectra) Bantam Bks.
—Last Puzzle & Testament. l.t. ed. 2001. (Senior Lifestyles Ser.). 511p. 28.95 (*0-7862-2944-6*) Thorndike Pr.
—With This Puzzle, I Thee Kill. 2003. 336p. 23.95 (*0-553-80241-0*) Bantam Bks.

**FEN, GERVASE (FICTITIOUS CHARACTER)—FICTION**

Chekhov, Anton. Swan Song. 1999. E-Book 0.99 (*1-58515-027-4*) MesaView, Inc.
Crispin, Edmund. Buried for Pleasure. 191p. reprint ed. lib. bdg. 20.95 (*0-89190-691-6*, Rivercity Pr.) Amereon, Ltd.
—Buried for Pleasure. Barzum, Jacques & Taylor, Wendell H., eds. 1976. (Crime Fiction Ser.). reprint ed. lib. bdg. 21.00 o.p. (*0-8240-2362-5*) Garland Publishing, Inc.
—Buried for Pleasure. 1980. mass mkt. 3.50 o.p. (*0-06-080506-4*, P 506, Perennial) HarperTrade.
—The Case of the Gilded Fly. l.t. ed. 1980. (YA). (gr. 7-12). lib. bdg. 13.95 o.p. (*0-8161-3018-3*, Macmillan Reference USA) Gale Group.
—The Case of the Gilded Fly. 1992. 224p. pap. 8.95 o.p. (*1-55882-108-2*) International Polygonics, Ltd.
—The Case of the Gilded Fly. 1980. pap. 2.95 o.p. (*0-380-50187-2*, 63552-6, Avon Bks.) Morrow/Avon.
—The Case of the Gilded Fly. 1979. (Walker Mystery Ser.). 223p. reprint ed. 8.95 o.s.i (*0-8027-5410-4*) Walker & Co.
—Frequent Hearses. l.t. ed. 1994. (General Ser.). 311p. lib. bdg. 16.95 (*0-8161-5860-6*, Macmillan Reference USA) Gale Group.
—Frequent Hearses. 1982. pap. 2.95 o.p. (*0-14-006325-0*) Penguin Group (USA) Inc.
—Frequent Hearses. 1987. (Classic Crime Ser.). 224p. pap. 5.95 o.p. (*0-14-009355-9*, Penguin Bks.) Viking Penguin.
—The Glimpses of the Moon. 23.95 (*0-89190-695-9*) Amereon, Ltd.
—The Glimpses of the Moon. 1979. pap. 2.95 o.p. (*0-380-45062-3*, 69021-7, Avon Bks.) Morrow/Avon.
—The Glimpses of the Moon. 1978. 8.95 o.s.i (*0-8027-5391-4*) Walker & Co.
—Holy Disorders. 1976. 22.95 (*0-8488-0468-6*) Amereon, Ltd.
—Holy Disorders. 1980. (General Ser.). lib. bdg. 13.95 o.p. (*0-8161-3111-2*, Macmillan Reference USA) Gale Group.
—Holy Disorders. 1980. 240p. pap. 2.95 o.p. (*0-380-51508-3*, Avon Bks.) Morrow/Avon.
—Holy Disorders. 1979. (Walker Mystery Ser.). 254p. 9.95 o.s.i (*0-8027-5411-2*) Walker & Co.
—The Long Divorce. 1981. (Crime Monthly Ser.). 256p. pap. 3.95 o.p. (*0-14-001304-0*, Penguin Bks.) Viking Penguin.
—Love Lies Bleeding. 20.95 (*0-89190-693-2*) Amereon, Ltd.
—Love Lies Bleeding. 1982. (Crime Monthly Ser.). pap. 3.95 o.p. (*0-14-000974-4*, Penguin Bks.) Viking Penguin.
—Love Lies Bleeding. 1981. 9.95 o.s.i (*0-8027-5444-9*) Walker & Co.
—The Moving Toy Shop. 20.95 (*0-8488-0104-0*) Amereon, Ltd.
—The Moving Toy Shop. 1989. (Penguin Classic Crime Ser.). 208p. pap. 6.99 (*0-14-008817-2*, Penguin Bks.) Penguin Group (USA) Inc.
—Swan Song. 1980. 192p. 16.95 (*0-8027-5420-1*) Boulevard Bks.
—Swan Song. 1993. reprint ed. lib. bdg. 16.95 (*1-56849-195-6*) Buccaneer Bks., Inc.
—Swan Song. 1982. 192p. pap. 2.50 o.p. (*0-380-55145-4*, 70020, Avon Bks.) Morrow/Avon.
—Swan Song. l.t. ed. 1987. (Linford Mystery Library). 336p. pap. 17.99 o.p. (*0-7089-6361-7*, Linford) Thorpe, F. A. Pubs. GBR. *Dist:* Ulverscroft Large Print Bks., Ltd., Ulverscroft Large Print Canada, Ltd.

**FENDER, MARTIN (FICTITIOUS CHARACTER)—FICTION**

Sublett, Jesse. Boiled in Concrete. 1999. pap. 3.95 (*0-14-015230-X*); 1992. 320p. 20.00 o.p. (*0-670-83888-8*) Viking Penguin. (Viking).
—Rock Critic Murders. 1990. 240p. mass mkt. 3.50 o.s.i (*0-440-20703-7*) Dell Publishing.
—Rock Critic Murders. 1989. pap. 3.95 o.p. (*0-14-011208-1*) Penguin Group (USA) Inc.
—Rock Critic Murders. 1989. 240p. 16.95 o.p. (*0-670-82302-3*) Viking Penguin.
—Tough Baby. 1999. pap. 4.95 (*0-14-012397-0*); 1990. 256p. 16.95 o.p. (*0-670-83325-8*) Viking Penguin. (Viking).
Sublett, Jessie. Never the Same Again. 2004. 300p. 24.00 (*1-58008-598-9*) Ten Speed Pr.

**FENTON, HILARY (FICTITIOUS CHARACTER)—FICTION**

Werner, Patricia. Hidden Gold of Widow's Mountain. 1993. 304p. mass mkt. 3.99 o.s.i (*0-8217-4134-9*, Zebra Bks.) Kensington Publishing Corp.

**FERGUSON, CHARLES (FICTITIOUS CHARACTER)—FICTION**

Higgins, Jack. Angel of Death. 1996. 352p. mass mkt. 7.99 (*0-425-15223-5*) Berkley Publishing Group.
—Angel of Death. unabr. ed. 1995. 24.95 o.p. (*0-7871-0391-8*, 692879) NewStar Media, Inc.
—Angel of Death. 2001. 23.95 (*0-399-14274-6*); 1995. 311p. 23.95 (*0-399-14042-5*, G. P. Putnam's Sons) Penguin Group (USA) Inc.
—Angel of Death. l.t. ed. 1996. (Paperback Bestsellers Ser.). 402p. lib. bdg. 24.95 (*0-7862-0465-6*) Thorndike Pr.
—Drink with the Devil. 1997. 336p. mass mkt. 7.99 (*0-425-15754-7*); mass mkt. 6.99 o.s.i (*0-425-16049-1*) Berkley Publishing Group.
—Drink with the Devil, Set. unabr. ed. 1999. audio 29.95 Highsmith Inc.
—Drink with the Devil. abr. ed. 1996. 2 cass. audio 17.95 o.p. (*0-7871-0966-5*); Set. 29.95 o.p. (*0-7871-0872-3*, 893923) NewStar Media, Inc.
—Drink with the Devil. 1996. 320p. 24.95 o.p. (*0-399-14154-5*, G. P. Putnam's Sons) Penguin Group (USA) Inc.
—Drink with the Devil. 1998. 5.98 o.p. (*0-7651-0898-4*) Smithmark Pubs., Inc.
—Drink with the Devil. l.t. ed. 1999. 430p. pap. 26.95 (*0-7862-0797-3*) Thorndike Pr.
—Edge of Danger. 2001. 304p. 25.95 o.s.i (*0-399-14701-2*) Penguin Group (USA) Inc.
—Edge of Danger. abr. unabr. ed. 2001. audio 24.95 o.s.i (*0-399-14721-7*, Putnam Berkley Audio) Putnam Publishing Group, The.
—Edge of Danger. unabr. ed. 2001. audio 48.00 (*0-7887-5259-6*) Recorded Bks., LLC.
—Edge of Danger. l.t. ed. 2001. 341p. 29.95 (*0-7862-3171-8*); 32.95 (*0-7862-3170-X*); (*0-7540-1608-0*); (*0-7540-2464-4*) Thorndike Pr.
—On Dangerous Ground. 1995. 336p. mass mkt. 7.99 (*0-425-14828-9*) Berkley Publishing Group.
—On Dangerous Ground. 1995. reprint ed. lib. bdg. 26.95 (*1-56849-595-1*) Buccaneer Bks., Inc.
—On Dangerous Ground. unabr. ed. 1999. audio 29.95 Highsmith Inc.
—On Dangerous Ground. abr. ed. 1993. 17.95 o.p. (*0-7871-0026-9*); 29.95 o.p. (*0-7871-0043-9*) NewStar Media, Inc.
—On Dangerous Ground. 1994. 320p. 22.95 o.p. (*0-399-13933-8*, G. P. Putnam's Sons) Penguin Group (USA) Inc.
—The President's Daughter. 2003. 320p. pap. 14.95 (*0-425-19294-6*); 1998. 320p. mass mkt. 7.99 (*0-425-16341-5*); 1998. mass mkt. 6.99 (*0-425-16542-6*) Berkley Publishing Group.
—The President's Daughter. l.t. ed. 1997. (Large Print Book Ser.). 26.95 o.p. (*1-56895-495-6*, Wheeler Publishing, Inc.) Gale Group.
—The President's Daughter. unabr. ed. 1999. audio 35.00 Highsmith Inc.
—The President's Daughter. abr. ed. 1997. 25.00 o.p. (*0-7871-1358-1*, 695116); 35.00 o.p. (*0-7871-1458-8*, 895269) NewStar Media, Inc.
—The President's Daughter. 1997. 320p. 23.95 o.s.i (*0-399-14239-8*, G. P. Putnam's Sons) Penguin Group (USA) Inc.
—Thunder Point. 1994. 368p. reprint ed. mass mkt. 7.99 (*0-425-14357-0*) Berkley Publishing Group.
—Thunder Point. unabr. ed. 1994. audio 72.00 (*0-7366-2651-4*, 3388) Books on Tape, Inc.
—Thunder Point. 1995. reprint ed. lib. bdg. 26.95 (*1-56849-594-3*) Buccaneer Bks., Inc.
—Thunder Point. l.t. ed. 1993. 26.95 o.p. (*1-56895-037-3*, Wheeler Publishing, Inc.) Gale Group.
—Thunder Point. unabr. ed. 2003. audio 34.95 (*1-59007-378-9*, New Millennium Audio) New Millennium Entertainment.
—Thunder Point. abr. ed. 1993. audio 16.95 o.p. (*1-55800-786-5*) NewStar Media, Inc.
—Thunder Point. 1993. 320p. 22.95 o.p. (*0-399-13835-8*, G. P. Putnam's Sons) Penguin Group (USA) Inc.
—Thunder Point. 5.98 o.s.i (*0-8317-6524-0*) Smithmark Pubs., Inc.
—The White House Connection. 2000. 304p. mass mkt. 7.99 (*0-425-17541-3*) Berkley Publishing Group.
—The White House Connection. unabr. ed. 1999. 7p. audio 57.25 (*1-56740-676-9*, 1797, Unabridged Library Editions); audio 35.95 (*1-56740-450-2*, 1796, Brilliance Audio Unabridged) Brilliance Audio.
—The White House Connection. unabr. ed. 1999. audio 57.25 Highsmith Inc.
—The White House Connection. 1999. 323p. 25.95 o.p. (*0-399-14489-7*, G. P. Putnam's Sons); 24.95 (*0-399-14528-1*, Putnam Berkley Audio) Penguin Group (USA) Inc.
—The White House Connection. l.t. ed. (Thorndike/G. K. Hall Paperback Bestsellers Ser.). 2000. 377p. 27.95 (*0-7862-2023-6*); 1999. 413p. 30.95 (*0-7862-2022-8*); 1999. (*0-7540-1328-6*); 1999. (*0-7540-2244-7*) Thorndike Pr.

**FERGUSSON, CLARE (FICTITIOUS CHARACTER)—FICTION**

Spencer-Fleming, Julia. A Fountain Filled with Blood. E-Book 23.95 (*0-312-71002-X*); 2004. mass mkt. 6.99 (*0-312-99543-1*, St. Martin's Paperbacks); 2003. 304p. 23.95 (*0-312-30410-2*, Saint Martin's Minotaur) St. Martin's Pr.
—In the Bleak Midwinter. E-Book 17.95 (*0-312-70446-1*); 2003. 384p. mass mkt. 6.99 (*0-312-98676-9*, St. Martin's Paperbacks); 2002. 272p. 23.95 (*0-312-28847-6*, Saint Martin's Minotaur) St. Martin's Pr.
—Out of the Deep I Cry. 2004. 304p. 23.95 (*0-312-31262-8*) St. Martin's Pr.

**FERMOYLE, MARIE (FICTITIOUS CHARACTER)—FICTION**

Morris, Mary McGarry. Songs in Ordinary Time. unabr. ed. 1997. Pt. 1. audio 80.00; Pt. 2. audio 80.00 Books on Tape, Inc.
—Songs in Ordinary Time. unabr. ed. 1997. audio 29.95 (*1-56100-781-1*, 272, Bookcassette); audio 169.25 (*1-56740-560-6*, 1053, Unabridged Library Editions) Brilliance Audio.
—Songs in Ordinary Time. 1996. 752p. pap. 13.95 (*0-14-024482-4*, Penguin Bks.) Penguin Group (USA) Inc.
—Songs in Ordinary Time. 1997. 26.95 (*0-670-87907-X*); 1995. 752p. 24.95 o.s.i (*0-670-86014-X*, Viking); 1997. audio 24.95 Viking Penguin.

**FERRAMI, JEANNIE (FICTITIOUS CHARACTER)—FICTION**

Follett, Ken. The Third Twin. 1998. pap. 7.99 (*0-449-45862-8*); 1997. pap. text 7.99 (*0-449-45794-X*); 1997. 480p. mass mkt. 7.99 (*0-449-22742-1*); 1997. mass mkt. 6.99 o.s.i (*0-449-22761-8*) Ballantine Bks. (Fawcett).
—The Third Twin, Set. abr. ed. 1996. audio 24.00 o.s.i (*0-679-45272-9*, 494389, RH Audio) Random Hse. Audio Publishing Group.
—The Third Twin. l.t. ed. 1996. 672p. pap. 25.95 o.p. (*0-7838-1923-4*) Random Hse. Large Print.
—The Third Twin. l.t. ed. 1996. (Large Print Ser.). 25.95 o.s.i (*0-679-75897-6*) Random Hse., Inc.

**FERRARO, GENE (FICTITIOUS CHARACTER)—FICTION**

DeChancie, John. Bride of the Castle. 1994. 192p. (Orig.). mass mkt. 4.99 o.s.i (*0-441-00120-3*) Ace Bks.
—Bride of the Castle. 2002. 176p. (Orig.). per. 14.95 (*0-7592-3240-7*) ereads.com.
—Castle Dreams. 1992. mass mkt. 4.99 o.s.i (*0-441-09414-7*) Ace Bks.
—Castle for Rent. 1989. mass mkt. 4.99 o.s.i (*0-441-09406-6*) Ace Bks.
—Castle for Rent. 2002. 200p. per. 14.95 (*0-7592-3204-0*) ereads.com.
—Castle Kidnapped. 1989. mass mkt. 4.99 o.s.i (*0-441-09408-2*) Ace Bks.
—Castle Kidnapped. 2002. 220p. per. 15.95 (*0-7592-3216-4*) ereads.com.
—Castle Murders. 1991. mass mkt. 4.99 o.s.i (*0-441-09273-X*) Ace Bks.
—Castle Perilous. 1988. mass mkt. 4.99 o.s.i (*0-441-09418-X*) Ace Bks.
—Castle Perilous. 1999. 212p. per. 15.95 (*0-7592-3198-2*) ereads.com.
—Castle Spellbound. 1992. 240p. (Orig.). mass mkt. 4.99 o.s.i (*0-441-09407-4*) Ace Bks.
—Castle War. 1990. mass mkt. 4.99 o.s.i (*0-441-09270-5*) Ace Bks.
—Castle War. 2002. 240p. per. 15.95 (*0-7592-3222-9*) ereads.com.

**FERRIS, NICOLA (FICTITIOUS CHARACTER)—FICTION**

Stewart, Mary. The Moon-Spinners, unabr. ed. 1993. audio 69.95 (*0-7451-6307-6*, CAB 197) BBC Audiobooks America.

—The Moon-Spinners. 1989. pap. 3.95 o.p. (*0-449-44824-X*); 1984. mass mkt. 4.95 o.s.i (*0-449-20609-2*) Ballantine Bks. (Fawcett).

—The Moon-Spinners. l.t. ed. 1968. (Ulverscroft Large Print Ser.). 12.00 o.p. (*0-85456-708-9*, Ulverscroft) Thorpe, F. A. Pubs. GBR. *Dist:* Ulverscroft Large Print Bks., Ltd., Ulverscroft Large Print Canada, Ltd.

**FETT, BOBA (FICTITIOUS CHARACTER)—FICTION**

Anderson, Kevin J., ed. Tales from Jabba's Palace. 1995. (Star Wars Ser.). 464p. mass mkt. 6.99 (*0-553-56815-9*, Spectra) Bantam Bks.

—Tales from Jabba's Palace. 1996. (Star Wars Ser.). 12.04 (*0-606-09892-5*) Turtleback Bks.

Golden, Christopher. Shadows of the Empire. 1996. (Star Wars Ser.). (Illus.). 176p. (J). (gr. 4-7). pap. text 4.50 o.s.i (*0-440-41303-6*) Dell Publishing.

—Shadows of the Empire: A Junior Novelization. 1996. (Star Wars Ser.). 10.55 (*0-606-11835-7*) Turtleback Bks.

Jeter, K. W. The Mandalorian Armor. 1998. (Star Wars: Bk. 1). 416p. (gr. 5). mass mkt. 6.99 (*0-553-57885-5*, Spectra) Bantam Bks.

—The Mandalorian Armor. abr. ed. 1998. (Star Wars: Bk. 1). audio 16.99 (*0-553-52496-8*, RH Audio) Random Hse. Audio Publishing Group.

—Slave Ship. 1998. (Star Wars: Bk. 2). 336p. mass mkt. 6.99 (*0-553-57888-X*) Bantam Bks.

Jeter, K. W. & Zahn, Timothy. Hard Merchandise. 1999. (Star Wars: Bk. 3). 368p. mass mkt. 6.99 (*0-553-57891-X*) Bantam Bks.

Manning, Russ & Goodwin, Archie. The Early Adventures. 1997. (Classic Star Wars Ser.). (Illus.). 240p. (J). (gr. 3 up). pap. 19.95 (*1-56971-178-X*) Dark Horse Comics.

Perry, Steve. Shadows of the Empire. 1996. (Star Wars Ser.). 12.04 (*0-606-11895-0*) Turtleback Bks.

Truman, Timothy, et al. The Bounty Hunters. 2000. (Star Wars Ser.). (Illus.). 112p. (YA). (gr. 7 up). pap. 12.95 (*1-56971-467-3*) Dark Horse Comics.

Wagner, John & Kennedy, Cam. Boba Fett: Death, Lies & Treachery. 1998. (Star Wars Ser.). (Illus.). 144p. (YA). (gr. 7 up). pap. 12.95 (*1-56971-311-1*) Dark Horse Comics.

Wagner, John, et al. Star Wars Boba Fett: Enemy of the Empire. 1999. (Star Wars Ser.). 112p. (YA). (gr. 7 up). pap. 12.95 (*1-56971-407-X*) Dark Horse Comics.

**FIDDLER (FICTITIOUS CHARACTER)—FICTION**

Maxwell, A. E. Art of Survival. 1993. 336p. mass mkt. 4.99 o.p. (*0-06-104115-7*, HarperTorch) Morrow/Avon.

—The Art of Survival. 1990. mass mkt. 4.50 o.s.i (*0-553-28479-7*) Bantam Bks.

—Frog & the Scorpion. 1986. 264p. 16.95 o.p. (*0-385-19260-6*) Doubleday Publishing.

—The Frog & the Scorpion. 1987. 224p. mass mkt. 3.50 o.s.i (*0-553-26876-7*) Bantam Bks.

—The Frog & the Scorpion. 1993. 320p. mass mkt. 4.99 o.p. (*0-06-104113-0*, HarperTorch) Morrow/Avon.

—Gatsby's Vineyard. 1988. 240p. mass mkt. 3.50 o.s.i (*0-553-27409-0*) Bantam Bks.

—Gatsby's Vineyard. 1987. 240p. 15.95 o.s.i (*0-385-23712-X*) Doubleday Publishing.

—Gatsby's Vineyard. 1993. 320p. mass mkt. 4.99 o.p. (*0-06-104112-2*, HarperTorch) Morrow/Avon.

—The Golden Empire. 1979. (Orig.). mass mkt. 2.50 o.s.i (*0-449-14267-1*, Fawcett) Ballantine Bks.

—Just Another Day in Paradise. 1986. mass mkt. 2.95 o.s.i (*0-553-25789-7*) Bantam Bks.

—Just Another Day in Paradise. 1985. 240p. 14.95 o.p. (*0-385-19259-2*) Doubleday Publishing.

—Just Another Day in Paradise. 1993. 304p. mass mkt. 4.99 o.p. (*0-06-104114-9*, HarperTorch) Morrow/Avon.

—Just Enough Light to Kill. 1989. mass mkt. 3.95 o.s.i (*0-553-28213-1*) Bantam Bks.

—Just Enough Light to Kill. 1993. 336p. mass mkt. 4.99 o.s.i (*0-06-104111-4*, HarperTorch) Morrow/Avon.

—The King of Nothing. 1994. 320p. mass mkt. 5.50 o.p. (*0-06-104230-7*, HarperTorch) Morrow/Avon.

—Money Burns. 1993. 368p. mass mkt. 5.50 o.p. (*0-06-104123-8*, HarperTorch) Morrow/Avon.

—Money Burns. 1993. 3.99 o.p. (*0-517-10621-3*) Random Hse. Value Publishing.

—Murder Hurts. 1995. 352p. mass mkt. 4.99 o.p. (*0-06-104318-4*, HarperTorch) Morrow/Avon.

—Redwood Empire. (Harlequin Historicals Ser.). 1995. 440p. per. (*0-373-28867-0*, 1-28867-9); 1987. 416p. mass mkt. (*0-373-97049-8*) Harlequin Enterprises, Ltd. (Harlequin Bks.).

**FIDELMA OF KILDAIRE, SISTER (FICTITIOUS CHARACTER)—FICTION**

Tremayne, Peter. Absolution by Murder: A Sister Fidelma Mystery. l.t. ed. 1996. (Magna Large Print Ser.). 351p. 29.99 o.p. (*0-7505-0929-5*) Magna Large Print Bks. GBR. *Dist:* Ulverscroft Large Print Bks., Ltd., Ulverscroft Large Print Canada, Ltd.

—Absolution by Murder: A Sister Fidelma Mystery. 1997. (Sister Fidelma Mysteries Ser.). 272p. mass mkt. 6.50 (*0-451-19299-0*, Signet Bks.) NAL.

—Absolution by Murder: A Sister Fidelma Mystery. 1995. 288p. 21.95 o.p. (*0-312-13918-7*, Saint Martin's Minotaur) St. Martin's Pr.

—Hemlock at Vespers: Fifteen Sister Fidelma Mysteries. 2000. xiii, 398p. pap. 15.95 (*0-312-25288-9*, Saint Martin's Griffin) St. Martin's Pr.

—Shroud for the Archbishop: A Sister Fidelma Mystery. l.t. ed. 1996. (Magna Large Print Ser.). (Illus.). 436p. 29.99 (*0-7505-0930-9*) Magna Large Print Bks. GBR. *Dist:* Ulverscroft Large Print Bks., Ltd.

—Shroud for the Archbishop: A Sister Fidelma Mystery. 1998. (Sister Fidelma Mysteries Ser.). 304p. mass mkt. 6.99 (*0-451-19300-8*, Signet Bks.) NAL.

—Shroud for the Archbishop: A Sister Fidelma Mystery. 1996. (Sister Fidelma Mysteries Ser.). 352p. 23.95 (*0-312-14734-1*, Saint Martin's Minotaur) St. Martin's Pr.

—Smoke in the Wind: A Mystery of Ancient Ireland. 2002. xxvi, 358p. mass mkt. 9.95 (*0-7472-6434-1*) Headline Bk. Publishing, Ltd. GBR. *Dist:* Trafalgar Square.

—The Spider's Web: A Celtic Mystery. l.t. ed. 1998. (Magna Large Print Ser.). 512p. (*0-7505-1245-8*) Magna Large Print Bks. GBR. *Dist:* Ulverscroft Large Print Canada, Ltd.

—The Spider's Web: A Celtic Mystery. 1999. (Celtic Mysteries Ser.). (Illus.). 352p. 23.95 (*0-312-20589-9*, Saint Martin's Minotaur) St. Martin's Pr.

—The Subtle Serpent. l.t. ed. 1998. (Magna Large Print Ser.). 488p. o.p. (*0-7505-1244-X*) Magna Large Print Bks. GBR. *Dist:* Ulverscroft Large Print Canada, Ltd.

—The Subtle Serpent: A Celtic Mystery. 1998. (Sister Fidelma Mysteries Ser.). 352p. 23.95 (*0-312-18670-3*, Saint Martin's Minotaur) St. Martin's Pr.

—The Subtle Serpent: A Mystery of Ancient Ireland, 1, 4. 1999. (Sister Fidelma Mysteries Ser.). 320p. mass mkt. 6.99 (*0-451-19558-2*, Signet Bks.) NAL.

—Suffer Little Children: A Sister Fidelma Mystery, 1 vol. 1999. (Sister Fidelma Mysteries Ser.). 320p. mass mkt. 6.50 (*0-451-19557-4*) NAL.

—Suffer Little Children: A Sister Fidelma Mystery. 1997. (Sister Fidelma Mysteries Ser.). 352p. 23.95 (*0-312-15665-0*, Saint Martin's Minotaur) St. Martin's Pr.

—Valley of the Shadow. (Sister Fidelma Mysteries Ser.). 2001. 320p. mass mkt. 5.99 (*0-451-20330-5*); 1999. reprint ed. pap. 5.99 (*0-451-26330-8*, Signet Bks.) NAL.

**FIELDING, JOHN, SIR, 1721-1780—FICTION**

Alexander, Bruce. Blind Justice. unabr. ed. 1998. (Sir John Fielding Mystery Ser.: Vol. 1). audio 56.00 (*0-7366-4081-9*, 4590) Books on Tape, Inc.

—Blind Justice: A Sir John Fielding Mystery. 1995. (Sir John Fielding Mystery Ser.). 336p. mass mkt. 6.50 (*0-425-15007-0*) Berkley Publishing Group.

—Blind Justice: A Sir John Fielding Mystery. 1994. (Sir John Fielding Ser.). 224p. 19.95 o.p. (*0-399-13978-8*, G. P. Putnam's Sons) Penguin Group (USA) Inc.

—Blind Justice: A Sir John Fielding Mystery. l.t. ed. 1996. (Large Print Ser.). 576p. 29.99 o.p. (*0-7089-3606-7*, Ulverscroft) Thorpe, F. A. Pubs. GBR. *Dist:* Ulverscroft Large Print Bks., Ltd., Ulverscroft Large Print Canada, Ltd.

—The Color of Death. 2001. 320p. reprint ed. mass mkt. 6.50 (*0-425-18203-7*, Prime Crime) Berkley Publishing Group.

—The Color of Death. l.t. ed. 2004. 416p. (*0-06-072687-3*, HarperLargePrint) HarperTrade.

—The Color of Death. 2004. (*0-06-050413-7*, Morrow, William & Co.) Morrow/Avon.

—The Color of Death: A Sir John Fielding Mystery. 2000. (Sir John Fielding Mystery Ser.). 288p. 24.95 o.s.i (*0-399-14648-2*) Penguin Group (USA) Inc.

—Death of a Colonial: A Sir John Fielding Mystery. 1999. (Sir John Fielding Mystery Ser.). 288p. 23.95 o.p. (*0-399-14564-8*, G. P. Putnam's Sons) Penguin Group (USA) Inc.

—The Death of a Colonial: A Sir John Fielding Mystery. 2000. (Sir John Fielding Ser.). 304p. mass mkt. 6.50 (*0-425-17702-5*) Berkley Publishing Group.

—Death of a Colonial: A Sir John Fielding Mystery. l.t. ed. 1999. (Core Ser.). 402p. 28.95 (*0-7838-8823-6*) Thorndike Pr.

—An Experiment in Treason: A Sir John Fielding Mystery. 2002. 288p. 24.95 o.s.i (*0-399-14923-6*) Putnam Publishing Group, The.

—An Experiment in Treason: A Sir John Fielding Mystery. l.t. ed. 2003. (Core Ser.). 415p. 29.95 (*0-7862-4992-7*) Thorndike Pr.

—Jack, Knave & Fool. unabr. ed. 1999. (Sir John Fielding Mystery Ser.). audio 64.00 Books on Tape, Inc.

—Jack, Knave & Fool: A Sir John Fielding Mystery. 1999. (Sir John Fielding Ser.). 416p. reprint ed. mass mkt. 6.99 (*0-425-17120-5*, Prime Crime) Berkley Publishing Group.

—Jack, Knave & Fool: A Sir John Fielding Mystery. l.t. ed. 1999. (Basic Ser.). 631p. 28.95 (*0-7862-1798-7*) Thorndike Pr.

—Jack Knave the Fool. 1998. (Sir John Fielding Mystery Ser.). 288p. 22.95 o.p. (*0-399-14419-6*, G. P. Putnam's Sons) Penguin Group (USA) Inc.

—Murder in Grub Street. unabr. ed. 1998. (Sir John Fielding Mystery Ser.: Vol. 2). audio 56.00 (*0-7366-3998-5*, 4498) Books on Tape, Inc.

—Murder in Grub Street: A Sir John Fielding Mystery. 1996. (Sir John Fielding Mystery Ser.). 320p. reprint ed. mass mkt. 6.99 (*0-425-15550-1*, Prime Crime) Berkley Publishing Group.

—Murder in Grub Street: A Sir John Fielding Mystery. 1995. (Sir John Fielding Ser.). 256p. 21.95 o.p. (*0-399-14085-9*, G. P. Putnam's Sons) Penguin Group (USA) Inc.

—Murder in Grub Street: A Sir John Fielding Mystery. l.t. ed. 1997. (Ulverscroft Large Print Ser.). 608p. 29.99 (*0-7089-3749-7*, Ulverscroft) Thorpe, F. A. Pubs. GBR. *Dist:* Ulverscroft Large Print Bks., Ltd., Ulverscroft Large Print Canada, Ltd.

—Person or Persons Unknown. unabr. ed. 1999. (Sir John Fielding Mystery Ser.). audio 56.00 (*0-7366-4337-0*, 4826) Books on Tape, Inc.

—Person or Persons Unknown: A Sir John Fielding Mystery. 1998. (Sir John Fielding Mystery Ser.: Bk. 4). 336p. reprint ed. mass mkt. 6.99 (*0-425-16566-3*, Prime Crime) Berkley Publishing Group.

—Person or Persons Unknown: A Sir John Fielding Mystery. 1997. (Sir John Fielding Ser.). 256p. 22.95 o.s.i (*0-399-14309-2*, G. P. Putnam's Sons) Penguin Group (USA) Inc.

—Smuggler's Moon. 2002. (Sir John Fielding Mystery Ser.: Vol. 8). 304p. reprint ed. mass mkt. 6.50 (*0-425-18690-3*, Prime Crime) Berkley Publishing Group.

—Smuggler's Moon. 1998. 23.95 o.p. (*0-399-14778-0*, Putnam & Grosset) Penguin Group (USA) Inc.

—Smuggler's Moon. 2002. 491p. 29.95 (*0-7862-4141-1*) Thorndike Pr.

—Smuggler's Moon: A Sir John Fielding Mystery. 2001. 288p. 24.95 o.s.i (*0-399-14774-8*) Penguin Group (USA) Inc.

—Watery Grave. 1997. (Sir John Fielding Mystery Ser.). 320p. mass mkt. 6.99 (*0-425-16036-X*, Prime Crime) Berkley Publishing Group.

—Watery Grave. unabr. ed. 1998. (Sir John Fielding Mystery Ser.: Vol. 3). audio 56.00 (*0-7366-3997-7*, 4497) Books on Tape, Inc.

—Watery Grave. 1996. (Sir John Fielding Mystery Ser.). 272p. 22.95 o.p. (*0-399-14155-3*, G. P. Putnam's Sons) Penguin Group (USA) Inc.

—Watery Grave. l.t. ed. 1998. (Ulverscroft Large Print Ser.). 544p. 29.99 o.p. (*0-7089-3984-8*, Ulverscroft) Thorpe, F. A. Pubs. GBR. *Dist:* Ulverscroft Large Print Bks., Ltd., Ulverscroft Large Print Canada, Ltd.

**FIELDING, KIT (FICTITIOUS CHARACTER)—FICTION**

Francis, Dick. Bolt. 1996. audio 29.95 (*0-7451-2842-4*) BBC Audiobooks America.

—Bolt. 1988. 336p. mass mkt. 5.95 o.s.i (*0-449-21239-4*, Fawcett) Ballantine Bks.

—Bolt. unabr. ed. 1993. (Kit Fielding Adventure Ser.: Bk. 2). audio 49.95 (*0-7451-4169-2*, CAB 852) Chivers Audio Bks. GBR. *Dist:* BBC Audiobooks America.

—Bolt. abr. ed. 1990. 2p. audio 16.99 (*0-88646-219-3*, 7219) Durkin Hayes Publishing Ltd.

—Bolt. l.t. ed. 1988. 388p. 19.95 o.p. (*0-8161-4329-3*); 12.95 o.p. (*0-8161-4330-7*) Gale Group. (Macmillan Reference USA).

—Bolt. 1987. 320p. 17.95 o.s.i (*0-399-13226-0*, G. P. Putnam's Sons) Penguin Putnam Bks. for Young Readers.

—Bolt. unabr. ed. 1999. audio 51.00 (*0-7887-2937-3*, 95719E7); audio compact disk 66.00 (*0-7887-3435-0*, C1041E7) Recorded Bks., LLC.

—Break In. unabr. ed. 1994. audio 69.95 (*0-7451-4225-7*, CAB 908); Set. 1998. (Chivers Word for Word Audio Ser.: Vol. 168). audio 34.95 (*0-7540-7520-6*) BBC Audiobooks America.

—Break In. 1987. 384p. mass mkt. 5.99 o.s.i (*0-449-20755-2*, Fawcett) Ballantine Bks.

—Break In. abr. ed. 1987. (gr. 8-10). pap. 29.99 incl. audio (*0-88646-824-8*, R7128); 1986. 2p. audio 16.99 (*0-88646-128-6*, 7128) Durkin Hayes Publishing Ltd.

—Break In. l.t. ed. 1987. (General Ser.). 18.95 o.p. (*0-8161-4161-4*); pap. 11.95 o.p. (*0-8161-4162-2*) Gale Group. (Macmillan Reference USA).

—Break In. 2001. 17.95 (*0-399-13685-1*) Penguin Group (USA) Inc.

—Break In. 1986. 17.95 o.p. (*0-399-13121-3*, G. P. Putnam's Sons) Penguin Putnam Bks. for Young Readers.

—Break In. unabr. ed. 1999. audio compact disk 73.00 (*0-7887-3717-1*, C1074E7) Recorded Bks., LLC.

**FIELDS, TESSA (FICTITIOUS CHARACTER)—FICTION**

Cannell, Dorothy. Down the Garden Path: A Pastoral Mystery. 1989. 272p. mass mkt. 3.95 o.s.i (*0-553-26895-3*) Bantam Bks.

—Down the Garden Path: A Pastoral Mystery. 1998. (Tessa Fields Mystery Ser.). 288p. pap. 5.99 (*0-14-026623-2*) Penguin Group (USA) Inc.

—Down the Garden Path: A Pastoral Mystery. 1985. 304p. 14.95 o.p. (*0-312-21869-9*) St. Martin's Pr.

**FIGUEROA, SUZE (FICTITIOUS CHARACTER)—FICTION**

D'Amato, Barbara. Killer.app. 350p. 1997. mass mkt. 5.99 (*0-8125-5391-8*); 1996. 22.95 o.p. (*0-312-85991-0*) Doherty, Tom Assocs., LLC. (Forge Bks.).

**FINCH, SEPTIMUS (FICTITIOUS CHARACTER)—FICTION**

Erskine, Margaret. Case with Three Husbands. l.t. ed. 1988. (Linford Mystery Library). 288p. pap. 17.99 o.p. (*0-7089-6505-9*, Linford) Thorpe, F. A. Pubs. GBR. *Dist:* Ulverscroft Large Print Bks., Ltd., Ulverscroft Large Print Canada, Ltd.

—The Ewe Lamb. 1995. 160p. 16.95 o.p. (*0-7451-8652-1*, Black Dagger) BBC Audiobooks America.

—Harriet Farewell. 1984. 176p. pap. 2.50 o.p. (*0-553-23780-2*) Bantam Bks.

—Harriet Farewell. l.t. ed. 1988. (Linford Mystery Library). 288p. pap. 17.99 o.p. (*0-7089-6513-X*, Ulverscroft) Thorpe, F. A. Pubs. GBR. *Dist:* Ulverscroft Large Print Bks., Ltd., Ulverscroft Large Print Canada, Ltd.

—The House in Hook Street. 1977. 6.95 o.p. (*0-385-13137-2*) Doubleday Publishing.

—The Woman at Belguardo. l.t. ed. 1989. (Linford Mystery Library). 371p. pap. 17.99 o.p. (*0-7089-6632-2*, Linford) Thorpe, F. A. Pubs. GBR. *Dist:* Ulverscroft Large Print Bks., Ltd., Ulverscroft Large Print Canada, Ltd.

**FINE, MISTY (FICTITIOUS CHARACTER)—FICTION**

Files, Lolita. Getting to the Good Part. 2000. 352p. pap. 13.95 (*0-446-67548-2*); 1999. 334p. 24.00 (*0-446-52420-4*) Warner Bks., Inc.

—Scenes from a Sistah. 1998. 288p. pap. 13.99 (*0-446-67442-7*); 1998. 320p. mass mkt. 6.50 (*0-446-60539-5*); 1997. 288p. 22.00 o.p. (*0-446-52100-0*) Warner Bks., Inc.

**FINK, MEL (FICTITIOUS CHARACTER)—FICTION**

Salinger, Steven D. Behold the Fire. 1998. 432p. mass mkt. 6.99 (*0-446-60620-0*); 1997. 384p. 23.00 o.p. (*0-446-52079-9*) Warner Bks., Inc.

**FINLEY, PETER (FICTITIOUS CHARACTER)—FICTION**

Lupica, Mike. Dead Air. 1987. 288p. mass mkt. 3.95 o.s.i (*0-345-30813-1*) Ballantine Bks.

—Extra Credits. 1990. mass mkt. 3.95 o.s.i (*0-345-36029-X*) Ballantine Bks.

—Limited Partner. 1991. mass mkt. 3.99 o.s.i (*0-345-37237-9*, Ballantine Bks.) Ballantine Bks.

**FINN, HUCKLEBERRY (FICTITIOUS CHARACTER)—FICTION**

Marx, Leo, ed. Mark Twain: Adventures of Huckleberry Finn. 1967. 391p. (C). pap. text 28.00 o.p. (*0-02-376890-8*, Macmillan College) Prentice Hall PTR.

Seelye, John, as told by. The True Adventures of Huckleberry Finn. 2nd ed. 1987. 368p. text 34.95 (*0-252-01446-4*); 339p. pap. text 18.95 (*0-252-01432-4*) Univ. of Illinois Pr.

Stewart, Stephen. Huck Finn & Tom Sawyer Collaboration: The Sequel to: Adventures of Huckleberry Finn. 2002. (Adventures of Huckleberry Finn Ser.). (Illus.). 289p. 26.95 (*0-9711335-0-6*) New Mill Publishing.

Twain, Mark. The Adventures of Huckleberry Finn. 1992. (Children's Classics Ser.). (Illus.). 224p. (YA). 12.99 o.s.i (*0-517-08128-8*) Crown Publishing Group.

—The Adventures of Huckleberry Finn. 1988. mass mkt. 4.95 (*0-938819-86-0*, Aerie) Doherty, Tom Assocs., LLC.

—The Adventures of Huckleberry Finn. Harris, Susan K., ed. 1999. (Riverside Editions, A125 Ser.). (Illus.). viii, 392p. pap. 6.25 (*0-395-98078-X*) Houghton Mifflin Co.

—The Adventures of Huckleberry Finn. E-Book 2.95 (*1-57799-800-6*) Logos Research Systems, Inc.

—The Adventures of Huckleberry Finn. Eyre, A. G., ed. 1982. (Simplified English Ser.). (Illus.). 110p. pap. text 5.95 o.p. (*0-582-52824-0*, 73957) Longman Publishing Group.
—The Adventures of Huckleberry Finn. E-Book 1.95 (*1-58515-201-3*) MesaView, Inc.
—The Adventures of Huckleberry Finn. 1985. (Read-Along Ser.). pap. 34.95 incl. audio (*0-88432-961-5*, S23927) Norton Pubs., Inc., Jeffrey /Audio-Forum.
—The Adventures of Huckleberry Finn. 2001. (Paperback Classics Ser.). 304p. pap. 5.95 (*0-375-75737-6*, Modern Library) Random House Adult Trade Publishing Group.
—The Adventures of Huckleberry Finn. (Literary Classics Ser.). 240p. 2001. 6.00 o.p. (*0-7624-0541-4*); 1990. text 5.98 o.p. (*0-89471-880-0*, Courage Bks.) Running Pr. Bk. Pubs.
—The Adventures of Huckleberry Finn. 1982. pap. 2.75 (*0-671-46198-2*, Washington Square Pr.) Simon & Schuster.
—The Adventures of Huckleberry Finn. Fischer, Victor et al, eds. 2002. (Illus.). 950p. text 75.00 (*0-520-23771-4*) Univ. of California Pr.
—The Adventures of Huckleberry Finn. Blair, Walter & Fischer, Victor, eds. 1996. (Mark Twain Library: No. 6). (Illus.). 432p. pap. 14.95 (*0-520-05520-9*) Univ. of California Pr.
—The Adventures of Huckleberry Finn. Blair, Walter et al, eds. 1988. (Pennyroyal-California Edition Ser.: No. 8). (Illus.). 930p. text 75.00 (*0-520-05965-4*) Univ. of California Pr.
—The Adventures of Huckleberry Finn. 1985. (Pennyroyal-California Edition Ser.). (Illus.). 417p. 45.00 (*0-520-05338-9*) Univ. of California Pr.
—The Adventures of Huckleberry Finn. 1990. E-Book 5.98 (*0-585-24751-X*) netLibrary, Inc.
—The Adventures of Huckleberry Finn. Fishkin, Shelley Fisher, ed. 1996. (Oxford Mark Twain Ser.). (Illus.). 464p. 19.95 (*0-19-510140-5*) Oxford Univ. Pr., Inc.
—The Adventures of Huckleberry Finn. reprint ed. lib. bdg. 48.00 (*0-7426-1051-9*) Classic Bks.
—The Adventures of Huckleberry Finn. l.t. unabr. ed. 2001. (Large Print Classics). ix, 387p. pap. 14.95 (*0-486-41780-8*) Dover Pubns., Inc.
—The Adventures of Huckleberry Finn. abr. ed. 1993. audio 19.95 o.p. (*1-55800-670-2*) NewStar Media, Inc.
—The Adventures of Huckleberry Finn. Bradley, E. Sculley et al, eds. 2nd ed. 1977. (Critical Editions Ser.). (C). pap. text o.p. (*0-393-09146-5*) Norton, W. W. & Co., Inc.
—The Adventures of Huckleberry Finn: Critical Controversies. Graff, Gerald & Phelan, James, eds. 1995. 550p. pap. text 8.50 (*0-312-11225-4*) Bedford/Saint Martin's.
—The Adventures of Huckleberry Finn: Tom Sawyer's Comrade. 2001. 340p. 26.99 (*1-58827-432-2*); 300p. 125.99 (*1-58827-910-3*); 300p. 25.99 (*1-58827-434-9*); 300p. 19.99 (*1-58827-436-5*); 340p. 126.99 (*1-58827-908-1*); 300p. per. 120.99 (*1-58827-911-1*); 340p. per. 121.99 (*1-58827-909-X*); 300p. per. 14.99 (*1-58827-437-3*); 300p. per. 20.99 (*1-58827-435-7*); 340p. per. 21.99 (*1-58827-433-0*) IndyPublish.com.
—The Adventures of Huckleberry Finn: Tom Sawyer's Comrade. 1997. 11.00 (*0-606-00100-X*) Turtleback Bks.
—The Annotated Huckleberry Finn: Adventures of Huckleberry Finn (Tom Sawyer's Comrade) Hearn, Michael Patrick, ed. 2003. (Illus.). 512p. 39.95 (*0-393-02039-8*) Norton, W. W. & Co., Inc.
—CliffsNotes on Twain's Huckleberry Finn. unabr. ed. 2003. (CliffsNotes Audio Ser.). (YA). audio compact disk 9.95 (*1-59125-223-7*) Penton Overseas, Inc.
—Huck Finn & Tom Sawyer among the Indians & Other Unfinished Stories. 1989. (Mark Twain Library). 392p. pap. 14.95 (*0-520-05110-6*); text 45.00 (*0-520-05090-8*) Univ. of California Pr.
—Huckleberry Finn. Date not set. pap. text (*0-17-557047-7*) Addison-Wesley Longman, Inc.
—Huckleberry Finn. unabr. ed. 2003. audio 24.95 (*0-563-49687-8*, BBCS 034); audio compact disk 39.95 (*0-563-49688-6*, BBCD 034) BBC Worldwide Americas.
—Huckleberry Finn. 1997. (Cyber Classics Ser.). 317p. pap. 14.95 incl. disk (*1-55701-199-0*); 435p. pap. 19.95 (*1-55701-228-8*) BNI Pubns., Inc.
—Huckleberry Finn. l.t. ed. 1997. 435p. pap. 19.95 (*1-58855-015-X*) Cyber Classics, Inc.
—Huckleberry Finn. 1942. 112p. pap. 5.60 (*0-87129-839-2*, H35) Dramatic Publishing Co.
—Huckleberry Finn. 1998. (SPA.). 384p. (*84-08-00303-8*) GeoPlaneta, Editorial, S. A.
—Huckleberry Finn, Set. abr. ed. 1992. audio 17.00 (*1-55994-630-X*, DCN 2038, HarperAudio) HarperTrade.
—Huckleberry Finn. 1989. audio 44.00 Jimcin Recordings.
—Huckleberry Finn. 1993. audio. audio 47.20 (*1-56544-030-7*, 350039) Literate Ear, Inc.
—Huckleberry Finn. l.t. ed. 1995. 507p. lib. bdg. 26.00 (*0-939495-76-7*); 1998. 320p. reprint ed. lib. bdg. 25.00 (*1-58287-038-1*) North Bks.
—Huckleberry Finn. Teresa Agnes, ed. Heller, Rudolf, tr. 1979. (SPA., Illus.). 64p. pap. text 3.95 (*0-88301-450-5*) Pendulum Pr., Inc.
—Huckleberry Finn. 1985. 366p. 14.50 o.s.i (*0-394-60521-7*) Random Hse., Inc.
—Huckleberry Finn. unabr. ed. 2002. (YA). (gr. 7 up). audio compact disk 88.00 (*1-58472-160-X*, Commuters Library) Sound Room Pubs., Inc.
—Huckleberry Finn: Custom Edition. deluxe ed. 1983. 1000.00 o.p. (*0-8103-1636-6*, 00000512) Gale Group.
—Huckleberry Finn Readalong. 1994. (Illustrated Classics Collection: No. 1). 64p. pap. 14.95 incl. audio (*0-7854-0708-1*, 40348); pap. 13.50 o.p. incl. audio (*1-56103-431-2*) American Guidance Service, Inc.
—Tom Sawyer & Huckleberry Finn. 1972. reprint ed. 14.95 o.p. (*0-460-00976-1*); 2.95 o.p. (*0-460-01976-7*) Biblio Distribution.
—Tom Sawyer & Huckleberry Finn. 1991. (Everyman's Library). 608p. 20.00 (*0-679-40584-4*) Random Hse., Inc.
—Tom Sawyer & Huckleberry Finn. 1943. 448p. pap. 5.95 o.p. (*0-460-87111-0*, Everyman's Classic Library in Paperback) Tuttle Publishing.
—Tom Sawyer & Huckleberry Finn. 1998. (Wordsworth Collection). 400p. pap. 3.95 (*1-85326-011-8*, 0118WW) Wordsworth Editions, Ltd. GBR. *Dist:* Casemate Pubs. & Bk. Distributors, LLC.
Twain, Mark & Nelson, Lee. Huck Finn & Tom Sawyer among the Indians. 2003. 268p. 18.95 (*1-55517-680-1*, 76801, Council Pr.) Cedar Fort, Inc./CFI Distribution.

### FINN, ROB (FICTITIOUS CHARACTER)—FICTION

Francis, Dick. Dead Cert; Nerve; For Kicks. 1996. mass mkt. 7.99 o.s.i (*0-449-28768-8*, Fawcett) Ballantine Bks.
—Nerve. l.t. ed. 1994. 18.95 o.p. (*0-7927-1755-4*); 1994. pap. o.p. (*0-7927-1754-6*); 1993. 54.95 o.p. incl. audio (*0-7451-5953-2*) BBC Audiobooks America.
—Nerve. 1987. mass mkt. 5.95 o.s.i (*0-449-21266-1*, Fawcett) Ballantine Bks.
—Nerve. 1998. 320p. reprint ed. mass mkt. 6.99 (*0-515-12346-3*, Jove) Berkley Publishing Group.
—Nerve. unabr. ed. 1991. audio 48.00 (*0-7366-1928-3*, 2751) Books on Tape, Inc.
—Nerve. 1965. mass mkt. 0.60 o.p. (*0-451-02607-1*, Signet Bks.) NAL.
—Nerve. 1984. mass mkt. 3.50 (*0-671-52522-0*); 1982. mass mkt. 2.95 (*0-671-45072-7*) Simon & Schuster. (Pocket).
—Nerve. 1987. audio 53.95 o.p. (*0-8161-9670-2*) Thorndike Pr.
—Nerve. l.t. ed. 1978. o.p. (*0-7089-0171-9*, Ulverscroft) Thorpe, F. A. Pubs.

### FINNEGAN, JACK (FICTITIOUS CHARACTER)—FICTION

Hand, Elizabeth. Glimmering. 1998. 560p. mass mkt. 6.99 o.s.i (*0-06-101216-5*); 1997. 400p. mass mkt. 22.00 o.p. (*0-06-100805-2*) Morrow/Avon. (Eos).

### FIORA (FICTITIOUS CHARACTER)—FICTION

Maxwell, A. E. Art of Survival. 1993. 336p. mass mkt. 4.99 o.p. (*0-06-104115-7*, HarperTorch) Morrow/Avon.
—The Art of Survival. 1990. mass mkt. 4.50 o.s.i (*0-553-28479-7*) Bantam Bks.
—Frog & the Scorpion. 1986. 264p. 16.95 o.p. (*0-385-19260-6*) Doubleday Publishing.
—The Frog & the Scorpion. 1987. 224p. mass mkt. 3.50 o.s.i (*0-553-26876-7*) Bantam Bks.
—The Frog & the Scorpion. 1993. 320p. mass mkt. 4.99 o.p. (*0-06-104113-0*, HarperTorch) Morrow/Avon.
—Gatsby's Vineyard. 1988. 240p. mass mkt. 3.50 o.s.i (*0-553-27409-0*) Bantam Bks.
—Gatsby's Vineyard. 1987. 240p. 15.95 o.s.i (*0-385-23712-X*) Doubleday Publishing.
—Gatsby's Vineyard. 1993. 320p. mass mkt. 4.99 o.p. (*0-06-104112-2*, HarperTorch) Morrow/Avon.
—The Golden Empire. 1979. (Orig.). mass mkt. 2.50 o.s.i (*0-449-14267-1*, Fawcett) Ballantine Bks.
—Just Another Day in Paradise. 1986. mass mkt. 2.95 o.s.i (*0-553-25789-7*) Bantam Bks.
—Just Another Day in Paradise. 1985. 240p. 14.95 o.p. (*0-385-19259-2*) Doubleday Publishing.
—Just Another Day in Paradise. 1993. 304p. mass mkt. 4.99 o.p. (*0-06-104114-9*, HarperTorch) Morrow/Avon.
—Just Enough Light to Kill. 1989. mass mkt. 3.95 o.s.i (*0-553-28213-1*) Bantam Bks.
—Just Enough Light to Kill. 1993. 336p. mass mkt. 4.99 o.s.i (*0-06-104111-4*, HarperTorch) Morrow/Avon.
—The King of Nothing. 1994. 320p. mass mkt. 5.50 o.p. (*0-06-104230-7*, HarperTorch) Morrow/Avon.
—Money Burns. 1993. 368p. mass mkt. 5.50 o.p. (*0-06-104123-8*, HarperTorch) Morrow/Avon.
—Money Burns. 1993. 3.99 o.p. (*0-517-10621-3*) Random Hse. Value Publishing.
—Murder Hurts. 1995. 352p. mass mkt. 4.99 o.p. (*0-06-104318-4*, HarperTorch) Morrow/Avon.
—Redwood Empire. (Harlequin Historicals Ser.). 1995. 440p. per. (*0-373-28867-0*, 1-28867-9); 1987. 416p. mass mkt. (*0-373-97049-8*) Harlequin Enterprises, Ltd. (Harlequin Bks.).

### FISCHMAN, NINA (FICTITIOUS CHARACTER)—FICTION

Piesman, Marissa. Alternate Sides. 1996. 304p. mass mkt. 5.50 o.s.i (*0-440-22240-0*) Dell Publishing.
—Close Quarters. 1995. 304p. mass mkt. 4.99 o.s.i (*0-440-21162-X*) Dell Publishing.
—Heading Uptown: A Nina Fischman Mystery. l.t. ed. 1993. 21.95 o.p. (*0-7927-1658-2*); pap. 19.95 o.p. (*0-7927-1657-4*) BBC Audiobooks America.
—Heading Uptown: A Nina Fischman Mystery. 1994. 320p. mass mkt. 5.50 o.s.i (*0-440-21161-1*) Dell Publishing.
—Personal Effects. Chelius, Jane, ed. 1991. 224p. (Orig.). mass mkt. 4.50 (*0-671-74275-2*, Pocket) Simon & Schuster.
—Survival Instincts. 1997. (Nina Fischman Mystery Ser.). 224p. mass mkt. 5.99 o.s.i (*0-440-22453-5*, Dell Bks.) Dell Publishing.
—Unorthodox Practices. 1989. 224p. mass mkt. 4.99 (*0-671-67315-7*, Pocket) Simon & Schuster.

### FISH, SYD (FICTITIOUS CHARACTER)—FICTION

Geason, Susan. Dogfish. 1993. 208p. (Orig.). pap. 9.95 o.p. (*1-86373-088-5*) Allen & Unwin Pty., Ltd. AUS. *Dist:* Independent Pubs. Group.
—Sharkbait. 1994. 176p. pap. 9.95 o.p. (*1-86373-632-8*) Independent Pubs. Group.
—Shaved Fish. 1993. 168p. (Orig.). pap. 9.95 o.p. (*0-04-442274-1*) Allen & Unwin Pty., Ltd. AUS. *Dist:* Independent Pubs. Group.

### FISHER (FICTITIOUS CHARACTER: GREEN)—FICTION

Green, Simon R. Bones of Haven. 1992. (Hawk & Fisher Ser.: 6). mass mkt. 3.99 o.s.i (*0-441-31837-1*) Ace Bks.
—God Killer. 1991. (Hawk & Fisher Ser.: 3). mass mkt. 3.95 o.s.i (*0-441-29460-X*) Ace Bks.
—Guard Against Dishonor. 1991. (Hawk & Fisher Ser.: 5). mass mkt. 3.99 o.s.i (*0-441-31836-3*) Ace Bks.
—Guards of Haven: The Adventures of Hawk & Fisher, Bk. 2. 1999. 576p. reprint ed. mass mkt. 7.99 (*0-451-45755-2*, ROC) NAL.
—Hawk & Fisher. 1990. (Hawk & Fisher Ser.: 1). mass mkt. 4.50 o.s.i (*0-441-58417-9*) Ace Bks.
—Swords of Haven. 1999. (Hawk & Fisher Omnibus Ser.: No. 1). 512p. reprint ed. mass mkt. 7.99 (*0-451-45750-1*, ROC) NAL.
—Winner Takes All. 1991. (Hawk & Fisher Ser.: 2). mass mkt. 3.95 o.s.i (*0-441-14291-5*) Ace Bks.
—Wolf in the Fold. 1991. (Hawk & Fisher Ser.: 4). mass mkt. 3.95 o.s.i (*0-441-31835-5*) Ace Bks.

### FISHER, PHRYNE (FICTITIOUS CHARACTER)—FICTION

Greenwood, Kerry. Flying Too High. 1992. mass mkt. 3.99 o.s.i (*0-449-14777-0*, Fawcett) Ballantine Bks.
—Murder on the Ballarat Train. 1993. (Orig.). mass mkt. 4.50 o.s.i (*0-449-14832-7*, Fawcett) Ballantine Bks.

### FITZDUANE, HUGO (FICTITIOUS CHARACTER)—FICTION

O'Reilly, Victor. The Devil's Footprint. 1998. 448p. mass mkt. 7.50 o.s.i (*0-425-16186-2*) Berkley Publishing Group.
—The Devil's Footprint. 1997. 400p. 24.95 o.p. (*0-399-14137-5*, G. P. Putnam's Sons) Penguin Group (USA) Inc.
—Games of the Hangman. 1992. 512p. mass mkt. 7.50 o.s.i (*0-425-13456-3*) Berkley Publishing Group.
—Games of the Hangman. 1991. 512p. 19.95 o.p. (*0-8021-1431-8*) Grove/Atlantic, Inc.
—Rules of the Hunt. 1995. 512p. mass mkt. 6.99 o.s.i (*0-425-15097-6*) Berkley Publishing Group.
—Rules of the Hunt. abr. ed. 1996. audio 7.99 o.p. (*1-56740-104-X*, 694, Paperback Nova Audio Bks.); 1995. audio 16.95 o.p. (*1-56100-413-8*, 1358, Nova Audio Bks.); 1995. audio 89.25 o.p. (*1-56100-244-5*, 1020, Unabridged Library Editions); 1995. audio 25.95 o.p. (*1-56100-619-X*, 242, Bookcassette) Brilliance Audio.
—Rules of the Hunt. 1995. 416p. 23.95 o.p. (*0-399-13869-2*, G. P. Putnam's Sons) Penguin Group (USA) Inc.
—Rules of the Hunt. 402p. pap. 4.98 o.p. (*0-7651-0430-X*) Smithmark Pubs., Inc.

### FITZGEOFFREY, CORMAC (FICTITIOUS CHARACTER)—FICTION

Howard, Robert E. Hawks of Outremer. 1979. 15.00 o.p. (*0-937986-11-9*) Grant, Donald M. Pub., Inc.

### FITZGERALD, COLLEEN (FICTITIOUS CHARACTER)—FICTION

Johnson, Barbara. Bad Moon Rising: A Colleen Fitzgerald Mystery. 1998. (Colleen Fitzgerald Mysteries Ser.). 224p. pap. 11.95 (*1-56280-211-9*) Naiad Pr., Inc.
—The Beach Affair. 1995. (Colleen Fitzgerald Mysteries Ser.). 224p. pap. 10.95 (*1-56280-090-6*) Naiad Pr., Inc.

### FITZGERALD, EDWARD (FICTITIOUS CHARACTER)—FICTION

Brown, Molly. Cracker: To Say I Love You. (Cracker Ser.). 1996. 249p. mass mkt. 5.99 (*0-312-95996-6*, St. Martin's Paperbacks); 1995. 256p. 21.95 o.p. (*0-312-13951-9*) St. Martin's Pr.
Holliday, Liz & McGovern, Jimy. Cracker: One Day a Lemming Will Fly. 1997. (Cracker Ser.). 272p. 22.95 o.p. (*0-312-18072-1*, Saint Martin's Minotaur) St. Martin's Pr.
McGovern, Jimmy. Cracker to Be a Somebody. 2000. mass mkt. (*0-312-96998-8*, St. Martin's Paperbacks) St. Martin's Pr.
McGovern, Jimmy & Holliday, Liz. Cracker: One Day a Lemming Will Fly. 1999. (Cracker Ser.). 272p. mass mkt. 5.99 (*0-312-96817-5*, St. Martin's Paperbacks) St. Martin's Pr.
Mortimore, Jim. Cracker: The Mad Woman in the Attic. 1996. 256p. 21.95 o.p. (*0-312-14576-4*, Saint Martin's Minotaur); Vol. 1. 1998. (Cracker Ser.: Vol. 1). mass mkt. 5.99 (*0-312-96337-8*, St. Martin's Paperbacks) St. Martin's Pr.
Roberts, G. Cracker Best Boys. 2000. 247p. 22.95 (*0-312-20498-1*, Saint Martin's Minotaur) St. Martin's Pr.

### FITZGERALD, FIONA (FICTITIOUS CHARACTER)—FICTION

Adler, Warren. American Quartet: A Fiona FitzGerald Mystery. 1982. 13.95 o.p. (*0-87795-365-1*, Morrow, William & Co.) Morrow/Avon.
—American Sextet: A Fiona FitzGerald Mystery. 1983. 256p. 13.95 o.p. (*0-87795-414-3*, Morrow, William & Co.) Morrow/Avon.
—Immaculate Deception: A Fiona FitzGerald Mystery. 1991. 18.95 o.p. (*1-55611-229-7*) Fine, Donald I. Bks.
—Immaculate Deception: A Fiona FitzGerald Mystery. 1992. 288p. mass mkt. 3.99 o.s.i (*0-8217-3935-2*, Zebra Bks.) Kensington Publishing Corp.
—Senator Love: A Fiona FitzGerald Mystery. 1991. 18.95 o.p. (*1-55611-244-0*) Fine, Donald I. Bks.
—Senator Love: A Fiona FitzGerald Mystery. 1992. 256p. reprint ed. mass mkt. 3.99 o.s.i (*0-8217-3998-0*, Zebra Bks.) Kensington Publishing Corp.
—The Ties That Bind: A Fiona FitzGerald Mystery. 1994. 224p. 19.95 o.p. (*1-55611-395-1*) Fine, Donald I. Bks.
—The Ties That Bind: A Fiona FitzGerald Mystery. 2001. E-Book 6.95 (*1-931304-20-3*); E-Book 6.95 (*1-931304-44-0*) Stonehouse Pr.
—The Ties That Bind: A Fiona FitzGerald Mystery. 2001. 0272p. 26.95 (*1-59006-020-2*) Stonehouse Pubns.
—The Witch of Watergate: A Fiona FitzGerald Mystery. 1992. 256p. 19.95 o.p. (*1-55611-296-3*) Fine, Donald I. Bks.

### FITZGERALD, STEPHANIE (FICTITIOUS CHARACTER)—FICTION

Garrison, Leslie Ann. Mental Graffiti: Tall Tales Trilogy. l.t. ed. 1999. (Tall Tales Ser.: No. 2). E-Book 24.95 incl. cd-rom (*1-929077-27-0*, Books OnScreen) PageFree Publishing, Inc.
—Sniper's Candy: Tall Tales Trilogy. l.t. ed. 2000. (Tall Tales Ser.: No. 3). E-Book 24.95 incl. cd-rom (*1-929077-28-9*, Books OnScreen) PageFree Publishing, Inc.
—Visions of Murder: Tall Tales Trilogy. l.t. ed. 1999. (Tall Tales Ser.). E-Book 14.99 incl. cd-rom (*1-929077-26-2*, Books OnScreen) PageFree Publishing, Inc.

### FITZGIBBON, ZELDA (FICTITIOUS CHARACTER)—FICTION

Monninger, Joe. Incident at Potter's Bridge. 1992. 272p. 21.00 o.p. (*1-55611-307-2*) Fine, Donald I. Bks.
—Razor's Song. 1993. 256p. mass mkt. 4.99 (*0-380-71874-X*, Avon Bks.) Morrow/Avon.

### FITZHUGH, ALACRITY (FICTITIOUS CHARACTER)—FICTION

Daley, Brian. The Fall of the White Ship Avatar: A Hobart Floyt-Alacrity Fitzhugh Adventure. 1986. (Orig.). mass mkt. 3.95 o.s.i (*0-345-32919-8*, Del Rey) Ballantine Bks.
—Jinx on a Terran Inheritance. 1985. 416p. (Orig.). mass mkt. 3.50 o.s.i (*0-345-31488-3*) Ballantine Bks.
—Requiem for a Ruler of Worlds, No. 1. 1985. 304p. (Orig.). mass mkt. 3.95 o.s.i (*0-345-31487-5*, Ballantine Bks.) Ballantine Bks.

**FITZROY, HENRY (FICTITIOUS CHARACTER)—FICTION**

Huff, Tanya. Blood Debt. 1997. (Victory Nelson Ser.). 336p. mass mkt. 6.99 (*0-88677-739-9*) DAW Bks., Inc.

—Blood Lines, Bk. 3. 1993. (Daw Book Collectors Ser.: Vol. 901). 272p. (Orig.). mass mkt. 5.99 o.s.i (*0-88677-530-2*) DAW Bks., Inc.

—Blood Pact. 1993. (Daw Book Collectors Ser.: Vol. 931). 336p. mass mkt. 5.99 o.s.i (*0-88677-582-5*) DAW Bks., Inc.

—Blood Trail. 1992. (Victor Nelson Investigator Ser.: Vol. 3). 304p. (Orig.). mass mkt. 6.99 (*0-88677-502-7*) DAW Bks., Inc.

**FLAGG, CONAN (FICTITIOUS CHARACTER)—FICTION**

Wren, M. K. Curiosity Didn't Kill the Cat. 1988. 272p. mass mkt. 4.95 o.s.i (*0-345-35002-2*) Ballantine Bks.

—Dead Matter. 1993. (Northwest Mysteries Ser.). 283p. mass mkt. 4.99 o.s.i (*0-345-37821-0*) Ballantine Bks.

—King of the Mountain. 1994. mass mkt. 4.99 o.s.i (*0-345-39019-9*) Ballantine Bks.

—A Multitude of Sins. 1989. mass mkt. 3.50 o.s.i (*0-345-35001-4*) Ballantine Bks.

—Nothing's Certain but Death. 1989. 256p. mass mkt. 3.95 o.s.i (*0-345-35000-6*) Ballantine Bks.

—Nothing's Certain but Death. 1978. 6.95 o.p. (*0-385-13283-2*) Doubleday Publishing.

—Oh, Bury Me Not! 1989. 256p. mass mkt. 4.99 o.s.i (*0-345-35004-9*) Ballantine Bks.

—Seasons of Death. 1989. 192p. mass mkt. 4.99 o.s.i (*0-345-35003-0*) Ballantine Bks.

—Seasons of Death. 1981. (Crime Club Ser.). 192p. 9.95 o.p. (*0-385-17413-6*) Doubleday Publishing.

—Wake up, Darlin' Corey. 1990. 224p. mass mkt. 4.95 o.s.i (*0-345-35071-5*) Ballantine Bks.

—Wake up, Darlin' Corey. 1984. (Crime Club Ser.). 192p. 11.95 o.p. (*0-385-19292-4*) Doubleday Publishing.

**FLANNERY, JIMMY (FICTITIOUS CHARACTER)—FICTION**

Campbell, Robert. The Cat's Meow. (Jimmy Flannery Mystery Ser.). 1990. 208p. mass mkt. 4.50 o.p. (*0-451-16431-8*, Signet Bks.); 1988. 240p. 16.95 o.p. (*0-453-00615-9*) NAL.

—A Flannery Trilogy: Featuring The Junkyard Dog, 600-Pound Gorilla & Hip-Deep in Alligators. rev. ed. 1999. (Flannery Trilogies Ser.: Vol. 1). 384p. pap. 24.95 (*1-58444-073-2*) Disc-Us Bks., Inc.

—A Flannery Trilogy: Featuring the Junkyard Dog, 600-Pound Gorilla & Hip-Deep in Alligators, 1. 2003. (Jimmy Flannery Mystery Ser.). E-Book 16.95 incl. cd-rom (*1-58444-084-8*) Disc-Us Bks., Inc.

—The Gift Horse's Mouth. Chelius, Jane, ed. 208p. 1990. 17.95 o.p. (*0-671-67586-9*, Atria); 1991. reprint ed. mass mkt. 4.99 (*0-671-74340-6*, Pocket) Simon & Schuster.

—Hip Deep in Alligators. 1988. 208p. mass mkt. 3.95 o.p. (*0-451-40096-8*, Onyx); 1987. 16.95 o.p. (*0-453-00577-2*) NAL.

—In a Pig's Eye. Chelius, Jane, ed. 224p. 1991. 19.00 (*0-671-70327-7*, Atria); 1992. reprint ed. mass mkt. 4.99 (*0-671-70328-5*, Pocket) Simon & Schuster.

—The Junkyard Dog. 2000. E-Book 14.50 o.p. incl. cd-rom (*1-58444-047-3*) Disc-Us Bks., Inc.

—The Junkyard Dog. 1986. mass mkt. 2.95 o.p. (*0-451-14396-5*); 192p. mass mkt. 3.99 o.s.i (*0-451-15899-7*) NAL. (Signet Bks.).

—The Junkyard Dog. unabr. ed. 1991. (Jimmy Flannery Mystery Ser.: Vol. 1). audio 35.00 (*1-55690-277-8*, 91231E7) Recorded Bks., LLC.

—The Lion's Share. 1996. 82p. 21.95 o.s.i (*0-89296-609-2*) Mysterious Pr.

—The Lion's Share. 1997. 224p. mass mkt. 5.99 o.s.i (*0-446-40464-0*) Warner Bks., Inc.

—Nibbled to Death by Ducks. unabr. ed. 1992. (Jimmy Flannery Mystery Ser.: Vol. 6). audio 44.00 (*1-55690-703-6*, 92105E7) Recorded Bks., LLC.

—Nibbled to Death by Ducks. 1989. 208p. 17.95 o.p. (*0-671-67585-0*, Atria) Simon & Schuster.

—Nibbled to Death by Ducks. Chelius, Jane, ed. 1990. 288p. reprint ed. mass mkt. 4.99 (*0-671-67583-4*, Pocket) Simon & Schuster.

—Pigeon Pie. 1998. (Jimmy Flannery Mystery Ser.: Vol. 27). 240p. 22.00 o.s.i (*0-89296-665-3*) Mysterious Pr.

—Pigeon Pie. l.t. ed. 1999. (Cloak & Dagger Ser.). 301p. 29.95 (*0-7862-1528-3*) Thorndike Pr.

—Sauce for the Goose. 1995. 240p. 18.95 o.s.i (*0-89296-608-4*) Mysterious Pr.

—Sauce for the Goose. 1996. 208p. mass mkt. 5.99 o.p. (*0-446-40463-2*) Warner Bks., Inc.

—Thinning the Turkey Herd. 1989. mass mkt. 3.50 o.p. (*0-451-15920-9*, Signet Bks.); 1988. 16.95 o.p. (*0-453-00583-7*) NAL.

—600-Pound Gorilla. 1987. 240p. mass mkt. 3.95 o.p. (*0-451-15390-1*, Signet Bks.) NAL.

—The 600-Pound Gorilla. unabr. ed. 1991. (Jimmy Flannery Mystery Ser.: Vol. 2). audio 35.00 (*1-55690-582-3*, 91307E7) Recorded Bks., LLC.

**FLANNIGAN, DIXIE (FICTITIOUS CHARACTER)—FICTION**

Rogers, Chris. Bitch Factor. 1998. 336p. mass mkt. 5.99 (*0-553-58001-9*) Bantam Bks.

—The Chill Factor. 2001. 416p. reprint ed. mass mkt. 6.50 o.s.i (*0-553-58073-6*) Bantam Bks.

—The Rage Factor. 2000. 400p. mass mkt. 5.99 (*0-553-58070-1*) Bantam Bks.

**FLASHMAN, HARRY PAGET (FICTITIOUS CHARACTER)—FICTION**

Fraser, George MacDonald. Black Ajax. 256p. 1999. pap. 12.95 (*0-7867-0618-X*); 1998. 23.00 o.p. (*0-7867-0553-1*) Avalon Publishing Group. (Carroll & Graf Pubs.).

—Flash for Freedom! unabr. ed. 1993. audio 69.95 o.p. (*0-7451-4208-7*, CAB 891) BBC Audiobooks America.

—Flash for Freedom! unabr. ed. 1994. (Flashman Ser.). audio 64.00 (*0-7366-2724-3*, 3454) Books on Tape, Inc.

—Flash for Freedom! 1985. (Flashman Ser.). pap. 6.95 o.p. (*0-452-25677-1*); 304p. pap. 14.00 (*0-452-26089-2*) Dutton/Plume. (Plume).

—Flash for Freedom! 1973. (Flashman Ser.). mass mkt. 1.50 o.p. (*0-451-06933-1*); mass mkt. 1.25 o.p. (*0-451-05491-1*) NAL. (Signet Bks.).

—Flashman. unabr. ed. 1994. (Flashman Ser.). audio 56.00 (*0-7366-2675-1*, 3412) Books on Tape, Inc.

—Flashman. 1984. (Flashman Ser.). 256p. pap. 14.00 (*0-452-25961-4*); pap. 6.95 o.p. (*0-452-25588-0*) Dutton/Plume. (Plume).

—Flashman. (Flashman Ser.). 1974. mass mkt. 1.25 o.p. (*0-451-06116-0*); 1970. mass mkt. 2.50 o.p. (*0-451-11658-5*); 1970. mass mkt. 1.50 o.p. (*0-451-06932-3*); 1970. mass mkt. 1.75 o.p. (*0-451-08009-2*); 1970. mass mkt. 0.95 o.p. (*0-451-04264-6*) NAL. (Signet Bks.).

—Flashman. l.t. ed. 1982. (Ulverscroft Large Print Ser.). 476p. 29.99 o.p. (*0-7089-0810-1*, Ulverscroft) Thorpe, F. A. Pubs. GBR. *Dist:* Ulverscroft Large Print Bks., Ltd., Ulverscroft Large Print Canada, Ltd.

—Flashman & the Angel of the Lord: From the Flashman Papers, 1958-59. unabr. ed. 1995. (Flashman Ser.). audio 80.00 (*0-7366-3131-3*, 3806) Books on Tape, Inc.

—Flashman & the Angel of the Lord: From the Flashman Papers, 1958-59. 1996. 400p. pap. 13.95 (*0-452-27440-0*, Plume) Dutton/Plume.

—Flashman & the Angel of the Lord: From the Flashman Papers, 1958-59. 1995. 394p. 24.00 o.s.i (*0-679-44172-7*) Knopf, Alfred A. Inc.

—Flashman & the Dragon. unabr. ed. 1995. (Flashman Ser.). audio 72.00 (*0-7366-3053-8*, 3735) Books on Tape, Inc.

—Flashman & the Dragon. 1987. (Flashman Ser.). 336p. pap. 13.95 (*0-452-26191-0*); pap. 7.95 o.p. (*0-452-25930-4*) Dutton/Plume. (Plume).

—Flashman & the Mountain of Light. unabr. ed. 1995. (Flashman Ser.). audio 80.00 (*0-7366-3096-1*, 3772) Books on Tape, Inc.

—Flashman & the Mountain of Light. 1992. (Flashman Ser.). 368p. reprint ed. pap. 13.95 (*0-452-26785-4*, Plume) Dutton/Plume.

—Flashman & the Redskins. unabr. ed. 1995. (Flashman Ser.). audio 96.00 (*0-7366-3007-4*, 3693) Books on Tape, Inc.

—Flashman & the Redskins. 1983. (Flashman Ser.). 480p. pap. 14.00 (*0-452-26487-1*); 480p. pap. 8.95 o.p. (*0-452-26066-3*); pap. 7.95 o.p. (*0-452-25431-0*) Dutton/Plume. (Plume).

—Flashman & the Redskins. l.t. ed. 1983. (Charnwood Large Print Ser.). 708p. 29.99 o.p. (*0-7089-8127-5*, Ulverscroft) Thorpe, F. A. Pubs. GBR. *Dist:* Ulverscroft Large Print Bks., Ltd., Ulverscroft Large Print Canada, Ltd.

—Flashman at the Charge. unabr. ed. 1994. audio 69.95 o.p. (*0-7451-4300-8*, CAB 983) BBC Audiobooks America.

—Flashman at the Charge. unabr. ed. 1994. (Flashman Ser.). audio 64.00 (*0-7366-2775-8*, 3494) Books on Tape, Inc.

—Flashman at the Charge. 1986. (Flashman Ser.). 288p. pap. 14.00 (*0-452-26413-8*); pap. 7.95 o.p. (*0-452-25957-6*); pap. 6.95 o.p. (*0-452-25765-4*) Dutton/Plume. (Plume).

—Flashman at the Charge. (Flashman Ser.). 1975. mass mkt. 1.50 o.p. (*0-451-06931-5*); 1974. mass mkt. 1.25 o.p. (*0-451-06094-6*) NAL. (Signet Bks.).

—Flashman in the Great Game. unabr. collector's ed. 1995. (Flashman Ser.). audio 72.00 (*0-7366-2908-4*, 3605) Books on Tape, Inc.

—Flashman in the Great Game. 1989. (Flashman Ser.). 336p. pap. 13.95 (*0-452-26303-4*, Plume) Dutton/Plume.

—Flashman in the Great Game. 1977. (Flashman Ser.). mass mkt. 2.50 o.p. (*0-451-09688-6*, E9688); mass mkt. 1.95 o.p. (*0-451-07429-7*) NAL. (Signet Bks.).

—Flashman in the Great Game. 1975. 8.95 o.p. (*0-394-49893-3*, Knopf Bks. for Young Readers) Random Hse. Children's Bks.

—Flashman in the Great Game. l.t. ed. 1985. (Charnwood Large Print Ser.). 512p. 29.99 o.p. (*0-7089-8264-6*, Ulverscroft) Thorpe, F. A. Pubs. GBR. *Dist:* Ulverscroft Large Print Bks., Ltd., Ulverscroft Large Print Canada, Ltd.

—Flashman's Lady. unabr. collector's ed. 1995. (Flashman Ser.). audio 72.00 (*0-7366-3008-2*, 3694) Books on Tape, Inc.

—Flashman's Lady. 1988. (Flashman Ser.). pap. 8.95 o.p. (*0-452-26080-9*); 336p. pap. 13.95 (*0-452-26489-8*) Dutton/Plume. (Plume).

—Flashman's Lady. 1979. (Flashman Ser.). mass mkt. 2.95 o.p. (*0-451-11660-7*, AE1660); mass mkt. 2.25 o.p. (*0-451-08514-0*) NAL. (Signet Bks.).

—Flashman's Lady. 1978. 8.95 o.p. (*0-394-50135-7*, Knopf Bks. for Young Readers) Random Hse. Children's Bks.

—Royal Flash. 1985. (Flashman Ser.). 256p. pap. 14.00 (*0-452-26112-0*, Plume) Dutton/Plume.

—Royal Flash. (Flashman Ser.). 1975. mass mkt. 1.50 o.p. (*0-451-06748-7*); 1971. mass mkt. 1.25 o.p. (*0-451-04831-8*) NAL. (Signet Bks.).

—Royal Flash. l.t. ed. 1985. (Ulverscroft Large Print Ser.). 528p. 29.99 o.p. (*0-7089-1362-8*, Ulverscroft) Thorpe, F. A. Pubs. GBR. *Dist:* Ulverscroft Large Print Bks., Ltd., Ulverscroft Large Print Canada, Ltd.

**FLEMING, JACK (FICTITIOUS CHARACTER)—FICTION**

Elrod, P. N. A Chill in the Blood. (Vampire Files Ser.: Vol. 7). 336p. 1998. 20.95 o.s.i (*0-441-00501-2*); 1999. reprint ed. mass mkt. 6.50 o.s.i (*0-441-00627-2*) Ace Bks.

—Cold Streets. 2003. 384p. mass mkt. 6.99 (*0-441-01103-9*); (Vampire Files Ser.: Bk. 9). 22.95 (*0-441-01009-1*) Ace Bks.

—Dark Sleep. (Vampire Files Ser.: Vol. 8). 368p. 2000. mass mkt. 6.99 (*0-441-00723-6*); 1999. 21.95 o.s.i (*0-441-00591-8*) Ace Bks.

—Lady Crymsyn: A Novel of the Vampire Files. 2000. (Vampire Files Ser.: Vol. 9). (Illus.). 416p. 22.95 o.s.i (*0-441-00724-4*) Ace Bks.

—Vampire Files: Blood Art. 1991. (Vampire Files Ser.: Vol. 4). 208p. mass mkt. 5.99 o.s.i (*0-441-85945-3*) Ace Bks.

—Vampire Files: Blood on the Water. 1992. (Vampire Files Ser.: Vol. 6). 208p. mass mkt. 5.99 o.s.i (*0-441-85947-X*) Ace Bks.

—Vampire Files: Fire in the Blood. 1991. (Vampire Files Ser.: Vol. 5). mass mkt. 5.99 o.s.i (*0-441-85946-1*) Ace Bks.

—Vampire Files: The Bloodlist, No. 1. 2003. 464p. pap. 14.00 (*0-441-01090-3*) Ace Bks.

—Vampire Files No. 01: Bloodlist. 1990. (Vampire Files Ser.). 208p. mass mkt. 6.50 o.s.i (*0-441-06795-6*) Ace Bks.

—Vampire Files No. 2: Lifeblood. 1990. (Vampire Files Ser.: Vol. 2). 208p. mass mkt. 5.99 o.s.i (*0-441-84776-5*) Ace Bks.

—Vampire Files No. 3: Bloodcircle. 1990. (Vampire Files Ser.: Vol. 3). mass mkt. 5.99 o.s.i (*0-441-06717-4*) Ace Bks.

**FLEMING, JAMES (FICTITIOUS CHARACTER)—FICTION**

Fallon, Ann C. Blood Is Thicker. 1990. 256p. (Orig.). mass mkt. 3.95 (*0-671-70623-3*, Pocket) Simon & Schuster.

—Dead Ends. Isaacson, Dana, ed. 1992. 256p. (Orig.). mass mkt. 4.99 (*0-671-75134-4*, Pocket) Simon & Schuster.

—Hour of Our Death. Chelius, Jane, ed. 1995. 256p. (Orig.). mass mkt. 5.50 (*0-671-88515-4*, Pocket) Simon & Schuster.

—Potter's Field. Isaacson, Dana, ed. 1993. 256p. (Orig.). mass mkt. 4.99 (*0-671-75136-0*, Pocket) Simon & Schuster.

—Where Death Lies. Isaacson, Dana, ed. 1991. 256p. mass mkt. 4.99 (*0-671-70624-1*, Pocket) Simon & Schuster.

**FLEMING, LAURA (FICTITIOUS CHARACTER)—FICTION**

Kelner, Toni L. P. Country Comes to Town: A Laura Fleming Mystery. (Laura Fleming Mystery Ser.). 336p. 1998. mass mkt. 5.99 (*1-57566-244-2*); 1996. 18.95 o.s.i (*1-57566-083-0*, Kensington Bks.) Kensington Publishing Corp.

—Dead Ringer. 1994. 304p. mass mkt. 3.99 o.s.i (*0-8217-4469-0*, Zebra Bks.) Kensington Publishing Corp.

—Death of a Damn Yankee. 2001. 32p. mass mkt. 5.99 o.s.i (*1-57566-686-3*); 1999. 295p. 20.00 o.s.i (*1-57566-431-3*, Kensington Bks.) Kensington Publishing Corp.

—Down Home Murder. 304p. 1999. mass mkt. 5.99 (*1-57566-429-1*); 1993. mass mkt. 3.99 o.s.i (*0-8217-4196-9*, Zebra Bks.) Kensington Publishing Corp.

—Mad As the Dickens. 2002. 320p. mass mkt. 5.99 (*1-57566-839-4*); 2001. 288p. 22.00 o.s.i (*1-57566-838-6*, Kensington Bks.) Kensington Publishing Corp.

—Tight As a Tick. 1998. (Laura Fleming Mystery Ser.). 320p. 18.95 o.s.i (*1-57566-242-6*) Kensington Publishing Corp.

—Tight as a Tick, 1. 1999. (Laura Fleming Mystery Ser.). 320p. mass mkt. 5.99 o.s.i (*1-57566-434-8*) Kensington Publishing Corp.

—Tight As a Tick. unabr. ed. 1999. audio 69.95 (*0-7927-2274-4*, CSL163, Chivers Sound Library) BBC Audiobooks America.

—Trouble Looking for a Place to Happen: A Laura Fleming Mystery. 1996. 352p. mass mkt. 4.99 o.s.i (*1-57566-007-5*); 1995. 336p. mass mkt. 16.95 o.p. (*0-8217-4855-6*) Kensington Publishing Corp.

—Wed & Buried: A Laura Fleming Mystery. 2003. (Laura Fleming Mystery Ser.). 272p. 22.00 (*1-57566-840-8*) Kensington Publishing Corp.

**FLETCH (FICTITIOUS CHARACTER)—FICTION**

Mcdonald, Gregory. Carioca Fletch. unabr. ed. 1989. audio 42.00 (*0-7366-1538-5*, 2408) Books on Tape, Inc.

—Carioca Fletch. 2002. (Illus.). 192p. pap. 12.00 (*0-375-71347-6*) Random Hse., Inc.

—Carioca Fletch. 1988. 288p. mass mkt. 4.99 o.s.i (*0-446-34899-6*) Warner Bks., Inc.

—Confess, Fletch. unabr. ed. 1988. audio 42.00 (*0-7366-1323-4*, 2227) Books on Tape, Inc.

—Confess, Fletch. 1976. 272p. mass mkt. 4.99 (*0-380-00814-9*, Avon Bks.) Morrow/Avon.

—Fletch. unabr. ed. 1988. audio 36.00 (*0-7366-1352-8*, 2253) Books on Tape, Inc.

—Fletch. 1976. 256p. mass mkt. 4.99 (*0-380-00645-6*, Avon Bks.) Morrow/Avon.

—Fletch & the Man Who. unabr. ed. 1988. audio 42.00 (*0-7366-1380-3*, 2273) Books on Tape, Inc.

—Fletch & the Man Who. l.t. ed. 1988. (General Ser.). 352p. pap. 17.95 o.p. (*0-8161-4654-3*, Macmillan Reference USA) Gale Group.

—Fletch & the Man Who. 1988. 288p. mass mkt. 4.99 o.s.i (*0-446-35560-7*) Warner Bks., Inc.

—Fletch & the Widow Bradley. unabr. ed. 1988. audio 36.00 (*0-7366-1418-4*, 2304) Books on Tape, Inc.

—Fletch & the Widow Bradley. 2000. E-Book (*1-930351-09-7*) FairHillBooks.com.

—Fletch & the Widow Bradley. 1982. (General Ser.). 11.95 o.p. (*0-8161-3377-8*, Macmillan Reference USA) Gale Group.

—Fletch & the Widow Bradley. 2002. (Vintage Crime/Black Lizard Ser.). 160p. pap. 11.00 (*0-375-71351-4*) Knopf, Alfred A. Inc.

—Fletch & the Widow Bradley. 1989. mass mkt. 4.99 o.s.i (*0-446-35997-1*) Warner Bks., Inc.

—The Fletch Chronicle Vol. 1: Fletch Won; Fletch, Too; Fletch & the Widow Bradley. 1989. 8.99 o.p. (*0-517-00308-2*) Random Hse. Value Publishing.

—The Fletch Chronicle Vol. 2: Fletch; Carioca Fletch; Confess, Fletch. 1989. 8.99 o.p. (*0-517-00307-4*) Random Hse. Value Publishing.

—The Fletch Chronicle Vol. 3: Fletch's Fortune; Fletch's Moxie; Fletch & the Man Who. 1989. 8.99 o.p. (*0-517-00309-0*) Random Hse. Value Publishing.

—Fletch Reflected. 1995. 288p. mass mkt. 6.50 o.s.i (*0-515-11676-9*, Jove) Berkley Publishing Group.

—Fletch Reflected. unabr. ed. 1996. audio 36.00 (*0-7366-3287-5*, 3942) Books on Tape, Inc.

—Fletch Reflected. 1994. 240p. 21.95 o.p. (*0-399-13983-4*, G. P. Putnam's Sons) Penguin Group (USA) Inc.

—Fletch Reflected. 224p. 4.98 o.p. (*0-7651-0180-7*) Smithmark Pubs., Inc.

—Fletch, Too. 2000. E-Book (*1-930351-06-2*) FairHillBooks.com.

—Fletch, Too. 2002. 256p. pap. 12.00 (*0-375-71353-0*, Vintage) Knopf Publishing Group.

—Fletch, Too. 1987. o.s.i (*0-446-51326-1*); mass mkt. 4.99 o.s.i (*0-446-34614-4*) Warner Bks., Inc.

—Fletch, Too. unabr. ed. 1989. audio 36.00 (*0-7366-1492-3*, 2368) Books on Tape, Inc.

—Fletch Won. unabr. ed. 1988. audio 42.00 (*0-7366-1452-4*, 2334) Books on Tape, Inc.

—Fletch Won. 2002. (Vintage Crime/Black Lizard Ser.). 272p. pap. 12.00 (*0-375-71352-2*) Knopf, Alfred A. Inc.

—Fletch Won. 272p. 1986. mass mkt. 4.99 o.s.i (*0-446-34095-2*); 1985. 14.45 o.p. (*0-446-51325-3*) Warner Bks., Inc.

—Fletch's Fortune. unabr. ed. 1988. audio 36.00 (*0-7366-1398-6*, 2287) Books on Tape, Inc.

—Fletch's Fortune. 1988. pap. 4.99 (*0-380-37978-3*, Avon Bks.) Morrow/Avon.

—Fletch's Moxie. unabr. ed. 1988. audio 42.00 (*0-7366-1442-7*, 2325) Books on Tape, Inc.

—Fletch's Moxie. 2000. E-Book (*1-930351-08-9*) FairHillBooks.com.

—Fletch's Moxie. 1989. 288p. mass mkt. 4.99 o.s.i (*0-446-35976-9*) Warner Bks., Inc.

—Son of Fletch. 1994. 272p. mass mkt. 5.99 o.s.i (*0-515-11470-7*, Jove) Berkley Publishing Group.
—Son of Fletch. 1993. 240p. 19.95 o.p. (*0-399-13831-5*, G. P. Putnam's Sons) Penguin Group (USA) Inc.
—Son of Fletch. 4.98 o.s.i (*0-8317-6523-2*) Smithmark Pubs., Inc.

**FLETCHER, JACK (FICTITIOUS CHARACTER)—FICTION**

Nunn, Kem. The Dogs of Winter. 1998. 368p. pap. 14.00 o.s.i (*0-671-79334-9*); 1997. 400p. 23.50 (*0-684-82647-X*) Simon & Schuster. (Scribner).

**FLETCHER, JESSICA (FICTITIOUS CHARACTER)—FICTION**

Bain, Donald. Brandy & Bullets: Murder, She Wrote. l.t. ed. 1999. (G. K. Hall Nightingale Ser.). 288p. pap. 20.95 (*0-7838-8596-2*) Thorndike Pr.
—Gin & Daggers: A Murder, She Wrote Mystery. l.t. ed. 2001. 329p. pap. 23.95 (*0-7838-9444-9*) Thorndike Pr.
—Knock 'em Dead: A Murder, She Wrote Mystery. l.t. ed. 2002. 264p. pap. 24.45 (*0-7862-4051-2*) Gale Group.
—Murder She Wrote. 1924. o.s.i (*0-688-09989-0*, Morrow, William & Co.) Morrow/Avon.
—Murder She Wrote: A Palette for Murder. l.t. ed. 2001. (G. K. Hall Nightingale Ser.). 274p. 23.95 (*0-7838-9319-1*) Thorndike Pr.
—Murder, She Wrote: A Palette for Murder. l.t. ed. 2001. 274p. (*0-7540-4395-9*); (*0-7540-4396-7*) Gale Group. (Macmillan Reference USA).
—Murder, She Wrote: Destination Murder. 2003. 288p. 19.95 (*0-451-21048-4*) NAL.
—Murder, She Wrote: Manhattans & Murder. l.t. ed. 1998. (Murder She Wrote Ser.). 288p. pap. 21.95 (*0-7838-0133-5*) Thorndike Pr.
—Trick or Treachery: A Murder, She Wrote Mystery. l.t. ed. 2001. (Large Print Mystery Ser.). 252p. pap. 23.95 (*0-7838-9496-1*, Macmillan Reference USA) Gale Group.

Bain, Donald & Fletcher, Jessica. A Little Yuletide Murder. 1998. (Murder She Wrote Ser.: Vol. 10). 304p. mass mkt. 6.50 (*0-451-19475-6*, Signet Bks.) NAL.
—A Little Yuletide Murder: A Murder, She Wrote, Mystery. l.t. ed. 2000. (Nightingale Ser.). 279p. pap. 21.95 (*0-7838-9101-6*) Thorndike Pr.
—Murder at the Powderhorn Ranch: A Murder, She Wrote Mystery. l.t. ed. 2000. (G. K. Hall Nightingale Ser.). 256p. pap. 21.95 (*0-7838-8926-7*, Macmillan Reference USA) Gale Group.
—Murder, She Wrote: Martinis & Mayhem. l.t. ed. 1999. (Nightingale Ser.). 280p. pap. 21.95 (*0-7838-8665-9*) Thorndike Pr.

Fletcher, Jessica. Gin & Daggers: Jessica Fletcher & Donald Bain Mystery. 2000. (Murder She Wrote Ser.). 272p. mass mkt. 6.50 (*0-451-19998-7*, Signet Bks.) NAL.
—Murder on the QE2. 1997. (Murder She Wrote Ser.: Vol. 8). 304p. mass mkt. 6.50 (*0-451-19291-5*, Signet Bks.) NAL.
—Murder, She Wrote: Dying to Retire By. 2004. 272p. mass mkt. 6.99 (*0-451-21171-5*, Signet Bks.) NAL.
—Murder She Wrote: Knock 'em Dead, Vol. 12. 1999. (Murder She Wrote Ser.). 288p. mass mkt. 6.50 (*0-451-19477-2*, Signet Bks.) NAL.
—Murder She Wrote: Trick or Treachery. 2000. (Murder She Wrote Ser.). 272p. mass mkt. 6.50 (*0-451-20152-3*, Signet Bks.) NAL.
—A Palette for Murder: A Murder, She Wrote Mystery. 1996. (Murder She Wrote Ser.: Vol. 6). 304p. mass mkt. 6.50 (*0-451-18820-9*, Signet Bks.) NAL.
—You Bet Your Life. 2002. (Murder She Wrote Ser.). 272p. mass mkt. 6.50 (*0-451-20721-1*, Signet Bks.) NAL.

Fletcher, Jessica & Bain, Donald. Blood on the Vine. 2001. (Murder She Wrote Ser.). 272p. mass mkt. 6.50 (*0-451-20275-9*, Signet Bks.) NAL.
—Brandy & Bullets. 1995. (Murder She Wrote Ser.: Vol. 3). 288p. (Orig.). mass mkt. 6.50 (*0-451-18491-2*, Signet Bks.) NAL.
—Deadly Judgement. 1996. (Murder She Wrote Ser.). 304p. mass mkt. 6.50 (*0-451-18771-7*) NAL.
—A Deadly Judgement. unabr. ed. 1999. (Murder She Wrote Ser.). audio 54.95 (*0-7927-2310-4*, CSL199, Chivers Sound Library) BBC Audiobooks America.
—Gin & Daggers. 1990. reprint ed. pap. 3.50 (*0-380-71166-4*, Avon Bks.) Morrow/Avon.
—Gin & Daggers: A Murder, She Wrote Mystery. 1989. 272p. text 17.95 o.p. (*0-07-003239-4*) McGraw-Hill Cos., The.
—The Highland Fling Murders. 1997. (Murder She Wrote Ser.: 7). 304p. mass mkt. 6.50 (*0-451-18851-9*, Signet Bks.) NAL.
—Manhattans & Murder. 1994. (Murder She Wrote Ser.: Vol. 1). 304p. mass mkt. 6.50 (*0-451-18142-5*, Signet Bks.) NAL.
—Manhattans & Murder. abr. ed. 1994. (Murder She Wrote Ser.). pap. 16.00 o.p. incl. audio (*0-453-00901-8*) Penguin/HighBridge.
—Murder at the Powderhorn Ranch. 1999. (Murder She Wrote Ser.: Vol. 11). 272p. mass mkt. 6.50 (*0-451-19476-4*) NAL.
—Murder in a Minor Key: A Murder, She Wrote Mystery. l.t. ed. 2003. 366p. pap. 24.45 (*0-7862-5357-6*) Thorndike Pr.
—Murder in Moscow. 1998. (Murder She Wrote Ser.: Vol. 9). 304p. mass mkt. 6.50 (*0-451-19474-8*, Signet Bks.) NAL.
—Murder, She Wrote: Martinis & Mayhem. 1995. (Murder She Wrote Ser.: Vol. 4). 304p. mass mkt. 6.50 (*0-451-18512-9*, Signet Bks.) NAL.
—Rum & Razors. l.t. ed. 1995. (Murder She Wrote Ser.). (Orig.). 22.95 o.p. (*1-56895-219-8*, Wheeler Publishing, Inc.) Gale Group.
—Rum & Razors. 1995. (Murder She Wrote Ser.: Vol. 2). 304p. (Orig.). mass mkt. 6.50 (*0-451-18383-5*) NAL.

Foxwell, Elizabeth & Greenberg, Martin H., eds. Murder, They Wrote, No. 2. 1998. (Murder She Wrote Anthology Ser.: No. 2). 352p. mass mkt. 6.99 o.s.i (*1-57297-339-0*) Boulevard Bks.

Greenberg, Martin H., ed. Murder, They Wrote. 1997. (Jessica Fletcher Presents Ser.). 368p. mass mkt. 6.99 o.s.i (*1-57297-194-0*) Boulevard Bks.

**FLETCHER, MARTIN (FICTITIOUS CHARACTER)—FICTION**

Miller, John Ramsey. The Last Family: A Suspense Novel. 1997. 480p. reprint ed. mass mkt. 6.99 (*0-553-57496-5*) Bantam Bks.

**FLETCHER, PHILIP (FICTITIOUS CHARACTER)—FICTION**

Shaw, Simon. The Company of Knaves. 1997. (Philip Fletcher Mystery Ser.). 224p. 22.95 (*0-312-18069-1*, Saint Martin's Minotaur) St. Martin's Pr.
—Dead for a Ducat. 1996. 224p. 20.95 o.p. (*0-312-14309-5*, Saint Martin's Minotaur) St. Martin's Pr.
—Murder Out of Tune. unabr. ed. 1993. audio 54.95 (*0-7451-4094-7*, CAB 782) BBC Audiobooks America.
—Murder Out of Tune. 1992. 256p. mass mkt. 4.50 o.s.i (*0-553-29592-6*) Bantam Bks.
—Murder Out of Tune. 1988. 192p. o.s.i (*0-385-24602-1*) Doubleday Publishing.
—The Villain of the Earth. 1995. 189p. 19.95 o.p. (*0-312-13201-8*, Saint Martin's Minotaur) St. Martin's Pr.

**FLINX OF THE COMMONWEALTH (FICTITIOUS CHARACTER)—FICTION**

Foster, Alan Dean. Bloodhype. 1995. (Flinx & Pip Novels Ser.). mass mkt. 5.99 o.p. (*0-345-90863-5*, Del Rey); 1983. mass mkt. 2.75 o.p. (*0-345-31021-7*, Del Rey); 1981. mass mkt. 2.50 o.p. (*0-345-30578-7*, Del Rey); 1980. mass mkt. 2.25 o.p. (*0-345-29476-9*, Del Rey); 1978. mass mkt. 1.95 o.p. (*0-345-28037-7*, Del Rey); No. 4. 1985. (Bloodhype Ser.: Vol. 4). mass mkt. 5.99 o.s.i (*0-345-33285-7*) Ballantine Bks.
—The End of the Matter. 1995. (Flinx & Pip Novels Ser.). mass mkt. 5.99 o.p. (*0-345-90861-9*, Del Rey); 1980. mass mkt. 2.25 o.p. (*0-345-29594-3*, Del Rey); 1977. mass mkt. 1.75 o.p. (*0-345-25861-4*, Del Rey); Vol.. 3. 1985. (End of the Matter Ser.: Vol. 3). 246p. mass mkt. 5.99 o.s.i (*0-345-33465-5*) Ballantine Bks.
—Flinx in Flux. 1988. 336p. mass mkt. 5.99 o.s.i (*0-345-34363-8*); 1995. reprint ed. mass mkt. 5.99 o.p. (*0-345-90867-8*) Ballantine Bks. (Del Rey).
—Flinx of the Commonwealth, 3 vols. 1982. mass mkt. 6.25 o.p. (*0-345-26200-X*, Del Rey) Ballantine Bks.
—For Love of Mother-Not. 1988. pap. 3.50 o.p. (*0-345-00891-X*); 1987. 256p. mass mkt. 5.99 o.s.i (*0-345-34689-0*); 1983. mass mkt. 2.95 o.p. (*0-345-30511-6*) Ballantine Bks. (Del Rey).
—For Love of Mother-Not. 1992. reprint ed. 18.00 o.p. (*0-7278-4403-2*) Severn Hse. Pubs., Ltd.
—Mid-Flinx. 1996. 352p. mass mkt. 7.99 (*0-345-40644-3*); 1995. 336p. 22.00 o.s.i (*0-345-38374-5*, Del Rey) Ballantine Bks.
—Orphan Star. 2003. 240p. pap. 6.99 (*0-345-46104-5*); 1995. mass mkt. 5.99 o.p. (*0-345-90859-7*); 1985. 240p. mass mkt. 5.99 o.s.i (*0-345-32449-8*); 1983. mass mkt. 2.75 o.p. (*0-345-31001-2*); 1981. mass mkt. 2.50 o.p. (*0-345-29903-5*); 1980. mass mkt. 2.25 o.p. (*0-345-29233-2*) Ballantine Bks. (Del Rey).
—Reunion. 2001. (Pip & Flinx Novel Ser.). 336p. 24.00 (*0-345-41867-0*, Del Rey) Ballantine Bks.
—The Tar-Aiym Krang. 1981. 256p. mass mkt. 6.50 (*0-345-30280-X*, Del Rey); 1980. mass mkt. 2.25 o.p. (*0-345-29232-4*, Del Rey); 1979. mass mkt. 1.95 o.p. (*0-345-28165-9*, Del Rey); 1975. mass mkt. 1.50 o.p. (*0-345-24085-5*); 1995. reprint ed. mass mkt. 5.99 (*0-345-90857-0*, Del Rey) Ballantine Bks.

**FLIPPO, JACK (FICTITIOUS CHARACTER)—FICTION**

Swanson, Doug J. Big Town. 1995. 288p. mass mkt. 4.50 o.p. (*0-06-109213-4*, HarperTorch) Morrow/Avon.
—Big Town: A Novel of Suspense. 1994. 224p. 18.00 o.p. (*0-06-017749-7*) HarperTrade.
—Dreamboat. 1996. 256p. mass mkt. 4.99 o.p. (*0-06-109214-2*); 1995. 288p. 20.00 o.p. (*0-06-017748-9*) HarperCollins Pubs.
—House of Corrections. 2001. (Jack Flippo Mysteries Ser.). 240p. mass mkt. 6.50 o.s.i (*0-425-17947-8*) Berkley Publishing Group.
—The House of Corrections. 2000. (Jack Flippo Mysteries Ser.). 304p. 24.95 o.s.i (*0-399-14615-6*) Penguin Group (USA) Inc.
—Umbrella Man. 1999. (Jack Flippo Mysteries Ser.: Vol. 4). 273p. 23.95 o.p. (*0-399-14503-6*, G. P. Putnam's Sons) Penguin Group (USA) Inc.
—96 Tears. 1996. 208p. 22.50 o.p. (*0-06-017511-7*) HarperCollins Pubs.

**FLINT, MIKE (FICTITIOUS CHARACTER)—FICTION**

Healy, R. Austin. The Ninth Race. 224p. 1995. pap. 12.95 o.p. (*0-8338-0217-8*); 1994. 21.95 o.p. (*0-8338-0211-9*) Marshall Jones Co.
—Sweetfeed: A Mike Flint Murder Mystery. 1996. 256p. 24.95 o.p. (*0-8338-0230-5*) Marshall Jones Co.

**FLINT, SAM (FICTITIOUS CHARACTER)—FICTION**

Wheeler, Richard S. Flint's Gift. unabr. ed. 1999. audio 56.95 (*0-7861-1355-3*, 106028) Blackstone Audio Bks., Inc.
—Flint's Gift. 1999. 351p. mass mkt. 5.99 (*0-8125-5019-6*); 1997. 384p. 23.95 o.p. (*0-312-86366-7*) Doherty, Tom Assocs., LLC. (Forge Bks.).
—Flint's Gift. unabr. ed. 1998. audio 70.00 (*0-7887-2280-8*, 95449E7 ) Recorded Bks., LLC.
—Flint's Gift. l.t. ed. 1998. (Western Ser.). 479p. 25.95 (*0-7838-0270-6*) Thorndike Pr.
—Flint's Honor. unabr. ed. 2000. audio 56.95 (*0-7861-1780-X*, 2579); audio compact disk 80.00 (*0-7861-9875-3*, z2579) Blackstone Audio Bks., Inc.
—Flint's Honor. 2001. 384p. mass mkt. 6.99 (*0-8125-5022-6*); 2nd ed. 1999. 320p. 23.95 (*0-312-86368-3*) Doherty, Tom Assocs., LLC. (Forge Bks.).
—Flint's Honor. l.t. ed. 2001. (G. K. Hall Western Ser.). 462p. 25.95 (*0-7838-9503-8*, Macmillan Reference USA) Gale Group.
—Flint's Truth. unabr. ed. 1998. audio 56.95 (*0-7861-1373-1*, 2280) Blackstone Audio Bks., Inc.
—Flint's Truth. 1998. (Sam Flint Novels Ser.). 352p. 23.95 o.p. (*0-312-86367-5*, Forge Bks.) Doherty, Tom Assocs., LLC.
—Flint's Truth. l.t. ed. 1998. (Western Ser.). 432p. 25.95 (*0-7838-0333-8*) Thorndike Pr.

**FLOYD, C. J. (FICTITIOUS CHARACTER)—FICTION**

Greer, Robert. The Devil's Backbone. 1998. 368p. 22.00 o.p. (*0-89296-653-X*) Mysterious Pr.
—The Devil's Backbone. 1999. (C J Floyd Mystery Ser.). 320p. mass mkt. 6.99 (*0-446-60711-8*) Warner Bks., Inc.
—The Devil's Hatband. 1996. 82p. 21.95 o.p. (*0-89296-634-3*) Mysterious Pr.
—The Devil's Hatband. 1997. 304p. reprint ed. mass mkt. 5.99 (*0-446-40485-3*) Warner Bks., Inc.
—The Devil's Red Nickel. 1997. 368p. 22.00 o.p. (*0-89296-652-1*) Mysterious Pr.
—The Devil's Red Nickel. 1998. mass mkt. 5.99 (*0-446-40529-9*, Mysterious Pr. Paperback Bks.); 352p. mass mkt. 5.99 (*0-446-60592-1*) Warner Bks., Inc.
—Heat Shock: A Novel. 2003. 320p. 24.95 (*0-89296-753-6*) Mysterious Pr.

**FLOYT, HOBART (FICTITIOUS CHARACTER)—FICTION**

Daley, Brian. The Fall of the White Ship Avatar: A Hobart Floyt-Alacrity Fitzhugh Adventure. 1986. (Orig.). mass mkt. 3.95 o.s.i (*0-345-32919-8*, Del Rey) Ballantine Bks.
—Jinx on a Terran Inheritance. 1985. 416p. (Orig.). mass mkt. 3.50 o.s.i (*0-345-31488-3*) Ballantine Bks.
—Requiem for a Ruler of Worlds, No. 1. 1985. 304p. (Orig.). mass mkt. 3.95 o.s.i (*0-345-31487-5*, Ballantine Bks.) Ballantine Bks.

**FLYNN, FRANCIS XAVIER (FICTITIOUS CHARACTER)—FICTION**

Mcdonald, Gregory. The Buck Passes Flynn. 1986. 224p. mass mkt. 4.95 o.s.i (*0-345-33690-9*); 1983. mass mkt. 2.50 o.s.i (*0-345-31610-X*); 1981. mass mkt. 2.25 o.s.i (*0-345-30029-7*) Ballantine Bks.
—The Buck Passes Flynn. 2000. E-Book (*1-930351-03-8*) FairHillBooks.com.
—The Buck Passes Flynn. l.t. ed. 1993. 12.95 o.p. (*0-8161-3394-8*, Macmillan Reference USA) Gale Group.
—The Buck Passes Flynn. 2004. 224p. pap. 12.00 (*0-375-71360-3*, Vintage) Knopf Publishing Group.
—Flynn. 2000. E-Book (*1-930351-04-6*) FairHillBooks.com.
—Flynn. 2003. (Vintage Crime/Black Lizard Ser.). 256p. pap. 12.00 (*0-375-71357-3*, Vintage) Knopf Publishing Group.
—Flynn. 1977. 1977p. pap. 3.95 (*0-380-01764-4*, Avon Bks.) Morrow/Avon.
—Flynn's In. 2000. E-Book (*1-930351-02-X*) FairHillBooks.com.
—Flynn's In. 2004. 208p. pap. 12.00 (*0-375-71361-1*, Vintage) Knopf Publishing Group.
—Flynn's In. ("Flynn" Ser.). 1999. 15.45 o.s.i (*0-89296-085-X*); 1987. 45.00 o.p. (*0-89296-086-8*) Mysterious Pr.
—Flynn's In. 1988. mass mkt. 4.95 o.s.i (*0-445-20864-3*) Warner Bks., Inc.
—Flynn's World. E-Book 23.50 (*1-930351-05-4*) FairHillBooks.com.
—Flynn's World. 224p. 2004. pap. 12.00 (*0-375-71358-1*, Vintage); 2003. 23.00 (*0-375-42236-6*, Pantheon) Knopf Publishing Group.

**FLYNN, JUDITH MCMONIGLE (FICTITIOUS CHARACTER)—FICTION**

Daheim, Mary R. Auntie Mayhem. 1996. (Bed-and-Breakfast Mysteries Ser.). 272p. mass mkt. 6.99 (*0-380-77878-5*, Avon Bks.) Morrow/Avon.
—Bantam of the Opera. 1993. 256p. (Orig.). mass mkt. 6.99 (*0-380-76934-4*, Avon Bks.) Morrow/Avon.
—Creeps Suzette. 2000. (Bed & Breakfast Mystery Ser.). 336p. mass mkt. 6.99 (*0-380-80079-9*, Avon Bks.) Morrow/Avon.
—Dune to Death. 1993. (Bed-and-Breakfast Mysteries Ser.). 240p. (Orig.). mass mkt. 6.99 (*0-380-76933-6*, Avon Bks.) Morrow/Avon.
—A Fit of Tempera. 1994. (Bed-and-Breakfast Mysteries Ser.). 256p. reprint ed. mass mkt. 6.99 (*0-380-77490-9*, Avon Bks.) Morrow/Avon.
—Fowl Prey. 1991. (Bed-and-Breakfast Mysteries Ser.). 272p. (Orig.). mass mkt. 6.99 (*0-380-76296-X*, Avon Bks.) Morrow/Avon.
—Hocus Croakus. 2003. 314p. 6.99 (*0-380-81564-8*); 320p. 23.95 (*0-380-97868-7*) Morrow/Avon. (Morrow, William & Co.).
—Holy Terrors. 1999. (Bed-and-Breakfast Mysteries Ser.). 256p. (Orig.). mass mkt. 6.99 (*0-380-76297-8*, Avon Bks.) Morrow/Avon.
—Just Desserts. l.t. ed. 2001. (Beeler Large Print Mystery Ser.). 240p. 25.95 (*1-57490-351-9*, Beeler Large Print Bks.) Beeler, Thomas T. Publisher.
—Just Desserts. 1999. (Bed & Breakfast Mystery Ser.). 256p. mass mkt. 6.99 (*0-380-76295-1*, Avon Bks.) Morrow/Avon.
—Legs Benedict: A Bed-and-Breakfast Mystery. 1999. (Bed-and-Breakfast Mysteries Ser.). 320p. mass mkt. 6.50 (*0-380-80078-0*, Avon Bks.) Morrow/Avon.
—Major Vices. 1995. (Bed-and-Breakfast Mysteries Ser.). 256p. (Orig.). mass mkt. 6.50 (*0-380-77491-7*, Avon Bks.) Morrow/Avon.
—Murder, My Suite. l.t. ed. 2002. 26.95 (*1-57490-414-0*) Beeler, Thomas T. Publisher.
—Murder, My Suite. 1995. (Bed-and-Breakfast Mysteries Ser.). 272p. mass mkt. 6.50 (*0-380-77877-7*, Avon Bks.) Morrow/Avon.
—Nutty as a Fruitcake. 1996. (Bed-and-Breakfast Mysteries Ser.). 272p. mass mkt. 6.99 (*0-380-77879-3*, Avon Bks.) Morrow/Avon.
—September Mourn. 1997. (Bed-and-Breakfast Mysteries Ser.). (Illus.). 320p. mass mkt. 6.50 (*0-380-78518-8*, Avon Bks.) Morrow/Avon.
—Silver Scream. 2002. 320p. 23.95 (*0-380-97867-9*, Morrow, William & Co.) Morrow/Avon.
—Silver Scream. l.t. ed. 2002. 28.95 (*0-7862-4612-X*) Thorndike Pr.
—Snow Place to Die: Where There's Ice... There's Vice. 1998. (Bed & Breakfast Mystery Ser.: No. 13). 304p. mass mkt. 6.99 (*0-380-78521-8*, Avon Bks.) Morrow/Avon.
—A Streetcar Named Expire. 2001. (Bed-and-Breakfast Mysteries Ser.). 320p. mass mkt. 6.99 (*0-380-80080-2*, Avon Bks.) Morrow/Avon.
—Suture Self. 2002. 352p. mass mkt. 6.99 (*0-380-81561-3*, Avon Bks.); 2001. 304p. 23.00 (*0-380-97866-0*, Morrow, William & Co.) Morrow/Avon.
—Wed & Buried. 1998. (Bed-and-Breakfast Mysteries Ser.). 304p. mass mkt. 6.50 (*0-380-78520-X*, Avon Bks.) Morrow/Avon.

**FLYNN, LAURA (FICTITIOUS CHARACTER)—FICTION**

Grant-Adamson, Lesley. Too Many Questions. 1993. mass mkt. 4.50 o.s.i (*0-449-22104-0*, Fawcett) Ballantine Bks.
—Too Many Questions. 1991. 15.95 o.p. (*0-312-05434-3*, Saint Martin's Minotaur) St. Martin's Pr.

**FLYNN, MAGGIE (FICTITIOUS CHARACTER)—FICTION**

Power, Margo. Image of Conspiracy: A Mystery Adventure. abr. ed. 1999. audio 10.95 (*1-894188-03-9*) APG Sales and Fulfillment.
—Image of Conspiracy: A Mystery Adventure. 1997. pap. text 5.99 (*1-886199-02-7*) Deadly Alibi Pr., Ltd.

**FOG, DUSTY (FICTITIOUS CHARACTER)—FICTION**

Edson, J. T. The Code of Dusty Fog. 1989. 2.95 (*1-55773-288-4*, Diamond Bks.) Berkley Publishing Group.
—Cure the Texas Fever. 1996. 208p. mass mkt. 4.50 o.s.i (*0-440-22215-X*) Dell Publishing.
—Cure the Texas Fever. 1997. 192p. 22.00 (*0-7278-5130-6*) Severn Hse. Pubs., Ltd.
—Go Back to Hell. (Orig.). 1986. 192p. mass mkt. 2.50 o.s.i (*0-425-09101-5*); 1982. mass mkt. 1.95 o.s.i (*0-425-05618-X*); 1979. mass mkt. 1.75 o.s.i (*0-425-04110-7*) Berkley Publishing Group.
—Go Back to Hell. 1992. 192p. (Orig.). mass mkt. 3.50 o.s.i (*0-440-21033-X*) Dell Publishing.
—The Small Texan. 1985. 192p. mass mkt. 2.50 o.p. (*0-425-07594-X*) Berkley Publishing Group.
—The Small Texan. l.t. ed. 1983. (Ulverscroft Large Print Ser.). 304p. 29.99 o.p. (*0-7089-0956-6*, Ulverscroft) Thorpe, F. A. Pubs. GBR. *Dist:* Ulverscroft Large Print Bks., Ltd., Ulverscroft Large Print Canada, Ltd.
—The Trouble Busters. 1990. 2.95 (*1-55773-297-3*, Diamond Bks.); 1984. 192p. mass mkt. 2.25 o.s.i (*0-425-06849-8*); 1982. mass mkt. 1.95 o.s.i (*0-425-05227-3*) Berkley Publishing Group.

**FOGARTY, LUANNE (FICTITIOUS CHARACTER)—FICTION**

Alam, Glynn Marsh. Cold Water Corpse: A Luanne Fogarty Mystery. 2003. (Illus.). 254p. 12.95 (*0-9725078-0-9*) Avocet Pr., Inc.
—Dive Deep & Deadly. 2000. 236p. pap. 12.95 (*0-9661072-9-2*) Avocet Pr., Inc.

**FOLEY, MALACHY (FICTITIOUS CHARACTER)—FICTION**

Walker, David J. Applaud the Hollow Ghost. 1997. 288p. 23.95 (*0-312-18041-1*, Saint Martin's Minotaur) St. Martin's Pr.
—Fixed in His Folly. 1999. (WWL Mystery Ser.: Bk. 315). 256p. per. (*0-373-26315-5*, 1-26315-1, Worldwide Library) Harlequin Enterprises, Ltd.
—Fixed in His Folly: A Malachy Foley Mystery. 1995. 262p. 21.95 o.p. (*0-312-13074-0*, Saint Martin's Minotaur) St. Martin's Pr.
—Half the Truth. 1996. 288p. 22.95 (*0-312-14611-6*, Saint Martin's Minotaur) St. Martin's Pr.
—No Show of Remorse: A Malachy Foley Mystery. E-Book 23.95 (*0-312-70467-4*); 2002. 304p. 23.95 (*0-312-25240-4*, Saint Martin's Minotaur) St. Martin's Pr.

**FOLGER, MERRY (FICTITIOUS CHARACTER)—FICTION**

Mathews, Francine. Death in a Cold Hard Light. 1999. (Indigo Ser.). 352p. reprint ed. mass mkt. 5.99 (*0-553-57625-9*) Bantam Bks.
—Death in a Cold Hard Light. unabr. collector's ed. 1998. (Merry Folger Ser.). audio 64.00 (*0-7366-4262-5*, 4761) Books on Tape, Inc.
—Death in a Mood Indigo. 1998. 352p. mass mkt. 5.99 (*0-553-57624-0*) Bantam Bks.
—Death in a Mood Indigo. unabr. collector's ed. 1997. (Merry Folger Ser.). audio 64.00 (*0-7366-4006-1*, 4504) Books on Tape, Inc.
—Death in Rough Water. unabr. collector's ed. 1997. (Merry Folger Ser.: Vol. 2). audio 56.00 (*0-7366-3631-5*, 4292) Books on Tape, Inc.
—Death in Rough Water: A Merry Folger Mystery. 1996. 288p. mass mkt. 5.50 (*0-380-72335-2*, Avon Bks.); 1995. 320p. 22.00 o.p. (*0-688-13473-4*, Morrow, William & Co.) Morrow/Avon.
—Death in the Off-Season. unabr. collector's ed. 1997. (Merry Folger Ser.: Vol. 1). audio 64.00 (*0-7366-3600-5*, 4255) Books on Tape, Inc.
—Death in the Off-Season. 1995. 352p. mass mkt. 4.99 (*0-380-72334-4*, Avon Bks.); 1994. 318p. 23.00 o.p. (*0-688-13443-2*, Morrow, William & Co.) Morrow/Avon.

**FOLLOWS, NATHANIEL (FICTITIOUS CHARACTER)—FICTION**

Piccirilli, Tom. Shards. 1997. mass mkt. 5.95 o.p. (*1-885173-41-5*); 1996. 214p. 20.95 o.p. (*1-885173-23-7*) Write Way Publishing.

**FOLLY, SUPERINTENDENT (FICTITIOUS CHARACTER)—FICTION**

Creasey, John. Let's Kill Uncle Lionel. 1976. 6.95 o.p. (*0-679-50589-X*) McKay, David Co., Inc.
—Murder in the Family. 1976. 190p. 6.95 o.p. (*0-679-50609-8*) McKay, David Co., Inc.

**FONTAINE, FELICIA (FICTITIOUS CHARACTER)—FICTION**

Close, Ellis. The Best Defense. 1999. 432p. mass mkt. 6.99 o.s.i (*0-06-093087-X*); 1998. 272p. 24.00 (*0-06-017496-X*) HarperCollins Pubs.

**FONTANA, MAC (FICTITIOUS CHARACTER)—FICTION**

Emerson, Earl. Black Hearts & Slow Dancing. 1997. 256p. mass mkt. 5.99 (*0-380-72937-7*, Avon Bks.); 1988. 320p. 17.95 o.p. (*0-688-07533-9*, Morrow, William & Co.) Morrow/Avon.
—Black Hearts & Slow Dancing. 1989. 272p. pap. 5.95 o.p. (*0-14-011732-6*, Penguin Bks.) Viking Penguin.
—The Dead Horse Paint Company. 1997. (Mac Fontana Mystery Ser.: No. 5). 272p. 24.00 (*0-688-13751-2*, Morrow, William & Co.); 1998. (Mac Fontana Mystery Ser.). 288p. reprint ed. mass mkt. 5.99 o.s.i (*0-380-72438-3*, Avon Bks.) Morrow/Avon.
—Going Crazy in Public. 1997. 288p. mass mkt. 5.99 (*0-380-72437-5*, Avon Bks.); 1996. 256p. 24.00 o.p. (*0-688-13750-4*, Morrow, William & Co.) Morrow/Avon.
—Help Wanted: Orphans Preferred. 1990. 320p. 17.95 o.p. (*0-688-09333-7*, Morrow, William & Co.); 1991. 288p. reprint ed. mass mkt. 4.99 o.p. (*0-380-71047-1*, Avon Bks.) Morrow/Avon.
—Morons & Madmen: A Mac Fontana Mystery. 1993. 18.00 o.p. (*0-688-09334-5*, Morrow, William & Co.); 1994. 256p. reprint ed. mass mkt. 4.99 (*0-380-72075-2*, Avon Bks.) Morrow/Avon.
—Morons & Madmen: A Mac Fontana Mystery. 268p. pap. 3.98 o.p. (*0-7651-0494-6*) Smithmark Pubs., Inc.

**FORD, ASHTON (FICTITIOUS CHARACTER)—FICTION**

Pendleton, Don. Eye to Eye. 1986. 224p. (Orig.). pap. 3.50 o.s.i (*0-445-20252-1*) Warner Bks., Inc.
—Heart to Heart. 1987. (Ashton Ford Ser.: No. 5). 256p. (Orig.). mass mkt. 3.95 o.s.i (*0-445-20258-0*) Warner Bks., Inc.
—Life to Life. 1987. (Ashton Ford Ser.: No. 4). 256p. (Orig.). mass mkt. 3.95 o.s.i (*0-445-20256-4*) Warner Bks., Inc.
—Mind to Mind. 1987. 256p. pap. 3.50 o.s.i (*0-445-20254-8*) Warner Bks., Inc.
—Time to Time. 1988. (Ashton Ford Ser.: No. 6). 256p. mass mkt. 3.95 o.s.i (*0-445-20260-2*) Warner Bks., Inc.
—Time to Time. 2000. (Ashton Ford Ser.). 215p. pap. 14.95 (*0-595-16396-3*) iUniverse, Inc.

**FORD, DOC (FICTITIOUS CHARACTER)—FICTION**

White, Randy Wayne. Captiva. 1997. 336p. reprint ed. mass mkt. 6.99 (*0-425-15854-3*, Prime Crime) Berkley Publishing Group.
—Captiva. 1996. 256p. 21.95 o.s.i (*0-399-14140-5*, G. P. Putnam's Sons) Penguin Group (USA) Inc.
—Everglades. l.t. ed. 2003. 469p. 30.95 (*1-58724-468-3*, Wheeler Publishing, Inc.) Gale Group.
—Everglades. 2003. 352p. 21.95 (*0-399-15058-7*, Putnam & Grosset) Putnam Publishing Group, The.
—The Heat Islands. (Doc Ford Novel Ser.). 1993. 307p. mass mkt. 6.99 (*0-312-92977-3*, St. Martin's Paperbacks); 1992. 336p. 19.95 (*0-312-06993-6*, Saint Martin's Minotaur) St. Martin's Pr.
—The Man Who Invented Florida. 1993. 288p. 20.95 o.p. (*0-312-09866-9*, Saint Martin's Minotaur); 1997. 294p. reprint ed. pap. 6.99 (*0-312-95398-4*, St. Martin's Paperbacks) St. Martin's Pr.
—The Mangrove Coast. 1999. (Prime Crime Mysteries Ser.). 336p. reprint ed. mass mkt. 6.99 (*0-425-17194-9*, Prime Crime) Berkley Publishing Group.
—The Mangrove Coast. 1998. 256p. 22.95 o.p. (*0-399-14372-6*, G. P. Putnam's Sons) Penguin Group (USA) Inc.
—North of Havana. 1998. 272p. mass mkt. 6.99 (*0-425-16294-X*, Prime Crime) Berkley Publishing Group.
—North of Havana. 1997. 256p. 22.95 o.p. (*0-399-14242-8*, G. P. Putnam's Sons) Penguin Group (USA) Inc.
—Sanibel Flats. 320p. 1990. 17.95 (*0-312-03926-3*, Saint Martin's Minotaur); 1991. reprint ed. mass mkt. 6.99 (*0-312-92602-2*, St. Martin's Paperbacks) St. Martin's Pr.
—Shark River. l.t. ed. 2002. 332p. lib. bdg. 28.95 (*1-58547-160-7*) Ctr. Point Large Print.
—Shark River. 2001. 320p. 24.95 o.p. (*0-399-14729-2*, Putnam & Grosset) Penguin Group (USA) Inc.
—Ten Thousand Islands. 2001. 320p. reprint ed. mass mkt. 6.99 (*0-425-18043-3*, Prime Crime) Berkley Publishing Group.
—Ten Thousand Islands. l.t. ed. 2001. xiv, 331p. 29.95 (*1-58724-110-2*, Wheeler Publishing, Inc.) Gale Group.
—Ten Thousand Islands. 2000. xvi, 320p. 23.95 o.s.i (*0-399-14620-2*) Penguin Group (USA) Inc.
—Twelve Mile Limit. 2003. 368p. mass mkt. 6.99 (*0-425-19073-0*, Prime Crime) Berkley Publishing Group.
—Twelve Mile Limit. 2002. 304p. 24.95 o.s.i (*0-399-14873-6*) Penguin Group (USA) Inc.
—Twelve Mile Limit. 2003. (Mystery Ser.). 30.95 (*0-7862-4812-2*) Thorndike Pr.

**FORD, LOU (FICTITIOUS CHARACTER)—FICTION**

Thompson, Jim. The Killer Inside Me. ltd. ed. 1989. 225p. 125.00 (*0-940941-07-4*) Blood & Guts Pr.
—The Killer Inside Me. 1984. (Quill Mysterious Classic Ser.). 256p. pap. 3.95 o.p. (*0-688-03922-7*, Quill) HarperTrade.
—The Killer Inside Me. 1991. 256p. pap. 11.00 (*0-679-73397-3*, Vintage) Knopf Publishing Group.

**FORESTER, ROBERT (FICTITIOUS CHARACTER)—FICTION**

Highsmith, Patricia. Cry of the Owl. 1989. 276p. pap. 12.00 (*0-87113-290-7*, Atlantic Monthly Pr.) Grove/Atlantic, Inc.

**FORRESTER, LILY (FICTITIOUS CHARACTER)—FICTION**

Rosenberg, Nancy Taylor. Buried Evidence. abr. ed. 2000. audio 24.95 o.p. (*1-56740-747-1*, 2175, Nova Audio Bks.); audio 35.95 (*1-56740-380-8*, 2173, Brilliance Audio Unabridged); 11p. audio 73.25 (*1-56740-922-9*, 2174, Unabridged Library Editions) Brilliance Audio.
—Buried Evidence. 2000. 359p. 24.95 (*0-7868-6619-5*) Disney Pr.
—Buried Evidence. 2002. E-Book 5.95 (*0-7868-6986-0*); 2003. 368p. reprint ed. mass mkt. 7.99 (*0-7868-8983-7*) Hyperion Pr.
—Buried Evidence. l.t. ed. 2000. (Americana Ser.). 575p. 30.95 (*0-7862-2924-1*) Thorndike Pr.
—Mitigating Circumstances. l.t. ed. 1994. 21.95 o.p. (*0-7927-1753-8*); pap. 21.95 o.p. (*0-7927-1752-X*) BBC Audiobooks America.
—Mitigating Circumstances. unabr. ed. 1996. audio 72.00 (*0-7366-3476-2*, 4119) Books on Tape, Inc.
—Mitigating Circumstances. 1993. 368p. 21.00 o.p. (*0-525-93587-8*) Dutton/Plume.
—Mitigating Circumstances. 1993. 448p. mass mkt. 7.99 o.s.i (*0-451-17672-3*, Signet Bks.) NAL.
—Mitigating Circumstances. abr. ed. 1993. audio 16.00 o.p. (*0-453-00817-8*) Penguin/HighBridge.
—Mitigating Circumstances, unabr. ed. 1997. audio 78.00 (*0-7887-0822-8*, 94972E7) Recorded Bks., LLC.

**FORSYTE FAMILY (FICTITIOUS CHARACTERS)—FICTION**

Galsworthy, John. The Complete Forsyte Saga. unabr. ed. audio 194.00 o.p. Recorded Bks., LLC.
—Flowering Wilderness. 23.95 (*0-89190-659-2*) Amereon, Ltd.
—Flowering Wilderness, , unabr. collector's ed. 1999. (End of Chapter Ser.: Vol. 2). audio 48.00 (*0-7366-4383-4*, 4849) Books on Tape, Inc.
—The Forsyte Saga. l.t. ed. 1996. (Perennial Bestseller Collection). 432p. (*0-7451-3813-6*, Black Dagger) BBC Audiobooks America.
—The Forsyte Saga. 1983. 540p. reprint ed. lib. bdg. 32.95 o.s.i (*0-89966-443-1*) Buccaneer Bks., Inc.
—The Forsyte Saga. 1982. 878p. pap. 18.00 (*0-684-17653-X*); 1977. 25.00 o.s.i (*0-684-15368-8*) Gale Group. (Macmillan Reference USA).
—The Forsyte Saga. 1999. (Oxford World's Classics Ser.). 912p. pap. 14.95 (*0-19-283862-8*) Oxford Univ. Pr., Inc.
—The Forsyte Saga. Harvey, Geoffrey, ed. & intro. by. 1997. (Oxford World's Classics Ser.). 902p. pap. 14.95 o.p. (*0-19-282298-5*) Oxford Univ. Pr., Inc.
—The Forsyte Saga. 1999. 1122p. 49.95 (*0-7351-0122-1*) Replica Bks.
—The Forsyte Saga. 1996. 896p. reprint ed. pap. 16.00 (*0-684-81889-2*, Touchstone) Simon & Schuster.
—The Forsyte Saga. 1997. (Penguin Twentieth-Century Classics Ser.). 912p. pap. 14.95 o.p. (*0-14-018399-X*, Penguin Classics) Viking Penguin.
—In Chancery, Vol. 2. 1996. (Forsyte Saga Ser.: Bk. II). audio 59.95 (*1-55685-428-5*) Audio Bk. Contractors, Inc.
—In Chancery. reprint ed. lib. bdg. 98.00 (*0-7426-2777-2*); 2001. 273p. pap. text 28.00 (*0-7426-7777-X*) Classic Bks.
—In Chancery. abr. ed. audio 15.95 o.p. (*0-88646-191-X*, 7192) Durkin Hayes Publishing Ltd.
—In Chancery, unabr. ed. 1988. (Forsyte Saga Ser.: Vol. 2). audio 70.00 (*1-55690-182-8*, 88040E7) Recorded Bks., LLC.
—In Chancery. l.t. ed. 1996. (Forsyte Saga Ser.: Vol. 2). 521p. lib. bdg. 23.95 (*0-7838-1505-0*) Thorndike Pr.
—In Chancery & Awakening, unabr. ed. 1998. (Forsyte Saga Ser.). audio 64.00 (*0-7366-4195-5*, 4693) Books on Tape, Inc.
—Maid in Waiting, unabr. collector's ed. 1999. (Forsyte Saga Ser.). audio 56.00 (*0-7366-4382-6*, 4848) Books on Tape, Inc.
—The Man of Property. E-Book 3.95 (*0-594-02239-8*) 1873 Pr.
—The Man of Property, Set. 1987. (Forsyte Saga Ser.: Bk. I). audio 53.95 (*1-55685-092-1*) Audio Bk. Contractors, Inc.
—The Man of Property. 1972. mass mkt. 1.50 o.p. (*0-345-22564-3*) Ballantine Bks.
—The Man of Property. reprint ed. lib. bdg. 98.00 (*0-7426-2747-0*); 2001. 386p. pap. text 28.00 (*0-7426-7747-8*) Classic Bks.
—The Man of Property. abr. ed. 1986. (YA). (gr. 7-9). audio 29.95 o.p. (*0-88646-817-5*, R 7154); audio 15.95 o.p. (*0-88646-153-7*, 7154) Durkin Hayes Publishing Ltd.
—The Man of Property. 2002. 332p. 26.99 (*1-4043-1634-5*); per. 21.99 (*1-4043-1635-3*) IndyPublish-.com.
—The Man of Property, unabr. ed. 1988. (Forsyte Saga Ser.: Vol. 1). audio 85.00 (*1-55690-183-6*, 88030E7) Recorded Bks., LLC.
—The Man of Property. l.t. ed. 1995. (Forsyte Saga Ser.: Vol. 1). 500p. 24.95 (*0-7838-1504-2*) Thorndike Pr.
—The Man of Property. 1977. pap. 3.95 o.p. (*0-14-003196-0*, Penguin Bks.) Viking Penguin.
—The Man of Property & Indian Summer of a Forsyte, unabr. collector's ed. 1998. audio 80.00 (*0-7366-4030-4*, 4529) Books on Tape, Inc.
—A Modern Comedy. 1920. 12.50 o.s.i (*0-684-10197-1*, Macmillan Reference USA) Gale Group.
—A Modern Comedy. 2002. 336p. pap. 32.95 (*0-7432-3774-9*, Scribner) Simon & Schuster.
—One More River, , unabr. collector's ed. 1999. (Forsyte Saga Ser.). audio 56.00 (*0-7366-4384-2*, 4850) Books on Tape, Inc.
—Salvation of a Forsyte & More. unabr. ed. 1992. (Forsyte Saga Ser.). audio 29.95 (*1-55685-224-X*) Audio Bk. Contractors, Inc.
—The Silver Spoon & Passers By. 23.95 (*0-8488-0064-8*) Amereon, Ltd.
—The Silver Spoon & Passers By. unabr. collector's ed. 1999. (Forsyte Saga Ser.). audio 56.00 (*0-7366-4385-0*, 4846) Books on Tape, Inc.
—Swan Song, unabr. collector's ed. 1999. (Forsyte Saga Ser.). audio 64.00 (*0-7366-4386-9*, 4847) Books on Tape, Inc.
—To Let, Set. 1996. (Forsyte Saga Ser.: Bk. III). audio 47.95 (*1-55685-429-3*) Audio Bk. Contractors, Inc.
—To Let. unabr. collector's ed. 1998. audio 56.00 (*0-7366-4196-3*, 4694) Books on Tape, Inc.
—To Let. reprint ed. lib. bdg. 98.00 (*0-7426-2780-2*); 2001. 317p. pap. text 28.00 (*0-7426-7780-X*) Classic Bks.
—To Let, unabr. ed. 1988. (Forsyte Saga Ser.: Vol. 3). audio 60.00 (*1-55690-184-4*, 88050E7) Recorded Bks., LLC.
—To Let. l.t. ed. 1996. (Forsyte Saga Ser.: Vol. 3). 455p. 24.95 (*0-7838-1506-9*) Thorndike Pr.
—The White Monkey. Date not set. 336p. 25.95 (*0-8488-2271-4*) Amereon, Ltd.
—The White Monkey & A Silent Wooing, unabr. collector's ed. 1998. (Forsyte Saga Ser.). audio 56.00 (*0-7366-4349-4*, 4809) Books on Tape, Inc.

**FORSYTHE, ROBERT (FICTITIOUS CHARACTER)—FICTION**

Giroux, E. X. A Death for a Dancer: A Robert Forsythe Mystery. 1986. mass mkt. 2.95 o.s.i (*0-345-33408-6*) Ballantine Bks.
—A Death for a Dancer: A Robert Forsythe Mystery. 1985. 192p. 12.95 o.p. (*0-312-18868-4*) St. Martin's Pr.
—A Death for a Dancing Doll. 1992. mass mkt. 3.99 o.s.i (*0-345-37609-9*) Ballantine Bks.
—A Death for a Dancing Doll. 1991. 17.95 o.p. (*0-312-05848-9*, Saint Martin's Minotaur) St. Martin's Pr.
—A Death for a Darling. 1986. 192p. mass mkt. 3.50 o.s.i (*0-345-33024-2*) Ballantine Bks.
—A Death for a Darling. 1985. 192p. 13.95 o.p. (*0-312-18607-X*) St. Martin's Pr.
—A Death for a Dietician. 1989. 192p. mass mkt. 3.95 o.s.i (*0-345-35767-1*) Ballantine Bks.
—A Death for a Dietitian. 1988. 176p. 13.95 o.p. (*0-312-01417-1*, Saint Martin's Minotaur) St. Martin's Pr.
—A Death for a Dilettante. 1987. 176p. mass mkt. 3.50 o.s.i (*0-345-34758-7*) Ballantine Bks.
—A Death for a Dilettante. 1987. (Robert Forsythe Mystery Ser.). 208p. 13.95 o.p. (*0-312-00044-8*) St. Martin's Pr.
—A Death for a Doctor: A Robert Forsythe Mystery. 1986. 208p. 13.95 o.p. (*0-312-18603-7*) St. Martin's Pr.
—A Death for a Dodo. 1993. 17.95 o.p. (*0-312-08762-4*, Saint Martin's Minotaur) St. Martin's Pr.
—A Death for a Double. 1991. 192p. mass mkt. 3.95 o.s.i (*0-345-36833-9*) Ballantine Bks.
—A Death for a Double. 1992. 2.99 o.p. (*0-517-09039-2*) Random Hse. Value Publishing.
—A Death for a Double. 1990. 208p. 15.95 o.p. (*0-312-03809-7*, Saint Martin's Minotaur) St. Martin's Pr.
—A Death for a Dreamer. 1990. (Death Ser.). 192p. mass mkt. 3.95 o.s.i (*0-345-36528-3*) Ballantine Bks.
—A Death for a Dreamer. 1989. 14.95 o.p. (*0-312-02901-2*, Saint Martin's Minotaur) St. Martin's Pr.
—A Death for Adonis. 1985. 160p. mass mkt. 4.95 o.s.i (*0-345-32889-2*) Ballantine Bks.
—A Death for Adonis. 1984. 160p. 11.95 o.p. (*0-312-18610-X*) St. Martin's Pr.

Giroux, E. X. & Giroux, Leo. A Death for a Doctor: A Robert Forsythe Mystery. 1987. 192p. mass mkt. 4.95 o.s.i (*0-345-34231-3*) Ballantine Bks.

**FORTIER, MARGO (FICTITIOUS CHARACTER)—FICTION**

Fennelly, Tony. The Hippie in the Wall. 1994. 240p. 19.95 o.p. (*0-312-10475-8*, Saint Martin's Minotaur) St. Martin's Pr.

—1 (900) D-E-A-D: A Margo Fortier Mystery. 1996. 240p. 21.95 (*0-312-14267-6*, Saint Martin's Minotaur) St. Martin's Pr.

**FORTLOW, SOCRATES (FICTITIOUS CHARACTER)—FICTION**

Mosley, Walter. Always Outnumbered, Always Outgunned. abr. ed. 1997. (Easy Rawlins Mystery Ser.). 25.00 o.p. (*0-7871-1646-7*, 695538) NewStar Media, Inc.

—Always Outnumbered, Always Outgunned. 1997. 224p. 23.00 (*0-393-04539-0*) Norton, W. W. & Co., Inc.

—Always Outnumbered, Always Outgunned. 1998. 208p. pap. 14.00 (*0-671-01499-4*, Washington Square Pr.) Simon & Schuster.

—Always Outnumbered, Always Outgunned. l.t. ed. 1998. (Basic Ser.). 360p. 30.95 (*0-7862-1268-3*) Thorndike Pr.

—Walkin' the Dog. unabr. ed. 2001. audio compact disk 56.00; 2000. audio 36.00 (*0-7366-4779-1*, 5124) Books on Tape, Inc.

—Walkin' the Dog. l.t. ed. 2000. (Core Ser.). 301p. 31.95 (*0-7838-8961-5*, Macmillan Reference USA) Gale Group.

—Walkin' the Dog, abr. ed. 1999. audio 17.98 Highsmith Inc.

—Walkin' the Dog. 2000. 288p. pap. 13.95 (*0-316-88171-6*, Back Bay); 2000. 14.95 (*0-316-57054-0*); 1999. 272p. 24.95 o.p. (*0-316-96620-7*) Little Brown & Co.

—Walkin' the Dog. 2000. audio compact disk 69.00 (*0-7887-4743-6*, C1229E7); 1999. audio 51.00 (*0-7887-3768-6*, 95985E7) Recorded Bks., LLC.

—Walkin' the Dog. l.t. ed. 2001. (G. K. Hall Paperback Ser.). 301p. pap. 29.95 (*0-7838-8962-3*) Thorndike Pr.

—Walkin' the Dog. abr. ed. 1999. 3p. audio 17.98 (*1-57042-710-0*) Time Warner AudioBooks.

**FORTUNATO, THERESA (FICTITIOUS CHARACTER)—FICTION**

Green, Kate. Black Dreams: A Theresa Fortunato Mystery. 1993. 288p. 20.00 o.p. (*0-06-017984-8*) HarperTrade.

—Black Dreams: A Theresa Fortunato Mystery. 1994. 464p. mass mkt. 5.99 o.p. (*0-06-109103-0*, HarperTorch) Morrow/Avon.

**FORTUNE, DAN (FICTITIOUS CHARACTER)—FICTION**

Collins, Michael. The Blood-Red Dream. l.t. ed. 1991. 17.95 o.p. (*0-7451-8144-9*, AH0180); pap. 15.95 o.p. (*0-7927-0664-1*, AS0216) BBC Audiobooks America.

—The Cadillac Cowboy. 1995. 288p. 20.95 o.p. (*1-55611-461-3*) Fine, Donald I. Bks.

—Cassandra in Red. 1992. 256p. 19.95 o.p. (*1-55611-316-1*) Fine, Donald I. Bks.

—Castrato. 1991. 416p. reprint ed. pap. 4.99 (*0-8439-3131-0*) Dorchester Publishing Co., Inc.

—Castrato. 1989. 288p. 17.95 o.p. (*1-55611-113-4*) Fine, Donald I. Bks.

—Chasing Eights. 1992. 400p. reprint ed. pap. 4.99 (*0-8439-3274-0*) Dorchester Publishing Co., Inc.

—Chasing Eights. 1990. 18.95 o.p. (*1-55611-145-2*) Fine, Donald I. Bks.

—Crime, Punishment - & Resurrection. 1992. 272p. 19.95 o.p. (*1-55611-295-5*) Fine, Donald I. Bks.

—Freak. 1990. mass mkt. (*0-373-26050-4*, Harlequin Bks.) Harlequin Enterprises, Ltd.

—The Irishman's Horse. 1991. 18.95 o.p. (*1-55611-185-1*) Fine, Donald I. Bks.

—Minnesota Strip. 1987. 264p. 17.95 o.p. (*1-55611-032-4*) Fine, Donald I. Bks.

—Minnesota Strip. 1988. pap. (*0-373-97093-5*, Harlequin Bks.) Harlequin Enterprises, Ltd.

—Red Rosa. 1988. 264p. 17.95 o.p. (*1-55611-052-9*) Fine, Donald I. Bks.

—Red Rosa. 1989. 304p. reprint ed. mass mkt. (*0-373-97099-4*, Harlequin Bks.) Harlequin Enterprises, Ltd.

—Silent Scream. 1989. mass mkt. (*0-373-28000-9*, Harlequin Bks.) Harlequin Enterprises, Ltd.

—The Slasher. 1989. mass mkt. (*0-373-27999-X*, Harlequin Bks.) Harlequin Enterprises, Ltd.

**FORTUNE, SARAH (FICTITIOUS CHARACTER)—FICTION**

Fyfield, Frances. Perfectly Pure & Good. unabr. ed. 1994. (Attorney Sarah Fortune Mysteries Ser.). audio 54.95 (*0-7451-4340-7*, CAB 1023) BBC Audiobooks America.

—Perfectly Pure & Good. 1995. (Mysteries Around the World Promotion Ser.). mass mkt. 5.99 o.s.i (*0-345-38279-X*, Ivy Bks.) Ballantine Bks.

—Perfectly Pure & Good. 1994. 224p. 20.00 o.s.i (*0-679-42665-5*, Pantheon) Knopf Publishing Group.

—Perfectly Pure & Good. l.t. ed. 1995. (Magna Large Print Ser.). 359p. o.p. (*0-7505-0797-7*) Magna Large Print Bks. GBR. *Dist:* Ulverscroft Large Print Canada, Ltd.

—Perfectly Pure & Good. 2000. 256p. pap. 5.99 (*0-14-029195-4*) Penguin Group (USA) Inc.

—Shadows on the Mirror. unabr. ed. 1994. audio 49.95 (*0-7451-4287-7*, CAB 970) Chivers Audio Bks. GBR. *Dist:* BBC Audiobooks America.

—Shadows on the Mirror. Chelius, Jane, ed. 1991. 17.95 o.p. (*0-671-70161-4*, Atria); 1992. 224p. reprint ed. mass mkt. 4.50 (*0-671-70162-2*, Pocket) Simon & Schuster.

—Staring at the Light, Set. unabr. ed. 1999. audio 69.95 (*0-7540-0364-7*, CAB1787) BBC Audiobooks America.

—Staring at the Light. unabr. ed. 2000. (Attorney Sarah Fortune Ser.). 10p. audio compact disk 94.95 (*0-7540-5313-X*, CCD 004) Chivers Audio Bks. GBR. *Dist:* BBC Audiobooks America.

—Staring at the Light. l.t. ed. 2000. (Basic Ser.). 511p. 27.95 (*0-7862-2514-9*) Thorndike Pr.

—Staring at the Light. 2000. (Attorney Sarah Fortune Mysteries Ser.). 288p. 23.95 o.s.i (*0-670-88730-7*) Viking Penguin.

Fyfield, Frances, ed. Staring at the Light. 2001. 288p. mass mkt. 5.99 (*0-14-029845-2*) Penguin Group (USA) Inc.

**FOSTER, STICK (FICTITIOUS CHARACTER)—FICTION**

Robinson, Kevin. Mall Rats: A Stick Foster Mystery. 1992. 202p. 19.95 o.p. (*0-8027-3215-1*) Walker & Co.

—A Matter of Perspective. 1993. (Stick Foster Mystery Ser.). 217p. 19.95 o.p. (*0-8027-3242-9*) Walker & Co.

—Split Seconds. 1991. 208p. 18.95 (*0-8027-5785-5*) Walker & Co.

**FOUCHEROUX, JEAN-PIERRE (FICTITIOUS CHARACTER)—FICTION**

Monbrun, Estelle. Murder Chez Proust. 1996. 240p. pap. 10.95 (*1-55970-341-5*) Arcade Publishing, Inc.

—Murder Chez Proust. Martyn, David, tr. 1995. (ENG & FRE.). 240p. 19.95 (*1-55970-283-4*) Arcade Publishing, Inc.

**FOX, TECUMSEH (FICTITIOUS CHARACTER)—FICTION**

Stout, Rex. Bad for Business. 1995. (Orig.). 240p. pap. 15.00 (*0-553-76302-4*); 176p. reprint ed. mass mkt. 4.99 (*0-553-25810-9*) Bantam Bks.

—The Broken Vase. 1995. (Mystery Ser.). 160p. (Orig.). mass mkt. 4.99 o.s.i (*0-553-25632-7*) Bantam Bks.

—The Broken Vase. 1976. (Orig.). pap. 1.25 o.s.i (*0-515-04065-7*, Jove) Berkley Publishing Group.

—The Broken Vase. l.t. ed. 1988. (Nightingale Ser.). 284p. (Orig.). pap. 11.95 o.p. (*0-8161-4392-7*, Macmillan Reference USA) Gale Group.

—Double for Death. 1995. (Orig.). 272p. pap. 19.00 (*0-553-76300-8*); 192p. mass mkt. 4.99 (*0-553-26059-6*) Bantam Bks.

**FOX, TRAVIS (FICTITIOUS CHARACTER)—FICTION**

Norton, Andre. Echoes in Time. 2000. (Time Traders Adventure Ser.). 320p. mass mkt. 5.99 (*0-8125-5274-1*, Tor Bks.) Doherty, Tom Assocs., LLC.

—The Time Traders. 1987. 224p. mass mkt. 3.99 o.s.i (*0-441-81255-4*); 1984. mass mkt. 2.50 o.s.i (*0-441-81254-6*); 1980. mass mkt. 1.95 o.s.i (*0-441-81253-8*) Ace Bks.

—The Time Traders. 2000. 384p. (J). 24.00 (*0-671-31952-3*) Baen Bks.

—The Time Traders. 1979. lib. bdg. 9.95 o.p. (*0-8398-2421-1*, Macmillan Reference USA) Gale Group.

Norton, Andre & Griffin, P. M. Fire Hand. 1995. 288p. mass mkt. 4.99 (*0-8125-1984-1*); 1994. 224p. 19.95 o.p. (*0-312-85313-0*) Doherty, Tom Assocs., LLC. (Tor Bks.).

Norton, Andre & Smith, Sherwood. Echoes in Time. 1999. (Time Traders Adventure Ser.). 319p. 23.95 (*0-312-85921-X*, Tor Bks.) Doherty, Tom Assocs., LLC.

**FRADE, CLETUS (FICTITIOUS CHARACTER)—FICTION**

Griffin, W. E. B. Blood & Honor. 1997. (Honor Bound Ser.: No. 2). 736p. mass mkt. 7.99 (*0-515-12194-0*, Jove) Berkley Publishing Group.

—Blood & Honor, Pt. 1. unabr. ed. 1996. (Honor Bound Ser.: No. 2). audio 80.00 (*0-7366-3594-7*, 4246A ) Books on Tape, Inc.

—Blood & Honor. l.t. ed. 1997. (Honor Bound Ser.: No. 2). 1105p. 28.95 (*0-7838-8125-8*, Macmillan Reference USA) Gale Group.

—Blood & Honor. 2001. 34.95 (*0-399-14481-1*); 1996. (Honor Bound Ser.: No. 2). 480p. 24.95 o.s.i (*0-399-14190-1*, G. P. Putnam's Sons); Set. 1996. (Honor Bound Ser.: No. 2). 4p. 24.95 o.p. (*0-399-14226-6*, 694560, Putnam Berkley Audio) Penguin Group (USA) Inc.

—Honor Bound. 1994. (Honor Bound Ser.: No. 1). 560p. mass mkt. 7.99 (*0-515-11486-3*, Jove) Berkley Publishing Group.

—Honor Bound, Pt. 1. unabr. ed. (Honor Bound Ser.: No. 1). audio 64.00 (*0-7366-2732-4*, 3460-A/B) Books on Tape, Inc.

—Honor Bound. unabr. ed. 1994. (Honor Bound Ser.: No. 1). audio 130.55 (*1-56100-184-8*, 901, Unabridged Library Editions); audio 29.95 (*1-56100-558-4*, 138, Bookcassette) Brilliance Audio.

—Honor Bound. l.t. ed. 1994. (Honor Bound Ser.: No. 1). 25.95 o.p. (*1-56895-100-0*, Wheeler Publishing, Inc.) Gale Group.

—Honor Bound. abr. ed. 2000. (Honor Bound Ser.: No. 1). audio 7.95 (*1-57815-012-4*, 1002, Media Bks. Audio Publishing) Media Bks., L. L. C.

—Honor Bound. 1994. (Honor Bound Ser.: No. 1). 384p. 22.95 o.p. (*0-399-13862-5*, G. P. Putnam's Sons) Penguin Group (USA) Inc.

—Honor Bound. 22.95 o.s.i (*0-399-14117-0*) Putnam Publishing Group, The.

—Secret Honor. 2000. (Honor Bound Ser.: No. 3). 624p. mass mkt. 7.99 (*0-515-13009-5*, Jove) Berkley Publishing Group.

—Secret Honor. 2000. audio compact disk 128.00 (*0-7366-7129-3*); (Honor Bound Ser.: No. 3). audio 104.00. (Honor Bound Ser.: Vol. 3). audio 104.00 (*0-7366-4833-X*, 5179) Books on Tape, Inc.

—Secret Honor. l.t. ed. 2000. (Honor Bound Ser.: No. 3). 28.95 (*1-56895-868-4*, Wheeler Publishing, Inc.) Gale Group.

—Secret Honor. 2000. (Honor Bound Ser.: No. 3). 544p. 25.95 o.s.i (*0-399-14568-0*); audio 24.95 o.s.i (*0-399-14580-X*, Putnam Berkley Audio) Penguin Group (USA) Inc.

—Secret Honor. (Honor Bound Ser.: No. 3). 512p. (*0-7278-5504-2*) Severn Hse. Pubs., Ltd.

**FRALEIGH, OFFICER (FICTITIOUS CHARACTER)—FICTION**

McNamara, Joseph D. The Blue Mirage. 1991. 320p. mass mkt. 5.99 o.s.i (*0-449-14755-X*, Fawcett) Ballantine Bks.

—The Blue Mirage. 1990. 324p. 19.95 o.p. (*0-688-09518-6*, Morrow, William & Co.) Morrow/Avon.

—Fatal Command. 1988. 288p. mass mkt. 5.99 o.s.i (*0-449-13393-1*, Fawcett) Ballantine Bks.

—Fatal Command. 1987. 17.95 o.p. (*0-87795-874-2*, Morrow, William & Co.) Morrow/Avon.

—The First Directive. 1985. 320p. mass mkt. 5.99 o.s.i (*0-449-12863-6*, Fawcett) Ballantine Bks.

—The First Directive. 1988. 320p. 2.99 o.p. (*0-517-55454-2*) Random Hse. Value Publishing.

**FRAME, MAX (FICTITIOUS CHARACTER)—FICTION**

Smith, Guy N. Dead End. 1996. 256p. mass mkt. 4.99 o.s.i (*0-8217-5263-4*) Kensington Publishing Corp.

**FRANCK, CESAR (FICTITIOUS CHARACTER)—FICTION**

Pyle, A. M. Murder Moves In. 1987. 256p. mass mkt. 3.50 o.p. (*0-451-14889-4*, Signet Bks.) NAL.

—Murder Moves In. 1986. 216p. 14.95 o.s.i (*0-8027-5635-2*) Walker & Co.

—Pure Murder. 1990. 256p. 16.95 o.p. (*0-312-03917-4*, Saint Martin's Minotaur) St. Martin's Pr.

—Trouble Making Toys. 1986. 256p. mass mkt. 2.95 o.p. (*0-451-14570-4*, Signet Bks.) NAL.

—Trouble Making Toys. 1985. 192p. 13.95 (*0-8027-5610-7*) Walker & Co.

**FRANK, LANE (FICTITIOUS CHARACTER)—FICTION**

Philpin, John. Dreams in the Key of Blue. 2000. 368p. mass mkt. 6.50 (*0-553-58006-X*) Bantam Bks.

—The Prettiest Feathers. 1997. 336p. pap. 23.00 (*0-553-76244-3*) Bantam Bks.

—Tunnel of Night. 1999. 384p. pap. 19.00 (*0-553-76201-X*) Bantam Bks.

Philpin, John & Sierra, Patricia. The Prettiest Feathers. 1997. 336p. mass mkt. 5.50 o.s.i (*0-553-57555-4*) Bantam Bks.

—Tunnel of Night. 1999. 384p. mass mkt. 6.50 o.s.i (*0-553-57954-1*) Bantam Bks.

**FRANK, LUCAS (FICTITIOUS CHARACTER)—FICTION**

Philpin, John. Dreams in the Key of Blue. 2000. 368p. mass mkt. 6.50 (*0-553-58006-X*) Bantam Bks.

—The Prettiest Feathers. 1997. 336p. pap. 23.00 (*0-553-76244-3*) Bantam Bks.

—Tunnel of Night. 1999. 384p. pap. 19.00 (*0-553-76201-X*) Bantam Bks.

Philpin, John & Sierra, Patricia. The Prettiest Feathers. 1997. 336p. mass mkt. 5.50 o.s.i (*0-553-57555-4*) Bantam Bks.

—Tunnel of Night. 1999. 384p. mass mkt. 6.50 o.s.i (*0-553-57954-1*) Bantam Bks.

**FRANKENSTEIN (FICTITIOUS CHARACTER)—FICTION**

Aldiss, Brian W. Frankenstein Unbound. 1974. 10.00 o.p. (*0-394-49079-7*) Random Hse., Inc.

—Frankenstein Unbound. 1990. mass mkt. 4.95 (*0-446-36036-8*) Warner Bks., Inc.

The Bride of Frankenstein. 1977. 1.25 o.s.i (*0-425-03414-3*) Berkley Publishing Group.

Haining, Peter, ed. The Frankenstein Omnibus. 1994. 10.98 (*0-7858-0041-7*) Book Sales, Inc.

Kay, Jeremy. The Secret Laboratory Journals of Dr. Victor Frankenstein. (Illus.). 1998. 208p. pap. 17.95 (*0-87951-867-7*); 1996. 176p. 29.95 (*0-87951-511-2*) Overlook Pr., The.

Price, Vincent & Lewis, Cathy. The Lodger: Story of Jack the Ripper. audio National Recording Co.

Shelley, Mary Wollstonecraft. Bernie Wrightson's Frankenstein: Or the Modern Prometheus. 2nd ed. 1995. (Illus.). 200p. 24.95 (*0-88733-194-7*) Miller, Charles F. Pub.

—The Essential Frankenstein. Wolf, Leonard, ed. 1993. (Essentials Ser.). 368p. (Orig.). pap. 15.95 o.p. (*0-452-26968-7*, Plume) Dutton/Plume.

—Frankenstein. 2000. 252p. E-Book 9.95 (*0-594-04128-7*) 1873 Pr.

—Frankenstein. Doyle, Debra & Roche, Ruth A., eds. 1997. (Classics Illustrated Study Guides). (Illus.). mass mkt. 4.99 (*1-57840-044-9*) Acclaim Bks.

—Frankenstein. 2000. (SPA.). 320p. 8.95 (*84-406-1953-7*) B Ediciones S.A. ESP. *Dist:* Distribooks, Inc.

—Frankenstein. E-Book (*0-7607-1308-1*) Barnes & Noble, Inc.

—Frankenstein. audio 26.95 (*1-885546-03-3*) Big Ben Audio, Inc.

—Frankenstein. 2001. per. 14.00 (*1-891355-53-8*) Blue Unicorn Editions.

—Frankenstein. Macdonald, D. L. & Scherf, Kathleen, eds. 1994. 280p. pap. (*1-55111-038-5*) Broadview Pr.

—Frankenstein. 1997. (Cambridge Literature Ser.). audio 14.95 o.p. (*0-521-59793-5*); audio compact disk 18.95 o.p. (*0-521-59794-3*) Cambridge Univ. Pr.

—Frankenstein. 1999. (Bloom's Reviews Comprehensive Research & Study Guides). 72p. pap. 4.95 (*0-7910-4121-2*) Chelsea Hse. Pubs.

—Frankenstein. 1994. (Illus.). 304p. 3.99 o.s.i (*0-517-11880-7*) Crown Publishing Group.

—Frankenstein. 1989. mass mkt. 3.25 o.s.i (*0-8125-0458-5*, Tor Classics); 1988. mass mkt. 4.95 (*0-938819-80-1*, Aerie) Doherty, Tom Assocs., LLC.

—Frankenstein. 1961. 2.95 o.p. (*0-460-01616-4*, Dutton) Dutton/Plume.

—Frankenstein. E-Book 2.49 (*1-58627-519-4*) Electric Umbrella Publishing.

—Frankenstein. 2003. (Barnes & Noble Classics Ser.). 288p. pap. 3.95 (*1-59308-005-0*) Fine Communications.

—Frankenstein. 2003. pap. 6.50 (*1-59456-236-9*) GreatUNpublished.com.

—Frankenstein. abr. ed. 2000. (Illus.). audio 13.95 (*1-84032-441-4*) Hodder Headline Audiobooks GBR. *Dist:* Trafalgar Square.

—Frankenstein. Stemach, Jerry, ed. 2000. audio compact disk 200.00 (*1-58702-512-4*) Johnston, Don Inc.

—Frankenstein. 1998. (Cloth Bound Pocket Ser.). (Illus.). 240p. 7.95 (*3-89508-089-6*, 520014) Konemann.

—Frankenstein. 1989. (English As a Second Language Bk.). pap. text 5.95 o.p. (*0-582-52546-2*) Longman Publishing Group.

—Frankenstein. 1992. (Everyman's Library). (Illus.). 272p. 15.00 (*0-679-40999-8*) McKay, David Co., Inc.

—Frankenstein. (Signet Classics). 2000. 240p. mass mkt. 3.95 (*0-451-52771-2*, Signet Classics); 1994. 224p. mass mkt. 3.99 o.s.i (*0-451-18377-0*, Signet Bks.); 1965. mass mkt. 0.95 o.p. (*0-451-50839-4*, Signet Classics); 1965. mass mkt. 1.25 o.p. (*0-451-50975-7*, Signet Classics); 1965. mass mkt. 1.50 o.p. (*0-451-51132-8*, Signet Classics); 1965. mass mkt. 0.75 o.p. (*0-451-50695-2*, Signet Classics); 1965. mass mkt. 0.60 o.p. (*0-451-50618-9*, Signet Classics); 1965. mass mkt. 0.50 o.p. (*0-451-50329-5*, Signet Classics); 1965. mass mkt. 1.75 o.p. (*0-451-52009-2*) NAL.

—Frankenstein. abr. ed. 1996. audio 13.98 (*962-634-503-9*, NA200314); 1994. audio compact disk 15.98 (*962-634-003-7*, NA200312) Naxos of America, Inc. (Naxos AudioBooks).

—Frankenstein. abr. ed. 2001. audio 18.00 (*1-59007-009-7*, New Millennium Audio) New Millennium Entertainment.

—Frankenstein. abr. ed. 1993. 16.95 o.p. (*1-55800-647-8*) NewStar Media, Inc.

—Frankenstein. (C). pap. (*0-393-97938-5*); pap. o.p. (*0-393-10028-6*) Norton, W. W. & Co., Inc.

—Frankenstein. 1988. 256p. pap. 6.00 (*0-914061-07-0*) Orchises Pr.
—Frankenstein. Kinsley, James & Joseph, M. K., eds. 1980. xx, 239 p. (*0-19-251010-X*) Oxford Univ. Pr., Inc.
—Frankenstein. 1995. (New Casebooks Ser.). ix, 271p. 69.95 (*0-312-12461-9*) Palgrave Macmillan.
—Frankenstein. Smith, Johanna M., ed. 1992. text 39.95 o.p. (*0-312-06525-6*) Palgrave Macmillan.
—Frankenstein. Teresa Agnes, ed. Heller, Rudolf, tr. 1979. (SPA., Illus.). 64p. stu. ed. 1.50 (*0-88301-568-4*); pap. text 3.95 (*0-88301-448-3*) Pendulum Pr., Inc.
—Frankenstein. 2003. (Penguin Classics Ser.). 336p. pap. 8.00 (*0-14-143947-5*) Penguin Group (USA) Inc.
—Frankenstein. Hindle, Maurice, ed. (Penguin Classics Ser.). 1990. 224p. pap. 3.99 o.p. (*0-14-035107-8*); 1986. 272p. pap. 2.95 o.p. (*0-14-043237-X*) Penguin Putnam Bks. for Young Readers. (Puffin Bks.).
—Frankenstein. 1995. (SPA.). 304p. (*84-01-46253-3*) Plaza & Janés Editories, S.A.
—Frankenstein. (FRE.). pap. 10.95 (*2-266-00354-2*) Presses Pocket FRA. *Dist:* Distribooks, Inc.
—Frankenstein. 2000. E-Book 4.95 (*0-679-64006-1*); 1999. 352p. pap. 7.95 (*0-375-75341-9*) Random House Adult Trade Publishing Group. (Modern Library).
—Frankenstein. 1988. xiv, 259p. 5.99 o.s.i (*0-517-66842-4*) Random Hse. Value Publishing.
—Frankenstein. (Learning Channel's Great Bks.). 1993. pap. 5.00 o.s.i (*0-679-74954-3*); 1993. (Illus.). 352p. 15.95 o.s.i (*0-679-60059-0*); 1984. 14.00 o.s.i (*0-394-60506-3*) Random Hse., Inc.
—Frankenstein. (Literary Classics Ser.). 1990. 224p. text 5.98 o.p. (*0-89471-882-7*, Courage Bks.); 1987. 224p. pap. 5.98 o.p. (*0-89471-520-8*); 1987. 184p. lib. bdg. 12.90 o.p. (*0-89471-521-6*) Running Pr. Bk. Pubs.
—Frankenstein. 2004. 304p. mass mkt. 3.95 (*0-7434-8758-3*, Pocket) Simon & Schuster.
—Frankenstein. 1999. pap. 9.98 (*0-671-04459-1*, Simon & Schuster Audioworks) Simon & Schuster Audio.
—Frankenstein, 2 cass. abr. ed. 1983. pap. 11.95 o.p. incl. audio (*0-88142-323-8*) Soundelux Audio Publishing.
—Frankenstein. abr. ed. audio 10.95 (*0-8045-1088-1*, SAC 1088) Spoken Arts, Inc.
—Frankenstein. 1996. pap. text 14.95 o.p. (*0-312-13840-7*) St. Martin's Pr.
—Frankenstein. Murfin, Ross C. & Smith, Johanna M., eds. 1991. (Case Studies in Contemporary Criticism: Vol. 1). 358p. (C). pap. text 11.95 o.p. (*0-312-04469-0*) St. Martin's Pr.
—Frankenstein. audio Thorsons.
—Frankenstein. Lyons, Paddy & Gooden, Philip, eds. 1994. (Illus.). 267p. pap. 5.95 (*0-460-87528-0*, Everyman's Classic Library in Paperback) Tuttle Publishing.
—Frankenstein. 2001. 125p. pap. 8.95 (*1-57002-165-1*) University Publishing Hse., Inc.
—Frankenstein. (English Library). Viking Penguin.
—Frankenstein. 1997. (Classics Library). (Illus.). 192p. pap. 3.95 (*1-85326-023-1*, 0231WW) Wordsworth Editions, Ltd. GBR. *Dist:* Casemate Pubs. & Bk. Distributors, LLC.
—Frankenstein. abr. ed. 1999. (Mystery Theatre Ser.). (Illus.). audio 16.95 (*1-56994-513-6*, 348844, Monterey SoundWorks) Monterey Media, Inc.
—Frankenstein. reprint ed. lib. bdg. 21.95 (*0-88411-130-X*) Amereon, Ltd.
—Frankenstein, Set. unabr. ed. 1998. 35.95 incl. audio (*1-55685-552-4*) Audio Bk. Contractors, Inc.
—Frankenstein. unabr. ed. audio 31.95 o.p. (*1-55656-087-7*, DAB 027) BBC Audiobooks America.
—Frankenstein. l.t. ed. 1998. 343p. pap. 19.95 (*1-55701-224-5*) BNI Pubns., Inc.
—Frankenstein. 1984. (Bantam Classics Ser.). (Illus.). 256p. reprint ed. mass mkt. 4.95 (*0-553-21247-8*) Bantam Dell Publishing Group.
—Frankenstein. Smith, Johanna M., ed. 2nd ed. 2000. (Case Studies in Contemporary Criticism). x, 470p. pap. text 8.50 (*0-312-19126-X*) Bedford/Saint Martin's.
—Frankenstein. l.t. ed. 2001. per. 15.50 (*1-58396-220-4*) Blue Unicorn Editions.
—Frankenstein. unabr. ed. 2002. audio 56.00 (*0-7366-8470-0*); 2002. audio compact disk 72.00 (*0-7366-8598-7*); 2001. audio 29.95 (*0-7366-6817-9*) Books on Tape, Inc.
—Frankenstein. unabr. ed. 2002. audio 29.95 (*1-59086-281-3*, 3867, Brilliance Audio Unabridged); 1993. audio 57.25 (*1-56100-120-1*, 843); 1993. (Illus.). audio 17.95 o.p. (*1-56100-486-3*, 115, Bookcassette) Brilliance Audio.
—Frankenstein. 1990. (Illus.). reprint ed. lib. bdg. 21.95 (*0-89966-693-0*) Buccaneer Bks., Inc.
—Frankenstein. l.t. ed. 1998. 343p. pap. 19.95 (*1-58855-029-X*) Cyber Classics, Inc.
—Frankenstein. unabr. ed. 1986. audio 26.95 o.p. (*1-55656-024-9*) Dercum Audio.
—Frankenstein. l.t. unabr. ed. (Large Print Classics Ser.). 2001. xv, 283p. pap. 9.95 (*0-486-41562-7*); 1994. 176p. pap. 1.50 (*0-486-28211-2*) Dover Pubns., Inc.
—Frankenstein. l.t. ed. 2001. 315p. 27.95 (*0-7838-9622-0*, Hall, G. K. & Co.) Gale Group.
—Frankenstein. l.t. ed. 1087p. pap. 82.38 (*0-7583-0911-2*); 872p. pap. 69.19 (*0-7583-0910-4*); 748p. pap. 56.13 (*0-7583-0909-0*); 203p. pap. 18.74 (*0-7583-0904-X*); 464p. pap. 36.06 (*0-7583-0907-4*); 258p. pap. 22.60 (*0-7583-0905-8*); 359p. pap. 28.72 (*0-7583-0906-6*); 604p. pap. 46.88 (*0-7583-0908-2*); 258p. lib. bdg. 30.60 (*0-7583-0897-3*); 872p. lib. bdg. 85.45 (*0-7583-0902-3*); 203p. lib. bdg. 26.48 (*0-7583-0896-5*); 1087p. lib. bdg. 94.38 (*0-7583-0903-1*); 604p. lib. bdg. 52.88 (*0-7583-0900-7*); 359p. lib. bdg. 36.72 (*0-7583-0898-1*); 464p. lib. bdg. 44.06 (*0-7583-0899-X*); 748p. lib. bdg. 62.13 (*0-7583-0901-5*) Huge Print Pr.
—Frankenstein. l.t. ed. 1987. (Mainstream Ser.). 275p. 15.95 o.p. (*1-85089-164-8*) ISIS Large Print Bks. GBR. *Dist:* Transaction Pubs.
—Frankenstein. unabr. ed. 1980. audio 42.00 Jimcin Recordings.
—Frankenstein. Stemach, Jerry, ed. l.t. ed. 2000. (Illus.). text 50.00 (*1-58702-514-0*); 100p. text 65.00 incl. audio, cd-rom (*1-58702-396-2*) Johnston, Don Inc.
—Frankenstein, Vol. 5. Stemach, Jerry & Venable, Gail Portnuff, eds. 2002. (Start-to-Finish Books). audio 100.00 (*1-58702-950-2*) Johnston, Don Inc.
—Frankenstein. l.t. ed. 1998. (Large Print Heritage Ser.). 337p. lib. bdg. 31.95 (*1-58118-020-9*, 22002) LRS.
—Frankenstein. l.t. ed. (Large Print Ser.). 1996. 420p. lib. bdg. 26.00 (*0-939495-93-7*); 1998. 210p. reprint ed. lib. bdg. 25.00 (*1-58287-030-6*) North Bks.
—Frankenstein, Set. 1992. audio 48.95 Olivia & Hill Pr., The.
—Frankenstein. 2nd ed. 2000. 416p. 49.95 (*0-312-22762-0*) Palgrave Macmillan.
—Frankenstein. adapted collector's ed. 1999. 12.95 o.p. incl. audio (*1-57019-160-3*, 4180) Radio Spirits, Inc.
—Frankenstein. 1987. (Radiobook Ser.). Pt. 1. audio 4.98 (*0-929541-16-2*); Pt. 2. audio 4.98 (*0-929541-17-0*) Radiola Co.
—Frankenstein. unabr. ed. 1993. audio 60.00 (*1-55690-771-0*, 93108E7) Recorded Bks., LLC.
—Frankenstein. Mellor, Anne K. & Reyes, Teresa, eds. 1995. (Enriched Classics Ser.). (Illus.). 304p. reprint ed. mass mkt. 4.99 (*0-671-53150-6*, Pocket) Simon & Schuster.
—Frankenstein. unabr. ed. 2003. audio 19.99 (*1-59335-194-1*, 30290) Soulmate Audio Bks., Inc.
—Frankenstein. unabr. ed. 2002. audio compact disk 18.95 (*1-58472-387-4*); audio compact disk 33.95 (*1-58472-252-5*, 091) Sound Room Pubs., Inc. (In Audio).
—Frankenstein. Lyons, Paddy, ed. & intro. by. 18th ed. 1992. 256p. pap. 2.95 o.p. (*0-460-87149-8*, Everyman's Classic Library in Paperback) Tuttle Publishing.
—Frankenstein. Hindle, Maurice, ed. & intro. by. rev. ed. 1992. (Classics Ser.). (Illus.). 320p. pap. 7.95 o.s.i (*0-14-043362-7*, Penguin Classics) Viking Penguin.
—Frankenstein, 2 vols. in 1. 2003. 148p. reprint ed. (*1-85477-117-5*) Woodstock Books.
—Frankenstein: An Another Time, Another Place Recording. unabr. ed. audio 44.95 (*0-7861-0877-0*, 1540) Blackstone Audio Bks., Inc.
—Frankenstein: High School Edition. 2nd ed. 2000. text 10.00 (*0-312-24948-9*) Bedford/Saint Martin's.
—Frankenstein: Or, the Modern Prometheus. 1973. 224 p. (*0-09-907920-8*) Arrow Bks., Ltd.
—Frankenstein: Or, the Modern Prometheus. 1998. 242p. pap. text 7.00 (*0-7881-5237-8*) DIANE Publishing Co.
—Frankenstein: Or, the Modern Prometheus. unabr. ed. 1991. audio 40.00 (*0-9631737-0-7*) French, Edward Inc.
—Frankenstein: Or, the Modern Prometheus. 1989. (Illus.). 125p. 12.95 o.p. (*0-87226-197-2*, Bedrick, Peter Bks.) McGraw-Hill Children's Publishing.
—Frankenstein: Or, the Modern Prometheus. 2001. (Oxford World's Classics Ser.). 224p. 15.00 (*0-19-514901-7*) Oxford Univ. Pr., Inc.
—Frankenstein: Or, the Modern Prometheus. Kinsley, James & Joseph, M. K., eds. 1982. (Oxford World's Classics Ser.). 270p. pap. 4.95 o.p. (*0-19-281532-6*) Oxford Univ. Pr., Inc.
—Frankenstein: Or, the Modern Prometheus. 1971. xxii, 241p. (*0-19-281116-9*) Oxford Univ. Pr., Inc.
—Frankenstein: Or, the Modern Prometheus. 1993. (*0-679-42789-9*, Modern Library) Random House Adult Trade Publishing Group.
—Frankenstein: Or, the Modern Prometheus. 1986. (Illus.). 304p. 9.98 o.p. (*1-85079-070-1*) Sterling Publishing Co., Inc.
—Frankenstein: Or, the Modern Prometheus. 1963. 10.00 (*0-606-00693-1*) Turtleback Bks.
—Frankenstein: Or, the Modern Prometheus. 1994. (Illus.). pap. 15.95 (*0-520-20179-5*); pap. 13.95 o.p. (*0-520-08942-1*) Univ. of California Pr.
—Frankenstein: Or, the Modern Prometheus. Rieger, James H., ed. & intro. by. 1982. xliv, 334p. reprint ed. pap. text 12.00 (*0-226-75227-5*) Univ. of Chicago Pr.
—Frankenstein: Or, the Modern Prometheus: The 1818 Text. Butler, Marilyn, ed. & intro. by. (Oxford World's Classics Ser.). 1998. 328p. pap. 6.95 (*0-19-283366-9*); 1994. 322p. pap. 4.95 o.p. (*0-19-282283-7*) Oxford Univ. Pr., Inc.
—Frankenstein: The Creator. audio 7.95 National Recording Co.
—Frankenstein: The 1818 Edition. Butler, Marilyn, ed. 1994. 352p. 55.00 (*1-85196-051-1*) Pickering & Chatto Pubs., Ltd. GBR. *Dist:* Ashgate Publishing Co.
—Frankenstein: Unabridged & Unadapted from the Original Text, & with Thirteen Related Readings. 2002. (Illus.). 324p. (*0-9710756-3-8*) Everbind/Marco Bk. Co.
—Frankenstein & Dracula. 1990. 25.00 o.p. (*0-87226-423-8*, Bedrick, Peter Bks.) McGraw-Hill Children's Publishing.
—Frankenstein: or The Modern Prometheus. 1999. (New York Public Library Collector's Edition Ser.). (Illus.). 320p. 18.95 o.s.i (*0-385-48732-0*) Doubleday Publishing.
—Frankenstein or the Modern Prometheus: The 1818 Text in Three Volumes. 1984. (Illus.). 272p. (C). 40.00 o.p. (*0-520-05281-1*); 254p. o.p. (*0-520-05317-6*) Univ. of California Pr.
—Frankenstein Readalong. 1994. (Illustrated Classics Collection). 64p. pap. 14.95 incl. audio (*0-7854-0707-3*, 40345); audio 13.50 o.p. (*1-56103-428-2*) American Guidance Service, Inc.
—Mary Shelley's Frankenstein. abr. ed. 1994. (Classics on Cassette). pap. 16.00 o.s.i incl. audio (*0-453-00912-3*) Penguin/HighBridge.
Shelley, Mary Wollstonecraft & Joseph, M. K. Frankenstein: Or, the Modern Prometheus. 1969. xxv, 241 p. (*0-19-255325-9*) Oxford Univ. Pr., Inc.
Shelley, Mary Wollstonecraft & Wells, H. G. Making Humans: Complete Texts with Introduction, Historical Contexts, Critical Essays. Wilt, Judith, ed. 2003. (New Riverside Editions Ser.). (Illus.). viii, 359p. 8.76 (*0-618-08489-4*) Houghton Mifflin Co.
Shelley, Mary Wollstonecraft, et al. Frankenstein: Or, the Modern Prometheus. 2nd ed. 1999. (Literary Texts Ser.). (Illus.). 364p. pap. (*1-55111-308-2*) Broadview Pr.
Stoker, Bram & Shelley, Mary Wollstonecraft. Dracula - Frankenstein. 1973. xiii, 655p. o.p. (*0-385-09580-5*) Doubleday Publishing.
—Dracula - Frankenstein. l.t. ed. 1999. (Illus.). E-Book 24.95 incl. cd-rom (*1-929077-39-4*, Books OnScreen) PageFree Publishing, Inc.
—Frankenstein, Dracula, Dr. Jekyll & Mr. Hyde. 1978. mass mkt. 4.50 o.p. (*0-451-52170-6*, Signet Classics) NAL.
Wolfson, Susan J. Frankenstein: A Cultural Edition. 2002. (Longman Cultural Edition Ser.). 384p. pap. 16.00 (*0-321-09698-3*) Longman Publishing Group.

**FRANKLIN, ALTON BENJAMIN (FICTITIOUS CHARACTER)—FICTION**

Russell, Randy. Blind Spot. 1991. 224p. mass mkt. 3.95 o.s.i (*0-553-28926-8*) Bantam Bks.
—Blind Spot. 1990. 14.95 o.s.i (*0-385-41563-X*) Doubleday Publishing.

**FRANKLIN, BENJAMIN, 1706-1790—FICTION**

Hall, Robert L. Benjamin Franklin & a Case of Artful Murder. 1995. mass mkt. 4.99 (*0-312-95419-0*, St. Martin's Paperbacks) St. Martin's Pr.
—Benjamin Franklin & a Case of Christmas Murder. l.t. ed. 1998. 413p. reprint ed. text 15.00 (*0-7881-5175-4*) DIANE Publishing Co.
—Benjamin Franklin & a Case of Christmas Murder. 1991. 288p. mass mkt. 3.99 o.p. (*0-312-92670-7*, St. Martin's Paperbacks); 1990. 17.95 o.p. (*0-312-05383-5*, Saint Martin's Minotaur) St. Martin's Pr.
—Benjamin Franklin Takes the Case: The American Agent Investigates Murder in the Dark Byways of London. 1993. mass mkt. 3.99 o.p. (*0-312-95047-0*, St. Martin's Paperbacks) St. Martin's Pr.
—London Blood: Further Adventures of the American Agent Abroad: A Benjamin Franklin Mystery. 1997. (Benjamin Franklin Mystery Ser.). 256p. 21.95 (*0-312-16908-6*, Saint Martin's Minotaur) St. Martin's Pr.
—Murder at Drury Lane: Further Adventures of the American Agent in London. 1993. mass mkt. 4.50 (*0-312-95112-4*, St. Martin's Paperbacks); 1992. 288p. 18.95 o.p. (*0-312-08266-5*, Saint Martin's Minotaur) St. Martin's Pr.
—Murder by the Waters: A Benjamin Franklin Mystery. pap. 15.95 (*0-312-30104-9*, Saint Martin's Griffin); 1995. 272p. 21.95 (*0-312-13568-8*, Saint Martin's Minotaur) St. Martin's Pr.
Heimerdinger, Chris. Ben Franklin & the Chamber of Time. 1995. (Orig.). pap. 11.95 (*0-87579-878-0*, Shadow Mountain) Deseret Bk. Co.
Keyes, J. Gregory. A Calculus of Angels. (Age of Unreason Ser.: 2). 2000. 448p. mass mkt. 6.99 (*0-345-40608-7*, Del Rey); 1999. (Illus.). 416p. pap. 14.00 o.s.i (*0-345-40607-9*) Ballantine Bks.
—Empire of Unreason. 2001. (Age of Unreason Ser.: Vol. 3). 416p. mass mkt. 6.99 (*0-345-40610-9*, Del Rey) Ballantine Bks.
—Newton's Cannon. (Age of Unreason Ser.: Vol. 1). 1999. 384p. mass mkt. 6.99 (*0-345-43378-5*, Del Rey); 1998. 480p. pap. 14.00 o.s.i (*0-345-40605-2*) Ballantine Bks.
O'Toole, G. J. Poor Richard's Game. 1983. 320p. pap. 3.50 o.p. (*0-440-17028-1*); 1982. 16.95 o.s.i (*0-385-28796-8*, Delacorte Pr.) Dell Publishing.
Wright, Esmond, ed. Benjamin Franklin: His Life As He Wrote It. 1996. (Illus.). 312p. pap. 18.95 (*0-674-06655-3*) Harvard Univ. Pr.
Zochert, Donald. Murder in the Hellfire Club. 1979. o.p. (*0-03-022441-1*) Holt, Henry & Co.
—Murder in the Hellfire Club. 1980. pap. 2.95 o.p. (*0-14-005504-5*, Penguin Bks.) Viking Penguin.

**FRANKLIN, CLYDE WAYNE (FICTITIOUS CHARACTER)—FICTION**

Grossman, Richard. The Alphabet Man: A Novel. 1993. 443p. 22.95 o.p. (*0-932511-76-7*); pap. 11.95 (*0-932511-77-5*) Fiction Collective Two, Inc.

**FRANKLIN, DEREK (FICTITIOUS CHARACTER)—FICTION**

Francis, Dick. Straight. 1998. mass mkt. 5.99 (*0-449-45788-5*); 1991. 320p. mass mkt. 5.95 o.p. (*0-449-45310-3*); 1991. 320p. mass mkt. 5.99 o.s.i (*0-449-21720-5*) Ballantine Bks. (Fawcett).
—Straight. 2003. 320p. mass mkt. 6.99 (*0-515-13465-1*, Jove) Berkley Publishing Group.
—Straight. l.t. ed. 1990. (General Ser.). 437p. 15.95 o.p. (*0-8161-4995-X*); lib. bdg. 21.95 o.p. (*0-8161-4991-7*) Gale Group. (Macmillan Reference USA).
—Straight. abr. ed. 1989. audio 15.95 (*1-55994-118-9*, CPN 2128, Caedmon) HarperTrade.
—Straight. 1989. 324p. 18.95 o.p. (*0-399-13470-0*, G. P. Putnam's Sons) Penguin Putnam Bks. for Young Readers.
—Straight. unabr. ed. 1994. audio 70.00 (*1-55690-993-4*, 94132E7) Recorded Bks., LLC.

**FRANKLYN, KIT (FICTITIOUS CHARACTER)—FICTION**

Donaldson, D. J. Blood on the Bayou. 1991. 16.95 o.p. (*0-312-05387-8*, Saint Martin's Minotaur) St. Martin's Pr.
—Cajun Nights. 1989. pap. 3.95 o.p. (*0-312-91610-8*, St. Martin's Paperbacks); 1988. 256p. 16.95 o.p. (*0-312-02175-5*, Saint Martin's Minotaur) St. Martin's Pr.
—Louisiana Fever. (Andy Broussard/Kit Franklyn Mysteries Ser.). 288p. 1997. mass mkt. 5.99 o.p. (*0-312-96257-6*, St. Martin's Paperbacks); 1996. 21.95 o.p. (*0-312-14362-1*, Saint Martin's Minotaur) St. Martin's Pr.
—New Orleans Requiem. 1995. (Mystery Ser.). 250p. per. (*0-373-26188-8*, 1-26188-2, Worldwide Library) Harlequin Enterprises, Ltd.
—New Orleans Requiem. 1994. 240p. 19.95 o.p. (*0-312-10495-2*, Saint Martin's Minotaur) St. Martin's Pr.
—No Mardi Gras for the Dead. 1995. (WWL Mystery Ser.). mass mkt. (*0-373-26163-2*, 1-26163-5, Harlequin Bks.) Harlequin Enterprises, Ltd.
—No Mardi Gras for the Dead. 1992. (Andy Broussard - Kit Franklyn Mystery Ser.). 216p. 17.95 o.p. (*0-312-08271-1*) St. Martin's Pr.
—Sleeping with the Crawfish: An Andy Broussard & Kit Franklyn Mystery. (Andy Broussard/Kit Franklyn Mysteries Ser.). 272p. 1998. mass mkt. 5.99 (*0-312-96681-4*, St. Martin's Paperbacks); 1997. 21.95 o.p. (*0-312-17025-4*, Saint Martin's Minotaur) St. Martin's Pr.

**FRASER, JAMIE (FICTITIOUS CHARACTER)—FICTION**

Gabaldon, Diana. Diana Gabaldon, 3 vols., Set. 1995. pap. 17.97 (*0-440-36066-8*) Dell Publishing.
—Dragonfly in Amber. 1993. 960p. mass mkt. 7.99 (*0-440-21562-5*); 1992. 752p. 27.95 (*0-385-30231-2*, Delacorte Pr.) Dell Publishing.
—Dragonfly in Amber. abr. ed. 1995. audio 25.95 o.s.i (*0-553-47330-1*, 692850, RH Audio) Random Hse. Audio Publishing Group.
—Dragonfly in Amber. unabr. ed. 1998. audio 186.00 (*0-7887-2170-4*, 95466E7);Set. audio 87.00 (*0-7887-2472-X*, 95587) Recorded Bks., LLC.
—Drums of Autumn. 1997. 1088p. mass mkt. 9.99 (*0-7704-2775-8*) Bantam Bks.
—Drums of Autumn. 1997. 1088p. mass mkt. 7.99 (*0-440-22425-X*); 1996. 896p. 27.95 (*0-385-31140-0*, Delacorte Pr.) Dell Publishing.
—Drums of Autumn. abr. ed. 1996. audio 25.95 (*0-553-47332-8*, 694515, RH Audio) Random Hse. Audio Publishing Group.

—Drums of Autumn. unabr. ed. 1999. audio 198.00 (*0-7887-3473-3*, 95755E7) Recorded Bks., LLC.
—The Fiery Cross. 2002. 992p. pap. 14.95 (*0-385-33676-4*); 2002. E-Book 13.95 (*0-440-33388-1*, Delta); 2001. 992p. 27.95 (*0-385-31527-9*, Delacorte Pr.) Dell Publishing.
—The Fiery Cross. 2002. 992p. pap. (*0-385-65943-1*, Anchor Canada) Doubleday Canada, Ltd. CAN. *Dist:* Random Hse., Inc.
—The Fiery Cross. abr. ed. 2001. audio 29.95 (*0-553-52861-0*); audio compact disk 34.95 (*0-553-71447-3*) Random Hse. Audio Publishing Group. (RH Audio).
—Outlander. 1998. 640p. pap. 14.95 (*0-385-31995-9*, Delacorte Pr.); 1996. 864p. mass mkt. 3.99 o.s.i (*0-440-22291-5*); 1992. 864p. mass mkt. 7.99 (*0-440-21256-1*); 1991. 640p. 27.95 (*0-385-30230-4*, Delacorte Pr.) Dell Publishing.
—Outlander. 2001. 640p. pap. (*0-385-65868-0*) Doubleday Canada, Ltd. CAN. *Dist:* Random Hse., Inc.
—Outlander. abr. ed. 1994. audio 21.98 o.s.i (*0-553-74580-8*); audio 25.95 (*0-553-47329-8*, 692279) Random Hse. Audio Publishing Group. (RH Audio).
—Outlander. unabr. ed. 1997. audio 175.00 (*0-7887-1298-5*, 95132E7) Recorded Bks., LLC.
—The Outlandish Companion: In Which Much Is Revealed Regarding Claire & Jamie Fraser, Their Lives & Times, Antecedents, Adventures, Companions & Progeny, with Learned Commentary (and Many Footnotes) by Their Humble Creator. 1999. (Illus.). 608p. 27.95 (*0-385-32413-8*, Delacorte Pr.) Dell Publishing.
—Voyager. 1994. 1072p. mass mkt. 7.99 (*0-440-21756-3*); 1993. 880p. 27.95 (*0-385-30232-0*, Delacorte Pr.) Dell Publishing.
—Voyager. abr. ed. 1994. audio 25.95 o.s.i (*0-553-47331-X*, 693353, RH Audio) Random Hse. Audio Publishing Group.
—Voyager. unabr. ed. 2000. (Claire Randall Ser.: Vol. 3). audio 186.00 (*0-7887-2926-8*, 95657E7) Recorded Bks., LLC.

**FRASER, ROBERT (FICTITIOUS CHARACTER)—FICTION**

Gibson, Graeme. Gentleman Death. 1995. 256p. pap. 12.95 (*0-7710-3312-5*) McClelland & Stewart/ Tundra Bks.
—Perpetual Motion. 1998. (New Canadian Library). 272p. mass mkt. 8.95 (*0-7710-3462-8*) McClelland & Stewart/Tundra Bks.
—Perpetual Motion. 1983. 283p. 12.95 o.p. (*0-312-60132-8*) St. Martin's Pr.
—Perpetual Motion. 1988. 288p. pap. 6.95 o.p. (*0-14-010382-1*, Penguin Bks.) Viking Penguin.

**FRASIER, GEORGE (FICTITIOUS CHARACTER)—FICTION**

Whitten, Les. A Killing Pace. 1996. 400p. reprint ed. pap. 4.99 (*0-8439-4017-4*) Dorchester Publishing Co., Inc.
—A Killing Pace. 1984. 420p. mass mkt. 3.50 o.p. (*0-8217-1418-X*, Zebra Bks.) Kensington Publishing Corp.
—A Killing Pace. 1983. 320p. 14.95 o.s.i (*0-689-11369-2*, Scribner) Simon & Schuster.

**FREDRICKSON, ROBERT, DOCTOR (FICTITIOUS CHARACTER)—FICTION**

*see Mongo (Fictitious Character)—Fiction*

**FREEMAN, GILES (FICTITIOUS CHARACTER)—FICTION**

Rickman, Phil. Candlenight. 1995. 480p. mass mkt. 5.99 o.s.i (*0-515-11715-3*, Jove) Berkley Publishing Group.

**FREEMAN, LAUREN (FICTITIOUS CHARACTER)—FICTION**

Shapiro, Barbara. See No Evil. 1996. 304p. (Orig.). mass mkt. 5.99 (*0-380-77421-6*, Avon Bks.) Morrow/Avon.

**FREEMAN, MAX (FICTITIOUS CHARACTER)—FICTION**

King, Jonathon. The Blue Edge of Midnight. 2003. 54.95 (*0-7927-2876-9*); 74.95 (*0-7927-2877-7*) BBC Audiobooks America.
—The Blue Edge of Midnight. 2002. 320p. 22.95 (*0-525-94643-8*, Dutton) Dutton/Plume.
—The Blue Edge of Midnight. 2004. 288p. mass mkt. 6.99 (*0-451-41078-5*, Onyx) NAL.
—The Blue Edge of Midnight. l.t. ed. 2002. (Mystery Ser.). 415p. 30.45 (*0-7862-4698-7*) Thorndike Pr.
—Shadow Men. unabr. ed. 2004. (Max Freeman Ser.). audio 27.95 (*1-59355-306-4*, 4918, Brilliance Audio Unabridged); audio 69.25 (*1-59355-307-2*, 4919, Brilliance Audio Unabridged Lib Ed); audio compact disk 82.25 (*1-59355-309-9*, 4921, Brilliance Audio on CD Unabridged Lib Ed); audio compact disk 29.95 (*1-59355-308-0*, 4920, Brilliance Audio on CD Unabridged) Brilliance Audio.
—Shadow Men. 2004. 288p. 23.95 (*0-525-94807-4*, Dutton) Dutton/Plume.
—A Visible Darkness. 2003. 64.95 (*0-7927-2869-6*); 49.95 (*0-7927-2868-8*) BBC Audiobooks America.
—A Visible Darkness. l.t. ed. 2003. lib. bdg. 28.95 (*1-58547-349-9*, Platinum) Ctr. Point Large Print.
—A Visible Darkness. 2003. 256p. 23.95 (*0-525-94714-0*) Dutton/Plume.
—A Visible Darkness. 2004. 288p. mass mkt. 6.99 (*0-451-41135-8*, Onyx) NAL.

**FREEMARK, NEST (FICTITIOUS CHARACTER)—FICTION**

Brooks, Terry. Angel Fire East. 2000. 384p. mass mkt. 7.99 (*0-345-43525-7*, Del Rey) Ballantine Bks.
—Angel Fire East. unabr. ed. 1999. audio 80.00 (*0-7887-4052-0*, 96159E7, Clipper Audio) Recorded Bks., LLC.
—A Knight of the Word. E-Book 6.99 (*1-58945-521-5*) Adobe Systems, Inc.
—A Knight of the Word. 1999. mass mkt. (*0-345-42942-7*, Ballantine Bks.); 1999. (Trolltown Ser.: Vol. 2). 408p. mass mkt. 6.99 (*0-345-42464-6*); 1998. 25.95 o.s.i (*0-345-43005-0*) Ballantine Bks.
—A Knight of the Word. 2001. E-Book 6.99 (*0-345-44459-0*) Random Hse., Inc.
—A Knight of the Word. unabr. ed. 2000. audio 75.00 (*0-7887-2516-5*, 95589E7) Recorded Bks., LLC.
—Running with the Demon. 1998. (Trolltown Ser.: Vol. 1). 448p. mass mkt. 7.99 (*0-345-42258-9*); 1997. 432p. 5.99 o.s.i (*0-345-37962-4*) Ballantine Bks. (Del Rey).
—Running with the Demon. unabr. ed. 1998. audio 97.00 (*0-7887-2168-2*, 95464E7) Recorded Bks., LLC.

**FREER, FELIX (FICTITIOUS CHARACTER)—FICTION**

Ferrars, E. X. Beware of the Dog. l.t. ed. 1993. (Mystery Ser.). 304p. 29.99 o.p. (*0-7505-0490-0*) Magna Large Print Bks. GBR. *Dist:* Ulverscroft Large Print Bks., Ltd., Ulverscroft Large Print Canada, Ltd.
—Death of a Minor Character. 1983. (Crime Club Ser.). 192p. 11.95 o.p. (*0-385-18839-0*) Doubleday Publishing.
—Death of a Minor Character. l.t. ed. 1984. (Ulverscroft Large Print Ser.). 320p. 12.50 o.p. (*0-7089-1225-7*, Ulverscroft) Thorpe, F. A. Pubs. GBR. *Dist:* Ulverscroft Large Print Bks., Ltd., Ulverscroft Large Print Canada, Ltd.
—Frog in the Throat. 1981. 112p. pap. 1.95 o.p. (*0-553-20040-2*) Bantam Bks.
—Frog in the Throat. 1980. (Crime Club Ser.). 192p. 8.95 o.p. (*0-385-17207-9*) Doubleday Publishing.
—Frog in the Throat. unabr. ed. 1998. audio 54.95 (*0-7531-0239-0*, 980209) ISIS Audio Bks. GBR. *Dist:* Ulverscroft Large Print Bks., Ltd.
—Frog in the Throat. l.t. ed. 1986. (Ulverscroft Large Print Ser.). 304p. 12.50 o.p. (*0-7089-1430-6*, Ulverscroft) Thorpe, F. A. Pubs. GBR. *Dist:* Ulverscroft Large Print Bks., Ltd., Ulverscroft Large Print Canada, Ltd.
—I Met Murder. 1986. (Crime Club Ser.). 192p. 12.95 o.p. (*0-385-23367-1*) Doubleday Publishing.
—I Met Murder. unabr. ed. 1998. audio 49.95 (*0-7531-0408-3*, 970704) ISIS Audio Bks. GBR. *Dist:* Ulverscroft Large Print Bks., Ltd.
—I Met Murder. l.t. ed. 1987. (Ulverscroft Large Print Ser.). 320p. 14.50 o.p. (*0-7089-1586-8*, Ulverscroft) Thorpe, F. A. Pubs. GBR. *Dist:* Ulverscroft Large Print Bks., Ltd., Ulverscroft Large Print Canada, Ltd.
—In at the Kill. 1979. 9.95 o.p. (*0-385-14913-1*) Doubleday Publishing.
—In at the Kill. 1980. 192p. pap. 3.95 o.p. (*0-14-005644-0*, Penguin Bks.) Viking Penguin.
—Last Will & Testament. 1981. 160p. pap. 1.95 o.p. (*0-553-14795-1*) Bantam Bks.
—Last Will & Testament. 1978. 7.95 o.p. (*0-385-14455-5*) Doubleday Publishing.
—Last Will & Testament. unabr. ed. 2001. audio 39.95 (*1-85496-692-8*, 980704) Soundings, Ltd. GBR. *Dist:* Ulverscroft Large Print Bks., Ltd.
—Last Will & Testament. l.t. ed. 1980. 284p. 12.00 o.p. (*0-7089-0505-6*, Ulverscroft) Thorpe, F. A. Pubs. GBR. *Dist:* Ulverscroft Large Print Bks., Ltd.
—Thinner Than Water. unabr. ed. 1993. 39.95 incl. audio (*0-7451-5925-7*, CAT 4063) BBC Audiobooks America.
—Thinner Than Water. 1982. (Crime Club Ser.). 192p. 10.95 o.p. (*0-385-17946-4*) Doubleday Publishing.
—Woman Slaughter. unabr. ed. 2001. audio 49.95 (*1-85089-823-5*, 20891) ISIS Audio Bks. GBR. *Dist:* Ulverscroft Large Print Bks., Ltd.

**FREER, VIRGINIA (FICTITIOUS CHARACTER)—FICTION**

Ferrars, E. X. Beware of the Dog. l.t. ed. 1993. (Mystery Ser.). 304p. 29.99 o.p. (*0-7505-0490-0*) Magna Large Print Bks. GBR. *Dist:* Ulverscroft Large Print Bks., Ltd., Ulverscroft Large Print Canada, Ltd.
—Death of a Minor Character. 1983. (Crime Club Ser.). 192p. 11.95 o.p. (*0-385-18839-0*) Doubleday Publishing.
—Death of a Minor Character. l.t. ed. 1984. (Ulverscroft Large Print Ser.). 320p. 12.50 o.p. (*0-7089-1225-7*, Ulverscroft) Thorpe, F. A. Pubs. GBR. *Dist:* Ulverscroft Large Print Bks., Ltd., Ulverscroft Large Print Canada, Ltd.
—Frog in the Throat. 1981. 112p. pap. 1.95 o.p. (*0-553-20040-2*) Bantam Bks.
—Frog in the Throat. 1980. (Crime Club Ser.). 192p. 8.95 o.p. (*0-385-17207-9*) Doubleday Publishing.
—Frog in the Throat. unabr. ed. 1998. audio 54.95 (*0-7531-0239-0*, 980209) ISIS Audio Bks. GBR. *Dist:* Ulverscroft Large Print Bks., Ltd.
—Frog in the Throat. l.t. ed. 1986. (Ulverscroft Large Print Ser.). 304p. 12.50 o.p. (*0-7089-1430-6*, Ulverscroft) Thorpe, F. A. Pubs. GBR. *Dist:* Ulverscroft Large Print Bks., Ltd., Ulverscroft Large Print Canada, Ltd.
—I Met Murder. 1986. (Crime Club Ser.). 192p. 12.95 o.p. (*0-385-23367-1*) Doubleday Publishing.
—I Met Murder. unabr. ed. 1998. audio 49.95 (*0-7531-0408-3*, 970704) ISIS Audio Bks. GBR. *Dist:* Ulverscroft Large Print Bks., Ltd.
—I Met Murder. l.t. ed. 1987. (Ulverscroft Large Print Ser.). 320p. 14.50 o.p. (*0-7089-1586-8*, Ulverscroft) Thorpe, F. A. Pubs. GBR. *Dist:* Ulverscroft Large Print Bks., Ltd., Ulverscroft Large Print Canada, Ltd.
—In at the Kill. 1979. 9.95 o.p. (*0-385-14913-1*) Doubleday Publishing.
—In at the Kill. 1980. 192p. pap. 3.95 o.p. (*0-14-005644-0*, Penguin Bks.) Viking Penguin.
—Last Will & Testament. 1981. 160p. pap. 1.95 o.p. (*0-553-14795-1*) Bantam Bks.
—Last Will & Testament. 1978. 7.95 o.p. (*0-385-14455-5*) Doubleday Publishing.
—Last Will & Testament. unabr. ed. 2001. audio 39.95 (*1-85496-692-8*, 980704) Soundings, Ltd. GBR. *Dist:* Ulverscroft Large Print Bks., Ltd.
—Last Will & Testament. l.t. ed. 1980. 284p. 12.00 o.p. (*0-7089-0505-6*, Ulverscroft) Thorpe, F. A. Pubs. GBR. *Dist:* Ulverscroft Large Print Bks., Ltd.
—Thinner Than Water. unabr. ed. 1993. 39.95 incl. audio (*0-7451-5925-7*, CAT 4063) BBC Audiobooks America.
—Thinner Than Water. 1982. (Crime Club Ser.). 192p. 10.95 o.p. (*0-385-17946-4*) Doubleday Publishing.
—Woman Slaughter. unabr. ed. 2001. audio 49.95 (*1-85089-823-5*, 20891) ISIS Audio Bks. GBR. *Dist:* Ulverscroft Large Print Bks., Ltd.

**FREERS, LUCY (FICTITIOUS CHARACTER)—FICTION**

Maracotta, Lindsay. The Dead Celeb. 1998. mass mkt. 5.99 (*0-380-72689-0*, Avon Bks.); 1997. 288p. 24.00 o.p. (*0-688-14499-3*, Morrow, William & Co.) Morrow/Avon.
—The Dead Hollywood Moms Society. 320p. 1997. mass mkt. 5.99 (*0-380-72688-2*, Avon Bks.); 1996. 24.00 o.p. (*0-688-14498-5*, Morrow, William & Co.) Morrow/Avon.
—Playing Dead: A Hollywood Mystery. 1999. 288p. 24.00 (*0-688-15867-6*, Morrow, William & Co.) Morrow/Avon.

**FRENCH, NED (FICTITIOUS CHARACTER)—FICTION**

Keating, H. R. F. The Good Detective. unabr. ed. 1995. audio 32.95 (*0-7861-0823-1*, 1646) Blackstone Audio Bks., Inc.
—The Good Detective. l.t. ed. 1996. pap. 21.95 (*1-56895-294-5*, Wheeler Publishing, Inc.) Gale Group.
—The Good Detective. 1995. 208p. 21.00 (*0-684-81522-2*); 20.00 (*1-883402-81-6*) Simon & Schuster. (Scribner).

**FRESHOUR, TOM (FICTITIOUS CHARACTER)—FICTION**

Morgan, Speer. The Freshour Cylinders. 2000. 345p. pap. 13.00 (*1-878448-99-4*); 1998. 245p. 23.00 (*1-878448-84-6*) MacMurray & Beck, Inc.

**FREVISSE, SISTER (FICTITIOUS CHARACTER)—FICTION**

Frazer, Margaret. The Bastard's Tale. 2003. 320p. mass mkt. 6.99 (*0-425-19329-2*) Berkley Publishing Group.
—The Bastard's Tale: A Dame Frevisse Mystery. 2003. (Dame Frevisse Mystery Ser.). 320p. 22.95 (*0-425-18649-0*, Prime Crime) Berkley Publishing Group.
—The Bishop's Tale. 1994. 208p. mass mkt. 6.50 (*0-425-14492-5*, Prime Crime) Berkley Publishing Group.
—The Boy's Tale. 1995. (Dame Frevisse Mystery Ser.). 240p. (Orig.). mass mkt. 6.50 (*0-425-14899-8*) Berkley Publishing Group.
—The Clerk's Tale. 2002. (Dame Frevisse Mystery Ser.). 320p. 22.95 (*0-425-18324-6*); reprint ed. mass mkt. 6.99 (*0-425-18738-1*) Berkley Publishing Group. (Prime Crime).
—The Hunter's Tale. 2004. 336p. 23.95 (*0-425-19401-9*) Berkley Publishing Group.
—The Maiden's Tale. 1998. (Dame Frevisse Mystery Ser.). 256p. mass mkt. 6.99 (*0-425-16407-1*, Prime Crime) Berkley Publishing Group.
—The Murderer's Tale. 1996. 240p. mass mkt. 5.99 o.s.i (*0-425-15406-8*, Prime Crime) Berkley Publishing Group.
—The Novice's Tale. 1993. (Dame Frevisse Mystery Ser.). 240p. (Orig.). mass mkt. 6.99 (*0-425-14321-X*) Berkley Publishing Group.
—The Outlaw's Tale. 224p. 1995. mass mkt. 5.99 o.s.i (*0-425-15119-0*); 1994. mass mkt. 4.50 o.s.i (*0-515-11335-2*, Jove) Berkley Publishing Group.
—The Prioress' Tale. 1997. (Dame Frevisse Mystery Ser.). 256p. mass mkt. 6.99 (*0-425-15944-2*, Prime Crime) Berkley Publishing Group.
—The Reeve's Tale. (Dame Frevisse Mystery Ser.). 288p. 1999. 21.95 o.s.i (*0-425-17232-5*, Prime Crime); 2000. reprint ed. mass mkt. 6.99 (*0-425-17667-3*) Berkley Publishing Group.
—The Reeve's Tale. l.t. ed. 2000. (Basic Ser.). 424p. 27.95 (*0-7862-2548-3*) Thorndike Pr.
—The Servant's Tale. 1993. (Dame Frevisse Mystery Ser.). mass mkt. 6.99 (*0-425-14389-9*); 240p. mass mkt. 4.50 o.s.i (*0-515-11163-5*, Jove) Berkley Publishing Group.
—The Squire's Tale. 2000. (Dame Frevisse Mystery Ser.). 288p. 21.95 o.s.i (*0-425-17678-9*) Berkley Publishing Group.
Frazer, Margaret, et al. The Novice's Tale. 1992. (Orig.). mass mkt. 4.50 o.s.i (*0-515-10900-2*, Jove) Berkley Publishing Group.

**FREY, NATHAN (FICTITIOUS CHARACTER)—FICTION**

Dixon, Stephen. Interstate: A Novel. 1997. 384p. pap. 14.00 o.s.i (*0-8050-5028-0*, Owl Bks.); 1995. 88p. 25.00 o.p. (*0-8050-2654-1*) Holt, Henry & Co.

**FRIEDMAN, KINKY—FICTION**

Friedman, Kinky. Armadillos & Old Lace. 1995. 256p. mass mkt. 7.50 (*0-553-57447-7*) Bantam Bks.
—Armadillos & Old Lace. 1994. 240p. 21.00 (*0-671-86923-X*, Simon & Schuster) Simon & Schuster.
—Blast from the Past. abr. ed. 2002. audio 17.95 (*1-56511-593-7*) HighBridge Co.
—Blast from the Past. 1999. 256p. pap. 15.00 (*0-345-41630-9*) Random Hse., Inc.
—Blast from the Past. 1998. 256p. 23.00 (*0-684-80379-8*, Simon & Schuster) Simon & Schuster.
—Blast from the Past. abr. ed. 1998. audio 17.95 (*1-55935-282-5*, 282-5BK) Soundelux Audio Publishing.
—A Case of Lone Star. 1988. mass mkt. 3.95 o.p. (*0-425-11185-7*) Berkley Publishing Group.
—A Case of Lone Star. 1987. 204p. 14.95 o.p. (*0-688-06410-8*, Morrow, William & Co.) Morrow/Avon.
—Elvis, Jesus & Coca Cola. 1994. 272p. mass mkt. 6.99 (*0-553-56891-4*) Bantam Bks.
—Elvis, Jesus & Coca Cola. 1993. 304p. 20.00 o.p. (*0-671-86922-1*, Simon & Schuster) Simon & Schuster.
—Frequent Flyer. 1990. mass mkt. 6.50 o.s.i (*0-425-12345-6*) Berkley Publishing Group.
—Frequent Flyer. 1989. 204p. 16.95 o.p. (*0-688-08166-5*, Morrow, William & Co.) Morrow/Avon.
—God Bless John Wayne. 1996. 256p. mass mkt. 6.99 (*0-553-57633-X*) Bantam Bks.
—God Bless John Wayne. 1995. 253p. 22.00 o.p. (*0-684-81051-4*, Simon & Schuster) Simon & Schuster.
—Greenwich Killing Time: A Thrilling Murder Mystery. 1987. 240p. mass mkt. 3.95 o.p. (*0-425-10497-4*) Berkley Publishing Group.
—Greenwich Killing Time: A Thrilling Murder Mystery. 1986. 13.95 o.p. (*0-688-06409-4*, Morrow, William & Co.) Morrow/Avon.
—The Love Song of J. Edgar Hoover. abr. ed. 1996. audio 16.95 (*1-55927-412-3*) Audio Renaissance.
—The Love Song of J. Edgar Hoover. 1998. mass mkt. o.p. (*0-345-41510-8*); 1997. 240p. pap. 12.95 (*0-345-41509-4*) Ballantine Bks.
—The Love Song of J. Edgar Hoover. l.t. ed. 1996. pap. 23.95 (*1-56895-394-1*, Wheeler Publishing, Inc.) Gale Group.
—The Love Song of J. Edgar Hoover. 1996. 23.00 (*0-684-80377-1*, Simon & Schuster) Simon & Schuster.
—Meanwhile Back at the Ranch. 2003. (Illus.). 272p. mass mkt. 6.99 (*0-671-04745-0*, Pocket Star); 2002. 208p. 24.00 (*0-684-86488-6*, Simon & Schuster) Simon & Schuster.
—The Mile High Club. unabr. ed. 2000. audio 24.95 (*1-56740-397-2*, 2229, Brilliance Audio Unabridged); 10p. audio 44.25 (*1-56740-943-1*, 2230, Unabridged Library Editions) Brilliance Audio.
—The Mile High Club. 224p. 2000. 23.00 o.s.i (*0-684-86486-X*, Simon & Schuster); 2001. reprint ed. pap. 13.00 (*0-671-04743-4*, Pocket) Simon & Schuster.
—Musical Chairs. 1991. 288p. 18.95 o.p. (*0-688-09148-2*, Morrow, William & Co.) Morrow/Avon.

—Musical Chairs. 1993. 3.99 o.p. (*0-517-10872-0*) Random Hse. Value Publishing.
—Roadkill, abr. ed. 1997. audio 16.95 o.p. (*1-55927-456-5*) Audio Renaissance.
—Roadkill. 1998. 256p. pap. 12.95 (*0-345-41632-5*) Ballantine Bks.
—Roadkill. unabr. ed. 1998. audio 32.00 (*0-7366-4130-0*, 4633) Books on Tape, Inc.
—Roadkill. 1997. 256p. 23.00 o.p. (*0-684-80378-X*, Simon & Schuster) Simon & Schuster.
—Spanking Watson. 224p. 2000. pap. 12.95 (*0-671-04742-6*, Pocket); 1999. 23.00 o.s.i (*0-684-85061-3*, Simon & Schuster); 1999. 23.00 (*0-684-86531-9*, Simon & Schuster) Simon & Schuster.
—Steppin' on a Rainbow. 2001. 208p. 23.00 (*0-684-86487-8*, Simon & Schuster) Simon & Schuster.
—When the Cat's Away. 1989. mass mkt. 3.95 o.p. (*0-425-11830-4*) Berkley Publishing Group.
—When the Cat's Away. 1988. 224p. 16.95 o.p. (*0-688-07555-X*, Morrow, William & Co.) Morrow/Avon.
—When the Cat's Away. 1991. 3.99 o.p. (*0-517-07564-4*) Random Hse. Value Publishing.

**FROST, CYNTHIA (FICTITIOUS CHARACTER)—FICTION**

Murphy, Haughton. A Very Venetian Murder. 1993. mass mkt. 4.50 o.s.i (*0-449-22066-4*, Fawcett) Ballantine Bks.
—A Very Venetian Murder. 1992. 256p. 19.00 o.p. (*0-671-70664-0*, Simon & Schuster) Simon & Schuster.

**FROST, JACK (FICTITIOUS CHARACTER)—FICTION**

Wingfield, R. D. Frost at Christmas. 1995. 288p. mass mkt. 6.50 (*0-553-57168-0*, Crimeline) Bantam Bks.
—Frost at Christmas. unabr. ed. 1997. audio 69.95 ISIS Audio Bks. GBR. *Dist:* Ulverscroft Large Print Bks., Ltd.
—Frost at Christmas. l.t. ed. 1993. (Magna Large Print Ser.). 433p. o.p. (*0-7505-0564-8*) Magna Large Print Bks. GBR. *Dist:* Ulverscroft Large Print Canada, Ltd.
—Frost at Christmas. 2000. (J). pap. 10.95 (*0-552-13981-5*) Transworld Publishers Ltd. GBR. *Dist:* Trafalgar Square.
—Hard Frost. 1995. (Jack Frost Mystery Ser.). 464p. mass mkt. 6.50 (*0-553-57170-2*, Crimeline) Bantam Bks.
—Hard Frost. unabr. ed. 1997. audio 94.95 (*0-7531-0099-1*, 970613) ISIS Audio Bks. GBR. *Dist:* Ulverscroft Large Print Bks., Ltd.
—Hard Frost. l.t. ed. 1997. (Magna Large Print Ser.). 560p. o.p. (*0-7505-1072-2*) Magna Large Print Bks. GBR. *Dist:* Ulverscroft Large Print Canada, Ltd.
—Night Frost. 1995. 368p. mass mkt. 6.99 (*0-553-57167-2*) Bantam Bks.
—Night Frost. l.t. ed. 1993. (Magna Large Print Ser.). 583p. o.p. (*0-7505-0566-4*) Magna Large Print Bks. GBR. *Dist:* Ulverscroft Large Print Canada, Ltd.
—A Touch of Frost. 1995. 368p. mass mkt. 6.50 (*0-553-57169-9*) Bantam Bks.
—A Touch of Frost. unabr. ed. 1997. audio 84.95 ISIS Audio Bks. GBR. *Dist:* Ulverscroft Large Print Bks., Ltd.
—A Touch of Frost. l.t. ed. 1993. (Magna Large Print Ser.). 597p. o.p. (*0-7505-0565-6*) Magna Large Print Bks. GBR. *Dist:* Ulverscroft Large Print Canada, Ltd.
—A Touch of Frost. unabr. ed. 2002. audio compact disk 99.95 (*0-7531-1493-3*) Soundings, Ltd. GBR. *Dist:* Ulverscroft Large Print Bks., Ltd.
—A Touch of Frost. 2000. 426p. pap. 10.95 (*0-552-14555-6*) Transworld Publishers Ltd. GBR. *Dist:* Trafalgar Square.
—Winter Frost. 2000. audio 94.95 (*0-7531-0689-2*, 000202); 14p. audio compact disk 99.95 (*0-7531-0886-0*, 108860) ISIS Audio Bks. GBR. *Dist:* Ulverscroft Large Print Bks., Ltd.
—Winter Frost. l.t. ed. 2000. (Magna Large Print Ser.). 592p. o.p. (*0-7505-1559-7*) Magna Large Print Bks. GBR. *Dist:* Ulverscroft Large Print Canada, Ltd.
—Winter Frost. 2001. 508p. pap. 9.95 (*0-552-14778-8*) Transworld Publishers Ltd. GBR. *Dist:* Trafalgar Square.

**FROST, REUBEN (FICTITIOUS CHARACTER)—FICTION**

Murphy, Haughton. Murder for Lunch. 1987. mass mkt. 2.95 o.s.i (*0-449-21276-9*, Fawcett) Ballantine Bks.
—Murder for Lunch. 1986. 240p. 14.70 o.p. (*0-671-60628-X*, Simon & Schuster) Simon & Schuster.
—Murder for Lunch. l.t. ed. 1990. (Ulverscroft Large Print Ser.). 29.99 o.p. (*0-7089-2225-2*, Ulverscroft) Thorpe, F. A. Pubs. GBR. *Dist:* Ulverscroft Large Print Bks., Ltd., Ulverscroft Large Print Canada, Ltd.
—Murder Keeps a Secret. 1990. 240p. mass mkt. 4.99 o.s.i (*0-449-21788-4*, Fawcett) Ballantine Bks.
—Murder Keeps a Secret. 1989. 16.95 o.p. (*0-671-66981-8*, Simon & Schuster) Simon & Schuster.
—Murder Saves Face. 1992. reprint ed. mass mkt. 3.99 o.s.i (*0-449-22065-6*, Fawcett) Ballantine Bks.
—Murder Saves Face. 1991. 288p. 18.95 o.p. (*0-671-70663-2*, Simon & Schuster) Simon & Schuster.
—Murder Takes a Partner. 1987. 288p. reprint ed. mass mkt. 3.50 o.s.i (*0-449-21434-6*, Fawcett) Ballantine Bks.
—Murder Takes a Partner. 1987. 240p. 15.45 o.p. (*0-671-63422-4*, Simon & Schuster) Simon & Schuster.
—Murder Takes a Partner. l.t. ed. 1990. (Ulverscroft Large Print Ser.). 29.99 o.p. (*0-7089-2158-2*, Ulverscroft) Thorpe, F. A. Pubs. GBR. *Dist:* Ulverscroft Large Print Bks., Ltd., Ulverscroft Large Print Canada, Ltd.
—Murder Times Two. 1990. 17.95 o.p. (*0-671-66982-6*, Simon & Schuster) Simon & Schuster.
—Murder Times Two: A Ruben Frost Mystery. 1991. 256p. mass mkt. 3.95 o.s.i (*0-449-21947-X*, Fawcett) Ballantine Bks.
—Murders & Acquisitions. 1989. mass mkt. 3.95 o.s.i (*0-449-21643-8*, Fawcett) Ballantine Bks.
—Murders & Acquisitions. 1988. 224p. 16.45 o.p. (*0-671-63735-5*, Simon & Schuster) Simon & Schuster.
—A Very Venetian Murder. 1993. mass mkt. 4.50 o.s.i (*0-449-22066-4*, Fawcett) Ballantine Bks.
—A Very Venetian Murder. 1992. 256p. 19.00 o.p. (*0-671-70664-0*, Simon & Schuster) Simon & Schuster.

**FU MANCHU, DOCTOR (FICTITIOUS CHARACTER)—FICTION**

Rohmer, Sax, pseud. The Bride of Fu Manchu. 1976. reprint ed. lib. bdg. 21.95 (*0-89190-801-3*, Rivercity Pr.) Amereon, Ltd.
—Daughter of Fu Manchu. lib. bdg. 22.95 (*0-8488-2112-2*) Amereon, Ltd.
—Drums of Fu Manchu. 20.95 (*0-8488-0619-0*) Amereon, Ltd.
—The Fu Manchu Omnibus. Vol. 1. 1996. 650p. pap. 16.95 (*0-7490-0271-9*); Vol. II. 1997. 656p. pap. 16.95 (*0-7490-0222-0*); Vol. 3. 1998. 650p. pap. 16.95 o.p. (*0-7490-0227-1*); Vol. 4. 1999. pap. 9.95 (*0-7490-0328-6*) Allison & Busby, Ltd. GBR. *Dist:* International Publishers Marketing.
—The Hand of Fu Manchu. Date not set. reprint ed. lib. bdg. 20.95 (*0-89190-802-1*, American Reprint Co.) Amereon, Ltd.
—The Hand of Fu Manchu. unabr. ed. 1994. audio 44.95 (*0-7861-0794-4*, 2132) Blackstone Audio Bks., Inc.
—The Hand of Fu Manchu, Set. unabr. ed. 1994. audio 29.00 Jimcin Recordings.
—The Hand of Fu Manchu. unabr. ed. 2002. audio compact disk 20.00 (*1-4001-5052-3*) Tantor Media, Inc.
—The Hand of Fu Manchu. 2001. 308p. pap. 14.95 (*1-58715-219-3*) Wildside Pr.
—The Insidious Dr. Fu-Manchu. 1976. lib. bdg. 13.95 o.s.i (*0-89968-143-3*, Lightyear Pr.) Buccaneer Bks., Inc.
—The Insidious Dr. Fu-Manchu. 1997. (Dover Classic Mystery Ser.). (Illus.). 224p. pap. 2.00 (*0-486-29898-1*) Dover Pubns., Inc.
—The Insidious Dr. Fu-Manchu. 2002. 244p. 18.99 (*1-4043-0924-1*); per. 13.99 (*1-4043-0925-X*) IndyPublish.com.
—The Insidious Dr. Fu-Manchu. 1985. mass mkt. 3.50 o.s.i (*0-8217-1668-9*) Kensington Publishing Corp.
—The Insidious Dr. Fu-Manchu. E-Book 1.95 (*1-57799-899-5*) Logos Research Systems, Inc.
—The Insidious Dr. Fu-Manchu. E-Book 5.00 (*0-7410-0442-9*) SoftBook Pr.
—The Island of Fu Manchu. 1986. 320p. mass mkt. 3.50 o.p. (*0-8217-1912-2*, Zebra Bks.) Kensington Publishing Corp.
—The Mask of Fu Manchu. 1976. reprint ed. lib. bdg. 21.95 (*0-89190-803-X*, Rivercity Pr.) Amereon, Ltd.
—The Mask of Fu Manchu. 1985. 362 p. (*0-89621-588-1*) BBC Audiobooks America.
—The Mystery of Dr. Fu Manchu. Date not set. pap. text (*0-17-556692-5*) Addison-Wesley Longman, Inc.
—The Mystery of Dr. Fu Manchu. l.t. ed. 1994. 18.95 o.p. (*0-7451-6454-4*); 1992. 248p. reprint ed. 14.95 o.p. (*0-86220-837-8*, Black Dagger) BBC Audiobooks America.
—The Return of Dr. Fu-Manchu. 20.95 (*0-89190-828-5*) Amereon, Ltd.
—The Return of Dr. Fu-Manchu. 1976. lib. bdg. 13.95 (*0-89968-141-7*, Lightyear Pr.) Buccaneer Bks., Inc.
—The Return of Dr. Fu-Manchu. E-Book 1.95 (*1-57799-900-2*) Logos Research Systems, Inc.
—Shadow of Fu Manchu. 1986. 272p. mass mkt. 3.50 o.p. (*0-8217-1870-3*, Zebra Bks.) Kensington Publishing Corp.
—Trail of Fu Manchu. 25.95 (*0-8488-0317-5*) Amereon, Ltd.
—Trail of Fu Manchu. 1985. mass mkt. 3.50 o.s.i (*0-8217-1619-0*) Kensington Publishing Corp.

**FULLER, JOSEPHINE (FICTITIOUS CHARACTER)—FICTION**

Murray, Lynne. At Large. 2002. 288p. mass mkt. 6.50 (*0-312-98004-3*, St. Martin's Paperbacks); 2001. 260p. 23.95 (*0-312-28029-7*, Saint Martin's Minotaur); 2001. 287.40 (*0-312-28026-2*, Saint Martin's Minotaur) St. Martin's Pr.
—Large Target: A Josephine Fuller Mystery. E-Book 6.50 (*0-312-27388-6*); 2001. 304p. mass mkt. 6.50 (*0-312-97537-6*, St. Martin's Paperbacks); 2000. viii, 258p. 23.95 (*0-312-25456-3*, Saint Martin's Minotaur) St. Martin's Pr.
—Larger Than Death: A Josephine Fuller Mystery. 1997. 300p. 23.00 (*0-9642949-0-7*) Orloff Pr.
—Larger Than Death: A Josephine Fuller Mystery. 2000. (Josephine Fuller Mystery Ser.). 304p. mass mkt. 5.99 (*0-312-97277-6*, St. Martin's Paperbacks) St. Martin's Pr.
—A Ton of Trouble. mass mkt. (*0-312-98467-7*, St. Martin's Paperbacks); E-Book 21.95 (*0-312-70744-4*); 2002. 160p. 22.95 (*0-312-30077-8*, Saint Martin's Minotaur) St. Martin's Pr.

**FURNESS, JACK (FICTITIOUS CHARACTER)—FICTION**

Kerr, Philip. Esau. 1998. 448p. mass mkt. 8.99 o.s.i (*0-7704-2762-6*) Bantam Bks.
—Esau. 1996. (Illus.). 356 p. (*0-7011-6281-3*) Chatto & Windus.
—Esau. l.t. ed. 1997. (Wheeler Large Print Book Ser.). 26.95 (*1-56895-447-6*, Wheeler Publishing, Inc.) Gale Group.
—Esau. 1997. 384p. 22.50 o.s.i (*0-8050-5175-9*) Holt, Henry & Co.
—Esau. 1998. 406p. mass mkt. 6.99 (*0-671-01992-9*, Pocket) Simon & Schuster.

**FURY, NELL (FICTITIOUS CHARACTER)—FICTION**

Pincus, Elizabeth. The Hangdog Hustle. 1995. (Neil Fury Ser.). 205p. (Orig.). pap. 9.95 (*1-883523-05-2*) Spinsters Ink Bks.
—The Solitary Twist. 1993. (Neil Fury Ser.). 225p. (Orig.). pap. 9.95 (*0-933216-93-9*) Spinsters Ink Bks.
—The Two Bit Tango. 1992. (Neil Fury Ser.). (Illus.). 193p. (Orig.). pap. 9.95 (*0-933216-88-2*) Spinsters Ink Bks.

**FURY, NICK (FICTITIOUS CHARACTER)—FICTION**

Goodwin, Archie & Chaykin, Howard. Wolverine - Nick Fury: Scorpio Connection. 64p. 1989. 16.95 (*0-87135-577-9*); 1990. (Illus.). reprint ed. pap. 12.95 o.p. (*0-87135-662-7*) Marvel Enterprises.
Harras, Bob, et al. Nick Fury vs. S. H. I. E. L. D. 1989. (Illus.). 276p. pap. 15.95 o.p. (*0-87135-554-X*) Marvel Enterprises.
Murray, Will. Nick Fury, Agent of Shield: Empyre. 2000. (Nick Fury, Agent of Shield Ser.). (Illus.). 304p. mass mkt. 6.50 (*0-425-16816-6*) Berkley Publishing Group.
Steranko, Jim. Nick Fury: Scorpio. 2000. (Illus.). 96p. 14.95 (*0-7851-0766-5*) Marvel Enterprises.
—Nick Fury, Agent of S. H. I. E. L. D. 2000. (Marvels Finest Ser.). (Illus.). 248p. pap. 17.95 (*0-7851-0747-9*, Marvel's Finest) Marvel Enterprises.

**FYFE, DAVID (FICTITIOUS CHARACTER)—FICTION**

Paul, William. Sleeping Dogs. 1995. 192p. 19.95 o.p. (*0-312-13603-X*, Saint Martin's Minotaur) St. Martin's Pr.
—Sleeping Partner. 1997. 192p. 19.95 o.p. (*0-312-15208-6*, Saint Martin's Minotaur) St. Martin's Pr.
—Sleeping Pretty. 1996. 192p. 19.95 o.p. (*0-312-14418-0*, Saint Martin's Minotaur) St. Martin's Pr.

## G

**G-8 (FICTITIOUS CHARACTER)—FICTION**

Hogan, Robert J. High Adventure: G-8 & His Battle Aces - White Wings for the Dead. Gunnison, John P., ed. & intro. by. 41st num. ed. 1998. (High Adventure Ser.: Vol. 41). (Illus.). 96p. per. 6.00 (*1-886937-28-1*) Adventure Hse.

**GABLE, CLARK, 1901-1960—FICTION**

Baxt, George. The Clark Gable & Carole Lombard Murder Case. 1997. 208p. 20.95 o.p. (*0-312-16799-7*, Saint Martin's Minotaur) St. Martin's Pr.

**GABRIEL, MATT (FICTITIOUS CHARACTER)—FICTION**

Gosling, Paula. The Body in Blackwater Bay. 1992. 304p. 17.95 (*0-89296-459-6*) Mysterious Pr.
—The Body in Blackwater Bay. 1993. 288p. mass mkt. 4.99 o.s.i (*0-446-40319-9*) Warner Bks., Inc.
—The Dead of Winter. 1997. 316p. mass mkt. o.s.i (*0-7515-1678-3*); 1995. 320p. o.s.i (*0-316-91238-7*) Little Brown & Co.
—The Dead of Winter. 1996. 82p. 21.95 o.p. (*0-89296-511-8*) Mysterious Pr.
—The Dead of Winter. 1997. 304p. mass mkt. 5.99 (*0-446-40499-3*) Warner Bks., Inc.
—A Few Dying Words. l.t. ed. 1994. 460p. pap. 19.95 (*0-8161-7482-2*, Macmillan Reference USA) Gale Group.
—A Few Dying Words. 1994. 352p. 18.95 o.s.i (*0-89296-510-X*) Mysterious Pr.
—A Few Dying Words. 1996. 320p. mass mkt. 5.99 o.s.i (*0-446-40460-8*) Warner Bks., Inc.

**GAIRDEN FAMILY (FICTITIOUS CHARACTERS)—FICTION**

Johnston, Coleen L. Guardians. 1994. (Gairden Legacy Ser.: No. 2). mass mkt. 4.99 o.p. (*0-312-95125-6*, St. Martin's Paperbacks) St. Martin's Pr.
—Inheritors. 1994. 340p. pap. text 4.99 o.p. (*0-312-95284-8*, St. Martin's Paperbacks) St. Martin's Pr.
Johnston, Colleen L. Founders. 1993. mass mkt. 4.99 o.p. (*0-312-95060-8*, St. Martin's Paperbacks) St. Martin's Pr.

**GALERAN DE LESNEVEN (FICTITIOUS CHARACTER)—FICTION**

Moore, Viviane. A Black Romance. 2002. (Illus.). 197p. mass mkt. 7.95 (*0-7528-4417-2*) Trafalgar Square.
—Blue Blood. 2002. (Illus.). v, 215p. mass mkt. 7.95 (*0-575-40319-5*) Trafalgar Square.
—The Darkest Red. 2002. (Illus.). 230p. mass mkt. 7.95 (*0-7528-4475-X*) Trafalgar Square.
—The White Path. Hunter, Adriana, tr. from FRE. 2003. (Illus.). 226p. pap. 13.95 (*0-575-07327-6*) Orion Publishing Group, Ltd. GBR. *Dist:* Trafalgar Square.

**GALINDO, DANIEL (FICTITIOUS CHARACTER)—FICTION**

Parker, Barbara. Criminal Justice. 1997. 320p. 22.95 o.p. (*0-525-93977-6*) Dutton/Plume.
—Criminal Justice. l.t. ed. 1997. 26.95 (*1-56895-498-0*, Wheeler Publishing, Inc.) Gale Group.
—Criminal Justice. 1998. 448p. mass mkt. 6.99 (*0-451-18474-2*, Signet Bks.) NAL.

**GALLAGHER, GORDON (FICTITIOUS CHARACTER)—FICTION**

Savarin, Julian J. Naja: A "Gallagher" Novel. 1993. 336p. mass mkt. 4.99 o.p. (*0-06-100475-8*, HarperTorch) Morrow/Avon.
—Naja: A "Gallagher" Novel. 1989. 256p. 16.95 o.p. (*0-312-03969-7*) St. Martin's Pr.
—Queensland File. 1994. 432p. mass mkt. 4.50 o.p. (*0-06-100683-1*, HarperTorch) Morrow/Avon.
—Queensland File. 1999. 420p. 26.00 (*0-7278-5445-3*) Severn Hse. Pubs., Ltd.
—Quiraing List. 1993. 432p. mass mkt. 4.99 o.p. (*0-06-100431-6*, HarperTorch) Morrow/Avon.
—Villiger. 384p. 26.00 (*0-7278-5517-4*) Severn Hse. Pubs., Ltd.
—Villiger. 1991. 18.95 o.p. (*0-312-05532-3*) St. Martin's Pr.
—Water Hole. 1993. 448p. mass mkt. 4.99 o.p. (*0-06-100654-8*, HarperTorch) Morrow/Avon.
—Water Hole. 1984. 13.95 o.p. (*0-312-85768-3*) St. Martin's Pr.
—Windshear. 1992. 352p. mass mkt. 4.50 o.p. (*0-06-100432-4*, HarperTorch) Morrow/Avon.
—Wolf Run. 1992. 464p. mass mkt. 4.50 o.p. (*0-06-100474-X*, HarperTorch) Morrow/Avon.
—Wolf Run. 1994. 2.99 o.p. (*0-517-12527-7*) Random Hse. Value Publishing.
—Wolf Run. 1991. 288p. 19.95 (*0-8027-1148-0*) Walker & Co.

**GALLAGHER, MARTIN (FICTITIOUS CHARACTER)—FICTION**

Lindsey, David L. Black Gold, Red Death. 1986. 256p. mass mkt. 5.99 o.s.i (*0-449-13121-1*, Fawcett) Ballantine Bks.

**GALLEGO, GEORGE (FICTITIOUS CHARACTER)—FICTION**

Riker, H. J. Duty's Call. 2000. (SEALs, the Warrior Breed Ser.: Vol. 8). 416p. mass mkt. 6.99 (*0-380-79508-6*, Avon Bks.) Morrow/Avon.

**GALLOWAY, THERESA (FICTITIOUS CHARACTER)—FICTION**

Grimes, Terris M. Blood Will Tell. 1997. 272p. mass mkt. 5.50 o.s.i (*0-451-40696-6*, Onyx) NAL.
—Somebody Else's Child. 1996. 272p. mass mkt. 5.99 o.s.i (*0-451-18672-9*, Signet Bks.) NAL.

**GALLOWAY, TILLER (FICTITIOUS CHARACTER)—FICTION**

Poyer, David. Bahamas Blue: A Tiller Galloway Thriller. 1992. mass mkt. 5.99 (*0-312-92846-7*, St. Martin's Paperbacks); 1991. 17.95 o.p. (*0-312-04858-0*) St. Martin's Pr.

—Down to a Sunless Sea: A Tiller Galloway Underwater Thriller. 1998. (Down to a Sunless Sea Ser.: Vol. 1). 368p. mass mkt. 5.99 (*0-312-96407-2*, St. Martin's Paperbacks); 1996. 352p. 23.95 o.p. (*0-312-14589-6*) St. Martin's Pr.

—Hatteras Blue: A Tiller Galloway Underwater Thriller. 1992. 288p. mass mkt. 5.99 (*0-312-92749-5*, St. Martin's Paperbacks); 1989. 16.95 o.p. (*0-312-02926-8*) St. Martin's Pr.

—Louisiana Blue: A Tiller Gallaway Underwater Thriller. 1994. 304p. 22.00 o.p. (*0-312-10494-4*); Vol. 1. 1995. (Louisiana Blue Ser.: Vol. 1). mass mkt. 5.99 (*0-312-95422-0*, St. Martin's Paperbacks) St. Martin's Pr.

## GALLOWGLASS, MAGNUS (FICTITIOUS CHARACTER)—FICTION

Stasheff, Christopher. M'Lady Witch. 1994. 256p. (Orig.). mass mkt. 5.99 o.s.i (*0-441-00113-0*) Ace Bks.

—Quicksilver's Knight. 1995. (Ace Fantasy Ser.). 288p. (Orig.). mass mkt. 5.50 o.s.i (*0-441-00229-3*) Ace Bks.

—A Wizard in Absentia. 1993. 272p. (Orig.). mass mkt. 5.99 o.s.i (*0-441-51569-X*) Ace Bks.

—A Wizard in Chaos. 1997. (Chronicles of the Rogue Wizard Ser.: Vol. 5). 256p. 21.95 (*0-312-86032-3*, Tor Bks.) Doherty, Tom Assocs., LLC.

—A Wizard in Midgard. 256p. 1999. mass mkt. 5.99 (*0-8125-4927-9*); 1998. (Chronicles of the Rogue Wizard Ser.: Vol. 6). 21.95 (*0-312-86033-1*) Doherty, Tom Assocs., LLC. (Tor Bks.).

## GALLOWGLASS, ROD (FICTITIOUS CHARACTER)—FICTION

Stasheff, Christopher. Escape Velocity. 1987. 256p. mass mkt. 4.99 o.s.i (*0-441-21603-X*); 1986. mass mkt. 2.95 o.s.i (*0-441-21602-1*); 1984. mass mkt. 2.95 o.s.i (*0-441-21600-5*); 1983. mass mkt. 2.95 o.s.i (*0-441-21599-8*) Ace Bks.

—Escape Velocity. 1984. 256p. mass mkt. 2.95 o.s.i (*0-441-21601-3*, Diamond Bks.) Berkley Publishing Group.

—King Kobold Revived. 1986. 224p. mass mkt. 4.99 o.s.i (*0-441-44491-1*); 1985. mass mkt. 2.95 o.s.i (*0-441-44489-X*); 1984. mass mkt. 2.95 o.s.i (*0-441-44488-1*) Ace Bks.

—King Kobold Revived. 1986. 224p. mass mkt. 2.95 o.s.i (*0-441-44490-3*, Diamond Bks.) Berkley Publishing Group.

—Warlock & Son. 1991. mass mkt. 5.99 o.s.i (*0-441-87314-6*) Ace Bks.

—The Warlock Enraged. 1986. 256p. reprint ed. mass mkt. 5.50 o.s.i (*0-441-87334-0*) Ace Bks.

—The Warlock Enraged. 1985. 256p. mass mkt. 2.95 o.s.i (*0-441-87340-5*, Diamond Bks.) Berkley Publishing Group.

—The Warlock Heretical. 1987. 224p. mass mkt. 4.99 o.s.i (*0-441-87286-7*) Ace Bks.

—The Warlock in Spite of Himself. mass mkt. 3.50 o.s.i (*0-441-87306-5*); 1986. mass mkt. 5.50 o.s.i (*0-441-87337-5*); 1985. 384p. mass mkt. 3.50 o.s.i (*0-441-87305-7*); 1984. mass mkt. 2.95 o.s.i (*0-441-87304-9*); 1982. mass mkt. 2.95 o.s.i (*0-441-87303-0*); 1982. 384p. mass mkt. 2.75 (*0-441-87302-2*); 1998. (Illus.). 384p. reprint ed. pap. 13.00 o.s.i (*0-441-00560-8*) Ace Bks.

—The Warlock in Spite of Himself. Del Ray, Lester, ed. 1975. (Library of Science Fiction). lib. bdg. 21.00 o.p. (*0-8240-1436-7*) Garland Publishing, Inc.

—The Warlock Insane. 1989. 256p. mass mkt. 4.99 o.s.i (*0-441-87364-2*) Ace Bks.

—The Warlock Missing. 1986. (Warlock Ser.: Vol. 7). 208p. reprint ed. mass mkt. 4.99 o.s.i (*0-441-84826-5*) Ace Bks.

—The Warlock Rock. 1990. 288p. mass mkt. 5.99 o.s.i (*0-441-87313-8*) Ace Bks.

—The Warlock Unlocked. 1986. 288p. mass mkt. 4.99 o.s.i (*0-441-87332-4*); 1984. mass mkt. 2.95 o.s.i (*0-441-87329-4*); 1983. mass mkt. 2.95 o.s.i (*0-441-87328-6*); 1982. mass mkt. 2.75 o.s.i (*0-441-87325-1*) Ace Bks.

—The Warlock Unlocked. 1985. 288p. mass mkt. 2.95 o.s.i (*0-441-87330-8*, Diamond Bks.) Berkley Publishing Group.

—The Warlock Wandering. 304p. 1987. mass mkt. 4.99 o.s.i (*0-441-87362-6*); 1986. mass mkt. 3.50 o.s.i (*0-441-87361-8*) Ace Bks.

—The Warlock's Companion. 1988. 240p. mass mkt. 4.99 o.s.i (*0-441-87341-3*) Ace Bks.

## GAMADGE, CLARA (FICTITIOUS CHARACTER)—FICTION

Boylan, Eleanor. Murder Crossed: A Clara Gamadge Mystery. 1996. 88p. 20.00 o.p. (*0-8050-3922-8*) Holt, Henry & Co.

—Murder Machree. 1993. (Florida Mysteries Ser.). reprint ed. mass mkt. 4.50 o.s.i (*0-8041-1012-3*, Ivy Bks.) Ballantine Bks.

—Murder Machree: A Clara Gamadge Mystery. 1992. (Clara Gamadge Mystery Ser.). 176p. 18.95 o.p. (*0-8050-1969-3*) Holt, Henry & Co.

—Murder Observed. 1992. mass mkt. 4.99 o.s.i (*0-8041-0812-9*, Ivy Bks.) Ballantine Bks.

—Murder Observed: A Clara Gamadge Mystery. 1990. 176p. 16.95 o.p. (*0-8050-1276-1*) Holt, Henry & Co.

—Pushing Murder. 1994. (Florida Mysteries Ser.). mass mkt. 4.99 o.s.i (*0-8041-1251-7*, Ivy Bks.) Ballantine Bks.

—Pushing Murder: A Clara Gamadge Mystery. 1993. 160p. 19.95 o.p. (*0-8050-1970-7*) Holt, Henry & Co.

—Working Murder. 1992. mass mkt. 5.99 o.s.i (*0-8041-0813-7*, Ivy Bks.) Ballantine Bks.

—Working Murder. 1989. 160p. 16.95 o.p. (*0-8050-1030-0*) Holt, Henry & Co.

—Working Murder. 1993. audio. audio 35.40 (*1-56544-002-1*, 250001) Literate Ear, Inc.

## GAMADGE, HENRY (FICTITIOUS CHARACTER)—FICTION

Daly, Elizabeth. And Dangerous to Know. 1984. 176p. pap. 2.95 o.p. (*0-553-24616-X*) Bantam Bks.

—And Dangerous to Know. 1991. 9.95 o.p. (*0-8050-0805-5*) Holt, Henry & Co.

—Any Shape or Form. 1981. (Murder Ink Mystery Ser.: No. 27). pap. 2.25 o.p. (*0-440-10108-5*) Dell Publishing.

—Arrow Pointing Nowhere. 1983. pap. 3.25 o.p. (*0-440-10021-6*) Dell Publishing.

—The Book of the Lion. 1985. 160p. pap. 2.95 o.p. (*0-553-24883-9*) Bantam Bks.

—The Book of the Lion. 1950. 9.95 o.p. (*0-8050-0806-3*) Holt, Henry & Co.

—Deadly Nightshade. 1993. audio 44.20 (*1-56544-034-X*, 250013); audio Literate Ear, Inc.

—Death & Letters. 1981. pap. 2.25 o.p. (*0-440-11791-7*) Dell Publishing.

—Death & Letters. Barzun, Jacques & Taylor, W. H., eds. 1982. (Crime Fiction 1950-1975 Ser.). 131p. lib. bdg. 18.00 o.p. (*0-8240-4979-9*) Garland Publishing, Inc.

—The House Without the Door. 1984. 192p. pap. 2.95 o.p. (*0-553-24610-0*) Bantam Bks.

—Murders in Volume Two: A Henry Gamadge Mystery. 1993. audio 41.00 (*1-56544-054-4*, 250016); audio Literate Ear, Inc.

—Murders in Volume Two: A Henry Gamadge Mystery. 1994. 320p. reprint ed. pap. 6.95 (*1-883402-52-2*, Scribner) Simon & Schuster.

—Night Walk. 1982. (Murder Ink Mystery Ser.: No. 55). pap. 2.50 o.p. (*0-440-16609-8*) Dell Publishing.

—Nothing Can Rescue Me. 1984. 192p. pap. 2.95 o.p. (*0-553-24605-4*) Bantam Bks.

—Somewhere in the House. 1984. 192p. pap. 2.95 o.p. (*0-553-24267-9*) Bantam Bks.

—Unexpected Night: A Henry Gamadge Mystery. 1986. (Mystery Ser.). 224p. pap. 2.95 o.p. (*0-553-25129-5*) Bantam Bks.

—Unexpected Night: A Henry Gamadge Mystery. 1991. 9.95 o.p. (*0-8050-0807-1*) Holt, Henry & Co.

—Unexpected Night: A Henry Gamadge Mystery. 1993. audio. audio 39.20 (*1-56544-033-1*, 250003) Literate Ear, Inc.

—Unexpected Night: A Henry Gamadge Mystery. 1995. pap. 6.95 (*1-883402-14-X*); 1994. 240p. reprint ed. per. 7.00 (*1-883402-51-4*) Simon & Schuster. (Scribner).

—The Wrong Way Down. 1986. mass mkt. 9.95 o.p. (*0-553-06515-7*) Bantam Bks.

## GAMBAR, JIMMY (FICTITIOUS CHARACTER)—FICTION

Carillo, Charles. My Ride with Gus. 256p. 1997. pap. 5.99 (*0-671-53569-2*, Pocket Star); 1996. 22.00 (*0-671-53568-4*, Atria) Simon & Schuster.

## GARAK (FICTITIOUS CHARACTER)—FICTION

Robinson, Andrew J. A Stitch in Time. (Star Trek Deep Space Nine Ser.: No. 27). E-Book 6.95 (*0-7434-2058-6*); 2000. (Illus.). 432p. pap. 6.50 (*0-671-03885-0*) Simon & Schuster. (Star Trek).

A Stitch in Time. 2000. per. 6.50 (*0-7434-1111-0*, Pocket) Simon & Schuster.

## GARCIA, LUPE (FICTITIOUS CHARACTER)—FICTION

Allyn, Doug. The Cheerio Killings. 1989. 256p. 22.95 o.p. (*0-312-03302-8*, Saint Martin's Minotaur) St. Martin's Pr.

—Motown Underground. 1993. 233p. 17.95 o.p. (*0-312-08851-5*, Saint Martin's Minotaur) St. Martin's Pr.

## GARCIA, RICHARD (FICTITIOUS CHARACTER)—FICTION

Stekel, Peter. The Flower Lover. pap. 17.11 (*0-7596-1163-7*) 1stBooks Library.

## GARCIA FAMILY (FICTITIOUS CHARACTERS)—FICTION

Alvarez, Julia. How the Garcia Girls Lost Their Accents. 1999. 308p. (YA). (ps up). 17.95 (*0-945575-57-2*, 71557) Algonquin Bks. of Chapel Hill.

—How the Garcia Girls Lost Their Accents. 1992. (Contemporary Fiction Ser.). (Illus.). 304p. pap. 14.00 (*0-452-26806-0*) Dutton/Plume.

—How the Garcia Girls Lost Their Accents. 1997. (C). pap. text o.p. (*0-8013-3147-1*) Longman Publishing Group.

—Yo! 1999. 350p. tchr. ed. 18.95 (*1-56512-157-0*, 72157) Algonquin Bks. of Chapel Hill.

—Yo! 1999. (SPA.). 416p. pap. 16.95 (*0-452-28140-7*); 1997. 320p. pap. 14.00 (*0-452-27918-6*, Plume) Dutton/Plume.

—Yo! l.t. ed. 2003. (Spanish Language Ser.). (SPA.). 28.95 (*0-7862-5190-5*) Thorndike Pr.

—Yo! 1997. 19.00 (*0-606-22212-X*) Turtleback Bks.

## GARDNER, ERLE STANLEY, 1889-1970—FICTION

Nolan, William F. Marble Orchard. 1995. 224p. 20.95 o.p. (*0-312-14011-8*, Saint Martin's Minotaur) St. Martin's Pr.

—Sharks Never Sleep. unabr. ed. 1999. audio 44.95 (*0-7861-1629-3*, 2457) Blackstone Audio Bks., Inc.

—Sharks Never Sleep. 1998. 288p. 22.95 o.p. (*0-312-19331-9*, Saint Martin's Minotaur) St. Martin's Pr.

Nolan, William F., ed. The Black Mask Boys: Masters in the Hard-Boiled School of Detective Fiction. 1984. 288p. 16.95 o.p. (*0-688-03966-9*, Morrow, William & Co.) Morrow/Avon.

—The Black Mask Boys: Masters in the Hard-Boiled School of Detective Fiction. 1987. 272p. reprint ed. 8.95 o.p. (*0-89296-931-8*) Mysterious Pr.

—The Black Mask Murders. 1994. 224p. 19.95 o.p. (*0-312-10942-3*, Saint Martin's Minotaur) St. Martin's Pr.

## GARDNER, NICK (FICTITIOUS CHARACTER)—FICTION

Lankford, Terrill. Shooters. 224p. 1998. mass mkt. 5.99 (*0-8125-5538-4*); 1996. 20.95 o.p. (*0-312-86272-5*) Doherty, Tom Assocs., LLC. (Forge Bks.).

—Shooters. abr. ed. 1997. audio 17.00 (*1-56876-068-X*) Soundlines Entertainment, Inc.

## GARDNER, STEVE (FICTITIOUS CHARACTER)—FICTION

Harper, Brian. Deadly Pursuit. 1995. 400p. (Orig.). mass mkt. 5.99 o.s.i (*0-451-18198-0*, Signet Bks.) NAL.

## GARFIELD (FICTITIOUS CHARACTER)—FICTION

Acey, Mark. Garfield's Christmas Tales. 1995. 10.15 o.p. (*0-606-07557-7*) Turtleback Bks.

Braun, Debra S. Garfield Collectibles. 1998. (Illus.). 152p. pap. 29.95 (*0-7643-0547-6*) Schiffer Publishing, Ltd.

Davis, Jim. Crazy about Numbers: Games & Sticker Fun. 1998. pap. (*2-922148-27-0*) Modus Vivendi.

—The Eighth Garfield Treasury. 1995. 128p. pap. 13.95 (*0-345-39778-9*) Ballantine Bks.

—The Fifth Garfield Treasury. 1989. (Illus.). 128p. pap. 14.00 (*0-345-36268-3*) Ballantine Bks.

—The Fourth Garfield Treasury. 1987. 128p. pap. 14.00 (*0-345-34726-9*) Ballantine Bks.

—Garfield: Food for Thought. 1987. (Garfield Ser.: Vol. 13). 128p. pap. 7.95 (*0-345-34129-5*) Ballantine Bks.

—Garfield: Food for Thought. 1987. (Illus.). (J). pap. 2.95 o.s.i (*0-440-82192-4*) Dell Publishing.

—Garfield: Survival of the Fattest: His 40th Book. 2004. (Garfield Ser.: Bk. 40). 96p. pap. 10.95 (*0-345-46458-3*) Ballantine Bks.

—Garfield: The Best Things in Life Are Edible. 1995. (Cartoon Bks.). (Illus.). 80p. 4.95 (*0-8362-0563-4*) Andrews McMeel Publishing.

—Garfield A to Z Zoo. 1984. (Garfield Mini-Storybook Ser.). (Illus.). 24p. (J). (ps-5). 1.25 o.s.i (*0-394-86483-2*, Random Hse. Bks. for Young Readers) Random Hse. Children's Bks.

—Garfield Activity Book. 1996. (Happy House Coloring Ser.). pap. 10.00 o.p. (*0-394-88551-1*, Random Hse. Bks. for Young Readers) Random Hse. Children's Bks.

—Garfield Alphabet Soup: Games & Sticker Fun. 1998. (Garfield Ser.). (J). pap. text (*2-922148-26-2*) Presses aventure/Adventure Pr.

—Garfield America, 8, Set. 1992. (J). 79.60 o.s.i (*0-448-40409-5*, Grosset & Dunlap) Penguin Putnam Bks. for Young Readers.

—Garfield & the Beast in the Basement. 1998. (J). 9.10 (*0-606-13411-5*) Turtleback Bks.

—Garfield & the Mysterious Mummy. 1998. (J). 9.10 (*0-606-13412-3*) Turtleback Bks.

—Garfield & the Tiger. 1990. (Golden Easy Readers Ser.: Level 2). (Illus.). 40p. (J). (gr. k-2). pap. 4.50 o.s.i (*0-307-11688-3*, Golden Bks.) Random Hse. Children's Bks.

—Garfield & the Tooth Fairy. 1998. (Garfield Ser.). (Illus.). 52p. (ps-4). pap. text (*2-922148-37-8*) Presses aventure/Adventure Pr.

—Garfield & the Wicked Wizard. 2001. (Planet Reader Ser.). (Illus.). (J). 9.10 (*0-606-21208-6*) Turtleback Bks.

—Garfield at Large: His First Book. 1984. (Garfield Ser.: Vol. 1). 128p. pap. 6.95 o.s.i (*0-345-32013-1*) Ballantine Bks.

—Garfield at Large: His First Book. 1980. (J). 13.00 (*0-606-03063-8*) Turtleback Bks.

—Garfield-Beach Key Lock Diary. 1988. (J). 9.98 o.p. (*0-89954-900-4*) Antioch Publishing Co.

—Garfield-Beach Photo Album. 1988. (J). 8.98 o.p. (*0-89954-901-2*) Antioch Publishing Co.

—Garfield Beefs Up: His 37th Book. 2000. (Garfield Ser.: Vol. 37). (Illus.). 96p. pap. 10.95 (*0-345-44109-5*, Ballantine Bks.) Ballantine Bks.

—Garfield Bigger & Better. 1996. (Garfield Ser.: Vol. 30). 128p. pap. 7.95 (*0-345-40770-9*) Ballantine Bks.

—Garfield, Bigger Than Life. 1981. (J). 13.00 (*0-606-02987-7*) Turtleback Bks.

—Garfield Bigger Than Life: His Third Book, Vol. 3. 1984. (Garfield Ser.: Vol. 3). 128p. pap. 6.95 o.s.i (*0-345-32007-7*) Ballantine Bks.

—Garfield Birthday Greetings, Vol. 3. 1990. (Postcard Bks.: No. 3). (Illus.). 64p. pap. 7.95 o.s.i (*0-345-36771-5*) Ballantine Bks.

—Garfield by the Pound. 1992. (Garfield Ser.: Vol. 22). 128p. pap. 7.95 (*0-345-37579-3*) Ballantine Bks.

—Garfield Chews the Fat. 1989. (Garfield Ser.: Vol. 17). 128p. pap. 7.95 (*0-345-35956-9*) Ballantine Bks.

—A Garfield Christmas. (Garfield Ser.). (Illus.). 1997. 192p. pap. 10.95 o.s.i (*0-345-42042-X*); 1987. 64p. pap. 5.95 o.s.i (*0-345-35368-4*) Ballantine Bks.

—Garfield Discovers America. 1992. 32p. (J). 9.95 o.s.i (*0-448-40257-2*, Grosset & Dunlap) Penguin Putnam Bks. for Young Readers.

—Garfield Dishes It Out. 1995. (Garfield Ser.: Vol. 27). (Illus.). 128p. pap. 7.95 (*0-345-39287-6*) Ballantine Bks.

—Garfield Eats His Heart Out. 2003. 96p. pap. 10.95 (*0-345-46459-1*); 1984. (Garfield Ser.: Vol. 6). (Illus.). 128p. pap. 7.95 (*0-345-32018-2*); 1983. pap. 4.95 o.s.i (*0-345-30912-X*) Ballantine Bks.

—Garfield Eats His Heart Out. 1983. (J). 13.00 (*0-606-02986-9*) Turtleback Bks.

—Garfield Fat Cat, 3 vols. (Garfield Ser.: Vol. 3). 384p. Vol. 1. 1993. (Illus.). pap. 9.95 o.s.i (*0-345-38385-0*); Vol. 2. 1994. (Illus.). pap. 10.95 (*0-345-39192-6*); Vol. 3. 1995. pap. 9.95 o.s.i (*0-345-39393-7*); Vol. 3. 1995. (Illus.). pap. 10.95 (*0-345-39493-3*); Vol. 4. 1995. (Illus.). pap. 10.95 (*0-345-40238-3*); Vol. 5. 1996. (Illus.). pap. 10.95 (*0-345-40404-1*) Ballantine Bks.

—Garfield Fat Cat: Takes His Licks; Keeps His Chins Up; By the Pound, 3 vols., Set. 1998. (Garfield Ser.: Vol. 8). (Illus.). 384p. pap. 10.95 (*0-345-42601-0*, Ballantine Bks.) Ballantine Bks.

—Garfield Fat Cat Three Pack: Takes His Licks; Keeps His Chins Up; By the Pound. (Garfield Ser.: Vol. 6). (Illus.). 384p. Vol. 6. 1996. pap. 10.95 (*0-345-40884-5*); Vol. VII. 1997. pap. 10.95 (*0-345-41449-7*) Ballantine Bks.

—Garfield Fat Cat 3-Pack No. 10: Garfield in the Fat Lane; Garfield Tons of Fun; Garfield Bigger & Better. 1999. (Illus.). 384p. pap. 10.95 (*0-345-43458-7*) Ballantine Bks.

—Garfield Gains Weight: His Second Book, Vol. 2. 1984. (Garfield Ser.: Vol. 2). (Illus.). 128p. pap. 7.95 o.s.i (*0-345-32008-5*) Ballantine Bks.

—Garfield Gains Weight: His Second Book. 1981. (J). 13.00 (*0-606-02927-3*) Turtleback Bks.

—Garfield Gets a Life. 1991. pap. 6.95 o.s.i (*0-345-37375-8*) Ballantine Bks.

—Garfield Goes to Waist. 1990. (Garfield Ser.: Vol. 18). 128p. pap. 7.95 (*0-345-36430-9*) Ballantine Bks.

—Garfield Hams It Up, No. 31. 1997. (Garfield Ser.: Vol. 31). 128p. pap. 7.95 (*0-345-41241-9*) Ballantine Bks.

—Garfield Hangs Out. 1990. (Garfield Ser.: Vol. 19). (Illus.). 128p. pap. 7.95 (*0-345-36835-5*) Ballantine Bks.

—Garfield Hits the Big Time. 1993. (Garfield Ser.: Vol. 25). (Illus.). 128p. pap. 7.95 (*0-345-38332-X*) Ballantine Bks.

—Garfield Hop, Skip & Jump: Games & Sticker Fun. 1998. (Garfield Ser.). (Illus.). (J). pap. (*2-922148-29-7*) Presses aventure/Adventure Pr.

—Garfield in Paradise. 1986. 64p. pap. 7.95 (*0-345-33796-4*) Ballantine Bks.

—Garfield in Paradise. 1986. (J). 13.10 (*0-606-01871-9*) Turtleback Bks.

—Garfield in the Rough. 1984. 64p. pap. 6.95 o.s.i (*0-345-32242-8*) Ballantine Bks.

—Garfield in the Rough. 1984. (J). 13.10 (*0-606-00284-7*) Turtleback Bks.

—Garfield Keeps His Chins Up, Vol. 23. 1992. (Garfield Ser.: Vol. 23). (Illus.). 128p. (Orig.). pap. 7.95 (*0-345-37959-4*) Ballantine Bks.

—Garfield Learning to Tell. 1998. pap. text (*2-922148-21-1*) Modus Vivendi.
—Garfield Loses His Feet. 1984. (Garfield Ser.: Vol. 9). 128p. pap. 7.95 (*0-345-31805-6*, Ballantine Bks.) Ballantine Bks.
—Garfield Makes It Big. 1985. (Garfield Ser.: Vol. 10). 128p. pap. 7.95 (*0-345-31928-1*) Ballantine Bks.
—Garfield Makes It Big. 1985. (J). 13.00 (*0-606-00283-9*) Turtleback Bks.
—Garfield on the Town. 1983. 64p. pap. 6.95 o.s.i (*0-345-31542-1*, Ballantine Bks.) Ballantine Bks.
—Garfield on the Town. 1983. (J). 13.10 (*0-606-03270-3*) Turtleback Bks.
—Garfield Out to Lunch. 1986. (Garfield Ser.: Vol. 12). (Illus.). 128p. pap. 7.95 (*0-345-33118-4*) Ballantine Bks.
—Garfield Out to Lunch. 1986. (J). 12.05 o.p. (*0-606-01872-7*) Turtleback Bks.
—Garfield Predicts! Fearless Forecasts for a Brave New Millennium. 1999. (Cartoon Bks.). 80p. 4.95 (*0-8362-3282-8*) Andrews McMeel Publishing.
—Garfield Predicts! Mini Edition: Fearless Forecasts for a Brave New Millennium. 1999. o.p. (*0-8362-7499-7*) Andrews McMeel Publishing.
—Garfield Pulls His Weight. (Garfield Ser.: No. 26). 1996. (Illus.). (J). pap. (*0-345-91033-8*, Ballantine Bks.); 1994. 128p. pap. 7.95 (*0-345-38666-3*) Ballantine Bks.
—Garfield Rolls On. 1985. (Garfield Ser.: Vol. 11). 128p. pap. 7.95 (*0-345-32634-2*) Ballantine Bks.
—Garfield Rounds Out. 1988. (Garfield Ser.: Vol. 16). (Illus.). 128p. pap. 7.95 (*0-345-35388-9*) Ballantine Bks.
—Garfield Says a Mouthful. 1991. (Garfield Ser.: Vol. 21). (Illus.). 128p. pap. 7.95 (*0-345-37368-5*) Ballantine Bks.
—Garfield Sits Around the House. 2003. 96p. pap. 10.95 (*0-345-46463-X*); 1984. (Garfield Ser.: Vol. 7). 128p. pap. 7.95 (*0-345-32011-5*); 1983. pap. 4.95 o.s.i (*0-345-31226-0*) Ballantine Bks.
—Garfield Sits Around the House. 1983. (J). 13.00 (*0-606-03273-8*) Turtleback Bks.
—Garfield Swallows His Pride. 1987. (Garfield Ser.: Vol. 14). 128p. pap. 7.95 (*0-345-34725-0*) Ballantine Bks.
—Garfield Takes His Licks. 1993. (Garfield Ser.: Vol. 24). 128p. pap. 7.95 (*0-345-38170-X*) Ballantine Bks.
—Garfield Takes the Cake: Games & Sticker Fun. 1984. (Garfield Ser.: Vol. 5). 128p. pap. 7.95 (*0-345-32009-3*) Ballantine Bks.
—Garfield Takes the Cake: Games & Sticker Fun. 1998. (Garfield Ser.). (J). pap. text (*2-922148-38-6*) Presses aventure/Adventure Pr.
—Garfield Takes the Cake: Games & Sticker Fun. 1982. (J). 13.00 (*0-606-02926-5*) Turtleback Bks.
—Garfield Takes up Space. 1991. (Garfield Ser.: Vol. 20). 128p. pap. 7.95 (*0-345-37029-5*, Ballantine Bks.) Ballantine Bks.
—Garfield, the Easter Bunny? 1989. (Illus.). 32p. (J). 8.95 o.p. (*0-448-09297-2*, Grosset & Dunlap) Penguin Putnam Bks. for Young Readers.
—Garfield Thinks Big. 1997. (Garfield Ser.: Vol. 32). 128p. pap. 7.95 (*0-345-41671-6*) Ballantine Bks.
—Garfield Throws His Weight Around. 1998. (Garfield Ser.: Vol. 33). (Illus.). 128p. pap. 7.95 (*0-345-42749-1*) Ballantine Bks.
—Garfield Tips the Scales: His 8th Book. 1986. (Garfield Ser.: Vol. 8). 128p. pap. 7.95 o.s.i (*0-345-33580-5*) Ballantine Bks.
—Garfield Tips the Scales: His 8th Book. 1984. (J). 12.05 o.p. (*0-606-03274-6*) Turtleback Bks.
—Garfield Tons of Fun. 1996. (Garfield Ser.: Vol. 29). (Illus.). 128p. pap. 7.95 (*0-345-40386-X*) Ballantine Bks.
—The Garfield Treasury. 1984. 128p. pap. 14.00 (*0-345-32106-5*) Ballantine Bks.
—The Garfield Treasury. 1982. (J). 18.55 (*0-606-02922-2*) Turtleback Bks.
—Garfield Twentieth Anniversary Collection. 1998. 224.25 o.s.i (*0-345-42658-4*) Ballantine Bks.
—Garfield Weighs In: His Fourth Book. 1984. (Garfield Ser.: Vol. 4). 128p. pap. 7.95 o.s.i (*0-345-32010-7*) Ballantine Bks.
—Garfield Weighs In: His Fourth Book. 1982. 13.00 (*0-606-00281-2*) Turtleback Bks.
—Garfield Worldwide. 1988. (Garfield Ser.: Vol. 15). 128p. pap. 7.95 (*0-345-35158-4*) Ballantine Bks.
—Garfield's Big Book of Excellent Excuses. 2000. (Illus.). (J). 9.65 (*0-606-18664-6*) Turtleback Bks.
—Garfield's Big Fat Hairy Joke Book. 1994. 39.90 o.s.i (*0-345-80148-2*); 1993. (Illus.). 144p. mass mkt. 5.99 (*0-345-38640-X*) Ballantine Bks.
—Garfield's Feline Fantasies. 1990. 141p. pap. 6.95 o.s.i (*0-345-36902-5*) Ballantine Bks.
—Garfield's Furry Tales. 1989. (Illus.). 48p. (J). (gr. k up). 10.95 o.s.i (*0-448-09286-7*, Grosset & Dunlap) Penguin Putnam Bks. for Young Readers.
—Garfield's Halloween Adventure. 1985. 64p. pap. 6.95 o.s.i (*0-345-33045-5*) Ballantine Bks.
—Garfield's Insults. 1994. mass mkt. 3.99 (*0-345-80147-4*) Ballantine Bks.
—Garfield's Night Before Christmas. 1988. (J). (gr. 2 up). 8.95 o.s.i (*0-448-09283-2*, Grosset & Dunlap) Penguin Putnam Bks. for Young Readers.
—Garfield's Top Ten Tom Cat Foolery. 1997. (Main Street Editions Ser.). (Illus.). 48p. 6.95 (*0-8362-2875-8*) Andrews McMeel Publishing.
—Grip It & Rip It! Garfield's Guide to Golf. 1999. (Little Bks.). (Illus.). 80p. 4.95 (*0-8362-8757-6*) Andrews McMeel Publishing.
—Here Comes Garfield. 1984. 128p. pap. 6.95 o.s.i (*0-345-32012-3*) Ballantine Bks.
—How to Draw Garfield & the Gang. 1999. (Illus.). pap. text 9.90 (*0-613-15823-7*) Econo-Clad Bks.
—Never Accept a Gift with Air Holes: Garfield's Holiday Tips & Quips. 1998. (Cartoon Bks.). (Illus.). 48p. 4.95 (*0-8362-5280-2*) Andrews McMeel Publishing.
—The Ninth Garfield Fat Cat, 3 bks., Vols. 25-27. 1998. (Garfield Ser.: Vol. 9). (Illus.). 384p. pap. 10.95 (*0-345-42903-6*) Ballantine Bks.
—The Ninth Garfield Treasury. 1997. (Illus.). 120p. pap. 14.00 (*0-345-41670-8*) Ballantine Bks.
—The Outrageous Origin. 1998. (Garfield's Pet Force Ser.: Vol. 1). (J). (gr. 3-7). mass mkt. 4.50 (*0-590-05908-4*) Scholastic, Inc.
—Pie-Rat's Revenge. 1998. (Garfield's Pet Force Ser.: Vol. 2). (Illus.). (J). (gr. 3-7). mass mkt. 4.50 (*0-590-05909-2*) Scholastic, Inc.
—Save the Rivers, Rain Forests & Ravioli. 1997. (Cartoon Bks.). (Illus.). 80p. 4.95 (*0-8362-2876-6*) Andrews McMeel Publishing.
—The Second Garfield Treasury. 1985. 120p. pap. 12.50 o.s.i (*0-345-33276-8*) Ballantine Bks.
—The Seventh Garfield Treasury. 1993. (Illus.). 128p. pap. 14.00 (*0-345-38427-X*) Ballantine Bks.
—The Sixth Garfield Treasury. 1991. (Illus.). 128p. pap. 14.00 (*0-345-37367-7*) Ballantine Bks.
—The Tenth Garfield Treasury. 1999. (Garfield Ser.). (Illus.). 128p. pap. 14.00 (*0-345-43674-1*) Ballantine Bks.
—The Third Garfield Treasury. 1985. 128p. pap. 14.00 (*0-345-32635-0*) Ballantine Bks.
—The Third Garfield Treasury. 1985. 18.55 (*0-606-00446-7*) Turtleback Bks.
Davis, Jim & Golden Books Staff. Garfield at the Cat Show. 1991. (Golden Story Book & Tape Ser.). (Illus.). 24p. (J). (ps-3). pap. 5.99 o.s.i (*0-307-14173-X*, 14173, Golden Bks.) Random Hse. Children's Bks.
Davis, Jim & Wallace, Carol M. The Garfield Book of Cat Names. 1988. 64p. pap. 6.95 (*0-345-35082-0*) Ballantine Bks.
Davis, Jim, et al. Garfield's Big Fat Holiday Joke Book. 1994. 144p. (Orig.). mass mkt. 3.99 o.s.i (*0-345-38955-7*) Ballantine Bks.
—Garfield's Big Fat Scary Joke Book. 1994. 144p. (Orig.). mass mkt. 4.99 (*0-345-38954-9*) Ballantine Bks.
The Garfield Assassination. (Presidency Ser.). audio 10.00 Esstee Audios.
Gipson, Robert. Garfield & the Gang: Collectors Guide. 2000. (Schiffer Book for Collectors Ser.). (Illus.). 160p. pap. 29.95 (*0-7643-1117-4*) Schiffer Publishing, Ltd.
Huge, Tom. Garfield & Arlene Go Picnicking. 1985. (Illus.). Random Hse. Children's Bks.
—Garfield & Friends, Set. Incl. Garfield & Arlene Go Picnicking. Garfield & Nermal Play Hide-and-Seek. Garfield & Odie Go Fishing. Garfield & Pooky Feel Lazy. (Illus.). 32p. 1985. 6.95 o.s.i (*0-394-87350-5*, Random Hse. Bks. for Young Readers) Random Hse. Children's Bks.
—Garfield & Nermal Play Hide-and-Seek. 1985. (Illus.). Random Hse. Children's Bks.
—Garfield & Odie Go Fishing. 1985. (Illus.). Random Hse. Children's Bks.
—Garfield & Pooky Feel Lazy. 1985. (Illus.). Random Hse. Children's Bks.
Kraft, Jim. Garfield & the Haunted Diner: A Lift-the-Flap Book. 1989. (Illus.). 24p. (J). 10.95 o.s.i (*0-448-00398-8*, Grosset & Dunlap) Penguin Putnam Bks. for Young Readers.
—Garfield at the Gym. 1991. (Golden Easy Readers Ser.). (Illus.). (J). (gr. k-2). pap. 4.50 o.s.i (*0-307-11696-4*, Golden Bks.) Random Hse. Children's Bks.
—Garfield's Tales of Mystery. 1991. (Garfield Ser.). (Illus.). 32p. (J). 9.95 o.s.i (*0-448-40132-0*, Grosset & Dunlap) Penguin Putnam Bks. for Young Readers.
Kraft, Jim & Davis, Jim. Garfield at the Gym. 1992. (Golden Book Ser.: Level 2). (Illus.). 32p. (J). (ps-2). pap. 3.25 o.s.i (*0-307-15960-4*, 15960, Golden Bks.) Random Hse. Children's Bks.
Kraft, Jim, et al. Garfield's Ghost Stories. 1992. (Garfield Ser.). (Illus.). 32p. (J). (ps-3). 10.95 o.s.i (*0-448-40577-6*, Grosset & Dunlap) Penguin Putnam Bks. for Young Readers.
Merriam-Webster, Inc. Staff. The Merriam-Webster & Garfield Dictionary: With Comics! 1999. (Illus.). 816p. (C). (gr. k up). pap. 12.95 (*0-87779-626-2*, MER-626) Merriam-Webster, Inc.

**GARION (FICTITIOUS CHARACTER)—FICTION**

Eddings, David. The Castle of Wizardry. (Belgariad Ser.: Bk. 4). 1997. pap. 11.95 o.s.i (*0-345-41885-9*); 1985. 384p. mass mkt. 7.50 (*0-345-33570-8*) Ballantine Bks.
—The Castle of Wizardry. 1984. (Belgariad: Bk. 4). 13.04 (*0-606-01242-7*) Turtleback Bks.
—Demon Lord of Karanda. (Mallorean Ser.: Bk. 3). 1997. pap. 12.95 o.s.i (*0-345-41918-9*); 1989. 416p. mass mkt. 7.50 (*0-345-36331-0*) Ballantine Bks. (Del Rey).
—Demon Lord of Karanda. 1991. 3.99 o.p. (*0-517-06775-7*) Random Hse. Value Publishing.
—Demon Lord of Karanda. 1989. (Malloreon: Bk. 3). 13.04 (*0-606-01247-8*) Turtleback Bks.
—Enchanters' End Game. 1997. (Belgariad Ser.: Bk. 5). pap. 11.95 o.s.i (*0-345-41886-7*); 1988. (Belgariad Ser.: Bk. 5). (Illus.). 384p. pap. o.p. (*0-345-00688-7*, Del Rey); 1986. (Belgariad Ser.: Bk. 5). (Illus.). 384p. mass mkt. 7.50 (*0-345-33871-5*, Del Rey); 1984. mass mkt. 3.50 o.p. (*0-345-30078-5*, Del Rey) Ballantine Bks.
—Enchanters' End Game. 1984. (Belgariad: Bk. 5). 13.04 (*0-606-01244-3*) Turtleback Bks.
—Guardians of the West. (Mallorean Ser.: Bk. 1). 1997. pap. 12.95 o.s.i (*0-345-41919-7*); 1988. 448p. mass mkt. 7.50 (*0-345-35266-1*); 1987. 16.95 o.s.i (*0-345-33000-5*) Ballantine Bks. (Del Rey).
—Guardians of the West. 1988. (Malloreon: Bk. 1). 13.04 (*0-606-01245-1*) Turtleback Bks.
—King of the Murgos. (Mallorean Ser.: Bk. 2). 1997. pap. 12.95 o.s.i (*0-345-41920-0*); 1989. 416p. mass mkt. 7.50 (*0-345-35880-5*) Ballantine Bks. (Del Rey).
—King of the Murgos. 1989. (Malloreon: Bk. 2). 13.04 (*0-606-01246-X*) Turtleback Bks.
—Magician's Gambit. 1997. (Belgariad Ser.: Bk. 3). pap. 11.95 o.s.i (*0-345-41887-5*); 1986. (Belgariad Ser.: Bk. 3). 320p. mass mkt. 6.99 (*0-345-33545-7*, Del Rey); 1985. mass mkt. 3.50 o.p. (*0-345-32731-4*, Del Rey); 1983. mass mkt. 2.95 o.p. (*0-345-30077-7*, Del Rey) Ballantine Bks.
—Magician's Gambit. 1983. (Belgariad: Bk. 3). 13.04 (*0-606-01241-9*) Turtleback Bks.
—Pawn of Prophecy. 2004. 304p. pap. 6.99 (*0-345-46864-3*); 1997. (Belgariad Ser.: Bk. 1). pap. 11.95 o.s.i (*0-345-41888-3*); 1986. (Belgariad Ser.: Bk. 1). 272p. mass mkt. 6.99 (*0-345-33551-1*); 1985. mass mkt. 3.50 o.p. (*0-345-32356-4*); 1982. mass mkt. 2.95 o.p. (*0-345-30997-9*); 1982. mass mkt. 2.95 o.p. (*0-345-29637-0*) Ballantine Bks. (Del Rey).
—Pawn of Prophecy. 1982. (Belgariad: Bk. 1). 13.04 (*0-606-01238-9*) Turtleback Bks.
—The Queen of Sorcery. (Belgariad Ser.: Bk. 2). 1997. pap. 11.95 o.s.i (*0-345-41889-1*); 1986. 336p. mass mkt. 7.50 (*0-345-33565-1*, Del Rey) Ballantine Bks.
—The Queen of Sorcery. 1982. (Belgariad: Bk. 2). 13.04 (*0-606-01240-0*) Turtleback Bks.
—The Seeress of Kell. (Mallorean Ser.: Bk. 5). 1997. pap. 12.95 o.s.i (*0-345-41922-7*); 1992. 384p. mass mkt. 6.99 (*0-345-37759-1*) Ballantine Bks. (Del Rey).
—Sorceress of Darshiva. (Mallorean Ser.: Bk. 4). 1997. 227p. pap. 12.95 o.s.i (*0-345-41921-9*); 1990. 384p. mass mkt. 7.50 (*0-345-36935-1*) Ballantine Bks. (Del Rey).
—Sorceress of Darshiva. 1991. 3.99 o.p. (*0-517-06791-9*) Random Hse. Value Publishing.

**GARLIN, KELRIC (FICTITIOUS CHARACTER)—FICTION**

Asaro, Catherine. Ascendant Sun. 2000. (Management & Leadership in Education Ser.). (Illus.). 380p. 24.95 (*0-312-86824-3*, Tor Bks.) Doherty, Tom Assocs., LLC.
—Catch the Lightning. 1997. 320p. pap. 6.99 (*0-8125-5102-8*); 1996. 496p. 24.95 o.p. (*0-312-86043-9*) Doherty, Tom Assocs., LLC. (Tor Bks.).
—The Last Hawk. (Tor Science Fiction Ser.). 1998. (Illus.). 463p. pap. 7.99 (*0-8125-5110-9*); 1997. 448p. 25.95 o.p. (*0-312-86044-7*) Doherty, Tom Assocs., LLC. (Tor Bks.).
—Primary Inversion. 1996. 369p. pap. 6.99 (*0-8125-5023-4*); 1995. 320p. 14.30 o.p. (*0-312-85764-0*) Doherty, Tom Assocs., LLC. (Tor Bks.).
—The Radiant Seas. (Saga of the Skolian Empire Ser.). (Illus.). 1999. 512p. mass mkt. 6.99 (*0-8125-8036-2*); 1998. 463p. 26.95 (*0-312-86714-X*) Doherty, Tom Assocs., LLC. (Tor Bks.).

**GARNET, EARL (FICTITIOUS CHARACTER)—FICTION**

Clement, Peter. Death Rounds. 1999. 345p. mass mkt. 6.99 (*0-449-00450-3*, Fawcett) Ballantine Bks.
—Lethal Practice. 1998. mass mkt. 6.99 (*0-8041-1781-0*, Ivy Bks.); 1998. 352p. mass mkt. 7.99 (*0-449-00281-0*, Fawcett); 1997. mass mkt. 6.99 (*0-345-40776-8*) Ballantine Bks.

**GARNISH, HARRY (FICTITIOUS CHARACTER)—FICTION**

McConnell, Frank. Blood Lake: A Harry Garnish/Bridget O'Toole Mystery. l.t. ed. 1988. 19.95 o.p. (*1-55504-590-1*); pap. 17.95 o.p. (*1-55504-573-1*) BBC Audiobooks America.
—Blood Lake: A Harry Garnish/Bridget O'Toole Mystery. 1988. (Crime Ser.). 256p. pap. 3.95 o.p. (*0-14-010755-X*, Penguin Bks.); 39.50 o.p. (*0-14-778359-3*) Viking Penguin.
—Blood Lake: A Harry Garnish/Bridget O'Toole Mystery. 1987. 256p. 16.95 o.s.i (*0-8027-5673-5*) Walker & Co.
—The Frog King: A Harry Garnish/Bridget O'Toole Mystery. l.t. ed. 1992. pap. 19.95 o.p. (*0-7927-1175-0*); 21.95 o.p. (*0-7927-1149-1*, CH0241) BBC Audiobooks America.
—The Frog King: A Harry Garnish/Bridget O'Toole Mystery. 1990. 192p. 18.95 o.p. (*0-8027-5748-0*) Walker & Co.
—Liar's Poker: A Harry Garnish/Bridget O'Toole Mystery. 1993. 234p. 19.95 (*0-8027-3229-1*) Walker & Co.
—Murder among Friends: A Harry Garnish/Bridget O'Toole Mystery. l.t. ed. 1986. pap. 13.95 o.p. (*0-7451-9149-5*) BBC Audiobooks America.
—Murder among Friends: A Harry Garnish/Bridget O'Toole Mystery. 1988. pap. 39.50 o.p. (*0-14-778313-5*); 192p. mass mkt. 3.95 o.p. (*0-451-82189-0*, Penguin Bks.) Viking Penguin.
—Murder among Friends: A Harry Garnish/Bridget O'Toole Mystery. 1983. 192p. 12.95 o.s.i (*0-8027-5567-4*) Walker & Co.

**GARON, SETH (FICTITIOUS CHARACTER)—FICTION**

Bachman, Richard, pseud. The Regulators. 1996. 480p. 24.95 o.s.i (*0-525-94190-8*); 325.00 o.s.i (*0-525-94224-6*) Dutton/Plume.
—The Regulators. 1997. (Illus.). 512p. mass mkt. 7.99 (*0-451-19101-3*, Signet Bks.) NAL.
—The Regulators, unabr. ed. 1997. audio 80.00 (*0-7887-1163-6*, 95006E7) Recorded Bks., LLC.
—The Regulators. l.t. ed. 1997. (Thorndike/G. K. Hall Paperback Bestsellers Ser.). 598p. pap. 26.95 (*0-7862-0845-7*) Thorndike Pr.
—The Regulators. 1996. (Illus.). 466p. text 24.95 (*0-670-87281-4*); 6p. pap. 29.95 o.p. incl. audio (*0-14-086322-2*, Penguin AudioBooks) Viking Penguin.

**GARRETT (FICTITIOUS CHARACTER: COOK)—FICTION**

Cook, Glen. Angry Lead Skies. 2002. 368p. mass mkt. 6.99 (*0-451-45875-3*, ROC) NAL.
—Bitter Gold Hearts. 1990. (Garrett Files Ser.). 256p. reprint ed. mass mkt. 3.95 o.p. (*0-451-45072-8*, ROC) NAL.
—Cold Copper Tears. 1988. (Garrett Files Ser.). 256p. mass mkt. 3.50 o.p. (*0-451-15773-7*, ROC) NAL.
—Deadly Quicksilver Lies. 1994. (Garrett Files Ser.). 352p. (Orig.). mass mkt. 4.99 o.s.i (*0-451-45305-0*, ROC) NAL.
—Dread Brass Shadows. 1990. (Garrett Files Ser.). 256p. mass mkt. 5.50 o.s.i (*0-451-45008-6*, ROC) NAL.
—Faded Steel Heat. 1999. (Garrett Files Ser.). 368p. mass mkt. 6.99 o.s.i (*0-451-45479-0*, ROC) NAL.
—Old Tin Sorrows. 1989. (Glen Garrett Files Ser.). 256p. mass mkt. 3.99 o.s.i (*0-451-45157-0*, ROC) NAL.
—Petty Pewter Gods. 1995. (Garrett Files Ser.). 304p. mass mkt. 5.99 o.s.i (*0-451-45478-2*, ROC) NAL.
—Red Iron Nights. 1991. (Garrett Files Ser.). 272p. (Orig.). mass mkt. 5.50 o.s.i (*0-451-45108-2*, ROC) NAL.
—Sweet Silver Blues. 1990. (Garrett Files Ser.). 256p. reprint ed. mass mkt. 5.50 o.s.i (*0-451-45070-1*, ROC) NAL.

**GARRETT, AMANDA LEE (FICTITIOUS CHARACTER)—FICTION**

Cobb, James H. Choosers of the Slain. l.t. ed. 1996. lib. bdg. 24.95 (*1-57490-076-5*, Beeler Large Print Bks.) Beeler, Thomas T. Publisher.
—Choosers of the Slain. 1997. 352p. mass mkt. 6.99 o.s.i (*0-425-16053-X*) Berkley Publishing Group.
—Choosers of the Slain. 1996. 352p. 23.95 o.p. (*0-399-14197-9*, G. P. Putnam's Sons) Penguin Group (USA) Inc.
—The Sea Fighter. 2000. 368p. 24.95 o.s.i (*0-399-14593-1*) Penguin Group (USA) Inc.
—Sea Strike. 1999. 368p. reprint ed. mass mkt. 6.99 (*0-425-16616-3*) Berkley Publishing Group.
—Sea Strike. 1997. 480p. 24.95 o.p. (*0-399-14324-6*, G. P. Putnam's Sons) Penguin Group (USA) Inc.

**GARRETT, DAVE (FICTITIOUS CHARACTER)—FICTION**

Albert, Neil. An Appointment in May: A Dave Garrett Mystery. 1996. (Dave Garrett Mystery Ser.). 288p. 20.95 (*0-8027-3279-8*) Walker & Co.



 

—Burning March. 1994. (Dave Garrett Mystery Ser.). 256p. 18.95 o.p. (*0-525-93718-8*, Dutton) Dutton/Plume.
—Burning March. 1995. (Dave Garrett Mystery Ser.). 256p. mass mkt. 4.50 o.s.i (*0-451-17860-2*, Signet Bks.) NAL.
—Cruel April: A Dave Garrett Mystery. 1995. (Dave Garrett Mystery Ser.). 272p. 19.95 o.s.i (*0-525-93719-6*, Dutton) Dutton/Plume.
—Cruel April: A Dave Garrett Mystery. 1996. (Dave Garrett Mystery Ser.). 272p. mass mkt. 5.50 o.s.i (*0-451-17861-0*, Signet Bks.) NAL.
—Cruel April: A Dave Garrett Mystery. l.t. ed. 1996. (Niagara Large Print Ser.). 336p. 29.50 o.p. (*0-7089-5826-5*, Ulverscroft) Thorpe, F. A. Pubs. GBR. *Dist:* Ulverscroft Large Print Bks., Ltd.
—The February Trouble: A Dave Garrett Mystery. 1994. (Dave Garrett Mystery Ser.). 256p. mass mkt. 3.99 o.s.i (*0-451-40417-3*, Signet Bks.) NAL.
—The February Trouble: A Dave Garrett Mystery. 1992. 235p. 19.95 (*0-8027-1244-4*) Walker & Co.
—The January Corpse. 1993. (Dave Garrett Mystery Ser.). 256p. mass mkt. 3.99 o.s.i (*0-451-40377-0*) NAL.
—The January Corpse. 1991. 192p. 18.95 (*0-8027-3206-2*) Walker & Co.
—Tangled June: A Dave Garrett Mystery. 1997. (Dave Garrett Mystery Ser.). 246p. 20.95 (*0-8027-3305-0*) Walker & Co.

### GARRETT, MAGGIE (FICTITIOUS CHARACTER)—FICTION

Taylor, Jean. The Last of Her Lies: A Maggie Garrett Mystery. 1996. 238p. (Orig.). pap. 10.95 (*1-878067-75-3*, Seal Pr.) Avalon Publishing Group.
—We Know Where You Live. 1995. 240p. pap. 9.95 (*1-878067-62-1*, Seal Pr.) Avalon Publishing Group.

### GARRISON, RICHARD (FICTITIOUS CHARACTER)—FICTION

Lumley, Brian. Psychamok. Date not set. pap. 15.95 (*0-312-85671-7*); 2002. 304p. 26.95 (*0-7653-0481-3*); 1993. 512p. mass mkt. 5.99 (*0-8125-2032-7*) Doherty, Tom Assocs., LLC. (Tor Bks.).
—Psychomech. 1992. 448p. mass mkt. 5.99 (*0-8125-2023-8*, Tor Bks.) Doherty, Tom Assocs., LLC.
—Psychosphere. (Orig.). 1992. 448p. mass mkt. 5.99 (*0-8125-2030-0*); 2001. 304p. reprint ed. pap. 15.95 (*0-312-85191-X*) Doherty, Tom Assocs., LLC. (Tor Bks.).

### GARRITY, JULIA CALLAHAN (FICTITIOUS CHARACTER)—FICTION

Trocheck, Kathy Hogan. Every Crooked Nanny. 1992. 208p. 19.00 o.p. (*0-06-017923-6*) HarperTrade.
—Every Crooked Nanny. 1993. (Callahan Garrity Mystery Ser.). 336p. mass mkt. 6.50 (*0-06-109170-7*, HarperTorch) Morrow/Avon.
—Every Crooked Nanny. l.t. ed. 1997. (Ulverscroft Large Print Ser.). 544p. 29.99 o.p. (*0-7089-3748-9*, Ulverscroft) Thorpe, F. A. Pubs. GBR. *Dist:* Ulverscroft Large Print Bks., Ltd., Ulverscroft Large Print Canada, Ltd.
—Happy Never After. 1995. 306p. 22.00 o.p. (*0-06-017637-7*) HarperCollins Pubs.
—Happy Never After. 1996. (Callahan Garrity Mystery Ser.). 320p. mass mkt. 5.99 (*0-06-109360-2*, HarperTorch) Morrow/Avon.
—Heart Trouble. 1996. (Callahan Garrity Mystery Ser.). 304p. 22.00 o.p. (*0-06-017638-5*) HarperCollins Pubs.
—Heart Trouble. 1997. 304p. mass mkt. 5.99 (*0-06-109585-0*, HarperTorch) Morrow/Avon.
—Heart Trouble. l.t. ed. 1998. (Ulverscroft Large Print Ser.). 448p. 29.99 (*0-7089-3947-3*, Ulverscroft) Thorpe, F. A. Pubs. GBR. *Dist:* Ulverscroft Large Print Bks., Ltd., Ulverscroft Large Print Canada, Ltd.
—Homemade Sin. l.t. ed. 1994. 379p. pap. 19.95 (*0-7838-1163-2*, Macmillan Reference USA) Gale Group.
—Homemade Sin. 1994. 256p. 20.00 o.p. (*0-06-017765-9*) HarperTrade.
—Homemade Sin. 1995. (Callahan Garrity Mystery Ser.). 304p. mass mkt. 5.99 (*0-06-109256-8*, HarperTorch) Morrow/Avon.
—Irish Eyes. 2000. (Callahan Garrity Mystery Ser.). 304p. 24.00 (*0-06-019421-9*) HarperCollins Pubs.
—Irish Eyes. 2001. (Callahan Garrity Mystery Ser.). 320p. mass mkt. 5.99 (*0-06-109869-8*, Avon Bks.) Morrow/Avon.
—Irish Eyes. l.t. ed. 2000. (Mystery Ser.). 473p. 28.95 (*0-7862-2837-7*) Thorndike Pr.
—Midnight Clear. l.t. ed. 2000. 360p. 26.95 (*1-57490-323-3*, Beeler Large Print Bks.) Beeler, Thomas T. Publisher.
—Midnight Clear. 1998. (Callahan Garrity Mystery Ser.). 288p. 23.00 o.s.i (*0-06-017543-5*) HarperCollins Pubs.
—Midnight Clear. 1999. (Callahan Garrity Mystery Ser.). 416p. mass mkt. 5.99 (*0-06-109800-0*, HarperTorch) Morrow/Avon.
—Strange Brew. l.t. ed. 1999. 24.95 (*1-57490-219-9*, Beeler Large Print Bks.) Beeler, Thomas T. Publisher.
—Strange Brew. 1997. (Callahan Garrity Mystery Ser.). 288p. 23.00 o.s.i (*0-06-017542-7*) HarperCollins Pubs.
—Strange Brew. 1998. (Callahan Garrity Mystery Ser.). 336p. reprint ed. mass mkt. 5.99 (*0-06-109173-1*, HarperTorch) Morrow/Avon.
—To Live & Die in Dixie. 1993. 288p. 20.00 o.p. (*0-06-017924-4*) HarperTrade.
—To Live & Die in Dixie. 1994. (Callahan Garrity Mystery Ser.). 320p. mass mkt. 5.99 (*0-06-109171-5*, HarperTorch) Morrow/Avon.
—To Live & Die in Dixie. l.t. ed. 1997. (Ulverscroft Large Print Ser.). 496p. 29.99 o.p. (*0-7089-3837-X*, Ulverscroft) Thorpe, F. A. Pubs. GBR. *Dist:* Ulverscroft Large Print Bks., Ltd., Ulverscroft Large Print Canada, Ltd.

### GASTNER, BILL (FICTITIOUS CHARACTER)—FICTION

Havill, Steven F. Bag Limit: A Sheriff Bill Gastner Mystery. 2001. (Illus.). 336p. 24.95 (*0-312-25183-1*, Saint Martin's Minotaur) St. Martin's Pr.
—Before She Dies. 1996. 288p. 21.95 o.p. (*0-312-13927-6*, Saint Martin's Minotaur) St. Martin's Pr.
—Bitter Recoil. 1992. 240p. 17.95 o.p. (*0-312-07656-8*, Saint Martin's Minotaur) St. Martin's Pr.
—Dead Weight. 2000. (Undersheriff Bill Gastner Mysteries Ser.). (Illus.). 280p. 23.95 (*0-312-25203-X*, Saint Martin's Minotaur) St. Martin's Pr.
—Heartshot. 2000. (Missing Mysteries Ser.: Vol. 16). 210p. pap. 14.95 (*1-890208-29-9*) Poisoned Pen Pr.
—Heartshot. 1991. text 16.95 o.p. (*0-312-05442-4*, Saint Martin's Minotaur) St. Martin's Pr.
—Out of Season. 2001. (WWL Mystery Ser.: No. 382). 251p. mass mkt. (*0-373-26382-1*, 1-26382-1, Worldwide Library) Harlequin Enterprises, Ltd.
—Out of Season. 1999. 304p. 23.95 (*0-312-24414-2*, Saint Martin's Minotaur) St. Martin's Pr.
—Privileged to Kill. 1996. 224p. 21.95 o.p. (*0-312-15196-9*, Saint Martin's Minotaur) St. Martin's Pr.
—Prolonged Exposure. 1998. (Undersheriff Bill Gastner Mysteries Ser.). 272p. 21.95 o.p. (*0-312-18158-2*, Saint Martin's Minotaur) St. Martin's Pr.
—The Scavengers: A Posadas County Mystery. 2002. (Illus.). 352p. 24.95 (*0-312-28833-6*, Saint Martin's Minotaur) St. Martin's Pr.
—Twice Buried. 1994. 224p. 19.95 o.p. (*0-312-10566-5*, Saint Martin's Minotaur) St. Martin's Pr.
Iakovou, Takis, et al. Deadly Morsels: Another Curse/Red or Green?/Cake Job/Sheep in Wolf's Clothing, 4 bks. in 1. 2003. (WWL Mystery Ser.: No. 452). 384p. mass mkt. (*0-373-26452-6*, Worldwide Library) Harlequin Enterprises, Ltd.

### GAUNT, JONATHAN (FICTITIOUS CHARACTER)—FICTION

Knox, Bill. A Burial in Portugal. l.t. ed. 1997. (Ulverscroft Large Print Ser.). 352p. 29.99 (*0-7089-3704-7*, Ulverscroft) Thorpe, F. A. Pubs. GBR. *Dist:* Ulverscroft Large Print Bks., Ltd., Ulverscroft Large Print Canada, Ltd.
—An Incident in Iceland. l.t. ed. 1996. (Linford Mystery Library). 320p. pap. 17.99 (*0-7089-7936-X*, Ulverscroft) Thorpe, F. A. Pubs. GBR. *Dist:* Ulverscroft Large Print Bks., Ltd., Ulverscroft Large Print Canada, Ltd.
—A Pay-Off in Switzerland. l.t. ed. 1997. (Linford Mystery Library). 320p. pap. 17.99 (*0-7089-5061-2*, Ulverscroft) Thorpe, F. A. Pubs. GBR. *Dist:* Ulverscroft Large Print Bks., Ltd., Ulverscroft Large Print Canada, Ltd.
—A Problem in Prague. l.t. ed. 1998. (Ulverscroft Large Print Ser.). 320p. 29.99 (*0-7089-3968-6*, Ulverscroft) Thorpe, F. A. Pubs. GBR. *Dist:* Ulverscroft Large Print Bks., Ltd., Ulverscroft Large Print Canada, Ltd.
MacLeod, Robert. A Killing in Malta. l.t. ed. 1979. (Ulverscroft Large Print Ser.). 29.99 o.p. (*0-7089-0320-7*, Ulverscroft) Thorpe, F. A. Pubs. GBR. *Dist:* Ulverscroft Large Print Bks., Ltd., Ulverscroft Large Print Canada, Ltd.
—A Legacy from Tenerife. l.t. ed. 1985. (Ulverscroft Large Print Ser.). 29.99 o.p. (*0-7089-1351-2*, Ulverscroft) Thorpe, F. A. Pubs. GBR. *Dist:* Ulverscroft Large Print Bks., Ltd., Ulverscroft Large Print Canada, Ltd.
—The Money Mountain. l.t. ed. 1988. (Ulverscroft Large Print Ser.). 400p. 29.99 o.p. (*0-7089-1838-7*, Ulverscroft) Thorpe, F. A. Pubs. GBR. *Dist:* Ulverscroft Large Print Bks., Ltd., Ulverscroft Large Print Canada, Ltd.
—A Property in Cyprus. l.t. ed. 1978. (Ulverscroft Large Print Ser.). 29.99 o.p. (*0-7089-0092-5*, Ulverscroft) Thorpe, F. A. Pubs. GBR. *Dist:* Ulverscroft Large Print Bks., Ltd., Ulverscroft Large Print Canada, Ltd.
—The Spanish Maze Game. l.t. ed. 1991. (Magna Large Print Ser.). 367p. o.p. (*0-7505-0171-5*) Magna Large Print Bks. GBR. *Dist:* Ulverscroft Large Print Canada, Ltd.
—A Witchdance in Bavaria. l.t. ed. 1977. (Ulverscroft Large Print Ser.). 29.99 o.p. (*0-7089-0010-0*, Ulverscroft) Thorpe, F. A. Pubs. GBR. *Dist:* Ulverscroft Large Print Bks., Ltd., Ulverscroft Large Print Canada, Ltd.
Webster, Noah. Flight from Paris. 1987. (Crime Club Ser.). 192p. 12.95 o.s.i (*0-385-23560-7*) Doubleday Publishing.
—An Incident in Iceland. 1979. (Crime Club Ser.). 7.95 o.p. (*0-385-15478-X*) Doubleday Publishing.
—Legacy from Tenerife. 1984. (Crime Club Ser.). 192p. 11.95 o.p. (*0-385-19556-7*) Doubleday Publishing.
—A Pay-Off in Switzerland. 1977. 6.95 o.p. (*0-385-13246-8*) Doubleday Publishing.
—A Problem in Prague. 1982. (Crime Club Ser.). 192p. 10.95 o.p. (*0-385-17944-8*) Doubleday Publishing.

### GAUNT, LELAND (FICTITIOUS CHARACTER)—FICTION

King, Stephen. Needful Things. l.t. ed. 1992. (General Ser.). 1044p. pap. 19.95 o.p. (*0-8161-5477-5*); lib. bdg. 25.95 o.p. (*0-8161-5476-7*) Gale Group. (Macmillan Reference USA).
—Needful Things. abr. unabr. ed. Pt. 1. 1991. 704p. 29.95 o.p. incl. audio (*0-453-00759-7*, Penguin Bks.); Pt. 2. 1991. 704p. 29.95 o.p. incl. audio (*0-453-00760-0*, Penguin Bks.); Pt. 2. audio 29.95 o.p.; Pt. 3. 1991. audio 29.95 o.p. (*0-453-00761-9*); Pt. 3. audio 29.95 o.p. HighBridge Co.
—Needful Things. 752p. 1993. mass mkt. 6.99 o.p. (*0-451-17859-9*); 1992. mass mkt. 7.99 (*0-451-17281-7*) NAL. (Signet Bks.).
—Needful Things. abr. unabr. ed. 1993. 49.95 incl. audio (*0-453-00859-3*) Penguin/HighBridge.
—Needful Things. 1992. 14.04 (*0-606-01485-3*) Turtleback Bks.
—Needful Things. 1991. 704p. text 35.00 (*0-670-83953-1*, Penguin Bks.) Viking Penguin.

### GAUTIER, JEAN-PAUL (FICTITIOUS CHARACTER)—FICTION

Grayson, Richard. Death au Gratin. 1995. 192p. 19.95 o.p. (*0-312-13047-3*, Saint Martin's Minotaur) St. Martin's Pr.
—Death off Stage. 1992. 192p. 16.95 o.p. (*0-312-06951-0*, Saint Martin's Minotaur) St. Martin's Pr.
—Death on the Cards. 2001. audio 54.95 (*1-85496-746-0*, 67460) Soundings, Ltd. GBR. *Dist:* Ulverscroft Large Print Bks., Ltd.
—Death on the Cards. 1988. 176p. 13.95 o.p. (*0-312-01758-8*, Saint Martin's Minotaur) St. Martin's Pr.
—Death on the Cards. l.t. ed. 1990. (Ulverscroft Large Print Ser.). 29.99 (*0-7089-2190-6*, Ulverscroft) Thorpe, F. A. Pubs. GBR. *Dist:* Ulverscroft Large Print Bks., Ltd., Ulverscroft Large Print Canada, Ltd.

### GED (FICTITIOUS CHARACTER)—FICTION

Le Guin, Ursula K. The Farthest Shore. 1984. mass mkt. 2.95 o.s.i (*0-553-23828-0*); (Earthsea Trilogy Ser.: Vol. 3). 208p. (gr. 6 up). mass mkt. 6.99 o.s.i (*0-553-26847-3*) Bantam Bks.
—The Farthest Shore. l.t. unabr. ed. 1988. 400p. (J). (gr. 5 up). 13.95 o.p. (*0-8161-4434-6*, Macmillan Reference USA) Gale Group.
—The Farthest Shore. 1993. (Earthsea Ser.: Vol. 3). (J). audio 44.20 (*1-56544-028-5*, 550009); audio Literate Ear, Inc.
—The Farthest Shore. unabr. ed. 1995. (J). (gr. 6). audio 53.00 (*0-7887-0181-9*, 94406E7) Recorded Bks., LLC.
—The Farthest Shore. rev. ed. (YA). 1990. (Illus.). 240p. (gr. 6 up). 21.00 (*0-689-31683-6*, Atheneum); Vol. 3. 2001. 272p. pap. 4.99 (*0-689-84782-3*, Aladdin); Vol. 3. 2001. 272p. mass mkt. 6.99 (*0-689-84534-0*, Simon Pulse) Simon & Schuster Children's Publishing.
—The Farthest Shore. 2001. 13.04 (*0-606-22122-0*); 1975. 13.04 (*0-606-00601-X*) Turtleback Bks.
—Tales from Earthsea. 2002. 336p. (YA). pap. 13.95 (*0-441-00932-8*) Ace Bks.
—Tehanu: The Last Book of Earthsea, No. 4. 1997. (Earthsea Cycle Ser.). 288p. mass mkt. 6.99 o.s.i (*0-553-28873-3*, Spectra) Bantam Bks.
—Tehanu: The Last Book of Earthsea. (ps up). 1990. 240p. (J). 21.00 (*0-689-31595-3*, Atheneum); Vol. 4. 2001. 288p. (YA). mass mkt. 6.99 (*0-689-84533-2*, Simon Pulse) Simon & Schuster Children's Publishing.
—Tehanu: The Last Book of Earthsea. 2001. 13.04 (*0-606-22123-9*); 1991. (J). 13.04 (*0-606-04825-1*) Turtleback Bks.
—The Tombs of Atuan. 1984. 160p. (Earthsea Trilogy Ser.: Vol. 2). mass mkt. 6.99 o.s.i (*0-553-27331-0*, Bantam Classics); (J). mass mkt. 2.95 o.s.i (*0-553-23903-1*) Bantam Bks.
—The Tombs of Atuan. l.t. ed. 1988. (Children's Ser.). 216p. (J). (gr. 5 up). 13.95 o.p. (*0-8161-4430-3*, Macmillan Reference USA) Gale Group.
—The Tombs of Atuan. 1993. (Earthsea Ser.: Vol. 2). audio 39.80 (*1-56544-027-7*, 550008); audio Literate Ear, Inc.
—The Tombs of Atuan. unabr. ed. 1994. (YA). (gr. 7). audio 36.00 (*0-7887-0067-7*, 94300E7) Recorded Bks., LLC.
—The Tombs of Atuan. 1990. (Illus.). 176p. (J). (gr. 4-7). 21.00 (*0-689-31684-4*, Atheneum) Simon & Schuster Children's Publishing.
—The Tombs of Atuan. 1975. (Earthsea Trilogy Ser.). (J). 13.04 (*0-606-00442-4*) Turtleback Bks.
—A Wizard of Earthsea. l.t. ed. 1986. (YA). (gr. 5 up). 16.95 o.p. (*0-7451-0337-5*, Galaxy Children's Large Print) BBC Audiobooks America.
—A Wizard of Earthsea. 1990. mass mkt. o.s.i (*0-553-54006-8*); 1984. mass mkt. 2.95 o.s.i (*0-553-23461-7*); 1984. (Earthsea Trilogy Ser.; Vol. 1). 192p. (gr. 9-12). mass mkt. 7.50 (*0-553-26250-5*, Spectra) Bantam Bks.
—A Wizard of Earthsea, 001. 1968. (Illus.). (YA). (gr. 5 up). 13.95 o.p. (*0-395-27653-5*) Houghton Mifflin Co.
—A Wizard of Earthsea. 1993. (Earthsea Ser.: Vol. 1). audio. audio 39.80 (*1-56544-008-0*, 550007) Literate Ear, Inc.
—A Wizard of Earthsea. unabr. ed. (YA). (gr. 7). 1997. (Earthsea Ser.: Bk. 1). audio 46.00 (*1-55690-611-0*, 92304E7); 1992. audio 42.00; 1992. audio 42.00 (*1-55690-745-1*, 92304) Recorded Bks., LLC.
—A Wizard of Earthsea. 1991. 208p. (YA). (gr. 7 up). 18.00 (*0-689-31720-4*, Atheneum) Simon & Schuster Children's Publishing.
—A Wizard of Earthsea. 1975. (Earthsea Trilogy Ser.). (YA). 13.04 (*0-606-00573-0*) Turtleback Bks.
Le Guin, Ursula K. & Garraty, Gail. The Tombs of Atuan. 1971. (Illus.). (J). (gr. 5-9). 15.95 o.s.i (*0-689-20680-1*, 558618, Atheneum) Simon & Schuster Children's Publishing.

### GEIGER, ROLF (FICTITIOUS CHARACTER)—FICTION

Hynd, Noel. The Prodigy. 1999. 352p. mass mkt. 5.99 o.s.i (*0-7860-0614-5*); 1998. 336p. 23.00 o.s.i (*1-57566-240-X*) Kensington Publishing Corp.

### GENNARO, ANGELA (FICTITIOUS CHARACTER)—FICTION

Lehane, Dennis. Darkness, Take My Hand. 1997. 400p. mass mkt. 7.99 (*0-380-72628-9*, Avon Bks.); 1996. 320p. 24.00 (*0-688-14380-6*, Morrow, William & Co.) Morrow/Avon.
—A Drink Before the War. 2003. 300p. pap. 14.00 (*0-15-602902-2*, Harvest Bks.); 1994. 288p. 22.95 (*0-15-100093-X*) Harcourt Trade Pubs.
—A Drink Before the War. 1996. 320p. mass mkt. 7.99 (*0-380-72623-8*, Avon Bks.) Morrow/Avon.
—A Drink Before the War. 336p. (*0-7278-5537-9*) Severn Hse. Pubs., Ltd.
—Gone, Baby, Gone. abr. ed. 1999. audio 7.99 o.s.i (*1-56740-305-0*, 1869, Paperback Nova Audio Bks.); 1998. audio 17.95 o.p. (*1-56740-783-8*, 450, Nova Audio Bks.); 1998. audio 26.95 (*1-56740-058-2*, 18, Bookcassette); 1998. audio 73.25 (*1-56740-587-8*, 881, Unabridged Library Editions) Brilliance Audio.
—Gone, Baby, Gone. 1999. 448p. mass mkt. 7.99 (*0-380-73035-9*, Avon Bks.); 1998. 256p. 24.00 (*0-688-15332-1*, Morrow, William & Co.) Morrow/Avon.
—Prayers for Rain. abr. ed. 2003. (Patrick Kenzie/Angela Gennaro Ser.: Vol. 0). audio compact disk 14.99 (*1-59086-517-0*, 4108); 2000. audio 7.99 (*1-56740-345-X*, 2044, Paperback Nova Audio Bks.); 1999. audio 17.95 o.p. (*1-56740-840-0*, 1698, Nova Audio Bks.); 2003. (Patrick Kenzie/Angela Gennaro Ser.: Vol. 0). audio compact disk 62.25 (*1-59086-555-3*, 4145); 1999. audio 35.95 (*1-56740-428-6*, 1696, Brilliance Audio Unabridged); 1999. audio 57.25 (*1-56740-654-8*, 1697, Unabridged Library Editions) Brilliance Audio.
—Prayers for Rain, Set. abr. ed. 1999. audio 17.95. audio 35.95 Highsmith Inc.
—Prayers for Rain. 2000. 416p. mass mkt. 7.99 (*0-380-73036-7*); 1999. 352p. 25.00 (*0-688-15333-X*, Morrow, William & Co.) Morrow/Avon.
—Prayers for Rain. l.t. ed. 1999. (Core Ser.). 570p. 29.95 (*0-7838-8786-8*) Thorndike Pr.
—Sacred. abr. ed. 1998. audio 7.99 o.p. (*1-56740-238-0*, 1650, Nova Audio Bks.); 1997. audio 16.95 o.p. (*1-56100-979-2*, 505, Nova Audio Bks.); 1997. audio 73.25 o.p. (*1-56100-829-X*, 1022, Unabridged Library Editions); 1997. audio 23.95 (*1-56100-754-4*, 244, Bookcassette) Brilliance Audio.
—Sacred. 1998. 400p. mass mkt. 7.99 (*0-380-72629-7*, Avon Bks.); 1997. 256p. 23.00 (*0-688-14381-4*, Morrow, William & Co.) Morrow/Avon.

### GENTLY, DIRK (FICTITIOUS CHARACTER)—FICTION

Adams, Douglas. Dirk Gently's Holistic Detective Agency. unabr. ed. 1997. 25.00 o.p. (*0-7871-1107-4*, 695351) NewStar Media, Inc.
—Dirk Gently's Holistic Detective Agency. 1990. 4.99 o.s.i (*0-517-02337-7*) Random Hse. Value Publishing.

—Dirk Gently's Holistic Detective Agency. 1991. 320p. mass mkt. 6.99 (*0-671-74672-3*, Pocket); 1989. 320p. mass mkt. 4.95 o.s.i (*0-671-69267-4*, Pocket); 1987. (Illus.). 264p. bds. 14.70 o.p. (*0-671-62582-9*, Simon & Schuster) Simon & Schuster.
—Dirk Gently's Holistic Detective Agency. abr. ed. 1987. audio 14.95 (*0-671-64724-5*, Simon & Schuster Audioworks) Simon & Schuster Audio.
—Dirk Gently's Holistic Detective Agency. 1987. 12.09 o.p. (*0-606-03771-3*) Turtleback Bks.
—The Long Dark Tea-Time of the Soul. unabr. ed. 1993. audio 24.95 o.p. (*1-55800-159-X*, Dove Audio) NewStar Media, Inc.
—The Long Dark Tea-Time of the Soul. 1991. 320p. mass mkt. 7.99 (*0-671-74251-5*, Pocket); 1990. 320p. mass mkt. 4.95 o.s.i (*0-671-69404-9*, Pocket); 1989. 17.95 o.p. (*0-671-62583-7*, Simon & Schuster) Simon & Schuster.
—The Long Dark Tea-Time of the Soul. abr. ed. 1989. audio 16.00 (*0-671-67852-3*, 391094, Simon & Schuster Audioworks) Simon & Schuster Audio.
—The Long Dark Tea-Time of the Soul. 1988. 13.04 (*0-606-01764-X*) Turtleback Bks.
—The Salmon of Doubt: Hitchhiking the Galaxy One Last Time. 2003. 336p. pap. 13.95 (*0-345-46095-2*) Ballantine Bks.
—The Salmon of Doubt: Hitchhiking the Galaxy One Last Time. 2002. 336p. 24.00 (*1-4000-4508-8*, Harmony) Crown Publishing Group.
—The Salmon of Doubt: Hitchhiking the Galaxy One Last Time. abr. ed. 1997. pap. 24.95 o.s.i incl. audio (*0-7871-0401-9*, NewStar Pr.) NewStar Media, Inc.
—The Salmon of Doubt: Hitchhiking the Galaxy One Last Time. 1995. o.p. (*0-517-70117-0*) Random Hse., Inc.
—Two Complete Novels. 1994. 608p. 5.99 o.s.i (*0-517-11912-9*) Random Hse. Value Publishing.

**GENTLY, GEORGE (FICTITIOUS CHARACTER)—FICTION**

Hunter, Alan. Death on the Broadlands: A Superintendent Gently Novel. 192p. 1986. pap. 2.95 o.p. (*0-8027-3156-2*); 1984. 12.95 o.s.i (*0-8027-5590-9*) Walker & Co.
—Death on the Heath. 1983. (Scene of the Crime Ser.: No. 58). pap. 2.75 o.p. (*0-440-11686-4*) Dell Publishing.
—Death on the Heath. 1982. 160p. 10.95 o.s.i (*0-8027-5468-6*) Walker & Co.
—Gently Between the Tides. 1985. (Walker's British Paperback Mysteries Ser.). pap. 2.95 o.p. (*0-8027-3145-7*) Walker & Co.
—Gently Between Tides. l.t. ed. 1986. lib. bdg. 14.95 o.p. (*0-7451-0321-9*, Macmillan Reference USA) Gale Group.
—Gently Between Tides. 1982. 11.95 o.s.i (*0-8027-5480-5*) Walker & Co.
—Gently by the Shore. l.t. ed. 1996. 304p. pap. 20.95 o.p. (*0-7862-0881-3*) Thorndike Pr.
—Gently Does It. l.t. ed. 1996. (G. K. Hall Nightingale Ser.). 287p. 17.95 (*0-7838-1879-3*, Macmillan Reference USA) Gale Group.
—Gently Floating. (Black Dagger Crime Ser.). 1992. 192p. 16.50 o.p. (*0-86220-848-3*, Black Dagger); 1993. 18.95 o.p. (*0-7451-6450-1*) BBC Audiobooks America.
—Gently Mistaken: An Inspector Gently Mystery, Set. unabr. ed. 1999. audio 39.95 (*0-7540-0369-8*, CAB1792) BBC Audiobooks America.
—Gently Scandalous. l.t. ed. 1992. 240p. 15.95 o.p. (*0-7451-1558-6*, Macmillan Reference USA) Gale Group.
—Gently Through the Woods. 1982. (Scene of the Crime Mystery Ser.: No. 46). pap. 2.25 o.p. (*0-440-13055-7*) Dell Publishing.
—Gently to the Summit. 1999. 208p. 21.95 (*0-7540-8553-8*, Black Dagger) BBC Audiobooks America.
—Gently with the Innocents. 1981. (Scene of the Crime Mystery Ser.: No. 28). pap. 2.25 o.p. (*0-440-12834-X*) Dell Publishing.
—Gently with the Millions. unabr. ed. 2001. audio 49.95 (*1-85695-472-2*, 92104) ISIS Audio Bks. GBR. *Dist:* Ulverscroft Large Print Bks., Ltd.
—Gently with the Painters. 1996. 208p. 19.50 (*0-7451-8675-0*, Black Dagger) BBC Audiobooks America.
—The Honfleur Decision. 1984. 182p. pap. 2.95 o.p. (*0-8027-3084-1*); 1981. 9.95 o.s.i (*0-8027-5437-6*) Walker & Co.
—Landed Gently. 1995. 224p. 19.50 o.p. (*0-7451-8663-7*, Black Dagger) BBC Audiobooks America.
—Landed Gently. 1982. (Scene of the Crime Ser.: No. 38). pap. 2.25 o.p. (*0-440-14711-5*) Dell Publishing.
—Over Here. l.t. ed. 2003. 245p. pap. 24.45 (*0-7862-5411-4*) Thorndike Pr.
—The Scottish Decision. 1981. 145p. 9.95 o.s.i (*0-8027-5456-2*); 1985. 192p. reprint ed. pap. 2.95 o.s.i (*0-8027-3113-9*) Walker & Co.
—The Unhanged Man. 1984. 192p. 12.95 o.s.i (*0-8027-5602-6*) Walker & Co.

**GENTRY, MEG (FICTITIOUS CHARACTER)—FICTION**

Huges, Charlotte. Valley of the Shadow. 1998. mass mkt. 5.99 (*0-380-78454-8*, Avon Bks.) Morrow/Avon.

**GENTRY, MERRY (FICTITIOUS CHARACTER)—FICTION**

Hamilton, Laurell K. A Caress of Twilight. 2003. 368p. mass mkt. 7.50 (*0-345-42342-9*, Fawcett); 2002. 336p. 23.95 o.s.i (*0-345-43527-3*) Ballantine Bks.
—A Kiss of Shadows. 2002. 480p. mass mkt. 6.99 (*0-345-42340-2*, Ballantine Bks.) Ballantine Bks.
—A Kiss of Shadows. unabr. ed. 2000. (Meredith Gentry Ser.). audio 34.95 (*1-58788-124-1*, 2380, Brilliance Audio Unabridged); audio 89.25 (*1-58788-125-X*, 2381, Unabridged Library Editions) Brilliance Audio.
—A Kiss of Shadows. l.t. ed. 2001. (Wheeler Large Print Book Ser.). 637p. 26.95 (*1-58724-014-9*, Wheeler Publishing, Inc.) Gale Group.
—Seduced by Moonlight. 2004. 336p. 23.95 (*0-345-44356-X*) Ballantine Bks.

**GHOTE, GANESH, INSPECTOR (FICTITIOUS CHARACTER)—FICTION**

Keating, H. R. F. Asking Questions. unabr. ed. 1997. audio 54.95 ISIS Audio Bks. GBR. *Dist:* Ulverscroft Large Print Bks., Ltd.
—Asking Questions. 1997. 282p. text 20.95 o.p. (*0-312-15057-1*, Saint Martin's Minotaur) St. Martin's Pr.
—Bats Fly up for Inspector Ghote. 1984. (Inspector Ghote Mystery Ser.). 190p. pap. 7.95 (*0-89733-120-6*) Academy Chicago Pubs., Ltd.
—The Body in the Billiard Room. 1988. 39.50 o.p. (*0-14-778384-4*) Penguin Group (USA) Inc.
—The Body in the Billiard Room. (Crime Ser.). 1988. 256p. pap. 3.95 o.p. (*0-14-010171-3*, Penguin Bks.); 1987. 224p. 15.95 o.p. (*0-670-81744-9*) Viking Penguin.
—Body in the Billiard Room. l.t. ed. 1988. (Mainstream Ser.). 19.95 o.p. (*1-85089-133-8*) ISIS Large Print Bks. GBR. *Dist:* Transaction Pubs.
—The Body in the Billiard Room. unabr. ed. 1988. audio 49.00 (*1-55690-064-3*, 88990) Recorded Bks., LLC.
—Breaking & Entering. unabr. ed. 2001. (Inspector Ghote Mystery Ser.). audio 54.95 (*0-7531-0991-3*, 010306) ISIS Audio Bks. GBR. *Dist:* ISIS Publishing.
—Breaking & Entering: An Inspector Ghote Mystery. 2001. 272p. 23.95 (*0-312-26952-8*, Saint Martin's Minotaur) St. Martin's Pr.
—Bribery, Corruption Also. 1999. 256p. 23.95 o.p. (*0-312-20502-3*, Saint Martin's Minotaur) St. Martin's Pr.
—Bribery, Corruption Also. l.t. ed. 1999. (Ulverscroft Large Print Ser.). 368p. 31.99 o.p. (*0-7089-4149-4*, Ulverscroft) Thorpe, F. A. Pubs. GBR. *Dist:* Ulverscroft Large Print Bks., Ltd., Ulverscroft Large Print Canada, Ltd.
—Cheating Death. unabr. ed. 2001. audio 49.95 (*1-85695-835-3*, 940810) ISIS Audio Bks. GBR. *Dist:* Ulverscroft Large Print Bks., Ltd.
—Cheating Death. l.t. ed. 1993. (Magna Large Print Ser.). 352p. o.p. (*0-7505-0480-3*) Magna Large Print Bks. GBR. *Dist:* Ulverscroft Large Print Canada, Ltd.
—Cheating Death. 1994. 176p. 18.95 o.s.i (*0-89296-512-6*) Mysterious Pr.
—Dead on Time. l.t. ed. 1990. 16.95 o.p. (*0-7451-9762-0*, C0078); pap. 15.95 o.p. (*0-7927-0218-2*) BBC Audiobooks America.
—Dead on Time. l.t. ed. 1989. 288p. reprint ed. 19.95 o.p. (*1-85089-283-0*) ISIS Large Print Bks. GBR. *Dist:* Transaction Pubs.
—Dead on Time. 1990. 208p. mass mkt. 4.95 (*0-445-40800-6*, Mysterious Pr. Paperback Bks.) Warner Bks., Inc.
—Dead on Time: An Inspector Ghote Mystery. 1989. 208p. 16.45 o.p. (*0-89296-386-7*) Mysterious Pr.
—Doing Wrong. 1995. 218p. 44.00 o.p. (*0-333-60413-X*); pap. 24.00 (*0-330-34004-2*) Pan Bks. Ltd. GBR. *Dist:* Trans-Atlantic Pubns., Inc.
—Doing Wrong: An Inspector Ghote Novel. 1994. 192p. 20.00 o.s.i (*1-883402-80-8*, Scribner) Simon & Schuster.
—Filmi, Filmi, Inspector Ghote. 1985. (Inspector Ghote Mystery Ser.). 192p. pap. 7.95 (*0-89733-138-9*) Academy Chicago Pubs., Ltd.
—Go West, Inspector Ghote. 1982. pap. 3.95 o.p. (*0-14-006319-6*, Penguin Bks.) Viking Penguin.
—Go West Inspector Ghote. 1981. (Crime Club Ser.). 192p. 10.95 o.p. (*0-385-17683-X*) Doubleday Publishing.
—The Iciest Sin. l.t. ed. 1992. (Magna Large Print Ser.). 323p. 29.99 o.p. (*0-7505-0421-8*) Magna Large Print Bks. GBR. *Dist:* Ulverscroft Large Print Bks., Ltd., Ulverscroft Large Print Canada, Ltd.
—The Iciest Sin. 1990. 176p. 18.45 o.p. (*0-89296-427-8*) Mysterious Pr.
—The Iciest Sin. unabr. ed. 1993. audio 42.00 (*1-55690-891-1*, 93333) Recorded Bks., LLC.
—The Iciest Sin. 1991. 192p. mass mkt. 4.99 o.s.i (*0-446-40062-9*, Mysterious Pr. Paperback Bks.) Warner Bks., Inc.
—Inspector Ghote Breaks an Egg. 1985. (Inspector Ghote Mystery Ser.). 192p. reprint ed. pap. 7.95 (*0-89733-177-X*) Academy Chicago Pubs., Ltd.
—Inspector Ghote Breaks an Egg. 1997. pap. text o.p. (*0-17-556422-1*) Addison-Wesley Longman, Inc.
—Inspector Ghote Breaks an Egg. 1974. pap. 1.25 o.p. (*0-14-003839-6*) Penguin Group (USA) Inc.
—Inspector Ghote Caught in Meshes. 1985. (Inspector Ghote Mystery Ser.). 224p. reprint ed. pap. 7.95 (*0-89733-178-8*) Academy Chicago Pubs., Ltd.
—Inspector Ghote Draws a Line. 1985. (Inspector Ghote Mystery Ser.). 195p. pap. 7.95 (*0-89733-139-7*) Academy Chicago Pubs., Ltd.
—Inspector Ghote Draws a Line. 2002. 192p. (*0-7540-8613-5*, Black Dagger) BBC Audiobooks America.
—Inspector Ghote Draws a Line. 1979. 7.95 o.p. (*0-385-14873-9*) Doubleday Publishing.
—Inspector Ghote Hunts the Peacock. 1985. (Inspector Ghote Mystery Ser.). 192p. reprint ed. pap. 7.95 (*0-89733-179-6*) Academy Chicago Pubs., Ltd.
—Inspector Ghote Hunts the Peacock. l.t. ed. 1992. pap. 20.95 o.p. (*0-7927-1136-X*, CS0303); 1991. 22.95 o.p. (*0-7927-1135-1*, CH0232) BBC Audiobooks America.
—Inspector Ghote Plays a Joker. 1984. (Inspector Ghote Mystery Ser.). 189p. reprint ed. pap. 5.95 o.s.i (*0-89733-096-X*) Academy Chicago Pubs., Ltd.
—Inspector Ghote Trusts the Heart. 1983. (Inspector Ghote Mystery Ser.). 250p. reprint ed. pap. 5.95 o.s.i (*0-89733-083-8*) Academy Chicago Pubs., Ltd.
—The Perfect Murder. 1997. (Inspector Ghote Mystery Ser.). 256p. pap. 10.95 (*0-89733-078-1*) Academy Chicago Pubs., Ltd.
—The Perfect Murder. 2003. 224p. 21.95 (*0-7540-8635-6*, Black Dagger); 1991. 22.95 o.p. (*0-7927-0980-2*, CH0156); 1991. pap. 20.95 o.p. (*0-7927-0981-0*, CS0255) BBC Audiobooks America.
—The Perfect Murder. unabr. ed. 1995. audio 44.95 (*0-7861-0813-4*, 1636) Blackstone Audio Bks., Inc.
—The Sheriff of Bombay. 1984. (Crime Club Ser.). 192p. 11.95 o.p. (*0-385-19461-7*) Doubleday Publishing.
—Under a Monsoon Cloud. l.t. ed. 1988. (Mainstream Ser.). 283p. reprint ed. lib. bdg. 18.95 o.p. (*1-85089-233-4*) ISIS Large Print Bks. GBR. *Dist:* Transaction Pubs.
—Under a Monsoon Cloud. unabr. ed. 1990. audio 42.00 (*1-55690-536-X*, 90040) Recorded Bks., LLC.
—Under a Monsoon Cloud. 224p. 1987. pap. 3.95 o.p. (*0-14-009209-9*, Penguin Bks.); 1986. 15.95 o.p. (*0-670-80367-7*) Viking Penguin.

**GIBBONS, CUTHBERT (FICTITIOUS CHARACTER)—FICTION**

Bruno, Anthony. Bad Apple. 1995. 336p. mass mkt. 4.99 o.s.i (*0-440-21121-2*) Dell Publishing.
—Bad Blood. 1990. 288p. reprint ed. mass mkt. 4.99 o.s.i (*0-440-20705-3*) Dell Publishing.
—Bad Blood. 1989. 256p. 19.95 o.p. (*0-399-13432-8*, G. P. Putnam's Sons) Penguin Putnam Bks. for Young Readers.
—Bad Business. 1992. 304p. mass mkt. 4.99 o.s.i (*0-440-21120-4*) Dell Publishing.
—Bad Guys. 1992. 288p. mass mkt. 4.99 o.s.i (*0-440-21363-0*) Dell Publishing.
—Bad Guys. 1988. 256p. 17.95 o.p. (*0-399-13340-2*) Putnam Publishing Group, The.
—Bad Luck. 1991. 288p. mass mkt. 4.99 o.s.i (*0-440-20924-2*) Dell Publishing.
—Bad Moon. 1993. 336p. mass mkt. 4.99 o.s.i (*0-440-21559-5*) Dell Publishing.

**GIBBS, BOB (FICTITIOUS CHARACTER)—FICTION**

Leonard, Elmore. Maximum Bob. 1998. 304p. pap. 10.95 o.s.i (*0-385-32396-4*, Delta); 1992. 352p. mass mkt. 6.99 o.s.i (*0-440-21218-9*); 1991. 304p. 100.00 o.s.i (*0-385-30493-5*, Delacorte Pr.) Dell Publishing.
—Maximum Bob. l.t. ed. 1994. 335p. pap. 18.95 o.p. (*0-8161-5808-8*, Macmillan Reference USA) Gale Group.
—Maximum Bob: International Edition. 1992. 352p. mass mkt. 5.99 o.s.i (*0-440-29520-3*) Dell Publishing.

**GIBBS, CONOR (FICTITIOUS CHARACTER)—FICTION**

Atkins, Leo. Dead Run. 2000. 288p. mass mkt. 5.99 o.s.i (*0-425-17777-7*, Prime Crime) Berkley Publishing Group.
—Deadbeat. 1999. (P. I. Mysteries Ser.). 320p. mass mkt. 5.99 o.s.i (*0-425-16781-X*, Prime Crime) Berkley Publishing Group.
—Play Dead. 2000. (P. I. Mysteries Ser.). 257p. mass mkt. 5.99 o.s.i (*0-425-17362-3*, Prime Crime) Berkley Publishing Group.

**GIBSON, CAROL (FICTITIOUS CHARACTER)—FICTION**

Mickelbury, Penny. One Must Wait. 1998. 256p. 22.00 (*0-684-83741-2*, Simon & Schuster) Simon & Schuster.
—One Must Wait. 1999. 304p. mass mkt. 6.50 (*0-312-97186-9*, St. Martin's Paperbacks) St. Martin's Pr.
—Paradise Interrupted. 2001. 288p. 23.00 (*0-684-85991-2*, Simon & Schuster) Simon & Schuster.
—The Step Between. 240p. 2002. pap. 17.95 (*0-7432-4636-5*); 2000. 22.00 (*0-684-85990-4*) Simon & Schuster. (Simon & Schuster).
—Where to Choose. 1999. 256p. 22.00 (*0-684-83742-0*, Simon & Schuster) Simon & Schuster.
—Where to Choose. 2001. 240p. reprint ed. mass mkt. 6.50 (*0-312-97708-5*, 20-3261, St. Martin's Paperbacks) St. Martin's Pr.

**GIBSON, TOM (FICTITIOUS CHARACTER)—FICTION**

Munson, Ronald. Night Vision. 1995. 336p. 21.95 o.p. (*0-525-93781-1*, Dutton) Dutton/Plume.
—Night Vision. 1996. pap. 5.99 o.s.i (*0-451-40659-1*, Onyx); 416p. mass mkt. 5.99 o.s.i (*0-451-18013-5*, Signet Bks.) NAL.

**GIDEON, GEORGE (FICTITIOUS CHARACTER)—FICTION**

Marric, J. J. Gideon's Art. 1990. mass mkt. 3.50 o.s.i (*0-8217-3149-1*, Zebra Bks.) Kensington Publishing Corp.
—Gideon's Badge. l.t. ed. 1980. (Ulverscroft Large Print Ser.). 354p. 29.99 o.p. (*0-7089-0535-8*, Ulverscroft) Thorpe, F. A. Pubs. GBR. *Dist:* Ulverscroft Large Print Bks., Ltd., Ulverscroft Large Print Canada, Ltd.
—Gideon's Day. 1989. mass mkt. 3.95 o.p. (*0-8217-2721-4*, Zebra Bks.) Kensington Publishing Corp.
—Gideon's Day. 1985. 304p. pap. 2.95 o.p. (*0-8128-8197-4*, Scarborough Hse.) Madison Bks., Inc.
—Gideon's Day. l.t. ed. 1972. (Ulverscroft Large Print Ser.). 29.99 o.p. (*0-85456-138-2*, Ulverscroft) Thorpe, F. A. Pubs. GBR. *Dist:* Ulverscroft Large Print Bks., Ltd., Ulverscroft Large Print Canada, Ltd.
—Gideon's Drive. 2003. 192p. 21.95 (*0-7540-8640-2*, Black Dagger) BBC Audiobooks America.
—Gideon's Drive. 1976. (Harper Novel of Suspense Ser.). 7.95 o.p. (*0-06-012821-6*) HarperCollins Pubs.
—Gideon's Drive. 1991. 224p. mass mkt. 3.50 o.p. (*0-8217-3322-2*, Zebra Bks.) Kensington Publishing Corp.
—Gideon's Drive. l.t. ed. 1978. (Ulverscroft Large Print Ser.). 29.99 o.p. (*0-7089-0164-6*, Ulverscroft) Thorpe, F. A. Pubs. GBR. *Dist:* Ulverscroft Large Print Bks., Ltd., Ulverscroft Large Print Canada, Ltd.
—Gideon's Fire. (Black Dagger Crime Ser.). 16.50 o.p. (*0-86220-814-9*, BD013, Black Dagger); 1992. audio 54.95 (*0-7451-2405-4*, CD 006) BBC Audiobooks America.
—Gideon's Fire. 1989. mass mkt. 3.50 o.s.i (*0-8217-2845-8*, Zebra Bks.) Kensington Publishing Corp.
—Gideon's Fire. l.t. ed. 1974. (Ulverscroft Large Print Ser.). 29.99 o.p. (*0-85456-264-8*, Ulverscroft) Thorpe, F. A. Pubs. GBR. *Dist:* Ulverscroft Large Print Bks., Ltd., Ulverscroft Large Print Canada, Ltd.
—Gideon's Fog. 1974. (Harper Novel of Suspense Ser.). 188p. 7.95 o.p. (*0-06-012798-8*) HarperCollins Pubs.
—Gideon's Fog. 1991. 224p. mass mkt. 3.50 o.s.i (*0-8217-3276-5*, Zebra Bks.) Kensington Publishing Corp.
—Gideon's Fog. l.t. ed. 1976. o.p. (*0-85456-422-5*, Ulverscroft) Thorpe, F. A. Pubs.
—Gideon's Force. 1985. 192p. 12.95 o.p. (*0-8128-3027-X*) Holt, Henry & Co.
—Gideon's Force. l.t. ed. 1980. (Ulverscroft Large Print Ser.). 29.99 o.p. (*0-7089-0422-X*, Ulverscroft) Thorpe, F. A. Pubs. GBR. *Dist:* Ulverscroft Large Print Bks., Ltd., Ulverscroft Large Print Canada, Ltd.
—Gideon's Law. 1991. 192p. 14.95 o.p. (*0-8128-3042-3*) Holt, Henry & Co.
—Gideon's Lot. 1990. mass mkt. 3.50 o.s.i (*0-8217-2927-6*, Zebra Bks.) Kensington Publishing Corp.
—Gideon's March. 1994. 192p. 16.95 o.p. (*0-7451-8640-8*, Black Dagger) BBC Audiobooks America.
—Gideon's March. 1990. mass mkt. 3.50 o.s.i (*0-8217-2876-8*, Zebra Bks.) Kensington Publishing Corp.
—Gideon's Men. 1990. mass mkt. 3.50 o.s.i (*0-8217-3219-6*, Zebra Bks.) Kensington Publishing Corp.
—Gideon's Men. l.t. ed. 1975. (Ulverscroft Large Print Ser.). 29.99 o.p. (*0-85456-325-3*, Ulverscroft) Thorpe, F. A. Pubs. GBR. *Dist:* Ulverscroft Large Print Bks., Ltd., Ulverscroft Large Print Canada, Ltd.

—Gideon's Month. 1989. mass mkt. 3.95 o.s.i (0-8217-2766-4, Zebra Bks.) Kensington Publishing Corp.
—Gideon's Month. pap. 2.95 o.p. (0-8128-8207-5, Scarborough Hse.) Madison Bks., Inc.
—Gideon's Month. l.t. ed. 1975. (Ulverscroft Large Print Ser.). 29.99 o.p. (0-85456-313-X, Ulverscroft) Thorpe, F. A. Pubs. GBR. Dist: Ulverscroft Large Print Bks., Ltd., Ulverscroft Large Print Canada, Ltd.
—Gideon's Night. 1989. mass mkt. 3.50 o.s.i (0-8217-2734-6, Zebra Bks.) Kensington Publishing Corp.
—Gideon's Night. 1985. 192p. pap. 2.95 o.p. (0-8128-8198-2, Scarborough Hse.) Madison Bks., Inc.
—Gideon's Power. 1990. mass mkt. 3.50 o.p. (0-8217-3105-X, Zebra Bks.) Kensington Publishing Corp.
—Gideon's Power. 1986. pap. 2.95 o.p. (0-8128-8307-1, Scarborough Hse.) Madison Bks., Inc.
—Gideon's Press. 1973. (Harper Novel of Suspense Ser.). 192p. 7.95 o.p. (0-06-012787-2) HarperCollins Pubs.
—Gideon's Press. 1990. mass mkt. 3.50 o.s.i (0-8217-3243-9, Zebra Bks.) Kensington Publishing Corp.
—Gideon's Press. l.t. ed. 1977. (Ulverscroft Large Print Ser.). 29.99 o.p. (0-7089-0031-3, Ulverscroft) Thorpe, F. A. Pubs. GBR. Dist: Ulverscroft Large Print Bks., Ltd., Ulverscroft Large Print Canada, Ltd.
—Gideon's Ride. 1990. mass mkt. 3.50 o.s.i (0-8217-2900-4, Zebra Bks.) Kensington Publishing Corp.
—Gideon's Ride. l.t. ed. 1974. (Ulverscroft Large Print Ser.). 29.99 o.p. (0-85456-234-6, Ulverscroft) Thorpe, F. A. Pubs. GBR. Dist: Ulverscroft Large Print Bks., Ltd., Ulverscroft Large Print Canada, Ltd.
—Gideon's Risk. 1989. mass mkt. 3.50 o.s.i (0-8217-2823-7, Zebra Bks.) Kensington Publishing Corp.
—Gideon's Risk. pap. 2.95 o.p. (0-8128-8226-1, Scarborough Hse.) Madison Bks., Inc.
—Gideon's River. 1995. 224p. 18.50 o.p. (0-7451-8654-8, Black Dagger) BBC Audiobooks America.
—Gideon's River. Barzun, Jacques & Taylor, W. H., eds. 1983. (Crime Fiction 1950-1975 Ser.). 143p. lib. bdg. 18.00 o.p. (0-8240-4956-X) Garland Publishing, Inc.
—Gideon's River. 1990. mass mkt. 3.50 o.s.i (0-8217-3079-7, Zebra Bks.) Kensington Publishing Corp.
—Gideon's River. 1986. pap. 2.95 o.p. (0-8128-8286-5, Scarborough Hse.) Madison Bks., Inc.
—Gideon's River. l.t. ed. 1973. (Ulverscroft Large Print Ser.). 29.99 o.p. (0-85456-179-X, Ulverscroft) Thorpe, F. A. Pubs. GBR. Dist: Ulverscroft Large Print Bks., Ltd., Ulverscroft Large Print Canada, Ltd.
—Gideon's Sport. 1990. mass mkt. 3.50 o.p. (0-8217-3128-9, Zebra Bks.) Kensington Publishing Corp.
—Gideon's Sport. 1987. pap. 2.95 o.p. (0-8128-8331-4, Scarborough Hse.) Madison Bks., Inc.
—Gideon's Sport. l.t. ed. 1980. (Ulverscroft Large Print Ser.). 334p. 29.99 o.p. (0-7089-0462-9, Ulverscroft) Thorpe, F. A. Pubs. GBR. Dist: Ulverscroft Large Print Bks., Ltd., Ulverscroft Large Print Canada, Ltd.
—Gideon's Staff. l.t. ed. 1991. pap. 16.95 o.p. (0-7927-0628-5, CS052); 1990. 18.95 o.p. (0-7927-0627-7, C0589) BBC Audiobooks America.
—Gideon's Staff. 1989. mass mkt. 3.50 o.s.i (0-8217-2797-4, Zebra Bks.) Kensington Publishing Corp.
—Gideon's Vote. 1990. mass mkt. 3.50 o.s.i (0-8217-2971-3, Zebra Bks.) Kensington Publishing Corp.
—Gideon's Vote. l.t. ed. 1982. 360p. 15.95 o.p. (0-7089-0745-8, Ulverscroft) Thorpe, F. A. Pubs. GBR. Dist: Ulverscroft Large Print Bks., Ltd.
—Gideon's Way. 1991. 192p. 14.95 o.p. (0-8128-3075-X) Holt, Henry & Co.
—Gideon's Way. 1987. pap. 3.50 o.s.i (0-8128-8329-2, Scarborough Hse.) Madison Bks., Inc.
—Gideon's Week. 1989. mass mkt. 3.95 o.s.i (0-8217-2722-2, Zebra Bks.) Kensington Publishing Corp.
—Gideon's Week. 1985. 192p. pap. 2.95 o.p. (0-8128-8199-0, Scarborough Hse.) Madison Bks., Inc.
—Gideon's Week. l.t. ed. 1969. (Ulverscroft Large Print Ser.). 29.99 o.p. (0-85456-659-7, Ulverscroft) Thorpe, F. A. Pubs. GBR. Dist: Ulverscroft Large Print Bks., Ltd., Ulverscroft Large Print Canada, Ltd.
—Gideon's Wrath. 1990. mass mkt. 3.50 o.p. (0-8217-3050-9, Zebra Bks.) Kensington Publishing Corp.
—Gideon's Wrath. l.t. ed. 1975. (Ulverscroft Large Print Ser.). 29.99 o.p. (0-85456-342-3, Ulverscroft) Thorpe, F. A. Pubs. GBR. Dist: Ulverscroft Large Print Bks., Ltd., Ulverscroft Large Print Canada, Ltd.
May, Gideon S. Gideon's Way. 1980. pap. 30.00 (0-907526-61-6) Alloway Publishing, Ltd. GBR. Dist: State Mutual Bk. & Periodical Service, Ltd.

### GILLARD, PATRICK (FICTITIOUS CHARACTER)—FICTION

Duffy, Margaret. Brass Eagle. 1990. 256p. mass mkt. 3.95 o.s.i (0-449-21887-2, Fawcett) Ballantine Bks.
—Brass Eagle. unabr. ed. 1998. audio 83.95 (1-85903-017-3) Magna Story Sound GBR. Dist: Ulverscroft Large Print Bks., Ltd.
—Brass Eagle. 1989. 15.95 o.p. (0-312-02880-6, Saint Martin's Minotaur) St. Martin's Pr.
—Brass Eagle. l.t. ed. 1991. (Ulverscroft Large Print Ser.). 29.99 o.p. (0-7089-2347-X, Ulverscroft) Thorpe, F. A. Pubs. GBR. Dist: Ulverscroft Large Print Bks., Ltd., Ulverscroft Large Print Canada, Ltd.
—Death of a Raven. 1989. 240p. mass mkt. 3.50 o.s.i (0-449-21741-8, Fawcett) Ballantine Bks.
—Death of a Raven. 1988. 224p. 15.95 o.p. (0-312-02567-X, Saint Martin's Minotaur) St. Martin's Pr.
—Death of a Raven. l.t. ed. 1990. (Ulverscroft Large Print Ser.). 29.99 o.p. (0-7089-2202-3, Ulverscroft) Thorpe, F. A. Pubs. GBR. Dist: Ulverscroft Large Print Bks., Ltd., Ulverscroft Large Print Canada, Ltd.
—A Murder of Crows. 1988. mass mkt. 3.50 o.s.i (0-449-21563-6, Fawcett) Ballantine Bks.
—A Murder of Crows. 1988. 240p. 15.95 o.p. (0-312-01483-X, Saint Martin's Minotaur) St. Martin's Pr.
—A Murder of Crows. l.t. ed. 1989. (Ulverscroft Large Print Ser.). 531p. 29.99 o.p. (0-7089-1929-4, Ulverscroft) Thorpe, F. A. Pubs. GBR. Dist: Ulverscroft Large Print Bks., Ltd., Ulverscroft Large Print Canada, Ltd.
—Rook-Shoot. l.t. ed. 1993. (Dales Mystery Ser.). 392p. pap. 19.99 (1-85389-399-4) Dales Large Print Bks. GBR. Dist: Ulverscroft Large Print Bks., Ltd.
—Rook-Shoot. 1991. 240p. 17.95 o.p. (0-312-06456-X, Saint Martin's Minotaur) St. Martin's Pr.
—Who Killed Cock Robin? 1990. 224p. 16.95 o.p. (0-312-04988-9, Saint Martin's Minotaur) St. Martin's Pr.

### GILLESPIE, CLAIRE (FICTITIOUS CHARACTER)—FICTION

Smith, Taylor. Random Acts. abr. ed. 1998. audio 7.99 (1-55204-154-9) Durkin Hayes Publishing Ltd.
—Random Acts. 1998. (Mira Bks.). 441p. mass mkt. (1-55166-431-3, 1-66431-7, Mira Bks.) Harlequin Enterprises, Ltd.

### GILLIS, MEG (FICTITIOUS CHARACTER)—FICTION

Songer, C. J. Bait. 1999. 384p. mass mkt. 6.99 (0-06-101424-9, HarperTorch) Morrow/Avon.
—Bait. 1998. 320p. 23.00 (0-684-85042-7, Scribner) Simon & Schuster.
—Hook. 1999. 304p. 24.00 o.s.i (0-684-85043-5, Scribner) Simon & Schuster.
—The Hook: A Meg Gillis Crime Novel. 2001. 320p. mass mkt. 6.99 (0-06-109874-4, HarperTorch) Morrow/Avon.

### GIORDANO, TEDDY (FICTITIOUS CHARACTER)—FICTION

Hoff, B. J. The Tangled Web. unabr. ed. 1998. (Daybreak Mystery Ser.: Bk. 3). audio 39.95 (1-55686-838-3) Books in Motion.
—The Tangled Web. 1991. (Daybreak Mystery Ser.: No. 3). 207p. pap. 6.95 o.p. (0-89636-242-6) Cook Communications Ministries.
—The Tangled Web. l.t. ed. 1998. (Christian Mystery Ser.). 279p. 23.95 (0-7862-1473-2) Thorndike Pr.
—The Tangled Web. 1997. (Daybreak Mysteries Ser.). 189p. pap. 8.99 o.p. (0-8423-7194-X) Tyndale Hse. Pubs.

### GIRARD, TERRY (FICTITIOUS CHARACTER)—FICTION

Kunz, Kathleen. Murder Once Removed. 1995. (WWL Mystery Ser.). 252p. per. (0-373-26175-6, 1-26175-9, Harlequin Bks.) Harlequin Enterprises, Ltd.
—Murder Once Removed. 1993. (Terry Girard Mystery Ser.). 216p. 19.95 o.p. (0-8027-3230-5) Walker & Co.

### GIRAUD, JULES (FICTITIOUS CHARACTER)—FICTION

Lescroart, John. Rasputin's Revenge. 1988. 288p. reprint ed. pap. 3.50 (0-8439-2671-6) Dorchester Publishing Co., Inc.
—Rasputin's Revenge. 2003. 288p. pap. 14.00 (0-451-20981-8) NAL.
—Rasputin's Revenge: The Further Startling Adventures of Auguste Lupa—Son of Holmes. 1987. 288p. 17.95 o.s.i (1-55611-011-1) Fine, Donald I. Bks.
—Son of Holmes. l.t. ed. 1991. 19.95 o.p. (0-7927-0735-4, CH018); pap. 17.95 o.p. (0-7927-0736-2, CS0122) BBC Audiobooks America.
—Son of Holmes. 1987. 256p. reprint ed. pap. 3.25 o.s.i (0-8439-2461-6) Dorchester Publishing Co., Inc.
—Son of Holmes. 1986. 223p. 15.95 o.s.i (0-917657-64-0) Fine, Donald I. Bks.
—Son of Holmes. 2003. 256p. pap. 14.00 (0-451-20875-7) NAL.
—Son of Holmes & Rasputin's Revenge: The Early Works of John T. Lescroart. 1995. 544p. pap. 16.95 o.s.i (1-55611-437-0) Fine, Donald I. Bks.

### GIVEN, SUSAN (FICTITIOUS CHARACTER)—FICTION

Barrett, Margaret & Dennis, Charles. Given the Evidence. 1999. 400p. reprint ed. mass mkt. 6.50 o.s.i (0-671-00154-X, Pocket) Simon & Schuster.
Barrett, Margaret, et al. Given the Evidence. 1998. 320p. 23.00 (0-671-00153-1, Atria) Simon & Schuster.
Rudman, Anne Beane, et al. Given the Crime. 1998. 336p. pap. 6.50 (0-671-00152-3, Pocket); 320p. 22.00 (0-671-00151-5, Atria) Simon & Schuster.

### GIVENS, RAYLAN (FICTITIOUS CHARACTER)—FICTION

Leonard, Elmore. Pronto. 1994. 384p. mass mkt. 6.50 o.s.i (0-440-21443-2) Dell Publishing.
—Pronto. 1998. 272p. pap. 9.95 o.s.i (0-385-33290-4) Doubleday Publishing.
—Riding the Rap. 1998. 304p. pap. 10.95 o.s.i (0-385-32417-0, Delta); 1996. 352p. mass mkt. 6.50 o.s.i (0-440-21441-6); 1995. 336p. mass mkt. 6.50 (0-440-29539-4) Dell Publishing.
—Riding the Rap. l.t. ed. 1995. (Large Print Bks.). 27.95 (1-56895-224-4, Wheeler Publishing, Inc.) Gale Group.
—Riding the Rap. 2002. 352p. mass mkt. 7.50 (0-06-008218-6) HarperCollins Pubs.

### GLAUBERMAN, ALEX (FICTITIOUS CHARACTER)—FICTION

Cluster, Dick. Obligations of the Bone. 1992. 18.95 o.p. (0-312-08274-6, Saint Martin's Minotaur) St. Martin's Pr.

### GLEASON, IZZY (FICTITIOUS CHARACTER)—FICTION

Hamill, Denis. Three Quarters. 1999. 352p. pap. 6.99 (0-671-00250-3, Pocket Star); 1998. 320p. 23.00 o.s.i (0-671-00249-X, Atria) Simon & Schuster.
—Throwing 7's. 1999. 319p. 24.00 (0-671-02614-3, Atria); 2000. (Illus.). 592p. reprint ed. pap. 6.99 (0-671-02615-1, Pocket Star) Simon & Schuster.

### GLENDOWER, HARRY, LORD (FICTITIOUS CHARACTER)—FICTION

Roberts, Meg-Lynn. Lord Diablo's Demise. 1996. mass mkt. 4.50 o.s.i (0-8217-5338-X, Zebra Bks.) Kensington Publishing Corp.

### GLENDOWER, TOBY (FICTITIOUS CHARACTER)—FICTION

Arnold, Margot, pseud. The Cape Cod Caper. 1982. (Murder Mystery Ser.). 192p. 2.50 (0-86721-206-3, Jove) Berkley Publishing Group.
—The Cape Cod Caper. 1988. (Penny Spring & Sir Toby Glendower Mystery Ser.). 192p. pap. 7.95 (0-88150-116-6, Foul Play) Norton, W. W. & Co., Inc.
—The Cape Cod Conundrum. (Penny Spring & Sir Toby Glendower Mystery Ser.). 224p. 1992. text 20.00 o.p. (0-88150-244-8); 1994. reprint ed. pap. 7.95 (0-88150-293-6) Norton, W. W. & Co., Inc. (Foul Play).
—The Catacomb Conspiracy. 1992. (Penny Spring & Sir Toby Glendower Mystery Ser.). 260p. 18.95 o.p. (0-88150-208-1) Countryman Pr.
—The Catacomb Conspiracy. 1993. (Penny Spring & Sir Toby Glendower Mystery Ser.). 240p. pap. 7.95 (0-88150-255-3, Foul Play) Norton, W. W. & Co., Inc.
—Death of a Voodoo Doll. 1989. 220p. reprint ed. pap. 7.95 (0-88150-132-8, Foul Play) Norton, W. W. & Co., Inc.
—Death on the Dragon's Tongue. 1982. 224p. 2.50 (0-86721-150-4, Jove) Berkley Publishing Group.
—Death on the Dragon's Tongue. 1990. (Penny Spring & Sir Toby Glendower Mystery Ser.). 224p. reprint ed. pap. 7.95 (0-88150-158-1, Foul Play) Norton, W. W. & Co., Inc.
—Dirge for a Dorset Druid. (Penny Spring & Sir Toby Glendower Mystery Ser.). 240p. 1995. pap. 7.95 (0-88150-334-7); 1993. 20.00 (0-88150-266-9) Norton, W. W. & Co., Inc. (Foul Play).
—Exit Actors, Dying. 1982. 176p. 2.50 (0-86721-181-4, Jove) Berkley Publishing Group.
—Exit Actors, Dying. 1988. (Penny Spring & Sir Toby Glendower Mystery Ser.). 176p. reprint ed. pap. 7.95 (0-88150-115-8, Foul Play) Norton, W. W. & Co., Inc.
—Lament for a Lady Laird. 1982. 224p. 2.50 (0-86721-132-6, Jove) Berkley Publishing Group.
—Lament for a Lady Laird. 1990. (Penny Spring & Sir Toby Glendower Mystery Ser.). 224p. reprint ed. pap. 7.95 (0-88150-159-X, Foul Play) Norton, W. W. & Co., Inc.
—The Menehune Murders. 1989. (Penny Spring & Sir Toby Glendower Mystery Ser.). 240p. 17.95 o.p. (0-88150-149-2) Countryman Pr.
—The Menehune Murders. 1991. (Penny Spring & Sir Toby Glendower Mystery Ser.). 260p. pap. 7.95 (0-88150-196-4, Foul Play) Norton, W. W. & Co., Inc.
—The Midas Murders. 1995. (Penny Spring & Sir Toby Glendower Mystery Ser.). 224p. 20.00 (0-88150-340-1, Foul Play) Norton, W. W. & Co., Inc.
—The Midas Murders: A Penny Spring & Sir Toby Glendower Mystery. 1997. (Penny Spring & Sir Toby Glendower Mystery Ser.). 224p. pap. 7.95 (0-88150-394-0) Norton, W. W. & Co., Inc.
—Toby's Folly. 1990. 256p. 18.95 o.p. (0-88150-177-8) Countryman Pr.
—Toby's Folly. 1992. (Penny Spring & Sir Toby Glendower Mystery Ser.). 256p. pap. 7.95 (0-88150-228-6, Foul Play) Norton, W. W. & Co., Inc.
—Zadok's Treasure. 1982. 192p. 2.50 (0-86721-228-4, Jove) Berkley Publishing Group.
—Zadok's Treasure. 1989. (Penny Spring & Sir Toby Glendower Mystery Ser.). 192p. reprint ed. pap. 7.95 (0-88150-133-6, Foul Play) Norton, W. W. & Co., Inc.

### GLENNING, PAULA (FICTITIOUS CHARACTER)—FICTION

Clarke, Anna. Cabin Three Thousand Thirty-Three. 1989. 3.50 (1-55773-251-5, Diamond Bks.) Berkley Publishing Group.
—Cabin Three Thousand Thirty-Three. 1986. (Crime Club Ser.). 192p. 12.95 o.p. (0-385-23264-0) Doubleday Publishing.
—Cabin Three Thousand Thirty-Three. l.t. ed. 1988. (Nightingale Ser.). 285p. 12.95 o.p. (0-8161-4387-0, Macmillan Reference USA) Gale Group.
—The Case of the Anxious Aunt. 1996. 208p. mass mkt. 5.99 o.p. (0-425-15311-8) Berkley Publishing Group.
—The Case of the Ludicrous Letters. 1994. 208p. (Orig.). mass mkt. 4.50 o.p. (0-425-14048-2) Berkley Publishing Group.
—The Case of the Paranoid Patient. 1993. 192p. mass mkt. 3.99 o.p. (0-425-13858-5) Berkley Publishing Group.
—The Case of the Paranoid Patient. l.t. ed. 1993. (Nightingale Ser.). 300p. lib. bdg. 15.95 (0-8161-5845-2, Macmillan Reference USA) Gale Group.
—Last Judgment. 1985. (Crime Club Ser.). 192p. 11.95 o.p. (0-385-19666-0) Doubleday Publishing.
—Last Seen in London. 1987. (Crime Club Ser.). 192p. o.s.i (0-385-23559-3) Doubleday Publishing.
—Last Seen in London. l.t. ed. 1992. 340p. pap. 14.95 o.p. (0-8161-5452-X, Macmillan Reference USA) Gale Group.
—Murder in Writing. 1990. 3.50 (1-55773-326-0, Diamond Bks.) Berkley Publishing Group.
—Murder in Writing. 1988. (Crime Club Ser.). 192p. pap. 15.00 (0-385-24325-1) Doubleday Publishing.
—Mystery Lady. 1986. (Crime Club Ser.). 192p. 12.95 o.p. (0-385-23546-1) Doubleday Publishing.
—The Whitelands Affair. 1992. mass mkt. 3.99 o.p. (0-425-13268-4) Berkley Publishing Group.

### GLICK, MURRAY (FICTITIOUS CHARACTER)—FICTION

Katz, Michael J. The Big Freeze. 1991. 256p. 21.95 o.p. (0-399-13558-8, G. P. Putnam's Sons) Penguin Group (USA) Inc.
—Last Dance in Redondo Beach. 1989. 256p. 17.95 o.p. (0-399-13445-X, G. P. Putnam's Sons) Penguin Putnam Bks. for Young Readers.
—Last Dance in Redondo Beach. 1990. 288p. bds. 3.95 (0-671-67913-9, Pocket) Simon & Schuster.
—Murder off the Glass. 1987. 16.95 o.p. (0-8027-5667-0) Walker & Co.

### GLITSKY, ABE (FICTITIOUS CHARACTER)—FICTION

Lescroart, John. A Certain Justice. 1996. pap. 6.99 (0-440-29547-5) Bantam Bks.
—A Certain Justice. 1996. 544p. mass mkt. 7.99 (0-440-22104-8) Dell Publishing.
—A Certain Justice. 1995. 448p. 22.95 o.p. (1-55611-445-1) Fine, Donald I. Bks.
—A Certain Justice. l.t. ed. 1996. 756p. 25.95 (0-7838-1565-4, Macmillan Reference USA) Gale Group.

### GOD SQUAD (FICTITIOUS CHARACTERS)—FICTION

Meyer, Charles. Beside the Still Waters. 1997. (Reverend Lucas Holt Mystery Ser.). 232p. pap. 6.50 (0-9631149-4-8) Stone Angel Bks.
—Blessed Are the Merciless. 1996. 272p. mass mkt. 5.50 o.s.i (0-425-15140-9) Berkley Publishing Group.
—Blessed Are the Merciless. 2nd ed. 1997. (Reverend Lucas Holt Mystery Ser.). 266p. reprint ed. pap. 6.50 (0-9631149-5-6) Stone Angel Bks.
—The Saints of God Murders. 1995. 256p. (Orig.). mass mkt. 5.99 o.s.i (0-425-14869-6, Prime Crime) Berkley Publishing Group.

### GODZILLA (FICTITIOUS CHARACTER)—FICTION

Bynum, Edward B. Godzillananda: His Life & Visions. 1996. 72p. pap. (1-57579-042-4) Pine Hill Pr., Inc.

Cerasini, Marc. Godzilla & the Lost Continent. 2000. (Godzilla Ser.). (J). pap. 5.99 (*0-679-88829-2*, Random Hse. Bks. for Young Readers) Random Hse. Children's Bks.

Godzilla. 1998. 80p. per. 16.95 (*0-7935-9834-6*) Leonard, Hal Corp.

Harmon, Jim. The Godzilla Book. 1986. 96p. lib. bdg. 19.95 o.p. (*0-8095-8080-2*) Millefleurs.

HarperCollins Staff. Godzilla Movie Postcard Book. 1998. (Illus.). 60p. mass mkt. 9.99 o.s.i (*0-06-107509-4*) HarperCollins Pubs.

Iwata, Kazuhisa. Godzilla. Stradley, Randy & Richardson, Mike, trs. from JPN. 1990. (Illus.). 192p. pap. 10.95 o.p. (*1-56971-035-X*) Dark Horse Comics.

—Godzilla. 2nd ed. 1995. (Illus.). 200p. (YA). (gr. 5 up). pap. 17.95 (*1-56971-063-5*) Dark Horse Comics.

Lees, J. D., et al. The Official Godzilla Compendium: A 40 Year Retrospective. 1998. (Illus.). 144p. (YA). (gr. 9-12). pap. 16.00 o.s.i (*0-679-88822-5*) Random Hse., Inc.

Marrero, Robert G. Godzilla-King of the Movie Monsters: An Illustrated Guide to Japanese Monster Movies. Winick, Margot, ed. 1996. (Illus.). 144p. (Orig.). pap. 15.95 o.s.i (*1-888214-01-5*) Fantasma Bks.

Molstad, Stephen. Godzilla. 1998. 240p. 23.00 o.p. (*0-06-105056-3*); 320p. mass mkt. 5.99 o.s.i (*0-06-105915-3*) Morrow/Avon. (Eos).

Scholastic, Inc. Staff. Godzilla: A Novelization. novel ed. 1998. (Godzilla Ser.). (Illus.). 152p. (J). (gr. 3-7). mass mkt. 3.99 (*0-590-28243-3*) Scholastic, Inc.

Sullivan, Robert E., Jr. Godzilla Discovers America. Tamalpais, Sal, ed. 1988. (Illus.). 48p. (Orig.). pap. 10.95 o.p. (*0-945223-00-5*) Nevraumont Publishing Co.

**GOFF, JAMES (FICTITIOUS CHARACTER)—FICTION**

Clarke, Anna. Cabin Three Thousand Thirty-Three. 1989. 3.50 (*1-55773-251-5*, Diamond Bks.) Berkley Publishing Group.

—Cabin Three Thousand Thirty-Three. 1986. (Crime Club Ser.). 192p. 12.95 o.p. (*0-385-23264-0*) Doubleday Publishing.

—Cabin Three Thousand Thirty-Three. l.t. ed. 1988. (Nightingale Ser.). 285p. 12.95 o.p. (*0-8161-4387-0*, Macmillan Reference USA) Gale Group.

—The Case of the Anxious Aunt. 1996. 208p. mass mkt. 5.99 o.p. (*0-425-15311-8*) Berkley Publishing Group.

—The Case of the Ludicrous Letters. 1994. 208p. (Orig.). mass mkt. 4.50 o.p. (*0-425-14048-2*) Berkley Publishing Group.

—The Case of the Paranoid Patient. 1993. 192p. mass mkt. 3.99 o.p. (*0-425-13858-5*) Berkley Publishing Group.

—The Case of the Paranoid Patient. l.t. ed. 1993. (Nightingale Ser.). 300p. lib. bdg. 15.95 (*0-8161-5845-2*, Macmillan Reference USA) Gale Group.

—Last Judgment. 1985. (Crime Club Ser.). 192p. 11.95 o.p. (*0-385-19666-0*) Doubleday Publishing.

—Last Seen in London. 1987. (Crime Club Ser.). 192p. o.s.i (*0-385-23559-3*) Doubleday Publishing.

—Last Seen in London. l.t. ed. 1992. 340p. pap. 14.95 o.p. (*0-8161-5452-X*, Macmillan Reference USA) Gale Group.

—Murder in Writing. 1990. 3.50 (*1-55773-326-0*, Diamond Bks.) Berkley Publishing Group.

—Murder in Writing. 1988. (Crime Club Ser.). 192p. pap. 15.00 (*0-385-24325-1*) Doubleday Publishing.

—Mystery Lady. 1986. (Crime Club Ser.). 192p. 12.95 o.p. (*0-385-23546-1*) Doubleday Publishing.

—The Whitelands Affair. 1992. mass mkt. 3.99 o.p. (*0-425-13268-4*) Berkley Publishing Group.

**GOICOCHEA, MARTA (FICTITIOUS CHARACTER)—FICTION**

Allen, Kate. I Knew You Would Call. 1995. 202p. (Orig.). pap. 10.95 (*0-934678-70-7*) New Victoria Pubs., Inc.

**GOLD, ARIEL (FICTITIOUS CHARACTER)—FICTION**

Mercer, Judy. Blind Spot. 2000. 480p. 23.95 (*0-671-03424-3*, Atria) Simon & Schuster.

—Double Take. l.t. ed. 1997. (G. K. Hall Mystery Ser.). 561p. 26.95 o.p. (*0-7838-8368-4*, Macmillan Reference USA) Gale Group.

—Double Take. 1997. 352p. 22.00 (*0-671-55707-6*, Atria) Simon & Schuster.

—Fast Forward. l.t. ed. 1996. (G. K. Hall Mystery Ser.). 593p. 22.95 o.p. (*0-7838-1495-X*, Macmillan Reference USA) Gale Group.

—Fast Forward. Date not set. pap. 3.99 (*0-671-02431-0*); 1997. (Illus.). 400p. pap. 6.99 (*0-671-89961-9*) Simon & Schuster. (Pocket).

—Fast Forward. Chernoff, Dona, ed. 1995. 352p. 22.00 o.p. (*0-671-89960-0*, Atria) Simon & Schuster.

—Split Image. l.t. ed. 1999. 26.95 (*1-56895-780-7*, Wheeler Publishing, Inc.) Gale Group.

—Split Image. 1999. (Illus.). 464p. pap. 6.99 (*0-671-55603-7*, Pocket); 1998. 340p. 23.00 (*0-671-55602-9*, Atria) Simon & Schuster.

**GOLD, NATALIE (FICTITIOUS CHARACTER)—FICTION**

Jaffe, Jody. Chestnut Mare, Beware. 1997. mass mkt. 5.99 o.s.i (*0-8041-1552-4*, Ivy Bks.); 1996. 288p. 21.00 o.s.i (*0-449-90998-0*, Fawcett) Ballantine Bks.

—Chestnut Mare, Beware. unabr. collector's ed. 1997. audio 64.00 (*0-7366-3599-8*, 4250) Books on Tape, Inc.

—Horse of a Different Killer. 1996. mass mkt. 5.99 o.s.i (*0-8041-1472-2*, Ivy Bks.); 1995. 288p. 21.00 o.s.i (*0-449-90997-2*) Ballantine Bks.

—Horse of a Different Killer. unabr. collector's ed. 1997. audio 48.00 (*0-913369-53-5*, 4265) Books on Tape, Inc.

—In Colt Blood. 1999. mass mkt. 5.99 o.s.i (*0-8041-1711-X*, Ivy Bks.) Ballantine Bks.

—In Colt Blood. collector's ed. 1999. audio 56.00 (*0-7366-4787-2*, 5134) Books on Tape, Inc.

**GOLD, RACHEL (FICTITIOUS CHARACTER)—FICTION**

Kahn, Michael A. Bearing Witness. 2000. (Rachel Gold Novels Ser.). 316p. 23.95 (*0-312-84883-8*, Forge Bks.) Doherty, Tom Assocs., LLC.

—Bearing Witness. 1999. pap. 21.95 (*0-525-94305-6*) NAL.

—Death Benefits: A Rachel Gold Mystery. 1992. (Rachel Gold Mystery Ser.). 320p. 19.00 o.p. (*0-525-93456-1*, Dutton) Dutton/Plume.

—Death Benefits: A Rachel Gold Mystery. 1994. (Rachel Gold Mystery Ser.). 320p. mass mkt. 4.99 o.s.i (*0-451-17687-1*, Signet Bks.) NAL.

—Due Diligence. 1996. (Rachel Gold Mystery Ser.). 400p. mass mkt. 5.99 o.s.i (*0-451-17970-6*, Signet Bks.) NAL.

—Due Dilligence: A Rachel Gold Mystery. 1995. (Rachel Gold Mystery Ser.). 336p. 20.95 o.s.i (*0-525-93743-9*, Dutton) Dutton/Plume.

—Firm Ambitions. 1995. 320p. mass mkt. 5.99 o.s.i (*0-451-17961-7*, Onyx) NAL.

—Firm Ambitions: A Rachel Gold Mystery. 1994. (Rachel Gold Mystery Ser.). 320p. 18.95 o.p. (*0-525-93742-0*, Dutton) Dutton/Plume.

—Grave Designs: A Rachel Gold Mystery. 1992. (Rachel Gold Mystery Ser.). 352p. mass mkt. 5.50 o.s.i (*0-451-40293-6*, Signet Bks.) NAL.

—Sheer Gall. 1996. (Rachel Gold Mystery Ser.). 320p. 23.95 o.s.i (*0-525-94188-6*) Dutton/Plume.

—Sheer Gall. 1998. (Rachel Gold Mystery Ser.). 368p. mass mkt. 5.99 o.s.i (*0-451-40733-4*, Onyx) NAL.

—Trophy Widow. E-Book 25.95 (*0-312-70732-0*, Tor Bks.); 2002. 432p. 25.95 (*0-7653-0218-7*, Forge Bks.) Doherty, Tom Assocs., LLC.

**GOLD, SHELDON (FICTITIOUS CHARACTER)—FICTION**

Devane, Terry. Juror Number Eleven: A Novel. 2003. 336p. mass mkt. 6.99 (*0-425-19066-8*) Berkley Publishing Group.

—Juror Number Eleven: A Novel. 2002. 320p. 24.95 o.s.i (*0-399-14886-8*) Penguin Group (USA) Inc.

—A Stain upon the Robe. 2004. 352p. mass mkt. 6.99 (*0-425-19742-5*) Berkley Publishing Group.

—A Stain upon the Robe. 2003. 304p. 24.95 (*0-399-15108-7*) Putnam Publishing Group, The.

—Uncommon Justice. 2002. 352p. reprint ed. mass mkt. 6.99 (*0-425-18424-2*) Berkley Publishing Group.

—Uncommon Justice. 2001. 240p. 24.95 o.p. (*0-399-14717-9*) Penguin Group (USA) Inc.

**GOLDMAN, DAVEY (FICTITIOUS CHARACTER)—FICTION**

Love, William F. Bishop's Revenge: A Bishop Regan & Davey Goldman Myster. 1993. 276p. 20.00 o.p. (*1-55611-351-X*) Fine, Donald I. Bks.

—Bloody Ten. 1992. 19.95 o.p. (*1-55611-275-0*) Fine, Donald I. Bks.

—Bloody Ten. 1994. mass mkt. (*0-373-26140-3*, Harlequin Bks.) Harlequin Enterprises, Ltd.

—The Chartreuse Clue. 1990. 18.95 o.p. (*1-55611-211-4*) Fine, Donald I. Bks.

—The Chartreuse Clue. 1991. 352p. reprint ed. mass mkt. 5.50 o.p. (*0-451-40273-1*, Onyx) NAL.

—The Fundamentals of Murder. 1991. 18.95 o.p. (*1-55611-233-5*) Fine, Donald I. Bks.

—The Ruby-Red Clue. 1992. Orig. Title: The Fundamentals of Murder. 288p. mass mkt. 4.99 o.s.i (*0-451-40329-0*, Onyx) NAL.

**GOMEZ, MISS (FICTITIOUS CHARACTER)—FICTION**

Trevor, William. Miss Gomez & the Brethren. 1997. 256p. pap. 11.95 (*0-14-025264-9*, Penguin Bks.) Penguin Group (USA) Inc.

**GOMEZ, SULLY (FICTITIOUS CHARACTER)—FICTION**

Cebulash, Mel. Dirty Money. 1993. 3.95 (*1-56420-002-7*) New Readers Pr.

—Dirty Money: A Sully Gomez Mystery. 1993. (J). audio 10.95 (*1-56420-003-5*) New Readers Pr.

—Knockout Punch: A Sully Gomez Mystery. 1993. audio 9.95 o.p. (*1-56420-009-4*); 3.95 o.p. (*1-56420-008-6*) New Readers Pr.

—Set to Explode: A Sully Gomez Mystery. 1993. 3.95 o.p. (*1-56420-004-3*) New Readers Pr.

—Set to Explode: A/Sully Gomez Mystery. 1993. (J). audio 10.00 o.p. (*1-56420-005-1*) New Readers Pr.

—A Sucker for Redheads: A Sully Gomez Mystery. 1993. audio 9.95 o.p. (*1-56420-007-8*); 3.95 o.p. (*1-56420-006-X*) New Readers Pr.

**GOOD, SALLY (FICTITIOUS CHARACTER)—FICTION**

Crider, Bill. Murder Is an Art. 1999. 256p. 21.95 o.p. (*0-312-19927-9*, Saint Martin's Minotaur) St. Martin's Pr.

**GOODMAN, JONATHAN (FICTITIOUS CHARACTER)—FICTION**

Oran, Daniel. Ulterior Motive. 1999. 384p. mass mkt. 5.99 o.s.i (*0-7860-0657-9*); 1998. 320p. mass mkt. 22.95 o.s.i (*1-57566-302-3*, Kensington Bks.) Kensington Publishing Corp.

—Ulterior Motive. 2001. E-Book 6.99 (*0-7592-1210-4*); 1998. 284p. per. 19.96 (*0-7592-1215-5*) eread-s.com.

**GOODMAN, RAYFORD (FICTITIOUS CHARACTER)—FICTION**

Cutler, Stan. Best Performance by a Patsy. 1991. (Goodman-Bradley Mystery Ser.). 352p. 18.95 o.p. (*0-525-93317-4*) Dutton/Plume.

—Best Performance by a Patsy. 1993. (Goodman-Bradley Mystery Ser.). 336p. mass mkt. 4.50 o.p. (*0-451-40359-2*, Onyx) NAL.

—The Face on the Cutting Room Floor. 1991. 320p. 18.95 o.p. (*0-525-93381-6*, Dutton) Dutton/Plume.

—The Face on the Cutting Room Floor. 1993. (Goodman-Bradley Mystery Ser.). 272p. mass mkt. 4.50 o.s.i (*0-451-40394-0*, Signet Bks.) NAL.

—Rough Cut. 1994. 336p. (Orig.). mass mkt. 4.99 o.s.i (*0-451-18253-7*) NAL.

—Shot on Location. 1993. (Goodman-Bradley Mystery Ser.). 352p. 19.00 o.p. (*0-525-93576-2*) Dutton/Plume.

—Shot on Location. 1994. (Goodman-Bradley Mystery Ser.). 336p. mass mkt. 4.99 o.p. (*0-451-40391-6*, Signet Bks.) NAL.

**GOODNIGHT, AUGUSTA (FICTITIOUS CHARACTER)—FICTION**

Ballard, Mignon F. Angel at Troublesome Creek. l.t. ed. 2000. (Beeler Large Print Mystery Ser.). 209p. 25.95 (*1-57490-275-X*, Beeler Large Print Bks.) Beeler, Thomas T. Publisher.

—Angel at Troublesome Creek. 2001. 224p. mass mkt. 5.99 (*0-425-17854-4*, Prime Crime) Berkley Publishing Group.

—Angel at Troublesome Creek. 1999. (Augusta Goodnight Mysteries Ser.). 213p. 22.95 (*0-312-24175-5*, Saint Martin's Minotaur) St. Martin's Pr.

—Angel at Troublesome Creek. 2001. 12.04 (*0-606-20547-0*) Turtleback Bks.

—An Angel to Die For. l.t. ed. 2001. (Beeler Large Print Mystery Ser.). 246p. 26.95 (*1-57490-337-3*, Beeler Large Print Bks.) Beeler, Thomas T. Publisher.

—An Angel to Die For. 2001. 208p. mass mkt. 5.99 o.s.i (*0-425-18208-8*) Berkley Publishing Group.

—The Angel Whispered Danger: An Augusta Goodnight Mystery. Date not set. pap. (*0-312-30814-0*, Saint Martin's Griffin); mass mkt. (*0-312-98643-2*, St. Martin's Paperbacks); 2003. 288p. 23.95 (*0-312-30813-2*, Saint Martin's Minotaur) St. Martin's Pr.

—Shadow of an Angel: An Augusta Goodnight Mystery. 2003. 256p. mass mkt. 5.99 (*0-425-18948-1*, Prime Crime) Berkley Publishing Group.

—Shadow of an Angel: An Augusta Goodnight Mystery. 2002. 304p. 23.95 (*0-312-28168-4*, Saint Martin's Minotaur) St. Martin's Pr.

**GORDIANUS THE FINDER (FICTITIOUS CHARACTER)—FICTION**

Saylor, Steven. Arms of Nemesis. 1993. 336p. reprint ed. mass mkt. 5.99 o.s.i (*0-8041-1127-8*, Ivy Bks.) Ballantine Bks.

—Arms of Nemesis. unabr. ed. 1997. audio 56.95 Blackstone Audio Bks., Inc.

—Arms of Nemesis. 1992. 320p. 19.95 o.p. (*0-312-08135-9*, Saint Martin's Minotaur) St. Martin's Pr.

—Catilina's Riddle. unabr. ed. 1997. audio 85.95 (*0-7861-1177-1*, 1920) Blackstone Audio Bks., Inc.

—Catilina's Riddle. 1993. 22.95 o.p. (*0-312-09763-8*) St. Martin's Pr.

—The House of the Vestals: The Investigations of Gordianus the Finder. 1998. mass mkt. (*0-312-96628-8*, St. Martin's Paperbacks); 1998. (House of Vestals Ser.: Vol. 1). 272p. mass mkt. 6.99 (*0-312-96452-8*, St. Martin's Paperbacks); 1997. 288p. 22.95 (*0-312-15444-5*, Saint Martin's Minotaur) St. Martin's Pr.

—Last Seen in Massilia. 2000. 277p. 23.95 (*0-312-20928-2*, Saint Martin's Minotaur); 2001. 288p. reprint ed. mass mkt. 6.50 (*0-312-97787-5*, St. Martin's Paperbacks) St. Martin's Pr.

—A Mist of Prophecies: A Novel of Ancient Rome. 2002. 288p. 24.95 (*0-312-27121-2*, Saint Martin's Minotaur) St. Martin's Pr.

—A Murder on the Appian Way. unabr. ed. 1996. audio 83.95 (*0-7861-0983-1*, 1760) Blackstone Audio Bks., Inc.

—A Murder on the Appian Way. 1996. 384p. 23.95 o.p. (*0-312-14377-X*, Saint Martin's Minotaur); 1997. 432p. reprint ed. mass mkt. 6.99 (*0-312-96173-1*, St. Martin's Paperbacks) St. Martin's Pr.

—Roman Blood. 1992. 416p. mass mkt. 6.50 o.s.i (*0-8041-1039-5*, Ivy Bks.) Ballantine Bks.

—Roman Blood. unabr. ed. 1996. audio 76.95 (*0-7861-1058-9*, 1829) Blackstone Audio Bks., Inc.

—Roman Blood. (St. Martin's Minotaur Mysteries Ser.). 2000. 416p. mass mkt. 6.99 (*0-312-97296-2*, St. Martin's Paperbacks); 1991. 288p. 19.95 (*0-312-06454-3*, Saint Martin's Minotaur) St. Martin's Pr.

—Rubicon. 2000. 301p. mass mkt. 6.50 (*0-312-97118-4*, St. Martin's Paperbacks); 1999. 288p. 23.95 o.p. (*0-312-20576-7*, Saint Martin's Minotaur) St. Martin's Pr.

—The Venus Throw. unabr. ed. 1997. audio 62.95 (*0-7861-1218-2*, 1998) Blackstone Audio Bks., Inc.

—The Venus Throw. l.t. ed. 1995. 587p. 25.95 o.p. (*0-7838-1443-7*, Macmillan Reference USA) Gale Group.

—The Venus Throw. 1995. x, 308p. 22.95 o.p. (*0-312-11912-7*, Saint Martin's Minotaur); 1996. 400p. reprint ed. pap. text 6.99 (*0-312-95778-5*, St. Martin's Paperbacks) St. Martin's Pr.

Saylor, Steven W. Catalina's Riddle. 1994. 480p. mass mkt. 6.50 (*0-8041-1269-X*, Ivy Bks.) Ballantine Bks.

**GORDON, LINDSAY (FICTITIOUS CHARACTER)—FICTION**

McDermid, Val. Booked for Murder. 2nd ed. 2000. (Lindsay Gordon Mystery Ser.). 260p. pap. 12.00 (*1-883523-37-0*) Spinsters Ink Bks.

—Common Murder. 2nd ed. 1995. 264p. pap. 10.95 (*1-883523-08-7*) Spinsters Ink Bks.

—Common Murder. l.t. ed. 2001. 286p. 32.50 (*0-7531-6538-4*) Thorpe, F. A. Pubs. GBR. *Dist:* Ulverscroft Large Print Bks., Ltd., Ulverscroft Large Print Canada, Ltd.

—Conferences Are Murder: A Lindsay Gordon Mystery. 1999. (Lindsay Gordon Mystery Ser.: Vol. 4). (Illus.). 264p. pap. 12.00 (*1-883523-30-3*) Spinsters Ink Bks.

—Deadline for Murder: A Lindsay Gordon Mystery. 2nd ed. 1997. (Kate Brannigan Mystery Ser.). 264p. (Orig.). pap. 10.95 (*1-883523-17-6*) Spinsters Ink Bks.

—Final Edition. unabr. ed. 2003. audio compact disk 71.95 (*0-7531-2214-6*) ISIS Audio Bks. GBR. *Dist:* Ulverscroft Large Print Bks., Ltd.

—Final Edition. l.t. ed. 2001. 288p. 32.50 (*0-7531-6540-6*) Thorpe, F. A. Pubs. GBR. *Dist:* Ulverscroft Large Print Bks., Ltd., Ulverscroft Large Print Canada, Ltd.

—Report for Murder. l.t. ed. 2001. (Magna Large Print Ser.). 400p. 32.50 (*0-7505-1699-2*) Magna Large Print Bks. GBR. *Dist:* Ulverscroft Large Print Bks., Ltd., Ulverscroft Large Print Canada, Ltd.

—Report for Murder. 224p. 25.00 (*0-7278-5554-9*) Severn Hse. Pubs., Ltd.

—Report for Murder. 2nd ed. 1998. 264p. pap. 10.95 (*1-883523-24-9*) Spinsters Ink Bks.

—Report for Murder. 1989. 208p. 16.95 o.p. (*0-312-03888-7*, Saint Martin's Minotaur) St. Martin's Pr.

McDermid, Val & Sylvester, Vari. Final Edition. unabr. ed. 2002. audio 54.95 (*0-7531-1155-1*) Soundings, Ltd. GBR. *Dist:* Ulverscroft Large Print Bks., Ltd.

**GORMENGHAST FAMILY (FICTITIOUS CHARACTER)—FICTION**

Peake, Mervyn. Gormenghast. 1978. mass mkt. 2.50 o.s.i (*0-345-27699-X*); 1973. mass mkt. 1.25 o.s.i (*0-345-23519-3*); 1970. mass mkt. 0.95 o.s.i (*0-345-21118-9*) Ballantine Bks.

—Gormenghast. 2000. 24.95 (*1-58567-082-0*); 1982. (Gormenghast Trilogy: Vol. II). (Illus.). 524p. 30.00 (*0-87951-144-3*) Overlook Pr., The.

—The Gormenghast Novels: Titus Groan, Gormenghast, Titus Alone. 2000. 1168p. 28.95 (*0-87951-628-3*) Overlook Pr., The.

—The Gormenghast Trilogy. 1991. (Gormenghast Trilogy: Vol. II). (Illus.). 264p. pap. 16.95 (*0-87951-426-4*); 1988. 1032p. 40.00 (*0-87951-974-6*); Vol. III. 1991. (Illus.). 262p. pap. 16.95 (*0-87951-427-2*) Overlook Pr., The.

—Titus Alone. 1978. mass mkt. 2.50 o.s.i (*0-345-28193-4*); 1977. mass mkt. 1.95 o.s.i (*0-345-25791-X*); 1974. mass mkt. 1.50 o.s.i (*0-345-24323-4*); 1973. mass mkt. 1.25 o.s.i (*0-345-23520-7*); 1970. mass mkt. 0.95 o.s.i (*0-345-21119-7*) Ballantine Bks.

—Titus Alone. 1982. (Gormenghast Trilogy: Vol. III). (Illus.). 264p. 30.00 (*0-87951-145-1*) Overlook Pr., The.

—Titus Groan. 1977. mass mkt. 2.25 o.s.i (*0-345-27096-7*); 1973. mass mkt. 1.25 o.s.i (*0-345-23518-5*) Ballantine Bks.

—Titus Groan. (Gormenghast Trilogy: Vol. I). (Illus.). 1991. 408p. pap. 16.95 (*0-87951-425-6*); 1982. 512p. 30.00 (*0-87951-143-5*) Overlook Pr., The.

**GORODISH, SERGE (FICTITIOUS CHARACTER)—FICTION**

Delacorta. Alba. 1990. 208p. pap. 7.95 o.p. (*0-87113-387-3*, Atlantic Monthly Pr.) Grove/Atlantic, Inc.

—Alba. Texier, Catherine, tr. 1989. 288p. 17.95 o.p. (*0-87113-324-5*) Grove/Atlantic, Inc.

—Diva. 1984. 192p. mass mkt. 3.50 o.s.i (*0-345-31265-1*, Ballantine Bks.) Ballantine Bks.

—Diva. Bair, Lowell, tr. from FRE. 1983. 9.50 o.p. (*0-671-47056-6*) Summit Bks.

—Lola. 1985. 176p. mass mkt. 2.95 o.s.i (*0-345-31268-6*, Ballantine Bks.) Ballantine Bks.

—Lola. 1985. 9.70 o.p. (*0-671-47752-8*) Summit Bks.

—Luna. 1985. 176p. mass mkt. 2.95 o.s.i (*0-345-31266-X*, Ballantine Bks.) Ballantine Bks.

—Luna. Reiter, Victoria, tr. 1984. (Gorodish-Alba Ser.). 128p. 9.70 o.p. (*0-671-49379-5*) Summit Bks.

—Nana. 1984. 192p. mass mkt. 2.75 o.s.i (*0-345-31267-8*, Ballantine Bks.) Ballantine Bks.

—Nana. Reiter, Victoria, tr. from FRE. 1984. (Gorodish-Alba Ser.: No. 2). 128p. 9.50 o.p. (*0-671-49210-1*) Summit Bks.

—Vida. Reiter, Victoria, tr. from FRE. 1985. 12.70 o.p. (*0-671-60424-4*) Summit Bks.

**GORZACK, ELEANOR (FICTITIOUS CHARACTER)—FICTION**

Mikulski, Barbara & Oates, Marylouise. Capitol Offense. abr. ed. 1997. audio 7.99 o.p. (*1-56740-184-8*, 632, Paperback Nova Audio Bks.); 1996. audio 16.95 o.p. (*1-56100-903-2*, 820, Nova Audio Bks.); 1996. audio 23.95 o.p. (*1-56100-693-9*, 58, Bookcassette); 1996. audio 73.25 o.p. (*1-56100-318-2*, 1149, Unabridged Library Editions) Brilliance Audio.

—Capitol Offense. 1996. 320p. 23.95 o.s.i (*0-525-94214-9*) Dutton/Plume.

—Capitol Offense. 1997. 416p. mass mkt. 6.99 o.s.i (*0-451-19032-7*, Signet Bks.) NAL.

—Capitol Venture. 1997. 320p. 24.95 o.p. (*0-525-94277-7*) Dutton/Plume.

—Capitol Venture. 1999. 384p. mass mkt. 6.99 o.s.i (*0-451-19183-8*) NAL.

**GOSSINGER, HENRY, SIR (FICTITIOUS CHARACTER)—FICTION**

Cannell, Dorothy. God Save the Queen. 1997. 224p. 22.95 o.s.i (*0-553-10163-3*); 1998. 272p. reprint ed. mass mkt. 6.50 (*0-553-57468-X*, Crimeline) Bantam Bks.

—God Save the Queen. l.t. ed. 1998. pap. 23.95 o.p. (*1-56895-542-1*, Wheeler Publishing, Inc.) Gale Group.

**GOULD, JAMES (FICTITIOUS CHARACTER)—FICTION**

Price, Eugenia. Lighthouse. 1999. mass mkt. (*0-553-23158-8*); 1985. 352p. mass mkt. 3.95 o.s.i (*0-553-24137-0*); 1972. 352p. mass mkt. 6.99 o.s.i (*0-553-26910-0*) Bantam Bks.

—Lighthouse. 1999. (St. Simons Trilogy Ser.: Vol. 1). 344p. pap. 14.95 (*1-57736-154-7*) Providence Hse. Pubs.

—Lighthouse. 1985. (St. Simons Island Trilogy Ser.). 356p. reprint ed. 14.95 o.p. (*0-934395-08-X*); 39.95 o.p. (*0-934395-09-8*) Rutledge Hill Pr.

**GOURMET DETECTIVE (FICTITIOUS CHARACTER)—FICTION**

King, Peter. Death Al Dente: A Gourmet Detective Mystery. 2000. (Culinary Mysteries Ser.). 256p. mass mkt. 5.99 (*0-312-97038-2*, St. Martin's Paperbacks); 1999. (Gourmet Detective Mystery Ser.: Vol. 4). 240p. 22.95 o.p. (*0-312-19891-4*, Saint Martin's Minotaur) St. Martin's Pr.

—Death & the Celestial Spice. 1997. (*0-312-15137-3*) St. Martin's Pr.

—Dine & Die on the Danube Express. l.t. ed. 2003. (Gourmet Detective Mystery Ser.). 411p. 28.95 (*0-7862-5554-4*) Thorndike Pr.

—Dine & Die on the Danube Express: A Gourmet Detective Mystery. 2003. 240p. 23.95 (*0-312-28366-0*, Saint Martin's Minotaur) St. Martin's Pr.

—Dying on the Vine: A Further Adventure of the Gourmet Detective. (Culinary Mysteries Ser.). 1999. 288p. mass mkt. 5.99 (*0-312-96683-0*, St. Martin's Paperbacks); 1998. 304p. 22.95 o.p. (*0-312-18090-X*, Saint Martin's Minotaur) St. Martin's Pr.

—Eat Drink & Be Dead: A Gourmet Detective Mystery. 2001. 215p. 22.95 (*0-312-24270-0*, Saint Martin's Minotaur) St. Martin's Pr.

—The Gourmet Detective. 256p. 1996. 22.95 (*0-312-14346-X*, Saint Martin's Minotaur); Vol. 1. 1997. mass mkt. 5.99 o.s.i (*0-312-96260-6*, St. Martin's Paperbacks) St. Martin's Pr.

—A Healthy Place to Die: A Gourmet Detective Mystery. (Gourmet Detective Mystery Ser.). 2001. 240p. mass mkt. 5.99 (*0-312-97683-6*, St. Martin's Paperbacks); 2000. 230p. 22.95 (*0-312-24269-7*, Saint Martin's Minotaur) St. Martin's Pr.

—Roux the Day: A Gourmet Detective Mystery. 2002. 288p. 23.95 (*0-312-28365-2*, Saint Martin's Minotaur) St. Martin's Pr.

—Roux the Day: A Gourmet Detective Mystery. 2003. (Mystery Ser.). 28.95 (*0-7862-4781-9*) Thorndike Pr.

—Spiced to Death. (Culinary Mysteries Ser.). 1998. 304p. mass mkt. 5.99 (*0-312-96500-1*, St. Martin's Paperbacks); 1997. 352p. text 23.95 o.p. (*0-312-15661-8*, Saint Martin's Minotaur) St. Martin's Pr.

**GRAFTON, JAKE (FICTITIOUS CHARACTER)—FICTION**

Coonts, Stephen. America: A Jake Grafton Novel. abr. ed. 2001. (Jake Grafton Ser.). audio 24.95 o.p. (*1-58788-555-7*, 2828, Nova Audio Bks.); audio compact disk 69.25 (*1-58788-557-3*, 2830, CD Library Edition); audio compact disk 29.95 (*1-58788-556-5*, 2829, CD); audio 34.95 (*1-58788-549-2*, 2826, Brilliance Audio Unabridged); audio 96.25 (*1-58788-554-9*, 2827, CD Unabridged Library Edition) Brilliance Audio.

—America: A Jake Grafton Novel. 2002. 464p. mass mkt. 7.99 (*0-312-98250-X*, St. Martin's Paperbacks); 2002. mass mkt. 7.99 (*0-312-98450-2*, St. Martin's Paperbacks); 2001. 390p. 25.95 (*0-312-25341-9*) St. Martin's Pr.

—America: A Jake Grafton Novel. l.t. ed. 2001. 657p. 31.95 (*0-7862-3641-8*); 28.95 (*0-7862-3645-0*) Thorndike Pr.

—Cuba. abr. ed. 2001. audio 25.00 (*1-59040-052-6*, Phoenix Audio) American International Publishing Group.

—Cuba. 1999. audio 96.00 (*0-7366-4645-0*); audio compact disk 112.00 (*0-7366-7127-7*); audio 96.00 Books on Tape, Inc.

—Cuba. l.t. ed. 1999. 25.95 (*1-56895-801-3*, Wheeler Publishing, Inc.) Gale Group.

—Cuba, Set. abr. ed. 1999. audio 25.00 Highsmith Inc.

—Cuba. 2002. audio compact disk 14.99 (*1-57815-550-9*, 4439CD5, Media Bks. Audio Publishing) Media Bks., L. L. C.

—Cuba. abr. ed. 1999. audio 25.00 (*0-7871-1967-9*, Dove Audio) NewStar Media, Inc.

—Cuba. 2000. 480p. mass mkt. 7.99 (*0-312-97139-7*, St. Martin's Paperbacks); 2nd ed. 1999. 384p. 24.95 (*0-312-20521-X*) St. Martin's Pr.

—Final Flight. unabr. ed. 1988. audio 72.00 (*0-7366-1525-3*, 2396) Books on Tape, Inc.

—Final Flight. 1989. 400p. mass mkt. 7.99 (*0-440-20447-X*) Dell Publishing.

—Final Flight. l.t. ed. 1990. (Magna Large Print Ser.). 601p. o.p. (*1-85057-718-8*) Magna Large Print Bks. GBR. *Dist:* Ulverscroft Large Print Canada, Ltd.

—Flight of the Intruder. abr. ed. 1990. audio 9.95 (*0-88690-314-9*, A20203, Audio Editions Bks. on Cassette) Audio Partners Publishing Corp.

—Flight of the Intruder. unabr. collector's ed. 1987. audio 72.00 (*0-7366-1175-4*, 2097) Books on Tape, Inc.

—Flight of the Intruder. unabr. ed. 1987. audio 19.95 o.p. (*0-930435-32-X*, 110, Bookcassette);Set. audio 73.25 o.p. (*1-56100-027-2*, 840) Brilliance Audio.

—Flight of the Intruder. l.t. ed. 1987. 523p. 19.95 o.p. (*0-8161-4295-5*); 11.95 o.p. (*0-8161-4296-3*) Gale Group. (Macmillan Reference USA).

—Flight of the Intruder. 1986. 329p. 26.95 (*0-87021-200-1*) Naval Institute Pr.

—Flight of the Intruder. unabr. ed. 1986. audio 70.00 (*1-55690-180-1*, 86980E7) Recorded Bks., LLC.

—Flight of the Intruder. 1991. mass mkt. 5.95 (*0-671-72470-3*, Pocket) Simon & Schuster.

—Flight of the Intruder. McCarthy, Paul, ed. 1990. 448p. mass mkt. 6.99 o.s.i (*0-671-70960-7*, Pocket) Simon & Schuster.

—Flight of the Intruder. 1987. mass mkt. 4.95 (*0-671-64012-7*, Pocket) Simon & Schuster.

—Hong Kong: A Jake Grafton Novel. unabr. ed. 2000. audio 80.00 (*0-7366-5629-4*) Books on Tape, Inc.

—Hong Kong: A Jake Grafton Novel. l.t. ed. 2000. (Wheeler Hardcover Ser.). 522p. 27.95 (*1-56895-985-0*, Wheeler Publishing, Inc.) Gale Group.

—Hong Kong: A Jake Grafton Novel. abr. ed. 2000. (Jake Grafton Novels Ser.). audio 25.95 (*0-694-52390-9*); audio compact disk 29.95 (*0-694-52389-5*); 15p. audio 39.95 (*0-694-52388-7*) HarperTrade. (HarperAudio).

—Hong Kong: A Jake Grafton Novel. 2001. 416p. mass mkt. 7.99 (*0-312-97837-5*, St. Martin's Paperbacks); 2000. 350p. 25.95 (*0-312-25339-7*) St. Martin's Pr.

—The Intruders. unabr. ed. 1995. audio 88.00 (*0-7366-2915-7*) Books on Tape, Inc.

—The Intruders. l.t. ed. 26.95 (*1-56895-164-7*, Wheeler Publishing, Inc.) Gale Group.

—The Intruders. 400p. 2002. mass mkt. 6.99 (*0-7434-5651-3*); 1995. (Illus.). mass mkt. 7.99 (*0-671-87061-0*) Simon & Schuster. (Pocket).

—The Intruders. McCarthy, Paul, ed. 1995. mass mkt. 6.50 (*0-671-51953-0*, Pocket); 1994. 352p. 23.00 o.p. (*0-671-87060-2*, Atria) Simon & Schuster.

—The Intruders, Set. abr. ed. 1994. audio 17.00 (*0-671-50144-5*, 390986, Simon & Schuster Audioworks) Simon & Schuster Audio.

—Liberty. l.t. ed. 2003. 688p. 32.95 (*1-58724-442-X*, Wheeler Publishing, Inc.) Gale Group.

—Liberty. 2004. 544p. mass mkt. 7.99 (*0-312-98970-9*); 2003. mass mkt. 7.99 (*0-312-99062-6*) St. Martin's Pr. (St. Martin's Paperbacks).

—Liberty: A Jake Grafton Novel. 2003. (Jake Grafton Novels Ser.). 352p. 25.95 (*0-312-28361-X*) St. Martin's Pr.

—The Minotaur. unabr. ed. 1990. audio 88.00 (*0-7366-1830-9*, 2666) Books on Tape, Inc.

—The Minotaur. 448p. 1993. mass mkt. 3.99 o.s.i (*0-440-21517-X*); 1990. mass mkt. 7.99 (*0-440-20742-8*) Dell Publishing.

—The Minotaur. 1989. 18.95 o.s.i (*0-385-26736-3*) Doubleday Publishing.

—The Minotaur. l.t. ed. 1991. (Magna Large Print Ser.). 719p. o.p. (*0-7505-0042-5*) Magna Large Print Bks. GBR. *Dist:* Ulverscroft Large Print Canada, Ltd.

—The Minotaur. 1993. 4.99 o.p. (*0-517-09881-4*) Random Hse. Value Publishing.

—The Red Horseman. unabr. ed. 1993. audio 80.00 (*0-7366-2541-0*, 3292) Books on Tape, Inc.

—The Red Horseman. l.t. ed. 1993. 25.95 o.p. (*1-56895-032-2*, Wheeler Publishing, Inc.) Gale Group.

—The Red Horseman. 1994. mass mkt. 6.50 (*0-671-89489-7*); 1993. pap. 6.50 (*0-671-88413-1*) Simon & Schuster. (Pocket).

—The Red Horseman. McCarthy, Paul, ed. 1993. 352p. 23.00 (*0-671-74887-4*, Atria); 1994. 432p. reprint ed. mass mkt. 7.99 (*0-671-74888-2*, Pocket) Simon & Schuster.

—The Red Horseman. abr. ed. 1993. audio 17.00 (*0-671-79067-6*, 391458, Simon & Schuster Audioworks) Simon & Schuster Audio.

—Under Siege. unabr. ed. 1991. audio 96.00 (*0-7366-1906-2*, 2732) Books on Tape, Inc.

—Under Siege. 1990. audio 12.79 o.s.i (*0-553-19958-7*); audio 15.99 o.s.i (*0-553-45264-9*) Random Hse. Audio Publishing Group. (RH Audio).

—Under Siege. 2002. 544p. mass mkt. 7.99 (*0-7434-5720-X*, Pocket) Simon & Schuster.

—Under Siege. McCarthy, Paul, ed. 1991. 544p. mass mkt. 7.99 (*0-671-74294-9*, Pocket); 1990. 416p. 19.95 o.p. (*0-671-72229-8*, Atria) Simon & Schuster.

**GRAHAM, ALAN (FICTITIOUS CHARACTER)—FICTION**

Shuman, Malcolm. Assassin's Blood. 1999. 224p. mass mkt. 5.99 (*0-380-80485-9*) Morrow/Avon.

—Burial Ground. 1998. 224p. mass mkt. 5.50 (*0-380-79423-3*, Avon Bks.) Morrow/Avon.

—Meriweather Murder. 1998. (Alan Graham Mysteries Ser.: No. 2). 272p. mass mkt. 5.99 (*0-380-79424-1*, Avon Bks.) Morrow/Avon.

—Past Dying. 2000. (Alan Graham Mysteries Ser.). 224p. mass mkt. 5.99 (*0-380-80486-7*, Avon Bks.) Morrow/Avon.

**GRAHAM, CHARLOTTE (FICTITIOUS CHARACTER)—FICTION**

Matteson, Stefanie. Murder among the Angels. 1996. 256p. mass mkt. 5.99 o.s.i (*0-425-15548-X*); 19.95 o.p. (*0-425-15149-2*) Berkley Publishing Group. (Prime Crime).

—Murder at Teatime. 1991. 3.95 (*1-55773-477-1*) Ace Bks.

—Murder at Teatime. 1994. mass mkt. 4.50 o.s.i (*0-425-14789-4*) Berkley Publishing Group.

—Murder at the Falls. 1993. 240p. (Orig.). mass mkt. 5.50 o.s.i (*0-425-14008-3*) Berkley Publishing Group.

—Murder at the Spa. 1990. mass mkt. 4.50 o.s.i (*0-425-14609-X*); 3.95 (*1-55773-411-9*) Berkley Publishing Group.

—Murder on High. l.t. ed. 2000. (Beeler Large Print Mystery Ser.). 25.95 (*1-57490-261-X*, Beeler Large Print Bks.) Beeler, Thomas T. Publisher.

—Murder on High. 1995. 272p. mass mkt. 5.99 o.s.i (*0-425-15050-X*); 1994. 18.95 o.p. (*0-425-14355-4*, Prime Crime) Berkley Publishing Group.

—Murder on the Cliff. 1991. 3.99 (*1-55773-596-4*) Ace Bks.

—Murder on the Cliff. 1991. mass mkt. 4.50 o.s.i (*0-425-14821-1*) Berkley Publishing Group.

—Murder on the Silk Road. 1992. 240p. 3.99 o.p. (*1-55773-814-9*, Diamond Bks.) Ace Bks.

—Murder on the Silk Road. 1992. mass mkt. 5.50 o.s.i (*0-425-14820-3*, Prime Crime) Berkley Publishing Group.

—Murder under the Palms. l.t. ed. 1998. (Beeler Large Print Mystery Ser.). 25.95 (*1-57490-137-0*, Beeler Large Print Bks.) Beeler, Thomas T. Publisher.

—Murder under the Palms. 1997. 256p. (Charlotte Graham Mystery Ser.: Vol. 3). 21.95 o.s.i (*0-425-15628-1*); reprint ed. mass mkt. 5.99 o.s.i (*0-425-16035-1*) Berkley Publishing Group. (Prime Crime).

—Murder under the Palms. unabr. ed. 1999. audio 44.95 (*0-7861-1653-6*, 2481) Blackstone Audio Bks., Inc.

**GRAHAM, EMMA (FICTITIOUS CHARACTER)—FICTION**

Grimes, Martha. Cold Flat Junction. 2001. audio 80.00 (*0-7366-6361-4*); audio 29.95 (*0-7366-5832-7*) Books on Tape, Inc.

—Cold Flat Junction. 448p. 2002. pap. 12.00 (*0-451-20523-5*); 2001. pap. 7.99 (*0-451-41007-6*) NAL. (Signet Bks.).

—Cold Flat Junction. 2001. 352p. 24.95 o.p. (*0-670-89491-5*, Viking) Viking Penguin.

—Hotel Paradise. 1997. 448p. mass mkt. 6.99 (*0-345-39425-9*); 1996. mass mkt. 6.99 o.s.i (*0-345-41202-8*) Ballantine Bks.

—Hotel Paradise. unabr. ed. 1996. audio 72.00 (*0-7366-3470-3*, 4114) Books on Tape, Inc.

—Hotel Paradise. l.t. ed. 1996. 538p. 24.00 o.p. (*0-7838-1682-0*, Macmillan Reference USA) Gale Group.

—Hotel Paradise. l.t. ed. 1996. 24.00 o.s.i (*0-679-75879-8*) Knopf, Alfred A. Inc.

—Hotel Paradise. abr. ed. 1996. audio 18.00 o.s.i (*0-679-45209-5*, RH Audio) Random Hse. Audio Publishing Group.

—Hotel Paradise. 1996. 368p. 24.00 o.s.i (*0-679-44187-5*) Random Hse., Inc.

**GRAHAM, LIZ (FICTITIOUS CHARACTER)—FICTION**

Bannister, Jo. A Bleeding of Innocents. 1999. 304p. (*0-7540-3481-X*); pap. (*0-7540-3482-8*) BBC Audiobooks America.

—A Bleeding of Innocents. 1997. (WWL Mystery Ser.: No. 241). per. (*0-373-26241-8*, 1-26241-9, Worldwide Library) Harlequin Enterprises, Ltd.

—A Bleeding of Innocents. unabr. ed. 1998. audio 69.95 (*1-872672-97-3*) Magna Story Sound GBR. *Dist:* Ulverscroft Large Print Bks., Ltd.

—A Bleeding of Innocents. 1993. 224p. 18.95 o.p. (*0-312-09750-6*, Saint Martin's Minotaur) St. Martin's Pr.

—A Bleeding of Innocents. l.t. ed. 1998. (General Ser.). 304p. pap. 24.95 (*0-7862-1610-7*) Thorndike Pr.

—Broken Lines. 2000. (Castlemere Mystery Ser.). 272p. per. (*0-373-26338-4*, Harlequin Bks.) Harlequin Enterprises, Ltd.

—Broken Lines. 1999. 304p. 22.95 (*0-312-19842-6*, Saint Martin's Minotaur) St. Martin's Pr.

—Broken Lines. l.t. ed. 1999. (General Ser.). 336p. pap. 23.95 (*0-7862-1682-4*) Thorndike Pr.

—Changelings. 2002. (WWL Mystery Ser.: No. 410). mass mkt. (*0-373-26410-0*, 1-26410-0, Worldwide Library) Harlequin Enterprises, Ltd.

—Changelings. 2000. 374p. (*0-333-90189-4*) Macmillan Pr.

—Changelings. l.t. ed. 2001. (Magna Large Print Ser.). 368p. (*0-7505-1761-1*) Magna Large Print Bks. GBR. *Dist:* Ulverscroft Large Print Canada, Ltd.

—Changelings. 2000. 384p. 23.95 (*0-312-26567-0*, Saint Martin's Minotaur) St. Martin's Pr.

—Charisma. 1997. per. (*0-373-26253-1*, 1-26253-4, Worldwide Library) Harlequin Enterprises, Ltd.

—Charisma. 1994. 208p. 18.95 o.p. (*0-312-11252-1*, Saint Martin's Minotaur) St. Martin's Pr.

—The Hireling's Tale. 1999. 316p. 23.95 (*0-312-24400-2*, Saint Martin's Minotaur) St. Martin's Pr.

—The Hireling's Tale. l.t. ed. 1999. (General Ser.). 352p. pap. 22.95 (*0-7862-2163-1*) Thorndike Pr.

—No Birds Sing. 1998. (WWL Mystery Ser.). per. (*0-373-26283-3*, 1-26283-1, Worldwide Library) Harlequin Enterprises, Ltd.

—No Birds Sing. 1996. 240p. 21.95 (*0-312-14382-6*, Saint Martin's Minotaur) St. Martin's Pr.

—No Birds Sing. l.t. ed. 1997. (Ulverscroft Large Print Ser.). 464p. 29.99 o.p. (*0-7089-3732-2*, Ulverscroft) Thorpe, F. A. Pubs. GBR. *Dist:* Ulverscroft Large Print Bks., Ltd., Ulverscroft Large Print Canada, Ltd.

—A Taste for Burning. 1997. (Castlemere Mystery Ser.). per. (*0-373-26259-0*, 1-26259-1, Worldwide Library) Harlequin Enterprises, Ltd.

—A Taste for Burning. 1995. 208p. 19.95 o.p. (*0-312-13191-7*, Saint Martin's Minotaur) St. Martin's Pr.

**GRAHAM, WILL (FICTITIOUS CHARACTER)—FICTION**

Harris, Thomas. Red Dragon. 1982. mass mkt. 3.95 o.s.i (*0-553-22746-7*); 368p. mass mkt. 4.50 o.s.i (*0-553-26485-0*); mass mkt. 4.95 o.s.i (*0-553-27522-4*) Bantam Bks.

—Red Dragon. 1991. 352p. reprint ed. lib. bdg. 24.95 o.p. (*0-89966-877-1*) Buccaneer Bks., Inc.

—Red Dragon. 2002. lib. bdg. 29.95 (*1-58547-237-9*, Premier) Ctr. Point Large Print.
—Red Dragon. 1990. 480p. reprint ed. mass mkt. 7.99 (*0-440-20615-4*) Dell Publishing.
—Red Dragon. 1998. 352p. pap. 12.95 (*0-385-31967-3*); 1997. pap. 11.95 (*0-385-31906-1*) Doubleday Publishing.
—Red Dragon. 2000. 368p. 26.95 (*0-525-94556-3*, Abrahams, William Bks.) Dutton/Plume.
—Red Dragon. 1981. 352p. 13.95 o.p. (*0-399-12442-X*, G. P. Putnam's Sons) Penguin Putnam Bks. for Young Readers.
—Red Dragon. abr. ed. 1989. audio 16.00 (*0-671-67854-X*, Simon & Schuster Audioworks) Simon & Schuster Audio.
—Red Dragon. l.t. ed. 1984. (Charnwood Large Print Ser.). 496p. 29.99 o.p. (*0-7089-8169-0*, Ulverscroft) Thorpe, F. A. Pubs. GBR. *Dist:* Ulverscroft Large Print Bks., Ltd., Ulverscroft Large Print Canada, Ltd.

**GRANNY WEATHERWAX (FICTITIOUS CHARACTER)—FICTION**

Pratchett, Terry. Carpe Jugulum. 1999. 432p. (YA). (gr. 9). mass mkt. (*0-552-14615-3*, Corgi) Bantam Bks.
—Carpe Jugulum. unabr. ed. 2000. (Discworld Ser.). 8p. audio 69.95 (*0-7531-0838-0*, 000603) ISIS Audio Bks. GBR. *Dist:* Ulverscroft Large Print Bks., Ltd.
—Carpe Jugulum. (Discworld Ser.). 2000. 400p. mass mkt. 6.99 (*0-06-102039-7*, HarperTorch); 1999. 296p. (J). 24.00 (*0-06-105158-6*, Eos) Morrow/Avon.
—Equal Rites. 1987. (Discworld Ser.). 256p. 18.95 o.p. (*0-575-03950-7*) Gollancz, Victor GBR. *Dist:* Trafalgar Square.
—Equal Rites. 2000. (Discworld Ser.). 240p. mass mkt. 6.99 (*0-06-102069-9*, Perennial) HarperTrade.
—Equal Rites. unabr. ed. 1998. (Discworld Ser.). audio 54.95 (*1-85695-828-0*, 951001) ISIS Audio Bks. GBR. *Dist:* Ulverscroft Large Print Bks., Ltd.
—Equal Rites. l.t. ed. (Discworld Ser.). 23.95 (*1-85695-387-4*) ISIS Large Print Bks. GBR. *Dist:* Transaction Pubs.
—Equal Rites. 1988. (Discworld Ser.). mass mkt. 3.50 o.p. (*0-451-15704-4*); 256p. mass mkt. 5.99 o.p. (*0-451-45092-2*) NAL. (ROC).
—Equal Rites. 2000. audio 16.95 (*0-552-14016-3*) Transworld Publishers Ltd. GBR. *Dist:* Trafalgar Square.
—Lords & Ladies. 1994. (Discworld Ser.). 384p. (YA). (gr. 9). mass mkt. 6.99 (*0-552-13891-6*) Bantam Bks.
—Lords & Ladies. unabr. ed. 1998. (Discworld Ser.). audio 69.95 (*0-7531-0018-5*, 960703) ISIS Audio Bks. GBR. *Dist:* Ulverscroft Large Print Bks., Ltd.
—Lords & Ladies. (Discworld Ser.). 1996. 400p. mass mkt. 6.99 (*0-06-105692-8*, Eos); 1995. 320p. pap. 12.00 o.p. (*0-06-109216-9*, HarperTorch) Morrow/Avon.
—Lords & Ladies. abr. ed. 2000. audio 16.95 (*0-552-14417-7*) Trafalgar Square.
—Maskerade. 1997. 380p. mass mkt. (*0-552-14236-0*, Corgi) Bantam Bks.
—Maskerade. unabr. ed. 1999. (Discworld Ser.). audio 69.95 (*0-7531-0518-7*, 990504) ISIS Audio Bks. GBR. *Dist:* Ulverscroft Large Print Bks., Ltd.
—Maskerade. l.t. unabr. ed. 1998. 24.95 (*0-7531-5156-1*, 151561) ISIS Large Print Bks. GBR. *Dist:* ISIS Publishing.
—Maskerade. (Discworld Ser.). 1998. 384p. mass mkt. 6.99 (*0-06-105691-X*, HarperTorch); 1997. 278p. 22.00 o.s.i (*0-06-105251-5*, Eos) Morrow/Avon.
—Witches Abroad. 1998. 285p. mass mkt. (*0-552-13465-1*, Corgi) Bantam Bks.
—Witches Abroad. unabr. ed. 1998. (Discworld Ser.). audio 69.95 (*0-7531-0020-7*, 960908) ISIS Audio Bks. GBR. *Dist:* Ulverscroft Large Print Bks., Ltd.
—Witches Abroad. 1993. (Discworld Ser.). 320p. mass mkt. 6.99 o.p. (*0-451-45225-9*, ROC) NAL.
—Wyrd Sisters. 1998. 331p. mass mkt. (*0-552-13460-0*, Corgi) Bantam Bks.
—Wyrd Sisters. 2001. (Discworld Ser.). 288p. mass mkt. 6.99 (*0-06-102066-4*) HarperCollins Pubs.
—Wyrd Sisters. unabr. ed. 1998. (Discworld Ser.). audio 69.95 (*0-7531-0021-5*, 960108) ISIS Audio Bks. GBR. *Dist:* Ulverscroft Large Print Bks., Ltd.
—Wyrd Sisters. 1990. (Discworld Ser.). 320p. mass mkt. 6.50 o.p. (*0-451-45012-4*, ROC) NAL.
—Wyrd Sisters. abr. ed. 2000. audio (*0-552-14014-7*) Transworld Publishers Ltd.
—Wyrd Sisters. 2000. (Discworld Ser.). xviii, 154p. pap. 9.95 (*0-552-14430-4*) Transworld Publishers Ltd. GBR. *Dist:* Trafalgar Square.

**GRANT, ALAN, INSPECTOR (FICTITIOUS CHARACTER)—FICTION**

Tey, Josephine. The Daughter of Time. unabr. ed. 2000. audio 24.95 (*1-57270-138-2*, N41138u, Audio Editions Mystery Masters) Audio Partners Publishing Corp.
—The Daughter of Time. 1985. 224p. mass mkt. 9.95 o.p. (*0-553-06510-6*) Bantam Bks.
—The Daughter of Time. 1976. 1.50 o.s.i (*0-425-03223-X*) Berkley Publishing Group.
—The Daughter of Time. 1976. 220p. lib. bdg. 27.95 (*0-89966-184-X*) Buccaneer Bks., Inc.
—The Daughter of Time. l.t. ed. 1984. (General Ser.). 320p. 12.95 o.p. (*0-8161-3634-3*); 9.95 o.p. (*0-8161-3688-2*) Gale Group. (Macmillan Reference USA).
—The Daughter of Time. 2003. 224p. (*0-434-76670-4*) Heinemann, William Ltd. GBR. *Dist:* Random Hse. of Canada, Ltd.
—The Daughter of Time. 2003. (Best Mysteries of All Time Ser.). ix, 224p. (*0-7621-8888-X*, Impress) Scriptorium Pr., The.
—The Daughter of Time. 1995. 208p. pap. 12.00 (*0-684-80386-0*, Touchstone) Simon & Schuster.
—The Daughter of Time. 1986. audio 49.95 o.p. (*0-8161-9726-1*) Thorndike Pr.
—The Franchise Affair. 1981. reprint ed. lib. bdg. 16.00 (*0-8376-0446-X*) Bentley Pubs.
—The Franchise Affair. unabr. ed. 2000. (Inspector Grant Mystery Ser.: Bk. 3). audio 59.95 (*0-7451-6324-6*, CAB 578) Chivers Audio Bks. GBR. *Dist:* BBC Audiobooks America.
—The Franchise Affair. 1993. pap. 5.95 o.p. (*0-87129-257-2*, F52) Dramatic Publishing Co.
—The Franchise Affair. 1998. 304p. pap. 11.00 (*0-684-84256-4*, Touchstone); 1988. 289p. pap. 6.00 o.s.i (*0-02-008823-X*, Scribner Paper Fiction); 1983. reprint ed. mass mkt. 3.95 o.s.i (*0-671-50812-1*, Pocket) Simon & Schuster.
—The Man in the Queue. 1981. reprint ed. lib. bdg. 16.00 (*0-8376-0450-8*) Bentley Pubs.
—The Man in the Queue. 1976. 1.25 o.p. (*0-425-03220-5*) Berkley Publishing Group.
—The Man in the Queue. unabr. ed. 2000. (Inspector Grant Mystery Ser.: Bk. 1). audio 49.95 (*0-7451-4161-7*, CAB 844) Chivers Audio Bks. GBR. *Dist:* BBC Audiobooks America.
—The Man in the Queue. 1995. 256p. pap. 12.00 (*0-684-81502-8*, Touchstone); 1986. 224p. mass mkt. 3.95 o.s.i (*0-671-41493-3*, Pocket); 1982. mass mkt. 2.95 o.s.i (*0-671-43524-8*, Pocket) Simon & Schuster.
—The Man in the Queue. l.t. ed. 2000. (Mystery Ser.). 392p. 26.95 o.p. (*0-7862-2345-6*) Thorndike Pr.
—A Shilling for Candles. 22.95 (*0-8488-1203-4*) Amereon, Ltd.
—A Shilling for Candles. 1976. 1.25 o.p. (*0-425-03221-3*) Berkley Publishing Group.
—A Shilling for Candles, unabr. ed. 1991. audio 39.95 (*0-7861-0224-1*, 1197) Blackstone Audio Bks., Inc.
—A Shilling for Candles. 1998. 240p. pap. 11.00 (*0-684-84238-6*, Touchstone); 1988. 240p. pap. 6.00 o.s.i (*0-02-054530-4*, Scribner Paper Fiction); 1984. mass mkt. 3.95 o.s.i (*0-671-55179-5*, Pocket); 1983. mass mkt. 2.95 o.s.i (*0-671-47625-4*, Pocket) Simon & Schuster.
—The Singing Sands. l.t. ed. 1975. 1.25 o.p. (*0-425-02948-4*) Berkley Publishing Group.
—The Singing Sands. Barzun, Jacques & Taylor, W. H., eds. 1982. (Crime Fiction 1950-1975 Ser.). 192p. lib. bdg. 5.00 o.p. (*0-8240-5000-2*) Garland Publishing, Inc.
—The Singing Sands. 1996. 224p. pap. 12.00 (*0-684-81892-2*, Touchstone); 1988. 240p. pap. 6.00 o.s.i (*0-02-008825-6*, Scribner Paper Fiction); 1983. 224p. mass mkt. 3.95 o.s.i (*0-671-49456-2*, Pocket) Simon & Schuster.
—The Singing Sands. l.t. ed. 1999. (Mystery Ser.). 341p. 27.95 (*0-7862-1916-5*) Thorndike Pr.
—To Love & Be Wise. l.t. ed. 1975. 1.25 o.s.i (*0-425-02898-4*) Berkley Publishing Group.
—To Love & Be Wise. unabr. ed. 2000. (Inspector Grant Mystery Ser.: Bk. 4). audio 49.95 (*0-7451-4259-1*, CAB 942) Chivers Audio Bks. GBR. *Dist:* BBC Audiobooks America.
—To Love & Be Wise. 1998. 224p. per. 12.00 (*0-684-00631-6*, Touchstone); 1987. mass mkt. 3.95 (*0-671-64547-1*, Pocket); 1984. mass mkt. 3.95 o.s.i (*0-671-50979-9*, Pocket); 1982. mass mkt. 2.95 o.s.i (*0-671-44191-4*, Pocket) Simon & Schuster.

**GRANT, CELIA (FICTITIOUS CHARACTER)—FICTION**

Sherwood, John. Bones Gather No Moss. 1994. 256p. 20.00 (*0-684-19738-3*); 1995. 288p. pap. 18.95 o.p. (*0-7838-1349-X*) Gale Group. (Macmillan Reference USA).
—A Botanist at Bay. 1986. mass mkt. 2.95 o.s.i (*0-345-33023-4*) Ballantine Bks.
—A Botanist at Bay. 1985. 176p. 13.95 o.s.i (*0-684-18432-X*); 1989. lib. bdg. 11.95 o.p. (*1-85057-559-2*) Gale Group. (Macmillan Reference USA).
—A Bouquet of Thorns. 1991. mass mkt. 3.95 o.s.i (*0-345-36525-9*) Ballantine Bks.
—A Bouquet of Thorns. 1989. 224p. 16.95 o.s.i (*0-684-19091-5*, Macmillan Reference USA) Gale Group.
—Creeping Jenny: A Celia Grant Mystery. 1993. 256p. 20.00 o.p. (*0-684-19613-1*, Macmillan Reference USA) Gale Group.
—Flowers of Evil. 1990. 224p. mass mkt. 3.95 o.s.i (*0-345-35342-0*) Ballantine Bks.
—Flowers of Evil. 1988. (Celia Grant Mystery Ser.). 204p. 14.95 o.p. (*0-684-18867-8*, Macmillan Reference USA) Gale Group.
—Flowers of Evil. l.t. ed. 1989. (Ulverscroft Large Print Ser.). 379p. 29.99 o.p. (*0-7089-1980-4*, Ulverscroft) Thorpe, F. A. Pubs. GBR. *Dist:* Ulverscroft Large Print Bks., Ltd., Ulverscroft Large Print Canada, Ltd.
—Green Trigger Finger. 1986. 176p. mass mkt. 2.95 o.s.i (*0-345-32890-6*) Ballantine Bks.
—The Hanging Garden: A Celia Grant Mystery. 1993. 192p. 20.00 o.p. (*0-684-19429-5*); 1994. 375p. lib. bdg. 16.95 (*0-8161-5903-3*) Gale Group. (Macmillan Reference USA).
—The Mantrap Garden. 1987. 192p. mass mkt. 2.95 o.s.i (*0-345-34306-9*) Ballantine Bks.
—The Mantrap Garden. 1986. 224p. 13.95 o.p. (*0-684-18726-4*, Macmillan Reference USA) Gale Group.
—The Mantrap Garden. l.t. ed. 1990. (Magna Large Print Ser.). 327p. o.p. (*1-85057-560-6*) Magna Large Print Bks. GBR. *Dist:* Ulverscroft Large Print Canada, Ltd.
—Menacing Groves. 1990. (Garden Mystery Ser.: No. 5). 208p. mass mkt. 3.95 o.s.i (*0-345-35975-5*) Ballantine Bks.
—Menacing Groves. 1989. 192p. 15.95 o.s.i (*0-684-18967-4*, Macmillan Reference USA) Gale Group.
—Menacing Groves. l.t. ed. 1990. (Magna Large Print Ser.). 320p. o.p. (*1-85057-661-0*) Magna Large Print Bks. GBR. *Dist:* Ulverscroft Large Print Canada, Ltd.
—A Shot in the Arm: Death at the BBC. 1983. 176p. 12.95 o.s.i (*0-684-17990-3*, Macmillan Reference USA) Gale Group.
—A Shot in the Arm: Death at the BBC. 1985. 172p. pap. 4.95 (*0-930330-25-0*) International Polygonics, Ltd.
—The Sunflower Plot. l.t. ed. 1992. 18.95 o.p. (*0-7451-8332-8*); pap. 16.95 o.p. (*0-7927-1018-5*) BBC Audiobooks America.
—The Sunflower Plot. 1991. 256p. 18.95 o.s.i (*0-684-19270-5*, Scribner) Simon & Schuster.

**GRANT, JOCELYN (FICTITIOUS CHARACTER)—FICTION**

Erskine, Barbara. House of Echoes. abr. ed. 1996. 448p. 24.95 o.s.i (*0-525-93867-2*) Dutton/Plume.
—House of Echoes. l.t. ed. 1996. (G. K. Hall Core Ser.). 662p. 25.95 (*0-7838-1851-3*, Macmillan Reference USA) Gale Group.
—House of Echoes. 1997. 480p. mass mkt. 6.50 o.s.i (*0-451-18195-6*, Signet Bks.) NAL.
—House of Echoes. 1996. 448p. text 29.99 (*0-670-85651-7*) Viking Penguin.

**GRANT, MARTIN (FICTITIOUS CHARACTER)—FICTION**

Lilliefors, Jim. Bananaville. 1996. 288p. text 22.95 o.p. (*0-312-14548-9*, Saint Martin's Minotaur) St. Martin's Pr.

**GRANT, PATRICK (FICTITIOUS CHARACTER)—FICTION**

Yorke, Margaret. Cast for Death. 1996. 18.50 o.p. (*0-7451-8685-8*, Black Dagger) BBC Audiobooks America.
—Cast for Death. 1983. pap. 2.25 o.p. (*0-553-22828-5*) Bantam Bks.
—Cast for Death. l.t. unabr. ed. 1999. 214p. 25.95 (*0-7531-6029-3*, 160293) ISIS Large Print Bks. GBR. *Dist:* ISIS Publishing.
—Cast for Death. l.t. ed. 1980. 12.00 o.p. (*0-7089-0408-4*, Ulverscroft) Thorpe, F. A. Pubs. GBR. *Dist:* Ulverscroft Large Print Bks., Ltd.
—Cast for Death. 1976. 6.95 o.p. (*0-8027-5353-1*) Walker & Co.
—Dead in the Morning. 2000. 224p. 21.95 (*0-7540-8560-0*, Black Dagger) BBC Audiobooks America.
—Dead in the Morning. 1982. pap. 2.25 (*0-553-22858-7*) Bantam Bks.
—Dead in the Morning. unabr. ed. 2000. audio 34.95 (*0-7451-6378-5*, CSL 079) Chivers Audio Bks. GBR. *Dist:* BBC Audiobooks America.
—Dead in the Morning. l.t. ed. 2000. (G. K. Hall Nightingale Ser.). 253p. 30.00 (*0-7838-8760-4*, Macmillan Reference USA) Gale Group.
—Dead in the Morning. l.t. ed. 1975. (Ulverscroft Large Print Ser.). 29.99 o.p. (*0-85456-390-3*, Ulverscroft) Thorpe, F. A. Pubs. GBR. *Dist:* Ulverscroft Large Print Bks., Ltd., Ulverscroft Large Print Canada, Ltd.
—Grave Matters. 1983. pap. 2.50 (*0-553-22914-1*) Bantam Bks.
—Grave Matters. l.t. ed. 1975. (Ulverscroft Large Print Ser.). 29.99 o.p. (*0-85456-333-4*, Ulverscroft) Thorpe, F. A. Pubs. GBR. *Dist:* Ulverscroft Large Print Bks., Ltd., Ulverscroft Large Print Canada, Ltd.
—Mortal Remains. l.t. ed. 1990. 18.95 o.p. (*0-7089-2163-9*, Ulverscroft) Thorpe, F. A. Pubs. GBR. *Dist:* Ulverscroft Large Print Bks., Ltd.
—Silent Witness. l.t. unabr. ed. 1999. 208p. 32.50 o.p. (*0-7531-6028-5*, 160285) ISIS Large Print Bks. GBR. *Dist:* Ulverscroft Large Print Bks., Ltd., Ulverscroft Large Print Canada, Ltd.
—Silent Witness. l.t. ed. 1976. o.p. (*0-85456-455-1*, Ulverscroft) Thorpe, F. A. Pubs.
—Silent Witness. 1975. 5.95 (*0-8027-5318-3*) Walker & Co.

**GRANT, SPENCER (FICTITIOUS CHARACTER)—FICTION**

Koontz, Dean. Dark Rivers of the Heart. 1997. pap. 12.95 o.s.i (*0-345-41946-4*); 1995. 592p. mass mkt. 7.99 o.s.i (*0-345-39657-X*) Ballantine Bks.

**GRAVE DIGGER JONES (FICTITIOUS CHARACTER)—FICTION**

*see Jones, Grave Digger (Fictitious Character)—Fiction*

**GRAVES, BRENT (FICTITIOUS CHARACTER)—FICTION**

Donoghue, P. S. The Sankov Confession. 1989. 18.95 o.p. (*1-55611-161-4*) Fine, Donald I. Bks.
—The Sankov Confession. 1992. 352p. mass mkt. 4.50 o.s.i (*0-8217-3800-3*, Zebra Bks.) Kensington Publishing Corp.

**GRAY, CORDELIA (FICTITIOUS CHARACTER)—FICTION**

James, P. D. Murder in Triplicate. 1982. 720p. pap. 12.95 o.p. (*0-684-17646-7*); 1980. 4.95 o.p. (*0-684-16748-4*) Gale Group. (Macmillan Reference USA).
—P. D. James in Murderous Company: Unnatural Causes, An Unsuitable Job for a Woman, The Black Tower. 1988. 9.99 o.s.i (*0-517-65994-8*); 1992. 688p. reprint ed. 13.99 o.s.i (*0-517-07228-9*) Random Hse. Value Publishing.
—The Skull Beneath the Skin. unabr. ed. 1994. audio 88.00 (*0-7366-2647-6*, 3384) Books on Tape, Inc.
—The Skull Beneath the Skin. unabr. ed. 2000. (Cordelia Gray Mystery Ser.: Bk. 2). audio 69.95 (*0-7451-6838-8*, CAB 330) Chivers Audio Bks. GBR. *Dist:* BBC Audiobooks America.
—The Skull Beneath the Skin. l.t. ed. 1983. 571p. 18.95 o.p. (*0-8161-3508-8*); 9.95 o.p. (*0-8161-3569-X*) Gale Group. (Macmillan Reference USA).
—The Skull Beneath the Skin. 1988. mass mkt. 4.95 (*0-446-35272-1*) Little Brown & Co.
—The Skull Beneath the Skin, Set. abr. ed. 1994. audio 15.99 o.s.i (*0-553-47223-2*, 391595, RH Audio) Random Hse. Audio Publishing Group.
—The Skull Beneath the Skin. 2001. 448p. pap. 12.00 (*0-7432-1956-2*, Touchstone); 1982. 352p. 13.95 o.s.i (*0-684-17773-0*, Scribner) Simon & Schuster.
—The Skull Beneath the Skin. 1988. 432p. mass mkt. 7.99 o.p. (*0-446-35372-8*) Warner Bks., Inc.
—Trilogy of Death. 1984. 976p. 19.95 o.s.i (*0-684-18243-2*, Scribner) Simon & Schuster.
—An Unsuitable Job for a Woman. unabr. ed. 1993. audio 56.00 (*0-7366-2497-X*, 3255) Books on Tape, Inc.
—An Unsuitable Job for a Woman. unabr. ed. 2000. (Cordelia Gray Mystery Ser.: Bk. 1). audio 49.95 (*0-7451-6064-6*, CAB 180) Chivers Audio Bks. GBR. *Dist:* BBC Audiobooks America.
—An Unsuitable Job for a Woman. 1980. (General Ser.). lib. bdg. 13.95 o.p. (*0-8161-6788-5*, Macmillan Reference USA) Gale Group.
—An Unsuitable Job for a Woman. unabr. ed. 1992. audio 51.00 (*1-55690-737-0*, 92110E7) Recorded Bks., LLC.
—An Unsuitable Job for a Woman. 2001. (Classic Ser.). 208p. 25.00 (*0-7432-2204-0*, Scribner); 256p. pap. 12.00 (*0-7432-1955-4*, Touchstone); 320p. 25.00 o.p. (*0-7432-2492-2*, Scribner) Simon & Schuster.
—An Unsuitable Job for a Woman. 1988. 288p. reprint ed. mass mkt. 6.99 o.p. (*0-446-31517-6*) Warner Bks., Inc.

**GRAY, HELEN (FICTITIOUS CHARACTER)—FICTION**

Bond, Larry. Day of Wrath. unabr. ed. 1998. audio 96.00 (*0-7366-4187-4*, 4685) Books on Tape, Inc.
—Day of Wrath. abr. ed. 1998. 5p. audio 25.00 (*0-671-58224-0*, 495728, Simon & Schuster Audioworks) Simon & Schuster Audio.
—Day of Wrath. l.t. ed. 1999. (Mystery Ser.). 725p. 30.95 o.p. (*0-7862-1616-6*) Thorndike Pr.
—Day of Wrath. 1999. 528p. mass mkt. 7.99 (*0-446-60705-3*); 1998. 496p. 25.00 (*0-446-51677-5*) Warner Bks., Inc.
—The Enemy Within. abr. ed. audio. 1999. audio 12.98 (*0-671-04632-2*, Simon & Schuster Audioworks) ;Set. 1996. 192p. pap. 23.00 incl. audio (*0-671-57054-4*, 493929, Simon & Schuster Audioworks) Simon & Schuster Audio.
—The Enemy Within. 1997. 528p. mass mkt. 7.99 (*0-446-60385-6*); 1996. 496p. 32.00 (*0-446-51676-7*) Warner Bks., Inc.
Bond, Larry & Larkin, Patrick. The Enemy Within. unabr. ed. 1996. audio 104.00 (*0-7366-3388-X*, 4038) Books on Tape, Inc.

Characters

**GRAY, JENNIFER (FICTITIOUS CHARACTER)—FICTION**

Livingston, Georgette. The Unlucky Collie Caper. 1995. (Jennifer Gray Mystery Ser.: Bk. 1). 192p. 18.95 (*0-8034-9139-5*, Avalon Bks.) Bouregy, Thomas & Co., Inc.

**GRAY, P. J. (FICTITIOUS CHARACTER)—FICTION**

Kennett, Shirley. Firecracker. 1998. 320p. mass mkt. 5.99 o.s.i (*0-7860-0525-4*, Pinnacle Bks.) Kensington Publishing Corp.

Kennett, Shirley. Chameleon. 1999. 384p. mass mkt. 5.99 (*0-7860-0638-2*) Kensington Publishing Corp.

—Chameleon: A Novel of Suspense. 1998. 320p. 22.00 o.s.i (*1-57566-347-3*) Kensington Publishing Corp.

—Fire Cracker. 1997. 320p. pap. 21.95 o.p. (*1-57566-181-0*) Kensington Publishing Corp.

—Gray Matter. 1997. 320p. mass mkt. 5.99 o.s.i (*0-7860-0389-8*, Pinnacle Bks.); 1996. 224p. 21.95 o.s.i (*1-57566-079-2*, Kensington Bks.) Kensington Publishing Corp.

**GRAYSON, GALE (FICTITIOUS CHARACTER)—FICTION**

Holbrook, Teri. A Far & Deadly Cry. 1995. 400p. mass mkt. 5.99 (*0-553-56859-0*, Crimeline) Bantam Bks.

—The Grass Widow. 1996. 320p. mass mkt. 5.99 o.s.i (*0-553-56860-4*, Crimeline) Bantam Bks.

—The Mother Tongue. 2001. 320p. (Orig.). mass mkt. 5.99 (*0-553-57719-0*) Bantam Bks.

**GREEN, BEN (FICTITIOUS CHARACTER)—FICTION**

Berrenson, Marc. Bodily Harm. 1992. 224p. (Orig.). mass mkt. 4.50 (*0-380-76613-2*, Avon Bks.) Morrow/Avon.

—L. A. Snitch. 1991. 256p. (Orig.). pap. 3.95 (*0-380-76324-9*, Avon Bks.) Morrow/Avon.

**GREEN, DETECTIVE INSPECTOR (FICTITIOUS CHARACTER)—FICTION**

Clark, Douglas. The Big Grouse: A Masters & Green Mystery. 1987. 224p. 18.95 o.p. (*0-575-03909-4*) Gollancz, Victor GBR. *Dist:* Trafalgar Square.

—The Big Grouse: A Masters & Green Mystery. 1988. 272p. reprint ed. pap. 3.95 o.p. (*0-06-080918-3*, P-918, Perennial) HarperTrade.

—Bitter Water: A Masters & Green Mystery. 1990. 256p. (Orig.). pap. 4.95 o.p. (*0-06-081024-6*, Perennial) HarperTrade.

—Bouquet Garni. l.t. ed. 1986. 368p. 12.50 o.p. (*0-7089-1415-2*, Ulverscroft) Thorpe, F. A. Pubs. GBR. *Dist:* Ulverscroft Large Print Bks., Ltd.

—Dead Letter: A Masters & Green Mystery. l.t. ed. 1989. (Ulverscroft Large Print Ser.). 379p. 29.99 o.p. (*0-7089-1972-3*, Ulverscroft) Thorpe, F. A. Pubs. GBR. *Dist:* Ulverscroft Large Print Bks., Ltd., Ulverscroft Large Print Canada, Ltd.

—Doone Walk. l.t. ed. 1987. (Linford Mystery Library). 336p. pap. 17.99 o.p. (*0-7089-6394-3*, Linford) Thorpe, F. A. Pubs. GBR. *Dist:* Ulverscroft Large Print Bks., Ltd., Ulverscroft Large Print Canada, Ltd.

—Dread & Water. l.t. ed. 1991. 17.95 o.p. (*0-7451-9999-2*, AH035); pap. 15.95 o.p. (*0-7927-0463-0*, AS071) BBC Audiobooks America.

—The Gimmel Flask. 1982. (Murder Ink Mystery Ser.: No. 41). pap. 2.25 o.p. (*0-440-13160-X*) Dell Publishing.

—Golden Rain. 1982. (Murder Ink Mystery Ser.: No. 47). 224p. pap. 2.50 o.p. (*0-440-12932-X*) Dell Publishing.

—Heberden's Seat. l.t. ed. 1991. 17.95 o.p. (*0-7451-8118-X*, AH0167); pap. 15.95 o.p. (*0-7927-0618-8*, AS0203) BBC Audiobooks America.

—Heberden's Seat. 1985. 192p. mass mkt. 3.50 o.p. (*0-06-080724-5*, P724, Perennial) HarperTrade.

—Jewelled Eye: A Masters & Green Mystery. l.t. ed. 1987. pap. 13.95 o.p. (*1-55504-251-1*) BBC Audiobooks America.

—Jewelled Eye: A Masters & Green Mystery. 1986. 189p. 17.95 o.p. (*0-575-03728-8*) Gollancz, Victor GBR. *Dist:* Trafalgar Square.

—Jewelled Eye: A Masters & Green Mystery. 1988. 272p. reprint ed. pap. 3.95 o.p. (*0-06-080919-1*, P-919, Perennial) HarperTrade.

—The Longest Pleasure. 1984. 192p. reprint ed. pap. 2.95 o.p. (*0-06-080689-3*, P689) HarperCollins Pubs.

—The Monday Theory. 1985. 208p. mass mkt. 3.50 o.p. (*0-06-080737-7*, P737, Perennial) HarperTrade.

—Nobody's Perfect. l.t. ed. (Atlantic Mystery Ser.). pap. 8.95 o.p. (*1-55504-561-8*, 844) BBC Audiobooks America.

—Nobody's Perfect. 1986. 192p. reprint ed. mass mkt. 3.50 o.p. (*0-06-080796-2*, P 796, Perennial) HarperTrade.

—Performance. 1986. 224p. reprint ed. mass mkt. 3.50 o.p. (*0-06-080810-1*, P 810, Perennial) HarperTrade.

—Plain Sailing: A Masters & Green Mystery. 1988. 272p. reprint ed. pap. 3.95 o.p. (*0-06-080917-5*, P-917, Perennial) HarperTrade.

—Plain Sailing: A Masters & Green Mystery. l.t. ed. 1989. (Ulverscroft Large Print Ser.). 384p. 29.99 o.p. (*0-7089-2008-X*, Ulverscroft) Thorpe, F. A. Pubs. GBR. *Dist:* Ulverscroft Large Print Bks., Ltd., Ulverscroft Large Print Canada, Ltd.

—Poacher's Bag. l.t. ed. 1989. (Atlantic Mystery Ser.). pap. 14.95 o.p. (*1-55504-716-5*, 149) BBC Audiobooks America.

—Poacher's Bag. 1983. 176p. pap. o.p. (*0-06-080643-5*, P 643) HarperCollins Pubs.

—Roast Eggs. 1983. 176p. pap. o.p. (*0-06-080644-3*, P 644) HarperCollins Pubs.

—Shelf Life. l.t. ed. 1992. 18.95 o.p. (*0-7451-8252-6*, AH0262); pap. 16.95 o.p. (*0-7927-0812-1*, AS0298) BBC Audiobooks America.

—Shelf Life. 1983. 176p. pap. o.p. (*0-06-080675-3*, P675) HarperCollins Pubs.

—Sick to Death. l.t. ed. 1990. 17.95 o.p. (*0-7451-9897-X*, C0628); pap. 15.95 o.p. (*0-7927-0360-X*, C0822) BBC Audiobooks America.

—Sick to Death. 1983. 176p. pap. o.p. (*0-06-080676-1*, P676) HarperCollins Pubs.

—Storm Centre. 1986. 18.95 o.p. (*0-575-03833-0*) Gollancz, Victor GBR. *Dist:* Trafalgar Square.

—Storm Centre. 1988. (Master & Green Mystery Ser.). 240p. reprint ed. pap. 3.95 o.p. (*0-06-080920-5*, P-920, Perennial) HarperTrade.

—Storm Centre. l.t. ed. 1987. (Linford Mystery Library). 368p. pap. 17.99 o.p. (*0-7089-6388-9*, Linford) Thorpe, F. A. Pubs. GBR. *Dist:* Ulverscroft Large Print Bks., Ltd., Ulverscroft Large Print Canada, Ltd.

—Table d'Hote. 1985. 208p. mass mkt. 3.50 o.p. (*0-06-080723-7*, P723, Perennial) HarperTrade.

—Table d'Hote. l.t. ed. 1981. (Ulverscroft Large Print Ser.). 315p. 29.99 o.p. (*0-7089-0603-6*, Ulverscroft) Thorpe, F. A. Pubs. GBR. *Dist:* Ulverscroft Large Print Bks., Ltd., Ulverscroft Large Print Canada, Ltd.

—Vicious Circle: A Masters & Green Mystery. l.t. ed. 1988. pap. 14.95 o.p. (*1-55504-629-0*, 313) BBC Audiobooks America.

—Vicious Circle: A Masters & Green Mystery. 1985. 208p. reprint ed. mass mkt. 3.50 o.p. (*0-06-080778-4*, P 778, Perennial) HarperTrade.

Fradkin, Barbara Fraser. Once upon a Time: An Inspector Green Mystery. 2002. 304p. pap. 10.95 (*0-929141-84-9*, Rendezvous Press) Napoleon Publishing/Rendezvous Pr. CAN. *Dist:* Words Distributing Co.

**GREENE, CHARLIE (FICTITIOUS CHARACTER)—FICTION**

Millhiser, Marlys. Death of the Office Witch. 1995. (Charlie Green Mystery Ser.). 304p. pap. 5.95 o.p. (*0-14-024340-2*, Penguin Bks.) Penguin Group (USA) Inc.

—Death of the Office Witch. 1993. 289p. 20.00 (*1-883402-02-6*, Scribner) Simon & Schuster.

—It's Murder Going Home. 1997. (Charlie Greene Mystery Ser.). 288p. mass mkt. 6.95 o.s.i (*0-14-026586-4*) Penguin Group (USA) Inc.

—It's Murder Going Home. 1996. 304p. 22.95 (*0-312-14628-0*, Saint Martin's Minotaur) St. Martin's Pr.

—Killer Commute: A Charlie Greene Mystery. 2000. (Charlie Greene Mysteries Ser.). 275p. 23.95 (*0-312-26610-3*, Saint Martin's Minotaur) St. Martin's Pr.

—Murder at Moot Point. 2001. 272p. pap. 19.00 (*0-385-50405-5*) Doubleday Publishing.

—Murder in a Hot Flash: A Charlie Greene Mystery. 1996. (Charlie Greene Ser.). 256p. pap. 5.95 o.s.i (*0-14-025138-3*) Penguin Group (USA) Inc.

—Murder in a Hot Flash: A Charlie Greene Mystery. 1995. 252p. 20.50 (*1-883402-29-8*, Scribner) Simon & Schuster.

—Nobody Dies in a Casino. 1999. 288p. 22.95 (*0-312-20344-6*, Saint Martin's Minotaur) St. Martin's Pr.

—Rampant Reaper. E-Book 23.95 (*0-312-70742-8*) St. Martin's Pr.

—The Rampant Reaper. 2003. (WWL Mystery Ser.: No. 478). 288p. mass mkt. (*0-373-26478-X*, Worldwide Library) Harlequin Enterprises, Ltd.

—The Rampant Reaper: A Charlie Greene Mystery. 2002. 288p. 23.95 (*0-312-29096-9*, Saint Martin's Minotaur) St. Martin's Pr.

**GREENE, DAVID (FICTITIOUS CHARACTER)—FICTION**

Harmetz, Aljean. Off the Face of the Earth. 1998. 320p. per. 6.99 (*0-671-00465-4*, Pocket); 1997. 288p. 22.00 (*0-684-83617-3*, Scribner) Simon & Schuster.

**GREENE, TERENCE (FICTITIOUS CHARACTER)—FICTION**

Cantwell, Aston. Double Delight. 1983. 256p. pap. 2.75 o.s.i (*0-446-30298-8*) Warner Bks., Inc.

Smith, Rosamond, pseud. Double Delight. 1999. 368p. pap. 12.95 o.s.i (*0-452-28041-9*, Plume); 1997. 336p. 23.95 o.p. (*0-525-94299-8*) Dutton/Plume.

—Double Delight. 1999. pap. 6.99 (*0-451-40782-2*, Signet Bks.) NAL.

**GREENFIELD, C. B. (FICTITIOUS CHARACTER)—FICTION**

Kallen, Lucille. C. B. Greenfield: A Little Madness. 1987. mass mkt. 3.50 o.s.i (*0-345-31119-1*, Ballantine Bks.) Ballantine Bks.

—C. B. Greenfield: No Lady in the House. 1984. 208p. mass mkt. 3.95 o.s.i (*0-345-32396-3*) Ballantine Bks.

—C. B. Greenfield: No Lady in the House. 1982. 12.95 o.p. (*0-671-43240-0*, Simon & Schuster) Simon & Schuster.

—C. B. Greenfield: No Lady in the House. l.t. ed. 1982. 374p. reprint ed. 10.95 o.p. (*0-89621-365-X*) Thorndike Pr.

—C. B. Greenfield: The Piano Bird. 1985. 224p. mass mkt. 3.95 o.s.i (*0-345-31118-3*, Ballantine Bks.) Ballantine Bks.

—C. B. Greenfield: The Piano Bird. 1984. 175p. 13.95 o.p. (*0-394-53081-0*) Random Hse., Inc.

—C. B. Greenfield: The Tanglewood Murder. 1985. mass mkt. 3.95 o.s.i (*0-345-33143-5*) Ballantine Bks.

—Introducing C. B. Greenfield. 1985. 208p. mass mkt. 3.95 o.s.i (*0-345-33426-4*); 1984. mass mkt. 2.50 o.p. (*0-345-32159-6*) Ballantine Bks.

—Introducing C. B. Greenfield. l.t. ed. 1980. 363p. reprint ed. 11.95 o.p. (*0-89621-260-2*) Thorndike Pr.

**GREENWAY, SOPHIE (FICTITIOUS CHARACTER)—FICTION**

Hart, Ellen. For Every Evil. 1995. (Jane Lawless Mysteries Ser.). 272p. mass mkt. 5.99 o.s.i (*0-345-38190-4*) Ballantine Bks.

—Murder in the Air. 1997. (Culinary Mysteries Ser.). 352p. mass mkt. 6.50 (*0-345-40203-0*, Ballantine Bks.) Ballantine Bks.

—The Oldest Sin. 1996. (Sophie Greenway Mystery Ser.: Bk. 3). 288p. mass mkt. 5.99 (*0-345-40202-2*) Ballantine Bks.

—Slice & Dice. 2000. (Culinary Mystery Ser.). 368p. mass mkt. 6.50 (*0-345-42153-1*, Fawcett) Ballantine Bks.

—This Little Piggy Went to Murder. 1994. (Midwest Mysteries Ser.). 230p. (Orig.). mass mkt. 5.99 o.s.i (*0-345-38189-0*) Ballantine Bks.

**GREER, DANIEL (FICTITIOUS CHARACTER)—FICTION**

Brandon, Jay. Predator's Waltz. Isaacson, Dana, ed. 1992. 304p. reprint ed. mass mkt. 4.99 (*0-671-70889-9*, Pocket) Simon & Schuster.

—Predator's Waltz. 1989. 288p. 17.95 o.p. (*0-312-03413-X*, Saint Martin's Minotaur) St. Martin's Pr.

**GREGORY, ALAN (FICTITIOUS CHARACTER)—FICTION**

White, Stephen. Blinded. 2004. 400p. 24.95 (*0-385-33620-9*, Delacorte Pr.) Dell Publishing.

—Cold Case. 2000. (Illus.). 368p. 24.95 (*0-525-94526-1*, Dutton) Dutton/Plume.

—Cold Case. 2001. 432p. mass mkt. 7.99 (*0-451-20155-8*, Signet Bks.) NAL.

—Cold Case. l.t. ed. 2000. (Mystery Ser.). 623p. 29.95 (*0-7862-2530-0*) Thorndike Pr.

—Critical Conditions. l.t. ed. 2000. 27.95 (*1-57490-280-6*, Beeler Large Print Bks.) Beeler, Thomas T. Publisher.

—Critical Conditions. unabr. ed. 1998. (Alan Gregory Ser.). audio 64.00 (*0-7366-4184-X*, 4682) Books on Tape, Inc.

—Critical Conditions. 1998. (Alan Gregory Ser.). 320p. 24.95 o.p. (*0-525-94270-X*) Dutton/Plume.

—Critical Conditions. 1999. (Alan Gregory Ser.). 416p. mass mkt. 7.99 (*0-451-19170-6*, Signet Bks.) NAL.

—Harm's Way. l.t. ed. 1996. lib. bdg. 24.95 (*1-57490-066-8*, Beeler Large Print Bks.) Beeler, Thomas T. Publisher.

—Harm's Way. unabr. collector's ed. 1997. (Alan Gregory Ser.). audio 56.00 (*0-913369-39-X*, 4215) Books on Tape, Inc.

—Harm's Way. 1997. 432p. mass mkt. 7.99 (*0-451-18368-1*, Signet Bks.) NAL.

—Harm's Way. 1996. 352p. 22.95 o.p. (*0-670-85861-7*, Viking) Viking Penguin.

—Higher Authority. unabr. collector's ed. 1995. (Alan Gregory Ser.). audio 80.00 (*0-7366-3042-2*, 3724) Books on Tape, Inc.

—Higher Authority. 1996. 432p. mass mkt. 7.99 (*0-451-18511-0*, Signet Bks.) NAL.

—Higher Authority. 1994. 464p. 22.95 o.p. (*0-670-85040-3*) Viking Penguin.

—Manner of Death. l.t. ed. 1999. 450p. 26.95 (*1-57490-177-X*) Beeler, Thomas T. Publisher.

—Manner of Death. 1999. audio compact disk 88.00 (*0-7366-5158-6*); 1999. audio 72.00 (*0-7366-4403-2*, 4864); 2001. audio compact disk 88.00 Books on Tape, Inc.

—Manner of Death. 1999. (Alan Gregory Ser.). 416p. 23.95 o.p. (*0-525-94440-0*) Dutton/Plume.

—Manner of Death. 2000. 416p. reprint ed. mass mkt. 7.50 (*0-451-19703-8*, Signet Bks.) NAL.

—Private Practices. unabr. collector's ed. 1993. (Alan Gregory Ser.). audio 80.00 (*0-7366-2592-5*, 3337) Books on Tape, Inc.

—Private Practices. 1994. 432p. mass mkt. 7.99 (*0-451-40431-9*, Signet Bks.) NAL.

—Private Practices. 1999. pap. (*0-14-017328-5*); 1993. 432p. 20.00 o.p. (*0-670-84673-2*) Viking Penguin. (Viking).

—Privileged Information. unabr. collector's ed. 1992. (Alan Gregory Ser.). audio 72.00 (*0-7366-2262-4*, 3050) Books on Tape, Inc.

—Privileged Information. 2001. 384p. mass mkt. 6.99 (*0-7860-1356-7*, Pinnacle Bks.); 1999. 383p. mass mkt. 5.99 o.s.i (*0-7860-0624-2*); 1992. 384p. reprint ed. mass mkt. 5.99 o.s.i (*0-8217-3951-4*, Zebra Bks.) Kensington Publishing Corp.

—Privileged Information. 1991. 368p. 19.95 o.p. (*0-670-83765-2*) Viking Penguin.

—The Program. abr. ed. 2001. audio 24.95 o.s.i (*1-58788-359-7*, 2545, Nova Audio Bks.); audio 34.95 (*1-58788-357-0*, 2543, Brilliance Audio Unabridged); audio 87.25 (*1-58788-358-9*, 2544) Brilliance Audio.

—The Program. l.t. ed. 2002. pap. 28.95 (*0-7862-3412-1*); 2001. 480p. 31.95 (*0-7862-3411-3*) Thorndike Pr.

—Remote Control. unabr. ed. 1997. (Alan Gregory Ser.). audio 64.00 (*0-7366-3769-9*, 4442) Books on Tape, Inc.

—Remote Control. 1997. (Alan Gregory Ser.). 320p. 22.95 o.s.i (*0-525-94269-6*) Dutton/Plume.

—Remote Control. 1998. (Alan Gregory Ser.). 432p. mass mkt. 6.99 (*0-451-19169-2*, Signet Bks.) NAL.

—Remote Control. abr. ed. 1997. (Alan Gregory Ser.). audio 16.95 o.s.i (*0-14-086549-7*, Penguin AudioBooks) Viking Penguin.

—Warning Signs. abr. ed. 2003. (Dr. Alan Gregory Series: Vol. 10). audio 12.99 (*1-59086-573-1*, 4163, Brilliance Audio Paperback Audiobooks); 2002. audio 24.95 o.p. (*1-58788-362-7*, 2548, Nova Audio Bks.); 2002. audio 34.95 (*1-58788-360-0*, 2546, Brilliance Audio Unabridged); 2002. audio 73.25 (*1-58788-361-9*, 2547, Unabridged Library Editions) Brilliance Audio.

—Warning Signs. 2002. lib. bdg. 29.95 (*1-58547-186-0*, Platinum) Ctr. Point Large Print.

—Warning Signs. 2003. 512p. mass mkt. 7.99 (*0-440-23741-6*); 2003. E-Book 7.99 (*0-440-33406-3*, Dell Bks.); 2002. 432p. 24.95 (*0-385-33618-7*, Delacorte Pr.) Dell Publishing.

—Warning Signs. unabr. ed. 2003. audio 19.99 (*1-59335-120-8*, 30216) Soulmate Audio Bks., Inc.

**GREGORY, JOE (FICTITIOUS CHARACTER)—FICTION**

Dee, Edward. Bronx Angel. 1995. 304p. 21.95 o.p. (*0-446-51774-7*); 1996. 384p. reprint ed. mass mkt. 6.50 (*0-446-60337-6*) Warner Bks., Inc.

—Little Boy Blue. l.t. ed. 1997. (Wheeler Large Print Book Ser.). pap. 23.95 (*1-56895-452-2*, Wheeler Publishing, Inc.) Gale Group.

—Little Boy Blue. abr. ed. 2001. audio 7.95 (*1-57815-217-8*, Media Bks. Audio Publishing) Media Bks., L. L. C.

—Little Boy Blue. abr. ed. 1997. audio 12.98 (*1-57042-475-6*, 394925) Time Warner AudioBooks.

—Little Boy Blue. 1997. 272p. 22.50 o.p. (*0-446-52038-1*); 1998. 320p. reprint ed. mass mkt. 6.99 o.s.i (*0-446-60522-0*) Warner Bks., Inc.

—14 Peck Slip. 1994. 304p. 19.95 o.s.i (*0-446-51770-4*); 1995. 336p. reprint ed. mass mkt. 5.99 (*0-446-60238-8*) Warner Bks., Inc.

Dee, Edward. Nightbird. 2000. 352p. E-Book 4.95 (*0-446-92362-1*) Time Warner Bk. Group.

—Nightbird. 2001. 352p. E-Book 4.95 (*0-446-96023-3*); 2000. 352p. mass mkt. 6.99 (*0-446-60913-7*); 2000. E-Book 4.95 (*0-446-91510-6*); 1999. 304p. 23.95 (*0-446-52039-X*) Warner Bks., Inc.

**GREY, ANA (FICTITIOUS CHARACTER)—FICTION**

Smith, April. Good Morning, Killer. 2003. 368p. 24.00 (*0-375-41240-9*) Knopf, Alfred A. Inc.

—North of Montana. 1995. 368p. mass mkt. 6.99 (*0-449-22502-X*, Fawcett) Ballantine Bks.

—North of Montana. l.t. ed. 1995. (Large Print Ser.). 352p. lib. bdg. 23.95 (*1-57490-035-8*, Beeler Large Print Bks.) Beeler, Thomas T. Publisher.

—North of Montana. abr. ed. 1994. audio 17.00 o.s.i (*0-679-43652-9*, RH Audio) Random Hse. Audio Publishing Group.

**GREY, BRUCE (FICTITIOUS CHARACTER)—FICTION**

Coben, Harlan. Miracle Cure: A Novel. 1991. 440p. 20.00 o.s.i (*0-945167-39-3*) British American Publishing, Ltd.

—Miracle Cure: A Novel. 1992. pap. 5.50 (*1-56171-126-8*) SPI Bks.

**GREY, HENRY (FICTITIOUS CHARACTER)—FICTION**

Francis, Dick. Flying Finish. 1997. mass mkt. 6.99 *(0-449-45726-5)*; 1987. mass mkt. 6.99 o.s.i *(0-449-21265-3)* Ballantine Bks. (Fawcett).
—Flying Finish. 1999. 288p. mass mkt. 6.99 *(0-515-12560-1*, Jove) Berkley Publishing Group.
—Flying Finish. unabr. ed. 1994. audio 48.00 *(0-7366-2676-X*, 3413) Books on Tape, Inc.
—Flying Finish. l.t. ed. 1995. 349p. reprint ed. 23.95 o.p. *(0-7838-1141-1*, Macmillan Reference USA) Gale Group.
—Flying Finish. abr. ed. audio 15.95 o.p. *(1-55994-137-5*, CPN 2137, HarperAudio) HarperTrade.
—Flying Finish. unabr. ed. 1997. audio 51.00 *(0-7887-0252-1*, 94461E7) Recorded Bks., LLC.
—Flying Finish. 1984. mass mkt. 3.50 *(0-671-50926-8)*; 1983. mass mkt. 2.95 *(0-671-47020-5)* Simon & Schuster. (Pocket).
—Flying Finish. l.t. ed. 1979. 12.00 o.p. *(0-7089-0298-7*, Ulverscroft) Thorpe, F. A. Pubs. GBR. *Dist:* Ulverscroft Large Print Bks., Ltd.

**GREY, JOE (FICTITIOUS CHARACTER)—FICTION**

Murphy, Shirley Rousseau. Cat Fear No Evil: A Joe Grey Mystery. 2004. 336p. 24.95 *(0-06-620949-8)* HarperCollins Pubs.
—Cat in the Dark. 1999. 272p. 22.00 o.s.i *(0-06-105096-2)* HarperCollins Pubs.
—Cat in the Dark. 1999. (Joe Grey Mysteries Ser.). 320p. mass mkt. 6.99 *(0-06-105947-1*, Eos) Morrow/Avon.
—Cat Laughing Last. 2002. (Joe Grey Mysteries Ser.). 368p. mass mkt. 6.99 *(0-06-101562-8*, Avon Bks.) Morrow/Avon.
—Cat Laughing Last: A Joe Grey Mystery. 2002. 288p. 23.95 *(0-06-620951-X)* HarperCollins Pubs.
—Cat on the Edge. 1996. 288p. mass mkt. 6.99 *(0-06-105600-6*, Eos) Morrow/Avon.
—Cat Raise the Dead. 1997. 304p. mass mkt. 6.99 *(0-06-105602-2*, Eos) Morrow/Avon.
—Cat Seeing Double: A Joe Grey Mystery. 2003. 304p. 24.95 *(0-06-620950-1)* HarperCollins Pubs.
—Cat Seeing Double: A Joe Grey Mystery. l.t. ed. 2003. (Americana Ser.). 28.95 *(0-7862-5436-X)* Thorndike Pr.
—Cat Spitting Mad. l.t. ed. 2002. (Wheeler Large Print Book Ser.). 281p. pap. 23.95 o.p. *(1-58724-158-7*, Wheeler Publishing, Inc.) Gale Group.
—Cat Spitting Mad. 2000. (Joe Grey Mysteries Ser.). 240p. 23.00 *(0-06-105098-9)* HarperCollins Pubs.
—Cat Spitting Mad. 2001. 304p. mass mkt. 6.99 *(0-06-105989-7*, Avon Bks.) Morrow/Avon.
—Cat to the Dogs: A Joe Grey Mystery. l.t. ed. 2000. 243p. 24.95 *(1-57490-264-4*, Beeler Large Print Bks.) Beeler, Thomas T. Publisher.
—Cat to the Dogs: A Joe Grey Mystery. 1999. (Joe Grey Mysteries Ser.). 256p. 23.00 *(0-06-105097-0)* HarperCollins Pubs.
—Cat to the Dogs: A Joe Grey Mystery. 2000. (Joe Grey Mysteries Ser.). 304p. mass mkt. 6.99 *(0-06-105988-9*, Avon Bks.) Morrow/Avon.
—Cat under Fire. l.t. ed. 2001. 265p. 25.95 *(1-57490-341-1)* Beeler, Thomas T. Publisher.
—Cat under Fire. 1997. 256p. mass mkt. 6.99 *(0-06-105601-4*, Eos) Morrow/Avon.

**GREY, LAVINIA, MOTHER (FICTITIOUS CHARACTER)—FICTION**

Gallison, Kate. Grave Misgivings: A Mother Lavinia Grey Mystery. 1999. (Mother Lavinia Grey Mysteries Ser.). 256p. mass mkt. 5.99 o.s.i *(0-440-22413-6)* Dell Publishing.
—Hasty Retreat: A Mother Lavinia Grey Mystery. 1998. (Mother Lavinia Grey Mysteries Ser.). 256p. mass mkt. 5.99 o.s.i *(0-440-22410-1*, Dell Bks.) Dell Publishing.
—Unholy Angels: A Mother Lavinia Grey Mystery. 1996. (Mother Lavinia Grey Mysteries Ser.). 272p. mass mkt. 5.99 o.s.i *(0-440-22220-6)* Dell Publishing.

**GREY MOUSER (FICTITIOUS CHARACTER)—FICTION**

Leiber, Fritz. The Knight & Knave of Swords. 1990. mass mkt. 3.95 o.s.i *(0-441-45125-X)* Ace Bks.
—Swords Against Death. (Fafhrd & Grey Mouser Ser.). 1986. mass mkt. 3.95 o.p. *(0-441-79193-X)*; 1984. mass mkt. 2.75 o.s.i *(0-441-79190-5)*; 1983. mass mkt. 2.75 o.s.i *(0-441-79158-1)*; 1982. mass mkt. 2.50 o.s.i *(0-441-79157-3)*; 1981. mass mkt. 2.25 o.s.i *(0-441-79156-5)* Ace Bks.
—Swords Against Death. 1977. (Science Fiction Ser.). lib. bdg. 9.95 o.p. *(0-8398-2399-1*, Macmillan Reference USA) Gale Group.
—Swords Against Death. 2003. 304p. mass mkt. 6.99 *(0-7434-5828-1)* ibooks, Inc.
—Swords Against Wizardry. 1986. (Fafhrd & Grey Mouser Ser.). mass mkt. 3.95 o.s.i *(0-441-79194-8)* Ace Bks.
—Swords Against Wizardry. 1977. (Science Fiction Ser.). lib. bdg. 9.95 o.p. *(0-8398-2401-7*, Macmillan Reference USA) Gale Group.
—Swords Against Wizardry. E-Book 6.99 *(1-58586-363-7)*; 2001. E-Book 6.99 *(0-7592-0913-8)* ereads.com.
—Swords Against Wizardry. 2003. 240p. mass mkt. 6.99 *(0-7434-7537-2)* ibooks, Inc.
—Swords & Deviltry. 1986. (Fafhrd & Grey Mouser Ser.: No. 1). 256p. mass mkt. 2.95 o.s.i *(0-441-79198-0)*; 1985. mass mkt. 2.95 o.s.i *(0-441-79197-2)*; 1985. mass mkt. 2.95 o.s.i *(0-441-79191-3)*; 1983. mass mkt. 2.75 o.s.i *(0-441-79179-4)*; 1982. mass mkt. 2.50 o.s.i *(0-441-79177-8)*; 1981. mass mkt. 2.25 o.s.i *(0-441-79176-X)* Ace Bks.
—Swords & Deviltry. 1977. (Fafhrd & Grey Mouser Ser.). lib. bdg. 9.95 o.p. *(0-8398-2398-3*, Macmillan Reference USA) Gale Group.
—Swords & Deviltry. 2003. 224p. mass mkt. 6.99 *(0-7434-4558-9)* ibooks, Inc.
—Swords & Ice Magic. 1986. mass mkt. 3.95 o.s.i *(0-441-79196-4)*; 1984. mass mkt. 2.75 o.s.i *(0-441-79189-1)*; 1983. mass mkt. 2.50 o.s.i *(0-441-79178-6)*; 1981. mass mkt. 2.25 o.s.i *(0-441-79169-7)* Ace Bks.
—Swords & Ice Magic. 1977. lib. bdg. 9.95 o.p. *(0-8398-2403-3*, Macmillan Reference USA) Gale Group.
—Swords in the Mist. mass mkt. 3.95 o.s.i *(0-441-79129-8)*; 1985. mass mkt. 3.95 o.s.i *(0-441-79192-1)*; 1983. mass mkt. 2.50 o.s.i *(0-441-79186-7)*; 1981. mass mkt. 2.25 o.s.i *(0-441-79185-9)* Ace Bks.
—Swords in the Mist. 1977. (Science Fiction Ser.). lib. bdg. 9.95 o.p. *(0-8398-2400-9*, Macmillan Reference USA) Gale Group.
—Swords in the Mist. E-Book 6.99 *(1-58586-366-1)*; E-Book 6.99 *(0-7592-0914-6)* ereads.com.
—Swords in the Mist. 2003. pap. 6.99 *(0-7434-7465-1)* ibooks, Inc.
—The Swords of Lankhmar. 1986. (Fafhrd & Grey Mouser Ser.: No. 4). 320p. mass mkt. 3.95 o.s.i *(0-441-79195-6)* Ace Bks.
—The Swords of Lankhmar. Date not set. 224p. 21.95 *(0-8488-2352-4)* Amereon, Ltd.

**GRIFFIN (FICTITIOUS CHARACTER: BANTOCK)—FICTION**

Bantock, Nick. Alexandria: In Which the Extraordinary Correspondence of Griffin & Sabine Unfolds. 19.95 o.s.i *(0-8118-3699-1)* Chronicle Bks. LLC.
—The Golden Mean: In Which the Extraordinary Correspondence of Griffin & Sabine Concludes. 1993. (Illus.). 48p. 17.95 *(0-8118-0298-1)* Chronicle Bks. LLC.
—The Golden Mean: In Which the Extraordinary Correspondence of Griffin & Sabine Concludes. unabr. ed. 1993. (Griffin & Sabine Trilogy). 40p. audio 10.95 *(1-879371-49-9)* Publishing Mills, Inc., The.
—Griffin & Sabine: An Extraordinary Address Book. 1994. (Illus.). 100p. 18.95 o.p. *(0-8118-0616-2)* Chronicle Bks. LLC.
—Griffin & Sabine: An Extraordinary Correspondence. (Illus.). 48p. 1991. 19.95 *(0-87701-788-3)*; 10th anniv. ltd. ed. 2001. 19.95 o.p. *(0-8118-3200-7)* Chronicle Bks. LLC.
—Griffin & Sabine: An Extraordinary Correspondence. 1991. audio 10.95 *(1-879371-42-1*, 30000) Publishing Mills, Inc., The.
—Griffin & Sabine Art Cards. 1994. 13.95 o.p. *(0-8118-0729-0)* Chronicle Bks. LLC.
—The Griffin & Sabine Trilogy, 3 bks. 1994. (Illus.). 49.95 *(0-8118-0696-0)* Chronicle Bks. LLC.
—The Griffin & Sabine Trilogy. unabr. ed. 1994. 2p. audio 24.95 *(1-879371-58-8*, 70000) Publishing Mills, Inc., The.
—The Gryphon: In Which the Extraordinary Correspondence of Griffin & Sabine Is Rediscovered. 2001. 19.95 o.s.i *(0-8118-3384-4)*; (Illus.). 56p. 19.95 *(0-8118-3162-0)* Chronicle Bks. LLC.
—Sabine's Notebook: In Which the Extraordinary Correspondence of Griffin & Sabine Continues. 1992. (Illus.). 48p. 17.95 *(0-8118-0180-2)* Chronicle Bks. LLC.
—Sabine's Notebook: In Which the Extraordinary Correspondence of Griffin & Sabine Continues. 1992. audio 10.95 *(1-879371-41-3*, 30010) Publishing Mills, Inc., The.
Bantock, Nick, illus. Alexandria: In Which the Extraordinary Correspondence of Griffin & Sabine Unfolds. 2002. 56p. 19.95 *(0-8118-3140-X)* Chronicle Bks. LLC.

**GRIFFIN, DEIRDRE (FICTITIOUS CHARACTER)—FICTION**

Taylor, Karen E. Bitter Blood. (Vampire Legacy). 352p. 1998. mass mkt. 4.99 o.s.i *(0-8217-6021-1)*; 1994. mass mkt. 4.50 o.s.i *(0-8217-4722-3*, Zebra Bks.) Kensington Publishing Corp.
—Blood Secrets. (Vampire Legacy). 304p. 1998. mass mkt. 4.99 o.s.i *(0-8217-6022-X)*; 1994. mass mkt. 4.50 o.s.i *(0-8217-4437-2*, Zebra Bks.) Kensington Publishing Corp.
—Blood Ties. (Vampire Legacy). 1998. 352p. mass mkt. 4.99 o.s.i *(0-8217-6023-8)*; 1996. 352p. mass mkt. 2.99 o.p. *(0-8217-5496-3)*; 1995. mass mkt. 4.99 o.s.i *(0-8217-5114-X)* Kensington Publishing Corp.

**GRIFFIN, JIMMY (FICTITIOUS CHARACTER)—FICTION**

Pairo, Preston. Bright Eyes. 1996. 320p. mass mkt. 5.99 o.s.i *(0-451-40706-7*, Onyx) NAL.
Pairo, Preston A., III. Angel's Crime. 1998. 416p. mass mkt. 6.50 o.s.i *(0-451-40710-5*, Onyx) NAL.

**GRIFFIN, LEW (FICTITIOUS CHARACTER)—FICTION**

Sallis, James. Black Hornet. 1994. 208p. 18.95 o.p. *(0-7867-0118-8*, Carroll & Graf Pubs.) Avalon Publishing Group.
—Black Hornet. 1996. (New Orleans Mystery Ser.: No. 3). 192p. mass mkt. 5.50 *(0-380-72515-0*, Avon Bks.) Morrow/Avon.
—Bluebottle. (Lew Griffin Mysteries Ser.). 161p. 2000. pap. 8.95 *(0-8027-7595-0)*; 1999. (Illus.). pap. 22.95 *(0-8027-3323-9)* Walker & Co.
—Eye of the Cricket. 2000. (Lew Griffin Mysteries Ser.). 196p. reprint ed. pap. 8.95 *(0-8027-7581-0)* Walker & Co.
—Eye of the Cricket: A Lew Griffin Mystery. 1997. (Lew Griffin Mysteries Ser.). 204p. 21.95 *(0-8027-3313-1)* Walker & Co.
—Ghost of a Flea: A Lew Griffin Novel. 2002. 252p. 23.95 *(0-8027-3369-7)* Walker & Co.
—The Long-Legged Fly. 1992. 208p. 17.95 o.p. *(0-88184-810-7*, Carroll & Graf Pubs.) Avalon Publishing Group.
—The Long-Legged Fly. 1994. 192p. mass mkt. 4.99 *(0-380-72242-9*, Avon Bks.) Morrow/Avon.
—The Long-Legged Fly. 183p. pap. 15.00 *(1-901982-41-6)* No Exit Pr. GBR. *Dist:* Trafalgar Square.
—Moth. 1993. 208p. 18.95 o.p. *(0-88184-945-6*, Carroll & Graf Pubs.) Avalon Publishing Group.
—Moth. 1995. (Lew Griffin Ser.). reprint ed. pap. 4.99 o.p. *(0-380-72377-8*, Avon Bks.) Morrow/Avon.

**GRIFFO, SIMONA (FICTITIOUS CHARACTER)—FICTION**

Crespi, Camilla T. The Trouble with a Bad Fit. 1996. 272p. 21.00 o.p. *(0-06-017661-X)* HarperCollins Pubs.
—The Trouble with a Bad Fit. 1997. 320p. mass mkt. 4.99 *(0-06-109408-0*, HarperTorch) Morrow/Avon.
—The Trouble with a Hot Summer: A Simona Griffo Mystery. 1997. 320p. 23.00 o.p. *(0-06-017662-8)* HarperCollins Pubs.
—The Trouble with a Hot Summer: A Simona Griffo Mystery. mass mkt. o.s.i *(0-06-109409-9)*; 1998. 368p. mass mkt. 5.99 o.s.i *(0-06-104464-4)* Morrow/Avon. (HarperTorch).
—The Trouble with a Small Raise. 1991. 288p. mass mkt. 3.95 o.s.i *(0-8217-3274-9*, Zebra Bks.) Kensington Publishing Corp.
—The Trouble with Going Home. 1996. 224p. mass mkt. 4.99 o.s.i *(0-06-109153-7)* HarperCollins Pubs.
—The Trouble with Going Home. 1994. 288p. 20.00 o.p. *(0-06-017725-X)* HarperTrade.
—The Trouble with Moonlighting. 1991. 224p. mass mkt. 3.95 o.s.i *(0-8217-3452-0*, Zebra Bks.) Kensington Publishing Corp.
—The Trouble with Thin Ice. 1994. 288p. 18.00 o.p. *(0-06-017726-8)* HarperTrade.
—The Trouble with Thin Ice. 1994. 304p. mass mkt. 4.50 o.p. *(0-06-109154-5*, HarperTorch) Morrow/Avon.
—The Trouble with Too Much Sun. 1992. (Simona Griffo Mystery Ser.). mass mkt. 3.99 o.s.i *(0-8217-3776-7*, Zebra Bks.) Kensington Publishing Corp.

**GRIFFON, NEIL (FICTITIOUS CHARACTER)—FICTION**

Francis, Dick. Bonecrack. l.t. ed. 1993. pap. 16.95 o.p. *(0-7927-1598-5)*; 18.95 o.p. *(0-7927-1599-3)*; audio 54.95 *(0-7451-5948-6)* BBC Audiobooks America.
—Bonecrack. 1993. 256p. mass mkt. 6.99 o.s.i *(0-449-22115-6*, Fawcett) Ballantine Bks.
—Bonecrack. unabr. ed. 1991. audio 42.00 *(0-7366-2039-7*, 2853) Books on Tape, Inc.
—Bonecrack. 1972. (Harper Novel of Suspense Ser.). 208p. 8.95 o.p. *(0-06-011319-7)* HarperCollins Pubs.
—Bonecrack. 1991. mass mkt. 4.95 *(0-671-74671-5)*; 1990. mass mkt. 4.50 *(0-671-70467-2)*; 1983. mass mkt. 3.50 *(0-671-50739-7)*; 1982. mass mkt. 2.95 o.s.i *(0-671-45459-5)* Simon & Schuster. (Pocket).
—Bonecrack. l.t. ed. 1974. 12.00 o.p. *(0-85456-292-3*, Ulverscroft) Thorpe, F. A. Pubs. GBR. *Dist:* Ulverscroft Large Print Bks., Ltd.

**GRIJPSTRA, HENK (FICTITIOUS CHARACTER)—FICTION**

Van de Wetering, Janwillem. The Amsterdam Cops: Collected Stories. 2000. 240p. pap. 12.00 *(1-56947-210-6)*; 1999. 254p. 22.00 *(1-56947-171-1)* Soho Pr., Inc.
—The Blond Baboon. 1987. 224p. mass mkt. 2.95 o.s.i *(0-345-34497-9)* Ballantine Bks.
—The Blond Baboon. l.t. ed. 1993. 12.50 o.p. *(0-8161-6646-3*, Macmillan Reference USA) Gale Group.
—The Blond Baboon, 001. 1978. 7.95 o.p. *(0-395-26307-7)* Houghton Mifflin Co.
—The Blond Baboon. 1979. (gr. 12). pap. 1.95 o.s.i *(0-671-82318-3*, Pocket) Simon & Schuster.
—The Blond Baboon. 1996. 218p. pap. 12.00 *(1-56947-063-4)* Soho Pr., Inc.
—The Corpse on the Dike. 1987. 224p. mass mkt. 3.50 o.s.i *(0-345-33130-3)* Ballantine Bks.
—The Corpse on the Dike, 001. 1976. 6.95 o.p. *(0-395-24675-X)* Houghton Mifflin Co.
—The Corpse on the Dike. 1982. mass mkt. 2.95 o.s.i *(0-671-43527-2*, Pocket) Simon & Schuster.
—The Corpse on the Dike. 1995. 232p. pap. 12.00 *(1-56947-049-9)* Soho Pr., Inc.
—Death of a Hawker. 1987. 256p. mass mkt. 3.50 o.s.i *(0-345-33131-1)* Ballantine Bks.
—Death of a Hawker. 1977. 6.95 o.p. *(0-395-25171-0)* Houghton Mifflin Co.
—Death of a Hawker. 1980. (gr. 12). pap. 2.25 o.s.i *(0-671-83557-2*, Pocket) Simon & Schuster.
—Hard Rain. 1987. pap. o.s.i *(0-345-00732-8)*; mass mkt. 3.95 o.s.i *(0-345-33964-9)* Ballantine Bks.
—Hard Rain. 1986. 288p. 15.95 o.s.i *(0-394-54924-4*, Pantheon) Knopf Publishing Group.
—Hard Rain. 1997. 313p. pap. 12.00 *(1-56947-104-5)* Soho Pr., Inc.
—The Hollow-Eyed Angel. 282p. 1997. pap. 13.00 *(1-56947-091-X)*; 1996. 22.00 *(1-56947-056-1)* Soho Pr., Inc.
—The Japanese Corpse. 1987. mass mkt. 3.50 o.s.i *(0-345-33128-1)* Ballantine Bks.
—The Japanese Corpse, 001. 1977. 7.95 o.p. *(0-395-25777-8)* Houghton Mifflin Co.
—The Japanese Corpse. 1982. mass mkt. 2.95 o.s.i *(0-671-43528-0*, Pocket) Simon & Schuster.
—The Japanese Corpse. 1996. 296p. pap. 12.00 *(1-56947-057-X)* Soho Pr., Inc.
—Just a Corpse at Twilight. unabr. ed. 1998. (Grijpstra & De Gier Mystery Ser.). audio 44.00 *(0-7887-2181-X*, 95477E7) Recorded Bks., LLC.
—Just a Corpse at Twilight. 1995. 266p. pap. 12.00 *(1-56947-075-8)*; 1994. 265p. 20.00 *(1-56947-016-2)* Soho Pr., Inc.
—The Maine Massacre. 1988. 240p. reprint ed. mass mkt. 3.95 o.s.i *(0-345-34496-0)* Ballantine Bks.
—The Maine Massacre, 001. 1978. 8.95 o.p. *(0-395-27395-1)* Houghton Mifflin Co.
—The Maine Massacre. unabr. ed. 1998. (Grijpstra & De Gier Mystery Ser.). audio 51.00 *(0-7887-2025-2*, 95400E7) Recorded Bks., LLC.
—The Maine Massacre. 1980. pap. 2.50 o.s.i *(0-671-82865-7*, Pocket) Simon & Schuster.
—The Maine Massacre. 1996. 231p. pap. 12.00 *(1-56947-064-2)* Soho Pr., Inc.
—The Mind-Murders. 1988. 208p. mass mkt. 3.95 o.s.i *(0-345-34495-2)* Ballantine Bks.
—The Mind-Murders, 001. 1981. 9.95 o.p. *(0-395-30544-6)* Houghton Mifflin Co.
—The Mind-Murders. 1984. mass mkt. 3.95 o.s.i *(0-671-54065-3*, Pocket) Simon & Schuster.
—The Mind-Murders. 1997. 224p. pap. 12.00 *(1-56947-092-8)* Soho Pr., Inc.
—Outsider in Amsterdam. 1986. mass mkt. 3.50 o.s.i *(0-345-33126-5)* Ballantine Bks.
—Outsider in Amsterdam. 1976. ix, 245p. *(0-434-85920-6*, Butterworth-Heinemann) Elsevier Science & Technology Bks.
—Outsider in Amsterdam, 001. 1975. 256p. 6.95 o.p. *(0-395-20705-3)* Houghton Mifflin Co.
—Outsider in Amsterdam. 1978. pap. 2.50 o.s.i *(0-671-43471-3*, Pocket) Simon & Schuster.
—Outsider in Amsterdam. 1994. 304p. pap. 12.00 *(1-56947-017-0)* Soho Pr., Inc.
—The Perfidious Parrot. 280p. 1998. (Amsterdam Cops Ser.: No. 14). pap. 12.00 *(1-56947-130-4)*; 1997. 22.00 *(1-56947-102-9)* Soho Pr., Inc.
—The Rattle-Rat. 1986. mass mkt. 3.50 o.s.i *(0-345-32872-8)* Ballantine Bks.
—The Rattle-Rat. l.t. ed. 1986. 392p. 17.95 o.p. *(0-8161-4121-5*, Macmillan Reference USA) Gale Group.
—The Rattle-Rat. 1985. 14.95 o.s.i *(0-394-54710-1*, Pantheon) Knopf Publishing Group.
—The Rattle-Rat. 1997. 294p. pap. 12.00 *(1-56947-103-7)* Soho Pr., Inc.
—The Sergeant's Cat. l.t. ed. 1991. 8.95 o.p. *(0-7451-9503-2*, 78) BBC Audiobooks America.
—The Streetbird. 1983. 288p. 13.95 o.p. *(0-399-12808-5*, G. P. Putnam's Sons) Penguin Putnam Bks. for Young Readers.
—The Streetbird. 1985. mass mkt. 3.50 o.s.i *(0-671-47521-5*, Pocket) Simon & Schuster.
—The Streetbird. 1997. 288p. pap. 12.00 *(1-56947-093-6)* Soho Pr., Inc.
—Tumbleweed. 1987. mass mkt. 3.50 o.s.i *(0-345-33127-3)* Ballantine Bks.

—Tumbleweed. l.t. ed. 1978. lib. bdg. 11.50 o.p. (0-8161-6569-6, Macmillan Reference USA) Gale Group.
—Tumbleweed, 001. 1976. 6.95 o.p. (0-395-24352-1) Houghton Mifflin Co.
—Tumbleweed. 1994. (Crime Ser.). 224p. pap. 12.00 (1-56947-018-9) Soho Pr., Inc.

GRIST, SIMEON (FICTITIOUS CHARACTER)—FICTION

Hallinan, Timothy. The Bone Polisher. 1996. (Simeon Grist Mystery Ser.). 304p. mass mkt. 5.99 o.p. (0-380-71372-1, Avon Bks.) Morrow/Avon.
—Everything but the Squeal: A Simeon Grist Suspense Novel. (Simeon Grist Mystery Ser.). 352p. 1991. mass mkt. 4.99 o.p. (0-451-40261-8, Onyx); 1990. 17.95 o.p. (0-453-00694-9) NAL.
—Incinerator. 1993. 304p. mass mkt. 4.99 (0-380-71370-5, Avon Bks.) Morrow/Avon.
—Incinerator: A Simeon Grist Mystery. 1992. 288p. 19.00 o.p. (0-688-10343-X, Morrow, William & Co.) Morrow/Avon.
—The Man with No Time. 1995. 336p. mass mkt. 4.99 (0-380-71371-3, Avon Bks.) Morrow/Avon.
—The Man with No Time: A Simeon Grist Mystery. 1993. 22.00 o.p. (0-688-10344-8, Morrow, William & Co.) Morrow/Avon.
—Skin Deep. 1992. (Simeon Grist Suspense Novel Ser.). 336p. reprint ed. mass mkt. 4.99 o.s.i (0-451-40309-6, Onyx) NAL.
—Skin Deep: A Simeon Grist Suspense Novel. 1991. (Simeon Grist Mystery Ser.). 336p. 18.95 o.p. (0-525-24978-8, Dutton) Dutton/Plume.

GUARNACCIA, MARSHAL (FICTITIOUS CHARACTER)—FICTION

Nabb, Magdalen. Death in Autumn. l.t. ed. 1986. 13.95 o.p. (0-89340-954-5, 291) BBC Audiobooks America.
—Death in Autumn. 2002. 158p. pap. 11.00 (1-56947-296-3) Soho Pr., Inc.
—Death in Autumn. 1987. (Crime Ser.). 160p. pap. 3.50 o.p. (0-14-009480-6, Penguin Bks.) Viking Penguin.
—Death in Autumn: A Florentine Mystery. 1985. (Marshall Guarnacci Mystery Ser.). 160p. 12.95 o.s.i (0-684-18337-4, Macmillan Reference USA) Gale Group.
—Death in Springtime. l.t. ed. 1985. 13.95 o.p. (0-89340-816-6, 932) BBC Audiobooks America.
—Death in Springtime. 1985. (Crime Ser.). 160p. pap. 3.95 o.p. (0-14-007770-7, Penguin Bks.) Viking Penguin.
—Death in Springtime: A Florentine Mystery. 1984. 168p. 11.95 o.s.i (0-684-18133-9, Macmillan Reference USA) Gale Group.
—Death of a Dutchman. 1984. (Crime Monthly Ser.). 224p. pap. 4.95 o.p. (0-14-006935-6, Penguin Bks.) Viking Penguin.
—Death of a Dutchman: A Novel of Murder in Florence. 1983. 176p. 11.95 o.p. (0-684-17847-8, Macmillan Reference USA) Gale Group.
—Death of an Englishman. 1982. 176p. 10.95 o.s.i (0-684-17757-9, Macmillan Reference USA) Gale Group.
—Death of an Englishman. 1984. (Crime Monthly Ser.). 176p. pap. 3.95 o.p. (0-14-006893-7, Penguin Bks.) Viking Penguin.
—The Marshal & the Madwoman. l.t. ed. 1989. (Atlantic Mystery Ser.). pap. 14.95 o.p. (1-55504-663-0, 824) BBC Audiobooks America.
—The Marshal & the Madwoman. 1988. 224p. 16.95 o.s.i (0-684-18984-4, Macmillan Reference USA) Gale Group.
—The Marshal & the Madwoman. 2003. 224p. pap. 12.00 (1-56947-340-4) Soho Pr., Inc.
—The Marshal & the Madwoman. 1989. (Crime Ser.). 224p. pap. 3.95 o.p. (0-14-011881-0, Penguin Bks.) Viking Penguin.
—The Marshal & the Murderer. 1987. (Marshall Guarnacci Mystery Ser.). 160p. 14.95 o.s.i (0-684-18884-8, Macmillan Reference USA) Gale Group.
—The Marshal & the Murderer. 1988. (Crime Ser.). 208p. pap. 3.95 o.p. (0-14-010678-2, Penguin Bks.) Viking Penguin.
—The Marshal at the Villa Torrini. 1994. 192p. 20.00 o.p. (0-06-016915-X) HarperCollins Pubs.
—Marshal Makes His Report: A Marshal Guarnaccia Mystery. 1992. 240p. 19.00 o.p. (0-06-016914-1) HarperTrade.
—The Marshall & the Murderer. 2002. 196p. pap. 12.00 (1-56947-297-1) Soho Pr., Inc.
—The Marshal's Own Case. l.t. ed. 1990. 17.95 o.p. (0-7451-9921-6, C0640); pap. 15.95 o.p. (0-7927-0372-3, C0834) BBC Audiobooks America.
—The Marshal's Own Case. 1991. (Crime Monthly Ser.). 176p. pap. 4.95 o.p. (0-14-014323-8, Penguin Bks.) Penguin Group (USA) Inc.
—The Marshal's Own Case: A Marshal Guarnaccia Mystery. 1990. 224p. 17.95 o.s.i (0-684-19201-2, Macmillan Reference USA) Gale Group.
—Some Bitter Taste. 2003. pap. 12.00 (1-56947-339-0) Soho Pr., Inc.
—Some Bitter Taste. l.t. ed. 2003. 289p. pap. 24.95 (0-7862-5418-1) Thorndike Pr.
—Some Bitter Taste: A Marshal Guarnaccia Investigation. 2002. 272p. 24.00 (1-56947-317-X) Soho Pr., Inc.

GUENEVERE, QUEEN (LEGENDARY CHARACTER)—FICTION

Borchardt, Alice. The Dragon Queen. 2003. 512p. mass mkt. 7.50 (0-345-44400-0); 2001. (Tales of Guinevere Ser.: Vol. 1). 480p. 25.00 (0-345-44399-3) Ballantine Bks. (Del Rey).
Godwin, Parke. Beloved Exile. 1984. 432p. (Orig.). pap. 3.95 o.s.i (0-553-24924-X, Spectra) Bantam Bks.
—Beloved Exile. 1994. 432p. (Orig.). mass mkt. 5.50 o.p. (0-380-77553-0, Avon Bks.) Morrow/Avon.
Miles, Rosalind. Guenevere, Queen of the Summer Country. (Guenevere Ser.: Bk. 1). 2000. (Illus.). 528p. pap. 11.95 (0-609-80650-5, Crown); 1999. 432p. 24.00 o.s.i (0-609-60362-0) Crown Publishing Group.
—The Knight of the Sacred Lake. 2001. (Guenevere Ser.: Bk. 2). 448p. pap. 11.95 (0-609-80802-8, Three Rivers Pr.) Crown Publishing Group.
Newman, Sharan. The Chessboard Queen. 1997. 320p. pap. 13.95 (0-312-86391-8, Tor Bks.) Doherty, Tom Assocs., LLC.
—The Chessboard Queen. 1984. 256p. pap. 5.95 o.p. (0-312-13177-1, Saint Martin's Griffin); 1983. 320p. 13.95 o.p. (0-312-13176-3) St. Martin's Pr.
—Guinevere. 1996. 256p. pap. 13.95 (0-312-86233-4, Tor Bks.) Doherty, Tom Assocs., LLC.
—Guinevere. l.t. ed. 1981. lib. bdg. 14.95 o.p. (0-8161-3254-2, Macmillan Reference USA) Gale Group.
—Guinevere. 1984. 296p. pap. 5.95 (0-312-35321-9, Saint Martin's Griffin); 1980. 256p. 10.95 o.p. (0-312-35318-9) St. Martin's Pr.
—Guinevere Evermore. 1998. 288p. pap. 13.95 (0-312-86641-0, Tor Bks.) Doherty, Tom Assocs., LLC.
—Guinevere Evermore. 1986. 288p. pap. 6.95 (0-312-35324-3, Saint Martin's Griffin); 1985. 320p. 15.95 o.p. (0-312-35322-7) St. Martin's Pr.
Snow, Alicia. The Song of Guinevere: A Defense of Arthur's Wife in Verse. 1999. (Illus.). 588p. pap. 29.95 (0-9660643-6-4) Belgrave Hse.
St. John, Nicole. Guinevere's Gift. 1978. 8.95 o.p. (0-394-41167-6) Random Hse., Inc.
—Guinevere's Gift. 1979. pap. 1.95 o.s.i (0-446-89881-3) Warner Bks., Inc.
Woolley, Persia. Child of the Northern Spring. 1988. 480p. mass mkt. 5.99 o.s.i (0-671-62199-8, Pocket) Simon & Schuster.
—Guinevere: The Legend in Autumn. 1991. 416p. 22.00 o.p. (0-671-70831-7, Simon & Schuster) Simon & Schuster.
—Guinevere: The Legend in Autumn. Rubenstein, Julie, ed. 1993. 448p. reprint ed. mass mkt. 5.99 (0-671-70832-5, Pocket) Simon & Schuster.
—Queen of the Summer Stars. 1990. 19.95 o.p. (0-671-62201-3, Simon & Schuster) Simon & Schuster.
—Queen of the Summer Stars. Rubenstein, Julie, ed. 1991. 448p. reprint ed. mass mkt. 6.50 (0-671-62202-1, Pocket) Simon & Schuster.

GUIDRY, JUNIOR (FICTITIOUS CHARACTER)—FICTION

Wells, Ken. Meely LaBauve: A Novel. 2001. 272p. pap. 11.95 (0-375-75816-X); 2000. 256p. 19.95 o.s.i (0-375-50311-0) Random Hse., Inc.
—Meely LaBauve: A Novel. l.t. ed. 2001. (Americana Ser.). 309p. 28.95 (0-7862-3023-1) Thorndike Pr.

GUIDRY, KARA (FICTITIOUS CHARACTER)—FICTION

Truscott, Lucian K., IV. Heart of War. 1997. 400p. 23.95 o.p. (0-525-94117-7) Dutton/Plume.
—Heart of War. 1998. 432p. mass mkt. 6.99 o.s.i (0-451-18770-9, Signet Bks.) NAL.
—Heart of War. abr. ed. 1997. 25.00 o.p. (0-7871-1512-6) NewStar Media, Inc.

GUILD, LEO (FICTITIOUS CHARACTER)—FICTION

Gorman, Ed. Dark Trail. 1990. (Novel of the West Ser.). 192p. 15.95 o.p. (0-87131-635-8) Evans, M. & Co., Inc.
—Dark Trail. 1992. 2.99 o.p. (0-517-09423-1) Random Hse. Value Publishing.
—The Dark Trail. 1997. (Evans Novel of the West Ser.). 215p. pap. 5.99 (0-8125-4826-4, Forge Bks.) Doherty, Tom Assocs., LLC.

GUIU, LONIA (FICTITIOUS CHARACTER)—FICTION

Oliver, Maria-Antonia. Antipodes. McNerney, Kathleen, tr. from SPA. 1989. (International Women's Crime Ser.). 224p. (Orig.). reprint ed. pap. 8.95 o.p. (0-931188-82-2, Seal Pr.) Avalon Publishing Group.
—Study in Lilac. McNerney, Kathleen, tr. from CAT. 1987. (International Women's Crime Ser.). 161p. pap. 16.95 o.p. (0-931188-53-9); pap. 8.95 o.p. (0-931188-52-0) Avalon Publishing Group. (Seal Pr.).

GUMP, FORREST (FICTITIOUS CHARACTER)—FICTION

Groom, Winston. Forrest Gump. 1988. mass mkt. 3.95 o.p. (0-425-10478-8) Berkley Publishing Group.
—Forrest Gump. unabr. ed. 1995. audio 42.00 (0-7366-3025-2, 3708) Books on Tape, Inc.
—Forrest Gump. 1986. 240p. 14.95 o.p. (0-385-23134-2) Doubleday Publishing.
—Forrest Gump. l.t. ed. 1995. pap. 21.95 o.p. (1-56895-087-X, Wheeler Publishing, Inc.) Gale Group.
—Forrest Gump. abr. ed. audio 17.00 o.p. Random Hse. Audio Publishing Group.
—Forrest Gump. unabr. ed. 1995. audio 51.00 (0-7887-0199-1, 94423E7) Recorded Bks., LLC.
—Forrest Gump. 1994. 240p. 20.00 o.p. (0-671-52606-5, Atria); 2002. 256p. reprint ed. pap. 13.00 (0-7434-5325-5, Washington Square Pr.) Simon & Schuster.
—Forrest Gump. Todd, Rebecca, ed. 1994. 256p. reprint ed. mass mkt. 6.99 (0-671-89445-5, Pocket) Simon & Schuster.
—Forrest Gump. abr. ed. 1994. audio 18.00 o.s.i (0-671-89681-4, 390802, Simon & Schuster Audioworks) Simon & Schuster Audio.
—Forrest Gump. 1994. 13.04 (0-606-19495-9) Turtleback Bks.
—Gump & Co. l.t. ed. 1996. (Wheeler Large Print Bks.). pap. 24.95 (1-56895-293-7, Wheeler Publishing, Inc.) Gale Group.
—Gump & Co. 1996. 256p. mass mkt. 6.99 (0-671-52264-7, Pocket); 1995. 256p. 22.00 o.p. (0-671-52170-5, Atria); 1995. per. 6.99 (0-671-56307-6, Pocket) Simon & Schuster.
—Gump & Co. abr. ed. 1999. audio 9.98 (0-671-04501-6); Set. 1995. 18.00 incl. audio (0-671-53680-X, 393274) Simon & Schuster Audio. (Simon & Schuster Audioworks).
—Gump & Co. 1997. 1.98 o.p. (0-7651-0699-X) Smithmark Pubs., Inc.

GUNNER, AARON (FICTITIOUS CHARACTER)—FICTION

Haywood, Gar Anthony. All the Lucky Ones Are Dead: An Aaron Gunner Mystery. 2000. 240p. 23.95 o.s.i (0-399-14540-0, G. P. Putnam's Sons) Penguin Group (USA) Inc.
—Fear of the Dark. 1988. 192p. 13.95 o.p. (0-312-01796-0, Saint Martin's Minotaur) St. Martin's Pr.
—Fear of the Dark. 1990. 192p. pap. 3.95 o.p. (0-14-013153-1, Penguin Bks.) Viking Penguin.
—It's Not a Pretty Sight: An Aaron Gunner Mystery. 1998. 256p. mass mkt. 5.99 o.s.i (0-425-16196-X, Prime Crime) Berkley Publishing Group.
—It's Not a Pretty Sight: An Aaron Gunner Mystery. 1996. 240p. 22.95 o.p. (0-399-14132-4, G. P. Putnam's Sons) Penguin Group (USA) Inc.
—Not Long for This World. 1991. (Crime Monthly Ser.). 272p. pap. 4.95 o.p. (0-14-015265-2, Penguin Bks.) Penguin Group (USA) Inc.
—Not Long for This World. 1990. 17.95 o.p. (0-312-04398-8, Saint Martin's Minotaur) St. Martin's Pr.
—When Last Seen Alive. 1999. 256p. mass mkt. 5.99 o.s.i (0-425-17027-6) Berkley Publishing Group.
—When Last Seen Alive. 1997. 240p. 22.95 o.p. (0-399-14303-3, G. P. Putnam's Sons) Penguin Group (USA) Inc.
—You Can Die Trying. 1993. 224p. 17.95 o.p. (0-312-09425-6, Saint Martin's Minotaur) St. Martin's Pr.
—You Can Die Trying: An Aaron Gunner Mystery. 1994. (Crime Ser.). 224p. reprint ed. pap. 5.95 o.p. (0-14-023946-4, Penguin Bks.) Penguin Group (USA) Inc.

GUNSMITH (FICTITIOUS CHARACTER)—FICTION

Roberts, J. R. Archer's Revenge. 1986. (Gunsmith Ser.: No. 48). 2.50 o.s.i (0-441-30952-6, Diamond Bks.) Berkley Publishing Group.
—Arizona Ambush. 1991. (Gunsmith Ser.: No. 119). mass mkt. 3.99 o.s.i (0-515-10710-7, Jove) Berkley Publishing Group.
—Bandit Gold. 1984. (Gunsmith Ser.: No. 15). 192p. 2.50 o.s.i (0-441-30905-4, Diamond Bks.) Berkley Publishing Group.
—Boom Town Killer. 1987. (Gunsmith Ser.: No. 62). 192p. 2.50 o.s.i (0-441-30966-6, 30966-6) Ace Bks.
—Bounty Hunter. 1990. (Gunsmith Ser.: NO. 107). mass mkt. 2.95 o.s.i (0-515-10447-7, Jove) Berkley Publishing Group.
—The Bounty Women. 1984. (Gunsmith Ser.: No. 35). 192p. 2.50 o.s.i (0-441-30914-3) Ace Bks.
—Brothers of the Gun. 1989. (Gunsmith Ser.: No. 93). mass mkt. 2.95 o.s.i (0-515-10132-X, Jove) Berkley Publishing Group.
—Buckskin's Trail. 1990. (Gunsmith Ser.: NO. 104). mass mkt. 2.95 o.s.i (0-515-10387-X, Jove) Berkley Publishing Group.
—Bullets & Ballots. 1983. (Gunsmith Ser.: No. 22). 192p. 2.25 o.s.i (0-441-30893-7) Ace Bks.
—Champion with a Gun. 1994. (Gunsmith Ser.: No. 151). 192p. (Orig.). mass mkt. 3.99 o.s.i (0-515-11409-X, Jove) Berkley Publishing Group.
—Chinaville. 1995. (Gunsmith Ser.: No. 167). 192p. (Orig.). mass mkt. 4.50 o.s.i (0-515-11747-1, Jove) Berkley Publishing Group.
—Chinese Gunmen. 1982. (Gunsmith Ser.). 240p. 2.25 o.s.i (0-441-30857-0) Ace Bks.
—The Comstock Gold Fraud. 1987. (Gunsmith Ser.: No. 61). 192p. 2.50 o.s.i (0-441-30965-8, Diamond Bks.) Berkley Publishing Group.
—Crossfire Mountain. 1986. (Gunsmith Ser.: No. 57). 192p. 2.50 o.s.i (0-441-30961-5, Diamond Bks.) Berkley Publishing Group.
—Dead Man's Hand. 1983. (Gunsmith Ser.: No. 14). 208p. 2.50 o.s.i (0-441-30922-4) Ace Bks.
—The Deadly Derringer. 1992. (Gunsmith Ser.: No. 121). 192p. mass mkt. 3.50 o.s.i (0-515-10755-7, Jove) Berkley Publishing Group.
—The Deadly Healer. 1986. (Gunsmith Ser.: No. 58). 192p. 2.50 o.s.i (0-441-30962-3, Diamond Bks.) Berkley Publishing Group.
—Denver Duo. 1986. (Gunsmith Ser.: No. 53). 192p. (Orig.). 2.50 o.s.i (0-441-30957-7, Diamond Bks.) Berkley Publishing Group.
—The Denver Ripper. 1995. (Gunsmith Ser.: No. 165). 192p. (Orig.). mass mkt. 3.99 o.s.i (0-515-11703-X, Jove) Berkley Publishing Group.
—Desert Hell. 1986. (Gunsmith Ser.: No. 51). 192p. (Orig.). 2.50 o.s.i (0-441-30955-0, Diamond Bks.) Berkley Publishing Group.
—The Diamond Gun. 1986. (Gunsmith Ser.: No. 52). 192p. (Orig.). 2.50 o.s.i (0-441-30956-9, Diamond Bks.) Berkley Publishing Group.
—The Dodge City Gang. 1984. (Gunsmith Ser.: No. 20). 192p. 2.50 o.s.i (0-441-30929-1, Diamond Bks.) Berkley Publishing Group.
—Draw to an Inside Death. 1983. (Gunsmith Ser.: No. 13). 208p. 2.25 o.s.i (0-441-30868-6, Diamond Bks.) Berkley Publishing Group.
—Dynamite Justice. 1984. (Gunsmith Ser.: No. 32). 192p. 2.50 o.s.i (0-441-30911-9) Ace Bks.
—The El Paso Salt War. 1985. (Gunsmith Ser.: No. 39). 192p. 2.50 o.s.i (0-441-30940-2, Diamond Bks.) Berkley Publishing Group.
—The Elliott Bay Murder. 1996. (Gunsmith Ser.: No. 170). 192p. (Orig.). mass mkt. 4.50 o.s.i (0-515-11918-0, Jove) Berkley Publishing Group.
—The Fast Draw League. 1987. (Gunsmith Ser.: No. 64). 192p. 2.50 o.s.i (0-441-30968-2, Diamond Bks.) Berkley Publishing Group.
—Five Against Death. 1992. (Gunsmith Ser.: No. 123). mass mkt. 3.99 o.s.i (0-515-10810-3, Jove) Berkley Publishing Group.
—Gambler's Blood. 1993. (Gunsmith Ser.: No. 141). 192p. (Orig.). mass mkt. 3.99 o.s.i (0-515-11196-1, Jove) Berkley Publishing Group.
—Game of Death. 1991. (Gunsmith Ser.: No. 115). mass mkt. 3.50 o.s.i (0-515-10615-1, Jove) Berkley Publishing Group.
—Geronimo's Trail. 1986. (Gunsmith Ser.: No. 60). 192p. 2.50 o.s.i (0-441-30964-X, Diamond Bks.) Berkley Publishing Group.
—Ghost Town. unabr. ed. 1996. (Gunsmith Ser.). audio 12.95 (1-882071-41-7) B&B Audio, Inc.
—Gillett's Rangers. 1994. (Gunsmith Ser.: No. 145). 192p. mass mkt. 3.99 o.s.i (0-515-11285-2, Jove) Berkley Publishing Group.
—Good or Bad. 1993. (Gunsmith Ser.: No. 124). 176p. (Orig.). mass mkt. 3.99 o.s.i (0-515-11258-5, Jove) Berkley Publishing Group.
—Grand Canyon Gold. 1991. (Gunsmith Ser.: No. 111). mass mkt. 2.95 o.s.i (0-515-10528-7, Jove) Berkley Publishing Group.
—The Guns of Abilene. 1982. (Gunsmith Ser.: No. 4). 224p. 2.25 o.s.i (0-441-30859-7) Ace Bks.
—Gunsmith: Homestead Law, No. 184. 1997. (Gunsmith Ser.: No. 184). 192p. mass mkt. 4.99 o.s.i (0-515-12051-0, Jove) Berkley Publishing Group.
—Gunsmith: Lady on the Run, No. 190. 1997. (Gunsmith Ser.: No. 190). 192p. mass mkt. 4.99 o.s.i (0-515-12163-0, Jove) Berkley Publishing Group.
—Gunsmith: Legend of the Bird, No. 206. 1999. (Gunsmith Ser.: No. 206). 192p. mass mkt. 4.99 o.s.i (0-515-12469-9, Jove) Berkley Publishing Group.
—Gunsmith: The Biloxi Queen, No. 185. 1997. (Gunsmith Ser.: No. 185). 192p. mass mkt. 4.99 o.s.i (0-515-12071-5, Jove) Berkley Publishing Group.
—Gunsmith: The French Models, No. 168. 1995. (Gunsmith Ser.: No. 168). 192p. (Orig.). mass mkt. 4.50 o.s.i (0-515-11767-6, Jove) Berkley Publishing Group.

—Gunsmith: The Orient Express, No. 188. 1997. (Gunsmith Ser.: No. 188). 192p. mass mkt. 4.99 o.s.i (*0-515-12133-9*, Jove) Berkley Publishing Group.
—Gunsmith Giant: Trouble in Tombstone. 1993. (Gunsmith Ser.: No. 1). mass mkt. 4.50 o.s.i (*0-515-11212-7*, Jove) Berkley Publishing Group.
—Hands of the Strangler. unabr. ed. 1996. (Gunsmith Ser.). audio 12.95 (*1-882071-40-9*) B&B Audio, Inc.
—The Hanging Woman. 1996. (Gunsmith Ser.: No. 172). 192p. (Orig.). mass mkt. 4.99 o.s.i (*0-515-11844-3*, Jove) Berkley Publishing Group.
—Hell on Wheels. 1986. (Gunsmith Ser.: No. 54). 192p. (Orig.). 2.50 o.s.i (*0-441-30958-5*, Diamond Bks.) Berkley Publishing Group.
—The Huntsville Trip. 1995. (Gunsmith Ser.: No. 159). 192p. (Orig.). mass mkt. 3.99 o.s.i (*0-515-11571-1*, Jove) Berkley Publishing Group.
—The James Boys. 1998. (Gunsmith Ser.: No. 200). 192p. mass mkt. 4.99 o.s.i (*0-515-12357-9*, Jove) Berkley Publishing Group.
—Jersey Lily. 1996. (Gunsmith Ser.: No. 173). 192p. mass mkt. 4.99 o.s.i (*0-515-11862-1*, Jove) Berkley Publishing Group.
—Judgement at Firecreek. 1989. (Gunsmith Ser.: No. 95). mass mkt. 2.95 o.s.i (*0-515-10176-1*, Jove) Berkley Publishing Group.
—Kansas City Killing. 1999. (Gunsmith Ser.: No. 207). 192p. mass mkt. 4.99 o.s.i (*0-515-12486-9*, Jove) Berkley Publishing Group.
—Killer's Race. 1991. (Gunsmith Ser.: No. 109). mass mkt. 2.95 o.s.i (*0-515-10496-5*, Jove) Berkley Publishing Group.
—King of the Border. 1985. (Gunsmith Ser.: No. 38). 192p. 2.50 o.s.i (*0-441-30936-4*) Ace Bks.
—Leadtown. 1982. (Gunsmith Ser.: No. 6). 208p. 2.25 o.s.i (*0-441-30861-9*) Ace Bks.
—Legbreakers & Heartbreakers. 1997. (Gunsmith Ser.: No. 187). 192p. mass mkt. 4.99 o.s.i (*0-515-12105-3*, Jove) Berkley Publishing Group.
—Legend Maker. 1986. (Gunsmith Ser.: No. 55). 192p. 2.50 o.s.i (*0-441-30959-3*, Diamond Bks.) Berkley Publishing Group.
—Lethal Ladies. 1994. (Gunsmith Ser.: No. 152). 192p. (Orig.). mass mkt. 3.99 o.s.i (*0-515-11437-5*, Jove) Berkley Publishing Group.
—The Life & Times of Clint Adams. 1995. (Gunsmith Ser.: No. 2). 288p. mass mkt. 4.99 o.s.i (*0-515-11728-5*, Jove) Berkley Publishing Group.
—The Longhorn War. 1985. (Gunsmith Ser.: No. 7). 224p. (Orig.). 2.50 o.s.i (*0-441-30930-5*, Diamond Bks.) Berkley Publishing Group.
—Macklin's Women. 1985. (Gunsmith Ser.: No. 1). 2.50 o.s.i (*0-441-30932-1*) Ace Bks.
—Macklin's Women. 1988. (Gunsmith Ser.: No. 1). 192p. mass mkt. 3.99 o.s.i (*0-515-10145-1*, Jove) Berkley Publishing Group.
—Massacre at Rock Springs. 1998. (Gunsmith Ser.: No. 194). 192p. mass mkt. 4.99 o.s.i (*0-515-12245-9*, Jove) Berkley Publishing Group.
—Night of the Gila. 1984. (Gunsmith Ser.: No. 34). 192p. 2.50 o.s.i (*0-441-30913-5*, Diamond Bks.) Berkley Publishing Group.
—Night of the Wolf. 1994. (Gunsmith Ser.: No. 150). 192p. (Orig.). mass mkt. 3.99 o.s.i (*0-515-11393-X*, Jove) Berkley Publishing Group.
—The Omaha Heat. 1995. (Gunsmith Ser.: No. 164). 192p. (Orig.). mass mkt. 3.99 o.s.i (*0-515-11688-2*, Jove) Berkley Publishing Group.
—One-Handed Gun. 1984. (Gunsmith Ser.: No. 11). 224p. 2.50 o.s.i (*0-441-30931-3*, Diamond Bks.) Berkley Publishing Group.
—The Oregon Strangler. 1991. (Gunsmith Ser.: No. 116). mass mkt. 3.50 o.s.i (*0-515-10651-8*, Jove) Berkley Publishing Group.
—Orphan Train. 1994. (Gunsmith Ser.: No. 154). 192p. (Orig.). mass mkt. 3.99 o.s.i (*0-515-11478-2*, Jove) Berkley Publishing Group.
—Outbreak. 1997. (Gunsmith Ser.: No. 191). 192p. mass mkt. 4.99 o.s.i (*0-515-12179-7*, Jove) Berkley Publishing Group.
—The Ponderosa War. 1984. (Gunsmith Ser.: No. 30). 192p. 2.50 o.s.i (*0-441-30903-8*) Ace Bks.
—The Posse. 1984. (Gunsmith Ser.: No. 33). 192p. 2.50 o.s.i (*0-441-30912-7*) Ace Bks.
—The Posse from Elsinore. 1997. (Gunsmith Ser.: No. 189). 192p. mass mkt. 4.99 o.s.i (*0-515-12145-2*, Jove) Berkley Publishing Group.
—Quanah's Revenge. 1983. (Gunsmith Ser.; No. 8). 224p. 2.50 o.s.i (*0-441-30901-1*) Ace Bks.
—The Ransom. 1995. (Gunsmith Ser.: No. 158). 192p. (Orig.). mass mkt. 3.99 o.s.i (*0-515-11553-3*, Jove) Berkley Publishing Group.
—Ride for Revenge. 1990. (Gunsmith Ser.: No. 100). 2.95 o.s.i (*0-515-10394-2*, Jove) Berkley Publishing Group.
—Ride the Revenge. 1990. (Gunsmith Ser.: No. 100). mass mkt. 2.95 o.s.i (*0-515-10288-1*, Jove) Berkley Publishing Group.
—Riverboat Gang. 1983. (Gunsmith Ser.: No. 23). 192p. 2.25 o.s.i (*0-441-30894-5*) Ace Bks.
—Samurai Hunt. 1993. (Gunsmith Ser.: No. 140). 192p. (Orig.). mass mkt. 3.99 o.s.i (*0-515-11168-6*, Jove) Berkley Publishing Group.
—Sasquatch Hunt. 1984. (Gunsmith Ser.: No. 21). 192p. 2.50 o.s.i (*0-441-30910-0*, Diamond Bks.) Berkley Publishing Group.
—Showdown in Raton. 1986. (Gunsmith Ser.: No. 49). 192p. (Orig.). 2.50 o.s.i (*0-441-30953-4*, Diamond Bks.) Berkley Publishing Group.
—Showdown in Rio Malo. 1987. (Gunsmith Ser.: NO. 65). 192p. 2.50 o.s.i (*0-441-30969-0*, Diamond Bks.) Berkley Publishing Group.
—Silver War. 1984. (Gunsmith Ser.: No. 17). 192p. 2.50 o.s.i (*0-441-30907-0*) Ace Bks.
—Six for the Money, Vol. 186. 1997. (Gunsmith Ser.: No. 186). 192p. mass mkt. 4.99 o.s.i (*0-515-12082-0*, Jove) Berkley Publishing Group.
—Spanish Gold. 1994. (Gunsmith Ser.: No. 149). 192p. (Orig.). mass mkt. 3.99 o.s.i (*0-515-11377-8*, Jove) Berkley Publishing Group.
—The Stagecoach Killers. 1992. (Gunsmith Ser.: No. 122). mass mkt. 3.99 o.s.i (*0-515-10792-1*, Jove) Berkley Publishing Group.
—The Ten Year Hunt. 1995. (Gunsmith Ser.: No. 160). 192p. (Orig.). mass mkt. 3.99 o.s.i (*0-515-11593-2*, Jove) Berkley Publishing Group.
—Texas Wind, Vol. 193. 1998. (Gunsmith Ser.: No. 194). 192p. mass mkt. 4.99 o.s.i (*0-515-12231-9*, Jove) Berkley Publishing Group.
—Three Guns for Glory. 1983. (Gunsmith Ser.: No. 5). 224p. 2.50 o.s.i (*0-441-30925-9*) Ace Bks.
—Tolliver's Deputies. 1994. (Gunsmith Ser.: No. 153). 192p. (Orig.). mass mkt. 3.99 o.s.i (*0-515-11456-1*, Jove) Berkley Publishing Group.
—Tombstone at Little Horn. 1990. (Gunsmith Ser.: No. 108). mass mkt. 2.95 o.s.i (*0-515-10474-4*) Berkley Publishing Group.
—The Trail Drive War. 1986. (Gunsmith Ser.: No. 59). 192p. 2.50 o.s.i (*0-441-30963-1*) Ace Bks.
—Trouble Rides a Fast Horse. 1984. (Gunsmith Ser.: No. 31). 192p. 2.50 o.s.i (*0-441-30904-6*) Ace Bks.
—Vengeance Town. 1988. (Gunsmith Ser.: No. 84). mass mkt. 2.95 o.s.i (*0-515-09849-3*, Jove) Berkley Publishing Group.
—The Vengeance Trail. 1991. (Gunsmith Ser.: No. 120). mass mkt. 3.99 o.s.i (*0-515-10735-2*, Jove) Berkley Publishing Group.
—Vigilante Hunt. 1993. (Gunsmith Ser.: No. 139). 192p. (Orig.). mass mkt. 3.99 o.s.i (*0-515-11138-4*, Jove) Berkley Publishing Group.
—Walking Dead Man. 1986. (Gunsmith Ser.: No. 56). 2.50 o.s.i (*0-441-30960-7*, Diamond Bks.) Berkley Publishing Group.
—When Legends Meet. 1986. (Gunsmith Ser.: No. 50). 192p. (Orig.). 2.50 o.s.i (*0-441-30954-2*, Diamond Bks.) Berkley Publishing Group.
—The Wild Women of Glitter Gulch. 1995. (Gunsmith Ser.: No. 163). 192p. (Orig.). mass mkt. 3.99 o.s.i (*0-515-11656-4*, Jove) Berkley Publishing Group.
—The Woman Hunt. 1982. (Gunsmith Ser.: No. 3). (Illus.). 224p. 2.25 o.s.i (*0-441-30858-9*, Diamond Bks.) Berkley Publishing Group.
—Wyoming Justice. 1993. (Gunsmith Ser.: No. 142). 192p. mass mkt. 3.99 o.s.i (*0-515-11218-6*, Jove) Berkley Publishing Group.

**GUNTHER, BERNHARD (FICTITIOUS CHARACTER)—FICTION**

Kerr, Philip. Berlin Noir: March Violets - The Pale Criminal - A German Requiem. 1994. (Penguin Crime/Mystery Ser.). 848p. 15.95 (*0-14-023170-6*) Viking Penguin.
—A German Requiem. 1993. (Crime Ser.). 320p. pap. 4.95 o.p. (*0-14-017561-X*, Penguin Bks.) Penguin Group (USA) Inc.
—A German Requiem. 1991. 320p. 19.95 o.p. (*0-670-83516-1*, Viking) Viking Penguin.
—March Violets. (Crime Ser.). 256p. 1990. pap. 4.95 o.p. (*0-14-011466-1*, Penguin Bks.); 1989. 17.95 o.p. (*0-670-82431-3*) Viking Penguin.
—The Pale Criminal. 1991. (Crime Monthly Ser.). 288p. reprint ed. pap. 4.95 o.p. (*0-14-015393-4*, Penguin Bks.) Penguin Group (USA) Inc.
—The Pale Criminal. 1990. 288p. 18.95 o.p. (*0-670-82433-X*) Viking Penguin.

**GUNTHER, JOE (FICTITIOUS CHARACTER)—FICTION**

Mayor, Archer. Bellows Falls. 1997. 224p. 22.00 o.p. (*0-89296-637-8*) Mysterious Pr.
—Bellows Falls. l.t. ed. 1998. (Mystery Ser.). 392p. 27.95 (*0-7838-8405-2*) Thorndike Pr.
—Bellows Falls. 1998. 352p. reprint ed. mass mkt. 6.99 (*0-446-60630-8*) Warner Bks., Inc.
—Borderlines. 1991. 320p. mass mkt. 4.50 (*0-380-71600-3*, Avon Bks.) Morrow/Avon.
—Borderlines. 1990. 256p. 19.95 o.s.i (*0-399-13553-7*, G. P. Putnam's Sons) Penguin Putnam Bks. for Young Readers.
—Borderlines. 1994. 336p. reprint ed. mass mkt. 6.99 (*0-446-40443-8*) Warner Bks., Inc.
—The Dark Root. 1995. 82p. 19.95 o.p. (*0-89296-558-4*) Mysterious Pr.
—The Dark Root. 1996. 400p. reprint ed. mass mkt. 6.99 (*0-446-40376-8*) Warner Bks., Inc.
—The Disposable Man. 1998. (Joe Gunther Mysteries Ser.). 294p. 22.00 o.p. (*0-89296-685-8*) Mysterious Pr.
—The Disposable Man. 1999. 336p. reprint ed. mass mkt. 6.99 (*0-446-60768-1*) Warner Bks., Inc.
—Fruits of the Poisonous Tree. 1994. 224p. 19.95 o.s.i (*0-89296-557-6*) Mysterious Pr.
—Fruits of the Poisonous Tree. 1995. (Joe Gunther Mysteries Ser.). 304p. reprint ed. mass mkt. 6.99 (*0-446-40374-1*) Warner Bks., Inc.
—Gatekeeper. 2003. (Joe Gunther Mysteries Ser.). 23.95 (*0-89296-766-8*) Mysterious Pr.
—The Marble Mask. l.t. ed. 2001. (Large Print Bks.). 347p. pap. 23.95 (*1-58724-129-3*, Wheeler Publishing, Inc.) Gale Group.
—The Marble Mask. 2001. 336p. reprint ed. mass mkt. 6.99 (*0-446-61029-1*) Warner Bks., Inc.
—Occam's Razor. l.t. ed. 2000. (Core Ser.). 544p. 30.00 o.p. (*0-7838-8814-7*, Macmillan Reference USA) Gale Group.
—Occam's Razor. 1999. 304p. 23.95 (*0-89296-682-3*) Mysterious Pr.
—Occam's Razor. 2000. 480p. reprint ed. mass mkt. 6.99 (*0-446-60887-4*) Warner Bks., Inc.
—Open Season. 1989. 320p. pap. 3.95 (*0-380-70756-X*, Avon Bks.) Morrow/Avon.
—Open Season. 1988. 304p. 18.95 o.p. (*0-399-13398-4*, G. P. Putnam's Sons) Penguin Putnam Bks. for Young Readers.
—Open Season. 1994. (Joe Gunther Mysteries Ser.). 320p. reprint ed. mass mkt. 6.99 (*0-446-40414-4*) Warner Bks., Inc.
—The Ragman's Memory. l.t. ed. 1997. (G. K. Hall Mystery Ser.). 483p. lib. bdg. 25.95 o.p. (*0-7838-8208-4*, Macmillan Reference USA) Gale Group.
—The Ragman's Memory. 1997. 368p. 6.50 (*0-446-40524-8*) Mysterious Pr.
—The Ragman's Memory. 1996. 336p. 22.00 o.p. (*0-89296-636-X*); 1997. 368p. reprint ed. mass mkt. 6.99 (*0-446-60590-5*) Warner Bks., Inc.
—Scent of Evil. 1992. 368p. 18.95 o.p. (*0-89296-471-5*) Mysterious Pr.
—Scent of Evil. 1993. (Joe Gunther Mysteries Ser.). 416p. reprint ed. mass mkt. 6.99 (*0-446-40335-0*) Warner Bks., Inc.
—The Skeleton's Knee. 1993. 320p. 18.95 (*0-89296-470-7*) Mysterious Pr.
—The Skeleton's Knee. 1994. (Joe Gunther Mysteries Ser.). 320p. reprint ed. mass mkt. 6.99 (*0-446-40099-8*) Warner Bks., Inc.
—Tucker Peak. 2001. 304p. 23.45 o.p. (*0-89296-724-2*) Mysterious Pr.
—Tucker Peak. 2002. 352p. reprint ed. mass mkt. 6.99 (*0-446-61208-1*) Warner Bks., Inc.

**GUTHRIE, ANSON (FICTITIOUS CHARACTER)—FICTION**

Anderson, Poul. The Fleet of Stars. 1998. 403p. mass mkt. 6.99 (*0-8125-4598-2*); 1997. 352p. 24.95 (*0-312-86036-6*) Doherty, Tom Assocs., LLC. (Tor Bks.).
—Harvest of Stars. 1994. 531p. mass mkt. 6.99 (*0-8125-1946-9*); 1993. 448p. 14.99 o.p. (*0-312-85277-0*); 1992. 544p. mass mkt. 91.64 (*0-8125-2946-4*) Doherty, Tom Assocs., LLC. (Tor Bks.).
—Harvest the Fire. 1995. 192p. 19.95 o.p. (*0-312-85943-0*); Vol. 1. 1997. (Illus.). 190p. pap. 5.99 (*0-8125-5375-6*) Doherty, Tom Assocs., LLC. (Tor Bks.).
—The Stars Are Also Fire. 1995. 544p. pap. 6.99 (*0-8125-3022-5*); 1994. 446p. 14.99 o.p. (*0-312-85534-6*) Doherty, Tom Assocs., LLC. (Tor Bks.).

**GUTIERREZ, VINCE (FICTITIOUS CHARACTER)—FICTION**

Lapierre, Janet. Baby Mine: A Port Silva Mystery. 1999. (Port Silva Mysteries Ser.). (Illus.). 255p. pap. 12.95 (*1-880284-32-4*) Daniel, John & Co., Pubs.
—Children's Games. 1989. 16.95 o.s.i (*0-684-19064-8*, Macmillan Reference USA) Gale Group.
—Children's Games. 1990. mass mkt. (*0-373-26052-0*, Harlequin Bks.) Harlequin Enterprises, Ltd.
—Children's Games. 1990. pap. o.s.i (*1-85381-112-2*) Virago Pr., Ltd. GBR. *Dist:* Little Brown & Co.
—The Cruel Mother. 1991. reprint ed. per. (*0-373-26078-4*, Harlequin Bks.) Harlequin Enterprises, Ltd.
—The Cruel Mother: A Meg Halloran Mystery. 1990. 224p. 18.95 o.s.i (*0-684-19170-9*, Macmillan Reference USA) Gale Group.
—Grandmother's House. 1991. 288p. 19.95 o.s.i (*0-684-19382-5*, Macmillan Reference USA) Gale Group.
—Grandmother's House. 1993. (Mystery Ser.). per. (*0-373-26120-9*, 1-26120-5, Harlequin Bks.) Harlequin Enterprises, Ltd.
—The Unquiet Grave. 1987. 240p. 15.95 o.p. (*0-312-01102-4*, Saint Martin's Minotaur) St. Martin's Pr.

**GWEN, LADY (FICTITIOUS CHARACTER)—FICTION**

Mansfield, Elizabeth. My Lord Murderer. 1986. 256p. mass mkt. 4.99 o.s.i (*0-515-08743-2*, Jove); 1981. mass mkt. 2.25 o.s.i (*0-425-05029-7*); 1978. mass mkt. 1.95 o.s.i (*0-425-03806-8*) Berkley Publishing Group.

# H

**HAAGEN, ANNEKE (FICTITIOUS CHARACTER)—FICTION**

Holtzer, Susan. Better Than Sex. 240p. 2002. mass mkt. 6.50 (*0-312-98005-1*, St. Martin's Paperbacks); 2001. 22.95 (*0-312-25345-1*, Saint Martin's Minotaur) St. Martin's Pr.
—Black Diamond. 1998. (Dead Letter Mysteries Ser.). 336p. mass mkt. 5.99 (*0-312-96629-6*, St. Martin's Paperbacks) St. Martin's Pr.
—Black Diamond: An Anneke Haagen Mystery. 1997. 272p. text 21.95 o.p. (*0-312-17174-9*, Saint Martin's Minotaur) St. Martin's Pr.
—Bleeding Maize & Blue. 304p. 1996. text 22.95 o.p. (*0-312-14552-7*, Saint Martin's Minotaur); Vol. 1. 1997. mass mkt. 5.99 (*0-312-96284-3*, St. Martin's Paperbacks) St. Martin's Pr.
—Curly Smoke: An Anneke Haagen Mystery. (Anneke Haagen Mystery Ser.). 1996. 213p. mass mkt. 5.99 o.s.i (*0-312-95943-5*, St. Martin's Paperbacks); 1995. 256p. 20.95 o.p. (*0-312-13458-4*, Saint Martin's Minotaur) St. Martin's Pr.
—The Silly Season: A Mystery at the University of Michigan. 2000. 288p. mass mkt. 5.99 (*0-312-97039-0*, St. Martin's Paperbacks) St. Martin's Pr.
—The Silly Season: An Entr'acte. 1998. 272p. 22.95 o.p. (*0-312-20010-2*, Saint Martin's Minotaur) St. Martin's Pr.
—Something to Kill For. 1995. 242p. mass mkt. 5.99 (*0-312-95589-8*, St. Martin's Paperbacks); 1994. 240p. 19.95 o.p. (*0-312-11117-7*, Saint Martin's Minotaur) St. Martin's Pr.
—Wedding Game: A Mystery at the University of Michigan. 2000. ix, 275p. (YA). 23.95 (*0-312-25228-5*, Saint Martin's Minotaur) St. Martin's Pr.

**HACKSHAW, ELIAS (FICTITIOUS CHARACTER)—FICTION**

Wilcox, Stephen F. The Jericho Flower: A Hackshaw Mystery. 2002. 295p. pap. 18.95 (*0-595-21509-2*, Mystery & Suspense Pr.) iUniverse, Inc.
—The Nimby Factor. 1992. 256p. 18.95 o.p. (*0-312-08270-3*, Saint Martin's Minotaur) St. Martin's Pr.
—The Painted Lady. 1993. 272p. 21.95 o.p. (*0-312-10520-7*, Saint Martin's Minotaur) St. Martin's Pr.
—The Twenty-Acre Plot. 1991. 16.95 o.p. (*0-312-05846-2*, Saint Martin's Minotaur) St. Martin's Pr.

**HAGGERTY, LEO (FICTITIOUS CHARACTER)—FICTION**

Schutz, Benjamin M. All the Old Bargains. 1987. 208p. mass mkt. 2.95 o.s.i (*0-553-26335-8*) Bantam Bks.
—All the Old Bargains. 1985. (Leo Haggerty Thriller Ser.). 208p. 13.95 o.p. (*0-312-94014-9*) Bluejay Bks.
—Embrace the Wolf. (Mystery Ser.). 208p. 1990. mass mkt. 2.25 o.s.i (*0-553-18508-X*); 1986. mass mkt. 2.95 o.s.i (*0-553-26106-1*) Bantam Bks.
—Embrace the Wolf. 1985. (Leo Haggerty Thriller Ser.). 208p. 13.95 o.p. (*0-312-94137-4*) Bluejay Bks.
—A Fistful of Empty. 1999. pap. 4.95 (*0-14-012890-5*); 1991. 208p. 17.95 o.p. (*0-670-83111-5*) Viking Penguin.
—Mexico Is Forever. 1994. 256p. 18.95 o.p. (*0-312-10502-9*, Saint Martin's Minotaur) St. Martin's Pr.
—Mexico Is Forever. 1999. pap. 3.95 (*0-14-012891-3*, Viking) Viking Penguin.
—A Tax in Blood. 1989. mass mkt. 3.95 o.s.i (*0-553-28291-3*) Bantam Bks.
—A Tax in Blood. 1987. (Leo Haggerty Thriller Ser.). 288p. 14.95 o.p. (*0-312-94421-7*, Tor Bks.) Doherty, Tom Assocs., LLC.
—The Things We Do for Love. 1990. mass mkt. 3.95 o.s.i (*0-553-28489-4*) Bantam Bks.
—The Things We Do for Love. 1989. 224p. 16.95 o.s.i (*0-684-18990-9*, Scribner) Simon & Schuster.

**HAGGERTY, LINDY (FICTITIOUS CHARACTER)—FICTION**

Freydont, Shelley. Backstage Murder: A Lindy Haggerty Mystery. 1999. 326p. reprint ed. 20.00 (*0-7567-5291-4*) DIANE Publishing Co.
—Backstage Murder: A Lindy Haggerty Mystery. (Lindy Haggerty Mystery Ser.). 2000. 336p. mass mkt. 5.99 o.s.i (*1-57566-590-5*); 1999. 316p. 20.00 o.s.i (*1-57566-458-5*) Kensington Publishing Corp.
—High Seas Murder: A Lindy Haggerty Mystery. 2000. (Linda Haggerty Mysteries Ser. ). 336p. 20.00 o.s.i (*1-57566-627-8*) Kensington Publishing Corp.

—A Merry Little Murder: A Lindy Haggerty Mystery. 2003. 240p. 22.00 (*0-7582-0126-5*) Kensington Publishing Corp.

—Midsummer Murder. 2002. 34p. mass mkt. 5.99 o.s.i (*1-57566-730-4*); 2001. 288p. 22.00 (*1-57566-674-X*) Kensington Publishing Corp. (Kensington Bks.).

**HAKIM ARIF (FICTITIOUS CHARACTER)—FICTION**

Ing, Dean. Soft Targets. Baen, Jim, ed. 1986. mass mkt. 2.95 o.s.i (*0-441-77407-5*) Ace Bks.

—Soft Targets. 1980. mass mkt. 2.50 o.s.i (*0-441-77406-7*) Ace Bks.

—Soft Targets. 1996. 247p. mass mkt. 5.99 (*0-8125-1947-7*, Tor Bks.) Doherty, Tom Assocs., LLC.

**HALE, PETER (FICTITIOUS CHARACTER)—FICTION**

Margolin, Phillip. The Burning Man. 1997. 384p. mass mkt. 7.99 (*0-553-57495-7*) Bantam Bks.

—The Burning Man. unabr. ed. 1996. audio 72.00 (*0-913369-24-1*, 4175) Books on Tape, Inc.

—The Burning Man. l.t. ed. 1997. (Wheeler Large Print Book Ser.). 27.95 (*1-56895-415-8*, Wheeler Publishing, Inc.) Gale Group.

**HALE, PRICH (FICTITIOUS CHARACTER)—FICTION**

Nienkemper, Robert C. Fatal Games. 2nd ed. 1998. 341p. reprint ed. mass mkt. 7.50 (*1-892614-00-6*, BWP-FG-2) Briarwood Pubns.

—Fatal Genes. 1999. 351p. pap. 7.50 (*1-892614-15-4*, BWP-FG) Briarwood Pubns.

**HALEY, ERIN (FICTITIOUS CHARACTER)—FICTION**

Mazza, Cris. Your Name Here. 1995. 280p. (Orig.). pap. 12.95 (*1-56689-031-4*) Coffee Hse. Pr.

**HALFHYDE, ST. VINCENT (FICTITIOUS CHARACTER)—FICTION**

McCutchan, Philip. Halfhyde & the Admiral. l.t. ed. 1991. (Lythway Ser.). 288p. 21.95 (*0-7451-1259-5*, Macmillan Reference USA) Gale Group.

—Halfhyde & the Admiral. 1990. 14.95 o.p. (*0-312-04323-6*) St. Martin's Pr.

—Halfhyde & the Chain Gangs. l.t. ed. 1986. lib. bdg. 17.50 o.p. (*0-7451-0406-1*, Macmillan Reference USA) Gale Group.

—Halfhyde & the Chain Gangs. unabr. ed. 2002. audio 54.95 (*1-84283-146-1*) Soundings, Ltd. GBR. *Dist:* Ulverscroft Large Print Bks., Ltd.

—Halfhyde & the Chain Gangs. 1985. 192p. 12.95 o.p. (*0-312-35662-5*) St. Martin's Pr.

—Halfhyde & the Flag Captain. unabr. ed. 2001. audio 54.95 (*1-86042-835-5*) Soundings, Ltd. GBR. *Dist:* Ulverscroft Large Print Bks., Ltd.

—Halfhyde & the Flag Captain. 1981. 183p. 9.95 o.p. (*0-312-35684-6*) St. Martin's Pr.

—Halfhyde & the Fleet Review. l.t. ed. 1998. (Dales Large Print Ser.). 385p. pap. 19.99 o.p. (*1-85389-835-X*) Dales Large Print Bks. GBR. *Dist:* Ulverscroft Large Print Bks., Ltd., Ulverscroft Large Print Canada, Ltd.

—Halfhyde & the Fleet Review. 1991. 224p. 17.95 o.p. (*0-312-06991-X*) St. Martin's Pr.

—Halfhyde for the Queen. 2001. audio 54.95 (*1-86042-771-5*, 27715) Soundings, Ltd. GBR. *Dist:* Ulverscroft Large Print Bks., Ltd.

—Halfhyde for the Queen. 1978. 7.95 o.p. (*0-312-35687-0*) St. Martin's Pr.

—Halfhyde Goes to War. l.t. ed. 1998. (Dales Large Print Ser.). 304p. pap. 19.99 o.p. (*1-85389-834-1*) Dales Large Print Bks. GBR. *Dist:* Ulverscroft Large Print Bks., Ltd., Ulverscroft Large Print Canada, Ltd.

—Halfhyde Goes to War. 1987. 176p. 12.95 o.p. (*0-312-00603-9*) St. Martin's Pr.

—Halfhyde on the Amazon. l.t. ed. 1990. 288p. lib. bdg. 22.95 o.p. (*0-7451-1164-5*, Macmillan Reference USA) Gale Group.

—Halfhyde on the Amazon. 1988. 224p. 14.95 o.p. (*0-312-01769-3*) St. Martin's Pr.

—Halfhyde on Zanatu. l.t. ed. 2002. (Magna Large Print Ser.). 288p. 32.50 (*0-7505-1856-1*) Magna Large Print Bks. GBR. *Dist:* Ulverscroft Large Print Bks., Ltd., Ulverscroft Large Print Canada, Ltd.

—Halfhyde on Zanatu. unabr. ed. 2002. audio 44.95 (*1-86042-974-2*) Soundings, Ltd. GBR. *Dist:* Ulverscroft Large Print Bks., Ltd.

—Halfhyde on Zanatu. 1982. 176p. 10.95 o.p. (*0-312-35688-9*) St. Martin's Pr.

—Halfhyde Ordered South. 1979. 9.95 o.p. (*0-312-35689-7*) St. Martin's Pr.

—Halfhyde Outward Bound. 1984. 176p. 10.95 o.p. (*0-312-35691-9*) St. Martin's Pr.

—Halfhyde to the Narrows. 1977. 7.95 o.p. (*0-312-35690-0*) St. Martin's Pr.

—Halfhyde's Island. 2004. 224p. pap. 13.95 (*1-59013-079-0*) McBooks Pr., Inc.

—Halfhyde's Island. 1976. 184p. 7.95 o.p. (*0-312-35700-1*) St. Martin's Pr.

—Halfhyde's Island. l.t. ed. 1978. (Ulverscroft Large Print Ser.). 29.99 o.p. (*0-7089-0159-X*, Ulverscroft) Thorpe, F. A. Pubs. GBR. *Dist:* Ulverscroft Large Print Bks., Ltd., Ulverscroft Large Print Canada, Ltd.

—Halfhyde's Island. 1985. 240p. mass mkt. 2.95 o.s.i (*0-446-32940-1*) Warner Bks., Inc.

**HALL, ADAM (FICTITIOUS CHARACTER)—FICTION**

Grisham, John. Camara de Gas. 1998. (Illus.). (J). 15.30 (*0-606-18346-9*) Turtleback Bks.

—The Chamber. 1995. mass mkt. 8.99 (*0-440-91084-6*); 688p. mass mkt. 7.99 (*0-440-22060-2*); mass mkt. (*0-440-29533-5*) Dell Publishing.

—The Chamber. 1994. 496p. 27.95 (*0-385-42472-8*); 880p. 29.95 o.s.i (*0-385-47439-3*); 496p. 250.00 o.s.i (*0-385-47440-7*) Doubleday Publishing.

—The Chamber, Level 6. 2000. (Penguin Reader Ser.). pap. 7.93 (*0-582-36411-6*) Longman Publishing Group.

—The Chamber. 1995. 14.04 (*0-606-17119-3*) Turtleback Bks.

**HALL, MASON (FICTITIOUS CHARACTER)—FICTION**

Murray, Earl P. Thunder in the Dawn. 1994. 413p. mass mkt. 5.99 (*0-8125-1319-3*, Tor Bks.); 1993. 416p. 22.95 o.p. (*0-312-85675-X*, Forge Bks.) Doherty, Tom Assocs., LLC.

**HALL, SATAN (FICTITIOUS CHARACTER)—FICTION**

Daly, Carroll J. The Adventures of Satan Hall. 1988. 304p. 8.95 (*0-89296-938-5*) Mysterious Pr.

**HALLAM, LUCAS (FICTITIOUS CHARACTER)—FICTION**

Washburn, L. J. Dead-Stick. l.t. ed. 1992. pap. 20.95 o.p. (*0-7927-1177-7*); 22.95 o.p. (*0-7927-1176-9*, CH0242) BBC Audiobooks America.

—Dead-Stick, Vol. 1. 1989. 16.95 o.p. (*0-312-93133-6*, Tor Bks.) Doherty, Tom Assocs., LLC.

—Dog Heavies: A Lucas Hallam Mystery. 1990. 288p. 17.95 o.p. (*0-312-93160-3*, Tor Bks.) Doherty, Tom Assocs., LLC.

—Wild Night. l.t. ed. 1991. 12.95 o.p. (*0-7927-0188-7*, 4718); pap. 10.95 o.p. (*0-7927-0189-5*, C0086) BBC Audiobooks America.

—Wild Night. 1987. 320p. pap. 3.95 o.p. (*0-8125-1041-0*, Tor Bks.) Doherty, Tom Assocs., LLC.

—Wild Night. 1998. (Mystery Ser.). 253p. 20.95 (*0-7862-1658-1*, Five Star) Gale Group.

**HALLECK, BILLY (FICTITIOUS CHARACTER)—FICTION**

Bachman, Richard, pseud. Thinner. abr. ed. 1985. audio 16.99 (*0-88646-127-8*, 7127) Durkin Hayes Publishing Ltd.

—Thinner. l.t. ed. 1986. (General Ser.). 438p. 16.95 o.p. (*0-8161-4020-0*); 9.95 o.p. (*0-8161-4021-9*) Gale Group. (Macmillan Reference USA).

—Thinner, Set. unabr. ed. 1999. audio 30.00 Highsmith Inc.

—Thinner. 1996. 320p. mass mkt. 6.99 o.s.i (*0-451-19075-0*, Signet Bks.); 1985. mass mkt. 4.50 o.p. (*0-451-13796-5*, Signet Bks.); 1984. 256p. text 12.95 o.p. (*0-453-00468-7*); 1985. 320p. reprint ed. mass mkt. 7.99 (*0-451-16134-3*, Signet Bks.) NAL.

—Thinner. 1984. 14.04 (*0-606-00776-8*) Turtleback Bks.

—Thinner. abr. unabr. ed. 1997. pap. 34.95 o.s.i incl. audio (*0-14-086629-9*); 1997. pap. 34.95 o.s.i incl. audio (*0-14-086629-9*); 1996. 8p. pap. 34.95 o.s.i incl. audio (*0-14-086266-8*); 1996. 8p. pap. 34.95 o.s.i incl. audio (*0-14-086266-8*) Viking Penguin. (Penguin AudioBooks).

**HALLEY, SID (FICTITIOUS CHARACTER)—FICTION**

Francis, Dick. Come to Grief. 1996. 384p. mass mkt. 6.99 (*0-515-11952-0*, Jove) Berkley Publishing Group.

—Come to Grief. unabr. ed. 1996. audio 56.00 (*0-7366-3274-3*, 3930) Books on Tape, Inc.

—Come to Grief. 1995. 320p. 23.95 o.p. (*0-399-14082-4*, G. P. Putnam's Sons); o.p. (*0-399-19295-6*) Penguin Group (USA) Inc.

—Come to Grief. unabr. ed. audio. 2000. audio 70.00 (*0-7887-0467-2*, 94660E7) Recorded Bks., LLC.

—Come to Grief. abr. ed. 1999. pap. 9.98 incl. audio (*0-671-04422-2*); 1999. pap. 9.98 incl. audio (*0-671-04422-2*); 1995. audio 18.00 (*0-671-53629-X*, 393277) Simon & Schuster Audio. (Simon & Schuster Audioworks).

—Come to Grief. l.t. ed. 1996. (Paperback Bestsellers Ser.). 402p. pap. 26.95 (*0-7838-1509-3*) Thorndike Pr.

—Come to Grief: International Edition. 1996. 6.99 o.s.i (*0-515-11937-7*, Jove) Berkley Publishing Group.

—Come to Grief: International Edition. l.t. ed. 1995. (Core Collection). 402p. 29.95 (*0-7838-1508-5*) Thorndike Pr.

—Comeback. 1993. 336p. mass mkt. 6.99 o.s.i (*0-449-21956-9*); mass mkt. 5.99 o.s.i (*0-449-45308-1*) Ballantine Bks. (Fawcett).

—Comeback. l.t. ed. (General Ser.). 1993. 420p. pap. 17.95 o.p. (*0-8161-5419-8*); 1992. 23.95 o.p. (*0-8161-5418-X*) Gale Group. (Macmillan Reference USA).

—Comeback. 1991. 320p. 21.95 o.s.i (*0-399-13670-3*, G. P. Putnam's Sons) Penguin Group (USA) Inc.

—Comeback. pap. 4.98 o.p. (*0-8317-5042-1*) Smithmark Pubs., Inc.

—Odds Against. unabr. ed. audio 54.95 o.p. (*1-85549-031-5*); 1998. audio 69.95 (*0-7540-0086-9*, CAB1509) BBC Audiobooks America.

—Odds Against. 1987. 320p. mass mkt. 5.99 o.s.i (*0-449-21269-6*, Fawcett) Ballantine Bks.

—Odds Against. 2000. 288p. mass mkt. 6.99 (*0-515-12551-2*, Jove) Berkley Publishing Group.

—Odds Against. unabr. ed. 1999. audio 39.95 Blackstone Audio Bks., Inc.

—Odds Against. unabr. ed. 2000. (Sid Halley Adventure Ser.: Bk. 1). audio 59.95 Chivers Audio Bks. GBR. *Dist:* BBC Audiobooks America.

—Odds Against. l.t. ed. 1991. (General Ser.). 272p. 15.95 o.s.i (*0-8161-5034-6*); lib. bdg. 21.95 o.p. (*0-8161-5033-8*) Gale Group. (Macmillan Reference USA).

—Odds Against. abr. ed. 1991. audio 15.95 o.s.i (*1-55994-138-3*, CPN 2138, HarperAudio) HarperTrade.

—Odds Against, unabr. ed. 1999. audio 39.95 Highsmith Inc.

—Odds Against. 1982. mass mkt. 2.95 o.s.i (*0-671-45076-X*, Pocket) Simon & Schuster.

—Whip Hand. unabr. ed. 1989. audio 64.95 o.s.i (*0-8161-9460-2*) BBC Audiobooks America.

—Whip Hand. 1996. pap. 5.99 (*0-449-45617-X*); 1987. mass mkt. 5.99 o.s.i (*0-449-21274-2*) Ballantine Bks. (Fawcett).

—Whip Hand. 1999. 304p. mass mkt. 6.99 (*0-515-12504-0*, Jove) Berkley Publishing Group.

—Whip Hand. unabr. ed. 2000. (Sid Halley Adventure Ser.: Bk. 2). audio 59.95; 1993. audio 69.95 (*0-7451-5960-5*, CAB 358) Chivers Audio Bks. GBR. *Dist:* BBC Audiobooks America.

—Whip Hand. l.t. ed. 1995. 376p. 21.95 (*0-8161-5785-5*, Macmillan Reference USA) Gale Group.

—Whip Hand. 2001. (Best Mysteries of All Time Ser.). 288p. (*0-7621-8871-5*, IM Pr.) Reader's Digest Assn., Inc., The.

—Whip Hand. unabr. ed. 1991. audio 51.00 (*1-55690-560-2*, 91109E7) Recorded Bks., LLC.

—Whip Hand. 1982. 336p. mass mkt. 3.50 o.s.i (*0-671-46404-3*, Pocket) Simon & Schuster.

—Whip Hand. 1984. audio o.s.i. audio 39.95 o.s.i (*0-8161-9785-7*, 91109) Thorndike Pr.

—Whip Hand. l.t. ed. 1980. (Ulverscroft Large Print Ser.). 459p. o.p. (*0-7089-0542-0*, Ulverscroft) Thorpe, F. A. Pubs. GBR. *Dist:* Ulverscroft Large Print Canada, Ltd.

—Whip Hand. abr. ed. 1996. audio 16.95 o.s.i (*0-14-086223-4*, Penguin AudioBooks) Viking Penguin.

**HALLIGAN, NINA (FICTITIOUS CHARACTER)—FICTION**

Kelley, Norman. The Big Mango. 2000. (Illus.). 270p. pap. 14.95 (*1-888451-10-6*) Akashic Bks.

—Black Heat. 228p. 1997. 22.00 o.p. (*1-887276-02-5*); 1996. (Illus.). pap. 12.95 (*1-887276-03-3*) Cool Grove Publishing, Inc. (Coolgrove Pr.).

—Black Heat: A Nina Halligan Mystery. 2001. 320p. 23.00 (*0-06-018542-2*) HarperTrade.

—A Phat Death: A Nina Halligan Mystery. 2003. 260p. pap. 14.95 (*1-888451-48-3*) Akashic Bks.

**HALLORAN, MEG (FICTITIOUS CHARACTER)—FICTION**

Lapierre, Janet. Baby Mine: A Port Silva Mystery. 1999. (Port Silva Mysteries Ser.). (Illus.). 255p. pap. 12.95 (*1-880284-32-4*) Daniel, John & Co., Pubs.

—Children's Games. 1989. 16.95 o.s.i (*0-684-19064-8*, Macmillan Reference USA) Gale Group.

—Children's Games. 1990. mass mkt. (*0-373-26052-0*, Harlequin Bks.) Harlequin Enterprises, Ltd.

—Children's Games. 1990. pap. o.s.i (*1-85381-112-2*) Virago Pr., Ltd. GBR. *Dist:* Little Brown & Co.

—The Cruel Mother. 1991. reprint ed. per. (*0-373-26078-4*, Harlequin Bks.) Harlequin Enterprises, Ltd.

—The Cruel Mother: A Meg Halloran Mystery. 1990. 224p. 18.95 o.s.i (*0-684-19170-9*, Macmillan Reference USA) Gale Group.

—Grandmother's House. 1991. 288p. 19.95 o.s.i (*0-684-19382-5*, Macmillan Reference USA) Gale Group.

—Grandmother's House. 1993. (Mystery Ser.). per. (*0-373-26120-9*, 1-26120-5, Harlequin Bks.) Harlequin Enterprises, Ltd.

—Old Enemies. 1993. 256p. text 20.00 (*0-684-19614-X*, Macmillan Reference USA) Gale Group.

—The Unquiet Grave. 1987. 240p. 15.95 o.p. (*0-312-01102-4*, Saint Martin's Minotaur) St. Martin's Pr.

**HALVORSEN, W. T. (FICTITIOUS CHARACTER)—FICTION**

Poyer, David. As the Wolf Loves Winter. 1997. 432p. mass mkt. 6.99 (*0-8125-3433-6*); 1996. 352p. 23.95 o.p. (*0-312-85601-6*) Doherty, Tom Assocs., LLC. (Forge Bks.).

—As the Wolf Loves Winter. l.t. ed. 1996. 25.95 (*1-56895-379-8*, Wheeler Publishing, Inc.) Gale Group.

—The Dead of Winter. 1988. 320p. pap. 5.99 (*0-8125-0787-8*, Tor Bks.) Doherty, Tom Assocs., LLC.

—Thunder on the Mountain: A Novel of 1936, Set. unabr. ed. 2000. audio 84.95 (*0-7927-2323-6*, CSL 212, Chivers Sound Library) BBC Audiobooks America.

—Thunder on the Mountain: A Novel of 1936. (Hemlock County Ser.). 2000. 419p. mass mkt. 6.99 (*0-8125-4004-2*); 1999. (Illus.). 384p. 25.95 (*0-312-86494-9*) Doherty, Tom Assocs., LLC. (Forge Bks.).

—Winter in the Heart. 1994. 416p. mass mkt. 5.99 o.p. (*0-8125-2298-2*); 1993. 352p. 21.95 o.p. (*0-312-85421-8*) Doherty, Tom Assocs., LLC. (Tor Bks.).

—Winter in the Heart. 4.98 o.s.i (*0-8317-4649-1*) Smithmark Pubs., Inc.

**HAMEL, NEIL (FICTITIOUS CHARACTER)—FICTION**

Van Gieson, Judith. Ditch Rider: A Neil Hamel Mystery. (Neil Hamel Mystery Ser.). 240p. 1999. mass mkt. 5.99 (*0-06-109515-X*); 1998. 23.00 (*0-06-017513-3*) HarperCollins Pubs.

—Hotshots. 1996. (Neil Hamel Mystery Ser.). 256p. 22.00 o.p. (*0-06-017512-5*) HarperCollins Pubs.

—The Lies That Bind: A Neil Hamel Mystery. 1994. 304p. mass mkt. 4.99 o.p. (*0-06-109051-4*) HarperCollins Pubs.

—The Lies That Bind: A Neil Hamel Mystery. 1993. 256p. 20.00 o.p. (*0-06-017705-5*) HarperTrade.

—North of the Border: A Neil Hamel Mystery. 1993. 176p. mass mkt. 4.99 (*0-671-76967-7*, Pocket) Simon & Schuster.

—North of the Border: A Neil Hamel Mystery. 2002. 178p. pap. 13.95 (*0-8263-2886-5*) Univ. of New Mexico Pr.

—North of the Border: A Neil Hamel Mystery. 1988. 16.95 o.p. (*0-8027-5706-5*) Walker & Co.

—The Other Side of Death. 1991. 224p. 18.95 o.p. (*0-06-016581-2*) HarperTrade.

—The Other Side of Death. 2003. 224p. pap. 13.95 (*0-8263-3207-2*) Univ. of New Mexico Pr.

—Parrot Blues. 1995. 256p. 20.00 o.p. (*0-06-017706-3*) HarperTrade.

—Parrot Blues. 1995. 272p. mass mkt. 4.99 o.p. (*0-06-109048-4*, HarperTorch) Morrow/Avon.

—Raptor. 1990. 17.95 o.p. (*0-06-016167-1*) HarperTrade.

—Raptor. Isaacson, Dana, ed. 1991. 256p. reprint ed. mass mkt. 4.99 (*0-671-73243-9*, Pocket) Simon & Schuster.

—Raptor. 2002. 252p. pap. 13.95 (*0-8263-2974-8*) Univ. of New Mexico Pr.

—The Wolf Path: A Neil Hamel Mystery. 1992. 224p. 19.00 o.p. (*0-06-016804-8*) HarperTrade.

—The Wolf Path: A Neil Hamel Mystery. 1993. 256p. mass mkt. 4.50 o.p. (*0-06-109139-1*, HarperTorch) Morrow/Avon.

**HAMILTON, ETHAN (FICTITIOUS CHARACTER)—FICTION**

Scott, Jefferson. Virtually Eliminated. 1996. 336p. pap. 9.99 o.p. (*0-88070-885-9*, Multnomah Bks.) Multnomah Pubs., Inc.

**HAMILTON, LISA (FICTITIOUS CHARACTER)—FICTION**

Marklin, Megan. The Summoned. Zion, Claire, ed. 1993. 320p. (Orig.). mass mkt. 4.99 (*0-671-76098-X*, Pocket) Simon & Schuster.

**HAMILTON, STEFIE (FICTITIOUS CHARACTER)—FICTION**

Brown, Richard E. & Brown, Beverly A. The Rose Engagement. exp. ed. 1996. (Orig.). 205p. (C). pap. text 12.00 (*0-9654000-2-6*); 203p. pap. 12.00 (*0-9654000-1-8*) Kent Information Services, Inc.

Hamilton, Scott. Landing It: My Life on & off the Ice. 2000. (Illus.). 48p. mass mkt. 6.99 o.s.i (*0-7860-1149-1*, Pinnacle Bks.) Kensington Publishing Corp.

**HAMLIN, MICHAEL (FICTITIOUS CHARACTER)—FICTION**

Kaiser, Janice. Last Night in Rio. 1996. 441p. per. (*1-55166-174-8*, 1-66174-3, Mira Bks.) Harlequin Enterprises, Ltd.

**HAMMER, JUDY (FICTITIOUS CHARACTER)—FICTION**

Cornwell, Patricia. Hornet's Nest. l.t. ed. 1998. 384p. mass mkt. 7.99 (*0-425-16098-X*) Berkley Publishing Group.

—Hornet's Nest. unabr. ed. 1997. (Judy Hammer Mystery Ser.). audio 72.00 (*0-913369-52-7*, 4264) Books on Tape, Inc.

—Hornet's Nest. l.t. ed. 1997. 523p. lib. bdg. 27.95 o.p. (*0-7838-8085-5*, Macmillan Reference USA) Gale Group.
—Hornet's Nest. 2000. 25.95 o.s.i (*0-399-14554-0*); 1997. 384p. 25.95 o.s.i (*0-399-14228-2*, G. P. Putnam's Sons); Set. 1997. audio 24.95 (*0-399-14282-7*, 694558) Penguin Group (USA) Inc.
—Hornet's Nest. l.t. ed. 1998. (Paperback Bestsellers Ser.). 490p. pap. 27.95 (*0-7838-8086-3*) Thorndike Pr.
—Southern Cross. 1999. audio compact disk (*0-7540-5316-4*, CCD007) BBC Audiobooks America.
—Southern Cross. 1999. 400p. mass mkt. 7.99 (*0-425-17254-6*) Berkley Publishing Group.
—Southern Cross. l.t. ed. (Wheeler Press Paperback Ser.). 2000. pap. 11.95 (*1-56895-973-7*); 1999. 458p. 29.95 (*1-56895-709-2*) Gale Group. (Wheeler Publishing, Inc.).
—Southern Cross, abr. ed. 1999. audio 24.95. audio 39.95 Highsmith Inc.
—Southern Cross. 1999. 25.95 o.s.i (*0-399-14771-3*); 368p. 25.95 o.p. (*0-399-14465-X*); 24.95 o.p. (*0-399-14478-1*, 696063); 39.95 o.p. (*0-399-14472-2*, 106043, Putnam Berkley Audio) Penguin Group (USA) Inc.
—Southern Cross. 1999. 39.95 o.s.i (*0-399-14772-1*, Putnam Berkley Audio); 24.95 o.s.i (*0-399-14773-X*) Putnam Publishing Group, The.
—Southern Cross. unabr. ed. 1999. audio 83.00 (*0-7887-2591-2*, 95612E7) Recorded Bks., LLC.
—Southern Cross. abr. ed. 1999. audio 16.85 (*1-85686-611-4*) Ulverscroft Audio (U.S.A.).

**HAMMER, MIKE (FICTITIOUS CHARACTER)—FICTION**

Spillane, Mickey. Black Alley. 1996. 240p. 23.95 o.s.i (*0-525-94229-7*) Dutton/Plume.
—Black Alley. l.t. ed. 1996. (G. K. Hall Core Ser.). 316p. 24.95 (*0-7838-1959-5*, Macmillan Reference USA) Gale Group.
—Black Alley. 1997. (Mike Hammer Ser.). 320p. mass mkt. 6.99 o.s.i (*0-451-19102-1*, Signet Bks.) NAL.
—Body Lovers. l.t. ed. 1999. (Mike Hammer Ser.). 248p. pap. 24.95 (*0-7838-8540-7*) Thorndike Pr.
—The Hammer Strikes Again: Five Complete Mike Hammer Novels. 1989. 784p. 9.99 o.s.i (*0-517-67578-1*) Random Hse. Value Publishing.
—The Killing Man. 1989. (Mike Hammer Ser.). 17.95 o.p. (*0-525-24827-7*, Dutton) Dutton/Plume.
—The Killing Man. l.t. ed. 1993. (Mike Hammer Ser.). 363p. lib. bdg. 19.95 o.p. (*0-8161-5552-6*, Macmillan Reference USA) Gale Group.
—The Killing Man. 1990. (Mike Hammer Ser.). 320p. mass mkt. 4.95 o.p. (*0-451-16784-8*, Signet Bks.) NAL.
—The Killing Man. 1992. 2.99 o.p. (*0-517-07997-6*) Random Hse. Value Publishing.
—Kiss Me Deadly. 1953. mass mkt. 2.95 o.p. (*0-451-13602-0*); reprint ed. mass mkt. 3.95 o.p. (*0-451-16593-4*) NAL. (Signet Bks.).
—Mickey Spillane: Five Complete Mike Hammer Novels. 1987. 9.99 o.s.i (*0-517-62950-X*) Random Hse. Value Publishing.
—Mike Hammer: The Comic Strip, Vol. 1. Collins, Max Allan & Robbins, Ed, eds. 1982. (U. S. Classics Ser.). (Illus.). 64p. pap. 5.95 o.p. (*0-912277-11-4*) Pierce, Ken Bks.
—Mike Hammer: The Comic Strip, Vol. 2. Collins, Max Allan & Yronwode, Catherine, eds. 1985. (U. S. Classics Ser.). (Illus.). 64p. pap. 5.95 (*0-912277-26-2*) Pierce, Ken Bks.
—The Mike Hammer Collection, 2 vols. 2001. 448p. pap. 15.00 (*0-451-20352-6*);Vol. 2. 528p. reprint ed. pap. 15.00 (*0-451-20425-5*) NAL.
—One Lonely Night. l.t. ed. 1994. (Mike Hammer Ser.). o.p. (*0-7927-2105-5*); pap. o.p. (*0-7927-2104-7*) BBC Audiobooks America.
—One Lonely Night. unabr. ed. 1991. (Mike Hammer Ser.). audio 48.00 (*0-7366-2020-6*, 2836) Books on Tape, Inc.
—One Lonely Night. l.t. ed. 1996. 21.95 (*0-7838-1229-9*, Macmillan Reference USA) Gale Group.
—One Lonely Night. 1951. (Mike Hammer Ser.). mass mkt. 3.50 o.p. (*0-451-15349-9*); mass mkt. 2.95 o.p. (*0-451-13710-8*, Signet Bks.); mass mkt. 3.95 o.p. (*0-451-16597-7*, AE2165, Signet Bks.) NAL.
—One Lonely Night. abr. ed. 1991. (Mike Hammer Ser.). audio 15.95 (*0-671-72605-6*, 326314, Simon & Schuster Audioworks) Simon & Schuster Audio.
—The Snake. (Mike Hammer Ser.). 19.95 (*0-89190-837-4*) Amereon, Ltd.
—The Snake. 1999. (Mike Hammer Ser.). 240p. (*0-7540-3617-0*) BBC Audiobooks America.
—The Snake. l.t. ed. 1999. (Mike Hammer Ser.). 240p. pap. (*0-7540-3618-9*, Macmillan Reference USA) Gale Group.
—The Snake. 1964. (Mike Hammer Ser.). 160p. mass mkt. 3.95 o.p. (*0-451-13715-9*, AE2209, Signet Bks.) NAL.
—The Snake. l.t. ed. 1998. (Mike Hammer Ser.). 240p. pap. 23.95 (*0-7838-0412-1*) Thorndike Pr.
—Survival— Zero! l.t. ed. 1999. (Mike Hammer Ser.). 264p. (*0-7540-3955-2*, Macmillan Reference USA) Gale Group.
—Survival-Zero. 1971. (Mike Hammer Ser.). 160p. mass mkt. 4.50 o.p. (*0-451-13704-3*, Signet Bks.) NAL.
—Survival Zero! l.t. ed. 1999. (Mike Hammer Ser.). 264p. pap. 24.95 (*0-7838-8735-3*) Wiley, John & Sons, Inc.
—The Twisted Thing. l.t. ed. 1994. (Mike Hammer Ser.). lib. bdg. 17.95 (*0-8161-5557-7*, Macmillan Reference USA) Gale Group.
—Vengeance Is Mine. 1951. (Mike Hammer Ser.). mass mkt. 2.95 o.p. (*0-451-14687-5*) NAL.

**HAMPTON, JAKE (FICTITIOUS CHARACTER)—FICTION**

Kraus, Harry L., Jr. Lethal Mercy. 1997. 384p. pap. 12.99 (*0-89107-921-1*) Crossway Bks.

**HANKS, ARLY (FICTITIOUS CHARACTER)—FICTION**

Hess, Joan. Madness in Maggody. 1992. (Arly Hanks Mystery Ser.). 240p. mass mkt. 5.99 o.s.i (*0-451-40299-5*, Onyx) NAL.
—Madness in Maggody. 1990. 16.95 o.p. (*0-312-05465-3*, Saint Martin's Minotaur) St. Martin's Pr.
—Maggody & the Moonbeams. 2001. 256p. 23.00 (*0-7432-0229-5*, Simon & Schuster) Simon & Schuster.
—Maggody in Manhattan. 1992. (Arly Hanks Mystery Ser.). 272p. 18.00 o.p. (*0-525-93519-3*, Dutton) Dutton/Plume.
—Maggody in Manhattan. 1993. (Arly Hanks Mystery Ser.). 256p. reprint ed. mass mkt. 5.50 o.s.i (*0-451-40376-2*, Onyx) NAL.
—The Maggody Militia. 1997. (Arly Hanks Mystery Ser.). 320p. 21.95 o.s.i (*0-525-94236-X*) Dutton/Plume.
—The Maggody Militia. 1998. (Arly Hanks Mystery Ser.). 224p. mass mkt. 5.99 o.s.i (*0-451-40726-1*, Onyx) NAL.
—Malice in Maggody. 1991. (Arly Hanks Mystery Ser.). 240p. mass mkt. 5.99 o.s.i (*0-451-40236-7*, Onyx) NAL.
—Martians in Maggody. 1994. (Arly Hanks Mystery Ser.). 256p. 18.95 o.s.i (*0-525-93840-0*) Dutton/Plume.
—Martians in Maggody. 1995. (Arly Hanks Mystery Ser.). 304p. mass mkt. 5.50 o.s.i (*0-451-40592-7*, Onyx) NAL.
—Miracles in Maggody, unabr. ed. 1999. audio 39.95 Blackstone Audio Bks., Inc.
—Miracles in Maggody. 1995. (Arly Hanks Mystery Ser.). 288p. 20.95 o.p. (*0-525-94051-0*, Dutton) Dutton/Plume.
—Miracles in Maggody. 1996. (Arly Hanks Mystery Ser.). 288p. mass mkt. 5.99 o.s.i (*0-451-40656-7*) NAL.
—Mischief in Maggody. 1991. (Arly Hanks Mystery Ser.). 256p. mass mkt. 5.99 o.s.i (*0-451-40253-7*, Onyx) NAL.
—Mischief in Maggody. 1988. 176p. 14.95 o.p. (*0-312-01792-8*, Saint Martin's Minotaur) St. Martin's Pr.
—Misery Loves Maggody. 1999. 288p. 22.00 (*0-684-84562-8*, Simon & Schuster); 2000. (Illus.). 304p. reprint ed. pap. 6.99 (*0-671-01684-9*, Pocket) Simon & Schuster.
—Mortal Remains in Maggody. 1991. (Arly Hanks Mystery Ser.). 304p. 18.95 o.p. (*0-525-93368-9*, Dutton) Dutton/Plume.
—Mortal Remains in Maggody. 1992. (Arly Hanks Mystery Ser.). 272p. mass mkt. 4.50 o.s.i (*0-451-40326-6*, Onyx) NAL.
—Much Ado in Maggody. 1991. (Arly Hanks Mystery Ser.). 256p. mass mkt. 5.99 o.s.i (*0-451-40268-5*, Onyx) NAL.
—Much Ado in Maggody. 1989. 15.95 o.p. (*0-312-02952-7*, Saint Martin's Minotaur) St. Martin's Pr.
—Muletrain to Maggody. 2004. 288p. 23.00 (*0-7432-2638-0*, Simon & Schuster) Simon & Schuster.
—Murder@Maggody.com. l.t. ed. 2000. (Wheeler Large Print Book Ser.). 312p. pap. 24.95 (*1-56895-886-2*, Wheeler Publishing, Inc.) Gale Group.
—Murder@Maggody.com. 2000. 256p. 22.00 o.s.i (*0-684-84563-6*, Simon & Schuster); 2001. (Illus.). 304p. reprint ed. mass mkt. 6.99 (*0-671-01685-7*, Pocket) Simon & Schuster.
—O Little Town of Maggody. 1993. (Arly Hanks Mystery Ser.). 256p. 19.00 o.p. (*0-525-93654-8*, Dutton) Dutton/Plume.
—O Little Town of Maggody. abr. ed. 1994. (Arly Hanks Mystery Ser.). audio 16.00 o.p. (*0-453-00871-2*, Penguin AudioBooks) HighBridge Co.
—O Little Town of Maggody. 1994. (Arly Hanks Mystery Ser.). 256p. mass mkt. 4.50 o.s.i (*0-451-40457-2*, Onyx) NAL.

**HANNAFORD, BENNIS (FICTITIOUS CHARACTER)—FICTION**

Haddam, Jane. Act of Darkness. 1991. 288p. mass mkt. 4.50 o.s.i (*0-553-29086-X*) Bantam Bks.
—And One to Die On: A Birthday Mystery. 1997. 304p. mass mkt. 5.99 o.s.i (*0-553-56448-X*) Bantam Bks.
—Baptism in Blood. 1996. 352p. mass mkt. 5.99 o.s.i (*0-553-57464-7*, Crimeline) Bantam Bks.
—Bleeding Hearts. 1995. 368p. mass mkt. 5.50 o.s.i (*0-553-56936-8*) Bantam Bks.
—Deadly Beloved. 1998. 336p. mass mkt. 5.99 o.s.i (*0-553-57200-8*) Bantam Bks.
—Dear Old Dead. 1994. 352p. mass mkt. 5.50 o.s.i (*0-553-56447-1*) Bantam Bks.
—Feast of Murder. 1992. 336p. mass mkt. 5.50 o.s.i (*0-553-29389-3*) Bantam Bks.
—A Festival of Deaths. 1994. 384p. mass mkt. 5.99 o.s.i (*0-553-56085-9*) Bantam Bks.
—The Fountain of Death. 1995. 352p. (Orig.). mass mkt. 5.50 o.s.i (*0-553-56449-8*, Crimeline) Bantam Bks.
—A Great Day for the Deadly. 1992. 288p. mass mkt. 5.50 o.s.i (*0-553-29388-5*) Bantam Bks.
—Murder Superior. 1993. 304p. mass mkt. 5.99 o.s.i (*0-553-56084-0*) Bantam Bks.
—Not a Creature Was Stirring: A Gregor Demarkian Holiday Mystery. 1990. 320p. mass mkt. 5.99 o.s.i (*0-553-28792-3*) Bantam Bks.
—Precious Blood. 1991. 336p. mass mkt. 5.99 o.s.i (*0-553-28913-6*) Bantam Bks.
—Quoth the Raven. 1991. 288p. mass mkt. 5.99 o.s.i (*0-553-29255-2*) Bantam Bks.
—Skeleton Key. 2000. 276p. 23.95 o.p. (*0-312-20909-6*, Saint Martin's Minotaur) St. Martin's Pr.
—A Stillness in Bethlehem. 1993. (Gregor Demarkian Holiday Mystery Ser.). 368p. mass mkt. 5.50 o.s.i (*0-553-29390-7*) Bantam Bks.

**HANNAY, RICHARD (FICTITIOUS CHARACTER)—FICTION**

Buchan, John. Greenmantle. lib. bdg. 20.95 (*0-8488-0925-4*) Amereon, Ltd.
—Greenmantle. unabr. ed. 1997. audio 69.95 (*0-7451-5813-7*, CAB 229) BBC Audiobooks America.
—Greenmantle. unabr. ed. 1996. audio 49.95 (*0-7861-1015-5*, 1793) Blackstone Audio Bks., Inc.
—Greenmantle. 1999. E-Book 2.49 (*1-58627-246-2*) Electric Umbrella Publishing.
—Greenmantle. 1986. pap. 9.95 o.p. (*0-87923-598-5*); 1988. 345p. reprint ed. 19.95 o.p. (*0-933852-84-3*) Godine, David R. Pub.
—Greenmantle. 2002. 244p. 24.99 (*1-4043-0500-9*); per. 20.99 (*1-4043-0501-7*) IndyPublish.com.
—Greenmantle. Macdonald, Kate, ed. (Oxford World's Classics Ser.). 320p. 1999. pap. 9.95 (*0-19-283684-6*); 1994. pap. 8.95 o.p. (*0-19-282953-X*) Oxford Univ. Pr., Inc.
—Greenmantle. 1992. (Classic Crime Ser.). (Illus.). 272p. pap. 5.95 o.p. (*0-14-001132-3*, Penguin Bks.) Penguin Group (USA) Inc.
—Greenmantle. (Ebook Classic Ser.). E-Book 5.00 (*0-7410-0825-4*) SoftBook Pr.
—Greenmantle. 1998. (Classics Library). 225p. pap. 3.95 (*1-85326-204-8*, 2048WW) Wordsworth Editions, Ltd. GBR. *Dist:* Casemate Pubs. & Bk. Distributors, LLC.
—The Island of Sheep. 22.95 (*0-8488-0926-2*) Amereon, Ltd.
—The Island of Sheep. unabr. ed. 2001. audio 61.95 (*1-85695-769-1*, 940503) ISIS Audio Bks. GBR. *Dist:* Ulverscroft Large Print Bks., Ltd.
—The Island of Sheep. Duncan, Ian, ed. 1997. (Oxford World's Classics Ser.). (Illus.). 268p. pap. (*0-19-282433-3*) Oxford Univ. Pr., Inc.
—The Island of Sheep. l.t. ed. 1970. (Ulverscroft Large Print Ser.). 432p. 29.99 o.p. (*0-85456-003-3*, Ulverscroft) Thorpe, F. A. Pubs. GBR. *Dist:* Ulverscroft Large Print Bks., Ltd., Ulverscroft Large Print Canada, Ltd.
—Mr. Standfast. 19.95 (*0-8488-0927-0*) Amereon, Ltd.
—Mr. Standfast. 1999. E-Book 2.49 (*1-58627-244-6*) Electric Umbrella Publishing.
—Mr. Standfast. 2002. 304p. 25.99 (*1-4043-1982-4*); per. 21.99 (*1-4043-1983-2*) IndyPublish.com.
—Mr. Standfast. 1994. (Oxford World's Classics Ser.). 384p. pap. 11.95 o.p. (*0-19-283116-X*) Oxford Univ. Pr., Inc.
—Mr. Standfast. 1988. reprint ed. lib. bdg. 69.00 (*0-7812-0165-9*) Reprint Services Corp.
—Mr. Standfast. 1928. 374p. reprint ed. 69.00 (*0-403-00879-4*) Scholarly Pr., Inc.
—Mr. Standfast. E-Book 5.00 (*0-7410-1241-3*) SoftBook Pr.
—Mr. Standfast. 1998. (Classics Library). 400p. pap. 3.95 (*1-85326-225-0*, 2250WW) Wordsworth Editions, Ltd. GBR. *Dist:* Casemate Pubs. & Bk. Distributors, LLC.
—The Power-Hourse & the 39 Steps. 2002. xxviii, 233p. pap. 11.95 (*1-873631-95-2*) B & W Publishing GBR. *Dist:* Interlink Publishing Group, Inc.
—The Thirty-Nine Steps. Date not set. (Nelson Readers Ser.). (J). pap. text (*0-17-557053-1*) Addison-Wesley Longman, Inc.
—The Thirty-Nine Steps. 1967. pap. text 61.25 (*0-582-53752-5*) Addison-Wesley Longman, Ltd. GBR. *Dist:* Trans-Atlantic Pubns., Inc.
—The Thirty-Nine Steps. 1976. reprint ed. lib. bdg. 19.95 (*0-89190-243-0*, Rivercity Pr.) Amereon, Ltd.
—The Thirty-Nine Steps, Set. unabr. ed. 1998. audio 24.95 (*1-55685-547-8*) Audio Bk. Contractors, Inc.
—The Thirty-Nine Steps. 1915. E-Book (*1-58734-003-8*) Bartleby.com.
—The Thirty-Nine Steps. unabr. ed. 1994. audio 23.95 (*0-7861-0689-1*, 1474) Blackstone Audio Bks., Inc.
—The Thirty-Nine Steps. 2002. pap. 3.50 (*1-59109-021-0*) Booksurge, LLC.
—The Thirty-Nine Steps. 1990. reprint ed. lib. bdg. 13.95 (*0-89968-487-4*) Buccaneer Bks., Inc.
—The Thirty-Nine Steps. unabr. ed. 2000. audio 34.95 (*0-7451-5812-9*, CAB 024) Chivers Audio Bks. GBR. *Dist:* BBC Audiobooks America.
—The Thirty-Nine Steps. l.t. ed. 2003. (Dales Large Print Ser.). 208p. pap. 21.99 (*1-84262-215-3*) Dales Large Print Bks. GBR. *Dist:* Ulverscroft Large Print Bks., Ltd., Ulverscroft Large Print Canada, Ltd.
—The Thirty-Nine Steps. unabr. ed. 1994. (Illus.). 96p. pap. text 1.50 (*0-486-28201-5*) Dover Pubns., Inc.
—The Thirty-Nine Steps. E-Book 2.49 (*1-58627-240-3*) Electric Umbrella Publishing.
—The Thirty-Nine Steps. 1991. 160p. reprint ed. pap. 6.95 o.s.i (*0-87923-838-0*) Godine, David R. Pub.
—The Thirty-Nine Steps. abr. ed. 1986. audio 15.95 o.p. (*1-55994-070-0*, CPN 2098, Caedmon) HarperTrade.
—The Thirty-Nine Steps. 2000. (Penguin Readers Ser.: Level 3). (C). pap. 7.66 (*0-582-41641-8*); 1995. (Fiction Ser.). (YA). pap. text 7.88 o.p. (*0-582-08467-9*, 79834) Longman Publishing Group.
—The Thirty-Nine Steps. Harvie, Christopher, ed. 1999. (Oxford World's Classics Ser.). 160p. pap. 8.95 (*0-19-283931-4*) Oxford Univ. Pr., Inc.
—The Thirty-Nine Steps. Hedge, Tricia, ed. 1995. (Illus.). 80p. pap. text 5.95 o.p. (*0-19-421677-2*) Oxford Univ. Pr., Inc.
—The Thirty-Nine Steps. 1994. (Oxford World's Classics Ser.). 150p. pap. 8.95 o.p. (*0-19-282991-2*) Oxford Univ. Pr., Inc.
—The Thirty-Nine Steps, Level 4. Hedge, Tricia, ed. 2000. (Bookworms Ser.). (Illus.). 96p. (J). pap. text 5.95 (*0-19-423048-1*) Oxford Univ. Pr., Inc.
—The Thirty-Nine Steps. 2000. audio compact disk (*1-894003-19-5*) Scenario Productions.
—The Thirty-Nine Steps. E-Book 5.00 (*0-7410-0618-9*) SoftBook Pr.
—The Thirty-Nine Steps. 1993. (Pocket Classics Ser.). pap. 4.95 (*0-7509-0482-8*) Sutton Publishing, Ltd. GBR. *Dist:* International Publishers Marketing.
—The Thirty-Nine Steps. l.t. ed. 1998. 132p. text 27.95 (*1-56000-497-5*) Transaction Pubs.
—The Thirty-Nine Steps. 1991. (World's Classics Ser.). 132p. 6.95 (*0-14-001130-7*) Viking Penguin.
—The Thirty-Nine Steps. Kraus, Josef, ed. 2001. per. 14.95 (*0-9709917-3-8*) Wexford College Pr.
—The Thirty-Nine Steps. 2002. 140p. pap. 15.95 (*1-59224-968-X*); lib. bdg. 27.95 (*1-59224-969-8*) Wildside Pr.
—The Thirty-Nine Steps. 1998. (Classics Library). 100p. pap. 3.95 (*1-85326-080-0*, 0800WW) Wordsworth Editions, Ltd. GBR. *Dist:* Casemate Pubs. & Bk. Distributors, LLC.
—The Thirty-Nine Steps & Greenmantle. unabr. collector's ed. 1994. audio 72.00 (*0-7366-2649-2*, 3386) Books on Tape, Inc.
—The Three Hostages. Miller, Karl, ed. 1995. (Oxford World's Classics Ser.). (Illus.). 330p. pap. (*0-19-282419-8*) Oxford Univ. Pr., Inc.
Hitchcock, Alfred & Buchan, John. The Thirty-Nine Steps. 1984. (Masterworks Collections). pap. 8.95 o.p. (*0-8044-6267-4*) Continuum International Publishing Group, Inc.

**HANRAHAN, MAC (FICTITIOUS CHARACTER)—FICTION**

Truman, Margaret. Murder in the Smithsonian. (Capital Crime Myteries Ser.). 1985. 304p. mass mkt. 6.99 (*0-449-20959-8*, Fawcett); 1984. mass mkt. 3.50 o.s.i (*0-449-20502-9*) Ballantine Bks.
—Murder in the Smithsonian. l.t. ed. 1983. (General Ser.). 9.95 o.p. (*0-8161-3631-9*); 383p. lib. bdg. 14.95 o.p. (*0-8161-3601-7*) Gale Group. (Macmillan Reference USA).
—Murder in the Smithsonian. 1993. audio 44.20 (*1-56544-035-8*, 250024); audio Literate Ear, Inc.
—Murder in the Smithsonian. 1983. 304p. 14.95 o.p. (*0-87795-475-5*, Morrow, William & Co.) Morrow/Avon.

**HANSEN, ANNIKA (FICTITIOUS CHARACTER)—FICTION**

*see Seven of Nine (Fictitious Character)—Fiction*

**HANSEN, EM (FICTITIOUS CHARACTER)—FICTION**

Andrews, Sarah. Bone Hunter. 2nd ed. 1999. 320p. 24.95 (*0-312-20381-0*, Saint Martin's Minotaur) St. Martin's Pr.

—Bone Hunter: An Em Hansen Mystery. 2000. (Em Hansen Mysteries Ser.). 353p. mass mkt. 6.50 (*0-312-97317-9*, St. Martin's Paperbacks) St. Martin's Pr.
—An Eye for Gold. E-Book 24.95 (*0-312-27607-9*); 2000. ix, 387p. 24.95 (*0-312-25349-4*, Saint Martin's Minotaur) St. Martin's Pr.
—A Fall in Denver: An Em Hansen Mystery. 1996. (Em Hansen Mystery Ser.). 272p. mass mkt. 5.50 o.s.i (*0-451-18793-8*) NAL.
—A Fall in Denver: An Em Hansen Mystery. 1995. 288p. 20.00 o.p. (*0-684-81523-0*); 20.00 (*1-883402-34-4*) Simon & Schuster. (Scribner).
—Fault Line. 2003. 336p. mass mkt. 6.50 (*0-312-98445-6*, St. Martin's Paperbacks); 2002. 304p. 23.95 (*0-312-25350-8*, Saint Martin's Minotaur) St. Martin's Pr.
—Killer Dust: A Mystery Featuring Forensic Geologist Em Hansen. 2003. 320p. 24.95 (*0-312-30196-0*, Saint Martin's Minotaur) St. Martin's Pr.
—Mother Nature. 1997. 352p. 23.95 (*0-312-15591-3*, Saint Martin's Minotaur) St. Martin's Pr.
—Only Flesh & Bones. 1999. (Dead Letter Mysteries Ser.: Vol. 1). 368p. mass mkt. 6.50 (*0-312-96702-0*, St. Martin's Paperbacks); 1998. 336p. 23.95 (*0-312-18642-8*, Saint Martin's Minotaur) St. Martin's Pr.
—Tensleep: An Em Hansen Mystery. 1995. (Em Hansen Mystery Ser.). 304p. mass mkt. 4.99 o.s.i (*0-451-18606-0*, Signet Bks.) NAL.
—Tensleep: An Em Hansen Mystery. 1994. 288p. 20.00 (*1-883402-33-6*, Scribner) Simon & Schuster.

### HANSON, BOMBER (FICTITIOUS CHARACTER)—FICTION

Champion, David. Celebrity Trouble: A Bomber Hanson Mystery. 1997. 200p. 20.00 (*1-888310-97-9*) Knoll, Allen A. Pubs.
—The Mountain Massacres: A Bomber Hanson Mystery. 1995. 161p. 14.95 (*0-9627297-4-4*) Knoll, Allen A. Pubs.
—Phantom Virus: A Bomber Hanson Mystery. 1999. 275p. 23.00 (*1-888310-93-6*) Knoll, Allen A. Pubs.
—She Died for Her Sins: A Bomber Hanson Mystery. 2002. 278p. 23.00 (*1-888310-51-0*) Knoll, Allen A. Pubs.
—Too Rich & Too Thin: A Bomber Hanson Mystery. 2000. (Bomber Hanson Mystery Ser.: Vol. 5). 233p. 22.00 (*1-888310-50-2*) Knoll, Allen A. Pubs.

### HANSON, WILLY (FICTITIOUS CHARACTER)—FICTION

Arnote, Ralph. Fallen Idols. 1992. 312p. pap. text 4.99 o.p. (*0-8125-1612-5*, Tor Bks.) Doherty, Tom Assocs., LLC.
—A Rage in Paradise. 288p. 1999. mass mkt. 5.99 (*0-8125-6263-1*, Tor Bks.); 1997. 23.95 (*0-312-86198-2*, Forge Bks.) Doherty, Tom Assocs., LLC.
—The Weekenders' Club. 1996. 400p. mass mkt. 5.99 o.p. (*0-8125-3880-3*, Forge Bks.) Doherty, Tom Assocs., LLC.

### HARALD, SIGRID (FICTITIOUS CHARACTER)—FICTION

Maron, Margaret. Baby Doll Games. 1988. 224p. mass mkt. 3.50 o.s.i (*0-553-27281-0*) Bantam Bks.
—Baby Doll Games. l.t. ed. 1992. (Mystery Ser.). 448p. 29.99 (*0-7089-2775-0*, Ulverscroft) Thorpe, F. A. Pubs. GBR. *Dist:* Ulverscroft Large Print Bks., Ltd., Ulverscroft Large Print Canada, Ltd.
—Baby Doll Games. 1995. (Sigrid Harald Mystery Ser.). 224p. mass mkt. 5.99 o.s.i (*0-446-40418-7*) Warner Bks., Inc.
—Bloody Kin. 1992. 224p. mass mkt. 4.50 o.s.i (*0-553-29514-4*) Bantam Bks.
—Bloody Kin. 1985. (Crime Club Ser.). 192p. 12.95 o.p. (*0-385-23231-4*) Doubleday Publishing.
—Bloody Kin. 1995. 224p. mass mkt. 5.99 (*0-446-40416-0*) Warner Bks., Inc.
—Corpus Christmas. 1990. 224p. mass mkt. 3.95 o.s.i (*0-553-27410-4*) Bantam Bks.
—Corpus Christmas. 2001. 288p. reprint ed. pap. 12.95 (*0-446-67766-3*) Warner Bks., Inc.
—Death in Blue Folders. 1992. (Crime Line Ser.). 224p. mass mkt. 4.50 o.s.i (*0-553-29498-9*) Bantam Bks.
—Death in Blue Folders. l.t. ed. 1992. (Mystery Ser.). 400p. 29.99 o.p. (*0-7089-2665-7*, Ulverscroft) Thorpe, F. A. Pubs. GBR. *Dist:* Ulverscroft Large Print Bks., Ltd., Ulverscroft Large Print Canada, Ltd.
—Death of a Butterfly. 1991. 192p. mass mkt. 3.99 o.s.i (*0-553-29121-1*) Bantam Bks.
—Death of a Butterfly. 1984. (Crime Club Ser.). 192p. 11.95 o.p. (*0-385-19554-0*) Doubleday Publishing.
—Death of a Butterfly. l.t. ed. 1991. (Ulverscroft Large Print Ser.). 29.99 o.p. (*0-7089-2465-4*, Ulverscroft) Thorpe, F. A. Pubs. GBR. *Dist:* Ulverscroft Large Print Bks., Ltd., Ulverscroft Large Print Canada, Ltd.
—Fugitive Colors. 1995. 272p. 18.95 o.s.i (*0-89296-567-3*) Mysterious Pr.
—Fugitive Colors. 260p. pap. 3.98 o.p. (*0-7651-0363-X*) Smithmark Pubs., Inc.
—Fugitive Colors. 1996. (Sigrid Harald Mystery Ser.). 256p. mass mkt. 5.99 (*0-446-40393-8*) Warner Bks., Inc.
—One Coffee With. 1988. mass mkt. 3.50 o.s.i (*0-553-27479-1*) Bantam Bks.
—One Coffee With. l.t. ed. 1991. (Ulverscroft Large Print Ser.). 29.99 o.p. (*0-7089-2433-6*, Ulverscroft) Thorpe, F. A. Pubs. GBR. *Dist:* Ulverscroft Large Print Bks., Ltd., Ulverscroft Large Print Canada, Ltd.
—One Coffee With. 1995. (Sigrid Harald Mystery Ser.). 192p. mass mkt. 5.99 o.s.i (*0-446-40415-2*) Warner Bks., Inc.
—Past Imperfect. 1992. 256p. mass mkt. 4.99 o.s.i (*0-553-29546-2*) Bantam Bks.
—Past Imperfect. 1991. 192p. 14.95 o.s.i (*0-385-41364-5*) Doubleday Publishing.
—The Right Jack. 1987. 224p. mass mkt. 3.50 o.s.i (*0-553-26859-7*) Bantam Bks.
—The Right Jack. l.t. ed. 1992. (Mystery Ser.). 480p. 29.99 o.p. (*0-7089-2730-0*, Ulverscroft) Thorpe, F. A. Pubs. GBR. *Dist:* Ulverscroft Large Print Bks., Ltd., Ulverscroft Large Print Canada, Ltd.
—The Right Jack. 1995. (Sigrid Harald Mystery Ser.). 224p. mass mkt. 5.99 o.s.i (*0-446-40417-9*) Warner Bks., Inc.
—Shoveling Smoke: Selected Mystery Stories. 1997. 248p. pap. 16.00 (*1-885941-15-3*); 240p. 40.00 o.p. (*1-885941-14-5*) Crippen & Landru, Pubs.

### HARDAWAY, ANNE (FICTITIOUS CHARACTER)—FICTION

Sherman, Beth. The Dead Man's Float. l.t. ed. 2003. (Mystery Ser.). 27.95 (*1-57490-489-2*, Beeler Large Print Bks.) Beeler, Thomas T. Publisher.
—The Dead Man's Float. 1998. (Jersey Shore Mysteries Ser.). 288p. mass mkt. 6.50 (*0-380-73107-X*, Avon Bks.) Morrow/Avon.
—Death at High Tide: A Jersey Shore Mystery. 1999. 256p. mass mkt. 6.50 (*0-380-73108-8*, Avon Bks.) Morrow/Avon.
—Death's a Beach. Grader, T. L., ed. 2000. (Jersey Shore Mysteries Ser.). 256p. mass mkt. 5.99 (*0-380-73109-6*, Avon Bks.) Morrow/Avon.

### HARDESTY, WIL (FICTITIOUS CHARACTER)—FICTION

Barre, Richard. Bearing Secrets: A Wil Hardesty Mystery. 1998. (Wil Hardesty Ser.: Vol. 2). 288p. reprint ed. mass mkt. 5.99 o.s.i (*0-425-16641-4*) Berkley Publishing Group.
—Bearing Secrets: A Wil Hardesty Mystery. 1996. (Wil Hardesty Ser.). 312p. 22.95 (*0-8027-3280-1*) Walker & Co.
—Blackheart Highway. (Wil Hardesty Ser.: Vol. 4). 2000. 326p. mass mkt. 6.99 o.s.i (*0-425-17467-0*); 1999. 336p. 21.95 o.s.i (*0-425-16903-0*, Prime Crime) Berkley Publishing Group.
—Burning Moon: A Wil Hardesty Novel. 2003. (Illus.). 330p. 25.95 (*1-59266-011-8*) Capra Pr.
—The Ghosts of Morning: A Will Hardesty Mystery. 1998. 336p. 21.95 o.s.i (*0-425-16300-8*); 1999. 320p. reprint ed. mass mkt. 6.50 o.s.i (*0-425-16931-6*, Prime Crime) Berkley Publishing Group.
—The Innocents. 1997. (Wil Hardesty Ser.: Vol. 1). 288p. mass mkt. 6.50 o.s.i (*0-425-16109-9*, Prime Crime) Berkley Publishing Group.
—The Innocents. 1995. 332p. 19.95 (*0-8027-3261-5*) Walker & Co.

### HARDING (FICTITIOUS CHARACTER)—FICTION

Wessel, John. Kiss It Goodbye: A Novel. 2002. 336p. E-Book 24.00 (*0-7432-2605-4*, Simon & Schuster) Simon & Schuster.
—Pretty Ballerina. 1998. 240p. 23.50 (*0-684-81464-1*, Simon & Schuster) Simon & Schuster.
—This Far, No Further. 1997. 384p. mass mkt. 6.99 o.s.i (*0-440-22490-X*) Dell Publishing.
—This Far, No Further. l.t. ed. 1997. (Large Print Book Ser.). 25.95 (*1-56895-418-2*, Wheeler Publishing, Inc.) Gale Group.
—This Far, No Further, unabr. ed. 1997. audio 75.00 (*0-7887-0803-1*, 94952E7) Recorded Bks., LLC.
—This Far, No Further. 1996. 336p. 23.00 (*0-684-81463-3*, Simon & Schuster) Simon & Schuster.
—This Far, No Further. 1999. pap. 9.98 (*0-671-04467-2*); Set. 1988. audio 18.00 (*0-671-57433-7*, 394372) Simon & Schuster Audio. (Simon & Schuster Audioworks).

### HARDY, ANNABELLE (FICTITIOUS CHARACTER)—FICTION

Jackson, Hialeah. The Alligator's Farewell. 1998. (Annabelle Hardy Mystery Ser.: No. 1). 368p. mass mkt. 5.99 o.s.i (*0-440-22660-0*) Dell Publishing.

### HARDY, CLIFF (FICTITIOUS CHARACTER)—FICTION

Corris, Peter. Beware of the Dog. 1994. 288p. mass mkt. 4.99 o.s.i (*0-440-21753-9*) Dell Publishing.
—The Big Drop & Other Cliff Hardy Stories. 1988. 208p. mass mkt. 3.50 o.s.i (*0-449-13228-5*, Fawcett) Ballantine Bks.
—Deal Me Out. l.t. ed. 1991. 11.95 o.p. (*0-947072-56-X*, C0376); pap. 17.95 o.p. (*1-86340-123-7*, AUS058) BBC Audiobooks America.
—Deal Me Out. 1987. mass mkt. 2.95 o.s.i (*0-449-13229-3*, Fawcett) Ballantine Bks.
—The Dying Trade. 1986. 256p. mass mkt. 2.95 o.s.i (*0-449-13030-4*, Fawcett) Ballantine Bks.
—The Empty Beach. l.t. ed. 1988. pap. 9.95 o.p. (*1-86340-081-8*) BBC Audiobooks America.
—The Empty Beach. 1986. mass mkt. 2.95 o.s.i (*0-449-13029-0*, Fawcett) Ballantine Bks.
—The Greenwich Apartments. 1986. 173p. pap. (*0-04-820030-1*) Allen & Unwin Pty., Ltd. AUS. *Dist:* Paul & Co. Pubs. Consortium, Inc.
—The Greenwich Apartments. 1988. mass mkt. 3.50 o.s.i (*0-449-14514-X*, Fawcett) Ballantine Bks.
—Heroin Annie. l.t. ed. 1990. pap. 9.95 o.p. (*1-86340-071-0*); 1988. lib. bdg. 15.95 o.p. (*0-947072-17-9*) BBC Audiobooks America.
—Heroine Annie & Other Cliff Hardy Stories. 1987. 256p. mass mkt. 2.95 o.s.i (*0-449-13031-2*, Fawcett) Ballantine Bks.
—The January Zone. l.t. ed. 1991. 21.95 o.p. (*1-86340-200-4*, AUH082); 12.95 o.p. (*0-7451-9609-8*, AUS150) BBC Audiobooks America.
—The January Zone. 1988. mass mkt. 3.50 o.s.i (*0-449-14513-1*, Fawcett) Ballantine Bks.
—Make Me Rich. 1987. 192p. mass mkt. 2.95 o.s.i (*0-449-13021-5*, Fawcett) Ballantine Bks.
—Man in the Shadows, Vol. 5. 1991. (Spanish Bit Saga). 176p. mass mkt. 3.99 o.s.i (*0-553-29087-8*) Bantam Bks.
—The Marvellous Boy. 1986. mass mkt. 2.95 o.s.i (*0-449-13028-2*, Fawcett) Ballantine Bks.
—Matrimonial Causes: A Cliff Hardy Mystery. 1994. 288p. mass mkt. 4.99 o.s.i (*0-440-21747-4*) Dell Publishing.
—O'Fear. 1991. 208p. 15.00 o.s.i (*0-385-42119-2*) Doubleday Publishing.
—Wet Graves. unabr. ed. 2001. audio (*1-86442-312-9*, 590376) Bolinda Publishing Pty. Ltd.
—Wet Graves. 1995. 288p. mass mkt. 4.99 o.s.i (*0-440-21750-4*) Dell Publishing.
—White Meat. 1986. mass mkt. 2.95 o.s.i (*0-449-13027-4*, Fawcett) Ballantine Bks.

### HARDY, DISMAS (FICTITIOUS CHARACTER)—FICTION

Lescroart, John. A Certain Justice. 1996. pap. 6.99 (*0-440-29547-5*) Bantam Bks.
—A Certain Justice. 1996. 544p. mass mkt. 7.99 (*0-440-22104-8*) Dell Publishing.
—A Certain Justice. 1995. 448p. 22.95 o.p. (*1-55611-445-1*) Fine, Donald I. Bks.
—A Certain Justice. l.t. ed. 1996. 756p. 25.95 (*0-7838-1565-4*, Macmillan Reference USA) Gale Group.
—Dead Irish. 1996. 416p. mass mkt. 7.99 (*0-440-20783-5*) Dell Publishing.
—Dead Irish. 1990. 18.95 o.p. (*1-55611-159-2*) Fine, Donald I. Bks.
—Dead Irish. 1996. audio 16.98 o.s.i (*0-553-74643-X*); 2000. audio 9.99 o.s.i (*0-553-52702-9*) Random Hse. Audio Publishing Group. (RH Audio).
—The First Law. abr. ed. 2003. (Dismas Hardy Ser.: Vol. 11). audio 24.95 (*1-59086-371-2*, 3959); audio 12.99 (*1-59086-374-7*, 3962, Brilliance Audio Paperback Audiobooks); audio 92.25 (*1-59086-370-4*, 3958); audio 34.95 (*1-59086-369-0*, 3957); audio compact disk 42.95 (*1-59086-372-0*, 3960); audio compact disk 107.25 (*1-59086-373-9*, 3961) Brilliance Audio.
—The First Law. 2003. 384p. 25.95 (*0-525-94705-1*) Dutton/Plume.
—The First Law. 2004. 757p. pap. 13.95 (*1-4104-0171-5*, Wheeler Publishing, Inc.) Gale Group.
—The First Law. 2004. 448p. mass mkt. 7.99 (*0-451-21022-0*, Signet Bks.) NAL.
—The First Law. 2003. 31.95 (*0-7862-5187-5*) Thorndike Pr.
—Hard Evidence. 1994. (Northern California Mysteries Ser.). 512p. mass mkt. 6.99 o.s.i (*0-8041-1275-4*, Ivy Bks.) Ballantine Bks.
—Hard Evidence. 1993. 478p. 21.95 o.p. (*1-55611-344-7*) Fine, Donald I. Bks.
—The Hearing. abr. ed. (Dismas Hardy Ser.). 2002. audio 12.99 (*1-58788-655-3*, 3021, Paperback Nova Audio Bks.); 2001. audio 24.95 o.s.i (*1-58788-177-2*, 2436, Nova Audio Bks.); 2001. audio 107.25 (*1-58788-176-4*, 2435); 2001. audio 34.95 (*1-58788-175-6*, 2434, Brilliance Audio Unabridged) Brilliance Audio.
—The Hearing. 2001. (Illus.). 464p. 25.95 o.s.i (*0-525-94575-X*, Dutton) Dutton/Plume.
—The Hearing. l.t. ed. 2002. 655p. pap. 29.95 (*0-7838-9394-9*, Macmillan Reference USA); 2001. 480p. 32.95 (*0-7838-9393-0*, Hall, G. K. & Co.) Gale Group.
—The Hearing. 2001. 544p. pap. 7.99 (*0-451-20450-6*); 2002. 560p. reprint ed. mass mkt. 7.99 (*0-451-20489-1*) NAL. (Signet Bks.).
—The Hearing. unabr. ed. 2003. (Dismas Hardy Ser.). audio 19.99 (*1-59335-088-0*, 30180) Soulmate Audio Bks., Inc.
—The Mercy Rule. 1999. 640p. mass mkt. 7.99 (*0-440-22282-6*) Dell Publishing.
—The Mercy Rule. l.t. ed. (Paperback Bestsellers Ser.). 684p. 1999. pap. 27.95 (*0-7838-0394-X*); 1998. 30.95 (*0-7838-0344-3*) Thorndike Pr.
—Nothing but the Truth. 1999. mass mkt. 7.99 (*0-440-29574-2*) Bantam Dell Publishing Group.
—Nothing but the Truth. 2000. mass mkt. 7.99 (*0-440-22664-3*); 448p. 24.95 o.s.i (*0-385-33353-6*, Delacorte Pr.) Dell Publishing.
—Nothing but the Truth. l.t. ed. 2000. 27.95 (*1-56895-813-7*, Wheeler Publishing, Inc.) Gale Group.
—Nothing but the Truth. 2001. 464p. mass mkt. 7.99 (*0-451-20285-6*) NAL.
—Nothing but the Truth. abr. ed. 2000. audio 25.95 (*0-553-52662-6*, RH Audio) Random Hse. Audio Publishing Group.
—The Oath. unabr. ed. 2002. (Dismas Hardy Ser.: Vol. 10). audio 34.95 (*1-58788-981-1*, 3501, Brilliance Audio Unabridged); audio 87.25 (*1-58788-982-X*, 3502, Unabridged Library Editions) Brilliance Audio.
—The Oath. 2002. 480p. 25.95 o.s.i (*0-525-94576-8*, Dutton) Dutton/Plume.
—The Oath. l.t. ed. 2002. 653p. 32.95 (*0-7862-4193-4*) Gale Group.
—The Oath. l.t. ed. 2002. 598p. pap. 13.95 (*0-7862-4194-2*) Thorndike Pr.
—The Second Chair. 2004. 400p. 25.95 (*0-525-94775-2*, Dutton) Dutton/Plume.
—The Vig. 1998. 384p. mass mkt. 7.99 (*0-440-20986-2*) Dell Publishing.
—The Vig. 1991. 18.95 o.p. (*1-55611-221-1*) Fine, Donald I. Bks.
—The Vig. abr. ed. 1998. audio 16.99 o.p. Random Hse. Audio Publishing Group.
—The 13th Juror. 1995. 560p. mass mkt. 7.99 (*0-440-22079-3*) Dell Publishing.
—The 13th Juror. 1994. 480p. 22.95 o.s.i (*1-55611-402-8*) Fine, Donald I. Bks.
—The 13th Juror. l.t. ed. 1994. 803p. lib. bdg. 24.95 o.p. (*0-8161-7448-2*, Macmillan Reference USA) Gale Group.

### HARISTEEN, HARRY (FICTITIOUS CHARACTER)—FICTION

Brown, Rita Mae. Cat on the Scent. 336p. 1999. (Illus.). 23.95 o.s.i (*0-553-09971-X*); 2000. reprint ed. mass mkt. 7.50 (*0-553-57541-4*) Bantam Bks.
—Cat on the Scent. l.t. ed. 1999. 26.95 o.p. (*1-56895-749-1*, Wheeler Publishing, Inc.) Gale Group.
—Catch as Cat Can. l.t. ed. 2002. 504p. 31.95 (*0-7862-4045-8*) Gale Group.
—Catch as Cat Can. l.t. ed. 2003. (Paperback Bestsellers Ser.). pap. 13.95 (*0-7862-4044-X*) Thorndike Pr.
—Claws & Effect. 2002. (Mrs. Murphy Mystery Ser.). (Illus.). 320p. reprint ed. mass mkt. 7.50 (*0-553-58090-6*) Bantam Bks.
—Claws & Effect. l.t. ed. 2001. (Illus.). 433p. 30.95 (*0-7862-3484-9*) Thorndike Pr.
—Murder at Monticello, or, Old Sins. 1995. (Mrs. Murphy Mystery Ser.). 320p. mass mkt. 7.50 (*0-553-57235-0*, Crimeline) Bantam Bks.
—Murder on the Prowl. 1999. 400p. reprint ed. mass mkt. 7.50 (*0-553-57540-6*) Bantam Bks.
—Murder on the Prowl. l.t. ed. 1998. (Basic Ser.). 467p. 30.95 (*0-7862-1458-9*) Thorndike Pr.
—Murder, She Meowed. 1997. (Mrs. Murphy Mystery Ser.). (Illus.). 336p. mass mkt. 7.50 (*0-553-57237-7*) Bantam Bks.
—Pawing Through the Past. 2001. (Mrs. Murphy Mystery Ser.). 352p. mass mkt. 7.50 (*0-553-58025-6*) Bantam Bks.
—Pawing Through the Past. l.t. ed. 2000. (Wheeler Large Print Book Ser.). (Illus.). 360p. 28.95 o.p. (*1-56895-134-5*, Wheeler Publishing, Inc.) Gale Group.
—Pay Dirt. 1996. (Mrs. Murphy Mystery Ser.). 288p. mass mkt. 7.50 (*0-553-57236-9*, Crimeline) Bantam Bks.
—Rest in Pieces. 1993. (Mrs. Murphy Mystery Ser.). 368p. mass mkt. 7.50 (*0-553-56239-8*) Bantam Bks.
—The Tail of the Tip-Off. 2004. (Illus.). 400p. mass mkt. 7.50 (*0-553-58285-2*) Bantam Bks.
—Whisker of Evil. 2004. (Illus.). 320p. 24.95 (*0-553-80161-9*) Bantam Bks.
—Wish You Were Here. l.t. ed. 1992. pap. 20.95 o.p. (*0-7927-1189-0*); 22.95 o.p. (*0-7927-1188-2*, CH0250) BBC Audiobooks America.
—Wish You Were Here. 1991. (Mrs. Murphy Mystery Ser.). 304p. mass mkt. 7.50 (*0-553-28753-2*) Bantam Bks.
Brown, Rita Mae & Brown, Sneaky Pie. Catch As Cat Can. 2003. (Illus.). 368p. mass mkt. 7.50 (*0-553-58028-0*, Bantam) Bantam Bks.
—Catch As Cat Can. 2002. (Illus.). 304p. 24.95 (*0-553-10744-5*) Bantam Dell Publishing Group.

—Catch as Cat Can. l.t. ed. 13.95 (*1-4104-0084-0*, Large Print Pr.) Thorndike Pr.
—The Tail of the Tip-Off. 2003. (Mrs. Murphy Mystery Ser.). E-Book 19.95 (*0-553-89725-X*); (Illus.). 320p. 24.95 (*0-553-80158-9*) Bantam Bks.
—The Tail of the Tip-Off. audio 29.99 (*1-4025-3628-3*) Recorded Bks., LLC.
—The Tail of the Tip-Off. l.t. ed. 2003. 32.95 (*0-7862-4991-9*) Thorndike Pr.

**HARPER, BENNI (FICTITIOUS CHARACTER)—FICTION**

Fowler, Earlene. Arkansas Traveler. 2001. 304p. 21.95 o.s.i (*0-425-17808-0*, Prime Crime) Berkley Publishing Group.
—Dove in the Window. l.t. ed. 2001. (Beeler Large Print Mystery Ser.). 310p. 25.95 (*1-57490-368-3*, Beeler Large Print Bks.) Beeler, Thomas T. Publisher.
—Dove in the Window. 1999. (Benni Harper Mystery Ser.). 320p. reprint ed. mass mkt. 6.99 (*0-425-16894-8*, Prime Crime) Berkley Publishing Group.
—Dove in the Window. 1999. 12.55 (*0-606-22164-6*) Turtleback Bks.
—Dove in the Window: A Benni Harper Mystery, No. 5. 1998. (Benni Harper Mystery Ser.). 304p. 21.95 o.s.i (*0-425-16299-0*) Berkley Publishing Group.
—Fool's Puzzle. l.t. ed. 1999. (Beeler Large Print Mystery Ser.). 25.95 (*1-57490-211-3*, Beeler Large Print Bks.) Beeler, Thomas T. Publisher.
—Fool's Puzzle. (Benni Harper Mystery Ser.). 1995. 256p. mass mkt. 6.99 (*0-425-14545-X*); 1994. 17.95 o.p. (*0-425-14041-5*) Berkley Publishing Group. (Prime Crime).
—Fool's Puzzle. 1995. 12.55 (*0-606-22783-0*) Turtleback Bks.
—Goose in the Pond. l.t. ed. 2001. (Beeler Large Print Mystery Ser.). 320p. 26.95 (*1-57490-335-7*, Beeler Large Print Bks.) Beeler, Thomas T. Publisher.
—Goose in the Pond. (Benni Harper Mystery Ser.: Vol. 4). 320p. 1998. mass mkt. 6.99 (*0-425-16239-7*); 1997. 21.95 o.s.i (*0-425-15782-2*) Berkley Publishing Group. (Prime Crime).
—Irish Chain. 320p. 1996. mass mkt. 6.99 (*0-425-15137-9*); 1995. 18.95 o.p. (*0-425-14619-7*, Prime Crime) Berkley Publishing Group.
—Kansas Troubles. l.t. ed. 2000. (Beeler Large Print Mystery Ser.). 329p. 25.95 (*1-57490-293-8*, Beeler Large Print Bks.) Beeler, Thomas T. Publisher.
—Kansas Troubles. 320p. 1996. 19.95 o.p. (*0-425-15148-4*); 1997. reprint ed. mass mkt. 6.99 (*0-425-15696-6*, Prime Crime) Berkley Publishing Group.
—Mariner's Compass: A Benni Harper Mystery. l.t. ed. 2001. (Beeler Large Print Mystery Ser.). 338p. 26.95 (*1-57490-401-9*, Beeler Large Print Bks.) Beeler, Thomas T. Publisher.
—Mariner's Compass: A Benni Harper Mystery. (Benni Harper Mystery Ser.: Vol. 6). 336p. 2000. mass mkt. 6.99 (*0-425-17408-5*); 1999. 21.95 o.s.i (*0-425-16891-3*, Prime Crime) Berkley Publishing Group.
—Seven Sisters. 2003. (Mystery Ser.). 27.95 (*1-57490-467-1*) Beeler, Thomas T. Publisher.
—Seven Sisters. 2000. (Benni Harper Mystery Ser.). 308p. 21.95 o.s.i (*0-425-17296-1*, Prime Crime) Berkley Publishing Group.
—Seven Sisters. 2001. 12.55 (*0-606-21883-1*) Turtleback Bks.
—Steps to the Altar. 2003. 320p. mass mkt. 6.99 (*0-425-18944-9*, Prime Crime) Berkley Publishing Group.
—Steps to the Altar. l.t. ed. 2002. (Wheeler Hardcover Ser.). 423p. 28.95 (*1-58724-280-X*, Wheeler Publishing, Inc.) Gale Group.
—Steps to the Altar: A Benni Harper Mystery. 2002. 320p. 22.95 (*0-425-18349-1*) Berkley Publishing Group.
—Sunshine & Shadow. 304p. 2004. mass mkt. 6.99 (*0-425-19528-7*); 2003. 22.95 (*0-425-18855-8*, Prime Crime) Berkley Publishing Group.
—Sunshine & Shadow. l.t. ed. 2003. 446p. 28.95 (*1-58724-475-6*, Wheeler Publishing, Inc.) Gale Group.

**HARPER, GOODWIN (FICTITIOUS CHARACTER)—FICTION**

*see Gourmet Detective (Fictitious Character)—Fiction*

**HARPER, NANCY (FICTITIOUS CHARACTER)—FICTION**

Babson, Marian. Paws for Alarm. 1998. (Dead Letter Mysteries Ser.). 272p. reprint ed. pap. 6.50 (*0-312-96513-3*, St. Martin's Paperbacks) St. Martin's Pr.

**HARPUR, COLIN (FICTITIOUS CHARACTER)—FICTION**

James, Bill, pseud. Astride a Grave. 1996. (Detective Colin Harpur Novel Ser.). 208p. reprint ed. 21.00 o.p. (*0-88150-361-4*, Foul Play) Norton, W. W. & Co., Inc.
—Club. 1995. (Detective Colin Harpur Novel Ser.). 224p. 20.00 o.p. (*0-88150-331-2*, Foul Play) Norton, W. W. & Co., Inc.
—Come Clean. 1992. (Detective Colin Harpur Novel Ser.). 256p. 20.00 (*0-88150-243-X*, Foul Play) Norton, W. W. & Co., Inc.
—The Detective Is Dead. 2001. (Harpur & Iles Ser.). 215p. 22.95 (*0-393-05019-X*) Norton, W. W. & Co., Inc.
—Eton Crop: A Harpur & Iles Mystery. (Harpur & Iles Ser.). 2000. 288p. pap. 7.95 (*0-393-32098-7*, Norton Paperbacks); 1999. 284p. 22.95 (*0-393-04761-X*) Norton, W. W. & Co., Inc.
—Gospel. l.t. ed. 1997. (G. K. Hall Core Ser.). 384p. lib. bdg. 25.95 (*0-7838-8236-X*, Macmillan Reference USA) Gale Group.
—Gospel. l.t. ed. (Harpur & Iles Ser.). 1998. 208p. pap. 10.00 (*0-393-31781-1*); 1997. 206p. 22.95 (*0-88150-383-5*) Norton, W. W. & Co., Inc.
—Halo Parade: A Harpur & Iles Mystery. (Harpur & Iles Ser.). 176p. 1998. pap. 10.00 (*0-393-31831-1*); 1991. reprint ed. 17.95 o.p. (*0-88150-204-9*) Norton, W. W. & Co., Inc. (Foul Play).
—In Good Hands. 2000. (Harpur & Iles Ser.). 214p. 22.95 (*0-393-05005-X*) Norton, W. W. & Co., Inc.
—Kill Me. (Harpur & Iles Ser.). 2001. (Illus.). 352p. pap. 15.95 (*0-393-32165-7*); 2000. 267p. 22.95 (*0-393-04920-5*) Norton, W. W. & Co., Inc.
—The Lolita Man. (Harpur & Iles Ser.). 1998. 160p. pap. 10.00 (*0-393-31782-X*); 1991. 158p. 17.95 (*0-88150-198-0*, Foul Play) Norton, W. W. & Co., Inc.
—Lovely Mover: A Harpur & Iles Mystery. (Harpur & Iles Ser.). 2000. 272p. pap. 7.95 (*0-393-32034-0*); 1999. 264p. 23.00 o.p. (*0-393-04763-6*, Foul Play) Norton, W. W. & Co., Inc.
—Lovely Mover: A Harpur & Iles Mystery. l.t. ed. 1998. (Mystery Ser.). 343p. 26.95 (*0-7862-1680-8*) Thorndike Pr.
—Naked at the Window: A Harpur & Iles Mystery. 2002. 224p. 23.95 (*0-393-05198-6*) Norton, W. W. & Co., Inc.
—Panicking Ralph. 2002. pap. 8.95 (*0-393-32306-4*); 2001. 288p. 24.95 (*0-393-04762-8*) Norton, W. W. & Co., Inc.
—Pay Days: A Harpur & Iles Mystery. 2001. 256p. 24.00 (*0-393-04214-6*) Norton, W. W. & Co., Inc.
—Protection. 1992. (Detective Colin Harpur Novel Ser.). 188p. 18.95 o.p. (*0-88150-231-6*) Norton, W. W. & Co., Inc.
—Roses, Roses: A Harpur & Iles Mystery. (Harpur & Iles Ser.). 1999. 208p. pap. 7.95 (*0-393-31925-3*); 1998. 216p. 23.00 o.p. (*0-393-04637-0*) Norton, W. W. & Co., Inc.
—Take. 1994. (Harpur & Iles Ser.). 240p. reprint ed. 20.00 (*0-88150-294-4*, Foul Play) Norton, W. W. & Co., Inc.
—Top Banana: A Harpur & Iles Mystery. l.t. ed. 1999. (Core Ser.). 306p. 27.95 (*0-7838-8717-5*, Macmillan Reference USA) Gale Group.
—Top Banana: A Harpur & Iles Mystery. (Harpur & Iles Ser.). 2000. 288p. pap. 7.95 (*0-393-31969-5*, Norton Paperbacks); 1999. 284p. 23.00 o.p. (*0-393-04718-0*) Norton, W. W. & Co., Inc.
—You'd Better Believe It. 1991. (Detective Chief Superintendent Colin Harper Novels / By Bill Ser.). 158p. pap. 4.95 (*0-88150-197-2*, Foul Play) Norton, W. W. & Co., Inc.
—You'd Better Believe It. 1985. 192p. pap. 12.95 o.p. (*0-312-89683-2*) St. Martin's Pr.

**HARRIGAN, PETER (FICTITIOUS CHARACTER)—FICTION**

Blum, Bill. The Last Appeal. 1997. 416p. mass mkt. 6.99 o.s.i (*0-451-18311-8*, Signet Bks.) NAL.

**HARRINGTON, HONOR (FICTITIOUS CHARACTER)—FICTION**

Pournelle, Jerry, et al. The Houses of the Kzinti. 2002. 448p. pap. 15.00 (*0-7434-3577-X*) Baen Bks.
Robinson, Spider. Lady Slings the Booze. 2002. 352p. pap. 7.99 (*0-7434-3578-8*) Baen Bks.
Weber, David. Ashes of Victory: An Honor Harrington Novel. 2000. (Honor Harrington Ser.). (Illus.). 576p. 25.00 (*0-671-57854-5*) Baen Bks.
—Echoes of Honor. (Honor Harrington Ser.). 1998. (Illus.). 592p. 24.00 (*0-671-87892-1*); 1999. 736p. reprint ed. pap. 7.99 (*0-671-57833-2*) Baen Bks.
—Field of Dishonor. 2002. 416p. pap. 7.99 (*0-7434-3574-5*); 1994. (Honor Harrington Ser.: Vol. 4). 384p. mass mkt. 6.99 (*0-671-87624-4*) Baen Bks.
—Field of Dishonor: Special Edition. 1999. (Honor Harrington Ser.). 320p. 4.99 o.s.i (*0-671-57820-0*) Baen Bks.
—Flag in Exile. 2002. 480p. pap. 7.99 (*0-7434-3575-3*); 2001. 416p. 10.00 (*0-671-31980-9*); 2002. 448p. reprint ed. mass mkt. 7.99 (*0-671-87681-3*) Baen Bks.
—The Honor of the Queen. 2002. 464p. mass mkt. 7.99 (*0-7434-3572-9*); 2000. (Illus.). 384p. 5.99 o.s.i (*0-671-57864-2*); 1993. 432p. mass mkt. 7.99 (*0-671-72172-0*) Baen Bks.
—In Enemy Hands. 1998. (Honor Harrington Ser.). 544p. pap. 7.99 (*0-671-57770-0*) Baen Bks.
—In Enemy Hands: An Honor Harrington Novel. 1997. (Honor Harrington Ser.: Vol. 7). 544p. 22.00 (*0-671-87793-3*) Baen Bks.
—On Basilisk Station. 2002. 464p. pap. 7.99 (*0-7434-3571-0*); 1993. 432p. mass mkt. 6.99 (*0-671-72163-1*); 1998. 352p. mass mkt. 1.99 (*0-671-57772-7*) Baen Bks.
—On Basilisk Station: Collectors Edition. deluxe ed. 1999. 336p. 18.00 (*0-671-57793-X*) Baen Bks.
—The Service of the Sword. 2003. (Worlds of Honor Ser.: Bk. 4). 496p. 26.00 (*0-7434-3599-0*) Baen Bks.
—The Short Victorious War. 2002. 352p. pap. 14.00 (*0-7434-3546-X*); (Honor Harrington Ser.: Vol. 3). 384p. mass mkt. 6.99 o.s.i (*0-671-87596-5*) Baen Bks.
—War of Honor. 2002. audio 35.00 (*0-7435-0700-2*); audio compact disk 39.95 (*0-7435-0701-0*) Simon & Schuster Audio. (Simon & Schuster Audioworks).
—Worlds of Honor. 2000. (Honor Harrington Ser.). 416p. pap. 6.99 (*0-671-57855-3*) Baen Bks.
Weber, David & Flint, Eric. Worlds of Honor: Changer of Worlds, 2 vols., Vol. 3. 2001. 374p. 25.00 (*0-671-31975-2*) Baen Bks.
Weber, David Martin. Honor among Enemies. (Honor Harrington Ser.: Vol. 6). 544p. 1996. 21.00 (*0-671-87723-2*); 1997. reprint ed. pap. 7.99 (*0-671-87783-6*) Baen Bks.

**HARRISON, CATHERINE (FICTITIOUS CHARACTER)—FICTION**

Sauter, Stacey. Immaculate Deception. 1997. 416p. mass mkt. 5.99 o.s.i (*0-451-19135-8*, Signet Bks.) NAL.

**HARRISON, CHIP (FICTITIOUS CHARACTER)—FICTION**

Block, Lawrence. Chip Harrison Scores Again. 1997. (Chip Harrison Mysteries Ser.). 256p. mass mkt. 5.99 o.s.i (*0-451-18797-0*, Signet Bks.) NAL.
—Make Out with Murder. unabr. ed. 1999. (Chip Harrison Mystery Ser.). audio 39.95 (*0-7927-2291-4*, CSL180, Chivers Sound Library) BBC Audiobooks America.
—Make Out with Murder. 1997. (Chip Harrison Mystery Ser.). 240p. mass mkt. 5.99 o.s.i (*0-451-18798-9*, Signet Bks.) NAL.
—No Score. unabr. ed. 2000. (Chip Harrison Mystery Ser.: Bk. 1). audio 54.95 (*0-7927-2262-0*, CSL 151) Chivers Audio Bks. GBR. *Dist:* BBC Audiobooks America.
—No Score. 1996. (Chip Harrison Mystery Ser.). 277p. mass mkt. 5.50 o.s.i (*0-451-18796-2*, Signet Bks.) NAL.
—The Topless Tulip Caper: A Chip Harrison Mystery. unabr. ed. 1999. (Chip Harrison Mystery Ser.). audio 39.95 (*0-7927-2303-1*, CSL192, Chivers Sound Library) BBC Audiobooks America.
—The Topless Tulip Caper: A Chip Harrison Mystery. 1998. (Chip Harrison Mystery Ser.). 272p. mass mkt. 5.99 o.s.i (*0-451-18799-7*, Signet Bks.) NAL.

**HARRISON, EMALINE (FICTITIOUS CHARACTER)—FICTION**

Kirkland, Martha. The Ruby Necklace. 1996. 224p. mass mkt. 4.99 o.s.i (*0-451-18720-2*, Signet Bks.) NAL.

**HARRISON, RICHARD (FICTITIOUS CHARACTER)—FICTION**

Anthony, Michael D. Becket Factor. 1991. 17.95 o.p. (*0-312-05821-7*, Saint Martin's Minotaur) St. Martin's Pr.
—Dark Provenance. 1995. 256p. 21.00 o.p. (*0-312-11767-1*, Saint Martin's Minotaur) St. Martin's Pr.
—Dark Provenance. l.t. ed. 1995. (Ulverscroft Large Print Ser.). 528p. 29.99 o.p. (*0-7089-3324-6*, Ulverscroft) Thorpe, F. A. Pubs. GBR. *Dist:* Ulverscroft Large Print Bks., Ltd., Ulverscroft Large Print Canada, Ltd.
—Midnight Come. 1999. 302p. 22.95 (*0-312-20058-7*, Saint Martin's Minotaur) St. Martin's Pr.

**HARROD, KATE (FICTITIOUS CHARACTER)—FICTION**

Coburn, Laura. Lying Silence. 1997. 416p. mass mkt. 5.99 o.s.i (*0-451-40641-9*, Onyx) NAL.
—Uncertain Death. 1996. 368p. mass mkt. 5.99 o.s.i (*0-451-40640-0*, Onyx) NAL.

**HARTE, EMMA (FICTITIOUS CHARACTER)—FICTION**

Bradford, Barbara Taylor. Hold the Dream. 1986. mass mkt. 4.50 o.s.i (*0-553-25621-1*); 688p. mass mkt. 6.99 o.s.i (*0-553-26554-7*) Bantam Bks.
—Hold the Dream. l.t. ed. 1985. (General Ser.). 1074p. 19.95 o.p. (*0-8161-3980-6*); 11.95 o.p. (*0-8161-3981-4*) Gale Group. (Macmillan Reference USA).
—Hold the Dream. unabr. ed. 2001. audio 69.95 (*1-85695-995-3*, 950903) ISIS Audio Bks. GBR. *Dist:* Ulverscroft Large Print Bks., Ltd.
—Hold the Dream. 1994. 768p. mass mkt. 7.50 (*0-06-100808-7*, HarperTorch) Morrow/Avon.
—To Be the Best. 1989. 448p. mass mkt. 6.99 o.s.i (*0-553-27953-X*); 1988. mass mkt. o.s.i (*0-553-17324-3*) Bantam Bks.
—To Be the Best. unabr. ed. 2000. 14p. audio compact disk 97.95 (*0-7531-0975-1*, 109751); 1998. audio 94.95 (*1-85695-710-1*, 940203) ISIS Audio Bks. GBR. *Dist:* Ulverscroft Large Print Bks., Ltd.
—To Be the Best. 1994. 496p. mass mkt. 6.50 (*0-06-100809-5*, HarperTorch) Morrow/Avon.
—A Woman of Substance. 1987. mass mkt. 4.50 o.s.i (*0-553-26534-2*); 832p. mass mkt. 6.99 o.s.i (*0-553-27790-1*) Bantam Bks.
—A Woman of Substance. 1984. 768p. 25.00 o.s.i (*0-385-12050-8*) Doubleday Publishing.
—A Woman of Substance. l.t. ed. 1987. 1286p. 21.95 o.p. (*0-8161-4240-8*); 14.95 o.p. (*0-8161-4239-4*) Gale Group. (Macmillan Reference USA).
—A Woman of Substance. 1994. 928p. mass mkt. 7.99 (*0-06-100807-9*, HarperTorch); 1980. 832p. pap. 4.50 (*0-380-49163-X*, Avon Bks.) Morrow/Avon.

**HARTRIGHT, WALTER (FICTITIOUS CHARACTER)—FICTION**

Collins, Wilkie. The Woman in White. 1976. reprint ed. lib. bdg. 35.95 (*0-89190-242-2*, Rivercity Pr.) Amereon, Ltd.
—The Woman in White, Set. unabr. ed. 1998. 89.95 incl. audio (*1-55685-525-7*) Audio Bk. Contractors, Inc.
—The Woman in White. unabr. ed. audio 114.95 o.p. (*1-85549-918-5*, CTC 018) BBC Audiobooks America.
—The Woman in White. 1985. mass mkt. 3.50 o.s.i (*0-553-21186-2*); 576p. mass mkt. 5.95 (*0-553-21263-X*) Bantam Bks. (Bantam Classics).
—The Woman in White. unabr. collector's ed. 1987. Pt. 1. audio 80.00 (*0-7366-3931-4*, 9169-A); Pt. 2. audio 72.00 (*0-7366-3932-2*, 9169-B) Books on Tape, Inc.
—The Woman in White. 1990. reprint ed. lib. bdg. 30.95 (*0-89968-499-8*) Buccaneer Bks., Inc.
—The Woman in White. reprint ed. Pt. 1. 2001. 575p. pap. text 28.00 (*0-7426-5022-7*); Pt. 1. 1999. (Works of Wilkie Collins: Vol. 1). 575p. lib. bdg. 98.00 (*1-58201-022-6*); Pt. 2. 1999. (Works of Wilkie Collins: Vol. 2). 556p. lib. bdg. 98.00 (*1-58201-023-4*) Classic Bks.
—The Woman in White. audio 97.95 Cover to Cover Cassettes, Ltd.
—The Woman in White. 1972. 2.95 o.p. (*0-460-01464-1*); 1955. 6.00 o.p. (*0-460-00464-6*) Dutton/Plume. (Dutton).
—The Woman in White. E-Book 2.49 (*0-7574-0472-3*) Electric Umbrella Publishing.
—The Woman in White, 001. Tillotson, Kathleen, ed. 1969. (C). mass mkt. 3.95 o.p. (*0-395-05211-4*, B116, Riverside Editions) Houghton Mifflin Co.
—The Woman in White. l.t. ed. 1990. 734p. 27.95 (*1-85089-470-1*) ISIS Large Print Bks. GBR. *Dist:* Transaction Pubs., Ulverscroft Large Print Canada, Ltd.
—The Woman in White. 1989. audio 89.00 Jimcin Recordings.
—The Woman in White. 1991. (Everyman's Library). 656p. 20.00 (*0-679-40563-1*, Everyman's Library) Knopf Publishing Group.
—The Woman in White. 1985. 630p. mass mkt. 5.95 o.s.i (*0-451-52437-3*, Signet Classics) NAL.
—The Woman in White. Sutherland, John, ed. & intro. by. 1998. (Oxford World's Classics Ser.). 736p. pap. 7.95 (*0-19-283429-0*) Oxford Univ. Pr., Inc.
—The Woman in White. Sucksmith, Harvey P., ed. 1981. (Oxford World's Classics Ser.). 662p. reprint ed. pap. 5.95 o.p. (*0-19-281534-2*) Oxford Univ. Pr., Inc.
—The Woman in White. Sutherland, John, ed. 2nd ed. 1996. (Oxford World's Classics Ser.). 734p. (C). pap. 6.95 o.p. (*0-19-282403-1*) Oxford Univ. Pr., Inc.
—The Woman in White. 2002. (Modern Library Classics). 704p. pap. 7.95 (*0-375-75906-9*, Modern Library) Random House Adult Trade Publishing Group.
—The Woman in White. 1998. (Works of Wilkie Collins: Vol. 1). 575p. reprint ed. lib. bdg. 90.00 (*0-7812-7716-7*) Reprint Services Corp.
—The Woman in White. (Classics Ser.). 720p. 2003. pap. 8.00 (*0-14-143961-0*, Penguin Classics); 2000. 7.95 (*0-14-043731-2*) Viking Penguin.
—The Woman in White. Symons, Julian, ed. 1982. pap. 3.95 o.p. (*0-14-005980-6*, Penguin Bks.); 1975. 656p. pap. 7.95 o.s.i (*0-14-043096-2*, Penguin Classics) Viking Penguin.
—The Woman in White. abr. ed. 1995. 4p. 23.95 o.s.i incl. audio (*0-14-086061-4*, Penguin AudioBooks) Viking Penguin.
—The Woman in White. 1998. (Wordsworth Collection). 512p. pap. 3.95 (*1-85326-077-0*, 0770WW) Wordsworth Editions, Ltd. GBR. *Dist:* Combined Publishing.

**HARWICK, EMERALD (FICTITIOUS CHARACTER)—FICTION**

Chaikin, Linda L. The Pirate & His Lady. 1997. (Buccaneers Ser.: No. 2). 384p. pap. 11.99 (*0-8024-1072-3*, 251) Moody Pr.

**HASKELL, BENTLEY (FICTITIOUS CHARACTER)—FICTION**

Cannell, Dorothy. Femmes Fatal. 1994. 304p. mass mkt. 6.99 (*0-553-29684-1*) Bantam Bks.
—Femmes Fatal. l.t. ed. 1993. (General Ser.). 385p. 21.95 o.p. (*0-8161-5654-9*, Macmillan Reference USA) Gale Group.
—How to Murder the Man of Your Dreams. 1996. 304p. mass mkt. 6.99 (*0-553-57360-8*) Bantam Bks.
—How to Murder the Man of Your Dreams. l.t. ed. 1996. 428p. 23.95 o.p. (*0-7838-1493-3*, Macmillan Reference USA) Gale Group.
—How to Murder Your Mother-in-Law. 1995. 288p. mass mkt. 6.50 (*0-553-56951-1*); 1994. 272p. 19.95 o.s.i (*0-553-07493-8*) Bantam Bks.
—How to Murder Your Mother-in-Law. unabr. ed. 1994. audio 57.25 o.p. (*1-56100-178-3*, 904, Unabridged Library Editions); audio 21.95 o.p. (*1-56100-552-5*, 141, Bookcassette) Brilliance Audio.
—How to Murder Your Mother-in-Law. l.t. ed. 1994. 385p. lib. bdg. 23.95 (*0-8161-5930-0*, Macmillan Reference USA) Gale Group.
—Mum's the Word. 1991. 272p. mass mkt. 6.50 o.s.i (*0-553-28686-2*) Bantam Bks.
—Mum's the Word. l.t. ed. 2001. (Beeler Large Print Mystery Ser.). 324p. 26.95 (*1-57490-352-7*, Beeler Large Print Bks.) Beeler, Thomas T. Publisher.
—The Spring Cleaning Murders: An Ellie Haskell Mystery. l.t. ed. 1998. (Beeler Large Print Mystery Ser.). 26.95 (*1-57490-162-1*, Beeler Large Print Bks.) Beeler, Thomas T. Publisher.
—The Spring Cleaning Murders: An Ellie Haskell Mystery. 1999. (Ellie Haskell Mysteries Ser.). 288p. pap. 6.99 (*0-14-027615-7*) Penguin Group (USA) Inc.
—The Spring Cleaning Murders: An Ellie Haskell Mystery. 1998. (Ellie Haskell Mysteries Ser.). 256p. 21.95 o.p. (*0-670-87571-6*, Viking) Viking Penguin.
—The Thin Woman: An Epicurean Mystery. 1992. 304p. mass mkt. 6.99 (*0-553-29195-5*) Bantam Bks.
—The Thin Woman: An Epicurean Mystery. l.t. ed. 2000. 376p. lib. bdg. 28.95 (*1-58547-008-2*) Ctr. Point Large Print.
—The Thin Woman: An Epicurean Mystery. 1984. 288p. 13.95 o.p. (*0-312-80005-3*) St. Martin's Pr.
—The Thin Woman: An Epicurean Mystery. 1985. (Crime Monthly Ser.). 256p. pap. 4.50 o.p. (*0-14-007947-5*, Penguin Bks.) Viking Penguin.
—The Widows' Club. 1989. 352p. mass mkt. 6.99 (*0-553-27794-4*) Bantam Bks.

**HASKELL, ELLIE (FICTITIOUS CHARACTER)—FICTION**

*see Simons, Ellie (Fictitious Character)—Fiction*

**HASKELL, VEJAY (FICTITIOUS CHARACTER)—FICTION**

Dunlap, Susan. The Bohemian Connection. 1994. 240p. pap. 15.00 o.s.i (*0-440-61356-6*); mass mkt. 5.50 o.s.i (*0-440-21569-2*) Dell Publishing.
—The Bohemian Connection. 1985. 192p. 12.95 o.p. (*0-312-08745-4*, 087454) St. Martin's Pr.
—An Equal Opportunity Death. 1994. 240p. mass mkt. 5.50 o.s.i (*0-440-21566-8*) Dell Publishing.
—An Equal Opportunity Death: A Mystery. 1984. 192p. 12.95 o.p. (*0-312-25775-9*) St. Martin's Pr.
—The Last Annual Slugfest. 1994. 256p. mass mkt. 4.99 o.s.i (*0-440-21558-7*) Dell Publishing.
—The Last Annual Slugfest. 1986. 224p. 14.95 o.p. (*0-312-46969-1*) St. Martin's Pr.

**HASTINGS, ARTHUR, CAPTAIN (FICTITIOUS CHARACTER)—FICTION**

Christie, Agatha. Black Coffee. l.t. ed. 1999. 26.95 o.p. (*1-56895-625-8*, Wheeler Publishing, Inc.) Gale Group.
—Black Coffee. unabr. ed. 1998. (Hercule Poirot Mystery Ser.). 6p. audio 24.95 (*1-55935-281-7*, 696051) Soundelux Audio Publishing.
—Black Coffee. (Hercule Poirot Mystery Ser.). 1998. (Illus.). 221p. 22.95 o.p. (*0-312-19241-X*, Saint Martin's Minotaur); 3rd ed. 1999. 290p. mass mkt. 6.99 (*0-312-97007-2*, St. Martin's Paperbacks) St. Martin's Pr.
—Black Coffee. abr. ed. 1998. audio 24.35 (*0-00-105536-4*) Ulverscroft Audio (U.S.A.).
—Curtain. 1976. 22.95 (*0-88411-386-8*) Amereon, Ltd.
—Curtain. 2000. (Hercule Poirot Mystery Ser.). 224p. mass mkt. 5.99 (*0-425-17374-7*) Berkley Publishing Group.
—Curtain. pap. 14.95 (*0-8161-4540-7*); 1992. 289p. lib. bdg. 19.95 o.p. (*0-8161-4539-3*) Gale Group. (Macmillan Reference USA).
—Curtain. 1995. 24.95 (*0-399-14016-6*, Philomel) Penguin Group (USA) Inc.
—Curtain. 1985. 288p. mass mkt. 4.99 o.p. (*0-671-54717-8*, Pocket) Simon & Schuster.
—Curtain. 1993. 12.04 (*0-606-12235-4*) Turtleback Bks.
—The Mysterious Affair at Styles. 22.95 (*0-88411-385-X*) Amereon, Ltd.
—The Mysterious Affair at Styles, 1995. audio 29.95 (*1-55685-373-4*) Audio Bk. Contractors, Inc.
—The Mysterious Affair at Styles. unabr. ed. 2004. audio compact disk 29.95 (*1-57270-297-4*); 1996. audio 22.95 (*1-57270-017-3*, N51017u, Audio Editions Mystery Masters) Audio Partners Publishing Corp.
—The Mysterious Affair at Styles. abr. ed. 2003. (Agatha Christie Audio Mystery Ser.). (Illus.). audio 12.95 (*1-55927-906-0*); audio 12.95 (*1-55927-906-0*) Audio Renaissance.
—The Mysterious Affair at Styles. 1992. 19.95 incl. audio (*1-882071-21-2*); 1992. 19.95 incl. audio (*1-882071-21-2*); 1998. audio 19.95 (*1-882071-59-X*, 023) B&B Audio, Inc.
—The Mysterious Affair at Styles. 1983. mass mkt. 2.95 o.s.i (*0-553-24093-5*); mass mkt. 3.50 o.s.i (*0-553-26547-4*); 192p. mass mkt. 3.50 o.s.i (*0-553-26587-3*) Bantam Bks.
—The Mysterious Affair at Styles. 1920. E-Book (*1-58734-006-2*) Bartleby.com.
—The Mysterious Affair at Styles. 1991. 208p. mass mkt. 5.99 (*0-425-12961-6*) Berkley Publishing Group.
—The Mysterious Affair at Styles. audio 26.95 (*1-885546-07-6*) Big Ben Audio, Inc.
—The Mysterious Affair at Styles. unabr. ed. 2000. audio compact disk 48.00 (*0-7861-9928-8*, z1362); 1996. audio 39.95 (*0-7861-0410-4*, 1362) Blackstone Audio Bks., Inc.
—The Mysterious Affair at Styles. unabr. collector's ed. 1996. audio 48.00 (*0-7366-3226-3*, 3887) Books on Tape, Inc.
—The Mysterious Affair at Styles. 1997. (Dover Mystery Classics Ser.). 160p. reprint ed. pap. text 2.00 (*0-486-29695-4*) Dover Pubns., Inc.
—The Mysterious Affair at Styles. E-Book 2.49 (*0-7574-0366-2*) Electric Umbrella Publishing.
—The Mysterious Affair at Styles. 1980. pap. 8.95 o.p. (*0-8161-3105-8*); 1976. lib. bdg. 10.95 o.p. (*0-8161-6343-X*); 1992. lib. bdg. 19.95 o.p. (*0-8161-4575-X*) Gale Group. (Macmillan Reference USA).
—The Mysterious Affair at Styles, unabr. ed. 1999. audio 39.95 Highsmith Inc.
—The Mysterious Affair at Styles. 2002. 208p. 94.99 (*1-4043-1778-3*); per. 89.99 (*1-4043-1779-1*) IndyPublish.com.
—The Mysterious Affair at Styles. E-Book 2.95 (*1-57799-964-9*); E-Book 2.95 (*1-57799-806-5*) Logos Research Systems, Inc.
—The Mysterious Affair at Styles. 2001. (Twelve-Point Ser.). 205p. lib. bdg. 25.00 (*1-58287-171-X*); 310p. lib. bdg. 26.00 (*1-58287-654-1*) North Bks.
—The Mysterious Affair at Styles. 1985. (Agatha Christie Ser.). 236p. 12.95 o.s.i (*0-396-08703-5*, G. P. Putnam's Sons) Penguin Putnam Bks. for Young Readers.
—The Mysterious Affair at Styles. 1999. E-Book 8.99 incl. cd-rom (*1-891595-60-1*) Quiet Vision Publishing.
—The Mysterious Affair at Styles. 2003. (Illus.). 240p. pap. 9.95 (*0-8129-7010-1*, Modern Library) Random House Adult Trade Publishing Group.
—The Mysterious Affair at Styles. (Ebook Classic Ser.). E-Book 5.00 (*0-7410-0495-X*) SoftBook Pr.
—The Mysterious Affair at Styles. l.t. ed. 2001. (Ulverscroft Large Print Ser.). 32.50 o.p. (*0-7089-1955-3*) Ulverscroft Large Print Bks., Ltd.
—The Mysterious Affair at Styles. 2002. 188p. pap. 16.95 (*1-59224-889-6*); lib. bdg. 29.95 (*1-59224-888-8*) Wildside Pr.
—The Mysterious Affair at Styles & The Secret Adversary: An Agatha Christie Omnibus. 1998. 464p. pap. 12.95 (*0-7867-0434-9*, Carroll & Graf Pubs.) Avalon Publishing Group.

**HASTINGS, FRANK (FICTITIOUS CHARACTER)—FICTION**

Pronzini, Bill & Wilcox, Collin. Two-Spot. 1993. 272p. mass mkt. 12.95 (*0-7867-0042-4*, Carroll & Graf Pubs.) Avalon Publishing Group.
—Two-Spot. 1978. 8.95 o.p. (*0-399-12129-3*) Putnam Publishing Group, The.
Wilcox, Collin. Aftershock. unabr. ed. 1997. (Frank Hastings Ser.). audio 48.00 (*0-7366-3554-8*, 4199) Books on Tape, Inc.
—Dead Aim. unabr. ed. 1996. (Frank Hastings Ser.). audio 48.00 (*0-7366-3373-1*, 4023) Books on Tape, Inc.
—Dead Center. unabr. ed. 1993. (Frank Hastings Ser.). audio 48.00 (*0-7366-2519-4*, 3274) Books on Tape, Inc.
—Dead Center. 1995. pap. 5.95 o.p. (*0-8050-4232-6*, Owl Bks.); 1992. 256p. 18.95 o.p. (*0-8050-1615-5*) Holt, Henry & Co.
—A Death Before Dying. unabr. ed. 1992. (Frank Hastings Ser.). audio 56.00 (*0-7366-2212-8*, 3005) Books on Tape, Inc.
—A Death Before Dying. 1994. 231p. pap. 5.95 o.p. (*0-8050-3122-7*, Owl Bks.) Holt, Henry & Co.
—A Death Before Dying: A Lt. Hastings Mystery. 1990. 240p. 18.95 o.p. (*0-8050-0979-5*) Holt, Henry & Co.
—The Disappearance. 19.95 (*0-89190-580-4*) Amereon, Ltd.
—The Disappearance. unabr. ed. 1996. (Frank Hastings Ser.). audio 48.00 (*0-7366-3346-4*, 3996) Books on Tape, Inc.
—Doctor, Lawyer ... 1981. (Mystery Ser.). 192p. 1.95 o.s.i (*0-515-05194-2*, Jove) Berkley Publishing Group.
—Doctor, Lawyer ... 1977. 6.95 o.p. (*0-394-40061-5*) Random Hse., Inc.
—Doctor, Lawyer... unabr. ed. 1997. (Frank Hastings Ser.). audio 48.00 (*0-7366-3530-0*, 4168) Books on Tape, Inc.
—Hiding Place. 20.95 (*0-89190-581-2*) Amereon, Ltd.
—Hiding Place. unabr. ed. 1996. (Frank Hastings Ser.). audio 48.00 (*0-7366-3404-5*, 4050) Books on Tape, Inc.
—Hire a Hangman. 1994. 248p. pap. 5.95 o.p. (*0-8050-3121-9*, Owl Bks.) Holt, Henry & Co.
—Hire a Hangman: A Lt. Hastings Mystery. Haun, Joann, ed. 1991. 256p. 18.95 o.p. (*0-8050-0980-9*) Holt, Henry & Co.
—The Lonely Hunter. unabr. ed. 1996. (Frank Hastings Ser.). audio 48.00 (*0-7366-3325-1*, 3977) Books on Tape, Inc.
—Long Way Down. unabr. ed. 1996. (Frank Hastings Ser.). audio 48.00 (*0-7366-3474-6*, 4117) Books on Tape, Inc.
—Mankiller. unabr. ed. 1997. (Frank Hastings Ser.). audio 48.00 (*0-7366-3788-5*, 4462) Books on Tape, Inc.
—Mankiller. 1980. 224p. 8.95 o.p. (*0-394-50550-6*) Random Hse., Inc.
—Night Games. 1986. 240p. 15.45 o.p. (*0-89296-160-0*) Mysterious Pr.
—Night Games. 1987. 240p. mass mkt. 3.95 o.s.i (*0-445-40590-2*, Mysterious Pr. Paperback Bks.) Warner Bks., Inc.
—The Pariah. 1988. 15.45 o.p. (*0-89296-280-1*) Mysterious Pr.
—The Pariah. 1989. mass mkt. 4.95 (*0-445-40790-5*, Mysterious Pr. Paperback Bks.) Warner Bks., Inc.
—Power Plays. 21.95 (*0-89190-582-0*) Amereon, Ltd.
—Power Plays. unabr. ed. 1997. (Frank Hastings Ser.). audio 48.00 (*0-7366-3737-0*, 4414) Books on Tape, Inc.
—Power Plays. 1979. 7.95 o.p. (*0-394-50172-1*) Random Hse., Inc.
—Stalking Horse: A Mystery. 1982. 10.50 o.p. (*0-394-51173-5*) Random Hse., Inc.
—Switchback. unabr. ed. 1994. (Frank Hastings Ser.). audio 56.00 (*0-7366-2701-4*, 3435) Books on Tape, Inc.
—Switchback. 1995. 89p. pap. 5.95 o.p. (*0-8050-4233-4*, Owl Bks.) Holt, Henry & Co.
—Switchback: A Lt. Hastings Mystery. 1993. 256p. 19.95 o.p. (*0-8050-2104-3*) Holt, Henry & Co.
—Victims. 1986. 14.95 o.p. (*0-89296-066-3*); pap. 3.95 o.p. (*0-445-40252-0*) Mysterious Pr.

**HASTINGS, STANLEY (FICTITIOUS CHARACTER)—FICTION**

Hall, Parnell. Actor. 1993. 288p. 19.95 (*0-89296-520-7*) Mysterious Pr.
—Actor. 1994. 304p. mass mkt. 5.50 (*0-446-40364-4*, Mysterious Pr. Paperback Bks.) Warner Bks., Inc.
—Blackmail. 1994. 288p. 19.95 o.p. (*0-89296-521-5*) Mysterious Pr.
—Blackmail. 1995. 304p. mass mkt. 5.99 o.s.i (*0-446-40365-2*) Warner Bks., Inc.
—Client. 1990. 18.95 o.p. (*1-55611-169-X*) Fine, Donald I. Bks.
—Client. 1991. 272p. mass mkt. 4.50 o.p. (*0-451-40249-9*, Onyx) NAL.
—Cozy: A Stanley Hastings Mystery. l.t. ed. 2002. 26.95 (*1-57490-417-5*) Beeler, Thomas T. Publisher.
—Detective. 1987. 300p. 17.95 o.p. (*1-55611-026-X*) Fine, Donald I. Bks.
—Detective. 1988. 256p. mass mkt. 3.95 o.p. (*0-451-40070-4*, Onyx) NAL.
—Favor. 1988. 17.95 o.p. (*1-55611-096-0*) Fine, Donald I. Bks.
—Favor. 1989. mass mkt. 3.95 o.p. (*0-451-40161-1*, 035, Onyx) NAL.
—Favor. 2002. 186p. pap. 6.99 (*0-7592-1854-4*); E-Book 6.99 (*0-7592-1849-8*); E-Book 6.99 (*0-7592-1851-X*); E-Book 6.99 (*0-7592-1850-1*) ereads.com.
—Juror. 1990. 18.95 o.p. (*1-55611-230-0*) Fine, Donald I. Bks.
—Juror. 1992. 304p. mass mkt. 4.99 o.p. (*0-451-40316-9*, Onyx) NAL.
—Manslaughter: A Stanley Hastings Mystery. 2003. (Otto Penzler Book Ser.). 320p. 25.00 (*0-7867-1127-2*, Carroll & Graf Pubs.) Avalon Publishing Group.
—Movie. 1995. 82p. 19.95 o.p. (*0-89296-569-X*) Mysterious Pr.
—Movie. 1996. 288p. mass mkt. 5.99 (*0-446-40395-4*) Warner Bks., Inc.
—Murder. 1988. 256p. 17.95 o.s.i (*1-55611-058-8*) Fine, Donald I. Bks.
—Murder. 2002. 256p. reprint ed. pap. 13.95 (*1-58754-111-4*, Olmstead Pr.) Moyer Bell.
—Murder. 1989. mass mkt. 3.95 o.p. (*0-451-40110-7*, Onyx) NAL.
—Murder. E-Book 6.99 (*0-7592-1545-6*) ereads.com.
—Scam. 1998. 336p. pap. 6.50 (*0-446-40469-1*, Mysterious Pr. Paperback Bks.) Warner Bks., Inc.
—Scam: A Stanley Hastings Mystery. l.t. ed. 1997. (Americana Ser.). 463p. 26.95 (*0-7862-1210-1*) Thorndike Pr.
—Scam: A Stanley Hastings Mystery. 1997. 320p. 21.50 o.p. (*0-89296-623-8*) Warner Bks., Inc.
—Shot. 1993. 320p. mass mkt. 4.99 o.p. (*0-451-40354-1*, Onyx) NAL.
—Shot: A Stanley Hastings Novel of Suspense. 1991. 18.95 o.p. (*1-55611-239-4*) Fine, Donald I. Bks.
—Strangler. 1989. 304p. 16.95 o.p. (*1-55611-125-8*) Fine, Donald I. Bks.
—Strangler. 1990. mass mkt. 4.50 o.p. (*0-451-40217-0*, Onyx) NAL.
—Suspense: A Stanley Hastings Mystery Novel. 1998. 320p. 23.00 o.p. (*0-89296-624-6*) Mysterious Pr.
—Trial. 1996. 82p. 21.95 o.s.i (*0-89296-570-3*) Mysterious Pr.
—Trial. 1997. 288p. mass mkt. 5.99 (*0-446-40396-2*) Warner Bks., Inc.

**HATCH, JAKE (FICTITIOUS CHARACTER)—FICTION**

Campbell, Robert. Red Cent. Chelius, Jane, ed. 1991. mass mkt. 4.50 (*0-671-74586-7*, Pocket) Simon & Schuster.
Campbell, Robert & Chelius, Jane, eds. Plugged Nickel. 1988. mass mkt. 4.99 (*0-671-64363-0*, Pocket) Simon & Schuster.

**HATCHER, CHRISTIAN (FICTITIOUS CHARACTER)—FICTION**

Diehl, William. Thai Horse. 1996. mass mkt. 5.99 (*0-345-90985-2*); 1989. 416p. mass mkt. 7.99 (*0-345-32745-4*); 1988. mass mkt. 4.95 o.s.i (*0-345-35782-5*) Ballantine Bks.

**HATFIELD, JIM (FICTITIOUS CHARACTER)—FICTION**

Cole, Jackson. The Death Riders. 1999. 167 p. (*0-7540-3651-0*); pap. (*0-7540-3652-9*) BBC Audiobooks America.
—The Death Riders. l.t. ed. 1999. (Nightingale Ser.). 176p. pap. 20.95 (*0-7838-0445-8*) Thorndike Pr.
—Fast Draw. l.t. ed. 2002. 180p. pap. 22.95 (*0-7862-3941-7*) Gale Group.
—Hell in Paradise. l.t. ed. 2001. 195p. pap. 22.95 (*0-7838-9566-6*) Thorndike Pr.
—Thunder Range: A Jim Hatfield Texas Ranger Western. l.t. ed. 1998. (Nightingale Ser.). 168p. pap. 20.95 (*0-7838-0244-7*) Thorndike Pr.
—Two-Gun Devil. l.t. ed. 2000. (G. K. Hall Nightingale Ser.). 208p. pap. 20.95 (*0-7838-8847-3*); (*0-7540-4015-1*) Gale Group. (Macmillan Reference USA).

**HAVERS, BARBARA (FICTITIOUS CHARACTER)—FICTION**

George, Elizabeth. Deception on His Mind. 1998. 752p. mass mkt. 7.99 (*0-553-57509-0*); mass mkt. 6.99 (*0-553-84018-5*) Bantam Bks.
—Deception on His Mind, Pt. A. unabr. ed. 1997. audio 64.00 (*0-7366-3827-X*, 4495-A) Books on Tape, Inc.
—Deception on His Mind. abr. ed. 1997. audio 24.95 (*0-553-47818-4*, 695229, RH Audio) Random Hse. Audio Publishing Group.
—Deception on His Mind. l.t. ed. 1997. (Basic Ser.). 1021p. 29.95 (*0-7862-1144-X*) Thorndike Pr.
—For the Sake of Elena. 1993. 464p. mass mkt. 7.99 (*0-553-56127-8*) Bantam Bks.
—For the Sake of Elena. unabr. ed. 1993. audio 88.00 (*0-7366-2385-X*, 3156) Books on Tape, Inc.
—For the Sake of Elena. l.t. ed. 1993. (Magna Large Print Ser.). 659p. o.p. (*0-7505-0497-8*) Magna Large Print Bks. GBR. *Dist:* Ulverscroft Large Print Canada, Ltd.
—For the Sake of Elena. abr. ed. 1992. audio 15.99 (*0-553-47034-5*, 390797, RH Audio) Random Hse. Audio Publishing Group.
—A Great Deliverance. 1989. 432p. mass mkt. 7.50 (*0-553-27802-9*) Bantam Bks.
—A Great Deliverance. unabr. ed. 1994. audio 64.00 (*0-7366-2624-7*, 3364) Books on Tape, Inc.
—A Great Deliverance. abr. ed. 1992. 180p. pap. 15.99 incl. audio (*0-553-47056-6*, RH Audio) Random Hse. Audio Publishing Group.
—In Pursuit of the Proper Sinner. 2000. 752p. mass mkt. 7.99 (*0-553-57510-4*) Bantam Bks.
—In Pursuit of the Proper Sinner. 1999. Pt. 1. audio 64.00 (*0-7366-4652-3*, 5033-A); Pt. 2. audio 64.00 (*0-7366-4722-8*, 5033-B) Books on Tape, Inc.

—In Pursuit of the Proper Sinner. l.t. ed. 1999. pap. 25.95 o.p. (*0-7838-8692-6*, Macmillan Reference USA) Gale Group.
—In Pursuit of the Proper Sinner, Set. abr. ed. 1999. audio 25.95 Highsmith Inc.
—In Pursuit of the Proper Sinner. abr. ed. 1999. audio 25.95 (*0-553-47819-2*, RH Audio) Random Hse. Audio Publishing Group.
—In Pursuit of the Proper Sinner. l.t. ed. 912p. 2000. pap. 14.95 (*0-375-72799-X*); 1999. 25.95 (*0-375-40846-0*) Random Hse. Large Print.
—In the Presence of the Enemy. 1997. 656p. mass mkt. 7.99 (*0-553-57608-9*) Bantam Bks.
—In the Presence of the Enemy. unabr. ed. 1996. audio 120.00 (*0-7366-3278-6*, 3934) Books on Tape, Inc.
—In the Presence of the Enemy. unabr. ed. 2000. (Inspector Thomas Lynley Mystery Ser.: Vol. 8). audio 128.00 (*0-7887-0523-7*, 94718E7) Recorded Bks., LLC.
—Missing Joseph. 1994. 592p. mass mkt. 7.99 (*0-553-56604-0*) Bantam Bks.
—Missing Joseph. unabr. ed. 1993. audio 104.00 (*0-7366-2533-X*, 3285) Books on Tape, Inc.
—Missing Joseph. l.t. ed. 1993. 12.95 o.p. (*1-56895-038-1*, Wheeler Publishing, Inc.) Gale Group.
—Payment in Blood. 1990. 432p. mass mkt. 7.99 (*0-553-28436-3*) Bantam Bks.
—Payment in Blood. unabr. ed. 1994. audio 72.00 (*0-7366-2637-9*, 3376) Books on Tape, Inc.
—Payment in Blood. unabr. ed. 2001. audio 69.95 (*1-85089-779-4*, 30691) ISIS Audio Bks. GBR. *Dist:* Ulverscroft Large Print Bks., Ltd.
—Payment in Blood. unabr. ed. 1992. (Inspector Thomas Lynley Mystery Ser.: Vol. 2). audio 85.00 (*1-55690-762-1*, 92426E7) Recorded Bks., LLC.
—Playing for the Ashes. 1995. 704p. mass mkt. 7.99 (*0-553-57251-2*, Crimeline) Bantam Bks.
—Playing for the Ashes, Pt. 1. unabr. ed. 1994. audio 64.00 (*0-7366-2885-1*, 3587-A) Books on Tape, Inc.
—A Suitable Vengeance. 1992. 464p. mass mkt. 7.99 (*0-553-29560-8*) Bantam Bks.
—A Suitable Vengeance. unabr. ed. 1994. audio 80.00 (*0-7366-2796-0*, 3511) Books on Tape, Inc.
—A Suitable Vengeance. l.t. ed. 1993. (Magna Large Print Ser.). 653p. o.p. (*0-7505-0456-0*) Magna Large Print Bks. GBR. *Dist:* Ulverscroft Large Print Canada, Ltd.
—A Suitable Vengeance. abr. ed. 1991. audio 15.99 (*0-553-45286-X*, RH Audio) Random Hse. Audio Publishing Group.
—A Suitable Vengeance. unabr. ed. 1993. (Inspector Thomas Lynley Mystery Ser.: Vol. 4). audio 97.00 (*1-55690-812-1*, 93121E7) Recorded Bks., LLC.
—A Traitor to Memory. 2002. mass mkt. 7.99 (*0-553-84037-1*) Bantam Bks.
—Well-Schooled in Murder. 1991. 432p. mass mkt. 7.99 (*0-553-28734-6*); 1990. 368p. 17.95 o.s.i (*0-553-07000-2*) Bantam Bks.
—Well-Schooled in Murder. unabr. ed. 1993. audio 80.00 (*0-7366-2602-6*, 3346) Books on Tape, Inc.
—Well-Schooled in Murder. abr. ed. 1991. audio 15.99 (*0-553-45278-9*, 391880, RH Audio) Random Hse. Audio Publishing Group.

**HAVOC, JOHNNY (FICTITIOUS CHARACTER)—FICTION**

Jakes, John. Holiday for Havoc. l.t. ed. 1992. 18.95 o.p. (*0-7927-1276-5*); pap. 16.95 o.p. (*0-7927-1277-3*) BBC Audiobooks America.
—Johnny Havoc. l.t. ed. 1991. 21.95 o.p. (*0-7927-0798-2*, CH079); pap. 19.95 o.p. (*0-7927-0799-0*, CS0175) BBC Audiobooks America.

**HAWK (FICTITIOUS CHARACTER: GREEN)—FICTION**

Green, Simon R. Bones of Haven. 1992. (Hawk & Fisher Ser.: 6). mass mkt. 3.99 o.s.i (*0-441-31837-1*) Ace Bks.
—God Killer. 1991. (Hawk & Fisher Ser.: 3). mass mkt. 3.95 o.s.i (*0-441-29460-X*) Ace Bks.
—Guard Against Dishonor. 1991. (Hawk & Fisher Ser.: 5). mass mkt. 3.99 o.s.i (*0-441-31836-3*) Ace Bks.
—Guards of Haven: The Adventures of Hawk & Fisher, Bk. 2. 1999. 576p. reprint ed. mass mkt. 7.99 (*0-451-45755-2*, ROC) NAL.
—Hawk & Fisher. 1990. (Hawk & Fisher Ser.: 1). mass mkt. 4.50 o.s.i (*0-441-58417-9*) Ace Bks.
—Swords of Haven. 1999. (Hawk & Fisher Omnibus Ser.: No. 1). 512p. reprint ed. mass mkt. 7.99 (*0-451-45750-1*, ROC) NAL.
—Winner Takes All. 1991. (Hawk & Fisher Ser.: 2). mass mkt. 3.95 o.s.i (*0-441-14291-5*) Ace Bks.
—Wolf in the Fold. 1991. (Hawk & Fisher Ser.: 4). mass mkt. 3.95 o.s.i (*0-441-31835-5*) Ace Bks.

**HAWK, JASON (FICTITIOUS CHARACTER: PARKER)—FICTION**

Parker, Robert B. Hush Money. 2000. (Spenser Mystery Ser.). 336p. pap. 7.99 (*0-425-17401-8*) Berkley Publishing Group.
—Hush Money. l.t. ed. 1999. (Spenser Mystery Ser.). 27.95 (*1-56895-739-4*, Wheeler Publishing, Inc.) Gale Group.
—Hush Money. unabr. ed. 1999. (Spenser Mystery Ser.). audio 30.00 (*0-7871-1870-2*, 890100) NewStar Media, Inc.
—Hush Money. 1999. (Spenser Mystery Ser.). 336p. 22.95 o.p. (*0-399-14458-7*) Penguin Group (USA) Inc.
—Hush Money. 2000. 13.55 (*0-606-20394-X*); 13.55 (*0-606-20098-3*) Turtleback Bks.

**HAWKINS, GENE (FICTITIOUS CHARACTER)—FICTION**

Francis, Dick. Blood Sport. 1995. audio 29.95 (*0-7451-2831-9*) BBC Audiobooks America.
—Blood Sport. 1988. mass mkt. 5.95 o.s.i (*0-449-21262-9*, Fawcett) Ballantine Bks.
—Blood Sport. 1999. 288p. mass mkt. 6.99 (*0-515-12651-9*, Jove) Berkley Publishing Group.
—Blood Sport, unabr. ed. 1996. 5p. audio 39.95 (*0-7861-0941-6*, 753865) Blackstone Audio Bks., Inc.
—Blood Sport. 1994. reprint ed. lib. bdg. 32.95 o.p. (*1-56849-282-0*) Buccaneer Bks., Inc.
—Blood Sport. unabr. ed. 2000. audio 49.95 (*0-7451-5947-8*, CAB 087) Chivers Audio Bks. GBR. *Dist:* BBC Audiobooks America.
—Blood Sport. l.t. ed. 1991. 16.95 o.p. (*0-8161-5227-6*); lib. bdg. 22.95 (*0-8161-5226-8*) Gale Group. (Macmillan Reference USA).
—Blood Sport. unabr. ed. 1991. audio 51.00 (*1-55690-059-7*, 91116E7) Recorded Bks., LLC.
—Blood Sport. 1984. mass mkt. 5.95 (*0-671-55694-0*); 1983. mass mkt. 3.50 o.s.i (*0-671-50738-9*) Simon & Schuster. (Pocket).
—Blood Sport. l.t. ed. 1972. 12.00 o.p. (*0-85456-106-4*, Ulverscroft) Thorpe, F. A. Pubs. GBR. *Dist:* Ulverscroft Large Print Bks., Ltd.

**HAWKINS, MACKENZIE (FICTITIOUS CHARACTER)—FICTION**

Ludlum, Robert. The Road to Omaha. 1993. 608p. mass mkt. 7.99 (*0-553-56044-1*) Bantam Bks.

**HAWKMOON, DORIAN (FICTITIOUS CHARACTER)—FICTION**

Moorcock, Michael. The Champion of Garathorm. 1986. (Chronicles of Castle Brass Ser.: No. 2). 160p. 2.95 o.s.i (*0-425-09042-6*); 1985. 2.75 o.s.i (*0-425-07646-6*) Berkley Publishing Group.
—The Champion of Garathorm. 1981. pap. 2.25 o.p. (*0-440-11173-0*) Dell Publishing.
—Count Brass, No. 1. 1988. (Chronicles of Castle Brass Ser.). mass mkt. 2.95 o.s.i (*0-441-11775-9*) Ace Bks.
—Count Brass. 1985. (Chronicles of Castle Brass Ser.: No. 1). 160p. 2.75 o.s.i (*0-425-07514-1*) Berkley Publishing Group.
—Count Brass. 1981. pap. 2.25 o.p. (*0-440-11541-8*) Dell Publishing.
—Count Brass. 2000. (Eternal Champion Ser.: Vol. 15). (Illus.). 339p. 24.99 (*1-56504-987-X*) White Wolf Publishing, Inc.
—Jewel in the Skull. 1977. mass mkt. 1.25 o.p. (*0-87997-276-9*); mass mkt. 1.95 o.p. (*0-87997-712-4*); mass mkt. 2.50 o.p. (*0-87997-841-4*); mass mkt. 2.75 o.p. (*0-88677-043-2*); mass mkt. 1.50 o.p. (*0-87997-419-2*); mass mkt. 1.75 o.p. (*0-87997-547-4*); (Runestaff Ser.: Bk. 1). 224p. mass mkt. 2.95 o.p. (*0-88677-175-7*) DAW Bks., Inc.
—The Mad God's Amulet. 1977. mass mkt. 1.25 o.p. (*0-87997-289-0*); 1977. mass mkt. 2.75 o.p. (*0-88677-044-0*); 1977. mass mkt. 1.95 o.p. (*0-87997-688-8*); 1977. mass mkt. 1.50 o.p. (*0-87997-391-9*); Bk. 2. 1985. mass mkt. 2.95 o.p. (*0-88677-216-8*, UJ2216) DAW Bks., Inc.
—The Quest for Tanelorn, No. 3. 1987. (Chronicles of Castle Brass Ser.). mass mkt. 2.95 o.s.i (*0-441-69712-7*) Ace Bks.
—The Quest for Tanelorn. 1985. (Chronicles of Castle Brass Ser.: No. 3). 160p. 2.75 o.s.i (*0-425-07707-1*) Berkley Publishing Group.
—The Quest for Tanelorn. 1981. pap. 2.25 o.p. (*0-440-17193-8*) Dell Publishing.
—The Runestaff. 1991. mass mkt. 4.50 o.s.i (*0-441-31848-7*) Ace Bks.
—The Runestaff. 1977. mass mkt. 1.75 o.p. (*0-87997-616-0*); 1977. mass mkt. 2.75 o.p. (*0-88677-046-7*); 1977. mass mkt. 1.50 o.p. (*0-87997-422-2*); 1977. mass mkt. 1.25 o.p. (*0-87997-324-2*); Bk. 4. 1985. mass mkt. 2.95 o.p. (*0-88677-218-4*, UE2218) DAW Bks., Inc.
—The Runestaff No. 1: Jewel in the Skull. 1990. mass mkt. 3.50 o.s.i (*0-441-31847-9*) Ace Bks.
—The Runestaff No. 2: Mad God's Amulet. 1990. mass mkt. 3.95 o.s.i (*0-441-51388-3*) Ace Bks.
—The Sword of the Dawn. 1977. (Science Fiction Ser.: No. 3). 224p. mass mkt. 2.95 o.p. (*0-88677-173-0*) DAW Bks., Inc.

**HAWLEY, BILL (FICTITIOUS CHARACTER)—FICTION**

Axler, Leo. Double Plot. 1994. 240p. mass mkt. 4.99 o.s.i (*0-425-14407-0*) Berkley Publishing Group.
—Final Viewing: A Bill Hawley Undertaking. 1994. 256p. (Orig.). mass mkt. 4.50 o.s.i (*0-425-14244-2*, Prime Crime) Berkley Publishing Group.
—Grave Matters: A Bill Hawley Undertaking. 1995. 256p. (Orig.). mass mkt. 4.99 o.s.i (*0-425-14581-6*, Prime Crime) Berkley Publishing Group.
—Separated at Death. 1996. 272p. mass mkt. 5.99 o.s.i (*0-425-15257-X*) Berkley Publishing Group.

**HAWTHORNE, HELEN (FICTITIOUS CHARACTER)—FICTION**

Viets, Elaine. Murder between the Covers: A Dead-End Job Mystery. 2003. 288p. mass mkt. 5.99 (*0-451-21081-6*, Signet Bks.) NAL.
—Shop Till You Drop: A Dead-End Job Mystery. 2003. 288p. mass mkt. 5.99 (*0-451-20855-2*, Signet Bks.) NAL.

**HAWTHORNE, TYRELL (FICTITIOUS CHARACTER)—FICTION**

Ludlum, Robert. The Scorpio Illusion. 1994. 672p. mass mkt. 7.99 (*0-553-56603-2*); 1994. 544p. mass mkt. 8.99 o.s.i (*0-553-56838-8*); 1993. mass mkt. 6.99 o.s.i (*0-553-18109-2*) Bantam Bks.
—The Scorpio Illusion. l.t. ed. 1993. 928p. 29.95 o.s.i (*0-385-47039-8*, Bantam Large Type) Bantam Doubleday Dell Large Print Group, Inc.
—The Scorpio Illusion. l.t. ed. pap. 18.95 o.p. (*0-7451-3550-1*) Chivers Large Print GBR. *Dist:* BBC Audiobooks America.
—The Scorpio Illusion. 1993. audio 23.98 o.s.i (*0-553-74541-7*); audio 19.20 o.s.i (*0-553-70057-X*) Random Hse. Audio Publishing Group. (RH Audio).
—The Scorpio Illusion. 6.98 o.p. (*0-8317-4693-9*) Smithmark Pubs., Inc.

**HAYCASTLE, MATILDA (FICTITIOUS CHARACTER)—FICTION**

Bailey, Michele. The Cuckoo Case. l.t. ed. 1997. (Ulverscroft Large Print Ser.). 304p. 31.50 o.p. (*0-7089-3695-4*, Ulverscroft) Thorpe, F. A. Pubs. GBR. *Dist:* Ulverscroft Large Print Bks., Ltd., Ulverscroft Large Print Canada, Ltd.
—Dreadful Lies. 1996. 192p. 19.95 o.p. (*0-312-14323-0*, Saint Martin's Minotaur) St. Martin's Pr.

**HAYDON, STUART (FICTITIOUS CHARACTER)—FICTION**

Lindsey, David L. Body of Truth. 1993. 480p. mass mkt. 6.99 (*0-553-28964-0*) Bantam Bks.
—A Cold Mind. 1994. 368p. mass mkt. 6.99 (*0-553-56081-6*) Bantam Bks.
—A Cold Mind. 1996. pap. o.s.i (*0-385-48406-2*) Doubleday Publishing.
—A Cold Mind. 1990. 352p. mass mkt. 5.99 (*0-671-73338-9*); 1984. mass mkt. 3.95 (*0-671-49933-5*) Simon & Schuster. (Pocket).
—Heat from Another Sun. 1996. 384p. mass mkt. 6.99 (*0-553-56790-X*) Bantam Bks.
—Heat from Another Sun. 1984. 256p. 14.95 o.p. (*0-06-015346-6*) HarperTrade.
—Heat from Another Sun. 1985. mass mkt. 5.95 (*0-671-54632-5*, Pocket) Simon & Schuster.
—In the Lake of the Moon. 1990. 400p. mass mkt. 6.50 o.s.i (*0-553-28344-8*) Bantam Bks.
—In the Lake of the Moon. 1988. 320p. 17.95 o.s.i (*0-689-11626-8*, Scribner) Simon & Schuster.
—Spiral. (Orig.). 1990. mass mkt. 5.99 (*0-671-73337-0*, Pocket); 1988. 416p. mass mkt. 4.50 (*0-671-64666-4*, Pocket); 1986. 320p. pap. 16.95 o.p. (*0-689-11625-X*, Scribner) Simon & Schuster.

**HAYES, JACK (FICTITIOUS CHARACTER)—FICTION**

Green, Vincent S. The Price of Victory. 1992. 240p. 19.95 (*0-8027-1200-2*) Walker & Co.

**HAYES, JESSE (FICTITIOUS CHARACTER)—FICTION**

Frey, Stephen. Inner Sanctum. 1997. 336p. 23.95 o.p. (*0-525-94206-8*) Dutton/Plume.
—Inner Sanctum. 1998. 448p. mass mkt. 7.99 (*0-451-19014-9*, Signet Bks.) NAL.
—The Inner Sanctum. l.t. ed. 1998. (Large Print Book Ser.). pap. 24.95 (*1-56895-533-2*, Wheeler Publishing, Inc.) Gale Group.

**HAYES, JUDITH (FICTITIOUS CHARACTER)—FICTION**

Porter, Anna. Hidden Agenda. 1986. 280p. 14.95 o.p. (*0-525-24427-1*, Dutton) Dutton/Plume.
—Hidden Agenda. 1987. mass mkt. 3.95 o.p. (*0-451-40025-9*, Onyx) NAL.
—Mortal Sins. 1989. mass mkt. 4.50 o.p. (*0-451-40153-0*, Onyx); 1988. 288p. 17.95 o.p. (*0-453-00616-7*) NAL.

**HAYES, KAREN (FICTITIOUS CHARACTER)—FICTION**

Biehl, Michael. Doctored Evidence: A Suspense Novel. 2003. 320p. mass mkt. 6.99 (*0-425-19311-X*) Berkley Publishing Group.
—Doctored Evidence: A Suspense Novel. 2002. 278p. pap. 24.95 (*1-882593-55-3*); 2003. 272p. reprint ed. pap. (*1-882593-70-7*) Bridge Works Publishing Co., Inc.
—Lawyered to Death: A Karen Hayes Mystery. 2003. 320p. 23.95 (*1-882593-76-6*) Bridge Works Publishing Co., Inc.

**HAYES, LUCINDA (FICTITIOUS CHARACTER)—FICTION**

Wesson, Marianne. Render Up the Body. l.t. ed. 1998. 336p. 24.00 o.s.i (*0-06-018292-X*) HarperCollins Pubs.
—Render up the Body: A Novel of Suspense. l.t. ed. 1998. 432p. mass mkt. 6.99 (*0-06-109392-0*, HarperTorch) Morrow/Avon.

**HAYES, NANETTE (FICTITIOUS CHARACTER)—FICTION**

Carter, Charlotte. Coq Au Vin. 1999. (Nanette Hayes Mystery Ser.). 200p. 22.00 o.s.i (*0-89296-678-5*) Mysterious Pr.
—Coq Au Vin. 2000. (Nanette Hayes Mysteries Ser.). 224p. mass mkt. 6.50 (*0-446-60787-8*) Warner Bks., Inc.
—Drumsticks. 2000. (Nanette Hayes Mystery Ser.). 208p. 22.95 (*0-89296-679-3*) Mysterious Pr.
—Rhode Island Red. (Mask Noir Ser.). 1998. 176p. pap. (*1-85242-591-1*); Vol. 1. 1997. 250p. (*1-85242-564-4*) Serpent's Tail Ltd.
—Rhode Island Red. 1999. (Nanette Hayes Mysteries Ser.). 224p. mass mkt. 5.99 (*0-446-60664-2*) Warner Bks., Inc.

**HAYLE, TAMARA (FICTITIOUS CHARACTER)—FICTION**

Wesley, Valerie Wilson. The Devil Riding. l.t. ed. 2001. (Softcover Ser.). 240p. pap. 23.95 o.p. (*1-58724-084-X*, Wheeler Publishing, Inc.) Gale Group.
—The Devil Riding. 2002. 304p. mass mkt. 6.99 (*0-380-73208-4*) HarperCollins Pubs.
—The Devil Riding. 2000. 208p. 23.95 o.s.i (*0-399-14617-2*) Penguin Group (USA) Inc.
—Devil's Gonna Get Him. 1996. (Tamara Hayle Mystery Ser.: Vol. 2). 288p. mass mkt. 6.99 (*0-380-72492-8*, Avon Bks.) Morrow/Avon.
—Devil's Gonna Get Him. 1995. 212p. 19.95 o.p. (*0-399-14027-1*, G. P. Putnam's Sons) Penguin Group (USA) Inc.
—Easier to Kill. l.t. ed. 1999. pap. 23.95 o.p. (*1-56895-704-1*, Wheeler Publishing, Inc.) Gale Group.
—Easier to Kill. 1999. (Tamara Hayle Mystery Ser.). 304p. mass mkt. 6.99 (*0-380-72910-5*, Avon Bks.) Morrow/Avon.
—Easier to Kill. 1998. (Tamara Hayle Mystery Ser.: Vol. 5). 193p. 23.95 o.p. (*0-399-14445-5*) Penguin Group (USA) Inc.
—The Hiding Place. 1998. (Tamara Hayle Mystery Ser.). 288p. mass mkt. 6.99 (*0-380-72909-1*, Avon Bks.) Morrow/Avon.
—No Hiding Place. unabr. ed. 1998. audio 40.00 (*0-7366-4214-5*, 4712) Books on Tape, Inc.
—No Hiding Place: A Tamara Hayle Mystery. 1997. 207p. 21.95 o.s.i (*0-399-14318-1*, G. P. Putnam's Sons) Penguin Group (USA) Inc.
—When Death Comes Stealin. 1995. (Tamara Hayle Mystery Ser.: Vol. 1). 320p. reprint ed. mass mkt. 6.99 (*0-380-72491-X*, Avon Bks.) Morrow/Avon.
—When Death Comes Stealing. 1994. 224p. 19.95 o.p. (*0-399-13949-4*, G. P. Putnam's Sons) Penguin Group (USA) Inc.
—When Death Comes Stealing. 1998. audio (*1-57042-666-X*); 1994. audio 17.00 (*1-57042-186-2*, 4-521862) Time Warner AudioBooks.
—Where Evil Sleeps. unabr. ed. 1998. audio 40.00 (*0-7366-4120-3*, 4624) Books on Tape, Inc.
—Where Evil Sleeps. 1997. 288p. mass mkt. 6.50 (*0-380-72908-3*, Avon Bks.) Morrow/Avon.
—Where Evil Sleeps. 1996. 224p. 21.95 o.p. (*0-399-14145-6*, G. P. Putnam's Sons) Penguin Group (USA) Inc.

**HAYS, SHARON (FICTITIOUS CHARACTER)—FICTION**

Gregory, Sarah. Capitol Scandal. 1999. 384p. mass mkt. 6.99 o.s.i (*0-451-19009-2*, Signet Bks.) NAL.
—Public Trust. 1997. 400p. mass mkt. 5.99 o.s.i (*0-451-19076-9*) NAL.

**HAZARD, AMANDA (FICTITIOUS CHARACTER)—FICTION**

Feddersen, Connie. Dead in the Cellar. 1995. mass mkt. 4.99 o.s.i (*0-8217-5245-6*); 1994. 288p. mass mkt. 3.99 o.s.i (*0-8217-4569-7*) Kensington Publishing Corp.
—Dead in the Dirt. 1996. mass mkt. 4.99 o.s.i (*1-57566-046-6*) Kensington Publishing Corp.
—Dead in the Driver's Seat. 1998. (Amanda Hazard Mysteries Ser.). 256p. mass mkt. 5.99 (*1-57566-297-3*) Kensington Publishing Corp.
—Dead in the Hay: An Amanda Hazard Mystery. 1999. (Amanda Hazard Mysteries Ser.). 256p. mass mkt. 5.99 o.s.i (*1-57566-463-1*, Kensington Bks.) Kensington Publishing Corp.

—Dead in the Melon Patch. 1995. (Amanda Hazard Mysteries Ser.). 288p. mass mkt. 4.99 o.s.i (*0-8217-4872-6*, Zebra Bks.) Kensington Publishing Corp.

—Dead in the Mud. 1997. (Amanda Hazard Mysteries Ser.). 264p. mass mkt. 5.50 o.s.i (*1-57566-156-X*) Kensington Publishing Corp.

—Dead in the Pumpkin Patch. 2000. (Amanda Pepper Mysteries Ser.). (Illus.). 256p. (J). mass mkt. 5.99 o.s.i (*1-57566-612-X*) Kensington Publishing Corp.

—Dead in the Water. (Amanda Hazard Mysteries Ser.). 1995. mass mkt. 4.99 o.s.i (*0-8217-5244-8*); 1993. 304p. mass mkt. 3.99 o.s.i (*0-8217-4267-1*, Zebra Bks.) Kensington Publishing Corp.

### HAZARD, PHILLIP HORATIO (FICTITIOUS CHARACTER)—FICTION

Stuart, V. A. The Brave Captains. 2003. (Philip Hazard Novels Ser.: No. 2). 272p. pap. 14.95 (*1-59013-040-5*) McBooks Pr., Inc.

—The Brave Captains: Hazard 2. l.t. ed. 1991. (Ulverscroft Large Print Ser.). 29.99 o.p. (*0-7089-2560-X*, Ulverscroft) Thorpe, F. A. Pubs. GBR. *Dist:* Ulverscroft Large Print Bks., Ltd., Ulverscroft Large Print Canada, Ltd.

—The Cannons of Lucknow. 2003. (Alexander Sheridan Novels: No. 4). 272p. (Orig.). pap. 14.95 (*1-59013-029-4*) McBooks Pr., Inc.

—Hazard in Circassia: Hazard 5. l.t. ed. 1993. (Ulverscroft Large Print Ser.). 416p. 29.99 o.p. (*0-7089-2962-1*, Ulverscroft) Thorpe, F. A. Pubs. GBR. *Dist:* Ulverscroft Large Print Bks., Ltd., Ulverscroft Large Print Canada, Ltd.

—Hazard of Huntress. 2004. (Phillip Hazard Novels Ser.: 4). 256p. pap. 13.95 (*1-59013-082-0*) McBooks Pr., Inc.

—Hazard of Huntress: Hazard 4. l.t. ed. 1993. (Ulverscroft Large Print Ser.). 432p. 29.99 o.p. (*0-7089-2903-6*, Ulverscroft) Thorpe, F. A. Pubs. GBR. *Dist:* Ulverscroft Large Print Bks., Ltd., Ulverscroft Large Print Canada, Ltd.

—Hazard's Command. 2004. (Phillip Hazard Novels Ser.: Vol. 3). 256p. pap. 13.95 (*1-59013-081-2*) McBooks Pr., Inc.

—Hazard's Command. l.t. ed. 1992. (Ulverscroft Large Print Ser.). 432p. 29.99 o.p. (*0-7089-2740-8*, Ulverscroft) Thorpe, F. A. Pubs. GBR. *Dist:* Ulverscroft Large Print Bks., Ltd., Ulverscroft Large Print Canada, Ltd.

—The Heroic Garrison. 1975. (Adventures of Alexander Sheridan Ser., No. 5). 224p. pap. 1.25 o.p. (*0-523-22628-4*, Pinnacle Bks.) Kensington Publishing Corp.

—Sailors on Horseback. l.t. ed. 1994. (Ulverscroft Large Print Ser.). 416p. 29.99 o.p. (*0-7089-3195-2*, Ulverscroft) Thorpe, F. A. Pubs. GBR. *Dist:* Ulverscroft Large Print Bks., Ltd., Ulverscroft Large Print Canada, Ltd.

—Shannon's Brigade: Hazard 7. l.t. ed. 1994. (Ulverscroft Large Print Ser.). 400p. 29.99 o.p. (*0-7089-3100-6*, Ulverscroft) Thorpe, F. A. Pubs. GBR. *Dist:* Ulverscroft Large Print Bks., Ltd., Ulverscroft Large Print Canada, Ltd.

—The Valiant Sailors. 1979. (Hazard: No. 1). pap. 1.75 o.p. (*0-523-40481-6*, Pinnacle Bks.) Kensington Publishing Corp.

—The Valiant Sailors. 2003. (Philip Hazard Novels Ser.: No. 1). 272p. pap. 14.95 (*1-59013-039-1*) McBooks Pr., Inc.

—The Valiant Sailors. 2001. audio 44.95 (*1-85496-197-7*, 61977) Soundings, Ltd. GBR. *Dist:* Ulverscroft Large Print Bks., Ltd.

—The Valiant Sailors: Hazard 1. l.t. ed. 1991. (Ulverscroft Large Print Ser.). 29.99 o.p. (*0-7089-2470-0*, Ulverscroft) Thorpe, F. A. Pubs. GBR. *Dist:* Ulverscroft Large Print Bks., Ltd., Ulverscroft Large Print Canada, Ltd.

—Victory at Sebastopol. 1973. (Hazard Ser.: No. 5). 208p. pap. text 0.95 o.p. (*0-523-21151-1*, Pinnacle Bks.) Kensington Publishing Corp.

—Victory at Sebastopol: Hazard 6. l.t. ed. 1993. (Ulverscroft Large Print Ser.). 368p. 29.99 o.p. (*0-7089-2995-8*, Ulverscroft) Thorpe, F. A. Pubs. GBR. *Dist:* Ulverscroft Large Print Bks., Ltd., Ulverscroft Large Print Canada, Ltd.

### HE WHO HEARS LIKE A COYOTE (FICTITIOUS CHARACTER)—FICTION

Camp, Will. Tony Hillerman's Frontier: Cold Justice. 1998. 256p. mass mkt. 5.99 o.s.i (*0-06-101292-0*, Eos) Morrow/Avon.

### HEARTWOOD, LEANDER (FICTITIOUS CHARACTER)—FICTION

Caputo, Philip. Equation for Evil. 1996. 416p. 25.00 o.p. (*0-06-018360-8*) HarperCollins Pubs.

—Equation for Evil. 1997. 496p. pap. 13.50 o.p. (*0-06-098411-2*, Perennial) HarperTrade.

—Equation for Evil. 488p. pap. 4.98 o.p. (*0-7651-0610-8*) Smithmark Pubs., Inc.

### HEATHCLIFF (FICTITIOUS CHARACTER)—FICTION

Bronte, Emily. Wuthering Heights. abr. ed. audio 12.95 (*0-89926-118-3*, 806) Audio Bk. Co.

—Wuthering Heights, Set. unabr. ed. 1994. audio 53.95 (*1-55685-334-3*) Audio Bk. Contractors, Inc.

—Wuthering Heights. unabr. ed. 1998. audio 39.95 (*1-57270-068-8*, F91068u, Cover to Cover Classics) Audio Partners Publishing Corp.

—Wuthering Heights. unabr. ed. audio 84.95 o.p. (*1-85549-917-7*, CTC 002) BBC Audiobooks America.

—Wuthering Heights. unabr. ed. 1992. audio 56.95 (*0-7861-0360-4*, 103863) Blackstone Audio Bks., Inc.

—Wuthering Heights. 2002. audio 64.00 (*0-7366-8796-3*); 2002. audio compact disk 80.00 (*0-7366-8797-1*); 2001. audio compact disk 88.00; 1981. (YA). audio 72.00 (*0-7366-0501-0*, 1475) Books on Tape, Inc.

—Wuthering Heights. unabr. ed. 2002. audio 29.95 (*1-59086-298-8*, 3884, Brilliance Audio Unabridged); 2001. audio compact disk 121.25 (*1-58788-615-4*, 2896, CD Unabridged Library Edition); 2001. audio compact disk 44.95 (*1-58788-614-6*, 2895, CD Unabridged); 1992. audio 19.95 o.p. (*1-56100-483-9*, 324, Bookcassette); 1992. audio 59.25 (*1-56100-117-1*, 1116, Unabridged Library Editions) Brilliance Audio.

—Wuthering Heights. 1997. (Cambridge Literature Ser.). audio 16.95 o.p. (*0-521-59798-6*); audio 16.95 o.p. (*0-521-59798-6*); audio compact disk 22.95 o.p. (*0-521-59797-8*) Cambridge Univ. Pr.

—Wuthering Heights. Hoyes, Richard, ed. 1997. (Cambridge Literature Ser.). (Illus.). 416p. pap. text 11.95 o.p. (*0-521-58949-5*) Cambridge Univ. Pr.

—Wuthering Heights. unabr. ed. 2000. 10p. audio compact disk 94.95 (*0-7540-5342-3*, CCD 033); audio 69.95 (*0-7451-2759-2*, SAB 125) Chivers Audio Bks. GBR. *Dist:* BBC Audiobooks America.

—Wuthering Heights. audio 59.95 Cover to Cover Cassettes, Ltd.

—Wuthering Heights. abr. ed. 1994. (gr. 7-9). pap. 29.99 incl. audio (*0-88646-846-9*, LSR 7358); 1993. audio 16.99 (*0-88646-358-0*, 7358); 1986. (YA). (gr. 7-9). audio 29.95 o.p. (*0-88646-786-1*, R 7017) Durkin Hayes Publishing Ltd.

—Wuthering Heights. abr. ed. 1994. audio (*0-00-104640-3*) HarperCollins Pubs. Ltd.

—Wuthering Heights. audio. audio 17.00 o.s.i (*1-55994-632-6*, DCN 2086, HarperAudio); audio 15.95 o.p. (*0-89845-395-X*, A 2086, Caedmon) HarperTrade.

—Wuthering Heights, Set. unabr. ed. 1999. audio 49.95 Highsmith Inc.

—Wuthering Heights. abr. ed. 2000. audio 13.95 (*1-84032-466-X*) Hodder Headline Audiobooks GBR. *Dist:* Trafalgar Square.

—Wuthering Heights. Pritchett, V. S., ed. 1956. (YA). pap. 16.36 (*0-395-05102-9*, Riverside Editions) Houghton Mifflin Co.

—Wuthering Heights. abr. ed. 2001. (Classics Collection). audio 7.95 (*1-57815-240-2*, Media Bks. Audio Publishing) Media Bks., L. L. C.

—Wuthering Heights. 1959. mass mkt. 0.60 o.p. (*0-451-50610-3*, Signet Classics) NAL.

—Wuthering Heights. abr. ed. 1995. (Classic Fiction Ser.). audio 17.98 (*962-634-563-2*, NA306314, Naxos AudioBooks) Naxos of America, Inc.

—Wuthering Heights. 1997. (Thornes Classic Novels Ser.). (Illus.). 354p. pap. 16.95 (*0-7487-2978-X*) Nelson Thornes GBR. *Dist:* Trans-Atlantic Pubns., Inc.

—Wuthering Heights. abr. ed. 2001. (Ultimate Classics Ser.). audio 25.00 (*1-931056-50-1*, New Millennium Audio) New Millennium Entertainment.

—Wuthering Heights. abr. ed. 2001. audio 25.00 New Millennium Publishing.

—Wuthering Heights. abr. ed. (Ultimate Classics Ser.). 1996. audio 19.95 o.p. (*0-7871-0673-9*, Dove Audio); 1994. audio 29.95 o.p. (*0-7871-0064-1*, Dove Audio); 1993. audio 16.95 o.p. (*1-55800-853-5*) NewStar Media, Inc.

—Wuthering Heights. (Read-along Ser.). 34.95 incl. audio Norton Pubs., Inc., Jeffrey /Audio-Forum.

—Wuthering Heights. abr. ed. 1993. (Classics on Cassette). 16.00 incl. audio (*0-453-00819-4*) Penguin/HighBridge.

—Wuthering Heights. 1987. (Radiobook Ser.). audio 4.98 (*0-929541-36-7*) Radiola Co.

—Wuthering Heights. 1987. audio 14.95 o.p. (*0-394-56409-X*); 1996. audio 21.99 o.s.i (*0-553-47776-5*); 1986. audio 16.00 o.s.i (*0-394-55733-6*) Random Hse. Audio Publishing Group. (RH Audio).

—Wuthering Heights, unabr. ed. 1981. audio 70.00 (*1-55690-575-0*, 81150E7) Recorded Bks., LLC.

—Wuthering Heights. 1992. 416p. mass mkt. 3.50 o.p. (*0-590-46030-7*, Scholastic Paperbacks) Scholastic, Inc.

—Wuthering Heights. unabr. ed. 2003. audio 19.99 (*1-59335-134-8*, 30230) Soulmate Audio Bks., Inc.

—Wuthering Heights. unabr. ed. 2002. audio compact disk 18.95 (*1-58472-408-0*, In Audio) Sound Room Pubs., Inc.

—Wuthering Heights. abr. ed. 1994. (A+ Audio Ser.). audio 8.00 (*1-57042-116-1*, 4-521161) Time Warner AudioBooks.

—Wuthering Heights. abr. ed. 1999. audio 11.95 (*1-85998-485-1*, Trafalgar Square Publishing) Trafalgar Square.

—Wuthering Heights. abr. ed. 1997. 4p. audio 23.95 (*0-14-086205-6*, Penguin AudioBooks) Viking Penguin.

—Wuthering Heights: Complete Text with Introduction, Contexts, Critical Essays. Hoeveler, Diane Long, ed. 2002. (New Riverside Edtions Ser.). (Illus.). viii, 456p. pap. 8.76 (*0-618-08486-X*) Houghton Mifflin Co.

—Wuthering Heights: Norton Critical Edition. Sale, William M., Jr. & Dunn, Richard J., eds. 3rd rev. ed. 1990. (Critical Editions Ser.). 396p. pap. text (*0-393-95760-8*) Norton, W. W. & Co., Inc.

—Wuthering Heights: Study Text. Adams, Richard & Cookson, Linda, eds. 1989. (Study Texts Ser.). (Illus.). 338p. pap. text 5.95 o.p. (*0-582-33098-X*, TG7232) Longman Publishing Group.

—Wuthering Heights: 1818 Version. Jack, Ian, ed. 2nd ed. 1995. (Oxford World's Classics Ser.). 428p. pap. 4.95 o.p. (*0-19-282350-7*) Oxford Univ. Pr., Inc.

—Wuthering Heights & Poems. Drabble, Margaret, ed. 1993. 432p. pap. 4.95 o.p. (*0-460-87311-3*, Everyman's Classic Library in Paperback) Tuttle Publishing.

—Wuthering Heights & Poems. 1991. 403p. pap. 5.95 o.p. (*0-460-87036-X*, Everyman's Classic Library in Paperback) Tuttle Publishing.

—Wuthering Heights with Connections. 2000. (HRW Library). 399p. 17.90 (*0-03-095770-2*) Holt, Rinehart & Winston.

Bronte, Emily & Bronte, Charlotte. Wuthering Heights & Jane Eyre. abr. ed. 2001. (gr. 10 up). audio 12.99 (*1-57815-260-7*, 4433, Media Bks. Audio Publishing) Media Bks., L. L. C.

Figes, Eva. Nelly's Version. 2002. 218p. pap. 12.50 (*1-56478-313-8*) Dalkey Archive Pr.

Wheatcroft, John. Catherine, Her Book. 1983. 13.95 (*0-8453-4742-X*, Cornwall Bks.) Associated Univ. Presses.

### HEENAN, MATTHEW (FICTITIOUS CHARACTER)—FICTION

Barnard, Robert. The Masters of the House: A Novel of Suspense. 1994. 224p. 20.00 (*0-684-19728-6*, Macmillan Reference USA) Gale Group.

—The Masters of the House: A Novel of Suspense. 1996. 224p. mass mkt. 4.99 (*0-380-72511-8*, Avon Bks.) Morrow/Avon.

### HEFFERMAN, HOOKY (FICTITIOUS CHARACTER)—FICTION

Meynell, Laurence. The Fairly Innocent Little Man. 1992. (Mystery Ser.: No. 102). per. (*0-373-26102-0*, Harlequin Bks.) Harlequin Enterprises, Ltd.

—The Fairly Innocent Little Man. (Jubilee Mystery Ser.). 192p. 7.95 o.s.i (*0-8128-2421-0*, Scarborough Hse.) Madison Bks., Inc.

### HEHZI OF NHOL, PRINCESS (FICTITIOUS CHARACTER)—FICTION

Keyes, J. Gregory. The Blackgod. 1998. (Chosen of the Changeling Ser.: 2). 512p. mass mkt. 6.99 (*0-345-41880-8*, Del Rey) Ballantine Bks.

—The Waterborn. 1997. (Waterborn Ser.: 1). 384p. mass mkt. 6.99 (*0-345-39670-7*, Del Rey) Ballantine Bks.

### HEIMRICH, M. L. (FICTITIOUS CHARACTER)—FICTION

Lockridge, Richard & Lockridge, Frances. Let Dead Enough Alone: A Captain Heimrich Mystery. l.t. ed. 1995. 232p. pap. 18.95 (*0-7838-1159-4*, Macmillan Reference USA) Gale Group.

### HELLER, NATHAN (FICTITIOUS CHARACTER)—FICTION

Collins, Max Allan. Angel in Black. 2001. (Nathan Heller Ser.). 352p. 21.95 o.s.i (*0-451-20263-5*, Signet Bks.) NAL.

—Blood & Thunder. Landt, Fran, ed. abr. ed. 1999. audio 16.95 (*1-882071-57-3*) B&B Audio, Inc.

—Blood & Thunder, Set. unabr. ed. 1997. audio 69.95 (*0-7927-2211-6*, CSL 100, Chivers Sound Library) BBC Audiobooks America.

—Blood & Thunder. 1999. 320p. reprint ed. text 22.00 (*0-7881-6601-8*) DIANE Publishing Co.

—Blood & Thunder. 1995. 336p. 21.95 o.s.i (*0-525-93759-5*, Dutton) Dutton/Plume.

—Blood & Thunder. 1996. 368p. mass mkt. 5.99 o.s.i (*0-451-17976-5*, Signet Bks.) NAL.

—Carnal Hours. abr. ed. 1999. audio 16.95 (*1-882071-71-9*) B&B Audio, Inc.

—Carnal Hours. 1994. (Nathan Heller Ser.). 336p. 20.95 o.p. (*0-525-93758-7*) Dutton/Plume.

—Carnal Hours. 1995. (Nathan Heller Ser.). 400p. mass mkt. 5.99 o.s.i (*0-451-17975-7*, Signet Bks.) NAL.

—Chicago Confidential. 2002. 304p. 22.95 (*0-451-20650-9*) NAL.

—Damned in Paradise. 1996. (Nathan Heller Ser.). 320p. 23.95 o.p. (*0-525-94225-4*) Dutton/Plume.

—Damned in Paradise. 1998. (Nathan Heller Ser.: Vol. 8). 320p. mass mkt. 5.99 o.s.i (*0-451-19104-8*, Signet Bks.) NAL.

—Damned in Paradise. unabr. ed. 1997. audio 70.00 (*0-7887-0855-4*, 95001E7) Recorded Bks., LLC.

—Dying in the Post-War World: A Nathan Heller Casebook. 1991. (Nate Heller Ser.). 280p. 19.95 o.p. (*0-88150-210-3*) Countryman Pr.

—Dying in the Post-War World: A Nathan Heller Casebook. 1993. 3.99 o.p. (*0-517-10403-2*) Random Hse. Value Publishing.

—Flying Blind. 1998. (Nathan Heller Ser.). 304p. 24.95 o.p. (*0-525-94311-0*) Dutton/Plume.

—Flying Blind. 1999. 384p. mass mkt. 5.99 o.s.i (*0-451-19262-1*) NAL.

—Kisses of Death: A Nathan Heller Casebook. 2001. (Illus.). 208p. pap. (*1-885941-56-0*); 223p. o.p. (*1-885941-55-2*) Crippen & Landru, Pubs.

—Majic Man. 1999. 304p. 23.95 o.p. (*0-525-94515-6*) Dutton/Plume.

—Majic Man. 2000. (Nathan Heller Ser.). 384p. mass mkt. 5.99 o.s.i (*0-451-19945-6*, Signet Bks.) NAL.

—Majic Man. l.t. ed. 2000. (Basic Ser.). 527p. 28.95 (*0-7862-2529-7*) Thorndike Pr.

—The Million Dollar Wound. 1987. 320p. reprint ed. pap. 3.95 o.p. (*0-8125-0159-4*, Tor Bks.) Doherty, Tom Assocs., LLC.

—The Million Dollar Wound. 1986. (Illus.). 400p. 16.95 o.p. (*0-312-53252-0*) St. Martin's Pr.

—The Million Dollar Wound. 2003. (Illus.). 352p. mass mkt. 6.99 (*0-7434-7463-5*) ibooks, Inc.

—Neon Mirage. 1991. 288p. mass mkt. 4.99 o.s.i (*0-553-28548-3*) Bantam Bks.

—Neon Mirage. 1988. (Illus.). 384p. 18.95 o.p. (*0-312-01484-8*, Saint Martin's Minotaur) St. Martin's Pr.

—Stolen Away: A Novel of the Lindbergh Kidnapping. 528p. 1992. mass mkt. 5.99 o.s.i (*0-553-29614-0*); 1991. 22.50 o.s.i (*0-553-07133-5*) Bantam Bks.

—True Crime. 1986. 384p. reprint ed. pap. 3.95 o.p. (*0-8125-0152-7*, Tor Bks.) Doherty, Tom Assocs., LLC.

—True Crime. 1984. 15.95 o.p. (*0-312-82045-3*) St. Martin's Pr.

—True Crime. 2003. (Illus.). 368p. mass mkt. 6.99 (*0-7434-5900-8*) ibooks, Inc.

—True Detective. 1986. 384p. reprint ed. pap. 3.95 o.p. (*0-8125-0150-0*, Tor Bks.) Doherty, Tom Assocs., LLC.

—True Detective. 1983. (Illus.). 368p. 14.95 o.p. (*0-312-82051-8*) St. Martin's Pr.

### HELLER, SHERI (FICTITIOUS CHARACTER)—FICTION

De Borchgrave, Sheri. A Dangerous Liaison. 1994. (Illus.). 336p. reprint ed. mass mkt. 4.99 o.s.i (*0-451-40509-9*, Onyx) NAL.

### HELM, MATT (FICTITIOUS CHARACTER)—FICTION

Hamilton, Donald. The Ambushers. 1985. 192p. (Orig.). mass mkt. 2.95 o.s.i (*0-449-12841-5*, Fawcett) Ballantine Bks.

—The Annihilators. 1983. mass mkt. 3.50 o.s.i (*0-449-12504-1*, Fawcett) Ballantine Bks.

—The Betrayers. 1986. mass mkt. 2.95 o.s.i (*0-449-13036-3*, Fawcett) Ballantine Bks.

—The Damagers. 1993. mass mkt. 4.99 o.s.i (*0-449-14847-5*, Fawcett) Ballantine Bks.

—Death of a Citizen. 1984. mass mkt. 1.95 o.s.i (*0-449-14087-3*, Fawcett); 1984. mass mkt. 3.50 o.s.i (*0-449-12798-2*, Fawcett); 1977. mass mkt. 1.50 o.s.i (*0-449-13922-0*); 1975. mass mkt. 1.25 o.s.i (*0-449-13338-9*) Ballantine Bks.

—The Demolishers. 1987. 352p. mass mkt. 3.95 o.s.i (*0-449-13233-1*, Fawcett) Ballantine Bks.

—The Detonators. 1985. 336p. mass mkt. 3.50 o.s.i (*0-449-12755-9*, Fawcett) Ballantine Bks.

—The Devastators. 1980. (Matt Helm Ser.). mass mkt. 1.95 o.s.i (*0-449-14084-9*, Fawcett) Ballantine Bks.

—The Frighteners. 1989. mass mkt. 4.50 o.s.i (*0-449-14521-2*, Fawcett) Ballantine Bks.

—The Infiltrators. 1984. 352p. mass mkt. 3.50 o.s.i (*0-449-12517-3*, Fawcett) Ballantine Bks.

—Interlopers. (Matt Helm Ser.). 1985. 224p. mass mkt. 2.95 o.s.i (*0-449-12907-1*); 1980. mass mkt. 1.95 o.s.i (*0-449-13994-8*); 1976. mass mkt. 1.50 o.s.i (*0-449-13498-9*) Ballantine Bks. (Fawcett).

—The Intimidators. 1985. (Matt Helm Ser.). 288p. (Orig.). mass mkt. 3.50 o.s.i (*0-449-12842-3*, Fawcett) Ballantine Bks.

—Intimidators. 1980. mass mkt. 1.95 o.s.i (*0-449-14110-1*, Fawcett); 1976. mass mkt. 1.50 o.s.i (*0-449-13489-X*) Ballantine Bks.

—The Intriguers. 1988. pap. 2.95 o.p. (*0-449-44510-0*, Fawcett) Ballantine Bks.

—Intriguers. 1981. mass mkt. 2.95 o.s.i (*0-449-13999-9*); 1976. mass mkt. 1.50 o.s.i (*0-449-13757-0*) Ballantine Bks.

—The Menacers. 1978. (Matt Helm Ser.). 192p. mass mkt. 1.75 o.s.i (*0-449-14077-6*, Fawcett) Ballantine Bks.

—Murderers' Row. 1981. (Matt Helm Ser.). mass mkt. 1.95 o.s.i (*0-449-14088-1*, Fawcett) Ballantine Bks.

—Murderer's Row. 1987. 192p. mass mkt. 2.95 o.s.i (*0-449-13274-9*, Fawcett) Ballantine Bks.

—The Poisoners. 1984. 224p. mass mkt. 2.95 o.s.i (*0-449-12693-5*, Fawcett) Ballantine Bks.

—The Ravagers. 1978. (Matt Helm Ser.). 144p. mass mkt. 1.75 o.s.i (*0-449-14078-4*, Fawcett) Ballantine Bks.

—Ravagers. 1977. mass mkt. 1.50 o.s.i (*0-449-13921-2*) Ballantine Bks.

—The Removers. 1986. (Matt Helm Ser.). mass mkt. 2.95 o.s.i (*0-449-13037-1*, Fawcett) Ballantine Bks.

—The Retaliators. 1984. 224p. mass mkt. 2.95 o.s.i (*0-449-12694-3*, Fawcett) Ballantine Bks.

—The Revengers. (Orig.). 1986. 352p. mass mkt. 3.50 o.s.i (*0-449-13093-2*); 1982. mass mkt. 2.95 o.s.i (*0-449-14487-9*) Ballantine Bks. (Fawcett).

—The Shadowers. 1986. mass mkt. 2.95 o.s.i (*0-449-13193-9*, Fawcett) Ballantine Bks.

—The Silencers. 1979. (Matt Helm Ser.). mass mkt. 1.75 o.s.i (*0-449-14136-5*, Fawcett) Ballantine Bks.

—Silencers. 1974. mass mkt. 0.95 o.s.i (*0-449-13000-2*) Ballantine Bks.

—The Terminators. 1980. (Matt Helm Ser.). 224p. mass mkt. 1.95 o.s.i (*0-449-14035-0*, Fawcett) Ballantine Bks.

—Terminators. 1977. mass mkt. 1.50 o.s.i (*0-449-13665-5*); 1975. mass mkt. 1.25 o.s.i (*0-449-13214-5*) Ballantine Bks.

—The Terrorizers. 1983. (Matt Helm Ser.). mass mkt. 2.50 o.s.i (*0-449-12597-1*, Fawcett) Ballantine Bks.

—The Threateners. 1992. mass mkt. 5.99 o.p. (*0-449-14681-2*, Fawcett) Ballantine Bks.

—The Vanishers. 1986. (Orig.). mass mkt. 3.50 o.s.i (*0-449-12967-5*, Fawcett) Ballantine Bks.

—The Wrecking Crew. 1979. (Matt Helm Ser.). mass mkt. 1.75 o.s.i (*0-449-14053-9*, Fawcett) Ballantine Bks.

—Wrecking Crew. 1977. mass mkt. 1.50 o.s.i (*0-449-13838-0*, Fawcett) Ballantine Bks.

**HEMLOCK, JONATHAN (FICTITIOUS CHARACTER)—FICTION**

Trevanian. The Loo Sanction. 1984. 352p. mass mkt. 5.99 o.s.i (*0-345-31738-6*, Ballantine Bks.) Ballantine Bks.

—The Loo Sanction. 1976. mass mkt. 2.50 o.p. (*0-380-00175-6*, 65383-4, Avon Bks.) Morrow/Avon.

—The Loo Sanction. l.t. ed. 1983. (Charnwood Large Print Ser.). 400p. 29.99 o.p. (*0-7089-8095-3*, Charnwood) Thorpe, F. A. Pubs. GBR. *Dist:* Ulverscroft Large Print Bks., Ltd., Ulverscroft Large Print Canada, Ltd.

**HENNING, KAREN (FICTITIOUS CHARACTER)—FICTION**

Daley, Robert. Tainted Evidence. 1995. pap. 5.99 (*0-446-36083-X*); 1994. 448p. mass mkt. 5.99 o.s.i (*0-446-60083-0*) Warner Bks., Inc.

**HENRIE O (FICTITIOUS CHARACTER)—FICTION**

Hart, Carolyn G. Crime on Her Mind: A Collection of Short Stories. 1999. (Mystery Ser.). 268p. 21.95 (*0-7862-1735-9*, Five Star) Gale Group.

—Dead Man's Island. 1994. 352p. mass mkt. 6.99 (*0-553-56607-5*) Bantam Bks.

—Dead Man's Island. unabr. ed. 1997. (Henrie O Mysteries Ser.). audio 48.00 (*0-7366-3837-7*, 4557) Books on Tape, Inc.

—Dead Man's Island. l.t. ed. 1994. (G. K. Hall Mystery Ser.). 355p. lib. bdg. 23.95 o.p. (*0-8161-5874-6*, Macmillan Reference USA) Gale Group.

—Death in Lovers' Lane. unabr. ed. 1998. (Henrie O Mysteries Ser.). audio 48.00 (*0-7366-4168-8*, 4670) Books on Tape, Inc.

—Death in Lovers' Lane. l.t. ed. 1997. (Wheeler Large Print Book Ser.). 25.95 (*1-56895-467-0*, Wheeler Publishing, Inc.) Gale Group.

—Death in Lovers' Lane. 1997. 288p. mass mkt. 20.00 o.p. (*0-380-97413-4*); 1998. 320p. reprint ed. mass mkt. 6.50 (*0-380-79002-5*) Morrow/Avon. (Avon Bks.).

—Death in Paradise. unabr. ed. 1998. (Henrie O Mysteries Ser.). audio 48.00 (*0-7366-4263-3*, 4762) Books on Tape, Inc.

—Death in Paradise. 1999. 304p. mass mkt. 6.50 (*0-380-79003-3*); 1998. 288p. 20.00 (*0-380-97414-2*) Morrow/Avon. (Avon Bks.).

—Death in Paradise, Set. abr. ed. 1998. audio 18.00 (*0-7871-1704-8*, Dove Audio) NewStar Media, Inc.

—Death in Paradise. l.t. ed. 2000. (Mystery Ser.). 415p. 29.95 (*0-7862-2679-X*) Thorndike Pr.

—Death on the River Walk. l.t. ed. 2000. (Large Print Book Ser.). pap. 23.95 (*1-56895-822-6*, Wheeler Publishing, Inc.) Gale Group.

—Death on the River Walk. 2000. 336p. mass mkt. 6.99 (*0-380-79005-X*); 1999. 256p. 22.00 (*0-380-97415-0*) Morrow/Avon. (Avon Bks.).

—Resort to Murder. 2001. 304p. 24.00 (*0-380-97773-7*, Morrow, William & Co.) Morrow/Avon.

—Resort to Murder. l.t. ed. 2001. 456p. 29.95 (*0-7862-3490-3*) Thorndike Pr.

—Scandal in Fair Haven. 1995. 352p. mass mkt. 6.99 (*0-553-56537-0*) Bantam Bks.

—Scandal in Fair Haven. unabr. ed. 1998. (Henrie O Mysteries Ser.). audio 56.00 (*0-7366-4144-0*, 4648) Books on Tape, Inc.

—Scandal in Fair Haven. l.t. ed. 1994. 414p. lib. bdg. 20.95 o.p. (*0-8161-7406-7*, Macmillan Reference USA) Gale Group.

**HENRY, DALLAS (FICTITIOUS CHARACTER)—FICTION**

Pairo, Preston. Beach Money. 1991. 208p. 18.95 o.p. (*0-8027-5786-3*) Walker & Co.

—One Dead Judge. 1993. 204p. 19.95 o.p. (*0-8027-1250-9*) Walker & Co.

**HENRY, KATHERINE (FICTITIOUS CHARACTER)—FICTION**

Bowen, Gail. Striking Out. 1996. 256p. mass mkt. 5.99 (*0-7710-3415-6*) McClelland & Stewart/Tundra Bks.

Gordon, Alison. The Dead Pull Hitter. 1991. 256p. mass mkt. 3.99 o.p. (*0-451-40240-5*, Onyx) NAL.

—The Dead Pull Hitter. 1989. 224p. 15.95 o.p. (*0-312-03319-2*, Saint Martin's Minotaur) St. Martin's Pr.

—The Dead Pull Hitter: A Kate Henry Mystery. 1996. 224p. mass mkt. 6.99 (*0-7710-3420-2*) McClelland & Stewart/Tundra Bks.

—Night Game. 1993. 269p. 18.95 o.p. (*0-312-09062-5*, Saint Martin's Minotaur) St. Martin's Pr.

—Night Games: A Kate Henry Mystery. 1993. 271p. mass mkt. 6.99 (*0-7710-3424-5*) McClelland & Stewart/Tundra Bks.

—Prairie Hardball. 1998. (Kate Henry Mysteries Ser.: Bk. 5). 288p. mass mkt. 6.95 (*0-7710-3413-X*) McClelland & Stewart/Tundra Bks.

—Prairie Hardball: A Kate Henry Mystery. 1998. (Kate Henry Mystery Ser.). 288p. 20.95 o.p. (*0-7710-3412-1*) McClelland & Stewart/Tundra Bks.

—Safe at Home. 1991. 17.95 o.p. (*0-312-05959-0*, Saint Martin's Minotaur) St. Martin's Pr.

—Safe at Home: A Kate Henry Mystery. 1996. 248p. mass mkt. 5.95 (*0-7710-3417-2*) McClelland & Stewart/Tundra Bks.

—Striking Out: A Kate Henry Mystery. 1995. 240p. 19.95 o.p. (*0-7710-3423-7*) McClelland & Stewart/Tundra Bks.

**HENRY, VICTOR (FICTITIOUS CHARACTER)—FICTION**

Wouk, Herman. War & Remembrance. unabr. ed. 1982. Pt. 1. audio 88.00 (*0-7366-0611-4*, 1575-A); Pt. 2. audio 96.00; Pt. 3. audio 88.00 Books on Tape, Inc.

—War & Remembrance. 1995. mass mkt. (*0-316-95591-4*); 1992. 1392p. mass mkt. 8.99 (*0-316-95515-9*); 1978. 1042p. (YA). (gr. 8 up). 29.95 o.p. (*0-316-95501-9*) Little Brown & Co.

—War & Remembrance. 1989. mass mkt. 5.95 o.p. (*0-671-67288-6*); 1983. mass mkt. 5.95 o.s.i (*0-671-46314-4*) Simon & Schuster. (Pocket).

—War & Remembrance. 1992. 15.04 (*0-606-12567-1*) Turtleback Bks.

—The Winds of War. unabr. ed. 1981. Pt. 1. audio 80.00 (*0-7366-0608-4*, 1574-A); Pt. II. audio 72.00; Pt. III. audio 72.00 Books on Tape, Inc.

—The Winds of War. 1995. mass mkt. (*0-316-95590-6*); 1992. (Illus.). 1056p. mass mkt. 8.99 (*0-316-95516-7*); 1971. 885p. (gr. 8). 35.00 o.p. (*0-316-95500-0*); 2002. 896p. reprint ed. pap. 15.95 (*0-316-95266-4*, Back Bay) Little Brown & Co.

—The Winds of War. 1989. mass mkt. 5.95 o.p. (*0-671-67287-8*); 1986. mass mkt. 5.95 o.s.i (*0-671-63472-0*) Simon & Schuster. (Pocket).

—The Winds of War. 1992. 14.04 (*0-606-12577-9*) Turtleback Bks.

—The Winds of War: T. V. Tie-In Edition. 1983. mass mkt. 4.95 o.s.i (*0-671-46319-5*, Pocket) Simon & Schuster.

—The Winds of War & War & Remembrance. 1978. 45.00 o.s.i (*0-316-95502-7*) Little Brown & Co.

**HENSHAW, SUSAN (FICTITIOUS CHARACTER)—FICTION**

Wolzien, Valerie. All Hallows' Evil. 1992. 256p. (Orig.). mass mkt. 6.99 (*0-449-14745-2*, Fawcett) Ballantine Bks.

—Death at a Discount. 2000. (Susan Henshaw Mysteries Ser.). 288p. mass mkt. 6.50 (*0-449-00630-1*, Fawcett) Ballantine Bks.

—Elected for Death. 1996. mass mkt. 5.99 o.s.i (*0-449-14959-5*, Fawcett) Ballantine Bks.

—The Fortieth Birthday Body: A Suburban Mystery. 1990. 240p. mass mkt. 6.50 (*0-449-14685-5*, Fawcett) Ballantine Bks.

—The Fortieth Birthday Body: A Suburban Mystery. 1992. 1.99 o.p. (*0-517-08392-2*) Random Hse. Value Publishing.

—The Fortieth Birthday Body: A Suburban Mystery. 1989. 266p. 16.95 o.p. (*0-312-02917-9*, Saint Martin's Minotaur) St. Martin's Pr.

—A Good Year for a Corpse. 1994. mass mkt. 5.99 o.s.i (*0-449-14833-5*, Fawcett) Ballantine Bks.

—Murder at the PTA Luncheon. 1990. 240p. mass mkt. 6.99 (*0-449-14639-1*, Fawcett) Ballantine Bks.

—Murder at the PTA Luncheon. 1988. 256p. 16.95 o.p. (*0-312-01480-5*, Saint Martin's Minotaur) St. Martin's Pr.

—An Old Faithful Murder. 1995. 256p. pap. 19.00 (*0-449-00743-X*); 1992. mass mkt. 5.99 (*0-449-14744-4*) Ballantine Bks. (Fawcett).

—Remodeled to Death. 1995. mass mkt. 5.99 o.s.i (*0-449-14921-8*, Fawcett) Ballantine Bks.

—A Star-Spangled Murder. 1993. 224p. mass mkt. 6.99 (*0-449-14834-3*, Fawcett) Ballantine Bks.

—The Student Body. 1999. (Susan Henshaw Mysteries Ser.). 240p. mass mkt. 6.99 (*0-449-15037-2*, Fawcett) Ballantine Bks.

—'Tis the Season to Be Murdered. 240p. (Orig.). 1995. pap. 15.00 (*0-449-00741-3*); 1994. mass mkt. 6.50 (*0-449-14920-X*) Ballantine Bks. (Fawcett).

—We Wish You a Merry Murder. 1993. mass mkt. 4.50 o.p. (*0-449-45259-X*); 1991. 288p. mass mkt. 6.99 (*0-449-14723-1*) Ballantine Bks. (Fawcett).

—Weddings Are Murder. 1998. (Susan Henshaw Mysteries Ser.). 240p. mass mkt. 6.99 (*0-449-15035-6*, Fawcett) Ballantine Bks.

**HEPBURN, ALAN (FICTITIOUS CHARACTER)—FICTION**

Carr, John Dickson. Captain Cut-Throat. 1980. 232p. 1.95 o.s.i (*0-441-09134-2*) Ace Bks.

—Captain Cut-Throat. 1998. 240p. mass mkt. 4.95 (*0-7867-0547-7*); 1988. 306p. pap. 3.95 o.p. (*0-88184-437-3*) Avalon Publishing Group. (Carroll & Graf Pubs.).

—Captain Cut-Throat. 1996. 21.50 o.p. (*0-7451-8689-0*, Black Dagger) BBC Audiobooks America.

**HERCULES (ROMAN MYTHOLOGY)—FICTION**

Boggs, Timothy. By the Sword. 1996. (Hercules: The Legendary Journeys Ser.). 224p. mass mkt. 5.99 o.s.i (*1-57297-198-3*) Boulevard Bks.

Fenster, Julie. Hercules: The Heart of the Hunter. unabr. ed. 1997. (Immortal Adventures Ser.). 16.95 o.p. incl. audio (*1-882071-90-5*) B&B Audio, Inc.

HarperCollins Staff. Hercules: The Legendary Journeys Postcard Book. 1998. (Illus.). 60p. mass mkt. 9.99 o.s.i (*0-06-107510-8*) HarperCollins Pubs.

Morreale, Marie T. Hercules: The Legendary Journey Scrapbook. 1996. (J). (gr. 4-7). mass mkt. 3.99 (*0-590-87104-8*) Scholastic, Inc.

Odom, Mel. Young Hercules: TV Tie In. 1999. (Young Hercules Ser.: Vol. 1). 160p. (J). (gr. 4-7). mass mkt. 3.99 (*0-671-03551-7*, Simon Pulse) Simon & Schuster Children's Publishing.

Saberhagen, Fred. The Arms of Hercules. 2000. (Book of the Gods Ser.: Vol. 3). 384p. pap. 14.95 (*0-312-87776-5*);Vol.3. 25.95 o.p. (*0-312-86774-3*) Doherty, Tom Assocs., LLC. (Tor Bks.).

Skolnick, Evan. Hercules Movie Adaptation. 1997. 23.95 (*1-57840-072-4*); pap. text 4.50 (*1-57840-073-2*) Acclaim Bks.

van Hise, James. Hercules & Xena: The Unofficial Companion. 1998. (Illus.). 272p. pap. 15.95 o.p. (*1-58063-001-4*, Renaissance Bks.) St. Martin's Pr.

**HERNANDEZ QUINTO, GIMIENDO (FICTITIOUS CHARACTER)—FICTION**

Norman, James. Murder, Chop Chop. 1997. reprint ed. pap. 13.00 (*0-915230-16-X*) Rue Morgue Pr.

**HERRICK, ROBERT (FICTITIOUS CHARACTER)—FICTION**

Macaulay, Rose. They Were Defeated. 1986. (Twentieth Century Classics Ser.). 445p. pap. 6.95 o.p. (*0-19-281316-1*) Oxford Univ. Pr., Inc.

**HERSHEY, CLAUDIA (FICTITIOUS CHARACTER)—FICTION**

Belgrave, Laura. Deadly Associations. 2003. (Claudia Hershey Mysteries Ser.). 220p. 23.95 (*1-57072-247-1*); 208p. pap. 13.95 (*1-57072-248-X*) Overmountain Pr. (Silver Dagger Mysteries).

—In the Spirit of Murder. 2000. (Claudia Hershey Mysteries Ser.). 204p. 24.50 (*1-57072-108-4*); pap. 15.00 (*1-57072-124-6*, Silver Dagger Mysteries) Overmountain Pr.

—Quietly Dead. 2001. (Claudia Hershey Mysteries Ser.: Vol. 2). v, 200p. 23.95 (*1-57072-172-6*); pap. 13.95 (*1-57072-173-4*) Overmountain Pr. (Silver Dagger Mysteries).

**HICKOK, WILD BILL, 1837-1876—FICTION**

Dexter, Pete. Deadwood. 1989. 384p. pap. 13.95 o.s.i (*0-14-012729-1*, Penguin Bks.) Penguin Group (USA) Inc.

—Deadwood. l.t. ed. 1997. (Niagara Large Print Ser.). 584p. 29.50 o.p. (*0-7089-5862-1*, Linford) Thorpe, F. A. Pubs. GBR. *Dist:* Ulverscroft Large Print Bks., Ltd.

—Deadwood. 1987. 512p. pap. 4.95 o.p. (*0-14-009910-7*, Penguin Bks.) Viking Penguin.

**HIGGINS, BRETT (FICTITIOUS CHARACTER)—FICTION**

Szymanski, Therese. When Good Girls Go Bad: A Motor City Thriller Featuring Brett Higgins. 2003. 274p. pap. 12.95 (*1-931513-11-2*) Bella Bks., Inc.

—When Some Body Disappears: A Brett Higgins Mystery. 1999. (Brett Higgins Mysteries Ser.). 173p. pap. 11.95 (*1-56280-227-5*) Naiad Pr., Inc.

—When the Dancing Stops: A Brett Higgins Mystery. 1997. (Brett Higgins Mysteries Ser.). 272p. (Orig.). pap. 11.95 (*1-56280-186-4*) Naiad Pr., Inc.

—When the Dead Speak: A Brett Higgins Mystery. 1998. (Brett Higgins Mysteries Ser.). 224p. (Orig.). pap. 11.95 (*1-56280-198-8*) Naiad Pr., Inc.

**HIGHLANDER (FICTITIOUS CHARACTER)—FICTION**

*see MacLeod, Duncan (Fictitious Character)—Fiction*

**HIGHTOWER, KAREN (FICTITIOUS CHARACTER)—FICTION**

*see Bast (Fictitious Character)—Fiction*

**HILDRETH, JANE (FICTITIOUS CHARACTER)—FICTION**

Spicer, Michael. The Cotswold Murder. 1990. 15.95 o.p. (*0-312-04285-X*, Saint Martin's Minotaur) St. Martin's Pr.

—The Cotswold Murders. l.t. ed. 1992. 248p. 15.95 o.p. (*0-7451-1543-8*, Macmillan Reference USA) Gale Group.

**HILL, JUDY (FICTITIOUS CHARACTER)—FICTION**

McGown, Jill. Death in the Family. 2004. 336p. mass mkt. 6.99 (*0-345-45849-4*, Fawcett); 2003. 320p. 22.95 (*0-345-45848-6*, Ballantine Bks.) Ballantine Bks.

—Death in the Family. l.t. ed. 2003. 30.45 (*0-7862-5380-0*) Thorndike Pr.

—An Evil Hour. 1987. 256p. 16.95 o.p. (*0-312-00592-X*) St. Martin's Pr.

—Gone to Her Death. 1991. mass mkt. 4.99 (*0-449-21966-6*, Fawcett) Ballantine Bks.

—Gone to Her Death. l.t. ed. 1991. (General Ser.). 330p. lib. bdg. 22.95 o.p. (*0-8161-5094-X*, Macmillan Reference USA) Gale Group.

—Gone to Her Death. 1989. 256p. 16.95 o.p. (*0-312-03839-9*, Saint Martin's Minotaur) St. Martin's Pr.

—Murder . . . Now & Then. 1993. 304p. 20.95 o.p. (*0-312-10006-X*, Saint Martin's Minotaur) St. Martin's Pr.

—Murder at the Old Vicarage. 1991. (Mysteries Around the World Promotion Ser.). 256p. mass mkt. 6.50 (*0-449-21819-8*, Ivy Bks.) Ballantine Bks.

—Murder at the Old Vicarage. l.t. ed. 1990. (General Ser.). 348p. lib. bdg. 18.95 o.p. (*0-8161-4838-4*, Macmillan Reference USA) Gale Group.

—Murder at the Old Vicarage. 1988. 256p. 16.95 o.p. (*0-312-02615-3*, Saint Martin's Minotaur) St. Martin's Pr.

—Murder Movie. 1992. mass mkt. 4.99 o.s.i (*0-449-22070-2*, Fawcett) Ballantine Bks.

—Murder Movie. 1990. 17.95 o.p. (*0-312-05475-0*, Saint Martin's Minotaur) St. Martin's Pr.

—Murder Movie. l.t. ed. 2001. (Ulverscroft Large Print Ser.). 448p. 32.50 (*0-7089-4435-3*) Ulverscroft Large Print Bks., Ltd.

—Murder... Now & Then. 1995. (Mysteries Around the World Promotion). mass mkt. 5.99 o.s.i (*0-449-22311-6*, Fawcett) Ballantine Bks.

—Murder... Now & Then. 1993. 407p. pap. 13.95 (*0-330-33243-0*) Pan Bks. Ltd. GBR. *Dist:* Trans-Atlantic Pubns., Inc.

—The Murders of Mrs. Austin & Mrs. Beale. 1993. 256p. reprint ed. mass mkt. 6.50 (*0-449-22162-8*, Fawcett) Ballantine Bks.

—The Murders of Mrs. Austin & Mrs. Beale. 1991. 224p. 17.95 o.p. (*0-312-06422-5*, Saint Martin's Minotaur) St. Martin's Pr.

—The Other Woman. 1994. mass mkt. 5.99 (*0-449-22272-1*, Fawcett) Ballantine Bks.

—The Other Woman. l.t. ed. 1997. 477p. (*0-7505-1065-X*) Magna Large Print Bks. GBR. *Dist:* Ulverscroft Large Print Bks., Ltd.

—The Other Woman. 1993. 236p. 17.95 o.p. (*0-312-08868-X*, Saint Martin's Minotaur) St. Martin's Pr.

—A Perfect Match. 1990. 192p. mass mkt. 6.50 (*0-449-21820-1*, Fawcett) Ballantine Bks.

—A Perfect Match. 1983. 192p. 11.95 o.p. (*0-312-60069-0*) St. Martin's Pr.

—Picture of Innocence. (British Mystery Ser.). 1999. 352p. mass mkt. 6.99 (*0-449-00251-9*); 1998. 336p. 22.00 o.p. (*0-449-00250-0*) Ballantine Bks. (Fawcett).

—Picture of Innocence. l.t. ed. 1998. (Mystery Ser.). 560p. 27.95 (*0-7862-1670-0*) Thorndike Pr.

—Plots & Errors. 2000. (Detective Chief Inspector Lloyd & Judy Hill Mysteries Ser.). 384p. mass mkt. 6.99 (*0-449-00253-5*, Fawcett) Ballantine Bks.

—Scene of Crime. l.t. ed. 2001. 391p. 29.95 (*0-7862-3647-7*) Thorndike Pr.

—A Shred of Evidence. 1997. 304p. mass mkt. 6.99 (0-449-22499-6) Ballantine Bks.
—Verdict Unsafe. 1998. 336p. mass mkt. 6.99 (0-449-22501-1); 1997. 327p. 22.00 o.p. (0-449-91067-9) Ballantine Bks. (Fawcett).
—Verdict Unsafe. l.t. ed. 1997. (Myst-Hall Ser.). 522p. lib. bdg. 23.95 (0-7838-8287-4, Macmillan Reference USA) Gale Group.

**HILL, MAGGIE (FICTITIOUS CHARACTER)—FICTION**

Howe, Melodie J. Beauty Dies. 1996. (Crime Ser.). 272p. pap. 5.95 o.s.i (0-14-023565-5) Penguin Group (USA) Inc.
—Beauty Dies: A Claire Conrad - Maggie Hill Mystery. 1994. 272p. 19.95 o.p. (0-670-85449-2, Viking) Viking Penguin.

**HILL, TONY (FICTITIOUS CHARACTER)—FICTION**

McDermid, Val. The Mermaids Singing. unabr. ed. 1999. 14p. audio compact disk 104.95 (0-7531-0710-4, 107104); audio 84.95 (0-7531-0075-4, 960808) ISIS Audio Bks. GBR. *Dist:* Ulverscroft Large Print Bks., Ltd.
—The Mermaids Singing. 1997. 480p. mass mkt. 6.50 o.p. (0-06-101175-4); 1996. 288p. mass mkt. 22.00 o.p. (0-06-101174-6) Morrow/Avon. (HarperTorch).
—The Wire in the Blood. unabr. ed. 1998. audio 94.95 (0-7531-0350-8, 980504) ISIS Audio Bks. GBR. *Dist:* Ulverscroft Large Print Bks., Ltd.
—The Wire in the Blood. ltd. ed. 1998. xii, 372p. 50.00 (1-890208-21-3) Poisoned Pen Pr.
—The Wire in the Blood. 2002. 528p. mass mkt. 6.99 (0-312-98365-4, St. Martin's Paperbacks) St. Martin's Pr.

**HILLSDEN, ALEC (FICTITIOUS CHARACTER)—FICTION**

Forbes, Bryan. A Spy at Twilight. 1991. 432p. reprint ed. mass mkt. 5.99 o.s.i (0-451-40263-4, Onyx) NAL.
—A Spy at Twilight. 1993. 3.99 o.p. (0-517-09107-0) Random Hse. Value Publishing.

**HINES, JAKE (FICTITIOUS CHARACTER)—FICTION**

Gunn, Elizabeth. Five Card Stud. 2000. (Jake Hines Mysteries Ser.). 195p. (YA). 23.95 (0-8027-3343-3) Walker & Co.
—Par Four: A Jake Hines Mystery. 2000. (Jake Hines Mysteries Ser.). 304p. mass mkt. 5.99 o.s.i (0-440-22636-8) Dell Publishing.
—Par Four: A Jake Hines Mystery. 1999. (Jake Hines Mysteries Ser.). (Illus.). 291p. pap. 22.95 (0-8027-3324-7) Walker & Co.
—Seventh-Inning Stretch. 2003. (WWL Mystery Ser.: No. 458). 256p. mass mkt. (0-373-26458-5, Worldwide Library) Harlequin Enterprises, Ltd.
—Seventh-Inning Stretch. l.t. ed. 2002. (Mystery Ser.). 353p. 29.95 (0-7862-4732-0) Thorndike Pr.
—Seventh-Inning Stretch: A Jake Hines Mystery. 2002. 228p. 23.95 (0-8027-3374-3) Walker & Co.
—Six-Pound Walleye. 2002. (WWL Mystery Ser.). mass mkt. (0-373-26425-9, Worldwide Library) Harlequin Enterprises, Ltd.
—Six-Pound Walleye: A Jake Hines Mystery. l.t. ed. 2001. 341p. 27.95 (0-7862-3616-7) Thorndike Pr.
—Six-Pound Walleye: A Jake Hines Mystery. 2001. (Jake Hines Mysteries Ser.). 216p. 23.95 (0-8027-3356-5) Walker & Co.
—Triple Play: A Jake Hines Mystery. 1998. (Jake Hines Mysteries Ser.). 224p. mass mkt. 5.99 o.s.i (0-440-22635-X) Dell Publishing.
—Triple Play: A Jake Hines Mystery. 1997. (Jake Hines Mysteries Ser.). 240p. 21.95 (0-8027-3307-7) Walker & Co.

**HIRSCH, MARTI (FICTITIOUS CHARACTER)—FICTION**

Moore, Miriam Ann. Last Dance. 1997. (Orig.). mass mkt. 5.99 (0-380-79118-8, Avon Bks.) Morrow/Avon.
—Stayin' Alive. 1998. (Marti Hirsch Mystery Ser.). mass mkt. 5.99 (0-380-79119-6, Avon Bks.) Morrow/Avon.

**HO KUM MENON (FICTITIOUS CHARACTER)—FICTION**

Baratham, Gopal. Moonrise, Sunset. 1996. (Mask Noir Ser.). 256p. (Orig.). pap. o.p. (1-85242-501-6) Serpent's Tail Ltd.

**HOAG, STEWART (FICTITIOUS CHARACTER)—FICTION**

Handler, David. The Boy Who Never Grew Up. 1993. 384p. mass mkt. 4.99 o.s.i (0-553-29739-2) Bantam Bks.
—The Boy Who Never Grew Up. unabr. ed. 1998. (Stewart Hoag Mystery Ser.: Vol. 5). audio 85.00 (0-7887-2283-2, 95534E7) Recorded Bks., LLC.
—The Girl Who Ran off with Daddy. 1996. 304p. mass mkt. 4.99 o.s.i (0-553-56902-3) Bantam Bks.
—The Man Who Cancelled Himself: A Stewart Hoag Mystery. 1995. 256p. mass mkt. 4.99 o.s.i (0-553-29397-4, Crimeline) Bantam Bks.
—The Man Who Cancelled Himself: A Stewart Hoag Mystery. 1995. 416p. 19.95 o.s.i (0-385-42160-5) Doubleday Publishing.
—The Man Who Cancelled Himself: A Stewart Hoag Mystery. unabr. ed. 1999. (Stewart Hoag Mystery Ser.: Vol. 6). audio 85.00 (0-7887-1992-0, 95379E7) Recorded Bks., LLC.
—The Man Who Died Laughing. 1990. 208p. mass mkt. 2.25 o.s.i (0-553-18520-9); 1988. 192p. mass mkt. 3.50 o.s.i (0-553-27469-4) Bantam Bks.
—The Man Who Lived by Night. 1989. 181p. mass mkt. 3.50 o.s.i (0-553-27935-1) Bantam Bks.
—The Man Who Loved Women to Death. 1998. 336p. mass mkt. 5.50 o.s.i (0-553-57480-9, Crimeline) Bantam Bks.
—The Man Who Loved Women to Death. 1997. 304p. 23.95 o.s.i (0-385-48052-0) Doubleday Publishing.
—The Man Who Loved Women to Death. unabr. ed. 2001. audio 61.00 (0-7887-4877-7, 96453x7) Recorded Bks., LLC.
—The Man Who Would Be F. Scott Fitzgerald. 1995. 224p. mass mkt. 4.99 o.s.i (0-553-27848-7) Bantam Bks.
—The Man Who Would Be F. Scott Fitzgerald. 1993. 256p. 17.00 o.s.i (0-385-46782-6) Doubleday Publishing.
—The Man Who Would Be F. Scott Fitzgerald. unabr. ed. 1998. (Stewart Hoag Mystery Ser.: Vol. 3). audio 51.00 (0-7887-0929-1, 95069E7) Recorded Bks., LLC.
—The Woman Who Fell from Grace. 1992. 240p. mass mkt. 4.99 o.s.i (0-553-28914-4) Bantam Bks.
—The Woman Who Fell from Grace. 1991. 240p. 15.00 o.s.i (0-385-42115-X) Doubleday Publishing.
—The Woman Who Fell from Grace. l.t. ed. 1992. (General Ser.). 19.95 o.p. (0-8161-5511-9); pap. 17.95 (0-8161-5512-7) Gale Group. (Macmillan Reference USA).
—The Woman Who Fell from Grace. unabr. ed. 1998. (Stewart Hoag Mystery Ser.: Vol. 4). audio 51.00 (0-7887-2024-4, 95399E7) Recorded Bks., LLC.

**HOARE, BARTHOLOMEW (FICTITIOUS CHARACTER)—FICTION**

Perkins, Wilder. Hoare & the Headless Captains: A Maritime Mystery Featuring Captain Bartholomew Hoare. 2000. 247p. 22.95 (0-312-25248-X, Saint Martin's Minotaur) St. Martin's Pr.
—Hoare & the Matter of Treason. 2001. 215p. 22.95 (0-312-27291-X, Saint Martin's Minotaur) St. Martin's Pr.
—Hoare & the Portsmouth Atrocities. 1998. 224p. 21.95 (0-312-19283-5, Saint Martin's Minotaur) St. Martin's Pr.

**HOARE, DIDO (FICTITIOUS CHARACTER)—FICTION**

MacDonald, Marianne. Blood Lies: A Dido Hoare Mystery. 2002. 259p. 23.95 (0-312-28305-9, Saint Martin's Minotaur) St. Martin's Pr.
—Death's Autograph. abr. ed. 1998. audio 54.95 (0-7540-0089-3, CAB1512) BBC Audiobooks America.
—Death's Autograph: A Mystery. 1999. (Antiquarian Book Mysteries Ser.). 352p. mass mkt. 5.99 (0-06-109742-X, HarperTorch) Morrow/Avon.
—Death's Autograph: A Mystery. 1997. (Dido Hoare Mysteries Ser.). 224p. 22.95 o.p. (0-312-16815-2, Saint Martin's Minotaur) St. Martin's Pr.
—Die Once: A Dido Hoare Mystery. 2003. 272p. 23.95 (0-312-28360-1, Saint Martin's Minotaur) St. Martin's Pr.
—Ghost Walk. 2000. (Antiquarian Book Mysteries Ser.). 304p. mass mkt. 5.99 (0-06-101426-5) HarperCollins Pubs.
—Ghost Walk. 1998. (Dido Hoare Mysteries Ser.). 256p. 21.95 o.p. (0-312-19417-X, Saint Martin's Minotaur) St. Martin's Pr.
—Smoke Screen. 1999. 255p. 23.95 o.p. (0-312-24243-3, Saint Martin's Minotaur) St. Martin's Pr.

**HOBBY, PAT (FICTITIOUS CHARACTER)—FICTION**

Fitzgerald, F. Scott. The Pat Hobby Stories. 1981. 17.50 o.s.i (0-684-16477-9, Macmillan Reference USA) Gale Group.
—The Pat Hobby Stories. 1995. 192p. pap. 10.00 (0-684-80442-5, Scribner) Simon & Schuster.

**HOCKADAY, NEIL (FICTITIOUS CHARACTER)—FICTION**

Adcock, Thomas. Dark Maze. Chelius, Jane, ed. 1991. 320p. (Orig.). mass mkt. 5.50 (0-671-72909-8, Pocket) Simon & Schuster.
—Devil's Heaven. 1996. 288p. mass mkt. 5.99 (0-671-77043-8, Pocket) Simon & Schuster.
—Devil's Heaven. Chelius, Jane, ed. 1995. 336p. 20.00 o.p. (0-671-89778-0, Atria) Simon & Schuster.
—Drown All the Dogs. Chelius, Jane, ed. 1995. 368p. mass mkt. 5.99 (0-671-88329-1, Pocket) Simon & Schuster.
—Drown All the Dogs: A Neil Hockaday Mystery. 1994. 352p. 20.00 o.p. (0-671-77041-1, Atria) Simon & Schuster.
—Grief Street. 1998. (Neil Hockaday Mystery Ser.). 304p. per. 6.50 (0-671-51987-5, Pocket) Simon & Schuster.
—Grief Street: A Neil Hockaday Mystery. 1997. (Neil Hockaday Mystery Ser.). 304p. 22.00 (0-671-51986-7, Atria) Simon & Schuster.
—Thrown Away Child. (Neil Hockaday Mystery Ser.). 1997. 400p. per. 5.99 (0-671-51984-0, Pocket); 1996. 352p. 21.00 o.p. (0-671-51985-9, Atria) Simon & Schuster.

**HOFFMAN, NICK (FICTITIOUS CHARACTER)—FICTION**

Raphael, Lev. Burning down the House: A Nick Hoffman Novel. 2001. 256p. 23.95 (0-8027-3365-4) Walker & Co.
—Death of a Constant Lover. 2000. (Nick Hoffman Mystery Ser.). 288p. pap. 12.95 (0-312-26496-8, Saint Martin's Griffin) St. Martin's Pr.
—Death of a Constant Lover. 1999. (Nick Hoffman Mystery Ser.). 288p. 22.95 (0-8027-3326-3) Walker & Co.
—The Edith Wharton Murders: A Nick Hoffman Mystery. (Stonewall Inn Editions Ser.). 1998. 240p. pap. 11.95 (0-312-19863-9, Saint Martin's Griffin); 1997. 208p. 21.95 o.p. (0-312-15519-0, Saint Martin's Minotaur) St. Martin's Pr.
—Let's Get Criminal. 1996. 240p. 20.95 o.p. (0-312-13999-3, Saint Martin's Minotaur); 2nd ed. 1997. 244p. pap. 11.95 (0-312-15160-8, Saint Martin's Griffin) St. Martin's Pr.
—Little Miss Evil: A Nick Hoffman Mystery. 2000. (Nick Hoffman Mystery Ser.). 184p. 23.95 (0-8027-3342-5) Walker & Co.

**HOFFMAN, SAM (FICTITIOUS CHARACTER)—FICTION**

Ignatius, David. The Bank of Fear. l.t. ed. 1995. (G. K. Hall Core Ser.). 576p. 23.95 (0-7838-1185-3, Macmillan Reference USA) Gale Group.
—The Bank of Fear. 1994. 20.00 o.p. (0-688-13136-0, Morrow, William & Co.); 1995. 400p. reprint ed. mass mkt. 5.99 (0-380-72280-1, Avon Bks.) Morrow/Avon.
—The Bank of Fear. unabr. ed. audio 78.00 (0-7887-0300-5, 94493E7) Recorded Bks., LLC.

**HOITT, JIMMY (FICTITIOUS CHARACTER)—FICTION**

Rawson, David. Murder on Mount Desert. 304p. 1996. pap. 15.95 (0-89272-363-7); 1995. 24.95 o.p. (0-89272-373-4) Down East Bks.

**HOLDEN, SIDNEY (FICTITIOUS CHARACTER)—FICTION**

Charyn, Jerome. Elsinore. 1991. 18.95 o.p. (0-89296-361-1) Mysterious Pr.
—Elsinore. 1992. 256p. mass mkt. 4.99 (0-446-40111-0, Mysterious Pr. Paperback Bks.) Warner Bks., Inc.

**HOLDEN, VICKY (FICTITIOUS CHARACTER)—FICTION**

Coel, Margaret. The Dream Stalker. 1997. 256p. 21.95 o.s.i (0-425-15967-1); 1998. 272p. reprint ed. mass mkt. 6.50 (0-425-16533-7) Berkley Publishing Group. (Prime Crime).
—The Dream Stalker. unabr. ed. 1999. (O'Malley Mystery Ser.). audio 39.95 (1-55686-873-1) Books in Motion.
—The Eagle Catcher. 1996. (Arapaho Indian Mysteries Ser.). 256p. mass mkt. 6.50 (0-425-15463-7) Berkley Publishing Group.
—The Eagle Catcher. Set. unabr. ed. 1999. (O'Malley Mystery Ser.). audio 36.95 Books in Motion.
—The Eagle Catcher. 16th l.t. ed. 2002. 248p. lib. bdg. 28.95 (1-58547-159-3) Ctr. Point Large Print.
—The Eagle Catcher. 1995. (Arapaho Indian Mysteries Ser.). 224p. 22.50 (0-87081-367-6) Univ. Pr. of Colorado.
—The Eagle Catcher. 1995. E-Book 22.50 (0-585-02336-0) netLibrary, Inc.
—The Ghost Walker. 256p. 1996. 21.95 o.p. (0-425-15468-8); 1997. reprint ed. mass mkt. 6.50 (0-425-15961-2) Berkley Publishing Group. (Prime Crime).
—The Ghost Walker. unabr. ed. 1999. (O'Malley Mystery Ser.). audio 39.95 (1-55686-865-0) Books in Motion.
—Killing Raven. 2004. 304p. mass mkt. 6.99 (0-425-19750-6); 2003. 288p. 22.95 (0-425-19261-X, Prime Crime) Berkley Publishing Group.
—The Lost Bird. 2000. 304p. mass mkt. 6.50 (0-425-17030-6) Berkley Publishing Group.
—The Lost Bird. l.t. ed. 2000. (G. K. Hall Core Ser.). 332p. 28.95 (0-7838-8958-5, Macmillan Reference USA) Gale Group.
—The Lost Bird: A Mystery. 1999. 304p. 21.95 o.s.i (0-425-17059-4, Prime Crime) Berkley Publishing Group.
—The Shadow Dancer. 2002. 304p. 22.95 (0-425-18640-7, Prime Crime) Berkley Publishing Group.
—The Shadow Dancer. l.t. ed. 2003. lib. bdg. 28.95 (1-58547-284-0, Platinum) Ctr. Point Large Print.
—The Spirit Woman. 2000. 272p. 21.95 o.s.i (0-425-17597-9); 2001. 304p. reprint ed. mass mkt. 6.50 (0-425-18090-5, Prime Crime) Berkley Publishing Group.
—The Spirit Woman. l.t. ed. 2001. 294p. lib. bdg. 28.95 (1-58547-063-5) Ctr. Point Large Print.
—The Story Teller. (Wind River Arapaho Ser.). 256p. 1998. 21.95 o.s.i (0-425-16538-8); 1999. reprint ed. mass mkt. 6.50 (0-425-17025-X) Berkley Publishing Group. (Prime Crime).
—The Story Teller. unabr. ed. 1999. (O'Malley Mystery Ser.). audio 49.95 (1-55686-891-X) Books in Motion.
—The Thunder Keeper. 2001. 256p. 22.95 o.s.i (0-425-18188-X, Prime Crime) Berkley Publishing Group.

**HOLIDAY, BEN (FICTITIOUS CHARACTER)—FICTION**

Brooks, Terry. The Black Unicorn. 1988. (Magic Kingdom of Landover Ser.: No. 2). 320p. mass mkt. 7.99 (0-345-33528-7, Del Rey) Ballantine Bks.
—The Black Unicorn. 1988. (Magic Kingdom of Landover Ser.: No. 2). 13.04 (0-606-01234-6) Turtleback Bks.
—Magic Kingdom for Sale - Sold! 1987. (Magic Kingdom of Landover Ser.: No. 1). 384p. mass mkt. 7.99 (0-345-31758-0, Ballantine Bks.) Ballantine Bks.
—Magic Kingdom for Sale - Sold! 1988. 3.99 o.p. (0-517-67355-X) Random Hse. Value Publishing.
—Magic Kingdom for Sale - Sold! 1986. (Magic Kingdom of Landover Ser.: No. 1). 13.04 (0-606-02550-2) Turtleback Bks.
—The Tangle Box. 1995. (Magic Kingdom of Landover Ser.: No. 4). 368p. reprint ed. mass mkt. 7.99 (0-345-38700-7, Del Rey) Ballantine Bks.
—Witches' Brew. 1996. (Magic Kingdom of Landover Ser.: No. 5). 352p. mass mkt. 6.99 (0-345-38702-3) Ballantine Bks.
—Wizard at Large. 1989. (Magic Kingdom of Landover Ser.: No. 3K.). 320p. mass mkt. 7.99 (0-345-36227-6, Del Rey) Ballantine Bks.
—Wizard at Large. 1989. (Magic Kingdom of Landover Ser.: No. 3). 13.04 (0-606-01235-4) Turtleback Bks.

**HOLLAND, BILLY BOB (FICTITIOUS CHARACTER)—FICTION**

Burke, James Lee. Bitterroot: A Novel. l.t. ed. 2002. 552p. pap. 25.00 (0-7432-3640-8, Simon & Schuster) Simon & Schuster.
—Cimarron Rose. l.t. ed. 1998. (Large Print Book Ser.). 27.95 (1-56895-527-8, Wheeler Publishing, Inc.) Gale Group.
—Cimarron Rose. (Dave Robicheaux Mysteries Ser.). 1998. 406p. mass mkt. 7.99 (0-7868-8930-6); 1997. 304p. 24.95 (0-7868-6258-0) Hyperion Pr.
—Cimarron Rose. 1997. 278p. (0-7528-0486-3) Orion Media.
—Cimarron Rose. unabr. ed. 1998. audio 75.00 (0-7887-1746-4, 95224E7) Recorded Bks., LLC.
—Cimarron Rose. abr. ed. 1997. (Dave Robicheaux Mystery Ser.). 5p. audio 25.00 (0-671-57630-5, 495292, Simon & Schuster Audioworks) Simon & Schuster Audio.
—Cimarron Rose. ltd. ed. 1997. 288p. 150.00 (0-9631925-9-0) Trice, B.E. Publishing.
—Heartwood. unabr. ed. 2000. 8p. audio 69.95 (0-7927-2363-5, CSL 252, Chivers Sound Library) BBC Audiobooks America.
—Heartwood. 2000. (Dave Robicheaux Mysteries Ser.). 400p. mass mkt. 7.50 (0-440-22401-2) Dell Publishing.
—Heartwood. l.t. ed. 1999. pap. 24.95 o.p. (0-7838-8690-X, Macmillan Reference USA) Gale Group.
—Heartwood, Set. abr. ed. 1999. audio 25.00 Highsmith Inc.
—Heartwood. l.t. ed. 1999. 560p. 24.95 (0-375-40849-5) Random Hse. Large Print.
—Heartwood. abr. ed. 1999. (Dave Robicheaux Mystery Ser.). audio 25.00 (0-671-58107-4, Simon & Schuster Audioworks) Simon & Schuster Audio.
—Heartwood. ltd. ed. 1999. 341p. 150.00 (1-890885-08-8) Trice, B.E. Publishing.

**HOLLAND, JAMES (FICTITIOUS CHARACTER)—FICTION**

Nance, John J. Pandora's Clock. l.t. ed. 1996. 630p. 25.95 (0-7838-1577-8, Macmillan Reference USA) Gale Group.
—Pandora's Clock. abr. ed. 1995. 24.95 o.p. (0-7871-0534-1) NewStar Media, Inc.
—Pandora's Clock. 1996. 438p. mass mkt. 6.99 (0-312-96034-4, St. Martin's Paperbacks) St. Martin's Pr.

**HOLLAND, PRIMROSE (FICTITIOUS CHARACTER)—FICTION**

Bannister, Jo. The Primrose Convention. l.t. ed. 1998. (0-7540-3254-X); 263p. pap. (0-7540-3253-1) BBC Audiobooks America.

—The Primrose Convention. 1998. 272p. 22.95 o.p. (*0-312-18157-4*, Saint Martin's Minotaur) St. Martin's Pr.
—The Primrose Convention. l.t. ed. 1998. (General Ser.). 272p. pap. 24.95 (*0-7862-1383-3*) Thorndike Pr.

**HOLLISTER, DEVIN (FICTITIOUS CHARACTER)—FICTION**

White, Charlotte. Deadly Medicine. 1993. 288p. mass mkt. 4.50 o.s.i (*1-55817-681-0*, Pinnacle Bks.) Kensington Publishing Corp.

**HOLLISTER, LAURA (FICTITIOUS CHARACTER)—FICTION**

Pine, Nicholas. Spring Break. 1993. (Terror Academy Ser.: No. 4). 208p. (Orig.). (YA). mass mkt. 3.50 o.s.i (*0-425-13969-7*) Berkley Publishing Group.

**HOLLOWAY, BARBARA (FICTITIOUS CHARACTER)—FICTION**

Wilhelm, Kate. Best Defense. 1995. mass mkt. 6.99 o.s.i (*0-449-22314-0*, Fawcett) Ballantine Bks.
—Best Defense. 1994. 352p. 21.95 o.p. (*0-312-10937-7*) St. Martin's Pr.
—Death Qualified. 1992. (Northwest Mysteries Ser.). mass mkt. 5.99 o.s.i (*0-449-22155-5*, Fawcett) Ballantine Bks.
—Death Qualified. 1991. 22.95 o.p. (*0-312-05853-5*) St. Martin's Pr.
—Defense for the Devil. 2000. 448p. mass mkt. (*1-55166-628-6*, 1-66628-8, Mira Bks.) Harlequin Enterprises, Ltd.
—Defense for the Devil. E-Book 24.95 (*0-312-26451-8*); 1999. 400p. 24.95 o.p. (*0-312-19854-X*) St. Martin's Pr.
—Desperate Measures. 2001. 384p. 24.95 (*0-312-27663-X*, Saint Martin's Minotaur) St. Martin's Pr.
—For the Defense. 1997. 472p. mass mkt. 6.99 (*0-449-22556-9*, Fawcett) Ballantine Bks.
—Malice Prepense. 1996. 368p. text 24.95 o.p. (*0-312-14364-8*) St. Martin's Pr.
—No Defense. l.t. ed. 2003. (Large Print Ser.). 29.95 (*1-57490-503-1*) Beeler, Thomas T. Publisher.
—No Defense. 2001. 448p. mass mkt. (*1-55166-785-1*, 1-66785-6, Mira Bks.) Harlequin Enterprises, Ltd.
—No Defense. 2000. 376p. 24.95 (*0-312-20953-3*) St. Martin's Pr.

**HOLLOWAY, SABRINA (FICTITIOUS CHARACTER)—FICTION**

Pozzessere, Heather G. Never Sleep with Strangers. 1998. 384p. mass mkt. (*1-55166-445-3*, Mira Bks.) Harlequin Enterprises, Ltd.

**HOLLOWELL, PATRICIA ANNE (FICTITIOUS CHARACTER)—FICTION**

*see Patricia Anne (Fictitious Character)—Fiction*

**HOLMES, HARRY (FICTITIOUS CHARACTER)—FICTION**

Farrow, David A. The Root of All Evil. 2002. E-Book 20.00 o.p. (*0-941711-54-4*); 1997. 350p. 23.95 (*0-941711-36-6*) Wyrick & Co.

**HOLMES, MYCROFT (FICTITIOUS CHARACTER)—FICTION**

Berger, Arthur A. Durkheim Is Dead! Sherlock Holmes Is Introduced to Social Theory. 2003. 200p. pap. 24.95 (*0-7591-0298-8*) AltaMira Pr.
Downing, Noel. Doctor Watson & the Invisible Man. 1992. 200p. 25.00 (*0-86025-275-2*) Henry, Ian Pubns. GBR. *Dist:* Empire Publishing Service.
Doyle, Arthur Conan. The Adventure of the Bruce-Partington Plans. abr. ed. 1997. audio 9.99 (*0-88646-908-2*, 7908) Durkin Hayes Publishing Ltd.
—The Adventure of the Bruce-Partington Plans. E-Book 2.49 (*0-7574-2897-5*) Electric Umbrella Publishing.
Fawcett, Quinn. Against the Brotherhood. (Mycroft Holmes Novels Ser.). 1998. 320p. mass mkt. 6.99 (*0-8125-4523-0*, Tor Bks.); 1997. 352p. 23.95 (*0-312-86362-4*, Forge Bks.) Doherty, Tom Assocs., LLC.
—Against the Brotherhood. 2001. audio compact disk 94.00 (*0-7887-3981-6*, C1143E7); 1999. audio 71.00 (*0-7887-4079-2*, H1073E7, Clipper Audio) Recorded Bks., LLC.
—Embassy Row. (Mycroft Holmes Novels Ser.). 384p. 1999. pap. 6.99 (*0-8125-4522-2*, Tor Bks.); 1998. 24.95 o.p. (*0-312-86363-2*, Forge Bks.) Doherty, Tom Assocs., LLC.
—The Flying Scotsman. 1999. (Mycroft Holmes Novels Ser.). (Illus.). 320p. 23.95 (*0-312-86364-0*, Forge Bks.) Doherty, Tom Assocs., LLC.
—The Flying Scotsman: A Mycroft Holmes Novel Authorized by Dame Jean Conan Coyle. 2000. (Mycroft Holmes Novels Ser.). 320p. pap. 14.95 (*0-312-87689-0*, Tor Bks.) Doherty, Tom Assocs., LLC.
—The Scottish Ploy. 2001. 352p. reprint ed. pap. 15.95 (*0-312-87628-9*, Forge Bks.) Doherty, Tom Assocs., LLC.
—The Scottish Ploy: The A. Mycroft Holmes Novel Authorized by Dame Jean Conan Doyle. 2000. (Mycroft Holmes Novels Ser.). 352p. 24.95 (*0-312-87282-8*, Forge Bks.) Doherty, Tom Assocs., LLC.
Hodel, Michael P. & Wright, Sean M., eds. Enter the Lion: A Posthumous Memoir of Mycroft Holmes. 1979. 9.95 o.p. (*0-8015-5286-9*, Dutton) Dutton/Plume.
Pearlman, Gilbert. The Adventures of Sherlock Holmes' Smarter Brother. Wilder, Gene, ed. 1975. pap. 1.75 o.p. (*0-345-25282-9*) Ballantine Bks.
Theroux, Marcel. The Confessions of Mycroft Holmes: A Paper Chase. 2001. (Illus.). 224p. 23.00 o.s.i (*0-15-100647-4*); 2002. 228p. reprint ed. pap. 14.00 (*0-15-600743-6*, Harvest Bks.) Harcourt Trade Pubs.

**HOLMES, SHERLOCK (FICTITIOUS CHARACTER)—FICTION**

Accardo, Pasquale J. The Infernal Holmes: Dante in Baker Street. 1999. (Sherlockian Scholarship Ser.). (Illus.). 264p. (*1-55246-190-4*) Battered Silicon Dispatch Box, The.
The Adventures of Sherlock Holmes. audio Audio Bk. Co.
The Adventures of Sherlock Holmes. unabr. collector's ed. Incl. Adventure of the Blue Carbuncle. Doyle, Arthur Conan. audio Beryl Coronet. audio Boscombe Valley Mystery. audio Case of Identity. audio Case of the Five Orange Pips. Doyle, Arthur Conan. audio Copper Beeches. Brett, Jeremy. audio Engineer's Thumb. audio Man with the Twisted Lip. Doyle, Arthur Conan. audio Noble Bachelor. audio Red-Headed League. Doyle, Arthur Conan. audio Scandal in Bohemia. Doyle, Arthur Conan. audio Speckled Band. audio 1984. (Sherlock Holmes Ser.). 1978. Set audio 56.00 (*0-7366-0101-5*, 1109) Books on Tape, Inc.
Andrews, Val. Sherlock Holmes & the Baker Street Dozen: A Collection of Thirteen Short Stories. 1997. 126p. pap. 13.95 (*0-947533-41-9*) Breese Bks., Ltd. GBR. *Dist:* Midpoint Trade Bks., Inc.
—Sherlock Holmes & the Brighton Pavilion Mystery. 1991. 124p. 25.00 (*0-86025-269-8*) Henry, Ian Pubns. GBR. *Dist:* Empire Publishing Service.
—Sherlock Holmes & the Circus of Fear. 1997. 112p. pap. 13.95 o.s.i (*0-947533-17-6*) Breese Bks., Ltd. GBR. *Dist:* Midpoint Trade Bks., Inc.
—Sherlock Holmes & the Egyptian Hall Adventure. 1997. 112p. pap. 9.95 (*0-947533-43-5*) Breese Bks., Ltd. GBR. *Dist:* Midpoint Trade Bks., Inc.
—Sherlock Holmes & the Egyptian Hall Adventure. l.t. ed. 1998. (Linford Mystery Large Print Ser.). 208p. pap. 17.99 (*0-7089-5346-8*, Linford) Thorpe, F. A. Pubs. GBR. *Dist:* Ulverscroft Large Print Bks., Ltd., Ulverscroft Large Print Canada, Ltd.
—Sherlock Holmes & the Eminent Thespian. 1991. 124p. 25.00 (*0-86025-268-X*) Henry, Ian Pubns. GBR. *Dist:* Empire Publishing Service.
—Sherlock Holmes & the Greyfriars School Mystery. 1997. 109p. pap. 10.95 (*0-947533-55-9*) Breese Bks., Ltd. GBR. *Dist:* Midpoint Trade Bks., Inc.
—Sherlock Holmes & the Greyfriars School Mystery. l.t. ed. 1999. (Linford Mystery Large Print Ser.). 192p. pap. 18.99 (*0-7089-5442-1*, Ulverscroft) Thorpe, F. A. Pubs. GBR. *Dist:* Ulverscroft Large Print Bks., Ltd., Ulverscroft Large Print Canada, Ltd.
—Sherlock Holmes & the Houdini Birthright. 1997. (Sherlock Holmes Mysteries Ser.). 160p. pap. 10.95 (*0-947533-91-5*) Breese Bks., Ltd. GBR. *Dist:* Midpoint Trade Bks., Inc.
—Sherlock Holmes & the Long Acre Vampire: A Sherlock Holmes Mystery. 2000. (Sherlock Holmes Mysteries Ser.). 128p. pap. 14.95 (*0-947533-29-X*) Breese Bks., Ltd. GBR. *Dist:* Midpoint Trade Bks., Inc.
—Sherlock Holmes & the Man Who Lost Himself. 1997. 112p. pap. 10.95 (*0-947533-70-2*) Breese Bks., Ltd. GBR. *Dist:* Midpoint Trade Bks., Inc.
—Sherlock Holmes & the Man Who Lost Himself. l.t. ed. 1998. (Linford Mystery Large Print Ser.). 224p. pap. 17.99 (*0-7089-5334-4*, Linford) Thorpe, F. A. Pubs. GBR. *Dist:* Ulverscroft Large Print Bks., Ltd., Ulverscroft Large Print Canada, Ltd.
—Sherlock Holmes & the Sandringham House Mystery. 1999. pap. (*0-947533-53-2*) Breese Bks., Ltd.
—Sherlock Holmes & the Sandringham House Mystery. l.t. ed. 2000. (Linford Mystery Large Print Ser.). 200p. pap. 18.99 o.p. (*0-7089-5772-2*, Linford) Thorpe, F. A. Pubs. GBR. *Dist:* Ulverscroft Large Print Bks., Ltd., Ulverscroft Large Print Canada, Ltd.
—Sherlock Holmes & the Secret Seven: A Sherlock Holmes Mystery. 2001. 128p. pap. 12.95 (*0-947533-09-5*) Breese Bks., Ltd. GBR. *Dist:* Midpoint Trade Bks., Inc.
—Sherlock Holmes & the Theatre of Death. 1997. 125p. pap. 13.95 (*0-947533-12-5*) Breese Bks., Ltd. GBR. *Dist:* Midpoint Trade Bks., Inc.
—Sherlock Holmes & the Theatre of Death. l.t. ed. 2000. (Linford Mystery Large Print Ser.). 216p. pap. 18.99 o.p. (*0-7089-5900-8*, Linford) Thorpe, F. A. Pubs. GBR. *Dist:* Ulverscroft Large Print Bks., Ltd., Ulverscroft Large Print Canada, Ltd.
—Sherlock Holmes & the Tomb of Terror. 2000. (Sherlock Holmes Ser.). 160p. pap. 14.95 (*0-947533-72-9*) Breese Bks., Ltd. GBR. *Dist:* Midpoint Trade Bks., Inc.
—Sherlock Holmes & the Yule-Tide Mystery. 1996. 112p. pap. 10.95 (*0-947533-11-7*) Breese Bks., Ltd. GBR. *Dist:* Midpoint Trade Bks., Inc.
—Sherlock Holmes & the Yule-Tide Mystery. l.t. ed. 1998. (Linford Mystery Large Print Ser.). 224p. pap. 17.99 (*0-7089-5394-8*, Linford) Thorpe, F. A. Pubs. GBR. *Dist:* Ulverscroft Large Print Bks., Ltd., Ulverscroft Large Print Canada, Ltd.
—Sherlock Holmes at the Varieties. 2000. (Sherlock Holmes Ser.). 196p. pap. 12.95 (*0-947533-82-6*) Breese Bks., Ltd. GBR. *Dist:* Midpoint Trade Bks., Inc.
—Sherlock Holmes on the Western Front. 2000. (Sherlock Holmes Ser.). 128p. pap. 14.95 (*0-947533-87-7*) Breese Bks., Ltd. GBR. *Dist:* Midpoint Trade Bks., Inc.
—Torment of Sherlock Holmes. 2000. (Sherlock Holmes Ser.). 112p. pap. 12.95 (*0-947533-23-0*) Breese Bks., Ltd. GBR. *Dist:* Midpoint Trade Bks., Inc.
Ariel Books Staff. Baker Street Companion. 1996. (Tiny Tomes Ser.). 128p. 3.95 (*0-8362-1008-5*) Andrews McMeel Publishing.
Asimov, Isaac, et al, eds. Sherlock Holmes Through Time & Space. (Illus.). 368p. 1984. 14.95 o.p. (*0-312-94400-4*); 1986. reprint ed. pap. 8.95 o.p. (*0-312-94401-2*) Bluejay Bks.
Baker, Abbey P. In the Dead of Winter. 1994. 240p. 19.95 o.p. (*0-312-11413-3*, Saint Martin's Minotaur) St. Martin's Pr.
Berger, Arthur Asa. Durkheim Is Dead! A Sherlock Holmes Mystery of Social Theory. 2003. (Illus.). 272p. 19.95 (*0-7591-0300-3*); 200p. pap. 70.00 o.s.i (*0-7591-0299-6*) AltaMira Pr.
Booth, Matthew. Sherlock Holmes & the Giant's Hand & Other Stories: A Sherlock Holmes Mystery. Date not set. (Sherlock Holmes Ser.). 176p. pap. 14.95 (*0-947533-14-1*) Breese Bks., Ltd. GBR. *Dist:* Midpoint Trade Bks., Inc.
Boucher, Anthony. The New Adventures of Sherlock Holmes, Vol. 5. abr. ed. 1994. (New Adventures of Sherlock Holmes Gift Edition Ser.: Vol. 5). 25.00 o.s.i incl. audio (*0-671-50143-7*, Simon & Schuster Audioworks) Simon & Schuster Audio.
—The New Adventures of Sherlock Holmes Vol. 1: The Unfortunate Tobacconist & the Paradol Chamber. abr. ed. 1999. (New Adventures of Sherlock Holmes Ser.: Vol. 1). audio (*0-671-04341-2*, Simon & Schuster Audioworks) Simon & Schuster Audio.
—The New Adventures of Sherlock Holmes Vol. 2: The Viennese Strangler & the Notorious Canary Trainer. abr. ed. 1999. audio (*0-671-04342-0*, Simon & Schuster Audioworks) Simon & Schuster Audio.
—The New Adventures of Sherlock Holmes Vol. 3: The April Fool's Day Adventure & the Strange Adventure of the Uneasy Chair. abr. ed. 1999. audio (*0-671-04343-9*, Simon & Schuster Audioworks) Simon & Schuster Audio.
—The New Adventures of Sherlock Holmes Vol. 4: The Strange Case of the Demon Barber & the Mystery of the Headless Monk. abr. ed. 1999. audio (*0-671-04344-7*, Simon & Schuster Audioworks) Simon & Schuster Audio.
—The New Adventures of Sherlock Holmes Vol. 5: The Amateur Mendicant Society & the Case of the Vanishing White Elephant. abr. ed. 1999. (New Adventures of Sherlock Holmes Ser.: Vol. 5). audio (*0-671-04346-3*, Simon & Schuster Audioworks) Simon & Schuster Audio.
—The New Adventures of Sherlock Holmes Vol. 6: The Case of the Limping Ghost & the Girl with the Gazelle. abr. ed. 1999. audio 5.98 (*0-671-04340-4*, Simon & Schuster Audioworks); 1998. audio 5.98 Simon & Schuster Audio.
—The New Adventures of Sherlock Holmes Vol. 7: The Case of the Out of Date Murder & the Waltz of Death. abr. ed. 1999. (New Adventures of Sherlock Holmes Ser.: Vol. 7). audio (*0-671-04347-1*, Simon & Schuster Audioworks) Simon & Schuster Audio.
—The New Adventures of Sherlock Holmes Vol. 8: Colonel Warburton's Madness. abr. ed. 1999. (New Adventures of Sherlock Holmes Ser.: Vol. 8). audio (*0-671-04348-X*, Simon & Schuster Audioworks) Simon & Schuster Audio.
—The New Adventures of Sherlock Holmes Vol. 9: A Scandal in Bohemia & the Second Generation. 1999. (New Adventures of Sherlock Holmes Ser.: Vol. 9). audio (*0-671-04349-8*, Simon & Schuster Audioworks) Simon & Schuster Audio.
—The New Adventures of Sherlock Holmes Vol. 10: In Flanders Fields & the Eyes of Mr. Leyton. abr. ed. 1999. (New Adventures of Sherlock Holmes Ser.: Vol. 10). audio (*0-671-04350-1*, Simon & Schuster Audioworks) Simon & Schuster Audio.
—The New Adventures of Sherlock Holmes Vol. 11: The Tell Tale Pigeon Feathers & the Indiscretion of Mr. Edwards. abr. ed. 1999. audio (*0-671-04351-X*, Simon & Schuster Audioworks) Simon & Schuster Audio.
—The New Adventures of Sherlock Holmes Vol. 11: The Tell Tale Pigeon Feathers & The Indiscretion of Mr. Edwards. abr. ed. 1991. audio 9.95 (*0-671-69083-3*, Simon & Schuster Audioworks) Simon & Schuster Audio.
—The New Adventures of Sherlock Holmes Vol. 12: The Problem of Thor Bridge & the Double Zero. 1999. audio (*0-671-04352-8*, Simon & Schuster Audioworks) Simon & Schuster Audio.
—The New Adventures of Sherlock Holmes Vol. 13: Murder in the Casbah & the Tankerville Club. abr. ed. 1999. (New Adventures of Sherlock Holmes Ser.: Vol. 13). audio (*0-671-04353-6*, Simon & Schuster Audioworks) Simon & Schuster Audio.
—The New Adventures of Sherlock Holmes Vol. 14: The Strange Case of the Murderer in Wax & the Man with the Twisted Lip. abr. ed. 1999. audio (*0-671-04354-4*, Simon & Schuster Audioworks) Simon & Schuster Audio.
—The New Adventures of Sherlock Holmes Vol. 15: The Guileless Gypsy & the Camberville Poisoners. abr. ed. 1999. (New Adventures of Sherlock Holmes Ser.: Vol. 15). audio (*0-671-04355-2*, Simon & Schuster Audioworks) Simon & Schuster Audio.
—The New Adventures of Sherlock Holmes Vol. 16: The Terrifying Cats & the Submarine Club. abr. ed. 1999. (New Adventures of Sherlock Holmes Ser.: Vol. 16). audio (*0-671-04356-0*, Simon & Schuster Audioworks) Simon & Schuster Audio.
—The New Adventures of Sherlock Holmes Vol. 17: The Living Doll & the Disappearing Scientists. abr. ed. 1999. audio (*0-671-04357-9*, Simon & Schuster Audioworks) Simon & Schuster Audio.
—The New Adventures of Sherlock Holmes Vol. 18: The Adventure of the Speckled Band & the Purloined Ruby. abr. ed. 1999. audio (*0-671-04358-7*, Simon & Schuster Audioworks) Simon & Schuster Audio.
—The New Adventures of Sherlock Holmes Vol. 19: The Book of Tobit & Murder Beyond the Mountains. abr. ed. 1999. audio (*0-671-04359-5*, Simon & Schuster Audioworks) Simon & Schuster Audio.
—The New Adventures of Sherlock Holmes Vol. 20: The Manor House Case & the Adventure of the Stuttering Ghost. abr. ed. 1999. audio (*0-671-04360-9*, Simon & Schuster Audioworks) Simon & Schuster Audio.
—The New Adventures of Sherlock Holmes Vol. 21: The Great Gandolfo & the Adventure of the Original Hamlet. abr. ed. 1999. audio (*0-671-04361-7*, Simon & Schuster Audioworks) Simon & Schuster Audio.
—The New Adventures of Sherlock Holmes Vol. 22: Murder by Moonlight & the Singular Affair of the Coptic Compass. 1999. (New Adventures of Sherlock Holmes Ser.). audio (*0-671-04362-5*, Simon & Schuster Audioworks) Simon & Schuster Audio.
—The New Adventures of Sherlock Holmes Vol. 23: The Gunpowder Plot & the Babbling Butler. abr. ed. 1999. audio (*0-671-04363-3*, Simon & Schuster Audioworks) Simon & Schuster Audio.
—The New Adventures of Sherlock Holmes Vol. 24: The Accidental Murderess & the Adventure of the Blarney Stone. abr. ed. 1999. (New Adventures of Sherlock Holmes Ser.). audio (*0-671-04364-1*, Simon & Schuster Audioworks) Simon & Schuster Audio.
—The New Adventures of Sherlock Holmes Vol. 25: The Night Before Christmas & the Darlington Substitution. abr. ed. 1999. (New Adventures of Sherlock Holmes Ser.). audio (*0-671-04365-X*, Simon & Schuster Audioworks) Simon & Schuster Audio.
—The New Adventures of Sherlock Holmes Vol. 26: The Haunting of Sherlock Holmes & the Baconian Cipher. abr. ed. 1999. audio (*0-671-04366-8*, Simon & Schuster Audioworks) Simon & Schuster Audio.
Boucher, Anthony & Green, Denis. The Haunting of Sherlock Holmes & Baconian Cipher. abr. ed. 1994. (New Adventures of Sherlock Holmes Ser.: Vol. 26). audio 12.00 (*0-671-79417-5*, Simon & Schuster Audioworks) Simon & Schuster Audio.
—The New Adventures of Sherlock Holmes. abr. ed. 1990. (Sherlock Holmes Ser.). audio 25.00 o.s.i (*0-671-72702-8*); 1993. (Sherlock Holmes Ser.). audio 25.00 o.s.i (*0-671-87587-6*); 2001. audio 49.95 (*0-7435-2045-9*); Set. 1992. (New Adventures of Sherlock Holmes Gift Edition Ser.: Vol. 3). audio 25.00 o.s.i (*0-671-79367-5*); Vol. 5-18.

Characters

1991. (New Adventures of Sherlock Holmes Ser.: Vol. 2). audio 25.00 o.s.i (*0-671-74750-9*); Vol. 10. 1990. audio 9.95 (*0-671-69082-5*) Simon & Schuster Audio. (Simon & Schuster Audioworks).

—The New Adventures of Sherlock Holmes Vol. 1: The Unfortunate Tobacconist & The Paradol Chamber. abr. ed. 1988. 9.95 incl. audio (*0-671-66076-4*, Simon & Schuster Audioworks) Simon & Schuster Audio.

—The New Adventures of Sherlock Holmes Vol. 3: The Aprl Fool's Day Adventure & The Strange Adventure of the Uneasy Easy Chair. abr. ed. 1989. 9.95 incl. audio (*0-671-67785-3*, Simon & Schuster Audioworks) Simon & Schuster Audio.

—The New Adventures of Sherlock Holmes Vol. 4: The Strange Case of the Demon Barber & The Mystery of the Headless Monk. abr. ed. 1989. 9.95 incl. audio (*0-671-68088-9*, Simon & Schuster Audioworks) Simon & Schuster Audio.

—The New Adventures of Sherlock Holmes Vol. 5: The Amateur Mendicant Society & The Case of the Vanishing White Elephant. abr. ed. 1990. audio 9.95 (*0-671-68423-X*, Simon & Schuster Audioworks) Simon & Schuster Audio.

—The New Adventures of Sherlock Holmes Vol. 6: Eight Classic Radio Mysteries. gif. ed. 1995. (New Adventures of Sherlock Holmes Gift Edition Ser.: Vol. 6). audio 25.00 o.s.i (*0-671-53703-2*, Simon & Schuster Audioworks) Simon & Schuster Audio.

—The New Adventures of Sherlock Holmes Vol. 6: The Case of the Limping Ghost & The Girl with the Gazelle. abr. ed. 1989. audio 9.95 (*0-671-68772-7*, Simon & Schuster Audioworks) Simon & Schuster Audio.

—The New Adventures of Sherlock Holmes Vol. 7: The Case of the Out of Date Murder & The Waltz of Death. abr. ed. 1990. audio 9.95 (*0-671-68773-5*, Simon & Schuster Audioworks) Simon & Schuster Audio.

—The New Adventures of Sherlock Holmes Vol. 8: Colonel Warburton's Madness & The Iron Box. abr. ed. 1990. (New Adventures of Sherlock Holmes Ser.: Vol. 8). 60p. audio 9.95 (*0-671-68774-3*, Simon & Schuster Audioworks) Simon & Schuster Audio.

—The New Adventures of Sherlock Holmes Vol. 9: A Scandal in Bohemia & The Second Generation. abr. ed. 1990. audio 9.95 (*0-671-69081-7*, Simon & Schuster Audioworks) Simon & Schuster Audio.

—The New Adventures of Sherlock Holmes Vol. 12: The Problem of Thor Bridge & The Double Zero. abr. ed. 1991. audio 9.95 (*0-671-70744-2*, 326340, Simon & Schuster Audioworks) Simon & Schuster Audio.

—The New Adventures of Sherlock Holmes Vol. 14: The Strange Case of the Murderer in Wax & The Man with the Twisted Lip. abr. ed. 1991. audio 9.95 (*0-671-70746-9*, Simon & Schuster Audioworks) Simon & Schuster Audio.

—The New Adventures of Sherlock Holmes Vol. 20: The Manor House Case & The Adventure of the Stuttering Ghost. abr. ed. 1993. audio 11.00 (*0-671-79411-6*, Simon & Schuster Audioworks) Simon & Schuster Audio.

Boucher, Anthony & Greene, Denis. The New Adventures of Sherlock Holmes Slip Case, Vols. 1-13. unabr. ed. audio 129.35 Simon & Schuster Audio.

Brown, Russell A. Sherlock Holmes & the Mysterious Friend of Oscar Wilde. (Stonewall Inn Editions Ser.). 1990. 192p. pap. 8.95 (*0-312-03932-8*, Saint Martin's Griffin); 1988. 176p. 14.95 o.p. (*0-312-02280-8*, Saint Martin's Minotaur) St. Martin's Pr.

Bruce, Colin. Einstein Paradox: And Other Science Mysteries Solved by Sherlock Holmes. 1963. 272p. text 3.00 o.p. (*0-465-09311-6*) Basic Bks.

—Einstein Paradox: And Other Science Mysteries Solved by Sherlock Holmes. 1998. 272p. reprint ed. pap. text 15.95 (*0-7382-0023-9*) Perseus Publishing.

Bugge, Carole. Haunting of Torre Abbey. 2000. 258p. 22.95 (*0-312-24557-2*, Saint Martin's Minotaur) St. Martin's Pr.

—Star of India. 1997. 256p. 21.95 (*0-312-18034-9*) St. Martin's Pr.

Campbell, Mark. Sherlock Holmes. 2001. 78p. pap. 6.95 (*1-903047-68-4*) Pocket Essentials GBR. *Dist:* Trafalgar Square.

Cannon, P. H. Pulptime. 1985. (Illus.). 96p. reprint ed. pap. 5.00 o.p. (*0-932445-06-3*) Ganley Pub.

—Pulptime. 1985. (Illus.). 96p. reprint ed. 15.00 (*0-932445-07-1*) Necronomicon Pr.

Caplan, Richard M. Dr. Watson, Mr. Sherlock Holmes. 1996. (Illus.). 172p. 24.00 (*1-896648-53-3*) Battered Silicon Dispatch Box, The.

Carraher, Philip J. Sherlock Holmes: The Adventure of the Dead Rabbits Society. 2001. 152p. 24.53 (*0-7596-0514-9*); pap. 13.98 (*0-7596-0513-0*) 1stBooks Library.

Champlin, Tim. Deadly Season. 2003. 256p. mass mkt. 4.99 (*0-8439-5131-1*) Dorchester Publishing Co., Inc.

—Deadly Season. 1997. (Western Ser.). 256p. lib. bdg. 18.95 o.p. (*0-7862-0783-3*, Five Star) Gale Group.

—Deadly Season. l.t. ed. 1998. (Western Ser.). 360p. 21.95 (*0-7862-0777-9*) Thorndike Pr.

Charnock, Ian. Elementary Cases of Sherlock Holmes. 1999. (Sherlock Holmes Ser.). 160p. pap. text o.s.i (*0-947533-97-4*) Breese Bks., Ltd.

—Watson's Last Case. 2000. (Adventures of Sherlock Holmes Ser.). 192p. pap. 14.95 (*0-947533-92-3*) Breese Bks., Ltd. GBR. *Dist:* Midpoint Trade Bks., Inc.

Churchill & Fewell. Musgrave Ritual in Latin. 1998. (Sherlockian Scholarship Ser.). 8.00 (*1-55246-136-X*) Battered Silicon Dispatch Box, The.

Conway, Tom & Bruce, Nigel. More New Adventures of Sherlock Holmes: Original Radio Drama. abr. ed. 1996. (New Adventures of Sherlock Holmes Ser.: Vol. 5). audio 9.95 o.p. (*1-56100-898-2*, 484); 1996. (New Adventures of Sherlock Holmes Ser.: Vol. 6). audio 9.95 o.p. (*1-56100-899-0*, 485); 1996. (New Adventures of Sherlock Holmes Ser.: Vol. 7). audio 9.95 o.p. (*1-56100-900-8*, 486); 1996. (New Adventures of Sherlock Holmes Ser.: Vol. 8). audio 9.95 o.p. (*1-56100-901-6*, 487); Vol. 1. 1996. (New Adventures of Sherlock Holmes Ser.: Vol. 1). audio 9.95 o.p. (*1-56100-875-3*, 480); Vol. 2. 1996. (New Adventures of Sherlock Holmes Ser.: Vol. 2). audio 9.95 o.p. (*1-56100-876-1*, 481); Vol. 3. 1996. (New Adventures of Sherlock Holmes Ser.: Vol. 3). audio 9.95 o.p. (*1-56100-877-X*, 482); Vol. 4. 1996. (New Adventures of Sherlock Holmes Ser.: Vol. 4). audio 9.95 o.p. (*1-56100-878-8*, 483); Vol. 9. 1996. (More New Adventures of Sherlock Holmes Ser.). audio 9.95 o.p. (*1-56100-923-7*, 521); Vol. 10. 1996. (More New Adventures of Sherlock Holmes Ser.). audio 9.95 o.p. (*1-56100-924-5*, 488); Vol. 11. 1996. (More New Adventures of Sherlock Holmes Ser.). audio 9.95 o.p. (*1-56100-950-4*, 489); Vol. 12. 1996. (More New Adventures of Sherlock Holmes Ser.). audio 9.95 o.p. (*1-56100-951-2*, 490); Vol. 13. 1997. (More New Adventures of Sherlock Holmes Ser.: Vol. 13). audio 9.95 o.p. (*1-56100-943-1*, 491); Vol. 14. 1997. (More New Adventures of Sherlock Holmes Ser.: Vol. 14). audio 9.95 o.p. (*1-56100-944-X*, 492); Vol. 15. 1997. (More New Adventures of Sherlock Holmes Ser.: Vol. 15). audio 9.95 o.p. (*1-56100-945-8*, 493); Vol. 16. 1997. (More New Adventures of Sherlock Holmes Ser.: Vol. 16). audio 9.95 o.p. (*1-56100-946-6*, 494) Brilliance Audio. (Nova Audio Bks.).

Cooper-Posey, Tracy & Doyle, Arthur Conan. The Case of the Reluctant Agent: A Sherlock Holmes Mystery. 2001. (Illus.). 256p. pap. 12.95 (*0-88801-263-2*) Turnstone Pr. CAN. *Dist:* General Distribution Services, Inc.

Daly, Lorraine. Sherlock Holmes & the Lusitania. Wilks, Ian, ed. 1998. 192p. 30.00 (*0-86025-291-4*) Henry, Ian Pubns. GBR. *Dist:* Empire Publishing Service.

Dare, M. P. The Shadow of the Rat: A Sherlock Holmes Adventure. 1999. 162p. pap. (*1-899562-71-0*) Ash-Tree Pr.

Dartagnan, Robert. Sherlock Holmes' Last Case. 2001. 330p. pap. 22.99 (*0-7388-6828-0*) Xlibris Corp.

Davies, David S. Fixed Point: The Life & Death of Sherlock Holmes. 1996. audio 7.95 (*1-888728-03-5*) Classic Specialties.

—Sherlock Holmes & the Hentzau Affair. 1991. 160p. 25.00 (*0-86025-274-4*) Henry, Ian Pubns. GBR. *Dist:* Empire Publishing Service.

Davies, David Stuart. The Scroll of the Dead: A Sherlock Holmes Adventure. 1998. 147p. o.p. (*1-899562-43-5*); pap. (*1-899562-47-8*) Ash-Tree Pr. (Calabash Pr.).

—The Shadow of the Rat: A Sherlock Holmes Adventure. 1999. 162p. (*1-899562-70-2*, Calabash Pr.) Ash-Tree Pr.

—Sherlock Holmes - The Last Act! 1999. 68p. pap. (*1-899562-77-X*, Calabash Pr.) Ash-Tree Pr.

Dibdin, Michael. The Last Sherlock Holmes Story. 1978. 7.95 o.s.i (*0-394-50065-2*, Pantheon) Knopf Publishing Group.

—The Last Sherlock Holmes Story. 1996. 192p. pap. 12.00 (*0-679-76658-8*) Random Hse., Inc.

Donat, Peter C. & Gould, Barney. Sherlock Holmes & the Shakespeare Solution. 1997. 90p. 24.00 (*1-55246-016-9*); pap. 10.00 (*1-55246-017-7*) Battered Silicon Dispatch Box, The.

Douglas, Carole Nelson. The Adventuress. 2004. 416p. mass mkt. 6.99 (*0-7653-4715-6*, Forge Bks.) Doherty, Tom Assocs., LLC.

—Castle Rouge: A Novel of Suspense Featuring Sherlock Holmes, Irene Adler, & Jack the Ripper. 2002. (Irene Adler Novel Ser.). (Illus.). 544p. 25.95 (*0-312-86941-X*, Forge Bks.) Doherty, Tom Assocs., LLC.

—Femme Fatale. Date not set. mass mkt. (*0-7653-4595-1*); 2003. 554p. 25.95 (*0-7653-0682-4*) Doherty, Tom Assocs., LLC. (Forge Bks.).

—Good Morning, Irene. (Irene Adler Adventure Ser.). 1992. (Illus.). 374p. mass mkt. 4.99 (*0-8125-0949-8*); 1991. 19.95 o.p. (*0-312-93211-1*) Doherty, Tom Assocs., LLC. (Tor Bks.).

—Good Morning, Irene. unabr. ed. 1999. audio 80.00 (*0-7887-2487-8*, 95562E7) Recorded Bks., LLC.

—Good Night, Mr. Holmes. 1991. 408p. mass mkt. 4.99 o.s.i (*0-8125-1430-0*); 1990. 18.95 o.p. (*0-312-93210-3*) Doherty, Tom Assocs., LLC. (Tor Bks.).

—Good Night, Mr. Holmes. unabr. ed. 1998. audio 78.00 (*0-7887-2489-4*, 95564E7) Recorded Bks., LLC.

—Irene at Large. 1993. (Irene Adler Adventure Ser.). 395p. mass mkt. 5.99 (*0-8125-1702-4*, Tor Bks.) Doherty, Tom Assocs., LLC.

—Irene at Large. unabr. ed. 2000. audio 91.00 (*0-7887-2492-4*, 95567E7) Recorded Bks., LLC.

—Irene's Last Waltz. 1994. (Irene Adler Adventure Ser.). 480p. 22.95 o.p. (*0-312-85224-X*, Forge Bks.) Doherty, Tom Assocs., LLC.

—Irene's Last Waltz. unabr. ed. 2000. audio 97.00 (*0-7887-2493-2*, 95568E7) Recorded Bks., LLC.

Doyle, Arthur Conan. The Adventure of the Beryl Coronet. E-Book 0.99 (*1-58515-033-9*) MesaView, Inc.

—The Adventure of the Blue Carbuncle. E-Book 0.99 (*1-58515-034-7*) MesaView, Inc.

—The Adventure of the Blue Carbuncle. 1983. (Radio Ser.). pap. 5.95 o.p. incl. audio (*0-88142-353-X*, 353) Soundelux Audio Publishing.

—The Adventure of the Bruce-Partington Plans. abr. ed. 1997. audio 9.99 (*0-88646-908-2*, 7908) Durkin Hayes Publishing Ltd.

—The Adventure of the Bruce-Partington Plans. E-Book 2.49 (*0-7574-2897-5*) Electric Umbrella Publishing.

—The Adventure of the Copper Beeches. E-Book 0.99 (*1-58515-035-5*) MesaView, Inc.

—The Adventure of the Dancing Men. 1996. (Sherlock Holmes Ser.). 18p. pap. 3.50 (*1-57514-202-3*, 3065) Encore Performance Publishing.

—The Adventure of the Dancing Men & Other Sherlock Holmes Stories. 1997. 80p. (Orig.). pap. 1.00 (*0-486-29558-3*) Dover Pubns., Inc.

—The Adventure of the Empty House. unabr. ed. 1995. (Stories from the Return of Sherlock Holmes Ser.). audio 16.99 (*0-88646-387-4*, 7387) Durkin Hayes Publishing Ltd.

—The Adventure of the Empty House. 1981. audio. audio 7.95 Jimcin Recordings.

—The Adventure of the Engineer's Thumb. E-Book 0.99 (*1-58515-036-3*) MesaView, Inc.

—The Adventure of the Musgrave Ritual. unabr. ed. 1979. audio 7.95 Jimcin Recordings.

—The Adventure of the Noble Bachelor. E-Book 0.99 (*1-58515-037-1*) MesaView, Inc.

—The Adventures & Memoirs of Sherlock Holmes. 2002. (World Digital Library). E-Book 3.95 (*0-594-09740-1*) 1873 Pr.

—The Adventures & Memoirs of Sherlock Holmes. 2002. (Modern Library Classics). 528p. pap. 12.95 (*0-375-76002-4*, Modern Library) Random House Adult Trade Publishing Group.

—The Adventures & Memoirs of Sherlock Holmes. 2001. (Classics Ser.). 576p. 13.00 (*0-14-043771-1*, Penguin Classics) Viking Penguin.

—The Adventures of Sherlock Holmes. 1985. 304p. mass mkt. 4.99 o.s.i (*0-345-32712-8*) Ballantine Bks.

—The Adventures of Sherlock Holmes. Green, Richard Lancelyn, ed. 1993. 438p. (C). 13.95 o.p. (*0-19-212318-1*, 14613) Oxford Univ. Pr., Inc.

—The Adventures of Sherlock Holmes. Green, Richard Lancelyn, ed. & intro. by. 1995. (Oxford World's Classics Ser.). 438p. reprint ed. pap. 5.95 o.p. (*0-19-282378-7*) Oxford Univ. Pr., Inc.

—The Adventures of Sherlock Holmes. l.t. ed. 2003. (Perennial Bestsellers Ser.). 28.95 (*0-7862-5631-1*) Thorndike Pr.

—The Adventures of Sherlock Holmes. Incl. Red-Headed League. audio Scandal in Bohemia. audio Speckled Band. audio Set audio 12.95 (*0-89926-125-6*, 813) Audio Bk. Co.

—The Adventures of Sherlock Holmes: A Scandal in Bohemia. 1970. 7.95 (*0-02-732920-8*, Simon & Schuster Children's Publishing) Simon & Schuster Children's Publishing.

—The Adventures of Sherlock Holmes: BBC, Vol. 3. abr. ed. 1997. (BBC Radio Presents Ser.: Vol. 3). audio 16.99 o.s.i (*0-553-47845-1*, RH Audio) Random Hse. Audio Publishing Group.

—The Adventures of Sherlock Holmes I: The Speckled Band; the Adventure of Copper Beeches; the Stock-Broker's Clerk; the Red-Headed League. abr. ed. (Sherlock Holmes Stories). (YA). 1999. audio compact disk 19.98 (*962-634-152-1*, NA315212); 1998. audio 17.98 (*962-634-652-3*, NA315214) Naxos of America, Inc. (Naxos AudioBooks).

—The Adventures of Sherlock Holmes II: A Scandal in Bohemia; The Five Orange Pips; The Adventure of the Engineer's Thumb; Silver Blaze. unabr. ed. 1999. (Sherlock Holmes Stories). audio 17.98 (*962-634-670-1*, NA317014, Naxos AudioBooks) Naxos of America, Inc.

—The Adventures of Sherlock Holmes III: The Man with the Twisted Lip; The Musgrave Ritual; The Adventure of the Cardboard Box; The Adventure of the Blue Carbuncle. unabr. ed. 2000. (Sherlock Holmes Stories). audio 17.98 (*962-634-691-4*, NA319114, Naxos AudioBooks) Naxos of America, Inc.

—The Adventures of Sherlock Holmes III: The Man with the Twisted Lip; the Musgrave Ritual; the Adventure of the Cardboard Box; the Adventure of the Blue Carbuncle. unabr. ed. 2000. (Sherlock Holmes Stories). (YA). audio compact disk 19.98 (*962-634-191-2*, NA319112, Naxos AudioBooks) Naxos of America, Inc.

—The Adventures of Sherlock Holmes V. unabr. ed. 2002. audio 17.98 (*962-634-766-X*, NA326614, Naxos AudioBooks); audio compact disk 19.98 Naxos of America, Inc.

—The Annotated Sherlock Holmes: The Four Novels & the Fifty-Six Short Stories Complete. Baring-Gould, William S., ed. 1988. (Illus.). 39.95 o.s.i (*0-517-50291-7*, Crown) Crown Publishing Group.

—The Annotated Sherlock Holmes: The Four Novels & the Fifty-Six Short Stories Complete, 2 vols. in 1. 1992. (Illus.). 824p. 22.99 o.s.i (*0-517-48102-2*) Random Hse. Value Publishing.

—The Best of Sherlock Holmes. 2001. 419p. pap. 3.95 (*1-85326-748-1*) Wordsworth Editions, Ltd. GBR. *Dist:* Combined Publishing.

—The Case-Book of Sherlock Holmes. 1986. mass mkt. 3.50 o.p. (*0-425-10194-0*); 1984. mass mkt. 2.50 o.s.i (*0-425-07175-8*) Berkley Publishing Group.

—The Case-Book of Sherlock Holmes. 2001. vi, 296p. pap. 8.95 (*0-7551-0647-4*) House of Stratus, Inc. GBR. *Dist:* Midpoint Trade Bks., Inc.

—The Case-Book of Sherlock Holmes. Robson, W. W., ed. (Oxford World's Classics Ser.). 336p. 2000. pap. 10.00 (*0-19-283917-9*); 1993. (C). 13.95 o.p. (*0-19-212311-4*, 14608) Oxford Univ. Pr., Inc.

—The Case-Book of Sherlock Holmes. Robson, W. W., ed. & intro. by. 1995. (Oxford Sherlock Holmes Ser.). 334p. reprint ed. pap. 6.95 o.p. (*0-19-282374-4*) Oxford Univ. Pr., Inc.

—The Case-Book of Sherlock Holmes. 1999. 353p. E-Book 3.99 incl. cd-rom (*1-57646-185-8*) Quiet Vision Publishing.

—The Case-Book of Sherlock Holmes, Vol. 1. abr. ed. 1998. (BBC Radio Presents Ser.). 355p. 16.99 o.s.i incl. audio (*0-553-47904-0*, RH Audio) Random Hse. Audio Publishing Group.

—The Case-Book of Sherlock Holmes. l.t. ed. 1967. 12.00 o.p. (*0-85456-590-6*, Ulverscroft) Thorpe, F. A. Pubs. GBR. *Dist:* Ulverscroft Large Print Bks., Ltd.

—The Case-Book of Sherlock Holmes. unabr. ed. 2000. audio 14.95 (*0-00-105478-3*) Trafalgar Square.

—The Case-Book of Sherlock Holmes. 1998. (Classics Library). 400p. pap. 3.95 (*1-85326-070-3*, 0703WW) Wordsworth Editions, Ltd. GBR. *Dist:* Casemate Pubs. & Bk. Distributors, LLC.

—The Case of Mr. George Edalji. reprint ed. lib. bdg. 98.00 (*0-7426-2716-0*); 2001. pap. text 28.00 (*0-7426-7716-8*) Classic Bks.

—The Complete Sherlock Holmes, 2 vols. 1986. mass mkt. 13.90 (*0-553-32825-5*, Bantam Classics) Bantam Bks.

—The Complete Sherlock Holmes. 1960. 1136p. 27.95 (*0-385-00689-6*) Doubleday Publishing.

—The Complete Sherlock Holmes. 2003. Vol. 1. 816p. pap. 7.95 (*1-59308-034-4*); Vol. II. 800p. pap. 7.95 (*1-59308-040-9*) Fine Communications.

—The Complete Sherlock Holmes. 2002. 480p. 14.99 (*0-517-22078-4*) Random Hse., Inc.

—The Crooked Man. 1989. audio 7.95 Jimcin Recordings.

—The Doings of Raffles Haw. 1977. (Short Story Index Reprint Ser.). 16.95 (*0-8369-3249-8*) Ayer Co. Pubs., Inc.

—The Doings of Raffles Haw. (Collected Works of Sir Arthur Conan Doyle). 2001. 199p. pap. text 28.00 (*0-7426-7686-2*); reprint ed. lib. bdg. 98.00 (*0-7426-2686-5*) Classic Bks.

—The Doings of Raffles Haw. 2002. 144p. per. 29.95 (*1-58963-866-2*) Fredonia Bks.

—The Doings of Raffles Haw. 1981. (Conan Doyle Centennial Ser.). (Illus.). 157p. 28.00 (*0-934468-43-5*) Gaslight Pubns.

—The Doings of Raffles Haw. 1986. 256p. 15.00 o.p. (*0-947898-37-9*) Periodicals Service Co.

—A Duet, with an Occasional Chorus. reprint ed. lib. bdg. 98.00 (*0-7426-2710-1*); lib. bdg. 98.00 (*0-7426-2702-0*); 2001. (Collected Works of Sir Arthur Conan Doyle: Vol. 2). pap. text 28.00 (*0-7426-7702-8*); 2001. (Collected Works of Sir Arthur Conan Doyle: Vol. 2). pap. text 28.00 (*0-7426-7710-9*) Classic Bks.

—A Duet, with an Occasional Chorus. 2001. 340p. per. 24.95 (*1-58963-461-6*) Fredonia Bks.

—A Duet, with an Occasional Chorus. 1990. (Conan Doyle Centennial Ser.). (Illus.). 270p. 28.00 (*0-934468-48-6*) Gaslight Pubns.

—The Final Adventures of Sherlock Holmes. 2002. (Illus.). 251p. 27.50 (0-7090-6738-0) Hale, Robert Ltd. GBR. Dist: Trafalgar Square.
—The Final Problem. abr. ed. 1983. (Radio Ser.). pap. 5.95 o.p. incl. audio (0-88142-355-6, 355) Soundelux Audio Publishing.
—The Firm of Girdlestone. (Collected Works of Sir Arthur Conan Doyle). 2001. 381p. pap. text 28.00 (0-7426-7682-X); reprint ed. lib. bdg. 98.00 (0-7426-2682-2) Classic Bks.
—The Firm of Girdlestone. 2001. (Illus.). 380p. per. 24.95 (1-58963-392-X) Fredonia Bks.
—The Firm of Girdlestone. 1981. (Conan Doyle Centennial Ser.). (Illus.). 364p. 16.95 o.p. (0-934468-42-7) Gaslight Pubns.
—The Further Adventures of Sherlock Holmes. Green, Richard Lancelyn, ed. 1986. (Fiction Ser.). 272p. pap. 6.95 o.s.i (0-14-007907-6, Penguin Bks.) Penguin Group (USA) Inc.
—The Great Adventures of Sherlock Holmes. 1994. (Illustrated Classics Collection). 64p. pap. 4.95 (0-7854-0715-4, 40391) American Guidance Service, Inc.
—The Great Adventures of Sherlock Holmes. 1995. (Puffin Classics Ser.). (Illus.). 288p. (YA). (gr. 4-7). pap. 4.99 (0-14-036689-X, Puffin Bks.) Penguin Putnam Bks. for Young Readers.
—The Great Adventures of Sherlock Holmes Readalong. 1994. (Illustrated Classics Collection). 64p. pap. 14.95 incl. audio (0-7854-0681-6, 40393) American Guidance Service, Inc.
—His Last Bow: Some Reminiscences of Sherlock Holmes. Date not set. (Heritage Literary Ser.). pap. text 31.50 (0-582-34914-1) Addison-Wesley Longman, Ltd. GBR. Dist: Trans-Atlantic Pubns., Inc.
—His Last Bow: Some Reminiscences of Sherlock Holmes. 1987. mass mkt. 2.50 o.p. (0-425-10491-5); 1986. mass mkt. 2.50 o.s.i (0-425-09579-7); 1984. mass mkt. 2.50 o.s.i (0-425-07502-8); 1981. mass mkt. 1.95 o.s.i (0-425-04870-5); 1980. mass mkt. 1.75 o.s.i (0-425-04534-X); 1978. mass mkt. 1.50 o.s.i (0-425-04003-8); 1976. mass mkt. 1.25 o.s.i (0-425-03129-2); 1974. mass mkt. 0.95 o.s.i (0-425-02804-6) Berkley Publishing Group.
—His Last Bow: Some Reminiscences of Sherlock Holmes. unabr. ed. 2000. audio compact disk 48.00 (0-7861-9939-3, z2471) Blackstone Audio Bks., Inc.
—His Last Bow: Some Reminiscences of Sherlock Holmes. unabr. collector's ed. 1993. audio 48.00 (0-7366-2335-3, 3114) Books on Tape, Inc.
—His Last Bow: Some Reminiscences of Sherlock Holmes. 1990. reprint ed. lib. bdg. 18.95 o.p. (0-89966-666-3) Buccaneer Bks., Inc.
—His Last Bow: Some Reminiscences of Sherlock Holmes. reprint ed. lib. bdg. 98.00 (0-7426-2735-7); 2001. 212p. pap. text 28.00 (0-7426-7735-4) Classic Bks.
—His Last Bow: Some Reminiscences of Sherlock Holmes. 2001. v, 236p. pap. 8.95 (0-7551-0646-6) House of Stratus, Inc. GBR. Dist: Midpoint Trade Bks., Inc.
—His Last Bow: Some Reminiscences of Sherlock Holmes. unabr. ed. 1994. audio 29.00 Jimcin Recordings.
—His Last Bow: Some Reminiscences of Sherlock Holmes. Edwards, Owen D., ed. 1993. (Oxford Sherlock Holmes Ser.). 302p. (C). 13.95 o.p. (0-19-212315-7) Oxford Univ. Pr., Inc.
—His Last Bow: Some Reminiscences of Sherlock Holmes. Edwards, Owen D., ed. & intro. by. 1995. (Oxford World's Classics Ser.). 304p. reprint ed. pap. 6.95 o.p. (0-19-282381-7) Oxford Univ. Pr., Inc.
—His Last Bow: Some Reminiscences of Sherlock Holmes. 1993. 208p. pap. 6.95 o.p. (0-14-005709-9) Penguin Group (USA) Inc.
—His Last Bow: Some Reminiscences of Sherlock Holmes. collector's ed. 2002. (Illus.). im. lthr. 38.85 (1-4115-1256-1); pap. 19.95 (1-4115-0526-3); 25.95 (1-4115-0884-X); pap. 17.95 (1-4115-0315-5) Polyglot Pr., Inc.
—His Last Bow: Some Reminiscences of Sherlock Holmes. 2001. E-Book 2.95 (1-58882-433-0) PublishingOnline.
—His Last Bow: Some Reminiscences of Sherlock Holmes. 1999. 292p. E-Book 3.99 incl. cd-rom (1-57646-183-1) Quiet Vision Publishing.
—His Last Bow: Some Reminiscences of Sherlock Holmes. l.t. ed. 1977. (Ulverscroft Large Print Ser.). 29.99 o.p. (0-7089-0076-3, Ulverscroft) Thorpe, F. A. Pubs. GBR. Dist: Ulverscroft Large Print Bks., Ltd., Ulverscroft Large Print Canada, Ltd.
—The Hound of the Baskervilles. 1976. 19.95 (0-8488-1286-7) Amereon, Ltd.
—The Hound of the Baskervilles. 1994. (Illustrated Classics Collection). 64p. pap. 4.95 (0-7854-0696-4, 40450); pap. 3.60 o.p. (1-56103-528-9) American Guidance Service, Inc.
—The Hound of the Baskervilles. ltd. ed. 1985. (Illus.). 200p. 300.00 o.p. (0-910457-06-9) Arion Pr.
—The Hound of the Baskervilles. abr. ed. audio 12.95 (0-89926-154-X, 842) Audio Bk. Co.
—The Hound of the Baskervilles, Set. unabr. ed. 1986. audio 29.95 (1-55685-008-5) Audio Bk. Contractors, Inc.
—The Hound of the Baskervilles. Klinger, Leslie Hawthorne, ed. anniv. ed. 2001. (The Baker Street Irregulars Manuscript Series: Vol. 2). (Illus.). 109p. 35.00 (0-9648788-3-6) Baker Street Irregulars, The.
—The Hound of the Baskervilles. 1987. 192p. mass mkt. 6.50 (0-345-35052-9) Ballantine Bks.
—The Hound of the Baskervilles. l.t. ed. Date not set. reprint ed. 24.00 (1-55246-292-7) Battered Silicon Dispatch Box, The.
—The Hound of the Baskervilles. 1986. mass mkt. 2.50 o.s.i (0-425-09592-4); 1984. mass mkt. 2.50 o.s.i (0-425-08090-0); 1983. mass mkt. 2.50 o.s.i (0-425-06587-1); 1982. mass mkt. 2.25 o.s.i (0-425-05219-2); 1980. mass mkt. 1.95 o.s.i (0-425-04421-1); 1979. mass mkt. 1.95 o.s.i (0-425-04535-8); 1978. mass mkt. 1.50 o.s.i (0-425-04000-3); 1977. mass mkt. 1.25 o.s.i (0-425-03336-8); 1974. mass mkt. 0.95 o.s.i (0-425-02805-4) Berkley Publishing Group.
—The Hound of the Baskervilles. Bennett, S. A., ed. 1992. (Adventures of Sherlock Holmes Ser.). (Illus.). 64p. pap. (0-944099-17-3) Bill Barry's Compass Bks.
—The Hound of the Baskervilles. unabr. ed. 1994. audio 32.95 (0-7861-0499-6, 1450) Blackstone Audio Bks., Inc.
—The Hound of the Baskervilles. unabr. ed. 1986. audio 39.95 (1-55686-238-5, 692234) Books in Motion.
—The Hound of the Baskervilles. unabr. collector's ed. 1993. (J). audio 36.00 (0-7366-2454-6, 3218) Books on Tape, Inc.
—The Hound of the Baskervilles. 2002. pap. 3.50 (1-59109-028-8) Booksurge, LLC.
—The Hound of the Baskervilles. 1986. lib. bdg. 19.95 (0-89966-229-3) Buccaneer Bks., Inc.
—The Hound of the Baskervilles. reprint ed. lib. bdg. 98.00 (0-7426-2707-1); lib. bdg. 48.00 (0-7426-1122-1); 2001. (Best Sellers of 1902 Ser.). pap. text 28.00 (0-7426-6122-9); 2001. (Collected Works of Sir Arthur Conan Doyle: Vol. 4). pap. text 28.00 (0-7426-7707-9) Classic Bks.
—The Hound of the Baskervilles. l.t. ed. 2003. (Dales Large Print Ser.). 320p. pap. 21.99 (1-84262-219-6) Dales Large Print Bks. GBR. Dist: Ulverscroft Large Print Bks., Ltd., Ulverscroft Large Print Canada, Ltd.
—The Hound of the Baskervilles. adapted ed. 1977. per. 6.50 (0-8222-0536-X) Dramatists Play Service, Inc.
—The Hound of the Baskervilles. abr. ed. audio 16.99 (0-88646-005-0, 7333); 1986. (YA). (gr. 6-8). audio 29.95 o.p. (0-88646-809-4, R 7007) Durkin Hayes Publishing Ltd.
—The Hound of the Baskervilles. (Illus.). 208p. 1988. pap. 10.95 o.p. (0-86547-264-5, North Point Pr.); 1986. 17.50 o.p. (0-86547-263-7) Farrar, Straus & Giroux.
—The Hound of the Baskervilles. 1976. (Crime Fiction Ser). reprint ed. lib. bdg. 21.00 o.p. (0-8240-2364-1) Garland Publishing, Inc.
—The Hound of the Baskervilles. abr. ed. 1996. audio 17.00 (1-55994-073-5, CPN 505, HarperAudio) HarperTrade.
—The Hound of the Baskervilles, unabr. ed. 1999. audio 32.95 Highsmith Inc.
—The Hound of the Baskervilles. 2001. v, 378p. pap. 8.95 (0-7551-0642-3) House of Stratus, Inc. GBR. Dist: Midpoint Trade Bks., Inc.
—The Hound of the Baskervilles. l.t. ed. 210p. pap. 21.88 (0-7583-1057-9); 167p. pap. 18.46 (0-7583-1056-0); 287p. pap. 27.46 (0-7583-1058-7); 370p. pap. 33.68 (0-7583-1059-5); 848p. pap. 67.50 (0-7583-1063-3); 474p. pap. 41.04 (0-7583-1060-9); 585p. pap. 48.89 (0-7583-1061-7); 683p. pap. 55.82 (0-7583-1062-5); 585p. lib. bdg. 56.61 (0-7583-1053-6); 370p. lib. bdg. 40.15 (0-7583-1051-X); 210p. lib. bdg. 27.88 (0-7583-1049-8); 167p. lib. bdg. 24.46 (0-7583-1048-X); 287p. lib. bdg. 33.46 (0-7583-1050-1); 474p. lib. bdg. 48.18 (0-7583-1052-8); 848p. lib. bdg. 87.24 (0-7583-1055-2); 683p. lib. bdg. 65.10 (0-7583-1054-4) Huge Print Pr.
—The Hound of the Baskervilles. 2002. 176p. 23.99 (1-4043-0972-1); per. 18.99 (1-4043-0973-X) IndyPublish.com.
—The Hound of the Baskervilles. unabr. ed. 1979. audio 28.00 Jimcin Recordings.
—The Hound of the Baskervilles. 1975. (Illus.). 4.95 o.p. (0-8052-3602-3); pap. 2.95 o.p. (0-8052-0505-5) Knopf Publishing Group. (Schocken).
—The Hound of the Baskervilles. l.t. ed. 1997. (Large Print Heritage Ser.). 282p. lib. bdg. 28.95 (1-58118-001-2, 21486) LRS.
—The Hound of the Baskervilles. Goodenough, Simon, ed. 1984. (Illus.). 192p. pap. o.p. (0-316-32002-1) Little Brown & Co.
—The Hound of the Baskervilles. Eyre, A. G., ed. 2000. (Longman Simplified English Ser.). 72p. pap. text 5.95 o.p. (0-582-52910-7, 73976) Longman Publishing Group.
—The Hound of the Baskervilles. 1997. pap. 3.95 (0-89375-410-2); 1986. mass mkt. 2.50 o.p. (0-451-52221-4); 1986. mass mkt. 2.25 o.p. (0-451-51983-3, Signet Classics); 1967. mass mkt. 0.50 o.p. (0-451-50337-6, Signet Classics); 100th anniv. ed. 2001. 256p. mass mkt. 4.95 (0-451-52801-8) NAL.
—The Hound of the Baskervilles. unabr. ed. 34.95 incl. audio Norton Pubs., Inc., Jeffrey /Audio-Forum.
—The Hound of the Baskervilles. 2002. E-Book (1-59342-019-6) Outrigger Publishing.
—The Hound of the Baskervilles. Robson, W. W., ed. 1993. (Oxford Sherlock Holmes Ser.). 232p. (C). 13.95 o.p. (0-19-212310-6, 8954) Oxford Univ. Pr., Inc.
—The Hound of the Baskervilles. Robson, W. W., ed. & intro. by. (Oxford World's Classics Ser.). 232p. reprint ed. 1998. pap. 8.95 (0-19-283519-X); 1995. pap. 6.95 o.p. (0-19-282377-9) Oxford Univ. Pr., Inc.
—The Hound of the Baskervilles. 1981. (Sherlock Holmes Ser.). 176p. (C). pap. 5.95 (0-14-000111-5, Penguin Bks.) Penguin Group (USA) Inc.
—The Hound of the Baskervilles. 1996. (Sherlock Holmes Ser.). (Illus.). 120p. 9.98 (1-879582-15-5) Platinum Pr., Inc.
—The Hound of the Baskervilles. collector's ed. 2002. (Illus.). im. lthr. 38.85 (1-4115-1252-9); pap. 19.95 (1-4115-0525-5); 25.95 (1-4115-0885-8); pap. 17.95 (1-4115-0317-1) Polyglot Pr., Inc.
—The Hound of the Baskervilles. abr. ed. 2000. (BBC Radio Presents Ser.). audio 18.00 o.s.i (0-553-52688-X, RH Audio) Random Hse. Audio Publishing Group.
—The Hound of the Baskervilles. unabr. ed. 1991. (Sherlock Holmes Mystery Ser.). audio 44.00 (1-55690-237-9, 91333E7) Recorded Bks., LLC.
—The Hound of the Baskervilles. unabr. ed. audio 24.95 (1-883049-79-2, Commuters Library) Sound Room Pubs., Inc.
—The Hound of the Baskervilles. (Mind's Eye Classic Ser.). 1996. audio 10.95 o.p. (1-55935-211-6); 1975. pap. 5.95 o.p. incl. audio (0-88142-334-3) Soundelux Audio Publishing.
—The Hound of the Baskervilles. l.t. ed. 2003. (Sherlock Holmes Ser.). 259p. 29.95 (0-7862-5870-5) Thorndike Pr.
—The Hound of the Baskervilles. 1986. 11.00 (0-606-01869-7) Turtleback Bks.
—The Hound of the Baskervilles. 2002. E-Book 2.95 (0-9712910-5-5) Twenty Penny Pr., Inc.
—The Hound of the Baskervilles. (Illus.). 150p. pap. 8.95 (1-57002-152-X) University Publishing Hse., Inc.
—The Hound of the Baskervilles. (Classics Ser.). 2001. 256p. pap. 8.00 (0-14-043786-X, Penguin Classics); 1995. 2p. audio 16.95 o.s.i (0-14-086164-5, Penguin AudioBooks) Viking Penguin.
—The Hound of the Baskervilles. 2001. 160p. pap. 3.95 (1-84022-400-2) Wordsworth Editions, Ltd. GBR. Dist: Combined Publishing.
—Maajabu Ya Utepe Wenye Madoadoa. Gateno, George, tr. 1993. Orig. Title: The Adventure of the Speckled Band. (SWA., Illus.). 31p. (Orig.). pap. 8.00 (0-9695673-3-2) Battered Silicon Dispatch Box, The.
—Mbwa Wa Familia Ya Baskerville. Mosotf, Zachary Mumbo & Ali, Hassan O., trs. (Sherlockian Scholarship Ser.).Tr. of Hound of the Baskervilles. (SWA.). pap. 12.00 (1-55246-059-2) Battered Silicon Dispatch Box, The.
—The Memoirs of Sherlock Holmes. 1986. mass mkt. 2.50 o.s.i (0-425-09576-2); 1984. mass mkt. 2.50 o.s.i (0-425-07315-7); 1976. mass mkt. 1.75 o.s.i (0-425-04400-9) Berkley Publishing Group.
—The Memoirs of Sherlock Holmes. 1982. reprint ed. lib. bdg. 21.95 o.p. (0-89966-428-8) Buccaneer Bks., Inc.
—The Memoirs of Sherlock Holmes. reprint ed. lib. bdg. 98.00 (0-7426-2692-X); 2001. (Collected Works of Sir Arthur Conan Doyle: Vol. 6). pap. text 28.00 (0-7426-7692-7) Classic Bks.
—The Memoirs of Sherlock Holmes. 2001. (Illus.). 300p. pap. 8.95 (0-7551-0644-X) House of Stratus, Inc. GBR. Dist: Midpoint Trade Bks., Inc.
—The Memoirs of Sherlock Holmes. 2002. 240p. 18.99 (1-4043-1910-7); per. 13.99 (1-4043-1911-5) IndyPublish.com.
—The Memoirs of Sherlock Holmes. 1976. (Illus.). 176p. 5.95 o.p. (0-8052-3622-8, Schocken) Knopf Publishing Group.
—The Memoirs of Sherlock Holmes. E-Book 2.95 (1-57799-810-3) Logos Research Systems, Inc.
—The Memoirs of Sherlock Holmes. l.t. ed. (Large Print Ser.). reprint ed. 1986. 421p. lib. bdg. 26.00 (0-939495-31-7); 1998. 270p. lib. bdg. 25.00 (1-58287-049-7) North Bks.
—The Memoirs of Sherlock Holmes. Roden, Christopher, ed. (Oxford World's Classics Ser.). 2000. 384p. pap. 9.95 (0-19-283811-3); 1993. 378p. (C). 13.95 o.p. (0-19-212309-2) Oxford Univ. Pr., Inc.
—The Memoirs of Sherlock Holmes. Roden, Christopher, ed. & intro. by. 1995. (Oxford World's Classics Ser.). 378p. reprint ed. pap. 6.95 o.p. (0-19-282375-2) Oxford Univ. Pr., Inc.
—The Memoirs of Sherlock Holmes. 1996. (Sherlock Holmes Ser.). (Illus.). 160p. 9.98 (1-879582-14-7) Platinum Pr., Inc.
—The Memoirs of Sherlock Holmes. collector's ed. 2002. (Illus.). im. lthr. 38.85 (1-4115-1248-0); pap. 19.95 (1-4115-0518-2); 25.95 (1-4115-0886-6); pap. 19.95 (1-4115-0314-7) Polyglot Pr., Inc.
—The Memoirs of Sherlock Holmes. 1999. 375p. E-Book 3.99 incl. cd-rom (1-57646-178-5) Quiet Vision Publishing.
—The Memoirs of Sherlock Holmes. 1994. audio 15.95 o.s.i (0-553-74577-8); 1994. audio 15.95 o.s.i (0-553-74612-X); 1993. audio 15.95 o.s.i (0-553-74550-6); 1993. audio 12.79 o.s.i (0-553-70054-5); Vol. 2. 1994. audio 16.99 o.s.i (0-553-47249-6); Vols. 1-3. 1997. 29.95 o.s.i incl. audio (0-553-47954-7) Random Hse. Audio Publishing Group. (RH Audio).
—The Memoirs of Sherlock Holmes. l.t. ed. 1966. (Ulverscroft Large Print Ser.). 29.99 o.p. (0-85456-573-6, Ulverscroft) Thorpe, F. A. Pubs. GBR. Dist: Ulverscroft Large Print Bks., Ltd., Ulverscroft Large Print Canada, Ltd.
—The Memoirs of Sherlock Holmes. 2001. (Classics of Mystery & Suspense Ser.). 318p. (1-58279-190-2) Trident Pr. International.
—The Memoirs of Sherlock Holmes. 1951. 256p. pap. 3.95 o.p. (0-14-000785-7, Penguin Bks.) Viking Penguin.
—The Memoirs of Sherlock Holmes. 2001. 230p. pap. 12.95 (0-595-01467-4) iUniverse, Inc.
—The Memoirs of Sherlock Holmes. unabr. collector's ed. Incl. Adventures of Silver Blaze. audio Crooked Man. audio Final Problem. audio Gloria Scott. audio Greek Interpreter. audio Musgrave Ritual. audio Naval Treaty. audio Reigate Squires. audio Resident Patient. audio Stockbroker's Clerk. audio Yellow Face. audio 1984. (Sherlock Holmes Ser.). 1980. Set audio 48.00 (0-7366-0320-4, 1308) Books on Tape, Inc.
—The Memoirs of Sherlock Holmes. unabr. ed. Incl. Adventure of the Crooked Man. audio Adventure of the Gloria Scott. audio Adventure of the Greek Interpreter. audio Adventure of the Musgrave Ritual. audio Adventure of the Naval Treaty. audio Adventure of the Reigate Squire. audio Adventure of the Resident Patient. audio Adventure of the Stockbroker's Clerk. audio Adventure of the Yellow Face. audio Adventures of Silver Blaze. audio Set audio 49.00 Jimcin Recordings.
—My Life with Sherlock Holmes: Conversations in Baker Street. Hamilton, J. R., ed. 1970. (Illus.). 5.75 o.p. (0-7195-1837-7) Transatlantic Arts, Inc.
—The Mysteries of Sherlock Holmes. 1996. (Illustrated Junior Library). (Illus.). 240p. (YA). (gr. 4-7). 16.99 (0-448-40957-7, Grosset & Dunlap) Penguin Putnam Bks. for Young Readers.
—The Mysteries of Sherlock Holmes. Conaway, Judith, ed. 1982. (Step into Classics Ser.). (Illus.). 96p. (gr. 3-5). pap. text 3.99 (0-394-85086-6, Random Hse. Bks. for Young Readers) Random Hse. Children's Bks.
—The Original Illustrated Sherlock Holmes: The Strand Facsimile Edition. 2001. (Illus.). 636p. 25.00 (0-7881-9933-1) DIANE Publishing Co.
—The Original Illustrated Strand Sherlock Holmes. 2001. (Complete Works Ser.). (Illus.). 1136p. pap. 7.95 (1-85326-896-8) Wordsworth Editions, Ltd. GBR. Dist: Advanced Global Distribution Services.
—The Original Illustrated Strand Sherlock Holmes: The Complete Facsimile Edition. 2000. (Illus.). 1126p. reprint ed. pap. text 25.00 (0-7881-9173-X) DIANE Publishing Co.
—The Oxford Sherlock Holmes, 9 vols., Set. Edwards, Owen D., ed. 1993. 2926p. (C). 125.00 o.p. (0-19-212329-7) Oxford Univ. Pr., Inc.
—The Red-Headed League. 1996. (Sherlock Holmes Ser.). 27p. pap. 3.50 (1-57514-260-0, 3068) Encore Performance Publishing.
—The Red-Headed League. 1995. (Jamestown Classics Ser.). pap., tchr. ed. 7.32 (0-89061-061-4) Jamestown.
—The Return of Sherlock Holmes. Date not set. (Heritage Literary Ser.). pap. text 31.50 (0-582-34913-3) Addison-Wesley Longman, Ltd. GBR. Dist: Trans-Atlantic Pubns., Inc.
—The Return of Sherlock Holmes. 1985. 320p. mass mkt. 2.95 o.s.i (0-345-32713-6) Ballantine Bks.
—The Return of Sherlock Holmes. 1986. 320p. mass mkt. 2.95 o.p. (0-425-10151-7); 1986. mass mkt. 2.50 o.s.i (0-425-09578-9); 1985. mass mkt. 2.50 o.s.i (0-425-08005-6); 1983. mass mkt. 2.50 o.s.i (0-425-07125-1); 1982. mass mkt. 2.25 o.s.i (0-425-04871-3); 1979. mass mkt. 1.75 o.s.i

(*0-425-04536-6*); 1978. mass mkt. 1.50 o.s.i (*0-425-04071-2*); 1976. mass mkt. 1.25 o.s.i (*0-425-03334-1*); 1973. mass mkt. 0.75 o.p. (*0-425-02353-2*) Berkley Publishing Group.

—The Return of Sherlock Holmes. unabr. ed. 1983. audio 56.95 (*0-7861-0592-5*, 2081) Blackstone Audio Bks., Inc.

—The Return of Sherlock Holmes. unabr. collector's ed. 1982. (J). audio 64.00 (*0-7366-3854-7*, 9051) Books on Tape, Inc.

—The Return of Sherlock Holmes. reprint ed. lib. bdg. 98.00 (*0-7426-2711-X*); 2001. 344p. pap. text 28.00 (*0-7426-7711-7*) Classic Bks.

—The Return of Sherlock Holmes. E-Book 2.49 (*0-7574-0391-3*) Electric Umbrella Publishing.

—The Return of Sherlock Holmes. unabr. ed. 1999. audio 56.95 Highsmith Inc.

—The Return of Sherlock Holmes. 2001. iv, 378p. pap. 8.95 (*0-7551-0643-1*) House of Stratus, Inc. GBR. *Dist:* Midpoint Trade Bks., Inc.

—The Return of Sherlock Holmes. 1975. (Illus.). 5.95 o.p. (*0-8052-3603-1*); pap. 2.95 o.p. (*0-8052-0506-3*) Knopf Publishing Group. (Schocken).

—The Return of Sherlock Holmes. E-Book 2.95 (*1-57799-838-3*); E-Book 2.95 (*1-57799-975-4*) Logos Research Systems, Inc.

—The Return of Sherlock Holmes. (English As a Second Language Bk.). 1981. pap. 5.95 o.p. (*0-582-52411-3*); Level 3. 2001. pap. 7.66 (*0-582-42697-9*) Longman Publishing Group.

—The Return of Sherlock Holmes. 1987. (Illus.). 320p. 25.00 o.p. (*0-89296-248-8*) Mysterious Pr.

—The Return of Sherlock Holmes. 2003. (Twelve-Point Ser.). lib. bdg. 25.00 (*1-58287-207-4*); lib. bdg. 26.00 (*1-58287-691-6*) North Bks.

—The Return of Sherlock Holmes. Green, Richard Lancelyn, ed. 1993. (Sherlock Holmes Ser.). 474p. (C). 13.95 o.p. (*0-19-212317-3*, 8952) Oxford Univ. Pr., Inc.

—The Return of Sherlock Holmes. Green, Richard Lancelyn, ed. & intro. by. 1995. (Oxford World's Classics Ser.). 456p. reprint ed. pap. 5.95 o.p. (*0-19-282376-0*) Oxford Univ. Pr., Inc.

—The Return of Sherlock Holmes. 1996. (Sherlock Holmes Ser.). (Illus.). 200p. 9.98 (*1-879852-13-9*) Platinum Pr., Inc.

—The Return of Sherlock Holmes. 1999. 482p. E-Book 3.99 incl. cd-rom (*1-57646-179-3*) Quiet Vision Publishing.

—The Return of Sherlock Holmes. 1995. audio 16.98 o.s.i (*0-553-74557-3*); Vol. 1. 1995. audio 16.99 o.s.i (*0-553-47349-2*); Vol. 2. 1995. audio 16.98 o.s.i (*0-553-74666-9*); Vol. 3. 1996. audio 16.99 o.s.i (*0-553-47655-6*) Random Hse. Audio Publishing Group. (RH Audio).

—The Return of Sherlock Holmes. 2001. audio 29.95 (*1-931102-46-5*, CA-051) TOPICS Entertainment.

—The Return of Sherlock Holmes. l.t. ed. 1967. (Ulverscroft Large Print Ser.). 29.99 o.p. (*0-85456-574-4*, Ulverscroft) Thorpe, F. A. Pubs. GBR. *Dist:* Ulverscroft Large Print Bks., Ltd., Ulverscroft Large Print Canada, Ltd.

—The Return of Sherlock Holmes. 2002. E-Book 2.95 (*0-9712910-8-X*) Twenty Penny Pr., Inc.

—The Return of Sherlock Holmes. 1987. 192p. pap. 3.50 o.p. (*0-14-010026-1*); 1982. 336p. pap. 5.95 o.p. (*0-14-005708-0*) Viking Penguin. (Penguin Bks.).

—The Return of Sherlock Holmes. 1997. (Classics Library). 320p. pap. 3.95 (*1-85326-058-4*, 0584WW) Wordsworth Editions, Ltd. GBR. *Dist:* Combined Publishing.

—The Return of Sherlock Holmes. unabr. ed. Incl. Abbey Grange. audio Adventure of Black Peter. audio Adventure of Charles Augustus Milverton. audio Adventure of the Six Napoleons. audio Dancing Men. audio Empty House. audio Golden Pince-Nez. audio Missing Three-Quarter. audio Norwood Builder. audio Priory School. audio Second Stain. audio Solitary Cyclist. audio Three Students. audio 1981. 1981. Set audio 49.00 Jimcin Recordings.

—The Return of Sherlock Holmes: The Oxford Sherlock Holmes. 1999. (Oxford World's Classics Ser.). pap. text 5.95 (*0-19-283761-3*) Oxford Univ. Pr., Inc.

—A Scandal in Bohemia. 1996. (Sherlock Holmes Ser.). 20p. pap. 3.50 (*1-57514-261-9*, 3069) Encore Performance Publishing.

—A Scandal in Bohemia. Stemach, Jerry, ed. l.t. ed. (Illus.). 100p. 2002. text 150.00 (*1-58702-042-4*); 2000. text 50.00 (*1-58702-499-3*) Johnston, Don Inc.

—A Scandal in Bohemia. 1999. E-Book 1.95 (*1-58515-031-2*) MesaView, Inc.

—Sherlock Holmes. unabr. ed. 1991. (Best of Sherlock Holmes Ser.: Vol. 2). audio 21.95 o.p. (*1-55656-016-8*, DAB041) BBC Audiobooks America.

—Sherlock Holmes. unabr. ed. 1986. audio 17.95 (*1-55569-116-1*, 5770-06) Great American Audio Corp.

—Sherlock Holmes. abr. ed. audio HarperTrade.

—Sherlock Holmes. abr. ed. 2001. audio 26.95 (*1-56511-557-0*) HighBridge Co.

—Sherlock Holmes, Vol. 3. 1991. audio 14.95 Minds Eye.

—Sherlock Holmes. unabr. ed. Incl. Case of Identity. audio Musgrave Ritual. audio Red-Headed League. audio Scandal in Bohemia. audio 1986. 1986. Set audio 16.95 (*1-55656-003-6*) Dercum Audio.

—Sherlock Holmes. abr. ed. Incl. Adventures of the Speckled Band. audio Redheaded League. audio Scandal in Bohemia. audio Silver Blaze. audio 1985. Set audio 29.95 (*0-89845-032-2*, SBC 107, Caedmon) HarperTrade.

—Sherlock Holmes: Selected Stories. Date not set. lib. bdg. 29.95 (*0-8488-1672-2*) Amereon, Ltd.

—Sherlock Holmes: Selected Stories. Roberts, S. C., ed. & intro. by. 1998. (Oxford World's Classics Ser.). 464p. pap. 10.95 (*0-19-283537-8*) Oxford Univ. Pr., Inc.

—Sherlock Holmes: Selected Stories. 1982. (Oxford World's Classics Ser.). 460p. pap. 7.95 o.p. (*0-19-281530-X*) Oxford Univ. Pr., Inc.

—Sherlock Holmes: The Complete Novels & Stories, 2 vols., 2003. (Bantam Classics Ser.). E-Book 6.95 (*0-553-89744-6*, Bantam Classics) Bantam Bks.

—Sherlock Holmes: The Complete Novels & Stories. 1986. (Bantam Classics Ser.). reprint ed. Vol. I. 1088p. mass mkt. 6.95 (*0-553-21241-9*); Vol. II. 768p. mass mkt. 6.95 (*0-553-21242-7*) Bantam Dell Publishing Group.

—Sherlock Holmes: The Complete Novels & Stories. 1986. 12.55 (*0-606-03127-8*) Turtleback Bks.

—Sherlock Holmes: The Hound of the Baskervilles. abr. ed. 2001. (Great Mystery Ser.). audio compact disk 14.99 (*1-57815-531-2*, Media Bks. Audio Publishing) Media Bks., L. L. C.

—Sherlock Holmes: The Hound of the Baskervilles. abr. ed. 2001. audio (*1-894003-26-8*) Scenario Productions.

—Sherlock Holmes: The Hound of the Baskervilles. unabr. ed. 2002. (YA). audio compact disk 29.95 (*1-58472-328-9*, 018, In Audio) Sound Room Pubs., Inc.

—The Sherlock Holmes Apocrypha. 1993. pap. 18.95 o.p. (*0-934468-51-6*) Gaslight Pubns.

—The Sherlock Holmes Collection: Study in Scarlet & The Sign of Four. 1999. audio 17.95; 1994. audio 17.95 (*1-56100-592-4*, 263) Brilliance Audio. (Bookcassette).

—The Sherlock Holmes Collection: Study in Scarlet & The Sign of Four. 1999. 2832p. E-Book 19.99 incl. cd-rom (*1-891595-13-X*) Quiet Vision Publishing.

—The Sherlock Holmes Mysteries: New Expanded Edition. exp. ed. 1985. 536p. (YA). mass mkt. 5.95 (*0-451-52431-4*, Signet Classics) NAL.

—Sherlock Holmes Reader. 1975. 3.95 o.s.i (*0-425-03010-5*) Berkley Publishing Group.

—Sherlock Holmes Strangest Cases. 2001. (Cottage Classics). (Illus.). 120p. 48.00 (*1-892847-02-7*); pap. 17.95 (*1-892847-03-5*) Word Play Pubns.

—Sherlock Holmes's Mysteries. unabr. ed. 2002. (YA). audio compact disk 18.95 (*1-58472-402-1*, In Audio) Sound Room Pubs., Inc.

—The Sign of the Four. Date not set. 112p. 16.95 (*0-8488-2550-0*) Amereon, Ltd.

—The Sign of the Four. 1994. (Library of Congress Centennial Bestseller Ser.). 160p. 24.95 (*1-55709-301-6*) Applewood Bks.

—The Sign of the Four. unabr. ed. 1991. (Best of Sherlock Holmes Ser.). audio 26.95 o.p. (*1-55656-140-7*, DAB042) BBC Audiobooks America.

—The Sign of the Four. 1987. (Illus.). 160p. mass mkt. 3.95 o.s.i (*0-345-35290-4*) Ballantine Bks.

—The Sign of the Four. 2000. (Encore Editions Ser.). 167p. (C). pap. (*1-55111-392-9*) Broadview Pr.

—The Sign of the Four. unabr. ed. (Best of Sherlock Holmes Ser.). 1998. pap. 21.95 o.s.i incl. audio (*1-55656-228-4*); 1990. audio 21.95 o.s.i (*1-55656-139-3*) Dercum Audio.

—The Sign of the Four. 1977. 9.95 o.p. (*0-385-12285-3*) Doubleday Publishing.

—The Sign of the Four. abr. ed. 1986. (J). (gr. 5-7). audio 29.95 o.p. (*0-88646-811-6*, R 7094); 1983. audio 15.95 o.p. (*0-88646-072-7*, TC-LFP 7094) Durkin Hayes Publishing Ltd.

—The Sign of the Four. 2001. iv, 144p. pap. 8.95 (*0-7551-0639-3*) House of Stratus, Inc. GBR. *Dist:* Midpoint Trade Bks., Inc.

—The Sign of the Four. Goodenough, Simon, ed. 1985. (Illus.). 192p. pap. o.p. (*0-316-32009-9*) Little Brown & Co.

—The Sign of the Four. Roden, Christopher, ed. 1993. (Oxford Sherlock Holmes Ser.). 192p. (C). 13.95 o.p. (*0-19-212316-5*, 14614) Oxford Univ. Pr., Inc.

—The Sign of the Four. Roden, Christopher, ed. & intro. by. 1995. (Oxford World's Classics Ser.). 192p. reprint ed. pap. 5.95 o.p. (*0-19-282379-5*) Oxford Univ. Pr., Inc.

—The Sign of the Four. 1999. 185p. E-Book 3.99 incl. cd-rom (*1-57646-181-5*) Quiet Vision Publishing.

—The Sign of the Four. unabr. ed. 1986. (Sherlock Holmes Mystery Ser.). audio 26.00 (*1-55690-477-0*, 86240E7) Recorded Bks., LLC.

—The Sign of the Four. 2002. E-Book 2.95 (*0-9712910-4-7*) Twenty Penny Pr., Inc.

—The Sign of the Four. 2001. (Classics Ser.). 160p. 7.00 (*0-14-043907-2*, Penguin Classics) Viking Penguin.

—Six Great Sherlock Holmes Stories. 1992. (Thrift Editions Ser.). 112p. (Orig.). pap. 1.50 (*0-486-27055-6*) Dover Pubns., Inc.

—A Study in Scarlet. 1984. 192p. mass mkt. 2.50 o.s.i (*0-425-08004-8*) Ace Bks.

—A Study in Scarlet. Date not set. 121p. 17.95 (*0-8488-2554-3*) Amereon, Ltd.

—A Study in Scarlet. unabr. ed. 1998. (C). audio 24.95 (*1-55685-608-3*) Audio Bk. Contractors, Inc.

—A Study in Scarlet. unabr. ed. 1991. (Best of Sherlock Holmes Ser.: Vol. 4). audio 26.95 o.p. (*1-55656-062-1*, DAB043) BBC Audiobooks America.

—A Study in Scarlet. 1975. 160p. mass mkt. 1.25 o.p. (*0-345-24714-0*) Ballantine Bks.

—A Study in Scarlet. Bennett, S. A., ed. 1992. (Adventures of Sherlock Holmes Ser.). (Illus.). 64p. pap. (*0-944099-18-1*) Bill Barry's Compass Bks.

—A Study in Scarlet. abr. ed. 1999. audio 23.95 (*0-7861-1604-8*); audio 23.95 Blackstone Audio Bks., Inc.

—A Study in Scarlet. 2001. per. 9.90 (*1-891355-68-6*); per. 15.50 (*1-58396-234-4*) Blue Unicorn Editions.

—A Study in Scarlet. unabr. collector's ed. 1982. (J). audio 30.00 (*0-7366-3965-9*, 9504) Books on Tape, Inc.

—A Study in Scarlet. 1989. lib. bdg. 15.95 (*0-89966-231-5*) Buccaneer Bks., Inc.

—A Study in Scarlet. (Collected Works of Sir Arthur Conan Doyle). 2001. pap. text 28.00 (*0-7426-7676-5*); reprint ed. lib. bdg. 98.00 (*0-7426-2676-8*) Classic Bks.

—A Study in Scarlet. unabr. ed. audio 21.95 o.p. (*1-55656-104-0*); 1997. (Best of Sherlock Holmes Ser.: Vol. 4). pap. 21.95 o.p. incl. audio (*1-55656-229-2*) Dercum Audio.

—A Study in Scarlet. 1977. 7.95 o.p. (*0-385-12283-7*) Doubleday Publishing.

—A Study in Scarlet. abr. ed. 1986. (J). (gr. 5-7). audio 29.95 o.p. (*0-88646-784-5*, R 7011); 1984. audio 15.95 o.p. (*0-88646-087-5*, TC-LFP 7011) Durkin Hayes Publishing Ltd.

—A Study in Scarlet. E-Book 2.49 (*0-7574-0260-7*) Electric Umbrella Publishing.

—A Study in Scarlet. 2001. iv, 156p. pap. 8.95 (*0-7551-0638-5*) House of Stratus, Inc. GBR. *Dist:* Midpoint Trade Bks., Inc.

—A Study in Scarlet. 1989. audio 18.00 Jimcin Recordings.

—A Study in Scarlet. E-Book 2.95 (*1-57799-808-1*) Logos Research Systems, Inc.

—A Study in Scarlet. Edwards, Owen Dudley, ed. 2000. (Oxford World's Classics Ser.). 256p. pap. 6.95 (*0-19-283765-6*) Oxford Univ. Pr., Inc.

—A Study in Scarlet. Edwards, Owen D., ed. 1993. (Oxford Sherlock Holmes Ser.). 254p. (C). 13.95 o.p. (*0-19-212313-0*, 14615) Oxford Univ. Pr., Inc.

—A Study in Scarlet. Edwards, Dudley, ed. & intro. by. 1995. (Oxford World's Classics Ser.). 254p. reprint ed. pap. 5.95 o.p. (*0-19-282380-9*) Oxford Univ. Pr., Inc.

—A Study in Scarlet. 1982. (Classic Crime Ser.). 144p. pap. 6.95 (*0-14-005707-2*, Penguin Bks.) Penguin Group (USA) Inc.

—A Study in Scarlet. collector's ed. 2002. (Illus.). im. lthr. 38.85 (*1-4115-1254-5*); pap. 19.95 (*1-4115-0521-2*); 25.95 (*1-4115-0889-0*); pap. 17.95 (*1-4115-0319-8*) Polyglot Pr., Inc.

—A Study in Scarlet. 1999. 191p. E-Book 3.99 incl. cd-rom (*1-57646-180-7*) Quiet Vision Publishing.

—A Study in Scarlet. 2003. 160p. pap. 6.95 (*0-8129-6854-9*, Modern Library) Random House Adult Trade Publishing Group.

—A Study in Scarlet. abr. ed. 1999. (Sherlock Holmes Ser.). audio 18.00 o.s.i (*0-553-52553-0*, RH Audio) Random Hse. Audio Publishing Group.

—A Study in Scarlet. unabr. ed. 1984. (Sherlock Holmes Mystery Ser.). audio 26.00 (*1-55690-498-3*, 84071E7) Recorded Bks., LLC.

—A Study in Scarlet. E-Book 5.00 (*0-7410-1416-5*) SoftBook Pr.

—A Study in Scarlet, 1. 1998. pap. text 6.95 (*0-9666443-1-X*) Thorby Enterprises, Inc.

—A Study in Scarlet. l.t. ed. 2001. (Perennial Bestsellers Ser.). 191p. 27.95 (*0-7838-9350-7*) Thorndike Pr.

—A Study in Scarlet. E-Book 2.00 (*1-58505-984-6*) Treeless Pr.

—A Study in Scarlet. 2001. (Classics Ser.). 192p. 7.00 (*0-14-043908-0*, Penguin Classics) Viking Penguin.

—A Study in Scarlet. 2001. (New Millennium Library). 109p. pap. 9.95 (*0-595-01428-3*) iUniverse, Inc.

—A Study in Scarlet & The Sign of the Four. 1986. mass mkt. 2.50 o.s.i (*0-425-09577-0*); 1983. mass mkt. 2.25 o.s.i (*0-425-05209-5*); 1978. mass mkt. 1.75 o.s.i (*0-425-04117-4*); 1975. mass mkt. 1.25 o.s.i (*0-425-02838-0*) Berkley Publishing Group.

—A Study in Scarlet & The Sign of the Four. 2003. (Dover Thrift Editions Ser.). 208p. 2.50 (*0-486-43166-5*) Dover Pubns., Inc.

—A Study in Scarlet & The Sign of the Four. l.t. ed. 1969. o.p. (*0-7089-0190-5*, Ulverscroft) Thorpe, F. A. Pubs.

—Tales for a Winter's Night. 1989. (Academy Book Ser.). 207p. pap. 14.95 (*0-89733-309-8*) Academy Chicago Pubs., Ltd.

—The Valley of Fear. 1976. 17.95 (*0-8488-1288-3*) Amereon, Ltd.

—The Valley of Fear. unabr. ed. 2003. (YA). (gr. 10 up). audio 29.95 (*1-55685-676-8*, ) Audio Bk. Contractors, Inc.

—The Valley of Fear. l.t. ed. 1990. pap. 16.95 o.p. (*0-7927-0475-4*, C0775) BBC Audiobooks America.

—The Valley of Fear. 1987. 176p. mass mkt. 2.50 o.p. (*0-425-10330-7*); 1986. mass mkt. 2.50 o.s.i (*0-425-09580-0*); 1984. mass mkt. 2.50 o.s.i (*0-425-07140-5*); 1981. mass mkt. 2.25 o.s.i (*0-425-05221-4*); 1980. mass mkt. 1.95 o.s.i (*0-425-04911-6*); 1979. mass mkt. 1.75 o.s.i (*0-425-04537-4*); 1978. mass mkt. 1.50 o.s.i (*0-425-03981-1*); 1976. mass mkt. 1.25 o.s.i (*0-425-03136-5*) Berkley Publishing Group.

—The Valley of Fear. unabr. ed. 1991. audio 39.95 (*0-7861-0612-3*, 2102) Blackstone Audio Bks., Inc.

—The Valley of Fear. unabr. collector's ed. 1991. audio 36.00 (*0-7366-2030-3*, 2844) Books on Tape, Inc.

—The Valley of Fear. 1988. lib. bdg. 16.95 (*0-89966-232-3*) Buccaneer Bks., Inc.

—The Valley of Fear. 1977. 7.95 o.p. (*0-385-12284-5*) Doubleday Publishing.

—The Valley of Fear. unabr. ed. 1991. audio 16.99 (*0-88646-296-7*, 7296) Durkin Hayes Publishing Ltd.

—The Valley of Fear, Set. unabr. ed. 1999. audio 39.95 Highsmith Inc.

—The Valley of Fear. 2001. iv, 200p. pap. 8.95 (*0-7551-0645-8*) House of Stratus, Inc. GBR. *Dist:* Midpoint Trade Bks., Inc.

—The Valley of Fear. unabr. ed. 1991. (YA). (gr. 9-12). audio 29.00 Jimcin Recordings.

—The Valley of Fear. Edwards, Owen D., ed. 1993. (Oxford Sherlock Holmes Ser.). 292p. (C). 13.95 o.p. (*0-19-212314-9*, 8951) Oxford Univ. Pr., Inc.

—The Valley of Fear. Edwards, Owen D., ed. & intro. by. 1995. (Oxford World's Classics Ser.). 292p. reprint ed. pap. 6.95 o.p. (*0-19-282382-5*) Oxford Univ. Pr., Inc.

—The Valley of Fear. 1991. (Classic Crime Ser.). 192p. pap. 6.00 o.p. (*0-14-005710-2*, Penguin Bks.) Penguin Group (USA) Inc.

—The Valley of Fear. collector's ed. 2002. (Illus.). im. lthr. 38.85 (*1-4115-1255-3*); pap. 19.95 (*1-4115-0524-7*); 25.95 (*1-4115-0890-4*); pap. 17.95 (*1-4115-0320-1*) Polyglot Pr., Inc.

—The Valley of Fear. 1999. 256p. E-Book 3.99 incl. cd-rom (*1-57646-184-X*) Quiet Vision Publishing.

—The Valley of Fear. abr. ed. 1999. (BBC Radio Presents Ser.). audio 18.00 o.s.i (*0-553-52622-7*, RH Audio) Random Hse. Audio Publishing Group.

—The Valley of Fear. unabr. ed. 1986. (Sherlock Holmes Mystery Ser.). audio 35.00 (*1-55690-539-4*, 86250E7) Recorded Bks., LLC.

—The Valley of Fear. unabr. ed. 2002. audio compact disk 20.00 (*1-4001-5040-X*); audio compact disk 33.00 (*1-4001-0040-2*) Tantor Media, Inc.

—The Valley of Fear. l.t. ed. 1978. (Ulverscroft Large Print Ser.). 29.99 o.p. (*0-7089-0086-0*, Ulverscroft) Thorpe, F. A. Pubs. GBR. *Dist:* Ulverscroft Large Print Bks., Ltd., Ulverscroft Large Print Canada, Ltd.

—The Valley of Fear. 2001. (Classics Ser.). 448p. 11.00 (*0-14-043772-X*, Penguin Classics) Viking Penguin.

—The White Company & Sir Nigel. 2000. (Common Reader Edition Ser.). 618p. pap. 24.95 (*1-888173-90-4*) Akadine Pr., The.

Doyle, Arthur Conan, as told by. A Study in Scarlet. 2002. E-Book 2.95 (*0-9712910-3-9*) Twenty Penny Pr., Inc.

Doyle, Arthur Conan, ed. The Adventures of Sherlock Holmes. 1985. 288p. mass mkt. 2.95 o.s.i (*0-553-26772-8*, Bantam Classics); mass mkt. 2.50 o.s.i (*0-553-24996-7*) Bantam Bks.

—The Adventures of Sherlock Holmes, Vol. 3. l.t. ed. 2000. reprint ed. 28.00 (*1-55246-290-0*) Battered Silicon Dispatch Box, The.

—The Adventures of Sherlock Holmes. 1984. mass mkt. 2.95 o.s.i (*0-425-08089-7*); 1984. mass mkt. 2.50 o.s.i (*0-425-07501-X*); 1983. mass mkt. 2.25 o.s.i (*0-425-04869-1*); 1980. mass mkt. 1.95 o.s.i (*0-425-04337-1*); 1977. mass mkt. 1.50 o.s.i (*0-425-03518-2*); 1975. mass mkt. 0.95 o.s.i (*0-425-02802-X*) Berkley Publishing Group.

—The Adventures of Sherlock Holmes. 2002. pap. 4.95 (*1-59109-027-X*) Booksurge, LLC.

—The Adventures of Sherlock Holmes. 1982. lib. bdg. 31.95 (*0-89966-385-0*) Buccaneer Bks., Inc.

—The Adventures of Sherlock Holmes. (Collected Works of Sir Arthur Conan Doyle). 2001. pap. text 28.00 (*0-7426-7687-0*); reprint ed. lib. bdg. 48.00 (*0-7426-1019-5*); reprint ed. lib. bdg. 98.00 (*0-7426-2687-3*); 2001. (Illus.). reprint ed. pap. text 28.00 (*0-7426-6019-2*) Classic Bks.

—The Adventures of Sherlock Holmes. 1989. mass mkt. 3.25 o.s.i (*0-8125-0425-9*, Tor Classics); 1988. mass mkt. 4.95 (*0-938819-89-5*, Aerie) Doherty, Tom Assocs., LLC.

—The Adventures of Sherlock Holmes. E-Book 3.49 (*1-929120-40-0*) Electric Umbrella Publishing.

—The Adventures of Sherlock Holmes. l.t. ed. 1999. 400p. pap. 22.00 (*0-06-093322-4*); 1901. reprint ed. o.p. (*0-06-011070-8*) HarperCollins Pubs.

—The Adventures of Sherlock Holmes. unabr. ed. 1999. audio 49.95Set. audio 24.95 Highsmith Inc.

—The Adventures of Sherlock Holmes. 2001. iv, 336p. pap. 8.95 (*0-7551-0637-7*) House of Stratus, Inc. GBR. *Dist:* Midpoint Trade Bks., Inc.

—The Adventures of Sherlock Holmes. 2001. 312p. 26.99 (*1-58827-348-2*); 19.99 (*1-58827-352-0*); 126.99 (*1-58827-960-X*); per. 21.99 (*1-58827-349-0*); per. 14.99 (*1-58827-353-9*); per. 121.99 (*1-58827-961-8*) IndyPublish.com.

—The Adventures of Sherlock Holmes. 1976. (Illus.). 192p. 5.95 o.p. (*0-8052-3621-X*, Schocken) Knopf Publishing Group.

—The Adventures of Sherlock Holmes. l.t. ed. 2000. (Large Print Heritage Ser.). 502p. lib. bdg. 35.95 (*1-58118-067-5*, 23664) LRS.

—The Adventures of Sherlock Holmes. abr. ed. 2001. (Great Mystery Ser.). audio compact disk 14.99 (*1-57815-530-4*, Media Bks. Audio Publishing) Media Bks., L. L. C.

—The Adventures of Sherlock Holmes. abr. ed. 1998. (National Public Radio Ser.). audio 24.95 (*1-56994-503-9*, Monterey SoundWorks) Monterey Media, Inc.

—The Adventures of Sherlock Holmes. 1997. pap. 2.95 (*0-89375-402-1*) NAL.

—The Adventures of Sherlock Holmes. l.t. ed. (Large Print Ser.). reprint ed. 1986. 494p. lib. bdg. 26.00 (*0-939495-30-9*); 1998. 308p. lib. bdg. 25.00 (*1-58287-011-X*) North Bks.

—The Adventures of Sherlock Holmes. (Oxford Progressive English Readers Ser.). (Illus.). 1982. pap. 4.95 o.p. (*0-19-581280-8*); 2nd ed. 1993. 78p. pap. text 5.95 (*0-19-585257-5*) Oxford Univ. Pr., Inc.

—The Adventures of Sherlock Holmes. 2002. Vol. 1. audio compact disk (*0-14-180388-6*); Vol. 2. audio compact disk (*0-14-180389-4*) Penguin Bks., Ltd.

—The Adventures of Sherlock Holmes. 1981. (Classic Crime Ser.). 288p. pap. 6.95 (*0-14-005724-2*, Penguin Bks.) Penguin Group (USA) Inc.

—The Adventures of Sherlock Holmes. 1996. (Sherlock Holmes Ser.). (Illus.). 172p. 9.98 (*1-879582-12-0*) Platinum Pr., Inc.

—The Adventures of Sherlock Holmes. collector's ed. 2002. (Illus.). im. lthr. 38.85 (*1-4115-1249-9*); pap. 19.95 (*1-4115-0522-0*); 25.95 (*1-4115-0882-3*); pap. 17.95 (*1-4115-0313-9*) Polyglot Pr., Inc.

—The Adventures of Sherlock Holmes. 1999. 442p. E-Book 3.99 incl. cd-rom (*1-57646-177-7*) Quiet Vision Publishing.

—The Adventures of Sherlock Holmes. unabr. ed. 1985. (Cassette Bookshelf Ser.). audio 15.98 (*0-8072-3415-X*, CB 105CX, Listening Library); Vol. 1. 1996. (BBC Radio Presents Ser.). audio 16.99 o.s.i (*0-553-47763-3*, RH Audio); Vol. 2. 1997. (Adventures of Sherlock Holmes Ser.: Vol. II). audio 16.99 o.s.i (*0-553-47778-1*, RH Audio) Random Hse. Audio Publishing Group.

—The Adventures of Sherlock Holmes. 1987. (Illus.). 320p. 12.95 o.p. (*0-89577-277-9*) Reader's Digest Assn., Inc., The.

—The Adventures of Sherlock Holmes. unabr. ed. 1986. (Sherlock Holmes Mystery Ser.). audio 60.00 (*1-55690-004-X*, 86950E7) Recorded Bks., LLC.

—The Adventures of Sherlock Holmes. 1995. (Ebook Classic Ser.). E-Book 5.00 (*0-7410-1456-4*) SoftBook Pr.

—The Adventures of Sherlock Holmes. 2002. E-Book 2.95 (*0-9712910-6-3*) Twenty Penny Pr., Inc.

—The Adventures of Sherlock Holmes. 1997. (Classics Library). 464p. pap. 3.95 (*1-85326-033-9*, 0339WW) Wordsworth Editions, Ltd. GBR. *Dist:* Combined Publishing.

—The Adventures of Sherlock Holmes. 2001. 260p. per. 12.95 (*0-595-01468-2*) iUniverse, Inc.

—The Adventures of Sherlock Holmes V. 2003. audio compact disk 19.98 (*962-634-266-8*) Naxos of America, Inc.

—The Adventures of Sherlock Holmes VI. unabr. ed. 2003. audio 17.98 (*962-634-780-5*); (YA). audio compact disk 19.98 (*962-634-280-3*) Naxos of America, Inc. (Naxos AudioBooks).

Doyle, Arthur Conan & Barry, William. Sherlock Holmes, a Graphic Novel: 100 Year Anniversary Edition. Harryman, Joan, ed. anniv. ed. 1987. (Illus.). 80p. (Orig.). pap. 8.95 (*0-944099-00-9*) Bill Barry's Compass Bks.

Doyle, Arthur Conan & Earlson, Ian M. Beeton's Christmas Annual—1987: Sherlock Holmes. 1987. (Illus.). 80p. pap. 9.95 (*0-9619318-1-7*); 19.95 o.p. (*0-9619318-0-9*) Pencil Productions, Ltd.

Doyle, Arthur Conan & Green, Richard Lancelyn, eds. The Adventures of Sherlock Holmes. 1998. (Oxford World's Classics Ser.). 448p. reprint ed. pap. 9.95 (*0-19-283508-4*) Oxford Univ. Pr., Inc.

Doyle, Arthur Conan & Howe, D. H. The Further Adventures of Sherlock Holmes. 2nd ed. 1993. (Illus.). 94p. pap. text 5.95 (*0-19-585335-0*) Oxford Univ. Pr., Inc.

Doyle, Arthur Conan & Reyburn, Stanley. The Valley of Fear. Landes, William-Alan, ed. 1998. 55p. pap. 10.00 (*0-88734-742-8*) Players Pr., Inc.

Dudley, Ernest. The Return of Sherlock Holmes: Based upon the Play by J. E. Harold Terry & Arthur Rose. 1993. 54p. (Orig.). (J). (gr. 6-12). pap. 10.00 (*0-88734-272-8*) Players Pr., Inc.

Estleman, Loren D. Dr. Jekyll & Mr. Holmes. 2001. 224p. pap. 12.00 (*0-7434-2392-5*) ibooks, Inc.

—Dr. Jekyll & Mr. Holmes. E-Book 6.99 (*1-59019-599-X*) ipicturebooks, LLC.

—Sherlock Holmes vs. Dracula or, The Adventure of the Sanguinary Count. 2000. 224p. pap. 14.00 (*0-7434-0714-8*) ibooks, Inc.

Estleman, Loren D. & Watson, John H. Dr. Jekyll & Mr. Holmes. 1979. 8.95 o.p. (*0-385-15257-4*) Doubleday Publishing.

—Dr. Jekyll & Mr. Holmes. 1980. 256p. pap. 3.95 o.p. (*0-14-005665-3*, Penguin Bks.) Viking Penguin.

—Sherlock Holmes vs. Dracula or, The Adventure of the Sanguinary Count. 1978. 7.95 o.p. (*0-385-14051-7*) Doubleday Publishing.

—Sherlock Holmes vs. Dracula or, The Adventure of the Sanguinary Count. 1979. 224p. pap. 3.95 o.p. (*0-14-005262-3*, Penguin Bks.) Viking Penguin.

Eustace, Grant. Absolute Discretion. 1997. 189p. pap. (*1-899562-31-1*, Calabash Pr.) Ash-Tree Pr.

Farmer, Philip Jose. The Adventure of the Peerless Peer. 1974. 112p. 5.50 o.p. (*0-915230-06-2*) Rue Morgue Pr.

Feuer, Lewis S. The Case of the Revolutionist's Daughter: Sherlock Holmes Meets Karl Marx. 1983. (Illus.). 159p. 15.50 (*0-87975-245-9*) Prometheus Bks., Pubs.

Fruttero, Carl & Lucentini, Franco. The D. Case: The Truth about the Mystery of Edwin Drood. Dowling, Gregory, tr. 1992. 587p. 23.95 (*0-15-113732-3*) Harcourt Trade Pubs.

Gardner, John E. The Return of Moriarty. 1981. 304p. mass mkt. 3.50 o.s.i (*0-425-05093-9*) Berkley Publishing Group.

—The Revenge of Moriarty. 1981. 272p. mass mkt. 3.50 o.s.i (*0-425-05092-0*) Berkley Publishing Group.

Green, Denis & Boucher, Anthony. The New Adventures of Sherlock Holmes Vol. 2: The Viennese Strangler & The Notorious Canary Trainer. abr. ed. 1988. 9.95 incl. audio (*0-671-66433-6*, Simon & Schuster Audioworks) Simon & Schuster Audio.

Greenberg, Martin H., et al, eds. Holmes for the Holidays. 304p. 1996. 21.95 o.s.i (*0-425-15473-4*); 1998. reprint ed. pap. 13.00 o.s.i (*0-425-16754-2*) Berkley Publishing Group. (Prime Crime).

—More Holmes for the Holidays. 1999. 272p. 21.95 o.s.i (*0-425-17033-0*, Prime Crime) Berkley Publishing Group.

—Murder in Baker Street: New Tales of Sherlock Holmes. 2001. 288p. 25.00 (*0-7867-0898-0*, Carroll & Graf Pubs.) Avalon Publishing Group.

—Murder, My Dear Watson: New Tales of Sherlock Holmes. 2003. 240p. pap. 14.00 (*0-7867-1244-9*); 2002. 288p. 24.00 (*0-7867-1081-0*, Carroll & Graf Pubs.) Avalon Publishing Group.

Greenberg, Martin H. & Lellenberg, J., eds. Murder in Baker Street: New Tales of Sherlock Holmes. 2002. 288p. pap. 14.00 (*0-7867-1074-8*, Carroll & Graf Pubs.) Avalon Publishing Group.

Greenberg, Martin H. & Rossel-Waugh, Carol-Lynn, eds. The New Adventures of Sherlock Holmes. 1987. (Illus.). 18.95 o.p. (*0-88184-344-X*, Carroll & Graf Pubs.) Avalon Publishing Group.

Greenberg, Martin H. & Waugh, Carol-Lynn Rossel, eds. The New Adventures of Sherlock Holmes. 1999. (Illus.). 344p. pap. 13.95 (*0-7867-0698-8*, Carroll & Graf Pubs.) Avalon Publishing Group.

Greenwood, L. B. Sherlock Holmes & the Case of Sabina Hall. 2001. 192p. pap. 14.95 (*0-7432-3528-2*, Simon & Schuster); 1989. mass mkt. 3.95 (*0-671-65915-4*, Pocket); 1988. 16.95 o.p. (*0-671-65914-6*, Simon & Schuster) Simon & Schuster.

—Sherlock Holmes & the Case of the Raleigh Legacy. l.t. ed. 1988. (Nightingale Ser.). 241p. 12.95 o.p. (*0-8161-4381-1*, Macmillan Reference USA) Gale Group.

—Sherlock Holmes & the Case of the Raleigh Legacy. 192p. 2001. pap. 14.95 (*0-7432-3530-4*, Scribner Paper Fiction); 1986. bds. 13.95 o.s.i (*0-689-11832-5*, Scribner) Simon & Schuster.

—Sherlock Holmes & the Case of the Raleigh Legacy. 1987. mass mkt. 2.95 (*0-312-90843-1*, St. Martin's Paperbacks) St. Martin's Pr.

—Sherlock Holmes & the Thistle of Scotland. 2000. 205p. pap. 14.95 (*0-7432-0552-9*); 1989. 17.95 o.p. (*0-671-65916-2*) Simon & Schuster. (Simon & Schuster).

—Sherlock Holmes & the Thistle of Scotland. Isaacson, Dana, ed. 1990. 208p. reprint ed. mass mkt. 3.95 (*0-671-70823-6*, Pocket) Simon & Schuster.

—Sherlock Holmes & the Thistle of Scotland Yard. l.t. ed. 1991. 19.95 o.p. (*0-7927-0890-3*, CH0100); pap. 17.95 o.p. (*0-7927-0891-1*, CS0200) BBC Audiobooks America.

Gregson, J. M. Sherlock Holmes & the Frightened Golfer. 1999. (Sherlock Holmes... Ser.). (*0-947533-68-0*) Breese Bks., Ltd.

—Sherlock Holmes & the Frightened Golfer. 2000. (Sherlock Holmes Ser.). 176p. pap. 12.95 (*0-947533-63-X*) Breese Bks., Ltd. GBR. *Dist:* Midpoint Trade Bks., Inc.

Hall, John. Sherlock Holmes & the Abbey School Mystery: A Sherlock Holmes Mystery. 2001. 176p. pap. 12.95 (*0-947533-24-9*) Breese Bks., Ltd. GBR. *Dist:* Midpoint Trade Bks., Inc.

—Sherlock Holmes & the Adler Papers: A Sherlock Holmes Mystery. 2001. 176p. pap. 14.95 (*0-947533-59-1*) Breese Bks., Ltd. GBR. *Dist:* Midpoint Trade Bks., Inc.

—Sherlock Holmes & the Boulevard Assassin. 1998. 174p. pap. 14.95 (*0-947533-52-4*) Breese Bks., Ltd. GBR. *Dist:* Midpoint Trade Bks., Inc.

—Sherlock Holmes & the Disgraced Inspector. 1998. 140p. pap. 14.95 (*0-947533-88-5*) Breese Bks., Ltd. GBR. *Dist:* Midpoint Trade Bks., Inc.

—Sherlock Holmes & the Disgraced Inspector. l.t. ed. 2000. (Linford Mystery Large Print Ser.). 248p. pap. 18.99 (*0-7089-5783-8*, Linford) Thorpe, F. A. Pubs. GBR. *Dist:* Ulverscroft Large Print Bks., Ltd., Ulverscroft Large Print Canada, Ltd.

—Sherlock Holmes & the Hammerford Will: A Sherlock Holmes Mystery. 2000. (Sherlock Holmes Mysteries Ser.). 212p. pap. 14.95 (*0-947533-98-2*) Breese Bks., Ltd. GBR. *Dist:* Midpoint Trade Bks., Inc.

—Sherlock Holmes & the Holborn Emporium: A Sherlock Holmes Mystery. 2001. 128p. pap. 12.95 (*0-947533-39-7*) Breese Bks., Ltd. GBR. *Dist:* Midpoint Trade Bks., Inc.

—Sherlock Holmes & the Telephone Murder Mystery. 1998. 189p. pap. 14.95 (*0-947533-47-8*) Breese Bks., Ltd. GBR. *Dist:* Midpoint Trade Bks., Inc.

Hall, John, ed. The Abominable Wife & Other Unrecorded Cases of Mr. Sherlock Holmes. 1998. 114p. pap. (*1-899562-61-3*, Calabash Pr.) Ash-Tree Pr.

Hammer, David L. The Twenty-Second Man. 1989. (Illus.). 125p. 15.95 (*0-938501-08-9*) Wessex Pr.

Hammer, David L. & MacLaren, Angus. The Quest. 1993. (Illus.). 125p. 15.95 (*0-938501-19-4*) Wessex Pr.

Hammer, David L., et al. My Dear Watson: Being the Annals of Sherlock Holmes. 1995. (Illus.). 104p. (Orig.). pap. 12.95 (*0-938501-22-4*) Wessex Pr.

Hanna, Edward B. The Whitechapel Horrors. 1993. 400p. pap. 10.95 (*0-7867-0019-X*, Carroll & Graf Pubs.) Avalon Publishing Group.

Hardwick, Michael & Hardwick, Mollie. The Private Life of Sherlock Holmes. 1993. 200p. 25.00 (*0-86025-277-9*) Henry, Ian Pubns. GBR. *Dist:* Empire Publishing Service.

Hardwicke, Edward, reader. The Adventures of Sherlock Holmes. abr. ed. 1994. audio 12.00 (*1-878427-38-5*, XC422) Cimino Publishing Group.

Harmidarow, Walter J. The Final Solution. 2001. 158p. pap. 18.99 (*1-55316-544-6*); E-Book 5.00 (*1-55316-035-5*) LTDBooks CAN. *Dist:* Baker & Taylor Bks., Lightning Source, Inc.

Hastie, Edmund. Sherlock Holmes & the Disappearing Prince & Other Stories: A Sherlock Holmes Mystery. 2000. (Sherlock Holmes Mysteries Ser.). 112p. pap. 12.95 (*0-947533-34-6*) Breese Bks., Ltd. GBR. *Dist:* Midpoint Trade Bks., Inc.

Highbridge. Sherlock Holmes Baker Street. abr. ed. 2015. audio 29.95 (*1-56511-625-9*) HighBridge Co.

Holmes, Donald W. Indian River Trilogy: From Sherlock to Shuttle. 2001. 242p. pap. 21.99 (*1-4010-1194-2*) Xlibris Corp.

Jack, Alex. Inspector Ginkgo Tips His Hat to Sherlock Holmes: A Romantic Thriller Featuring the Macrobiotic Detective. 1994. 240p. pap. 12.95 (*1-882984-01-3*) One Peaceful World Pr.

Jack, Colin. The Strange Case of Mrs. Hudson's Cat: And Other Science Mysteries Solved by Sherlock Holmes. 1997. 272p. (C). text 23.00 o.p. (*0-201-46139-0*) Perseus Bks. Group.

Janda, Anita. The Secret Diary of Dr. Watson. 2001. 280p. 27.95 (*0-7490-0570-X*) Allison & Busby, Ltd. GBR. *Dist:* International Publishers Marketing.

Jaynes, Roger. Sherlock Holmes A Duel with the Devil. 2002. 144p. 19.95 (*0-947533-85-0*); 192p. pap. 7.95 (*0-947533-75-3*) Breese Bks., Ltd. GBR. *Dist:* Midpoint Trade Bks., Inc.

Jeffers, H. Paul. The Adventure of the Stalwart Companions. 1978. 7.95 o.p. (*0-06-012248-X*) HarperCollins Pubs.

Kaye, Marvin. The Confidential Casebook of Sherlock Holmes. E-Book 14.95 (*0-312-27984-1*); 1999. E-Book 23.95 o.s.i (*0-312-20713-1*) St. Martin's Pr.

—The Game Is Afoot: Parodies, Pastiches & Ponderings of Sherlock Holmes. 1995. reprint ed. pap. 15.95 (*0-312-11797-3*, NPB 0274, Saint Martin's Griffin) St. Martin's Pr.

—The Resurrected Holmes. 1997. 352p. pap. 14.95 (*0-312-15639-1*, Saint Martin's Griffin) St. Martin's Pr.

Kaye, Marvin, ed. The Confidential Casebook of Sherlock Holmes. 368p. 1999. (Illus.). pap. 14.95 (*0-312-20638-0*, Saint Martin's Griffin); 1997. 23.95 (*0-312-18071-3*, Saint Martin's Minotaur) St. Martin's Pr.

—The Game Is Afoot: Parodies, Pastiches & Ponderings of Sherlock Holmes. 1994. 448p. 24.95 o.p. (*0-312-10468-5*, Saint Martin's Minotaur) St. Martin's Pr.

—The Resurrected Holmes: New Cases from the Notes of John H. Watson, M. D. 1996. 353p. 24.95 o.p. (*0-312-14037-1*, Saint Martin's Minotaur) St. Martin's Pr.

Kelley, Gordon E. Sherlock Holmes: Screen & Sound Guide. 1994. (Illus.). 343p. 42.00 (*0-8108-2859-6*) Scarecrow Pr., Inc.

Kendrick, Stephen. Night Watch. 2003. 272p. pap. 13.00 (*0-425-19167-2*, Prime Crime) Berkley Publishing Group.

—Night Watch: A Long-Lost Adventure in Which Sherlock Holmes Meets Father Brown. 2001. (Illus.). 272p. 23.00 (*0-375-40367-1*, Pantheon) Knopf Publishing Group.

Kent. The Irregular, Pt. III. 1998. (New Adventures of Sherlock Holmes Ser.). 24.00 (*1-55246-106-8*) Battered Silicon Dispatch Box, The.

King, Laurie R. The Beekeeper's Apprentice. reprint ed. 2002. 384p. pap. 11.95 (*0-553-38152-0*); 1996. 448p. mass mkt. 6.99 (*0-553-57165-6*) Bantam Bks.

—The Beekeeper's Apprentice. abr. ed. 1996. 6p. audio 16.99 (*0-88646-388-2*, 7388) Durkin Hayes Publishing Ltd.

—The Beekeeper's Apprentice. l.t. ed. 1996. 574p. 24.95 (*0-7838-1932-3*, Macmillan Reference USA) Gale Group.

—The Beekeeper's Apprentice. unabr. ed. (Mary Russell Mystery Ser.: Vol. 1). 2001. audio compact disk 124.00; 1995. audio 85.00 (*0-7887-0319-6*, 94511E7) Recorded Bks., LLC.

—The Beekeeper's Apprentice. 1994. xvii, 347p. 23.95 (*0-312-10423-5*, Saint Martin's Minotaur) St. Martin's Pr.

—The Game. 2004. 384p. 23.95 (*0-553-80194-5*) Bantam Bks.

—Justice Hall. 2003. 464p. mass mkt. 6.99 (*0-553-58111-2*); 2002. 352p. 23.95 (*0-553-11113-2*) Bantam Bks.

—Justice Hall. l.t. ed. 2002. 625p. 30.95 (*0-7862-3953-0*) Thorndike Pr.

—A Letter of Mary. 1998. (Mary Russell Novels Ser.). 336p. reprint ed. mass mkt. 6.99 (*0-553-57780-8*) Bantam Bks.

—A Letter of Mary. abr. ed. 1997. audio 16.99 (*0-88646-420-X*, 7420) Durkin Hayes Publishing Ltd.

—A Letter of Mary. l.t. ed. 1997. (G. K. Hall Mystery Ser.). 384p. lib. bdg. 26.95 o.p. (*0-7838-8067-7*, Macmillan Reference USA) Gale Group.

—A Letter of Mary. unabr. ed. 1997. (Mary Russell Mystery Ser.: Vol. 3). audio 70.00 (*0-7887-0649-7*, 94826E7) Recorded Bks., LLC.

—A Letter of Mary. 1999. E-Book 23.95 (*0-312-20728-X*); 1996. viii, 276p. 23.95 (*0-312-14670-1*, Saint Martin's Minotaur) St. Martin's Pr.

—A Monstrous Regiment of Women. 1996. (Mary Russell Ser.: No. 2). 368p. mass mkt. 6.99 (*0-553-57456-6*, Crimeline) Bantam Bks.

—A Monstrous Regiment of Women. abr. ed. 1995. audio 16.99 (*0-88646-390-4*, 7390) Durkin Hayes Publishing Ltd.

—A Monstrous Regiment of Women. unabr. ed. 1996. (Mary Russell Mystery Ser.: Vol. 2). audio 78.00 (*0-7887-0493-1*, 94685E7) Recorded Bks., LLC.

—A Monstrous Regiment of Women. 1995. viii, 326p. 22.95 (*0-312-13565-3*, Saint Martin's Minotaur) St. Martin's Pr.

—The Moor. 1999. (Mary Russell Novels Ser.). 400p. (gr. 5 up). mass mkt. 6.99 (*0-553-57952-5*) Bantam Bks.

—The Moor. l.t. ed. 1998. (G. K. Hall Mystery Ser.). 419p. 27.95 (*0-7838-0162-9*, Macmillan Reference USA) Gale Group.

—The Moor. unabr. ed. 1998. (Mary Russell Mystery Ser.: Vol. 4). audio 75.00 (*0-7887-1979-3*, 95366E7 ) Recorded Bks., LLC.

—The Moor. 1999. E-Book 23.95 (*0-312-20731-X*); 1997. (Illus.). 307p. 23.95 o.p. (*0-312-16934-5*, Saint Martin's Minotaur) St. Martin's Pr.

—O Jerusalem. 2000. (Mary Russell Novels Ser.). 464p. mass mkt. 6.99 (*0-553-58105-8*) Bantam Bks.

—O Jerusalem. 1999. (Mary Russell Novels Ser.). (Illus.). 384p. 23.95 o.s.i (*0-553-11093-4*) Broadway Bks.

—O Jerusalem. unabr. ed. 1999. (Mary Russell Mystery Ser.: Vol. 5). audio 83.00 (*0-7887-3746-5*, 95781E7) Recorded Bks., LLC.

King, Stephen, et al. The New Adventures of Sherlock Holmes. Greenberg, Martin H. & Rossel Waugh, Carol-Lynn, eds. 1988. (Illus.). 344p. pap. 11.95 o.p. (*0-88184-435-7*, Carroll & Graf Pubs.) Avalon Publishing Group.

Kurland, Michael, ed. My Sherlock Holmes: Untold Stories of the Great Detective. 2004. 384p. pap. 14.95 (*0-312-32595-9*); 2003. 368p. 24.95 (*0-312-28093-9*) St. Martin's Pr.

Leppek, Chris. Surrogate Assassin. 1998. (Sherlock Holmes Mysteries Ser.). 418p. 24.95 (*1-885173-54-7*) Write Way Publishing.

Maguire, Eddie. Sherlock Holmes & the Tandridge Hall Murder & Other Stories: A Sherlock Holmes Mystery. 2000. (Sherlock Holmes Mysteries Ser.). 176p. pap. 14.95 (*0-947533-19-2*) Breese Bks., Ltd. GBR. *Dist:* Midpoint Trade Bks., Inc.

Meiser, Edith. The Adventures of Sherlock Holmes. abr. collector's ed. 1998. (Smithsonian Historical Performances Ser.). 60p. pap. 24.98 incl. audio (*1-57019-034-8*, 5016); (Illus.). pap. 39.98 incl. audio compact disk (*1-57019-035-6*, 5017) Radio Spirits, Inc.

Meyer, Nicholas. Canary Trainer: From the Memoirs of John H. Watson. 1995. 224p. pap. 10.95 (*0-393-31241-0*) Norton, W. W. & Co., Inc.

—The Seven-Percent Solution. l.t. ed. 1977. (Ulverscroft Large Print Ser.). 29.99 o.p. (*0-7089-0052-6*, Ulverscroft) Thorpe, F. A. Pubs. GBR. *Dist:* Ulverscroft Large Print Bks., Ltd., Ulverscroft Large Print Canada, Ltd.

Meyer, Nicholas, ed. The Seven-Percent Solution: Being a Reprint from the Reminiscences of John H. Watson, M. D. 1993. 256p. pap. 13.00 (*0-393-31119-8*) Norton, W. W. & Co., Inc.

Millett, Larry. The Disappearance of Sherlock Holmes: A Mystery Featuring Shadwell Rafferty. 2002. 352p. 23.95 o.s.i (*0-670-03140-2*, Viking) Viking Penguin.

—Sherlock Holmes & the Ice Palace Murders: From the American Chronicles of John H. Watson, M.D. 1998. 336p. 23.95 o.p. (*0-670-87944-4*) Viking Penguin.

—Sherlock Holmes & the Rune Stone Mystery: From the American Chronicles of John H. Watson, M.D. 2000. (Sherlock Holmes Mysteries Ser.). 368p. pap. 5.99 (*0-14-029645-X*) Penguin Group (USA) Inc.

—Sherlock Holmes & the Rune Stone Mystery: From the American Chronicles of John H. Watson, M.D. 1999. (Sherlock Holmes Ser.). (Illus.). 317p. (J). 23.95 o.s.i (*0-670-88821-4*, Viking) Viking Penguin.

—Sherlock Holmes & the Secret Alliance. 2002. 336p. mass mkt. 6.99 (*0-14-200155-4*) Penguin Group (USA) Inc.

—Sherlock Holmes & the Secret Alliance. 2001. 336p. 24.95 o.s.i (*0-670-03015-5*, Viking) Viking Penguin.

Mitchelson, Austin. The Baker Street Irregular: The Unauthorized Biography of Sherlock Holmes. 1994. 35.00 (*0-88734-905-6*) Players Pr., Inc.

Mitchelson, Austin & Utechin, Nicholas. Sherlock Holmes & the Earthquake Machine. 1994. 25.00 (*0-86025-283-3*) Henry, Ian Pubns. GBR. *Dist:* Empire Publishing Service.

—Sherlock Holmes & the Earthquake Machine. 1994. 25.00 (*0-88734-903-X*) Players Pr., Inc.

—Sherlock Holmes & the Hellbirds. 1995. 35.00 (*0-86025-284-1*) Players Pr., Inc.

Naslund, Sena Jeter. Sherlock in Love: A Novel. 2001. 240p. pap. 13.00 (*0-688-17844-8*, Perennial) HarperTrade.

Norbu, Jamyang. Sherlock Holmes - The Missing Years: The Adventures of the Great Detective in India & Tibet. 2001. 288p. 23.95 (*1-58234-132-X*) Bloomsbury Publishing.

Paul, Jeremy. The Naval Treaty: The Adventures of Sherlock Holmes. 1991. (Illus.). 48p. (Orig.). pap. 11.00 (*0-86025-435-6*) Henry, Ian Pubns. GBR. *Dist:* Empire Publishing Service.

Paxton, Bill. The Hidden Adventures of Sherlock Holmes. 2001. (Illus.). 239p. 25.00 (*0-9702298-1-X*) Omnibus Enterprises, Ltd.

Pearlman, Gilbert. The Adventures of Sherlock Holmes' Smarter Brother. Wilder, Gene, ed. 1975. pap. 1.75 o.p. (*0-345-25282-9*) Ballantine Bks.

Queen, Ellery. A Study in Terror. l.t. ed. 2001. 192p. pap. 24.95 (*0-7838-9485-6*); (*0-7540-4586-2*); (*0-7540-4585-4*) Gale Group. (Macmillan Reference USA).

Rathbone, Basil & Bruce, Nigel. The New Adventures of Sherlock Holmes. 1998. Vol. 1 24.98 incl. audio; Vol. 2 24.98 incl. audio; Vol. 3 24.98 incl. audio; Vol. 4. 24.98 incl. audio; Vol. 5. 24.98 incl. audio; Vol. 6. 24.98 incl. audio Radio Spirits, Inc.

Riccardi, Theodore. The Oriental Casebook of Sherlock Holmes. 2003. 320p. 23.95 (*1-4000-6065-6*) Random House Adult Trade Publishing Group.

Roberts, Barrie. Sherlock Holmes & the Crosby Murder. 2002. 224p. 24.00 (*0-7867-1016-0*, Carroll & Graf Pubs.) Avalon Publishing Group.

—Sherlock Holmes & the Devil's Grail. 2000. 190p. pap. 9.95 (*0-7490-0470-3*, London Hse.) Allison & Busby, Ltd. GBR. *Dist:* International Publishers Marketing.

—Sherlock Holmes & the Railway Maniac. 2001. 192p. pap. 10.95 (*0-7490-0546-7*) Allison & Busby, Ltd. GBR. *Dist:* International Publishers Marketing.

Roberts, Lora. The Affair of the Incognito Tenant: A Mystery with Sherlock Holmes. 2003. 264p. pap. 13.95 (*1-880284-67-7*) Daniel, John & Co., Pubs.

Sand, George. The Mammoth Book of New Sherlock Holmes Adventures. Ashley, Mike, ed. 1997. (Mammoth Bks.). 512p. pap. 11.95 (*0-7867-0477-2*, Carroll & Graf Pubs.) Avalon Publishing Group.

Scarlet Pimpernal. 1988. mass mkt. 4.95 (*1-55902-008-3*, Aerie) Doherty, Tom Assocs., LLC.

Scarlet Pimpernel. 1988. mass mkt. 2.25 (*1-55902-010-5*, Aerie) Doherty, Tom Assocs., LLC.

Scott, David. Holmes Redux Vol. 1: New Adventures of Sherlock Holmes. 1997. 120p. pap. 9.95 (*1-880222-28-0*) Red Apple Publishing.

Seil, William. Sherlock Holmes & the Titanic Tragedy. 1996. 253p. pap. 14.95 (*0-947533-35-4*) Breese Bks., Ltd. GBR. *Dist:* Midpoint Trade Bks., Inc.

Senuta, Michael. Second Thoughts about Sherlock Holmes. 2002. (Illus.). 32p. (YA). (gr. 4-12). pap. 8.00 (*0-934468-55-9*) Gaslight Pubns.

Shepherd, Walter. On the Scent with Sherlock Holmes. Date not set. (Illus.). 85p. 15.95 (*0-934468-18-4*) Gaslight Pubns.

Showler, Peter. Sherlock Holmes & the Watson Pastiche. 2001. (Sherlockian Scholarship Ser.). pap. 12.00 (*1-55246-180-7*) Battered Silicon Dispatch Box, The.

Siciliano, Sam. The Angel of the Opera: Sherlock Holmes Meets the Phantom of the Opera. 1994. 272p. 21.95 (*1-883402-46-8*, Scribner) Simon & Schuster.

Soares, Jo. A Samba for Sherlock. Landers, Clifford E., tr. from POR. 1997. 288p. 3.99 o.s.i (*0-375-40065-6*, Pantheon) Knopf Publishing Group.

—A Samba for Sherlock: A Novel. 1998. 288p. pap. 19.00 (*0-375-70066-8*, Vintage) Knopf Publishing Group.

Templeman, Roy. Sherlock Holmes & the Chinese Junk Affair & Other Stories. 1999. (Sherlock Holmes... Ser.). pap. o.s.i (*0-947533-73-7*) Breese Bks., Ltd.

Thomas, Donald. The Secret Cases of Sherlock Holmes. 352p. 1999. pap. 12.95 (*0-7867-0636-8*); 1998. 24.00 o.p. (*0-7867-0516-7*) Avalon Publishing Group. (Carroll & Graf Pubs.).

—Sherlock Holmes & the Voice from the Crypt: And Other Tales. 2002. 352p. 25.00 (*0-7867-0973-1*, Carroll & Graf Pubs.) Avalon Publishing Group.

—Sherlock Holmes & Voices from the Crypt. 2004. pap. 14.00 (*0-7867-1325-9*, Carroll & Graf Pubs.) Avalon Publishing Group.

Thomson, June. Holmes & Watson: A Study in Friendship. 2001. 288p. 24.00 (*0-7867-0827-1*, Carroll & Graf Pubs.) Avalon Publishing Group.

—The Secret Files of Sherlock Holmes. l.t. ed. 1994. 21.95 o.p. (*0-7927-2042-3*); pap. 20.95 o.p. (*0-7927-2041-5*) BBC Audiobooks America.

—The Secret Journals of Sherlock Holmes. 1995. 20.00 (*1-883402-38-7*, Scribner) Simon & Schuster.

Tolins. Sherlockian Twaddle. 1999. (Sherlockian Scholarship Ser.). 22.00 (*1-55246-186-6*) Battered Silicon Dispatch Box, The.

Vanneman, Alan. Sherlock Holmes & the Hapsburg Tiara. 2004. 320p. 25.00 (*0-7867-1297-X*, Carroll & Graf Pubs.) Avalon Publishing Group.

Vaughan, Ralph E. Sherlock Holmes: In the Dreaming Detective. 1997. reprint ed. pap. 9.95 (*0-936071-65-6*) Gryphon Bks.

Walker, Jan. The Singular Case of the Duplicate Holmes. 1994. text 30.00 (*0-86025-278-7*) Henry, Ian Pubns. GBR. *Dist:* Empire Publishing Service.

Watson, John H. Sherlock Holmes & the Red Demon. Millett, Larry, ed. 1997. 336p. pap. 9.95 o.s.i (*0-14-025882-5*); 366p. pap. 9.95 Penguin Group (USA) Inc.

—Sherlock Holmes & the Red Demon. Millett, Larry, ed. & intro. by. 1996. (Illus.). 336p. 22.95 (*0-670-87039-0*, Viking) Viking Penguin.

Watson, John H. & Meyer, Nicholas. The Seven-Percent Solution. 1985. mass mkt. 3.95 o.s.i (*0-345-33156-7*) Ballantine Bks.

Weighell, Ron. The Irregular Casebook of Sherlock Holmes. 2000. 152p. (*1-55310-001-8*); pap. (*1-55310-003-4*) Ash-Tree Pr. (Calabash Pr.).

Welles, Orson, et al. The Adventures of Sherlock Holmes: The Napoleon of Crime. audio 7.95 National Recording Co.

Weyman, Ronald C. Sherlock Holmes: Travels in the Canadian West. Paton, Jean, ed. 1994. (Illus.). 218p. pap. 17.00 o.p. (*0-88924-245-3*) Simon & Pierre Publishing Co., Ltd. CAN. *Dist:* Empire Publishing Service.

Worcester, Wayne. The Jewel of Covent Garden. 2000. 336p. mass mkt. 5.99 o.s.i (*0-451-20195-7*) NAL.

## HOLOGRAPHIC DOCTOR (FICTITIOUS CHARACTER)—FICTION

Friedman, Michael Jan. The Television Episode: Day of Honor. 1997. (Star Trek Voyager). 224p. mass mkt. 5.99 (*0-671-01981-3*, Star Trek) Simon & Schuster.

Galanter, Dave & Brodeur, Greg. Battle Lines. 1999. (Star Trek Voyager Ser.: No. 18). 264p. mass mkt. 6.50 o.s.i (*0-671-00259-7*, Star Trek) Simon & Schuster.

Golden, Christie. Seven of Nine. 1998. (Star Trek Voyager Ser.: No. 16). 233p. mass mkt. 6.50 (*0-671-02491-4*, Star Trek) Simon & Schuster.

Hugh, Dafydd ab. The Final Fury No. 4: Invasion! 1996. (Star Trek Voyager Ser.: No. 9). 320p. (J). mass mkt. 6.50 (*0-671-54181-1*, Star Trek) Simon & Schuster.

—Invasion! No. 4: The Final Fury. 1999. (Star Trek Voyager Ser.: No. 9). E-Book 6.99 (*0-671-04098-7*, Star Trek) Simon & Schuster.

Kotani, Eric & Smith, Dean Wesley. Death of a Neutron Star. 1999. (Star Trek Voyager Ser.: No. 17). 263p. mass mkt. 6.50 o.s.i (*0-671-00425-5*, Star Trek) Simon & Schuster.

## HOLSTROM, CLARK (FICTITIOUS CHARACTER)—FICTION

McColley, Kevin. Praying to a Laughing God: A Novel. 1998. 352p. 24.00 (*0-684-83761-7*, Simon & Schuster) Simon & Schuster.

## HOLT, LUCAS, REVEREND (FICTITIOUS CHARACTER)—FICTION

Meyer, Charles. Beside the Still Waters. 1997. (Reverend Lucas Holt Mystery Ser.). 232p. pap. 6.50 (*0-9631149-4-8*) Stone Angel Bks.

—Blessed Are the Merciless. 1996. 272p. mass mkt. 5.50 o.s.i (*0-425-15140-9*) Berkley Publishing Group.

—Blessed Are the Merciless. 2nd ed. 1997. (Reverend Lucas Holt Mystery Ser.). 266p. reprint ed. pap. 6.50 (*0-9631149-5-6*) Stone Angel Bks.

—The Saints of God Murders. 1995. 256p. (Orig.). mass mkt. 5.99 o.s.i (*0-425-14869-6*, Prime Crime) Berkley Publishing Group.

## HOLT, MITCH (FICTITIOUS CHARACTER)—FICTION

Hoag, Tami. Guilty As Sin. 1997. 624p. mass mkt. 7.99 (*0-553-56452-8*) Bantam Bks.

—Guilty As Sin. l.t. ed. 1996. 825p. 25.95 o.p. (*0-7838-1821-1*, Macmillan Reference USA) Gale Group.

—Guilty As Sin. abr. ed. 1996. 6p. audio 23.00 (*1-56876-057-4*) Soundlines Entertainment, Inc.

—Night Sins. 1995. 576p. mass mkt. 7.99 (*0-553-56451-X*, Fanfare) Bantam Bks.

—Night Sins. l.t. ed. 1995. 821p. 25.95 o.p. (*0-7838-1348-1*, Macmillan Reference USA) Gale Group.

—Night Sins, abr. ed. 1996. audio 17.00 (*1-56876-058-2*, 394501) Soundlines Entertainment, Inc.

## HOLT, SAMANTHA (FICTITIOUS CHARACTER)—FICTION

Wilson, Karen A. Beware of Sleeping Dogs. 1996. 304p. mass mkt. 5.99 o.p. (*0-425-15337-1*, Prime Crime) Berkley Publishing Group.

## HOLT, WHIP (FICTITIOUS CHARACTER)—FICTION

Ross, Dana Fuller, pseud. California! 1984. mass mkt. 3.99 o.s.i (*0-553-80006-X*); 384p. mass mkt. 4.99 o.s.i (*0-553-26377-3*); mass mkt. 3.95 o.s.i (*0-553-24655-0*) Bantam Bks.

—California! l.t. ed. 1982. (Reader's Request Ser.). lib. bdg. 17.95 o.p. (*0-8161-3319-0*, Macmillan Reference USA) Gale Group.

—Nebraska! 1984. mass mkt. 3.99 o.s.i (*0-553-80002-7*); 400p. mass mkt. 4.95 o.s.i (*0-553-26162-2*) Bantam Bks.

—Nebraska! (Reader's Request Ser.). 1982. lib. bdg. 18.95 o.p. (*0-8161-3315-8*); 1993. 64.95 o.p. incl. audio (*0-7838-1105-5*) Gale Group. (Macmillan Reference USA).

—Oregon! 1983. mass mkt. 3.99 o.s.i (*0-553-80004-3*); 384p. mass mkt. 4.99 o.s.i (*0-553-26072-3*) Bantam Bks.

—Oregon! l.t. ed. 1982. (Reader's Request Ser.). lib. bdg. 16.95 o.p. (*0-8161-3317-4*, Macmillan Reference USA) Gale Group.

—Texas! 1984. mass mkt. 3.99 o.s.i (*0-553-80005-1*); 368p. mass mkt. 4.99 o.s.i (*0-553-26070-7*) Bantam Bks.

—Texas! 1982. (Reader's Request Ser.). lib. bdg. 16.95 o.p. (*0-8161-3318-2*, Macmillan Reference USA) Gale Group.

—Wyoming! 1983. mass mkt. 3.99 o.s.i (*0-553-80003-5*); 384p. mass mkt. 4.95 o.s.i (*0-553-26242-4*) Bantam Bks.

—Wyoming! (Reader's Request Ser.). 1982. lib. bdg. 16.95 o.p. (*0-8161-3316-6*); 1993. 50.95 o.p. (*0-7838-1107-1*) Gale Group. (Macmillan Reference USA).

## HOLT FAMILY (FICTITIOUS CHARACTERS)—FICTION

Ross, Dana Fuller, pseud. Carolina Courage! 1990. (Holts: An American Dynasty Ser.: No. 3). 368p. mass mkt. 5.99 o.s.i (*0-553-28756-7*) Bantam Bks.

—Carolina Courage! l.t. ed. 1991. (Holts, an American Dynasty Ser.: Vol. 3). 400p. 21.95 (*0-8161-5309-4*, Macmillan Reference USA) Gale Group.

—Homecoming! 1994. (Holts: An American Dynasty Ser.: Bk. 9). 384p. mass mkt. 5.99 o.s.i (*0-553-56150-2*) Bantam Bks.

—Homecoming! l.t. ed. 1995. (G. K. Hall Core Ser.). 455p. 23.95 (*0-7838-1173-X*, Macmillan Reference USA) Gale Group.

—Honor! 1998. (Wagons West: The Empire Trilogy : Bk. 1). (Illus.). 400p. mass mkt. 5.99 o.s.i (*0-553-57764-6*) Bantam Bks.

—Honor! l.t. ed. 2001. (Thorndike Western Ser.). (Illus.). 576p. (J). 26.95 (*0-7862-3116-5*) Thorndike Pr.

—Justice!, No. 3. 1999. (Wagons West: The Empire Trilogy : Bk. 3). 400p. mass mkt. 6.50 (*0-553-57766-2*) Bantam Bks.

—Justice! l.t. ed. 2001. (Wagons West: The Empire Trilogy : Bk. 3). (Illus.). 387p. 26.95 (*0-7862-3117-3*) Thorndike Pr.

—Pacific Destiny. 1994. 368p. mass mkt. 5.99 o.s.i (*0-553-56149-9*) Bantam Bks.

—Pacific Destiny. l.t. ed. 1994. 507p. lib. bdg. 23.95 (*0-8161-7466-0*, Macmillan Reference USA) Gale Group.

—Vengeance! l.t. ed. 2001. (Wagons West: The Empire Trilogy : Bk. 2). (Illus.). 560p. 26.95 (*0-7862-3118-1*) Thorndike Pr.

—Yukon Justice. 1992. (Holts: An American Dynasty Ser.: No. 7). 368p. mass mkt. 5.99 o.s.i (*0-553-29763-5*) Bantam Bks.

—Yukon Justice. l.t. ed. 1992. (General Ser.). 18.95 o.p. (*0-8161-5488-0*); lib. bdg. 21.95 o.p. (*0-8161-5487-2*) Gale Group. (Macmillan Reference USA).

## HOLYHANDS, DION (FICTITIOUS CHARACTER)—FICTION

Routley, Jane. Aramaya. 2000. 352p. mass mkt. 6.99 (*0-380-79460-8*); 1999. 288p. pap. 13.50 (*0-380-79428-4*) Morrow/Avon. (Eos).

—Fire Angels. 1999. 512p. mass mkt. 6.99 (*0-380-79427-6*, Avon Bks.); 1998. 448p. pap. 13.00 o.p. (*0-380-79425-X*, Eos) Morrow/Avon.

—Mage Heart. 2000. reprint ed. pap. 6.99 o.s.i (*0-380-78127-1*, Avon Bks.) Morrow/Avon.

## HOOLIHAN, MIKE (FICTITIOUS CHARACTER)—FICTION

Amis, Martin. Night Train. 1997. 149p. (*0-224-05018-4*) Cape, Jonathan Ltd. GBR. *Dist:* National Geographic Society, Trafalgar Square.

—Night Train. l.t. ed. 1998. 26.95 o.p. (*1-56895-570-7*, Wheeler Publishing, Inc.) Gale Group.

—Night Train. 1999. 176p. pap. 12.00 (*0-375-70114-1*, Vintage) Knopf Publishing Group.

—Night Train, abr. ed. 1998. audio 25.00 (*0-7871-1724-2*, 395703, Dove Audio) NewStar Media, Inc.

## HOPE, ALISON (FICTITIOUS CHARACTER)—FICTION

Kelly, Susan B. Hope Against Hope. 1991. 256p. 19.95 o.s.i (*0-684-19387-6*, Macmillan Reference USA) Gale Group.

—Hope Against Hope. 1993. per. (*0-373-26118-7*, 1-26118-9, Harlequin Bks.) Harlequin Enterprises, Ltd.

—Hope Against Hope. l.t. ed. 1991. (Magna Large Print Ser.). 345p. o.p. (*0-7505-0163-4*) Magna Large Print Bks. GBR. *Dist:* Ulverscroft Large Print Canada, Ltd.

—Hope Will Answer: An Inspector Nick Trevellyan - Alison Hope Mystery. 1993. 256p. 20.00 o.p. (*0-684-19523-2*, Macmillan Reference USA) Gale Group.

—Hope Will Answer: An Inspector Nick Trevellyan - Alison Hope Mystery. l.t. ed. 1994. (Magna Large Print Ser.). 428p. 29.99 o.p. (0-7505-0594-X) Magna Large Print Bks. GBR. Dist: Ulverscroft Large Print Bks., Ltd., Ulverscroft Large Print Canada, Ltd.
—Kids' Stuff. 1994. 256p. 20.00 (0-684-19649-2, Macmillan Reference USA) Gale Group.
—Time of Hope. 1994. (WWL Mystery Ser.). mass mkt. (0-373-26141-1, 1-26141-1, Harlequin Bks.) Harlequin Enterprises, Ltd.
—Time of Hope. 1992. 224p. 20.00 o.s.i (0-684-19423-6, Scribner) Simon & Schuster.
—A Time of Hope. l.t. ed. 1993. (Magna Large Print Ser.). 346p. 29.99 o.p. (0-7505-0487-0) Magna Large Print Bks. GBR. Dist: Ulverscroft Large Print Bks., Ltd., Ulverscroft Large Print Canada, Ltd.

HOPE, FRED (FICTITIOUS CHARACTER)—FICTION

Llewellyn, Sam. Maelstrom. 1996. 384p. mass mkt. 5.99 (0-671-78997-X, Pocket) Simon & Schuster.
—Maelstrom. Chelius, Jane, ed. 1994. 416p. 20.00 o.p. (0-671-78995-3, Atria) Simon & Schuster.

HOPE, MATTHEW (FICTITIOUS CHARACTER)—FICTION

McBain, Ed, pseud. Beauty & the Beast. unabr. ed. 1985. (Matthew Hope Ser.). audio 42.00 (0-7366-1034-0, 1964) Books on Tape, Inc.
—Beauty & the Beast. 1983. 228p. o.p. (0-03-062198-4) Holt, Henry & Co.
—Beauty & the Beast. 1988. 256p. mass mkt. 3.99 o.s.i (1-55817-662-4); mass mkt. 3.95 o.p. (1-55817-134-7) Kensington Publishing Corp. (Pinnacle Bks.).
—Beauty & the Beast. 1994. 224p. mass mkt. 5.99 o.s.i (0-446-60131-4) Warner Bks., Inc.
—Cinderella. unabr. ed. 1992. (Matthew Hope Ser.). audio 48.00 (0-7366-2245-4, 3035) Books on Tape, Inc.
—Cinderella. 1986. (Matthew Hope Ser.). 256p. (J). o.p. (0-03-004959-8) Holt, Henry & Co.
—Cinderella. 1993. 15.95 o.p. (1-55800-396-7); audio 8.95 o.p. (1-55800-494-7, Dove Audio) NewStar Media, Inc.
—Cinderella. 272p. 1994. mass mkt. 5.99 o.s.i (0-446-60134-9); 1989. mass mkt. 4.99 (0-445-40898-7, Mysterious Pr. Paperback Bks.); 1987. mass mkt. 3.95 o.s.i (0-445-40618-6) Warner Bks., Inc.
—Gladly the Cross-Eyed Bear. unabr. ed. 1997. (Matthew Hope Ser.). audio 48.00 (0-913369-38-1, 4214) Books on Tape, Inc.
—Gladly the Cross-Eyed Bear, Set. abr. ed. 1996. (Matthew Hope Mystery Ser.). 3p. audio 16.99 (0-88646-423-4, 394439) Durkin Hayes Publishing Ltd.
—Gladly the Cross-Eyed Bear. l.t. ed. 1996. (G. K. Hall Core Ser.). 424p. 25.95 (0-7838-1899-8, Macmillan Reference USA) Gale Group.
—Gladly the Cross-Eyed Bear. l.t. ed. 1998. (Paperback Bestsellers Ser.). 424p. pap. 25.95 (0-7838-1900-5) Thorndike Pr.
—Gladly the Cross-Eyed Bear. (Matthew Hope Novels Ser.). 336p. 1998. mass mkt. 6.50 o.s.i (0-446-60494-1); 1996. 22.50 o.p. (0-446-51989-8) Warner Bks., Inc.
—Goldilocks. 1979. pap. 2.25 o.p. (0-553-12158-8, 13158-3) Bantam Bks.
—Goldilocks. unabr. ed. 1985. (Matthew Hope Ser.). audio 36.00 (0-7366-1032-4, 1962) Books on Tape, Inc.
—Goldilocks. 224p. 1988. mass mkt. 3.95 o.s.i (1-55817-108-8); 1985. pap. 3.50 o.p. (0-523-42452-3) Kensington Publishing Corp. (Pinnacle Bks.).
—Goldilocks. 1978. 8.95 o.p. (0-87795-177-2, Morrow, William & Co.) Morrow/Avon.
—Goldilocks. 1996. 224p. mass mkt. 5.99 o.s.i (0-446-60305-8) Warner Bks., Inc.
—The House That Jack Built. unabr. ed. 1992. (Matthew Hope Ser.). audio 48.00 (0-7366-2177-6, 2974) Books on Tape, Inc.
—The House That Jack Built. l.t. ed. 1989. (General Ser.). 320p. 13.95 o.p. (0-8161-4934-8); lib. bdg. 20.95 (0-8161-4758-2) Gale Group. (Macmillan Reference USA).
—The House That Jack Built. 1988. 16.95 o.p. (0-8050-0787-3) Holt, Henry & Co.
—The House That Jack Built. 256p. 1994. mass mkt. 5.99 o.s.i (0-446-60136-5); 1989. mass mkt. 4.99 (0-445-40623-2, Mysterious Pr. Paperback Bks.) Warner Bks., Inc.
—Jack & the Beanstalk. unabr. ed. 1985. (Matthew Hope Ser.). audio 48.00 Books on Tape, Inc.
—Jack & the Beanstalk. 1984. o.p. (0-03-062197-6) Holt, Henry & Co.
—Jack & the Beanstalk. 288p. 1992. mass mkt. 3.99 o.s.i (1-55817-663-2); 1985. pap. 3.50 o.p. (0-523-42559-7) Kensington Publishing Corp. (Pinnacle Bks.).
—Jack & the Beanstalk. 1994. 256p. mass mkt. 5.99 (0-446-60132-2) Warner Bks., Inc.
—The Last Best Hope. unabr. ed. 1998. (Matthew Hope Ser.). audio 40.00 (0-7366-4215-3, 4713) Books on Tape, Inc.
—The Last Best Hope. l.t. ed. 1998. (Basic Ser.). 397p. pap. 29.95 (0-7862-1605-0) Thorndike Pr.
—The Last Best Hope. (Matthew Hope Novels Ser.). 1999. 304p. mass mkt. 7.50 o.s.i (0-446-60673-1); 1998. 320p. 24.00 o.p. (0-446-51990-1) Warner Bks., Inc.
—Mary, Mary. l.t. ed. 1993. 24.95 o.p. (0-7927-1662-0); pap. 22.95 o.p. (0-7927-1661-2) BBC Audiobooks America.
—Mary, Mary. unabr. ed. 1993. (Matthew Hope Ser.). audio 72.00 (0-7366-2480-5, 3242) Books on Tape, Inc.
—Mary, Mary. unabr. ed. 1993. 73.25 o.p. incl. audio (1-56100-137-6, 1280, Unabridged Library Editions); audio 23.95 o.p. (1-56100-508-8, 173, Bookcassette) Brilliance Audio.
—Mary, Mary. 384p. 1994. mass mkt. 5.99 o.s.i (0-446-60054-7); 1993. 19.95 o.s.i (0-446-51738-0) Warner Bks., Inc.
—Puss in Boots. unabr. ed. 1992. (Matthew Hope Ser.). audio 48.00 (0-7366-2193-8, 2988) Books on Tape, Inc.
—Puss in Boots. 1987. 15.95 o.p. (0-8050-0371-1) Holt, Henry & Co.
—Puss in Boots. 1993. audio 15.95 o.p. (1-55800-259-6) NewStar Media, Inc.
—Puss in Boots. 1994. 224p. mass mkt. 5.99 o.s.i (0-446-60135-7); 1988. mass mkt. 4.95 o.s.i (0-445-40621-6) Warner Bks., Inc.
—Rumpelstiltskin. 1985. 240p. mass mkt. 4.95 o.s.i (0-345-33149-4); 1982. mass mkt. 2.50 o.p. (0-345-30436-5) Ballantine Bks.
—Rumpelstiltskin. 1981. (Matthew Hope Mystery Ser.). 12.95 o.p. (0-670-61059-3) Viking Penguin.
—Rumpelstiltskin. 1994. 240p. mass mkt. 5.99 o.s.i (0-446-60130-6) Warner Bks., Inc.
—Snow White & Rose Red. unabr. ed. 1995. audio 54.95 (0-7451-6155-3, CAB 162) BBC Audiobooks America.
—Snow White & Rose Red. unabr. ed. 1986. (Matthew Hope Ser.). audio 48.00 (0-7366-1036-7, 1966) Books on Tape, Inc.
—Snow White & Rose Red. 1985. o.p. (0-03-002603-2) Holt, Henry & Co.
—Snow White & Rose Red. abr. ed. 1993. audio 15.95 o.p. (1-55800-256-1, Dove Audio) NewStar Media, Inc.
—Snow White & Rose Red. 256p. 1994. mass mkt. 5.99 o.s.i (0-446-60133-0); 1986. reprint ed. mass mkt. 4.99 o.s.i (0-445-40513-9) Warner Bks., Inc.
—There Was a Little Girl. unabr. ed. 1995. (Matthew Hope Ser.). audio 56.00 (0-7366-2972-6, 3663) Books on Tape, Inc.
—There Was a Little Girl. l.t. ed. 1995. 424p. pap. 19.95 o.p. (0-7838-1181-0); 480p. 24.95 o.p. (0-7838-1180-2) Gale Group. (Macmillan Reference USA).
—There Was a Little Girl. 1999. audio (1-57042-777-1); 1994. audio 12.98 (1-57042-197-8, 4-521978) Time Warner AudioBooks.
—There Was a Little Girl. 1995. 352p. mass mkt. 6.50 (0-446-60214-0); 1994. 336p. 21.95 o.s.i (0-446-51739-9) Warner Bks., Inc.
—Three Blind Mice. l.t. ed. 1991. (General Ser.). 396p. lib. bdg. 21.95 (0-8161-5169-5, Macmillan Reference USA) Gale Group.
—Three Blind Mice. abr. ed. (Super Sound Buy, Dove Ser.). 1994. audio 8.99 o.p. (0-7871-0233-4); 1993. 15.95 o.p. (1-55800-392-4, 41460) NewStar Media, Inc.
—Three Blind Mice. 1994. 304p. mass mkt. 5.99 o.s.i (0-446-60137-3); 1991. mass mkt. 4.99 o.s.i (0-446-40035-1) Warner Bks., Inc.

HOPKINS, LLOYD (FICTITIOUS CHARACTER)—FICTION

Ellroy, James. Because the Night. 1987. pap. 5.99 (0-380-70063-8, Avon Bks.) Morrow/Avon.
—Because the Night. 1986. 15.95 (0-89296-071-X) Mysterious Pr.
—L. A. Noir. 2000. 648p. 25.00 (0-89296-686-6); 600p. E-Book 14.95 (0-7595-9046-X); 600p. E-Book 14.95 (0-7595-0040-1); 600p. E-Book 14.95 (0-7595-4041-1); 600p. E-Book 14.95 (0-7595-8042-1); E-Book 14.95 (0-7595-6040-4) Mysterious Pr.

HOPKINS, MARTY (FICTITIOUS CHARACTER)—FICTION

Carlson, Pat M. Bloodstream. 1996. 336p. mass mkt. 5.99 (0-671-76978-2, Pocket) Simon & Schuster.
—Bloodstream. Chelius, Jane, ed. 1995. 336p. 20.00 o.p. (0-671-76977-4, Atria) Simon & Schuster.
—Gravestone. Chelius, Jane, ed. 336p. 1993. 20.00 (0-671-76974-X, Atria); 1994. reprint ed. mass mkt. 5.50 (0-671-76975-8, Pocket) Simon & Schuster.

HOPPER, TURING (FICTITIOUS CHARACTER)—FICTION

Andrews, Donna. Click Here for Murder. 304p. 2004. mass mkt. 6.50 (0-425-19529-5); 2003. 22.95 (0-425-18856-6, Prime Crime) Berkley Publishing Group.
—You've Got Murder. 304p. 2003. mass mkt. 6.50 (0-425-18945-7, Prime Crime); 2002. 21.95 (0-425-18191-X) Berkley Publishing Group.

HORN, CORRAN (FICTITIOUS CHARACTER)—FICTION

Schweighofer, Peter. Tales from the Empire: Stories from Star Wars Adventure Journal. 1997. (Star Wars Ser.). 368p. mass mkt. 6.99 (0-553-57876-6) Bantam Bks.
Stackpole, Michael A. The Bacta War. 1997. (Star Wars: Bk. 4). 384p. mass mkt. 6.99 (0-553-56804-3, Spectra) Bantam Bks.
—The Bacta War. abr. ed. 1997. (Star Wars Ser.: Bk. 4). audio 16.99 (0-553-47425-1, RH Audio) Random Hse. Audio Publishing Group.
—The Bacta War. 1997. (Star Wars: No. 4). (J). (gr. 3-7). 12.04 (0-606-11900-0) Turtleback Bks.
—Dark Tide: Onslaught. abr. ed. 2000. (Star Wars: Bk. 2). audio 18.00 (0-375-40956-4, RH Audio) Random Hse. Audio Publishing Group.
—Dark Tide I: Onslaught. 2000. (Star Wars Ser.: Bk. 2). 125.82 o.s.i (0-345-43891-4); 304p. mass mkt. 6.99 (0-345-42854-4, Del Rey) Ballantine Bks.
—Dark Tide II: Ruin. abr. ed. 2000. (Star Wars: Bk. 3). audio 18.00 (0-375-40969-6, RH Audio) Random Hse. Audio Publishing Group.
—I, Jedi. abr. ed. 1998. (Star Wars Ser.). audio 16.99 (0-553-47948-2, 391211, RH Audio) Random Hse. Audio Publishing Group.
—I, Jedi: Star Wars. 1999. (Star Wars Ser.). 608p. mass mkt. 6.99 (0-553-57873-1) Broadway Bks.
—Isard's Revenge. 1999. (Star Wars: Bk. 8). (Illus.). 352p. mass mkt. 6.99 (0-553-57903-7) Bantam Bks.
—Isard's Revenge. abr. ed. 1999. (Star Wars Ser.: Bk. 8). audio 18.00 (0-553-52546-8, RH Audio) Random Hse. Audio Publishing Group.
—The Kryptos Trap. 1996. (Star Wars: Bk. 3). 384p. mass mkt. 6.99 (0-553-56803-5, Spectra) Bantam Bks.
—The Krytos Trap. abr. ed. 1996. (Star Wars Ser.: Bk. 3). audio 16.99 o.s.i (0-553-47420-0, 394343, RH Audio) Random Hse. Audio Publishing Group.
—The Krytos Trap. 1996. (Star Wars: Bk. 3). 12.04 (0-606-11899-3) Turtleback Bks.
—Rogue Squadron. 1996. (Star Wars: Bk. 1). 416p. mass mkt. 6.99 (0-553-56801-9, Spectra) Bantam Bks.
—Rogue Squadron. abr. ed. 1996. (Star Wars Ser.: Bk. 1). audio 16.99 (0-553-47418-9, 394341, RH Audio) Random Hse. Audio Publishing Group.
—Rogue Squadron. 1996. (Star Wars: Bk. 1). 12.04 (0-606-11897-7) Turtleback Bks.
—Ruin: Dark Tide II. 2000. (Star Wars Ser.: No.3). 304p. mass mkt. 6.99 (0-345-42856-0) Ballantine Bks.
—Wedge's Gamble. 1996. (Star Wars: Bk. 2). 384p. mass mkt. 6.99 (0-553-56802-7, Spectra) Bantam Bks.
—Wedge's Gamble. abr. ed. 1996. (Star Wars Ser.: Bk. 2). audio 16.99 (0-553-47419-7, 394342, RH Audio) Random Hse. Audio Publishing Group.
—Wedge's Gamble. 1996. (Star Wars: Bk. 2). 12.04 (0-606-11898-5) Turtleback Bks.
Stackpole, Michael A., et al. Blood & Honor. 1999. (Star Wars Ser.: Bk. 6). 96p. (YA). (gr. 5 up). pap. 12.95 (1-56971-387-1) Dark Horse Comics.

HORNBLOWER, HORATIO (FICTITIOUS CHARACTER)—FICTION

Forester, C. S. Admiral Hornblower in the West Indies. unabr. ed. 1980. (Hornblower Ser.: No. 10). audio 48.00 Books on Tape, Inc.
—Admiral Hornblower in the West Indies. 1989. 17.95 o.p. (0-316-28901-9); 1963. 29.95 o.s.i (0-316-28904-3); 1989. (Hornblower Ser.: No. 11). 336p. reprint ed. pap. 13.00 (0-316-28941-8, Back Bay) Little Brown & Co.
—Beat to Quarters. 2002. audio compact disk 56.00 (0-7366-9128-6); 2002. audio 48.00 (0-7366-8898-6); 2001. audio 29.95 (0-7366-6755-5); 1984. audio 64.00 (0-7366-0654-8, 1615) Books on Tape, Inc.
—Beat to Quarters. 1974. (Hornblower Ser.: No. 5). pap. 1.25 o.p. (0-523-22385-4, Pinnacle Bks.) Kensington Publishing Corp.
—Beat to Quarters. 1985. (Hornblower Ser.: No. 6). 288p. pap. 13.00 (0-316-28932-9, Back Bay) Little Brown & Co.
—Commodore Hornblower. 1976. (Hornblower Ser.: No. 8). 24.95 (0-88411-928-9) Amereon, Ltd.
—Commodore Hornblower. 2002. audio 56.00 (0-7366-9118-9); 2002. audio compact disk 64.00 (0-7366-9119-7); 1980. (Hornblower Ser.: No. 8). audio 56.00 (0-7366-3095-3, 1347-A) Books on Tape, Inc.
—Commodore Hornblower. 1975. (Hornblower Ser.: No. 8). 320p. pap. 1.50 o.p. (0-523-23388-4, Pinnacle Bks.) Kensington Publishing Corp.
—Commodore Hornblower. 1945. (YA). (gr. 7 up). 17.95 o.p. (0-316-28894-2); 1989. (Hornblower Ser.: No. 9). 320p. reprint ed. pap. 13.00 (0-316-28938-8, Back Bay) Little Brown & Co.
—Commodore Hornblower. abr. ed. 1999. (Hornblower Ser.: No. 8). mass mkt. 16.85 incl. audio (1-85998-999-3) Ulverscroft Audio (U.S.A.).
—Flying Colours. 1975. (Hornblower Ser.: No. 7). 192p. pap. 1.25 o.p. (0-523-22387-0, Pinnacle Bks.) Kensington Publishing Corp.
—Flying Colours. 1989. (Hornblower Ser.: No. 8). 256p. pap. 13.00 (0-316-28939-6, Back Bay) Little Brown & Co.
—Hornblower & the Atropos. 1976. (Hornblower Ser.: No. 4). 25.95 (0-8488-0487-2, Queens Hse., Inc.) Amereon, Ltd.
—Hornblower & the Atropos. 2002. audio 56.00 (0-7366-8900-1); 2002. audio compact disk 56.00 (0-7366-9127-8); 2001. audio 29.95 (0-7366-6760-1); 1984. audio 56.00 (0-7366-0653-X, 1614) Books on Tape, Inc.
—Hornblower & the Atropos. 1953. 17.95 o.p. (0-316-28911-6); 1985. (Hornblower Ser.: No. 5). 352p. reprint ed. pap. 13.00 (0-316-28929-9, Back Bay) Little Brown & Co.
—Hornblower & the Atropos. abr. ed. 1999. (Hornblower Ser.: No. 4). audio 25.00 (0-7871-1960-1, Dove Audio) NewStar Media, Inc.
—Hornblower & the Atropos. abr. ed. 2000. mass mkt. 16.95 incl. audio (1-85998-977-2) Trafalgar Square.
—Hornblower & the Hotspur. 1976. (Hornblower Ser.: No. 3). 25.95 (0-8488-0488-0, Queens Hse., Inc.) Amereon, Ltd.
—Hornblower & the Hotspur. unabr. collector's ed. 1984. (Hornblower Ser.: No. 3). audio 64.00 (0-7366-0652-1, 1613) Books on Tape, Inc.
—Hornblower & the Hotspur. 1981. (Hornblower Ser.: No. 3). 352p. pap. 2.75 o.p. (0-523-41790-X, Pinnacle Bks.) Kensington Publishing Corp.
—Hornblower & the Hotspur. 1998. (Hornblower Ser.: No. 3). 400p. pap. 13.00 (0-316-29046-7, Back Bay); 1985. 344p. pap. 14.95 o.p. (0-316-28928-0, Back Bay); 1962. 17.95 o.p. (0-316-28899-3) Little Brown & Co.
—Hornblower & the Hotspur. abr. ed. 1999. (Hornblower Ser.: No. 3). audio 25.00 (0-7871-1959-8, Dove Audio) NewStar Media, Inc.
—Hornblower During the Crisis. unabr. collector's ed. 1988. (Hornblower Ser.: No. 11). audio 30.00 (0-7366-1354-4, 2255) Books on Tape, Inc.
—Hornblower During the Crisis. 1967. (Illus.). 162p. 17.95 o.p. (0-316-28915-9); 1990. (Hornblower Ser.: No. 4). 176p. reprint ed. pap. 13.00 (0-316-28944-2, Back Bay) Little Brown & Co.
—Lieutenant Hornblower. 1976. (Hornblower Ser.: No. 2). 24.95 (0-8488-0489-9, Queens Hse., Inc.) Amereon, Ltd.
—Lieutenant Hornblower. unabr. collector's ed. 1984. (Hornblower Ser.: No. 2). audio 48.00 (0-7366-0651-3, 1612) Books on Tape, Inc.
—Lieutenant Hornblower. (Hornblower Ser.: No. 2). 1980. 320p. pap. 2.50 o.p. (0-523-41387-4); 1974. pap. 1.50 o.p. (0-523-00382-X) Kensington Publishing Corp. (Pinnacle Bks.).
—Lieutenant Hornblower. 1998. (Hornblower Ser.: No. 2). 320p. pap. 13.00 (0-316-29063-7); 1984. 306p. pap. 14.95 o.p. (0-316-28921-3) Little Brown & Co. (Back Bay).
—Lieutenant Hornblower. abr. ed. 1999. (Hornblower Ser.: No. 2). audio 25.00 (0-7871-1961-X, Dove Audio) NewStar Media, Inc.
—Lieutenant Hornblower. abr. ed. 1998. (Hornblower Ser.: No. 2). audio 16.95 (1-85998-976-4) Trafalgar Square.
—Lord Hornblower. Date not set. (Hornblower Ser.: No. 9). 320p. (0-8488-1324-3) Amereon, Ltd.
—Lord Hornblower, Set. unabr. ed. 1999. (Hornblower Ser.: No. 9). 20p. audio 69.95 (0-7540-0363-9, CAB1786) BBC Audiobooks America.
—Lord Hornblower. 2001. audio compact disk 56.00 (0-7366-9117-0); 1980. (Hornblower Ser.: No. 9). audio 48.00 (0-7366-0362-X, 1347-B) Books on Tape, Inc.
—Lord Hornblower. 1991. (Hornblower Ser.: No. 9). lib. bdg. 21.95 (1-56849-052-6) Buccaneer Bks., Inc.
—Lord Hornblower. 1981. (Hornblower Ser.: No. 9). 256p. pap. 2.50 o.p. (0-523-41394-7, Pinnacle Bks.) Kensington Publishing Corp.
—Lord Hornblower. 1946. (J). (gr. 7 up). 17.95 o.p. (0-316-28908-6); 1989. (Hornblower Ser.: No. 10). 336p. reprint ed. pap. 13.00 (0-316-28943-4, Back Bay) Little Brown & Co.
—Lord Hornblower. abr. ed. 2000. audio 16.95 (1-84032-100-8) Trafalgar Square.
—Mr. Midshipman Hornblower. unabr. ed. 1992. (Hornblower Ser.: No. 1). audio 69.95 (0-7451-5940-0, CAB 654) BBC Audiobooks America.

Characters

—Mr. Midshipman Hornblower. unabr. collector's ed. 1983. (Hornblower Ser.: No. 1). audio 64.00 (*0-7366-0650-5*, 1611) Books on Tape, Inc.
—Mr. Midshipman Hornblower. 1991. (Hornblower Ser.: No. 1). lib. bdg. 21.95 (*1-56849-053-4*) Buccaneer Bks., Inc.
—Mr. Midshipman Hornblower. (Hornblower Ser.: No. 1). 1981. 172p. pap. 2.50 o.p. (*0-523-41672-5*); 1974. pap. 1.50 o.p. (*0-523-23381-7*) Kensington Publishing Corp. (Pinnacle Bks.).
—Mr. Midshipman Hornblower. 1998. 320p. 18.95 o.p. (*0-316-29060-2*); 1950. (YA). 17.95 o.p. (*0-316-28909-4*); 1984. (Hornblower Ser.: No. 1). 320p. reprint ed. pap. 13.00 (*0-316-28912-4*, Back Bay) Little Brown & Co.
—Mr. Midshipman Hornblower. Hedge, Tricia, ed. 2000. (Hornblower Ser.: No. 1). (Illus.). 96p. (J). pap. text 5.95 (*0-19-423041-4*) Oxford Univ. Pr., Inc.
—Mr. Midshipman Hornblower. abr. ed. 1998. (Hornblower Ser.: No. 1). audio 16.95 (*1-85998-975-6*) Trafalgar Square.
—Ship of the Line. unabr. ed. 1998. (Hornblower Ser.: No. 6). audio 69.95 (*0-7540-0195-4*, CAB 1618) BBC Audiobooks America.
—Ship of the Line. 2002. audio 48.00 (*0-7366-8899-4*); 2001. audio 29.95 (*0-7366-6756-3*); 1987. audio 48.00 (*0-7366-1228-9*, 2146) Books on Tape, Inc.
—Ship of the Line. abr. ed. 1998. (Hornblower Ser.: No. 6). mass mkt. incl. audio (*1-85998-997-7*) Hodder Headline Audiobooks.
—Ship of the Line. 1980. (Hornblower Ser.: No. 6). 256p. pap. 2.50 o.p. (*0-523-41391-2*, Pinnacle Bks.) Kensington Publishing Corp.
—Ship of the Line. 1985. (Hornblower Ser.: No. 7). 304p. (gr. 8). pap. 13.00 (*0-316-28936-1*, Back Bay) Little Brown & Co.
—Ship of the Line. l.t. ed. 1999. (Hornblower Ser.: No. 6). 336p. 31.99 o.p. (*0-7089-4157-5*, Ulverscroft) Thorpe, F. A. Pubs. GBR. *Dist:* Ulverscroft Large Print Bks., Ltd., Ulverscroft Large Print Canada, Ltd.
Forester, C. S. & Gruffudd, Ioan. Hornblower & the Hotspur. abr. ed. 1998. (Hornblower Ser.: No. 3). audio 16.85 (*1-85998-995-0*) Ulverscroft Audio (U.S.A.).
Parkinson, C. Northcote. The Life & Times of Horatio Hornblower. 1994. reprint ed. lib. bdg. 32.95 (*1-56849-318-5*) Buccaneer Bks., Inc.
—The Life & Times of Horatio Hornblower. l.t. ed. 2000. (Charnwood Large Print Ser.). 432p. 31.99 (*0-7089-9193-9*, Ulverscroft) Thorpe, F. A. Pubs. GBR. *Dist:* Ulverscroft Large Print Bks., Ltd., Ulverscroft Large Print Canada, Ltd.
—The Life & Times of Horatio Hornblower. 1970. 304p. (*0-7181-0787-X*, Joseph, Michael) Viking Penguin.
—The Life & Times of Horatio Hornblower: A Fictional Biography. 1998. 320p. pap. 10.95 (*0-7509-2109-9*) Sutton Publishing.

### HORNE, EVAN (FICTITIOUS CHARACTER)—FICTION

Moody, Bill. Bird Lives! An Evan Horne Mystery. 2000. (Evan Horne Mysteries Ser.: Bk. 350). per. (*0-373-26350-3*, 1-26350-8, Worldwide Library) Harlequin Enterprises, Ltd.
—Bird Lives! An Evan Horne Mystery. 1999. (Evan Horne Mysteries Ser.). 256p. 22.95 (*0-8027-3327-1*) Walker & Co.
—Death of A Tenor Man: An Evan Horne Mystery. 1995. 240p. 21.95 (*0-8027-3269-0*) Walker & Co.
—Death of a Tenor Man: An Evan Horne Mystery. 1997. 288p. mass mkt. 5.50 o.s.i (*0-440-22324-5*) Dell Publishing.
—Looking for Chet Baker: An Evan Horne Mystery. 2003. (WWL Mystery Ser.: No. 450). 272p. mass mkt. (*0-373-26450-X*, Worldwide Library) Harlequin Enterprises, Ltd.
—Looking for Chet Baker: An Evan Horne Mystery. 2002. 253p. 23.95 (*0-8027-3368-9*) Walker & Co.
—Solo Hand. 1996. 304p. mass mkt. 5.50 o.s.i (*0-440-22322-9*) Dell Publishing.
—Solo Hand. 2003. 193p. pap. 13.95 (*0-9644138-3-3*, Dark City Bks.) OffByOne Pr.
—Solo Hand. 1994. 19.95 (*0-8027-3248-8*) Walker & Co.
—The Sound of the Trumpet: An Evan Horne Mystery. 1998. (Evan Horne Mysteries Ser.: Vol. 3). 304p. mass mkt. 5.99 o.s.i (*0-440-22194-3*) Dell Publishing.
—The Sound of the Trumpet: An Evan Horne Mystery. 1997. (Evan Horne Mysteries Ser.). 240p. 21.95 (*0-8027-3291-7*) Walker & Co.
Sherman. The Jazz Musician. 1994. pap. (*0-312-09318-7*, Saint Martin's Griffin) St. Martin's Pr.

### HOUSE, DUFFY (FICTITIOUS CHARACTER)—FICTION

Evers, Crabbe. Bleeding Dodger Blue. 1991. 224p. mass mkt. 4.50 o.s.i (*0-553-29177-7*) Bantam Bks.
—Fear in Fenway: A Duffy House Mystery. 1994. 256p. mass mkt. 4.99 (*0-380-71865-0*, Avon Bks.); 1993. 238p. 18.00 o.p. (*0-688-11468-7*, Morrow, William & Co.) Morrow/Avon.
—Murder in Wrigley Field. 1991. 256p. mass mkt. 3.95 o.s.i (*0-553-28915-2*) Bantam Bks.
—Murderer's Row. 1991. 288p. mass mkt. 3.99 o.s.i (*0-553-29088-6*) Bantam Bks.
—Tigers Burning: A Duffy House Mystery. 1995. 272p. mass mkt. 4.99 (*0-380-71866-9*, Avon Bks.); 1994. 246p. 20.00 o.p. (*0-688-11469-5*, Morrow, William & Co.) Morrow/Avon.

### HOUSTON, STEVIE (FICTITIOUS CHARACTER)—FICTION

Richardson, Tracey. Last Rites: A Stevie Houston Mystery. 1997. (Stevie Houston Mysteries Ser.). 176p. pap. 11.95 (*1-56280-164-3*) Naiad Pr., Inc.
—Over the Line: A Stevie Houston Mystery. 1998. (Stevie Houston Mysteries Ser.: Vol. 2). 240p. (Orig.). pap. 11.95 (*1-56280-202-X*) Naiad Pr., Inc.

### HOWARD, ED (FICTITIOUS CHARACTER)—FICTION

Mason, David S. Shadow over Babylon. l.t. ed. 1994. pap. 22.95 o.p. (*0-7927-1893-3*); 24.95 o.p. (*0-7927-1894-1*) BBC Audiobooks America.
—Shadow over Babylon. 1993. 496p. 22.95 o.p. (*0-525-93709-9*, Dutton) Dutton/Plume.
—Shadow over Babylon. 1995. 480p. pap. o.s.i (*0-451-17671-5*); 528p. mass mkt. 5.99 o.s.i (*0-451-18063-1*) NAL. (Signet Bks.).

### HOWARD, JASON (FICTITIOUS CHARACTER)—FICTION

Cook, Robin. Mortal Fear. 1989. 368p. mass mkt. 7.99 (*0-425-11388-4*) Berkley Publishing Group.
—Mortal Fear. 17.95 o.s.i (*0-399-13690-8*) Penguin Group (USA) Inc.
—Mortal Fear. 1988. 368p. 17.95 o.p. (*0-399-13318-6*, G. P. Putnam's Sons) Penguin Putnam Bks. for Young Readers.
—Mortal Fear. 1989. 14.04 (*0-606-00930-2*) Turtleback Bks.

### HOWARD, JERI (FICTITIOUS CHARACTER)—FICTION

Dawson, Janet. A Credible Threat. (Jeri Howard Mystery Ser.). 1997. mass mkt. 5.99 o.s.i (*0-449-22357-4*); 1996. 256p. 21.00 o.p. (*0-449-90977-8*) Ballantine Bks. (Fawcett).
—Don't Turn Your Back on the Ocean. 1994. 336p. 20.00 o.p. (*0-449-90766-X*, Fawcett) Ballantine Bks.
—Kindred Crimes. 1992. mass mkt. 4.99 o.s.i (*0-449-22014-1*, Fawcett) Ballantine Bks.
—Kindred Crimes. 1990. 17.95 o.p. (*0-312-04464-X*, Saint Martin's Minotaur) St. Martin's Pr.
—Kindred Crimes. l.t. ed. 1993. (Ulverscroft Large Print Ser.). 480p. 29.99 o.p. (*0-7089-2929-X*, Ulverscroft) Thorpe, F. A. Pubs. GBR. *Dist:* Ulverscroft Large Print Bks., Ltd., Ulverscroft Large Print Canada, Ltd.
—Nobody's Child. 1995. 352p. 21.00 o.s.i (*0-449-90976-X*, Fawcett) Ballantine Bks.
—Nobody's Child: A Jeri Howard Mystery. 1996. 320p. mass mkt. 6.99 o.s.i (*0-449-22356-6*, Fawcett) Ballantine Bks.
—Take a Number. (Northern California Mysteries Ser.). 1994. mass mkt. 4.99 o.s.i (*0-449-22183-0*); 1993. 352p. 20.00 o.s.i (*0-449-90765-1*) Ballantine Bks. (Fawcett).
—Till the Old Men Die. 1993. 275p. mass mkt. 4.50 o.s.i (*0-449-22133-4*, Fawcett) Ballantine Bks.
—Where the Bodies Are Buried. (Jeri Howard Mystery Ser.). 1999. 304p. mass mkt. 6.50 o.s.i (*0-449-00322-1*); 1998. 288p. 23.50 o.s.i (*0-449-00198-9*) Ballantine Bks. (Fawcett).
—Witness to Evil. 1998. 21.95 (*0-449-91060-1*); 1998. 304p. mass mkt. 6.50 (*0-449-22471-6*); 1997. 304p. 21.95 o.s.i (*0-449-00042-7*) Ballantine Bks. (Fawcett).

### HOWARD, ROZ (FICTITIOUS CHARACTER)—FICTION

Kenney, Susan. Garden of Malice. 1984. 288p. mass mkt. 2.95 o.s.i (*0-345-31712-2*, Ballantine Bks.) Ballantine Bks.
—Garden of Malice. 1992. (Crime Ser.). 288p. reprint ed. pap. 5.95 o.p. (*0-14-016966-0*, Penguin Bks.) Penguin Group (USA) Inc.
—Graves in Academe. 1990. 28p. pap. 5.95 o.p. (*0-14-013349-6*, Penguin Bks.); 1986. 224p. pap. 3.95 o.p. (*0-14-009386-9*, Penguin Bks.); 1985. 288p. 14.95 o.p. (*0-670-80734-6*) Viking Penguin.
—One Fell Sloop. 1991. (Crime Monthly Ser.). 304p. reprint ed. pap. 5.95 o.p. (*0-14-015406-X*, Penguin Bks.) Penguin Group (USA) Inc.
—One Fell Sloop. 1990. 288p. 16.95 o.p. (*0-670-83537-4*) Viking Penguin.

### HOWE, EMMA (FICTITIOUS CHARACTER)—FICTION

Roberts, Gillian. Time & Trouble. 1999. 336p. mass mkt. 5.99 (*0-312-96996-1*, St. Martin's Paperbacks); 1998. 384p. 24.95 (*0-312-18673-8*, Saint Martin's Minotaur) St. Martin's Pr.
—Whatever Doesn't Kill You: An Emma Howe & Billie August Mystery. 2001. 312p. 23.95 (*0-312-26269-8*, Saint Martin's Minotaur) St. Martin's Pr.

### HOWELL, NOAH (FICTITIOUS CHARACTER)—FICTION

Baxter, Mary L. Lightning Strikes. 1997. (Thirty-Six Hours Ser.: No. 1). per. (*0-373-65006-X*, 1-65006-8, Harlequin Bks.) Harlequin Enterprises, Ltd.

### HOWL, THE MAGICIAN (FICTITIOUS CHARACTER)—FICTION

Jones, Diana Wynne. Castle in the Air. 1991. (Illus.). 208p. (J). (gr. 7 up). 15.95 (*0-688-09686-7*, Greenwillow Bks.) HarperCollins Children's Bk. Group.
—Howl's Moving Castle. 1989. mass mkt. 3.50 o.s.i (*0-441-34664-2*) Ace Bks.
—Howl's Moving Castle. 1986. 224p. (YA). (gr. 7 up). 16.95 (*0-688-06233-4*, Greenwillow Bks.) HarperCollins Children's Bk. Group.

### HOWLAND, EDITH (FICTITIOUS CHARACTER)—FICTION

Highsmith, Patricia. Edith's Diary. 1989. 320p. pap. 13.50 (*0-87113-296-6*, Atlantic Monthly Pr.) Grove/Atlantic, Inc.
—Edith's Diary. 1978. pap. 1.95 o.s.i (*0-671-82042-7*, Pocket); 1977. 8.95 o.s.i (*0-671-22686-X*, Simon & Schuster) Simon & Schuster.

### HOYLAND, TAMARA (FICTITIOUS CHARACTER)—FICTION

Mann, Jessica. Death Beyond the Nile. l.t. ed. 1991. 15.95 o.p. (*0-7927-9582-2*, 5055); pap. 15.95 o.p. (*0-7927-0010-4*, 4617) BBC Audiobooks America.
—Death Beyond the Nile. 1989. 192p. 14.95 o.p. (*0-312-02564-5*, Saint Martin's Minotaur) St. Martin's Pr.

### HUBBERT, T. S. (FICTITIOUS CHARACTER)—FICTION

Gray, Gallagher. A Cast of Killers. 1994. (Partners in Crime Ser.). mass mkt. 4.99 o.s.i (*0-8041-1146-4*, Ivy Bks.) Ballantine Bks.
—A Cast of Killers. 1992. 256p. 20.95 o.p. (*1-55611-328-5*) Fine, Donald I. Bks.
—Death of a Dream Maker. 1995. mass mkt. 5.50 o.s.i (*0-8041-1247-9*, Ivy Bks.) Ballantine Bks.
—Hubbert & Lil: Partners in Crime. 1993. mass mkt. 4.99 o.s.i (*0-8041-0948-6*, Ivy Bks.) Ballantine Bks.
—Hubbert & Lil: Partners in Crime. 1991. 256p. 18.95 o.p. (*1-55611-308-0*) Fine, Donald I. Bks.
—A Motive for Murder. 1996. (Partners in Crime Ser.). mass mkt. 5.50 o.s.i (*0-8041-1248-7*, Ivy Bks.) Ballantine Bks.

### HUBBLEY, HARRIET (FICTITIOUS CHARACTER)—FICTION

Manthorne, Jackie. The Deadly Reunion. 1995. 252p. pap. 10.95 (*0-921881-32-0*) Ragweed Pr. CAN. *Dist:* General Distribution Services, Inc.
—The Final Take: A Harriet Hubbley Mystery. 1996. 256p. pap. 10.95 (*0-921881-41-X*) Ragweed Pr. CAN. *Dist:* Univ. of Toronto Pr.
—The Last Resort: A Harriet Hubbley Mystery, Vol. 3. 1995. 252p. pap. 10.95 (*0-921881-34-7*) Ragweed Pr. CAN. *Dist:* Univ. of Toronto Pr.
—Sudden Death. 1997. 264p. pap. 10.95 (*0-921881-43-6*) Ragweed Pr. CAN. *Dist:* Univ. of Toronto Pr.

### HUBER, RACHEL (FICTITIOUS CHARACTER)—FICTION

Chamberlain, Diane. Reflection. 1996. 384p. 24.00 o.p. (*0-06-017652-0*) HarperCollins Pubs.
—Reflection. 1997. 416p. mass mkt. 5.99 o.s.i (*0-06-109396-3*, HarperTorch) Morrow/Avon.

### HUCKLEBERRY, HONEY (FICTITIOUS CHARACTER)—FICTION

Moseley, Margaret. The Fourth Steven. 1998. 272p. mass mkt. 5.99 o.s.i (*0-425-16406-3*, Prime Crime) Berkley Publishing Group.
—Grinning in His Mashed Potatoes. 1999. 304p. mass mkt. 6.50 o.s.i (*0-425-16982-0*, Prime Crime) Berkley Publishing Group.

### HUDSON, EMMA (FICTITIOUS CHARACTER)—FICTION

Hosier, Sydney. Elementary, Mrs. Hudson. 1996. (Introducing Emma Hudson, the Other Sleuth of Baker Street Ser.: No. 1). 224p. (Orig.). mass mkt. 5.50 (*0-380-78175-1*, Avon Bks.) Morrow/Avon.
—Game's Afoot, Mrs. Hudson. 1998. mass mkt. 5.99 (*0-380-79217-6*, Avon Bks.) Morrow/Avon.
—Most Baffling, Mrs. Hudson: An Emma Hudson Mystery. 1998. mass mkt. 5.50 (*0-380-79216-8*, Avon Bks.) Morrow/Avon.
—Murder, Mrs. Hudson. 1997. mass mkt. 5.50 (*0-380-78176-X*, Avon Bks.) Morrow/Avon.

### HUDSON, OLIVIA (FICTITIOUS CHARACTER)—FICTION

Armstrong, Charlotte. The Dream Walker. 1992. 320p. mass mkt. 3.99 o.s.i (*0-8217-3908-5*, Zebra Bks.) Kensington Publishing Corp.

### HUDSON, ROBIN (FICTITIOUS CHARACTER)—FICTION

Hayter, Sparkle. The Chelsea Girl Murders. 2000. (Robin Hudson Mysteries Ser.). 240p. 23.00 (*0-688-15518-9*, Morrow, William & Co.) Morrow/Avon.
—The Last Manly Man. 1999. (Robin Hudson Mysteries Ser.). 256p. reprint ed. pap. 9.95 o.s.i (*0-688-16972-4*, Quill) HarperTrade.
—The Last Manly Man: A Robin Hudson Mystery. 1998. (Robin Hudson Mysteries Ser.). 256p. 22.00 (*0-688-15517-0*, Morrow, William & Co.) Morrow/Avon.
—The Last Manly Man: A Robin Hudson Mystery. 2001. 272p. 5.99 (*0-14-200039-6*) Viking Penguin.
—Nice Girls Finish Last. 1997. (Viking Mystery Suspense Ser.). 256p. pap. 5.95 (*0-14-024516-2*) Penguin Group (USA) Inc.
—Nice Girls Finish Last: A Robin Hudson Mystery. 1996. (Robin Hudson Mystery Ser.). 256p. 20.95 o.p. (*0-670-86039-5*) Viking Penguin.
—Revenge of the Cootie Girls. 1997. (Robin Hudson Mystery Ser.). 240p. 20.95 o.s.i (*0-670-86940-6*) Viking Penguin.
—What's a Girl Gotta Do? 1995. (Robin Hudson Mystery Ser.). 288p. pap. 6.99 (*0-14-024481-6*, Penguin Bks.) Penguin Group (USA) Inc.
—What's a Girl Gotta Do? 1994. 270p. 19.95 o.p. (*1-56947-000-6*) Soho Pr., Inc.

### HUFF, WALTER (FICTITIOUS CHARACTER)—FICTION

Cain, James M. Double Indemnity. Date not set. lib. bdg. 14.95 (*0-8488-1754-0*) Amereon, Ltd.
—Double Indemnity. l.t. ed. 1985. (Nightingale Ser.). 184p. 9.95 o.p. (*0-8161-3830-3*, Macmillan Reference USA) Gale Group.
—Double Indemnity, Set. abr. ed. 1996. audio 17.00 (*0-89845-777-7*, 390675, HarperAudio) HarperTrade.
—Double Indemnity. 1992. pap. 8.00 (*0-394-23901-6*); 1989. 128p. pap. 10.00 (*0-679-72322-6*); 1978. pap. 2.95 o.p. (*0-394-72581-6*) Knopf Publishing Group. (Vintage).
—Double Indemnity. mass mkt. 0.25 o.p. (*0-451-01427-8*); 1950. mass mkt. 0.25 o.p. (*0-451-00784-0*) NAL. (Signet Bks.).
—Double Indemnity. 1992. pap. 8.00 (*0-679-74096-1*) Random Hse., Inc.

### HUGHES, KELLY (FICTITIOUS CHARACTER)—FICTION

Francis, Dick. Enquiry. 1987. 280p. mass mkt. 6.99 o.s.i (*0-449-21268-8*, Fawcett) Ballantine Bks.
—Enquiry. 2000. 272p. mass mkt. 6.99 (*0-515-12867-8*, Jove) Berkley Publishing Group.
—Enquiry. unabr. ed. 2000. audio compact disk 49.99 (*0-7861-9933-4*, z1736); 1996. audio 32.95 (*0-7861-0959-9*, 1736) Blackstone Audio Bks., Inc.
—Enquiry. unabr. ed. 1993. audio 49.95 (*0-7451-5949-4*, CAB 051) Chivers Audio Bks. GBR. *Dist:* BBC Audiobooks America.
—Enquiry. l.t. ed. 1995. 305p. lib. bdg. 22.95 o.p. (*0-7838-1142-X*, Macmillan Reference USA) Gale Group.
—Enquiry. unabr. ed. 1990. audio 44.00 (*1-55690-169-0*, 90088E7) Recorded Bks., LLC.
—Enquiry. 1984. mass mkt. 3.50 (*0-671-54362-8*); 1981. pap. 2.95 o.s.i (*0-671-44926-5*) Simon & Schuster. (Pocket).
—Enquiry. unabr. ed. 1983. audio 53.95 o.p. (*0-8161-9771-7*) Thorndike Pr.
—Enquiry. l.t. ed. 1980. (Ulverscroft Large Print Ser.). 12.00 o.p. (*0-7089-0399-1*, Ulverscroft) Thorpe, F. A. Pubs. GBR. *Dist:* Ulverscroft Large Print Bks., Ltd., Ulverscroft Large Print Canada, Ltd.

### HULL, JAKE (FICTITIOUS CHARACTER)—FICTION

Reaves, Michael. Night Hunter. 1997. 276p. mass mkt. 5.99 (*0-8125-1994-9*); 1995. 256p. 21.95 o.p. (*0-312-85318-1*) Doherty, Tom Assocs., LLC. (Tor Bks.).

### HUNT, BESSIE (FICTITIOUS CHARACTER)—FICTION

Gilman, Charlotte Perkins. Unpunished: A Mystery. Golden, Catherine & Knight, Denise D., eds. 1998. 256p. pap. 10.95 (*1-55861-185-1*) Feminist Pr. at The City Univ. of New York.
—Unpunished: A Mystery. Golden, Cathrine & Knight, Denise D., eds. 1997. 256p. 18.95 (*1-55861-170-3*) Feminist Pr. at The City Univ. of New York.

**HUNT, CLAIRE (FICTITIOUS CHARACTER)—FICTION**

Matthews, Christine & Randisi, Robert J. The Masks of Auntie Laveau: A Gil & Claire Hunt Mystery. 2002. 208p. 23.95 (*0-312-26898-X*, Saint Martin's Minotaur) St. Martin's Pr.

—Murder Is the Deal of the Day. 2003. (WWL Mystery Ser.: No. 472). 256p. mass mkt. (*0-373-26472-0*, Worldwide Library) Harlequin Enterprises, Ltd.

—Murder Is the Deal of the Day. 1998. 240p. 22.95 o.p. (*0-312-19928-7*, Saint Martin's Minotaur) St. Martin's Pr.

**HUNT, GIL (FICTITIOUS CHARACTER)—FICTION**

Matthews, Christine & Randisi, Robert J. The Masks of Auntie Laveau: A Gil & Claire Hunt Mystery. 2002. 208p. 23.95 (*0-312-26898-X*, Saint Martin's Minotaur) St. Martin's Pr.

—Murder Is the Deal of the Day. 2003. (WWL Mystery Ser.: No. 472). 256p. mass mkt. (*0-373-26472-0*, Worldwide Library) Harlequin Enterprises, Ltd.

—Murder Is the Deal of the Day. 1998. 240p. 22.95 o.p. (*0-312-19928-7*, Saint Martin's Minotaur) St. Martin's Pr.

**HUNT, MORGAN (FICTITIOUS CHARACTER)—FICTION**

Norman, Geoffrey. Deep End. 1995. 256p. mass mkt. 4.99 (*0-380-71912-6*, Avon Bks.) Morrow/Avon.

**HUNTER, HAWK (FICTITIOUS CHARACTER)—FICTION**

Maloney, Mack. The Circle War. 1996. (Wingman Ser.: 2). 416p. mass mkt. 4.99 o.s.i (*0-7860-0346-4*, Pinnacle Bks.) Kensington Publishing Corp.

—The Death Orbit. 1997. (Wingman Ser.: No. 13). 416p. mass mkt. 4.99 o.s.i (*0-7860-0357-X*, Pinnacle Bks.) Kensington Publishing Corp.

—The Final Storm. 1998. (Wingman Ser.: No. 6). 352p. mass mkt. 4.99 o.s.i (*0-7860-0505-X*, Pinnacle Bks.) Kensington Publishing Corp.

—Freedom Express. 1998. (Wingman Ser.: No. 7). 384p. mass mkt. 4.99 o.s.i (*0-7860-0548-3*, Pinnacle Bks.) Kensington Publishing Corp.

—The Ghost War. 1993. 448p. mass mkt. 4.50 o.s.i (*0-8217-4223-X*, Zebra Bks.) Kensington Publishing Corp.

—The Lucifer Crusade. (Wingman Ser.: No. 3). 1997. 416p. mass mkt. 4.99 o.s.i (*0-7860-0388-X*, Pinnacle Bks.); 1987. 432p. mass mkt. 3.95 o.s.i (*0-8217-2232-8*, Zebra Bks.) Kensington Publishing Corp.

—Return from the Inferno. (Wingman Ser.: No. 9). 1999. 352p. mass mkt. 4.99 o.s.i (*0-7860-0645-5*); 1991. mass mkt. 3.95 o.s.i (*0-8217-3510-1*, Zebra Bks.) Kensington Publishing Corp.

—Return of Sky Ghost. 1998. (Wingman Ser.: No. 15). 352p. mass mkt. 4.99 o.s.i (*0-7860-0510-6*, Pinnacle Bks.) Kensington Publishing Corp.

—The Sky Ghost. 1997. (Wingman Ser.: No. 14). 384p. mass mkt. 4.99 o.s.i (*0-7860-0452-5*, Pinnacle Bks.) Kensington Publishing Corp.

—Skyfire. (Wingman Ser.: No. 8). 1998. 352p. mass mkt. 4.99 o.s.i (*0-7860-0605-6*, Pinnacle Bks.); 1990. mass mkt. 3.95 o.s.i (*0-8217-3121-1*, Zebra Bks.) Kensington Publishing Corp.

—Target: Point Zero. 1996. (Wingman Ser.). 384p. mass mkt. 4.99 o.s.i (*0-7860-0299-9*, Pinnacle Bks.) Kensington Publishing Corp.

—Thunder in the East. 1988. (Wingman Ser.: No. 4). 432p. mass mkt. 3.95 o.s.i (*0-8217-2453-3*, Zebra Bks.) Kensington Publishing Corp.

—The Twisted Cross. 1997. (Wingman Ser.: No. 5). 384p. mass mkt. 4.99 o.s.i (*0-7860-0467-3*, Pinnacle Bks.) Kensington Publishing Corp.

—War of the Sun. (Wingman Ser.: No. 10). 1999. 448p. mass mkt. 4.99 o.s.i (*0-7860-0665-X*); 1999. 441p. (J). mass mkt. 4.99 o.s.i (*0-7860-1033-9*, Pinnacle Bks.); 1992. mass mkt. 3.99 o.s.i (*0-8217-3773-2*, Zebra Bks.) Kensington Publishing Corp.

**HUNTER, LEAH (FICTITIOUS CHARACTER)—FICTION**

Lacey, Sarah. File under Arson. unabr. ed. 1998. audio 63.95 (*1-85903-172-2*) Magna Story Sound GBR. *Dist:* Ulverscroft Large Print Bks., Ltd.

—File under Arson. 1996. 224p. 20.95 o.p. (*0-312-13972-1*, Saint Martin's Minotaur) St. Martin's Pr.

—File under Deceased. l.t. ed. 1994. (Dales Large Print Ser.). 321p. pap. 19.99 o.p. (*1-85389-475-3*) Dales Large Print Bks. GBR. *Dist:* Ulverscroft Large Print Bks., Ltd., Ulverscroft Large Print Canada, Ltd.

—File under Deceased. unabr. ed. 1998. audio 57.95 (*1-85903-171-4*) Magna Story Sound GBR. *Dist:* Ulverscroft Large Print Bks., Ltd.

—File under Deceased. 1993. 192p. 17.95 o.p. (*0-312-09807-3*, Saint Martin's Minotaur) St. Martin's Pr.

—File under Jeopardy. unabr. ed. audio 63.95 (*1-85903-173-0*) Magna Story Sound GBR. *Dist:* Ulverscroft Large Print Bks., Ltd.

—File under Jeopardy. 1997. 21.95 o.p. (*0-312-15127-6*, Saint Martin's Minotaur) St. Martin's Pr.

—File under Missing. l.t. ed. 1994. (Dales Large Print Ser.). 393p. pap. 19.99 o.p. (*1-85389-499-0*) Dales Large Print Bks. GBR. *Dist:* Ulverscroft Large Print Bks., Ltd., Ulverscroft Large Print Canada, Ltd.

—File under Missing, Set. unabr. ed. 1998. audio 63.95 (*1-85903-176-5*) Magna Story Sound GBR. *Dist:* Ulverscroft Large Print Bks., Ltd.

—File under Missing. 1994. 224p. 19.95 o.p. (*0-312-10982-2*, Saint Martin's Minotaur) St. Martin's Pr.

**HUNTER, MATT (FICTITIOUS CHARACTER)—FICTION**

Frash, Bill. Imminent Engagement. 1999. 200p. pap. 14.95 (*1-882897-33-1*) Lost Coast Pr.

—Imminent Engagement. 1997. 300p. pap. 6.95 o.p. (*1-56550-072-5*) Vision Bks. International.

—Impending Peril. 1998. 240p. pap. 14.95 (*1-882897-22-6*) Lost Coast Pr.

—Impending Peril. 2nd rev. ed. 1997. 310p. reprint ed. pap. 6.95 o.p. (*1-56550-071-7*) Vision Bks. International.

—Is the Red Witch Dead? 1998. 320p. pap. 14.95 (*1-882897-23-4*) Lost Coast Pr.

—Is the Red Witch Dead? 1997. 431p. pap. 6.95 o.p. (*1-56550-070-9*) Vision Bks. International.

**HUTCHINSON, SANDY (FICTITIOUS CHARACTER)—FICTION**

Johnson-Hodge, Margaret. Butterscotch Blues. 2000. 295p. 23.95 o.p. (*0-312-26484-4*); E-Book 6.50 (*0-312-27429-7*) St. Martin's Pr.

—Butterscotch Blues: A Novel. 2001. 320p. mass mkt. 6.50 (*0-312-97630-5*, St. Martin's Paperbacks) St. Martin's Pr.

**HUTTON, CLAIRE (FICTITIOUS CHARACTER)—FICTION**

Gorman, Ed. First Lady, Vol. 1. 1996. 370p. pap. text 6.99 o.p. (*0-8125-5041-2*, Forge Bks.) Doherty, Tom Assocs., LLC.

**HYATT, LEXY (FICTITIOUS CHARACTER)—FICTION**

Miller, Carlene. Killing at the Cat: A Lexy Hyatt Mystery. 1998. 200p. pap. 10.95 (*0-934678-95-2*) New Victoria Pubs., Inc.

—Mayhem at the Marina: A Lexy Hyatt Mystery. 1999. (Lexy Hyatt Mysteries Ser.). 220p. pap. 11.95 (*1-892281-05-8*) New Victoria Pubs., Inc.

—Reporter on the Run: A Lexy Hyatt Mystery. 2001. (Lexy Hyatt Mysteries Ser.). 200p. pap. 11.95 (*1-892281-14-7*) New Victoria Pubs., Inc.

**HYDE, PATRICK (FICTITIOUS CHARACTER)—FICTION**

Thomas, Craig. Playing with Cobras. unabr. ed. 1995. (ACE.). audio 79.95 (*0-7451-4365-2*, CAB 1048) Chivers Audio Bks. GBR. *Dist:* BBC Audiobooks America.

—Playing with Cobras. 1994. 432p. mass mkt. 5.99 o.p. (*0-06-109168-5*, HarperTorch) Morrow/Avon.

—Playing with Cobras. pap. 5.98 o.p. (*0-8317-3494-9*) Smithmark Pubs., Inc.

—Playing with Cobras, Set. 1994. (Studio Ser.). audio 89.95 o.p. (*0-7862-9983-5*) Thorndike Pr.

—Playing with Cobras: A Novel. 1993. 416p. 18.00 o.p. (*0-06-017955-4*) HarperTrade.

**HYLAND, MORN (FICTITIOUS CHARACTER)—FICTION**

Stephens, Reed, pseud. The Gap into Conflict: The Real Story. (Gap Ser.: No. 1). 1992. 272p. mass mkt. 7.50 (*0-553-29509-8*); 1991. 224p. 6.00 o.s.i (*0-553-08049-0*) Bantam Bks.

—The Gap into Madness: Chaos & Order. 1995. (Gap Ser.: No. 4). 688p. mass mkt. 6.99 (*0-553-57253-9*) Bantam Bks.

—The Gap into Power: A Dark & Hungry God Arises. 1993. (Gap Ser.: No. 3). 528p. mass mkt. 7.50 (*0-553-56260-6*) Bantam Bks.

—The Gap into Vision: Forbidden Knowledge. (Gap Ser.: No. 2). 1992. 480p. mass mkt. 7.50 (*0-553-29760-0*); 1991. 416p. 125.00 o.s.i (*0-553-07387-7*) Bantam Bks.

Stephens, Reed, pseud & Donaldson, Stephen R. The Gap into Ruin: This Day All Gods Die. 1997. (Gap Ser.: No. 5). 704p. mass mkt. 6.99 (*0-553-57328-4*) Bantam Bks.

# I

**ICHIRO, SANO (FICTITIOUS CHARACTER)—FICTION**

Rowland, Laura Joh. Bundori. 1997. 432p. mass mkt. 6.99 (*0-06-101197-5*, HarperTorch) Morrow/Avon.

—The Concubine's Tattoo. 2000. 384p. mass mkt. 6.99 (*0-312-96922-8*, St. Martin's Paperbacks); 1999. E-Book 6.50 (*0-312-24607-2*); 1998. 336p. 23.95 o.p. (*0-312-19252-5*, Saint Martin's Minotaur) St. Martin's Pr.

—The Dragon King's Palace. 2004. mass mkt. 6.99 (*0-312-99003-0*, St. Martin's Paperbacks) St. Martin's Pr.

—The Samurai's Wife. 2000. 203p. 23.95 (*0-312-20325-X*, Saint Martin's Minotaur) St. Martin's Pr.

—Shinju. Date not set. 384p. mass mkt. (*0-06-101035-9*); 1996. 448p. mass mkt. 6.99 (*0-06-100950-4*) Morrow/Avon. (HarperTorch).

—The Way of the Traitor. 1998. 384p. mass mkt. 6.99 (*0-06-101090-1*) HarperCollins Pubs.

**IL MORO (FICTITIOUS CHARACTER)—FICTION**

Ennis, Michael. Duchess of Milan. 1993. 576p. reprint ed. mass mkt. 5.99 o.s.i (*0-451-40428-9*, Signet Bks.) NAL.

—Duchess of Milan. 1999. pap. 9.00 (*0-14-014799-3*); 1992. (Illus.). 592p. 22.50 o.p. (*0-670-83783-0*) Viking Penguin. (Viking).

**ILES, DESMOND (FICTITIOUS CHARACTER)—FICTION**

James, Bill, pseud. Astride a Grave. 1996. (Detective Colin Harpur Novel Ser.). 208p. reprint ed. 21.00 o.p. (*0-88150-361-4*, Foul Play) Norton, W. W. & Co., Inc.

—Club. 1995. (Detective Colin Harpur Novel Ser.). 224p. 20.00 o.p. (*0-88150-331-2*, Foul Play) Norton, W. W. & Co., Inc.

—Come Clean. 1992. (Detective Colin Harpur Novel Ser.). 256p. 20.00 (*0-88150-243-X*, Foul Play) Norton, W. W. & Co., Inc.

—The Detective Is Dead. 2001. (Harpur & Iles Ser.). 215p. 22.95 (*0-393-05019-X*) Norton, W. W. & Co., Inc.

—Eton Crop: A Harpur & Iles Mystery. (Harpur & Iles Ser.). 2000. 288p. pap. 7.95 (*0-393-32098-7*, Norton Paperbacks); 1999. 284p. 22.95 (*0-393-04761-X*) Norton, W. W. & Co., Inc.

—Gospel. l.t. ed. 1997. (G. K. Hall Core Ser.). 384p. lib. bdg. 25.95 (*0-7838-8236-X*, Macmillan Reference USA) Gale Group.

—Gospel. l.t. ed. (Harpur & Iles Ser.). 1998. 208p. pap. 10.00 (*0-393-31781-1*); 1997. 206p. 22.95 (*0-88150-383-5*) Norton, W. W. & Co., Inc.

—Halo Parade: A Harpur & Iles Mystery. (Harpur & Iles Ser.). 176p. 1998. pap. 10.00 (*0-393-31831-1*); 1991. reprint ed. 17.95 o.p. (*0-88150-204-9*) Norton, W. W. & Co., Inc. (Foul Play).

—In Good Hands. 2000. (Harpur & Iles Ser.). 214p. 22.95 (*0-393-05005-X*) Norton, W. W. & Co., Inc.

—Kill Me. 2000. (Harpur & Iles Ser.). 267p. 22.95 (*0-393-04920-5*) Norton, W. W. & Co., Inc.

—The Lolita Man. (Harpur & Iles Ser.). 1998. 160p. pap. 10.00 (*0-393-31782-X*); 1991. 158p. 17.95 (*0-88150-198-0*, Foul Play) Norton, W. W. & Co., Inc.

—Lovely Mover: A Harpur & Iles Mystery. (Harpur & Iles Ser.). 2000. 272p. pap. 7.95 (*0-393-32034-0*); 1999. 264p. 23.00 o.p. (*0-393-04763-6*, Foul Play) Norton, W. W. & Co., Inc.

—Lovely Mover: A Harpur & Iles Mystery. l.t. ed. 1998. (Mystery Ser.). 343p. 26.95 (*0-7862-1680-8*) Thorndike Pr.

—Naked at the Window: A Harpur & Iles Mystery. 2002. 224p. 23.95 (*0-393-05198-6*) Norton, W. W. & Co., Inc.

—Panicking Ralph. 2002. pap. 8.95 (*0-393-32306-4*); 2001. 288p. 24.95 (*0-393-04762-8*) Norton, W. W. & Co., Inc.

—Pay Days: A Harpur & Iles Mystery. 2001. 256p. 24.00 (*0-393-04214-6*) Norton, W. W. & Co., Inc.

—Protection. 1992. (Detective Colin Harpur Novel Ser.). 188p. 18.95 o.p. (*0-88150-231-6*) Norton, W. W. & Co., Inc.

—Roses, Roses: A Harpur & Iles Mystery. (Harpur & Iles Ser.). 1999. 208p. pap. 7.95 (*0-393-31925-3*); 1998. 216p. 23.00 o.p. (*0-393-04637-0*) Norton, W. W. & Co., Inc.

—Take. 1994. (Harpur & Iles Ser.). 240p. reprint ed. 20.00 (*0-88150-294-4*, Foul Play) Norton, W. W. & Co., Inc.

—Top Banana: A Harpur & Iles Mystery. l.t. ed. 1999. (Core Ser.). 306p. 27.95 (*0-7838-8717-5*, Macmillan Reference USA) Gale Group.

—Top Banana: A Harpur & Iles Mystery. (Harpur & Iles Ser.). 2000. 288p. pap. 7.95 (*0-393-31969-5*, Norton Paperbacks); 1999. 284p. 23.00 o.p. (*0-393-04718-0*) Norton, W. W. & Co., Inc.

—You'd Better Believe It. 1991. (Detective Chief Superintendent Colin Harper Novels / By Bill Ser.). 158p. pap. 4.95 (*0-88150-197-2*, Foul Play) Norton, W. W. & Co., Inc.

—You'd Better Believe It. 1985. 192p. pap. 12.95 o.p. (*0-312-89683-2*) St. Martin's Pr.

**IMANISHI EITARO —FICTITIOUS CHARACTER)—FICTION**

Matsumoto, Seicho. Inspector Imanishi Investigates. 310p. 1994. pap. 13.00 (*1-56947-019-7*); 1990. pap. 9.95 o.p. (*0-939149-43-5*); 1989. 18.95 o.p. (*0-939149-28-1*) Soho Pr., Inc.

**INDERMILL, BONNIE (FICTITIOUS CHARACTER)—FICTION**

Berry, Carole. The Death of a Dancing Fool. 1996. (Orig.). mass mkt. 5.99 o.s.i (*0-425-15513-7*); 272p. 21.95 o.p. (*0-425-15143-3*, Prime Crime); 272p. pap. 9.00 o.p. (*0-425-15142-5*) Berkley Publishing Group.

—The Death of a Difficult Woman. 272p. 1995. mass mkt. 4.99 o.s.i (*0-425-15008-9*); 1994. 18.95 o.p. (*0-425-14356-2*) Berkley Publishing Group. (Prime Crime).

—The Death of a Dimpled Darling. 1997. 272p. mass mkt. 5.99 o.s.i (*0-425-16097-1*, Prime Crime) Berkley Publishing Group.

—Death of a Downsizer. 1999. (Bonnie Indermill Mystery Ser.). 272p. mass mkt. 5.99 o.s.i (*0-425-16614-7*, Prime Crime) Berkley Publishing Group.

—Good Night, Sweet Prince. 1995. 240p. mass mkt. 4.99 o.s.i (*0-425-14773-8*) Berkley Publishing Group.

—Good Night Sweet Prince. 1991. 256p. mass mkt. 3.95 o.s.i (*0-440-20784-3*) Dell Publishing.

—Island Girl. 1991. 256p. 18.95 o.p. (*0-312-06381-4*, Saint Martin's Minotaur) St. Martin's Pr.

—The Letter of the Law. 1990. 224p. mass mkt. 3.95 o.s.i (*0-440-20524-7*) Dell Publishing.

—The Letter of the Law. 1987. 208p. 15.95 o.p. (*0-312-01059-1*, Saint Martin's Minotaur) St. Martin's Pr.

—The Letter of the Law: Bonnie Indermill Mystery. 1995. 224p. mass mkt. 4.99 o.s.i (*0-425-15105-0*) Berkley Publishing Group.

—The Year of the Monkey. 1996. 256p. mass mkt. 5.50 o.s.i (*0-425-15184-0*) Berkley Publishing Group.

—The Year of the Monkey. 1990. 256p. reprint ed. mass mkt. 3.50 o.s.i (*0-440-20672-3*) Dell Publishing.

—The Year of the Monkey. 1988. 288p. 16.95 o.p. (*0-312-01850-9*, Saint Martin's Minotaur) St. Martin's Pr.

**INGOLD INGLORION (FICTITIOUS CHARACTER)—FICTION**

Hambly, Barbara. The Armies of Daylight. (Darwath Trilogy Ser.). 1997. mass mkt. 5.99 (*0-345-91172-5*); 1983. 309p. mass mkt. 5.99 o.s.i (*0-345-29671-0*) Ballantine Bks. (Del Rey).

—Icefalcon's Quest. 1995. 368p. pap. 19.00 (*0-345-47035-4*, Del Rey) Ballantine Bks.

—Mother of Winter. 1997. (Darwath Trilogy Ser.). 384p. mass mkt. 6.99 (*0-345-39723-1*, Del Rey) Ballantine Bks.

—The Time of the Dark. (Darwath Trilogy Ser.). 1997. mass mkt. 5.99 (*0-345-91168-7*); 1984. 272p. mass mkt. 5.99 o.s.i (*0-345-31965-6*) Ballantine Bks. (Del Rey).

—The Walls of Air. (Darwath Trilogy Ser.). (Orig.). 1997. mass mkt. 5.99 (*0-345-91170-9*); 1983. (Illus.). 297p. mass mkt. 5.99 o.s.i (*0-345-29670-2*) Ballantine Bks. (Del Rey).

**INNES, RACHEL (FICTITIOUS CHARACTER)—FICTION**

Rinehart, Mary Roberts. The Circular Staircase. Date not set. lib. bdg. 20.95 (*0-8488-2159-9*) Amereon, Ltd.

—The Circular Staircase. 1991. 368p. 4.95 o.p. (*0-88184-772-0*); 1985. 272p. pap. 3.50 o.p. (*0-88184-106-4*) Avalon Publishing Group. (Carroll & Graf Pubs.).

—The Circular Staircase. 1976. lib. bdg. 19.95 (*0-89968-181-6*, Lightyear Pr.) Buccaneer Bks., Inc.

—The Circular Staircase. E-Book 2.49 (*1-58627-657-3*) Electric Umbrella Publishing.

—The Circular Staircase. 1989. audio 32.00 Jimcin Recordings.

—The Circular Staircase. 1997. 288p. mass mkt. 5.50 o.s.i (*1-57566-180-2*); 1985. mass mkt. 3.95 o.s.i (*0-8217-3528-4*, Zebra Bks.); 1985. mass mkt. 3.50 o.p. (*0-8217-1723-5*, Zebra Bks.) Kensington Publishing Corp.

—Circular Staircase. 2004. 288p. mass mkt. 5.99 (*0-7582-0528-7*, Kensington Bks.) Kensington Publishing Corp.

—The Circular Staircase, Set. unabr. ed. 1989. audio 35.95 (*1-55685-151-0*) Audio Bk. Contractors, Inc.

—The Circular Staircase. unabr. ed. 1992. audio 44.95 (*0-7861-0619-0*, 2109) Blackstone Audio Bks., Inc.

—The Circular Staircase. unabr. ed. 1993. audio 39.95 (*1-55686-469-8*, 469) Books in Motion.

—The Circular Staircase. 1997. (Dover Mystery Classics Ser.). (Illus.). 160p. reprint ed. pap. text 2.00 (*0-486-29713-6*) Dover Pubns., Inc.

—The Circular Staircase. l.t. ed. 1980. lib. bdg. 13.95 o.p. (*0-8161-6641-2*, Macmillan Reference USA) Gale Group.

**INTERNATIONAL INVESTIGATION-RESCUE COMMITTEE (FICTITIOUS CHARACTERS)—FICTION**

Scott, Barbara A. Always in a Foreign Land. 1993. 410p. pap. 11.50 (*0-9637134-0-X*) Zenar Bks.

—Caught in the Web. 1996. 360p. (Orig.). pap. 12.50 (*0-9637134-1-8*) Zenar Bks.

**IQBAL, DETECTIVE (FICTITIOUS CHARACTER)—FICTION**

Bernard, Cheryl. Moghul Buffet. 1998. 208p. 22.00 o.p. (*0-374-21179-5*) Farrar, Straus & Giroux.

**ISAAC OF GIRONA (FICTITIOUS CHARACTER)—FICTION**

Roe, Caroline. An Antidote for Avarice. 1999. (Prime Crime Mysteries Ser.: 3). 288p. mass mkt. 6.50 o.s.i (*0-425-17260-0*, Prime Crime) Berkley Publishing Group.

—Cure for a Charlatan. 1999. (Chronicles of Issac of Girona Ser.: 2). 272p. mass mkt. 6.50 (*0-425-16734-8*, Prime Crime) Berkley Publishing Group.

—A Draught for a Dead Man. 336p. 2003. mass mkt. 6.50 (*0-425-19308-X*); 2002. (Illus.). 22.95 (*0-425-18648-2*, Prime Crime) Berkley Publishing Group.

—Remedy for Treason. 1998. (Chronicles of Issac of Girona Ser.: Vol. 1). 272p. mass mkt. 5.99 o.s.i (*0-425-16295-8*, Prime Crime) Berkley Publishing Group.

—Solace for a Sinner. 2000. (Isaac of Gerona Ser.). 288p. mass mkt. 6.50 o.s.i (*0-425-17776-9*, Prime Crime) Berkley Publishing Group.

**ISEN, MARK (FICTITIOUS CHARACTER)—FICTION**

Ruggero, Ed. The Common Defense. McCarthy, Paul, ed. 1992. 352p. 20.00 (*0-671-73008-8*, Atria); 432p. reprint ed. mass mkt. 5.99 (*0-671-73009-6*, Pocket) Simon & Schuster.

**IVES, HANNAH (FICTITIOUS CHARACTER)—FICTION**

Talley, Marcia. Sing It to Her Bones. l.t. ed. 2000. 27.95 (*1-57490-301-2*, Beeler Large Print Bks.) Beeler, Thomas T. Publisher.

—Sing It to Her Bones: A Hannah Ives Mystery. 1999. (Hannah Ives Mysteries Ser.). 304p. mass mkt. 5.99 (*0-440-23517-0*) Dell Publishing.

—Unbreathed Memories. l.t. ed. 2002. 26.95 (*1-57490-396-9*) Beeler, Thomas T. Publisher.

—Unbreathed Memories. 2000. (Hannah Ives Mysteries Ser.). 288p. mass mkt. 5.99 (*0-440-23518-9*) Dell Publishing.

**IVORY, KATE (FICTITIOUS CHARACTER)—FICTION**

Stallwood, Veronica. Death & the Oxford Box: A Mystery Introducing Kate Ivory. 1994. 224p. 20.00 o.p. (*0-684-19596-8*, Macmillan Reference USA) Gale Group.

—Deathspell. l.t. ed. 1994. 21.95 o.p. (*0-7927-1989-1*); pap. 19.95 o.p. (*0-7927-1988-3*) BBC Audiobooks America.

—Deathspell. 1992. 224p. text 20.00 (*0-684-19517-8*, Macmillan Reference USA) Gale Group.

—Oxford Exit. 1995. 192p. 20.00 o.s.i (*0-684-19729-4*, Scribner) Simon & Schuster.

—Oxford Mourning: A Kate Ivory Mystery. 1996. 208p. 20.00 o.p. (*0-684-19730-8*, Scribner) Simon & Schuster.

—Oxford Mourning: A Kate Ivory Mystery. l.t. ed. 1997. (Ulverscroft Large Print Ser.). 448p. 31.50 o.p. (*0-7089-3710-1*, Ulverscroft) Thorpe, F. A. Pubs. GBR. *Dist:* Ulverscroft Large Print Bks., Ltd., Ulverscroft Large Print Canada, Ltd.

**IVORY, MALCOLM (FICTITIOUS CHARACTER)—FICTION**

London, Mary. Un Crime Chinois. 1999. (FRE.). 288p. reprint ed. pap. 14.95 (*1-58348-148-6*) iUniverse, Inc.

—Le Crime Etrange de Greenwich: Une Enquetge de Sir Malcolm Ivory. 1999. (FRE.). 292p. reprint ed. pap. 14.95 (*1-58348-154-0*) iUniverse, Inc.

—La Double Mort de Thomas Stuart. Baudricourt, J. P., tr. 1999. (FRE., Illus.). 308p. reprint ed. pap. 14.95 (*1-58348-146-X*) iUniverse, Inc.

—Un Meurtre Chez les Francs-Macons. 1999. (FRE.). 220p. reprint ed. pap. 12.95 (*1-58348-153-2*) iUniverse, Inc.

—Sept Ladies pour un Meurtre: Une Enquete de Sir Malcolm Ivory. 1999. (FRE.). 208p. reprint ed. pap. 11.95 (*1-58348-149-4*) iUniverse, Inc.

# J

**JACK OF KINROWEN (FICTITIOUS CHARACTER)—FICTION**

De Lint, Charles. Drink down the Moon. 1990. mass mkt. 3.95 o.s.i (*0-441-16861-2*) Ace Bks.

—Jack the Giant Killer. 1990. mass mkt. 3.50 o.s.i (*0-441-37970-2*); 1987. 16.95 o.p. (*0-441-37969-9*) Ace Bks.

**JACK, SASSELA (FICTITIOUS CHARACTER)—FICTION**

James, Chris K. Fling with a Demon Lover. 1997. 256p. pap. 12.00 o.p. (*0-06-092827-1*, Perennial) HarperTrade.

**JACK, THE RIPPER—FICTION**

Andrews, Mark. The Return of Jack the Ripper. 1977. pap. 1.75 o.p. (*0-8439-0476-3*) Dorchester Publishing Co., Inc.

Ball, Nicholas. The Diary of Jack the Ripper. abr. ed. 1993. audio 16.95 o.p. (*1-55800-980-9*, Dove Audio) NewStar Media, Inc.

Borowitz, Albert. The Jack the Ripper Walking Tour Murder. 1986. 256p. 15.95 o.p. (*0-312-43944-X*) St. Martin's Pr.

Daniel, Mark. Jack the Ripper. 1988. 272p. mass mkt. 3.95 o.p. (*0-451-16018-5*, Signet Bks.) NAL.

Douglas, Carole Nelson. Castle Rouge: A Novel of Suspense Featuring Sherlock Holmes, Irene Adler, & Jack the Ripper. 2002. (Irene Adler Novel Ser.). (Illus.). 544p. 25.95 (*0-312-86941-X*, Forge Bks.) Doherty, Tom Assocs., LLC.

Dozois, Gardner. Ripper! 1988. 488p. mass mkt. 3.95 (*0-8125-1700-8*, Tor Bks.) Doherty, Tom Assocs., LLC.

Farjeon, Clanash. A Handbook for the Attendants on the Insane: The Autobiography of Jack the Ripper As Revealed to Clanash Farjeon. 2003. 332p. pap. (*1-55395-792-X*) Trafford Publishing.

Flowers, R. Barri. In the Dark of Night. 2001. 252p. pap. 14.95 (*0-595-17650-X*) iUniverse, Inc.

Geary, Rick. A Treasury of Victorian Murder. 1987. 64p. (Orig.). pap. 6.95 o.s.i (*0-918348-41-2*, Comics Lit) NBM Publishing Co.

—A Treasury of Victorian Murder Vol. 2: Jack the Ripper. 1995. (Treasury of Victorian Murder Ser.). (Illus.). 64p. 15.95 (*1-56163-124-8*, Comics Lit) NBM Publishing Co.

Gordon, Richard. Jack the Ripper. 1980. 9.95 o.p. (*0-689-11101-0*, Scribner) Simon & Schuster.

Moore, Alan. From Hell. 2002. (Illus.). 560p. pap. 35.00 (*0-9585783-4-6*) Campbell Comics, Eddie AUS. *Dist:* Top Shelf Productions.

—From Hell. Amara, Philip, ed. (Illus.). Vol. 1. 1994. 64p. reprint ed. pap. 4.95 (*0-87816-286-0*); Vol. 2. 1994. 64p. pap. 4.95 (*0-87816-287-9*); Vol. 3. 1993. 80p. reprint ed. pap. 4.95 (*0-87816-252-6*) Kitchen Sink Pr., Inc.

—From Hell, Vol. 4. Vance, James, ed. 1994. (Illus.). 48p. pap. 4.95 o.p. (*0-87816-270-4*) Kitchen Sink Pr., Inc.

—From Hell, Vol. 5. Amara, Philip & Campbell, Eddie, eds. 1994. (Illus.). 60p. pap. 4.95 o.p. (*0-87816-300-X*) Kitchen Sink Pr., Inc.

—From Hell, Vol. 8. Amara, Philip, ed. 1995. (Illus.). 58p. pap. 4.95 o.p. (*0-87816-360-3*) Kitchen Sink Pr., Inc.

—From Hell, Vol. 9. Amara, Philip & Couch, Chris, eds. 1996. (Illus.). 58p. pap. 4.95 o.p. (*0-87816-418-9*) Kitchen Sink Pr., Inc.

—From Hell, Vol. 10. 1997. pap. text 4.95 o.p. (*0-87816-506-1*); 1996. (Illus.). 48p. pap. 4.95 o.p. (*0-87816-438-3*) Kitchen Sink Pr., Inc.

Price, Vincent & Lewis, Cathy. The Lodger: Story of Jack the Ripper. audio National Recording Co.

Queen, Ellery. A Study in Terror. l.t. ed. 2001. 192p. (*0-7540-4586-2*); (*0-7540-4585-4*) Gale Group. (Macmillan Reference USA).

Thor, Raymond. Bloodguilty. 1997. Orig. Title: Blood Guilty. 256p. 23.95 (*0-9658727-7-7*) Danger Publishing.

—Bloodguilty: The Crime of Two Centuries. 256p. 2002. E-Book 5.50 (*0-9658727-5-0*); 1998. pap. 14.95 (*0-9658727-6-9*) Danger Publishing.

West, Pamela. Yours Truly, Jack the Ripper. 1989. (YA). reprint ed. mass mkt. 3.50 o.s.i (*0-440-20259-0*) Dell Publishing.

—Yours Truly, Jack the Ripper. 1987. 320p. 17.95 o.p. (*0-312-00868-6*, Saint Martin's Minotaur) St. Martin's Pr.

West, Paul. The Women of Whitechapel & Jack the Ripper. 1992. 428p. pap. 14.95 (*0-87951-478-7*) Overlook Pr., The.

**JACKSON, JACKO (FICTITIOUS CHARACTER)—FICTION**

Palmer, Frank. Bent Grasses: An Inspector "Jacko" Jackson Mystery. 1994. 191p. 18.95 o.p. (*0-312-11752-3*, Saint Martin's Minotaur) St. Martin's Pr.

—Blood Brother. l.t. ed. 1995. 282p. pap. 20.95 o.p. (*0-7838-1544-1*, Macmillan Reference USA) Gale Group.

—Blood Brother: An Inspector "Jacko" Jackson Mystery. 1995. 192p. 19.95 o.p. (*0-312-13435-5*, Saint Martin's Minotaur) St. Martin's Pr.

—Nightwatch. 1996. 208p. 20.95 o.p. (*0-312-14381-8*, Saint Martin's Minotaur) St. Martin's Pr.

**JACKSON, JEFF (FICTITIOUS CHARACTER)—FICTION**

Craig, Philip R. A Beautiful Place to Die: A Martha's Vineyard Mystery. 1989. 224p. 18.95 o.s.i (*0-684-19122-9*, Macmillan Reference USA) Gale Group.

—A Beautiful Place to Die: A Martha's Vineyard Mystery. 1991. 224p. mass mkt. 6.99 (*0-380-71155-9*, Avon Bks.) Morrow/Avon.

—A Case of Vineyard Poison. 1996. 224p. mass mkt. 5.99 (*0-380-72679-3*, Avon Bks.) Morrow/Avon.

—A Case of Vineyard Poison: A Martha's Vineyard Mystery. 1995. 253p. 20.00 o.p. (*0-684-19616-6*, Scribner) Simon & Schuster.

—Cliff Hanger: A Martha's Vineyard Mystery. 1993. 256p. 20.00 o.p. (*0-684-19552-6*, Macmillan Reference USA) Gale Group.

—Cliff Hanger: A Martha's Vineyard Mystery. 1994. 224p. mass mkt. 4.99 (*0-380-72240-2*, Avon Bks.) Morrow/Avon.

—A Deadly Vineyard Holiday. 1998. (Martha's Vineyard Mysteries Ser.). 240p. mass mkt. 6.50 (*0-380-73110-X*, Avon Bks.) Morrow/Avon.

—A Deadly Vineyard Holiday: A Martha's Vineyard Mystery. 1997. 282p. 20.50 (*0-684-19718-9*, Scribner) Simon & Schuster.

—A Deadly Vineyard Holiday: A Martha's Vineyard Mystery. l.t. ed. 1997. (Core Ser.). 344p. lib. bdg. 26.95 (*0-7838-8278-5*) Thorndike Pr.

—Death on a Vineyard Beach. 1997. 224p. mass mkt. 6.50 (*0-380-72873-7*, Avon Bks.) Morrow/Avon.

—Death on a Vineyard Beach: A Martha's Vineyard Mystery. 1996. 288p. 21.00 o.p. (*0-684-19717-0*, Scribner) Simon & Schuster.

—The Double Minded Men: A Martha's Vineyard Mystery. 1992. (Martha's Vineyard Mystery Ser.: No. 3). 256p. text 20.00 (*0-684-19396-5*, Macmillan Reference USA) Gale Group.

—The Double Minded Men: A Martha's Vineyard Mystery. 1993. 256p. pap. 4.99 (*0-380-71973-8*, Avon Bks.) Morrow/Avon.

—A Fatal Vineyard Season. 2000. (Martha's Vineyard Mysteries Ser.). 224p. mass mkt. 5.99 (*0-380-73289-0*, Avon Bks.) Morrow/Avon.

—A Fatal Vineyard Season: A Martha's Vineyard Mystery. 1999. (Martha's Vineyard Mysteries Ser.). (Illus.). 224p. 22.00 o.s.i (*0-684-85544-5*, Scribner) Simon & Schuster.

—A Fatal Vineyard Season: A Martha's Vineyard Mystery. l.t. ed. 1999. (Mystery Ser.). (Illus.). 324p. 28.95 (*0-7862-2207-7*) Thorndike Pr.

—Off Season. 1996. (Martha's Vineyard Ser.: No. 5). 224p. mass mkt. 5.99 (*0-380-72588-6*, Avon Bks.) Morrow/Avon.

—Off Season: A Martha's Vineyard Mystery. 1994. 256p. 20.00 (*0-684-19617-4*, Macmillan Reference USA) Gale Group.

—A Shoot on Martha's Vineyard. 1999. (Martha's Vineyard Mysteries Ser.). 256p. mass mkt. 5.99 (*0-380-73201-7*, Avon Bks.) Morrow/Avon.

—Shoot on Martha's Vineyard: A Martha's Vineyard Mystery. 1998. (Martha's Vineyard Mysteries Ser.). 288p. 22.00 (*0-684-83454-5*, Scribner) Simon & Schuster.

—A Shoot on Martha's Vineyard: A Martha's Vineyard Mystery. l.t. ed. 1999. (Mystery Ser.). 427p. 27.95 (*0-7862-1614-X*) Thorndike Pr.

—Vineyard Blues: A Martha's Vineyard Mystery. 2001. 224p. mass mkt. 5.99 (*0-380-81859-0*, Avon Bks.) Morrow/Avon.

—Vineyard Blues: A Martha's Vineyard Mystery. 2000. (Martha's Vineyard Mysteries Ser.). (Illus.). 224p. 23.00 o.s.i (*0-684-83455-3*, Scribner) Simon & Schuster.

—Vineyard Blues: A Martha's Vineyard Mystery. l.t. ed. 2000. (Mystery Ser.). (Illus.). 339p. 29.95 (*0-7862-2591-2*) Thorndike Pr.

—Vineyard Enigma: A Martha Vineyard Mystery. 2002. (Illus.). 256p. 24.00 (*0-7432-0523-5*, Scribner) Simon & Schuster.

—A Vineyard Killing: A Martha's Vineyard Mystery. 2003. (Illus.). 240p. 24.00 (*0-7432-0524-3*, Scribner) Simon & Schuster.

—Vineyard Shadows. 2001. (Martha's Vineyard Mysteries Ser.). 256p. 24.00 o.s.i (*0-684-85545-3*, Scribner) Simon & Schuster.

—Vineyard Shadows: A Martha's Vineyard Mystery. 2002. 256p. mass mkt. 6.50 (*0-380-82099-4*) Morrow/Avon.

—Vineyard Shadows: A Martha's Vineyard Mystery. l.t. ed. 2001. 334p. 29.95 (*0-7862-3646-9*) Thorndike Pr.

—The Woman Who Walked into the Sea: A Martha's Vineyard Mystery. 1993. 224p. reprint ed. mass mkt. 4.99 (*0-380-71536-8*, Avon Bks.) Morrow/Avon.

—The Woman Who Walked into the Sea: A Martha's Vineyard Mystery. 1991. 224p. 17.95 o.s.i (*0-684-19228-4*, Scribner) Simon & Schuster.

Craig, Philip R. & Tapply, William G. First Light. l.t. ed. 2002. 443p. 29.95 (*0-7862-4185-3*) Gale Group.

—First Light: The First Ever Brady Coyne/J. W. Jackson Novel. 2002. 352p. E-Book 24.00 (*0-7432-3484-7*); 24.00 (*0-7432-2208-3*) Simon & Schuster. (Scribner).

**JACKSON, KEN (FICTITIOUS CHARACTER)—FICTION**

Fraser, Anthea. The April Rainers. 1990. 14.95 o.s.i (*0-385-41088-3*) Doubleday Publishing.

—Death Speaks Softly. 1987. (Crime Club Ser.). 192p. 12.95 o.s.i (*0-385-24147-X*) Doubleday Publishing.

—Death Speaks Softly. l.t. ed. 1988. 336p. (*0-7089-1846-8*, Ulverscroft) Thorpe, F. A. Pubs.

—The Gospel Makers. 1994. 224p. 14.99 (*0-00-232490-3*) HarperSanFrancisco.

—The Gospel Makers. 1996. 208p. 20.95 o.p. (*0-312-13979-9*, Saint Martin's Minotaur) St. Martin's Pr.

—Home Through the Dark. 2000. 21.95 (*0-7540-8575-9*, Black Dagger) BBC Audiobooks America.

—Home Through the Dark. l.t. ed. 2002. (Dales Large Print Ser.). 304p. pap. 21.99 o.p. (*1-84262-204-8*) Dales Large Print Bks. GBR. *Dist:* Ulverscroft Large Print Bks., Ltd., Ulverscroft Large Print Canada, Ltd.

—Home Through the Dark. 1977. (General Ser.). lib. bdg. 10.95 o.p. (*0-8161-6442-8*, Macmillan Reference USA) Gale Group.

—A Necessary End. 1986. 192p. 13.95 o.s.i (*0-8027-5641-7*) Walker & Co.

—The Nine Bright Shiners. 1988. (Crime Club Ser.). 192p. pap. 12.95 o.s.i (*0-385-24323-5*) Doubleday Publishing.

—The Nine Bright Shiners. l.t. ed. 1990. (Ulverscroft Large Print Ser.). 29.99 o.p. (*0-7089-2173-6*, Ulverscroft) Thorpe, F. A. Pubs. GBR. *Dist:* Ulverscroft Large Print Bks., Ltd., Ulverscroft Large Print Canada, Ltd.

—One Is One & All Alone. 1998. 192p. 20.95 (*0-312-19309-2*, Saint Martin's Minotaur) St. Martin's Pr.

—Pretty Maids All in a Row. l.t. ed. 2001. (Dales Large Print Ser.). 272p. pap. 21.99 (*1-84262-075-4*) Dales Large Print Bks. GBR. *Dist:* Ulverscroft Large Print Bks., Ltd., Ulverscroft Large Print Canada, Ltd.

—Pretty Maids All in a Row. 1987. (Crime Club Ser.). 192p. 12.95 o.s.i (*0-385-23798-7*) Doubleday Publishing.

—Pretty Maids All in a Row. l.t. ed. 1987. (Ulverscroft Large Print Ser.). 336p. o.p. (*0-7089-1624-4*, Ulverscroft) Thorpe, F. A. Pubs. GBR. *Dist:* Ulverscroft Large Print Canada, Ltd.

—The Seven Stars. 1997. 224p. 20.95 o.p. (*0-312-15650-2*, Saint Martin's Minotaur) St. Martin's Pr.

—A Shroud for Delilah. 1986. (Crime Club Ser.). 192p. 12.95 o.p. (*0-385-23543-7*) Doubleday Publishing.

—A Shroud for Delilah. l.t. ed. 1985. 368p. 15.95 o.p. (*0-7089-1377-6*, Ulverscroft) Thorpe, F. A. Pubs. GBR. *Dist:* Ulverscroft Large Print Bks., Ltd.

—Six Proud Walkers. 1989. (Crime Club Ser.). 12.95 o.s.i (*0-385-24615-3*) Doubleday Publishing.

—Six Proud Walkers. l.t. ed. 1989. (Ulverscroft Large Print Ser.). 29.99 o.p. (*0-7089-2181-7*, Ulverscroft) Thorpe, F. A. Pubs. GBR. *Dist:* Ulverscroft Large Print Bks., Ltd., Ulverscroft Large Print Canada, Ltd.

—Symbols at Your Door. 1991. 192p. 15.00 o.s.i (*0-385-41685-7*) Doubleday Publishing.

—The Ten Commandments. unabr. ed. 1998. audio 49.95 (*0-7540-0172-5*, CAB 1595) Chivers Audio Bks. GBR. *Dist:* BBC Audiobooks America.

—The Ten Commandments. 2000. (DCI Webb Mysteries Ser.). 190p. 22.95 (*0-312-20915-0*); 192p. text 20.95 (*0-312-18672-X*) St. Martin's Pr. (Saint Martin's Minotaur).

—The Ten Commandments. l.t. ed. 2000. 279p. (*0-7540-4070-4*); (*0-7540-4071-2*) Thorndike Pr.

—Three, Three, the Rivals. 1992. 13.99 (*0-00-232380-X*) HarperSanFrancisco.

—Three, Three, the Rivals. 1995. 188p. 18.95 o.p. (*0-312-11902-X*, Saint Martin's Minotaur) St. Martin's Pr.

—Three, Three, the Rivals. l.t. ed. 1993. (Mystery Ser.). 368p. 29.99 o.p. (*0-7089-2984-2*, Ulverscroft) Thorpe, F. A. Pubs. GBR. *Dist:* Ulverscroft Large Print Bks., Ltd., Ulverscroft Large Print Canada, Ltd.

**JACOB, MATT (FICTITIOUS CHARACTER)—FICTION**

Klein, Zachery. Two Way Toll. 1993. (Boston Mysteries Ser.). mass mkt. 4.99 o.s.i (*0-8041-1005-0*, Ivy Bks.) Ballantine Bks.

**JACOBS, CALISTA (FICTITIOUS CHARACTER)—FICTION**

Knight, Kathryn L. Dark Swan. 1996. (WWL Mystery Ser.). per. (*0-373-26203-5*, 1-26203-9, Worldwide Library) Harlequin Enterprises, Ltd.

—Dark Swan. 1994. 224p. 19.95 o.p. (*0-312-10961-X*, Saint Martin's Minotaur) St. Martin's Pr.

—Mortal Words. 1990. 17.95 o.p. (*0-671-68446-9*, Simon & Schuster) Simon & Schuster.

—Mortal Words. Chelius, Jane, ed. 1991. 352p. reprint ed. mass mkt. 4.50 (*0-671-68449-3*, Pocket) Simon & Schuster.

—Mumbo Jumbo. 1991. 17.95 o.p. (*0-671-68448-5*, Simon & Schuster) Simon & Schuster.

—Mumbo Jumbo. Chelius, Jane, ed. 1992. 224p. reprint ed. mass mkt. 4.99 (*0-671-68447-7*, Pocket) Simon & Schuster.

—Trace Elements. 1986. 15.95 o.p. (*0-393-02333-8*) Norton, W. W. & Co., Inc.

—Trace Elements. 1987. mass mkt. 3.50 (*0-671-64089-5*, Pocket) Simon & Schuster.

**JACOBS, CHARLEY (FICTITIOUS CHARACTER)—FICTION**

Knight, Kathryn L. Mumbo Jumbo. 1991. 17.95 o.p. (*0-671-68448-5*, Simon & Schuster) Simon & Schuster.

—Mumbo Jumbo. Chelius, Jane, ed. 1992. 224p. reprint ed. mass mkt. 4.99 (*0-671-68447-7*, Pocket) Simon & Schuster.

**JACOBS, PETER (FICTITIOUS CHARACTER)—FICTION**

Pike, Christopher, pseud. The Cold One. 1995. 394p. pap. text 5.99 o.s.i (*0-8125-1245-6*); 1994. 352p. 21.00 o.p. (*0-312-85117-0*) Doherty, Tom Assocs., LLC. (Tor Bks.).

**JACOBY, MILES (FICTITIOUS CHARACTER)—FICTION**

Randisi, Robert J. Eye in the Ring. 1986. 256p. pap. 2.75 o.p. (*0-380-81455-2*, 81455-2, Avon Bks.) Morrow/Avon.

—Full Contact: A Miles Jacoby Mystery. l.t. ed. 1988. pap. 14.95 o.p. (*1-55504-699-1*, 827) BBC Audiobooks America.

—Full Contact: A Miles Jacoby Mystery. 2000. mass mkt. 2.95 (*0-380-69984-2*, Avon Bks.) Morrow/Avon.

—Full Contact: A Miles Jacoby Mystery. 1984. 256p. 13.95 o.p. (*0-312-30966-X*) St. Martin's Pr.

—Hard Look: A Miles Jacoby Mystery. 1993. (Miles Jacoby Mystery Ser.). 252p. 21.00 o.s.i (*0-8027-1251-7*) Walker & Co.

—Separate Cases. 1990. 192p. 18.95 (*0-8027-5723-5*) Walker & Co.

—Stand-Up: A Miles Jacoby Mystery. 1994. 246p. 20.95 o.p. (*0-8027-3196-1*) Walker & Co.

—The Steinway Collection. 1986. 272p. pap. 2.75 o.p. (*0-380-85175-X*, 85175, Avon Bks.) Morrow/Avon.

**JACOBY, PAMELA (FICTITIOUS CHARACTER)—FICTION**

Gruenfeld, Lee. Irreparable Harm. 388p. 4.98 o.p. (*0-8317-7883-0*) Smithmark Pubs., Inc.

—Irreparable Harm. 1994. 432p. mass mkt. 5.99 o.s.i (*0-446-60059-8*); 1993. 400p. 18.95 o.s.i (*0-446-51713-5*) Warner Bks., Inc.

**JACOVICH, MILAN (FICTITIOUS CHARACTER)—FICTION**

Roberts, Les. The Best-Kept Secret. (Milan Jacovich Mysteries Ser.). 2000. 311p. mass mkt. 5.99 (*0-312-97126-5*, St. Martin's Paperbacks); 1999. 308p. 23.95 (*0-312-20499-X*, Saint Martin's Minotaur) St. Martin's Pr.

—The Cleveland Connection. (Milan Jacovich Mysteries Ser.). 1997. 336p. mass mkt. 5.99 o.s.i (*0-312-96218-5*, St. Martin's Paperbacks); 1993. 294p. 19.95 (*0-312-08746-2*, Saint Martin's Minotaur) St. Martin's Pr.

—Cleveland Local. 1998. (Milan Jacovich Mysteries Ser.). 288p. mass mkt. 5.99 (*0-312-96678-4*, St. Martin's Paperbacks) St. Martin's Pr.

—The Cleveland Local. 1997. (Milan Jacovich Mysteries Ser.). 288p. 22.95 o.p. (*0-312-16801-2*, Saint Martin's Minotaur) St. Martin's Pr.

—Collision Bend. (Milan Jacovich Mysteries Ser.). 1997. 288p. mass mkt. 5.99 (*0-312-96399-8*, St. Martin's Paperbacks); 1996. 320p. 22.95 o.p. (*0-312-14570-5*, Saint Martin's Minotaur) St. Martin's Pr.

—Deep Shaker. 1992. mass mkt. 3.99 (*0-312-92795-9*, St. Martin's Paperbacks); 1991. 17.95 o.p. (*0-312-05855-1*, Saint Martin's Minotaur) St. Martin's Pr.

—The Duke of Cleveland. 2002. 240p. mass mkt. 6.50 (*0-312-98366-2*, St. Martin's Paperbacks) St. Martin's Pr.

—The Duke of Cleveland: A Milan Jacovich Mystery. 1995. 272p. 21.95 o.p. (*0-312-13473-8*, Saint Martin's Minotaur) St. Martin's Pr.

—The Dutch. l.t. ed. 2002. 28.95 (*0-7862-4096-2*) Gale Group.

—The Dutch. mass mkt. (*0-312-98028-0*, St. Martin's Paperbacks); 2001. 293p. 23.95 (*0-312-26579-4*, Saint Martin's Minotaur) St. Martin's Pr.

—Full Cleveland. 1990. mass mkt. 3.95 (*0-312-92345-7*, St. Martin's Paperbacks); 1989. 224p. 15.95 o.p. (*0-312-03349-4*, Saint Martin's Minotaur) St. Martin's Pr.

—Full Cleveland: A Milan Jacovich Mystery. 1991. 2.99 o.p. (*0-517-07803-1*) Random Hse. Value Publishing.

—The Indian Sign. E-Book 23.95 (*0-312-27594-3*); 2001. 304p. mass mkt. 6.50 (*0-312-97646-1*, St. Martin's Paperbacks); 2000. 274p. 23.95 (*0-312-25217-X*, Saint Martin's Minotaur) St. Martin's Pr.

—Irish Sports Pages. mass mkt. (*0-312-98380-8*, St. Martin's Paperbacks); 2002. 304p. 23.95 (*0-312-28661-9*, Saint Martin's Minotaur) St. Martin's Pr.

—The Lake Effect: A Milan Jacovich Mystery. 1994. 352p. 21.95 (*0-312-11537-7*, Saint Martin's Minotaur) St. Martin's Pr.

—Pepper Pike. (Milan Jacovich Mysteries Ser.). 1988. 240p. 15.95 o.p. (*0-312-02266-2*, Saint Martin's Minotaur); Vol. 1. 1990. 232p. mass mkt. 5.99 o.s.i (*0-312-92213-2*, St. Martin's Paperbacks) St. Martin's Pr.

—A Shoot in Cleveland. (Milan Jacovich Mysteries Ser.). 1999. 336p. mass mkt. 5.99 (*0-312-96694-6*, St. Martin's Paperbacks); 1999. E-Book 5.99 o.s.i (*0-312-20742-5*); 1998. 368p. 23.95 o.p. (*0-312-18663-0*, Saint Martin's Minotaur) St. Martin's Pr.

**JACOWICZ, ISADORA 'JAKE' (FICTITIOUS CHARACTER)—FICTION**

Kerr, Philip. A Philosophical Investigation. 1995. 384p. mass mkt. 8.99 o.s.i (*0-7704-2592-5*) Bantam Bks.

—A Philosophical Investigation. 1994. 336p. pap. 14.00 o.s.i (*0-452-27140-1*, Plume) Dutton/Plume.

—A Philosophical Investigation. 1993. 329p. 20.00 o.p. (*0-374-23176-1*) Farrar, Straus & Giroux.

**JADE, MARA (FICTITIOUS CHARACTER)—FICTION**

Baron, Mike, et al. Dark Force Rising. 1998. (Star Wars Ser.). (Illus.). 160p. (YA). (gr. 7 up). pap. 17.95 (*1-56971-269-7*) Dark Horse Comics.

Lucasfilm Ltd. Staff. The Last Command. unabr. ed. 1996. (Star Wars: Bk. 3). audio 104.00. audio Books on Tape, Inc.

Salvatore, R. A. Vector Prime. (Star Wars Ser.). 2003. E-Book 2.99 (*0-345-46740-X*, Ballantine Bks.); 2000. 416p. mass mkt. 7.50 (*0-345-42845-5*); 1999. 400p. 24.95 (*0-345-42844-7*) Ballantine Bks.

—Vector Prime. abr. ed. 1999. (Star Wars: Bk. 1). audio 18.00 (*0-375-40689-1*, RH Audio) Random Hse. Audio Publishing Group.

Schweighofer, Peter. Tales from the Empire: Stories from Star Wars Adventure Journal. 1997. (Star Wars Ser.). 368p. mass mkt. 6.99 (*0-553-57876-6*) Bantam Bks.

Stackpole, Michael A. I, Jedi. abr. ed. 1998. (Star Wars Ser.). audio 16.99 (*0-553-47948-2*, 391211, RH Audio) Random Hse. Audio Publishing Group.

—I, Jedi: Star Wars. 1999. (Star Wars Ser.). 608p. mass mkt. 6.99 (*0-553-57873-1*) Broadway Bks.

Stackpole, Michael A., et al. The Union. 2000. (Star Wars Ser.). (Illus.). 96p. (J). (gr. 7 up). pap. 12.95 (*1-56971-464-9*) Dark Horse Comics.

Zahn, Timothy. Dark Force Rising. (Star Wars: Bk. 2). 1993. 448p. mass mkt. 6.99 (*0-553-56071-9*); 1992. 368p. 18.50 o.s.i (*0-553-08574-3*); Vol. 2. 1992. 384p. 125.00 o.s.i (*0-553-08907-2*, Spectra) Bantam Bks.

—Dark Force Rising. unabr. ed. 1995. (Star Wars: Bk. 2). audio 96.00 Books on Tape, Inc.

—Dark Force Rising. abr. ed. 1992. (Star Wars: Bk. 2). audio 16.99 (*0-553-47055-8*, RH Audio) Random Hse. Audio Publishing Group.

—Heir to the Empire. (Star Wars: Bk. 1). 9999. pap. 9.90 o.s.i (*0-593-02481-8*); 1992. 432p. mass mkt. 6.99 (*0-553-29612-4*); 1991. 368p. 22.95 o.s.i (*0-553-07327-3*); 1991. 368p. 125.00 o.s.i (*0-553-07340-0*, Spectra) Bantam Bks.

—Heir to the Empire. unabr. ed. 1995. (Star Wars: Bk. 1). audio 88.00 Books on Tape, Inc.

—Heir to the Empire. abr. ed. 1991. (Star Wars: Bk. 1). audio 16.99 (*0-553-45296-7*, 391663, RH Audio) Random Hse. Audio Publishing Group.

—Heir to the Empire. 1993. (Star Wars: Bk. 1). 64.95 o.p. incl. audio (*0-7838-1100-4*); 64.95 o.p. incl. audio (*0-7838-1100-4*) Thorndike Pr.

—Heir to the Empire. 1991. (Star Wars: Bk. 1). 12.04 (*0-606-00751-2*) Turtleback Bks.

—The Last Command. (Star Wars: Bk. 3). 1994. 496p. mass mkt. 6.99 (*0-553-56492-7*, Spectra); 1993. 416p. 125.00 o.s.i (*0-553-09500-5*) Bantam Bks.

—The Last Command. abr. ed. 1993. (Star Wars: Bk. 3). audio 16.99 (*0-553-47157-0*, RH Audio) Random Hse. Audio Publishing Group.

—The Last Command. 1994. (Star Wars: Bk. 3). 12.04 (*0-606-08205-0*) Turtleback Bks.

—Specter of the Past. 1998. (Star Wars Hand of Thrawn Ser.: No. 1). 416p. (gr. 5 up). mass mkt. 6.99 (*0-553-29804-6*) Bantam Bks.

—Specter of the Past. abr. ed. 1997. (Star Wars Ser.: Vol. 1). (gr. 5 up). audio 16.99 (*0-553-47893-1*, RH Audio) Random Hse. Audio Publishing Group.

—Specter of the Past. l.t. ed. 1998. (Star Wars). 512p. 25.95 (*0-7838-8434-6*) Thorndike Pr.

—The Thrawn Trilogy. abr. ed. 2000. (Star Wars: Bk. 1,2,3). 29.95 incl. audio (*0-553-52699-5*);Set. (YA). 29.95 incl. audio Random Hse. Audio Publishing Group.

—Vision of the Future. 1999. (Star Wars Hand of Thrawn Ser.: No. 2). 720p. (gr. 5 up). mass mkt. 6.99 (*0-553-57879-0*) Bantam Bks.

—Vision of the Future. abr. ed. 1998. (Star Wars Ser.: Vol. 2). (gr. 5 up). audio 16.99 (*0-553-47921-0*, 392221, RH Audio) Random Hse. Audio Publishing Group.

Zahn, Timothy, et al. Heir to the Empire. 1996. (Star Wars Ser.). (Illus.). 160p. (YA). (gr. 7 up). pap. 19.95 (*1-56971-202-6*) Dark Horse Comics.

**JAELLYN (FICTITIOUS CHARACTER: LOGSTON)—FICTION**

Logston, Anne. Dagger's Edge. 1994. 240p. (Orig.). mass mkt. 4.99 o.s.i (*0-441-00036-3*) Ace Bks.

—Dagger's Point. 1995. 272p. (Orig.). mass mkt. 4.99 o.s.i (*0-441-00134-3*) Ace Bks.

**JAENELLE (FICTITIOUS CHARACTER)—FICTION**

Bishop, Anne. Daughter of the Blood. 1998. (Black Jewels Trilogy Ser.: 1). 416p. mass mkt. 6.99 (*0-451-45671-8*, ROC) NAL.

—Heir to the Shadows. 1999. (Black Jewels Trilogy Ser.: 2). 496p. mass mkt. 6.99 (*0-451-45672-6*) NAL.

—Queen of the Darkness, Vol. 3. 2000. (Black Jewels Trilogy Ser.: Vol. 3). 448p. (J). mass mkt. 6.99 (*0-451-45673-4*, ROC) NAL.

**JAKE (FICTITIOUS CHARACTER: CLEARY)—FICTION**

Cleary, Melissa. And Your Little Dog, Too. 1998. (Dog Lover's Mysteries Ser.). 208p. mass mkt. 5.99 o.s.i (*0-425-16242-7*, Prime Crime) Berkley Publishing Group.

—Dead & Buried. 1994. 208p. (Orig.). mass mkt. 4.99 o.s.i (*0-425-14547-6*, Prime Crime) Berkley Publishing Group.

—Dog Collar Crime. 1993. 192p. (Orig.). 3.99 o.s.i (*1-55773-896-3*, Diamond Bks.) Ace Bks.

—A Dog Collar Crime. 1994. (Orig.). mass mkt. 4.99 o.s.i (*0-425-14857-2*, Prime Crime) Berkley Publishing Group.

—First Pedigree Murder: A Dog Lover's Mystery. 1994. 208p. (Orig.). mass mkt. 4.99 o.s.i (*0-425-14299-X*, Prime Crime) Berkley Publishing Group.

—Hounded to Death. 1993. 192p. mass mkt. 4.99 o.s.i (*0-425-14324-4*) Berkley Publishing Group.

—The Maltese Puppy. 1995. 256p. (Orig.). mass mkt. 4.99 o.s.i (*0-425-14721-5*, Prime Crime) Berkley Publishing Group.

—A Murder Most Beastly. 1996. 208p. (Orig.). mass mkt. 4.99 o.s.i (*0-425-15139-5*) Berkley Publishing Group.

—Old Dogs. 1997. (Dog Lover's Mysteries Ser.). 224p. mass mkt. 5.99 o.s.i (*0-425-15858-6*, Prime Crime) Berkley Publishing Group.

—Skull & Dog Bones. 1994. (Orig.). mass mkt. 4.99 o.s.i (*0-425-14541-7*); 208p. mass mkt. 4.50 o.s.i (*0-515-11279-8*, Jove) Berkley Publishing Group.

—Tail of Two Murders. 1993. 192p. (Orig.). mass mkt. 4.99 o.s.i (*0-425-15809-8*, Prime Crime) Berkley Publishing Group.

Cleary, Melissa & Jove Publications Staff. Hounded to Death. 1993. (Dog Lover's Mysteries Ser.). 184p. mass mkt. 3.99 o.s.i (*0-515-11190-2*, Jove) Berkley Publishing Group.

Minear, Lola F. In the Dog House: A Collection of Short Stories. 1981. 47p. 6.95 o.p. (*0-533-04878-8*) Vantage Pr., Inc.

**JAMES, CASSIDY (FICTITIOUS CHARACTER)—FICTION**

Calloway, Kate. Fifth Wheel: A Cassidy James Mystery. 1998. (Cassidy James Mysteries Ser.: No. 5). 256p. pap. 11.95 (*1-56280-218-6*) Naiad Pr., Inc.

—First Impressions: A Cassidy James Mystery. 1996. (Cassidy James Mysteries Ser.). 208p. (Orig.). pap. 11.95 (*1-56280-133-3*) Naiad Pr., Inc.

—Fourth Down: A Cassidy James Mystery. 1998. (Cassidy James Mysteries Ser.). 240p. (Orig.). pap. 11.95 (*1-56280-193-7*) Naiad Pr., Inc.

—Second Fiddle: A Cassidy James Mystery. 1996. (Cassidy James Mysteries Ser.). 224p. (Orig.). pap. 11.95 (*1-56280-161-9*) Naiad Pr., Inc.

—Seventh Heaven: A Cassidy James Mystery. 1999. (Cassidy James Mysteries Ser.). 230p. pap. 11.95 (*1-56280-262-3*) Naiad Pr., Inc.

—Sixth Sense: A Cassidy James Mystery. 1999. (Cassidy James Mysteries Ser.). 215p. pap. 11.95 (*1-56280-228-3*) Naiad Pr., Inc.

—Third Degree: A Cassidy James Mystery. 1997. (Cassidy James Mysteries Ser.). 256p. (Orig.). pap. 11.95 (*1-56280-185-6*) Naiad Pr., Inc.

—8th Day: A Cassidy James Mystery. 2001. 240p. pap. 12.95 (*1-931513-04-X*) Bella Bks., Inc.

**JAMES, DEWEY (FICTITIOUS CHARACTER)—FICTION**

Morgan, Kate. Days of Crime & Roses. 1992. 192p. (Orig.). mass mkt. 3.99 o.p. (*0-425-13471-7*) Berkley Publishing Group.

—Home Sweet Homicide. 1991. mass mkt. 3.95 o.p. (*0-425-12895-4*) Berkley Publishing Group.

—Murder Most Fowl. 1991. mass mkt. 3.50 o.p. (*0-425-12610-2*) Berkley Publishing Group.

—Mystery Loves Company. 1992. mass mkt. 3.99 o.p. (*0-425-13237-4*) Berkley Publishing Group.

—The Old School Dies. 1996. 240p. (Orig.). mass mkt. 5.99 o.s.i (*0-425-15552-8*, Prime Crime) Berkley Publishing Group.

—Slay at the Races. 1990. mass mkt. 3.50 o.p. (*0-425-12166-6*) Berkley Publishing Group.

—Wanted: Dude or Alive. 1994. 208p. (Orig.). mass mkt. 4.50 o.p. (*0-425-14330-9*, Prime Crime) Berkley Publishing Group.

**JAMES, DUKE (FICTITIOUS CHARACTER)—FICTION**

Rizzi, Timothy. The Phalanx Dragon. 2000. 480p. reprint ed. pap. 6.99 (*0-8439-3885-4*, Leisure Bks.) Dorchester Publishing Co., Inc.

—The Phalanx Dragon. 1994. (Illus.). 432p. 21.95 o.p. (*1-55611-391-9*) Fine, Donald I. Bks.

—The Phalanx Dragon. 1995. E-Book 9.95 (*0-585-29807-6*) netLibrary, Inc.

**JAMES, GEMMA (FICTITIOUS CHARACTER)—FICTION**

Crombie, Deborah. All Shall Be Well. 1995. 272p. mass mkt. 6.99 (*0-425-14771-1*) Berkley Publishing Group.

—All Shall Be Well. 2004. 288p. mass mkt. 6.99 (*0-06-053439-7*, Avon Bks.) Morrow/Avon.

—All Shall Be Well: A Superintendent Duncan Kincaid - Sergeant Gemma James Mystery. 1994. 256p. text 20.00 (*0-684-19654-9*, Macmillan Reference USA) Gale Group.

—And Justice There is None. 2002. E-Book 19.50 (*0-553-89707-1*) Bantam Bks.

—And Justice There Is None. 2003. 416p. mass mkt. 6.99 (*0-553-57930-4*); 2002. 336p. 23.95 (*0-553-10973-1*) Bantam Bks.

—And Justice There Is None. l.t. ed. 2003. 29.95 (*1-58724-400-4*, Wheeler Publishing, Inc.) Gale Group.

—Dreaming of the Bones. 1998. 416p. mass mkt. 6.99 (*0-553-57931-2*) Bantam Bks.

—Dreaming of the Bones. l.t. ed. 2000. pap. 25.95 (*1-56895-899-4*, Wheeler Publishing, Inc.) Gale Group.

—Dreaming of the Bones. l.t. ed. 1998. (Magna Large Print Ser.). 480p. o.p. (*0-7505-1315-2*) Magna Large Print Bks. GBR. *Dist:* Ulverscroft Large Print Canada, Ltd.

—Dreaming of the Bones. 2001. audio compact disk 116.00 (*0-7887-5203-0*, C1360E7); 2000. audio 85.00 (*0-7887-4085-7*, 95946E7) Recorded Bks., LLC.

—Dreaming of the Bones. 1997. 350p. 21.50 (*0-684-84720-5*); 21.50 (*0-684-80141-8*) Simon & Schuster. (Scribner).

—A Finer End. l.t. ed. 2001. (Illus.). 526p. 30.95 (*0-7862-3581-0*) Thorndike Pr.

—Kissed a Sad Goodbye. 1999. 336p. 23.95 o.s.i (*0-553-10943-X*) Bantam Bks.

—Kissed a Sad Goodbye. l.t. ed. 1999. (Large Print Book Ser.). pap. 24.95 (*1-56895-731-9*, Wheeler Publishing, Inc.) Gale Group.

—Kissed a Sad Goodbye. unabr. ed. 1999. audio 87.00 (*0-7887-3751-1*, 95869E7) Recorded Bks., LLC.

—Leave the Grave Green. 1996. 304p. mass mkt. 6.50 (*0-425-15308-8*) Berkley Publishing Group.

—Leave the Grave Green. l.t. ed. 2000. pap. 23.95 (*1-56895-846-3*, Wheeler Publishing, Inc.) Gale Group.

—Leave the Grave Green. l.t. ed. 1997. (Magna Large Print Ser.). 400p. (*0-7505-1114-1*) Magna Large Print Bks. GBR. *Dist:* Ulverscroft Large Print Canada, Ltd.

—Leave the Grave Green. 1995. 224p. 20.00 o.p. (*0-684-19770-7*, Scribner) Simon & Schuster.

—Mourn Not Your Dead. 1997. 304p. reprint ed. mass mkt. 6.99 (*0-425-15778-4*, Prime Crime) Berkley Publishing Group.

—Mourn Not Your Dead. l.t. ed. 1997. (Magna Large Print Ser.). 412p. (*0-7505-1175-3*) Magna Large Print Bks. GBR. *Dist:* Ulverscroft Large Print Canada, Ltd.

—Mourn Not Your Dead: A Duncan Kincaid/Gemma James Crime Novel. l.t. ed. 1996. 25.95 (*1-56895-367-4*, Wheeler Publishing, Inc.) Gale Group.

—Mourn Not Your Dead: A Duncan Kincaid/Gemma James Crime Novel. 1996. 288p. 21.00 o.p. (*0-684-80131-0*, Scribner) Simon & Schuster.

—Now May You Weep. l.t. ed. 2004. lib. bdg. 29.95 (*1-58547-409-6*, Platinum) Ctr. Point Large Print.

Characters

—Now May You Weep. 2003. 384p. 23.95 (*0-06-052523-1*, Morrow, William & Co.) Morrow/Avon.
—A Share in Death: A Mystery Introducing Superintendent Duncan Kincaid & Sergeant Gemma James. 1994. 208p. reprint ed. mass mkt. 6.50 (*0-425-14197-7*, Prime Crime) Berkley Publishing Group.
—A Share in Death: A Mystery Introducing Superintendent Duncan Kincaid & Sergeant Gemma James. l.t. ed. 1995. (Magna Large Print Ser.). 259p. (*0-7505-0833-7*) Magna Large Print Bks. GBR. *Dist:* Ulverscroft Large Print Canada, Ltd.
—A Share in Death: A Mystery Introducing Superintendent Duncan Kincaid & Sergeant Gemma James. 1993. 256p. 20.00 o.p. (*0-684-19527-5*, Scribner) Simon & Schuster.

**JAMES, HILTON (FICTITIOUS CHARACTER)—FICTION**

Due, Tananarive. The Between: A Novel. 288p. 1996. pap. 13.00 (*0-06-092726-7*, Perennial); 1995. 22.00 o.p. (*0-06-017250-9*) HarperTrade.

**JAMES, JESSE, 1847-1882—FICTION**

Barry, Desmond. The Chivalry of Crime: A Novel. 480p. 2001. pap. 14.95 (*0-316-12084-7*); 2000. (gr. 8). 24.95 o.p. (*0-316-12038-3*) Little Brown & Co. (Back Bay).
Cotton, Ralph W. While Angels Dance: The Life & Times of Jeston Nash. 1995. 344p. pap. text 5.50 o.p. (*0-312-95461-1*, St. Martin's Paperbacks); 1994. 352p. 21.95 o.p. (*0-312-11098-7*) St. Martin's Pr.
Dodd, Susan. Mamaw. 1990. 288p. mass mkt. 3.95 o.s.i (*0-345-36297-7*) Ballantine Bks.
—Mamaw. 1988. 368p. 18.95 o.p. (*0-670-82180-2*, Viking) Viking Penguin.
—Mamaw: A Novel of an Outlaw Mother. 1999. 368p. reprint ed. pap. 13.00 (*0-688-17001-3*, Quill) HarperTrade.
Hansen, Ron. The Assassination of Jesse James by the Coward Robert Ford. 1984. 368p. mass mkt. 3.95 o.s.i (*0-345-29626-5*) Ballantine Bks.
—The Assassination of Jesse James by the Coward Robert Ford. 1997. 320p. pap. 13.00 (*0-06-097699-3*, Perennial) HarperTrade.
—The Assassination of Jesse James by the Coward Robert Ford. 1990. pap. 8.95 o.p. (*0-393-30679-8*) Norton, W. W. & Co., Inc.
Henry, Will. Death of a Legend. l.t. ed. 2003. lib. bdg. 27.95 (*1-58547-296-4*, Western) Ctr. Point Large Print.
—Death of a Legend. 1996. 336p. reprint ed. mass mkt. 4.99 (*0-8439-3990-7*) Dorchester Publishing Co., Inc.
—Jesse James: Death of a Legend. 1996. E-Book 9.95 (*0-585-30149-2*) netLibrary, Inc.
Lewis, Preston. The Redemption of Jesse James. Lewis, Preston, ed. 1995. 368p. mass mkt. 5.50 o.s.i (*0-553-56542-7*) Bantam Bks.
—The Redemption of Jesse James. l.t. ed. 1995. 496p. 20.95 o.p. (*0-7838-1500-X*, Macmillan Reference USA) Gale Group.
Marvin, Isabel R. The Tenth Rifle & the Jesse James Gang. 1994. (Illus.). (J). pap. 5.00 (*0-932433-12-X*) Windswept Hse. Pubs.
Taylor, Robert. Loving Belle Starr. 1984. 224p. 14.95 o.p. (*0-912697-07-5*) Algonquin Bks. of Chapel Hill.

**JAMES, JESSE (FICTITIOUS CHARACTER)—FICTION**

O'Brien, Meg. Eagles Die Too: A Jessica James Mystery. 1992. 256p. 16.50 o.s.i (*0-385-42265-2*) Doubleday Publishing.
—Salmon in the Soup. 1990. 256p. (Orig.). mass mkt. 3.95 o.s.i (*0-553-28617-X*) Bantam Bks.
—Thin Ice. 1994. 416p. mass mkt. 4.99 o.s.i (*0-553-56962-7*) Bantam Bks.

**JAMES, JESSICA (FICTITIOUS CHARACTER)—FICTION**

*see James, Jesse (Fictitious Character)—Fiction*

**JAMES, LIZ (FICTITIOUS CHARACTER)—FICTION**

Stuyck, Karen H. Lethal Lessons. 1997. 272p. mass mkt. 5.99 o.s.i (*0-425-15723-7*, Prime Crime) Berkley Publishing Group.

**JAMESON, CASS (FICTITIOUS CHARACTER)—FICTION**

Wheat, Carolyn. Dead Man's Thoughts. 1995. 240p. mass mkt. 4.99 o.p. (*0-425-14933-1*) Berkley Publishing Group.
—Dead Man's Thoughts. 1983. 256p. 14.95 o.p. (*0-312-18501-4*) St. Martin's Pr.
—Fresh Kills. 240p. (Orig.). 1996. mass mkt. 5.50 o.s.i (*0-425-15276-6*); 1995. 19.95 o.p. (*0-425-14785-1*, Prime Crime); 1995. pap. 9.00 o.p. (*0-425-14920-X*, Prime Crime) Berkley Publishing Group.
—Mean Streak. (Cass Jameson Legal Mysteries Ser.). 240p. 1997. mass mkt. 5.99 o.s.i (*0-425-15577-3*); 1996. 19.95 o.p. (*0-425-15317-7*) Berkley Publishing Group. (Prime Crime).
—Sworn to Defend. (Cass Jameson Legal Mysteries Ser.). 320p. 1998. 22.95 o.s.i (*0-425-16303-2*); 1999. reprint ed. mass mkt. 5.99 o.s.i (*0-425-16932-4*) Berkley Publishing Group. (Prime Crime).
—Troubled Waters. (Cass Jameson Legal Mysteries Ser.). 1998. 256p. mass mkt. 5.99 o.s.i (*0-425-16380-6*); 1997. 240p. 21.95 o.s.i (*0-425-15784-9*) Berkley Publishing Group. (Prime Crime).
—Troubled Waters. 1998. 12.04 (*0-606-15743-3*) Turtleback Bks.
—Where Nobody Dies. 1988. 240p. mass mkt. 3.50 o.s.i (*0-553-27369-8*) Bantam Bks.
—Where Nobody Dies. 1996. (Cass Jameson Legal Mysteries Ser.). 272p. mass mkt. 5.99 o.s.i (*0-425-15408-4*, Prime Crime) Berkley Publishing Group.
—Where Nobody Dies. 1986. 288p. 15.95 o.p. (*0-312-86700-X*) St. Martin's Pr.

**JAMESON, MARGARET (FICTITIOUS CHARACTER)—FICTION**

Robinson, Lillian S. Murder Most Puzzling: A Literary Mystery. 1998. 320p. 21.95 (*0-941968-09-X*) Wildcat Publishing Co., Inc.

**JAMMU, S. (FICTITIOUS CHARACTER)—FICTION**

Franzen, Jonathan. The Twenty-Seventh City. 1997. 528p. pap. 15.00 o.s.i (*0-374-52505-6*); 1988. 544p. 19.95 o.s.i (*0-374-27972-1*) Farrar, Straus & Giroux.
—The Twenty-Seventh City. 1990. pap. 8.95 (*0-380-70840-X*, Avon Bks.) Morrow/Avon.
—The Twenty-Seventh City. 2001. 528p. pap. 14.00 (*0-312-42014-5*) Picador.
—The Twenty-Seventh City. 1992. 1.99 o.p. (*0-517-08590-9*); 1991. 2.99 o.p. (*0-517-06299-2*) Random Hse. Value Publishing.

**JANEK, FRANK (FICTITIOUS CHARACTER)—FICTION**

Bayer, William. Mirror Maze. 1995. 400p. mass mkt. 5.99 o.s.i (*0-515-11523-1*, Jove) Berkley Publishing Group.
—Switch. 1985. 352p. mass mkt. 4.99 o.s.i (*0-451-15356-1*, Signet Bks.) NAL.
—Wallflower. 1992. mass mkt. 5.99 o.s.i (*0-515-10843-X*, Jove) Berkley Publishing Group.
—Wallflower. 1993. 3.99 o.p. (*0-517-10959-X*) Random Hse. Value Publishing.

**JANEWAY, CLIFF (FICTITIOUS CHARACTER)—FICTION**

Dunning, John. Booked to Die. l.t. ed. 1998. (Niagara Large Print Ser.). 552p. 29.50 o.p. (*0-7089-5836-2*, Ulverscroft) Thorpe, F. A. Pubs. GBR. *Dist:* Ulverscroft Large Print Bks., Ltd., Ulverscroft Large Print Canada, Ltd.
—The Bookman's Promise. 2005. 384p. mass mkt. (*0-7434-7629-8*, Pocket) Simon & Schuster.
—The Bookman's Promise: A Cliff Janeway Novel. 2004. 384p. 25.00 (*0-7432-4992-5*, Scribner) Simon & Schuster.
—The Bookman's Wake. 1996. 448p. mass mkt. 7.99 (*0-671-56782-9*, Pocket Star); 1995. (Illus.). 352p. 21.00 (*0-684-80003-9*, Scribner) Simon & Schuster.

**JANEWAY, KATHRYN MARGARET (FICTITIOUS CHARACTER)—FICTION**

Archer, Nathan. Ragnarok. 1995. (Star Trek Voyager Ser.: No. 3). 288p. mass mkt. 5.99 (*0-671-52044-X*, Star Trek) Simon & Schuster.
Betancourt, John G. Incident at Arbuk. 1995. (Star Trek Voyager Ser.: No. 5). 224p. mass mkt. 5.99 o.s.i (*0-671-52048-2*, Star Trek) Simon & Schuster.
The Captain's Table. 2000. (Star Trek, The Next Generation Ser.). E-Book 16.95 (*0-7434-0670-2*, Star Trek) Simon & Schuster.
Carey, Diane L. Equinox. 1999. (Star Trek Voyager Ser.). 272p. (J). pap. 6.99 (*0-671-04295-5*, Star Trek) Simon & Schuster.
—Flashback. 1996. (Star Trek Voyager Ser.). 288p. per. 5.99 (*0-671-00383-6*, Star Trek) Simon & Schuster.
Carey, Diane L., et al. Invasion Omnibus: First Strike; The Soldiers of Fear; Time's Enemy; The Final Fury. 1998. (Star Trek Ser.). 960p. mass mkt. 14.00 (*0-671-02185-0*, Star Trek) Simon & Schuster.
Cox, Greg. The Black Shore. 1997. (Star Trek Voyager Ser.: No. 13). (Illus.). 288p. mass mkt. 5.99 (*0-671-56061-1*, Star Trek) Simon & Schuster.
Galanter, Dave & Brodeur, Greg. Battle Lines. 1999. (Star Trek Voyager Ser.: No. 18). 264p. mass mkt. 6.50 o.s.i (*0-671-00259-7*, Star Trek) Simon & Schuster.
Garland, Mark A. & McGraw, Charles G. Ghost of a Chance. 1996. (Star Trek Voyager Ser.: No. 7). 288p. pap. 5.99 (*0-671-56798-5*, Star Trek) Simon & Schuster.
Golden, Christie. Cloak & Dagger Vol. 1: Dark Matters Trilogy. 2000. (Star Trek Voyager Ser.: No. 19). 256p. pap. 6.99 o.s.i (*0-671-03582-7*, Star Trek) Simon & Schuster.
—Ghost Dance Vol. 2: Dark Matters Trilogy. 2000. (Star Trek Voyager Ser.: No. 20). 288p. pap. 6.99 (*0-671-03583-5*, Star Trek) Simon & Schuster.
—Homecoming. 2003. (Star Trek Voyager Ser.). 288p. mass mkt. 6.99 (*0-7434-6754-X*);Bk. 1. E-Book 5.99 (*0-7434-7563-1*) Simon & Schuster. (Star Trek).
—Marooned. 1997. (Star Trek Voyager Ser.: No. 14). (Illus.). 304p. pap. 5.99 (*0-671-01423-4*, Star Trek) Simon & Schuster.
—The Murdered Sun. 1996. (Star Trek Voyager Ser.: No. 6). 288p. mass mkt. 5.99 o.s.i (*0-671-53783-0*, Star Trek) Simon & Schuster.
—Seven of Nine. 1998. (Star Trek Voyager Ser.: No. 16). 233p. mass mkt. 6.50 (*0-671-02491-4*, Star Trek) Simon & Schuster.
—Shadow of Heaven No. 3: Dark Matters Trilogy. 2000. (Star Trek Voyager Ser.: No. 21). (Illus.). 288p. mass mkt. 6.99 o.s.i (*0-671-03584-3*, Star Trek) Simon & Schuster.
Graf, L. A. Caretaker. abr. ed. 1995. (Star Trek Voyager Ser.: No. 1). 17.00 o.s.i incl. audio (*0-671-52142-X*) Baen Bks.
—Caretaker. Ordover, John, ed. 1995. (Star Trek Voyager Ser.: No. 1). 288p. mass mkt. 5.99 Simon & Schuster.
Graf, L. A., et al. The Captain's Table Omnibus. 2000. (Star Trek Ser.). 1152p. pap. 16.95 (*0-671-04052-9*, Star Trek) Simon & Schuster.
Haber, Karen. Bless the Beasts. 1996. (Star Trek Voyager Ser.: No. 10). 288p. pap. 5.99 (*0-671-56780-2*, Star Trek) Simon & Schuster.
Hugh, Dafydd ab. The Final Fury No. 4: Invasion! 1996. (Star Trek Voyager Ser.: No. 9). 320p. (J). mass mkt. 6.50 (*0-671-54181-1*, Star Trek) Simon & Schuster.
—Invasion! No. 4: The Final Fury. 1999. (Star Trek Voyager Ser.: No. 9). E-Book 6.99 (*0-671-04098-7*, Star Trek) Simon & Schuster.
Janeway, Kathryn Margaret. Fire Ship: The Captain's Table. 1998. (Star Trek: Vol. 4). (Illus.). 288p. pap. 6.50 (*0-671-01467-6*, Star Trek) Simon & Schuster.
Kotani, Eric & Smith, Dean Wesley. Death of a Neutron Star. 1999. (Star Trek Voyager Ser.: No. 17). 263p. mass mkt. 6.50 o.s.i (*0-671-00425-5*, Star Trek) Simon & Schuster.
Lewitt, S. N. Cybersong. 1996. (Star Trek Voyager Ser.: No. 8). 288p. mass mkt. 5.99 (*0-671-56783-7*, Star Trek) Simon & Schuster.
Scott, Melissa. The Garden. 1997. (Star Trek Voyager Ser.: No. 11). (Illus.). 288p. mass mkt. 5.99 (*0-671-56799-3*, Star Trek) Simon & Schuster.
Smith, Dean Wesley & Rusch, Kristine K. The Escape. 1995. (Star Trek Voyager Ser.: No. 2). 256p. mass mkt. 5.50 (*0-671-52096-2*, Star Trek) Simon & Schuster.
Smith, Dean Wesley, et al. Echoes. 1998. (Star Trek Voyager Ser.: No. 15). 304p. pap. 5.99 (*0-671-00200-7*, Star Trek) Simon & Schuster.
Taylor, Jeri. Mosaic. (Star Trek Voyager Ser.). 320p. 1997. pap. 5.99 (*0-671-56312-2*); 1996. 22.00 (*0-671-56311-4*) Simon & Schuster. (Star Trek).
—Mosaic. abr. ed. 1996. (Star Trek Ser.). audio 18.00 (*0-671-57400-0*, Simon & Schuster Audioworks) Simon & Schuster Audio.
—Pathways. (Star Trek Voyager Ser.: Vol. 2). 1999. 528p. pap. 6.50 o.s.i (*0-671-02626-7*); 1998. (Illus.). 448p. 23.00 o.s.i (*0-671-00346-1*) Simon & Schuster. (Star Trek).
—Pathways. abr. ed. 1998. (Star Trek Voyager Ser.: Vol. 2). 24.00 incl. audio (*0-671-58230-5*, Simon & Schuster Audioworks) Simon & Schuster Audio.
—Pathways. 1999. (Star Trek Voyager Ser.). 12.55 (*0-606-19503-3*) Turtleback Bks.
—Star Trek Voyager: Pathways. abr. ed. 1999. (Star Trek Voyager Ser.). audio 24.35 (*0-671-01115-4*) Ulverscroft Audio (U.S.A.).
Wilson, David N. Chrysalis. 1997. (Star Trek Voyager Ser.: No. 12). (Illus.). 304p. mass mkt. 5.99 (*0-671-00150-7*, Star Trek) Simon & Schuster.
Wright, Susan. Badlands. 1999. (Star Trek Ser.: Vol. 2). (Illus.). 288p. pap. 6.99 (*0-671-03958-X*, Star Trek) Simon & Schuster.
—The Badlands, No. 2. 2000. (Star Trek Ser.). E-Book 6.99 (*0-7434-0675-3*, Star Trek) Simon & Schuster.
—Violations. 1995. (Star Trek Voyager Ser.: No. 4). 288p. mass mkt. 5.99 (*0-671-52046-6*, Star Trek) Simon & Schuster.

**JANSSON, WILLA (FICTITIOUS CHARACTER)—FICTION**

Matera, Lia. Havana Twist: A Willa Jansson Mystery. abr. ed. 1998. (Willa Jansson Mystery Ser.). 3p. audio 18.00 (*0-7871-1735-8*, Dove Audio) NewStar Media, Inc.
—Havana Twist: A Willa Jansson Mystery. (Willa Jansson Mystery Ser.). 1999. 352p. pap. 6.99 o.s.i (*0-671-00421-2*, Pocket); 1998. 256p. 22.00 (*0-684-83470-7*, Simon & Schuster) Simon & Schuster.
—Hidden Agenda. 1992. (Willa Jansson Ser.). mass mkt. 5.99 o.s.i (*0-345-37128-3*, Ballantine Bks.) Ballantine Bks.
—Hidden Agenda. 1988. mass mkt. 3.50 o.s.i (*0-553-27721-9*) Bantam Bks.
—Last Chants. (Willa Jansson Mystery Ser.). 1997. 320p. pap. 5.99 (*0-671-88096-9*, Pocket); 1996. 240p. 21.00 (*0-684-81085-9*, Simon & Schuster) Simon & Schuster.
—Prior Convictions. 1992. (Northern California Mysteries Ser.). mass mkt. 5.99 o.s.i (*0-345-37445-2*) Ballantine Bks.
—Prior Convictions. 1991. 224p. 17.95 o.p. (*0-671-68560-0*, Simon & Schuster) Simon & Schuster.
—A Radical Departure. 1988. mass mkt. 3.50 o.s.i (*0-553-27072-9*) Bantam Bks.
—Star Witness. (Willa Jansson Mystery Ser.). 1998. 336p. pap. 6.50 (*0-671-00420-4*, Pocket); 1997. 240p. 21.50 (*0-684-83469-3*, Simon & Schuster) Simon & Schuster.
—Where Lawyers Fear to Tread. 1991. (Willa Jansson Ser.). mass mkt. 5.99 o.s.i (*0-345-37125-9*) Ballantine Bks.
—Where Lawyers Fear to Tread. 1987. mass mkt. 3.50 o.s.i (*0-553-27588-7*) Bantam Bks.
—Where Lawyers Fear to Tread. 1999. (Mystery Ser.). 209p. 20.95 o.p. (*0-7862-1814-2*, Five Star) Gale Group.

**JANUARY, BENJAMIN (FICTITIOUS CHARACTER)—FICTION**

Hambly, Barbara. Days of the Dead. 2004. 448p. mass mkt. 6.99 (*0-553-58162-7*); 2003. (Illus.). 336p. 23.95 (*0-553-10954-5*) Bantam Bks.
—Days of the Dead. l.t. ed. 2004. 544p. 25.95 (*0-375-43250-7*) Random Hse. Large Print.
—Die upon a Kiss. 2002. 480p. mass mkt. 5.99 (*0-553-58165-1*) Bantam Bks.
—Die upon a Kiss. l.t. ed. 2003. 608p. 25.95 (*0-375-43266-3*) Random Hse. Large Print.
—A Free Man of Color. 1998. 432p. reprint ed. mass mkt. 6.99 (*0-553-57526-0*) Bantam Bks.
—Wet Grave. 2003. 384p. mass mkt. 6.50 (*0-553-58159-7*); 2002. (Illus.). 304p. 23.95 (*0-553-10935-9*) Bantam Bks.
—Wet Grave. l.t. ed. 2003. 486p. 25.95 (*0-375-43274-4*, Random House Large Print) Random Hse. Large Print.

**JARRETT, DAN (FICTITIOUS CHARACTER)—FICTION**

Friedman, Hal. Over the Edge. 1999. 416p. mass mkt. 6.99 o.s.i (*0-06-109367-X*); 1998. 320p. 24.00 (*0-06-018265-2*) HarperCollins Pubs.

**JARVIS, DEREK (FICTITIOUS CHARACTER)—FICTION**

Yorke, Margaret. Almost the Truth. 1995. 294p. mass mkt. o.s.i (*0-7515-1216-8*) Little Brown & Co.
—Almost the Truth. 1995. (Cloak & Dagger Ser.). 278p. 18.95 o.p. (*0-89296-582-7*) Mysterious Pr.
—Almost the Truth. 1996. 240p. mass mkt. 5.99 o.s.i (*0-446-40479-9*) Warner Bks., Inc.

**JARVIS, ELENA (FICTITIOUS CHARACTER)—FICTION**

Herndon, Nancy. Acid Bath. 1995. 272p. (Orig.). mass mkt. 4.99 o.s.i (*0-425-14551-4*, Prime Crime) Berkley Publishing Group.
—C. O. P. Out. 1998. (Elena Jarvis Ser.). 304p. mass mkt. 5.99 o.s.i (*0-425-16293-1*, Prime Crime) Berkley Publishing Group.
—Casanova Crimes. 1999. 288p. mass mkt. 5.99 o.s.i (*0-425-16812-3*, Prime Crime) Berkley Publishing Group.
—Hunting Game. 1996. 288p. (Orig.). mass mkt. 5.99 o.s.i (*0-425-15579-X*, Prime Crime) Berkley Publishing Group.
—Lethal Statues. 1996. 304p. mass mkt. 5.99 o.s.i (*0-425-15384-3*) Berkley Publishing Group.
—Time Bombs. 1997. 320p. mass mkt. 5.99 o.s.i (*0-425-15965-5*, Prime Crime) Berkley Publishing Group.
—Widow's Watch. 1995. 304p. mass mkt. 5.50 o.s.i (*0-425-14900-5*) Berkley Publishing Group.
—Widow's Watch. 2002. pap. 6.99 (*0-7592-3636-4*); 2002. E-Book 6.99 (*0-7592-3632-1*); 2002. E-Book 6.99 (*0-7592-3633-X*); 2001. E-Book 6.99 (*0-7592-3631-3*) ereads.com.

**JASPER, ELLEN (FICTITIOUS CHARACTER)—FICTION**

Michener, James A. Caravans. 1986. mass mkt. 5.95 o.p. (*0-449-44521-6*); 1986. 448p. mass mkt. 7.99 (*0-449-21380-3*); 1985. mass mkt. 4.95 o.p. (*0-449-21051-0*); 1983. mass mkt. 3.95 o.p. (*0-449-20415-4*); 1983. mass mkt. 3.75 o.p. (*0-449-20285-2*) Ballantine Bks. (Fawcett).
—Caravans. l.t. ed. 1993. 16.95 o.p. (*0-8161-3261-5*, Macmillan Reference USA) Gale Group.
—Caravans. 2003. (Illus.). 352p. pap. 14.95 (*0-8129-6982-0*, Random Hse. Trade Paperbacks) Random House Adult Trade Publishing Group.
—Caravans. 1963. 29.95 o.s.i (*0-394-41849-2*) Random Hse., Inc.

**JASPER, JAZZ (FICTITIOUS CHARACTER)—FICTION**

McQuillan, Karin. The Cheetah Chase. 1995. mass mkt. 5.99 o.s.i (*0-345-39780-0*); 1994. 304p. 20.00 o.s.i (*0-345-38183-1*) Ballantine Bks.

—Deadly Safari. 1991. (Boston Mysteries Ser.). 272p. mass mkt. 4.99 o.s.i (*0-345-37057-0*, Ballantine Bks.) Ballantine Bks.

—Deadly Safari. 1990. 304p. 17.95 o.p. (*0-312-03808-9*, Saint Martin's Minotaur) St. Martin's Pr.

—Deadly Safari. l.t. ed. 1994. (Ulverscroft Large Print Ser.). 512p. 29.99 o.p. (*0-7089-3189-8*, Ulverscroft) Thorpe, F. A. Pubs. GBR. *Dist:* Ulverscroft Large Print Bks., Ltd., Ulverscroft Large Print Canada, Ltd.

—Elephants' Graveyard. 1994. (Boston Mysteries Ser.). 272p. mass mkt. 4.99 o.s.i (*0-345-38862-3*) Ballantine Bks.

**JASPER, KATE (FICTITIOUS CHARACTER)—FICTION**

Girdner, Jaqueline. Adjusted to Death. 1991. 3.99 (*1-55773-453-4*) Ace Bks.

—Adjusted to Death. 1994. mass mkt. 4.99 o.s.i (*0-425-14706-1*) Berkley Publishing Group.

—A Cry for Self-Help. (Kate Jasper Mysteries Ser.). 288p. 1998. mass mkt. 5.99 o.s.i (*0-425-16265-6*); 1997. 21.95 o.s.i (*0-425-15630-3*, Prime Crime) Berkley Publishing Group.

—Death Hits the Fan. 1999. (Kate Jasper Mystery Ser.). 288p. reprint ed. mass mkt. 5.99 o.s.i (*0-425-16808-5*, Prime Crime) Berkley Publishing Group.

—Death Hits the Fan: A Kate Jasper Mystery. 1998. (Kate Jasper Mysteries Ser.). 288p. 21.95 o.s.i (*0-425-16148-X*) Berkley Publishing Group.

—Fat-Free & Fatal. 1993. (Orig.). 3.99 o.s.i (*1-55773-917-X*) Ace Bks.

—Fat-Free & Fatal. 1993. 224p. (Orig.). mass mkt. 5.99 o.s.i (*0-425-15811-X*, Prime Crime) Berkley Publishing Group.

—The Last Resort. 1991. 3.95 (*1-55773-525-5*) Ace Bks.

—The Last Resort. 1991. mass mkt. 5.50 o.s.i (*0-425-14431-3*, Prime Crime) Berkley Publishing Group.

—Most Likely to Die. (Mistery Ser.). 288p. 1996. 21.95 o.s.i (*0-425-15145-X*, Prime Crime); 1996. pap. 10.00 o.p. (*0-425-15146-8*); 1997. reprint ed. mass mkt. 5.99 o.s.i (*0-425-15721-0*, Prime Crime) Berkley Publishing Group.

—Murder Most Mellow. 1992. 3.99 o.s.i (*1-55773-721-5*, Diamond Bks.) Ace Bks.

—Murder Most Mellow. 1992. mass mkt. 5.50 o.s.i (*0-425-14707-X*, Prime Crime) Berkley Publishing Group.

—Murder, My Deer: A Kate Jasper Mystery. 2000. (Kate Jasper Mysteries Ser.). (Illus.). 275p. 21.95 o.s.i (*0-425-17328-3*) Berkley Publishing Group.

—Murder on the Astral Plane. 2000. (Kate Jasper Mysteries Ser.: Vol. 10). 309p. mass mkt. 5.99 o.s.i (*0-425-17359-3*, Prime Crime) Berkley Publishing Group.

—Murder on the Astral Plane: A Kate Jasper Mystery. 1999. (Kate Jasper Ser.). 320p. 21.95 o.s.i (*0-425-16701-1*, Prime Crime) Berkley Publishing Group.

—A Stiff Critique. 1995. 272p. (Orig.). mass mkt. 4.99 o.s.i (*0-425-14719-3*, Prime Crime) Berkley Publishing Group.

—Tea-Totally Dead. 1994. mass mkt. 4.99 o.s.i (*0-425-14210-8*) Berkley Publishing Group.

**JAVERT, INSPECTOR (FICTITIOUS CHARACTER)—FICTION**

Center for Learning Network Staff & Hugo, Victor. Les Miserables: Curriculum Unit. 1992. (Novel Ser.). 98p. reprint ed. tchr. ed., spiral bd. 18.95 (*1-56077-255-7*) Ctr. for Learning, The.

Hugo, Victor. Les Miserables. 1997. (Classics Illustrated Study Guides). (Illus.). 64p. (YA). (gr. 7 up). mass mkt., stu. ed. 4.99 o.p. (*1-57840-017-1*) Acclaim Bks.

—Les Miserables. 1976. (J). 25.95 (*0-8488-0535-6*) Amereon, Ltd.

—Les Miserables. 1998. (J). mass mkt. 5.99 (*0-449-45834-2*) Ballantine Bks.

—Les Miserables. Wilbour, Charles E., tr. 1996. 336p. pap. 12.95 (*0-449-91167-5*, Fawcett) Ballantine Bks.

—Les Miserables. 1987. (J). mass mkt. 3.95 o.s.i (*0-449-30057-9*); 1982. (Illus.). 416p. mass mkt. 5.99 (*0-449-30002-1*) Ballantine Bks. (Fawcett).

—Les Miserables. abr. ed. audio 62.95 Blackstone Audio Bks., Inc.

—Les Miserables. unabr. collector's ed. 1993. (J). audio 72.00 (*0-7366-2339-6*, 116013) Books on Tape, Inc.

—Les Miserables. 1990. 528p. (J). reprint ed. lib. bdg. 49.95 (*0-89966-452-0*) Buccaneer Bks., Inc.

—Les Miserables. 1987. (J). pap. 5.60 (*0-87129-287-4*, L57) Dramatic Publishing Co.

—Les Miserables. Allem, Maurice, ed. 1976. (FRE.). 1808p. (J). lib. bdg. 125.00 (*0-7859-3757-9*, 2070102645) French & European Pubns., Inc.

—Les Miserables. Wilbour, Charles E., tr. 1998. (Everyman's Library). 1472p. (J). 23.00 (*0-375-40317-5*) Knopf, Alfred A. Inc.

—Les Miserables. E-Book 2.95 (*1-57799-952-5*) Logos Research Systems, Inc.

—Les Miserables. abr. ed. 2000. audio 7.95 (*1-57815-117-1*, 1079, Media Bks. Audio Publishing) Media Bks., L. L. C.

—Les Miserables. E-Book 1.95 (*1-58515-009-6*) MesaView, Inc.

—Les Miserables. 1987. 19.95 o.p. (*0-453-00579-9*); 1408p. (J). mass mkt. 7.95 (*0-451-52526-4*, Signet Classics); (J). mass mkt. 6.95 o.p. (*0-451-52157-9*, Signet Classics); mass mkt. 5.95 o.p. (*0-451-52082-3*) NAL.

—Les Miserables. abr. ed. 1996. audio 22.98 (*962-634-605-1*, NA410514); audio compact disk 26.98 (*962-634-105-X*, NA410512) Naxos of America, Inc. (Naxos AudioBooks).

—Les Miserables. abr. ed. 1993. audio 16.95 o.p. (*1-55800-036-4*, Dove Audio) NewStar Media, Inc.

—Les Miserables. Fahnestock, Lee & MacAfee, Norman, trs. abr. ed. (Classics on Cassette). 1998. audio compact disk 34.95 (*0-453-00966-2*); 1992. 23.95 incl. audio (*0-453-00785-6*, 693468) Penguin/HighBridge.

—Les Miserables. 1987. (Radiola 3-CMR 5). audio 16.95 (*0-929541-48-0*); audio 4.98 (*0-929541-22-7*) Radiola Co.

—Les Miserables. Wilbour, Charles E., tr. 1992. (Modern Library Ser.). 1280p. 22.95 (*0-679-60012-4*) Random Hse., Inc.

—Les Miserables. deluxe ed. (Pleiade Ser.). (FRE.). (J). 84.95 (*2-07-010264-5*) Schoenhof's Foreign Bks., Inc.

—Les Miserables. Benichou, Paul, ed. Wilbour, Charles E., tr. abr. ed. 1983. 544p. (gr. 11 up). mass mkt. 5.99 (*0-671-50439-8*, Pocket) Simon & Schuster.

—Les Miserables. abr. ed. 1998. audio 22.95 (*1-55935-273-6*) Soundelux Audio Publishing.

—Les Miserables. audio Spoken Arts, Inc.

—Les Miserables. 1964. (J). 12.04 (*0-606-02836-6*) Turtleback Bks.

—Les Miserables. abr. ed. 1997. (Penguin Classics Ser.). 4p. (J). pap. 18.95 o.p. incl. audio (*0-14-086261-7*, Penguin AudioBooks) Viking Penguin.

—Les Miserables. Denny, Norman, tr. from FRE. & intro. by. rev. ed. 1982. (Classics Ser.). 1232p. (J). pap. 11.95 (*0-14-044430-0*, Penguin Classics) Viking Penguin.

—Les Miserables. 1997. (Classics Ser.: Vol. 2). (J). 512p. pap. 3.95 (*1-85326-050-9*, 0509WW); 496p. pap. 3.95 (*1-85326-085-1*, 0851WW) Wordsworth Editions, Ltd. GBR. *Dist:* Casemate Pubs. & Bk. Distributors, LLC.

—Los Miserables. 6th ed. 1998. (Clasicos Universales Ser.: Vol. 18). (SPA., Illus.). 1392p. 23.95 (*84-08-01939-2*) Planeta Publishing Corp.

—Les Miserables. unabr. ed. Pt. 1. 1996. audio 99.95 (*0-7861-0534-8*, 1810-A); Pt. 2. 1996. audio 85.95 (*0-7861-0535-6*, 1810-B); Pt. 3. audio 83.95 Blackstone Audio Bks., Inc.

—Les Miserables. unabr. ed. 1996. (FRE.). (J). Vol. I. pap. 8.95 (*2-87714-296-5*); Vol. II. pap. 7.95 (*2-87714-301-5*); Vol. III. pap. 7.95 (*2-87714-302-3*) Bookking International FRA. *Dist:* Distribooks, Inc.

—Les Miserables. Vol. 1. 1990. pap. 12.95 (*0-7859-2876-6*); Vol. 1. 1973. (FRE.). pap. 11.95 (*0-7859-2306-3*, 2070363481); Vol. 2. 1990. (FRE.). (J). pap. 12.95 (*0-7859-3385-9*); Vol. 2. 1973. (FRE.). pap. 11.95 (*0-7859-2633-X*, 207036349X); Vol. 3. 1973. (FRE.). pap. 11.95 (*0-7859-2307-1*, 2070363503) French & European Pubns., Inc.

—Les Miserables, Set. abr. ed. 1998. audio compact disk 29.95; 1995. 29.95 o.p. (*0-7871-0289-X*) NewStar Media, Inc.

—Les Miserables, 3 tomes. 1951. (Folio Ser.: Nos. 348, 349, & 350). (FRE.). I. (J). pap. 10.95 (*2-07-036348-1*); II. (J). pap. 10.95 (*2-07-036349-X*); III. pap. 10.95 (*2-07-036350-3*) Schoenhof's Foreign Bks., Inc.

—Les Miserables, 5 vols., Set. Hapgood, Isabel F., tr. from FRE. 1993. (Illus.). reprint ed. o.p. (*1-877767-87-5*) University Publishing Hse., Inc.

—Les Miserables: Parts I & II. abr. ed. 1989. audio 120.00 Jimcin Recordings.

—Romans Complets: Les Miserables, Vol. 2. 1970. (FRE.). pap. 49.95 (*0-7859-3933-4*) French & European Pubns., Inc.

—Victor Hugo's Les Miserables. 1998. pap. (*0-345-42502-2*); mass mkt. (*0-345-42503-0*) Ballantine Bks.

—Works of Victor Hugo: The Hunchback of Notre-Dame, Les Miserables. 1991. (Classics - Bonded Leather Fibers Ser.). 763p. 24.95 o.p. (*0-681-41056-6*) Borders Pr.

Hugo, Victor & Dawson, Michael. Les Miserables. adapted collector's ed. 1998. (Smithsonian Historical Performances Ser.). 29p. (Illus.). pap. 24.98 incl. audio compact disk (*1-57019-066-6*, 4035); pap. 9.99 incl. audio (*1-57019-065-8*, 4034) Radio Spirits, Inc.

Hugo, Victor & Kulling, Monica. Les Miserables. 1995. (Step into Classics Ser.). (Illus.). 112p. (gr. 3-5). pap. text 3.99 (*0-679-86668-X*) Random Hse., Inc.

Monarch Staff & Hugo, Victor. Les Miserables. (C). 3.95 (*0-671-00844-7*, Arco) Peterson's.

**JAZEN (FICTITIOUS CHARACTER)—FICTION**

McConnell, Ashley. The Courts of Sorcery. 1997. (Demon Wars Trilogy Ser.: 3). 224p. mass mkt. 5.99 o.s.i (*0-441-00393-1*) Ace Bks.

—The Fountains of Mirlacca. 1995. (Demon Wars Trilogy Ser.: 1). 86p. (Orig.). mass mkt. 4.99 o.s.i (*0-441-00206-4*) Ace Bks.

—The Itinerant Exorcist. 1996. (Demon Wars Trilogy Ser.: 2). 208p. (Orig.). mass mkt. 5.99 o.s.i (*0-441-00312-5*) Ace Bks.

**JEEVES (FICTITIOUS CHARACTER)—FICTION**

Eckhardt, Jason C. & Cannon, P. H. Scream for Jeeves: A Parody. 1994. (Illus.). 86p. 20.00 (*0-940884-61-5*); pap. 7.50 (*0-940884-60-7*) Necronomicon Pr.

Parkinson, C. Northcote. Jeeves: A Gentleman's Personal Gentleman. 1981. 191p. 8.95 o.p. (*0-312-44144-4*) St. Martin's Pr.

Wodehouse, P. G. Aunts Aren't Gentlemen. unabr. ed. 2000. (Wooster & Jeeves Comedy Ser.). audio 34.95 (*0-7451-4098-X*, CAB 786) Chivers Audio Bks. GBR. *Dist:* BBC Audiobooks America.

—Bertie Wooster Sees It Through. 18.95 (*0-8488-0671-9*) Amereon, Ltd.

—Bertie Wooster Sees It Through. 2000. 240p. pap. 13.00 (*0-7432-0361-5*, Touchstone) Simon & Schuster.

—Carry On, Jeeves! 19.95 (*0-89190-296-1*) Amereon, Ltd.

—Carry On, Jeeves! unabr. ed. 2000. audio compact disk 48.00 (*0-7861-9949-0*, z2442) Blackstone Audio Bks., Inc.

—Carry On, Jeeves! 1990. reprint ed. lib. bdg. 15.95 (*0-89968-559-5*) Buccaneer Bks., Inc.

—Carry On, Jeeves! 2003. 17.95 (*1-58567-392-7*) Overlook Pr., The.

—Carry On, Jeeves! 240p. 2000. 7.95 (*0-14-028408-7*); 1975. pap. 8.95 o.s.i (*0-14-001174-9*, Penguin Bks.) Viking Penguin.

—Carry on, Jeeves! 8 Complete Stories. unabr. ed. 1999. audio 22.95 (*1-57270-109-9*, C41109u, Audio Editions Bks. on Cassette) Audio Partners Publishing Corp.

—The Cat-Nappers. unabr. ed. 2001. audio compact disk 19.95; 2000. audio compact disk 32.00 (*0-7861-6897-8*, z1783); 1996. audio 23.95 (*0-7861-1006-6*, 1783); 1996. audio 23.95 (*0-7861-1393-6*, 1783) Blackstone Audio Bks., Inc.

—The Cat-Nappers. reprint ed. 1990. 240p. pap. 11.00 o.p. (*0-06-097250-5*); 1985. 192p. mass mkt. 3.95 o.p. (*0-06-080769-5*, P 769) HarperTrade. (Perennial).

—The Cat-Nappers. 1975. 192p. 7.95 o.s.i (*0-671-21972-3*, Simon & Schuster) Simon & Schuster.

—The Code of the Woosters. reprint ed. lib. bdg. 21.95 (*0-89190-291-0*, Rivercity Pr.) Amereon, Ltd.

—The Code of the Woosters. unabr. ed. 2000. (Wooster & Jeeves Comedy Ser.). audio 49.95 (*0-7451-6372-6*, CAB 497) Chivers Audio Bks. GBR. *Dist:* BBC Audiobooks America.

—The Code of the Woosters. 1975. 240p. mass mkt. 9.00 (*0-394-72028-8*, Vintage) Knopf Publishing Group.

—The Code of the Woosters. unabr. ed. 1997. (Wodehouse's Bertie & Jeeves Ser.). audio 22.95 (*1-58081-060-8*, CTA60) L. A. Theatre Works.

—The Code of the Woosters. 2000. (Collector's Wodehouse Ser.). 224p. 17.95 (*1-58567-057-X*) Overlook Pr., The.

—The Code of the Woosters. unabr. ed. 1989. audio 51.00 (*1-55690-109-7*, 89600E7) Recorded Bks., LLC.

—Enter Jeeves: 15 Early Stories. 1997. 288p. reprint ed. pap. 8.95 (*0-486-29717-9*) Dover Pubns., Inc.

—How Right You Are, Jeeves. reprint ed. lib. bdg. 21.95 (*0-89190-293-7*, Rivercity Pr.) Amereon, Ltd.

—How Right You Are, Jeeves. 1990. reprint ed. lib. bdg. 17.95 (*0-89968-560-9*) Buccaneer Bks., Inc.

—How Right You Are, Jeeves. 1985. 192p. reprint ed. pap. 3.95 o.p. (*0-06-080770-9*, P 770, Perennial) HarperTrade.

—How Right You Are, Jeeves. 2000. 208p. pap. 12.00 (*0-7432-0359-3*, Touchstone); 1960. 3.50 o.p. (*0-671-32460-8*, Simon & Schuster) Simon & Schuster.

—How Right You Are, Jeeves: A Jeeves & Bertie Novel. 1990. 205p. reprint ed. pap. 11.00 o.p. (*0-06-096499-5*, Perennial) HarperTrade.

—The Inimitable Jeeves. 21.95 (*0-8488-0676-X*) Amereon, Ltd.

—The Inimitable Jeeves. unabr. ed. 2000. audio 29.95 (*1-57270-150-1*, C61150u, Audio Editions Bks. on Cassette) Audio Partners Publishing Corp.

—The Inimitable Jeeves. unabr. ed. 2000. audio 27.95 (*0-7861-1775-3*); audio 39.95 (*0-7861-1740-0*, 2545); audio compact disk 48.00 (*0-7861-9903-2*, z2545) Blackstone Audio Bks., Inc.

—The Inimitable Jeeves. unabr. ed. 2000. (Wooster & Jeeves Comedy Ser.). audio 49.95 (*0-7451-6373-4*, CSL 061) Chivers Audio Bks. GBR. *Dist:* BBC Audiobooks America.

—The Inimitable Jeeves. 2000. 240p. pap. 7.95 (*0-14-028412-5*) Penguin Group (USA) Inc.

—The Inimitable Jeeves. unabr. ed. 2000. audio 27.95 Penton Overseas, Inc.

—The Inimitable Jeeves. 1975. 224p. pap. 8.95 o.s.i (*0-14-000933-7*, Penguin Bks.) Viking Penguin.

—Introducing Jeeves: 6 Classic Stories. 2004. pap. 12.95 (*0-486-43361-7*) Dover Pubns., Inc.

—Jeeves & the Feudal Spirit: A Jeeves & Bertie Novel. 19.95 (*0-8488-0673-5*) Amereon, Ltd.

—Jeeves & the Feudal Spirit: A Jeeves & Bertie Novel. 1996. audio 29.95 (*0-7451-2847-5*) BBC Audiobooks America.

—Jeeves & the Feudal Spirit: A Jeeves & Bertie Novel, unabr. ed. 1996. audio 39.95 (*0-7861-0916-5*, 1723) Blackstone Audio Bks., Inc.

—Jeeves & the Feudal Spirit: A Jeeves & Bertie Novel. 1990. 246p. pap. 10.00 o.p. (*0-06-096500-2*); 1983. 176p. mass mkt. 3.95 o.p. (*0-06-080666-4*, P666) HarperTrade. (Perennial).

—Jeeves & the Feudal Spirit: A Jeeves & Bertie Novel. 2002. (Illus.). 231p. 16.95 (*1-58567-229-7*) Overlook Pr., The.

—Jeeves & the Tie That Binds. 20.95 (*0-8488-0674-3*) Amereon, Ltd.

—Jeeves & the Tie That Binds. audio 24.95 (*0-7861-1398-7*); 1992. audio 32.95 (*0-7861-0291-8*, 1255) Blackstone Audio Bks., Inc.

—Jeeves & the Tie That Binds. 1983. 192p. mass mkt. 3.95 o.p. (*0-06-080667-2*, P667); 1990. 79p. reprint ed. pap. 10.00 o.p. (*0-06-097283-1*) HarperTrade. (Perennial).

—Jeeves & the Tie That Binds, Set. unabr. ed. 1999. audio 32.95 Highsmith Inc.

—Jeeves & the Tie That Binds. 1971. 5.95 o.s.i (*0-671-21038-6*, Simon & Schuster) Simon & Schuster.

—Jeeves in the Morning. unabr. ed. 2000. audio compact disk 69.99 (*0-7861-9941-5*, z1740); 1996. audio 39.95 (*0-7861-0963-7*, 1740) Blackstone Audio Bks., Inc.

—Jeeves in the Morning. 1983. reprint ed. pap. 3.95 o.p. (*0-06-080658-3*, P 658, Perennial) HarperTrade.

—Jeeves in the Offing. 2002. 16.95 (*1-58567-325-0*) Penguin Group (USA) Inc.

—Jeeves in the Offing. 1984. audio 53.95 o.p. (*0-8161-9784-9*) Thorndike Pr.

—Jeeves Omnibus 2, Vol. 2. 1994. pap. (*0-09-174574-8*) Random Hse. of Canada, Ltd. CAN. *Dist:* Random Hse., Inc.

—Joy in the Morning. 2002. 296p. 16.95 (*1-58567-276-9*) Overlook Pr., The.

—Life with Jeeves. 1983. 560p. pap. 15.95 (*0-14-005902-4*, Penguin Bks.) Penguin Group (USA) Inc.

—Mating Season. 22.95 (*0-8488-0677-8*) Amereon, Ltd.

—The Mating Season. unabr. ed. 1995. audio 44.95 (*0-7861-0761-8*, 1610) Blackstone Audio Bks., Inc.

—The Mating Season. 1989. 224p. reprint ed. pap. 10.00 o.p. (*0-06-097248-3*, Perennial) HarperTrade.

—P. G. Wodehouse: Five Complete Novels. annuals 1995. (Avenel Readers Library). 688p. 12.99 o.s.i (*0-517-40538-5*) Random Hse. Value Publishing.

—The Return of Jeeves. 21.95 (*0-8488-0332-9*) Amereon, Ltd.

—The Return of Jeeves. 1985. 240p. reprint ed. pap. 3.95 o.p. (*0-06-080768-7*, P 768, Perennial) HarperTrade.

—The Return of Jeeves. mass mkt. 0.50 o.p. (*0-451-02843-0*, Signet Bks.) NAL.

—The Return of Jeeves: A Jeeves & Bertie Novel. 1990. 231p. reprint ed. pap. 11.00 o.p. (*0-06-096502-9*, Perennial) HarperTrade.

—Right Ho, Jeeves. 22.95 (*0-8488-0680-8*) Amereon, Ltd.

—Right Ho, Jeeves. 1999. audio 29.95 (*0-7451-2814-9*) BBC Audiobooks America.

—Right Ho, Jeeves. unabr. ed. 1992. audio 44.95 (*0-7861-0363-9*, 1320) Blackstone Audio Bks., Inc.

—Right Ho, Jeeves. unabr. ed. 2000. (Wooster & Jeeves Comedy Ser.). audio 49.95 (*0-7451-6371-8*, CAB 414) Chivers Audio Bks. GBR. *Dist:* BBC Audiobooks America.

—Right Ho, Jeeves. 2000. (Collector's Wodehouse Ser.). 224p. 17.95 (*1-58567-058-8*) Overlook Pr., The.

—Right Ho, Jeeves. 2000. 272p. pap. 7.95 (*0-14-028409-5*) Penguin Group (USA) Inc.

—Right Ho, Jeeves. unabr. ed. 1988. audio 44.00 (*1-55690-444-4*, 88070E7) Recorded Bks., LLC.
—Right Ho, Jeeves. 2001. 2p. audio (*0-14-180315-0*, Penguin AudioBooks); 1975. 256p. pap. 9.95 o.s.i (*0-14-000934-5*, Penguin Bks.) Viking Penguin.
—Stiff Upper Lip, Jeeves. 20.95 (*0-8488-0682-4*) Amereon, Ltd.
—Stiff Upper Lip, Jeeves. unabr. ed. 1991. audio 39.95 (*0-7861-0279-9*, 1245) Blackstone Audio Bks., Inc.
—Stiff Upper Lip, Jeeves. unabr. ed. 2000. (Wooster & Jeeves Comedy Ser.). audio 49.95 (*0-7451-4043-2*, CAB 740) Chivers Audio Bks. GBR. *Dist:* BBC Audiobooks America.
—Stiff Upper Lip, Jeeves. 192p. 1983. mass mkt. 3.95 o.p. (*0-06-080668-0*, P668); 1990. reprint ed. pap. 10.00 o.p. (*0-06-097284-X*) HarperTrade. (Perennial).
—Stiff Upper Lip, Jeeves. mass mkt. 0.50 o.p. (*0-451-02841-4*, Signet Bks.) NAL.
—Stiff Upper Lip, Jeeves. 2000. 224p. pap. 12.00 (*0-7432-0360-7*, Touchstone); (Illus.). 24.00 (*0-7432-0410-7*, Simon & Schuster) Simon & Schuster.
—Thank You, Jeeves. reprint ed. lib. bdg. 23.95 (*0-89190-294-5*, Rivercity Pr.) Amereon, Ltd.
—Thank You, Jeeves. unabr. ed. 1989. audio 39.95 (*0-7861-0174-1*, 1155) Blackstone Audio Bks., Inc.
—Thank You, Jeeves. 1983. 480p. mass mkt. 3.95 o.p. (*0-06-080657-5*) HarperCollins Pubs.
—Thank You, Jeeves. 1989. 288p. reprint ed. pap. 10.00 o.p. (*0-06-097249-1*, Perennial) HarperTrade.
—Thank You, Jeeves. unabr. ed. 1998. audio 19.95 (*1-58081-119-1*, TPT117) L. A. Theatre Works.
—Thank You, Jeeves. 2003. 288p. 17.95 (*1-58567-434-6*) Overlook Pr., The.
—Thank You, Jeeves. unabr. ed. 1984. audio 35.00 (*1-55690-509-2*, 84130E7) Recorded Bks., LLC.
—Very Good, Jeeves. 1998. (Bertie Wooster & Jeeves Ser.). audio 34.95 (*0-7540-7524-9*) BBC Audiobooks America.
—Very Good, Jeeves. 1975. (ACE.). 256p. pap. 8.95 o.s.i (*0-14-001173-0*, Penguin Bks.) Viking Penguin.
—Very Good, Jeeves! 2000. 288p. 7.95 (*0-14-028410-9*) Viking Penguin.
—Very Good, Jeeves. reprint ed. lib. bdg. 22.95 (*0-89190-295-3*, Rivercity Pr.) Amereon, Ltd.
—Very Good, Jeeves. unabr. ed. 1992. audio 44.95 (*0-7861-0310-8*, 1272) Blackstone Audio Bks., Inc.
—Very Good, Jeeves. 1990. reprint ed. lib. bdg. 18.95 (*0-89968-561-7*) Buccaneer Bks., Inc.
—The World of Jeeves. 672p. 1988. 25.00 o.p. (*0-06-015968-5*); 1989. reprint ed. pap. 18.00 o.s.i (*0-06-097244-0*, Perennial) HarperTrade.
Wodehouse, P. G., et al. Jeeves & the Feudal Spirit: A Jeeves & Bertie Novel. 1991. (BBC Humor Ser.). audio 14.95 Minds Eye.

**JEFFERS, ANNE (FICTITIOUS CHARACTER)—FICTION**

Brightwell, Emily. Mrs. Jeffries Sweeps the Chimney. 2004. 224p. mass mkt. 6.50 (*0-425-19391-8*) Berkley Publishing Group.
Saul, John. Black Lightning. Grey, Linda, ed. 1996. 448p. mass mkt. 7.99 (*0-449-22504-6*, Fawcett) Ballantine Bks.

**JEFFERSON, ART (FICTITIOUS CHARACTER)—FICTION**

Pearson, Ryne Douglas. Capitol Punishment. 1996. 352p. mass mkt. 5.99 (*0-380-72228-3*, Avon Bks.); 1995. 320p. 22.00 o.p. (*0-688-12983-8*, Morrow, William & Co.) Morrow/Avon.
—Cloudburst. 1993. 23.00 o.p. (*0-688-12246-9*, Morrow, William & Co.) Morrow/Avon.
—Cloudburst. unabr. ed. 1993. audio 85.00 (*1-55690-901-2*, 93343E7) Recorded Bks., LLC.
—Mercury Rising. 1998. 326p. mass mkt. 6.50 (*0-380-80294-5*, Avon Bks.) Morrow/Avon.
—Mercury Rising. abr. ed. 1998. audio 18.00 (*0-671-58253-4*, Simon & Schuster Audioworks) Simon & Schuster Audio.
—October's Ghost. 1994. 312p. 23.00 o.p. (*0-688-12984-6*, Morrow, William & Co.); 1995. 464p. reprint ed. mass mkt. 5.99 (*0-380-72227-5*, Avon Bks.) Morrow/Avon.
—October's Ghost. unabr. ed. 1995. audio 91.00 (*0-7887-0101-0*, 94342E7) Recorded Bks., LLC.
—Simple Simon. 1997. pap. 5.99 (*0-380-72574-6*, Avon Bks.); 1996. 288p. 24.00 o.p. (*0-688-14296-6*, Morrow, William & Co.) Morrow/Avon.
—Simple Simon. unabr. ed. 1997. audio 51.00 (*0-7887-0814-7*, 94964E7) Recorded Bks., LLC.
—Simple Simon. abr. ed. 1980. 192p. pap. 18.00 o.s.i incl. audio (*0-671-57040-4*, 638847, Simon & Schuster Audioworks) Simon & Schuster Audio.

**JEFFRIES, ELISE (FICTITIOUS CHARACTER)—FICTION**

Bunkley, Anita Richmond. Balancing Act. 1997. 352p. 23.95 o.p. (*0-525-94010-3*) Dutton/Plume.
—Balancing Act. 1998. 400p. mass mkt. 6.99 o.s.i (*0-451-18483-1*, Signet Bks.) NAL.

**JEFFRIES, HARRIET (FICTITIOUS CHARACTER)—FICTION**

Sale, Medora. Murder in a Good Cause. 1990. 224p. 18.95 o.s.i (*0-684-19216-0*) Macmillan Information.
—Murder in Focus. 1989. 288p. 17.95 o.s.i (*0-684-19082-6*, Macmillan Reference USA) Gale Group.
—Murder on the Run. unabr. ed. 1998. (Inspector John Sanders Mystery Ser.). audio 39.95 (*1-55686-825-1*) Books in Motion.
—Pursued by Shadows. 1992. (Inspector John Sanders Mystery Ser.). 256p. text 20.00 (*0-684-19505-4*, Scribner) Simon & Schuster.
—Shortcut to Santa Fe. 1994. 256p. 20.00 (*0-684-19680-8*, Scribner) Simon & Schuster.
—Sleep of the Innocent. unabr. ed. 1999. (Inspector John Sanders Mystery Ser.). audio 49.95 (*1-55686-906-1*) Books in Motion.
—Sleep of the Innocent. 1991. 256p. 18.95 o.s.i (*0-684-19305-1*, Scribner) Simon & Schuster.

**JEFFRIES, MRS. (FICTITIOUS CHARACTER)—FICTION**

Brightwell, Emily. The Ghost & Mrs. Jeffries. 1993. (Victorian Mystery Ser.). mass mkt. 5.50 o.s.i (*0-425-13949-2*) Berkley Publishing Group.
—The Ghost & Mrs. Jeffries. l.t. ed. 1999. (Paperback Ser.). 279p. pap. 24.95 (*0-7838-8602-0*) Thorndike Pr.
—The Inspector & Mrs. Jeffries. 1993. (Victorian Mystery Ser.). 192p. mass mkt. 5.99 (*0-425-13622-1*) Berkley Publishing Group.
—The Inspector & Mrs. Jeffries. l.t. ed. 1999. (Paperback Ser.). 256p. pap. 23.95 (*0-7838-0417-2*) Thorndike Pr.
—Mrs. Jeffries & the Missing Alibi. 1996. (Victorian Mystery Ser.). 240p. mass mkt. 5.99 o.s.i (*0-425-15256-1*) Berkley Publishing Group.
—Mrs. Jeffries Dusts for Clues. 1993. (Victorian Mystery Ser.). 192p. mass mkt. 5.50 o.s.i (*0-425-13704-X*) Berkley Publishing Group.
—Mrs. Jeffries Dusts for Clues. 1999. (G. K. Hall Paperback Ser.). 253p. pap. 23.95 (*0-7838-8721-3*, Macmillan Reference USA) Gale Group.
—Mrs. Jeffries on the Ball. l.t. ed. 1995. (Nightingale Ser.). 282p. reprint ed. pap. 18.95 o.p. (*0-7838-1284-1*, Macmillan Reference USA) Gale Group.
—Mrs. Jeffries on the Ball: A Victorian Mystery. 1994. (Victorian Mystery Ser.). 208p. mass mkt. 5.99 o.s.i (*0-425-14491-7*, Prime Crime) Berkley Publishing Group.
—Mrs. Jeffries on the Trail. 1995. (Victorian Mystery Ser.). 240p. mass mkt. 5.50 o.s.i (*0-425-14691-X*, Prime Crime) Berkley Publishing Group.
—Mrs. Jeffries Plays the Cook. 1995. (Victorian Mystery Ser.). 240p. mass mkt. 5.50 o.s.i (*0-425-15053-4*) Berkley Publishing Group.
—Mrs. Jeffries Pleads Her Case. 2003. 208p. (Orig.). mass mkt. 5.99 (*0-425-18947-3*, Prime Crime) Berkley Publishing Group.
—Mrs. Jeffries Questions the Answer. 1997. (Victorian Mystery Ser.). 240p. mass mkt. 5.99 o.s.i (*0-425-16093-9*, Prime Crime) Berkley Publishing Group.
—Mrs. Jeffries Questions the Answer. l.t. ed. 2000. (G. K. Hall Paperback Ser.). 287p. pap. 23.95 (*0-7838-9266-7*, Macmillan Reference USA) Gale Group.
—Mrs. Jeffries Reveals Her Art. 1998. (Victorian Mystery Ser.). 240p. mass mkt. 5.99 o.s.i (*0-425-16243-5*, Prime Crime) Berkley Publishing Group.
—Mrs. Jeffries Reveals Her Art. l.t. ed. 2000. (G. K. Hall Paperback Ser.). 272p. pap. 23.95 (*0-7838-9104-0*, Macmillan Reference USA) Gale Group.
—Mrs. Jeffries Rocks the Boat. 1999. (Victorian Mystery Ser.: Vol. 12). 208p. mass mkt. 5.99 o.s.i (*0-425-16934-0*) Berkley Publishing Group.
—Mrs. Jeffries Rocks the Boat. l.t. ed. 2002. pap. 24.95 (*0-7862-4463-1*) Thorndike Pr.
—Mrs. Jeffries Stands Corrected. 1996. (Victorian Mystery Ser.). 224p. mass mkt. 5.99 o.s.i (*0-425-15580-3*, Prime Crime) Berkley Publishing Group.
—Mrs. Jeffries Takes Stock. 1994. (Victorian Mystery Ser.). 208p. mass mkt. 4.99 o.s.i (*0-425-14282-5*, Prime Crime) Berkley Publishing Group.
—Mrs. Jeffries Takes Stock. l.t. ed. 2000. (Paperback Ser.). 261p. pap. 23.95 (*0-7838-9157-1*) Thorndike Pr.
—Mrs. Jeffries Takes the Cake. 1998. (Victorian Mystery Ser.). 240p. mass mkt. 5.99 o.s.i (*0-425-16569-8*, Prime Crime) Berkley Publishing Group.
—Mrs. Jeffries Takes the Cake. l.t. ed. 1999. (Paperback Ser.). 282p. pap. 24.95 (*0-7838-8798-1*, Macmillan Reference USA) Gale Group.
—Mrs. Jeffries Takes the Stage. 1997. (Victorian Mystery Ser.). 240p. mass mkt. 5.99 o.s.i (*0-425-15724-5*, Prime Crime) Berkley Publishing Group.
—Mrs. Jeffries Takes the Stage. l.t. ed. 2000. (G. K. Hall Paperback Ser.). 280p. pap. 23.95 (*0-7838-9035-4*, Macmillan Reference USA) Gale Group.
—Mrs. Jeffries Weeds the Plot. l.t. ed. 2002. 304p. pap. 24.95 (*0-7862-4464-X*) Thorndike Pr.

**JEFFRY, JANE (FICTITIOUS CHARACTER)—FICTION**

Churchill, Jill. Bell, Book, & Scandal. l.t. ed. 2004. (Jane Jeffry Mystery Ser.). 226p. 30.95 (*1-58724-578-7*, Wheeler Publishing, Inc.) Gale Group.
—Bell, Book, & Scandal. 2003. 224p. 23.95 (*0-06-009797-3*, Morrow, William & Co.) Morrow/Avon.
—Class Menagerie. 1999. (Jane Jeffry Mystery Ser.). 224p. mass mkt. 6.99 (*0-380-77380-5*, Avon Bks.) Morrow/Avon.
—Farewell to Yarns. 1991. (Jane Jeffry Mystery Ser.). 256p. mass mkt. 6.99 (*0-380-76399-0*, Avon Bks.) Morrow/Avon.
—Fear of Frying. (Jane Jeffry Mystery Ser.). 1998. 256p. mass mkt. 6.99 (*0-380-78707-5*); 1997. 224p. pap. 22.00 (*0-380-97324-3*) Morrow/Avon. (Avon Bks.).
—From Here to Paternity. 1995. (Jane Jeffry Mystery Ser.). 256p. (Orig.). mass mkt. 6.99 (*0-380-77715-0*, Avon Bks.) Morrow/Avon.
—Grime & Punishment. 1989. 208p. (Orig.). mass mkt. 3.50 o.s.i (*0-553-27646-8*) Bantam Bks.
—Grime & Punishment. 1992. (Jane Jeffry Mystery Ser.). 256p. (Orig.). mass mkt. 6.99 (*0-380-76400-8*, Avon Bks.) Morrow/Avon.
—A Groom with a View: A Jane Jeffry Mystery. (Jane Jeffry Mystery Ser.). 2000. 288p. mass mkt. 6.50 (*0-380-79450-0*); Bk. C. 1999. 224p. 22.00 (*0-380-97570-X*) Morrow/Avon. (Avon Bks.).
—A Groom with a View: A Jane Jeffry Mystery. l.t. ed. 2000. (Americana Ser.). 293p. 27.95 (*0-7862-2454-1*) Thorndike Pr.
—The House of Seven Mabels: A Jane Jeffry Mystery. 2002. 240p. 23.95 (*0-380-97736-2*, Morrow, William & Co.) Morrow/Avon.
—A Knife to Remember. 1999. (Jane Jeffry Mystery Ser.). 224p. mass mkt. 6.99 (*0-380-77381-3*, Avon Bks.) Morrow/Avon.
—The Merchant of Menace: A Jane Jeffry Mystery. 1999. 256p. mass mkt. 6.99 (*0-380-79449-7*); 1998. 224p. 21.00 (*0-380-97569-6*) Morrow/Avon. (Avon Bks.).
—Mulch Ado about Nothing: A Jane Jeffry Mystery. 2001. 272p. mass mkt. 6.50 (*0-380-80491-3*); 2000. 216p. 23.00 (*0-380-97735-4*, Morrow, William & Co.) Morrow/Avon.
—Quiche Before Dying. 1993. (Jane Jeffry Mystery Ser.). 192p. mass mkt. 6.99 (*0-380-76932-8*, Avon Bks.) Morrow/Avon.
—Silence of the Hams. 1996. (Jane Jeffry Mystery Ser.). 288p. mass mkt. 6.99 (*0-380-77716-9*, Avon Bks.) Morrow/Avon.
—War & Peas. (Jane Jeffry Mystery Ser.). 1997. 288p. mass mkt. 6.99 (*0-380-78706-7*); 1996. 224p. mass mkt. 20.00 (*0-380-97323-5*) Morrow/Avon. (Avon Bks.).

**JEKYLL, DOCTOR (FICTITIOUS CHARACTER)—FICTION**

Dalmatian Press Staff, adapted by. Dr. Jekyll & Mr. Hyde. 1994. (Review Ser.: No. 3). 136p. pap. 6.00 (*0-9641292-5-6*) Global City Pr.
Edgar, David. The Strange Case of Dr. Jekyll & Mr. Hyde. 1992. 112p. pap. 13.95 o.p. (*1-85459-121-5*) Hern, Nick Bks. GBR. *Dist:* Theatre Communications Group, Inc.
Estleman, Loren D. Dr. Jekyll & Mr. Holmes. 2001. 224p. pap. 12.00 (*0-7434-2392-5*) ibooks, Inc.
—Dr. Jekyll & Mr. Holmes. E-Book 6.99 (*1-59019-599-X*) ipicturebooks, LLC.
Estleman, Loren D. & Watson, John H. Dr. Jekyll & Mr. Holmes. 1979. 8.95 o.p. (*0-385-15257-4*) Doubleday Publishing.
—Dr. Jekyll & Mr. Holmes. 1980. 256p. pap. 3.95 o.p. (*0-14-005665-3*, Penguin Bks.) Viking Penguin.
Hedge, Tricia, ed. Jekyll & Hyde. 1991. (Illus.). 80p. pap. text 5.95 o.p. (*0-19-421661-6*) Oxford Univ. Pr., Inc.
Jekyll & Hyde: The Musical. 1999. 48p. pap. 9.95 (*1-57560-152-4*) Cherry Lane Music Co.
Jekyll & Hyde Vocal Selections - Broadway Edition. 1997. 100p. otabind 17.95 (*1-57560-071-4*, HL02502211, Cherry Lane Music) Cherry Lane Music Co.
Oldknow, Antony, ed. Four Short Novels: Carmilla, the Strange Case of Dr. Jekyll & Mr. Hyde, the Sign of the Four, & the Snows of Kilimanjaro. 1998. 295p. pap. text 18.00 (*1-881604-32-2*) Scopcraeft Pr.
Slout, William L. The Trial of Dr. Jekyll: An Adaptation of Robert Louis Stevenson's "The Strange Case of Dr. Jekyll & Mr. Hyde", a Play in two Acts. 1993. (Clipper Studies in the Theatre: No. 7). viii, 75p. pap. 15.00 o.p. (*0-8095-6253-7*); lib. bdg. 25.00 o.p. (*0-8095-6252-9*) Millefleurs.
Stevenson, Robert Louis. Dr. Jekyll & Mr. Hyde. Date not set. pap. text (*0-17-556567-8*) Addison-Wesley Longman, Inc.
—Dr. Jekyll & Mr. Hyde. 1964. (Airmont Classics Ser.). (YA). (gr. 8 up). mass mkt. 2.25 (*0-8049-0042-6*, CL-42) Airmont Publishing Co., Inc.
—Dr. Jekyll & Mr. Hyde. (Illus.). lib. bdg. 19.95 (*0-88411-994-7*, Aeonian Pr.) Amereon, Ltd.
—Dr. Jekyll & Mr. Hyde. 1994. (Illustrated Classics Collection). 64p. pap. 4.95 (*0-7854-0664-6*, 40337); pap. 3.60 o.p. (*1-56103-420-7*) American Guidance Service, Inc.
—Dr. Jekyll & Mr. Hyde. unabr. ed. 1991. audio 21.95 o.p. (*1-55656-088-5*, DAB028) BBC Audiobooks America.
—Dr. Jekyll & Mr. Hyde. 1985. (gr. 7 up). pap. 1.25 o.p. (*0-553-15402-8*); 1982. 128p. mass mkt. 3.95 (*0-553-21277-X*, Bantam Classics) Bantam Bks.
—Dr. Jekyll & Mr. Hyde. 1990. (Illus.). 48p. 3.75 o.s.i (*0-425-12025-2*, Classics Illustrated) Berkley Publishing Group.
—Dr. Jekyll & Mr. Hyde. Danahay, Martin A., ed. 1999. (Literary Texts Ser.). 325p. pap. (*1-55111-245-0*) Broadview Pr.
—Dr. Jekyll & Mr. Hyde. 1990. reprint ed. lib. bdg. 16.95 (*0-89968-552-8*) Buccaneer Bks., Inc.
—Dr. Jekyll & Mr. Hyde. unabr. ed. audio 16.95 o.p. (*1-55656-036-2*); 1997. pap. 16.95 incl. audio (*1-55656-222-5*) Dercum Audio.
—Dr. Jekyll & Mr. Hyde. unabr. ed. 1994. audio 4.99 (*0-88646-712-8*) Durkin Hayes Publishing Ltd.
—Dr. Jekyll & Mr. Hyde. 2002. (Illus.). 48p. pap. 7.95 (*0-237-52281-0*) Evans Brothers, Ltd. GBR. *Dist:* Trafalgar Square.
—Dr. Jekyll & Mr. Hyde. abr. ed. 2015. audio 16.95 (*1-56511-644-5*) HighBridge Co.
—Dr. Jekyll & Mr. Hyde. 1991. (Vintage Bks.). 112p. pap. 8.00 (*0-679-73476-7*, Vintage) Knopf Publishing Group.
—Dr. Jekyll & Mr. Hyde. 1992. (Everyman's Library). 272p. 17.00 (*0-679-40538-0*) McKay, David Co., Inc.
—Dr. Jekyll & Mr. Hyde. 1987. (Signet Classics). 128p. mass mkt. 3.95 o.p. (*0-451-52393-8*, Signet Classics); mass mkt. 2.25 o.p. (*0-451-52138-2*) NAL.
—Dr. Jekyll & Mr. Hyde. abr. ed. 2001. audio 18.00 (*1-931056-77-3*, New Millennium Audio) New Millennium Entertainment.
—Dr. Jekyll & Mr. Hyde. abr. ed. 1994. 17.95 o.p. (*1-55800-691-5*) NewStar Media, Inc.
—Dr. Jekyll & Mr. Hyde. abr. ed. 1995. (Classics on Cassette). pap. 16.95 o.s.i incl. audio (*0-453-00940-9*) Penguin/HighBridge.
—Dr. Jekyll & Mr. Hyde. 1999. E-Book 3.99 incl. cd-rom (*1-891595-92-X*) Quiet Vision Publishing.
—Dr. Jekyll & Mr. Hyde. unabr. ed. 1999. audio 18.00 (*1-55690-155-0*, 80050E7) Recorded Bks., LLC.
—Dr. Jekyll & Mr. Hyde. 1987. (Running Press Classics Ser.). 63p. pap. 2.95 o.p. (*0-89471-491-0*); lib. bdg. 12.90 o.p. (*0-89471-492-9*) Running Pr. Bk. Pubs.
—Dr. Jekyll & Mr. Hyde. Shefter, Harry, ed. 1980. (Enriched Classics Ser.). 176p. mass mkt. 1.95 o.s.i (*0-671-48957-7*, Pocket) Simon & Schuster.
—Dr. Jekyll & Mr. Hyde. unabr. ed. 2002. audio compact disk 25.00 (*1-58472-101-4*, Commuters Library); (YA). pap. incl. audio compact disk (*1-58472-245-2*, In Audio); (YA). pap. incl. audio compact disk (*1-58472-245-2*, In Audio) Sound Room Pubs., Inc.
—Dr. Jekyll & Mr. Hyde. abr. ed. 1973. pap. 5.95 o.p. incl. audio (*0-88142-337-8*) Soundelux Audio Publishing.
—Dr. Jekyll & Mr. Hyde. 1998. 135p. text 27.95 (*1-56000-517-3*) Transaction Pubs.
—Dr. Jekyll & Mr. Hyde. (Stepping Stone Adventures Ser.). 2000. 10.04 (*0-606-19893-8*); 1985. 10.00 (*0-606-02457-3*) Turtleback Bks.
—Dr. Jekyll & Mr. Hyde. 1997. (Classics Library). 256p. pap. 3.95 (*1-85326-061-4*, 0614WW) Wordsworth Editions, Ltd. GBR. *Dist:* Casemate Pubs. & Bk. Distributors, LLC.
—Dr. Jekyll & Mr. Hyde. unabr. ed. 1991. audio 16.95 (*1-55686-217-2*, 217) Books in Motion.
—Dr. Jekyll & Mr. Hyde, Set. unabr. ed. 1994. audio 20.95 (*1-55685-344-0*) Audio Bk. Contractors, Inc.
—Dr. Jekyll & Mr. Hyde, Set. 1992. audio 26.95 Olivia & Hill Pr., The.
—Dr. Jekyll & Mr. Hyde & Other Stories. E-Book 5.00 (*0-7607-1297-2*) Barnes & Noble, Inc.
—Dr. Jekyll & Mr. Hyde & Other Stories. 1982. (Oxford Progressive English Readers Ser.). (Illus.). pap. 4.95 o.p. (*0-19-581056-2*) Oxford Univ. Pr., Inc.
—Dr. Jekyll & Mr. Hyde & Other Stories. 1994. (Literary Classics Ser.). 221p. (YA). text 5.98 o.p. (*1-56138-474-7*, Courage Bks.) Running Pr. Bk. Pubs.
—Dr. Jekyll & Mr. Hyde & Other Stories. Calder, Jenni, ed. 1981. (English Library). pap. 2.95 o.p. (*0-14-005776-5*) Viking Penguin.
—Dr. Jekyll & Mr. Hyde & Other Stories. Calder, Jenni, ed. & intro. by. 1980. (Penguin English Library). 304p. pap. 6.95 o.s.i (*0-14-043117-9*, Penguin Classics) Viking Penguin.
—Dr. Jekyll & Mr. Hyde & Other Tales of the Macabre. unabr. ed. 1980. audio 42.00 Jimcin Recordings.

—Dr. Jekyll & Mr. Hyde & Travels with a Donkey. abr. ed. 1995. audio 26.95 (*1-885546-04-1*) Big Ben Audio, Inc.

—Dr. Jekyll & Mr. Hyde & Weir of Hermiston. Letley, Emma, ed. & intro. by. 1987. (Oxford World's Classics Ser.). 256p. pap. 5.95 o.p. (*0-19-281740-X*) Oxford Univ. Pr., Inc.

—Dr. Jekyll & Mr. Hyde Readalong. 1994. (Illustrated Classics Collection). 64p. pap. 14.95 incl. audio (*0-7854-0705-7*, 40339) American Guidance Service, Inc.

—El Extrano Casa de Dr. Jekyll y Mister Hyde. Teresa Agnes, ed. Heller, Rudolf, tr. 1979. Orig. Title: Dr. Jekyll & Mr. Hyde. (SPA., Illus.). 64p. stu. ed. 1.50 (*0-88301-567-6*); pap. text 3.95 (*0-88301-447-5*) Pendulum Pr., Inc.

—The Strange Case of Dr. Jekyll & Mr. Hyde. abr. ed. audio 12.95 (*0-89926-144-2*, 832) Audio Bk. Co.

—The Strange Case of Dr. Jekyll & Mr. Hyde. audio 12.00 (*1-878427-41-5*, XC437) Cimino Publishing Group.

—The Strange Case of Dr. Jekyll & Mr. Hyde. Wolfson, Susan J. & Qualls, Barry V., eds. 2000. 107p. (C). pap. text 8.95 (*1-58390-010-1*, Copley Editions) Copley Publishing Group, Inc.

—The Strange Case of Dr. Jekyll & Mr. Hyde. 1991. (Dover Thrift Editions Ser.). 64p. pap. 1.00 (*0-486-26688-5*) Dover Pubns., Inc.

—The Strange Case of Dr. Jekyll & Mr. Hyde. abr. ed. 1996. audio 9.95 o.s.i (*1-55994-102-2*, CPN 1283, HarperAudio) HarperTrade.

—The Strange Case of Dr. Jekyll & Mr. Hyde, Set. abr. ed. 1999. audio 16.95 Highsmith Inc.

—The Strange Case of Dr. Jekyll & Mr. Hyde. l.t. ed. 87p. pap. 15.57 (*0-7583-2409-X*); 343p. pap. 36.19 (*0-7583-2415-4*); 153p. pap. 20.85 (*0-7583-2411-1*); 195p. pap. 24.30 (*0-7583-2412-X*); 240p. pap. 27.92 (*0-7583-2413-8*); 295p. pap. 32.38 (*0-7583-2414-6*); 70p. pap. 14.16 (*0-7583-2408-1*); 119p. pap. 18.16 (*0-7583-2410-3*); 70p. lib. bdg. 21.47 (*0-7583-2400-6*); 295p. lib. bdg. 39.65 (*0-7583-2406-5*); 119p. lib. bdg. 27.18 (*0-7583-2402-2*); 343p. lib. bdg. 43.00 (*0-7583-2407-3*); 240p. lib. bdg. 35.74 (*0-7583-2405-7*); 87p. lib. bdg. 23.92 (*0-7583-2401-4*); 153p. lib. bdg. 29.54 (*0-7583-2403-0*); 195p. lib. bdg. 32.57 (*0-7583-2404-9*) Huge Print Pr.

—The Strange Case of Dr. Jekyll & Mr. Hyde. l.t. ed. 1998. (Large Print Heritage Ser.). 120p. lib. bdg. (*1-58118-024-1*, 22016) LRS.

—The Strange Case of Dr. Jekyll & Mr. Hyde, Level 5. 2000. (C). pap. 7.93 (*0-582-42745-2*) Longman Publishing Group.

—The Strange Case of Dr. Jekyll & Mr. Hyde. 1999. Bk. 1. E-Book 1.95 (*1-58515-237-4*); Bk. 2. E-Book 1.95 (*1-58515-238-2*) MesaView, Inc.

—The Strange Case of Dr. Jekyll & Mr. Hyde, Set. abr. ed. 1999. (Mystery Theatre Ser.). audio 16.95 (*1-56994-514-4*, 32904, Monterey SoundWorks) Monterey Media, Inc.

—The Strange Case of Dr. Jekyll & Mr. Hyde. abr. ed. 1996. (Classic Fiction Ser.). (YA). audio 13.98 (*962-634-590-X*, NA209014, Naxos AudioBooks) Naxos of America, Inc.

—The Strange Case of Dr. Jekyll & Mr. Hyde. Seely, John, ed. 1995. (Thornes Classic Novels Ser.). (Illus.). 195p. pap. 14.95 (*0-7487-1829-X*) Nelson Thornes GBR. *Dist:* Trans-Atlantic Pubns., Inc.

—The Strange Case of Dr. Jekyll & Mr. Hyde. unabr. ed. 2001. audio 42.95 NorthStar Audio Bks.

—The Strange Case of Dr. Jekyll & Mr. Hyde. Letley, Emma, ed. & intro. by. 1998. (Oxford World's Classics Ser.). 272p. pap. 6.95 (*0-19-283431-2*) Oxford Univ. Pr., Inc.

—The Strange Case of Dr. Jekyll & Mr. Hyde. 2nd ed. 1993. (Illus.). 110p. pap. text 5.95 (*0-19-585429-2*) Oxford Univ. Pr., Inc.

—The Strange Case of Dr. Jekyll & Mr. Hyde. 1996. (Classic Ser.). 96p. pap. 0.95 o.p. (*0-14-600177-X*) Penguin Group (USA) Inc.

—The Strange Case of Dr. Jekyll & Mr. Hyde. unabr. ed. 1987. (Cassette Bookshelf Ser.). audio 15.98 (*0-8072-3448-6*, CB116CX, Listening Library) Random Hse. Audio Publishing Group.

—The Strange Case of Dr. Jekyll & Mr. Hyde. Qualls, Barry V., ed. & intro. by. 1995. 144p. mass mkt. 3.99 (*0-671-53210-3*, Pocket) Simon & Schuster.

—The Strange Case of Dr. Jekyll & Mr. Hyde. unabr. ed. 2000. audio compact disk 18.95; 1996. 16.95 incl. audio (*1-883049-69-5*, 394107) Sound Room Pubs., Inc. (Commuters Library).

—The Strange Case of Dr. Jekyll & Mr. Hyde. audio 10.95 Spoken Arts, Inc.

—The Strange Case of Dr. Jekyll & Mr. Hyde. unabr. ed. 2002. audio compact disk 26.00 (*1-4001-0076-3*); audio compact disk 20.00 (*1-4001-5076-0*) Tantor Media, Inc.

—The Strange Case of Dr. Jekyll & Mr. Hyde. 1996. 272p. reprint ed. pap. 6.95 (*0-460-87792-5*, Everyman's Classic Library in Paperback) Tuttle Publishing.

—The Strange Case of Dr. Jekyll & Mr. Hyde. 1990. (Illus.). 164p. pap. 10.00 (*0-8032-9240-6*, Bison Bks.); reprint ed. 25.00 o.p. (*0-8032-4212-3*) Univ. of Nebraska Pr.

—The Strange Case of Dr. Jekyll & Mr. Hyde. 1999. 110p. reprint ed. pap. 8.95 (*1-57002-097-3*) University Publishing Hse., Inc.

—The Strange Case of Dr. Jekyll & Mr. Hyde & Other Stories. 2001. per. 14.00 (*1-891355-88-0*) Blue Unicorn Editions.

—The Strange Case of Dr. Jekyll & Mr. Hyde & Other Stories. 2003. (Barnes & Noble Classics Ser.). 304p. mass mkt. 3.95 (*1-59308-054-9*) Fine Communications.

—The Strange Case of Dr. Jekyll & Mr. Hyde & Other Stories. 1998. (Cloth Bound Pocket Ser.). 240p. 7.95 (*3-89508-079-9*, 521294) Konemann.

—The Strange Case of Dr. Jekyll & Mr. Hyde & Other Stories. 1963. (Illus.). 8.00 o.p. (*0-399-20040-1*) Putnam Publishing Group, The.

—The Strange Case of Dr. Jekyll & Mr. Hyde & Other Stories. 1994. xx, 252p. reprint ed. pap. text 6.95 o.p. (*0-460-87197-8*, Everyman's Classic Library in Paperback) Tuttle Publishing.

Stevenson, Robert Louis & James, Henry. Dr. Jekyll & Mr. Hyde, collector's ed. 1977. audio 42.00 (*0-7366-0058-2*, 1070) Books on Tape, Inc.

Tennant, Emma. Two Women of London: The Strange Case of Ms. Jekyll & Mrs. Hyde. 1992. 121p. (Orig.). pap. 6.95 o.p. (*0-571-14330-X*) Faber & Faber, Inc.

Thomas, Donald. Jekyll, Alias Hyde: A Variation. 1988. 224p. 15.95 o.p. (*0-312-02592-0*, Saint Martin's Minotaur) St. Martin's Pr.

Wolf, Leonard, ed. The Essential Dr. Jekyll & Mr. Hyde: The Definitive, Annotated Edition of Robert Louis Stevenson's Classic Novel. annot. ed. 1995. (Essentials Ser.). (Illus.). 304p. (Orig.). pap. 14.95 o.p. (*0-452-26969-5*, Plume) Dutton/Plume.

**JEKYLL, HESTER (FICTITIOUS CHARACTER)—FICTION**

Bloch, Robert. The Jekyll Legacy. 1990. 17.95 o.p. (*0-312-85037-9*, Tor Bks.) Doherty, Tom Assocs., LLC.

Bloch, Robert & Norton, Andre. The Jekyll Legacy. 1991. mass mkt. 4.99 (*0-8125-1583-8*, Tor Bks.) Doherty, Tom Assocs., LLC.

**JENNER, JIMMY (FICTITIOUS CHARACTER)—FICTION**

Milne, John. Daddy's Girl. 201p. pap. 13.00 (*1-874061-90-4*) No Exit Pr. GBR. *Dist:* Trafalgar Square.

—Daddy's Girl. 1989. 15.95 o.p. (*0-312-02893-8*, Saint Martin's Minotaur) St. Martin's Pr.

—Dead Birds. l.t. ed. 1988. pap. 13.95 o.p. (*1-55504-546-4*) BBC Audiobooks America.

—Dead Birds. 202p. pap. 13.00 (*1-874061-87-4*) No Exit Pr. GBR. *Dist:* Trafalgar Square.

—Dead Birds. 1990. 20p. pap. 3.95 o.p. (*0-14-013911-7*); 1988. 208p. pap. 3.95 o.p. (*0-14-009704-X*, Penguin Bks.); 1987. 208p. 14.95 o.p. (*0-670-81444-X*) Viking Penguin.

—The Moody Man. 249p. pap. 13.00 (*1-874061-89-0*) No Exit Pr. GBR. *Dist:* Trafalgar Square.

—The Moody Man. 1989. 256p. pap. 3.95 o.p. (*0-14-010145-4*, Penguin Bks.); 1988. 15.95 o.p. (*0-670-81728-7*) Viking Penguin.

**JENNER, VICTOR (FICTITIOUS CHARACTER)—FICTION**

Rendell, Ruth. Live Flesh. 1987. pap. o.p. (*0-345-00727-1*); 352p. mass mkt. 6.99 (*0-345-34485-5*) Ballantine Bks.

—Live Flesh. l.t. ed. 1987. 331p. 18.95 o.p. (*0-8161-4280-7*, Macmillan Reference USA) Gale Group.

**JENNINGS, MARILEE (FICTITIOUS CHARACTER)—FICTION**

Hoag, Tami. Dark Paradise. 1994. 544p. mass mkt. 7.99 (*0-553-56161-8*) Bantam Bks.

**JENSEN, ALEX (FICTITIOUS CHARACTER)—FICTION**

Henry, Sue. Deadfall: An Alaska Mystery. unabr. ed. 2000. (Alaska Mystery Ser.). audio 29.95 (*0-7366-4428-8*) Books on Tape, Inc.

—Deadfall: An Alaska Mystery. (Alaska Mysteries Ser.). 1999. 320p. mass mkt. 6.99 (*0-380-79891-3*); 1998. 304p. 22.00 (*0-380-97661-7*) Morrow/Avon. (Avon Bks.).

—Death Takes Passage: An Alex Jensen Mystery. (Alaska Mysteries Ser.). 1998. (Illus.). 352p. mass mkt. 6.99 (*0-380-78863-2*); 1997. 272p. (YA). mass mkt. 22.00 o.p. (*0-380-97469-X*) Morrow/Avon. (Avon Bks.).

—Murder on the Iditarod Trail. unabr. collector's ed. 1999. audio 48.00 (*0-7366-4413-X*, 4874) Books on Tape, Inc.

—Murder on the Iditarod Trail. 1991. 18.95 o.p. (*0-87113-440-3*) Grove/Atlantic, Inc.

—Murder on the Iditarod Trail. 1993. (Alaska Mysteries Ser.). 320p. reprint ed. mass mkt. 6.99 (*0-380-71758-1*, Avon Bks.) Morrow/Avon.

—Sleeping Lady. unabr. ed. 1999. audio 48.00 (*0-7366-4458-X*, 4903) Books on Tape, Inc.

—Sleeping Lady. 320p. 1996. 22.00 o.p. (*0-688-13747-4*, Morrow, William & Co.); 1997. reprint ed. mass mkt. 6.99 (*0-380-72407-3*, Avon Bks.) Morrow/Avon.

—Termination Dust. (Alex Jensen Ser.). 1996. 320p. mass mkt. 6.99 (*0-380-72406-5*, Avon Bks.); 1995. 305p. 23.00 o.p. (*0-688-13746-6*, Morrow, William & Co.) Morrow/Avon.

**JENSEN, POUL (FICTITIOUS CHARACTER)—FICTION**

Davidsen, Leif. The Sardine Deception. Nunnally, Tiina & Murray, Steven T., trs. from DAN. 1986. Tr. of Uhellige Allianсer. 199p. pap. 6.95 (*0-940242-15-X*) Fjord Pr.

**JENSEN, SMOKE (FICTITIOUS CHARACTER)—FICTION**

Johnstone, William W. Absaroka Ambush. (First Mountain Man Ser.). 288p. 1996. mass mkt. 4.99 o.s.i (*0-8217-5538-2*, Zebra Bks.); 1993. mass mkt. 3.99 o.s.i (*1-55817-689-6*, Pinnacle Bks.) Kensington Publishing Corp.

—Battle of the Mountain Man. 1998. 256p. mass mkt. 4.99 o.s.i (*0-8217-5925-6*, Zebra Bks.) Kensington Publishing Corp.

—Blood of the Mountain Man. l.t. ed. 2001. (G. K. Hall Western Ser.). 297p. 24.95 o.p. (*0-7838-9487-2*, Macmillan Reference USA) Gale Group.

—Blood of the Mountain Man. 1995. 255p. mass mkt. 4.99 o.s.i (*0-8217-5324-X*); 1992. 256p. mass mkt. 3.50 o.s.i (*0-8217-3931-X*) Kensington Publishing Corp. (Zebra Bks.).

—Blood on the Divide. 1996. (First Mountain Man Ser.). 320p. mass mkt. 4.99 o.s.i (*0-8217-5511-0*, Zebra Bks.) Kensington Publishing Corp.

—Cheyenne Challenge No. 5: First Mountain Man. 352p. 1995. mass mkt. 4.50 o.s.i (*0-8217-5048-8*); 1997. (First Mountain Man Ser.: Vol. 5). reprint ed. mass mkt. 4.99 o.s.i (*0-8217-5607-9*, Zebra Bks.) Kensington Publishing Corp.

—Code of the Mountain Man. 2001. 288p. mass mkt. 5.99 (*0-7860-1304-4*); 1998. 288p. mass mkt. 4.99 (*0-8217-5944-2*); 1995. mass mkt. 4.99 o.s.i (*0-8217-5365-7*, Zebra Bks.); 1991. 288p. mass mkt. 3.50 o.s.i (*0-8217-3342-7*, Zebra Bks.) Kensington Publishing Corp.

—Code of the Mountain Man. l.t. ed. 2000. (G. K. Hall Western Ser.). (Illus.). 328p. 24.95 o.p. (*0-7838-9130-X*) Thorndike Pr.

—Courage of the Mountain Man. l.t. ed. 2001. (G. K. Hall Western Ser.). 309p. 24.95 (*0-7838-9409-0*, Macmillan Reference USA) Gale Group.

—Courage of the Mountain Man. 2001. 256p. mass mkt. 5.99 (*0-7860-1306-0*); 1995. 256p. mass mkt. 4.99 o.s.i (*0-8217-5366-5*, Zebra Bks.); 1995. 224p. mass mkt. 4.99 (*0-8217-5058-5*); 1992. mass mkt. 3.50 o.s.i (*0-8217-3720-1*, Zebra Bks.) Kensington Publishing Corp.

—Creed of the Mountain Man, 1. 1999. 256p. mass mkt. 4.99 o.s.i (*0-8217-6258-3*) Kensington Publishing Corp.

—Cunning of the Mountain Man. 320p. 1995. mass mkt. 4.99 o.s.i (*0-8217-5362-2*); 1994. mass mkt. 3.99 o.s.i (*0-8217-4723-1*) Kensington Publishing Corp. (Zebra Bks.).

—Cunning of the Mountain Man. l.t. ed. 2003. 25.95 (*0-7862-4630-8*) Thorndike Pr.

—The First Mountain Man. (Mountain Man Ser.). 1996. 320p. mass mkt. 4.99 o.s.i (*0-8217-5510-2*, Zebra Bks.); 1991. mass mkt. 3.99 o.s.i (*1-55817-565-2*, Pinnacle Bks.); No. 1. 1997. 208p. mass mkt. 4.99 (*0-8217-5701-6*, Zebra Bks.) Kensington Publishing Corp.

—The First Mountain Man: Blood on the Divide. 1992. 320p. mass mkt. 3.99 o.s.i (*1-55817-609-8*, Pinnacle Bks.) Kensington Publishing Corp.

—The First Mountain Man: Forty Guns West. 1993. 288p. mass mkt. 3.99 o.s.i (*1-55817-775-2*) Kensington Publishing Corp.

—Fury of the Mountain Man. 1995. 352p. mass mkt. 5.99 (*0-7860-1308-7*); 1995. mass mkt. 4.99 o.s.i (*0-8217-5364-9*, Zebra Bks.); 1995. 352p. mass mkt. 4.50 o.s.i (*0-8217-4920-X*, Zebra Bks.); 1993. 352p. mass mkt. 3.50 o.s.i (*0-8217-4328-7*, Zebra Bks.) Kensington Publishing Corp.

—Fury of the Mountain Man. 2002. (Western Ser.). 25.95 (*0-7862-4631-6*) Thorndike Pr.

—Guns of the Mountain Man. 1999. (Zebra Bks.). 256p. mass mkt. 4.99 o.s.i (*0-8217-6407-1*, Zebra Bks.) Kensington Publishing Corp.

—Heart of the Mountain Man. 2000. 256p. mass mkt. 5.99 o.s.i (*0-8217-6618-X*) Kensington Publishing Corp.

—Honor of the Mountain Man, No. 19. 1998. (Mountain Man Ser.). 288p. mass mkt. 4.99 o.s.i (*0-8217-5820-9*, Zebra Bks.) Kensington Publishing Corp.

—Journey of the Mountain Man. l.t. ed. 1999. (Western Ser.). 349p. 24.95 (*0-7838-8808-2*, Macmillan Reference USA) Gale Group.

—Journey of the Mountain Man. 2000. 256p. mass mkt. 5.99 (*0-7860-1302-8*); 1998. 224p. mass mkt. 4.99 o.s.i (*0-8217-5893-4*); 1997. 192p. mass mkt. 4.99 o.s.i (*0-8217-5702-4*); 1995. mass mkt. 4.50 o.s.i (*0-8217-5015-1*, Zebra Bks.); 1995. 224p. mass mkt. 4.99 o.s.i (*0-8217-5771-7*); 1989. mass mkt. 3.50 o.s.i (*0-8217-4244-2*, Zebra Bks.); 1989. mass mkt. 2.95 o.s.i (*0-8217-2602-1*); 1986. mass mkt. 2.25 o.p. (*0-8217-1816-9*, Zebra Bks.) Kensington Publishing Corp.

—The Last Mountain Man. 208p. 2000. mass mkt. 5.99 (*0-8217-6856-5*); 1996. mass mkt. 4.99 o.s.i (*0-8217-5274-X*); 1984. mass mkt. 3.50 o.s.i (*0-8217-4084-9*, Zebra Bks.) Kensington Publishing Corp.

—The Last Mountain Man. l.t. ed. 1998. (Western Ser.). 228p. 24.95 (*0-7838-8391-9*) Thorndike Pr.

—Law of the Mountain Man. l.t. ed. 1999. (Western Ser.). 319p. 24.95 o.p. (*0-7838-8730-2*, Macmillan Reference USA) Gale Group.

—Law of the Mountain Man. 1998. 256p. mass mkt. 4.99 o.s.i (*0-8217-5854-3*, Zebra Bks.); 1995. mass mkt. 4.50 o.s.i (*0-8217-5117-4*); 1989. mass mkt. 3.50 o.s.i (*0-8217-4085-7*, Zebra Bks.); 1995. 256p. mass mkt. 4.99 o.s.i (*0-8217-5367-3*) Kensington Publishing Corp.

—Ordeal of the Mountain Man. 1996. 288p. mass mkt. 4.99 o.s.i (*0-8217-5373-8*, Zebra Bks.) Kensington Publishing Corp.

—Power of the Mountain Man. 1995. (Zebra Bks.). mass mkt. 4.99 o.s.i (*0-8217-5363-0*, Zebra Bks.); 256p. mass mkt. 3.99 o.s.i (*0-8217-4871-8*) Kensington Publishing Corp.

—Preacher & the Mountain Caesar. 1997. (First Mountain Man Ser.). 304p. mass mkt. 5.99 (*0-8217-6585-X*) Kensington Publishing Corp.

—Preacher & the Mountain Caesar No. 6: First Mountain Man. 1997. 416p. reprint ed. mass mkt. 4.99 o.s.i (*0-8217-5636-2*, Zebra Bks.) Kensington Publishing Corp.

—Pursuit of the Mountain Man. l.t. ed. 2000. (G. K. Hall Western Ser.). 320p. 25.95 (*0-7838-9274-8*, Macmillan Reference USA) Gale Group.

—Pursuit of the Mountain Man. 2001. 256p. mass mkt. 5.99 (*0-7860-1305-2*); 1998. 256p. mass mkt. 4.99 o.s.i (*0-8217-6011-4*); 1996. 256p. mass mkt. 4.99 o.s.i (*0-8217-5246-4*); 1991. mass mkt. 3.50 o.s.i (*0-8217-3515-2*, Zebra Bks.) Kensington Publishing Corp.

—Rage of the Mountain Man. 1996. mass mkt. 4.99 o.s.i (*0-8217-5361-4*); 1994. 288p. mass mkt. 3.99 o.s.i (*0-8217-4567-0*) Kensington Publishing Corp. (Zebra Bks.).

—Rage of the Mountain Man. 2003. (Western Ser.). 25.95 (*0-7862-4633-2*) Thorndike Pr.

—Return of the Mountain Man. 2000. 192p. mass mkt. 5.99 (*0-7860-1296-X*); 1996. mass mkt. 4.99 o.s.i (*0-8217-5298-7*, Zebra Bks.); 1989. mass mkt. 3.50 o.s.i (*0-8217-4018-0*, Zebra Bks.); 1989. mass mkt. 2.95 o.p. (*0-8217-2940-3*) Kensington Publishing Corp.

—Return of the Mountain Man. l.t. ed. 1998. (Western Ser.). 223p. 24.95 (*0-7838-0334-6*) Thorndike Pr.

—Revenge of the Mountain Man. l.t. ed. 1999. (Western Ser.). 325p. 24.95 o.p. (*0-7838-8607-1*, Macmillan Reference USA) Gale Group.

—Revenge of the Mountain Man. 1997. 256p. mass mkt. 4.99 o.s.i (*0-8217-5815-2*); 1995. mass mkt. 4.50 o.s.i (*0-8217-5176-X*); 1988. 256p. mass mkt. 3.50 o.s.i (*0-8217-3821-6*, Zebra Bks.) Kensington Publishing Corp.

—Spirit of the Mountain Man. 1995. 256p. mass mkt. 4.99 o.s.i (*0-8217-5191-3*, Zebra Bks.); mass mkt. 5.99 (*0-7860-1450-4*, Pinnacle Bks.) Kensington Publishing Corp.

—Trail of the Mountain Man. 2000. 272p. mass mkt. 5.99 (*0-7860-1297-8*); 1996. 272p. mass mkt. 4.99 o.s.i (*0-8217-5609-5*); 1995. mass mkt. 4.50 o.s.i (*0-8217-5151-4*); 1987. mass mkt. 3.50 o.s.i (*0-8217-3676-0*, Zebra Bks.) Kensington Publishing Corp.

—Trail of the Mountain Man. l.t. ed. 1999. (Western Ser.). 356p. 24.95 (*0-7838-8541-5*) Thorndike Pr.

—Triumph of the Mountain Man. abr. ed. 1999. audio 16.95 (*1-882071-92-1*) B&B Audio, Inc.

—Triumph of the Mountain Man. 1997. 288p. mass mkt. 4.99 o.s.i (*0-8217-5551-X*, Zebra Bks.) Kensington Publishing Corp.

—Valor of the Mountain Man. l.t. ed. 2001. (G.K. Hall Large Print Western Ser.). 325p. 25.95 (*0-7838-9539-9*, Macmillan Reference USA) Gale Group.

—Valor of the Mountain Man. 2001. 256p. mass mkt. 5.99 (*0-7860-1299-4*, Pinnacle Bks.) Kensington Publishing Corp.

—Vengeance of the Mountain Man, No. 18. 1997. 256p. mass mkt. 4.99 o.s.i (*0-8217-5681-8*) Kensington Publishing Corp.

—War of the Mountain Man. l.t. ed. 2000. (G. K. Hall Western Ser.). 343p. 24.95 (*0-7838-8940-2*, Macmillan Reference USA) Gale Group.

—War of the Mountain Man. 2001. 256p. mass mkt. 5.99 (*0-7860-1303-6*); 1996. 256p. mass mkt. 4.99 o.s.i (*0-8217-5610-9*); 1995. 288p. mass mkt. 4.50 o.s.i (*0-8217-5083-6*); 1990. mass mkt. 3.50 o.p. (*0-8217-3618-3*, Zebra Bks.) Kensington Publishing Corp.

**JESS, LADY (FICTITIOUS CHARACTER)—FICTION**

Durgin, Doranna. Changespell. rev. ed. 1997. 352p. pap. 5.99 (*0-671-87765-8*) Baen Bks.

—Dun Lady's Jess. 1994. per. 4.99 (*0-671-87617-1*) Baen Bks.

**JESUS CHRIST—FICTION**

Ashcroft, Mary Ellen. The Magdalene Gospel. 1995. 144p. 16.95 o.s.i (*0-385-47855-0*) Doubleday Publishing.

—The Magdalene Gospel: Meeting the Women Who Followed Jesus. 2004. xix, 144p. 12.99 (*0-8066-4358-7*, Augsburg Bks.) Augsburg Fortress, Pubs.

Balzac, Honoré de. Christ in Flanders. E-Book 2.49 (*1-58627-005-2*) Electric Umbrella Publishing.

—Christ in Flanders. E-Book 2.00 (*0-7410-0679-0*) SoftBook Pr.

Beavers, Marion C. The Wedding. 1997. 208p. (Orig.). pap. 10.99 (*1-883893-83-6*) WinePress Publishing.

Blaylock, James P. The Last Coin. 1996. 336p. mass mkt. 5.99 o.s.i (*0-441-47075-0*); 1988. 17.95 o.p. (*0-441-11381-8*) Ace Bks.

—The Last Coin. ltd. ed. 1988. 60.00 (*0-929480-00-7*) Ziesing, Mark V.

Byrne, Matthew. Heaven Looked Upwards. 1997. (*1-86059-066-7*) Town Hse.

Carse, James P. The Gospel of the Beloved Disciple. 1997. 144p. 18.00 (*0-06-061576-1*); pap. 13.00 (*0-06-061577-X*) HarperSanFrancisco.

Cordy, Michael. The Miracle Strain. 1998. 484p. mass mkt. (*0-552-14578-5*, Corgi) Bantam Bks.

—The Miracle Strain. 1997. 384p. 24.00 o.p. (*0-688-15508-1*, Morrow, William & Co.) Morrow/Avon.

Crace, Jim. Quarantine. 2002. E-Book 9.00 (*0-374-70334-5*); 2002. E-Book (*0-374-70335-3*); 2002. E-Book 15.00 (*0-374-70331-0*); 2002. E-Book o.p. (*0-374-70333-7*); 1998. 256p. 23.00 o.s.i (*0-374-23962-2*) Farrar, Straus & Giroux.

—Quarantine. 1999. 256p. pap. 13.00 (*0-312-19951-1*) Picador.

—Quarantine, Set. 1999. pap. (*0-312-20702-6*, Saint Martin's Griffin) St. Martin's Pr.

—Quarantine. l.t. ed. 1998. (Core Ser.). 323p. 30.95 (*0-7838-0113-0*) Thorndike Pr.

—Quarantine: Palm/Peanut. 2002. E-Book (*0-374-70332-9*) Farrar, Straus & Giroux.

Dillon, Sally Pierson. Victory of the Warrior King: The Story of the Life of Jesus. 2001. 224p. pap. 9.99 (*0-8280-1604-6*) Review & Herald Publishing Assn.

Dorr, Roberta Kells. Honored. 2003. 96p. 10.99 (*0-8007-1817-8*) Revell, Fleming H. Co.

Douglas, Lloyd Cassel. The Robe. Date not set. 476p. 30.95 (*0-8488-2252-8*) Amereon, Ltd.

—The Robe. 1985. 544p. 11.95 o.p. (*0-553-06400-2*) Bantam Bks.

—The Robe. unabr. ed. 1984. Pt. 1. audio 64.00 (*0-7366-0377-8*, 1356-A); Pt. 2. audio 64.00 Books on Tape, Inc.

—The Robe. 1952. 77p. pap. 5.60 (*0-87129-941-0*, R19) Dramatic Publishing Co.

—The Robe. 1999. 520p. pap. 14.00 (*0-395-95775-3*); 1986. pap. 9.95 (*0-395-40299-9*); 1986. 528p. pap. 14.95 o.p. (*0-395-40799-0*); 1942. 528p. 24.95 o.p. (*0-395-07635-8*) Houghton Mifflin Co.

—The Robe. l.t. ed. 1995. 889p. lib. bdg. 22.95 (*0-7838-1362-7*) Thorndike Pr.

Drummond, Richard H. Life of Jesus the Christ: An Edgar Cayce Guide. 1996. (Edgar Cayce Guides). 222p. mass mkt. 5.99 (*0-312-96057-3*, St. Martin's Paperbacks) St. Martin's Pr.

Enumah, Festus I. The Innocent Blood & Judas Iscariot. 2002. (Illus.). 269p. (*1-55306-344-9*); pap. (*1-55306-296-5*) Essence Publishing. (Guardian Bks.).

Galli, Guy M. Lifted Up: A Novel. 2003. vi, 232p. 14.95 (*1-59156-179-5*) Covenant Communications.

Griffiths, W. G. Malchus. 2002. (Illus.). 384p. pap. 14.99 (*1-58919-967-7*) RiverOak Publishing.

Groot, Tracy. The Brother's Keeper. 2003. 320p. pap. 11.99 (*0-8024-3105-4*) Moody Pr.

Gruber, Louis N. Jay: A Spiritual Fantasy. 2001. 280p. pap. 22.95 (*0-7596-5891-9*) 1stBooks Library.

Ignacio, Jose & Ignacio, Maria Lopez Vigil. Just Jesus: The Message of a Better World, 3 vols. 2000. (Scandalous Gospel Jesus of Nazareth Ser.: Vol. 2). 384p. pap. 18.95 (*0-8245-1849-7*, Crossroad Classic) Crossroad Publishing Co.

Ignacio, Jose & Lopez Vigil, Maria. Just Jesus: The Passion Book, 3 vols. 2000. 416p. pap. 18.95 (*0-8245-1857-8*, Crossroad 8 Avenue) Crossroad Publishing Co.

Kemp, Kenny. The Welcoming Door: Parables of the Carpenter. 2002. (Parables of the Carpenter Ser.). (Illus.). 304p. 18.95 (*0-06-008264-X*) HarperSanFrancisco.

LaCroix, Mary. The Remnant: A Novel. 6th ed. 1987. 544p. reprint ed. pap. 14.95 (*0-87604-201-9*, 544) A.R.E. Pr.

Lliteras, D. S. The Thieves of Golgotha. 1998. 192p. 19.95 (*1-57174-085-6*) Hampton Roads Publishing Co., Inc.

Lucado, Max. Cosmic Christmas. 1997. 128p. 12.99 (*0-8499-1530-9*) W Publishing Group.

Lund, Gerald N. Behold the Man. 2002. xx, 682p. 26.95 (*1-57008-853-5*, Shadow Mountain) Deseret Bk. Co.

Montreuil, Margaret. God in Sandals: When Jesus Walked among Us. 2003. 458p. pap. 22.99 (*1-59160-718-3*) Xulon Pr., Inc.

Moore, Christopher. Lamb: The Gospel According to Biff, Christ's Childhood Pal. 2003. 464p. pap. 13.95 (*0-380-81381-5*, Perennial) HarperTrade.

Morris, Tony, illus. The Fourth Wise Man. 1995. 32p. (J). (gr. 5-7). 12.99 o.p. (*0-8066-2713-1*, 9-2713) Augsburg Fortress, Pubs.

Omartian, Stormie. Child of Promise. gif. ed. 2000. (Illus.). 109p. 24.99 o.p. (*0-7369-0250-3*) Harvest Hse. Pubs.

Podrug, Junius. Dark Passage. Date not set. pap. (*0-7653-0580-1*, Forge Bks.); E-Book 24.95 (*0-312-70836-X*, Tor Bks.); 2004. 320p. mass mkt. 6.99 (*0-8125-7850-3*, Tor Bks.); 2002. 464p. 24.95 (*0-312-87514-2*, Forge Bks.) Doherty, Tom Assocs., LLC.

Read, P. Anne Atkins Recommends. 2001. x, 307p. pap. 11.00 (*0-340-75625-X*) Hodder & Stoughton, Ltd. GBR. *Dist:* Trafalgar Square.

Reece, Colleen L. Belated Follower. 1996. pap. text 2.97 o.p. (*1-55748-973-4*) Barbour Publishing, Inc.

—Belated Follower. l.t. ed. 2000. (Christian Fiction Ser.). 278p. 24.95 (*0-7862-2861-X*) Thorndike Pr.

Ricci, Nino. Testament. 2003. 464p. pap. (*0-385-65855-9*, Anchor Canada) Doubleday Canada, Ltd. CAN. *Dist:* Random Hse., Inc.

—Testament. 2003. (Illus.). 464p. tchr. ed. 25.00 (*0-618-27353-0*) Houghton Mifflin Co.

Sheldon, Charles Monroe. Jesus Is Here! Continuing the Story of in His Steps. 1984. 235 P. ;p. (*0-941678-06-7*) Capper's Bks.

Torrey, Michele. Beloved Rabbi: A Story of Jesus. 2000. 196p. E-Book 8.00 (*0-7388-8416-2*) Xlibris Corp.

Truman, Ruth. Not of This Fold. 2001. 168p. pap. 13.98 (*0-7596-1948-4*) 1stBooks Library.

Venter, Frans. Simon of Cyrene: The Man Who Carried the Cross of Christ. Bell, James S., ed. 1993. (Christian Epics Ser.). 330p. pap. 9.99 o.p. (*0-8024-7100-5*) Moody Pr.

Wise, Charles C., Jr. The Magian Gospel of Brother Yeshua. 1979. (Illus.). 306p. 11.95 (*0-917023-05-6*); pap. 5.95 (*0-917023-06-4*) Magian Pr., The.

Zacharias, Ravi K. Sense & Sensuality: Jesus Talks with Oscar Wilde on the Pursuit of Pleasure. 2003. (Great Conversations Ser.). 96p. 9.99 (*1-59052-014-9*) Multnomah Pubs., Inc.

**JIN, JOSHUA (FICTITIOUS CHARACTER)—FICTION**

Lee, Gus. No Physical Evidence. 1998. 400p. 24.95 o.s.i (*0-449-91139-X*, Fawcett) Ballantine Bks.

—No Physical Evidence. abr. ed. 1998. audio 17.95 o.p. (*1-56740-785-4*, 1462, Nova Audio Bks.); audio 28.95 (*1-56740-060-4*, 1460, Bookcassette); audio 89.25 (*1-56740-589-4*, 1461, Unabridged Library Editions) Brilliance Audio.

—No Physical Evidence: A Courtroom Novel. 2000. 384p. mass mkt. 6.99 o.s.i (*0-8041-1779-9*, Ivy Bks.) Ballantine Bks.

**JIREL OF JOIRY (FICTITIOUS CHARACTER)—FICTION**

Moore, C. L. Jirel of Joiry. 1982. 224p. mass mkt. 5.50 o.s.i (*0-441-38570-2*) Ace Bks.

**JOAN, SISTER (FICTITIOUS CHARACTER)—FICTION**

Black, Veronica. A Vow of Adoration: A Sister Joan Mystery. 1997. (Sister Joan Mystery Ser.: Vol. 9). 190p. 20.95 (*0-312-18205-8*, Saint Martin's Minotaur) St. Martin's Pr.

—A Vow of Chastity: A Sister Joan Mystery. 1993. mass mkt. 4.50 o.s.i (*0-8041-1055-7*, Ivy Bks.) Ballantine Bks.

—A Vow of Chastity: A Sister Joan Mystery. 1992. 192p. 16.95 o.p. (*0-312-07112-4*, Saint Martin's Minotaur) St. Martin's Pr.

—A Vow of Chastity: A Sister Joan Mystery. l.t. ed. 1992. (Linford Mystery Library). 400p. pap. 17.99 o.p. (*0-7089-7262-4*, Linford) Thorpe, F. A. Pubs. GBR. *Dist:* Ulverscroft Large Print Bks., Ltd., Ulverscroft Large Print Canada, Ltd.

—A Vow of Compassion: A Sister Joan Mystery. 1998. (Sister Joan Mystery Ser.: Vol. 10). 208p. 20.95 (*0-312-19354-8*, Saint Martin's Minotaur) St. Martin's Pr.

—A Vow of Compassion: A Sister Joan Mystery. l.t. ed. 1998. (Ulverscroft Large Print Ser.). 336p. 29.99 (*0-7089-3972-4*, Ulverscroft) Thorpe, F. A. Pubs. GBR. *Dist:* Ulverscroft Large Print Bks., Ltd., Ulverscroft Large Print Canada, Ltd.

—A Vow of Devotion: A Sister Joan Mystery. (Sister Joan Mystery Ser.). 1997. mass mkt. 5.50 o.s.i (*0-312-96005-0*, St. Martin's Paperbacks); 1995. 186p. 20.95 o.p. (*0-312-13206-9*, Saint Martin's Minotaur) St. Martin's Pr.

—A Vow of Devotion: A Sister Joan Mystery. l.t. ed. 1998. (Nightingale Ser.). 276p. pap. 20.95 (*0-7838-8388-9*) Thorndike Pr.

—A Vow of Fidelity: A Sister Joan Mystery. 1996. 208p. text 19.95 o.p. (*0-312-14064-9*, Saint Martin's Minotaur); Vol. 1. 1997. (Vow of Fidelity Ser.: Vol. 1). 192p. mass mkt. 5.50 (*0-312-96259-2*, St. Martin's Paperbacks) St. Martin's Pr.

—A Vow of Fidelity: A Sister Joan Mystery. l.t. ed. 1997. (Ulverscroft Large Print Ser.). 352p. 29.99 (*0-7089-3697-0*, Ulverscroft) Thorpe, F. A. Pubs. GBR. *Dist:* Ulverscroft Large Print Bks., Ltd., Ulverscroft Large Print Canada, Ltd.

—A Vow of Obedience: A Sister Joan Mystery. 1995. (Sister Joan Mystery Ser.). mass mkt. 5.50 o.s.i (*0-8041-1245-2*, Ivy Bks.) Ballantine Bks.

—A Vow of Obedience: A Sister Joan Mystery. l.t. ed. 1994. 298p. pap. 19.95 (*0-8161-7472-5*, Macmillan Reference USA) Gale Group.

—A Vow of Obedience: A Sister Joan Mystery. 1996. mass mkt. 143.76 (*0-312-95718-1*); 1994. 192p. 18.95 o.p. (*0-312-10573-8*, Saint Martin's Minotaur) St. Martin's Pr.

—A Vow of Penance: A Sister Joan Mystery. 1996. mass mkt. 5.50 (*0-312-95850-1*, St. Martin's Paperbacks); 1994. 270p. 19.95 o.p. (*0-312-11092-8*, Saint Martin's Minotaur) St. Martin's Pr.

—A Vow of Penance: A Sister Joan Mystery. l.t. ed. 1995. (Ulverscroft Large Print Ser.). 352p. 29.99 (*0-7089-3326-2*, Ulverscroft) Thorpe, F. A. Pubs. GBR. *Dist:* Ulverscroft Large Print Bks., Ltd., Ulverscroft Large Print Canada, Ltd.

—A Vow of Poverty: A Sister Joan Mystery. 1996. 208p. 20.95 o.p. (*0-312-14756-2*, Saint Martin's Minotaur) St. Martin's Pr.

—A Vow of Poverty: A Sister Joan Mystery. l.t. ed. 1997. (Ulverscroft Large Print Ser.). 388p. 29.99 (*0-7089-3733-0*, Ulverscroft) Thorpe, F. A. Pubs. GBR. *Dist:* Ulverscroft Large Print Bks., Ltd., Ulverscroft Large Print Canada, Ltd.

—A Vow of Sanctity: A Sister Joan Mystery. 1994. mass mkt. 4.99 o.s.i (*0-8041-1244-4*, Ivy Bks.) Ballantine Bks.

—A Vow of Sanctity: A Sister Joan Mystery. 1993. 192p. 16.95 (*0-312-09408-6*, Saint Martin's Minotaur) St. Martin's Pr.

—A Vow of Sanctity: A Sister Joan Mystery. l.t. ed. 1994. (Ulverscroft Large Print Ser.). 400p. 29.99 o.p. (*0-7089-3197-9*, Ulverscroft) Thorpe, F. A. Pubs. GBR. *Dist:* Ulverscroft Large Print Bks., Ltd., Ulverscroft Large Print Canada, Ltd.

—A Vow of Silence: A Sister Joan Mystery. 1991. mass mkt. 4.99 o.s.i (*0-8041-0814-5*, Ivy Bks.) Ballantine Bks.

—A Vow of Silence: A Sister Joan Mystery. 1990. 15.95 o.p. (*0-312-04441-0*, Saint Martin's Minotaur) St. Martin's Pr.

—A Vow of Silence: A Sister Joan Mystery. l.t. ed. 1991. (Ulverscroft Large Print Ser.). 29.99 (*0-7089-2529-4*, Ulverscroft) Thorpe, F. A. Pubs. GBR. *Dist:* Ulverscroft Large Print Bks., Ltd., Ulverscroft Large Print Canada, Ltd.

**JOEY ONE WAY (FICTITIOUS CHARACTER)—FICTION**

Rose, Joel. Kill Kill Faster Faster. 1998. 224p. pap. 11.95 o.s.i (*0-14-027329-8*) Penguin Group (USA) Inc.

**JOHANNSON, HILDA (FICTITIOUS CHARACTER)—FICTION**

Dams, Jeanne M. Death in Lacquer Red: A Hilda Johansson Mystery. l.t. ed. 1999. (Beeler Large Print Mystery Ser.). 225p. 25.95 (*1-57490-240-7*, Beeler Large Print Bks.) Beeler, Thomas T. Publisher.

—Death in Lacquer Red: A Hilda Johansson Mystery. 1999. (Hilda Johansson Mysteries Ser.). vii, 225p. 22.95 (*0-8027-3329-8*) Walker & Co.

—Green Grow the Victims: A Hilda Johansson Mystery. l.t. ed. 2001. (Beeler Large Print Mystery Ser.). x, 236p. 25.95 (*1-57490-369-1*, Beeler Large Print Bks.) Beeler, Thomas T. Publisher.

—Red, White & Blue Murders: A Hilda Johannson Mystery. 2000. (Hilda Johansson Mysteries Ser.). 189p. 23.95 (*0-8027-3341-7*) Walker & Co.

**JOHNSON, AVA (FICTITIOUS CHARACTER)—FICTION**

Cleage, Pearl. I Wish I Had a Red Dress. l.t. ed. 2001. (Hardcover Ser.). 340p. 30.95 (*1-58724-062-9*, Wheeler Publishing, Inc.) Gale Group.

—I Wish I Had a Red Dress. Gaudinier, ed. abr. ed. 2001. audio 25.95 (*0-694-52418-2*, HarperAudio) HarperTrade.

—I Wish I Had a Red Dress. 2001. 336p. 24.00 (*0-380-97733-8*, Morrow, William & Co.) Morrow/Avon.

—What Looks Like Crazy on an Ordinary Day. unabr. ed. 2001. audio 54.95 (*0-7927-2439-9*, CSL 328, Chivers Sound Library) BBC Audiobooks America.

—What Looks Like Crazy on an Ordinary Day. 2000. mass mkt. (*0-380-81771-3*, Avon Bks.); 1998. 256p. pap. 13.00 (*0-380-79487-X*, Avon Bks.); 1997. 256p. 20.00 (*0-380-97584-X*, Morrow, William & Co.) Morrow/Avon.

—What Looks Like Crazy on an Ordinary Day. abr. ed. 1998. audio 23.00 (*0-671-04470-2*, 593654, Simon & Schuster Audioworks) Simon & Schuster Audio.

—What Looks Like Crazy on an Ordinary Day. l.t. ed. (Americana Ser.). 416p. 2000. pap. 26.95 (*0-7862-1760-X*); 1999. 29.95 (*0-7862-1759-6*) Thorndike Pr.

**JOHNSON, COFFIN ED (FICTITIOUS CHARACTER)—FICTION**

Himes, Chester B. All Shot up. 1973. 160p. reprint ed. 7.95 o.p. (*0-911860-29-0*) Chatham Bookseller.

—All Shot Up. 2nd ed. 1996. 170p. reprint ed. pap. 12.95 (*1-56025-103-4*, Thunder's Mouth Pr.) Avalon Publishing Group.

—The Big Gold Dream. 2nd ed. 1996. 156p. reprint ed. pap. 12.95 (*1-56025-104-2*, Thunder's Mouth Pr.) Avalon Publishing Group.

—The Big Gold Dream. 1973. 160p. reprint ed. 7.95 o.p. (*0-911860-30-4*) Chatham Bookseller.

—Blind Man with a Pistol. 1989. (Vintage Crime Ser.). 192p. pap. 11.00 (*0-394-75998-2*, Vintage) Knopf Publishing Group.

—Cotton Comes to Harlem. 1994. (Illus.). lib. bdg. 11.95 (*1-56849-422-X*) Buccaneer Bks., Inc.

—Cotton Comes to Harlem. 1975. reprint ed. 8.95 o.p. (*0-911860-55-X*) Chatham Bookseller.

—Cotton Comes to Harlem. 1988. (Crime Ser.). (Illus.). 160p. pap. 11.00 (*0-394-75999-0*, Vintage) Knopf Publishing Group.

—The Crazy Kill. 1973. 160p. reprint ed. 7.95 o.p. (*0-911860-32-0*) Chatham Bookseller.

—The Crazy Kill. 160p. 1995. pap. 25.00 o.s.i (*0-8052-8217-3*, Schocken); 1989. pap. 11.00 (*0-679-72572-5*, Vintage) Knopf Publishing Group.

—For Love of Imabelle. 1973. 192p. reprint ed. 7.95 o.p. (*0-911860-33-9*) Chatham Bookseller.

—The Heat's On. 1975. 220p. reprint ed. 17.00 (*0-911860-57-6*) Chatham Bookseller.

—The Heat's On. 1988. (Vintage Crime Ser.). 176p. pap. 15.00 (*0-394-75997-4*, Vintage) Knopf Publishing Group.

—A Rage in Harlem. 1989. (Vintage Crime Ser.). Orig. Title: For Love of Imabelle. 160p. pap. 10.00 (*0-679-72040-5*, Vintage) Knopf Publishing Group.

—The Real Cool Killers. 1973. 160p. reprint ed. 7.95 o.p. (*0-911860-36-3*) Chatham Bookseller.

—The Real Cool Killers. 1988. (Vintage Crime Ser.). 160p. pap. 10.95 (*0-679-72039-1*, Pantheon) Knopf Publishing Group.

**JOHNSON, DAVID (FICTITIOUS CHARACTER)—FICTION**

Ashbaugh, Regan C. Downtick. 1998. 568p. pap. 6.99 (*0-671-01889-2*, Pocket) Simon & Schuster.

**JOHNSON, MAUREEN (FICTITIOUS CHARACTER)—FICTION**

Heinlein, Robert A. Time Enough for Love. 1987. 608p. mass mkt. 7.99 (*0-441-81076-4*) Ace Bks.

—Time Enough for Love. 1986. 608p. 4.50 o.s.i (*0-425-10224-6*); 1984. 3.95 o.s.i (*0-425-07990-2*); 1983. 3.95 o.s.i (*0-425-07050-6*); 1982. 3.75 o.s.i (*0-425-06126-4*); 1981. 3.25 o.s.i (*0-425-05490-X*); 1980. 2.75 o.s.i (*0-425-04684-2*); 1978. 2.50 o.s.i (*0-425-04373-8*); 1976. 2.25 o.s.i (*0-425-03471-2*); 1974. 1.95 o.p. (*0-425-02493-8*) Berkley Publishing Group.

—Time Enough for Love. 1973. 7.95 o.p. (*0-399-11151-4*) Putnam Publishing Group, The.

—To Sail Beyond the Sunset. 1988. 448p. mass mkt. 7.99 (*0-441-74860-0*) Ace Bks.

—To Sail Beyond the Sunset. 1987. 448p. 18.95 o.p. (*0-399-13267-8*) Putnam Publishing Group, The.

**JOHNSON, TOY (FICTITIOUS CHARACTER)—FICTION**

Rosenberg, Nancy Taylor. California Angel. 1995. 272p. (J). 17.95 o.p. (*0-525-93945-8*, Dutton Children's Bks.) Dutton/Plume.

—California Angel. l.t. ed. 1995. 25.95 o.p. (*1-56895-214-7*, Wheeler Publishing, Inc.) Gale Group.

—California Angel. abr. ed. 1995. 16.95 o.p. incl. audio (*0-453-00925-5*) HighBridge Co.

—California Angel. 1995. pap. 6.50 o.s.i (*0-451-18757-1*); 1995. 400p. mass mkt. 6.50 o.p. (*0-451-18628-1*); 1996. 400p. mass mkt. 6.99 o.s.i (*0-451-19177-3*) NAL. (Signet Bks.).

**JOKER (FICTITIOUS CHARACTER)—FICTION**

Dixon, Chuck. The Joker: Devil's Advocate. 1995. (Illus.). 96p. 24.95 o.p. (*1-56389-240-5*) DC Comics.

Dixon, Chuck & Nolan, Graham. The Joker: Devil's Advocate. 1996. (Illus.). 96p. pap. 12.95 (*1-56389-280-4*, Vertigo) DC Comics.

**JONES, ABEL (FICTITIOUS CHARACTER)—FICTION**

Parry, Owen. Bold Sons of Erin: A Novel of Suspense. 2003. 352p. 24.95 (*0-06-051390-X*, Morrow, William & Co.) Morrow/Avon.

—Faded Coat of Blue. 2000. audio 56.00 (*0-7366-5920-X*) Books on Tape, Inc.

—Faded Coat of Blue. 2002. 352p. pap. 13.95 (*0-06-093766-1*, Perennial) HarperTrade.

—Faded Coat of Blue. 2000. 368p. mass mkt. 6.99 (*0-380-79739-9*); 1999. 352p. 23.00 (*0-380-97642-0*, Avon Bks.) Morrow/Avon.

—Faded Coat of Blue. abr. ed. 1999. audio 25.00 (*0-7871-2006-5*) NewStar Media, Inc.

—Honor's Kingdom. 2003. 448p. mass mkt. 7.99 (*0-06-051079-X*, HarperTorch); 2002. 336p. 25.95 (*0-06-018634-8*, Morrow, William & Co.) Morrow/Avon.

—Honor's Kingdom. 2002. (Adventure Ser.). 28.95 (*0-7862-4852-1*) Thorndike Pr.

—Shadows of Glory. 2001. 384p. mass mkt. 6.99 (*0-380-82087-0*); 2000. 311p. 24.00 (*0-380-97643-9*, Morrow, William & Co.) Morrow/Avon.

**JONES, AMELIA (FICTITIOUS CHARACTER)—FICTION**

Gilman, Dorothy. The Tightrope Walker. l.t. ed. 1992. pap. 15.95 o.p. (*0-7927-0863-6*); 18.95 o.p. (*0-7927-0862-8*, E0017) BBC Audiobooks America.

—The Tightrope Walker. 1980. 224p. mass mkt. 2.50 o.p. (*0-449-24305-2*, Fawcett) Ballantine Bks.

—The Tightrope Walker. 1979. 9.95 o.p. (*0-385-14959-X*) Doubleday Publishing.

**JONES, BRIDGET (FICTITIOUS CHARACTER)—FICTION**

Fielding, Helen. Bridget Jones: The Edge of Reason. l.t. ed. 2000. (Wheeler Large Print Book Ser.). 458p. 28.95 (*1-56895-893-5*, Wheeler Publishing, Inc.) Gale Group.

—Bridget Jones: The Edge of Reason. abr. ed. 2001. audio (*0-333-74611-2*) Macmillan U.K. GBR. *Dist:* Macmillan Publishing Co., Inc.

—Bridget Jones: The Edge of Reason. 2001. 352p. pap. 14.00 (*0-14-029847-9*) Penguin Group (USA) Inc.

—Bridget Jones: The Edge of Reason. abr. ed. 2000. audio 25.95 (*0-375-41604-8*, RH Audio) Random Hse. Audio Publishing Group.

—Bridget Jones: The Edge of Reason. unabr. ed. 2001. audio compact disk 97.00 (*0-7887-6169-2*, C1393) Recorded Bks., LLC.

—Bridget Jones: The Edge of Reason. 2000. 352p. 24.95 (*0-670-89296-3*, Penguin Bks.) Viking Penguin.

—Bridget Jones' Diary: A Novel. l.t. ed. (Thorndike/G. K. Hall Paperback Bestsellers Ser.). 413p. 1999. pap. 26.95 (*0-7862-1637-9*); 1998. 29.95 (*0-7862-1636-0*) Thorndike Pr.

—Bridget Jones's Diary: A Novel. 2001. audio (*0-333-72217-5*); audio compact disk (*0-333-90353-6*) Macmillan U.K. GBR. *Dist:* Macmillan Publishing Co., Inc.

—Bridget Jones's Diary: A Novel. movie tie-in ed. 2001. 288p. pap. 12.95 (*0-14-100019-8*) Penguin Group (USA) Inc.

—Bridget Jones's Diary: A Novel. abr. ed. 1998. audio 18.00 (*0-375-40478-3*, 396075); 2001. audio compact disk 21.00 (*0-375-41681-1*) Random Hse. Audio Publishing Group. (RH Audio).

—Bridget Jones's Diary: A Novel. unabr. ed. 2001. audio compact disk 78.00 (*0-7887-6175-7*, C1399); 1999. audio 54.00 (*0-7887-2917-9*, 95709E5) Recorded Bks., LLC.

—Bridget Jones's Diary: A Novel. 1999. 288p. 14.00 (*0-14-028009-X*); 1998. 320p. 22.95 (*0-670-88072-8*) Viking Penguin.

—Diario de Bridget Jones. 2000. Tr. of Bridget Jones's Diary: A Novel. (SPA.). 320p. 10.95 (*84-01-46117-0*) Distribooks, Inc.

—Le Journal de Bridget Jones. 2000. Tr. of Bridget Jones's Diary: A Novel. (FRE.). pap. 13.95 (*2-290-30039-X*) Distribooks, Inc.

—Das Tagebuch der Bridget Jones. 2000. Tr. of Bridget Jones's Diary: A Novel. (GER.). pap. 18.95 (*3-442-44392-X*) Distribooks, Inc.

**JONES, CASEY (FICTITIOUS CHARACTER)—FICTION**

Munger, Katy. Legwork. 1997. (Casey Jones Mysteries Ser.). 224p. mass mkt. 5.99 (*0-380-79136-6*, Avon Bks.) Morrow/Avon.

—Out of Time. 1998. (Casey Jones Mysteries Ser.). 272p. mass mkt. 6.50 (*0-380-79138-2*, Avon Bks.) Morrow/Avon.

**JONES, CREIGHTON (FICTITIOUS CHARACTER)—FICTION**

Goodrum, Charles. The Best Cellar: A Werner-Bok Library Mystery. 1988. 288p. reprint ed. mass mkt. 3.95 o.p. (*0-06-080931-0*, P 931, Perennial) HarperTrade.

—Carnage of the Realm: A Werner-Bok Library Mystery. 1988. 240p. reprint ed. mass mkt. 3.95 o.p. (*0-06-080932-9*, Perennial) HarperTrade.

—Dewey Decimated: A Werner-Bok Library Mystery. 1988. 304p. reprint ed. mass mkt. 3.95 o.p. (*0-06-080933-7*, P 933, Perennial) HarperTrade.

—A Slip of the Tong. 1992. 192p. 16.95 o.p. (*0-312-07806-4*); Vol. 1. 1958. 17.95 o.p. (*0-312-08296-7*) St. Martin's Pr. (Saint Martin's Minotaur).

Goodrum, Charles A. The Best Cellar: Murder & Mystery at the Werner-Bok Library. 1987. 160p. 13.95 o.p. (*0-312-00008-1*) St. Martin's Pr.

—Carnage of the Realm. 1988. 1.99 o.p. (*0-517-53504-1*) Random Hse. Value Publishing.

**JONES, DAVID (FICTITIOUS CHARACTER)—FICTION**

Lutz, John. The Ex. 1999. 320p. mass mkt. 4.99 o.s.i (*0-7860-0186-0*); 1997. 304p. mass mkt. 5.50 o.s.i (*1-57566-178-0*); 1996. 256p. 21.00 o.s.i (*1-57566-078-4*, Kensington Bks.) Kensington Publishing Corp.

**JONES, DEMARY (FICTITIOUS CHARACTER)—FICTION**

Larkin, E. L. Dead Men Die. 1999. 192p. lib. bdg. 18.95 (*0-8034-9348-7*, Avalon Bks.) Bouregy, Thomas & Co., Inc.

—Hear Me Die. 1998. 192p. 18.95 (*0-8034-9309-6*, Avalon Bks.) Bouregy, Thomas & Co., Inc.

**JONES, ELIZABETH (FICTITIOUS CHARACTER)—FICTION**

Peters, Elizabeth, pseud. The Copenhagen Connection. unabr. ed. 2001. audio 27.95 (*0-7861-1928-4*) Blackstone Audio Bks., Inc.

—The Copenhagen Connection. 1992. mass mkt. 4.99 (*0-8125-2227-3*); 1990. mass mkt. 4.50 o.s.i (*0-8125-0914-5*) Doherty, Tom Assocs., LLC. (Tor Bks.).

—The Copenhagen Connection. 1982. (General Ser.). lib. bdg. 13.95 o.p. (*0-8161-3467-7*, Macmillan Reference USA) Gale Group.

—The Copenhagen Connection. 2001. 384p. mass mkt. 6.99 (*0-380-73338-2*, Avon Bks.) Morrow/Avon.

—The Copenhagen Connection. 1994. 224p. mass mkt. 5.50 (*0-446-36483-5*) Warner Bks., Inc.

**JONES, FREMONT (FICTITIOUS CHARACTER)—FICTION**

Day, Dianne. Beacon Street Mourning: A Fremont Jones Mystery. 2001. 304p. mass mkt. 5.99 (*0-553-58061-2*) Bantam Bks.

—Beacon Street Mourning: A Fremont Jones Mystery. 2000. (Fremont Jones Mystery Ser.). 288p. 22.95 o.s.i (*0-385-48610-3*) Doubleday Publishing.

—The Bohemian Murders. 1998. (Fremont Jones Mystery Ser.). 288p. reprint ed. mass mkt. 6.50 (*0-553-57412-4*, Crimeline) Bantam Bks.

—The Bohemian Murders: A Fremont Jones Mystery. l.t. ed. 1999. 25.95 (*1-57490-217-2*) Beeler, Thomas T. Publisher.

—The Bohemian Murders: A Fremont Jones Mystery. 1997. 256p. 21.95 o.s.i (*0-385-47923-9*) Doubleday Publishing.

—Death Train to Boston. 2000. (Fremont Jones Mystery Ser.). 272p. mass mkt. 5.99 (*0-553-58055-8*) Bantam Bks.

—Emperor Norton's Ghost. 1999. (Fremont Jones Mystery Ser.). 336p. mass mkt. 6.50 (*0-553-58078-7*) Bantam Bks.

—Emperor Norton's Ghost, , unabr. ed. 1999. (Fremont Jones Mystery Ser.). audio 56.00 (*0-7366-4505-5*, 4920) Books on Tape, Inc.

—Fire & Fog. 1997. 288p. mass mkt. 6.50 (*0-553-56922-8*, Crimeline) Bantam Bks.

—Fire & Fog. 2000. audio 48.00 (*0-7366-4839-9*); (Fremont Jones Mystery Ser.: 2). audio 36.00 Books on Tape, Inc.

—Fire & Fog. 1996. 320p. 21.00 o.s.i (*0-385-47550-0*) Doubleday Publishing.

—The Strange Files of Fremont Jones. 1996. (Fremont Jones Mystery Ser.: Vol. 1). 272p. mass mkt. 5.99 (*0-553-56921-X*, Crimeline) Bantam Bks.

—The Strange Files of Fremont Jones. 1999. audio 48.00 (*0-7366-4788-0*); Set. 2000. audio 48.00 Books on Tape, Inc.

—The Strange Files of Fremont Jones. 1995. 240p. 19.95 o.s.i (*0-385-47549-7*) Doubleday Publishing.

—The Strange Files of Fremont Jones. l.t. ed. 1996. (Niagara Large Print Ser.). 336p. 29.50 o.p. (*0-7089-5824-9*, Ulverscroft) Thorpe, F. A. Pubs. GBR. *Dist:* Ulverscroft Large Print Bks., Ltd.

**JONES, GENENE (FICTITIOUS CHARACTER)—FICTION**

Moore, Kelly. Deadly Medicine. 1989. 561p. mass mkt. 4.99 (*0-312-91579-9*, St. Martin's Paperbacks) St. Martin's Pr.

**JONES, GRAVE DIGGER (FICTITIOUS CHARACTER)—FICTION**

Himes, Chester B. All Shot up. 1973. 160p. reprint ed. 7.95 o.p. (*0-911860-29-0*) Chatham Bookseller.

—All Shot Up. 2nd ed. 1996. 170p. reprint ed. pap. 12.95 (*1-56025-103-4*, Thunder's Mouth Pr.) Avalon Publishing Group.

—The Big Gold Dream. 2nd ed. 1996. 156p. reprint ed. pap. 12.95 (*1-56025-104-2*, Thunder's Mouth Pr.) Avalon Publishing Group.

—The Big Gold Dream. 1973. 160p. reprint ed. 7.95 o.p. (*0-911860-30-4*) Chatham Bookseller.

—Blind Man with a Pistol. 1989. (Vintage Crime Ser.). 192p. pap. 11.00 (*0-394-75998-2*, Vintage) Knopf Publishing Group.

—Cotton Comes to Harlem. 1994. (Illus.). lib. bdg. 11.95 (*1-56849-422-X*) Buccaneer Bks., Inc.

—Cotton Comes to Harlem. 1975. reprint ed. 8.95 o.p. (*0-911860-55-X*) Chatham Bookseller.

—Cotton Comes to Harlem. 1988. (Crime Ser.). (Illus.). 160p. pap. 11.00 (*0-394-75999-0*, Vintage) Knopf Publishing Group.

—The Crazy Kill. 1973. 160p. reprint ed. 7.95 o.p. (*0-911860-32-0*) Chatham Bookseller.

—The Crazy Kill. 160p. 1995. pap. 25.00 o.s.i (*0-8052-8217-3*, Schocken); 1989. pap. 11.00 (*0-679-72572-5*, Vintage) Knopf Publishing Group.

—For Love of Imabelle. 1973. 192p. reprint ed. 7.95 o.p. (*0-911860-33-9*) Chatham Bookseller.

—The Heat's On. 1975. 220p. reprint ed. 17.00 (*0-911860-57-6*) Chatham Bookseller.

—The Heat's On. 1988. (Vintage Crime Ser.). 176p. pap. 15.00 (*0-394-75997-4*, Vintage) Knopf Publishing Group.

—A Rage in Harlem. 1989. (Vintage Crime Ser.). Orig. Title: For Love of Imabelle. 160p. pap. 10.00 (*0-679-72040-5*, Vintage) Knopf Publishing Group.

—The Real Cool Killers. 1973. 160p. reprint ed. 7.95 o.p. (*0-911860-36-3*) Chatham Bookseller.

—The Real Cool Killers. 1988. (Vintage Crime Ser.). 160p. pap. 10.95 (*0-679-72039-1*, Pantheon) Knopf Publishing Group.

**JONES, INDIANA (FICTITIOUS CHARACTER)—FICTION**

Artifacts. 2001. 27p. 3.00 net. (*0-9708750-0-2*) Sick Puppy Pr.

Artifacts. (Indiana Jones Ser.). 18.00 (*0-87431-434-8*, 45010) West End Games, Inc.

Caidin, Martin. Indiana Jones & the Sky Pirates. 1993. 320p. mass mkt. 5.50 (*0-553-56192-8*) Bantam Bks.

—Indiana Jones & the White Witch. 1994. 336p. mass mkt. 5.50 (*0-553-56194-4*) Bantam Bks.

Huyck, Willard & Katz, Gloria. Indiana Jones & the Temple of Doom. 1984. pap. 17.95 o.s.i (*0-345-31878-1*) Ballantine Bks.

Huyck, Willard, et al. Indiana Jones & the Temple of Doom: The Illustrated Screenplay. 1984. (Illus.). 176p. 30.00 o.s.i (*0-345-31879-X*) Ballantine Bks.

Indiana Jones & Lands of Adventure. (Indiana Jones Ser.). 15.00 (*0-87431-430-5*, 45005) West End Games, Inc.

Indiana Jones & the Golden Vampires. (Indiana Jones Ser.). 20.00 (*0-87431-431-3*, 45006) West End Games, Inc.

Indiana Jones & the Rising Sun. (Indiana Jones Ser.). 15.00 (*0-87431-427-5*, 45002) West End Games, Inc.

Indiana Jones & Tomb of the Templars. (Indiana Jones Ser.). 18.00 (*0-87431-429-1*, 45004) West End Games, Inc.

Indiana Jones Find Your Fate, 5 vols. 1985. pap. 12.65 o.s.i (*0-345-32969-4*, Del Rey) Ballantine Bks.

Indy's Adventures. (Indiana Jones Ser.). 15.00 (*0-87431-436-4*, 45009) West End Games, Inc.

Kahn, James. Indiana Jones & the Temple of Doom. 1984. 224p. mass mkt. 4.99 o.s.i (*0-345-31457-3*, Ballantine Bks.) Ballantine Bks.

MacGregor, Rob. Indiana Jones & the Dance of the Giants. 1991. 256p. mass mkt. 5.50 (*0-553-29035-5*) Bantam Bks.

—Indiana Jones & the Interior World. 1992. 272p. mass mkt. 5.50 (*0-553-29966-2*) Bantam Bks.

—Indiana Jones & the Last Crusade. 1989. 224p. mass mkt. 4.99 o.s.i (*0-345-36161-X*) Ballantine Bks.

—Indiana Jones & the Last Crusade. abr. ed. 1993. audio 14.95 o.p. (*1-55800-207-3*) NewStar Media, Inc.

—Indiana Jones & the Seven Veils. 1991. 304p. mass mkt. 5.50 (*0-553-29334-6*) Bantam Bks.

—Indiana Jones & the Unicorn's Legacy. 1992. 304p. mass mkt. 5.50 (*0-553-29666-3*) Bantam Bks.

—The Peril at Delphi. 1991. (Indiana Jones Ser.: No. 1). 272p. mass mkt. 4.99 o.s.i (*0-553-28931-4*) Bantam Bks.

Malam, John. Indiana Jones Explores Ancient Greece. 1996. (Illus.). 47p. (J). (gr. 5-8). 19.95 (*0-237-51221-1*) Evans Brothers, Ltd. GBR. *Dist:* Trafalgar Square.

McCoy, Max. Indiana Jones & the Dinosaur Eggs, Vol. 10. 1996. 240p. mass mkt. 5.99 (*0-553-56193-6*) Bantam Bks.

—Indiana Jones & the Hollow Earth, No. 11. 1997. (Indiana Jones Ser.: Vol. 11). 288p. mass mkt. 5.99 (*0-553-56195-2*) Bantam Bks.

—Indiana Jones & the Philosopher's Stone. 1995. 256p. mass mkt. 5.50 (*0-553-56196-0*) Bantam Bks.

—Indiana Jones & the Secret of the Sphinx. 1999. 208p. mass mkt. 5.99 (*0-553-56197-9*) Bantam Bks.

Raiders of the Lost Ark. (Indiana Jones Ser.). 25.00 (*0-87431-428-3*, 45003) West End Games, Inc.

Richardson, Mike, et al. Indiana Jones & the Fate of Atlantis. 1995. (Illus.). 112p. pap. 13.95 o.p. (*1-878574-36-1*) Dark Horse Comics.

Sky Pirates & Other Tales. (Indiana Jones Ser.). 15.00 (*0-87431-437-2*, 45015) West End Games, Inc.

Stine, Megan & Stine, William. Indiana Jones & the Mask of the Elephant, No. 17. 1987. mass mkt. 2.25 o.s.i (*0-345-33883-9*) Ballantine Bks.

Temple of Doom. (Indiana Jones Ser.). 25.00 (*0-87431-435-6*, 45008) West End Games, Inc.

The World of Indiana Jones. (Indiana Jones Ser.). 20.00 (*0-87431-426-7*, 45001); 30.00 (*0-87431-425-9*, 45000) West End Games, Inc.

**JONES, JACOB (FICTITIOUS CHARACTER)—FICTION**

Jakubowski, Maxim. It's You That I Want to Kiss. 1997. 222p. pap. 16.95 (*1-899344-15-2*) Do-Not Pr., The GBR. *Dist:* Dufour Editions, Inc.

**JONES, JOY-IN-THE-LORD (FICTITIOUS CHARACTER)—FICTION**

Black, Veronica. My Pilgrim Love. l.t. ed. 1997. pap. 18.95 o.p. (*0-7838-1971-4*, Macmillan Reference USA) Gale Group.

**JONES, NEELY (FICTITIOUS CHARACTER)—FICTION**

Wren, M. K. Neely Jones: The Medusa Pool. 1999. 313p. 24.95 (*0-312-24223-9*, Saint Martin's Minotaur) St. Martin's Pr.

**JONES, NICCOLO (FICTITIOUS CHARACTER)—FICTION**

Stansberry, Domenic. The Last Days of Il Duce. 1998. 168p. 22.00 (*1-57962-004-3*) Permanent Pr., The.

**JONES, SAM (FICTITIOUS CHARACTER)—FICTION**

Henderson, Lauren. Black Rubber Dress. E-Book 11.50 (*1-58945-549-5*) Adobe Systems, Inc.

—Black Rubber Dress. 1999. E-Book 11.50 (*0-609-60715-4*) Random Hse., Inc.

—Black Rubber Dress: A Sam Jones Novel. 1999. 304p. pap. 12.95 (*0-609-80438-3*, Three Rivers Pr.) Crown Publishing Group.

—Chained! 2000. 249p. (*0-09-180045-5*) Hutchinson, Fred Cancer Research Ctr.

—Chained! 2000. 256p. pap. o.p. (*0-09-180050-1*) Random Hse. of Canada, Ltd. CAN. *Dist:* Random Hse., Inc.

—Chained! A Novel. 2002. 336p. pap. 12.95 (*0-609-80865-6*, Three Rivers Pr.) Crown Publishing Group.

—Freeze My Margarita. E-Book 11.50 (*1-58945-594-0*) Adobe Systems, Inc.

—Freeze My Margarita. 2000. E-Book 11.50 (*0-609-60882-7*, Crown); 22.00 (*0-609-60744-8*); 288p. pap. 12.95 (*0-609-80487-1*, Crown) Crown Publishing Group.

—Freeze My Margarita: A Sam Jones Novel. 2000. 320p. pap. 13.00 (*0-609-80684-X*, Three Rivers Pr.) Crown Publishing Group.

—Pretty Boy: A Novel. 2002. 352p. pap. 12.95 (*0-609-80866-4*) Random Hse., Inc.

—The Strawberry Tattoo. 2000. (Sam Jones Novel Ser.). (Illus.). 316p. pap. 12.95 (*0-609-80685-8*, Three Rivers Pr.) Crown Publishing Group.

**JONES, TEXANA (FICTITIOUS CHARACTER)—FICTION**

Martin, Allana. Death of a Healing Woman: A Texana Jones Mystery. l.t. ed. 1997. (G. K. Hall Mystery Ser.). 290p. lib. bdg. 25.95 o.p. (*0-7838-8216-5*, Macmillan Reference USA) Gale Group.

—Death of a Healing Woman: A Texana Jones Mystery. 1998. (WWL Mystery Ser.). per. (*0-373-26281-7*, 1-26281-5, Worldwide Library) Harlequin Enterprises, Ltd.

—Death of a Healing Woman: A Texana Jones Mystery. l.t. ed. 1996. 224p. 20.95 (*0-312-14581-0*, Saint Martin's Minotaur) St. Martin's Pr.

—Death of a Myth Maker: A Texana Jones Mystery. 2001. (WWL Mystery Ser.: No. 380). 252p. mass mkt. (*0-373-26380-5*, 1-26380-5, Worldwide Library) Harlequin Enterprises, Ltd.

—Death of a Myth Maker: A Texana Jones Mystery. 2000. (Texana Jones Mystery Ser.). (Illus.). 272p. 23.95 (*0-312-25241-2*, Saint Martin's Minotaur) St. Martin's Pr.

—Death of a Saint Maker. 1999. (gr. 3). per. (*0-373-26299-X*, Harlequin Bks.) Harlequin Enterprises, Ltd.

Characters

—Death of a Saint Maker: A Texana Jones Mystery. 1997. (Texana Jones Mystery Ser.). 288p. 22.95 o.p. (0-312-18083-7, Saint Martin's Minotaur) St. Martin's Pr.
—Death of an Evangelista. 2000. (WWL Mystery Ser.: No. 335). mass mkt. (0-373-26335-X, 1-26335-9, Worldwide Library) Harlequin Enterprises, Ltd.
—Death of an Evangelista. 1999. 272p. 22.95 o.p. (0-312-19853-1, Saint Martin's Minotaur) St. Martin's Pr.
—Death of the Last Villista. 2002. (WWL Mystery Ser.: No. 434). 256p. mass mkt. (0-373-26434-8, Worldwide Library) Harlequin Enterprises, Ltd.
—Death of the Last Villista. 2001. (Texana Jones Mystery Ser.). 224p. 22.95 (0-312-26573-5, Saint Martin's Minotaur) St. Martin's Pr.

### JONES, TYLER (FICTITIOUS CHARACTER)—FICTION

Drury, Joan M. Closed in Silence. 1998. (Tyler Jones Feminist Mystery Ser.: No. 3). 224p. pap. 10.95 (1-883523-29-X) Spinsters Ink Bks.
—The Other Side of Silence. 1993. 256p. pap. 9.95 (0-933216-92-0) Spinsters Ink Bks.
—Silent Words. 1996. 224p. pap. 10.95 (1-883523-13-3) Spinsters Ink Bks.

### JORDAN, ALICE (FICTITIOUS CHARACTER)—FICTION

Beck, K. K. We Interrupt This Broadcast. 1997. 240p. 20.00 o.p. (0-89296-642-4) Mysterious Pr.

### JORDAN, CAROL (FICTITIOUS CHARACTER)—FICTION

McDermid, Val. The Mermaids Singing. unabr. ed. 1999. 14p. audio compact disk 104.95 (0-7531-0710-4, 107104); audio 84.95 (0-7531-0075-4, 960808) ISIS Audio Bks. GBR. Dist: Ulverscroft Large Print Bks., Ltd.
—The Mermaids Singing. 1997. 480p. mass mkt. 6.50 o.p. (0-06-101175-4); 1996. 288p. mass mkt. 22.00 o.p. (0-06-101174-6) Morrow/Avon. (HarperTorch).
—The Wire in the Blood. unabr. ed. 1998. audio 94.95 (0-7531-0350-8, 980504) ISIS Audio Bks. GBR. Dist: Ulverscroft Large Print Bks., Ltd.
—The Wire in the Blood. ltd. ed. 1998. xii, 372p. 50.00 (1-890208-21-3) Poisoned Pen Pr.
—The Wire in the Blood. 2002. 528p. mass mkt. 6.99 (0-312-98365-4, St. Martin's Paperbacks) St. Martin's Pr.

### JORDAN, EMILY (FICTITIOUS CHARACTER)—FICTION

Riselman, Brian. Where Darkness Sleeps. 1995. mass mkt. 5.99 o.p. (0-312-95682-7, St. Martin's Paperbacks) St. Martin's Pr.

### JORDAN, HARRY (FICTITIOUS CHARACTER)—FICTION

Adler, Elizabeth A. Now or Never. l.t. ed. 1997. 448p. mass mkt. 6.99 (0-440-22464-0) Dell Publishing.

### JORDAN, JOHN (FICTITIOUS CHARACTER)—FICTION

Lister, Michael. Power in the Blood: A John Jordan Mystery. 1997. (John Jordan Mystery Ser.). 326p. 18.95 o.p. (1-56164-137-5) Pineapple Pr., Inc.

### JORIAN, KING OF XYLAR (FICTITIOUS CHARACTER)—FICTION

de Camp, L. Sprague. The Clocks of Iraz. 1987. (Reluntant King Ser.: Vol. 2). 176p. mass mkt. 3.95 o.s.i (0-345-35212-2); 1983. mass mkt. 2.50 o.s.i (0-345-29841-1) Ballantine Bks. (Del Rey).
—The Goblin Tower. 1985. (Reluntant King Ser.: Vol. 1). 272p. mass mkt. 3.95 o.s.i (0-345-32812-4); 1983. mass mkt. 2.75 o.p. (0-345-29842-X) Ballantine Bks. (Del Rey).
—The Honorable Barbarian. 1990. 208p. mass mkt. 4.95 o.s.i (0-345-36652-2, Del Rey) Ballantine Bks.
—The Unbeheaded King. 1986. 192p. mass mkt. 3.95 o.s.i (0-345-33837-5); 1983. mass mkt. 2.50 o.s.i (0-345-29840-3) Ballantine Bks. (Del Rey).

### JORY (FICTITIOUS CHARACTER: BASS)—FICTION

Bass, Milton. Gunfighter Jory. 1987. 192p. mass mkt. 2.75 o.p. (0-451-15053-8, Signet Bks.) NAL.
—Jory. 1987. mass mkt. 2.75 o.p. (0-451-14932-7); 224p. mass mkt. 2.95 o.p. (0-451-16130-0) NAL. (Signet Bks.).
—Sheriff Jory. 1987. mass mkt. 2.75 o.p. (0-451-14817-7, Signet Bks.) NAL.
Bass, Milton R. Mister Jory. 1987. 192p. mass mkt. 2.75 o.p. (0-451-14965-3, Signet Bks.) NAL.
—Mister Jory. 1976. 7.95 o.p. (0-399-11702-4) Putnam Publishing Group, The.

### JOSEPH, TREVOR (FICTITIOUS CHARACTER)—FICTION

John, Katherine. Murder of a Dead Man. 1996. 314p. 23.95 o.p. (0-312-15369-4, Saint Martin's Minotaur) St. Martin's Pr.
—Six Foot Under. 1996. 384p. 23.95 o.p. (0-312-14416-4, Saint Martin's Minotaur) St. Martin's Pr.
—Six Foot Under. l.t. ed. 1996. (Large Print Ser.). 752p. 29.99 o.p. (0-7089-3554-0, Ulverscroft) Thorpe, F. A. Pubs. GBR. Dist: Ulverscroft Large Print Bks., Ltd., Ulverscroft Large Print Canada, Ltd.
—Without Trace. 1995. 426p. 24.95 o.p. (0-312-13218-2, Saint Martin's Minotaur) St. Martin's Pr.

### JOSHUA (FICTITIOUS CHARACTER: GIRZONE)—FICTION

Girzone, Joseph F. Joshua. 1994. o.s.i (0-385-47480-6) Doubleday Publishing.
—Joshua. l.t. ed. 1993. (General Ser.). 401p. lib. bdg. 16.95 o.p. (0-8161-5737-5); 18.95 o.s.i (0-8161-5736-7) Gale Group. (Macmillan Reference USA).
—Joshua. 1991. pap. o.p. (0-7710-3318-4) McClelland & Stewart/Tundra Bks.
—Joshua. unabr. ed. 2000. audio compact disk 63.00 (0-7887-3966-2, C1121E7); 1993. audio 51.00 (1-55690-908-X, 93404E7) Recorded Bks., LLC.
—Joshua. 1995. 288p. pap. 12.00 (0-684-81346-7, Touchstone) Simon & Schuster.
—Joshua, 3 vols. Incl. 288p. pap. 12.00 (0-684-81346-7); Joshua & the Children. 240p. pap. 11.00 (0-684-81345-9); Joshua in the Holy Land. 224p. pap. 11.00 (0-684-81344-0); , Touchstone 1995. Set per. 27.00 (0-684-00054-7, Scribner Paper Fiction) Simon & Schuster.
—Joshua: A Parable for Today. 1994. 320p. 16.95 (0-385-47421-0) Doubleday Publishing.
—Joshua: A Parable for Today. 1989. 301p. 15.95 o.p. (0-911519-16-5); 1983. 320p. 14.95 (0-911519-03-3); 1990. 14.95 o.p. (0-911519-24-6) Richelieu Court Pubns., Inc.
—Joshua: A Parable for Today. movie tie-in ed. 2002. 288p. pap. 12.00 o.s.i (0-7432-3566-5, Touchstone) Simon & Schuster.
—Joshua: The Homecoming. 272p. 1999. (Illus.). 19.95 (0-385-49509-9); 2000. reprint ed. pap. 11.95 (0-385-49510-2) Doubleday Publishing.
—Joshua: The Homecoming. l.t. ed. 1999. (Core Ser.). 296p. 31.95 (0-7838-8825-2, Macmillan Reference USA) Gale Group.
—Joshua & the Children. l.t. ed. 1994. 255p. lib. bdg. 16.95 o.p. (0-8161-5739-1, Macmillan Reference USA) Gale Group.
—Joshua & the Children. 1991. mass mkt. 5.95 (0-7710-3319-2) McClelland & Stewart/Tundra Bks.
—Joshua & the Children. abr. ed. 1991. audio 15.99 o.s.i (0-553-45285-1, RH Audio) Random Hse. Audio Publishing Group.
—Joshua & the Children. 240p. 1995. pap. 11.00 (0-684-81345-9, Touchstone); 1991. pap. 8.95 o.s.i (0-02-019905-8, Scribner Paper Fiction) Simon & Schuster.
—Joshua & the Children. l.t. ed. 1993. (Inspirational Ser.). 255p. lib. bdg. 25.95 (0-8161-5738-3) Thorndike Pr.
—Joshua & the City. 1996. (Illus.). 256p. pap. 12.95 (0-385-48569-7) Doubleday Publishing.
—Joshua & the City. l.t. ed. 1996. pap. 18.95 o.p. (0-7838-1215-9); 1995. 280p. 24.95 (0-7838-1214-0) Gale Group. (Macmillan Reference USA).
—Joshua & the Shepherd. 1996. 256p. pap. 11.00 (0-684-82504-X, Touchstone) Simon & Schuster.
—Joshua II. 1986. 320p. 12.00 o.p. (0-911519-08-4) Richelieu Court Pubns., Inc.
—Joshua in the Holy Land. l.t. ed. 1995. 17.95 (0-8161-5743-X); 1994. 271p. lib. bdg. 23.95 (0-8161-5742-1) Gale Group. (Macmillan Reference USA).
—Joshua in the Holy Land. abr. ed. 1992. audio 15.99 o.s.i (0-553-47117-1, RH Audio) Random Hse. Audio Publishing Group.
—Joshua in the Holy Land. 1995. 224p. pap. 11.00 (0-684-81344-0, Touchstone); 1992. 16.00 o.s.i (0-02-543445-4, Scribner) Simon & Schuster.
—Joshua, the Journey Home: Includes Joshua, Joshua & the Children & Joshua in the Holy Land, 3 vols. in 1. 1997. 608p. 12.99 (0-88486-179-1, Arrowood Pr.) BBS Publishing Corp.

### JOURDEMAYNE, TRUTH (FICTITIOUS CHARACTER)—FICTION

Bradley, Marion Zimmer. Ghostlight. (Light Ser.). 2003. 384p. mass mkt. 6.99 (0-7653-4666-4); 1995. 304p. 22.95 o.p. (0-312-85881-7); 4th ed. 1996. 304p. pap. 15.95 (0-312-86218-0) Doherty, Tom Assocs., LLC. (Tor Bks.).
—Gravelight. (Light Ser.). 2003. 416p. mass mkt. 6.99 (0-7653-4667-2); 1998. 352p. pap. 14.95 (0-312-86507-4); 1997. 352p. 24.95 o.p. (0-312-86503-1) Doherty, Tom Assocs., LLC. (Tor Bks.).
—Heartlight. 416p. 1999. pap. 15.95 (0-312-86509-0); 1998. 25.95 (0-312-86508-2) Doherty, Tom Assocs., LLC. (Tor Bks.).
—Witchlight. 2004. mass mkt. 6.99 (0-7653-4714-8); 1996. 304p. 23.95 o.p. (0-312-86104-4); 3rd ed. 1997. 304p. pap. 14.95 (0-312-85831-0) Doherty, Tom Assocs., LLC. (Tor Bks.).
—Witchlight. abr. ed. 2000. audio 7.95 (1-57815-177-5, 1120, Media Bks. Audio Publishing) Media Bks., L. L. C.
—Witchlight, Set. abr. ed. 1996. audio 16.95 o.p. (1-55935-234-5) Soundelux Audio Publishing.

### JURNET, BENJAMIN (FICTITIOUS CHARACTER)—FICTION

Haymon, S. T. A Beautiful Death. 1993. 19.95 o.p. (0-312-10420-0, Saint Martin's Minotaur) St. Martin's Pr.
—Death & the Pregnant Virgin. 208p. 1991. mass mkt. 2.50 o.s.i (0-553-18513-6); 1984. pap. text 2.95 o.p. (0-553-23703-9) Bantam Bks.
—Death & the Pregnant Virgin. unabr. ed. 1993. audio 61.95 (1-85089-848-0, 40791) ISIS Audio Bks. GBR. Dist: Ulverscroft Large Print Bks., Ltd.
—Death & the Pregnant Virgin. 1980. 224p. 9.95 o.p. (0-312-18592-8) St. Martin's Pr.
—Death of a God. 1990. 256p. mass mkt. 3.95 o.s.i (0-553-27266-7) Bantam Bks.
—Death of a God. 1992. 1.99 o.p. (0-517-08388-4) Random Hse. Value Publishing.
—Death of a God. 1987. 224p. 14.95 o.p. (0-312-00119-3) St. Martin's Pr.
—Death of a Hero. l.t. ed. 2000. pap. 21.99 (0-7531-6225-3) ISIS Large Print Bks. GBR. Dist: Ulverscroft Large Print Bks., Ltd., Ulverscroft Large Print Canada, Ltd.
—Death of a Hero. 1996. 256p. 21.95 o.p. (0-312-14582-9, Saint Martin's Minotaur) St. Martin's Pr.
—Death of a Warrior Queen. l.t. ed. 1996. 352p. 24.95 (1-85695-334-3) ISIS Large Print Bks. GBR. Dist: Transaction Pubs.
—Death of a Warrior Queen. 1991. 224p. 17.95 o.p. (0-312-06950-2, Saint Martin's Minotaur) St. Martin's Pr.
—Ritual Murder. 1991. 256p. mass mkt. 4.50 o.s.i (0-553-29385-0) Bantam Bks.
—Ritual Murder. 1984. 256p. pap. 2.50 o.p. (0-523-42175-3, Pinnacle Bks.) Kensington Publishing Corp.
—Ritual Murder. 1982. 224p. 11.95 o.p. (0-312-68478-9) St. Martin's Pr.
—Stately Homicide. 1984. 11.95 o.p. (0-312-75708-5) St. Martin's Pr.
—Stately Homicide. 1985. 256p. mass mkt. 3.50 o.s.i (0-445-20161-4) Warner Bks., Inc.
—A Very Particular Murder. 1991. 288p. mass mkt. 4.50 o.s.i (0-553-28880-6) Bantam Bks.
—A Very Particular Murder. 1992. 2.99 o.p. (0-517-09061-9) Random Hse. Value Publishing.
—A Very Particular Murder. 1989. 16.95 o.p. (0-312-02998-5) St. Martin's Pr.

### JURY, RICHARD (FICTITIOUS CHARACTER)—FICTION

Grimes, Martha. The Anodyne Necklace. 1990. 256p. reprint ed. mass mkt. 5.99 o.s.i (0-440-10280-4) Dell Publishing.
—The Anodyne Necklace. 1983. 252p. 15.95 o.p. (0-316-32882-0) Little Brown & Co.
—The Anodyne Necklace. 2004. 320p. mass mkt. 7.99 (0-451-41089-0, Onyx) NAL.
—The Anodyne Necklace. abr. ed. 1999. audio 9.98 (0-671-04429-X, Simon & Schuster Audioworks) Simon & Schuster Audio.
—The Anodyne Necklace. l.t. ed. 1983. 420p. reprint ed. 13.95 o.p. (0-89621-486-9) Thorndike Pr.
—The Blue Last: A Richard Jury Mystery. 16th l.t. ed. 2002. 472p. lib. bdg. 29.95 (1-58547-166-6) Ctr. Point Large Print.
—The Blue Last: A Richard Jury Mystery. 2002. 464p. reprint ed. mass mkt. 7.99 (0-451-41055-6, Onyx) NAL.
—The Blue Last: A Richard Jury Mystery. 2002. 464p. pap. 7.99 (0-451-41025-4) Penguin Group (USA) Inc.
—The Blue Last: A Richard Jury Mystery. 2001. 384p. 24.95 o.p. (0-670-03004-X, Viking) Viking Penguin.
—The Case Has Altered: A Richard Jury Mystery. unabr. ed. 1998. audio 72.00 (0-7366-4072-X, 4581) Books on Tape, Inc.
—The Case Has Altered: A Richard Jury Mystery. l.t. ed. 1998. (Wheeler Large Print Book Ser.). 515p. 27.95 o.p. (1-56895-546-4, Wheeler Publishing, Inc.) Gale Group.
—The Case Has Altered: A Richard Jury Mystery. 1997. 384p. 24.00 o.s.i (0-8050-5620-3) Holt, Henry & Co.
—The Case Has Altered: A Richard Jury Mystery. 1998. 432p. mass mkt. 7.99 (0-451-40868-3, Onyx) NAL.
—The Case Has Altered: A Richard Jury Mystery. abr. ed. 1997. audio 24.00 (0-671-57756-5, 595585, Simon & Schuster Audioworks) Simon & Schuster Audio.
—The Deer Leap. 1986. 256p. mass mkt. 6.99 o.s.i (0-440-11938-3) Dell Publishing.
—The Deer Leap. 1985. 15.95 o.p. (0-316-32886-3) Little Brown & Co.
—The Dirty Duck. 1990. 256p. mass mkt. 6.99 o.s.i (0-440-12050-0) Dell Publishing.
—The Dirty Duck. 1984. 252p. 14.95 o.s.i (0-316-32883-9) Little Brown & Co.
—The Dirty Duck. abr. ed. 1993. (Inspector Richard Jury Ser.). audio 16.00 (0-671-75989-2, 390661, Simon & Schuster Audioworks) Simon & Schuster Audio.
—The Five Bells & Bladebone. 1988. 384p. mass mkt. 6.99 o.s.i (0-440-20133-0) Dell Publishing.
—The Five Bells & Bladebone. 1987. 15.95 o.p. (0-316-32889-8) Little Brown & Co.
—The Five Bells & Bladebone. 2002. 352p. reprint ed. mass mkt. 6.99 (0-451-41038-6, Onyx) NAL.
—The Grave Maurice: A Richard Jury Mystery. 2003. 400p. mass mkt. 7.99 (0-451-41101-3, Onyx) NAL.
—The Grave Maurice: A Richard Jury Mystery. l.t. ed. 2003. (Core Ser.). 574p. 31.95 (0-7862-4929-3) Thorndike Pr.
—The Grave Maurice: A Richard Jury Mystery. 2002. 432p. 25.95 o.s.i (0-670-03045-7); 4p. audio 25.95 (0-14-280011-2, Penguin AudioBooks) Viking Penguin.
—Help the Poor Struggler. 1986. 240p. mass mkt. 6.99 o.s.i (0-440-13584-2) Dell Publishing.
—Help the Poor Struggler. 1985. 288p. 15.95 o.p. (0-316-32884-7) Little Brown & Co.
—The Horse You Came in On. 1994. 384p. mass mkt. 7.99 (0-345-38755-4) Ballantine Bks.
—The Horse You Came in On. l.t. ed. 1993. 19.00 o.s.i (0-679-74770-2) Random Hse. Large Print.
—The Horse You Came in On. unabr. ed. 1994. audio 70.00 (0-7887-0003-0, 94142E7) Recorded Bks., LLC.
—The Horse You Came in On. abr. ed. 1993. (Inspector Richard Jury Ser.). audio 17.00 (0-671-87223-0, 390934, Simon & Schuster Audioworks) Simon & Schuster Audio.
—I Am the Only Running Footman. 1990. 320p. mass mkt. 5.99 o.s.i (0-440-13924-4) Dell Publishing.
—I Am the Only Running Footman. 1986. 15.95 o.s.i (0-316-32887-1) Little Brown & Co.
—I Am the Only Running Footman. 2001. 320p. mass mkt. 6.99 (0-451-41002-5, Onyx) NAL.
—I Am the Only Running Footman. 1992. 4.99 o.p. (0-517-09217-4) Random Hse. Value Publishing.
—Jerusalem Inn. 1990. 288p. reprint ed. mass mkt. 6.99 o.s.i (0-440-14181-8) Doubleday Publishing.
—Jerusalem Inn. 1984. 288p. 15.95 o.s.i (0-316-32879-0) Little Brown & Co.
—The Lamorna Wink: A Richard Jury Mystery. 2000. 432p. reprint ed. mass mkt. 6.99 (0-451-40936-1, Onyx) NAL.
—The Lamorna Wink: A Richard Jury Mystery. l.t. ed. 2000. (Basic Ser.). 515p. 29.95 (0-7862-2324-3) Thorndike Pr.
—The Lamorna Wink: A Richard Jury Mystery. 1999. 3384p. 22.95 o.s.i (0-670-88870-2, Viking) Viking Penguin.
—The Man with a Load of Mischief. 1990. 320p. mass mkt. 5.99 o.s.i (0-440-15327-1) Dell Publishing.
—The Man with a Load of Mischief. 1981. 255p. 15.95 o.s.i (0-316-32880-4) Little Brown & Co.
—The Man with a Load of Mischief. 2003. 288p. mass mkt. 6.99 (0-451-41081-5, Onyx) NAL.
—The Man with a Load of Mischief. abr. ed. 1992. audio 16.00 (0-671-75960-4, Simon & Schuster Audioworks) Simon & Schuster Audio.
—The Man with a Load of Mischief. l.t. ed. 1984. 455p. reprint ed. 13.95 o.p. (0-89621-514-8) Thorndike Pr.
—The Old Contemptibles. 1992. 304p. mass mkt. 6.99 (0-345-37456-8); 1991. mass mkt. 5.99 o.s.i (0-345-37515-7) Ballantine Bks.
—The Old Contemptibles. unabr. ed. 1991. audio 56.00 (0-7366-1954-2, 2775) Books on Tape, Inc.
—The Old Contemptibles. 1991. 19.95 o.s.i (0-316-32894-4); 22.95 o.s.i (0-316-32898-7) Little Brown & Co.
—The Old Contemptibles. l.t. ed. 1995. (Magna Large Print Ser.). 531p. o.p. (0-7505-0835-3) Magna Large Print Bks. GBR. Dist: Ulverscroft Large Print Canada, Ltd.
—The Old Contemptibles. abr. ed. 1999. audio 9.98 (0-671-04500-8); 1991. audio 15.95 (0-671-73569-1, 391301) Simon & Schuster Audio. (Simon & Schuster Audioworks).
—The Old Fox Deceiv'd. 1991. 304p. mass mkt. 5.99 o.s.i (0-440-16747-7) Dell Publishing.
—The Old Fox Deceiv'd. 1982. 288p. 16.95 o.p. (0-316-32881-2) Little Brown & Co.
—The Old Fox Deceiv'd. 2003. 320p. mass mkt. 7.99 (0-451-41068-8) NAL.
—The Old Fox Deceiv'd. 1999. pap. 9.98 (0-671-04430-3); 1992. audio 16.00 (0-671-75991-4, 391302) Simon & Schuster Audio. (Simon & Schuster Audioworks).
—The Old Silent. unabr. ed. 1990. audio 72.00 (0-7366-1833-3, 2668) Books on Tape, Inc.
—The Old Silent. 448p. 1993. mass mkt. 3.99 o.s.i (0-440-21519-6); 1990. mass mkt. 6.99 o.s.i (0-440-20492-5) Dell Publishing.
—The Old Silent. 1989. 296p. 18.95 o.p. (0-316-32318-7) Little Brown & Co.

—The Old Silent. 1992. 5.99 o.p. (*0-517-07973-9*) Random Hse. Value Publishing.
—The Old Silent. abr. ed. 1992. audio 16.00 (*0-671-73617-5*, Simon & Schuster Audioworks) Simon & Schuster Audio.
—Rainbow's End. 1996. 448p. mass mkt. 7.50 (*0-345-39426-7*) Ballantine Bks.
—Rainbow's End. unabr. ed. 1995. audio 60.00 (*0-7366-3138-0*, 3813) Books on Tape, Inc.
—Rainbow's End. l.t. ed. 1995. 22.00 o.s.i (*0-679-76228-0*) Random Hse. Large Print.
—Rainbow's End. abr. ed. 1995. (Inspector Richard Jury Ser.). audio 17.00 (*0-671-53450-5*, 392985, Simon & Schuster Audioworks) Simon & Schuster Audio.
—The Stargazey: A Richard Jury Mystery. unabr. ed. 1999. audio 64.00 (*0-7366-4463-6*, 4908) Books on Tape, Inc.
—The Stargazey: A Richard Jury Mystery. 1998. 384p. 25.00 o.s.i (*0-8050-5622-X*) Holt, Henry & Co.
—The Stargazey: A Richard Jury Mystery. 1999. 432p. reprint ed. mass mkt. 7.99 (*0-451-40897-7*, Onyx) NAL.
—The Stargazey: A Richard Jury Mystery. l.t. ed. (Thorndike/G. K. Hall Paperback Bestsellers Ser.). 2000. 647p. pap. 27.95 (*0-7862-1789-8*); 1999. 581p. 30.95 (*0-7862-1788-X*) Thorndike Pr.

**JUSTICE, BENJAMIN (FICTITIOUS CHARACTER)—FICTION**

Wilson, John Morgan. Blind Eye: A Benjamin Justice Novel. 2003. 288p. 23.95 (*0-312-30919-8*, Saint Martin's Minotaur) St. Martin's Pr.
—Justice at Risk: A Benjamin Justice Mystery. 2000. (Benjamin Justice Mystery Ser.). 368p. mass mkt. 6.50 (*0-553-57860-X*) Bantam Bks.
—Justice at Risk: A Benjamin Justice Mystery. 1999. (Benjamin Justice Mystery Ser.). 304p. 22.95 o.s.i (*0-385-49116-6*) Doubleday Publishing.
—Revision of Justice: A Benjamin Justice Mystery. 1999. (Benjamin Justice Mystery Ser.). 416p. mass mkt. 5.99 (*0-553-57533-3*) Bantam Bks.
—Simple Justice: A Benjamin Justice Mystery. 1997. (Benjamin Justice Mystery Ser.). 304p. mass mkt. 6.50 o.s.i (*0-553-57532-5*) Bantam Bks.
—Simple Justice: A Benjamin Justice Mystery. 1996. 256p. 21.00 o.s.i (*0-385-48234-5*) Doubleday Publishing.

# K

**KACHIGAN, MILO (FICTITIOUS CHARACTER)—FICTION**

Cercone, Karen R. Blood Tracks. 1998. (American Historical Mysteries Ser.). 256p. mass mkt. 5.99 o.s.i (*0-425-16241-9*, Prime Crime) Berkley Publishing Group.
—Coal Bones. 1999. 288p. mass mkt. 5.99 o.s.i (*0-425-16698-8*, Prime Crime) Berkley Publishing Group.
—Steel Ashes. 1997. 272p. mass mkt. 5.99 o.s.i (*0-425-15856-X*, Prime Crime) Berkley Publishing Group.

**KAI LUNG (FICTITIOUS CHARACTER)—FICTION**

Bramah, Ernest. Kai Lung Beneath the Mulberry-Tree. Reginald, R. & Melville, Douglas, eds. 1978. (Lost Race & Adult Fantasy Ser.). reprint ed. lib. bdg. 28.95 (*0-405-10959-8*) Ayer Co. Pubs., Inc.
—Kai Lung Unrolls His Mat. 1974. mass mkt. 1.25 o.s.i (*0-345-23787-0*) Ballantine Bks.
—The Wallet of Kai Lung. 1977. 337p. lib. bdg. 15.95 (*0-89966-269-2*) Buccaneer Bks., Inc.

**KAINE, ALLISON (FICTITIOUS CHARACTER)—FICTION**

Allen, Kate. Give My Secrets Back: An Alison Kaine Mystery. 1995. 200p. (Orig.). pap. 9.95 (*0-934678-64-2*) New Victoria Pubs., Inc.
—Just a Little Lie: An Alison Kaine Mystery. 1998. (Alison Kaine Mysteries Ser.: Vol. 4). 224p. pap. 12.95 (*0-934678-94-4*) New Victoria Pubs., Inc.
—Takes One to Know One: An Alison Kaine Mystery. 1996. 200p. (Orig.). pap. 10.95 (*0-934678-74-X*) New Victoria Pubs., Inc.
—Tell Me What You Like: An Alison Kaine Mystery. 1993. 219p. (Orig.). pap. 11.95 (*0-934678-48-0*) New Victoria Pubs., Inc.

**KAINE, DANIEL (FICTITIOUS CHARACTER)—FICTION**

Hoff, B. J. The Captive Voice. unabr. ed. 1998. (Daybreak Mystery Ser.: Bk. 2). audio 39.95 (*1-55686-835-9*) Books in Motion.
—The Captive Voice. l.t. ed. 1998. (Christian Mystery Ser.). 279p. 23.95 o.p. (*0-7862-1411-2*) Thorndike Pr.
—The Captive Voice. 1996. (Daybreak Mysteries Ser.: Vol. 2). 187p. pap. 8.99 o.p. (*0-8423-7193-1*) Tyndale Hse. Pubs.
—Dark River Legacy. unabr. ed. 1999. (Daybreak Mystery Ser.: Bk. 5). audio 39.95 (*1-55686-859-6*) Books in Motion.
—Dark River Legacy. 1992. 208p. pap. 6.99 o.p. (*0-7814-0479-7*); (Daybreak Mystery Ser.: No. 5). 192p. pap. 6.95 o.p. (*0-89636-248-5*) Cook Communications Ministries.
—Dark River Legacy. l.t. ed. 1999. (Christian Mystery Ser.). 272p. 24.95 (*0-7862-1677-8*) Thorndike Pr.
—Dark River Legacy. 1997. (Daybreak Mysteries Ser.). 179p. pap. 8.99 o.p. (*0-8423-7196-6*) Tyndale Hse. Pubs.
—The Domino Image. 1992. 208p. pap. 6.99 o.p. (*0-7814-0520-3*); 1987. (Daybreak Mystery Ser.: No. 2). 196p. pap. 6.95 o.p. (*0-89636-218-3*) Cook Communications Ministries.
—Mists of Danger. 1986. 196p. pap. 6.99 o.p. (*0-89636-206-X*) Cook Communications Ministries.
—Storm at Daybreak. unabr. ed. 1998. (Daybreak Mystery Ser.: Bk. 1). audio 39.95 (*1-55686-830-8*) Books in Motion.
—Storm at Daybreak. 1992. 208p. pap. 6.99 o.p. (*0-7814-0519-X*); 196p. pap. 6.95 o.p. (*0-89636-217-5*) Cook Communications Ministries.
—Storm at Daybreak. l.t. ed. 1998. (Christian Mystery Ser.). 280p. 23.95 (*0-7862-1317-5*) Thorndike Pr.
—Storm at Daybreak. 1996. (Daybreak Mysteries Ser.: Vol. 1). 195p. pap. 8.99 o.p. (*0-8423-7192-3*) Tyndale Hse. Pubs.
—The Tangled Web. unabr. ed. 1998. (Daybreak Mystery Ser.: Bk. 3). audio 39.95 (*1-55686-838-3*) Books in Motion.
—The Tangled Web. 1991. (Daybreak Mystery Ser.: No. 3). 207p. pap. 6.95 o.p. (*0-89636-242-6*) Cook Communications Ministries.
—The Tangled Web. l.t. ed. 1998. (Christian Mystery Ser.). 279p. 23.95 (*0-7862-1473-2*) Thorndike Pr.
—The Tangled Web. 1997. (Daybreak Mysteries Ser.). 189p. pap. 8.99 o.p. (*0-8423-7194-X*) Tyndale Hse. Pubs.
—Vow of Silence. 1992. 208p. pap. 6.99 o.p. (*0-7814-0528-9*); (Daybreak Mystery Ser.: No. 4). 194p. pap. 6.95 o.p. (*0-89636-234-5*) Cook Communications Ministries.
—Vow of Silence. l.t. ed. 1998. (Christian Mystery Ser.). 280p. 23.95 (*0-7862-1563-1*) Thorndike Pr.
—Vow of Silence. l.t. ed. 1990. (Linford Mystery Large Print Ser.). pap. 17.99 o.p. (*0-7089-6902-X*, Ulverscroft) Thorpe, F. A. Pubs. GBR. *Dist:* Ulverscroft Large Print Bks., Ltd., Ulverscroft Large Print Canada, Ltd.
—Vow of Silence. 1997. (Daybreak Mysteries Ser.: No. 4). 193p. pap. 8.99 o.p. (*0-8423-7195-8*) Tyndale Hse. Pubs.

**KAISER, BILL (FICTITIOUS CHARACTER)—FICTION**

Hall, Matthew. The Art of Breaking Glass. 1998. 400p. mass mkt. 6.99 (*0-446-60580-8*) Warner Bks., Inc.
—The Art of Breaking Glass: A Novel. 1997. 336p. 23.95 o.p. (*0-316-33924-5*) Little Brown & Co.

**KAMAL, BEN (FICTITIOUS CHARACTER)—FICTION**

Land, Jon. Blood Diamonds. E-Book 25.95 (*0-312-70604-9*, Tor Bks.); 2002. 384p. 25.95 (*0-7653-0226-8*, Forge Bks.); 2003. 416p. reprint ed. mass mkt. 7.99 (*0-7653-4148-4*, Forge Bks.) Doherty, Tom Assocs., LLC.
—The Blue Widows. Date not set. mass mkt. (*0-7653-4526-9*); 2003. 384p. 24.95 (*0-7653-0599-2*) Doherty, Tom Assocs., LLC. (Forge Bks.).
—The Pillars of Solomon. 2000. 438p. mass mkt. 6.99 (*0-8125-6672-6*); 1999. (Illus.). 352p. 24.95 (*0-312-86819-7*) Doherty, Tom Assocs., LLC. (Forge Bks.).
—A Walk in the Darkness. 2000. 352p. 25.95 (*0-312-87265-8*, Forge Bks.) Doherty, Tom Assocs., LLC.
—The Walls of Jericho. 1998. 480p. mass mkt. 6.99 (*0-8125-6456-1*, Tor Bks.); 1997. 304p. 23.95 (*0-312-86267-9*, Forge Bks.) Doherty, Tom Assocs., LLC.
—The Walls of Jericho. abr. ed. 1997. audio 17.00 (*1-56876-066-3*) Soundlines Entertainment, Inc.

**KAMIYA FAMILY (FICTITIOUS CHARACTERS)—FICTION**

Sakamoto, Edward. Hawai'i No Ka Oi: The Kamiya Family Trilogy. 1995. 176p. pap. 18.00 (*0-8248-1726-5*) Univ. of Hawaii Pr.

**KANE, GAVIN (FICTITIOUS CHARACTER)—FICTION**

Higgins, Jack. Sheba. 1995. 272p. mass mkt. 7.99 (*0-425-14670-7*) Berkley Publishing Group.
—Sheba. l.t. ed. 1995. (Large Print Bks.). pap. 22.95 o.p. (*1-56895-126-4*, Wheeler Publishing, Inc.) Gale Group.
—Sheba. abr. ed. 1995. 17.95 o.p. (*0-7871-0230-X*); 24.95 o.p. (*0-7871-0225-3*, 692954) NewStar Media, Inc.

**KANTOR, ALEXANDER (FICTITIOUS CHARACTER)—FICTION**

Bunn, T. Davis. The Amber Room. 1992. (Priceless Collection). 336p. pap. 9.99 o.p. (*1-55661-285-0*) Bethany Hse. Pubs.
—The Amber Room. l.t. ed. 2001. (Christian Mystery Ser.). 519p. 24.95 o.p. (*0-7862-3070-3*) Thorndike Pr.
—Florian's Gate. 1992. (Priceless Collection). 352p. (ps up). pap. 9.99 o.p. (*1-55661-244-3*) Bethany Hse. Pubs.
—Florian's Gate. l.t. ed. 2000. (Christian Mystery Ser.). 563p. 24.95 (*0-7862-2877-6*) Thorndike Pr.
—Winter Palace. 1993. (Priceless Collection: No. 3). 352p. pap. 9.99 o.p. (*1-55661-324-5*) Bethany Hse. Pubs.
—Winter Palace. 2001. audio 50.95 NorthStar Audio Bks.
—Winter Palace. l.t. ed. 2001. (Thorndike Christian Mystery Ser.). (Illus.). 512p. 24.95 (*0-7862-3179-3*) Thorndike Pr.

**KARDON, DAN (FICTITIOUS CHARACTER)—FICTION**

Katz, Jamie. Dead Low Tide. 1998. (Dan Kardon Mysteries Ser.). 384p. mass mkt. 5.99 (*0-06-109711-X*, HarperTorch) Morrow/Avon.

**KARP, BUTCH (FICTITIOUS CHARACTER)—FICTION**

Tanenbaum, Robert K. Absolute Rage. 2003. (Illus.). 480p. mass mkt. 7.99 (*0-7434-0345-2*, Pocket) Simon & Schuster.
—Act of Revenge. unabr. ed. 1999. (Butch Karp Mystery Ser.). audio 88.00 (*0-7366-4742-2*, 5080) Books on Tape, Inc.
—Act of Revenge. l.t. ed. 2001. (Large Print Book Ser.). 575p. 28.95 (*1-58724-025-4*, Wheeler Publishing, Inc.) Gale Group.
—Act of Revenge. 1999. 416p. o.p. (*0-06-019218-6*, HarperFlamingo) HarperCollins Pubs. Canada, Ltd.
—Act of Revenge. 2000. 544p. mass mkt. 7.50 (*0-06-109730-6*, HarperTorch) Morrow/Avon.
—Corruption of Blood. unabr. ed. 1998. (Butch Karp Mystery Ser.). audio 80.00 (*0-7366-4045-2*, 4544) Books on Tape, Inc.
—Corruption of Blood. 1995. 368p. 22.95 o.p. (*0-525-93870-2*, Dutton) Dutton/Plume.
—Corruption of Blood. 1996. 416p. mass mkt. 7.99 (*0-451-18196-4*, Signet Bks.) NAL.
—Depraved Indifference. 1989. 18.95 o.p. (*0-453-00679-5*); 1990. 400p. reprint ed. mass mkt. 7.99 (*0-451-16842-9*, Signet Bks.) NAL.
—Enemy Within. 2001. (Illus.). 368p. 24.95 (*0-7434-0342-8*, Atria) Simon & Schuster.
—Falsely Accused. unabr. ed. 1998. (Butch Karp Mystery Ser.). audio 56.00 (*0-7366-4026-6*, 452511.95) Books on Tape, Inc.
—Falsely Accused. 1996. 320p. 23.95 o.s.i (*0-525-94168-1*) Dutton/Plume.
—Falsely Accused. 1997. 448p. mass mkt. 7.99 (*0-451-19000-9*, Signet Bks.) NAL.
—Immoral Certainty. unabr. ed. 1997. (Butch Karp Mystery Ser.). audio 64.00 (*0-7366-3689-7*, 4368) Books on Tape, Inc.
—Immoral Certainty. 1991. 304p. 18.95 o.p. (*0-525-24941-9*, Dutton) Dutton/Plume.
—Immoral Certainty. 1992. 400p. reprint ed. mass mkt. 7.99 (*0-451-17186-1*, Signet Bks.) NAL.
—Irresistible Impulse. unabr. ed. 1998. (Butch Karp Mystery Ser.). audio 64.00 (*0-7366-4134-3*, 4639) Books on Tape, Inc.
—Irresistible Impulse. 1997. 352p. 24.95 o.p. (*0-525-94310-2*) Dutton/Plume.
—Irresistible Impulse. 1998. 445p. mass mkt. 6.99 (*0-451-19261-3*, Signet Bks.) NAL.
—Justice Denied. unabr. ed. 1997. (Butch Karp Mystery Ser.). audio 64.00 (*0-7366-3688-9*, 4367) Books on Tape, Inc.
—Justice Denied. 1994. 320p. 18.95 o.p. (*0-525-93814-1*) Dutton/Plume.
—Justice Denied. abr. ed. 1994. pap. 16.00 o.p. incl. audio (*0-453-00903-4*, 25024-33894) Penguin/HighBridge.
—Material Witness. unabr. ed. 1997. (Butch Karp Mystery Ser.). audio 64.00 (*0-7366-3687-0*, 4366) Books on Tape, Inc.
—Material Witness. 1993. 320p. 20.00 o.p. (*0-525-93579-7*, Dutton) Dutton/Plume.
—Material Witness. 1994. 416p. mass mkt. 7.99 (*0-451-18020-8*, Signet Bks.) NAL.
—No Lesser Plea. 1988. 368p. reprint ed. mass mkt. 7.99 (*0-451-15496-7*, Signet Bks.) NAL.
—No Lesser Plea. 1987. 17.95 o.p. (*0-531-09783-8*, Watts, Franklin) Scholastic Library Publishing.
—Reckless Endangerment. unabr. ed. 1999. (Butch Karp Mystery Ser.). audio 88.00 (*0-7366-4351-6*, 4828) Books on Tape, Inc.
—Reckless Endangerment. abr. ed. 1998. audio 17.95 o.p. (*1-56740-784-6*, 443, Nova Audio Bks.); audio 26.95 (*1-56740-059-0*, 10, Bookcassette); audio 73.25 o.p. (*1-56740-588-6*, 1001) Brilliance Audio.
—Reckless Endangerment. 1998. 352p. 23.95 o.p. (*0-525-94347-1*) Dutton/Plume.
—Reckless Endangerment. 1999. 448p. reprint ed. mass mkt. 7.99 (*0-451-19328-8*, Signet Bks.) NAL.
—Reversible Error. unabr. ed. 1997. (Butch Karp Mystery Ser.). audio 56.00 (*0-7366-3686-2*, 4365) Books on Tape, Inc.
—Reversible Error. 1992. 288p. 20.00 o.p. (*0-525-93423-5*, Dutton) Dutton/Plume.
—Reversible Error. 1993. 448p. reprint ed. mass mkt. 7.99 (*0-451-17519-0*, Signet Bks.) NAL.
—True Justice. unabr. ed. 2001. 10p. audio 84.95 (*0-7927-2397-X*, CSL 286); audio compact disk 115.95 (*0-7927-9984-4*, SLD 035) BBC Audiobooks America. (Chivers Sound Library).
—True Justice. 2000. 384p. 24.95 o.s.i (*0-7434-0589-7*, Atria); 2001. (Illus.). 464p. reprint ed. mass mkt. 7.99 (*0-7434-0590-0*, Pocket) Simon & Schuster.
—True Justice. 2002. audio 14.95 (*0-7435-2759-3*, Encore); 2000. audio 25.00 (*0-7435-0553-0*, Simon & Schuster Audioworks) Simon & Schuster Audio.
—True Justice. l.t. ed. 2001. (Thorndike Mystery Ser.). 681p. 30.95 (*0-7862-3032-0*) Thorndike Pr.

**KASDAN, DAN (FICTITIOUS CHARACTER)—FICTION**

Gold, Herbert. She Took My Arm As If She Loved Me. 256p. 1998. pap. 12.95 (*0-312-19525-7*, Saint Martin's Griffin); 1997. 21.95 (*0-312-15653-7*) St. Martin's Pr.

**KEAN, MAGGIE (FICTITIOUS CHARACTER)—FICTION**

Davis, Nageeba. A Dying Art: A Maggie Kean Mystery. 272p. 2001. 22.95 o.s.i (*0-425-17951-6*); 2002. reprint ed. mass mkt. 6.99 o.s.i (*0-425-18548-6*) Berkley Publishing Group. (Prime Crime).
—An Opening for Murder: A Maggie Kean Mystery. 2002. 320p. 22.95 (*0-425-18493-5*) Berkley Publishing Group.

**KEANE, OWEN (FICTITIOUS CHARACTER)—FICTION**

Faherty, Terence. Deadstick. 1995. (WWL Mystery Ser.). per. (*0-373-26167-5*, 1-26167-6, Harlequin Bks.) Harlequin Enterprises, Ltd.
—Deadstick. 1991. 240p. 11.99 o.p. (*0-312-06332-6*, Saint Martin's Minotaur) St. Martin's Pr.
—Die Dreaming: An Owen Keane Mystery. 1996. pap. (*0-373-28207-9*, Harlequin Bks.); per. (*0-373-26207-8*, 1-26207-0, Worldwide Library) Harlequin Enterprises, Ltd.
—Die Dreaming: An Owen Keane Mystery. 1994. 272p. 20.95 o.p. (*0-312-11045-6*, Saint Martin's Minotaur) St. Martin's Pr.
—Live to Regret. 1995. 251p. per. (*0-373-26180-2*, 1-26180-9, Harlequin Bks.) Harlequin Enterprises, Ltd.
—Live to Regret. 1992. 224p. 17.95 o.p. (*0-312-08255-X*, Saint Martin's Minotaur) St. Martin's Pr.
—The Lost Keats: An Owen Keane Mystery. 1996. (Mystery Ser.). 250p. per. (*0-373-26192-6*, 1-26192-4, Worldwide Library) Harlequin Enterprises, Ltd.
—The Lost Keats: An Owen Keane Mystery. 1993. 272p. 18.95 o.p. (*0-312-09329-2*, Saint Martin's Minotaur) St. Martin's Pr.
—The Ordained: An Owen Keane Mystery. 1998. per. (*0-373-26296-5*, 1-26296-3, Mira Bks.) Harlequin Enterprises, Ltd.
—The Ordained: An Owen Keane Mystery. 1997. (Owen Keane Mysteries Ser.). 240p. 21.95 o.p. (*0-312-16958-2*, Saint Martin's Minotaur) St. Martin's Pr.
—Orion Rising: An Owen Keane Mystery. 1999. (Owen Keane Mysteries Ser.). 256p. 22.95 (*0-312-20351-9*, Saint Martin's Minotaur) St. Martin's Pr.
—Prove the Nameless: An Owen Keane Mystery. 1998. (WWL Mystery Ser.). per. (*0-373-26269-8*, 1-26269-0, Worldwide Library) Harlequin Enterprises, Ltd.
—Prove the Nameless: An Owen Keane Mystery. 1996. (Owen Keane Mysteries Ser.). 304p. 22.95 (*0-312-14706-6*, Saint Martin's Minotaur) St. Martin's Pr.

**KEARNEY, DANIEL (FICTITIOUS CHARACTER)—FICTION**

Gores, Joe. Contract Null & Void. 1996. 82p. 21.95 o.s.i (*0-89296-592-4*) Mysterious Pr.
—Contract Null & Void. 1997. (Dka File Novel Ser.). 336p. mass mkt. 6.50 o.s.i (*0-446-40447-0*) Warner Bks., Inc.
—Final Notice. 1992. 208p. reprint ed. mass mkt. 4.99 (*0-446-40314-8*, Mysterious Pr. Paperback Bks.) Warner Bks., Inc.

**KEARNY, NEEVE (FICTITIOUS CHARACTER)—FICTION**

Clark, Mary Higgins. While My Pretty One Sleeps. Rubenstein, Julie, ed. 1990. 320p. reprint ed. mass mkt. 7.99 (*0-671-67368-8*, Pocket) Simon & Schuster.

Characters

**KEATE, SARAH (FICTITIOUS CHARACTER)—FICTION**

Eberhart, Mignon G. Man Missing. 1992. (Black Dagger Crime Ser.). 192p. 16.50 o.p. (*0-86220-845-9*, Black Dagger) BBC Audiobooks America.

—Man Missing. 1988. 192p. pap. 2.95 (*0-446-32737-9*); mass mkt. 5.50 o.s.i (*0-446-35212-8*) Warner Bks., Inc.

—The Mystery of Hunting's End. 1998. (Illus.). 341p. pap. 15.00 (*0-8032-6737-1*, Bison Bks.) Univ. of Nebraska Pr.

—The Mystery of Huntings End. 1976. reprint ed. lib. bdg. 25.95 (*0-88411-764-2*) Amereon, Ltd.

—The Patient in Room 18. 1976. reprint ed. lib. bdg. 23.95 (*0-88411-765-0*) Amereon, Ltd.

—The Patient in Room 18. 1995. 304p. pap. 9.95 o.p. (*0-8032-6727-4*, Bison Bks.) Univ. of Nebraska Pr.

—While the Patient Slept. 1976. reprint ed. lib. bdg. 24.95 (*0-88411-759-6*) Amereon, Ltd.

—While the Patient Slept. 1995. 315p. pap. 11.00 (*0-8032-6726-6*, Bison Bks.) Univ. of Nebraska Pr.

—Wolf in Man's Clothing. Date not set. 221p. 21.95 (*0-8488-2256-0*) Amereon, Ltd.

—Wolf in Man's Clothing. 1996. 294p. pap. 13.00 (*0-8032-6732-0*, Bison Bks.) Univ. of Nebraska Pr.

—Wolf in Man's Clothing. 1993. mass mkt. 4.99 o.s.i (*0-446-77818-4*); 1987. 224p. mass mkt. 4.99 (*0-446-31470-6*) Warner Bks., Inc.

**KEATING, NICKY (FICTITIOUS CHARACTER)—FICTION**

Rosemoor, Patricia. After the Dark: Seven Sins. 1997. (Harlequin Intrigue Ser.: No. 451). per. (*0-373-22451-6*, 1-22451-8, Harlequin Bks.) Harlequin Enterprises, Ltd.

**KEBRON, ZAK (FICTITIOUS CHARACTER)—FICTION**

David, Peter. Dark Allies. 1999. (Star Trek Ser.: No. 8). (Illus.). 288p. pap. 6.50 (*0-671-02080-3*, Star Trek) Simon & Schuster.

—End Game. 1997. (Star Trek Ser.: No. 4). (Illus.). 208p. pap. 3.99 (*0-671-01398-X*, Star Trek) Simon & Schuster.

—Excalibur: Requiem. 2000. (Star Trek Ser.: No. 9). 288p. pap. 6.99 (*0-671-04238-6*, Star Trek) Simon & Schuster.

—House of Cards; Into the Void; The Two-Front War; End Game. abr. ed. 1997. (Star Trek Ser.: Nos. 1-4). audio 22.00 (*0-671-57625-9*, Simon & Schuster Audioworks) Simon & Schuster Audio.

—The Quiet Place. (Star Trek Ser.: No. 7). 288p. 2002. E-Book 6.99 (*0-7434-5574-6*); 1999. pap. 6.50 (*0-671-02079-X*) Simon & Schuster. (Star Trek).

—The Two-Front War. 1997. (Star Trek Ser.: No. 3). 304p. per. 3.99 (*0-671-01397-1*, Star Trek) Simon & Schuster.

**KEDRIGERN (FICTITIOUS CHARACTER)—FICTION**

Morressy, John. Kedrigern & Charming Couple. 1990. mass mkt. 3.50 o.s.i (*0-441-43265-4*) Ace Bks.

—Kedrigern in Wanderland. 1988. mass mkt. 3.50 o.s.i (*0-441-43264-6*) Ace Bks.

—The Questing of Kedrigern. 1987. 208p. mass mkt. 2.95 o.s.i (*0-441-69721-6*) Ace Bks.

—Remembrance for Kedrigern. 1990. mass mkt. 3.95 o.s.i (*0-441-71244-4*) Ace Bks.

—A Voice for Princess. 1986. 224p. mass mkt. 2.95 o.s.i (*0-441-84800-1*) Ace Bks.

**KEENER, RYDAL (FICTITIOUS CHARACTER)—FICTION**

Highsmith, Patricia. The Two Faces of January. 1988. 288p. pap. 13.00 (*0-87113-209-5*, Atlantic Monthly Pr.) Grove/Atlantic, Inc.

**KELLEHER, BOBBY (FICTITIOUS CHARACTER)—FICTION**

Feinstein, John. Running Mates. 1993. 336p. mass mkt. 4.50 o.p. (*0-06-104248-X*, HarperTorch) Morrow/Avon.

—Running Mates. 1994. 3.99 o.p. (*0-517-11763-0*) Random Hse. Value Publishing.

—Winter Games: A Mystery. 1995. 288p. 21.95 o.p. (*0-316-27721-5*) Little Brown & Co.

—Winter Games: A Mystery. 1997. 277p. mass mkt. 5.99 o.p. (*0-312-96149-9*, St. Martin's Paperbacks) St. Martin's Pr.

**KELLER, LINCOLN (FICTITIOUS CHARACTER)—FICTION**

Meadows, Lee E. Silent Conspiracy. 2002. (Lincoln Keller Mystery Ser.). pap. 16.95 (*1-928623-06-9*) Proctor Pubns.

—Silent Conspiracy: A Lincoln Keller Mystery. 1997. 270p. 24.95 o.p. (*1-882792-38-6*) Proctor Pubns.

—Silent Suspicion: A Lincoln Keller Mystery. 2000. (Lincoln Keller Mystery Ser.). 437p. 24.95 (*1-882792-93-9*) Proctor Pubns.

**KELLING, SARAH (FICTITIOUS CHARACTER)—FICTION**

MacLeod, Charlotte. The Balloon Man. 1998. (Sarah Kelling & Max Bittersohn Mysteries Ser.). 240p. 23.00 o.s.i (*0-89296-657-2*) Mysterious Pr.

—The Balloon Man. 2000. 288p. mass mkt. 6.50 (*0-446-60835-1*) Warner Bks., Inc.

—The Bilbao Looking Glass. 1983. (Crime Club Ser.). 192p. 11.95 o.p. (*0-385-18336-4*) Doubleday Publishing.

—The Bilbao Looking Glass. 1984. 208p. pap. 3.50 (*0-380-67454-8*, Avon Bks.) Morrow/Avon.

—The Bilbao Looking Glass. 2003. 192p. pap. 6.99 (*0-7434-7492-9*) ibooks, Inc.

—The Convivial Codfish. 1984. (Crime Club Ser.). 192p. 11.95 o.p. (*0-385-19333-5*) Doubleday Publishing.

—The Convivial Codfish. 1985. 224p. pap. 3.50 (*0-380-69865-X*, Avon Bks.) Morrow/Avon.

—The Convivial Codfish. 2003. 208p. mass mkt. 6.99 (*0-7434-7493-7*) ibooks, Inc.

—The Family Vault. 1979. 10.95 o.p. (*0-385-14871-2*) Doubleday Publishing.

—The Family Vault. 1980. 240p. mass mkt. 4.50 (*0-380-49080-3*, Avon Bks.) Morrow/Avon.

—The Gladstone Bag: A Sarah Kelling Mystery. 1990. 16.95 o.p. (*0-89296-370-0*) Mysterious Pr.

—The Gladstone Bag: A Sarah Kelling Mystery. 1992. 3.99 o.p. (*0-517-08076-1*) Random Hse. Value Publishing.

—The Gladstone Bag: A Sarah Kelling Mystery. 1991. mass mkt. 5.99 o.p. (*0-446-40002-5*, Mysterious Pr. Paperback Bks.) Warner Bks., Inc.

—The Odd Job. l.t. ed. 1995. 352p. reprint ed. 21.95 o.p. (*0-7838-1374-0*, Macmillan Reference USA) Gale Group.

—The Odd Job. 1995. 288p. 18.95 o.s.i (*0-89296-571-1*) Mysterious Pr.

—The Odd Job. 1996. 272p. mass mkt. 5.99 o.p. (*0-446-40397-0*) Warner Bks., Inc.

—The Palace Guard. 1981. 192p. 10.95 o.p. (*0-385-17533-7*) Doubleday Publishing.

—The Palace Guard. 1982. 176p. mass mkt. 3.99 (*0-380-59857-4*, Avon Bks.) Morrow/Avon.

—The Palace Guard. l.t. ed. 1982. 325p. reprint ed. 11.95 o.p. (*0-89621-345-5*) Thorndike Pr.

—The Palace Guard. 2003. 192p. mass mkt. 6.99 (*0-7434-5912-1*) ibooks, Inc.

—The Plain Old Man. 1985. (Crime Club Ser.). 192p. 12.95 o.p. (*0-385-23003-6*) Doubleday Publishing.

—The Plain Old Man. l.t. ed. 1986. (Nightingale Ser.). 336p. 10.95 o.p. (*0-8161-4025-1*, Macmillan Reference USA) Gale Group.

—The Plain Old Man. 1986. 224p. mass mkt. 3.99 (*0-380-70148-0*, Avon Bks.) Morrow/Avon.

—The Plain Old Man. 2003. 224p. mass mkt. 6.99 (*0-7434-7479-1*) ibooks, Inc.

—The Recycled Citizen. l.t. ed. 1989. (General Ser.). 352p. lib. bdg. 19.95 o.p. (*0-8161-4777-9*, Macmillan Reference USA) Gale Group.

—The Recycled Citizen. 1988. 208p. 15.45 o.p. (*0-89296-187-2*) Mysterious Pr.

—The Recycled Citizen. 1992. 4.50 (*0-446-77518-5*); 1989. 272p. mass mkt. 4.99 o.p. (*0-445-40689-5*, Mysterious Pr. Paperback Bks.) Warner Bks., Inc.

—The Resurrection Man: A Sarah Kelling & Max Bittersohn Mystery. l.t. ed. 1993. (Magna Large Print Ser.). 381p. o.p. (*0-7505-0496-X*) Magna Large Print Bks. GBR. *Dist:* Ulverscroft Large Print Canada, Ltd.

—The Resurrection Man: A Sarah Kelling & Max Bittersohn Mystery. 1992. 256p. 17.95 o.p. (*0-89296-443-X*) Mysterious Pr.

—The Resurrection Man: A Sarah Kelling & Max Bittersohn Mystery. 1993. 256p. mass mkt. 5.99 o.p. (*0-446-40332-6*, Mysterious Pr. Paperback Bks.) Warner Bks., Inc.

—The Resurrection Man: A Sarah Kelling & Max Bittersohn Mystery. 2001. 256p. mass mkt. 6.99 (*0-7434-2377-1*) ibooks, Inc.

—The Silver Ghost: A Sarah Kelling Mystery. l.t. ed. 1990. (Magna Large Print Ser.). 339p. 29.99 o.p. (*1-85057-592-4*) Magna Large Print Bks. GBR. *Dist:* Ulverscroft Large Print Bks., Ltd., Ulverscroft Large Print Canada, Ltd.

—The Silver Ghost: A Sarah Kelling Mystery. 1988. (Sarah Kelling Mystery Ser.). 224p. 15.95 (*0-89296-189-9*) Mysterious Pr.

—The Silver Ghost: A Sarah Kelling Mystery. 1989. 224p. reprint ed. mass mkt. 4.99 o.p. (*0-445-40828-6*, Mysterious Pr. Paperback Bks.) Warner Bks., Inc.

—The Withdrawing Room. 1980. (Crime Club Ser.). 192p. 8.95 o.p. (*0-385-17181-1*) Doubleday Publishing.

—The Withdrawing Room. 1982. 192p. mass mkt. 3.99 (*0-380-56473-4*, Avon Bks.) Morrow/Avon.

—The Withdrawing Room. 2002. 192p. pap. 6.99 (*0-7434-5258-5*) ibooks, Inc.

**KELLY, ANDRE (FICTITIOUS CHARACTER)—FICTION**

Mayle, Peter. Chasing Cezanne. l.t. ed. 1997. pap. 23.00 o.p. (*0-7838-8133-9*, Macmillan Reference USA) Gale Group.

—Chasing Cezanne. 1997. 295p. 23.00 (*0-679-45511-6*) Knopf, Alfred A. Inc.

—Chasing Cezanne. l.t. ed. 1997. 23.00 o.s.i (*0-679-77440-8*) Random Hse. Large Print.

—Chasing Cezanne. aut. ed. 1997. 23.00 o.p. (*0-676-53421-X*) Random Hse., Inc.

—Chasing Cezanne: A Novel. 1998. 304p. reprint ed. pap. 12.00 (*0-679-78120-X*, Vintage) Knopf Publishing Group.

—Chasing Cezanne: A Novel. l.t. ed. 1997. (Large Print Ser.). pap. 23.00 o.s.i (*0-679-77432-7*) Random Hse., Inc.

**KELLY, HOMER (FICTITIOUS CHARACTER)—FICTION**

Langton, Jane. The Dante Game: A Homer Kelly Mystery. 1992. (Homer Kelly Mystery Ser.). (Illus.). 336p. pap. 6.99 o.s.i (*0-14-013887-0*, Penguin Bks.) Penguin Group (USA) Inc.

—The Dante Game: A Homer Kelly Mystery. 1991. (Homer Kelly Mystery Ser.). (Illus.). 336p. 18.95 o.p. (*0-670-83439-4*) Viking Penguin.

—Dark Nantucket Noon. 1993. (Black Dagger Crime Ser.). (Illus.). 304p. 16.50 o.p. (*0-7451-8604-1*, Black Dagger) BBC Audiobooks America.

—Dark Nantucket Noon. unabr. ed. 1982. audio 48.00 (*0-7366-0630-0*, 1591) Books on Tape, Inc.

—Dark Nantucket Noon. 1981. (Fiction Ser.). 304p. pap. 5.99 (*0-14-005836-2*, Penguin Bks.) Penguin Group (USA) Inc.

—Dead as a Dodo: A Homer Kelly Mystery. 1997. (Homer Kelly Mystery Ser.). (Illus.). 256p. pap. 6.95 o.s.i (*0-14-024795-5*) Penguin Group (USA) Inc.

—Dead as a Dodo: A Homer Kelly Mystery. 1996. (Homer Kelly Mystery Ser.). 352p. 21.95 o.s.i (*0-670-86221-5*) Viking Penguin.

—Dead As a Dodo: A Homer Kelly Mystery. unabr. ed. 1997. audio 56.00 (*0-913369-62-4*, 4295) Books on Tape, Inc.

—The Deserter: Murder at Gettysburg. 2003. (Illus.). 256p. 23.95 (*0-312-30186-3*, Saint Martin's Minotaur) St. Martin's Pr.

—Divine Inspiration: A Homer Kelly Mystery. unabr. collector's ed. 1994. audio 56.00 (*0-7366-2722-7*, 3452) Books on Tape, Inc.

—Divine Inspiration: A Homer Kelly Mystery. abr. ed. 1994. (Homer Kelly Mystery Ser.). audio 16.00 o.p. (*0-453-00888-7*, Penguin AudioBooks) HighBridge Co.

—Divine Inspiration: A Homer Kelly Mystery. 1994. (Homer Kelly Mystery Ser.). (Illus.). 416p. reprint ed. pap. 5.99 o.s.i (*0-14-017376-5*, Penguin Bks.) Penguin Group (USA) Inc.

—Divine Inspiration: A Homer Kelly Mystery. 1993. (Homer Kelly Mystery Ser.). (Illus.). 416p. 20.00 o.p. (*0-670-84709-7*, Viking) Viking Penguin.

—Emily Dickinson Is Dead. unabr. collector's ed. 1987. audio 48.00 (*0-7366-1077-4*, 2004) Books on Tape, Inc.

—Emily Dickinson Is Dead. 1984. 256p. 13.95 o.p. (*0-312-24434-7*) St. Martin's Pr.

—Emily Dickinson Is Dead. l.t. ed. 1992. (Linford Mystery Large Print Ser.). 448p. pap. 17.99 o.p. (*0-7089-7162-8*, Ulverscroft) Thorpe, F. A. Pubs. GBR. *Dist:* Ulverscroft Large Print Bks., Ltd., Ulverscroft Large Print Canada, Ltd.

—Emily Dickinson Is Dead. 1985. (Crime Ser.). 256p. pap. 5.95 o.p. (*0-14-007771-5*, Penguin Bks.) Viking Penguin.

—The Escher Twist: A Homer Kelly Mystery. 2002. (Homer Kelly Mystery Ser.). (Illus.). 256p. 22.95 o.s.i (*0-670-03067-8*, Viking) Viking Penguin.

—Escher Twist: A Homer Kelly Mystery. 2002. 256p. mass mkt. 6.99 (*0-14-200184-8*) Penguin Group (USA) Inc.

—The Face on the Wall: A Homer Kelly Mystery. l.t. ed. 1999. (Large Print Mystery Ser.). 25.95 (*1-57490-205-9*, Beeler Large Print Bks.) Beeler, Thomas T. Publisher.

—The Face on the Wall: A Homer Kelly Mystery, , unabr. ed. 1999. audio 48.00 (*0-7366-4369-9*, 4827) Books on Tape, Inc.

—The Face on the Wall: A Homer Kelly Mystery. 1999. (Homer Kelly Mystery Ser.). (Illus.). 304p. pap. 5.99 o.s.i (*0-14-028157-6*) Penguin Group (USA) Inc.

—The Face on the Wall: A Homer Kelly Mystery. 1998. (Homer Kelly Mystery Ser.). (Illus.). 288p. 21.95 o.p. (*0-670-87674-7*) Viking Penguin.

—God in Concord: A Homer Kelly Mystery. 1993. (Homer Kelly Mystery Ser.). (Illus.). 352p. pap. 6.99 (*0-14-016594-0*, Penguin Bks.) Penguin Group (USA) Inc.

—God in Concord: A Homer Kelly Mystery. 1992. (Homer Kelly Mystery Ser.). 384p. 19.00 o.p. (*0-670-84260-5*, Viking) Viking Penguin.

—Good & Dead. unabr. collector's ed. 1992. audio 48.00 (*0-7366-2223-3*, 3013) Books on Tape, Inc.

—Good & Dead. 1986. 320p. 15.95 o.p. (*0-312-33865-1*) St. Martin's Pr.

—Good & Dead. (Homer Kelly Mystery Ser.). 256p. 1989. pap. 5.95 o.s.i (*0-14-012687-2*); 1987. pap. 3.95 o.p. (*0-14-010088-1*) Viking Penguin. (Penguin Bks.).

—The Memorial Hall Murder. unabr. ed. 1982. audio 48.00 (*0-7366-0631-9*, 1592) Books on Tape, Inc.

—The Memorial Hall Murder. 1996. pap. (*0-14-771166-5*) Penguin Group (USA) Inc.

—The Memorial Hall Murder. 1981. (Fiction Ser.). 272p. pap. 5.95 o.p. (*0-14-005704-8*, Penguin Bks.) Viking Penguin.

—Murder at Monticello: A Homer Kelly Mystery. 2001. (Homer Kelly Mystery Ser.). (Illus.). 256p. 22.95 o.s.i (*0-670-89462-1*, Viking) Viking Penguin.

—Murder at the Gardner. unabr. collector's ed. 1990. audio 56.00 (*0-7366-1741-8*, 2581) Books on Tape, Inc.

—Murder at the Gardner. 1989. (Penguin Crime Fiction Ser.). 368p. pap. 6.99 (*0-14-011382-7*, Penguin Bks.) Penguin Group (USA) Inc.

—Murder at the Gardner. 1988. (Illus.). 288p. 17.95 o.p. (*0-312-01479-1*, Saint Martin's Minotaur) St. Martin's Pr.

—Natural Enemy. unabr. collector's ed. 1992. audio 48.00 (*0-7366-2231-4*, 3021) Books on Tape, Inc.

—Natural Enemy. 1982. (Joan Kahn Bk.). (Illus.). 288p. 11.95 o.p. (*0-89919-081-2*) Houghton Mifflin Co.

—Natural Enemy. (Homer Kelly Mystery Ser.). 1990. 28p. pap. 5.95 o.p. (*0-14-013393-3*); 1987. (Illus.). 228p. pap. 3.95 o.p. (*0-14-009345-1*) Viking Penguin. (Penguin Bks.).

—The Shortest Day: Murder at the Revels. unabr. collector's ed. 1996. (Homer Kelly Mystery Ser.). audio 42.00 (*0-7366-3331-6*, 3982) Books on Tape, Inc.

—The Shortest Day: Murder at the Revels. 1996. (Homer Kelly Mystery Ser.). (Illus.). 272p. pap. 5.95 o.s.i (*0-14-017377-3*, Viking) Penguin Group (USA) Inc.

—The Shortest Day: Murder at the Revels. 1995. (Homer Kelly Mystery Ser.). (Illus.). 272p. 19.95 o.p. (*0-670-84710-0*) Viking Penguin.

—The Thief of Venice: A Homer Kelly Mystery. 2000. (Homer Kelly Mystery Ser.). (Illus.). 256p. pap. 5.99 (*0-14-029189-X*) Penguin Group (USA) Inc.

—The Thief of Venice: A Homer Kelly Mystery. 1999. (Homer Kelly Mystery Ser.). 256p. 22.95 o.p. (*0-670-88210-0*, Viking) Viking Penguin.

—The Transcendental Murder. unabr. collector's ed. 1982. audio 48.00 (*0-7366-0499-5*, 1473) Books on Tape, Inc.

—The Transcendental Murder. (Homer Kelly Mystery Ser.). 1990. 36p. pap. 6.95 o.p. (*0-14-014852-3*); 1989. 288p. pap. 3.95 o.p. (*0-14-011384-3*) Viking Penguin. (Penguin Bks.).

**KELLY, IRENE (FICTITIOUS CHARACTER)—FICTION**

Burke, Jan. Bones: An Irene Kelly Novel. l.t. ed. 2000. (Wheeler Large Print Book Ser.). 561p. pap. 25.95 (*1-56895-940-0*, Wheeler Publishing, Inc.) Gale Group.

—Bones: An Irene Kelly Novel. 2001. 448p. mass mkt. 6.99 (*0-451-20247-3*, Signet Bks.) NAL.

—Bones: An Irene Kelly Novel. 1999. (Irene Kelly Mystery Ser.: No. 7). 384p. 23.00 o.s.i (*0-684-85551-8*, Simon & Schuster) Simon & Schuster.

—Dear Irene, An Irene Kelly Novel. 1996. pap. 5.50 (*0-380-72556-8*, Avon Bks.) Morrow/Avon.

—Dear Irene, An Irene Kelly Novel. 1995. 288p. 20.00 o.s.i (*0-671-78216-9*, Simon & Schuster) Simon & Schuster.

—Flight: A Novel of Suspense. l.t. ed. 2001. 601p. 28.95 o.p. (*1-58724-051-3*, Wheeler Publishing, Inc.) Gale Group.

—Flight: A Novel of Suspense. 2001. 400p. 24.00 (*0-684-85552-6*); 24.00 (*0-7432-0170-1*) Simon & Schuster. (Simon & Schuster).

—Goodnight, Irene: An Irene Kelly Novel. 1994. (Irene Kelly Mystery Ser.). 256p. pap. 5.99 (*0-380-72279-8*, Avon Bks.) Morrow/Avon.

—Goodnight, Irene: An Irene Kelly Novel. 2002. (Illus.). 384p. pap. 6.99 (*0-7434-4451-5*, Pocket); 1993. 18.00 o.p. (*0-671-78200-2*, Simon & Schuster) Simon & Schuster.

—Goodnight, Irene: An Irene Kelly Novel. l.t. ed. 1995. (Ulverscroft Large Print Ser.). 528p. 29.99 o.p. (*0-7089-3287-8*, Ulverscroft) Thorpe, F. A. Pubs. GBR. *Dist:* Ulverscroft Large Print Bks., Ltd., Ulverscroft Large Print Canada, Ltd.

—Hocus: An Irene Kelly Novel. l.t. ed. 1997. lib. bdg. 24.95 (*1-57490-106-0*, Beeler Large Print Bks.) Beeler, Thomas T. Publisher.

—Hocus: An Irene Kelly Novel. 1998. (Irene Kelly Mystery Ser.). 480p. mass mkt. 6.99 o.p. (*0-06-104439-3*) HarperCollins Pubs.

—Hocus: An Irene Kelly Novel. 1997. 336p. 22.00 (*0-684-80344-5*); 22.00 (*0-684-00492-5*) Simon & Schuster. (Simon & Schuster).

—Liar: An Irene Kelly Mystery. 1999. (Irene Kelly Mystery Ser.). 400p. mass mkt. 7.50 (*0-06-104440-7*) HarperCollins Pubs.

—Liar: An Irene Kelly Mystery. 1998. (Irene Kelly Mystery Ser.). 352p. 23.00 (*0-684-80345-3*, Simon & Schuster) Simon & Schuster.

—Remember Me, Irene: An Irene Kelly Novel. 1997. 352p. mass mkt. 5.50 o.s.i (*0-06-104438-5*, HarperTorch) Morrow/Avon.

—Remember Me, Irene: An Irene Kelly Novel. 1996. 304p. 21.00 o.p. (*0-684-80343-7*, Simon & Schuster) Simon & Schuster.

—Sweet Dreams, Irene: An Irene Kelly Novel. 1995. pap. 4.99 (*0-380-72350-6*, Avon Bks.) Morrow/Avon.

—Sweet Dreams, Irene: An Irene Kelly Novel. 1994. 287p. 18.00 (*0-671-78210-X*, Simon & Schuster) Simon & Schuster.

**KELLY, JOHN (FICTITIOUS CHARACTER)—FICTION**

*see Clark, John (Fictitious Character)—Fiction*

**KELLY, LUTHER SAGE, 1849-1928—FICTION**

Bowen, Peter. Imperial Kelly. 1993. 3.99 o.p. (*0-517-11272-8*) Random Hse. Value Publishing.

—Yellowstone Kelly. 1990. 320p. mass mkt. 3.95 o.s.i (*0-553-28597-1*) Bantam Bks.

—Yellowstone Kelly. 1988. (Frontier Library). 260p. 17.95 o.s.i (*0-915463-40-7*, Frontier Library, The) Jameson Bks., Inc.

**KELLY, PAUL (FICTITIOUS CHARACTER)—FICTION**

Sweeney, Eamonn. Waiting for the Healer. 1999. 320p. pap. 13.00 (*0-312-20046-3*); 1998. 308p. 23.00 (*0-312-18206-6*) Picador.

**KELLY, VIRGINIA (FICTITIOUS CHARACTER)—FICTION**

Baker, Nikki. In the Game. 1991. (Virginia Kelly Mystery Ser.). 224p. (Orig.). pap. 9.95 (*1-56280-004-3*) Naiad Pr., Inc.

—The Lavender House Murder. 1992. (Virginia Kelly Mystery Ser.). 224p. pap. 9.95 o.p. (*1-56280-012-4*) Naiad Pr., Inc.

—The Long Goodbyes. 1993. (Virginia Kelly Mystery Ser.: No. 3). 208p. pap. 9.95 o.p. (*1-56280-042-6*) Naiad Pr., Inc.

—The Ultimate Exit Strategy: A Virginia Kelly Mystery. 2001. 240p. pap. 11.95 (*1-931513-03-1*) Bella Bks., Inc.

**KELTNER, JASON (FICTITIOUS CHARACTER)—FICTION**

Snyder, Keith. Coffin's Got the Dead Guy on the Inside. 1999. mass mkt. 5.99 (*0-440-23536-7*); 320p. mass mkt. 5.99 o.s.i (*0-440-23541-3*) Dell Publishing.

—Coffin's Got the Dead Guy on the Inside. l.t. ed. 1998. (Jason Keltner Mysteries Ser.). 300p. 22.95 (*0-8027-3320-4*) Walker & Co.

—The Night Men: A Jason Keltner Mystery. 2001. 312p. 23.95 (*0-8027-3370-0*) Walker & Co.

—Show Control. 1996. 267p. 20.95 o.p. (*1-885173-11-3*) Write Way Publishing.

—Trouble Comes Back. 1999. (Jason Keltner Mysteries Ser.). 318p. 22.95 (*0-8027-3338-7*) Walker & Co.

**KELVIN OF RUD (FICTITIOUS CHARACTER)—FICTION**

Anthony, Piers. Dragon's Gold. 1991. 282p. (Orig.). mass mkt. 4.99 (*0-8125-1384-3*, Tor Bks.) Doherty, Tom Assocs., LLC.

—Orc's Opal. 1992. 3.99 o.p. (*0-517-09031-7*) Random Hse. Value Publishing.

—Serpent's Silver. 1992. 3.99 o.p. (*0-517-09032-5*) Random Hse. Value Publishing.

Anthony, Piers & Margroff, Robert E. Chimaera's Copper. (Xanth Novels Ser.). 1991. 311p. mass mkt. 4.95 (*0-8125-0915-3*); 1990. 320p. 17.95 o.p. (*0-312-93213-8*) Doherty, Tom Assocs., LLC. (Tor Bks.).

—Dragon's Gold. 1987. (Orig.). mass mkt. 3.95 o.s.i (*0-8125-3125-6*, Tor Bks.) Doherty, Tom Assocs., LLC.

—Mouvar's Magic. 1993. 310p. mass mkt. 5.99 (*0-8125-1982-5*); 1992. 320p. 18.95 o.p. (*0-312-85305-X*) Doherty, Tom Assocs., LLC. (Tor Bks.).

—Orc's Opal. 1991. mass mkt. 4.99 o.p. (*0-8125-1177-8*); 1990. 18.95 o.p. (*0-312-85107-3*) Doherty, Tom Assocs., LLC. (Tor Bks.).

—Orc's Opal. 1994. 20.00 o.p. (*0-7278-4534-9*) Severn Hse. Pubs., Ltd.

—Serpent's Silver. 1988. 320p. 17.95 o.p. (*0-312-93103-4*); Vol. 2. 1989. (Serpent's Silver Ser.: Vol. 2). 313p. mass mkt. 4.95 (*0-8125-0257-4*) Doherty, Tom Assocs., LLC. (Tor Bks.).

**KEMP, JOHN MASON (FICTITIOUS CHARACTER)—FICTION**

McCutchan, Philip. Convoy of Fear. l.t. ed. 1992. (Lythway Ser.). 273p. 15.95 o.p. (*0-7451-1617-5*, Macmillan Reference USA) Gale Group.

—Convoy of Fear. 1997. 192p. pap. 11.95 o.p. (*0-312-16607-9*, Saint Martin's Griffin); 1990. 15.95 o.p. (*0-312-05065-8*) St. Martin's Pr.

**KEMP, LENNOX (FICTITIOUS CHARACTER)—FICTION**

Meek, M. R. D. A House to Die For. l.t. ed. 2000. (Dales Large Print Ser.). 368p. pap. 20.99 o.p. (*1-84262-044-4*) Dales Large Print Bks. GBR. *Dist:* Ulverscroft Large Print Bks., Ltd., Ulverscroft Large Print Canada, Ltd.

—A House to Die For. l.t. ed. 2000. pap. 20.99 (*1-84137-069-X*) Magna Large Print Bks. GBR. *Dist:* Ulverscroft Large Print Bks., Ltd.

—A House to Die For. 1999. 219p. 25.00 (*0-7278-5442-9*) Severn Hse. Pubs., Ltd.

—Postscript to Murder, Vol. 1. 1997. (PostScript to Murder Ser.: Vol. 1). 224p. text 21.95 o.p. (*0-312-15626-X*, Saint Martin's Minotaur) St. Martin's Pr.

—This Blessed Plot. 1992. (WWL Mystery Ser.: No. 93). mass mkt. (*0-373-26093-8*, 1-26093-4, Harlequin Bks.) Harlequin Enterprises, Ltd.

—Touch & Go. 1994. per. (*0-373-26146-2*, 1-26146-0, Harlequin Bks.) Harlequin Enterprises, Ltd.

—The Vanishing Point. 2002. 256p. 26.99 (*0-7278-5840-8*) Severn Hse. Pubs., Ltd.

—A Worm of Doubt: A Lennox Kemp Mystery. l.t. ed. 1988. lib. bdg. 11.95 o.p. (*1-85057-487-1*, Macmillan Reference USA) Gale Group.

—A Worm of Doubt: A Lennox Kemp Mystery. 1990. mass mkt. (*0-373-26048-2*, Harlequin Bks.) Harlequin Enterprises, Ltd.

—A Worm of Doubt: A Lennox Kemp Mystery. 1988. 208p. 14.95 o.s.i (*0-684-18939-9*, Scribner) Simon & Schuster.

**KENDALL, CORAL (FICTITIOUS CHARACTER)—FICTION**

Chaikin, Linda L. Kingscote. 1994. (Heart of India Ser.: No. 3). 400p. pap. 10.99 o.p. (*1-55661-378-4*) Bethany Hse. Pubs.

**KENDALL, JOHN (FICTITIOUS CHARACTER)—FICTION**

Francis, Dick. Longshot. 1999. mass mkt. (*0-449-45825-3*); 1992. 336p. mass mkt. 6.99 o.s.i (*0-449-21955-0*); 1992. mass mkt. 5.99 o.p. (*0-449-45309-X*) Ballantine Bks. (Fawcett).

—Longshot. unabr. ed. 1994. audio 56.00 (*0-7366-2739-1*, 3465) Books on Tape, Inc.

—Longshot. l.t. ed. 1992. (General Ser.). 412p. pap. 16.95 o.p. (*0-8161-5417-1*); lib. bdg. 21.95 o.p. (*0-8161-5416-3*) Gale Group. (Macmillan Reference USA).

—Longshot. abr. ed. audio 15.95 o.p. (*1-55994-345-9*, CPN 2187, HarperAudio) HarperTrade.

—Longshot. abr. ed. 2000. audio 7.95 (*1-57815-047-7*, 1019, Media Bks. Audio Publishing) Media Bks., L. L. C.

—Longshot. 1990. 324p. 19.95 o.s.i (*0-399-13581-2*, G. P. Putnam's Sons) Penguin Putnam Bks. for Young Readers.

—Longshot. 1992. 4.99 o.p. (*0-517-09581-5*) Random Hse. Value Publishing.

—Longshot: Open Market. 1991. mass mkt. 5.99 o.s.i (*0-449-22084-2*, Fawcett) Ballantine Bks.

**KENDRICK, JONATHAN (FICTITIOUS CHARACTER)—FICTION**

Piccirilli, Tom. The Dead Past, Vol. 1. 1999. (Felicity Grove Mysteries Ser.). 208p. reprint ed. mass mkt. 5.99 o.s.i (*0-425-16696-1*, Prime Crime) Berkley Publishing Group.

—The Dead Past. l.t. ed. 1999. (Thorndike Senior Lifestyle Ser.). 285p. 26.95 (*0-7862-1833-9*) Thorndike Pr.

—The Dead Past. 1997. (Felicity Grove Mysteries Ser.). 212p. 21.95 o.p. (*1-885173-28-8*) Write Way Publishing.

—Sorrow's Crown. 1999. (Felicity Grove Mysteries Ser.). 208p. mass mkt. 5.99 o.s.i (*0-425-17028-4*, Prime Crime) Berkley Publishing Group.

—Sorrow's Crown. 1999. 240p. 21.95 o.p. (*1-885173-53-9*) Write Way Publishing.

**KENDRY, VEIL (FICTITIOUS CHARACTER)—FICTION**

Chesbro, George C. Jungle of Steel & Stone. 3rd ed. 2000. 208p. reprint ed. pap. 16.99 (*1-930253-08-7*) Apache Beach Pubns.

—Jungle of Steel & Stone. 1987. 208p. 16.95 (*0-89296-204-6*) Mysterious Pr.

—Jungle of Steel & Stone. 1988. mass mkt. 3.95 (*0-445-40522-8*, Mysterious Pr. Paperback Bks.) Warner Bks., Inc.

**KENNEDY, CHRISTY (FICTITIOUS CHARACTER)—FICTION**

Charles, Paul. The Ballad of Sean & Wilko. 2000. (Inspector Christy Kennedy Mystery Ser.: No. 4). 284p. 31.00 (*1-899344-58-6*); 283p. pap. 15.95 (*1-899344-57-8*) Do-Not Pr., The GBR. *Dist:* Dufour Editions, Inc.

—The Ballad of Sean & Wilko. 2000. 283p. (*1-902602-02-1*) New Island Bks. IRL. *Dist:* Dufour Editions, Inc.

—Fountain of Sorrow. 1999. 230p. 31.00 (*1-899344-38-1*); pap. 14.95 (*1-899344-39-X*) Do-Not Pr., The GBR. *Dist:* Dufour Editions, Inc.

—The Hissing of the Silent Lonely Room. 2002. (Inspector Christy Kennedy Mystery Ser.: No. 5). 286p. 29.95 (*1-899344-70-5*); pap. 15.95 (*1-899344-71-3*) Do-Not Pr., The GBR. *Dist:* Dufour Editions, Inc.

—I Love the Sound of Breaking Glass: An Inspector Christy Kennedy Mystery. 1997. (Bloodlines Ser.). 232p. pap. 14.95 (*1-899344-16-0*) Do-Not Pr., The GBR. *Dist:* Dufour Editions, Inc.

—Last Boat to Camden Town: An Inspector Christy Kennedy Mystery. 1998. (Illus.). 168p. pap. 15.95 (*1-899344-30-6*); 34.95 (*1-899344-29-2*) Do-Not Pr., The GBR. *Dist:* Dufour Editions, Inc.

**KENNEDY, JERRY (FICTITIOUS CHARACTER)—FICTION**

Higgins, George V. Defending Billy Ryan. unabr. ed. 1997. audio 39.95 (*0-7861-1234-4*) Blackstone Audio Bks., Inc.

—Defending Billy Ryan. l.t. ed. 1993. 50.95 (*0-7838-1112-8*, Macmillan Reference USA) Gale Group.

—Defending Billy Ryan. 1992. 320p. 21.95 o.p. (*0-8050-1677-5*) Holt, Henry & Co.

—Defending Billy Ryan. 1994. 304p. mass mkt. 4.99 o.s.i (*0-8217-4586-7*) Kensington Publishing Corp.

—Kennedy for the Defense. 1985. 224p. mass mkt. 2.95 o.p. (*0-345-32612-1*) Ballantine Bks.

—Kennedy for the Defense. 1992. mass mkt. 4.50 o.s.i (*0-8217-3724-4*, Zebra Bks.) Kensington Publishing Corp.

—Kennedy for the Defense. 1980. 9.95 o.p. (*0-394-42406-9*, Knopf Bks. for Young Readers) Random Hse. Children's Bks.

—Kennedy for the Defense: A Novel. 1995. pap. 12.00 o.p. (*0-8050-4182-6*, Owl Bks.) Holt, Henry & Co.

—Penance for Jerry Kennedy. 1986. 320p. pap. 3.50 o.p. (*0-88184-224-9*, Carroll & Graf Pubs.) Avalon Publishing Group.

—Sandra Nichols Found Dead: A Jerry Kennedy Novel. 1997. 256p. pap. 12.00 o.s.i (*0-8050-5222-4*, Owl Bks.); 1996. 89p. 23.00 o.p. (*0-8050-3747-0*) Holt, Henry & Co.

**KENOBI, OBI-WAN (FICTITIOUS CHARACTER)—FICTION**

Allston, Aaron. Star Wars. 1999. (Star Wars Ser.). mass mkt. 5.99 (*0-553-58125-2*) Bantam Bks.

Anderson, Kevin J. Darksaber. 1996. (Star Wars Ser.). 464p. mass mkt. 6.99 (*0-553-57611-9*, Spectra); (YA). mass mkt. 10.95 o.s.i (*0-553-84011-8*) Bantam Bks.

—Darksaber. 1995. audio 16.98 o.s.i (*0-553-74672-3*); audio 16.99 (*0-553-47423-5*, 393257) Random Hse. Audio Publishing Group. (RH Audio).

Ashburn, Jo. Star Wars: Episode I: The Phantom Menace. 1999. (Prima's Official Strategy Guides). (Illus.). 96p. pap. 9.99 o.s.i (*0-7615-2148-8*, Prima Lifestyles) Crown Publishing Group.

Bear, Greg. Rogue Planet. 2000. (Star Wars Ser.). 352p. 26.00 (*0-345-43538-9*, Del Rey) Ballantine Bks.

—Rogue Planet. abr. ed. 2000. (Star Wars Ser.). audio 25.00 (*0-375-41563-7*); audio compact disk 29.95 (*0-375-41586-6*) Random Hse. Audio Publishing Group. (RH Audio).

Brooks, Terry. Star Wars Episode I: The Phantom Menace. 2000. 352p. mass mkt. o.s.i (*0-345-43975-9*, Del Rey); 2000. 352p. mass mkt. 7.50 (*0-345-43411-0*, Del Rey); 1999. (*0-345-43754-3*); 1999. 324p. 25.00 (*0-345-42765-3*, Del Rey) Ballantine Bks.

—Star Wars Episode I: The Phantom Menace. abr. ed. 1999. (Star Wars Ser.). audio 19.95 (*0-375-40635-2*); audio compact disk 49.95 (*0-375-40743-X*); audio compact disk 24.95 (*0-375-40637-9*);Set. audio 39.95 (*0-375-40655-7*) Random Hse. Audio Publishing Group. (RH Audio).

—Star Wars Episode I: The Phantom Menace. 1999. (Star Wars Episode I Ser.). 13.55 (*0-606-19372-3*) Turtleback Bks.

Daley, Brian. Star Wars: The National Public Radio Dramatization. 1994. (Star Wars Ser.). (Illus.). 352p. pap. 19.00 o.s.i (*0-345-39109-8*, Del Rey) Ballantine Bks.

Dorling Kindersley Publishing Staff. Star Wars: The Power of Myth. 2000. (Star Wars Ser.). (Illus.). 48p. (J). pap. 12.95 (*0-7894-5591-9*, D K Ink) Dorling Kindersley Publishing, Inc.

—Star Wars: The Power of Myth. l.t. ed. 2000. (Illus.). 48p. 11.55 o.p. (*0-7513-6679-X*) Thorpe, F. A. Pubs. GBR. *Dist:* Ulverscroft Large Print Bks., Ltd., Ulverscroft Large Print Canada, Ltd.

Gardner, J. J. Star Wars Movie Story. 1997. (Star Wars Ser.). (J). (gr. 5-7). mass mkt. 5.99 (*0-590-06654-4*) Scholastic, Inc.

Hamill, Mark, et al. Star Wars: The Original Radio Drama. abr. unabr. ed. 1993. (Star Wars Ser.). audio 39.95 (*0-942110-99-4*, 692313); audio compact disk 64.95 (*1-56511-005-6*) HighBridge Co.

Jones, Bruce, et al. Star Wars: A New Hope. 1997. (Star Wars Ser.). 104p. (YA). (gr. 3 up). pap. 9.95 (*1-56971-213-1*) Dark Horse Comics.

—Star Wars Trilogy: A New Hope, Empire Strikes Back, Return of the Jedi. 2nd ed. 1997. (Star Wars Ser.). (Illus.). (J). (gr. 3 up). pap. 29.85 o.p. (*1-56971-257-3*) Dark Horse Comics.

Lucas, George. Star Wars: A New Hope. 1995. (Star Wars Ser.). 272p. 16.00 o.s.i (*0-345-40077-1*, Del Rey) Ballantine Bks.

—Star Wars: A New Hope. 1996. (YA). (gr. 7-12). audio 17.00 o.p. (*1-57042-248-6*) Time Warner AudioBooks.

—Star Wars: A New Hope. 1998. (Star Wars Manga Ser.: Bk. 4). (Illus.). 96p. (YA). (gr. 3 up). pap. 9.95 (*1-56971-365-0*); pap. 9.95 (*1-56971-364-2*); pap. 9.95 (*1-56971-362-6*) Dark Horse Comics.

—Star Wars: A New Hope, Script Facsimiles. deluxe ed. 1998. (Star Wars Ser.). (Illus.). 176p. pap. 18.95 (*0-345-42080-2*, Del Rey) Ballantine Bks.

—Star Wars: A New Hope: The Illustrated Screenplay. 1998. (Star Wars Trilogy Ser.). (Illus.). 208p. pap. 12.00 o.s.i (*0-345-42069-1*, Del Rey) Ballantine Bks.

—Star Wars: Episode I: The Phantom Menace Facsimile Script. 2000. (Star Wars Ser.). (Illus.). 144p. pap. 18.95 (*0-345-43123-5*, Del Rey) Ballantine Bks.

—Star Wars: Episode I: The Phantom Menace Illustrated Screenplay. 1999. (Star Wars Ser.). (Illus.). vii, 150p. (Orig.). pap. 14.95 (*0-345-43110-3*, Del Rey) Ballantine Bks.

Lucas, George. Star Wars Trilogy: Star Wars; The Empire Strikes Back; Return of the Jedi. unabr. ed. 1994. (Star Wars Ser.). audio 50.00 o.p. (*1-57042-157-9*, 4-521579); audio 75.00 o.p. (*1-57042-169-2*, 2-521579) Time Warner AudioBooks.

Lucas, George, et al. Star Wars: Episode I: The Phantom Menace. 1999. (Star Wars Ser.). (Illus.). 112p. pap. 12.95 (*1-56971-359-6*) Dark Horse Comics.

—Star Wars Trilogy: Star Wars; The Empire Strikes Back; Return of the Jedi. (Star Wars Ser.). 1997. mass mkt. 6.99 (*0-345-91126-1*); 1993. 480p. mass mkt. 7.99 (*0-345-38438-5*, Del Rey); 1987. 480p. pap. 12.95 (*0-345-34806-0*, Del Rey) Ballantine Bks.

—Star Wars Trilogy: Star Wars; The Empire Strikes Back; Return of the Jedi. 1987. (J). (gr. 3-7). 16.05 (*0-606-01231-1*) Turtleback Bks.

Lucasfilm Ltd. The Complete Trilogy Cassette Gift-Pack: Star Wars, The Empire Strikes Back, & Return of the Jedi. abr. ed. 1996. (Star Wars Ser.). audio 105.85 o.p. (*1-56511-173-7*) HighBridge Co.

Lucasfilm Ltd. Staff. Star Wars. 1999. pap. 0.90 o.s.i (*0-375-80892-2*, Random Hse. Bks. for Young Readers) Random Hse. Children's Bks.

—Star Wars: Episode I: The Phantom Menace. 1999. pap. 1.94 o.s.i (*0-375-80898-1*, Random Hse. Bks. for Young Readers) Random Hse. Children's Bks.

—Star Wars: Episode I: The Phantom Menace. 1999. pap. 1.80 o.s.i (*0-375-80897-3*) Random Hse., Inc.

Lund, Kristin. Inside the Worlds of Star Wars: Episode 1. Dorling Kindersley Publishing Staff, ed. l.t. ed. 2000. (Illus.). 48p. 21.45 o.p. (*0-7513-6222-0*) Thorpe, F. A. Pubs. GBR. *Dist:* Ulverscroft Large Print Bks., Ltd., Ulverscroft Large Print Canada, Ltd.

Rhino Records Staff, ed. Star Wars: Episode I: The Phantom Menace. 1999. (Star Wars Ser.). 24p. (J). 9.98 incl. audio compact disk. (Illus.). 5.98 incl. audio (*1-56826-996-X*, R4 75642) Rhino Entertainment.

Schultz, Mark, et al. Star Wars: Episode I: The Phantom Menace Adventures. 2000. (Star Wars Ser.). (Illus.). 112p. (YA). (gr. 5 up). pap. 12.95 (*1-56971-443-6*) Dark Horse Comics.

Star Wars Trilogy: Star Wars; The Empire Strikes Back; Return of the Jedi, 3 vols. 1987. (Star Wars Ser.). pap. 8.65 o.p. (*0-345-32964-3*, Del Rey) Ballantine Bks.

Thomas, Jim K. Star Wars: Luke's Fate. 1996. (Step into Reading Step 3 Bks.). (J). (gr. 2-3). 10.14 (*0-606-11893-4*) Turtleback Bks.

Whitman, John. Star Wars: Episode I: The Phantom Menace. 1999. (Star Wars Ser.). (Illus.). 344p. (YA). (gr. 3 up). 9.95 o.p. (*0-8118-2315-6*) Chronicle Bks. LLC.

Whitman, John & Lucas, George. Star Wars. 1996. (Mighty Chronicles Ser.). (Illus.). 432p. (gr. 4-7). 9.95 o.s.i (*0-8118-1480-7*) Chronicle Bks. LLC.

Zahn, Timothy. Star Wars. 1994. (Star Wars Ser.). pap. 17.95 o.s.i (*0-553-63485-2*) Bantam Bks.

**KENT, CHARLOTTE (FICTITIOUS CHARACTER)—FICTION**

Kittredge, Mary. Dead & Gone: A Charlotte Kent Mystery. 1991. 224p. reprint ed. mass mkt. (*0-373-26075-X*, Harlequin Bks.) Harlequin Enterprises, Ltd.

—Poison Pen. 1992. mass mkt. (*0-373-26099-7*, Harlequin Bks.) Harlequin Enterprises, Ltd.

—Poison Pen. 1990. 182p. 18.95 o.s.i (*0-8027-5768-5*) Walker & Co.

**KENWOOD, CHRISTA (FICTITIOUS CHARACTER)—FICTION**

Booth, Pat. Miami. 1992. mass mkt. 5.99 o.s.i (*0-345-38165-3*) Ballantine Bks.

—Miami. 1991. 384p. 20.00 o.s.i (*0-517-58415-8*, Crown) Crown Publishing Group.

—Miami. 1994. 4.99 o.p. (*0-517-11672-3*) Random Hse. Value Publishing.

**KENZIE, PATRICK (FICTITIOUS CHARACTER)—FICTION**

Lehane, Dennis. Darkness, Take My Hand. 1997. 400p. mass mkt. 7.99 (*0-380-72628-9*, Avon Bks.); 1996. 320p. 24.00 (*0-688-14380-6*, Morrow, William & Co.) Morrow/Avon.

—A Drink Before the War. 2003. 300p. pap. 14.00 (*0-15-602902-2*, Harvest Bks.); 1994. 288p. 22.95 (*0-15-100093-X*) Harcourt Trade Pubs.

—A Drink Before the War. 1996. 320p. mass mkt. 7.99 (*0-380-72623-8*, Avon Bks.) Morrow/Avon.

—A Drink Before the War. 336p. (*0-7278-5537-9*) Severn Hse. Pubs., Ltd.

—Gone, Baby, Gone. abr. ed. 1999. audio 7.99 o.s.i (*1-56740-305-0*, 1869, Paperback Nova Audio Bks.); 1998. audio 17.95 o.p. (*1-56740-783-8*, 450, Nova Audio Bks.); 1998. audio 26.95 (*1-56740-058-2*, 18, Bookcassette); 1998. audio 73.25 (*1-56740-587-8*, 881, Unabridged Library Editions) Brilliance Audio.

—Gone, Baby, Gone. 1999. 448p. mass mkt. 7.99 (*0-380-73035-9*, Avon Bks.); 1998. 256p. 24.00 (*0-688-15332-1*, Morrow, William & Co.) Morrow/Avon.

—Prayers for Rain. abr. ed. 2003. (Patrick Kenzie/Angela Gennaro Ser.: Vol. 0). audio compact disk 14.99 (*1-59086-517-0*, 4108); 2000. audio 7.99 (*1-56740-345-X*, 2044, Paperback Nova Audio Bks.); 1999. audio 17.95 o.p. (*1-56740-840-0*, 1698, Nova Audio Bks.); 2003. (Patrick Kenzie/Angela Gennaro Ser.: Vol. 0). audio compact disk 62.25 (*1-59086-555-3*, 4145); 1999. audio 35.95 (*1-56740-428-6*, 1696, Brilliance Audio Unabridged); 1999. audio 57.25 (*1-56740-654-8*, 1697, Unabridged Library Editions) Brilliance Audio.

—Prayers for Rain, Set. abr. ed. 1999. audio 17.95. audio 35.95 Highsmith Inc.

—Prayers for Rain. 2000. 416p. mass mkt. 7.99 (*0-380-73036-7*); 1999. 352p. 25.00 (*0-688-15333-X*, Morrow, William & Co.); 1999. 352p. 25.00 (*0-688-15333-X*, Morrow, William & Co.) Morrow/Avon.

—Prayers for Rain. l.t. ed. 1999. (Core Ser.). 570p. 29.95 (*0-7838-8786-8*) Thorndike Pr.

—Sacred. abr. ed. 1998. audio 7.99 o.p. (*1-56740-238-0*, 1650, Nova Audio Bks.); 1997. audio 16.95 o.p. (*1-56100-979-2*, 505, Nova Audio Bks.); 1997. audio 73.25 o.p. (*1-56100-829-X*, 1022, Unabridged Library Editions); 1997. audio 23.95 (*1-56100-754-4*, 244, Bookcassette) Brilliance Audio.

—Sacred. 1998. 400p. mass mkt. 7.99 (*0-380-72629-7*, Avon Bks.); 1997. 256p. 23.00 (*0-688-14381-4*, Morrow, William & Co.) Morrow/Avon.

**KEOGH, HARRY (FICTITIOUS CHARACTER)—FICTION**

Lumley, Brian. Harry Keogh: Necroscope & Other Heroes! 2003. 320p. 25.95 (*0-7653-0847-9*, Tor Bks.) Doherty, Tom Assocs., LLC.

—Necroscope: The Lost Years. (Necroscope Ser.: Vol. 9). 1996. 593p. mass mkt. 7.99 (*0-8125-5363-2*); 1994. 384p. 23.95 (*0-312-85787-X*); 1992. mass mkt. 6.99 (*0-8125-2137-4*) Doherty, Tom Assocs., LLC. (Tor Bks.).

—Necroscope Vol. II: Resurgence: The Lost Years. 1996. (Necroscope Ser.: Vol. 10). 448p. 25.95 o.p. (*0-312-85948-1*, Tor Bks.) Doherty, Tom Assocs., LLC.

**KEOUGH, JOE (FICTITIOUS CHARACTER)—FICTION**

Randisi, Robert J. Alone with the Dead. unabr. ed. 1999. audio 69.95 (*0-7927-2267-1*, CSL156, Chivers Sound Library) BBC Audiobooks America.

—Alone with the Dead. (Joe Keough Mysteries Ser.). 368p. reprint ed. 1999. mass mkt. 6.99 (*0-8439-4641-5*); 1998. pap. 5.50 (*0-8439-4435-8*) Dorchester Publishing Co., Inc. (Leisure Bks.).

—Alone with the Dead. 1995. 262p. 21.95 o.p. (*0-312-13022-8*, Saint Martin's Minotaur) St. Martin's Pr.

—Alone with the Dead. 1999. E-Book 9.95 (*0-585-29635-9*) netLibrary, Inc.

—Blood on the Arch: A Joe Keough Mystery. E-Book 22.95 (*0-312-27407-6*); 2000. 280p. 22.95 (*0-312-24179-8*, Saint Martin's Minotaur) St. Martin's Pr.

—East of the Arch: A Joe Keough Mystery. 2002. 336p. 24.95 (*0-312-28398-9*, Saint Martin's Minotaur) St. Martin's Pr.

—In the Shadow of the Arch. 2000. (Joe Keough Mysteries Ser.). 368p. mass mkt. 4.99 (*0-8439-4761-6*, Leisure Bks.) Dorchester Publishing Co., Inc.

—In the Shadow of the Arch. 1997. (Joe Keough Mysteries Ser.). 368p. 24.95 (*0-312-18115-9*, Saint Martin's Minotaur) St. Martin's Pr.

**KEREMOS, HELEN (FICTITIOUS CHARACTER)—FICTION**

Zaremba, Eve. Beyond Hope. 1990. 184p. pap. 11.95 (*0-921299-02-8*) Second Story Pr. CAN. *Dist:* SCB Distributors.

—The Butterfly Effect: A Helen Keremos Detective Novel. 1994. 332p. pap. 9.95 (*0-929005-56-2*) Second Story Pr. CAN. *Dist:* SCB Distributors.

—Uneasy Lies: A Helen Keremos Mystery. 1994. 255p. pap. 11.95 (*0-929005-17-1*) Second Story Pr. CAN. *Dist:* LPC/InBook.

—White Noise: A Helen Keremos Mystery Novel. 1997. 248p. pap. 11.95 (*0-929005-97-X*) Second Story Pr. CAN. *Dist:* SCB Distributors.

—Work for a Million. (NFS Canada Ser.). 200p. pap. 11.95 o.p. (*0-921299-00-1*) Second Story Pr. CAN. *Dist:* SCB Distributors.

**KERGULIN, ZOE (FICTITIOUS CHARACTER)—FICTION**

Labovitz, Trudy. Deadly Embrace: A Zoe Kergulin Mystery. 2000. (Zoe Kergulin Mystery Ser.: Vol. 1). vi, 200p. pap. 12.00 (*1-883523-38-9*) Spinsters Ink Bks.

—Ordinary Justice: A Zoe Kergulin Mystery. 1999. 248p. pap. 12.00 (*1-883523-31-1*) Spinsters Ink Bks.

**KERN, KAREN (FICTITIOUS CHARACTER)—FICTION**

Sloan, Susan R. Guilt by Association. 1995. 512p. 22.95 o.s.i (*0-446-51857-3*); 1996. 544p. reprint ed. mass mkt. 7.99 (*0-446-60306-6*) Warner Bks., Inc.

**KERN, LINDSEY (FICTITIOUS CHARACTER)—FICTION**

Shapiro, Barbara. Shattered Echoes. 1993. (Orig.). pap. 4.99 o.p. (*0-380-76747-3*, Avon Bks.) Morrow/Avon.

**KERNEY, KEVIN (FICTITIOUS CHARACTER)—FICTION**

McGarrity, Michael. Everyone Dies. abr. ed. (Kevin Kerney Ser.). 2004. audio 9.99 (*1-59086-782-3*, 4375, Brilliance Audio Paperback Audiobooks); 2003. audio 19.95 (*1-59086-781-5*, 4374); 2003. audio 29.95 (*1-59086-779-3*, 4372, Brilliance Audio Unabridged); 2003. audio 74.25 (*1-59086-780-7*, 4373, Brilliance Audio Unabridged Lib Ed) Brilliance Audio.

—Everyone Dies. l.t. ed. 2004. lib. bdg. 28.95 (*1-58547-374-X*, Platinum) Ctr. Point Large Print.

—Everyone Dies. 2003. (Kevin Kerney Novel Ser.). 336p. 23.95 (*0-525-94761-2*, Dutton) Dutton/Plume.

—Everyone Dies. 2004. 352p. mass mkt. 6.99 (*0-451-41147-1*, Onyx) NAL.

—Hermit's Peak. l.t. ed. 2001. (Illus.). 310p. 27.95 (*1-57490-338-1*) Beeler, Thomas T. Publisher.

—Hermit's Peak. (Kevin Kerney Novels Ser.). 1999. (Illus.). 320p. 24.00 o.s.i (*0-684-85078-8*, Scribner); 2000. 368p. reprint ed. mass mkt. 6.99 (*0-671-02147-8*, Pocket) Simon & Schuster.

—Hermit's Peak. abr. ed. 1999. (Kevin Kerney Novels Ser.). 320p. audio 24.00 o.s.i (*0-671-04577-6*, 591045, Simon & Schuster Audioworks) Simon & Schuster Audio.

—The Judas Judge. abr. ed. 2000. (Kevin Kerney Novels Ser.). audio 25.00 o.s.i (*0-7435-0627-8*, Simon & Schuster Audioworks) Simon & Schuster Audio.

—The Judas Judge: A Kevin Kerney Novel. 2000. (Kevin Kerney Novels Ser.). 288p. 23.95 o.s.i (*0-525-94547-4*, Dutton) Dutton/Plume.

—Mexican Hat. l.t. ed. 2001. (Illus.). 302p. 26.95 (*1-57490-379-9*, Beeler Large Print Bks.) Beeler, Thomas T. Publisher.

—Mexican Hat. unabr. ed. 1998. (Kevin Kerney Mystery Ser.: Vol. 2). audio 51.00 (*0-7887-1892-4*, 95314E7) Recorded Bks., LLC.

—Mexican Hat. 1998. (Kevin Kerney Novels Ser.). (Illus.). 336p. mass mkt. 6.50 (*0-671-00253-8*, Pocket Star) Simon & Schuster.

—The Mexican Hat: A Novel. 1997. 304p. 22.95 (*0-393-04063-1*) Norton, W. W. & Co., Inc.

—Serpent Gate. l.t. ed. 2000. 307p. 27.95 (*1-57490-326-8*, Beeler Large Print Bks.) Beeler, Thomas T. Publisher.

—Serpent Gate. unabr. ed. 1998. (Kevin Kerney Mystery Ser.: Vol. 3). audio 53.00 (*0-7887-2598-X*, 95497E7) Recorded Bks., LLC.

—Serpent Gate. (Kevin Kerney Novels Ser.). 1999. (Illus.). 368p. mass mkt. 6.99 (*0-671-02146-X*, Pocket Star); 1998. 320p. 23.00 o.s.i (*0-684-85076-1*, Scribner); 1998. 22.50 o.p. (*0-684-85345-0*, Scribner) Simon & Schuster.

—Serpent Gate. 2000. audio 15.99 (*0-7435-0557-3*); 1998. audio 23.00 (*0-671-58242-9*) Simon & Schuster Audio. (Simon & Schuster Audioworks).

—Serpent Gate. 1999. 12.55 (*0-606-19062-7*) Turtleback Bks.

—Slow Kill. 2004. 23.95 (*0-525-94799-X*, Dutton) Dutton/Plume.

—Tularosa. l.t. ed. 1996. pap. 23.95 (*1-56895-372-0*, Wheeler Publishing, Inc.) Gale Group.

—Tularosa. 1996. 304p. 25.00 (*0-393-03922-6*) Norton, W. W. & Co., Inc.

—Tularosa. unabr. ed. 2000. (Kevin Kerney Mystery Ser.: Vol. 1). audio 51.00 (*0-7887-1767-7*, 95245E7) Recorded Bks., LLC.

—Tularosa. 1998. 3.99 (*0-671-02373-X*, Pocket); 1997. (Illus.). 336p. mass mkt. 6.99 (*0-671-00252-X*, Pocket Star) Simon & Schuster.

—Under the Color of Law: A Kevin Kerney Novel. 2001. 320p. 23.95 o.p. (*0-525-94604-7*, Dutton) Dutton/Plume.

—Under the Color of Law: A Kevin Kerney Novel. 2002. 400p. mass mkt. 6.99 (*0-451-41044-0*, Onyx) NAL.

—Under the Color of Law: A Kevin Kerney Novel. abr. ed. 2001. audio 26.00 o.s.i (*0-7435-0755-X*); audio compact disk 32.00 o.s.i (*0-7435-0756-8*) Simon & Schuster Audio. (Simon & Schuster Audioworks).

**KERRIGAN, JOSH (FICTITIOUS CHARACTER)—FICTION**

Sheffield, Charles. Putting up Roots. 2003. (Jupiter Ser.). 256p. (YA). mass mkt. 5.99 (*0-7653-4569-2*, Starscape); 1998. (Tor Science Fiction Ser.). 256p. mass mkt. 5.99 (*0-8125-3892-7*, Tor Bks.); 1998. (Tor Science Fiction Ser.: 3). 288p. mass mkt. 5.99 (*0-8125-5392-6*, Tor Bks.); 1997. 256p. (gr. 7). 21.95 (*0-312-86241-5*, Tor Bks.) Doherty, Tom Assocs., LLC.

**KES (FICTITIOUS CHARACTER)—FICTION**

Cox, Greg. The Black Shore. 1997. (Star Trek Voyager Ser.: No. 13). (Illus.). 288p. mass mkt. 5.99 (*0-671-56061-1*, Star Trek) Simon & Schuster.

Friedman, Michael Jan. Day of Honor No. 3: Her Klingon Soul. 1997. (Star Trek Voyager: Vol. 3). (Illus.). 304p. mass mkt. 5.99 (*0-671-00240-6*, Star Trek) Simon & Schuster.

Golden, Christie. Marooned. 1997. (Star Trek Voyager Ser.: No. 14). (Illus.). 304p. pap. 5.99 (*0-671-01423-4*, Star Trek) Simon & Schuster.

Wright, Susan. Violations. 1995. (Star Trek Voyager Ser.: No. 4). 288p. mass mkt. 5.99 (*0-671-52046-6*, Star Trek) Simon & Schuster.

**KESSINGER, MEG (FICTITIOUS CHARACTER)—FICTION**

Gleiter, Jan. A House by the Side of the Road. (Dead Letter Mysteries Ser.: Vol. 1). 1999. 272p. mass mkt. 5.99 (*0-312-96693-8*, St. Martin's Paperbacks); Vol. 1. 1998. 288p. 22.95 (*0-312-18596-0*, Saint Martin's Minotaur) St. Martin's Pr.

**KESTREL, JULIAN (FICTITIOUS CHARACTER)—FICTION**

Ross, Kate. A Broken Vessel. 1995. (Crime Ser.). 304p. pap. 6.99 (*0-14-023453-5*, Penguin Bks.) Penguin Group (USA) Inc.

—A Broken Vessel. 1994. (Julian Kestrel Mystery Ser.). 304p. 18.95 o.p. (*0-670-84999-5*, Viking) Viking Penguin.

—Cut to the Quick. 1994. (Crime Ser.). 352p. pap. 6.99 (*0-14-023394-6*, Penguin Bks.) Penguin Group (USA) Inc.

—Cut to the Quick. 1993. 352p. 19.00 o.p. (*0-670-84847-6*, Viking) Viking Penguin.

—The Devil in Music. 1998. (Julian Kestrel Mystery Ser.). 480p. pap. 6.99 (*0-14-026364-0*) Penguin Group (USA) Inc.

—The Devil in Music. 1997. (Julian Kestrel Mystery Ser.). 464p. 24.95 o.s.i (*0-670-86359-9*) Viking Penguin.

—Whom the Gods Love. 1996. (Julian Kestrel Mystery Ser.). 400p. pap. 6.99 (*0-14-024767-X*, Penguin Bks.) Penguin Group (USA) Inc.

—Whom the Gods Love. 1995. (Julian Kestrel Mystery Ser.). 400p. 20.95 o.p. (*0-670-86207-X*, Viking) Viking Penguin.

**KETTERLING, KATE (FICTITIOUS CHARACTER)—FICTION**

Pykare, Nina Coombs. Death Comes for Desdemona. 1999. (First Edition Romance Ser.). 136p. 24.95 (*0-7862-2042-2*, Five Star) Gale Group.

**KEYES, BRIAN (FICTITIOUS CHARACTER)—FICTION**

Hiaasen, Carl. Tourist Season. l.t. ed. 1996. (G. K. Hall Mystery Ser.). 524p. lib. bdg. 23.95 o.p. (*0-7838-1647-2*, Macmillan Reference USA) Gale Group.

—Tourist Season. 1986. 295p. 15.95 o.p. (*0-399-13145-0*, G. P. Putnam's Sons) Penguin Putnam Bks. for Young Readers.

—Tourist Season. 1989. mass mkt. 3.95 (*0-446-73857-3*); 1987. 384p. reprint ed. mass mkt. 7.99 (*0-446-34345-5*) Warner Bks., Inc.

**KHAAVREN (FICTITIOUS CHARACTER)—FICTION**

Brust, Steven. Five Hundred Years After. (Tor Fantasy Ser.). 1995. 576p. mass mkt. 6.99 (*0-8125-1522-6*); 1994. 448p. 23.95 o.p. (*0-312-85179-0*) Doherty, Tom Assocs., LLC. (Tor Bks.).

—The Phoenix Guards. 1992. 491p. mass mkt. 7.99 (*0-8125-0689-8*); 1991. 16.95 o.p. (*0-312-85157-X*) Doherty, Tom Assocs., LLC. (Tor Bks.).

**KI (FICTITIOUS CHARACTER)—FICTION**

Ellis, Wesley. The Chicago Showdown. 1993. (Lone Star Ser.: No. 126). 192p. (Orig.). mass mkt. 3.99 o.s.i (*0-515-11044-2*, Jove) Berkley Publishing Group.

—Lone Star & a Comstock Crossfire, No. 78. 1989. mass mkt. 2.95 o.s.i (*0-515-09925-2*, Jove) Berkley Publishing Group.

—Lone Star & a Saloon Called Hell. 1994. (Lone Star Ser.: No. 143). 192p. (Orig.). mass mkt. 3.99 o.s.i (*0-515-11408-1*, Jove) Berkley Publishing Group.

—Lone Star & Deep Water Princess. 1992. (Lone Star Ser.: No. 116). 192p. mass mkt. 3.50 o.s.i (*0-515-10833-2*, Jove) Berkley Publishing Group.

—Lone Star & Hickok's Ghost. 1988. mass mkt. 2.95 o.s.i (*0-515-09586-9*, Jove) Berkley Publishing Group.

—Lone Star & the Alaskan Guns. 1985. (Lone Star Ser.: No. 40). 192p. mass mkt. 2.50 o.s.i (*0-515-08423-9*, Jove) Berkley Publishing Group.

—Lone Star & the Alaskan Renegades No. 104. 1991. mass mkt. 2.95 o.s.i (*0-515-10592-9*, Jove) Berkley Publishing Group.

—Lone Star & the Amarillo Rifles, No. 29. 1985. 192p. mass mkt. 2.50 o.s.i (*0-515-08082-9*, Jove) Berkley Publishing Group.

—Lone Star & the Apache Revenge, No. 21. 1984. 192p. mass mkt. 2.50 o.s.i (*0-515-07533-7*, Jove) Berkley Publishing Group.

—Lone Star & the Apache Warrior. 1985. (Lone Star Ser.: No. 37). 192p. mass mkt. 2.50 o.s.i (*0-515-08344-5*, Jove) Berkley Publishing Group.

—Lone Star & the Arizona Gunmen. 1990. (Lone Star Ser.: No. 91). mass mkt. 2.95 o.s.i (*0-515-10271-7*, Jove) Berkley Publishing Group.

—Lone Star & the Arizona Stranger. 1989. (Lone Star Ser.: No. 87). mass mkt. 2.95 o.s.i (*0-515-10174-5*, Jove) Berkley Publishing Group.

—Lone Star & the Aztec Treasure. 1992. (Lone Star Ser.: No. 123). 192p. mass mkt. 3.99 o.s.i (*0-515-10981-9*, Jove) Berkley Publishing Group.

—Lone Star & the Babary Killers, No. 80. 1989. mass mkt. 2.95 o.s.i (*0-515-09986-4*, Jove) Berkley Publishing Group.

—Lone Star & the Badlands War, No. 16. 1984. 192p. mass mkt. 2.50 o.s.i (*0-515-08199-X*, Jove) Berkley Publishing Group.

—Lone Star & the Bank Robbers. 1990. (Lone Star Ser.: No. 99). mass mkt. 2.95 o.s.i (*0-515-10446-9*, Jove) Berkley Publishing Group.

—Lone Star & the Bellwether Kid. 1993. (Lone Star Ser.: No. 133). 192p. (Orig.). mass mkt. 3.99 o.s.i (*0-515-11195-3*, Jove) Berkley Publishing Group.

—Lone Star & the Biggest Gun in the West. 1985. (Lone Star Ser.: No. 36). 192p. mass mkt. 2.50 o.s.i (*0-515-08332-1*, Jove) Berkley Publishing Group.

—Lone Star & the Black Bandana Gang. 1992. (Lone Star Ser.: No. 117). mass mkt. 3.50 o.s.i (*0-515-10850-2*, Jove) Berkley Publishing Group.

—Lone Star & the Bogus Banker. 1995. (Lone Star Ser.: No. 152). 192p. (Orig.). mass mkt. 3.99 o.s.i (*0-515-11592-4*, Jove) Berkley Publishing Group.

—Lone Star & the Border Bandits, No. 3. 1983. 192p. mass mkt. 2.50 o.s.i (*0-515-07540-X*, Jove) Berkley Publishing Group.

—Lone Star & the Bounty Hunters. 1990. (Lone Star Ser.: No. 97). mass mkt. 2.95 o.s.i (*0-515-10402-7*, Jove) Berkley Publishing Group.

—Lone Star & the Brutus Gang. 1993. (Lone Star Ser.: No. 127). 192p. (Orig.). mass mkt. 3.99 o.s.i (*0-515-11062-0*, Jove) Berkley Publishing Group.

—Lone Star & the Buccaneers. 1992. (Lone Star Ser.: No. 122). 192p. (Orig.). mass mkt. 3.99 o.s.i (*0-515-10956-8*, Jove) Berkley Publishing Group.

—Lone Star & the Buffalo Hunters. 1985. (Lone Star Ser.: No. 35). 192p. mass mkt. 2.50 o.s.i (*0-515-08233-3*, Jove) Berkley Publishing Group.

—Lone Star & the California Gold. 1991. (Lone Star Ser.: No. 105). mass mkt. 2.95 o.s.i (*0-515-10571-6*, Jove) Berkley Publishing Group.

—Lone Star & the California Oil War. 1985. (Lone Star Ser.: No. 39). 192p. mass mkt. 2.50 o.s.i (*0-515-08397-6*, Jove) Berkley Publishing Group.

—Lone Star & the Cheyenne Showdown. 1990. (Lone Star Ser.: No. 100). 192p. mass mkt. 3.50 o.s.i (*0-515-10473-6*, Jove) Berkley Publishing Group.

—Lone Star & the Cheyenne Trackdown, No. 67. 1988. mass mkt. 2.75 o.s.i (*0-515-09492-7*, Jove) Berkley Publishing Group.

—Lone Star & the Colorado Ambush. 1990. (Lone Star Ser.: No. 98). mass mkt. 2.95 o.s.i (*0-515-10427-2*, Jove) Berkley Publishing Group.

—Lone Star & the Comancheros, No. 69. 1988. mass mkt. 2.75 o.s.i (*0-515-09549-4*, Jove) Berkley Publishing Group.

—Lone Star & the Con Man's Ransom, No. 52. 1986. 192p. mass mkt. 2.75 o.s.i (*0-515-08797-1*, Jove) Berkley Publishing Group.

—Lone Star & the Deadly Stranger No. 71. 1988. mass mkt. 2.95 o.s.i (*0-515-09648-2*, Jove) Berkley Publishing Group.

—Lone Star & the Deadly Vigilantes No. 111. 1991. mass mkt. 3.50 o.s.i (*0-515-10709-3*, Jove) Berkley Publishing Group.

—Lone Star & the Deadly Vixens. 1994. (Lone Star Ser.: No. 142). 192p. (Orig.). mass mkt. 3.99 o.s.i (*0-515-11376-X*, Jove) Berkley Publishing Group.

—Lone Star & the Death Chase. 1994. (Lone Star Ser.: No. 138). 192p. (Orig.). mass mkt. 3.99 o.s.i (*0-515-11314-X*, Jove) Berkley Publishing Group.

—Lone Star & the Death Merchants No. 77. 1989. mass mkt. 2.95 o.s.i (*0-515-09876-0*, Jove) Berkley Publishing Group.

—Lone Star & the Death Mine, No. 136. 1993. 192p. (Orig.). mass mkt. 3.99 o.s.i (*0-515-11256-9*, Jove) Berkley Publishing Group.

—Lone Star & the Death Train, No. 57. 1987. 192p. mass mkt. 2.75 o.s.i (*0-515-08960-5*, Jove) Berkley Publishing Group.

—Lone Star & the Denver Madam, No. 13. 1985. 192p. mass mkt. 2.50 o.s.i (*0-515-08219-8*, Jove) Berkley Publishing Group.

—Lone Star & the Devil Worshipers No. 96. 1990. mass mkt. 2.95 o.s.i (*0-515-10386-1*, Jove) Berkley Publishing Group.

—Lone Star & the Devil's Playground No. 106. 1991. mass mkt. 2.95 o.s.i (*0-515-10598-8*, Jove) Berkley Publishing Group.

—Lone Star & the Diamond Swindlers, No. 85. 1989. mass mkt. 2.95 o.s.i (*0-515-10131-1*, Jove) Berkley Publishing Group.

—Lone Star & the Galvanized Yankees. 1995. (Lone Star Ser.: No. 150). 192p. (Orig.). mass mkt. 3.99 o.s.i (*0-515-11552-5*, Jove) Berkley Publishing Group.

—Lone Star & the Gamble of Death. 1990. (Lone Star Ser.: No. 89). mass mkt. 2.95 o.s.i (*0-515-10213-X*, Jove) Berkley Publishing Group.

—Lone Star & the Gemstone Robbers, Vol. 102. 1991. mass mkt. 2.95 o.s.i (*0-515-10513-9*, Jove) Berkley Publishing Group.

—Lone Star & the Ghost Dancers No. 112. 1991. mass mkt. 3.50 o.s.i (*0-515-10734-4*, Jove) Berkley Publishing Group.

—Lone Star & the Ghost Pirates, No. 18. 1984. 192p. mass mkt. 2.50 o.s.i (*0-515-08095-0*, Jove) Berkley Publishing Group.

—Lone Star & the Ghost Ship Pirates No. 130. 1993. 192p. (Orig.). mass mkt. 3.99 o.s.i (*0-515-11120-1*, Jove) Berkley Publishing Group.

—Lone Star & the Gold Mine. 1993. (Lone Star Ser.: No 128). 192p. (Orig.). mass mkt. 3.99 o.s.i (*0-515-11083-3*, Jove) Berkley Publishing Group.

—Lone Star & the Gold Mine War. 1985. (Lone Star Ser.: No. 38). 192p. mass mkt. 2.50 o.s.i (*0-515-08368-2*, Jove) Berkley Publishing Group.

—Lone Star & the Gold Raiders, No. 12. 1984. 192p. mass mkt. 2.50 o.s.i (*0-515-08162-0*, Jove) Berkley Publishing Group.

—Lone Star & the Golden Mesa, No. 33. 1985. 192p. mass mkt. 2.50 o.s.i (*0-515-08191-4*, Jove) Berkley Publishing Group.

—Lone Star & the Great Pilgrim Heist. 1993. (Lone Star Ser.: No. 134). mass mkt. 3.99 o.s.i (*0-515-11217-8*, Jove) Berkley Publishing Group.

—Lone Star & the Gulf Pirates, No. 49. 1986. 192p. mass mkt. 2.75 o.s.i (*0-515-08676-2*, Jove) Berkley Publishing Group.

—Lone Star & the Gunpowder Cure, No. 47. 1986. 192p. mass mkt. 2.50 o.s.i (*0-515-08608-8*, Jove) Berkley Publishing Group.

—Lone Star & the Gunrunners. 1992. (Lone Star Ser.: No. 121). 192p. (Orig.). mass mkt. 3.99 o.s.i (*0-515-10930-4*, Jove) Berkley Publishing Group.

—Lone Star & the Hangrope Heritage, No. 23. 1984. 192p. mass mkt. 2.50 o.s.i (*0-515-07734-8*, Jove) Berkley Publishing Group.

—Lone Star & the Hardrock Payoff, No. 9. 1984. 192p. mass mkt. 2.50 o.s.i (*0-515-08260-0*, Jove) Berkley Publishing Group.

—Lone Star & the Hellbound Pilgrims. 1992. (Lone Star Ser.: No. 113). 192p. mass mkt. 3.50 o.s.i (*0-515-10754-9*, Jove) Berkley Publishing Group.

—Lone Star & the Horse Thieves, No. 115. 1992. mass mkt. 3.50 o.s.i (*0-515-10809-X*, Jove) Berkley Publishing Group.

—Lone Star & the Indian Gold. 1990. (Lone Star Ser.: No. 94). mass mkt. 2.95 o.s.i (*0-515-10335-7*, Jove) Berkley Publishing Group.

—Lone Star & the Indian Rebellion, No. 50. 1986. 192p. mass mkt. 2.75 o.s.i (*0-515-08716-5*, Jove) Berkley Publishing Group.

—Lone Star & the James Gang's Loot, No. 65. 1988. 192p. mass mkt. 2.75 o.s.i (*0-515-09379-3*, Jove) Berkley Publishing Group.

—Lone Star & the Kansas Wolves, No. 4. 1983. 192p. mass mkt. 2.50 o.s.i (*0-515-07419-5*, Jove) Berkley Publishing Group.

—Lone Star & the Land Barons, No. 48. 1986. 192p. mass mkt. 2.50 o.s.i (*0-515-08649-5*, Jove) Berkley Publishing Group.

—Lone Star & the Land Grabbers, No. 6. 1984. 192p. mass mkt. 2.50 o.s.i (*0-515-08258-9*, Jove) Berkley Publishing Group.

—Lone Star & the Lost Gold Mine, No. 68. 1988. mass mkt. 2.75 o.s.i (*0-515-09522-2*, Jove) Berkley Publishing Group.

—Lone Star & the Medicine Lodge Shoot-Out, No. 79. 1989. mass mkt. 2.95 o.s.i (*0-515-09960-0*, Jove) Berkley Publishing Group.

—Lone Star & the Mescalero Outlaws, No. 28. 1984. 192p. mass mkt. 2.50 o.s.i (*0-515-08055-1*, Jove) Berkley Publishing Group.

—Lone Star & the Mexican Muskets. 1992. (Lone Star Ser.: No. 119). 192p. (Orig.). mass mkt. 3.50 o.s.i (*0-515-10881-2*, Jove) Berkley Publishing Group.

—Lone Star & the Mexican Standoff, No. 15. 1984. 192p. mass mkt. 2.50 o.s.i (*0-515-07887-5*, Jove) Berkley Publishing Group.

—Lone Star & the Mission War, No. 46. 1986. 192p. mass mkt. 2.50 o.s.i (*0-515-08581-2*, Jove) Berkley Publishing Group.

—Lone Star & the Montana Land Grab, No. 64. 1987. mass mkt. 2.75 o.s.i (*0-515-09328-9*, Jove) Berkley Publishing Group.

—Lone Star & the Montana Marauders. 1994. (Lone Star Ser.: No. 140). 192p. (Orig.). mass mkt. 3.99 o.s.i (*0-515-11357-3*, Jove) Berkley Publishing Group.

—Lone Star & the Montana Troubles, No. 24. 1984. 192p. (Orig.). mass mkt. 2.50 o.s.i (*0-515-07748-8*, Jove) Berkley Publishing Group.

—Lone Star & the Moon Trail Feud, No. 32. 1985. 192p. mass mkt. 2.50 o.s.i (*0-515-08174-4*, Jove) Berkley Publishing Group.

—Lone Star & the Mountain Man, No. 25. 1984. 192p. mass mkt. 2.50 o.s.i (*0-515-07880-8*, Jove) Berkley Publishing Group.

—Lone Star & the Mountain of Fire. 1995. (Lone Star Ser.: No. 153). 192p. (Orig.). mass mkt. 3.99 o.s.i (*0-515-11613-0*, Jove) Berkley Publishing Group.

—Lone Star & the Mountain of Gold No. 84. 1989. mass mkt. 2.95 o.s.i (*0-515-10108-7*, Jove) Berkley Publishing Group.

—Lone Star & the Nevada Bloodbath. 1988. (Lone Star Ser.: No. 73). mass mkt. 2.95 o.s.i (*0-515-09708-X*, Jove) Berkley Publishing Group.

—Lone Star & the Nevada Gold. 1994. (Lone Star Ser.: No. 147). 192p. (Orig.). mass mkt. 3.99 o.s.i (*0-515-11494-4*, Jove) Berkley Publishing Group.

—Lone Star & the Nevada Mustangs, No. 51. 1986. 192p. mass mkt. 2.75 o.s.i (*0-515-08755-6*, Jove) Berkley Publishing Group.

—Lone Star & the Oklahoma Ambush No. 103. 1991. mass mkt. 2.95 o.s.i (*0-515-10527-9*, Jove) Berkley Publishing Group.

—Lone Star & the Oklahoma Rustlers No. 110. 1991. mass mkt. 3.50 o.s.i (*0-515-10690-9*, Jove) Berkley Publishing Group.

—Lone Star & the Opium Rustlers, No. 2. 1983. 192p. mass mkt. 2.50 o.s.i (*0-515-07520-5*, Jove) Berkley Publishing Group.

—Lone Star & the Oregon Rail Sabotage, No. 45. 1986. 192p. mass mkt. 2.50 o.s.i (*0-515-08570-7*, Jove) Berkley Publishing Group.

—Lone Star & the Outlaw Posse, No. 60. 1987. 192p. mass mkt. 2.75 o.s.i (*0-515-09114-6*, Jove) Berkley Publishing Group.

—Lone Star & the Phantom Gunmen, No. 63. 1987. mass mkt. 2.75 o.s.i (*0-515-09257-6*, Jove) Berkley Publishing Group.

—Lone Star & the Railroad Killers. 1990. (Lone Star Ser.: No. 95). mass mkt. 2.95 o.s.i (*0-515-10353-5*, Jove) Berkley Publishing Group.

—Lone Star & the Railroad War, No. 14. 1984. 192p. mass mkt. 2.50 o.s.i (*0-515-07888-3*, Jove) Berkley Publishing Group.

—Lone Star & the Redemption Massacre, No. 137. 1994. 192p. (Orig.). mass mkt. 3.99 o.s.i (*0-515-11284-4*, Jove) Berkley Publishing Group.

—Lone Star & the Renegade Comanches, No. 10. 1983. 192p. mass mkt. 2.25 o.s.i (*0-515-06235-9*, Jove) Berkley Publishing Group.

—Lone Star & the Renegade Rancher. 1990. (Lone Star Ser.: No. 92). mass mkt. 2.95 o.s.i (*0-515-10287-3*, Jove) Berkley Publishing Group.

—Lone Star & the Rio Grande Bandits, No. 34. 1985. 192p. mass mkt. 2.50 o.s.i (*0-515-08255-4*, Jove) Berkley Publishing Group.

—Lone Star & the Ripper. 1990. (Lone Star Ser.: No. 93). mass mkt. 2.95 o.s.i (*0-515-10309-8*, Jove) Berkley Publishing Group.

—Lone Star & the River of No Return. 1993. (Lone Star Ser.: No. 135). mass mkt. 3.99 o.s.i (*0-515-11239-9*, Jove) Berkley Publishing Group.

—Lone Star & the River Pirates. 1991. (Lone Star Ser.: No. 107). mass mkt. 3.50 o.s.i (*0-515-10614-3*, Jove) Berkley Publishing Group.

—Lone Star & the River Queen. 1994. (Lone Star Ser.: No. 145). 192p. mass mkt. 3.99 o.s.i (*0-515-11455-3*, Jove) Berkley Publishing Group.

—Lone Star & the Riverboat. 1984. (Gamblers Ser.: No. 27). 192p. mass mkt. 2.50 o.s.i (*0-515-07916-2*, Jove) Berkley Publishing Group.

—Lone Star & the Rogue Grizzlies, No. 81. 1989. mass mkt. 2.95 o.s.i (*0-515-10016-1*, Jove) Berkley Publishing Group.

—Lone Star & the Rustler's Ambush, No. 58. 1987. 192p. (Orig.). mass mkt. 2.75 o.s.i (*0-515-09008-5*, Jove) Berkley Publishing Group.

—Lone Star & the San Antonio Rais, No. 17. 1983. 192p. mass mkt. 2.50 o.s.i (*0-515-07353-9*, Jove) Berkley Publishing Group.

—Lone Star & the San Diego Bonanza No. 129. 1993. 192p. (Orig.). mass mkt. 3.99 o.s.i (*0-515-11104-X*, Jove) Berkley Publishing Group.

—Lone Star & the Santa Fe Showdown. 1992. (Lone Star Ser.: No. 120). 192p. (Orig.). mass mkt. 3.99 o.s.i (*0-515-10902-9*, Jove) Berkley Publishing Group.

—Lone Star & the School for Outlaws. 1985. (Lone Star Ser.: No. 30). mass mkt. 2.50 o.s.i (*0-515-08110-8*, Jove) Berkley Publishing Group.

—Lone Star & the Scorpion. 1995. 192p. mass mkt. 3.99 o.s.i (*0-515-11570-3*, Jove) Berkley Publishing Group.

—Lone Star & the Shadow Catcher. 1989. (Lone Star Ser.: No. 88). mass mkt. 2.95 o.s.i (*0-515-10194-X*, Jove) Berkley Publishing Group.

—Lone Star & the Showdowners, No. 8. 1983. 192p. mass mkt. 2.50 o.s.i (*0-515-07521-3*, Jove) Berkley Publishing Group.

—Lone Star & the Sierra Sabotage. 1991. (Lone Star Ser.: No. 101). mass mkt. 2.95 o.s.i (*0-515-10495-7*, Jove) Berkley Publishing Group.

—Lone Star & the Sierra Swindlers, No. 55. 1987. mass mkt. 2.75 o.s.i (*0-515-08908-7*, Jove) Berkley Publishing Group.

—Lone Star & the Silver Bandits No. 72. 1988. mass mkt. 2.95 o.s.i (*0-515-09683-0*, Jove) Berkley Publishing Group.

—Lone Star & the Sky Warriors, No. 61. 1987. mass mkt. 2.75 o.s.i (*0-515-09170-7*, Jove) Berkley Publishing Group.

—Lone Star & the Slaughter Showdown. 1994. (Lone Star Ser.: No. 139). 192p. (Orig.). mass mkt. 3.99 o.s.i (*0-515-11339-5*, Jove) Berkley Publishing Group.

—Lone Star & the Stagecoach War, No. 53. 1987. 192p. mass mkt. 2.75 o.s.i (*0-515-08839-0*, Jove) Berkley Publishing Group.

—Lone Star & the Steel Rail No. 132. 1993. (Lone Star Ser.: No. 132). 192p. (Orig.). mass mkt. 3.99 o.s.i (*0-515-11167-8*, Jove) Berkley Publishing Group.

—Lone Star & the Stockyard Showdown, No. 26. 1984. 192p. mass mkt. 2.50 o.s.i (*0-515-07920-0*, Jove) Berkley Publishing Group.

—Lone Star & the Suicide Spread, No. 75. 1988. mass mkt. 2.95 o.s.i (*0-515-09808-6*, Jove) Berkley Publishing Group.

—Lone Star & the Temperance Army. 1995. (Lone Star Ser.: No. 149). 192p. (Orig.). mass mkt. 3.99 o.s.i (*0-515-11529-0*, Jove) Berkley Publishing Group.

—Lone Star & the Texas Gambler, No. 22. 1984. 192p. mass mkt. 2.50 o.s.i (*0-515-07628-7*, Jove) Berkley Publishing Group.

—Lone Star & the Texas Killers, No. 86. 1989. mass mkt. 2.95 o.s.i (*0-515-10155-9*, Jove) Berkley Publishing Group.

—Lone Star & the Texas Rangers No. 76. 1988. mass mkt. 2.95 o.s.i (*0-515-09848-5*, Jove) Berkley Publishing Group.

—Lone Star & the Texas Tornado. 1994. (Lone Star Ser.: No. 148). 192p. mass mkt. 3.99 o.s.i (*0-515-11506-1*, Jove) Berkley Publishing Group.

—Lone Star & the Timber Pirates, No. 5. 1983. 192p. mass mkt. 2.50 o.s.i (*0-515-07415-2*, Jove) Berkley Publishing Group.

—Lone Star & the Timberland Terror, No. 43. 1986. 192p. mass mkt. 2.50 o.s.i (*0-515-08496-4*, Jove) Berkley Publishing Group.

—Lone Star & the Tombstone Gamble, No. 42. 1986. 192p. mass mkt. 2.50 o.s.i (*0-515-08462-X*, Jove) Berkley Publishing Group.

—Lone Star & the Tong's Revenge, No. 59. 1987. mass mkt. 2.75 o.s.i (*0-515-09057-3*, Jove) Berkley Publishing Group.

—Lone Star & the Trail of Blood. 1994. (Lone Star Ser.: No. 141). 192p. (Orig.). mass mkt. 3.99 o.s.i (*0-515-11392-1*, Jove) Berkley Publishing Group.

—Lone Star & the Trail of Murder No. 124. 1992. 192p. (Orig.). mass mkt. 3.99 o.s.i (*0-515-10998-3*, Jove) Berkley Publishing Group.

—Lone Star & the Trail to Abilene. 1992. (Lone Star Ser.: No. 114). 192p. mass mkt. 3.50 o.s.i (*0-515-10791-3*, Jove) Berkley Publishing Group.

—Lone Star & the Utah Kid, No. 5. 1982. 192p. mass mkt. 2.25 o.s.i (*0-515-06230-8*, Jove) Berkley Publishing Group.

—Lone Star & the Warpath No. 83. 1989. mass mkt. 2.95 o.s.i (*0-515-10062-5*, Jove) Berkley Publishing Group.

—Lone Star & the White River Curse, No. 41. 1986. 192p. mass mkt. 2.50 o.s.i (*0-515-08446-8*, Jove) Berkley Publishing Group.

—Lone Star & the Wolf Pack No. 125. 1993. 192p. (Orig.). mass mkt. 3.99 o.s.i (*0-515-11019-1*, Jove) Berkley Publishing Group.

—Lone Star & the Yuma Prison Break No. 109. 1991. mass mkt. 3.50 o.s.i (*0-515-10670-4*, Jove) Berkley Publishing Group.

—Lone Star in a Range War, No. 62. 1987. 192p. mass mkt. 2.75 o.s.i (*0-515-09216-9*, Jove) Berkley Publishing Group.

—Lone Star in Cripple Creek. 1990. (Lone Star Ser.: No. 90). mass mkt. 2.95 o.s.i (*0-515-10242-3*, Jove) Berkley Publishing Group.

—Lone Star in Hell's Canyon, No. 82. 1989. mass mkt. 2.95 o.s.i (*0-515-10036-6*, Jove) Berkley Publishing Group.

—Lone Star in the Big Horn Mountains, No. 56. 1987. 192p. mass mkt. 2.75 o.s.i (*0-515-08935-4*, Jove) Berkley Publishing Group.

—Lone Star in the Big Thicket. 1988. (Lone Star Ser.: No. 74). mass mkt. 2.95 o.s.i (*0-515-09759-4*, Jove) Berkley Publishing Group.

—Lone Star in the Cherokee Strip, No. 44. 1986. 192p. mass mkt. 2.50 o.s.i (*0-515-08515-4*, Jove) Berkley Publishing Group.

—Lone Star in the Choctaw Nation, No. 108. 1991. mass mkt. 3.50 o.s.i (*0-515-10650-X*, Jove) Berkley Publishing Group.

—Lone Star in the Sierra Diablos, No. 144. 1994. (Lone Star Ser.). 192p. (Orig.). mass mkt. 3.99 o.s.i (*0-515-11436-7*, Jove) Berkley Publishing Group.

—Lone Star in the Timberlands. 1992. (Lone Star Ser.: No. 118). mass mkt. 3.50 o.s.i (*0-515-10866-9*, Jove) Berkley Publishing Group.

—Lone Star on Outlaw Mountain, No. 11. 1984. 192p. mass mkt. 2.50 o.s.i (*0-515-08198-1*, Jove) Berkley Publishing Group.

—Lone Star on the Devil's Trail, No. 20. 1984. 192p. mass mkt. 2.50 o.s.i (*0-515-07436-5*, Jove) Berkley Publishing Group.

—Lone Star on the Hangman's Tale. 1993. (Lone Star Ser.: No. 131). 192p. (Orig.). mass mkt. 3.99 o.s.i (*0-515-11137-6*, Jove) Berkley Publishing Group.

—Lone Star on the Owlhoot Trail, No. 19. 1984. 192p. mass mkt. 2.50 o.s.i (*0-515-07409-8*, Jove) Berkley Publishing Group.

—Lone Star on the Treasure River, No. 31. 1985. 192p. mass mkt. 2.50 o.s.i (*0-515-08043-8*, Jove) Berkley Publishing Group.

—Lone Star On Treachery Trail. 1986. (Lone Star Ser.: No. 1). 192p. mass mkt. 3.99 o.s.i (*0-515-08708-4*, Jove) Berkley Publishing Group.

**KICKAHA (FICTITIOUS CHARACTER)—FICTION**

Farmer, Philip Jose. More Than Fire: A World of Tiers Novel. 1995. 320p. pap. 5.99 (*0-8125-1959-0*); 1993. 304p. 20.95 o.p. (*0-312-85280-0*) Doherty, Tom Assocs., LLC. (Tor Bks.).

—Red Orc's Rage. 1991. 18.95 o.p. (*0-312-85036-0*); 1992. 288p. reprint ed. mass mkt. 4.99 (*0-8125-0890-4*) Doherty, Tom Assocs., LLC. (Tor Bks.).

**KICKLIGHTER, TRUMAN (FICTITIOUS CHARACTER)—FICTION**

Trocheck, Kathy Hogan. Crash Course. 1997. 272p. 22.50 o.p. (*0-06-017642-3*) HarperCollins Pubs.

—Crash Course. 1998. (Truman Kicklighter Mysteries Ser.). 320p. mass mkt. 5.99 o.s.i (*0-06-109172-3*, HarperTorch) Morrow/Avon.

—Lickety-Split. 1996. 288p. 22.00 o.p. (*0-06-017641-5*) HarperCollins Pubs.

—Lickety-Split. 1997. 272p. mass mkt. 5.99 o.s.i (*0-06-109361-0*, HarperTorch) Morrow/Avon.

**KIDD AND LUELLEN (FICTITIOUS CHARACTERS)—FICTION**

Sandford, John, pseud. The Devil's Code. l.t. ed. 2001. 375p. (*0-7540-1583-1*, Macmillan Reference USA) Gale Group.

—The Devil's Code. 2000. (Kidd Ser.). 320p. 25.95 o.s.i (*0-399-14650-4*) Penguin Group (USA) Inc.

—The Devil's Code. abr. ed. 2000. audio 24.95 o.s.i (*0-399-14676-8*, Putnam Berkley Audio) Putnam Publishing Group, The.

—The Devil's Code. unabr. ed. 2001. audio compact disk 78.00 (*0-7887-6171-4*, C1395); 2000. audio 59.00 (*0-7887-4946-3*, 96464E7) Recorded Bks., LLC.

—The Devil's Code. l.t. ed. 375p. 2002. pap. 29.95 (*0-7838-9371-X*); 2001. 32.95 (*0-7838-9370-1*) Thorndike Pr.

—The Fool's Run. 1996. 352p. mass mkt. 7.99 (*0-425-15572-2*) Berkley Publishing Group.

—The Fool's Run. l.t. ed. 2003. lib. bdg. 29.95 (*1-58547-297-2*, Premier) Ctr. Point Large Print.

—The Hanged Man's Song. 2003. 336p. 25.95 (*0-399-15139-7*, Putnam & Grosset) Putnam Publishing Group, The.

### KIET, BAMSAN (FICTITIOUS CHARACTER)—FICTION

Alexander, Gary. Kiet & the Golden Peacock: A Superintendent Bamsan Kiet Mystery. 1989. 192p. 14.95 o.p. (*0-312-03372-9*, Saint Martin's Minotaur) St. Martin's Pr.

### KILBOURN, JOANNE (FICTITIOUS CHARACTER)—FICTION

Bowen, Gail. Burying Ariel. (Joanne Kilbourn Mystery Ser.). 2001. 272p. mass mkt. 7.99 (*0-7710-1498-8*); 2000. 264p. 24.95 o.s.i (*0-7710-1490-2*) McClelland & Stewart/Tundra Bks.

—A Colder Kind of Death. 2001. (Joanne Kilbourn Mystery Ser.). 224p. mass mkt. 7.95 (*0-7710-1495-3*) McClelland & Stewart/Tundra Bks.

—A Colder Kind of Death: A Joanne Kilbourn Mystery. 1999. 240p. 19.95 o.p. (*0-7710-1482-1*); 1995. 232p. mass mkt. 7.99 (*0-7710-1483-X*) McClelland & Stewart/Tundra Bks.

—Deadly Appearances. 2000. (Joanne Kilbourn Mystery Ser.). 280p. mass mkt. 7.99 (*0-7710-1491-0*) McClelland & Stewart/Tundra Bks.

—Deadly Appearances: A Joanne Kilbourn Mystery. 1992. mass mkt. 5.99 o.s.i (*0-7704-2433-3*) Bantam Bks.

—Deadly Appearances: A Joanne Kilbourn Mystery. (*0-88894-703-8*) Douglas & McIntyre, Ltd.

—Deadly Appearances: A Joanne Kilbourn Mystery. 1997. 280p. mass mkt. 7.99 (*0-7710-1485-6*) McClelland & Stewart/Tundra Bks.

—A Killing Spring. 1997. (Joanne Kilbourn Mystery Ser.). 272p. mass mkt. 5.95 (*0-7710-1486-4*) McClelland & Stewart/Tundra Bks.

—A Killing Spring: A Joanne Kilburn Mystery. 1997. 264p. 22.95 o.p. (*0-7710-1484-8*) McClelland & Stewart/Tundra Bks.

—Love & Murder. 1993. 224p. 17.95 o.p. (*0-312-09344-6*, Saint Martin's Minotaur) St. Martin's Pr.

—Murder at the Mendel: A Joanne Kilbourn Mystery. 1992. mass mkt. 7.99 o.s.i (*0-7710-1480-5*) McClelland & Stewart/Tundra Bks.

—Verdict in Blood. (Joanne Kilbourn Mystery Ser.). 264p. 1999. mass mkt. 7.95 (*0-7710-1489-9*); 1998. 20.95 o.s.i (*0-7710-1487-2*) McClelland & Stewart/Tundra Bks.

—The Wandering Soul Murders: A Joanne Kilbourn Mystery. 1993. 216p. mass mkt. 7.99 (*0-7710-1481-3*) McClelland & Stewart/Tundra Bks.

—The Wandering Soul Murders: A Joanne Kilbourn Mystery. 1994. 207p. 19.95 o.p. (*0-312-10574-6*, Saint Martin's Minotaur) St. Martin's Pr.

### KILDARE, DOCTOR (FICTITIOUS CHARACTER)—FICTION

Brand, Max. Dr. Kildare Takes Charge. 160p. reprint ed. lib. bdg. 18.95 (*0-88411-531-3*) Amereon, Ltd.

—Dr. Kildare Takes Charge. l.t. ed. 1997. (G. K. Hall Nightingale Ser.). pap. 17.95 o.p. (*0-7838-1847-5*, Macmillan Reference USA) Gale Group.

—Dr. Kildare's Search & Dr. Kildare's Hardest Case. l.t. ed. 1994. 173p. lib. bdg. 16.95 (*0-8161-5896-7*, Macmillan Reference USA) Gale Group.

—The Secret of Dr. Kildare. 180p. reprint ed. lib. bdg. 19.95 (*0-88411-530-5*, Rivercity Pr.) Amereon, Ltd.

### KILKENNY, NOLAN (FICTITIOUS CHARACTER)—FICTION

Grace, Tom. Quantum. 2000. audio 48.00 Books on Tape, Inc.

—Quantum. abr. ed. 2000. audio 24.98 (*1-57042-868-9*) Time Warner AudioBooks.

—Quantum. 2000. 384p. 24.95 o.s.i (*0-446-52410-7*) Warner Bks., Inc.

—Spyder Web. unabr. ed. 1999. audio 64.00 (*0-7366-4461-X*, 4906) Books on Tape, Inc.

—Spyder Web, Set. abr. ed. 1999. audio 22.00 Highsmith Inc.

—Spyder Web. 1997. 305p. 24.95 o.p. (*0-9656040-0-4*) Seanachaoi Pr.

—Spyder Web. abr. ed. 1999. audio 22.00 (*1-57042-624-4*, 696062) Time Warner AudioBooks.

—Spyder Web. 2000. 448p. mass mkt. 7.50 (*0-446-60789-4*); 1999. 480p. 25.00 o.p. (*0-446-52407-7*) Warner Bks., Inc.

### KILLEBREW, COLEY (FICTITIOUS CHARACTER)—FICTION

Shoemaker, Bill. Dark Horse. 1997. 312p. mass mkt. 6.99 (*0-449-15003-8*); 1996. 304p. 22.00 o.p. (*0-449-90597-7*) Ballantine Bks. (Fawcett).

—Fire Horse. 1996. mass mkt. 5.99 o.s.i (*0-449-14974-9*, Fawcett) Ballantine Bks.

—Fire Horse. l.t. ed. 1995. (Niagara Large Print Ser.). 415p. 29.50 o.p. (*0-7089-5802-8*, Ulverscroft) Thorpe, F. A. Pubs. GBR. *Dist:* Ulverscroft Large Print Bks., Ltd.

—Stalking Horse. 1994. (Los Angeles Mysteries Ser.). mass mkt. 5.99 o.s.i (*0-449-14936-6*, Fawcett) Ballantine Bks.

—Stalking Horse. l.t. ed. 1995. 481p. pap. 19.95 o.p. (*0-7838-1296-5*, Macmillan Reference USA) Gale Group.

—Stalking Horse. abr. ed. 1993. 16.95 o.p. (*0-7871-0025-0*) NewStar Media, Inc.

### KILLIGAN, MICHAEL (FICTITIOUS CHARACTER)—FICTION

Dooling, Richard. White Man's Grave: A Novel. 1994. 356p. 22.00 o.p. (*0-374-28951-4*) Farrar, Straus & Giroux.

—White Man's Grave: A Novel. 1995. 400p. pap. 15.00 (*0-312-13214-X*) Picador.

### KILMER, JAKE (FICTITIOUS CHARACTER)—FICTION

Diehl, William. Hooligans. 1996. mass mkt. 5.99 (*0-345-90987-9*); 1985. 448p. mass mkt. 7.99 (*0-345-31201-5*, Ballantine Bks.) Ballantine Bks.

—Hooligans. 1984. 15.95 o.p. (*0-394-53049-7*) Random Hse., Inc.

### KIM, HARRY (FICTITIOUS CHARACTER)—FICTION

Carey, Diane L., et al. Day of Honor Omnibus: Ancient Blood; Armageddon Sky; Her Klingon Soul; Treaty's Law; Day of Honor, Honor Bound. 1999. (Star Trek Ser.). (Illus.). 1104p. pap. 16.00 (*0-671-02813-8*, Pocket) Simon & Schuster.

Friedman, Michael Jan. Day of Honor No. 3: Her Klingon Soul. 1997. (Star Trek Voyager: Vol. 3). (Illus.). 304p. mass mkt. 5.99 (*0-671-00240-6*, Star Trek) Simon & Schuster.

—The Television Episode: Day of Honor. 1997. (Star Trek Voyager). 224p. mass mkt. 5.99 (*0-671-01981-3*, Star Trek) Simon & Schuster.

Garland, Mark A. & McGraw, Charles G. Ghost of a Chance. 1996. (Star Trek Voyager Ser.: No. 7). 288p. pap. 5.99 (*0-671-56798-5*, Star Trek) Simon & Schuster.

Graf, L. A. Caretaker. abr. ed. 1995. (Star Trek Voyager Ser.: No. 1). 17.00 o.s.i incl. audio (*0-671-52142-X*) Baen Bks.

—Caretaker. Ordover, John, ed. 1995. (Star Trek Voyager Ser.: No. 1). 288p. mass mkt. 5.99 Simon & Schuster.

Haber, Karen. Bless the Beasts. 1996. (Star Trek Voyager Ser.: No. 10). 288p. pap. 5.99 (*0-671-56780-2*, Star Trek) Simon & Schuster.

Smith, Dean Wesley, et al. Echoes. 1998. (Star Trek Voyager Ser.: No. 15). 304p. pap. 5.99 (*0-671-00200-7*, Star Trek) Simon & Schuster.

Taylor, Jeri. Pathways. (Star Trek Voyager Ser.: Vol. 2). 1999. 528p. pap. 6.50 o.s.i (*0-671-02626-7*); 1998. (Illus.). 448p. 23.00 o.s.i (*0-671-00346-1*) Simon & Schuster. (Star Trek).

—Pathways. abr. ed. 1998. (Star Trek Voyager Ser.: Vol. 2). 24.00 incl. audio (*0-671-58230-5*, Simon & Schuster Audioworks) Simon & Schuster Audio.

—Pathways. 1999. (Star Trek Voyager Ser.). 12.55 (*0-606-19503-3*) Turtleback Bks.

—Star Trek Voyager: Pathways. abr. ed. 1999. (Star Trek Voyager Ser.). audio 24.35 (*0-671-01115-4*) Ulverscroft Audio (U.S.A.).

Wright, Susan. Violations. 1995. (Star Trek Voyager Ser.: No. 4). 288p. mass mkt. 5.99 (*0-671-52046-6*, Star Trek) Simon & Schuster.

### KIM, SISTER (FICTITIOUS CHARACTER)—FICTION

Quill, Monica. Nun Plussed: A Sister Mary Teresa Mystery. 1995. 250p. per. (*0-373-26187-X*, Worldwide Library) Harlequin Enterprises, Ltd.

—Nun Plussed: A Sister Mary Teresa Mystery. 1993. 224p. 18.95 o.p. (*0-312-09890-1*, Saint Martin's Minotaur) St. Martin's Pr.

—Sister Hood: A Sister Mary Teresa Mystery. 1991. 16.95 o.p. (*0-312-04602-2*, Saint Martin's Minotaur) St. Martin's Pr.

—The Veil of Ignorance: A Sister Mary Teresa Mystery. 1988. 208p. 15.95 o.p. (*0-312-02308-1*, Saint Martin's Minotaur) St. Martin's Pr.

### KIMBERLAIN, JARED (FICTITIOUS CHARACTER)—FICTION

Land, Jon. The Eighth Trumpet. 1989. mass mkt. 5.95 o.s.i (*0-449-13398-2*, Fawcett) Ballantine Bks.

—The Ninth Dominion. 1991. (Orig.). mass mkt. 5.99 o.s.i (*0-449-14775-4*, Fawcett) Ballantine Bks.

### KINCAID, BEN (FICTITIOUS CHARACTER)—FICTION

Bernhardt, William. Blind Justice. 1997. mass mkt. 3.50 o.s.i (*0-345-41806-9*); 1992. 320p. mass mkt. 6.99 (*0-345-37483-5*) Ballantine Bks.

—Blind Justice. unabr. ed. 1998. (Justice Ser.: Vol. 2). audio 48.00 (*0-7366-4106-8*, 4611) Books on Tape, Inc.

—Blind Justice. unabr. ed. 2001. (Attorney Ben Kincaid Mystery Ser.). audio Chivers Audio Bks. GBR. *Dist:* BBC Audiobooks America.

—Blind Justice. l.t. ed. 1993. 80.95 o.p. (*0-7862-9989-4*, Macmillan Reference USA) Gale Group.

—Criminal Intent. 2003. 416p. mass mkt. 7.50 (*0-345-44175-3*, Fawcett); 2002. E-Book 16.95 (*0-345-45862-1*, Ballantine Bks.); 2002. 368p. 23.95 (*0-345-44173-7*, Ballantine Bks.) Ballantine Bks.

—Criminal Intent. l.t. ed. 2004. 592p. 25.95 (*0-375-43262-0*) Random Hse. Large Print.

—Cruel Justice. 1997. mass mkt. 3.50 o.s.i (*0-345-41807-7*); 1996. 480p. mass mkt. 7.50 (*0-345-40803-9*) Ballantine Bks.

—Cruel Justice. unabr. ed. 1998. (Justice Ser.). audio 72.00 (*0-7366-4180-7*, 4678) Books on Tape, Inc.

—Cruel Justice. l.t. ed. 1996. pap. 23.95 (*1-56895-323-2*, Wheeler Publishing, Inc.) Gale Group.

—Dark Justice. 1999. 448p. mass mkt. 6.99 (*0-345-43476-5*) Ballantine Bks.

—Deadly Justice. 1997. mass mkt. 3.50 o.s.i (*0-345-41808-5*); 1993. 320p. mass mkt. 7.50 (*0-345-38027-4*) Ballantine Bks.

—Deadly Justice. unabr. ed. 1998. (Justice Ser.: Vol. 3). audio 48.00 (*0-7366-4107-6*, 4612) Books on Tape, Inc.

—Deadly Justice. l.t. ed. 1994. 65.95 o.p. (*0-7862-9988-6*, Macmillan Reference USA) Gale Group.

—Death Row. 2004. 416p. mass mkt. 7.50 (*0-345-44176-1*, Fawcett); 2003. 320p. 25.95 (*0-345-44174-5*, Ballantine Bks.) Ballantine Bks.

—Death Row. l.t. ed. 2004. 544p. 27.95 (*0-375-43316-3*) Random Hse. Large Print.

—Double Jeopardy. 1996. 416p. mass mkt. 7.99 (*0-345-39784-3*) Ballantine Bks.

—Double Jeopardy. l.t. ed. 1996. (Niagara Large Print Ser.). 431p. 29.50 o.p. (*0-7089-5828-1*, Ulverscroft) Thorpe, F. A. Pubs. GBR. *Dist:* Ulverscroft Large Print Bks., Ltd.

—Extreme Justice. 1998. (Ben Kincaid Ser.). 384p. mass mkt. 6.99 (*0-345-42481-6*) Ballantine Bks.

—Hate Crime. 2004. 368p. 25.95 (*0-345-45147-3*, Ballantine Bks.) Ballantine Bks.

—Hate Crime. l.t. ed. 2004. 592p. 27.95 (*0-375-43341-4*) Random Hse. Large Print.

—Murder One. 2001. 416p. reprint ed. mass mkt. 7.50 (*0-345-42815-3*, Ballantine Bks.) Ballantine Bks.

—Naked Justice. 1997. 448p. mass mkt. 6.99 (*0-449-00087-7*, Fawcett) Ballantine Bks.

—Naked Justice. unabr. ed. 1997. (Justice Ser.). audio 88.00 (*0-7366-3789-3*, 4463) Books on Tape, Inc.

—Naked Justice. l.t. ed. 1997. (Niagara Large Print Ser.). 688p. 29.50 o.p. (*0-7089-5879-6*, Ulverscroft) Thorpe, F. A. Pubs. GBR. *Dist:* Ulverscroft Large Print Bks., Ltd.

—Perfect Justice. 1997. mass mkt. 3.50 o.s.i (*0-345-41809-3*) Ballantine Bks.

—Perfect Justice. unabr. ed. 1998. (Justice Ser.: Vol. 4). audio 56.00 (*0-7366-4108-4*, 4613) Books on Tape, Inc.

—Perfect Justice, Set. l.t. ed. 1994. (Studio Ser.). 64.95 o.p. incl. audio (*0-7862-9987-8*, Macmillan Reference USA) Gale Group.

—Perfect Justice. 1995. 416p. mass mkt. 6.99 (*0-345-39133-0*, House of Collectibles) Random Hse. Information Group.

—Primary Justice. 1997. mass mkt. 3.50 o.s.i (*0-345-41810-7*); 1991. 320p. mass mkt. 6.99 (*0-345-37479-7*) Ballantine Bks.

—Primary Justice. unabr. ed. 1998. (Justice Ser.: Vol. 1). audio 48.00 (*0-7366-4105-X*, 4610) Books on Tape, Inc.

—Primary Justice. (Mystery Ser.). 1998. 309p. 22.95 (*0-7862-1659-X*, Five Star); Set. 1993. 79.95 o.p. incl. audio (*0-7862-9991-6*, Macmillan Reference USA) Gale Group.

### KINCAID, BIFF (FICTITIOUS CHARACTER)—FICTION

Barton, Dan. Dead Crowd. E-Book 23.95 (*0-312-70622-7*); 2002. 272p. 23.95 (*0-312-29034-9*, Saint Martin's Minotaur) St. Martin's Pr.

### KINCAID, CYNTHIA (FICTITIOUS CHARACTER)—FICTION

Davis, Thulani. Maker of Saints. 1997. 256p. pap. 15.00 (*0-14-026735-2*) Penguin Group (USA) Inc.

—Maker of Saints. 1996. 256p. 22.00 (*0-684-81225-8*, Scribner) Simon & Schuster.

### KINCAID, DUNCAN (FICTITIOUS CHARACTER)—FICTION

Crombie, Deborah. All Shall Be Well. 1995. 272p. mass mkt. 6.99 (*0-425-14771-1*) Berkley Publishing Group.

—All Shall Be Well. 2004. 288p. mass mkt. 6.99 (*0-06-053439-7*, Avon Bks.) Morrow/Avon.

—All Shall Be Well: A Superintendent Duncan Kincaid - Sergeant Gemma James Mystery. 1994. 256p. text 20.00 (*0-684-19654-9*, Macmillan Reference USA) Gale Group.

—And Justice There is None. 2002. E-Book 19.50 (*0-553-89707-1*) Bantam Bks.

—And Justice There Is None. 2003. 416p. mass mkt. 6.99 (*0-553-57930-4*); 2002. 336p. 23.95 (*0-553-10973-1*) Bantam Bks.

—And Justice There Is None. l.t. ed. 2003. 29.95 (*1-58724-400-4*, Wheeler Publishing, Inc.) Gale Group.

—Dreaming of the Bones. 1998. 416p. mass mkt. 6.99 (*0-553-57931-2*) Bantam Bks.

—Dreaming of the Bones. l.t. ed. 2000. pap. 25.95 (*1-56895-899-4*, Wheeler Publishing, Inc.) Gale Group.

—Dreaming of the Bones. l.t. ed. 1998. (Magna Large Print Ser.). 480p. o.p. (*0-7505-1315-2*) Magna Large Print Bks. GBR. *Dist:* Ulverscroft Large Print Canada, Ltd.

—Dreaming of the Bones. 2001. audio compact disk 116.00 (*0-7887-5203-0*, C1360E7); 2000. audio 85.00 (*0-7887-4085-7*, 95946E7) Recorded Bks., LLC.

—Dreaming of the Bones. 1997. 350p. 21.50 (*0-684-84720-5*); 21.50 (*0-684-80141-8*) Simon & Schuster. (Scribner).

—A Finer End. l.t. ed. 2001. (Illus.). 526p. 30.95 (*0-7862-3581-0*) Thorndike Pr.

—Kissed a Sad Goodbye. 1999. 336p. 23.95 o.s.i (*0-553-10943-X*) Bantam Bks.

—Kissed a Sad Goodbye. l.t. ed. 1999. (Large Print Book Ser.). pap. 24.95 (*1-56895-731-9*, Wheeler Publishing, Inc.) Gale Group.

—Kissed a Sad Goodbye. unabr. ed. 1999. audio 87.00 (*0-7887-3751-1*, 95869E7) Recorded Bks., LLC.

—Leave the Grave Green. 1996. 304p. mass mkt. 6.50 (*0-425-15308-8*) Berkley Publishing Group.

—Leave the Grave Green. l.t. ed. 2000. pap. 23.95 (*1-56895-846-3*, Wheeler Publishing, Inc.) Gale Group.

—Leave the Grave Green. l.t. ed. 1997. (Magna Large Print Ser.). 400p. (*0-7505-1114-1*) Magna Large Print Bks. GBR. *Dist:* Ulverscroft Large Print Canada, Ltd.

—Leave the Grave Green. 1995. 224p. 20.00 o.p. (*0-684-19770-7*, Scribner) Simon & Schuster.

—Mourn Not Your Dead. 1997. 304p. reprint ed. mass mkt. 6.99 (*0-425-15778-4*, Prime Crime) Berkley Publishing Group.

—Mourn Not Your Dead. l.t. ed. 1997. (Magna Large Print Ser.). 412p. (*0-7505-1175-3*) Magna Large Print Bks. GBR. *Dist:* Ulverscroft Large Print Canada, Ltd.

—Mourn Not Your Dead: A Duncan Kincaid/Gemma James Crime Novel. l.t. ed. 1996. 25.95 (*1-56895-367-4*, Wheeler Publishing, Inc.) Gale Group.

—Mourn Not Your Dead: A Duncan Kincaid/Gemma James Crime Novel. 1996. 288p. 21.00 o.p. (*0-684-80131-0*, Scribner) Simon & Schuster.

—Now May You Weep. l.t. ed. 2004. lib. bdg. 29.95 (*1-58547-409-6*, Platinum) Ctr. Point Large Print.

—Now May You Weep. 2003. 384p. 23.95 (*0-06-052523-1*, Morrow, William & Co.) Morrow/Avon.

—A Share in Death: A Mystery Introducing Superintendent Duncan Kincaid & Sergeant Gemma James. 1994. 208p. reprint ed. mass mkt. 6.50 (*0-425-14197-7*, Prime Crime) Berkley Publishing Group.

—A Share in Death: A Mystery Introducing Superintendent Duncan Kincaid & Sergeant Gemma James. l.t. ed. 1995. (Magna Large Print Ser.). 259p. (*0-7505-0833-7*) Magna Large Print Bks. GBR. *Dist:* Ulverscroft Large Print Canada, Ltd.

—A Share in Death: A Mystery Introducing Superintendent Duncan Kincaid & Sergeant Gemma James. 1993. 256p. 20.00 o.p. (*0-684-19527-5*, Scribner) Simon & Schuster.

### KINCAID, LIBBY (FICTITIOUS CHARACTER)—FICTION

Tucker, Kerry. Cold Feet: A Libby Kincaid Mystery. 1992. 208p. 19.00 o.p. (*0-06-016530-8*) HarperTrade.

—Cold Feet: A Libby Kincaid Mystery. 1993. 304p. mass mkt. 4.50 o.p. (*0-06-109985-6*, HarperTorch) Morrow/Avon.

—Death Echo: A Libby Kincaid Mystery. 1993. 224p. 19.00 o.p. (*0-06-017700-4*) HarperTrade.

—Death Echo: A Libby Kincaid Mystery. 1994. 288p. mass mkt. 4.50 o.p. (*0-06-109986-4*, HarperTorch) Morrow/Avon.

—Drift Away: A Libby Kincaid Mystery. 1995. 240p. mass mkt. 4.99 o.p. (*0-06-109176-6*); 1994. 224p. 20.00 o.p. (*0-06-017999-6*) HarperCollins Pubs.

—Still Waters. l.t. ed. 1992. 18.95 o.p. (*0-7451-8356-5*); pap. 16.95 o.p. (*0-7927-1104-1*) BBC Audiobooks America.

—Still Waters. 1991. 208p. 18.95 o.p. (*0-06-016529-4*) HarperTrade.

—Still Waters. 1992. 272p. mass mkt. 3.99 o.p. (*0-06-109095-6*, HarperTorch) Morrow/Avon.

**KINCAID FAMILY (FICTITIOUS CHARACTERS)—FICTION**

Brady, Taylor. Westward Winds. 2000. (Kincaids Ser.: Vol. 4). 280p. 26.95 (*0-7862-2727-3*, Five Star) Gale Group.

**KING, JESSE (FICTITIOUS CHARACTER)—FICTION**

Hardwick, Gary. Double Dead. 1997. 368p. 23.95 o.s.i (*0-525-93920-2*) Dutton/Plume.

—Double Dead. 1998. 400p. mass mkt. 6.99 o.s.i (*0-451-18276-6*, Onyx) NAL.

**KING, NATE (FICTITIOUS CHARACTER)—FICTION**

Thompson, David. Black Powder. 1995. (Wilderness Ser.: Vol. 21). 176p. mass mkt. 3.99 (*0-8439-3820-X*) Dorchester Publishing Co., Inc.

—Blood Feud. 1999. (Wilderness Ser.: No. 26). 176p. pap. 3.99 (*0-8439-4477-3*, Leisure Bks.) Dorchester Publishing Co., Inc.

—Blood Feud. 1999. E-Book 9.95 (*0-585-28565-9*) netLibrary, Inc.

—Blood Truce. 1993. (Wilderness Ser.: No. 16). 176p. (Orig.). mass mkt. 3.50 (*0-8439-3525-1*) Dorchester Publishing Co., Inc.

—Vengeance Trail - Death Hunt, 2 vols. in 1, Set. 2000. (Wilderness Ser.: Nos. 7 & 8). 352p. pap. 4.99 (*0-8439-4297-5*, Leisure Bks.) Dorchester Publishing Co., Inc.

**KING, WILLOW (FICTITIOUS CHARACTER)—FICTION**

Cooper, Natasha. Bitter Herbs. l.t. ed. 1995. (Ulverscroft Large Print Ser.). 528p. 29.99 o.p. (*0-7089-3291-6*, Ulverscroft) Thorpe, F. A. Pubs. GBR. *Dist:* Ulverscroft Large Print Bks., Ltd., Ulverscroft Large Print Canada, Ltd.

—Bloody Roses. 1993. 256p. 20.00 o.s.i (*0-517-59022-0*, Crown) Crown Publishing Group.

—A Common Death. l.t. ed. 1991. (Ulverscroft Large Print Ser.). Orig. Title: Festering Lillies. 29.99 o.p. (*0-7089-2458-1*, Ulverscroft) Thorpe, F. A. Pubs. GBR. *Dist:* Ulverscroft Large Print Bks., Ltd., Ulverscroft Large Print Canada, Ltd.

—The Drowning Pool. 1998. (WWL Mystery Ser.). per. (*0-373-26271-X*, 1-26271-6, Worldwide Library) Harlequin Enterprises, Ltd.

—The Drowning Pool: A Willow King Mystery. 1997. (Willow King Mysteries Ser.). 240p. 21.95 (*0-312-15130-6*, Saint Martin's Minotaur) St. Martin's Pr.

—Poison Flowers. unabr. ed. 1998. audio 83.95 (*1-85903-128-5*) Magna Story Sound GBR. *Dist:* Ulverscroft Large Print Bks., Ltd.

—Poison Flowers. 1993. 3.99 o.p. (*0-517-09845-8*) Random Hse. Value Publishing.

—Poison Flowers. l.t. ed. 1992. (Mystery Ser.). 544p. 29.99 o.p. (*0-7089-2726-2*, Ulverscroft) Thorpe, F. A. Pubs. GBR. *Dist:* Ulverscroft Large Print Bks., Ltd., Ulverscroft Large Print Canada, Ltd.

—Rotten Apples. 1997. (WWL Mystery Ser.: No. 244). per. (*0-373-26244-2*, 1-26244-3, Worldwide Library) Harlequin Enterprises, Ltd.

—Rotten Apples. unabr. ed. 1998. audio 76.95 (*1-85903-141-2*) Magna Story Sound GBR. *Dist:* Ulverscroft Large Print Bks., Ltd.

—Rotten Apples. 1995. 288p. 21.95 o.p. (*0-312-13161-5*, Saint Martin's Minotaur) St. Martin's Pr.

—Sour Grapes. 1999. (WWL Mystery Ser.: Vol. 319). pap. (*0-373-26319-8*, Worldwide Library) Harlequin Enterprises, Ltd.

—Sour Grapes. 1998. (Willow King Mysteries Ser.). 304p. 22.95 (*0-312-18666-5*, Saint Martin's Minotaur) St. Martin's Pr.

Cooper, Natasha & Myers, Tanya. Festering Lillies. unabr. ed. 1996. audio 69.95 o.p. (*1-85903-111-0*, 31110) Magna Story Sound GBR. *Dist:* Ulverscroft Large Print Bks., Ltd.

**KING KONG (FICTITIOUS CHARACTER)—FICTION**

Berenstain, Michael, illus. King Kong. 1983. (Step-up Adventures Ser.). 96p. (J). (gr. 2-5). 4.99 o.s.i (*0-394-95617-6*, Random Hse. Bks. for Young Readers) Random Hse. Children's Bks.

**KINGSLEY, LUCY (FICTITIOUS CHARACTER)—FICTION**

Charles, Kate. Appointed to Die. 1994. 368p. 19.95 o.s.i (*0-89296-548-7*) Mysterious Pr.

—Appointed to Die. 1995. 352p. mass mkt. 5.99 o.s.i (*0-446-40361-X*) Warner Bks., Inc.

—A Dead Man Out of Mind. l.t. ed. 1996. (G. K. Hall Mystery Ser.). 429p. 22.95 o.p. (*0-7838-1706-1*, Macmillan Reference USA) Gale Group.

—A Dead Man Out of Mind. 1995. 82p. 19.95 o.p. (*0-89296-585-1*) Mysterious Pr.

—A Dead Man Out of Mind. 1996. 288p. mass mkt. 5.99 o.p. (*0-446-40432-2*) Warner Bks., Inc.

—A Drink of Deadly Wine. 1992. 336p. 17.95 (*0-89296-501-0*) Mysterious Pr.

—A Drink of Deadly Wine. 1993. (Book of Psalms Mysteries Ser.). 304p. mass mkt. 5.99 o.s.i (*0-446-40194-3*) Warner Bks., Inc.

—Evil Angels among Them. l.t. ed. 1997. (G. K. Hall Mystery Ser.). 371p. lib. bdg. 25.95 o.p. (*0-7838-2024-0*, Macmillan Reference USA) Gale Group.

—Evil Angels among Them. 352p. 1997. mass mkt. 6.50 (*0-446-40521-3*, Mysterious Pr. Paperback Bks.); 1996. 21.50 o.p. (*0-89296-639-4*) Warner Bks., Inc.

—The Snares of Death. 1993. 368p. 18.95 (*0-89296-498-7*) Mysterious Pr.

—The Snares of Death. 1994. 352p. mass mkt. 5.50 (*0-446-40195-1*) Warner Bks., Inc.

—Unruly Passions. 2001. 440p. pap. 8.95 (*0-7515-2437-9*) Warner Bks. GBR. *Dist:* Trafalgar Square.

**KINGSLEY, SARA (FICTITIOUS CHARACTER)—FICTION**

Wilson, Anne. Truth or Dare: A Sara Kingsley Mystery. 1997. 164p. pap. 13.95 (*0-7043-4461-0*) Women's Pr., Ltd., The GBR. *Dist:* Trafalgar Square.

**KINLEY, JACKSON (FICTITIOUS CHARACTER)—FICTION**

Cook, Thomas H. Evidence of Blood. 1998. 400p. reprint ed. mass mkt. 5.99 (*0-553-57836-7*) Bantam Bks.

—Evidence of Blood. 1993. 384p. mass mkt. 5.99 o.s.i (*0-8217-4123-3*, Zebra Bks.) Kensington Publishing Corp.

—Evidence of Blood. 1991. 320p. 19.95 o.p. (*0-399-13668-1*, G. P. Putnam's Sons) Penguin Group (USA) Inc.

**KINLOCH, ALEXANDER (FICTITIOUS CHARACTER)—FICTION**

Francis, Dick. To the Hilt. 1997. 352p. mass mkt. 6.99 (*0-515-12148-7*, Jove) Berkley Publishing Group.

—To the Hilt. unabr. ed. 1997. audio 56.00 (*0-913369-59-4*, 4287) Books on Tape, Inc.

—To the Hilt. 2015. 24.95 o.s.i (*0-399-14486-2*); 1996. 320p. 24.95 o.p. (*0-399-14185-5*, G. P. Putnam's Sons) Penguin Group (USA) Inc.

—To the Hilt. unabr. ed. 1997. audio 60.00 (*0-7887-0805-8*, 94954E7) Recorded Bks., LLC.

—To the Hilt. abr. ed. 1998. audio 14.40 (*0-671-57734-4*, 908766); 1996. audio 18.00 (*0-671-53630-3*, 394243) Simon & Schuster Audio. (Simon & Schuster Audioworks).

—To the Hilt. l.t. ed. (Paperback Bestsellers Ser.). 492p. 1998. pap. 26.95 (*0-7862-0893-7*); 1996. 28.95 (*0-7862-0892-9*) Thorndike Pr.

**KINNEY, MICHAEL (FICTITIOUS CHARACTER)—FICTION**

Hall, Karen. Dark Debts. 1997. 501p. mass mkt. 6.99 o.s.i (*0-8041-1655-5*, Ivy Bks.) Ballantine Bks.

**KINSELLA, KATE (FICTITIOUS CHARACTER)—FICTION**

Green, Christine. Deadly Admirer. 1996. per. (*0-373-26223-X*, 1-26223-7, Worldwide Library) Harlequin Enterprises, Ltd.

—Deadly Admirer. l.t. ed. 1994. (Magna Large Print Ser.). 351p. 29.99 o.p. (*0-7505-0699-7*) Magna Large Print Bks. GBR. *Dist:* Ulverscroft Large Print Bks., Ltd., Ulverscroft Large Print Canada, Ltd.

—Deadly Admirer: A Kate Kinsella Mystery. 1993. 197p. 19.95 (*0-8027-3244-5*) Walker & Co.

—Deadly Bond. 2002. 288p. 25.99 (*0-7278-5783-5*); 29.99 (*0-7278-7207-9*) Severn Hse. Pubs., Ltd.

—Deadly Echo: A Kate Kunsella Mystery. 2002. 256p. 25.99 (*0-7278-5916-1*) Severn Hse. Pubs., Ltd.

—Deadly Errand. l.t. ed. 1993. (Magna Large Print Ser.). 384p. 29.99 (*0-7505-0434-X*) Magna Large Print Bks. GBR. *Dist:* Ulverscroft Large Print Bks., Ltd.

—Deadly Errand. 1992. 206p. 19.95 (*0-8027-3219-4*) Walker & Co.

—Deadly Partners. 1998. (Kate Kinsella Mysteries Ser.). per. (*0-373-26274-4*, 1-26274-0, Worldwide Library) Harlequin Enterprises, Ltd.

—Deadly Partners. l.t. ed. 1998. (Magna Large Print Ser.). 336p. (*0-7505-1240-7*) Magna Large Print Bks. GBR. *Dist:* Ulverscroft Large Print Canada, Ltd.

—Deadly Partners: A Kate Kinsella Mystery. 1997. (Kate Kinsella Mystery Ser.). 240p. 21.95 (*0-8027-3297-6*) Walker & Co.

—Deadly Practice. 1997. per. (*0-373-26232-9*, 1-23232-8, Worldwide Library) Harlequin Enterprises, Ltd.

—Deadly Practice. l.t. ed. 1998. (Magna Large Print Ser.). 352p. o.p. (*0-7505-1324-1*) Magna Large Print Bks. GBR. *Dist:* Ulverscroft Large Print Canada, Ltd.

—Deadly Practice. 1995. 200p. 19.95 (*0-8027-3257-7*) Walker & Co.

**KIRA NERYS (FICTITIOUS CHARACTER)—FICTION**

Archer, Nathan. Valhalla. (Star Trek Deep Space Nine Ser.: No. 10). E-Book 6.99 (*0-7434-2041-1*, Star Trek) Simon & Schuster.

—Valhalla. Ordover, John, ed. 1995. (Star Trek Deep Space Nine Ser.: No. 10). 288p. mass mkt. 5.50 (*0-671-88115-9*, Star Trek) Simon & Schuster.

Betancourt, John. Devil in the Sky. (Star Trek Deep Space Nine Ser.: No. 11). E-Book 6.95 (*0-7434-2042-X*, Star Trek) Simon & Schuster.

Betancourt, John G. The Heart of the Warrior. 1996. (Star Trek Deep Space Nine Ser.: No. 17). 288p. pap. 5.99 (*0-671-00239-2*, Star Trek) Simon & Schuster.

Carey, Diane L. The Search. 1994. (Star Trek Deep Space Nine Ser.). 272p. mass mkt. 5.50 (*0-671-50604-8*, Star Trek) Simon & Schuster.

—Station Rage. 1995. (Star Trek Deep Space Nine Ser.: No. 13). 288p. mass mkt. 5.99 (*0-671-88561-8*, Star Trek) Simon & Schuster.

—What You Leave Behind. 1999. (Star Trek Deep Space Nine Ser.). 224p. pap. 6.50 (*0-671-03476-6*, Star Trek) Simon & Schuster.

Cox, Greg. Devil in the Sky. 1995. (Star Trek Deep Space Nine Ser.: No. 11). (Illus.). 288p. (J). mass mkt. 5.50 (*0-671-88114-0*, Star Trek) Simon & Schuster.

David, Peter, et al. Wrath of the Prophets. 1997. (Star Trek Deep Space Nine Ser.: No. 20). 304p. pap. 5.99 (*0-671-53817-9*, Star Trek) Simon & Schuster.

Dillard, J. M., et al. Emissary; The Siege; Bloodletter; The Big Game; Betrayal, 5 bks. 1997. (Star Trek). pap. text 0.95 o.p. (*0-8359-1492-5*) Globe Fearon Educational Publishing.

Graf, L. A. Armageddon Sky: Day of Honor. Keenan, Randall, ed. 1997. (Star Trek, The Next Generation: Vol. 2). 304p. pap. 5.99 o.s.i (*0-671-00675-4*, Star Trek) Simon & Schuster.

Hugh, Dafydd ab. The Conquered No. 1: Rebels. 1999. (Star Trek Deep Space Nine Ser.: No. 24). 256p. pap. 6.50 o.s.i (*0-671-01140-5*, Star Trek) Simon & Schuster.

—The Liberated No. 3: Rebels. 1999. (Resistance Trilogy Ser.: No. 26). 256p. mass mkt. 6.50 o.s.i (*0-671-01142-1*, Star Trek) Simon & Schuster.

Jeter, K. W. Bloodletter. 1993. (Star Trek Deep Space Nine Ser.: No. 3). 288p. mass mkt. 5.50 (*0-671-87275-3*, Star Trek) Simon & Schuster.

—The Bloodletter. 1993. (Star Trek Deep Space Nine Ser.: No. 3). E-Book 6.99 (*0-7434-1222-2*, Star Trek) Simon & Schuster.

Peel, John. Objective: Bajor. 1996. (Star Trek Deep Space Nine Ser.: No. 15). 288p. per. 5.99 (*0-671-56811-6*, Star Trek) Simon & Schuster.

Reeves-Stevens, Judith & Reeves-Stevens, Garfield. Millennium No. 2: The War of the Prophets. 2000. (Star Trek Deep Space Nine Ser.). E-Book 6.99 (*0-7434-0680-X*, Star Trek) Simon & Schuster.

—Millennium Vol. 2: The War of the Prophets. 2000. (Star Trek Deep Space Nine: Vol. 2). 432p. pap. 6.50 o.s.i (*0-671-02402-7*, Star Trek) Simon & Schuster.

Schofield, Sandy. The Big Game. 1994. (Star Trek Deep Space Nine Ser.: No. 4). E-Book 6.99 (*0-7434-1223-0*, Star Trek) Simon & Schuster.

—The Big Game. Ordover, John, ed. 1993. (Star Trek Deep Space Nine Ser.: No. 4). 288p. mass mkt. 5.50 (*0-671-88030-6*, Star Trek) Simon & Schuster.

Sheckley, Robert. Laertian Gamble. 1995. (Star Trek Deep Space Nine Ser.: No. 12). 288p. mass mkt. 5.99 (*0-671-88690-8*, Star Trek) Simon & Schuster.

Smith, Dean Wesley & Rusch, Kristine K. Vectors No. 2: Double Helix. 1999. (Star Trek, The Next Generation: No. 52). (Illus.). 304p. pap. 6.50 (*0-671-03256-9*, Star Trek) Simon & Schuster.

Sutcliffe, Katherine. Fever. 2001. 416p. pap. 6.99 (*0-7434-1197-8*); E-Book 6.99 (*0-7434-1774-7*) Simon & Schuster. (Pocket).

Wright, Susan. Dark Passions. 2001. (Star Trek Ser.: Bk. 2). 224p. pap. 6.99 (*0-671-78786-1*); 256p. pap. 6.99 (*0-671-78785-3*) Simon & Schuster. (Star Trek).

**KIRBY, JACK (FICTITIOUS CHARACTER)—FICTION**

Elliott, James. Nowhere to Hide. 1998. 400p. mass mkt. 5.99 o.s.i (*0-7860-0538-6*, Pinnacle Bks.) Kensington Publishing Corp.

—Nowhere to Hide. 1997. 272p. 23.00 (*0-684-82362-4*, Simon & Schuster) Simon & Schuster.

**KIRBY, JACQUELINE (FICTITIOUS CHARACTER)—FICTION**

Peters, Elizabeth, pseud. Die for Love. unabr. ed. 1999. audio 49.95 (*0-7861-1476-2*, 108962) Blackstone Audio Bks., Inc.

—Die for Love. 1992. 288p. mass mkt. 4.50 (*0-8125-2470-5*, Forge Bks.); 1988. pap. 3.95 o.s.i (*0-8125-0791-6*, Tor Bks.) Doherty, Tom Assocs., LLC.

—Die for Love, Set. unabr. ed. 1999. audio 49.95 Highsmith Inc.

—Die for Love. unabr. ed. 2001. audio 54.95 (*1-85695-829-9*, 941203); 2000. audio compact disk 89.95 (*0-7531-0694-9*, 106949) ISIS Audio Bks. GBR. *Dist:* Ulverscroft Large Print Bks., Ltd., ISIS Publishing.

—Die for Love. 1993. 288p. reprint ed. lib. bdg. 20.00 o.p. (*0-7278-4491-1*) Severn Hse. Pubs., Ltd.

—Die for Love. 1990. mass mkt. 3.95 o.s.i (*0-312-92137-3*, St. Martin's Paperbacks) St. Martin's Pr.

—The Murders of Richard III. unabr. ed. 1995. audio 39.95 (*0-7861-0869-X*, 1667) Blackstone Audio Bks., Inc.

—The Murders of Richard III. unabr. ed. 1995. audio 54.95 (*1-85695-869-8*, 950211) ISIS Audio Bks. GBR. *Dist:* Ulverscroft Large Print Bks., Ltd.

—The Murders of Richard III. 1986. 240p. mass mkt. 6.99 (*0-445-40229-6*) Warner Bks., Inc.

—Naked Once More. unabr. ed. 1995. audio 62.95 (*0-7861-0809-6*, 1632) Blackstone Audio Bks., Inc.

—Naked Once More. l.t. ed. 1990. (General Ser.). 550p. pap. 13.95 o.p. (*0-8161-4940-2*); lib. bdg. 20.95 o.p. (*0-8161-4939-9*) Gale Group. (Macmillan Reference USA).

—Naked Once More. 1991. 3.99 o.p. (*0-517-07443-5*) Random Hse. Value Publishing.

—Naked Once More. unabr. ed. 1997. audio 85.00 (*0-7887-0928-3*, 95068E7) Recorded Bks., LLC.

—Naked Once More. 1990. 368p. mass mkt. 6.99 (*0-446-36032-5*); 1989. 17.45 o.s.i (*0-446-51482-9*) Warner Bks., Inc.

—The Seventh Sinner. unabr. ed. 2001. audio compact disk 19.95; 2000. audio compact disk 40.00 (*0-7861-9942-3*, z2249); 1998. audio 32.95 (*0-7861-1467-3*, 2249); 1998. audio 32.95 (*0-7861-1324-3*, 696025) Blackstone Audio Bks., Inc.

—The Seventh Sinner. l.t. ed. 2002. lib. bdg. 27.95 (*1-58547-188-7*, Premier) Ctr. Point Large Print.

—The Seventh Sinner. 1991. reprint ed. 18.95 o.p. (*0-7278-4195-5*) Severn Hse. Pubs., Ltd.

—The Seventh Sinner. 1990. mass mkt. 3.95 o.s.i (*0-445-77323-5*); 1989. 256p. mass mkt. 6.99 (*0-445-40778-6*); 1986. mass mkt. 3.95 o.s.i (*0-445-40225-3*) Warner Bks., Inc.

**KIRK, DEVLIN (FICTITIOUS CHARACTER)—FICTION**

Burns, Rex. Parts Unknown: A Devlin Kirk Mystery. 1991. (Crime Monthly Ser.). 272p. reprint ed. pap. 4.95 o.p. (*0-14-012396-2*, Penguin Bks.) Penguin Group (USA) Inc.

—Parts Unknown: A Devlin Kirk Mystery. 1990. 272p. 17.95 o.p. (*0-670-82912-9*) Viking Penguin.

**KIRK, JAMES T. (FICTITIOUS CHARACTER)—FICTION**

Barr, Mike W. Gemini. 2003. (Star Trek). 320p. pap. 6.99 (*0-7434-0074-7*, Star Trek) Simon & Schuster.

Bear, Greg. Corona. (Star Trek: No. 15). 2000. 192p. pap. 3.99 o.s.i (*0-7434-0372-X*); 2000. E-Book 6.95 (*0-7434-1966-9*); 1990. mass mkt. 4.50 o.s.i (*0-671-70798-1*); 1986. mass mkt. 3.50 o.s.i (*0-671-62749-X*); 1984. mass mkt. 2.95 o.s.i (*0-671-47390-5*); 1991. reprint ed. mass mkt. 5.50 (*0-671-74353-8*) Simon & Schuster. (Star Trek).

—Corona. 1985. (Star Trek Ser.: No. 15). 192p. 20.00 o.p. (*0-89366-246-1*) Ultramarine Publishing Co., Inc.

Black Fire. 2000. E-Book 6.99 (*0-7434-1959-6*, Star Trek) Simon & Schuster.

Bloodthirst. 2000. (Star Trek Ser.). E-Book 6.99 (*0-7434-1988-X*, Star Trek) Simon & Schuster.

Bonanno, Margaret W. Dwellers in the Crucible. 1991. (Star Trek: No. 25). 320p. mass mkt. 4.95 (*0-671-74147-0*, Star Trek) Simon & Schuster.

—Probe. Stern, Dave, ed. (Star Trek Ser.). 352p. 1992. 18.95 (*0-671-72420-7*); 1993. reprint ed. mass mkt. 5.99 (*0-671-79065-X*) Simon & Schuster. (Star Trek).

—Probe. abr. ed. 1992. (Star Trek Ser.: Vol. 2). audio 17.00 (*0-671-73727-9*, 297233, Simon & Schuster Audioworks) Simon & Schuster Audio.

—Strangers from the Sky. 1990. (Star Trek Ser.). mass mkt. 5.99 (*0-671-73481-4*, Star Trek) Simon & Schuster.

—Strangers from the Sky. abr. ed. (Star Trek Ser.). 1990. audio 11.00; 1987. audio 11.00 (*0-671-64718-0*, Simon & Schuster Audioworks) Simon & Schuster Audio.

The Captain's Table. 2000. (Star Trek, The Next Generation Ser.). E-Book 16.95 (*0-7434-0670-2*, Star Trek) Simon & Schuster.

Carey, Diane L. Battlestations! (Star Trek: No. 31). 2000. E-Book 6.99 (*0-7434-1982-0*); 1999. 288p. pap. 3.99 (*0-671-03858-3*) Simon & Schuster. (Star Trek).

—Best Destiny. 1999. (Star Trek Ser.). E-Book 6.99 (*0-671-04111-8*, Star Trek) Simon & Schuster.

—Best Destiny. Ryan, Kevin, ed. 1992. (Star Trek Ser.). 416p. 20.00 o.p. (*0-671-79587-2*, Star Trek) Simon & Schuster.

—Best Destiny. 1900. (Star Trek Ser.). per. 12.99 (*0-671-01945-7*, Star Trek) Simon & Schuster.

—Best Destiny. Ripin, Kevin, ed. 1993. (Star Trek Ser.). 416p. reprint ed. mass mkt. 5.99 (*0-671-79588-0*, Pocket) Simon & Schuster.

—Best Destiny. (Star Trek Ser.). 1999. pap. 9.98 (*0-671-04410-9*); 1992. audio 17.00 (*0-671-79103-6*) Simon & Schuster Audio. (Simon & Schuster Audioworks).

—Challenger No. 6: New Earth. 2000. (Star Trek: No. 94). 416p. pap. 6.99 (*0-671-04298-X*, Star Trek) Simon & Schuster.

—Dreadnought! (Star Trek: No. 29). 2000. E-Book 6.99 (*0-7434-1980-4*); 1999. 256p. pap. 3.99 (*0-671-03852-4*) Simon & Schuster. (Star Trek).

—First Strike No. 1: Invasion. 1996. (Star Trek: No. 79). 304p. (J). pap. 6.50 (*0-671-54002-5*, Star Trek) Simon & Schuster.

—Fortunes of War No. 1: Dreadnought. 1990. (Star Trek: No. 29). mass mkt. 5.50 o.s.i (*0-671-72567-X*, Star Trek) Simon & Schuster.

—Fortunes of War No. 2: Battlestations! (Star Trek: No. 31). 1991. mass mkt. 4.99 (*0-671-74025-3*); 1989. mass mkt. 4.50 o.s.i (*0-671-70183-5*) Simon & Schuster. (Star Trek).

—The Great Starship Race. 1993. (Star Trek: No. 67). 320p. mass mkt. 5.99 (*0-671-87250-8*, Star Trek) Simon & Schuster.

—Invasion! No. 1: First Strike. (Star Trek: No. 79). 2000. E-Book 6.99 (*0-7434-2030-6*); 1999. E-Book 6.99 (*0-671-04095-2*) Simon & Schuster. (Star Trek).

—New Earth No. 1: Wagon Train to the Stars. 2000. (Star Trek: No. 89). mass mkt. 6.50 (*0-7434-1114-5*, Star Trek) Simon & Schuster.

—Trials & Tribble-ations. 1996. (Star Trek Deep Space Nine Ser.). 144p. mass mkt. 3.99 (*0-671-00902-8*, Star Trek) Simon & Schuster.

—Wagon Train to the Stars No. 1: New Earth. 2000. (Star Trek: No. 89). (Illus.). 400p. mass mkt. 6.99 o.s.i (*0-671-04296-3*, Star Trek) Simon & Schuster.

Carey, Diane L. & Kirkland, James I. First Frontier. 1995. (Star Trek: No. 75). 400p. mass mkt. 5.99 (*0-671-52045-8*, Star Trek) Simon & Schuster.

Carey, Diane L. & Smith, Dean Wesley. Belle Terre No. 2: New Earth. 2000. (Star Trek: No. 90). (Illus.). 288p. pap. 6.50 (*0-671-04297-1*, Star Trek) Simon & Schuster.

—New Earth No. 2: Belle Terre. 2000. (Star Trek: No. 90). mass mkt. 6.50 (*0-7434-1115-3*, Star Trek) Simon & Schuster.

Carey, Diane L., et al. Day of Honor Omnibus: Ancient Blood; Armageddon Sky; Her Klingon Soul; Treaty's Law; Day of Honor; Honor Bound. 1999. (Star Trek Ser.). (Illus.). 1104p. pap. 16.00 (*0-671-02813-8*, Pocket) Simon & Schuster.

—Invasion Omnibus: First Strike; The Soldiers of Fear; Time's Enemy; The Final Fury. 1998. (Star Trek Ser.). 960p. mass mkt. 14.00 (*0-671-02185-0*, Star Trek) Simon & Schuster.

Carter, Carmen. Dreams of the Raven. (Star Trek: No. 34). 2000. E-Book 6.99 (*0-7434-1985-5*); 1991. mass mkt. 5.50 o.s.i (*0-671-74356-2*) Simon & Schuster. (Star Trek).

Claremont, Chris. Debt of Honor. Greenberger, Bob, ed. 1992. (Star Trek Ser.). (Illus.). 96p. (YA). 24.95 o.s.i (*1-56389-023-2*) DC Comics.

Clowes, Carolyn. The Pandora Principle. (Star Trek: No. 49). 2000. E-Book 6.99 (*0-7434-2000-4*); 1990. 288p. mass mkt. 4.99 (*0-671-65815-8*) Simon & Schuster. (Star Trek).

Cooper, Sonni. Black Fire. 1986. (Star Trek Ser.: No. 8). pap. 1.95 o.s.i (*0-440-82036-7*) Dell Publishing.

—Black Fire. (Star Trek: No. 8). 1989. mass mkt. 4.50 o.s.i (*0-671-70548-2*); 1986. per. 3.50 (*0-671-62747-3*); 1985. mass mkt. 3.50 o.s.i (*0-671-61758-3*); 1983. mass mkt. 2.95 o.s.i (*0-671-83632-3*) Simon & Schuster. (Star Trek).

Correy, Lee, pseud. The Abode of Life. (Star Trek: No. 6). 1989. mass mkt. 4.99 o.s.i (*0-671-70596-2*, Star Trek); 1986. mass mkt. 3.50 o.s.i (*0-671-62746-5*, Star Trek); 1984. 11.80 o.p. (*0-671-90086-2*, Pocket); 1983. mass mkt. 2.95 o.s.i (*0-671-47719-6*, Star Trek) Simon & Schuster.

Cox, Greg. Assignment Eternity. 1998. (Star Trek Ser.: No. 84). 304p. (J). per. 5.99 o.s.i (*0-671-00117-5*, Star Trek) Simon & Schuster.

—The Eugenics Wars. (Star Trek). Vol. 2. 2003. (Illus.). 464p. pap. 6.99 (*0-7434-0644-3*); Vol. 2. 2002. 352p. 24.95 (*0-7434-0643-5*); Vol. 3. 2005. mass mkt. 6.99 (*0-7434-5712-9*) Simon & Schuster. (Star Trek).

—The Rise & Fall of Khan Noonien Singh. 2001. (Eugenics Wars Ser.: Vol. 1). 416p. 24.95 (*0-671-02127-3*); reprint ed. E-Book 24.95 (*0-7434-2259-7*) Simon & Schuster. (Star Trek).

Crandall, Melissa. Shell Game. Stern, Dave, ed. 1993. (Star Trek: No. 63). 288p. mass mkt. 5.50 (*0-671-79572-4*, Star Trek) Simon & Schuster.

Crispin, A. C. Sarek. Ryan, Kevin, ed. (Star Trek Ser.). 1999. E-Book 6.99 (*0-671-04112-6*); 1995. 416p. (J). mass mkt. 5.99 (*0-671-79562-7*) Simon & Schuster. (Star Trek).

—Sarek. (Star Trek Ser.). 1994. 448p. 22.00 o.p. (*0-671-79561-9*); 2000. 416p. pap. 3.99 (*0-7434-0374-6*) Simon & Schuster. (Star Trek).

—Sarek. abr. ed. (Star Trek Ser.). 1999. audio 9.98 (*0-671-04480-X*); 1996. audio 17.00 (*0-671-88591-X*) Simon & Schuster Audio. (Simon & Schuster Audioworks).

—Time for Yesterday. 2000. E-Book 6.99 (*0-7434-1990-1*); 1999. (Star Trek Ser.: No. 39). 320p. pap. 3.99 (*0-671-03857-5*); 1989. (Star Trek: No. 39). 288p. mass mkt. 5.50 (*0-671-70094-4*) Simon & Schuster. (Star Trek).

—Time for Yesterday. abr. ed. 1989. (Star Trek Ser.: No. 39). audio 11.00 (*0-671-67017-4*, Simon & Schuster Audioworks) Simon & Schuster Audio.

—Yesterday's Son. (Star Trek: No. 11). 2000. E-Book 6.99 (*0-7434-1962-6*); 1999. 192p. pap. 3.99 (*0-671-03851-6*); 1990. 192p. mass mkt. 4.50 o.s.i (*0-671-72449-5*) Simon & Schuster. (Star Trek).

Culbreath, Myrna & Culbreath, Marshak. Triangle. 2000. (Star Trek: No. 9). E-Book 6.99 (*0-7434-1960-X*, Star Trek) Simon & Schuster.

David, Peter. The Captain's Daughter. (Star Trek: No. 76). 2000. E-Book 6.99 (*0-7434-2027-6*); 1995. 288p. mass mkt. 5.99 o.s.i (*0-671-52047-4*) Simon & Schuster. (Star Trek).

—The Rift. Stern, Dave, ed. 1991. (Star Trek: No. 57). 288p. mass mkt. 4.99 (*0-671-74796-7*, Star Trek) Simon & Schuster.

—Vendetta. abr. ed. 1991. (Star Trek Ser.). audio 15.95 (*0-671-74342-2*, Simon & Schuster Audioworks) Simon & Schuster Audio.

—Who Killed Captain Kirk? Kahan, Bob, ed. 1993. (Star Trek Ser.). (Illus.). 176p. pap. 16.95 o.s.i (*1-56389-096-8*) DC Comics.

David, Peter, et al. Disinherited. 1992. (Star Trek: No. 59). 272p. mass mkt. 4.99 (*0-671-77958-3*, Star Trek) Simon & Schuster.

—The Disinherited. (Star Trek: No. 59). E-Book 6.99 (*0-7434-2010-1*, Star Trek) Simon & Schuster.

DeCandido, Keith R. A. The Brave & the Bold, Bk. 1. 2002. (Star Trek Ser.: Bk. 1). (Illus.). 288p. pap. 6.99 (*0-7434-1922-7*, Star Trek) Simon & Schuster.

DeWeese, Gene. Chain of Attack. (Star Trek: No. 32). 2000. E-Book 6.99 (*0-7434-1983-9*); 1988. 256p. mass mkt. 5.50 (*0-671-66658-4*) Simon & Schuster. (Star Trek).

—The Final Nexus. (Star Trek: No. 43). 2000. E-Book 6.99 (*0-7434-1994-4*); 1991. mass mkt. 4.95 o.s.i (*0-671-74148-9*) Simon & Schuster. (Star Trek).

—Renegade. 2000. (Star Trek: No. 55). E-Book 6.99 (*0-7434-2006-3*, Star Trek) Simon & Schuster.

—Renegade. Stern, Dave, ed. 1991. (Star Trek: No. 55). 256p. mass mkt. 4.95 (*0-671-65814-X*, Star Trek) Simon & Schuster.

Dillard, J. M. Bloodthirst. Stern, Dave, ed. 1990. (Star Trek: No. 37). mass mkt. 5.50 (*0-671-70876-7*, Star Trek) Simon & Schuster.

—Demons. (Star Trek: No. 30). 2000. E-Book 6.99 (*0-7434-1981-2*); 1990. mass mkt. 4.50 (*0-671-70877-5*) Simon & Schuster. (Star Trek).

—The Final Frontier. abr. ed. (Star Trek Ser.: No. 5). audio 7.95. 1990. audio 7.95 (*0-671-68507-4*, Simon & Schuster Audioworks) Simon & Schuster Audio.

—Generations. (Star Trek Ser.: No. 7). 1995. (Illus.). 304p. mass mkt. 5.99 (*0-671-53753-9*); 1994. 288p. 20.00 o.p. (*0-671-51742-2*) Simon & Schuster. (Star Trek).

—Generations. 1994. (Star Trek Ser.: No. 7). pap. 17.00 incl. audio (*0-671-51996-4*, Simon & Schuster Audioworks) Simon & Schuster Audio.

—The Lost Years. 1989. (Star Trek Ser.). (Illus.). 320p. 17.95 o.p. (*0-671-68293-8*, Star Trek) Simon & Schuster.

—The Lost Years. Stern, David, ed. 1990. (Star Trek). 448p. reprint ed. mass mkt. 5.99 (*0-671-70795-7*, Star Trek) Simon & Schuster.

—The Lost Years. abr. ed. 1989. (Star Trek Ser.: Vol. 2). audio 15.95 o.s.i (*0-671-68632-1*, Simon & Schuster Audioworks) Simon & Schuster Audio.

—Mindshadow. (Star Trek: No. 27). 2000. E-Book 6.99 (*0-7434-1978-2*); 1989. 256p. mass mkt. 5.50 (*0-671-70420-6*) Simon & Schuster. (Star Trek).

—Recovery. Ryan, Kevin, ed. 1995. (Star Trek: No. 73). 288p. mass mkt. 5.50 (*0-671-88342-9*, Star Trek) Simon & Schuster.

—Star Trek 5: The Final Frontier. 1989. (Star Trek Ser.: No. 5). mass mkt. 4.50 (*0-671-68008-0*, Star Trek) Simon & Schuster.

—The Undiscovered Country. Stern, Dave, ed. 1992. (Star Trek Ser.: No. 6). 320p. mass mkt. 5.50 (*0-671-75883-7*, Pocket) Simon & Schuster.

—The Undiscovered Country. abr. ed. 1992. (Star Trek Ser.: No. 6). audio 11.00 (*0-671-75873-X*, Simon & Schuster Audioworks) Simon & Schuster Audio.

Duane, Diane. Doctor's Orders. (Star Trek: No. 50). 2000. E-Book 6.99 (*0-7434-2001-2*); 1990. 288p. mass mkt. 5.50 (*0-671-66189-2*) Simon & Schuster. (Star Trek).

—My Enemy, My Ally, Bk. 1. 2000. (Star Trek Ser.: No. 18). 320p. pap. 6.99 (*0-7434-0369-X*, Star Trek) Simon & Schuster.

—Rihannsu: My Enemy, My Ally, No. 1. Stern, Dave, ed. 1989. (Star Trek: No. 18). 320p. mass mkt. 5.50 (*0-671-70421-4*, Star Trek) Simon & Schuster.

—Rihannsu Bk. 4: Honor Blade. 2000. (Star Trek Ser.: No. 96). 240p. mass mkt. 6.99 (*0-671-04210-6*, Star Trek) Simon & Schuster.

—Rihannsu No. 1: My Enemy, My Ally. 2000. (Star Trek: No. 18). E-Book 6.99 (*0-7434-1969-3*, Star Trek) Simon & Schuster.

—Spock's World. (Star Trek Ser.). 1989. 400p. mass mkt. 6.50 (*0-671-66773-4*); 1988. pap. 16.95 o.p. (*0-671-66851-X*); 2000. 400p. pap. 3.99 (*0-7434-0371-1*) Simon & Schuster. (Star Trek).

—Spock's World. abr. ed. 1989. (Star Trek Ser.). audio 16.00 (*0-671-67917-1*, Simon & Schuster Audioworks) Simon & Schuster Audio.

—The Wounded Sky. (Star Trek: No. 13). 2000. E-Book 6.99 (*0-7434-1964-2*); 1991. 224p. mass mkt. 5.50 o.s.i (*0-671-74352-X*) Simon & Schuster. (Star Trek).

Dvorkin, David. Timetrap. 1988. (Star Trek: No. 40). 288p. (Orig.). mass mkt. 4.95 (*0-671-64870-5*, Star Trek) Simon & Schuster.

—The Trellisane Confrontation. 2000. E-Book 6.99 (*0-7434-1965-0*); 1989. (Star Trek: No. 14). mass mkt. 4.50 (*0-671-70095-2*) Simon & Schuster. (Star Trek).

Dwellers in the Crucible. 2000. E-Book 6.99 (*0-7434-1976-6*, Star Trek) Simon & Schuster.

Ecklar, Julia. The Kobayashi Maru. 1989. (Star Trek: No. 47). mass mkt. 5.50 (*0-671-65817-4*, Star Trek) Simon & Schuster.

—The Kobayashi Maru. (Star Trek Ser.: No. 47). 1999. audio 5.98 (*0-671-04486-9*); 1990. audio 11.00 (*0-671-70895-3*) Simon & Schuster Audio. (Simon & Schuster Audioworks).

Eklund, Gordon. Devil World. 1995. (Star Trek Ser.). 160p. mass mkt. 4.99 o.s.i (*0-553-24677-1*, Spectra) Bantam Bks.

Fantasimulations Associates Staff. Triangle. 1985. (Star Trek Ser.: No. 9). 92p. (Orig.). pap. 12.00 o.p. (*0-931787-25-4*) FASA Corp.

Ferguson, Brad. Crisis on Centaurus. 2000. (Star Trek: No. 28). E-Book 6.99 (*0-7434-1979-0*, Star Trek) Simon & Schuster.

—Crisis on Centaurus. Stern, Dave, ed. 1990. (Star Trek: No. 28). mass mkt. 4.99 (*0-671-70799-X*, Star Trek) Simon & Schuster.

—A Flag Full of Stars. Stern, Dave, ed. 1991. (Star Trek: No. 54). 240p. mass mkt. 5.99 (*0-671-73918-2*, Star Trek) Simon & Schuster.

The First Frontier. 2000. No. 75. E-Book 6.99 (*0-7434-2026-8*, Star Trek) Simon & Schuster.

Flinn, Denny Martin. Fearful Summons. 1995. (Star Trek: No. 74). 288p. mass mkt. 5.50 (*0-671-89007-7*, Star Trek) Simon & Schuster.

—The Fearful Summons. 2000. (Star Trek: No. 74). E-Book 6.99 (*0-7434-2025-X*, Star Trek) Simon & Schuster.

Fontana, D. C. Vulcan's Glory. 2000. (Star Trek Ser.). E-Book 6.99 (*0-7434-1995-2*, Star Trek) Simon & Schuster.

Ford, John M. How Much for Just the Planet?, No. 2. 1999. (Star Trek Ser.: No. 36). 256p. pap. 3.99 (*0-671-03859-1*, Star Trek) Simon & Schuster.

—Worlds Apart No. 2: How Much for Just the Planet? 2000. (Star Trek: No. 36). E-Book 6.99 (*0-7434-1987-1*, Star Trek) Simon & Schuster.

—Worlds Apart No. 2: How Much for Just the Planet? Stern, Dave, ed. 1990. (Star Trek: No. 36). mass mkt. 4.99 o.s.i (*0-671-72214-X*, Star Trek) Simon & Schuster.

Foster, Alan Dean. Star Trek Log One. 1975. (Star Trek Ser.). reprint ed. lib. bdg. 22.95 (*0-88411-081-8*) Amereon, Ltd.

—Star Trek Logs Four, Five & Six. 1993. (Star Trek Ser.). mass mkt. 5.99 o.s.i (*0-345-38522-5*, Del Rey) Ballantine Bks.

—Star Trek Logs One, Two & Three. 1992. (Star Trek Ser.). mass mkt. 4.99 o.s.i (*0-345-38247-1*, Del Rey) Ballantine Bks.

—Star Trek Logs Seven, Eight & Nine. 1993. (Star Trek Ser.). mass mkt. 5.99 o.s.i (*0-345-38561-6*, Del Rey) Ballantine Bks.

Friedman, Michael Jan. Constitution No. 2: My Brother's Keeper. 1998. (Star Trek My Brother's Keeper Ser.: No. 86). 288p. mass mkt. 6.50 (*0-671-01919-8*, Star Trek) Simon & Schuster.

—Double, Double. 1989. (Star Trek: No. 45). mass mkt. 4.99 (*0-671-66130-2*, Star Trek) Simon & Schuster.

—Enterprise No. 3: My Brother's Keeper. 1999. (Star Trek My Brother's Keeper Ser.: No. 87). 288p. pap. 6.50 (*0-671-01920-1*, Star Trek) Simon & Schuster.

—Faces of Fire. 2000. (Star Trek: No. 58). E-Book 6.99 (*0-7434-2009-8*, Star Trek) Simon & Schuster.

—Faces of Fire. Stern, Dave, ed. 1992. (Star Trek: No. 58). 320p. mass mkt. 5.50 (*0-671-74992-7*, Star Trek) Simon & Schuster.

—Faces of Fire. 1992. (Star Trek Ser.: No. 58). audio 16.00 o.s.i (*0-671-77802-1*, Simon & Schuster Audioworks) Simon & Schuster Audio.

—Legacy. 2000. (Star Trek: No. 56). E-Book 6.99 (*0-7434-2007-1*, Star Trek) Simon & Schuster.

—Legacy. Stern, Dave, ed. 1991. (Star Trek: No. 56). 256p. mass mkt. 4.95 (*0-671-74468-2*, Star Trek) Simon & Schuster.

—Republic No. 1: My Brother's Keeper. 1998. (Star Trek My Brother's Keeper Ser.: No. 85). 288p. mass mkt. 6.50 (*0-671-01914-7*, Star Trek) Simon & Schuster.

—Shadows on the Sun. 1993. (Star Trek Ser.). 352p. 22.00 (*0-671-86909-4*, Star Trek) Simon & Schuster.

—Shadows on the Sun. Ryan, Kevin, ed. 1994. (Star Trek Ser.). 352p. reprint ed. mass mkt. 5.99 (*0-671-86910-8*, Star Trek) Simon & Schuster.

—Star Trek: Modala Imperative. Kahan, Bob, ed. 1992. (Star Trek Ser.). (Illus.). 208p. pap. 19.95 (*1-56389-040-2*) DC Comics.

Gilden, Mel. The Starship Trap. (Star Trek: No. 64). 2000. E-Book 6.99 (*0-7434-2015-2*, Star Trek); 1993. mass mkt. 5.50 (*0-671-97754-7*, Pocket) Simon & Schuster.

—The Starship Trap. Stern, Dave, ed. 1993. (Star Trek: No. 64). 256p. mass mkt. 5.50 (*0-671-79324-1*, Star Trek) Simon & Schuster.

Golden, Christie. Last Roundup. 2003. (Star Trek). 352p. pap. 6.99 (*0-7434-4910-X*, Star Trek) Simon & Schuster.

—Star Trek the Last Roundup. 2002. (Star Trek Ser.). audio 18.00 (*0-7435-2495-0*); audio compact disk 24.00 (*0-7435-2496-9*) Simon & Schuster Audio. (Simon & Schuster Audioworks).

Graf, L. A. Death Count. 2000. (Star Trek: No. 62). E-Book 6.99 (*0-7434-2013-6*, Star Trek) Simon & Schuster.

—Death Count. Stern, Dave, ed. 1992. (Star Trek Ser.: No. 62). 288p. mass mkt. 4.99 (*0-671-79322-5*, Star Trek) Simon & Schuster.

—Firestorm. (Star Trek: No. 68). 2000. E-Book 6.99 (*0-7434-2019-5*); 1994. 288p. mass mkt. 5.50 (*0-671-86588-9*) Simon & Schuster. (Star Trek).

—Ice Trap. 2000. (Star Trek: No. 60). E-Book 6.99 (*0-7434-2011-X*, Star Trek) Simon & Schuster.

—New Earth No. 3: Rough Trails. 2000. (Star Trek: No. 91). reprint ed. E-Book 6.50 (*0-7434-1117-X*, Star Trek) Simon & Schuster.

—New Earth No. 33: Rough Trails. 2000. (Star Trek: No. 91). 400p. pap. 6.50 (*0-671-03600-9*, Star Trek) Simon & Schuster.

—Traitor Winds. 2000. (Star Trek: No. 70). E-Book 6.99 (*0-7434-2021-7*, Star Trek) Simon & Schuster.

—Traitor Winds. Ryan, Kevin, ed. 1994. (Star Trek Ser.: No. 70). 288p. mass mkt. 5.50 (*0-671-86913-2*, Star Trek) Simon & Schuster.

Graf, L. A. & Ecklar, Julia. Ice Trap. Stern, Dave, ed. 1992. (Star Trek: No. 60). 288p. mass mkt. 4.99 (*0-671-78068-9*, Star Trek) Simon & Schuster.

Graf, L. A., et al. The Captain's Table Omnibus. 2000. (Star Trek Ser.). 1152p. pap. 16.95 (*0-671-04052-9*, Star Trek) Simon & Schuster.

The Great Starship Race. 2000. (Star Trek Ser.: No. 67). E-Book 6.99 (*0-7434-2018-7*, Star Trek) Simon & Schuster.

Gunn, James & Sturgeon, Theodore. The Joy Machine. 1996. (Star Trek: No. 80). 288p. pap. 5.99 (*0-671-00221-X*, Star Trek) Simon & Schuster.

Hambly, Barbara. Crossroad. Ordover, John, ed. (Star Trek: No. 71). 2000. E-Book 6.99 (*0-7434-2022-5*); 1994. 288p. mass mkt. 5.99 (*0-671-79323-3*) Simon & Schuster. (Star Trek).

—Ghost-Walker. (Star Trek: No. 53). 2000. E-Book 6.99 (*0-7434-2004-7*); 1991. 13p. mass mkt. 4.95 o.s.i (*0-671-64398-3*) Simon & Schuster. (Star Trek).

—Ishmael. (Star Trek: No. 23). 2000. E-Book 6.99 (*0-7434-1974-X*); 1991. 256p. mass mkt. 5.50 (*0-671-74355-4*); 1990. mass mkt. 4.50 o.s.i (*0-671-73587-X*) Simon & Schuster. (Star Trek).

Hawke, Simon. The Patrian Transgression. 1994. (Star Trek: No. 69). 288p. mass mkt. 5.50 (*0-671-88044-6*, Star Trek) Simon & Schuster.

The Joy Machine. 2000. No. 80. E-Book 6.99 (*0-7434-2031-4*, Star Trek) Simon & Schuster.

Kagan, Janet. Uhura's Song. (Star Trek: No. 21). 384p. 1985. mass mkt. 3.50 o.s.i (*0-671-54730-5*); 2000. pap. 3.99 (*0-7434-0373-8*) Simon & Schuster. (Star Trek).

L. A. Graf. War Dragons No. 1: The Captain Table. 1998. (Star Trek: Vol. 1). 288p. pap. 6.50 (*0-671-01463-3*, Star Trek) Simon & Schuster.

Klass, Judy. Cry of the Onlies. (Star Trek: No. 46). 1991. 336p. mass mkt. 4.95 (0-671-74078-4); 1989. bds. 4.50 o.s.i (0-671-68167-2) Simon & Schuster. (Star Trek).
—The Cry of the Onlies. 2000. (Star Trek: No. 46). E-Book 6.99 (0-7434-1997-9, Star Trek) Simon & Schuster.
Kramer-Rolls, Dana. Home Is the Hunter. 2000. (Star Trek: No. 52). E-Book 6.99 (0-7434-2003-9, Star Trek) Simon & Schuster.
—Home Is the Hunter. Stern, David, ed. 1990. (Star Trek: No. 52). 288p. mass mkt. 4.99 (0-671-66662-2, Star Trek) Simon & Schuster.
Larson, Majliss. Pawns & Symbols. 2000. (Star Trek: No. 26). E-Book 6.99 (0-7434-1977-4, Star Trek) Simon & Schuster.
Lorrah, Jean. The Idic Epidemic. (Star Trek: No. 38). 1990. mass mkt. 4.50 (0-671-70768-X); 1988. 274p. mass mkt. 3.95 o.s.i (0-671-63574-3) Simon & Schuster. (Star Trek).
—The IDIC Epidemic. 2000. (Star Trek: No. 38). E-Book 6.99 (0-7434-1989-8, Star Trek) Simon & Schuster.
—The Vulcan Academy Murders. (Star Trek: No. 20). 2000. E-Book 6.99 (0-7434-1971-5); 1991. mass mkt. 4.95 (0-671-74283-3); 1990. mass mkt. 4.50 o.s.i (0-671-72367-7) Simon & Schuster. (Star Trek).
Marshak, Sondra & Culbreath, Myrna. The Prometheus Design. (Star Trek: No. 5). 1990. mass mkt. 5.50 (0-671-72366-9); 1982. mass mkt. 2.50 o.s.i (0-671-83398-7); 1982. E-Book 6.99 (0-7434-1212-5) Simon & Schuster. (Star Trek).
—Triangle. (Star Trek: No. 9). 1991. mass mkt. 5.50 (0-671-74351-1); 1986. per. 3.50 (0-671-62748-1); 1985. mass mkt. 3.50 o.s.i (0-671-60548-8); 1983. mass mkt. 2.95 o.s.i (0-671-49298-5) Simon & Schuster. (Star Trek).
McIntyre, Vonda N. Enterprise: The First Adventure. (Star Trek Ser.). 1990. mass mkt. 5.99 (0-671-73032-0); 1988. 320p. mass mkt. 4.50 o.s.i (0-671-65912-X) Simon & Schuster. (Star Trek).
—Enterprise: The First Adventure. 1988. (Star Trek Ser.). audio 11.00 (0-671-62951-4, Simon & Schuster Audioworks) Simon & Schuster Audio.
—The Entropy Effect. (Star Trek: No. 2). 1990. mass mkt. 5.50 (0-671-72416-9); 1986. pap. 3.50 (0-671-62743-0); 1985. mass mkt. 3.50 o.s.i (0-671-62229-3); 1983. 224p. mass mkt. 2.95 o.s.i (0-671-49300-0); 1981. E-Book 6.99 (0-7434-1209-5); 1981. mass mkt. 2.50 o.s.i (0-671-83692-7) Simon & Schuster. (Star Trek).
—The Entropy Effect. abr. ed. 1988. (Star Trek: No. 2). audio 11.00 (0-671-66864-1, Simon & Schuster Audioworks) Simon & Schuster Audio.
—The Search for Spock. 1990. (Star Trek: No. 17). mass mkt. 5.50 (0-671-73133-5, Star Trek) Simon & Schuster.
—The Wrath of Khan. (Star Trek: No. 7). 1991. mass mkt. 5.50 (0-671-74149-7); 1984. mass mkt. 2.95 o.s.i (0-671-55248-1) Simon & Schuster. (Star Trek).
McIntyre, Vonda N., et al. Star Trek Boxed Set: The Entropy Effect; The Covenant of the Crown; Yesterday's Son; The IDIC Epidemic. 1991. (Star Trek: Nos. 2, 4, 11, 38). pap. 18.00 (0-671-96368-6, Pocket) Simon & Schuster.
Milan, Victor. From the Depths. (Star Trek: No. 66). 2000. E-Book 6.99 (0-7434-2017-9); 1993. 288p. mass mkt. 5.50 (0-671-86911-6) Simon & Schuster. (Star Trek).
Mitchell, V. E. Enemy Unseen. Stern, David, ed. 1990. (Star Trek: No. 51). 288p. mass mkt. 4.99 (0-671-68403-5, Star Trek) Simon & Schuster.
—Windows on a Lost World. Stern, Dave, ed. 1993. (Star Trek: No. 65). 288p. mass mkt. 5.99 (0-671-79512-0, Star Trek) Simon & Schuster.
—Windows on a Lost World. abr. ed. 1993. (Star Trek Ser.: No. 65). audio 17.00 (0-671-86962-0, 391662, Simon & Schuster Audioworks) Simon & Schuster Audio.
Morwood, Peter. Rules of Engagement. (Star Trek: No. 48). 2000. E-Book 6.99 (0-7434-1999-5); 1990. 240p. mass mkt. 4.99 (0-671-66129-9) Simon & Schuster. (Star Trek).
Murdock, M. S. Web of the Romulans. 2000. E-Book 6.99 (0-7434-1961-8); 1989. (Star Trek: No. 10). mass mkt. 5.50 o.s.i (0-671-70093-6) Simon & Schuster. (Star Trek).
—Web of the Romulans. abr. ed. 1988. (Star Trek Ser.: No. 10). audio 9.95 (0-671-64719-9, Simon & Schuster Audioworks) Simon & Schuster Audio.
Nelson, Majliss. Pawns & Symbols. 1988. (Star Trek: No. 26). 288p. (Orig.). mass mkt. 5.50 o.s.i (0-671-66497-2, Star Trek) Simon & Schuster.
Oltion, Jerry. Mudd in Your Eye. (Star Trek: No. 81). 2000. E-Book 6.99 (0-7434-2032-2); 1997. 304p. pap. 5.99 (0-671-00260-0) Simon & Schuster. (Star Trek).
—Twilight's End. 1996. (Star Trek Ser.: No. 77). 288p. mass mkt. 5.99 (0-671-53873-X, Star Trek) Simon & Schuster.
—The Twilight's End. 2000. E-Book 6.99 (0-7434-2028-4, Star Trek) Simon & Schuster.
Oltion, Jerry & Oltion, Kathy. The Flaming Arrow, Bk. 4. 2000. (Star Trek Ser.: No. 92). (Illus.). 336p. pap. 6.50 (0-671-78562-1, Star Trek) Simon & Schuster.
Oltion, Kathy & Oltion, Jerry. New Earth No. 4: The Flaming Arrow. 2000. (Star Trek: No. 92). (Illus.). (J). reprint ed. E-Book 6.50 (0-7434-1118-8, Star Trek) Simon & Schuster.
The Patrian Transgression. 2000. (Star Trek Ser.: No. 69). E-Book 6.99 (0-7434-2020-9, Star Trek) Simon & Schuster.
Paul, Barbara. The Three-Minute Universe. 1991. (Star Trek: No. 41). mass mkt. 4.95 o.s.i (0-671-74358-9, Star Trek) Simon & Schuster.
Peel, John. Where No Man Has Gone Before. 1986. (Star Trek Ser.). 96p. lib. bdg. 19.95 o.p. (0-8095-8019-5) Millefleurs.
Reeves-Stevens, Garfield. Memory Prime. 2000. (Star Trek: No. 42). E-Book 6.99 (0-7434-1993-6, Star Trek) Simon & Schuster.
Reeves-Stevens, Garfield & Reeves-Stevens, Judith. Memory Prime. 1991. (Star Trek: No. 42). 320p. mass mkt. 5.50 (0-671-74359-7, Star Trek) Simon & Schuster.
Reeves-Stevens, Judith. Prime Directive. abr. ed. 2001. (Star Trek Ser.). audio 9.98 (0-671-04465-6, Simon & Schuster Audioworks) Simon & Schuster Audio.
Reeves-Stevens, Judith & Reeves-Stevens, Garfield. Federation. 1995. (Star Trek Ser.). 480p. mass mkt. 6.50 (0-671-89423-4, Star Trek) Simon & Schuster.
—Federation. Ryan, Kevin, ed. 1994. (Star Trek Ser.). 480p. 22.00 o.p. (0-671-89422-6, Star Trek) Simon & Schuster.
—Federation. abr. ed. 1994. (Star Trek Ser.). audio 17.00 (0-671-50575-0, Simon & Schuster Audioworks) Simon & Schuster Audio.
—Federation. (Star Trek Ser.). 470p. pap. 4.98 o.p. (0-7651-0507-1) Smithmark Pubs., Inc.
—Prime Directive. Stern, David, ed. 1990. (Star Trek Ser.). 416p. 18.95 (0-671-70772-8, Star Trek) Simon & Schuster.
—Prime Directive. Stern, Dave, ed. 1991. (Star Trek Ser.). 416p. reprint ed. mass mkt. 5.99 (0-671-74466-6, Star Trek) Simon & Schuster.
—Prime Directive. abr. ed. 1990. (Star Trek Ser.). audio 15.95 (0-671-72631-5, Simon & Schuster Audioworks) Simon & Schuster Audio.
Reynolds, Mack. Mission to Horatius. 1999. (Star Trek Ser.). (Illus.). 208p. 16.00 o.s.i (0-671-02812-X, Atria) Simon & Schuster.
—Well Meet Again. unabr. ed. 1999. (Star Trek Ser.). audio 39.95 (0-671-04380-3, Simon & Schuster Audioworks) Simon & Schuster Audio.
The Rift. 2000. E-Book 6.99 (0-7434-2008-X, Star Trek) Simon & Schuster.
Roddenberry, Gene. The Motion Picture. 1979. (Star Trek: No. 1). E-Book 6.99 (0-7434-1208-7, Star Trek) Simon & Schuster.
—Star Trek: The Motion Picture. (Star Trek: No. 1). 1984. mass mkt. 2.95 o.s.i (0-671-54685-6); 1980. mass mkt. 2.95 o.s.i (0-671-83089-9) Simon & Schuster. (Star Trek).
Roddenberry, Gene, et al. Star Trek: The Motion Picture. 1979. (Star Trek: No. 1). 252 p. o.p. (0-671-25324-7, Simon & Schuster) Simon & Schuster.
Rotsler, William. Distress Call. Barish, Wendy, ed. 1982. (Star Trek Ser.). (Illus.). (Orig.). (J). (gr. 3-7). pap. 2.85 o.s.i (0-671-46389-6, Simon & Schuster Children's Publishing) Simon & Schuster Children's Publishing.
Rusch, Kristine K. & Smith, Dean Wesley. Thin Air, No. 5. 2000. (Star Trek Ser.: No. 93). 256p. pap. 6.50 (0-671-78577-X, Star Trek) Simon & Schuster.
Sargent, Pamela & Zebrowski, George. Across the Universe. 1999. (Star Trek Ser.: No. 88). 256p. pap. 6.50 (0-671-01989-9, Star Trek) Simon & Schuster.
—Garth of Izar. 2003. (Star Trek). 288p. pap. 6.99 (0-7434-0641-9, Star Trek) Simon & Schuster.
—Heart of the Sun. 1997. (Star Trek Ser.: No. 83). 304p. per. 5.99 (0-671-00237-6, Star Trek) Simon & Schuster.
Shatner, William. Ashes of Eden. Ryan, Kevin, ed. 1995. (Star Trek Ser.). 320p. 23.00 o.p. (0-671-52035-0, Star Trek) Simon & Schuster.
—The Captain's Peril: A Novel. 2002. (Star Trek Ser.: No. 7). 352p. 25.00 (0-7434-4819-7, Star Trek) Simon & Schuster.
—Preserver. (Star Trek Ser.). reprint ed. 2001. 448p. pap. 6.99 (0-671-02126-5); 2001. E-Book 23.95 (0-7434-1955-3); 2000. (Illus.). (J). E-Book 23.95 (0-7434-1119-6) Simon & Schuster. (Star Trek).
—Preserver. abr. ed. 2000. (Star Trek Ser.). audio 18.00 (0-7435-0031-8, Simon & Schuster Audioworks) Simon & Schuster Audio.
—Spectre. 1998. (Star Trek Ser.). 384p. mass mkt. 6.99 (0-671-02053-6, Pocket) Simon & Schuster.
—Spectre. abr. ed. 1998. (Star Trek Ser.: Vol. 2). audio 18.00 (0-671-57998-3, AF09R, Simon & Schuster Audioworks) Simon & Schuster Audio.
—Star Trek: The Captain's Peril. abr. ed. 2002. audio compact disk 24.00 (0-7435-2648-1, Simon & Schuster Audioworks) Simon & Schuster Audio.
Shatner, William, et al. Ashes of Eden. 1996. (Star Trek Ser.). 320p. mass mkt. 6.99 (0-671-52036-9, Star Trek) Simon & Schuster.
—Ashes of Eden. abr. ed. 1995. (Star Trek Ser.). audio 18.00 o.s.i (0-671-52892-0, 392990, Simon & Schuster Audioworks) Simon & Schuster Audio.
—Avenger. (Star Trek Ser.). 1998. (Illus.). 416p. pap. 7.99 (0-671-55131-0, Star Trek); 1997. per. 6.99 (0-671-01744-6, Pocket); 1997. 384p. 23.00 o.s.i (0-671-55132-9, Star Trek) Simon & Schuster.
—Avenger. abr. ed. 1989. (Star Trek Ser.). audio 18.00 (0-671-57524-4, 395166, Simon & Schuster Audioworks) Simon & Schuster Audio.
—Dark Victory. (Star Trek Ser.). 320p. 1999. 23.00 o.s.i (0-671-00882-X); 2000. reprint ed. pap. 6.99 (0-671-00884-6) Simon & Schuster. (Star Trek).
—Odyssey: The Ashes of Eden; The Return; Avenger. 1998. (Star Trek Ser.). 1072p. pap. 14.00 (0-671-02547-3, Star Trek) Simon & Schuster.
—Preserver. 2000. (Star Trek Ser.). 384p. 23.95 o.s.i (0-671-02125-7, Star Trek) Simon & Schuster.
—The Return. (Star Trek Ser.). 1997. 400p. mass mkt. 6.99 (0-671-52609-X, Star Trek); 1996. 384p. 22.00 o.p. (0-671-52610-3, Atria) Simon & Schuster.
—The Return. abr. ed. 1996. (Star Trek Ser.). audio 18.00 o.s.i (0-671-56848-5, 393928, Simon & Schuster Audioworks) Simon & Schuster Audio.
—Spectre. 384p. 2002. E-Book 6.99 (0-7434-5408-1); 1998. (Illus.). 23.00 o.s.i (0-671-00878-1); 1999. reprint ed. pap. 6.50 (0-671-00880-3) Simon & Schuster. (Star Trek).
—Star Trek: The Ashes of Eden. 2001. (Star Trek Ser.). (Illus.). 94p. pap. 14.95 (1-56389-235-9) DC Comics.
—Star Trek: The Return. l.t. ed. 1996. (Star Trek Ser.). 456p. 24.95 (1-56895-359-3, Wheeler Publishing, Inc.) Gale Group.
Shell Game. 2000. E-Book 6.99 (0-7434-2014-4, Star Trek) Simon & Schuster.
Smith, Dean W., et al. Rings of Tautee, No. 078. 1996. (Star Trek Ser.: No. 78). 256p. pap. 5.99 (0-671-00171-X, Star Trek) Simon & Schuster.
Smith, Dean Wesley. The Rings of Tautee. 2000. E-Book 6.99 (0-7434-2029-2, Star Trek) Simon & Schuster.
Smith, Dean Wesley & Rusch, Kristine K. Day of Honor No. 4: Treaty's Law. 1997. (Star Trek Voyager: Vol. 4). 304p. pap. 5.99 (0-671-00424-7, Star Trek) Simon & Schuster.
Snodgrass, Melinda. The Tears of the Singers. 2000. (Star Trek: No. 19). E-Book 6.99 (0-7434-1970-7, Star Trek) Simon & Schuster.
Snodgrass, Melinda M. Tears of the Singers. 1989. (Star Trek: No. 19). mass mkt. 5.50 (0-671-69654-8, Star Trek) Simon & Schuster.
The Tears of the Singers. 2000. (Star Trek: No. 19). E-Book 6.99 (0-7434-2005-5, Star Trek) Simon & Schuster.
Van Hise, Della. Killing Time. (Star Trek: No. 24). 2000. E-Book 6.99 (0-7434-1975-8); 1989. mass mkt. 4.99 (0-671-70597-0) Simon & Schuster. (Star Trek).
Vardeman, Robert E. The Klingon Gambit. (Star Trek: No. 3). 1990. mass mkt. 4.50 (0-671-70767-1); 1987. mass mkt. 3.95 o.s.i (0-671-66342-9); 1986. per. 3.50 (0-671-62744-9); 1985. mass mkt. 3.50 o.s.i (0-671-62231-5); 1983. mass mkt. 2.95 o.s.i (0-671-47720-X); 1981. E-Book 6.99 (0-7434-1210-9) Simon & Schuster. (Star Trek).
—Mutiny on the Enterprise. (Star Trek: No. 12). 2000. E-Book 6.99 (0-7434-1963-4); 1990. mass mkt. 5.50 (0-671-70800-7); 1988. mass mkt. 3.95 o.s.i (0-671-67073-5); 1983. 192p. mass mkt. 2.95 o.s.i (0-671-46541-4) Simon & Schuster. (Star Trek).
Vornholt, John. Sanctuary. 2000. (Star Trek: No. 61). E-Book 6.99 (0-7434-2012-8, Star Trek) Simon & Schuster.
—Sanctuary. Stern, Dave, ed. 1992. (Star Trek Ser.: No. 61). 288p. mass mkt. 4.99 (0-671-76994-4, Star Trek) Simon & Schuster.
Weinstein, Howard. The Better Man. 2000. (Star Trek: No. 72). E-Book 6.99 (0-7434-2023-3, Star Trek) Simon & Schuster.
—The Better Man. Ordover, John, ed. 1994. (Star Trek: No. 72). 288p. mass mkt. 5.50 (0-671-86912-4, Pocket) Simon & Schuster.
—Deep Domain. (Star Trek: No. 33). 2000. E-Book 6.99 (0-7434-1984-7); 1989. mass mkt. 5.50 (0-671-70549-0); 1988. 288p. mass mkt. 3.95 o.s.i (0-671-67077-8) Simon & Schuster. (Star Trek).
Weinstein, Howard, et al. Star Trek: Revisitations. Kahan, Bob, ed. 1996. (Star Trek Ser.). (Illus.). 176p. pap. 19.95 (1-56389-223-5) DC Comics.
Windows on a Lost World. 2000. (Star Trek Ser.: No. 65). E-Book 6.99 (0-7434-2016-0, Star Trek) Simon & Schuster.
Wright, Susan. Badlands. 1999. (Star Trek Ser.: Bk. 1). (Illus.). 304p. pap. 6.50 (0-671-03957-1, Star Trek) Simon & Schuster.
—The Badlands, No. 1. 2000. (Star Trek Ser.). E-Book 6.99 (0-7434-0674-5, Star Trek) Simon & Schuster.

**KITOLOGITAK, MATTEESIE (FICTITIOUS CHARACTER)—FICTION**

Young, Scott. Murder in a Cold Climate. 1989. mass mkt. o.s.i (0-449-21746-9) Ballantine Bks.
—Murder in a Cold Climate. (Crime Ser.). 1990. 240p. pap. 4.50 o.p. (0-14-012336-9, Penguin Bks.); 1989. 256p. 16.95 o.p. (0-670-82889-0) Viking Penguin.
—The Shaman's Knife. 1994. (Crime Ser.). 288p. pap. 5.95 o.p. (0-14-014353-X, Penguin Bks.) Penguin Group (USA) Inc.
—The Shaman's Knife. 1993. 288p. 20.00 o.p. (0-670-83555-2, Viking) Viking Penguin.

**KLEIN, DAVID (FICTITIOUS CHARACTER)—FICTION**

Ellroy, James. White Jazz. 1997. 368p. pap. 13.00 o.s.i (0-449-00088-5, Fawcett) Ballantine Bks.
—White Jazz. unabr. collector's ed. 1992. (L. A. Quartet). audio 64.00 (0-7366-2323-X, 3103) Books on Tape, Inc.
—White Jazz. 2001. 368p. pap. 13.00 (0-375-72736-1, Vintage) Knopf Publishing Group.
—White Jazz: A Novel. 1993. (Los Angeles Mysteries Ser.). 368p. mass mkt. 5.99 o.s.i (0-449-14841-6, Fawcett) Ballantine Bks.

**KLEIN, DYLAN (FICTITIOUS CHARACTER)—FICTION**

Coleman, Reed F. Life Goes Sleeping. 1991. 271p. 28.00 (1-877946-05-2) Permanent Pr., The.
—Little Easter. 1993. 221p. 24.00 (1-877946-23-0) Permanent Pr., The.
—They Don't Play Stickball in Milwaukee. 208p. 1997. 24.00 (1-877946-95-8); 1998. reprint ed. pap. 16.00 (1-57962-016-7) Permanent Pr., The.

**KLEIN, RAY (FICTITIOUS CHARACTER)—FICTION**

Willocks, Tim. Green River Rising. abr. ed. 1994. audio 16.95 o.p. (1-56100-380-8, 1314, Nova Audio Bks.); audio 23.95 o.p. (1-56100-581-9, 128, Bookcassette); audio 57.25 o.p. (1-56100-206-2, 884, Unabridged Library Editions) Brilliance Audio.
—Green River Rising. abr. ed. 2000. audio 7.95 (1-57815-034-5, 1051, Media Bks. Audio Publishing) Media Bks., L. L. C.
—Green River Rising. 1995. 400p. mass mkt. 5.99 (0-380-72357-3, Avon Bks.); 1994. 23.00 o.p. (0-688-13571-4, Morrow, William & Co.) Morrow/Avon.

**KLICK, CHRIS (FICTITIOUS CHARACTER)—FICTION**

McCall, Wendell. Aim for the Heart. l.t. ed. 2002. 224p. lib. bdg. 28.95 (1-58547-142-9) Ctr. Point Large Print.
—Aim for the Heart. 1991. 192p. mass mkt. 4.50 o.s.i (0-440-21082-8) Dell Publishing.
—Aim for the Heart. 1999. (Chris Klick Mysteries Ser.). 155p. pap. 14.95 (1-890208-23-X) Poisoned Pen Pr.
—Aim for the Heart. 1990. 192p. 15.95 o.p. (0-312-04669-3, Saint Martin's Minotaur) St. Martin's Pr.
—Concerto in Dead Flat. l.t. ed. 2002. lib. bdg. 28.95 (1-58547-157-7, Premier) Ctr. Point Large Print.
—Concerto in Dead Flat. 2000. pap. 12.95 (1-890208-52-3); 1999. 277p. 23.95 (1-890208-18-3) Poisoned Pen Pr.
—Dead Aim. l.t. ed. 2001. 400p. lib. bdg. 28.95 (1-58547-141-0); 319p. (1-74030-542-6) Ctr. Point Large Print.
—Dead Aim. 1990. 272p. reprint ed. mass mkt. 3.95 o.s.i (0-440-20510-7) Dell Publishing.
—Dead Aim. 1999. (Chris Klick Mysteries Ser.: Vol. 11). 250p. pap. 14.95 (1-890208-20-5) Poisoned Pen Pr.
—Dead Aim. 1991. 2.99 o.p. (0-517-07670-5) Random Hse. Value Publishing.
—Dead Aim. 1988. 272p. 16.95 o.p. (0-312-02184-4, Saint Martin's Minotaur) St. Martin's Pr.

**KLINE, HARRY (FICTITIOUS CHARACTER)—FICTION**

Luber, Philip. Deliver Us from Evil. 1997. 324p. mass mkt. 5.99 (0-449-14940-4, Fawcett) Ballantine Bks.
—Forgive Us Our Sins. 1994. (Boston Mysteries Ser.). mass mkt. 5.99 o.s.i (0-449-14849-1, Fawcett) Ballantine Bks.
—Pray for Us Sinners. 1997. 294p. (Orig.). mass mkt. 5.99 o.s.i (0-449-18329-7, Fawcett) Ballantine Bks.

**KLOTSKY, SONIA 'SONNY' (FICTITIOUS CHARACTER)—FICTION**

Turow, Scott. The Burden of Proof. 1990. audio 8.95 American Audio Prose Library, Inc.

—The Burden of Proof. unabr. collector's ed. 1990. audio 96.00 (*0-7366-1786-8*, 2623) Books on Tape, Inc.
—The Burden of Proof. 1990. 367.20 o.p. (*0-374-11735-7*); 640p. 30.00 (*0-374-11734-9*); E-Book 22.92 (*0-374-70092-3*); 640p. E-Book 9.95 o.p. (*0-374-70091-5*); E-Book 22.95 (*0-374-70093-1*) Farrar, Straus & Giroux.
—The Burden of Proof. l.t. ed. 1991. (General Ser.). 690p. 14.95 o.p. (*0-8161-5125-3*); 14.95 o.p. (*0-8161-5132-6*) Gale Group. (Macmillan Reference USA).
—The Burden of Proof. abr. ed. 1990. audio 17.00 (*0-671-70743-4*, Simon & Schuster Audioworks) Simon & Schuster Audio.
—The Burden of Proof. reprint ed. 2000. 608p. pap. 14.95 (*0-446-67712-4*); 1991. 576p. mass mkt. 7.99 (*0-446-36058-9*) Warner Bks., Inc.
—The Laws of Our Fathers. unabr. ed. 1997. Pt. 1. audio 64.00 (*0-7366-3642-0*, 4304-A); Pt. 2. (Illus.). audio 64.00 (*0-7366-3643-9*, 4304-B) Books on Tape, Inc.
—The Laws of Our Fathers. 1996. 817p. 26.95 (*0-374-18423-2*) Farrar, Straus & Giroux.
—The Laws of Our Fathers. abr. ed. 1996. audio 26.00 (*0-671-57432-9*); audio 20.80 (*0-671-57741-7*, 908770) Simon & Schuster Audio. (Simon & Schuster Audioworks).
—The Laws of Our Fathers. l.t. ed. (Paperback Bestsellers Ser.). 931p. 1997. pap. 26.95 (*0-7838-1946-3*); 1996. 29.95 (*0-7838-1945-5*) Thorndike Pr.
—The Laws of Our Fathers. 1997. 832p. reprint ed. mass mkt. 7.99 (*0-446-60440-2*) Warner Bks., Inc.

**KNIGHT, JERRY (FICTITIOUS CHARACTER)—FICTION**

Nessen, Ron. Knight & Day. audio 24.95 (*0-7861-1399-5*) Blackstone Audio Bks., Inc.
—Knight & Day. 1996. 256p. mass mkt. 5.99 (*0-8125-5053-6*, Forge Bks.) Doherty, Tom Assocs., LLC.
—Press Corpse. 1997. (Knight & Day Mysteries Ser.). 215p. pap. 5.99 (*0-8125-6793-5*, Forge Bks.) Doherty, Tom Assocs., LLC.
Nessen, Ron & Neuman, Johanna. Death with Honors. unabr. ed. 1999. (Knight & Day Mystery Ser.: Vol. 3). audio 29.95 (*0-7861-1534-3*);Pt. 3. audio 44.95 (*0-7861-1484-3*, 2336) Blackstone Audio Bks., Inc.
—Death with Honors, No. 3. 1998. (Knight & Day Mysteries Ser.). 288p. 22.95 o.p. (*0-312-85594-X*, Forge Bks.) Doherty, Tom Assocs., LLC.
—Knight & Day. unabr. ed. 1996. audio 32.95 (*0-7861-1009-0*, 1788) Blackstone Audio Bks., Inc.
—Knight & Day. 1995. 256p. 21.95 o.p. (*0-312-85588-5*, Forge Bks.) Doherty, Tom Assocs., LLC.
—Press Corpse. unabr. ed. 2000. audio 27.95 (*0-7861-1545-9*); 1999. audio 39.95 Blackstone Audio Bks., Inc.
—Press Corpse. 1996. 256p. 21.95 o.p. (*0-312-85592-3*, Forge Bks.) Doherty, Tom Assocs., LLC.

**KNIGHT, MICKY (FICTITIOUS CHARACTER)—FICTION**

Redmann, J. M. Death by the Riverside. 1990. 256p. (Orig.). pap. 9.95 o.p. (*0-934678-27-8*) New Victoria Pubs., Inc.
—Death by the Riverside: The First Micky Knight Mystery. 2001. 256p. pap. 11.95 (*1-931513-05-8*) Bella Bks., Inc.
—Death of Jocasta. 1992. 288p. (Orig.). pap. 10.95 o.p. (*0-934678-39-1*) New Victoria Pubs., Inc.
—Deaths of Jocasta: The Second Micky Knight Mystery. 2002. 330p. pap. 12.95 (*1-931513-10-4*) Bella Bks., Inc.
—The Intersection of Law & Desire. 1997. mass mkt. 5.99 (*0-380-72819-2*, Avon Bks.) Morrow/Avon.
—The Intersection of Law & Desire. 1995. 336p. 22.00 o.p. (*0-393-03793-2*) Norton, W. W. & Co., Inc.
—Lost Daughters: A Micky Knight Mystery. 1999. (Mickey Knight Mystery Ser.). 320p. text 24.95 o.p. (*0-393-04028-3*) Norton, W. W. & Co., Inc.

**KNIGHT, PHILIP (FICTITIOUS CHARACTER)—FICTION**

McInerny, Ralph. The Book of Kills: A Mystery Set at the University of Notre Dame. E-Book 23.95 (*0-312-27604-4*); 2000. 275p. 23.95 o.p. (*0-312-20346-2*, Saint Martin's Minotaur); 2001. 288p. reprint ed. mass mkt. 6.50 o.s.i (*0-312-97922-3*, St. Martin's Paperbacks) St. Martin's Pr.
—The Book of Kills: A Mystery Set at the University of Notre Dame. 2001. (Basic Ser.). 375p. 28.95 o.p. (*0-7862-3642-6*) Thorndike Pr.
—Celt & Pepper: A Mystery Set at the University of Notre Dame. 2002. 240p. 22.95 (*0-312-29117-5*, Saint Martin's Minotaur) St. Martin's Pr.
—Celt & Pepper: A Mystery Set at the University of Notre Dame. 2003. 28.95 (*0-7862-5179-4*) Thorndike Pr.
—Emerald Aisle: A Mystery Set at the University of Notre Dame. 2002. E-Book 23.95 (*1-59061-743-6*) Adobe Systems, Inc.
—Emerald Aisle: A Mystery Set at the University of Notre Dame. l.t. ed. 2002. 344p. 28.95 (*0-7862-4345-7*) Gale Group.
—Emerald Aisle: A Mystery Set at the University of Notre Dame. mass mkt. (*0-312-98277-1*, St. Martin's Paperbacks); E-Book 23.95 (*0-312-70326-0*); 2001. 288p. 22.95 (*0-312-26938-2*, Saint Martin's Minotaur) St. Martin's Pr.
—Irish Coffee. Date not set. pap. (*0-312-30902-3*, Saint Martin's Griffin); mass mkt. (*0-312-98691-2*, St. Martin's Paperbacks); 2003. 288p. 23.95 (*0-312-30901-5*, Saint Martin's Minotaur) St. Martin's Pr.
—Irish Tenure: A Mystery Set at the University of Notre Dame. 2000. 263p. mass mkt. 5.99 (*0-312-97320-9*, St. Martin's Paperbacks); 1999. 246p. 22.95 o.p. (*0-312-20345-4*, Saint Martin's Minotaur) St. Martin's Pr.
—Irish Tenure: A Mystery Set at the University of Notre Dame. l.t. ed. 2000. (Basic Ser.). 336p. 28.95 (*0-7862-2667-6*) Thorndike Pr.
—Lack of the Irish: A Mystery Set at the University of Notre Dame. (Notre Dame Mystery Ser.). 1999. 240p. mass mkt. 5.99 (*0-312-96927-9*, St. Martin's Paperbacks); 1998. 224p. 21.95 o.p. (*0-312-19294-0*, Saint Martin's Minotaur) St. Martin's Pr.
—On This Rockne: A Notre Dame Mystery. (Notre Dame Mystery Ser.). 1998. 320p. pap. 5.99 (*0-312-96738-1*, St. Martin's Paperbacks); 1997. 224p. 20.95 o.p. (*0-312-17054-8*, 749186, Saint Martin's Minotaur) St. Martin's Pr.

**KNIGHT, ROGER (FICTITIOUS CHARACTER)—FICTION**

McInerny, Ralph. The Book of Kills: A Mystery Set at the University of Notre Dame. E-Book 23.95 (*0-312-27604-4*); 2000. 275p. 23.95 o.p. (*0-312-20346-2*, Saint Martin's Minotaur); 2001. 288p. reprint ed. mass mkt. 6.50 o.s.i (*0-312-97922-3*, St. Martin's Paperbacks) St. Martin's Pr.
—The Book of Kills: A Mystery Set at the University of Notre Dame. 2001. (Basic Ser.). 375p. 28.95 o.p. (*0-7862-3642-6*) Thorndike Pr.
—Celt & Pepper: A Mystery Set at the University of Notre Dame. 2002. 240p. 22.95 (*0-312-29117-5*, Saint Martin's Minotaur) St. Martin's Pr.
—Celt & Pepper: A Mystery Set at the University of Notre Dame. 2003. 28.95 (*0-7862-5179-4*) Thorndike Pr.
—Emerald Aisle: A Mystery Set at the University of Notre Dame. 2002. E-Book 23.95 (*1-59061-743-6*) Adobe Systems, Inc.
—Emerald Aisle: A Mystery Set at the University of Notre Dame. l.t. ed. 2002. 344p. 28.95 (*0-7862-4345-7*) Gale Group.
—Emerald Aisle: A Mystery Set at the University of Notre Dame. mass mkt. (*0-312-98277-1*, St. Martin's Paperbacks); E-Book 23.95 (*0-312-70326-0*); 2001. 288p. 22.95 (*0-312-26938-2*, Saint Martin's Minotaur) St. Martin's Pr.
—Irish Coffee. Date not set. pap. (*0-312-30902-3*, Saint Martin's Griffin); mass mkt. (*0-312-98691-2*, St. Martin's Paperbacks); 2003. 288p. 23.95 (*0-312-30901-5*, Saint Martin's Minotaur) St. Martin's Pr.
—Irish Tenure: A Mystery Set at the University of Notre Dame. 2000. 263p. mass mkt. 5.99 (*0-312-97320-9*, St. Martin's Paperbacks); 1999. 246p. 22.95 o.p. (*0-312-20345-4*, Saint Martin's Minotaur) St. Martin's Pr.
—Irish Tenure: A Mystery Set at the University of Notre Dame. l.t. ed. 2000. (Basic Ser.). 336p. 28.95 (*0-7862-2667-6*) Thorndike Pr.
—Lack of the Irish: A Mystery Set at the University of Notre Dame. (Notre Dame Mystery Ser.). 1999. 240p. mass mkt. 5.99 (*0-312-96927-9*, St. Martin's Paperbacks); 1998. 224p. 21.95 o.p. (*0-312-19294-0*, Saint Martin's Minotaur) St. Martin's Pr.
—On This Rockne: A Notre Dame Mystery. (Notre Dame Mystery Ser.). 1998. 320p. pap. 5.99 (*0-312-96738-1*, St. Martin's Paperbacks); 1997. 224p. 20.95 o.p. (*0-312-17054-8*, 749186, Saint Martin's Minotaur) St. Martin's Pr.

**KNOTT, DEBORAH (FICTITIOUS CHARACTER)—FICTION**

Maron, Margaret. Bootlegger's Daughter. 1992. 272p. 18.95 (*0-89296-445-6*) Mysterious Pr.
—Bootlegger's Daughter. audio o.p. National Humanities Ctr.
—Bootlegger's Daughter. unabr. ed. 1994. (Deborah Knott Mystery Ser.: Vol. 1). audio 60.00 (*0-7887-0086-3*, 94326E7) Recorded Bks., LLC.
—Bootlegger's Daughter. l.t. ed. 2000. (Mystery Ser.). 426p. 29.95 o.p. (*0-7862-2327-8*) Thorndike Pr.
—Bootlegger's Daughter. 1993. 272p. reprint ed. mass mkt. 6.99 (*0-446-40323-7*) Warner Bks., Inc.
—Home Fires: A Deborah Knott Mystery. 1998. (Deborah Knott Mysteries Ser.: Vol. 6). 245p. 22.00 o.p. (*0-89296-655-6*) Mysterious Pr.
—Home Fires: A Deborah Knott Mystery. unabr. ed. 1999. (Deborah Knott Mystery Ser.: Vol. 6). audio 46.00 (*0-7887-3212-9*, 95726E7) Recorded Bks., LLC.
—Home Fires: A Deborah Knott Mystery. l.t. ed. 1999. (Mystery Ser.). 325p. 29.95 (*0-7862-1620-4*) Thorndike Pr.
—Home Fires: A Deborah Knott Mystery. 2001. 304p. E-Book 4.95 (*0-7595-4387-9*); 2001. 304p. E-Book 4.95 (*0-7595-9427-9*); 2001. 304p. E-Book 4.95 (*0-7595-8391-9*); 2001. 304p. E-Book 4.95 (*0-7595-6385-3*); 2000. 288p. reprint ed. mass mkt. 6.50 (*0-446-60810-6*) Warner Bks., Inc.
—Killer Market. 1997. 288p. 22.00 o.p. (*0-89296-654-8*) Mysterious Pr.
—Killer Market. unabr. ed. 2000. (Deborah Knott Ser.: Vol. 5). audio 51.00 (*0-7887-2944-6*, 95724E7) Recorded Bks., LLC.
—Killer Market. l.t. ed. 1998. (*0-7540-3329-5*); (*0-7540-3330-9*) Thorndike Pr.
—Killer Market. 2001. 288p. E-Book 4.95 (*0-7595-9428-7*); 2001. 288p. E-Book 4.95 (*0-7595-4388-7*); 2001. 288p. E-Book 4.95 (*0-7595-8392-7*); 2001. 288p. E-Book 4.95 (*0-7595-6386-1*); 1999. 304p. reprint ed. mass mkt. 6.99 (*0-446-60619-7*) Warner Bks., Inc.
—Shooting at Loons. l.t. ed. 1994. pap. 19.95 o.p. (*1-56895-083-7*, Wheeler Publishing, Inc.) Gale Group.
—Shooting at Loons. 1994. 240p. 18.95 (*0-89296-447-2*) Mysterious Pr.
—Shooting at Loons. audio o.p. National Humanities Ctr.
—Shooting at Loons. unabr. ed. 2000. (Deborah Knott Mystery Ser.: Vol. 3). audio 44.00 (*0-7887-0665-9*, 94842E7) Recorded Bks., LLC.
—Shooting at Loons. 1995. 256p. reprint ed. mass mkt. 6.99 (*0-446-40424-1*) Warner Bks., Inc.
—Shoveling Smoke: Selected Mystery Stories. 1997. 248p. pap. 16.00 (*1-885941-15-3*); 240p. 40.00 o.p. (*1-885941-14-5*) Crippen & Landru, Pubs.
—Slow Dollar. l.t. ed. 2002. (Basic Ser.). 344p. 29.95 o.p. (*0-7862-4670-7*) Thorndike Pr.
—Southern Discomfort, Bk. II. 1993. 256p. 17.95 (*0-89296-446-4*) Mysterious Pr.
—Southern Discomfort. unabr. ed. 1994. (Deborah Knott Mystery Ser.: Vol. 2). audio 51.00 (*0-7887-0032-4*, 94231E7) Recorded Bks., LLC.
—Southern Discomfort. l.t. ed. 2000. (Mystery Ser.). 351p. 29.95 (*0-7862-2330-8*) Thorndike Pr.
—Southern Discomfort. 1994. 224p. reprint ed. mass mkt. 6.99 (*0-446-40080-7*) Warner Bks., Inc.
—Storm Track. 2000. (Deborah Knott Mysteries Ser.). 272p. 22.95 (*0-89296-656-4*) Mysterious Pr.
—Storm Track. l.t. ed. 2000. (Mystery Ser.). 349p. 29.95 (*0-7862-2465-7*) Thorndike Pr.
—Uncommon Clay. 2001. (Deborah Knott Mysteries Ser.). 304p. 23.95 o.p. (*0-89296-720-X*) Mysterious Pr.
—Uncommon Clay. l.t. ed. 2001. 371p. 30.95 o.p. (*0-7862-3370-2*) Thorndike Pr.
—Uncommon Clay. 2002. 336p. mass mkt. 6.99 (*0-446-61087-9*) Warner Bks., Inc.
—Up Jumps the Devil. unabr. ed. 2000. (Deborah Knott Mystery Ser.: Vol. 4). audio 51.00 (*0-7887-1310-8*, 95152E7) Recorded Bks., LLC.
—Up Jumps the Devil. 1996. 256p. 20.00 o.s.i (*0-89296-568-1*); 1997. 304p. reprint ed. mass mkt. 6.99 (*0-446-60406-2*) Warner Bks., Inc.

**KOCH, ED, 1924—FICTION**

Koch, Edward I. Murder at City Hall. 1995. 208p. mass mkt. 19.95 o.p. (*0-8217-5087-9*, Zebra Bks.) Kensington Publishing Corp.
—Murder on Broadway. 1997. 320p. mass mkt. 5.99 o.s.i (*1-57566-186-1*) Kensington Publishing Corp.
—Murder on 34th Street. 1998. 288p. mass mkt. 5.99 o.s.i (*1-57566-355-4*); 1997. 192p. 19.95 o.s.i (*1-57566-232-9*) Kensington Publishing Corp.
—The Senator Must Die. 1998. 224p. 22.00 o.s.i (*1-57566-325-2*, Kensington Bks.) Kensington Publishing Corp.
Koch, Edward I. & Resnicow, Herbert. Murder at City Hall. 1996. 224p. mass mkt. 5.99 o.s.i (*1-57566-053-9*) Kensington Publishing Corp.
Koch, Edward I. & Staub, Wendy Corsi. Murder on Broadway. 1996. 192p. 19.95 o.s.i (*1-57566-049-0*) Kensington Publishing Corp.

**KODIAK, ATTICUS (FICTITIOUS CHARACTER)—FICTION**

Rucka, Greg. Keeper. 1997. 368p. mass mkt. 6.99 (*0-553-57428-0*, Crimeline) Bantam Bks.
—Keeper: An Atticus Kodiac Novel. unabr. ed. 1998. audio 60.00 (*0-7887-1876-2*, 95298E7) Recorded Bks., LLC.
—Shooting at Midnight. 2000. 400p. mass mkt. 6.99 (*0-553-57827-8*) Bantam Bks.
—Smoker. 1999. 432p. mass mkt. 6.99 (*0-553-57829-4*) Bantam Bks.
Rucka, Gregory. Finder. 1999. audio 60.00 Recorded Bks., LLC.
—Finder: An Atticus Kodiac Novel. 1998. 352p. mass mkt. 6.99 (*0-553-57429-9*) Bantam Bks.
—Finder: An Atticus Kodiac Novel. unabr. ed. 1999. audio 62.00 (*0-7887-3994-8*, 96082E7) Recorded Bks., LLC.

**KOERNEY, KATHRYN (FICTITIOUS CHARACTER)—FICTION**

Sumners, Cristina. Crooked Heart. 2003. 336p. mass mkt. 6.99 (*0-553-58430-8*); 2002. 304p. 23.95 (*0-553-80303-4*); 2002. E-Book 19.50 (*0-553-89710-1*) Bantam Bks.

**KOESLER, ROBERT, FATHER (FICTITIOUS CHARACTER)—FICTION**

Kienzle, William X. Assault with Intent. 1987. (Father Koesler Mystery Ser.: No. 4). 273p. 9.95 o.p. (*0-8362-6117-8*) Andrews McMeel Publishing.
—Assault with Intent. 1985. (Father Koesler Mystery Ser.: No. 4). 320p. mass mkt. 5.99 o.s.i (*0-345-33283-0*); 1983. mass mkt. 2.95 o.p. (*0-345-30812-3*) Ballantine Bks.
—Assault with Intent. unabr. collector's ed. 1997. (Father Koesler Mystery Ser.). audio 56.00 (*0-7366-3994-2*, 4459) Books on Tape, Inc.
—Bishop As Pawn. 1994. (Father Koesler Mystery Ser.: No. 16). xiii, 266p. 18.95 o.p. (*0-8362-6130-5*) Andrews McMeel Publishing.
—Bishop As Pawn. 1995. (Father Koesler Mystery Ser.: No. 16). mass mkt. 5.99 o.s.i (*0-345-38800-3*) Ballantine Bks.
—Body Count. 1992. (Father Koesler Mystery Ser.: No. 14). viii, 266p. 18.95 o.p. (*0-8362-6128-3*) Andrews McMeel Publishing.
—Body Count. 1993. (Father Koesler Mystery Ser.: No. 14). reprint ed. mass mkt. 5.99 o.s.i (*0-345-37767-2*) Ballantine Bks.
—Call No Man Father. 1995. (Father Koesler Mystery Ser.: No. 17). 272p. 18.95 o.p. (*0-8362-6131-3*) Andrews McMeel Publishing.
—Call No Man Father. 1996. (Father Koesler Mystery Ser.: No. 17). mass mkt. 5.99 o.s.i (*0-345-38801-1*) Ballantine Bks.
—Chameleon. 1991. (Father Koesler Mystery Ser.: No. 13). 289p. pap. 16.95 o.p. (*0-8362-6127-5*) Andrews McMeel Publishing.
—Chameleon. 1992. (Father Koesler Mystery Ser.: No. 13). mass mkt. 5.99 o.s.i (*0-345-36621-2*) Ballantine Bks.
—Dead Wrong. 1993. (Father Koesler Mystery Ser.: No. 15). 269p. 18.95 o.p. (*0-8362-6129-1*) Andrews McMeel Publishing.
—Dead Wrong. 1994. (Father Koesler Mystery Ser.: No. 15). mass mkt. 5.99 o.s.i (*0-345-37766-4*) Ballantine Bks.
—Deadline for a Critic. 1987. (Father Koesler Mystery Ser.: No. 9). 263p. 14.95 o.p. (*0-8362-6123-2*) Andrews McMeel Publishing.
—Deadline for a Critic. 1988. (Father Koesler Mystery Ser.: No. 9). 352p. mass mkt. 5.99 o.s.i (*0-345-33190-7*) Ballantine Bks.
—Deadline for a Critic. 1990. (Father Koesler Mystery Ser.: No. 9). 2.99 o.p. (*0-517-05975-4*) Random Hse. Value Publishing.
—Death Bed. 1987. (Father Koesler Mystery Ser.: No. 8). mass mkt. 5.99 o.s.i (*0-345-33189-3*) Ballantine Bks.
—Death Wears a Red Hat. 1980. (Father Koesler Mystery Ser.: No. 2). 304p. 9.95 o.p. (*0-8362-6111-9*) Andrews McMeel Publishing.
—Death Wears a Red Hat. 1989. (Father Koesler Mystery Ser.: No. 2). mass mkt. 5.99 o.s.i (*0-345-35669-1*) Ballantine Bks.
—Death Wears a Red Hat. 1981. (Father Koesler Mystery Ser.: No. 2). 288p. pap. 3.50 o.p. (*0-553-26524-5*) Bantam Bks.
—Death Wears a Red Hat. unabr. collector's ed. 1997. (Father Koesler Mystery Ser.). audio 56.00 (*0-7366-4063-0*, 4574) Books on Tape, Inc.
—Death Wears a Red Hat. l.t. ed. 1981. (Father Koesler Mystery Ser.: No. 2). 553p. 29.99 o.p. (*0-7089-0647-8*, Ulverscroft) Thorpe, F. A. Pubs. GBR. *Dist:* Ulverscroft Large Print Bks., Ltd., Ulverscroft Large Print Canada, Ltd.
—Deathbed. 1985. (Father Koesler Mystery Ser.: No. 8). 258p. 14.95 o.p. (*0-8362-6122-4*) Andrews McMeel Publishing.
—Eminence. 1989. (Father Koesler Mystery Ser.: No. 11). 312p. 15.95 o.p. (*0-8362-6125-9*) Andrews McMeel Publishing.
—Eminence. 1990. (Father Koesler Mystery Ser.: No. 11). 368p. mass mkt. 5.99 o.s.i (*0-345-35395-1*) Ballantine Bks.
—Eminence. 1990. 3.99 o.p. (*0-517-05976-2*) Random Hse. Value Publishing.
—The Gathering. 2002. 288p. 22.95 (*0-7407-2229-8*) Andrews McMeel Publishing.
—The Gathering. 2003. 304p. mass mkt. 6.99 (*0-345-45794-3*, Fawcett) Ballantine Bks.
—The Greatest Evil. 1998. (Father Koesler Mystery Ser.: No. 20). vii, 278p. 19.95 o.p. (*0-8362-5206-3*) Andrews McMeel Publishing.
—The Greatest Evil. 1999. (Father Koesler Mystery Ser.: No. 20). 294p. mass mkt. 6.99 (*0-345-42638-X*) Ballantine Bks.
—The Greatest Evil. unabr. collector's ed. 1998. (Father Koesler Mystery Ser.). audio 56.00 (*0-7366-4529-2*, 4720) Books on Tape, Inc.

—Kill & Tell. 1984. (Father Koesler Mystery Ser.: No. 6). 250p. 12.95 o.p. (*0-8362-6120-8*) Andrews McMeel Publishing.
—Kill & Tell. 1985. (Father Koesler Mystery Ser.: No. 6). mass mkt. 5.99 o.s.i (*0-345-31856-0*) Ballantine Bks.
—Kill & Tell. l.t. ed. 1984. (Father Koesler Mystery Ser.: No. 6). 378p. 15.95 o.p. (*0-8161-3779-X*, Macmillan Reference USA) Gale Group.
—The Man Who Loved God. 1997. (Father Koesler Mystery Ser.: No. 19). 274p. 19.95 (*0-8362-2754-9*) Andrews McMeel Publishing.
—The Man Who Loved God. 1998. (Father Koesler Mystery Ser.: No. 19). 304p. mass mkt. 6.99 o.s.i (*0-345-40290-1*) Ballantine Bks.
—Marked for Murder. 1988. (Father Koesler Mystery Ser.: No. 10). 281p. 14.95 o.p. (*0-8362-6124-0*) Andrews McMeel Publishing.
—Marked for Murder. 1989. (Father Koesler Mystery Ser.: No. 10). mass mkt. 5.99 o.s.i (*0-345-35397-8*) Ballantine Bks.
—Masquerade. 1990. (Father Koesler Mystery Ser.: No. 12). 267p. 15.95 o.p. (*0-8362-6126-7*) Andrews McMeel Publishing.
—Masquerade. 1991. (Father Koesler Mystery Ser.: No. 12). 384p. mass mkt. 5.99 o.s.i (*0-345-36620-4*) Ballantine Bks.
—Mind over Murder. 1981. (Father Koesler Mystery Ser.: No. 3). v, 296p. 9.95 o.p. (*0-8362-6114-3*) Andrews McMeel Publishing.
—Mind over Murder. 1989. (Father Koesler Mystery Ser.: No. 3). mass mkt. 5.99 o.s.i (*0-345-35667-5*) Ballantine Bks.
—Mind over Murder. 1982. (Father Koesler Mystery Ser.: No. 3). pap. 3.50 o.p. (*0-553-25008-6*) Bantam Bks.
—Mind over Murder. unabr. collector's ed. 1997. (Father Koesler Mystery Ser.). audio 64.00 (*0-7366-4064-9*, 4575) Books on Tape, Inc.
—No Greater Love. 1999. (Father Koesler Mystery Ser.: No. 21). 292p. 19.95 o.p. (*0-8362-7865-8*) Andrews McMeel Publishing.
—No Greater Love. 2000. (Father Koesler Mystery Ser.). 304p. mass mkt. 6.99 (*0-345-42639-8*, Fawcett) Ballantine Bks.
—Requiem for Moses. 1996. (Father Koesler Mystery Ser.: No. 18). 272p. 19.95 o.p. (*0-8362-1042-5*) Andrews McMeel Publishing.
—Requiem for Moses. 1997. (Father Koesler Mystery Ser.: No. 19). 322p. mass mkt. 5.99 o.s.i (*0-345-40291-X*) Ballantine Bks.
—The Rosary Murders. 1979. (Father Koesler Mystery Ser.: No. 1). 257p. 9.95 o.p. (*0-8362-6101-1*) Andrews McMeel Publishing.
—The Rosary Murders. 1989. (Father Koesler Mystery Ser.: No. 1). 304p. mass mkt. 5.99 o.s.i (*0-345-35668-3*) Ballantine Bks.
—The Rosary Murders. 1984. mass mkt. 3.50 o.s.i (*0-553-25084-1*); 1980. (Father Koesler Mystery Ser.: No. 1). 304p. mass mkt. 3.50 o.s.i (*0-553-26406-0*) Bantam Bks.
—The Sacrifice. 1999. 288p. 22.95 (*0-7407-1226-8*) Andrews McMeel Publishing.
—Shadow of Death. 1983. (Father Koesler Mystery Ser.: No. 5). 252p. 10.95 o.p. (*0-8362-6119-4*) Andrews McMeel Publishing.
—Shadow of Death. (Father Koesler Mystery Ser.: No. 5). 1985. mass mkt. 5.99 o.s.i (*0-345-33110-9*); 1984. mass mkt. 2.95 o.p. (*0-345-31251-1*) Ballantine Bks.
—Shadow of Death. unabr. collector's ed. 1999. (Father Koesler Mystery Ser.). audio 56.00 (*0-7366-4330-3*, 4824) Books on Tape, Inc.
—Shadow of Death. l.t. ed. 1983. (Father Koesler Mystery Ser.: No. 5). lib. bdg. 16.95 o.p. (*0-8161-3582-7*, Macmillan Reference USA) Gale Group.
—Sudden Death. 1985. (Father Koesler Mystery Ser.: No. 7). 257p. 12.95 o.p. (*0-8362-6121-6*) Andrews McMeel Publishing.
—Sudden Death. 1986. (Father Koesler Mystery Ser.: No. 7). mass mkt. 5.99 o.s.i (*0-345-32851-5*) Ballantine Bks.
—Sudden Death. l.t. ed. 1986. (Father Koesler Mystery Ser.: No. 7). 416p. 16.95 o.p. (*0-8161-3965-2*, Macmillan Reference USA) Gale Group.
—Till Death. 2000. 279p. 19.95 (*0-7407-0489-3*) Andrews McMeel Publishing.
—Till Death. 2001. 304p. mass mkt. 6.99 (*0-449-00713-8*, Fawcett) Ballantine Bks.

**KOHLER, HERMANN (FICTITIOUS CHARACTER)—FICTION**

Janes, J. Robert. Carousel. 1993. 20.00 o.p. (*1-55611-357-9*) Fine, Donald I. Bks.
—Carousel. 1999. (St-Cyr & Kohler Ser.). 288p. pap. 12.00 (*1-56947-175-4*) Soho Pr., Inc.
—Dollmaker. 2003. pap. 12.00 (*1-56947-346-3*); 2002. 258p. 23.00 (*1-56947-285-8*) Soho Pr., Inc.
—Mannequin. (St-Cyr & Kohler Ser.). 1999. 272p. pap. 12.00 (*1-56947-176-2*); 1998. 266p. 22.00 (*1-56947-129-0*) Soho Pr., Inc.
—Mayhem. 1999. 272p. pap. 12.00 (*1-56947-158-4*) Soho Pr., Inc.
—Mirage. 1992. 272p. 20.00 o.p. (*1-55611-340-4*) Fine, Donald I. Bks.
—Salamander. (Crime Ser.). 1999. 314p. pap. 12.00 (*1-56947-157-6*); 1998. 322p. 22.00 (*1-56947-119-3*) Soho Pr., Inc.
—Sandman. (St-Cyr & Kohler Ser.). 272p. 1998. pap. 12.00 (*1-56947-120-7*); 1997. 22.00 (*1-56947-106-1*) Soho Pr., Inc.
—Stonekiller. 1997. 261p. pap. 12.00 (*1-56947-107-X*); 22.00 o.p. (*1-56947-083-9*) Soho Pr., Inc.

**KOKO (FICTITIOUS CHARACTER)—FICTION**

Braun, Lilian Jackson. The Cat Who Ate Danish Modern. 1986. (Cat Who Ser.). 192p. mass mkt. 6.99 (*0-515-08712-2*, Jove) Berkley Publishing Group.
—The Cat Who Ate Danish Modern. 1989. (Black Dagger Crime Ser.). 200p. reprint ed. text 12.95 o.p. (*0-86220-755-X*) Chivers Pr. GBR. *Dist:* BBC Audiobooks America.
—The Cat Who Ate Danish Modern. l.t. ed. 1990. (Nightingale Ser.). 274p. 14.95 o.p. (*0-8161-4914-3*, Macmillan Reference USA) Gale Group.
—The Cat Who Ate Danish Modern. unabr. ed. 1990. (Cat Who Ser.). audio 35.00 (*1-55690-090-2*, 90081E7) Recorded Bks., LLC.
—The Cat Who Ate Danish Modern. 1986. 13.04 (*0-606-13246-5*) Turtleback Bks.
—The Cat Who Blew the Whistle. 1996. (Cat Who Ser.). 320p. mass mkt. 6.99 (*0-515-11824-9*, Jove) Berkley Publishing Group.
—The Cat Who Blew the Whistle. abr. ed. 1995. (J). audio 17.95 o.p. (*0-7871-0229-6*, 393238) NewStar Media, Inc.
—The Cat Who Blew the Whistle. 1995. 240p. 21.95 o.p. (*0-399-13981-8*, G. P. Putnam's Sons) Penguin Group (USA) Inc.
—The Cat Who Blew the Whistle. l.t. ed. (Paperback Bestsellers Ser.). 270p. 1996. lib. bdg. 18.95 (*0-7838-1253-1*); 1995. lib. bdg. 24.95 (*0-7838-1252-3*) Thorndike Pr.
—The Cat Who Blew the Whistle. 1996. 13.04 (*0-606-12643-0*) Turtleback Bks.
—The Cat Who Brought down the House. 2003. 256p. mass mkt. 6.99 (*0-515-13655-7*, Jove) Berkley Publishing Group.
—The Cat Who Brought down the House. 2003. 240p. 23.95 (*0-399-14942-2*); audio 24.95 (*0-399-14993-7*, Putnam Berkley Audio) Putnam Publishing Group, The.
—The Cat Who Brought down the House. 2003. 299p. 32.95 (*0-7862-5036-4*); 2004. 304p. pap. 13.95 (*1-59413-011-6*, Large Print Pr.) Thorndike Pr.
—The Cat Who Came to Breakfast. 1995. (Cat Who Ser.). 272p. (J). pap. 6.99 (*0-515-11564-9*, Jove) Berkley Publishing Group.
—The Cat Who Came to Breakfast. l.t. ed. 296p. 1995. 17.95 o.p. (*0-8161-5935-1*); 1994. lib. bdg. 23.95 o.p. (*0-8161-5934-3*) Gale Group. (Macmillan Reference USA).
—The Cat Who Came to Breakfast. abr. ed. 1993. audio 16.95 o.p. (*1-55800-937-X*, 393255, Dove Audio) NewStar Media, Inc.
—The Cat Who Came to Breakfast. 1994. 240p. 19.95 o.p. (*0-399-13868-4*, G. P. Putnam's Sons) Penguin Group (USA) Inc.
—The Cat Who Came to Breakfast. 1995. 13.04 (*0-606-12644-9*) Turtleback Bks.
—The Cat Who Could Read Backwards. l.t. ed. 1991. 12.95 o.p. (*0-7927-0098-8*, C0139) BBC Audiobooks America.
—The Cat Who Could Read Backwards. 256p. 2003. pap. 10.00 (*0-425-19520-1*); 1986. mass mkt. 6.99 (*0-515-09017-4*, Jove) Berkley Publishing Group.
—The Cat Who Could Read Backwards. l.t. ed. 1997. (Large Print Book Ser.). 25.95 o.p. (*1-56895-470-0*, Wheeler Publishing, Inc.) Gale Group.
—The Cat Who Could Read Backwards. 1997. (Cat Who. . . Ser.). 240p. 19.95 o.p. (*0-399-14286-X*, G. P. Putnam's Sons) Penguin Group (USA) Inc.
—The Cat Who Could Read Backwards. unabr. ed. 1990. (Cat Who Ser.). audio 19.95 (*1-55690-091-0*, 90082) Recorded Bks., LLC.
—The Cat Who Had 14 Tales. 1988. (Cat Who Ser.). 256p. mass mkt. 6.99 (*0-515-09497-8*, Jove) Berkley Publishing Group.
—The Cat Who Had 14 Tales. l.t. ed. 1991. (Nightingale Ser.). 241p. 14.95 o.p. (*0-8161-4915-1*, Macmillan Reference USA) Gale Group.
—The Cat Who Had 14 Tales. unabr. ed. 2000. (Cat Who Ser.). (J). audio 35.00 (*0-7887-0312-9*, 94504E7) Recorded Bks., LLC.
—The Cat Who Had 14 Tales. 1988. 13.04 (*0-606-13247-3*) Turtleback Bks.
—The Cat Who Knew a Cardinal. 1992. (Cat Who Ser.). 288p. mass mkt. 6.99 (*0-515-10786-7*, Jove) Berkley Publishing Group.
—The Cat Who Knew a Cardinal. l.t. ed. 1992. (General Ser.). 316p. 18.95 (*0-8161-5279-9*); lib. bdg. 19.95 o.p. (*0-8161-5278-0*) Gale Group. (Macmillan Reference USA).
—The Cat Who Knew a Cardinal. abr. ed. 1993. 15.95 o.p. (*1-55800-444-0*, 390492) NewStar Media, Inc.
—The Cat Who Knew a Cardinal. 1991. (Cat Who Ser.). 240p. 16.95 o.p. (*0-399-13664-9*, G. P. Putnam's Sons) Penguin Group (USA) Inc.
—The Cat Who Knew a Cardinal. 1992. 13.04 (*0-606-12645-7*) Turtleback Bks.
—The Cat Who Knew a Cardinal; The Cat Who Moved a Mountain; The Cat Who Wasn't There. unabr. ed. 1993. audio 19.95 o.p. (*1-55800-782-2*) NewStar Media, Inc.
—The Cat Who Knew Shakespeare. 1988. (Cat Who Ser.). 256p. mass mkt. 6.99 (*0-515-09582-6*, Jove) Berkley Publishing Group.
—The Cat Who Knew Shakespeare. l.t. ed. 1989. 284p. 12.95 o.p. (*0-8161-4790-6*, Macmillan Reference USA) Gale Group.
—The Cat Who Knew Shakespeare. unabr. ed. 1991. (Cat Who Ser.). (YA). (gr. 10 up). audio 24.95 (*1-55690-092-9*, 91115E7) Recorded Bks., LLC.
—The Cat Who Knew Shakespeare. 1991. 13.04 (*0-606-13248-1*) Turtleback Bks.
—The Cat Who Lived High. 1991. (Cat Who Ser.). 304p. mass mkt. 6.99 (*0-515-10566-X*, Jove) Berkley Publishing Group.
—The Cat Who Lived High. l.t. ed. 1991. lib. bdg. 19.95 o.p. (*0-8161-5126-1*, Macmillan Reference USA) Gale Group.
—The Cat Who Lived High. 1990. 240p. 17.95 o.p. (*0-399-13554-5*, G. P. Putnam's Sons) Penguin Putnam Bks. for Young Readers.
—The Cat Who Lived High. unabr. ed. 1994. (Cat Who Ser.: No. 11). audio 32.95 (*1-55690-992-6*, 94131) Recorded Bks., LLC.
—The Cat Who Lived High. 1991. 13.04 (*0-606-12646-5*) Turtleback Bks.
—The Cat Who Moved a Mountain. 1992. (Cat Who Ser.). 272p. mass mkt. 6.99 (*0-515-10950-9*, Jove) Berkley Publishing Group.
—The Cat Who Moved a Mountain. l.t. ed. 1993. (General Ser.). 379p. 18.95 o.p. (*0-8161-5551-8*); 20.95 o.p. (*0-8161-5550-X*) Gale Group. (Macmillan Reference USA).
—The Cat Who Moved a Mountain. abr. ed. 1993. 15.95 o.p. (*1-55800-470-X*, 390493) NewStar Media, Inc.
—The Cat Who Moved a Mountain. 1992. (Cat Who Ser.). 240p. 18.95 o.p. (*0-399-13646-0*, G. P. Putnam's Sons) Penguin Group (USA) Inc.
—The Cat Who Moved a Mountain. 1992. 13.04 (*0-606-12647-3*) Turtleback Bks.
—The Cat Who Played Brahms. l.t. ed. 1990. 18.95 o.p. (*0-7927-0335-9*, C0029); pap. 16.95 o.p. (*0-7927-0345-6*) BBC Audiobooks America.
—The Cat Who Played Brahms. 1987. (Cat Who Ser.). 256p. mass mkt. 6.99 (*0-515-09050-6*, Jove) Berkley Publishing Group.
—The Cat Who Played Brahms. unabr. ed. 1992. (Cat Who Ser.). audio 24.95 (*1-55690-651-X*, 92133) Recorded Bks., LLC.
—The Cat Who Played Brahms. 1990. 13.04 (*0-606-13249-X*) Turtleback Bks.
—The Cat Who Played Post Office. 1987. (Cat Who Ser.). 272p. pap. 6.99 (*0-515-09320-3*, Jove) Berkley Publishing Group.
—The Cat Who Played Post Office. l.t. ed. 2000. (Wheeler Large Print Book Ser.). (Illus.). 230p. 27.95 o.p. (*1-56895-840-4*, Wheeler Publishing, Inc.) Gale Group.
—The Cat Who Played Post Office. unabr. ed. 2001. audio 24.95 (*0-7887-5432-7*); 2000. audio 24.95 (*1-55690-689-7*, 92343) Recorded Bks., LLC.
—The Cat Who Played Post Office. 1987. 13.04 (*0-606-13250-3*) Turtleback Bks.
—The Cat Who Robbed a Bank. l.t. ed. 2000. pap. 22.95 o.p. (*0-7838-8710-8*, Macmillan Reference USA) Gale Group.
—The Cat Who Robbed a Bank. 2000. (Cat Who Ser.). 256p. 23.95 o.p. (*0-399-14570-2*) Penguin Group (USA) Inc.
—The Cat Who Robbed a Bank, No. 2. abr. ed. 2000. (Cat Who Ser.: Vol. 22). 3p. 17.95 o.s.i (*0-399-14582-6*, Putnam Berkley Audio) Putnam Publishing Group, The.
—The Cat Who Robbed a Bank. l.t. ed. 2000. 400p. 23.95 (*0-375-40878-9*) Random Hse. Large Print.
—The Cat Who Robbed a Bank. unabr. ed. 1999. (Cat Who Ser.). audio 29.95 (*0-7887-4032-6*, 96010 ) Recorded Bks., LLC.
—The Cat Who Said Cheese. 1997. (Cat Who Ser.). 272p. reprint ed. pap. 6.99 (*0-515-12027-8*, Jove) Berkley Publishing Group.
—The Cat Who Said Cheese. l.t. ed. 1997. pap. 23.95 o.p. (*0-7838-1632-4*, Macmillan Reference USA) Gale Group.
—The Cat Who Said Cheese. abr. ed. 1996. 17.95 o.p. (*0-7871-0610-0*) NewStar Media, Inc.
—The Cat Who Said Cheese. 1996. (Cat Who Ser.). (*0-399-19300-6*); 256p. 22.95 o.p. (*0-399-14075-1*, G. P. Putnam's Sons) Penguin Group (USA) Inc.
—The Cat Who Said Cheese. l.t. ed. 1996. (Core Collection). 303p. 27.95 (*0-7838-1631-6*) Thorndike Pr.
—The Cat Who Said Cheese. 1997. 13.04 (*0-606-12648-1*) Turtleback Bks.
—The Cat Who Sang for the Birds. 1999. (Cat Who Ser.). (Illus.). 272p. reprint ed. mass mkt. 6.99 (*0-515-12463-X*, Jove) Berkley Publishing Group.
—The Cat Who Sang for the Birds. l.t. ed. 1998. 26.95 o.p. (*1-56895-555-3*, Wheeler Publishing, Inc.) Gale Group.
—The Cat Who Sang for the Birds. 1998. (Cat Who. . . Ser.). 256p. (YA). 22.95 o.p. (*0-399-14333-5*, G. P. Putnam's Sons);Set. 3p. (J). 17.95 o.s.i (*0-399-14350-5*, 395411, Putnam Berkley Audio) Penguin Group (USA) Inc.
—The Cat Who Sang for the Birds. unabr. ed. (Cat Who Ser.). 1999. audio compact disk 54.00 (*0-7887-3428-8*, C1034E7); 1998. audio 32.95 (*0-7887-1971-8*, 95358) Recorded Bks., LLC.
—The Cat Who Saw Red. 1986. (Cat Who Ser.). 256p. mass mkt. 6.99 (*0-515-09016-6*); mass mkt. 2.95 o.s.i (*0-515-08491-3*) Berkley Publishing Group. (Jove).
—The Cat Who Saw Red. l.t. ed. 1989. 13.95 o.p. (*0-8161-4388-9*, Macmillan Reference USA) Gale Group.
—The Cat Who Saw Red. unabr. ed. 1990. (Cat Who Ser.). (YA). (gr. 10 up). audio 35.00 (*1-55690-093-7*, 90083E7) Recorded Bks., LLC.
—The Cat Who Saw Red. 1986. 13.04 (*0-606-13251-1*) Turtleback Bks.
—The Cat Who Saw Stars. 2000. (Cat Who Ser.). 304p. reprint ed. mass mkt. 6.99 (*0-515-12739-6*, Jove) Berkley Publishing Group.
—The Cat Who Saw Stars. l.t. ed. 2000. 11.95 (*1-56895-980-X*); 1999. 27.95 (*1-56895-595-2*) Gale Group. (Wheeler Publishing, Inc.).
—The Cat Who Saw Stars, abr. ed. 1999. audio 17.95 Highsmith Inc.
—The Cat Who Saw Stars. 1999. (Cat Who. . . Ser.). 240p. 22.95 o.p. (*0-399-14431-5*); 17.95 o.p. (*0-399-14455-2*, 393651, Putnam Berkley Audio) Penguin Group (USA) Inc.
—The Cat Who Saw Stars. unabr. ed. (Cat Who Ser.: Vol. 21). 2001. audio compact disk 38.00 (*0-7887-3971-9*, C1090E7); 1999. audio 32.95 (*0-7887-2913-6*, 95706 ) Recorded Bks., LLC.
—The Cat Who Smelled a Rat. 2002. (Cat Who Ser.). 304p. reprint ed. mass mkt. 6.99 (*0-515-13226-8*, Jove) Berkley Publishing Group.
—The Cat Who Smelled a Rat. 2001. (Cat Who. . . Ser.). (Illus.). 256p. 23.95 o.s.i (*0-399-14665-2*, G. P. Putnam's Sons) Penguin Group (USA) Inc.
—The Cat Who Smelled a Rat. abr. ed. 2001. (Cat Who Ser.). audio 17.95 o.s.i (*0-399-14681-4*, Putnam Berkley Audio) Putnam Publishing Group, The.
—The Cat Who Smelled a Rat. unabr. ed. 2001. audio 29.95 (*0-7887-4977-3*, 964417); audio compact disk 48.00 Recorded Bks., LLC.
—The Cat Who Smelled a Rat. l.t. ed. 293p. 2002. pap. 29.95 (*0-7862-2823-7*); 2001. 32.95 (*0-7862-2822-9*) Thorndike Pr.
—The Cat Who Sniffed Glue. 1989. (Cat Who Ser.). 288p. mass mkt. 6.99 (*0-515-09954-6*, Jove) Berkley Publishing Group.
—The Cat Who Sniffed Glue. l.t. ed. 1990. (Nightingale Ser.). 312p. 13.95 o.p. (*0-8161-4864-3*, Macmillan Reference USA) Gale Group.
—The Cat Who Sniffed Glue. 1988. (Cat Who. . . Ser.). 192p. 14.95 o.p. (*0-399-13381-X*, G. P. Putnam's Sons) Penguin Putnam Bks. for Young Readers.
—The Cat Who Sniffed Glue. unabr. ed. 2000. audio 44.00 (*1-55690-837-7*, 93205E7) Recorded Bks., LLC.
—The Cat Who Sniffed Glue. 1989. 13.04 (*0-606-13252-X*) Turtleback Bks.
—The Cat Who Tailed a Thief. 1998. (Cat Who. . . Ser.). 272p. mass mkt. 6.99 (*0-515-12240-8*, Jove) Berkley Publishing Group.
—The Cat Who Tailed a Thief. l.t. ed. 1997. 293p. 27.95 o.p. (*0-7838-8046-4*, Macmillan Reference USA) Gale Group.
—The Cat Who Tailed a Thief. abr. ed. 1997. 17.95 o.p. (*0-7871-1352-2*, 394616) NewStar Media, Inc.
—The Cat Who Tailed a Thief. 1997. (Cat Who. . . Ser.). 256p. 22.95 o.p. (*0-399-14210-X*, G. P. Putnam's Sons) Penguin Group (USA) Inc.
—The Cat Who Tailed a Thief. l.t. ed. 1998. (Paperback Bestsellers Ser.). 293p. pap. 27.95 (*0-7838-8047-2*) Thorndike Pr.
—The Cat Who Tailed a Thief. 1998. 13.04 (*0-606-13253-8*) Turtleback Bks.
—The Cat Who Talked to Ghosts. 1990. (Cat Who Ser.). 288p. pap. 6.99 (*0-515-10265-2*, Jove) Berkley Publishing Group.
—The Cat Who Talked to Ghosts. l.t. ed. 1991. (General Ser.). 300p. 21.95 (*0-8161-5081-8*, Macmillan Reference USA) Gale Group.
—The Cat Who Talked to Ghosts. 1990. 224p. 15.95 o.p. (*0-399-13477-8*, G. P. Putnam's Sons) Penguin Putnam Bks. for Young Readers.
—The Cat Who Talked to Ghosts. unabr. ed. 1994. (Cat Who Ser.). audio 32.95 (*0-7887-0050-2*, 94249E7); audio 42.00 Recorded Bks., LLC.

—The Cat Who Talked to Ghosts. 1990. 13.04 (*0-606-13254-6*) Turtleback Bks.
—The Cat Who Talked Turkey. 2003. 288p. 23.95 (*0-399-15107-9*) Putnam Publishing Group, The.
—The Cat Who Turned on & Off. 1986. (Cat Who Ser.). 272p. mass mkt. 6.99 (*0-515-08794-7*, Jove) Berkley Publishing Group.
—The Cat Who Turned on & Off. l.t. ed. 1992. (Nightingale Ser.). 285p. 14.95 o.p. (*0-8161-4815-5*, Macmillan Reference USA) Gale Group.
—The Cat Who Turned on & Off. unabr. ed. 1991. (Cat Who Ser.). audio 44.00 (*1-55690-094-5*, 91402E7) Recorded Bks., LLC.
—The Cat Who Turned on & Off. 1986. 11.60 o.p. (*0-606-13255-4*) Turtleback Bks.
—The Cat Who Wasn't There. 1993. (Cat Who Ser.). 288p. mass mkt. 6.99 (*0-515-11127-9*, Jove) Berkley Publishing Group.
—The Cat Who Wasn't There. l.t. ed. 1993. (General Ser.). 367p. 17.95 o.p. (*0-8161-5694-8*); lib. bdg. 21.95 (*0-8161-5693-X*) Gale Group. (Macmillan Reference USA).
—The Cat Who Wasn't There. abr. ed. (Super Sound Buy, Dove Ser.). 1994. audio 8.99 o.p. (*0-7871-0071-4*, 390494, Dove Audio); 1993. 16.95 o.p. (*1-55800-667-2*) NewStar Media, Inc.
—The Cat Who Wasn't There. 1992. 240p. 18.95 o.p. (*0-399-13780-7*, G. P. Putnam's Sons) Penguin Group (USA) Inc.
—The Cat Who Wasn't There. 1993. 13.04 (*0-606-12649-X*) Turtleback Bks.
—The Cat Who Wasn't There; The Cat Who Blew the Whistle. abr. ed. 1999. audio 25.00 (*0-7871-1901-6*, Dove Audio) NewStar Media, Inc.
—The Cat Who Went into the Closet. 1994. (Cat Who Ser.). 288p. mass mkt. 6.99 (*0-515-11332-8*, Jove) Berkley Publishing Group.
—The Cat Who Went into the Closet. l.t. ed. 1993. 24.95 o.p. (*1-56895-050-0*, Wheeler Publishing, Inc.) Gale Group.
—The Cat Who Went into the Closet. abr. ed. 1993. (Jim Qwilleran Mystery Ser.). audio 16.95 o.p. (*1-55800-785-7*, 390495) NewStar Media, Inc.
—The Cat Who Went into the Closet. 1993. (Cat Who Ser.). 240p. 19.95 o.p. (*0-399-13830-7*, G. P. Putnam's Sons) Penguin Group (USA) Inc.
—The Cat Who Went into the Closet. 5.98 o.p. (*0-8317-5327-7*) Smithmark Pubs., Inc.
—The Cat Who Went into the Closet. 1994. 13.04 (*0-606-13256-2*) Turtleback Bks.
—The Cat Who Went Underground. 1989. (Cat Who Ser.). 288p. mass mkt. 6.99 (*0-515-10123-0*, Jove) Berkley Publishing Group.
—The Cat Who Went Underground. l.t. ed. 1990. (General Ser.). 324p. 19.95 o.p. (*0-8161-4941-0*, Macmillan Reference USA) Gale Group.
—The Cat Who Went Underground. 1989. (Cat Who. . . Ser.). 224p. 14.95 o.p. (*0-399-13431-X*, G. P. Putnam's Sons) Penguin Putnam Bks. for Young Readers.
—The Cat Who Went Underground. unabr. ed. 2000. (Cat Who Ser.). audio 32.95 (*1-55690-803-2*, 93112) Recorded Bks., LLC.
—The Cat Who Went Underground. 1989. 13.04 (*0-606-13257-0*) Turtleback Bks.
—The Cat Who Went up the Creek. 2002. 240p. 23.95 o.s.i (*0-399-14675-X*) Penguin Group (USA) Inc.
—The Cat Who Went up the Creek. abr. ed. 2002. audio 17.95 o.s.i (*0-399-14819-1*, Putnam Berkley Audio) Putnam Publishing Group, The.
—El Gato Que Leia del Reves. 1997. Tr. of Cat Who Could Read Backwards. (SPA.). 248p. 14.58 (*84-01-47431-0*) Plaza & Janés Editories, S.A. ESP. *Dist:* Distribooks, Inc., Lectorum Pubns., Inc.
—The Private Life of the Cat Who... Tales of Koko & Yum Yum from the Journal of James Macintosh Quilleran. l.t. ed. 2003. 109p. 32.95 (*0-7862-5692-3*) Thorndike Pr.
—The Private Life of the Cat Who... Tales of Koko & Yum Yum from the Journals of James Mackintosh Qwilleran. 2003. 144p. 10.95 (*0-399-15132-X*, Putnam & Grosset) Putnam Publishing Group, The.
—Three Complete Novels. 2002. 803p. 14.98 (*0-399-14813-2*) Penguin Group (USA) Inc.
The Cat Who Could Read Backwards. 2002. audio 19.95 (*0-7887-5430-0*, 00144) Recorded Bks., LLC.

**KOSCUISKO, ANDREJ (FICTITIOUS CHARACTER)—FICTION**

Matthews, Susan R. Exchange of Hostages. 1997. pap. 5.99 (*0-380-78913-2*, Avon Bks.) Morrow/Avon.
—The Hour of Judgement. 1999. 272p. mass mkt. 5.99 (*0-380-80314-3*, Eos) Morrow/Avon.
—Prisoner of Conscience. 1998. mass mkt. 3.99 (*0-380-78914-0*, Eos) Morrow/Avon.

**KOSLOW, LEIGH (FICTITIOUS CHARACTER)—FICTION**

Claire, Edie. Never Buried. 1999. 256p. mass mkt. 5.99 o.s.i (*0-451-19788-7*, Signet Bks.) NAL.
—Never Buried. l.t. ed. 2002. (Mystery Ser.). 333p. 28.95 (*0-7862-4737-1*) Thorndike Pr.
—Never Preach Past Noon. 2000. (Leigh Koslow Mysteries Ser.). 272p. mass mkt. 5.99 (*0-451-20144-2*, Signet Bks.) NAL.
—Never Preach Past Noon: A Leigh Koslow Mystery. l.t. ed. 2001. (Thorndike Mystery Ser.). 392p. 28.95 (*0-7862-3177-7*) Thorndike Pr.
—Never Sorry. 1999. (Leigh Koslow Mysteries Ser.). 272p. mass mkt. 5.99 o.s.i (*0-451-19885-9*, Signet Bks.) NAL.
—Never Tease a Siamese. l.t. ed. 2002. (Paperback Ser.). 424p. pap. 25.95 (*0-7862-4980-3*) Gale Group.
—Never Tease a Siamese. 2002. (Leigh Koslow Mysteries Ser.). 272p. mass mkt. 5.99 (*0-451-20683-5*, Signet Bks.) NAL.

**KOVAK, MILTON (FICTITIOUS CHARACTER)—FICTION**

Cooper, Susan Rogers. Chasing Away the Devil. 1993. (Mystery Ser.). per. (*0-373-26129-2*, 1-26129-6, Harlequin Bks.) Harlequin Enterprises, Ltd.
—Chasing Away the Devil. 1991. 192p. 16.95 o.p. (*0-312-06316-4*, Saint Martin's Minotaur) St. Martin's Pr.
—Doctors & Lawyers & Such. 1995. 256p. 21.95 o.p. (*0-312-13468-1*, Saint Martin's Minotaur) St. Martin's Pr.
—Houston in the Rearview Mirror. 1992. (WWL Mystery Ser.: No. 95). per. (*0-373-26095-4*, 1-26095-9, Harlequin Bks.) Harlequin Enterprises, Ltd.
—Houston in the Rearview Mirror. 1990. 160p. 14.95 o.p. (*0-312-03843-7*, Saint Martin's Minotaur) St. Martin's Pr.
—Lying Wonders: A Sheriff Milt Kovak Mystery. 2003. 224p. 22.95 (*0-312-29056-X*, Saint Martin's Minotaur) St. Martin's Pr.
—The Man in the Green Chevy. 1991. reprint ed. per. (*0-373-26071-7*, Harlequin Bks.) Harlequin Enterprises, Ltd.
—The Man in the Green Chevy. abr. ed. 1997. audio 17.00 (*1-883268-46-X*) Spellbinders, Inc.
—The Man in the Green Chevy. 1989. 208p. 15.95 o.p. (*0-312-02604-8*, Saint Martin's Minotaur) St. Martin's Pr.
—Other People's Houses. 1992. per. (*0-373-26112-8*, 1-26112-2, Harlequin Bks.) Harlequin Enterprises, Ltd.
—Other People's Houses. pap. 3.99 (*0-373-05139-5*); 1990. 176p. 14.95 o.p. (*0-312-05139-5*, Saint Martin's Minotaur) St. Martin's Pr.

**KOZAK, THEA (FICTITIOUS CHARACTER)—FICTION**

Clark, Katharine. Steal Away. 368p. 1999. mass mkt. 6.50 o.s.i (*0-449-00319-1*); 1998. 24.00 o.s.i (*0-449-00276-4*) Ballantine Bks. (Fawcett).
Flora, Kate. Chosen for Death. 2003. 256p. pap. 13.00 (*1-932325-00-X*) Crum Creek Pr.
—Chosen for Death. 288p. 1995. mass mkt. 4.99 (*0-8125-3429-8*); 1994. 20.95 o.p. (*0-312-85598-2*) Doherty, Tom Assocs., LLC. (Forge Bks.).
—Death at the Wheel. (Thea Kozak Mystery Ser.). 320p. 1998. mass mkt. 5.99 (*0-8125-6484-7*); 1996. 22.95 o.p. (*0-312-85599-0*) Doherty, Tom Assocs., LLC. (Forge Bks.).
—Death in a Funhouse Mirror. 1995. 352p. 23.95 o.p. (*0-312-85600-8*); Vol. 1. 1996. mass mkt. 5.99 o.p. (*0-8125-3432-8*) Doherty, Tom Assocs., LLC. (Forge Bks.).
—Death in Paradise. 2000. (Thea Kozak Mystery Ser.). 352p. mass mkt. 6.99 (*0-8125-7157-6*, Tor Bks.); 24.95 (*0-312-86398-5*, Forge Bks.) Doherty, Tom Assocs., LLC.
—An Educated Death. 384p. 1999. mass mkt. 6.99 (*0-8125-7156-8*); 1997. 23.95 (*0-312-86079-X*) Doherty, Tom Assocs., LLC. (Forge Bks.).
—Liberty or Death: A Thea Kozack Mystery. 2003. (Thea Kozak Ser.). 336p. 24.95 (*0-312-87791-9*, Forge Bks.) Doherty, Tom Assocs., LLC.

**KOZOL, TONY (FICTITIOUS CHARACTER)—FICTION**

Ripley, J. R. The Body from Ipanema: A Tony Kozol Mystery. 2002. (Tony Kozol Mystery Ser.: Vol. 4). 244p. (YA). kivar 22.95 (*1-892695-08-1*) Long Wind Publishing.
—Lost in Austin. 2002. (WWL Mystery Ser.: No. 417). 253p. mass mkt. (*0-373-26417-8*, 1-26417-5, Worldwide Library) Harlequin Enterprises, Ltd.
—Lost in Austin: Tony Kozol Mystery. 2001. (Tony Kozol Mystery Ser.: Vol. 3). 246p. 19.95 (*1-892695-06-5*) Long Wind Publishing.
—Stiff in the Freezer: A Tony Kozol Mystery. 1998. 159p. 19.95 (*1-892339-04-8*) Beachfront Publishing.

**KRAMER, MERRY (FICTITIOUS CHARACTER)—FICTION**

Roper, Gayle G. Caught in a Bind. 2000. (Amhearst Mystery Ser.). 320p. pap. 10.99 (*0-310-21850-0*) Zondervan.
—Caught in the Act. 2000. (Five Star Christian Fiction Ser.). 311p. 24.95 (*0-7862-2776-1*, Five Star) Gale Group.
—Caught in the Act? 1998. (Amhearst Mystery Ser.: 2). 272p. pap. 10.99 (*0-310-21909-4*) Zondervan.
—Caught in the Middle. 1997. (Amhearst Mystery Ser.: Vol. 1). 240p. pap. 10.99 (*0-310-20995-1*) Zondervan.

**KRAMER, TROMPIE (FICTITIOUS CHARACTER)—FICTION**

McClure, James. The Artful Egg. l.t. ed. 1986. 19.95 o.p. (*1-55504-011-X*, 247) BBC Audiobooks America.
—The Artful Egg. 1985. 283p. 13.95 o.p. (*0-394-53472-7*, Pantheon) Knopf Publishing Group.
—The Artful Egg. 1986. 5.95 (*0-07-544541-7*) McGraw-Hill Cos., The.
—The Blood of an Englishman. 1981. 288p. 11.00 o.p. (*0-06-013046-6*) HarperCollins Pubs.
—The Blood of an Englishman. l.t. ed. 1982. (Ulverscroft Large Print Ser.). 498p. 29.99 o.p. (*0-7089-0744-X*, Ulverscroft) Thorpe, F. A. Pubs. GBR. *Dist:* Ulverscroft Large Print Bks., Ltd., Ulverscroft Large Print Canada, Ltd.
—The Caterpillar Cop. 1973. (Harper Novel of Suspense Ser.). 240p. 7.95 o.p. (*0-06-012897-6*) HarperCollins Pubs.
—The Caterpillar Cop. 1982. reprint ed. pap. 2.95 o.s.i (*0-394-71058-4*, Pantheon) Knopf Publishing Group.
—Four & Twenty Virgins. l.t. ed. 1990. (Magna Large Print Ser.). 258p. o.p. (*1-85057-723-4*) Magna Large Print Bks. GBR. *Dist:* Ulverscroft Large Print Canada, Ltd.
—The Gooseberry Fool. 1974. (Novel of Suspense Ser.). 224p. 7.95 o.p. (*0-06-012898-4*) HarperCollins Pubs.
—Imago. 1988. 16.95 o.p. (*0-89296-273-9*) Mysterious Pr.
—Imago. 1989. mass mkt. 4.50 o.s.i (*0-445-40729-8*, Mysterious Pr. Paperback Bks.) Warner Bks., Inc.
—Rogue Eagle. 1976. 256p. 8.95 o.p. (*0-06-012949-2*) HarperCollins Pubs.
—Snake. 1976. (Harper Novel of Suspense Ser.). 224p. o.p. (*0-06-012884-4*) HarperCollins Pubs.
—The Song Dog. l.t. ed. 1992. (General Ser.). 408p. 20.95 o.p. (*0-8161-5344-2*, Macmillan Reference USA) Gale Group.
—The Song Dog. 1991. 17.95 (*0-89296-274-7*) Mysterious Pr.
—The Song Dog. 1992. 304p. mass mkt. 4.99 o.s.i (*0-446-40186-2*, Mysterious Pr. Paperback Bks.) Warner Bks., Inc.
—The Steam Pig. 1972. (Harper Novel of Suspense Ser.). 256p. 7.95 o.p. (*0-06-012896-8*) HarperCollins Pubs.
—The Steam Pig. l.t. ed. 1990. (Magna Large Print Ser.). 373p. o.p. (*1-85057-635-1*) Magna Large Print Bks. GBR. *Dist:* Ulverscroft Large Print Canada, Ltd.
—The Sunday Hangman. 1977. (Harper Novel of Suspense Ser.). o.p. (*0-06-012859-3*) HarperCollins Pubs.

**KRAYCHIK, STAN (FICTITIOUS CHARACTER)—FICTION**

Michaels, Grant. Body to Dye For. 1991. (Stonewall Inn Editions Ser.: Vol. 1). 241p. pap. 11.95 (*0-312-05825-X*, Saint Martin's Griffin); 1990. 17.95 o.p. (*0-312-04273-6*, Saint Martin's Minotaur) St. Martin's Pr.
—Dead As a Doornail. (Stan Kraychik Mystery Ser.). 256p. 1999. pap. 12.95 (*0-312-20644-5*, Saint Martin's Griffin); 1998. 22.95 o.p. (*0-312-18077-2*, Saint Martin's Minotaur) St. Martin's Pr.
—Dead on Your Feet. 256p. 1993. 12.99 o.p. (*0-312-09781-6*, Saint Martin's Minotaur); 4th ed. 1994. (Stonewall Inn Editions Ser.: Vol. 1). pap. 11.95 (*0-312-11457-5*, Saint Martin's Griffin) St. Martin's Pr.
—Love You to Death. (Stonewall Inn Editions Ser.). 1993. 10.95 (*0-312-08841-8*, Saint Martin's Griffin); 1992. 256p. 18.95 (*0-312-07027-6*, Saint Martin's Minotaur) St. Martin's Pr.
—Mask for a Diva. 1996. 304p. pap. 10.95 (*0-312-14120-3*, Saint Martin's Griffin); 1994. 272p. 20.95 o.p. (*0-312-11462-1*, Saint Martin's Minotaur) St. Martin's Pr.
—Time to Check Out: A Stan Kraychik Mystery. 1996. 272p. 21.95 o.p. (*0-312-14434-2*, Saint Martin's Minotaur); 1997. 256p. reprint ed. pap. 12.95 (*0-312-15673-1*, NPB 0273, Saint Martin's Griffin) St. Martin's Pr.

**KREIZLER, LASZLO (FICTITIOUS CHARACTER)—FICTION**

Carr, Caleb. The Alienist. 1995. 608p. mass mkt. 7.99 (*0-553-57299-7*); mass mkt. 6.99 o.s.i (*0-553-84001-0*) Bantam Bks.
—The Alienist. unabr. ed. 1995. audio 104.00 (*0-7366-2898-3*, 3598) Books on Tape, Inc.
—The Alienist. l.t. ed. 1994. pap. 22.95 o.p. (*1-56895-078-0*, Wheeler Publishing, Inc.) Gale Group.
—The Alienist. 1994. 496p. 29.95 o.s.i (*0-679-41779-6*) Random Hse., Inc.
—The Alienist. abr. ed. 1994. audio 22.00 (*0-671-88757-2*, 492028, Simon & Schuster Audioworks) Simon & Schuster Audio.
—The Angel of Darkness. 1998. mass mkt. 7.99 o.s.i (*0-345-42514-6*); 768p. mass mkt. 7.99 (*0-345-42763-7*) Ballantine Bks.
—The Angel of Darkness. unabr. ed. 1998. audio 72.00 (*0-7366-4114-9*, 4619-A); audio 72.00 (*0-7366-4115-7*, 4619-B) Books on Tape, Inc.
—The Angel of Darkness. l.t. ed. 1999. pap. 25.95 o.p. (*0-7838-8242-4*, Macmillan Reference USA) Gale Group.
—The Angel of Darkness. abr. ed. 1997. audio 25.00 (*0-671-57748-4*, 595482, Simon & Schuster Audioworks) Simon & Schuster Audio.

**KRISTOS, BROTHER (FICTITIOUS CHARACTER)—FICTION**

Sanders, Lawrence. Capital Crimes. 1990. 352p. mass mkt. 7.50 o.s.i (*0-425-12164-X*) Berkley Publishing Group.
—Capital Crimes. l.t. ed. 1990. (General Ser.). 432p. 16.95 o.p. (*0-8161-4929-1*); lib. bdg. 21.95 o.p. (*0-8161-4924-0*) Gale Group. (Macmillan Reference USA).
—Capital Crimes. 1989. 19.95 o.p. (*0-399-13426-3*, G. P. Putnam's Sons) Penguin Putnam Bks. for Young Readers.

**KRUEGER, FREDDY (FICTITIOUS CHARACTER)—FICTION**

Spencer, James. The Nightmare Never Ends: The Official History of Freddy Krueger & the Nightmare on Elm Street Films. 1992. (Illus.). 224p. pap. 17.95 o.s.i (*0-8065-1368-3*, Citadel Pr.) Kensington Publishing Corp.

**KRUGER, DAN (FICTITIOUS CHARACTER)—FICTION**

Cormany, Michael. Lost Daughter. 1991. 224p. reprint ed. pap. 3.50 (*0-8439-3063-2*) Dorchester Publishing Co., Inc.
—Polaroid Man. 1993. 240p. reprint ed. pap. 3.99 (*0-8439-3542-1*) Dorchester Publishing Co., Inc.
—Red Winter. 1991. 224p. (Orig.). reprint ed. pap. 3.50 (*0-8439-3142-6*) Dorchester Publishing Co., Inc.
—Red Winter. 1991. (Orig.). 2.99 o.p. (*0-517-06332-8*) Random Hse. Value Publishing.
—Rich or Dead. 1991. 208p. reprint ed. pap. 3.50 (*0-8439-3186-8*) Dorchester Publishing Co., Inc.

**KRUGER, HERBIE (FICTITIOUS CHARACTER)—FICTION**

Gardner, John E. Confessor. l.t. ed. 1995. 25.95 (*1-56895-280-5*, Wheeler Publishing, Inc.) Gale Group.
—Confessor. 1995. 560p. 22.50 (*1-883402-25-5*, Scribner) Simon & Schuster.
—Confessor. 2000. 349p. 27.50 (*0-593-01913-X*); 445p. pap. 10.95 (*0-552-14472-X*) Transworld Publishers Ltd. GBR. *Dist:* Trafalgar Square.

**KRUSE, KIMMY (FICTITIOUS CHARACTER)—FICTION**

Cooper, Susan Rogers. Funny As a Dead Comic. 1993. 224p. 18.95 o.p. (*0-312-09815-4*, Saint Martin's Minotaur) St. Martin's Pr.
—Funny as a Dead Relative. 1994. 224p. 19.95 o.p. (*0-312-11438-9*, Saint Martin's Minotaur) St. Martin's Pr.

## L

**LABATARDE, MAGDALENE (FICTITIOUS CHARACTER)—FICTION**

Gellis, Roberta. Bone of Contention: A Magdalene la Batarde Mystery. mass mkt. (*0-7653-4007-0*, Tor Bks.); 2002. 432p. 25.95 (*0-7653-0019-2*, Forge Bks.) Doherty, Tom Assocs., LLC.
—A Mortal Bane. 2001. 352p. mass mkt. 6.99 (*0-8125-7236-X*, Tor Bks.) Doherty, Tom Assocs., LLC.
—A Personal Devil. 2001. 320p. 23.95 (*0-312-86998-3*, Forge Bks.) Doherty, Tom Assocs., LLC.

**LACEY, MEG (FICTITIOUS CHARACTER)—FICTION**

Bowers, Elisabeth. Ladies' Night. 1988. (International Women's Crime Ser.). 238p. pap. 8.95 o.p. (*0-931188-65-2*, Seal Pr.) Avalon Publishing Group.
—No Forwarding Address. 288p. 1991. 18.95 o.p. (*1-878067-13-3*); 1994. reprint ed. pap. 10.95 o.p. (*1-878067-46-X*) Avalon Publishing Group. (Seal Pr.).

**LA FORGE, GEORDI (FICTITIOUS CHARACTER)—FICTION**

Carey, Diane L. Ghost Ship. (Star Trek, The Next Generation Ser.: No. 1). 1991. mass mkt. 5.50 (*0-671-74608-1*); 1990. mass mkt. 4.50 o.s.i (*0-671-73515-2*); 1988. E-Book 6.99 (*0-7434-1213-3*) Simon & Schuster. (Star Trek).

DeWeese, Gene. The Peacekeepers. (Star Trek, The Next Generation Ser.: No. 2). 1990. mass mkt. 5.50 (*0-671-73653-1*); 1988. E-Book 6.99 (*0-7434-1214-1*); 1988. mass mkt. 3.95 o.s.i (*0-671-66929-X*) Simon & Schuster. (Star Trek).

Dillard, J. M. First Contact. abr. ed. 1996. (Star Trek Ser.: No. 8). audio 18.00 (*0-671-57391-8*, Simon & Schuster Audioworks) Simon & Schuster Audio.

—Generations. (Star Trek Ser.: No. 7). 1995. (Illus.). 304p. mass mkt. 5.99 (*0-671-53753-9*); 1994. 288p. 20.00 o.p. (*0-671-51742-2*) Simon & Schuster. (Star Trek).

—Generations. 1994. (Star Trek Ser.: No. 7). pap. 17.00 incl. audio (*0-671-51996-4*, Simon & Schuster Audioworks) Simon & Schuster Audio.

Dillard, J. M. & Berman, Rick. Insurrection. 1998. (Star Trek Ser.: No. 9). 304p. 22.00 o.s.i (*0-671-02447-7*, Star Trek) Simon & Schuster.

Duane, Diane. Dark Mirror. 1993. (Star Trek, The Next Generation Ser.). 352p. 22.00 o.p. (*0-671-79377-2*, Star Trek) Simon & Schuster.

—Dark Mirror. Ryan, Kevin, ed. 1994. (Star Trek, The Next Generation Ser.). 352p. reprint ed. mass mkt. 5.99 (*0-671-79438-8*, Star Trek) Simon & Schuster.

—Dark Mirror. abr. ed. 1996. (Star Trek Ser.). audio 17.00 (*0-671-87974-X*, Simon & Schuster Audioworks) Simon & Schuster Audio.

Friedman, Michael Jan. All Good Things. 1994. (Star Trek Ser.). 256p. o.p. (*0-671-50014-7*, Atria) Simon & Schuster.

—Relics. (Star Trek, The Next Generation Ser.). E-Book 6.99 (*0-7434-2074-8*, Star Trek) Simon & Schuster.

—Relics. Stern, Dave, ed. 1992. (Star Trek, The Next Generation Ser.). 256p. mass mkt. 5.50 (*0-671-86476-9*, Star Trek) Simon & Schuster.

—Relics. abr. ed. 1995. (Star Trek Ser.). audio 17.00 (*0-671-86528-5*, Simon & Schuster Audioworks) Simon & Schuster Audio.

—Stargazer: Three, Bk. 3. 2003. (Star Trek, The Next Generation Ser.). 288p. mass mkt. 6.99 (*0-7434-4852-9*, Star Trek) Simon & Schuster.

Friesner, Esther M. To Storm Heaven. 1997. (Star Trek, The Next Generation Ser.: No. 46). (Illus.). 304p. pap. 5.99 (*0-671-56838-8*, Star Trek) Simon & Schuster.

Hugh, Dafydd ab. Balance of Power. Ryan, Kevin, ed. 1994. (Star Trek, The Next Generation Ser.: No. 33). 304p. mass mkt. 5.50 (*0-671-52003-2*, Star Trek) Simon & Schuster.

Somtow, S. P. Do Comets Dream? 2003. (Star Trek, The Next Generation Ser.). 288p. pap. 6.99 (*0-7434-1130-7*, Star Trek) Simon & Schuster.

Thompson, W. R. Infiltrator. 1996. (Star Trek, The Next Generation Ser.: No. 42). 288p. mass mkt. 5.99 (*0-671-56831-0*, Star Trek) Simon & Schuster.

Vornholt, John. Rogue Saucer. 1996. (Star Trek, The Next Generation Ser.: No. 39). 288p. mass mkt. 5.99 (*0-671-54917-0*, Star Trek) Simon & Schuster.

**LAIDLAW, JACK (FICTITIOUS CHARACTER)—FICTION**

McIlvanney, William. The Big Man. 1986. 320p. 16.95 o.p. (*0-688-06405-1*, Morrow, William & Co.) Morrow/Avon.

—Laidlaw. 1993. 224p. pap. 15.00 (*0-15-648109-X*) Harcourt Trade Pubs.

—Laidlaw. (International Crime Ser.). 1982. pap. 2.95 o.s.i (*0-394-73338-X*); 1977. 7.95 o.p. (*0-394-41253-2*) Knopf Publishing Group. (Pantheon).

—The Papers of Tony Veitch. 1993. 256p. pap. 9.95 (*0-15-670828-0*, Harvest Bks.) Harcourt Trade Pubs.

—The Papers of Tony Veitch. 1983. 256p. 12.95 o.p. (*0-394-42437-9*, Pantheon) Knopf Publishing Group.

—Strange Loyalties. 1993. (Harvest Book Ser.). 288p. pap. 9.95 (*0-15-685644-1*, Harvest Bks.) Harcourt Trade Pubs.

—Strange Loyalties. 1992. 20.00 o.p. (*0-688-11413-X*, Morrow, William & Co.) Morrow/Avon.

**LAIRD, ANNIE (FICTITIOUS CHARACTER)—FICTION**

Green, George Dawes. The Juror. unabr. ed. 1997. audio 69.95 Eye in the Ear Inc.

—The Juror. l.t. ed. 1995. 27.95 (*1-56895-220-1*, Wheeler Publishing, Inc.) Gale Group.

—The Juror. 2001. audio 69.95 (*0-7531-0043-6*, 960307); 1999. audio compact disk 99.95 (*0-7531-0709-0*, 107090) ISIS Audio Bks. GBR. *Dist:* Ulverscroft Large Print Bks., Ltd.

—The Juror. 415p. pap. 5.98 o.p. (*0-7651-0302-8*) Smithmark Pubs., Inc.

—The Juror. abr. ed. 1995. audio 17.00 (*1-57042-135-8*, 391401) Time Warner AudioBooks.

—The Juror. 1995. 432p. 21.95 o.s.i (*0-446-51885-9*); 464p. reprint ed. mass mkt. 6.99 o.s.i (*0-446-60269-8*) Warner Bks., Inc.

**LAKE, BARRETT (FICTITIOUS CHARACTER)—FICTION**

Erickson, Lynn. Searching for Sarah. 1999. 352p. mass mkt. 5.99 o.s.i (*0-515-12699-3*, Jove) Berkley Publishing Group.

Singer, Shelley. Following Jane. 1993. (Barrett Lake Mystery Ser.). 256p. (Orig.). mass mkt. 4.50 o.s.i (*0-451-17523-9*, Signet Bks.) NAL.

—Interview with Mattie: A Barrett Lake Mystery. 1995. (Barrett Lake Mystery Ser.). 288p. mass mkt. 4.99 o.s.i (*0-451-18492-0*, Signet Bks.) NAL.

—Picture of David. 1993. (Barrett Lake Mystery Ser.: No. 2). 256p. (Orig.). mass mkt. 4.50 o.p. (*0-451-17699-5*, Signet Bks.) NAL.

—Searching for Sara. 1994. (Barrett Lake Mystery Ser.: No. 3). 256p. (Orig.). mass mkt. 4.50 o.p. (*0-451-17985-4*, Signet Bks.) NAL.

**LAKE, CONNIE (FICTITIOUS CHARACTER)—FICTION**

Truman, Margaret. Murder on Embassy Row. 1985. (Capital Crime Myteries Ser.). 352p. mass mkt. 6.99 (*0-449-20621-1*, Fawcett) Ballantine Bks.

—Murder on Embassy Row. l.t. ed. 1984. (General Ser.). 16.95 o.p. (*0-8161-3727-7*); 9.95 o.p. (*0-8161-3765-X*) Gale Group. (Macmillan Reference USA).

—Murder on Embassy Row. 1993. audio 49.00 (*1-56544-042-0*, 250027); audio Literate Ear, Inc.

—Murder on Embassy Row. 1984. 297p. 15.95 o.p. (*0-87795-594-8*, Morrow, William & Co.) Morrow/Avon.

**LAKEN, DARCY (FICTITIOUS CHARACTER)—FICTION**

Bennett, Cherie. Sunset after Hours. 1993. (Sunset After Dark Ser.). 224p. (gr. 7 up). mass mkt. 3.50 o.s.i (*0-425-13666-3*) Berkley Publishing Group.

**LAMAR, KATLIN (FICTITIOUS CHARACTER)—FICTION**

Board, Sherri L. Angels of Anguish. 1999. (Katlin Lamar Mystery Ser.). 304p. pap. 11.95 (*0-9634767-5-0*) Crime-Zone Bks.

—Blind Belief. 2002. ("A Katlin LaMar Mystery" —Cover Ser.). 284p. pap. 12.95 (*0-9705049-6-9*) Avocet Pr., Inc.

**LAMB, ELIZABETH (FICTITIOUS CHARACTER)—FICTION**

Morison, B. J. The Martini Effect. 1992. (Little Maine Murder Ser.). 17.95 (*0-945980-38-8*) North Country Pr.

**LAMB, MATTHEW (FICTITIOUS CHARACTER)—FICTION**

Maynard, Kenneth. First Lieutenant. 1986. pap. 3.50 o.p. (*0-312-90510-6*, St. Martin's Paperbacks); 1985. 224p. 13.95 o.p. (*0-312-29244-9*) St. Martin's Pr.

—Lamb in Command. 1986. mass mkt. 3.50 (*0-312-90618-8*, St. Martin's Paperbacks); 208p. 13.95 o.p. (*0-312-46435-5*) St. Martin's Pr.

—Lamb in Command. 1986. 199p. (*0-297-78790-X*) Weidenfeld & Nicolson, Ltd. GBR. *Dist:* Trafalgar Square.

—Lieutenant Lamb. 1984. 176p. 10.95 o.p. (*0-312-48371-6*) St. Martin's Pr.

**LAMBROS, JULIA (FICTITIOUS CHARACTER)—FICTION**

Iakovou, Takis & Iakovou, Judy. Go Close Against the Enemy. 1999. (WWL Mystery Ser.: Bk. 314). 256p. per. (*0-373-26314-7*, 1-26314-4, Worldwide Library) Harlequin Enterprises, Ltd.

—Go Close Against the Enemy. 1998. 288p. 23.95 o.p. (*0-312-18587-1*, Saint Martin's Minotaur) St. Martin's Pr.

—So Dear to Wicked Men. 1998. (WWL Mystery Ser.). per. (*0-373-26277-9*, 1-26277-3, Worldwide Library) Harlequin Enterprises, Ltd.

—So Dear to Wicked Men, Vol. 1. 1996. (So Dear to Wicked Men Ser.: Vol. 1). 320p. 22.95 (*0-312-14740-6*, Saint Martin's Minotaur) St. Martin's Pr.

Iakovou, Takis, et al. Deadly Morsels: Another Curse/Red or Green?/Cake Job/Sheep in Wolf's Clothing, 4 bks. in 1. 2003. (WWL Mystery Ser.: No. 452). 384p. mass mkt. (*0-373-26452-6*, Worldwide Library) Harlequin Enterprises, Ltd.

**LAMBROS, NICK (FICTITIOUS CHARACTER)—FICTION**

Iakovou, Takis & Iakovou, Judy. Go Close Against the Enemy. 1999. (WWL Mystery Ser.: Bk. 314). 256p. per. (*0-373-26314-7*, 1-26314-4, Worldwide Library) Harlequin Enterprises, Ltd.

—Go Close Against the Enemy. 1998. 288p. 23.95 o.p. (*0-312-18587-1*, Saint Martin's Minotaur) St. Martin's Pr.

—So Dear to Wicked Men. 1998. (WWL Mystery Ser.). per. (*0-373-26277-9*, 1-26277-3, Worldwide Library) Harlequin Enterprises, Ltd.

—So Dear to Wicked Men, Vol. 1. 1996. (So Dear to Wicked Men Ser.: Vol. 1). 320p. 22.95 (*0-312-14740-6*, Saint Martin's Minotaur) St. Martin's Pr.

Iakovou, Takis, et al. Deadly Morsels: Another Curse/Red or Green?/Cake Job/Sheep in Wolf's Clothing, 4 bks. in 1. 2003. (WWL Mystery Ser.: No. 452). 384p. mass mkt. (*0-373-26452-6*, Worldwide Library) Harlequin Enterprises, Ltd.

**LAMERINO, GLORIA (FICTITIOUS CHARACTER)—FICTION**

Minichino, Camille. The Beryllium Murder. 2000. 272p. 24.00 (*0-688-17207-5*, Morrow, William & Co.) Morrow/Avon.

—The Boric Acid Murder. 2002. (Gloria Lamerino Mystery Ser.). 288p. 23.95 (*0-312-28502-7*, Saint Martin's Minotaur) St. Martin's Pr.

—The Boric Acid Murder. 2002. (Senior Lifestyles Ser.). 28.95 (*0-7862-4810-6*) Thorndike Pr.

—The Helium Murder. 1998. (Periodic Table Mystery Ser.: Bk. 2). 192p. 18.95 (*0-8034-9298-7*, Avalon Bks.) Bouregy, Thomas & Co., Inc.

—The Hydrogen Murder. 1997. (Periodic Table Mystery Ser.: Bk. 1). 228p. 18.95 (*0-8034-9268-5*, Avalon Bks.) Bouregy, Thomas & Co., Inc.

—The Hydrogen Murder. 2003. (WWL Mystery Ser.: No. 467). 256p. mass mkt. (*0-373-26467-4*, Worldwide Library) Harlequin Enterprises, Ltd.

—The Lithium Murder: A Gloria Lamerino Mystery. 1999. 231p. 24.00 (*0-688-16784-5*, Morrow, William & Co.) Morrow/Avon.

**LANDIS, WOODLEY (FICTITIOUS CHARACTER)—FICTION**

Kihn, Greg. The Horror Show. 1997. 274p. pap. text 5.99 (*0-8125-5108-7*); 1996. 352p. 23.95 (*0-312-86045-5*) Doherty, Tom Assocs., LLC. (Tor Bks.).

**LANDON, ARNOLD (FICTITIOUS CHARACTER)—FICTION**

Lewis, Roy. Angel of Death. l.t. ed. 1997. (Magna Large Print Ser.). 335p. o.p. (*0-7505-1204-0*) Magna Large Print Bks. GBR. *Dist:* Ulverscroft Large Print Canada, Ltd.

—Angel of Death. unabr. ed. 1999. audio 69.95 (*1-85903-264-8*) Ulverscroft Audio (U.S.A.).

—Bloodeagle. l.t. ed. 1994. 22.95 o.p. (*0-7927-1928-X*); pap. 20.95 o.p. (*0-7927-1927-1*) BBC Audiobooks America.

—The Cross Bearer. l.t. ed. 1995. (Magna Large Print Ser.). 378p. o.p. (*0-7505-0846-9*) Magna Large Print Bks. GBR. *Dist:* Ulverscroft Large Print Canada, Ltd.

—Cross Bearer: An Arnold Landon Mystery. 1994. 205p. 18.95 o.p. (*0-312-11765-5*, Saint Martin's Minotaur) St. Martin's Pr.

—Dead Secret. l.t. ed. 2002. (Magna Large Print Ser.). 288p. 32.50 (*0-7505-1823-5*) Magna Large Print Bks. GBR. *Dist:* Ulverscroft Large Print Bks., Ltd., Ulverscroft Large Print Canada, Ltd.

—Dead Secret. unabr. ed. 2002. audio 49.95 (*1-85903-513-2*) Soundings, Ltd. GBR. *Dist:* Ulverscroft Large Print Bks., Ltd.

—Dead Secret: An Arnold Landon Mystery. 2001. 256p. 24.00 (*0-7867-0885-9*, Carroll & Graf Pubs.) Avalon Publishing Group.

—The Devil Is Dead. l.t. ed. 1990. 17.95 o.p. (*0-7451-9920-8*, C0638); pap. 15.95 o.p. (*0-7927-0370-7*, C0832) BBC Audiobooks America.

—The Devil Is Dead. 1990. 208p. 15.95 o.p. (*0-312-04851-3*, Saint Martin's Minotaur) St. Martin's Pr.

—A Gathering of Ghosts. 1983. 192p. 10.95 o.p. (*0-312-31788-3*) St. Martin's Pr.

—Men of Subtle Craft. 1988. 192p. 13.95 (*0-312-81789-4*) St. Martin's Pr.

—Most Cunning Workmen. 1986. (Atlantic Ser.). 274 p. (*0-89340-966-9*) BBC Audiobooks America.

—Most Cunning Workmen. 1985. 182 p. 10.95 o.p. (*0-312-54907-5*) St. Martin's Pr.

—A Secret Dying: An Arthur Landon Mystery. l.t. ed. 1993. 21.95 o.p. (*0-7927-1546-2*); pap. 19.95 o.p. (*0-7927-1545-4*) BBC Audiobooks America.

—A Secret Dying: An Arthur Landon Mystery. 1993. 17.95 o.p. (*0-312-08887-6*, Saint Martin's Minotaur) St. Martin's Pr.

—A Wisp of Smoke. 1991. 208p. 17.95 o.p. (*0-312-07123-X*, Saint Martin's Minotaur) St. Martin's Pr.

Lewis, Roy H. Bloodeagle: An Arnold Landon Mystery. 1993. 224p. 19.95 o.p. (*0-312-10431-6*, Saint Martin's Minotaur) St. Martin's Pr.

—Men of Subtle Craft. l.t. ed. 1988. pap. 14.95 o.p. (*1-55504-661-4*, 462) BBC Audiobooks America.

—A Trout in the Milk: An Arnold Landon Novel. l.t. ed. 1988. (Atlantic Large Print Ser.). 285 p. (*1-55504-562-6*) BBC Audiobooks America.

—A Trout in the Milk: An Arnold Landon Novel. 1986. 208p. 13.95 o.p. (*0-312-82009-7*) St. Martin's Pr.

—A Wisp of Smoke. l.t. ed. 1992. (Magna Large Print Ser.). 326p. 29.99 (*0-7505-0355-6*) Magna Large Print Bks. GBR. *Dist:* Ulverscroft Large Print Bks., Ltd.

**LANDRY FAMILY (FICTITIOUS CHARACTERS)—FICTION**

Andrews, V. C. All That Glitters. l.t. ed. 2000. 26.95 (*1-56895-236-8*, Wheeler Publishing, Inc.) Gale Group.

—All That Glitters. 1995. (Landry Ser.). 352p. mass mkt. 7.99 (*0-671-87319-9*, Pocket) Simon & Schuster.

—All That Glitters. Marrow, Linda, ed. 1995. 352p. 23.00 o.p. (*0-671-87574-4*, Atria) Simon & Schuster.

—Hidden Jewel. l.t. ed. (Paperback Bestsellers Ser.). 1997. 459p. pap. 24.95 o.p. (*0-7838-1696-0*); 1996. 26.95 o.p. (*0-7838-1695-2*) Gale Group. (Macmillan Reference USA).

—Hidden Jewel. Marrow, Linda, ed. 1995. 384p. 23.00 o.p. (*0-671-87575-2*, Atria) Simon & Schuster.

—Hidden Jewel. l.t. ed. 1995. (Landry Ser.). 384p. mass mkt. 7.99 (*0-671-87320-2*, Pocket) Simon & Schuster.

—Pearl in the Mist. l.t. ed. 1995. 555p. 19.95 o.p. (*0-7838-1165-9*); 514p. 24.95 (*0-7838-1164-0*) Gale Group. (Macmillan Reference USA).

—Pearl in the Mist. Marrow, Linda, ed. 1994. 384p. 23.00 (*0-671-75937-X*, Atria); mass mkt. 7.99 (*0-671-75936-1*, Pocket) Simon & Schuster.

—Pearl in the Mist. 1994. 14.04 (*0-606-07067-2*) Turtleback Bks.

—Ruby. l.t. ed. 2000. 25.95 o.p. (*1-56895-074-8*, Wheeler Publishing, Inc.) Gale Group.

—Ruby. 1998. (SPA., Illus.). 544p. 12.95 (*84-01-49795-7*, PJ9450) Plaza & Janés Editories, S.A. ESP. *Dist:* Lectorum Pubns., Inc.

—Ruby, unabr. ed. 1997. (Landry Ser.: Vol. 1). audio 97.00 (*0-7887-1088-5*, 94981E7) Recorded Bks., LLC.

—Ruby. 1994. 448p. 22.00 (*0-671-75935-3*, Atria) Simon & Schuster.

—Ruby. Marrow, Linda, ed. 1994. (Landry Ser.). 448p. mass mkt. 7.99 (*0-671-75934-5*, Pocket) Simon & Schuster.

—Ruby. 1994. 14.04 (*0-606-05989-X*) Turtleback Bks.

—Tarnished Gold. l.t. ed. 2000. (Large Print Bks.). 26.95 o.p. (*1-56895-338-0*, Wheeler Publishing, Inc.) Gale Group.

—Tarnished Gold. 1996. (Landry Ser.). 352p. mass mkt. 6.99 (*0-671-87321-0*, Pocket) Simon & Schuster.

—Tarnished Gold. Marrow, Linda, ed. 1996. 320p. 23.00 o.p. (*0-671-87576-0*, Atria) Simon & Schuster.

**LANE, MARK (FICTITIOUS CHARACTER)—FICTION**

Williamson, Kathryn. The Secret in the Rose Room. 1997. 192p. (Orig.). mass mkt. 5.99 o.p. (*1-56315-076-X*) SterlingHouse Pubs., Inc.

**LANGDON, ROBERT (FICTITIOUS CHARACTER)—FICTION**

Brown, Dan. Angels & Demons: A Novel. 2000. E-Book 24.95 (*1-930161-13-1*) Adobe Systems, Inc.

—Angels & Demons: A Novel. l.t. ed. 2003. 768p. 26.95 (*0-375-43318-X*) Random Hse. Large Print.

—Angels & Demons: A Novel. 2003. 592p. 17.95 (*0-7434-8622-6*, Atria); 2000. 448p. 24.95 o.s.i (*0-671-02735-2*, Atria); 2000. E-Book 6.29 (*0-7434-1239-7*, Atria); 2001. (Illus.). 608p. reprint ed. mass mkt. 7.99 (*0-671-02736-0*, Pocket Star) Simon & Schuster.

—Angels & Demons: A Novel. abr. ed. 2003. audio 26.00 (*0-7435-3576-6*); audio compact disk 30.00 (*0-7435-3577-4*) Simon & Schuster Audio. (Simon & Schuster Audioworks).

—The Da Vinci Code: A Novel. 2004. 512p. mass mkt. 7.99 (*0-345-45151-1*, Fawcett) Ballantine Bks.

—The Da Vinci Code: A Novel. unabr. ed. 2003. audio 80.00 (*0-7366-8970-2*) Books on Tape, Inc.

—The Da Vinci Code: A Novel. 2003. 464p. 24.95 (*0-385-50420-9*); E-Book 12.00 (*0-385-50421-7*) Doubleday Publishing.

—The Da Vinci Code: A Novel. abr. ed. 2003. audio 25.95 (*0-7393-0731-2*, Listening Library); audio compact disk 29.95 (*0-7393-0204-3*, RH Audio) Random Hse. Audio Publishing Group.

—The Da Vinci Code: A Novel. l.t. ed. 2003. 752p. 26.95 (*0-375-43230-2*) Random Hse. Large Print.

**LANGDON, SKIP (FICTITIOUS CHARACTER)—FICTION**

Smith, Julie. The Axeman's Jazz. 1992. (Skip Langdon Novel Ser.). 368p. mass mkt. 6.99 (*0-8041-0954-0*, Ivy Bks.) Ballantine Bks.

—The Axeman's Jazz. 1991. 384p. 19.95 o.p. (*0-312-06295-8*, Saint Martin's Minotaur) St. Martin's Pr.

—Crescent City Kill. (Skip Langdon Novel Ser.). 1998. 368p. mass mkt. 6.50 o.s.i (*0-8041-1397-1*, Ivy Bks.); 1997. 326p. 4.99 o.s.i (*0-449-91000-8*, Fawcett) Ballantine Bks.

—House of Blues. 1996. (Skip Langdon Novel Ser.). 352p. reprint ed. mass mkt. 6.99 o.s.i (*0-8041-1342-4*, Ivy Bks.) Ballantine Bks.

—Jazz Funeral. 1994. (Skip Langdon Novel Ser.). 368p. mass mkt. 5.99 o.s.i (*0-8041-1252-5*, Ivy Bks.) Ballantine Bks.

—The Kindness of Strangers. 1997. (Skip Langdon Novel Ser.). mass mkt. 5.99 o.s.i (*0-8041-1273-8*, Ivy Bks.) Ballantine Bks.

—Mean Rooms: A Short Story Collection. 2000. (Five Star Mystery Ser.). 196p. 21.95 (*0-7862-2364-2*, Five Star) Gale Group.
—Mean Woman Blues. mass mkt. (*0-7653-4465-3*, Forge Bks.); E-Book (*0-312-71094-1*, Tor Bks.); 2003. 304p. 24.95 (*0-7653-0552-6*, Forge Bks.) Doherty, Tom Assocs., LLC.
—New Orleans Beat: A Skip Langdon Mystery. 1995. (Skip Langdon Novel Ser.). 368p. mass mkt. 6.50 o.s.i (*0-8041-1336-X*, Ivy Bks.) Ballantine Bks.
—New Orleans Mourning. 1990. (Skip Langdon Novel Ser.). 352p. mass mkt. 6.99 (*0-8041-0738-6*, Ivy Bks.) Ballantine Bks.
—New Orleans Mourning, unabr. ed. 1999. (Skip Langdon Mysteries Ser. ). audio 87.00 (*0-7887-3480-6*, 95775E7) Recorded Bks., LLC.
—New Orleans Mourning. 1990. 384p. 17.95 o.p. (*0-312-03892-5*, Saint Martin's Minotaur) St. Martin's Pr.
—82 Desire. (Skip Langdon Novel Ser.). 1999. 352p. mass mkt. 6.99 (*0-8041-1699-7*, Ivy Bks.); 1998. 320p. 24.00 o.s.i (*0-449-00060-5*, Fawcett) Ballantine Bks.
—82 Desire. l.t. ed. 1999. (Large Print Book Ser.). pap. 24.95 (*1-56895-628-2*, Wheeler Publishing, Inc.) Gale Group.

**LANGE, ELIZABETH (FICTITIOUS CHARACTER)—FICTION**

Clark, Mary Higgins. Weep No More, My Lady. E-Book 9.95 (*1-930161-66-2*) Adobe Systems, Inc.
—Weep No More, My Lady. unabr. ed. 1993. audio 48.00 (*0-7366-2601-8*, 3345) Books on Tape, Inc.
—Weep No More, My Lady. 1993. reprint ed. lib. bdg. 37.95 (*0-89968-446-7*, Lightyear Pr.) Buccaneer Bks., Inc.
—Weep No More, My Lady. 1993. 384p. mass mkt. 3.99 o.s.i (*0-440-21473-4*); reprint ed. mass mkt. 6.99 o.s.i (*0-440-20098-9*) Dell Publishing.
—Weep No More, My Lady. 1997. 384p. pap. 11.95 o.s.i (*0-385-31921-5*) Doubleday Publishing.
—Weep No More, My Lady. l.t. ed. 1988. (General Ser.). 441p. 19.95 o.p. (*0-8161-4367-6*, Macmillan Reference USA) Gale Group.
—Weep No More, My Lady. 2000. E-Book 9.95 (*0-7432-0616-9*, Simon & Schuster); 1998. (Illus.). 336p. mass mkt. 7.99 (*0-671-02558-9*, Pocket); 1987. (Illus.). 320p. bds. 17.45 o.p. (*0-671-55664-9*, Simon & Schuster) Simon & Schuster.
—Weep No More, My Lady. 1987. 12.09 o.p. (*0-606-04108-7*) Turtleback Bks.

**LANGE, LIZBET (FICTITIOUS CHARACTER)—FICTION**

Thrasher, L. L. Charlie's Bones. l.t. ed. 2000. (Dales Large Print Ser.). 304p. pap. (*1-84137-000-2*) Magna Large Print Bks. GBR. *Dist:* Ulverscroft Large Print Bks., Ltd., Ulverscroft Large Print Canada, Ltd.
—Charlie's Bones. 1998. 224p. 21.95 (*1-885173-47-4*) Write Way Publishing.
—Charlie's Web. 2000. 225p. 23.95 (*1-885173-66-0*) Write Way Publishing.

**LANGLEY, INGRID (FICTITIOUS CHARACTER)—FICTION**

Duffy, Margaret. Brass Eagle. 1990. 256p. mass mkt. 3.95 o.s.i (*0-449-21887-2*, Fawcett) Ballantine Bks.
—Brass Eagle. unabr. ed. 1998. audio 83.95 (*1-85903-017-3*) Magna Story Sound GBR. *Dist:* Ulverscroft Large Print Bks., Ltd.
—Brass Eagle. 1989. 15.95 o.p. (*0-312-02880-6*, Saint Martin's Minotaur) St. Martin's Pr.
—Brass Eagle. l.t. ed. 1991. (Ulverscroft Large Print Ser.). 29.99 o.p. (*0-7089-2347-X*, Ulverscroft) Thorpe, F. A. Pubs. GBR. *Dist:* Ulverscroft Large Print Bks., Ltd., Ulverscroft Large Print Canada, Ltd.
—Death of a Raven. 1989. 240p. mass mkt. 3.50 o.s.i (*0-449-21741-8*, Fawcett) Ballantine Bks.
—Death of a Raven. 1988. 224p. 15.95 o.p. (*0-312-02567-X*, Saint Martin's Minotaur) St. Martin's Pr.
—Death of a Raven. l.t. ed. 1990. (Ulverscroft Large Print Ser.). 29.99 o.p. (*0-7089-2202-3*, Ulverscroft) Thorpe, F. A. Pubs. GBR. *Dist:* Ulverscroft Large Print Bks., Ltd., Ulverscroft Large Print Canada, Ltd.
—A Murder of Crows. 1988. mass mkt. 3.50 o.s.i (*0-449-21563-6*, Fawcett) Ballantine Bks.
—A Murder of Crows. 1988. 240p. 15.95 o.p. (*0-312-01483-X*, Saint Martin's Minotaur) St. Martin's Pr.
—A Murder of Crows. l.t. ed. 1989. (Ulverscroft Large Print Ser.). 531p. 29.99 o.p. (*0-7089-1929-4*, Ulverscroft) Thorpe, F. A. Pubs. GBR. *Dist:* Ulverscroft Large Print Bks., Ltd., Ulverscroft Large Print Canada, Ltd.
—Rook-Shoot. l.t. ed. 1993. (Dales Mystery Ser.). 392p. pap. 19.99 (*1-85389-399-4*) Dales Large Print Bks. GBR. *Dist:* Ulverscroft Large Print Bks., Ltd.
—Rook-Shoot. 1991. 240p. 17.95 o.p. (*0-312-06456-X*, Saint Martin's Minotaur) St. Martin's Pr.
—Who Killed Cock Robin? 1990. 224p. 16.95 o.p. (*0-312-04988-9*, Saint Martin's Minotaur) St. Martin's Pr.

**LANGSLOW, MEG (FICTITIOUS CHARACTER)—FICTION**

Andrews, Donna. Crouching Buzzard, Leaping Loon. 2004. 320p. mass mkt. 6.99 (*0-312-99001-4*, St. Martin's Paperbacks); 2003. 304p. 23.95 (*0-312-27731-8*, Saint Martin's Minotaur) St. Martin's Pr.
—Crouching Buzzard, Leaping Loon. l.t. ed. 2003. (Mystery Ser.). 30.45 (*0-7862-5488-2*) Thorndike Pr.
—Murder with Peacocks. l.t. ed. 2002. (Mystery Ser.). 26.95 (*1-57490-388-8*, Beeler Large Print Bks.) Beeler, Thomas T. Publisher.
—Murder with Peacocks. (Meg Langslow Mysteries Ser.). 2000. 320p. mass mkt. 6.50 (*0-312-97063-3*, St. Martin's Paperbacks); 1998. 332p. 23.95 (*0-312-19929-5*, Saint Martin's Minotaur) St. Martin's Pr.
—Murder with Puffins. l.t. ed. 2002. 26.95 (*1-57490-415-9*) Beeler, Thomas T. Publisher.
—Murder with Puffins. 2001. 320p. mass mkt. 6.50 o.s.i (*0-312-97886-3*, St. Martin's Paperbacks); 2000. 281p. 24.95 (*0-312-26221-3*, Saint Martin's Minotaur) St. Martin's Pr.
—Revenge of the Wrought-Iron Flamingos. l.t. ed. 2002. (Mystery Ser.). 419p. 29.95 (*0-7862-3925-5*) Gale Group.
—Revenge of the Wrought-Iron Flamingos. mass mkt. (*0-312-98022-1*, St. Martin's Paperbacks); 2002. 288p. mass mkt. 6.50 (*0-312-98319-0*, St. Martin's Paperbacks); 2001. 304p. 23.95 (*0-312-27729-6*, Saint Martin's Minotaur) St. Martin's Pr.
—We'll Always Have Parrots: A Meg Langslow Mystery. 2004. 304p. 23.95 (*0-312-27732-6*, Saint Martin's Minotaur) St. Martin's Pr.

**LANGSTON, TOM (FICTITIOUS CHARACTER)—FICTION**

Blair, Clifford. The Guns of Sacred Heart. 1991. 192p. 18.95 (*0-8027-4123-1*) Walker & Co.
—Storm over the Lightning L. 1993. 192p. 19.95 (*0-8027-1236-3*) Walker & Co.

**LANNAT, CAPTAIN (FICTITIOUS CHARACTER)—FICTION**

McQuinn, Donald E. The Prisoner Within, Vol. 2. 1997. (Prisoner Within Ser.: Vol. 2). mass mkt. 6.99 o.s.i (*0-345-40044-5*, Del Rey) Ballantine Bks.
—With Full Honors. 1996. (With Full Honors Ser.: Vol. 1). mass mkt. 5.99 o.s.i (*0-345-40045-3*, Del Rey) Ballantine Bks.

**LANNIHAN, WOLF (FICTITIOUS CHARACTER)—FICTION**

Sanders, Lawrence. Tales of the Wolf. 20.95 (*0-8488-0356-6*) Amereon, Ltd.
—Tales of the Wolf. 1986. 240p. mass mkt. 4.50 (*0-380-75145-3*, Avon Bks.) Morrow/Avon.
—Tales of the Wolf: The Cases of Wolf Lannihan. l.t. ed. 1987. 332p. 18.95 o.p. (*0-8161-4289-0*, Macmillan Reference USA) Gale Group.

**LANOIS, ADELE (FICTITIOUS CHARACTER)—FICTION**

MacColl, Mary-Rose. No Safe Place: A Novel about Sex & Power. 1997. 180p. pap. 12.95 o.p. (*1-86448-174-9*) Allen & Unwin Pty., Ltd. AUS. *Dist:* Independent Pubs. Group.

**LANSING, CLIFF (FICTITIOUS CHARACTER)—FICTION**

Hackler, Micah S. Coyote Returns: A Sherrif Lansing Mystery. 1996. 336p. mass mkt. 5.50 o.s.i (*0-440-22094-7*) Dell Publishing.
—The Dark Canyon, Vol. 4. 1997. (Sheriff Lansing Mystery Ser.: Vol. 4). 384p. mass mkt. 5.99 o.s.i (*0-440-22358-X*, Dell Bks.) Dell Publishing.
—Legend of the Dead: A Sheriff Lansing Mystery. 1995. 256p. mass mkt. 5.50 o.s.i (*0-440-22093-9*) Dell Publishing.
—The Shadowcatcher: A Sherrif Lansing Mystery. 1997. (Sheriff Lansing Mystery Ser.: Vol. 3). 320p. mass mkt. 5.99 o.s.i (*0-440-22339-3*) Dell Publishing.

**LARCH, MARIAN (FICTITIOUS CHARACTER)—FICTION**

Paul, Barbara. The Apostrophe Thief. 1994. mass mkt. (*0-373-26155-1*, 1-26155-1, Harlequin Bks.) Harlequin Enterprises, Ltd.
—The Apostrophe Thief: A Mystery with Marian Larch. 1993. 256p. 20.00 o.p. (*0-684-19553-4*, Macmillan Reference USA) Gale Group.
—Fare Play. 1995. 256p. 20.00 (*0-684-19715-4*, Scribner) Simon & Schuster.
—Fare Play. l.t. ed. 1997. (Ulverscroft Large Print Ser.). 400p. 31.50 o.p. (*0-7089-3690-3*, Ulverscroft) Thorpe, F. A. Pubs. GBR. *Dist:* Ulverscroft Large Print Bks., Ltd., Ulverscroft Large Print Canada, Ltd.
—Fare Play: A Mystery with Marian Larch. l.t. ed. 1995. 314p. pap. 20.95 o.p. (*0-7838-1413-5*, Macmillan Reference USA) Gale Group.
—Full Frontal Murder. 1998. (WWL Mystery Ser.). per. (*0-373-26284-1*, 1-26284-9, Worldwide Library) Harlequin Enterprises, Ltd.
—Full Frontal Murder, Bk. 2. 1997. (Full Frontal Murder Ser.: Vol. 2). 256p. 20.50 (*0-684-19716-2*, Scribner) Simon & Schuster.
—Full Frontal Murder: A Mystery with Marian Larch. l.t. ed. 1998. (Mystery Ser.). 319p. 27.95 (*0-7838-8363-3*) Thorndike Pr.
—The Renewable Virgin. 1986. (Mystery Ser.). 192p. mass mkt. 2.95 o.s.i (*0-553-26234-3*) Bantam Bks.
—Renewable Virgin. l.t. ed. 1985. (Nightingale Ser.). 360p. 9.95 o.p. (*0-8161-3888-5*, Macmillan Reference USA) Gale Group.
—Renewable Virgin. 1985. 12.95 o.p. (*0-684-18300-5*, Scribner) Simon & Schuster.
—You Have the Right to Remain Silent. 1993. (Mystery Ser.). mass mkt. (*0-373-26132-2*, 1-26132-0, Harlequin Bks.) Harlequin Enterprises, Ltd.
—You Have the Right to Remain Silent, unabr. ed. 1993. audio 51.00 (*1-55690-836-9*, 93204E7) Recorded Bks., LLC.
—You Have the Right to Remain Silent: A Mystery with Marian Larch. 1992. 256p. 20.00 o.s.i (*0-684-19380-9*, Scribner) Simon & Schuster.

**LARKIN, ELDON (FICTITIOUS CHARACTER)—FICTION**

Kohler, Vincent. Banjo Boy. 1994. 226p. 19.95 o.p. (*0-312-11475-3*, Saint Martin's Minotaur) St. Martin's Pr.
—Rainy North Woods. Isaacson, Dana, ed. 1990. 320p. reprint ed. mass mkt. 3.95 (*0-671-72971-3*, Pocket) Simon & Schuster.
—Rainy North Woods. 1990. 256p. 16.95 o.p. (*0-312-03918-2*, Saint Martin's Minotaur) St. Martin's Pr.
—Raven's Widows. 1997. 256p. text 22.95 o.p. (*0-312-14714-7*, Saint Martin's Minotaur) St. Martin's Pr.
—Rising Dog. 1992. 288p. 18.95 o.p. (*0-312-07075-6*, Saint Martin's Minotaur) St. Martin's Pr.

**LARKIN, POP (FICTITIOUS CHARACTER)—FICTION**

Bates, H. E. The Darling Buds of May. l.t. ed. 1992. (Magna Large Print Ser.). 208p. o.p. (*0-7505-0426-9*) Magna Large Print Bks. GBR. *Dist:* Ulverscroft Large Print Canada, Ltd.
—The Darling Buds of May: A Comedy. 1996. (*0-573-01751-4*) French, Samuel Inc.
—The Darling Buds of May: The Pop Larkin Chronicles, 3 vols. 1993. 352p. reprint ed. pap. 11.00 o.p. (*0-06-097596-2*, Perennial) HarperTrade.
—The Darling Buds of May: The Pop Larkin Chronicles. 1993. 333p. 20.00 o.p. (*0-688-11960-3*, Morrow, William & Co.) Morrow/Avon.
—A Little of What You Fancy, unabr. ed. 1994. audio 54.95 (*0-7451-4221-4*, CAB 904) BBC Audiobooks America.
—When the Green Woods Laugh. unabr. ed. 1992. 39.95 incl. audio (*0-7451-4044-0*, CAB 741) BBC Audiobooks America.

**LARKIN FAMILY (FICTITIOUS CHARACTERS)—FICTION**

Bates, H. E. The Darling Buds of May, Set. unabr. ed. 2001. (Larkin Family Ser.: Bk. 1). audio 34.95 (*0-7451-5780-7*, CAB 178) Chivers Audio Bks. GBR. *Dist:* BBC Audiobooks America.
—The Darling Buds of May. l.t. ed. 1992. (Magna Large Print Ser.). 208p. o.p. (*0-7505-0426-9*) Magna Large Print Bks. GBR. *Dist:* Ulverscroft Large Print Canada, Ltd.
—The Darling Buds of May: A Comedy. 1996. (*0-573-01751-4*) French, Samuel Inc.
—The Darling Buds of May: The Pop Larkin Chronicles, 3 vols. 1993. 352p. reprint ed. pap. 11.00 o.p. (*0-06-097596-2*, Perennial) HarperTrade.
—The Darling Buds of May: The Pop Larkin Chronicles. 1993. 333p. 20.00 o.p. (*0-688-11960-3*, Morrow, William & Co.) Morrow/Avon.
—A Little of What You Fancy, unabr. ed. 1994. audio 54.95 (*0-7451-4221-4*, CAB 904) BBC Audiobooks America.
—When the Green Woods Laugh. unabr. ed. 1992. 39.95 incl. audio (*0-7451-4044-0*, CAB 741) BBC Audiobooks America.

**LAROCHE, RENEE (FICTITIOUS CHARACTER)—FICTION**

LaFavor, Carole. Along the Journey River. 1996. 192p. pap. 10.95 (*1-56341-070-2*); lib. bdg. 22.95 (*1-56341-071-0*) Firebrand Bks.
—Evil Dead Center: A Mystery. 1997. 224p. pap. 11.95 (*1-56341-088-5*); 216p. lib. bdg. 24.95 (*1-56341-089-3*) Firebrand Bks.

**LARSON, JACK (FICTITIOUS CHARACTER)—FICTION**

Geller, Shari P. Fatal Convictions. 1996. 416p. 24.00 o.p. (*0-06-039181-2*) HarperCollins Pubs.
—Fatal Convictions. 1998. 544p. mass mkt. 6.50 o.s.i (*0-06-101223-8*, HarperTorch) Morrow/Avon.

**LARUE, CHARLOTTE (FICTITIOUS CHARACTER)—FICTION**

Colley, Barbara. Death Tidies Up. 2004. 288p. mass mkt. 6.50 (*1-57566-876-9*, Kensington Bks.) Kensington Publishing Corp.
—Death Tidies Up: A Charlotte LaRue Mystery. 2003. 256p. 22.00 (*1-57566-875-0*) Kensington Publishing Corp.
—Death Tidies Up: A Charlotte LaRue Mystery. l.t. ed. 2003. (Senior Lifestyles Ser.). 28.95 (*0-7862-5223-5*) Thorndike Pr.
—Maid for Murder: A Squeaky Clean Charlotte la Rue Mystery. l.t. ed. 2002. 461p. 28.95 o.p. (*0-7862-3947-6*) Gale Group.
—Maid for Murder: A Squeaky Clean Charlotte la Rue Mystery. 288p. 2003. mass mkt. 5.99 (*1-57566-874-2*); 2002. 22.00 (*1-57566-873-4*) Kensington Publishing Corp.
—Polished Off. 2004. 288p. 22.00 (*1-57566-877-7*, Kensington Bks.) Kensington Publishing Corp.

**LASH, ERNEST (FICTITIOUS CHARACTER)—FICTION**

Yalom, Irvin D. Lying on the Couch. 1996. 384p. text 25.00 o.p. (*0-465-04295-3*) Basic Bks.
—Lying on the Couch: A Novel. 1997. 384p. pap. 14.00 (*0-06-092851-4*, Perennial) HarperTrade.

**LASLOW, DEBRA (FICTITIOUS CHARACTER)—FICTION**

Krich, Rochelle Majer. Speak No Evil. 1996. 82p. 21.95 o.p. (*0-89296-584-3*) Mysterious Pr.
—Speak No Evil. 1997. 384p. mass mkt. 6.50 o.p. (*0-446-40505-1*) Warner Bks., Inc.

**LASSIE (FICTITIOUS CHARACTER)—FICTION**

Wells, Rosemary. Lassie Come Home, ERS. 1995. (Illus.). 48p. (J). (gr. 2 up). reprint ed. 16.95 (*0-8050-3794-2*, Holt, Henry & Co. Bks. For Young Readers) Holt, Henry & Co.
—Lassie Come Home: Eric Knight's Original Classic, ERS. 1998. (Illus.). 48p. (YA). (ps up). reprint ed. pap. 7.95 (*0-8050-5995-4*, Holt, Henry & Co. Bks. For Young Readers) Holt, Henry & Co.
Wells, Rosemary & Knight, Eric. Lassie Come Home, ERS. 2000. (Illus.). 64p. (J). (gr. 2-5). 15.95 (*0-8050-6423-0*, Holt, Henry & Co. Bks. For Young Readers) Holt, Henry & Co.

**LASSITER, DANE (FICTITIOUS CHARACTER)—FICTION**

Palmer, Diana. The Case of the Mesmerizing Boss. 1997. (And the Winner Is...Ser.). mass mkt. (*0-373-48343-0*, 1-48343-7, Harlequin Bks.) Harlequin Enterprises, Ltd.

**LASSITER, JAKE (FICTITIOUS CHARACTER)—FICTION**

Levine, Paul. False Dawn. 1993. 320p. 21.95 o.s.i (*0-553-08995-1*) Bantam Bks.
—False Dawn. 1993. audio 15.99 o.s.i (*0-553-47136-8*, RH Audio) Random Hse. Audio Publishing Group.
—The False Dawn. 1994. 368p. mass mkt. 5.99 o.s.i (*0-553-56504-4*) Bantam Bks.
—Flesh & Bones. 1998. (Jake Lassiter Mystery Ser.). 352p. mass mkt. 5.99 (*0-380-72591-6*, Avon Bks.) Morrow/Avon.
—Flesh & Bones: A Jake Lassiter Novel. l.t. ed. 1997. (G. K. Hall Core Ser.). 468p. 26.95 (*0-7838-8065-0*, Macmillan Reference USA) Gale Group.
—Flesh & Bones: A Jake Lassiter Novel. l.t. ed. 1997. 336p. 23.00 (*0-688-14305-9*, Morrow, William & Co.) Morrow/Avon.
—Fool Me Twice. 1996. 352p. mass mkt. 5.99 (*0-380-72590-8*, Avon Bks.) Morrow/Avon.
—Fool Me Twice: A Jake Lassiter Novel. 1996. 356p. 22.00 o.p. (*0-688-14304-0*, Morrow, William & Co.) Morrow/Avon.
—Mortal Sin. 1995. 352p. mass mkt. 5.50 (*0-380-72161-9*, Avon Bks.); 1994. 20.00 o.p. (*0-688-12717-7*, Morrow, William & Co.) Morrow/Avon.
—Night Vision. 1992. 448p. mass mkt. 5.99 o.s.i (*0-553-29762-7*); 1991. 352p. 20.00 o.s.i (*0-553-07796-1*) Bantam Bks.
—Slashback. abr. ed. 1995. audio 16.95 o.p. (*1-56100-415-4*, 1375, Nova Audio Bks.); audio 57.25 o.p. (*1-56100-246-1*, 1049, Unabridged Library Editions) Brilliance Audio.
—Slashback. abr. ed. 2000. audio 7.95 (*1-57815-144-9*, 1103, Media Bks. Audio Publishing) Media Bks., L. L. C.
—Slashback. 1995. pap. 5.99 o.p. (*0-380-72162-7*, Avon Bks.) Morrow/Avon.
—Slashback: A Jake Lassiter Novel. 1995. 350p. 22.00 o.p. (*0-688-12718-5*, Morrow, William & Co.) Morrow/Avon.
—To Speak for the Dead. 1991. 400p. mass mkt. 5.99 o.s.i (*0-553-29172-6*) Bantam Bks.
—9 Scorpions. abr. ed. 1998. audio 25.00 (*0-671-58231-3*, 496022, Simon & Schuster Audioworks) Simon & Schuster Audio.

Levine, Paul J. To Speak for the Dead. 1990. 304p. 17.95 o.s.i (*0-553-05747-2*) Bantam Bks.

**LASTANZA, DINO (FICTITIOUS CHARACTER)—FICTION**

De Noux, O'Neil. Big Kiss. 1990. mass mkt. 4.50 o.s.i (*0-8217-3531-4*, Zebra Bks.) Kensington Publishing Corp.
—The Big Show. 1998. 320p. pap. 5.95 (*0-9653145-8-8*, Autumn Bks.) Pontalba Pr.
—Crescent City Kills. 1992. mass mkt. 4.50 o.s.i (*0-8217-3752-X*, Zebra Bks.) Kensington Publishing Corp.

**LATHAM, DREW (FICTITIOUS CHARACTER)—FICTION**

Ludlum, Robert. The Apocalypse Watch. 1996. 768p. mass mkt. 7.99 (*0-553-56957-0*); mass mkt. 7.50 o.s.i (*0-553-84005-3*) Bantam Bks.
—The Apocalypse Watch. l.t. ed. 1995. 28.95 o.p. (*1-56895-238-4*, Wheeler Publishing, Inc.) Gale Group.

**LATIMER, CHARLES (FICTITIOUS CHARACTER)—FICTION**

Ambler, Eric. A Coffin for Dimitrios. 214p. reprint ed. lib. bdg. 22.95 (*0-89190-461-1*, Rivercity Pr.) Amereon, Ltd.
—A Coffin for Dimitrios. 1996. 216p. pap. 8.95 (*0-7867-0364-4*); 1990. pap. 3.95 o.p. (*0-88184-619-8*) Avalon Publishing Group. (Carroll & Graf Pubs.).
—A Coffin for Dimitrios. 1990. reprint ed. lib. bdg. 18.95 (*0-89968-471-8*) Buccaneer Bks., Inc.

**LATIN, MAX (FICTITIOUS CHARACTER)—FICTION**

Davis, Norbert. The Adventures of Max Latin. 1988. 272p. 8.95 (*0-89296-932-6*) Mysterious Pr.

**LATTERLY, HESTER (FICTITIOUS CHARACTER)—FICTION**

Perry, Anne. A Breach of Promise. (William Monk Novels Ser.). 1999. 384p. mass mkt. 6.99 (*0-8041-1855-8*, Ivy Bks.); 1998. 384p. 25.00 o.s.i (*0-449-90849-6*, Fawcett); 1998. mass mkt. 6.99 (*0-8041-1888-4*, Ivy Bks.) Ballantine Bks.
—A Breach of Promise. abr. ed. 1998. audio 18.00 o.s.i (*0-375-40275-6*, 396111, RH Audio) Random Hse. Audio Publishing Group.
—A Breach of Promise. l.t. ed. 1998. (Basic Ser.). 639p. 29.95 (*0-7862-1465-1*) Thorndike Pr.
—Cain His Brother. 1996. 416p. mass mkt. 7.50 (*0-8041-1507-9*); mass mkt. 6.99 o.s.i (*0-8041-1504-4*) Ballantine Bks. (Ivy Bks.).
—Cain His Brother. abr. ed. 1997. (William Monk Mystery Ser.). audio 8.99 o.s.i (*0-679-46025-X*, 393145, RH Audio) Random Hse. Audio Publishing Group.
—Cain His Brother. l.t. ed. 1996. (Cloak & Dagger Ser.). 629p. 26.95 (*0-7862-0607-1*) Thorndike Pr.
—A Dangerous Mourning. 1992. 352p. mass mkt. 6.99 (*0-8041-1037-9*, Ivy Bks.) Ballantine Bks.
—A Dangerous Mourning. unabr. ed. 1995. (Inspector Monk Ser.: Vol. 2). audio 91.00 (*0-7887-0417-6*, 94609E7) Recorded Bks., LLC.
—Defend & Betray. 1993. 448p. mass mkt. 7.50 (*0-8041-1188-X*, Ivy Bks.); 1992. 18.00 o.p. (*0-449-90555-1*, Fawcett); 1992. 368p. 18.00 o.p. (*0-449-90755-4*, Fawcett) Ballantine Bks.
—Defend & Betray. unabr. ed. 2000. (Inspector Monk Ser.: Vol. 3). audio 97.00 (*0-7887-0403-6*, 94595E7) Recorded Bks., LLC.
—The Face of a Stranger. 1998. mass mkt. 3.99 o.s.i (*0-8041-1885-X*); 1991. 352p. mass mkt. 6.99 (*0-8041-0858-7*) Ballantine Bks. (Ivy Bks.).
—The Face of a Stranger. unabr. ed. 1995. (Inspector Monk Ser.: Vol. 1). audio 78.00 (*0-7887-0321-8*, 94513E7) Recorded Bks., LLC.
—Funeral in Blue. 2001. 352p. 25.00 (*0-345-44001-3*, Ballantine Bks.) Ballantine Bks.
—Funeral in Blue. l.t. ed. 2002. (Basic Ser.). 574p. 30.95 (*0-7862-3640-X*) Gale Group.
—The Silent Cry. 368p. 1998. (William Monk Novels Ser.: Vol. 8). mass mkt. 6.99 (*0-8041-1793-4*, Ivy Bks.); 1997. 24.95 o.s.i (*0-449-90848-8*, Fawcett) Ballantine Bks.
—The Silent Cry. l.t. ed. 1998. (Basic Ser.). 616p. 30.95 (*0-7862-1301-9*) Thorndike Pr.
—The Sins of the Wolf. 1995. 448p. mass mkt. 6.99 (*0-8041-1383-1*, Ivy Bks.) Ballantine Bks.
—The Sins of the Wolf. unabr. ed. 2000. (Inspector Monk Ser.: Vol. 5). audio 91.00 (*0-7887-0272-6*, 94481E7) Recorded Bks., LLC.
—A Sudden, Fearful Death. 1994. 464p. mass mkt. 6.99 (*0-8041-1283-5*, Ivy Bks.) Ballantine Bks.
—A Sudden, Fearful Death. unabr. ed. 2000. (Inspector Monk Ser.: Vol. 4). audio 97.00 (*0-7887-0499-0*, 94692E7) Recorded Bks., LLC.
—The Twisted Root. 2000. (William Monk Novels Ser.). 368p. mass mkt. 7.50 (*0-8041-1936-8*, Ballantine Bks.) Ballantine Bks.
—The Twisted Root. l.t. ed. 1999. pap. 25.00 o.p. (*0-7838-8698-5*, Macmillan Reference USA) Gale Group.
—The Twisted Root, Set. abr. ed. 1999. audio 25.00 Highsmith Inc.
—The Twisted Root, Set. abr. ed. 1999. audio 25.00 o.s.i (*0-375-40810-X*, RH Audio) Random Hse. Audio Publishing Group.
—The Twisted Root. l.t. ed. 1999. 496p. 25.00 (*0-375-40857-6*) Random Hse. Large Print.
—Weighed in the Balance. 1996. mass mkt. 6.99 o.s.i (*0-8041-1619-9*); 1997. 384p. mass mkt. 7.50 (*0-8041-1562-1*) Ballantine Bks. (Ivy Bks.).

**LAUGHTON, MITCH (FICTITIOUS CHARACTER)—FICTION**

Browne, Gerald A. West 47th. 1997. 416p. mass mkt. 6.99 o.p. (*0-446-60413-5*, Warner Vision); 1996. 82p. 23.95 o.s.i (*0-446-51662-7*) Warner Bks., Inc.

**LAURANO, LAUREN (FICTITIOUS CHARACTER)—FICTION**

Scoppettone, Sandra. Everything You Have Is Mine. 1992. (Lauren Laurano Mystery Ser.). 320p. mass mkt. 6.99 o.s.i (*0-345-37682-X*) Ballantine Bks.
—Everything You Have Is Mine. 1991. 261p. 19.95 o.p. (*0-316-77646-7*) Little Brown & Co.
—Gonna Take a Homicidal Journey: A Lauren Laurano Mystery. 1999. (Lauren Laurano Mystery Ser.). 288p. mass mkt. 6.99 (*0-345-43118-9*) Ballantine Bks.
—Gonna Take a Homicidal Journey: A Lauren Laurano Mystery. 1998. 240p. (gr. 8). 22.95 o.p. (*0-316-77665-3*) Little Brown & Co.
—I'll Be Leaving You Always: A Lauren Laurano Mystery. 1994. 288p. mass mkt. 6.50 (*0-345-38269-2*) Ballantine Bks.
—I'll Be Leaving You Always: A Lauren Laurano Mystery. 1993. 251p. 19.95 o.p. (*0-316-77647-5*) Little Brown & Co.
—Let's Face the Music & Die: A Lauren Laurano Mystery. 1997. (Lauren Laurano Mystery Ser.). 320p. mass mkt. 6.50 (*0-345-41225-7*) Ballantine Bks.
—Let's Face the Music & Die: A Lauren Laurano Mystery. 1996. 249p. 21.95 o.p. (*0-316-77664-5*) Little Brown & Co.
—My Sweet Untraceable You. 1995. 320p. mass mkt. 6.50 o.s.i (*0-345-39162-4*) Ballantine Bks.
—My Sweet Untraceable You. 1994. 275p. 19.95 o.p. (*0-316-77648-3*) Little Brown & Co.

**LAVINE, ROSIE (FICTITIOUS CHARACTER)—FICTION**

Michaels, Melisa. Cold Iron. E-Book 5.99 (*1-58787-097-5*) Electric Umbrella Publishing.
—Cold Iron. 1997. 368p. mass mkt. 5.99 o.s.i (*0-451-45654-8*, ROC) NAL.
—Sister to the Rain. E-Book 5.99 (*1-58787-099-1*) Electric Umbrella Publishing.
—Sister to the Rain. 1998. 320p. mass mkt. 5.99 o.s.i (*0-451-45730-7*, ROC) NAL.

**LAVOTINI, SIERRA (FICTITIOUS CHARACTER)—FICTION**

Bartholomew, Nancy. Drag Strip. 1999. (Sierra Lavotini Mysteries Ser.). 272p. 23.95 (*0-312-20295-4*, Saint Martin's Minotaur) St. Martin's Pr.
—Drag Strip: A Sierra Lavotini Mystery. 2000. 288p. mass mkt. 5.99 (*0-312-97579-1*, St. Martin's Paperbacks) St. Martin's Pr.
—Film Strip: A Sierra Lavotini Mystery. 2000. 262p. 23.95 o.p. (*0-312-26161-6*, Saint Martin's Minotaur) St. Martin's Pr.
—The Miracle Strip. 1998. (Sierra Lavotini Mysteries Ser.). 256p. 22.95 (*0-312-19299-1*, Saint Martin's Minotaur) St. Martin's Pr.
—The Miracle Strip: A Sierra Lavotini Mystery. 1999. (Sierra Lavotini Mysteries Ser.). 256p. mass mkt. 5.99 (*0-312-97095-1*, St. Martin's Paperbacks) St. Martin's Pr.
—Strip Poker: A Sierra Lavotini Mystery. 2001. 272p. 23.95 (*0-312-26259-0*, Saint Martin's Minotaur) St. Martin's Pr.

**LAWLESS, JANE (FICTITIOUS CHARACTER)—FICTION**

Hart, Ellen. Faint Praise. 1997. (Jane Lawless Mysteries Ser.). 321p. mass mkt. 5.99 o.s.i (*0-345-40493-9*) Ballantine Bks.
—Faint Praise: A Jane Lawless Mystery. 1995. (Jane Lawless Mysteries Ser.). 272p. text 20.95 (*1-878067-67-2*, Seal Pr.) Avalon Publishing Group.
—Hallowed Murder. 1989. 224p. pap. 8.95 o.p. (*0-931188-83-0*, Seal Pr.) Avalon Publishing Group.
—Hallowed Murder. 2003. 256p. pap. 13.95 (*0-312-31931-2*, Saint Martin's Minotaur) St. Martin's Pr.
—A Hallowed Murder. 1993. (Jane Lawless Mysteries Ser.). 256p. reprint ed. mass mkt. 6.99 (*0-345-38140-8*) Ballantine Bks.
—Hallowed Murder. unabr. ed. 1995. (Jane Lawless Mysteries Ser.: No. 1). audio 39.95 (*1-888348-00-3*, HCB101) Hall Closet Bk. Co.
—Hunting the Witch. 1999. 384p. 24.95 (*0-312-20386-1*, Saint Martin's Minotaur) St. Martin's Pr.
—Immaculate Midnight: A Jane Lawless Mystery. E-Book 24.95 (*0-312-70728-2*); 2003. 336p. pap. 13.95 (*0-312-31365-9*, Saint Martin's Griffin); 2002. 384p. 24.95 (*0-312-26676-6*, Saint Martin's Minotaur) St. Martin's Pr.
—An Intimate Ghost: A Jane Lawless Mystery. 2004. 320p. 24.95 (*0-312-31747-6*, Saint Martin's Minotaur) St. Martin's Pr.
—A Killing Cure. 1993. 304p. 19.95 (*1-878067-36-2*, Seal Pr.) Avalon Publishing Group.
—A Killing Cure. 1995. (Jane Lawless Mysteries Ser.). 304p. mass mkt. 5.99 o.s.i (*0-345-39112-8*) Ballantine Bks.
—Merchant of Venus. mass mkt. (*0-312-97991-6*, St. Martin's Paperbacks); 2001. 389p. 24.95 (*0-312-26618-9*, Saint Martin's Minotaur) St. Martin's Pr.
—Robber's Wine: A Jane Lawless Mystery. 1996. (Jane Lawless Mysteries Ser.). 304p. 21.95 (*1-878067-80-X*, Seal Pr.) Avalon Publishing Group.
—Robber's Wine: A Jane Lawless Mystery. 1998. (Jane Lawless Mysteries Ser.). mass mkt. 5.99 o.s.i (*0-345-40494-7*) Ballantine Bks.
—A Small Sacrifice. 1994. (Jane Lawless Mysteries Ser.). 300p. 20.95 (*1-878067-55-9*, Seal Pr.) Avalon Publishing Group.
—A Small Sacrifice. 1995. (Jane Lawless Mysteries Ser.). mass mkt. 5.99 o.s.i (*0-345-39113-6*) Ballantine Bks.
—Stage Fright. 1992. 261p. 9.95 (*1-878067-21-4*, Seal Pr.) Avalon Publishing Group.
—Stage Fright. 1994. (Midwest Mysteries Ser.). mass mkt. 5.99 o.s.i (*0-345-38142-4*) Ballantine Bks.
—Stage Fright. Date not set. pap. (*0-312-31765-4*); pap. (*0-312-32020-5*) St. Martin's Pr. (St. Martin's Paperbacks).
—Vital Lies. 1991. 200p. (Orig.). pap. 9.95 o.s.i (*1-878067-02-8*, Seal Pr.) Avalon Publishing Group.
—Vital Lies. 1993. (Jane Lawless Mysteries Ser.). 256p. (Orig.). reprint ed. mass mkt. 5.99 o.s.i (*0-345-38141-6*) Ballantine Bks.
—Vital Lies. Date not set. (Orig.). pap. (*0-312-31766-2*); pap. (*0-312-32046-9*) St. Martin's Pr. (St. Martin's Paperbacks).
—Wicked Games. (Jane Lawless Mysteries Ser.). 368p. 1998. 24.95 (*0-312-18680-0*, Saint Martin's Minotaur); Vol. 1. 3rd ed. 1999. mass mkt. 5.99 (*0-312-96707-1*, St. Martin's Paperbacks) St. Martin's Pr.

**LAWRENCE, MAGGIE (FICTITIOUS CHARACTER)—FICTION**

Handberg, Ron. Malice Intended. 1997. 608p. mass mkt. 6.50 (*0-06-101246-7*, HarperTorch) Morrow/Avon.

**LAWSON, GARDNER (FICTITIOUS CHARACTER)—FICTION**

Warfield, Gallatin. Raising Cain. 1998. 400p. mass mkt. 6.99 (*0-446-60513-1*); 1996. 352p. 23.45 o.p. (*0-446-51850-6*) Warner Bks., Inc.
—Silent Son. 1994. 336p. 21.95 o.s.i (*0-446-51725-9*) Warner Bks., Inc.
—The Silent Son. 1995. 384p. mass mkt. 5.99 o.s.i (*0-446-60199-3*) Warner Bks., Inc.
—State vs. Justice, Set. unabr. ed. 1998. audio 103.95 (*1-85903-130-7*) Magna Story Sound GBR. *Dist:* Ulverscroft Large Print Bks., Ltd.
—State vs. Justice. 1993. 384p. mass mkt. 5.99 o.s.i (*0-446-36477-0*); 1992. 336p. 18.95 o.p. (*0-446-51688-0*) Warner Bks., Inc.

**LAWSON, LORETTA (FICTITIOUS CHARACTER)—FICTION**

Smith, Joan. Don't Leave Me This Way. 1991. mass mkt. 5.99 o.s.i (*0-449-21964-X*, Fawcett) Ballantine Bks.
—Don't Leave Me This Way. 1991. 288p. 18.95 o.s.i (*0-684-19233-0*, Macmillan Reference USA) Gale Group.
—Full Stop. (Loretta Lawson Mystery Ser.). 1997. 262p. mass mkt. 5.99 o.s.i (*0-449-22300-0*); 1996. 288p. 21.00 o.s.i (*0-449-91048-2*) Ballantine Bks. (Fawcett).
—A Masculine Ending. 1989. 224p. mass mkt. 5.99 o.s.i (*0-449-21688-8*, Fawcett) Ballantine Bks.
—A Masculine Ending. 1988. 186p. 15.95 o.s.i (*0-684-18938-0*, Macmillan Reference USA) Gale Group.
—What Men Say. 1995. mass mkt. 5.99 o.s.i (*0-449-22297-7*, Fawcett) Ballantine Bks.
—What Men Say: A Loretta Lawson Mystery. 1994. 224p. 20.00 o.s.i (*0-449-90920-4*, Fawcett) Ballantine Bks.
—Why Aren't They Screaming? 1990. 224p. mass mkt. 4.99 o.s.i (*0-449-21777-9*, Fawcett) Ballantine Bks.
—Why Aren't They Screaming? 1989. 208p. 16.95 o.s.i (*0-684-19028-1*, Scribner) Simon & Schuster.

**LAZARUS, RINA (FICTITIOUS CHARACTER)—FICTION**

Kellerman, Faye. Day of Atonement: A Peter Decker & Rina Lazarus Novel. 1998. 368p. mass mkt. 6.99 o.s.i (*0-449-00323-X*); 1992. mass mkt. 6.99 o.s.i (*0-449-14824-6*) Ballantine Bks. (Fawcett).
—Day of Atonement: A Peter Decker & Rina Lazarus Novel. l.t. ed. 1992. (Large Print Bks.). 401p. lib. bdg. 21.95 (*0-8161-5351-5*, Macmillan Reference USA) Gale Group.
—Day of Atonement: A Peter Decker & Rina Lazarus Novel. 2004. 400p. mass mkt. 7.99 (*0-06-055489-4*, HarperTorch); 1991. 359p. 20.00 o.p. (*0-688-08604-7*, Morrow, William & Co.) Morrow/Avon.
—False Prophet: A Peter Decker & Rina Lazarus Novel. 1998. 416p. mass mkt. 7.99 (*0-449-00329-9*); 1994. mass mkt. 5.99 o.p. (*0-449-45337-5*); 1993. mass mkt. 5.99 o.s.i (*0-449-14840-8*); 1993. mass mkt. 5.99 o.s.i (*0-449-14898-X*) Ballantine Bks. (Fawcett).
—False Prophet: A Peter Decker & Rina Lazarus Novel. l.t. ed. 1994. (Large Print Bks.). 554p. lib. bdg. 23.95 (*0-8161-7458-X*, Macmillan Reference USA) Gale Group.
—False Prophet: A Peter Decker & Rina Lazarus Novel. 1992. 367p. 20.00 o.p. (*0-688-10553-X*, Morrow, William & Co.) Morrow/Avon.
—The Forgotten: A Peter Decker & Rina Lazarus Novel. l.t. ed. 2001. 592p. pap. 25.00 (*0-06-620958-7*) HarperCollins Pubs.
—The Forgotten: A Peter Decker & Rina Lazarus Novel. 2001. 384p. 26.00 (*0-688-15614-2*, Morrow, William & Co.) Morrow/Avon.
—The Forgotten: A Peter Decker & Rina Lazarus Novel. abr. ed. 2001. audio 25.00 (*0-671-58271-2*); audio compact disk 30.00 o.s.i (*0-7435-0761-4*) Simon & Schuster Audio. (Simon & Schuster Audioworks).
—Grievous Sin. unabr. ed. 2003. audio 19.99 (*1-59335-087-2*, 30179) Soulmate Audio Bks., Inc.
—Grievous Sin: A Peter Decker & Rina Lazarus Novel. 1998. 400p. mass mkt. 7.99 (*0-449-00330-2*); 1994. mass mkt. 6.99 o.s.i (*0-449-14839-4*) Ballantine Bks. (Fawcett).
—Grievous Sin: A Peter Decker & Rina Lazarus Novel. unabr. ed. 1996. audio 72.00 (*0-7366-3321-9*, 3973) Books on Tape, Inc.
—Grievous Sin: A Peter Decker & Rina Lazarus Novel. unabr. ed. 1993. audio 23.95 o.p. (*1-56100-518-5*, 129, Bookcassette); audio 73.25 (*1-56100-150-3*, 885, Unabridged Library Editions) Brilliance Audio.
—Grievous Sin: A Peter Decker & Rina Lazarus Novel. l.t. ed. 1994. (Large Print Bks.). 552p. lib. bdg. 24.95 (*0-8161-7460-1*, Macmillan Reference USA) Gale Group.
—Grievous Sin: A Peter Decker & Rina Lazarus Novel. 1993. 368p. 20.00 o.p. (*0-688-10554-8*, Morrow, William & Co.) Morrow/Avon.
—Jupiter's Bones: A Peter Decker & Rina Lazarus Novel. l.t. ed. 552p. 2000. pap. 28.95 (*0-7838-8783-3*); 1999. 31.95 (*0-7838-8782-5*) Gale Group. (Macmillan Reference USA).
—Jupiter's Bones: A Peter Decker & Rina Lazarus Novel. Feron, C. F., ed. 2000. 448p. mass mkt. 7.50 (*0-380-73082-0*, Avon Bks.) Morrow/Avon.
—Jupiter's Bones: A Peter Decker & Rina Lazarus Novel. 1999. 375p. 25.00 o.p. (*0-688-15612-6*, Morrow, William & Co.) Morrow/Avon.
—Jupiter's Bones: A Peter Decker & Rina Lazarus Novel. abr. ed. 1999. audio 25.00 (*0-671-57759-X*, Simon & Schuster Audioworks) Simon & Schuster Audio.
—Justice: A Peter Decker & Rina Lazarus Novel. unabr. ed. 1996. audio 80.00 (*0-7366-3275-1*, 3931) Books on Tape, Inc.
—Justice: A Peter Decker & Rina Lazarus Novel. abr. ed. 1996. audio 7.99 o.p. (*1-56740-129-5*, 665, Paperback Nova Audio Bks.); 1995. audio 16.95 o.p. (*1-56100-850-8*, 1258, Nova Audio Bks.); 1995. audio 89.25 o.p. (*1-56100-283-6*, 914, Unabridged Library Editions); 1995. audio 25.95 o.p. (*1-56100-658-0*, 150, Bookcassette) Brilliance Audio.
—Justice: A Peter Decker & Rina Lazarus Novel. l.t. ed. 1995. 563p. 26.95 (*0-7838-1494-1*, Macmillan Reference USA) Gale Group.
—Justice: A Peter Decker & Rina Lazarus Novel. abr. ed. 2000. audio 7.95 (*1-57815-172-4*, 1115, Media Bks. Audio Publishing) Media Bks., L. L. C.
—Justice: A Peter Decker & Rina Lazarus Novel. 1996. 465p. mass mkt. 7.99 (*0-380-72498-7*); 1995. 388p. 23.00 o.p. (*0-688-04613-4*, Morrow, William & Co.) Morrow/Avon.
—Milk & Honey: A Peter Decker & Rina Lazarus Novel. 384p. 1998. mass mkt. 6.99 o.s.i (*0-449-00313-2*); 1991. mass mkt. 5.99 o.s.i (*0-449-14728-2*) Ballantine Bks. (Fawcett).
—Milk & Honey: A Peter Decker & Rina Lazarus Novel. 1990. 384p. 18.95 o.p. (*0-688-08603-9*, Morrow, William & Co.) Morrow/Avon.
—Prayers for the Dead: A Peter Decker & Rina Lazarus Novel. unabr. ed. 1997. audio 80.00 Books on Tape, Inc.
—Prayers for the Dead: A Peter Decker & Rina Lazarus Novel. abr. ed. 1997. audio 7.99 o.p. (*1-56740-181-3*, 689, Nova Audio Bks.); 1996. audio 16.95 o.p. (*1-56100-919-9*, 1349, Nova

Audio Bks.); 1996. audio 89.25 o.p. (1-56100-334-4, 991, Unabridged Library Editions); 1996. audio 25.95 o.p. (1-56100-709-9, 218, Bookcassette) Brilliance Audio.

—Prayers for the Dead: A Peter Decker & Rina Lazarus Novel. l.t. ed. 1996. (Large Print Bks.). 586p. 26.95 (0-7838-1910-2, Macmillan Reference USA) Gale Group.

—Prayers for the Dead: A Peter Decker & Rina Lazarus Novel. 1997. 424p. mass mkt. 7.99 (0-380-72624-6); 1996. 406p. 24.00 o.p. (0-688-14367-9, Morrow, William & Co.) Morrow/Avon.

—The Quality of Mercy. 1990. 544p. mass mkt. 6.99 o.s.i (0-449-21892-9, Fawcett) Ballantine Bks.

—The Quality of Mercy. 1989. 607p. 19.95 o.p. (1-55710-027-6, Morrow, William & Co.) Morrow/Avon.

—The Ritual Bath: A Peter Decker & Rina Lazarus Novel. 1998. mass mkt. 6.99 (0-449-45814-8); 1987. 288p. mass mkt. 6.99 o.s.i (0-449-21373-0) Ballantine Bks. (Fawcett).

—The Ritual Bath: A Peter Decker & Rina Lazarus Novel. l.t. ed. 2000. (G. K. Hall Core Ser.). 368p. 30.95 (0-7838-9046-X, Macmillan Reference USA) Gale Group.

—The Ritual Bath: A Peter Decker & Rina Lazarus Novel. 1999. 384p. mass mkt. 6.99 (0-380-73266-1) Morrow/Avon.

—Sacred & Profane: A Peter Decker & Rina Lazarus Novel. 1998. mass mkt. 6.99 (0-449-45815-6); 1988. mass mkt. 6.99 o.s.i (0-449-21502-4, Fawcett) Ballantine Bks.

—Sacred & Profane: A Peter Decker & Rina Lazarus Novel. l.t. ed. 2001. (Magna Large Print Ser.). 400p. (0-7505-1667-4) Magna Large Print Bks. GBR. *Dist:* Ulverscroft Large Print Canada, Ltd.

—Sacred & Profane: A Peter Decker & Rina Lazarus Novel. 1999. 384p. mass mkt. 6.99 (0-380-73267-X, Avon Bks.); 1987. 311p. 16.95 o.p. (0-87795-887-4, Morrow, William & Co.) Morrow/Avon.

—Sacred & Profane: A Peter Decker & Rina Lazarus Novel. 1990. 3.99 o.p. (0-517-05799-9) Random Hse. Value Publishing.

—Sanctuary: A Peter Decker & Rina Lazarus Novel. unabr. ed. 1996. audio 72.00 (0-7366-3355-3, 4006) Books on Tape, Inc.

—Sanctuary: A Peter Decker & Rina Lazarus Novel. abr. ed. 1994. audio 16.95 o.p. (1-56100-386-7, 1359, Nova Audio Bks.); audio 89.25 o.p. (1-56100-221-6, 1023, Unabridged Library Editions); audio 25.95 o.p. (1-56100-596-7, 246, Bookcassette) Brilliance Audio.

—Sanctuary: A Peter Decker & Rina Lazarus Novel. l.t. ed. 1995. 509p. pap. 23.95 o.p. (1-56895-090-X, Wheeler Publishing, Inc.) Gale Group.

—Sanctuary: A Peter Decker & Rina Lazarus Novel. abr. ed. 2000. audio 7.95 (1-57815-022-1, 1006, Media Bks. Audio Publishing) Media Bks., L. L. C.

—Sanctuary: A Peter Decker & Rina Lazarus Novel. 1994. 396p. 22.00 o.p. (0-688-04612-6, Morrow, William & Co.); 1995. 428p. reprint ed. pap. 6.99 (0-380-72497-9, Avon Bks.) Morrow/Avon.

—Serpent's Tooth: A Peter Decker & Rina Lazarus Novel. unabr. ed. 1997. audio 72.00 (0-7366-4049-5, 4548) Books on Tape, Inc.

—Serpent's Tooth: A Peter Decker & Rina Lazarus Novel. l.t. ed. 539p. 2001. pap. 30.00 (0-7838-8323-4); 1997. lib. bdg. 28.95 o.p. (0-7838-8322-6) Gale Group. (Macmillan Reference USA).

—Serpent's Tooth: A Peter Decker & Rina Lazarus Novel. 1998. 432p. mass mkt. 6.99 (0-380-72625-4, Avon Bks.); 1997. 416p. 24.50 (0-688-14368-7, Morrow, William & Co.); 1997. 416p. 294.00 (0-688-15649-5, Morrow, William & Co.) Morrow/Avon.

—Serpent's Tooth: A Peter Decker & Rina Lazarus Novel. abr. ed. 1997. audio 24.00 (0-671-57757-3, 495448, Simon & Schuster Audioworks) Simon & Schuster Audio.

—Stalker: A Peter Decker & Rina Lazarus Novel. unabr. ed. 2001. audio compact disk 115.95 (0-7927-9987-9, SLD 038, Chivers Sound Library) BBC Audiobooks America.

—Stalker: A Peter Decker & Rina Lazarus Novel. l.t. ed. 2000. 624p. pap. 25.00 (0-06-019729-3, HarperLargePrint) HarperTrade.

—Stalker: A Peter Decker & Rina Lazarus Novel. 2001. 448p. mass mkt. 7.99 (0-380-81769-1, Avon Bks.); 2001. 448p. mass mkt. 7.99 (0-380-81854-X, Avon Bks.); 2000. 416p. 25.00 (0-688-15613-4, Morrow, William & Co.) Morrow/Avon.

—Stalker: A Peter Decker & Rina Lazarus Novel. abr. ed. 2000. audio 25.00 (0-671-57760-3, Simon & Schuster Audioworks) Simon & Schuster Audio.

—Stone Kiss. 2003. 528p. mass mkt. 7.99 (0-446-61147-6, Warner Vision); 2002. 400p. 25.95 (0-446-53038-7); 2002. 668p. 25.95 (0-446-53078-6) Warner Bks., Inc.

**LEAPHORN, JOE, LT. (FICTITIOUS CHARACTER)—FICTION**

Hillerman, Tony. The Blessing Way. unabr. ed. 1993. audio 36.00 (0-7366-2510-0, 3266) Books on Tape, Inc.

—The Blessing Way. l.t. ed. 1992. (General Ser.). 304p. pap. 17.95 o.p. (0-8161-5431-7); lib. bdg. 20.95 o.p. (0-8161-5430-9) Gale Group. (Macmillan Reference USA).

—The Blessing Way. (Harper Novel of Suspense Ser.). 1970. 10.00 o.p. (0-06-011896-2); 1990. 304p. reprint ed. mass mkt. 6.99 (0-06-100001-9) HarperCollins Pubs.

—The Blessing Way. abr. ed. 1995. (Joe Leaphorn Mystery Ser.). 3p. audio 18.00 (1-55994-160-X, 394151, HarperAudio) HarperTrade.

—The Blessing Way. 1993. audio 39.80 (1-56544-006-4, 250020); audio Literate Ear, Inc.

—The Blessing Way. 1978. (gr. 7 up). pap. 2.95 o.p. (0-380-39941-5, Avon Bks.) Morrow/Avon.

—The Blessing Way. unabr. ed. 1990. (Joe Leaphorn Mystery Ser.: Vol. 1). audio 44.00 (1-55690-058-9, 90080E7) Recorded Bks., LLC.

—The Blessing Way. 1990. 12.55 (0-606-16174-0) Turtleback Bks.

—Coyote Waits. unabr. ed. 1990. audio 42.00 (0-7366-1788-4, 2625) Books on Tape, Inc.

—Coyote Waits. 1990. 292p. 75.00 o.p. (0-06-016422-0); 1990. 292p. 19.95 o.p. (0-06-016370-4); 1995. 3p. audio 18.00 o.s.i (1-55994-198-7, 390569, HarperAudio); 1990. pap. 19.95 o.p. (0-06-016423-9) HarperTrade.

—Coyote Waits. 1992. 368p. mass mkt. 6.99 (0-06-109932-5, HarperTorch) Morrow/Avon.

—Coyote Waits. 1990. audio 10.00 New Letters on Air.

—Coyote Waits. 1990. (J). 13.04 (0-606-01125-0) Turtleback Bks.

—Dance Hall of the Dead. abr. ed. 1986. audio 15.95 (0-88690-127-8, N20024, Audio Editions Bks. on Cassette) Audio Partners Publishing Corp.

—Dance Hall of the Dead. unabr. ed. 1994. audio 36.00 (0-7366-2610-7, 3352) Books on Tape, Inc.

—Dance Hall of the Dead. 1997. lib. bdg. 37.95 (1-56849-695-8) Buccaneer Bks., Inc.

—Dance Hall of the Dead. 2004. 224p. pap. 11.95 (0-06-056374-5); 1990. 272p. reprint ed. mass mkt. 6.99 (0-06-100002-7) HarperTrade. (Perennial).

—Dance Hall of the Dead. 1993. audio. audio 37.20 (1-56544-025-0, 250021) Literate Ear, Inc.

—Dance Hall of the Dead. 1982. (YA). (gr. 9 up). mass mkt. 2.95 o.p. (0-380-00217-5, 60093-5, Avon Bks.) Morrow/Avon.

—Dance Hall of the Dead. unabr. ed. 1991. (Joe Leaphorn Mystery Ser.: Vol. 2). (YA). (gr. 10). audio 44.00 (1-55690-134-8, 91122E7) Recorded Bks., LLC.

—Dance Hall of the Dead. l.t. ed. (Paperback Bestsellers Ser.). 239p. 1994. pap. 20.95 (0-8161-5433-3); 1993. lib. bdg. 25.95 (0-8161-5432-5) Thorndike Pr.

—Dance Hall of the Dead. 1990. 12.55 (0-606-16124-4) Turtleback Bks.

—The Fallen Man. unabr. ed. 1997. audio 42.00 (0-913369-37-3, 4211) Books on Tape, Inc.

—The Fallen Man. 1996. 304p. 24.00 o.p. (0-06-017773-X) HarperCollins Pubs.

—The Fallen Man, Set. abr. ed. 1996. (Joe Leaphorn Mystery Ser.). audio 25.00 (1-55994-978-3, 694496, HarperAudio) HarperTrade.

—The Fallen Man. 1997. 320p. mass mkt. 6.99 (0-06-109288-6, HarperTorch) Morrow/Avon.

—The Fallen Man. unabr. ed. 1997. (Jim Chee Mystery Ser.: Vol. 9). audio 51.00 (0-7887-0907-0, 94961E7) Recorded Bks., LLC.

—The Fallen Man. 1998. 5.98 o.p. (0-7651-0823-2) Smithmark Pubs., Inc.

—The First Eagle. 1998. 224p. 25.00 (0-00-224569-8); 288p. 25.00 o.s.i (0-06-017581-8); 25.00 o.s.i (0-06-099536-X) HarperCollins Pubs.

—The First Eagle. unabr. ed. 1998. audio 34.95 (0-694-52051-9, 896038);Set. audio 25.00 (0-694-52011-X, 696034) HarperTrade. (HarperAudio).

—The First Eagle. 1999. 336p. mass mkt. 6.99 (0-06-109785-3, HarperTorch) Morrow/Avon.

—The First Eagle. unabr. ed. (Joe Leaphorn Mystery Ser.). 1999. audio compact disk 58.00 (0-7887-3445-8, C1051E7); 1998. audio 56.00 (0-7887-2160-7, 95456E7) Recorded Bks., LLC.

—The First Eagle. l.t. ed. (Paperback Bestsellers Ser.). 360p. 1999. pap. 28.95 o.p. (0-7862-1625-5); 1998. 30.95 (0-7862-1624-7) Thorndike Pr.

—The First Eagle. 1999. 13.04 (0-606-16536-3) Turtleback Bks.

—Hunting Badger. 1999. 288p. 26.00 (0-06-019289-5); 26.00 (0-00-224550-7) HarperCollins Pubs.

—Hunting Badger. l.t. ed. 1999. 256p. pap. 26.00 (0-06-095564-3, HarperLargePrint); 2000. audio compact disk 29.95 (0-694-52287-2, HarperAudio); Set. 2000. 30p. audio 25.00 (0-694-52057-8, HarperAudio) HarperTrade.

—Hunting Badger. 2001. 352p. mass mkt. 7.50 (0-06-109786-1, HarperTorch) Morrow/Avon.

—Hunting Badger. unabr. ed. 1999. (Joe Leaphorn Mystery Ser.). audio 29.95 (0-7887-3894-1, 96076) Recorded Bks., LLC.

—The Joe Leaphorn Mysteries: Three Classic Hillerman Mysteries Featuring Lt. Joe Leaphorn: The Blessing Way, Dance Hall of the Dead, Listening Woman. 1989. 448p. 19.00 o.p. (0-06-016174-4) HarperTrade.

—Leaphorn & Chee: Three Classic Mysteries Featuring Lt. Joe Leaphorn & Officer Jim Chee. 1992. 512p. 19.00 o.p. (0-06-016909-5) HarperTrade.

—Listening Woman. unabr. ed. 1994. audio 36.00 (0-7366-2671-9, 3408) Books on Tape, Inc.

—Listening Woman. l.t. ed. (General Ser.). 303p. 1994. pap. 18.95 o.p. (0-8161-5435-X); 1993. lib. bdg. 22.95 (0-8161-5434-1) Gale Group. (Macmillan Reference USA).

—Listening Woman. 1978. (Harper Novel of Suspense Ser.). o.p. (0-06-011901-2) HarperCollins Pubs.

—Listening Woman. 1993. audio. audio 44.20 (1-56544-036-6, 250022) Literate Ear, Inc.

—Listening Woman. 1990. 336p. mass mkt. 6.99 (0-06-100029-9, HarperTorch); 1979. pap. 3.95 (0-380-43554-3, Avon Bks.) Morrow/Avon.

—Listening Woman. unabr. ed. 1990. (Joe Leaphorn Mystery Ser.: Vol. 3). audio 44.00 (1-55690-310-3, 90073E7) Recorded Bks., LLC.

—Sacred Clowns. unabr. ed. 1994. audio 48.00 (0-7366-2645-X, 3382) Books on Tape, Inc.

—Sacred Clowns. 1994. 368p. mass mkt. 6.99 (0-06-109260-6) HarperCollins Pubs.

—Sacred Clowns. 1993. 304p. 100.00 o.p. (0-06-016830-7); 304p. 23.00 o.p. (0-06-016767-X); audio 17.00 (1-55994-549-4, 391505, HarperAudio) HarperTrade.

—Sacred Clowns. unabr. ed. 1993. (Jim Chee Mystery Ser.: Vol. 8). audio 51.00 (1-55690-910-1, 93406E7) Recorded Bks., LLC.

—Sacred Clowns. 1994. 13.04 (0-606-16175-9) Turtleback Bks.

—Sacred Clowns: A Novel. 2003. 320p. pap. 11.95 (0-06-053805-8, Perennial) HarperTrade.

—The Sinister Pig. 2003. (0-06-601944-3) HarperCollins Pubs.

—The Sinister Pig. 2003. 240p. 25.95 (0-06-019443-X, HarperCollins); E-Book 19.95 (0-06-055860-1, HarperCollins); 320p. pap. 25.95 (0-06-054543-7, HarperLargePrint) HarperTrade.

—The Sinister Pig. 2004. mass mkt. (0-06-109878-7, HarperTorch) Morrow/Avon.

—Skinwalkers. unabr. ed. 1994. audio 36.00 (0-7366-2795-2, 3510) Books on Tape, Inc.

—Skinwalkers. 1990. 320p. mass mkt. 6.99 (0-06-100017-5); 1987. mass mkt. 4.95 o.p. (0-06-080893-4, P/893) HarperCollins Pubs.

—Skinwalkers. 1990. audio 15.95; 1987. 224p. 19.95 o.p. (0-06-015695-3); 1991. audio 18.00 (1-55994-166-9, CPN 2152, HarperAudio) HarperTrade.

—Skinwalkers. 1993. audio 39.80 (1-56544-007-2, 250032); audio Literate Ear, Inc.

—Skinwalkers. unabr. ed. 1990. (Jim Chee Mystery Ser.: Vol. 4). audio 44.00 (1-55690-480-0, 90074E7) Recorded Bks., LLC.

—Skinwalkers. 1987. 13.04 (0-606-03655-5) Turtleback Bks.

—Talking God. unabr. ed. 1989. audio 42.00 (0-7366-1656-X, 2507) Books on Tape, Inc.

—Talking God. 2003. E-Book 6.99 (0-06-054725-1) HarperCollins Pubs.

—Talking God. 1991. 368p. mass mkt. 6.99 (0-06-109918-X, Perennial); 1989. 17.95 o.p. (0-06-016118-3) HarperTrade.

—Talking God. 1989. 13.04 (0-606-04823-5) Turtleback Bks.

—A Thief of Time. unabr. ed. 1994. audio 36.00 (0-7366-2841-X, 3549) Books on Tape, Inc.

—A Thief of Time. l.t. ed. 1990. 14.95 o.p. (0-8161-5061-3); 1989. 344p. 18.95 o.p. (0-8161-4699-3) Gale Group. (Macmillan Reference USA).

—A Thief of Time. 2002. E-Book 6.99 (0-06-054713-8); E-Book (0-06-054720-0) HarperCollins Pubs.

—A Thief of Time. 1988. 224p. 15.45 o.p. (0-06-015938-3); 2002. 176p. audio 9.99 (0-06-008296-8, HarperAudio); Set. 1995. audio 18.00 (0-89845-794-7, 391761, HarperAudio) HarperTrade.

—A Thief of Time. 1990. 352p. reprint ed. mass mkt. 6.99 (0-06-100004-3, HarperTorch) Morrow/Avon.

—A Thief of Time. 1989. 13.04 (0-606-04346-2) Turtleback Bks.

—The Wailing Wind. 2002. (Illus.). 240p. 25.95 (0-06-019444-8); E-Book 19.95 (0-06-054703-0); E-Book (0-06-054708-1) HarperCollins Pubs.

—The Wailing Wind. l.t. ed. 2002. 320p. pap. 25.95 (0-06-009388-9, HarperLargePrint); 384p. 29.95 (0-06-009258-0, Caedmon); audio 26.95 (0-694-52348-8, HarperAudio) HarperTrade.

—The Wailing Wind. 2003. 368p. mass mkt. 7.99 (0-06-109879-5, HarperTorch) Morrow/Avon.

—The Wailing Wind. unabr. ed. 2002. audio 29.95 (1-4025-2394-7, RG087); audio compact disk 66.00 (1-4025-2904-X, C1816); audio 48.00 (1-4025-2393-9) Recorded Bks., LLC.

Hillerman, Tony, reader. Talking God, , abr. ed. 1995. audio 18.00 (0-89845-956-7, CPN 2122, HarperAudio) HarperTrade.

**LEARY-PARKER, TIMMIE (FICTITIOUS CHARACTER)—FICTION**

Dreyer, Eileen. Brain Dead. 1997. 416p. mass mkt. 22.00 o.p. (0-06-101095-2) HarperCollins Pubs.

—Brain Dead. 1998. 512p. mass mkt. 6.99 (0-06-101096-0, HarperTorch) Morrow/Avon.

**LECTER, HANNIBAL (FICTITIOUS CHARACTER)—FICTION**

Harris, Thomas. Hannibal. unabr. ed. 1999. audio 32.00. audio 44.95 (0-7366-4568-3, 4975) Books on Tape, Inc.

—Hannibal. 1999. 496p. 27.95 (0-385-29929-X) Broadway Bks.

—Hannibal. 2000. 560p. mass mkt. 7.99 (0-440-22467-5) Dell Publishing.

—Hannibal, abr. ed. 1999. audio 27.95. audio 39.95 Highsmith Inc.

—Hannibal. abr. ed. 2004. audio 17.99 (0-7393-1246-4, RH Audio Price-Less); 1999. audio 27.95 (0-553-52677-4, RH Audio); 1999. audio compact disk 31.95 (0-553-45663-6, RH Audio); 1999. audio 39.95 (0-553-50244-1, RH Audio) Random Hse. Audio Publishing Group.

—Red Dragon. 1982. mass mkt. 3.95 o.s.i (0-553-22746-7); mass mkt. 4.95 o.s.i (0-553-27522-4); 368p. mass mkt. 4.50 o.s.i (0-553-26485-0) Bantam Bks.

—Red Dragon. 1991. 352p. reprint ed. lib. bdg. 24.95 o.p. (0-89966-877-1) Buccaneer Bks., Inc.

—Red Dragon. 2002. lib. bdg. 29.95 (1-58547-237-9, Premier) Ctr. Point Large Print.

—Red Dragon. 1990. 480p. reprint ed. mass mkt. 7.99 (0-440-20615-4) Dell Publishing.

—Red Dragon. 1998. 352p. pap. 12.95 (0-385-31967-3); 1997. pap. 11.95 (0-385-31906-1) Doubleday Publishing.

—Red Dragon. 2000. 368p. 26.95 (0-525-94556-3, Abrahams, William Bks.) Dutton/Plume.

—Red Dragon. 1981. 352p. 13.95 o.p. (0-399-12442-X, G. P. Putnam's Sons) Penguin Putnam Bks. for Young Readers.

—Red Dragon. abr. ed. 2003. audio 19.95 (0-7435-2705-4); 2003. audio compact disk 19.95 (0-7435-2706-2); 1989. audio 16.00 (0-671-67854-X); 2003. audio 49.95 (0-7435-2707-0) Simon & Schuster Audio. (Simon & Schuster Audioworks).

—Red Dragon. l.t. ed. 1984. (Charnwood Large Print Ser.). 496p. 29.99 o.p. (0-7089-8169-0, Ulverscroft) Thorpe, F. A. Pubs. GBR. *Dist:* Ulverscroft Large Print Bks., Ltd., Ulverscroft Large Print Canada, Ltd.

—The Silence of the Lambs. l.t. ed. 2001. 367p. lib. bdg. 28.95 (1-58547-110-0) Ctr. Point Large Print.

—The Silence of the Lambs. 1989. 4.99 o.p. (0-517-00503-4) Random Hse. Value Publishing.

—The Silence of the Lambs, unabr. ed. 1989. audio 70.00 (1-55690-830-X, 93142E7) Recorded Bks., LLC.

—The Silence of the Lambs. abr. ed. 2002. audio compact disk 19.95 (0-7435-2710-0); 1988. audio 17.00 (0-671-67351-3) Simon & Schuster Audio. (Simon & Schuster Audioworks).

—The Silence of the Lambs. 1991. 384p. mass mkt. 7.99 (0-312-92458-5, St. Martin's Paperbacks); 1989. mass mkt. 5.95 o.s.i (0-312-91543-8, St. Martin's Paperbacks); 1988. 352p. 24.95 (0-312-02282-4); 1998. 352p. pap. 13.95 (0-312-19526-5, Saint Martin's Griffin) St. Martin's Pr.

**LEDUC, AIMEE (FICTITIOUS CHARACTER)—FICTION**

Black, Cara. Murder in Belleville: An Aimee Leduc Investigation. 2000. (Aimee Leduc Investigation Ser.). (Illus.). 341p. 23.00 (1-56947-211-4) Soho Pr., Inc.

—Murder in the Bastille. 2003. 304p. 24.00 (1-56947-324-2) Soho Pr., Inc.

—Murder in the Marais. 1999. (Aimee Leduc Investigation Ser.). 354p. 22.00 (1-56947-159-2) Soho Pr., Inc.

—Murder in the Marais: An Aimee Leduc Investigation. 2000. (Illus.). 360p. pap. 13.00 (1-56947-212-2) Soho Pr., Inc.

—Murder in the Sentier. (Illus.). 2003. 336p. pap. 13.00 (1-56947-331-5); 2002. 304p. 24.00 (1-56947-278-5) Soho Pr., Inc.

**LEE, ANNA (FICTITIOUS CHARACTER)—FICTION**

Cody, Liza. Backhand. 1992. 288p. mass mkt. 4.99 o.s.i (0-553-29627-2); mass mkt. 5.99 o.s.i (0-7704-2531-3) Bantam Bks.

—Backhand. unabr. ed. 1993. (Anna Lee Mystery Ser.: Vol. 6). audio 60.00 (1-55690-808-3, 93117E7) Recorded Bks., LLC.

—Backhand: An Anna Lee Mystery. 1992. 288p. 18.50 o.s.i (0-385-42231-8) Doubleday Publishing.

—Bad Company. 1983. 260p. 11.95 o.p. (*0-684-17760-9*, Macmillan Reference USA) Gale Group.
—Bad Company. 1992. pap. o.p. (*0-09-982120-6*) Hutchinson GBR. *Dist:* Random Hse. of Canada, Ltd.
—Bad Company. unabr. ed. 2000. audio compact disk 64.95 (*0-7531-0906-9*, 109069); 1997. audio 54.95 (*1-85695-740-3*, 940506) ISIS Audio Bks. GBR. *Dist:* Ulverscroft Large Print Bks., Ltd.
—Bad Company. 1984. 288p. mass mkt. 2.95 o.s.i (*0-446-30738-6*) Warner Bks., Inc.
—Dupe. 1992. mass mkt. 4.99 o.s.i (*0-7704-2439-2*); 256p. mass mkt. 4.99 o.s.i (*0-553-29641-8*) Bantam Bks.
—Dupe. 1981. 252p. 10.95 o.s.i (*0-684-17153-8*, Macmillan Reference USA) Gale Group.
—Dupe. 1992. pap. o.p. (*0-09-982110-9*) Hutchinson GBR. *Dist:* Random Hse. of Canada, Ltd.
—Dupe. 1984. mass mkt. 2.95 o.s.i (*0-446-30527-8*) Warner Bks., Inc.
—Head Case. l.t. ed. 1992. 18.95 o.p. (*0-7451-8282-8*, AH0274); pap. 16.95 o.p. (*0-7927-0951-9*, AS0310) BBC Audiobooks America.
—Head Case. 1989. 192p. reprint ed. mass mkt. 3.95 o.s.i (*0-553-27645-X*) Bantam Bks.
—Head Case. unabr. ed. 1997. audio 54.95 (*1-85695-745-4*, 940201) ISIS Audio Bks. GBR. *Dist:* Ulverscroft Large Print Bks., Ltd.
—Head Case: An Anna Lee Mystery. 1986. 196p. 13.95 o.s.i (*0-684-18586-5*, Macmillan Reference USA) Gale Group.
—Stalker. 1986. 208p. mass mkt. 3.50 o.s.i (*0-446-32807-3*) Warner Bks., Inc.
—The Stalker. 1989. mass mkt. 1.95 o.s.i (*0-553-18503-9*) Bantam Bks.
—Stalker: A Mystery. 1985. 168p. 11.95 o.s.i (*0-684-18234-3*, Scribner) Simon & Schuster.
—Under Contract. 1990. 208p. mass mkt. 3.95 o.s.i (*0-553-28345-6*) Bantam Bks.
—Under Contract. unabr. ed. 1993. (Anna Lee Mystery Ser.: Vol. 5). audio 51.00 (*1-55690-929-2*, 93425E7) Recorded Bks., LLC.
—Under Contract: An Anna Lee Mystery. 1987. 16.95 o.p. (*0-684-18780-9*, Scribner) Simon & Schuster.

**LEE, HEAVEN (FICTITIOUS CHARACTER)—FICTION**

Temple, Lou Jane. Bread on Arrival. l.t. ed. 2003. (Mystery Ser.). 27.95 (*1-57490-486-8*, Beeler Large Print Bks.) Beeler, Thomas T. Publisher.
—Bread on Arrival. (St. Martin's Minotaur Mysteries Ser.). 1999. 288p. mass mkt. 6.50 (*0-312-96942-2*, St. Martin's Paperbacks); 1998. 272p. 22.95 o.p. (*0-312-19244-4*, Saint Martin's Minotaur) St. Martin's Pr.
—The Cornbread Killer. 2000. 272p. mass mkt. 5.99 (*0-312-97427-2*, St. Martin's Paperbacks); 1999. 242p. 22.95 o.p. (*0-312-20605-4*, Saint Martin's Minotaur) St. Martin's Pr.
—The Cornbread Killer: A Heaven Lee Mystery. l.t. ed. 2001. (Beeler Large Print Mystery Ser.). 245p. 25.95 (*1-57490-336-5*, Beeler Large Print Bks.) Beeler, Thomas T. Publisher.
—Death Is a Semisweet: A Heaven Lee Mystery. 2002. 288p. 23.95 (*0-312-30122-7*, Saint Martin's Minotaur) St. Martin's Pr.
—Death of Rhubarb. 1996. 220p. mass mkt. 6.50 (*0-312-95891-9*, St. Martin's Paperbacks) St. Martin's Pr.
—Red Beans & Vice. mass mkt. o.p. (*0-312-98100-7*, St. Martin's Paperbacks); 2001. 288p. 23.95 (*0-312-28013-0*, Saint Martin's Minotaur) St. Martin's Pr.
—Revenge of the Barbeque Queens. 1997. (Dead Letter Mysteries Ser.). 217p. mass mkt. 6.50 (*0-312-96074-3*, St. Martin's Paperbacks) St. Martin's Pr.
—Stiff Risotto. 1997. 224p. mass mkt. 6.50 (*0-312-96321-1*, St. Martin's Paperbacks) St. Martin's Pr.

**LEE, ROBERT E. (ROBERT EDWARD), 1807-1870—FICTION**

Adams, Richard. Traveller. 1989. 368p. reprint ed. mass mkt. 4.95 o.s.i (*0-440-20493-3*) Dell Publishing.
—Traveller. 1993. audio 53.20 (*1-56544-000-5*, 450001); audio Literate Ear, Inc.
—Traveller. 1990. 4.99 o.p. (*0-517-05728-X*) Random Hse. Value Publishing.
Goldsboro, Bobby. Ribbit E. Lee. 1997. (J). 24.99 (*1-58083-025-0*) Animazing Entertainment, Inc.
Harper, M. A. For the Love of Robert E. Lee. 1994. 325p. pap. 13.00 (*1-56947-002-2*); 1992. 330p. 20.00 o.s.i (*0-939149-63-X*) Soho Pr., Inc.
Herrin, Lamar. The Unwritten Chronicles of Robert E. Lee. 1991. pap. 9.95 o.p. (*0-312-05983-3*, Saint Martin's Griffin); 1989. 256p. 17.95 o.p. (*0-312-03448-2*) St. Martin's Pr.
McIntire, Dennis P. Lee at Chattanooga: A Novel of What Might Have Been. 2002. (Illus.). 320p. pap. 16.95 (*1-58182-257-X*) Cumberland Hse. Publishing.
Savage, Douglas. The Court-Martial of Robert E. Lee: A Historical Novel. 1995. 480p. pap. 21.99 (*0-446-67056-1*) Warner Bks., Inc.
—Court-Martial of Robert E. Lee: A Historical Novel. 1993. 448p. text o.p. (*0-938289-26-8*, 289268, Combined Publishing) Da Capo Pr., Inc.
Shaara, Jeff. Gone for Soldiers: A Novel of the Mexican War. 2000. (Illus.). 448p. 26.95 (*0-345-42750-5*, Ballantine Bks.) Ballantine Bks.
—Gone for Soldiers: A Novel of the Mexican War. abr. ed. 2000. audio 25.95 (*0-553-52720-7*); audio compact disk 29.95 (*0-553-71198-9*); audio 39.95 (*0-553-50254-9*) Random Hse. Audio Publishing Group. (RH Audio).
—Gone for Soldiers: A Novel of the Mexican War. l.t. ed. 2000. 688p. 26.95 (*0-375-43057-1*) Random Hse. Large Print.
—The Last Full Measure. 1998. 576p. 27.95 (*0-345-40491-2*) Ballantine Bks.
—The Last Full Measure: A Novel. l.t. ed. 1998. pap. 25.00 o.s.i (*0-375-70291-1*) Random Hse. Large Print.
Shaara, Jeff, ed. The Last Full Measure. 2000. 640p. mass mkt. 7.99 (*0-345-43481-1*, Ballantine Bks.); 1999. (Illus.). 576p. pap. 14.95 (*0-345-42548-0*); 1998. 25.95 o.s.i (*0-345-43003-4*) Ballantine Bks.
—The Last Full Measure. unabr. collector's ed. 1998. Pt. 1. audio 64.00 (*0-7366-4209-9*, 4708-A); Pt. 2. audio 64.00 (*0-7366-4210-2*, 4708-B) Books on Tape, Inc.
—The Last Full Measure. l.t. ed. 1998. pap. 25.00 o.p. (*0-7838-0155-6*, Macmillan Reference USA) Gale Group.
—The Last Full Measure. abr. ed. 1999. audio 25.95 Highsmith Inc.
—The Last Full Measure. 2000. E-Book 12.50 (*0-345-43850-7*) Random Hse., Inc.
Shaara, Jeff & Shaara, Michael. Gods & Generals. 1996. 512p. 26.95 (*0-345-40492-0*) Ballantine Bks.
Shaara, Michael. Gods & Generals. 1997. (Illus.). 512p. pap. 14.95 (*0-345-40957-4*) Ballantine Bks.
—Gods & Generals. l.t. ed. 1996. 784p. 25.00 o.p. (*0-7838-1686-3*, Macmillan Reference USA) Gale Group.
Shaara, Michael & Shaara, Jeff. Gods & Generals. l.t. ed. 1996. 784p. pap. 25.95 (*0-679-75885-2*) Random Hse. Large Print.

**LEE, WILL (FICTITIOUS CHARACTER)—FICTION**

Woods, Stuart. Capital Crimes. unabr. ed. 2003. (Will Lee Ser.). audio 29.95 (*1-59086-736-X*, 4328, Brilliance Audio Unabridged); audio 69.25 (*1-59086-737-8*, 4329, Library Edition); audio compact disk 82.25 (*1-59086-739-4*, 4331, Brilliance Audio on CD Lib Ed); audio compact disk 29.95 (*1-59086-738-6*, 4330, Brilliance Audio on CD Unabridged) Brilliance Audio.
—Capital Crimes. l.t. ed. 2003. 408p. 32.95 (*1-58724-561-2*, Wheeler Publishing, Inc.) Gale Group.
—Capital Crimes. 2004. 368p. mass mkt. 7.99 (*0-451-21156-1*, Signet Bks.) NAL.
—Capital Crimes. 2003. 304p. 25.95 (*0-399-15090-0*, Putnam & Grosset) Putnam Publishing Group, The.
—Chiefs. 1982. pap. 3.95 o.p. (*0-553-24080-3*) Bantam Bks.
—Chiefs. 1999. 432p. mass mkt. 7.99 (*0-380-70347-5*, Avon Bks.) Morrow/Avon.
—Chiefs. 1981. 14.95 o.s.i (*0-393-01461-4*) Norton, W. W. & Co., Inc.
—Chiefs. 2000. audio compact disk 142.00; 1981. audio 97.00 (*0-7887-4055-5*, 96105E7) Recorded Bks., LLC.
—Grass Roots. l.t. ed. 1990. (General Ser.). 548p. 24.95 (*0-8161-4993-3*, Macmillan Reference USA) Gale Group.
—Grass Roots. 2002. 496p. mass mkt. 7.99 (*0-06-101422-2*); 1990. pap. 6.99 (*0-380-71169-9*) Morrow/Avon. (Avon Bks.).
—Grass Roots. 1989. 19.95 o.p. (*0-671-66739-4*, Simon & Schuster) Simon & Schuster.
—The Run. 2000. 368p. 26.00 (*0-06-019187-2*); 448p. pap. 26.00 (*0-06-019720-X*) HarperCollins Pubs.
—The Run. unabr. ed. 2000. audio 34.95 (*0-694-52318-6*, HarperAudio) HarperTrade.
—The Run. 2001. 400p. mass mkt. 7.99 (*0-06-101343-9*) Morrow/Avon.
—Run Before the Wind. 1999. 320p. mass mkt. 7.99 (*0-380-70507-9*, Avon Bks.) Morrow/Avon.
—Run Before the Wind. 1983. 16.50 o.p. (*0-393-01651-X*) Norton, W. W. & Co., Inc.
—Run Before the Wind. l.t. ed. 1989. (Ulverscroft Large Print Ser.). 624p. 29.99 o.p. (*0-7089-2003-9*, Ulverscroft) Thorpe, F. A. Pubs. GBR. *Dist:* Ulverscroft Large Print Bks., Ltd., Ulverscroft Large Print Canada, Ltd.

**LEFLER, ROBIN (FICTITIOUS CHARACTER)—FICTION**

David, Peter. End Game. 1997. (Star Trek Ser.: No. 4). (Illus.). 208p. pap. 3.99 (*0-671-01398-X*, Star Trek) Simon & Schuster.
—Excalibur: Renaissance. 2000. (Star Trek Ser.: No. 10). 288p. pap. 6.99 (*0-671-04239-4*, Star Trek) Simon & Schuster.
—Fire on High. 1998. (Star Trek Ser.: No. 6). 288p. pap. 6.50 (*0-671-02037-4*, Star Trek) Simon & Schuster.
—House of Cards; Into the Void; The Two-Front War; End Game. abr. ed. 1997. (Star Trek Ser.: Nos. 1-4). audio 22.00 (*0-671-57625-9*, Simon & Schuster Audioworks) Simon & Schuster Audio.

**LEIA, PRINCESS (FICTITIOUS CHARACTER)—FICTION**

Allen, Roger Macbride. Ambush at Corellia. 1995. (Star Wars: Bk. 1). 320p. mass mkt. 6.99 (*0-553-29803-8*, Spectra) Bantam Bks.
—Ambush at Corellia. abr. ed. 1995. (Star Wars: Bk. 1). audio 16.99 (*0-553-47202-X*, 392779, RH Audio) Random Hse. Audio Publishing Group.
—Ambush at Corellia. 1995. (Star Wars: Bk. 1). 12.04 (*0-606-08197-6*) Turtleback Bks.
—Assault at Selonia. 1995. (Star Wars: Bk. 2). 320p. mass mkt. 6.99 (*0-553-29805-4*, Spectra) Bantam Bks.
—Assault at Selonia. abr. ed. 1995. (Star Wars: Bk. 2). (J). (gr. k). audio 16.99 (*0-553-47203-8*, RH Audio) Random Hse. Audio Publishing Group.
—Assault at Selonia. 1995. (Star Wars: Bk. 2). 12.04 (*0-606-08198-4*) Turtleback Bks.
—The Corellian Trilogy Boxed Set: Ambush at Corellia; Assault at Selonia; Showdown at Centerpoint. 1997. (Star Wars). (YA). (gr. 5 up). mass mkt. 17.97 o.s.i (*0-553-94083-X*, Spectra) Bantam Bks.
—The Corellian Trilogy Boxed Set: Ambush at Corellia; Assault at Selonia; Showdown at Centerpoint. 1999. (Star Wars). (YA). (gr. 5 up). incl. audio Random Hse. Audio Publishing Group.
—Showdown at Centerpoint. 1995. (Star Wars: Bk. 3). 336p. mass mkt. 6.99 (*0-553-29806-2*, Spectra) Bantam Bks.
—Showdown at Centerpoint. abr. ed. 1995. (Star Wars: Bk. 3 ). audio 16.99 (*0-553-47204-6*, RH Audio) Random Hse. Audio Publishing Group.
—Showdown at Centerpoint. 1995. (Star Wars: Bk. 3). 11.09 o.p. (*0-606-09891-7*) Turtleback Bks.
Allston, Aaron. Star Wars. 1999. (Star Wars Ser.). mass mkt. 5.99 (*0-553-58125-2*) Bantam Bks.
Anderson, Kevin J. Champions of the Force. 1994. (Star Wars: Vol. 3). 368p. mass mkt. 6.99 (*0-553-29802-X*) Bantam Bks.
—Champions of the Force. abr. ed. 1994. (star wars: Vol. 3). audio 16.99 (*0-553-47201-1*, RH Audio) Random Hse. Audio Publishing Group.
—Champions of the Force. 1994. (Star Wars: Vol. 3). 12.04 (*0-606-08204-2*) Turtleback Bks.
—Dark Apprentice. 1994. (Star Wars: Vol. 2). 368p. mass mkt. 6.99 (*0-553-29799-6*) Bantam Bks.
—Dark Apprentice. abr. ed. 1994. (star wars: Vol. 2). audio 16.99 (*0-553-47200-3*); audio 16.98 o.s.i (*0-553-74564-6*) Random Hse. Audio Publishing Group. (RH Audio).
—Dark Apprentice. 1994. (Star Wars: Vol. 2). 12.04 (*0-606-08203-4*) Turtleback Bks.
—The Jedi Academy Trilogy Omnibus. abr. ed. 1997. (Star Wars Ser.). (gr. 5 up). 29.95 incl. audio (*0-553-47848-6*, RH Audio) Random Hse. Audio Publishing Group.
—Jedi Search. 1994. (Star Wars: Vol. 1). 384p. mass mkt. 6.99 (*0-553-29798-8*) Bantam Bks.
—Jedi Search. abr. ed. 1994. (star wars: Vol. 1). audio 16.98 o.s.i (*0-553-74512-3*); audio 16.99 (*0-553-47199-6*) Random Hse. Audio Publishing Group. (RH Audio).
—Jedi Search. 1994. (Star Wars: Vol. 1). 12.04 (*0-606-08202-6*) Turtleback Bks.
—Jedi Trilogy: Jedi Search; Dark Apprentice; Champions of the Force, 3 vols. 1997. (Star Wars). (YA). (gr. 5). 20.97 (*0-553-64839-X*) Bantam Bks.
Austin, Terry, et al. Splinter of the Mind's Eye. 1996. (Star Wars Ser.). (Illus.). 112p. (YA). (gr. 5 up). pap. 14.95 (*1-56971-223-9*) Dark Horse Comics.
Baron, Mike, et al. Dark Force Rising. 1998. (Star Wars Ser.). (Illus.). 160p. (YA). (gr. 7 up). pap. 17.95 (*1-56971-269-7*) Dark Horse Comics.
Daley, Brian. The Empire Strikes Back: The National Public Radio Dramatization. 1995. (Star Wars Ser.). (Illus.). 320p. pap. 19.00 o.s.i (*0-345-39605-7*, Del Rey) Ballantine Bks.
—Return of the Jedi: The National Public Radio Dramatization. 1996. 208p. pap. 15.00 o.s.i (*0-345-40782-2*) Ballantine Bks.
—Star Wars: The National Public Radio Dramatization. 1994. (Star Wars Ser.). (Illus.). 352p. pap. 19.00 o.s.i (*0-345-39109-8*, Del Rey) Ballantine Bks.
Dark Horse Comics Staff, et al. Empires End. 1997. (Star Wars Ser.). (Illus.). 56p. (YA). (gr. 7 up). pap. 5.95 (*1-56971-306-5*) Dark Horse Comics.
—Shadows of the Empire. 1997. (Star Wars Ser.). (Illus.). 160p. (YA). (gr. 7 up). pap. 17.95 (*1-56971-183-6*) Dark Horse Comics.
Foster, Alan Dean. Splinter of the Mind's Eye. 1994. mass mkt. 4.99 o.s.i (*0-345-90332-3*); 1986. 304p. mass mkt. 6.99 (*0-345-32023-9*); 1978. 7.95 o.p. (*0-345-27566-7*) Ballantine Bks. (Del Rey).
Gardner, J. J. The Empire Strikes Back. 1997. (Star Wars Ser.). (Illus.). (J). (gr. 5-7). mass mkt. 5.99 (*0-590-06656-0*) Scholastic, Inc.
—Star Wars Movie Story. 1997. (Star Wars Ser.). (J). (gr. 5-7). mass mkt. 5.99 (*0-590-06654-4*) Scholastic, Inc.
Glut, Donald F. The Empire Strikes Back. 1997. (Star Wars Ser.). pap. 5.99 (*0-345-91183-0*); 1995. (Star Wars Ser.). 224p. 16.00 o.s.i (*0-345-40078-X*); 1985. (Star Wars Ser.: Vol. 2). 224p. mass mkt. 5.99 (*0-345-32022-0*); 1980. mass mkt. 2.25 o.p. (*0-345-28392-9*) Ballantine Bks. (Del Rey).
Golden, Christopher. Shadows of the Empire. 1996. (Star Wars Ser.). (Illus.). 176p. (J). (gr. 4-7). pap. text 4.50 o.s.i (*0-440-41303-6*) Dell Publishing.
—Shadows of the Empire: A Junior Novelization. 1996. (Star Wars Ser.). 10.55 (*0-606-11835-7*) Turtleback Bks.
Goodwin, Archie. The Empire Strikes Back: Classic Star Wars. 1995. (Star Wars Ser.). (Illus.). 104p. pap. 9.95 o.p. (*1-56971-088-0*) Dark Horse Comics.
Goodwin, Archie, et al. The Empire Strikes Back: Special Edition. 1997. (Star Wars Ser.). 104p. (J). (gr. 3 up). pap. 9.95 (*1-56971-234-4*) Dark Horse Comics.
—Return of the Jedi: Special Edition. 1997. (Star Wars Ser.). 104p. (YA). (gr. 3 up). pap. 9.95 (*1-56971-235-2*) Dark Horse Comics.
Hambly, Barbara. Children of the Jedi. 1996. (Star Wars Ser.). mass mkt. 10.95 o.s.i (*0-553-84008-8*); 432p. reprint ed. mass mkt. 6.99 (*0-553-57293-8*, Spectra) Bantam Bks.
—Children of the Jedi. 1995. audio 16.98 o.s.i (*0-553-74566-2*); audio 16.99 (*0-553-47195-3*) Random Hse. Audio Publishing Group. (RH Audio).
—Children of the Jedi. 1996. (Star Wars Ser.). 12.04 (*0-606-11887-X*) Turtleback Bks.
—Night Lily: The Lover's Tale. abr. ed. 1995. (Star Wars Ser.). audio compact disk 13.99 o.s.i (*0-553-45541-9*, , RH Audio) Random Hse. Audio Publishing Group.
—Nightlily: The Lover's Tale. abr. ed. 1995. (Star Wars Ser.). audio 12.00 o.p. (*0-553-45413-7*, RH Audio) Random Hse. Audio Publishing Group.
—Planet of Twilight. 1998. (Star Wars Ser.). 416p. reprint ed. mass mkt. 6.99 (*0-553-57517-1*) Bantam Bks.
—Planet of Twilight. abr. ed. 1997. (Star Wars Ser.). audio 16.99 (*0-553-47196-1*, RH Audio) Random Hse. Audio Publishing Group.
Hamill, Mark, et al. Star Wars: The Original Radio Drama. abr. unabr. ed. 1993. (Star Wars Ser.). audio 39.95 (*0-942110-99-4*, 692313); audio compact disk 64.95 (*1-56511-005-6*) HighBridge Co.
Jones, Bruce, et al. Star Wars: A New Hope. 1997. (Star Wars Ser.). 104p. (YA). (gr. 3 up). pap. 9.95 (*1-56971-213-1*) Dark Horse Comics.
—Star Wars Trilogy: A New Hope, Empire Strikes Back, Return of the Jedi. 2nd ed. 1997. (Star Wars Ser.). (Illus.). (J). (gr. 3 up). pap. 29.85 o.p. (*1-56971-257-3*) Dark Horse Comics.
Kahn, James. Return of the Jedi. (Star Wars Ser.). 1997. mass mkt. 5.99 (*0-345-91184-9*, Del Rey); 1995. 240p. 16.00 (*0-345-40079-8*, Del Rey); 1983. (Illus.). 224p. mass mkt. 5.95 o.p. (*0-345-30960-X*); 1983. 192p. mass mkt. 5.99 (*0-345-30767-4*, Del Rey) Ballantine Bks.
Kube-McDowell, Michael P. Before the Storm. 1996. (Star Wars: Bk. 1). 336p. mass mkt. 6.99 (*0-553-57273-3*, Spectra) Bantam Bks.
—Before the Storm. abr. ed. 1996. (Star Wars: Bk. 1). audio 16.99 (*0-553-47422-7*, 394259, RH Audio) Random Hse. Audio Publishing Group.
—Before the Storm. 1996. (Star Wars: Bk. 1). 12.04 (*0-606-11884-5*) Turtleback Bks.
—Shield of Lies. 1996. (Star Wars: Bk. 2). pap. 10.95 o.s.i (*0-553-84010-X*); 368p. mass mkt. 6.99 (*0-553-57277-6*, Spectra) Bantam Bks.
—Shield of Lies. abr. ed. 1996. (Star Wars: Bk. 2). audio 16.99 o.s.i (*0-553-47424-3*, 394260, RH Audio) Random Hse. Audio Publishing Group.
—Shield of Lies. 1996. (Star Wars: Bk. 2). 12.04 (*0-606-11885-3*) Turtleback Bks.
—Tyrant's Test. 1996. (Star Wars: Bk. 3). (Illus.). 400p. (gr. 5 up). mass mkt. 6.99 (*0-553-57275-X*, Spectra) Bantam Bks.
—Tyrant's Test. abr. ed. 1996. (Star Wars: Bk. 3). audio 16.99 (*0-553-47421-9*, 394598, RH Audio) Random Hse. Audio Publishing Group.
—Tyrant's Test. 1997. (Star Wars: Bk. 3). 12.04 (*0-606-11886-1*) Turtleback Bks.
Levy, Elizabeth, adapted by. Return of the Jedi. 1995. (Illus.). 64p. (J). (gr. 4-7). pap. 3.99 (*0-679-87205-1*) Random Hse., Inc.
Lucas, George. The Empire Strikes Back. 1994. 8.98 (*1-57042-172-2*) Warner Bks., Inc.

—The Empire Strikes Back: The Original Radio Drama. abr. unabr. ed. 1993. (Star Wars Ser.). audio 39.95 (*1-56511-000-5*, 492026); audio compact disk 59.95 (*1-56511-007-2*) HighBridge Co.

—Return of the Jedi. 1997. mass mkt. 5.99 o.s.i (*0-345-41356-3*, Del Rey) Ballantine Bks.

—Return of the Jedi. 1995. 8.98 (*1-57042-208-7*) Warner Bks., Inc.

—Return of the Jedi: The Original Radio Drama. abr. unabr. ed. 1996. (Star Wars Ser.). audio 25.95 (*1-56511-157-5*); audio compact disk 34.95 (*1-56511-158-3*) HighBridge Co.

—Star Wars: A New Hope. 1995. (Star Wars Ser.). 272p. 16.00 o.s.i (*0-345-40077-1*, Del Rey) Ballantine Bks.

—Star Wars: A New Hope. 1996. (YA). (gr. 7-12). audio 17.00 o.p. (*1-57042-248-6*) Time Warner AudioBooks.

—Star Wars: A New Hope. 1998. (Star Wars Manga Ser.: Bk. 4). (Illus.). 96p. (YA). (gr. 3 up). pap. 9.95 (*1-56971-365-0*); pap. 9.95 (*1-56971-364-2*); pap. 9.95 (*1-56971-362-6*) Dark Horse Comics.

—Star Wars: A New Hope, Script Facsimiles. deluxe ed. 1998. (Star Wars Ser.). (Illus.). 176p. pap. 18.95 (*0-345-42080-2*, Del Rey) Ballantine Bks.

—Star Wars: A New Hope: The Illustrated Screenplay. 1998. (Star Wars Trilogy Ser.). (Illus.). 208p. pap. 12.00 o.s.i (*0-345-42069-1*, Del Rey) Ballantine Bks.

—Star Wars Adventures. abr. ed. 1994. (Star Wars Ser.). audio 8.98 o.p. Time Warner AudioBooks.

Lucas, George. Star Wars Trilogy: Star Wars; The Empire Strikes Back; Return of the Jedi. unabr. ed. 1994. (Star Wars Ser.). audio 50.00 o.p. (*1-57042-157-9*, 4-521579); audio 75.00 o.p. (*1-57042-169-2*, 2-521579) Time Warner AudioBooks.

Lucas, George & Kasdan, Lawrence. Return of the Jedi. deluxe ed. 1998. (Star Wars Ser.). (Illus.). 144p. pap. 18.95 (*0-345-42082-9*, Ballantine Bks.) Ballantine Bks.

—Return of the Jedi: The Illustrated Screenplay. 1998. (Illus.). 208p. pap. 12.00 (*0-345-42079-9*, Del Rey) Ballantine Bks.

Lucas, George, et al. The Empire Strikes Back. deluxe ed. 1998. (Star Wars Ser.). (Illus.). 160p. pap. 18.95 o.s.i (*0-345-42081-0*, Del Rey) Ballantine Bks.

—Star Wars Trilogy: Star Wars; The Empire Strikes Back; Return of the Jedi. (Star Wars Ser.). 1997. mass mkt. 6.99 (*0-345-91126-1*); 1993. 480p. mass mkt. 7.99 (*0-345-38438-5*, Del Rey); 1987. 480p. pap. 12.95 (*0-345-34806-0*, Del Rey) Ballantine Bks.

—Star Wars Trilogy: Star Wars; The Empire Strikes Back; Return of the Jedi. 1987. (J). (gr. 3-7). 16.05 (*0-606-01231-1*) Turtleback Bks.

Lucasfilm Ltd. The Complete Trilogy Cassette Gift-Pack: Star Wars, The Empire Strikes Back, & Return of the Jedi. abr. ed. 1996. (Star Wars Ser.). audio 105.85 o.p. (*1-56511-173-7*) HighBridge Co.

Lucasfilm Ltd. Staff. The Last Command. unabr. ed. 1996. (Star Wars: Bk. 3). audio 104.00. audio Books on Tape, Inc.

—Star Wars. 1999. pap. 0.90 o.s.i (*0-375-80892-2*, Random Hse. Bks. for Young Readers) Random Hse. Children's Bks.

Luceno, James. Agents of Chaos II: Jedi Eclipse. 2000. (Star Wars Ser.: Bk. 5). 368p. mass mkt. 6.99 (*0-345-42859-5*, Ballantine Bks.) Ballantine Bks.

Manning, Russ & Goodwin, Archie. The Early Adventures. 1997. (Classic Star Wars Ser.). (Illus.). 240p. (J). (gr. 3 up). pap. 19.95 (*1-56971-178-X*) Dark Horse Comics.

McIntyre, Vonda N. The Crystal Star. 1994. audio 13.59 o.s.i (*0-553-70082-0*, RH Audio) Random Hse. Audio Publishing Group.

—Crystal Star. abr. ed. 1994. (Star Wars Ser.). audio 16.99 (*0-553-47194-5*, RH Audio) Random Hse. Audio Publishing Group.

—The Crystal Star. 1995. (Star Wars Ser.). 448p. reprint ed. mass mkt. 6.99 (*0-553-57174-5*) Bantam Bks.

Perry, Steve. Shadows of the Empire. 1997. (Star Wars Ser.). 416p. (gr. 5 up). mass mkt. 6.99 (*0-553-57413-2*, Spectra) Bantam Bks.

—Shadows of the Empire. abr. ed. 1996. (Star Wars Ser.). audio 16.99 (*0-553-47438-3*, 393956, RH Audio) Random Hse. Audio Publishing Group.

—Shadows of the Empire. 1996. (Star Wars Ser.). 12.04 (*0-606-11895-0*) Turtleback Bks.

Perry, Steve, et al. Evolution: Shadows of the Empire. 2000. (Star Wars Ser.). (Illus.). 120p. (YA). (gr. 7 up). pap. 14.95 (*1-56971-441-X*) Dark Horse Comics.

Rusch, Kristine K. The New Rebellion. 1997. (Star Wars Ser.). 560p. mass mkt. 6.99 (*0-553-57414-0*, Spectra) Bantam Bks.

—The New Rebellion. 1997. (Star Wars Ser.). 12.04 (*0-606-11894-2*) Turtleback Bks.

—New Rebellion. abr. ed. 1996. (Star Wars Ser.). audio 16.99 (*0-553-47743-9*, RH Audio) Random Hse. Audio Publishing Group.

Salvatore, R. A. Vector Prime. (Star Wars Ser.). 2003. E-Book 2.99 (*0-345-46740-X*, Ballantine Bks.); 2000. 416p. mass mkt. 7.50 (*0-345-42845-5*); 1999. 400p. 24.95 (*0-345-42844-7*) Ballantine Bks.

—Vector Prime. abr. ed. 1999. (Star Wars: Bk. 1). audio 18.00 (*0-375-40689-1*, RH Audio) Random Hse. Audio Publishing Group.

Star Wars Trilogy: Star Wars; The Empire Strikes Back; Return of the Jedi, 3 vols. 1987. (Star Wars Ser.). pap. 8.65 o.p. (*0-345-32964-3*, Del Rey) Ballantine Bks.

Tyers, Kathy. Balance Point. 2000. (Star Wars Ser.: Bk. 6). 352p. 25.95 (*0-345-42857-9*, Del Rey) Ballantine Bks.

—Star Wars - The New Jedi Order: Balance Point. abr. ed. 2000. (Star Wars). audio 18.00 (*0-375-41624-2*, RH Audio) Random Hse. Audio Publishing Group.

—The Truce at Bakura. 1994. (Star Wars Ser.). 352p. mass mkt. 6.99 (*0-553-56872-8*) Bantam Bks.

—The Truce at Bakura. 1993. audio 13.59 o.s.i (*0-553-70065-0*, RH Audio) Random Hse. Audio Publishing Group.

—The Truce at Bakura. 1994. (Star Wars Ser.). 11.09 o.p. (*0-606-08201-8*) Turtleback Bks.

Veitch, Tom. Dark Empire. 2nd ed. 1993. (Star Wars Ser.). (Illus.). 184p. (YA). (gr. 7 up). pap. 17.95 (*1-56971-073-2*) Dark Horse Comics.

—Dark Empire I. abr. ed. 1994. (Star Wars Ser.). audio 17.00 o.p. (*1-57042-083-1*, 4-520831) Time Warner AudioBooks.

—Dark Empire II. 1995. (Star Wars Ser.). (Illus.). 168p. (YA). (gr. 7 up). pap. 17.95 (*1-56971-119-4*) Dark Horse Comics.

—Dark Empire II. abr. ed. 1995. (Star Wars Ser.). audio 17.00 o.p. (*1-57042-309-1*, 4-523091) Time Warner AudioBooks.

—Star Wars: Dark Empire. abr. ed. 1997. (Star Wars Ser.). audio 16.95 (*1-56511-200-8*) HighBridge Co.

—Star Wars: Dark Empire II. abr. ed. 1997. (Star Wars Ser.). pap. 16.95 incl. audio (*1-56511-201-6*) HighBridge Co.

Veitch, Tom & Kennedy, Cam. Dark Empire: The Collected Edition. 1993. (Star Wars Ser.). (Illus.). pap. 16.95 o.p. (*1-878574-56-6*); 99.95 o.p. (*1-878574-57-4*) Dark Horse Comics.

Weinberg, Larry. The Empire Strikes Back: Classic Star Wars. 1995. (Star Wars Ser.). (Illus.). 54p. (J). (gr. 4-7). pap. 3.99 o.s.i (*0-679-87204-3*) Random Hse., Inc.

Whitman, John & Lucas, George. Star Wars. 1996. (Mighty Chronicles Ser.). (Illus.). 432p. (gr. 4-7). 9.95 o.s.i (*0-8118-1480-7*) Chronicle Bks. LLC.

Wolverton, Dave. The Courtship of Princess Leia. 1995. (Star Wars Ser.). 400p. mass mkt. 6.99 (*0-553-56937-6*) Bantam Bks.

—The Courtship of Princess Leia. abr. ed. 1994. (Star Wars Ser.). audio 16.99 (*0-553-47193-7*, RH Audio) Random Hse. Audio Publishing Group.

—The Courtship of Princess Leia. 1994. (Star Wars Ser.). 12.04 (*0-606-08199-2*) Turtleback Bks.

Zahn, Timothy. Dark Force Rising. (Star Wars: Bk. 2). 1993. 448p. mass mkt. 6.99 (*0-553-56071-9*); 1992. 368p. 18.50 o.s.i (*0-553-08574-3*); Vol. 2. 1992. 384p. 125.00 o.s.i (*0-553-08907-2*, Spectra) Bantam Bks.

—Dark Force Rising. unabr. ed. 1995. (Star Wars: Bk. 2). audio 96.00 Books on Tape, Inc.

—Dark Force Rising. abr. ed. 1992. (Star Wars: Bk. 2). audio 16.99 (*0-553-47055-8*, RH Audio) Random Hse. Audio Publishing Group.

—Heir to the Empire. (Star Wars: Bk. 1). 9999. pap. 9.90 o.s.i (*0-593-02481-8*); 1992. 432p. mass mkt. 6.99 (*0-553-29612-4*); 1991. 368p. 22.95 o.s.i (*0-553-07327-3*); 1991. 368p. 125.00 o.s.i (*0-553-07340-0*, Spectra) Bantam Bks.

—Heir to the Empire. unabr. ed. 1995. (Star Wars: Bk. 1). audio 88.00 Books on Tape, Inc.

—Heir to the Empire. abr. ed. 1991. (Star Wars: Bk. 1). audio 16.99 (*0-553-45296-7*, 391663, RH Audio) Random Hse. Audio Publishing Group.

—Heir to the Empire. 1993. (Star Wars: Bk. 1). 64.95 o.p. incl. audio (*0-7838-1100-4*); 64.95 o.p. incl. audio (*0-7838-1100-4*) Thorndike Pr.

—Heir to the Empire. 1991. (Star Wars: Bk. 1). 12.04 (*0-606-00751-2*) Turtleback Bks.

—The Last Command. (Star Wars: Bk. 3). 1994. 496p. mass mkt. 6.99 (*0-553-56492-7*, Spectra); 1993. 416p. 125.00 o.s.i (*0-553-09500-5*) Bantam Bks.

—The Last Command. abr. ed. 1993. (Star Wars: Bk. 3). audio 16.99 (*0-553-47157-0*, RH Audio) Random Hse. Audio Publishing Group.

—The Last Command. 1994. (Star Wars: Bk. 3). 12.04 (*0-606-08205-0*) Turtleback Bks.

—Specter of the Past. 1998. (Star Wars Hand of Thrawn Ser.: No. 1). 416p. (gr. 5 up). mass mkt. 6.99 (*0-553-29804-6*) Bantam Bks.

—Specter of the Past. abr. ed. 1997. (Star Wars Ser.: Vol. 1). (gr. 5 up). audio 16.99 (*0-553-47893-1*, RH Audio) Random Hse. Audio Publishing Group.

—Specter of the Past. l.t. ed. 1998. (Star Wars). 512p. 25.95 (*0-7838-8434-6*) Thorndike Pr.

—Star Wars. 1994. (Star Wars Ser.). pap. 17.95 o.s.i (*0-553-63485-2*) Bantam Bks.

—The Thrawn Trilogy. abr. ed. 2000. (Star Wars: Bk. 1,2,3). 29.95 incl. audio (*0-553-52699-5*);Set. (YA). 29.95 incl. audio Random Hse. Audio Publishing Group.

—Vision of the Future. 1999. (Star Wars Hand of Thrawn Ser.: No. 2). 720p. (gr. 5 up). mass mkt. 6.99 (*0-553-57879-0*) Bantam Bks.

—Vision of the Future. abr. ed. 1998. (Star Wars Ser.: Vol. 2). (gr. 5 up). audio 16.99 (*0-553-47921-0*, 392221, RH Audio) Random Hse. Audio Publishing Group.

Zahn, Timothy, et al. Heir to the Empire. 1996. (Star Wars Ser.). (Illus.). 160p. (YA). (gr. 7 up). pap. 19.95 (*1-56971-202-6*) Dark Horse Comics.

## LEIDL, CONSTANCE (FICTITIOUS CHARACTER)—FICTION

Wilhelm, Kate. The Casebook of Constance & Charlie. Vol. 1. 1999. 614p. pap. 18.95 (*0-312-24501-7*); Vol. 2. 2000. 595p. pap. 16.95 (*0-312-25378-8*) St. Martin's Pr. (Saint Martin's Griffin).

—The Dark Door. 1993. 352p. pap. 4.50 (*0-8439-3416-6*) Dorchester Publishing Co., Inc.

—The Dark Door. 1988. 256p. 16.95 o.p. (*0-312-02182-8*) St. Martin's Pr.

—A Flush of Shadows: Five Short Novels. 1996. mass mkt. 5.99 o.s.i (*0-449-22434-1*, Fawcett) Ballantine Bks.

—A Flush of Shadows: Five Short Novels. 1995. 352p. 22.95 o.p. (*0-312-13075-9*, Saint Martin's Minotaur) St. Martin's Pr.

—Hamlet Trap: A Charlie Meiklejohn & Constance Leidl Mystery. 1988. mass mkt. 4.50 (*0-312-91125-4*, St. Martin's Paperbacks) St. Martin's Pr.

—The Hamlet Trap: A Constance & Charlie Meiklejohn Mystery. 1987. 240p. 15.95 o.p. (*0-312-94000-9*, Saint Martin's Minotaur) St. Martin's Pr.

—A Sense of Shadow, 001. 1981. 9.95 o.p. (*0-395-30545-4*) Houghton Mifflin Co.

—Seven Kinds of Death. 1994. 256p. reprint ed. pap. 4.50 (*0-8439-3570-7*) Dorchester Publishing Co., Inc.

—Seven Kinds of Death. 1992. 256p. 18.95 o.p. (*0-312-08290-8*, Saint Martin's Minotaur) St. Martin's Pr.

—Smart House. l.t. ed. 1991. 16.95 o.p. (*0-7451-9790-6*, C0300); pap. 15.95 o.p. (*0-7927-0255-7*, C0434) BBC Audiobooks America.

—Smart House. 1991. 272p. reprint ed. pap. 3.95 (*0-8439-3043-8*) Dorchester Publishing Co., Inc.

—Smart House: A Charlie Meiklejohn-Constance Leidl Mystery. 1989. 272p. 16.95 o.p. (*0-312-02642-0*, Saint Martin's Minotaur) St. Martin's Pr.

—Sweet, Sweet Poison. 1991. 272p. reprint ed. pap. 3.99 (*0-8439-3163-9*) Dorchester Publishing Co., Inc.

—Sweet, Sweet Poison. 1990. 16.95 o.p. (*0-312-04433-X*, Saint Martin's Minotaur) St. Martin's Pr.

## LEIGH, MARTHA (FICTITIOUS CHARACTER)—FICTION

Holt, Victoria. Mistress of Mellyn. 1992. mass mkt. 5.99 o.p. (*0-449-45002-3*, Fawcett); 1988. mass mkt. o.s.i (*0-449-20227-5*); 1981. 240p. mass mkt. 3.50 o.s.i (*0-449-23924-1*, Fawcett); 1978. mass mkt. 1.75 o.s.i (*0-449-23124-0*) Ballantine Bks.

—Mistress of Mellyn. 1988. 12.95 o.p. (*0-385-00912-7*) Doubleday Publishing.

—Mistress of Mellyn. l.t. ed. 1969. (Ulverscroft Large Print Ser.). o.p. (*0-85456-705-4*, Ulverscroft) Thorpe, F. A. Pubs. GBR. *Dist:* Ulverscroft Large Print Canada, Ltd.

—Mistress of Mellyn. unabr. ed. 1999. audio 54.95 BBC Audiobooks America.

## LEIGH, ROSALIND (FICTITIOUS CHARACTER)—FICTION

Walters, Minette. The Sculptress. l.t. ed. 1994. (Magna Large Print Ser.). 488p. 29.99 o.p. (*0-7505-0625-3*) Magna Large Print Bks. GBR. *Dist:* Ulverscroft Large Print Bks., Ltd., Ulverscroft Large Print Canada, Ltd.

—The Sculptress. 1993. (Illus.). 308p. 21.95 o.p. (*0-312-09909-6*, Saint Martin's Minotaur); Vol. 1. 1994. mass mkt. 7.99 (*0-312-95361-5*, St. Martin's Paperbacks) St. Martin's Pr.

## LENAHAN, KIERAN (FICTITIOUS CHARACTER)—FICTION

Daly, Conor. Buried Lies. (Kieran Lenahan Mystery Ser.). 1997. 304p. mass mkt. 5.50 o.s.i (*1-57566-168-3*); 1996. 320p. 18.95 o.p. (*1-57566-033-4*) Kensington Publishing Corp.

—Local Knowledge. 1997. pap. 9.95 o.s.i (*1-57566-153-5*); 1996. mass mkt. 4.99 o.s.i (*1-57566-036-9*) Kensington Publishing Corp.

## LENNOX, BILL (FICTITIOUS CHARACTER)—FICTION

Traylor, James L., ed. Hollywood Troubleshooter: W. T. Ballards Bill Lennox Stories. 1985. 156p. 19.95 (*0-87972-316-5*, Popular Pr.) Univ. of Wisconsin Pr.

## LENNOX, TORY (FICTITIOUS CHARACTER)—FICTION

Gibbs, Tony. Fade to Black. 1997. 256p. 22.50 o.p. (*0-89296-602-5*); 1996. 328p. 21.95 o.p. (*0-89296-603-3*) Mysterious Pr.

—Shot in the Dark. 1997. 320p. mass mkt. 5.99 (*0-446-40519-1*) Warner Bks., Inc.

## LENSON, DAN (FICTITIOUS CHARACTER)—FICTION

Poyer, David. Black Storm: A David Lenson Novel. 384p. 2003. (Illus.). mass mkt. 6.99 (*0-312-98385-9*, St. Martin's Paperbacks); 2002. 24.95 (*0-312-26969-2*) St. Martin's Pr.

—China Sea: A Dan Lenson Novel. 2000. (Dan Lenson Novels Ser.). (Illus.). 352p. 24.95 (*0-312-20287-3*) St. Martin's Pr.

—The Circle. 1993. 543p. mass mkt. 6.99 (*0-312-92964-1*, St. Martin's Paperbacks); 1992. 416p. 21.95 o.p. (*0-312-07671-1*) St. Martin's Pr.

—The Gulf. 442p. 1991. (Illus.). mass mkt. 7.99 (*0-312-92577-8*, St. Martin's Paperbacks); 1990. 19.95 o.p. (*0-312-05096-8*) St. Martin's Pr.

—The Med. (Illus.). 1991. 576p. mass mkt. 6.99 (*0-312-92722-3*, St. Martin's Paperbacks); 1988. 512p. 19.95 o.p. (*0-312-01788-X*) St. Martin's Pr.

—The Passage. 1997. 560p. mass mkt. 6.99 (*0-312-95450-6*, St. Martin's Paperbacks); 1994. (*0-312-11381-1*); 1994. 516p. 22.95 o.p. (*0-312-11874-0*) St. Martin's Pr.

—Tomahawk. (Dan Lenson Novels Ser.). 2000. 480p. mass mkt. 6.99 (*0-312-96561-3*, St. Martin's Paperbacks); 1998. 384p. 24.95 (*0-312-17975-8*) St. Martin's Pr.

—Tomahawk. l.t. ed. 1998. (Americana Ser.). 672p. 28.95 (*0-7862-1457-0*) Thorndike Pr.

## LEONARDO, DA VINCI, 1452-1519—FICTION

Berry, R. M. Leonardo's Horse. 1997. (Illus.). 317p. (Orig.). pap. 13.95 (*1-57366-031-0*) Fiction Collective Two, Inc.

Dann, Jack. The Memory Cathedral: A Secret History of Leonardo da Vinci. 1995. 512p. 22.95 o.s.i (*0-553-09637-0*); 1996. 508p. reprint ed. pap. 27.00 (*0-553-37857-0*) Bantam Bks.

Defirenze, Rina. Mystery of the Mona Lisa: Leonardo Da Vinci's Greatest Painting. 1996. 354p. 22.95 o.p. (*0-8038-9381-7*) Hastings Hse. Daytrips Pubs.

Herman, George. A Comedy of Murders. 1994. 448p. 23.95 o.p. (*0-7867-0064-5*, Carroll & Graf Pubs.) Avalon Publishing Group.

—The Tears of the Madonna. 1996. 288p. 22.95 o.p. (*0-7867-0243-5*, Carroll & Graf Pubs.) Avalon Publishing Group.

Perutz, Leo. Leonardo's Judas. Mosbacher, Eric, tr. from GER. 1989. 160p. lib. bdg. 16.95 o.s.i (*1-55970-002-5*) Arcade Publishing, Inc.

West, Cameron. The Medici Dagger. 2002. E-Book 5.99 (*0-7434-2451-4*); 2001. (Illus.). 256p. 25.00 (*0-7434-2035-7*) Simon & Schuster. (Atria).

## LEROY, PETER (FICTITIOUS CHARACTER)—FICTION

Kraft, Eric. At Home with the Glynns: The Personal History, Experiences & Observations of Peter Leroy (Continued) 1996. pap. 11.00 (*0-312-14279-X*) Picador.

—Do Clams Bite? 1982. (Peter Leroy Ser.: Vol. 1, No. 2). (Illus.). 96p. pap. 4.95 o.p. (*0-918222-45-1*) Applewood Bks.

—Do Clams Bite? 1986. 96p. mass mkt. 4.95 o.p. (*0-446-38353-8*) Warner Bks., Inc.

—The Fox & the Clam. 1984. (Personal History, Adventures, Experiences & Observations of Peter Leroy Ser.). pap. 4.95 o.p. (*0-918222-53-2*) Applewood Bks.

—Leaving Small's Hotel. 1999. 352p. pap. 14.00 (*0-312-20660-7*); 1998. 336p. 23.00 o.p. (*0-312-18689-4*) Picador.

—Life on the Bolotomy. 1983. (Peter Leroy Ser.: Vol. 1, No. 3). (Illus.). 96p. pap. 4.95 o.p. (*0-918222-48-6*) Applewood Bks.

—Life on the Bolotomy. 1986. 96p. mass mkt. 4.95 o.p. (*0-446-38354-6*) Warner Bks., Inc.

—The Little Follies: The Personal History, Adventure, Experiences & Observations of Peter Leroy (So Far) 1995. pap. 13.00 (*0-312-11928-3*) Picador.

—Mutiny!, No. 10. 1985. 96p. pap. 4.95 o.p. (*0-918222-76-1*) Applewood Bks.

—My Mother Takes a Tumble. 1982. (Portable Peter Leroy Ser.: Vol. 1 No. 1). 96p. pap. 4.95 o.p. (*0-918222-40-0*) Applewood Bks.

—My Mother Takes a Tumble. 1986. 96p. mass mkt. 4.95 o.p. (*0-446-38350-3*) Warner Bks., Inc.

—The Personal History, Adventures, Experiences, & Observations of Peter Leroy, Vol. 1. 1983. (Peter Leroy Ser.). 400p. 17.95 o.p. (*0-918222-50-8*) Applewood Bks.

—Peter Leroy: Take the Long Way Home. 1984. (Peter Leroy Ser.: No. 7). pap. 4.95 o.p. (*0-918222-61-3*) Applewood Bks.

—The Static of the Spheres. 1983. (Peter Leroy Ser.: Vol. 1, No. 4). pap. 4.95 o.p. (*0-918222-49-4*) Applewood Bks.

—The Static of the Spheres. 1986. 96p. mass mkt. 4.95 o.p. (0-446-38356-2) Warner Bks., Inc.
—What a Piece of Work I Am. 3rd ed. 1995. 288p. pap. 11.00 (0-312-13211-5) Picador.
—What a Piece of Work I Am: A Novel. 1994. 275p. 22.00 o.s.i (0-517-59612-1, Crown) Crown Publishing Group.
—Where Do You Stop? The Personal History, Adventures, Experiences, & Observations of Peter Leroy. 1992. (Illus.). 192p. 15.00 o.s.i (0-517-58544-8, Crown) Crown Publishing Group.
—Where Do You Stop? The Personal History, Adventures, Experiences & Observations of Peter Leroy. 1995. pap. 10.00 (0-312-11932-1) Picador.
—The Young Tars, No. 9. 1985. 96p. pap. 4.95 o.p. (0-918222-68-0) Applewood Bks.

**LESTAT (FICTITIOUS CHARACTER)—FICTION**

Rice, Anne. Blackwood Farm. 2003. 640p. mass mkt. 7.99 (0-345-44368-3) Ballantine Bks.
—Blackwood Farm. audio compact disk (0-7366-8866-8); 2002. audio 96.00 (0-7366-8865-X) Books on Tape, Inc.
—Blackwood Farm. 2002. (Vampire Chronicles). 544p. 26.95 (0-375-41199-2); (0-676-97542-9) Knopf, Alfred A. Inc.
—Blackwood Farm. abr. ed. 2002. (Vampire Chronicles). audio compact disk 29.95 (0-553-71417-1); audio 39.95 (0-553-71416-3) Random Hse. Audio Publishing Group.
—Blackwood Farm: The Vampire Chronicles. 2002. E-Book 6.99 (1-4000-4020-5) Knopf Publishing Group.
—Blood Canticle. 2003. (Vampire Chronicles). E-Book 25.95 (1-4000-4194-5) Knopf Publishing Group.
—Blood Canticle. 2003. (Vampire Chronicles). 320p. 25.95 (0-375-41200-X) Knopf, Alfred A. Inc.
—Blood Canticle. abr. ed. 2003. audio 25.95 (0-7393-0467-4, Listening Library); audio compact disk 29.95 (0-7393-0630-8, Listening Library); audio 39.95 (0-7393-0631-6) Random Hse. Audio Publishing Group.
—Entrevista con el Vampiro. 2000. (SPA.). pap. 11.95 (84-406-4149-4) B Ediciones S.A. ESP. Dist: Distribooks, Inc.
—Entrevista con el Vampiro. 4th ed. 2000. (SPA., Illus.). 464p. 9.00 (84-95501-25-2, SN12818) Suma de Letras, S.L. ESP. Dist: Lectorum Pubns., Inc., Santillana USA Publishing Co., Inc.
—Interview with the Vampire. 1997. (Vampire Chronicles: Bk. 1). pap. 14.00 o.s.i (0-345-91272-1); 1994. (Vampire Chronicles: Bk. 1). pap. 6.99 o.p. (0-345-90444-3); 1994. (Vampire Chronicles: Bk. 1). mass mkt. 6.99 o.p. (0-345-90333-1); 1991. (Vampire Chronicles: Bk. 1). 352p. mass mkt. 7.99 (0-345-33766-2); 1985. mass mkt. 3.50 o.p. (0-345-32899-X); 1982. mass mkt. 2.95 o.p. (0-345-31059-4); 1981. mass mkt. 2.75 o.p. (0-345-29882-9); 1979. mass mkt. 2.25 o.p. (0-345-28126-8); 20th ed. 1997. (Vampire Chronicles: Bk. 1). 352p. pap. 14.95 (0-345-40964-7) Ballantine Bks.
—Interview with the Vampire. 1991. (Vampire Chronicles: Bk. 1). 320p. reprint ed. lib. bdg. 35.95 (0-89966-781-3) Buccaneer Bks., Inc.
—Interview with the Vampire. (Vampire Chronicles: Bk. 1). 1994. 23.00 o.s.i (0-394-26725-7); 1993. o.s.i (0-394-25662-X); 1976. 352p. 27.95 (0-394-49821-6); 1996. 384p. 35.00 o.s.i (0-679-45084-X) Knopf, Alfred A. Inc.
—Interview with the Vampire. 1987. audio 14.95 o.p. (0-394-55747-6); Set. 1995. audio compact disk 25.00 (0-679-44764-4); Set. 1986. audio 17.00 (0-394-55617-8, 390985) Random Hse. Audio Publishing Group. (RH Audio).
—Interview with the Vampire. unabr. ed. (Vampire Chronicles: Bk. 1). 1999. audio compact disk 114.00 (0-7887-3442-3, C1048E7); 1994. audio 85.00 (0-7887-0065-0, 94321E7) Recorded Bks., LLC.
—Memnoch, the Devil. (Vampire Chronicles: Bk. 5). 1997. pap. 14.00 o.s.i (0-345-91273-X); 1996. mass mkt. 7.50 o.s.i (0-345-40499-8); 1996. 464p. pap. 14.95 (0-345-38940-9) Ballantine Bks.
—Memnoch, the Devil. 1995. (Vampire Chronicles: Bk. 5). 368p. 29.95 (0-679-44101-8) Knopf, Alfred A. Inc.
—Memnoch, the Devil. abr. ed. 1995. (Vampire Chronicles). audio 23.50 (0-679-43832-7, 493006, RH Audio) Random Hse. Audio Publishing Group.
—Memnoch, the Devil. deluxe ltd. num. ed. 1995. (Vampire Chronicles: Vol. 5). 354p. 195.00 (0-9631925-4-X) Trice, B.E. Publishing.
—The Queen of the Damned. 1997. (Vampire Chronicles: Bk. 3). 464p. pap. 15.00 (0-345-41962-6); 1994. (Vampire Chronicles: Bk. 3). mass mkt. 6.99 o.p. (0-345-90335-8); 1989. (Vampire Chronicles: Bk. 3). 512p. mass mkt. 7.99 (0-345-35152-5); 1989. mass mkt. 5.95 o.s.i (0-345-36260-8); 1988. (Vampire Chronicles: Bk. 3). 464p. 27.95 (0-394-55823-5) Ballantine Bks.
—The Queen of the Damned. 1993. (Vampire Chronicles: Bk. 3). o.s.i (0-394-25660-3) Knopf, Alfred A. Inc.
—The Queen of the Damned. abr. ed. 1988. (Critical Edition Ser.). audio 18.00 (0-394-57318-8, 391430, RH Audio) Random Hse. Audio Publishing Group.
—The Queen of the Damned. 1990. 5.99 o.p. (0-517-05227-X) Random Hse. Value Publishing.
—The Queen of the Damned. unabr. ed. 1995. (Vampire Chronicles: Bk. 3). audio 120.00 (0-7887-0100-2, 94341E7) Recorded Bks., LLC.
—The Tale of the Body Thief. 1997. 448p. pap. 15.00 (0-345-41963-4); 1994. (Vampire Chronicles: Bk. 4). mass mkt. 6.99 o.p. (0-345-90336-6); 1993. (Vampire Chronicles: Bk. 4). 448p. mass mkt. 7.99 (0-345-38475-X); 1993. mass mkt. 5.99 o.s.i (0-345-38388-5) Ballantine Bks.
—The Tale of the Body Thief. 1992. (Vampire Chronicles). 428p. 23.50 o.s.i (0-394-22317-9) Knopf, Alfred A. Inc.
—The Tale of the Body Thief, Set. abr. ed. 1992. (Vampire Chronicles: No. 4). pap. 18.00 incl. audio (0-679-41162-3, RH Audio) Random Hse. Audio Publishing Group.
—The Tale of the Body Thief. unabr. ed. 1995. (Vampire Chronicles: Bk. 4). audio 112.00 (0-7887-0096-0, 94337E7) Recorded Bks., LLC.
—The Tale of the Body Thief: The Vampire Chronicles. 1992. (Vampire Chronicles: Bk. 4). 448p. 30.00 (0-679-40528-3) Knopf, Alfred A. Inc.
—The Vampire Armand. (New Tales of the Vampires Ser.: Bk. 2). mass mkt. 7.50 o.s.i (0-345-42930-3); 2002. (Vampire Chronicles). E-Book 7.99 (0-345-46453-2, Ballantine Bks.); 2000. (Vampire Chronicles). 480p. mass mkt. 7.99 (0-345-43480-3, Ballantine Bks.); 1999. (Vampire Chronicles: Bk. 2). 400p. pap. 14.95 (0-345-40927-2) Ballantine Bks.
—The Vampire Armand. unabr. ed. 1998. (New Tales of the Vampires Ser.: Bk. 2). audio 88.00 (0-7366-4225-0, 4726) Books on Tape, Inc.
—The Vampire Armand. l.t. ed. 1999. (New Tales of the Vampires Ser.: Bk. 2). pap. 26.95 o.p. (0-7838-0263-3, Macmillan Reference USA) Gale Group.
—The Vampire Armand. abr. ed. 1999. audio 24.00. audio 44.95 Highsmith Inc.
—The Vampire Armand. 1998. (Vampire Chronicles: Bk. 2). 384p. 26.95 (0-679-45447-0) Knopf, Alfred A. Inc.
—The Vampire Armand. abr. ed. 1998. audio 24.00 (0-375-40181-4, 493414); audio compact disk 27.50 (0-375-40433-3); audio 44.95 (0-375-40434-1, 134535) Random Hse. Audio Publishing Group. (RH Audio).
—The Vampire Armand. l.t. ed. 1998. (Vampire Chronicles). 576p. pap. 26.95 (0-375-70415-9) Random Hse. Large Print.
—The Vampire Armand. ltd. ed. 1998. (Vampire Chronicles: Bk. 6). 150.00 (1-890885-06-1) Trice, B.E. Publishing.
—The Vampire Chronicles, 4 vols. (Vampire Chronicles). 1993. 31.96 (0-345-38540-3); Set. 1989. 20.97 (0-345-36422-8) Ballantine Bks.
—The Vampire Chronicles, 3 vols. 1990. (Vampire Chronicles). 99.50 o.s.i (0-394-58186-5) Random Hse., Inc.
—The Vampire Lestat. (Vampire Chronicles: Bk. 2). 1997. 496p. pap. 15.95 (0-345-41964-2); 1994. mass mkt. 6.99 o.p. (0-345-90334-X); 1986. 560p. mass mkt. 7.99 (0-345-31386-0) Ballantine Bks.
—The Vampire Lestat. (Vampire Chronicles: Bk. 2). 1993. o.s.i (0-394-25661-1); 1985. 496p. 27.95 (0-394-53443-3) Knopf, Alfred A. Inc.
—The Vampire Lestat, Set. abr. ed. 1989. (Vampire Chronicles). audio 18.00 (0-394-57705-1, 391846, RH Audio) Random Hse. Audio Publishing Group.
—The Vampire Lestat. unabr. ed. 1994. (Vampire Chronicles: Bk. 2). audio 128.00 (0-7887-0098-7, 94339E7) Recorded Bks., LLC.

Rice, Anne, reader. Blackwood Farm. abr. ed. 2002. (Vampire Chronicles). audio 25.95 (0-553-71381-7) Random Hse. Audio Publishing Group.

**LESTRADE, INSPECTOR (FICTITIOUS CHARACTER)—FICTION**

Hall, John. Sherlock Holmes & the Disgraced Inspector. 1998. 140p. pap. 14.95 (0-947533-88-5) Breese Bks., Ltd. GBR. Dist: Midpoint Trade Bks., Inc.
—Sherlock Holmes & the Disgraced Inspector. l.t. ed. 2000. (Linford Mystery Large Print Ser.). 248p. pap. 18.99 (0-7089-5783-8, Linford) Thorpe, F. A. Pubs. GBR. Dist: Ulverscroft Large Print Bks., Ltd., Ulverscroft Large Print Canada, Ltd.

Trow, M. J. The Adventures of Inspector Lestrade. (Lestrade Mysteries Ser.: Vol. 1). 2000. 224p. pap. 9.95 (0-89526-291-6); 1998. 208p. 19.95 (0-89526-343-2) Regnery Publishing, Inc., An Eagle Publishing Co. (Gateway Editions).
—Brigade: The Further Adventures of Lestrade. (Lestrade Mystery Ser.: Vol. 2). 2000. 219p. pap. 9.95 (0-89526-290-8); 1998. 208p. 19.95 (0-89526-342-4) Regnery Publishing, Inc., An Eagle Publishing Co. (Gateway Editions).
—Lestrade & the Brother of Death. 1999. (Lestrade Mysteries Ser.: Vol. 7). 224p. 19.95 (0-89526-268-1) Regnery Publishing, Inc., An Eagle Publishing Co.
—Lestrade & the Dead Man's Hand. 2000. (Gateway Mystery Ser.: Vol. XI). 237p. 19.95 (0-89526-288-6, Gateway Editions) Regnery Publishing, Inc., An Eagle Publishing Co.
—Lestrade & the Deadly Game. 1999. (Lestrade Mysteries Ser.: Vol. 5). 224p. 19.95 (0-89526-312-2, Gateway Editions) Regnery Publishing, Inc., An Eagle Publishing Co.
—Lestrade & the Devil's Own. 2001. (Lestrade Mystery Ser.: Vol. 16). 190p. 19.95 (0-89526-215-0) Regnery Publishing, Inc., An Eagle Publishing Co.
—Lestrade & the Gift of the Prince. 2000. (Lestrade Mysteries Ser.). 208p. 19.95 (0-89526-253-3, Gateway Editions) Regnery Publishing, Inc., An Eagle Publishing Co.
—Lestrade & the Guardian Angel. 1999. (Lestrade Mysteries Ser.: Vol. 8). 240p. 19.95 (0-89526-267-3) Regnery Publishing, Inc., An Eagle Publishing Co.
—Lestrade & the Hallowed House. 208p. 2001. (Lestrade Mystery Ser.). pap. 12.95 (0-89526-213-4); 1999. (Lestrade Mysteries Ser.: Vol. 3). 19.95 (0-89526-341-6, Gateway Editions) Regnery Publishing, Inc., An Eagle Publishing Co.
—Lestrade & the Kiss of Horus. 2001. (Lestrade Mystery Ser.: Vol. 15). (Illus.). 235p. (J). 19.95 (0-89526-214-2) Regnery Publishing, Inc., An Eagle Publishing Co.
—Lestrade & the Leviathan. 1999. (Lestrade Mysteries Ser.: Vol. 4). 208p. 19.95 (0-89526-340-8, Gateway Editions) Regnery Publishing, Inc., An Eagle Publishing Co.
—Lestrade & the Magpie. 2000. (Gateway Mystery Ser.: Vol. X). 224p. 19.95 (0-89526-289-4, Gateway Editions) Regnery Publishing, Inc., An Eagle Publishing Co.
—Lestrade & the Mirror of Murder. 2001. (Lestrade Mystery Ser.: Vol. 14). 250p. 19.95 (0-89526-233-9) Regnery Publishing, Inc., An Eagle Publishing Co.
—Lestrade & the Ripper. 1999. (Lestrade Mysteries Ser.: Vol. 6). 287p. 19.95 (0-89526-311-4, Gateway Editions) Regnery Publishing, Inc., An Eagle Publishing Co.
—Lestrade & the Sawdust Ring. 2000. (Lestrade Mystery Ser.: Vol. 13). 224p. 19.95 (0-89526-245-2, Gateway Editions) Regnery Publishing, Inc., An Eagle Publishing Co.
—Lestrade & the Sign of Nine. 2000. (Lestrade Mystery Ser.: Vol. 12). 224p. 19.95 (0-89526-246-0) Regnery Publishing, Inc., An Eagle Publishing Co.
—The Supreme Adventure of Inspector Lestrade. 1987. pap. 3.95 o.s.i (0-8128-8313-6); 1985. 224p. 14.95 o.p. (0-8128-3036-9) Madison Bks., Inc. (Scarborough Hse.).

**LEVENDEUR, CATHERINE (FICTITIOUS CHARACTER)—FICTION**

Newman, Sharan. Cursed in the Blood. 2000. 370p. mass mkt. 6.99 (0-8125-9020-1, Forge Bks.); 1999. 23.95 (0-312-87153-8, Tor Bks.); 1998. 352p. 23.95 (0-312-86567-8, Forge Bks.) Doherty, Tom Assocs., LLC.
—Death Comes As Epiphany. 1995. 322p. mass mkt. 5.99 (0-8125-2293-1, Forge Bks.); 1993. 320p. 19.95 (0-312-85419-6, Tor Bks.); 2002. reprint ed. pap. 14.95 (0-7653-0374-4, Forge Bks.) Doherty, Tom Assocs., LLC.
—The Devil's Door. 1995. 416p. mass mkt. 6.99 (0-8125-2295-8); 1994. 384p. 21.95 o.p. (0-312-85420-X) Doherty, Tom Assocs., LLC. (Forge Bks.).
—The Difficult Saint. 2000. (Catherine Levendeur Mystery Ser.). 352p. mass mkt. 6.99 (0-8125-8433-3, Forge Bks.) Doherty, Tom Assocs., LLC.
—Heresy: A Catherine LeVendeur Mystery. mass mkt. (0-7653-4287-1); 2008. 352p. pap. 14.95 (0-7653-0247-0); 2002. (Illus.). 352p. 24.95 (0-7653-0246-2) Doherty, Tom Assocs., LLC. (Forge Bks.).
—Strong As Death. unabr. collector's ed. 1999. (Catherine LeVendeur Ser.: 4). audio 72.00 (0-7366-4862-3, 5189) Books on Tape, Inc.
—Strong As Death. (Catherine Levendeur Mystery Ser.). 384p. 1997. mass mkt. 5.99 (0-8125-3935-4); 1996. 23.95 o.p. (0-312-86179-6) Doherty, Tom Assocs., LLC. (Forge Bks.).
—The Wandering Arm. 2001. pap. 14.95 (0-312-87733-1); 1996. 372p. mass mkt. 5.99 (0-8125-5089-7); 1995. 352p. 23.95 o.p. (0-312-85829-9) Doherty, Tom Assocs., LLC. (Forge Bks.).

**LEVINE, DANNY (FICTITIOUS CHARACTER)—FICTION**

Handler, David. The Boss. 1988. 224p. pap. 15.00 (0-345-34929-6) Ballantine Bks.
—Kiddo. 1988. 256p. mass mkt. 3.95 o.s.i (0-345-35230-0) Ballantine Bks.

**LEVINE, MICHAEL (FICTITIOUS CHARACTER)—FICTION**

Levine, Michael. Triangle of Death: Deep Cover II. 1997. mass mkt. 6.99 (0-440-22111-0); 512p. mass mkt. 6.99 o.s.i (0-440-22367-9) Dell Publishing.

**LEWIS, MELDRICK (FICTITIOUS CHARACTER)—FICTION**

Preisler, Jerome. Homicide No. 2: Violent Delights, No. 2. 2nd ed. 1997. 288p. mass mkt. 5.99 o.s.i (1-57297-340-4) Boulevard Bks.

**LEWIS, MORDECAI (FICTITIOUS CHARACTER)—FICTION**

Early, Tom. The Bold. 1992. (Sons of Texas Ser.: No. 5). 256p. (Orig.). mass mkt. 4.99 o.p. (0-425-13334-6) Berkley Publishing Group.
—The Defiant. 1993. (Sons of Texas Ser.: No. 6). 272p. (Orig.). mass mkt. 4.99 o.p. (0-425-13706-6) Berkley Publishing Group.
—The Proud. 1992. (Sons of Texas Ser.: No. 4). mass mkt. 4.50 o.p. (0-425-12967-5) Berkley Publishing Group.
—The Raiders. 1989. (Sons of Texas Ser.: No. 2). mass mkt. 4.99 o.p. (0-425-11874-6) Berkley Publishing Group.
—The Rebels. 1990. (Sons of Texas Ser.: No. 3). mass mkt. 4.99 o.p. (0-425-12215-8) Berkley Publishing Group.
—Sons of Texas. 1989. mass mkt. 4.99 o.p. (0-425-11474-0) Berkley Publishing Group.

**LEWIS, REBECCA (FICTITIOUS CHARACTER)—FICTION**

Zelman, Anita. Dead down Under: A Rebecca Lewis Mystery. 2002. 188p. 12.95 (1-56474-398-5) Fithian Pr.

**LEWIS, SERGEANT (FICTITIOUS CHARACTER)—FICTION**

Dexter, Colin. The Daughters of Cain. 1996. 320p. mass mkt. 6.99 (0-8041-1364-5) Ballantine Bks.
—The Daughters of Cain. unabr. ed. 1995. audio 49.95 (0-7861-0714-6, 1591) Blackstone Audio Bks., Inc.
—The Daughters of Cain. unabr. ed. 1995. (Inspector Morse Mystery Ser.: Bk. 11). audio 59.95 (0-7451-6555-9, CAB 1171) Chivers Audio Bks. GBR. Dist: BBC Audiobooks America.
—The Daughters of Cain, Set. abr. ed. 1996. (Inspector Morse Mystery Ser.). 3p. audio 16.99 (0-88646-407-2, 393852) Durkin Hayes Publishing Ltd.
—The Daughters of Cain. o.p. (0-517-70153-7) Random Hse. Value Publishing.
—The Daughters of Cain. unabr. ed. 2000. (Inspector Morse Mystery Ser.: Vol. 11). audio 70.00 (0-7887-0297-1, 94490E7) Recorded Bks., LLC.
—The Daughters of Cain. l.t. ed. 1995. (Charnwood Large Print Ser.). 448p. 29.99 o.p. (0-7089-8869-5, Charnwood) Thorpe, F. A. Pubs. GBR. Dist: Ulverscroft Large Print Bks., Ltd., Ulverscroft Large Print Canada, Ltd.
—The Dead of Jericho, Set. 1998. (Inspector Morse Mystery Ser.). audio 29.95 (0-7540-7519-2) BBC Audiobooks America.
—The Dead of Jericho. 1996. (Inspector Morse Mystery Ser.). 304p. mass mkt. 6.99 (0-8041-1486-2, Ivy Bks.) Ballantine Bks.
—The Dead of Jericho. 1988. 224p. mass mkt. 4.50 o.s.i (0-553-27237-3) Bantam Bks.
—The Dead of Jericho. 1981. 168p. 9.95 o.p. (0-312-18511-1) St. Martin's Pr.
—The Dead of Jericho. 1990. audio 53.95 o.p. (0-8161-9623-0) Thorndike Pr.
—The Dead of Jericho. l.t. ed. 1984. 416p. 15.95 o.p. (0-7089-1098-X, Ulverscroft) Thorpe, F. A. Pubs. GBR. Dist: Ulverscroft Large Print Bks., Ltd.
—Death Is Now My Neighbor: An Inspector Morse Novel. 1998. (Illus.). 336p. mass mkt. 6.99 (0-8041-1572-9, Ivy Bks.) Ballantine Bks.
—Death Is Now My Neighbor: An Inspector Morse Novel. unabr. ed. (Inspector Morse Mystery Ser.). 2000. 8p. audio compact disk 79.95 (0-7540-5349-0, CCD 040); 1998. audio 59.95 (0-7451-6775-6, CAB 1391) Chivers Audio Bks. GBR. Dist: BBC Audiobooks America.
—Death Is Now My Neighbor: An Inspector Morse Novel. aut. ed. 1997. 24.00 o.s.i (0-517-70824-8) Crown Publishing Group.
—The Jewel That Was Ours: An Inspector Morse Mystery. 1993. 256p. mass mkt. 6.99 (0-8041-0981-8, Ivy Bks.) Ballantine Bks.
—The Jewel That Was Ours: An Inspector Morse Mystery. unabr. ed. 1996. audio 44.95 (0-7861-0980-7, 1757) Blackstone Audio Bks., Inc.
—The Jewel That Was Ours: An Inspector Morse Mystery. unabr. ed. 2000. (Inspector Morse Mystery Ser.: Bk. 9). audio 59.95 (0-7451-4090-4, CAB 778) Chivers Audio Bks. GBR. Dist: BBC Audiobooks America.
—The Jewel That Was Ours: An Inspector Morse Mystery. abr. ed. 1994. audio 16.99 (0-88646-369-6, LFP 7369) Durkin Hayes Publishing Ltd.

—The Jewel That Was Ours: An Inspector Morse Mystery. 2001. audio (*0-333-90435-4*) Macmillan U.K. GBR. *Dist:* Macmillan Publishing Co., Inc.

—The Jewel That Was Ours: An Inspector Morse Mystery. unabr. ed. 1992. (Inspector Morse Mystery Ser.: Vol. 9). audio 60.00 (*1-55690-683-8*, 92315E7) Recorded Bks., LLC.

—Last Bus to Woodstock. 1996. 288p. mass mkt. 6.99 (*0-8041-1490-0*, Ivy Bks.) Ballantine Bks.

—Last Bus to Woodstock. 1988. 224p. mass mkt. 3.95 o.s.i (*0-553-27777-4*) Bantam Bks.

—Last Bus to Woodstock. l.t. ed. 1990. o.p. (*0-7089-2298-8*, Ulverscroft) Thorpe, F. A. Pubs.

—Last Seen Wearing: An Inspector Morse Mystery. unabr. ed. 2000. (Inspector Morse Mystery Ser.). audio 29.95 (*1-57270-145-5*, N61145u, Audio Editions Mystery Masters) Audio Partners Publishing Corp.

—Last Seen Wearing: An Inspector Morse Mystery. 1997. 336p. mass mkt. 6.99 (*0-8041-1491-9*, Ivy Bks.) Ballantine Bks.

—Last Seen Wearing: An Inspector Morse Mystery. 1988. 272p. mass mkt. 5.99 o.s.i (*0-553-28003-1*) Bantam Bks.

—Last Seen Wearing: An Inspector Morse Mystery. unabr. ed. 2000. (Inspector Morse Mystery Ser.: Bk. 2). audio 59.95 (*0-7451-4122-6*, CAB 805) Chivers Audio Bks. GBR. *Dist:* BBC Audiobooks America.

—Last Seen Wearing: An Inspector Morse Mystery. l.t. ed. 1989. 17.95 o.p. (*0-7089-2184-1*, Ulverscroft) Thorpe, F. A. Pubs. GBR. *Dist:* Ulverscroft Large Print Bks., Ltd.

—Morse's Greatest Mystery. unabr. ed. 1996. audio 39.95 (*0-7861-0957-2*, 1734) Blackstone Audio Bks., Inc.

—Morse's Greatest Mystery & Other Stories. 1996. (Inspector Morse Mystery Ser.). 304p. mass mkt. 6.99 (*0-8041-1309-2*, Ivy Bks.) Ballantine Bks.

—Morse's Greatest Mystery & Other Stories. abr. ed. 1996. audio 24.99 (*0-88646-410-2*, 7410) Durkin Hayes Publishing Ltd.

—Morse's Greatest Mystery & Other Stories. unabr. ed. 1996. audio 51.00 (*0-7887-0481-8*, 94674E7) Recorded Bks., LLC.

—The Remorseful Day. 2001. 336p. mass mkt. 6.99 (*0-8041-1954-6*, Fawcett) Ballantine Bks.

—The Remorseful Day. 2000. (Inspector Morse Mystery Ser.). 384p. 24.00 o.s.i (*0-609-60622-0*); 24.00 (*0-609-50295-6*) Crown Publishing Group. (Crown).

—The Remorseful Day. l.t. ed. 2000. (Wheeler Large Print Book Ser.). 442p. 27.95 (*1-56895-883-8*, Wheeler Publishing, Inc.) Gale Group.

—The Remorseful Day. abr. ed. 2000. audio 18.00 (*0-7871-2521-0*) NewStar Media, Inc.

—The Riddle of the Third Mile. 1999. 55p. audio 29.95 (*0-7451-2815-7*) BBC Audiobooks America.

—The Riddle of the Third Mile. 1997. (Inspector Morse Mystery Ser.). 272p. mass mkt. 6.99 (*0-8041-1488-9*, Ivy Bks.) Ballantine Bks.

—The Riddle of the Third Mile. 1988. 224p. mass mkt. 5.99 o.s.i (*0-553-27363-9*) Bantam Bks.

—The Riddle of the Third Mile. unabr. ed. 2000. (Inspector Morse Mystery Ser.: Bk. 6). audio 49.95 (*0-7451-5895-1*, CAB 672) Chivers Audio Bks. GBR. *Dist:* BBC Audiobooks America.

—The Riddle of the Third Mile. 1984. 224p. 11.95 o.p. (*0-312-68228-X*) St. Martin's Pr.

—The Riddle of the Third Mile. l.t. ed. 2001. 349p. 28.95 (*0-7862-3343-5*); (*0-7540-2473-3*); (*0-7540-1619-6*) Thorndike Pr.

—The Secret of Annexe 3. unabr. ed. 2000. (Inspector Morse Mystery Ser.). audio 29.95 (*1-57270-155-2*, N61155u, Audio Editions Mystery Masters) Audio Partners Publishing Corp.

—The Secret of Annexe 3. unabr. ed. 1994. (Inspector Morse Mystery Ser.). audio 54.95 (*0-7451-4321-0*, CAB 1004) BBC Audiobooks America.

—The Secret of Annexe 3, Vol. 3. 1997. (Inspector Morse Mystery Ser.). 304p. mass mkt. 6.99 (*0-8041-1489-7*, Ivy Bks.) Ballantine Bks.

—The Secret of Annexe 3. 1988. 224p. reprint ed. mass mkt. 5.99 o.s.i (*0-553-27549-6*) Bantam Bks.

—The Secret of Annexe 3. unabr. ed. 2000. (Inspector Morse Mystery Ser.: Bk. 7). audio 49.95 Chivers Audio Bks. GBR. *Dist:* BBC Audiobooks America.

—The Secret of Annexe 3. 1987. 224p. 15.95 o.p. (*0-312-01089-3*, Saint Martin's Minotaur) St. Martin's Pr.

—The Secret of Annexe 3. l.t. ed. 2000. (Mystery Ser.). 371p. pap. 26.95 (*0-7862-2676-5*); (*0-7540-4235-9*); (*0-7540-4236-7*) Thorndike Pr.

—Service of All the Dead. 1996. 304p. mass mkt. 6.99 (*0-8041-1485-4*, Ivy Bks.) Ballantine Bks.

—Service of All the Dead. 1988. 224p. mass mkt. 3.95 o.s.i (*0-553-27239-X*) Bantam Bks.

—Service of All the Dead. unabr. ed. 2000. (Inspector Morse Mystery Ser.: Bk. 4). audio 49.95 (*0-7451-6497-8*, CAB 1113) Chivers Audio Bks. GBR. *Dist:* BBC Audiobooks America.

—Service of All the Dead. 1982. (Murder Ink Mystery Ser.: No. 43). pap. 2.50 o.p. (*0-440-18026-0*) Dell Publishing.

—Service of All the Dead. 1979. 9.95 o.p. (*0-312-71316-9*) St. Martin's Pr.

—Service of All the Dead. l.t. ed. 2000. (Mystery Ser.). 402p. 27.95 (*0-7862-3040-1*); (*0-7540-2405-9*); (*0-7540-1531-9*) Thorndike Pr.

—The Silent World of Nicholas Quinn. 1997. (Inspector Morse Mystery Ser.). 288p. mass mkt. 6.99 (*0-8041-1487-0*, Ivy Bks.) Ballantine Bks.

—The Silent World of Nicholas Quinn. 1988. 224p. mass mkt. 5.99 o.s.i (*0-553-27238-1*) Bantam Bks.

—The Silent World of Nicholas Quinn. unabr. ed. 2000. (Inspector Morse Mystery Ser.: Bk. 3). audio 49.95 (*0-7451-6607-5*, CAB 1223) Chivers Audio Bks. GBR. *Dist:* BBC Audiobooks America.

—The Silent World of Nicholas Quinn. 2001. audio (*0-333-90440-0*) Macmillan U.K. GBR. *Dist:* Macmillan Publishing Co., Inc.

—The Silent World of Nicholas Quinn. (Mystery Bookshelf Selection Ser.). 1978. pap. 3.50 o.p. (*0-312-72468-3*, Saint Martin's Griffin); 1977. 7.95 o.p. (*0-312-72467-5*) St. Martin's Pr.

—The Silent World of Nicholas Quinn. l.t. ed. 1992. (Mystery Ser.). 432p. 29.99 o.p. (*0-7089-2620-7*, Ulverscroft) Thorpe, F. A. Pubs. GBR. *Dist:* Ulverscroft Large Print Bks., Ltd., Ulverscroft Large Print Canada, Ltd.

—The Way Through the Woods: An Inspector Morse Mystery. 1994. 336p. mass mkt. 6.99 (*0-8041-1142-1*, Ivy Bks.) Ballantine Bks.

—The Way Through the Woods: An Inspector Morse Mystery. unabr. ed. 1996. audio 49.95 (*0-7861-0931-9*, 1686) Blackstone Audio Bks., Inc.

—The Way Through the Woods: An Inspector Morse Mystery. unabr. ed. 2000. (Inspector Morse Mystery Ser.: Bk. 10). audio 59.95 (*0-7451-4167-6*, CAB 850) Chivers Audio Bks. GBR. *Dist:* BBC Audiobooks America.

—The Way Through the Woods: An Inspector Morse Mystery. abr. ed. 1993. audio 16.99 (*0-88646-352-1*, LFP 7352) Durkin Hayes Publishing Ltd.

—The Way Through the Woods: An Inspector Morse Mystery. 1995. 4.99 o.p. (*0-517-14495-6*) Random Hse. Value Publishing.

—The Way Through the Woods: An Inspector Morse Mystery. unabr. ed. 1993. (Inspector Morse Mystery Ser.: Vol. 10). audio 70.00 (*1-55690-883-0*, 93325E7) Recorded Bks., LLC.

—The Wench Is Dead. unabr. ed. 2000. (Inspector Morse Mystery Ser.). audio 29.95 (*1-57270-130-7*, N61130u, Audio Editions Mystery Masters) Audio Partners Publishing Corp.

—The Wench Is Dead. 1999. (Inspector Morse Mystery Ser.). 290p. mass mkt. 6.99 o.s.i (*0-8041-1889-2*, Ivy Bks.) Ballantine Bks.

—The Wench Is Dead. 1991. 208p. mass mkt. 5.99 o.s.i (*0-553-29120-3*) Bantam Bks.

—The Wench Is Dead. 1992. 3.99 o.p. (*0-517-09062-7*) Random Hse. Value Publishing.

—The Wench Is Dead. 1990. 15.95 o.p. (*0-312-04444-5*, Saint Martin's Minotaur) St. Martin's Pr.

—The Wench Is Dead. l.t. ed. 1991. (Ulverscroft Large Print Ser.). 29.99 o.p. (*0-7089-2512-X*, Ulverscroft) Thorpe, F. A. Pubs. GBR. *Dist:* Ulverscroft Large Print Bks., Ltd., Ulverscroft Large Print Canada, Ltd.

—The Wench Is Dead. abr. ed. 1998. audio 15.00 (*0-333-74612-0*) Ulverscroft Audio (U.S.A.).

Thaw, John. Deceived by Flight. 1998. (Inspector Morse Mystery Ser.). audio 14.95 o.p. (*1-56938-257-3*, AMP-2573) Acorn Media Publishing, Inc.

—The Ghost in the Machine. 1998. (Inspector Morse Mystery Ser.). audio 14.95 o.p. (*1-56938-256-5*, AMP-2565) Acorn Media Publishing, Inc.

—Infernal Serpent. 1998. (Inspector Morse Mystery Ser.). audio 14.95 o.p. (*1-56938-258-1*, AMP-2581) Acorn Media Publishing, Inc.

—Inspector Morse Series, 4 vols. 1998. audio 59.80 (*1-56938-255-7*, AMP-2557) Acorn Media Publishing, Inc.

—Masonic Mysteries. 1998. (Inspector Morse Mystery Ser.). audio 14.95 o.p. (*1-56938-259-X*, AMP-8259) Acorn Media Publishing, Inc.

## LEWIS, WYN (FICTITIOUS CHARACTER)—FICTION

Kaufelt, David A. The Fat Boy Murders. 1993. 240p. 20.00 (*0-671-76092-0*, Atria) Simon & Schuster.

—The Fat Boy Murders. Grose, Bill, ed. 1994. 256p. reprint ed. mass mkt. 5.50 (*0-671-76093-9*, Pocket) Simon & Schuster.

—The Fat Boy Murders. 230p. 3.98 o.p. (*0-8317-2355-6*) Smithmark Pubs., Inc.

—The Ruthless Realtor Murders: A Wyn Lewis Mystery. 1998. per. 6.50 (*0-671-51148-3*, Pocket); 1997. 240p. 22.00 o.s.i (*0-671-51147-5*, Atria) Simon & Schuster.

—The Winter Women Murders. 1995. 256p. mass mkt. 5.50 (*0-671-76095-5*, Pocket) Simon & Schuster.

—The Winter Women Murders: A Wyn Lewis Mystery. Grose, Bill, ed. 1994. 224p. 20.00 o.p. (*0-671-76094-7*, Atria) Simon & Schuster.

## LEWRIE, ALAN (FICTITIOUS CHARACTER)—FICTION

Lambdin, Dewey. For King & Country: The Naval Adventures of Alan Lewrie. 1994. 1088p. pap. 19.95 o.s.i (*1-55611-413-3*, Fine, Donald I.) Fine, Donald I. Bks.

—The French Admiral. 1999. mass mkt. (*0-449-00359-0*, Fawcett) Ballantine Bks.

—The French Admiral. 1990. (Midshipman Alan Lewrie Adventure Ser.). 19.95 o.p. (*1-55611-208-4*) Fine, Donald I. Bks.

—The French Admiral. l.t. ed. 1999. (G. K. Hall Core Ser.). 637p. 27.95 (*0-7838-8788-4*, Macmillan Reference USA) Gale Group.

—The French Admiral. 1991. mass mkt. 4.95 o.s.i (*1-55817-491-5*, Pinnacle Bks.) Kensington Publishing Corp.

—The Gun Ketch: An Alan Lewrie Naval Adventure. 1996. (Alan Lewrie Navel Adventures Ser.). 336p. mass mkt. 6.99 (*0-449-22450-3*, Fawcett) Ballantine Bks.

—The Gun Ketch: An Alan Lewrie Naval Adventure. 1993. 21.95 o.s.i (*1-55611-356-0*) Fine, Donald I. Bks.

—Havoc's Sword: An Alan Lewrie Naval Adventure. 2003. (Illus.). 384p. 25.95 (*0-312-28688-0*) St. Martin's Pr.

—H.M.S. Cockerel: An Alan Lewrie Naval Adventure. 1997. (Alan Lewrie Navel Adventures Ser.). 416p. mass mkt. 6.50 (*0-449-22448-1*, Fawcett) Ballantine Bks.

—H.M.S. Cockerel: An Alan Lewrie Naval Adventure. 1995. (Alan Lewrie Ser.). 368p. 23.95 o.s.i (*1-55611-446-X*) Fine, Donald I. Bks.

—H.M.S. Cockerel: An Alan Lewrie Naval Adventure. 1996. text 23.95 (*0-07-036237-8*) McGraw-Hill Cos., The.

—Jester's Fortune: An Alan Lewrie Naval Adventure. 1999. (Alan Lewrie Navel Adventures Ser.). (Illus.). 384p. 26.95 o.p. (*0-525-94482-6*) Dutton/Plume.

—Jester's Fortune: An Alan Lewrie Naval Adventure. l.t. ed. 1999. (Core Ser.). (Illus.). 618p. pap. 27.95 (*0-7838-8681-0*, Macmillan Reference USA) Gale Group.

—King's Captain. 2000. (Alan Lewrie Navel Adventures Ser.). 358p. 25.95 (*0-312-26885-8*) St. Martin's Pr.

—The King's Coat. 1998. (Alan Lewrie Navel Adventures Ser.: Vol. 1). 384p. mass mkt. 6.99 (*0-449-00360-4*, Fawcett) Ballantine Bks.

—The King's Coat. 1989. 384p. 19.95 o.s.i (*1-55611-142-8*) Fine, Donald I. Bks.

—The King's Coat. 1990. mass mkt. 3.95 o.p. (*1-55817-389-7*, Pinnacle Bks.) Kensington Publishing Corp.

—The King's Coat. 1991. 3.99 o.p. (*0-517-07481-8*) Random Hse. Value Publishing.

—The King's Coat. l.t. ed. 1999. (G. K. Hall Core Ser.). 573p. 28.95 (*0-7838-0440-7*) Thorndike Pr.

—A King's Commander. 1998. (Alan Lewrie Navel Adventures Ser.). (Illus.). 384p. mass mkt. 6.99 (*0-449-00022-2*, Fawcett) Ballantine Bks.

—A King's Commander. 1997. (Alan Lewrie Ser.). 384p. 24.95 o.s.i (*1-55611-504-0*) Fine, Donald I. Bks.

—The King's Commission. 1996. (Alan Lewrie Navel Adventures Ser.). 384p. mass mkt. 6.99 (*0-449-22452-X*, Fawcett) Ballantine Bks.

—The King's Commission. 1991. 21.95 o.p. (*1-55611-187-8*) Fine, Donald I. Bks.

—The King's Privateer: An Alan Lewrie Naval Adventure. 1996. (Alan Lewrie Navel Adventures Ser.). 368p. mass mkt. 5.99 (*0-449-22451-1*, Fawcett) Ballantine Bks.

—The King's Privateer: An Alan Lewrie Naval Adventure. 1992. 21.95 o.s.i (*1-55611-324-2*) Fine, Donald I. Bks.

—Sea of Grey. (Alan Lewrie Navel Adventures Ser.). 2003. 400p. pap. 14.95 (*0-312-32016-7*, Saint Martin's Griffin); 2002. (Illus.). 416p. 25.95 (*0-312-28685-6*) St. Martin's Pr.

—Sea of Grey. 2002. (Alan Lewrie Naval Adventure Ser.: Bk. 10). 29.95 (*0-7862-4891-2*) Thorndike Pr.

## LIDENBROCK, PROFESSOR (FICTITIOUS CHARACTER)—FICTION

Verne, Jules. Journey to the Center of the Earth. (Illus.). 72p. pap. 7.95 (*1-55576-081-3*, EDN505B) AV Concepts Corp.

—Journey to the Center of the Earth. 1997. (Classics Illustrated Study Guides). (Illus.). mass mkt. 4.99 (*1-57840-034-1*) Acclaim Bks.

—Journey to the Center of the Earth. (J). (gr. 3-7). 23.95 (*0-88411-918-1*) Amereon, Ltd.

—Journey to the Center of the Earth. 1991. 272p. (J). (gr. 3-7). mass mkt. 3.95 o.s.i (*0-553-21397-0*) Bantam Bks.

—Journey to the Center of the Earth. 1992. 260p. (J). (gr. 3-7). mass mkt. 3.99 (*0-8125-0471-2*, Tor Classics) Doherty, Tom Assocs., LLC.

—Journey to the Center of the Earth. 2002. 252p. 95.99 (*1-4043-1148-3*); per. 90.99 (*1-4043-1149-1*) IndyPublish.com.

—Journey to the Center of the Earth. 1989. (J). (gr. 3-7). audio 42.00 Jimcin Recordings.

—Journey to the Center of the Earth. 1999. 304p. pap. 20.00 o.s.i (*1-57566-532-8*); mass mkt. 5.50 o.s.i (*1-57566-533-6*) Kensington Publishing Corp.

—Journey to the Center of the Earth. 1996. pap. 2.95 (*0-89375-417-X*); 1986. (J). (gr. 3-7). mass mkt. 3.50 o.p. (*0-451-52343-1*); 1986. (J). (gr. 3-7). mass mkt. 2.75 o.p. (*0-451-51982-5*); 1986. 304p. (J). (gr. 3-7). mass mkt. 5.95 (*0-451-52450-0*, Signet Classics) NAL.

—Journey to the Center of the Earth. Butcher, William, tr. & intro. by. 1998. 272p. (J). (gr. 3-7). pap. 8.95 (*0-19-283675-7*) Oxford Univ. Pr., Inc.

—Journey to the Center of the Earth. 1965. 256p. (J). (gr. 3-7). pap. 4.95 (*0-14-002265-1*, Penguin Bks.) Penguin Group (USA) Inc.

—Journey to the Center of the Earth. 1999. 225p. (J). pap. 7.95 (*1-902058-08-9*) Pulp Fictions GBR. *Dist:* 7 Hills Bk. Distributors.

—Journey to the Center of the Earth. 2001. 178p. pap. 14.99 (*1-57646-283-8*); 1999. (J). (gr. 3-7). E-Book 3.99 incl. cd-rom (*1-57646-043-6*) Quiet Vision Publishing.

—Journey to the Center of the Earth. 2003. 224p. pap. 8.95 (*0-8129-7009-8*, Modern Library) Random House Adult Trade Publishing Group.

—Journey to the Center of the Earth. 1986. 12.00 (*0-606-01887-5*) Turtleback Bks.

—Journey to the Center of the Earth. 1998. (Classics Library). 208p. pap. 3.95 (*1-85326-287-0*, 280WW) Wordsworth Editions, Ltd. GBR. *Dist:* Casemate Pubs. & Bk. Distributors, LLC.

—A Journey to the Center of the Earth. 2003. 304p. mass mkt. 5.95 (*0-451-52896-4*, Signet Classics) NAL.

—Journey to the Center of the Earth. unabr. ed. 1996. audio 49.95 (*0-7451-2527-1*, CCA3368, Chivers Children's Audio Bks.) BBC Audiobooks America.

—Journey to the Center of the Earth. unabr. ed. 1980. (J). (gr. 3-7). audio 49.95 (*0-7861-0585-2*, 2074) Blackstone Audio Bks., Inc.

—Journey to the Center of the Earth. unabr. collector's ed. 1998. (J). (gr. 3-7). audio 64.00 (*0-7366-3849-0*, 9023) Books on Tape, Inc.

—Journey to the Center of the Earth. unabr. ed. 1993. (gr. 3-7). audio 17.95 (*1-56100-503-7*, 149, Bookcassette); audio 57.25 (*1-56100-141-4*, 912, Unabridged Library Editions) Brilliance Audio.

—Journey to the Center of the Earth. abr. ed. 1984. (J). (gr. 3-7). audio 12.95 (*0-694-50313-4*, SWC 1581, Caedmon) HarperTrade.

—Journey to the Center of the Earth. l.t. ed. 1083p. pap. 76.98 (*0-7583-1206-7*); 566p. pap. 40.24 (*0-7583-1203-2*); 260p. pap. 21.85 (*0-7583-1200-8*); 325p. pap. 26.11 (*0-7583-1201-6*); 444p. pap. 32.53 (*0-7583-1202-4*); 1257p. pap. 86.35 (*0-7583-1207-5*); 882p. pap. 67.20 (*0-7583-1205-9*); 722p. pap. 49.49 (*0-7583-1204-0*); 444p. lib. bdg. 38.53 (*0-7583-1194-X*); 325p. lib. bdg. 32.11 (*0-7583-1193-1*); 722p. lib. bdg. 55.49 (*0-7583-1196-6*); 1083p. lib. bdg. 88.98 (*0-7583-1198-2*); 260p. lib. bdg. 27.85 (*0-7583-1192-3*); 566p. lib. bdg. 46.24 (*0-7583-1195-8*); 1257p. lib. bdg. 98.35 (*0-7583-1199-0*); 882p. lib. bdg. 79.20 (*0-7583-1197-4*) Huge Print Pr.

—Journey to the Center of the Earth. l.t. ed. 2000. (LRS Large Print Heritage Ser.). 441p. (YA). (gr. 6-12). lib. bdg. 34.95 (*1-58118-074-8*, 23666) LRS.

—Journey to the Center of the Earth. abr. ed. 1995. (J). (gr. 3-7). audio 13.98 o.p. (*962-634-554-3*, NA205414); audio compact disk 15.98 o.p. (*962-634-054-1*, NA205412) Naxos of America, Inc. (Naxos AudioBooks).

—Journey to the Center of the Earth. abr. ed. 1997. audio 25.00 (*0-7871-1452-9*); (J). audio 7.00 (*0-7871-1453-7*) NewStar Media, Inc. (Dove Audio).

—Journey to the Center of the Earth. unabr. ed. 1988. (J). (gr. 3-7). audio 70.00 (*1-55690-271-9*, 88490E7) Recorded Bks., LLC.

—Journey to the Center of the Earth. unabr. ed. 2002. (YA). audio compact disk 18.95 (*1-58472-388-2*, In Audio) Sound Room Pubs., Inc.

—Journey to the Center of the Earth. Baldick, Robert, tr. from FRE. l.t. ed. 1998. (Science Fiction Ser.). 328p. 23.00 (*0-7838-0319-2*) Thorndike Pr.

—Journey to the Center of the Earth. unabr. ed. 1997. 246p. reprint ed. pap. 14.95 o.p. (*1-57002-054-X*) University Publishing Hse., Inc.

—Journey to the Center of the Earth. abr. ed. 1996. (Classic Ser.). audio 10.95 o.s.i (*0-14-086240-4*, Penguin AudioBooks) Viking Penguin.

**LIEBERMAN, ABE (FICTITIOUS CHARACTER)—FICTION**

Kaminsky, Stuart M. The Big Silence. 2000. 288p. 23.95 (0-312-86926-6, Forge Bks.) Doherty, Tom Assocs., LLC.
—The Big Silence. l.t. ed. 2001. (Thorndike Basic Ser.). 411p. 29.95 (0-7862-3148-3) Thorndike Pr.
—Lieberman's Choice. l.t. ed. 1994. 222p. 24.95 o.p. (0-7927-2109-8); pap. 23.95 o.p. (0-7927-2108-X) BBC Audiobooks America.
—Lieberman's Choice. 1994. (Midwest Mysteries Ser.). mass mkt. 4.99 o.s.i (0-8041-1176-6, Ivy Bks.) Ballantine Bks.
—Lieberman's Choice. abr. ed. 1995. (Abe Lieberman Mystery Ser.). audio 16.99 (0-88646-384-X, 391066) Durkin Hayes Publishing Ltd.
—Lieberman's Choice. 1993. 216p. 18.95 o.p. (0-312-08836-1, Saint Martin's Minotaur) St. Martin's Pr.
—Lieberman's Day. 1994. mass mkt. 4.99 o.s.i (0-8041-1286-X, Ivy Bks.) Ballantine Bks.
—Lieberman's Day. abr. ed. 1994. (Abe Lieberman Mystery Ser.). audio 16.99 (0-88646-346-7, 391067) Durkin Hayes Publishing Ltd.
—Lieberman's Day. l.t. ed. 1994. 286p. 23.95 o.p. (1-56895-115-9, Wheeler Publishing, Inc.) Gale Group.
—Lieberman's Day. 1994. (Henry Holt Mystery Ser.). 260p. 19.95 o.p. (0-8050-2575-8) Holt, Henry & Co.
—Lieberman's Day. unabr. ed. 2000. (Abe Lieberman Mystery Ser.). audio 51.00 (0-7887-0418-4, 94610E7) Recorded Bks., LLC.
—Lieberman's Folly. l.t. ed. 1994. 290p. 20.95 o.p. (0-7927-1979-4); pap. 19.95 o.p. (0-7927-1978-6) BBC Audiobooks America.
—Lieberman's Folly. 1992. (Midwest Mysteries Ser.). mass mkt. 4.99 o.s.i (0-8041-0924-9, Ivy Bks.) Ballantine Bks.
—Lieberman's Folly. 1991. 216p. 15.95 o.p. (0-312-05398-3, Saint Martin's Minotaur) St. Martin's Pr.
—Lieberman's Law. unabr. ed. 1999. audio 49.95 Blackstone Audio Bks., Inc.
—Lieberman's Law. 1996. (Henry Holt Mystery Ser.). 309p. 22.50 o.p. (0-8050-3749-7) Holt, Henry & Co.
—Lieberman's Law. unabr. ed. 1996. (Abe Lieberman Mystery Ser.). audio 60.00 (0-7887-0586-5, 94705E7) Recorded Bks., LLC.
—Lieberman's Thief. 1996. mass mkt. 5.50 o.s.i (0-8041-1287-8, Ivy Bks.) Ballantine Bks.
—Lieberman's Thief. abr. ed. 1996. audio 7.99 o.p. (1-56740-112-0, 1321, Paperback Nova Audio Bks.); 1995. (Abe Lieberman Mystery Ser.: Bk. 4). audio 16.95 o.p. (1-56100-430-8, 1320, Nova Audio Bks.); 1995. (Abe Lieberman Mystery Ser.: Vol. 4). audio 57.25 o.p. (1-56100-263-1, 1266, Unabridged Library Editions); 1995. (Abe Lieberman Mystery Ser.: Vol. Bk. 4). audio 23.95 o.p. (1-56100-638-6, 162, Bookcassette) Brilliance Audio.
—Lieberman's Thief. 1995. (Henry Holt Mystery Ser.). 238p. 22.50 o.p. (0-8050-2576-6) Holt, Henry & Co.
—Not Quite Kosher. 2002. (Abe Lieberman Ser.). 256p. 23.95 (0-312-87453-7, Forge Bks.) Doherty, Tom Assocs., LLC.

**LIFFEY, JACK (FICTITIOUS CHARACTER)—FICTION**

Shannon, John. The Concrete River. 1998. (Jack Liffey Mystery Ser.). 240p. reprint ed. mass mkt. 5.99 o.s.i (0-425-16193-5, Prime Crime) Berkley Publishing Group.
—The Concrete River. 1996. 192p. pap. 12.00 o.p. (0-9639050-5-8, West Coast Crime) Blue Heron Publishing.
—The Cracked Earth. 1999. (Jack Liffey Mystery Ser.). 288p. mass mkt. 5.99 o.s.i (0-425-16732-1) Berkley Publishing Group.
—The Poison Sky. 2000. (Jack Liffey Mystery Ser.). 241p. mass mkt. 5.99 o.s.i (0-425-17424-7, Prime Crime) Berkley Publishing Group.
—Streets on Fire: A Jack Liffey Mystery. Penzler, Otto, ed. 2002. 240p. 24.00 (0-7867-1018-7, Carroll & Graf Pubs.) Avalon Publishing Group.

**LIGHT, ROBIN (FICTITIOUS CHARACTER)—FICTION**

Block, Barbara. Blowing Smoke. 2002. 34p. mass mkt. 5.99 (1-57566-723-1, Kensington Bks.); 2001. 368p. 22.00 o.s.i (1-57566-670-7) Kensington Publishing Corp.
—Chutes & Adders. 1995. mass mkt. 4.99 o.s.i (0-8217-4997-8) Kensington Publishing Corp.
—Chutes & Adders: A Robin Light Mystery. 1994. 320p. mass mkt. 16.95 o.s.i (0-8217-4533-6) Kensington Publishing Corp.
—Endangered Species: A Robin Light Mystery. 1999. (Robin Light Mystery Ser.). 320p. 20.00 o.s.i (1-57566-449-6, Kensington Bks.) Kensington Publishing Corp.
—In Plain Sight: A Robin Light Mystery. (Robin Light Mystery Ser.). 1997. 336p. mass mkt. 5.50 o.s.i (1-57566-199-3); 1996. 321p. 18.95 o.p. (1-57566-059-8, Kensington Bks.) Kensington Publishing Corp.
—Rubbed Out. 2003. 304p. mass mkt. 5.99 (1-57566-724-X, Kensington Bks.) Kensington Publishing Corp.
—Rubbed Out: A Robin Light Thriller. 2002. (Robin Light Thriller Ser.). 368p. 22.00 (1-57566-709-6, Kensington Bks.) Kensington Publishing Corp.
—The Scent of Murder. 336p. 1999. mass mkt. 5.99 o.s.i (1-57566-331-7); 1997. 18.95 o.s.i (1-57566-195-0) Kensington Publishing Corp.
—Twister. 1996. (Robin Light Mystery Ser.). 304p. mass mkt. 4.99 (1-57566-062-8, Kensington Bks.) Kensington Publishing Corp.
—Twister: A Robin Light Mystery. 1995. mass mkt. 16.95 o.p. (0-8217-4989-7, Zebra Bks.) Kensington Publishing Corp.
—Vanishing Act. 1998. (Robin Light Mystery Ser.). 352p. 20.00 o.s.i (1-57566-326-0, Kensington Bks.) Kensington Publishing Corp.
—Vanishing Act: A Robin Light Mystery. 1999. (Robin Light Mystery Ser.). 320p. mass mkt. 5.99 (1-57566-442-9) Kensington Publishing Corp.

**LIGHTFOOT, MARIE (FICTITIOUS CHARACTER)—FICTION**

Pickard, Nancy. Ring of Truth. l.t. ed. 2002. (Marie Lightfoot Mysteries Ser.). 29.95 (0-7862-3743-0) Gale Group.
—Ring of Truth. (Marie Lightfoot Mysteries Ser.). 2001. 23.95 (0-7434-1205-2, Atria); 2001. (Illus.). 272p. 23.95 (0-671-88797-1, Atria); 2002. (Illus.). 384p. reprint ed. pap. 6.99 (0-671-88796-3, Pocket); 2001. reprint ed. E-Book 23.95 (0-7434-1805-0, Atria) Simon & Schuster.
—The Truth Hurts. (Marie Lightfoot Mysteries Ser.). 2003. 400p. mass mkt. 6.99 (0-7434-1204-4, Pocket); 2002. 336p. 24.00 (0-7434-1203-6, Atria) Simon & Schuster.
—The Truth Hurts. l.t. ed. 2002. (Marie Lightfoot Mysteries Ser.). 29.95 (0-7862-4675-8) Thorndike Pr.
—The Whole Truth. (Marie Lightfoot Mysteries Ser.). E-Book 22.95 (1-58945-297-6) Adobe Systems, Inc.
—The Whole Truth. (Marie Lightfoot Mysteries Ser.). 2000. 272p. 22.95 o.s.i (0-671-88795-5, Atria); 2001. reprint ed. E-Book 22.95 (0-7434-1804-2, Atria); 2001. (Illus.). 368p. reprint ed. mass mkt. 6.99 o.s.i (0-671-88794-7, Pocket) Simon & Schuster.
—The Whole Truth. l.t. ed. 2000. (Marie Lightfoot Mysteries Ser.). 439p. 29.95 (0-7862-2577-7) Thorndike Pr.

**LIGHTSTONE, HARRY (FICTITIOUS CHARACTER)—FICTION**

Goddard, Ken. Double Blind. 1998. (Henry Lightstone Ser.: 3). 460p. mass mkt. 6.99 (0-8125-5061-7); 1997. 384p. 24.95 o.p. (0-312-85796-9) Doherty, Tom Assocs., LLC. (Forge Bks.).
—Prey. 1993. 398p. mass mkt. 5.99 (0-8125-1198-0); 1992. 336p. 21.95 o.p. (0-312-85112-X) Doherty, Tom Assocs., LLC. (Tor Bks.).
—Wildfire. 1995. 460p. pap. text 5.99 o.p. (0-8125-2302-4); 1994. 384p. 22.95 o.p. (0-312-85424-2) Doherty, Tom Assocs., LLC. (Forge Bks.).

**LI'L ABNER (FICTITIOUS CHARACTER)—FICTION**

Capp, Al. Li'l Abner. Kitchen, Denis, ed. 1988. (Li'l Abner Dailies Ser.: Vol. I). (Illus.). 232p. pap. 16.95 o.s.i (0-87816-037-X) Kitchen Sink Pr., Inc.
—Lil Abner, No. 24. Couch, N. C. Christopher, ed. 1997. (Illus.). 176p. pap. 18.95 (0-87816-316-6); 2nd ed. 34.95 (0-87816-317-4) Kitchen Sink Pr., Inc.
—Li'l Abner. No. 26. 1998. 184p. pap. 22.95 (0-87816-290-9); No. 27. 1999. (0-87816-296-8); No. 27. 1998. 176p. pap. 22.95 (0-87816-295-X) Kitchen Sink Pr., Inc.
—Li'l Abner, Vol. I. Kitchen, Denis, ed. 1988. (Complete Li'l Abner Ser.). (Illus.). 232p. 27.95 o.p. (0-87816-036-1) Kitchen Sink Pr., Inc.
—Li'l Abner, Vol. 17. Vance, James, ed. 1993. (Illus.). 160p. 34.95 (0-87816-209-7) Kitchen Sink Pr., Inc.
—Li'l Abner, Vol. 18. Vance, Jim, ed. 1994. (Illus.). 176p. reprint ed. pap. 18.95 o.p. (0-87816-241-0) Kitchen Sink Pr., Inc.
—Li'l Abner, Vol. 19. Vance, James, ed. 2nd ed. 1994. (Illus.). 160p. 34.95 (0-87816-249-6) Kitchen Sink Pr., Inc.
—Li'l Abner. 1995. (Illus.). Vol. 21. 2nd ed. 176p. 34.95 (0-87816-263-1); Vol. 22. 192p. 40.00 (0-87816-272-0); Vol. 23. 176p. 34.95 (0-87816-305-0) Kitchen Sink Pr., Inc.
—Li'l Abner: Li'l Abner Meets the Shmoo, No. 27. 1998. (Li'l Abner Dailies Ser.). (Illus.). 180p. reprint ed. pap. 22.95 (0-87816-116-3) Kitchen Sink Pr., Inc.
—Li'l Abner Dailies. 1995. (Li'l Abner Dailies Ser.: Vol. XXI). pap. 18.95 (0-87816-262-3); 1995. (Li'l Abner Dailies Ser.: Vol. XXII). (Illus.). pap. 20.95 (0-87816-271-2); Vol. 23. 1996. (Illus.). 176p. pap. text 18.95 (0-87816-304-2) Kitchen Sink Pr., Inc.
—Li'l Abner Dailies, 1938: Abner in the Orphanage, Strange Gal in the Swamp. Schreiner, Dave, ed. 1989. (Li'l Abner Dailies Ser.: Vol. IV). (Illus.). 168p. 27.95 (0-87816-051-5); pap. 16.95 (0-87816-052-3) Kitchen Sink Pr., Inc.
—Li'l Abner Dailies 1939, Vol. 5. Schreiner, Dave & Cairol, Julie C., eds. 1989. (Illus.). 176p. 27.95 (0-87816-056-6) Kitchen Sink Pr., Inc.
—Li'l Abner Dailies 1939, Vol. 5. Schreiner, Dave, ed. 1988. (Illus.). 176p. pap. 16.95 o.p. (0-87816-057-4) Kitchen Sink Pr., Inc.
—Li'l Abner Dailies 1940, Vol.VI. Schreiner, Dave, ed. 1989. (Li'l Abner Dailies Ser.: Vol. VI). (Illus.). 174p. 27.95 o.p. (0-87816-058-2) Kitchen Sink Pr., Inc.
—Li'l Abner Dailies, 1940, Vol.VI. Schreiner, Dave, ed. 1989. (Li'l Abner Dailies Ser.). (Illus.). 174p. pap. 16.95 (0-87816-059-0) Kitchen Sink Pr., Inc.
—Li'l Abner Dailies 1941, Vol. VII. Schreiner, Dave, ed. 1990. (Li'l Abner Dailies Ser.). (Illus.). 27.95 (0-87816-064-7); pap. 16.95 o.p. (0-87816-065-5) Kitchen Sink Pr., Inc.
Capp, AL. Li'l Abner Dailies 1942, Vol. VIII. Schreiner, Dave, ed. 1990. (Li'l Abner Dailies Ser.). (Illus.). 29.95 o.p. (0-87816-068-X) Kitchen Sink Pr., Inc.
Capp, Al. Li'l Abner Dailies, 1942, Vol. VIII. Schreiner, Dave, ed. 1990. (Li'l Abner Dailies Ser.). (Illus.). pap. 16.95 o.p. (0-87816-069-8) Kitchen Sink Pr., Inc.
—Li'l Abner Dailies 1943. Schreiner, Dave, ed. 1990. (Illus.). (Li'l Abner Dailies Ser.: Vol. IX). pap. 16.95 o.s.i (0-87816-074-4);Vol. IX. 29.95 (0-87816-073-6) Kitchen Sink Pr., Inc.
—Li'l Abner Dailies 1944, Vol. 10. Schreiner, Dave, ed. 1990. (Li'l Abner Dailies Ser.: Vol. X). (Illus.). 168p. 29.95 o.p. (0-87816-078-7) Kitchen Sink Pr., Inc.
—Li'l Abner Dailies, 1944, Vol. 10. Schreiner, Dave, ed. 1990. (Li'l Abner Dailies Ser.: Vol. X). (Illus.). pap. 18.95 o.p. (0-87816-079-5) Kitchen Sink Pr., Inc.
—Li'l Abner Dailies, 1945, Vol. 11. Schreiner, Dave & Gardner, Madeline, eds. 1991. (Al Capp's Li'l Abner Ser.). (Illus.). reprint ed. pap. 18.95 o.p. (0-87816-083-3) Kitchen Sink Pr., Inc.
—Li'l Abner Dailies 1945, Vol. 11. Schreiner, Dave, ed. 2nd ed. 1991. (Al Capp's Li'l Abner Ser.). (Illus.). 168p. reprint ed. 29.95 o.p. (0-87816-082-5) Kitchen Sink Pr., Inc.
—Li'l Abner Dailies 1946. 1991. (Illus.). 168p. (Li'l Abner Dailies Ser.: Vol. XII). 29.95 o.p. (0-87816-091-4);Vol. 12. pap. 18.95 (0-87816-092-2) Kitchen Sink Pr., Inc.
—Li'l Abner Dailies 1947. Schreiner, Dave, ed. 1992. (Illus.). 180p. (Al Capp's Li'l Abner Ser.: Vol. 13). 24.95 o.p. (0-87816-098-1); (Li'l Abner Dailies Ser.: Vol. XIII). pap. 16.95 o.p. (0-87816-099-X) Kitchen Sink Pr., Inc.
—Li'l Abner Dailies 1949 Vol. 15: Kick in the Kigmies! Schreiner, Dave, ed. 1993. (Illus.). 176p. (Li'l Abner Dailies Ser.: Vol. XV). pap. 18.95 o.p. (0-87816-127-9); 34.95 (0-87816-126-0) Kitchen Sink Pr., Inc.
—Li'l Abner Dailies, 1950: In Search of the Perfect Woman. Schreiner, Dave, ed. 1993. (Li'l Abner Dailies Ser.: Vol. 16). (Illus.). 184p. pap. 18.95 o.p. (0-87816-144-9); 34.95 (0-87816-143-0) Kitchen Sink Pr., Inc.
—Li'l Abner Dailies, 1959. 1996. (Li'l Abner Dailies Ser.: Vol. 25). (Illus.). 184p. 34.95 (0-87816-279-8); pap. 18.95 (0-87816-278-X) Kitchen Sink Pr., Inc.
—Li'l Abner Daily Strips, 1951. Schreiner, Dave, ed. 1993. (Li'l Abner Dailies Ser.: Vol. 17). (Illus.). 180p. pap. 18.95 (0-87816-210-0) Kitchen Sink Pr., Inc.
—Li'l Abner, 1952, Vol. 18. Schriener, Dave, ed. 1994. (Illus.). 176p. (YA). (gr. 6 up). reprint ed. 34.95 (0-87816-242-9) Kitchen Sink Pr., Inc.
—Li'l Abner, 1953, Vol. 19. Vance, Jim, ed. 1994. (Illus.). 160p. (YA). (gr. 6 up). pap. 18.95 o.p. (0-87816-248-8) Kitchen Sink Pr., Inc.
—Li'l Abner 1954, Vol. 20. Couch, Chris, ed. 1995. (Illus.). 160p. 34.95 o.p. (0-87816-255-0); pap. 18.95 o.p. (0-87816-254-2) Kitchen Sink Pr., Inc.
Schreiner, Dave, ed. Li'l Abner. 1988. (Li'l Abner Dailies Ser.: Vol. II). (Illus.). 160p. 27.95 o.p. (0-87816-040-X); 168p. 27.95 o.p. (0-87816-042-6); 168p. pap. 16.95 o.p. (0-87816-043-4);2. 160p. pap. 16.95 (0-87816-041-8) Kitchen Sink Pr., Inc.

**LIL, AUNTIE (FICTITIOUS CHARACTER)—FICTION**

Gray, Gallagher. A Cast of Killers. 1994. (Partners in Crime Ser.). mass mkt. 4.99 o.s.i (0-8041-1146-4, Ivy Bks.) Ballantine Bks.
—A Cast of Killers. 1992. 256p. 20.95 o.p. (1-55611-328-5) Fine, Donald I. Bks.
—Death of a Dream Maker. 1995. mass mkt. 5.50 o.s.i (0-8041-1247-9, Ivy Bks.) Ballantine Bks.
—Hubbert & Lil: Partners in Crime. 1993. mass mkt. 4.99 o.s.i (0-8041-0948-6, Ivy Bks.) Ballantine Bks.
—Hubbert & Lil: Partners in Crime. 1991. 256p. 18.95 o.p. (1-55611-308-0) Fine, Donald I. Bks.
—A Motive for Murder. 1996. (Partners in Crime Ser.). mass mkt. 5.50 o.s.i (0-8041-1248-7, Ivy Bks.) Ballantine Bks.

**LINCOLN, EDWARD (FICTITIOUS CHARACTER)—FICTION**

Francis, Dick. Smokescreen. l.t. ed. 1993. 19.95 o.p. (0-7927-1664-7); 1993. pap. 17.95 o.p. (0-7927-1663-9); 1995. audio 54.95 (0-7451-6832-9, CAB 486) BBC Audiobooks America.
—Smokescreen. 1993. 272p. mass mkt. 6.99 (0-449-22111-3, Fawcett) Ballantine Bks.
—Smokescreen. unabr. ed. 1999. audio 32.95 (0-7861-1514-9, 2364) Blackstone Audio Bks., Inc.
—Smokescreen. unabr. ed. 1994. audio 42.00 (0-7366-2838-X, 3546) Books on Tape, Inc.
—Smokescreen. unabr. ed. 2000. audio 49.95 Chivers Audio Bks. GBR. *Dist:* BBC Audiobooks America.
—Smokescreen. 1973. (Harper Novel of Suspense Ser.). 224p. 8.95 o.p. (0-06-011334-0) HarperCollins Pubs.
—Smokescreen. 1990. audio 15.95; audio 15.95 o.p. (1-55994-130-8, CPN 2130) HarperTrade. (HarperAudio).
—Smokescreen. unabr. ed. 1999. audio 32.95 Highsmith Inc.
—Smokescreen. abr. ed. 2000. audio 7.95 (1-57815-049-3, 1046, Media Bks. Audio Publishing) Media Bks., L. L. C.
—Smokescreen. unabr. ed. 2000. audio 44.00 (0-7887-0231-9, 94456E7) Recorded Bks., LLC.
—Smokescreen. 1990. mass mkt. 4.95 (0-671-70470-2); 1984. 224p. mass mkt. 3.50 (0-671-50737-0); 1982. mass mkt. 2.95 o.s.i (0-671-45911-2) Simon & Schuster. (Pocket).
—Smokescreen. l.t. ed. 1978. 12.00 o.p. (0-7089-0126-3, Ulverscroft) Thorpe, F. A. Pubs. GBR. *Dist:* Ulverscroft Large Print Bks., Ltd.

**LINDSEY, HOBART (FICTITIOUS CHARACTER)—FICTION**

Lupoff, Richard A. The Bessie Blue Killer: A Hobart Lindsey - Marvia Plum Mystery. 1994. 304p. 20.95 o.p. (0-312-10425-1, Saint Martin's Minotaur) St. Martin's Pr.
—The Classic Car Killer. 1992. 288p. (Orig.). mass mkt. 4.99 o.s.i (0-553-29607-8) Bantam Bks.
—The Comic Book Killer. 1989. mass mkt. 3.95 o.s.i (0-553-27781-2) Bantam Bks.
—The Cover Girl Killer: A Hobart Lindsey - Marvia Plum Mystery. 1995. 224p. 21.95 o.p. (0-312-13455-X, Saint Martin's Minotaur) St. Martin's Pr.
—The Radio Red Killer. 1997. (Marvia Plum Mystery Ser.). 268p. text 22.95 o.p. (0-312-17181-1, Saint Martin's Minotaur) St. Martin's Pr.
—The Sepia Siren Killer. 1994. (Hobart Lidsey-Mariva Plum Mystery Ser.). 304p. 20.95 o.p. (0-312-11332-3, Saint Martin's Minotaur) St. Martin's Pr.
—The Silver Chariot Killer. 1996. 192p. text 21.95 o.p. (0-312-14736-8, Saint Martin's Minotaur) St. Martin's Pr.

**LINNEAR, NICHOLAS (FICTITIOUS CHARACTER)—FICTION**

Van Lustbader, Eric. Floating City. abr. ed. 1994. 24.95 o.p. (0-7871-0162-1) NewStar Media, Inc.
—Floating City. 1995. (Illus.). 512p. (J). mass mkt. 6.99 (0-671-86809-8, Pocket); 1994. 416p. 22.00 o.p. (0-671-86808-X, Atria) Simon & Schuster.
—Floating City. Zion, Claire, ed. 1994. reprint ed. pap. 6.50 o.s.i (0-671-89857-4, Pocket) Simon & Schuster.
—The Kaisho. abr. ed. 1993. audio 16.95 o.p. (1-55800-889-6) NewStar Media, Inc.
—The Kaisho. 1998. 3.99 (0-671-02329-2, Pocket) Simon & Schuster.
—The Kaisho. Zion, Claire, ed. 1993. 496p. 22.00 (0-671-86806-3, Atria); 1994. 592p. reprint ed. mass mkt. 6.99 (0-671-86807-1, Pocket Star) Simon & Schuster.
—The Miko. 1985. 560p. mass mkt. 6.99 (0-449-20596-7, Fawcett) Ballantine Bks.
—The Miko. 1984. 16.95 o.p. (0-394-53929-X, Villard Bks.) Random House Adult Trade Publishing Group.
—The Ninja. 1985. 512p. mass mkt. 6.99 (0-449-20916-4, Fawcett) Ballantine Bks.
—The Ninja. 1980. 448p. 12.95 o.p. (0-87131-314-6) Evans, M. & Co., Inc.
—The Ninja. l.t. ed. 1983. (Charnwood Large Print Ser.). 800p. 29.99 o.p. (0-7089-8149-6, Charnwood) Thorpe, F. A. Pubs. GBR. *Dist:* Ulverscroft Large Print Bks., Ltd., Ulverscroft Large Print Canada, Ltd.
—Second Skin. abr. ed. 1995. 24.95 o.p. (0-7871-0397-7) NewStar Media, Inc.


Characters

—Second Skin. 1996. 528p. mass mkt. 6.99 (*0-671-70349-8*); pap. 6.50 o.s.i (*0-671-53782-2*) Simon & Schuster. (Pocket).

—Second Skin. Zion, Claire, ed. 1995. 464p. 22.00 o.p. (*0-671-86810-1*, Atria) Simon & Schuster.

—White Ninja. 1995. 512p. pap. 27.00 (*0-345-46677-2*, Fawcett); 1993. mass mkt. 3.99 o.p. (*0-449-22265-9*); 1991. 512p. mass mkt. 6.99 (*0-449-21851-1*, Fawcett); 1990. mass mkt. 5.95 o.s.i (*0-449-21972-0*) Ballantine Bks.

—White Ninja. abr. ed. 1993. audio 15.95 o.p. (*1-55800-249-9*, 40990); audio 8.99 o.p. (*1-55800-903-5*) NewStar Media, Inc. (Dove Audio).

—White Ninja. 1991. 4.99 o.p. (*0-517-07909-7*) Random Hse. Value Publishing.

**LISAN, MAGALIE (FICTITIOUS CHARACTER)—FICTION**

Brunel, Sigrid. Woman with Red Hair. 1991. 200p. (Orig.). pap. 8.95 (*0-934678-30-8*) New Victoria Pubs., Inc.

**LISLE, DARINA (FICTITIOUS CHARACTER)—FICTION**

Laurence, Janet. Death & the Epicure. l.t. ed. 1994. (Magna Large Print Ser.). 384p. (*0-7505-0702-0*) Magna Large Print Bks. GBR. *Dist:* Ulverscroft Large Print Canada, Ltd.

—Death & the Epicure. 1993. 208p. 18.95 o.p. (*0-312-10451-0*, Saint Martin's Minotaur) St. Martin's Pr.

—Death at the Table. l.t. ed. 1997. (Paperback Ser.). 360p. lib. bdg. 21.95 (*0-7838-8255-6*, Macmillan Reference USA) Gale Group.

—Death at the Table. 1999. (Mystery Ser.: Bk. 316). per. (*0-373-26316-3*, 1-26316-9, Worldwide Library) Harlequin Enterprises, Ltd.

—Death at the Table. l.t. ed. 1997. 224p. 20.95 o.p. (*0-312-15105-5*, Saint Martin's Minotaur) St. Martin's Pr.

—A Deep Coffyn. 1989. 14.95 o.s.i (*0-385-26626-X*) Doubleday Publishing.

—Hotel Morgue. l.t. ed. 1992. (Mystery Ser.). 431p. 29.99 o.p. (*0-7505-0298-3*) Magna Large Print Bks. GBR. *Dist:* Ulverscroft Large Print Bks., Ltd., Ulverscroft Large Print Canada, Ltd.

—Recipe for Death. l.t. ed. 1994. (Magna Large Print Ser.). 415p. (*0-7505-0640-7*) Magna Large Print Bks. GBR. *Dist:* Ulverscroft Large Print Canada, Ltd.

**LITTLE ORPHAN ANNIE (FICTITIOUS CHARACTER)—FICTION**

Gray, Harold. Little Orphan Annie. 1982. (Illus.). 64p. (J). (gr. 2 up). reprint ed. pap. 2.95 o.p. (*0-486-24420-2*) Dover Pubns., Inc.

—Little Orphan Annie in Cosmic City. 1982. (Illus.). 64p. (J). (gr. 2 up). pap. 1.95 o.p. (*0-486-24421-0*) Dover Pubns., Inc.

—Little Orphan Annie in the Great Depression. 1979. (Illus.). 58p. (Orig.). (J). (gr. 5 up). pap. 3.95 o.p. (*0-486-23737-0*) Dover Pubns., Inc.

Little Orphan Annie. (J). audio National Recording Co.

Riley, James Whitcomb & Stanley, Diane. Little Orphan Annie. 1983. (Illus.). 32p. (J). (ps-3). 9.95 o.s.i (*0-399-20904-2*, G. P. Putnam's Sons) Penguin Putnam Bks. for Young Readers.

**LITTLEJOHN, ELDON (FICTITIOUS CHARACTER)—FICTION**

Maxwell, Jan. Baptism by Murder. 1995. 224p. (Orig.). mass mkt. 4.99 (*0-380-77621-9*, Avon Bks.) Morrow/Avon.

**LIU, HULAN (FICTITIOUS CHARACTER)—FICTION**

See, Lisa. Flower Net. 1998. 480p. mass mkt. 6.99 o.s.i (*0-06-109543-5*); 1997. 352p. 24.00 o.p. (*0-06-017527-3*) HarperCollins Pubs.

—The Interior. 1999. 400p. 25.00 o.s.i (*0-06-019261-5*) HarperCollins Pubs.

**LIVESAY, PETER (FICTITIOUS CHARACTER)—FICTION**

Hunter, Fred. Capital Queers. (Alex Reynolds Mysteries Ser.). 2000. 232p. pap. 12.95 (*0-312-26301-5*, Saint Martin's Griffin); 1999. 224p. 23.95 o.p. (*0-312-20463-9*, Saint Martin's Minotaur) St. Martin's Pr.

—Federal Fag. (Alex Reynolds Mysteries Ser.). 272p. 1999. pap. 11.95 (*0-312-20649-6*, Saint Martin's Griffin); 1998. 22.95 o.p. (*0-312-18580-4*, Saint Martin's Minotaur) St. Martin's Pr.

—Government Gay. (Alex Reynolds Mysteries Ser.). 1998. 224p. pap. 11.95 (*0-312-18721-1*, Saint Martin's Griffin); 1997. 215p. text 21.95 o.p. (*0-312-15536-0*, Saint Martin's Minotaur) St. Martin's Pr.

—National Nancys. 2000. (Alex Reynolds Mysteries Ser.). 240p. 22.95 (*0-312-25233-1*, Saint Martin's Minotaur) St. Martin's Pr.

**LLOYD, HILARY (FICTITIOUS CHARACTER)—FICTION**

Radley, Sheila. Blood on the Happy Highway. l.t. ed. 1984. 384p. 16.95 o.p. (*0-7089-1316-4*, Ulverscroft) Thorpe, F. A. Pubs. GBR. *Dist:* Ulverscroft Large Print Bks., Ltd.

—The Chief Inspector's Daughter. 1987. (Mystery Ser.). 224p. mass mkt. 3.50 o.s.i (*0-553-26942-9*) Bantam Bks.

—The Chief Inspector's Daughter. 1982. (Nightingale Ser.). pap. 9.95 o.p. (*0-8161-3413-8*, Macmillan Reference USA) Gale Group.

—The Chief Inspector's Daughter. l.t. ed. 1982. (Ulverscroft Large Print Ser.). 432p. 29.99 o.p. (*0-7089-1033-5*, Ulverscroft) Thorpe, F. A. Pubs. GBR. *Dist:* Ulverscroft Large Print Bks., Ltd., Ulverscroft Large Print Canada, Ltd.

—Cross My Heart & Hope to Die: An Inspector Quantrill Mystery. 1992. (Quantrill Ser.: No. 8). 288p. text 19.00 (*0-684-19410-4*, Macmillan Reference USA) Gale Group.

—Cross My Heart & Hope to Die: An Inspector Quantrill Mystery. l.t. ed. 1998. (Ulverscroft Large Print Ser.). 416p. 29.99 o.p. (*0-7089-3956-2*, Ulverscroft) Thorpe, F. A. Pubs. GBR. *Dist:* Ulverscroft Large Print Bks., Ltd., Ulverscroft Large Print Canada, Ltd.

—Death in the Morning. 1987. 224p. reprint ed. mass mkt. 3.50 o.s.i (*0-553-26857-0*) Bantam Bks.

—Death in the Morning. 1980. pap. 3.50 o.p. (*0-440-11785-2*) Dell Publishing.

—Death in the Morning. 1981. (General Ser.). lib. bdg. 13.95 o.p. (*0-8161-3199-6*, Macmillan Reference USA) Gale Group.

—Fair Game. l.t. ed. 1999. (Ulverscroft Large Print Ser.). 416p. 31.99 o.p. (*0-7089-4028-5*, Ulverscroft) Thorpe, F. A. Pubs. GBR. *Dist:* Ulverscroft Large Print Bks., Ltd., Ulverscroft Large Print Canada, Ltd.

—Fate Worse Than Death. 1987. 208p. mass mkt. 2.95 o.s.i (*0-553-26538-5*) Bantam Bks.

—Fate Worse Than Death. 1986. 224p. 13.95 o.p. (*0-684-18582-2*, Macmillan Reference USA) Gale Group.

—Fate Worse Than Death. l.t. ed. 1986. (Mystery Ser.). 448p. 29.99 o.p. (*0-7089-1630-9*, Ulverscroft) Thorpe, F. A. Pubs. GBR. *Dist:* Ulverscroft Large Print Bks., Ltd., Ulverscroft Large Print Canada, Ltd.

—The Quiet Road to Death. 1984. 176p. 11.95 o.s.i (*0-684-18124-X*, Scribner) Simon & Schuster.

—The Quiet Road to Death. 1985. (Crime Monthly Ser.). 192p. pap. 3.95 o.p. (*0-14-007746-4*, Penguin Bks.) Viking Penguin.

—A Talent for Destruction. 1984. mass mkt. 2.50 o.s.i (*0-345-31250-3*) Ballantine Bks.

—A Talent for Destruction. 1982. 224p. 10.95 o.p. (*0-684-17663-7*, Scribner) Simon & Schuster.

—This Way Out. 1992. 2.99 o.p. (*0-517-08033-8*) Random Hse. Value Publishing.

—This Way Out. 1989. 256p. 16.95 o.s.i (*0-684-19125-3*, Scribner) Simon & Schuster.

—This Way Out. 1990. 224p. reprint ed. pap. 4.50 o.p. (*0-14-014453-6*, Penguin Bks.) Viking Penguin.

—Who Saw Him Die? 1988. 224p. mass mkt. 3.50 o.s.i (*0-553-27607-7*) Bantam Bks.

—Who Saw Him Die? 1988. (Inspector Douglas Quantrill Mystery Ser.). 224p. 14.95 o.s.i (*0-684-18883-X*, Scribner) Simon & Schuster.

**LLOYD, INSPECTOR (FICTITIOUS CHARACTER)—FICTION**

McGown, Jill. Death in the Family. 2004. 336p. mass mkt. 6.99 (*0-345-45849-4*, Fawcett); 2003. 320p. 22.95 (*0-345-45848-6*, Ballantine Bks.) Ballantine Bks.

—Death in the Family. l.t. ed. 2003. 30.45 (*0-7862-5380-0*) Thorndike Pr.

—An Evil Hour. 1987. 256p. 16.95 o.p. (*0-312-00592-X*) St. Martin's Pr.

—Gone to Her Death. 1991. mass mkt. 4.99 (*0-449-21966-6*, Fawcett) Ballantine Bks.

—Gone to Her Death. l.t. ed. 1991. (General Ser.). 330p. lib. bdg. 22.95 o.p. (*0-8161-5094-X*, Macmillan Reference USA) Gale Group.

—Gone to Her Death. 1989. 256p. 16.95 o.p. (*0-312-03839-9*, Saint Martin's Minotaur) St. Martin's Pr.

—Murder . . . Now & Then. 1993. 304p. 20.95 o.p. (*0-312-10006-X*, Saint Martin's Minotaur) St. Martin's Pr.

—Murder at the Old Vicarage. 1991. (Mysteries Around the World Promotion Ser.). 256p. mass mkt. 6.50 (*0-449-21819-8*, Ivy Bks.) Ballantine Bks.

—Murder at the Old Vicarage. l.t. ed. 1990. (General Ser.). 348p. lib. bdg. 18.95 o.p. (*0-8161-4838-4*, Macmillan Reference USA) Gale Group.

—Murder at the Old Vicarage. 1988. 256p. 16.95 o.p. (*0-312-02615-3*, Saint Martin's Minotaur) St. Martin's Pr.

—Murder Movie. 1992. mass mkt. 4.99 o.s.i (*0-449-22070-2*, Fawcett) Ballantine Bks.

—Murder Movie. 1990. 17.95 o.p. (*0-312-05475-0*, Saint Martin's Minotaur) St. Martin's Pr.

—Murder Movie. l.t. ed. 2001. (Ulverscroft Large Print Ser.). 448p. 32.50 (*0-7089-4435-3*) Ulverscroft Large Print Bks., Ltd.

—Murder... Now & Then. 1995. (Mysteries Around the World Promotion). mass mkt. 5.99 o.s.i (*0-449-22311-6*, Fawcett) Ballantine Bks.

—Murder... Now & Then. 1993. 407p. pap. 13.95 (*0-330-33243-0*) Pan Bks. Ltd. GBR. *Dist:* Trans-Atlantic Pubns., Inc.

—The Murders of Mrs. Austin & Mrs. Beale. 1993. 256p. reprint ed. mass mkt. 6.50 (*0-449-22162-8*, Fawcett) Ballantine Bks.

—The Murders of Mrs. Austin & Mrs. Beale. 1991. 224p. 17.95 o.p. (*0-312-06422-5*, Saint Martin's Minotaur) St. Martin's Pr.

—The Other Woman. 1994. mass mkt. 5.99 (*0-449-22272-1*, Fawcett) Ballantine Bks.

—The Other Woman. l.t. ed. 1997. 477p. (*0-7505-1065-X*) Magna Large Print Bks. GBR. *Dist:* Ulverscroft Large Print Bks., Ltd.

—The Other Woman. 1993. 236p. 17.95 o.p. (*0-312-08868-X*, Saint Martin's Minotaur) St. Martin's Pr.

—A Perfect Match. 1990. 192p. mass mkt. 6.50 (*0-449-21820-1*, Fawcett) Ballantine Bks.

—A Perfect Match. 1983. 192p. 11.95 o.p. (*0-312-60069-0*) St. Martin's Pr.

—Picture of Innocence. (British Mystery Ser.). 1999. 352p. mass mkt. 6.99 (*0-449-00251-9*); 1998. 336p. 22.00 o.p. (*0-449-00250-0*) Ballantine Bks. (Fawcett).

—Picture of Innocence. l.t. ed. 1998. (Mystery Ser.). 560p. 27.95 (*0-7862-1670-0*) Thorndike Pr.

—Plots & Errors. 2000. (Detective Chief Inspector Lloyd & Judy Hill Mysteries Ser.). 384p. mass mkt. 6.99 (*0-449-00253-5*, Fawcett) Ballantine Bks.

—Scene of Crime. l.t. ed. 2001. 391p. 29.95 (*0-7862-3647-7*) Thorndike Pr.

—A Shred of Evidence. 1997. 304p. mass mkt. 6.99 (*0-449-22499-6*) Ballantine Bks.

—Verdict Unsafe. 1998. 336p. mass mkt. 6.99 (*0-449-22501-1*); 1997. 327p. 22.00 o.p. (*0-449-91067-9*) Ballantine Bks. (Fawcett).

—Verdict Unsafe. l.t. ed. 1997. (Myst-Hall Ser.). 522p. lib. bdg. 23.95 (*0-7838-8287-4*, Macmillan Reference USA) Gale Group.

**LOCKE, JOHN (FICTITIOUS CHARACTER)—FICTION**

Barnao, Jack. Hammerlocke. 1987. 256p. 3.50 o.s.i (*0-441-31609-3*, Diamond Bks.) Berkley Publishing Group.

—Hammerlocke. 1986. 240p. 13.95 o.s.i (*0-684-18683-7*, Macmillan Reference USA) Gale Group.

—Lockestep. 1989. 3.50 (*1-55773-159-4*, Diamond Bks.) Berkley Publishing Group.

—Lockestep. 1988. (John Locke Mystery Ser.). 240p. 15.95 o.s.i (*0-684-18782-5*, Macmillan Reference USA) Gale Group.

—Lockestep. 186p. 2002. pap. 6.99 (*0-7592-1432-8*); 2002. E-Book 6.99 (*0-7592-1429-8*); 2002. E-Book 6.99 (*0-7592-1430-1*); 2001. E-Book 6.99 (*0-7592-1428-X*) ereads.com.

—Timelocke: A John Locke Mystery. 1991. 256p. 18.95 o.s.i (*0-684-19298-5*, Scribner) Simon & Schuster.

**LOCKWOOD, JOHN (FICTITIOUS CHARACTER)—FICTION**

Cannell, Stephen J. Final Victim. 1997. 384p. mass mkt. 7.99 (*0-380-72816-8*, Avon Bks.); 1996. 416p. 25.00 o.p. (*0-688-14775-5*, Morrow, William & Co.) Morrow/Avon.

—Final Victim. abr. ed. 1996. 24.95 o.p. (*0-7871-1111-2*, 694124) NewStar Media, Inc.

**LOGAN (FICTITIOUS CHARACTER: NOLAN)—FICTION**

Nolan, William F. Logan's Run. Amereon Ltd. Staff, ed. 1985. 18.95 (*0-8488-0103-2*) Amereon, Ltd.

—Logan's Run. abr. ed. 1993. audio 15.95 o.p. (*1-55800-140-9*, Dove Audio) NewStar Media, Inc.

—Logan's Search. 1980. 160p. pap. 1.95 (*0-553-13805-7*) Bantam Bks.

Nolan, William F. & Johnson, George C. Logan: A Trilogy. 1992. 384p. pap. 12.00 o.s.i (*0-440-50404-X*, Dell Bks.) Dell Publishing.

—Logan: A Trilogy. 1986. (Illus.). 384p. 16.95 o.p. (*0-940776-23-5*) Maclay & Assocs.

—Logan's Run. 1976. 18.95 (*0-8488-0102-4*) Amereon, Ltd.

—Logan's Run. 1992. 160p. reprint ed. lib. bdg. 25.95 (*0-89966-896-8*) Buccaneer Bks., Inc.

**LOGAN, BRIDGETT (FICTITIOUS CHARACTER)—FICTION**

Rucka, Greg. Shooting at Midnight. 2000. 400p. mass mkt. 6.99 (*0-553-57827-8*) Bantam Bks.

Rucka, Gregory. Finder. 1999. audio 60.00 Recorded Bks., LLC.

—Finder: An Atticus Kodiac Novel. 1998. 352p. mass mkt. 6.99 (*0-553-57429-9*) Bantam Bks.

—Finder: An Atticus Kodiac Novel, unabr. ed. 1999. audio 62.00 (*0-7887-3994-8*, 96082E7) Recorded Bks., LLC.

**LOGAN, KATE (FICTITIOUS CHARACTER)—FICTION**

Heggan, Christine. Suspicion. 1997. 378p. per. (*1-55166-305-8*, 0-66305-4, Mira Bks.) Harlequin Enterprises, Ltd.

**LOGAN, WHITNEY (FICTITIOUS CHARACTER)—FICTION**

Lambert, Mercedes. Dogtown: A Whitney Logan Mystery. 1992. (Whitney Logan Mystery Ser.). 272p. pap. 6.95 o.p. (*0-14-013928-1*, Penguin Bks.) Penguin Group (USA) Inc.

—Soultown. 1997. (Whitney Logan Mystery Ser.). 256p. pap. 5.95 o.s.i (*0-14-025492-7*) Penguin Group (USA) Inc.

—Soultown: A Whitney Logan Mystery. 1996. (Whitney Logan Mystery Ser.). 256p. 21.95 o.s.i (*0-670-86684-9*, Viking) Viking Penguin.

**LOGAN FAMILY (FICTITIOUS CHARACTERS)—FICTION**

Andrews, V. C. Melody. 1999. 15.70 (*0-613-01437-5*) CRC Pr. LLC.

—Melody. l.t. ed. 1996. (G. K. Hall Core Ser.). 451p. 25.95 (*0-7838-1906-4*, Macmillan Reference USA) Gale Group.

—Melody. 1996. 384p. 23.00 o.p. (*0-671-53470-X*, Atria); pap. 7.99 (*0-671-53471-8*, Pocket) Simon & Schuster.

—Melody. 1996. 14.04 (*0-606-13603-7*) Turtleback Bks.

—Music in the Night. 1998. (Logan Ser.). 320p. 24.00 o.s.i (*0-671-53467-X*, Atria); (Illus.). 336p. pap. 7.99 (*0-671-53474-2*, Pocket) Simon & Schuster.

—Music in the Night. l.t. ed. 1999. (Core Ser.). 436p. 29.95 (*0-7838-8533-4*) Thorndike Pr.

—Music in the Night. 1998. 14.04 (*0-606-13627-4*) Turtleback Bks.

—Olivia. 1999. (Logan Ser.). 384p. 24.00 (*0-671-00760-2*, Atria); pap. 7.99 (*0-671-00761-0*, Pocket) Simon & Schuster.

—Olivia. l.t. ed. 1999. (Core Ser.). 456p. 28.95 (*0-7838-8592-X*) Thorndike Pr.

—Olivia. 1999. 14.04 (*0-606-17529-6*) Turtleback Bks.

—Unfinished Symphony. 1997. (Logan Ser.). 352p. 24.00 o.s.i (*0-671-53469-6*, Atria); 384p. mass mkt. 7.99 (*0-671-53473-4*, Pocket) Simon & Schuster.

—Unfinished Symphony. l.t. ed. 1998. (Core Ser.). 479p. 30.95 (*0-7838-8407-9*) Thorndike Pr.

—Unfinished Symphony. 1997. 14.04 (*0-606-13883-8*) Turtleback Bks.

**LONDON, ED (FICTITIOUS CHARACTER)—FICTION**

Block, Lawrence. Coward's Kiss. 1996. 160p. mass mkt. 3.95 (*0-7867-0334-2*, Carroll & Graf Pubs.) Avalon Publishing Group.

—Coward's Kiss. 1987. 160p. reprint ed. pap. 4.95 o.p. (*0-88150-085-2*) Countryman Pr.

—Coward's Kiss. 1999. (Mystery Ser.). 184p. pap. 19.95 (*0-7862-2075-9*, Five Star) Gale Group.

—Coward's Kiss. 2003. 224p. mass mkt. 4.99 (*0-7434-5899-0*) ibooks, Inc.

**LONDON, TEDDY (FICTITIOUS CHARACTER)—FICTION**

Morgan, Robert. All Things under the Moon. 1994. 224p. (Orig.). mass mkt. 4.99 o.p. (*0-425-14302-3*, Prime Crime) Berkley Publishing Group.

—The Only Thing to Fear. 1994. 256p. mass mkt. 4.99 o.s.i (*0-425-14468-2*, Prime Crime) Berkley Publishing Group.

—Some Things Come Back. 1995. 256p. (Orig.). mass mkt. 4.99 o.s.i (*0-425-14690-1*, Prime Crime) Berkley Publishing Group.

—Some Things Never Die. 1993. 208p. (Orig.). 3.99 o.p. (*1-55773-887-4*, Diamond Bks.) Ace Bks.

—Thing That Darkness Hides. 1993. 4.50 o.p. (*1-55773-960-9*, Diamond Bks.) Ace Bks.

—Things That Are Not There. 1992. 208p. (Orig.). 3.99 o.p. (*1-55773-827-0*, Diamond Bks.) Ace Bks.

**LONG, LAZARUS (FICTITIOUS CHARACTER)—FICTION**

Heinlein, Robert A. The Cat Who Walks Through Walls. 1988. 400p. mass mkt. 7.99 (*0-441-09499-6*) Ace Bks.

—The Cat Who Walks Through Walls. 1986. 400p. 3.95 o.s.i (*0-425-09332-8*) Berkley Publishing Group.

—The Cat Who Walks Through Walls. 1985. 384p. 17.95 o.s.i (*0-399-13103-5*); 75.00 o.p. (*0-399-13116-7*) Putnam Publishing Group, The.

—The Cat Who Walks Through Walls. unabr. ed. 1999. audio 91.00 (*0-7887-2940-3*, 95721E7) Recorded Bks., LLC.

—Methuselah's Children. 21.95 (*0-88411-883-5*) Amereon, Ltd.

—Methuselah's Children. 1986. 288p. pap. 3.50 o.s.i (*0-671-65597-3*) Baen Bks.
—Methuselah's Children. 1980. mass mkt. 1.75 o.p. (*0-451-09083-7*, ROC); 1970. mass mkt. 0.35 o.p. (*0-451-01752-8*, Signet Bks.); 1970. mass mkt. 0.50 o.p. (*0-451-02621-7*, Signet Bks.); 1970. mass mkt. 0.50 o.p. (*0-451-02191-6*, Signet Bks.); 1970. mass mkt. 0.75 o.p. (*0-451-04226-3*, ROC); 1960. mass mkt. 2.50 o.p. (*0-451-13089-8*, AE3089, Signet Bks.); 1960. mass mkt. 2.25 o.p. (*0-451-09875-7*, ROC); 1960. mass mkt. 1.50 o.p. (*0-451-07591-9*, ROC); 1960. mass mkt. 1.25 o.p. (*0-451-06382-1*, ROC) NAL.
—The Notebooks of Lazarus Long. 1985. pap. 10.95 o.p. (*0-399-51184-9*) Berkley Publishing Group.
—The Notebooks of Lazarus Long. 1995. (Illus.). 64p. reprint ed. pap. 15.95 o.p. (*0-87654-473-1*, A801) Pomegranate Communications, Inc.
—The Notebooks of Lazarus Long. 1978. (Illus.). 7.95 o.p. (*0-399-12242-7*) Putnam Publishing Group, The.
—Revolt in 2100. 1986. 352p. reprint ed. mass mkt. 4.99 o.s.i (*0-671-65589-2*) Baen Bks.
—Revolt in 2100. 1979. mass mkt. 1.75 o.p. (*0-451-08674-0*); 1969. mass mkt. 0.25 o.p. (*0-451-01194-5*); 1969. mass mkt. 0.50 o.p. (*0-451-02638-1*); 1969. mass mkt. 0.60 o.p. (*0-451-03563-1*); 1969. mass mkt. 0.35 o.p. (*0-451-01699-8*); 1969. mass mkt. 0.75 o.p. (*0-451-04236-0*); 1955. mass mkt. 1.95 o.p. (*0-451-09139-6*); 1955. mass mkt. 1.50 o.p. (*0-451-07234-0*); 1955. mass mkt. 0.95 o.p. (*0-451-05340-0*); 1955. mass mkt. 1.25 o.p. (*0-451-06232-9*) NAL. (ROC).
—Revolt in 2100 & Methuselah's Children. 1998. 496p. pap. 6.99 (*0-671-57780-8*) Baen Bks.
—Time Enough for Love. 1987. 608p. mass mkt. 7.99 (*0-441-81076-4*) Ace Bks.
—Time Enough for Love. 1986. 608p. 4.50 o.s.i (*0-425-10224-6*); 1984. 3.95 o.s.i (*0-425-07990-2*); 1983. 3.95 o.s.i (*0-425-07050-6*); 1982. 3.75 o.s.i (*0-425-06126-4*); 1981. 3.25 o.s.i (*0-425-05490-X*); 1980. 2.75 o.s.i (*0-425-04684-2*); 1978. 2.50 o.s.i (*0-425-04373-8*); 1976. 2.25 o.s.i (*0-425-03471-2*); 1974. 1.95 o.p. (*0-425-02493-8*) Berkley Publishing Group.
—Time Enough for Love. 1973. 7.95 o.p. (*0-399-11151-4*) Putnam Publishing Group, The.
—To Sail Beyond the Sunset. 1988. 448p. mass mkt. 7.99 (*0-441-74860-0*) Ace Bks.
—To Sail Beyond the Sunset. 1987. 448p. 18.95 o.p. (*0-399-13267-8*) Putnam Publishing Group, The.

**LONG, MAYLAND (FICTITIOUS CHARACTER)—FICTION**

MacAvoy, R. A. Tea with the Black Dragon. 1983. mass mkt. 2.95 o.s.i (*0-553-25403-0*); 192p. mass mkt. 3.95 o.s.i (*0-553-27992-0*) Bantam Bks.
—Tea with the Black Dragon. E-Book 6.99 (*1-58586-195-2*) ereads.com.
—Twisting the Rope. 1986. 256p. mass mkt. 3.50 o.s.i (*0-553-26026-X*, Spectra) Bantam Bks.
—Twisting the Rope. 2002. 179p. pap. 6.99 (*1-58586-059-X*); 2000. E-Book 6.99 (*1-58586-057-3*); 2000. E-Book 6.99 (*1-58586-310-6*); 2000. E-Book 6.99 (*1-58586-058-1*) ereads.com.

**LONGARM (FICTITIOUS CHARACTER)—FICTION**

Evans, Tabor. The Arizona Flame, No. 294. 2003. (Longarm Ser.). 192p. (Orig.). mass mkt. 4.99 (*0-515-13532-1*, Jove) Berkley Publishing Group.
—Bank, No. 301. 2003. (Longarm Ser.). 192p. mass mkt. 4.99 (*0-515-13641-7*, Jove) Berkley Publishing Group.
—The Contrary Cowgirls. 2002. (Longarm Giant Ser.). 304p. mass mkt. 5.99 (*0-515-13383-3*, Jove) Berkley Publishing Group.
—Desert Rose, Vol. 290. 2002. (Longarm Ser.). 192p. mass mkt. 4.99 (*0-515-13442-2*, Jove) Berkley Publishing Group.
—Druid Sisters, No. 286. 2002. (Carrier Ser.: Vol. 286). 192p. (Orig.). mass mkt. 4.99 (*0-515-13368-X*, Jove) Berkley Publishing Group.
—Longarm. 2004. 192p. mass mkt. 4.99 (*0-515-13685-9*, J#303); 1986. mass mkt. 4.50 o.s.i (*0-515-08965-6*); 1983. mass mkt. 2.50 o.s.i (*0-515-07524-8*); 1982. mass mkt. 2.25 o.s.i (*0-515-06576-5*); 1981. mass mkt. 1.95 o.s.i (*0-515-06154-9*); 1981. mass mkt. 1.95 o.s.i (*0-515-05983-8*); 1979. mass mkt. 1.75 o.s.i (*0-515-05360-0*); 1978. mass mkt. 1.50 o.s.i (*0-515-04750-3*); No. 295. 2003. 192p. mass mkt. 4.99 (*0-515-13549-6*); No. 300. 2003. 192p. mass mkt. 4.99 (*0-515-13633-6*); Vol. 287. 2002. 192p. mass mkt. 4.99 (*0-515-13390-6*) Berkley Publishing Group. (Jove).
—Longarm, Vol. 288. 2002. 192p. mass mkt. 4.99 o.s.i (*0-515-13406-6*) Penguin Group (USA) Inc.
—Longarm & Big Trouble in Bodie. 1995. (Longarm Ser.: No. 201). 192p. mass mkt. 4.50 o.s.i (*0-515-11702-1*, Jove) Berkley Publishing Group.
—Longarm & Santa Anna's Gold. 1984. (Longarm Ser.: No. 60). 192p. mass mkt. 2.50 o.s.i (*0-515-08259-7*, Jove) Berkley Publishing Group.
—Longarm & the Apache Plunder. 1994. (Longarm Ser.: No. 189). 192p. (Orig.). mass mkt. 3.99 o.s.i (*0-515-11454-5*, Jove) Berkley Publishing Group.
—Longarm & the Avenging Angels. 1987. (Longarm Ser.: No. 3). mass mkt. 2.75 o.s.i (*0-515-08967-2*, 04791-0, Jove) Berkley Publishing Group.
—Longarm & the Backwoods Baroness. 1997. (Longarm Ser.: No. 222). 192p. mass mkt. 4.99 o.s.i (*0-515-12080-4*, Jove) Berkley Publishing Group.
—Longarm & the Bad Girls of Rio Blanco. 2003. (Longarm Ser.: No. 296). 192p. mass mkt. 4.99 (*0-515-13577-1*, Jove) Berkley Publishing Group.
—Longarm & the Bandit Queen. 1980. (Longarm Ser.: No. 17). 256p. mass mkt. 1.75 o.s.i (*0-515-05309-0*, Jove) Berkley Publishing Group.
—Longarm & the Barbed Wire Bullies, No. 190. 1994. (Longarm Ser.). 192p. (Orig.). mass mkt. 3.99 o.s.i (*0-515-11476-6*, Jove) Berkley Publishing Group.
—Longarm & the Big Outfit. 1984. (Longarm Ser.: No. 13). 192p. mass mkt. 2.50 o.s.i (*0-515-07886-7*, Jove) Berkley Publishing Group.
—Longarm & the Big Posse, No. 105. 1987. (Longarm Ser.). mass mkt. 2.75 o.s.i (*0-515-09169-3*, Jove) Berkley Publishing Group.
—Longarm & the Big Shoot-Out, No. 85. 1986. (Longarm Ser.). 192p. mass mkt. 2.50 o.s.i (*0-515-08445-X*, Jove) Berkley Publishing Group.
—Longarm & the Bitterroots. 1985. (Longarm Ser.: No. 82). mass mkt. 2.50 o.s.i (*0-515-08367-4*, Jove) Berkley Publishing Group.
—Longarm & the Black Widow, Vol. 259. 2000. (Longarm Ser.: Vol. 259). 192p. mass mkt. 4.99 o.s.i (*0-515-12839-2*, Jove) Berkley Publishing Group.
—Longarm & the Blackfoot Guns. (Longarm Ser.). 1985. mass mkt. 2.50 o.s.i (*0-515-08190-6*); No. 77. 1987. mass mkt. 2.75 o.s.i (*0-515-09282-7*) Berkley Publishing Group. (Jove).
—Longarm & the Blindman's Vengeance. 1984. (Longarm Ser.: No. 72). 192p. mass mkt. 2.50 o.s.i (*0-515-06273-1*, Jove) Berkley Publishing Group.
—Longarm & the Blood Harvest, No. 108. 1987. (Longarm Ser.). mass mkt. 2.75 o.s.i (*0-515-09325-4*, Jove) Berkley Publishing Group.
—Longarm & the Bloody Trackdown, No. 109. 1988. (Longarm Ser.). 192p. mass mkt. 2.75 o.s.i (*0-515-09378-5*, Jove) Berkley Publishing Group.
—Longarm & the Blossom Rock Banshee. 1998. (Longarm Ser.: Vol. 238). 192p. mass mkt. 4.99 o.s.i (*0-515-12372-2*, Jove) Berkley Publishing Group.
—Longarm & the Blue-Eyed Squaw. 2000. (Longarm Ser.: Vol. 19). 304p. mass mkt. 5.99 o.s.i (*0-515-12705-1*, Jove) Berkley Publishing Group.
—Longarm & the Blue Norther. (Longarm Ser.). 1983. mass mkt. 2.50 o.s.i (*0-515-07727-5*); 1981. mass mkt. 1.95 o.s.i (*0-515-05592-1*) Berkley Publishing Group. (Jove).
—Longarm & the Boardinghouse Widow. 1997. (Longarm Ser.: No. 218). 192p. mass mkt. 4.99 o.s.i (*0-515-12016-2*, Jove) Berkley Publishing Group.
—Longarm & the Bone Skinners. 1986. (Longarm Ser.: No. 96). 192p. mass mkt. 2.75 o.s.i (*0-515-08796-3*, Jove) Berkley Publishing Group.
—Longarm & the Boot Hillers. (Longarm Ser.). (Orig.). 1984. mass mkt. 2.50 o.s.i (*0-515-08059-4*); 1982. 208p. mass mkt. 2.25 o.s.i (*0-515-06584-6*) Berkley Publishing Group. (Jove).
—Longarm & the Border Showdown. 1993. (Longarm Ser.: No. 174). 192p. (Orig.). mass mkt. 3.99 o.s.i (*0-515-11119-8*, Jove) Berkley Publishing Group.
—Longarm & the Border Wildcat. 1998. (Longarm Ser.: Vol. 229). 192p. mass mkt. 4.99 o.s.i (*0-515-12209-2*, Jove) Berkley Publishing Group.
—Longarm & the Bounty Hunters. (Longarm Ser.: No. 187). 192p. 1994. mass mkt. 3.99 o.s.i (*0-515-11407-3*); No. 57. 1983. mass mkt. 2.50 o.s.i (*0-515-07859-X*) Berkley Publishing Group. (Jove).
—Longarm & the Bounty Huntress, No. 148. 1991. (Longarm Ser.). mass mkt. 2.95 o.s.i (*0-515-10547-3*, Jove) Berkley Publishing Group.
—Longarm & the Bounty of Blood, No. 181. 1994. (Longarm Ser.). 192p. (Orig.). mass mkt. 3.99 o.s.i (*0-515-11283-6*, Jove) Berkley Publishing Group.
—Longarm & the Branded Beauty. 1998. (Longarm Ser.: Vol. 233). 192p. mass mkt. 4.99 o.s.i (*0-515-12278-5*, Jove) Berkley Publishing Group.
—Longarm & the Buckskin Rogue. (Longarm Ser.). 1983. mass mkt. 2.50 o.s.i (*0-515-07619-8*); No. 53. 1984. 192p. mass mkt. 2.50 o.s.i (*0-515-08101-9*) Berkley Publishing Group. (Jove).
—Longarm & the Calgary Kid. 1998. (Longarm Ser.: Vol. 17). 272p. mass mkt. 5.50 o.s.i (*0-515-12276-9*, Jove) Berkley Publishing Group.
—Longarm & the Calico Kid, No. 54. 1984. 192p. mass mkt. 2.50 o.s.i (*0-515-07723-2*, Jove) Berkley Publishing Group.
—Longarm & the Captive Women. 1993. (Longarm Ser.: No. 176). 192p. (Orig.). mass mkt. 3.99 o.s.i (*0-515-11166-X*, Jove) Berkley Publishing Group.
—Longarm & the Carnival Killer. 1993. (Longarm Ser.: No. 175). 192p. (Orig.). mass mkt. 3.99 o.s.i (*0-515-11136-8*, Jove) Berkley Publishing Group.
—Longarm & the Cattle Baron, No. 64. 1984. (Longarm Ser.). 192p. mass mkt. 2.50 o.s.i (*0-515-06265-0*, Jove) Berkley Publishing Group.
—Longarm & the Chain Gang Women. 1999. (Longarm Ser.: Vol. 250). 192p. mass mkt. 4.99 o.s.i (*0-515-12614-4*, Jove) Berkley Publishing Group.
—Longarm & the Church Ladies. 2000. (Longarm Ser.: Vol. 260). 192p. mass mkt. 4.99 o.s.i (*0-515-12872-4*, Jove) Berkley Publishing Group.
—Longarm & the Colorado Counterfeiter. 1999. (Longarm Ser.: Vol. 241). 192p. mass mkt. 4.99 o.s.i (*0-515-12437-0*, Jove) Berkley Publishing Group.
—Longarm & the Colorado Counterfeiter. abr. ed. 2000. (Longarm Ser.). 3p. audio 9.99 (*0-88646-591-5*) Durkin Hayes Publishing Ltd.
—Longarm & the Comancheros. 1984. (Longarm Ser.). mass mkt. 2.50 o.s.i (*0-515-08064-0*, Jove) Berkley Publishing Group.
—Longarm & the Cottonwood Curse. 1987. (Longarm Ser.: No. 101). 192p. mass mkt. 2.75 o.s.i (*0-515-08959-1*, Jove) Berkley Publishing Group.
—Longarm & the Counterfeit Corpse. 1996. (Longarm Ser.: No. 212). 192p. mass mkt. 4.99 o.s.i (*0-515-11925-3*, Jove) Berkley Publishing Group.
—Longarm & the Cowboy Revenge. 1987. (Longarm Ser.: No. 79). 192p. mass mkt. 2.75 o.s.i (*0-515-09284-3*, Jove) Berkley Publishing Group.
—Longarm & the Crooked Railman. 1986. (Longarm Ser.: No. 92). 192p. mass mkt. 2.50 o.s.i (*0-515-08648-7*, Jove) Berkley Publishing Group.
—Longarm & the Cursed Corpse. 1999. (Longarm Ser.: Vol. 246). 192p. mass mkt. 4.99 o.s.i (*0-515-12519-9*, Jove) Berkley Publishing Group.
—Longarm & the Custer County War, No. 61. 1985. (Longarm Ser.). 192p. mass mkt. 2.50 o.s.i (*0-515-08388-7*, Jove) Berkley Publishing Group.
—Longarm & the Danish Dames. 1999. (Longarm Ser.). 304p. mass mkt. 5.50 o.s.i (*0-515-12435-4*, Jove) Berkley Publishing Group.
—Longarm & the Dead Man's Play. 1997. (Longarm Ser.: Vol. 225). 192p. mass mkt. 4.99 o.s.i (*0-515-12144-4*, Jove) Berkley Publishing Group.
—Longarm & the Dead Man's Reward. 1997. (Longarm Ser.: No. 221). 192p. mass mkt. 4.99 o.s.i (*0-515-12069-3*, Jove) Berkley Publishing Group.
—Longarm & the Dead Ringers, No. 180. 1993. (Longarm Ser.). 192p. (Orig.). mass mkt. 3.99 o.s.i (*0-515-11255-0*, Jove) Berkley Publishing Group.
—Longarm & the Deadly Dead Man, No. 22. 2003. (Longarm Giant Ser.). 288p. (Orig.). mass mkt. 5.99 (*0-515-13547-X*, Jove) Berkley Publishing Group.
—Longarm & the Deadly Prisoner. 1996. (Longarm Ser.: No. 210). 192p. mass mkt. 4.99 o.s.i (*0-515-11879-6*, Jove) Berkley Publishing Group.
—Longarm & the Deadly Thaw. 1995. (Longarm Ser.: No. 198). 192p. (Orig.). mass mkt. 3.99 o.s.i (*0-515-11634-3*, Jove) Berkley Publishing Group.
—Longarm & the Denver Bustout, No. 149. 1991. (Longarm Ser.). mass mkt. 2.95 o.s.i (*0-515-10570-8*, Jove) Berkley Publishing Group.
—Longarm & the Denver Executioners. 2001. (Longarm Ser.: No. 276). 192p. mass mkt. 4.99 o.s.i (*0-515-13171-7*, Jove) Berkley Publishing Group.
—Longarm & the Desert Duchess. 1984. (Longarm Ser.: No. 68). 192p. mass mkt. 2.50 o.s.i (*0-515-08369-0*, Jove) Berkley Publishing Group.
—Longarm & the Desert Spirits. 1987. (Longarm Ser.: No. 99). mass mkt. 2.75 o.s.i (*0-515-08907-9*, Jove) Berkley Publishing Group.
—Longarm & the Desperate Manhunt. 1987. (Longarm Ser.: No. 102). 192p. (Orig.). mass mkt. 2.75 o.s.i (*0-515-09007-7*, Jove) Berkley Publishing Group.
—Longarm & the Devil's Railroad. 1983. (Longarm Ser.: No. 39). mass mkt. 2.50 o.s.i (*0-515-07412-8*, Jove) Berkley Publishing Group.
—Longarm & the Devil's Sister. 1999. (Longarm Ser.: Vol. 244). 192p. mass mkt. 4.99 o.s.i (*0-515-12485-0*, Jove) Berkley Publishing Group.
—Longarm & the Diamond Snatchers. 1993. (Longarm Ser.: No. 173). 192p. (Orig.). mass mkt. 3.99 o.s.i (*0-515-11103-1*, Jove) Berkley Publishing Group.
—Longarm & the Diary of Madame Velvet. 1999. (Longarm Ser.: Vol. 251). 192p. mass mkt. 4.99 o.s.i (*0-515-12660-8*, Jove) Berkley Publishing Group.
—Longarm & the Doomed Witness, No. 126. 1989. (Longarm Ser.). mass mkt. 2.95 o.s.i (*0-515-10035-8*, Jove) Berkley Publishing Group.
—Longarm & the Double-Barrel Blowout. 1997. (Longarm Ser.: Vol. 223). 192p. mass mkt. 4.99 o.s.i (*0-515-12104-5*, Jove) Berkley Publishing Group.
—Longarm & the Double Eagles. 1992. (Longarm Ser.: No. 166). 192p. (Orig.). mass mkt. 3.99 o.s.i (*0-515-10955-X*, Jove) Berkley Publishing Group.
—Longarm & the Dragon Hunters. (Longarm Ser.: No. 26). 1982. 255p. mass mkt. 2.25 o.s.i (*0-515-06952-3*); 1981. mass mkt. 1.95 o.s.i (*0-515-06103-4*) Berkley Publishing Group. (Jove).
—Longarm & the Durango Double-Cross. 1998. (Longarm Ser.: Vol. 231). 192p. mass mkt. 4.99 o.s.i (*0-515-12244-0*, Jove) Berkley Publishing Group.
—Longarm & the Durango Payroll. 1985. (Longarm Ser.: No. 74). 192p. mass mkt. 2.50 o.s.i (*0-515-08109-4*, Jove) Berkley Publishing Group.
—Longarm & the Dynamite Damsel, Vol. 256. 2000. (Longarm Ser.: No. 256). 184p. mass mkt. 4.99 o.s.i (*0-515-12770-1*, Jove) Berkley Publishing Group.
—Longarm & the Eastern Dudes. 1983. (Longarm Ser.). mass mkt. 2.50 o.s.i (*0-515-07522-1*);No. 49. 192p. mass mkt. 2.50 o.s.i (*0-515-07425-X*) Berkley Publishing Group. (Jove).
—Longarm & the Escape Artist. 1986. (Longarm Ser.: No. 95). 192p. mass mkt. 2.75 o.s.i (*0-515-08754-8*, Jove) Berkley Publishing Group.
—Longarm & the Fool Killer. 1992. (Longarm Ser.: No. 167). 192p. (Orig.). mass mkt. 3.99 o.s.i (*0-515-10980-0*, Jove) Berkley Publishing Group.
—Longarm & the Four Corners Gang. 1999. (Longarm Ser.: Vol. 252). 192p. mass mkt. 4.99 o.s.i (*0-515-12687-X*, Jove) Berkley Publishing Group.
—Longarm & the French Actress. 1983. (Longarm Ser.). mass mkt. 2.50 o.s.i (*0-515-07545-0*); 192p. mass mkt. 2.50 o.s.i (*0-515-07861-1*) Berkley Publishing Group. (Jove).
—Longarm & the Frontier Duchess. 1987. (Longarm Ser.: No. 81). 192p. mass mkt. 2.75 o.s.i (*0-515-09287-8*, Jove) Berkley Publishing Group.
—LongArm & the Gallagher Gang. 1994. (Longarm Ser.: No. 188). 192p. (Orig.). mass mkt. 3.99 o.s.i (*0-515-11435-9*, Jove) Berkley Publishing Group.
—Longarm & the Ghost Dancers. 1982. (Longarm Ser.). mass mkt. 2.25 o.s.i (*0-515-07141-2*, Jove) Berkley Publishing Group.
—Longarm & the Golden Lady. 1982. (Longarm Ser.: No. 32). mass mkt. 2.25 o.s.i (*0-515-06582-X*, Jove) Berkley Publishing Group.
—Longarm & the Grand Slam Heist. 1996. (Longarm Ser.: No. 209). 192p. mass mkt. 4.99 o.s.i (*0-515-11861-3*, Jove) Berkley Publishing Group.
—Longarm & the Grave Robbers. 1993. 17.50 o.p. (*0-7451-4561-2*, Gunsmoke) BBC Audiobooks America.
—Longarm & the Grave Robbers. 1998. (Longarm Ser.: Vol. 239). 192p. mass mkt. 4.99 o.s.i (*0-515-12392-7*, Jove) Berkley Publishing Group.
—Longarm & the Grave Robbers. abr. ed. 2000. (Longarm Ser.). 3p. audio 9.99 (*0-88646-583-4*) Durkin Hayes Publishing Ltd.
—Longarm & the Great Cattle Kill. 1986. (Longarm Ser.: No. 91). 192p. mass mkt. 2.50 o.s.i (*0-515-08607-X*, Jove) Berkley Publishing Group.
—Longarm & the Great Train Robbery, No. 46. 1982. (Longarm Ser.). 192p. mass mkt. 2.25 o.s.i (*0-515-05602-2*, Jove) Berkley Publishing Group.
—Longarm & the Hangman's Daughter, Vol. 20. 2001. (Longarm Ser.: Vol. 20). 320p. mass mkt. 5.99 o.s.i (*0-515-12999-2*, Jove) Berkley Publishing Group.
—Longarm & the Hangman's Noose, No. 66. 1984. (Longarm Ser.). 192p. mass mkt. 2.50 o.s.i (*0-515-06267-7*, Jove) Berkley Publishing Group.
—Longarm & the Hangman's Vengeance. 1988. (Longarm Ser.: No. 110). mass mkt. 2.75 o.s.i (*0-515-09445-5*, Jove) Berkley Publishing Group.
—Longarm & the Hatchet Men. 1980. (Longarm Ser.: No. 9). mass mkt. 1.95 o.s.i (*0-515-05973-0*, Jove) Berkley Publishing Group.
—Longarm & the Hatchet Woman. 1998. (Longarm Ser.: Vol. 237). 192p. mass mkt. 4.99 o.s.i (*0-515-12356-0*, Jove) Berkley Publishing Group.
—Longarm & the Hatchet Woman. abr. ed. 2000. (Longarm Ser.). 3p. audio 9.99 (*0-88646-575-3*) Durkin Hayes Publishing Ltd.
—Longarm & the Haunted Whorehouse. 2002. (Longarm Ser.: No. 284). 192p. mass mkt. 4.99 (*0-515-13337-X*, Jove) Berkley Publishing Group.
—Longarm & the Helldorado. 1995. (Longarm Ser.: No. 196). 192p. (Orig.). mass mkt. 3.99 o.s.i (*0-515-11591-6*, Jove) Berkley Publishing Group.
—Longarm & the High Rollers. 1994. (Longarm Ser.: No. 186). 192p. (Orig.). mass mkt. 3.99 o.s.i (*0-515-11391-3*, Jove) Berkley Publishing Group.
—Longarm & the Highgraders. 1987. (Longarm Ser.: No. 7). (Orig.). mass mkt. 2.75 o.s.i (*0-515-08971-0*, Jove) Berkley Publishing Group.
—Longarm & the Hostage Woman. 1996. (Longarm Ser.: No. 215). 192p. mass mkt. 4.99 o.s.i (*0-515-11968-7*, Jove) Berkley Publishing Group.
—Longarm & the Indian War. 1997. (Longarm Ser.: No. 220). 192p. mass mkt. 4.99 o.s.i (*0-515-12050-2*, Jove) Berkley Publishing Group.
—Longarm & the Island Passage, No. 89. 1986. (Longarm Ser.). 192p. mass mkt. 2.50 o.s.i (*0-515-08569-3*, Jove) Berkley Publishing Group.

—Longarm & the James County War, No. 63. 1984. (Longarm Ser.). 192p. mass mkt. 2.50 o.s.i (*0-515-06264-2*, Jove) Berkley Publishing Group.

—Longarm & the Jerkwater Bustout. 1995. (Longarm Ser.: No. 194). 192p. (Orig.). mass mkt. 3.99 o.s.i (*0-515-11551-7*, Jove) Berkley Publishing Group.

—Longarm & the John Bull Feud, Vol. 199. 1995. (Longarm Ser.). 192p. (Orig.). mass mkt. 4.50 o.s.i (*0-515-11655-6*, Jove) Berkley Publishing Group.

—Longarm & the Kansas Jailbird. 1999. (Longarm Ser.: 243). 192p. mass mkt. 4.99 o.s.i (*0-515-12468-0*, Jove) Berkley Publishing Group.

—Longarm & the Kansas Killer, No. 200. 1995. (Longarm Ser.). 192p. (Orig.). mass mkt. 4.50 o.s.i (*0-515-11681-5*, Jove) Berkley Publishing Group.

—Longarm & the Killer's Shadow No. 145. 1991. (Longarm Ser.). mass mkt. 2.95 o.s.i (*0-515-10494-9*, Jove) Berkley Publishing Group.

—Longarm & the Kissin' Cousins. 2003. (Longarm Ser.: No. 298). 192p. mass mkt. 4.99 (*0-515-13599-2*, Jove) Berkley Publishing Group.

—Longarm & the Lady Bandit. 2001. (Longarm Ser.: Vol. 270). 192p. mass mkt. 4.99 o.s.i (*0-515-13057-5*, Jove) Berkley Publishing Group.

—Longarm & the Lady Faire. 1997. (Longarm Ser.: Vol. 226). 192p. mass mkt. 4.99 o.s.i (*0-515-12162-2*, Jove) Berkley Publishing Group.

—Longarm & the Lady from Tombstone. 1999. (Longarm Ser.: Vol. 247). 192p. mass mkt. 4.99 o.s.i (*0-515-12533-4*, Jove) Berkley Publishing Group.

—Longarm & the Lady Hustlers. 2003. (Longarm Ser.: No. 292). 192p. mass mkt. 4.99 (*0-515-13493-7*, Jove) Berkley Publishing Group.

—Longarm & the Laredo Loop. 1984. (Longarm Ser.: No. 33). 224p. mass mkt. 2.50 o.s.i (*0-515-08062-4*, Jove) Berkley Publishing Group.

—Longarm & the Last Man. 1994. (Longarm Ser.: No. 184). 192p. (Orig.). mass mkt. 3.99 o.s.i (*0-515-11356-5*, Jove) Berkley Publishing Group.

—Longarm & the Loggers. 1987. (Longarm Ser.: No. 6). (Orig.). mass mkt. 2.75 o.s.i (*0-515-08970-2*, Jove) Berkley Publishing Group.

—Longarm & the Lone Star Bounty. (Longarm Ser.). 1986. 320p. mass mkt. 3.50 o.s.i (*0-515-08517-0*); 1984. mass mkt. 2.95 o.s.i (*0-515-08168-X*); 1984. mass mkt. 3.50 o.s.i (*0-515-07706-2*); 1984. mass mkt. 2.95 o.s.i (*0-515-07611-2*) Berkley Publishing Group. (Jove).

—Longarm & the Lone Star Captive. 1991. (Longarm Ser.). mass mkt. 4.50 o.s.i (*0-515-10646-1*, Jove) Berkley Publishing Group.

—Longarm & the Lone Star Frame. 1988. (Longarm Ser.). mass mkt. 3.50 o.s.i (*0-515-09752-7*, Jove) Berkley Publishing Group.

—Longarm & the Lone Star Legend. 1986. (Longarm Ser.). mass mkt. 3.50 o.s.i (*0-515-08768-8*, Jove) Berkley Publishing Group.

—Longarm & the Lone Star Mission. 1987. (Longarm Ser.). 288p. (Orig.). mass mkt. 3.50 o.s.i (*0-515-08880-3*, Jove) Berkley Publishing Group.

—Longarm & the Lone Star Rescue. 1987. (Longarm Ser.). 288p. mass mkt. 3.50 o.s.i (*0-515-09294-0*, Jove) Berkley Publishing Group.

—Longarm & the Lone Star Rustlers. (Longarm Ser.). 1990. mass mkt. 3.95 o.s.i (*0-515-10381-0*); 1987. mass mkt. 3.50 o.s.i (*0-515-09295-9*) Berkley Publishing Group. (Jove).

—Longarm & the Lone Star Showdown. (Longarm Ser.). 1987. 304p. mass mkt. 3.50 o.s.i (*0-515-09292-4*); 1986. mass mkt. 3.50 o.s.i (*0-515-08644-4*) Berkley Publishing Group. (Jove).

—Longarm & the Lone Star Vengeance. (Longarm Ser.). 1986. 320p. mass mkt. 3.50 o.s.i (*0-515-08518-9*); 1983. mass mkt. 2.95 o.s.i (*0-515-07085-8*) Berkley Publishing Group. (Jove).

—Longarm & the Lusty Lady. 1996. (Longarm Ser.: No. 16). 256p. mass mkt. 5.50 o.s.i (*0-515-11923-7*, Jove) Berkley Publishing Group.

—Longarm & the Maiden Medusa. 1997. (Longarm Ser.: Vol. 224). 192p. mass mkt. 4.99 o.s.i (*0-515-12132-0*, Jove) Berkley Publishing Group.

—Longarm & the Man-Eaters. 1994. (Longarm Ser.: No. 192). 192p. (Orig.). mass mkt. 3.99 o.s.i (*0-515-11505-3*, Jove) Berkley Publishing Group.

—Longarm & the Maximilian's Gold. 2003. (Longarm Ser.: No. 299). 192p. mass mkt. 4.99 (*0-515-13624-7*, Jove) Berkley Publishing Group.

—Longarm & the Mexican Line-Up. 1987. (Longarm Ser.: No. 97). 192p. mass mkt. 2.75 o.s.i (*0-515-08838-2*, Jove) Berkley Publishing Group.

—Longarm & the Minute Men. 1996. (Longarm Ser.: No. 213). 192p. mass mkt. 4.99 o.s.i (*0-515-11942-3*, Jove) Berkley Publishing Group.

—Longarm & the Molly Maguires. 1981. (Longarm Ser.: No. 10). 1.95 o.s.i (*0-515-06064-X*, Jove) Berkley Publishing Group.

—Longarm & the Montana Massacre, Vol. 146. 1991. (Longarm Ser.). mass mkt. 2.95 o.s.i (*0-515-10512-0*, Jove) Berkley Publishing Group.

—Longarm & the Moonshiners. (Longarm Ser.: No. 42). 1983. 192p. mass mkt. 2.50 o.s.i (*0-515-07538-8*); 1982. mass mkt. 2.25 o.s.i (*0-515-07127-7*) Berkley Publishing Group. (Jove).

—Longarm & the Mountain Bandit. 2001. (Longarm Ser.: Vol. 267). 192p. mass mkt. 4.99 o.s.i (*0-515-13018-4*, Jove) Berkley Publishing Group.

—Longarm & the Mounties. 1981. (Longarm Ser.: No. 16). 252p. 1.95 o.s.i (*0-515-06104-2*, Jove) Berkley Publishing Group.

—Longarm & the Mustang Gang, Vol. 255. 2000. (Longarm Ser.: Vol. 255). 192p. mass mkt. 4.99 o.s.i (*0-515-12755-8*, Jove) Berkley Publishing Group.

—Longarm & the Mysterious Mistress. 2002. (Longarm Ser.: No. 285). 192p. mass mkt. 4.99 (*0-515-13351-5*, Jove) Berkley Publishing Group.

—Longarm & the Navaho Drums. 1993. (Longarm Ser.: No. 13). 288p. (Orig.). mass mkt. 4.50 o.s.i (*0-515-11164-3*, Jove) Berkley Publishing Group.

—Longarm & the Nesters. 1987. (Longarm Ser.: No. 8). (Orig.). mass mkt. 2.75 o.s.i (*0-515-08972-9*, Jove) Berkley Publishing Group.

—Longarm & the Nevada Belly Dancer, Vol. 257. 2000. (Longarm Ser.: No. 257). 192p. mass mkt. 4.99 o.s.i (*0-515-12790-6*, Jove) Berkley Publishing Group.

—Longarm & the Nevada Nymphs. 1998. (Longarm Ser.: Vol. 240). 192p. mass mkt. 4.99 o.s.i (*0-515-12411-7*, Jove) Berkley Publishing Group.

—Longarm & the Nevada Swindle. 1993. (Longarm Ser.: No. 171). 192p. (Orig.). mass mkt. 3.99 o.s.i (*0-515-11061-2*, Jove) Berkley Publishing Group.

—Longarm & the New Mexico Shoot Out. 1988. (Longarm Ser.: No. 118). mass mkt. 2.95 o.s.i (*0-515-09758-6*, Jove) Berkley Publishing Group.

—Longarm & the Omaha Tinhorns, No. 67. 1984. (Longarm Ser.). 192p. mass mkt. 2.50 o.s.i (*0-515-08304-6*, Jove) Berkley Publishing Group.

—Longarm & the Outlaw Lawman. (Longarm Ser.). 1983. mass mkt. 2.50 o.s.i (*0-515-07528-0*); No. 56. 1984. 192p. mass mkt. 2.50 o.s.i (*0-515-08099-3*) Berkley Publishing Group. (Jove).

—Longarm & the Pistolero Princess, Vol. 258. 2000. (Longarm Ser.: Vol. 258). 192p. mass mkt. 4.99 o.s.i (*0-515-12808-2*, Jove) Berkley Publishing Group.

—Longarm & the Poisoners. 2003. (Longarm Ser.: No. 293). 192p. (Orig.). mass mkt. 4.99 (*0-515-13513-5*, Jove) Berkley Publishing Group.

—Longarm & the Quiet Guns, No. 114. 1988. (Longarm Ser.). mass mkt. 2.95 o.s.i (*0-515-09585-0*, Jove) Berkley Publishing Group.

—Longarm & the Racy Ladies. 1996. (Longarm Ser.: No. 214). 192p. mass mkt. 4.99 o.s.i (*0-515-11956-3*, Jove) Berkley Publishing Group.

—Longarm & the Railroaders. 1983. (Longarm Ser.: No. 24). 252p. mass mkt. 2.25 o.s.i (*0-515-07363-6*, Jove) Berkley Publishing Group.

—Longarm & the Rancher's Showdown, No. 88. 1986. (Longarm Ser.). 192p. mass mkt. 2.50 o.s.i (*0-515-08514-6*, Jove) Berkley Publishing Group.

—Longarm & the Rebel Brand. 1992. (Longarm Ser.: No. 165). 192p. (Orig.). mass mkt. 3.99 o.s.i (*0-515-10929-0*, Jove) Berkley Publishing Group.

—Longarm & the Rebel Executioner, No. 227. 1997. (Longarm Ser.). 192p. mass mkt. 4.99 o.s.i (*0-515-12178-9*, Jove) Berkley Publishing Group.

—Longarm & the Red-Light Ladies. 1999. (Longarm Ser.: Vol. 242). 192p. mass mkt. 4.99 o.s.i (*0-515-12450-8*, Jove) Berkley Publishing Group.

—Longarm & the Redhead's Ransom, Vol. 254. 2000. (Longarm Ser.: Vol. 54 ). 192p. mass mkt. 4.99 o.s.i (*0-515-12734-5*, Jove) Berkley Publishing Group.

—Longarm & the Renegade Assassins. 1998. (Longarm Ser.: Vol. 234). 192p. mass mkt. 4.99 o.s.i (*0-515-12292-0*, Jove) Berkley Publishing Group.

—Longarm & the Renegade Sergeant. 1988. (Longarm Ser.: No. 119). mass mkt. 2.95 o.s.i (*0-515-09807-8*, Jove) Berkley Publishing Group.

—Longarm & the River of Death, No. 152. 1991. (Longarm Ser.). mass mkt. 3.50 o.s.i (*0-515-10649-6*, Jove) Berkley Publishing Group.

—Longarm & the River Pirates. 1998. (Longarm Ser.: Vol. 236). 192p. mass mkt. 4.99 o.s.i (*0-515-12340-4*, Jove) Berkley Publishing Group.

—Longarm & the River Pirates. abr. ed. 2000. (Longarm Ser.). 3p. audio 9.99 (*0-88646-571-0*) Durkin Hayes Publishing Ltd.

—Longarm & the Rocky Mountain Chase, No. 103. 1987. (Longarm Ser.). mass mkt. 2.75 o.s.i (*0-515-09056-5*, Jove) Berkley Publishing Group.

—Longarm & the Runaway Thieves. 1986. (Longarm Ser.: No. 94). 192p. mass mkt. 2.75 o.s.i (*0-515-08715-7*, Jove) Berkley Publishing Group.

—Longarm & the Rurales. 1983. (Longarm Ser.: No. 27). mass mkt. 2.25 o.s.i (*0-515-07265-6*, Jove) Berkley Publishing Group.

—Longarm & the Saddle Rock Spook. 1995. (Longarm Ser.: Vol. 203). 192p. mass mkt. 4.50 o.s.i (*0-515-11746-3*, Jove) Berkley Publishing Group.

—Longarm & the San Angelo Showdown. 1995. (Longarm Ser.: No. 193). 192p. (Orig.). mass mkt. 3.99 o.s.i (*0-515-11528-2*, Jove) Berkley Publishing Group.

—Longarm & the San Joaquin War. 1992. (Longarm Ser.: No. 12). 288p. (Orig.). mass mkt. 3.99 o.s.i (*0-515-10897-9*, Jove) Berkley Publishing Group.

—Longarm & the Secret Assassin. 1996. (Longarm Ser.: No. 216). 192p. mass mkt. 4.99 o.s.i (*0-515-11982-2*, Jove) Berkley Publishing Group.

—Longarm & the Sheep War. 1999. (Longarm Ser.: Vol. 249). 192p. mass mkt. 4.99 o.s.i (*0-515-12572-5*, Jove) Berkley Publishing Group.

—Longarm & the Sheepherders. 1980. (Longarm Ser.: No. 21). 256p. mass mkt. 1.95 o.s.i (*0-515-05906-4*, Jove) Berkley Publishing Group.

—Longarm & the Shivaree Riders, No. 202. 1995. (Longarm Ser.). 192p. (Orig.). mass mkt. 4.50 o.s.i (*0-515-11730-7*, Jove) Berkley Publishing Group.

—Longarm & the Shoshoni River. 1992. (Longarm Ser.: No. 168). 192p. (Orig.). mass mkt. 3.99 o.s.i (*0-515-10997-5*, Jove) Berkley Publishing Group.

—Longarm & the Sidesaddle Assassin. 2001. (Longarm Ser.: No. 278). 192p. mass mkt. 4.99 o.s.i (*0-515-13232-2*, Jove) Berkley Publishing Group.

—Longarm & the Silver Mine Marauders. 1995. (Longarm Ser.: No. 197). (Orig.). mass mkt. 3.99 o.s.i (*0-515-11612-2*, Jove) Berkley Publishing Group.

—Longarm & the Skull Canyon Gang, No. 150. 1991. (Longarm Ser.). mass mkt. 2.95 o.p. (*0-515-10597-X*, Jove) Berkley Publishing Group.

—Longarm & the Snake Dancers. 1983. (Longarm Ser.: No. 51). 192p. mass mkt. 2.50 o.s.i (*0-515-07523-X*, Jove) Berkley Publishing Group.

—Longarm & the Stagecoach Bandits. 1985. (Longarm Ser.: No. 84). 192p. mass mkt. 2.75 o.s.i (*0-515-09289-4*, Jove) Berkley Publishing Group.

—Longarm & the Stalking Corpse. 1982. (Longarm Ser.: No. 37). mass mkt. 2.25 o.s.i (*0-515-06954-X*, Jove) Berkley Publishing Group.

—Longarm & the Steer Swindlers, No. 65. 1984. (Longarm Ser.). 192p. mass mkt. 2.50 o.s.i (*0-515-06266-9*, Jove) Berkley Publishing Group.

—Longarm & the Tenderfoot. 1987. (Longarm Ser.: No. 83). 192p. mass mkt. 2.75 o.s.i (*0-515-09288-6*, Jove) Berkley Publishing Group.

—Longarm & the Texas Hijackers. 1994. (Longarm Ser.: No. 191). 192p. mass mkt. 3.99 o.s.i (*0-515-11493-6*, Jove) Berkley Publishing Group.

—Longarm & the Texas Rangers. 1980. (Longarm Ser.: No. 11). mass mkt. 1.95 o.s.i (*0-515-05902-1*, Jove) Berkley Publishing Group.

—Longarm & the Town Tamer. 1983. (Longarm Ser.: No. 23). 269p. mass mkt. 2.25 o.s.i (*0-515-07142-0*, Jove) Berkley Publishing Group.

—Longarm & the Trail Drive Sham. 1987. (Longarm Ser.: No. 98). 192p. (Orig.). mass mkt. 2.75 o.s.i (*0-515-08883-8*, Jove) Berkley Publishing Group.

—Longarm & the Train Robbers. 1994. (Longarm Ser.: No. 182). 192p. (Orig.). mass mkt. 3.99 o.s.i (*0-515-11313-1*, Jove) Berkley Publishing Group.

—Longarm & the Treacherous Trial. 1988. (Longarm Ser.: No. 117). mass mkt. 2.95 o.s.i (*0-515-09707-1*, Jove) Berkley Publishing Group.

—Longarm & the Unwritten Law. 1995. (Longarm Ser.: No. 15). 288p. (Orig.). mass mkt. 4.99 o.s.i (*0-515-11680-7*, Jove) Berkley Publishing Group.

—Longarm & the Vanishing Virgin. 1999. (Longarm Ser.: Vol. 245). 192p. mass mkt. 4.99 o.s.i (*0-515-12511-3*, Jove) Berkley Publishing Group.

—Longarm & the Voodoo Queen, No. 228. 1997. (Longarm Ser.). 192p. mass mkt. 4.99 o.s.i (*0-515-12191-6*, Jove) Berkley Publishing Group.

—Longarm & the Wendigo. 1987. (Longarm Ser.: No. 4). 256p. (Orig.). mass mkt. 2.75 o.s.i (*0-515-08968-0*, Jove) Berkley Publishing Group.

—Longarm & the Whiskey Creek Widow. 1998. (Longarm Ser.: Vol. 232). 192p. mass mkt. 4.99 o.s.i (*0-515-12265-3*, Jove) Berkley Publishing Group.

—Longarm & the Whiskey Woman. 1997. (Longarm Ser.: No. 217). 192p. mass mkt. 4.99 o.s.i (*0-515-11998-9*, Jove) Berkley Publishing Group.

—Longarm & the Wicked Schoolmarm. 1998. (Longarm Ser.: Vol. 235). 192p. mass mkt. 4.99 o.s.i (*0-515-12302-1*, Jove) Berkley Publishing Group.

—Longarm & the Widow's Spite. 2001. (Longarm Ser.: No. 275). 192p. mass mkt. 4.99 o.s.i (*0-515-13184-9*, Jove) Berkley Publishing Group.

—Longarm & the Wronged Woman. 1999. (Longarm Ser.: No. 248). 192p. mass mkt. 4.99 o.s.i (*0-515-12556-3*, Jove) Berkley Publishing Group.

—Longarm & the Wyoming Wildwomen. 1998. (Longarm Ser.: Vol. 230). 192p. mass mkt. 4.99 o.s.i (*0-515-12230-0*, Jove) Berkley Publishing Group.

—Longarm & the Wyoming Wildwomen. abr. ed. 2000. (Longarm Ser.). audio 9.99 (*0-88646-550-8*, DHA-6550) Durkin Hayes Publishing Ltd.

—Longarm & the Yukon Queen. 2001. (Longarm Ser.: No. 277). 192p. mass mkt. 4.99 o.s.i (*0-515-13206-3*, Jove) Berkley Publishing Group.

—Longarm & the Yuma Prison Girls. (Longarm Ser.: No. 195). (Orig.). 1995. 192p. mass mkt. 3.99 o.s.i (*0-515-11569-X*); 1982. mass mkt. 2.25 o.s.i (*0-515-07091-2*) Berkley Publishing Group. (Jove).

—Longarm & Town-Taming Tess. 2003. (Longarm Ser.: No. 297). 192p. mass mkt. 4.99 (*0-515-13585-2*, Jove) Berkley Publishing Group.

—Longarm at Fort Reno, No. 73. 1985. (Longarm Ser.). 192p. mass mkt. 2.50 o.s.i (*0-515-06274-X*, Jove) Berkley Publishing Group.

—Longarm at Robber's Roost. 1980. (Longarm Ser.: No. 20). 256p. mass mkt. 1.95 o.s.i (*0-515-05931-5*, Jove) Berkley Publishing Group.

—Longarm in Boulder Canyon. 1983. (Longarm Ser.: No. 44). mass mkt. 2.50 o.s.i (*0-515-07431-4*, Jove) Berkley Publishing Group.

—Longarm in Deadwood. 1983. (Longarm Ser.: No. 45). mass mkt. 2.50 o.s.i (*0-515-07543-4*, Jove) Berkley Publishing Group.

—Longarm in Leadville. (Longarm Ser.: No. 14). 1981. mass mkt. 1.95 o.s.i (*0-515-06070-4*); 1979. mass mkt. 1.75 o.s.i (*0-515-05306-6*) Berkley Publishing Group. (Jove).

—Longarm in Lincoln County. 1982. (Longarm Ser.: No. 12). 254p. mass mkt. 2.25 o.s.i (*0-515-06950-7*, Jove) Berkley Publishing Group.

—Longarm in No Man's Land. 1984. (Longarm Ser.: No. 58). 192p. mass mkt. 2.50 o.s.i (*0-515-07858-1*, Jove) Berkley Publishing Group.

—Longarm in Northfield. 1982. (Longarm Ser.: No. 31). 208p. mass mkt. 2.25 o.s.i (*0-515-06580-3*, Jove) Berkley Publishing Group.

—Longarm in Silver City. 1983. (Longarm Ser.: No. 40). 192p. mass mkt. 2.50 o.s.i (*0-515-07413-6*, Jove) Berkley Publishing Group.

—Longarm in the Badlands. 1983. (Longarm Ser.: No. 47). 192p. mass mkt. 2.50 o.s.i (*0-515-07418-7*, Jove) Berkley Publishing Group.

—Longarm in the Big Bend. 1983. (Longarm Ser.: No. 50). 192p. mass mkt. 2.50 o.s.i (*0-515-07854-9*, Jove) Berkley Publishing Group.

—Longarm in the Big Burnout, No. 113. 1988. (Longarm Ser.). mass mkt. 2.75 o.s.i (*0-515-09548-6*, Jove) Berkley Publishing Group.

—Longarm in the Big Thicket. 1983. (Longarm Ser.: No. 48). 192p. (Orig.). 2.50 o.s.i (*0-515-07414-4*, Jove) Berkley Publishing Group.

—Longarm in the Bighorn Basin, No. 107. 1987. (Longarm Ser.). mass mkt. 2.75 o.s.i (*0-515-09256-8*, Jove) Berkley Publishing Group.

—Longarm in the Cross Fire. 1993. (Longarm Ser.: No. 177). 192p. (Orig.). mass mkt. 3.99 o.s.i (*0-515-11194-5*, Jove) Berkley Publishing Group.

—Longarm in the Four Corners. 1982. (Longarm Ser.: No. 19). 224p. mass mkt. 2.25 o.s.i (*0-515-06628-1*, Jove) Berkley Publishing Group.

—Longarm in the Hard Rock Country, No. 86. 1987. (Longarm Ser.). 192p. mass mkt. 2.75 o.s.i (*0-515-09290-8*, Jove) Berkley Publishing Group.

—Longarm in the Indian Nation. 1987. (Longarm Ser.: No. 5). 272p. (Orig.). mass mkt. 2.75 o.s.i (*0-515-08969-9*, Jove) Berkley Publishing Group.

—Longarm in the Ruby Range Country, No. 90. 1986. (Longarm Ser.). 192p. mass mkt. 2.50 o.s.i (*0-515-08580-4*, Jove) Berkley Publishing Group.

—Longarm in the Sand Hills. 1981. (Longarm Ser.: No. 13). 1.95 o.s.i (*0-515-06153-0*, Jove) Berkley Publishing Group.

—Longarm in the Texas Panhandle, No. 87. 1987. (Longarm Ser.). mass mkt. 2.75 o.s.i (*0-515-09291-6*, Jove) Berkley Publishing Group.

—Longarm in the Valley of Death. 1988. (Longarm Ser.: No. 115). mass mkt. 2.95 o.s.i (*0-515-09647-4*, Jove) Berkley Publishing Group.

—Longarm in the Valley of Sin. 1999. (Longarm Ser.: Vol. 253). 192p. mass mkt. 4.99 o.s.i (*0-515-12707-8*, Jove) Berkley Publishing Group.

—Longarm in Virginia City, No. 62. 1984. (Longarm Ser.). 192p. mass mkt. 2.50 o.s.i (*0-515-06263-4*, Jove) Berkley Publishing Group.

—Longarm in Yuma. 1983. (Longarm Ser.: No. 43). mass mkt. 2.50 o.s.i (*0-515-07525-6*, Jove) Berkley Publishing Group.

—Longarm of the Painted Desert, No. 69. 1984. (Longarm Ser.). 192p. mass mkt. 2.50 o.s.i (*0-515-08374-7*, Jove) Berkley Publishing Group.

—Longarm on Deadman's Trail, No. 106. 1987. (Longarm Ser.). 192p. mass mkt. 2.75 o.s.i (*0-515-09215-0*, Jove) Berkley Publishing Group.

—Longarm on the Arkansas. 1984. (Divide Ser.: No. 71). 192p. mass mkt. 2.50 o.s.i (*0-515-07915-4*, Jove) Berkley Publishing Group.

—Longarm on the Barbary Coast. 1982. (Longarm Ser.: No. 41). 192p. mass mkt. 2.25 o.s.i (*0-515-07070-X*, Jove) Berkley Publishing Group.

—Longarm on the Big Muddy. 1982. (Longarm Ser.: No. 29). 224p. mass mkt. 2.25 o.s.i (*0-515-07067-X*, Jove) Berkley Publishing Group.

—Longarm on the Border. 1987. (Longarm Ser.: No. 2). (Orig.). mass mkt. 2.75 o.s.i (*0-515-08966-4*, Jove) Berkley Publishing Group.
—Longarm on the Devil's Highway. 1992. (Longarm Ser.: No. 162). mass mkt. 3.50 o.s.i (*0-515-10865-0*, Jove) Berkley Publishing Group.
—Longarm on the Devil's Trail. 1980. (Longarm Ser.: No. 15). 224p. 1.95 o.s.i (*0-515-05904-8*, Jove) Berkley Publishing Group.
—Longarm on the Fever Coast. 1994. (Longarm Ser.: No. 183). 192p. (Orig.). mass mkt. 3.99 o.s.i (*0-515-11338-7*, Jove) Berkley Publishing Group.
—Longarm on the Great Divide, No. 52. 1983. (Longarm Ser.). 192p. mass mkt. 2.50 o.s.i (*0-515-07722-4*, Jove) Berkley Publishing Group.
—Longarm on the Humboldt. 1983. (Longarm Ser.: No. 28). 256p. mass mkt. 2.25 o.s.i (*0-515-06629-X*, Jove) Berkley Publishing Group.
—Longarm on the Nevada Line, No. 76. 1985. (Longarm Ser.). 192p. mass mkt. 2.50 o.s.i (*0-515-08173-6*, Jove) Berkley Publishing Group.
—Longarm on the Ogallala Trail. 1984. (Longarm Ser.: No. 70). 192p. mass mkt. 2.50 o.s.i (*0-515-06271-5*, Jove) Berkley Publishing Group.
—Longarm on the Old Mission Trail. 1982. (Longarm Ser.: No. 25). 253p. mass mkt. 2.25 o.s.i (*0-515-07066-1*, Jove) Berkley Publishing Group.
—Longarm on the Overland Trail, No. 104. 1987. (Longarm Ser.). 192p. mass mkt. 2.75 o.s.i (*0-515-09113-8*, Jove) Berkley Publishing Group.
—Longarm on the Santa Cruz, No. 78. 1987. (Longarm Ser.). 192p. mass mkt. 2.75 o.s.i (*0-515-09283-5*, Jove) Berkley Publishing Group.
—Longarm on the Santa Fe. 1984. (Longarm Ser.: No.36). 256p. mass mkt. 2.50 o.s.i (*0-515-08063-2*, Jove) Berkley Publishing Group.
—Longarm on the Santee Killing Grounds. 1994. (Longarm Ser.: No. 14). 288p. (Orig.). mass mkt. 4.99 o.s.i (*0-515-11459-6*, Jove) Berkley Publishing Group.
—Longarm on the Siwash Trail. 1986. (Longarm Ser.: No. 93). 192p. mass mkt. 2.75 o.s.i (*0-515-08675-4*, Jove) Berkley Publishing Group.
—Longarm on the Thunderbird Run. 1988. (Longarm Ser.: No. 111). mass mkt. 2.75 o.s.i (*0-515-09491-9*, Jove) Berkley Publishing Group.
—Longarm on the Yellowstone. 1981. (Longarm Ser.: No. 18). 256p. mass mkt. 1.95 o.s.i (*0-515-06155-7*, Jove) Berkley Publishing Group.
—Longarm South of the Gila. 1982. (Longarm Ser.: No. 30). 256p. mass mkt. 2.25 o.s.i (*0-515-06581-1*, Jove) Berkley Publishing Group.
—Longarm West of the Pecos. 1987. (Longarm Ser.). mass mkt. 2.75 o.s.i (*0-515-09280-0*, Jove) Berkley Publishing Group.
—Paradise, Vol. 289. 2002. (Longarm Ser.). 192p. mass mkt. 4.99 o.s.i (*0-515-13419-8*) Penguin Group (USA) Inc.
—Rancher's Daughter, Vol. 291. 2003. (Longarm Ser.). 192p. mass mkt. 4.99 o.s.i (*0-515-13472-4*, Jove) Berkley Publishing Group.

**LONGCHAMP, DAWN (FICTITIOUS CHARACTER)—FICTION**

Andrews, V. C. Dawn. unabr. ed. 1991. (Cutler Ser.). audio 64.00 (*0-7366-1944-5*, 2765) Books on Tape, Inc.
—Dawn. l.t. ed. 1991. (General Ser.). 472p. pap. 17.95 (*0-8161-5186-5*); lib. bdg. 20.95 (*0-8161-5184-9*) Gale Group. (Macmillan Reference USA).
—Dawn. 2003. audio 76.95 (*0-7531-1772-X*); audio compact disk 89.95 (*0-7531-2231-6*) ISIS Audio Bks. GBR. *Dist:* Ulverscroft Large Print Bks., Ltd.
—Dawn. 1990. 19.95 (*0-671-67067-0*, Atria) Simon & Schuster.
—Dawn. Marrow, Linda, ed. 1990. (Cutler Ser.). 416p. mass mkt. 7.99 (*0-671-67068-9*, Pocket) Simon & Schuster.
—Dawn. 1990. 14.04 (*0-606-04649-6*) Turtleback Bks.
—Midnight Whispers, unabr. ed. 1993. audio 72.00 (*0-7366-2532-1*, 3284) Books on Tape, Inc.
—Midnight Whispers. l.t. ed. 1993. (G. K. Hall Large Print Book Ser.). 515p. 19.95 o.p. (*0-8161-5656-5*); lib. bdg. 23.95 (*0-8161-5655-7*) Gale Group. (Macmillan Reference USA).
—Midnight Whispers. Marrow, Linda, ed. 1992. 448p. (Midnight Whispers Ser.: Vol. 5). mass mkt. 7.99 (*0-671-69516-9*, Pocket);Vol. 5. 22.00 (*0-671-69517-7*, Atria) Simon & Schuster.
—Midnight Whispers. 1992. 14.04 (*0-606-02201-5*) Turtleback Bks.
—Secrets of the Morning. unabr. ed. 1993. (Cutler Ser.). audio 64.00 (*0-7366-2356-6*, 3131) Books on Tape, Inc.
—Secrets of the Morning. l.t. ed. 1992. (General Ser.). 487p. pap. 17.95 (*0-8161-5386-8*); lib. bdg. 20.95 (*0-8161-5385-X*) Gale Group. (Macmillan Reference USA).
—Secrets of the Morning. unabr. ed. 2003. audio 84.95 (*0-7531-1773-8*) ISIS Audio Bks. GBR. *Dist:* Ulverscroft Large Print Bks., Ltd.
—Secrets of the Morning. Marrow, Linda, ed. 1991. (Cutler Ser.). 416p. mass mkt. 7.99 (*0-671-69512-6*, Pocket);Vol. 2. 384p. 21.95 (*0-671-69513-4*, Atria) Simon & Schuster.
—Secrets of the Morning. 1991. 14.04 (*0-606-05012-4*) Turtleback Bks.
—Twilight's Child. unabr. ed. 1993. (Dawn Ser.: Vol. 3). audio 72.00 (*0-7366-2406-6*, 3175) Books on Tape, Inc.
—Twilight's Child. l.t. ed. 1993. (General Ser.). 555p. pap. 17.95 (*0-8161-5525-9*); lib. bdg. 20.95 (*0-8161-5524-0*) Gale Group. (Macmillan Reference USA).
—Twilight's Child. Marrow, Linda, ed. 1992. 416p. (Twilight's Child Ser.: Vol. 3). mass mkt. 7.99 (*0-671-69514-2*, Pocket);Vol. 3. 22.00 o.p. (*0-671-69515-0*, Atria) Simon & Schuster.
—Twilight's Child. 1992. 14.04 (*0-606-00810-1*) Turtleback Bks.

**LONGINUS, CASCA (FICTITIOUS CHARACTER)—FICTION**

Dengelegi, Paul. The Liberator, Vol. 1. 1999. (Barry Sadler's Casca Ser.). 288p. mass mkt. 5.99 o.s.i (*0-515-12689-6*, Jove) Berkley Publishing Group.
Sadler, Barry. African Mercenary. (Casca Ser.: No. 12). 1985. 2.95 o.s.i (*0-441-09330-2*); 1984. 2.75 o.s.i (*0-441-09260-8*) Ace Bks.
—African Mercenary. 1986. (Casca: No. 12). 224p. 2.95 o.s.i (*0-441-09346-9*, Diamond Bks.) Berkley Publishing Group.
—The Assassin. 1985. (Casca Ser.: No. 13). 2.75 o.s.i (*0-441-09327-2*) Ace Bks.
—The Assassin. (Casca: No. 13). 192p. 1988. mass mkt. 3.99 o.s.i (*0-515-09911-2*, Jove); 1985. 2.95 o.s.i (*0-441-09337-X*, Diamond Bks.) Berkley Publishing Group.
—The Barbarian. (Casca: No. 5). 1985. 192p. 2.95 o.s.i (*0-441-09348-5*, Diamond Bks.); Bk. 5. 1987. mass mkt. 3.99 o.s.i (*0-515-09147-2*, Jove) Berkley Publishing Group.
—Casca Conquistador. 1984. 2.75 o.s.i (*0-441-09322-1*) Ace Bks.
—Casca the Barbarian. 1984. 2.75 o.s.i (*0-441-09326-4*); 1983. 2.50 o.s.i (*0-441-09225-X*); 1981. 2.25 o.s.i (*0-441-09217-9*) Ace Bks.
—Casca the Damned. 1984. 2.75 o.s.i (*0-441-09324-8*) Ace Bks.
—Casca the Damned. 1987. (Casca: No. 7). mass mkt. 3.99 o.s.i (*0-515-09474-9*); mass mkt. 3.99 o.s.i (*0-515-09473-0*) Berkley Publishing Group. (Jove).
—Casca the Persian. 1983. 2.50 o.s.i (*0-441-09219-5*) Ace Bks.
—Casca the Warlord. 1984. 2.75 o.s.i (*0-441-09262-4*); 1981. 2.25 o.s.i (*0-441-09218-7*) Ace Bks.
—The Conquistador. (Casca Ser.: No. 10). 1985. 2.95 o.s.i (*0-441-09334-5*); 1984. 2.50 o.s.i (*0-441-09241-1*) Ace Bks.
—The Conquistador. abr. ed. 2004. audio compact disk (*1-58807-715-2*); 2004. (Illus.). audio compact disk 25.00 (*1-58807-284-3*); 2003. (Casca Ser.: No. 10). audio 18.00 (*1-58807-110-3*); 2003. audio (*1-58807-539-7*) Americana Publishing, Inc.
—The Conquistador. (Casca: No. 10). 1987. mass mkt. 3.99 o.s.i (*0-515-09601-6*, Jove); 1986. 176p. 2.95 o.s.i (*0-441-09351-5*, Diamond Bks.) Berkley Publishing Group.
—The Conquistador. abr. ed. 2001. (Casca Ser.: No. 10). audio 9.99 (*1-55204-509-9*, GOL3509) Durkin Hayes Publishing Ltd.
—Cry Havoc. 1985. 3.50 o.p. (*0-8125-8827-4*); 1983. 352p. pap. 3.50 o.p. (*0-523-48057-1*) Doherty, Tom Assocs., LLC. (Tor Bks.).
—Cursed. 1987. (Casca: No. 18). 192p. mass mkt. 3.99 o.s.i (*0-515-09109-X*, Jove) Berkley Publishing Group.
—Damned. 1985. (Casca Ser.: No. 7). 2.95 o.s.i (*0-441-09332-9*) Ace Bks.
—Desert Mercenary. 1986. (Casca Ser.: No. 16). 2.95 o.s.i (*0-441-09356-6*) Ace Bks.
—Desert Mercenary. (Casca: No. 16). 192p. 1987. mass mkt. 3.99 o.s.i (*0-515-09556-7*, Jove); 1986. 2.95 o.s.i (*0-441-09336-1*, Diamond Bks.) Berkley Publishing Group.
—The Eternal Mercenary. 1985. (Casca Ser.: No. 1). 2.95 o.s.i (*0-441-09338-8*) Ace Bks.
—The Eternal Mercenary. (Casca: No. 1). 1987. mass mkt. 3.95 o.s.i (*0-515-09535-4*, Jove); 1986. 256p. 2.95 o.s.i (*0-441-09361-2*, Diamond Bks.) Berkley Publishing Group.
—God of Death. (Casca Ser.: No. 2). 1985. 2.95 o.s.i (*0-441-09335-3*); 1985. pap. 2.50 o.s.i (*0-441-09249-7*); 1984. 2.75 o.s.i (*0-441-09325-6*); 1983. 2.50 o.s.i (*0-441-09221-7*) Ace Bks.
—God of Death. 1988. mass mkt. 3.95 o.s.i (*0-515-09919-8*, Jove); 1986. (Casca: No. 2). 224p. 2.95 o.s.i (*0-441-09362-0*, Diamond Bks.) Berkley Publishing Group.
—The Legionnaire. 1984. (Casca Ser.: No. 11). 2.75 o.s.i (*0-441-09328-0*); 2.50 o.s.i (*0-441-09244-6*) Ace Bks.
—The Legionnaire. (Casca: No. 10). 1987. mass mkt. 3.99 o.s.i (*0-515-09602-4*, Jove); 1985. 176p. 2.95 o.s.i (*0-441-09339-6*, Diamond Bks.) Berkley Publishing Group.
—The Mongol. 1990. (Casca: No. 22). 176p. mass mkt. 3.99 o.s.i (*0-515-10240-7*, Jove) Berkley Publishing Group.
—Morituri. 1982. 320p. (Orig.). mass mkt. 2.95 (*0-523-48045-8*, Tor Bks.) Doherty, Tom Assocs., LLC.
—Panzer Soldier. (Casca Ser.: No. 4). 1985. 2.75 o.s.i (*0-441-09314-0*); 1984. 2.50 o.s.i (*0-441-09252-7*); 1983. 2.50 o.s.i (*0-441-09222-5*) Ace Bks.
—Panzer Soldier. 1987. (Casca: No. 4). mass mkt. 3.99 o.s.i (*0-515-09472-2*, Jove) Berkley Publishing Group.
—The Persian. 1984. (Casca Ser.: No. 6). 2.75 o.s.i (*0-441-09263-2*) Ace Bks.
—The Persian. (Casca: No. 6). 1992. mass mkt. 3.99 o.s.i (*0-515-10796-4*); 1985. 224p. 2.95 o.s.i (*0-441-09264-0*) Berkley Publishing Group. (Jove).
—The Phoenix. 1985. (Casca Ser.: No. 14). 2.95 o.s.i (*0-441-09329-9*) Ace Bks.
—The Phoenix. (Casca: No. 14). 192p. 1987. mass mkt. 3.99 o.s.i (*0-515-09471-4*, Jove); 1986. 2.95 o.s.i (*0-441-09350-7*, Diamond Bks.) Berkley Publishing Group.
—Pirate. 1987. (Casca: No. 15). 176p. mass mkt. 3.99 o.s.i (*0-515-09599-0*, Jove) Berkley Publishing Group.
—The Pirate. (Casca Ser.: No. 15). 1986. 2.95 o.s.i (*0-441-09354-X*); 1985. 176p. 2.95 o.s.i (*0-441-09347-7*); 1985. 2.95 o.s.i (*0-441-09331-0*) Ace Bks.
—Razor. 1988. 3.95 (*1-55773-002-4*, Diamond Bks.) Berkley Publishing Group.
—Rescue. 1991. mass mkt. 4.50 o.s.i (*0-515-10490-6*, Jove) Berkley Publishing Group.
—Run for the Sun. 1986. 256p. (Orig.). pap. 3.50 o.p. (*0-8125-8829-0*, Tor Bks.) Doherty, Tom Assocs., LLC.
—Samurai. 1988. (Casca: No. 19). 176p. mass mkt. 3.99 o.s.i (*0-515-09516-8*, Jove) Berkley Publishing Group.
—The Sentinel. (Casca Ser.: No. 9). 1984. 2.75 o.s.i (*0-441-09259-4*); 1983. 2.50 o.s.i (*0-441-09237-3*) Ace Bks.
—The Sentinel. (Casca: No. 9). 1988. mass mkt. 3.99 o.s.i (*0-515-09997-X*, Jove); 1985. 176p. 2.95 o.s.i (*0-441-09269-1*, Diamond Bks.) Berkley Publishing Group.
—Seppuku. 1988. 224p. mass mkt. 3.95 (*0-8125-8845-2*, Tor Bks.) Doherty, Tom Assocs., LLC.
—The Shooter. 1987. 288p. (Orig.). pap. 3.50 o.p. (*0-8125-8831-2*, Tor Bks.) Doherty, Tom Assocs., LLC.
—Soldier of Fortune. (Casca Ser.: No. 8). 1985. 2.95 o.s.i (*0-441-09333-7*); 1984. 2.75 o.s.i (*0-441-09323-X*); 1983. 2.50 o.s.i (*0-441-09226-8*) Ace Bks.
—Soldier of Fortune. (Casca: NO. 8). 1987. mass mkt. 3.99 o.s.i (*0-515-09723-3*, Jove); 1986. 192p. 2.95 o.s.i (*0-441-09352-3*, Diamond Bks.) Berkley Publishing Group.
—Soldier of Gideon. 1988. (Casca: No. 20). mass mkt. 3.99 o.s.i (*0-515-09701-2*, Jove) Berkley Publishing Group.
—The Trench Soldier. 1989. (Casca: No. 21). 176p. mass mkt. 3.99 o.s.i (*0-515-09931-7*, Jove) Berkley Publishing Group.
—The Warlord. 1986. (Casca Ser.: No. 3). pap. 2.95 o.s.i (*0-441-09996-3*); 2.95 o.s.i (*0-441-09343-4*) Ace Bks.
—The Warlord. (Casca: No. 3). 1988. mass mkt. 3.99 o.s.i (*0-515-09996-1*, Jove); 1987. 196p. 2.95 o.s.i (*0-441-09363-9*, Diamond Bks.) Berkley Publishing Group.
—The Warrior. 1987. (Casca Ser.: No. 17). 192p. 2.95 o.s.i (*0-441-09353-1*) Ace Bks.
—The Warrior. 1987. (Casca: No. 17). 192p. mass mkt. 3.99 o.s.i (*0-515-09603-2*, Jove) Berkley Publishing Group.
Sapler. Damned. 1985. (Casca Ser.: No. 7). 2.95 o.s.i (*0-441-09349-3*) Ace Bks.

**LONGMIRE, HARRY (FICTITIOUS CHARACTER)—FICTION**

Thomas, Ross. Yellow-Dog Contract. 272p. reprint ed. 1987. pap. 3.50 o.p. (*0-06-080847-0*, P 847); 1984. pap. 2.95 o.p. (*0-06-080704-0*, P 704) Harper-Trade. (Perennial).
—Yellow-Dog Contract. 1983. pap. 1.75 o.p. (*0-380-01828-4*, 36186, Avon Bks.) Morrow/Avon.
—Yellow-Dog Contract. 1993. 224p. mass mkt. 4.99 o.p. (*0-446-40174-9*) Warner Bks., Inc.

**LONIGAN, STUDS (FICTITIOUS CHARACTER)—FICTION**

Farrell, James T. Studs Lonigan. Date not set. lib. bdg. 38.95 (*0-8488-1974-8*) Amereon, Ltd.
—Studs Lonigan. 1979. pap. 2.75 o.p. (*0-380-00934-X*, 59758-6, Avon Bks.) Morrow/Avon.
—Studs Lonigan. 1993. (Prairie State Bks.). 912p. pap. 21.95 (*0-252-06282-5*); text 49.95 o.p. (*0-252-02062-6*) Univ. of Illinois Pr.
—Studs Lonigan: A Trilogy. 2004. (Library of America: Vol. 148). 1024p. 35.00 (*1-931082-55-3*) Library of America, The.
—Young Lonigan. 2003. 224p. mass mkt. 7.95 (*0-451-52913-8*, Signet Classics) NAL.
—Young Lonigan. 2003. 224p. pap. 13.00 (*0-14-218007-6*, Penguin Classics) Viking Penguin.

**LOOMIS, TUCKER (FICTITIOUS CHARACTER)—FICTION**

MacDonald, John D. Barrier Island. 1987. (Florida Mysteries Ser.). 272p. reprint ed. mass mkt. 5.99 o.s.i (*0-449-13179-3*, Fawcett) Ballantine Bks.
—Barrier Island. l.t. ed. 1987. (General Ser.). 288p. 18.95 o.p. (*0-8161-4262-9*); 11.95 o.p. (*0-8161-4263-7*) Gale Group. (Macmillan Reference USA).
—Barrier Island. 1986. 16.95 o.s.i (*0-394-55427-2*) Knopf, Alfred A. Inc.

**LORD, EMMA (FICTITIOUS CHARACTER)—FICTION**

Daheim, Mary R. The Alpine Advocate. 1992. (Emma Lord Mysteries Ser.). 240p. mass mkt. 6.99 (*0-345-37672-2*) Ballantine Bks.
—The Alpine Betrayal. 1993. (Emma Lord Mysteries Ser.). 240p. mass mkt. 6.99 (*0-345-37937-3*) Ballantine Bks.
—The Alpine Christmas. 1993. (Emma Lord Mysteries Ser.). 272p. mass mkt. 6.99 (*0-345-38270-6*) Ballantine Bks.
—The Alpine Decoy. 1994. (Emma Lord Mysteries Ser.). 256p. mass mkt. 6.99 (*0-345-38841-0*) Ballantine Bks.
—The Alpine Escape. 1995. (Emma Lord Mysteries Ser.). 288p. (Orig.). mass mkt. 6.99 (*0-345-38842-9*) Ballantine Bks.
—The Alpine Fury. 1995. 320p. (Orig.). mass mkt. 6.99 (*0-345-38843-7*) Ballantine Bks.
—The Alpine Gamble. 1996. (Emma Lord Mysteries Ser.). 304p. mass mkt. 6.99 (*0-345-39641-3*) Ballantine Bks.
—The Alpine Gamble. l.t. ed. 1999. (Beeler Large Print Mystery Ser.). (*1-57490-210-5*, Beeler Large Print Bks.) Beeler, Thomas T. Publisher.
—The Alpine Hero. 1996. (Emma Lord Mysteries Ser.). 320p. mass mkt. 6.99 (*0-345-39642-1*) Ballantine Bks.
—The Alpine Hero. l.t. ed. 1999. (Beeler Large Print Mystery Ser.). 25.95 (*1-57490-203-2*, Beeler Large Print Bks.) Beeler, Thomas T. Publisher.
—The Alpine Icon. 1997. (Emma Lord Mysteries Ser.). 336p. mass mkt. 6.99 (*0-345-39643-X*) Ballantine Bks.
—The Alpine Icon. l.t. ed. 1998. 353p. 24.95 (*1-57490-138-9*, Beeler Large Print Bks.) Beeler, Thomas T. Publisher.
—The Alpine Journey. 1998. (Emma Lord Mysteries Ser.). 320p. mass mkt. 6.99 (*0-345-39644-8*) Ballantine Bks.
—Alpine Journey. l.t. ed. 2003. 512p. 25.95 (*0-375-43268-X*, Random House Large Print) Random Hse. Large Print.
—The Alpine Kindred. l.t. ed. 2004. 448p. 25.95 (*0-375-43253-1*) Random Hse. Large Print.
—The Alpine Kindred: An Emma Lord Mystery. 1998. (Emma Lord Mysteries Ser.). 320p. mass mkt. 6.99 (*0-345-42122-1*) Ballantine Bks.
—The Alpine Legacy. 1999. (Emma Lord Mysteries Ser.). 320p. mass mkt. 6.99 (*0-345-42123-X*, Ballantine Bks.) Ballantine Bks.
—The Alpine Menace. Blades, Joe, ed. 2000. (Emma Lord Mysteries Ser.). 304p. mass mkt. 6.99 (*0-345-42124-8*, Fawcett) Ballantine Bks.
—The Alpine Nemesis. 2001. (Emma Lord Mystery Ser.). 320p. mass mkt. 6.99 (*0-345-42125-6*) Ballantine Bks.

**LORD WESTFIELD'S MEN (FICTITIOUS CHARACTERS)—FICTION**

Marston, Edward. The Vagabond Clown: An Elizabethan Theater Mystery Featuring Nicholas Bracewell. Date not set. pap. (*0-312-30790-X*, Saint Martin's Griffin); mass mkt. (*0-312-98612-2*, St. Martin's Paperbacks); E-Book (*0-312-70591-3*); 2003. 352p. 24.95 (*0-312-30789-6*, Saint Martin's Minotaur) St. Martin's Pr.

**LORING, HELEN, LADY (FICTITIOUS CHARACTER)—FICTION**

Dickson, Carter, pseud. The Curse of the Bronze Lamp. 1997. 192p. mass mkt. 4.95 (*0-7867-0440-3*, Carroll & Graf Pubs.) Avalon Publishing Group.

**LOUDERMILK, DOTTIE (FICTITIOUS CHARACTER)—FICTION**

Haywood, Gar Anthony. Bad News Travels Fast. 1996. mass mkt. 5.99 o.s.i (*0-425-15464-5*) Berkley Publishing Group.

Characters

—Bad News Travels Fast. abr. ed. 1996. audio 7.99 o.p. (*1-56740-122-8*, 623, Paperback Nova Audio Bks.); 1995. audio 16.95 o.p. (*1-56100-424-3*, 1147, Nova Audio Bks.); 1995. audio 23.95 o.p. (*1-56100-636-X*, 36, Bookcassette); 1995. audio 57.25 o.p. (*1-56100-261-5*, 800, Unabridged Library Editions) Brilliance Audio.

—Bad News Travels Fast. 1995. 240p. 21.95 o.p. (*0-399-14017-4*, G. P. Putnam's Sons) Penguin Group (USA) Inc.

—Bad News Travels Fast. l.t. ed. 1996. (Niagara Large Print Ser.). 139p. 29.50 o.p. (*0-7089-5837-0*, Ulverscroft) Thorpe, F. A. Pubs. GBR. *Dist:* Ulverscroft Large Print Bks., Ltd.

—Going Nowhere Fast. 1995. 224p. mass mkt. 5.99 o.s.i (*0-425-15051-8*, Prime Crime) Berkley Publishing Group.

—Going Nowhere Fast. abr. ed. 1994. audio 16.95 o.p. (*1-56100-378-6*, 1312, Nova Audio Bks.); audio 57.25 o.p. (*1-56100-204-6*, 1222, Unabridged Library Editions); audio 23.95 o.p. (*1-56100-578-9*, 124, Bookcassette) Brilliance Audio.

—Going Nowhere Fast. abr. ed. 2000. audio 7.95 (*1-57815-010-8*, 1063, Media Bks. Audio Publishing) Media Bks., L. L. C.

—Going Nowhere Fast. 1994. 240p. 19.95 o.p. (*0-399-13917-6*, G. P. Putnam's Sons) Penguin Group (USA) Inc.

**LOUDERMILK, JOE (FICTITIOUS CHARACTER)—FICTION**

Haywood, Gar Anthony. Bad News Travels Fast. 1996. mass mkt. 5.99 o.s.i (*0-425-15464-5*) Berkley Publishing Group.

—Bad News Travels Fast. abr. ed. 1996. audio 7.99 o.p. (*1-56740-122-8*, 623, Paperback Nova Audio Bks.); 1995. audio 16.95 o.p. (*1-56100-424-3*, 1147, Nova Audio Bks.); 1995. audio 23.95 o.p. (*1-56100-636-X*, 36, Bookcassette); 1995. audio 57.25 o.p. (*1-56100-261-5*, 800, Unabridged Library Editions) Brilliance Audio.

—Bad News Travels Fast. 1995. 240p. 21.95 o.p. (*0-399-14017-4*, G. P. Putnam's Sons) Penguin Group (USA) Inc.

—Bad News Travels Fast. l.t. ed. 1996. (Niagara Large Print Ser.). 139p. 29.50 o.p. (*0-7089-5837-0*, Ulverscroft) Thorpe, F. A. Pubs. GBR. *Dist:* Ulverscroft Large Print Bks., Ltd.

—Going Nowhere Fast. 1995. 224p. mass mkt. 5.99 o.s.i (*0-425-15051-8*, Prime Crime) Berkley Publishing Group.

—Going Nowhere Fast. abr. ed. 1994. audio 16.95 o.p. (*1-56100-378-6*, 1312, Nova Audio Bks.); audio 57.25 o.p. (*1-56100-204-6*, 1222, Unabridged Library Editions); audio 23.95 o.p. (*1-56100-578-9*, 124, Bookcassette) Brilliance Audio.

—Going Nowhere Fast. abr. ed. 2000. audio 7.95 (*1-57815-010-8*, 1063, Media Bks. Audio Publishing) Media Bks., L. L. C.

—Going Nowhere Fast. 1994. 240p. 19.95 o.p. (*0-399-13917-6*, G. P. Putnam's Sons) Penguin Group (USA) Inc.

**LOVE, PHAROAH (FICTITIOUS CHARACTER)—FICTION**

Baxt, George. A Queer Kind of Death. 1998. 300p. pap. 10.00 o.p. (*1-55583-448-5*) Alyson Pubns.

—A Queer Kind of Death: A Pharoah Love Mystery. 1986. (Library of Crime Classics). pap. 4.95 o.p. (*0-930330-46-3*) International Polygonics, Ltd.

—A Queer Kind of Death: A Pharoah Love Mystery. 1979. pap. 4.95 o.p. (*0-312-66022-7*, Saint Martin's Griffin) St. Martin's Pr.

—A Queer Kind of Love: A Pharoah Love Mystery. 1994. 288p. 20.00 (*1-883402-01-8*, Scribner) Simon & Schuster.

—A Queer Kind of Love: A Pharoah Love Mystery. pap. (*0-312-29217-1*); 1995. pap. 8.95 (*0-312-13152-6*) St. Martin's Pr. (Saint Martin's Griffin).

—A Queer Kind of Umbrella: A Pharoah Love Mystery. 1995. 240p. 20.50 (*0-684-81496-X*, Simon & Schuster); 21.00 (*1-883402-35-2*, Scribner) Simon & Schuster.

—Topsy & Evil. 1987. 232p. reprint ed. pap. 4.95 o.p. (*0-930330-66-8*) International Polygonics, Ltd.

**LOVEJOY (FICTITIOUS CHARACTER)—FICTION**

Gash, Jonathan. Firefly Gadroon. 1985. (Lovejoy Mystery Ser.). 12.95 o.p. (*0-525-24135-3*, Dutton) Dutton/Plume.

—Firefly Gadroon. 1984. 208p. 11.95 o.p. (*0-312-29205-8*) St. Martin's Pr.

—Firefly Gadroon. l.t. ed. 1983. 352p. 15.95 o.p. (*0-7089-1012-2*, Ulverscroft) Thorpe, F. A. Pubs. GBR. *Dist:* Ulverscroft Large Print Bks., Ltd.

—Firefly Gadroon. 1985. (Lovejoy Mystery Ser.). 208p. pap. 5.95 o.s.i (*0-14-008007-4*, Penguin Bks.) Viking Penguin.

—Gold by Gemini. 1982. (Scene of the Crime Mystery Ser.: No. 36). pap. 2.25 o.p. (*0-440-12749-1*) Dell Publishing.

—Gold by Gemini. 1978. 186p. 8.95 (*0-06-011463-0*) HarperCollins Pubs.

—Gold by Gemini. 1988. (Lovejoy Mystery Ser.). 192p. mass mkt. 3.95 o.p. (*0-451-82185-8*) NAL.

—Gold by Gemini. unabr. ed. 1999. (Lovejoy Mystery Ser.). audio 53.00 (*1-84197-020-4*, H1020E7, Clipper Audio); audio compact disk 59.00 (*1-84197-090-5*, C1126E7);Set. audio 53.00 Recorded Bks., LLC.

—Gold by Gemini. l.t. ed. 1981. (Ulverscroft Large Print Ser.). 29.99 o.p. (*0-7089-0575-7*, Ulverscroft) Thorpe, F. A. Pubs. GBR. *Dist:* Ulverscroft Large Print Bks., Ltd., Ulverscroft Large Print Canada, Ltd.

—Gold by Gemini. 1988. (Lovejoy Mystery Ser.). 224p. pap. 5.95 o.p. (*0-14-023014-9*, Penguin Bks.); 224p. pap. 3.95 o.p. (*0-14-010529-8*, Penguin Bks.); pap. 39.50 o.p. (*0-14-778299-6*) Viking Penguin.

—The Gondola Scam. 1984. 256p. 12.95 o.p. (*0-312-33828-7*) St. Martin's Pr.

—The Gondola Scam. 1985. (Lovejoy Mystery Ser.). 256p. pap. 5.99 o.p. (*0-14-007656-5*, Penguin Bks.) Viking Penguin.

—The Grace in Older Women: A Lovejoy Novel. 1996. (Lovejoy Mystery Ser.). 288p. pap. 5.95 o.p. (*0-14-024662-2*, Penguin Bks.) Penguin Group (USA) Inc.

—The Grace in Older Women: A Lovejoy Novel. 1995. (Lovejoy Mystery Ser.). 288p. 19.95 o.p. (*0-670-86128-6*, Viking) Viking Penguin.

—The Grail Tree. 21.95 (*0-88411-559-3*) Amereon, Ltd.

—The Grail Tree. 1982. (Scene of the Crime Ser.: No. 48). 288p. pap. 2.50 o.p. (*0-440-13022-0*) Dell Publishing.

—The Grail Tree. 1980. o.p. (*0-06-011462-2*) HarperCollins Pubs.

—The Grail Tree. 1988. (Lovejoy Mystery Ser.). 224p. mass mkt. 3.95 o.p. (*0-451-82186-6*) NAL.

—The Grail Tree. unabr. ed. (Lovejoy Mystery Ser.). 2001. audio compact disk 67.00 (*1-84197-098-0*, C1142E7); 1999. audio 53.00 (*1-84197-028-X*, H1027E7) Recorded Bks., LLC. (Clipper Audio).

—The Grail Tree. l.t. ed. 1983. (Ulverscroft Large Print Ser.). 368p. 29.99 o.p. (*0-7089-0958-2*, Ulverscroft) Thorpe, F. A. Pubs. GBR. *Dist:* Ulverscroft Large Print Bks., Ltd., Ulverscroft Large Print Canada, Ltd.

—The Grail Tree. 1988. (Lovejoy Mystery Ser.). 224p. pap. 5.95 o.s.i (*0-14-023015-7*, Penguin Bks.); 224p. pap. 3.95 o.p. (*0-14-010530-1*, Penguin Bks.); pap. 39.50 o.p. (*0-14-778300-3*) Viking Penguin.

—The Great California Game. 1992. (Lovejoy Mystery Ser.). 256p. reprint ed. pap. 5.95 o.p. (*0-14-017224-6*, Penguin Bks.) Penguin Group (USA) Inc.

—The Great California Game. 1991. 288p. 19.95 o.p. (*0-312-06363-6*, Saint Martin's Minotaur) St. Martin's Pr.

—The Great California Game. l.t. ed. 1993. (Mystery Ser.). 512p. 29.99 o.p. (*0-7089-2930-3*, Ulverscroft) Thorpe, F. A. Pubs. GBR. *Dist:* Ulverscroft Large Print Bks., Ltd., Ulverscroft Large Print Canada, Ltd.

—Jade Woman. 1988. 288p. 17.95 o.p. (*0-312-02224-7*, Saint Martin's Minotaur) St. Martin's Pr.

—Jade Woman. l.t. ed. 1990. 18.95 o.p. (*0-7089-2189-2*, Ulverscroft) Thorpe, F. A. Pubs. GBR. *Dist:* Ulverscroft Large Print Bks., Ltd.

—Jade Woman. 1990. (Lovejoy Mystery Ser.). 288p. pap. 5.95 o.p. (*0-14-012280-X*, Penguin Bks.) Viking Penguin.

—The Judas Pair. 1981. (Scene of the Crime Mystery Ser.: No. 30). pap. 2.25 o.p. (*0-440-14354-3*) Dell Publishing.

—The Judas Pair. 1988. 39.50 o.p. (*0-14-778245-7*) Penguin Group (USA) Inc.

—The Judas Pair. 1999. (Lovejoy Mystery Ser.). audio 53.00 (*1-84197-004-2*, H1004E7); audio compact disk 61.00Set. audio 53.00 Recorded Bks., LLC.

—The Judas Pair. l.t. ed. 1982. (Ulverscroft Large Print Ser.). 368p. 29.99 o.p. (*0-7089-0856-X*, Ulverscroft) Thorpe, F. A. Pubs. GBR. *Dist:* Ulverscroft Large Print Bks., Ltd., Ulverscroft Large Print Canada, Ltd.

—The Judas Pair. (Lovejoy Mystery Ser.). 1989. 22p. pap. 6.95 o.p. (*0-14-012688-0*); 1988. 224p. pap. 3.95 o.p. (*0-14-010528-X*) Viking Penguin. (Penguin Bks.).

—The Lies of Fair Ladies. 1993. (Lovejoy Mystery Ser.). 272p. pap. 5.95 o.p. (*0-14-017630-6*, Penguin Bks.) Penguin Group (USA) Inc.

—The Lies of Fair Ladies. 1992. 288p. 19.95 o.p. (*0-312-07620-7*, Saint Martin's Minotaur) St. Martin's Pr.

—The Lies of Fair Ladies. l.t. ed. 1994. (Large Print Ser.). 592p. 29.99 o.p. (*0-7089-3006-9*, Ulverscroft) Thorpe, F. A. Pubs. GBR. *Dist:* Ulverscroft Large Print Bks., Ltd., Ulverscroft Large Print Canada, Ltd.

—Moonspender. 1987. 240p. 14.95 o.p. (*0-312-00156-8*) St. Martin's Pr.

—Moonspender. (Lovejoy Mystery Ser.). 1990. 224p. pap. 5.99 o.p. (*0-14-014339-4*); 1988. 272p. pap. 4.50 o.p. (*0-14-010646-4*) Viking Penguin. (Penguin Bks.).

—Paid & Loving Eyes. 1994. (Lovejoy Mystery Ser.). 272p. pap. 5.99 o.s.i (*0-14-023557-4*, Penguin Bks.) Penguin Group (USA) Inc.

—Paid & Loving Eyes. 1993. (Lovejoy Novel of Suspense Ser.). 288p. 19.95 o.p. (*0-312-09361-6*, Saint Martin's Minotaur) St. Martin's Pr.

—Paid & Loving Eyes. l.t. ed. 1994. (Ulverscroft Large Print Ser.). 608p. 29.99 o.p. (*0-7089-3164-2*, Ulverscroft) Thorpe, F. A. Pubs. GBR. *Dist:* Ulverscroft Large Print Bks., Ltd., Ulverscroft Large Print Canada, Ltd.

—Pearlhanger. 1985. 256p. 14.95 o.p. (*0-312-59970-6*) St. Martin's Pr.

—Pearlhanger. l.t. ed. 2000. (Mystery Ser.). 319p. 26.95 (*0-7862-2456-8*); (*0-7540-4138-7*); (*0-7540-4139-5*) Thorndike Pr.

—Pearlhanger. 1986. (Lovejoy Mystery Ser.). 24p. pap. 5.95 o.p. (*0-14-008468-1*, Penguin Bks.) Viking Penguin.

—The Possessions of a Lady. 1997. (Lovejoy Mystery Ser.). 336p. pap. 5.95 o.s.i (*0-14-025792-6*) Penguin Group (USA) Inc.

—The Possessions of a Lady. 1996. (Lovejoy Mystery Ser.). 332p. 21.95 o.s.i (*0-670-86933-3*, Viking) Viking Penguin.

—A Rag, a Bone & a Hank of Hair. 2001. (Lovejoy Mystery Ser.). 352p. pap. 5.99 o.s.i (*0-14-029857-6*) Penguin Group (USA) Inc.

—A Rag, a Bone & a Hank of Hair. 2000. (Lovejoy Mystery Ser.). 256p. 23.95 o.s.i (*0-670-88598-3*, Viking) Viking Penguin.

—The Rich & the Profane. l.t. ed. 1999. pap. 23.95 (*1-56895-794-7*, Wheeler Publishing, Inc.) Gale Group.

—The Rich & the Profane. 2000. (Lovejoy Mystery Ser.). 352p. pap. 5.99 (*0-14-028622-5*, Penguin Bks.) Penguin Group (USA) Inc.

—The Rich & the Profane. 1999. (Lovejoy Mystery Ser.). 288p. 22.95 o.s.i (*0-670-88346-8*) Viking Penguin.

—The Sin Within Her Smile. l.t. ed. 1994. 385p. 20.95 (*0-8161-1115-4*); lib. bdg. 21.95 (*0-7838-1115-2*) Gale Group. (Macmillan Reference USA).

—The Sin Within Her Smile. 1995. (Lovejoy Mystery Ser.). 240p. pap. 5.99 o.s.i (*0-14-023839-5*, Penguin Bks.) Penguin Group (USA) Inc.

—The Sin Within Her Smile. 1994. (Lovejoy Mystery Ser.). 240p. 18.95 o.p. (*0-670-85608-8*, Viking) Viking Penguin.

—The Sleepers of Erin. 1983. (Lovejoy Mystery Ser.). 228p. 13.95 o.p. (*0-525-24163-9*, 01354-410, Dutton) Dutton/Plume.

—The Sleepers of Erin. l.t. ed. 1985. 384p. 15.95 o.p. (*0-7089-1363-6*, Ulverscroft) Thorpe, F. A. Pubs. GBR. *Dist:* Ulverscroft Large Print Bks., Ltd.

—The Sleepers of Erin. 1984. (Crime Monthly Ser.). 224p. pap. 5.99 o.p. (*0-14-006970-4*, Penguin Bks.) Viking Penguin.

—Spend Game. 1981. (Joan Kahn Bk.). 204p. 9.95 o.p. (*0-89919-030-8*) Houghton Mifflin Co.

—Spend Game. unabr. ed. 2000. (Lovejoy Mystery Ser.). audio 53.00 (*1-84197-045-X*, H1050E7, Clipper Audio) Recorded Bks., LLC.

—Spend Game. l.t. ed. 1981. 360p. 12.00 o.p. (*0-7089-0673-7*, Ulverscroft) Thorpe, F. A. Pubs. GBR. *Dist:* Ulverscroft Large Print Bks., Ltd.

—Spend Game. 1982. (Crime Monthly Ser.). 208p. pap. 5.95 o.p. (*0-14-006190-8*, Penguin Bks.) Viking Penguin.

—The Tartan Sell. 1990. (Lovejoy Mystery Ser.). 24p. pap. 5.99 (*0-14-014596-6*, Penguin Bks.) Penguin Group (USA) Inc.

—The Tartan Sell. 1986. 240p. 14.95 o.p. (*0-312-78614-X*) St. Martin's Pr.

—The Tartan Sell. 1987. (Lovejoy Mystery Ser.). 240p. pap. 3.95 o.p. (*0-14-009745-7*, Penguin Bks.) Viking Penguin.

—The Vatican Rip. 1982. (Joan Kahn Bk.). 228p. 10.95 o.p. (*0-89919-080-4*) Houghton Mifflin Co.

—The Vatican Rip. l.t. ed. 1984. 368p. 15.95 o.p. (*0-7089-1101-3*, Ulverscroft) Thorpe, F. A. Pubs. GBR. *Dist:* Ulverscroft Large Print Bks., Ltd.

—The Vatican Rip. 1983. (Lovejoy Mystery Ser.). 224p. pap. 5.99 o.s.i (*0-14-006431-1*, Penguin Bks.) Viking Penguin.

—The Very Last Gambado. 1991. (Crime Monthly Ser.). 288p. reprint ed. pap. 5.95 o.p. (*0-14-014738-1*, Penguin Bks.) Penguin Group (USA) Inc.

—The Very Last Gambado. 1990. 18.95 o.p. (*0-312-05175-1*) St. Martin's Pr.

—The Very Last Gambado. l.t. ed. 1991. (Ulverscroft Large Print Ser.). 29.99 o.p. (*0-7089-2532-4*, Ulverscroft) Thorpe, F. A. Pubs. GBR. *Dist:* Ulverscroft Large Print Bks., Ltd., Ulverscroft Large Print Canada, Ltd.

**LOVELACE, CLARISSE (FICTITIOUS CHARACTER)—FICTION**

Aldyne, Nathan. The Canary. 1986. (Orig.). mass mkt. 3.50 o.s.i (*0-345-33167-2*) Ballantine Bks.

—Canary: A Daniel Valentine & Clarisse Lovelace Mystery. 1999. 188p. (Orig.). reprint ed. pap. 10.00 o.p. (*1-55583-443-4*, Alyson Bks.) Alyson Pubns.

—Cobalt. 1998. (Daniel Valentine & Clarisse Lovelace Mystery Ser.: Vol. 2). 200p. pap. 10.00 o.p. (*1-55583-441-8*) Alyson Pubns.

—Cobalt. 1985. 208p. mass mkt. 2.95 o.s.i (*0-345-32705-5*) Ballantine Bks.

—Cobalt. 1982. 224p. pap. 2.75 o.p. (*0-380-81117-0*, 81117-0, Avon Bks.) Morrow/Avon.

—Cobalt. 1982. 168p. 9.95 o.p. (*0-312-14515-2*) St. Martin's Pr.

—Slate: A Daniel Valentine & Clarissa Lovelace Mystery. 1999. 234p. reprint ed. pap. 10.00 (*1-55583-442-6*) Alyson Pubns.

—Slate: A Daniel Valentine & Clarissa Walker Mystery. 1985. 192p. mass mkt. 3.50 o.s.i (*0-345-31366-6*, Ballantine Bks.) Ballantine Bks.

—Slate: A Daniel Valentine & Clarissa Walker Mystery. 1984. 12.95 o.p. (*0-394-53697-5*, Villard Bks.) Random House Adult Trade Publishing Group.

—Vermilion. 1997. 220p. pap. 10.95 o.p. (*1-55583-434-5*) Alyson Pubns.

—Vermilion. 1980. pap. 2.25 o.p. (*0-380-76596-9*, 81570-2, Avon Bks.) Morrow/Avon.

**LOWELL, CRAIG (FICTITIOUS CHARACTER)—FICTION**

Griffin, W. E. B. The Aviators. 1989. (Brotherhood of War Ser.: No. 8). 464p. mass mkt. 7.99 (*0-515-10053-6*, Jove) Berkley Publishing Group.

—The Aviators. unabr. collector's ed. 1995. (Brotherhood of War Ser.: No. 8). audio 88.00 (*0-7366-3086-4*, 133384) Books on Tape, Inc.

—The Aviators. 2001. (Brotherhood of War Ser.: No. 8). 18.95 (*0-399-13683-5*) Penguin Group (USA) Inc.

—The Aviators. 1988. (Brotherhood of War Ser.: No. 8). 416p. 18.95 o.p. (*0-399-13380-1*, G. P. Putnam's Sons) Penguin Putnam Bks. for Young Readers.

—The Aviators. abr. ed. 1989. (Brotherhood of War Ser.: No. 8). audio 14.95 (*0-671-67501-X*, Simon & Schuster Audioworks) Simon & Schuster Audio.

—The Berets. 1986. (Brotherhood of War Ser.: No. 5). 416p. mass mkt. 7.99 (*0-515-09020-4*, Jove) Berkley Publishing Group.

—The Berets. unabr. ed. 1995. (Brotherhood of War Ser.: No. 5). audio 88.00 Books on Tape, Inc.

—The Berets. 1992. (Brotherhood of War Ser.: No. 5). o.p. (*0-7126-2515-1*) Random Hse. UK, Ltd. GBR. *Dist:* Random Hse. of Canada, Ltd.

—Brotherhood of War Bk. 4: The Generals. unabr. collector's ed. 1995. audio 72.00 (*0-7366-3028-7*, 3710) Books on Tape, Inc.

—Brotherhood of War Boxed Set: The Berets; The Generals; The New Breed; The Aviators. (Brotherhood of War Ser.: Nos. 5-8). 1992. 23.96 o.s.i (*0-515-11026-4*); 1991. 22.90 o.s.i (*0-515-10773-5*); 1989. 19.35 o.s.i (*0-515-10228-8*) Berkley Publishing Group. (Jove).

—Brotherhood of War Boxed Set: The Captains; The Majors. 1987. (Brotherhood of War Ser.: Nos. 2-3). 13.50 o.s.i (*0-515-09435-8*, Jove) Berkley Publishing Group.

—Brotherhood of War Boxed Set: The Colonels; The Generals; The New Breed. 1988. (Brotherhood of War Ser.: Nos. 4, 6, 7). 13.50 o.s.i (*0-515-09891-4*, Jove) Berkley Publishing Group.

—Brotherhood of War Boxed Set: The Lieutenants; The Captains; The Majors. 1987. (Brotherhood of War Ser.: Nos. 1-3). 13.50 o.s.i (*0-515-09433-1*, Jove) Berkley Publishing Group.

—Brotherhood of War Boxed Set: The Lieutenants; The Captains; The Majors; The Colonels. (Brotherhood of War Ser.: Nos. 1-4). 1992. 23.96 o.s.i (*0-515-11024-8*); 1991. 22.90 o.s.i (*0-515-10771-9*); 1989. 19.80 o.s.i (*0-515-10226-1*) Berkley Publishing Group. (Jove).

—The Captains. (Brotherhood of War Ser.: No. 2). (*0-515-09013-1*); 1986. 416p. mass mkt. 7.99 (*0-515-09138-3*); 1982. mass mkt. 3.95 o.s.i (*0-515-06444-0*); 1982. mass mkt. 3.50 o.s.i (*0-515-05644-8*) Berkley Publishing Group. (Jove).

—The Colonels. 1986. (Brotherhood of War Ser.: No. 4). 480p. mass mkt. 7.99 (*0-515-09022-0*, Jove) Berkley Publishing Group.

—The Colonels. 1992. (Brotherhood of War Ser.: No. 4). o.p. (*0-7126-2510-0*) Random Hse. UK, Ltd. GBR. *Dist:* Random Hse. of Canada, Ltd.

—The Generals. 1986. (Brotherhood of War Ser.: No. 6). 384p. mass mkt. 7.99 (*0-515-08455-7*, Jove) Berkley Publishing Group.

—The Lieutenants. (Brotherhood of War Ser.: No. 1). 1986. 416p. mass mkt. 7.99 (0-515-09021-2); 1982. mass mkt. 3.95 o.s.i (0-515-06443-2); 1982. mass mkt. 3.50 o.s.i (0-515-05643-X) Berkley Publishing Group. (Jove).
—The Lieutenants. unabr. collector's ed. 1995. (Brotherhood of War Ser.: No. 1). audio 88.00 (0-7366-2916-5, 3613) Books on Tape, Inc.
—The Majors. (Brotherhood of War Ser.: No. 3). 1986. 384p. mass mkt. 7.99 (0-515-08995-8); 1983. mass mkt. 3.95 o.s.i (0-515-06447-5); 1983. mass mkt. 3.50 o.s.i (0-515-05645-6) Berkley Publishing Group. (Jove).
—The Majors. unabr. collector's ed. 1995. (Brotherhood of War Ser.: No. 4). audio 80.00 (0-7366-2981-5, 3672) Books on Tape, Inc.
—The New Breed. 1988. (Brotherhood of War Ser.: No. 7). 384p. mass mkt. 7.99 (0-515-09226-6, Jove) Berkley Publishing Group.
—The New Breed. unabr. ed. 1996. (Brotherhood of War Ser.: No. 7). audio 88.00. audio Books on Tape, Inc.
—The New Breed. 1987. (Brotherhood of War Ser.: No. 7). 416p. 16.95 o.p. (0-399-13305-4, G. P. Putnam's Sons) Penguin Putnam Bks. for Young Readers.

**LOWELL, TONY (FICTITIOUS CHARACTER)—FICTION**

Ayres, E. C. Eye of the Gator. 1995. 320p. 22.95 o.p. (0-312-13490-8, Saint Martin's Minotaur) St. Martin's Pr.
—Hour of the Manatee Vol. 1. 1995. (Tony Lowell Mysteries Ser.). 296p. mass mkt. 4.99 (0-312-95406-9, St. Martin's Paperbacks) St. Martin's Pr.
—Night of the Panther. 1997. (Tony Lowell Mysteries Ser.). 272p. 22.95 o.p. (0-312-15607-3, Saint Martin's Minotaur) St. Martin's Pr.

**LOWENKOPF, SHELLY (FICTITIOUS CHARACTER)—FICTION**

Fliegel, Richard. The Man Who Murdered Himself. Chelius, Jane, ed. 1994. 288p. (Orig.). mass mkt. 4.99 (0-671-74451-8, Pocket) Simon & Schuster.

**LOWRY, GIDEON (FICTITIOUS CHARACTER)—FICTION**

Leslie, John. Blue Moon. 1998. (Gideon Lowry Mystery Ser.: Vol. 4). 256p. 23.00 o.s.i (0-671-53514-5, Atria) Simon & Schuster.
—Killing Me Softly. Grose, Bill, ed. (Orig.). 1995. 272p. mass mkt. 5.50 (0-671-86421-1, Pocket); 1994. 256p. 20.00 (0-671-86420-3, Atria) Simon & Schuster.
—Love for Sale. 1997. (Gideon Lowry Mystery Ser.). 272p. pap. 6.50 (0-671-51126-2, Pocket) Simon & Schuster.
—Love for Sale: A Gideon Lowry Mystery. 1997. 272p. 22.00 (0-671-51127-0, Atria) Simon & Schuster.
—Night & Day. 256p. 2002. pap. 17.95 (0-7434-7025-7); 1996. mass mkt. 5.99 (0-671-86423-8) Simon & Schuster. (Pocket).
—Night & Day: A Gideon Lowry Mystery. Grose, William, ed. 1995. 256p. (Orig.). pap. 20.00 o.p. (0-671-86422-X, Atria) Simon & Schuster.

**LUCIA (FICTITIOUS CHARACTER)—FICTION**

Benson, E. F. Lucia in London. (Make Way for Lucia Ser.: Pt. 2). 1984. 320p. pap. 3.95 o.p. (0-06-080695-8, P695); Pt. II. 1987. 256p. pap. 12.00 o.p. (0-06-091373-8, PL 1373) HarperTrade. (Perennial).
—Lucia in London. unabr. ed. 2002. audio compact disk 84.95 (0-7531-1537-9) ISIS Audio Bks. GBR. *Dist:* Ulverscroft Large Print Bks., Ltd.
—Lucia in London. 1999. 232p. pap. 11.95 (1-55921-277-2) Moyer Bell.
—Lucia's Progress. 2000. (Lucia Ser.). 230p. pap. 11.95 (1-55921-233-0) Moyer Bell.
—Mapp & Lucia. 1986. pap. o.s.i (0-552-99084-1, Corgi) Bantam Bks.
—Mapp & Lucia. (Make Way for Lucia Ser.: Pt. 4). 320p. 1984. mass mkt. 3.95 o.p. (0-06-080714-8, P 714); Pt. IV. 1986. reprint ed. pap. 12.00 o.p. (0-06-091328-2, PL 1328) HarperTrade. (Perennial).
—Mapp & Lucia. 2000. (Illus.). 277p. pap. 12.95 (1-55921-232-2) Moyer Bell.
—Mapp & Lucia. 2000. (Humour Classics Ser.). 315p. 14.95 (1-85375-390-4) Prion GBR. *Dist:* Trafalgar Square.
—Miss Mapp. unabr. ed. 1999. audio 41.95 (1-55685-587-7) Audio Bk. Contractors, Inc.
—Miss Mapp. 1986. pap. o.s.i (0-552-99083-3, Corgi) Bantam Bks.
—Miss Mapp, Pt. III. (Make Way for Lucia Ser.). 1987. 272p. pap. 5.95 o.p. (0-06-091374-6); 1984. mass mkt. 3.95 o.p. (0-06-080696-6) HarperTrade. (Perennial).
—Miss Mapp. 1999. 232p. pap. 11.95 (1-55921-275-6) Moyer Bell.
Holt, Tom. Lucia Triumphant. 2004. (Lucia Ser.). 224p. pap. 12.95 (1-55921-310-8) Moyer Bell.

**LUCKS, JOLAYNE (FICTITIOUS CHARACTER)—FICTION**

Hiaasen, Carl. Lucky You. aut. ed. 1997. 24.00 o.s.i (0-676-54009-0) Random Hse., Inc.
—Lucky You. deluxe ltd. ed. 1997. 368p. 150.00 (1-890885-01-0) Trice, B.E. Publishing.
—Lucky You. 1998. 496p. reprint ed. mass mkt. 7.99 (0-446-60465-8) Warner Bks., Inc.

**LUFT, BUNNY (FICTITIOUS CHARACTER)—FICTION**

Cohen, Martin S. The Truth about Marvin Kalish. 1992. 288p. lib. bdg. 22.95 o.p. (0-914539-04-3) Ben-Simon Pubns.
—The Truth about Marvin Kalish: A Mystery. 1992. 280p. pap. 13.95 (0-914539-05-1) Ben-Simon Pubns.

**LUGER, DAVID (FICTITIOUS CHARACTER)—FICTION**

Brown, Dale. Flight of the Old Dog. Breslin, Ed, ed. 1988. 416p. reprint ed. mass mkt. 7.99 (0-425-10893-7); mass mkt. 4.50 o.s.i (0-425-11089-3) Berkley Publishing Group.
—Flight of the Old Dog. 1987. 352p. 18.95 o.p. (1-55611-034-0) Fine, Donald I. Bks.
—Night of the Hawk. 1993. 576p. mass mkt. 7.99 (0-425-13661-2) Berkley Publishing Group.
—Night of the Hawk. 1992. 400p. 22.95 o.p. (0-399-13739-4, G. P. Putnam's Sons) Penguin Group (USA) Inc.
—Night of the Hawk. 22.95 o.s.i (0-399-13904-4) Putnam Publishing Group, The.

**LUMSEY, NORA (FICTITIOUS CHARACTER)—FICTION**

Schanker, D. R. A Criminal Appeal. 2000. 352p. mass mkt. 5.99 o.s.i (0-440-23581-2) Dell Publishing.
—A Criminal Appeal. 1998. 288p. 23.95 (0-312-19253-3, Saint Martin's Minotaur) St. Martin's Pr.
—Natural Law. 2001. 242p. 22.95 (0-312-26684-7, Saint Martin's Minotaur) St. Martin's Pr.

**LUNT, HENRY (FICTITIOUS CHARACTER)—FICTION**

McNamara, Tom. Henry Lunt & the Ranger. 1992. pap. 5.95 (0-9625632-2-6) NUVENTURES Publishing.
—Henry Lunt & the Ranger: A Novel of Espionage & High Adventure During the American Revolution. McNamara, Ellen, ed. 1991. (Illus.). 352p. 18.95 (0-9625632-3-4) NUVENTURES Publishing.
—Henry Lunt & the Spymaster. 1994. (Henry Lunt Adventures Ser.: No. 2). 429p. pap. 10.95 (0-9625632-5-0) NUVENTURES Publishing.

**LUPA, AUGUST (FICTITIOUS CHARACTER)—FICTION**

Lescroart, John. Rasputin's Revenge. 1988. 288p. reprint ed. pap. 3.50 (0-8439-2671-6) Dorchester Publishing Co., Inc.
—Rasputin's Revenge. 2003. 288p. pap. 14.00 (0-451-20981-8) NAL.
—Rasputin's Revenge: The Further Startling Adventures of Auguste Lupa—Son of Holmes. 1987. 288p. 17.95 o.s.i (1-55611-011-1) Fine, Donald I. Bks.
—Son of Holmes. l.t. ed. 1991. 19.95 o.p. (0-7927-0735-4, CH018); pap. 17.95 o.p. (0-7927-0736-2, CS0122) BBC Audiobooks America.
—Son of Holmes. 1987. 256p. reprint ed. pap. 3.25 o.s.i (0-8439-2461-6) Dorchester Publishing Co., Inc.
—Son of Holmes. 1986. 223p. 15.95 o.s.i (0-917657-64-0) Fine, Donald I. Bks.
—Son of Holmes. 2003. 256p. pap. 14.00 (0-451-20875-7) NAL.
—Son of Holmes & Rasputin's Revenge: The Early Works of John T. Lescroart. 1995. 544p. pap. 16.95 o.s.i (1-55611-437-0) Fine, Donald I. Bks.

**LUTHER, DOC (FICTITIOUS CHARACTER)—FICTION**

Thompson, Jim. Recoil. 1985. 192p. reprint ed. pap. 3.95 o.p. (0-916870-89-8, Black Mask) Creative Arts Bk. Co.
—Recoil. 1992. 192p. pap. 10.00 o.s.i (0-679-73308-6, Vintage) Knopf Publishing Group.

**LYNCH, JACK (FICTITIOUS CHARACTER)—FICTION**

Womack, Steven. Murphy's Fault. 1990. 320p. 17.95 o.p. (0-312-03896-8, Saint Martin's Minotaur); Vol. 1. 1991. mass mkt. 3.99 o.p. (0-312-92539-5, St. Martin's Paperbacks) St. Martin's Pr.
—Smash Cut. 3.98 o.s.i (0-8317-4629-7) Smithmark Pubs., Inc.
—Smash Cut. 1991. 304p. 18.95 o.p. (0-312-06467-5, Saint Martin's Minotaur) St. Martin's Pr.
—The Software Bomb. 3.98 o.p. (0-8317-4632-7) Smithmark Pubs., Inc.
—The Software Bomb. 1993. 288p. 19.95 o.p. (0-312-09390-X, Saint Martin's Minotaur) St. Martin's Pr.

**LYNDHURST, JOANNA (FICTITIOUS CHARACTER)—FICTION**

Smith, Carol. Charmed Circle. 1998. 355p. 24.00 o.p. (0-446-52238-4) Warner Bks., Inc.
—The Charmed Circle. 1999. 352p. mass mkt. 6.99 (0-446-60704-5) Warner Bks., Inc.

**LYNLEY, THOMAS (FICTITIOUS CHARACTER)—FICTION**

George, Elizabeth. Deception on His Mind. 1998. 752p. mass mkt. 7.99 (0-553-57509-0); mass mkt. 6.99 (0-553-84018-5) Bantam Bks.
—Deception on His Mind, Pt. A. unabr. ed. 1997. audio 64.00 (0-7366-3827-X, 4495-A) Books on Tape, Inc.
—Deception on His Mind. abr. ed. 1997. audio 24.95 (0-553-47818-4, 695229, RH Audio) Random Hse. Audio Publishing Group.
—Deception on His Mind. l.t. ed. 1997. (Basic Ser.). 1021p. 29.95 (0-7862-1144-X) Thorndike Pr.
—For the Sake of Elena. 1993. 464p. mass mkt. 7.99 (0-553-56127-8) Bantam Bks.
—For the Sake of Elena. unabr. ed. 1993. audio 88.00 (0-7366-2385-X, 3156) Books on Tape, Inc.
—For the Sake of Elena. l.t. ed. 1993. (Magna Large Print Ser.). 659p. o.p. (0-7505-0497-8) Magna Large Print Bks. GBR. *Dist:* Ulverscroft Large Print Canada, Ltd.
—For the Sake of Elena. abr. ed. 1992. audio 15.99 (0-553-47034-5, 390797, RH Audio) Random Hse. Audio Publishing Group.
—A Great Deliverance. 1989. 432p. mass mkt. 7.50 (0-553-27802-9) Bantam Bks.
—A Great Deliverance. unabr. ed. 1994. audio 64.00 (0-7366-2624-7, 3364) Books on Tape, Inc.
—A Great Deliverance. abr. ed. 1992. 180p. pap. 15.99 incl. audio (0-553-47056-6, RH Audio) Random Hse. Audio Publishing Group.
—In Pursuit of the Proper Sinner. 2000. 752p. mass mkt. 7.99 (0-553-57510-4) Bantam Bks.
—In Pursuit of the Proper Sinner. 1999. Pt. 1. audio 64.00 (0-7366-4652-3, 5033-A); Pt. 2. audio 64.00 (0-7366-4722-8, 5033-B) Books on Tape, Inc.
—In Pursuit of the Proper Sinner. l.t. ed. 1999. pap. 25.95 o.p. (0-7838-8692-6, Macmillan Reference USA) Gale Group.
—In Pursuit of the Proper Sinner, Set. abr. ed. 1999. audio 25.95 Highsmith Inc.
—In Pursuit of the Proper Sinner. abr. ed. 1999. audio 25.95 (0-553-47819-2, RH Audio) Random Hse. Audio Publishing Group.
—In Pursuit of the Proper Sinner. l.t. ed. 912p. 2000. pap. 14.95 (0-375-72799-X); 1999. 25.95 (0-375-40846-0) Random Hse. Large Print.
—In the Presence of the Enemy. 1997. 656p. mass mkt. 7.99 (0-553-57608-9) Bantam Bks.
—In the Presence of the Enemy. unabr. ed. 1996. audio 120.00 (0-7366-3278-6, 3934) Books on Tape, Inc.
—In the Presence of the Enemy. unabr. ed. 2000. (Inspector Thomas Lynley Mystery Ser.: Vol. 8). audio 128.00 (0-7887-0523-7, 94718E7) Recorded Bks., LLC.
—Missing Joseph. 1994. 592p. mass mkt. 7.99 (0-553-56604-0) Bantam Bks.
—Missing Joseph. unabr. ed. 1993. audio 104.00 (0-7366-2533-X, 3285) Books on Tape, Inc.
—Missing Joseph. l.t. ed. 1993. 12.95 o.p. (1-56895-038-1, Wheeler Publishing, Inc.) Gale Group.
—Payment in Blood. 1990. 432p. mass mkt. 7.99 (0-553-28436-3) Bantam Bks.
—Payment in Blood. unabr. ed. 1994. audio 72.00 (0-7366-2637-9, 3376) Books on Tape, Inc.
—Payment in Blood. unabr. ed. 2001. audio 69.95 (1-85089-779-4, 30691) ISIS Audio Bks. GBR. *Dist:* Ulverscroft Large Print Bks., Ltd.
—Payment in Blood. unabr. ed. 1992. (Inspector Thomas Lynley Mystery Ser.: Vol. 2). audio 85.00 (1-55690-762-1, 92426E7) Recorded Bks., LLC.
—Playing for the Ashes. 1995. 704p. mass mkt. 7.99 (0-553-57251-2, Crimeline) Bantam Bks.
—Playing for the Ashes, Pt. 1. unabr. ed. 1994. audio 64.00 (0-7366-2885-1, 3587-A) Books on Tape, Inc.
—A Suitable Vengeance. 1992. 464p. mass mkt. 7.99 (0-553-29560-8) Bantam Bks.
—A Suitable Vengeance. unabr. ed. 1994. audio 80.00 (0-7366-2796-0, 3511) Books on Tape, Inc.
—A Suitable Vengeance. l.t. ed. 1993. (Magna Large Print Ser.). 653p. o.p. (0-7505-0456-0) Magna Large Print Bks. GBR. *Dist:* Ulverscroft Large Print Canada, Ltd.
—A Suitable Vengeance. abr. ed. 1991. audio 15.99 (0-553-45286-X, RH Audio) Random Hse. Audio Publishing Group.
—A Suitable Vengeance. unabr. ed. 1993. (Inspector Thomas Lynley Mystery Ser.: Vol. 4). audio 97.00 (1-55690-812-1, 93121E7) Recorded Bks., LLC.
—A Traitor to Memory. 2002. mass mkt. 7.99 (0-553-84037-1) Bantam Bks.
—Well-Schooled in Murder. 1991. 432p. mass mkt. 7.99 (0-553-28734-6); 1990. 368p. 17.95 o.s.i (0-553-07000-2) Bantam Bks.
—Well-Schooled in Murder. unabr. ed. 1993. audio 80.00 (0-7366-2602-6, 3346) Books on Tape, Inc.
—Well-Schooled in Murder. abr. ed. 1991. audio 15.99 (0-553-45278-9, 391880, RH Audio) Random Hse. Audio Publishing Group.

**LYNX, JASON (FICTITIOUS CHARACTER)—FICTION**

Orde, A. J., pseud. Dead on Sunday. 1994. (Southwest Mysteries Ser.). mass mkt. 4.99 o.s.i (0-449-22282-9, Fawcett) Ballantine Bks.
—Dead on Sunday. l.t. ed. 1995. (Dales Large Print Ser.). 400p. pap. o.p. (1-85389-529-6) Dales Large Print Bks. GBR. *Dist:* Ulverscroft Large Print Canada, Ltd.
—Death & the Dogwalker. 1993. mass mkt. 4.50 o.s.i (0-449-22027-3, Fawcett) Ballantine Bks.
—Death for Old Times' Sake. 1993. mass mkt. 4.50 o.s.i (0-449-22193-8, Fawcett) Ballantine Bks.
—Death for Old Times' Sake. 1992. 240p. 16.50 o.s.i (0-385-41941-4) Doubleday Publishing.
—A Little Neighborhood Murder. 1992. mass mkt. 4.50 o.s.i (0-449-22026-5, Fawcett) Ballantine Bks.
—A Little Neighborhood Murder. l.t. ed. 1992. (Linford Mystery Library). 448p. pap. 17.99 o.p. (0-7089-7163-6, Linford) Thorpe, F. A. Pubs. GBR. *Dist:* Ulverscroft Large Print Bks., Ltd., Ulverscroft Large Print Canada, Ltd.
—A Long Time Dead. 1995. mass mkt. 5.50 o.s.i (0-449-22359-0, Fawcett) Ballantine Bks.
Orde, A. J., pseud & Tepper, Sheri S. Death of Innocents. 1997. (Jason Lynx Mystery Ser.). mass mkt. 5.99 o.s.i (0-449-22519-4, Fawcett) Ballantine Bks.

**LYNX, PHILIP (FICTITIOUS CHARACTER)—FICTION**

*see Flinx of the Commonwealth (Fictitious Character)—Fiction*

**LYON, THOMAS (FICTITIOUS CHARACTER)—FICTION**

Francis, Dick. Wild Horses. 352p. 2004. mass mkt. 6.99 (0-425-19674-7); 1995. mass mkt. 6.99 (0-515-11723-4, Jove); 1995. pap. 5.99 o.s.i (0-515-11789-7, Jove) Berkley Publishing Group.
—Wild Horses. unabr. ed. 1995. audio 56.00 (0-7366-2970-X, 3631) Books on Tape, Inc.
—Wild Horses. l.t. ed. 1994. (Large Print Bks.). 26.95 o.p. (1-56895-123-X, Wheeler Publishing, Inc.) Gale Group.
—Wild Horses. 1994. 320p. 22.95 o.p. (0-399-13974-5, G. P. Putnam's Sons) Penguin Group (USA) Inc.
—Wild Horses. unabr. ed. 2000. audio 60.00 (0-7887-0265-3, 94474E7) Recorded Bks., LLC.
—Wild Horses. 1999. pap. 9.98 (0-671-04424-9); Set. 1994. audio 17.00 (0-671-87971-5, 391913) Simon & Schuster Audio. (Simon & Schuster Audioworks).

## M

**MABRY, BUBBA (FICTITIOUS CHARACTER)—FICTION**

Brewer, Steve. Baby Face. 2000. (Bubba Mabry Mystery Ser.). 256p. mass mkt. 5.95 (1-890768-20-0, Intrigue Pr.) Corvus Publishing.
—Baby Face. 1995. (Illus.). 256p. (J). mass mkt. 5.50 (0-671-74735-5, Pocket) Simon & Schuster.
—Crazy Love. 2001. (Bubba Mabry Mystery Ser.: No. 6). 252p. 23.95 (1-890768-31-6, Intrigue Pr.) Corvus Publishing.
—Crazy Love. 2003. (WWL Mystery Ser.: No. 477). 256p. mass mkt. (0-373-26477-1, Worldwide Library) Harlequin Enterprises, Ltd.
—Dirty Pool. 2003. (WWL Mystery Ser.: No. 462). 272p. mass mkt. (0-373-26462-3, Worldwide Library) Harlequin Enterprises, Ltd.
—Dirty Pool. 1999. 272p. 23.95 o.p. (0-312-20203-2, Saint Martin's Minotaur) St. Martin's Pr.
—Lonely Street. unabr. ed. 1999. (Bubba Mabry Mystery Ser.). audio 39.95 (1-55686-867-7) Books in Motion.
—Lonely Street. 1999. (Bubba Mabry Mystery Ser.: No. 1). 256p. mass mkt. 5.95 (1-890768-19-7, Intrigue Pr.) Corvus Publishing.
—Lonely Street. Grad, Doug, ed. 1994. 224p. mass mkt. 4.99 (0-671-74734-7, Pocket) Simon & Schuster.
—Shaky Ground. 2003. (WWL Mystery Ser.: No. 454). 256p. mass mkt. (0-373-26454-2, Worldwide Library) Harlequin Enterprises, Ltd.
—Shaky Ground. 1997. 233p. 22.95 o.p. (0-312-15652-9, Saint Martin's Minotaur) St. Martin's Pr.
—Witchy Woman. 1996. 208p. 21.95 o.p. (0-312-14076-2, Saint Martin's Minotaur) St. Martin's Pr.
—Witchy Woman: A Bubba Mabry P. I. Mystery. 1999. (Bubba Mabry Mystery Ser.). 256p. reprint ed. mass mkt. 5.95 (1-890768-13-8, Intrigue Pr.) Corvus Publishing.

**MCALISTER, HALEY (FICTITIOUS CHARACTER)—FICTION**

Kiecolt-Glaser, Janice K. Detecting Lies. 1997. 256p. (Orig.). mass mkt. 5.50 (*0-380-78991-4*, Avon Bks.) Morrow/Avon.

—Unconscious Truths. 1998. mass mkt. 5.99 (*0-380-78992-2*, Avon Bks.) Morrow/Avon.

**MACALISTER, MARTI (FICTITIOUS CHARACTER)—FICTION**

Bland, Eleanor Taylor. Dead Time. 1993. 304p. mass mkt. 4.99 o.s.i (*0-451-40427-0*, Signet Bks.) NAL.

—Dead Time: A Marti MacAlister Mystery. 1992. 224p. 17.95 o.p. (*0-312-07053-5*, Saint Martin's Minotaur) St. Martin's Pr.

—Done Wrong. 1996. mass mkt. 5.99 (*0-312-95794-7*, St. Martin's Paperbacks); 1995. 216p. 20.95 o.p. (*0-312-13053-8*, Saint Martin's Minotaur) St. Martin's Pr.

—Fatal Remains. 2003. 288p. 23.95 (*0-312-30097-2*, Saint Martin's Minotaur) St. Martin's Pr.

—Gone Quiet. 1995. 336p. mass mkt. 4.99 o.s.i (*0-451-18267-7*, Signet Bks.) NAL.

—Gone Quiet: A Marti MacAlister Mystery. 1994. 224p. 19.95 o.p. (*0-312-11018-9*, Saint Martin's Minotaur) St. Martin's Pr.

—Keep Still. l.t. ed. 1996. (G. K. Hall Mystery Ser.). 316p. 21.95 o.p. (*0-7838-1931-5*, Macmillan Reference USA) Gale Group.

—Keep Still. 1996. 224p. 20.95 o.p. (*0-312-14318-4*, Saint Martin's Minotaur); Vol. 1. 1998. 240p. mass mkt. 5.99 (*0-312-96172-3*, St. Martin's Paperbacks) St. Martin's Pr.

—Scream in Silence. 2001. 320p. reprint ed. mass mkt. 6.50 (*0-312-97494-9*, 20-3259, St. Martin's Paperbacks) St. Martin's Pr.

—Scream in Silence: A Marti MacAlister Mystery. 2000. 290p. 23.95 (*0-312-20378-0*, Saint Martin's Minotaur) St. Martin's Pr.

—See No Evil. (Marti MacAlister Ser.). 288p. 1999. mass mkt. 5.99 (*0-312-96818-3*, St. Martin's Paperbacks); 1998. 22.95 o.p. (*0-312-16910-8*, Saint Martin's Minotaur) St. Martin's Pr.

—See No Evil. l.t. ed. 1998. (Core Ser.). 392p. 29.95 (*0-7838-0112-2*) Thorndike Pr.

—Slow Burn. 1994. 320p. mass mkt. 4.99 o.s.i (*0-451-17944-7*, Signet Bks.) NAL.

—Slow Burn: A Marti MacAlister Mystery. 1993. 224p. 17.95 (*0-312-09237-7*, Saint Martin's Minotaur) St. Martin's Pr.

—Tell No Tales: A Marti MacAlister Mystery. l.t. ed. 1999. (Wheeler Large Print Book Ser.). 352p. pap. 23.95 (*1-56895-756-4*, Wheeler Publishing, Inc.) Gale Group.

—Tell No Tales: A Marti MacAlister Mystery. (Marti MacAlister Ser.). 2000. 288p. mass mkt. 5.99 (*0-312-97113-3*, St. Martin's Paperbacks); 1999. vii, 264p. 22.95 o.p. (*0-312-20067-6*, Saint Martin's Minotaur) St. Martin's Pr.

—Whispers in the Dark. l.t. ed. 2002. 28.95 o.p. (*1-58724-187-0*, Wheeler Publishing, Inc.) Gale Group.

—Whispers in the Dark. mass mkt. (*0-312-97990-8*, St. Martin's Paperbacks); 2001. 244p. 23.95 (*0-312-20379-9*, Saint Martin's Minotaur) St. Martin's Pr.

—Windy City Dying: A Marti MacAlister Mystery. 320p. 2003. pap. 13.95 (*0-312-32048-5*, Saint Martin's Griffin); 2002. 24.95 (*0-312-30098-0*, Saint Martin's Minotaur) St. Martin's Pr.

**MACALPIN, ALASTAIR (FICTITIOUS CHARACTER)—FICTION**

Stuart, Anne. Prince of Swords. 1997. (Romance Ser.). 270p. lib. bdg. 22.95 (*0-7862-1116-4*, Five Star) Gale Group.

—Prince of Swords. 1996. 384p. mass mkt. 5.99 o.s.i (*0-8217-5397-5*, Zebra Bks.) Kensington Publishing Corp.

**MCAULIFF, ALEX (FICTITIOUS CHARACTER)—FICTION**

Ludlum, Robert. The Cry of the Halidon. 1996. 448p. mass mkt. 7.99 (*0-553-57614-3*) Bantam Bks.

—The Cry of the Halidon. l.t. ed. 1997. (Wheeler Large Print Book Ser.). 26.95 o.p. (*1-56895-445-X*, Wheeler Publishing, Inc.) Gale Group.

—The Cry of the Halidon, Set. abr. ed. 1996. 24.95 o.p. (*0-7871-1264-X*, 694324) NewStar Media, Inc.

**MCAULIFFE, LARRY (FICTITIOUS CHARACTER)—FICTION**

Greeley, Andrew M. The Cardinal Virtues. 1990. 19.45 o.s.i (*0-446-51478-0*) Warner Bks., Inc.

—Cardinal Virtues. 1991. mass mkt. 5.95 o.s.i (*0-446-36094-5*) Warner Bks., Inc.

—The Cardinal Virtues. l.t. ed. 1992. 16.95 o.p. (*0-7927-0650-1*); 1991. 21.95 o.p. (*0-7927-0624-2*, E0009) BBC Audiobooks America.

**MACBETH, HAMISH (FICTITIOUS CHARACTER)—FICTION**

Beaton, M. C., pseud. Death of a Cad. 1988. mass mkt. 4.99 o.s.i (*0-8041-0225-2*, Ivy Bks.) Ballantine Bks.

—Death of a Cad. l.t. ed. 1995. 265p. pap. 17.95 (*0-7838-1457-7*, Macmillan Reference USA) Gale Group.

—Death of a Cad. unabr. ed. 1999. audio 46.00 (*0-7887-4080-6*, H1074E7, Clipper Audio) Recorded Bks., LLC.

—Death of a Cad. 1986. 208p. 13.95 o.p. (*0-312-00118-5*) St. Martin's Pr.

—Death of a Cad. 2000. 222p. pap. 6.95 o.p. (*0-553-40792-9*) Transworld Publishers Ltd. GBR. *Dist:* Trafalgar Square.

—Death of a Cad. 2004. mass mkt. (*0-446-60714-2*) Warner Bks., Inc.

—Death of a Celebrity. l.t. ed. 2002. 264p. 26.95 (*1-58724-152-8*, Wheeler Publishing, Inc.) Gale Group.

—Death of a Celebrity. 2002. 272p. 23.95 (*0-89296-676-9*) Mysterious Pr.

—Death of a Celebrity. 2003. 304p. mass mkt. 6.99 (*0-446-61204-9*) Warner Bks., Inc.

—Death of a Charming Man. 2001. 208p. 18.95 (*0-89296-529-0*) Mysterious Pr.

—Death of a Charming Man. unabr. ed. 1997. (Hamish Macbeth Mystery Ser.). audio 44.00 (*0-7887-1084-2*, 95088E7) Recorded Bks., LLC.

—Death of a Charming Man. 1995. (Hamish Macbeth Mystery Ser.). 176p. reprint ed. mass mkt. 6.99 (*0-446-40338-5*) Warner Bks., Inc.

—Death of a Dentist. 2001. 256p. 22.00 (*0-89296-643-2*); E-Book 4.95 (*0-446-92301-X*); E-Book 4.95 (*0-446-91295-6*) Mysterious Pr.

—Death of a Dentist. unabr. ed. 1998. (Hamish Macbeth Mystery Ser.). audio 44.00 (*0-7887-2044-9*, 95408E7) Recorded Bks., LLC.

—Death of a Dentist. 1998. (Hamish Macbeth Mystery Ser.). 256p. mass mkt. 6.99 (*0-446-60601-4*); mass mkt. (*0-446-40494-2*, Mysterious Pr. Paperback Bks.) Warner Bks., Inc.

—Death of a Dustman. 2001. (Hamish Macbeth Mystery Ser.). 215p. 22.95 o.p. (*0-89296-631-9*) Mysterious Pr.

—Death of a Dustman. 2002. (Hamish Macbeth Mystery Ser.). 256p. reprint ed. mass mkt. 6.99 (*0-446-60931-5*) Warner Bks., Inc.

—Death of a Glutton. 1995. 176p. mass mkt. 6.50 (*0-8041-1212-6*, Ivy Bks.) Ballantine Bks.

—Death of a Glutton. l.t. ed. 1996. 17.95 o.p. (*0-7838-1484-4*, Macmillan Reference USA) Gale Group.

—Death of a Glutton. 1993. 152p. 16.95 o.p. (*0-312-08761-6*, Saint Martin's Minotaur) St. Martin's Pr.

—Death of a Glutton. 187p. pap. 6.95 o.p. (*0-553-40972-7*) Transworld Publishers Ltd. GBR. *Dist:* Trafalgar Square.

—Death of a Gossip. l.t. ed. 1986. 13.95 o.p. (*0-89340-955-3*, 254) BBC Audiobooks America.

—Death of a Gossip. 1988. 160p. reprint ed. mass mkt. 4.99 o.s.i (*0-8041-0226-0*, Ivy Bks.) Ballantine Bks.

—Death of a Gossip. l.t. ed. 1996. (Nightingale Ser.). 194p. pap. 17.95 o.p. (*0-7838-1472-0*, Macmillan Reference USA) Gale Group.

—Death of a Gossip. 1985. 192p. 12.95 o.p. (*0-312-18637-1*) St. Martin's Pr.

—Death of a Gossip. 1999. (Hamish Macbeth Mystery Ser.). 192p. reprint ed. mass mkt. 6.99 (*0-446-60713-4*) Warner Bks., Inc.

—Death of a Hussy. 1991. 160p. mass mkt. 6.99 (*0-8041-0768-8*, Ivy Bks.) Ballantine Bks.

—Death of a Hussy. 1990. 160p. 14.95 o.p. (*0-312-05071-2*, Saint Martin's Minotaur) St. Martin's Pr.

—Death of a Hussy. l.t. ed. 1999. (Nightingale Ser.). 208p. pap. 21.95 (*0-7838-8664-0*) Thorndike Pr.

—Death of a Hussy. 2000. pap. 6.95 (*0-553-40967-0*) Transworld Publishers Ltd. GBR. *Dist:* Trafalgar Square.

—Death of a Macho Man. 1996. (Hamish Macbeth Mystery Ser.). 224p. 4.95 o.p. (*0-89296-531-2*) Mysterious Pr.

—Death of a Macho Man. unabr. ed. 1997. (Hamish Macbeth Mystery Ser.: Vol. 12). audio 44.00 (*0-7887-1749-9*, 95227E7) Recorded Bks., LLC.

—Death of a Macho Man. 1997. (Hamish Macbeth Mystery Ser.). 240p. mass mkt. 6.99 (*0-446-40340-7*) Warner Bks., Inc.

—Death of a Nag. 2001. 192p. E-Book 4.95 (*0-446-91296-4*); 18.95 (*0-89296-530-4*); E-Book 4.95 (*0-446-92302-8*) Mysterious Pr.

—Death of a Nag. unabr. ed. 1997. (Hamish Macbeth Mystery Ser.). audio 44.00 (*0-7887-1285-3*, 95147E7) Recorded Bks., LLC.

—Death of a Nag. 1996. (Hamish Macbeth Mystery Ser.). 192p. mass mkt. 5.99 (*0-446-40339-3*) Warner Bks., Inc.

—Death of a Perfect Wife. 1990. mass mkt. 4.99 o.s.i (*0-8041-0593-6*, Ivy Bks.) Ballantine Bks.

—Death of a Perfect Wife. 1989. 224p. 15.95 o.p. (*0-312-03322-2*, Saint Martin's Minotaur) St. Martin's Pr.

—Death of a Perfect Wife. 2000. 202p. pap. 6.95 o.p. (*0-553-40794-5*) Transworld Publishers Ltd. GBR. *Dist:* Trafalgar Square.

—Death of a Poison Pen. 2004. 23.95 (*0-89296-788-9*) Mysterious Pr.

—Death of a Prankster. 1993. (Hamish Macbeth Mystery Ser.: Vol. 7). 176p. mass mkt. 6.50 (*0-8041-1102-2*, Ivy Bks.) Ballantine Bks.

—Death of a Prankster. l.t. ed. 1998. (Hamish Macbeth Mystery Ser.). pap. 19.95 o.p. (*0-7838-8417-6*, Macmillan Reference USA) Gale Group.

—Death of a Prankster. 1992. 160p. 16.95 o.p. (*0-312-07701-7*, Saint Martin's Minotaur) St. Martin's Pr.

—Death of a Prankster. 187p. pap. 6.95 o.p. (*0-553-40969-7*) Transworld Publishers Ltd. GBR. *Dist:* Trafalgar Square.

—Death of a Scriptwriter. 224p. 2001. 22.00 (*0-89296-644-0*); 2001. E-Book 4.95 (*0-446-92314-1*); 1999. E-Book 4.95 (*0-446-91297-2*) Mysterious Pr.

—Death of a Scriptwriter. unabr. ed. 1998. (Hamish Macbeth Mystery Ser.). audio 44.00 (*0-7887-2175-5*, 95471E7) Recorded Bks., LLC.

—Death of a Scriptwriter. 1999. (Hamish Macbeth Mystery Ser.). 224p. reprint ed. mass mkt. 6.99 (*0-446-60698-7*) Warner Bks., Inc.

—Death of a Snob. 1992. (Hamish Macbeth Mystery Ser.). 160p. mass mkt. 6.99 (*0-8041-0912-5*, Ivy Bks.) Ballantine Bks.

—Death of a Snob. l.t. ed. 2000. (G. K. Hall Nightingale Ser.). 210p. 30.00 (*0-7838-8755-8*, Macmillan Reference USA) Gale Group.

—Death of a Snob. 1991. 15.95 o.p. (*0-312-05851-9*, Saint Martin's Minotaur) St. Martin's Pr.

—Death of a Snob. 186p. pap. 6.95 o.p. (*0-553-40968-9*) Transworld Publishers Ltd. GBR. *Dist:* Trafalgar Square.

—Death of a Travelling Man. 1996. 176p. mass mkt. 6.99 (*0-8041-1211-8*, Ivy Bks.) Ballantine Bks.

—Death of a Travelling Man. 1993. (Hamish Macbeth Mystery Ser.). 208p. 17.95 o.p. (*0-312-09783-2*, Saint Martin's Minotaur) St. Martin's Pr.

—Death of a Village. 2003. 274p. 30.95 (*1-58724-441-1*) Gale Group.

—Death of a Village. 2003. (Hamish Macbeth Mystery Ser.). 256p. 23.95 (*0-89296-677-7*) Mysterious Pr.

—Death of a Village. 2004. 272p. mass mkt. 6.99 (*0-446-61371-1*) Warner Bks., Inc.

—Death of an Addict. 2001. (Hamish Macbeth Mystery Ser.). 224p. 22.00 o.p. (*0-89296-675-0*) Mysterious Pr.

—Death of an Addict. unabr. ed. 1999. (Hamish Macbeth Mystery Ser.). audio 46.00 (*0-7887-3486-5*, 95690E7) Recorded Bks., LLC.

—Death of an Outsider. 1990. (Hamish Macbeth Mystery Ser.). 160p. mass mkt. 4.99 o.s.i (*0-8041-0487-5*, Ivy Bks.) Ballantine Bks.

—Death of an Outsider. l.t. ed. 1998. (Hamish Macbeth Mystery Ser.). pap. 19.95 o.p. (*0-7838-8299-8*); (*0-7540-3136-5*) Gale Group. (Macmillan Reference USA).

—Death of an Outsider. unabr. ed. 1999. (Hamish Macbeth Mystery Ser.). audio 38.00 (*1-84197-009-3*, H1009E7);Set. audio 38.00 Recorded Bks., LLC.

—Death of an Outsider. 1988. (Hamish Macbeth Mystery Ser.). 192p. 14.95 o.p. (*0-312-02188-7*, Saint Martin's Minotaur) St. Martin's Pr.

—Death of an Outsider. 2000. (Hamish Macbeth Mystery Ser.). 218p. pap. 6.95 o.p. (*0-553-40793-7*) Transworld Publishers Ltd. GBR. *Dist:* Trafalgar Square.

—Death of an Outsider: A Hamish Macbeth Mystery. 1991. (Hamish Macbeth Mystery Ser.). 3.99 o.p. (*0-517-06864-8*) Random Hse. Value Publishing.

—A Highland Christmas. (Hamish Macbeth Mystery Ser.). 2001. (Illus.). 128p. 16.95 o.p. (*0-89296-699-8*); 2000. E-Book 16.95 (*0-446-96000-4*); 1999. 128p. E-Book 9.95 (*0-446-91480-0*) Mysterious Pr.

—A Highland Christmas. 2002. 160p. mass mkt. 4.99 (*0-446-60919-6*) Warner Bks., Inc.

**MCCABE, CASSIDY (FICTITIOUS CHARACTER)—FICTION**

Matthews, Alex. Cat's Claw. (Cassidy McCabe Mystery Ser.: No. 5). 2001. 325p. mass mkt. 6.99 (*1-890768-35-9*); 2000. 272p. 22.95 (*1-890768-22-7*) Corvus Publishing. (Intrigue Pr.).

—Death's Domain: Sixth Cassidy McCabe Mystery. 2001. 320p. 23.95 (*1-890768-37-5*, Intrigue Pr.) Corvus Publishing.

—Satan's Silence. 1998. (Cassidy McCabe Mysteries Ser.: No. 2). 368p. mass mkt. 5.50 (*1-890768-04-9*, Intrigue Pr.) Corvus Publishing.

—Satan's Silence. Ellison, Lee, ed. 1997. (Cassidy McCabe Mystery Ser.: No. 2). 304p. 22.50 o.p. (*0-9643161-5-3*, Intrigue Pr.) Corvus Publishing.

—Secret's Shadow. unabr. ed. 1998. (Cassidy McCabe Mystery Ser.). audio 49.95 (*1-55686-745-X*) Books in Motion.

—Secret's Shadow: The First Cassidy McCabe Mystery. 1998. (Cassidy McCabe Mysteries Ser.: Vol. 1). 352p. mass mkt. 5.50 (*1-890768-03-0*, Intrigue Pr.) Corvus Publishing.

—Secret's Shadow: The First Cassidy McCabe Mystery. Ellison, Lee, ed. 1996. 296p. 22.50 o.p. (*0-9643161-3-7*, Intrigue Pr.) Corvus Publishing.

—Vendetta's Victim: The Third Cassidy McCabe Mystery. (Cassidy McCabe Mysteries Ser.). 1999. 256p. mass mkt. 5.95 (*1-890768-14-6*); 1998. 222p. 22.95 o.p. (*0-9643161-9-6*) Corvus Publishing. (Intrigue Pr.).

—Wanton's Web. 2001. (Cassidy McCabe Mystery Ser.: No. 4). 304p. mass mkt. 6.99 (*1-890768-34-0*); 1999. (Cassidy McCabe Mysteries Ser.). 316p. 22.95 (*1-890768-12-X*) Corvus Publishing. (Intrigue Pr.).

—Wedding's Widow: The Seventh Cassidy McCabe Mystery. 2003. (Cassidy McCabe Mystery Ser.: 7). 24.95 (*1-890768-49-9*, Intrigue Pr.) Corvus Publishing.

**MCCABE, MURDOCK (FICTITIOUS CHARACTER)—FICTION**

Howard, Gil. The Chaos Chip. Keene, James A., ed. 1999. 350p. 24.95 (*0-944435-46-7*) Glenbridge Publishing, Ltd.

**MCCADDEN, CARL (FICTITIOUS CHARACTER)—FICTION**

Lusby, Jim. Making the Cut. 2003. 254p. pap. 7.95 (*0-7528-4375-3*) Orion Publishing Group, Ltd. GBR. *Dist:* Trafalgar Square.

—Serial. 2002. 224p. 29.95 (*0-7528-5694-4*); pap. (*0-7528-5695-2*) Orion Publishing Group, Ltd. GBR. *Dist:* Trafalgar Square.

**MCCAIN, SAM (FICTITIOUS CHARACTER)—FICTION**

Gorman, Ed. Breaking Up Is Hard to Do: A Sam McCain Mystery. 2004. 240p. 25.00 (*0-7867-1296-1*, Carroll & Graf Pubs.) Avalon Publishing Group.

—The Day the Music Died. 1999. 212p. 22.95 (*0-7867-0569-8*, Carroll & Graf Pubs.) Avalon Publishing Group.

—The Day the Music Died. 2000. (Sam McCain Mystery Ser.). 258p. mass mkt. 5.99 o.s.i (*0-425-17411-5*) Berkley Publishing Group.

—The Day the Music Died. l.t. ed. 1999. (Mystery Ser.). 323p. 27.95 (*0-7862-2032-5*) Thorndike Pr.

—The Day the Music Died. 2000. (Illus.). 12.04 (*0-606-18007-9*) Turtleback Bks.

—Everybody's Somebody's Fool: A Sam McCain Mystery. 2003. 224p. 24.00 (*0-7867-1114-0*, Carroll & Graf Pubs.) Avalon Publishing Group.

—Save the Last Dance for Me. 2001. 224p. 24.00 (*0-7867-0968-5*, Carroll & Graf Pubs.) Avalon Publishing Group.

—Save the Last Dance for Me. 2003. (WWL Mystery Ser.: No. 461). 256p. mass mkt. (*0-373-26461-5*, Worldwide Library) Harlequin Enterprises, Ltd.

—Save the Last Dance for Me. l.t. ed. 2002. (Mystery Ser.). 335p. 29.95 (*0-7862-4398-8*) Thorndike Pr.

—Wake up Little Susie: A Sam McCain Mystery. 2000. 225p. 22.95 (*0-7867-0665-1*, Carroll & Graf Pubs.) Avalon Publishing Group.

—Will You Still Love Me Tomorrow? 2001. 256p. 22.95 (*0-7867-0775-5*, Carroll & Graf Pubs.) Avalon Publishing Group.

—Will You Still Love Me Tomorrow? 2002. 208p. reprint ed. mass mkt. 5.99 (*0-425-18716-0*, Prime Crime) Berkley Publishing Group.

—Will You Still Love Me Tomorrow? l.t. ed. 2001. 301p. 29.95 (*0-7862-3672-8*); 280p. (*0-7540-4739-3*); 280p. (*0-7540-4738-5*) Thorndike Pr.

**MACCALLISTER FAMILY (FICTITIOUS CHARACTER)—FICTION**

Johnstone, William W. Dreams of Eagles. 1998. 412p. mass mkt. 5.99 (*0-8217-6086-6*); 1994. 416p. mass mkt. 4.99 o.s.i (*0-8217-4619-7*) Kensington Publishing Corp.

—Eyes of Eagles. 2000. mass mkt. 5.99 (*0-7860-1364-8*, Pinnacle Bks.); 1993. 480p. mass mkt. 4.99 o.s.i (*0-8217-4285-X*, Zebra Bks.) Kensington Publishing Corp.

—Rage of Eagles. 1998. (Arabesque Ser.). 320p. mass mkt. 5.99 (*0-7860-0507-6*, Pinnacle Bks.) Kensington Publishing Corp.

—Scream of Eagles. 1997. 320p. mass mkt. 5.99 o.s.i (*0-7860-0447-9*, Pinnacle Bks.); 1996. 320p. pap. 19.95 o.p. (*1-57566-016-4*); 1996. mass mkt. 19.95 o.s.i (*0-8217-5253-7*) Kensington Publishing Corp.

—Song of Eagles. 1999. 320p. mass mkt. 5.99 (*0-7860-1012-6*); 304p. mass mkt. 5.99 o.s.i (*0-7860-0639-0*) Kensington Publishing Corp.

—Talons of Eagles. 1996. mass mkt. 5.99 (*0-7860-0249-2*, Pinnacle Bks.); 1995. 352p. mass mkt. 18.95 o.p. (*0-8217-4890-4*) Kensington Publishing Corp.

**MCCARRON, BLUE (FICTITIOUS CHARACTER)—FICTION**

Padgett, Abigail. Blue. 1998. 288p. 22.00 (*0-89296-671-8*) Mysterious Pr.

—Blue. 1999. mass mkt. (*0-446-60763-0*) Warner Bks., Inc.

**MCCARTHY, GAIL (FICTITIOUS CHARACTER)—FICTION**

Crum, Laura. Breakaway. 2001. (Gail McCarthy Mysteries Ser.). 224p. 22.95 (*0-312-27181-6*, Saint Martin's Minotaur) St. Martin's Pr.

—Cutter. (Gail McCarthy Mysteries Ser.). 1995. 196p. mass mkt. 4.99 (*0-312-95674-6*, St. Martin's Paperbacks); 1994. 208p. 18.95 o.p. (*0-312-10960-1*, Saint Martin's Minotaur) St. Martin's Pr.

—Hayburner: A Gail McCarthy Mystery. 2003. 208p. 22.95 (*0-312-29047-0*, Saint Martin's Minotaur) St. Martin's Pr.

—Hoofprints. 1995. 208p. 21.95 o.p. (*0-312-13983-7*, Saint Martin's Minotaur); Vol. 1. 1996. mass mkt. 5.99 (*0-312-96040-9*, St. Martin's Paperbacks) St. Martin's Pr.

—Roughstock. 1997. 224p. text 20.95 o.p. (*0-312-15643-X*, Saint Martin's Minotaur) St. Martin's Pr.

—Slickrock. 1999. (Gail McCarthy Mysteries Ser.). 256p. 22.95 (*0-312-20910-X*, Saint Martin's Minotaur) St. Martin's Pr.

**MCCARTHY, JAMES (FICTITIOUS CHARACTER)—FICTION**

Gerrold, David. A Day for Damnation. (War Against the Chtorr Ser.: Vol. II). 1985. mass mkt. 3.95 o.s.i (*0-671-45121-9*, Pocket); 1984. 400p. 16.45 (*0-671-47553-3*, Atria) Simon & Schuster.

—A Matter for Men: War Against the Chtorr, Vol. 1. 1984. (Science Fiction Ser.). 416p. mass mkt. 3.95 o.s.i (*0-671-45120-0*, Pocket) Simon & Schuster.

—Season for Slaughter, No. 4. 1992. (War Against the Chtorr Ser.: Bk. 4). 560p. mass mkt. 5.99 o.s.i (*0-553-28976-4*, Spectra) Bantam Bks.

**MCCAULEY, QUINT (FICTITIOUS CHARACTER)—FICTION**

Brod, D. C. Brothers in Blood: A Quint McCauley Mystery. 1993. 288p. 21.95 (*0-8027-3239-9*) Walker & Co.

—Error in Judgment. 1991. 4.50 o.p. (*1-55773-584-0*, Diamond Bks.) Ace Bks.

—Error in Judgment. l.t. ed. 1993. (General Ser.). 544p. 29.99 o.p. (*0-7089-2855-2*, Ulverscroft) Thorpe, F. A. Pubs. GBR. *Dist:* Ulverscroft Large Print Bks., Ltd., Ulverscroft Large Print Canada, Ltd.

—Error in Judgment. 1990. 192p. 18.95 (*0-8027-5763-4*) Walker & Co.

—Masquerade in Blue. 1991. 208p. 19.95 (*0-8027-5792-8*) Walker & Co.

**MCCHANDLER, DOAN (FICTITIOUS CHARACTER)—FICTION**

Outland, Orland. Death Wore a Fabulous New Fragrance. 1998. (Doan & Binky Mysteries Ser.). 208p. mass mkt. 5.99 o.s.i (*0-425-16197-8*, Prime Crime) Berkley Publishing Group.

—Death Wore a Smart Little Outfit. 1997. 224p. mass mkt. 5.50 o.s.i (*0-425-15855-1*, Prime Crime) Berkley Publishing Group.

**MCCLEARY, MIKE (FICTITIOUS CHARACTER)—FICTION**

MacGregor, T. J. Blue Pearl. 1994. 384p. 21.95 (*0-7868-6061-8*) Hyperion Pr.

—Dark Fields. 9999. 4.95 o.p. (*0-345-22756-5*); 1986. mass mkt. 5.99 o.s.i (*0-345-33756-5*) Ballantine Bks.

—Death Flats. 1991. (Florida Mysteries Ser.). (Orig.). mass mkt. 4.99 o.s.i (*0-345-35768-X*) Ballantine Bks.

—Death Sweet. 1988. 384p. mass mkt. 4.99 o.s.i (*0-345-33753-0*) Ballantine Bks.

—Kill Flash. 1987. pap. 3.95 o.p. (*0-345-00751-4*); mass mkt. 4.99 o.s.i (*0-345-33754-9*) Ballantine Bks.

—Kin Dread. 1990. 320p. (Orig.). mass mkt. 4.95 o.s.i (*0-345-35766-3*) Ballantine Bks.

—Mistress of the Bones. 1995. 352p. 21.95 (*0-7868-6106-1*) Hyperion Pr.

—On Ice. 1989. mass mkt. 4.99 o.s.i (*0-345-35045-6*) Ballantine Bks.

—Spree. 1992. (Florida Mysteries Ser.). (Orig.). mass mkt. 4.99 o.s.i (*0-345-37346-4*) Ballantine Bks.

—Storm Surge. 1993. 336p. (YA). 19.95 o.p. (*1-56282-789-8*) Hyperion Pr.

**MCCLEARY, WILTON (FICTITIOUS CHARACTER)—FICTION**

Graham, Mark. The Black Maria. 2000. (Mysteries of Old Philadelphia Ser.). 384p. mass mkt. 6.50 (*0-380-80068-3*, Avon Bks.) Morrow/Avon.

—The Killing Breed. 1998. (Mysteries of Old Philadelphia Ser.). 272p. mass mkt. 5.99 (*0-380-80066-7*, Avon Bks.) Morrow/Avon.

—The Resurrectionist. 1999. (Mysteries of Old Philadelphia Ser.). 320p. mass mkt. 5.99 (*0-380-80067-5*, Avon Bks.) Morrow/Avon.

**MCCLEET, ADAM (FICTITIOUS CHARACTER)—FICTION**

Hanson, Rick. Extreme Odds. 1998. 240p. 22.00 o.s.i (*1-57566-333-3*) Kensington Publishing Corp.

—Mortal Remains. 1996. mass mkt. 4.99 o.s.i (*0-7860-0284-0*, Pinnacle Bks.); 1995. 256p. mass mkt. 18.95 o.p. (*0-8217-4955-2*, Zebra Bks.) Kensington Publishing Corp.

—Spare Parts. 1995. 256p. mass mkt. 4.99 o.s.i (*0-7860-0156-9*, Pinnacle Bks.); 1995. 256p. mass mkt. 4.99 (*0-8217-0156-8*, Zebra Bks.); 1994. 288p. mass mkt. 20.00 o.s.i (*0-8217-4738-X*, Zebra Bks.) Kensington Publishing Corp.

—Splitting Heirs. (Adam McCleet Mysteries Ser. ). 1998. 256p. mass mkt. 5.99 o.s.i (*1-57566-365-1*); 1997. 240p. 21.95 o.p. (*1-57566-194-2*, Kensington Bks.) Kensington Publishing Corp.

—Still Life. (Adam McCleet Mysteries Ser. ). 1997. 256p. mass mkt. 5.50 o.s.i (*1-57566-200-0*); 1996. 204p. 19.95 o.s.i (*1-57566-041-5*) Kensington Publishing Corp.

**MCCLENDON, ROSE (FICTITIOUS CHARACTER)—FICTION**

King, Stephen. Rose Madder. l.t. ed. 1995. 652p. 27.95 o.p. (*1-56895-261-9*, Wheeler Publishing, Inc.) Gale Group.

—Rose Madder. 1996. mass mkt. 7.50 (*0-451-18876-4*); 480p. mass mkt. 7.99 (*0-451-18636-2*) NAL. (Signet Bks.).

—Rose Madder. pap. 6.98 o.p. (*0-7651-0399-0*) Smithmark Pubs., Inc.

—Rose Madder. 1996. 14.04 (*0-606-09798-8*) Turtleback Bks.

—Rose Madder. 1995. (Illus.). 432p. 25.95 (*0-670-85869-2*, Viking); 16p. audio 59.95 o.s.i (*0-14-086158-0*) Viking Penguin.

**MCCLINTOCH, LARA (FICTITIOUS CHARACTER)—FICTION**

Hamilton, Lyn. The African Quest: An Archaeological Mystery. 2001. (Archaeological Mystery Ser.). (Illus.). 304p. 21.95 o.s.i (*0-425-17806-4*) Berkley Publishing Group.

—The Celtic Riddle. 2000. 304p. mass mkt. 6.50 (*0-425-17775-0*, Prime Crime) Berkley Publishing Group.

—The Celtic Riddle: An Archaeological Mystery. 2000. 296p. 21.95 o.s.i (*0-425-17235-X*, Prime Crime) Berkley Publishing Group.

—The Etruscan Chimera. 2003. 304p. mass mkt. 6.50 (*0-425-18908-2*, Prime Crime) Berkley Publishing Group.

—The Magyar Venus. 2004. 256p. 22.95 (*0-425-19429-9*) Berkley Publishing Group.

—The Maltese Goddess: An Archaeological Mystery. 1998. (Archaeological Mystery Ser.). 256p. mass mkt. 6.50 (*0-425-16240-0*, Prime Crime) Berkley Publishing Group.

—The Moche Warrior: An Archaeological Mystery. (Archaeological Mystery Ser.). 336p. 1999. 21.95 o.s.i (*0-425-16809-3*); 2000. reprint ed. mass mkt. 6.50 (*0-425-17308-9*) Berkley Publishing Group. (Prime Crime).

—The Thai Amulet. 2004. 288p. mass mkt. 6.99 (*0-425-19487-6*); 2003. 256p. 22.95 (*0-425-19006-4*, Prime Crime) Berkley Publishing Group.

—The Xibalba Murders: An Archeological Mystery. 1997. (Archaeological Mystery Ser.). 304p. mass mkt. 6.50 (*0-425-15722-9*, Prime Crime) Berkley Publishing Group.

**MCCLINTOCK, SHIRLEY (FICTITIOUS CHARACTER)—FICTION**

Oliphant, B. J., pseud. A Ceremonial Death. 1995. mass mkt. 5.99 o.s.i (*0-449-14897-1*, Fawcett) Ballantine Bks.

—Dead in the Scrub. 1990. 240p. mass mkt. 4.95 o.s.i (*0-449-14653-7*, Fawcett) Ballantine Bks.

—Death & the Delinquent. 1992. (Southwest Mysteries Ser.). (Orig.). mass mkt. 4.50 o.s.i (*0-449-14718-5*, Fawcett) Ballantine Bks.

—Death Served up Cold. 1994. (Orig.). mass mkt. 4.99 o.s.i (*0-449-14896-3*, Fawcett) Ballantine Bks.

—Deservedly Dead, No. 1. 1992. (Deservedly Dead Ser.: Vol. 1). mass mkt. 4.99 o.s.i (*0-449-14717-7*, Fawcett) Ballantine Bks.

—The Haunting at Lost Lake. l.t. ed. 1991. (Orig.). pap. 19.95 o.p. (*0-7927-0745-1*, CH023); pap. 17.95 o.p. (*0-7927-0746-X*, CS0129) BBC Audiobooks America.

—The Unexpected Corpse. 1990. 224p. (Orig.). mass mkt. 4.99 o.s.i (*0-449-14674-X*, Fawcett) Ballantine Bks.

**MCCONE, SHARON (FICTITIOUS CHARACTER)—FICTION**

Muller, Marcia. Ask the Cards a Question. unabr. ed. 1996. (Sharon McCone Ser.). audio 36.00 (*0-7366-3454-1*, 4098) Books on Tape, Inc.

—Ask the Cards a Question: A Sharon McCone Mystery. l.t. ed. 1996. 239p. pap. 19.95 o.p. (*0-7838-1480-1*, Macmillan Reference USA) Gale Group.

—Ask the Cards a Question: A Sharon McCone Mystery. 1982. 168p. 10.95 o.p. (*0-312-05653-2*) St. Martin's Pr.

—Ask the Cards a Question: A Sharon McCone Mystery. 1990. 224p. reprint ed. mass mkt. 6.99 (*0-445-40849-9*) Warner Bks., Inc.

—Both Ends of the Night. unabr. ed. 1997. (Sharon McCone Ser.). audio 48.00 (*0-7366-3802-4*, 4473) Books on Tape, Inc.

—Both Ends of the Night. abr. ed. (Sharon Mccone Ser.). 1998. audio 7.99 o.p. (*1-56740-250-X*, 629, Paperback Nova Audio Bks.); 1997. audio 16.95 o.p. (*1-56100-985-7*, 1137); 1997. audio 73.25 o.p. (*1-56100-834-6*, 814, Unabridged Library Editions); 1997. audio 23.95 (*1-56100-759-5*, 51, Bookcassette) Brilliance Audio.

—Both Ends of the Night. l.t. ed. 1997. (Wheeler Large Print Book Ser.). pap. 24.95 (*1-56895-463-8*, Wheeler Publishing, Inc.) Gale Group.

—Both Ends of the Night. 1997. 368p. 22.50 o.p. (*0-89296-622-X*) Mysterious Pr.

—Both Ends of the Night. 1998. (Sharon McCone Mysteries Ser.). 384p. reprint ed. mass mkt. 6.99 (*0-446-60550-6*) Warner Bks., Inc.

—The Broken Promise Land. unabr. ed. 1996. (Sharon McCone Ser.). audio 64.00 (*0-7366-3383-9*, 4033) Books on Tape, Inc.

—The Broken Promise Land. abr. ed. (Sharon Mccone Ser.). 1997. audio 7.99 o.p. (*1-56740-177-5*, 630, Paperback Nova Audio Bks.); 1996. audio 16.95 o.p. (*1-56100-956-3*, 817, Nova Audio Bks.); 1996. audio 73.25 o.p. (*1-56100-343-3*, 816, Unabridged Library Editions); 1996. audio 23.95 o.p. (*1-56100-718-8*, 53, Bookcassette) Brilliance Audio.

—The Broken Promise Land. 1996. 82p. 22.95 o.s.i (*0-89296-621-1*) Mysterious Pr.

—The Broken Promise Land. 1997. (Sharon McCone Mysteries Ser.). 400p. reprint ed. mass mkt. 6.50 (*0-446-60410-0*) Warner Bks., Inc.

—The Cheshire Cat's Eye: A Sharon McCone Mystery. unabr. ed. 1996. (Sharon McCone Ser.). audio 36.00 (*0-7366-3490-8*, 4130) Books on Tape, Inc.

—The Cheshire Cat's Eye: A Sharon McCone Mystery. l.t. ed. 1988. (Nightingale Ser.). 278p. pap. 12.95 o.p. (*0-8161-4396-X*, Macmillan Reference USA) Gale Group.

—The Cheshire Cat's Eye: A Sharon McCone Mystery. 1983. 160p. 10.95 o.p. (*0-312-13175-5*) St. Martin's Pr.

—The Cheshire Cat's Eye: A Sharon McCone Mystery. 1990. 224p. reprint ed. mass mkt. 6.99 (*0-445-40850-2*) Warner Bks., Inc.

—Edwin of the Iron Shoes. 1993. (Black Dagger Crime Ser.). 184p. 16.50 o.p. (*0-7451-8617-3*, Black Dagger) BBC Audiobooks America.

—Edwin of the Iron Shoes. unabr. ed. 1996. (Sharon McCone Ser.). audio 36.00 (*0-7366-3408-8*, 4054) Books on Tape, Inc.

—Edwin of the Iron Shoes. 1977. (McKay-Washburn Mystery Ser.). 7.95 o.p. (*0-679-50782-5*) McKay, David Co., Inc.

—Edwin of the Iron Shoes. 1978. (Crime Ser.). pap. 1.95 o.p. (*0-14-004915-0*, Penguin Bks.) Viking Penguin.

—Edwin of the Iron Shoes. 1990. 224p. reprint ed. mass mkt. 6.99 (*0-445-40902-9*) Warner Bks., Inc.

—Eye of the Storm. unabr. ed. 1998. (Sharon McCone Ser.). audio 56.00 (*0-7366-4135-1*, 4640) Books on Tape, Inc.

—Eye of the Storm. 1988. 15.95 o.p. (*0-89296-269-0*) Mysterious Pr.

—Eye of the Storm. 1989. 256p. reprint ed. mass mkt. 6.99 o.s.i (*0-445-40625-9*) Warner Bks., Inc.

—Games to Keep the Dark Away: A Sharon McCone Mystery. unabr. ed. 1997. (Sharon McCone Ser.). audio 36.00 (*0-7366-3566-1*, 4212) Books on Tape, Inc.

—Games to Keep the Dark Away: A Sharon McCone Mystery. l.t. ed. 1986. (Nightingale Ser.). 278p. 11.95 o.p. (*0-8161-3903-2*, Macmillan Reference USA) Gale Group.

—Games to Keep the Dark Away: A Sharon McCone Mystery. 2003. 320p. pap. 14.95 (*0-312-31620-8*, L. A. Weekly Bks.) St. Martin's Pr.

—Games to Keep the Dark Away: A Sharon McCone Mystery. 1990. reprint ed. mass mkt. 6.99 (*0-445-40851-0*) Warner Bks., Inc.

—Leave a Message for Willie: A Sharon McCone Mystery. unabr. ed. 1997. (Sharon McCone Ser.). audio 42.00 (*0-7366-3779-6*, 4452) Books on Tape, Inc.

—Leave a Message for Willie: A Sharon McCone Mystery. l.t. ed. 1995. 266p. pap. 20.95 o.p. (*0-7838-1481-X*, Macmillan Reference USA) Gale Group.

—Leave a Message for Willie: A Sharon McCone Mystery. 1984. 192p. 11.95 o.p. (*0-312-47728-7*) St. Martin's Pr.

—Leave a Message for Willie: A Sharon McCone Mystery. 1990. 224p. reprint ed. mass mkt. 6.99 (*0-445-40900-2*) Warner Bks., Inc.

—Listen to the Silence. abr. ed. 2000. audio 17.95 (*1-56740-883-4*, Nova Audio Bks.); audio 24.95 (*1-56740-487-1*, 1982, Brilliance Audio Unabridged); audio 44.25 (*1-56740-705-6*, 1983, Unabridged Library Editions) Brilliance Audio.

—Listen to the Silence. l.t. ed. 2000. (Wheeler Large Print Book Ser.). 328p. 28.95 o.p. (*1-56895-908-7*, Wheeler Publishing, Inc.) Gale Group.

—Listen to the Silence. 2000. 304p. 23.95 (*0-89296-689-0*) Mysterious Pr.

—McCone & Friends. 2000. 202p. (Illus.). (J). pap. 16.00 (*1-885941-38-2*); 40.00 o.p. (*1-885941-37-4*) Crippen & Landru, Pubs.

—Pennies on a Dead Woman's Eyes. 1992. 304p. 18.95 (*0-89296-454-5*) Mysterious Pr.

—Pennies on a Dead Woman's Eyes. 1993. 366p. reprint ed. mass mkt. 6.99 (*0-446-40033-5*) Warner Bks., Inc.

—The Shape of Dread. unabr. ed. 1999. audio 48.00 (*0-7366-4455-5*, 4900) Books on Tape, Inc.

—The Shape of Dread. 1989. 16.95 o.p. (*0-89296-271-2*) Mysterious Pr.

—The Shape of Dread. 1990. 288p. reprint ed. mass mkt. 6.99 (*0-445-40916-9*) Warner Bks., Inc.

—There's Nothing to Be Afraid Of. unabr. ed. 1997. (Sharon McCone Ser.). audio 48.00 (*0-7366-3780-X*, 4453) Books on Tape, Inc.

—There's Nothing to Be Afraid Of. 1985. 256p. 14.95 o.p. (*0-312-79955-1*) St. Martin's Pr.

—There's Nothing to Be Afraid Of. 1990. 224p. reprint ed. mass mkt. 6.99 o.s.i (*0-445-40901-0*) Warner Bks., Inc.

—There's Something in a Sunday: A Sharon McCone Mystery. unabr. ed. 1998. (Sharon McCone Ser.). audio 48.00 (*0-7366-4136-X*, 4641) Books on Tape, Inc.

—There's Something in a Sunday: A Sharon McCone Mystery. 1989. 15.95 o.p. (*0-89296-270-4*) Mysterious Pr.

—There's Something in a Sunday: A Sharon McCone Mystery. 1990. 224p. reprint ed. mass mkt. 6.99 (*0-445-40865-0*) Warner Bks., Inc.

—Till the Butchers Cut Him Down: A Sharon McCone Mystery. 1994. 352p. 18.95 o.s.i (*0-89296-455-3*) Mysterious Pr.

—Till the Butchers Cut Him Down: A Sharon McCone Mystery. 1995. pap. (*0-446-40034-3*, Mysterious Pr. Paperback Bks.); 336p. reprint ed. mass mkt. 5.99 (*0-446-60302-3*) Warner Bks., Inc.

—Trophies & Dead Things: A Sharon McCowe Mystery. unabr. ed. 1999. audio 48.00 Books on Tape, Inc.

—Trophies & Dead Things: A Sharon McCowe Mystery. l.t. ed. 1991. (General Ser.). 379p. lib. bdg. 19.95 o.p. (*0-8161-5134-2*, Macmillan Reference USA) Gale Group.

—Trophies & Dead Things: A Sharon McCowe Mystery. 1990. 272p. 16.95 o.p. (*0-89296-417-0*) Mysterious Pr.

—Trophies & Dead Things: A Sharon McCowe Mystery. 1991. 272p. reprint ed. mass mkt. 5.99 o.s.i (*0-446-40039-4*) Warner Bks., Inc.

—A Walk Through the Fire. 1999. 362p. 23.00 o.s.i (*0-89296-688-2*) Mysterious Pr.

—Where Echoes Live. 1991. 17.95 o.p. (*0-89296-418-9*) Mysterious Pr.

—Where Echoes Live. 1992. 368p. reprint ed. mass mkt. 6.99 (*0-446-40161-7*) Warner Bks., Inc.

—While Other People Sleep. unabr. ed. 1999. (Sharon McCone Ser.). audio 48.00 (*0-7366-4318-4*, 4790) Books on Tape, Inc.

—While Other People Sleep. unabr. ed. 1998. (Sharon McCone Ser.). audio 25.95 (*1-56740-061-2*, 1, Bookcassette); audio 57.25 (*1-56740-590-8*, 1095, Unabridged Library Editions);Set. audio 17.95 o.p. (*1-56740-786-2*, 448, Nova Audio Bks.) Brilliance Audio.

—While Other People Sleep. 1998. (Sharon McCone Mysteries Ser.). 344p. 23.00 o.p. (*0-89296-650-5*) Mysterious Pr.

—While Other People Sleep. l.t. ed. 1998. (Mystery Ser.). 432p. 28.95 o.p. (*0-7862-1615-8*) Thorndike Pr.

—While Other People Sleep. 1999. 304p. reprint ed. mass mkt. 6.99 (*0-446-60721-5*) Warner Bks., Inc.

—A Wild & Lonely Place: A Sharon McCone Mystery. unabr. ed. 2000. (Sharon McCone Ser.: 16). audio 48.00 Books on Tape, Inc.

—A Wild & Lonely Place: A Sharon McCone Mystery. 1995. 300p. 19.95 o.s.i (*0-89296-526-6*) Mysterious Pr.

—A Wild & Lonely Place: A Sharon McCone Mystery. 1996. 336p. reprint ed. mass mkt. 6.99 (*0-446-60328-7*) Warner Bks., Inc.

—Wolf in the Shadows. 1993. 368p. 18.95 (*0-89296-525-8*) Mysterious Pr.

—Wolf in the Shadows. 1994. 384p. reprint ed. mass mkt. 5.50 (*0-446-40383-0*) Warner Bks., Inc.

Muller, Marcia & Pronzini, Bill. Double. unabr. ed. 1997. audio 64.00 (*0-7366-3710-9*, 4394) Books on Tape, Inc.

—Double. 1984. 288p. 13.95 o.p. (*0-312-21807-9*) St. Martin's Pr.

—Double. 1995. 288p. reprint ed. mass mkt. 5.50 o.s.i (*0-446-40413-6*) Warner Bks., Inc.

**MCCONNELL, JAMES (FICTITIOUS CHARACTER)—FICTION**

Couch, Dick. Seal Team 1. 1991. 288p. (Orig.). mass mkt. 5.99 o.p. (*0-380-76115-7*, Avon Bks.) Morrow/Avon.

**MCCORKLE, MAC (FICTITIOUS CHARACTER)—FICTION**

Thomas, Ross. The Backup Men: A McCorkle & Padillo Novel. 224p. reprint ed. 1986. pap. 3.50 o.p. (*0-06-080833-0*, P 833); 1984. pap. 2.95 o.p. (*0-06-080726-1*, P726) HarperTrade. (Perennial).

—The Backup Men: A McCorkle & Padillo Novel. 1978. pap. 1.75 o.p. (*0-671-81934-8*, Pocket) Simon & Schuster.

—The Backup Men: A McCorkle & Padillo Novel. 1992. 256p. mass mkt. 5.99 o.p. (*0-446-40170-6*) Warner Bks., Inc.

—Cast a Yellow Shadow. 1986. 192p. pap. 2.25 o.p. (*0-380-02391-1*, 57711-9, Avon Bks.) Morrow/Avon.

—Cast a Yellow Shadow. 1987. 272p. reprint ed. mass mkt. 5.99 o.s.i (*0-445-40556-2*) Warner Bks., Inc.

—The Cold War Swap. mass mkt. (*0-312-99036-7*, St. Martin's Paperbacks) St. Martin's Pr.

—The Cold War Swap. l.t. ed. 2003. 356p. 29.95 (*0-7862-5576-5*) Thorndike Pr.

—The Cold War Swap: A McCorkle & Padillo Novel. 224p. 1984. pap. 2.95 o.p. (*0-06-080686-9*, P686); 1986. reprint ed. mass mkt. 3.50 o.p. (*0-06-080834-9*, P 834) HarperTrade. (Perennial).

—The Cold War Swap: A McCorkle & Padillo Novel. 1978. pap. 1.75 o.p. (*0-671-81898-8*, Pocket) Simon & Schuster.

—The Cold War Swap: A McCorkle & Padillo Novel. 1992. mass mkt. 5.99 o.p. (*0-446-40168-4*) Warner Bks., Inc.

—Twilight at Mac's Place. 1990. 352p. 19.95 o.p. (*0-89296-214-3*); 75.00 (*0-89296-434-0*) Mysterious Pr.

—Twilight at Mac's Place. mass mkt. (*0-312-99038-3*, St. Martin's Paperbacks); 2003. 320p. pap. 13.95 (*0-312-31584-8*, Saint Martin's Griffin) St. Martin's Pr.

—Twilight at Mac's Place. 1991. 352p. mass mkt. 5.99 o.s.i (*0-446-40059-9*) Warner Bks., Inc.

**MCCOSKEY, SUNNY (FICTITIOUS CHARACTER)—FICTION**

Gordon, Nadia. Sharpshooter: A Napa Valley Mystery. 2002. 224p. pap. 11.95 (*0-8118-3462-X*) Chronicle Bks. LLC.

Seelig, Tina L. Games for Your Brain: Dinosaur Cards. 2003. (Illus.). 61p. (YA). 9.95 (*0-8118-3498-0*) Chronicle Bks. LLC.

**MCCOY, DOC (FICTITIOUS CHARACTER)—FICTION**

Carey, Diane L. Double Helix No. 3: Red Sector. 1999. (Star Trek, The Next Generation Ser.: No. 53). (Illus.). 336p. mass mkt. 6.50 (*0-671-03257-7*, Star Trek) Simon & Schuster.

Golden, Christie. Last Roundup. 2003. (Star Trek). 352p. pap. 6.99 (*0-7434-4910-X*, Star Trek) Simon & Schuster.

Sherman, Josepha & Shwartz, Susan. Vulcan's Forge. 1998. (Star Trek Ser.). 288p. pap. 6.50 (*0-671-00927-3*, Star Trek) Simon & Schuster.

—Vulcan's Forge. abr. ed. 1995. (Star Trek Ser.: Vol. 2). audio 18.00 (*0-671-57621-6*, Simon & Schuster Audioworks) Simon & Schuster Audio.

Thompson, Jim. The Getaway. 1984. 192p. reprint ed. pap. 3.95 o.p. (*0-916870-75-8*, Black Mask) Creative Arts Bk. Co.

—The Getaway. 1990. (Vintage Crime/Black Lizard Ser.). 192p. pap. 11.00 (*0-679-73250-0*, Vintage) Knopf Publishing Group.

**MCCOY, KEN (FICTITIOUS CHARACTER)—FICTION**

Griffin, W. E. B. Battleground. 1991. (Corps Ser.: No. 4). 496p. mass mkt. 7.99 (*0-515-10640-2*, Jove) Berkley Publishing Group.

—Battleground. unabr. ed. 1993. (Corps Ser.: No. 4). audio 96.00 (*0-7366-2240-3*, 3030) Books on Tape, Inc.

—Battleground. 2001. 19.95 (*0-399-13794-7*); 1991. (Corps Ser.: No. 4). 416p. 19.95 o.s.i (*0-399-13550-2*, G. P. Putnam's Sons) Penguin Group (USA) Inc.

—Behind the Lines. 1996. (Corps Ser.: No. 7). 576p. mass mkt. 7.99 (*0-515-11938-5*, Jove) Berkley Publishing Group.

—Behind the Lines. unabr. ed. 1996. (Corps Ser.: No. 7). audio 104.00 (*0-7366-3307-3*, 3961) Books on Tape, Inc.

—Behind the Lines. unabr. ed. (Corps Ser.: No. 7). 1996. audio 27.95 (*1-56100-683-1*, 42, Bookcassette); 1996. audio 105.25 (*1-56100-308-5*, 807, Unabridged Library Editions); Set. 1997. audio 7.99 o.s.i (*1-56740-147-3*, 626, Nova Audio Bks.) Brilliance Audio.

—Behind the Lines. l.t. ed. 1996. (Corps Ser.: No. 7). 800p. 26.95 (*0-7838-1722-3*, Macmillan Reference USA) Gale Group.

—Behind the Lines. 2001. 23.95 (*0-399-14336-X*); 1996. (Corps Ser.: No. 7). 384p. 23.95 o.p. (*0-399-14086-7*, G. P. Putnam's Sons) Penguin Group (USA) Inc.

—Call to Arms. 1987. (Corps Ser.: No. 2). 384p. mass mkt. 7.99 (*0-515-09349-1*, Jove) Berkley Publishing Group.

—Call to Arms. unabr. collector's ed. 1992. (Corps Ser.: No. 2). audio 80.00 (*0-7366-2206-3*, 3001) Books on Tape, Inc.

—Close Combat. l.t. ed. 1994. (Corps Ser.: No. 6). 22.95 o.p. (*0-7927-1660-4*) BBC Audiobooks America.

—Close Combat. 1993. (Corps Ser.: No. 6). 416p. mass mkt. 7.99 (*0-515-11269-0*, Jove) Berkley Publishing Group.

—Close Combat. unabr. ed. 1993. (Corps Ser.: No. 6). audio 80.00 (*0-7366-2423-6*, 112719) Books on Tape, Inc.

—Close Combat. 1993. (Corps Ser.: No. 6). 416p. 22.95 o.p. (*0-399-13766-1*, G. P. Putnam's Sons) Penguin Group (USA) Inc.

—The Corps: Semper Fi. 1986. (Corps Ser.: No. 1). 352p. mass mkt. 7.99 (*0-515-08749-1*, Jove) Berkley Publishing Group.

—The Corps Boxed Set: Battleground, Line of Fire, Close Combat. 1995. (Corps Ser.: Nos. 4-6). 11.98 o.s.i (*0-399-14013-1*) Penguin Group (USA) Inc.

—The Corps Boxed Set: Semper Fi, Call to Arms, Counterattack, Battleground. 1991. (Corps Ser.: Nos. 1-4). 22.45 o.s.i (*0-515-10775-1*, Jove) Berkley Publishing Group.

—Counterattack. 1990. (Corps Ser.: No. 3). 512p. mass mkt. 7.99 (*0-515-10417-5*, Jove) Berkley Publishing Group.

—Counterattack. unabr. collector's ed. 1992. (Corps Ser.: No. 3). audio 104.00 (*0-7366-2211-X*, 3004) Books on Tape, Inc.

—Counterattack. 1990. (Corps Ser.: No. 3). 400p. 16.95 o.p. (*0-399-13493-X*, G. P. Putnam's Sons) Penguin Putnam Bks. for Young Readers.

—In Danger's Path, Vol. 8. 1999. (Corps Ser.: No. 8). 736p. reprint ed. mass mkt. 7.99 (*0-515-12698-5*, Jove) Berkley Publishing Group.

—In Danger's Path. l.t. ed. 1999. (Corps Ser.: No. 8). 883p. 31.95 (*1-56895-724-6*, Wheeler Publishing, Inc.) Gale Group.

—In Danger's Path, Set. abr. ed. 1999. (Corps Ser.: No. 8). audio 24.95 Highsmith Inc.

—In Danger's Path. 1999. (Corps Ser.: No. 8). 560p. 24.95 o.p. (*0-399-14421-8*);No. 8. 24.95 o.s.i (*0-399-14454-4*, 752354) Penguin Group (USA) Inc.

—Line of Fire. 1993. (Corps Ser.: No. 5). 480p. mass mkt. 7.99 (*0-515-11013-2*, Jove) Berkley Publishing Group.

—Line of Fire. unabr. ed. 1992. (Corps Ser.: No. 5). audio 96.00 (*0-7366-2255-1*, 3044) Books on Tape, Inc.

—Line of Fire. 1992. (Corps Ser.: No. 5). 416p. 21.95 o.p. (*0-399-13671-1*, G. P. Putnam's Sons) Penguin Group (USA) Inc.

—Semper Fi. unabr. collector's ed. 1992. (Corps Ser.: No. 1). audio 72.00 (*0-7366-2196-2*, 2991) Books on Tape, Inc.

**MCCOY, LEONARD (FICTITIOUS CHARACTER)—FICTION**

Bonanno, Margaret W. Strangers from the Sky. 1990. (Star Trek Ser.). mass mkt. 5.99 (*0-671-73481-4*, Star Trek) Simon & Schuster.

—Strangers from the Sky. abr. ed. (Star Trek Ser.). 1990. audio 11.00; 1987. audio 11.00 (*0-671-64718-0*, Simon & Schuster Audioworks) Simon & Schuster Audio.

Carter, Carmen. Dreams of the Raven. (Star Trek: No. 34). 2000. E-Book 6.99 (*0-7434-1985-5*); 1991. mass mkt. 5.50 o.s.i (*0-671-74356-2*) Simon & Schuster. (Star Trek).

Crispin, A. C. Time for Yesterday. 2000. E-Book 6.99 (*0-7434-1990-1*); 1999. (Star Trek Ser.: No. 39). 320p. pap. 3.99 (*0-671-03857-5*); 1989. (Star Trek: No. 39). 288p. mass mkt. 5.50 (*0-671-70094-4*) Simon & Schuster. (Star Trek).

—Time for Yesterday. abr. ed. 1989. (Star Trek Ser.: No. 39). audio 11.00 (*0-671-67017-4*, Simon & Schuster Audioworks) Simon & Schuster Audio.

—Yesterday's Son. (Star Trek: No. 11). 2000. E-Book 6.99 (*0-7434-1962-6*); 1999. 192p. pap. 3.99 (*0-671-03851-6*); 1990. 192p. mass mkt. 4.50 o.s.i (*0-671-72449-5*) Simon & Schuster. (Star Trek).

DeWeese, Gene. Renegade. 2000. (Star Trek: No. 55). E-Book 6.99 (*0-7434-2006-3*, Star Trek) Simon & Schuster.

—Renegade. Stern, Dave, ed. 1991. (Star Trek: No. 55). 256p. mass mkt. 4.95 (*0-671-65814-X*, Star Trek) Simon & Schuster.

Dillard, J. M. Demons. (Star Trek: No. 30). 2000. E-Book 6.99 (*0-7434-1981-2*); 1990. mass mkt. 4.50 (*0-671-70877-5*) Simon & Schuster. (Star Trek).

—The Final Frontier. abr. ed. (Star Trek Ser.: No. 5). audio 7.95. 1990. audio 7.95 (*0-671-68507-4*, Simon & Schuster Audioworks) Simon & Schuster Audio.

—The Lost Years. 1989. (Star Trek Ser.). (Illus.). 320p. 17.95 o.p. (*0-671-68293-8*, Star Trek) Simon & Schuster.

—The Lost Years. Stern, David, ed. 1990. (Star Trek). 448p. reprint ed. mass mkt. 5.99 (*0-671-70795-7*, Star Trek) Simon & Schuster.

—The Lost Years. abr. ed. 1989. (Star Trek Ser.: Vol. 2). audio 15.95 o.s.i (*0-671-68632-1*, Simon & Schuster Audioworks) Simon & Schuster Audio.

—Recovery. Ryan, Kevin, ed. 1995. (Star Trek: No. 73). 288p. mass mkt. 5.50 (*0-671-88342-9*, Star Trek) Simon & Schuster.

—Star Trek 5: The Final Frontier. 1989. (Star Trek Ser.: No. 5). mass mkt. 4.50 (*0-671-68008-0*, Star Trek) Simon & Schuster.

—The Undiscovered Country. Stern, Dave, ed. 1992. (Star Trek Ser.: No. 6). 320p. mass mkt. 5.50 (*0-671-75883-7*, Pocket) Simon & Schuster.

—The Undiscovered Country. abr. ed. 1992. (Star Trek Ser.: No. 6). audio 11.00 (*0-671-75873-X*, Simon & Schuster Audioworks) Simon & Schuster Audio.

Duane, Diane. Doctor's Orders. (Star Trek: No. 50). 2000. E-Book 6.99 (*0-7434-2001-2*); 1990. 288p. mass mkt. 5.50 (*0-671-66189-2*) Simon & Schuster. (Star Trek).

—Rihannsu Bk. 3: Swordhunt. 2000. (Star Trek Ser.: No. 95). 256p. pap. 6.99 (*0-671-04209-2*, Star Trek) Simon & Schuster.

—Spock's World. (Star Trek Ser.). 1989. 400p. mass mkt. 6.50 (*0-671-66773-4*); 1988. pap. 16.95 o.p. (*0-671-66851-X*); 2000. 400p. pap. 3.99 (*0-7434-0371-1*) Simon & Schuster. (Star Trek).

—Spock's World. abr. ed. 1989. (Star Trek Ser.). audio 16.00 (*0-671-67917-1*, Simon & Schuster Audioworks) Simon & Schuster Audio.

Duane, Diane & Morwood, Peter. Rihannsu: The Romulan Way, No. 2. 1991. (Star Trek: No. 35). mass mkt. 4.99 (*0-671-74357-0*, Star Trek) Simon & Schuster.

—Rihannsu No. 2: The Romulan Way. 2000. (Star Trek: No. 35). E-Book 6.99 (*0-7434-1986-3*, Star Trek) Simon & Schuster.

—The Romulan Way. (Star Trek: No. 35). 1988. mass mkt. 3.95 o.s.i (*0-671-68085-4*); Bk. 2. 2000. 256p. pap. 6.99 (*0-7434-0370-3*) Simon & Schuster. (Star Trek).

Ecklar, Julia. The Kobayashi Maru. 1989. (Star Trek: No. 47). mass mkt. 5.50 (*0-671-65817-4*, Star Trek) Simon & Schuster.

—The Kobayashi Maru. (Star Trek Ser.: No. 47). 1999. audio 5.98 (*0-671-04486-9*); 1990. audio 11.00 (*0-671-70895-3*) Simon & Schuster Audio. (Simon & Schuster Audioworks).

Ferguson, Brad. Crisis on Centaurus. 2000. (Star Trek: No. 28). E-Book 6.99 (*0-7434-1979-0*, Star Trek) Simon & Schuster.

—Crisis on Centaurus. Stern, Dave, ed. 1990. (Star Trek: No. 28). mass mkt. 4.99 (*0-671-70799-X*, Star Trek) Simon & Schuster.

Foster, Alan Dean. Star Trek Logs One, Two & Three. 1992. (Star Trek Ser.). mass mkt. 4.99 o.s.i (*0-345-38247-1*, Del Rey) Ballantine Bks.

Friedman, Michael Jan. Crossover. (Star Trek, The Next Generation Ser.). E-Book 6.99 (*0-7434-2066-7*); 1996. 320p. mass mkt. 5.99 (*0-671-89676-8*); 1995. 320p. 23.00 o.p. (*0-671-89677-6*) Simon & Schuster. (Star Trek).

—Crossover. abr. ed. 1995. (Star Trek Ser.). audio 17.00 o.s.i (*0-671-53628-1*, Simon & Schuster Audioworks) Simon & Schuster Audio.

—Faces of Fire. 2000. (Star Trek: No. 58). E-Book 6.99 (*0-7434-2009-8*, Star Trek) Simon & Schuster.

—Faces of Fire. Stern, Dave, ed. 1992. (Star Trek: No. 58). 320p. mass mkt. 5.50 (*0-671-74992-7*, Star Trek) Simon & Schuster.

—Faces of Fire. 1992. (Star Trek Ser.: No. 58). audio 16.00 o.s.i (*0-671-77802-1*, Simon & Schuster Audioworks) Simon & Schuster Audio.

—Shadows on the Sun. 1993. (Star Trek Ser.). 352p. 22.00 (*0-671-86909-4*, Star Trek) Simon & Schuster.

—Shadows on the Sun. Ryan, Kevin, ed. 1994. (Star Trek Ser.). 352p. reprint ed. mass mkt. 5.99 (*0-671-86910-8*, Star Trek) Simon & Schuster.

—Shadows on the Sun. abr. ed. 1993. (Star Trek Ser.). audio 17.00 (*0-671-86974-4*, Simon & Schuster Audioworks) Simon & Schuster Audio.

—Star Trek: Modala Imperative. Kahan, Bob, ed. 1992. (Star Trek Ser.). (Illus.). 208p. pap. 19.95 (*1-56389-040-2*) DC Comics.

Graf, L. A. Death Count. 2000. (Star Trek: No. 62). E-Book 6.99 (*0-7434-2013-6*, Star Trek) Simon & Schuster.

—Ice Trap. 2000. (Star Trek: No. 60). E-Book 6.99 (*0-7434-2011-X*, Star Trek) Simon & Schuster.

Graf, L. A. & Ecklar, Julia. Ice Trap. Stern, Dave, ed. 1992. (Star Trek: No. 60). 288p. mass mkt. 4.99 (*0-671-78068-9*, Star Trek) Simon & Schuster.

McIntyre, Vonda N. The Entropy Effect. (Star Trek: No. 2). 1990. mass mkt. 5.50 (*0-671-72416-9*); 1986. pap. 3.50 (*0-671-62743-0*); 1985. mass mkt. 3.50 o.s.i (*0-671-62229-3*); 1983. 224p. mass mkt. 2.95 o.s.i (*0-671-49300-0*); 1981. E-Book 6.99 (*0-7434-1209-5*); 1981. mass mkt. 2.50 o.s.i (*0-671-83692-7*) Simon & Schuster. (Star Trek).

—The Entropy Effect. abr. ed. 1988. (Star Trek: No. 2). audio 11.00 (*0-671-66864-1*, Simon & Schuster Audioworks) Simon & Schuster Audio.

—The Search for Spock. 2000. (Star Trek Ser.: No. 3). E-Book 6.99 (*0-7434-1968-5*); 1990. (Star Trek: No. 17). mass mkt. 5.50 (*0-671-73133-5*) Simon & Schuster. (Star Trek).

—The Wrath of Khan. (Star Trek: No. 7). 1991. mass mkt. 5.50 (*0-671-74149-7*); 1984. mass mkt. 2.95 o.s.i (*0-671-55248-1*) Simon & Schuster. (Star Trek).

McIntyre, Vonda N., et al. Star Trek Boxed Set: The Entropy Effect; The Covenant of the Crown; Yesterday's Son; The IDIC Epidemic. 1991. (Star Trek: Nos. 2, 4, 11, 38). pap. 18.00 (*0-671-96368-6*, Pocket) Simon & Schuster.

Mitchell, V. E. Enemy Unseen. Stern, David, ed. 1990. (Star Trek: No. 51). 288p. mass mkt. 4.99 (*0-671-68403-5*, Star Trek) Simon & Schuster.

—Windows on a Lost World. Stern, Dave, ed. 1993. (Star Trek: No. 65). 288p. mass mkt. 5.99 (*0-671-79512-0*, Star Trek) Simon & Schuster.

—Windows on a Lost World. abr. ed. 1993. (Star Trek Ser.: No. 65). audio 17.00 (*0-671-86962-0*, 391662, Simon & Schuster Audioworks) Simon & Schuster Audio.

Peel, John. Where No Man Has Gone Before. 1986. (Star Trek Ser.). 96p. lib. bdg. 19.95 o.p. (*0-8095-8019-5*) Millefleurs.

Reeves-Stevens, Judith. Prime Directive. abr. ed. 2001. (Star Trek Ser.). audio 9.98 (*0-671-04465-6*, Simon & Schuster Audioworks) Simon & Schuster Audio.

Reeves-Stevens, Judith & Reeves-Stevens, Garfield. Prime Directive. Stern, David, ed. 1990. (Star Trek Ser.). 416p. 18.95 (*0-671-70772-8*, Star Trek) Simon & Schuster.

—Prime Directive. Stern, Dave, ed. 1991. (Star Trek Ser.). 416p. reprint ed. mass mkt. 5.99 (*0-671-74466-6*, Star Trek) Simon & Schuster.

—Prime Directive. abr. ed. 1990. (Star Trek Ser.). audio 15.95 (*0-671-72631-5*, Simon & Schuster Audioworks) Simon & Schuster Audio.

Reynolds, Mack. Mission to Horatius. 1999. (Star Trek Ser.). (Illus.). 208p. 16.00 o.s.i (*0-671-02812-X*, Atria) Simon & Schuster.

—Well Meet Again. unabr. ed. 1999. (Star Trek Ser.). audio 39.95 (*0-671-04380-3*, Simon & Schuster Audioworks) Simon & Schuster Audio.

Roddenberry, Gene. The Motion Picture. 1979. (Star Trek: No. 1). E-Book 6.99 (*0-7434-1208-7*, Star Trek) Simon & Schuster.

—Star Trek: The Motion Picture. (Star Trek: No. 1). 1984. mass mkt. 2.95 o.s.i (*0-671-54685-6*); 1980. mass mkt. 2.95 o.s.i (*0-671-83089-9*) Simon & Schuster. (Star Trek).

Roddenberry, Gene, et al. Star Trek: The Motion Picture. 1979. (Star Trek: No. 1). 252 p. o.p. (*0-671-25324-7*, Simon & Schuster) Simon & Schuster.

Shatner, William. Ashes of Eden. Ryan, Kevin, ed. 1995. (Star Trek Ser.). 320p. 23.00 o.p. (*0-671-52035-0*, Star Trek) Simon & Schuster.

—Preserver. (Star Trek Ser.). reprint ed. 2001. 448p. pap. 6.99 (*0-671-02126-5*); 2001. E-Book 23.95 (*0-7434-1955-3*); 2000. (Illus.). (J). E-Book 23.95 (*0-7434-1119-6*) Simon & Schuster. (Star Trek).

—Preserver. abr. ed. 2000. (Star Trek Ser.). audio 18.00 (*0-7435-0031-8*, Simon & Schuster Audioworks) Simon & Schuster Audio.

Shatner, William, et al. Ashes of Eden. 1996. (Star Trek Ser.). 320p. mass mkt. 6.99 (*0-671-52036-9*, Star Trek) Simon & Schuster.

—Ashes of Eden. abr. ed. 1995. (Star Trek Ser.). audio 18.00 o.s.i (*0-671-52892-0*, 392990, Simon & Schuster Audioworks) Simon & Schuster Audio.

—Dark Victory. (Star Trek Ser.). 320p. 1999. 23.00 o.s.i (*0-671-00882-X*); 2000. reprint ed. pap. 6.99 (*0-671-00884-6*) Simon & Schuster. (Star Trek).

—Preserver. 2000. (Star Trek Ser.). 384p. 23.95 o.s.i (*0-671-02125-7*, Star Trek) Simon & Schuster.

—Star Trek: The Ashes of Eden. 2001. (Star Trek Ser.). (Illus.). 94p. pap. 14.95 (*1-56389-235-9*) DC Comics.

Smith, Dean W., et al. Rings of Tautee, No. 078. 1996. (Star Trek Ser.: No. 78). 256p. pap. 5.99 (*0-671-00171-X*, Star Trek) Simon & Schuster.

Smith, Dean Wesley. The Rings of Tautee. 2000. E-Book 6.99 (*0-7434-2029-2*, Star Trek) Simon & Schuster.

Vardeman, Robert E. The Klingon Gambit. 1981. (Star Trek: No. 3). E-Book 6.99 (*0-7434-1210-9*, Star Trek) Simon & Schuster.

Vornholt, John. Sanctuary. 2000. (Star Trek: No. 61). E-Book 6.99 (*0-7434-2012-8*, Star Trek) Simon & Schuster.

—Sanctuary. Stern, Dave, ed. 1992. (Star Trek Ser.: No. 61). 288p. mass mkt. 4.99 (*0-671-76994-4*, Star Trek) Simon & Schuster.

Weinstein, Howard. The Covenant of the Crown. (Star Trek: No. 4). 1989. mass mkt. 4.50 (*0-671-70078-2*); 1988. mass mkt. 3.95 o.s.i (*0-671-67072-7*); 1983. 192p. mass mkt. 2.95 o.s.i (*0-671-49297-7*); 1981. E-Book 6.99 (*0-7434-1211-7*) Simon & Schuster. (Star Trek).

Windows on a Lost World. 2000. (Star Trek Ser.: No. 65). E-Book 6.99 (*0-7434-2016-0*, Star Trek) Simon & Schuster.

### MCCRACKEN, BLAINE (FICTITIOUS CHARACTER)—FICTION

Land, Jon. Day of the Delphi. 1993. 432p. (Orig.). mass mkt. 5.99 (*0-8125-3434-4*, Tor Bks.) Doherty, Tom Assocs., LLC.

—Dead Simple. 1999. 404p. mass mkt. 6.99 (*0-8125-4001-8*); 1998. 320p. 23.95 (*0-312-86489-2*) Doherty, Tom Assocs., LLC. (Forge Bks.).

—Fires of Midnight. 1996. 361p. pap. text 6.99 (*0-8125-5252-0*); 1995. 320p. 22.95 o.p. (*0-312-85971-6*) Doherty, Tom Assocs., LLC. (Forge Bks.).

—The Omicron Legion. 1991. 352p. (Orig.). mass mkt. 5.95 o.s.i (*0-449-14635-9*, Fawcett) Ballantine Bks.

—The Vengeance of the Tau. 1993. (Orig.). mass mkt. 5.99 o.s.i (*0-449-14776-2*, Fawcett) Ballantine Bks.

### MCCRAE, AUGUSTUS (FICTITIOUS CHARACTER)—FICTION

McMurtry, Larry. Comanche Moon. unabr. ed. 1999. Pt. 1. audio 72.00; Pt. 2. (Lonesome Dove Ser.: No. 2). audio 64.00 Books on Tape, Inc.

—Comanche Moon, Set. unabr. ed. 1999. (Lonesome Dove Ser.: No. 2). audio 45.00 Highsmith Inc.

—Comanche Moon. 2000. (Lonesome Dove Ser.: No. 2). 720p. pap. 16.00 (*0-684-85755-3*, Simon & Schuster); 1998. (Lonesome Dove Ser.: No. 2). 816p. pap. 7.99 (*0-671-02064-1*, Pocket); 1998. mass mkt. 6.99 (*0-671-02049-8*, Pocket); 1997. (Lonesome Dove Ser.: No. 2). 752p. 28.50 (*0-684-80754-8*, Simon & Schuster) Simon & Schuster.

—Comanche Moon. unabr. ed. 1997. (Lonesome Dove Ser.: No. 2). 24p. audio 60.00 (*0-671-57730-1*, 135489, Simon & Schuster Audioworks) Simon & Schuster Audio.

—Comanche Moon. l.t. ed. 1999. (Paperback Bestsellers Ser.: No. 2). 921p. pap. 28.95 (*0-7862-1392-2*) Thorndike Pr.

—Comanche Moon. 1998. 14.04 (*0-606-16182-1*) Turtleback Bks.

—Dead Man's Walk. unabr. ed. 1996. audio 80.00 (*0-7366-3211-5*, 3874) Books on Tape, Inc.

—Dead Man's Walk. l.t. ed. (Lonesome Dove Ser.: No. 1). 1999. 800p. 27.95 o.p. (*0-7838-1510-7*); 1996. pap. 25.95 o.p. (*0-7838-1511-5*) Gale Group. (Macmillan Reference USA).

—Dead Man's Walk. (Lonesome Dove Ser.: No. 1). 2000. 464p. pap. 15.00 (*0-684-85754-5*, Simon & Schuster); 1995. 480p. 26.00 (*0-684-80753-X*, Simon & Schuster); 1996. 528p. pap. 7.99 (*0-671-00116-7*, Pocket) Simon & Schuster.

—Dead Man's Walk. unabr. ed. 1995. (Lonesome Dove Ser.: No. 1). audio 45.00 (*0-671-55169-8*, 113285, Simon & Schuster Audioworks) Simon & Schuster Audio.

—Dead Man's Walk. l.t. ed. 1998. (Lonesome Dove Ser.: No. 1). 5.98 o.p. (*0-7651-0771-6*) Smithmark Pubs., Inc.

—Dead Man's Walk. 2000. 21.05 (*0-606-20274-9*) Turtleback Bks.

—Lonesome Dove, Pt. 1. unabr. collector's ed. 1986. audio 56.00 (*0-7366-0582-7*, 1552-A) Books on Tape, Inc.

—Lonesome Dove. unabr. ed. 1993. (Lonesome Dove Ser.: No. 3). Vol. 1. 49.95 o.p. (*1-55800-481-5*); Vol. 2. 49.95 o.p. (*1-55800-622-2*); Vols. 1 & 2. audio 69.95 o.p. (*1-55800-719-9*) NewStar Media, Inc.

—Lonesome Dove. Grose, Bill, ed. 2000. (Lonesome Dove Ser.: No. 3). 960p. mass mkt. 7.99 (*0-671-79589-9*, Pocket) Simon & Schuster.

—Lonesome Dove. 2000. (Simon & Schuster Classic Editions: No. 3). (Illus.). 864p. 30.00 (*0-684-87122-X*, Simon & Schuster); 2000. (Lonesome Dove Ser.: No. 3). 864p. pap. 16.00 (*0-684-85752-9*, Simon & Schuster); 1993. (Lonesome Dove Ser.: No. 3). mass mkt. 6.99 (*0-671-74471-2*, Pocket); 1985. (Lonesome Dove Ser.: No. 3). 848p. 28.00 (*0-671-50420-7*, Simon & Schuster); No. 3. 1988. 960p. mass mkt. 7.99 (*0-671-68390-X*, Pocket) Simon & Schuster.

Smith, Julie. New Orleans Mourning. 1990. 384p. 17.95 o.p. (*0-312-03892-5*, Saint Martin's Minotaur) St. Martin's Pr.

### MCCUNN, DICKSON (FICTITIOUS CHARACTER)—FICTION

Buchan, John. Castle Gay. 1993. pap. 7.00 (*0-7509-0483-6*) Sutton Publishing, Ltd. GBR. *Dist:* International Publishers Marketing.

—Huntingtower. Stonehouse, Ann F., ed. 1997. (Oxford World's Classics Ser.). (Illus.). 260p. pap. 8.95 o.p. (*0-19-283229-8*) Oxford Univ. Pr., Inc.

—Huntingtower. 1993. pap. 7.00 (*0-7509-0484-4*) Sutton Publishing, Ltd. GBR. *Dist:* International Publishers Marketing.

### MCCUSKER, KATE (FICTITIOUS CHARACTER)—FICTION

Elm, Joanna. Delusion. 1999. 374p. mass mkt. 6.99 (*0-8125-6480-4*, Tor Bks.); 1997. 384p. 23.95 (*0-312-86064-1*, Forge Bks.) Doherty, Tom Assocs., LLC.

### MACDONALD, DEVON (FICTITIOUS CHARACTER)—FICTION

Jacobs, Nancy B. The Silver Scalpel. 1993. (Devon McDonald Ser.). 240p. 21.95 o.p. (*0-399-13834-X*, G. P. Putnam's Sons) Penguin Group (USA) Inc.

—A Slash of Scarlet. 1992. 240p. 19.95 o.p. (*0-399-13733-5*, G. P. Putnam's Sons) Penguin Group (USA) Inc.

—A Slash of Scarlet. Rubenstein, Julie, ed. 1993. 256p. reprint ed. mass mkt. 4.99 (*0-671-86504-8*, Pocket) Simon & Schuster.

—The Turquoise Tattoo. 1992. 256p. reprint ed. mass mkt. 4.99 (*0-671-75535-8*, Pocket) Simon & Schuster.

—The Turquoise Tattoo: A Devon MacDonald Mystery. 1991. 240p. 19.95 o.p. (*0-399-13551-0*, G. P. Putnam's Sons) Penguin Group (USA) Inc.

### MCDONALD, PAUL (FICTITIOUS CHARACTER)—FICTION

Smith, Julie. Huckleberry Fiend. 1987. (Paul McDonald Mystery Ser.). 224p. 15.95 (*0-89296-237-2*) Mysterious Pr.

—Huckleberry Fiend. 1988. 224p. mass mkt. 5.50 (*0-445-40696-8*, Mysterious Pr. Paperback Bks.) Warner Bks., Inc.

—True-Life Adventure. 1986. 15.45 o.p. (*0-89296-120-1*) Mysterious Pr.

—True-Life Adventure. 1986. 256p. reprint ed. mass mkt. 4.99 o.s.i (*0-445-40505-8*, Mysterious Pr. Paperback Bks.) Warner Bks., Inc.

### MCDOWELL, SCOTT (FICTITIOUS CHARACTER)—FICTION

Palmer, Jessica. Cradlesong. Todd, Rebecca, ed. 1993. 320p. (Orig.). mass mkt. 4.99 (*0-671-73421-0*, Pocket) Simon & Schuster.

### MCEVOY, JACK (FICTITIOUS CHARACTER)—FICTION

Connelly, Michael. The Poet. l.t. ed. 2000. pap. 25.95 o.p. (*1-56895-330-5*, Wheeler Publishing, Inc.) Gale Group.

—The Poet. 1996. 440p. 22.95 o.p. (*0-316-15398-2*) Little Brown & Co.

—The Poet. 1997. 528p. reprint ed. mass mkt. 7.99 (*0-446-60261-2*) Warner Bks., Inc.

### MCGAMMON, CLYDE (FICTITIOUS CHARACTER)—FICTION

Clements, Mark A. Lorelei. 1995. 304p. pap. 4.99 (*0-8439-3867-6*) Dorchester Publishing Co., Inc.

—Lorelei. 1994. 304p. 20.95 o.p. (*1-55611-410-9*) Fine, Donald I. Bks.

—Lorelei. 1995. E-Book 9.95 (*0-585-28857-7*) netLibrary, Inc.

### MCGARR, PETER (FICTITIOUS CHARACTER)—FICTION

Gill, Bartholomew. Death in Dublin. 2003. 368p. mass mkt. 6.99 (*0-06-000850-4*, Avon Bks.); 304p. 24.95 (*0-06-000849-0*, Morrow, William & Co.) Morrow/Avon.

—The Death of a Joyce Scholar. 1990. (Peter McGarr Mystery Ser.). 336p. reprint ed. mass mkt. 6.99 (*0-380-71129-X*, Avon Bks.) Morrow/Avon.

—The Death of a Joyce Scholar: A Peter McGarr Mystery. 1989. 310p. 18.95 o.p. (*0-688-08713-2*, Morrow, William & Co.) Morrow/Avon.

—The Death of an Ardent Bibliophile: A Peter McGarr Mystery. 1996. 256p. mass mkt. 5.50 (*0-380-72206-2*, Avon Bks.); 1995. 288p. 20.00 o.p. (*0-688-12909-9*, Morrow, William & Co.) Morrow/Avon.

—The Death of an Irish Lover: A Peter McGarr Mystery. 2001. 320p. mass mkt. 6.50 (*0-380-80863-3*, Avon Bks.) Morrow/Avon.

—The Death of an Irish Politician. 2000. (Inspector Peter McGarr Mysteries Ser.). 240p. mass mkt. 6.99 (*0-380-73273-4*, Avon Bks.) Morrow/Avon.

—The Death of an Irish Sea Wolf. 1997. (Peter McGarr Mystery Ser.). 304p. mass mkt. 6.50 (*0-380-72578-9*, Avon Bks.) Morrow/Avon.

—The Death of an Irish Sea Wolf: A Peter McGarr Mystery. 1996. 288p. 23.00 o.p. (*0-688-14183-8*, Morrow, William & Co.) Morrow/Avon.

—The Death of an Irish Sinner. 2001. (Inspector Peter McGarr Mysteries Ser.). 288p. 24.00 (*0-380-97798-2*, Morrow, William & Co.) Morrow/Avon.

—The Death of an Irish Sinner: A Peter McGarr Mystery. 2002. 368p. mass mkt. 6.99 (*0-380-80864-1*, Avon Bks.) Morrow/Avon.

—The Death of an Irish Tinker. 1998. (Inspector Peter McGarr Mysteries Ser.). 256p. mass mkt. 6.99 (*0-380-72579-7*, Avon Bks.) Morrow/Avon.

—The Death of an Irish Tinker: A Peter McGarr Mystery. 1997. 288p. 23.00 (*0-688-14184-6*, Morrow, William & Co.) Morrow/Avon.

—The Death of an Irish Tradition. 2003. 368p. mass mkt. 6.99 (*0-06-052261-5*, Avon Bks.) Morrow/Avon.

—The Death of Love: A Peter McGarr Mystery. 1993. 352p. mass mkt. 4.99 (*0-380-71982-7*, Avon Bks.); 1992. 356p. 20.00 o.p. (*0-688-08715-9*, Morrow, William & Co.) Morrow/Avon.

—Death on a Cold, Wild River: A Peter McGarr Mystery. Date not set. 256p. mass mkt. 4.99 (*0-380-72205-4*, Avon Bks.); 1993. 251p. 20.00 o.p. (*0-688-12881-5*, Morrow, William & Co.) Morrow/Avon.

—McGarr & the Legacy of a Woman Scorned. 224p. 1987. mass mkt. 3.50 o.p. (*0-14-009609-4*, Penguin Bks.); 1986. 14.95 o.p. (*0-670-80673-0*) Viking Penguin.

—McGarr & the Method of Descartes. (Crime Monthly Ser.). 1985. 304p. pap. 3.95 o.p. (*0-14-008405-3*, Penguin Bks.); 1984. 288p. 14.95 o.p. (*0-670-46432-5*) Viking Penguin.

—McGarr & the P. M. of Belgrave Square. (Crime Monthly Ser.). 1984. 256p. pap. 3.95 o.p. (*0-14-007323-X*, Penguin Bks.); 1983. 240p. 13.95 o.p. (*0-670-46430-9*) Viking Penguin.

—McGarr & the Politician's Wife. 1982. (Crime Monthly Ser.). pap. 3.95 o.p. (*0-14-005984-9*, Penguin Bks.) Viking Penguin.

—McGarr & the Sienese Conspiracy. 1980. pap. 2.25 o.p. (*0-440-15784-6*) Dell Publishing.

—McGarr & the Sienese Conspiracy. 1977. 7.95 o.s.i (*0-684-15185-5*, Macmillan Reference USA) Gale Group.

—McGarr & the Sienese Conspiracy. 1986. (Crime Ser.). 224p. pap. 3.95 o.p. (*0-14-008580-7*, Penguin Bks.) Viking Penguin.

—McGarr at the Dublin Horse Show. 1981. pap. 2.25 o.p. (*0-440-15379-4*) Dell Publishing.

—McGarr on the Cliffs of Moher. 1982. (Crime Monthly Ser.). 252p. pap. 3.50 o.p. (*0-14-006197-5*, Penguin Bks.) Viking Penguin.

Maxwell, Cathy. The Marriage Contract. 2001. 384p. mass mkt. 6.50 (*0-380-80833-1*, Avon Bks.) Morrow/Avon.

—The Marriage Contract. unabr. ed. 2001. audio 54.00 Recorded Bks., LLC.

### MCGARVEY, JACK (FICTITIOUS CHARACTER)—FICTION

Koontz, Dean. Winter Moon. 1997. pap. 12.95 o.p. (*0-345-41949-9*); 1993. 480p. mass mkt. 7.99 o.s.i (*0-345-38610-8*) Ballantine Bks.

### MCGARVEY, KIRK (FICTITIOUS CHARACTER)—FICTION

Hagberg, David. High Flight. 1996. 879p. mass mkt. 7.99 (*0-8125-1012-7*, Tor Bks.); 1995. 640p. 24.95 o.p. (*0-312-85092-1*, Forge Bks.) Doherty, Tom Assocs., LLC.

—Joshua's Hammer. (Kirk McGarvey Novels Ser.). 2000. (Illus.). 352p. 25.95 (*0-312-86128-1*, Forge Bks.); 2001. 544p. reprint ed. mass mkt. 7.99 (*0-8125-4439-0*, Tor Bks.) Doherty, Tom Assocs., LLC.

—White House. 2001. 422p. mass mkt. 6.99 (*0-8125-5064-1*); 1999. 384p. 25.95 (*0-312-86682-8*) Doherty, Tom Assocs., LLC. (Forge Bks.).

### MCGEE, TRAVIS (FICTITIOUS CHARACTER)—FICTION

MacDonald, John D. Bright Orange for the Shroud. (Travis McGee Novel Ser.). 1987. 224p. mass mkt. 5.99 o.s.i (*0-449-13358-3*, Fawcett); 1996. reprint ed. mass mkt. 5.99 (*0-449-45615-3*, Fawcett); 1996. 352p. reprint ed. mass mkt. 6.99 (*0-449-22444-9*, Ballantine Bks.) Ballantine Bks.

—Bright Orange for the Shroud. unabr. collector's ed. 1978. (Travis McGee Ser.: No. 6). audio 48.00 (*0-7366-0174-0*, 1176) Books on Tape, Inc.

—Bright Orange for the Shroud. l.t. ed. 1985. 14.95 o.p. (*0-8161-3979-2*, Macmillan Reference USA) Gale Group.

—Cinnamon Skin. (Travis McGee Novel Ser.). 1996. 336p. mass mkt. 7.50 (*0-449-22484-8*); 1986. 288p. mass mkt. 5.95 o.s.i (*0-449-12873-3*) Ballantine Bks. (Fawcett).

—Cinnamon Skin. unabr. collector's ed. 1982. (Travis McGee Ser.: No. 20). audio 48.00 (*0-7366-0689-0*, 1649) Books on Tape, Inc.

—Cinnamon Skin. 1983. (General Ser.). lib. bdg. 14.95 o.p. (*0-8161-3504-5*, Macmillan Reference USA) Gale Group.

—Cinnamon Skin. 1982. 288p. o.p. (*0-06-014990-6*) HarperCollins Pubs.

—Cinnamon Skin. abr. ed. 2000. (Travis McGee Ser.). audio 9.99 (*0-375-41014-7*, RH Audio) Random Hse. Audio Publishing Group.

—Cinnamon Skin. 1990. 3.99 o.p. (*0-517-05439-6*) Random Hse. Value Publishing.

—The Damned. 1985. (Travis McGee Novel Ser.). mass mkt. 3.95 o.s.i (*0-449-12887-3*, Fawcett) Ballantine Bks.

—Darker Than Amber. 1997. mass mkt. 5.99 (*0-449-45637-4*); 1996. 320p. mass mkt. 6.99 (*0-449-22446-5*); 1987. 192p. mass mkt. 5.99 o.s.i (*0-449-13339-7*); 1984. 192p. mass mkt. 2.95 o.p. (*0-449-12752-4*) Ballantine Bks. (Fawcett).

—Darker Than Amber. unabr. collector's ed. 1978. (Travis McGee Ser.: No. 7). audio 42.00 (*0-7366-0216-X*, 1214) Books on Tape, Inc.

—Darker Than Amber. l.t. ed. 1988. (General Ser.). 319p. 16.95 o.p. (*0-8161-4008-1*, Macmillan Reference USA) Gale Group.

—A Deadly Shade of Gold. (Travis McGee Novel Ser.). 1996. 448p. mass mkt. 6.99 (*0-449-22442-2*); 1987. 288p. mass mkt. 5.99 o.s.i (*0-449-13313-3*) Ballantine Bks. (Fawcett).

—A Deadly Shade of Gold. unabr. collector's ed. 1978. (Travis McGee Ser.: No. 5). audio 64.00 (*0-7366-0106-6*, 1114) Books on Tape, Inc.

—A Deadly Shade of Gold. l.t. ed. 1987. 447p. 16.95 o.p. (*0-8161-4004-9*, Macmillan Reference USA) Gale Group.

—The Deep Blue Goodbye. 1995. 320p. mass mkt. 6.99 (*0-449-22383-3*); 1986. 256p. mass mkt. 4.95 o.s.i (*0-449-13252-8*); 1984. mass mkt. 2.95 o.p. (*0-449-12673-0*) Ballantine Bks. (Fawcett).

—The Deep Blue Goodbye. unabr. collector's ed. 1983. (Travis McGee Ser.: No. 1). audio 36.00 (*0-7366-0699-8*, 1662) Books on Tape, Inc.

—The Deep Blue Goodbye. l.t. ed. 1984. (General Ser.). 296p. 12.95 o.p. (*0-8161-3626-2*); 8.95 o.p. (*0-8161-3740-4*) Gale Group. (Macmillan Reference USA).

—The Dreadful Lemon Sky. (Travis McGee Novel Ser.). 1996. 320p. mass mkt. 6.99 (*0-449-22479-1*); 1987. 272p. mass mkt. 5.99 o.s.i (*0-449-13404-0*); 1985. 272p. mass mkt. 3.50 o.p. (*0-449-12964-0*) Ballantine Bks. (Fawcett).

—The Dreadful Lemon Sky. unabr. collector's ed. 1977. (Travis McGee Ser.: No. 16). audio 42.00 (*0-7366-0047-7*, 1059) Books on Tape, Inc.

—The Dreadful Lemon Sky. (Travis McGee Ser.). 2001. audio 9.99 (*0-375-41672-2*); 1988. audio 15.95 o.p. (*0-394-57084-7*) Random Hse. Audio Publishing Group. (RH Audio).

—Dress Her in Indigo. 1997. pap. text 5.99 (*0-449-45716-8*); 1996. 336p. mass mkt. 7.50 (*0-449-22462-7*); 1987. 256p. mass mkt. 5.99 o.s.i (*0-449-13293-5*); 1985. mass mkt. 3.50 o.p. (*0-449-12984-5*) Ballantine Bks. (Fawcett).

—Dress Her in Indigo. unabr. collector's ed. 1980. (Travis McGee Ser.: No. 11). audio 56.00 (*0-7366-0243-7*, 1239) Books on Tape, Inc.

—Dress Her in Indigo. l.t. ed. 1985. (General Ser.). 360p. 13.95 o.p. (*0-8161-3822-2*); 9.95 o.p. (*0-8161-3820-6*) Gale Group. (Macmillan Reference USA).

—The Empty Copper Sea. 21.95 (*0-89190-778-5*) Amereon, Ltd.

—The Empty Copper Sea. 1996. 320p. mass mkt. 7.50 (*0-449-22480-5*); 1987. 256p. mass mkt. 4.99 o.s.i (*0-449-13333-8*); 1985. mass mkt. 3.50 o.p. (*0-449-12913-6*) Ballantine Bks. (Fawcett).

—The Empty Copper Sea. unabr. collector's ed. 1979. (Travis McGee Ser.: No. 17). audio 48.00 (*0-7366-0331-X*, 1318) Books on Tape, Inc.

—The Empty Copper Sea. 1979. lib. bdg. 13.50 o.p. (*0-8161-6702-8*, Macmillan Reference USA) Gale Group.

—The Empty Copper Sea. abr. ed. 1987. audio 15.95 o.s.i (*0-394-56085-X*, RH Audio) Random Hse. Audio Publishing Group.

—Five Complete Travis McGee Novels. 1988. 8.99 o.s.i (*0-517-47671-1*) Random Hse. Value Publishing.

—Free Fall in Crimson. 1996. 320p. mass mkt. 7.50 (*0-449-22482-1*); 1987. 288p. mass mkt. 4.95 o.s.i (*0-449-13253-6*); 1985. 288p. mass mkt. 3.50 o.p. (*0-449-12894-6*) Ballantine Bks. (Fawcett).

—Free Fall in Crimson. unabr. collector's ed. 1981. (Travis McGee Ser.: No. 19). audio 48.00 (*0-7366-0632-7*, 1593) Books on Tape, Inc.

—Free Fall in Crimson. l.t. ed. 1981. 13.50 o.p. (*0-8161-3272-0*, Macmillan Reference USA) Gale Group.

—Free Fall in Crimson. 1981. 224p. 15.00 o.p. (*0-06-014833-0*) HarperTrade.

—Free Fall in Crimson. 1992. audio 16.00 o.s.i (*0-394-55989-4*, RH Audio) Random Hse. Audio Publishing Group.

—The Girl in the Plain Brown Wrapper. 1997. mass mkt. 5.99 (0-449-45715-X); 1996. 352p. mass mkt. 7.50 (0-449-22461-9); 1987. 256p. mass mkt. 5.99 o.s.i (0-449-13341-9); 1985. mass mkt. 3.50 o.p. (0-449-12915-2) Ballantine Bks. (Fawcett).
—The Girl in the Plain Brown Wrapper. unabr. collector's ed. 1984. (Travis McGee Ser.: No. 10). audio 56.00 (0-7366-0704-8, 1667) Books on Tape, Inc.
—The Girl in the Plain Brown Wrapper. l.t. ed. 1984. (General Ser.). lib. bdg. 12.95 o.p. (0-8161-3627-0, Macmillan Reference USA) Gale Group.
—The Green Ripper. 21.95 (0-89190-779-3) Amereon, Ltd.
—The Green Ripper. (Travis McGee Novel Ser.). 1996. 320p. mass mkt. 7.50 (0-449-22481-3); 1987. 288p. mass mkt. 5.99 o.s.i (0-449-13246-3); 1985. 228p. mass mkt. 3.50 o.p. (0-449-13042-8) Ballantine Bks. (Fawcett).
—The Green Ripper. unabr. collector's ed. 1980. (Travis McGee Ser.: No. 18). audio 42.00 (0-7366-0474-X, 1449) Books on Tape, Inc.
—The Green Ripper. 1980. (General Ser.). lib. bdg. 12.95 o.p. (0-8161-3023-X, Macmillan Reference USA) Gale Group.
—The Green Ripper. 1979. 15.00 o.p. (0-397-01362-0) HarperCollins Pubs.
—The Green Ripper. abr. ed. (Travis McGee Ser.). 1994. audio 8.99 o.s.i (0-679-43407-0); 1991. audio 16.00 o.p. (0-394-55988-6); Set. 2000. audio 9.99 o.s.i (0-375-41581-5) Random Hse. Audio Publishing Group. (RH Audio).
—The Lonely Silver Rain. 1996. 320p. mass mkt. 7.50 (0-449-22485-6); 1986. 256p. mass mkt. 5.95 o.s.i (0-449-12509-2) Ballantine Bks. (Fawcett).
—The Lonely Silver Rain. unabr. collector's ed. 1986. (Travis McGee Ser.: No. 21). audio 42.00 (0-7366-0476-6, 1451) Books on Tape, Inc.
—The Long Lavender Look. (Travis McGee Novel Ser.). 1998. mass mkt. 5.99 (0-449-45717-6); 1996. 352p. mass mkt. 6.99 (0-449-22474-0); 1987. 256p. mass mkt. 4.95 o.s.i (0-449-13334-6) Ballantine Bks. (Fawcett).
—The Long Lavender Look. unabr. collector's ed. 1984. (Travis McGee Ser.: No. 12). audio 48.00 (0-7366-0705-6, 1668) Books on Tape, Inc.
—The Long Lavender Look. l.t. ed. 1986. (General Ser.). 363p. 15.95 o.p. (0-8161-4007-3, Macmillan Reference USA) Gale Group.
—The Long Lavender Look. abr. ed. (Travis McGee Ser.). 1994. audio 8.99 o.s.i (0-679-43406-2); 1990. audio 15.95 o.p. (0-394-55982-7) Random Hse. Audio Publishing Group. (RH Audio).
—Nightmare in Pink. (Travis McGee Novel Ser.). 1995. 304p. mass mkt. 6.99 (0-449-22414-7); 1987. 144p. mass mkt. 4.95 o.s.i (0-449-13312-5) Ballantine Bks. (Fawcett).
—Nightmare in Pink. unabr. collector's ed. 1983. (Travis McGee Ser.: No. 2). audio 36.00 (0-7366-0700-5, 1663) Books on Tape, Inc.
—Nightmare in Pink. 1976. (Adult Ser.). reprint ed. lib. bdg. 9.95 o.p. (0-8161-6382-0, Macmillan Reference USA) Gale Group.
—One Fearful Yellow Eye. 1997. mass mkt. 5.99 (0-449-45639-0); 1996. 336p. mass mkt. 7.50 (0-449-22458-9); 1987. 244p. mass mkt. 4.95 o.s.i (0-449-13292-7); 1985. mass mkt. 3.50 o.p. (0-449-12933-0) Ballantine Bks. (Fawcett).
—One Fearful Yellow Eye. 1983. (General Ser.). lib. bdg. 14.95 o.p. (0-8161-3380-8, Macmillan Reference USA) Gale Group.
—Pale Gray for Guilt. 1997. mass mkt. 5.99 (0-449-45721-4); 1996. 320p. mass mkt. 6.99 (0-449-22460-0); 1987. 224p. mass mkt. 5.99 o.s.i (0-449-13331-1); 1985. mass mkt. 3.95 o.p. (0-449-12897-0) Ballantine Bks. (Fawcett).
—Pale Gray for Guilt. unabr. collector's ed. 1984. (Travis McGee Ser.: No. 9). audio 48.00 (0-7366-0703-X, 1666) Books on Tape, Inc.
—Pale Gray for Guilt. l.t. ed. 1986. (Large Print Bks.). 357p. lib. bdg. 15.95 o.p. (0-8161-4006-5, Macmillan Reference USA) Gale Group.
—A Purple Place for Dying. 1995. 320p. mass mkt. 7.50 (0-449-22438-4); 1987. 160p. mass mkt. 5.99 o.s.i (0-449-13336-2); 1980. mass mkt. 2.25 o.p. (0-449-14219-1) Ballantine Bks. (Fawcett).
—A Purple Place for Dying. unabr. collector's ed. 1977. (Travis McGee Ser.: No. 3). audio 36.00 (0-7366-0052-3, 1064) Books on Tape, Inc.
—A Purple Place for Dying. l.t. ed. 1984. (General Ser.). 312p. 9.95 o.p. (0-8161-3690-4); lib. bdg. 13.95 o.p. (0-8161-3625-4) Gale Group. (Macmillan Reference USA).
—A Purple Place for Dying. 1976. 15.00 o.p. (0-397-01166-0) HarperCollins Pubs.
—The Quick Red Fox. 1996. mass mkt. 5.99 (0-449-45613-7); 1995. 320p. mass mkt. 7.50 (0-449-22440-6); 1987. 160p. mass mkt. 4.95 o.s.i (0-449-13403-2); 1981. mass mkt. 2.50 o.p. (0-449-14264-7) Ballantine Bks. (Fawcett).
—The Quick Red Fox. unabr. collector's ed. 1983. (Travis McGee Ser.: No. 4). audio 36.00 (0-7366-0701-3, 1664) Books on Tape, Inc.
—The Quick Red Fox. l.t. ed. 1993. 12.95 o.p. (0-8161-3382-4, Macmillan Reference USA) Gale Group.
—The Quick Red Fox. abr. ed. 1999. audio 9.99 o.s.i (0-375-41593-9, RH Audio) Random Hse. Audio Publishing Group.
—The Scarlet Ruse. 1996. 352p. mass mkt. 7.50 (0-449-22477-5); 1987. 320p. mass mkt. 4.95 o.s.i (0-449-13247-1); 1985. mass mkt. 3.50 o.p. (0-449-13040-1) Ballantine Bks. (Fawcett).
—The Scarlet Ruse. unabr. collector's ed. 1985. (Travis McGee Ser.: No. 14). audio 48.00 (0-7366-0707-2, 1670) Books on Tape, Inc.
—The Scarlet Ruse. 1980. (General Ser.). lib. bdg. 13.95 o.p. (0-8161-3118-X, Macmillan Reference USA) Gale Group.
—The Scarlet Ruse. abr. ed. 1994. (Travis McGee Ser.). audio 8.99 o.s.i (0-679-43405-4, RH Audio) Random Hse. Audio Publishing Group.
—A Tan & Sandy Silence. (Travis McGee Novel Ser.). 1996. 336p. mass mkt. 7.50 (0-449-22476-7, Fawcett); 1986. 256p. mass mkt. 4.95 o.s.i (0-449-13250-1, Fawcett); 1985. 256p. mass mkt. 3.50 o.p. (0-449-12969-1, Fawcett); 1984. mass mkt. 2.95 o.p. (0-449-12707-9); 1983. mass mkt. 2.95 o.p. (0-449-12677-3); 1982. mass mkt. 2.75 o.p. (0-449-12404-5); 1981. mass mkt. 2.50 o.p. (0-449-14220-5); 1978. mass mkt. 1.75 o.p. (0-449-13635-3) Ballantine Bks.
—A Tan & Sandy Silence. unabr. collector's ed. 1984. (Travis McGee Ser.: No. 13). audio 48.00 (0-7366-0706-4, 1669) Books on Tape, Inc.
—A Tan & Sandy Silence. l.t. ed. 1982. 360p. lib. bdg. 13.95 o.p. (0-8161-3381-6, Macmillan Reference USA) Gale Group.
—A Tan & Sandy Silence. abr. ed. 1994. audio 8.99 o.s.i (0-679-43408-9); 1993. audio 16.00 o.p. (0-394-55983-5) Random Hse. Audio Publishing Group. (RH Audio).
—The Turquoise Lament. 1996. 320p. mass mkt. 6.99 (0-449-22478-3); 1987. 256p. mass mkt. 5.99 o.s.i (0-449-13249-8); 1982. 256p. mass mkt. 2.95 o.p. (0-449-14200-0) Ballantine Bks. (Fawcett).
—The Turquoise Lament. unabr. collector's ed. 1983. (Travis McGee Ser.: No. 15). audio 48.00 (0-7366-0708-0, 1671) Books on Tape, Inc.
—The Turquoise Lament. l.t. ed. 1982. lib. bdg. 13.95 o.p. (0-8161-3383-2, Macmillan Reference USA) Gale Group.
—The Turquoise Lament. 1973. 15.00 (0-397-00987-9, Lippincott) Lippincott Williams & Wilkins.
—The Turquoise Lament. abr. ed. 1991. (Travis McGee Ser.). audio 16.00 o.s.i (0-394-55985-1, RH Audio) Random Hse. Audio Publishing Group.

### MCGOWAN, JOHN (FICTITIOUS CHARACTER)—FICTION

Benig, Irving. The Messiah Stones: A Tale of Our Times. l.t. ed. 1996. 25.95 (1-56895-318-6, Wheeler Publishing, Inc.) Gale Group.

### MACGOWEN, MAGGIE (FICTITIOUS CHARACTER)—FICTION

Hornsby, Wendy. Bad Intent: A Maggie MacGowen Mystery. 1994. (Maggie MacGowen Mystery Ser.). 304p. 18.95 o.p. (0-525-93817-6, Dutton) Dutton/ Plume.
—Bad Intent: A Maggie MacGowen Mystery. 1995. (Maggie MacGowen Mystery Ser.). 384p. mass mkt. 5.50 o.s.i (0-451-18501-3, Onyx) NAL.
—A Hard Light: A Maggie MacGowen Mystery. 1997. (Maggie MacGowen Mystery Ser.). 272p. 22.95 o.p. (0-525-94067-7) Dutton/Plume.
—A Hard Light: A Maggie MacGowen Mystery. 1998. (Maggie Macgowen Mystery Ser.). 272p. mass mkt. 5.99 o.s.i (0-451-18690-7, Signet Bks.) NAL.
—Midnight Baby: A Maggie MacGowen Mystery. 1993. (Maggie MacGowen Mystery Ser.). 272p. 19.00 o.p. (0-525-93615-7, Dutton) Dutton/Plume.
—Midnight Baby: A Maggie MacGowen Mystery. 1994. (Maggie MacGowen Mystery Ser.). 304p. mass mkt. 5.99 o.s.i (0-451-18136-0, Signet Bks.) NAL.
—Telling Lies: A Maggie MacGowen Mystery. 1992. 256p. 18.00 o.p. (0-525-93472-3, Dutton) Dutton/ Plume.
—Telling Lies: A Maggie MacGowen Mystery. 1993. (Maggie MacGowen Mystery Ser.). 288p. mass mkt. 5.99 o.s.i (0-451-40380-0, Onyx) NAL.
—77th Street Requiem: A Maggie MacGowan Mystery. 1996. (Maggie MacGowen Mystery Ser.). 384p. mass mkt. 5.99 o.s.i (0-451-40675-3, Signet Bks.) NAL.
—77th Street Requiem: A Maggie MacGowen Mystery. 1995. (Maggie MacGowen Mystery Ser.). 288p. 21.95 o.p. (0-525-93998-9, Dutton) Dutton/Plume.
—77th Street Requiem: A Maggie MacGowen Mystery. l.t. ed. 1996. (Large Print Bks.). pap. 21.95 (1-56895-334-8, Wheeler Publishing, Inc.) Gale Group.

### MCGRAIL, NUALA ANNE (FICTITIOUS CHARACTER)—FICTION

Greeley, Andrew M. Irish Eyes: A Nuala Anne McGrail Novel. 2000. 320p. 24.95 (0-312-86570-8); 2001. 352p. reprint ed. mass mkt. 6.99 (0-8125-9024-4) Doherty, Tom Assocs., LLC. (Forge Bks.).
—Irish Eyes: A Nuala Anne McGrail Novel. l.t. ed. 2001. 525p. 29.95 (0-7862-3091-6); (0-7540-1621-8) Thorndike Pr.
—Irish Gold: A Nuala Anne McGrail Novel. (Nuala Anne McGrail Novel Ser.). 1995. 493p. pap. 7.99 (0-8125-5076-5); 1994. 336p. 14.29 o.p. (0-312-85813-2) Doherty, Tom Assocs., LLC. (Forge Bks.).
—Irish Gold: A Nuala Anne McGrail Novel. abr. ed. 1994. 17.95 o.p. (0-7871-0332-2, 390987) NewStar Media, Inc.
—Irish Lace: A Nuala Anne McGrail Novel. (Nuala Anne McGrail Novel Ser.). 1997. 345p. pap. 6.99 (0-8125-5077-3, Tor Bks.); 1996. 304p. 23.95 o.p. (0-312-86234-2, Forge Bks.) Doherty, Tom Assocs., LLC.
—Irish Lace: A Nuala Anne McGrail Novel. abr. ed. 1996. 17.95 o.p. (0-7871-1022-1, 394462) NewStar Media, Inc.
—Irish Lace: A Nuala Anne McGrail Novel. 1998. 4.98 o.p. (0-7651-1156-X) Smithmark Pubs., Inc.
—Irish Love: A Nuala Anne McGrail Novel. 2001. 304p. 24.95 (0-312-87187-2); 2002. 368p. reprint ed. mass mkt. 6.99 (0-8125-7606-3) Doherty, Tom Assocs., LLC. (Forge Bks.).
—Irish Love: A Nuala Anne McGrail Novel. l.t. ed. 2001. (Wheeler Large Print Book Ser.). 386p. 29.95 o.p. (1-58724-058-0, Wheeler Publishing, Inc.) Gale Group.
—Irish Mist: A Nuala Anne McGrail Novel. E-Book 6.99 (0-312-87113-9, Tor Bks.); 2000. 384p. mass mkt. 6.99 (0-8125-9023-6, Forge Bks.); 1999. (Illus.). 319p. 23.95 (0-312-86569-4, Forge Bks.) Doherty, Tom Assocs., LLC.
—Irish Mist: A Nuala Anne McGrail Novel. abr. ed. 1999. audio 16.99 (0-88646-491-9); audio 39.99 (0-88646-530-3, DHA-6530) Durkin Hayes Publishing Ltd.
—Irish Mist: A Nuala Anne McGrail Novel. l.t. ed. 2001. (Basic Ser.). 517p. 28.95 (0-7862-3085-1) Thorndike Pr.
—Irish Stew: A Nuala Anne McGrail Novel. 2002. 304p. 25.95 (0-312-87188-0, Forge Bks.) Doherty, Tom Assocs., LLC.
—Irish Stew: A Nuala Anne McGrail Novel. l.t. ed. 2003. 25.95 (1-58724-413-6, Wheeler Publishing, Inc.) Gale Group.
—Irish Whiskey: A Nuala Anne McGrail Novel. 1998. (Nuala Anne McGrail Novel Ser.). 309p. pap. 6.99 (0-8125-7770-1, Tor Bks.); 304p. 23.95 o.p. (0-312-85596-6, Forge Bks.) Doherty, Tom Assocs., LLC.
—Irish Whiskey: A Nuala Anne McGrail Novel, Set. abr. ed. 1998. audio 18.00 (0-7871-1684-X, Dove Audio) NewStar Media, Inc.
—Irish Whiskey: A Nuala Anne McGrail Novel. l.t. ed. 2000. (Basic Ser.). 549p. 28.95 (0-7862-2930-6) Thorndike Pr.

### MCGRATH, BILLY (FICTITIOUS CHARACTER)—FICTION

Rayner, Richard. Murder Book. 1999. 432p. mass mkt. 5.99 o.s.i (0-06-109737-3) HarperCollins Pubs.
—Murder Book. 2001. 384p. pap. 14.00 (0-06-093828-5, Perennial) HarperTrade.
—Murder Book. 1997. 384p. tchr. ed. 25.00 o.p. (0-395-83625-5) Houghton Mifflin Co.

### MCGRATH, KERRY (FICTITIOUS CHARACTER)—FICTION

Clark, Mary Higgins. Let Me Call You Sweetheart. 2000. E-Book 9.95 (0-7432-0623-1, Simon & Schuster); 1996. 320p. pap. 7.99 (0-671-56817-5, Pocket); 1995. 26.00 o.s.i (0-684-80395-X, Simon & Schuster) Simon & Schuster.
—Let Me Call You Sweetheart. abr. ed. 1995. audio 18.00 (0-671-52128-4, 393021, Simon & Schuster Audioworks) Simon & Schuster Audio.
—Let Me Call You Sweetheart. 1996. 14.04 (0-606-09540-3) Turtleback Bks.

### MACGREGOR, LAKE (FICTITIOUS CHARACTER)—FICTION

Dare, Justine. Dangerous Games, 1 vol. 1999. 336p. mass mkt. 5.99 o.s.i (0-451-40773-3, Signet Bks.) NAL.
—Dangerous Ground. 1998. 384p. mass mkt. 5.99 o.s.i (0-451-40765-2, Signet Bks.) NAL.

### MACGREGOR FAMILY (FICTITIOUS CHARACTERS)—FICTION

Roberts, Nora. All the Possibilities. 1992. mass mkt. (0-373-51015-2, 5-51015-1); 1987. mass mkt. (0-373-48210-8); 1985. (0-373-09247-4) Harlequin Enterprises, Ltd. (Harlequin Bks.).
—For Now, Forever. 1992. (NR Flowers Ser.: No. 19). mass mkt. (0-373-51019-5, 5-51019-3); 1987. mass mkt. (0-373-09361-6) Harlequin Enterprises, Ltd. (Harlequin Bks.).
—The MacGregor Brides. l.t. ed. 2002. (Wheeler Large Print Book Ser.). 28.95 (1-58724-191-9, Wheeler Publishing, Inc.) Gale Group.
—The MacGregor Brides. 384p. 2002. mass mkt. (0-373-21847-8); 1997. per. (0-373-48350-3) Harlequin Enterprises, Ltd. (Harlequin Bks.).
—The MacGregor Grooms. 2002. (Wheeler Hardcover Ser.). 29.95 (1-58724-279-6, Wheeler Publishing, Inc.) Gale Group.
—The MacGregor Grooms. (Silhouette Special Releases Ser.). 384p. 2002. mass mkt. (0-373-21855-9); 1998. (Illus.). per. (0-373-48369-4, 1-48369-2) Harlequin Enterprises, Ltd. (Silhouette).
—The MacGregors: Alan & Grant. 1999. (Silhouette Special Releases Ser.). (Illus.). 512p. mass mkt. (0-373-48389-9, 1-48389-0, Silhouette) Harlequin Enterprises, Ltd.
—The MacGregors: Daniel & Ian. 1999. (Macgregors Ser.). (Illus.). 347p. mass mkt. (0-373-48390-2, 1-48390-8, Harlequin Bks.) Harlequin Enterprises, Ltd.
—The MacGregors: Serena & Caine. 1998. (Macgregors Ser.). (Illus.). 505p. mass mkt. (0-373-48388-0, 1-48388-2, Harlequin Bks.) Harlequin Enterprises, Ltd.
—One Man's Art. 1992. (NR Flowers Ser.: No. 17). mass mkt. (0-373-51017-9, 5-51017-7); 1987. mass mkt. (0-373-48211-6); 1985. (0-373-09259-8) Harlequin Enterprises, Ltd. (Harlequin Bks.).
—The Perfect Neighbor. 1999. (Silhouette Special Edition Ser.: No. 1232). (Illus.). 256p. mass mkt. (0-373-24232-8, 1-24232-0, Harlequin Bks.) Harlequin Enterprises, Ltd.
—Playing the Odds. 1992. (NR Flowers Ser.: No. 12). mass mkt. (0-373-51012-8); 1987. mass mkt. (0-373-48208-6); 1985. mass mkt. (0-373-09225-3) Harlequin Enterprises, Ltd. (Harlequin Bks.).
—Rebellion. 1999. 298p. mass mkt. (0-373-83428-4, 1-83428-2); 1998. mass mkt. (0-373-83403-9, 1-83403-5); 1988. mass mkt. (0-373-28604-X) Harlequin Enterprises, Ltd. (Harlequin Bks.).
—Tempting Fate. 1992. (NR Flowers Ser.: No. 13). mass mkt. (0-373-51013-6, Silhouette); 1987. mass mkt. (0-373-48209-4, Harlequin Bks.); 1985. (0-373-09235-0, Harlequin Bks.) Harlequin Enterprises, Ltd.
—The Winning Hand. 2002. 256p. mass mkt. (0-373-23995-5); 1998. (Silhouette Special Edition Ser.: No. 1202). (Illus.). 250p. per. (0-373-24202-6, 1-24202-3) Harlequin Enterprises, Ltd. (Harlequin Bks.).

### MCGROGAN, ANNIE (FICTITIOUS CHARACTER)—FICTION

Farrell, Gillian B. Alibi for an Actress. Chelius, Jane, ed. 256p. 1992. 19.00 (0-671-75707-5, Atria); 1993. reprint ed. mass mkt. 5.50 (0-671-75708-3, Pocket) Simon & Schuster.
—Murder & a Muse. 1995. 288p. mass mkt. 5.99 (0-671-75711-3, Pocket); 1994. 256p. 20.00 (0-671-75710-5, Atria) Simon & Schuster.

### MCGUFFIN, AMOS (FICTITIOUS CHARACTER)—FICTION

Upton, Robert. Dead on the Stick. 256p. 1987. pap. 3.50 o.p. (0-14-007601-8, Penguin Bks.); 1986. 15.95 o.p. (0-670-80331-6) Viking Penguin.
—The Faberge Egg. 1988. 208p. 16.95 o.p. (0-525-24692-4, Dutton) Dutton/Plume.
—Fade Out. 1984. (Amos McGuffin Mystery Ser.). 13.95 o.p. (0-670-30469-7) Viking Penguin.
—Fade Out: An Amos McGuffin Mystery. 1986. 192p. pap. 3.95 o.p. (0-14-008312-X, Penguin Bks.) Viking Penguin.
—A Golden Fleecing. 1979. 10.95 o.p. (0-312-33730-2) St. Martin's Pr.
—A Killing in Real Estate: An Amos McGuffin Mystery. 1990. 192p. 17.95 o.p. (0-525-24927-3, Dutton) Dutton/Plume.
—Who'd Want to Kill Old George? 1982. 224p. pap. 2.50 o.p. (0-523-41537-0, Pinnacle Bks.) Kensington Publishing Corp.
—Who'd Want to Kill Old George? 1976. 7.95 o.p. (0-399-11867-5) Putnam Publishing Group, The.

### MCGUIRE, AMY (FICTITIOUS CHARACTER)—FICTION

Gorman, Ed. Senatorial Privilege. 1999. 382p. mass mkt. 6.99 (0-8125-5042-0); 1997. 384p. 23.95 (0-312-85778-0) Doherty, Tom Assocs., LLC. (Forge Bks.).

### MCGUIRE, JOSEPH PETER (FICTITIOUS CHARACTER)—FICTION

Reynolds, John L. And Leave Her Lay Dying. 1992. (Crime Ser.). 272p. pap. 4.95 o.p. (0-14-012298-2, Penguin Bks.) Penguin Group (USA) Inc.
—And Leave Her Lay Dying. 1990. 304p. 16.95 o.p. (0-670-82875-0) Viking Penguin.
—The Man Who Murdered God. 272p. 1989. 16.95 o.p. (0-670-82736-3); 1990. reprint ed. pap. 4.50 o.p. (0-14-012037-8, Penguin Bks.) Viking Penguin.

—Whisper Death. 1992. 256p. 18.95 o.p. (*0-670-83669-9*, Viking) Viking Penguin.
Smith, Julie. Death Turns a Trick. 1993. pap. 3.99 o.p. (*0-8041-9805-5*); 1992. reprint ed. mass mkt. 5.99 o.s.i (*0-8041-0856-0*) Ballantine Bks. (Ivy Bks.).
—Other People's Skeletons. 1995. 240p. pap. 15.00 (*0-345-47164-4*); 1994. pap. 4.99 o.p. (*0-8041-9820-9*, Ivy Bks.); 1993. mass mkt. 5.99 o.s.i (*0-8041-1086-7*, Ivy Bks.) Ballantine Bks.
—Other People's Skeletons. 1999. (Mystery Ser.). 232p. 20.95 (*0-7862-1953-X*, Five Star) Gale Group.
—The Sourdough Wars. 1993. pap. 4.99 o.p. (*0-8041-9807-1*); 1992. mass mkt. 5.99 o.s.i (*0-8041-0929-X*) Ballantine Bks. (Ivy Bks.).
—Tourist Trap. 1993. pap. 4.99 o.p. (*0-8041-9806-3*); 1992. mass mkt. 5.99 o.s.i (*0-8041-0930-3*) Ballantine Bks. (Ivy Bks.).
—Tourist Trap. 1986. 240p. 15.45 o.p. (*0-89296-162-7*) Mysterious Pr.
—Tourist Trap. 1987. 240p. mass mkt. 3.95 o.s.i (*0-445-40640-2*, Mysterious Pr. Paperback Bks.) Warner Bks., Inc.

**MCGUIRE, MADISON (FICTITIOUS CHARACTER)—FICTION**

Williams, Amanda K. Club Twelve. 1990. 288p. pap. 9.95 (*0-941483-64-9*) Naiad Pr., Inc.
—The Providence File. 1991. 250p. (Orig.). pap. 8.95 (*0-941483-92-4*) Naiad Pr., Inc.
—A Singular Spy. 1992. 192p. pap. 8.95 o.p. (*1-56280-008-6*) Naiad Pr., Inc.
—The Spy in Question. 1993. (Madison McGuire Novel Ser.). 234p. pap. 9.95 o.p. (*1-56280-037-X*) Naiad Pr., Inc.

**MCGUIRE, ROWLAND (FICTITIOUS CHARACTER)—FICTION**

Beauman, Sally. Danger Zones. 1997. mass mkt. 6.99 o.s.i (*0-449-22561-5*, Fawcett) Ballantine Bks.
—Danger Zones. l.t. ed. 1996. pap. 22.95 o.p. (*1-56895-343-7*, Wheeler Publishing, Inc.) Gale Group.

**MCHENRY, MARK (FICTITIOUS CHARACTER)—FICTION**

David, Peter. Dark Allies. 1999. (Star Trek Ser.: No. 8). (Illus.). 288p. pap. 6.50 (*0-671-02080-3*, Star Trek) Simon & Schuster.
—Excalibur: Requiem. 2000. (Star Trek Ser.: No. 9). 288p. pap. 6.99 (*0-671-04238-6*, Star Trek) Simon & Schuster.

**MCILVAIN, BILLY (FICTITIOUS CHARACTER)—FICTION**

Van Meter, David A. Necessary Evil. 1994. 282p. 19.95 o.p. (*0-316-89729-9*) Little Brown & Co.
—Necessary Evil. 1997. 313p. mass mkt. 5.99 (*0-312-95924-9*, St. Martin's Paperbacks); 1996. pap. (*0-312-95715-7*) St. Martin's Pr.

**MACINTYRE, URBINO (FICTITIOUS CHARACTER)—FICTION**

Sklepowich, Edward. Black Bridge: A Mystery of Venice. 1995. 224p. 20.50 (*0-684-81520-6*); o.s.i (*1-883402-84-0*) Simon & Schuster. (Scribner).
—Death in a Serene City. 1992. 304p. pap. 4.50 (*0-380-71636-4*, Avon Bks.); 1990. 18.95 o.p. (*0-688-09180-6*, Morrow, William & Co.) Morrow/Avon.
—Death in the Palazzo: A Venetian Mystery. 1997. 250p. 21.50 o.p. (*0-684-83031-0*, Scribner) Simon & Schuster.
—Farewell to the Flesh: An Urbino Macintyre Mystery. 1993. 288p. pap. 4.99 (*0-380-71814-6*, Avon Bks.); 1991. 352p. 19.00 o.p. (*0-688-11006-1*, Morrow, William & Co.) Morrow/Avon.
—The Last Gondola: A Mystery of Venice. 2003. 384p. 24.95 (*0-312-29049-7*, Saint Martin's Minotaur) St. Martin's Pr.
—Liquid Desires: An Urbino Macintyre Mystery. 1993. 315p. 22.00 o.p. (*0-688-11165-3*, Morrow, William & Co.); 1994. 320p. reprint ed. mass mkt. 4.99 (*0-380-72150-3*, Avon Bks.) Morrow/Avon.
—Liquid Desires: An Urbino Macintyre Mystery. 316p. 4.98 o.p. (*0-7651-0268-4*) Smithmark Pubs., Inc.

**MACK, RUDYARD (FICTITIOUS CHARACTER)—FICTION**

Beasley, David. The Grand Conspiracy: A New York Library Mystery. 1997. 176p. pap. 10.95 (*0-915317-06-0*) Davus Publishing.
—The Jenny: A New York Library Detective Novel. 1994. 120p. pap. 7.95 (*0-915317-03-6*) Davus Publishing.

**MACKADE FAMILY (FICTITIOUS CHARACTERS)—FICTION**

Roberts, Nora. The Fall of Shane MacKade: The MacKade Brothers. 1996. (Silhouette Special Edition Ser.: Vol. 1022). 248p. per. (*0-373-24022-8*, 1-24022-5, Silhouette) Harlequin Enterprises, Ltd.
—The Heart of Devin Mackade. 1996. (Silhouette Intimate Moments Ser.: Vol. 697). (Illus.). 242p. per. (*0-373-07697-5*, 1-07697-5, Silhouette); 1998. (Silhouette Ser.). (*0-373-59859-9*, Harlequin Bks.) Harlequin Enterprises, Ltd.
—The Pride of Jared Mackade. 1995. (Silhouette Special Edition Ser.: Vol. 1000). 249p. per. (*0-373-24000-7*, 1-24000-1, Silhouette) Harlequin Enterprises, Ltd.
—The Return of Rafe Mackade. 1995. (Mackade Brothers Ser.: Vol. 631). (Illus.). 251p. per. (*0-373-07631-2*, 1-07631-4, Silhouette) Harlequin Enterprises, Ltd.

**MACKAY, KATHERYN (FICTITIOUS CHARACTER)—FICTION**

McGuire, Christine. Until Death Do Us Part. 1996. 352p. pap. 6.50 (*0-671-53618-4*, Pocket) Simon & Schuster.
—Until Judgment Day. 2003. 368p. mass mkt. 6.99 (*0-7434-2230-9*, Pocket) Simon & Schuster.

**MCKAY, KEVIN (FICTITIOUS CHARACTER)—FICTION**

McNamara, Joseph D. Code 211 Blue. 1996. mass mkt. 5.99 o.s.i (*0-449-14894-7*, Fawcett) Ballantine Bks.

**MACKENDRICK, ARIELLA (FICTITIOUS CHARACTER)—FICTION**

Monk, Karyn. Once a Warrior. 1997. 384p. mass mkt. 6.50 (*0-553-57422-1*, Fanfare) Bantam Bks.

**MCKENNA, BRIAN (FICTITIOUS CHARACTER)—FICTION**

Mahoney, Dan. Black & White. E-Book 24.95 (*0-312-26442-9*); 2000. 528p. mass mkt. 6.99 (*0-312-97149-4*, St. Martin's Paperbacks); 1999. 356p. 24.95 o.p. (*0-312-20278-4*) St. Martin's Pr.
—Detective First Grade. 1994. 443p. mass mkt. 6.99 (*0-312-95313-5*, St. Martin's Paperbacks); 1993. 384p. 21.95 o.p. (*0-312-09288-1*) St. Martin's Pr.
—The Edge of the City. 1996. 514p. mass mkt. 6.99 (*0-312-95788-2*, St. Martin's Paperbacks); 1995. 22.95 (*0-312-11812-0*); 1995. 464p. 14.99 o.p. (*0-312-13058-9*) St. Martin's Pr.
—Gibraltar. 2003. 416p. mass mkt. 6.99 (*0-312-98387-5*, St. Martin's Paperbacks) St. Martin's Pr.
—Hyde. unabr. ed. 2000. audio 83.95 (*0-7861-1755-9*, 2559) Blackstone Audio Bks., Inc.
—Hyde. 1999. E-Book 6.99 (*0-312-20723-9*); 1997. 560p. mass mkt. 6.99 (*0-312-96392-0*, St. Martin's Paperbacks); 1996. 384p. 24.95 (*0-312-15146-2*) St. Martin's Pr.
—Justice: A Novel of the NYPD. 2003. 352p. 24.95 (*0-312-30957-0*) St. Martin's Pr.
—Once in, Never Out. unabr. ed. 1999. audio 76.95 (*0-7861-1509-2*, 2359) Blackstone Audio Bks., Inc.
—Once in, Never Out. 1999. 480p. mass mkt. 6.99 (*0-312-96676-8*, St. Martin's Paperbacks); 1998. 352p. 24.95 (*0-312-18228-7*) St. Martin's Pr.
—The Protectors. E-Book 18.95 (*0-312-70763-0*); 2002. 352p. 24.95 (*0-312-28450-0*) St. Martin's Pr.

**MCKENNA, KATE (FICTITIOUS CHARACTER)—FICTION**

O'Brien, Meg. Take My Breath Away. 1997. 306p. mass mkt. 5.99 (*0-312-96158-8*, St. Martin's Paperbacks) St. Martin's Pr.

**MCKENNA, MICHAEL (FICTITIOUS CHARACTER)—FICTION**

Preston, Fayrene. In Guilty Night. 1998. 352p. mass mkt. 5.99 o.s.i (*0-553-57582-1*) Bantam Bks.

**MCKENNA, PATIENCE (FICTITIOUS CHARACTER)—FICTION**

Haddam, Jane. Sweet, Savage Death. 2000. 192p. pap. 7.95 (*1-55882-033-7*) International Polygonics, Ltd.
—Wicked, Loving Murder: A Patience McKenna Mystery. 2000. (Patience McKenna Mysteries Ser.). 182p. pap. 8.95 (*1-55882-034-5*, Library of Crime Classics) International Polygonics, Ltd.
Papazoglou, Orania, pseud. Death's Savage Passion. 1986. (Crime Club Ser.). 192p. 12.95 o.p. (*0-385-19954-6*) Doubleday Publishing.
—Death's Savage Passion. 1987. 192p. pap. 3.50 o.p. (*0-14-009967-0*, Penguin Bks.) Viking Penguin.
—Once & Always Murder. 1990. 14.95 o.s.i (*0-385-24843-1*) Doubleday Publishing.
—Rich, Radiant Slaughter. 1988. (Crime Club Ser.). 12.95 o.s.i (*0-385-24612-9*) Doubleday Publishing.
—Sweet, Savage Death. l.t. ed. 1985. lib. bdg. 14.95 o.p. (*0-89340-791-7*, 262) BBC Audiobooks America.
—Sweet, Savage Death. 1984. (Crime Club Ser.). 192p. 11.95 o.p. (*0-385-19255-X*) Doubleday Publishing.
—Sweet, Savage Death. 1985. (Crime Monthly Ser.). 192p. pap. 3.50 o.p. (*0-14-007745-6*, Penguin Bks.) Viking Penguin.
—Wicked, Loving Murder. l.t. ed. 1986. o.p. (*1-55504-125-6*); pap. o.p. (*1-55504-111-6*) BBC Audiobooks America.
—Wicked, Loving Murder. 1985. (Crime Club Ser.). 192p. 12.95 o.p. (*0-385-19953-8*) Doubleday Publishing.
—Wicked, Loving Murder. 1986. 35.00 o.p. (*0-14-779207-X*) Penguin Group (USA) Inc.
—Wicked, Loving Murder. 1986. 192p. pap. 3.50 o.p. (*0-14-008548-3*, Penguin Bks.) Viking Penguin.
Papzoglou, Orania. Death's Savage Passion. 2001. 182p. reprint ed. pap. 8.95 (*1-55882-036-1*, Library of Crime Classics) International Polygonics, Ltd.

**MACKENZIE, AGNES (FICTITIOUS CHARACTER)—FICTION**

Lamb, Arnette. Beguiled. 1996. (Clan MacKenzie Trilogy Ser.). 320p. pap. 6.50 (*0-671-88219-8*, Pocket) Simon & Schuster.

**MCKENZIE, ALEX (FICTITIOUS CHARACTER)—FICTION**

Borthwick, J. S. Bodies of Water. 1991. 287p. mass mkt. 5.99 (*0-312-92603-0*, St. Martin's Paperbacks); 1990. 17.95 o.p. (*0-312-04269-8*, Saint Martin's Minotaur) St. Martin's Pr.
—The Bridled Groom: A Dead Letter Mystery. 1995. 336p. mass mkt. 6.50 (*0-312-95505-7*, St. Martin's Paperbacks) St. Martin's Pr.
—The Bridled Groom: A Mystery. 1994. 304p. 20.95 o.p. (*0-312-10435-9*, Saint Martin's Minotaur) St. Martin's Pr.
—The Case of the Hook-Billed Kites. (Dead Letter Mysteries Ser.). 256p. 1991. (Illus.). mass mkt. 5.99 (*0-312-92604-9*, St. Martin's Paperbacks); 1982. 12.95 o.p. (*0-312-12335-3*) St. Martin's Pr.
—The Case of the Hook-Billed Kites. 1983. 256p. pap. 3.95 o.p. (*0-14-006785-X*, Penguin Bks.) Viking Penguin.
—Coup de Grace. 2000. (Illus.). x, 335p. 24.95 (*0-312-25313-3*, Saint Martin's Minotaur) St. Martin's Pr.
—The Down-East Murders. 1991. 296p. mass mkt. 6.50 (*0-312-92606-5*, St. Martin's Paperbacks) St. Martin's Pr.
—The Down-East Murders: A Mystery Set on the Coast of Maine. 1985. 288p. 14.95 o.p. (*0-312-21855-9*) St. Martin's Pr.
—Dude on Arrival: A Christmas Mystery. 1992. 306p. mass mkt. 6.50 (*0-312-92955-2*, St. Martin's Paperbacks); 1991. 320p. 19.95 o.p. (*0-312-06341-5*, Saint Martin's Minotaur) St. Martin's Pr.
—The Garden Plot. (Dead Letter Mysteries Ser.). 1998. 336p. pap. 6.50 (*0-312-96291-6*, St. Martin's Paperbacks); 1997. 352p. 23.95 (*0-312-15131-4*, Saint Martin's Minotaur) St. Martin's Pr.
—Murder in the Rough. 2003. 352p. mass mkt. 6.50 (*0-312-98453-7*, St. Martin's Paperbacks); 2002. (Illus.). 336p. 24.95 (*0-312-28829-8*, Saint Martin's Minotaur) St. Martin's Pr.
—My Body Lies over the Ocean. (Sarah Deane Mysteries Ser.). 304p. 2000. mass mkt. 6.50 (*0-312-97040-4*, St. Martin's Paperbacks); 1998. 22.95 o.p. (*0-312-19991-0*, Saint Martin's Minotaur) St. Martin's Pr.
—The Student Body. 1991. 293p. mass mkt. 6.50 (*0-312-92605-7*, St. Martin's Paperbacks); 1987. mass mkt. 3.50 o.s.i (*0-312-90738-9*, St. Martin's Paperbacks); 1986. 320p. 16.95 o.p. (*0-312-76934-2*) St. Martin's Pr.

**MCKENZIE, MAC (FICTITIOUS CHARACTER)—FICTION**

Guthrie, Al. Murder by Tarot. 1992. mass mkt. 3.99 o.s.i (*0-8217-3637-X*, Zebra Bks.) Kensington Publishing Corp.

**MACKENZIE FAMILY (FICTITIOUS CHARACTER)—FICTION**

Howard, Linda. The Mackenzie Family. 1998. (Promo Ser.). per. (*0-373-48376-7*, 1-48376-7, Silhouette) Harlequin Enterprises, Ltd.
—The Mackenzies. 1996. mass mkt. (*1-55166-246-9*, 1-66246-9, Mira Bks.) Harlequin Enterprises, Ltd.
—Mackenzie's Mission. 2000. 256p. mass mkt. (*0-373-48408-9*); 1992. mass mkt. (*0-373-07445-X*, 5-07445-5) Harlequin Enterprises, Ltd. (Silhouette).
—Mackenzie's Mountain. l.t. ed. 1993. (Senses Ser.). 17.95 o.p. (*0-373-58800-3*) BBC Audiobooks America.
—Mackenzie's Mountain. 2000. 256p. mass mkt. (*1-55166-574-3*); 1989. mass mkt. (*0-373-07281-3*) Harlequin Enterprises, Ltd. (Harlequin Bks.).
—Mackenzie's Pleasure. (Silhouette Intimate Moments Ser.). 1996. 248p. per. (*0-373-07691-6*, 1-07691-8, Silhouette); 1999. (*0-373-59540-9*, Harlequin Bks.) Harlequin Enterprises, Ltd.
Howard, Linda, et al. Christmas Kisses: Mackenzie's Magic, Silver Bells, A Wild West Christmas. 1996. 377p. per. (*0-373-48328-7*, 1-48328-8, Harlequin Bks.) Harlequin Enterprises, Ltd.

**MCKINNEY, LEE (FICTITIOUS CHARACTER)—FICTION**

Carl, Joanna. The Chocolate Cat Caper. 2002. 240p. mass mkt. 5.99 (*0-451-20556-1*, Signet Bks.) NAL.
—The Chocolate Cat Caper. l.t. ed. 2002. (Mystery Ser.). 328p. 28.95 (*0-7862-4405-4*) Thorndike Pr.
—The Chocolate Frog Frame-Up. 2003. 240p. mass mkt. 5.99 (*0-451-20985-0*, Signet Bks.) NAL.

**MCKINNON, RACHEL (FICTITIOUS CHARACTER)—FICTION**

Miller, Linda Lael. Fletcher's Woman. 1997. mass mkt. 3.99 (*0-671-01004-2*); 1991. 320p. mass mkt. 6.99 (*0-671-73768-6*); 1990. mass mkt. 4.50 (*0-671-70632-2*) Simon & Schuster. (Pocket).

**MCKINNON, SAVANNAH (FICTITIOUS CHARACTER)—FICTION**

Summer, Mark. The Monster of Minnesota. 1997. (News from the Edge Ser.: Vol. 1). 208p. mass mkt. 6.50 o.s.i (*0-441-00459-8*) Ace Bks.
Sumner, Mark. News from the Edge. 1999. (News from the Edge Ser.). 208p. mass mkt. 6.50 o.s.i (*0-441-00628-0*) Ace Bks.
—News from the Edge: Insanity, Illinois, No. 2. 1998. 208p. mass mkt. 6.50 o.s.i (*0-441-00511-X*) Ace Bks.

**MACKLIN, PETER (FICTITIOUS CHARACTER)—FICTION**

Estleman, Loren D. Any Man's Death. l.t. ed. 1990. (Magna Large Print Ser.). 310p. 29.99 o.p. (*1-85057-645-9*) Magna Large Print Bks. GBR. *Dist:* Ulverscroft Large Print Bks., Ltd., Ulverscroft Large Print Canada, Ltd.
—Any Man's Death. 1987. 224p. mass mkt. 3.95 o.s.i (*0-445-40588-0*, Mysterious Pr. Paperback Bks.) Warner Bks., Inc.
—Kill Zone. l.t. ed. 1991. 23.95 o.p. (*0-7927-1027-4*, CH0167); pap. 21.95 o.p. (*0-7927-1028-2*, CS0268) BBC Audiobooks America.
—Kill Zone. 1986. mass mkt. 2.95 o.s.i (*0-449-12839-3*, Fawcett) Ballantine Bks.
—Kill Zone. 1986. 224p. 14.95 o.p. (*0-89296-065-5*) Mysterious Pr.
—Roses Are Dead. l.t. ed. 1991. pap. 17.95 o.p. (*0-7927-0589-0*, CS045); 1990. 19.95 o.p. (*0-7927-0588-2*, C0582) BBC Audiobooks America.
—Roses Are Dead. 240p. 1987. pap. 3.95 o.s.i (*0-445-40574-0*); 1986. 15.95 (*0-89296-136-8*) Mysterious Pr.
—Something Borrowed, Something Black. E-Book 24.95 (*0-312-70606-5*, Tor Bks.); 2003. 224p. mass mkt. 6.99 (*0-8125-4546-X*, Tor Bks.); 2002. 236p. 24.95 (*0-312-87863-X*, CPHC0630, Forge Bks.) Doherty, Tom Assocs., LLC.

**MCKNIGHT, ALEX (FICTITIOUS CHARACTER)—FICTION**

Hamilton, Steve. Blood Is the Sky: An Alex McKnight Mystery. 2003. 304p. 21.95 (*0-312-30115-4*, Saint Martin's Minotaur) St. Martin's Pr.
—A Cold Day in Paradise. l.t. ed. 2001. 354p. lib. bdg. 28.95 (*1-58547-136-4*) Ctr. Point Large Print.
—A Cold Day in Paradise. (Alex McKnight Mysteries Ser.). 2000. 320p. mass mkt. 6.99 (*0-312-96919-8*, St. Martin's Paperbacks); 1998. 288p. 22.95 (*0-312-19248-7*, Saint Martin's Minotaur) St. Martin's Pr.
—A Cold Day in Paradise: A Mystery, Set. unabr. ed. 1999. (Chivers Sound Library American Collections). audio 54.95 (*0-7927-2326-0*, CSL 215, Chivers Sound Library) BBC Audiobooks America.
—The Hunting Wind. 2001. E-Book 23.95 (*1-58945-851-6*) Adobe Systems, Inc.
—The Hunting Wind. E-Book 23.95 (*0-312-70180-2*) St. Martin's Pr.
—North of Nowhere: An Alex McKnight Mystery. unabr. ed. 2002. 8p. audio compact disk 79.95 (*0-7927-2632-4*, SLD 463, Chivers Sound Library) BBC Audiobooks America.
—North of Nowhere: An Alex McKnight Mystery. 2003. 352p. mass mkt. 6.99 (*0-312-98381-6*, St. Martin's Paperbacks); 2002. 288p. 23.95 (*0-312-26897-1*, Saint Martin's Minotaur) St. Martin's Pr.
—Winter of the Wolf Moon. E-Book 6.50 (*0-312-27360-6*) St. Martin's Pr.
—Winter of the Wolf Moon: An Alex McKnight Mystery. 2000. (Alex McKnight Mysteries Ser.). 274p. 23.95 (*0-312-25295-1*, Saint Martin's Minotaur) St. Martin's Pr.

**MCLAIN, MACE (FICTITIOUS CHARACTER)—FICTION**

Frey, Stephen. The Vulture Fund. 1996. 384p. 23.95 o.s.i (*0-525-93986-5*, Dutton) Dutton/Plume.
—The Vulture Fund. l.t. ed. 1996. 26.95 (*1-56895-390-9*, Wheeler Publishing, Inc.) Gale Group.
—The Vulture Fund. 1997. 416p. mass mkt. 7.99 (*0-451-18479-3*, Onyx) NAL.
—The Vulture Fund. 1998. 4.98 o.p. (*0-7651-0895-X*) Smithmark Pubs., Inc.

**MACLANAHAN, PATRICK (FICTITIOUS CHARACTER)—FICTION**

Brown, Dale. Battle Born. 1999. 416p. 24.95 o.s.i (*0-553-11123-X*) Bantam Bks.

Characters

—Battle Born. unabr. ed. 2000. audio 96.00 (*0-7366-4780-5*, 5125) Books on Tape, Inc.
—Battle Born. abr. ed. 1999. audio 25.95 (*0-553-52649-9*, RH Audio) Random Hse. Audio Publishing Group.
—Battle Born. l.t. ed. 1999. 720p. 24.95 (*0-375-40861-4*) Random Hse. Large Print.
—The Day of the Cheetah. 1990. 528p. mass mkt. 7.99 (*0-425-12043-0*) Berkley Publishing Group.
—The Day of the Cheetah. 1989. 384p. 18.95 o.p. (*1-55611-121-5*) Fine, Donald I. Bks.
—Fatal Terrain. 1998. 496p. mass mkt. 7.99 (*0-425-16260-5*) Berkley Publishing Group.
—Fatal Terrain. abr. ed. 1997. 25.00 o.p. (*0-7871-1466-9*) NewStar Media, Inc.
—Fatal Terrain. 1997. 448p. 24.95 o.s.i (*0-399-14241-X*, G. P. Putnam's Sons) Penguin Group (USA) Inc.
—Fatal Terrain. 24.95 o.s.i (*0-399-14556-7*) Putnam Publishing Group, The.
—Flight of the Old Dog. Breslin, Ed, ed. 1988. 416p. reprint ed. mass mkt. 7.99 (*0-425-10893-7*); mass mkt. 4.50 o.s.i (*0-425-11089-3*) Berkley Publishing Group.
—Flight of the Old Dog. 1987. 352p. 18.95 o.p. (*1-55611-034-0*) Fine, Donald I. Bks.
—Night of the Hawk. 1993. 576p. mass mkt. 7.99 (*0-425-13661-2*) Berkley Publishing Group.
—Night of the Hawk. 1992. 400p. 22.95 o.p. (*0-399-13739-4*, G. P. Putnam's Sons) Penguin Group (USA) Inc.
—Night of the Hawk. 22.95 o.s.i (*0-399-13904-4*) Putnam Publishing Group, The.
—Shadows of Steel. 1997. 384p. mass mkt. 7.99 (*0-425-15716-4*) Berkley Publishing Group.
—Shadows of Steel. 24.95 o.s.i (*0-399-14485-4*) Putnam Publishing Group, The.
—Shadows of Steel. l.t. ed. 1996. (Basic Ser.). 575p. 28.95 (*0-7862-0779-5*) Thorndike Pr.
—Sky Masters. 1992. 496p. mass mkt. 7.99 (*0-425-13262-5*) Berkley Publishing Group.
—Sky Masters. abr. ed. 1993. 15.95 o.p. (*1-55800-352-5*, 41410) NewStar Media, Inc.
—Sky Masters. 1991. 512p. 21.95 o.p. (*0-399-13705-X*, G. P. Putnam's Sons) Penguin Group (USA) Inc.
—Sky Masters. 21.95 o.s.i (*0-399-13852-8*); 1991. 21.95 o.p. (*1-55611-232-7*) Putnam Publishing Group, The.
—The Tin Man. 1999. 464p. reprint ed. mass mkt. 7.99 (*0-553-58000-0*, Bantam Classics) Bantam Bks.
—The Tin Man. l.t. ed. 1998. (Large Print Book Ser.). 26.95 (*1-56895-684-3*, Wheeler Publishing, Inc.) Gale Group.

**MACLAREN, NEIL (FICTITIOUS CHARACTER)—FICTION**

Grant, Charles. Raven. 1995. 256p. mass mkt. 5.99 (*0-8125-2080-7*, Tor Bks.) Doherty, Tom Assocs., LLC.

**MACLEAN, KATE, DETECTIVE (FICTITIOUS CHARACTER)—FICTION**

Gilpatrick, Noreen. Final Design. 1995. 384p. mass mkt. 5.50 o.s.i (*0-446-40324-5*) Warner Bks., Inc.
—Shadow of Death. 1995. 400p. 19.95 o.s.i (*0-89296-515-0*); 1993. 384p. 17.95 (*0-89296-514-2*) Mysterious Pr.
—Shadow of Death. 1996. 400p. mass mkt. 5.99 (*0-446-40325-3*) Warner Bks., Inc.

**MACLEAN, TOM (FICTITIOUS CHARACTER)—FICTION**

Maas, Peter. China White. l.t. ed. 1995. (Large Print Bks.). pap. 23.95 (*1-56895-096-9*, Wheeler Publishing, Inc.) Gale Group.
—China White. 1995. 320p. mass mkt. 5.99 o.s.i (*0-7860-0204-2*, Pinnacle Bks.) Kensington Publishing Corp.
—China White. 1994. 272p. 23.00 o.s.i (*0-671-69417-0*, Simon & Schuster) Simon & Schuster.

**MCLEES, KELLY (FICTITIOUS CHARACTER)—FICTION**

Gorman, Carol. Graveyard Moon. 1993. 160p. (Orig.). pap. 3.50 (*0-380-76991-3*, Avon Bks.) Morrow/Avon.

**MACLEISH, COOPER (FICTITIOUS CHARACTER)—FICTION**

Reaves, Sam. A Long Cold Fall. 1992. 304p. pap. 4.50 (*0-380-71641-0*, Avon Bks.) Morrow/Avon.

**MCLEISH, JOHN (FICTITIOUS CHARACTER)—FICTION**

Neel, Janet. Death among the Dons. l.t. ed. 1994. 369p. lib. bdg. 21.95 (*0-8161-7439-3*, Macmillan Reference USA) Gale Group.
—Death among the Dons. 1995. (Illus.). 272p. (J). mass mkt. 5.50 (*0-671-89952-X*, Pocket) Simon & Schuster.
—Death among the Dons. 1993. 240p. 19.95 o.p. (*0-312-10450-2*, Saint Martin's Minotaur) St. Martin's Pr.
—Death of a Partner. l.t. ed. 1996. 384p. pap. 20.95 (*0-7838-1641-3*, Macmillan Reference USA) Gale Group.
—Death of a Partner. Chelius, Jane, ed. 1994. 256p. reprint ed. mass mkt. 4.99 (*0-671-74839-4*, Pocket) Simon & Schuster.
—Death of a Partner. 1991. 16.95 o.p. (*0-312-05411-4*, Saint Martin's Minotaur) St. Martin's Pr.
—Death on Site. l.t. ed. 1996. 363p. pap. 20.95 o.p. (*0-7838-1640-5*, Macmillan Reference USA) Gale Group.
—Death on Site. Chelius, Jane, ed. 1993. 288p. reprint ed. mass mkt. 4.99 (*0-671-73581-0*, Pocket) Simon & Schuster.
—Death on Site. 1990. 256p. 16.95 o.p. (*0-312-04298-1*, Saint Martin's Minotaur) St. Martin's Pr.
—Death's Bright Angel. Chelius, Jane, ed. 1991. 288p. reprint ed. mass mkt. 4.99 (*0-671-73579-9*, Pocket) Simon & Schuster.
—Death's Bright Angel. 1988. 224p. 15.95 o.p. (*0-312-02568-8*, Saint Martin's Minotaur) St. Martin's Pr.
—Death's Bright Angel. l.t. ed. 1998. (General Ser.). 365p. pap. 23.95 (*0-7862-1289-6*) Thorndike Pr.
—A Timely Death. l.t. ed. 1997. 382p. pap. 21.95 (*0-7838-8140-1*, Macmillan Reference USA) Gale Group.
—A Timely Death. 1996. 219p. text 21.95 o.p. (*0-312-15223-X*, Saint Martin's Minotaur) St. Martin's Pr.
—To Die for: A Mystery. 1999. 240p. 21.95 o.p. (*0-312-20598-8*, Saint Martin's Minotaur) St. Martin's Pr.

**MACLEOD, DUNCAN (FICTITIOUS CHARACTER)—FICTION**

Buchanan, Ginjer. White Silence. 1999. (Highlander Ser.). 240p. mass mkt. 5.99 (*0-446-60634-0*) Warner Bks., Inc.
Henderson, Jason. The Element of Fire, No. 1. 1995. (Highlander Ser.: Vol. 1). 224p. reprint ed. mass mkt. 5.99 (*0-446-60283-3*) Warner Bks., Inc.
Holder, Nancy. The Measure of a Man. 1997. (Highlander Ser.). 224p. reprint ed. mass mkt. 5.99 (*0-446-60455-0*) Warner Bks., Inc.
Horvath, Gillian, ed. An Evening at Joe's: Fiction by the Cast & Crew of Highlander. 2000. (Highlander Ser.). (Illus.). 304p. (YA). pap. 12.95 o.s.i (*0-425-17749-1*) Berkley Publishing Group.
Lettow, Donna. Highlander: Barricades. 1999. 224p. (Orig.). mass mkt. 6.50 (*0-446-60573-5*, Aspect) Warner Bks., Inc.
—Zealot. 1997. (Highlander Ser.). 256p. (Orig.). reprint ed. mass mkt. 5.99 o.s.i (*0-446-60457-7*) Warner Bks., Inc.
McConnell, Ashley. Scimitar. 1996. (Highlander Ser.). 224p. reprint ed. mass mkt. 5.99 o.s.i (*0-446-60284-1*) Warner Bks., Inc.
Neason, Rebecca. The Path. 1997. (Highlander Ser.). 224p. (Orig.). reprint ed. mass mkt. 5.99 (*0-446-60456-9*) Warner Bks., Inc.
—Shadow of Obsession No. 7. 1998. (Highlander Ser.: Vol. 7). 240p. (Orig.). mass mkt. 5.99 (*0-446-60547-6*) Warner Bks., Inc.
Roberson, Jennifer. Scotland the Brave. 1996. (Highlander Ser.). 224p. (Orig.). reprint ed. mass mkt. 5.99 o.s.i (*0-446-60286-8*) Warner Bks., Inc.
Sherman, Josepha. The Captive Soul. 1998. (Highlander Ser.). 224p. mass mkt. 5.99 o.s.i (*0-446-60571-9*) Warner Bks., Inc.

**MCLEOD, ORLA (FICTITIOUS CHARACTER)—FICTION**

Scott, Manda. No Good Deed. 2003. 432p. mass mkt. 5.99 (*0-553-58468-5*); 2002. 320p. 22.95 (*0-553-80267-4*) Bantam Bks.

**MCMILLEN, BEN (FICTITIOUS CHARACTER)—FICTION**

Brown, Mark. Game Face. 1992. (Ben McMillen Hawaiian Mystery Ser.). 302p. 19.95 (*0-918024-92-7*) Ox Bow Pr.
—The Puna Kahuna: A Ben McMillen Hawaiian Mystery. 1993. 19.95 (*1-881987-02-7*) Ox Bow Pr.
—Yellowfin. 1992. (Ben McMillen Hawaiian Mystery Ser.). 256p. 19.95 (*0-918024-93-5*) Ox Bow Pr.

**MCMORROW, JACK (FICTITIOUS CHARACTER)—FICTION**

Boyle, Gerry. Bloodline. 1996. 336p. mass mkt. 5.99 o.s.i (*0-425-15182-4*) Berkley Publishing Group.
—Bloodline. 1995. 21.95 o.p. (*0-399-14030-1*, G. P. Putnam's Sons) Penguin Group (USA) Inc.
—Borderline. (Jack McMorrow Mystery Ser.). 368p. 1998. 22.95 o.s.i (*0-425-16147-1*); 2000. reprint ed. mass mkt. 6.99 o.s.i (*0-425-16964-2*, Prime Crime) Berkley Publishing Group.
—Cover Story. 2000. (Jack McMorrow Mystery Ser.: No. 7). 371p. 22.95 o.s.i (*0-425-16893-X*, Prime Crime) Berkley Publishing Group.
—The Cover Story. 2001. (Jack McMorrow Mystery Ser.: No. 7). 384p. 6.99 (*0-425-17852-8*, Prime Crime) Berkley Publishing Group.
—Deadline: A Jack McMorrow Mystery. 1995. 288p. mass mkt. 6.50 o.s.i (*0-425-14637-5*, Prime Crime) Berkley Publishing Group.
—Deadline: A Jack McMorrow Mystery. 1993. 17.95 (*0-945980-44-2*) North Country Pr.
—Lifeline. 1997. (Jack McMorrow Mystery Ser.). 368p. mass mkt. 5.99 o.s.i (*0-425-15688-5*) Berkley Publishing Group.
—Lifeline. 1996. 288p. 22.95 o.s.i (*0-399-14150-2*, G. P. Putnam's Sons) Penguin Group (USA) Inc.
—Potshot. 1998. (Jack McMorrow Mystery Ser.). 336p. mass mkt. 5.99 o.s.i (*0-425-16233-8*) Berkley Publishing Group.
—Potshot. 1997. 304p. 23.95 o.p. (*0-399-14259-2*, G. P. Putnam's Sons) Penguin Group (USA) Inc.

**MCNALLY, ARCHY (FICTITIOUS CHARACTER)—FICTION**

Lardo, Vincent. McNally's Chance. l.t. ed. (Paperback Bestsellers Ser.). 2003. 416p. pap. 13.95 (*0-7862-3361-3*); 2001. 447p. 31.95 (*0-7862-3360-5*); 2001. 416p. (*0-7540-1697-8*) Thorndike Pr.
—McNally's Folly. abr. ed. 2000. (Archy McNally Mystery Ser.). audio compact disk 23.50 (*0-7435-0540-9*, Simon & Schuster Audioworks) Simon & Schuster Audio.
—McNally's Folly. l.t. ed. 431p. 2001. pap. 29.95 (*0-7862-2644-7*); 2000. (*0-7540-1532-7*) Thorndike Pr.
Lardo, Vincent & Sanders, Lawrence. McNally's Chance. 2001. 320p. 24.95 o.p. (*0-399-14732-2*) Penguin Group (USA) Inc.
—McNally's Chance. abr. ed. 2001. (Archy McNally Mystery Ser.). audio 18.00 (*0-7435-0529-8*); audio compact disk 24.00 (*0-7435-0541-7*) Simon & Schuster Audio. (Simon & Schuster Audioworks).
—McNally's Folly. abr. ed. 2000. (Archy McNally Mystery Ser.). audio 18.00 (*0-7435-0528-X*, Simon & Schuster Audioworks) Simon & Schuster Audio.
Sanders, Lawrence. McNally's Alibi. abr. ed. 2002. audio compact disk 30.00 (*0-7435-0542-5*, Simon & Schuster Audioworks) Simon & Schuster Audio.
—McNally's Caper. 1995. (Archy McNally Mystery Ser.). 352p. mass mkt. 7.99 (*0-425-14530-1*) Berkley Publishing Group.
—McNally's Caper. l.t. ed. 384p. reprint ed. 1995. pap. 18.95 o.p. (*0-8161-5975-0*); 1994. lib. bdg. 24.95 (*0-8161-5974-2*) Gale Group. (Macmillan Reference USA).
—McNally's Caper. l.t. ed. 1995. (Magna Large Print Ser.). 403p. o.p. (*0-7505-0837-X*) Magna Large Print Bks. GBR. *Dist:* Ulverscroft Large Print Canada, Ltd.
—McNally's Caper. 1994. 320p. 22.95 o.p. (*0-399-13919-2*, G. P. Putnam's Sons) Penguin Group (USA) Inc.
—McNally's Caper. abr. ed. 1994. (Archy McNally Mystery Ser.). audio 17.00 (*0-671-87164-1*, 391157, Simon & Schuster Audioworks) Simon & Schuster Audio.
—McNally's Chance. 2002. pap. 7.99 (*0-425-18445-5*) Berkley Publishing Group.
—McNally's Dilemma. 2000. (Archy McNally Mystery Ser.). 336p. mass mkt. 7.99 (*0-425-17536-7*) Berkley Publishing Group.
—McNally's Dilemma. 1999. 320p. 24.95 o.s.i (*0-399-14490-0*) Penguin Group (USA) Inc.
—McNally's Dilemma. abr. ed. 1999. audio 18.00 (*0-671-57692-5*, Simon & Schuster Audioworks) Simon & Schuster Audio.
—McNally's Dilemma. l.t. ed. (Thorndike/G. K. Hall Paperback Bestsellers Ser.). 2000. 407p. 28.95 (*0-7862-2247-6*); 1999. 432p. 31.95 (*0-7862-2246-8*) Thorndike Pr.
—McNally's Folly. unabr. ed. 2000. 10p. audio 69.95 (*0-7927-2392-9*, CSL 281, Chivers Sound Library) BBC Audiobooks America.
—McNally's Gamble. 1998. (Archy McNally Mystery Ser.). 368p. mass mkt. 7.50 (*0-425-16259-1*) Berkley Publishing Group.
—McNally's Gamble. l.t. ed. 1997. 26.95 o.p. (*1-56895-487-5*, Wheeler Publishing, Inc.) Gale Group.
—McNally's Gamble. 1997. 307p. 24.95 o.s.i (*0-399-14248-7*, G. P. Putnam's Sons) Penguin Group (USA) Inc.
—McNally's Gamble. 24.95 o.s.i (*0-399-14560-5*) Putnam Publishing Group, The.
—McNally's Gamble. 1998. audio 9.98 (*0-671-58153-8*); 1997. audio 18.00 (*0-671-53793-8*, 394532) Simon & Schuster Audio. (Simon & Schuster Audioworks).
—McNally's Luck. 1993. (Archy McNally Mystery Ser.). 336p. mass mkt. 7.99 (*0-425-13745-7*) Berkley Publishing Group.
—McNally's Luck. l.t. ed. (G. K. Hall Large Print Book Ser.). 350p. 1994. pap. 19.95 o.p. (*0-8161-5678-6*); 1993. 24.95 (*0-8161-5677-8*) Gale Group. (Macmillan Reference USA).
—McNally's Luck. l.t. ed. 1994. (Magna Large Print Ser.). 406p. o.p. (*0-7505-0679-2*) Magna Large Print Bks. GBR. *Dist:* Ulverscroft Large Print Canada, Ltd.
—McNally's Luck. 1992. 320p. 22.95 o.p. (*0-399-13762-9*, G. P. Putnam's Sons) Penguin Group (USA) Inc.
—McNally's Luck. 1994. 5.99 o.p. (*0-517-12590-0*) Random Hse. Value Publishing.
—McNally's Luck, abr. ed. 1992. (Archy McNally Mystery Ser.). audio 17.00 (*0-671-76989-8*, Simon & Schuster Audioworks) Simon & Schuster Audio.
—McNally's Puzzle. l.t. ed. 1997. (Archy McNally Mystery Ser.). 352p. mass mkt. 7.99 (*0-425-15746-6*) Berkley Publishing Group.
—McNally's Puzzle. l.t. ed. 1996. 26.95 o.p. (*0-7838-1712-6*, Macmillan Reference USA) Gale Group.
—McNally's Puzzle. 1996. 320p. 24.95 o.p. (*0-399-14135-9*, G. P. Putnam's Sons) Penguin Group (USA) Inc.
—McNally's Puzzle, abr. ed. 1996. (Archy McNally Mystery Ser.). audio 18.00 (*0-671-53792-X*, 393484, Simon & Schuster Audioworks) Simon & Schuster Audio.
—McNally's Puzzle. l.t. ed. 1997. (Paperback Bestsellers Ser.). pap. 26.95 (*0-7838-1713-4*) Thorndike Pr.
—McNally's Risk. 1994. (Archy McNally Mystery Ser.). 336p. reprint ed. pap. 7.99 (*0-425-14286-8*) Berkley Publishing Group.
—McNally's Risk. l.t. ed. 1993. 322p. 26.95 o.p. (*1-56895-042-X*, Wheeler Publishing, Inc.) Gale Group.
—McNally's Risk. l.t. ed. 1994. (Magna Large Print Ser.). 420p. (*0-7505-0680-6*) Magna Large Print Bks. GBR. *Dist:* Ulverscroft Large Print Canada, Ltd.
—McNally's Risk. 1993. 320p. 22.95 o.p. (*0-399-13816-1*, G. P. Putnam's Sons) Penguin Group (USA) Inc.
—McNally's Risk, abr. ed. 1993. (Archy McNally Mystery Ser.). audio 17.00 (*0-671-79743-3*, 391159, Simon & Schuster Audioworks) Simon & Schuster Audio.
—McNally's Secret. 1993. (Archy McNally Mystery Ser.). 352p. pap. 7.99 (*0-425-13572-1*) Berkley Publishing Group.
—McNally's Secret. l.t. ed. 1993. (General Ser.). 381p. pap. 17.95 o.p. (*0-8161-5540-2*); lib. bdg. 22.95 o.p. (*0-8161-5539-9*) Gale Group. (Macmillan Reference USA).
—McNally's Secret. 1992. 320p. 21.95 o.p. (*0-399-13675-4*, G. P. Putnam's Sons) Penguin Group (USA) Inc.
—McNally's Secret. abr. ed. 1992. (Archy McNally Mystery Ser.). audio 17.00 (*0-671-74472-0*, 391160, Simon & Schuster Audioworks) Simon & Schuster Audio.
—McNally's Trial. 1996. (Archy McNally Mystery Ser.). 352p. pap. 7.99 (*0-425-14755-X*) Berkley Publishing Group.
—McNally's Trial. unabr. ed. 1996. audio 48.00 (*0-7366-3260-3*, 3917) Books on Tape, Inc.
—McNally's Trial. l.t. ed. 1995. (Large Print Bks.). 26.95 o.p. (*1-56895-208-2*, Wheeler Publishing, Inc.) Gale Group.
—McNally's Trial. 1995. 309p. 23.95 o.p. (*0-399-14006-9*) Penguin Group (USA) Inc.
—McNally's Trial, unabr. ed. audio 51.00 (*0-7887-0487-7*, 94680E7) Recorded Bks., LLC.
—McNally's Trial. 2003. audio 9.95 (*0-7435-3244-9*, Encore); 2003. audio compact disk 9.95 (*0-7435-3263-5*, Encore); 1999. pap. 12.98 (*0-671-04455-9*, Simon & Schuster Audioworks); 1999. audio 9.98 (*0-671-04639-X*, Simon & Schuster Audioworks); 1995. audio 17.00 (*0-671-87165-X*, 391161, Simon & Schuster Audioworks) Simon & Schuster Audio.
—Three Complete Novels: McNally's Caper; McNally's Trial; McNally's Puzzle. 1998. 800p. 12.98 o.p. (*0-399-14435-8*, G. P. Putnam's Sons) Penguin Group (USA) Inc.
—Three Complete Novels: McNally's Secret; McNally's Luck; McNally's Risk. 1997. 576p. 12.98 o.p. (*0-399-14307-6*, G. P. Putnam's Sons) Penguin Group (USA) Inc.
Sanders, Lawrence & Lardo, Vincent. McNally's Dare. 2003. 304p. 24.95 (*0-399-15055-2*) Penguin Group (USA) Inc.
—McNally's Folly. 2000. (Archy McNally Ser.). 320p. 24.95 o.s.i (*0-399-14618-0*) Penguin Group (USA) Inc.
—McNally's Folly. l.t. ed. 2000. (Basic Ser.). 431p. 31.95 (*0-7862-2643-9*) Thorndike Pr.

**MCNEAL, AARON (FICTITIOUS CHARACTER)—FICTION**

Dobyns, Stephen. The Church of Dead Girls. l.t. ed. 1997. (Large Print Book Ser.). 26.95 (*1-56895-478-6*, Wheeler Publishing, Inc.) Gale Group.
—The Church of Dead Girls. 400p. 1998. pap. 14.00 o.s.i (*0-8050-5104-X*, Owl Bks.); 1997. 23.00 o.s.i (*0-8050-5103-1*, Metropolitan Bks.) Holt, Henry & Co.
—The Church of Dead Girls. 2001. 432p. reprint ed. mass mkt. 6.99 (*0-312-97736-0*, St. Martin's Paperbacks) St. Martin's Pr.

MCNEELY, KATHY (FICTITIOUS CHARACTER)—FICTION

Charbonneau, Louis. The Ice: A Novel of Antarctica. 1991. 19.95 o.p. (*1-55611-177-0*) Fine, Donald I. Bks.
—The Ice: A Novel of Antarctica. 1993. 320p. reprint ed. mass mkt. 5.50 (*0-671-74714-2*, Pocket) Simon & Schuster.

MCNULTY, ENEAS (FICTITIOUS CHARACTER)—FICTION

Barry, Sebastian. The Whereabouts of Eneas McNulty. l.t. ed. 1998. (Basic Ser.). 429p. 28.95 (*0-7862-1709-X*) Thorndike Pr.
—The Whereabouts of Eneas McNulty. 320p. 1999. 12.95 (*0-14-028018-9*); 1998. 23.95 o.p. (*0-670-87828-6*) Viking Penguin.

MCPHEE, SUTTON (FICTITIOUS CHARACTER)—FICTION

English, Brenda H. Corruption of Faith. 1997. 272p. mass mkt. 5.99 o.s.i (*0-425-16091-2*, Prime Crime) Berkley Publishing Group.
—Corruption of Justice. 1999. 272p. mass mkt. 5.99 o.s.i (*0-425-16811-5*, Prime Crime) Berkley Publishing Group.
—Corruption of Power. 1998. (Sutton McPhee Mystery Ser.). 288p. mass mkt. 5.99 o.s.i (*0-425-16398-9*, Prime Crime) Berkley Publishing Group.

MACPHERSON, ANNIE (FICTITIOUS CHARACTER)—FICTION

Smith, Janet L. Practice to Deceive. 1993. (Northwest Mysteries Ser.). mass mkt. 4.99 o.s.i (*0-8041-0978-8*, Ivy Bks.) Ballantine Bks.
—Sea of Troubles. 1991. 224p. mass mkt. 4.99 o.s.i (*0-8041-0759-9*, Ivy Bks.) Ballantine Bks.
—Sea of Troubles. 1990. 197p. pap. 8.95 o.p. (*0-9602676-9-7*, Perseverance Pr.) Daniel, John & Co., Pubs.
—Sea of Troubles. 1990. 200p. (C). reprint ed. lib. bdg. 29.00 o.p. (*0-8095-4208-0*) Millefleurs.
—A Vintage Murder. 1995. mass mkt. 5.99 o.s.i (*0-8041-1385-8*, Ivy Bks.); 1994. 240p. 20.00 o.s.i (*0-449-90871-2*, Fawcett) Ballantine Bks.

MACPHERSON, ELIZABETH (FICTITIOUS CHARACTER)—FICTION

McCrumb, Sharyn. Highland Laddie Gone. 1999. mass mkt. 5.99 o.s.i (*0-345-91575-5*); 1998. mass mkt. o.s.i (*0-345-42948-6*); 1991. 224p. mass mkt. 5.99 (*0-345-36036-2*, Ivy Bks.) Ballantine Bks.
—Highland Laddie Gone. l.t. ed. 2002. 28.95 (*1-58547-213-1*, Premier) Ctr. Point Large Print.
—Highland Laddie Gone. 1986. 192p. pap. 2.95 o.p. (*0-380-89910-8*, Avon Bks.) Morrow/Avon.
—Highland Laddie Gone. unabr. ed. 1992. audio 44.00 (*1-55690-678-1*, 92220E7) Recorded Bks., LLC.
—Highland Laddie Gone. 1993. 19.00 o.p. (*0-7278-4418-0*) Severn Hse. Pubs., Ltd.
—If I'd Killed Him When I Met Him... Date not set. pap. (*0-449-22537-2*, Fawcett); 1996. mass mkt. o.p. (*0-345-40451-3*); 1996. 288p. mass mkt. 6.99 (*0-449-14998-6*, Fawcett); 1995. 277p. 20.00 o.s.i (*0-345-38229-3*) Ballantine Bks.
—If I'd Killed Him When I Met Him... l.t. ed. 1997. (Large Print Book Ser.). pap. 24.95 (*1-56895-472-7*, Wheeler Publishing, Inc.) Gale Group.
—If I'd Killed Him When I Met Him... unabr. ed. 1996. audio 51.00 (*0-7887-0506-7*, 94699E7) Recorded Bks., LLC.
—Lovely in Her Bones. 1999. 5.99 (*0-345-91574-7*); 1998. mass mkt. o.s.i (*0-345-42947-8*); 1990. 224p. reprint ed. mass mkt. 5.99 (*0-345-36035-4*) Ballantine Bks.
—Lovely in Her Bones. l.t. ed. 2000. (Wheeler Large Print Book Ser.). 249p. pap. 23.95 (*1-56895-859-5*, Wheeler Publishing, Inc.) Gale Group.
—Lovely in Her Bones. 1985. 224p. pap. 2.95 o.p. (*0-380-89592-7*, Avon Bks.) Morrow/Avon.
—Lovely in Her Bones. 1993. 224p. lib. bdg. 20.00 o.p. (*0-7278-4495-4*) Severn Hse. Pubs., Ltd.
—MacPherson's Lament. (Elizabeth MacPherson Ser.). 304p. 1993. mass mkt. 6.99 (*0-345-38474-1*); 1992. 17.00 o.p. (*0-345-36576-3*) Ballantine Bks.
—MacPherson's Lament. l.t. ed. 2002. 30.95 (*1-58724-230-3*, Wheeler Publishing, Inc.) Gale Group.
—MacPherson's Lament. unabr. ed. 2000. audio 46.00 (*0-7887-3109-2*, 95820E7) Recorded Bks., LLC.
—Missing Susan. 2000. mass mkt. 6.99 (*0-345-91578-X*); 1992. 256p. reprint ed. mass mkt. 5.99 (*0-345-37945-4*) Ballantine Bks.
—Missing Susan. l.t. ed. 1993. (General Ser.). 408p. pap. 18.95 (*0-8161-5566-6*, Macmillan Reference USA) Gale Group.
—Missing Susan. unabr. ed. 1998. audio 51.00 (*0-7887-1993-9*, 95380E7) Recorded Bks., LLC.
—Paying the Piper. 1999. 5.99 (*0-345-91576-3*); 1988. 192p. mass mkt. 5.99 (*0-345-34518-5*) Ballantine Bks.
—Paying the Piper. unabr. ed. 1993. audio 35.00 (*1-55690-709-5*, 93109E7) Recorded Bks., LLC.
—Paying the Piper. 1991. reprint ed. 18.95 o.p. (*0-7278-4247-1*) Severn Hse. Pubs., Ltd.
—The PMS Outlaws. l.t. ed. 2000. (Large Print Book Ser.). 328p. 28.95 o.p. (*1-56895-935-4*, Wheeler Publishing, Inc.) Gale Group.
—Sick of Shadows. 1999. 5.99 (*0-345-91573-9*); 1998. mass mkt. o.s.i (*0-345-42946-X*); 1989. 240p. mass mkt. 6.99 (*0-345-35653-5*) Ballantine Bks.
—Sick of Shadows. 240p. 1984. pap. 2.95 o.p. (*0-380-87189-0*, 87189); 1992. reprint ed. 19.00 o.p. (*0-7278-4334-6*) Severn Hse. Pubs., Ltd.
—Sick of Shadows. l.t. ed. 2000. (Basic Ser.). 352p. 29.95 (*0-7862-2370-7*) Thorndike Pr.
—The Windsor Knot. 2000. mass mkt. 6.50 (*0-345-91577-1*); 1991. 224p. mass mkt. 6.99 (*0-345-36427-9*) Ballantine Bks.
—The Windsor Knot. l.t. ed. 2001. 267p. 29.95 (*0-7838-9407-4*, Macmillan Reference USA) Gale Group.
—The Windsor Knot. unabr. ed. 1993. audio 44.00 (*1-55690-890-3*, 93332E7) Recorded Bks., LLC.

MACPHERSON, SKY (FICTITIOUS CHARACTER)—FICTION

Purcell, Deirdre. Sky. 1997. 432p. mass mkt. 5.99 o.s.i (*0-451-19089-0*, Signet Bks.) NAL.

MCTAVISH, STONER (FICTITIOUS CHARACTER)—FICTION

Dreher, Sarah. Bad Company: A Stoner McTavish Mystery. 1995. 235p. pap. 10.95 (*0-934678-66-9*); trans. 19.95 (*0-934678-67-7*) New Victoria Pubs., Inc.
—A Captive in Time. 1990. (Stoner McTavish Mystery Ser.). 256p. (Orig.). pap. 10.95 (*0-934678-22-7*) New Victoria Pubs., Inc.
—Gray Magic. 1987. (Stoner McTavish Mystery Ser.). 282p. (Orig.). pap. 9.95 (*0-934678-11-1*) New Victoria Pubs., Inc.
—Otherworld. 1993. (Stoner McTavish Mystery Ser.). 256p. (Orig.). pap. 10.95 (*0-934678-44-8*) New Victoria Pubs., Inc.
—Shaman's Moon. 1998. (Stoner McTavish Mystery Ser.). 197p. pap. 12.95 (*0-934678-91-X*) New Victoria Pubs., Inc.
—Something Shady. 1986. (Stoner McTavish Mystery Ser.). 272p. pap. 8.95 (*0-934678-07-3*) New Victoria Pubs., Inc.
—Stoner McTavish. 1985. (Stoner McTavish Mystery Ser.). 200p. pap. 9.95 (*0-934678-06-5*) New Victoria Pubs., Inc.

MCVAY, LIZZIE (FICTITIOUS CHARACTER)—FICTION

Stine, R. L. The Prom Queen. 1992. (Fear Street Ser.: No. 11). 176p. (YA). (gr. 7 up). pap. 4.99 (*0-671-72485-1*, Simon Pulse) Simon & Schuster Children's Publishing.
—The Prom Queen. 1992. (Fear Street Ser.: No. 11). (YA). (gr. 7 up). 10.04 (*0-606-02008-X*) Turtleback Bks.

MCWHINNY, TISH (FICTITIOUS CHARACTER)—FICTION

Comfort, Barbara. The Cashmere Kid. (Tish McWhinny Mystery Ser.). 224p. 1994. pap. 6.95 (*0-88150-321-5*); 1993. text 18.00 o.p. (*0-88150-254-5*) Norton, W. W. & Co., Inc. (Foul Play).
—Elusive Quarry. (Tish McWhinny Mystery Ser.). 224p. 1996. pap. 7.50 (*0-88150-370-3*); 1995. 19.00 o.p. (*0-88150-332-0*) Norton, W. W. & Co., Inc. (Foul Play).
—Grave Consequences. (Vermont Village Murders Ser.). (Orig.). 1989. 233p. pap. 5.95 (*0-9608726-4-7*); 1994. 240p. reprint ed. pap. 6.00 o.p. (*0-88150-296-0*, Foul Play) Norton, W. W. & Co., Inc.
—A Pair for the Queen. 1999. 221p. pap. 7.95 (*0-393-31913-X*); 1998. (Tish McWhinny Mystery Ser.: Vol. 5). 192p. 22.00 (*0-393-04627-3*) Norton, W. W. & Co., Inc.
—Phoebe's Knee. (Tish McWhinny Mystery Ser.). (Orig.). 1994. 224p. pap. 7.95 (*0-88150-295-2*, Foul Play); 1986. 220p. pap. 3.95 (*0-9608726-3-9*) Norton, W. W. & Co., Inc.
Comfort, Barbara, contrib. by. A Pair for the Queen. l.t. ed. 1999. (Senior Lifestyles Ser.). 320p. o.p. (*0-7862-2297-2*) Thorndike Pr.

MADDOCK, JOREY (FICTITIOUS CHARACTER)—FICTION

Fabio. Mysterious. 1998. 352p. mass mkt. 6.99 o.s.i (*0-7860-0491-6*, Pinnacle Bks.) Kensington Publishing Corp.

MADDOCK, YANABA (FICTITIOUS CHARACTER)—FICTION

McCaffrey, Anne & Scarborough, Elizabeth. Power Play. 1992. 5.99 o.s.i (*0-345-38175-0*) Ballantine Bks.
McCaffrey, Anne & Scarborough, Elizabeth Ann. Power Lines. 1995. 336p. mass mkt. 6.99 (*0-345-38780-5*, Del Rey) Ballantine Bks.
—Power Play. 1996. 352p. mass mkt. 6.99 (*0-345-38781-3*, Del Rey) Ballantine Bks.
—The Powers That Be. 2002. E-Book 6.99 (*0-345-45755-2*); 1994. 384p. mass mkt. 6.99 (*0-345-38779-1*, Del Rey) Ballantine Bks.
—The Powers That Be. abr. ed. 1993. audio 16.95 o.p. (*1-55800-855-1*) NewStar Media, Inc.

MADDOX, JUDY (FICTITIOUS CHARACTER)—FICTION

Follett, Ken. The Hammer of Eden. 1999. 448p. mass mkt. 7.99 (*0-449-22754-5*, Fawcett) Ballantine Bks.
—The Hammer of Eden. l.t. ed. 1998. 672p. 25.95 o.p. (*0-7838-0265-X*, Macmillan Reference USA) Gale Group.
—The Hammer of Eden: A Novel. l.t. ed. 1998. 672p. pap. 25.95 o.s.i (*0-375-70419-1*) Random Hse., Inc.

MADRIANI, PAUL (FICTITIOUS CHARACTER)—FICTION

Martini, Steve. The Arraignment. 2003. 416p. 25.95 (*0-399-14878-7*) Putnam Publishing Group, The.
—The Arraignment. 2003. audio compact disk 30.00 (*0-7435-2480-2*); audio 26.00 (*0-671-04694-2*) Simon & Schuster Audio. (Simon & Schuster Audioworks).
—The Attorney. unabr. ed. 2001. audio compact disk 110.95 (*0-7927-9952-6*, SLD 003); 2000. audio 84.95 (*0-7927-2408-9*, CSL 297) BBC Audiobooks America. (Chivers Sound Library).
—The Attorney. 2001. 448p. mass mkt. 7.99 (*0-515-13004-4*, Jove) Berkley Publishing Group.
—The Attorney. 2000. 448p. 25.95 o.s.i (*0-399-14536-2*) Penguin Group (USA) Inc.
—The Attorney. abr. ed. 2000. (Paul Madriani Novels Ser.). 5p. audio 25.00 (*0-671-04696-9*); audio compact disk 32.00 (*0-7435-0006-7*) Simon & Schuster Audio. (Simon & Schuster Audioworks).
—The Attorney. l.t. ed. 2000. (Basic Ser.). 613p. 31.95 (*0-7862-2433-9*) Thorndike Pr.
—Compelling Evidence. 1993. 448p. mass mkt. 7.99 (*0-515-11039-6*, Jove) Berkley Publishing Group.
—Compelling Evidence. l.t. ed. 1992. (General Ser.). 608p. lib. bdg. 23.95 o.p. (*0-8161-5548-8*, Macmillan Reference USA) Gale Group.
—Compelling Evidence. abr. ed. 1993. (Super Sound Buy, Dove Ser.). audio 8.99 o.p. (*1-55800-802-0*); 15.95 o.p. (*1-55800-613-3*) NewStar Media, Inc.
—Compelling Evidence. 1992. 384p. 21.95 o.p. (*0-399-13712-2*, G. P. Putnam's Sons) Penguin Group (USA) Inc.
—Compelling Evidence. l.t. ed. 1993. (G. K. Hall Large Print Book Ser.). 657p. pap. 19.95 (*0-8161-5549-6*) Thorndike Pr.
—Compelling Evidence & Prime Witness. abr. ed. 1998. (Steve Martini Collections). audio 25.00 (*0-7871-1759-5*, Dove Audio) NewStar Media, Inc.
—Double Tap. 2003. 384p. 25.95 (*0-399-15092-7*) Putnam Publishing Group, The.
—The Judge. 1996. 512p. mass mkt. 6.99 o.s.i (*0-515-11915-6*, Jove); reprint ed. pap. 7.99 (*0-515-11964-4*) Berkley Publishing Group.
—The Judge. 1996. 400p. 23.95 o.p. (*0-399-14043-3*, G. P. Putnam's Sons) Penguin Group (USA) Inc.
—The Judge. unabr. ed. audio 85.00 (*0-7887-0466-4*, 94659E7) Recorded Bks., LLC.
—The Judge. abr. ed. 1996. audio 24.00 (*0-671-53453-X*); Set. 1998. audio 12.98 (*0-671-58209-7*, 493061) Simon & Schuster Audio. (Simon & Schuster Audioworks).
—The Judge. l.t. ed. 1996. (Thorndike/G. K. Hall Paperback Bestsellers Ser.). 567p. pap. 27.95 (*0-7838-1611-1*); lib. bdg. 28.95 (*0-7838-1610-3*) Thorndike Pr.
—Prime Witness. 1994. 416p. mass mkt. 7.99 (*0-515-11264-X*, Jove) Berkley Publishing Group.
—Prime Witness. l.t. ed. 590p. 1994. 19.95 o.p. (*0-8161-5870-3*); 1993. 23.95 o.p. (*0-8161-5869-X*) Gale Group. (Macmillan Reference USA).
—Prime Witness. abr. ed. 1993. audio 16.95 o.p. (*1-55800-813-6*, 391400) NewStar Media, Inc.
—Prime Witness. 1993. 384p. 21.95 o.p. (*0-399-13802-1*, G. P. Putnam's Sons) Penguin Group (USA) Inc.
—Undue Influence. 480p. 1995. mass mkt. 7.99 (*0-515-11605-X*); 1996. pap. 6.99 o.s.i (*0-515-12072-3*) Berkley Publishing Group. (Jove).
—Undue Influence. l.t. ed. 1996. 567p. 19.95 o.p. (*0-7838-1129-2*); 1994. 714p. lib. bdg. 25.95 o.p. (*0-7838-1128-4*) Gale Group. (Macmillan Reference USA).
—Undue Influence. 1994. 400p. 22.95 o.p. (*0-399-13932-X*) Penguin Group (USA) Inc.
—Undue Influence. unabr. ed. 1995. audio 85.00 (*0-7887-0190-8*, 94425E7) Recorded Bks., LLC.
—Undue Influence. abr. ed. 1994. audio 17.00 (*0-671-89520-6*); Set. 1998. audio 9.98 (*0-671-58129-5*, 391836) Simon & Schuster Audio. (Simon & Schuster Audioworks).
—Undue Influence, Compelling Evidence, Prime Witness. 1995. 20.97 o.s.i (*0-515-11795-1*, Jove) Berkley Publishing Group.

MAGARACZ, NICK (FICTITIOUS CHARACTER)—FICTION

Gallison, Kate. Jersey Monkey. 1992. 224p. 17.95 o.p. (*0-312-07006-3*, Saint Martin's Minotaur) St. Martin's Pr.

MAGLIONE, GIANNA (FICTITIOUS CHARACTER)—FICTION

Micklebury, Penny. Keeping Secrets. 1994. 240p. pap. 9.95 o.p. (*1-56280-052-3*) Naiad Pr., Inc.
—Night Songs. 1995. 224p. pap. 10.95 o.p. (*1-56280-097-3*) Naiad Pr., Inc.

MAGNUM, CUDDY (FICTITIOUS CHARACTER)—FICTION

Malone, Michael. First Lady. l.t. ed. 2003. (Magna Large Print Ser.). 545p. (*0-7505-1985-1*) Magna Large Print Bks. GBR. *Dist:* Ulverscroft Large Print Canada, Ltd.
—First Lady. 448p. 2002. pap. 15.00 (*1-57071-971-3*); 2001. 24.00 (*1-57071-743-5*) Sourcebooks, Inc. (Sourcebooks Landmark).
—Time's Witness. Rosenman, Jane, ed. 1994. 592p. pap. (*0-671-87527-2*, Washington Square Pr.) Simon & Schuster.
—Times Witness. Peters, Sally, ed. 1991. 592p. reprint ed. mass mkt. 5.95 (*0-671-70318-8*, Pocket) Simon & Schuster.
—Time's Witness: A Novel. 1989. 540p. 19.95 o.s.i (*0-316-54480-9*) Little Brown & Co.

MAGRUDER, TOMBSTONE (FICTITIOUS CHARACTER)—FICTION

Douglass, Keith. Alpha Strike. 1997. (Carrier Ser.: No. 8). 336p. mass mkt. 6.99 o.s.i (*0-515-12018-9*, Jove) Berkley Publishing Group.

MAGUIRE, MAGGIE (FICTITIOUS CHARACTER)—FICTION

Bryan, Kate. Murder at Bent Elbow. 1998. (Maggie Maguire Mysteries Ser.: Vol. 1). 224p. mass mkt. 5.99 o.s.i (*0-425-16194-3*, Prime Crime) Berkley Publishing Group.
—A Record of Death. 1998. (Maggie Maguire Mysteries Ser.: Vol. 2). 224p. mass mkt. 5.99 o.s.i (*0-425-16537-X*) Berkley Publishing Group.

MAGUIRE, TRISH (FICTITIOUS CHARACTER)—FICTION

Cooper, Natasha. Creeping Ivy. 1999. 342p. 23.95 o.p. (*0-312-20520-1*, Saint Martin's Minotaur) St. Martin's Pr.
—Creeping Ivy. l.t. ed. 1999. (Ulverscroft Large Print Ser.). 376p. 31.99 o.p. (*0-7089-4144-3*, Ulverscroft) Thorpe, F. A. Pubs. GBR. *Dist:* Ulverscroft Large Print Bks., Ltd., Ulverscroft Large Print Canada, Ltd.
—Fault Lines. 2000. 346p. 23.95 (*0-312-25316-8*, Saint Martin's Minotaur) St. Martin's Pr.
—Fault Lines. l.t. ed. 2000. (Ulverscroft Large Print Ser.). 480p. 31.99 (*0-7089-4276-8*, Ulverscroft) Thorpe, F. A. Pubs. GBR. *Dist:* Ulverscroft Large Print Bks., Ltd., Ulverscroft Large Print Canada, Ltd.
—Out of the Dark. 320p. pap. (*0-671-03765-X*, Free Pr.) Simon & Schuster.
—Out of the Dark: A Trish Maguire Mystery. 2002. 320p. 23.95 (*0-312-30061-1*, Saint Martin's Minotaur) St. Martin's Pr.
—A Place of Safety: A Trish Maguire Mystery. 2003. 320p. 24.95 (*0-312-31936-3*, Saint Martin's Minotaur) St. Martin's Pr.

MAGWITCH, ABEL (FICTITIOUS CHARACTER)—FICTION

Carey, Peter. Jack Maggs. 1999. 368p. pap. 13.00 (*0-679-76037-7*, Vintage) Knopf Publishing Group.
—Jack Maggs. 1998. 309p. 24.00 (*0-679-44008-9*) Knopf, Alfred A. Inc.
—Jack Maggs. 1998. 417p. pap. 16.95 (*0-7022-3049-9*) Univ. of Queensland Pr. AUS. *Dist:* International Specialized Bk. Services.

MAIGRET, JULES (FICTITIOUS CHARACTER)—FICTION

Courtine, Robert J. Madame Maigret's Recipes. Manheim, Mary, tr. 1987. pap. 5.95 o.p. (*0-15-650172-4*, Harvest Bks.) Harcourt Trade Pubs.
Four on Maigret. unabr. ed. Incl. Drowned Men's Inn. audio o.s.i Maigret's Mistake. audio o.s.i Maigret's Pipe. audio o.s.i Mr. Monday. audio o.s.i 1985. 1985. Set audio 16.95 o.s.i (*1-55656-002-8*) Dercum Audio.
Simenon. Maigret & the Wine Merchant. 2003. pap. 8.00 (*0-15-602844-1*) Harcourt Trade Pubs.
Simenon, Georges. The Accomplices. Frechtman, Bernard, tr. 1977. pap. 2.25 o.p. (*0-15-602670-8*, Harvest Bks.) Harcourt Trade Pubs.
—The Accomplices. mass mkt. 0.50 o.p. (*0-451-02751-5*, Signet Bks.) NAL.
—Across the Street. 1992. 18.95 (*0-15-103266-1*) Harcourt Trade Pubs.
—African Trio: Talatala, Tropic Moon, Aboard the Aquitaine. 1979. 9.95 o.p. (*0-15-103955-0*) Harcourt Trade Pubs.


Characters

—Aine des Ferchaux. 1985. (Folio Ser.: No. 930). (FRE.). 4332p. (Orig.). pap. 10.95 o.p. (2-07-036930-7) Schoenhof's Foreign Bks., Inc.
—L' Aine des Ferchaux. 1977. (FRE.). pap. 13.95 (0-7859-4076-6) French & European Pubns., Inc.
—L' Ami d'Enfance de Maigret. pap. 10.95 (0-8288-6099-8, F126480) French & European Pubns., Inc.
—L' Ami d'Enfance de Maigret. 2000. (Maigret Mystery Ser.). (FRE.). pap. 12.95 (2-253-14213-1) Librairie Generale Francaise, LGF FRA. Dist: Distribooks, Inc.
—L' Amie de Madame Maigret. (FRE.). pap. 10.95 (0-8288-6156-0, F126404) French & European Pubns., Inc.
—L' Amie de Madame Maigret. 2000. (Maigret Mystery Ser.). (FRE.). pap. 12.95 (2-253-14225-5) Librairie Generale Francaise, LGF FRA. Dist: Distribooks, Inc.
—Aunt Jeanne. Sainsbury, Geoffrey, tr. from FRE. 1983. 160p. 13.95 o.p. (0-15-109792-5) Harcourt Trade Pubs.
—Les Autres. 1992. (FRE.). pap. 11.95 (0-7859-3261-5, 2266053019) French & European Pubns., Inc.
—Betty. 1992. (FRE.). pap. 11.95 (0-7859-3255-0, 2266049801) French & European Pubns., Inc.
—Big Bob. Lowe, Eileen M., tr. 1981. 180p. 11.95 o.p. (0-15-112075-7) Harcourt Trade Pubs.
—Le Blanc a Lunettes. 1978. (FRE.). pap. 10.95 (0-7859-4093-6) French & European Pubns., Inc.
—The Blue Room. Ellenbogen, Eileen, tr. 1978. 141p. reprint ed. pap. 2.95 o.s.i (0-15-613267-2, Harvest Bks.) Harcourt Trade Pubs.
—Le Bourgmestre de Fumes, Malempin, les Inconnus Dans la Masion. 1992. (FRE.). 1148p. 49.95 (0-7859-0494-8, 2258035279) French & European Pubns., Inc.
—Le Bourgmestre de Furnes. 1977. (FRE.). pap. 10.95 (0-7859-4077-4) French & European Pubns., Inc.
—The Cat. Frechtman, Bernard, tr. from FRE. 1976. (Helen & Kurt Wolff Bk.). 182p. pap. 2.95 o.s.i (0-15-615549-4, Harvest Bks.) Harcourt Trade Pubs.
—Le Cercle des Mahe. 1981. (FRE.). pap. 10.95 (0-7859-4161-4) French & European Pubns., Inc.
—Ceux de la Soif. 1978. (FRE.). pap. 10.95 (0-7859-4098-7) French & European Pubns., Inc.
—Le Chat. 1992. (FRE.). pap. 11.95 (0-7859-3254-2, 2266049798) French & European Pubns., Inc.
—Chemin sans Issue. 1979. (FRE.). pap. 10.95 (0-7859-4118-5) French & European Pubns., Inc.
—Le Chien Jaune. Katz, Eve & Hall, Donald R., eds. 1967. (FRE.). (C). pap. text 18.12 o.p. (0-06-046163-2) Addison-Wesley Educational Pubs., Inc.
—Le Chien Jaune. 1967. (College French Ser.). (FRE.). pap. 21.95 o.p. (0-8384-3771-0) Heinle.
—Choix De Simenon. Lindsay, Frank W. & Nazzaro, Anthony M., eds. 1972. (Illus.). pap. o.p. (0-13-133033-0) Prentice-Hall.
—Les Clients d'Avrenos. 1966. (FRE.). pap. 11.95 (0-7859-3962-8) French & European Pubns., Inc.
—The Clockmaker. Benny, Norman, tr. 1977. 124p. pap. 2.95 o.s.i (0-15-618170-3, Harvest Bks.) Harcourt Trade Pubs.
—Colere de Maigret. 1963. (FRE.). 192p. pap. 11.95 (0-7859-1472-2, 2258001730) French & European Pubns., Inc.
—Confidence de Maigret. 1992. (FRE.). 192p. pap. 11.95 (0-7859-1605-9, 226604978X) French & European Pubns., Inc.
—Le Coup de Vague. 1978. (FRE.). pap. 10.95 (0-7859-4100-2) French & European Pubns., Inc.
—The Couple from Poitiers. Ellenbogen, Eileen, tr. 1986. 144p. 13.95 (0-15-122700-4) Harcourt Trade Pubs.
—La Dansuese Du Gai-Moulin, la Guinguette a Deux Sous, l'Ombre Chinoise. 1991. (FRE.). 928p. 49.95 (0-7859-0486-7, 2258032725) French & European Pubns., Inc.
—The Delivery. Ellenbogen, Eileen, ed. 1981. (Helen & Kurt Wolff Bk.). 10.95 o.p. (0-15-124655-6) Harcourt Trade Pubs.
—Demoiselles de Concarneau. 1936. (Folio Ser.: No. 933). (FRE.). 148p. pap. 6.95 (2-07-036933-1) Schoenhof's Foreign Bks., Inc.
—Les Demoiselles de Concarneau. 1977. (FRE.). pap. 10.95 (0-7859-4078-2) French & European Pubns., Inc.
—The Disappearance of Odile. 1972. (Helen & Kurt Wolff Bk.). 6.95 o.p. (0-15-125720-5) Harcourt Trade Pubs.
—Donadieu's Will. Gilbert, Stuart, tr. 2nd ed. 1991. 343p. 22.95 (0-15-126310-8) Harcourt Trade Pubs.
—The Door. Woodward, Daphne, tr. 1990. 138p. 18.95 o.s.i (0-15-126370-1) Harcourt Trade Pubs.
—Echec de Maigret. 1990. (FRE.). 192p. pap. 11.95 (0-7859-1494-3, 2285002475) French & European Pubns., Inc.
—Enigmes, Level B. (FRE.). text 8.95 (0-88436-058-X, 40269) EMC/Paradigm Publishing.
—The Family Lie. Hillier, Caroline & Quigly, Isabel, trs. 1978. (Helen & Kurt Wolff Bk.). 7.95 o.p. (0-15-156247-4) Harcourt Trade Pubs.
—Les Fantomes du Chapelier. 1992. (FRE.). pap. 11.95 (0-7859-3256-9, 2266050877) French & European Pubns., Inc.
—Faubourg. 1978. (FRE.). pap. 8.95 (0-7859-4094-4) French & European Pubns., Inc.
—Fils Cardinaud. 1943. (Folio Ser.: No. 1047). (FRE.). 148p. pap. 6.95 (2-07-037047-X) Schoenhof's Foreign Bks., Inc.
—Le Fils, le Negre, Maigret Voyage, Strip-Tease, les Scruples de Maigret, le President, le Passage de la Ligne, 23 vols., Set. 1989. (FRE.). 832p. 49.95 (0-7859-0555-3, 225803003X) French & European Pubns., Inc.
—La Folle de Maigret. 1990. (FRE.). 186p. pap. 11.95 (0-7859-1495-1, 2285003846) French & European Pubns., Inc.
—Four on Maigret. unabr. ed. (Inspector Maigret Mystery Ser.). audio 21.95 o.p. (1-55656-077-X, DAB056) BBC Audiobooks America.
—Four on Maigret. unabr. ed. 1997. (Mystery Library). pap. 16.95 o.p. incl. audio (1-55656-254-3) Dercum Audio.
—The Girl with a Squint. Thomson, Helen, tr. 1978. 7.95 o.p. (0-15-135692-0) Harcourt Trade Pubs.
—The Glass Cage. 1973. (Helen & Kurt Wolff Bk.). 5.50 o.p. (0-15-135800-1) Harcourt Trade Pubs.
—The Grandmother. Stewart, Jean, tr. 1980. (Helen & Kurt Wolff Bk.). 192p. reprint ed. 8.95 o.p. (0-15-136738-8) Harcourt Trade Pubs.
—The Hatter's Phantoms. 19.95 (0-89190-428-X) Amereon, Ltd.
—The Hatter's Phantoms. Trask, Willard R., tr. (Helen & Kurt Wolff Bk.). 1981. 176p. pap. 3.95 o.s.i (0-15-639342-5, Harvest Bks.); 1976. 6.95 o.p. (0-15-139270-6) Harcourt Trade Pubs.
—L' Homme Qui Regardait Passer les Trains. 1967. (FRE.). pap. 15.95 (0-7859-3963-6) French & European Pubns., Inc.
—L' Horloger d'Everton. 1992. (FRE.). pap. 16.95 (0-7859-3304-2, 2804007790) French & European Pubns., Inc.
—The House on the Quai Notre-Dame. Hamilton, Alastair, tr. 1975. (Helen & Kurt Wolff Bk.). 160p. 6.95 o.p. (0-15-142181-1) Harcourt Trade Pubs.
—Inconnus Dans la Maison. 1975. (Folio Ser.: No. 664). (FRE.). pap. 8.95 (2-07-036664-2) Schoenhof's Foreign Bks., Inc.
—Les Inconnus dans la Maison. 1975. (FRE.). pap. 10.95 (0-7859-4041-3) French & European Pubns., Inc.
—The Innocents. 1974. (Helen & Kurt Wolff Bk.). 6.50 o.p. (0-15-144430-7) Harcourt Trade Pubs.
—Inspector Maigret & the Strangled Stripper. unabr. collector's ed. 1983. audio 30.00 (0-7366-0533-9, 1507) Books on Tape, Inc.
—Inspector Maigret's Case Files: Murder a la Carte. 1992. 9.98 (0-88365-810-0, Galahad Bks.) BBS Publishing Corp.
—Intimate Memoirs: Including Marie-Jo's Book. Salemson, Harold J., tr. 1984. 800p. 22.95 o.s.i (0-15-144892-2) Harcourt Trade Pubs.
—Intimate Memoirs: Including Marie-Jo's Book. Salemson, Harold J., tr. 1984. 815 p. o.p. (0-241-11219-2, Hamilton, Hamish) Viking Penguin.
—The Iron Staircase. Date not set. lib. bdg. 18.95 (0-8488-2161-0) Amereon, Ltd.
—The Iron Staircase. Ellenbogen, Eileen, tr. 1981. 192p. pap. 2.95 o.s.i (0-15-645484-X, Harvest Bks.) Harcourt Trade Pubs.
—Justice. Sainsbury, Geoffrey, tr. from FRE. 1985. (Helen & Kurt Wolff Bk.). 176p. reprint ed. 13.95 (0-15-146585-1) Harcourt Trade Pubs.
—Letter to My Mother. Manheim, Ralph, tr. 1976. (Helen & Kurt Wolff Bk.). 96p. 5.95 o.p. (0-15-150445-8) Harcourt Trade Pubs.
—The Little Doctor. Stewart, Jean, tr. from FRE. 1981. (Helen & Kurt Wolff Bk.). 10.95 o.p. (0-15-152768-7) Harcourt Trade Pubs.
—Le Locataire. 1978. (FRE.). pap. 10.95 (0-7859-4091-X, 2070369986) French & European Pubns., Inc.
—Le Locataire. 1934. (Folio Ser.: No. 998). (FRE.). 181p. pap. 6.95 (2-07-036998-6) Schoenhof's Foreign Bks., Inc.
—Le Locataire, les Suicides, les Pitard. 1992. (FRE.). 990p. 49.95 (0-7859-0491-3, 2258035244) French & European Pubns., Inc.
—The Lodger. Gilbert, Stuart, tr. from FRE. 1983. (Helen & Kurt Wolff Bk.). 176p. reprint ed. 12.95 o.p. (0-15-152960-4) Harcourt Trade Pubs.
—The Long Exile. Ellenbogen, Eileen, tr. 1983. (Helen & Kurt Wolff Bk.). 372p. 15.95 o.s.i (0-15-152997-3) Harcourt Trade Pubs.
—Madame Maigret's Own Case. 2003. 180p. pap. 8.00 (0-15-602849-2); 2nd ed. 1991. 182p. (C). pap. 6.00 o.s.i (0-15-655106-3, Harvest Bks.); 2nd ed. 1990. 192p. 17.95 o.s.i (0-15-154968-0) Harcourt Trade Pubs.
—Maigret a New York. 1996. (FRE.). audio 21.95 Olivia & Hill Pr., The.
—Maigret a Vichy. 2000. (Maigret Mystery Ser.). (FRE.). pap. 12.95 (2-253-14216-6) Librairie Generale Francaise, LGF FRA. Dist: Distribooks, Inc.
—Maigret a Vichy. 1992. (FRE.). audio 32.95 Olivia & Hill Pr., The.
—Maigret Afraid. Duff, Margaret, tr. (Helen & Kurt Wolff Bk.). 1996. 170p. pap. 6.00 o.s.i (0-15-655142-X, Harvest Bks.); 1983. 176p. 13.95 o.s.i (0-15-155560-5) Harcourt Trade Pubs.
—Maigret among the Rich. 1978. mass mkt. 5.95 o.p. (0-671-79051-X, Pocket) Simon & Schuster.
—Maigret & the Apparition. Ellenbogen, Eileen, tr. 1978. (Adult Ser.). lib. bdg. 9.95 o.p. (0-8161-6503-3, Macmillan Reference USA) Gale Group.
—Maigret & the Apparition. 168p. 2003. pap. 8.00 (0-15-602838-7); 1991. pap. 6.00 o.s.i (0-15-655127-6) Harcourt Trade Pubs. (Harvest Bks.).
—Maigret & the Apparition. Ellenbogen, Eileen, tr. 1976. (Helen & Kurt Wolff Bk.). 6.95 o.p. (0-15-155125-1) Harcourt Trade Pubs.
—Maigret & the Black Sheep. l.t. ed. 2001. (Dales Large Print Ser.). 208p. pap. 21.99 (1-84262-061-4) Dales Large Print Bks. GBR. Dist: Ulverscroft Large Print Bks., Ltd., Ulverscroft Large Print Canada, Ltd.
—Maigret & the Black Sheep. Thompson, Helen, tr. 1976. (Helen & Kurt Wolff Bk.). 168p. 6.95 o.p. (0-15-155146-4) Harcourt Trade Pubs.
—Maigret & the Black Sheep. Thomson, Helen, tr. 1983. 168p. reprint ed. pap. 3.95 o.s.i (0-15-655138-1, Harvest Bks.) Harcourt Trade Pubs.
—Maigret & the Bum. unabr. collector's ed. 1984. audio 24.00 (0-7366-0540-1, 1514) Books on Tape, Inc.
—Maigret & the Bum. 2003. 160p. pap. 8.00 (0-15-602839-5, Harvest Bks.) Harcourt Trade Pubs.
—Maigret & the Bum. Stewart, Jean, tr. 1996. 156p. (C). pap. 3.95 o.s.i (0-15-655130-6, Harvest Bks.) Harcourt Trade Pubs.
—Maigret & the Bum. 1995. pap. 6.00 (0-15-600249-3) Harcourt Trade Pubs.
—Maigret & the Burglar's Wife. 2003. 176p. pap. 8.00 (0-15-602840-9); 1992. 167p. pap. 5.95 o.s.i (0-15-655167-5, Harvest Bks.) Harcourt Trade Pubs.
—Maigret & the Burglar's Wife. Maclaren-Ross, J., tr. 1990. 18.95 o.s.i (0-15-155572-9) Harcourt Trade Pubs.
—Maigret & the Calame Report. Budberg, Moura, tr. 1996. 192p. pap. 6.00 (0-15-655153-5, Harvest Bks.) Harcourt Trade Pubs.
—Maigret & the Calame Report. 1995. pap. o.s.i (0-15-600248-5) Harcourt Trade Pubs.
—Maigret & the Death of a Harbor-Master. Gilbert, Stuart, tr. 1989. 182p. pap. 6.00 (0-15-655161-6, Harvest Bks.) Harcourt Trade Pubs.
—Maigret & the Enigmatic Letter. 1964. pap. 2.95 o.p. (0-14-002023-3, Penguin Bks.) Viking Penguin.
—Maigret & the Flemish Shop. Sainsbury, Geoffrey, tr. 1990. 182p. pap. 5.95 o.p. (0-15-655118-7) Harcourt Trade Pubs.
—Maigret & the Fortuneteller. 1990. 140p. pap. 5.95 o.s.i (0-15-655163-2) Harcourt Trade Pubs.
—Maigret & the Fortuneteller. Sainsbury, Geoffrey, tr. 1989. 144p. 16.95 o.s.i (0-15-155571-0) Harcourt Trade Pubs.
—Maigret & the Gangsters. Varese, Louise, tr. from FRE. 1986. 162p. 14.95 (0-15-155565-6) Harcourt Trade Pubs.
—Maigret & the Gangsters. Varese, Louise, tr. 1988. 160p. pap. 3.50 (0-380-70414-5, Avon Bks.) Morrow/Avon.
—Maigret & the Headless Corpse. Ellenbogen, Eileen, tr. l.t. ed. 1989. (Nightingale Ser.). 274p. 13.95 o.p. (0-8161-4664-0, Macmillan Reference USA) Gale Group.
—Maigret & the Headless Corpse. Ellenbogen, Eileen, tr. 1985. (Helen & Kurt Wolff Bk.). 196p. (C). pap. 6.00 (0-15-655144-6, Harvest Bks.) Harcourt Trade Pubs.
—Maigret & the Hotel Majestic. Hillier, Caroline, tr. 1991. 182p. pap. 6.00 o.s.i (0-15-655133-0, Harvest Bks.) Harcourt Trade Pubs.
—Maigret & the Hundred Gibbets. 1963. pap. 2.95 o.p. (0-14-002025-X, Penguin Bks.) Viking Penguin.
—Maigret & the Informer. lib. bdg. 18.95 (0-8488-2033-9) Amereon, Ltd.
—Maigret & the Informer. 1973. 5.95 o.p. (0-15-155140-5) Harcourt Trade Pubs.
—Maigret & the Killer. lib. bdg. 19.95 (0-8488-2034-7) Amereon, Ltd.
—Maigret & the Killer. unabr. ed. 1993. (Inspector Maigret Mystery Ser.). audio 39.95 (0-7451-6284-3, CAB 600) BBC Audiobooks America.
—Maigret & the Killer. unabr. ed. 2000. (Inspector Maigret Mystery Ser.). audio 34.95 Chivers Audio Bks. GBR. Dist: BBC Audiobooks America.
—Maigret & the Killer. abr. ed. 1997. (Maigret Ser.). audio 16.99 (0-88646-452-8, 7452) Durkin Hayes Publishing Ltd.
—Maigret & the Killer. Moir, Lyn, tr. l.t. ed. 1991. (Nightingale Ser.). 239p. pap. 14.95 o.p. (0-8161-5117-2, Macmillan Reference USA) Gale Group.
—Maigret & the Killer. 2003. 168p. pap. 8.00 (0-15-602841-7, Harvest Bks.) Harcourt Trade Pubs.
—Maigret & the Killer. Moir, Lyn, tr. 1991. (Helen & Kurt Wolff Bk.). 165p. pap. 5.95 o.s.i (0-15-655124-1, Harvest Bks.) Harcourt Trade Pubs.
—Maigret & the Loner. 166p. 19.95 (0-89190-429-8) Amereon, Ltd.
—Maigret & the Loner. 1983. 168p. pap. 3.95 o.s.i (0-15-655139-X, Harvest Bks.) Harcourt Trade Pubs.
—Maigret & the Madwoman. unabr. ed. 1999. audio 21.95 (1-57270-125-0, N31125u, Audio Editions Mystery Masters) Audio Partners Publishing Corp.
—Maigret & the Madwoman. unabr. ed. 1995. (Inspector Maigret Mystery Ser.). audio 31.95 (0-7451-6520-6, CAB 1136) BBC Audiobooks America.
—Maigret & the Madwoman. 2003. 180p. pap. 8.00 (0-15-602850-6, Harvest Bks.) Harcourt Trade Pubs.
—Maigret & the Madwoman. Ellenbogen, Eileen, tr. 1992. (Helen & Kurt Wolff Bk.). 176p. pap. 5.95 o.s.i (0-15-655122-5, Harvest Bks.) Harcourt Trade Pubs.
—Maigret & the Man on the Bench. 2003. 192p. pap. 8.00 (0-15-602837-9, Harvest Bks.) Harcourt Trade Pubs.
—Maigret & the Man on the Bench. Ellenbogen, Eileen, tr. from FRE. (Helen & Kurt Wolff Bk.). 1993. 181p. pap. 5.95 o.s.i (0-15-655123-3, Harvest Bks.); 1975. 9.95 o.p. (0-15-155145-6) Harcourt Trade Pubs.
—Maigret & the Millionaires. l.t. ed. 2002. (Dales Large Print Ser.). 224p. pap. 21.99 (1-84262-097-5) Dales Large Print Bks. GBR. Dist: Ulverscroft Large Print Bks., Ltd., Ulverscroft Large Print Canada, Ltd.
—Maigret & the Millionaires. Stewart, Jean, tr. 1992. 182p. pap. 5.95 o.s.i (0-15-655150-0, Harvest Bks.); 1974. 168p. 5.95 o.p. (0-15-155143-X) Harcourt Trade Pubs.
—Maigret & the Nahour Case. Hamilton, Alastair, tr. l.t. ed. 1992. (Nightingale Ser.). 229p. pap. 14.95 o.p. (0-8161-5274-8, Macmillan Reference USA) Gale Group.
—Maigret & the Nahour Case. Hamilton, Alastair, tr. 1993. 168p. pap. 5.95 (0-15-655149-7, Harvest Bks.) Harcourt Trade Pubs.
—Maigret & the Nahour Case. 1983. (Helen & Kurt Wolff Bk.). 168p. 10.95 o.p. (0-15-155559-1) Harcourt Trade Pubs.
—Maigret & the Pickpocket. unabr. ed. 1992. (Inspector Maigret Mystery Ser.). 39.95 incl. audio (0-7451-4030-0, CAB 727) BBC Audiobooks America.
—Maigret & the Pickpocket. unabr. ed. 2000. (Inspector Maigret Mystery Ser.). audio 34.95 Chivers Audio Bks. GBR. Dist: BBC Audiobooks America.
—Maigret & the Pickpocket. Ryan, Nigel, tr. l.t. ed. 1990. (Nightingale Ser.). 13.95 o.p. (0-8161-4666-7, Macmillan Reference USA) Gale Group.
—Maigret & the Pickpocket. Ryan, Nigel, tr. from FRE. 1995. (Helen & Kurt Wolff Bk.). 156p. pap. 6.00 (0-15-655145-4, Harvest Bks.) Harcourt Trade Pubs.
—Maigret & the Reluctant Witness. abr. ed. 1998. audio 16.99 (0-88646-458-7, 7458) Durkin Hayes Publishing Ltd.
—Maigret & the Saturday Caller. 2003. 128p. pap. 8.00 (0-15-602842-5); 1992. 132p. pap. 6.00 o.s.i (0-15-655175-6, Harvest Bks.) Harcourt Trade Pubs.
—Maigret & the Saturday Caller. White, Tony, tr. 1991. 124p. 17.95 (0-15-155566-4) Harcourt Trade Pubs.
—Maigret & the Spinster. 2003. 168p. pap. 8.00 (0-15-602843-3, Harvest Bks.) Harcourt Trade Pubs.
—Maigret & the Spinster. Ellenbogen, Eileen, tr. 1996. 168p. (C). pap. 6.00 o.s.i (0-15-655129-2, Harvest Bks.); 1977. reprint ed. 6.95 o.p. (0-15-155550-8) Harcourt Trade Pubs.
—Maigret & the Tavern by the Seine. Sainsbury, Geoffrey, tr. 1990. 182p. pap. 6.00 (0-15-655164-0, Harvest Bks.) Harcourt Trade Pubs.
—Maigret & the Toy Village. unabr. ed. 1992. (Inspector Maigret Mystery Ser.). audio 39.95 (0-7451-6283-5, CAB 666) BBC Audiobooks America.
—Maigret & the Toy Village. Ellenbogen, Eileen, tr. l.t. ed. 1989. 216p. pap. 12.95 o.p. (0-8161-4427-3, Macmillan Reference USA) Gale Group.
—Maigret & the Toy Village. Ellenbogen, Eileen, tr. 1994. pap. 5.95 (0-15-655154-3, Harvest Bks.); 1979. 7.95 o.p. (0-15-155554-0) Harcourt Trade Pubs.
—Maigret & the Wine Merchant. unabr. collector's ed. 1984. audio 30.00 (0-7366-0544-4, 1518) Books on Tape, Inc.
—Maigret & the Wine Merchant. Ellenbogen, Eileen, tr. 1993. 187p. pap. 6.00 o.s.i (0-15-655125-X, Harvest Bks.) Harcourt Trade Pubs.
—Maigret & the Yellow Dog. 1995. (Helen & Kurt Wolff Bk.). 140p. pap. 6.00 (0-15-655157-8) Harcourt Trade Pubs.

—Maigret & the Yellow Dog. Asher, Linda, tr. 1987. 15.95 o.s.i (*0-15-155564-8*) Harcourt Trade Pubs.

—Maigret at the Coroner's. Keene, Frances, tr. (Helen & Kurt Wolff Bk.). 1992. 176p. (C). pap. 5.95 o.s.i (*0-15-655143-8*, Harvest Bks.); 1980. 180p. reprint ed. 8.95 o.p. (*0-15-155556-7*) Harcourt Trade Pubs.

—Maigret at the Crossroads. 1963. pap. 2.95 o.p. (*0-14-002028-4*, Penguin Bks.) Viking Penguin.

—Maigret at the Crossroads (Omnibus) 1984. (Crime Ser.). 320p. pap. 6.95 o.p. (*0-14-006652-7*, Penguin Bks.) Viking Penguin.

—Maigret at the Gai-Moulin.Tr. of Danseuse du Gai-Moulin. 2003. 176p. pap. 8.00 (*0-15-602845-X*); 1993. 182p. pap. 6.00 (*0-15-655176-4*) Harcourt Trade Pubs.

—Maigret at the Gai-Moulin. Sainsbury, Geoffrey, tr. 2nd ed. 1991. Tr. of Danseuse du Gai-Moulin. 166p. 17.95 o.s.i (*0-15-155568-0*) Harcourt Trade Pubs.

—Maigret au Picratt's. 2000. (Maigret Mystery Ser.). (FRE.). pap. 12.95 (*2-253-14219-0*) Librairie Generale Francaise, LGF FRA. *Dist:* Distribooks, Inc.

—Maigret Bides His Time. Hamilton, Alastair, tr. 160p. 1992. pap. 5.95 (*0-15-655151-9*, Harvest Bks.); 1985. 12.95 o.p. (*0-15-155563-X*) Harcourt Trade Pubs.

—Maigret et la Grande Perche. 2000. (Maigret Mystery Ser.). (FRE.). pap. 12.95 (*2-253-14223-9*) Librairie Generale Francaise, LGF FRA. *Dist:* Distribooks, Inc.

—Maigret et l'Affaire Nahour. 2000. (Maigret Mystery Ser.). (FRE.). pap. 12.95 (*2-253-14220-4*) Librairie Generale Francaise, LGF FRA. *Dist:* Distribooks, Inc.

—Maigret et le Clochard, Level B. (FRE.). text 8.95 (*0-88436-047-4*, 40270) EMC/Paradigm Publishing.

—Maigret et le Clochard. l.t. ed. 1997. (French Ser.). (FRE.). 236p. pap. 30.99 o.p. (*2-84011-186-1*) Feryane, SA, Editions FRA. *Dist:* Ulverscroft Large Print Bks., Ltd., Ulverscroft Large Print Canada, Ltd.

—Maigret et le Clochard. 2000. (Maigret Mystery Ser.). (FRE.). pap. 12.95 (*2-253-14228-X*) Librairie Generale Francaise, LGF FRA. *Dist:* Distribooks, Inc.

—Maigret et le Clochard. 1995. (FRE.). audio 28.95 Olivia & Hill Pr., The.

—Maigret et le Corps Sans Tete. 1992. (FRE.). pap. 11.95 (*0-7859-3257-7*, 2266051032) French & European Pubns., Inc.

—Maigret et le Corps Sans Tete, La Boule Noire, Maigret Tend un Piege, Les Complices, En Cas de Malheur, Un Echec de Maigret, Le Petit Homme d'Arkhangelsh, Maigret S'Amuse. 1989. (FRE.). 49.95 (*0-7859-0482-4*, 2258027977) French & European Pubns., Inc.

—Maigret et le Fantome, Level B. 2000. (FRE.). text 8.95 (*0-8219-1470-7*, 40271) EMC/Paradigm Publishing.

—Maigret et le Fantome. l.t. ed. 1996. (French Ser.). (FRE.). 224p. pap. 30.99 o.p. (*2-84011-152-7*) Feryane, SA, Editions FRA. *Dist:* Ulverscroft Large Print Bks., Ltd., Ulverscroft Large Print Canada, Ltd.

—Maigret et les Braves Gens. l.t. ed. 2002. (French Ser.). 221p. pap. 30.99 o.p. (*2-84011-459-3*) Feryane, SA, Editions FRA. *Dist:* Ulverscroft Large Print Bks., Ltd., Ulverscroft Large Print Canada, Ltd.

—Maigret et les Braves Gens: Student Edition. Daudon, Rene, ed. 1969. (FRE.). (Orig.). (C). pap. text, stu. ed. 4.95 o.p. (*0-15-551287-0*) Harcourt College Pubs.

—Maigret et les Temoins Recalcitrants, La Vielle, L'Ours en Peluche, Une Confidence de Maigret, Le Veuf, Maigret aux Assises, Maigret et les Viellards, Betty. 1990. (FRE.). 830p. 49.95 (*0-7859-0483-2*, 2258031532) French & European Pubns., Inc.

—Maigret et l'Inspecteur Maigrecieux, la Passager Clandestin, le Temoignage de l'Enfant Du Choeur, le Client le Plus Obstine Du Monde, On Ne Tue Pas les Pauvres Types, la Jument Perdue, Maigret et Son Mort, Pedigree. 1988. (FRE.). 49.95 (*0-7859-0477-8*, 2258021154) French & European Pubns., Inc.

—Maigret Goes Home. Baldick, Robert, tr. 1989. 16.95 (*0-15-155150-2*) Harcourt Trade Pubs.

—Maigret Goes Home. Baldick, Robert, tr. 1967. 139p. pap. 1.95 o.p. (*0-14-001901-4*, Penguin Bks.) Viking Penguin.

—Maigret Goes to School. Woodward, Daphne, tr. 1992. Tr. of Maigret a l'Ecole. 196p. pap. 5.95 o.s.i (*0-15-655156-X*) Harcourt Trade Pubs.

—Maigret Has Doubts. Moir, Lyn, tr. 1982. 144p. 10.95 o.p. (*0-15-155558-3*) Harcourt Trade Pubs.

—Maigret Has Doubts. 1988. 160p. pap. 3.50 (*0-380-70410-2*, Avon Bks.) Morrow/Avon.

—Maigret Has Scruples. Eglesfield, Robert, tr. 1996. (Helen & Kurt Wolff Bk.). 192p. pap. 6.00 (*0-15-655160-8*) Harcourt Trade Pubs.

—Maigret Has Scruples. 1995. pap. 6.00 (*0-15-600247-7*) Harcourt Trade Pubs.

—Maigret Hesitates. Moir, Lyn, tr. 1993. 182p. pap. 5.95 (*0-15-655152-7*, Harvest Bks.) Harcourt Trade Pubs.

—Maigret in Court. Brain, Robert, tr. 1983. (Helen & Kurt Wolff Bk.). 160p. reprint ed. 11.95 o.s.i (*0-15-155561-3*) Harcourt Trade Pubs.

—Maigret in Court. Brain, Robert, tr. 1988. 160p. pap. 3.50 (*0-380-70411-0*, Avon Bks.) Morrow/Avon.

—Maigret in Exile. Ellenbogen, Eileen, tr. from FRE. (Harvest Book Ser.). 1994. 168p. pap. 5.95 (*0-15-655136-5*, Harvest Bks.); 1979. 7.95 o.p. (*0-15-155147-2*) Harcourt Trade Pubs.

—Maigret in Holland. 2003. 180p. pap. 8.00 (*0-15-602852-2*); 2nd ed. 1994. 182p. pap. 5.95 o.s.i (*0-15-600084-9*) Harcourt Trade Pubs. (Harvest Bks.).

—Maigret in Holland. Sainsbury, Geoffrey, tr. 2nd ed. 1993. 165p. 18.95 o.s.i (*0-15-155159-6*) Harcourt Trade Pubs.

—Maigret in Montmartre. Woodward, Daphne, tr. 1989. 202p. pap. 6.00 (*0-15-655162-4*) Harcourt Trade Pubs.

—Maigret in Vichy. Ellenbogen, Eileen, tr. 1995. (Harvest Book Ser.). 182p. pap. 6.00 o.s.i (*0-15-655140-3*, Harvest Bks.) Harcourt Trade Pubs.

—Maigret Loses His Temper. 2003. 144p. pap. 8.00 (*0-15-602847-6*, Harvest Bks.) Harcourt Trade Pubs.

—Maigret Loses His Temper. Eglesfield, Robert, tr. 1993. (Helen & Kurt Wolff Bk.). 144p. pap. 5.95 o.s.i (*0-15-655128-4*, Harvest Bks.) Harcourt Trade Pubs.

—Maigret Meets a Milord. 1963. pap. 2.95 o.p. (*0-14-002027-6*, Penguin Bks.) Viking Penguin.

—Maigret Meets a Milord (Omnibus) 1983. pap. 6.95 o.p. (*0-14-006651-9*, Penguin Bks.) Viking Penguin.

—Maigret Mystified. 1964. Orig. Title: Shadow in the Courtyard. pap. 1.95 o.p. (*0-14-002024-1*, Penguin Bks.) Viking Penguin.

—Maigret on the Defensive. Hamilton, Alastair, tr. 1981. (Helen & Kurt Wolff Bk.). 144p. 10.95 o.p. (*0-15-155557-5*) Harcourt Trade Pubs.

—Maigret on the Defensive. 1987. 160p. pap. 3.50 (*0-380-70409-9*, Avon Bks.) Morrow/Avon.

—Maigret on the Riviera. 1989. 140p. pap. 6.00 o.s.i (*0-15-655158-6*, Harvest Bks.) Harcourt Trade Pubs.

—Maigret on the Riviera. Sainsbury, Geoffrey, tr. 1988. 144p. 14.95 o.s.i (*0-15-155149-9*) Harcourt Trade Pubs.

—Maigret S'Amuse. l.t. ed. 1999. (French Ser.). (FRE.). 275p. pap. 30.99 (*2-84011-329-5*) Feryane, SA, Editions FRA. *Dist:* Ulverscroft Large Print Bks., Ltd., Ulverscroft Large Print Canada, Ltd.

—Maigret Se Trompe. 2000. (Maigret Mystery Ser.). (FRE.). pap. 12.95 (*2-253-14227-1*) Librairie Generale Francaise, LGF FRA. *Dist:* Distribooks, Inc.

—Maigret Se Trompe, Crime Impuni, Maigret a l'Ecole, Maigret et la Jeun Morte. 1990. (FRE.). 860p. 49.95 (*0-7859-0480-8*, 2258025966) French & European Pubns., Inc.

—Maigret Sets a Trap. 20.95 (*0-89190-427-1*) Amereon, Ltd.

—Maigret Sets a Trap. unabr. ed. 2000. audio 21.95 (*1-57270-152-8*, N31152u, Audio Editions Mystery Masters) Audio Partners Publishing Corp.

—Maigret Sets a Trap. (Black Dagger Crime Ser.). 16.50 o.p. (*0-86220-825-4*, BD024, Black Dagger) BBC Audiobooks America.

—Maigret Sets a Trap. unabr. collector's ed. 1983. audio 30.00 (*0-7366-0534-7*, 1508) Books on Tape, Inc.

—Maigret Sets a Trap. unabr. ed. 2000. (Inspector Maigret Mystery Ser.). audio 34.95 (*0-7451-4118-8*, CAB 801) Chivers Audio Bks. GBR. *Dist:* BBC Audiobooks America.

—Maigret Sets a Trap. Woodward, Daphne, tr. l.t. ed. 1990. (Nightingale Ser.). 230p. pap. 13.95 o.p. (*0-8161-4665-9*, Macmillan Reference USA) Gale Group.

—Maigret Sets a Trap. 2003. 192p. pap. 8.00 (*0-15-602848-4*, Harvest Bks.) Harcourt Trade Pubs.

—Maigret Sets a Trap. Woodward, Daphne, tr. 1992. (Helen & Kurt Wolff Bk.). 182p. pap. 5.95 o.s.i (*0-15-655126-8*, Harvest Bks.) Harcourt Trade Pubs.

—Maigret Stonewalled. 1963. pap. 2.95 o.p. (*0-14-002026-8*, Penguin Bks.) Viking Penguin.

—Maigret Tend un Piege. l.t. ed. 1994. (French Ser.). (FRE.). pap. 30.99 o.p. (*2-84011-095-4*) Feryane, SA, Editions FRA. *Dist:* Ulverscroft Large Print Bks., Ltd., Ulverscroft Large Print Canada, Ltd.

—A Maigret Trio: Maigret's Failure, Maigret in Society, & Maigret & the Lazy Burglar. 23.95 (*0-89190-425-5*) Amereon, Ltd.

—A Maigret Trio: Maigret's Failure, Maigret in Society, & Maigret & the Lazy Burglar. Woodward, Daphne & Eglesfield, Robert, trs. 1994. (Harvest Book Ser.). 288p. pap. 10.00 o.s.i (*0-15-655137-3*, Harvest Bks.) Harcourt Trade Pubs.

—Maigret's Boyhood Friend. 19.95 (*0-89190-426-3*) Amereon, Ltd.

—Maigret's Boyhood Friend. unabr. collector's ed. 1984. audio 36.00 (*0-7366-0543-6*, 1517) Books on Tape, Inc.

—Maigret's Boyhood Friend. Ellenbogen, Eileen, tr. l.t. ed. 1991. (Nightingale Ser.). 260p. pap. 14.95 o.p. (*0-8161-5116-4*, Macmillan Reference USA) Gale Group.

—Maigret's Boyhood Friend. 2003. 192p. pap. 8.00 (*0-15-602851-4*, Harvest Bks.) Harcourt Trade Pubs.

—Maigret's Boyhood Friend. Ellenbogen, Eileen, tr. (Harvest Book Ser.). 1996. 196p. pap. 6.00 o.s.i (*0-15-655131-4*, Harvest Bks.); 1970. 4.95 o.p. (*0-15-155135-9*) Harcourt Trade Pubs.

—Maigret's Christmas. unabr. collector's ed. 1979. audio 80.00 (*0-7366-0226-7*, 1223) Books on Tape, Inc.

—Maigret's Christmas: 9 Stories. Stewart, Jean, tr. (Helen & Kurt Wolff Bk.). 1992. 336p. pap. 12.00 o.s.i (*0-15-655132-2*, Harvest Bks.); 1977. 8.95 o.p. (*0-15-155551-6*) Harcourt Trade Pubs.

—Maigret's Memoirs. Stewart, Jean, tr. from FRE. 1985. (Helen & Kurt Wolff Bk.). 160p. reprint ed. 13.95 (*0-15-155148-0*) Harcourt Trade Pubs.

—Maigret's Memoirs. Stewart, Jean, tr. 1989. 144p. reprint ed. pap. 3.50 (*0-380-70412-9*, Avon Bks.) Morrow/Avon.

—Maigret's Mistake. Hodge, Alan, tr. 1988. 188p. pap. 6.00 (*0-15-655155-1*) Harcourt Trade Pubs.

—Maigret's Pipe. Stewart, Jean, tr. from FRE. (Harvest Book Ser.). 1994. 336p. pap. 11.00 (*0-15-655146-2*, Harvest Bks.); 1978. 8.95 o.p. (*0-15-155553-2*) Harcourt Trade Pubs.

—Maigret's Revolver. Ryan, Nigel, tr. from FRE. l.t. ed. 1992. (Nightingale Ser.). 241p. pap. 14.95 o.p. (*0-8161-5316-7*, Macmillan Reference USA) Gale Group.

—Maigret's Revolver. Ryan, Nigel, tr. from FRE. (Helen & Kurt Wolff Bk.). 1991. 182p. (C). pap. 5.95 o.s.i (*0-15-659556-7*, Harvest Bks.); 1984. (FRE.). 176p. 12.95 o.s.i (*0-15-155562-1*) Harcourt Trade Pubs.

—Maigret's Rival. Thomson, Helen, tr. l.t. ed. 1988. (Nightingale Ser.). 244p. 12.95 o.p. (*0-8161-4426-5*, Macmillan Reference USA) Gale Group.

—Maigret's Rival. Thomson, Helen, tr. 1994. 182p. pap. 5.95 (*0-15-655141-1*, Harvest Bks.); 1980. 180p. reprint ed. 7.95 o.p. (*0-15-155555-9*) Harcourt Trade Pubs.

—Maigret's War of Nerves. Sainsbury, Geoffrey, tr. l.t. ed. 1987. (Nightingale Ser.). 280p. 10.95 o.p. (*0-8161-4309-9*, Macmillan Reference USA) Gale Group.

—Maigret's War of Nerves. Sainsbury, Geoffrey, tr. 1986. (Helen & Kurt Wolff Bk.). 180p. 13.95 (*0-15-155570-2*) Harcourt Trade Pubs.

—Maigret's War of Nerves. Sainsbury, Geoffrey, tr. 1989. 160p. pap. 3.50 (*0-380-70413-7*, Avon Bks.) Morrow/Avon.

—The Man on the Bench in the Barn. Budberg, Moura, tr. 1970. (Helen & Kurt Wolff Bk.). 188p. 5.95 o.p. (*0-15-156928-2*) Harcourt Trade Pubs.

—The Man with the Little Dog. Stewart, Jean, tr. 1989. 176p. 16.95 (*0-15-156933-9*) Harcourt Trade Pubs.

—Le Meurtre d'un Etudiant. Ernst, ed. 1971. (FRE.). 240p. (C). pap. text 39.00 o.p. (*0-03-084993-4*) Harcourt College Pubs.

—Mon Ami Maigret, 1996. (FRE.). audio 28.95 Olivia & Hill Pr., The.

—Monsieur Gallet, Decede, le Pendu De Saint-Pholien, le Charretier De la Providence. 1991. (FRE.). 924p. 49.95 (*0-7859-0485-9*, 2258032458) French & European Pubns., Inc.

—Monsieur Monde Vanishes. Stewart, Jean, tr. 1977. (Helen & Kurt Wolff Bk.). 6.95 o.p. (*0-15-162098-9*) Harcourt Trade Pubs.

—Monsieur Monde Vanishes. 2004. 144p. pap. 12.95 (*1-59017-096-2*) New York Review of Bks., Inc., The.

—La Mort de Belle, le Revolver de Maigret, les Freres Rico, Maigret et l'Homme du Banc, Antoine et Julie, Maigret a Peur, l'Escalier de Fer, Feux Rouges. 1989. (FRE.). 49.95 (*0-7859-0481-6*, 2258027098) French & European Pubns., Inc.

—La Morte d'August. 1991. (FRE.). pap. 11.95 (*0-7859-3249-6*, 2266045911) French & European Pubns., Inc.

—The Murderer. Sainsbury, Geoffrey, tr. 1986. 144p. 15.95 (*0-15-163270-7*) Harcourt Trade Pubs.

—Mystery: Four Great Inspector Maigret Novels. 1996. 12.98 o.p. (*0-88365-948-4*, Galahad Bks.) BBS Publishing Corp.

—The Nightclub. Stewart, Jean, tr. 1979. (Helen & Kurt Wolff Bk.). 7.95 o.p. (*0-15-165589-8*) Harcourt Trade Pubs.

—None of Maigret's Business. unabr. collector's ed. 1983. audio 30.00 (*0-7366-0535-5*, 1509) Books on Tape, Inc.

—Un Nouveau Dans la Ville, Maigret et la Vielle Dame, l'Amie de Madame Maigret, l'Enterrement de Monsieur Bouvet, Maigret et les Petits Cochons Sans Queue, les Voles Verts, Tante Jeanne, les Memoires de Maigret, 23 vols., Set. 1988. (FRE.). 860p. 49.95 (*0-7859-0554-5*, 225802353X) French & European Pubns., Inc.

—November. Stewart, Jean, tr. 1978. 185p. pap. 2.95 o.s.i (*0-15-667582-X*, Harvest Bks.); 1970. 9.95 o.p. (*0-15-167560-0*) Harcourt Trade Pubs.

—Oncle Charles S'est Enferme, la Veuve Couderc, Cecile Est Morte. 1992. (FRE.). 1018p. 49.95 (*0-7859-0495-6*, 2258035287) French & European Pubns., Inc.

—The Outlaw. Curtis, Howard, tr. 1987. 15.95 (*0-15-170509-7*) Harcourt Trade Pubs.

—La Patience de Maigret. 2000. (Maigret Mystery Ser.). (FRE.). pap. 12.95 (*2-253-14221-2*) Librairie Generale Francaise, LGF FRA. *Dist:* Distribooks, Inc.

—La Patience de Maigret, le Confessional, la Morte d'Auguste. 1990. (FRE.). 896p. 49.95 (*0-7859-0488-3*, 2258033039) French & European Pubns., Inc.

—The Patience of Maigret. unabr. ed. 1996. (Inspector Maigret Mystery Ser.). audio 31.95 (*0-7451-6564-8*, CAB1180) BBC Audiobooks America.

—Il Peut Bergere. 1966. (FRE.). pap. 11.95 (*0-7859-3964-4*) French & European Pubns., Inc.

—La Pipe de Maigret. Goodall, Geoffrey, ed. 1969. (FRE.). 70p. pap. text 6.95 o.p. (*0-312-46235-2*) St. Martin's Pr.

—La Pipe de Maigret, Maigret Se Fache, Maigret a New York, Lettre a Mon Juge, le Destin Des Malou. 1988. (FRE.). 49.95 (*0-7859-0476-X*, 2258020980) French & European Pubns., Inc.

—La Porte. 1993. (FRE.). pap. 11.95 (*0-7859-3258-5*, 2266052683) French & European Pubns., Inc.

—La Premiere Enquete de Maigret, Les Fantomes du Chapelier, Mon Ami Maigret, Les Quatres Jours du Pauvre Homme, Maigret Chez le Coroner, Un Nouveau dans la Ville, La Neige Etait Sale, Le Fond de la Bouteille. (FRE.). 49.95 (*0-7859-0478-6*, 2258021421) French & European Pubns., Inc.

—La Prison, Maigret Hesite, la Main. 1991. (FRE.). 896p. 49.95 (*0-7859-0489-1*, 2258033047) French & European Pubns., Inc.

—The Reckoning. Read, Emily, tr. 1984. (Helen & Kurt Wolff Bk.). 128p. 12.95 o.p. (*0-15-175980-4*) Harcourt Trade Pubs.

—The Rich Man. Stewart, Jean, tr. from FRE. 1971. (Helen & Kurt Wolff Bk.). 5.95 o.p. (*0-15-177162-6*) Harcourt Trade Pubs.

—Le Riche Homme, la Folie de Maigret, la Disparition D'Odile. 1991. (FRE.). 864p. 49.95 (*0-7859-0490-5*, 2258033055) French & European Pubns., Inc.

—La Rue aux Trois Poussins. 1992. (FRE.). pap. 11.95 (*0-7859-3260-7*, 2266052993) French & European Pubns., Inc.

—La Rue aux Trois Poussins: Le Mari de Melie, Level A. (FRE.). text 7.95 (*0-88436-985-4*, 40301) EMC/Paradigm Publishing.

—The Rules of the Game. l.t. ed. 1991. 212p. reprint ed. lib. bdg. 11.95 o.p. (*1-85057-869-9*, Macmillan Reference USA) Gale Group.

—The Rules of the Game. Curtis, Howard, tr. 1988. (Helen & Kurt Wolff Bk.). 160p. 18.95 o.p. (*0-15-169475-3*) Harcourt Trade Pubs.

—The Rules of the Game. l.t. ed. 1991. (Magna Large Print Ser.). 212p. o.p. (*1-85057-868-0*) Magna Large Print Bks. GBR. *Dist:* Ulverscroft Large Print Canada, Ltd.

—Sailors' Rendezvous. 1970. pap. 1.95 o.p. (*0-14-003136-7*, Penguin Bks.) Viking Penguin.

—Soeurs Lacroix. (Folio Ser.: No. 1209). (FRE.). pap. 8.95 (*2-07-037209-X*) Schoenhof's Foreign Bks., Inc.

—Striptease. 1993. (FRE.). pap. 11.95 (*0-7859-3259-3*, 2266052691) French & European Pubns., Inc.

—Striptease. Brain, Robert, tr. 1989. 17.95 (*0-15-185910-8*) Harcourt Trade Pubs.

—Sunday. Ryan, Nigel, tr. 1976. (Helen & Kurt Wolff Bk.). pap. 2.50 o.p. (*0-15-686301-4*, Harvest Bks.) Harcourt Trade Pubs.

—The Survivors. Gilbert, Stuart, tr. from FRE. 1985. (Helen & Kurt Wolff Bk.). 180p. 14.95 o.s.i (*0-15-187047-0*) Harcourt Trade Pubs.

—The Suspect. Gilbert, Stuart, tr. 1991. 17.95 o.s.i (*0-15-137057-5*) Harcourt Trade Pubs.

—Tante Jeanne. 1991. (FRE.). pap. 11.95 (*0-7859-3244-5*, 2266045202) French & European Pubns., Inc.

—Le Temps de Anais, un Noel de Maigret, Maigret Au Picratt's, Maigret en Meuble, une Vie Comme Neuve, Maigret et la Grande Perche, Marie Qui Louche, Miagret Lognon et les Gangsters. 1988. (FRE.). 49.95 (*0-7859-0479-4*, 2258023564) French & European Pubns., Inc.

—Le Testament Donadieu, l'Assassin, le Blanc a Lunettes. 1992. (FRE.). 1000p. 49.95 (*0-7859-0492-1*, 2258035252) French & European Pubns., Inc.
—Le Train. 1991. (FRE.). pap. 11.95 (*0-7859-3248-8*, 2266045849) French & European Pubns., Inc.
—Les Treize Enigmes, la Folle d'Itteville, les Treize Mysteres. 1992. (FRE.). 1047p. 49.95 (*0-7859-0487-5*, 2258032733) French & European Pubns., Inc.
—Trois Crimes de Mes Amis. (Folio Ser.: No. 1112). (FRE.). pap. 8.95 (*2-07-037112-3*) Schoenhof's Foreign Bks., Inc.
—Les Trois Crimes de Mes Amis, le Suspect, les Soeurs Lacroix. 1992. (FRE.). 1021p. 49.95 (*0-7859-0493-X*, 2258035260) French & European Pubns., Inc.
—Trois Nouvelles de Georges Simenon. Lindsay, Frank W. & Nazzaro, Anthony M., eds. 1966. (gr. 10-12). pap. text o.p. (*0-13-930917-9*) Prentice-Hall.
—The Truth about Bebe Donge. Varese, Louise, tr. 2nd ed. 1992. 176p. 18.95 (*0-15-191319-6*) Harcourt Trade Pubs.
—Uncle Charles. l.t. unabr. ed. 1998. (Keating's Choice Ser.). 202p. 22.95 (*1-85089-418-3*, 894183) ISIS Large Print Bks. GBR. *Dist:* Transaction Pubs.
—Uncle Charles Has Locked Himself In. Curtis, Howard, tr. 1987. 19.95 o.s.i (*0-15-192685-9*) Harcourt Trade Pubs.
—The Venice Train. Hamilton, Alastair, tr. (Helen & Kurt Wolff Bk.). 1983. 160p. pap. 3.95 o.s.i (*0-15-693523-6*, Harvest Bks.); 1974. 168p. 6.50 o.p. (*0-15-193506-8*) Harcourt Trade Pubs.
—La Vieille. 1991. (FRE.). pap. 11.95 (*0-7859-3245-3*, 2266045210) French & European Pubns., Inc.
—Le Voleur de Maigret. 2000. (Maigret Mystery Ser.). (FRE.). pap. 12.95 (*2-253-14218-2*) Librairie Generale Francaise, LGF FRA. *Dist:* Distribooks, Inc.
—Voyageur de la Toussaint. 1941. (Folio Ser.: No. 932). (FRE.). 360p. pap. 9.95 (*2-07-036932-3*) Schoenhof's Foreign Bks., Inc.
—When I Was Old. 1971. (Helen & Kurt Wolff Bk.). (Illus.). 343p. 8.50 o.p. (*0-15-195950-1*) Harcourt Trade Pubs.
—The White Horse Inn. Denny, Norman, tr. 1980. (Helen & Kurt Wolff Bk.). 144p. 7.95 o.p. (*0-15-196240-5*) Harcourt Trade Pubs.
—The Widower. Baldick, Robert, tr. from FRE. 1982. 10.95 o.p. (*0-15-196644-3*) Harcourt Trade Pubs.

### MAITLAND, ANTONY (FICTITIOUS CHARACTER)—FICTION

Woods, Sara. Away with Them to Prison. 1989. 224p. pap. 3.50 (*0-380-70589-3*, Avon Bks.) Morrow/Avon.
—Away with Them to Prison. 1985. 12.95 o.p. (*0-312-06311-3*) St. Martin's Pr.
—Away with Them to Prison. l.t. ed. 1988. 464p. 17.95 o.p. (*0-7089-1811-5*, Ulverscroft) Thorpe, F. A. Pubs. GBR. *Dist:* Ulverscroft Large Print Bks., Ltd.
—The Bloody Book of the Law. 1984. 208p. 10.95 o.p. (*0-312-08489-7*) St. Martin's Pr.
—The Bloody Book of the Law. l.t. ed. 1987. (Ulverscroft Large Print Ser.). 384p. 29.99 o.p. (*0-7089-1735-6*, Ulverscroft) Thorpe, F. A. Pubs. GBR. *Dist:* Ulverscroft Large Print Bks., Ltd., Ulverscroft Large Print Canada, Ltd.
—Bloody Instructions. 1986. pap. 2.95 (*0-380-69858-7*, Avon Bks.) Morrow/Avon.
—Call Back Yesterday. 1983. 224p. 10.95 o.p. (*0-312-11424-9*) St. Martin's Pr.
—Call Back Yesterday. l.t. ed. 1985. (Ulverscroft Large Print Ser.). 368p. 12.50 o.p. (*0-7089-1358-X*, Ulverscroft) Thorpe, F. A. Pubs. GBR. *Dist:* Ulverscroft Large Print Bks., Ltd., Ulverscroft Large Print Canada, Ltd.
—Cry Guilty. 1981. 192p. 9.95 o.p. (*0-312-17802-6*) St. Martin's Pr.
—Dearest Enemy. 1981. 196p. 9.95 o.p. (*0-312-18546-4*) St. Martin's Pr.
—Dearest Enemy. l.t. ed. 1984. (Ulverscroft Large Print Ser.). 416p. 12.50 o.p. (*0-7089-1235-4*, Ulverscroft) Thorpe, F. A. Pubs. GBR. *Dist:* Ulverscroft Large Print Bks., Ltd., Ulverscroft Large Print Canada, Ltd.
—Defy the Devil. 1984. 304p. 11.95 o.p. (*0-312-19121-9*) St. Martin's Pr.
—Defy the Devil. l.t. ed. 1986. 328p. 15.95 o.p. (*0-7089-1481-0*, Ulverscroft) Thorpe, F. A. Pubs. GBR. *Dist:* Ulverscroft Large Print Bks., Ltd.
—Enter a Gentlewoman. 1982. 196p. 10.95 o.p. (*0-312-25691-4*) St. Martin's Pr.
—Enter a Gentlewoman. l.t. ed. 1984. 336p. 15.95 o.p. (*0-7089-1136-6*, Ulverscroft) Thorpe, F. A. Pubs. GBR. *Dist:* Ulverscroft Large Print Bks., Ltd.
—Error of the Moon. 1986. 176p. pap. 2.95 (*0-380-69859-5*, Avon Bks.) Morrow/Avon.
—Exit Murderer. (Fingerprint Mysteries Ser.). 1983. 192p. pap. 5.95 o.p. (*0-312-27588-9*, Saint Martin's Griffin); 1978. 7.95 o.p. (*0-312-27587-0*) St. Martin's Pr.
—The Law's Delay. 1977. 7.95 o.p. (*0-312-47565-9*) St. Martin's Pr.
—Let's Choose Executors. 1986. (Anthony Maitland Detective Ser.). 224p. pap. 2.95 o.p. (*0-380-69860-9*, Avon Bks.) Morrow/Avon.
—The Lie Direct. 1989. 160p. pap. 3.95 (*0-380-70588-5*, Avon Bks.) Morrow/Avon.
—The Lie Direct. 1983. 192p. 10.95 o.p. (*0-312-48369-4*) St. Martin's Pr.
—The Lie Direct. l.t. ed. 1986. 336p. o.p. (*0-7089-1551-5*, Ulverscroft) Thorpe, F. A. Pubs.
—Most Deadly Hate. 1987. 240p. pap. 3.50 (*0-380-70477-3*, Avon Bks.) Morrow/Avon.
—Most Deadly Hate. 1986. 224p. 13.95 o.p. (*0-312-54914-8*) St. Martin's Pr.
—Most Deadly Hate. l.t. ed. 1987. 496p. 14.95 o.p. (*0-7089-1663-5*, Ulverscroft) Thorpe, F. A. Pubs. GBR. *Dist:* Ulverscroft Large Print Bks., Ltd.
—Most Grievous Murder. 1982. 192p. 10.95 o.p. (*0-312-54908-3*) St. Martin's Pr.
—Most Grievous Murder. l.t. ed. 1984. (Ulverscroft Large Print Ser.). 288p. o.p. (*0-7089-1179-X*, Ulverscroft) Thorpe, F. A. Pubs. GBR. *Dist:* Ulverscroft Large Print Canada, Ltd.
—Murder's Out of Tune. l.t. ed. 1986. (Nightingale Ser.). 314p. pap. 10.95 o.p. (*0-8161-4002-2*, Macmillan Reference USA) Gale Group.
—Murder's Out of Tune. 1988. 192p. pap. 3.50 (*0-380-70586-9*, Avon Bks.) Morrow/Avon.
—Murder's Out of Tune. 1984. 208p. 11.95 o.p. (*0-312-55345-5*) St. Martin's Pr.
—Naked Villainy. l.t. ed. 1988. (General Ser.). 379p. 17.95 o.p. (*0-8161-4395-1*, Macmillan Reference USA) Gale Group.
—Naked Villainy. 1988. 288p. pap. 3.50 (*0-380-70479-X*, Avon Bks.) Morrow/Avon.
—Naked Villainy. 1987. 256p. 14.95 o.p. (*0-312-00163-0*) St. Martin's Pr.
—Nor Live So Long. l.t. ed. 1987. (Nightingale Ser.). 331p. 10.95 o.p. (*0-8161-4225-4*, Macmillan Reference USA) Gale Group.
—Nor Live So Long. 1988. 224p. pap. 3.50 (*0-380-70478-1*, Avon Bks.) Morrow/Avon.
—Nor Live So Long. 1986. 208p. 13.95 o.p. (*0-312-57740-0*) St. Martin's Pr.
—An Obscure Grave. 1985. 11.95 o.p. (*0-312-58053-3*) St. Martin's Pr.
—An Obscure Grave. l.t. ed. 1987. 384p. 14.95 o.p. (*0-7089-1607-4*, Ulverscroft) Thorpe, F. A. Pubs. GBR. *Dist:* Ulverscroft Large Print Bks., Ltd.
—Proceed to Judgment. 1980. 8.95 o.p. (*0-312-64776-X*) St. Martin's Pr.
—Put Out the Light. 1987. 240p. pap. 3.50 (*0-380-70476-5*, Avon Bks.) Morrow/Avon.
—Put Out the Light. 1985. 224p. 13.95 o.p. (*0-312-65702-1*) St. Martin's Pr.
—A Show of Violence. l.t. ed. 1980. 238p. o.p. (*0-7089-0436-X*, Ulverscroft) Thorpe, F. A. Pubs.
—They Stay for Death. 1988. 192p. mass mkt. 3.50 (*0-380-70587-7*, Avon Bks.) Morrow/Avon.
—They Stay for Death. 1980. 8.95 o.p. (*0-312-79983-7*) St. Martin's Pr.
—Third Encounter. 1986. pap. 3.50 (*0-380-69863-3*, Avon Bks.) Morrow/Avon.
—This Fatal Writ. 1979. 7.95 o.p. (*0-312-80050-9*) St. Martin's Pr.
—This Fatal Writ. l.t. ed. 1983. (Ulverscroft Large Print Ser.). 336p. 29.99 o.p. (*0-7089-0967-1*, Ulverscroft) Thorpe, F. A. Pubs. GBR. *Dist:* Ulverscroft Large Print Bks., Ltd., Ulverscroft Large Print Canada, Ltd.
—This Little Measure. 1986. (Anthony Maitland Detective Ser.). 192p. mass mkt. 2.95 (*0-380-69862-5*, Avon Bks.) Morrow/Avon.
—Villains by Necessity. 1982. 224p. 10.95 o.p. (*0-312-84683-5*) St. Martin's Pr.
—Villains by Necessity. l.t. ed. 1988. (Ulverscroft Large Print Ser.). 384p. 29.99 o.p. (*0-7089-1781-X*, Ulverscroft) Thorpe, F. A. Pubs. GBR. *Dist:* Ulverscroft Large Print Bks., Ltd., Ulverscroft Large Print Canada, Ltd.
—Weep for Her. 1981. 224p. 9.95 o.p. (*0-312-86019-6*) St. Martin's Pr.
—Where Should He Die? 1983. 224p. 10.95 o.p. (*0-312-86702-6*) St. Martin's Pr.
Woods, Sara, ed. Malice Domestic. 1986. pap. 3.50 (*0-380-69861-7*, Avon Bks.) Morrow/Avon.

### MAKER, ALVIN (FICTITIOUS CHARACTER)—FICTION

Card, Orson Scott. Alvin Journeyman. (Tales of Alvin Maker Ser.: No. 4). 1996. 416p. mass mkt. 6.99 (*0-8125-0923-4*); 1995. 384p. 23.95 o.p. (*0-312-85053-0*); 1995. 200.00 (*0-312-86005-6*) Doherty, Tom Assocs., LLC. (Tor Bks.).
—Alvin Journeyman. abr. ed. 1999. (Tales of Alvin Maker Ser.: No. 4). audio 25.00 (*0-7871-1879-6*, Dove Audio) NewStar Media, Inc.
—Alvin Journeyman. 1996. (Tales of Alvin Maker Ser.: No. 4). 13.04 (*0-606-11033-X*) Turtleback Bks.
—Heartfire. (Tales of Alvin Maker Ser.: No. 5). 1999. 352p. mass mkt. 6.99 (*0-8125-0924-2*); 1998. 304p. 24.95 o.p. (*0-312-85054-9*); 1999. 200.00 (*0-312-86728-X*) Doherty, Tom Assocs., LLC. (Tor Bks.).
—Heartfire, Set. abr. ed. 1998. (Tales of Alvin Maker Ser.: No. 5). audio 26.95 (*0-7871-1746-3*, Dove Audio) NewStar Media, Inc.
—Prentice Alvin. 1989. (Tales of Alvin Maker Ser.: No. 3). 352p. mass mkt. 6.99 (*0-8125-0212-4*); 17.95 o.p. (*0-312-93141-7*) Doherty, Tom Assocs., LLC. (Tor Bks.).
—Prentice Alvin. 1993. (Tales of Alvin Maker Ser.: No. 3). audio 50.60 (*1-56544-047-1*, 550005); audio Literate Ear, Inc.
—Prentice Alvin. abr. ed. 1999. (Tales of Alvin Maker Ser.: No. 3). audio 25.00 (*0-7871-1841-9*, Dove Audio) NewStar Media, Inc.
—Prentice Alvin. 1989. (Tales of Alvin Maker Ser.: No. 3). 13.04 (*0-606-11761-X*) Turtleback Bks.
—Red Prophet. (Tales of Alvin Maker Ser.: No. 2). 320p. 1992. mass mkt. 6.99 (*0-8125-2426-8*); 1987. 17.95 o.p. (*0-312-93043-7*) Doherty, Tom Assocs., LLC. (Tor Bks.).
—Red Prophet. 1993. (Tales of Alvin Maker Ser.: No. 2). audio 53.20 (*1-56544-048-X*, 550004); audio Literate Ear, Inc.
—Red Prophet. abr. ed. 1998. (Tales of Alvin Maker Ser.: No. 2). audio 25.00 (*0-7871-1812-5*, Dove Audio) NewStar Media, Inc.
—Red Prophet. 1988. (Tales of Alvin Maker Ser.: No. 2). 13.04 (*0-606-11784-9*) Turtleback Bks.
—Seventh Son. 2003. (Alvin Maker Ser.). 256p. (YA). mass mkt. 3.99 o.s.i (*0-7653-4775-X*, Tor Bks.); 2003. mass mkt. 6.99 (*0-7653-4565-X*, Tor Teen); 1993. (Tales of Alvin Maker Ser.: No. 1). 256p. mass mkt. 6.99 (*0-8125-3305-4*, Tor Bks.); 1988. (Tales of Alvin Maker Ser.: No. 1). (Illus.). 256p. pap. 3.95 o.s.i (*0-8125-3353-4*, Tor Bks.); 1987. (Tales of Alvin Maker Ser.: No. 1). 17.95 o.p. (*0-312-93019-4*, Tor Bks.) Doherty, Tom Assocs., LLC.
—Seventh Son. 1993. (Tales of Alvin Maker Ser.: No. 1). audio. audio 47.00 (*1-56544-018-8*, 550003) Literate Ear, Inc.
—Seventh Son, abr. ed. 1998. (Tales of Alvin Maker Ser.: No. 1). audio 25.00 (*0-7871-1679-3*, Dove Audio) NewStar Media, Inc.
—Seventh Son. 1987. (Tales of Alvin Maker Ser.: No. 1). 13.04 (*0-606-04134-6*) Turtleback Bks.

### MALAUSSENE, BENJAMIN (FICTITIOUS CHARACTER)—FICTION

Pennac, Daniel. Monsieur Malaussene. l.t. ed. 1996. (French Ser.). (FRE.). Vol. 1. 450p. pap. 30.99 o.p. (*2-84011-150-0*); Vol. 2. 419p. pap. 30.99 o.p. (*2-84011-151-9*) Feryane, SA, Editions FRA. *Dist:* Ulverscroft Large Print Bks., Ltd., Ulverscroft Large Print Canada, Ltd.
—Monsieur Malaussene. 2003. 368p. pap. (*1-84343-020-7*) Harvill Pr., The GBR. *Dist:* Trafalgar Square.

### MALCOLM, IAN (FICTITIOUS CHARACTER)—FICTION

Crichton, Michael. Jurassic Park. 1997. pap. 12.00 o.s.i (*0-345-41895-6*); 1995. pap. 6.99 o.p. (*0-345-90878-3*); 1993. (YA). mass mkt. 6.99 o.p. (*0-345-90231-9*); 1991. (YA). mass mkt. 6.99 (*0-345-01954-7*); 1991. (Illus.). 416p. mass mkt. 7.99 (*0-345-37077-5*, Ballantine Bks.); 1991. mass mkt. 5.99 o.s.i (*0-345-37473-8*) Ballantine Bks.
—Jurassic Park. l.t. ed. 1991. 592p. (YA). lib. bdg. 22.95 o.p. (*0-8161-5252-7*, Macmillan Reference USA) Gale Group.
—Jurassic Park. 1990. 416p. 27.95 (*0-394-58816-9*) Knopf, Alfred A. Inc.
—Jurassic Park. 2002. pap. 7.67 (*0-582-50382-5*) Longman Publishing Group.
—Jurassic Park. (FRE.). pap. 14.95 (*2-266-00566-9*) Presses Pocket FRA. *Dist:* Distribooks, Inc.
—Jurassic Park. 1992. 5.99 o.p. (*0-517-08349-3*) Random Hse. Value Publishing.
—Jurassic Park. 1991. (YA). 14.04 (*0-606-01181-1*) Turtleback Bks.
—Jurassic Park, Set. abr. ed. 1990. audio 17.00 (*0-394-58830-4*, 391009, RH Audio) Random Hse. Audio Publishing Group.
—The Lost World: A Novel. 1997. pap. 12.00 (*0-345-41900-6*); 1997. (YA). mass mkt. 7.99 (*0-345-91166-0*); 1996. (Illus.). 448p. mass mkt. 7.99 (*0-345-40288-X*, Ballantine Bks.); 1996. mass mkt. 7.50 o.s.i (*0-345-40507-2*) Ballantine Bks.
—The Lost World: A Novel. l.t. ed. 1995. 640p. (YA). 25.95 (*0-7838-1589-1*, Macmillan Reference USA) Gale Group.
—The Lost World: A Novel. 1995. 416p. 29.95 (*0-679-41946-2*); 1997. (YA). 14.95 o.s.i (*0-679-45540-X*) Knopf, Alfred A. Inc.
—The Lost World: A Novel. abr. ed. 1995. audio 24.00 (*0-679-44548-X*, 493139); audio compact disk 27.50 (*0-679-44763-6*) Random Hse. Audio Publishing Group. (RH Audio).
—The Lost World: A Novel. unabr. ed. 1999. audio compact disk 104.00 (*0-7887-3725-2*, C1082E7); audio 80.00 (*0-7887-3093-2*, 95804E7) Recorded Bks., LLC.
—The Lost World: A Novel. l.t. ed. 1996. (Charnwood Large Print Ser.). 608p. 29.99 (*0-7089-8922-5*, Charnwood) Thorpe, F. A. Pubs. GBR. *Dist:* Ulverscroft Large Print Bks., Ltd., Ulverscroft Large Print Canada, Ltd.

### MALCOLM, TRISH (FICTITIOUS CHARACTER)—FICTION

Petree, Sheree. Number, Please. 2002. 288p. pap. 9.95 (*1-892343-25-8*, Oak Tree Pr.) Oak Tree Publishing.

### MALLARD, TIMOTHY (FICTITIOUS CHARACTER)—FICTION

Beechey, Alan. An Embarrassment of Corpses. 1997. 265p. 22.95 (*0-312-16936-1*, Saint Martin's Minotaur) St. Martin's Pr.

### MALLEN FAMILY (FICTITIOUS CHARACTER)—FICTION

Marchant, Catherine, pseud. The Mallen Girl. 1981. 288p. pap. 2.50 o.p. (*0-553-13933-9*) Bantam Bks.
—The Mallen Girl. unabr. ed. 2001. audio 69.95 (*1-85496-274-4*, 62744) Soundings, Ltd. GBR. *Dist:* Ulverscroft Large Print Bks., Ltd.
—The Mallen Girl. l.t. ed. 2000. (Romance Ser.). 447p. 28.95 (*0-7862-2140-2*) Thorndike Pr.
—The Mallen Girl. l.t. ed. 1981. (Ulverscroft Large Print Ser.). 458p. 12.50 o.p. (*0-7089-0641-9*, Ulverscroft) Thorpe, F. A. Pubs. GBR. *Dist:* Ulverscroft Large Print Bks., Ltd., Ulverscroft Large Print Canada, Ltd.
—The Mallen Girl. 1988. 288p. mass mkt. 11.95 (*0-552-09896-5*) Transworld Publishers Ltd. GBR. *Dist:* Trafalgar Square.
—The Mallen Litter. unabr. ed. 1997. (Mallen Trilogy Ser.: Bk. 3). audio 39.95 o.p. Beeler, Thomas T. Publisher.
—The Mallen Litter. l.t. ed. 2000. (Romance Ser.). 504p. 28.95 (*0-7862-2139-9*, Macmillan Reference USA) Gale Group.
—The Mallen Litter. l.t. ed. 2000. 504p. (*0-7540-1502-5*); (*0-7540-2383-4*) Thorndike Pr.
—The Mallen Litter. l.t. ed. 1981. 529p. 12.00 o.p. (*0-7089-0669-9*, Ulverscroft) Thorpe, F. A. Pubs. GBR. *Dist:* Ulverscroft Large Print Bks., Ltd.
—The Mallen Litter. 1988. 320p. mass mkt. 11.95 (*0-552-10151-6*) Transworld Publishers Ltd. GBR. *Dist:* Trafalgar Square.
—The Mallen Lot. 1981. 320p. pap. 2.75 o.p. (*0-553-13934-7*) Bantam Bks.
—The Mallen Streak. 1981. 288p. pap. 2.50 o.p. (*0-553-13932-0*) Bantam Bks.
—The Mallen Streak. unabr. ed. 1997. audio 79.95 (*1-85496-267-1*, 62671) Soundings, Ltd. GBR. *Dist:* Ulverscroft Large Print Bks., Ltd.
—The Mallen Streak. l.t. ed. 1999. (Romance Ser.). 456p. 28.95 (*0-7862-2141-0*) Thorndike Pr.
—The Mallen Streak. 2000. 999p. (J). pap. 13.95 o.p. (*0-552-14699-4*); 1984. 256p. mass mkt. 10.95 (*0-552-09720-9*) Transworld Publishers Ltd. GBR. *Dist:* Trafalgar Square.

### MALLETT, DAN (FICTITIOUS CHARACTER)—FICTION

Parrish, Frank. Death in the Rain: A Dan Mallet Novel of Suspense. 1986. 160p. reprint ed. mass mkt. 3.50 o.p. (*0-06-080797-0*, P 797, Perennial) HarperTrade.

### MALLETT, INSPECTOR (FICTITIOUS CHARACTER)—FICTION

Hare, Cyril. Death Is No Sportsman: An Inspector Mallett Mystery. 1991. 320p. pap. 5.95 o.p. (*0-06-080555-2*, Perennial) HarperTrade.
—He Should Have Died Hereafter. 2000. (Black Dagger Crime Ser.). 21.95 (*0-7540-8569-4*, Black Dagger) BBC Audiobooks America.
—Suicide Excepted: An Inspector Mallett Mystery. 1982. (Illus.). 219p. (C). pap. 4.95 (*0-486-24245-5*) Dover Pubns., Inc.
—Suicide Excepted: An Inspector Mallett Mystery. 1983. 288p. pap. 5.95 o.p. (*0-06-080636-2*, Perennial) HarperTrade.
—Tenant for Death: An Inspector Mallet Mystery. 1981. 200p. reprint ed. pap. 4.95 o.p. (*0-486-24103-3*) Dover Pubns., Inc.
—Tenant for Death: An Inspector Mallet Mystery. 1991. 304p. pap. 5.95 o.p. (*0-06-080570-6*, Perennial) HarperTrade.
—Tragedy at Law: An Inspector Mallett & Francis Pettigrew Mystery. 1986. mass mkt. 9.95 o.p. (*0-553-06518-1*) Bantam Bks.
—Tragedy at Law: An Inspector Mallett & Francis Pettigrew Mystery. 1991. 400p. pap. 5.95 o.p. (*0-06-080522-6*, Perennial) HarperTrade.

—Untimely Death: An Inspector Mallett & Francis Pettigrew Mystery. 1992. 192p. reprint ed. pap. 8.00 o.p. (*0-06-092252-4*, Perennial) HarperTrade.

**MALLOREN FAMILY (FICTITIOUS CHARACTER)—FICTION**

Beverley, Jo. Devilish. 2000. 352p. mass mkt. 6.99 (*0-451-19997-9*, Signet Bks.) NAL.
—Devilish. l.t. ed. 2000. (Basic Ser.). 608p. 29.95 (*0-7862-2653-6*) Thorndike Pr.
—My Lady Notorious. 1993. pap. 4.50 (*0-380-76785-6*, Avon Bks.) Morrow/Avon.
—My Lady Notorious. 2002. 384p. reprint ed. mass mkt. 6.99 (*0-451-20644-4*, Signet Bks.) NAL.
—Secrets of the Night. l.t. ed. 1999. pap. 23.95 (*1-56895-770-X*, Wheeler Publishing, Inc.) Gale Group.
—Secrets of the Night. 352p. 2004. mass mkt. 6.99 (*0-451-21158-8*, Signet Bks.); 1999. mass mkt. 6.50 o.s.i (*0-451-40889-6*, Topaz) NAL.
—Something Wicked. 1998. (Star-Romance Ser.). 382p. 25.95 (*0-7862-1603-4*, Five Star) Gale Group.
—Something Wicked. 1997. 352p. mass mkt. 5.99 (*0-8217-5548-X*, Zebra Bks.) Kensington Publishing Corp.
—Something Wicked. 1997. 384p. mass mkt. 6.99 (*0-451-40780-6*, Onyx) NAL.
—Tempting Fortune. 2002. 432p. mass mkt. 6.99 (*0-8217-7347-X*); 1995. 448p. mass mkt. 4.99 o.s.i (*0-8217-4858-0*, Zebra Bks.) Kensington Publishing Corp.
—Tempting Fortune. 2003. (Basic Ser.). 28.95 (*0-7862-5311-8*) Thorndike Pr.

**MALLORY (FICTITIOUS CHARACTER: COLLINS)—FICTION**

Collins, Max Allan. The Baby Blue Rip-Off. 1987. 224p. pap. 2.95 o.p. (*0-8125-0154-3*, Tor Bks.) Doherty, Tom Assocs., LLC.
—The Baby Blue Rip-Off. 1983. 11.95 o.s.i (*0-8027-5475-9*) Walker & Co.
—Kill Your Darlings. 1988. 224p. pap. 3.95 o.p. (*0-8125-0161-6*, Tor Bks.) Doherty, Tom Assocs., LLC.
—Kill Your Darlings. 1984. 192p. 13.95 o.s.i (*0-8027-5594-1*) Walker & Co.
—Nice Weekend for a Murder. 1986. 192p. 15.95 o.s.i (*0-8027-5656-5*) Walker & Co.
—A Nice Weekend for a Murder. 1994. 208p. mass mkt. 3.99 (*0-8125-0138-1*, Tor Bks.) Doherty, Tom Assocs., LLC.
—No Cure for Death. 1987. 288p. reprint ed. pap. 3.50 o.p. (*0-8125-0157-8*, Tor Bks.) Doherty, Tom Assocs., LLC.
—No Cure for Death. 1983. 192p. 12.95 o.p. (*0-8027-5488-0*) Walker & Co.
—A Shroud for Aquarius. 1988. 256p. pap. 3.95 o.p. (*0-8125-0163-2*, Tor Bks.) Doherty, Tom Assocs., LLC.
—A Shroud for Aquarius. 1985. (Mallory Mystery Ser.). 175p. 14.95 o.p. (*0-8027-5629-8*) Walker & Co.

**MALLORY, KATHLEEN (FICTITIOUS CHARACTER)—FICTION**

O'Connell, Carol. Crime School. 2003. 416p. mass mkt. 7.99 (*0-515-13535-6*, Jove) Berkley Publishing Group.
—Crime School. l.t. ed. 2003. 30.95 (*1-58724-376-8*, Wheeler Publishing, Inc.) Gale Group.
—Crime School. 2002. 352p. 24.95 o.s.i (*0-399-14928-7*, Putnam & Grosset) Putnam Publishing Group, The.
—Dead Famous. 2004. (*1-58547-372-3*) Ctr. Point Large Print.
—Dead Famous. 2003. 304p. 24.95 (*0-399-15084-6*) Putnam Publishing Group, The.
—Killing Critics. 1997. (Kathleen Mallory Novels Ser.). 400p. mass mkt. 7.99 (*0-515-12086-3*, Jove) Berkley Publishing Group.
—Killing Critics. abr. ed. (Kathleen Mallory Mystery Ser.). 1997. audio 7.99 o.p. (*1-56740-170-8*, 667, Paperback Nova Audio Bks.); 1996. audio 16.95 o.p. (*1-56100-894-X*, 1260, Nova Audio Bks.); 1996. 11p. audio 73.25 o.p. (*1-56100-316-6*, 917); 1996. audio 23.95 o.p. (*1-56100-691-2*, 152, Bookcassette) Brilliance Audio.
—Killing Critics. l.t. ed. 1996. (G. K. Hall Mystery Ser.). 534p. 25.95 o.p. (*0-7838-1903-X*, Macmillan Reference USA) Gale Group.
—Killing Critics. 1996. 304p. 23.95 o.s.i (*0-399-14168-5*, G. P. Putnam's Sons) Penguin Group (USA) Inc.
—Mallory's Oracle. l.t. ed. 1995. (Large Print Ser.). 330p. lib. bdg. 25.95 (*1-57490-024-2*, Beeler Large Print Bks.) Beeler, Thomas T. Publisher.
—Mallory's Oracle. 1995. (Kathleen Mallory Novels Ser.). 336p. mass mkt. 7.99 (*0-515-11647-5*, Jove) Berkley Publishing Group.
—Mallory's Oracle. 1994. 288p. 21.95 o.p. (*0-399-13975-3*, G. P. Putnam's Sons) Penguin Group (USA) Inc.
—Mallory's Oracle. abr. ed. 1996. audio 8.99 o.s.i (*0-679-45593-0*, RH Audio) Random Hse. Audio Publishing Group.
—Mallory's Oracle. 4.98 o.p. (*0-7651-0181-5*) Smithmark Pubs., Inc.
—The Man Who Cast Two Shadows. 1996. (Kathleen Mallory Novels Ser.). 336p. mass mkt. 7.99 (*0-515-11890-7*, Jove) Berkley Publishing Group.
—The Man Who Cast Two Shadows. l.t. ed. 1995. pap. 20.95 o.p. (*1-56895-258-9*, Wheeler Publishing, Inc.) Gale Group.
—The Man Who Cast Two Shadows. abr. ed. 1998. 8.99 o.s.i incl. audio (*0-375-40328-0*) Knopf, Alfred A. Inc.
—The Man Who Cast Two Shadows. 1995. 23.95 o.p. (*0-399-14064-6*, G. P. Putnam's Sons) Penguin Group (USA) Inc.
—Shell Game. 1999. (James Bond Adventure Ser.). 374p. 24.95 o.p. (*0-399-14495-1*, G. P. Putnam's Sons) Penguin Group (USA) Inc.
—The Shell Game. 2000. (Kathleen Mallory Novels Ser.). 416p. mass mkt. 7.50 (*0-425-17603-7*) Berkley Publishing Group.
—Shell Game. unabr. ed. 1999. (Chivers Sound Library American Collections). audio 96.95 (*0-7927-2347-3*, CSL 236, Chivers Sound Library) BBC Audiobooks America.
—Shell Game. l.t. ed. 2001. (Wheeler Large Print Book Ser.). 547p. pap. 23.95 (*1-58724-008-4*, Wheeler Publishing, Inc.) Gale Group.
—Stone Angel. 1998. (Kathleen Mallory Novels Ser.). 400p. mass mkt. 7.99 (*0-515-12298-X*, Jove) Berkley Publishing Group.
—Stone Angel. abr. ed. (Kathleen Mallory Mystery Ser.). 1998. audio 7.99 o.p. (*1-56740-255-0*, 705, Paperback Nova Audio Bks.); 1997. audio 16.95 o.p. (*1-56100-935-0*, 1382, Nova Audio Bks.); 1997. audio 73.25 o.p. (*1-56100-824-9*, 1059, Unabridged Library Editions); 1997. audio 23.95 (*1-56100-749-8*, 278, Bookcassette) Brilliance Audio.
—Stone Angel. l.t. ed. 1997. 24.95 o.p. (*1-56895-507-3*, Wheeler Publishing, Inc.) Gale Group.
—Stone Angel. 1997. 341p. 24.95 o.s.i (*0-399-14234-7*, G. P. Putnam's Sons) Penguin Group (USA) Inc.

**MALLORY, STUART (FICTITIOUS CHARACTER)—FICTION**

Roat, Ronald C. Close Softly the Doors. (Stuart Mallory Mystery Ser.). 1993. 148p. pap. 12.95 (*0-934257-96-5*); 2nd ed. 1991. 160p. 18.95 (*0-934257-48-5*) Story Line Pr.
—High Walk. 1996. (Stuart Mallory Mystery Ser.). 288p. 17.95 (*1-885266-16-2*) Story Line Pr.
—A Still & Icy Silence. 1993. (Stuart Mallory Mystery Ser.). 303p. 21.95 (*0-934257-94-9*) Story Line Pr.

**MALLORY, WANDA (FICTITIOUS CHARACTER)—FICTION**

Frankel, Valerie. A Body to Die For. 1995. 240p. mass mkt. 5.50 (*0-671-79520-1*, Pocket) Simon & Schuster.
—A Deadline for Murder. Wells, Leslie, ed. 1991. 304p. (Orig.). bds. 3.95 (*0-671-73021-5*, Pocket) Simon & Schuster.
—Murder on Wheels. Isaacson, Dana, ed. 1992. 224p. (Orig.). mass mkt. 4.50 (*0-671-73195-5*, Pocket) Simon & Schuster.
—Prime Time for Murder. 1994. 256p. mass mkt. 4.99 (*0-671-79519-8*, Pocket) Simon & Schuster.

**MALLOY, CLAIRE (FICTITIOUS CHARACTER)—FICTION**

Hess, Joan. Busy Bodies. 1995. (Claire Malloy Mystery Ser.). 256p. 19.95 o.p. (*0-525-93910-5*) Dutton/Plume.
—Busy Bodies. 1996. (Claire Malloy Mystery Ser.). 272p. mass mkt. 5.50 o.s.i (*0-451-40560-9*, Onyx) NAL.
—Closely Akin to Murder. 1996. (Claire Malloy Mystery Ser.). 240p. 21.95 o.s.i (*0-525-93911-3*, Dutton) Dutton/Plume.
—Closely Akin to Murder. 1997. (Claire Malloy Mysteries Ser.). 272p. mass mkt. 5.99 o.s.i (*0-451-40561-7*, Onyx) NAL.
—A Conventional Corpse. l.t. ed. 2000. (Wheeler Softcover Ser.). 293p. pap. 24.95 (*1-56895-995-8*, Wheeler Publishing, Inc.) Gale Group.
—A Conventional Corpse. 2001. 304p. mass mkt. 6.50 o.s.i (*0-312-97726-3*, St. Martin's Paperbacks); 2000. 275p. 23.95 (*0-312-24662-5*, Saint Martin's Minotaur) St. Martin's Pr.
—Dear Miss Demeanor. 1990. (Claire Malloy Ser.: No. 3). 195p. mass mkt. 4.99 o.s.i (*0-345-34911-3*) Ballantine Bks.
—Dear Miss Demeanor. (Claire Malloy Mysteries Ser.). 2000. 208p. mass mkt. 5.99 (*0-312-97313-6*, St. Martin's Paperbacks); 1987. 192p. 13.95 o.p. (*0-312-00702-7*, Saint Martin's Minotaur) St. Martin's Pr.
—Death by the Light of the Moon. 208p. 1995. pap. 15.00 (*0-345-47171-7*); 1994. mass mkt. 6.50 (*0-345-37838-5*) Ballantine Bks.
—Death by the Light of the Moon. (Claire Malloy Mystery Ser.). 240p. 2003. mass mkt. 6.99 (*0-312-99101-0*, St. Martin's Paperbacks); 1992. 18.95 o.p. (*0-312-06949-9*, Saint Martin's Minotaur) St. Martin's Pr.
—A Diet to Die For. 1992. (Claire Mallory Mystery Ser.). reprint ed. mass mkt. 5.50 o.s.i (*0-345-36654-9*) Ballantine Bks.
—A Diet to Die For. 1989. 192p. 14.95 o.p. (*0-312-03326-5*, Saint Martin's Minotaur) St. Martin's Pr.
—A Holly, Jolly Murder. l.t. ed. 2003. (Mystery Ser.). 27.95 (*1-57490-531-7*) Beeler, Thomas T. Publisher.
—A Holly, Jolly Murder. 1997. (Claire Malloy Mystery Ser.). 272p. 22.95 o.s.i (*0-525-94240-8*) Dutton/Plume.
—A Holly, Jolly Murder. 1998. (Claire Malloy Mystery Ser.). 288p. mass mkt. 5.99 o.s.i (*0-451-40728-8*, Onyx) NAL.
—The Murder at the Murder at the Mimosa Inn. 1987. mass mkt. 4.99 o.s.i (*0-345-34324-7*) Ballantine Bks.
—The Murder at the Murder at the Mimosa Inn. 1999. 192p. mass mkt. 5.99 (*0-312-97178-8*, St. Martin's Paperbacks); 1986. 208p. 13.95 o.p. (*0-312-55293-9*) St. Martin's Pr.
—Out on a Limb. E-Book 17.95 (*0-312-70895-5*); 2003. 336p. mass mkt. 6.99 (*0-312-98632-7*, St. Martin's Paperbacks); 2003. mass mkt. o.p. (*0-312-98967-9*, St. Martin's Paperbacks); 2002. 304p. 23.95 (*0-312-26680-4*, Saint Martin's Minotaur) St. Martin's Pr.
—Out on a Limb. 2003. (Americana Ser.). 28.95 (*0-7862-5102-6*) Thorndike Pr.
—Poisoned Pins. 1993. (Claire Malloy Mystery Ser.). 256p. 18.00 o.p. (*0-525-93591-6*) Dutton/Plume.
—Poisoned Pins. 1994. (Claire Malloy Mystery Ser.). 256p. mass mkt. 5.99 o.s.i (*0-451-40390-8*, Onyx) NAL.
—A Really Cute Corpse. 1988. 192p. 14.95 o.p. (*0-312-02271-9*, Saint Martin's Minotaur) St. Martin's Pr.
—Roll over & Play Dead. 1992. reprint ed. mass mkt. 5.50 o.s.i (*0-345-37586-6*) Ballantine Bks.
—Roll over & Play Dead. (Claire Malloy Mystery Ser.). 2003. 208p. mass mkt. 5.99 (*0-312-98828-1*, St. Martin's Paperbacks); 1991. 17.95 o.p. (*0-312-05956-6*, Saint Martin's Minotaur) St. Martin's Pr.
—Strangled Prose. 1987. mass mkt. 5.99 o.s.i (*0-345-34059-0*) Ballantine Bks.
—Strangled Prose. 192p. 1998. mass mkt. 5.99 (*0-312-96864-7*, St. Martin's Paperbacks); 1985. 12.95 o.p. (*0-312-76428-6*) St. Martin's Pr.
—Tickled to Death. 1994. (Claire Malloy Mystery Ser.). 224p. 18.95 o.p. (*0-525-93810-9*) Dutton/Plume.
—Tickled to Death. l.t. ed. 1994. pap. 19.95 o.p. (*1-56895-079-9*, Wheeler Publishing, Inc.) Gale Group.
—Tickled to Death. 1995. (Claire Malloy Mystery Ser.). 304p. mass mkt. 5.99 o.s.i (*0-451-40550-1*, Onyx) NAL.

**MALLOY, FRANK (FICTITIOUS CHARACTER)—FICTION**

Thompson, Victoria. Murder on Astor Place. 1999. (Gaslight Mysteries Ser.). 288p. mass mkt. 6.99 (*0-425-16896-4*, Prime Crime) Berkley Publishing Group.
—Murder on St. Mark's Place. 2000. (Gaslight Mysteries Ser.). 288p. mass mkt. 6.99 (*0-425-17361-5*, Prime Crime) Berkley Publishing Group.

**MALLOY, HANNAH (FICTITIOUS CHARACTER)—FICTION**

Griffin, Annie. Date with the Perfect Dead Man. 1999. (Hannah & Kiki Mysteries Ser.: Vol. 2). 288p. mass mkt. 5.99 o.s.i (*0-425-16985-5*) Berkley Publishing Group.
—Love & the Single Corpse. 2000. (Hannah & Kiki Mysteries Ser.). 288p. mass mkt. 5.99 o.s.i (*0-425-17612-6*, Prime Crime) Berkley Publishing Group.
—A Very Eligible Corpse. 1998. (Hannah & Kiki Mysteries Ser.). 272p. mass mkt. 5.99 o.s.i (*0-425-16535-3*) Berkley Publishing Group.

**MALLOY, KIKI (FICTITIOUS CHARACTER)—FICTION**

Griffin, Annie. Date with the Perfect Dead Man. 1999. (Hannah & Kiki Mysteries Ser.: Vol. 2). 288p. mass mkt. 5.99 o.s.i (*0-425-16985-5*) Berkley Publishing Group.
—Love & the Single Corpse. 2000. (Hannah & Kiki Mysteries Ser.). 288p. mass mkt. 5.99 o.s.i (*0-425-17612-6*, Prime Crime) Berkley Publishing Group.
—A Very Eligible Corpse. 1998. (Hannah & Kiki Mysteries Ser.). 272p. mass mkt. 5.99 o.s.i (*0-425-16535-3*) Berkley Publishing Group.

**MALLOY, MACK (FICTITIOUS CHARACTER)—FICTION**

Turow, Scott. Pleading Guilty. unabr. ed. 1993. audio 64.00 (*0-7366-2605-0*, 3348) Books on Tape, Inc.
—Pleading Guilty. E-Book 4.95 (*0-374-70105-9*); E-Book 4.95 (*0-374-70118-0*); 2001. E-Book 4.95 o.p. (*0-374-70104-0*); 1993. 400p. 24.00 (*0-374-23457-4*); 1993. E-Book 24.00 (*0-374-70106-7*) Farrar, Straus & Giroux.
—Pleading Guilty. l.t. ed. 1993. 495p. pap. 19.95 o.p. (*0-8161-5747-2*); lib. bdg. 25.95 (*0-8161-5746-4*) Gale Group. (Macmillan Reference USA).
—Pleading Guilty. abr. ed. 1993. audio 24.00 (*0-671-87043-2*, Simon & Schuster Audioworks) Simon & Schuster Audio.
—Pleading Guilty. 1994. 480p. reprint ed. mass mkt. 7.99 (*0-446-36550-5*) Warner Bks., Inc.

**MALONE, SCOBIE (FICTITIOUS CHARACTER)—FICTION**

Cleary, Jon. Autumn Maze. l.t. ed. 1995. 422p. lib. bdg. 23.95 o.p. (*0-7838-1277-9*, Macmillan Reference USA) Gale Group.
—Autumn Maze: A Scobie Malone Mystery. 1995. 320p. 22.00 o.p. (*0-688-13697-4*, Morrow, William & Co.) Morrow/Avon.
—Babylon South. 1990. 352p. 19.95 o.p. (*0-688-08976-3*, Morrow, William & Co.) Morrow/Avon.
—Bleak Spring. l.t. ed. 1994. 416p. lib. bdg. 22.95 (*0-8161-7437-7*, Macmillan Reference USA) Gale Group.
—Bleak Spring. 1994. 22.00 o.p. (*0-688-12332-5*, Morrow, William & Co.) Morrow/Avon.
—Dark Summer. 1993. 269p. 20.00 o.p. (*0-688-11414-8*, Morrow, William & Co.) Morrow/Avon.
—A Different Turf. unabr. ed. 2001. audio (*1-86340-796-0*, 580336) Bolinda Publishing Pty, Ltd.
—Dilemma. l.t. ed. 2000. (G. K. Hall Core Ser.). 393p. 28.95 (*0-7838-9069-9*, Macmillan Reference USA) Gale Group.
—Dilemma. 2000. 272p. 23.00 (*0-688-17192-3*, Morrow, William & Co.) Morrow/Avon.
—Dragons at the Party. 1988. 320p. 17.95 o.p. (*0-688-07487-1*, Morrow, William & Co.) Morrow/Avon.
—Dragons at the Party. unabr. ed. 1999. audio 79.95 Soundings, Ltd. GBR. *Dist:* Ulverscroft Large Print Bks., Ltd.
—Dragons at the Party. l.t. ed. 1988. (Charnwood Large Print Ser.). 464p. 29.99 o.p. (*0-7089-8474-6*, Ulverscroft) Thorpe, F. A. Pubs. GBR. *Dist:* Ulverscroft Large Print Bks., Ltd., Ulverscroft Large Print Canada, Ltd.
—Endpeace: A Scobie Malone Mystery. 1997. 272p. 23.00 (*0-688-14710-0*, Morrow, William & Co.) Morrow/Avon.
—Endpeace: A Scobie Malone Mystery. l.t. ed. 1998. (Core Ser.). 421p. 28.95 (*0-7838-8369-2*) Thorndike Pr.
—Five Ring Circus. unabr. ed. 2001. audio (*1-86442-364-1*, 590270) Bolinda Publishing Pty, Ltd.
—Five-Ring Circus: Suspense Down Under. 1999. 256p. 23.00 (*0-688-16468-4*, Morrow, William & Co.) Morrow/Avon.
—Five-Ring Circus: Suspense down Under. l.t. ed. 1999. (Core Ser.). 399p. 28.95 (*0-7838-8617-9*) Thorndike Pr.
—The High Commissioner. audio 33.95 o.p. Ulverscroft Audio (U.S.A.).
—Murder Song. l.t. ed. 1992. pap. 21.95 o.p. (*0-7927-1183-1*); 23.95 o.p. (*0-7927-1182-3*, CH0243) BBC Audiobooks America.
—Murder Song. 1990. 288p. 18.95 o.p. (*0-688-09458-9*, Morrow, William & Co.) Morrow/Avon.
—Now & Then, Amen. 1989. 320p. 18.95 o.p. (*0-688-08390-0*, Morrow, William & Co.) Morrow/Avon.
—Now & Then, Amen. l.t. ed. 1989. (Charnwood Large Print Ser.). 29.99 o.p. (*0-7089-8528-9*, Charnwood) Thorpe, F. A. Pubs. GBR. *Dist:* Ulverscroft Large Print Bks., Ltd., Ulverscroft Large Print Canada, Ltd.
—Pride's Harvest. 1991. (Scobie Malone Mystery Ser.). 336p. 20.00 o.p. (*0-688-10408-8*, Morrow, William & Co.) Morrow/Avon.
—Pride's Harvest. unabr. ed. 2001. audio 69.95 (*1-85496-811-4*, 68114) Soundings, Ltd. GBR. *Dist:* Ulverscroft Large Print Bks., Ltd.
—Pride's Harvest. l.t. ed. 1993. (Charnwood Large Print Ser.). 432p. 29.99 o.p. (*0-7089-8690-0*, Charnwood) Thorpe, F. A. Pubs. GBR. *Dist:* Ulverscroft Large Print Bks., Ltd., Ulverscroft Large Print Canada, Ltd.
—Winter Chill. l.t. ed. 1996. 24.95 o.p. (*1-56895-331-3*, Wheeler Publishing, Inc.) Gale Group.
—Winter Chill: A Scobie Malone Mystery. 1996. 269p. 23.00 o.p. (*0-688-14311-3*, Morrow, William & Co.) Morrow/Avon.

**MALORY, SHEILA, MRS. (FICTITIOUS CHARACTER)—FICTION**

Holt, Hazel. The Cruellest Month. l.t. ed. 1992. 240p. 14.95 o.p. (*0-7451-1491-1*, Macmillan Reference USA) Gale Group.
—The Cruellest Month. 1992. (Mrs. Malory Mystery Ser.). 224p. mass mkt. 4.50 o.s.i (*0-451-40313-4*, Onyx) NAL.
—The Cruellest Month. 1991. 15.95 o.p. (*0-312-05840-3*, Saint Martin's Minotaur) St. Martin's Pr.

—Death among Friends, 1 vol. 1999. (Sheila Malory Mysteries Ser.). 256p. mass mkt. 5.99 o.s.i (*0-451-19691-0*) NAL.
—Death among Friends. l.t. ed. 1999. (General Ser.). 232p. pap. 24.95 (*0-7862-1979-3*); (*0-7540-3816-5*); (*0-7540-3815-7*) Thorndike Pr.
—Mrs. Malory: Death of a Dean. l.t. ed. 1996. (Mrs. Malory Mystery Ser.). 194p. 22.95 o.s.i (*0-525-94150-9*, Dutton) Dutton/Plume.
—Mrs. Malory: Death of a Dean. l.t. ed. 1996. pap. 23.95 (*1-56895-392-5*, Wheeler Publishing, Inc.) Gale Group.
—Mrs. Malory: Death of a Dean. 1997. (Sheila Malory Mysteries Ser.). 176p. mass mkt. 5.99 o.s.i (*0-451-19109-9*) NAL.
—Mrs. Malory: Detective in Residence. 1994. (Mrs. Malory Mystery Ser.). 192p. 18.95 o.p. (*0-525-93903-2*) Dutton/Plume.
—Mrs. Malory: Detective in Residence. 1995. (Sheila Malory Mysteries Ser.). 256p. mass mkt. 4.99 o.s.i (*0-451-18017-8*, Signet Bks.) NAL.
—Mrs. Malory & Death by Water. 2003. 256p. mass mkt. 5.99 (*0-451-20809-9*, Signet Bks.) NAL.
—Mrs. Malory & Death by Water. l.t. ed. 2003. 28.95 (*0-7862-5381-9*) Thorndike Pr.
—Mrs. Malory & the Delay of Execution. l.t. ed. 2002. (Mystery Ser.). 273p. 28.95 (*0-7862-4910-2*) Gale Group.
—Mrs. Malory & the Delay of Execution. 2002. 256p. mass mkt. 5.99 (*0-451-20627-4*) NAL.
—Mrs. Malory & the Fatal Legacy: A Sheila Malory Mystery. 2000. (Sheila Malory Mysteries Ser.). 256p. mass mkt. 5.99 (*0-451-20002-0*, Signet Bks.) NAL.
—Mrs. Malory & the Fatal Legacy: A Sheila Malory Mystery. l.t. ed. 2000. (Mystery Ser.). 344p. 27.95 (*0-7862-2842-3*) Thorndike Pr.
—Mrs. Malory & the Festival Murders. 1994. (Mrs. Malory Mystery Ser.). 224p. mass mkt. 3.99 o.s.i (*0-451-18015-1*, Signet Bks.) NAL.
—Mrs. Malory & the Festival Murders. 1993. 171p. 17.95 o.p. (*0-312-08852-3*, Saint Martin's Minotaur) St. Martin's Pr.
—Mrs. Malory & the Lilies That Fester. 2001. (Sheila Malory Mysteries Ser.). 256p. mass mkt. 5.99 o.s.i (*0-451-20354-2*, Signet Bks.) NAL.
—Mrs. Malory & the Lilies That Fester. 2001. 303p. 28.95 (*0-7862-3675-2*) Thorndike Pr.
—Mrs. Malory & the Only Good Lawyer. 1997. (Mrs. Malory Mystery Ser.). 192p. 22.95 o.p. (*0-525-94151-7*) Dutton/Plume.
—Mrs. Malory & the Only Good Lawyer. 1998. (Sheila Malory Mysteries Ser.). 256p. mass mkt. 5.99 o.s.i (*0-451-19264-8*, Signet Bks.) NAL.
—Mrs Malory & the Silent Killer. 2004. 256p. mass mkt. 5.99 (*0-451-21165-0*, Signet Bks.) NAL.
—Mrs. Malory Investigates. 1991. (Mrs. Malory Mystery Ser.). 224p. mass mkt. 5.50 o.s.i (*0-451-40269-3*, Onyx) NAL.
—Mrs. Malory Investigates. 1990. 192p. 14.95 o.p. (*0-312-03894-1*, Saint Martin's Minotaur) St. Martin's Pr.
—Mrs. Malory Wonders Why. 1995. (Mrs. Malory Mystery Ser.). 192p. 20.95 o.s.i (*0-525-93932-6*, Dutton) Dutton/Plume.
—Mrs. Malory Wonders Why. 1996. (Sheila Malory Mysteries Ser.). 256p. mass mkt. 5.50 o.s.i (*0-451-18286-3*) NAL.
—Mrs. Malory's Shortest Journey. 1995. (Mrs. Malory Mystery Ser.). 256p. mass mkt. 4.99 o.s.i (*0-451-18395-9*, Signet Bks.) NAL.
—The Shortest Journey: A Mrs. Malory Mystery. l.t. ed. 1995. 232p. pap. 17.95 o.p. (*0-7838-1138-1*, Macmillan Reference USA) Gale Group.
—The Shortest Journey: A Mrs. Malory Mystery. 1994. 224p. 19.95 o.p. (*0-312-11140-1*, Saint Martin's Minotaur) St. Martin's Pr.

**MALORY, TOM (FICTITIOUS CHARACTER)—FICTION**

Hawke, Simon. The Samurai Wizard. 1991. mass mkt. 4.99 (*0-446-36132-1*) Warner Bks., Inc.
—The Wizard of Camelot. 1993. 224p. (Orig.). mass mkt. 4.99 (*0-446-36242-5*, Aspect) Warner Bks., Inc.
—The Wizard of Lovecraft's Cafe. 1993. 224p. (Orig.). mass mkt. 4.99 (*0-446-36517-3*, Aspect) Warner Bks., Inc.
—The Wizard of Rue Morgue. 1990. 208p. mass mkt. 4.50 o.s.i (*0-445-20704-3*) Warner Bks., Inc.
—Wizard of Santa Fe. 1991. mass mkt. 4.99 o.s.i (*0-446-36194-1*) Warner Bks., Inc.
—The Wizard of Sunset Strip. 1989. 208p. mass mkt. 4.99 (*0-445-20702-7*) Warner Bks., Inc.
—The Wizard of Whitechapel. 1988. 224p. mass mkt. 4.99 (*0-445-20304-8*) Warner Bks., Inc.
—The Wizard of 4th Street. 1988. 247p. mass mkt. 4.50 (*0-445-20842-2*) Warner Bks., Inc.

**MALTRAVERS, AUGUSTUS (FICTITIOUS CHARACTER)—FICTION**

Richardson, Robert. The Lazarus Tree. l.t. ed. 1996. (G. K. Hall Nightingale Ser.). 303p. pap. 17.95 o.p. (*0-7838-1483-6*, Macmillan Reference USA) Gale Group.
—The Lazarus Tree. 1995. (WWL Mystery Ser.). per. (*0-373-26166-7*, 1-26166-8, Harlequin Bks.) Harlequin Enterprises, Ltd.

**MANCINI, MUNCH (FICTITIOUS CHARACTER)—FICTION**

Seranella, Barbara. No Human Involved. 1998. 304p. mass mkt. 6.99 o.s.i (*0-06-101361-7*, HarperTorch) Morrow/Avon.
—No Human Involved. 1997. 256p. 22.95 o.p. (*0-312-15614-6*, Saint Martin's Minotaur) St. Martin's Pr.
—No Man Standing. 2002. (Wheeler Hardcover Ser.). 28.95 (*1-58724-304-0*, Wheeler Publishing, Inc.) Gale Group.
—No Man Standing. 2003. (Illus.). 368p. pap. 6.99 (*0-7434-2033-0*, Pocket) Simon & Schuster.
—No Man Standing: A Munch Mancini Crime Novel. 2002. 304p. 24.00 (*0-7432-1386-6*, Scribner) Simon & Schuster.
—No Offense Intended. 1998. 272p. 24.00 o.p. (*0-06-019212-7*) HarperCollins Pubs.
—No Offense Intended. 1999. 336p. mass mkt. 6.99 o.s.i (*0-06-109724-1*, HarperTorch) Morrow/Avon.
—Unfinished Business. 2002. (Illus.). 336p. mass mkt. 6.99 (*0-7434-2209-0*, Pocket) Simon & Schuster.
—Unfinished Business: A Munch Mancini Crime Novel. 2001. 272p. 24.00 (*0-7432-1266-5*, Scribner) Simon & Schuster.
—Unpaid Dues. 2004. 320p. mass mkt. 6.99 (*0-7434-6637-3*, Pocket); 2003. 304p. 25.00 (*0-7432-4500-8*, Scribner) Simon & Schuster.
—Unwanted Company. 2000. 304p. 24.00 o.s.i (*0-06-019213-5*) HarperCollins Pubs.

**MANDEL, GREG (FICTITIOUS CHARACTER)—FICTION**

Hamilton, Peter F. Mindstar Rising. (Greg Mandel Ser.). 1997. 423p. mass mkt. 6.99 (*0-8125-9056-2*); 1996. 384p. 23.95 o.p. (*0-312-85955-4*) Doherty, Tom Assocs., LLC. (Tor Bks.).
—Mindstar Rising. 1993. 438p. pap. 16.95 (*0-330-32376-8*) Pan Bks. Ltd. GBR. *Dist:* Trans-Atlantic Pubns., Inc.
—The Nano Flower. 1999. (Greg Mandel Ser.: Vol. 3). 602p. mass mkt. 6.99 (*0-8125-7769-8*); 1998. 448p. 25.95 (*0-312-86580-5*) Doherty, Tom Assocs., LLC. (Tor Bks.).
—A Quantum Murder. 1998. 375p. mass mkt. 6.99 (*0-8125-5524-4*); 1997. 384p. 24.95 (*0-312-85954-6*) Doherty, Tom Assocs., LLC. (Tor Bks.).

**MANDELLA, WILLIAM (FICTITIOUS CHARACTER)—FICTION**

Haldeman, Joe. Forever Free. 288p. 1999. 21.95 o.s.i (*0-441-00697-3*); 2000. reprint ed. mass mkt. 6.99 (*0-441-00787-2*) Ace Bks.
—Forever Free. 2000. 13.04 (*0-606-19705-2*) Turtleback Bks.
—Forever Peace. 1998. 368p. mass mkt. 6.99 (*0-441-00566-7*); 1997. 336p. 21.95 o.s.i (*0-441-00406-7*) Ace Bks.
—Forever Peace. 1998. 13.04 (*0-606-15823-5*) Turtleback Bks.
—The Forever War. 1985. mass mkt. 3.50 o.s.i (*0-345-32489-7*); 1982. mass mkt. 2.75 o.s.i (*0-345-31020-9*, Del Rey); 1981. mass mkt. 2.50 o.s.i (*0-345-30148-X*, Del Rey); 1979. mass mkt. 2.25 o.s.i (*0-345-28914-5*, Del Rey); 1976. mass mkt. 1.75 o.s.i (*0-345-25798-7*) Ballantine Bks.
—The Forever War. 2003. 288p. pap. 13.95 (*0-06-051086-2*, Eos); 1991. 272p. mass mkt. 6.99 (*0-380-70821-3*, Avon Bks.) Morrow/Avon.
—The Forever War, Vol. 2. Marvano, ed. 1991. 56p. 45.00 o.p. (*1-56163-026-8*); pap. 8.95 o.p. (*1-56163-025-X*) NBM Publishing Co.
—The Forever War, Vol. 3. 1992. 56p. 45.00 o.p. (*1-56163-046-2*); pap. 2.99 o.p. (*1-56163-045-4*) NBM Publishing Co.
—The Forever War. unabr. ed. 2000. audio compact disk 75.00 (*0-7887-3983-2*, C1146E7); 1999. audio 60.00 (*0-7887-3773-2*, 95990E7) Recorded Bks., LLC.
—The Forever War. 1974. 8.95 o.p. (*0-312-29890-0*) St. Martin's Pr.
Haldeman, Joe & Hoffman, Joyce. When the Sirens Sang of War: Women Correspondents & the Vietnam Experience. 2004. 256p. text 25.00 (*0-306-81059-X*) Da Capo Pr., Inc.
Haldeman, Joe & Marvano. The Forever War, Vol. 1. 56p. 1991. 45.00 o.p. (*1-56163-004-7*); 1990. pap. 8.95 o.p. (*0-918348-95-1*) NBM Publishing Co.

**MANION, TERRY (FICTITIOUS CHARACTER)—FICTION**

Lochte, Dick. Blue Bayou. 1993. (Southern Mysteries Ser.). mass mkt. 4.99 o.s.i (*0-8041-1145-6*, Ivy Bks.) Ballantine Bks.
—Blue Bayou. 1992. 304p. 20.00 o.p. (*0-671-74711-8*, Simon & Schuster) Simon & Schuster.
—The Neon Smile. 1996. mass mkt. 5.99 o.s.i (*0-8041-1405-6*, Ivy Bks.) Ballantine Bks.
—The Neon Smile. 1995. (Illus.). 304p. 21.00 (*0-671-74712-6*, Simon & Schuster) Simon & Schuster.

**MANKIND (FICTITIOUS CHARACTER)—FICTION**

Castle, Dorothy R. The Diabolical Game to Win Man's Soul: A Rhetorical & Structural Approach to Mankind. 1990. (American University Studies: Ser. IV, Vol. 70). VI, 215p. (C). text 41.50 (*0-8204-1237-6*) Lang, Peter Publishing, Inc.

**MANKOWSKI, CHRIS (FICTITIOUS CHARACTER)—FICTION**

Leonard, Elmore. Freaky Deaky. unabr. collector's ed. 1997. audio 48.00 (*0-7366-3606-4*, 4260) Books on Tape, Inc.
—Freaky Deaky. unabr. ed. 2000. audio 59.95 (*1-56054-962-9*, SAB 016) Chivers Audio Bks. GBR. *Dist:* BBC Audiobooks America.
—Freaky Deaky. abr. ed. 1988. audio 16.99 (*0-88646-232-0*, LFP 7232) Durkin Hayes Publishing Ltd.
—Freaky Deaky. l.t. ed. 1989. 376p. 20.95 o.p. (*0-8161-4708-6*, Macmillan Reference USA) Gale Group.
—Freaky Deaky. 1998. 320p. pap. 12.00 (*0-688-16096-4*, Quill) HarperTrade.
—Freaky Deaky. 2002. 448p. mass mkt. 7.50 (*0-06-008955-5*); 1988. 18.95 o.p. (*0-87795-975-7*, Morrow, William & Co.) Morrow/Avon.
—Freaky Deaky. 1990. 4.99 o.p. (*0-517-03358-5*) Random Hse. Value Publishing.
—Freaky Deaky, unabr. ed. 1995. audio 51.00 (*0-7887-0324-2*, 94516E7) Recorded Bks., LLC.
—Freaky Deaky. 1989. mass mkt. 5.95 (*0-446-35039-7*) Warner Bks., Inc.

**MANLEY, GERARD (FICTITIOUS CHARACTER)—FICTION**

Lodge, Jeff. Where This Lake Is. 1997. (New American Voices Ser.: Vol. 1). 250p. (Orig.). pap. 14.00 (*1-877727-68-7*) White Pine Pr.

**MANN, JACK (FICTITIOUS CHARACTER)—FICTION**

Gross, Ken. Hell Bent. 288p. 1993. mass mkt. 4.99 (*0-8125-1756-3*); 1992. 18.95 o.p. (*0-312-85304-1*) Doherty, Tom Assocs., LLC. (Tor Bks.).

**MANNING, MARK (FICTITIOUS CHARACTER)—FICTION**

Craft, Michael. Body Language. (Mark Manning Mystery Ser.). 2000. 288p. pap. 13.00 (*1-57566-554-9*, Kensington Bks.); 1999. 273p. 22.00 o.s.i (*1-57566-419-4*) Kensington Publishing Corp.
—Boy Toy. 2002. 272p. pap. 13.95 o.s.i (*0-312-28709-7*, Saint Martin's Griffin) St. Martin's Pr.
—Boy Toy: A Mark Manning Mystery. 2001. (Mark Manning Mystery Ser.). 272p. 23.95 (*0-312-26917-X*) St. Martin's Pr.
—Eye Contact. (Mark Manning Mystery Ser.). 1999. 342p. pap. 12.00 (*1-57566-425-9*); 1998. 352p. 21.95 o.s.i (*1-57566-292-2*) Kensington Publishing Corp. (Kensington Bks.).
—Flight Dreams. 2000. (Mark Manning Mystery Ser.: Vol. 1). 24p. pap. 13.00 (*1-57566-854-8*); 1998. 256p. pap. 10.95 o.s.i (*1-57566-294-9*, Kensington Bks.); 1997. (Mark Manning Mystery Ser.: Vol. 1). 224p. 19.95 o.s.i (*1-57566-174-8*, Kensington Bks.) Kensington Publishing Corp.
—Hot Spot: A Mark Manning Mystery. 288p. 2003. pap. 13.95 (*0-312-31364-0*, Saint Martin's Griffin); 2002. 23.95 (*0-312-28900-6*, Saint Martin's Minotaur) St. Martin's Pr.
—Name Games: A Mark Manning Mystery. 2000. (Mark Manning Mystery Ser.). 312p. 23.95 (*0-312-24552-1*, Saint Martin's Minotaur) St. Martin's Pr.

**MANNING, RHODA KATHERINE (FICTITIOUS CHARACTER)—FICTION**

Gilchrist, Ellen. I, Rhoda Manning, Go Hunting with My Daddy: And Other Stories. 304p. 2002. 25.95 (*0-316-17358-4*); 2003. reprint ed. pap. 14.95 (*0-316-73868-9*, Back Bay) Little Brown & Co.

**MANNING BROTHERS (FICTITIOUS CHARACTERS)—FICTION**

Macomber, Debbie. Bride on the Loose. 1992. (Special Ser.: No. 756). per. (*0-373-09756-5*, Silhouette) Harlequin Enterprises, Ltd.
—Marriage of Inconvenience. 1992. (Silhouette Special Edition Ser.: No. 732). mass mkt. (*0-373-09732-8*, 5-09732-4, Harlequin Bks.) Harlequin Enterprises, Ltd.
—Stand-in Wife. 1992. (Silhouette Special Edition Ser.: No. 744). mass mkt. (*0-373-09744-1*, 5-09744-9, Harlequin Bks.) Harlequin Enterprises, Ltd.

**MANTRELL, MATT (FICTITIOUS CHARACTER)—FICTION**

Stasheff, Christopher. Her Majesty's Wizard. 1986. 352p. (Orig.). mass mkt. 6.99 (*0-345-27456-3*, Del Rey) Ballantine Bks.
—My Son, the Wizard. (Wizard in Rhyme Ser.: No. 5). 1999. 368p. mass mkt. 6.99 (*0-345-42480-8*, Del Rey); 1997. 352p. pap. 11.95 o.p. (*0-345-37602-1*) Ballantine Bks.
—The Oathbound Wizard. 2004. 416p. pap. 6.99 (*0-345-46117-7*); 1993. mass mkt. 5.99 o.s.i (*0-345-38547-0*) Ballantine Bks. (Del Rey).
—The Secular Wizard. 1995. (Wizard in Rhyme Ser.). 384p. mass mkt. 6.99 (*0-345-38854-2*, Del Rey) Ballantine Bks.
—The Witch Doctor, No. 3. 1994. (Wizard in Rhyme Ser.: Bk. III). 432p. mass mkt. 5.99 o.s.i (*0-345-38851-8*, Del Rey) Ballantine Bks.

**MAPP, MISS (FICTITIOUS CHARACTER)—FICTION**

Benson, E. F. Lucia's Progress. 2000. (Lucia Ser.). 230p. pap. 11.95 (*1-55921-233-0*) Moyer Bell.
—Mapp & Lucia. 1986. pap. o.s.i (*0-552-99084-1*, Corgi) Bantam Bks.
—Mapp & Lucia. (Make Way for Lucia Ser.: Pt. 4). 320p. 1984. mass mkt. 3.95 o.p. (*0-06-080714-8*, P 714); Pt. IV. 1986. reprint ed. pap. 12.00 o.p. (*0-06-091328-2*, PL 1328) HarperTrade. (Perennial).
—Mapp & Lucia. 2000. (Illus.). 277p. pap. 12.95 (*1-55921-232-2*) Moyer Bell.
—Mapp & Lucia. 2000. (Humour Classics Ser.). 315p. 14.95 (*1-85375-390-4*) Prion GBR. *Dist:* Trafalgar Square.
—Miss Mapp. unabr. ed. 1999. audio 41.95 (*1-55685-587-7*) Audio Bk. Contractors, Inc.
—Miss Mapp. 1986. pap. o.s.i (*0-552-99083-3*, Corgi) Bantam Bks.
—Miss Mapp, Pt. III. (Make Way for Lucia Ser.). 1987. 272p. pap. 5.95 o.p. (*0-06-091374-6*); 1984. mass mkt. 3.95 o.p. (*0-06-080696-6*) HarperTrade. (Perennial).
—Miss Mapp. 1999. 232p. pap. 11.95 (*1-55921-275-6*) Moyer Bell.
Holt, Tom. Lucia Triumphant. 2004. (Lucia Ser.). 224p. pap. 12.95 (*1-55921-310-8*) Moyer Bell.

**MARCH, CARMEL (FICTITIOUS CHARACTER)—FICTION**

Holt, Victoria. The Black Opal. 1997. mass mkt. 3.50 o.p. (*0-449-00056-7*); 1994. 384p. mass mkt. 6.99 (*0-449-22271-3*) Ballantine Bks. (Fawcett).
—The Black Opal. l.t. ed. 1993. 496p. 26.95 o.s.i (*0-385-47025-8*, Doubleday Large Type) Bantam Doubleday Dell Large Print Group, Inc.

**MARCH, LAURA (FICTITIOUS CHARACTER)—FICTION**

Eberhart, Mignon G. Postmark Murder. 1983. 208p. mass mkt. 5.50 (*0-446-31181-2*) Warner Bks., Inc.

**MARCH FAMILY (FICTITIOUS CHARACTERS)—FICTION**

Alcott, Louisa May. Jo's Boys. unabr. ed. 1996. audio 41.95 (*1-55685-437-4*) Audio Bk. Contractors, Inc.
—Jo's Boys. unabr. ed. 1999. audio 49.95 (*0-7861-1288-3*, 2188) Blackstone Audio Bks., Inc.
—Little Men: Life at Plumfield with Jo's Boys. unabr. ed. 1996. audio 49.95 (*0-7861-0956-4*, 1733) Blackstone Audio Bks., Inc.
—Little Women. 1981. mass mkt. 2.50 o.s.i (*0-441-05466-8*) Ace Bks.
—Little Women. unabr. ed. 1995. audio 69.95 (*0-7451-2740-1*, SAB 106, Sterling Audio Bks.) BBC Audiobooks America.
—Little Women. 2001. audio 85.95 (*0-7861-1880-6*, 2679); 1994. audio 95.95 (*0-7861-0489-9*, 1440) Blackstone Audio Bks., Inc.
—Little Women. unabr. ed. 2002. audio 104.00 (*0-7366-8608-8*); 1998. (YA). (gr. 8 up). audio 96.00 (*0-7366-4123-8*, 136011) Books on Tape, Inc.
—Little Women. unabr. ed. 2002. audio 34.95 (*1-59086-293-7*, 3879, Brilliance Audio Unabridged); 1998. audio 22.95 o.p. (*1-56740-090-6*, 1510, Bookcassette); 1998. 18p. audio 66.25 (*1-56740-619-X*, 1511, Unabridged Library Editions) Brilliance Audio.
—Little Women. audio 18.95 California Artists Radio Theater Productions.
—Little Women. (Early Best Sellers Ser.). reprint ed. lib. bdg. 48.00 (*0-7426-1003-9*) Classic Bks.
—Little Women. 1994. 461p. mass mkt. 3.99 (*0-8125-2333-4*, Tor Classics) Doherty, Tom Assocs., LLC.
—Little Women. abr. ed. 1992. (J). (gr. 4-7). audio 16.99 (*0-88646-315-7*, 7315) Durkin Hayes Publishing Ltd.
—Little Women. 1972. 2.95 o.p. (*0-460-01248-7*, Dutton) Dutton/Plume.
—Little Women. E-Book 2.49 (*1-929120-48-6*) Electric Umbrella Publishing.
—Little Women. 1997. pap. 5.50 (*1-57514-326-7*, 1051) Encore Performance Publishing.
—Little Women. 1997. (Classic Collection). 15.99 o.p. (*1-56179-552-6*) Focus on the Family Publishing.
—Little Women. abr. ed. 1999. audio 16.95 Highsmith Inc.

—Little Women, ERS. 1993. (Little Classics Ser.). (Illus.). 308p. (J). (gr. 4-8). 15.95 o.p. (*0-8050-2767-X*, Holt, Henry & Co. Bks. For Young Readers) Holt, Henry & Co.

—Little Women. 2001. audio 18.95 Lodestone Catalog, The.

—Little Women. E-Book 2.95 (*1-57799-829-4*) Logos Research Systems, Inc.

—Little Women. 1981. (English As a Second Language Bk.). pap. text 4.46 net. (*0-582-53489-5*, 74091) Longman Publishing Group.

—Little Women. 1998. (Little Brown Notebooks Ser.). (Illus.). 256p. 9.99 (*1-897954-77-8*) M Q Pubns. GBR. *Dist:* Independent Pubs. Group.

—Little Women. 1983. (Modern Library College Editions Ser.). 603p. (C). pap. 11.25 (*0-07-554389-3*, McGraw-Hill Humanities, Social Sciences & World Languages) McGraw-Hill Higher Education.

—Little Women. 1998. 98p. audio 16.95 (*1-56994-509-8*, 329314, Monterey SoundWorks) Monterey Media, Inc.

—Little Women. 1983. mass mkt. 3.50 o.p. (*0-451-52214-1*) NAL.

—Little Women. abr. ed. 2002. audio 25.00 (*1-59007-125-5*, New Millennium Audio) New Millennium Entertainment.

—Little Women. abr. ed. 1993. (Classic, Ultimate, Dove Ser.). (Illus.). audio 19.95 o.p. (*1-55800-945-0*, Dove Audio) NewStar Media, Inc.

—Little Women. l.t. ed. 1998. 665p. lib. bdg. 28.00 (*0-939495-51-1*) North Bks.

—Little Women. unabr. ed. (Read-along Ser.). pupil's gde. ed. 34.95 incl. audio Norton Pubs., Inc., Jeffrey /Audio-Forum.

—Little Women. 2003. audio 21.99 (*1-58926-180-1*, C05M-0040) Oasis Audio.

—Little Women. 1998. audio 17.95 (*0-19-422786-3*) Oxford Univ. Pr., Inc.

—Little Women. Alderson, Valerie, ed. & intro. by. (Oxford World's Classics Ser.). 1998. 530p. pap. 7.95 (*0-19-283434-7*); 1995. 526p. pap. 5.95 o.p. (*0-19-282765-0*) Oxford Univ. Pr., Inc.

—Little Women. 1998. pap. 7.00 (*0-582-40194-1*) Pearson Education.

—Little Women. 1987. audio 14.95 o.p. (*0-394-56410-3*, RH Audio) Random Hse. Audio Publishing Group.

—Little Women. 1995. (Literary Classics Giant Ser.). 688p. text 8.98 o.p. (*1-56138-566-2*, Courage Bks.) Running Pr. Bk. Pubs.

—Little Women. 1994. 592p. mass mkt. 5.99 (*0-671-51764-3*, Pocket) Simon & Schuster.

—Little Women. unabr. ed. 2003. audio 29.99 (*1-59335-015-5*, 30097) Soulmate Audio Bks., Inc.

—Little Women. 1995. (Little Brown Notebook Ser.). (Illus.). 256p. 6.95 (*0-8069-3975-3*) Sterling Publishing Co., Inc.

—Little Women. (Bullseye Step into Classics Ser.). 1994. 10.04 (*0-606-09566-7*); 1962. 10.10 o.p. (*0-606-00974-4*) Turtleback Bks.

—Little Women. abr. ed. 2p. 1997. audio 16.95 o.s.i (*0-14-086146-7*); 1996. audio 10.95 o.s.i (*0-14-086203-X*, Penguin AudioBooks) Viking Penguin.

—Little Women & Good Wives. 1992. 464p. reprint ed. pap. 7.95 (*0-460-87141-2*, Everyman's Classic Library in Paperback) Tuttle Publishing.

—Mujercitas. 5th ed. 1997. (SPA., Illus.). 248p. 12.95 (*84-392-8232-X*) Everest Publishing.

—Mujercitas. 1995. (SPA.). 304p. 13.50 (*84-01-00914-6*, PJ9396) Plaza & Janés Editories, S.A. ESP. *Dist:* Distribooks, Inc., Lectorum Pubns., Inc.

—Mujercitas. 2002. (SPA.). 304p. mass mkt. 7.95 (*1-4000-0080-7*) Random Hse., Inc.

Alcott, Louisa May, photos by. Little Men: Life at Plumfield with Jo's Boys. Date not set. 20.95 (*0-8488-1476-2*) Amereon, Ltd.

—Little Men: Life at Plumfield with Jo's Boys. 1986. 352p. mass mkt. 4.95 (*0-451-52275-3*, Signet Classics) NAL.

—Little Men: Life at Plumfield with Jo's Boys. 1994. (Puffin Classics). (J). 11.04 (*0-606-07797-9*) Turtleback Bks.

Emerson, Charlotte. Beth's Snow Dancer. 1999. (Little Women Journals Ser.). 10.04 (*0-606-16347-6*) Turtleback Bks.

—Meg's Dearest Wish. 1999. (Little Women Journals ). 10.04 (*0-606-16350-6*) Turtleback Bks.

Emerson, Charlotte & Alcott, Louisa May. Beth's Snow Dancer. (Little Women Journals). (J). 1999. (Illus.). 128p. (gr. 3-7). mass mkt. 3.99 (*0-380-79704-6*); 1998. 144p. 10.00 o.p. (*0-380-97632-3*) Morrow/Avon. (Avon Bks.).

—Jo's Troubled Heart. (Little Women Journals). (J). 1999. (Illus.). 128p. (gr. 3-7). pap. 3.99 (*0-380-79669-4*); 1998. 119p. (gr. 4-7). 10.00 o.p. (*0-380-97629-3*) Morrow/Avon. (Avon Bks.).

—Meg's Dearest Wish. (Little Women Journals). (Illus.). (J). 1999. 128p. (gr. 3-7). pap. 3.99 (*0-380-79705-4*); 1998. 144p. mass mkt. 10.00 o.p. (*0-380-97633-1*) Morrow/Avon. (Avon Bks.).

Pfeffer, Susan Beth. A Gift for Jo. 1999. (Portraits of Little Women Ser.: No. 10). (Illus.). 112p. (gr. 3-7). text 9.95 o.s.i (*0-385-32668-8*, Dell Books for Young Readers) Random Hse. Children's Bks.

Pfeffer, Susan Beth & Alcott, Louisa May. Amy Makes a Friend. 1998. (Portraits of Little Women Ser.). (Illus.). 112p. (gr. 3-7). text 9.95 o.s.i (*0-385-32584-3*, Dell Books for Young Readers) Random Hse. Children's Bks.

—Amy's Story. 1997. (Portraits of Little Women Ser.). 112p. (gr. 3-7). text 9.95 o.s.i (*0-385-32529-0*, Delacorte Pr.) Dell Publishing.

—Beth's Story. 1997. (Portraits of Little Women Ser.). 112p. (gr. 3-7). text 9.95 o.s.i (*0-385-32526-6*, Delacorte Pr.) Dell Publishing.

—A Gift for Beth. 1999. (Portraits of Little Women Ser.: No. 11). (Illus.). 112p. (gr. 3-7). text 9.95 o.s.i (*0-385-32667-X*, Dell Books for Young Readers) Random Hse. Children's Bks.

—Jo Makes a Friend. 1998. (Portraits of Little Women Ser.). (Illus.). 112p. (gr. 3-7). text 9.95 (*0-385-32581-9*, Dell Books for Young Readers) Random Hse. Children's Bks.

—Jo's Story. 1997. (Portraits of Little Women Ser.). 112p. (gr. 3-7). text 9.95 o.s.i (*0-385-32523-1*, Dell Books for Young Readers) Random Hse. Children's Bks.

—Meg Makes a Friend. 1998. (Portraits of Little Women Ser.). (Illus.). 112p. (gr. 3-7). text 9.95 (*0-385-32580-0*, Delacorte Pr.) Dell Publishing.

**MARETTO, SUZANNE (FICTITIOUS CHARACTER)—FICTION**

Maynard, Joyce. To Die For. 1992. 304p. 20.00 o.p. (*0-525-93396-4*, Dutton) Dutton/Plume.

—To Die For. 1995. 368p. mass mkt. 5.99 o.s.i (*0-451-18607-9*); 1993. 366p. pap. o.s.i (*0-451-18373-8*); 1993. 368p. mass mkt. 5.99 o.s.i (*0-451-17327-9*, Signet Bks.) NAL.

**MARIANNE (FICTITIOUS CHARACTER: TEPPER)—FICTION**

Tepper, Sheri S. Marianne, the Madam, & the Momentary Gods. 1988. mass mkt. 2.95 o.s.i (*0-441-51962-8*) Ace Bks.

—Marianne, the Magus & the Manticore. 1988. mass mkt. 3.50 o.s.i (*0-441-51945-8*); 1985. mass mkt. 2.95 o.s.i (*0-441-51944-X*) Ace Bks.

—Marianne, the Matchbox & the Malachite Mouse. 1989. mass mkt. 3.50 o.s.i (*0-441-51964-4*) Ace Bks.

**MARIE, BETH (FICTITIOUS CHARACTER)—FICTION**

Owens, Virginia Stem. At Point Blank: A Suspense Novel. 1992. 240p. 14.99 o.p. (*0-8010-6724-3*); (gr. 10). pap. 9.99 o.p. (*0-8010-6752-9*) Baker Bks.

**MARK OF TASAVALTA (FICTITIOUS CHARACTER)—FICTION**

Saberhagen, Fred. Wayfinder's Story. (Lost Swords Ser.: Vol. 7). 256p. 1993. mass mkt. 4.99 (*0-8125-0575-1*); 1992. 17.95 o.p. (*0-312-85000-X*) Doherty, Tom Assocs., LLC. (Tor Bks.).

—Woundhealer's Story. (Lost Swords Ser.: Vol. 1). 1992. 320p. mass mkt. 4.50 (*0-8125-2356-3*); 1983. 309p. mass mkt. 6.95 (*0-523-48560-3*) Doherty, Tom Assocs., LLC. (Tor Bks.).

**MARKBY, ALAN (FICTITIOUS CHARACTER)—FICTION**

Granger, Ann. Beneath These Stones. 2000. (Meredith & Markby Mysteries Ser.). 250p. 22.95 (*0-312-24178-X*, Saint Martin's Minotaur) St. Martin's Pr.

—Call the Dead Again. l.t. ed. 1999. 30.00 o.p. (*0-7862-1817-7*, Macmillan Reference USA) Gale Group.

—Call the Dead Again. 2000. (Meredith & Markby Mysteries Ser.). 288p. mass mkt. 5.99 (*0-380-73297-1*, Avon Bks.) Morrow/Avon.

—Call the Dead Again. 1999. (Meredith & Markby Mysteries Ser.). 256p. 22.95 (*0-312-20505-8*, Saint Martin's Minotaur) St. Martin's Pr.

—Candle for a Corpse. 1997. (Meredith & Markby Mysteries Ser.: Vol. 8). 288p. mass mkt. 5.99 (*0-380-73012-X*, Avon Bks.) Morrow/Avon.

—Candle for a Corpse. 1996. 256p. text 21.95 o.p. (*0-312-14292-7*, Saint Martin's Minotaur) St. Martin's Pr.

—Cold in the Earth. 1994. 256p. mass mkt. 5.50 (*0-380-72213-5*, Avon Bks.) Morrow/Avon.

—Cold in the Earth. 1993. 218p. 17.95 o.p. (*0-312-08747-0*, Saint Martin's Minotaur) St. Martin's Pr.

—Cold in the Earth. l.t. ed. 1994. (Ulverscroft Large Print Ser.). 576p. 29.99 o.p. (*0-7089-3111-1*, Ulverscroft) Thorpe, F. A. Pubs. GBR. *Dist:* Ulverscroft Large Print Bks., Ltd., Ulverscroft Large Print Canada, Ltd.

—A Fine Place for Death. 1996. (New Meredith & Markby Mystery Ser.: No. 6). 288p. mass mkt. 5.50 (*0-380-72573-8*, Avon Bks.) Morrow/Avon.

—A Fine Place for Death. 1994. 249p. 21.00 o.p. (*0-312-11787-6*, Saint Martin's Minotaur) St. Martin's Pr.

—A Fine Place for Death. l.t. ed. 1995. (Ulverscroft Large Print Ser.). 528p. 29.99 o.p. (*0-7089-3346-7*, Ulverscroft) Thorpe, F. A. Pubs. GBR. *Dist:* Ulverscroft Large Print Bks., Ltd., Ulverscroft Large Print Canada, Ltd.

—Flowers for His Funeral. 1997. mass mkt. 5.50 (*0-380-72887-7*, Avon Bks.) Morrow/Avon.

—Flowers for His Funeral. 1995. 250p. 21.95 o.p. (*0-312-13495-9*, Saint Martin's Minotaur) St. Martin's Pr.

—Murder among Us. 1995. (Meredith & Markby Mysteries Ser.: No. 4). 304p. mass mkt. 5.99 (*0-380-72476-6*, Avon Bks.) Morrow/Avon.

—Murder among Us. 1993. 224p. 18.95 o.p. (*0-312-09875-8*); (*0-312-09343-8*) St. Martin's Pr. (Saint Martin's Minotaur).

—Murder among Us. l.t. ed. 1994. (Ulverscroft Large Print Ser.). 544p. 29.99 o.p. (*0-7089-3146-4*, Ulverscroft) Thorpe, F. A. Pubs. GBR. *Dist:* Ulverscroft Large Print Bks., Ltd., Ulverscroft Large Print Canada, Ltd.

—A Restless Evil: A Mitchell & Markby Mystery. Date not set. pap. (*0-312-30656-3*, Saint Martin's Griffin); Date not set. E-Book (*0-312-70514-X*); mass mkt. (*0-312-98553-3*, St. Martin's Paperbacks); 2002. (Illus.). 256p. 23.95 (*0-312-30655-5*, Saint Martin's Minotaur) St. Martin's Pr.

—A Restless Evil: A Mitchell & Markby Mystery. l.t. ed. 2003. lib. bdg. 25.95 (*0-7862-5096-8*) Thorndike Pr.

—Say It with Poison. 1993. 224p. mass mkt. 5.50 (*0-380-71823-5*, Avon Bks.) Morrow/Avon.

—Say It with Poison. 1991. 16.95 o.p. (*0-312-05506-4*, Saint Martin's Minotaur) St. Martin's Pr.

—A Season for Murder. 1993. (Meredith & Markby Mysteries Ser.: Vol. 2). 256p. mass mkt. 5.99 o.s.i (*0-380-71997-5*, Avon Bks.) Morrow/Avon.

—A Season for Murder. 1992. 256p. 18.95 o.p. (*0-312-07079-9*, Saint Martin's Minotaur) St. Martin's Pr.

—A Season for Murder. l.t. ed. 1992. (Magna Large Print Ser.). 361p. 29.99 o.p. (*0-7505-0483-8*, Ulverscroft) Thorpe, F. A. Pubs. GBR. *Dist:* Ulverscroft Large Print Bks., Ltd., Ulverscroft Large Print Canada, Ltd.

—Shades of Murder: A Mitchell & Markby Mystery. 2001. 288p. 23.95 (*0-312-28445-4*, Saint Martin's Minotaur) St. Martin's Pr.

—A Touch of Mortality. 1998. 288p. mass mkt. 5.99 (*0-380-73087-1*, Avon Bks.) Morrow/Avon.

—A Touch of Mortality. 1997. 256p. 21.95 (*0-312-15231-0*, Saint Martin's Minotaur) St. Martin's Pr.

—Where Old Bones Lie. 1995. (New Meredith & Markby Mystery Ser.: No. 5). 288p. mass mkt. 5.99 (*0-380-72477-4*, Avon Bks.) Morrow/Avon.

—Where Old Bones Lie. 1994. 224p. 19.95 o.p. (*0-312-11097-9*, Saint Martin's Minotaur) St. Martin's Pr.

—Where Old Bones Lie. l.t. ed. 1995. (Ulverscroft Large Print Ser.). 528p. 29.99 o.p. (*0-7089-3391-2*, Ulverscroft) Thorpe, F. A. Pubs. GBR. *Dist:* Ulverscroft Large Print Bks., Ltd., Ulverscroft Large Print Canada, Ltd.

—A Word After Dying. 1998. (Meredith & Markby Mysteries Ser.). 256p. 21.95 (*0-312-17067-X*, Saint Martin's Minotaur) St. Martin's Pr.

—A Word after Dying. 1999. (Meredith & Markby Mysteries Ser.). 304p. mass mkt. 5.99 (*0-380-73227-0*, Avon Bks.) Morrow/Avon.

—A Word after Dying. pap. 14.95 (*0-312-30475-7*, Saint Martin's Griffin) St. Martin's Pr.

—A Word after Dying. l.t. ed. 1997. (Ulverscroft Large Print Ser.). 560p. 29.99 o.p. (*0-7089-3809-4*, Ulverscroft) Thorpe, F. A. Pubs. GBR. *Dist:* Ulverscroft Large Print Bks., Ltd., Ulverscroft Large Print Canada, Ltd.

**MARKHAM, GEORGE (FICTITIOUS CHARACTER)—FICTION**

Connery, Tom. Honour Be Damned. 2003. 240p. pap. 14.00 (*0-425-19195-8*) Berkley Publishing Group.

—Honour Redeemed. 2003. 336p. pap. 13.00 (*0-425-18972-4*) Berkley Publishing Group.

—Honour Redeemed. 2000. (Markham of the Marines Ser.: Vol. 2). 328p. 21.95 (*0-89526-255-X*) Regnery Publishing, Inc., An Eagle Publishing Co.

—Shred of Honour: A Markham of the Marines Novel. 1999. (Markham of the Marines Ser.). (Illus.). 328p. 21.95 (*0-89526-269-X*) Regnery Publishing, Inc., An Eagle Publishing Co.

—A Shred of Honour: A Markham of the Marines Novel. 2002. (Illus.). 320p. pap. 13.00 (*0-425-18498-6*) Berkley Publishing Group.

**MARKHAM, ROY (FICTITIOUS CHARACTER)—FICTION**

Block, Lawrence. You Could Call It Murder. 1996. 240p. mass mkt. 4.95 o.p. (*0-7867-0342-3*, Carroll & Graf Pubs.) Avalon Publishing Group.

—You Could Call It Murder. 1987. 140p. reprint ed. pap. 4.95 o.p. (*0-88150-086-0*) Countryman Pr.

—You Could Call It Murder. l.t. ed. 1989. 240p. 11.95 o.p. (*0-8161-4628-4*, Macmillan Reference USA) Gale Group.

—You Could Call It Murder. 2002. 176p. pap. 6.99 (*0-7434-4515-5*) ibooks, Inc.

**MARLEY, CAL (FICTITIOUS CHARACTER)—FICTION**

Pomidor, Bill. Anatomy of a Murder. 1996. (Cal & Plato Marley Mystery Ser.). 272p. mass mkt. 5.50 o.s.i (*0-451-18417-3*, Signet Bks.) NAL.

—Mind over Murder. 1998. (Cal & Plato Marley Mystery Ser.). 288p. mass mkt. 5.99 o.s.i (*0-451-19216-8*, Signet Bks.) NAL.

—Murder by Prescription. 1995. (Cal & Plato Marley Ser.). 288p. mass mkt. 4.99 o.s.i (*0-451-18416-5*, Signet Bks.) NAL.

—Skeletons in the Closet. 1997. (Cal & Plato Marley Mystery Ser.). 288p. mass mkt. 5.50 o.s.i (*0-451-18418-1*, Signet Bks.) NAL.

—Ten Little Medicine Men. 1998. (Cal & Plato Marley Mystery Ser.). 288p. mass mkt. 5.99 o.s.i (*0-451-19214-1*, Signet Bks.) NAL.

**MARLEY, PLATO (FICTITIOUS CHARACTER)—FICTION**

Pomidor, Bill. Anatomy of a Murder. 1996. (Cal & Plato Marley Mystery Ser.). 272p. mass mkt. 5.50 o.s.i (*0-451-18417-3*, Signet Bks.) NAL.

—Mind over Murder. 1998. (Cal & Plato Marley Mystery Ser.). 288p. mass mkt. 5.99 o.s.i (*0-451-19216-8*, Signet Bks.) NAL.

—Murder by Prescription. 1995. (Cal & Plato Marley Ser.). 288p. mass mkt. 4.99 o.s.i (*0-451-18416-5*, Signet Bks.) NAL.

—Skeletons in the Closet. 1997. (Cal & Plato Marley Mystery Ser.). 288p. mass mkt. 5.50 o.s.i (*0-451-18418-1*, Signet Bks.) NAL.

—Ten Little Medicine Men. 1998. (Cal & Plato Marley Mystery Ser.). 288p. mass mkt. 5.99 o.s.i (*0-451-19214-1*, Signet Bks.) NAL.

**MARLIN, JOE (FICTITIOUS CHARACTER)—FICTION**

Block, Lawrence. Mona. 1994. 144p. pap. 3.95 o.p. (*0-7867-0105-6*, Carroll & Graf Pubs.) Avalon Publishing Group.

—Mona. deluxe ltd. ed. 1997. (Illus.). 138p. text 25.00 o.p. (*0-9640454-6-X*) Cahill, James Publishing.

—Mona. 1999. (Five Star Mystery Ser.). 171p. 21.95 o.p. (*0-7862-1705-7*, Five Star) Gale Group.

**MARLOWE, LISA (FICTITIOUS CHARACTER)—FICTION**

Clark-Cross, Barbara. Storm Front. 1992. 384p. mass mkt. 4.50 o.s.i (*1-55817-668-3*, Pinnacle Bks.) Kensington Publishing Corp.

**MARLOWE, PHILIP (FICTITIOUS CHARACTER)—FICTION**

Chandler, Raymond. Adieu, Ma Jolie. 1988. Orig. Title: Farewell, My Lovely. (FRE.). 301p. pap. 11.95 (*0-7859-2102-8*, 2070380793) French & European Pubns., Inc.

—The Adventures of Philip Marlowe, Vol. 1. collector's ed. 1999. 34.98 incl. audio Radio Spirits, Inc.

—The Big Sleep. deluxe ltd. ed. 1986. (Illus.). 250p. 425.00 o.p. (*0-910457-09-3*) Arion Pr.

—The Big Sleep. 1975. 224p. mass mkt. 1.50 o.s.i (*0-345-24565-2*); 1973. mass mkt. 0.95 o.s.i (*0-345-22201-6*) Ballantine Bks.

—The Big Sleep. 1986. (Mystery Ser.). mass mkt. 9.95 o.p. (*0-553-06513-0*) Bantam Bks.

—The Big Sleep. 1994. reprint ed. lib. bdg. 29.95 o.p. (*1-56849-261-8*) Buccaneer Bks., Inc.

—The Big Sleep. l.t. ed. 2002. 232p. lib. bdg. 27.95 (*1-58547-164-X*) Ctr. Point Large Print.

—The Big Sleep. abr. ed. audio 15.95 o.p. (*0-88646-007-7*, 7009) Durkin Hayes Publishing Ltd.

—The Big Sleep. 1989. (Illus.). 256p. reprint ed. 22.95 o.p. (*0-86547-402-8*, North Point Pr.) Farrar, Straus & Giroux.

—The Big Sleep. Garrett, George P. et al, eds. 1989. (Film Scripts Ser.). reprint ed. pap. 19.95 (*0-89197-677-9*) Irvington Pubs.

—The Big Sleep. 1992. pap. 9.00 (*0-394-23906-7*); 1988. 240p. reprint ed. pap. 12.00 (*0-394-75828-5*) Knopf Publishing Group. (Vintage).

—The Big Sleep. unabr. ed. 2002. audio compact disk 39.95 (*1-59007-090-9*, New Millennium Audio); audio 29.95 (*1-59007-089-5*) New Millennium Entertainment.

—The Big Sleep. abr. ed. 1993. 16.95 o.p. (*1-55800-690-7*); audio 29.95 o.p. (*1-55800-848-9*, 752391) NewStar Media, Inc.

—The Big Sleep. 1992. pap. 9.00 o.p. (*0-679-74091-0*); 1978. pap. 3.95 o.p. (*0-394-72631-6*) Random Hse., Inc.

—The Big Sleep. 2002. (Best Mysteries of All Time Ser.). 261p. (*0-7621-8880-4*, Impress) Scriptorium Pr., The.

—The Big Sleep. 1995. 288p. reprint ed. 35.00 (*1-883402-16-6*, Scribner) Simon & Schuster.

—The Big Sleep & Farewell, My Lovely. 1995. (Modern Library Ser.). 544p. 18.95 (*0-679-60140-6*) Random Hse., Inc.

—The Big Sleep & The High Window. abr. ed. 1999. audio 16.85 (0-563-55892-X) BBC Bk. Publishing GBR. *Dist:* Ulverscroft Large Print Bks., Ltd.

—La Dame du Lac. 1988. Orig. Title: Lady of the Lake. (FRE.). 258p. pap. 10.95 (0-7859-2088-9, 2070379434) French & European Pubns., Inc.

—Farewell, My Lovely. 1983. 256p. mass mkt. 2.25 o.s.i (0-345-31528-6, Ballantine Bks.); 1973. mass mkt. 0.95 o.s.i (0-345-22202-4) Ballantine Bks.

—Farewell, My Lovely. 1992. pap. 10.00 (0-394-23907-5); 1988. 304p. reprint ed. pap. 12.00 (0-394-75827-7) Knopf Publishing Group. (Vintage).

—Farewell, My Lovely. unabr. ed. 2002. audio 29.95 (1-59007-091-7); audio compact disk 45.00 (1-59007-092-5) New Millennium Entertainment. (New Millennium Audio).

—Farewell, My Lovely. abr. ed. 1993. 16.95 o.p. (1-55800-672-9); audio 29.95 o.p. (1-55800-769-5) NewStar Media, Inc.

—Farewell, My Lovely. 1986. audio 14.95 o.p. (0-394-55466-3); 1985. audio 16.00 o.p. (0-394-55048-X) Random Hse. Audio Publishing Group. (RH Audio).

—Farewell, My Lovely. 1992. pap. 10.00 (0-679-74090-2); 1976. pap. 3.95 o.p. (0-394-72138-1) Random Hse., Inc.

—Farewell, My Lovely & The Lady in the Lake. abr. ed. 1999. audio 16.85 (0-563-55897-0) BBC Bk. Publishing GBR. *Dist:* Ulverscroft Large Print Bks., Ltd.

—La Grande Fenetre. 1989. Orig. Title: High Window. (FRE.). 276p. pap. 10.95 (0-7859-2236-9, 207038103X) French & European Pubns., Inc.

—Le Grande Sommeil. 1987. Orig. Title: Big Sleep. (FRE.). 252p. pap. 10.95 (0-7859-2071-4, 2070378659) French & European Pubns., Inc.

—The High Window. 1971. mass mkt. 0.95 o.s.i (0-345-22203-2) Ballantine Bks.

—The High Window. l.t. ed. 23.95 (1-85695-367-X) ISIS Large Print Bks. GBR. *Dist:* Transaction Pubs.

—The High Window. 1992. pap. 10.00 (0-394-23908-3); 1976. pap. 3.95 o.p. (0-394-72141-1); 1988. 272p. reprint ed. pap. 12.00 (0-394-75826-9) Knopf Publishing Group. (Vintage).

—The High Window. abr. ed. 2003. audio 18.00 (1-59007-101-8); audio compact disk 25.00 (1-59007-102-6) New Millennium Entertainment. (New Millennium Audio).

—The High Window. abr. ed. 1993. audio 15.95 o.p. (1-55800-091-7, 40290, Dove Audio) NewStar Media, Inc.

—Killer in the Rain. 1987. mass mkt. 3.95 o.s.i (0-345-35185-1); 1986. mass mkt. 2.95 o.s.i (0-345-34195-3); 1984. mass mkt. 2.50 o.s.i (0-345-32020-4); 1980. mass mkt. 2.25 o.s.i (0-345-28858-0); 1977. mass mkt. 1.95 o.s.i (0-345-25728-6) Ballantine Bks.

—Killer in the Rain & Other Stories. abr. ed. 2002. audio 25.00 (1-59007-062-3, New Millennium Audio) New Millennium Entertainment.

—Killer in the Rain & Other Stories. abr. ed. 1996. 24.95 o.p. (0-7871-0555-4, 693446) NewStar Media, Inc.

—The Lady in the Lake. Date not set. lib. bdg. 20.95 (0-8488-2136-X) Amereon, Ltd.

—The Lady in the Lake. 1976. (Crime Fiction Ser). reprint ed. lib. bdg. 21.00 o.p. (0-8240-2358-7) Garland Publishing, Inc.

—The Lady in the Lake. l.t. ed. 23.95 (1-85695-362-9) ISIS Large Print Bks. GBR. *Dist:* Transaction Pubs.

—The Lady in the Lake. 1992. pap. 10.00 (0-394-23909-1); 1988. 272p. pap. 12.00 (0-394-75825-0); 1976. pap. 3.95 o.p. (0-394-72145-4) Knopf Publishing Group. (Vintage).

—The Lady in the Lake. abr. ed. 2002. audio 18.00 (1-59007-093-3); audio compact disk 25.00 (1-59007-094-1) New Millennium Entertainment. (New Millennium Audio).

—The Lady in the Lake. abr. ed. 1993. audio 15.95 o.p. (1-55800-069-0, 40240); audio 8.99 o.p. (1-55800-916-7) NewStar Media, Inc. (Dove Audio).

—The Lady in the Lake. 1992. pap. 10.00 (0-679-74088-0) Random Hse., Inc.

—The Lady in the Lake. 1994. 288p. 35.00 (1-883402-94-8, Scribner) Simon & Schuster.

—Later Novels & Other Writings: The Lady in the Lake; The Little Sister; The Long Goodbye; Playback; Double Indemnity; Essays & Letters. MacShane, Frank, ed. 1995. 1088p. 35.00 (1-883011-08-6) Library of America, The.

—The Little Sister. l.t. ed. 1993. 21.95 o.p. (0-7927-1654-X); pap. 19.95 o.p. (0-7927-1653-1); audio 54.95 (0-7451-5823-4, CAB 057) BBC Audiobooks America.

—The Little Sister. 1985. mass mkt. 2.95 o.s.i (0-345-32217-7); 1983. mass mkt. 2.25 o.s.i (0-345-31643-6); 1977. mass mkt. 1.95 o.s.i (0-345-25727-8) Ballantine Bks.

—The Little Sister. 1988. (Vintage Crime Ser.). 256p. pap. 12.00 (0-394-75767-X, Vintage) Knopf Publishing Group.

—The Little Sister. abr. ed. 2002. audio 18.00 (1-59007-099-2); audio compact disk 21.95 (1-59007-100-X) New Millennium Entertainment. (New Millennium Audio).

—The Little Sister. abr. ed. 1993. pap. 15.95 o.p. incl. audio (1-55800-082-8, 40270) NewStar Media, Inc.

—The Little Sister. 1994. 256p. 35.00 (1-883402-79-4, Scribner) Simon & Schuster.

—The Little Sister. unabr. ed. 1983. (J). audio 49.95 o.p. (0-8161-9777-6) Thorndike Pr.

—The Long Goodbye. 1987. mass mkt. 3.95 o.s.i (0-345-34938-5); 1985. mass mkt. 2.95 o.s.i (0-345-32132-4); 1982. mass mkt. 2.50 o.s.i (0-345-30582-5); 1980. mass mkt. 2.25 o.s.i (0-345-28859-9); 1977. mass mkt. 1.95 o.s.i (0-345-25734-0) Ballantine Bks.

—The Long Goodbye. 1992. pap. 10.00 (0-394-23910-5); 1988. 384p. pap. 13.00 (0-394-75768-8) Knopf Publishing Group. (Vintage).

—The Long Goodbye. abr. ed. 2002. audio 18.00 (1-59007-095-X); audio compact disk 21.95 (1-59007-096-8) New Millennium Entertainment. (New Millennium Audio).

—The Long Goodbye. abr. ed. 1993. audio 15.95 o.p. (1-55800-002-X, 40010, Dove Audio) NewStar Media, Inc.

—The Long Goodbye. 1992. pap. 10.00 (0-679-74087-2) Random Hse., Inc.

—The Long Goodbye & The Little Sister. abr. ed. 1999. audio 16.85 (0-563-55803-2) BBC Bk. Publishing GBR. *Dist:* Ulverscroft Large Print Bks., Ltd.

—Midnight Raymond Chandler, 001. 1971. 10.25 o.p. (0-395-13152-9) Houghton Mifflin Co.

—Other Side of Raymond Chandler. 23.95 (0-88411-421-X) Amereon, Ltd.

—Philip Marlowe. 1999. (Illus.). 416p. pap. 16.00 (0-671-03890-7) ibooks, Inc.

—Playback. 1987. mass mkt. 2.95 o.s.i (0-345-32226-6); 1987. mass mkt. 3.95 o.s.i (0-345-34933-4); 1984. mass mkt. 2.50 o.s.i (0-345-31961-3); 1980. mass mkt. 2.25 o.s.i (0-345-28857-2); 1976. mass mkt. 1.50 o.s.i (0-345-25169-5) Ballantine Bks.

—Playback. l.t. ed. 2001. (Dales Large Print Ser.). 240p. pap. 20.99 (1-84262-094-0) Dales Large Print Bks. GBR. *Dist:* Ulverscroft Large Print Bks., Ltd., Ulverscroft Large Print Canada, Ltd.

—Playback. 1988. (Vintage Crime Ser.). 176p. pap. 11.00 (0-394-75766-1, Vintage) Knopf Publishing Group.

—Playback. abr. ed. 2002. audio 18.00 (1-59007-097-6); audio compact disk 21.95 (1-59007-098-4) New Millennium Entertainment. (New Millennium Audio).

—Playback. unabr. ed. 1993. pap. 24.95 o.p. (1-55800-270-7) NewStar Media, Inc.

—Poodle Springs. abr. ed. 2002. audio 18.00 (1-59007-105-0); audio 25.00 (1-59007-106-9) New Millennium Entertainment. (New Millennium Audio).

—Raymond Chandler: Four Complete Philip Marlowe Novels. 1986. 8.99 o.s.i (0-517-61811-7) Random Hse. Value Publishing.

—Red Wind. unabr. ed. 2002. audio 15.00 (1-59007-107-7); audio compact disk 21.95 (1-59007-108-5) New Millennium Entertainment. (New Millennium Audio).

—Stories & Early Novels: Pulp Stories; The Big Sleep; Farewell, My Lovely; The High Window. MacShane, Frank, ed. 1995. 1216p. 35.00 (1-883011-07-8) Library of America, The.

—Trouble Is My Business. 1987. mass mkt. 3.95 o.s.i (0-345-35494-X); 1984. mass mkt. 2.50 o.s.i (0-345-32021-2); 1980. mass mkt. 2.25 o.s.i (0-345-28862-9) Ballantine Bks.

—Trouble Is My Business. 1992. pap. 9.00 (0-394-23911-3); 1988. 224p. pap. 12.00 (0-394-75764-5) Knopf Publishing Group. (Vintage).

—Trouble Is My Business. unabr. ed. 2002. audio 18.00 (1-59007-103-4); audio compact disk 21.95 (1-59007-104-2) New Millennium Entertainment. (New Millennium Audio).

—Trouble Is My Business. unabr. ed. 1993. audio 15.95 o.p. (1-55800-090-9, 40320, Dove Audio) NewStar Media, Inc.

—Trouble Is My Business. 1992. pap. 9.00 (0-679-74086-4) Random Hse., Inc.

—Un Tueur sous la Pluie. 1988. Orig. Title: Killer in the Rain. (FRE.). 245p. pap. 10.95 (0-7859-2082-X, 2070379108) French & European Pubns., Inc.

Chandler, Raymond & Parker, Robert B. Farewell, My Lovely & Poodle Springs. abr. ed. 1993. audio 17.95 (1-55800-778-4, Dove Audio) NewStar Media, Inc.

—Poodle Springs. 1990. (J). mass mkt. 7.50 o.s.i (0-425-12343-X) Berkley Publishing Group.

—Poodle Springs. abr. ed. 1993. audio 14.95 o.p. (1-55800-168-9, Dove Audio) NewStar Media, Inc.

—Poodle Springs. 1989. 18.95 o.p. (0-399-13482-4, G. P. Putnam's Sons) Penguin Putnam Bks. for Young Readers.

Lark, Michael. Graphic Comic Book: Raymond Chandler's 'The Little Sister' 1997. (Illus.). 136p. pap. 15.00 o.s.i (0-684-82933-9, Fireside) Simon & Schuster.

Parker, Robert B. Perchance to Dream. 1993. 288p. mass mkt. 6.99 o.s.i (0-425-13131-9) Berkley Publishing Group.

—Perchance to Dream. unabr. ed. 1994. (Spenser Ser.). audio 30.00 (0-7366-2694-8, 3428) Books on Tape, Inc.

—Perchance to Dream. abr. ed. 1993. 15.95 o.p. (1-55800-291-X, 41250) NewStar Media, Inc.

—Perchance to Dream. 1991. (Spenser Thriller Ser.). 272p. 19.95 o.p. (0-399-13580-4, G. P. Putnam's Sons) Penguin Group (USA) Inc.

—Philip Marlowe. E-Book 12.95 (1-58824-001-0) ibooks, Inc.

Parker, Robert B. & Chandler, Raymond. Poodle Springs & Pastime. abr. ed. 1999. audio 25.00 (0-7871-1894-X, Dove Audio) NewStar Media, Inc.

### MAROSI, LIEUTENANT (FICTITIOUS CHARACTER)—FICTION

Galgoczi, Erzsebet. Another Love. Rieder, Ines & Newman, Felice, trs. from GER. 1991. 160p. 24.95 o.p. (0-939416-52-2); pap. 8.95 o.p. (0-939416-51-4) Cleis Pr.

### MARPLE, JANE (FICTITIOUS CHARACTER)—FICTION

Christie, Agatha. At Bertram's Hotel. unabr. ed. 1997. (Miss Marple Mysteries Ser.). audio 54.95 o.p. (0-7451-6812-4, CAB 313) BBC Audiobooks America.

—At Bertram's Hotel. 1987. (HC Collection). 9.95 o.p. (0-553-82243-8) Bantam Bks.

—At Bertram's Hotel. l.t. ed. (Agatha Christie Ser.). 329p. 1992. 14.95 o.p. (0-8161-4532-6); 1991. lib. bdg. 19.95 o.p. (0-8161-4531-8) Gale Group. (Macmillan Reference USA).

—At Bertram's Hotel. 2000. (Miss Marple Mysteries Ser.). 224p. mass mkt. 5.99 (0-451-19993-6, Signet Bks.) NAL.

—At Bertram's Hotel. 1992. 208p. 22.95 o.s.i (0-399-13706-8, G. P. Putnam's Sons) Penguin Group (USA) Inc.

—At Bertram's Hotel. 1982. mass mkt. 2.75 o.s.i (0-671-45761-6); 1984. mass mkt. 3.50 o.s.i (0-671-54385-7) Simon & Schuster. (Pocket).

—At Bertram's Hotel. 1988. audio 53.95 o.p. (0-8161-9107-7) Thorndike Pr.

—At Bertram's Hotel. l.t. ed. 1968. (Ulverscroft Large Print Ser.). 367p. 12.00 o.p. (0-85456-586-8, Ulverscroft) Thorpe, F. A. Pubs. GBR. *Dist:* Ulverscroft Large Print Bks., Ltd., Ulverscroft Large Print Canada, Ltd.

—The Body in the Library. 1987. (HC Collection). 9.95 o.p. (0-553-35058-7) Bantam Bks.

—The Body in the Library. l.t. ed. (Popular Author Ser.). 249p. 1989. 10.95 o.p. (0-8161-4501-6); 1988. lib. bdg. 19.95 o.p. (0-8161-4458-3) Gale Group. (Macmillan Reference USA).

—The Body in the Library. 2000. (Miss Marple Mysteries Ser.). 224p. mass mkt. 5.99 (0-451-19987-1, Signet Bks.) NAL.

—The Body in the Library. 1985. (Agatha Christie Ser.). 240p. 14.95 o.s.i (0-399-15017-X, G. P. Putnam's Sons) Penguin Group (USA) Inc.

—The Body in the Library. 1985. 12.95 o.s.i (0-396-08699-3) Putnam Publishing Group, The.

—The Body in the Library. 1985. mass mkt. 3.50 o.s.i (0-671-60255-1); 1984. 11.80 o.p. (0-671-90084-6); 1983. mass mkt. 2.95 o.s.i (0-671-46496-5) Simon & Schuster. (Pocket).

—The Body in the Library. 1992. (Miss Marple Mysteries Ser.). 12.04 (0-606-12195-1) Turtleback Bks.

—A Caribbean Mystery. unabr. ed. 1997. (Miss Marple Mysteries Ser.). audio 54.95 o.p. (0-7451-6813-2, CAB 581) BBC Audiobooks America.

—A Caribbean Mystery. l.t. ed. (Agatha Christie Ser.). 1990. 312p. 12.95 o.p. (0-8161-4538-5); 1989. 273p. lib. bdg. 20.95 o.p. (0-8161-4537-7) Gale Group. (Macmillan Reference USA).

—A Caribbean Mystery. 2000. (Miss Marple Mysteries Ser.). 224p. mass mkt. 5.99 (0-451-19992-8, Signet Bks.) NAL.

—A Caribbean Mystery. 1987. (Agatha Christie Ser.). 224p. 14.95 o.s.i (0-396-09156-3, G. P. Putnam's Sons) Penguin Putnam Bks. for Young Readers.

—A Caribbean Mystery. 1990. 224p. mass mkt. 3.95 o.s.i (0-671-70598-9); 1982. mass mkt. 2.95 o.s.i (0-671-46920-7) Simon & Schuster. (Pocket).

—A Caribbean Mystery. l.t. ed. 1967. (Ulverscroft Large Print Ser.). 313p. 12.00 (0-85456-587-6, Ulverscroft) Thorpe, F. A. Pubs. GBR. *Dist:* Ulverscroft Large Print Bks., Ltd., Ulverscroft Large Print Canada, Ltd.

—A Caribbean Mystery. 1992. (Miss Marple Mysteries Ser.). 12.04 (0-606-12212-5) Turtleback Bks.

—A Caribbean Mystery: A Miss Marple Murder Mystery. unabr. ed. 2001. audio 24.95 (1-57270-110-2, N41110u, Audio Editions Bks. on Cassette) Audio Partners Publishing Corp.

—The Herb of Death & Other Stories. unabr. ed. 1989. 7p. audio 16.99 (0-88646-241-X) Durkin Hayes Publishing Ltd.

—The Mirror Crack'd. l.t. ed. 1993. pap. 12.95 o.p. (0-8161-4560-1, Macmillan Reference USA) Gale Group.

—The Mirror Crack'd. 2000. (Miss Marple Mysteries Ser.). 224p. mass mkt. 5.99 (0-451-19989-8, Signet Bks.) NAL.

—The Mirror Crack'd. 1985. 224p. mass mkt. 3.50 o.s.i (0-671-55701-7); 1983. mass mkt. 2.95 o.s.i (0-671-49352-3) Simon & Schuster. (Pocket).

—The Mirror Crack'd from Side to Side. unabr. ed. 1996. audio 54.95 (0-7451-4060-2, CAB 757) BBC Audiobooks America.

—The Mirror Crack'd from Side to Side. l.t. ed. 1966. (Ulverscroft Large Print Ser.). 401p. o.p. (0-85456-698-8, Ulverscroft) Thorpe, F. A. Pubs. GBR. *Dist:* Ulverscroft Large Print Canada, Ltd.

—Miss Marple: The Complete Short Stories. 1986. 352p. pap. 12.95 (0-425-09486-3) Berkley Publishing Group.

—Miss Marple Investigates. unabr. ed. 2000. audio 19.99 (0-88646-552-4, DHA-6552) Durkin Hayes Publishing Ltd.

—The Moving Finger. (Miss Marple Mysteries Ser.). 208p. 1987. mass mkt. 5.99 o.s.i (0-425-10569-5); 1985. mass mkt. 2.95 o.s.i (0-425-08796-4) Berkley Publishing Group.

—The Moving Finger. 1982. 192p. pap. 2.95 o.p. (0-440-15861-3) Dell Publishing.

—The Moving Finger. l.t. ed. (Agatha Christie Ser.). 264p. 1990. pap. 12.95 o.p. (0-8161-4562-8); 1989. lib. bdg. 19.95 o.p. (0-8161-4561-X) Gale Group. (Macmillan Reference USA).

—The Moving Finger. 1986. (Agatha Christie Ser.). 12.95 o.s.i (0-396-08803-1, G. P. Putnam's Sons) Penguin Putnam Bks. for Young Readers.

—The Moving Finger. 1991. 10.60 (0-606-12432-2) Turtleback Bks.

—The Moving Finger: A Miss Marple Murder Mystery. unabr. ed. 2001. audio 24.95 (1-57270-123-4, N41123u, Audio Editions Mystery Masters) Audio Partners Publishing Corp.

—The Moving Finger: A Miss Marple Mystery. unabr. ed. 1996. audio 54.95 (0-7451-4045-9, CAB742) BBC Audiobooks America.

—Murder at the Vicarage. unabr. ed. audio 69.95 o.p. (0-7451-6817-5, CAB 611) BBC Audiobooks America.

—Murder at the Vicarage. (Agatha Christie Ser.). 1986. 240p. mass mkt. 5.99 o.s.i (0-425-09453-7); 1984. mass mkt. 2.95 o.s.i (0-425-06790-4) Berkley Publishing Group.

—Murder at the Vicarage. 1970. 224p. pap. 2.50 o.s.i (0-440-15946-6) Dell Publishing.

—Murder at the Vicarage. l.t. ed. (Agatha Christie Ser.). 408p. 1990. 12.95 o.p. (0-8161-4566-0); 1989. 16.95 o.p. (0-8161-4565-2) Gale Group. (Macmillan Reference USA).

—Murder at the Vicarage. 2000. (Miss Marple Mysteries Ser.). 256p. mass mkt. 5.99 (0-451-20115-9); 70th anniv. ed. (Illus.). pap. 12.00 o.s.i (0-451-19978-2) NAL. (Signet Bks.).

—Murder at the Vicarage. 1986. (Agatha Christie Ser.). 12.95 (0-396-08804-X, G. P. Putnam's Sons) Penguin Putnam Bks. for Young Readers.

—Murder at the Vicarage. abr. ed. 1997. (BBC Radio Presents Ser.). audio 18.00 o.s.i (0-553-47767-6, RH Audio) Random Hse. Audio Publishing Group.

—A Murder Is Announced. 1986. mass mkt. 9.95 o.p. (0-553-35040-4) Bantam Bks.

—A Murder Is Announced. 1991. (Miss Marple Mysteries Ser.). 240p. mass mkt. 5.99 o.s.i (0-425-12962-4) Berkley Publishing Group.

—A Murder Is Announced. l.t. ed. 1988. (Popular Author Ser.). 368p. pap. 9.95 o.p. (0-8161-4572-5); lib. bdg. 19.95 o.p. (0-8161-4571-7) Gale Group. (Macmillan Reference USA).

—A Murder Is Announced. 2001. (Miss Marple Mysteries Ser.). 240p. mass mkt. 5.99 (0-451-20119-1) NAL.

—A Murder Is Announced. 1967. (Agatha Christie Ser.). 12.95 (0-396-08702-7, G. P. Putnam's Sons) Penguin Group (USA) Inc.

—A Murder Is Announced. 1985. mass mkt. 3.50 o.s.i (0-671-55267-8, Pocket) Simon & Schuster.

—A Murder Is Announced. 1988. (G. K. Hall Audio Bks.). audio 69.95 o.s.i (0-8161-9108-5) Thorndike Pr.

—A Murder Is Announced. 1991. (Miss Marple Mysteries Ser.). 12.04 (0-606-12436-5) Turtleback Bks.

—A Murder Is Announced: A Miss Marple Mystery. unabr. ed. 1996. audio 69.95 o.p. (0-7451-6818-3, CAB297) BBC Audiobooks America.

—Murder with Mirrors. 1985. 192p. 9.95 o.p. (0-553-35027-7) Bantam Bks.

—Murder with Mirrors. 1986. (Agatha Christie Ser.). 14.95 (*0-396-08867-8*, G. P. Putnam's Sons) Penguin Putnam Bks. for Young Readers.
—Murder with Mirrors. 1990. mass mkt. 3.95 o.p. (*0-671-70603-9*, Pocket) Simon & Schuster.
—Nemesis. abr. ed. 1998. audio 16.85 (*0-563-55728-1*) BBC Bk. Publishing GBR. *Dist:* Ulverscroft Large Print Bks., Ltd.
—Nemesis. (Agatha Christie Ser.). 1991. 400p. 12.95 o.p. (*0-8161-4582-2*); 1990. 368p. lib. bdg. 13.95 o.p. (*0-8161-4581-4*) Gale Group. (Macmillan Reference USA).
—Nemesis. (SPA.). 240p. 7.95 (*84-272-0294-6*) Molino, Editorial ESP. *Dist:* AIMS International Bks., Inc.
—Nemesis. 2000. 224p. mass mkt. 5.99 (*0-451-20018-7*, Signet Bks.) NAL.
—Nemesis. 1989. mass mkt. 4.99 o.p. (*0-671-70416-8*); 1984. mass mkt. 3.50 o.s.i (*0-671-54206-0*) Simon & Schuster. (Pocket).
—A Pocket Full of Pye: A Miss Marple Mystery. 1991. (Miss Marple Mysteries Ser.). 192p. mass mkt. 5.99 o.s.i (*0-425-13028-2*) Berkley Publishing Group.
—A Pocket Full of Rye. unabr. ed. 1995. audio 54.95 o.p. (*0-7451-5831-5*, CAB 099) BBC Audiobooks America.
—A Pocket Full of Rye. 2000. (Miss Marple Mysteries Ser.). 224p. mass mkt. 5.99 (*0-451-19986-3*, Signet Bks.) NAL.
—A Pocket Full of Rye. 1985. mass mkt. 3.50 o.s.i (*0-671-55796-3*); 1983. mass mkt. 2.95 o.s.i (*0-671-49203-9*); 1982. mass mkt. 2.75 o.s.i (*0-671-44727-0*) Simon & Schuster. (Pocket).
—A Pocket Full of Rye. l.t. ed. 1983. 384p. o.p. (*0-7089-1066-1*, Ulverscroft) Thorpe, F. A. Pubs.
—The Regatta Mystery & Other Stories. 1986. 176p. mass mkt. 5.99 (*0-425-10041-3*) Berkley Publishing Group.
—The Regatta Mystery & Other Stories. 1976. mass mkt. 2.95 o.s.i (*0-440-17336-1*) Dell Publishing.
—The Regatta Mystery & Other Stories. l.t. ed. (Agatha Christie Ser.). 280p. 1990. 12.95 o.p. (*0-8161-4596-2*); 1989. 12.95 o.p. (*0-8161-4595-4*) Gale Group. (Macmillan Reference USA).
—The Regatta Mystery & Other Stories. 1986. (Agatha Christie Ser.). 229p. 12.95 o.s.i (*0-396-08805-8*, G. P. Putnam's Sons) Penguin Putnam Bks. for Young Readers.
—The Secret Adversary. 1983. mass mkt. 2.95 o.s.i (*0-553-24035-8*) Bantam Bks.
—The Secret Adversary. E-Book 2.49 (*0-7574-0450-2*) Electric Umbrella Publishing.
—The Secret Adversary. 2002. 264p. pap. 19.95 (*1-59224-846-2*); lib. bdg. 29.95 (*1-59224-847-0*) Wildside Pr.
—Sleeping Murder. 22.95 (*0-88411-387-6*) Amereon, Ltd.
—Sleeping Murder. unabr. ed. 1997. (Miss Marple Mysteries Ser.). audio 54.95 o.p. (*0-7451-5834-X*, CAB 620) BBC Audiobooks America.
—Sleeping Murder. l.t. ed. (Agatha Christie Ser.). 1991. 336p. 13.95 o.p. (*0-8161-4600-4*); 1990. 298p. lib. bdg. 19.95 o.p. (*0-8161-4599-7*) Gale Group. (Macmillan Reference USA).
—Sleeping Murder. 2000. (Miss Marple Mysteries Ser.). 224p. mass mkt. 5.99 (*0-451-20019-5*, Signet Bks.) NAL.
—Sleeping Murder. l.t. ed. 1978. (Ulverscroft Large Print Ser.). 344p. 12.00 o.p. (*0-7089-0109-3*, Ulverscroft) Thorpe, F. A. Pubs. GBR. *Dist:* Ulverscroft Large Print Bks., Ltd., Ulverscroft Large Print Canada, Ltd.
—Sleeping Murder. 1992. 12.04 (*0-606-12521-3*) Turtleback Bks.
—They Do It with Mirrors. unabr. ed. 1995. audio 54.95 o.p. (*0-7451-5837-4*, CAB 086) BBC Audiobooks America.
—They Do It with Mirrors. 2000. (Miss Marple Mysteries Ser.). 224p. mass mkt. 5.99 (*0-451-19990-1*, Signet Bks.) NAL.
—They Do It with Mirrors. 1985. audio 53.95 o.p. (*0-8161-9897-7*) Thorndike Pr.
—They Do It with Mirrors. l.t. ed. 1987. (Ulverscroft Large Print Ser.). 16.95 o.p. (*0-7089-1737-2*, Ulverscroft) Thorpe, F. A. Pubs. GBR. *Dist:* Ulverscroft Large Print Bks., Ltd., Ulverscroft Large Print Canada, Ltd.
—They Do It with Mirrors. 1992. (Miss Marple Mysteries Ser.). 12.04 (*0-606-12440-3*) Turtleback Bks.
—They Do It with Mirrors: A Miss Marple Murder Mystery. unabr. ed. 2000. audio 24.95 (*1-57270-143-9*, N41143u, Audio Editions Mystery Masters) Audio Partners Publishing Corp.
—The Thirteen Problems. (Agatha Christie Ser.). 1998. mass mkt. 3.99 o.s.i (*0-425-16926-X*); 1985. 224p. mass mkt. 5.99 o.s.i (*0-425-08903-7*) Berkley Publishing Group.
—The Thirteen Problems. 2000. (Miss Marple Mysteries Ser.). 224p. mass mkt. 5.99 (*0-451-20020-9*, Signet Bks.) NAL.
—The Thirteen Problems. l.t. ed. 1968. (Ulverscroft Large Print Ser.). 358p. 12.00 o.p. (*0-85456-475-6*, Ulverscroft) Thorpe, F. A. Pubs. GBR. *Dist:* Ulverscroft Large Print Bks., Ltd., Ulverscroft Large Print Canada, Ltd.
—Three Blind Mice. abr. ed. 1990. audio 16.99 (*0-88646-172-3*, 7173) Durkin Hayes Publishing Ltd.
—Three Blind Mice & Other Stories. 1984. 224p. mass mkt. 5.99 o.s.i (*0-425-06806-4*) Berkley Publishing Group.
—Three Blind Mice & Other Stories. 1980. pap. 2.50 o.s.i (*0-440-15867-2*) Dell Publishing.
—Three Blind Mice & Other Stories. l.t. ed. (Popular Author Ser.). 338p. 1989. 10.95 o.p. (*0-8161-4462-1*); 1988. lib. bdg. 19.95 o.p. (*0-8161-4461-3*) Gale Group. (Macmillan Reference USA).
—Three Blind Mice & Other Stories. 1985. (Agatha Christie Ser.). 240p. 12.95 (*0-396-08707-8*, G. P. Putnam's Sons) Penguin Putnam Bks. for Young Readers.
—Three Blind Mice & Other Stories. 2001. 288p. reprint ed. mass mkt. 5.99 (*0-312-97976-2*, St. Martin's Paperbacks) St. Martin's Pr.
—Thumbmark of St. Peter. unabr. ed. 1993. (Miss Marple Mysteries Ser.). audio 4.99 (*0-88646-649-0*) Durkin Hayes Publishing Ltd.
—The Tuesday Club Murders. unabr. ed. 2004. audio 25.95 (*1-57270-359-8*); audio compact disk 29.95 (*1-57270-360-1*) Audio Partners Publishing Corp.
—The Tuesday Club Murders. 1984. mass mkt. 2.95 o.s.i (*0-425-06807-2*) Berkley Publishing Group.
—The Tuesday Club Murders. 1971. 192p. pap. 2.50 o.s.i (*0-440-19136-X*) Dell Publishing.
—The Tuesday Club Murders. unabr. ed. 1987. audio 16.99 (*0-88646-196-0*, 7197) Durkin Hayes Publishing Ltd.
—The Tuesday Club Murders. l.t. ed. 1992. lib. bdg. 19.95 o.p. (*0-8161-4613-6*); 1989. 328p. 12.95 o.p. (*0-8161-4612-8*) Gale Group. (Macmillan Reference USA).
—What Mrs. McGillicuddy Saw! l.t. ed. (Popular Author Ser.). 1991. 12.95 o.p. (*0-8161-4618-7*); 1990. 342p. lib. bdg. 12.95 o.p. (*0-8161-4617-9*) Gale Group. (Macmillan Reference USA).
—What Mrs. McGillicuddy Saw! 1987. (Agatha Christie Ser.). 14.95 o.s.i (*0-396-09014-1*, G. P. Putnam's Sons) Penguin Putnam Bks. for Young Readers.
—What Mrs. McGillicuddy Saw! 1991. mass mkt. 3.95 o.p. (*0-671-70602-0*); 1983. mass mkt. 2.95 o.s.i (*0-671-49454-6*) Simon & Schuster. (Pocket).
—4:50 from Paddington. 2000. (Miss Marple Mysteries Ser.). 224p. mass mkt. 5.99 (*0-451-20051-9*, Signet Bks.) NAL.
—4:50 from Paddington. 1982. (Agatha Christie Ser.). 9.95 (*0-396-08110-X*, G. P. Putnam's Sons) Penguin Putnam Bks. for Young Readers.
—4:50 from Paddington. l.t. ed. 1965. (Ulverscroft Large Print Ser.). 391p. (*0-85456-474-8*, Ulverscroft) Thorpe, F. A. Pubs. GBR. *Dist:* Ulverscroft Large Print Canada, Ltd.

Christie, Agatha & Leach, Rosemary. They Do It with Mirrors. abr. ed. 2002. (The/Agatha Christie Mystery Series). (Illus.). audio 12.95 (*1-55927-758-0*) Audio Renaissance.

**MARSALA, CAT (FICTITIOUS CHARACTER)—FICTION**

D'Amato, Barbara. Hard Bargain: A Cat Marsala Mystery. 1999. (Cat Marsala Ser.). 288p. mass mkt. 5.99 o.s.i (*0-425-16898-0*) Berkley Publishing Group.
—Hard Bargain: A Cat Marsala Mystery. 1997. (Illus.). 288p. 21.00 o.s.i (*0-684-83353-0*, Scribner) Simon & Schuster.
—Hard Case: A Cat Marsala Mystery. 1995. 240p. mass mkt. 4.99 o.s.i (*0-425-15009-7*, Prime Crime) Berkley Publishing Group.
—Hard Case: A Cat Marsala Mystery. 1994. 288p. 20.00 o.p. (*0-684-19686-7*, Macmillan Reference USA) Gale Group.
—Hard Christmas: A Cat Marsala Mystery. 1996. 288p. mass mkt. 5.99 o.s.i (*0-425-15465-3*, Prime Crime) Berkley Publishing Group.
—Hard Christmas: A Cat Marsala Mystery. 1995. 288p. 20.00 (*0-684-19687-5*, Scribner) Simon & Schuster.
—Hard Evidence: A Cat Marsala Mystery. 2000. (Cat Marsala Mysteries Ser.). (Illus.). 255p. mass mkt. 6.50 o.s.i (*0-425-17412-3*, Prime Crime) Berkley Publishing Group.
—Hard Evidence: A Cat Marsala Mystery. l.t. ed. 2000. (Wheeler Large Print Bks.). (Illus.). 247p. pap. 23.95 (*1-56895-861-7*, Wheeler Publishing, Inc.) Gale Group.
—Hard Evidence: A Cat Marsala Mystery. 1999. (Cat Marsala Mysteries Ser.). 256p. 22.00 (*0-684-83354-9*, Scribner) Simon & Schuster.
—Hard Luck: A Cat Marsala Mystery. 1992. 224p. text 20.00 (*0-684-19408-2*, Macmillan Reference USA) Gale Group.
—Hard Luck: A Cat Marsala Mystery. 1993. (Mystery Ser.). per. (*0-373-26124-1*, 1-26124-7, Harlequin Bks.) Harlequin Enterprises, Ltd.
—Hard Road: A Cat Marsala Mystery. 2001. (Cat Marsala Mysteries Ser.). E-Book 23.00 (*0-7432-1855-8*, Scribner) Simon & Schuster.
—Hard Tack: A Cat Marsala Mystery. 1991. 224p. 18.95 o.s.i (*0-684-19299-3*, Macmillan Reference USA) Gale Group.
—Hard Tack: A Cat Marsala Mystery. 1992. (WWL Mystery Ser.: No. 97). per. (*0-373-26097-0*, 1-26097-5, Harlequin Bks.) Harlequin Enterprises, Ltd.
—Hard Women: A Cat Marsala Mystery. 1993. 256p. 20.00 o.p. (*0-684-19564-X*, Macmillan Reference USA) Gale Group.
—Hard Women: A Cat Marsala Mystery. 1994. per. (*0-373-26150-0*, 1-26150-2, Harlequin Bks.) Harlequin Enterprises, Ltd.
—Hardball. 2003. 224p. pap. 13.00 (*1-932325-01-8*) Crum Creek Pr.
—Hardball. 1990. 224p. 17.95 o.s.i (*0-684-19140-7*, Macmillan Reference USA) Gale Group.
—Hardball. 1993. (Illus.). per. (*0-373-83302-4*, 1-83302-9); 1991. mass mkt. (*0-373-26066-0*) Harlequin Enterprises, Ltd. (Harlequin Bks.).

D'Amato, Barbara & D'Amato, Brian. Hard Road: A Cat Marsala Mystery. 2001. 288p. 23.00 (*0-7432-0095-0*, Scribner) Simon & Schuster.

**MARSH, EMMA (FICTITIOUS CHARACTER)—FICTION**

Dean, Elizabeth. Murder Is a Collector's Item. Schantz, Tom & Schantz, Enid, eds. 1998. (Emma Marsh Mysteries Ser.). 192p. reprint ed. pap. 14.00 (*0-915230-19-4*) Rue Morgue Pr.

**MARSH, JENNIFER (FICTITIOUS CHARACTER)—FICTION**

Fitzwater, Judy. Dying for a Clue. 1999. (Jennifer Marsh Mysteries Ser.). 240p. mass mkt. 7.99 (*0-449-00426-0*, Fawcett) Ballantine Bks.
—Dying for a Clue. l.t. ed. 2000. (G. K. Hall Paperback Ser.). 271p. pap. 23.95 (*0-7838-9113-X*, Macmillan Reference USA) Gale Group.
—Dying to Be Murdered. 2001. (Jennifer Marsh Mysteries Ser.). 240p. mass mkt. 6.50 (*0-449-00640-9*) Ballantine Bks.
—Dying to Get Even. 1999. (Jennifer Marsh Mysteries Ser.). 240p. mass mkt. 6.50 (*0-449-00386-8*, Fawcett) Ballantine Bks.
—Dying to Get Her Man. l.t. ed. 2002. 327p. pap. 24.95 (*0-7862-4587-5*) Thorndike Pr.
—Dying to Get Published. (Jennifer Marsh Mysteries Ser.). 240p. 1998. mass mkt. 5.99 (*0-449-00294-2*, Fawcett); 1995. pap. 15.00 (*0-345-46381-1*, Ballantine Bks.) Ballantine Bks.
—Dying to Get Published. l.t. ed. 2000. (G. K. Hall Paperback Ser.). 264p. pap. 23.95 (*0-7838-8855-4*, Macmillan Reference USA) Gale Group.
—Dying to Remember. 2000. (Jennifer Marsh Mysteries Ser.). 240p. mass mkt. 6.50 (*0-449-00639-5*, Fawcett) Ballantine Bks.
—Dying to Remember. l.t. ed. 2001. 272p. (*0-7540-4426-2*); (*0-7540-4425-4*) Gale Group. (Macmillan Reference USA).
—Dying to Remember. l.t. ed. 2001. (Paperback Ser.). 272p. pap. 24.95 (*0-7838-9333-7*) Thorndike Pr.

**MARSHALL, ANNA (FICTITIOUS CHARACTER)—FICTION**

Modesitt, L. E., Jr. Darksong Rising. (Spellsong Cycle Ser.: Bk. 3). 2001. 501p. mass mkt. 6.99 (*0-8125-6668-8*); 1999. 507p. 27.95 (*0-312-86822-7*) Doherty, Tom Assocs., LLC. (Tor Bks.).
—The Soprano Sorceress. (Spellsong Cycle Ser.: Bk. 1). 1998. 672p. mass mkt. 6.99 (*0-8125-4559-1*); 1997. 509p. 25.95 (*0-312-86022-6*) Doherty, Tom Assocs., LLC. (Tor Bks.).
—The Spellsong War. (Spellsong Cycle Ser.: 2). 1999. 657p. pap. text 6.99 (*0-8125-4002-6*); 1997. 464p. 25.95 o.p. (*0-312-86492-2*) Doherty, Tom Assocs., LLC. (Tor Bks.).
—The Spellsong War. 1999. (Spellsong Cycle Ser.: No. 2). E-Book 6.99 (*0-312-87151-1*) St. Martin's Pr.

**MARSHALL, JORDAN (FICTITIOUS CHARACTER)—FICTION**

Brandon, Jay. Local Rules. 1996. 320p. mass mkt. 5.99 (*0-671-88409-3*, Pocket); 1995. 304p. 22.00 o.p. (*0-671-88408-5*, Atria) Simon & Schuster.

**MARSHALL, NEIL (FICTITIOUS CHARACTER)—FICTION**

Hemlin, Tim. A Catered Christmas. 1998. (Culinary Mysteries Ser.). 272p. mass mkt. 5.99 o.s.i (*0-345-42001-2*) Ballantine Bks.
—Dead Man's Broth. 1999. (Culinary Mysteries Ser.). 304p. mass mkt. 5.99 o.s.i (*0-345-42002-0*) Ballantine Bks.
—If Wishes Were Horses. 1996. mass mkt. 5.50 o.s.i (*0-345-40318-5*) Ballantine Bks.
—People in Glass Houses. 1997. (Culinary Mysteries Ser.). 230p. mass mkt. 5.50 o.s.i (*0-345-40902-7*) Ballantine Bks.
—A Whisper of Rage. 1997. (Culinary Mysteries Ser.). mass mkt. 5.50 o.s.i (*0-345-40319-3*) Ballantine Bks.

**MARSHALL, SHARON (FICTITIOUS CHARACTER)—FICTION**

Christiansen, Nancy. Deadly Deep. 1995. 352p. mass mkt. 4.50 o.s.i (*0-8217-4811-4*, Pinnacle Bks.) Kensington Publishing Corp.

**MARTELLI, GERRY (FICTITIOUS CHARACTER)—FICTION**

Gleiter, Jan. Lie down with Dogs. (Dead Letter Mysteries Ser.). 240p. 1997. mass mkt. 5.99 o.p. (*0-312-96175-8*, St. Martin's Paperbacks); 1996. 21.95 o.p. (*0-312-14003-7*, Saint Martin's Minotaur) St. Martin's Pr.

**MARTIN, DOROTHY (FICTITIOUS CHARACTER)—FICTION**

Dams, Jeanne M. The Body in the Transept. 1996. (Dorothy Martin Mystery Ser.). 224p. mass mkt. 5.99 (*0-06-101133-9*, HarperTorch) Morrow/Avon.
—The Body in the Transept: A Dorothy Martin Mystery. unabr. collector's ed. 1996. audio 42.00 (*0-913369-23-3*, 4174) Books on Tape, Inc.
—The Body in the Transept: A Dorothy Martin Mystery. 1995. 216p. 19.95 (*0-8027-3275-5*) Walker & Co.
—Holy Terror in the Hebrides. 1999. (Dorothy Martin Mystery Ser.: Vol. 3). 272p. mass mkt. 5.99 (*0-06-101346-3*, HarperTorch) Morrow/Avon.
—Holy Terror in the Hebrides: A Dorothy Martin Mystery, , unabr. collector's ed. 1999. audio 40.00 (*0-7366-4296-X*, 4789) Books on Tape, Inc.
—Holy Terror in the Hebrides: A Dorothy Martin Mystery. l.t. ed. 2000. (Thorndike Senior Lifestyle Ser.). 333p. 27.95 o.p. (*0-7862-2407-X*, Macmillan Reference USA) Gale Group.
—Holy Terror in the Hebrides: A Dorothy Martin Mystery. 1997. (Dorothy Martin Mystery Ser.). 224p. 21.95 (*0-8027-3311-5*) Walker & Co.
—Killing Cassidy: A Dorothy Martin Mystery. l.t. ed. 2001. 344p. 28.95 (*0-7862-3332-X*) Thorndike Pr.
—Killing Cassidy: A Dorothy Martin Mystery. 2000. (Dorothy Martin Mystery Ser.). 210p. 23.95 (*0-8027-3347-6*) Walker & Co.
—Malice in Miniature. 2000. (Dorothy Martin Mystery Ser.). 272p. mass mkt. 5.99 (*0-06-101345-5*) HarperCollins Pubs.
—Malice in Miniature: A Dorothy Martin Mystery, , unabr. collector's ed. 1999. audio 40.00 (*0-7366-4506-3*, 4919) Books on Tape, Inc.
—Malice in Miniature: A Dorothy Martin Mystery. l.t. ed. 2001. (Senior Lifestyles Ser.). 344p. 28.95 (*0-7862-2408-8*) Thorndike Pr.
—Malice in Miniature: A Dorothy Martin Mystery. 1998. (Dorothy Martin Mystery Ser.). (Illus.). 220p. (gr. 8). 22.95 (*0-8027-3322-0*) Walker & Co.
—Sinning Out of School: A Dorothy Martin Mystery. 2003. 264p. 23.95 (*0-8027-3379-4*) Walker & Co.
—To Perish in Penzance: A Dorothy Martin Mystery. l.t. ed. 2002. 364p. 28.95 (*0-7862-3846-1*) Gale Group.
—To Perish in Penzance: A Dorothy Martin Mystery. 2001. 240p. 23.95 (*0-8027-3367-0*) Walker & Co.
—Trouble in the Town Hall. 1998. (Dorothy Martin Mystery Ser.). 256p. mass mkt. 5.99 (*0-06-101132-0*, HarperTorch) Morrow/Avon.
—Trouble in the Town Hall: A Dorothy Martin Mystery. unabr. collector's ed. 1997. audio 42.00 (*0-7366-3834-2*, 4554) Books on Tape, Inc.
—Trouble in the Town Hall: A Dorothy Martin Mystery. l.t. ed. 2000. (Thorndike Senior Lifestyle Ser.). 315p. 27.95 (*0-7862-2406-1*) Thorndike Pr.
—Trouble in the Town Hall: A Dorothy Martin Mystery. 1996. (Dorothy Martin Mystery Ser.). 256p. 20.95 (*0-8027-3285-2*) Walker & Co.
—The Victim in Victoria Station. l.t. ed. 2001. (Dorothy Martin Mystery Ser.). (Illus.). 295p. 27.95 (*0-7862-2409-6*) Thorndike Pr.
—The Victim in Victoria Station: A Dorothy Martin Mystery. 1999. (Dorothy Martin Mystery Ser.). (Illus.). 208p. 23.95 (*0-8027-3337-9*) Walker & Co.

**MARTIN, JAKE (FICTITIOUS CHARACTER)—FICTION**

Coughlin, William Jeremiah. In the Presence of Enemies. l.t. ed. 1993. (General Ser.). 575p. lib. bdg. 22.95 o.p. (*0-8161-5695-6*, Macmillan Reference USA) Gale Group.
—In the Presence of Enemies. 1994. mass mkt. 6.99 (*0-312-95164-7*, St. Martin's Paperbacks); 1993. 309p. 21.95 o.p. (*0-312-08818-3*) St. Martin's Pr.
—Presence of Enemies. 1924. o.s.i (*0-688-08192-4*, Morrow, William & Co.) Morrow/Avon.

**MARTIN, KAY (FICTITIOUS CHARACTER)—FICTION**

Adams, Deborah. All the Dark Disguises. 1993. mass mkt. 4.99 o.s.i (*0-345-37765-6*) Ballantine Bks.

### MARTIN, SAZ (FICTITIOUS CHARACTER)—FICTION

Duffy, Stella. Beneath the Blonde: A Saz Martin Mystery. 1997. (Mask Noir Ser.). 240p. pap. text o.p. (*1-85242-542-3*) Serpent's Tail Ltd.

—Calendar Girl. 2000. 224p. pap. (*1-85242-712-4*); 1995. 160p. pap. o.p. (*1-85242-367-6*) Serpent's Tail Ltd.

### MARTINDALE, THOMAS (FICTITIOUS CHARACTER)—FICTION

Lovell, Ron. Dead Whales Tell No Tales: A Thomas Martindale Mystery. 2003. 184p. pap. 18.95 (*0-86534-383-7*) Sunstone Pr.

—Murder at Yaquina Head: A Thomas Martindale Mystery. 2002. 184p. pap. 18.95 (*0-86534-369-1*); 256p. 22.95 (*0-86534-345-4*) Sunstone Pr.

### MARTINELLI, KATE (FICTITIOUS CHARACTER)—FICTION

King, Laurie R. A Grave Talent. 1995. 368p. mass mkt. 6.99 (*0-553-57399-3*, Crimeline) Bantam Bks.

—A Grave Talent. unabr. ed. 1996. (Kate Martinelli Mystery Ser.: Vol. 1). audio 85.00 (*0-7887-0395-1*, 94587E7) Recorded Bks., LLC.

—A Grave Talent. 1993. 310p. 19.95 (*0-312-08804-3*, Saint Martin's Minotaur) St. Martin's Pr.

—Night Work. 2000. (Kate Martinelli Mysteries Ser.). 416p. mass mkt. 6.99 (*0-553-57825-1*) Bantam Bks.

—To Play the Fool. 1996. 320p. mass mkt. 6.99 (*0-553-57455-8*, Crimeline) Bantam Bks.

—To Play the Fool. unabr. ed. 1996. (Kate Martinelli Mystery Ser.: Vol. 2). audio 60.00 (*0-7887-0406-0*, 94598E7); audio Recorded Bks., LLC.

—To Play the Fool. 1995. 260p. 21.00 o.p. (*0-312-11907-0*, Saint Martin's Minotaur) St. Martin's Pr.

—With Child. 1997. 320p. mass mkt. 6.99 (*0-553-57458-2*) Bantam Bks.

—With Child. unabr. ed. 1996. (Kate Martinelli Mystery Ser.: Vol. 3). audio 70.00 (*0-7887-0579-2*, 94757E7) Recorded Bks., LLC.

—With Child. 1996. 275p. 21.95 o.p. (*0-312-14077-0*, Saint Martin's Minotaur) St. Martin's Pr.

—With Child. l.t. ed. 1998. (Ulverscroft Large Print Ser.). 528p. 29.99 (*0-7089-3904-X*, Ulverscroft) Thorpe, F. A. Pubs. GBR. *Dist:* Ulverscroft Large Print Bks., Ltd., Ulverscroft Large Print Canada, Ltd.

### MARTINEZ, DOLPH (FICTITIOUS CHARACTER)—FICTION

Sanderson, Jim. El Camino del Rio: A Mystery. 221p. 1999. pap. 14.95 (*0-8263-2159-3*); 1998. 21.95 (*0-8263-1990-4*) Univ. of New Mexico Pr.

### MARX, GROUCHO, 1891-1977—FICTION

Goulart, Ron. Elementary My Dear Groucho. 1999. 261p. (J). 23.95 (*0-312-20892-8*, Saint Martin's Minotaur) St. Martin's Pr.

—Groucho Marx: Master Detective. 1998. 262p. (YA). 22.95 o.p. (*0-312-18106-X*, Saint Martin's Minotaur) St. Martin's Pr.

—Groucho Marx & the Broadway Murders. l.t. ed. 2002. (General Ser.). 265p. pap. 24.95 (*0-7862-3692-2*) Gale Group.

—Groucho Marx & the Broadway Murders. 2001. 213p. 22.95 (*0-312-26598-0*, Saint Martin's Minotaur) St. Martin's Pr.

—Groucho Marx, Private Eye. 1999. 263p. 23.95 (*0-312-19895-7*, Saint Martin's Minotaur) St. Martin's Pr.

### MARY ALICE (FICTITIOUS CHARACTER)—FICTION

George, Anne. Murder Boogies with Elvis. (Southern Sisters Mysteries Ser.). 2002. 288p. mass mkt. 6.99 (*0-06-103102-X*, Avon Bks.); 2001. 256p. 23.00 (*0-06-019870-2*, Morrow, William & Co.) Morrow/Avon.

—Murder Boogies with Elvis: A Southern Sisters Mystery. l.t. ed. 2001. (Mystery Ser.). 27.95 (*1-57490-380-2*, Beeler Large Print Bks.) Beeler, Thomas T. Publisher.

—Murder Carries a Torch. 2000. (Southern Sisters Mysteries Ser.). 272p. 23.00 (*0-380-97810-5*, Morrow, William & Co.) Morrow/Avon.

—Murder Carries a Torch: A Southern Sisters Mystery. l.t. ed. 2001. (Large Print Bks.). 274p. pap. 23.95 (*1-58724-127-7*, Wheeler Publishing, Inc.) Gale Group.

—Murder Carries a Torch: A Southern Sisters Mystery. 2001. 288p. mass mkt. 6.99 (*0-380-80938-9*, Avon Bks.) Morrow/Avon.

—Murder Gets a Life. l.t. ed. 2000. (Beeler Large Print Mystery Ser.). 234p. 26.95 (*1-57490-290-3*, Beeler Large Print Bks.) Beeler, Thomas T. Publisher.

—Murder Gets a Life: A Southern Sisters Mystery. (Southern Sisters Mysteries Ser.). 1999. 272p. mass mkt. 6.99 (*0-380-79366-0*); 1998. 256p. 20.00 o.p. (*0-380-97558-0*) Morrow/Avon. (Avon Bks.).

—Murder Makes Waves. l.t. ed. 2000. (Beeler Large Print Mystery Ser.). 246p. 26.95 (*1-57490-274-1*, Beeler Large Print Bks.) Beeler, Thomas T. Publisher.

—Murder Makes Waves. (Southern Sisters Mysteries Ser.). 1998. 272p. mass mkt. 6.99 (*0-380-78450-5*); 1997. 256p. 20.00 o.p. (*0-380-97527-0*) Morrow/Avon. (Avon Bks.).

—Murder on a Bad Hair Day. l.t. ed. 1999. (Beeler Large Print Mystery Ser.). 277p. 26.95 (*1-57490-238-5*, Beeler Large Print Bks.) Beeler, Thomas T. Publisher.

—Murder on a Bad Hair Day. 1996. (Southern Sisters Mysteries Ser.). 256p. mass mkt. 6.99 (*0-380-78087-9*, Avon Bks.) Morrow/Avon.

—Murder on a Girl's Night Out. 1996. (Southern Sisters Mysteries Ser.). 256p. mass mkt. 6.99 (*0-380-78086-0*, Avon Bks.) Morrow/Avon.

—Murder on a Girls' Night Out. l.t. ed. 1999. (Beeler Large Print Mystery Ser.). 26.95 (*1-57490-212-1*, Beeler Large Print Bks.) Beeler, Thomas T. Publisher.

—Murder Runs in the Family. l.t. ed. 2000. (Beeler Large Print Mystery Ser.). 243p. 26.95 (*1-57490-258-X*, Beeler Large Print Bks.) Beeler, Thomas T. Publisher.

—Murder Runs in the Family. 1997. (Southern Sisters Mysteries Ser.). 288p. mass mkt. 6.99 (*0-380-78449-1*, Avon Bks.) Morrow/Avon.

—Murder Shoots the Bull. 2000. (Southern Sisters Mysteries Ser.). 272p. mass mkt. 6.99 (*0-380-80149-3*, Avon Bks.) Morrow/Avon.

—Murder Shoots the Bull: A Southern Sisters Mystery. l.t. ed. 1999. (*0-07-862222-0*) McGraw-Hill Cos., The.

—Murder Shoots the Bull: A Southern Sisters Mystery. 1999. (Southern Sisters Mysteries Ser.). 247p. 22.00 (*0-380-97688-9*, Avon Bks.) Morrow/Avon.

—Murder Shoots the Bull: A Southern Sisters Mystery. l.t. ed. 1999. (Americana Ser.). 358p. 26.95 (*0-7862-2222-0*) Thorndike Pr.

### MARY HELEN, SISTER (FICTITIOUS CHARACTER)—FICTION

O'Marie, Carol Anne. Advent of Dying: A Sister Mary Helen Mystery. 1987. 256p. mass mkt. 4.99 o.s.i (*0-440-10052-6*); 1986. 288p. 14.95 o.p. (*0-385-29506-5*, Delacorte Pr.) Dell Publishing.

—The Corporal Works of Murder. 2002. (Sister Mary Helen Mystery Ser.). 208p. 22.95 (*0-312-20917-7*, Saint Martin's Minotaur) St. Martin's Pr.

—Death Goes on Retreat. unabr. ed. 2001. (Sister Mary Helen Mystery Ser.). audio 29.95 (*1-57270-187-0*, N61187u, Audio Editions Mystery Masters) Audio Partners Publishing Corp.

—Death Goes on Retreat. unabr. ed. 2000. (Sister Mary Helen Mystery Ser.). audio 49.95 (*0-7927-2213-2*, CSL 102) Chivers Audio Bks. GBR. *Dist:* BBC Audiobooks America.

—Death Goes on Retreat: A Sister Mary Helen Mystery. 1996. 272p. mass mkt. 5.50 o.s.i (*0-440-21610-9*) Dell Publishing.

—Death of an Angel: A Sister Mary Helen Mystery. unabr. ed. 1998. audio 39.95 (*0-7861-1452-5*, 2314) Blackstone Audio Bks., Inc.

—Death of an Angel: A Sister Mary Helen Mystery. l.t. ed. 1997. pap. 23.95 (*1-56895-442-5*, Wheeler Publishing, Inc.) Gale Group.

—Death of an Angel: A Sister Mary Helen Mystery. 1996. 256p. 21.95 (*0-312-15107-1*, Saint Martin's Minotaur); 3rd ed. 1997. 304p. mass mkt. 6.50 (*0-312-96396-3*, St. Martin's Paperbacks) St. Martin's Pr.

—Death Takes up a Collection: A Sister Mary Helen Mystery. (Sister Mary Helen Mystery Ser.: Vol. 8). 1998. 224p. 21.95 o.p. (*0-312-19256-8*, Saint Martin's Minotaur); 1999. 256p. reprint ed. mass mkt. 6.50 (*0-312-97193-1*, St. Martin's Paperbacks) St. Martin's Pr.

—Death Takes up a Collection: A Sister Mary Helen Mystery. l.t. ed. 1999. (Mystery Ser.). 347p. 27.95 (*0-7862-1663-8*) Thorndike Pr.

—The Missing Madonna: A Sister Mary Helen Mystery. 1989. 272p. reprint ed. mass mkt. 4.99 o.s.i (*0-440-20473-9*) Dell Publishing.

—The Missing Madonna: A Sister Mary Helen Mystery. l.t. ed. 1990. (General Ser.). 371p. lib. bdg. 20.95 o.p. (*0-8161-4814-7*, Macmillan Reference USA) Gale Group.

—Murder in Ordinary Time: A Sister Mary Helen Mystery. 256p. 1992. mass mkt. 4.99 o.s.i (*0-440-21353-3*); 1991. 18.00 o.s.i (*0-385-30226-6*, Delacorte Pr.) Dell Publishing.

—Murder in Ordinary Time: A Sister Mary Helen Mystery. l.t. ed. 1992. (General Ser.). 352p. lib. bdg. 20.95 o.p. (*0-8161-5425-2*); lib. bdg. 16.95 o.p. (*0-8161-5426-0*) Gale Group. (Macmillan Reference USA).

—Murder Makes a Pilgrimage: A Sister Mary Helen Mystery, unabr. ed. 2000. audio 69.95 (*0-7927-2325-2*, CSL 214, Chivers Sound Library) BBC Audiobooks America.

—Murder Makes a Pilgrimage: A Sister Mary Helen Mystery. 1994. 320p. mass mkt. 5.50 o.s.i (*0-440-21613-3*) Dell Publishing.

—Murder Makes a Pilgrimage: A Sister Mary Helen Mystery. l.t. ed. 1994. 336p. lib. bdg. 21.95 o.p. (*0-8161-5951-3*, Macmillan Reference USA) Gale Group.

—A Novena for Murder: A Sister Mary Helen Mystery. 1986. 192p. mass mkt. 4.99 o.s.i (*0-440-16469-9*) Dell Publishing.

—A Novena for Murder: A Sister Mary Helen Mystery. 1984. 224p. 12.95 o.s.i (*0-684-18087-1*, Macmillan Reference USA) Gale Group.

—Requiem at the Refuge: A Sister Mary Helen Mystery. 2000. (Sister Mary Helen Mystery Ser.). 276p. 23.95 (*0-312-20906-1*, Saint Martin's Minotaur) St. Martin's Pr.

—Requiem at the Refuge: A Sister Mary Helen Mystery. l.t. ed. 2000. (Mystery Ser.). 421p. 29.95 (*0-7862-2844-X*) Thorndike Pr.

### MARY TERESA, SISTER (FICTITIOUS CHARACTER)—FICTION

Quill, Monica. Half Past Nun: A Sister Mary Teresa Mystery. 1997. 198p. 20.95 o.p. (*0-312-15541-7*, Saint Martin's Minotaur) St. Martin's Pr.

—Nun Plussed: A Sister Mary Teresa Mystery. 1995. 250p. per. (*0-373-26187-X*, Worldwide Library) Harlequin Enterprises, Ltd.

—Nun Plussed: A Sister Mary Teresa Mystery. 1993. 224p. 18.95 o.p. (*0-312-09890-1*, Saint Martin's Minotaur) St. Martin's Pr.

—Sister Hood: A Sister Mary Teresa Mystery. 1991. 16.95 o.p. (*0-312-04602-2*, Saint Martin's Minotaur) St. Martin's Pr.

—The Veil of Ignorance: A Sister Mary Teresa Mystery. 1988. 208p. 15.95 o.p. (*0-312-02308-1*, Saint Martin's Minotaur) St. Martin's Pr.

### MASON, MIRIEL (FICTITIOUS CHARACTER)—FICTION

Little, Constance & Little, Gwenyth. The Black Honeymoon. Schantz, Tom & Schantz, Enid, eds. 2nd ed. 1998. 187p. reprint ed. pap. 14.00 (*0-915230-21-6*) Rue Morgue Pr.

### MASON, PERRY (FICTITIOUS CHARACTER)—FICTION

Chastain, Thomas. Perry Mason in the Case of Too Many Murders. 1990. 256p. pap. 3.95 (*0-380-70787-X*, Avon Bks.); 1989. 240p. 14.95 o.p. (*0-688-07164-3*, Morrow, William & Co.) Morrow/Avon.

Gardner, Erle Stanley. The Case of the Amorous Aunt. 1994. mass mkt. 4.50 o.s.i (*0-345-37878-4*) Ballantine Bks.

—The Case of the Amorous Aunt. l.t. ed. 1985. (Nightingale Ser.). 11.95 o.p. (*0-8161-3752-8*, Macmillan Reference USA) Gale Group.

—The Case of the Angry Mourner. 1989. (*1-55504-971-0*); 1991. 12.95 o.p. (*1-55504-970-2*, 215) BBC Audiobooks America.

—The Case of the Angry Mourner. 1993. mass mkt. 4.50 o.s.i (*0-345-37870-9*) Ballantine Bks.

—The Case of the Baited Hook. (Perry Mason Bks.). 288p. reprint ed. lib. bdg. 23.95 (*0-88411-416-3*) Amereon, Ltd.

—The Case of the Baited Hook. (Perry Mason Mysteries Ser.). 1999. mass mkt. 4.99 (*0-345-91478-3*); 1995. 224p. pap. 15.00 (*0-345-46896-1*); 1986. 224p. mass mkt. 5.99 (*0-345-32942-2*) Ballantine Bks.

—The Case of the Beautiful Beggar. 1976. 21.95 (*0-8488-0498-8*) Amereon, Ltd.

—The Case of the Beautiful Beggar. 1986. mass mkt. 3.50 o.s.i (*0-345-34318-2*) Ballantine Bks.

—The Case of the Beautiful Beggar. l.t. ed. 1998. (G. K. Hall Paperback Ser.). 272p. 22.95 o.p. (*0-7838-0269-2*, Macmillan Reference USA) Gale Group.

—The Case of the Beautiful Beggar. abr. ed. 1988. audio 14.95 (*1-55800-118-2*, 40450, Dove Audio) NewStar Media, Inc.

—The Case of the Bigamous Spouse. l.t. ed. 1988. pap. 18.95 o.p. (*1-55504-668-1*); lib. bdg. 20.95 o.p. (*1-55504-687-8*) BBC Audiobooks America.

—The Case of the Bigamous Spouse. 1987. mass mkt. 2.95 o.s.i (*0-345-34378-6*) Ballantine Bks.

—The Case of the Bigamous Spouse. 1972. pap. 0.95 o.p. (*0-671-77865-X*, Pocket) Simon & Schuster.

—The Case of the Black-Eyed Blonde. 1976. 21.95 (*0-8488-0271-3*) Amereon, Ltd.

—The Case of the Black-Eyed Blonde. 1985. 208p. mass mkt. 3.50 o.s.i (*0-345-32311-4*) Ballantine Bks.

—The Case of the Black-Eyed Blonde. 1975. pap. 1.50 o.p. (*0-671-78782-9*, Pocket) Simon & Schuster.

—The Case of the Blonde Bonanza. 1994. mass mkt. 4.50 o.s.i (*0-345-37877-6*) Ballantine Bks.

—The Case of the Blonde Bonanza. l.t. ed. 1987. (Nightingale Ser.). 291p. pap. 11.95 o.p. (*0-8161-4283-1*, Macmillan Reference USA) Gale Group.

—The Case of the Borrowed Brunette. 1987. 224p. mass mkt. 4.99 o.s.i (*0-345-34374-3*) Ballantine Bks.

—The Case of the Borrowed Brunette. 1976. pap. 1.95 o.p. (*0-671-80470-7*, Pocket) Simon & Schuster.

—The Case of the Buried Clock. 1976. 22.95 (*0-8488-0273-X*) Amereon, Ltd.

—The Case of the Buried Clock. 1997. mass mkt. 4.99 (*0-345-90799-X*); 1986. mass mkt. 3.95 o.s.i (*0-345-33691-7*); 1983. mass mkt. 4.99 o.s.i (*0-345-31013-6*, Ballantine Bks.) Ballantine Bks.

—The Case of the Buried Clock. l.t. ed. 1998. (Paperback Ser.). 312p. pap. 24.95 (*0-7838-0366-4*) Thorndike Pr.

—The Case of the Calendar Girl. 1976. 21.95 (*0-8488-0499-6*) Amereon, Ltd.

—The Case of the Calendar Girl. 1987. 224p. mass mkt. 4.99 o.s.i (*0-345-34375-1*) Ballantine Bks.

—The Case of the Careless Cupid. 1995. mass mkt. 4.99 o.s.i (*0-345-39226-4*) Ballantine Bks.

—The Case of the Careless Cupid. l.t. ed. 2003. (Dales Large Print Ser.). 304p. pap. 21.99 (*1-84262-216-1*) Dales Large Print Bks. GBR. *Dist:* Ulverscroft Large Print Bks., Ltd., Ulverscroft Large Print Canada, Ltd.

—The Case of the Careless Cupid. 1977. lib. bdg. 9.95 o.p. (*0-8161-6447-9*, Macmillan Reference USA) Gale Group.

—The Case of the Careless Kitten. 1976. 23.95 (*0-8488-0272-1*) Amereon, Ltd.

—The Case of the Careless Kitten. 1989. (Perry Mason Mysteries Ser.). 224p. mass mkt. 4.99 o.s.i (*0-345-36223-3*) Ballantine Bks.

—The Case of the Caretaker's Cat. 1976. (Perry Mason Bks.). reprint ed. lib. bdg. 24.95 (*0-88411-407-4*) Amereon, Ltd.

—The Case of the Caretaker's Cat. 1985. (Perry Mason Mysteries Ser.). reprint ed. mass mkt. 4.99 o.s.i (*0-345-32156-1*) Ballantine Bks.

—The Case of the Caretaker's Cat. l.t. ed. 1998. (Perry Mason Mysteries Ser.). 283p. 21.95 o.p. (*0-7838-8439-7*, Macmillan Reference USA) Gale Group.

—The Case of the Cautious Coquette. 1997. 18.95 (*0-88411-440-6*); 1976. 21.95 (*0-8488-0500-3*) Amereon, Ltd.

—The Case of the Cautious Coquette. l.t. ed. 1991. 19.95 o.p. (*0-7927-0847-4*, CSO189); pap. 17.95 o.p. (*0-7927-0848-2*) BBC Audiobooks America.

—The Case of the Cautious Coquette. 1988. 240p. reprint ed. mass mkt. 4.99 o.s.i (*0-345-35202-5*) Ballantine Bks.

—The Case of the Counterfeit Eye. 1976. (Perry Mason Books Ser.). reprint ed. lib. bdg. 24.95 (*0-88411-406-6*) Amereon, Ltd.

—The Case of the Counterfeit Eye. (*0-7540-3701-0*); 1999. 296 p. (*0-7540-3702-9*) BBC Audiobooks America.

—The Case of the Counterfeit Eye. (Perry Mason Mysteries Ser.). 1998. mass mkt. 4.99 (*0-345-91229-2*); 1986. 256p. mass mkt. 4.99 o.s.i (*0-345-33195-8*) Ballantine Bks.

—The Case of the Counterfeit Eye. 1974. pap. 0.95 o.p. (*0-671-77895-1*, Pocket) Simon & Schuster.

—The Case of the Counterfeit Eye. l.t. ed. 1999. (Paperback Ser.). 296p. pap. 23.95 o.p. (*0-7838-8522-9*) Thorndike Pr.

—The Case of the Crimson Kiss. 1972. pap. 0.95 o.p. (*0-671-77881-1*, Simon Pulse) Simon & Schuster Children's Publishing.

—The Case of the Crooked Candle. 1976. 21.95 (*0-8488-0275-6*) Amereon, Ltd.

—The Case of the Crooked Candle. l.t. ed. 1989. vi, 339 p. (*1-55504-787-4*) BBC Audiobooks America.

—The Case of the Crooked Candle. 1989. mass mkt. 3.99 o.p. (*0-345-01834-6*); 1987. mass mkt. 3.99 o.s.i (*0-345-34164-3*) Ballantine Bks.

—The Case of the Crooked Candle. 1976. (Crime Fiction Ser.). reprint ed. lib. bdg. 21.00 o.p. (*0-8240-2368-4*) Garland Publishing, Inc.

—The Case of the Crying Swallow: A Perry Mason Novelette & Other Stories. l.t. ed. 1987. (Nightingale Ser.). 295p. 11.95 o.p. (*0-8161-4284-X*, Macmillan Reference USA) Gale Group.

—The Case of the Curious Bride. 1976. (Perry Mason Bks.). reprint ed. lib. bdg. 23.95 (*0-88411-405-8*) Amereon, Ltd.

—The Case of the Curious Bride. (Perry Mason Mysteries Ser.). 2000. 192p. mass mkt. 5.99 o.s.i (*0-345-43783-7*, Fawcett); 1989. 224p. mass mkt. 4.99 o.s.i (*0-345-36222-5*) Ballantine Bks.

—The Case of the Curious Bride, abr. ed. 1992. audio 16.99 (*0-88646-300-9*, 7300) Durkin Hayes Publishing Ltd.

—The Case of the Curious Bride. l.t. ed. 2001. (G. K. Hall Paperback Ser.). 319p. pap. 24.95 (*0-7838-9432-5*); (*0-7540-4535-8*); (*0-7540-4536-6*) Gale Group. (Macmillan Reference USA).

—The Case of the Curious Bride. 1992. pap. 46.00 o.p. (*0-671-82708-1*, Pocket) Simon & Schuster.

—The Case of the Dangerous Dowager. 1976. (Perry Mason Bks.). reprint ed. lib. bdg. 19.95 (*0-88411-410-4*) Amereon, Ltd.

—The Case of the Dangerous Dowager. (Perry Mason Mysteries Ser.). 1998. mass mkt. 4.99 (*0-345-91231-4*); 1986. 224p. mass mkt. 4.99 o.s.i (*0-345-33192-3*) Ballantine Bks.

—The Case of the Dangerous Dowager. l.t. ed. 2000. (G. K. Hall Paperback Ser.). 299p. pap. 23.95 (0-7838-9225-X, Macmillan Reference USA) Gale Group.
—The Case of the Daring Decoy. 1989. (Perry Mason Mysteries Ser.). 224p. mass mkt. 4.99 o.s.i (0-345-36220-9) Ballantine Bks.
—The Case of the Daring Divorcee. 1984. 192p. mass mkt. 3.95 o.s.i (0-345-32003-4) Ballantine Bks.
—The Case of the Deadly Toy. (Perry Mason Mysteries Ser.). 224p. 2000. mass mkt. 6.99 (0-345-43784-5, Fawcett); 1985. mass mkt. 3.50 o.s.i (0-345-33494-9) Ballantine Bks.
—The Case of the Deadly Toy. 1981. 288p. reprint ed. lib. bdg. 18.00 (0-8376-0397-8) Bentley Pubs.
—The Case of the Deadly Toy. l.t. ed. 1993. (Nightingale Ser.). 378p. lib. bdg. 15.95 o.p. (0-8161-5632-8, Macmillan Reference USA) Gale Group.
—The Case of the Demure Defendant. 1991. 192p. mass mkt. 3.95 o.s.i (0-345-37148-8, Ballantine Bks.) Ballantine Bks.
—The Case of the Demure Defendant. l.t. ed. 1988. 336p. 15.95 o.p. (0-7089-1785-2, Ulverscroft) Thorpe, F. A. Pubs. GBR. *Dist:* Ulverscroft Large Print Bks., Ltd.
—The Case of the Drowning Duck. (Perry Mason Bks.). 284p. reprint ed. lib. bdg. 23.95 (0-88411-420-1) Amereon, Ltd.
—The Case of the Drowning Duck. l.t. ed. 1990. (Perry Mason Mystery Ser.). 21.95 o.p. (0-7927-0635-8, C0595); pap. 19.95 o.p. (0-7927-0636-6) BBC Audiobooks America.
—The Case of the Drowning Duck. 1993. reprint ed. mass mkt. 4.50 o.s.i (0-345-37868-7) Ballantine Bks.
—The Case of the Drowning Duck. 1976. pap. 1.95 o.p. (0-671-80281-X, Pocket) Simon & Schuster.
—The Case of the Drowsy Mosquito. 1976. 22.95 (0-8488-0274-8) Amereon, Ltd.
—The Case of the Drowsy Mosquito. 1994. reprint ed. mass mkt. 4.99 o.s.i (0-345-37869-5) Ballantine Bks.
—The Case of the Drowsy Mosquito. 1976. (Two-in-One Ser.). pap. 1.95 o.p. (0-671-80390-5, Pocket) Simon & Schuster.
—The Case of the Drowsy Mosquito. l.t. ed. 1978. 12.00 o.p. (0-7089-0235-9, Ulverscroft) Thorpe, F. A. Pubs. GBR. *Dist:* Ulverscroft Large Print Bks., Ltd.
—The Case of the Dubious Bridegroom. l.t. ed. 1994. 22.95 o.p. (0-7927-2103-9); pap. 21.95 o.p. (0-7927-2102-0) BBC Audiobooks America.
—The Case of the Dubious Bridegroom. 1986. 224p. mass mkt. 3.50 o.s.i (0-345-34186-4); 1984. mass mkt. 2.50 o.p. (0-345-31811-0); 1983. mass mkt. 4.99 o.s.i (0-345-30881-6) Ballantine Bks.
—The Case of the Duplicate Daughter. 1988. mass mkt. 3.50 o.s.i (0-345-35681-0) Ballantine Bks.
—The Case of the Duplicate Daughter. 1975. pap. 1.50 o.p. (0-671-78779-9, Pocket) Simon & Schuster.
—The Case of the Empty Tin. (Perry Mason Bks.). 282p. reprint ed. lib. bdg. 23.95 (0-88411-419-8) Amereon, Ltd.
—The Case of the Empty Tin. 1985. 240p. mass mkt. 4.99 o.s.i (0-345-33198-2); 1996. reprint ed. mass mkt. 4.99 (0-345-90798-1) Ballantine Bks.
—The Case of the Empty Tin. l.t. ed. 1979. (Ulverscroft Large Print Ser.). 12.00 o.p. (0-7089-0244-8, Ulverscroft) Thorpe, F. A. Pubs. GBR. *Dist:* Ulverscroft Large Print Bks., Ltd., Ulverscroft Large Print Canada, Ltd.
—The Case of the Fabulous Fake. l.t. ed. 1990. (Perry Mason Mystery Ser.). pap. 10.95 o.p. (0-89340-024-6, C0148) BBC Audiobooks America.
—The Case of the Fabulous Fake. 1986. mass mkt. 3.95 o.s.i (0-345-33548-1) Ballantine Bks.
—The Case of the Fabulous Fake. 1969. 7.95 o.p. (0-688-01276-0, Morrow, William & Co.) Morrow/Avon.
—The Case of the Fan-Dancer's Horse. 1992. reprint ed. mass mkt. 4.99 o.s.i (0-345-37144-5) Ballantine Bks.
—The Case of the Fan-Dancer's Horse & the Case of the Hesitant Hostess. 1977. pap. 1.95 o.p. (0-671-81386-2, Pocket) Simon & Schuster.
—The Case of the Fenced-In Woman. 1994. (Perry Mason Mysteries Ser.). 224p. mass mkt. 5.99 o.s.i (0-345-39223-X) Ballantine Bks.
—The Case of the Fiery Fingers. 1987. mass mkt. 3.50 o.s.i (0-345-35161-4) Ballantine Bks.
—The Case of the Fiery Fingers. 1975. pap. 1.50 o.p. (0-671-78783-7, Pocket) Simon & Schuster.
—The Case of the Foot-Loose Doll. 1986. 208p. mass mkt. 5.99 (0-345-33636-4); 1983. mass mkt. 2.50 o.p. (0-345-31273-2); Vol. 1. 1999. mass mkt. 4.99 (0-345-91479-1) Ballantine Bks.
—The Case of the Foot-Loose Doll. l.t. ed. 1989. (G. K. Hall Large Print Book Ser.). 320p. 13.95 o.p. (0-8161-4788-4, Macmillan Reference USA) Gale Group.
—The Case of the Foot-Loose Doll. 1975. pap. 24.95 o.p. (0-671-78787-X, Atria) Simon & Schuster.
—The Case of the Fugitive Nurse. 1993. mass mkt. 4.99 o.s.i (0-345-37873-3) Ballantine Bks.
—The Case of the Gilded Lily. l.t. ed. 1991. 8.95 o.p. (1-55504-899-4, 16) BBC Audiobooks America.
—The Case of the Gilded Lily. 1999. mass mkt. 4.99 (0-345-91480-5); 1985. 199p. mass mkt. 5.99 o.s.i (0-345-32318-1) Ballantine Bks.
—The Case of the Gilded Lily. 1981. (Perry Mason Mysteries Ser.). 256p. reprint ed. lib. bdg. 18.00 (0-8376-0396-X) Bentley Pubs.
—The Case of the Glamorous Ghost. l.t. ed. 1992. pap. 20.95 o.p. (0-7927-1044-4, CS0279); 1991. 22.95 o.p. (0-7927-1043-6, CH0211) BBC Audiobooks America.
—The Case of the Glamorous Ghost. 240p. 2000. mass mkt. 5.99 (0-345-43786-1, Fawcett); 1986. mass mkt. 3.95 o.s.i (0-345-34440-5) Ballantine Bks.
—The Case of the Glamorous Ghost. 1977. pap. 1.95 o.p. (0-671-81691-8, Pocket) Simon & Schuster.
—The Case of the Golddigger's Purse. 1997. mass mkt. 4.99 (0-345-90800-7); 1984. 224p. mass mkt. 4.99 o.s.i (0-345-31680-0, Ballantine Bks.) Ballantine Bks.
—The Case of the Golddigger's Purse. l.t. ed. 2002. 370p. pap. 25.95 (0-7862-4251-5) Gale Group.
—The Case of the Green-Eyed Sister. 1978. xii, 426p. (0-89340-140-4) BBC Audiobooks America.
—The Case of the Green-Eyed Sister. 1993. mass mkt. 4.50 o.s.i (0-345-37872-5) Ballantine Bks.
—The Case of the Green-Eyed Sister. 1975. pap. 1.50 o.p. (0-671-80074-4, Pocket) Simon & Schuster.
—The Case of the Grinning Gorilla. 1986. mass mkt. 2.95 o.s.i (0-345-34187-2) Ballantine Bks.
—The Case of the Grinning Gorilla. 1973. pap. 0.95 o.p. (0-671-77889-7, Star Trek) Simon & Schuster.
—The Case of the Half-Wakened Wife. 1991. 256p. mass mkt. 4.99 o.s.i (0-345-37147-X, Ballantine Bks.) Ballantine Bks.
—The Case of the Haunted Husband. 281p. reprint ed. lib. bdg. 23.95 (0-88411-418-X) Amereon, Ltd.
—The Case of the Haunted Husband. 1986. vii, 374 p. (1-55504-067-5) BBC Audiobooks America.
—The Case of the Haunted Husband. 1985. 208p. mass mkt. 4.99 o.s.i (0-345-33495-7) Ballantine Bks.
—The Case of the Haunted Husband. abr. ed. 1991. 2p. audio 16.99 (0-88646-299-1) Durkin Hayes Publishing Ltd.
—The Case of the Hesitant Hostess. 1993. mass mkt. 4.50 o.s.i (0-345-37871-7) Ballantine Bks.
—The Case of the Hesitant Hostess. l.t. ed. 1991. 377p. pap. 15.95 o.p. (0-8161-5064-8, Macmillan Reference USA) Gale Group.
—The Case of the Horrified Heirs. 1995. 192p. mass mkt. 5.99 (0-345-39227-2); pap. 15.00 (0-345-47043-5) Ballantine Bks.
—The Case of the Howling Dog. 1976. (Perry Mason Bks.). reprint ed. lib. bdg. 24.95 (0-88411-404-X) Amereon, Ltd.
—The Case of the Howling Dog. 1987. mass mkt. 4.99 o.s.i (0-345-34783-8); 1984. mass mkt. 2.50 o.p. (0-345-31679-7) Ballantine Bks.
—The Case of the Howling Dog. l.t. ed. 1999. (Paperback Ser.). 279p. pap. 23.95 (0-7838-8775-2, Macmillan Reference USA) Gale Group.
—The Case of the Ice-Cold Hands. 1989. mass mkt. 3.95 o.s.i (0-345-35939-9) Ballantine Bks.
—The Case of the Ice-Cold Hands. 1980. (General Ser.). lib. bdg. 11.95 o.p. (0-8161-3174-0, Macmillan Reference USA) Gale Group.
—The Case of the Irate Witness. 1973. pap. 0.95 o.p. (0-671-77883-8, Pocket) Simon & Schuster.
—The Case of the Lame Canary. (Perry Mason Bks.). 281p. reprint ed. lib. bdg. 23.95 (0-88411-411-2) Amereon, Ltd.
—The Case of the Lame Canary. 1996. mass mkt. 4.99 (0-345-90796-5); 1987. 256p. mass mkt. 4.99 o.s.i (0-345-35162-2); 1984. mass mkt. 2.50 o.s.i (0-345-31547-2) Ballantine Bks.
—The Case of the Lazy Lover. l.t. ed. 1982. vii, 438 p. (0-89340-362-8) BBC Audiobooks America.
—The Case of the Lazy Lover. 1997. mass mkt. 4.99 (0-345-90801-5); 1987. mass mkt. 2.95 o.s.i (0-345-35007-3); 1981. mass mkt. 4.99 o.s.i (0-345-29496-3) Ballantine Bks.
—The Case of the Lazy Lover. l.t. ed. 1997. 21.95 (0-7838-8348-X, Macmillan Reference USA) Gale Group.
—The Case of the Lazy Lover. abr. ed. 1989. audio 14.95 (1-55800-119-0, 40460, Dove Audio) NewStar Media, Inc.
—The Case of the Lonely Heiress. (Perry Mason Mysteries Ser.). 1997. mass mkt. 4.99 (0-345-90802-3); 1986. 224p. mass mkt. 3.95 o.s.i (0-345-34012-4); 1984. mass mkt. 2.50 o.p. (0-345-31797-1); 1983. 224p. mass mkt. 5.99 o.s.i (0-345-31012-8, Ballantine Bks.) Ballantine Bks.
—The Case of the Lonely Heiress. l.t. ed. 2001. 216p. pap. 24.95 (0-7838-9506-2, Macmillan Reference USA) Gale Group.
—The Case of the Lonely Heiress. 1973. pap. 0.95 o.p. (0-671-77886-2, Atria) Simon & Schuster.
—The Case of the Long-Legged Models. 1994. mass mkt. 4.99 o.s.i (0-345-37876-8) Ballantine Bks.
—The Case of the Long-Legged Models. 1971. pap. 0.75 o.p. (0-671-75556-0, Pimsleur) Simon & Schuster Audio.
—The Case of the Lucky Legs. 1976. (Perry Mason Bks.). reprint ed. lib. bdg. 23.95 (0-88411-403-1) Amereon, Ltd.
—The Case of the Lucky Legs. 1999. (0-7540-3827-0); (0-7540-3826-2) BBC Audiobooks America.
—The Case of the Lucky Legs. 1990. (Perry Mason Mysteries Ser.: No. 58). 224p. mass mkt. 3.95 o.s.i (0-345-36927-0) Ballantine Bks.
—The Case of the Lucky Legs. 1973. pap. 0.95 o.p. (0-671-77891-9, Simon & Schuster Audioworks) Simon & Schuster Audio.
—The Case of the Lucky Legs. l.t. ed. 1999. (G. K. Hall Paperback Ser.). 320p. pap. 23.95 (0-7838-8612-8) Thorndike Pr.
—The Case of the Lucky Loser. l.t. ed. 1991. 12.95 o.p. (0-7927-0227-1, 4764); 1990. pap. 17.95 o.p. (0-7927-0228-X, C0247) BBC Audiobooks America.
—The Case of the Lucky Loser. 1990. 192p. mass mkt. 4.99 o.s.i (0-345-36497-X) Ballantine Bks.
—The Case of the Mischievous Doll. 1989. mass mkt. 4.99 o.s.i (0-345-35940-2) Ballantine Bks.
—The Case of the Mischievous Doll. 1981. (General Ser.). lib. bdg. 11.95 o.p. (0-8161-3215-1, Macmillan Reference USA) Gale Group.
—The Case of the Moth-Eaten Mink. 1990. (Perry Mason Mysteries Ser.: No. 57). 240p. mass mkt. 3.95 o.p. (0-345-36928-9) Ballantine Bks.
—The Case of the Moth-Eaten Mink. l.t. ed. 1992. (General Ser.). 365p. lib. bdg. 19.95 o.p. (0-8161-5063-X, Macmillan Reference USA) Gale Group.
—The Case of the Moth-Eaten Mink. 1971. pap. 0.75 o.p. (0-671-75539-0, Star Trek) Simon & Schuster.
—The Case of the Mythical Monkeys. 1984. mass mkt. 3.95 o.s.i (0-345-31404-2) Ballantine Bks.
—The Case of the Mythical Monkeys. 1981. 288p. reprint ed. lib. bdg. 18.00 (0-8376-0398-6) Bentley Pubs.
—The Case of the Mythical Monkeys. l.t. ed. 1993. 13.95 o.p. (0-8161-3384-0, Macmillan Reference USA) Gale Group.
—The Case of the Negligent Nymph. 1986. 176p. mass mkt. 3.95 o.s.i (0-345-34013-2) Ballantine Bks.
—The Case of the Negligent Nymph. 1973. pap. 0.95 o.p. (0-671-77892-7, Pocket) Simon & Schuster.
—The Case of the Nervous Accomplice. 1992. mass mkt. 3.99 o.s.i (0-345-37874-1) Ballantine Bks.
—The Case of the Nervous Accomplice. 1974. pap. 0.95 o.p. (0-671-77926-5, Pocket) Simon & Schuster.
—The Case of the One-Eyed Witness. 1995. 240p. mass mkt. 5.99 (0-345-39225-6) Ballantine Bks.
—The Case of the One-Eyed Witness. l.t. ed. 1990. pap. 15.95 o.p. (0-8161-5062-1, Macmillan Reference USA) Gale Group.
—The Case of the One-Eyed Witness. 1971. pap. 0.75 o.p. (0-671-75536-6, Star Trek) Simon & Schuster.
—The Case of the Perjured Parrot. (Perry Mason Bks.). 288p. reprint ed. lib. bdg. 23.95 (0-88411-414-7) Amereon, Ltd.
—The Case of the Perjured Parrot. (Perry Mason Mysteries Ser.). 1987. mass mkt. 4.99 o.s.i (0-345-34685-8); 1982. mass mkt. 2.25 o.p. (0-345-30396-2) Ballantine Bks.
—The Case of the Perjured Parrot. l.t. ed. 2001. 253p. (0-7540-4401-7); (0-7540-4402-5) Gale Group. (Macmillan Reference USA).
—The Case of the Perjured Parrot. 1975. pap. 1.50 o.p. (0-671-78944-9, Pocket) Simon & Schuster.
—The Case of the Perjured Parrot. l.t. ed. 2001. (G. K. Hall Nightingale Ser.). 253p. pap. 23.95 (0-7838-9322-1) Thorndike Pr.
—The Case of the Phantom Fortune. 1986. mass mkt. 3.50 o.s.i (0-345-33191-5) Ballantine Bks.
—The Case of the Phantom Fortune. l.t. ed. 1984. (Nightingale Ser.). 9.95 o.p. (0-8161-3754-4, Macmillan Reference USA) Gale Group.
—The Case of the Phantom Fortune. 1974. pap. 0.95 o.p. (0-671-77896-X, Pocket) Simon & Schuster.
—The Case of the Postponed Murder. 1995. mass mkt. 4.99 o.s.i (0-345-39229-9) Ballantine Bks.
—The Case of the Postponed Murder. 1973. (General Ser.). reprint ed. lib. bdg. 8.95 o.p. (0-8161-6090-2, Macmillan Reference USA) Gale Group.
—The Case of the Postponed Murder. 1973. 7.95 o.p. (0-688-00033-9, Morrow, William & Co.) Morrow/Avon.
—The Case of the Postponed Murder. 1974. pap. 0.95 o.p. (0-671-77894-3, Pocket) Simon & Schuster.
—The Case of the Queenly Contestant. l.t. ed. 1990. (Perry Mason Mystery Ser.). pap. 18.95 o.p. (0-89340-025-4, C0160) BBC Audiobooks America.
—The Case of the Queenly Contestant. 1993. reprint ed. mass mkt. 4.50 o.s.i (0-345-37879-2) Ballantine Bks.
—The Case of the Reluctant Model. 1990. 208p. mass mkt. 3.95 o.s.i (0-345-36689-1) Ballantine Bks.
—The Case of the Reluctant Model. abr. ed. audio 16.99 (0-88646-301-7, DHA7301); 2000. audio 19.99 (0-88646-558-3, DHA-6558) Durkin Hayes Publishing Ltd.
—The Case of the Restless Redhead. 1980. xiv, 435 p. (0-89340-261-3) BBC Audiobooks America.
—The Case of the Restless Redhead. 1985. mass mkt. 3.95 o.s.i (0-345-33199-0) Ballantine Bks.
—The Case of the Rolling Bones. (Perry Mason Bks.). 288p. reprint ed. lib. bdg. 23.95 (0-88411-415-5) Amereon, Ltd.
—The Case of the Rolling Bones. 1999. 4.99 (0-345-91481-3); 1985. 208p. reprint ed. mass mkt. 4.99 o.s.i (0-345-32979-1) Ballantine Bks.
—The Case of the Rolling Bones. l.t. ed. 1986. (Nightingale Ser.). 350p. 11.95 o.p. (0-8161-4080-4, Macmillan Reference USA) Gale Group.
—The Case of the Rolling Bones. 1976. (Two-in-One Ser.). pap. 1.95 o.p. (0-671-80583-5, Pocket) Simon & Schuster.
—The Case of the Runaway Corpse. 1990. 224p. mass mkt. 4.99 o.s.i (0-345-36498-8) Ballantine Bks.
—The Case of the Runaway Corpse. l.t. ed. 1988. lib. bdg. 14.95 o.p. (1-85057-453-7, Macmillan Reference USA) Gale Group.
—The Case of the Screaming Woman. l.t. ed. 1992. pap. 18.95 o.p. (0-7927-0969-1) BBC Audiobooks America.
—The Case of the Screaming Woman. 1994. mass mkt. 4.99 o.s.i (0-345-37875-X); 1992. 20.95 o.p. (0-7927-1228-5, CH0260) Ballantine Bks.
—The Case of the Shapely Shadow. 1986. mass mkt. 3.50 o.s.i (0-345-33496-5) Ballantine Bks.
—The Case of the Shoplifter's Shoe. (Perry Mason Bks.). 312p. reprint ed. lib. bdg. 24.95 (0-88411-413-9) Amereon, Ltd.
—The Case of the Shoplifter's Shoe. 1998. mass mkt. 4.99 (0-345-91233-0); 1986. 224p. mass mkt. 5.99 o.s.i (0-345-32943-0) Ballantine Bks.
—The Case of the Shoplifter's Shoe. 1973. pap. 0.95 o.p. (0-671-77888-9, Pocket) Simon & Schuster.
—The Case of the Silent Partner. (Perry Mason Bks.). reprint ed. lib. bdg. 23.95 (0-88411-417-1) Amereon, Ltd.
—The Case of the Silent Partner. 1999. 4.99 (0-345-91482-1); 1986. 224p. mass mkt. 4.99 o.s.i (0-345-33684-4) Ballantine Bks.
—The Case of the Silent Partner. 2003. (Paperback Ser.). pap. 25.95 (0-7862-5047-X) Thorndike Pr.
—The Case of the Singing Skirt. 1992. mass mkt. 3.99 o.s.i (0-345-37149-6) Ballantine Bks.
—The Case of the Singing Skirt. 1981. 256p. reprint ed. 18.00 (0-8376-0399-4) Bentley Pubs.
—The Case of the Singing Skirt. l.t. ed. 1988. (Nightingale Ser.). 183p. 12.95 o.p. (0-8161-4515-6, Macmillan Reference USA) Gale Group.
—The Case of the Sleepwalker's Niece. 1976. (Perry Mason Bks.). reprint ed. lib. bdg. 21.95 (0-88411-408-2) Amereon, Ltd.
—The Case of the Sleepwalker's Niece. 1991. (Perry Mason Mysteries Ser.). mass mkt. 3.99 o.s.i (0-345-37146-1, Ballantine Bks.) Ballantine Bks.
—The Case of the Sleepwalker's Niece. l.t. ed. 1993. (Nightingale Ser.). 344p. 14.95 o.p. (0-8161-5633-6, Macmillan Reference USA) Gale Group.
—The Case of the Sleepwalker's Niece. 1973. pap. 0.95 o.p. (0-671-77893-5, Pocket) Simon & Schuster.
—The Case of the Smoking Chimney. l.t. ed. 1990. (Nightingale Ser.). 12.95 o.p. (0-8161-4789-2, Macmillan Reference USA) Gale Group.
—The Case of the Spurious Spinster. 1988. mass mkt. 3.50 o.s.i (0-345-35203-3) Ballantine Bks.
—The Case of the Stepdaughter's Secret. 1989. (Perry Mason Mysteries Ser.). 192p. mass mkt. 3.95 o.s.i (0-345-36221-7) Ballantine Bks.
—The Case of the Stepdaughter's Secret. l.t. ed. 1985. (Nightingale Ser.). 288p. 9.95 o.p. (0-8161-3753-6, Macmillan Reference USA) Gale Group.
—The Case of the Stepdaughter's Secret. 1977. pap. 1.95 o.p. (0-671-80968-7, Pocket) Simon & Schuster.
—The Case of the Stuttering Bishop. 1976. (Perry Mason Bks.). reprint ed. lib. bdg. 23.95 (0-88411-409-0) Amereon, Ltd.
—The Case of the Stuttering Bishop. l.t. ed. 1994. 21.95 o.p. (0-7927-1907-7); pap. 19.95 o.p. (0-7927-1906-9) BBC Audiobooks America.
—The Case of the Stuttering Bishop. 1998. mass mkt. 4.99 (0-345-91230-6); 1988. 192p. mass mkt. 6.99 (0-345-35680-2) Ballantine Bks.
—The Case of the Substitute Face. (Perry Mason Bks.). 310p. reprint ed. lib. bdg. 24.95 (0-88411-412-0) Amereon, Ltd.
—The Case of the Substitute Face. l.t. ed. 1993. 22.95 o.p. (0-7927-1562-4); pap. 20.95 o.p. (0-7927-1561-6) BBC Audiobooks America.
—The Case of the Substitute Face. (Perry Mason Mysteries Ser.). 1998. mass mkt. 4.99 (0-345-91232-2); 1987. pap. o.s.i (0-345-01849-4); 1987. 256p. mass mkt. 4.99 o.s.i (0-345-34377-8) Ballantine Bks.

Characters

—The Case of the Substitute Face. 1974. pap. 1.25 o.p. (0-671-78448-X, Pocket) Simon & Schuster.
—The Case of the Sulky Girl. 1976. (Perry Mason Books Ser.). reprint ed. lib. bdg. 24.95 (0-88411-402-3) Amereon, Ltd.
—The Case of the Sulky Girl. 1992. mass mkt. 4.99 o.s.i (0-345-37145-3) Ballantine Bks.
—The Case of the Sulky Girl, unabr. ed. 1991. (Listen for Pleasure Ser.). audio 16.99 (0-88646-298-3, LFP 7298) Durkin Hayes Publishing Ltd.
—The Case of the Sun Bather's Diary. 1995. 244p. pap. 15.00 (0-345-47042-7, Fawcett); 1985. 208p. mass mkt. 2.95 o.s.i (0-345-33503-1) Ballantine Bks.
—The Case of the Sun Bather's Diary. 1971. pap. 1.25 o.p. (0-671-82704-9, Pocket) Simon & Schuster.
—The Case of the Sun Bather's Diary. l.t. ed. 2001. (Paperback Ser.). 328p. 24.95 (0-7838-9338-8) Thorndike Pr.
—The Case of the Sun Bather's Diary: A Perry Mason Mystery. 2000. (Perry Mason Mysteries Ser.). 240p. mass mkt. 5.99 (0-345-43788-8, Fawcett) Ballantine Bks.
—The Case of the Terrified Typist. 1999. 4.99 (0-345-91483-X); 1987. 192p. mass mkt. 5.99 o.s.i (0-345-34165-1) Ballantine Bks.
—The Case of the Terrified Typist. l.t. ed. 1989. 296p. 14.95 o.p. (0-8161-4514-8, Macmillan Reference USA) Gale Group.
—The Case of the Terrified Typist. 1975. pap. 1.50 o.p. (0-671-78780-2, Simon Pulse) Simon & Schuster Children's Publishing.
—The Case of the Troubled Trustee. 1995. mass mkt. 4.99 o.s.i (0-345-39224-8) Ballantine Bks.
—The Case of the Vagabond Virgin. l.t. ed. 1990. pap. 17.95 o.p. (0-7927-0534-3, C0794); 19.95 o.p. (0-7927-0533-5, C0286) BBC Audiobooks America.
—The Case of the Vagabond Virgin. 1997. pap. 4.99 (0-345-90803-1); 1986. mass mkt. 3.50 o.s.i (0-345-34319-0); 1982. mass mkt. 4.99 o.s.i (0-345-30393-8) Ballantine Bks.
—The Case of the Vagabond Virgin. 1973. pap. 0.95 o.p. (0-671-77885-4, Simon Pulse) Simon & Schuster Children's Publishing.
—The Case of the Velvet Claws. 1976. (Perry Mason Books Ser.). reprint ed. lib. bdg. 24.95 (0-88411-401-5) Amereon, Ltd.
—The Case of the Velvet Claws. 1996. mass mkt. 4.99 (0-345-90793-0); 1985. 224p. mass mkt. 5.99 o.s.i (0-345-32317-3) Ballantine Bks.
—The Case of the Velvet Claws. 2002. (Best Mysteries of All Time Ser.). 261p. (0-7621-8878-2, IM Pr.) Reader's Digest Assn., Inc., The.
—The Case of the Waylaid Wolf. 1990. (Perry Mason Mysteries Ser.). 208p. mass mkt. 3.95 o.s.i (0-345-36690-5) Ballantine Bks.
—The Case of the Waylaid Wolf. 1976. pap. 1.95 o.p. (0-671-80860-5, Pocket) Simon & Schuster.
—The Case of the Worried Waitress. 1986. 160p. mass mkt. 2.95 o.s.i (0-345-33193-1) Ballantine Bks.
—Perry Mason: Seven Complete Novels. 19th ed. 1994. 832p. 13.99 o.s.i (0-517-29363-3) Random Hse. Value Publishing.

**MASON, TOM (FICTITIOUS CHARACTER)—FICTION**

Zubro, Mark Richard. Are You Nuts? (Tom & Scott Mystery Ser.). 256p. 1999. pap. 12.95 (0-312-20634-8, Saint Martin's Griffin); 1998. 21.95 (0-312-18528-6, Saint Martin's Minotaur) St. Martin's Pr.
—An Echo of Death: A Tom & Scott Mystery. (Tom & Scott Mystery Ser.). 1995. 208p. pap. 11.95 (0-312-13480-0, Saint Martin's Griffin); 1994. 192p. 18.95 o.p. (0-312-11268-8, Saint Martin's Minotaur) St. Martin's Pr.
—Here Comes the Corpse. 2002. (Tom & Scott Mystery Ser.: No. 9). 256p. 23.95 (0-312-28098-X, Saint Martin's Minotaur) St. Martin's Pr.
—One Dead Drag Queen. E-Book 22.95 (0-312-27586-2); 2001. 256p. pap. 12.95 (0-312-27702-4, Saint Martin's Griffin); 2000. 256p. 22.95 o.s.i (0-312-20937-1, Saint Martin's Minotaur) St. Martin's Pr.
—The Only Good Priest. (Tom & Scott Mystery Ser.). 1992. 192p. pap. 10.95 (0-312-07054-3, Saint Martin's Griffin); 1991. 8.99 o.p. (0-312-05486-6, Saint Martin's Minotaur) St. Martin's Pr.
—The Principal Cause of Death. (Tom & Scott Mystery Ser.). 1993. 192p. pap. 11.95 (0-312-09896-0, Saint Martin's Griffin); 1992. 208p. 11.99 o.p. (0-312-07767-X, Saint Martin's Minotaur) St. Martin's Pr.
—Rust on the Razor. (Tom & Scott Mystery Ser.). 224p. 1997. pap. 11.95 (0-312-15644-8, Saint Martin's Griffin); 1996. text 20.95 o.p. (0-312-14404-0, Saint Martin's Minotaur) St. Martin's Pr.
—A Simple Suburban Murder. (Stonewall Inn Editions Ser.). 1990. 6.50 o.p. (0-312-03887-9, Saint Martin's Minotaur); 1990. 224p. pap. 8.95 (0-312-03933-6, Saint Martin's Griffin); 1989. 224p. 15.95 o.p. (0-312-02640-4, Saint Martin's Minotaur) St. Martin's Pr.
—Why Isn't Becky Twitchell Dead? 1970. 208p. 15.00 o.p. (0-312-03955-7) Palgrave Macmillan.
—Why Isn't Becky Twitchell Dead? 1991. (Stonewall Inn Editions Ser.). 189p. pap. 12.95 (0-312-05996-5, Saint Martin's Griffin) St. Martin's Pr.

**MASTERS, CAROLINE (FICTITIOUS CHARACTER)—FICTION**

Patterson, Richard North. Degree of Guilt. 1998. pap. 7.99 (0-345-91454-6); 1997. pap. 12.00 o.s.i (0-345-41811-5); 1992. mass mkt. o.s.i (0-345-38408-3); 1993. 544p. reprint ed. mass mkt. 7.99 (0-345-38184-X) Ballantine Bks.
—Degree of Guilt. unabr. collector's ed. 1994. audio 104.00 (0-7366-2612-3, 3354) Books on Tape, Inc.
—Degree of Guilt. unabr. ed. 1993. audio 16.00 o.s.i (0-679-42131-9); Set. 1994. audio 8.99 o.s.i (0-679-43409-7) Random Hse. Audio Publishing Group. (RH Audio).
—Degree of Guilt. l.t. ed. 1993. 25.00 o.s.i (0-679-42211-0) Random Hse., Inc.
—Eyes of a Child. 1998. pap. 7.99 (0-345-91463-5); 1997. pap. 12.00 o.s.i (0-345-41813-1); 1995. 576p. mass mkt. 7.99 (0-345-38613-2); 1995. mass mkt. 6.99 o.s.i (0-345-40007-0); 1994. mass mkt. o.p. (0-345-39526-3) Ballantine Bks.
—Eyes of a Child. abr. ed. 2003. audio compact disk 14.99 (0-7393-0377-5, RH Audio Price-Less); 1995. audio 17.00 o.s.i (0-679-43952-8, RH Audio); Set. 1997. audio 8.99 o.s.i (0-679-46021-7, RH Audio) Random Hse. Audio Publishing Group.
—Eyes of a Child. l.t. ed. 1995. pap. 23.00 o.s.i (0-679-76031-8) Random Hse., Inc.
—The Final Judgment. 1998. pap. 7.99 (0-345-91462-7); 1996. 512p. mass mkt. 7.99 o.s.i (0-345-40761-X) Ballantine Bks.
—The Final Judgment. 1996. mass mkt. o.s.i (0-345-40498-X) Ballantine Bks. of Canada.
—The Final Judgment. l.t. ed. 1995. 640p. 25.95 o.p. (0-7838-1581-6, Macmillan Reference USA) Gale Group.
—The Final Judgment. 1995. 400p. 25.00 o.s.i (0-679-42989-1) Knopf, Alfred A. Inc.
—The Final Judgment, Set. abr. ed. 1998. audio 8.99 o.s.i (0-375-40299-3); 1995. audio 18.00 o.s.i (0-679-44765-2, 393153) Random Hse. Audio Publishing Group. (RH Audio).
—The Final Judgment: A Novel. l.t. ed. 1995. 640p. pap. 25.00 (0-679-76666-9) Random Hse. Large Print.

**MASTERS, CHUCK (FICTITIOUS CHARACTER)—FICTION**

McBain, Ed, pseud. Death of a Nurse. 1991. 192p. mass mkt. 4.50 (0-380-71125-7, Avon Bks.) Morrow/Avon.
—Death of a Nurse. 1982. mass mkt. 2.25 o.p. (0-451-11519-8); 1976. mass mkt. 1.25 o.p. (0-451-06903-X) NAL. (Signet Bks.).

**MASTERS, GEORGE, DETECTIVE SUPERINTENDENT (FICTITIOUS CHARACTER)—FICTION**

Clark, Douglas. The Big Grouse: A Masters & Green Mystery. 1987. 224p. 18.95 o.p. (0-575-03909-4) Gollancz, Victor GBR. Dist: Trafalgar Square.
—The Big Grouse: A Masters & Green Mystery. 1988. 272p. reprint ed. pap. 3.95 o.p. (0-06-080918-3, P-918, Perennial) HarperTrade.
—Bitter Water: A Masters & Green Mystery. 1990. 256p. (Orig.). pap. 4.95 o.p. (0-06-081024-6, Perennial) HarperTrade.
—Bouquet Garni. l.t. ed. 1986. 368p. 12.50 o.p. (0-7089-1415-2, Ulverscroft) Thorpe, F. A. Pubs. GBR. Dist: Ulverscroft Large Print Bks., Ltd.
—Dead Letter: A Masters & Green Mystery. l.t. ed. 1989. (Ulverscroft Large Print Ser.). 379p. 29.99 o.p. (0-7089-1972-3, Ulverscroft) Thorpe, F. A. Pubs. GBR. Dist: Ulverscroft Large Print Bks., Ltd., Ulverscroft Large Print Canada, Ltd.
—Doone Walk. l.t. ed. 1987. (Linford Mystery Library). 336p. pap. 17.99 o.p. (0-7089-6394-3, Linford) Thorpe, F. A. Pubs. GBR. Dist: Ulverscroft Large Print Bks., Ltd., Ulverscroft Large Print Canada, Ltd.
—Dread & Water. l.t. ed. 1991. 17.95 o.p. (0-7451-9999-2, AH035); pap. 15.95 o.p. (0-7927-0463-0, AS071) BBC Audiobooks America.
—The Gimmel Flask. 1982. (Murder Ink Mystery Ser.: No. 41). pap. 2.25 o.p. (0-440-13160-X) Dell Publishing.
—Golden Rain. 1982. (Murder Ink Mystery Ser.: No. 47). 224p. pap. 2.50 o.p. (0-440-12932-X) Dell Publishing.
—Heberden's Seat. l.t. ed. 1991. 17.95 o.p. (0-7451-8118-X, AH0167); pap. 15.95 o.p. (0-7927-0618-8, AS0203) BBC Audiobooks America.
—Heberden's Seat. 1985. 192p. mass mkt. 3.50 o.p. (0-06-080724-5, P724, Perennial) HarperTrade.
—Jewelled Eye: A Masters & Green Mystery. l.t. ed. 1987. pap. 13.95 o.p. (1-55504-251-1) BBC Audiobooks America.
—Jewelled Eye: A Masters & Green Mystery. 1986. 189p. 17.95 o.p. (0-575-03728-8) Gollancz, Victor GBR. Dist: Trafalgar Square.
—Jewelled Eye: A Masters & Green Mystery. 1988. 272p. reprint ed. pap. 3.95 o.p. (0-06-080919-1, P-919, Perennial) HarperTrade.
—The Longest Pleasure. 1984. 192p. reprint ed. pap. 2.95 o.p. (0-06-080689-3, P689) HarperCollins Pubs.
—The Monday Theory. 1985. 208p. mass mkt. 3.50 o.p. (0-06-080737-7, P737, Perennial) HarperTrade.
—Nobody's Perfect. l.t. ed. (Atlantic Mystery Ser.). pap. 8.95 o.p. (1-55504-561-8, 844) BBC Audiobooks America.
—Nobody's Perfect. 1986. 192p. reprint ed. mass mkt. 3.50 o.p. (0-06-080796-2, P 796, Perennial) HarperTrade.
—Performance. 1986. 224p. reprint ed. mass mkt. 3.50 o.p. (0-06-080810-1, P 810, Perennial) HarperTrade.
—Plain Sailing: A Masters & Green Mystery. 1988. 272p. reprint ed. pap. 3.95 o.p. (0-06-080917-5, P-917, Perennial) HarperTrade.
—Plain Sailing: A Masters & Green Mystery. l.t. ed. 1989. (Ulverscroft Large Print Ser.). 384p. 29.99 o.p. (0-7089-2008-X, Ulverscroft) Thorpe, F. A. Pubs. GBR. Dist: Ulverscroft Large Print Bks., Ltd., Ulverscroft Large Print Canada, Ltd.
—Poacher's Bag. l.t. ed. 1989. (Atlantic Mystery Ser.). pap. 14.95 o.p. (1-55504-716-5, 149) BBC Audiobooks America.
—Poacher's Bag. 1983. 176p. pap. o.p. (0-06-080643-5, P 643) HarperCollins Pubs.
—Roast Eggs. 1983. 176p. pap. o.p. (0-06-080644-3, P 644) HarperCollins Pubs.
—Shelf Life. l.t. ed. 1992. 18.95 o.p. (0-7451-8252-6, AH0262); pap. 16.95 o.p. (0-7927-0812-1, AS0298) BBC Audiobooks America.
—Shelf Life. 1983. 176p. pap. o.p. (0-06-080675-3, P675) HarperCollins Pubs.
—Sick to Death. l.t. ed. 1990. 17.95 o.p. (0-7451-9897-X, C0628); pap. 15.95 o.p. (0-7927-0360-X, C0822) BBC Audiobooks America.
—Sick to Death. 1983. 176p. pap. o.p. (0-06-080676-1, P676) HarperCollins Pubs.
—Storm Centre. 1986. 18.95 o.p. (0-575-03833-0) Gollancz, Victor GBR. Dist: Trafalgar Square.
—Storm Centre. 1988. (Master & Green Mystery Ser.). 240p. reprint ed. pap. 3.95 o.p. (0-06-080920-5, P-920, Perennial) HarperTrade.
—Storm Centre. l.t. ed. 1987. (Linford Mystery Library). 368p. pap. 17.99 o.p. (0-7089-6388-9, Linford) Thorpe, F. A. Pubs. GBR. Dist: Ulverscroft Large Print Bks., Ltd., Ulverscroft Large Print Canada, Ltd.
—Table d'Hote. 1985. 208p. mass mkt. 3.50 o.p. (0-06-080723-7, P723, Perennial) HarperTrade.
—Table d'Hote. l.t. ed. 1981. (Ulverscroft Large Print Ser.). 315p. 29.99 o.p. (0-7089-0603-6, Ulverscroft) Thorpe, F. A. Pubs. GBR. Dist: Ulverscroft Large Print Bks., Ltd., Ulverscroft Large Print Canada, Ltd.
—Vicious Circle: A Masters & Green Mystery. l.t. ed. 1988. pap. 14.95 o.p. (1-55504-629-0, 313) BBC Audiobooks America.
—Vicious Circle: A Masters & Green Mystery. 1985. 208p. reprint ed. mass mkt. 3.50 o.p. (0-06-080778-4, P 778, Perennial) HarperTrade.

**MASTERS, MOLLY (FICTITIOUS CHARACTER)—FICTION**

O'Kane, Leslie. The Cold, Hard Fax: A Molly Masters Mystery. 1998. (Molly Masters Mysteries Ser.). 288p. mass mkt. 5.99 o.s.i (0-449-00158-X, Fawcett) Ballantine Bks.
—The Cold, Hard Fax: A Molly Masters Mystery. l.t. ed. 2000. (Mystery Ser.). 381p. 26.95 (0-7862-2833-4) Thorndike Pr.
—Death & Faxes. 1997. per. (0-373-26248-5, 1-26248-4, Worldwide Library) Harlequin Enterprises, Ltd.
—Death & Faxes. 1996. 240p. 19.95 o.p. (0-312-13960-8, Saint Martin's Minotaur) St. Martin's Pr.
—Death of a PTA Goddess. 2002. 272p. mass mkt. 6.99 (0-449-00721-9) Ballantine Bks.
—Death of a PTA Goddess: A Molly Masters Mystery. 2003. (Mystery Ser.). 28.95 (0-7862-5118-2) Thorndike Pr.
—The Fax of Life, 1. 1999. 256p. mass mkt. 5.99 o.s.i (0-449-00160-1, Fawcett) Ballantine Bks.
—The Fax of Life. l.t. ed. 2000. (Mystery Ser.). 381p. 26.95 (0-7862-2328-6) Thorndike Pr.
—Just the Fax, Ma'am. 1997. per. (0-373-26254-X, 1-26254-2, Worldwide Library) Harlequin Enterprises, Ltd.
—Just the Fax, Ma'am. 1996. 256p. 21.95 o.p. (0-312-14637-X, Saint Martin's Minotaur) St. Martin's Pr.
—The School Board Murder. 2000. (Molly Masters Mysteries Ser.). 240p. mass mkt. 6.50 o.s.i (0-449-00567-4, Fawcett) Ballantine Bks.
—When the Fax Lady Sings: A Molly Masters Mystery. 2001. (Molly Masters Mysteries Ser.). 256p. mass mkt. 6.50 (0-449-00568-2, Fawcett) Ballantine Bks.
—When the Fax Lady Sings: A Molly Masters Mystery. l.t. ed. 2001. 351p. 27.95 (0-7862-3483-0) Thorndike Pr.

**MASUTO, MASAO (FICTITIOUS CHARACTER)—FICTION**

Cunningham, E. V., pseud. The Case of the Angry Actress. 1984. 192p. pap. 2.95 o.p. (0-440-11093-9) Dell Publishing.
—The Case of the Kidnapped Angel. 192p. 1983. (Masao Masuto Mystery Ser.: No. 5). pap. 2.95 o.p. (0-440-11224-9); 1982. 12.95 o.s.i (0-385-28118-8, Delacorte Pr.) Dell Publishing.
—The Case of the Kidnapped Angel. l.t. ed. 1983. 216p. pap. 7.95 o.p. (0-8161-3471-5, Macmillan Reference USA) Gale Group.
—The Case of the Murdered MacKenzie. 1984. (Masao Masuto Mystery Ser.). 192p. 11.95 o.s.i (0-385-29337-2, Delacorte Pr.) Dell Publishing.
—The Case of the Murdered MacKenzie. l.t. ed. 1985. (Nightingale Ser.). 386p. 9.95 o.p. (0-8161-3771-4, Macmillan Reference USA) Gale Group.
—The Case of the One-Penny Orange. l.t. ed. 1982. (Nightingale Ser.). lib. bdg. 11.95 o.p. (0-8161-3334-4, Macmillan Reference USA) Gale Group.
—The Case of the One-Penny Orange. 1982. (Masao Masuto Mystery Ser.). 176p. pap. o.p. (0-03-059858-3, Owl Bks.) Holt, Henry & Co.
—The Case of the Poisoned Eclairs. 1980. pap. 2.25 o.p. (0-440-11256-7) Dell Publishing.
—The Case of the Poisoned Eclairs. 1982. (Nightingale Ser.). pap. 9.95 o.p. (0-8161-3333-6, Macmillan Reference USA) Gale Group.
—The Case of the Poisoned Eclairs. 1979. o.p. (0-03-044721-6) Holt, Henry & Co.
—The Case of the Russian Diplomat. 1979. 1.75 o.s.i (0-515-04881-X, 04881-X, Jove) Berkley Publishing Group.
—The Case of the Russian Diplomat. (Masao Masuto Mystery Ser.). 1982. 176p. pap. o.p. (0-03-059857-5, Owl Bks.); 1978. o.p. (0-03-022456-X) Holt, Henry & Co.
—The Case of the Sliding Pool. 1983. pap. 2.95 o.p. (0-440-12092-6); 1981. 10.95 o.s.i (0-440-01114-0, Delacorte Pr.) Dell Publishing.
—The Case of the Sliding Pool. 1982. (Nightingale Ser.). pap. 9.95 o.p. (0-8161-3348-4, Macmillan Reference USA) Gale Group.

**MATELLI, ANGELA (FICTITIOUS CHARACTER)—FICTION**

Lee, Wendi. Crazy Like a Fox: An Angela Matelli Mystery. 2002. 240p. 22.95 (0-312-26139-X, Saint Martin's Minotaur) St. Martin's Pr.
—Deadbeat. 2000. 256p. mass mkt. (0-373-26339-2, Harlequin Bks.) Harlequin Enterprises, Ltd.
—Deadbeat. 1999. (Angela Matelli Mysteries Ser.). 256p. 22.95 o.p. (0-312-16812-8, Saint Martin's Minotaur) St. Martin's Pr.
—The Good Daughter. 1996. pap. 4.99 (0-312-95696-7, St. Martin's Paperbacks); 1994. 224p. 19.95 o.p. (0-312-11259-9, Saint Martin's Minotaur) St. Martin's Pr.
—Habeas Campus. 2003. (WWL Mystery Ser.: No. 447). 256p. mass mkt. (0-373-26447-X, Worldwide Library) Harlequin Enterprises, Ltd.
—He Who Dies. 2001. (WWL Mystery Ser.: No. 386). 252p. mass mkt. (0-373-26386-4, Worldwide Library) Harlequin Enterprises, Ltd.
—He Who Dies. E-Book 5.99 (0-312-27437-8) St. Martin's Pr.
—He Who Dies: An Angela Matelli Mystery. 2000. (Angela Matelli Mysteries Ser.). 247p. 23.95 (0-312-20894-4, Saint Martin's Minotaur) St. Martin's Pr.
—Missing Eden. 1999. per. (0-373-26301-5, Harlequin Bks.) Harlequin Enterprises, Ltd.
—Missing Eden. 1996. 240p. 21.95 o.p. (0-312-14370-2, Saint Martin's Minotaur) St. Martin's Pr.

**MATHIAS, MALCOLM 'MOON' (FICTITIOUS CHARACTER)—FICTION**

Hillerman, Tony. Finding Moon. 1995. ix, 319p. 24.00 o.p. (0-06-017772-1); 288p. 432.00 o.p. (0-06-017669-5); 336p. 150.00 o.p. (0-06-017287-8) HarperCollins Pubs.
—Finding Moon. 1996. 368p. mass mkt. 6.99 (0-06-109261-4, HarperTorch) Morrow/Avon.
—Finding Moon. l.t. ed. 1996. (Basic Ser.). 448p. 28.95 (0-7862-0574-1) Thorndike Pr.
—Finding Moon. 1996. lib. bdg. 13.04 (0-606-16176-7) Turtleback Bks.

**MATLOCK, JAMES BARBOUS (FICTITIOUS CHARACTER)—FICTION**

Ludlum, Robert. The Matlock Paper. 1989. 384p. mass mkt. 7.99 (0-553-27960-2); 400p. mass mkt. 3.99 o.s.i (0-553-19949-8) Bantam Bks.
—The Matlock Paper. 1974. 384p. mass mkt. 3.50 o.s.i (0-440-15538-X) Dell Publishing.

—The Matlock Paper. 1993. 3.49 o.p. *(0-517-10406-7)* Random Hse. Value Publishing.

**MATSUSHITA, DAIYU (FICTITIOUS CHARACTER)—FICTION**

Takagi, Akimitsu. The Tattoo Murder Case. Boehm, Deborah, tr. 1997. 240p. 23.00 *(1-56947-108-8)* Soho Pr., Inc.

**MATSUYAMA KAZE (FICTITIOUS CHARACTER)—FICTION**

Furutani, Dale. Death at the Crossroads: A Samurai Mystery. 1999. audio 24.95 *(0-7366-4703-1)* Books on Tape, Inc.

—Death at the Crossroads: A Samurai Mystery. 1998. 256p. 22.00 *(0-688-15817-X*, Morrow, William & Co.) Morrow/Avon.

—Jade Palace Vendetta: A Samurai Mystery. 1999. (Samurai Mysteries Ser.). 222p. 23.00 *(0-688-15818-8*, Morrow, William & Co.) Morrow/Avon.

—Kill the Shogun. collector's ed. 2000. audio 40.00 *(0-7366-5645-6)* Books on Tape, Inc.

—Kill the Shogun. 2000. (Samurai Mysteries Ser.). 240p. 23.00 o.s.i *(0-688-15819-6*, Morrow, William & Co.) Morrow/Avon.

—Kill the Shogun: A Samurai Mystery. l.t. ed. 2001. (Thorndike Mystery Ser.). 327p. 27.95 *(0-7862-3190-4)* Thorndike Pr.

**MATTHEWS, CHARLES (FICTITIOUS CHARACTER)—FICTION**

Meredith, Doris R. The Homefront Murders. 1994. (Southwest Mysteries Ser.). mass mkt. 4.99 o.s.i *(0-345-38050-9)* Ballantine Bks.

—The Sheriff & the Branding Iron Murders. 1992. mass mkt. 3.99 o.s.i *(0-345-36950-5)* Ballantine Bks.

—The Sheriff & the Branding Iron Murders. l.t. ed. 1997. (Nightingale Ser.). pap. 18.95 o.p. *(0-7838-2044-5*, Macmillan Reference USA) Gale Group.

—The Sheriff & the Branding Iron Murders. 1986. 160p. pap. 2.95 *(0-380-70050-6*, Avon Bks.) Morrow/Avon.

—The Sheriff & the Branding Iron Murders. Holland, Stephen, ed. abr. ed. 1994. audio 24.95 *(1-883268-12-5)* Spellbinders, Inc.

—The Sheriff & the Branding Iron Murders. 1985. 159p. 14.95 *(0-8027-4050-2)* Walker & Co.

—The Sheriff & the Folsom Man Murders. 1992. mass mkt. 3.99 o.s.i *(0-345-36949-1)* Ballantine Bks.

—The Sheriff & the Folsom Man Murders. 1987. 208p. pap. 2.95 *(0-380-70364-5*, Avon Bks.) Morrow/Avon.

—The Sheriff & the Folsom Man Murders. 1989. 2.99 o.p. *(0-517-00603-0)* Random Hse. Value Publishing.

—The Sheriff & the Folsom Man Murders. l.t. ed. 1999. 261p. pap. 24.95 *(0-7838-8582-2)* Thorndike Pr.

—The Sheriff & the Folsom Man Murders. 1987. 192p. 16.95 *(0-8027-5663-8)* Walker & Co.

—The Sheriff & the Panhandle Murders. l.t. ed. 1986. 13.95 o.p. *(1-55504-028-4*, 317) BBC Audiobooks America.

—The Sheriff & the Panhandle Murders. 1991. mass mkt. 4.99 o.s.i *(0-345-36951-3)* Ballantine Bks.

—The Sheriff & the Panhandle Murders. 1985. 224p. pap. 2.95 o.p. *(0-380-69929-X*, Avon Bks.) Morrow/Avon.

—The Sheriff & the Panhandle Murders. Holland, Stephen, ed. abr. ed. 1994. audio 24.95 *(1-883268-08-7)* Spellbinders, Inc.

—The Sheriff & the Panhandle Murders. 1984. 192p. 12.95 o.s.i *(0-8027-4036-7)* Walker & Co.

—The Sheriff & the Pheasant Hunt Murders. 1993. mass mkt. 4.50 o.s.i *(0-345-36948-3)* Ballantine Bks.

—The Sheriff & the Pheasant Hunt Murders. Holland, Stephen, ed. abr. ed. 1994. audio 24.95 *(1-883268-07-9)* Spellbinders, Inc.

**MATTHEWS, DAPHNE (FICTITIOUS CHARACTER)—FICTION**

Pearson, Ridley. The Angel Maker. 1994. 464p. mass mkt. 7.50 o.s.i *(0-440-21632-X)* Dell Publishing.

—The Angel Maker. 2003. (Illus.). 368p. reprint ed. mass mkt. 6.99 *(0-7868-9008-8)* Hyperion Pr.

—The Angel Maker. abr. ed. 1999. audio 9.99 o.s.i *(0-553-70195-9*, RH Audio) Random Hse. Audio Publishing Group.

—The Art of Deception. abr. ed. 2003. (Lou Boldt/Daphne Matthews Ser.). audio 12.99 *(1-59086-077-2*, 3630, Brilliance Audio Paperback Audiobooks); 2002. (Lou Boldt & Daphne Matthews Mystery Ser.: Vol. 8). audio 24.95 o.p. *(1-59086-076-4*, 3629, Nova Audio Bks.); 2002. (Lou Boldt & Daphne Matthews Mystery Ser.: Vol. 8). audio 87.25 *(1-59086-075-6*, 3628, Unabridged Library Editions); 2002. (Lou Boldt & Daphne Matthews Mystery Ser.: Vol. 8). audio 32.95 *(1-59086-074-8*, 3627, Brilliance Audio Unabridged); 2002. (Lou Boldt & Daphne Matthews Mystery Ser.: Vol. 8). audio compact disk 40.95 *(1-59086-226-0*, 3798, CD Unabridged); 2002. (Lou Boldt & Daphne Matthews Mystery Ser.: Vol. 8). audio compact disk 102.25 *(1-59086-227-9*, 3799, CD Unabridged Library Edition) Brilliance Audio.

—The Art of Deception. 2003. 464p. mass mkt. 7.99 *(0-7868-9000-2)*; 2003. E-Book *(1-4013-9841-3)*; 2003. E-Book 5.99 *(1-4013-9838-3)*; 2003. E-Book 5.99 *(1-4013-9837-5)*; 2003. E-Book 5.99 *(1-4013-9840-5)*; 2003. E-Book 5.99 *(1-4013-9839-1)*; 2002. 384p. 23.95 *(0-7868-6724-8)* Hyperion Pr.

—The Art of Deception. unabr. ed. 2003. (Lou Boldt/Daphne Matthews Ser.). audio 19.99 *(1-59335-200-X*, 30297) Soulmate Audio Bks., Inc.

—The Art of Deception. 2003. (Basic Ser.). 31.95 *(0-7862-4967-6)* Thorndike Pr.

—Beyond Recognition. unabr. ed. 1998. audio 96.00 *(0-7366-4092-4*, 4599) Books on Tape, Inc.

—Beyond Recognition. abr. ed. 1997. (Lou Boldt & Daphne Matthews Mystery Ser.). 3p. audio 7.99 *(1-56740-228-3*, 627, Paperback Nova Audio Bks.); audio 16.95 o.p. *(1-56100-970-9*, 1134, Nova Audio Bks.); audio 27.95 *(1-56100-733-1*, 45, Bookcassette); audio 105.25 *(1-56100-807-9*, 809) Brilliance Audio.

—Beyond Recognition. 1997. 496p. 22.95 o.p. *(0-7868-6240-8)*; 2003. 656p. reprint ed. mass mkt. 7.99 *(0-7868-8928-4)* Hyperion Pr.

—The Body of David Hayes. 2003. 23.95 *(0-7868-6725-6)* Hyperion Pr.

—The First Victim. abr. ed. (Lou Boldt/Daphne Matthews Ser.). 2000. audio 7.99 *(1-56740-980-6*, 2116, Paperback Nova Audio Bks.); 1999. audio 17.95 o.p. *(1-56740-836-2*, 1676, Nova Audio Bks.); 1999. audio 35.95 *(1-56740-423-5*, 1674, Brilliance Audio Unabridged); 1999. 9p. audio 57.25 *(1-56740-649-1*, 1675, Unabridged Library Editions) Brilliance Audio.

—The First Victim. aut. ltd. ed. 1999. 400p. 23.95 *(0-7868-6558-X)* Disney Pr.

—The First Victim. l.t. ed. 2001. (Large Print Bks.). 475p. pap. 23.95 *(1-58724-099-8*, Wheeler Publishing, Inc.) Gale Group.

—The First Victim, Set. abr. ed. 1999. audio 17.95 Highsmith Inc.

—The First Victim. 2001. 400p. E-Book 5.95 *(0-7868-7143-1)*; 2001. 400p. E-Book 5.95 *(0-7868-7146-6)*; 2001. 400p. E-Book 5.95 *(0-7868-7144-X)*; 2001. 400p. E-Book 5.95 *(0-7868-7142-3)*; 2001. 400p. E-Book 5.95 *(0-7868-7145-8)*; 1999. 381p. 23.95 *(0-7868-6440-0)*; 2003. 416p. reprint ed. mass mkt. 7.99 *(0-7868-8966-7)* Hyperion Pr.

—Middle of Nowhere. abr. ed. (Lou Boldt & Daphne Matthews Mystery Ser.). 2001. audio 12.99 *(1-58788-296-5*, 2657, Paperback Nova Audio Bks.); 2000. audio 24.95 o.p. *(1-56740-893-1*, 2053, Nova Audio Bks.); 2000. audio 73.25 *(1-56740-716-1*, 2052, Unabridged Library Editions); 2000. audio 32.95 *(1-56740-498-7*, 2051, Brilliance Audio Unabridged) Brilliance Audio.

—Middle of Nowhere. l.t. ed. 2001. (Large Print Book Ser.). 516p. 29.95 *(1-58724-013-0*, Wheeler Publishing, Inc.) Gale Group.

—Middle of Nowhere. 2001. 384p. E-Book 5.95 *(0-7868-7197-0)*; 2001. 384p. E-Book 5.95 *(0-7868-7149-0)*; 2001. 384p. E-Book 5.95 *(0-7868-7198-9)*; 2000. 375p. 23.95 *(0-7868-6563-6)*; 2003. 384p. reprint ed. mass mkt. 7.99 *(0-7868-8960-8)* Hyperion Pr.

—No Witnesses. unabr. ed. 1995. (Lou Boldt & Daphne Matthews Mystery Ser.). audio 72.00 *(0-7366-2950-5*, 3644) Books on Tape, Inc.

—No Witnesses. 1996. 480p. mass mkt. 7.50 o.s.i *(0-440-22142-0)* Dell Publishing.

—No Witnesses. 1994. 384p. 22.95 *(0-7868-6066-9)*; 2003. 480p. reprint ed. mass mkt. 6.99 *(0-7868-9006-1)* Hyperion Pr.

—No Witnesses. abr. ed. 1999. audio 9.99 o.s.i *(0-553-70215-7*, RH Audio) Random Hse. Audio Publishing Group.

—The Pied Piper. unabr. ed. 1999. audio 88.00 Books on Tape, Inc.

—The Pied Piper. abr. ed. (Lou Boldt & Daphne Matthews Mystery Ser.). 1999. audio 7.99 o.s.i *(1-56740-302-6*, 1864, Paperback Nova Audio Bks.); 1998. 10p. audio 89.25 *(1-56740-569-X*, 983); 1998. audio 28.95 *(1-56100-790-0*, 19, Bookcassette); Set. 1998. audio 17.95 o.p. *(1-56740-765-X*, 451, Nova Audio Bks.) Brilliance Audio.

—The Pied Piper. l.t. ed. 2000. pap. 23.95 *(1-56895-834-X*, Wheeler Publishing, Inc.) Gale Group.

—The Pied Piper. 1998. 497p. 23.95 *(0-7868-6300-5)*; 2003. 528p. reprint ed. mass mkt. 7.99 *(0-7868-8955-1)* Hyperion Pr.

—The Pied Piper & Beyond Recognition. 1998. *(0-7868-6433-8)* Disney Pr.

—Undercurrents. 2000. E-Book 4.99 *(1-58910-004-2)* PreviewPort.com.

—Undercurrents. 1992. mass mkt. 6.99 *(0-312-92958-7*, St. Martin's Paperbacks); 1989. mass mkt. 4.95 o.s.i *(0-312-91485-7*, St. Martin's Paperbacks); 1988. 416p. 18.95 o.p. *(0-312-01841-X)* St. Martin's Pr.

**MATTHEWS, MAREN (FICTITIOUS CHARACTER)—FICTION**

Fuchs, Jake. Death of a Dad: The Nursery School Murders. 1998. 180p. pap. 13.95 *(0-88739-159-1)* Creative Arts Bk. Co.

**MATTHEWS, NELL (FICTITIOUS CHARACTER)—FICTION**

Sandstrom, Eve K. Homicide Report. 1998. 368p. mass mkt. 5.99 o.s.i *(0-451-19034-3*, Onyx) NAL.

—The Smoking Gun: A Nell Matthews Mystery. 2000. (Neil Matthews Mysteries Ser.). 240p. mass mkt. 5.99 o.s.i *(0-451-19976-6*, Signet Bks.) NAL.

—The Smoking Gun: A Nell Matthews Mystery. l.t. ed. 2000. (Mystery Ser.). 365p. 26.95 *(0-7862-2977-2)* Thorndike Pr.

—Violence Beat. 1997. 384p. mass mkt. 5.99 o.s.i *(0-451-19033-5*, Signet Bks.) NAL.

**MATTHEWS, WYATT (FICTITIOUS CHARACTER)—FICTION**

Freedman, J. F. Key Witness. 1997. 544p. 23.95 o.s.i *(0-525-94334-X)* Dutton/Plume.

—Key Witness. 1998. 688p. mass mkt. 7.99 *(0-451-17990-0*, Signet Bks.) NAL.

**MATTISON, MATT (FICTITIOUS CHARACTER)—FICTION**

Darnton, John. Neanderthal: A Novel. 1998. (SPA.). 208p. *(84-08-02725-5)* GeoPlaneta, Editorial, S. A.

—Neanderthal: A Novel. l.t. ed. 1997. 416p. mass mkt. 7.99 *(0-312-96300-9*, St. Martin's Paperbacks) St. Martin's Pr.

—Neanderthal: A Novel. l.t. ed. 1996. (Americana Ser.). 607p. 29.95 *(0-7862-0824-4)* Thorndike Pr.

**MATURIN, STEPHEN (FICTITIOUS CHARACTER)—FICTION**

O'Brian, Patrick. Aubrey & Maturin, 18 vols. 1996. 432.00 *(0-393-04117-4)* Norton, W. W. & Co., Inc.

—The Aubrey-Maturin Series, 17 vols. (Aubrey-Maturin Ser.). (C). 1995. 408.00 *(0-393-03975-7)*; Set. 1994. 384.00 *(0-393-03749-5)* Norton, W. W. & Co., Inc.

—Blue at the Mizzen. 1999. audio compact disk 64.00 *(0-7366-5201-9)*; 2000. audio 29.95 *(0-7366-4686-8)*; 2000. audio compact disk 34.95 *(0-7366-4760-0)*; 1999. audio 48.00 *(0-7366-4737-6*, 5075) Books on Tape, Inc.

—Blue at the Mizzen. (Aubrey-Maturin Ser.). 1999. (Illus.). 288p. 24.00 *(0-393-04844-6)*; 250.00 *(0-393-04874-8)*; 2000. (Illus.). 272p. reprint ed. pap. 13.95 *(0-393-32107-X*, Norton Paperbacks) Norton, W. W. & Co., Inc.

—Blue at the Mizzen. abr. ed. 1999. (Aubrey-Maturin Ser.). audio 25.00 *(0-375-40876-2*, RH Audio) Random Hse. Audio Publishing Group.

—Blue at the Mizzen. unabr. ed. (Aubrey-Maturin Ser.). 2000. audio compact disk 81.00 *(0-7887-4204-3*, C1133E7); 1999. audio 60.00 *(0-7887-3769-4*, 95986E7) Recorded Bks., LLC.

—Blue at the Mizzen. l.t. ed. 2000. (Aubrey-Maturin Ser.). 393p. 27.95 *(0-7862-2047-3)*; 435p. 30.95 *(0-7862-2046-5)* Thorndike Pr.

—The Commodore. l.t. ed. 1995. (Aubrey-Maturin Ser.). 25.95 *(1-56895-271-6*, Wheeler Publishing, Inc.) Gale Group.

—The Commodore. (Aubrey-Maturin Ser.). 1996. 288p. pap. 13.95 *(0-393-31459-6*, Norton Paperbacks); 1995. 288p. 24.00 *(0-393-03760-6)*; 1995. 150.00 o.p. *(0-393-03886-6)* Norton, W. W. & Co., Inc.

—Desolation Island. 1979. (Aubrey-Maturin Ser.). 276p. 9.95 o.s.i *(0-8128-2590-X)*; pap. 2.50 o.p. *(0-8128-7066-2)* Madison Bks., Inc. (Scarborough Hse.).

—Desolation Island. (Aubrey-Maturin Ser.). 1994. 24.00 *(0-393-03705-3)*; 1991. (Illus.). 325p. pap. 13.95 *(0-393-30812-X)* Norton, W. W. & Co., Inc.

—The Far Side of the World. l.t. ed. 2002. (Aubrey-Maturin Ser.). 538p. 29.95 *(0-7862-1930-0*, Macmillan Reference USA) Gale Group.

—The Far Side of the World. 2003. 366p. pap. 13.95 *(0-393-32476-1)*; 1994. 24.00 *(0-393-03710-X)*; 1992. 368p. pap. 13.95 *(0-393-30862-6)* Norton, W. W. & Co., Inc.

—The Fortune of War. (Aubrey-Maturin Ser.). 1994. 24.00 *(0-393-03706-1)*; 1991. 329p. pap. 13.95 *(0-393-30813-8)* Norton, W. W. & Co., Inc.

—The Fortune of War. l.t. ed. 2001. (Illus.). 311p. *(0-7540-1588-2)*; *(0-7540-2449-0)* Thorndike Pr.

—HMS Surprise. (Aubrey-Maturin Ser.). 1994. 24.00 *(0-393-03703-7)*; 1991. 379p. pap. 13.95 *(0-393-30761-1)* Norton, W. W. & Co., Inc.

—HMS Surprise. l.t. ed. 2000. (Famous Authors Ser.). 608p. 28.95 *(0-7862-1934-3*, MML06400-170754); *(0-7540-1460-6)*; *(0-7540-2350-8)* Thorndike Pr.

—The Hundred Days. (Aubrey-Maturin Ser.). 288p. 1999. pap. 13.95 *(0-393-31979-2)*; 1998. 24.00 *(0-393-04674-5)* Norton, W. W. & Co., Inc.

—The Hundred Days. l.t. ed. (Aubrey-Maturin Ser.). 461p. 2000. 26.95 *(0-7862-1749-9)*; 1999. 29.95 *(0-7862-1748-0)* Thorndike Pr.

—The Ionian Mission. unabr. ed. 1993. (Aubrey-Maturin Ser.). audio 80.00 *(0-7366-2336-1*, 3115) Books on Tape, Inc.

—The Ionian Mission. (Aubrey-Maturin Ser.). 1994. 24.00 *(0-393-03708-8)*; 1992. 368p. pap. 13.95 *(0-393-30821-9)* Norton, W. W. & Co., Inc.

—The Ionian Mission. abr. ed. 2000. (Aubrey-Maturin Ser.). audio 25.00 *(0-375-41577-7*, RH Audio) Random Hse. Audio Publishing Group.

—The Ionian Mission. unabr. ed. 1994. (Aubrey-Maturin Ser.: No. 8). audio 91.00 *(1-55690-985-3*, 94124E7) Recorded Bks., LLC.

—The Ionian Mission. l.t. ed. 2001. (Aubrey-Maturin Ser.). (Illus.). 572p. 28.95 *(0-7862-1928-9)*; 576p. *(0-7540-1700-1)*; 576p. *(0-7540-9100-7)* Thorndike Pr.

—The Letter of Marque. (Aubrey-Maturin Ser.). 1992. 288p. pap. 13.95 *(0-393-30905-3)*; 1990. 284p. 24.00 *(0-393-02874-7)* Norton, W. W. & Co., Inc.

—The Letter of Marque. abr. ed. 2001. (Aubrey-Maturin Ser.: Vol. 12). audio 25.00 *(0-375-41598-X*, RH Audio) Random Hse. Audio Publishing Group.

—The Letter of Marque. l.t. ed. 1999. (Aubrey-Maturin Ser.). 495p. 29.95 *(0-7862-1925-4)* Thorndike Pr.

—Master & Commander. l.t. ed. 1999. *(0-7540-2248-X)*; *(0-7540-1334-0)* BBC Audiobooks America.

—Master & Commander. 2003. 412p. pap. 13.95 *(0-393-32517-2)*; 1994. 24.00 *(0-393-03701-0)*; 1990. (Illus.). 411p. pap. 13.95 *(0-393-30705-0)* Norton, W. W. & Co., Inc.

—Master & Commander. l.t. ed. 1999. (Aubrey-Maturin Ser.). 696p. 28.95 o.p. *(0-7862-1932-7)* Thorndike Pr.

—The Mauritius Command. unabr. ed. 1992. (Aubrey-Maturin Ser.). audio 72.00 *(0-7366-2248-9*, 3037) Books on Tape, Inc.

—The Mauritius Command. l.t. ed. 2000. (Aubrey-Maturin Ser.). (Illus.). 530p. 28.95 *(0-7862-1935-1*, Macmillan Reference USA) Gale Group.

—The Mauritius Command. 1978. (Aubrey-Maturin Ser.). 8.95 o.p. *(0-8128-2476-8)*; pap. 2.50 o.p. *(0-8128-7046-8)* Madison Bks., Inc. (Scarborough Hse.).

—The Mauritius Command. (Aubrey-Maturin Ser.). 1994. 24.00 *(0-393-03704-5)*; 1991. 348p. pap. 13.95 *(0-393-30762-X)* Norton, W. W. & Co., Inc.

—The Mauritius Command. abr. ed. 1999. (Aubrey-Maturin Ser.). audio 25.00 *(0-375-40875-4*, RH Audio) Random Hse. Audio Publishing Group.

—The Mauritius Command. unabr. ed. 1993. (Aubrey-Maturin Ser.: No. 4). audio 85.00 *(1-55690-804-0*, 93113E7) Recorded Bks., LLC.

—The Mauritius Command. l.t. ed. 2000. (Illus.). 530p. *(0-7540-1519-X)*; *(0-7540-2398-2)* Thorndike Pr.

—The Nutmeg of Consolation. (Aubrey-Maturin Ser.). 320p. 1993. pap. 13.95 *(0-393-30906-1)*; 1991. 24.00 *(0-393-03032-6)* Norton, W. W. & Co., Inc.

—The Nutmeg of Consolation. l.t. ed. 2002. (Famous Authors Ser.). 516p. 29.95 *(0-7862-1938-6)* Thorndike Pr.

—Post Captain. (Aubrey-Maturin Ser.). 1994. 24.00 *(0-393-03702-9)*; 1990. 496p. pap. 13.95 *(0-393-30706-9)* Norton, W. W. & Co., Inc.

—Post Captain. l.t. ed. 2000. (Aubrey-Maturin Ser.). (Illus.). 721p. 27.95 *(0-7862-1933-5*, MML06400-17053); *(0-7540-1423-1)*; *(0-7540-2320-6)* Thorndike Pr.

—The Reverse of the Medal. l.t. ed. 2002. (Aubrey-Maturin Ser.). 419p. 29.95 *(0-7862-1931-9*, Macmillan Reference USA) Gale Group.

—The Reverse of the Medal. (Aubrey-Maturin Ser.). 1994. 24.00 *(0-393-03711-8)*; 1992. 288p. pap. 13.95 *(0-393-30960-6)* Norton, W. W. & Co., Inc.

—The Surgeon's Mate. l.t. ed. 2001. (Aubrey-Maturin Ser.). (Illus.). 569p. 28.95 *(0-7862-1936-X*, Macmillan Reference USA) Gale Group.

—The Surgeon's Mate. (Aubrey-Maturin Ser.). 1994. 24.00 *(0-393-03707-X)*; 1992. 384p. pap. 13.95 *(0-393-30820-0)* Norton, W. W. & Co., Inc.

—The Surgeon's Mate. abr. ed. 2000. (Aubrey-Maturin Ser.). audio 25.00 *(0-375-41020-1*, RH Audio) Random Hse. Audio Publishing Group.

—The Surgeon's Mate. l.t. ed. 2001. (Thorndike Press Large Print Famous Authors Ser.). (Illus.). 624p. *(0-7540-1662-5)*; *(0-7540-9076-0)* Thorndike Pr.

—The Thirteen-Gun Salute. (Aubrey-Maturin Ser.). 1992. 336p. pap. 13.95 *(0-393-30907-X)*; 1991. 24.00 *(0-393-02974-3)* Norton, W. W. & Co., Inc.

—The Thirteen-Gun Salute. l.t. ed. 2002. (Famous Authors Ser.). 510p. 29.95 *(0-7862-1937-8)* Thorndike Pr.

—Treason's Harbour. (Aubrey-Maturin Ser.). 1994. 24.00 *(0-393-03709-6)*; 1992. 334p. pap. 13.95 *(0-393-30863-4)* Norton, W. W. & Co., Inc.

—Treason's Harbour. l.t. ed. 2002. 524p. 29.95 *(0-7862-1929-7)* Thorndike Pr.

—The Truelove. (Aubrey-Maturin Ser.). 1993. 256p. pap. 13.95 (0-393-31016-7); 1992. 192p. 24.00 (0-393-03109-8) Norton, W. W. & Co., Inc.
—The Wine-Dark Sea. (Aubrey-Maturin Ser.). 1994. 272p. pap. 13.95 (0-393-31244-5); 1993. 261p. 24.00 (0-393-03558-1) Norton, W. W. & Co., Inc.
—The Yellow Admiral. l.t. ed. 1997. (Aubrey-Maturin Ser.). 27.95 o.p. (1-56895-430-1, Wheeler Publishing, Inc.) Gale Group.
—The Yellow Admiral. (Aubrey-Maturin Ser.). 1997. (Illus.). 272p. pap. 13.95 (0-393-31704-8); 1996. 262p. 24.00 (0-393-04044-5) Norton, W. W. & Co., Inc.
—The Yellow Admiral. 1999. (Aubrey-Maturin Ser.). pap. 12.98 (0-671-04444-3, Simon & Schuster Audioworks) Simon & Schuster Audio.

**MAVIN MANYSHAPED (FICTITIOUS CHARACTER)—FICTION**

Tepper, Sheri S. The Flight of Mavin Manyshaped. 1985. 192p. mass mkt. 2.75 o.s.i (0-441-24092-5) Ace Bks.
—The Search of Mavin Manyshaped. 1985. 176p. mass mkt. 2.95 o.s.i (0-441-75712-X) Ace Bks.
—The Song of Mavin Manyshaped. 1985. 192p. mass mkt. 2.75 o.s.i (0-441-77523-3) Ace Bks.

**MAXIMILLIAN THE VAGUELY DISREPUTABLE (FICTITIOUS CHARACTER)—FICTION**

Brenner, Mayer A. Catastrophe's Spell. 1989. (Dance of Gods Ser.: 1). 320p. mass mkt. 4.99 o.p. (0-88677-357-1) DAW Bks., Inc.
—Spell of Apocalypse. 1994. (Dance of Gods Ser.: 4). 320p. (Orig.). mass mkt. 4.99 o.p. (0-88677-602-3) DAW Bks., Inc.
—Spell of Fate. 1992. (Dance of Gods Ser.: 3). 432p. (Orig.). mass mkt. 4.99 o.p. (0-88677-508-6) DAW Bks., Inc.
—Spell of Intrigue. 1990. (Dance of Gods Ser.: 2). 336p. mass mkt. 4.50 o.p. (0-88677-453-5) DAW Bks., Inc.

**MAXWELL, GEORGIA LEE (FICTITIOUS CHARACTER)—FICTION**

Friedman, Mickey. Magic Mirror. l.t. ed. 1990. (General Ser.). 354p. lib. bdg. 18.95 o.p. (0-8161-4823-6, Macmillan Reference USA) Gale Group.
—Magic Mirror. 256p. 1989. pap. 3.95 o.p. (0-14-010847-5, Penguin Bks.); 1988. 16.95 o.p. (0-670-82132-2) Viking Penguin.
—A Temporary Ghost. l.t. ed. 1991. (General Ser.). 285p. lib. bdg. 18.95 o.p. (0-8161-5012-5, Macmillan Reference USA) Gale Group.
—A Temporary Ghost. (Georgia Lee Maxwell Mystery Ser.). 224p. 1990. pap. 4.50 o.p. (0-14-010848-3, Penguin Bks.); 1989. 16.95 o.p. (0-670-82133-0) Viking Penguin.

**MAXWELL, JACQUES (FICTITIOUS CHARACTER)—FICTION**

Legg, John. Flintlock Trail. 1997. 256p. mass mkt. 4.99 o.p. (0-06-101064-2, HarperTorch) Morrow/Avon.

**MAXWELL, LAUREN (FICTITIOUS CHARACTER)—FICTION**

Quinn, Elizabeth. Killer Whale. 1997. 256p. pap. 5.99 (0-671-52770-3, Pocket) Simon & Schuster.
—Lamb to the Slaughter. 1996. 208p. mass mkt. 5.99 (0-671-52765-7, Pocket) Simon & Schuster.
—Murder Most Grizzly. Marrow, Linda, ed. 1993. 224p. (Orig.). mass mkt. 4.99 (0-671-74990-0, Pocket) Simon & Schuster.
—A Wolf in Death's Clothing. 1995. 224p. mass mkt. 5.50 (0-671-74991-9, Pocket) Simon & Schuster.

**MAXWELL, MAMA (FICTITIOUS CHARACTER)—FICTION**

Killough, Lee. Bridling Chaos. rev. ed. 1998. 624p. pap. 19.00 (0-9658345-3-0) Meisha Merlin Publishing, Inc.
—The Doppelganger Gambit. 1979. mass mkt. 1.95 o.s.i (0-345-28267-1) Ballantine Bks.
—Dragon's Teeth. 1990. mass mkt. 4.95 o.s.i (0-445-20906-2) Warner Bks., Inc.
—Spider Play. 1986. pap. 3.50 o.s.i (0-445-20273-4) Warner Bks., Inc.

**MAYFAIR WOMEN (FICTITIOUS CHARACTERS)—FICTION**

Rice, Anne. Blackwood Farm. 2002. 544p. (0-676-97542-9); 26.95 (0-375-41199-2) Knopf, Alfred A. Inc.
—Blackwood Farm: The Vampire Chronicles. 2002. E-Book 6.99 (1-4000-4020-5) Knopf Publishing Group.
—Blood Canticle. 2003. (Vampire Chronicles). E-Book 25.95 (1-4000-4194-5) Knopf Publishing Group.
—Blood Canticle. 2003. (Vampire Chronicles). 320p. 25.95 (0-375-41200-X) Knopf, Alfred A. Inc.
—Blood Canticle. abr. ed. 2003. audio 25.95 (0-7393-0467-4, Listening Library); audio compact disk 29.95 (0-7393-0630-8, Listening Library); audio 39.95 (0-7393-0631-6) Random Hse. Audio Publishing Group.
—Lasher. (SPA.). 26.95 (950-08-1316-5, AA9101) Atlantida ARG. *Dist:* Lectorum Pubns., Inc.
—Lasher. (Lives of the Mayfair Witches Ser.). 1995. 640p. mass mkt. 7.99 (0-345-39781-9); 1994. 592p. pap. 14.95 (0-345-37764-8) Ballantine Bks.
—Lasher. 1993. 592p. 30.00 (0-679-41295-6); 22.00 o.s.i (0-394-28021-0) Knopf, Alfred A. Inc.
—Lasher, abr. ed. 1993. audio 17.00 (0-679-42173-4, 391044, RH Audio) Random Hse. Audio Publishing Group.
—Taltos. 2000. 12.95 B Ediciones S.A. ESP. *Dist:* Distribooks, Inc.
—Taltos. 1996. 576p. mass mkt. 7.99 (0-345-40431-9); 1995. 480p. pap. 14.95 (0-345-39471-2); 1995. mass mkt. (0-345-40006-2, Ballantine Bks.) Ballantine Bks.
—Taltos. 1994. 467p. 25.00 (0-679-42573-X) Knopf, Alfred A. Inc.
—Taltos. (FRE.). pap. 12.95 (2-266-07477-6) Presses Pocket FRA. *Dist:* Distribooks, Inc.
—Taltos, Set. abr. ed. 1994. audio 22.50 (0-679-43654-5, 492019, RH Audio) Random Hse. Audio Publishing Group.
—Taltos. deluxe ltd. num. ed. 1994. 467p. 150.00 (0-9631925-1-5) Trice, B.E. Publishing.
—The Witching Hour. (Lives of the Mayfair Witches Ser.). 1993. 1056p. mass mkt. 7.99 (0-345-38446-6); 1991. 976p. pap. 15.95 (0-345-36789-8) Ballantine Bks.
—The Witching Hour. 1998. pap. o.s.i (0-394-25663-8); 1990. 976p. 29.95 (0-394-58786-3) Knopf, Alfred A. Inc.
—The Witching Hour. abr. ed. 2002. audio 9.99 (0-553-71352-3); Set. 1990. audio 18.00 o.s.i (0-394-58789-8) Random Hse. Audio Publishing Group. (RH Audio).

**MAYHEW, MISS (FICTITIOUS CHARACTER)—FICTION**

Naef, Adam. The Barbury Hall Murders: A Mystery Set in the England of Jane Austen. 1997. 216p. (Orig.). pap. 12.95 (0-9633494-8-1) Picardy Pr.

**MAYNARD, LOIS (FICTITIOUS CHARACTER)—FICTION**

Rinehart, Mary Roberts. The Swimming Pool. 1981. (Reader's Request Ser.). lib. bdg. 16.95 o.p. (0-8161-3233-X, Macmillan Reference USA) Gale Group.
—The Swimming Pool. 1997. 336p. mass mkt. 5.50 o.s.i (0-8217-5634-6); 1997. 336p. mass mkt. 5.50 o.s.i (1-57566-157-8); 1991. mass mkt. 3.95 o.s.i (0-8217-3679-5, Zebra Bks.); 1985. mass mkt. 3.50 o.p. (0-8217-1686-7, Zebra Bks.) Kensington Publishing Corp.

**MAYO, ASEY (FICTITIOUS CHARACTER)—FICTION**

Taylor, Phoebe Atwood. The Annulet of Gilt. 1986. (Asey Mayo Cape Cod Mystery Ser.). 288p. reprint ed. pap. 6.95 (0-88150-078-X, Foul Play) Norton, W. W. & Co., Inc.
—The Asey Mayo Trio. 1990. 256p. reprint ed. pap. 7.95 (0-88150-171-9, Foul Play) Norton, W. W. & Co., Inc.
—Banbury Bog. 1978. reprint ed. lib. bdg. 16.95 o.p. (0-89966-247-1) Buccaneer Bks., Inc.
—Banbury Bog. 1987. (Asey Mayo Cape Cod Mystery Ser.). 176p. reprint ed. pap. 5.95 (0-88150-090-9, Foul Play) Norton, W. W. & Co., Inc.
—The Cape Cod Mystery. 1985. (Asey Mayo Cape Cod Mystery Ser.). 192p. pap. 7.95 (0-88150-046-1, Foul Play) Norton, W. W. & Co., Inc.
—The Deadly Sunshade. l.t. ed. 1992. 19.95 o.p. (0-7927-1318-4); pap. 17.95 o.p. (0-7927-1317-6) BBC Audiobooks America.
—The Deadly Sunshade. 1989. (Asey Mayo Cape Cod Mystery Ser.). 300p. reprint ed. pap. 6.00 o.p. (0-88150-136-0) Countryman Pr.
—Death Lights a Candle. 1989. (Asey Mayo Cape Cod Mystery Ser.). 304p. reprint ed. pap. 7.95 (0-88150-145-X, Foul Play) Norton, W. W. & Co., Inc.
—Deathblow Hill. 1993. (Asey Mayo Cape Cod Mystery Ser.). 286p. pap. 6.50 (0-88150-262-6, Foul Play) Norton, W. W. & Co., Inc.
—Diplomatic Corpse. 1989. (Asey Mayo Cape Cod Mystery Ser.). 244p. reprint ed. pap. 5.95 o.p. (0-88150-146-8) Countryman Pr.
—Figure Away. 1979. (Foul Play Press Bks.). reprint ed. pap. 4.50 o.p. (0-914378-48-1) Countryman Pr.
—Figure Away. 1991. (Asey Mayo Cape Cod Mystery Ser.). 286p. reprint ed. pap. 5.95 o.p. (0-88150-206-5, Foul Play) Norton, W. W. & Co., Inc.
—Going, Going, Gone. 21.95 (0-8488-1201-8) Amereon, Ltd.
—Murder at the New York World's Fair. 1987. 265p. reprint ed. pap. 8.95 o.p. (0-88150-095-X) Countryman Pr.
—The Mystery of the Cape Cod Players. 1987. (Asey Mayo Cape Cod Mystyery Ser.). 272p. reprint ed. pap. 6.00 o.p. (0-88150-091-7) Countryman Pr.
—The Mystery of the Cape Cod Tavern. 1985. (Asey Mayo Cape Cod Mystery Ser.). 288p. pap. 7.95 (0-88150-047-X, Foul Play) Norton, W. W. & Co., Inc.
—Octagon House. 1983. pap. 4.50 o.p. (0-914378-47-3) Countryman Pr.
—Octagon House. 1991. (Asey Mayo Cape Cod Mystery Ser.). 296p. pap. 6.95 (0-88150-194-8, Foul Play) Norton, W. W. & Co., Inc.
—Octagon House. 1999. lib. bdg. 22.95 (1-56723-139-X, 148) Yestermorrow, Inc.
—Proof of the Pudding. 1979. (Foul Play Press Bks.). reprint ed. pap. 4.95 o.p. (0-914378-55-4) Countryman Pr.
—Proof of the Pudding. 1991. 192p. pap. 6.00 (0-88150-193-X, Foul Play) Norton, W. W. & Co., Inc.
—Punch with Care. 21.95 (0-8488-1202-6) Amereon, Ltd.
—Punch with Care. 1992. (Asey Mayo Cape Cod Mystery Ser.). 224p. pap. 7.95 (0-88150-229-4, Foul Play) Norton, W. W. & Co., Inc.
—The Six Iron Spiders. 1979. (Foul Play Press Bks.). reprint ed. pap. 4.95 o.p. (0-914378-53-8) Countryman Pr.
—The Six Iron Spiders. 1992. (Asey Mayo Cape Cod Mystery Ser.). 288p. pap. 6.95 (0-88150-230-8, Foul Play) Norton, W. W. & Co., Inc.
—Three Plots for Asey Mayo. 1969. 5.95 o.p. (0-393-08534-1); 1991. 320p. reprint ed. pap. 6.95 o.p. (0-88150-205-7, Foul Play) Norton, W. W. & Co., Inc.
—The Tinkling Symbol. 1993. (Asey Mayo Cape Cod Mystery Ser.). 288p. pap. 7.95 (0-88150-263-4, Foul Play) Norton, W. W. & Co., Inc.

**MAYO, GIL (FICTITIOUS CHARACTER)—FICTION**

Eccles, Marjorie. An Accidental Shroud: An Inspector Mayo Mystery. l.t. ed. 1996. (Magna Large Print Ser.). (Illus.). 327p. 29.99 (0-7505-0982-1) Magna Large Print Bks. GBR. *Dist:* Ulverscroft Large Print Bks., Ltd.
—An Accidental Shroud: An Inspector Mayo Mystery. 1996. 20.95 o.p. (0-312-15045-8, Saint Martin's Minotaur) St. Martin's Pr.
—The Company She Kept. l.t. ed. 1994. (Magna Large Print Ser.). 320p. 29.99 o.p. (0-7505-0642-3) Magna Large Print Bks. GBR. *Dist:* Ulverscroft Large Print Bks., Ltd., Ulverscroft Large Print Canada, Ltd.
—The Company She Kept. 1996. 192p. 21.95 o.p. (0-312-14297-8, Saint Martin's Minotaur) St. Martin's Pr.
—Death of a Good Woman. l.t. ed. 1991. (Ulverscroft Large Print Ser.). 29.99 o.p. (0-7089-2460-3, Ulverscroft) Thorpe, F. A. Pubs. GBR. *Dist:* Ulverscroft Large Print Bks., Ltd., Ulverscroft Large Print Canada, Ltd.
—A Death of Distinction. l.t. ed. 1996. (Magna Large Print Ser.). 337p. (0-7505-1021-8) Magna Large Print Bks. GBR. *Dist:* Ulverscroft Large Print Canada, Ltd.
—A Death of Distinction. 1998. (Gil Mayo Mysteries Ser.). 192p. 20.95 o.p. (0-312-18566-9, Saint Martin's Minotaur) St. Martin's Pr.
—Echoes of Silence. 2003. 224p. 22.95 (0-312-30880-9, Saint Martin's Minotaur) St. Martin's Pr.
—Killing Me Softly. l.t. ed. 1999. (Magna Large Print Ser.). 368p. (0-7505-1383-7) Magna Large Print Bks. GBR. *Dist:* Ulverscroft Large Print Canada, Ltd.
—Killing Me Softly. 2000. 205p. 22.95 (0-312-20469-8, Saint Martin's Minotaur) St. Martin's Pr.
—Late of This Parish. l.t. ed. 1993. (Magna Large Print Ser.). 380p. 29.99 o.p. (0-7505-0516-8) Magna Large Print Bks. GBR. *Dist:* Ulverscroft Large Print Bks., Ltd., Ulverscroft Large Print Canada, Ltd.
—Late of This Parish. 1994. 224p. 19.95 o.p. (0-312-11019-7, Saint Martin's Minotaur) St. Martin's Pr.
—More Deaths Than One. 1991. 192p. 15.00 o.s.i (0-385-41918-X) Doubleday Publishing.
—Requiem for a Dove. l.t. ed. 1992. (Mystery Ser.). 384p. 29.99 o.p. (0-7089-2603-7, Ulverscroft) Thorpe, F. A. Pubs. GBR. *Dist:* Ulverscroft Large Print Bks., Ltd., Ulverscroft Large Print Canada, Ltd.
—A Species of Revenge. l.t. ed. 1998. 315p. (0-7540-3425-9) BBC Audiobooks America.
—A Species of Revenge. 1998. (Gil Mayo Mysteries Ser.). 224p. 20.95 o.p. (0-312-19338-6, Saint Martin's Minotaur) St. Martin's Pr.
—A Species of Revenge. l.t. ed. 1998. (Nightingale Ser.). 320p. pap. 20.95 (0-7838-0288-9) Thorndike Pr.
—A Sunset Touch: A Mystery Featuring Superintendent Gil Mayo. 2002. 208p. 22.95 (0-312-28353-9, Saint Martin's Minotaur) St. Martin's Pr.

**MEADOWS, CHRIS (FICTITIOUS CHARACTER)—FICTION**

Hiaasen, Carl. Powder Burn. 1998. 288p. pap. 12.00 (0-375-70068-4, Vintage) Knopf Publishing Group.

**MEAGHER, FEARGAL (FICTITIOUS CHARACTER)—FICTION**

Olden, Marc. Fear's Justice. 1998. 352p. pap. 6.99 (0-671-00379-8, Pocket) Simon & Schuster.

**MEEHAN, ALVIRAH (FICTITIOUS CHARACTER)—FICTION**

Clark, Mary Higgins. The Lottery Winner. E-Book 9.95 (1-930161-64-6) Adobe Systems, Inc.
—The Lottery Winner. 1997. reprint ed. lib. bdg. 32.95 (1-56849-588-9) Buccaneer Bks., Inc.
—The Lottery Winner. 2000. E-Book 9.95 (0-7432-0626-6, Simon & Schuster); 1995. 304p. mass mkt. 7.99 (0-671-86717-2, Pocket); 1994. 26.00 o.s.i (0-684-80222-8, Simon & Schuster); 1994. (Illus.). 256p. 22.00 (0-671-86716-4, Simon & Schuster) Simon & Schuster.
—The Lottery Winner. 265p. pap. 5.98 o.p. (0-7651-0558-6) Smithmark Pubs., Inc.

**MEIKLEJOHN, CHARLIE (FICTITIOUS CHARACTER)—FICTION**

Wilhelm, Kate. The Casebook of Constance & Charlie. Vol. 1. 1999. 614p. pap. 18.95 (0-312-24501-7); Vol. 2. 2000. 595p. pap. 16.95 (0-312-25378-8) St. Martin's Pr. (Saint Martin's Griffin).
—The Dark Door. 1993. 352p. pap. 4.50 (0-8439-3416-6) Dorchester Publishing Co., Inc.
—The Dark Door. 1988. 256p. 16.95 o.p. (0-312-02182-8) St. Martin's Pr.
—A Flush of Shadows: Five Short Novels. 1996. mass mkt. 5.99 o.s.i (0-449-22434-1, Fawcett) Ballantine Bks.
—A Flush of Shadows: Five Short Novels. 1995. 352p. 22.95 o.p. (0-312-13075-9, Saint Martin's Minotaur) St. Martin's Pr.
—Hamlet Trap: A Charlie Meiklejohn & Constance Leidl Mystery. 1988. mass mkt. 4.50 (0-312-91125-4, St. Martin's Paperbacks) St. Martin's Pr.
—The Hamlet Trap: A Constance & Charlie Micklejohn Mystery. 1987. 240p. 15.95 o.p. (0-312-94000-9, Saint Martin's Minotaur) St. Martin's Pr.
—A Sense of Shadow, 001. 1981. 9.95 o.p. (0-395-30545-4) Houghton Mifflin Co.
—Seven Kinds of Death. 1994. 256p. reprint ed. pap. 4.50 (0-8439-3570-7) Dorchester Publishing Co., Inc.
—Seven Kinds of Death. 1992. 256p. 18.95 o.p. (0-312-08290-8, Saint Martin's Minotaur) St. Martin's Pr.
—Smart House. l.t. ed. 1991. 16.95 o.p. (0-7451-9790-6, C0300); pap. 15.95 o.p. (0-7927-0255-7, C0434) BBC Audiobooks America.
—Smart House. 1991. 272p. reprint ed. pap. 3.95 (0-8439-3043-8) Dorchester Publishing Co., Inc.
—Smart House: A Charlie Meiklejohn-Constance Leidl Mystery. 1989. 272p. 16.95 o.p. (0-312-02642-0, Saint Martin's Minotaur) St. Martin's Pr.
—Sweet, Sweet Poison. 1991. 272p. reprint ed. pap. 3.99 (0-8439-3163-9) Dorchester Publishing Co., Inc.
—Sweet, Sweet Poison. 1990. 16.95 o.p. (0-312-04433-X, Saint Martin's Minotaur) St. Martin's Pr.

**MELLORS, KRISTIN (FICTITIOUS CHARACTER)—FICTION**

King, Tabitha. Survivor. 1997. 448p. 24.95 o.p. (0-525-94241-6) Dutton/Plume.
—Survivor. 1998. 496p. mass mkt. 7.99 o.p. (0-451-19090-4, Signet Bks.) NAL.

**MELVILLE, HERMAN, 1819-1891—FICTION**

Busch, Frederick. The Night Inspector. E-Book 12.50 (1-58945-550-9) Adobe Systems, Inc.
—The Night Inspector. 2000. (Illus.). 304p. pap. 14.00 (0-449-00615-8, Ballantine Bks.) Ballantine Bks.
—The Night Inspector. 1999. E-Book 12.50 (0-609-60768-5, Harmony) Crown Publishing Group.
—The Night Inspector: A Novel. 1999. 288p. 23.00 o.s.i (0-609-60235-7, Harmony) Crown Publishing Group.
Duberstein, Larry. The Handsome Sailor. 1998. 240p. 25.00 (1-57962-007-8) Permanent Pr., The.
—The Handsome Sailor. l.t. ed. 1999. (Basic Ser.). 405p. 28.95 (0-7862-1685-9) Thorndike Pr.
—The Handsome Sailor. E-Book 6.99 (0-7592-2866-3); 2001. E-Book 6.99 (0-7592-2656-3) ereads.com.
Lentricchia, Frank. Lucchesi & the Whale. Fish, Stanley & Jameson, Fredric, eds. 2003. 128p. pap. 16.95 (0-8223-3171-3) Duke Univ. Pr.
—Lucchesi & the Whale. 2001. (Post-Contemporary Interventions Ser.). 104p. pap. 24.95 (0-8223-2654-X) Duke Univ. Pr.

**MELVILLE, SUSAN (FICTITIOUS CHARACTER)—FICTION**

Smith, Evelyn E. Miss Melville Regrets. 1987. mass mkt. 5.99 o.s.i (0-449-21259-9, Fawcett) Ballantine Bks.
—Miss Melville Regrets. 1986. 288p. 17.95 o.p. (0-917657-45-4) Fine, Donald I. Bks.

—Miss Melville Regrets. l.t. ed. 1989. (Ulverscroft Large Print Ser.). 29.99 o.p. (*0-7089-2110-8*, Ulverscroft) Thorpe, F. A. Pubs. GBR. *Dist:* Ulverscroft Large Print Bks., Ltd., Ulverscroft Large Print Canada, Ltd.
—Miss Melville Returns. 1988. mass mkt. 4.99 o.s.i (*0-449-21499-0*, Fawcett) Ballantine Bks.
—Miss Melville Returns. 1987. 272p. 17.95 o.s.i (*1-55611-015-4*) Fine, Donald I. Bks.
—Miss Melville Rides a Tiger. 1992. mass mkt. 4.99 o.s.i (*0-449-22105-9*, Fawcett) Ballantine Bks.
—Miss Melville Rides a Tiger. 1991. 18.95 o.p. (*1-55611-219-X*) Fine, Donald I. Bks.
—Miss Melville Rides a Tiger. l.t. ed. 1993. (General Ser.). 334p. 20.95 o.p. (*0-8161-5559-3*); pap. o.p. (*0-8161-5560-7*) Gale Group. (Macmillan Reference USA).
—Miss Melville Runs for Cover. 2015. 256p. 19.95 (*1-55611-361-7*) Fine, Donald I. Bks.
—Miss Melville's Revenge. 1990. 224p. mass mkt. 5.99 o.s.i (*0-449-21794-9*, Fawcett) Ballantine Bks.
—Miss Melville's Revenge. 1989. 288p. 17.95 o.p. (*1-55611-076-6*) Fine, Donald I. Bks.

**MENDOZA, DIANA (FICTITIOUS CHARACTER)—FICTION**

Lucas, Frances. If Looks Could Kill. 1995. 190p. (Orig.). pap. 9.95 (*0-934678-63-4*) New Victoria Pubs., Inc.

**MENDOZA, LUIS (FICTITIOUS CHARACTER)—FICTION**

Shannon, Dell. The Ace of Spades. l.t. ed. 1992. 18.95 o.p. (*0-7451-8385-9*); pap. 16.95 o.p. (*0-7927-1151-3*) BBC Audiobooks America.
—The Ace of Spades. 1984. reprint ed. pap. 3.95 o.p. (*0-89296-078-7*) Mysterious Pr.
—Appearances of Death. 1980. 208p. pap. 1.95 o.p. (*0-553-13953-3*) Bantam Bks.
—Appearances of Death. l.t. ed. 1981. 319p. reprint ed. 12.95 o.p. (*0-89621-319-6*) Thorndike Pr.
—Blood Count. 1988. 224p. mass mkt. (*0-373-26006-7*, Harlequin Bks.) Harlequin Enterprises, Ltd.
—Blood Count. 1989. 2.99 o.p. (*0-517-69441-7*) Random Hse. Value Publishing.
—Blood Count: The 37th Volume of a Detective Series. 1986. 224p. 15.95 o.p. (*0-688-06394-2*, Morrow, William & Co.) Morrow/Avon.
—Case Pending. l.t. ed. 1991. pap. 14.95 o.p. (*0-7927-0173-9*, C0214); 1990. 16.95 o.p. (*0-7451-9742-6*, C0066) BBC Audiobooks America.
—Case Pending. 1984. reprint ed. pap. 3.95 o.p. (*0-89296-076-0*) Mysterious Pr.
—Chaos of Crime. l.t. ed. 1988. lib. bdg. 14.95 o.p. (*1-85057-443-X*, Macmillan Reference USA) Gale Group.
—Chaos of Crime. 1988. 224p. reprint ed. pap. (*0-373-26015-6*, Harlequin Bks.) Harlequin Enterprises, Ltd.
—Chaos of Crime. 1985. 256p. 14.95 o.p. (*0-688-02297-9*, Morrow, William & Co.) Morrow/Avon.
—Cold Trail. 1989. 224p. reprint ed. mass mkt. (*0-373-26027-X*, Harlequin Bks.) Harlequin Enterprises, Ltd.
—The Death Bringers. l.t. ed. 1993. 21.95 o.p. (*0-7927-1513-6*) BBC Audiobooks America.
—The Death-Bringers. l.t. ed. 1993. pap. 19.95 o.p. (*0-7927-1512-8*); 1996. audio 54.95 (*0-7927-2205-1*, CSL094, Chivers Sound Library) BBC Audiobooks America.
—Death by Inches. l.t. ed. 1992. 18.95 o.p. (*0-7451-8425-1*); pap. 16.95 o.p. (*0-7927-1343-5*) BBC Audiobooks America.
—Death of a Busybody. l.t. ed. 1991. 17.95 o.p. (*0-7451-8024-8*, AH083); pap. 15.95 o.p. (*0-7927-0500-9*, AS0119) BBC Audiobooks America.
—Death of a Busybody. 1985. (Lt. Luis Mendoza Mystery Ser.). pap. 3.95 o.s.i (*0-89296-149-X*) Mysterious Pr.
—Destiny of Death. 1984. 227p. 14.95 o.p. (*0-688-03109-9*, Morrow, William & Co.) Morrow/Avon.
—Destiny of Death: A Luis Mendoza Mystery. 1991. 224p. reprint ed. mass mkt. (*0-373-26073-3*, Harlequin Bks.) Harlequin Enterprises, Ltd.
—The Dispossessed. 1988. 352p. 18.95 o.p. (*0-688-07998-9*, Morrow, William & Co.) Morrow/Avon.
—Double Bluff. l.t. ed. 1991. 17.95 o.p. (*0-7451-8173-2*, AH0227); pap. 15.95 o.p. (*0-7927-0708-7*, AS0263) BBC Audiobooks America.
—Double Bluff. 1985. (Lt. Luis Mendoza Mystery Ser.). pap. 3.95 o.p. (*0-89296-150-3*) Mysterious Pr.
—Exploit of Death. 1990. mass mkt. (*0-373-26061-X*, Harlequin Bks.) Harlequin Enterprises, Ltd.
—Exploit of Death. l.t. ed. 1983. (Luis Mendoza Mystery Ser.). 349p. reprint ed. 12.95 o.p. (*0-89621-493-1*) Thorndike Pr.
—Extra Kill. 1984. 256p. reprint ed. pap. 3.95 o.p. (*0-89296-080-9*) Mysterious Pr.
—Felony at Random. 1980. 224p. pap. 1.95 o.p. (*0-553-13954-1*) Bantam Bks.
—Felony at Random. l.t. ed. 1981. (Ulverscroft Large Print Ser.). 355p. 29.99 o.p. (*0-7089-0660-5*, Ulverscroft) Thorpe, F. A. Pubs. GBR. *Dist:* Ulverscroft Large Print Bks., Ltd., Ulverscroft Large Print Canada, Ltd.
—Felony File. l.t. ed. 1981. 374p. reprint ed. 10.95 o.p. (*0-89621-281-5*) Thorndike Pr.
—Knave of Hearts. 1984. reprint ed. pap. 3.95 o.p. (*0-89296-082-5*) Mysterious Pr.
—The Manson Curse. l.t. ed. 1992. 18.95 o.p. (*0-7451-8253-4*, AH0264); pap. 16.95 o.p. (*0-7927-0814-8*, AS0300) BBC Audiobooks America.
—The Manson Curse. 1990. 288p. 17.95 o.p. (*0-688-10119-4*, Morrow, William & Co.) Morrow/Avon.
—Mark of Murder. 1994. 256p. mass mkt. 4.50 o.p. (*0-7867-0043-2*, Carroll & Graf Pubs.) Avalon Publishing Group.
—Mark of Murder. l.t. ed. 1991. 12.95 o.p. (*0-7927-0147-X*, 4662); pap. 17.95 o.p. (*0-7927-0148-8*, C0079) BBC Audiobooks America.
—Mark of Murder: A Lieutenant Luis Mendoza Mystery. 1986. 240p. mass mkt. 3.95 (*0-445-40262-8*, Mysterious Pr. Paperback Bks.) Warner Bks., Inc.
—Motive on Record. 1990. mass mkt. (*0-373-26049-0*, Harlequin Bks.) Harlequin Enterprises, Ltd.
—The Motive on Record. l.t. ed. 1982. 364p. reprint ed. 12.95 o.p. (*0-89621-394-3*) Thorndike Pr.
—Murder by the Tale. 1987. 224p. 16.95 o.p. (*0-688-07538-X*, Morrow, William & Co.) Morrow/Avon.
—Murder by the Tale. 1989. 2.99 o.p. (*0-517-69454-9*) Random Hse. Value Publishing.
—Murder Most Strange. 1989. mass mkt. (*0-373-26037-7*, Harlequin Bks.) Harlequin Enterprises, Ltd.
—Murder Most Strange. l.t. ed. 1982. 354p. 12.95 o.p. (*0-89621-377-3*) Thorndike Pr.
—Root of All Evil. 1993. 208p. mass mkt. 3.95 o.p. (*0-88184-978-2*, Carroll & Graf Pubs.) Avalon Publishing Group.
—Root of All Evil. l.t. ed. 1993. 21.95 o.p. (*0-7927-1771-6*); pap. 19.95 o.p. (*0-7927-1770-8*) BBC Audiobooks America.
—Root of All Evil. 1986. 288p. reprint ed. mass mkt. 3.95 (*0-445-40259-8*, Mysterious Pr. Paperback Bks.) Warner Bks., Inc.
—The Scalpel & the Sword. 1987. 416p. 18.95 o.p. (*0-688-07216-X*, Morrow, William & Co.) Morrow/Avon.
—Sorrow to the Grave. 1992. 18.00 o.p. (*0-688-11577-2*, Morrow, William & Co.) Morrow/Avon.
—Streets of Death. 1980. 192p. pap. 1.95 o.p. (*0-553-13952-5*) Bantam Bks.
—Streets of Death. l.t. ed. 1980. 315p. reprint ed. 9.95 o.p. (*0-89621-250-5*) Thorndike Pr.

**MENLO, ANNIE (FICTITIOUS CHARACTER)—FICTION**

O'Callaghan, Maxine. Only in the Ashes. 1997. 320p. mass mkt. 5.99 o.s.i (*0-515-12077-4*, Jove) Berkley Publishing Group.
—Shadow of the Child. 1996. 336p. mass mkt. 5.99 o.s.i (*0-515-11822-2*, Jove) Berkley Publishing Group.

**MENSING, LOREN (FICTITIOUS CHARACTER)—FICTION**

Nevins, Francis M. Corrupt & Ensnare. 1978. 8.95 o.p. (*0-399-12203-6*) Putnam Publishing Group, The.
—Corrupt & Ensnare. 2000. 232p. pap. 14.95 (*1-58348-998-3*) iUniverse, Inc.
—Into the Same River Twice. 1996. 224p. 21.00 o.p. (*0-7867-0314-8*, Carroll & Graf Pubs.) Avalon Publishing Group.
—Into the Same River Twice. 2000. 228p. pap. 14.95 (*0-595-00001-0*, Authors Choice Pr.) iUniverse, Inc.
—Publish & Perish. 2000. 192p. pap. 12.95 (*0-595-00059-2*) iUniverse, Inc.

**MERCER, PHILIP (FICTITIOUS CHARACTER)—FICTION**

Du Brul, Jack. Charon's Landing. abr. ed. 1999. audio 17.95 o.p. (*1-56740-823-0*, 1569, Nova Audio Bks.); audio 30.95 (*1-56740-402-2*, 1567, Bookcassette); audio 105.25 (*1-56740-631-9*, 1571, Unabridged Library Editions) Brilliance Audio.
—Charon's Landing. 2000. 512p. mass mkt. 7.99 o.s.i (*0-8125-7550-4*, Tor Bks.); 1999. 384p. 24.95 (*0-312-86816-2*, Forge Bks.) Doherty, Tom Assocs., LLC.
—Charon's Landing. unabr. ed. 1999. audio 17.95 Highsmith Inc.
—The Medusa Stone. abr. ed. 2000. audio 24.95 o.p. (*1-56740-898-2*, 2069, Nova Audio Bks.); audio 89.25 (*1-56740-721-8*, 2068, Unabridged Library Editions) Brilliance Audio.
—The Medusa Stone. 2000. 464p. mass mkt. 6.99 (*0-451-40922-1*, Onyx) NAL.
—Vulcan's Forge. unabr. ed. 1998. audio 56.95 (*0-7861-1314-6*, 106031) Blackstone Audio Bks., Inc.
—Vulcan's Forge. abr. ed. 1998. audio 7.99 o.s.i (*1-56740-281-X*, 1691, Paperback Nova Audio Bks.); audio 17.95 o.p. (*1-56740-772-2*, 515, Nova Audio Bks.); audio 73.25 (*1-56740-577-0*, 1091, Unabridged Library Editions); audio 26.95 (*1-56100-798-6*, 312, Bookcassette) Brilliance Audio.
—Vulcan's Forge. 1999. 378p. mass mkt. 6.99 (*0-8125-6461-8*); 1998. 352p. 24.95 (*0-312-86481-7*) Doherty, Tom Assocs., LLC. (Forge Bks.).

**MERCURY, RYAN (FICTITIOUS CHARACTER)—FICTION**

Koke, Jak. Beyond the Pale. 1998. (Dragon Heart Saga Ser.). 288p. mass mkt. 5.99 o.s.i (*0-451-45674-2*) NAL.
—Clockwork Asylum: The Dragon Heart Saga. 1997. (Shadowrun Ser.: No. 28). 288p. mass mkt. 5.99 o.s.i (*0-451-45620-3*, Signet Bks.) NAL.
—Stranger Souls. 1997. (Shadowrun Ser.: No. 26). 288p. mass mkt. 5.99 o.s.i (*0-451-45610-6*, ROC) NAL.

**MEREDITH, CALLIOPE (FICTITIOUS CHARACTER)—FICTION**

Mildon, Marsha. Fighting for Air. 1995. 185p. (Orig.). pap. text 10.95 (*0-934678-69-3*) New Victoria Pubs., Inc.
—Stalking the Goddess Ship. 1999. 210p. pap. 10.95 (*1-892281-02-3*) New Victoria Pubs., Inc.

**MEREN, LORD (FICTITIOUS CHARACTER)—FICTION**

Robinson, Lynda S. Drinker of Blood. 1998. (Lord Meren Mystery Ser.). 290p. 22.00 (*0-89296-673-4*) Mysterious Pr.
—Eater of Souls: A Lord Meren Mystery. 1997. (Lord Meren Mystery Ser.). 228p. 21.95 (*0-8027-3294-1*) Walker & Co.
—Murder at the Feast of Rejoicing: A Lord Meren Mystery. 3rd ed. 1997. (Lord Meren Mystery Ser.). 256p. mass mkt. 6.50 (*0-345-39532-8*) Ballantine Bks.
—Murder at the Feast of Rejoicing: A Lord Meren Mystery. 1996. (Lord Meren Mystery Ser.). 240p. (YA). 20.95 (*0-8027-3274-7*) Walker & Co.
—Murder at the God's Gate. 1995. (Lord Meren Mystery Ser.). 288p. mass mkt. 6.50 (*0-345-39531-X*) Ballantine Bks.
—Murder at the God's Gate. 1995. 248p. 19.95 (*0-8027-3198-8*) Walker & Co.
—Murder in the Place of Anubis. 1994. (Lord Meren Mystery Ser.). 224p. mass mkt. 6.99 (*0-345-38922-0*) Ballantine Bks.
—Murder in the Place of Anubis. 1994. 203p. 18.95 (*0-8027-3249-6*) Walker & Co.
—Slayer of Gods. 2001. (Lord Meren Mystery Ser.). (Illus.). 256p. 23.45 o.p. (*0-89296-705-6*) Mysterious Pr.

**MERLIN (LEGENDARY CHARACTER)—FICTION**

Ashley, Mike, ed. The Merlin Chronicles. 1995. 448p. (Orig.). pap. 12.95 (*0-7867-0275-3*, Carroll & Graf Pubs.) Avalon Publishing Group.
Atwater, Richard-Merlin. The Three Degrees of Christmas: An Inspirational Christmas Classic. Atwater, Yekaterina A., tr. from RUS. 1997. (Illus.). 254p. 24.95 (*0-9661380-0-7*, 006-1001) Three Swans Publishing Co.
Barron, T. A. Fires of Merlin. 2002. 240p. mass mkt. 5.99 (*0-441-00957-3*) Ace Bks.
—The Lost Years of Merlin. 2002. 304p. mass mkt. 5.99 (*0-441-00930-1*) Ace Bks.
—Mirror of Merlin. 2001. (Lost Years of Merlin Ser.: No. 4). 304p. reprint ed. mass mkt. 6.99 (*0-441-00846-1*) Ace Bks.
—A T. A. Barron Collection: The Lost Years of Merlin; The Seven Songs of Merlin; The Fires of Merlin, 3 bks. in 1. 2001. (Illus.). (J). 14.98 (*0-399-23734-8*, Philomel) Penguin Putnam Bks. for Young Readers.
Chamberlin, Ann. The Merlin of Oak Wood. Date not set. pap. (*0-312-87659-9*, Tor Bks.) Doherty, Tom Assocs., LLC.
—The Merlin of St. Gilles' Well. 2000. mass mkt. 6.99 (*0-8125-9002-3*); 2000. (Joan of Arc Tapestries Ser.: Vol. 1). (Illus.). 320p. pap. 13.95 (*0-312-87591-6*); 2nd ed. 1999. (Joan of Arc Tapestries Ser.: Vol. 1). (Illus.). 320p. 23.95 (*0-312-86551-1*) Doherty, Tom Assocs., LLC. (Tor Bks.).
Chopra, Deepak. El Retorno de Merlin. 1998. (SPA.). 416p. (*84-270-2152-6*) Ediciones Martinez Roca.
—El Retorno de Merlin. (SPA.). pap. 25.00 (*958-04-3512-X*, NR9053) Norma S.A. COL. *Dist:* Lectorum Pubns., Inc.
—The Return of Merlin. 1996. 432p. pap. 14.95 (*0-449-91074-1*, Fawcett) Ballantine Bks.
—The Return of Merlin. l.t. ed. 1996. 24.95 (*1-56895-288-0*, Wheeler Publishing, Inc.) Gale Group.
Cunqueiro, Alvaro. Merlin & Company. Smith, Colin, tr. from SPA. 1996. 224p. pap. 6.95 o.p. (*0-460-87731-3*, Everyman's Classic Library in Paperback) Tuttle Publishing.
Drury, Neville. Merlin's Book of Magic & Enchantment. 1999. (Illus.). 160p. 8.98 (*0-7651-1026-1*) Smithmark Pubs., Inc.
Evans, Quinn Taylor. Daughter of the Mist. 1999. (Merlin's Legacy Ser.: Vol. 2). 416p. 26.95 (*0-7862-1768-5*, Five Star) Gale Group.
—Daughter of the Mist. 1999. mass mkt. 5.99 o.s.i (*0-8217-6753-4*) Kensington Publishing Corp.
—Dawn of Camelot. 1999. (Merlin's Legacy Ser.: Vol. 5). 433p. pap. 25.95 (*0-7862-2080-5*, Five Star) Gale Group.
—Merlin's Legacy. 1999. 25.95 o.p. (*0-7862-1923-8*, Five Star) Gale Group.
Fallingstar, Cerridwen. The Heart of the Fire. 1990. 521p. (Orig.). pap. 15.95 (*0-9621470-0-1*) Cauldron Pubns.
Felderman, Eric. This Prophecy Merlin Shall Make. 1991. (Illus.). 101p. 38.95 (*0-945942-14-1*) Portmanteau Editions.
Grenier, Roger. Another November. Kaplan, Alice Y., tr. from ENG. 1998. Orig. Title: Le Pierrot Noir. 86p. pap. 12.00 (*0-8032-7072-0*) Univ. of Nebraska Pr.
Gunson, Jonathan & Coombe, Marten. The Merlin Mystery. 1998. (Illus.). 48p. 21.00 o.p. (*0-446-52432-8*) Mysterious Pr.
Holdstock, Robert. The Iron Grail. Date not set. pap. (*0-7653-0727-8*); 2004. 320p. 24.95 (*0-7653-0726-X*) Doherty, Tom Assocs., LLC. (Tor Bks.).
King, J. Robert. Mad Merlin. 2000. 304p. 24.95 (*0-312-86963-0*, Tor Bks.) Doherty, Tom Assocs., LLC.
Kock, Ernst A., ed. Henry Lovelich's Merlin, Vol. II. 1963. (EETS Extra Ser.: Vol. 112). 625p. reprint ed. 75.00 (*0-19-722562-4*) Early English Text Society (EETS) GBR. *Dist:* Boydell & Brewer, Inc.
Kornaros, Vitzentzos. Erotocritos. 1984. (C). text 26.95 (*0-85036-335-7*) Merlin Pr. Ltd. GBR. *Dist:* Paul & Co. Pubs. Consortium, Inc.
Lawhead, Stephen R. Merlin. unabr. ed. 1995. audio 85.95 (*0-7861-0708-1*, 1585) Blackstone Audio Bks., Inc.
—Merlin. 1988. (Pendragon Cycle Ser.: Bk. 2). 448p. pap. 11.99 o.p. (*0-89107-436-8*) Crossway Bks.
—Merlin. 1990. (Pendragon Cycle Ser.: Bk. 2). 448p. reprint ed. mass mkt. 7.50 (*0-380-70889-2*, Avon Bks.) Morrow/Avon.
—Merlin. 1996. (Pendragon Cycle Ser.: Bk. 2). 480p. pap. 29.99 (*0-310-20506-9*) Zondervan.
—The Pendragon Cycle: Taliesin; Merlin; Arthur. 1989. pap. 35.97 o.p. (*0-89107-540-2*) Crossway Bks.
Loventhal, Milton & McDowell, Jennifer. Ronnie Goose Rhymes for Grown-Ups. 1984. (Mother Goose Rhymes for Grown-ups Ser.). 10.95 (*0-930142-07-1*) Merlin Pr.
Mallory, James. The End of Magic. 2000. (Merlin Ser.: Vol. 3). 304p. mass mkt. 6.99 (*0-446-60792-4*) Warner Bks., Inc.
—The King's Wizard. 1999. (Merlin Ser.: Vol. 2). 304p. mass mkt. 6.99 (*0-446-60791-6*) Warner Bks., Inc.
—Merlin: The End of Magic. 1999. 287p. (*0-00-651291-7*) HarperCollins Pubs.
—Merlin Pt. I: The Old Magic. l.t. ed. 1999. (G. K. Hall Science Fiction Ser.). 283p. 23.95 (*0-7838-8772-8*) Thorndike Pr.
—The Old Magic. 1999. (Merlin Ser.: Vol. 1). 288p. mass mkt. 6.99 (*0-446-60766-5*) Warner Bks., Inc.
Neill, Gene. I'm Gonna Bury You! 11th rev. ed. 1991. (Illus.). 210p. reprint ed. pap. 5.00 (*0-9608028-0-0*) Voice of Triumph, Inc., The.
Obrien, Judith. One Perfect Knight. 1998. 380p. pap. 6.50 (*0-671-00040-3*, Pocket) Simon & Schuster.
Radford, Irene. Guardian of the Trust. 2000. (Merlin's Descendants Ser.: Vol. 2). (Illus.). 480p. 23.95 o.s.i (*0-88677-874-3*) DAW Bks., Inc.
—Guardian of the Vision, Vol. 3. (Merlin's Descendants Ser.: Vol. 3). 2001. (Illus.). 480p. 23.95 (*0-88677-994-4*); 2002. 560p. reprint ed. mass mkt. 6.99 (*0-7564-0071-6*) DAW Bks., Inc.
Saberhagen, Fred. Merlin's Bones. 1995. 384p. 22.95 o.p. (*0-312-85563-X*, Tor Bks.) Doherty, Tom Assocs., LLC.
Spinner, Stephanie & Sokolova, Valerie. The Magic of Merlin. 2000. (Road to Reading Ser.). (Illus.). 48p. (J). (ps-3). pap. 3.99 (*0-307-26403-3*, Golden Bks.) Random Hse. Children's Bks.
Stewart, Mary. The Crystal Cave. (Book I of the Arthurian Saga Ser.). 1996. 544p. pap. 12.95 o.s.i (*0-449-91161-6*); 1984. pap. 3.95 o.p. (*0-449-44118-0*); 1984. 384p. mass mkt. 6.50 o.s.i (*0-449-20644-0*); 1983. mass mkt. 3.95 o.s.i (*0-449-20563-0*); 1978. mass mkt. 1.95 o.s.i (*0-449-23315-4*) Ballantine Bks. (Fawcett).
—The Crystal Cave. unabr. ed. 2000. (Merlin Ser.: Bk. 1). audio 79.95 (*0-7451-6305-X*, CAB 676) Chivers Audio Bks. GBR. *Dist:* BBC Audiobooks America.
—The Crystal Cave. l.t. ed. 1982. (Reader's Request Ser.). 19.95 o.p. (*0-8161-3338-7*, Macmillan Reference USA) Gale Group.

—The Crystal Cave. 2003. (Illus.). 512p. pap. 14.95 (*0-06-054825-8*, Morrow, William & Co.) Morrow/Avon.

—The Crystal Cave, Set. abr. ed. 1993. audio 16.95 o.p. (*1-55800-224-3*, Dove Audio) NewStar Media, Inc.

—The Crystal Cave. 1983. 19.00 (*0-606-18993-9*) Turtleback Bks.

—The Hollow Hills. 1996. (Arthurian Saga Ser.: Vol. 2). 512p. pap. 14.00 o.s.i (*0-449-91173-X*); 1984. pap. 3.95 o.p. (*0-449-44119-9*); 1984. mass mkt. 5.95 o.s.i (*0-449-20645-9*); 1978. mass mkt. 1.95 o.s.i (*0-449-23316-2*) Ballantine Bks. (Fawcett).

—The Hollow Hills. 1991. 400p. reprint ed. lib. bdg. 37.95 (*0-89966-855-0*) Buccaneer Bks., Inc.

—The Hollow Hills. l.t. ed. 1982. 19.95 o.p. (*0-8161-3339-5*, Macmillan Reference USA) Gale Group.

—The Hollow Hills. 2003. (Illus.). 496p. pap. 14.95 (*0-06-054826-6*); 1973. 512p. 9.95 o.p. (*0-688-00179-3*, Morrow, William & Co.) Morrow/Avon.

—The Hollow Hills. abr. ed. 1993. audio 15.95 o.p. (*1-55800-227-8*, Dove Audio) NewStar Media, Inc.

—The Hollow Hills. 1984. 19.00 (*0-606-18994-7*) Turtleback Bks.

—The Last Enchantment. 1996. (Arthurian Saga Ser.: Vol. 3). 544p. pap. 14.00 o.s.i (*0-449-91176-4*); 1984. pap. 3.95 o.s.i (*0-449-44120-2*); 1984. mass mkt. 5.95 o.s.i (*0-449-20646-7*) Ballantine Bks. (Fawcett).

—The Last Enchantment. unabr. ed. 2000. (Merlin Ser.: Bk. 3). audio 79.95 (*0-7451-4128-5*, CAB 811) Chivers Audio Bks. GBR. *Dist:* BBC Audiobooks America.

—The Last Enchantment. l.t. ed. 1982. 19.95 o.p. (*0-8161-3340-9*, Macmillan Reference USA) Gale Group.

—The Last Enchantment. 2003. (Illus.). 528p. pap. 14.95 (*0-06-054827-4*, Morrow, William & Co.) Morrow/Avon.

—The Last Enchantment. abr. ed. 1993. audio 15.95 o.p. (*1-55800-228-6*, Dove Audio) NewStar Media, Inc.

—The Last Enchantment. 1984. 20.05 (*0-606-18995-5*) Turtleback Bks.

—Mary Stewart's Merlin Trilogy. 1980. 928p. 29.95 (*0-688-00347-8*, Morrow, William & Co.) Morrow/Avon.

Whyte, Jack. The Fort at River's Bend. (Camulod Chronicles: Bk. 5). (Illus.). 2000. 480p. mass mkt. 6.99 (*0-8125-4418-8*, Tor Bks.); 1999. 352p. 24.95 (*0-312-86597-X*, Forge Bks.) Doherty, Tom Assocs., LLC.

—The Saxon Shore. 1998. (Camulod Chronicles: Bk. 4). (Illus.). 496p. 26.95 o.p. (*0-312-86596-1*, Forge Bks.) Doherty, Tom Assocs., LLC.

—The Sorcerer: Metamorphosis. 1999. (Camulod Chronicles: Bk. 6). (Illus.). 352p. 23.95 (*0-312-86598-8*, Forge Bks.) Doherty, Tom Assocs., LLC.

—Uther. 2001. (Camulod Chronicles: Bk. 7). (Illus.). viii, 916p. mass mkt. 7.99 (*0-8125-7102-9*, Tor Bks.) Doherty, Tom Assocs., LLC.

—Uther: Camulod Chronicles. 2001. (Camulod Chronicles: Bk. 7). (Illus.). 623p. 27.95 (*0-312-86443-4*, Forge Bks.) Doherty, Tom Assocs., LLC.

**MERRICK FAMILY (FICTITIOUS CHARACTERS)—FICTION**

Hill, Deborah. The House of Kingsley Merrick. 1979. mass mkt. 2.50 o.p. (*0-451-08918-9*, E8918, Signet Bks.) NAL.

—Kingsland. 1981. mass mkt. 2.95 o.p. (*0-451-11263-6*, AE 1263, Signet Bks.) NAL.

—This Is the House. 1981. mass mkt. 3.50 o.p. (*0-451-11272-5*, AE1272); 1979. mass mkt. 2.50 o.p. (*0-451-08877-8*); 1977. mass mkt. 1.95 o.p. (*0-451-07610-9*) NAL. (Signet Bks.).

**MERRIMAN, MAGNUS (FICTITIOUS CHARACTER)—FICTION**

Brown, George M. Magnus. 1999. 196p. pap. 11.95 (*0-86241-814-3*) Canongate Bks. GBR. *Dist:* Grove/Atlantic, Inc.

**MERRIVALE, HENRY, SIR (FICTITIOUS CHARACTER)—FICTION**

Carr, John Dickson. Merrivale, March & Murder. Greene, Douglas G., ed. 1992. 350p. 22.95 o.p. (*1-55882-101-5*) International Polygonics, Ltd.

Dickson, Carter, pseud. And So to Murder. l.t. ed. 18.95 o.p. (*0-7451-6426-9*); 1993. pap. 16.95 o.p. (*0-7451-6432-3*); 1989. audio 54.95 (*0-7451-5902-8*) BBC Audiobooks America.

—And So to Murder. 1988. mass mkt. 3.50 o.p. (*0-8217-2536-X*, Zebra Bks.) Kensington Publishing Corp.

—Behind the Crimson Blind. 1989. mass mkt. 3.50 o.p. (*0-8217-2607-2*, Zebra Bks.) Kensington Publishing Corp.

—The Cavalier's Cup. 1987. mass mkt. 3.50 o.s.i (*0-8217-2170-4*, Zebra Bks.) Kensington Publishing Corp.

—The Curse of the Bronze Lamp. 1997. 192p. mass mkt. 4.95 (*0-7867-0440-3*); 1984. 260p. pap. 3.50 o.p. (*0-88184-101-3*) Avalon Publishing Group. (Carroll & Graf Pubs.).

—The Curse of the Bronze Lamp. 1945. o.s.i (*0-688-05616-4*, Morrow, William & Co.) Morrow/Avon.

—Death in Five Boxes. 1977. reprint ed. pap. 1.50 o.s.i (*0-505-51203-3*) Dorchester Publishing Co., Inc.

—Death in Five Boxes. 1991. 192p. reprint ed. pap. text 5.95 o.p. (*1-55882-098-1*, Library of Crime Classics) International Polygonics, Ltd.

—The Gilded Man. 1988. 256p. reprint ed. pap. 4.95 o.p. (*0-930330-88-9*, Library of Crime Classics) International Polygonics, Ltd.

—A Graveyard to Let. 1978. reprint ed. pap. 1.50 o.s.i (*0-505-51222-X*) Dorchester Publishing Co., Inc.

—He Wouldn't Kill Patience. 1988. 192p. pap. 4.95 o.p. (*0-930330-86-2*) International Polygonics, Ltd.

—The Judas Window. 1987. 192p. pap. 5.95 o.p. (*0-930330-62-5*) International Polygonics, Ltd.

—Merrivale Holds the Key: Two Classic Locked-Room Mysteries. 1995. 628p. pap. 14.95 (*1-55882-027-2*) International Polygonics, Ltd.

—My Late Wives. 1988. 288p. mass mkt. 3.50 o.p. (*0-8217-2384-7*, Zebra Bks.) Kensington Publishing Corp.

—Night at the Mocking Widow. 1988. 320p. mass mkt. 3.50 o.p. (*0-8217-2463-0*, Zebra Bks.) Kensington Publishing Corp.

—Nine & Death Makes Ten. (Black Dagger Crime Ser.). 12.95 o.p. (*0-86220-797-5*, BD002) Chivers Pr. GBR. *Dist:* BBC Audiobooks America.

—Nine & Death Makes Ten. 1987. 175p. reprint ed. pap. 5.95 (*0-930330-69-2*) International Polygonics, Ltd.

—The Peacock Feather Murders. 1987. 192p. reprint ed. pap. 5.95 o.p. (*0-930330-68-4*) International Polygonics, Ltd.

—The Plague Court Murders. 1990. 285p. reprint ed. pap. 5.95 o.p. (*1-55882-062-0*) International Polygonics, Ltd.

—The Punch & Judy Murders. 1988. 192p. pap. 4.95 o.p. (*0-930330-85-4*) International Polygonics, Ltd.

—The Reader Is Warned. 1989. 192p. pap. 5.95 o.p. (*1-55882-019-1*, Library of Crime Classics) International Polygonics, Ltd.

—The Red Widow Murders. 1988. 302p. reprint ed. pap. 4.95 o.p. (*0-930330-87-0*, Library of Crime Classics) International Polygonics, Ltd.

—Seeing Is Believing. 1990. mass mkt. 3.50 o.p. (*0-8217-2928-4*, Zebra Bks.) Kensington Publishing Corp.

—She Died a Lady. 1987. 256p. mass mkt. 3.50 o.p. (*0-8217-2238-7*, Zebra Bks.) Kensington Publishing Corp.

—The Skeleton in the Clock. 1977. reprint ed. pap. 1.50 o.s.i (*0-505-51194-0*) Dorchester Publishing Co., Inc.

—The Skeleton in the Clock. 1992. 303p. pap. 5.95 o.p. (*1-55882-103-1*) International Polygonics, Ltd.

—The Unicorn Murders. 2000. 21.95 (*0-7540-8568-6*, Black Dagger) BBC Audiobooks America.

—The Unicorn Murders. 1989. 192p. reprint ed. pap. 5.95 o.p. (*1-55882-015-9*, Library of Crime Classics) International Polygonics, Ltd.

—The White Priory Murders. 1990. 214p. reprint ed. pap. 5.95 o.s.i (*1-55882-072-8*) International Polygonics, Ltd.

Dickson, Carter, pseud & Melling, John K. Behind the Crimson Blind. 1990. (Black Dagger Crime Ser.). 280p. reprint ed. text 16.50 o.p. (*0-86220-768-1*, Black Dagger) BBC Audiobooks America.

**MERSI, MICK (FICTITIOUS CHARACTER)—FICTION**

St. Edmunds, Anne. Red Right Returning. 1997. (New England Mystery Ser.). per. (*0-373-26258-2*, 1-26258-3, Worldwide Library) Harlequin Enterprises, Ltd.

—Red Right Returning. 1996. 224p. 20.95 o.p. (*0-312-14033-9*, Saint Martin's Minotaur) St. Martin's Pr.

**MESPIL, LUNZIE (FICTITIOUS CHARACTER)—FICTION**

McCaffrey, Anne & Moon, Elizabeth. Generation Warriors. 2002. 352p. reprint ed. pap. 6.99 (*0-671-72041-4*) Baen Bks.

McCaffrey, Anne & Nye, Jody L. The Death of Sleep. 1990. 384p. (Orig.). pap. 6.99 (*0-671-69884-2*) Baen Bks.

**METCALF, CONRAD (FICTITIOUS CHARACTER)—FICTION**

Lethem, Jonathan. Gun, with Occasional Music. 5th ed. 1995. 262p. pap. 12.95 (*0-312-85878-7*, CPB1189, Tor Bks.) Doherty, Tom Assocs., LLC.

—Gun, with Occasional Music. 1994. 262p. 19.95 o.s.i (*0-15-136458-3*) Harcourt Trade Pubs.

**METELLUS, DECIUS CAECILIUS (FICTITIOUS CHARACTER)—FICTION**

Roberts, John Maddox. The Catiline Conspiracy. 1991. (SPQR Ser. : No. 2). 224p. mass mkt. 3.50 (*0-380-75995-0*, Avon Bks.) Morrow/Avon.

—The Sacrilege. 1999. (SPQR Ser.: Vol. 3). 256p. pap. 13.95 (*0-312-24697-8*, Saint Martin's Griffin) St. Martin's Pr.

—The Sacrilege: An SPQR Mystery. 1992. 224p. (Orig.). mass mkt. 4.50 (*0-380-76627-2*, Avon Bks.) Morrow/Avon.

—The Temple of the Muses. 1992. (SPQR Ser. : No. 4). 224p. (Orig.). mass mkt. 4.50 (*0-380-76629-9*, Avon Bks.) Morrow/Avon.

—The Temple of the Muses. 3rd ed. 1999. (SPQR Ser.: Vol. 4). 240p. (Orig.). pap. 13.95 (*0-312-24698-6*, CPB1103, Saint Martin's Griffin) St. Martin's Pr.

—The Tribune's Curse. 2003. (SPQR Ser.: No. VII). (Illus.). 224p. 22.95 o.s.i (*0-312-30488-9*, Saint Martin's Minotaur) St. Martin's Pr.

**MIATHAN, ARCHMAGE (FICTITIOUS CHARACTER)—FICTION**

Furey, Maggie. Aurian. 1994. 608p. mass mkt. 6.99 (*0-553-56525-7*) Bantam Bks.

—Harp of Winds. 1995. 464p. mass mkt. 6.99 (*0-553-56526-5*, Spectra) Bantam Bks.

—Sword of the Flame. 1996. (Bantam Spectra Book Ser.). 464p. mass mkt. 7.50 (*0-553-56527-3*, Spectra) Bantam Bks.

**MICHAELS, LAURA (FICTITIOUS CHARACTER)—FICTION**

Miles, John. A Most Deadly Retirement. 1997. per. (*0-373-26252-3*, 1-26252-6, Worldwide Library) Harlequin Enterprises, Ltd.

—A Most Deadly Retirement: A Laura Michaels Mystery. 1995. 246p. 22.95 (*0-8027-3258-5*) Walker & Co.

—Murder in Retirement. 1997. (WWL Mystery Ser.: No. 243). per. (*0-373-26243-4*, 1-26243-5, Worldwide Library) Harlequin Enterprises, Ltd.

—Murder in Retirement: A Laura Michaels Mystery. 1994. 246p. 19.95 (*0-8027-3246-1*) Walker & Co.

—A Permanent Retirement. 1997. (Laura Michaels Mystery Ser.). 256p. per. (*0-373-26228-0*, 1-26228-6, Worldwide Library) Harlequin Enterprises, Ltd.

—A Permanent Retirement. 1992. 230p. 19.95 (*0-8027-1243-6*) Walker & Co.

**MICHAELSON, RICHARD (FICTITIOUS CHARACTER)—FICTION**

Bowen, Michael. Collateral Damage. pap. 15.95 (*0-312-29181-7*, Saint Martin's Griffin); 1999. 224p. 22.95 (*0-312-20289-X*, Saint Martin's Minotaur) St. Martin's Pr.

—Corruptly Procured: A Richard Michaelson Mystery. 1994. 256p. 20.95 o.p. (*0-312-10524-X*, Saint Martin's Minotaur) St. Martin's Pr.

—Coyote Wind: A Montana Mystery. 1995. (Montana Mystery Ser.). mass mkt. 4.50 (*0-312-95601-0*, St. Martin's Paperbacks) St. Martin's Pr.

—Faithfully Executed. 1991. 240p. 17.95 o.p. (*0-312-07018-7*, Saint Martin's Minotaur) St. Martin's Pr.

—Washington Deceased. 1990. 10.95 o.p. (*0-312-05179-4*, Saint Martin's Minotaur) St. Martin's Pr.

—Worst Case Scenario. 1996. 224p. 24.00 o.s.i (*0-517-70149-9*) Random Hse., Inc.

—Worst Case Scenario: A Washington, D. C. Mystery. l.t. ed. 1997. 257p. 23.95 o.p. (*0-7838-8072-3*, Macmillan Reference USA) Gale Group.

**MIDDLETON, MARIS (FICTITIOUS CHARACTER)—FICTION**

Davis, Kaye. Devil's Leg Crossing. 1997. (Maris Middleton Mysteries Ser.). 240p. pap. 11.95 o.p. (*1-56280-158-9*) Naiad Pr., Inc.

—Possessions: A Maris Middleton Mystery. 1998. (Maris Middleton Mysteries Ser.). 240p. (Orig.). pap. 11.95 (*1-56280-192-9*) Naiad Pr., Inc.

—Shattered Illusions: A Maris Middleton Mystery. 1999. (Maris Middleton Mysteries Ser.: No. 4). 240p. pap. 11.95 (*1-56280-252-6*) Naiad Pr., Inc.

—Until the End: A Maris Middleton Mystery. 1999. (Maris Middleton Mysteries Ser.: No. 3). 224p. pap. 11.95 (*1-56280-222-4*) Naiad Pr., Inc.

**MIDDLETON-BROWN, DAVID (FICTITIOUS CHARACTER)—FICTION**

Charles, Kate. Appointed to Die. 1994. 368p. 19.95 o.s.i (*0-89296-548-7*) Mysterious Pr.

—Appointed to Die. 1995. 352p. mass mkt. 5.99 o.s.i (*0-446-40361-X*) Warner Bks., Inc.

—A Dead Man Out of Mind. l.t. ed. 1996. (G. K. Hall Mystery Ser.). 429p. 22.95 o.p. (*0-7838-1706-1*, Macmillan Reference USA) Gale Group.

—A Dead Man Out of Mind. 1995. 82p. 19.95 o.p. (*0-89296-585-1*) Mysterious Pr.

—A Dead Man Out of Mind. 1996. 288p. mass mkt. 5.99 o.p. (*0-446-40432-2*) Warner Bks., Inc.

—A Drink of Deadly Wine. 1992. 336p. 17.95 (*0-89296-501-0*) Mysterious Pr.

—A Drink of Deadly Wine. 1993. (Book of Psalms Mysteries Ser.). 304p. mass mkt. 5.99 o.s.i (*0-446-40194-3*) Warner Bks., Inc.

—Evil Angels among Them. l.t. ed. 1997. (G. K. Hall Mystery Ser.). 371p. lib. bdg. 25.95 o.p. (*0-7838-2024-0*, Macmillan Reference USA) Gale Group.

—Evil Angels among Them. 352p. 1997. mass mkt. 6.50 (*0-446-40521-3*, Mysterious Pr. Paperback Bks.); 1996. 21.50 o.p. (*0-89296-639-4*) Warner Bks., Inc.

—The Snares of Death. 1993. 368p. 18.95 (*0-89296-498-7*) Mysterious Pr.

—The Snares of Death. 1994. 352p. mass mkt. 5.50 (*0-446-40195-1*) Warner Bks., Inc.

—Unruly Passions. 2001. 440p. pap. 8.95 (*0-7515-2437-9*) Warner Bks. GBR. *Dist:* Trafalgar Square.

**MIDNIGHT, BRENDA (FICTITIOUS CHARACTER)—FICTION**

Wilson, Barbara J. Accessory to Murder. 1998. (Brenda Midnight Mysteries Ser.). mass mkt. 5.50 (*0-380-78821-7*, Avon Bks.) Morrow/Avon.

—Capped Off. 1999. (Brenda Midnight Mysteries Ser.). 256p. mass mkt. 5.99 (*0-380-80355-0*, Avon Bks.) Morrow/Avon.

—Death Brims Over. 1997. (Brenda Midnight Mysteries Ser.). mass mkt. 5.50 (*0-380-78820-9*, Avon Bks.) Morrow/Avon.

—Death Flips It's Lid. 1998. (Brenda Midnight Mysteries Ser.). mass mkt. 5.99 (*0-380-78822-5*, Avon Bks.) Morrow/Avon.

—Murder & the Mad Hatter: A Brenda Midnight Mystery. 2001. (Brenda Midnight Mysteries Ser.). 256p. mass mkt. 5.99 (*0-380-80357-7*, Avon Bks.) Morrow/Avon.

**MIDNIGHT LOUIE (FICTITIOUS CHARACTER)—FICTION**

Douglas, Carole Nelson. The Cat & the King of Clubs. 1999. (Mystery Ser.). 227p. 20.95 (*0-7862-1920-3*, Five Star) Gale Group.

—The Cat & the Queen of Hearts. 1999. (Mystery Ser.). 223p. 21.95 (*0-7862-2173-9*, Five Star) Gale Group.

—Cat in a Crimson Haze: A Midnight Louie Mystery. (Midnight Louie Mystery Ser.). 1996. 408p. mass mkt. 6.99 (*0-8125-4414-5*, Forge Bks.); 1996. mass mkt. 219.68 (*0-8125-6330-1*); 1995. 352p. 22.95 o.p. (*0-312-85901-5*, Forge Bks.) Doherty, Tom Assocs., LLC.

—Cat in a Crimson Haze: A Midnight Louie Mystery. l.t. ed. 1995. (Midnight Louie Mystery Ser.). 604p. 24.95 o.p. (*0-7838-1390-2*, Macmillan Reference USA) Gale Group.

—Cat in a Crimson Haze: A Midnight Louie Mystery. 1996. mass mkt. 223.68 (*0-8125-6329-8*) Holtzbrinck Pubs.

—Cat in a Diamond Dazzle: A Midnight Louie Mystery. (Midnight Louie Mystery Ser.). 1997. 411p. mass mkt. 6.99 (*0-8125-5506-6*); 1996. 416p. 24.95 o.p. (*0-312-86085-4*) Doherty, Tom Assocs., LLC. (Forge Bks.).

—Cat in a Flamingo Fedora: A Midnight Louie Mystery. (Midnight Louie Mystery Ser.). 1998. 373p. mass mkt. 6.99 (*0-8125-6535-5*); 1997. 384p. 24.95 o.p. (*0-312-86329-2*) Doherty, Tom Assocs., LLC. (Forge Bks.).

—Cat in a Golden Garland: A Midnight Louie Mystery. (Midnight Louie Mystery Ser.). 1998. 406p. mass mkt. 6.99 (*0-8125-3036-5*); 1997. 352p. 23.95 (*0-312-86386-1*) Doherty, Tom Assocs., LLC. (Forge Bks.).

—Cat in a Golden Garland: A Midnight Louie Mystery. l.t. ed. 1998. (G. K. Hall Core Ser.). 576p. 25.95 o.p. (*0-7838-8419-2*, Macmillan Reference USA) Gale Group.

—Cat in a Jeweled Jumpsuit: A Midnight Louie Mystery. 2000. 432p. mass mkt. 6.99 (*0-8125-6674-2*); 1999. 384p. 24.95 (*0-312-86817-0*) Doherty, Tom Assocs., LLC. (Forge Bks.).

—Cat in a Jeweled Jumpsuit: A Midnight Louie Mystery. abr. ed. 1999. audio 25.00 (*0-7871-2353-6*, Dove Audio) NewStar Media, Inc.

—Cat in a Jeweled Jumpsuit: A Midnight Louie Mystery. l.t. ed. 2000. (Americana Ser.). 599p. 29.95 (*0-7862-2455-X*) Thorndike Pr.

—Cat in a Kiwi Con: A Midnight Louie Mystery. (Midnight Louie Mystery Ser.). 2001. 432p. mass mkt. 6.99 (*0-8125-8425-2*); 2000. 384p. 24.95 o.p. (*0-312-86955-X*) Doherty, Tom Assocs., LLC. (Forge Bks.).

—Cat in a Leopard Spot: A Midnight Louie Mystery. E-Book 24.95 (*0-312-70128-4*, Tor Bks.); 2002. 416p. pap. 6.99 (*0-8125-7022-7*, Forge Bks.); 2001. 384p. 24.95 (*0-312-85370-X*, Forge Bks.) Doherty, Tom Assocs., LLC.

—Cat in a Midnight Choir: A Midnight Louie Mystery. E-Book 24.95 (*0-312-70619-7*, Tor Bks.); 2003. 416p. mass mkt. 24.95 (*0-8125-7021-9*, Forge Bks.); 2002. 336p. 24.95 (*0-312-85797-7*, Forge Bks.) Doherty, Tom Assocs., LLC.

—Cat in a Neon Nightmare. Date not set. mass mkt. (*0-7653-4592-7*, Forge Bks.) Doherty, Tom Assocs., LLC.

—Cat in a Neon Nightmare. l.t. ed. 2003. 582p. 29.95 (*0-7862-5755-5*) Thorndike Pr.

—Cat in a Neon Nightmare: A Midnight Louie Mystery. 2003. (Midnight Louie Mystery Ser.). 384p. 24.95 (*0-7653-0680-8*, Forge Bks.) Doherty, Tom Assocs., LLC.

—Cat in an Indigo Mood: A Midnight Louie Mystery. l.t. ed. 2003. (Large Print Ser.). 29.95 (*1-57490-473-6*, Beeler Large Print Bks.) Beeler, Thomas T. Publisher.

—Cat in an Indigo Mood: A Midnight Louie Mystery. 1999. 384p. mass mkt. 6.99 (*0-8125-6187-2*); (Illus.). 381p. 24.95 (*0-312-86635-6*) Doherty, Tom Assocs., LLC. (Forge Bks.).

—Cat in an Indigo Mood: A Midnight Louie Mystery. abr. ed. 1999. (Midnight Louie Mysteries Ser.). audio 18.00 (*0-7871-1911-3*, Dove Audio) NewStar Media, Inc.

—Cat on a Blue Monday: A Midnight Louie Mystery. l.t. ed. 1994. o.p. (*0-7927-2111-X*); pap. o.p. (*0-7927-2110-1*) BBC Audiobooks America.

—Cat on a Blue Monday: A Midnight Louie Mystery. 1994. (Midnight Louie Mystery Ser.). 374p. mass mkt. 6.99 (*0-8125-3441-7*); 384p. 21.95 o.p. (*0-312-85607-5*) Doherty, Tom Assocs., LLC. (Forge Bks.).

—Cat on a Blue Monday: A Midnight Louie Mystery. l.t. ed. 1994. 540p. pap. 17.95 o.p. (*0-8161-7456-3*, Macmillan Reference USA) Gale Group.

—Cat on a Hyacinth Hunt: A Midnight Louie Mystery. (Midnight Louie Mystery Ser.). 384p. 1999. mass mkt. 6.99 (*0-8125-6186-4*); 1998. 23.95 (*0-312-86634-8*) Doherty, Tom Assocs., LLC. (Forge Bks.).

—Cat on a Hyacinth Hunt: A Midnight Louie Mystery. l.t. ed. 2000. pap. 23.95 (*1-56895-872-2*, Wheeler Publishing, Inc.) Gale Group.

—Cat on a Hyacinth Hunt: A Midnight Louie Mystery. abr. ed. 1998. (Midnight Louie Mysteries Ser.). 3p. audio 19.95 (*0-7871-1749-8*, Dove Audio) NewStar Media, Inc.

—Cat with an Emerald Eye: A Midnight Louie Mystery. (Midnight Louie Mystery Ser.). 384p. 1997. mass mkt. 6.99 (*0-8125-4012-3*); 1996. 24.95 o.p. (*0-312-86228-8*) Doherty, Tom Assocs., LLC. (Forge Bks.).

—Catnap: A Midnight Louie Mystery. l.t. ed. 1993. (Midnight Louie Mystery Ser.). 23.95 o.p. (*0-7927-1644-2*); pap. 21.95 o.p. (*0-7927-1643-4*) BBC Audiobooks America.

—Catnap: A Midnight Louie Mystery. (Midnight Louie Mystery Ser.). 1993. 241p. mass mkt. 6.99 (*0-8125-1682-6*, Forge Bks.); 1992. 256p. 17.95 o.p. (*0-312-85217-7*, Tor Bks.) Doherty, Tom Assocs., LLC.

—Pussyfoot: A Midnight Louie Mystery. l.t. ed. 1994. (Midnight Louie Mystery Ser.). 24.95 o.p. (*0-7927-1846-1*); pap. 22.95 o.p. (*0-7927-1845-3*) BBC Audiobooks America.

—Pussyfoot: A Midnight Louie Mystery. (Midnight Louie Mystery Ser.). 1994. 304p. mass mkt. 5.99 (*0-8125-1683-4*); 1993. 256p. 19.95 o.p. (*0-312-85218-5*) Doherty, Tom Assocs., LLC. (Tor Bks.).

**MILLER, ANNIK (FICTITIOUS CHARACTER)—FICTION**

Brahms, Ann. Run for Your Life. 1993. 352p. mass mkt. 4.50 o.s.i (*0-8217-4193-4*, Zebra Bks.) Kensington Publishing Corp.

**MILLER, CLAUDIA (FICTITIOUS CHARACTER)—FICTION**

Wallace, Marilyn. Current Danger. 1999. 320p. mass mkt. 5.99 o.s.i (*0-553-58072-8*) Bantam Bks.

—Current Danger. l.t. ed. 1998. 317p. 24.95 (*1-57490-140-0*, Beeler Large Print Bks.) Beeler, Thomas T. Publisher.

**MILLER, LYDIA (FICTITIOUS CHARACTER)—FICTION**

Hyde, Eleanor. Animal Instincts. 1996. 230p. mass mkt. 5.50 o.s.i (*0-449-14941-2*, Fawcett) Ballantine Bks.

—In Murder We Trust. 1995. mass mkt. 5.50 o.s.i (*0-449-14942-0*, Fawcett) Ballantine Bks.

**MILLER, PETER, LIEUTENANT (FICTITIOUS CHARACTER)—FICTION**

Dietz, Denise. Beat up a Cookie: An Ellie Bernstein Mystery. 2000. per. (*0-373-26340-6*, Harlequin Bks.) Harlequin Enterprises, Ltd.

—Beat up a Cookie: An Ellie Bernstein Mystery. 1994. 216p. 19.95 o.p. (*0-8027-3186-4*) Walker & Co.

—Footprints in the Butter: An Ingrid Beaumont Mystery Co-Starring Hitchcock the Dog. 1999. 224p. 21.95 (*0-9663397-2-X*, 16579330) Delphi Bks.

—Throw Darts at a Cheesecake. 1999. per. (*0-373-26334-1*, Harlequin Bks.) Harlequin Enterprises, Ltd.

—Throw Darts at a Cheesecake. 1992. 211p. 19.95 o.p. (*0-8027-1237-1*) Walker & Co.

**MILLER, RICHARD MILHOUS 'NIX' (FICTITIOUS CHARACTER)—FICTION**

Eversz, Robert M. Gypsy Hearts. 1997. 272p. 23.00 o.p. (*0-8021-1609-4*, Grove Pr.) Grove/Atlantic, Inc.

**MILLER, ROBIN (FICTITIOUS CHARACTER)—FICTION**

Maiman, Jaye. Baby, It's Cold: A Robin Miller Mystery. 1997. (Robin Miller Mysteries Ser.: Vol. 5). 256p. pap. 10.95 o.p. (*1-56280-156-2*); 1996. 288p. 19.95 (*1-56280-141-4*) Naiad Pr., Inc.

—Crazy for Loving. 1992. (Robin Miller Mysteries Ser.: No. 2). 320p. pap. 11.95 (*1-56280-025-6*) Naiad Pr., Inc.

—Every Time We Say Goodbye. 1999. (Robin Miller Mysteries Ser.: No. 7). 250p. pap. 11.95 (*1-56280-248-8*) Naiad Pr., Inc.

—I Left My Heart. 1991. (Robin Miller Mysteries Ser.: Vol. 1). 320p. pap. 11.95 o.p. (*0-941483-72-X*) Naiad Pr., Inc.

—Old Black Magic: A Robin Miller Mystery. 1997. (Robin Miller Mysteries Ser.: Vol. 6). 288p. pap. 11.95 o.p. (*1-56280-175-9*) Naiad Pr., Inc.

—Someone to Watch. 1995. (Robin Miller Mysteries Ser.: Vol. 4). 288p. pap. 10.95 (*1-56280-095-7*) Naiad Pr., Inc.

—Under My Skin. 1993. (Robin Miller Mysteries Ser.: No. 3). 336p. pap. 11.95 (*1-56280-049-3*) Naiad Pr., Inc.

**MILLHOLLAND, KATE (FICTITIOUS CHARACTER)—FICTION**

Hartzmark, Gini. A Bitter Business. (Kate Millholland Novel Ser.). 1997. 340p. mass mkt. 5.99 o.s.i (*0-8041-1241-X*, Ivy Bks.); 1995. 320p. 4.99 o.s.i (*0-449-90989-1*, Fawcett) Ballantine Bks.

—Dead Certain. 2000. (Kate Millholland Novel Ser.). 320p. mass mkt. 6.50 o.s.i (*0-8041-1900-7*, Ivy Bks.) Ballantine Bks.

—Fatal Reaction. 1998. (Kate Millholland Novel Ser.). 352p. mass mkt. 6.50 o.s.i (*0-8041-1743-8*, Ivy Bks.) Ballantine Bks.

—Final Option. 1994. (Midwest Mysteries Ser.). (Orig.). mass mkt. 5.99 o.s.i (*0-8041-1227-4*, Ivy Bks.) Ballantine Bks.

—Principal Defense. 1992. (Midwest Mysteries Ser.). mass mkt. 5.99 o.s.i (*0-8041-1074-3*, Ivy Bks.) Ballantine Bks.

—Rough Trade. 1999. 293p. mass mkt. 6.50 (*0-8041-1829-9*, Ivy Bks.) Ballantine Bks.

**MILLHONE, KINSEY (FICTITIOUS CHARACTER)—FICTION**

Grafton, Sue. A Is for Alibi. 1987. mass mkt. 3.50 o.s.i (*0-553-26563-6*); 224p. mass mkt. 7.99 (*0-553-27991-2*) Bantam Bks.

— A Is for Alibi, unabr. collector's ed. 1993. (Kinsey Millhone Mystery Ser.). audio 48.00 (*0-7366-2455-4*, 3219) Books on Tape, Inc.

— A Is for Alibi. 1994. (Kinsey Millhone Mystery Ser.). reprint ed. lib. bdg. 29.95 o.p. (*1-56849-284-7*) Buccaneer Bks., Inc.

— A Is for Alibi. l.t. ed. 1991. (Kinsey Millhone Mystery Ser.). 354p. 20.95 o.p. (*0-8161-5144-X*, Macmillan Reference USA) Gale Group.

— A Is for Alibi. 1982. (Kinsey Millhone Mystery Ser.). 256p. o.p. (*0-03-059048-5*); 288p. 27.00 (*0-8050-1334-2*) Holt, Henry & Co.

— A Is for Alibi. 1984. (Kinsey Millhone Mystery Ser.). 192p. mass mkt. 2.75 o.p. (*0-451-12862-1*) NAL.

— A Is for Alibi, Set. abr. ed. 1990. (Kinsey Millhone Mystery Ser.). audio 18.00 o.s.i (*0-394-57977-1*, 390310, RH Audio) Random Hse. Audio Publishing Group.

— A Is for Alibi. 2001. (Kinsey Millhone Mystery Ser.). 285p. (*0-7621-8860-X*) Reader's Digest Assn., Inc., The.

— A Is for Alibi. l.t. ed. 1988. (Kinsey Millhone Mystery Ser.). 432p. 15.95 o.p. (*0-7089-1744-5*, Ulverscroft) Thorpe, F. A. Pubs. GBR. *Dist:* Ulverscroft Large Print Bks., Ltd.

—B Is for Burglar. 1986. mass mkt. 3.50 o.s.i (*0-553-26061-8*); 224p. mass mkt. 7.99 (*0-553-28034-1*) Bantam Bks.

—B Is for Burglar. unabr. collector's ed. 1993. (Kinsey Millhone Mystery Ser.). audio 48.00 (*0-7366-2457-0*, 3221) Books on Tape, Inc.

—B Is for Burglar. 1994. (Kinsey Millhone Mystery Ser.). reprint ed. lib. bdg. 29.95 (*1-56849-283-9*) Buccaneer Bks., Inc.

—B Is for Burglar. l.t. ed. 1991. (Kinsey Millhone Mystery Ser.). 20.95 o.p. (*0-8161-5145-8*, Macmillan Reference USA) Gale Group.

—B Is for Burglar. 1985. (Kinsey Millhone Mystery Ser.). 240p. 27.00 (*0-8050-1632-5*) Holt, Henry & Co.

—B Is for Burglar. abr. ed. (Kinsey Millhone Mystery Ser.). 2001. audio compact disk 22.95 (*0-375-41718-4*); 1991. audio 18.00 (*0-394-57978-X*, 390367) Random Hse. Audio Publishing Group. (RH Audio).

—B Is for Burglar. l.t. ed. 1988. (Kinsey Millhone Mystery Ser.). 448p. 17.95 o.p. (*0-7089-1786-0*, Ulverscroft) Thorpe, F. A. Pubs. GBR. *Dist:* Ulverscroft Large Print Bks., Ltd.

—C Is for Corpse. 1987. mass mkt. 3.50 o.s.i (*0-553-26468-0*); 224p. mass mkt. 7.99 (*0-553-28036-8*) Bantam Bks.

—C Is for Corpse. unabr. collector's ed. 1993. (Kinsey Millhone Mystery Ser.). audio 48.00 (*0-7366-2512-7*, 3268) Books on Tape, Inc.

—C Is for Corpse. 1986. (Kinsey Millhone Mystery Ser.). 258p. 27.00 (*0-8050-2818-8*); 256p. 19.95 o.p. (*0-03-001888-9*) Holt, Henry & Co.

—C Is for Corpse. abr. ed. (Kinsey Millhone Mystery Ser.). 2001. audio compact disk 22.95 (*0-375-41719-2*); Set. 1992. audio 18.00 (*0-679-40189-X*, 390467) Random Hse. Audio Publishing Group. (RH Audio).

—C Is for Corpse. l.t. ed. 1991. (Kinsey Millhone Mystery Ser.). 371p. pap. 22.95 (*0-8161-5146-6*) Thorndike Pr.

—C Is for Corpse. l.t. ed. 1988. (Kinsey Millhone Mystery Ser.). 432p. 15.95 o.p. (*0-7089-1898-0*, Ulverscroft) Thorpe, F. A. Pubs. GBR. *Dist:* Ulverscroft Large Print Bks., Ltd.

—D Is for Deadbeat. 1988. (Kinsey Millhone Mystery Ser.). 256p. reprint ed. mass mkt. 7.99 (*0-553-27163-6*) Bantam Bks.

—D Is for Deadbeat. unabr. collector's ed. 1993. (Kinsey Millhone Mystery Ser.). audio 42.00 (*0-7366-2568-2*, 3317) Books on Tape, Inc.

—D Is for Deadbeat. l.t. ed. 1992. (Kinsey Millhone Mystery Ser.). 345p. 16.95 o.p. (*0-8161-5147-4*, Macmillan Reference USA) Gale Group.

—D Is for Deadbeat, Set. abr. ed. 1993. (Kinsey Millhone Mystery Ser.). audio 18.00 (*0-679-40354-X*, 390596, RH Audio) Random Hse. Audio Publishing Group.

—D Is for Deadbeat. l.t. ed. 1990. (Kinsey Millhone Mystery Ser.). 18.95 o.p. (*0-7089-2118-3*, Ulverscroft) Thorpe, F. A. Pubs. GBR. *Dist:* Ulverscroft Large Print Bks., Ltd.

—E Is for Evidence. 1989. (Kinsey Millhone Mystery Ser.). 208p. mass mkt. 7.99 (*0-553-27955-6*) Bantam Bks.

—E Is for Evidence. unabr. collector's ed. 1994. (Kinsey Millhone Mystery Ser.). audio 42.00 (*0-7366-2615-8*, 3357) Books on Tape, Inc.

—E Is for Evidence. l.t. ed. 1989. (Kinsey Millhone Mystery Ser.). 319p. 20.95 o.p. (*0-8161-4715-9*, Macmillan Reference USA) Gale Group.

—E Is for Evidence. 1988. (Kinsey Millhone Mystery Ser.). 240p. 27.00 (*0-8050-0459-9*) Holt, Henry & Co.

—E Is for Evidence. abr. ed. 1989. (Kinsey Millhone Mystery Ser.). audio 18.00 (*0-394-57982-8*, 390695, RH Audio) Random Hse. Audio Publishing Group.

—F Is for Fugitive. 1990. (Kinsey Millhone Mystery Ser.). 352p. mass mkt. 7.99 (*0-553-28478-9*) Bantam Bks.

—F Is for Fugitive. unabr. collector's ed. 1994. (Kinsey Millhone Mystery Ser.). audio 48.00 (*0-7366-2620-4*, 3360) Books on Tape, Inc.

—F Is for Fugitive. l.t. ed. 1990. (Kinsey Millhone Mystery Ser.). 368p. 21.95 (*0-8161-4901-1*, Macmillan Reference USA) Gale Group.

—F Is for Fugitive. 1989. (Kinsey Millhone Mystery Ser.). 272p. 25.00 (*0-8050-0460-2*) Holt, Henry & Co.

—F Is for Fugitive. abr. ed. 1989. (Kinsey Millhone Mystery Ser.). audio 18.00 (*0-394-57983-6*, 390742); audio 17.00 (*0-394-58173-3*) Random Hse. Audio Publishing Group. (RH Audio).

—G Is for Gumshoe. (Kinsey Millhone Mystery Ser.). 1997. pap. 12.95 o.s.i (*0-449-00062-1*); 1995. mass mkt. 6.99 o.p. (*0-449-45491-6*); 1993. mass mkt. 5.99 o.p. (*0-449-45161-5*); 1991. pap. 6.99 (*0-449-45764-8*); 1991. 352p. mass mkt. 7.99 (*0-449-21936-4*) Ballantine Bks. (Fawcett).

—G Is for Gumshoe. unabr. collector's ed. 1994. (Kinsey Millhone Mystery Ser.). audio 48.00 (*0-7366-2679-4*, 3415) Books on Tape, Inc.

—G Is for Gumshoe. l.t. ed. 1991. (Kinsey Millhone Mystery Ser.). 355p. 20.95 o.p. (*0-8161-5090-7*, Macmillan Reference USA) Gale Group.

—G Is for Gumshoe. 1990. (Kinsey Millhone Mystery Ser.). 272p. 27.00 (*0-8050-0461-0*) Holt, Henry & Co.

—G Is for Gumshoe. abr. ed. 1990. (Kinsey Millhone Mystery Ser.). audio 16.00 o.p. (*0-394-58632-8*);Set. audio 18.00 (*0-394-58563-1*, 390833) Random Hse. Audio Publishing Group. (RH Audio).

—G Is for Gumshoe. l.t. ed. 1991. (Kinsey Millhone Mystery Ser.). 355p. pap. 22.95 o.p. (*0-8161-5091-5*) Thorndike Pr.

—H Is for Homicide. (Kinsey Millhone Mystery Ser.). 1997. pap. 11.00 o.s.i (*0-449-00063-X*); 1995. mass mkt. 6.99 o.p. (*0-449-45492-4*); 1993. mass mkt. 5.99 o.p. (*0-449-45162-3*); 1992. pap. 6.99 (*0-449-45765-6*); 1992. 304p. mass mkt. 7.99 (*0-449-21946-1*) Ballantine Bks. (Fawcett).

—H Is for Homicide. unabr. collector's ed. 1994. (Kinsey Millhone Mystery Ser.). audio 48.00 (*0-7366-2728-6*, 3458) Books on Tape, Inc.

—H Is for Homicide. l.t. ed. 1992. (Kinsey Millhone Mystery Ser.). 390p. 16.95 o.p. (*0-8161-5281-0*, Macmillan Reference USA) Gale Group.

—H Is for Homicide. (Kinsey Millhone Mystery Ser.). 1991. 272p. 25.00 (*0-8050-1084-X*); 1992. 390p. lib. bdg. 20.95 (*0-8161-5280-2*) Holt, Henry & Co.

—H Is for Homicide, Set. abr. ed. 1991. (Kinsey Millhone Mystery Ser.). 18.00 incl. audio (*0-394-58698-0*, 390890, RH Audio) Random Hse. Audio Publishing Group.

—I Is for Innocent. (Kinsey Millhone Mystery Ser.). 1997. 304p. pap. 12.95 (*0-449-00064-8*); 1995. mass mkt. 6.99 o.p. (*0-449-45493-2*); 1994. mass mkt. 5.99 o.p. (*0-449-45335-9*); 1993. pap. 6.99 (*0-449-45766-4*); 1993. 352p. mass mkt. 7.99 (*0-449-22151-2*) Ballantine Bks. (Fawcett).

—I Is for Innocent. unabr. ed. 1993. (Kinsey Millhone Mystery Ser.). audio 56.00 (*0-7366-2433-3*, 3198) Books on Tape, Inc.

—I Is for Innocent. l.t. ed. 1994. (Kinsey Millhone Mystery Ser.). 373p. 16.95 o.p. (*0-8161-5538-0*, Macmillan Reference USA) Gale Group.

—I Is for Innocent. 1992. (Kinsey Millhone Mystery Ser.). 272p. 27.00 (*0-8050-1085-8*) Holt, Henry & Co.

—I Is for Innocent. abr. ed. 1992. (Kinsey Millhone Mystery Ser.). audio 18.00 (*0-679-41115-1*, 390946, RH Audio) Random Hse. Audio Publishing Group.

—I Is for Innocent. l.t. ed. 1993. (Kinsey Millhone Mystery Ser.). 373p. 24.95 (*0-8161-5537-2*) Thorndike Pr.

—J Is for Judgment. (Kinsey Millhone Mystery Ser.). 1997. pap. 11.00 o.s.i (*0-449-00065-6*); 1995. mass mkt. 6.99 o.p. (*0-449-45495-9*); 1994. pap. 6.99 (*0-449-45767-2*); 1994. 384p. mass mkt. 7.99 (*0-449-22148-2*) Ballantine Bks. (Fawcett).

—J Is for Judgment. unabr. ed. 1994. (Kinsey Millhone Mystery Ser.). audio 56.00 (*0-7366-2736-7*, 3463) Books on Tape, Inc.

—J Is for Judgment. l.t. ed. 1993. (Kinsey Millhone Mystery Ser.). lib. bdg. 23.95 o.p. (*0-8161-5750-2*, Macmillan Reference USA) Gale Group.

—J Is for Judgment. 1993. (Kinsey Millhone Mystery Ser.). 304p. 27.00 (*0-8050-1935-9*) Holt, Henry & Co.

—J Is for Judgment, Set. abr. ed. 1993. (Kinsey Millhone Mystery Ser.). audio 18.00 (*0-679-41368-5*, 390993, RH Audio) Random Hse. Audio Publishing Group.

—J Is for Judgment. l.t. ed. 1994. (Kinsey Millhone Mystery Ser.). 410p. pap. 20.95 (*0-8161-5751-0*) Thorndike Pr.

—K Is for Killer. (Kinsey Millhone Mystery Ser.). 1997. pap. 11.00 o.s.i (*0-449-00066-4*); 1995. pap. 6.99 (*0-449-45768-0*); 1995. 320p. mass mkt. 7.99 (*0-449-22150-4*) Ballantine Bks. (Fawcett).

—K Is for Killer. unabr. ed. 1995. (Kinsey Millhone Mystery Ser.). audio 56.00 (*0-7366-3043-0*, 3725) Books on Tape, Inc.

—K Is for Killer. l.t. ed. 1994. (Kinsey Millhone Mystery Ser.). 26.95 o.p. (*1-56895-101-9*, Wheeler Publishing, Inc.) Gale Group.

—K Is for Killer. 1994. (Kinsey Millhone Mystery Ser.). 304p. 27.00 (*0-8050-1936-7*) Holt, Henry & Co.

—Kinsey Millhone Mystery Series Boxed Set: G Is for Gumshoe; H Is for Homicide; I Is for Innocent, 3 vols. 1993. (Kinsey Millhone Mystery Ser.). 23.97 o.s.i (*0-449-22262-4*, Fawcett) Ballantine Bks.

—L Is for Lawless. (Kinsey Millhone Mystery Ser.). 1997. pap. 11.00 o.s.i (*0-449-00067-2*); 1996. pap. 6.99 (*0-449-45769-9*); 1996. 336p. mass mkt. 7.99 (*0-449-22149-0*) Ballantine Bks. (Fawcett).

—L Is for Lawless. unabr. ed. 1996. (Kinsey Millhone Mystery Ser.). audio 56.00 (*0-7366-3305-7*, 3959) Books on Tape, Inc.

—L Is for Lawless. 1995. (Kinsey Millhone Mystery Ser.). 304p. 24.00 (*0-8050-1937-5*) Holt, Henry & Co.

—L Is for Lawless, Set. abr. ed. 1995. (Kinsey Millhone Mystery Ser.). audio 18.00 (*0-679-42462-8*, 393143, RH Audio) Random Hse. Audio Publishing Group.

—L Is for Lawless. 1997. (Kinsey Millhone Mystery Ser.). 5.98 o.p. (*0-7651-0722-8*) Smithmark Pubs., Inc.

—L Is for Lawless. l.t. ed. (Kinsey Millhone Mystery Ser.). 384p. 1996. pap. 26.95 (*0-7838-1383-X*); 1995. 29.95 (*0-7838-1382-1*) Thorndike Pr.

—M Is for Malice. 1997. (Kinsey Millhone Mystery Ser.). 352p. mass mkt. 7.99 (*0-449-22360-4*, Fawcett) Ballantine Bks.

—M Is for Malice. unabr. collector's ed. 1997. (Kinsey Millhone Mystery Ser.). audio 56.00 (*0-913369-70-5*, 4322) Books on Tape, Inc.

—M Is for Malice. 1996. (Kinsey Millhone Mystery Ser.). (Illus.). 304p. 27.00 (*0-8050-3637-7*) Holt, Henry & Co.

—M Is for Malice. l.t. ed. 1997. (Kinsey Millhone Mystery Ser.). 458p. pap. 27.95 (*0-7838-1834-3*); lib. bdg. 29.95 (*0-7838-1833-5*) Thorndike Pr.

—N Is for Noose. 1999. (Kinsey Millhone Mystery Ser.). mass mkt. (*0-449-00457-0*); 336p. mass mkt. 7.99 (*0-449-22361-2*) Ballantine Bks. (Fawcett).

—N Is for Noose. unabr. ed. 1998. (Kinsey Millhone Mystery Ser.). audio 56.00 (*0-7366-4141-6*, 4645) Books on Tape, Inc.
—N Is for Noose. unabr. ed. 1999. (Kinsey Millhone Mystery Ser.). audio 39.95 Highsmith Inc.
—N Is for Noose. 1998. (Kinsey Millhone Mystery Ser.). 320p. 25.00 (*0-8050-3650-4*) Holt, Henry & Co.
—N Is for Noose. abr. ed. 2002. audio compact disk 25.95 (*0-553-71339-6*); 1998. audio 24.00 (*0-375-40289-6*, 495734); 1998. audio 34.95 (*0-375-40326-4*, AD37D) Random Hse. Audio Publishing Group. (RH Audio).
—N Is for Noose. l.t. ed. (Kinsey Millhone Mystery Ser.). 455p. 1999. pap. 27.95 (*0-7862-1297-7*); 1998. 30.95 (*0-7862-1296-9*) Thorndike Pr.
—O Is for Outlaw. 2001. (Kinsey Millhone Mystery Ser.). 368p. mass mkt. 7.99 (*0-449-00378-7*, Ballantine Bks.) Ballantine Bks.
—O Is for Outlaw. 2000. (Kinsey Millhone Mystery Ser.). audio 39.95 Blackstone Audio Bks., Inc.
—O Is for Outlaw. 1999. (Kinsey Millhone Mystery Ser.). audio 44.95 Books on Tape, Inc.
—O Is for Outlaw. abr. ed. 1999. (Kinsey Millhone Mystery Ser.). audio 25.95. audio 39.95 Highsmith Inc.
—O Is for Outlaw. 1999. (Kinsey Millhone Mystery Ser.). 336p. 26.00 (*0-8050-5955-5*) Holt, Henry & Co.
—O Is for Outlaw. abr. ed. 2004. audio 17.99 (*0-7393-1219-7*, RH Audio Price-Less); 1999. audio compact disk 29.95 (*0-375-40661-1*, RH Audio); 1999. audio 25.95 (*0-375-40415-5*, RH Audio); 1999. audio 39.95 (*0-375-40662-X*, N160, RH Audio) Random Hse. Audio Publishing Group.
—O Is for Outlaw. l.t. ed. (Kinsey Millhone Mystery Ser.). 534p. 2000. 28.95 (*0-7862-2045-7*); 1999. 31.95 (*0-7862-2044-9*) Thorndike Pr.
—P Is for Peril. 2001. (Kinsey Millhone Mystery Ser.). 304p. 26.95 (*0-399-14719-5*, Wood, Marian Bks.) Penguin Group (USA) Inc.
—P Is for Peril. l.t. ed. (Paperback Bestsellers Ser.). 2003. 557p. pap. 14.95 (*0-7862-2948-9*); 2001. 352p. 33.95 (*0-7862-2931-4*) Thorndike Pr.
—Q Is for Quarry. 2002. 400p. 26.95 (*0-399-14915-5*) Putnam Publishing Group, The.
—Q Is for Quarry. pap. o.p. (*0-7862-4369-4*); 2002. 640p. 33.95 (*0-7862-4370-8*) Thorndike Pr.
—Sue Grafton: D is for Deadbeat; E is for Evidence; F is for Fugitive, 3 vols. 2001. (Kinsey Millhone Mystery Ser.). 736p. 13.99 (*0-517-16271-7*) Random Hse. Value Publishing.

**MILLS, TODD (FICTITIOUS CHARACTER)—FICTION**

Zimmerman, R. D. Closet: A Todd Mills Mystery. 1995. 320p. mass mkt. 4.99 o.s.i (*0-440-21869-1*) Dell Publishing.
—Closet: A Todd Mills Mystery. 1997. 304p. pap. 10.95 o.s.i (*0-385-32004-3*) Doubleday Publishing.
—Hostage. 1998. 288p. pap. 10.95 o.s.i (*0-385-31892-8*, Delacorte Pr.) Dell Publishing.
—Innuendo. 2000. (Todd Mills Mysteries Ser.). 320p. pap. 11.95 (*0-385-31926-6*, Dial Bks.) Dell Publishing.
—Outburst: A Todd Mills Mystery. 1999. (Illus.). 304p. pap. 19.00 (*0-385-31923-1*, Delacorte Pr.) Dell Publishing.
—Tribe. 1996. 288p. mass mkt. 5.50 o.s.i (*0-440-21870-5*) Dell Publishing.
—Tribe: A Todd Mills Mystery. 1997. 272p. pap. 10.95 o.s.i (*0-385-32002-7*) Doubleday Publishing.

**MILLSAPS, LARRY (FICTITIOUS CHARACTER)—FICTION**

Blackstock, Terri. Justifiable Means. l.t. ed. 1998. (Christian Mystery Ser.). 499p. 23.95 o.p. (*0-7862-1471-6*) Thorndike Pr.
—Justifiable Means. 1996. (Sun Coast Chronicles Ser.: Bk. 2). 320p. pap. 12.99 (*0-310-20016-4*) Zondervan.

**MILODRAGOVITCH, MILO (FICTITIOUS CHARACTER)—FICTION**

Crumley, James. Bordersnakes. 1997. 288p. mass mkt. 6.50 (*0-446-60448-8*); 1996. 336p. 22.00 o.p. (*0-89296-573-8*) Warner Bks., Inc.
—Dancing Bear. unabr. ed. 1997. audio 48.00 (*0-7366-3819-9*, 4487) Books on Tape, Inc.
—Dancing Bear. 1984. (Vintage Contemporaries Ser.). 240p. pap. 13.00 (*0-394-72576-X*, Vintage) Knopf Publishing Group.
—Dancing Bear. 1983. 256p. 12.95 o.p. (*0-394-52195-1*) Random Hse., Inc.
—The Final Country. l.t. ed. 2003. 25.95 (*1-58724-412-8*, Wheeler Publishing, Inc.) Gale Group.
—The Final Country. 2001. 320p. 24.95 (*0-89296-666-1*) Mysterious Pr.
—The Final Country. 2002. 320p. pap. 12.95 (*0-446-67964-X*, Mysterious Pr. Paperback Bks.) Warner Bks., Inc.
—The Last Good Kiss. 1992. audio 13.95 (*1-55644-375-7*, 12021) American Audio Prose Library, Inc.
—The Last Good Kiss. 1988. (Vintage Contemporaries Ser.). 256p. pap. 11.95 (*0-394-75989-3*, Vintage) Knopf Publishing Group.
—The Last Good Kiss. 1978. 8.95 o.p. (*0-394-41946-4*) Random Hse., Inc.
—The Last Good Kiss. 1983. mass mkt. 3.50 o.s.i (*0-671-49889-4*, Pocket) Simon & Schuster.
—The Mexican Tree Duck. unabr. ed. 1997. audio 48.00 (*0-7366-3820-2*, 4488) Books on Tape, Inc.
—The Mexican Tree Duck. 1993. 256p. 19.95 (*0-89296-391-3*) Mysterious Pr.
—The Mexican Tree Duck. 1994. 272p. mass mkt. 5.99 (*0-446-40407-1*); 2001. 256p. reprint ed. pap. 11.95 (*0-446-67791-4*) Warner Bks., Inc.
—The Wrong Case. 1985. (Vintage Contemporaries Ser.). 288p. pap. 12.00 (*0-394-73558-7*) Random Hse., Inc.

**MILYUKIN, MIKHAIL (FICTITIOUS CHARACTER)—FICTION**

Kerr, Philip. Dead Meat. 1996. 228p. mass mkt. 7.99 o.s.i (*0-7704-2704-9*) Bantam Bks.
—Dead Meat. 1994. 256p. pap. 13.95 o.p. (*0-385-25466-0*) Doubleday Publishing.
—Dead Meat. 1994. 256p. 18.95 o.s.i (*0-89296-562-2*) Mysterious Pr.
—Dead Meat. 1995. 272p. mass mkt. 5.99 o.s.i (*0-446-40379-2*) Warner Bks., Inc.

**MINOGUE, MATT (FICTITIOUS CHARACTER)—FICTION**

Brady, John. All Souls. 1993. 304p. 20.95 o.p. (*0-312-09735-2*, Saint Martin's Minotaur) St. Martin's Pr.
—All Souls. 2002. (Matt Minogue Mystery Ser.). 306p. pap. 14.95 (*1-58642-043-7*) Steerforth Pr.
—A Carra King. 2000. 356p. pap. 21.95 (*1-55278-164-X*) McArthur & Co. CAN. *Dist:* HarperCollins Pubs. Canada, Ltd.
—The Good Life. 1995. 352p. 22.95 o.p. (*0-312-13083-X*, Saint Martin's Minotaur) St. Martin's Pr.
—Kaddish in Dublin. 1992. 288p. 18.95 o.p. (*0-312-08229-0*, Saint Martin's Minotaur) St. Martin's Pr.
—Kaddish in Dublin. 2002. (Matt Minogue Mystery Ser.). 253p. pap. 14.95 (*1-58642-042-9*) Steerforth Pr.
—A Stone of the Heart. 1988. 256p. 16.95 o.p. (*0-312-01829-0*, Saint Martin's Minotaur) St. Martin's Pr.
—A Stone of the Heart. 2001. (Matt Minogue Mystery Ser.). (Illus.). xxiii, 247p. pap. 14.95 (*1-58642-029-1*) Steerforth Pr.
—A Stone of the Heart. 1990. 256p. pap. 3.95 o.p. (*0-14-013847-1*, Penguin Bks.) Viking Penguin.
—Unholy Ground. 1991. 288p. 18.95 o.p. (*0-312-07109-4*, Saint Martin's Minotaur) St. Martin's Pr.
—Unholy Ground. 2002. (Matt Minogue Mystery Ser.). 208p. reprint ed. pap. 14.95 (*1-58642-037-2*) Steerforth Pr.

**MIRACLE, TORI (FICTITIOUS CHARACTER)—FICTION**

Malmont, Valerie S. Death, Bones & Stately Homes: A Tori Miracle Pennsylvania Dutch Mystery. 2003. 286p. pap. 13.95 (*1-880284-65-0*) Daniel, John & Co., Pubs.
—Death, Guns & Sticky Buns. 2000. (Tori Miracle Mysteries Ser.). 320p. mass mkt. 6.50 (*0-440-23598-7*) Bantam Dell Publishing Group.
—Death, Lies & Apple Pies. 1998. (Tori Miracle Mysteries Ser.). 288p. mass mkt. 5.99 (*0-440-22634-1*) Dell Publishing.
—Death, Lies & Apple Pies. l.t. ed. 1997. (Core Ser.). 326p. lib. bdg. 25.95 o.p. (*0-7838-8333-1*, Macmillan Reference USA) Gale Group.
—Death, Lies & Apple Pies. 1997. (Illus.). 224p. 22.00 o.s.i (*0-684-80189-2*, Simon & Schuster) Simon & Schuster.
—Death Pays the Rose Rent: A Tori Miracle Mystery. (Tori Miracle Mysteries Ser.). 1999. 304p. mass mkt. 6.50 (*0-440-22633-3*); 1998. 352p. mass mkt. 5.99 o.s.i (*0-440-22628-7*) Dell Publishing.
—Death Pays the Rose Rent: A Tori Miracle Mystery. 1994. 286p. 20.00 (*0-671-86967-1*, Simon & Schuster) Simon & Schuster.
—Death, Snow & Mistletoe. 2000. (Tori Miracle Mysteries Ser.). 320p. mass mkt. 5.99 (*0-440-23601-0*) Dell Publishing.

**MITCHELL, CASSANDRA (FICTITIOUS CHARACTER)—FICTION**

Wright, Laurali R. Acts of Murder. 1998. 288p. 22.00 (*0-684-81381-5*, Scribner) Simon & Schuster.
—Acts of Murder. l.t. ed. 1998. (Mystery Ser.). 381p. 27.95 (*0-7862-1678-6*) Thorndike Pr.
—A Chill Rain in January. 1991. 336p. mass mkt. 7.99 (*0-7704-2417-1*) Bantam Bks.
—A Chill Rain in January. 1991. (Crime Monthly Ser.). 288p. pap. 4.50 o.p. (*0-14-012982-0*, Penguin Bks.) Penguin Group (USA) Inc.
—A Chill Rain in January. 1990. 288p. 17.95 o.p. (*0-670-83129-8*, Viking) Viking Penguin.
—Fall from Grace. l.t. ed. 1992. pap. 17.95 o.p. (*0-7927-1270-6*); 19.95 o.p. (*0-7927-1271-4*) BBC Audiobooks America.
—Fall from Grace. 1999. pap. (*0-14-099717-2*) NAL.
—Fall from Grace. 1992. (Crime Ser.). 256p. reprint ed. pap. 5.95 o.p. (*0-14-012981-2*, Penguin Bks.) Penguin Group (USA) Inc.
—Fall from Grace. 1991. 256p. 18.95 o.p. (*0-670-83130-1*, Viking) Viking Penguin.
—Mother Love: A Karl Alberg Mystery with Cassandra Mitchell. 1996. 264p. mass mkt. 7.99 o.s.i (*0-7704-2716-2*) Bantam Bks.
—Mother Love: A Karl Alberg Mystery with Cassandra Mitchell. 1995. 288p. 26.95 o.p. (*0-385-25477-6*) Doubleday Publishing.
—Mother Love: A Karl Alberg Mystery with Cassandra Mitchell. 1995. (Illus.). 304p. 21.00 o.p. (*0-684-19673-5*, Scribner) Simon & Schuster.
—Prized Possessions, No. 5. 1997. 336p. mass mkt. 7.50 (*0-7704-2543-7*) Bantam Bks.
—Prized Possessions. 1994. (Crime Ser.). 272p. pap. 5.95 o.p. (*0-14-017146-0*, Penguin Bks.) Penguin Group (USA) Inc.
—Prized Possessions. 1993. 272p. 19.00 o.p. (*0-670-84565-5*, Viking) Viking Penguin.
—Sleep While I Sing. l.t. ed. 1991. 17.95 o.p. (*0-7451-8072-8*, AH0107); pap. 15.95 o.p. (*0-7927-0555-6*, AS0143) BBC Audiobooks America.
—Sleep While I Sing. 1988. 240p. mass mkt. 6.99 (*0-7704-2300-0*) Bantam Bks.
—Sleep While I Sing. 1988. o.s.i (*0-385-25042-8*) Doubleday Publishing.
—Sleep While I Sing. 1987. 224p. pap. 3.95 o.p. (*0-14-008880-6*, Penguin Bks.); 1987. 39.50 o.p. (*0-14-778226-0*); 1986. 224p. 15.95 o.p. (*0-670-81089-4*) Viking Penguin.
—Strangers among Us. 1997. 256p. mass mkt. 8.99 (*0-7704-2758-8*) Bantam Bks.
—Strangers among Us. 1996. 256p. 20.50 o.p. (*0-684-81382-3*, Scribner) Simon & Schuster.
—Strangers among Us. l.t. ed. 2000. (Mystery Ser.). 360p. 27.95 (*0-7862-2557-2*) Thorndike Pr.
—The Suspect. (Crime Ser.). 224p. 1987. pap. 5.95 o.p. (*0-14-010477-1*, Penguin Bks.); 1985. 15.95 o.p. (*0-670-80596-3*) Viking Penguin.
—A Touch of Panic: A Karl Alberg Mystery. 1995. 288p. mass mkt. 7.99 o.s.i (*0-7704-2620-4*) Bantam Bks.
—A Touch of Panic: A Karl Alberg Mystery. 1995. (Crime Ser.). 288p. pap. 5.95 o.s.i (*0-14-023300-8*, Penguin Bks.) Penguin Group (USA) Inc.
—A Touch of Panic: A Karl Alberg Mystery. 1994. 288p. 20.00 o.s.i (*0-684-19672-7*, Scribner) Simon & Schuster.

**MITCHELL, MEREDITH (FICTITIOUS CHARACTER)—FICTION**

Granger, Ann. Beneath These Stones. 2000. (Meredith & Markby Mysteries Ser.). 250p. 22.95 (*0-312-24178-X*, Saint Martin's Minotaur) St. Martin's Pr.
—Call the Dead Again. l.t. ed. 1999. 30.00 o.p. (*0-7862-1817-7*, Macmillan Reference USA) Gale Group.
—Call the Dead Again. 2000. (Meredith & Markby Mysteries Ser.). 288p. mass mkt. 5.99 (*0-380-73297-1*, Avon Bks.) Morrow/Avon.
—Call the Dead Again. 1999. (Meredith & Markby Mysteries Ser.). 256p. 22.95 (*0-312-20505-8*, Saint Martin's Minotaur) St. Martin's Pr.
—Candle for a Corpse. 1997. (Meredith & Markby Mysteries Ser.: Vol. 8). 288p. mass mkt. 5.99 (*0-380-73012-X*, Avon Bks.) Morrow/Avon.
—Candle for a Corpse. 1996. 256p. text 21.95 o.p. (*0-312-14292-7*, Saint Martin's Minotaur) St. Martin's Pr.
—Cold in the Earth. 1994. 256p. mass mkt. 5.50 (*0-380-72213-5*, Avon Bks.) Morrow/Avon.
—Cold in the Earth. 1993. 218p. 17.95 o.p. (*0-312-08747-0*, Saint Martin's Minotaur) St. Martin's Pr.
—Cold in the Earth. l.t. ed. 1994. (Ulverscroft Large Print Ser.). 576p. 29.99 o.p. (*0-7089-3111-1*, Ulverscroft) Thorpe, F. A. Pubs. GBR. *Dist:* Ulverscroft Large Print Bks., Ltd., Ulverscroft Large Print Canada, Ltd.
—A Fine Place for Death. 1996. (New Meredith & Markby Mystery Ser.: No. 6). 288p. mass mkt. 5.50 (*0-380-72573-8*, Avon Bks.) Morrow/Avon.
—A Fine Place for Death. 1994. 249p. 21.00 o.p. (*0-312-11787-6*, Saint Martin's Minotaur) St. Martin's Pr.
—A Fine Place for Death. l.t. ed. 1995. (Ulverscroft Large Print Ser.). 528p. 29.99 o.p. (*0-7089-3346-7*, Ulverscroft) Thorpe, F. A. Pubs. GBR. *Dist:* Ulverscroft Large Print Bks., Ltd., Ulverscroft Large Print Canada, Ltd.
—Flowers for His Funeral. 1997. mass mkt. 5.50 (*0-380-72887-7*, Avon Bks.) Morrow/Avon.
—Flowers for His Funeral. 1995. 250p. 21.95 o.p. (*0-312-13495-9*, Saint Martin's Minotaur) St. Martin's Pr.
—Murder among Us. 1995. (Meredith & Markby Mysteries Ser.: No. 4). 304p. mass mkt. 5.99 (*0-380-72476-6*, Avon Bks.) Morrow/Avon.
—Murder among Us. 1993. 224p. 18.95 o.p. (*0-312-09875-8*); (*0-312-09343-8*) St. Martin's Pr. (Saint Martin's Minotaur).
—Murder among Us. l.t. ed. 1994. (Ulverscroft Large Print Ser.). 544p. 29.99 o.p. (*0-7089-3146-4*, Ulverscroft) Thorpe, F. A. Pubs. GBR. *Dist:* Ulverscroft Large Print Bks., Ltd., Ulverscroft Large Print Canada, Ltd.
—Say It with Poison. 1993. 224p. mass mkt. 5.50 (*0-380-71823-5*, Avon Bks.) Morrow/Avon.
—Say It with Poison. 1991. 16.95 o.p. (*0-312-05506-4*, Saint Martin's Minotaur) St. Martin's Pr.
—A Season for Murder. 1993. (Meredith & Markby Mysteries Ser.: Vol. 2). 256p. mass mkt. 5.99 o.s.i (*0-380-71997-5*, Avon Bks.) Morrow/Avon.
—A Season for Murder. 1992. 256p. 18.95 o.p. (*0-312-07079-9*, Saint Martin's Minotaur) St. Martin's Pr.
—A Season for Murder. l.t. ed. 1992. (Magna Large Print Ser.). 361p. 29.99 o.p. (*0-7505-0483-8*, Ulverscroft) Thorpe, F. A. Pubs. GBR. *Dist:* Ulverscroft Large Print Bks., Ltd., Ulverscroft Large Print Canada, Ltd.
—Shades of Murder: A Mitchell & Markby Mystery. 2001. 288p. 23.95 (*0-312-28445-4*, Saint Martin's Minotaur) St. Martin's Pr.
—A Touch of Mortality. 1998. 288p. mass mkt. 5.99 (*0-380-73087-1*, Avon Bks.) Morrow/Avon.
—A Touch of Mortality. 1997. 256p. 21.95 (*0-312-15231-0*, Saint Martin's Minotaur) St. Martin's Pr.
—Where Old Bones Lie. 1995. (New Meredith & Markby Mystery Ser.: No. 5). 288p. mass mkt. 5.99 (*0-380-72477-4*, Avon Bks.) Morrow/Avon.
—Where Old Bones Lie. 1994. 224p. 19.95 o.p. (*0-312-11097-9*, Saint Martin's Minotaur) St. Martin's Pr.
—Where Old Bones Lie. l.t. ed. 1995. (Ulverscroft Large Print Ser.). 528p. 29.99 o.p. (*0-7089-3391-2*, Ulverscroft) Thorpe, F. A. Pubs. GBR. *Dist:* Ulverscroft Large Print Bks., Ltd., Ulverscroft Large Print Canada, Ltd.
—A Word After Dying. 1998. (Meredith & Markby Mysteries Ser.). 256p. 21.95 (*0-312-17067-X*, Saint Martin's Minotaur) St. Martin's Pr.
—A Word after Dying. 1999. (Meredith & Markby Mysteries Ser.). 304p. mass mkt. 5.99 (*0-380-73227-0*, Avon Bks.) Morrow/Avon.
—A Word after Dying. pap. 14.95 (*0-312-30475-7*, Saint Martin's Griffin) St. Martin's Pr.
—A Word after Dying. l.t. ed. 1997. (Ulverscroft Large Print Ser.). 560p. 29.99 o.p. (*0-7089-3809-4*, Ulverscroft) Thorpe, F. A. Pubs. GBR. *Dist:* Ulverscroft Large Print Bks., Ltd., Ulverscroft Large Print Canada, Ltd.

**MITCHELL, MICHELLE (MITCH) (FICTITIOUS CHARACTER)—FICTION**

Allyn, Doug. Black Water. 1996. 240p. 21.95 o.p. (*0-312-13932-2*, Saint Martin's Minotaur); Vol. 1. 1997. 217p. mass mkt. 5.99 (*0-312-96150-2*, St. Martin's Paperbacks) St. Martin's Pr.
—A Dance in Deep Water: A Mitch Mitchell Mystery. 1997. (Mitch Mitchell Mystery Ser.). 256p. 22.95 o.p. (*0-312-16807-1*, Saint Martin's Minotaur) St. Martin's Pr.
—Icewater Mansions. 247p. 1996. mass mkt. 5.50 (*0-312-95764-5*, St. Martin's Paperbacks); 1995. 21.00 o.p. (*0-312-11829-5*, Saint Martin's Minotaur) St. Martin's Pr.

**MITRY, DESIREE (FICTITIOUS CHARACTER)—FICTION**

Handler, David. The Bright Silver Star. Date not set. pap. (*0-312-30715-2*, Saint Martin's Griffin); Date not set. mass mkt. (*0-312-99461-3*, St. Martin's Paperbacks); Date not set. mass mkt. (*0-312-99620-9*, St. Martin's Paperbacks); mass mkt. (*0-312-98578-9*, St. Martin's Paperbacks); E-Book (*0-312-70566-2*); 2003. 320p. 24.95 (*0-312-30714-4*, Saint Martin's Minotaur) St. Martin's Pr.
—The Hot Pink Farmhouse. Date not set. mass mkt. (*0-312-98579-7*, St. Martin's Paperbacks); E-Book 17.95 (*0-312-70893-9*); 2002. 336p. 23.95 (*0-312-28015-7*, Saint Martin's Minotaur) St. Martin's Pr.

**MOFFETT, PIERCE (FICTITIOUS CHARACTER)—FICTION**

Crowley, John. AEgypt. 1994. 400p. pap. 13.95 o.s.i (*0-553-37430-3*) Bantam Bks.
—Love & Sleep. 1995. 512p. pap. 12.95 o.s.i (*0-553-37468-0*) Bantam Bks.

**MOLE, ADRIAN (FICTITIOUS CHARACTER)—FICTION**

Townsend, Sue. Adrian Mole: The Cappuccino Years. unabr. ed. 2000. audio compact disk 82.00 (*1-84197-136-7*, C1246E7); 1999. audio 60.00 (*0-7887-4054-7*, 96160E7) Recorded Bks., LLC.
—Adrian Mole: The Cappuccino Years. 2001. 400p. pap. 14.00 (*1-56947-247-5*); 2000. xv, 390p. 24.00 (*1-56947-204-1*) Soho Pr., Inc.
—Adrian Mole: The Cappuccino Years. abr. ed. 2000. 3p. audio compact disk (*0-14-180188-3*); 1999. audio (*0-14-180090-9*) Viking Penguin. (Penguin AudioBooks).
—Adrian Mole: The Lost Years. 309p. 1996. pap. 14.00 (*1-56947-055-3*); 1994. 22.00 (*1-56947-014-6*) Soho Pr., Inc.

—Adrian Mole: The Wilderness Years. unabr. ed. 1994. (Mini-CAB Audio Bks.). audio 39.95 (*0-7451-4281-8*, CAB 964) BBC Audiobooks America.

—Adrian Mole Diaries. 1986. 368p. 14.95 o.p. (*0-394-55298-9*) Grove/Atlantic, Inc.

—Adrian Mole Diaries. 1997. 304p. pap. 12.95 (*0-380-73044-8*, Perennial) HarperTrade.

**MOM (FICTITIOUS CHARACTER: YAFFE)—FICTION**

Yaffe, James. Mom among the Liars. 1994. (WWL Mystery Ser.). mass mkt. (*0-373-26142-X*, 1-26142-9, Harlequin Bks.) Harlequin Enterprises, Ltd.

—Mom among the Liars. 1992. 224p. 17.95 o.p. (*0-312-08264-9*, Saint Martin's Minotaur) St. Martin's Pr.

—Mom Doth Murder Sleep. 1992. (WWL Mystery Ser.: No. 98). mass mkt. (*0-373-26098-9*, 1-26098-3, Harlequin Bks.) Harlequin Enterprises, Ltd.

—Mom Doth Murder Sleep. 1991. 16.95 o.p. (*0-312-05898-5*, Saint Martin's Minotaur) St. Martin's Pr.

—Mom Meets Her Maker. 1991. 224p. mass mkt. (*0-373-26067-9*, Harlequin Bks.) Harlequin Enterprises, Ltd.

—Mom Meets Her Maker. 1990. 256p. 16.95 o.p. (*0-312-03893-3*, Saint Martin's Minotaur) St. Martin's Pr.

—My Mother, the Detective: The Complete "Mom" Short Stories. 1996. 175p. pap. 15.00 (*1-885941-11-0*); 40.00 o.p. (*1-885941-10-2*) Crippen & Landru, Pubs.

—A Nice Murder for Mom. 1990. mass mkt. (*0-373-26044-X*, Harlequin Bks.) Harlequin Enterprises, Ltd.

—A Nice Murder for Mom. 1988. 208p. 15.95 o.p. (*0-312-02260-3*, Saint Martin's Minotaur) St. Martin's Pr.

**MONAGHAN, TESS (FICTITIOUS CHARACTER)—FICTION**

Lippman, Laura. Baltimore Blues. 1997. 304p. mass mkt. 6.99 (*0-380-78875-6*, Avon Bks.) Morrow/Avon.

—Butcher's Hill. 1998. (Tess Monaghan Mysteries Ser.: Vol. 3). 288p. mass mkt. 5.99 (*0-380-79846-8*, Avon Bks.) Morrow/Avon.

—Charm City. l.t. ed. 2002. (Wheeler Large Print Book Ser.). 27.95 (*1-58724-214-1*, Wheeler Publishing, Inc.) Gale Group.

—Charm City. 1997. (Tess Monaghan Mysteries Ser.: Vol. 2). 304p. mass mkt. 6.99 (*0-380-78876-4*, Avon Bks.) Morrow/Avon.

—In a Strange City. 16th l.t. ed. 2002. 368p. lib. bdg. 27.95 (*1-58547-171-2*) Ctr. Point Large Print.

—In a Strange City. unabr. ed. 2002. audio 69.95 (*0-7531-1521-2*) ISIS Audio Bks. GBR. *Dist:* Ulverscroft Large Print Bks., Ltd.

—In a Strange City. 2002. 400p. mass mkt. 6.99 (*0-380-81023-9*); 2001. 320p. 24.00 (*0-380-97818-0*, Morrow, William & Co.) Morrow/Avon.

—In Big Trouble. 1999. (Tess Monaghan Mysteries Ser.). 352p. mass mkt. 6.99 (*0-380-79847-6*, Avon Bks.) Morrow/Avon.

—The Last Place. 2003. 432p. mass mkt. 7.50 (*0-380-81024-7*, Avon Bks.); 2002. 352p. 23.95 (*0-380-97819-9*, Morrow, William & Co.) Morrow/Avon.

—The Sugar House. 2000. (Tess Monaghan Mysteries Ser.). 320p. 24.00 (*0-380-97817-2*, Morrow, William & Co.) Morrow/Avon.

—The Sugar House: A Tess Monaghan Mystery. 2001. 384p. mass mkt. 6.99 (*0-380-81022-0*, Avon Bks.) Morrow/Avon.

—The Sugar House: A Tess Monaghan Mystery. l.t. ed. 2001. (Thorndike Americana Ser.). 483p. 28.95 (*0-7862-3288-9*) Thorndike Pr.

**MONGO (FICTITIOUS CHARACTER)—FICTION**

Chesbro, George C. An Affair of Sorcerers. 3rd ed. 1999. 352p. reprint ed. pap. 16.99 (*0-9674503-9-X*) Apache Beach Pubns.

—An Affair of Sorcerers. 1988. mass mkt. 3.50 o.s.i (*0-440-20047-4*) Dell Publishing.

—An Affair of Sorcerers. 1980. mass mkt. 2.25 o.p. (*0-451-09243-0*, E9243, Signet Bks.) NAL.

—An Affair of Sorcerers. 1979. 9.95 o.s.i (*0-671-24625-9*, Simon & Schuster) Simon & Schuster.

—The Beasts of Valhalla. 3rd ed. 1999. 336p. reprint ed. pap. 16.99 (*0-9674503-3-0*) Apache Beach Pubns.

—The Beasts of Valhalla. 1987. mass mkt. 3.95 o.s.i (*0-440-10484-X*) Dell Publishing.

—The Beasts of Valhalla. 1985. 352p. 15.95 o.s.i (*0-689-11516-4*, Scribner) Simon & Schuster.

—Bleeding in the Eye of a Brainstorm: A Mongo Mystery. 1995. 224p. 21.00 (*0-684-81495-1*, Simon & Schuster); 21.00 (*1-883402-67-0*, Scribner) Simon & Schuster.

—City of Whispering Stone. 3rd ed. 1999. 236p. reprint ed. pap. 16.99 (*0-9674503-1-4*) Apache Beach Pubns.

—City of Whispering Stone. 1988. pap. 3.50 o.s.i (*0-440-11259-1*) Dell Publishing.

—City of Whispering Stone. 1979. mass mkt. 1.95 o.p. (*0-451-08812-3*, J8812, Signet Bks.) NAL.

—City of Whispering Stone. 1978. 9.95 o.s.i (*0-671-24003-X*, Simon & Schuster) Simon & Schuster.

—The Cold Smell of Sacred Stone. 3rd ed. 1999. 304p. reprint ed. pap. 16.99 (*0-9674503-2-2*) Apache Beach Pubns.

—The Cold Smell of Sacred Stone. 1989. 304p. reprint ed. mass mkt. 4.50 o.s.i (*0-440-20394-5*) Dell Publishing.

—The Cold Smell of Sacred Stone. 1988. 320p. 16.95 o.s.i (*0-689-11913-5*, Scribner) Simon & Schuster.

—Dark Chant in a Crimson Key. 3rd ed. 1999. 224p. reprint ed. pap. 16.99 (*0-9674503-8-1*) Apache Beach Pubns.

—Dark Chant in a Crimson Key. 1992. 224p. 18.95 o.p. (*0-89296-463-4*) Mysterious Pr.

—Dark Chant in a Crimson Key. 1993. 224p. mass mkt. 5.99 o.p. (*0-446-40333-4*, Mysterious Pr. Paperback Bks.) Warner Bks., Inc.

—Dream of a Falling Eagle. 2002. 212p. per. 16.99 (*1-930253-14-1*) Apache Beach Pubns.

—The Fear in Yesterday's Rings. 3rd ed. 1999. 224p. reprint ed. pap. 16.99 (*0-9674503-5-7*) Apache Beach Pubns.

—The Fear in Yesterday's Rings. 1991. 18.95 o.p. (*0-89296-396-4*) Mysterious Pr.

—The Fear in Yesterday's Rings. abr. ed. 1991. audio 16.00 o.s.i Random Hse. Audio Publishing Group.

—The Fear in Yesterday's Rings. 1992. 224p. mass mkt. 4.99 (*0-446-40102-1*, Mysterious Pr. Paperback Bks.) Warner Bks., Inc.

—In the House of Secret Enemies. 1990. 240p. 18.95 o.p. (*0-89296-395-6*) Mysterious Pr.

—In the House of Secret Enemies. 1992. 240p. mass mkt. 4.99 o.p. (*0-446-40043-2*) Warner Bks., Inc.

—An Incident at Bloodtide. 3rd ed. 2000. 208p. reprint ed. 16.99 (*1-930253-00-1*) Apache Beach Pubns.

—An Incident at Bloodtide. 1993. 208p. 18.95 (*0-89296-464-2*) Mysterious Pr.

—An Incident at Bloodtide. 1994. 256p. mass mkt. 5.50 (*0-446-40054-8*, Mysterious Pr. Paperback Bks.) Warner Bks., Inc.

—The Language of Cannibals. 3rd ed. 1999. 208p. reprint ed. pap. 16.99 (*0-9674503-6-5*) Apache Beach Pubns.

—The Language of Cannibals. 1990. 208p. 18.95 o.p. (*0-89296-394-8*) Mysterious Pr.

—The Language of Cannibals. 1991. mass mkt. 4.95 o.p. (*0-446-40003-3*, Mysterious Pr. Paperback Bks.) Warner Bks., Inc.

—Second Horseman Out of Eden. 3rd ed. 1999. 256p. reprint ed. pap. 16.99 (*0-9674503-4-9*) Apache Beach Pubns.

—Second Horseman Out of Eden. 1989. 18.95 o.s.i (*0-689-11979-8*, Scribner) Simon & Schuster.

—Second Horseman Out of Eden. 1990. 256p. reprint ed. mass mkt. 4.95 (*0-445-40862-6*, Mysterious Pr. Paperback Bks.) Warner Bks., Inc.

—Shadow of a Broken Man. 3rd ed. 1999. 260p. reprint ed. pap. 16.99 (*0-9674503-7-3*) Apache Beach Pubns.

—Shadow of a Broken Man. 1987. mass mkt. 3.50 o.s.i (*0-440-17761-8*) Dell Publishing.

—Shadow of a Broken Man. 1983. mass mkt. 2.50 o.p. (*0-451-12013-2*, Signet Bks.) NAL.

—Shadow of a Broken Man. 1977. 7.95 o.p. (*0-671-22696-7*, Simon & Schuster) Simon & Schuster.

—Two Songs This Archangel Sings. 3rd ed. 1999. 256p. reprint ed. pap. 16.99 (*0-9674503-0-6*) Apache Beach Pubns.

—Two Songs This Archangel Sings. 1988. mass mkt. 3.95 o.s.i (*0-440-20105-5*) Dell Publishing.

—Two Songs This Archangel Sings. 1986. 320p. 14.95 o.p. (*0-689-11659-4*, Scribner) Simon & Schuster.

**MONK, DITTANY HENBIT (FICTITIOUS CHARACTER)—FICTION**

Craig, Alisa, pseud. The Grub & Stakers House a Haunt. l.t. ed. 1994. 21.95 o.p. (*0-7927-1919-0*); pap. 19.95 o.p. (*0-7927-1918-2*) BBC Audiobooks America.

—The Grub & Stakers House a Haunt. 224p. 1994. pap. 4.99 (*0-380-71044-7*, Avon Bks.); 1993. 18.00 o.p. (*0-688-08644-6*, Morrow, William & Co.) Morrow/Avon.

—The Grub-&-Stakers Move a Mountain. 1981. (Crime Club Ser.). 192p. 10.95 o.p. (*0-385-17411-X*) Doubleday Publishing.

—The Grub-&-Stakers Move a Mountain. 1987. 192p. pap. 3.50 o.p. (*0-380-70331-9*, Avon Bks.) Morrow/Avon.

—The Grub-&-Stakers Move a Mountain. l.t. ed. 1981. 332p. reprint ed. 9.95 o.p. (*0-89621-288-2*) Thorndike Pr.

—The Grub-&-Stakers Pinch a Poke. 1988. (Illus.). 208p. (Orig.). pap. 3.50 (*0-380-75538-6*, Avon Bks.) Morrow/Avon.

—The Grub-&-Stakers Quilt a Bee. 1985. (Crime Club Ser.). 192p. 11.95 o.p. (*0-385-19767-5*) Doubleday Publishing.

—The Grub-&-Stakers Quilt a Bee. 1987. 192p. pap. 3.50 (*0-380-70337-8*, Avon Bks.) Morrow/Avon.

—The Grub-&-Stakers Spin a Yarn. 1990. 224p. pap. 3.50 (*0-380-75540-8*, Avon Bks.) Morrow/Avon.

**MONK, IVAN (FICTITIOUS CHARACTER)—FICTION**

Phillips, Gary. Perdition, U. S. A. 1997. 272p. mass mkt. 5.99 o.s.i (*0-425-15900-0*, Prime Crime) Berkley Publishing Group.

—Perdition, U. S. A. 1994. 260p. pap. 13.00 o.p. (*0-9639050-6-6*, West Coast Crime) Blue Heron Publishing.

—Violent Spring. 1997. 27p. reprint ed. mass mkt. 5.99 o.s.i (*0-425-15625-7*, Prime Crime) Berkley Publishing Group.

—Violent Spring. 1994. 275p. pap. 9.00 o.p. (*1-883303-13-3*, West Coast Crime) Blue Heron Publishing.

**MONK, JASON (FICTITIOUS CHARACTER)—FICTION**

Forsyth, Frederick. Icon. 1997. 576p. mass mkt. (*0-552-13991-2*, Corgi); 1997. 576p. mass mkt. 7.99 (*0-553-57460-4*); 1997. 560p. mass mkt. 7.99 (*0-553-84012-6*); 1996. 400p. 32.95 o.p. (*0-593-02801-5*) Bantam Bks.

—Icon. l.t. ed. (Paperback Bestsellers Ser.). 765p. 1998. pap. 27.95 (*0-7838-1961-7*); 1996. 29.95 (*0-7838-1960-9*) Thorndike Pr.

**MONK, OSBERT (FICTITIOUS CHARACTER)—FICTION**

Craig, Alisa, pseud. The Grub & Stakers House a Haunt. l.t. ed. 1994. 21.95 o.p. (*0-7927-1919-0*); pap. 19.95 o.p. (*0-7927-1918-2*) BBC Audiobooks America.

—The Grub & Stakers House a Haunt. 224p. 1994. pap. 4.99 (*0-380-71044-7*, Avon Bks.); 1993. 18.00 o.p. (*0-688-08644-6*, Morrow, William & Co.) Morrow/Avon.

—The Grub-&-Stakers Move a Mountain. 1981. (Crime Club Ser.). 192p. 10.95 o.p. (*0-385-17411-X*) Doubleday Publishing.

—The Grub-&-Stakers Move a Mountain. 1987. 192p. pap. 3.50 o.p. (*0-380-70331-9*, Avon Bks.) Morrow/Avon.

—The Grub-&-Stakers Move a Mountain. l.t. ed. 1981. 332p. reprint ed. 9.95 o.p. (*0-89621-288-2*) Thorndike Pr.

—The Grub-&-Stakers Pinch a Poke. 1988. (Illus.). 208p. (Orig.). pap. 3.50 (*0-380-75538-6*, Avon Bks.) Morrow/Avon.

—The Grub-&-Stakers Quilt a Bee. 1985. (Crime Club Ser.). 192p. 11.95 o.p. (*0-385-19767-5*) Doubleday Publishing.

—The Grub-&-Stakers Quilt a Bee. 1987. 192p. pap. 3.50 (*0-380-70337-8*, Avon Bks.) Morrow/Avon.

—The Grub-&-Stakers Spin a Yarn. 1990. 224p. pap. 3.50 (*0-380-75540-8*, Avon Bks.) Morrow/Avon.

**MONK, WILLIAM (FICTITIOUS CHARACTER)—FICTION**

Perry, Anne. A Breach of Promise. (William Monk Novels Ser.). 1999. 384p. mass mkt. 6.99 (*0-8041-1855-8*, Ivy Bks.); 1998. 384p. 25.00 o.s.i (*0-449-90849-6*, Fawcett); 1998. mass mkt. 6.99 (*0-8041-1888-4*, Ivy Bks.) Ballantine Bks.

—A Breach of Promise. abr. ed. 1998. audio 18.00 o.s.i (*0-375-40275-6*, 396111, RH Audio) Random Hse. Audio Publishing Group.

—A Breach of Promise. l.t. ed. 1998. (Basic Ser.). 639p. 29.95 (*0-7862-1465-1*) Thorndike Pr.

—Cain His Brother. 1996. 416p. mass mkt. 7.50 (*0-8041-1507-9*); mass mkt. 6.99 o.s.i (*0-8041-1504-4*) Ballantine Bks. (Ivy Bks.).

—Cain His Brother. abr. ed. 1997. (William Monk Mystery Ser.). audio 8.99 o.s.i (*0-679-46025-X*, 393145, RH Audio) Random Hse. Audio Publishing Group.

—Cain His Brother. l.t. ed. 1996. (Cloak & Dagger Ser.). 629p. 26.95 (*0-7862-0607-1*) Thorndike Pr.

—A Dangerous Mourning. 1992. 352p. mass mkt. 6.99 (*0-8041-1037-9*, Ivy Bks.) Ballantine Bks.

—A Dangerous Mourning. unabr. ed. 1995. (Inspector Monk Ser.: Vol. 2). audio 91.00 (*0-7887-0417-6*, 94609E7) Recorded Bks., LLC.

—Death of a Stranger. 2003. 352p. mass mkt. 7.50 (*0-345-44006-4*); 2002. 352p. 25.95 (*0-345-44005-6*, Ballantine Bks.); 2002. E-Book 18.00 (*0-345-45865-6*, Ballantine Bks.) Ballantine Bks.

—Death of a Stranger. l.t. ed. 2003. (Basic Ser.). 570p. 32.95 (*0-7862-4939-0*) Thorndike Pr.

—Defend & Betray. 1993. 448p. mass mkt. 7.50 (*0-8041-1188-X*, Ivy Bks.); 1992. 18.00 o.p. (*0-449-90555-1*, Fawcett); 1992. 368p. 18.00 o.p. (*0-449-90755-4*, Fawcett) Ballantine Bks.

—Defend & Betray. unabr. ed. 2000. (Inspector Monk Ser.: Vol. 3). audio 97.00 (*0-7887-0403-6*, 94595E7) Recorded Bks., LLC.

—The Face of a Stranger. 1998. mass mkt. 3.99 o.s.i (*0-8041-1885-X*); 1991. 352p. mass mkt. 6.99 (*0-8041-0858-7*) Ballantine Bks. (Ivy Bks.).

—The Face of a Stranger. unabr. ed. 1995. (Inspector Monk Ser.: Vol. 1). audio 78.00 (*0-7887-0321-8*, 94513E7) Recorded Bks., LLC.

—Funeral in Blue. 2001. 352p. 25.00 (*0-345-44001-3*, Ballantine Bks.) Ballantine Bks.

—Funeral in Blue. l.t. ed. 2002. (Basic Ser.). 574p. 30.95 (*0-7862-3640-X*) Gale Group.

—The Silent Cry. 368p. 1998. (William Monk Novels Ser.: Vol. 8). mass mkt. 6.99 (*0-8041-1793-4*, Ivy Bks.); 1997. 24.95 o.s.i (*0-449-90848-8*, Fawcett) Ballantine Bks.

—The Silent Cry. l.t. ed. 1998. (Basic Ser.). 616p. 30.95 (*0-7862-1301-9*) Thorndike Pr.

—The Sins of the Wolf. 1995. 448p. mass mkt. 6.99 (*0-8041-1383-1*, Ivy Bks.) Ballantine Bks.

—The Sins of the Wolf. unabr. ed. 2000. (Inspector Monk Ser.: Vol. 5). audio 91.00 (*0-7887-0272-6*, 94481E7) Recorded Bks., LLC.

—Slaves of Obsession. 11th ed. 2001. 368p. mass mkt. 7.50 (*0-449-00592-5*, Fawcett) Ballantine Bks.

—A Sudden, Fearful Death. 1994. 464p. mass mkt. 6.99 (*0-8041-1283-5*, Ivy Bks.) Ballantine Bks.

—A Sudden, Fearful Death. unabr. ed. 2000. (Inspector Monk Ser.: Vol. 4). audio 97.00 (*0-7887-0499-0*, 94692E7) Recorded Bks., LLC.

—The Twisted Root. 2000. (William Monk Novels Ser.). 368p. mass mkt. 7.50 (*0-8041-1936-8*, Ballantine Bks.) Ballantine Bks.

—The Twisted Root. l.t. ed. 1999. pap. 25.00 o.p. (*0-7838-8698-5*, Macmillan Reference USA) Gale Group.

—The Twisted Root, Set. abr. ed. 1999. audio 25.00 Highsmith Inc.

—The Twisted Root, Set. abr. ed. 1999. audio 25.00 o.s.i (*0-375-40810-X*, RH Audio) Random Hse. Audio Publishing Group.

—The Twisted Root. l.t. ed. 1999. 496p. 25.00 (*0-375-40857-6*) Random Hse. Large Print.

—Weighed in the Balance. 1996. mass mkt. 6.99 o.s.i (*0-8041-1619-9*); 1997. 384p. mass mkt. 7.50 (*0-8041-1562-1*) Ballantine Bks. (Ivy Bks.).

**MONMOUTH, ROBERT CAREY, EARL OF, CA. 1560-1639—FICTION**

Chisholm, P. F. A Famine of Horses: A Sir Robert Carey Mystery. unabr. ed. 1997. audio 61.95 Eye in the Ear Inc.

—A Famine of Horses: A Sir Robert Carey Mystery. l.t. ed. 1995. (Magna Large Print Ser.). 447p. 29.99 (*0-7505-0838-8*) Magna Large Print Bks. GBR. *Dist:* Ulverscroft Large Print Bks., Ltd., Ulverscroft Large Print Canada, Ltd.

—A Famine of Horses: A Sir Robert Carey Mystery. 2000. (Sir Robert Carey Mysteries Ser.: Vol. 14). 400p. pap. 14.95 (*1-890208-27-2*) Poisoned Pen Pr.

—A Famine of Horses: A Sir Robert Carey Mystery. 1995. 270p. text 20.95 (*0-8027-3252-6*) Walker & Co.

—A Season of Knives: A Sir Robert Carey Mystery. unabr. ed. 2001. audio 69.95 (*0-7531-0036-3*, 970607) ISIS Audio Bks. GBR. *Dist:* Ulverscroft Large Print Bks., Ltd.

—A Season of Knives: A Sir Robert Carey Mystery. 2000. (Missing Mysteries Ser.: No. 18). 250p. pap. 14.95 (*1-890208-32-9*) Poisoned Pen Pr.

—A Season of Knives: A Sir Robert Carey Mystery. 1996. (Sir Robert Carey Mystery Ser.). 240p. 19.95 (*0-8027-3276-3*) Walker & Co.

—A Surfeit of Guns: A Sir Robert Carey Mystery, Vol. 20. 2000. (Missing Mysteries Ser.: Vol. 20). pap. 14.95 (*1-890208-35-3*) Poisoned Pen Pr.

—A Surfeit of Guns: A Sir Robert Carey Mystery. 1997. (Sir Robert Carey Mysteries Ser.). 233p. 20.95 (*0-8027-3304-2*) Walker & Co.

**MONTANA, KENT (FICTITIOUS CHARACTER)—FICTION**

Fenn, Lionel. Kent Montana & the Once & Future Thing. 1991. mass mkt. 3.95 o.s.i (*0-441-43537-8*) Ace Bks.

—Kent Montana & the Really Ugly Thing from Mars. 1990. mass mkt. 3.95 o.s.i (*0-441-43535-1*) Ace Bks.

—Kent Montana & the Reasonably Invisible Man. 1991. mass mkt. 3.95 o.s.i (*0-441-43536-X*) Ace Bks.

**MONTERO, BRITT (FICTITIOUS CHARACTER)—FICTION**

Buchanan, Edna. Act of Betrayal. unabr. collector's ed. 1996. (Britt Montero Ser.). audio 56.00 (*0-7366-3306-5*, 3960) Books on Tape, Inc.

—Act of Betrayal. abr. ed. (Britt Montero Mystery Ser.). 1997. 3p. audio 7.99 o.p. (*1-56740-148-1*, 617, Paperback Nova Audio Bks.); 1996. audio 17.95 o.p. (*1-56100-868-0*, 454, Nova Audio Bks.); 1996. 7p. audio 57.25 o.p. (*1-56100-296-8*, 786, Unabridged Library Editions); 1996. audio 23.95 o.p. (*1-56100-671-8*, 24, Bookcassette) Brilliance Audio.

—Act of Betrayal, Set. unabr. ed. 1999. audio 57.25 Highsmith Inc.

—Act of Betrayal. 1997. 448p. mass mkt. 5.99 (0-7868-8923-3); 1996. 320p. 21.95 o.p. (0-7868-6098-7) Hyperion Pr.
—Act of Betrayal. unabr. ed. 2000. (Britt Montero Mystery Ser.: Vol. 4). audio 60.00 (0-7887-0488-5, 94681E7) Recorded Bks., LLC.
—Contents under Pressure. unabr. collector's ed. 1993. (Britt Montero Ser.). audio 56.00 (0-7366-2378-7, 3150) Books on Tape, Inc.
—Contents under Pressure. 1992. 304p. (YA). 21.95 o.p. (1-56282-932-7) Hyperion Pr.
—Contents under Pressure. 1994. (Britt Montero Mysteries Ser.). 368p. mass mkt. 6.99 (0-380-72260-7, Avon Bks.) Morrow/Avon.
—Contents under Pressure. l.t. ed. 472p. pap. 2.99 o.s.i (0-7669-1026-1) World Pubns., Inc.
—Garden of Evil. abr. ed. 2000. audio 7.99 (1-58788-037-7, 2281, Paperback Nova Audio Bks.); 1999. audio 17.95 o.p. (1-56740-861-3, 1813, Nova Audio Bks.); 1999. 9p. audio 57.25 (1-56740-682-3, 1811, Unabridged Library Editions); 1999. audio 24.95 (1-56740-456-1, 1810, Bookcassette) Brilliance Audio.
—Garden of Evil, Set. abr. ed. 1999. audio 17.95. audio 57.25 Highsmith Inc.
—Garden of Evil. (Britt Montero Mysteries Ser.). 2000. 320p. mass mkt. 6.99 (0-380-79841-7); 1999. 319p. 24.00 (0-380-97654-4) Morrow/Avon. (Avon Bks.).
—Garden of Evil. unabr. ed. 2000. (Britt Montero Mystery Ser.: Vol. 6). audio 65.00 (0-7887-4420-8, 96128E7) Recorded Bks., LLC.
—Garden of Evil. l.t. ed. 2000. (Mystery Ser.). 437p. 29.95 (0-7862-2331-6) Thorndike Pr.
—The Ice Maiden. l.t. ed. 2003. lib. bdg. 29.95 (1-58547-309-X, Platinum) Ctr. Point Large Print.
—The Ice Maiden. 2003. 320p. mass mkt. 7.50 (0-380-72834-6, Avon Bks.); 2002. 304p. 23.95 (0-380-97332-4, Morrow, William & Co.) Morrow/Avon.
—Margin of Error. unabr. collector's ed. 1997. (Britt Montero Ser.). audio 56.00 (0-7366-3832-6, 4552) Books on Tape, Inc.
—Margin of Error. abr. ed. 1998. audio 7.99 o.p. (1-56740-253-4, 675, Paperback Nova Audio Bks.); 1997. 8p. audio 57.25 o.p. (1-56100-822-2, 937, Unabridged Library Editions); 1997. audio 23.95 (1-56100-747-1, 171) Brilliance Audio.
—Margin of Error. l.t. ed. 1998. pap. 24.95 (1-56895-563-4, Wheeler Publishing, Inc.) Gale Group.
—Margin of Error. 1997. 304p. 22.95 o.p. (0-7868-6232-7); 1998. 384p. reprint ed. mass mkt. 5.99 (0-7868-8931-4) Hyperion Pr.
—Margin of Error. unabr. ed. (Britt Montero Mystery Ser.: Vol. 5). 1999. audio compact disk 79.00 (0-7887-3424-5, C1030E7); 1997. audio 75.00 (0-7887-1777-4, 95251E7) Recorded Bks., LLC.
—Margin of Error. l.t. ed. 2000. (Ulverscroft Large Print Ser.). 488p. (0-7089-4189-3, Ulverscroft) Thorpe, F. A. Pubs. GBR. *Dist:* Ulverscroft Large Print Bks., Ltd., Ulverscroft Large Print Canada, Ltd.
—Miami, It's Murder. unabr. collector's ed. 1994. (Britt Montero Ser.). audio 48.00 (0-7366-2740-5, 3466) Books on Tape, Inc.
—Miami, It's Murder. unabr. ed. 1994. audio 57.25 o.p. (1-56100-175-9, 941, Unabridged Library Editions); audio 21.95 o.p. (1-56100-548-7, 175, Bookcassette) Brilliance Audio.
—Miami, It's Murder. abr. ed. audio 17.00 o.p. (1-55994-794-2, CPN 2383, HarperAudio) HarperTrade.
—Miami, It's Murder. 1994. 256p. 21.95 o.p. (1-56282-802-9) Hyperion Pr.
—Miami, It's Murder. 1995. (Britt Montero Mysteries Ser.). 320p. mass mkt. 6.99 (0-380-72261-5, Avon Bks.) Morrow/Avon.
—Nobody Lives Forever. 1997. 400p. mass mkt. 5.99 o.s.i (1-57566-123-3); 1992. mass mkt. 5.99 o.s.i (0-8217-3712-0, Zebra Bks.) Kensington Publishing Corp.
—Nobody Lives Forever. 1992. 3.99 o.p. (0-517-09448-7) Random Hse. Value Publishing.
—Suitable for Framing. unabr. collector's ed. 1995. (Britt Montero Ser.). audio 56.00 (0-7366-3072-4, 3754) Books on Tape, Inc.
—Suitable for Framing. abr. ed. 1995. audio 16.95 o.p. (1-56100-401-4, 1383, Nova Audio Bks.); 9p. audio 57.25 o.p. (1-56100-234-8, 1062, Unabridged Library Editions); audio 23.95 o.p. (1-56100-609-2, 281, Bookcassette) Brilliance Audio.
—Suitable for Framing. l.t. ed. 1995. 25.95 o.p. (1-56895-210-4, Wheeler Publishing, Inc.) Gale Group.
—Suitable for Framing. 1996. 368p. mass mkt. 4.99 (0-7868-8901-2); 1995. 256p. 21.95 (0-7868-6047-2) Hyperion Pr.
—Suitable for Framing. abr. ed. 2000. audio 7.95 (1-57815-028-0, 1033, Media Bks. Audio Publishing) Media Bks., L. L. C.
—Suitable for Framing. unabr. ed. 2000. (Britt Montero Mystery Ser.: Vol. 3). audio 60.00 (0-7887-0296-3, 94489E7) Recorded Bks., LLC.
—You Only Die Twice. l.t. ed. 2001. 396p. lib. bdg. 27.95 (1-58547-124-0) Ctr. Point Large Print.
—You Only Die Twice. 2002. 368p. mass mkt. 6.99 (0-380-79842-5); 2001. 304p. 24.00 (0-380-97655-2, Morrow, William & Co.) Morrow/Avon.

## MONTEZ, LUIS (FICTITIOUS CHARACTER)—FICTION

Ramos, Manuel. The Ballad of Gato Guerrero. 2004. (Latino Voices Ser.). 192p. pap. 14.00 (0-8101-2091-7) Northwestern Univ. Pr.
—The Ballad of Rocky Ruiz. 2004. (Latino Voices Ser.). 212p. pap. 14.00 (0-8101-2090-9) Northwestern Univ. Pr.

## MONTGOMERY, INSPECTOR (FICTITIOUS CHARACTER)—FICTION

Shepherd, Stella. Embers of Death: An Inspector Montgomery Mystery. l.t. ed. 1997. (Dales Large Print Ser.). 272p. pap. 19.99 (1-85389-757-4) Dales Large Print Bks. GBR. *Dist:* Ulverscroft Large Print Bks., Ltd.
—Embers of Death: An Inspector Montgomery Mystery. 1996. 224p. text 20.95 o.p. (0-312-15097-0, Saint Martin's Minotaur) St. Martin's Pr.

## MONTGOMERY, KAYLA (FICTITIOUS CHARACTER)—FICTION

Laundrie, Amy C. Deliver Us from Evil: A Kayla Montgomery Mystery. 1997. 109p. pap. 9.99 (0-88092-369-5, 3695) Royal Fireworks Publishing Co.
—Eye of Truth: A Kayla Montgomery Mystery. 1996. 119p. pap. 9.99 (0-88092-304-0); lib. bdg. o.p. (0-88092-305-9) Royal Fireworks Publishing Co.
—Lead Us Not into Temptation. 1999. (Kayla Montgomery Mystery Ser.: No. 4). 188p. pap. 9.99 (0-88092-454-3, 4543) Royal Fireworks Publishing Co.
—Thirty Pieces of Silver: A Kayla Montgomery Mystery. 1996. 156p. (gr. 6 up). pap. 9.99 (0-88092-364-4); lib. bdg. o.p. (0-88092-365-2) Royal Fireworks Publishing Co.
—Wolves in Sheep's Clothing. 2001. (Kayla Montgomery Mystery Ser.: Vol. 5). (Illus.). pap. 9.99 (0-88092-549-3, 5493) Royal Fireworks Publishing Co.

## MONTGOMERY, KELLIE (FICTITIOUS CHARACTER)—FICTION

Wilcox, Valerie. Sins of Betrayal: A Sailing Mystery. 1999. 304p. mass mkt. 6.50 o.s.i (0-425-16963-4, Prime Crime) Berkley Publishing Group.
—Sins of Deception. 2000. (Sailing Mystery Ser.). 288p. mass mkt. 5.99 o.s.i (0-425-17507-3, Prime Crime) Berkley Publishing Group.
—The Sins of Silence. 1998. (Elliot Bay Mysteries Ser.). 336p. mass mkt. 5.99 o.s.i (0-425-16396-2, Prime Crime) Berkley Publishing Group.

## MONTGOMERY FAMILY (FICTITIOUS CHARACTERS)—FICTION

Deveraux, Jude. The Awakening. l.t. ed. 1989. (General Ser.). 374p. 17.95 o.p. (0-8161-4739-6, Macmillan Reference USA) Gale Group.
—The Awakening. l.t. ed. 1990. (Magna Large Print Ser.). 443p. o.p. (1-85057-771-4) Magna Large Print Bks. GBR. *Dist:* Ulverscroft Large Print Canada, Ltd.
—The Awakening. 1991. 352p. mass mkt. 7.99 (0-671-74378-3); 1990. mass mkt. 4.95 (0-671-70679-9) Simon & Schuster. (Pocket).
—The Black Lyon. (Star-Romance Ser.). 1997. 339p. 23.95 o.p. (0-7862-0951-8, Five Star); 1987. 429p. 19.95 o.p. (0-8161-4177-0, Macmillan Reference USA) Gale Group.
—The Black Lyon. 2000. 352p. pap. 12.50 (0-380-81206-1); 1980. 288p. mass mkt. 7.99 (0-380-75911-X) Morrow/Avon. (Avon Bks.).
—The Black Lyon. 1991. reprint ed. 18.95 o.p. (0-7278-4049-5) Severn Hse. Pubs., Ltd.
—The Duchess. l.t. ed. 1992. (General Ser.). 494p. 21.95 o.p. (0-8161-5413-9); 17.95 o.p. (0-8161-5414-7) Gale Group. (Macmillan Reference USA).
—The Duchess. Marrow, Linda, ed. 1992. 368p. mass mkt. 7.99 (0-671-68972-X, Pocket); 1991. 320p. 21.00 o.p. (0-671-68971-1, Atria) Simon & Schuster.
—The Duchess. abr. ed. 1999. audio 9.98 (0-671-04415-X); Set. 1991. audio 16.00 (0-671-74751-7, 390693) Simon & Schuster Audio. (Simon & Schuster Audioworks).
—Eternity. l.t. ed. 1992. (General Ser.). 352p. pap. 16.95 o.p. (0-8161-5523-2); lib. bdg. 20.95 o.p. (0-8161-5522-4) Gale Group. (Macmillan Reference USA).
—Eternity. Marrow, Linda, ed. 1992. 352p. mass mkt. 7.99 (0-671-74457-7, Pocket) Simon & Schuster.
—The Heiress. 2002. E-Book 7.99 (1-59061-642-1) Adobe Systems, Inc.
—The Heiress. l.t. ed. 1996. 26.95 o.p. (1-56895-290-2, Wheeler Publishing, Inc.) Gale Group.
—The Heiress. 2001. E-Book 7.99 (0-7434-1739-9); 1995. 384p. mass mkt. 7.99 (0-671-74462-3) Simon & Schuster. (Pocket).
—High Tide. l.t. ed. 1999. 25.95 (1-56895-800-5, Wheeler Publishing, Inc.) Gale Group.
—High Tide, Set. abr. ed. 1999. audio 24.00 Highsmith Inc.
—High Tide. 2003. (Illus.). 368p. mass mkt. 5.99 (0-7434-6713-2, Pocket); 2000. (Illus.). 368p. mass mkt. 7.99 (0-671-01417-X, Pocket); 1999. 320p. 24.00 o.s.i (0-671-01416-1, Atria) Simon & Schuster.
—High Tide. abr. ed. 1999. audio 24.00 (0-671-04623-3, Simon & Schuster Audioworks) Simon & Schuster Audio.
—Highland Velvet. l.t. ed. 1985. (General Ser.). 16.95 o.p. (0-8161-3794-3, Macmillan Reference USA) Gale Group.
—Highland Velvet. 1997. (Illus.). 384p. mass mkt. 3.99 (0-671-01134-0, Pocket) Simon & Schuster.
—Highland Velvet. Marrow, Linda, ed. 1991. (Montgomery Annals Ser.: No. 3). 368p. mass mkt. 7.99 (0-671-73972-7, Pocket) Simon & Schuster.
—Highland Velvet. 1990. mass mkt. 4.95 (0-671-70668-3, Pocket) Simon & Schuster.
—Highland Velvet. Marrow, Linda, ed. 1985. (Montgomery Annals Ser.: No. 3). mass mkt. 3.95 (0-671-60073-7, Pocket) Simon & Schuster.
—Highland Velvet. 1982. (Montgomery Annals Ser.: No. 2). mass mkt. 2.95 (0-671-45034-4, Pocket) Simon & Schuster.
—The Invitation. l.t. ed. 524p. reprint ed. 1995. lib. bdg. 16.95 o.p. (0-8161-5663-8); 1994. lib. bdg. 24.95 o.p. (0-8161-5662-X) Gale Group. (Macmillan Reference USA).
—The Invitation. Marrow, Linda, ed. 1994. 384p. reprint ed. mass mkt. 7.99 (0-671-74458-5, Pocket) Simon & Schuster.
—A Knight in Shining Armor. l.t. ed. 1990. (General Ser.). 528p. lib. bdg. 20.95 o.p. (0-8161-4936-4, Macmillan Reference USA) Gale Group.
—A Knight in Shining Armor. 1996. 384p. mass mkt. 3.99 (0-671-00759-9, Pocket); 1990. 320p. mass mkt. 7.99 o.s.i (0-671-70509-1, Pocket); 1989. 17.95 o.p. (0-671-67857-4, Atria) Simon & Schuster.
—A Knight in Shining Armor. abr. ed. 1990. audio 15.95 (0-671-70742-6, Simon & Schuster Audioworks) Simon & Schuster Audio.
—The Maiden. l.t. ed. 1989. (General Ser.). 352p. 20.95 o.p. (0-8161-4844-9, Macmillan Reference USA) Gale Group.
—The Maiden. 1989. mass mkt. 4.50 (0-671-68886-3); 1991. 320p. reprint ed. mass mkt. 7.99 (0-671-74379-1) Simon & Schuster. (Pocket).
—Mountain Laurel. l.t. ed. 1991. (General Ser.). 405p. lib. bdg. 21.95 (0-8161-5124-5, Macmillan Reference USA) Gale Group.
—Mountain Laurel. Marrow, Linda, ed. 1990. 320p. 18.95 o.p. (0-671-68975-4, Atria); 1991. 384p. reprint ed. mass mkt. 7.99 (0-671-68976-2, Pocket) Simon & Schuster.
—Mountain Laurel. 2003. audio compact disk 9.95 (0-7435-3274-0, Encore); 2003. audio 9.95 (0-7435-3245-7, Encore); 1990. 14.95 incl. audio (0-671-70872-4, Simon & Schuster Audioworks) Simon & Schuster Audio.
—The Princess. l.t. ed. 1989. 14.95 o.p. (0-8161-4483-4); 554p. 20.95 o.p. (0-8161-4482-6) Gale Group. (Macmillan Reference USA).
—The Princess. 1991. 336p. mass mkt. 7.99 (0-671-74380-5); 1990. mass mkt. 4.95 (0-671-72754-0) Simon & Schuster. (Pocket).
—The Raider. l.t. ed. 1988. 395p. 17.95 o.p. (0-8161-4371-4, Macmillan Reference USA) Gale Group.
—The Raider. 1990. mass mkt. 4.95 (0-671-70681-0); 1991. 320p. reprint ed. mass mkt. 7.99 (0-671-74381-3) Simon & Schuster. (Pocket).
—The Temptress. l.t. ed. 1987. (General Ser.). 376p. 18.95 o.p. (0-8161-4259-9, Macmillan Reference USA) Gale Group.
—The Temptress. Morrow, Linda, ed. 1991. 352p. mass mkt. 7.99 (0-671-74384-8, Pocket) Simon & Schuster.
—The Temptress. 1990. mass mkt. 4.95 (0-671-70683-7); 1988. mass mkt. 4.50 (0-671-67452-8) Simon & Schuster. (Pocket).
—The Temptress. Morrow, Linda, ed. 1986. mass mkt. 3.95 (0-671-55683-5, Pocket) Simon & Schuster.
—Velvet Angel. l.t. ed. 1985. (General Ser.). 328p. 13.95 o.p. (0-8161-3793-5, Macmillan Reference USA) Gale Group.
—Velvet Angel. 1990. mass mkt. 4.95 (0-671-70671-3, Pocket) Simon & Schuster.
—Velvet Angel. Marrow, Linda, ed. 1991. 352p. reprint ed. mass mkt. 7.99 (0-671-73973-5, Pocket) Simon & Schuster.
—The Velvet Promise. l.t. ed. 1984. (General Ser.). 17.95 o.p. (0-8161-3783-8, Macmillan Reference USA) Gale Group.
—The Velvet Promise. 1990. mass mkt. 4.95 (0-671-70672-1); 1988. mass mkt. 4.50 (0-671-67040-9); 1984. mass mkt. 3.95 (0-671-54756-9) Simon & Schuster. (Pocket).
—The Velvet Promise. Marrow, Linda, ed. 1991. (Richard Gallen Bks.). 320p. reprint ed. mass mkt. 7.99 (0-671-73974-3, Pocket) Simon & Schuster.
—Velvet Song. l.t. ed. 1984. (General Ser.). lib. bdg. 13.95 o.p. (0-8161-3633-5, Macmillan Reference USA) Gale Group.
—Velvet Song. 1990. mass mkt. 4.95 (0-671-70673-X); 1988. mass mkt. 4.50 (0-671-67226-6) Simon & Schuster. (Pocket).
—Velvet Song. Marrow, Linda, ed. 1991. 352p. reprint ed. mass mkt. 7.99 (0-671-73975-1, Pocket) Simon & Schuster.
—Wishes. l.t. ed. 1991. (General Ser.). 324p. 19.95 o.p. (0-8161-5054-0); 15.95 o.p. (0-8161-5148-2) Gale Group. (Macmillan Reference USA).
—Wishes. 1990. 416p. mass mkt. 4.95 (0-671-73726-0); 1991. 320p. reprint ed. mass mkt. 7.99 (0-671-74385-6) Simon & Schuster. (Pocket).

## MONTONE, JAMES (FICTITIOUS CHARACTER)—FICTION

Bowman, Eric. Before I Wake. 1998. 336p. reprint ed. mass mkt. 6.99 o.s.i (0-515-12353-6, Jove) Berkley Publishing Group.
—Before I Wake, Set. abr. ed. 1997. 25.00 o.p. (0-7871-1463-4, 695277) NewStar Media, Inc.
—Before I Wake. 1997. 320p. 24.95 o.p. (0-399-14263-0, G. P. Putnam's Sons) Penguin Group (USA) Inc.

## MONTROSE, CLAIRE (FICTITIOUS CHARACTER)—FICTION

Henry, April. Circles of Confusion. 1998. (Claire Montrose Mysteries Ser.). 288p. 23.00 (0-06-019204-6) HarperCollins Pubs.
—Circles of Confusion. 1999. (Claire Montrose Mysteries Ser.). 368p. mass mkt. 5.99 (0-06-109715-2, HarperTorch) Morrow/Avon.
—Square in the Face. 2000. (Claire Montrose Mysteries Ser.). 272p. 24.00 (0-06-019205-4) HarperCollins Pubs.
—Square in the Face. 2001. (Claire Montrose Mysteries Ser.). 256p. mass mkt. 5.99 (0-06-109716-0, Avon Bks.) Morrow/Avon.

## MONTROSE, JEAN (FICTITIOUS CHARACTER)—FICTION

Roe, C. F. Bad Blood. l.t. ed. 1993. (Magna Large Print Ser.). 366p. (0-7505-0486-2) Magna Large Print Bks. GBR. *Dist:* Ulverscroft Large Print Canada, Ltd.
—A Bonny Case of Murder: Dr. Jean Montrose Mystery. 1994. (Dr. Jean Montrose Mystery Ser.). 256p. (Orig.). mass mkt. 3.99 o.s.i (0-451-18067-4) NAL.
—A Classy Touch of Murder. 1993. (Dr. Jean Montrose Mystery Ser.: No. 3). 256p. mass mkt. 5.99 o.s.i (0-451-17713-4, Signet Bks.) NAL.
—A Classy Touch of Murder. 256p. 24.00 (0-7278-5183-7) Severn Hse. Pubs., Ltd.
—Death by Fire. l.t. ed. 1992. (Magna Large Print Ser.). 345p. (0-7505-0128-6) Magna Large Print Bks. GBR. *Dist:* Ulverscroft Large Print Canada, Ltd.
—A Fiery Hint of Murder. 1993. (Dr. Jean Montrose Mystery Ser.: No. 2). 256p. reprint ed. mass mkt. 5.50 o.s.i (0-451-17606-5, Signet Bks.) NAL.
—The Hidden Cause of Murder. 1996. (Dr. Jean Montrose Mystery Ser.). 256p. mass mkt. 5.50 o.s.i (0-451-18633-8, Signet Bks.) NAL.
—A Nasty Bit of Murder. 1992. (Dr. Jean Montrose Mystery Ser.). 288p. mass mkt. 5.50 o.s.i (0-451-17468-2, Signet Bks.) NAL.
—A Relative Act of Murder. 1995. (Dr. Jean Montrose Mystery Ser.). 256p. (Orig.). mass mkt. 5.50 o.s.i (0-451-18183-2, Signet Bks.) NAL.
—Tangled Knot of Murder. 1996. (Dr. Jean Montrose Mystery Ser.). 256p. mass mkt. 5.50 o.s.i (0-451-19079-3, Signet Bks.) NAL.
—A Torrid Piece of Murder: A Dr. Jean Montrose Mystery. 1994. (Dr. Jean Montrose Mystery Ser.). 256p. (Orig.). mass mkt. 5.50 o.s.i (0-451-18182-4, Signet Bks.) NAL.

## MOODROW, STANLEY (FICTITIOUS CHARACTER)—FICTION

Solomita, Stephen. Bad to the Bone. 1992. 352p. mass mkt. 4.99 (0-380-71760-3, Avon Bks.) Morrow/Avon.
—Bad to the Bone. 1991. 256p. 21.95 o.p. (0-399-13593-6, G. P. Putnam's Sons) Penguin Group (USA) Inc.
—Damaged Goods: A Stanley Moodrow Novel. 1996. 384p. 22.00 o.p. (0-684-81584-2, Scribner) Simon & Schuster.
—Force of Nature. 1990. 352p. pap. 4.95 (0-380-70949-X, Avon Bks.) Morrow/Avon.
—Force of Nature. 1989. 288p. 19.95 o.s.i (0-399-13491-3, G. P. Putnam's Sons) Penguin Putnam Bks. for Young Readers.
—Forced Entry. 1991. 384p. pap. 4.99 (0-380-71361-6, Avon Bks.) Morrow/Avon.
—Forced Entry. 1990. 320p. 19.95 o.p. (0-399-13559-6, G. P. Putnam's Sons) Penguin Putnam Bks. for Young Readers.

—A Piece of the Action. 1994. 352p. mass mkt. 4.99 (*0-380-72103-1*, Avon Bks.) Morrow/Avon.
—A Piece of the Action. 1992. 256p. 22.95 o.p. (*0-399-13730-0*, G. P. Putnam's Sons) Penguin Group (USA) Inc.
—A Twist of the Knife. 1990. 336p. pap. 4.95 (*0-380-70997-X*, Avon Bks.) Morrow/Avon.
—A Twist of the Knife. 1988. 288p. 17.95 o.p. (*0-399-13401-8*, G. P. Putnam's Sons) Penguin Putnam Bks. for Young Readers.
Stephen, Solomita. Force of Nature. 1991. 4.99 o.p. (*0-517-07422-2*) Random Hse. Value Publishing.

**MOODY, KEITH (FICTITIOUS CHARACTER)—FICTION**

Matthews, Greg. Far from Heaven: A Keith Moody Mystery. 1997. (Keith Moody Mystery Ser.). 276p. 20.95 (*0-8027-3303-4*) Walker & Co.

**MOODY, SCOTT (FICTITIOUS CHARACTER)—FICTION**

Oliver, Steve. Moody Forever. 2003. 258p. pap. 13.95 (*0-9644138-1-7*, Dark City Bks.) OffByOne Pr.
—Moody Forever. (St. Martin's Minotaur Mysteries Ser.). 272p. 1999. mass mkt. 5.99 (*0-312-96923-6*, St. Martin's Paperbacks); 1998. 22.95 o.p. (*0-312-19301-7*, Saint Martin's Minotaur) St. Martin's Pr.

**MOON, CHARLIE (FICTITIOUS CHARACTER: DOSS)—FICTION**

Doss, James D. Dead Soul. Date not set. pap. (*0-312-31746-8*, St. Martin's Paperbacks); Date not set. mass mkt. (*0-312-99462-1*, St. Martin's Paperbacks); mass mkt. (*0-312-99109-6*, St. Martin's Paperbacks); 2003. 352p. 24.95 (*0-312-31744-1*, Saint Martin's Minotaur) St. Martin's Pr.
—Grandmother Spider: A Charlie Moon Mystery. 2001. 384p. mass mkt. 6.99 (*0-380-80394-1*) HarperCollins Pubs.
—The Shaman Laughs. 1995. 272p. 21.95 o.p. (*0-312-13601-3*, Saint Martin's Minotaur) St. Martin's Pr.
—Shaman Laughs. 1997. (Shaman Mysteries Ser.). 352p. mass mkt. 6.99 (*0-380-72690-4*, Avon Bks.) Morrow/Avon.
—The Shaman Sings. 1994. 272p. 3000.00 o.p. (*0-312-10547-9*, Saint Martin's Minotaur) St. Martin's Pr.
—Shaman Sings. 1995. (Shaman Mysteries Ser.). 256p. mass mkt. 6.99 (*0-380-72496-0*, Avon Bks.) Morrow/Avon.
—The Shaman's Bones. 1997. 288p. 22.00 (*0-380-97424-X*, Avon Bks.) Morrow/Avon.
—The Shaman's Game. (Shaman Mysteries Ser.). 1999. 352p. mass mkt. 6.50 (*0-380-79030-0*); 1998. 384p. 22.00 (*0-380-97425-8*) Morrow/Avon. (Avon Bks.).
—The Shaman's Mistake. 1998. (Shaman Mysteries Ser.). 352p. mass mkt. 6.99 (*0-380-79029-7*, Avon Bks.) Morrow/Avon.
—White Shell Woman: A Charlie Moon Mystery. 2002. 304p. 23.95 (*0-06-019932-6*, Morrow, William & Co.) Morrow/Avon.

**MOON, CHARLIE (FICTITIOUS CHARACTER: YARBRO)—FICTION**

Yarbro, Chelsea Quinn. Ogilvie, Tallant & Moon. 1976. (Red Mask Mystery Ser.). (Illus.). 214p. 6.95 o.p. (*0-399-11630-3*) Putnam Publishing Group, The.

**MOON, DONOVAN (FICTITIOUS CHARACTER)—FICTION**

Atkins, Peter. Morningstar. 1992. 304p. mass mkt. 4.50 o.p. (*0-06-100512-6*, HarperTorch) Morrow/Avon.

**MOON, JOHN (FICTITIOUS CHARACTER)—FICTION**

Jones, Matthew F. A Single Shot. 1997. 256p. pap. 11.95 o.s.i (*0-385-31833-2*, Delta) Dell Publishing.
—A Single Shot. 1996. 256p. 22.00 o.p. (*0-374-26465-1*) Farrar, Straus & Giroux.

**MOON, PHYLLIDA (FICTITIOUS CHARACTER)—FICTION**

Dewhurst, Eileen. Closing Stages. 192p. 25.99 (*0-7278-5698-7*); 27.00 (*0-7278-7078-5*) Severn Hse. Pubs., Ltd.
—Double Act. l.t. ed. 2001. (Magna Large Print Ser.). 320p. 31.99 (*0-7505-1601-1*) Magna Large Print Bks. GBR. *Dist:* Ulverscroft Large Print Bks., Ltd., Ulverscroft Large Print Canada, Ltd.
—Double Act. 2000. 218p. 26.00 (*0-7278-5533-6*) Severn Hse. Pubs., Ltd.
—Easeful Death. 2002. 224p. 25.99 (*0-7278-5906-4*) Severn Hse. Pubs., Ltd.
—No Love Lost. 2002. 256p. 25.99 (*0-7278-5816-5*) Severn Hse. Pubs., Ltd.

**MOONDARK, GAN (FICTITIOUS CHARACTER)—FICTION**

McQuinn, Donald E. Wanderer. 1994. 800p. mass mkt. 6.99 o.s.i (*0-345-39018-0*, Del Rey) Ballantine Bks.
—Warrior. 1995. pap. 6.99 o.p. (*0-345-90214-9*); 1991. 672p. mass mkt. 6.99 o.s.i (*0-345-37348-0*) Ballantine Bks. (Del Rey).
—Witch. (Orig.). 1995. mass mkt. 6.99 o.s.i (*0-345-39737-1*); 1994. 512p. pap. 10.00 o.p. (*0-345-37841-5*) Ballantine Bks. (Del Rey).

**MORA, VINCENT (FICTITIOUS CHARACTER)—FICTION**

Leonard, Elmore. Glitz. l.t. ed. 1985. (General Ser.). 407p. 15.95 o.p. (*0-8161-3834-6*); 9.95 o.p. (*0-8161-3835-4*) Gale Group. (Macmillan Reference USA).
—Glitz. 1998. 432p. pap. 12.00 (*0-688-16095-6*, Quill) HarperTrade.
—Glitz. 2002. 432p. mass mkt. 7.50 (*0-06-008953-9*); 1983. 14.95 o.p. (*0-87795-632-4*, Morrow, William & Co.) Morrow/Avon.
—Glitz. 1987. 368p. mass mkt. 6.99 (*0-446-34343-9*); 1986. mass mkt. 3.95 (*0-446-32920-7*) Warner Bks., Inc.

**MORAN, GEORGE (FICTITIOUS CHARACTER)—FICTION**

Leonard, Elmore. Cat Chaser. unabr. collector's ed. 1995. audio 48.00 (*0-7366-3117-8*, 3793) Books on Tape, Inc.
—Cat Chaser. abr. ed. (Audio Favorites Ser.). audio 9.99 (*1-55204-011-9*, 390491); 1989. audio 16.99 (*0-88646-239-8*) Durkin Hayes Publishing Ltd.
—Cat Chaser. l.t. ed. 1986. (General Ser.). 364p. 16.95 o.p. (*0-8161-3947-4*, Macmillan Reference USA) Gale Group.
—Cat Chaser. 1998. (Elmore Leonard Library). 288p. pap. 12.00 (*0-688-16341-6*, Perennial) HarperTrade.
—Cat Chaser. 2003. 384p. mass mkt. 7.50 (*0-06-051222-9*, HarperTorch); 1983. 288p. mass mkt. 6.50 (*0-380-64642-0*, Avon Bks.); 1982. 13.50 o.p. (*0-87795-398-8*, Morrow, William & Co.) Morrow/Avon.
—Cat Chaser. unabr. ed. 1995. audio 51.00 (*0-7887-0256-4*, 94465E7) Recorded Bks., LLC.

**MORAN, STOKES (FICTITIOUS CHARACTER)—FICTION**

McGaughey, Neil. And Then There Were Ten. 1995. 255p. 21.00 (*0-684-19760-X*, Scribner) Simon & Schuster.
—Best Money Murder Can Buy: A Stokes Moran Mystery. 1996. 256p. 21.00 (*0-684-19761-8*, Scribner) Simon & Schuster.
—A Corpse by Any Other Name: A Stokes Moran Mystery. 1998. (Stokes Moran Mystery Ser.). 240p. 22.00 (*0-684-19762-6*, Scribner) Simon & Schuster.
—Otherwise Known As Murder. 1994. 224p. text 20.00 (*0-684-19674-3*, Macmillan Reference USA) Gale Group.

**MORELL, CHARLIE (FICTITIOUS CHARACTER)—FICTION**

Abella, Alex. Dead of Night. 1998. 304p. 23.00 (*0-684-81426-9*, Simon & Schuster) Simon & Schuster.

**MORELLI, TEODORA (FICTITIOUS CHARACTER)—FICTION**

French, Linda. Coffee to Die For. 1998. (Professor Teodora Morelli Mystery Ser.: No. 2). 224p. mass mkt. 5.99 (*0-380-79575-2*, Avon Bks.) Morrow/Avon.
—Steeped in Murder. 1999. (Professor Teodora Morelli Mystery Ser.). 256p. mass mkt. 5.99 (*0-380-79576-0*, Avon Bks.) Morrow/Avon.
—Talking Rain: A Professor Teodora Morelli Mystery. 1998. (Professor Teodora Morelli Mystery Ser.). 224p. mass mkt. 5.99 (*0-380-79573-6*, Avon Bks.) Morrow/Avon.

**MORGAN, AVERY (FICTITIOUS CHARACTER)—FICTION**

Whitten, Leslie H. The Fangs of Morning - The Alchemist, 2 bks. in 1. 1994. 448p. pap. 5.99 (*0-8439-3685-1*) Dorchester Publishing Co., Inc.

**MORGAN, CORDELIA (FICTITIOUS CHARACTER)—FICTION**

Johnson, Bett Reece. The Woman Who Found Grace. 2003. 300p. pap. 12.95 (*1-57344-150-3*) Cleis Pr.
—The Woman Who Knew Too Much: A Cordelia Morgan Mystery. 1998. (Cordelia Morgan Mysteries Ser.). 250p. pap. 12.95 (*1-57344-045-0*) Cleis Pr.
—The Woman Who Rode to the Moon: A Cordelia Morgan Mystery. 1999. (Cordelia Morgan Mysteries Ser.). 321p. pap. 12.95 (*1-57344-086-8*) Cleis Pr.

**MORGAN, DANA (FICTITIOUS CHARACTER)—FICTION**

Reid, Sally H. Undertow. 1992. 320p. mass mkt. 4.50 o.s.i (*0-8217-3962-X*, Zebra Bks.) Kensington Publishing Corp.

**MORGAN, GREG (FICTITIOUS CHARACTER)—FICTION**

Garnett, Griffin T. The Sandscrapers: A Forgotten Navy. Pruett, Robert H., ed. 1995. (Illus.). 432p. pap. 14.95 o.p. (*1-883911-03-6*) Brandylane Pubs., Inc.
—The Sandscrapers: A Forgotten Navy. 2nd ed. 1996. 432p. pap. 15.95 o.p. (*1-883911-10-9*) Brandylane Pubs., Inc.
—The Sandscrapers: A Forgotten Navy. 1999. 394p. pap. 17.95 (*0-7414-0177-0*) Buy Bks. on the Web.Com.
—The Sandscrapers: A Forgotten Navy. 2003. (Illus.). 420p. pap. 17.95 (*1-929381-20-4*, Third Millennium Publishing) Sci Fi-Arizona, Inc.
—Taboo Avenged. 1997. 320p. pap. 14.95 (*1-883911-16-8*) Brandylane Pubs., Inc.

**MORGAN, JAMES (FICTITIOUS CHARACTER)—FICTION**

Coburn, Andrew. No Way Home. 1992. 288p. 20.00 o.p. (*0-525-93470-7*, Dutton) Dutton/Plume.
—No Way Home. 1993. 352p. mass mkt. 4.99 o.s.i (*0-451-17675-8*, Signet Bks.) NAL.
—Voices in the Dark. 1994. 304p. 19.95 o.p. (*0-525-93644-0*, Dutton) Dutton/Plume.
—Voices in the Dark. 1995. 304p. mass mkt. 4.99 o.p. (*0-451-40590-0*, Onyx) NAL.

**MORGAN, SARA (FICTITIOUS CHARACTER)—FICTION**

Stine, R. L. Superstitious. 1996. 400p. mass mkt. 6.99 (*0-446-60350-3*) Warner Bks., Inc.

**MORGAN, TAYLOR (FICTITIOUS CHARACTER)—FICTION**

Rust, Megan Mallory. Coffin Corner. 2000. (Alaskan Mystery Ser.). 224p. mass mkt. 5.99 o.s.i (*0-425-17508-1*) Berkley Publishing Group.
—Dead Stick. 1998. (New Alaskan Murder Mysteries Ser.). 208p. mass mkt. 5.99 o.s.i (*0-425-16296-6*, Prime Crime) Berkley Publishing Group.
—Red Line, 1 vol. 1999. 224p. mass mkt. 5.99 o.s.i (*0-425-16897-2*) Berkley Publishing Group.

**MORIARTY, PROFESSOR (FICTITIOUS CHARACTER)—FICTION**

Bugge, Carole. Star of India. 1997. 256p. 21.95 (*0-312-18034-9*) St. Martin's Pr.
Doyle, Arthur Conan. The Adventure of the Empty House. unabr. ed. 1995. (Stories from the Return of Sherlock Holmes Ser.). audio 16.99 (*0-88646-387-4*, 7387) Durkin Hayes Publishing Ltd.
—The Adventure of the Empty House. 1981. audio. audio 7.95 Jimcin Recordings.
—The Final Problem. abr. ed. 1983. (Radio Ser.). pap. 5.95 o.p. incl. audio (*0-88142-355-6*, 355) Soundelux Audio Publishing.
—The Valley of Fear. 1976. 17.95 (*0-8488-1288-3*) Amereon, Ltd.
—The Valley of Fear. unabr. ed. 2003. (YA). (gr. 10 up). audio 29.95 (*1-55685-676-8*, ) Audio Bk. Contractors, Inc.
—The Valley of Fear. l.t. ed. 1990. pap. 16.95 o.p. (*0-7927-0475-4*, C0775) BBC Audiobooks America.
—The Valley of Fear. 1987. 176p. mass mkt. 2.50 o.p. (*0-425-10330-7*); 1986. mass mkt. 2.50 o.s.i (*0-425-09580-0*); 1984. mass mkt. 2.50 o.s.i (*0-425-07140-5*); 1981. mass mkt. 2.25 o.s.i (*0-425-05221-4*); 1980. mass mkt. 1.95 o.s.i (*0-425-04911-6*); 1979. mass mkt. 1.75 o.s.i (*0-425-04537-4*); 1978. mass mkt. 1.50 o.s.i (*0-425-03981-1*); 1976. mass mkt. 1.25 o.s.i (*0-425-03136-5*) Berkley Publishing Group.
—The Valley of Fear. unabr. ed. 1991. audio 39.95 (*0-7861-0612-3*, 2102) Blackstone Audio Bks., Inc.
—The Valley of Fear. unabr. collector's ed. 1991. audio 36.00 (*0-7366-2030-3*, 2844) Books on Tape, Inc.
—The Valley of Fear. 1988. lib. bdg. 16.95 (*0-89966-232-3*) Buccaneer Bks., Inc.
—The Valley of Fear. 1977. 7.95 o.p. (*0-385-12284-5*) Doubleday Publishing.
—The Valley of Fear. unabr. ed. 1991. audio 16.99 (*0-88646-296-7*, 7296) Durkin Hayes Publishing Ltd.
—The Valley of Fear, Set. unabr. ed. 1999. audio 39.95 Highsmith Inc.
—The Valley of Fear. 2001. iv, 200p. pap. 8.95 (*0-7551-0645-8*) House of Stratus, Inc. GBR. *Dist:* Midpoint Trade Bks., Inc.
—The Valley of Fear. unabr. ed. 1991. (YA). (gr. 9-12). audio 29.00 Jimcin Recordings.
—The Valley of Fear. Edwards, Owen D., ed. 1993. (Oxford Sherlock Holmes Ser.). 292p. (C). 13.95 o.p. (*0-19-212314-9*, 8951) Oxford Univ. Pr., Inc.
—The Valley of Fear. Edwards, Owen D., ed. & intro. by. 1995. (Oxford World's Classics Ser.). 292p. reprint ed. pap. 6.95 o.p. (*0-19-282382-5*) Oxford Univ. Pr., Inc.
—The Valley of Fear. 1991. (Classic Crime Ser.). 192p. pap. 6.00 o.p. (*0-14-005710-2*, Penguin Bks.) Penguin Group (USA) Inc.
—The Valley of Fear. collector's ed. 2002. (Illus.). im. lthr. 38.85 (*1-4115-1255-3*); pap. 19.95 (*1-4115-0524-7*); 25.95 (*1-4115-0890-4*); pap. 17.95 (*1-4115-0320-1*) Polyglot Pr., Inc.
—The Valley of Fear. 1999. 256p. E-Book 3.99 incl. cd-rom (*1-57646-184-X*) Quiet Vision Publishing.
—The Valley of Fear. abr. ed. 1999. (BBC Radio Presents Ser.). audio 18.00 o.s.i (*0-553-52622-7*, RH Audio) Random Hse. Audio Publishing Group.
—The Valley of Fear. unabr. ed. 1986. (Sherlock Holmes Mystery Ser.). audio 35.00 (*1-55690-539-4*, 86250E7) Recorded Bks., LLC.
—The Valley of Fear. unabr. ed. 2002. audio compact disk 20.00 (*1-4001-5040-X*); audio compact disk 33.00 (*1-4001-0040-2*) Tantor Media, Inc.
—The Valley of Fear. l.t. ed. 1978. (Ulverscroft Large Print Ser.). 29.99 o.p. (*0-7089-0086-0*, Ulverscroft) Thorpe, F. A. Pubs. GBR. *Dist:* Ulverscroft Large Print Bks., Ltd., Ulverscroft Large Print Canada, Ltd.
Doyle, Arthur Conan & Reyburn, Stanley. The Valley of Fear. Landes, William-Alan, ed. 1998. 55p. pap. 10.00 (*0-88734-742-8*) Players Pr., Inc.
Gardner, John E. The Return of Moriarty. 1981. 304p. mass mkt. 3.50 o.s.i (*0-425-05093-9*) Berkley Publishing Group.
—The Revenge of Moriarty. 1981. 272p. mass mkt. 3.50 o.s.i (*0-425-05092-0*) Berkley Publishing Group.
Hall, John. Sherlock Holmes & the Boulevard Assassin. 1998. 174p. pap. 14.95 (*0-947533-52-4*) Breese Bks., Ltd. GBR. *Dist:* Midpoint Trade Bks., Inc.
Kurland, Michael. The Great Game: A Professor Moriarty Novel. 2003. 304p. pap. 13.95 (*0-312-30505-2*, Saint Martin's Griffin); 2001. 288p. 24.95 (*0-312-20891-X*, Saint Martin's Minotaur) St. Martin's Pr.
Meyer, Nicholas. The Seven-Percent Solution. l.t. ed. 1977. (Ulverscroft Large Print Ser.). 29.99 o.p. (*0-7089-0052-6*, Ulverscroft) Thorpe, F. A. Pubs. GBR. *Dist:* Ulverscroft Large Print Bks., Ltd., Ulverscroft Large Print Canada, Ltd.
Meyer, Nicholas, ed. The Seven-Percent Solution: Being a Reprint from the Reminiscences of John H. Watson, M. D. 1993. 256p. pap. 13.00 (*0-393-31119-8*) Norton, W. W. & Co., Inc.
Watson, John H. & Meyer, Nicholas. The Seven-Percent Solution. 1985. mass mkt. 3.95 o.s.i (*0-345-33156-7*) Ballantine Bks.

**MORIZIO, SAL (FICTITIOUS CHARACTER)—FICTION**

Truman, Margaret. Murder on Embassy Row. 1985. (Capital Crime Myteries Ser.). 352p. mass mkt. 6.99 (*0-449-20621-1*, Fawcett) Ballantine Bks.
—Murder on Embassy Row. l.t. ed. 1984. (General Ser.). 16.95 o.p. (*0-8161-3727-7*); 9.95 o.p. (*0-8161-3765-X*) Gale Group. (Macmillan Reference USA).
—Murder on Embassy Row. 1993. audio. audio 49.00 (*1-56544-042-0*, 250027) Literate Ear, Inc.
—Murder on Embassy Row. 1984. 297p. 15.95 o.p. (*0-87795-594-8*, Morrow, William & Co.) Morrow/Avon.

**MORLAND, REBECCA (FICTITIOUS CHARACTER)—FICTION**

Harrod-Eagles, Cynthia. The Flood-Tide. 1995. (Morland Dynasty Ser.: No. 9). 428p. mass mkt. 6.95 (*0-7515-0646-X*) Warner Futura GBR. *Dist:* Trafalgar Square.
Latt, Mimi. Pursuit of Justice. abr. ed. 1998. audio 7.99 o.s.i (*1-56740-277-1*, 1684, Paperback Nova Audio Bks.); audio 17.95 o.p. (*1-56740-767-6*, 503, Nova Audio Bks.); audio 26.95 (*1-56100-792-7*, 223, Bookcassette); audio 73.25 (*1-56740-571-1*, 996, Unabridged Library Editions) Brilliance Audio.
—Pursuit of Justice. l.t. ed. 1998. (Large Print Bks.). pap. 24.95 (*1-56895-589-8*, Wheeler Publishing, Inc.) Gale Group.
—Pursuit of Justice. 1999. (Illus.). 480p. mass mkt. 6.99 o.s.i (*0-671-03411-1*, Pocket); 1998. 384p. 23.00 (*0-684-81184-7*, Simon & Schuster) Simon & Schuster.

**MORLEY, IRISH (FICTITIOUS CHARACTER)—FICTION**

Cambray, C. K. Programmed for Peril. 1993. 336p. (Orig.). mass mkt. 4.99 (*0-671-73540-3*, Pocket) Simon & Schuster.

**MORLEY, SI (FICTITIOUS CHARACTER)—FICTION**

Finney, Jack. From Time to Time: The Sequel to Time & Again. l.t. ed. 1995. (G. K. Hall Core Ser.). 610p. 25.95 o.p. (*0-7838-1387-2*, Macmillan Reference USA) Gale Group.
—From Time to Time: The Sequel to Time & Again. unabr. ed. 1995. audio 70.00 (*0-7887-0338-2*, 94530E7) Recorded Bks., LLC.
—From Time to Time: The Sequel to Time & Again. 1996. (Illus.). 304p. pap. 12.00 (*0-684-81844-2*, Touchstone); 1995. 288p. 22.50 o.p. (*0-671-89884-1*, Simon & Schuster) Simon & Schuster.

—From Time to Time: The Sequel to Time & Again. abr. ed. 1995. audio 23.00 (*0-671-52118-7*, 492039, Simon & Schuster Audioworks) Simon & Schuster Audio.
—Time & Again. 1995. reprint ed. lib. bdg. 25.95 (*0-89968-403-3*, Lightyear Pr.) Buccaneer Bks., Inc.
—Time & Again. l.t. ed. 1995. 512p. 25.95 o.p. (*0-7838-1386-4*, Macmillan Reference USA) Gale Group.
—Time & Again. unabr. ed. 1996. audio 97.00 (*0-7887-0344-7*, 94536E7) Recorded Bks., LLC.
—Time & Again. 1995. 25.00 (*0-684-80117-5*, Simon & Schuster); 1995. (Illus.). 400p. pap. 13.00 (*0-684-80105-1*, Touchstone); 1986. 400p. pap. 10.95 o.s.i (*0-671-24295-4*, Fireside) Simon & Schuster.
—Time & Again. abr. ed. 1995. audio 23.00 o.s.i (*0-671-52139-X*, 492983, Simon & Schuster Audioworks) Simon & Schuster Audio.
—Time & Again: Broadway Edition. 1997. pap. 11.00 (*0-684-83594-0*, Scribner Paper Fiction) Simon & Schuster.

## MORRIS, JOHN (FICTITIOUS CHARACTER)—FICTION

Logue, John. The Feathery Touch of Death. 1996. 272p. mass mkt. 5.50 o.s.i (*0-440-22063-7*) Dell Publishing.
—On a Par with Murder. 1999. (Morris & Sullivan Mystery Ser.: Vol. 5). 288p. mass mkt. 5.99 o.s.i (*0-440-22400-4*) Dell Publishing.
—A Rain of Death. 1998. (Morris & Sullivan Mystery Ser.). 304p. mass mkt. 5.99 o.s.i (*0-440-22397-0*) Dell Publishing.

## MORRIS, LEE (FICTITIOUS CHARACTER)—FICTION

Francis, Dick. Decider. 1995. 352p. mass mkt. 6.99 (*0-515-11617-3*, Jove) Berkley Publishing Group.
—Decider. unabr. ed. 1994. audio 56.00 (*0-7366-2771-5*, 3491) Books on Tape, Inc.
—Decider. l.t. ed. 1995. 399p. pap. 19.95 o.p. (*0-8161-5914-9*); 1994. 429p. pap. 25.95 o.p. (*0-8161-5913-0*) Gale Group. (Macmillan Reference USA).
—Decider. 1993. 320p. 22.95 o.p. (*0-399-13871-4*, G. P. Putnam's Sons) Penguin Group (USA) Inc.
—Decider. unabr. ed. 1994. audio 60.00 (*0-7887-0022-7*, 94221E7) Recorded Bks., LLC.
—Decider. 1999. audio 9.98 (*0-671-04423-0*); Set. 1993. audio 17.00 (*0-671-87972-3*, 390637) Simon & Schuster Audio. (Simon & Schuster Audioworks).
—Decider: Open Market Edition. 1994. mass mkt. 5.99 o.p. (*0-449-22348-5*, Fawcett) Ballantine Bks.

## MORRIS, RUTHIE KANTOR (FICTITIOUS CHARACTER)—FICTION

Horowitz, Renee B. Deadly Rx. 2001. 172p. per. 13.75 (*0-7433-0363-6*) Clocktower Bks.
—Deadly Rx. 1997. mass mkt. 5.50 (*0-380-78620-6*, Avon Bks.) Morrow/Avon.
—Rx for Murder. 2001. 160p. per. 13.50 (*0-7433-0116-1*) Clocktower Bks.
—Rx for Murder. 1997. mass mkt. 5.50 (*0-380-78619-2*, Avon Bks.) Morrow/Avon.

## MORRISON, HUGH (FICTITIOUS CHARACTER)—FICTION

Orenstein, Frank. A Vintage Year for Dying. 1994. 256p. 20.95 o.p. (*0-312-10442-1*, Saint Martin's Minotaur) St. Martin's Pr.

## MORRISON, JOE (FICTITIOUS CHARACTER)—FICTION

Whittingham, Richard. Their Kind of Town. 1994. 384p. 22.50 o.p. (*1-55611-358-7*) Fine, Donald I. Bks.
—Their Kind of Town. 1996. mass mkt. 5.99 (*0-380-72502-9*, Avon Bks.) Morrow/Avon.

## MORRISON, MAY (FICTITIOUS CHARACTER)—FICTION

Star, Nancy. Up Next. (May Morrison Mysteries Ser.). 1999. 368p. mass mkt. 6.50 (*0-671-00894-3*, Pocket Star); 1998. 352p. 23.00 (*0-671-00893-5*, Atria) Simon & Schuster.
Star, Nancy & Gourlay, Jack. Now This: A May Morrison Mystery. 1999. (May Morrison Mysteries Ser.). 352p. 24.00 o.s.i (*0-671-00895-1*, Atria) Simon & Schuster.

## MORRISSEY, INSPECTOR (FICTITIOUS CHARACTER)—FICTION

Mitchell, Kay. In Stony Places. 1993. mass mkt. (*0-373-26126-8*, 1-26126-2, Harlequin Bks.) Harlequin Enterprises, Ltd.
—In Stony Places. 1992. 208p. 17.95 o.p. (*0-312-07001-2*, Saint Martin's Minotaur) St. Martin's Pr.
—In Stony Places. l.t. ed. 1994. (Ulverscroft Large Print Ser.). 336p. 29.99 o.p. (*0-7089-3115-4*, Ulverscroft) Thorpe, F. A. Pubs. GBR. *Dist:* Ulverscroft Large Print Bks., Ltd., Ulverscroft Large Print Canada, Ltd.
—A Lively Form of Death. 1992. (WWL Mystery Ser.). mass mkt. (*0-373-26106-3*, 1-26106-4, Harlequin Bks.) Harlequin Enterprises, Ltd.
—A Lively Form of Death. 1991. 15.95 o.p. (*0-312-05464-5*, Saint Martin's Minotaur) St. Martin's Pr.
—A Lively Form of Death. l.t. ed. 1993. (General Ser.). 336p. 29.99 o.p. (*0-7089-2864-1*, Ulverscroft) Thorpe, F. A. Pubs. GBR. *Dist:* Ulverscroft Large Print Bks., Ltd., Ulverscroft Large Print Canada, Ltd.
—A Portion for Foxes. 1997. per. (*0-373-26235-3*, 1-26235-1, Worldwide Library) Harlequin Enterprises, Ltd.
—A Portion for Foxes. 1995. 240p. 21.95 o.p. (*0-312-13589-0*, Saint Martin's Minotaur) St. Martin's Pr.
—A Rage of Innocents. 1999. (Chief Inspector Morrissey Mysteries Ser.: Vol. 318). 252p. per. (*0-373-26318-X*, Worldwide Library) Harlequin Enterprises, Ltd.
—A Rage of Innocents. 1998. (Chief Inspector Morrissey Mysteries Ser.). 224p. 20.95 (*0-312-18656-8*, Saint Martin's Minotaur) St. Martin's Pr.
—Roots of Evil. 1995. (WWL Mystery Ser.). per. (*0-373-26162-4*, 1-26162-7, Harlequin Bks.) Harlequin Enterprises, Ltd.
—Roots of Evil. 1993. (Chief Inspector Morrissey Mysteries Ser.). 176p. 17.95 o.p. (*0-312-09374-8*, Saint Martin's Minotaur) St. Martin's Pr.
—A Strange Desire. l.t. ed. 1995. (Ulverscroft Large Print Ser.). 432p. 29.99 o.p. (*0-7089-3244-4*, Ulverscroft) Thorpe, F. A. Pubs. GBR. *Dist:* Ulverscroft Large Print Bks., Ltd., Ulverscroft Large Print Canada, Ltd.

## MORRONE, RITA (FICTITIOUS CHARACTER)—FICTION

Scottoline, Lisa. Running from the Law. l.t. ed. 1996. 24.95 o.p. (*1-56895-319-4*, Wheeler Publishing, Inc.) Gale Group.
—Running from the Law. 1996. 464p. mass mkt. 7.99 (*0-06-109411-0*) HarperCollins Pubs.

## MORSE, INSPECTOR (FICTITIOUS CHARACTER)—FICTION

Dexter, Colin. The Daughters of Cain. 1996. 320p. mass mkt. 6.99 (*0-8041-1364-5*) Ballantine Bks.
—The Daughters of Cain. unabr. ed. 1995. audio 49.95 (*0-7861-0714-6*, 1591) Blackstone Audio Bks., Inc.
—The Daughters of Cain. unabr. ed. 1995. (Inspector Morse Mystery Ser.: Bk. 11). audio 59.95 (*0-7451-6555-9*, CAB 1171) Chivers Audio Bks. GBR. *Dist:* BBC Audiobooks America.
—The Daughters of Cain, Set. abr. ed. 1996. (Inspector Morse Mystery Ser.). 3p. audio 16.99 (*0-88646-407-2*, 393852) Durkin Hayes Publishing Ltd.
—The Daughters of Cain. o.p. (*0-517-70153-7*) Random Hse. Value Publishing.
—The Daughters of Cain. unabr. ed. 2000. (Inspector Morse Mystery Ser.: Vol. 11). audio 70.00 (*0-7887-0297-1*, 94490E7) Recorded Bks., LLC.
—The Daughters of Cain. l.t. ed. 1995. (Charnwood Large Print Ser.). 448p. 29.99 o.p. (*0-7089-8869-5*, Charnwood) Thorpe, F. A. Pubs. GBR. *Dist:* Ulverscroft Large Print Bks., Ltd., Ulverscroft Large Print Canada, Ltd.
—The Dead of Jericho, Set. 1998. (Inspector Morse Mystery Ser.). audio 29.95 (*0-7540-7519-2*) BBC Audiobooks America.
—The Dead of Jericho. 1996. (Inspector Morse Mystery Ser.). 304p. mass mkt. 6.99 (*0-8041-1486-2*, Ivy Bks.) Ballantine Bks.
—The Dead of Jericho. 1988. 224p. mass mkt. 4.50 o.s.i (*0-553-27237-3*) Bantam Bks.
—The Dead of Jericho. unabr. ed. 2000. (Inspector Morse Mystery Ser.: Bk. 5). audio 49.95 (*0-7451-5894-3*, CAB 442) Chivers Audio Bks. GBR. *Dist:* BBC Audiobooks America.
—The Dead of Jericho. 2001. audio (*0-333-90662-4*) Macmillan U.K. GBR. *Dist:* Macmillan Publishing Co., Inc.
—The Dead of Jericho. 1981. 168p. 9.95 o.p. (*0-312-18511-1*) St. Martin's Pr.
—The Dead of Jericho. 1990. audio 53.95 o.p. (*0-8161-9623-0*) Thorndike Pr.
—The Dead of Jericho. l.t. ed. 1984. 416p. 15.95 o.p. (*0-7089-1098-X*, Ulverscroft) Thorpe, F. A. Pubs. GBR. *Dist:* Ulverscroft Large Print Bks., Ltd.
—Death Is Now My Neighbor: An Inspector Morse Novel. 1998. (Illus.). 336p. mass mkt. 6.99 (*0-8041-1572-9*, Ivy Bks.) Ballantine Bks.
—Death Is Now My Neighbor: An Inspector Morse Novel. unabr. ed. (Inspector Morse Mystery Ser.). 2000. 8p. audio compact disk 79.95 (*0-7540-5349-0*, CCD 040); 1998. audio 59.95 (*0-7451-6775-6*, CAB 1391) Chivers Audio Bks. GBR. *Dist:* BBC Audiobooks America.
—Death Is Now My Neighbor: An Inspector Morse Novel. aut. ed. 1997. 24.00 o.s.i (*0-517-70824-8*) Crown Publishing Group.
—The Jewel That Was Ours: An Inspector Morse Mystery. 1993. 256p. mass mkt. 6.99 (*0-8041-0981-8*, Ivy Bks.) Ballantine Bks.
—The Jewel That Was Ours: An Inspector Morse Mystery. unabr. ed. 1996. audio 44.95 (*0-7861-0980-7*, 1757) Blackstone Audio Bks., Inc.
—The Jewel That Was Ours: An Inspector Morse Mystery. unabr. ed. 2000. (Inspector Morse Mystery Ser.: Bk. 9). audio 59.95 (*0-7451-4090-4*, CAB 778) Chivers Audio Bks. GBR. *Dist:* BBC Audiobooks America.
—The Jewel That Was Ours: An Inspector Morse Mystery. abr. ed. 1994. audio 16.99 (*0-88646-369-6*, LFP 7369) Durkin Hayes Publishing Ltd.
—The Jewel That Was Ours: An Inspector Morse Mystery. 2001. audio (*0-333-90435-4*) Macmillan U.K. GBR. *Dist:* Macmillan Publishing Co., Inc.
—The Jewel That Was Ours: An Inspector Morse Mystery. unabr. ed. 1992. (Inspector Morse Mystery Ser.: Vol. 9). audio 60.00 (*1-55690-683-8*, 92315E7) Recorded Bks., LLC.
—Last Bus to Woodstock. 1996. 288p. mass mkt. 6.99 (*0-8041-1490-0*, Ivy Bks.) Ballantine Bks.
—Last Bus to Woodstock. 1988. 224p. mass mkt. 3.95 o.s.i (*0-553-27777-4*) Bantam Bks.
—Last Bus to Woodstock. 2001. audio (*0-333-90663-2*) Macmillan U.K. GBR. *Dist:* Macmillan Publishing Co., Inc.
—Last Bus to Woodstock. l.t. ed. 1990. o.p. (*0-7089-2298-8*, Ulverscroft) Thorpe, F. A. Pubs.
—Last Seen Wearing: An Inspector Morse Mystery. unabr. ed. 2000. (Inspector Morse Mystery Ser.). audio 29.95 (*1-57270-145-5*, N61145u, Audio Editions Mystery Masters) Audio Partners Publishing Corp.
—Last Seen Wearing: An Inspector Morse Mystery. 1997. 336p. mass mkt. 6.99 (*0-8041-1491-9*, Ivy Bks.) Ballantine Bks.
—Last Seen Wearing: An Inspector Morse Mystery. 1988. 272p. mass mkt. 5.99 o.s.i (*0-553-28003-1*) Bantam Bks.
—Last Seen Wearing: An Inspector Morse Mystery. l.t. ed. 1989. 17.95 o.p. (*0-7089-2184-1*, Ulverscroft) Thorpe, F. A. Pubs. GBR. *Dist:* Ulverscroft Large Print Bks., Ltd.
—Morse's Greatest Mystery. unabr. ed. 1996. audio 39.95 (*0-7861-0957-2*, 1734) Blackstone Audio Bks., Inc.
—Morse's Greatest Mystery & Other Stories. 1996. (Inspector Morse Mystery Ser.). 304p. mass mkt. 6.99 (*0-8041-1309-2*, Ivy Bks.) Ballantine Bks.
—Morse's Greatest Mystery & Other Stories. abr. ed. 1996. audio 24.99 (*0-88646-410-2*, 7410) Durkin Hayes Publishing Ltd.
—Morse's Greatest Mystery & Other Stories. unabr. ed. 1996. audio 51.00 (*0-7887-0481-8*, 94674E7) Recorded Bks., LLC.
—The Remorseful Day. 2001. 336p. mass mkt. 6.99 (*0-8041-1954-6*, Fawcett) Ballantine Bks.
—The Remorseful Day. 2000. (Inspector Morse Mystery Ser.). 384p. 24.00 o.s.i (*0-609-60622-0*); 24.00 (*0-609-50295-6*) Crown Publishing Group. (Crown).
—The Remorseful Day. l.t. ed. 2000. (Wheeler Large Print Book Ser.). 442p. 27.95 (*1-56895-883-8*, Wheeler Publishing, Inc.) Gale Group.
—The Remorseful Day. abr. ed. 2000. audio 18.00 (*0-7871-2521-0*) NewStar Media, Inc.
—The Riddle of the Third Mile. 1999. 55p. audio 29.95 (*0-7451-2815-7*) BBC Audiobooks America.
—The Riddle of the Third Mile. 1997. (Inspector Morse Mystery Ser.). 272p. mass mkt. 6.99 (*0-8041-1488-9*, Ivy Bks.) Ballantine Bks.
—The Riddle of the Third Mile. 1988. 224p. mass mkt. 5.99 o.s.i (*0-553-27363-9*) Bantam Bks.
—The Riddle of the Third Mile. unabr. ed. 2000. (Inspector Morse Mystery Ser.: Bk. 6). audio 49.95 (*0-7451-5895-1*, CAB 672) Chivers Audio Bks. GBR. *Dist:* BBC Audiobooks America.
—The Riddle of the Third Mile. 1984. 224p. 11.95 o.p. (*0-312-68228-X*) St. Martin's Pr.
—The Riddle of the Third Mile. l.t. ed. 2001. 349p. 28.95 (*0-7862-3343-5*); (*0-7540-1619-6*); (*0-7540-2473-3*) Thorndike Pr.
—The Secret of Annexe 3. unabr. ed. 2000. (Inspector Morse Mystery Ser.). audio 29.95 (*1-57270-155-2*, N61155u, Audio Editions Mystery Masters) Audio Partners Publishing Corp.
—The Secret of Annexe 3. unabr. ed. 1994. (Inspector Morse Mystery Ser.). audio 54.95 (*0-7451-4321-0*, CAB 1004) BBC Audiobooks America.
—The Secret of Annexe 3, Vol. 3. 1997. (Inspector Morse Mystery Ser.). 304p. mass mkt. 6.99 (*0-8041-1489-7*, Ivy Bks.) Ballantine Bks.
—The Secret of Annexe 3. 1988. 224p. reprint ed. mass mkt. 5.99 o.s.i (*0-553-27549-6*) Bantam Bks.
—The Secret of Annexe 3. unabr. ed. 2000. (Inspector Morse Mystery Ser.: Bk. 7). audio 49.95 Chivers Audio Bks. GBR. *Dist:* BBC Audiobooks America.
—The Secret of Annexe 3. 1987. 224p. 15.95 o.p. (*0-312-01089-3*, Saint Martin's Minotaur) St. Martin's Pr.
—The Secret of Annexe 3. l.t. ed. 2000. (Mystery Ser.). 371p. pap. 26.95 (*0-7862-2676-5*); (*0-7540-4235-9*); (*0-7540-4236-7*) Thorndike Pr.
—Service of All the Dead. 1996. 304p. mass mkt. 6.99 (*0-8041-1485-4*, Ivy Bks.) Ballantine Bks.
—Service of All the Dead. 1988. 224p. mass mkt. 3.95 o.s.i (*0-553-27239-X*) Bantam Bks.
—Service of All the Dead. unabr. ed. 2000. (Inspector Morse Mystery Ser.: Bk. 4). audio 49.95 (*0-7451-6497-8*, CAB 1113) Chivers Audio Bks. GBR. *Dist:* BBC Audiobooks America.
—Service of All the Dead. 1982. (Murder Ink Mystery Ser.: No. 43). pap. 2.50 o.p. (*0-440-18026-0*) Dell Publishing.
—Service of All the Dead. 1979. 9.95 o.p. (*0-312-71316-9*) St. Martin's Pr.
—Service of All the Dead. l.t. ed. 2000. (Mystery Ser.). 402p. 27.95 (*0-7862-3040-1*); (*0-7540-1531-9*); (*0-7540-2405-9*) Thorndike Pr.
—The Silent World of Nicholas Quinn. 1997. (Inspector Morse Mystery Ser.). 288p. mass mkt. 6.99 (*0-8041-1487-0*, Ivy Bks.) Ballantine Bks.
—The Silent World of Nicholas Quinn. 1988. 224p. mass mkt. 5.99 o.s.i (*0-553-27238-1*) Bantam Bks.
—The Silent World of Nicholas Quinn. unabr. ed. 2000. (Inspector Morse Mystery Ser.: Bk. 3). audio 49.95 (*0-7451-6607-5*, CAB 1223) Chivers Audio Bks. GBR. *Dist:* BBC Audiobooks America.
—The Silent World of Nicholas Quinn. 2001. audio (*0-333-90440-0*) Macmillan U.K. GBR. *Dist:* Macmillan Publishing Co., Inc.
—The Silent World of Nicholas Quinn. (Mystery Bookshelf Selection Ser.). 1978. pap. 3.50 o.p. (*0-312-72468-3*, Saint Martin's Griffin); 1977. 7.95 o.p. (*0-312-72467-5*) St. Martin's Pr.
—The Silent World of Nicholas Quinn. l.t. ed. 1992. (Mystery Ser.). 432p. 29.99 o.p. (*0-7089-2620-7*, Ulverscroft) Thorpe, F. A. Pubs. GBR. *Dist:* Ulverscroft Large Print Bks., Ltd., Ulverscroft Large Print Canada, Ltd.
—The Way Through the Woods: An Inspector Morse Mystery. 1994. 336p. mass mkt. 6.99 (*0-8041-1142-1*, Ivy Bks.) Ballantine Bks.
—The Way Through the Woods: An Inspector Morse Mystery. unabr. ed. 1996. audio 49.95 (*0-7861-0931-9*, 1686) Blackstone Audio Bks., Inc.
—The Way Through the Woods: An Inspector Morse Mystery. unabr. ed. 2000. (Inspector Morse Mystery Ser.: Bk. 10). audio 59.95 (*0-7451-4167-6*, CAB 850) Chivers Audio Bks. GBR. *Dist:* BBC Audiobooks America.
—The Way Through the Woods: An Inspector Morse Mystery. abr. ed. 1993. audio 16.99 (*0-88646-352-1*, LFP 7352) Durkin Hayes Publishing Ltd.
—The Way Through the Woods: An Inspector Morse Mystery. 1995. 4.99 o.p. (*0-517-14495-6*) Random Hse. Value Publishing.
—The Way Through the Woods: An Inspector Morse Mystery. unabr. ed. 1993. (Inspector Morse Mystery Ser.: Vol. 10). audio 70.00 (*1-55690-883-0*, 93325E7) Recorded Bks., LLC.
—The Wench Is Dead. unabr. ed. 2000. (Inspector Morse Mystery Ser.). audio 29.95 (*1-57270-130-7*, N61130u, Audio Editions Mystery Masters) Audio Partners Publishing Corp.
—The Wench Is Dead. 1999. (Inspector Morse Mystery Ser.). 290p. mass mkt. 6.99 o.s.i (*0-8041-1889-2*, Ivy Bks.) Ballantine Bks.
—The Wench Is Dead. 1991. 208p. mass mkt. 5.99 o.s.i (*0-553-29120-3*) Bantam Bks.
—The Wench Is Dead. unabr. ed. 2000. (Inspector Morse Mystery Ser.: Bk. 8). audio 49.95 (*0-7451-5896-X*, CAB 582) Chivers Audio Bks. GBR. *Dist:* BBC Audiobooks America.
—The Wench Is Dead. 1992. 3.99 o.p. (*0-517-09062-7*) Random Hse. Value Publishing.
—The Wench Is Dead. 1990. 15.95 o.p. (*0-312-04444-5*, Saint Martin's Minotaur) St. Martin's Pr.
—The Wench Is Dead. l.t. ed. 1991. (Ulverscroft Large Print Ser.). 29.99 o.p. (*0-7089-2512-X*, Ulverscroft) Thorpe, F. A. Pubs. GBR. *Dist:* Ulverscroft Large Print Bks., Ltd., Ulverscroft Large Print Canada, Ltd.
—The Wench Is Dead. abr. ed. 1998. audio 15.00 (*0-333-74612-0*) Ulverscroft Audio (U.S.A.).
Thaw, John. Deceived by Flight. 1998. (Inspector Morse Mystery Ser.). audio 14.95 o.p. (*1-56938-257-3*, AMP-2573) Acorn Media Publishing, Inc.
—The Ghost in the Machine. 1998. (Inspector Morse Mystery Ser.). audio 14.95 o.p. (*1-56938-256-5*, AMP-2565) Acorn Media Publishing, Inc.
—Infernal Serpent. 1998. (Inspector Morse Mystery Ser.). audio 14.95 o.p. (*1-56938-258-1*, AMP-2581) Acorn Media Publishing, Inc.
—Inspector Morse Series, 4 vols. 1998. audio 59.80 (*1-56938-255-7*, AMP-2557) Acorn Media Publishing, Inc.
—Masonic Mysteries. 1998. (Inspector Morse Mystery Ser.). audio 14.95 o.p. (*1-56938-259-X*, AMP-8259) Acorn Media Publishing, Inc.

## MORSON, FELIX (FICTITIOUS CHARACTER)—FICTION

Mortimer, John. Felix in the Underwood. 1998. 256p. pap. 12.95 o.s.i (*0-14-027496-0*) Penguin Group (USA) Inc.

—Felix in the Underworld. l.t. ed. 1997. 308p. pap. 21.95 o.p. (0-7838-8307-2, Macmillan Reference USA) Gale Group.
—Felix in the Underworld. 1997. 247p. 22.95 o.s.i (0-670-86079-4); 2p. pap. 16.95 o.s.i incl. audio (0-14-086151-3, Penguin AudioBooks) Viking Penguin.

**MORTON, GLADYS BABBINGTON (FICTITIOUS CHARACTER)—FICTION**

Baxter, Glen. The Billiard Table Murders. 1991. 256p. pap. 10.00 (0-380-76668-X, Avon Bks.) Morrow/ Avon.

**MORTON, JAMES (FICTITIOUS CHARACTER)—FICTION**

Harrison, Ray. Akin to Murder. l.t. ed. 1995. (Magna Large Print Ser.). 468p. (0-7505-0873-6) Magna Large Print Bks. GBR. *Dist:* Ulverscroft Large Print Canada, Ltd.
—Counterfeit of Murder. 1989. mass mkt. 3.95 o.p. (0-425-11645-X) Berkley Publishing Group.
—Counterfeit of Murder. 1987. 320p. 15.95 o.p. (0-312-00585-7) St. Martin's Pr.
—Death of a Dancing Lady. 1988. mass mkt. 2.95 o.s.i (0-425-11047-8) Berkley Publishing Group.
—Death of a Dancing Lady: A Sargent Bragg-Constable Morton Mystery. 1986. 256p. 13.95 o.p. (0-684-18581-4, Macmillan Reference USA) Gale Group.
—Death of an Honourable Member. 1988. mass mkt. 3.50 o.p. (0-425-11189-X) Berkley Publishing Group.
—Death of an Honourable Member. 1985. 160p. 11.95 o.p. (0-684-18245-9, Macmillan Reference USA) Gale Group.
—Deathwatch. 1989. mass mkt. 3.50 o.p. (0-425-11392-2) Berkley Publishing Group.
—Deathwatch. 1986. 176p. 13.95 o.p. (0-684-18425-7, Macmillan Reference USA) Gale Group.
—Draught of Death. l.t. ed. 2000. (Dales Large Print Ser.). 352p. pap. (1-84137-009-6) Magna Large Print Bks. GBR. *Dist:* Ulverscroft Large Print Bks., Ltd., Ulverscroft Large Print Canada, Ltd.
—Facets of Murder. l.t. ed. 1998. (Ulverscroft Large Print Ser.). 368p. 29.99 (0-7089-3952-X, Ulverscroft) Thorpe, F. A. Pubs. GBR. *Dist:* Ulverscroft Large Print Bks., Ltd., Ulverscroft Large Print Canada, Ltd.
—Hallmark of Murder. l.t. ed. 1996. (Dales Large Print Ser.). (Illus.). 403p. pap. 19.99 (1-85389-663-2) Dales Large Print Bks. GBR. *Dist:* Ulverscroft Large Print Bks., Ltd.
—Harvest of Death. 1990. mass mkt. 3.95 o.s.i (0-425-11979-3) Berkley Publishing Group.
—Harvest of Death. 1988. 288p. 16.95 o.p. (0-312-02218-2, Saint Martin's Minotaur) St. Martin's Pr.
—Murder by Design. l.t. ed. 1997. (Linford Mystery Library). 416p. pap. 17.99 o.p. (0-7089-5071-X, Linford) Thorpe, F. A. Pubs. GBR. *Dist:* Ulverscroft Large Print Bks., Ltd., Ulverscroft Large Print Canada, Ltd.
—Patently Murder. l.t. ed. 1996. (Magna Large Print Ser.). 492p. 29.99 (0-7505-0922-8) Magna Large Print Bks. GBR. *Dist:* Ulverscroft Large Print Bks., Ltd.
—Patently Murder: A Sergeant Bragg & Constable Morton Mystery. 1991. 256p. 18.95 o.p. (0-312-07058-6, Saint Martin's Minotaur) St. Martin's Pr.
—A Season for Death. 1988. 288p. 15.95 o.p. (0-312-01815-0, Saint Martin's Minotaur) St. Martin's Pr.
—Sphere of Death. 1990. 17.95 o.p. (0-312-05161-1, Saint Martin's Minotaur) St. Martin's Pr.
—Tincture of Death. 1991. mass mkt. 3.95 o.p. (0-425-12550-5) Berkley Publishing Group.
—Tincture of Death. 1989. 240p. 15.95 o.p. (0-312-03442-3, Saint Martin's Minotaur) St. Martin's Pr.
—Why Kill Arthur Potter? 1984. 160p. 11.95 o.s.i (0-684-18131-2, Scribner) Simon & Schuster.
—Why Kill Arthur Potter? 1985. mass mkt. 2.95 o.s.i (0-445-20053-7) Warner Bks., Inc.

**MOSELEY, HOKE (FICTITIOUS CHARACTER)—FICTION**

Willeford, Charles. The Way We Die Now. 1989. mass mkt. 3.95 o.s.i (0-345-35332-3) Ballantine Bks.
—The Way We Die Now. 1996. mass mkt. 4.99 o.s.i (0-440-21885-3) Dell Publishing.

**MOSES, ZEN (FICTITIOUS CHARACTER)—FICTION**

Cosin, Elizabeth M. Zen & the Art of Murder. (St. Martin's Minotaur Mysteries Ser.). 1999. 304p. mass mkt. 5.99 (0-312-96948-1, St. Martin's Paperbacks); 1998. 288p. 22.95 o.p. (0-312-19376-9, Saint Martin's Minotaur) St. Martin's Pr.

**MOSS, GRIFFIN (FICTITIOUS CHARACTER: BANTOCK)—FICTION**

*see Griffin (Fictitious Character: Bantock)—Fiction*

**MOSS, WILEY (FICTITIOUS CHARACTER)—FICTION**

Barrett, Neal, Jr. Bad Eye Blues, Vol. 1. (Wiley Moss Mystery Ser.). 1999. 352p. mass mkt. 5.99 o.s.i (1-57566-484-4); 1997. 288p. 21.95 o.p. (1-57566-173-X) Kensington Publishing Corp.
—Skinny Annie Blues. (Wiley Moss Mystery Ser.). 1997. 304p. mass mkt. 5.50 (1-57566-134-9); 1996. 256p. 21.95 o.p. (1-57566-058-X) Kensington Publishing Corp. (Kensington Bks.).

**MOTO, MR. (FICTITIOUS CHARACTER)—FICTION**

Marquand, John P. Last Laugh, Mr. Moto. Date not set. 192p. 20.95 (0-8488-2363-X) Amereon, Ltd.
—Last Laugh, Mr. Moto. 1986. mass mkt. 4.95 o.p. (0-316-54705-0) Little Brown & Co.
—Mr. Moto Is So Sorry. 1976. 17.95 (0-89387-016-1) Amereon, Ltd.
—Mr. Moto Is So Sorry. 1986. mass mkt. 3.95 o.p. (0-316-54702-6) Little Brown & Co.
—Right You Are, Mr. Moto. Date not set. 256p. 22.95 (0-8488-2362-1) Amereon, Ltd.
—Right You Are, Mr. Moto. 1986. mass mkt. 4.95 o.p. (0-316-54706-9) Little Brown & Co.
—Thank You, Mr. Moto. reprint ed. lib. bdg. 23.95 (0-88411-142-3) Amereon, Ltd.
—Thank You, Mr. Moto. 1985. 288p. reprint ed. mass mkt. 3.95 o.p. (0-316-54698-4) Little Brown & Co.
—Think Fast, Mr. Moto. 150p. 18.95 (0-8488-2670-1) Amereon, Ltd.
—Think Fast, Mr. Moto. 1986. mass mkt. 3.95 o.p. (0-316-54703-4) Little Brown & Co.
—Your Turn, Mr. Moto. 128p. 17.95 (0-8488-2669-8) Amereon, Ltd.
—Your Turn, Mr. Moto. 1985. 288p. reprint ed. mass mkt. 3.95 o.p. (0-316-54697-6) Little Brown & Co.

**MOTT, ANGUS (FICTITIOUS CHARACTER)—FICTION**

Curzon, Clare. All Unwary. (0-7540-3467-4); 1999. 340p. pap. (0-7540-3468-2) BBC Audiobooks America.
—All Unwary. 1998. (Thames Valley Mystery Ser.). 256p. 21.95 o.p. (0-312-18037-3, Saint Martin's Minotaur) St. Martin's Pr.
—All Unwary. l.t. ed. 1999. (General Ser.). 352p. pap. 23.95 (0-7862-1544-5) Thorndike Pr.
—The Blue-Eyed Boy. 1991. 192p. 14.95 o.s.i (0-385-41668-7) Doubleday Publishing.
—The Blue-Eyed Boy. l.t. ed. 1992. (Ulverscroft Large Print Ser.). 416p. 29.99 o.p. (0-7089-2585-5, Ulverscroft) Thorpe, F. A. Pubs. GBR. *Dist:* Ulverscroft Large Print Bks., Ltd., Ulverscroft Large Print Canada, Ltd.
—Cat's Cradle. 1994. (WWL Mystery Ser.). per. (0-373-26151-9, 1-26151-0, Harlequin Bks.) Harlequin Enterprises, Ltd.
—Cat's Cradle. 1992. 224p. 17.95 o.p. (0-312-07664-9, Saint Martin's Minotaur) St. Martin's Pr.
—Close Quarters: A Thames Valley Mystery. l.t. ed. 1997. 357p. lib. bdg. 21.95 (0-7838-8214-9, Macmillan Reference USA) Gale Group.
—Close Quarters: A Thames Valley Mystery. l.t. ed. 1998. 256p. per. (0-373-26292-2, 1-26292-2, Worldwide Library) Harlequin Enterprises, Ltd.
—Close Quarters: A Thames Valley Mystery. l.t. ed. 1996. 192p. 20.95 (0-312-15079-2, Saint Martin's Minotaur) St. Martin's Pr.
—Cold Hands. 218p. 26.00 o.p. (0-7278-5462-3) Severn Hse. Pubs., Ltd.
—Cold Hands. l.t. ed. 2001. (Ulverscroft Large Print Ser.). 376p. 31.99 (0-7089-4329-2) Thorpe, F. A. Pubs. GBR. *Dist:* Ulverscroft Large Print Bks., Ltd., Ulverscroft Large Print Canada, Ltd.
—Cold Hands: A Mike Yeadings Mystery. 2001. 256p. 22.95 (0-312-20464-7, Saint Martin's Minotaur) St. Martin's Pr.
—Death Prone. 1995. (Mystery Ser.). 251p. per. (0-373-26189-6, 1-26189-0, Worldwide Library) Harlequin Enterprises, Ltd.
—Death Prone. 1994. 224p. 19.95 o.p. (0-312-10453-7, Saint Martin's Minotaur) St. Martin's Pr.
—First Wife, Twice Removed. 1995. (WWL Mystery Ser.). per. (0-373-26168-3, 1-26168-4, Harlequin Bks.) Harlequin Enterprises, Ltd.
—First Wife, Twice Removed. 1993. (Thames Valley Mystery Ser.). 224p. 17.95 o.p. (0-312-09289-X, Saint Martin's Minotaur) St. Martin's Pr.
—Guilty Knowledge. 2000. 256p. 23.95 (0-312-26169-1, Saint Martin's Minotaur) St. Martin's Pr.
—Nice People. 1995. 246p. 20.95 o.p. (0-312-13132-1, Saint Martin's Minotaur) St. Martin's Pr.
—Past Mischief. 1997. per. (0-373-26256-6, 1-26256-7, Worldwide Library) Harlequin Enterprises, Ltd.
—Past Mischief. 1995. 280p. mass mkt. o.s.i (0-7515-1301-6) Little Brown & Co.
—Past Mischief. 1996. 224p. text 21.95 o.p. (0-312-14388-5, Saint Martin's Minotaur) St. Martin's Pr.
—Three-Core Lead. 1990. 14.95 o.s.i (0-385-41139-1) Doubleday Publishing.
—Three-Core Lead. l.t. ed. 1992. (Lythway Ser.). 308p. 15.95 o.p. (0-7451-1615-9, Macmillan Reference USA) Gale Group.
—Trojan Hearse. l.t. ed. 1986. lib. bdg. 14.95 o.p. (0-7451-0318-9, Macmillan Reference USA) Gale Group.

**MOUNTAIN MAN (FICTITIOUS CHARACTER)—FICTION**

*see Jensen, Smoke (Fictitious Character)—Fiction*

**MOUNTFORD, SUZIE (FICTITIOUS CHARACTER)—FICTION**

Gardner, John. Bottled Spider. 29.99 (0-7278-7200-1); 2002. 384p. 26.99 (0-7278-5829-7) Severn Hse. Pubs., Ltd.
—The Streets of Town. 2003. 352p. 26.99 (0-7278-5921-8) Severn Hse. Pubs., Ltd.

**MOWGLI (FICTITIOUS CHARACTER)—FICTION**

Kipling, Rudyard. The Works of Rudyard Kipling. 2002. Vol. I. 452p. per. 23.99 (1-58827-815-8); Vol. I. 452p. 28.99 (1-58827-814-X); Vol. II. 548p. per. 25.99 (1-58827-817-4); Vol. II. 548p. 29.99 (1-58827-816-6) IndyPublish.com.
—The Works of Rudyard Kipling. 2001. (Poetry Library). 880p. pap. 6.95 (1-85326-405-9) Wordsworth Editions, Ltd. GBR. *Dist:* Advanced Global Distribution Services.

**MOZART, WOLFGANG AMADEUS, 1756-1791—FICTION**

Bastable, Bernard. Dead Mr. Mozart. 1996. 183p. mass mkt. o.s.i (0-7515-1092-0) Little Brown & Co.
—Dead Mr. Mozart. 1995. 19.95 o.p. (0-312-11771-X, Saint Martin's Minotaur) St. Martin's Pr.
—To Die Like a Gentleman. 1993. 192p. 16.95 o.p. (0-312-09402-7, Saint Martin's Minotaur) St. Martin's Pr.
—Too Many Notes, Mr. Mozart. 1996. 192p. 21.00 o.p. (0-7867-0315-6, Carroll & Graf Pubs.) Avalon Publishing Group.
—Too Many Notes, Mr. Mozart. 1998. 250p. mass mkt. o.s.i (0-7515-1806-9) Little Brown & Co.
Cowell, Stephanie. Marrying Mozart: A Novel. 2004. 368p. 24.95 (0-670-03268-9, Viking) Viking Penguin.
Montano, Mary. Loving Mozart: A Past Life Memory of the Composer's Final Years. 1995. 239p. pap. 21.00 (0-9642577-0-X) Cantus Verus Bks.
Neider, Charles. Mozart & the Archbooby. 1991. (Contemporary American Fiction Ser.). 96p. (Orig.). pap. 8.95 o.p. (0-14-015402-7, Penguin Bks.) Penguin Group (USA) Inc.
Rudel, Anthony J. Imagining Don Giovanni. 2001. 288p. 24.00 (0-87113-827-1, Atlantic Monthly Pr.) Grove/Atlantic, Inc.
Slater, Harrison Gradwell. Night Music. 2003. 576p. pap. 14.95 (0-451-20972-9) NAL.
Stafford, Joyce T. Mozart & Me. 2003. 720p. 29.95 (1-929490-05-4) Beil, Frederic C. Pub., Inc.

**MUFFIN, CHARLIE (FICTITIOUS CHARACTER)—FICTION**

Freemantle, Brian. Charlie Muffin. 2001. audio 49.95 (1-84283-021-X); 2002. audio compact disk 59.95 (1-84283-230-1) Soundings, Ltd. GBR. *Dist:* Ulverscroft Large Print Bks., Ltd.
—Charlie Muffin's Uncle Sam. unabr. ed. 2002. audio 61.95 (1-84283-189-5) Soundings, Ltd. GBR. *Dist:* Ulverscroft Large Print Bks., Ltd.
—Comrade Charlie: A Charlie Muffin Novel. 1992. 448p. 22.95 o.p. (0-312-08166-9) St. Martin's Pr.
—Dead Men Living. 2000. (Charlie Muffin Thrillers Ser.). 345p. 24.95 (0-312-24379-0) St. Martin's Pr.
—Kings of Many Castles. E-Book 24.95 (0-312-70931-5) St. Martin's Pr.
—Kings of Many Castles: A Charlie Muffin Thriller. 2002. 352p. 24.95 (0-312-30412-9) St. Martin's Pr.
—The Run Around. 1990. mass mkt. 4.95 o.s.i (0-553-28407-X) Bantam Bks.

**MULCAHANEY, NORAH (FICTITIOUS CHARACTER)—FICTION**

O'Donnell, Lillian. Blue Death. 1998. 224p. 22.95 o.p. (0-399-14367-X) Penguin Group (USA) Inc.
—Casual Affairs. 1987. mass mkt. 2.95 o.s.i (0-449-21064-2, Fawcett) Ballantine Bks.
—Casual Affairs. 1985. 240p. 16.95 o.p. (0-399-13100-0) Putnam Publishing Group, The.
—The Children's Zoo. 1982. mass mkt. 3.50 o.s.i (0-449-24498-9, Fawcett) Ballantine Bks.
—Cop Without a Shield. 1984. 256p. mass mkt. 2.95 o.s.i (0-449-20534-7, Fawcett) Ballantine Bks.
—Cop Without a Shield. 1983. 256p. 13.95 o.p. (0-399-12872-7, G. P. Putnam's Sons) Penguin Putnam Bks. for Young Readers.
—A Good Night to Kill. 1989. 224p. mass mkt. 4.99 o.s.i (0-449-21706-X, Fawcett) Ballantine Bks.
—A Good Night to Kill. 1989. 256p. 17.95 o.p. (0-399-13403-4, G. P. Putnam's Sons) Penguin Putnam Bks. for Young Readers.
—Ladykiller. 1985. 240p. mass mkt. 2.95 o.s.i (0-449-20744-7, Fawcett) Ballantine Bks.
—Leisure Dying. 1976. 6.95 o.p. (0-399-11741-5) Putnam Publishing Group, The.
—Lockout. 1995. (Norah Mulcahaney Ser.). mass mkt. 5.99 o.s.i (0-449-22329-9, Fawcett) Ballantine Bks.
—Lockout. 1994. 240p. 19.95 o.p. (0-399-13921-4, G. P. Putnam's Sons) Penguin Group (USA) Inc.
—No Business Being a Cop. 1987. mass mkt. 2.95 o.s.i (0-449-21322-6); 1980. mass mkt. 1.95 o.p. (0-449-24219-6) Ballantine Bks. (Fawcett).
—No Business Being a Cop. 1979. 8.95 o.p. (0-399-12276-1) Putnam Publishing Group, The.
—The Other Side of the Door. 1988. mass mkt. 2.95 o.s.i (0-449-21598-9, Fawcett) Ballantine Bks.
—The Other Side of the Door. 1988. 240p. 17.95 o.p. (0-399-13316-X, G. P. Putnam's Sons) Penguin Putnam Bks. for Young Readers.
—A Private Crime. 1992. mass mkt. 3.99 o.s.i (0-449-21989-5, Fawcett) Ballantine Bks.
—A Private Crime. l.t. ed. 1992. (General Ser.). 333p. lib. bdg. 21.95 o.p. (0-8161-5277-2, Macmillan Reference USA) Gale Group.
—A Private Crime. 1991. 240p. 19.95 o.p. (0-399-13585-5, G. P. Putnam's Sons) Penguin Group (USA) Inc.
—Pushover. 1993. mass mkt. 4.99 o.s.i (0-449-22152-0, Fawcett) Ballantine Bks.
—Pushover. 1992. 240p. 19.95 o.p. (0-399-13674-6, G. P. Putnam's Sons) Penguin Group (USA) Inc.
—Shadow in Red. 2015. 240p. 16.95 (0-399-13208-2, G. P. Putnam's Sons) Penguin Group (USA) Inc.

**MULCAY, KATE (FICTITIOUS CHARACTER)—FICTION**

Sibley, Celestine. Ah, Sweet Mystery: A Kate Mulcay Novel of Suspense. 1991. 224p. 19.00 o.p. (0-06-016304-6) HarperTrade.
—Ah, Sweet Mystery: A Kate Mulcay Novel of Suspense. 1992. 272p. mass mkt. 4.50 o.p. (0-06-109083-2, HarperTorch) Morrow/Avon.
—Dire Happenings at Scratch Ankle: A Kate Mulcay Mystery. 1993. 224p. 19.00 o.p. (0-06-017703-9) HarperTrade.
—Dire Happenings at Scratch Ankle: A Kate Mulcay Mystery. 1994. 224p. mass mkt. 4.50 o.p. (0-06-109050-6, HarperTorch) Morrow/Avon.
—A Plague of Kinfolks: A Kate Mulcay Mystery. 1996. 224p. mass mkt. 4.99 o.s.i (0-06-109049-2); 1995. 208p. 20.00 o.p. (0-06-017704-7) HarperCollins Pubs.
—Straight As an Arrow: A Kate Mulcay Mystery. 1992. 256p. 19.00 o.p. (0-06-016305-4) HarperTrade.
—Straight As an Arrow: A Kate Mulcay Mystery. 1994. 224p. mass mkt. 4.50 o.p. (0-06-109190-1, HarperTorch) Morrow/Avon.

**MULDER, FOX (FICTITIOUS CHARACTER)—FICTION**

Anderson, Kevin J. Antibodies. 1998. (X-Files Ser.: Vol. 5). 288p. mass mkt. 6.50 (0-06-105624-3, HarperEntertainment) Morrow/Avon.
—Ground Zero. 1996. 304p. mass mkt. 6.50 o.s.i (0-06-105677-4, HarperEntertainment); 1995. 80p. 22.00 o.p. (0-06-105223-X, Eos); 1995. 304p. 50.00 o.p. (0-06-105248-5, Eos) Morrow/Avon.
—Ground Zero: TV Guide Edition. 1995. (X-Files Ser.). 176p. mass mkt. 5.99 (0-06-105847-5) HarperCollins Pubs.
—Ruins. 1996. (X-Files Ser.). 304p. mass mkt. 22.00 o.p. (0-06-105247-7) HarperCollins Pubs.
—Ruins. (X-Files Ser.: Vol. 4). 1997. 272p. mass mkt. 6.50 o.s.i (0-06-105736-3, HarperEntertainment); 1996. 304p. 50.00 o.s.i (0-06-105273-6, Eos) Morrow/Avon.
—Skin. 2000. (X-Files Ser.). 336p. mass mkt. 6.50 (0-06-105644-8, HarperEntertainment) Morrow/ Avon.
Grant, Charles L. Goblins. 1994. (X-Files Ser.: Vol. 1). 288p. mass mkt. 6.50 (0-06-105414-3, HarperEntertainment) Morrow/Avon.
Hand, Elizabeth. Antibodies. 1997. 304p. mass mkt. 22.00 o.p. (0-06-105289-2, Eos) Morrow/Avon.
Martin, Les. Die, Bug, Die! 1996. (X-Files Ser.: No. 10). 112p. pap. 4.50 o.p. (0-06-440671-7, Harper Trophy) HarperCollins Children's Bk. Group.
—Die, Bug, Die! 1997. (X-Files Ser.: No. 10). 9.60 o.p. (0-606-10977-3) Turtleback Bks.
Mezrich, Ben. Skin. abr. ed. 1999. 272p. 23.95 (0-06-105041-5) HarperCollins Pubs.
—Skin. l.t. ed. 1999. (Science Fiction Ser.). 336p. 26.95 (0-7838-8778-7) Thorndike Pr.

**MULHEISEN, FANG, DETECTIVE SERGEANT (FICTITIOUS CHARACTER)—FICTION**

Jackson, Jon A. Badger Games: A Detective Sergeant Mulheisen Mystery. 2004. 336p. pap. 12.00 (0-8021-3983-3, Grove Pr.) Grove/Atlantic, Inc.
—The Blind Pig. 2001. (Detective Sergeant Mullheisen Mysteries Ser.). 228p. pap. 12.00 (0-8021-3706-7) Grove/Atlantic, Inc.
—The Blind Pig. 1988. (Modern Hard-Boiled Detective Ser.). 228p. reprint ed. pap. 7.95 o.p. (0-939767-07-4) McMillan, Dennis Pubns.

Characters

—The Blind Pig. 1979. 7.95 o.p. (0-394-42613-4) Random Hse., Inc.
—The Blind Pig. 1988. 228p. pap. 6.95 (0-89366-275-5) Ultramarine Publishing Co., Inc.
—The Blind Pig: A Detective Sergeant Mulheisen Novel. 1995. 288p. mass mkt. 4.99 o.s.i (0-440-21714-8) Dell Publishing.
—Dead Folks: A Detective Sergeant Mulheisen Mystery. 1996. 272p. 22.00 o.p. (0-87113-638-4, Atlantic Monthly Pr.) Grove/Atlantic, Inc.
—Dead Folks: A Detective Sergeant Mullheisen Mystery. 2001. (Detective Sergeant Mullheisen Mysteries Ser.). 264p. reprint ed. pap. 12.00 (0-8021-3602-8) Grove/Atlantic, Inc.
—Deadman. 1994. 272p. 20.00 o.p. (0-87113-562-0, Atlantic Monthly Pr.) Grove/Atlantic, Inc.
—Deadman: A Detective Sergeant Mulheisen Novel. 1995. 304p. mass mkt. 4.99 o.s.i (0-440-22047-5) Dell Publishing.
—The Die Hard. 2001. (Detective Sergeant Mullheisen Mysteries Ser.). 215p. pap. 12.00 (0-8021-3707-5) Grove/Atlantic, Inc.
—The Diehard. 1977. 6.95 o.p. (0-394-41030-0) Random Hse., Inc.
—The Diehard: A Detective Sergeant Mulheisen Novel. 1995. 272p. mass mkt. 4.99 o.s.i (0-440-21717-2) Dell Publishing.
—Grootka. 1990. 352p. 19.95 o.p. (0-88150-179-4) Countryman Pr.
—Grootka. 1992. 352p. mass mkt. 4.99 o.s.i (0-440-21151-4) Dell Publishing.
—Hit on the House. 1995. 304p. mass mkt. 4.99 o.s.i (0-440-21711-3) Dell Publishing.
—Hit on the House. (Detective Sergeant Mullheisen Mysteries Ser.). 2001. 256p. pap. 12.00 (0-8021-3705-9); 1993. 237p. 20.00 o.p. (0-87113-495-0) Grove/Atlantic, Inc.
—Man with an Axe: A Detective Sergeant Mulheisen Mystery. 1998. 240p. 23.00 o.p. (0-87113-708-9, Atlantic Monthly Pr.) Grove/Atlantic, Inc.

**MULLER, KURT (FICTITIOUS CHARACTER)—FICTION**

Zigal, Thomas. Hardrock Stiff: A Kurt Muller Mystery. 1997. (Kurt Muller Mysteries Ser.). 384p. mass mkt. 5.99 o.s.i (0-440-22452-7) Dell Publishing.
—Into Thin Air: A Novel. 1996. (Kurt Muller Mysteries Ser.). 368p. mass mkt. 5.50 o.s.i (0-440-22251-6) Dell Publishing.
—Pariah. 2000. (Kurt Muller Mysteries Ser.). 336p. mass mkt. 5.99 o.s.i (0-440-22443-8) Dell Publishing.

**MULLIGAN, DOYLE (FICTITIOUS CHARACTER)—FICTION**

Fox, Stuart. The Back of Beyond. 1995. 320p. mass mkt. 4.99 (0-8125-2081-5, Forge Bks.); 1994. 352p. 21.95 o.p. (0-312-85366-1, Tor Bks.) Doherty, Tom Assocs., LLC.
—Black Fire. 1994. 320p. mass mkt. 4.99 o.p. (0-8125-1643-5); 1992. 320p. 19.95 o.p. (0-312-85269-X); 1958. 19.95 o.p. (0-312-07657-6) Doherty, Tom Assocs., LLC. (Tor Bks.).

**MULLINS, BILL (FICTITIOUS CHARACTER)—FICTION**

Denhart, Jeffrey. Just Bones. 1997. mass mkt. 5.95 (1-885173-45-8); 1996. 225p. text 20.95 o.p. (1-885173-15-6) Write Way Publishing.

**MULLOY, DENNIS MICHAEL (FICTITIOUS CHARACTER)—FICTION**

Greeley, Andrew M. White Smoke: A Novel about the Next Papal Conclave. 1997. 466p. mass mkt. 6.99 (0-8125-9055-4); 1996. 384p. 24.95 o.p. (0-312-85814-0) Doherty, Tom Assocs., LLC. (Forge Bks.).
—White Smoke: A Novel about the Next Papal Conclave, Set. abr. ed. 1996. audio 24.99 (0-88646-413-7, 693997) Durkin Hayes Publishing Ltd.
—White Smoke: A Novel about the Next Papal Conclave. 1997. 6.99 (0-312-87118-X) St. Martin's Pr.

**MUNN, ALEX (FICTITIOUS CHARACTER)—FICTION**

Foy, George. The Shift. 1997. 544p. mass mkt. 5.99 o.s.i (0-553-57471-X); 1996. 480p. pap. 12.95 o.s.i (0-553-37544-X) Bantam Bks.

**MUNRO, ANNE (FICTITIOUS CHARACTER)—FICTION**

Conley, Martha. Growing Light. 1993. 224p. 18.95 o.p. (0-312-09823-5, Saint Martin's Minotaur) St. Martin's Pr.
—The Growing Light. 1995. 240p. mass mkt. 4.99 o.s.i (0-425-14792-4) Berkley Publishing Group.

**MUNRO, EWAN (FICTITIOUS CHARACTER)—FICTION**

Livesey, Margot. Criminals. 1997. 288p. pap. 11.95 (0-14-026277-6) Penguin Group (USA) Inc.

**MURDOCH, ROSS (FICTITIOUS CHARACTER)—FICTION**

Norton, Andre. Echoes in Time. 2000. (Time Traders Adventure Ser.). 320p. mass mkt. 5.99 (0-8125-5274-1, Tor Bks.) Doherty, Tom Assocs., LLC.
—The Time Traders. 1987. 224p. mass mkt. 3.99 o.s.i (0-441-81255-4); 1984. mass mkt. 2.50 o.s.i (0-441-81254-6); 1980. mass mkt. 1.95 o.s.i (0-441-81253-8) Ace Bks.
—The Time Traders. 2000. 384p. (J). 24.00 (0-671-31952-3) Baen Bks.
—The Time Traders. 1979. lib. bdg. 9.95 o.p. (0-8398-2421-1, Macmillan Reference USA) Gale Group.
Norton, Andre & Griffin, P. M. Fire Hand. 1995. 288p. mass mkt. 4.99 (0-8125-1984-1); 1994. 224p. 19.95 o.p. (0-312-85313-0) Doherty, Tom Assocs., LLC. (Tor Bks.).
Norton, Andre & Smith, Sherwood. Echoes in Time. 1999. (Time Traders Adventure Ser.). 319p. 23.95 (0-312-85921-X, Tor Bks.) Doherty, Tom Assocs., LLC.

**MURDOCH, WILLIAM (FICTITIOUS CHARACTER)—FICTION**

Jennings, Maureen. Except the Dying. 1997. 288p. 23.95 (0-312-16829-2, 737113, Saint Martin's Minotaur) St. Martin's Pr.
—Except the Dying: A Mystery. 1999. 336p. mass mkt. 5.99 (0-06-109739-X, HarperTorch) Morrow/Avon.
—Under the Dragon's Tail. 1999. 304p. mass mkt. 5.99 (0-06-109740-3, HarperTorch) Morrow/Avon.
—Under the Dragon's Tail. 1998. 256p. 21.95 o.p. (0-312-19348-3, Saint Martin's Minotaur) St. Martin's Pr.

**MURDOCK, PAGE (FICTITIOUS CHARACTER)—FICTION**

Estleman, Loren D. City of Widows. 1995. 254p. pap. text 5.99 (0-8125-3538-3); 1994. 256p. 20.95 o.p. (0-312-85667-9) Doherty, Tom Assocs., LLC. (Forge Bks.).
—High Rocks. 1996. pap. 4.99 (0-8125-3566-9, Forge Bks.) Doherty, Tom Assocs., LLC.
—High Rocks. 1979. 7.95 o.p. (0-385-14696-5) Doubleday Publishing.
—High Rocks. l.t. ed. 1988. lib. bdg. 14.95 o.p. (1-85057-425-1, Macmillan Reference USA) Gale Group.
—High Rocks. 1987. 192p. mass mkt. 2.75 o.s.i (0-671-63846-7, Pocket) Simon & Schuster.
—Murdock's Law. 1982. (Double D Western Ser.). 192p. pap. 11.95 o.p. (0-385-17957-X) Doubleday Publishing.
—Murdock's Law. 1987. 224p. mass mkt. 2.75 o.s.i (0-671-44951-6, Pocket) Simon & Schuster.
—Stamping Ground. 1997. 213p. pap. 5.99 (0-8125-3569-3, Forge Bks.) Doherty, Tom Assocs., LLC.
—Stamping Ground. 1980. (Double D Western Ser.). 10.95 o.p. (0-385-15563-8) Doubleday Publishing.
—White Desert. 240p. 2001. mass mkt. 5.99 (0-8125-8436-8); 2000. reprint ed. 22.95 o.p. (0-312-86969-X, NHC 0145) Doherty, Tom Assocs., LLC. (Forge Bks.).
—White Desert. l.t. ed. 2002. (Western Ser.). 324p. 26.95 (0-7862-3854-2) Thorndike Pr.

**MURPHY, AL (FICTITIOUS CHARACTER)—FICTION**

Paulsen, Gary. Murphy. 1988. 160p. mass mkt. 2.75 o.s.i (0-671-64432-7, Pocket) Simon & Schuster.
—Murphy. 1987. 192p. 14.95 o.s.i (0-8027-4068-5) Walker & Co.
—Murphy's Ambush. unabr. ed. 1999. audio 26.00 (0-7887-0485-0, 94678E7) Recorded Bks., LLC.
—Murphy's Gold. 1989. 144p. mass mkt. 2.75 o.s.i (0-671-66944-3, Pocket) Simon & Schuster.
—Murphy's Gold. 1988. 14.95 o.s.i (0-8027-4078-2) Walker & Co.
—Murphy's Herd. Grad, Doug, ed. 1992. 160p. reprint ed. mass mkt. 3.50 o.s.i (0-671-69561-4, Pocket) Simon & Schuster.
—Murphy's Herd. 1989. 192p. 17.95 o.s.i (0-8027-4094-4) Walker & Co.
—Murphy's Stand. 1993. 128p. 17.95 o.s.i (0-8027-1277-0) Walker & Co.
—Murphy's War. Grad, Doug, ed. 1990. 160p. bds. 2.95 o.s.i (0-671-66986-9, Pocket) Simon & Schuster.
Paulsen, Gary & Burks, Brian. Murphy's Ambush. 1995. 118p. 17.95 o.s.i (0-8027-4149-5) Walker & Co.
—Murphy's Trail. 1996. 137p. 18.95 (0-8027-4154-1) Walker & Co.

**MURPHY, FRANK (FICTITIOUS CHARACTER)—FICTION**

Westermann, John. Ladies of the Night. 1998. 288p. 23.00 (0-671-87124-2, Atria) Simon & Schuster.

**MURPHY, MRS. (FICTITIOUS CHARACTER)—FICTION**

Brown, Rita Mae. Cat on the Scent. 336p. 1999. (Illus.). 23.95 o.s.i (0-553-09971-X); 2000. reprint ed. mass mkt. 7.50 (0-553-57541-4) Bantam Bks.
—Cat on the Scent. l.t. ed. 1999. 26.95 o.p. (1-56895-749-1, Wheeler Publishing, Inc.) Gale Group.
—Catch as Cat Can. l.t. ed. 2002. 504p. 31.95 (0-7862-4045-8) Gale Group.
—Catch as Cat Can. l.t. ed. 2003. (Paperback Bestsellers Ser.). pap. 13.95 (0-7862-4044-X) Thorndike Pr.
—Claws & Effect. 2002. (Mrs. Murphy Mystery Ser.). (Illus.). 320p. reprint ed. mass mkt. 7.50 (0-553-58090-6) Bantam Bks.
—Claws & Effect. l.t. ed. 2001. (Illus.). 433p. 30.95 (0-7862-3484-9) Thorndike Pr.
—Murder at Monticello, or, Old Sins. 1995. (Mrs. Murphy Mystery Ser.). 320p. mass mkt. 7.50 (0-553-57235-0, Crimeline) Bantam Bks.
—Murder on the Prowl. 1999. 400p. reprint ed. mass mkt. 7.50 (0-553-57540-6) Bantam Bks.
—Murder on the Prowl. l.t. ed. 1998. (Basic Ser.). 467p. 30.95 (0-7862-1458-9) Thorndike Pr.
—Murder, She Meowed. 1997. (Mrs. Murphy Mystery Ser.). (Illus.). 336p. mass mkt. 7.50 (0-553-57237-7) Bantam Bks.
—Pawing Through the Past. 2001. (Mrs. Murphy Mystery Ser.). 352p. mass mkt. 7.50 (0-553-58025-6) Bantam Bks.
—Pawing Through the Past. l.t. ed. 2000. (Wheeler Large Print Book Ser.). (Illus.). 360p. 28.95 o.p. (1-56895-134-5, Wheeler Publishing, Inc.) Gale Group.
—Pay Dirt. 1996. (Mrs. Murphy Mystery Ser.). 288p. mass mkt. 7.50 (0-553-57236-9, Crimeline) Bantam Bks.
—Rest in Pieces. 1993. (Mrs. Murphy Mystery Ser.). 368p. mass mkt. 7.50 (0-553-56239-8) Bantam Bks.
—The Tail of the Tip-Off. 2004. (Illus.). 400p. mass mkt. 7.50 (0-553-58285-2) Bantam Bks.
—Wish You Were Here. l.t. ed. 1992. pap. 20.95 o.p. (0-7927-1189-0); 22.95 o.p. (0-7927-1188-2, CH0250) BBC Audiobooks America.
—Wish You Were Here. 1991. (Mrs. Murphy Mystery Ser.). 304p. mass mkt. 7.50 (0-553-28753-2) Bantam Bks.
Brown, Rita Mae & Brown, Sneaky Pie. Catch As Cat Can. 2003. (Illus.). 368p. mass mkt. 7.50 (0-553-58028-0, Bantam) Bantam Bks.
—Catch As Cat Can. 2002. (Illus.). 304p. 24.95 (0-553-10744-5) Bantam Dell Publishing Group.
—Catch as Cat Can. l.t. ed. 13.95 (1-4104-0084-0, Large Print Pr.) Thorndike Pr.
—The Tail of the Tip-Off. 2003. (Mrs. Murphy Mystery Ser.). E-Book 19.95 (0-553-89725-X); (Illus.). 320p. 24.95 (0-553-80158-9) Bantam Bks.
—The Tail of the Tip-Off. audio 29.99 (1-4025-3628-3) Recorded Bks., LLC.
—The Tail of the Tip-Off. l.t. ed. 2003. 32.95 (0-7862-4991-9) Thorndike Pr.

**MURPHY, RUBY (FICTITIOUS CHARACTER)—FICTION**

Estep, Maggie. Gargantuan: A Ruby Murphy Mystery. 2004. 240p. pap. 12.95 (0-609-61033-3, Three Rivers Pr.) Crown Publishing Group.
—Hex: A Ruby Murphy Mystery. 2003. 320p. pap. 14.00 (1-4000-4837-0, Three Rivers Pr.) Crown Publishing Group.

**MURPHY, SEAN (FICTITIOUS CHARACTER)—FICTION**

Cook, Robin. Terminal. 384p. 1996. mass mkt. 7.99 (0-425-15506-4); 1994. mass mkt. 6.99 o.s.i (0-425-14094-6) Berkley Publishing Group.
—Terminal. unabr. ed. 1993. audio 72.00 (0-7366-2447-3, 3211) Books on Tape, Inc.
—Terminal. 1993. 400p. 21.95 o.p. (0-399-13771-8, G. P. Putnam's Sons) Penguin Group (USA) Inc.
—Terminal, Set. abr. ed. 1993. audio 17.00 (0-671-79901-0, 391749, Simon & Schuster Audioworks) Simon & Schuster Audio.
—Terminal. pap. 6.98 o.p. (0-8317-4385-9) Smithmark Pubs., Inc.
—Terminal. 1994. 14.04 (0-606-06051-0) Turtleback Bks.

**MUSGRAVE, TOM (FICTITIOUS CHARACTER)—FICTION**

Tonkin, Peter. The Hound of the Borders. 2003. 256p. 26.99 (0-7278-5935-8) Severn Hse. Pubs., Ltd.

**MYER, MELANIE (FICTITIOUS CHARACTER)—FICTION**

Zanger, Molleen. Gardenias Where There Are None. 1994. 256p. pap. 9.95 o.p. (1-56280-056-6) Naiad Pr., Inc.

**MYLES, JORDAN (FICTITIOUS CHARACTER)—FICTION**

Navratilova, Martina & Nickels, Liz. The Total Zone. abr. ed. 1996. audio 7.99 o.p. (1-56740-211-9, 1393, Paperback Nova Audio Bks.); 1994. audio 79.25 o.p. (1-56100-224-0, 1082, Unabridged Library Editions); 1994. audio 23.95 o.p. (1-56100-599-1, 294, Bookcassette) Brilliance Audio.
Navratilova, Martina & Nickles, Liz. Breaking Point: A Novel of Suspense. 1997. 200p. mass mkt. 5.99 o.s.i (0-345-38868-2) Ballantine Bks.
—Killer Instinct. 1998. (Jordan Myles Mysteries Ser.). 322p. mass mkt. 6.99 o.s.i (0-345-38876-3) Ballantine Bks.
—The Total Zone. 1995. (Jordan Myles Mysteries Ser.). mass mkt. 6.99 o.s.i (0-345-38867-4) Ballantine Bks.

**MZAR, JEWEL (FICTITIOUS CHARACTER)—FICTION**

Ohio, Denise. End of the Empire. 160p. 1994. pap. 8.95 o.p. (0-312-10975-X, Saint Martin's Griffin); 1993. 10.99 o.p. (0-312-09282-2) St. Martin's Pr.

## N

**NAJARIAN, ERIC (FICTITIOUS CHARACTER)—FICTION**

Palmer, Michael. Extreme Measures. 1992. 448p. mass mkt. 7.50 (0-553-29577-2) Bantam Bks.

**NAMELESS DETECTIVE (FICTITIOUS CHARACTER)—FICTION**

Pronzini, Bill. Bindlestiff. 1983. 208p. 11.95 o.p. (0-312-07864-1) St. Martin's Pr.
—Bleeders. l.t. ed. 2002. 352p. 30.45 (0-7862-4119-5) Gale Group.
—Blowback. 1983. 149p. reprint ed. pap. 4.95 o.p. (0-88150-034-8) Countryman Pr.
—Blowback. 1977. 6.95 o.p. (0-394-40793-8) Random Hse., Inc.
—Bones. l.t. ed. 1991. 21.95 o.p. (0-7927-0937-3, CH0147); pap. 19.95 o.p. (0-7927-0938-1, CS0244) BBC Audiobooks America.
—Bones. 1985. (Nameless Detective Ser.). 224p. 12.95 o.p. (0-312-08769-1, 087691) St. Martin's Pr.
—Boobytrap: A "Nameless Detective" Mystery. 1998. (Nameless Detective Mystery Ser.). 256p. 23.00 (0-7867-0505-1, Carroll & Graf Pubs.) Avalon Publishing Group.
—Boobytrap: A "Nameless Detective" Mystery. unabr. ed. 1999. ("Nameless Detective" Mystery Ser.). audio 54.95 (0-7927-2269-8, CSL158, Chivers Sound Library) BBC Audiobooks America.
—Boobytrap: A "Nameless Detective" Mystery. l.t. ed. 1999. (Mystery Ser.). 317p. 28.95 (0-7862-1718-9) Thorndike Pr.
—Breakdown. l.t. ed. 1992. 19.95 o.p. (0-7927-1050-9); pap. 17.95 o.p. (0-7927-1051-7) BBC Audiobooks America.
—Breakdown. 1991. 256p. mass mkt. 4.50 o.s.i (0-440-21157-3) Dell Publishing.
—Crazybone: A "Nameless Detective" Mystery. l.t. ed. 2000. (Mystery Ser.). 317p. 29.95 (0-7862-2694-3) Thorndike Pr.
—Deadfall. 1986. 272p. 15.95 o.p. (0-312-18525-1) St. Martin's Pr.
—Demons: A "Nameless Detective" Mystery. 1994. 288p. mass mkt. 4.99 o.s.i (0-440-21118-2) Dell Publishing.
—Demons: A "Nameless Detective" Mystery. l.t. ed. 1994. 65.95 o.p. (0-7862-9982-7, Macmillan Reference USA) Gale Group.
—Dragonfire: A "Nameless Detective" Mystery. 1982. 208p. 10.95 o.p. (0-312-21893-1) St. Martin's Pr.
—Epitaphs: A "Nameless Detective" Mystery. 1993. 304p. mass mkt. 4.99 o.s.i (0-440-21117-4); 1992. 240p. 19.00 o.s.i (0-385-30504-4, Delacorte Pr.) Dell Publishing.
—Hoodwink: A "Nameless Detective" Mystery. l.t. ed. 1990. pap. 17.95 o.p. (0-7927-0193-3, C0242) BBC Audiobooks America.
—Hoodwink: A "Nameless Detective" Mystery. 1981. 238p. 10.95 o.p. (0-312-38969-8) St. Martin's Pr.
—Illusions: A "Nameless Detective" Mystery. 1997. 256p. 23.00 o.p. (0-7867-0403-9, Carroll & Graf Pubs.) Avalon Publishing Group.
—Illusions: A "Nameless Detective" Mystery. unabr. ed. 2000. (Nameless Detective Mystery Ser.). audio 49.95 (0-7927-2234-5, CSL 123) Chivers Audio Bks. GBR. *Dist:* BBC Audiobooks America.
—Illusions: A "Nameless Detective" Mystery. 1999. 254p. lib. bdg. 26.95 (0-7351-0222-8) Replica Bks.
—Jackpot. 1990. 240p. reprint ed. mass mkt. 3.95 o.s.i (0-440-20821-1) Dell Publishing.
—Jackpot. l.t. ed. 1991. (General Ser.). 342p. lib. bdg. 20.95 (0-8161-5037-0, Macmillan Reference USA) Gale Group.
—Labyrinth. 2001. 186p. pap. 12.95 (1-931755-01-9) Mystery Vault, Inc.
—Labyrinth. 1980. 8.95 o.p. (0-312-46352-9) St. Martin's Pr.
—The Nameless Detective: Dragonfire-Bindlestiff. 1990. pap. 5.95 (1-877961-15-9) Knightsbridge Publishing.
—The Nameless Detective: Hoodwink & Scattershot. 1990. 560p. reprint ed. pap. 5.95 (1-877961-94-9) Knightsbridge Publishing.

—The Nameless Detective: Labyrinth & Bones. 1990. 560p. pap. 5.95 (*1-877961-92-2*) Knightsbridge Publishing.

—Nightshades: A "Nameless Detective" Mystery. 1984. 208p. 11.95 o.p. (*0-312-57338-3*) St. Martin's Pr.

—Quarry: A "Nameless Detective" Mystery. l.t. ed. 1992. 22.95 o.p. (*0-7927-1392-3*); pap. 20.95 o.p. (*0-7927-1391-5*) BBC Audiobooks America.

—Quarry: A "Nameless Detective" Mystery. 1992. 224p. mass mkt. 4.99 o.s.i (*0-440-21116-6*) Dell Publishing.

—Quicksilver: A "Nameless Detective" Mystery. 1984. 192p. 11.95 o.p. (*0-312-66081-2*) St. Martin's Pr.

—Scattershot: A "Nameless Detective" Mystery. l.t. ed. 1989. 18.95 o.p. (*1-55504-833-1*, 296) BBC Audiobooks America.

—Scattershot: A "Nameless Detective" Mystery. 1983. 176p. pap. 5.95 o.p. (*0-312-70047-4*, Saint Martin's Griffin); 1982. 182p. 10.95 o.p. (*0-312-70046-6*) St. Martin's Pr.

—Sentinels: A "Nameless Detective" Mystery. 1996. 288p. 20.00 (*0-7867-0311-3*); 2002. 224p. reprint ed. pap. 11.00 (*0-7867-1014-4*) Avalon Publishing Group. (Carroll & Graf Pubs.).

—Sentinels: A "Nameless Detective" Mystery. l.t. ed. 1996. lib. bdg. 23.95 (*1-57490-074-9*, Beeler Large Print Bks.) Beeler, Thomas T. Publisher.

—Sentinels: A "Nameless Detective" Mystery. unabr. ed. 2000. (Nameless Detective Mystery Ser.). audio 49.95 (*0-7927-2207-8*, CSL 096) Chivers Audio Bks. GBR. *Dist:* BBC Audiobooks America.

—Shackles: A "Nameless Detective" Mystery. 1988. 272p. 16.95 o.p. (*0-312-01818-5*, Saint Martin's Minotaur) St. Martin's Pr.

—The Snatch. 1984. (Nameless Detective Mystery Ser.). reprint ed. pap. 4.95 o.p. (*0-88150-021-6*) Countryman Pr.

—Spadework: A Collection of "Nameless Detective" Stories. 1996. 192p. pap. 16.00 (*1-885941-07-2*); 30.00 o.p. (*1-885941-06-4*) Crippen & Landru, Pubs.

—Spook: A Nameless Detective Novel. 2002. 224p. 25.00 (*0-7867-1086-1*, Carroll & Graf Pubs.) Avalon Publishing Group.

—Undercurrent. 1984. 213p. pap. 4.95 o.p. (*0-88150-033-X*) Countryman Pr.

—The Vanished. 1984. (Nameless Detective Mystery Ser.). reprint ed. pap. 4.95 o.p. (*0-88150-022-4*) Countryman Pr.

—The Vanished. 1974. pap. 0.95 o.p. (*0-671-77714-9*, Pocket) Simon & Schuster.

—The Vanished. l.t. ed. 1999. (G. K. Hall Nightingale Ser.). 236p. pap. 20.95 (*0-7838-8766-3*) Thorndike Pr.

Pronzini, Bill & Wilcox, Collin. Two-Spot. 1993. 272p. mass mkt. 12.95 (*0-7867-0042-4*, Carroll & Graf Pubs.) Avalon Publishing Group.

—Two-Spot. 1978. 8.95 o.p. (*0-399-12129-3*) Putnam Publishing Group, The.

**NARMAN, SABRA (FICTITIOUS CHARACTER)—FICTION**

Tigges, John. The Curse. 1993. 400p. (Orig.). pap. 4.50 (*0-8439-3389-5*) Dorchester Publishing Co., Inc.

**NASH, DAVID (FICTITIOUS CHARACTER)—FICTION**

Margolin, Phillip, ed. The Last Innocent Man. 1995. 352p. reprint ed. mass mkt. 7.99 (*0-553-56979-1*) Bantam Bks.

—The Last Innocent Man. unabr. ed. 1996. audio 48.00 Books on Tape, Inc.

—The Last Innocent Man. 2002. lib. bdg. 29.95 (*1-58547-247-6*, Premier) Ctr. Point Large Print.

—The Last Innocent Man. 1981. 252p. 11.95 o.p. (*0-316-54617-8*) Little Brown & Co.

—The Last Innocent Man. l.t. ed. 1999. (Charnwood Large Print Ser.). 352p. 31.99 o.p. (*0-7089-9071-1*, Ulverscroft) Thorpe, F. A. Pubs. GBR. *Dist:* Ulverscroft Large Print Bks., Ltd., Ulverscroft Large Print Canada, Ltd.

**NASH, JESTON (FICTITIOUS CHARACTER)—FICTION**

Cotton, Ralph W. Cost of a Killing. 1996. 304p. mass mkt. 5.99 (*0-671-57032-3*, Pocket) Simon & Schuster.

**NAUGHTON, TERRY (FICTITIOUS CHARACTER)—FICTION**

Parker, T. Jefferson. Where Serpents Lie. 1999. mass mkt. 6.99 (*0-7868-8949-7*); 2003. 576p. reprint ed. mass mkt. 7.50 (*0-7868-8944-6*) Hyperion Pr.

—Where Serpents Lie. l.t. ed. 1998. (Cloak & Dagger Ser.). 655p. 28.95 (*0-7862-1526-7*) Thorndike Pr.

**NAVARRE, TRES (FICTITIOUS CHARACTER)—FICTION**

Riordan, Rick. Big Red Tequilla. 1997. 400p. mass mkt. 6.50 (*0-553-57644-5*) Bantam Bks.

—The Widower's Two-Step. 1998. 416p. mass mkt. 6.50 (*0-553-57645-3*) Bantam Bks.

**NAZHURET (FICTITIOUS CHARACTER)—FICTION**

MacAvoy, R. A. The Belly of the Wolf. (Lens of the World Ser.: 3). 1995. 224p. mass mkt. 4.99 (*0-380-71018-8*, Avon Bks.); 1994. 187p. 20.00 o.p. (*0-688-09601-8*, Morrow, William & Co.) Morrow/Avon.

—King of the Dead. (Lens of the World Ser.: 2). 288p. 1992. mass mkt. 4.50 (*0-380-71017-X*, Avon Bks.); 1991. 19.00 o.p. (*0-688-09600-X*, Morrow, William & Co.) Morrow/Avon.

—Lens of the World. (Lens of the World Ser.: 1). 1990. 18.95 o.p. (*0-688-09484-8*, Morrow, William & Co.); 1991. 288p. reprint ed. mass mkt. 4.99 (*0-380-71016-1*, Avon Bks.) Morrow/Avon.

**NEBRASKA (FICTITIOUS CHARACTER)—FICTION**

Reynolds, William J. Drive-By: A Nebraska Mystery. Emmel, Gayle, ed. 1995. 329p. pap. 5.95 (*0-944287-14-X*) Ex Machina.

**NEELIX (FICTITIOUS CHARACTER)—FICTION**

Betancourt, John G. Incident at Arbuk. 1995. (Star Trek Voyager Ser.: No. 5). 224p. mass mkt. 5.99 o.s.i (*0-671-52048-2*, Star Trek) Simon & Schuster.

Golden, Christie. Homecoming. 2003. (Star Trek Voyager Ser.). 288p. mass mkt. 6.99 (*0-7434-6754-X*);Bk. 1. E-Book 5.99 (*0-7434-7563-1*) Simon & Schuster. (Star Trek).

—Marooned. 1997. (Star Trek Voyager Ser.: No. 14). (Illus.). 304p. pap. 5.99 (*0-671-01423-4*, Star Trek) Simon & Schuster.

—Seven of Nine. 1998. (Star Trek Voyager Ser.: No. 16). 233p. mass mkt. 6.50 (*0-671-02491-4*, Star Trek) Simon & Schuster.

Hugh, Dafydd ab. The Final Fury No. 4: Invasion! 1996. (Star Trek Voyager Ser.: No. 9). 320p. (J). mass mkt. 6.50 (*0-671-54181-1*, Star Trek) Simon & Schuster.

—Invasion! No. 4: The Final Fury. 1999. (Star Trek Voyager Ser.: No. 9). E-Book 6.99 (*0-671-04098-7*, Star Trek) Simon & Schuster.

Scott, Melissa. The Garden. 1997. (Star Trek Voyager Ser.: No. 11). (Illus.). 288p. mass mkt. 5.99 (*0-671-56799-3*, Star Trek) Simon & Schuster.

**NEHMER, KURT (FICTITIOUS CHARACTER)—FICTION**

Sullivan, Thomas. The Martyring. 2000. 256p. pap. 13.95 (*0-312-87498-7*, Tor Bks.); 1999. mass mkt. (*0-8125-4543-5*, Tor Bks.); 1998. 256p. 22.95 (*0-312-86361-6*, Forge Bks.) Doherty, Tom Assocs., LLC.

**NELSON, VICKI (FICTITIOUS CHARACTER)—FICTION**

Huff, Tanya. Blood Debt. 1997. (Victory Nelson Ser.). 336p. mass mkt. 6.99 (*0-88677-739-9*) DAW Bks., Inc.

—Blood Lines, Bk. 3. 1993. (Daw Book Collectors Ser.: Vol. 901). 272p. (Orig.). mass mkt. 5.99 o.s.i (*0-88677-530-2*) DAW Bks., Inc.

—Blood Price. 1991. (Daw Book Collectors Ser.: Vol. 850). 272p. (Orig.). mass mkt. 6.99 (*0-88677-471-3*) DAW Bks., Inc.

—Blood Trail. 1992. (Victor Nelson Investigator Ser.: Vol. 3). 304p. (Orig.). mass mkt. 6.99 (*0-88677-502-7*) DAW Bks., Inc.

**NESS, ELIOT (FICTITIOUS CHARACTER)—FICTION**

Collins, Max Allan. Bullet Proof, Vol. 3. 1989. mass mkt. 3.50 o.s.i (*0-553-27982-3*) Bantam Bks.

—Butcher's Dozen. 1988. 224p. mass mkt. 3.50 o.s.i (*0-553-26151-7*) Bantam Bks.

—Butcher's Dozen. 1998. (Mystery Ser.). 263p. 20.95 o.p. (*0-7862-1662-X*, Five Star) Gale Group.

—The Dark City. 1987. mass mkt. 3.50 o.p. (*0-553-26539-3*) Bantam Bks.

—Murder by the Numbers. unabr. ed. 1998. audio 19.95 (*1-882071-47-6*) B&B Audio, Inc.

—Murder by the Numbers. 1993. 17.95 o.p. (*0-312-08856-6*, Saint Martin's Minotaur) St. Martin's Pr.

Tucker, Kenneth. Eliot Ness & the Untouchables: The Historical Reality & the Film & Television Depictions. 2000. (Illus.). 208p. per. 32.00 (*0-7864-0772-7*) McFarland & Co., Inc. Pubs.

**NESTLETON, ALICE (FICTITIOUS CHARACTER)—FICTION**

Adamson, Lydia. A Cat by Any Other Name. unabr. collector's ed. 1997. (Alice Nestleton Ser.). audio 30.00 (*0-7366-3597-1*, 4248) Books on Tape, Inc.

—A Cat by Any Other Name: An Alice Nestleton Mystery. 1992. (Alice Nestleton Mystery Ser.). 208p. mass mkt. 5.50 o.s.i (*0-451-17231-0*, Signet Bks.) NAL.

—A Cat in a Chorus Line. unabr. ed. 1997. (Alice Nestleton Ser.: Vol. 12). audio 24.00 (*0-7366-4052-5*, 4561) Books on Tape, Inc.

—A Cat in a Chorus Line. 1996. (Alice Nestleton Mystery Ser.). 256p. mass mkt. 5.50 o.s.i (*0-451-18084-4*, Signet Bks.) NAL.

—A Cat in a Glass House. unabr. ed. 1997. (Alice Nestleton Ser.). audio 30.00 (*0-7366-3675-7*, 4354) Books on Tape, Inc.

—A Cat in a Glass House. 1993. (Alice Nestleton Mystery Ser.). 208p. mass mkt. 3.99 o.s.i (*0-451-17706-1*, Signet Bks.) NAL.

—A Cat in Fine Style. unabr. ed. 1997. (Alice Nestleton Ser.: Vol. 10). audio 30.00 (*0-7366-3831-8*, 4551) Books on Tape, Inc.

—A Cat in Fine Style: An Alice Nestleton Mystery. 1995. (Alice Nestleton Mystery Ser.). 224p. mass mkt. 5.99 o.s.i (*0-451-18083-6*, Signet Bks.) NAL.

—A Cat in the Manger. l.t. ed. 1991. 17.95 o.p. (*0-7451-8142-2*, AH0179); pap. 15.95 o.p. (*0-7927-0663-3*, AS0215) BBC Audiobooks America.

—A Cat in the Manger. unabr. collector's ed. 1997. (Alice Nestleton Ser.: Vol. 1). audio 30.00 (*0-7366-3556-4*, 4201) Books on Tape, Inc.

—A Cat in the Manger. 1990. (Alice Nestleton Mystery Ser.). 208p. mass mkt. 5.50 o.s.i (*0-451-16787-2*, Signet Bks.) NAL.

—A Cat in the Wings. unabr. collector's ed. 1997. (Alice Nestleton Ser.). audio 36.00 (*0-7366-3598-X*, 4249) Books on Tape, Inc.

—A Cat in the Wings. 1992. (Alice Nestleton Mystery Ser.: No. 5). 208p. mass mkt. 5.99 o.s.i (*0-451-17336-8*, Signet Bks.) NAL.

—A Cat in the Wings: An Alice Nestleton Mystery. l.t. ed. 2001. 301p. 28.95 o.p. (*0-7862-3676-0*) Thorndike Pr.

—A Cat in Wolf's Clothing. unabr. collector's ed. 1997. (Alice Nestleton Ser.: Vol. 3). audio 30.00 (*0-7366-3558-0*, 4203) Books on Tape, Inc.

—A Cat in Wolf's Clothing. 1991. (Alice Nestleton Mystery Ser.). 208p. mass mkt. 4.99 o.s.i (*0-451-17085-7*, Signet Bks.) NAL.

—A Cat in Wolf's Clothing: An Alice Nestleton Mystery. l.t. ed. 1993. (General Ser.). 223p. pap. 16.95 (*0-8161-5401-5*); lib. bdg. 18.95 o.p. (*0-8161-5400-7*) Gale Group. (Macmillan Reference USA).

—A Cat Named Brat. unabr. ed. 2002. audio 39.95 (*0-7927-2627-8*, CSL 483, Chivers Children's Audio Bks.) BBC Audiobooks America.

—A Cat Named Brat. 2002. 208p. mass mkt. 5.99 (*0-451-20664-9*) NAL.

—A Cat Named Brat: An Alice Nestleton Mystery. 2003. (Mystery Ser.). 30.45 (*0-7862-4757-6*) Thorndike Pr.

—A Cat of a Different Color. unabr. collector's ed. 1997. (Alice Nestleton Ser.: Vol. 2). audio 30.00 (*0-7366-3557-2*, 4202) Books on Tape, Inc.

—A Cat of a Different Color. l.t. ed. 1992. (General Ser.). 200p. pap. 14.95 o.p. (*0-8161-5399-X*); lib. bdg. 18.95 o.p. (*0-8161-5398-1*) Gale Group. (Macmillan Reference USA).

—A Cat of a Different Color. 1991. (Alice Nestleton Mystery Ser.). 208p. mass mkt. 5.50 o.s.i (*0-451-16955-7*, Signet Bks.) NAL.

—A Cat of One's Own. 1999. (Alice Nestleton Mysteries Ser.: Bk. 17). 208p. 19.95 (*0-525-94428-1*) Dutton/Plume.

—A Cat of One's Own, 1. 2000. (Alice Nestleton Mysteries Ser.). 208p. mass mkt. 5.99 o.s.i (*0-451-19769-0*) NAL.

—A Cat of One's Own. l.t. ed. 1999. (Mystery Ser.). 216p. 28.95 (*0-7862-1884-3*) Thorndike Pr.

—A Cat on a Beach Blanket. unabr. ed. 1998. (Alice Nestleton Ser.). audio 30.00 (*0-7366-4260-9*, 4759) Books on Tape, Inc.

—A Cat on a Beach Blanket. 1997. (Alice Nestleton Mystery Ser.). (Illus.). 192p. 18.95 o.p. (*0-525-94304-8*) Dutton/Plume.

—A Cat on a Beach Blanket. 1998. (Alice Nestleton Mysteries Ser.). 256p. mass mkt. 5.99 o.s.i (*0-451-19259-1*, Signet Bks.) NAL.

—A Cat on a Beach Blanket: An Alice Nestleton Mystery. l.t. ed. 2001. 231p. 29.95 (*0-7862-2649-8*); (*0-7540-4552-8*) Thorndike Pr.

—A Cat on a Winning Streak. unabr. ed. 1997. (Alice Nestleton Ser.). audio 24.00 (*0-7366-3746-X*, 4421) Books on Tape, Inc.

—A Cat on a Winning Streak. 1995. (Alice Nestleton Mystery Ser.). 240p. mass mkt. 4.50 o.s.i (*0-451-18082-8*, Signet Bks.) NAL.

—A Cat on Jingle Bell Rock. unabr. ed. 1999. (Alice Nestleton Ser.). audio 24.95 (*0-7366-4336-2*, 4825) Books on Tape, Inc.

—A Cat on Jingle Bell Rock. 1997. (Alice Nestleton Mystery Ser.). 192p. 19.95 o.p. (*0-525-94375-7*) Dutton/Plume.

—A Cat on Jingle Bell Rock. 1998. (Alice Nestleton Mystery Ser.). 340p. mass mkt. 5.99 o.s.i (*0-451-19458-6*, Signet Bks.) NAL.

—A Cat on Jingle Bell Rock: An Alice Nestleton Mystery. l.t. ed. 2000. (Mystery Ser.). 216p. 28.95 (*0-7862-2650-1*) Thorndike Pr.

—A Cat on Stage Left. 1998. (Alice Nestleton Mysteries Ser.: Vol. 16). (Illus.). 176p. 19.95 o.p. (*0-525-94419-2*) Dutton/Plume.

—A Cat on Stage Left: An Alice Nestleton Mystery, 1 vol., Vol. 16. 1999. (Alice Nestleton Mysteries Ser.: Vol. 16). 256p. mass mkt. 5.99 o.s.i (*0-451-19734-8*) NAL.

—A Cat on Stage Left: An Alice Nestleton Mystery. l.t. ed. 1998. (Mystery Ser.). 232p. 27.95 (*0-7862-1559-3*) Thorndike Pr.

—A Cat on the Cutting Edge. unabr. ed. 1997. (Alice Nestleton Ser.: Vol. 9). audio 24.00 (*0-7366-3745-1*, 4420) Books on Tape, Inc.

—A Cat on the Cutting Edge. l.t. ed. 1995. (Alice Nestleton Mystery Ser.). 178p. lib. bdg. 21.95 o.p. (*0-7838-1243-4*, Macmillan Reference USA) Gale Group.

—A Cat on the Cutting Edge. 1994. (Alice Nestleton Mystery Ser.). 224p. mass mkt. 4.50 o.s.i (*0-451-18080-1*, Signet Bks.) NAL.

—A Cat under the Mistletoe. unabr. ed. 1998. (Alice Nestleton Ser.). audio 30.00 (*0-7366-4259-5*, 4758) Books on Tape, Inc.

—A Cat under the Mistletoe. 1997. (Alice Nestleton Mysteries Ser.). 256p. mass mkt. 5.99 o.s.i (*0-451-19105-6*, Signet Bks.) NAL.

—A Cat under the Mistletoe: A Christmas Cat Mystery. 1996. (Alice Nestleton Mystery Ser.). 224p. 18.95 o.p. (*0-525-94226-2*, Dutton) Dutton/Plume.

—A Cat under the Mistletoe: An Alice Nestleton Mystery. l.t. ed. 2000. (Mystery Ser.). 248p. 28.95 (*0-7862-2651-X*) Thorndike Pr.

—A Cat with a Fiddle. unabr. collector's ed. 1997. (Alice Nestleton Ser.: Vol. 6). audio 36.00 (*0-7366-3676-5*, 4355) Books on Tape, Inc.

—A Cat with a Fiddle. 1993. (Alice Nestleton Mystery Ser.: No. 6). 224p. mass mkt. 5.50 o.s.i (*0-451-17586-7*, Signet Bks.) NAL.

—A Cat with a Fiddle: An Alice Nestleton Mystery. l.t. ed. 2002. (Mystery Ser.). 270p. 29.45 (*0-7862-3895-X*) Gale Group.

—A Cat with No Regrets. unabr. ed. 1997. (Alice Nestleton Ser.). audio 30.00 (*0-7366-3744-3*, 4419) Books on Tape, Inc.

—A Cat with No Regrets. 1994. (Alice Nestleton Mystery Ser.: No. 8). 208p. mass mkt. 3.99 o.s.i (*0-451-18055-0*, Signet Bks.) NAL.

—A Cat with No Regrets. 1999. pap. (*0-525-93811-7*) Viking Penguin.

—A Cat with the Blues. 2000. (Alice Nestleton Mysteries Ser.: Vol. 10). 208p. mass mkt. 5.99 (*0-451-20196-5*) NAL.

—A Cat with the Blues: An Alice Nestleton Mystery. l.t. ed. 2001. (Thorndike Mystery Ser.). 200p. 29.95 (*0-7862-3076-2*); (*0-7540-4465-3*) Thorndike Pr.

**NEVELSON, JACK (FICTITIOUS CHARACTER)—FICTION**

Watson, Larry. White Crosses. 384p. 1998. pap. 14.00 (*0-671-56773-X*, Washington Square Pr.); 1997. 23.00 o.s.i (*0-671-56771-3*, Atria) Simon & Schuster.

**NEWCOMBE, CHLOE (FICTITIOUS CHARACTER)—FICTION**

Thornton, Betsy. The Cowboy Rides Away. 1997. 288p. mass mkt. 5.50 o.s.i (*0-440-22327-X*) Dell Publishing.

—The Cowboy Rides Away. 1996. 256p. 21.95 o.p. (*0-312-14301-X*, Saint Martin's Minotaur) St. Martin's Pr.

—Ghost Towns. 2003. 256p. reprint ed. mass mkt. 5.99 (*0-425-18889-2*, Prime Crime) Berkley Publishing Group.

—Ghost Towns. 2002. 272p. 23.95 (*0-312-28041-6*, Saint Martin's Minotaur) St. Martin's Pr.

—High Lonesome Road. E-Book 23.95 (*1-58945-672-6*) Adobe Systems, Inc.

—High Lonesome Road. 2001. 233p. 23.95 (*0-312-26861-0*, Saint Martin's Minotaur) St. Martin's Pr.

—The High Lonesome Road. 2002. 256p. mass mkt. 5.99 o.s.i (*0-425-18455-2*) Berkley Publishing Group.

**NEWTON, CASSIE (FICTITIOUS CHARACTER)—FICTION**

Smith, Joan. Brush with Death. 1990. mass mkt. 3.50 o.s.i (*0-515-10304-7*, Jove) Berkley Publishing Group.

—Capriccio. 1989. mass mkt. 3.50 o.s.i (*0-515-09984-8*, Jove) Berkley Publishing Group.

**NEXT, THURSDAY (FICTITIOUS CHARACTER)—FICTION**

Fforde, Jasper. The Eyre Affair. l.t. ed. 2002. 576p. 28.95 (*0-7862-4293-0*) Gale Group.

—The Eyre Affair. abr. ed. 2002. audio 34.95 (*1-56511-545-7*); audio compact disk 36.95 (*1-56511-546-5*) HighBridge Co.

—The Eyre Affair. 2003. 384p. pap. 14.00 (*0-14-200180-5*) Penguin Group (USA) Inc.

—The Eyre Affair. 2002. 272p. 23.95 (*0-670-03064-3*, Viking) Viking Penguin.

—Lost in a Good Book: A Thursday Next Novel. abr. ed. 2003. audio 36.95 (*1-56511-756-5*); audio compact disk 36.95 (*1-56511-757-3*) HighBridge Co.

—Lost in a Good Book: A Thursday Next Novel. 2004. 416p. pap. 14.00 (*0-14-200403-0*) Penguin Group (USA) Inc.
—Lost in a Good Book: A Thursday Next Novel. 2003. 416p. 24.95 (*0-670-03190-9*, Viking); pap. 249.50 o.p. (*0-670-78341-2*) Viking Penguin.
—The Well of Lost Plots: A Thursday Next Novel. 2004. 400p. 24.95 (*0-670-03289-1*) Viking Penguin.

**NEZ, LEE (FICTITIOUS CHARACTER)—FICTION**

Thurlo, David & Thurlo, Aimee. Second Sunrise: A Lee Nez Novel. 2002. (Lee Nez Novel Ser.). 336p. 24.95 (*0-7653-0441-4*, Forge Bks.) Doherty, Tom Assocs., LLC.

**NICHOLS, JANE (FICTITIOUS CHARACTER)—FICTION**

Tan, Maureen. A. K. A. Jane. 1999. 336p. mass mkt. 6.50 (*0-446-60667-7*) Warner Bks., Inc.
—AKA Jane. 1997. 304p. 22.00 o.p. (*0-89296-658-0*) Mysterious Pr.
—AKA Jane. abr. ed. 1998. audio 23.00 (*1-56876-070-1*) Soundlines Entertainment, Inc.
—Run Jane Run. 1999. 274p. 22.00 o.s.i (*0-89296-659-9*) Mysterious Pr.
—Run Jane Run. 2001. 304p. E-Book 4.95 (*0-446-92313-3*) Time Warner Bk. Group.
—Run Jane Run. 2001. 304p. E-Book 4.95 (*0-446-96064-0*); 2001. 304p. E-Book 4.95 (*0-446-92100-9*); 2000. 304p. mass mkt. 6.50 (*0-446-60904-8*); 1999. E-Book 4.95 (*0-446-91276-X*) Warner Bks., Inc.

**NICHOLS, NASON (FICTITIOUS CHARACTER)—FICTION**

Thomson, Maynard F. Breaking Faith. 1997. 352p. per. 6.50 (*0-671-86789-X*, Pocket) Simon & Schuster.
—Breaking Faith. Wolverton, Pete R., ed. 1996. 384p. 22.00 (*0-671-74900-5*, Atria) Simon & Schuster.
—Trade Secrets. Chelius, Jane, ed. 256p. 1994. mass mkt. 4.99 (*0-671-86788-1*, Pocket); 1993. 20.00 (*0-671-74899-8*, Atria) Simon & Schuster.
—Trade Secrets. 244p. 3.98 o.p. (*0-8317-2322-X*) Smithmark Pubs., Inc.

**NICHOLSON, ALIX (FICTITIOUS CHARACTER)—FICTION**

Gilligan, Sharon. Danger! Cross Currents: An Alix Nicholson Mystery. 1994. 170p. pap. 9.99 (*1-883061-01-6*) Rising Tide Pr.
—Danger in High Places: An Alix Nicholson Mystery. 1993. 156p. pap. 9.95 (*0-9628938-7-0*) Rising Tide Pr.

**NICKERSON, MARTHA (FICTITIOUS CHARACTER)—FICTION**

Connors, Rose. Absolute Certainty. 2003. 304p. E-Book 24.00 (*0-7432-3366-2*, Scribner); 2003. (Illus.). 320p. mass mkt. 6.99 (*0-7434-4881-2*, Pocket Star); 2002. 304p. 24.00 (*0-7432-2906-1*, Scribner) Simon & Schuster.
—Absolute Certainty. 2002. (Basic Ser.). 27.95 (*0-7862-4791-6*) Thorndike Pr.

**NICKLES, EDDIE (FICTITIOUS CHARACTER)—FICTION**

Pease, William D. The Monkey's Fist. 1997. 448p. mass mkt. 6.99 o.s.i (*0-451-18872-1*, Signet Bks.) NAL.
—The Monkey's Fist. 1996. 368p. 23.95 o.s.i (*0-670-85129-9*, Viking) Viking Penguin.
—Playing the Dozens. 1992. 432p. mass mkt. 5.99 o.s.i (*0-451-16986-7*, Signet Bks.) NAL.
—Playing the Dozens. 1990. 352p. 19.95 o.p. (*0-670-83518-8*) Viking Penguin.

**NIFFT THE LEAN (FICTITIOUS CHARACTER)—FICTION**

Shea, Michael. The A'Rak. 2000. 320p. mass mkt. 6.99 (*0-671-31947-7*) Baen Bks.
—Incompleat Nifft. 2000. 576p. mass mkt. 6.99 (*0-671-57869-3*) Baen Bks.
—Mines of Behemoth. 1997. 256p. mass mkt. 5.99 o.s.i (*0-671-87847-6*) Baen Bks.
—Nifft the Lean. 1982. 304p. mass mkt. 2.95 o.p. (*0-87997-783-3*) DAW Bks., Inc.

**NIGHTINGALE, DEIRDRE QUINN (FICTITIOUS CHARACTER)—FICTION**

Adamson, Lydia. Dr. Nightingale Chase. 1996. (Dr. Nightingale Mystery Ser.). 240p. mass mkt. 5.50 o.s.i (*0-451-18869-1*, Signet Bks.) NAL.
—Dr. Nightingale Comes Home. l.t. ed. 2003. (Mystery Ser.). (Orig.). 27.95 (*1-57490-490-6*, Beeler Large Print Bks.) Beeler, Thomas T. Publisher.
—Dr. Nightingale Comes Home. 1994. (Deirdre Quinn Nightingale Mystery Ser.). 224p. (Orig.). mass mkt. 3.99 o.s.i (*0-451-17872-6*, Signet Bks.) NAL.
—Dr. Nightingale Enters the Bear Cave. 1996. (Deirdre Quinn Nightingale Mystery Ser.). 272p. mass mkt. 5.50 o.s.i (*0-451-18673-7*, Signet Bks.) NAL.
—Dr. Nightingale Follows a Canine Clue. l.t. ed. 2001. (Beeler Large Print Mystery Ser.). 141p. 25.95 (*1-57490-409-4*, Beeler Large Print Bks.) Beeler, Thomas T. Publisher.
—Dr. Nightingale Follows a Canine Clue. 2001. (Dr. Nightingale Mystery Ser.). 208p. mass mkt. 5.99 o.s.i (*0-451-20366-6*, Signet Bks.) NAL.
—Dr. Nightingale Goes the Distance. 1995. (Deirdre Quinn Nightingale Mystery Ser.). 256p. (Orig.). mass mkt. 4.99 o.s.i (*0-451-18493-9*, Signet Bks.) NAL.
—Dr. Nightingale Goes to the Dogs. 1995. (Deirdre Quinn Nightingale Mystery Ser.). 224p. (Orig.). mass mkt. 4.50 o.s.i (*0-451-18290-1*, Signet Bks.) NAL.
—Dr. Nightingale Races the Outlaw Colt. 1998. (Deirdre Quinn Nightingale Mystery Ser.). 224p. mass mkt. 5.99 o.s.i (*0-451-18815-2*, Signet Bks.) NAL.
—Dr. Nightingale Races the Outlaw Colt: A Deirdre Quinn Nightingale Mystery. l.t. ed. 2000. (Mystery Ser.). 235p. 27.95 (*0-7862-2486-X*) Thorndike Pr.
—Dr. Nightingale Rides the Elephant. 1994. (Deirdre Quinn Nightingale Mystery Ser.). 208p. (Orig.). mass mkt. 5.50 o.s.i (*0-451-18134-4*, Signet Bks.) NAL.
—Dr. Nightingale Rides to the Hounds. 1997. (Dr. Nightingale Mystery Ser.). 224p. mass mkt. 5.99 o.s.i (*0-451-18813-6*, Signet Bks.) NAL.
—Dr. Nightingale Seeks Greener Pastures: A Deirdre Quinn Nightingale Mystery. l.t. ed. 2001. 216p. 27.95 (*0-7862-3471-7*) Thorndike Pr.

**NILSEN, PAM (FICTITIOUS CHARACTER)—FICTION**

Wilson, Barbara. The Dog Collar Murders. 1989. 203p. (Orig.). pap. 9.95 (*1-878067-25-7*, Seal Pr.) Avalon Publishing Group.
—Murder in the Collective. 1984. 183p. (Orig.). pap. 9.95 (*1-878067-23-0*, Seal Pr.) Avalon Publishing Group.
—Sisters of the Road. 1986. 202p. (Orig.). pap. 9.95 (*1-878067-24-9*, Seal Pr.) Avalon Publishing Group.

**NOBLE, KARA (FICTITIOUS CHARACTER)—FICTION**

Wilson, B. L. Bloody Waters. Silvestro, Denise, ed. 1993. 272p. (Orig.). mass mkt. 4.99 (*0-671-73908-5*, Pocket) Simon & Schuster.

**NOG (FICTITIOUS CHARACTER)—FICTION**

Reeves-Stevens, Judith & Reeves-Stevens, Garfield. Millennium No. 1: The Fall of Terok Nor. 2000. (Star Trek Deep Space Nine Ser.). E-Book 6.99 (*0-7434-0679-6*); (Star Trek Deep Space Nine: Vol. 1). 464p. pap. 6.50 o.s.i (*0-671-02401-9*) Simon & Schuster. (Star Trek).
—Millennium No. 1: The Fall of Terok Nor. abr. ed. 2000. (Star Trek Ser. ). audio 18.00 (*0-7435-0010-5*, Simon & Schuster Audioworks) Simon & Schuster Audio.

**NOLAN, LON (FICTITIOUS CHARACTER)—FICTION**

Shelley, Rick. Captain. 1999. (Dirigent Mercenary Corps Ser.). 288p. (Orig.). mass mkt. 6.50 (*0-441-00605-1*) Ace Bks.
—Colonel. 2000. (Dirigent Mercenary Corps Ser.). 272p. mass mkt. 5.99 (*0-441-00782-1*) Ace Bks.
—Lieutenant. 1998. (Dirigent Mercenary Corps Ser.). 272p. mass mkt. 5.99 (*0-441-00568-3*) Ace Bks.
—Major. 1999. (Dirigent Mercenary Corps Ser.). 272p. mass mkt. 6.50 (*0-441-00680-9*) Ace Bks.
—Officer-Cadet. 1998. (Dirigent Mercenary Corps Ser.). 288p. mass mkt. 5.99 (*0-441-00526-8*) Ace Bks.

**NOON, FREDDIE URBAN (FICTITIOUS CHARACTER)—FICTION**

Westlake, Donald E. Smoke. 1995. 454p. 21.95 o.s.i (*0-89296-534-7*) Mysterious Pr.
—Smoke. 1996. 448p. reprint ed. mass mkt. 7.50 (*0-446-40344-X*) Warner Bks., Inc.

**NOONAN, MIKE (FICTITIOUS CHARACTER)—FICTION**

King, Stephen. Bag of Bones. 2000. (RUS.). Vol. 1. pap. 14.95 (*5-237-01450-X*); Vol. 2. pap. 14.95 (*5-237-01451-8*) AST, Izdatel'stvo, OOO, firma RUS. *Dist:* Distribooks, Inc.
—Bag of Bones. 2002. E-Book 9.99 (*1-59061-785-1*) Adobe Systems, Inc.
—Bag of Bones. unabr. ed. 1999. audio 59.95 Highsmith Inc.
—Bag of Bones. unabr. ed. 1999. audio 56.00 (*1-84032-192-X*) Hodder Headline Audiobooks GBR. *Dist:* Ulverscroft Large Print Bks., Ltd.
—Bag of Bones. 1999. E-Book 28.00 (*0-684-83541-X*, Scribner); 1998. 544p. 28.00 (*0-684-85350-7*, Scribner); 1988. pap. 7.99 (*0-671-02607-0*, Pocket); 1999. 752p. reprint ed. mass mkt. 7.99 (*0-671-02423-X*, Pocket) Simon & Schuster.
—Bag of Bones. unabr. ed. 1998. audio 59.95 (*0-671-58234-8*, 136013); audio compact disk 79.95 (*0-671-04306-4*) Simon & Schuster Audio. (Simon & Schuster Audioworks).
—Bag of Bones. l.t. ed. 1999. (Thorndike/G. K. Hall Paperback Bestsellers Ser.). 901p. pap. 28.95 (*0-7862-1721-9*); 30.95 o.p. (*0-7862-1720-0*) Thorndike Pr.
—Bag of Bones. 1999. 14.04 (*0-606-17066-9*) Turtleback Bks.

**NOP (FICTITIOUS CHARACTER)—FICTION**

McCaig, Donald. Nop's Trials. l.t. ed. 1984. (General Ser.). 15.95 o.p. (*0-8161-3734-X*, Macmillan Reference USA) Gale Group.
—Nop's Trials. 1992. 336p. pap. 13.95 (*1-55821-185-3*, Lyons Pr.) Globe Pequot Pr., The.
—Nop's Trials. 1984. 2.99 o.p. (*0-517-55189-6*) Random Hse. Value Publishing.
—Nop's Trials. 1985. mass mkt. 3.95 o.s.i (*0-446-32641-0*) Warner Bks., Inc.
McCraig, Donald, ed. Nop's Hope. 1998. 224p. reprint ed. pap. 14.95 (*1-55821-574-3*, Lyons Pr.) Globe Pequot Pr., The.

**NORDEJOONG, CHICAGO (FICTITIOUS CHARACTER)—FICTION**

McKernan, Victoria. Crooked Island. 1994. 288p. 18.95 o.p. (*0-88184-998-7*, Carroll & Graf Pubs.) Avalon Publishing Group.
—Crooked Island. unabr. ed. 1994. audio 48.00 (*0-7366-2860-6*, 3567) Books on Tape, Inc.
—Osprey Reef. 1990. 224p. 17.95 o.p. (*0-88184-635-X*, Carroll & Graf Pubs.) Avalon Publishing Group.
—Point Deception. 1992. 288p. 19.95 o.p. (*0-88184-798-4*, Carroll & Graf Pubs.) Avalon Publishing Group.

**NORE, PHILIP (FICTITIOUS CHARACTER)—FICTION**

Francis, Dick. Reflex. unabr. ed. 2000. audio 34.95 (*1-57270-135-8*, N81135u, Audio Editions Mystery Masters) Audio Partners Publishing Corp.
—Reflex. 1997. mass mkt. (*0-449-45727-3*); 1986. 352p. mass mkt. 5.99 o.s.i (*0-449-21173-8*); 1986. mass mkt. 4.50 o.p. (*0-449-21036-7*); 1984. mass mkt. 3.95 o.p. (*0-449-20713-7*); 1982. mass mkt. 3.50 o.p. (*0-449-24500-4*) Ballantine Bks. (Fawcett).
—Reflex. 2003. 304p. mass mkt. 6.99 (*0-515-13509-7*, Jove) Berkley Publishing Group.
—Reflex. l.t. ed. 1981. (General Ser.). lib. bdg. 14.95 o.p. (*0-8161-3255-0*, Macmillan Reference USA) Gale Group.
—Reflex. 1981. 288p. 11.95 o.p. (*0-399-12598-1*) Putnam Publishing Group, The.

**NORGREN, CHRIS (FICTITIOUS CHARACTER)—FICTION**

Elkins, Aaron. A Deceptive Clarity. 1993. mass mkt. 5.99 o.s.i (*0-449-14900-5*, Fawcett) Ballantine Bks.
—A Deceptive Clarity. 1989. 2.99 o.p. (*0-517-00558-1*) Random Hse. Value Publishing.
—A Deceptive Clarity. 1987. 15.95 o.p. (*0-8027-5666-2*) Walker & Co.
—A Glancing Light. 1994. mass mkt. o.s.i (*0-449-45458-4*); 1992. mass mkt. 4.99 o.s.i (*0-449-14829-7*) Ballantine Bks. (Fawcett).
—A Glancing Light. 1991. 368p. 18.95 o.s.i (*0-684-19278-0*, Macmillan Reference USA) Gale Group.
—Old Scores. unabr. ed. 1995. (Chris Norgren Mystery Ser.: Vol. 3). audio 51.00 (*0-7887-0166-5*, 94391E7) Recorded Bks., LLC.
—Old Scores: A Chris Norgren Mystery. l.t. ed. 1994. 22.95 o.p. (*0-7927-1944-1*); pap. 20.95 o.p. (*0-7927-1943-3*) BBC Audiobooks America.
—Old Scores: A Chris Norgren Mystery. 1994. (Northwest Mysteries Ser.). mass mkt. 5.99 o.s.i (*0-449-14899-8*, Fawcett) Ballantine Bks.
—Old Scores: A Chris Norgren Mystery. 1993. 256p. 20.00 o.p. (*0-684-19551-8*, Macmillan Reference USA) Gale Group.

**NORSTROM, BRYNNA (FICTITIOUS CHARACTER)—FICTION**

Brooks, Betty. Warrior's Destiny. 1995. mass mkt. 4.99 o.s.i (*0-8217-4934-X*); 384p. mass mkt. 4.99 o.s.i (*0-8217-4999-4*) Kensington Publishing Corp.

**NORTH, HUGH (FICTITIOUS CHARACTER)—FICTION**

Mason, Francis Van Wyck. Saigon Singer. 1976. 24.95 (*0-89190-352-6*) Amereon, Ltd.
—Two Tickets for Tangier. 1976. 23.95 (*0-89190-354-2*) Amereon, Ltd.

**NORTH, JERRY (FICTITIOUS CHARACTER)—FICTION**

Lockeridge, Frances & Lockeridge, Richard. The Norths Meet Murder. 19.95 (*0-89190-916-8*) Amereon, Ltd.
Lockridge, Frances. Death Has a Small Voice. Date not set. 272p. pap. 8.00 (*0-06-092523-X*) HarperCollins Pubs.
—Death of an Angel. Date not set. 464p. pap. 8.00 (*0-06-092524-8*) HarperCollins Pubs.
—A Key to Death. Date not set. pap. 8.00 (*0-06-092522-1*) HarperCollins Pubs.
—Murder Comes First. Date not set. pap. 8.00 (*0-06-092521-3*) HarperCollins Pubs.
—Murder in a Hurry. Date not set. 352p. pap. 8.00 (*0-06-092520-5*) HarperCollins Pubs.
—Murder Is Served. 1987. mass mkt. 3.50 o.s.i (*0-671-63988-9*, Pocket) Simon & Schuster.
Lockridge, Frances & Lockridge, R. Death Takes a Bow. (Mr. & Mrs. North Mystery Ser.). 21.95 (*0-89190-918-4*) Amereon, Ltd.
Lockridge, Frances & Lockridge, Richard. Curtain for a Jester. 1975. (Mr. & Mrs. North Ser.). 222p. reprint ed. lib. bdg. 21.95 (*0-89190-904-4*, Rivercity Pr.) Amereon, Ltd.
—Dead As a Dinosaur. 1975. (Mr. & Mrs. North Ser.). 185p. reprint ed. lib. bdg. 21.95 (*0-89190-903-6*, Rivercity Pr.) Amereon, Ltd.
—Dead As a Dinosaur. 1993. reprint ed. lib. bdg. 17.95 (*1-56849-208-1*) Buccaneer Bks., Inc.
—Dead As a Dinosaur. 1994. (Mr. & Mrs. North Mystery Ser.). 192p. reprint ed. pap. 8.00 o.p. (*0-06-092510-8*) HarperCollins Pubs.
—Death Has a Small Voice. 1993. reprint ed. lib. bdg. 17.95 (*1-56849-209-X*) Buccaneer Bks., Inc.
—Death of a Tall Man. 1994. 256p. reprint ed. pap. 8.00 o.p. (*0-06-092513-2*, Perennial) HarperTrade.
—Death of an Angel. 1975. (Mr. & Mrs. North Ser.). reprint ed. lib. bdg. 21.95 (*0-89190-907-9*, Rivercity Pr.) Amereon, Ltd.
—Death Takes a Bow. 1994. 288p. reprint ed. pap. 8.00 o.p. (*0-06-092516-7*, Perennial) HarperTrade.
—The Dishonest Murderer. 1975. 223p. reprint ed. lib. bdg. 21.95 (*0-89190-901-X*) Amereon, Ltd.
—The Dishonest Murderer. 1994. (Mr. & Mrs. North Mystery Ser.). 224p. reprint ed. pap. 8.00 o.p. (*0-06-092509-4*) HarperCollins Pubs.
—Hanged for a Sheep. 1994. (Mr. & Mrs. North Mystery). 304p. reprint ed. pap. 8.00 o.p. (*0-06-092488-8*, Perennial) HarperTrade.
—The Judge Is Reversed. 1975. reprint ed. lib. bdg. 21.95 (*0-89190-910-9*, Rivercity Pr.) Amereon, Ltd.
—A Key to Death. 1975. 224p. reprint ed. lib. bdg. 21.95 (*0-89190-906-0*, Rivercity Pr.) Amereon, Ltd.
—Killing the Goose. 1994. 256p. reprint ed. pap. 8.00 o.p. (*0-06-092515-9*, Perennial) HarperTrade.
—Long Skeleton. 1975. reprint ed. lib. bdg. 21.95 (*0-89190-909-5*, Rivercity Pr.) Amereon, Ltd.
—Murder by the Book. 1983. mass mkt. 2.95 o.s.i (*0-671-47333-6*, Pocket) Simon & Schuster.
—Murder Comes First. 1975. 192p. reprint ed. lib. bdg. 22.95 (*0-89190-902-8*, Rivercity Pr.) Amereon, Ltd.
—Murder Is Served. 1994. (Mr. & Mrs. North Mystery Ser.). 240p. reprint ed. pap. 8.00 o.p. (*0-06-092511-6*, Perennial) HarperTrade.
—Murder Is Suggested. 1987. (Mr.and Mrs. North Mystery Ser.: No. 11). 224p. mass mkt. 3.50 o.s.i (*0-671-65728-3*, Pocket) Simon & Schuster.
—Murder Out of Turn. 18.95 (*0-89190-914-1*) Amereon, Ltd.
—Murder Out of Turn. 1994. (Mr. & Mrs. North Mystery). 304p. reprint ed. pap. 8.00 o.p. (*0-06-092489-6*, HarperTorch) Morrow/Avon.
—The Norths Meet Murder. 1994. (Mr. & Mrs. North Mystery Ser.). 320p. reprint ed. pap. 8.00 o.p. (*0-06-092490-X*, Perennial) HarperTrade.
—Payoff for the Banker. 1994. 224p. reprint ed. pap. 8.00 o.p. (*0-06-092514-0*, Perennial) HarperTrade.
—A Pinch of Poison. 18.95 (*0-89190-917-6*) Amereon, Ltd.
—A Pinch of Poison. 1994. (Mr. & Mrs. North Mystery). 320p. reprint ed. pap. 8.00 o.p. (*0-06-092498-5*, Perennial) HarperTrade.
—Voyage into Violence: A Mr. & Mrs. North Mystery. 1975. reprint ed. lib. bdg. 21.95 (*0-89190-908-7*, Rivercity Pr.) Amereon, Ltd.
Lockridge, Richard & Lockridge, Frances. Death of an Angel. 1988. (Mr.and Mrs. North Mystery Ser.). 224p. mass mkt. 3.50 o.s.i (*0-671-65665-1*, Pocket) Simon & Schuster.
—Death on an Aisle. 1986. pap. 9.95 o.p. (*0-553-06512-2*) Bantam Bks.
—Death Takes a Bow. 1982. (Mr. & Mrs. North Ser.: No. 4). 240p. mass mkt. 2.95 o.s.i (*0-671-44337-2*, Pocket) Simon & Schuster.
—The Judge Is Reversed. 1983. mass mkt. 2.95 o.s.i (*0-671-44338-0*, Pocket) Simon & Schuster.
—Killing the Goose. 22.95 (*0-89190-911-7*) Amereon, Ltd.
—Murder Comes First. 1982. (Mr.and Mrs. North Mystery Ser.). mass mkt. 2.95 o.s.i (*0-671-44335-6*, Pocket) Simon & Schuster.
—Murder Has Its Points. 1984. (Mr.and Mrs. North Mystery Ser.). 224p. mass mkt. 2.95 o.s.i (*0-671-47331-X*, Pocket) Simon & Schuster.
—Murder in a Hurry. 1983. mass mkt. 2.95 o.s.i (*0-671-44436-0*, Pocket) Simon & Schuster.

—Voyage into Violence: A Mr. & Mrs. North Mystery. 1983. (Mr.and Mrs. North Mystery Ser.). 224p. mass mkt. 2.95 o.s.i (*0-671-47329-8*, Pocket) Simon & Schuster.

Lockridge, Richard & Lockridge, Francis Louis Davis. Death Has a Small Voice. 1976. 20.95 (*0-89190-905-2*) Amereon, Ltd.

Mr. & Mrs. North: Case of the Missing Sparkler. audio National Recording Co.

**NORTH, PAM (FICTITIOUS CHARACTER)—FICTION**

Lockeridge, Frances & Lockeridge, Richard. The Norths Meet Murder. 19.95 (*0-89190-916-8*) Amereon, Ltd.

Lockridge, Frances. Death Has a Small Voice. Date not set. 272p. pap. 8.00 (*0-06-092523-X*) HarperCollins Pubs.

—Death of an Angel. Date not set. 464p. pap. 8.00 (*0-06-092524-8*) HarperCollins Pubs.

—A Key to Death. Date not set. pap. 8.00 (*0-06-092522-1*) HarperCollins Pubs.

—Murder Comes First. Date not set. pap. 8.00 (*0-06-092521-3*) HarperCollins Pubs.

—Murder in a Hurry. Date not set. 352p. pap. 8.00 (*0-06-092520-5*) HarperCollins Pubs.

—Murder Is Served. 1987. mass mkt. 3.50 o.s.i (*0-671-63988-9*, Pocket) Simon & Schuster.

Lockridge, Frances & Lockridge, R. Death Takes a Bow. (Mr. & Mrs. North Mystery Ser.). 21.95 (*0-89190-918-4*) Amereon, Ltd.

Lockridge, Frances & Lockridge, Richard. Curtain for a Jester. 1975. (Mr. & Mrs. North Ser.). 222p. reprint ed. lib. bdg. 21.95 (*0-89190-904-4*, Rivercity Pr.) Amereon, Ltd.

—Dead As a Dinosaur. 1975. (Mr. & Mrs. North Ser.). 185p. reprint ed. lib. bdg. 21.95 (*0-89190-903-6*, Rivercity Pr.) Amereon, Ltd.

—Dead As a Dinosaur. 1993. reprint ed. lib. bdg. 17.95 (*1-56849-208-1*) Buccaneer Bks., Inc.

—Dead As a Dinosaur. 1994. (Mr. & Mrs. North Mystery Ser.). 192p. reprint ed. pap. 8.00 o.p. (*0-06-092510-8*) HarperCollins Pubs.

—Death Has a Small Voice. 1993. reprint ed. lib. bdg. 17.95 (*1-56849-209-X*) Buccaneer Bks., Inc.

—Death of a Tall Man. 1994. 256p. reprint ed. pap. 8.00 o.p. (*0-06-092513-2*, Perennial) HarperTrade.

—Death of an Angel. 1975. (Mr. & Mrs. North Ser.). reprint ed. lib. bdg. 21.95 (*0-89190-907-9*, Rivercity Pr.) Amereon, Ltd.

—Death Takes a Bow. 1994. 288p. reprint ed. pap. 8.00 o.p. (*0-06-092516-7*, Perennial) HarperTrade.

—The Dishonest Murderer. 1975. 223p. reprint ed. lib. bdg. 21.95 (*0-89190-901-X*) Amereon, Ltd.

—The Dishonest Murderer. 1994. (Mr. & Mrs. North Mystery Ser.). 224p. reprint ed. pap. 8.00 o.p. (*0-06-092509-4*) HarperCollins Pubs.

—Hanged for a Sheep. 1994. (Mr. & Mrs. North Mystery). 304p. reprint ed. pap. 8.00 o.p. (*0-06-092488-8*, Perennial) HarperTrade.

—The Judge Is Reversed. 1975. reprint ed. lib. bdg. 21.95 (*0-89190-910-9*, Rivercity Pr.) Amereon, Ltd.

—A Key to Death. 1975. 224p. reprint ed. lib. bdg. 21.95 (*0-89190-906-0*, Rivercity Pr.) Amereon, Ltd.

—Killing the Goose. 1994. 256p. reprint ed. pap. 8.00 o.p. (*0-06-092515-9*, Perennial) HarperTrade.

—Long Skeleton. 1975. reprint ed. lib. bdg. 21.95 (*0-89190-909-5*, Rivercity Pr.) Amereon, Ltd.

—Murder by the Book. 1983. mass mkt. 2.95 o.s.i (*0-671-47333-6*, Pocket) Simon & Schuster.

—Murder Comes First. 1975. 192p. reprint ed. lib. bdg. 22.95 (*0-89190-902-8*, Rivercity Pr.) Amereon, Ltd.

—Murder Is Served. 1994. (Mr. & Mrs. North Mystery Ser.). 240p. reprint ed. pap. 8.00 o.p. (*0-06-092511-6*, Perennial) HarperTrade.

—Murder Is Suggested. 1987. (Mr.and Mrs. North Mystery Ser.: No. 11). 224p. mass mkt. 3.50 o.s.i (*0-671-65728-3*, Pocket) Simon & Schuster.

—Murder Out of Turn. 18.95 (*0-89190-914-1*) Amereon, Ltd.

—Murder Out of Turn. 1994. (Mr. & Mrs. North Mystery). 304p. reprint ed. pap. 8.00 o.p. (*0-06-092489-6*, HarperTorch) Morrow/Avon.

—The Norths Meet Murder. 1994. (Mr. & Mrs. North Mystery Ser.). 320p. reprint ed. pap. 8.00 o.p. (*0-06-092490-X*, Perennial) HarperTrade.

—Payoff for the Banker. 1994. 224p. reprint ed. pap. 8.00 o.p. (*0-06-092514-0*, Perennial) HarperTrade.

—A Pinch of Poison. 18.95 (*0-89190-917-6*) Amereon, Ltd.

—A Pinch of Poison. 1994. (Mr. & Mrs. North Mystery). 320p. reprint ed. pap. 8.00 o.p. (*0-06-092491-8*, Perennial) HarperTrade.

—Voyage into Violence: A Mr. & Mrs. North Mystery. 1975. reprint ed. lib. bdg. 21.95 (*0-89190-908-7*, Rivercity Pr.) Amereon, Ltd.

Lockridge, Richard & Lockridge, Frances. Death of an Angel. 1988. (Mr.and Mrs. North Mystery Ser.). 224p. mass mkt. 3.50 o.s.i (*0-671-65665-1*, Pocket) Simon & Schuster.

—Death on an Aisle. 1986. pap. 9.95 o.p. (*0-553-06512-2*) Bantam Bks.

—Death Takes a Bow. 1982. (Mr. & Mrs. North Ser.: No. 4). 240p. mass mkt. 2.95 o.s.i (*0-671-44337-2*, Pocket) Simon & Schuster.

—The Judge Is Reversed. 1983. mass mkt. 2.95 o.s.i (*0-671-44338-0*, Pocket) Simon & Schuster.

—Killing the Goose. 22.95 (*0-89190-911-7*) Amereon, Ltd.

—Murder Comes First. 1982. (Mr.and Mrs. North Mystery Ser.). mass mkt. 2.95 o.s.i (*0-671-44335-6*, Pocket) Simon & Schuster.

—Murder Has Its Points. 1984. (Mr.and Mrs. North Mystery Ser.). 224p. mass mkt. 2.95 o.s.i (*0-671-47331-X*, Pocket) Simon & Schuster.

—Murder in a Hurry. 1983. mass mkt. 2.95 o.s.i (*0-671-44436-0*, Pocket) Simon & Schuster.

—Voyage into Violence: A Mr. & Mrs. North Mystery. 1983. (Mr.and Mrs. North Mystery Ser.). 224p. mass mkt. 2.95 o.s.i (*0-671-47329-8*, Pocket) Simon & Schuster.

Lockridge, Richard & Lockridge, Francis Louis Davis. Death Has a Small Voice. 1976. 20.95 (*0-89190-905-2*) Amereon, Ltd.

Mr. & Mrs. North: Case of the Missing Sparkler. audio National Recording Co.

**NOVA, DAVID (FICTITIOUS CHARACTER)—FICTION**

Blum, Bill. The Face of Justice. 1999. pap. 19.95 (*0-525-93906-7*); 1998. 400p. mass mkt. 6.99 o.s.i (*0-451-40803-9*, Onyx) NAL.

**NOVA, LISA (FICTITIOUS CHARACTER)—FICTION**

Grimson, Todd. Brand New Cherry Flavor. 1996. 368p. mass mkt. 20.00 o.p. (*0-06-105233-7*) HarperCollins Pubs.

—Brand New Cherry Flavor. 1997. mass mkt. 13.00 o.s.i (*0-06-105320-1*, Eos) Morrow/Avon.

**NOVAK, JACK (FICTITIOUS CHARACTER)—FICTION**

Hunt, E. Howard. Islamorada. 1995. 240p. 20.95 o.s.i (*1-55611-438-9*) Fine, Donald I. Bks.

—Ixtapa. 1994. (Jack Novak Ser.). 224p. 19.95 o.p. (*1-55611-404-4*) Fine, Donald I. Bks.

—Izmir: A Jack Novak Adventure. 1996. (Jack Novak Adventure Ser.). 240p. 21.95 o.p. (*1-55611-474-5*) Fine, Donald I. Bks.

—Sonora. 2000. 315p. 23.95 (*0-312-87205-4*, Forge Bks.) Doherty, Tom Assocs., LLC.

—Sonora. 1999. pap. 24.95 (*1-55611-535-0*) Fine, Donald I. Bks.

**NOVAK, M. J. (FICTITIOUS CHARACTER)—FICTION**

Gerritsen, Tess. Peggy Sue Got Murdered. 1994. 288p. mass mkt. 5.99 o.p. (*0-06-108270-8*) HarperCollins Pubs.

—Peggy Sue Got Murdered. 1998. 288p. 24.00 o.p. (*0-7278-5304-X*) Severn Hse. Pubs., Ltd.

**NOVEMBER MAN (FICTITIOUS CHARACTER)—FICTION**

*see Devereaux (Fictitious Character: Granger)—Fiction*

**NOWEK, GREGORI (FICTITIOUS CHARACTER)—FICTION**

White, Robin. Siberian Light. 1998. 528p. mass mkt. 6.99 (*0-440-22460-8*) Dell Publishing.

**NUDGER, ALO (FICTITIOUS CHARACTER)—FICTION**

Lutz, John. Buyer Beware. 1992. (Mystery Scene Bk.). 192p. pap. 3.95 o.p. (*0-88184-840-9*, Carroll & Graf Pubs.) Avalon Publishing Group.

—Buyer Beware. l.t. ed. 1988. pap. 17.95 o.p. (*1-55504-671-1*); lib. bdg. 19.95 o.p. (*1-55504-690-8*) BBC Audiobooks America.

—Buyer Beware. 1976. 6.95 o.p. (*0-399-11811-X*) Putnam Publishing Group, The.

—Dancer's Debt. 1988. 256p. 16.95 o.p. (*0-312-00028-6*) St. Martin's Pr.

—Death by Jury: An Alo Nudger Mystery. 1995. 352p. 23.95 o.p. (*0-312-13613-7*, Saint Martin's Minotaur) St. Martin's Pr.

—Diamond Eyes. 1990. 224p. 15.95 o.p. (*0-312-05074-7*, Saint Martin's Minotaur) St. Martin's Pr.

—Nightlines: The First Alo Nudger Mystery. 1987. 352p. pap. 3.95 o.p. (*0-8125-0648-0*, Tor Bks.) Doherty, Tom Assocs., LLC.

—Nightlines: The First Alo Nudger Mystery. 1984. 13.95 o.p. (*0-312-57324-3*) St. Martin's Pr.

—Oops! unabr. ed. 1998. audio 40.00 (*0-7366-4221-8*, 4721) Books on Tape, Inc.

—Oops! l.t. ed. 1998. (Large Print Book Ser.). pap. 23.95 o.p. (*1-56895-653-3*, Wheeler Publishing, Inc.) Gale Group.

—Oops! 1997. 304p. 22.95 o.p. (*0-312-18152-3*, Saint Martin's Minotaur) St. Martin's Pr.

—Ride the Lightning. 1990. mass mkt. 3.95 (*0-8125-0642-1*, Tor Bks.) Doherty, Tom Assocs., LLC.

—Ride the Lightning. 1987. 256p. 15.95 o.p. (*0-312-00182-7*) St. Martin's Pr.

—The Right to Sing the Blues. 1988. 256p. pap. 2.95 o.p. (*0-8125-0646-4*, Tor Bks.) Doherty, Tom Assocs., LLC.

—The Right to Sing the Blues. 1985. 256p. 14.95 o.p. (*0-312-68235-2*) St. Martin's Pr.

—The Right to Sing the Blues. E-Book 9.99 (*1-58824-387-7*); 2001. 256p. pap. 14.00 (*0-7434-1288-5*) ibooks, Inc.

—Thicker Than Blood: An Alo Nudger Mystery. Set. unabr. ed. 1999. audio 54.95 (*0-7927-2314-7*, CSL203, Chivers Sound Library) BBC Audiobooks America.

—Thicker Than Blood: An Alo Nudger Mystery. 1993. 272p. 19.95 o.p. (*0-312-09922-3*, Saint Martin's Minotaur) St. Martin's Pr.

—Time Exposure. 1990. 2.99 o.p. (*0-517-05936-3*) Random Hse. Value Publishing.

—Time Exposure. 1989. 16.95 o.p. (*0-312-02990-X*, Saint Martin's Minotaur) St. Martin's Pr.

# O

**O., OPHELIA (FICTITIOUS CHARACTER)—FICTION**

*see Ophelia O. (Fictitious Character)—Fiction*

**OAKES, BLACKFORD (FICTITIOUS CHARACTER)—FICTION**

Buckley, William F., Jr. The Blackford Oakes Reader. 1995. 340p. 18.95 o.p. (*0-8362-8098-9*) Andrews McMeel Publishing.

—The Blackford Oakes Reader, Vol. 1. 1999. 312p. pap. 18.95 (*1-58348-383-7*) iUniverse, Inc.

—High Jinx. unabr. ed. 1990. audio 39.95 (*0-7861-0106-7*, 752369) Blackstone Audio Bks., Inc.

—High Jinx. unabr. collector's ed. 1995. (Blackford Oakes Ser.). audio 48.00 (*0-7366-2913-0*, 3610) Books on Tape, Inc.

—High Jinx. 1997. (Blackford Oakes Novel Ser.). 320p. reprint ed. pap. 10.95 (*1-888952-52-0*) Cumberland Hse. Publishing.

—High Jinx. 1987. 352p. mass mkt. 4.50 o.s.i (*0-440-13957-0*) Dell Publishing.

—High Jinx. 1986. 264p. 16.95 o.p. (*0-385-19443-9*) Doubleday Publishing.

—Marco Polo, If You Can. unabr. collector's ed. 1982. (Blackford Oakes Ser.). audio 48.00 (*0-7366-0683-1*, 1643) Books on Tape, Inc.

—Marco Polo, If You Can. 1996. (Blackford Oakes Novel Ser.). 288p. reprint ed. pap. 10.95 (*1-888952-11-3*) Cumberland Hse. Publishing.

—Marco Polo, If You Can. 1982. 275p. 13.95 o.p. (*0-385-15232-9*) Doubleday Publishing.

—Marco Polo, If You Can. 1983. pap. 3.95 (*0-380-61424-3*, Avon Bks.) Morrow/Avon.

—Marco Polo, If You Can. l.t. ed. 1982. 414p. reprint ed. 14.95 o.p. (*0-89621-361-7*) Thorndike Pr.

—Mongoose R. I. P. A Blackford Oakes Novel. unabr. ed. 1992. audio 56.95 (*0-7861-0097-4*, 1090) Blackstone Audio Bks., Inc.

—Mongoose R. I. P. A Blackford Oakes Novel. 1998. (Blackford Oakes Novel Ser.). 376p. reprint ed. pap. 12.95 (*1-888952-72-5*) Cumberland Hse. Publishing.

—Mongoose R. I. P. A Blackford Oakes Novel. 1989. 384p. reprint ed. mass mkt. 4.50 o.s.i (*0-440-20231-0*) Dell Publishing.

—Mongoose R. I. P. A Blackford Oakes Novel. 1993. 4.99 o.p. (*0-517-10701-5*) Random Hse. Value Publishing.

—Saving the Queen. 1997. (Blackford Oakes Novel Ser.). 320p. reprint ed. pap. 10.95 (*1-888952-27-X*) Cumberland Hse. Publishing.

—Saving the Queen. 1976. 7.95 o.s.i (*0-385-03800-3*) Doubleday Publishing.

—Saving the Queen. 1992. 79p. mass mkt. 5.50 o.p. (*0-06-104148-3*, HarperTorch); 1981. 288p. pap. 3.95 (*0-380-55111-X*, Avon Bks.) Morrow/Avon.

—Saving the Queen. 1977. pap. 2.25 o.s.i (*0-446-89164-9*) Warner Bks., Inc.

—See You Later, Alligator. unabr. collector's ed. 1985. (Blackford Oakes Ser.). audio 64.00 (*0-7366-0489-8*, 1464) Books on Tape, Inc.

—See You Later, Alligator. 1997. (Blackford Oakes Novel Ser.). 320p. reprint ed. pap. 10.95 (*1-888952-51-2*) Cumberland Hse. Publishing.

—See You Later, Alligator. 1986. mass mkt. 3.95 o.s.i (*0-440-17682-4*) Dell Publishing.

—See You Later, Alligator. 1985. 312p. 16.95 o.p. (*0-385-19442-0*) Doubleday Publishing.

—Stained Glass. unabr. ed. audio 47.60 Audio Bk. Co.

—Stained Glass. unabr. collector's ed. 1981. (Blackford Oakes Ser.). audio 48.00 (*0-7366-0338-7*, 1324) Books on Tape, Inc.

—Stained Glass. 1997. (Blackford Oakes Novel Ser.). 320p. reprint ed. pap. 10.95 (*1-888952-29-6*) Cumberland Hse. Publishing.

—Stained Glass. 1978. 13.95 o.p. (*0-385-12542-9*) Doubleday Publishing.

—Stained Glass. 1992. 288p. mass mkt. 5.50 o.p. (*0-06-104149-1*, HarperTorch); 1981. 352p. pap. 3.95 (*0-380-54791-0*, Avon Bks.) Morrow/Avon.

—The Story of Henri Tod. unabr. collector's ed. 1984. (Blackford Oakes Ser.). audio 48.00 (*0-7366-1003-0*, 1936) Books on Tape, Inc.

—The Story of Henri Tod. 1996. (Blackford Oakes Novel Ser.). 320p. reprint ed. pap. 10.95 (*1-888952-12-1*) Cumberland Hse. Publishing.

—The Story of Henri Tod. 1989. 272p. mass mkt. 4.50 o.s.i (*0-440-18327-8*) Dell Publishing.

—The Story of Henri Tod. 1984. 264p. 14.95 o.p. (*0-385-15234-5*) Doubleday Publishing.

—Tucker's Last Stand: A Blackford Oakes Novel. unabr. ed. 1991. audio 44.95 (*0-7861-0225-X*, 1198) Blackstone Audio Bks., Inc.

—Tucker's Last Stand: A Blackford Oakes Novel. unabr. collector's ed. 1991. audio 56.00 (*0-7366-2084-2*, 2890) Books on Tape, Inc.

—Tucker's Last Stand: A Blackford Oakes Novel. 1998. (Blackford Oakes Novel Ser.). 320p. reprint ed. pap. 10.95 (*1-888952-73-3*) Cumberland Hse. Publishing.

—Tucker's Last Stand: A Blackford Oakes Novel. 1992. 352p. mass mkt. 5.99 o.p. (*0-06-104165-3*, HarperTorch) Morrow/Avon.

—Tucker's Last Stand: A Blackford Oakes Novel. 1992. 3.99 o.p. (*0-517-09025-2*) Random Hse. Value Publishing.

—A Very Private Plot: A Blackford Oakes Novel. unabr. ed. 1995. audio 39.95 (*0-7861-0722-7*, 1598) Blackstone Audio Bks., Inc.

—A Very Private Plot: A Blackford Oakes Novel. 1998. (Blackford Oakes Novel Ser.). 256p. reprint ed. pap. 10.95 (*1-888952-74-1*) Cumberland Hse. Publishing.

—A Very Private Plot: A Blackford Oakes Novel. 1994. 272p. 20.00 o.p. (*0-688-12795-9*, Morrow, William & Co.) Morrow/Avon.

—Who's on First? unabr. collector's ed. 1982. (Blackford Oakes Ser.). audio 48.00 (*0-7366-0682-3*, 1642) Books on Tape, Inc.

—Who's on First? 1997. (Blackford Oakes Novel Ser.). 320p. reprint ed. pap. 10.95 (*1-888952-28-8*) Cumberland Hse. Publishing.

—Who's on First? 1980. 13.95 o.p. (*0-385-14681-7*) Doubleday Publishing.

—Who's on First? 1992. 304p. mass mkt. 5.50 o.p. (*0-06-104150-5*, HarperTorch); 1981. 288p. pap. 3.95 o.p. (*0-380-52555-0*, Avon Bks.) Morrow/Avon.

**OATLAND, SARAH (FICTITIOUS CHARACTER)—FICTION**

Carlon, Patricia. The Whispering Wall. 1998. 208p. pap. 12.00 (*1-56947-111-8*) Soho Pr., Inc.

**OBI-WAN KENOBI (FICTITIOUS CHARACTER)—FICTION**

*see Kenobi, Obi-Wan (Fictitious Character)—Fiction*

**O'BRIEN, KALI (FICTITIOUS CHARACTER)—FICTION**

Jacobs, Jonnie. Cold Justice. 2003. 480p. mass mkt. 6.99 (*0-7860-1543-8*, Pinnacle Bks.); 2002. 34p. 23.00 (*1-57566-827-0*, Kensington Bks.) Kensington Publishing Corp.

—Evidence of Guilt. (Kali O'Brien Mystery Ser.). 1998. 384p. mass mkt. 5.99 (*1-57566-279-5*); 1997. 368p. 18.95 o.p. (*1-57566-141-1*) Kensington Publishing Corp. (Kensington Bks.).

—Intent to Harm. 2003. 352p. 22.00 (*1-57566-829-7*, Kensington Bks.) Kensington Publishing Corp.

—Motion to Dismiss. (Kali O'Brien Mystery Ser.). 2000. 400p. mass mkt. 5.99 (*1-57566-543-3*); 1999. 304p. 22.00 (*1-57566-395-3*) Kensington Publishing Corp.

—Motion to Dismiss. 2002. 284p. per. 17.95 (*0-7592-1227-9*) ereads.com.

—Shadow of Doubt. (Kali O'Brien Mystery Ser.). 1997. 308p. mass mkt. 5.50 o.s.i (*1-57566-146-2*, Kensington Bks.); 1996. 304p. pap. 18.95 o.p. (*1-57566-017-2*); 1996. mass mkt. 18.95 o.s.i (*0-8217-5254-5*) Kensington Publishing Corp.

—Witness for the Defense. 2002. 432p. mass mkt. 6.99 (*1-57566-828-9*, Kensington Bks.); 2001. 336p. 23.00 o.s.i (*1-57566-643-X*) Kensington Publishing Corp.

**O'BRIEN, MILES (FICTITIOUS CHARACTER)—FICTION**

Carey, Diane L. What You Leave Behind. 1999. (Star Trek Deep Space Nine Ser.). 224p. pap. 6.50 (*0-671-03476-6*, Star Trek) Simon & Schuster.

Garland, Mark. Trial by Error. 1997. (Star Trek Deep Space Nine Ser.: No. 21). (Illus.). 304p. pap. 5.99 (*0-671-00251-1*, Star Trek) Simon & Schuster.

Hugh, Dafydd ab. Vengeance. 1998. (Star Trek Deep Space Nine Ser.: No. 22). 304p. pap. 6.50 (*0-671-00468-9*, Star Trek) Simon & Schuster.

Schofield, Sandy. The Big Game. 1994. (Star Trek Deep Space Nine Ser.: No. 4). E-Book 6.99 (*0-7434-1223-0*, Star Trek) Simon & Schuster.

—The Big Game. Ordover, John, ed. 1993. (Star Trek Deep Space Nine Ser.: No. 4). 288p. mass mkt. 5.50 (*0-671-88030-6*, Star Trek) Simon & Schuster.

**OCHS, CHARLIE (FICTITIOUS CHARACTER)—FICTION**

Abrahams, Peter. Revolution, No. 9. 2002. 320p. mass mkt. 6.99 (*0-345-44580-5*, Fawcett) Ballantine Bks.

—Revolution, No. 9. 1992. 336p. 18.95 o.p. (*0-89296-481-2*) Mysterious Pr.

—Revolution, No. 9. 1993. 320p. mass mkt. 5.50 o.p. (*0-446-40156-0*, Mysterious Pr. Paperback Bks.) Warner Bks., Inc.

**O'CLARE, MAIREAD (FICTITIOUS CHARACTER)—FICTION**

Devane, Terry. Juror Number Eleven: A Novel. 2003. 336p. mass mkt. 6.99 (*0-425-19066-8*) Berkley Publishing Group.

—Juror Number Eleven: A Novel. 2002. 320p. 24.95 o.s.i (*0-399-14886-8*) Penguin Group (USA) Inc.

—A Stain upon the Robe. 2004. 352p. mass mkt. 6.99 (*0-425-19742-5*) Berkley Publishing Group.

—A Stain upon the Robe. 2003. 304p. 24.95 (*0-399-15108-7*) Putnam Publishing Group, The.

—Uncommon Justice. 2002. 352p. reprint ed. mass mkt. 6.99 (*0-425-18424-2*) Berkley Publishing Group.

—Uncommon Justice. 2001. 240p. 24.95 o.p. (*0-399-14717-9*) Penguin Group (USA) Inc.

**O'CONNER, THUNDERBIRD (FICTITIOUS CHARACTER)—FICTION**

Deitz, Tom. Above the Lower Sky. 2000. 23.00 (*0-380-97244-1*); 1996. mass mkt. 5.99 (*0-380-77483-6*, Avon Bks.); 1994. 23.00 (*0-688-13716-4*, Avon Bks.) Morrow/Avon.

—The Demons in the Green. 1996. 432p. (Orig.). mass mkt. 5.99 (*0-380-78271-5*, Avon Bks.) Morrow/Avon.

**O'CONNOR, CORK (FICTITIOUS CHARACTER)—FICTION**

Krueger, William Kent. Boundary Waters. (Cork O'Connor Mysteries Ser.). 1999. 336p. 23.00 (*0-671-01698-9*, Atria); 2000. 416p. reprint ed. mass mkt. 6.99 (*0-671-01699-7*, Pocket Star) Simon & Schuster.

—Iron Lake: A Cork O'Connor Mystery. 1999. (Illus.). 464p. mass mkt. 6.99 (*0-671-01697-0*, Pocket Star); 1998. E-Book 23.00 (*0-671-03690-4*, Atria); 1998. (Cork O'Connor Mysteries Ser.: Vol. 1). 320p. 23.00 (*0-671-01696-2*, Atria) Simon & Schuster.

—Iron Lake: A Cork O'Connor Mystery. l.t. ed. 2001. 584p. 29.95 (*0-7862-3174-2*) Thorndike Pr.

—Purgatory Ridge: A Cork O'Connor Mystery. 2001. (Illus.). 368p. 23.95 (*0-671-04753-1*, Atria); 2002. 448p. reprint ed. mass mkt. 6.99 (*0-671-04754-X*, Pocket Star) Simon & Schuster.

—Purgatory Ridge: A Cork O'Connor Mystery. l.t. ed. 2001. (Americana Ser.). 627p. 30.95 (*0-7862-3213-7*) Thorndike Pr.

**O'CONNOR, DALLAS (FICTITIOUS CHARACTER)—FICTION**

Green, Chloe. Designed to Die. (Dallas O'Connor Mysteries Ser.). 2002. 288p. mass mkt. 5.99 o.s.i (*0-7582-0180-X*); 2001. (Illus.). 256p. 22.00 o.s.i (*1-57566-665-0*) Kensington Publishing Corp.

—Fashion Victim. 2003. mass mkt. 5.99 (*1-57566-716-9*); 2002. 288p. 22.00 (*1-57566-715-0*) Kensington Publishing Corp. (Kensington Bks.).

—Going Out in Style. 2000. (Dallas O'Connor Mysteries Ser.). 316p. 20.00 o.s.i (*1-57566-574-3*) Kensington Publishing Corp.

**O'CONNOR, KIERAN (FICTITIOUS CHARACTER)—FICTION**

Allman, Kevin. Hot Shot. 1998. 256p. 22.95 (*0-312-16866-7*, Saint Martin's Minotaur) St. Martin's Pr.

**O'CONNOR, RACHEL (FICTITIOUS CHARACTER)—FICTION**

Freeman, Mary. Bleeding Heart. 2000. (Gardening Mysteries Ser.). 288p. mass mkt. 5.99 o.s.i (*0-425-17669-X*) Berkley Publishing Group.

—Devil's Trumpet. 1999. (Gardening Mysteries Ser.). 272p. (Orig.). mass mkt. 5.99 o.s.i (*0-425-16821-2*, Prime Crime) Berkley Publishing Group.

Freeman, Mary E. Wilkins. Deadly Nightshade. 1999. (Gardening Mysteries Ser.). 224p. mass mkt. 5.99 o.s.i (*0-425-17196-5*, Prime Crime) Berkley Publishing Group.

**O'DELL, KENDALL (FICTITIOUS CHARACTER)—FICTION**

Nobel, Sylvia. Deadly Sanctuary. Lebowitz, Max, ed. 1998. (Kendall O'Dell Mysteries Ser.). (Illus.). iii, 360p. pap. 15.95 (*0-9661105-7-9*) Nite Owl Bks.

—The Devil's Cradle. Williams, Jerry R., ed. l.t. ed. 1999. (Kendall O'Dell Mystery Ser.). (Illus.). 445p. pap. 17.95 (*0-9661105-8-7*) Nite Owl Bks.

**ODO (FICTITIOUS CHARACTER)—FICTION**

Betancourt, John G. The Heart of the Warrior. 1996. (Star Trek Deep Space Nine Ser.: No. 17). 288p. pap. 5.99 (*0-671-00239-2*, Star Trek) Simon & Schuster.

Carey, Diane L. The Search. 1994. (Star Trek Deep Space Nine Ser.). 272p. mass mkt. 5.50 (*0-671-50604-8*, Star Trek) Simon & Schuster.

—What You Leave Behind. 1999. (Star Trek Deep Space Nine Ser.). 224p. pap. 6.50 (*0-671-03476-6*, Star Trek) Simon & Schuster.

David, Peter. The Siege. 1993. (Star Trek Deep Space Nine Ser.: No. 2). E-Book 6.99 (*0-7434-1221-4*); 288p. mass mkt. 5.50 (*0-671-87083-1*) Simon & Schuster. (Star Trek).

Dillard, J. M., et al. Emissary; The Siege; Bloodletter; The Big Game; Betrayal, 5 bks. 1997. (Star Trek). pap. text 0.95 o.p. (*0-8359-1492-5*) Globe Fearon Educational Publishing.

Hugh, Dafydd ab. The Conquered No. 1: Rebels. 1999. (Star Trek Deep Space Nine Ser.: No. 24). 256p. pap. 6.50 o.s.i (*0-671-01140-5*, Star Trek) Simon & Schuster.

—Fallen Heroes. (Star Trek Deep Space Nine Ser.: No. 5). 1999. E-Book 6.50 (*0-671-04114-2*); 1994. E-Book 6.99 (*0-7434-1224-9*) Simon & Schuster. (Star Trek).

—Fallen Heroes. Ordover, John, ed. 1994. (Star Trek Deep Space Nine Ser.: No. 5). 288p. mass mkt. 5.50 (*0-671-88459-X*, Star Trek) Simon & Schuster.

—Fallen Heroes. abr. ed. 1994. (Star Trek Deep Space Nine Ser.: No. 5). audio 16.00 (*0-671-89182-0*, Simon & Schuster Audioworks) Simon & Schuster Audio.

—Fallen Heroes Star Trek Continuity. 1999. 12.99 (*0-671-02166-4*, Star Trek) Simon & Schuster.

—Rebels: The Conquered. (Star Trek Deep Space Nine Ser.: No. 24). E-Book 6.99 (*0-7434-2055-1*, Star Trek) Simon & Schuster.

—Vengeance. 1998. (Star Trek Deep Space Nine Ser.: No. 22). 304p. pap. 6.50 (*0-671-00468-9*, Star Trek) Simon & Schuster.

Jeter, K. W. Warped. 1996. (Star Trek Deep Space Nine Ser.). 352p. mass mkt. 5.99 (*0-671-56781-0*, Star Trek) Simon & Schuster.

—Warped. Ryan, Kevin, ed. 1995. (Star Trek Deep Space Nine Ser.). 352p. 22.00 o.p. (*0-671-87252-4*, Star Trek) Simon & Schuster.

—Warped. abr. ed. (Star Trek Deep Space Nine Ser.). 1999. audio 9.98 (*0-671-04504-0*); 1995. 16.00 incl. audio (*0-671-52120-9*); 1995. 16.00 incl. audio (*0-671-52120-9*) Simon & Schuster Audio. (Simon & Schuster Audioworks).

Reeves-Stevens, Judith & Reeves-Stevens, Garfield. Millennium No. 1: The Fall of Terok Nor. 2000. (Star Trek Deep Space Nine Ser.). E-Book 6.99 (*0-7434-0679-6*); (Star Trek Deep Space Nine: Vol. 1). 464p. pap. 6.50 o.s.i (*0-671-02401-9*) Simon & Schuster. (Star Trek).

—Millennium No. 1: The Fall of Terok Nor. abr. ed. 2000. (Star Trek Ser. ). audio 18.00 (*0-7435-0010-5*, Simon & Schuster Audioworks) Simon & Schuster Audio.

Schofield, Sandy. The Big Game. 1994. (Star Trek Deep Space Nine Ser.: No. 4). E-Book 6.99 (*0-7434-1223-0*, Star Trek) Simon & Schuster.

—The Big Game. Ordover, John, ed. 1993. (Star Trek Deep Space Nine Ser.: No. 4). 288p. mass mkt. 5.50 (*0-671-88030-6*, Star Trek) Simon & Schuster.

Shimerman, Armin. The Merchant Prince. 2001. E-Book 23.95 (*1-58945-288-7*) Adobe Systems, Inc.

—The Merchant Prince. 2001. (Illus.). 368p. reprint ed. mass mkt. 6.99 (*0-671-03613-0*, Star Trek); Bk. 2. 2001. 320p. reprint ed. E-Book 6.99 (*0-7434-1748-8*, Star Trek); Bk. 3. 2003. 368p. mass mkt. 7.99 (*0-671-03594-0*, Pocket Star) Simon & Schuster.

Shimerman, Armin & George, David R., III. Star Trek Deep Space Nine: The 34th Rule. abr. ed. 1999. (Star Trek Deep Space Nine Ser.: No. 23). audio 16.85 (*0-671-03358-1*) Ulverscroft Audio (U.S.A.).

—The 34th Rule. 1999. (Star Trek Deep Space Nine Ser.: No. 23). 448p. pap. 6.50 (*0-671-00793-9*, Star Trek) Simon & Schuster.

—The 34th Rule. abr. ed. 1999. (Star Trek Ser. : No. 23). audio 18.00 (*0-671-04395-1*, Simon & Schuster Audioworks) Simon & Schuster Audio.

Shimerman, Armin & Scott, Michael. The Merchant Prince, Book 3. 2003. E-Book (*0-7434-8044-9*, Pocket) Simon & Schuster.

Wright, Susan. The Tempest. 1997. (Star Trek Deep Space Nine Ser.: No. 19). (Illus.). 304p. pap. 5.99 (*0-671-00227-9*, Star Trek) Simon & Schuster.

**O'DONNELL, DANTE (FICTITIOUS CHARACTER)—FICTION**

Leuci, Robert. Fence Jumpers: A Novel. 1996. 403p. pap. 5.99 o.p. (*0-312-95937-0*, St. Martin's Paperbacks); 1995. 338p. 22.95 o.p. (*0-312-13073-2*) St. Martin's Pr.

**O'FLAHERTY, DANNY (FICTITIOUS CHARACTER)—FICTION**

Harrington, Jonathan. The Death of Cousin Rose. 2000. mass mkt. (*0-373-26347-3*, Worldwide Library) Harlequin Enterprises, Ltd.

—The Death of Cousin Rose. 1996. (Danny O'Flaherty Mysteries Ser.). 215p. 19.95 o.p. (*1-885173-06-7*) Write Way Publishing.

—A Great Day for Dying. 2002. (WWL Mystery Ser.: No. 413). 256p. mass mkt. (*0-373-26413-5*, Worldwide Library) Harlequin Enterprises, Ltd.

—The Second Sorrowful Mystery. 2000. (Danny O'Flaherty Mysteries Ser.). 256p. mass mkt. (*0-373-26358-9*, 1-26358-1, Worldwide Library) Harlequin Enterprises, Ltd.

—The Second Sorrowful Mystery. 1999. 240p. 21.95 (*1-885173-37-7*) Write Way Publishing.

**OFSTED, LEE (FICTITIOUS CHARACTER)—FICTION**

Elkins, Charlotte & Elkins, Aaron. A Golf Mystery. 1924. (*0-688-16495-1*); (*0-688-16496-X*) Morrow/Avon. (Morrow, William & Co.).

—Nasty Breaks. unabr. ed. audio 27.95 (*0-7861-1384-7*); 1999. audio 39.95 (*0-7861-1244-1*, 2153) Blackstone Audio Bks., Inc.

—Nasty Breaks. 1997. 240p. 22.00 o.p. (*0-89296-596-7*) Mysterious Pr.

—Nasty Breaks. unabr. ed. 1998. audio 44.00 (*0-7887-2001-5*, 95388E7) Recorded Bks., LLC.

—Nasty Breaks. l.t. ed. 1998. (Cloak & Dagger Ser.). 335p. 27.95 (*0-7862-1445-7*) Thorndike Pr.

—Rotten Lies. 1995. 82p. 19.95 o.p. (*0-89296-598-3*) Mysterious Pr.

—Rotten Lies. 1997. 224p. mass mkt. 5.99 o.p. (*0-446-40452-7*, Mysterious Pr. Paperback Bks.) Warner Bks., Inc.

—A Wicked Slice. 1990. 192p. mass mkt. 5.50 o.s.i (*0-449-14686-3*, Fawcett) Ballantine Bks.

—A Wicked Slice. 1989. 14.95 o.p. (*0-312-03003-7*, Saint Martin's Minotaur) St. Martin's Pr.

**OGILVIE, JAMES (FICTITIOUS CHARACTER)—FICTION**

MacNeil, Duncan. By Command of the Viceroy. 1975. 224p. 8.95 o.p. (*0-312-11060-X*) St. Martin's Pr.

—By Command of the Viceroy. l.t. ed. 1979. (Ulverscroft Large Print Ser.). 29.99 o.p. (*0-7089-0341-X*, Ulverscroft) Thorpe, F. A. Pubs. GBR. *Dist:* Ulverscroft Large Print Bks., Ltd., Ulverscroft Large Print Canada, Ltd.

—Charge of Cowardice. 1978. 8.95 o.p. (*0-312-13006-6*) St. Martin's Pr.

—Cunningham's Revenge. l.t. ed. 1986. lib. bdg. 17.95 o.p. (*0-89340-949-9*, 113) BBC Audiobooks America.

—Cunningham's Revenge. 1985. 192p. 13.95 o.s.i (*0-8027-0847-1*) Walker & Co.

—The Red Daniel. 1977. reprint ed. pap. 1.50 o.s.i (*0-8439-0477-1*) Dorchester Publishing Co., Inc.

—The Restless Frontier. 1980. 8.95 o.p. (*0-312-67782-0*) St. Martin's Pr.

—Wolf in the Fold. 1977. 8.95 o.p. (*0-312-88637-3*) St. Martin's Pr.

McCutchan, Philip. Captain at Arms, 1. 1999. 286p. 25.00 o.p. (*0-7278-2231-4*) Severn Hse. Pubs., Ltd.

—Captain at Arms. l.t. ed. 1999. (General Ser.). 426p. pap. 23.95 (*0-7862-2094-5*); (*0-7540-3922-6*); (*0-7540-3921-8*) Thorndike Pr.

—The First Command. 1999. 315p. (*0-7540-3471-2*); pap. (*0-7540-3472-0*) BBC Audiobooks America.

—The First Command. 1998. 192p. 22.00 o.p. (*0-7278-5290-6*) Severn Hse. Pubs., Ltd.

—The First Command. l.t. ed. 1999. (General Ser.). 315p. pap. 23.95 (*0-7862-1589-5*) Thorndike Pr.

—Honour & Empire. 1999. 224p. 25.00 (*0-7278-2293-4*) Severn Hse. Pubs., Ltd.

—Honour & Empire. l.t. ed. 2000. (General Ser.). 324p. pap. 23.95 (*0-7862-2303-0*); (*0-7540-3987-0*); (*0-7540-3988-9*) Thorndike Pr.

—Ogilvie & the Mem'Sahib. 2002. 224p. 25.99 (*0-7278-5827-0*) Severn Hse. Pubs., Ltd.

—Ogilvie at War. 1999. 221p. 25.00 (*0-7278-5471-2*) Severn Hse. Pubs., Ltd.

—Ogilvie at War. l.t. ed. 2000. (General Ser.). 343p. pap. 23.95 (*0-7862-2567-X*); (*0-7540-4156-5*); (*0-7540-4157-3*) Thorndike Pr.

—Ogilvie's Dangerous Mission. 2003. 208p. 25.99 (*0-7278-5922-6*) Severn Hse. Pubs., Ltd.

—Soldier of the Queen. 1998. 224p. 24.00 o.p. (*0-7278-5345-7*) Severn Hse. Pubs., Ltd.

**O'GRADY, CANYON (FICTITIOUS CHARACTER)—FICTION**

Sharpe, Jon. Assassins Trail. 1991. (Canyon O'Grady Ser.: No. 13). 176p. mass mkt. 3.50 o.p. (*0-451-16964-6*, Signet Bks.) NAL.

—Bleeding Kansas. 1990. (Canyon O'Grady Ser.: No. 8). 176p. mass mkt. 3.50 o.p. (*0-451-16610-8*, Signet Bks.) NAL.

—Blood & Gold. 1991. (Canyon O'Grady Ser.: No. 16). 176p. (Orig.). mass mkt. 3.50 o.p. (*0-451-17094-6*, Signet Bks.) NAL.

—Blood Bounty. 1992. (Canyon O'Grady Ser.: No. 18). 176p. (Orig.). mass mkt. 3.50 o.s.i (*0-451-17198-5*, Signet Bks.) NAL.

—California Vengeance. 1992. (Canyon O'Grady Ser.: No. 20). 176p. (Orig.). mass mkt. 3.50 o.p. (*0-451-17305-8*, Signet Bks.) NAL.

—Canyon O'Grady. 1989. (Silver Slaughter Ser.: No. 2). mass mkt. 2.95 o.p. (*0-451-16070-3*) NAL.

—Chicago Six-Guns. 1993. (Canyon O'Grady Ser.: No. 24). 176p. (Orig.). mass mkt. 3.50 o.p. (*0-451-17529-8*, Signet Bks.) NAL.

—Colonel Death. 1991. (Canyon O'Grady Ser.: No. 14). (Illus.). 176p. mass mkt. 3.50 o.p. (*0-451-16997-2*, Signet Bks.) NAL.

—Colorado Ambush. 1992. (Canyon O'Grady Ser.: No. 22). 176p. (Orig.). mass mkt. 3.50 o.p. (*0-451-17373-2*, Signet Bks.) NAL.

—Comstock Crazy. 1990. (Canyon O'Grady Ser.: No. 6). 176p. mass mkt. 3.50 o.p. (*0-451-16442-3*, Signet Bks.) NAL.

—Counterfeit Madam. 1990. (Canyon O'Grady Ser.: No. 9). mass mkt. 3.50 o.p. (*0-451-16725-2*, Signet Bks.) NAL.

—Dead Men's Trails. 1989. (Canyon O'Grady Ser.: No. 1). 176p. (Orig.). mass mkt. 2.95 o.p. (*0-451-16068-1*, Signet Bks.) NAL.

—The Great Land Swindle. 1990. (Canyon O'Grady Ser.: No. 10). 176p. (Orig.). mass mkt. 3.50 o.p. (*0-451-16801-1*, Signet Bks.) NAL.

—The Killer's Club. 1992. (Canyon O'Grady Ser.: No. 17). 176p. mass mkt. 3.50 o.p. (*0-451-17131-4*, Signet Bks.) NAL.

—The Lincoln Assignment. 1990. (Canyon O'Grady Ser.: No. 5). 176p. mass mkt. 3.50 o.p. (*0-451-16368-0*) NAL.

—Louisiana Gold Race. 1993. (Canyon O'Grady Ser.: No. 23). 176p. (Orig.). mass mkt. 3.50 o.s.i (*0-451-17376-7*, Signet Bks.) NAL.

—Machine Gun Madness. 1989. (Canyon O'Grady Ser.: No. 3). 176p. mass mkt. 2.95 o.p. (*0-451-16152-1*, Signet Bks.) NAL.

—Railroad Renegades. 1991. (Canyon O'Grady Ser.: No. 12). 176p. mass mkt. 3.50 o.p. (*0-451-16921-2*, Signet Bks.) NAL.

—Rio Grande Ransom. 1992. (Canyon O'Grady Ser.: No. 19). 176p. (Orig.). mass mkt. 3.50 o.s.i (*0-451-17239-6*, Signet Bks.) NAL.

—Rocky Mountain Feud. 1993. (Canyon O'Grady Ser.: No. 25). 176p. (Orig.). mass mkt. 3.50 o.p. (*0-451-17595-6*, Signet Bks.) NAL.

—Shadow Guns. 1989. (Canyon O'Grady Ser.: No. 4). mass mkt. 3.50 o.p. (*0-451-16276-5*, 014) NAL.

—Soldier's Song. 1991. (Canyon O'Grady Ser.: No. 11). 176p. mass mkt. 3.50 o.p. (*0-451-16879-8*, Signet Bks.) NAL.

—Wyoming Conspiracy. 1992. (Canyon O'Grady Ser.: No. 21). 176p. (Orig.). mass mkt. 3.50 o.p. (*0-451-17370-8*, Signet Bks.) NAL.

**O'HALLORAN FAMILY (FICTITIOUS CHARACTERS)—FICTION**

Macomber, Debbie. Because of the Baby. 1996. (Harlequin Romance Ser.). 185p. per. (*0-373-03395-8*, 1-03395-0, Harlequin Bks.) Harlequin Enterprises, Ltd.

—Because of the Baby. l.t. ed. 1997. (Harlequin Romance Ser.). 20.95 (*0-263-15007-0*) Harlequin Mills & Boon, Ltd. GBR. *Dist:* Ulverscroft Large Print Bks., Ltd.

—Brides for Brothers. 1995. 187p. per. (*0-373-03379-6*, 1-03379-4, Harlequin Bks.) Harlequin Enterprises, Ltd.

—Brides for Brothers. l.t. ed. 1997. 20.95 o.s.i (*0-263-14919-6*) Harlequin Mills & Boon, Ltd. GBR. *Dist:* Ulverscroft Large Print Bks., Ltd.

—Daddy's Little Helper. 1995. 185p. per. (*0-373-03387-7*, 1-03387-7, Harlequin Bks.) Harlequin Enterprises, Ltd.

—Ending in Marriage. 1996. (Harlequin Romance Ser.). 186p. per. (*0-373-03403-2*, 1-03403-2, Harlequin Bks.) Harlequin Enterprises, Ltd.

—Falling for Him (Midnight Sons) 1996. (Harlequin Romance Ser.). 184p. per. (*0-373-03399-0*, 1-03399-2, Harlequin Bks.) Harlequin Enterprises, Ltd.

—Falling for Him (Midnight Sons) l.t. ed. 1997. (Harlequin Romance Ser.). 20.95 o.s.i (*0-263-15044-5*) Harlequin Mills & Boon, Ltd. GBR. *Dist:* Ulverscroft Large Print Bks., Ltd.

—Family Men: Daddy's Little Helper & Because of the Baby, 2 bks. in 1. 2000. (Harlequin Midnight Sons Ser.). 384p. mass mkt. (*0-373-83435-7*, 1-83435-7, Harlequin Bks.) Harlequin Enterprises, Ltd.

—Mail-Order Marriages. 2000. (Harlequin Midnight Sons Ser.: Vol. 1). 384p. mass mkt. (*0-373-83434-9*, Harlequin Bks.) Harlequin Enterprises, Ltd.

—The Marriage Risk. 1995. (Harlequin Romance Ser.: Vol. 3383). 189p. per. (*0-373-03383-4*, Harlequin Bks.) Harlequin Enterprises, Ltd.

Macomber, Debbie & Wisdom, Linda Randall. The Last Two Bachelors. 2000. (Harlequin Midnight Sons Ser.: Vol. 3). 384p. mass mkt. *(0-373-83436-5*, 1-83436-5, Harlequin Bks.) Harlequin Enterprises, Ltd.

**O'HARA, FRANK (FICTITIOUS CHARACTER)—FICTION**

Diehl, William. Chameleon. 1996. mass mkt. 5.99 *(0-345-90986-0)*; 1982. 480p. mass mkt. 6.99 *(0-345-29445-9)* Ballantine Bks.

—Chameleon. 1981. 14.50 o.p. *(0-394-51961-2)* Random Hse., Inc.

Hynd, Noel. A Room for the Dead. 1995. 416p. mass mkt. 5.99 o.s.i *(0-7860-0089-9*, Pinnacle Bks.); mass mkt. 5.99 *(0-8217-0089-8*, Zebra Bks.) Kensington Publishing Corp.

**OHARA, ISAMU (FICTITIOUS CHARACTER)—FICTION**

Hamilton, Nan. Killers Rights. 19.95 *(0-8027-5579-8)* Walker & Co.

**O'HARA, NICK (FICTITIOUS CHARACTER)—FICTION**

Uhnak, Dorothy. Codes of Betrayal. 1999. 320p. pap. 6.99 o.p. *(0-312-96531-1*, St. Martin's Paperbacks); 1997. 293p. 23.95 *(0-312-15582-4)* St. Martin's Pr.

**O'HARA, SCARLETT (FICTITIOUS CHARACTER)—FICTION**

Ripley, Alexandra. Scarlett: The Sequel to Margaret Mitchell's Gone with the Wind. 1991. (SPA.). *(84-406-2275-9)* B Ediciones S.A.

—Scarlett: The Sequel to Margaret Mitchell's Gone with the Wind. 1992. audio 80.00 *(0-7366-2309-4)*;Pt. A. audio 88.00 *(0-7366-2308-6*, 3091A);Pt. B. audio 80.00 Books on Tape, Inc.

—Scarlett: The Sequel to Margaret Mitchell's Gone with the Wind. l.t. ed. 1992. (General Ser.). 1184p. pap. 21.95 *(0-8161-5528-3)*; 1184p. lib. bdg. 28.95 o.p. *(0-8161-5527-5)*; lib. bdg. 11.97 *(0-8161-5535-6)*; lib. bdg. 11.97 *(0-8161-5536-4)* Gale Group. (Macmillan Reference USA).

—Scarlett: The Sequel to Margaret Mitchell's Gone with the Wind. abr. ed. 1992. audio 25.00 *(0-671-77966-4*, 692301, Simon & Schuster Audioworks) Simon & Schuster Audio.

—Scarlett: The Sequel to Margaret Mitchell's Gone with the Wind. 1991. 13.04 *(0-606-02212-0)* Turtleback Bks.

—Scarlett: The Sequel to Margaret Mitchell's Gone with the Wind. 1992. 896p. mass mkt. 7.99 *(0-446-36325-1)*; 1991. 823p. 24.45 o.p. *(0-446-51507-8)*; 1992. 100.00 *(0-446-51718-6)* Warner Bks., Inc.

**OHAYON, MICHAEL (FICTITIOUS CHARACTER)—FICTION**

Gur, Batya. Literary Murder: A Critical Case. 1994. Tr. of Mavet Ba-Hug Le-Sifrut. 368p. pap. 12.95 *(0-06-092548-5*, Perennial) HarperTrade.

—Literary Murder: A Critical Case. Bilu, Dalya, tr. from ENG. 1993. Tr. of Mavet Ba-Hug Le-Sifrut. 384p. 20.00 o.p. *(0-06-019023-X*, HarperCollins) HarperTrade.

—Murder Duet: A Musical Case. 1999. (Michael Ohayon Mysteries Ser.). 448p. 25.00 *(0-06-017268-1)* HarperCollins Pubs.

—Murder on a Kibbutz: A Communal Case. 1995. 368p. pap. 13.95 *(0-06-092654-6*, Perennial) HarperTrade.

—The Saturday Morning Murder: A Psychoanalytic Case. Bilu, Dalya, tr. from ENG. 1992. 320p. 20.00 o.p. *(0-06-019024-8)*; 1993. 304p. reprint ed. pap. 11.00 *(0-06-099508-4*, Perennial) HarperTrade.

**O'KEEFE, KATHERINE (FICTITIOUS CHARACTER)—FICTION**

Spruill, Steven. Rulers of Darkness. 1995. 357p. 22.95 o.p. *(0-312-13163-1)*; Vol. 1. 1998. (Rulers of Darkness Ser.: Vol. 1). 352p. mass mkt. 6.50 *(0-312-95668-1*, St. Martin's Paperbacks) St. Martin's Pr.

**OLIVAW, R. DANEEL (FICTITIOUS CHARACTER)—FICTION**

Asimov, Isaac. Caves of Steel. 1986. mass mkt. 4.95 o.s.i *(0-345-33820-0*, Del Rey); 1985. mass mkt. 3.50 o.s.i *(0-345-32900-7*, Del Rey); 1982. mass mkt. 2.25 o.s.i *(0-449-20063-9*, Fawcett); 1981. mass mkt. 2.25 o.s.i *(0-449-23782-6*, Fawcett); 1978. mass mkt. 1.50 o.s.i *(0-449-22858-4*, Fawcett) Ballantine Bks.

—Caves of Steel. 1991. 288p. mass mkt. 7.99 *(0-553-29340-0)* Bantam Bks.

—Caves of Steel. 1955. mass mkt. 0.35 o.p. *(0-451-01240-2*, Signet Bks.) NAL.

—Caves of Steel. 1991. 13.04 *(0-606-19272-7)* Turtleback Bks.

—The Naked Sun. 1986. mass mkt. 4.95 o.s.i *(0-345-33821-9)*; 1985. mass mkt. 3.50 o.s.i *(0-345-33031-5*, Del Rey); 1983. mass mkt. 2.95 o.s.i *(0-345-31390-9*, Del Rey); 1981. mass mkt. 2.25 o.s.i *(0-449-24243-9*, Fawcett); 1975. mass mkt. 1.50 o.s.i *(0-449-22648-4)* Ballantine Bks.

—The Naked Sun. 1991. 288p. mass mkt. 7.99 *(0-553-29339-7)* Bantam Bks.

—The Naked Sun. 1991. 13.04 *(0-606-19282-4)* Turtleback Bks.

—Robots & Empire. 1986. 512p. mass mkt. 5.99 o.s.i *(0-345-32894-9*, Del Rey); mass mkt. 3.95 o.s.i *(0-345-33769-7)* Ballantine Bks.

—The Robots of Dawn, Vol. 3. 1984. 416p. mass mkt. 5.95 o.s.i *(0-345-31571-5*, Ballantine Bks.) Ballantine Bks.

—The Robots of Dawn. 1983. 432p. 15.95 o.p. *(0-385-18400-X)* Doubleday Publishing.

—The Robots of Dawn. abr. ed. audio 12.95 o.p. *(0-89845-142-6*, SWC 1732, Caedmon) HarperTrade.

**OLIVER, ARIADNE (FICTITIOUS CHARACTER)—FICTION**

Christie, Agatha. Cards on the Table. mass mkt. 3.50 o.s.i *(0-425-12577-7)*; 2001. E-Book 5.99 *(0-425-17790-4)*; 1998. mass mkt. 3.99 o.s.i *(0-425-16924-3)*; 1986. mass mkt. 2.95 o.s.i *(0-425-09317-4)*; 1984. mass mkt. 2.95 o.s.i *(0-425-06778-5)* Berkley Publishing Group.

—Cards on the Table. 1980. pap. 2.95 o.p. *(0-440-11052-1)* Dell Publishing.

—Cards on the Table. 1987. (Agatha Christie Ser.). 14.95 *(0-396-09010-9*, G. P. Putnam's Sons) Penguin Putnam Bks. for Young Readers.

—Cards on the Table. 1984. (Hercule Poirot Mystery Ser.). 12.04 *(0-606-12211-7)* Turtleback Bks.

—The Cards on the Table. 1987. (Hercule Poirot Mystery Ser.). 224p. mass mkt. 5.99 *(0-425-10567-9)* Berkley Publishing Group.

—Cards on the Table. l.t. ed. 1983. 352p. 12.50 o.p. *(0-7089-1151-X*, Ulverscroft) Thorpe, F. A. Pubs. GBR. *Dist:* Ulverscroft Large Print Bks., Ltd.

—Dead Man's Folly. unabr. ed. 1997. audio 54.95 o.p. *(0-7451-6815-9*, CAB 314) BBC Audiobooks America.

—Dead Man's Folly. 2000. (Hercule Poirot Mystery Ser.). 240p. mass mkt. 5.99 *(0-425-17473-5)* Berkley Publishing Group.

—Dead Man's Folly. 1986. (Agatha Christie Ser.). 14.95 o.s.i *(0-396-08864-3*, G. P. Putnam's Sons) Penguin Putnam Bks. for Young Readers.

—Dead Man's Folly. 1990. 224p. mass mkt. 3.95 o.p. *(0-671-69484-7)*; 1984. mass mkt. 3.50 o.s.i *(0-671-54318-0)*; 1983. mass mkt. 2.95 o.s.i *(0-671-47317-4)* Simon & Schuster. (Pocket).

—Dead Man's Folly. 1988. audio 53.95 o.p. *(0-8161-9109-3)* Thorndike Pr.

—Dead Man's Folly. l.t. ed. 1983. 336p. 12.50 o.p. *(0-85456-772-0*, Ulverscroft) Thorpe, F. A. Pubs. GBR. *Dist:* Ulverscroft Large Print Bks., Ltd.

—Elephants Can Remember. 1984. (Agatha Christie Ser.). 224p. mass mkt. 5.99 *(0-425-06782-3)* Berkley Publishing Group.

—Elephants Can Remember. 1976. pap. 1.25 o.p. *(0-440-12329-1)* Dell Publishing.

—Elephants Can Remember. l.t. ed. (Agatha Christie Ser.). 1991. 291p. pap. 12.95 o.p. *(0-8161-4546-6)*; 1990. 328p. lib. bdg. 19.95 o.p. *(0-8161-4545-8)*; 1984. pap. 9.95 o.p. *(0-8161-3122-8)*; 1973. reprint ed. lib. bdg. 9.95 o.p. *(0-8161-6086-4)* Gale Group. (Macmillan Reference USA).

—Elephants Can Remember. 1972. (Agatha Christie Ser.). 8.95 *(0-396-07769-2*, G. P. Putnam's Sons) Penguin Group (USA) Inc.

—Elephants Can Remember. 1992. 12.04 *(0-606-12274-5)* Turtleback Bks.

—Elephants Can Remember. l.t. ed. 2001. (Ulverscroft Large Print Ser.). 368p. 32.50 *(0-7089-2657-6)* Ulverscroft Large Print Bks., Ltd.

—Elephants Can Remember: A Hercule Poirot Mystery. unabr. ed. 1999. audio 49.95 *(0-7540-0334-5*, CAB1757) Chivers Audio Bks. GBR. *Dist:* BBC Audiobooks America.

**OLIVER, GIDEON (FICTITIOUS CHARACTER)—FICTION**

Elkins, Aaron. Curses! 1989. 208p. 15.95 o.p. *(0-89296-263-1)* Mysterious Pr.

—Curses! 1990. 254p. mass mkt. 5.99 o.p. *(0-445-40864-2*, Mysterious Pr. Paperback Bks.) Warner Bks., Inc.

—The Dark Place. 1983. 192p. 13.95 o.s.i *(0-8027-5565-8)* Walker & Co.

—The Dark Place. 1994. 208p. mass mkt. 5.99 o.s.i *(0-446-40403-9)*; 1989. mass mkt. 4.50 o.s.i *(0-445-20955-0)* Warner Bks., Inc.

—Dead Men's Hearts. 1994. 240p. 18.95 o.s.i *(0-89296-466-9)* Mysterious Pr.

—Dead Men's Hearts. 1995. 256p. mass mkt. 6.99 *(0-446-40056-4)* Warner Bks., Inc.

—Fellowship of Fear. 1982. 256p. 11.95 o.s.i *(0-8027-5478-3)* Walker & Co.

—Fellowship of Fear. 1994. 216p. mass mkt. 5.99 o.s.i *(0-446-40402-0)*; 1989. pap. 4.99 *(0-445-20953-4)* Warner Bks., Inc.

—Icy Clutches. l.t. ed. 1992. (Mystery Ser.). 388p. 29.99 *(0-7505-0353-X)* Magna Large Print Bks. GBR. *Dist:* Ulverscroft Large Print Bks., Ltd.

—Icy Clutches. 1990. 304p. 16.95 o.p. *(0-89296-377-8)* Mysterious Pr.

—Icy Clutches. 1991. 304p. mass mkt. 5.99 o.p. *(0-446-40040-8*, Mysterious Pr. Paperback Bks.) Warner Bks., Inc.

—Make No Bones. l.t. ed. 1993. 22.95 o.p. *(0-7927-1505-5)*; pap. 20.95 o.p. *(0-7927-1504-7)* BBC Audiobooks America.

—Make No Bones. 1991. (Gideon Oliver Mystery Ser.). 304p. 17.95 o.p. *(0-89296-378-6)* Mysterious Pr.

—Make No Bones. 1993. 240p. mass mkt. 5.99 o.p. *(0-446-40308-3*, Mysterious Pr. Paperback Bks.) Warner Bks., Inc.

—Murder in the Queen's Arms. 1986. 208p. mass mkt. 2.95 o.s.i *(0-553-26235-1)* Bantam Bks.

—Murder in the Queen's Arms. 1985. 195p. 14.95 o.s.i *(0-8027-5626-3)* Walker & Co.

—Murder in the Queen's Arms. 1990. 224p. mass mkt. 5.99 *(0-445-40913-4*, Mysterious Pr. Paperback Bks.) Warner Bks., Inc.

—Old Bones: A Gideon Oliver Mystery. l.t. ed. 1991. pap. 8.95 o.p. *(1-55504-804-8*, 533) BBC Audiobooks America.

—Old Bones: A Gideon Oliver Mystery. 1987. 208p. 15.45 o.p. *(0-89296-262-3)* Mysterious Pr.

—Old Bones: A Gideon Oliver Mystery. 1988. 256p. mass mkt. 6.50 o.s.i *(0-445-40687-9)* Warner Bks., Inc.

—Skeleton Dance. (Gideon Oliver Mystery Ser.). 2001. 352p. mass mkt. 6.99 *(0-380-73163-0*, Avon Bks.); 2000. 256p. 23.00 *(0-688-15928-1*, Morrow, William & Co.) Morrow/Avon.

—Skeleton Dance: A Novel. l.t. ed. 2000. (G. K. Hall Core Ser.). 343p. 30.95 *(0-7838-9190-3*, Macmillan Reference USA) Gale Group.

—Twenty Blue Devils. unabr. ed. 2000. audio 59.95 *(0-7927-2218-3*, CSL 107) Chivers Audio Bks. GBR. *Dist:* BBC Audiobooks America.

—Twenty Blue Devils. l.t. ed. 1997. (Cloak & Dagger Ser.). 421p. 25.95 o.p. *(0-7862-1091-5)* Thorndike Pr.

—Twenty Blue Devils. 1997. 288p. mass mkt. 5.99 o.s.i *(0-446-40526-4)*; 22.00 o.p. *(0-89296-467-7)* Warner Bks., Inc.

**OLIVEREZ, ELENA (FICTITIOUS CHARACTER)—FICTION**

Muller, Marcia. The Legend of the Slain Soldiers: An Elena Oliverez Mystery. 1987. 224p. mass mkt. 3.50 o.p. *(0-451-15050-3*, Signet Bks.) NAL.

—The Legend of the Slain Soldiers: An Elena Oliverez Mystery. 1985. 181p. 13.95 o.p. *(0-8027-5617-4)* Walker & Co.

—The Legend of the Slain Soldiers: An Elena Oliverez Mystery. 1996. 192p. mass mkt. 5.99 *(0-446-40421-7)* Warner Bks., Inc.

—The Tree of Death. 1987. mass mkt. 3.50 o.p. *(0-451-14749-9*, Signet Bks.) NAL.

—The Tree of Death. 1983. (Mysteries Ser.). 192p. 12.95 o.s.i *(0-8027-5576-3)* Walker & Co.

—The Tree of Death. 1996. 208p. mass mkt. 5.99 o.s.i *(0-446-40420-9)* Warner Bks., Inc.

Muller, Marcia & Pronzini, Bill. Beyond the Grave. 240p. 1999. mass mkt. 5.95 *(0-7867-0650-3)*; 1991. mass mkt. 3.95 o.p. *(0-88184-731-3)* Avalon Publishing Group. (Carroll & Graf Pubs.).

—Beyond the Grave. l.t. ed. 2001. 388p. pap. 24.95 *(0-7838-9537-2*, Macmillan Reference USA) Gale Group.

—Beyond the Grave. 1986. 224p. 15.95 o.p. *(0-8027-5651-4)* Walker & Co.

**O'MALLEY, GRACE, 1530?-1600?—FICTION**

Asprin, Robert L. Another Fine Myth. l.t. ed. 2001. 256p. *(0-7540-4638-9*, Macmillan Reference USA) Gale Group.

Llywelyn, Morgan. Grania: She-King of the Irish Seas. 1987. 480p. mass mkt. 4.50 o.s.i *(0-8041-0116-7*, Ivy Bks.) Ballantine Bks.

—Grania: She-King of the Irish Seas. 2003. 416p. pap. 15.95 *(0-7653-0838-X*, Forge Bks.) Doherty, Tom Assocs., LLC.

—Grania: She-King of the Irish Seas. 1986. 422p. 3.99 o.s.i *(0-517-55951-X)* Random Hse. Value Publishing.

**O'MALLEY, JAN (FICTITIOUS CHARACTER)—FICTION**

Dart, Iris Rainer. Show Business Kills. 1995. 310p. 21.95 o.p. *(0-316-17334-7)* Little Brown & Co.

—Show Business Kills. 1996. 400p. mass mkt. 6.50 o.p. *(0-446-36511-4)* Warner Bks., Inc.

**O'MALLEY, JOHN (FICTITIOUS CHARACTER)—FICTION**

Coel, Margaret. The Dream Stalker. 1997. 256p. 21.95 o.s.i *(0-425-15967-1)*; 1998. 272p. reprint ed. mass mkt. 6.50 *(0-425-16533-7)* Berkley Publishing Group. (Prime Crime).

—The Dream Stalker. unabr. ed. 1999. (O'Malley Mystery Ser.). audio 39.95 *(1-55686-873-1)* Books in Motion.

—The Eagle Catcher. 1996. (Arapaho Indian Mysteries Ser.). 256p. mass mkt. 6.50 *(0-425-15463-7)* Berkley Publishing Group.

—The Eagle Catcher, Set. unabr. ed. 1999. (O'Malley Mystery Ser.). audio 36.95 Books in Motion.

—The Eagle Catcher. 16th l.t. ed. 2002. 248p. lib. bdg. 28.95 *(1-58547-159-3)* Ctr. Point Large Print.

—The Eagle Catcher. 1995. (Arapaho Indian Mysteries Ser.). 224p. 22.50 *(0-87081-367-6)* Univ. Pr. of Colorado.

—The Eagle Catcher. 1995. E-Book 22.50 *(0-585-02336-0)* netLibrary, Inc.

—The Ghost Walker. 256p. 1996. 21.95 o.p. *(0-425-15468-8)*; 1997. reprint ed. mass mkt. 6.50 *(0-425-15961-2)* Berkley Publishing Group. (Prime Crime).

—The Ghost Walker. unabr. ed. 1999. (O'Malley Mystery Ser.). audio 39.95 *(1-55686-865-0)* Books in Motion.

—Killing Raven. 2004. 304p. mass mkt. 6.99 *(0-425-19750-6)*; 2003. 288p. 22.95 *(0-425-19261-X*, Prime Crime) Berkley Publishing Group.

—The Lost Bird. 2000. 304p. mass mkt. 6.50 *(0-425-17030-6)* Berkley Publishing Group.

—The Lost Bird. l.t. ed. 2000. (G. K. Hall Core Ser.). 332p. 28.95 *(0-7838-8958-5*, Macmillan Reference USA) Gale Group.

—The Lost Bird: A Mystery. 1999. 304p. 21.95 o.s.i *(0-425-17059-4*, Prime Crime) Berkley Publishing Group.

—The Shadow Dancer. 2002. 304p. 22.95 *(0-425-18640-7*, Prime Crime) Berkley Publishing Group.

—The Shadow Dancer. l.t. ed. 2003. lib. bdg. 28.95 *(1-58547-284-0*, Platinum) Ctr. Point Large Print.

—The Spirit Woman. 2000. 272p. 21.95 o.s.i *(0-425-17597-9)*; 2001. 304p. reprint ed. mass mkt. 6.50 *(0-425-18090-5*, Prime Crime) Berkley Publishing Group.

—The Spirit Woman. l.t. ed. 2001. 294p. lib. bdg. 28.95 *(1-58547-063-5)* Ctr. Point Large Print.

—The Story Teller. (Wind River Arapaho Ser.). 256p. 1998. 21.95 o.s.i *(0-425-16538-8)*; 1999. reprint ed. mass mkt. 6.50 *(0-425-17025-X)* Berkley Publishing Group. (Prime Crime).

—The Story Teller. unabr. ed. 1999. (O'Malley Mystery Ser.). audio 49.95 *(1-55686-891-X)* Books in Motion.

—The Thunder Keeper. 2001. 256p. 22.95 o.s.i *(0-425-18188-X*, Prime Crime) Berkley Publishing Group.

**O'MALLEY, TOMMY (FICTITIOUS CHARACTER)—FICTION**

O'Reilly, Bill. Those Who Trespass: A Novel of Murder & Television. 1998. 332p. pap. 24.00 *(0-9631246-8-4)* Bancroft Pr.

—Those Who Trespass: A Novel of Murder & Television. 1999. 384p. reprint ed. mass mkt. 6.99 o.s.i *(0-451-40882-9*, Onyx) NAL.

—Those Who Trespass: A Novel of Murder & Television. l.t. ed. 2004. 464p. 24.95 *(0-375-43306-6)* Random Hse. Large Print.

**O'MALLEY DE MARISCO, SKYE (FICTITIOUS CHARACTER)—FICTION**

Small, Bertrice. All the Sweet Tomorrows. 1986. 608p. mass mkt. 6.99 *(0-345-33473-6)*; 1984. pap. 8.95 o.p. *(0-345-31050-0)* Ballantine Bks.

—Bedazzled. (Skye's Legacy Ser.). 2000. 445p. mass mkt. 6.99 o.s.i *(0-8217-6521-3*, Zebra Bks.); 1999. 374p. pap. 12.95 o.s.i *(1-57566-432-1)* Kensington Publishing Corp.

—Besieged. 352p. 2003. mass mkt. 6.99 *(0-7582-0430-2)*; 2000. pap. 14.00 *(1-57566-525-5*, Kensington Bks.) Kensington Publishing Corp.

—Darling Jasmine. (Zebra Historical Romance Ser.). 1998. 432p. mass mkt. 6.99 o.s.i *(0-8217-5919-1*, Zebra Bks.); 1997. 416p. pap. 12.95 o.s.i *(1-57566-208-6)* Kensington Publishing Corp.

—Lost Love Found. 1991. 512p. mass mkt. 6.99 *(0-345-37419-3)*; 1989. pap. 7.95 o.p. *(0-345-35275-0)* Ballantine Bks.

—A Love for All Time. 2001. 528p. pap. 14.00 *(0-451-20474-3*, Signet Bks.); 1994. 624p. mass mkt. 5.99 o.s.i *(0-451-40441-6*, Onyx); 1987. 624p. mass mkt. 5.99 o.p. *(0-451-15900-4*, Signet Bks.); 1987. mass mkt. 4.50 o.p. *(0-451-14725-1*, Signet Bks.); 1986. 704p. pap. 8.95 o.p. *(0-451-82141-6*, Signet Bks.) NAL.

—Skye O'Malley. 1984. 480p. mass mkt. 6.99 *(0-345-32364-5)*; 1981. mass mkt. 2.95 o.p. *(0-345-28680-4)* Ballantine Bks.

—Skye O'Malley. abr. ed. 1994. audio 5.99 *(1-57096-019-4*, RAZ 920) Romance Alive Audio.

—Skye O'Malley. 1990. 20.00 o.p. *(0-7278-4060-6)* Severn Hse. Pubs., Ltd.

—This Heart of Mine. 1988. 576p. (Orig.). mass mkt. 6.99 *(0-345-35673-X)* Ballantine Bks.

—Wild Jasmine. 1996. 544p. mass mkt. 6.99 *(0-345-40134-4)* Ballantine Bks.

**OMAR, THE STORYTELLER (FICTITIOUS CHARACTER)—FICTION**

Duncan, Dave. The Hunters' Haunt. 1995. 232p. (Orig.). per. 19.95 (*1-58586-114-6*) ereads.com.
—The Reaver Road. 1992. mass mkt. 4.99 o.s.i (*0-345-37481-9*, Del Rey) Ballantine Bks.
Duncan, David J. The Hunters' Haunt. 1995. 295p. (Orig.). mass mkt. 5.99 o.s.i (*0-345-38459-8*, Del Rey) Ballantine Bks.

**OMEGA, JAY (FICTITIOUS CHARACTER)—FICTION**

McCrumb, Sharyn. Bimbos of the Death Sun. 1996. 224p. mass mkt. 6.50 (*0-345-41215-X*) Ballantine Bks.
—Bimbos of the Death Sun. unabr. ed. 1988. audio 35.00 (*0-7887-3758-9*, 95942E7) Recorded Bks., LLC.
—Bimbos of the Death Sun. 1988. pap. 3.95 o.p. (*0-88038-455-7*) Wizards of the Coast.
—Zombies of the Gene Pool. 1993. 288p. mass mkt. 6.99 (*0-345-37914-4*) Ballantine Bks.

**ONE-EYED MACK (FICTITIOUS CHARACTER)—FICTION**

Lehrer, Jim. Crown Oklahoma. 1991. 208p. mass mkt. 3.95 o.s.i (*0-345-36124-5*) Ballantine Bks.
—Crown Oklahoma. 1997. (One-Eyed Mack Mystery Ser.). 324p. pap. 12.95 (*1-57178-040-8*) Council Oak Bks.
—Crown Oklahoma. 1989. 224p. 18.95 o.p. (*0-399-13434-4*, G. P. Putnam's Sons) Penguin Putnam Bks. for Young Readers.
—Kick the Can. 1997. 420p. (C). reprint ed. pap. 12.95 (*1-57178-059-9*) Council Oak Bks.
—Kick the Can. 1988. 256p. 17.95 o.p. (*0-399-13350-X*, G. P. Putnam's Sons) Penguin Putnam Bks. for Young Readers.
—Kick the Can. 1992. 3.99 o.p. (*0-517-09580-7*) Random Hse. Value Publishing.
—Lost & Found. abr. ed. audio 16.99 (*0-88646-293-2*, 7293) Durkin Hayes Publishing Ltd.
—Lost & Found. 1991. 224p. 19.95 o.p. (*0-399-13601-0*, G. P. Putnam's Sons) Penguin Group (USA) Inc.
—Lost & Found. 1992. 3.99 o.p. (*0-517-09582-3*) Random Hse. Value Publishing.
—Short List. abr. ed. 1992. (One-Eyed Mack Ser.: No. 2). audio 16.99 (*0-88646-314-9*, 7314) Durkin Hayes Publishing Ltd.
—Short List. 1992. 224p. 19.95 o.p. (*0-399-13665-7*, G. P. Putnam's Sons) Penguin Group (USA) Inc.
—The Sooner Spy. 1997. (One-Eyed Mack Mystery Ser.). 328p. pap. 12.95 (*1-57178-041-6*) Council Oak Bks.
—The Sooner Spy. 1990. 224p. 19.95 o.p. (*0-399-13536-7*, G. P. Putnam's Sons) Penguin Putnam Bks. for Young Readers.

**O'NEAL, FREDDIE (FICTITIOUS CHARACTER)—FICTION**

Dain, Catherine. Bet Against the House. 1995. 224p. (Orig.). mass mkt. 4.99 o.s.i (*0-425-14580-8*, Prime Crime) Berkley Publishing Group.
—Lament for a Dead Cowboy. 1994. 208p. (Orig.). mass mkt. 4.50 o.s.i (*0-425-14328-7*, Prime Crime) Berkley Publishing Group.
—Lay It on the Line. 1992. mass mkt. 3.99 o.s.i (*0-425-14325-2*); 208p. mass mkt. 3.99 o.s.i (*0-515-10926-6*, Jove) Berkley Publishing Group.
—Walk a Crooked Mile. 1994. 208p. mass mkt. 3.99 o.s.i (*0-515-11310-7*, Jove) Berkley Publishing Group.

**O'NEIL, ALLISON (FICTITIOUS CHARACTER)—FICTION**

Douglas, Lauren W. Death at Lavender Bay: An Allison O'Neil Mystery. 1996. (Allison O'Neil Mysteries Ser.). 256p. (Orig.). pap. 11.95 (*1-56280-085-X*) Naiad Pr., Inc.
—Swimming Cat Cove: An Allison O'Neil Mystery. 1997. (Allison O'Neil Mysteries Ser.). 224p. (Orig.). pap. 11.95 (*1-56280-168-6*) Naiad Pr., Inc.

**O'NEILL, CONNOR (FICTITIOUS CHARACTER)—FICTION**

Green, Christine. Die in My Dreams. 1995. 272p. mass mkt. 4.99 o.s.i (*0-553-56932-5*, Crimeline) Bantam Bks.
—Die in My Dreams. l.t. ed. 1996. pap. 20.95 (*0-7838-1727-4*, Macmillan Reference USA) Gale Group.

**O'NEILL, JIM (FICTITIOUS CHARACTER)—FICTION**

Disney, Doris M. Last Straw. 1988. mass mkt. 2.95 o.s.i (*0-8217-2286-7*, Zebra Bks.) Kensington Publishing Corp.

**O'NEILL, PEGGY (FICTITIOUS CHARACTER)—FICTION**

Lake, M. D. Amends for Murder. l.t. ed. 1991. pap. 15.95 o.p. (*0-7927-0801-6*, AS0288) BBC Audiobooks America.
—Amends for Murder. 1989. pap. 4.99 (*0-380-75865-2*, Avon Bks.) Morrow/Avon.
—Cold Comfort. 1990. pap. 5.99 (*0-380-76032-0*, Avon Bks.) Morrow/Avon.
—Flirting with Death. 1996. (Orig.). pap. 5.99 o.p. (*0-380-77522-0*, Avon Bks.) Morrow/Avon.
—A Gift for Murder. 1992. (Peggy O'Neill Mystery Ser.). 256p. mass mkt. 5.50 (*0-380-76855-0*, Avon Bks.) Morrow/Avon.
—Grave Choices: A Peggy O'Neill Mystery. 1995. pap. 5.99 o.p. (*0-380-77521-2*, Avon Bks.) Morrow/Avon.
—Midsummer Malice. 1997. (Peggy O'Neill Mystery Ser.). pap. 5.99 o.p. (*0-380-78759-8*, Avon Bks.) Morrow/Avon.
—Murder by Mail. 1993. (Orig.). pap. 5.99 o.p. (*0-380-76856-9*, Avon Bks.) Morrow/Avon.
—Once upon a Crime. 1995. (Peggy O'Neill Mystery Ser.). (Orig.). pap. 5.50 (*0-380-77520-4*, Avon Bks.) Morrow/Avon.
—Poisoned Ivy. 1992. (Peggy O'Neill Mystery Ser.). 256p. pap. 5.50 (*0-380-76573-X*, Avon Bks.) Morrow/Avon.

**OPARA, CHRISTIE (FICTITIOUS CHARACTER)—FICTION**

Uhnak, Dorothy. The Bait. 1976. pap. 1.95 o.s.i (*0-671-82326-4*, Pocket) Simon & Schuster.
—The Ledger. 1977. pap. 1.95 o.s.i (*0-671-82328-0*, Pocket) Simon & Schuster.

**OPERATOR 5 (FICTITIOUS CHARACTER)—FICTION**

Carr, Nick. America's Secret Service Ace: The Operator 5 Story. 1985. (Starmont Pulp & Dime Novel Studies: No. 2). reprint ed. 64p. lib. bdg. 19.95 o.p. (*0-89370-564-0*); (Illus.). 63p. 19.95 o.p. (*0-930261-70-4*); (Illus.). 63p. pap. 9.95 o.p. (*0-930261-73-9*) Millefleurs.

**OPHELIA O. (FICTITIOUS CHARACTER)—FICTION**

Jones, Tanya. Ophelia O. & the Antenatal Mysteries. 1996. 416p. pap. 13.95 (*0-7472-4912-1*) Headline Bk. Publishing, Ltd. GBR. *Dist:* Trafalgar Square.
—Ophelia O. & the Mortgage Bandits. 1996. 448p. pap. 13.95 (*0-7472-4867-2*) Headline Bk. Publishing, Ltd. GBR. *Dist:* Trafalgar Square.

**O'REILLY, PEGGY (FICTITIOUS CHARACTER)—FICTION**

Lake, M. D. Grave Choices: A Peggy O'Neill Mystery. 1995. pap. 5.99 o.p. (*0-380-77521-2*, Avon Bks.) Morrow/Avon.

**O'RILEY, JOE (FICTITIOUS CHARACTER)—FICTION**

Levy, Bob. Broken Hearts: A Novel of Suspense. 2000. 284p. 24.95 (*0-86534-312-8*) Sunstone Pr.
—Past Tense: A Novel of Crime & Suspense. 2002. 288p. 24.95 (*0-86534-341-1*) Sunstone Pr.

**O'ROARKE, JOCELYN (FICTITIOUS CHARACTER)—FICTION**

Dentinger, Jane. Dead Pan. 1994. (Jocelyn O'Roarke Mystery Ser.). 256p. pap. 5.95 o.s.i (*0-14-015834-0*, Penguin Bks.) Penguin Group (USA) Inc.
—Dead Pan: A Jocelyn O'Roarke Mystery. 1992. (Jocelyn O'Roarke Mystery Ser.). 256p. 19.00 o.p. (*0-670-84108-0*, Viking) Viking Penguin.
—Death Mask. 1988. 240p. 16.95 o.s.i (*0-684-18922-4*, Macmillan Reference USA) Gale Group.
—Death Mask. 1994. (Jocelyn O'Roarke Mystery Ser.). 304p. reprint ed. pap. 5.95 o.p. (*0-14-015843-X*, Penguin Bks.) Penguin Group (USA) Inc.
—First Hit of the Season. l.t. ed. 1985. lib. bdg. 13.95 o.p. (*0-89340-875-1*, 863) BBC Audiobooks America.
—First Hit of the Season. 1984. (Crime Club Ser.). 192p. 11.95 o.p. (*0-385-19409-9*) Doubleday Publishing.
—First Hit of the Season. 1993. (Jocelyn O'Roarke Mystery Ser.). 192p. pap. 4.95 o.p. (*0-14-015842-1*, Penguin Bks.) Penguin Group (USA) Inc.
—Murder on Cue. 1984. (Murder Ink Mystery Ser.: No. 71). pap. 2.95 o.p. (*0-440-16105-3*) Dell Publishing.
—Murder on Cue. 1983. 192p. 11.95 o.p. (*0-385-18411-5*) Doubleday Publishing.
—Murder on Cue. 1992. (Jocelyn O'Roarke Mystery Ser.). 192p. reprint ed. pap. 5.95 o.p. (*0-14-015841-3*, Penguin Bks.) Penguin Group (USA) Inc.
—The Queen Is Dead. 1995. (Jocelyn O'Roarke Mystery Ser.). 288p. pap. 5.95 o.s.i (*0-14-015835-9*, Penguin Bks.) Penguin Group (USA) Inc.
—The Queen Is Dead: A Jocelyn O'Roarke Mystery. 1994. (Jocelyn O'Roarke Mystery Ser.). 288p. 19.95 o.p. (*0-670-84109-9*, Viking) Viking Penguin.
—Who Dropped Peter Pan? A Jocelyn O'Roarke Mystery. 1996. (Penguin Crime Fiction Ser.). 288p. pap. 5.95 o.s.i (*0-14-024554-5*, Penguin Bks.) Penguin Group (USA) Inc.
—Who Dropped Peter Pan? A Jocelyn O'Roarke Mystery. 1995. (Jocelyn O'Roarke Mystery Ser.). 288p. 21.95 o.p. (*0-670-86070-0*, Viking) Viking Penguin.

**O'RYAN, JACK (FICTITIOUS CHARACTER)—FICTION**

Bova, Ben. Orion. 432p. 1989. pap. 3.95 o.s.i (*0-8125-3233-3*); 1992. reprint ed. mass mkt. 5.99 (*0-8125-3247-3*) Doherty, Tom Assocs., LLC. (Tor Bks.).
—Orion among the Stars. 1996. mass mkt. 5.99 (*0-8125-3511-1*); 1995. 320p. 14.95 o.p. (*0-312-85637-7*) Doherty, Tom Assocs., LLC. (Tor Bks.).
—Orion & the Conqueror. 1995. 350p. mass mkt. 5.99 (*0-8125-2376-8*); 1994. 384p. 22.95 o.p. (*0-312-85447-1*) Doherty, Tom Assocs., LLC. (Tor Bks.).
—Orion in the Dying Time. 1991. mass mkt. 4.99 (*0-8125-1429-7*); 1990. 18.95 o.p. (*0-312-93111-5*) Doherty, Tom Assocs., LLC. (Tor Bks.).
—Vengeance of Orion. 1989. 342p. mass mkt. 3.95 (*0-8125-3161-2*); 1988. 352p. 17.95 o.p. (*0-312-93049-6*) Doherty, Tom Assocs., LLC. (Tor Bks.).

**OSBOURNE, CRAIG (FICTITIOUS CHARACTER)—FICTION**

Higgins, Jack. Cold Harbour. 2003. 304p. mass mkt. 7.99 (*0-425-19320-9*) Berkley Publishing Group.
—Cold Harbour. 1990. 239.40 (*0-671-94343-X*); 19.95 o.p. (*0-671-68425-6*) Simon & Schuster. (Simon & Schuster).
—Cold Harbour. Grose, Bill, ed. 1990. reprint ed. mass mkt. 6.50 (*0-671-68426-4*, Pocket) Simon & Schuster.
—Cold Harbour. abr. ed. 1990. 15.95 incl. audio (*0-671-70194-0*, Simon & Schuster Audioworks) Simon & Schuster Audio.

**O'SHAUGHNESSY, KIERNAN (FICTITIOUS CHARACTER)—FICTION**

Dunlap, Susan. High Fall. 1995. (Kiernan O'Shaugnessy Mystery Ser.). 320p. mass mkt. 5.99 o.s.i (*0-440-21560-9*) Dell Publishing.
—High Fall. l.t. ed. 1995. (Large Print Bks.). pap. 20.95 (*1-56895-093-4*, Wheeler Publishing, Inc.) Gale Group.
—No Immunity: A Kiernan O'Shaughnessy Mystery. unabr. ed. 1999. audio 44.95 Blackstone Audio Bks., Inc.
—No Immunity: A Kiernan O'Shaughnessy Mystery. unabr. ed. 2000. audio 59.95 (*0-7927-2270-1*, CSL 159) Chivers Audio Bks. GBR. *Dist:* BBC Audiobooks America.
—No Immunity: A Kiernan O'Shaughnessy Mystery. 1999. (Kiernan O'Shaugnessy Mystery Ser.). 352p. mass mkt. 5.99 o.s.i (*0-440-22480-2*) Dell Publishing.
—No Immunity: A Kiernan O'Shaughnessy Mystery. l.t. ed. 1999. pap. 23.95 (*1-56895-782-3*, Wheeler Publishing, Inc.) Gale Group.
—Pious Deception. 1990. 256p. mass mkt. 5.99 o.s.i (*0-440-20746-0*) Dell Publishing.
—Rogue Wave. 1992. 272p. mass mkt. 5.99 o.s.i (*0-440-21197-2*) Dell Publishing.
—Rogue Wave. 1994. 3.99 o.p. (*0-517-13047-5*) Random Hse. Value Publishing.

**O'SHEA, VICTORY (FICTITIOUS CHARACTER)—FICTION**

MacPherson, Rett. A Comedy of Heirs. 2nd ed. 1999. (Torie O'Shea Mysteries Ser.). 214p. 21.95 (*0-312-20513-9*, Saint Martin's Minotaur) St. Martin's Pr.
—Family Skeletons. 1998. (Dead Letter Mysteries Ser.: Vol. 1). 224p. mass mkt. 6.50 (*0-312-96602-4*, St. Martin's Paperbacks); 1997. 208p. 21.95 o.p. (*0-312-15236-1*, Saint Martin's Minotaur) St. Martin's Pr.
—A Misty Mourning. l.t. ed. 2001. (Beeler Large Print Mystery Ser.). 251p. 25.95 (*1-57490-353-5*, Beeler Large Print Bks.) Beeler, Thomas T. Publisher.
—A Misty Mourning. (Torie O'Shea Mysteries Ser.). 2000. 244p. 22.95 (*0-312-26619-7*, Saint Martin's Minotaur); 2001. 272p. reprint ed. mass mkt. 6.50 (*0-312-97784-0*, St. Martin's Paperbacks) St. Martin's Pr.
—Veiled Antiquity. 1999. (Veiled Antiquity Ser.: Vol. 1). 240p. mass mkt. 5.99 (*0-312-96701-2*, St. Martin's Paperbacks); 1998. 224p. 20.95 (*0-312-18677-0*, Saint Martin's Minotaur) St. Martin's Pr.
MacPherson, Rett, contrib. by. A Comedy of Heirs: A Novel. l.t. ed. 2000. (Mystery Ser.). 349p. 27.95 o.p. (*0-7862-2346-4*) Thorndike Pr.
McPherson, Rett. A Comedy of Heirs: A Torie O'Shea Mystery. 2000. (Torie O'Shea Mysteries Ser.). 230p. mass mkt. 5.99 (*0-312-97133-8*, St. Martin's Paperbacks) St. Martin's Pr.

**O'SULLIVAN, MICHAEL (FICTITIOUS CHARACTER)—FICTION**

Collins, Max Allan. Road to Perdition. Heifer, Andrew, ed. 1998. (Illus.). 304p. pap. 13.95 (*1-56389-449-1*) DC Comics.
—Road to Perdition. 2002. 256p. mass mkt. 6.99 (*0-451-41029-7*) Penguin Group (USA) Inc.
—Road to Perdition. (Illus.). 304p. 2002. pap. 14.00 (*0-7434-4224-5*); 1998. per. 14.00 (*0-671-00921-4*) Simon & Schuster. (Pocket).

**OTANI, TETSUO, SUPERINTENDENT (FICTITIOUS CHARACTER)—FICTION**

Melville, James. The Body Wore Brocade: A Superintendent Otani Mystery. 1994. mass mkt. 4.99 o.s.i (*0-449-22189-X*, Fawcett) Ballantine Bks.
—The Body Wore Brocade: A Superintendent Otani Mystery. 1992. 224p. text 20.00 (*0-684-19413-9*, Macmillan Reference USA) Gale Group.
—The Body Wore Brocade: A Superintendent Otani Mystery. l.t. ed. 1994. (Ulverscroft Ser.). 304p. 29.99 o.p. (*0-7089-3064-6*, Ulverscroft) Thorpe, F. A. Pubs. GBR. *Dist:* Ulverscroft Large Print Bks., Ltd., Ulverscroft Large Print Canada, Ltd.
—The Bogus Buddha. 1991. mass mkt. 3.99 o.s.i (*0-449-21971-2*, Fawcett) Ballantine Bks.
—The Bogus Buddha. 1991. (Superintendent Otani Mystery Ser.). 224p. 17.95 o.s.i (*0-684-19247-0*, Macmillan Reference USA) Gale Group.
—The Bogus Buddha. l.t. ed. 1992. (Keating's Choice Ser.). 249p. 21.95 o.p. (*1-85089-569-4*) ISIS Large Print Bks. GBR. *Dist:* Transaction Pubs.
—The Chrysanthemum Chain. 1986. mass mkt. 2.95 o.s.i (*0-449-20822-2*, Fawcett) Ballantine Bks.
—The Chrysanthemum Chain. 1982. 182p. 9.95 o.p. (*0-312-13463-0*) St. Martin's Pr.
—The Chrysanthemum Chain. l.t. ed. 1982. (Ulverscroft Large Print Ser.). 370p. 29.99 o.p. (*0-7089-0758-X*, Ulverscroft) Thorpe, F. A. Pubs. GBR. *Dist:* Ulverscroft Large Print Bks., Ltd., Ulverscroft Large Print Canada, Ltd.
—The Death Ceremony. 1987. 208p. mass mkt. 2.95 o.s.i (*0-449-21131-2*, Fawcett) Ballantine Bks.
—The Death Ceremony. 1985. 192p. 12.95 o.p. (*0-312-18549-9*) St. Martin's Pr.
—Death of a Daimyo. 1986. mass mkt. 2.95 o.s.i (*0-449-20824-9*, Fawcett) Ballantine Bks.
—Death of a Daimyo. 1984. 152p. 10.95 o.p. (*0-312-18635-5*) St. Martin's Pr.
—Death of a Daimyo. l.t. ed. 1986. (Ulverscroft Large Print Ser.). 288p. 29.99 o.p. (*0-7089-1462-4*, Ulverscroft) Thorpe, F. A. Pubs. GBR. *Dist:* Ulverscroft Large Print Bks., Ltd., Ulverscroft Large Print Canada, Ltd.
—Diplomatic Baggage. 1996. 224p. 20.00 o.p. (*0-7278-4717-1*) Severn Hse. Pubs., Ltd.
—Go Gently, Gaijin. l.t. ed. 1991. pap. 8.95 o.p. (*1-55504-847-1*, 163); 1989. 19.95 o.p. (*1-55504-846-3*, 130) BBC Audiobooks America.
—Go Gently, Gaijin. 1988. (Superintendent Otani Mystery Ser.). 192p. mass mkt. 2.95 o.s.i (*0-449-21413-3*, Fawcett) Ballantine Bks.
—Go Gently, Gaijin. 1986. 192p. 12.95 o.p. (*0-312-32989-X*, Saint Martin's Minotaur) St. Martin's Pr.
—A Haiku for Hanae. 1990. 176p. mass mkt. 3.95 o.s.i (*0-449-21835-X*, Fawcett) Ballantine Bks.
—A Haiku for Hanae. 1989. 288p. 16.95 o.s.i (*0-684-19131-8*, Macmillan Reference USA) Gale Group.
—A Haiku for Hanae. l.t. ed. 1991. (Magna Large Print Ser.). 268p. o.p. (*1-85057-897-4*) Magna Large Print Bks. GBR. *Dist:* Ulverscroft Large Print Canada, Ltd.
—The Imperial Way. 1987. 240p. 18.95 o.p. (*0-233-97819-4*) Andre Deutsch GBR. *Dist:* Trafalgar Square, Trans-Atlantic Pubns., Inc.
—The Imperial Way. 1987. 304p. reprint ed. mass mkt. 3.95 o.s.i (*0-449-21374-9*, Fawcett) Ballantine Bks.
—Kimono for a Corpse. 1989. mass mkt. 3.50 o.s.i (*0-449-21644-6*, Fawcett) Ballantine Bks.
—Kimono for a Corpse. 1988. 208p. 14.95 o.p. (*0-312-01454-6*, Saint Martin's Minotaur) St. Martin's Pr.
—The Ninth Netsuke. 1986. mass mkt. 2.95 o.s.i (*0-449-20823-0*, Fawcett) Ballantine Bks.
—The Ninth Netsuke. 1982. 160p. 9.95 o.p. (*0-312-57476-2*) St. Martin's Pr.
—The Ninth Netsuke. l.t. ed. 1986. (Ulverscroft Large Print Ser.). 320p. 29.99 o.p. (*0-7089-1404-7*, Ulverscroft) Thorpe, F. A. Pubs. GBR. *Dist:* Ulverscroft Large Print Bks., Ltd., Ulverscroft Large Print Canada, Ltd.
—The Reluctant Ronin: A Superintendent Otani Mystery. 1989. 224p. mass mkt. 3.50 o.s.i (*0-449-21619-5*, Fawcett) Ballantine Bks.
—The Reluctant Ronin: A Superintendent Otani Mystery. l.t. ed. 1989. 304p. lib. bdg. 23.95 o.p. (*0-7451-0950-0*, Macmillan Reference USA) Gale Group.
—The Reluctant Ronin: A Superintendent Otani Mystery. 1988. 192p. 15.95 o.s.i (*0-684-18947-X*, Scribner) Simon & Schuster.
—Sayonara, Sweet Amaryllis. 1987. 208p. mass mkt. 2.95 o.s.i (*0-449-20825-7*, Fawcett) Ballantine Bks.
—Sayonara, Sweet Amaryllis. 1985. 160p. 10.95 o.p. (*0-312-69995-6*) St. Martin's Pr.
—Sayonara, Sweet Amaryllis. l.t. ed. 1986. (Ulverscroft Large Print Ser.). 320p. 29.99 o.p. (*0-7089-1433-0*, Ulverscroft) Thorpe, F. A. Pubs. GBR. *Dist:* Ulverscroft Large Print Bks., Ltd., Ulverscroft Large Print Canada, Ltd.

—A Sort of Samurai. 1985. 208p. mass mkt. 2.95 o.s.i (0-449-20821-4, Fawcett) Ballantine Bks.
—A Sort of Samurai. 1983. 176p. pap. 5.95 o.p. (0-312-74559-1, Saint Martin's Griffin); 1982. 168p. 9.95 o.p. (0-312-74558-3) St. Martin's Pr.
—A Tarnished Phoenix. l.t. ed. 1992. (Adventure Suspense Ser.). 432p. 29.99 o.p. (0-7089-2666-5, Ulverscroft) Thorpe, F. A. Pubs. GBR. *Dist:* Ulverscroft Large Print Bks., Ltd., Ulverscroft Large Print Canada, Ltd.
—The Wages of Zen. 1985. 224p. mass mkt. 3.50 o.s.i (0-449-20838-9, Fawcett) Ballantine Bks.

**OTHMAN, PEREVAL (FICTITIOUS CHARACTER)—FICTION**

Constantine, Storm. Scenting Hollowed Blood. 1999. (Grigori Trilogy Ser.: No. 2). 386p. pap. 16.00 (0-9658345-5-7) Meisha Merlin Publishing, Inc.
—Stalking Tender Prey. 1998. (Grigori Trilogy Ser.: Vol. 1). 488p. pap. 16.00 (0-9658345-4-9) Meisha Merlin Publishing, Inc.
—Stealing Sacred Fire. 2000. (Grigori Trilogy Ser.: Vol. 3). 456p. pap. 16.00 (0-9658345-6-5) Meisha Merlin Publishing, Inc.

**O'TOOLE, BRIDGET, SISTER (FICTITIOUS CHARACTER)—FICTION**

McConnell, Frank. Blood Lake: A Harry Garnish/Bridget O'Toole Mystery. l.t. ed. 1988. 19.95 o.p. (1-55504-590-1); pap. 17.95 o.p. (1-55504-573-1) BBC Audiobooks America.
—Blood Lake: A Harry Garnish/Bridget O'Toole Mystery. 1988. (Crime Ser.). 256p. pap. 3.95 o.p. (0-14-010755-X, Penguin Bks.); 39.50 o.p. (0-14-778359-3) Viking Penguin.
—Blood Lake: A Harry Garnish/Bridget O'Toole Mystery. 1987. 256p. 16.95 o.s.i (0-8027-5673-5) Walker & Co.
—The Frog King: A Harry Garnish/Bridget O'Toole Mystery. l.t. ed. 1992. pap. 19.95 o.p. (0-7927-1175-0); 21.95 o.p. (0-7927-1149-1, CH0241) BBC Audiobooks America.
—The Frog King: A Harry Garnish/Bridget O'Toole Mystery. 1990. 192p. 18.95 o.p. (0-8027-5748-0) Walker & Co.
—Liar's Poker: A Harry Garnish/Bridget O'Toole Mystery. 1993. 234p. 19.95 (0-8027-3229-1) Walker & Co.
—Murder among Friends: A Harry Garnish/Bridget O'Toole Mystery. l.t. ed. 1986. pap. 13.95 o.p. (0-7451-9149-5) BBC Audiobooks America.
—Murder among Friends: A Harry Garnish/Bridget O'Toole Mystery. 1988. pap. 39.50 o.p. (0-14-778313-5); 192p. mass mkt. 3.95 o.p. (0-451-82189-0, Penguin Bks.) Viking Penguin.
—Murder among Friends: A Harry Garnish/Bridget O'Toole Mystery. 1983. 192p. 12.95 o.s.i (0-8027-5567-4) Walker & Co.

**OWEN, GARETH CADWALLADER (FICTITIOUS CHARACTER)—FICTION**

Pearce, Michael. The Girl in the Nile. 2003. (Mamur Zapt Mystery Ser.). 230p. pap. 14.95 o.s.i (1-59058-053-2) Poisoned Pen Pr.
—The Mamur Zapt & the Donkey-Vous: A Suspense Tale of Old Cairo. 1992. 272p. 17.95 (0-89296-486-3) Mysterious Pr.
—The Mamur Zapt & the Donkey-Vous: A Suspense Tale of Old Cairo. 1993. 272p. mass mkt. 4.99 o.s.i (0-446-40181-1) Warner Bks., Inc.
—The Men Behind: A Mamur Zapt Mystery. 2003. (Mamur Zapt Mystery Ser.). 225p. pap. 14.95 o.s.i (1-59058-052-4) Poisoned Pen Pr.

**OXBY, INSPECTOR JACK (FICTITIOUS CHARACTER)—FICTION**

Swan, Thomas. The Cezanne Chase: A Novel of Suspense. 2004. 320p. 21.95 (1-55704-304-3) Newmarket Pr.
—The Da Vinci Deception: A Novel of Suspense. 1990. 304p. mass mkt. 4.95 o.s.i (0-553-28495-9) Bantam Bks.
—The Da Vinci Deception: A Novel of Suspense. 2004. 288p. 23.95 (1-55704-352-3) Newmarket Pr.
—The Final Faberge: A Novel of Suspense. 2001. 416p. mass mkt. 6.50 o.s.i (0-451-40964-7, Onyx) NAL.
—The Final Faberge: A Novel of Suspense. 2004. 320p. 24.95 (1-55704-382-5) Newmarket Pr.

# P

**PACE, STEVE (FICTITIOUS CHARACTER)—FICTION**

Heller, Jean. Maximum Impact. 1995. 627p. pap. 5.99 (0-8125-1619-2); 1993. 432p. 22.95 o.p. (0-312-85203-7) Doherty, Tom Assocs., LLC. (Forge Bks.).

**PAGAN, FRANK (FICTITIOUS CHARACTER)—FICTION**

Armstrong, Campbell. Jig. Congdon, Thomas, ed. 1987. 512p. 18.95 o.p. (0-688-06879-0, Morrow, William & Co.) Morrow/Avon.
—Jig. 1989. bds. 4.95 (0-671-66524-3, Pocket) Simon & Schuster.
—Jigsaw. 1996. 476p. mass mkt. 8.99 o.s.i (0-552-14168-2) Bantam Bks.
—Jigsaw. 1997. 352p. mass mkt. 5.99 o.s.i (0-7860-0412-6, Pinnacle Bks.) Kensington Publishing Corp.
—Jigsaw. 1995. 431p. 21.95 o.p. (0-316-04821-6) Little Brown & Co.
—White Light. 1988. 18.95 o.p. (0-688-07701-3, Morrow, William & Co.) Morrow/Avon.

**PAGE, GIDEON (FICTITIOUS CHARACTER)—FICTION**

Stockley, Grif. Blind Judgment. 1999. (Gideon Page Mystery Ser.). 384p. mass mkt. 6.50 o.s.i (0-06-101317-X) HarperCollins Pubs.
—Blind Judgment. 1997. 21.50 (0-684-81564-8, Simon & Schuster) Simon & Schuster.
—Expert Testimony. 1994. pap. 5.99 o.p. (0-8041-9832-2); 1993. pap. 5.99 o.p. (0-8041-9810-1); 1992. mass mkt. 5.99 o.s.i (0-8041-1094-8) Ballantine Bks. (Ivy Bks.).
—Expert Testimony. 1991. 19.95 o.p. (0-671-70920-8) Summit Bks.
—Illegal Motion: A Gideon Page Mystery. 1997. 408p. mass mkt. 6.99 o.s.i (0-449-18332-7, Fawcett); 1996. mass mkt. 6.99 o.p. (0-449-22557-7, Fawcett); 1995. mass mkt. 5.99 o.s.i (0-8041-1401-3, Ivy Bks.) Ballantine Bks.
—Illegal Motion: A Gideon Page Mystery. 1995. 301p. 21.00 (0-684-80355-0, Simon & Schuster) Simon & Schuster.
—Probable Cause. 1993. (Southern Mysteries Ser.). mass mkt. 5.99 o.s.i (0-8041-1133-2, Ivy Bks.) Ballantine Bks.
—Probable Cause. 1992. 287p. 19.00 o.p. (0-671-74601-4, Simon & Schuster) Simon & Schuster.
—Religious Conviction. 1995. reprint ed. mass mkt. 5.99 o.s.i (0-8041-1255-X, Ivy Bks.) Ballantine Bks.
—Religious Conviction. 1994. 286p. 21.00 (0-671-79869-3, Simon & Schuster) Simon & Schuster.

**PAGE, LORRAINE (FICTITIOUS CHARACTER)—FICTION**

La Plante, Lynda. Cold Blood. 1999. 480p. mass mkt. 6.99 o.s.i (0-515-12479-6, Jove) Berkley Publishing Group.
—Cold Blood. unabr. ed. 2000. (Lorraine Page Mystery Ser.). audio 89.95 (0-7451-8782-X, CAB 1417) Chivers Audio Bks. GBR. *Dist:* BBC Audiobooks America.
—Cold Heart. unabr. ed. 1998. audio 84.95 (0-7540-0213-6, CAB 1636) BBC Audiobooks America.
—Cold Shoulder. 1997. 464p. mass mkt. 6.99 o.s.i (0-515-12128-2, Jove) Berkley Publishing Group.
—Cold Shoulder. unabr. ed. 2000. (Lorraine Page Mystery Ser.). audio 79.95 (0-7451-6511-7, CAB 1127) Chivers Audio Bks. GBR. *Dist:* BBC Audiobooks America.

**PAGET, CHRISTOPHER (FICTITIOUS CHARACTER)—FICTION**

Patterson, Richard North. Degree of Guilt. 1998. pap. 7.99 (0-345-91454-6); 1997. pap. 12.00 o.s.i (0-345-41811-5); 1992. mass mkt. o.s.i (0-345-38408-3); 1993. 544p. reprint ed. mass mkt. 7.99 (0-345-38184-X) Ballantine Bks.
—Degree of Guilt. unabr. collector's ed. 1994. audio 104.00 (0-7366-2612-3, 3354) Books on Tape, Inc.
—Degree of Guilt. unabr. ed. 1993. audio 16.00 o.s.i (0-679-42131-9); Set. 1994. audio 8.99 o.s.i (0-679-43409-7) Random Hse. Audio Publishing Group. (RH Audio).
—Degree of Guilt. l.t. ed. 1993. 25.00 o.s.i (0-679-42211-0) Random Hse., Inc.
—Eyes of a Child. 1998. pap. 7.99 (0-345-91463-5); 1997. pap. 12.00 o.s.i (0-345-41813-1); 1995. 576p. mass mkt. 7.99 (0-345-38613-2); 1995. mass mkt. 6.99 o.s.i (0-345-40007-0); 1994. mass mkt. o.p. (0-345-39526-3) Ballantine Bks.
—Eyes of a Child. abr. ed. 2003. audio compact disk 14.99 (0-7393-0377-5, RH Audio Price-Less); 1995. audio 17.00 o.s.i (0-679-43952-8, RH Audio); Set. 1997. audio 8.99 o.s.i (0-679-46021-7, RH Audio) Random Hse. Audio Publishing Group.
—Eyes of a Child. l.t. ed. 1995. pap. 23.00 o.s.i (0-679-76031-8) Random Hse., Inc.
—The Lasko Tangent. 1997. pap. 12.00 o.s.i (0-345-41814-X); 1994. mass mkt. 5.99 o.p. (0-345-90128-2); 1985. 368p. mass mkt. 7.99 (0-345-32532-X); 1980. mass mkt. 1.95 o.p. (0-345-28705-3) Ballantine Bks.
—The Lasko Tangent. l.t. ed. 2000. 11.95 (1-56895-984-2); 26.95 o.p. (1-56895-830-7) Gale Group. (Wheeler Publishing, Inc.).
—The Lasko Tangent. 1979. 9.95 o.p. (0-393-01190-9) Norton, W. W. & Co., Inc.
—The Lasko Tangent, Set. abr. ed. 1999. audio 8.99 o.s.i (0-375-40571-2, RH Audio) Random Hse. Audio Publishing Group.

**PAIGE, JENNY (FICTITIOUS CHARACTER)—FICTION**

Koontz, Dean. Phantoms. 432p. 1997. mass mkt. 7.50 o.s.i (0-425-16202-8); 1986. mass mkt. 7.99 o.s.i (0-425-10145-2) Berkley Publishing Group.
—Phantoms. 1983. 352p. 15.95 o.p. (0-399-12655-4, G. P. Putnam's Sons) Penguin Putnam Bks. for Young Readers.
—Phantoms. 1983. 14.04 (0-606-03685-7) Turtleback Bks.

**PAKSENARRION (FICTITIOUS CHARACTER)—FICTION**

Moon, Elizabeth. The Deed of Paksenarrion. Baen, James, ed. 2003. 1136p. 26.00 (0-7434-7160-1) Baen Bks.
—The Deed of Paksenarrion. 1992. 1040p. reprint ed. pap. 18.00 (0-671-72104-6) Baen Bks.
—Divided Allegiance. 1988. (Deed of Paksenarrion Ser.: Bk. 2). 528p. (Orig.). pap. 7.99 (0-671-69786-2) Baen Bks.
—Oath of Gold. 2001. (Deed of Paksenarrion Ser.: Bk. III). 512p. pap. 6.99 (0-671-69798-6) Baen Bks.
—Sheepfarmer's Daughter. 1988. (Sheepfarmer's Daughter Ser.: Bk. 1). 512p. pap. 5.99 (0-671-65416-0) Baen Bks.

**PALFREY, PHILIPPA (FICTITIOUS CHARACTER)—FICTION**

James, P. D. Innocent Blood. 1980. 10.95 o.s.i (0-684-16591-0, Macmillan Reference USA) Gale Group.
—Innocent Blood. 2001. 400p. pap. 12.00 (0-7432-1963-5, Touchstone) Simon & Schuster.
—Innocent Blood. 1988. 352p. mass mkt. 6.99 o.p. (0-446-31177-4) Warner Bks., Inc.

**PALLARD, FRANK (FICTITIOUS CHARACTER)—FICTION**

Koontz, Dean. The Bad Place. 1990. 432p. mass mkt. 7.99 (0-425-12434-7) Berkley Publishing Group.
—The Bad Place. l.t. ed. 1991. (Magna Large Print Ser.). 612p. o.p. (0-7505-0103-0) Magna Large Print Bks. GBR. *Dist:* Ulverscroft Large Print Canada, Ltd.
—The Bad Place. 2001. 19.95 (0-399-13703-3) Penguin Group (USA) Inc.
—The Bad Place. 1990. 384p. 19.95 o.p. (0-399-13498-0); 75.00 o.p. (0-399-13510-3) Penguin Putnam Bks. for Young Readers. (G. P. Putnam's Sons).
—The Bad Place. 1990. 14.04 (0-606-00936-1) Turtleback Bks.

**PALMA, CARMEN (FICTITIOUS CHARACTER)—FICTION**

Lindsey, David L. Mercy. 1991. 608p. mass mkt. 7.50 (0-553-28972-1) Bantam Bks.
—Mercy. 1992. audio 12.79 o.s.i (0-553-70055-3); 1999. audio 9.99 o.s.i (0-553-70205-X) Random Hse. Audio Publishing Group. (RH Audio).

**PALMER, CHILI (FICTITIOUS CHARACTER)—FICTION**

Leonard, Elmore. Be Cool. 1999. (0-7540-1295-6) BBC Audiobooks America.
—Be Cool. 1999. audio compact disk 48.00 (0-7366-4761-9); 2000. audio compact disk (0-7366-5552-2); 1999. audio 40.00 (0-7366-4449-0, 4894) Books on Tape, Inc.
—Be Cool. 2000. 368p. mass mkt. 7.50 o.s.i (0-440-23505-7); 1999. mass mkt. 7.99 (0-440-29577-7) Dell Publishing.
—Be Cool. abr. ed. 1999. audio 25.00 o.s.i (0-553-52604-9, RH Audio) Random Hse. Audio Publishing Group.
—Be Cool. 2000. E-Book 7.50 (0-440-33423-3) Random Hse., Inc.
—Be Cool. unabr. ed. 2000. audio compact disk 59.00 (0-7887-3430-X, C1036E7); 1999. audio 51.00 (0-7887-2916-0, 95708E7) Recorded Bks., LLC.
—Be Cool. l.t. ed. (Thorndike/G. K. Hall Paperback Bestsellers Ser.). 383p. 2000. pap. 27.95 (0-7862-1839-8); 1999. lib. bdg. 30.95 (0-7862-1838-X) Thorndike Pr.
—Get Shorty. unabr. ed. 1992. audio 48.00 (0-7366-2222-5, 3012) Books on Tape, Inc.
—Get Shorty. 2000. 368p. mass mkt. 4.99 o.s.i (0-440-23614-2); 1998. 304p. pap. 9.95 o.s.i (0-385-32398-0); 1995. 304p. pap. 8.95 o.s.i (0-385-31567-8, Delacorte Pr.); 1991. 368p. mass mkt. 5.50 o.s.i (0-440-29515-7); 1991. 384p. mass mkt. 6.99 o.s.i (0-440-20980-3) Dell Publishing.
—Get Shorty. l.t. ed. 1993. pap. 18.95 (0-8161-5809-6, Macmillan Reference USA) Gale Group.
—Get Shorty. 1990. audio 14.98 o.s.i (0-553-74582-4); audio 12.79 o.s.i (0-553-19964-1) Random Hse. Audio Publishing Group. (RH Audio).
Leonard, Elmore, contrib. by. Be Cool. 1999. (0-7540-2221-8) BBC Audiobooks America.

**PALMER, HARRY (FICTITIOUS CHARACTER)—FICTION**

Deighton, Len. Spy Story. 1985. 272p. mass mkt. 4.95 o.s.i (0-345-31569-3, Ballantine Bks.) Ballantine Bks.
—Spy Story. 1974. 6.95 o.p. (0-15-184838-6) Harcourt Trade Pubs.
—Spy Story. 1991. 304p. mass mkt. 5.50 o.p. (0-06-100265-8, HarperTorch) Morrow/Avon.
—Spy Story. 1983. mass mkt. 3.50 o.s.i (0-671-47164-3, 80058, Pocket) Simon & Schuster.

**PALMER, JODY (FICTITIOUS CHARACTER)—FICTION**

Pine, Nicholas. Stalker. 1993. (Terror Academy Ser.: No. 2). 192p. (Orig.). (J). mass mkt. 3.50 o.s.i (0-425-13814-3) Berkley Publishing Group.

**PALMER-JONES, GEORGE (FICTITIOUS CHARACTER)—FICTION**

Cleeves, Ann. Another Man's Poison. 1993. mass mkt. 4.50 o.s.i (0-449-14850-5, Fawcett) Ballantine Bks.
—Another Man's Poison. l.t. ed. 1994. (Ulverscroft Large Print Ser.). 400p. 29.99 o.p. (0-7089-3038-7, Ulverscroft) Thorpe, F. A. Pubs. GBR. *Dist:* Ulverscroft Large Print Bks., Ltd., Ulverscroft Large Print Canada, Ltd.
—A Bird in the Hand. 1987. mass mkt. 4.99 o.s.i (0-449-13349-4, Fawcett) Ballantine Bks.
—A Bird in the Hand. l.t. ed. 1988. 416p. 15.95 o.p. (0-7089-1830-1, Ulverscroft) Thorpe, F. A. Pubs. GBR. *Dist:* Ulverscroft Large Print Bks., Ltd.
—Come Death & High Water. 1988. 224p. mass mkt. 4.50 o.s.i (0-449-13348-6, Fawcett) Ballantine Bks.
—Come Death & High Water. l.t. ed. 1989. (Ulverscroft Large Print Ser.). 29.99 o.p. (0-7089-2101-9, Ulverscroft) Thorpe, F. A. Pubs. GBR. *Dist:* Ulverscroft Large Print Bks., Ltd., Ulverscroft Large Print Canada, Ltd.
—High Island Blues. 1996. mass mkt. 5.50 o.s.i (0-449-14979-X) Ballantine Bks.
—The Mill on the Shore. 1994. mass mkt. 4.99 o.s.i (0-449-14918-8, Fawcett) Ballantine Bks.
—Murder in Paradise. 1988. mass mkt. 4.99 o.s.i (0-449-14540-9, Fawcett) Ballantine Bks.
—Murder in Paradise. l.t. ed. 1990. (Ulverscroft Large Print Ser.). 29.99 o.p. (0-7089-2200-7, Ulverscroft) Thorpe, F. A. Pubs. GBR. *Dist:* Ulverscroft Large Print Bks., Ltd., Ulverscroft Large Print Canada, Ltd.
—A Prey to Murder. 1989. 192p. mass mkt. 4.99 o.s.i (0-449-14575-1, Fawcett) Ballantine Bks.
—A Prey to Murder. l.t. ed. 1991. (Ulverscroft Large Print Ser.). 29.99 o.p. (0-7089-2386-0, Ulverscroft) Thorpe, F. A. Pubs. GBR. *Dist:* Ulverscroft Large Print Bks., Ltd., Ulverscroft Large Print Canada, Ltd.
—Sea Fever. 1991. (Illus.). 192p. mass mkt. 3.99 o.s.i (0-449-14707-X, Fawcett) Ballantine Bks.

**PALMER-JONES, MOLLY (FICTITIOUS CHARACTER)—FICTION**

Cleeves, Ann. Another Man's Poison. 1993. mass mkt. 4.50 o.s.i (0-449-14850-5, Fawcett) Ballantine Bks.
—Another Man's Poison. l.t. ed. 1994. (Ulverscroft Large Print Ser.). 400p. 29.99 o.p. (0-7089-3038-7, Ulverscroft) Thorpe, F. A. Pubs. GBR. *Dist:* Ulverscroft Large Print Bks., Ltd., Ulverscroft Large Print Canada, Ltd.
—A Bird in the Hand. 1987. mass mkt. 4.99 o.s.i (0-449-13349-4, Fawcett) Ballantine Bks.
—A Bird in the Hand. l.t. ed. 1988. 416p. 15.95 o.p. (0-7089-1830-1, Ulverscroft) Thorpe, F. A. Pubs. GBR. *Dist:* Ulverscroft Large Print Bks., Ltd.
—Come Death & High Water. 1988. 224p. mass mkt. 4.50 o.s.i (0-449-13348-6, Fawcett) Ballantine Bks.
—Come Death & High Water. l.t. ed. 1989. (Ulverscroft Large Print Ser.). 29.99 o.p. (0-7089-2101-9, Ulverscroft) Thorpe, F. A. Pubs. GBR. *Dist:* Ulverscroft Large Print Bks., Ltd., Ulverscroft Large Print Canada, Ltd.
—High Island Blues. 1996. mass mkt. 5.50 o.s.i (0-449-14979-X) Ballantine Bks.
—The Mill on the Shore. 1994. mass mkt. 4.99 o.s.i (0-449-14918-8, Fawcett) Ballantine Bks.
—Murder in Paradise. 1988. mass mkt. 4.99 o.s.i (0-449-14540-9, Fawcett) Ballantine Bks.
—Murder in Paradise. l.t. ed. 1990. (Ulverscroft Large Print Ser.). 29.99 o.p. (0-7089-2200-7, Ulverscroft) Thorpe, F. A. Pubs. GBR. *Dist:* Ulverscroft Large Print Bks., Ltd., Ulverscroft Large Print Canada, Ltd.
—A Prey to Murder. 1989. 192p. mass mkt. 4.99 o.s.i (0-449-14575-1, Fawcett) Ballantine Bks.
—A Prey to Murder. l.t. ed. 1991. (Ulverscroft Large Print Ser.). 29.99 o.p. (0-7089-2386-0, Ulverscroft) Thorpe, F. A. Pubs. GBR. *Dist:* Ulverscroft Large Print Bks., Ltd., Ulverscroft Large Print Canada, Ltd.
—Sea Fever. 1991. (Illus.). 192p. mass mkt. 3.99 o.s.i (0-449-14707-X, Fawcett) Ballantine Bks.

**PALMIERI, FELIX (FICTITIOUS CHARACTER)—FICTION**

Murano, Vincent & Hammer, Richard. The Thursday Club: A Novel. 1992. 304p. 21.00 o.p. (*0-671-73448-2*, Simon & Schuster) Simon & Schuster.

—The Thursday Club: A Novel. Rubenstein, Julie, ed. 1994. 304p. reprint ed. mass mkt. 5.50 (*0-671-73864-X*, Pocket) Simon & Schuster.

**PAMPLEMOUSSE, ARISTIDE (FICTITIOUS CHARACTER)—FICTION**

Bond, Michael. Monsieur Pamplemousse. 1986. 192p. mass mkt. 4.99 o.s.i (*0-449-20956-3*, Fawcett) Ballantine Bks.

—Monsieur Pamplemousse. 1985. 192p. 13.95 o.p. (*0-8253-0267-6*) Beaufort Bks., Inc.

—Monsieur Pamplemousse. l.t. ed. 1991. (Nightingale Series Large Print Bks.). 240p. pap. 14.95 o.p. (*0-8161-5111-3*, Macmillan Reference USA) Gale Group.

—Monsieur Pamplemousse. unabr. ed. 1991. (Monsieur Pamplemousse Mystery Ser.: Vol. 1). (YA). (gr. 10 up). audio 35.00 (*1-55690-346-4*, 91225E7) Recorded Bks., LLC.

—Monsieur Pamplemousse Afloat. 1999. 214p. pap. 9.95 (*0-7490-0347-2*) Allison & Busby, Ltd. GBR. *Dist:* International Publishers Marketing.

—Monsieur Pamplemousse Aloft. 1990. mass mkt. 4.99 o.s.i (*0-449-21673-X*, Fawcett) Ballantine Bks.

—Monsieur Pamplemousse Aloft. 1991. 2.99 o.p. (*0-517-07165-7*) Random Hse. Value Publishing.

—Monsieur Pamplemousse & the Secret Mission. 1987. mass mkt. 4.95 o.s.i (*0-449-21128-2*, Fawcett) Ballantine Bks.

—Monsieur Pamplemousse & the Secret Mission. 1986. 208p. 13.95 o.p. (*0-8253-0301-X*) Beaufort Bks., Inc.

—Monsieur Pamplemousse & the Secret Mission. l.t. ed. 1991. (Nightingale Ser.). 280p. pap. 14.95 o.p. (*0-8161-5110-5*, Macmillan Reference USA) Gale Group.

—Monsieur Pamplemousse & the Secret Mission. unabr. ed. 1991. (Monsieur Pamplemousse Mystery Ser.: Vol. 3). audio 35.00 (*1-55690-327-8*, 91311E7) Recorded Bks., LLC.

—Monsieur Pamplemousse Investigates. 1991. mass mkt. 3.99 o.s.i (*0-449-21899-6*, Fawcett) Ballantine Bks.

—Monsieur Pamplemousse Investigates. unabr. ed. 1991. (Monsieur Pamplemousse Mystery Ser.: Vol. 7). audio 44.00 (*1-55690-698-6*, 91408E7) Recorded Bks., LLC.

—Monsieur Pamplemousse Omnibus. 1999. Vol. 1. 191p. 16.95 o.p. (*0-7490-0352-9*); Vol. 2. 592p. pap. text 16.95 (*0-7490-0410-X*); Vol. 3. 704p. pap. 16.95 (*0-7490-0442-8*) Allison & Busby, Ltd. GBR. *Dist:* International Publishers Marketing.

—Monsieur Pamplemousse on Probation. 2000. 160p. pap. 9.95 (*0-7490-0463-0*, London Hse.) Allison & Busby, Ltd. GBR. *Dist:* International Publishers Marketing.

—Monsieur Pamplemousse on the Spot. 1988. reprint ed. mass mkt. 3.95 o.s.i (*0-449-21338-2*, Fawcett) Ballantine Bks.

—Monsieur Pamplemousse on the Spot. 1987. 160p. 14.95 o.p. (*0-8253-0389-3*) Beaufort Bks., Inc.

—Monsieur Pamplemousse on the Spot. l.t. unabr. ed. 1989. (Nightingale Ser.). 277p. 13.95 o.p. (*0-8161-4695-0*, Macmillan Reference USA) Gale Group.

—Monsieur Pamplemousse on Vacation. 2002. 191p. 25.95 (*0-7490-0532-7*) Allison & Busby, Ltd. GBR. *Dist:* International Publishers Marketing.

—Monsieur Pamplemousse on Vacation. 2003. (General Ser.). lib. bdg. 25.95 (*0-7862-4742-8*) Thorndike Pr.

—Monsieur Pamplemousse Rests His Case. 1993. mass mkt. 4.50 o.p. (*0-449-22045-1*); 1991. 176p. 17.00 o.s.i (*0-449-90639-6*) Ballantine Bks. (Fawcett).

—Monsieur Pamplemousse Rests His Case. l.t. ed. 1993. (Nightingale Ser.). 285p. lib. bdg. 15.95 o.p. (*0-8161-5768-5*, Macmillan Reference USA) Gale Group.

—Monsieur Pamplemousse Rests His Case. 1993. mass mkt. 3.99 o.p. (*0-517-09781-8*) Random Hse. Value Publishing.

—Monsieur Pamplemousse Rests His Case. unabr. ed. 1992. (Monsieur Pamplemousse Mystery Ser.: Vol. 8). audio 35.00 (*1-55690-759-1*, 92415E7) Recorded Bks., LLC.

—Monsieur Pamplemousse Stands Firm. 1994. mass mkt. 4.99 o.s.i (*0-449-22201-2*, Fawcett) Ballantine Bks.

—Monsieur Pamplemousse Takes the Cure. 1989. mass mkt. 3.95 o.s.i (*0-449-21674-8*, Fawcett) Ballantine Bks.

—Monsieur Pamplemousse Takes the Cure. l.t. ed. 1990. (Nightingale Ser.). 288p. pap. 14.95 o.p. (*0-8161-4893-7*, Macmillan Reference USA) Gale Group.

—More about Paddington. l.t. ed. 1991. (Paddington Ser.). (Illus.). 176p. (J). (ps-3). 13.95 o.p. (*0-7451-1297-8*, Galaxy Children's Large Print) BBC Audiobooks America.

—More about Paddington. rev. ed. 1979. (Paddington Ser.). (Illus.). 144p. (J). (gr. 4-6). 15.00 (*0-395-06640-9*) Houghton Mifflin Co.

—More about Paddington. 1979. (Paddington Ser.). (Illus.). 128p. (J). (ps-3). pap. 2.95 o.s.i (*0-440-45825-0*, Yearling) Random Hse. Children's Bks.

**PANTALOON (FICTITIOUS CHARACTER)—FICTION**

Barrie, J. M. Pantaloon. Landes, William-Alan, ed. 1993. 32p. (J). (gr. 6-12). pap. 6.00 (*0-88734-316-3*) Players Pr., Inc.

**PARET, IRY (FICTITIOUS CHARACTER)—FICTION**

Burke, James Lee. The Lost Get-Back Boogie. Date not set. lib. bdg. 24.95 (*0-8488-1780-X*) Amereon, Ltd.

—The Lost Get-Back Boogie. 1987. 256p. pap. 8.95 o.p. (*0-8050-0541-2*, Owl Bks.) Holt, Henry & Co.

—The Lost Get-Back Boogie. 256p. 1995. pap. 10.95 (*0-7868-8101-1*); 1997. reprint ed. mass mkt. 5.99 (*0-7868-8934-9*) Hyperion Pr.

—The Lost Get-Back Boogie. 1986. 241p. 16.95 (*0-8071-1334-4*) Louisiana State Univ. Pr.

**PARGETER, MRS. (FICTITIOUS CHARACTER)—FICTION**

Brett, Simon. Mrs. Pargeter's Package. 1991. 288p. 18.95 o.s.i (*0-684-19286-1*, Macmillan Reference USA) Gale Group.

—Mrs. Pargeter's Package. unabr. ed. 2001. audio 54.95 (*1-85089-648-8*, 91061); 1999. audio compact disk 59.95 (*0-7531-0711-2*, 107112) ISIS Audio Bks. GBR. *Dist:* Ulverscroft Large Print Bks., Ltd.

—Mrs. Pargeter's Package. l.t. ed. 1991. (Magna Large Print Ser.). 270p. o.p. (*0-7505-0130-8*) Magna Large Print Bks. GBR. *Dist:* Ulverscroft Large Print Canada, Ltd.

—Mrs. Pargeter's Package. 1992. 224p. mass mkt. 4.99 (*0-446-36204-2*) Warner Bks., Inc.

—Mrs. Pargeter's Plot. 1999. (WWL Mystery Ser.: No. 322). per. (*0-373-26322-8*, 1-26322-7, Worldwide Library) Harlequin Enterprises, Ltd.

—Mrs. Pargeter's Plot. unabr. ed. 2001. audio 49.95 (*0-7531-0103-3*, 961001); 2000. audio compact disk 59.95 (*0-7531-0904-2*, 109042) ISIS Audio Bks. GBR. *Dist:* Ulverscroft Large Print Bks., Ltd.

—Mrs. Pargeter's Plot. l.t. ed. 1998. (Magna Large Print Ser.). 320p. o.p. (*0-7505-1284-9*) Magna Large Print Bks. GBR. *Dist:* Ulverscroft Large Print Canada, Ltd.

—Mrs. Pargeter's Plot. 1998. (Mrs. Pargeter Mysteries Ser.). 256p. 22.00 (*0-684-83714-5*, Scribner) Simon & Schuster.

—Mrs. Pargeter's Plot. l.t. ed. 1998. (Mystery Ser.). 255p. 30.95 (*0-7838-0172-6*) Thorndike Pr.

—Mrs. Pargeter's Point of Honour. 2003. (Mystery Ser.). 28.95 (*1-57490-465-5*) Beeler, Thomas T. Publisher.

—Mrs. Pargeter's Point of Honour. 2000. (Mrs. Pargeter Mysteries Ser.). 256p. mass mkt. (*0-373-26361-9*, 1-26361-5, Worldwide Library) Harlequin Enterprises, Ltd.

—Mrs. Pargeter's Point of Honour. unabr. ed. 1999. audio 54.95 (*0-7531-0466-0*, 981201) ISIS Audio Bks. GBR. *Dist:* Ulverscroft Large Print Bks., Ltd.

—Mrs. Pargeter's Point of Honour. l.t. ed. 1999. (Magna Large Print Ser.). 320p. o.p. (*0-7505-1394-2*) Magna Large Print Bks. GBR. *Dist:* Ulverscroft Large Print Canada, Ltd.

—Mrs. Pargeter's Point of Honour. 272p. 2002. pap. 18.95 (*0-7432-4186-X*); 1999. 23.00 o.s.i (*0-684-86295-6*) Simon & Schuster. (Scribner).

—Mrs. Pargeter's Pound of Flesh. 1993. 224p. 20.00 o.p. (*0-684-19565-8*, Macmillan Reference USA) Gale Group.

—Mrs. Pargeter's Pound of Flesh. unabr. ed. 2001. audio 54.95 (*1-85695-571-0*, 93051) ISIS Audio Bks. GBR. *Dist:* Ulverscroft Large Print Bks., Ltd.

—Mrs. Pargeter's Pound of Flesh. l.t. ed. 1993. (Magna Large Print Ser.). 307p. (*0-7505-0579-6*) Magna Large Print Bks. GBR. *Dist:* Ulverscroft Large Print Canada, Ltd.

—Mrs. Pargeter's Pound of Flesh. 1994. (Crime Ser.). 208p. pap. 5.95 o.p. (*0-14-023485-3*, Penguin Bks.) Penguin Group (USA) Inc.

—Mrs., Presumed Dead. 1990. 256p. mass mkt. 3.95 o.s.i (*0-440-20552-2*) Dell Publishing.

—Mrs., Presumed Dead. 1989. 256p. 17.95 o.s.i (*0-684-18851-1*, Macmillan Reference USA) Gale Group.

—Mrs., Presumed Dead. unabr. ed. 2001. audio 54.95 (*1-85695-429-3*, 89042) ISIS Audio Bks. GBR. *Dist:* Ulverscroft Large Print Bks., Ltd.

—A Nice Class of Corpse. 1988. 224p. mass mkt. 3.50 o.s.i (*0-440-20113-6*) Dell Publishing.

—A Nice Class of Corpse. 1987. 196p. 14.95 o.p. (*0-684-18685-3*, Macmillan Reference USA) Gale Group.

—A Nice Class of Corpse. unabr. ed. 2001. audio 54.95 (*1-85089-755-7*, 87122) ISIS Audio Bks. GBR. *Dist:* Ulverscroft Large Print Bks., Ltd.

—A Nice Class of Corpse. l.t. ed. 1987. (Mainstream Ser.). 236p. reprint ed. lib. bdg. 17.95 o.p. (*1-85089-174-5*) ISIS Large Print Bks. GBR. *Dist:* Transaction Pubs.

**PARIS, CHARLES (FICTITIOUS CHARACTER)—FICTION**

Brett, Simon. An Amateur Corpse. l.t. ed. 1990. pap. 5.00 (*0-7451-1285-4*) BBC Audiobooks America.

—An Amateur Corpse. 1980. mass mkt. 1.95 o.p. (*0-425-04489-0*) Berkley Publishing Group.

—An Amateur Corpse. unabr. ed. 1994. audio 39.95 (*0-7861-0483-X*, 1435) Blackstone Audio Bks., Inc.

—An Amateur Corpse. unabr. ed. 2000. (Charles Paris Mystery Ser.: Bk. 4). audio 49.95 (*0-7451-6617-2*, CAB 1233) Chivers Audio Bks. GBR. *Dist:* BBC Audiobooks America.

—An Amateur Corpse. 1986. mass mkt. 3.50 o.s.i (*0-440-10185-9*) Dell Publishing.

—An Amateur Corpse. l.t. ed. 1990. (Nightingale Ser.). 300p. pap. 13.95 (*0-8161-5040-0*, Macmillan Reference USA) Gale Group.

—An Amateur Corpse. unabr. ed. 2000. (Charles Paris Mystery Ser. : Vol. 4). audio 44.00 (*0-7887-1286-1*, 95146E7) Recorded Bks., LLC.

—An Amateur Corpse. 1991. mass mkt. 3.95 o.p. (*0-446-35960-2*) Warner Bks., Inc.

—An Amateur Corpse. 2000. 196p. pap. 12.95 (*0-595-00359-1*) iUniverse, Inc.

—Cast, in Order of Disappearance. unabr. ed. 1993. audio 39.95 (*0-7451-5803-X*, CSL 052) BBC Audiobooks America.

—Cast, in Order of Disappearance. 1981. mass mkt. 2.25 o.p. (*0-425-04934-5*) Berkley Publishing Group.

—Cast, in Order of Disappearance. l.t. ed. 1990. (Nightingale Ser.). 279p. pap. 13.95 o.p. (*0-8161-4917-8*, Macmillan Reference USA) Gale Group.

—Cast, in Order of Disappearance. unabr. ed. 1997. (Charles Paris Mystery Ser. : Vol. 1). audio 35.00 (*0-7887-0858-9*, 94984E7) Recorded Bks., LLC.

—A Comedian Dies. 1980. mass mkt. 2.25 o.p. (*0-425-04702-4*) Berkley Publishing Group.

—A Comedian Dies. unabr. ed. 1999. audio 39.95 Blackstone Audio Bks., Inc.

—A Comedian Dies. unabr. ed. 1998. (Charles Paris Mystery Ser. : Vol. 5). audio 44.00 (*0-7887-1886-X*, 95308E7) Recorded Bks., LLC.

—A Comedian Dies. 1990. mass mkt. 3.95 o.p. (*0-446-35958-0*) Warner Bks., Inc.

—A Comedian Dies. 2000. 164p. pap. 11.95 (*0-595-00358-3*) iUniverse, Inc.

—Corporate Bodies. l.t. ed. 1993. 22.95 o.p. (*0-7927-1418-0*); pap. 20.95 o.p. (*0-7927-1417-2*) BBC Audiobooks America.

—Corporate Bodies. unabr. ed. 1993. audio 39.95 (*0-7861-0394-9*, 752393) Blackstone Audio Bks., Inc.

—Corporate Bodies. unabr. ed. 2000. (Charles Paris Mystery Ser.: Bk. 14). audio 49.95 (*0-7451-4131-5*, CAB 814) Chivers Audio Bks. GBR. *Dist:* BBC Audiobooks America.

—Corporate Bodies. abr. ed. 1992. 2p. audio 16.99 (*0-88646-323-8*, 7323); Set. 1996. audio 9.99 (*1-55204-012-7*, 393577) Durkin Hayes Publishing Ltd.

—Corporate Bodies. 1992. 256p. 19.00 (*0-684-19397-3*, Macmillan Reference USA) Gale Group.

—Corporate Bodies. 1993. (Mystery Ser.). mass mkt. (*0-373-26130-6*, 1-26130-4, Harlequin Bks.) Harlequin Enterprises, Ltd.

—Corporate Bodies. unabr. ed. 2000. (Charles Paris Mystery Ser. : Vol. 15). audio 44.00 (*1-55690-654-4*, 92406E7) Recorded Bks., LLC.

—Dead Giveaway. unabr. ed. 2000. (Charles Paris Mystery Ser.: Bk. 11). audio 49.95 (*0-7451-4210-9*, CAB 893) Chivers Audio Bks. GBR. *Dist:* BBC Audiobooks America.

—Dead Giveaway. 1987. 256p. mass mkt. 3.50 o.s.i (*0-440-11914-6*) Dell Publishing.

—Dead Giveaway. (Charles Paris Mystery Ser.). 1986. 169p. 13.95 o.p. (*0-684-18517-2*); 1987. 237p. 10.95 o.p. (*0-8161-4218-1*) Gale Group. (Macmillan Reference USA).

—Dead Giveaway. unabr. ed. 1993. audio 37.00 (*0-7887-8987-2*, H1223L8, Clipper Audio) Recorded Bks., LLC.

—Dead Giveaway. 2000. 180p. pap. 12.95 (*0-595-00357-5*) iUniverse, Inc.

—Dead Room Farce. unabr. ed. 1998. audio 54.95 (*0-7540-0150-4*, CAB 1573) BBC Audiobooks America.

—Dead Room Farce. unabr. ed. 1999. audio 39.95 (*0-7861-1642-0*, 2470) Blackstone Audio Bks., Inc.

—Dead Room Farce. 1998. 208p. 20.95 (*0-312-19251-7*, Saint Martin's Minotaur) St. Martin's Pr.

—Dead Room Farce. l.t. ed. 1998. (Mystery Ser.). 344p. 27.95 (*0-7862-1564-X*) Thorndike Pr.

—The Dead Side of the Mike. unabr. ed. 1997. audio 54.95 (*0-7451-6738-1*, CAB 1354) BBC Audiobooks America.

—The Dead Side of the Mike. unabr. ed. 1992. audio 39.95 (*0-7861-0340-X*, 1297) Blackstone Audio Bks., Inc.

—The Dead Side of the Mike. 1986. pap. 3.50 o.p. (*0-440-11763-1*) Dell Publishing.

—The Dead Side of the Mike. unabr. ed. 1998. (Charles Paris Mystery Ser. : No. 6). audio 44.00 (*0-7887-2520-3*, 95593E7) Recorded Bks., LLC.

—The Dead Side of the Mike. 1991. mass mkt. 3.95 o.p. (*0-446-35957-2*) Warner Bks., Inc.

—The Dead Side of the Mike. 2000. 180p. per. 11.95 (*0-595-00354-0*) iUniverse, Inc.

—Murder in the Title. unabr. ed. 2000. (Charles Paris Mystery Ser.: Bk. 9). audio 49.95 (*0-7451-4072-6*, CAB 769) Chivers Audio Bks. GBR. *Dist:* BBC Audiobooks America.

—Murder in the Title. 1986. pap. 3.50 o.p. (*0-440-16016-2*) Dell Publishing.

—Murder in the Title. 1983. 192p. 11.95 o.s.i (*0-684-17898-2*, Macmillan Reference USA) Gale Group.

—Murder in the Title. 1990. mass mkt. 3.95 o.p. (*0-446-35954-8*) Warner Bks., Inc.

—Murder in the Title. 2000. (Charles Paris Mystery Ser.). 196p. pap. 12.95 (*0-595-00353-2*) iUniverse, Inc.

—Murder Unprompted. unabr. ed. 1992. (Audio Bks.). audio 39.95 (*0-7451-5804-8*, CAB 686) BBC Audiobooks America.

—Murder Unprompted. unabr. ed. 1997. audio 32.95 (*0-7861-1081-3*, 1851) Blackstone Audio Bks., Inc.

—Murder Unprompted. 1986. (Murder Ink Mystery Ser.: No. 69). pap. 3.50 o.p. (*0-440-16145-2*) Dell Publishing.

—Murder Unprompted. (Nightingale Ser.). 1983. 290p. pap. 9.95 o.p. (*0-8161-3540-1*); 1982. 160p. 10.95 o.s.i (*0-684-17659-9*) Gale Group. (Macmillan Reference USA).

—Murder Unprompted. unabr. ed. 2001. audio compact disk 49.00 (*0-7887-3982-4*, C1145E7); 1999. audio 38.00 (*0-7887-4081-4*, H1075E7) Recorded Bks., LLC. (Clipper Audio).

—Murder Unprompted. 1990. mass mkt. 3.95 o.p. (*0-446-35955-6*) Warner Bks., Inc.

—Not Dead, Only Resting. l.t. ed. 1985. (Nightingale Ser.). 304p. 10.95 o.p. (*0-8161-3831-1*, Macmillan Reference USA) Gale Group.

—Not Dead, Only Resting. 1990. mass mkt. 3.95 o.p. (*0-446-35952-1*) Warner Bks., Inc.

—Not Dead, Only Resting. 2000. 180p. pap. 12.95 (*0-595-00356-7*) iUniverse, Inc.

—Not Dead, Only Resting: A Charles Paris Mystery. 1984. 176p. 11.95 o.s.i (*0-684-18193-2*, Macmillan Reference USA) Gale Group.

—A Reconstructed Corpse. unabr. ed. 2000. (Charles Paris Mystery Ser.: Bk. 15). audio (*0-7451-4357-1*, CAB 1040) Chivers Audio Bks. GBR. *Dist:* BBC Audiobooks America.

—A Reconstructed Corpse. l.t. ed. 1994. 234p. 24.95 (*1-56895-117-5*, Wheeler Publishing, Inc.) Gale Group.

—A Reconstructed Corpse. 1996. (WWL Mystery Ser.). per. (*0-373-26194-2*, 1-26194-0, Worldwide Library) Harlequin Enterprises, Ltd.

—A Reconstructed Corpse. l.t. ed. 1994. (Magna Large Print Ser.). 302p. o.p. (*0-7505-0717-9*) Magna Large Print Bks. GBR. *Dist:* Ulverscroft Large Print Canada, Ltd.

—A Reconstructed Corpse. unabr. ed. 1994. audio 44.00 (*0-7887-0110-X*, 94351E7) Recorded Bks., LLC.

—A Reconstructed Corpse. 1994. 192p. 20.00 (*0-684-19700-6*, Scribner) Simon & Schuster.

—A Series of Murders. unabr. ed. 1993. audio 39.95 (*0-7451-5801-3*, CAB 427) BBC Audiobooks America.

—A Series of Murders. 1989. 224p. 16.95 o.s.i (*0-684-19096-6*, Scribner) Simon & Schuster.

—A Series of Murders. 1990. mass mkt. 3.95 o.s.i (*0-446-35949-1*) Warner Bks., Inc.

—Sicken & So Die. unabr. ed. 1996. (Charles Paris Mystery Ser.). audio 54.95 (*0-7451-6698-9*, CAB1314) BBC Audiobooks America.

—Sicken & So Die. unabr. ed. (Charles Paris Mystery Ser.). 2000. audio compact disk 40.00 (*0-7861-9896-6*, z1874); 1997. audio 32.95 (*0-7861-1108-9*, 1874) Blackstone Audio Bks., Inc.

—Sicken & So Die. 1997. per. (*0-373-26262-0*, 1-26262-5, Worldwide Library) Harlequin Enterprises, Ltd.

—Sicken & So Die. 1997. 208p. 20.50 (*0-684-82459-0*, Scribner) Simon & Schuster.

—Situation Tragedy. unabr. ed. 1996. audio 32.95 (*0-7861-0965-3*, 1742) Blackstone Audio Bks., Inc.

—Situation Tragedy. 1986. pap. 3.50 o.p. (*0-440-18792-3*) Dell Publishing.

—Situation Tragedy. unabr. ed. 1998. audio 69.95 o.p. (*1-872672-11-6*) Magna Story Sound GBR. *Dist:* Ulverscroft Large Print Bks., Ltd.

—Situation Tragedy. 1981. (Charles Paris Mystery Ser. : Vol. 7). audio 44.00 (*0-7887-3491-1*, 95898E7) Recorded Bks., LLC.

—Situation Tragedy. 1981. 192p. 9.95 o.s.i (*0-684-17268-2*, Scribner) Simon & Schuster.

—Situation Tragedy. 1990. mass mkt. 3.95 o.s.i (*0-446-35956-4*) Warner Bks., Inc.

—So Much Blood. 1981. mass mkt. 2.25 o.s.i (*0-425-04935-3*); 1979. mass mkt. 1.75 o.s.i (*0-425-04159-X*) Berkley Publishing Group.

—So Much Blood. unabr. ed. 2000. (Charles Paris Mystery Ser.: Bk. 2). audio 49.95 (*0-7451-4251-6*, CAB 934) Chivers Audio Bks. GBR. *Dist:* BBC Audiobooks America.

—So Much Blood. 1986. mass mkt. 3.50 o.s.i (*0-440-18069-4*) Dell Publishing.

—So Much Blood. unabr. ed. 1997. (Charles Paris Mystery Ser. : Vol. 2). audio 44.00 (*0-7887-0931-3*, 95071E7) Recorded Bks., LLC.

—So Much Blood. 2000. 196p. pap. 12.95 (*0-595-00360-5*) iUniverse, Inc.

—Star Trap. unabr. ed. 1995. audio 54.95 (*0-7451-6481-1*, CAB 1097) BBC Audiobooks America.

—Star Trap. unabr. ed. 2000. audio 32.95 (*0-7861-1750-8*, 2554); audio compact disk 40.00 (*0-7861-9901-6*, z2554) Blackstone Audio Bks., Inc.

—Star Trap. 1986. mass mkt. 3.50 o.s.i (*0-440-18300-6*) Dell Publishing.

—Star Trap. l.t. ed. 1989. 315p. 13.95 o.p. (*0-8161-4774-4*, Macmillan Reference USA) Gale Group.

—Star Trap. unabr. ed. 1997. (Charles Paris Mystery Ser. : Vol. 3). audio 44.00 (*0-7887-1146-6*, 95084E7) Recorded Bks., LLC.

—Star Trap. 1990. mass mkt. 3.95 o.p. (*0-446-35959-9*) Warner Bks., Inc.

—What Bloody Man Is That? unabr. ed. 1993. 54.95 incl. audio (*0-7451-5805-6*, CAB 632) BBC Audiobooks America.

—What Bloody Man Is That? 1989. mass mkt. 3.50 o.s.i (*0-440-20344-9*) Dell Publishing.

—What Bloody Man Is That? l.t. ed. 1988. (Nightingale Ser.). 297p. 12.95 o.p. (*0-8161-4398-6*, Macmillan Reference USA) Gale Group.

—What Bloody Man Is That? unabr. ed. 2002. audio 40.00 (*1-4025-1944-3*, Clipper Audio) Recorded Bks., LLC.

—What Bloody Man Is That? 1987. 196p. 14.95 o.p. (*0-684-18824-4*, Scribner) Simon & Schuster.

—What Bloody Man Is That? 2000. 188p. pap. 12.95 (*0-595-00349-4*) iUniverse, Inc.

**PARIS, THOMAS (FICTITIOUS CHARACTER)—FICTION**

Carey, Diane L., et al. Day of Honor Omnibus: Ancient Blood; Armageddon Sky; Her Klingon Soul; Treaty's Law; Day of Honor; Honor Bound. 1999. (Star Trek Ser.). (Illus.). 1104p. pap. 16.00 (*0-671-02813-8*, Pocket) Simon & Schuster.

Cox, Greg. The Black Shore. 1997. (Star Trek Voyager Ser.: No. 13). (Illus.). 288p. mass mkt. 5.99 (*0-671-56061-1*, Star Trek) Simon & Schuster.

Friedman, Michael Jan. The Television Episode: Day of Honor. 1997. (Star Trek Voyager). 224p. mass mkt. 5.99 (*0-671-01981-3*, Star Trek) Simon & Schuster.

Garland, Mark A. & McGraw, Charles G. Ghost of a Chance. 1996. (Star Trek Voyager Ser.: No. 7). 288p. pap. 5.99 (*0-671-56798-5*, Star Trek) Simon & Schuster.

Golden, Christie. Ghost Dance Vol. 2: Dark Matters Trilogy. 2000. (Star Trek Voyager Ser.: No. 20). 288p. pap. 6.99 (*0-671-03583-5*, Star Trek) Simon & Schuster.

—Homecoming. 2003. (Star Trek Voyager Ser.). 288p. mass mkt. 6.99 (*0-7434-6754-X*);Bk. 1. E-Book 5.99 (*0-7434-7563-1*) Simon & Schuster. (Star Trek).

—Marooned. 1997. (Star Trek Voyager Ser.: No. 14). (Illus.). 304p. pap. 5.99 (*0-671-01423-4*, Star Trek) Simon & Schuster.

—The Murdered Sun. 1996. (Star Trek Voyager Ser.: No. 6). 288p. mass mkt. 5.99 o.s.i (*0-671-53783-0*, Star Trek) Simon & Schuster.

Graf, L. A. Caretaker. abr. ed. 1995. (Star Trek Voyager Ser.: No. 1). 17.00 o.s.i incl. audio (*0-671-52142-X*) Baen Bks.

—Caretaker. Ordover, John, ed. 1995. (Star Trek Voyager Ser.: No. 1). 288p. mass mkt. 5.99 Simon & Schuster.

Haber, Karen. Bless the Beasts. 1996. (Star Trek Voyager Ser.: No. 10). 288p. pap. 5.99 (*0-671-56780-2*, Star Trek) Simon & Schuster.

Kotani, Eric & Smith, Dean Wesley. Death of a Neutron Star. 1999. (Star Trek Voyager Ser.: No. 17). 263p. mass mkt. 6.50 o.s.i (*0-671-00425-5*, Star Trek) Simon & Schuster.

Shatner, William. Spectre. 1998. (Star Trek Ser.). 384p. mass mkt. 6.99 (*0-671-02053-6*, Pocket) Simon & Schuster.

—Spectre. abr. ed. 1998. (Star Trek Ser.: Vol. 2). audio 18.00 (*0-671-57998-3*, AF09R, Simon & Schuster Audioworks) Simon & Schuster Audio.

Shatner, William, et al. Spectre. 384p. 2002. E-Book 6.99 (*0-7434-5408-1*); 1998. (Illus.). 23.00 o.s.i (*0-671-00878-1*); 1999. reprint ed. pap. 6.50 (*0-671-00880-3*) Simon & Schuster. (Star Trek).

Smith, Dean Wesley, et al. Echoes. 1998. (Star Trek Voyager Ser.: No. 15). 304p. pap. 5.99 (*0-671-00200-7*, Star Trek) Simon & Schuster.

Taylor, Jeri. Mosaic. (Star Trek Voyager Ser.). 320p. 1997. pap. 5.99 (*0-671-56312-2*); 1996. 22.00 (*0-671-56311-4*) Simon & Schuster. (Star Trek).

—Mosaic. abr. ed. 1996. (Star Trek Ser.). audio 18.00 (*0-671-57400-0*, Simon & Schuster Audioworks) Simon & Schuster Audio.

—Pathways. (Star Trek Voyager Ser.: Vol. 2). 1999. 528p. pap. 6.50 o.s.i (*0-671-02626-7*); 1998. (Illus.). 448p. 23.00 o.s.i (*0-671-00346-1*) Simon & Schuster. (Star Trek).

—Pathways. abr. ed. 1998. (Star Trek Voyager Ser.: Vol. 2). 24.00 incl. audio (*0-671-58230-5*, Simon & Schuster Audioworks) Simon & Schuster Audio.

—Pathways. 1999. (Star Trek Voyager Ser.). 12.55 (*0-606-19503-3*) Turtleback Bks.

—Star Trek Voyager: Pathways. abr. ed. 1999. (Star Trek Voyager Ser.). audio 24.35 (*0-671-01115-4*) Ulverscroft Audio (U.S.A.).

**PARKER (FICTITIOUS CHARACTER: STARK)—FICTION**

Stark, Richard. Backflash. 1998. 292p. 20.00 o.p. (*0-89296-662-9*) Mysterious Pr.

—Backflash. 1998. audio 25.00 (*0-7871-7882-9*, Dove Audio) NewStar Media, Inc.

—Backflash. 1999. 304p. pap. 12.95 (*0-446-67526-1*) Warner Bks., Inc.

—Breakout. 2002. 304p. 23.95 (*0-89296-779-X*) Mysterious Pr.

—Breakout. 2003. 304p. pap. 12.95 (*0-446-67825-2*, Mysterious Pr. Paperback Bks.) Warner Bks., Inc.

—Butcher's Moon. 1985. 336p. pap. 2.95 o.p. (*0-380-69907-9*, Avon Bks.) Morrow/Avon.

—Butcher's Moon. 1974. 307 p. o.p. (*0-394-48343-X*) Random Hse., Inc.

—Comeback. 1997. 304p. 18.00 o.p. (*0-89296-661-0*) Mysterious Pr.

—Comeback. l.t. ed. 1998. (Cloak & Dagger Ser.). 315p. 27.95 (*0-7862-1348-5*) Thorndike Pr.

—Comeback. 1998. 304p. pap. 12.95 (*0-446-67465-6*) Warner Bks., Inc.

—Deadly Edge. l.t. ed. 1992. 18.95 o.p. (*0-7451-8354-9*); pap. 16.95 o.p. (*0-7927-1102-5*) BBC Audiobooks America.

—Deadly Edge. 1971. 214 p. o.p. (*0-394-46292-0*) Random Hse., Inc.

—Firebreak. 2001. 304p. 23.45 o.p. (*0-89296-711-0*) Mysterious Pr.

—Firebreak. 2002. 304p. pap. 12.95 (*0-446-67824-4*, Mysterious Pr. Paperback Bks.) Warner Bks., Inc.

—Flashfire. unabr. ed. 2001. audio 40.00 (*0-7366-6206-5*) Books on Tape, Inc.

—Flashfire. 2000. 288p. 22.95 o.p. (*0-89296-710-2*); 304p. E-Book 14.95 (*0-7595-9036-2*); 304p. E-Book 14.95 (*0-7595-4031-4*); 304p. E-Book 14.95 (*0-7595-8032-4*); E-Book 14.95 (*0-7595-6031-5*) Mysterious Pr.

—Flashfire. l.t. ed. 2001. (Mystery Ser.). 328p. 29.95 (*0-7862-2940-3*) Thorndike Pr.

—Flashfire. 2001. 288p. reprint ed. pap. 12.95 (*0-446-67790-6*) Warner Bks., Inc.

—The Jugger. 2002. 224p. pap. 12.95 (*0-446-67774-4*, Mysterious Pr. Paperback Bks.) Warner Bks., Inc.

—The Man with the Getaway Face. l.t. ed. 1988. pap. 13.95 o.p. (*1-55504-393-3*) BBC Audiobooks America.

—The Man with the Getaway Face. unabr. collector's ed. 1999. audio 32.00 (*0-7366-4410-5*, 4871) Books on Tape, Inc.

—The Man with the Getaway Face. 1998. (Parker Novels Ser.). 224p. pap. 12.95 (*0-446-67466-4*) Warner Bks., Inc.

—The Mourner. 2001. 224p. reprint ed. pap. 12.00 (*0-446-67772-8*) Warner Bks., Inc.

—The Outfit. l.t. ed. 1988. pap. 14.95 o.p. (*1-55504-697-5*, 755) BBC Audiobooks America.

—The Outfit. , unabr. collector's ed. 1999. audio 32.00 (*0-7366-4411-3*, 4872) Books on Tape, Inc.

—The Outfit. 1981. 142p. reprint ed. 25.00 (*0-89366-149-X*) Ultramarine Publishing Co., Inc.

—The Outfit. 1998. (Parker Novels Ser.). 224p. pap. 12.95 o.s.i (*0-446-67467-2*) Warner Bks., Inc.

—Payback. 1999. 208p. pap. 12.00 o.s.i (*0-446-67464-8*) Warner Bks., Inc.

—The Score. 2001. 224p. reprint ed. pap. 12.00 (*0-446-67773-6*) Warner Bks., Inc.

—Slayground. 1971. 183p. o.p. (*0-394-46430-3*) Random Hse., Inc.

**PARKER, CHARLIE (FICTITIOUS CHARACTER)—FICTION**

Connolly, John. Dark Hollow. 2002. 528p. reprint ed. mass mkt. 6.99 (*0-7434-1022-X*, Pocket) Simon & Schuster.

—Dark Hollow: A Novel. 2001. 448p. 25.00 (*0-7432-0332-1*, Simon & Schuster) Simon & Schuster.

—Every Dead Thing. 1999. 400p. 25.00 (*0-684-85714-6*, Simon & Schuster) Simon & Schuster.

—The Killing Kind. 2002. 384p. 25.00 (*0-7434-5334-4*, Atria) Simon & Schuster.

—The White Road. 2004. (Illus.). 528p. mass mkt. 25.00 (*0-7434-5639-4*, Pocket); 2003. 400p. 25.00 (*0-7434-5638-6*, Atria); 2003. E-Book 19.99 (*0-7434-6263-7*, Atria) Simon & Schuster.

Shelton, Connie. Deadly Gamble. unabr. ed. 1996. (Charlie Parker Ser.: Bk. 1). audio 39.95 (*1-55686-653-4*) Books in Motion.

—Honeymoons Can Be Murder. 2002. (WWL Mystery Ser.). 256p. mass mkt. (*0-373-26427-5*, Worldwide Library) Harlequin Enterprises, Ltd.

—Honeymoons Can Be Murder: A Charlie Parker Mystery. 2001. (The Charlie Parker Mystery Ser.: Vol. 6). 268p. 23.95 (*1-890768-30-8*, Intrigue Pr.) Corvus Publishing.

—Memories Can Be Murder. Ellison, Lee, ed. 1999. (The Charlie Parker Mystery Ser.: 5). 224p. 22.95 (*1-890768-18-9*, Intrigue Pr.) Corvus Publishing.

—Memories Can Be Murder. 2002. (WWL Mystery Ser.: No. 414). 250p. mass mkt. (*0-373-26414-3*, Worldwide Library) Harlequin Enterprises, Ltd.

—Partnerships Can Kill. unabr. ed. 1996. (Charlie Parker Ser.: Bk. 3). audio 26.95 (*1-55686-667-4*) Books in Motion.

—Reunions Can Be Murder. 2003. (WWL Mystery Ser.: No. 475). 256p. mass mkt. (*0-373-26475-5*, Worldwide Library) Harlequin Enterprises, Ltd.

—Reunions Can Be Murder: The Seventh Charlie Parker Mystery. 2002. (The Charlie Parker Mystery Ser.: No. 7). 255p. 23.95 (*1-890768-46-4*, Intrigue Pr.) Corvus Publishing.

—Small Towns Can Be Murder. (The Charlie Parker Mystery Ser.: No. 4). 1999. (Illus.). 256p. mass mkt. 5.95 (*1-890768-16-2*); 1998. 224p. 22.95 (*1-890768-05-7*) Corvus Publishing. (Intrigue Pr.).

—Vacations Can Be Murder. unabr. ed. 1996. (Charlie Parker Ser.: Bk. 2). audio 39.95 (*1-55686-660-7*) Books in Motion.

—Vacations Can Be Murder: The Second Charlie Parker Mystery. Lenz, Leslie, ed. 1995. (Charlie Parker Mysteries Ser.). 216p. 21.95 o.p. (*0-9643161-1-0*, Intrigue Pr.) Corvus Publishing.

—Vacations Can Be Murder: The Second Charlie Parker Mystery. 1997. (The Charlie Parker Mystery Ser.: Vol. 2). 272p. reprint ed. mass mkt. 5.50 (*1-890768-01-4*, Intrigue Pr.) Corvus Publishing.

**PARKER, CHARLOTTE (FICTITIOUS CHARACTER)—FICTION**

Shelton, Connie. Deadly Gamble: The First Charlie Parker Mystery. Lenz, Leslie, ed. 1995. 216p. 21.95 o.p. (*0-9643161-0-2*, Intrigue Pr.) Corvus Publishing.

—Deadly Gamble: The First Charlie Parker Mystery. 1997. (The Charlie Parker Mystery Ser.: Vol. 1). 288p. reprint ed. mass mkt. 5.50 (*1-890768-00-6*, Intrigue Pr.) Corvus Publishing.

—Partnerships Can Kill. 1998. (The Charlie Parker Mystery Ser.: No. 3). 240p. mass mkt. 5.50 (*1-890768-02-2*, Intrigue Pr.) Corvus Publishing.

—Partnerships Can Kill. Ellison, Lee, ed. 1997. 208p. 21.95 o.p. (*0-9643161-4-5*, Intrigue Pr.) Corvus Publishing.

**PARKER, CLAIRE (FICTITIOUS CHARACTER)—FICTION**

Gough, Laurence. Death on a No. 8 Hook. 2001. (Willows & Parker Mystery Ser.). 232p. mass mkt. 7.95 (*0-7710-3533-0*) McClelland & Stewart/Tundra Bks.

—The Goldfish Bowl. 2001. (Willows & Parker Mystery Ser.). 216p. mass mkt. 7.95 (*0-7710-3532-2*) McClelland & Stewart/Tundra Bks.

—The Goldfish Bowl. 1988. 192p. 13.95 o.p. (*0-312-01434-1*, Saint Martin's Minotaur) St. Martin's Pr.

—The Goldfish Bowl. 1990. 192p. pap. 3.95 o.p. (*0-14-011596-X*, Penguin Bks.) Viking Penguin.

—Heartbreaker. 1996. (Willows & Parker Mystery Ser.). 272p. mass mkt. 5.99 (*0-7710-3447-4*) McClelland & Stewart/Tundra Bks.

—Heartbreaker: A Willows & Parker Mystery. 1996. 272p. 22.95 o.p. (*0-7710-3438-5*) McClelland & Stewart/Tundra Bks.

—Hot Shots. 2002. 224p. mass mkt. 6.95 (*0-7710-3545-4*) McClelland & Stewart/Tundra Bks.

—Hot Shots. 1991. (Crime Monthly Ser.). 192p. pap. 4.95 o.p. (*0-14-015488-4*, Penguin Bks.) Penguin Group (USA) Inc.

—Hot Shots. 1990. 192p. 16.95 o.p. (*0-670-83014-3*) Viking Penguin.

—Karaoke Rap. 1998. (Willows & Parker Mystery Ser.). 368p. 20.95 o.p. (*0-7710-3403-2*) McClelland & Stewart/Tundra Bks.

—Killers. 1995. 256p. pap. 8.95 o.p. (*0-575-05782-3*) Gollancz, Victor GBR. *Dist:* Trafalgar Square.

—Killers. 1993. o.p. (*0-7710-3439-3*) McClelland & Stewart/Tundra Bks.

—Memory Lane. 1997. (Willows & Parker Mystery Ser.). 304p. mass mkt. 5.95 (*0-7710-3404-0*) McClelland & Stewart/Tundra Bks.

—Memory Lane: A Willows & Parker Mystery. 1997. 296p. 24.95 o.p. (*0-7710-3437-7*) McClelland & Stewart/Tundra Bks.

—Serious Crimes. 2002. 256p. mass mkt. 6.95 (*0-7710-3546-2*) McClelland & Stewart/Tundra Bks.

—Serious Crimes. 1999. pap. (*0-670-83675-3*) Viking Penguin.

—Shutterbug. 1999. (Willows & Parker Mystery Ser.). 288p. mass mkt. 7.95 (*0-7710-3429-6*) McClelland & Stewart/Tundra Bks.

—Shutterbug: A Willows & Parker Mystery. 1998. (Willows & Parker Mystery Ser.: Bk. 11). 288p. 20.95 o.p. (*0-7710-3531-4*) McClelland & Stewart/Tundra Bks.

—Silent Knives. 1988. 192p. 13.95 o.p. (*0-312-01747-2*, Saint Martin's Minotaur) St. Martin's Pr.

—Silent Knives. 1990. 192p. pap. 3.95 o.p. (*0-14-012189-7*, Penguin Bks.) Viking Penguin.

**PARKER, JENNY (FICTITIOUS CHARACTER)—FICTION**

Windle, Jeanette. Mystery at Death Canyon. 2002. (Parker Twins Ser.: No. 4). 176p. (J). (gr. 3-8). pap. 5.99 (*0-8254-4148-X*) Kregel Pubns.

—Mystery at Death Canyon. 1996. (Twin Pursuits Ser.: No. 1). 128p. pap. 4.99 o.p. (*0-88070-904-9*, Multnomah Bks.) Multnomah Pubs., Inc.

**PARKER, QUINN (FICTITIOUS CHARACTER)—FICTION**

Zimmerman, Bruce. Blood under the Bridge. 1989. 16.95 o.p. (*0-06-016087-X*) HarperTrade.

—Blood under the Bridge. 1990. mass mkt. 3.95 o.p. (*0-312-92244-2*, St. Martin's Paperbacks) St. Martin's Pr.

—Crimson Green: A Quinn Parker Novel of Suspense. 1994. 320p. 20.00 o.p. (*0-06-017069-7*) HarperCollins Pubs.

—Crimson Green: A Quinn Parker Suspense Novel. 1995. 368p. mass mkt. 4.50 o.p. (*0-06-109359-9*) HarperCollins Pubs.

—Thicker Than Water: A Novel of Suspense. 1991. 288p. 19.95 o.p. (*0-06-016387-9*) HarperTrade.

—Thicker Than Water: A Quinn Parker Mystery. 1993. 368p. mass mkt. 4.50 o.p. (*0-06-109026-3*, HarperTorch) Morrow/Avon.

**PARKMAN, TOBY (FICTITIOUS CHARACTER)—FICTION**

Washburn, Stan. Into Thin Air. 1996. 336p. mass mkt. 6.99 (*0-671-56246-0*, Pocket) Simon & Schuster.

**PARNELL, MEGAN (FICTITIOUS CHARACTER)—FICTION**

Biggar, Joan R. Missing on Castaway Island. 1997. (Megan Parnell Mysteries Ser.: Vol. 1). 160p. (J). (gr. 5-9). pap. text 5.99 (*0-570-05015-4*, 56-1842) Concordia Publishing Hse.

—Mystery at Camp Galena. 1997. (Megan Parnell Mysteries Ser.: Vol. 2). 160p. (J). (gr. 5-9). pap. text 5.99 (*0-570-05016-2*, 56-1843) Concordia Publishing Hse.

—Trouble in Yakima Valley. 1998. (Megan Parnell Mysteries Ser.: Vol. 3). 160p. (J). (gr. 5-9). 5.99 (*0-570-05031-6*, 56-1855) Concordia Publishing Hse.

**PARRISH, GEORGE (FICTITIOUS CHARACTER)—FICTION**

Barnard, Robert. A Little Local Murder. 1984. 192p. mass mkt. 2.95 o.s.i (*0-440-14882-0*) Dell Publishing.

—A Little Local Murder. 1983. 192p. 11.95 o.s.i (*0-684-17882-6*, Macmillan Reference USA) Gale Group.

—A Little Local Murder. 1995. 192p. pap. 7.95 (*0-88150-325-8*, Foul Play) Norton, W. W. & Co., Inc.

**PASCALE, LILY (FICTITIOUS CHARACTER)—FICTION**

Thomas, Scarlett. Dead Clever: A Lily Pascale Mystery. 2004. 296p. pap. 13.99 (*1-932112-19-7*); 2003. 288p. 24.95 (*1-932112-01-4*, Kate's Mystery Bks.) Justin, Charles & Co. Pubs.

—In Your Face: A Lily Pascale Mystery. 2004. 288p. 24.95 (*1-932112-08-1*) Justin, Charles & Co. Pubs.

**PASCOE, PETER (FICTITIOUS CHARACTER)—FICTION**

Hill, Reginald. An Advancement of Learning. unabr. ed. 2000. (Dalziel & Pascoe Mystery Ser.). audio 59.95 (*0-7451-6688-1*, CAB 1304) Chivers Audio Bks. GBR. *Dist:* BBC Audiobooks America.

—An Advancement of Learning. 1985. 254p. 14.95 o.s.i (*0-88150-053-4*) Countryman Pr.

—An Advancement of Learning. 1987. 256p. mass mkt. 4.50 o.p. (*0-451-14656-5*, Signet Bks.) NAL.

—An April Shroud. 1986. 256p. 15.95 o.p. (*0-88150-065-8*) Countryman Pr.

—An April Shroud. 1987. mass mkt. 3.50 o.p. (*0-451-14783-9*, Signet Bks.) NAL.

—An April Shroud. l.t. ed. 1999. (Charnwood Large Print Ser.). 320p. 31.99 o.p. (*0-7089-9084-3*, Ulverscroft) Thorpe, F. A. Pubs. GBR. *Dist:* Ulverscroft Large Print Bks., Ltd., Ulverscroft Large Print Canada, Ltd.

—Arms & the Women. (Dalziel & Pascoe Mystery Ser.). 2000. 512p. mass mkt. 6.99 (*0-440-22594-9*); 1999. 416p. 23.95 o.s.i (*0-385-33279-3*, Delacorte Pr.) Dell Publishing.

—Asking for the Moon. 1998. (Dalziel & Pascoe Mystery Ser.). 336p. reprint ed. mass mkt. 6.50 (*0-440-22583-3*) Doubleday Publishing.

—Asking for the Moon. l.t. ed. 1997. (Charnwood Large Print Ser.). 384p. 29.99 o.p. (*0-7089-8974-8*, Ulverscroft) Thorpe, F. A. Pubs. GBR. *Dist:* Ulverscroft Large Print Bks., Ltd., Ulverscroft Large Print Canada, Ltd.

—Bones & Silence. 1991. (Dalziel & Pascoe Mystery Ser.). 448p. mass mkt. 6.99 (*0-440-20935-8*) Dell Publishing.

—Bones & Silence. l.t. ed. 1992. (Mystery Ser.). 528p. 29.99 o.p. (*0-7089-8673-0*, Ulverscroft) Thorpe, F. A. Pubs. GBR. *Dist:* Ulverscroft Large Print Bks., Ltd., Ulverscroft Large Print Canada, Ltd.

—Child's Play. l.t. ed. 1988. (Ulverscroft Large Print Ser.). 560p. 29.99 o.p. (*0-7089-1912-X*, Ulverscroft) Thorpe, F. A. Pubs. GBR. *Dist:* Ulverscroft Large Print Bks., Ltd., Ulverscroft Large Print Canada, Ltd.

—Child's Play. 1988. mass mkt. 3.95 (*0-446-34533-4*) Warner Bks., Inc.

—A Clubbable Woman. unabr. ed. 2000. (Dalziel & Pascoe Mystery Ser.). audio 59.95 (*0-7451-6613-X*, CAB 1230) Chivers Audio Bks. GBR. *Dist:* BBC Audiobooks America.

—A Clubbable Woman. 1984. 256p. reprint ed. 12.95 o.p. (*0-88150-032-1*) Countryman Pr.

—A Clubbable Woman. 1985. mass mkt. 3.50 o.p. (*0-451-15516-5*); mass mkt. 2.95 o.p. (*0-451-13810-4*) NAL. (Signet Bks.).

—Deadheads, Set unabr. ed. 1999. (Superintendent Daiziel & Sergeant Pascoe Mysteries Ser.). audio 69.95 BBC Audiobooks America.

—Deadheads. 1985. mass mkt. 3.95 o.p. (*0-451-15895-4*, Signet Bks.); mass mkt. 3.50 o.p. (*0-451-13559-8*, ROC) NAL.

—Deadheads. l.t. ed. 1985. 512p. o.p. (*0-7089-1312-1*, Ulverscroft) Thorpe, F. A. Pubs.

—Deadheads: A Dalziel & Pascoe Mystery, Set unabr. ed. 1999. audio 69.95 (*0-7540-0286-1*, CAB 1709) BBC Audiobooks America.

—Death's Jest-Book. 2003. 512p. (*0-385-65963-6*) Doubleday Canada, Ltd. CAN. *Dist:* Random Hse., Inc.

—Death's Jest-Book. 2004. 704p. mass mkt. (*0-7704-2924-6*) Seal Bks. CAN. *Dist:* Random Hse. of Canada, Ltd.

—Death's Jest Book. 2003. 576p. 25.95 (*0-06-052805-2*) HarperCollins Pubs.

—Dialogues of the Dead. 2002. mass mkt. 6.99 (*0-440-23728-9*) Dell Publishing.

—Dialogues of the Dead. 2003. 528p. mass mkt. 7.50 (*0-06-052809-5*) HarperCollins Pubs.

—Dialogues of the Dead. 2003. 624p. mass mkt. (*0-7704-2892-4*) Seal Bks. CAN. *Dist:* Random Hse. of Canada, Ltd.

—Exit Lines. 1986. mass mkt. 3.50 o.p. (*0-451-14252-7*, Signet Bks.); 256p. mass mkt. 3.99 o.s.i (*0-451-16166-1*) NAL.

—Exit Lines. l.t. ed. 1985. (Charnwood Large Print Ser.). 400p. 29.99 o.p. (*0-7089-8266-2*, Ulverscroft) Thorpe, F. A. Pubs. GBR. *Dist:* Ulverscroft Large Print Bks., Ltd., Ulverscroft Large Print Canada, Ltd.

—A Killing Kindness. 1989. 269p. reprint ed. pap. 5.95 o.s.i (*1-55882-003-5*, Library of Crime Classics) International Polygonics, Ltd.

—A Killing Kindness. 1981. 10.95 o.p. (*0-394-51910-8*, Pantheon) Knopf Publishing Group.

—A Killing Kindness: A Dalziel & Pascoe Mystery, Set. unabr. ed. 1999. audio 69.95 (*0-7540-0382-5*, CAB1805) BBC Audiobooks America.

—On Beulah Height. 1999. (Dalziel & Pascoe Mystery Ser.). 560p. mass mkt. 6.99 (*0-440-22590-6*) Dell Publishing.

—On Beulah Height. 1998. 384p. o.s.i (*0-385-25734-1*) Doubleday Canada, Ltd. CAN. *Dist:* Random Hse., Inc.

—On Beulah Height. l.t. ed. 1999. (Charnwood Large Print Ser.). 624p. 31.99 o.p. (*0-7089-9056-8*, Charnwood) Thorpe, F. A. Pubs. GBR. *Dist:* Ulverscroft Large Print Bks., Ltd., Ulverscroft Large Print Canada, Ltd.

—On Beulah Height: A Dalziel-Pascoe Murder Mystery. 1998. 384p. 22.95 o.s.i (*0-385-33278-5*) Doubleday Publishing.

—Pictures of Perfection. 1995. (Dalziel & Pascoe Mystery Ser.). 352p. mass mkt. 6.99 (*0-440-21800-4*) Dell Publishing.

—Pictures of Perfection. l.t. ed. 1995. (Charnwood Large Print Ser.). 432p. 29.99 o.p. (*0-7089-8845-8*, Charnwood) Thorpe, F. A. Pubs. GBR. *Dist:* Ulverscroft Large Print Bks., Ltd., Ulverscroft Large Print Canada, Ltd.

—A Pinch of Snuff. 1990. 336p. mass mkt. 6.99 (*0-440-16912-7*) Dell Publishing.

—A Pinch of Snuff. 1978. (Harper Novel of Suspense Ser.). 9.95 o.p. (*0-06-011876-8*) HarperCollins Pubs.

—Recalled to Life. 1993. (Dalziel & Pascoe Mystery Ser.). 400p. mass mkt. 6.99 (*0-440-21573-0*) Dell Publishing.

—Ruling Passion. unabr. ed. 2000. (Dalziel & Pascoe Mystery Ser.). audio 69.95 (*0-7540-0042-7*, CAB 1465) Chivers Audio Bks. GBR. *Dist:* BBC Audiobooks America.

—Ruling Passion. 1990. 336p. mass mkt. 6.99 (*0-440-16889-9*) Dell Publishing.

—Ruling Passion. l.t. ed. 2001. (Charnwood Large Print Ser.). 376p. 31.99 o.p. (*0-7089-9230-7*, Ulverscroft) Thorpe, F. A. Pubs. GBR. *Dist:* Ulverscroft Large Print Bks., Ltd., Ulverscroft Large Print Canada, Ltd.

—Underworld. 1989. 288p. mass mkt. 4.50 (*0-446-34534-2*) Warner Bks., Inc.

—Underworld: A New Dalziel-Pascoe Murder Mystery. 1988. 288p. 14.95 o.s.i (*0-684-18931-3*, Scribner) Simon & Schuster.

—The Wood Beyond. 1997. (Dalziel & Pascoe Mystery Ser.). 448p. mass mkt. 6.99 (*0-440-21803-9*) Dell Publishing.

—The Wood Beyond, Set. unabr. ed. 1997. audio 94.95 Eye in the Ear Inc.

—The Wood Beyond. l.t. ed. 1996. 25.95 o.p. (*0-7838-1864-5*, Macmillan Reference USA) Gale Group.

**PASMORE, TOM (FICTITIOUS CHARACTER)—FICTION**

Straub, Peter. Mystery. 1990. 19.95 o.p. (*0-525-24818-8*, Dutton) Dutton/Plume.

—Mystery. 1991. 560p. mass mkt. 7.99 (*0-451-16869-0*, Signet Bks.) NAL.

—Mystery. abr. ed. 1990. audio 15.95 (*0-671-69268-2*, Simon & Schuster Audioworks) Simon & Schuster Audio.

—The Throat. 1993. 688p. 24.00 o.p. (*0-525-93503-7*) Dutton/Plume.

—The Throat. 1994. 704p. mass mkt. 7.99 (*0-451-17918-8*, Signet Bks.) NAL.

—The Throat. abr. ed. 1993. audio 25.00 (*0-671-72591-2*, 692323, Simon & Schuster Audioworks) Simon & Schuster Audio.

**PASSAU, LOUIS (FICTITIOUS CHARACTER)—FICTION**

Gardner, John E. Maestro. 1993. 280p. 23.00 (*1-883402-24-7*, Scribner) Simon & Schuster.

—Maestro. 1995. 656p. mass mkt. 6.50 o.s.i (*0-446-60168-3*) Warner Bks., Inc.

**PASTOR, DANNY (FICTITIOUS CHARACTER)—FICTION**

Waller, Robert James. Puerto Vallarta Squeeze. 1996. 256p. mass mkt. 5.99 o.s.i (*0-446-60360-0*); 1995. 214p. 18.95 o.p. (*0-446-51747-X*) Warner Bks., Inc.

**PATRICIA ANNE (FICTITIOUS CHARACTER)—FICTION**

George, Anne. Murder Boogies with Elvis. (Southern Sisters Mysteries Ser.). 2002. 288p. mass mkt. 6.99 (*0-06-103102-X*, Avon Bks.); 2001. 256p. 23.00 (*0-06-019870-2*, Morrow, William & Co.) Morrow/Avon.

—Murder Boogies with Elvis: A Southern Sisters Mystery. l.t. ed. 2001. (Mystery Ser.). 27.95 (*1-57490-380-2*, Beeler Large Print Bks.) Beeler, Thomas T. Publisher.

—Murder Carries a Torch. 2000. (Southern Sisters Mysteries Ser.). 272p. 23.00 (*0-380-97810-5*, Morrow, William & Co.) Morrow/Avon.

—Murder Carries a Torch: A Southern Sisters Mystery. l.t. ed. 2001. (Large Print Bks.). 274p. pap. 23.95 (*1-58724-127-7*, Wheeler Publishing, Inc.) Gale Group.

—Murder Carries a Torch: A Southern Sisters Mystery. 2001. 288p. mass mkt. 6.99 (*0-380-80938-9*, Avon Bks.) Morrow/Avon.

—Murder Gets a Life. l.t. ed. 2000. (Beeler Large Print Mystery Ser.). 234p. 26.95 (*1-57490-290-3*, Beeler Large Print Bks.) Beeler, Thomas T. Publisher.

—Murder Gets a Life: A Southern Sisters Mystery. (Southern Sisters Mysteries Ser.). 1999. 272p. mass mkt. 6.99 (*0-380-79366-0*); 1998. 256p. 20.00 o.p. (*0-380-97558-0*) Morrow/Avon. (Avon Bks.).

—Murder Makes Waves. l.t. ed. 2000. (Beeler Large Print Mystery Ser.). 246p. 26.95 (*1-57490-274-1*, Beeler Large Print Bks.) Beeler, Thomas T. Publisher.

—Murder Makes Waves. (Southern Sisters Mysteries Ser.). 1998. 272p. mass mkt. 6.99 (*0-380-78450-5*); 1997. 256p. 20.00 o.p. (*0-380-97527-0*) Morrow/Avon. (Avon Bks.).

—Murder on a Bad Hair Day. l.t. ed. 1999. (Beeler Large Print Mystery Ser.). 277p. 26.95 (*1-57490-238-5*, Beeler Large Print Bks.) Beeler, Thomas T. Publisher.

—Murder on a Bad Hair Day. 1996. (Southern Sisters Mysteries Ser.). 256p. mass mkt. 6.99 (*0-380-78087-9*, Avon Bks.) Morrow/Avon.

—Murder on a Girl's Night Out. 1996. (Southern Sisters Mysteries Ser.). 256p. mass mkt. 6.99 (*0-380-78086-0*, Avon Bks.) Morrow/Avon.

—Murder on a Girls' Night Out. l.t. ed. 1999. (Beeler Large Print Mystery Ser.). 26.95 (*1-57490-212-1*, Beeler Large Print Bks.) Beeler, Thomas T. Publisher.

—Murder Runs in the Family. l.t. ed. 2000. (Beeler Large Print Mystery Ser.). 243p. 26.95 (*1-57490-258-X*, Beeler Large Print Bks.) Beeler, Thomas T. Publisher.

—Murder Runs in the Family. 1997. (Southern Sisters Mysteries Ser.). 288p. mass mkt. 6.99 (*0-380-78449-1*, Avon Bks.) Morrow/Avon.

—Murder Shoots the Bull. 2000. (Southern Sisters Mysteries Ser.). 272p. mass mkt. 6.99 (*0-380-80149-3*, Avon Bks.) Morrow/Avon.

—Murder Shoots the Bull: A Southern Sisters Mystery. l.t. ed. 1999. (*0-07-862222-0*) McGraw-Hill Cos., The.

—Murder Shoots the Bull: A Southern Sisters Mystery. 1999. (Southern Sisters Mysteries Ser.). 247p. 22.00 (*0-380-97688-9*, Avon Bks.) Morrow/Avon.

—Murder Shoots the Bull: A Southern Sisters Mystery. l.t. ed. 1999. (Americana Ser.). 358p. 26.95 (*0-7862-2222-0*) Thorndike Pr.

**PATRICK, LARA (FICTITIOUS CHARACTER)—FICTION**

Podrug, Junius. Presumed Guilty. 1998. 576p. mass mkt. 6.99 (*0-8125-5507-4*); 1997. 384p. 24.95 (*0-312-86242-3*) Doherty, Tom Assocs., LLC. (Forge Bks.).

**PATTERSON, ASHLEY (FICTITIOUS CHARACTER)—FICTION**

Sheldon, Sidney. Tell Me Your Dreams. abr. ed. 1998. audio 24.95 (*1-55927-521-9*, 696017); 39.95 incl. audio (*1-55927-522-7*) Audio Renaissance.

—Tell Me Your Dreams. l.t. ed. 1998. 26.00 (*0-688-16691-1*); 352p. 26.00 o.p. (*0-688-16282-7*) Morrow/Avon. (Morrow, William & Co.).

—Tell Me Your Dreams. 1999. 384p. mass mkt. 7.99 (*0-446-60720-7*) Warner Bks., Inc.

**PATTERSON, JONELLE (FICTITIOUS CHARACTER)—FICTION**

Racina, Thom. Hidden Agenda. 1998. 368p. 24.95 o.p. (*0-525-94031-6*) Dutton/Plume.

—Hidden Agenda. 1999. 368p. reprint ed. mass mkt. 6.99 o.s.i (*0-451-18600-1*) NAL.

**PATTERSON, MARTHA (FICTITIOUS CHARACTER)—FICTION**

Sprague, Gretchen. Death in Good Company. 1999. (WWL Mystery Ser.: No. 303). mass mkt. (*0-373-26303-1*, 1-26303-7, Worldwide Library) Harlequin Enterprises, Ltd.

—Death in Good Company. 1997. 224p. 21.95 o.p. (*0-312-16813-6*, Saint Martin's Minotaur) St. Martin's Pr.

—Death in Good Company. l.t. ed. 1998. (Basic Ser.). 335p. 28.95 (*0-7862-1345-0*) Thorndike Pr.

—Maquette for Murder. 2001. (WWL Mystery Ser.: No. 378). 251p. mass mkt. (*0-373-26378-3*, Worldwide Library) Harlequin Enterprises, Ltd.

—Maquette for Murder. E-Book 5.99 (*0-312-27355-X*); 2000. 240p. 22.95 (*0-312-19920-1*, Saint Martin's Minotaur) St. Martin's Pr.

—Murder in a Heat Wave. 2004. (WWL Mystery Ser.: No. 489). 256p. mass mkt. (*0-373-26489-5*, Worldwide Library) Harlequin Enterprises, Ltd.

—Murder in a Heat Wave. 2003. (Martha Patterson Mysteries Ser.). 224p. 22.95 (*0-312-27662-1*, Saint Martin's Minotaur) St. Martin's Pr.

—Murder in a Heat Wave: A Martha Patterson Mystery. l.t. ed. 2003. (Mystery Ser.). 28.95 (*0-7862-5487-4*) Thorndike Pr.

**PAULING, ANDI (FICTITIOUS CHARACTER)—FICTION**

Roberts, Lillian. Almost Human. 1998. mass mkt. 5.99 o.s.i (*0-449-00228-4*, Fawcett) Ballantine Bks.

—The Hand That Feeds You. 1997. mass mkt. 5.50 o.s.i (*0-449-14986-2*, Fawcett) Ballantine Bks.

—Riding for a Fall. 1996. (Veterinarian Mystery Ser.). mass mkt. 5.50 o.s.i (*0-449-14985-4*, Fawcett) Ballantine Bks.

**PAYNE, MATTHEW (FICTITIOUS CHARACTER)—FICTION**

Griffin, W. E. B. The Assassin: A Badge of Honor Novel. 5th ed. 1993. (Badge of Honor Ser.). 464p. mass mkt. 7.99 (*0-515-11113-9*, Jove) Berkley Publishing Group.

—The Assassin: A Badge of Honor Novel. unabr. collector's ed. 1994. audio 96.00 (*0-7366-2851-7*, 133263) Books on Tape, Inc.

—Badge of Honor Boxed Set. (Badge of Honor Ser.). 1993. 23.96 o.s.i (*0-515-11301-8*); 1992. 19.84 o.s.i (*0-515-11030-2*); 1991. 14.85 o.s.i (*0-515-10777-8*) Berkley Publishing Group. (Jove).

—Badge of Honor Boxed Set: Men in Blue, Special Operations, the Victim. 1996. 12.98 o.s.i (*0-399-14152-9*) Penguin Group (USA) Inc.

—Badge of Honor Boxed Set: The Witness; the Assassin; the Murderers. 1997. 816p. 12.98 o.s.i (*0-399-14238-X*) Penguin Group (USA) Inc.

—Badge of Honor VIII: Final Justice. 2003. 528p. mass mkt. 7.99 (*0-515-13656-5*, Jove) Berkley Publishing Group.

—Final Justice: A Badge of Honor Novel. 2003. 480p. 26.95 (*0-399-14926-0*); 26.95 (*0-399-14926-0*) Putnam Publishing Group, The.

—Final Justice: A Badge of Honor Novel. 512p. (*0-7278-5917-X*) Severn Hse. Pubs., Ltd.

—Final Justice: A Badge of Honor Novel. l.t. ed. 2003. (Core Ser.). 32.95 (*0-7862-5571-4*) Thorndike Pr.

—The Investigators: A Badge of Honor Novel. 1998. 592p. reprint ed. mass mkt. 7.99 (*0-515-12406-0*, Jove) Berkley Publishing Group.

—The Investigators: A Badge of Honor Novel. unabr. ed. 1998. audio 104.00 (*0-7366-4084-3*, 4593) Books on Tape, Inc.

—The Investigators: A Badge of Honor Novel. l.t. ed. 1999. 735p. pap. 20.00 o.p. (*0-7838-0140-8*, Macmillan Reference USA) Gale Group.

—The Investigators: A Badge of Honor Novel. 1998. 448p. 24.95 o.p. (*0-399-14308-4*); 24.95 (*0-399-14349-1*, 695430) Penguin Group (USA) Inc.

—The Investigators: A Badge of Honor Novel. 416p. (*0-7278-5476-3*) Severn Hse. Pubs., Ltd.

—The Investigators: A Badge of Honor Novel. l.t. ed. 1998. 735p. 30.94 (*0-7838-0139-4*) Thorndike Pr.

—Men in Blue: A Badge of Honor Novel. 1988. (Badge of Honor Ser.). 352p. mass mkt. 7.99 (*0-515-09750-0*, Jove) Berkley Publishing Group.

—Men in Blue: A Badge of Honor Novel. unabr. collector's ed. 1993. audio 64.00 (*0-7366-2482-1*, 3244) Books on Tape, Inc.

—The Murderers: A Badge of Honor Novel. 1995. (Badge of Honor Ser.). 544p. mass mkt. 7.99 (*0-515-11742-0*, Jove) Berkley Publishing Group.

—The Murderers: A Badge of Honor Novel. unabr. ed. 1995. audio 96.00 (*0-7366-2949-1*, 3643) Books on Tape, Inc.

—The Murderers: A Badge of Honor Novel. unabr. ed. 1995. audio 25.95 (*1-56100-586-X*, 189, Bookcassette); audio 89.25 (*1-56100-211-9*, 957, Unabridged Library Editions) Brilliance Audio.

—The Murderers: A Badge of Honor Novel. l.t. ed. 1995. 24.95 o.p. (*1-56895-209-0*, Wheeler Publishing, Inc.) Gale Group.

—The Murderers: A Badge of Honor Novel. abr. ed. 2000. audio 7.95 (*1-57815-001-9*, 1017, Media Bks. Audio Publishing) Media Bks., L. L. C.

—The Murderers: A Badge of Honor Novel. 1995. 384p. 23.95 o.p. (*0-399-13976-1*) Putnam Publishing Group, The.

—The Murderers: A Badge of Honor Novel. 396p. pap. 5.98 o.p. (*0-7651-0428-8*) Smithmark Pubs., Inc.

—Special Operations: A Badge of Honor Novel. 1989. (Badge of Honor Ser.). (Illus.). 368p. mass mkt. 7.99 (*0-515-10148-6*, Jove) Berkley Publishing Group.

—Special Operations: A Badge of Honor Novel. unabr. collector's ed. 1993. audio 64.00 (*0-7366-2492-9*, 3251) Books on Tape, Inc.

—The Victim: A Badge of Honor Novel. 1991. (Badge of Honor Ser.). 352p. mass mkt. 7.99 (*0-515-10397-7*, Jove) Berkley Publishing Group.

—The Victim: A Badge of Honor Novel. unabr. collector's ed. 1993. audio 72.00 (*0-7366-2498-8*, 3256) Books on Tape, Inc.

—The Witness: A Badge of Honor Novel. 1992. (Badge of Honor Ser.). 432p. mass mkt. 7.99 (*0-515-10747-6*, Jove) Berkley Publishing Group.

—The Witness: A Badge of Honor Novel. unabr. collector's ed. 1993. audio 88.00 (*0-7366-2553-4*, 3304) Books on Tape, Inc.

**PAYNE, ROBERT (FICTITIOUS CHARACTER)—FICTION**

Barnard, Robert. A Little Local Murder. l.t. ed. 1985. (Nightingale Ser.). 320p. pap. 9.95 o.p. (*0-8161-3798-6*, Macmillan Reference USA) Gale Group.

**PEABODY, AMELIA (FICTITIOUS CHARACTER)—FICTION**

Peters, Elizabeth, pseud. The Ape Who Guards the Balance. abr. ed. 2001. audio 25.00 (*1-59040-136-0*, Phoenix Audio) American International Publishing Group.

—The Ape Who Guards the Balance. l.t. ed. 1999. (Amelia Peabody Mystery Ser.: No. 10). 26.95 (*1-56895-597-9*, Wheeler Publishing, Inc.) Gale Group.

—The Ape Who Guards the Balance. 2002. E-Book 7.50 (*0-06-052322-0*); E-Book 7.50 (*0-06-052323-9*); E-Book 7.50 (*0-06-052324-7*); E-Book 7.50 (*0-06-052325-5*) HarperCollins General Bks. Group. (PerfectBound).

—The Ape Who Guards the Balance. (Amelia Peabody Mystery Ser.: No. 10). 1999. 464p. (gr. 8 up). mass mkt. 7.50 (*0-380-79856-5*); 1998. 384p. 24.00 (*0-380-97657-9*) Morrow/Avon. (Avon Bks.).
—The Ape Who Guards the Balance. abr. ed. (Amelia Peabody Mystery Ser.: No. 10). 1999. audio 7.99 (*0-7871-2188-6*); 1998. audio 25.00 (*0-7871-1761-7*, 696052) NewStar Media, Inc.
—The Ape Who Guards the Balance, 1998. (Amelia Peabody Mystery Ser.: No. 10). audio 96.00 (*0-7887-2473-8*, 95548E7) Recorded Bks., LLC.
—Children of the Storm. 2003. (Amelia Peabody Mystery Ser.). 416p. 25.95 (*0-06-621476-9*) HarperCollins Pubs.
—Children of the Storm. l.t. ed. 2003. 640p. pap. 25.95 (*0-06-053333-1*, HarperLargePrint) HarperTrade.
—Children of the Storm. 2004. 480p. mass mkt. 7.50 (*0-06-103248-4*, Avon Bks.) Morrow/Avon.
—Crocodile on the Sandbank. 1978. (Amelia Peabody Mystery Ser.: No. 1). mass mkt. 1.75 o.s.i (*0-449-23713-3*, Fawcett) Ballantine Bks.
—Crocodile on the Sandbank. 1988. (Amelia Peabody Mystery Ser.: No. 1). reprint ed. pap. 3.95 o.p. (*0-89296-072-8*) Mysterious Pr.
—Crocodile on the Sandbank. unabr. ed. 1990. (Amelia Peabody Mystery Ser.: No. 1). (YA). audio 60.00 (*1-55690-127-5*, 90085E7) Recorded Bks., LLC.
—Crocodile on the Sandbank. 1988. (Amelia Peabody Mystery Ser.). 272p. reprint ed. mass mkt. 7.50 (*0-445-40651-8*) Warner Bks., Inc.
—The Curse of the Pharaohs. l.t. ed. 1993. (Amelia Peabody Mystery Ser.). 14.95 o.p. (*0-8161-3274-7*, Macmillan Reference USA) Gale Group.
—The Curse of the Pharaohs. unabr. ed. 1990. (Amelia Peabody Mystery Ser.: Vol. 2). (YA). (gr. 10). audio 70.00 (*1-55690-130-5*, 90095E7) Recorded Bks., LLC.
—The Curse of the Pharaohs. 1988. (Amelia Peabody Mystery Ser.). 304p. reprint ed. mass mkt. 7.50 (*0-445-40648-8*) Warner Bks., Inc.
—The Deeds of the Disturber. l.t. ed. 1989. (Amelia Peabody Mystery Ser.: No. 5). 512p. 20.95 o.p. (*0-8161-4694-2*, Macmillan Reference USA) Gale Group.
—The Deeds of the Disturber. 2000. (Amelia Peabody Mystery Ser.: No. 5). 400p. mass mkt. 7.50 (*0-380-73195-9*, Avon Bks.) Morrow/Avon.
—The Deeds of the Disturber. unabr. ed. 1993. (Amelia Peabody Mystery Ser.: No. 5). audio 85.00 (*1-55690-942-X*, 93438E7) Recorded Bks., LLC.
—The Deeds of the Disturber. 1988. (Amelia Peabody Mystery Ser.: No. 5). 320p. 16.95 o.s.i (*0-689-11907-0*, Scribner) Simon & Schuster.
—The Deeds of the Disturber. 1989. (Amelia Peabody Mystery Ser.: No. 5). 304p. mass mkt. 5.99 (*0-446-35333-7*) Warner Bks., Inc.
—The Falcon at the Portal. l.t. ed. 1999. (Amelia Peabody Mystery Ser.: No. 11). 27.95 (*1-56895-765-3*, Wheeler Publishing, Inc.) Gale Group.
—The Falcon at the Portal. 2002. (Amelia Peabody Mystery Ser.). E-Book 7.50 (*0-06-050440-4*); E-Book 7.50 (*0-06-621027-5*); E-Book 7.50 (*0-06-018905-3*); E-Book 7.50 (*0-06-621028-3*) HarperCollins General Bks. Group. (PerfectBound).
—The Falcon at the Portal. (Amelia Peabody Mystery Ser.: No. 11). 2000. 464p. mass mkt. 7.50 (*0-380-79857-3*, Avon Bks.); 1999. 384p. (gr. 8). 24.00 (*0-380-97658-7*, Morrow, William & Co.); 1999. 384p. (gr. 8). 24.00 (*0-380-97658-7*, Morrow, William & Co.) Morrow/Avon.
—The Falcon at the Portal. abr. ed. 1999. (Amelia Peabody Mystery Ser.: No. 11). audio 26.95 (*0-7871-1924-5*, Dove Audio) NewStar Media, Inc.
—The Falcon at the Portal. unabr. ed. (Amelia Peabody Mystery Ser.: No. 11). 2000. audio compact disk 119.00 (*0-7887-4206-X*, C1135E7); 1999. audio 96.00 (*0-7887-3744-9*, 95650E7) Recorded Bks., LLC.
—The Falcon at the Portal. 2000. (Amelia Peabody Mystery Ser.: No. 11). 13.04 (*0-606-18956-4*) Turtleback Bks.
—The Golden One: A Novel of Suspense. 2002. E-Book 19.95 (*0-06-009840-6*); E-Book 19.95 (*0-06-009892-9*) HarperCollins General Bks. Group. (PerfectBound).
—The Golden One: A Novel of Suspense. 2002. E-Book 19.95 (*0-06-009842-2*); E-Book 19.95 (*0-06-009841-4*) HarperCollins Pubs.
—The Golden One: A Novel of Suspense. 2002. audio 25.95 (*0-694-52509-X*, Caedmon); 688p. 25.95 (*0-06-009386-2*, HarperLargePrint) HarperTrade.
—The Golden One: A Novel of Suspense. 2003. 512p. mass mkt. 7.50 (*0-380-81715-2*, Avon Bks.); 2002. 448p. 25.95 (*0-380-97885-7*, Morrow, William & Co.) Morrow/Avon.
—He Shall Thunder in the Sky. 2001. (Amelia Peabody Mystery Ser.: Bk. 12). 512p. mass mkt. 7.50 (*0-380-79858-1*, Avon Bks.); 2000. (Amelia Peabody Mystery Ser.: Bk. 12). (Illus.). 416p. 25.00 (*0-380-97659-5*, Morrow, William & Co.); 2000. (*0-380-29962-3*) Morrow/Avon.
—He Shall Thunder in the Sky. abr. ed. 2000. (Amelia Peabody Mystery Ser.: Bk. 12). audio 25.00 (*0-7871-2513-X*, Dove Audio) NewStar Media, Inc.
—He Shall Thunder in the Sky. unabr. ed. 2001. audio compact disk 142.00 (*0-7887-6176-5*, C1400); 2000. (Amelia Peabody Mystery Ser.: Vol. 12). audio 103.00 (*0-7887-4850-5*, 96110E7) Recorded Bks., LLC.
—He Shall Thunder in the Sky. l.t. ed. (Illus.). 728p. 2001. (Amelia Peabody Mystery Ser.: Bk. 12). pap. 29.95 (*0-7862-2828-8*); 2000. (Amelia Peabody Mystery Ser.: Bk. 12). 31.95 (*0-7862-2827-X*); 2000. (*0-7540-1498-3*) Thorndike Pr.
—The Hippopotamus Pool. l.t. ed. 1996. (Amelia Peabody Mystery Ser.: No. 8). 571p. lib. bdg. 24.95 o.p. (*0-7838-1726-6*, Macmillan Reference USA) Gale Group.
—The Hippopotamus Pool. unabr. ed. 2000. (Amelia Peabody Mystery Ser.: No. 8). (J). audio 85.00 (*0-7887-0607-1*, 94617E7) Recorded Bks., LLC.
—The Hippopotamus Pool. abr. ed. 1996. (Amelia Peabody Mystery Ser.: No. 8). audio 21.95 o.p. (*1-55935-207-8*) Soundelux Audio Publishing.
—The Hippopotamus Pool. (Amelia Peabody Mystery Ser.: No. 8). 1996. 82p. 22.95 o.s.i (*0-446-51833-6*); 1997. 448p. reprint ed. mass mkt. 7.50 (*0-446-60398-8*) Warner Bks., Inc.
—The Last Camel Died at Noon. l.t. ed. 1992. (Amelia Peabody Mystery Ser.: No. 6). 576p. pap. 24.95 (*0-8161-5358-2*); 574p. lib. bdg. 21.95 o.p. (*0-8161-5357-4*) Gale Group. (Macmillan Reference USA).
—The Last Camel Died at Noon. unabr. ed. 1991. (Amelia Peabody Mystery Ser.: No. 6). audio 91.00 (*1-55690-300-6*, 91318E7) Recorded Bks., LLC.
—The Last Camel Died at Noon. 1992. 448p. mass mkt. 7.50 (*0-446-36338-3*); 1991. (Amelia Peabody Mystery Ser.: No. 6). 18.95 o.p. (*0-446-51483-7*) Warner Bks., Inc.
—Lion in the Valley. unabr. ed. 2001. audio 56.95 (*0-7861-2107-6*); audio compact disk 80.00 (*0-7861-9643-2*, ZR2869) Blackstone Audio Bks., Inc.
—Lion in the Valley. 1990. (Amelia Peabody Mystery Ser.: No. 4). 320p. reprint ed. mass mkt. 4.99 o.p. (*0-8125-1242-1*, Tor Bks.) Doherty, Tom Assocs., LLC.
—Lion in the Valley. 1999. (Amelia Peabody Mystery Ser.: No. 4). 384p. mass mkt. 7.50 (*0-380-73119-3*, Avon Bks.) Morrow/Avon.
—Lion in the Valley. unabr. ed. 1992. (Amelia Peabody Mystery Ser.: No. 4). audio 78.00 (*1-55690-690-0*, 92346E7) Recorded Bks., LLC.
—Lion in the Valley. 1986. (Amelia Peabody Mystery Ser.: No. 4). 288p. 14.95 o.p. (*0-689-11619-5*, Scribner) Simon & Schuster.
—Lord of the Silent. l.t. ed. 2001. 704p. pap. 25.00 (*0-06-620961-7*) HarperCollins Pubs.
—Lord of the Silent. abr. ed. 2001. audio 25.95 (*0-694-52510-3*, HarperAudio) HarperTrade.
—Lord of the Silent. 2002. 496p. mass mkt. 7.50 (*0-380-81714-4*); 2001. (Illus.). 416p. 25.00 (*0-380-97884-9*, Morrow, William & Co.) Morrow/Avon.
—Lord of the Silent. unabr. ed. 2001. audio 49.95 (*0-7887-9359-4*, 96726); audio compact disk 134.00 (*1-4025-0477-2*, C1533) Recorded Bks., LLC.
—The Mummy Case. (Amelia Peabody Mystery Ser.: No. 3). 1994. mass mkt. 4.50 (*0-8125-3214-7*); 1992. mass mkt. 3.99 o.s.i (*0-8125-2031-9*); 1988. pap. 3.95 o.s.i (*0-8125-0793-2*); 1986. pap. 3.50 o.s.i (*0-8125-0760-6*) Doherty, Tom Assocs., LLC. (Tor Bks.).
—The Mummy Case. l.t. ed. 1985. (Amelia Peabody Mystery Ser.: No. 3). 450p. pap. 17.95 o.p. (*0-8161-3934-2*, Macmillan Reference USA) Gale Group.
—The Mummy Case. unabr. ed. 1991. (Amelia Peabody Mystery Ser.: No. 3). audio 78.00 (*1-55690-631-5*, 91420E7) Recorded Bks., LLC.
—The Mummy Case. 1995. (Amelia Peabody Mystery Ser.). 336p. reprint ed. mass mkt. 7.50 (*0-446-60193-4*) Warner Bks., Inc.
—Seeing a Large Cat. unabr. ed. 1997. (Amelia Peabody Mystery Ser.: No. 9). audio 90.00 (*0-7887-1297-7*, 95131E7) Recorded Bks., LLC.
—Seeing a Large Cat. (Amelia Peabody Mystery Ser.: No. 9). 1997. 416p. 24.00 o.p. (*0-446-51834-4*); 1998. 432p. reprint ed. mass mkt. 7.50 (*0-446-60557-3*) Warner Bks., Inc.
—The Snake, the Crocodile & the Dog. l.t. ed. (Amelia Peabody Mystery Ser.: No. 7). 555p. 1994. pap. 17.95 (*0-8161-5682-4*); 1993. 24.95 (*0-8161-5681-6*) Gale Group. (Macmillan Reference USA).
—The Snake, the Crocodile & the Dog. unabr. ed. 1992. (Amelia Peabody Mystery Ser.: No. 7). audio 91.00 (*1-55690-783-4*, 92422E7) Recorded Bks., LLC.
—The Snake, the Crocodile & the Dog. (Amelia Peabody Mystery Ser.: No. 7). 1992. 340p. 28.00 (*0-446-51585-X*); 1994. 448p. reprint ed. mass mkt. 7.50 (*0-446-36478-9*) Warner Bks., Inc.

**PEACE, CHARLIE (FICTITIOUS CHARACTER)—FICTION**

Barnard, Robert. The Bad Samaritan. unabr. ed. 1997. audio 54.95 (*0-7531-0046-0*, 961104) ISIS Audio Bks. GBR. *Dist:* Ulverscroft Large Print Bks., Ltd.
—The Bad Samaritan. 1996. (Crime Ser.). 240p. pap. 5.95 o.p. (*0-14-025730-6*) Penguin Group (USA) Inc.
—The Bad Samaritan. 1995. 240p. 21.00 (*0-684-81334-3*, Scribner) Simon & Schuster.
—The Corpse at the Haworth Tandoori. l.t. ed. 1999. (Wheeler Large Print Book Ser.). (Illus.). 290p. pap. 24.95 (*1-56895-744-0*, Wheeler Publishing, Inc.) Gale Group.
—The Corpse at the Haworth Tandoori. l.t. ed. 2000. (Magna Large Print Ser.). 352p. o.p. (*0-7505-1502-3*) Magna Large Print Bks. GBR. *Dist:* Ulverscroft Large Print Bks., Ltd., Ulverscroft Large Print Canada, Ltd.
—The Corpse at the Haworth Tandoori. 2002. 288p. pap. 18.95 (*0-7432-2427-2*); 1999. (Illus.). 283p. 22.00 (*0-684-85532-1*) Simon & Schuster. (Scribner).
—A Hovering of Vultures. 1995. 224p. mass mkt. 6.99 o.p. (*0-552-14119-4*); 1994. 229p. 24.50 o.s.i (*0-593-03397-3*) Bantam Bks.
—A Hovering of Vultures. 1993. 224p. text 20.00 (*0-684-19625-5*, Macmillan Reference USA) Gale Group.
—A Hovering of Vultures. 1995. 224p. mass mkt. 4.99 (*0-380-77653-7*, Avon Bks.) Morrow/Avon.
—A Hovering of Vultures. 1993. 22.00 o.s.i (*0-684-19666-2*, Scribner) Simon & Schuster.
—No Place of Safety. 1998. 192p. 21.50 (*0-684-84503-2*, Scribner) Simon & Schuster.
—No Place of Safety. l.t. ed. 1998. (Basic Ser.). 312p. 28.95 (*0-7862-1452-X*); (*0-7540-3361-9*); (*0-7540-3362-7*) Thorndike Pr.

**PEACH, PERCY (FICTITIOUS CHARACTER)—FICTION**

Gregson, J. M. A Little Learning. 2002. 256p. 25.99 (*0-7278-5763-0*); 28.99 (*0-7278-7168-4*) Severn Hse. Pubs., Ltd.
—Murder at the Lodge. 2003. 224p. 26.99 (*0-7278-5813-0*) Severn Hse. Pubs., Ltd.
—To Kill a Wife. l.t. ed. 1999. (Magna Large Print Ser.). 384p. 31.99 o.p. (*0-7505-1409-4*) Magna Large Print Bks. GBR. *Dist:* Ulverscroft Large Print Bks., Ltd., Ulverscroft Large Print Canada, Ltd.
—To Kill a Wife. 1999. 224p. 25.00 (*0-7278-2273-X*) Severn Hse. Pubs., Ltd.

**PECKOVER, HENRY (FICTITIOUS CHARACTER)—FICTION**

Kenyon, Michael. The Elgar Variation. 1981. 360p. 13.95 o.p. (*0-698-11057-9*) Putnam Publishing Group, The.
—A Free-Range Wife. 1988. 208p. pap. 3.50 o.p. (*0-380-70382-3*, Avon Bks.) Morrow/Avon.
—A Free Range Wife. 1983. (Crime Club Ser.). (Illus.). 192p. 11.95 o.p. (*0-385-18838-2*) Doubleday Publishing.
—A Healthy Way to Die. 1986. (Crime Club Ser.). 192p. 12.95 o.p. (*0-385-23355-8*) Doubleday Publishing.
—A Healthy Way to Die. 1987. 192p. pap. 2.95 o.p. (*0-380-70380-7*, Avon Bks.) Morrow/Avon.
—Kill the Butler. 1993. 221p. 17.95 o.p. (*0-312-08833-7*, Saint Martin's Minotaur) St. Martin's Pr.
—Man at the Wheel. 1982. (Crime Club Ser.). 11.95 o.p. (*0-385-18299-6*) Doubleday Publishing.
—Man at the Wheel. 1988. 192p. pap. 3.50 (*0-380-70381-5*, Avon Bks.) Morrow/Avon.
—Peckover & the Bog Man: An Inspector Peckover Mystery. 1995. 208p. 20.95 o.p. (*0-312-13582-3*, Saint Martin's Minotaur) St. Martin's Pr.
—Peckover Holds the Baby. 1988. (Crime Club Ser.). 192p. pap. 12.95 o.s.i (*0-385-24324-3*) Doubleday Publishing.
—Peckover Holds the Baby. 1988. pap. 3.50 (*0-380-70636-9*, Avon Bks.) Morrow/Avon.
—Peckover Joins the Choir. 1994. 224p. 19.95 o.p. (*0-312-10523-1*, Saint Martin's Minotaur) St. Martin's Pr.

**PECOS, BEN (FICTITIOUS CHARACTER)—FICTION**

Slater, Susan. The Pumpkin Seed Massacre. Ellison, Lee, ed. 1999. (Ben Pecos Mysteries Ser.: Vol. 1). 240p. 22.95 o.p. (*1-890768-17-0*, Intrigue Pr.) Corvus Publishing.
—Thunderbird. 2002. (Ben Pecos Mysteries Ser.). 230p. 23.95 (*1-890768-41-3*, Intrigue Pr.) Corvus Publishing.
—Thunderbird. 2003. (WWL Mystery Ser.: No. 449). 272p. mass mkt. o.s.i (*0-373-26449-6*, Worldwide Library) Harlequin Enterprises, Ltd.
—Yellow Lies. 2002. (WWL Mystery Ser.: No. 422). mass mkt. (*0-373-26422-4*, 1-26422-5, Worldwide Library) Harlequin Enterprises, Ltd.
—Yellow Lies: A Ben Pecos Mystery. 2000. (Ben Pecos Mysteries Ser.). 297p. 22.95 (*1-890768-26-X*, Intrigue Pr.) Corvus Publishing.

**PEDERSEN, GUN (FICTITIOUS CHARACTER)—FICTION**

Enger, L. L. The Sinners' League: A Gun Pedersen Mystery. 1994. 288p. 21.00 (*1-883402-64-6*, Scribner) Simon & Schuster.

**PEEBLES, SAM (FICTITIOUS CHARACTER)—FICTION**

King, Stephen. The Library Policeman. abr. unabr. ed. 1991. (Four Past Midnight Ser.). audio 30.95 (*0-453-00748-1*, 892527) Penguin/HighBridge.
—Policia de la Biblioteca. 1999. Tr. of Library Policeman. (SPA.). mass mkt. 4.99 (*0-451-18660-5*, Signet Bks.) NAL.

**PEL, EVARISTE CLOVIS DESIRE (FICTITIOUS CHARACTER)—FICTION**

Hebden, Mark. Pel among the Pueblos. 1988. 16.95 o.p. (*0-8027-5690-5*) Walker & Co.
—Pel & the Bombers. 1986. pap. 2.95 o.p. (*0-8027-3169-4*); 1985. 13.95 o.p. (*0-8027-5608-5*) Walker & Co.
—Pel & the Faceless Corpse. 1984. 192p. pap. 2.95 o.p. (*0-8027-3100-7*); 1982. 190p. 11.95 o.s.i (*0-8027-5473-2*) Walker & Co.
—Pel & the Missing Persons. 1991. 208p. 17.95 o.p. (*0-312-06441-1*, Saint Martin's Minotaur) St. Martin's Pr.
—Pel & the Party Spirit. 1990. 15.95 o.p. (*0-312-05491-2*, Saint Martin's Minotaur) St. Martin's Pr.
—Pel & the Picture of Innocence. 1989. 192p. 14.95 o.p. (*0-312-02628-5*, Saint Martin's Minotaur) St. Martin's Pr.
—Pel & the Pirates. 1987. 192p. 15.95 o.p. (*0-8027-5672-7*) Walker & Co.
—Pel & the Predators. 1985. 192p. 14.95 o.p. (*0-8027-5624-7*) Walker & Co.
—Pel & the Promised Land. 1992. 17.95 o.p. (*0-312-08872-8*, Saint Martin's Minotaur) St. Martin's Pr.
—Pel & the Sepulchre Job. 1993. 160p. 17.95 o.p. (*0-312-09893-6*, Saint Martin's Minotaur) St. Martin's Pr.
—Pel & the Staghound. 1984. 192p. 12.95 o.s.i (*0-8027-5580-1*) Walker & Co.
—Pel & the Touch of Pitch. 1988. 16.95 o.p. (*0-8027-5720-0*) Walker & Co.
—Pel under Pressure. 1983. 192p. 12.95 o.s.i (*0-8027-5566-6*) Walker & Co.

**PELHAM, ELIZA (FICTITIOUS CHARACTER)—FICTION**

Horsley, Kate. A Killing in New Town. 1995. 286p. pap. 14.00 (*0-9631909-6-2*) La Alameda Pr.

**PELLAM, JOHN (FICTITIOUS CHARACTER)—FICTION**

Deaver, Jeffery. Shallow Graves. 2001. E-Book 6.99 (*0-7434-2401-8*, Pocket) Simon & Schuster.
Jeffries, William, pseud. Bloody River Blues. rev. ed. 2000. (Location Scout Mystery Ser.). (Illus.). 368p. mass mkt. 7.99 (*0-671-04750-7*, Pocket) Simon & Schuster.
—Bloody River Blues: A Location Scout Mystery. l.t. ed. 2002. 400p. pap. 29.95 (*0-7838-9310-8*, Macmillan Reference USA) Gale Group.
—Bloody River Blues: A Location Scout Mystery. 1993. 256p. mass mkt. 4.50 (*0-380-76670-1*, Avon Bks.) Morrow/Avon.
—Bloody River Blues: A Location Scout Mystery. l.t. ed. 2001. 400p. 32.95 (*0-7838-9309-4*) Thorndike Pr.
—Hell's Kitchen: A Location Scout Mystery. l.t. ed. 2000. (Wheeler Hardcover Ser.). 379p. (Orig.). 26.95 (*1-56895-136-1*, Wheeler Publishing, Inc.) Gale Group.
—Shallow Graves. E-Book 6.99 (*1-59061-257-4*) Adobe Systems, Inc.
—Shallow Graves: A Location Scout Mystery. l.t. ed. 2000. (G. K. Hall Core Ser.). 380p. 31.95 (*0-7838-9296-9*, Macmillan Reference USA) Gale Group.
—Shallow Graves: A Location Scout Mystery. 1992. (Location Scout Mystery Ser.). 272p. mass mkt. 4.50 (*0-380-76669-8*, Avon Bks.) Morrow/Avon.
—Shallow Graves: A Location Scout Mystery. 2000. (Illus.). 368p. pap. 6.99 (*0-671-04748-5*, Pocket) Simon & Schuster.

**PELLETIER, KAREN (FICTITIOUS CHARACTER)—FICTION**

Dobson, Joanne. Cold & Pure & Very Dead: A Karen Pelletier Mystery. 2000. 272p. 22.95 o.s.i (*0-385-49340-1*) Doubleday Publishing.
—Maltese Manuscript. 2003. 264p. 24.95 o.s.i (*1-59058-039-7*); 450p. pap. 22.95 o.s.i (*1-59058-087-7*) Poisoned Pen Pr.
—Maltese Manuscript. 2004. 272p. mass mkt. 6.99 (*0-7434-8005-8*) ibooks, Inc.

—The Northbury Papers. 1999. 352p. mass mkt. 6.50 (*0-553-57661-5*) Bantam Bks.
—The Northbury Papers. 1998. 288p. 21.95 o.s.i (*0-385-48693-6*) Doubleday Publishing.
—Quieter Than Sleep. 1998. 336p. reprint ed. mass mkt. 6.99 (*0-553-57660-7*) Bantam Bks.
—The Raven & the Nightingale. 2000. 320p. mass mkt. 5.99 (*0-553-57999-1*) Bantam Bks.
—The Raven & the Nightingale: A Modern Mystery of Edgar Allen Poe. 1999. 288p. 21.95 o.s.i (*0-385-49339-8*) Doubleday Publishing.

**PELLETIER, LIBBY (FICTITIOUS CHARACTER)—FICTION**

White, Michael C. A Brother's Blood: A Novel. 1996. 336p. 22.50 o.p. (*0-06-018667-4*) HarperCollins Pubs.
—A Brother's Blood: A Novel. 1997. 336p. pap. 13.00 (*0-06-092859-X*, Perennial) HarperTrade.

**PELMAN THE POWERSHAPER (FICTITIOUS CHARACTER)—FICTION**

Hughes, Robert Don. The Power & the Prophet, No. 3. 1985. 352p. mass mkt. 4.99 o.s.i (*0-345-30353-9*, Del Rey) Ballantine Bks.
—The Prophet of Lamath. 1985. mass mkt. 4.99 o.s.i (*0-345-32544-3*); 1979. mass mkt. 1.95 o.p. (*0-345-28211-6*) Ballantine Bks. (Del Rey).
—The Wizard in Waiting. 1987. 208p. mass mkt. 3.95 o.s.i (*0-345-34602-5*); 1982. mass mkt. 2.75 o.p. (*0-345-28574-3*) Ballantine Bks. (Del Rey).

**PEMBRIDGE, DIANA (FICTITIOUS CHARACTER)—FICTION**

D'Alpuget, Blanche. White Eye. 1994. 254p. pap. 22.00 (*0-671-62005-3*, Simon & Schuster) Simon & Schuster.

**PENDEL, HARRY (FICTITIOUS CHARACTER)—FICTION**

Le Carré, John. The Tailor of Panama. 1997. (George Smiley Novels Ser.). mass mkt. 6.99 o.p. (*0-449-22739-1*, Fawcett); 416p. mass mkt. 7.99 (*0-345-42043-8*, Ballantine Bks.) Ballantine Bks.
—The Tailor of Panama. unabr. collector's ed. 1997. (George Smiley Novels Ser.). audio 80.00 (*0-913369-86-1*, 4382) Books on Tape, Inc.
—The Tailor of Panama. 1996. (George Smiley Novels Ser.). 25.00 o.s.i (*0-679-45446-2*); 320p. 25.00 (*0-679-45480-2*); pap. 25.00 o.p. (*0-679-77413-0*) Knopf, Alfred A. Inc.
—The Tailor of Panama. abr. ed. 1996. (George Smiley Ser.). audio 25.95 (*0-679-45813-1*, 694392, RH Audio) Random Hse. Audio Publishing Group.
—The Tailor of Panama. l.t. ed. 1996. (George Smiley Ser.). 512p. pap. 25.00 o.p. (*0-7838-1933-1*) Random Hse. Large Print.

**PENETRATOR (FICTITIOUS CHARACTER)—FICTION**

Cunningham, Chet. Tokyo Purple - Northwest Contract. 1991. (Penetrator Double Ser.). 368p. pap. 4.50 (*0-8439-3020-9*) Dorchester Publishing Co., Inc.
Derrick, Lionel. The Hellbomb Flight. 1975. (Penetrator Ser.). 192p. pap. 1.25 o.p. (*0-523-22690-X*, Pinnacle Bks.) Kensington Publishing Corp.
—High Disaster: Penetrator No. 22. 1977. (Penetrator Ser). pap. 1.50 o.p. (*0-523-40067-5*, Pinnacle Bks.) Kensington Publishing Corp.
—Jungle Blitz. 1982. (Penetrator Ser.: No. 48). 192p. pap. 2.25 o.p. (*0-523-41680-6*, Pinnacle Bks.) Kensington Publishing Corp.
—Mankill Sport. 1976. (Penetrator Ser.: No. 14). 192p. pap. 1.25 o.p. (*0-523-22858-9*, Pinnacle Bks.) Kensington Publishing Corp.
—Oklahoma Firefight. 1979. (Penetrator Ser.: No. 31). pap. 1.50 o.p. (*0-523-40363-1*, Pinnacle Bks.) Kensington Publishing Corp.
—The Penetrator. 1977. (Penetrator Ser. : Vol. 18). pap. 1.25 o.p. (*0-523-22995-X*); 1973. (Penetrator Ser.). 160p. pap. 0.95 o.p. (*0-523-21237-2*); 1973. (Penetrator Ser.). 192p. pap. 1.25 o.p. (*0-523-40101-9*) Kensington Publishing Corp. (Pinnacle Bks.).
—Penetrator: Baja Bandidos. 1974. (Penetrator Ser. : Vol. 7). pap. 1.25 o.p. (*0-523-22502-4*, Pinnacle Bks.) Kensington Publishing Corp.
—Penetrator: Dodge City Bombers. 1975. (Penetrator Ser. : Vol. 9). 192p. pap. 1.25 o.p. (*0-523-22627-6*, Pinnacle Bks.) Kensington Publishing Corp.
—Penetrator: Hell's Hostages, No. 41. 1981. 192p. pap. 1.75 o.p. (*0-523-41116-2*, Pinnacle Bks.) Kensington Publishing Corp.
—Penetrator: Hijacking Manhattan. 1974. (Penetrator Ser. : Vol. 4). pap. 0.95 o.p. (*0-523-21338-7*, Pinnacle Bks.) Kensington Publishing Corp.
—Penetrator: Northwest Contract. 1975. (Penetrator Ser. : Vol. 8). 192p. pap. 1.25 o.p. (*0-523-22540-7*, Pinnacle Bks.) Kensington Publishing Corp.
—Penetrator: Orphan Army. 1982. (Penetrator Ser. : Vol. 47). 208p. pap. 2.25 o.p. (*0-523-41554-0*, Pinnacle Bks.) Kensington Publishing Corp.
—Penetrator: Panama Power Play. 1978. (Penetrator Ser. : Vol. 19). pap. 1.50 o.p. (*0-523-40429-8*, Pinnacle Bks.) Kensington Publishing Corp.
—Penetrator: Showbiz Wipeout, No. 32. 1979. pap. 1.50 o.p. (*0-523-40514-6*, Pinnacle Bks.) Kensington Publishing Corp.
—Penetrator: Terrorist Torment. 1982. (Penetrator Ser. : Vol. 46). 192p. pap. 1.95 o.p. (*0-523-41553-2*, Pinnacle Bks.) Kensington Publishing Corp.
—Penetrator: The Radiation Hit. 1977. (Penetrator Ser. : Vol. 20). 192p. pap. 1.50 o.p. (*0-523-40044-6*, Pinnacle Bks.) Kensington Publishing Corp.
—The Penetrator, No. 5. 1974. pap. 0.95 o.p. (*0-523-21378-6*, Pinnacle Bks.) Kensington Publishing Corp.
—The Penetrator, No. 6. 1974. 192p. pap. 1.25 o.p. (*0-523-22434-6*, Pinnacle Bks.) Kensington Publishing Corp.
—Plundered Paradise. 1983. (Penetrator Ser.: No. 51). 208p. pap. 2.25 o.p. (*0-523-41736-5*, Pinnacle Bks.) Kensington Publishing Corp.
—Satan's Swarm. 1983. (Penetrator Ser.: No. 49). 192p. pap. 2.25 o.p. (*0-523-41681-4*, Pinnacle Bks.) Kensington Publishing Corp.
—The Skyhigh Betrayers. 1978. (Penetrator Ser.: No. 28). pap. 1.50 o.p. (*0-523-40268-6*, Pinnacle Bks.) Kensington Publishing Corp.
—The Supergun Mission, No. 21. 1977. (Penetrator Ser.). pap. 1.25 o.p. (*0-523-40079-9*, Pinnacle Bks.) Kensington Publishing Corp.
—The Target Is H. 1983. (Penetrator Ser.: No. 1). 192p. pap. 1.95 o.p. (*0-523-42056-0*, Pinnacle Bks.) Kensington Publishing Corp.
Penetrator. Neutron Nightmare. 1983. (Penetrator Ser. : Vol. 50). pap. 2.25 o.p. (*0-523-41735-7*, Pinnacle Bks.) Kensington Publishing Corp.

**PENN, ALEX (FICTITIOUS CHARACTER)—FICTION**

Block, Lawrence. After the First Death. 1994. 268p. mass mkt. 4.50 o.p. (*0-7867-0167-6*, Carroll & Graf Pubs.) Avalon Publishing Group.
—After the First Death. 1984. 192p. reprint ed. pap. 4.95 o.p. (*0-88150-020-8*) Countryman Pr.
—After the First Death. l.t. ed. 1992. (Nightingale Ser.). 291p. pap. 14.95 o.p. (*0-8161-5408-2*, Macmillan Reference USA) Gale Group.
—After the First Death. 2002. 192p. mass mkt. 6.99 (*0-7434-4507-4*) ibooks, Inc.

**PENN, SIMON (FICTITIOUS CHARACTER)—FICTION**

Monahan, Brent. Blood of the Covenant. 1997. 320p. mass mkt. 5.99 (*0-312-96214-2*, St. Martin's Paperbacks) St. Martin's Pr.

**PEPPER, AMANDA (FICTITIOUS CHARACTER)—FICTION**

Roberts, Gillian. Adam & Evil. 2000. (Amanda Pepper Mysteries Ser.). 240p. mass mkt. 6.50 (*0-345-42935-4*, Ballantine Bks.) Ballantine Bks.
—Adam & Evil. l.t. ed. 2000. (Beeler Large Print Mystery Ser.). 260p. 26.95 (*1-57490-292-X*, Beeler Large Print Bks.) Beeler, Thomas T. Publisher.
—Adam & Evil. unabr. ed. 2000. (Amanda Pepper Mysteries Ser.: No. 9). audio 54.00 (*0-7887-4311-2*, 96107E7) Recorded Bks., LLC.
—The Bluest Blood, unabr. ed. 1998. (Amanda Pepper Mysteries Ser.: Vol. 8). audio 51.00 (*0-7887-2518-1*, 95591E7) Recorded Bks., LLC.
—The Bluest Blood: An Amanda Pepper Mystery. (Amanda Pepper Mysteries Ser.). 1999. 304p. mass mkt. 6.50 (*0-345-42315-1*); Vol. 8. 1998. 240p. 22.00 o.s.i (*0-345-40326-6*, Ballantine Bks.) Ballantine Bks.
—The Bluest Blood: An Amanda Pepper Mystery. l.t. ed. 2000. (Beeler Large Print Mystery Ser.). (Illus.). 261p. 25.95 (*1-57490-321-7*, Beeler Large Print Bks.) Beeler, Thomas T. Publisher.
—Caught Dead in Philadelphia. 1988. 208p. mass mkt. 6.50 (*0-345-35340-4*) Ballantine Bks.
—Caught Dead in Philadelphia. unabr. ed. 1993. (Amanda Pepper Mysteries Ser.: Vol. 1). audio 44.00 (*1-55690-900-4*, 93342E7) Recorded Bks., LLC.
—Caught Dead in Philadelphia: A Mystery Introducing Amanda Pepper. 1987. 224p. 16.95 o.s.i (*0-684-18809-0*, Macmillan Reference USA) Gale Group.
—Claire & Present Danger. 2003. 256p. 22.95 (*0-345-45490-1*, Ballantine Bks.) Ballantine Bks.
—Claire & Present Danger. l.t. ed. 2003. (Mystery Ser.). 28.95 (*1-57490-527-9*) Beeler, Thomas T. Publisher.
—Helen Hath No Fury: An Amanda Pepper Mystery. 2001. 256p. reprint ed. mass mkt. 6.99 (*0-345-42932-X*, Fawcett) Ballantine Bks.
—Helen Hath No Fury: An Amanda Pepper Mystery. l.t. ed. 2001. (Beeler Large Print Mystery Ser.). 240p. 25.95 (*1-57490-334-9*, Beeler Large Print Bks.) Beeler, Thomas T. Publisher.
—How I Spent My Summer Vacation. 1995. 256p. mass mkt. 5.99 (*0-345-38594-2*); pap. 19.00 o.s.i (*0-345-46533-4*) Ballantine Bks.
—I'd Rather Be in Philadelphia. 1993. 240p. mass mkt. 5.99 (*0-345-37782-6*) Ballantine Bks.
—In the Dead of Summer. 288p. 1996. mass mkt. 5.99 (*0-345-40650-8*); 1995. pap. 19.00 o.s.i (*0-345-46534-2*, Ballantine Bks.) Ballantine Bks.
—The Mummer's Curse. unabr. ed. 1996. (Amanda Pepper Mysteries Ser.: Vol. 7). audio 51.00 (*0-7887-0667-5*, 94844E7) Recorded Bks., LLC.
—The Mummers' Curse, Vol. 7. 1997. (Amanda Pepper Mysteries Ser.). 288p. mass mkt. 5.99 (*0-345-40324-X*, Ballantine Bks.) Ballantine Bks.
—Philly Stakes. 1990. 208p. mass mkt. 5.99 (*0-345-36266-7*) Ballantine Bks.
—Philly Stakes. unabr. ed. 1994. (Amanda Pepper Mysteries Ser.: Vol. 2). audio 51.00 (*1-55690-994-2*, 94133E7) Recorded Bks., LLC.
—Philly Stakes. 1989. 240p. 17.95 o.s.i (*0-684-19071-0*, Scribner) Simon & Schuster.
—With Friends Like These... 1995. 272p. pap. 19.00 o.s.i (*0-345-46535-0*) Ballantine Bks.
Roberts, Gillian & Foster, Alan Dean. With Friends Like These... 1994. 272p. mass mkt. 5.99 (*0-345-37784-2*); 1993. 256p. 18.00 o.s.i (*0-345-37783-4*) Ballantine Bks.

**PERCEVAL, LYDIA (FICTITIOUS CHARACTER)—FICTION**

Barnard, Robert. A Fatal Attachment. 1994. mass mkt. 5.99 o.s.i (*0-552-13932-7*) Bantam Bks.
—A Fatal Attachment. 1992. 288p. 20.00 (*0-684-19412-0*, Macmillan Reference USA) Gale Group.
—A Fatal Attachment. l.t. ed. 1993. (Magna Large Print Ser.). 348p. o.p. (*0-7505-0506-0*) Magna Large Print Bks. GBR. *Dist:* Ulverscroft Large Print Canada, Ltd.
—A Fatal Attachment. 1994. 240p. mass mkt. 4.99 (*0-380-71998-3*, Avon Bks.) Morrow/Avon.

**PEREGRINE FAMILY (FICTITIOUS CHARACTERS)—FICTION**

Deveraux, Jude. The Conquest. l.t. ed. 1991. (General Ser.). 408p. 17.95 o.p. (*0-8161-5230-6*); lib. bdg. 20.95 (*0-8161-5231-4*) Gale Group. (Macmillan Reference USA).
—The Conquest. Marrow, Linda, ed. 1991. 320p. mass mkt. 7.99 (*0-671-64447-5*, Pocket) Simon & Schuster.
—The Taming. l.t. ed. 1990. (General Ser.). 382p. lib. bdg. 20.95 o.p. (*0-8161-4937-2*, Macmillan Reference USA) Gale Group.
—The Taming. Morrow, Linda, ed. 1991. 384p. mass mkt. 7.99 (*0-671-74383-X*, Pocket) Simon & Schuster.
—The Taming. 1990. mass mkt. 4.95 (*0-671-72992-6*, Pocket) Simon & Schuster.

**PERKINS, ANDREA (FICTITIOUS CHARACTER)—FICTION**

Coker, Carolyn. Appearance of Evil. 1995. 250p. per. (*0-373-26185-3*, 1-26185-8, Worldwide Library) Harlequin Enterprises, Ltd.

**PERKINS, BEN (FICTITIOUS CHARACTER)—FICTION**

Kantner, Rob. Made in Detroit. 1990. mass mkt. 3.95 o.s.i (*0-553-28458-4*) Bantam Bks.

**PERKINS, DOUGLAS (FICTITIOUS CHARACTER)—FICTION**

Babson, Marian. Cover-up Story. 1991. 208p. mass mkt. 3.99 o.s.i (*0-553-29330-3*) Bantam Bks.
—Cover-up Story. l.t. ed. 1991. (Nightingale Ser.). 264p. pap. 14.95 o.p. (*0-8161-4926-7*, Macmillan Reference USA) Gale Group.
—Cover-up Story. 2003. 224p. mass mkt. 6.50 (*0-312-98822-2*, St. Martin's Paperbacks); 1988. 192p. 14.95 o.p. (*0-312-02180-1*, Saint Martin's Minotaur) St. Martin's Pr.
—In the Teeth of Adversity. 1992. 208p. mass mkt. 4.99 o.s.i (*0-553-29131-9*) Bantam Bks.
—In the Teeth of Adversity. l.t. ed. 1992. (Nightingale Ser.). 250p. 14.95 o.p. (*0-8161-5259-4*, Macmillan Reference USA) Gale Group.
—In the Teeth of Adversity. 2003. 176p. mass mkt. 6.50 (*0-312-99103-7*, St. Martin's Paperbacks); 1990. 14.95 o.p. (*0-312-04332-5*, Saint Martin's Minotaur) St. Martin's Pr.
—Murder at the Cat Show. 1990. 192p. reprint ed. mass mkt. 3.95 o.s.i (*0-553-28590-4*) Bantam Bks.
—Murder at the Cat Show. l.t. ed. 1992. (Nightingale Ser.). 264p. 14.95 o.p. (*0-8161-5258-6*, Macmillan Reference USA) Gale Group.
—Murder at the Cat Show. pap. 15.95 (*0-312-31278-4*, Saint Martin's Griffin); 2003. 192p. mass mkt. 5.99 (*0-312-98974-1*, St. Martin's Paperbacks); 1989. 14.95 o.p. (*0-312-02954-3*, Saint Martin's Minotaur) St. Martin's Pr.
—Tourists Are for Trapping. 1991. 192p. mass mkt. 3.99 o.s.i (*0-553-29031-2*) Bantam Bks.
—Tourists Are for Trapping. 1992. 2.99 o.p. (*0-517-09060-0*) Random Hse. Value Publishing.
—Tourists Are for Trapping. 2003. 208p. mass mkt. 5.99 (*0-312-99099-5*, St. Martin's Paperbacks); 1989. 192p. 14.95 o.p. (*0-312-03444-X*, Saint Martin's Minotaur) St. Martin's Pr.

**PERRIN, MICHAEL (FICTITIOUS CHARACTER)—FICTION**

Bear, Greg. Infinity Concerto. 1987. mass mkt. 3.95 o.s.i (*0-441-37059-4*) Ace Bks.
—Infinity Concerto. 1986. 352p. 3.50 o.s.i (*0-425-09536-3*); 1984. 2.95 o.s.i (*0-425-07308-4*) Berkley Publishing Group.
—The Serpent Mage. (Orig.). 1987. mass mkt. 3.95 o.s.i (*0-441-75910-6*); 1986. mass mkt. 2.75 o.s.i (*0-441-79066-6*) Ace Bks.
—The Serpent Mage. 1986. 352p. (Orig.). 3.50 o.s.i (*0-425-09337-9*) Berkley Publishing Group.
—Songs of Earth & Power. 1996. 695p. pap. text 6.99 (*0-8125-3603-7*); 1994. 560p. 24.95 o.p. (*0-312-85669-5*) Doherty, Tom Assocs., LLC. (Tor Bks.).
—Songs of Earth & Power. 1992. (*0-7126-5494-1*) Random Hse. UK, Ltd. GBR. *Dist:* Random Hse. of Canada, Ltd.

**PERRIN, REGINALD (FICTITIOUS CHARACTER)—FICTION**

Nobbs, David. The Better World of Reginald Perrin. l.t. unabr. ed. 1998. 400p. 32.50 (*0-7531-5506-0*, 155060) ISIS Large Print Bks. GBR. *Dist:* Ulverscroft Large Print Bks., Ltd., Ulverscroft Large Print Canada, Ltd.
—The Fall & Rise of Reginald Perrin. l.t. unabr. ed. 1998. 368p. 24.95 (*0-7531-5504-4*, 155044) Ulverscroft Large Print Bks., Ltd.
—The Legacy of Reginald Perrin. l.t. unabr. ed. 1999. 336p. 25.95 (*0-7531-5507-9*, 155079) ISIS Large Print Bks. GBR. *Dist:* ISIS Publishing.
—The Return of Reginald Perrin. l.t. unabr. ed. 1999. 342p. 26.95 (*0-7531-5505-2*, 155052) ISIS Large Print Bks. GBR. *Dist:* ISIS Publishing.

**PERROT, DICK (FICTITIOUS CHARACTER)—FICTION**

Morrison, Arthur. A Child of the Jago. (Academy Book Ser.). 208p. 1995. pap. 12.00 (*0-89733-392-6*); 1983. pap. 8.95 o.p. (*0-85115-203-1*) Academy Chicago Pubs., Ltd.

**PERRY, WILL (FICTITIOUS CHARACTER)—FICTION**

Pullman, Philip. The Golden Compass. unabr. ed. 1999. (His Dark Materials Ser.: Bk. 1). (YA). (gr. 7-12). audio Random Hse. Audio Publishing Group.

**PERRY-MONDORI, KAREN (FICTITIOUS CHARACTER)—FICTION**

Arnold, Catherine. Due Process. 1996. 368p. mass mkt. 5.99 o.s.i (*0-451-18614-1*, Signet Bks.) NAL.
—Imperfect Justice. 1997. 464p. mass mkt. 5.99 o.s.i (*0-451-19292-3*, Signet Bks.) NAL.

**PETERS, ANNA (FICTITIOUS CHARACTER)—FICTION**

Law, Janice. Backfire. 1996. (WWL Mystery Ser.). per. (*0-373-26201-9*, 1-26201-3, Worldwide Library) Harlequin Enterprises, Ltd.
—Backfire. 1994. (Anna Peters Mystery Ser.). 208p. 18.95 o.p. (*0-312-11474-5*, Saint Martin's Minotaur) St. Martin's Pr.
—The Big Payoff. 1976. 6.95 o.p. (*0-395-21900-0*) Houghton Mifflin Co.
—The Big Payoff. 1999. 192p. pap. 9.95 (*1-58348-697-6*) iUniverse, Inc.
—Cross-Check. 1998. (WWL Mystery Ser.). 256p. per. (*0-373-26291-4*, 1-26291-4, Worldwide Library) Harlequin Enterprises, Ltd.
—Cross-Check. 1997. 224p. 20.95 (*0-312-15504-2*, Saint Martin's Minotaur) St. Martin's Pr.
—Death Under Par, 001. 1981. 9.95 o.p. (*0-395-30227-7*) Houghton Mifflin Co.
—Death Under Par. 2000. 248p. pap. 12.95 (*0-595-00040-1*) iUniverse, Inc.
—Gemini Trip. 1977. 7.95 o.p. (*0-395-25703-4*) Houghton Mifflin Co.
—Gemini Trip. 2000. (Anna Peters Mystery Ser.). 188p. pap. 9.95 (*0-595-08851-1*) iUniverse, Inc.
—A Safe Place to Die. 1995. per. (*0-373-26179-9*, 1-26179-1, Harlequin Bks.) Harlequin Enterprises, Ltd.
—A Safe Place to Die. 1993. 208p. 17.95 o.p. (*0-312-09300-4*, Saint Martin's Minotaur) St. Martin's Pr.
—The Shadow of the Palms, 001. 1980. 8.95 o.p. (*0-395-28591-7*) Houghton Mifflin Co.
—The Shadow of the Palms. 2000. (Anna Peters Mystery Ser.). 228p. pap. 13.95 (*0-595-08938-0*) iUniverse, Inc.
—Time Lapse: An Anna Peters Mystery. 1998. (WWL Mystery Ser.). per. (*0-373-26267-1*, 1-26267-4, Worldwide Library) Harlequin Enterprises, Ltd.
—Time Lapse: An Anna Peters Mystery. 1992. 199p. 19.95 o.p. (*0-8027-3221-6*) Walker & Co.
—Under Orion, 001. 1978. 14.95 o.p. (*0-395-26484-7*) Houghton Mifflin Co.
—Under Orion. 2000. 192p. pap. 11.95 (*0-595-08852-X*) iUniverse, Inc.

**PETERS, TOBY (FICTITIOUS CHARACTER)—FICTION**

Kaminsky, Stuart M. Bullet for a Star. unabr. ed. 1994. audio 23.95 (*0-7861-0731-6*, 1482) Blackstone Audio Bks., Inc.

—Bullet for a Star. 1985. (Toby Peters Mystery Ser.). pap. 3.95 o.p. (*0-89296-147-3*) Mysterious Pr.

—Bullet for a Star. 1977. (Toby Peters Mystery Ser.). 188p. 7.95 o.p. (*0-312-10797-8*) St. Martin's Pr.

—Bullet for a Star. 1991. (Toby Peters Mystery Ser.). 192p. mass mkt. 4.99 (*0-446-40061-0*, Mysterious Pr. Paperback Bks.) Warner Bks., Inc.

—Buried Caesars. l.t. ed. 1991. (Toby Peters Mystery Ser.). 281p. 18.95 o.p. (*0-7927-0490-8*); pap. 16.95 o.p. (*0-7927-0491-6*, C0783) BBC Audiobooks America.

—Buried Caesars. 1989. (Toby Peters Mystery Ser.). 192p. 15.45 o.p. (*0-89296-374-3*) Mysterious Pr.

—Buried Caesars. unabr. ed. 1997. (Toby Peters Mystery Ser.: Vol. 14). audio 44.00 (*0-7887-0401-X*, 94593E7) Recorded Bks., LLC.

—Buried Caesars. 1990. (Toby Peters Mystery Ser.). 192p. mass mkt. 4.50 (*0-445-40878-2*, Mysterious Pr. Paperback Bks.) Warner Bks., Inc.

—Catch a Falling Clown. 1981. (Toby Peters Mystery Ser.). 182p. 10.95 o.p. (*0-312-12377-9*) St. Martin's Pr.

—Catch a Falling Clown. 1984. (Toby Peters Mystery Ser.). 182p. reprint ed. pap. 3.95 o.p. (*0-14-007022-2*, Penguin Bks.) Viking Penguin.

—Dancing in the Dark. unabr. ed. 1996. (Toby Peters Mystery Ser.). 30p. audio 39.95 (*0-7861-0961-0*, 754074) Blackstone Audio Bks., Inc.

—Dancing in the Dark. 1996. (Toby Peters Mystery Ser.). 228p. 19.95 o.s.i (*0-89296-528-2*) Mysterious Pr.

—Dancing in the Dark. unabr. ed. audio. 1996. (Toby Peters Mystery Ser.: Vol. 19). audio 44.00 (*0-7887-0621-7*, 94795E7) Recorded Bks., LLC.

—Dancing in the Dark. 224p. 2001. E-Book 4.95 (*0-7595-4429-8*); 2001. E-Book 4.95 (*0-7595-8325-0*); 2001. E-Book 4.95 (*0-7595-6319-5*); 2001. E-Book 4.95 (*0-7595-9352-3*); 2001. E-Book 4.95 (*0-7595-0320-6*); 1997. mass mkt. 5.99 o.p. (*0-446-40337-7*) Warner Bks., Inc.

—The Devil Met a Lady. unabr. ed. 1995. audio 39.95 (*0-7861-0881-9*, 1536) Blackstone Audio Bks., Inc.

—The Devil Met a Lady. 1993. (Toby Peters Mystery Ser.). 208p. 18.95 (*0-89296-436-7*) Mysterious Pr.

—The Devil Met a Lady. 1995. (Toby Peters Mystery Ser.). 208p. mass mkt. 5.50 (*0-446-40423-3*, Mysterious Pr. Paperback Bks.) Warner Bks., Inc.

—The Devil Met a Lady. 2000. (Toby Peters Mysteries Ser.). 240p. pap. 12.00 (*0-7434-0004-6*) ibooks, Inc.

—Down for the Count. l.t. ed. 1986. (Toby Peters Mystery Ser.). 307p. 11.95 o.p. (*0-8161-4000-6*, Macmillan Reference USA) Gale Group.

—Down for the Count. 1985. (Toby Peters Mystery Ser.). 192p. 12.95 o.p. (*0-312-21862-1*) St. Martin's Pr.

—Down for the Count. 1990. (Toby Peters Mystery Ser.). mass mkt. 4.50 o.s.i (*0-445-40908-8*, Mysterious Pr. Paperback Bks.) Warner Bks., Inc.

—The Fala Factor. 1985. (Toby Peters Mystery Ser.). pap. 3.95 o.p. (*0-89296-148-1*) Mysterious Pr.

—The Fala Factor. 1984. (Toby Peters Mystery Ser.). 174p. 11.95 o.p. (*0-312-27967-1*) St. Martin's Pr.

—The Fala Factor. 1993. (Toby Peters Mystery Ser.). 224p. mass mkt. 4.99 (*0-446-40065-3*, Mysterious Pr. Paperback Bks.) Warner Bks., Inc.

—A Fatal Glass of Beer. unabr. ed. 1998. (Toby Peters Mystery Ser.). audio 29.95 (*0-7861-1465-7*); audio 44.95 (*0-7861-1346-4*, 1766) Blackstone Audio Bks., Inc.

—A Fatal Glass of Beer, Set. unabr. ed. 1999. audio 44.95 Highsmith Inc.

—A Fatal Glass of Beer. 1997. (Toby Peters Mystery Ser.). (ACE.). 256p. 21.50 o.p. (*0-89296-630-0*) Mysterious Pr.

—A Fatal Glass of Beer. unabr. ed. 1997. (Toby Peters Mystery Ser.: Vol. 20). audio 51.00 (*0-7887-0650-0*, 94827E7) Recorded Bks., LLC.

—A Few Minutes Past Midnight. 2001. 240p. 24.00 (*0-7867-0862-X*, Carroll & Graf Pubs.) Avalon Publishing Group.

—A Few Minutes Past Midnight. l.t. ed. 2002. 347p. 29.95 (*0-7862-4118-7*) Gale Group.

—He Done Her Wrong. unabr. ed. 1998. audio 39.95 (*0-7861-1280-8*, 2175) Blackstone Audio Bks., Inc.

—He Done Her Wrong. 1984. (Toby Peters Mystery Ser.). reprint ed. pap. 3.95 o.p. (*0-89296-095-7*) Mysterious Pr.

—He Done Her Wrong. 1983. (Toby Peters Mystery Ser.). 168p. 10.95 o.p. (*0-312-36491-1*) St. Martin's Pr.

—He Done Her Wrong. 1995. (Toby Peters Mystery Ser.). 208p. mass mkt. 5.50 (*0-446-40191-9*, Mysterious Pr. Paperback Bks.) Warner Bks., Inc.

—High Midnight. unabr. ed. 1995. audio 32.95 (*0-7861-0765-0*, 1614) Blackstone Audio Bks., Inc.

—High Midnight. 1984. (Toby Peters Mystery Ser.). reprint ed. pap. 3.95 o.p. (*0-89296-091-4*) Mysterious Pr.

—High Midnight. 1981. (Toby Peters Mystery Ser.). 188p. 9.95 o.p. (*0-312-37234-5*) St. Martin's Pr.

—The Howard Hughes Affair. 1980. (Toby Peters Mystery Ser.). 192p. 2.25 o.s.i (*0-441-34462-3*) Ace Bks.

—The Howard Hughes Affair. unabr. ed. 1999. audio 32.95 (*0-7861-1397-9*, 1570); 1995. audio 32.95 (*0-7861-0668-9*, 1570) Blackstone Audio Bks., Inc.

—The Howard Hughes Affair. 1979. (Toby Peters Mystery Ser.). 207p. 8.95 o.p. (*0-312-39617-1*) St. Martin's Pr.

—The Howard Hughes Affair. 1990. (Toby Peters Mystery Ser.). 224p. mass mkt. 4.95 o.s.i (*0-445-40905-3*, Mysterious Pr. Paperback Bks.) Warner Bks., Inc.

—The Man Who Shot Lewis Vance. unabr. ed. 1998. audio 5.99 (*0-88646-963-5*, PAC-7963) Durkin Hayes Publishing Ltd.

—The Man Who Shot Lewis Vance. 1986. (Toby Peters Mystery Ser.). 224p. 14.95 o.p. (*0-312-51394-1*) St. Martin's Pr.

—The Man Who Shot Lewis Vance. 1990. (Toby Peters Mystery Ser.). 208p. mass mkt. 4.50 o.s.i (*0-445-40909-6*, Mysterious Pr. Paperback Bks.) Warner Bks., Inc.

—The Melting Clock. l.t. ed. 1992. (Toby Peters Mystery Ser.). 260p. 19.95 o.p. (*0-7927-1280-3*); pap. 17.95 o.p. (*0-7927-1281-1*) BBC Audiobooks America.

—The Melting Clock. unabr. ed. 1998. (Toby Peters Mystery Ser.). audio 32.95 (*0-7861-1468-1*, 2227) Blackstone Audio Bks., Inc.

—The Melting Clock. 1991. (Toby Peters Mystery Ser.). 192p. 17.45 o.p. (*0-89296-435-9*) Mysterious Pr.

—The Melting Clock. 1993. (Toby Peters Mystery Ser.). 208p. mass mkt. 4.99 (*0-446-40304-0*, Mysterious Pr. Paperback Bks.) Warner Bks., Inc.

—Mildred Pierced. 2003. (Otto Penzler Book Ser.). 224p. 24.00 (*0-7867-1182-5*, Carroll & Graf Pubs.) Avalon Publishing Group.

—Murder on the Yellow Brick Road. unabr. ed. 1994. audio 23.95 (*0-7861-0785-5*, 1511) Blackstone Audio Bks., Inc.

—Murder on the Yellow Brick Road. 1978. (Toby Peters Mystery Ser.). 197p. 7.95 o.p. (*0-312-55318-8*) St. Martin's Pr.

—Murder on the Yellow Brick Road. 1979. (Toby Peters Mystery Ser.). 208p. pap. 3.95 o.p. (*0-14-005124-4*, Penguin Bks.) Viking Penguin.

—Murder on the Yellow Brick Road. 2000. (Toby Peters Mysteries Ser.). 192p. pap. 12.00 (*0-7434-0000-3*) ibooks, Inc.

—Never Cross a Vampire. unabr. ed. 2000. audio compact disk 48.00 (*0-7861-9943-1*, z2256); 1999. audio compact disk 24.95 (*0-7861-1461-4*); 1998. audio 32.95 (*0-7861-1353-7*, 2256) Blackstone Audio Bks., Inc.

—Never Cross a Vampire. unabr. ed. 1999. audio 32.95 Highsmith Inc.

—Never Cross a Vampire. 1984. (Toby Peters Mystery Ser.). reprint ed. pap. 3.95 o.s.i (*0-89296-087-6*) Mysterious Pr.

—Never Cross a Vampire. 1980. (Toby Peters Mystery Ser.). 182p. 8.95 o.p. (*0-312-56471-6*) St. Martin's Pr.

—Never Cross a Vampire. 1995. (Toby Peters Mystery Ser.). 192p. mass mkt. 5.50 (*0-446-40190-0*, Mysterious Pr. Paperback Bks.) Warner Bks., Inc.

—Never Cross a Vampire. 2000. 224p. pap. 12.00 (*0-7434-0713-X*) ibooks, Inc.

—Poor Butterfly. unabr. ed. 1996. audio 32.95 (*0-7861-1018-X*, 1796) Blackstone Audio Bks., Inc.

—Poor Butterfly. 1990. (Toby Peters Mystery Ser.). 179p. 17.95 o.p. (*0-89296-411-1*) Mysterious Pr.

—Poor Butterfly. unabr. ed. 1997. (Toby Peters Mystery Ser.: Vol. 15). audio 35.00 (*0-7887-0833-3*, 94978E7) Recorded Bks., LLC.

—Poor Butterfly. 1991. (Toby Peters Mystery Ser.). mass mkt. 4.95 o.s.i (*0-446-40011-4*) Warner Bks., Inc.

—Smart Moves. unabr. ed. 1997. audio 39.95 (*0-7861-1167-4*, 1934) Blackstone Audio Bks., Inc.

—Smart Moves. 1987. (Toby Peters Mystery Ser.). 272p. 15.95 o.p. (*0-312-00190-8*) St. Martin's Pr.

—Smart Moves. 1996. (Toby Peters Mystery Ser.). 224p. reprint ed. mass mkt. 5.99 o.p. (*0-446-40438-1*, Mysterious Pr. Paperback Bks.) Warner Bks., Inc.

—Think Fast, Mr. Peters. 1996. (Toby Peters Mystery Ser.). 224p. mass mkt. 5.99 (*0-446-40440-3*, Mysterious Pr. Paperback Bks.) Warner Bks., Inc.

—To Catch a Spy. 2002. 240p. 24.00 (*0-7867-1023-3*, Carroll & Graf Pubs.) Avalon Publishing Group.

—Tomorrow Is Another Day. 1995. (Toby Peters Mystery Ser.). 208p. 18.95 o.s.i (*0-89296-527-4*) Mysterious Pr.

—Tomorrow Is Another Day. unabr. ed. 1995. (Toby Peters Mystery Ser.: Vol. 18). audio 51.00 (*0-7887-0354-4*, 94546E7) Recorded Bks., LLC.

—Tomorrow Is Another Day. 1996. (Toby Peters Mystery Ser.). 224p. mass mkt. 5.99 (*0-446-40336-9*, Mysterious Pr. Paperback Bks.) Warner Bks., Inc.

—You Bet Your Life. 1979. (Toby Peters Mystery Ser.). 215p. 8.95 o.p. (*0-312-89662-X*) St. Martin's Pr.

—You Bet Your Life. 1990. (Toby Peters Mystery Ser.). 224p. mass mkt. 4.95 o.s.i (*0-445-40906-1*, Mysterious Pr. Paperback Bks.) Warner Bks., Inc.

**PETERSON, MATTHEW (FICTITIOUS CHARACTER)—FICTION**

Arnold, N. Xavier. The Genocide Files. 2nd ed. 1997. 332p. reprint ed. 16.95 (*0-9651007-0-7*, 021-99) Tana Lake Publishing.

**PETERSON, WESLEY (FICTITIOUS CHARACTER)—FICTION**

Ellis, Kate. The Bone Garden. 2003. 240p. 23.95 (*0-312-30037-9*, Saint Martin's Minotaur) St. Martin's Pr.

**PETTIGREW, FRANCIS (FICTITIOUS CHARACTER)—FICTION**

Hare, Cyril. Death Walks the Woods: A Francis Pettigrew Mystery. 1991. 288p. reprint ed. pap. 8.00 o.p. (*0-06-092136-6*, Perennial) HarperTrade.

—He Should Have Died Hereafter. 2000. (Black Dagger Crime Ser.). 21.95 (*0-7540-8569-4*, Black Dagger) BBC Audiobooks America.

—Tragedy at Law: An Inspector Mallett & Francis Pettigrew Mystery. 1986. mass mkt. 9.95 o.p. (*0-553-06518-1*) Bantam Bks.

—Tragedy at Law: An Inspector Mallett & Francis Pettigrew Mystery. 1991. 400p. pap. 5.95 o.p. (*0-06-080522-6*, Perennial) HarperTrade.

—Untimely Death: An Inspector Mallett & Francis Pettigrew Mystery. 1992. 192p. reprint ed. pap. 8.00 o.p. (*0-06-092252-4*, Perennial) HarperTrade.

—When the Wind Blows. l.t. ed. 2001. (Dales Large Print Ser.). 304p. pap. 21.99 (*1-84262-104-1*) Dales Large Print Bks. GBR. *Dist:* Ulverscroft Large Print Bks., Ltd., Ulverscroft Large Print Canada, Ltd.

—When the Wind Blows. 1976. (Crime Fiction Ser.). reprint ed. lib. bdg. 21.00 o.p. (*0-8240-2373-0*) Garland Publishing, Inc.

—When the Wind Blows. 1978. reprint ed. pap. 1.95 o.p. (*0-06-080454-8*, P 454) HarperCollins Pubs.

—The Wind Blows Death: A Francis Pettigrew Mystery. 1991. 272p. reprint ed. pap. 8.00 o.p. (*0-06-092138-2*, Perennial) HarperTrade.

—With a Bare Bodkin: A Francis Pettigrew Mystery. 1991. 256p. reprint ed. pap. 8.00 o.p. (*0-06-092139-0*, Perennial) HarperTrade.

**PHANTOM OF THE OPERA (FICTITIOUS CHARACTER)—FICTION**

Bassett, Jennifer. The Phantom of the Opera. 1993. (Illus.). 48p. pap. text 5.95 o.p. (*0-19-422707-3*) Oxford Univ. Pr., Inc.

Forsyth, Frederick. The Phantom of Manhattan. 1999. audio 30.00 (*0-7871-2370-6*) NewStar Media, Inc.

—The Phantom of Manhattan. 2000. 320p. mass mkt. 6.50 (*0-312-97585-6*, St. Martin's Paperbacks); 1999. 192p. 19.95 o.p. (*0-312-24656-0*) St. Martin's Pr.

—Phantom of Manhattan. 2000. E-Book 19.95 (*0-312-26839-4*) St. Martin's Pr.

—The Phantom of Manhattan. unabr. collector's ed. 1999. audio 22.95 (*0-7366-4735-X*, 5073) Books on Tape, Inc.

—The Phantom of Manhattan. abr. ed. 1999. audio 25.00 (*0-7871-2161-4*) NewStar Media, Inc.

—The Phantom of Manhattan. l.t. ed. (Paperback Bestsellers Ser.). 232p. 2001. 28.95 (*0-7862-2203-4*); 2000. (*0-7540-1395-2*); 2000. (*0-7540-2297-8*); 2000. (Illus.). 30.95 (*0-7862-2202-6*) Thorndike Pr.

Leroux, Gaston. The Phantom of the Opera. 2002. (World Digital Library). E-Book 3.95 (*0-594-08398-2*) 1873 Pr.

—The Phantom of the Opera. Date not set. lib. bdg. 26.95 (*0-8488-1652-8*) Amereon, Ltd.

—The Phantom of the Opera, Set. unabr. ed. 1988. (Classic Books on Cassettes Ser.). audio 41.95 (*1-55685-118-9*) Audio Bk. Contractors, Inc.

—The Phantom of the Opera. 1986. 269p. reprint ed. pap. 3.95 o.p. (*0-88184-249-4*, Carroll & Graf Pubs.) Avalon Publishing Group.

—The Phantom of the Opera. 1990. (Bantam Classics Ser.). 288p. mass mkt. 4.95 (*0-553-21376-8*) Bantam Bks.

—The Phantom of the Opera. E-Book 5.00 (*0-7607-1322-7*) Barnes & Noble, Inc.

—The Phantom of the Opera. unabr. ed. 1988. audio 49.95 (*0-7861-0565-8*, 2057) Blackstone Audio Bks., Inc.

—The Phantom of the Opera. unabr. collector's ed. 2000. audio 56.00 (*0-7366-5139-X*, 9188); 1998. audio 48.00 (*0-7366-4154-8*, 4657) Books on Tape, Inc.

—The Phantom of the Opera. 2002. pap. 3.95 (*1-59109-403-8*) Booksurge, LLC.

—The Phantom of the Opera. 1975. lib. bdg. 28.95 (*0-89966-136-X*) Buccaneer Bks., Inc.

—The Phantom of the Opera. abr. ed. audio 15.95 o.p. (*0-88646-216-9*, 7216) Durkin Hayes Publishing Ltd.

—The Phantom of the Opera. E-Book 2.49 (*1-58627-839-8*) Electric Umbrella Publishing.

—The Phantom of the Opera, Set. abr. ed. 1998. audio 18.00 (*0-89845-776-9*, CPN 2108, HarperAudio) HarperTrade.

—The Phantom of the Opera. 1990. 300p. pap. 9.95 o.s.i (*0-87052-937-4*) Hippocrene Bks., Inc.

—The Phantom of the Opera. l.t. ed. 551p. pap. 44.00 (*0-7583-1803-0*); 429p. pap. 35.66 (*0-7583-1802-2*); 313p. pap. 28.72 (*0-7583-1801-4*); 710p. pap. 54.00 (*0-7583-1804-9*); 874p. pap. 69.34 (*0-7583-1805-7*); 1075p. pap. 83.07 (*0-7583-1806-5*); 249p. pap. 23.80 (*0-7583-1800-6*); 1262p. pap. 93.20 (*0-7583-1807-3*); 1262p. lib. bdg. 105.20 (*0-7583-1799-9*); 249p. lib. bdg. 29.80 (*0-7583-1792-1*); 313p. lib. bdg. 34.72 (*0-7583-1793-X*); 429p. lib. bdg. 41.66 (*0-7583-1794-8*); 551p. lib. bdg. 50.00 (*0-7583-1795-6*); 710p. lib. bdg. 60.00 (*0-7583-1796-4*); 874p. lib. bdg. 84.50 (*0-7583-1797-2*); 1075p. lib. bdg. 95.07 (*0-7583-1798-0*) Huge Print Pr.

—The Phantom of the Opera. l.t. ed. 1988. (Mainstream Ser.). 432p. reprint ed. lib. bdg. 18.95 o.p. (*1-85089-234-2*) ISIS Large Print Bks. GBR. *Dist:* Transaction Pubs.

—The Phantom of the Opera. 1989. audio 36.00 Jimcin Recordings.

—The Phantom of the Opera, Level 5. 2002. pap. 7.67 (*0-582-50502-X*) Longman Publishing Group.

—The Phantom of the Opera. 1988. (Illus.). 25.00 o.p. (*0-89296-279-8*) Mysterious Pr.

—The Phantom of the Opera. 2001. 288p. mass mkt. 4.95 (*0-451-52815-8*, Signet Classics); 1989. 288p. mass mkt. 4.95 o.s.i (*0-451-52482-9*, Signet Classics); 1987. mass mkt. 3.95 o.p. (*0-451-52173-0*); 1987. mass mkt. 4.50 o.p. (*0-451-52432-2*, Signet Classics) NAL.

—The Phantom of the Opera. abr. ed. 1997. audio 13.98 (*962-634-618-3*, NA211814); audio compact disk 15.98 o.p. (*962-634-118-1*, NA211812) Naxos of America, Inc. (Naxos AudioBooks).

—The Phantom of the Opera. abr. ed. 1993. (Classic, Ultimate, Dove Ser.). audio 29.95 o.p. (*0-7871-0110-9*);Set. audio 15.95 o.p. (*1-55800-007-0*, 390236, Dove Audio) NewStar Media, Inc.

—The Phantom of the Opera. 1989. (Bullseye Chillers Ser.). (Illus.). 96p. (J). (gr. 3-7). 5.99 o.s.i (*0-394-93847-X*, Random Hse. Bks. for Young Readers) Random Hse. Children's Bks.

—The Phantom of the Opera. 2002. (Modern Library Classics). 320p. pap. 8.95 (*0-375-76113-6*) Random Hse., Inc.

—The Phantom of the Opera, unabr. ed. 1988. audio 60.00 (*1-55690-410-X*, 88991E7) Recorded Bks., LLC.

—The Phantom of the Opera. 1938. 10.60 o.p. (*0-606-03258-4*) Turtleback Bks.

—The Phantom of the Opera. 1995. mass mkt. 5.95 (*0-352-31716-7*) Virgin Bks. GBR. *Dist:* London Bridge.

—The Phantom of the Opera. 1986. 272p. mass mkt. 5.99 (*0-446-30120-5*) Warner Bks., Inc.

—The Phantom of the Opera. 1998. (Classics Library). 224p. pap. 3.95 (*1-85326-273-0*, 2730WW) Wordsworth Editions, Ltd. GBR. *Dist:* Combined Publishing.

—The Phantom of the Opera: The Original Novel. 1988. 368p. reprint ed. mass mkt. 7.00 (*0-06-080924-8*, PL-7140, Perennial) HarperTrade.

—The Phantom of the Opera: The Play. 1979. pap. 5.60 (*0-87129-363-3*, P45) Dramatic Publishing Co.

The Phantom of the Opera. 1998. 16p. pap. 6.95 (*0-7935-9664-5*) Leonard, Hal Corp.

Riley, Philip J. The Phantom of the Opera: The Original Shooting Script. Conforti, John, ed. 1999. (Universal Filmscript Series: Classic Silents: 1). (Illus.). pap. text 24.95 (*1-882127-33-1*) Magicimage Filmbooks.

Robinette, Joseph & Chauls, Robert. The Phantom of the Opera: Musical. 1992. pap. 5.95 (*0-87129-173-8*, P08) Dramatic Publishing Co.

Siciliano, Sam. The Angel of the Opera: Sherlock Holmes Meets the Phantom of the Opera. 1994. 272p. 21.95 (*1-883402-46-8*, Scribner) Simon & Schuster.

**PHILLIPS, ALEX (FICTITIOUS CHARACTER)—FICTION**

Zimmerman, R. D. Blood Trance. 1994. 304p. mass mkt. 4.99 o.s.i (*0-440-21518-8*) Dell Publishing.

—Blood Trance. 1993. 236p. 20.00 o.p. (*0-688-12139-X*, Morrow, William & Co.) Morrow/Avon.

—Death Trance. 1993. 304p. mass mkt. 4.99 o.s.i (*0-440-21326-6*) Dell Publishing.

—Death Trance: A Novel of Hypnotic Detection. 1992. 256p. 20.00 o.p. (*0-688-11451-2*, Morrow, William & Co.) Morrow/Avon.

—Red Trance. 1995. 320p. mass mkt. 4.99 o.s.i (*0-440-21763-6*) Dell Publishing.

—Red Trance. 1994. 237p. 20.00 o.p. (*0-688-13030-5*, Morrow, William & Co.) Morrow/Avon.

### PHILLIPS, BINO (FICTITIOUS CHARACTER)—FICTION

Gray, A. W. Bino. 1988. 208p. 16.95 o.p. (*0-525-24590-1*, Dutton) Dutton/Plume.

—Bino. 1989. mass mkt. 3.95 o.p. (*0-451-40129-8*, Onyx) NAL.

—Bino's Blues. 1995. 256p. 20.00 (*0-671-88186-8*, Simon & Schuster) Simon & Schuster.

—In Defense of Judges. 1990. 18.95 o.p. (*0-525-24875-7*, Dutton) Dutton/Plume.

—In Defense of Judges. 1991. 368p. mass mkt. 5.99 o.s.i (*0-451-40271-5*, Onyx) NAL.

—Killings. 1993. 304p. 20.00 o.p. (*0-525-93625-4*, Dutton) Dutton/Plume.

—Killings. 1994. 384p. mass mkt. 4.99 o.p. (*0-451-40525-0*, Onyx) NAL.

### PHILLIPS, MADDY (FICTITIOUS CHARACTER)—FICTION

Zimmerman, R. D. Blood Trance. 1994. 304p. mass mkt. 4.99 o.s.i (*0-440-21518-8*) Dell Publishing.

—Blood Trance. 1993. 236p. 20.00 o.p. (*0-688-12139-X*, Morrow, William & Co.) Morrow/Avon.

—Death Trance. 1993. 304p. mass mkt. 4.99 o.s.i (*0-440-21326-6*) Dell Publishing.

—Death Trance: A Novel of Hypnotic Detection. 1992. 256p. 20.00 o.p. (*0-688-11451-2*, Morrow, William & Co.) Morrow/Avon.

—Red Trance. 1995. 320p. mass mkt. 4.99 o.s.i (*0-440-21763-6*) Dell Publishing.

—Red Trance. 1994. 237p. 20.00 o.p. (*0-688-13030-5*, Morrow, William & Co.) Morrow/Avon.

### PHULE, WILLARD, CAPTAIN (FICTITIOUS CHARACTER)—FICTION

Asprin, Robert L. Phule's Company. 1990. (Phule's Company Ser.: 1). 240p. mass mkt. 6.99 (*0-441-66251-X*) Ace Bks.

—Phule's Paradise. 1992. (Phule's Company Ser.: 2). 256p. mass mkt. 6.99 (*0-441-66253-6*) Ace Bks.

Asprin, Robert L. & Heck, Peter J. A Phule & His Money. 1999. (Phule's Company Ser.: 3). 288p. mass mkt. 6.99 (*0-441-00658-2*) Ace Bks.

—Phule Me Twice. 2000. (Phule's Company Ser.). 320p. mass mkt. 6.99 (*0-441-00791-0*) Ace Bks.

### PIBBLE, JIMMY (FICTITIOUS CHARACTER)—FICTION

Dickinson, Peter. The Glass-Sided Ant's Nest. 1991. 186p. reprint ed. pap. 7.95 o.s.i (*1-55882-089-2*, Library of Crime Classics) International Polygonics, Ltd.

—The Glass-Sided Ant's Nest. 1981. pap. 3.95 o.p. (*0-14-005864-8*, Penguin Bks.) Viking Penguin.

—Old English Peep Show. 1984. pap. 3.95 o.s.i (*0-394-72602-2*) Random Hse., Inc.

—One Foot in the Grave. 1980. 8.95 o.p. (*0-394-50894-7*, Pantheon) Knopf Publishing Group.

—One Foot in the Grave. 1981. 224p. pap. 2.95 o.p. (*0-14-005779-X*, Penguin Bks.) Viking Penguin.

—The Sinful Stones. 1992. 200p. pap. 8.95 o.p. (*1-55882-109-0*) International Polygonics, Ltd.

### PICARD, INSPECTOR (FICTITIOUS CHARACTER)—FICTION

Carey, Diane L. Ghost Ship. 1988. (Star Trek, The Next Generation Ser.: No. 1). E-Book 6.99 (*0-7434-1213-3*, Star Trek) Simon & Schuster.

Kotzwinkle, William. Fata Morgana. 1996. (Illus.). 209p. pap. 12.95 (*1-56924-787-0*, Marlowe & Co.) Avalon Publishing Group.

—Fata Morgana. 1980. 208p. pap. 2.95 o.p. (*0-553-11736-X*) Bantam Bks.

—Fata Morgana. 1983. 208p. pap. 3.50 o.p. (*0-380-64691-9*, 64691, Avon Bks.) Morrow/Avon.

—Fata Morgana. 1977. 7.95 o.p. (*0-394-40905-1*, Knopf Bks. for Young Readers) Random Hse. Children's Bks.

### PICARD, JEAN-LUC (FICTITIOUS CHARACTER)—FICTION

Betancourt, John Gregory. Infection Vol. 1: Double Helix. 1999. (Star Trek, The Next Generation Ser.: No. 51). (Illus.). 256p. pap. 6.50 (*0-671-03255-0*, Star Trek) Simon & Schuster.

Bischoff, David. Grounded. Stern, David, ed. 1993. (Star Trek, The Next Generation Ser.: No. 25). 288p. mass mkt. 5.50 (*0-671-79747-6*, Star Trek) Simon & Schuster.

The Captain's Table. 2000. (Star Trek, The Next Generation Ser.). E-Book 16.95 (*0-7434-0670-2*, Star Trek) Simon & Schuster.

Carey, Diane L. Day of Honor No. 1: Ancient Blood. 1997. (Star Trek, The Next Generation: Vol. 1). (Illus.). 304p. pap. 5.99 (*0-671-00238-4*, Star Trek) Simon & Schuster.

—Descent. 1993. (Star Trek, The Next Generation Ser.). 288p. mass mkt. 5.99 (*0-671-88267-8*, Star Trek) Simon & Schuster.

—Double Helix No. 3: Red Sector. 1999. (Star Trek, The Next Generation Ser.: No. 53). (Illus.). 336p. mass mkt. 6.50 (*0-671-03257-7*, Star Trek) Simon & Schuster.

—Ghost Ship. (Star Trek, The Next Generation Ser.: No. 1). 1991. mass mkt. 5.50 (*0-671-74608-1*); 1990. mass mkt. 4.50 o.s.i (*0-671-73515-2*) Simon & Schuster. (Star Trek).

—Ship of the Line. (Star Trek, The Next Generation Ser.). 1997. 320p. 22.00 (*0-671-00924-9*); 1999. 336p. reprint ed. pap. 6.50 (*0-671-00925-7*) Simon & Schuster. (Star Trek).

—Ship of the Line. abr. ed. (Star Trek Ser.). 1997. audio 18.00; 1995. audio 18.00 (*0-671-57712-3*, Simon & Schuster Audioworks) Simon & Schuster Audio.

Carey, Diane L., et al. Invasion Omnibus: First Strike; The Soldiers of Fear; Time's Enemy; The Final Fury. 1998. (Star Trek Ser.). 960p. mass mkt. 14.00 (*0-671-02185-0*, Star Trek) Simon & Schuster.

Carter, Carmen. The Children of Hamlin. Stern, Dave, ed. 1990. (Star Trek, The Next Generation Ser.: No. 3). mass mkt. 5.50 o.s.i (*0-671-73555-1*, Star Trek) Simon & Schuster.

—The Children of Hamlin. 1989. (Star Trek, The Next Generation Ser.: No. 3). E-Book 6.99 (*0-7434-1215-X*, Star Trek) Simon & Schuster.

—The Devil's Heart. (Star Trek, The Next Generation Ser.). E-Book 6.99 (*0-7434-2063-2*, Star Trek) Simon & Schuster.

—The Devil's Heart. Stern, Dave, ed. 1993. (Star Trek, The Next Generation Ser.). 320p. 20.00 (*0-671-79325-X*, Star Trek) Simon & Schuster.

—The Devil's Heart. Ryan, Kevin, ed. 1994. (Star Trek, The Next Generation Ser.). 320p. reprint ed. mass mkt. 5.99 (*0-671-79426-4*, Star Trek) Simon & Schuster.

—The Devil's Heart. abr. ed. 1993. (Star Trek Ser.). audio 17.00 (*0-671-79861-8*, Simon & Schuster Audioworks) Simon & Schuster Audio.

Carter, Carmen, et al. Doomsday World. Stern, David, ed. 1991. (Star Trek, The Next Generation Ser.: No. 12). 288p. (Orig.). mass mkt. 5.50 o.s.i (*0-671-74144-6*, Star Trek) Simon & Schuster.

—Doomsday World. 1990. (Star Trek, The Next Generation Ser.: No. 12). (Orig.). mass mkt. 4.50 o.s.i (*0-671-70237-8*, Star Trek) Simon & Schuster.

Cox, Greg. The Q-Continuum No. 1: Q-Space. 1999. (Star Trek, The Next Generation Ser.: No. 47). E-Book 6.99 (*0-671-04101-0*, Star Trek) Simon & Schuster.

—The Q Continuum No. 2: Q-Zone. (Star Trek, The Next Generation Ser.: No. 48). (J). 1999. E-Book 6.99 (*0-671-04102-9*); 1998. 270p. mass mkt. 6.50 o.s.i (*0-671-01921-X*) Simon & Schuster. (Star Trek).

—Q-Space No. 1: The Q-Continuum. 1998. (Star Trek, The Next Generation Ser.: No. 47). 288p. (J). pap. 6.50 (*0-671-01915-5*, Star Trek) Simon & Schuster.

—Q-Strike No. 3: The Q Continuum. (Star Trek, The Next Generation Ser.: No. 49). 1999. E-Book 6.99 (*0-671-04103-7*); 1998. 272p. (J). mass mkt. 6.99 o.s.i (*0-671-01922-8*) Simon & Schuster. (Star Trek).

Crispin, A. C. The Eyes of the Beholders. (Star Trek, The Next Generation Ser.: No. 13). E-Book 6.99 (*0-7434-2093-4*, Star Trek) Simon & Schuster.

—The Eyes of the Beholders. Stern, David, ed. 1990. (Star Trek, The Next Generation Ser.: No. 13). 256p. mass mkt. 5.50 (*0-671-70010-3*, Star Trek) Simon & Schuster.

David, Peter. Double or Nothing. 1999. (Star Trek, The Next Generation Ser.: Vol. 5). 277p. pap. 6.50 o.s.i (*0-671-03478-2*, Star Trek) Simon & Schuster.

—House of Cards. 1997. (Star Trek Ser.: No. 1). 168p. per. 3.99 o.s.i (*0-671-01395-5*, Star Trek) Simon & Schuster.

—Q-in-Law. pap. text 7.50 (*0-8359-1105-5*) Globe Fearon Educational Publishing.

—Q-in-Law. 1999. (Star Trek, The Next Generation Ser.: No. 18). E-Book 6.99 (*0-671-04099-5*, Star Trek) Simon & Schuster.

—Q-in-Law. Stern, Dave, ed. 1991. (Star Trek, The Next Generation Ser.: No. 18). 272p. (J). mass mkt. 5.99 o.s.i (*0-671-73389-3*, Star Trek) Simon & Schuster.

—Q-in-Law. abr. ed. 1992. (Star Trek Ser.: No. 18). audio 12.00 (*0-671-75958-2*, Simon & Schuster Audioworks) Simon & Schuster Audio.

—Q-Squared. (Star Trek, The Next Generation Ser.). E-Book 6.99 (*0-7434-2065-9*); 1999. E-Book 6.99 (*0-671-04100-2*); 1995. 448p. (J). mass mkt. 6.50 o.s.i (*0-671-89151-0*) Simon & Schuster. (Star Trek).

—Q-Squared. Ryan, Kevin, ed. 1994. (Star Trek, The Next Generation Ser.). 448p. 22.00 o.p. (*0-671-89152-9*, Star Trek) Simon & Schuster.

—Q-Squared. abr. ed. 1994. (Star Trek Ser.). audio 17.00 (*0-671-89180-4*, Simon & Schuster Audioworks) Simon & Schuster Audio.

—A Rock & a Hard Place. (Star Trek, The Next Generation Ser.: No. 10). E-Book 6.99 (*0-7434-2090-X*, Star Trek) Simon & Schuster.

—A Rock & a Hard Place. Stern, Dave, ed. 1991. (Star Trek, The Next Generation Ser.: No. 10). 256p. mass mkt. 5.50 (*0-671-74142-X*, Star Trek) Simon & Schuster.

—A Rock & a Hard Place. 1990. (Star Trek, The Next Generation Ser.: No. 10). mass mkt. 3.95 o.s.i (*0-671-69364-6*, Star Trek) Simon & Schuster.

—Star Trek: The Next Generation. 2002. (Star Trek Ser.). audio 9.98 (*0-7435-2772-0*, Simon & Schuster Audioworks) Simon & Schuster Audio.

—Strike Zone. (Star Trek, The Next Generation Ser.: No. 5). 1991. mass mkt. 5.99 (*0-671-74647-2*); 1990. mass mkt. 4.50 o.s.i (*0-671-73516-0*) Simon & Schuster. (Star Trek).

—The Strike Zone. 1989. (Star Trek, The Next Generation Ser.: No. 5). E-Book 6.99 (*0-7434-1217-6*, Star Trek) Simon & Schuster.

—Vendetta. 1991. (Star Trek, The Next Generation Ser.). mass mkt. 5.99 (*0-671-74145-4*, Star Trek) Simon & Schuster.

—Vendetta. Stern, Dave, ed. 1991. (Star Trek, The Next Generation Ser.). 416p. mass mkt. 5.99 (*0-671-73305-2*, Star Trek) Simon & Schuster.

De Lancie, John. I, Q. 2003. (Star Trek Ser.). audio 9.95 (*0-7435-3256-2*); audio compact disk 9.95 (*0-7435-3275-9*) Simon & Schuster Audio. (Encore).

De Lancie, John & David, Peter. I, Q. (Star Trek Ser.). 2000. 256p. pap. 6.99 (*0-671-02444-2*); 1999. E-Book 23.00 (*0-7434-0079-8*); 1999. 256p. 22.95 o.s.i (*0-671-02443-4*); 1900. 252p. mass mkt. (*0-671-03581-9*) Simon & Schuster. (Star Trek).

—I, Q. abr. ed. 1999. (Star Trek Ser.). audio 18.00 (*0-671-04378-1*, Simon & Schuster Audioworks) Simon & Schuster Audio.

DeWeese, Gene. Into the Nebula. (Star Trek, The Next Generation Ser.: No. 36). E-Book 6.99 (*0-7434-2137-X*); 1995. 288p. mass mkt. 5.99 (*0-671-89453-6*) Simon & Schuster. (Star Trek).

—The Peacekeepers. (Star Trek, The Next Generation Ser.: No. 2). 1990. mass mkt. 5.50 (*0-671-73653-1*); 1988. E-Book 6.99 (*0-7434-1214-1*); 1988. mass mkt. 3.95 o.s.i (*0-671-66929-X*) Simon & Schuster. (Star Trek).

Dillard, J. M. First Contact. abr. ed. 1996. (Star Trek Ser.: No. 8). audio 18.00 (*0-671-57391-8*, Simon & Schuster Audioworks) Simon & Schuster Audio.

—Generations. (Star Trek Ser.: No. 7). 1995. (Illus.). 304p. mass mkt. 5.99 (*0-671-53753-9*); 1994. 288p. 20.00 o.p. (*0-671-51742-2*) Simon & Schuster. (Star Trek).

—Generations. 1994. (Star Trek Ser.: No. 7). pap. 17.00 incl. audio (*0-671-51996-4*, Simon & Schuster Audioworks) Simon & Schuster Audio.

—Insurrection. abr. ed. (Star Trek Ser.: No. 9). 1998. audio 18.00 o.s.i (*0-671-58259-3*, 396208, Simon & Schuster Audioworks); 2003. audio 9.95 (*0-7435-3254-6*, Encore) Simon & Schuster Audio.

—The Movie. 1996. (Star Trek Ser.). (Illus.). 288p. 21.00 o.p. (*0-671-00316-X*, Star Trek) Simon & Schuster.

—Possession. 2000. (Star Trek, The Next Generation Ser.: No. 40). E-Book 6.99 (*0-7434-2117-5*, Star Trek) Simon & Schuster.

—Star Trek: Nemesis. abr. ed. 2002. (Star Trek Ser.). audio 19.95 (*0-7435-2688-0*); audio compact disk 19.95 (*0-7435-2689-9*) Simon & Schuster Audio. (Simon & Schuster Audioworks).

Dillard, J. M. & Berman, Rick. Insurrection. 1998. (Star Trek Ser.: No. 9). 304p. 22.00 o.s.i (*0-671-02447-7*, Star Trek) Simon & Schuster.

Dillard, J. M. & O'Malley, Kathleen. Possession. 1996. (Star Trek, The Next Generation Ser.: No. 40). 288p. mass mkt. 5.99 (*0-671-86485-8*, Star Trek) Simon & Schuster.

Duane, Diane. Dark Mirror. 1993. (Star Trek, The Next Generation Ser.). 352p. 22.00 o.p. (*0-671-79377-2*, Star Trek) Simon & Schuster.

—Dark Mirror. Ryan, Kevin, ed. 1994. (Star Trek, The Next Generation Ser.). 352p. reprint ed. mass mkt. 5.99 (*0-671-79438-8*, Star Trek) Simon & Schuster.

—Dark Mirror. abr. ed. 1996. (Star Trek Ser.). audio 17.00 (*0-671-87974-X*, Simon & Schuster Audioworks) Simon & Schuster Audio.

—Intellivore. 1997. (Star Trek, The Next Generation Ser.: No. 45). 272p. mass mkt. 6.50 o.s.i (*0-671-56832-9*, Star Trek) Simon & Schuster.

Dvorkin, David & Dvorkin, Daniel. The Captain's Honor. 1991. (Star Trek, The Next Generation Ser.: No. 8). mass mkt. 5.50 (*0-671-74140-3*, Star Trek) Simon & Schuster.

Ferguson, Brad. The Last Stand. (Star Trek, The Next Generation Ser.: No. 37). 2000. E-Book 6.99 (*0-7434-2139-6*); 1995. 288p. mass mkt. 5.99 (*0-671-50105-4*) Simon & Schuster. (Star Trek).

Forstchen, William R. The Forgotten War. (Star Trek, The Next Generation Ser.: No. 57). E-Book 6.99 (*0-7434-2138-8*); 1999. (Illus.). 304p. mass mkt. 6.50 o.s.i (*0-671-01159-6*) Simon & Schuster. (Star Trek).

Friedman, Michael Jan. All Good Things. Ryan, Kevin, ed. 1995. (Star Trek, The Next Generation Ser.). (Illus.). 256p. mass mkt. 5.99 (*0-671-52148-9*, Star Trek) Simon & Schuster.

—All Good Things. 1994. (Star Trek Ser.). 256p. o.p. (*0-671-50014-7*, Atria) Simon & Schuster.

—All Good Things... (Star Trek, The Next Generation Ser.). E-Book 6.99 (*0-7434-2076-4*, Star Trek) Simon & Schuster.

—All Good Things. abr. ed. 1994. (Star Trek Ser.). audio 17.00 o.s.i (*0-671-89482-X*, Simon & Schuster Audioworks) Simon & Schuster Audio.

—A Call to Darkness. (Star Trek, The Next Generation Ser.: No. 9). E-Book 6.99 (*0-7434-2089-6*); 1991. mass mkt. 5.50 (*0-671-74141-1*); 1989. 304p. mass mkt. 3.95 o.s.i (*0-671-68708-5*) Simon & Schuster. (Star Trek).

—Crossover. (Star Trek, The Next Generation Ser.). E-Book 6.99 (*0-7434-2066-7*); 1996. 320p. mass mkt. 5.99 (*0-671-89676-8*); 1995. 320p. 23.00 o.p. (*0-671-89677-6*) Simon & Schuster. (Star Trek).

—Crossover. abr. ed. 1995. (Star Trek Ser.). audio 17.00 o.s.i (*0-671-53628-1*, Simon & Schuster Audioworks) Simon & Schuster Audio.

—Doomsday World. (Star Trek, The Next Generation Ser.: No. 12). E-Book 6.99 (*0-7434-2092-6*, Star Trek) Simon & Schuster.

—The First Virtue No. 6: Double Helix. (Star Trek, The Next Generation Ser.: No. 56). E-Book 6.99 (*0-7434-2136-1*); 1999. 271p. pap. 6.50 o.s.i (*0-671-03258-5*) Simon & Schuster. (Star Trek).

—Fortune's Light. (Star Trek, The Next Generation Ser.: No. 15). E-Book 6.99 (*0-7434-2095-0*, Star Trek) Simon & Schuster.

—Fortune's Light. Stern, David, ed. 1991. (Star Trek, The Next Generation Ser.: No. 15). 288p. mass mkt. 5.50 (*0-671-70836-8*, Star Trek) Simon & Schuster.

—Kahless. (Star Trek, The Next Generation Ser.). 1997. (Illus.). 336p. mass mkt. 5.99 (*0-671-00887-0*); 1996. 320p. 23.00 (*0-671-54779-8*) Simon & Schuster. (Star Trek).

—Kahless. Set. 1996. (Star Trek Ser.). audio 18.00 o.s.i (*0-671-57068-4*, 394072, Simon & Schuster Audioworks) Simon & Schuster Audio.

—Planet X. (Star Trek, The Next Generation Ser.). E-Book 6.99 (*0-7434-2070-5*); 1998. (Illus.). 288p. mass mkt. 6.99 (*0-671-01916-3*) Simon & Schuster. (Star Trek).

—Relics. (Star Trek, The Next Generation Ser.). E-Book 6.99 (*0-7434-2074-8*, Star Trek) Simon & Schuster.

—Relics. Stern, Dave, ed. 1992. (Star Trek, The Next Generation Ser.). 256p. mass mkt. 5.50 (*0-671-86476-9*, Star Trek) Simon & Schuster.

—Relics. abr. ed. 1995. (Star Trek Ser.). audio 17.00 (*0-671-86528-5*, Simon & Schuster Audioworks) Simon & Schuster Audio.

—Reunion. Stern, Dave, ed. (Star Trek, The Next Generation Ser.). 352p. 1991. 19.00 (*0-671-74808-4*); 1992. reprint ed. mass mkt. 5.99 (*0-671-78755-1*) Simon & Schuster. (Star Trek).

—Reunion. abr. ed. 1991. (Star Trek, The Next Generation Ser.). audio 16.00 (*0-671-75036-4*, Simon & Schuster Audioworks) Simon & Schuster Audio.

—Star Lost. Kahan, Bob, ed. 1993. (Star Trek Ser.). (Illus.). 144p. (Orig.). (YA). pap. 14.95 o.p. (*1-56389-084-4*) DC Comics.

—Star Trek: Modala Imperative. Kahan, Bob, ed. 1992. (Star Trek Ser.). (Illus.). 208p. pap. 19.95 (*1-56389-040-2*) DC Comics.

—Star Trek: The Next Generation. 2002. audio 9.98 (*0-7435-2773-9*, Simon & Schuster Audioworks) Simon & Schuster Audio.

—Stargazer: Three, Bk. 3. 2003. (Star Trek, The Next Generation Ser.). 288p. mass mkt. 6.99 (*0-7434-4852-9*, Star Trek) Simon & Schuster.

—The Valiant. (Star Trek, The Next Generation Ser.). 2000. 288p. 23.95 o.s.i (*0-671-77522-7*); 2001. 304p. reprint ed. mass mkt. 6.99 (*0-671-77523-5*) Simon & Schuster. (Star Trek).

—The Valiant. abr. ed. 2000. (Star Trek Ser.). audio 18.00 o.s.i (*0-671-04786-8*, Simon & Schuster Audioworks) Simon & Schuster Audio.

Friedman, Michael Jan & Ryan, Kevin. Requiem. 1994. (Star Trek, The Next Generation Ser.: No. 32). 288p. mass mkt. 5.50 (*0-671-79567-8*, Star Trek) Simon & Schuster.

Friesner, Esther M. To Storm Heaven. 1997. (Star Trek, The Next Generation Ser.: No. 46). (Illus.). 304p. pap. 5.99 (*0-671-56838-8*, Star Trek) Simon & Schuster.

Galanter, Dave & Brodeur, Greg. Foreign Foes. (Star Trek, The Next Generation Ser.: No. 31). E-Book 6.99 (*0-7434-2114-0*); 1994. 288p. mass mkt. 5.50 (*0-671-88414-X*) Simon & Schuster. (Star Trek).

Gerrold, David. Encounter at Farpoint. (Star Trek, The Next Generation Ser.). E-Book 6.99 *(0-7434-2072-1,* Star Trek) Simon & Schuster.

—Encounter at Farpoint. Stern, Dave, ed. 1991. (Star Trek, The Next Generation Ser.). 192p. mass mkt. 5.99 *(0-671-74388-0,* Star Trek) Simon & Schuster.

—Encounter at Farpoint. 1987. (Star Trek, The Next Generation Ser.). mass mkt. 3.95 o.s.i *(0-671-65241-9,* Star Trek) Simon & Schuster.

Gilden, Mel. Boogeymen. (Star Trek, The Next Generation Ser.: No. 17). E-Book 6.99 *(0-7434-2097-7,* Star Trek) Simon & Schuster.

—Boogeymen. Stern, Dave, ed. 1991. (Star Trek, The Next Generation Ser.: No. 17). 288p. mass mkt. 5.50 *(0-671-70970-4,* Star Trek) Simon & Schuster.

Graf, L. A., et al. The Captain's Table Omnibus. 2000. (Star Trek Ser.). 1152p. pap. 16.95 *(0-671-04052-9,* Star Trek) Simon & Schuster.

Greenberger, Robert. The Romulan Stratagem. 1995. (Star Trek, The Next Generation Ser.: No. 35). 288p. mass mkt. 5.99 *(0-671-87997-9,* Star Trek) Simon & Schuster.

Hamilton, Laurell K. Nightshade. Stern, Dave, ed. 1992. (Star Trek, The Next Generation Ser.: No. 24). 288p. mass mkt. 5.50 *(0-671-79566-X,* Star Trek) Simon & Schuster.

Hawke, Simon. Blaze of Glory. 1995. (Star Trek, The Next Generation Ser.: No. 34). 288p. mass mkt. 5.50 *(0-671-88045-4,* Pocket) Simon & Schuster.

—The Romulan Prize. Stern, Dave, ed. 1993. (Star Trek, The Next Generation Ser.: No. 26). 288p. mass mkt. 5.50 o.s.i *(0-671-79746-8,* Star Trek) Simon & Schuster.

Hugh, Dafydd ab. Balance of Power. Ryan, Kevin, ed. 1994. (Star Trek, The Next Generation Ser.: No. 33). 304p. mass mkt. 5.50 *(0-671-52003-2,* Star Trek) Simon & Schuster.

Johnson, Kij & Cox, Greg. Dragon's Honor. Ordover, John, ed. 1996. (Star Trek, The Next Generation Ser.: No. 38). 288p. mass mkt. 5.99 *(0-671-50107-0,* Star Trek) Simon & Schuster.

Lorrah, Jean. Metamorphosis. 1990. (Star Trek, The Next Generation Ser.). 416p. mass mkt. 5.99 *(0-671-68402-7,* Star Trek) Simon & Schuster.

—Survivors. Stern, Dave, ed. 1991. (Star Trek, The Next Generation Ser.: No. 4). 256p. mass mkt. 5.50 *(0-671-74290-6,* Star Trek) Simon & Schuster.

—Survivors. 1989. (Star Trek, The Next Generation Ser.: No. 4). E-Book 6.99 *(0-7434-1216-8,* Star Trek) Simon & Schuster.

Mancour, T. L. Spartacus. (Star Trek, The Next Generation Ser.: No. 20). E-Book 6.99 *(0-7434-2100-0,* Star Trek) Simon & Schuster.

—Spartacus. Stern, Dave, ed. 1992. (Star Trek, The Next Generation Ser.: No. 20). 288p. mass mkt. 5.50 *(0-671-76051-3,* Star Trek) Simon & Schuster.

McCay, W. A. Chains of Command. (Star Trek, The Next Generation Ser.: No. 21). E-Book 6.99 *(0-7434-2101-9,* Star Trek) Simon & Schuster.

McCay, W. A. & Flood, E. L. Chains of Command. Stern, David, ed. 1992. (Star Trek, The Next Generation Ser.: No. 21). 288p. mass mkt. 5.50 *(0-671-74264-7,* Star Trek) Simon & Schuster.

Mitchell, V. E. Imbalance. (Star Trek, The Next Generation Ser.: No. 22). E-Book 6.99 *(0-7434-2102-7,* Star Trek) Simon & Schuster.

—Imbalance. Stern, Dave, ed. 1992. (Star Trek, The Next Generation Ser.: No. 22). 288p. mass mkt. 5.50 *(0-671-77571-5,* Star Trek) Simon & Schuster.

Neason, Rebecca. Guises of the Mind. Ryan, Kevin, ed. 1993. (Star Trek, The Next Generation Ser.: No. 27). 288p. (Orig.). mass mkt. 5.50 *(0-671-79831-6,* Star Trek) Simon & Schuster.

Peel, John. Death of Princes. 1996. (Star Trek, The Next Generation Ser.: No. 44). 304p. pap. 5.99 *(0-671-56808-6,* Star Trek) Simon & Schuster.

—Death of Princes. 2000. (Star Trek, The Next Generation Ser.: No. 44). E-Book 6.99 *(0-7434-2122-1,* Star Trek) Simon & Schuster.

—Here There Be Dragons. Ryan, Kevin, ed. 1993. (Star Trek, The Next Generation Ser.: No. 28). 288p. (Orig.). mass mkt. 5.99 *(0-671-86571-4,* Star Trek) Simon & Schuster.

Pellegrino, Charles R. Dyson Sphere. 2000. (Star Trek, The Next Generation Ser.: No. 50). E-Book 6.99 *(0-7434-2129-9,* Star Trek) Simon & Schuster.

Pellegrino, Charles R. & Zebrowski, George. Dyson Sphere. 1999. (Star Trek, The Next Generation Ser.: No. 50). 235p. pap. 6.50 o.s.i *(0-671-54173-0,* Star Trek) Simon & Schuster.

Picard, Jean-Luc. Dujonia Hoard No. 2: The Captain's Table. 1998. (Star Trek: Vol. 2). 288p. mass mkt. 6.50 *(0-671-01465-X,* Star Trek) Simon & Schuster.

Reeves-Stevens, Judith & Reeves-Stevens, Garfield. Federation. 1995. (Star Trek Ser.). 480p. mass mkt. 6.50 *(0-671-89423-4,* Star Trek) Simon & Schuster.

—Federation. Ryan, Kevin, ed. 1994. (Star Trek Ser.). 480p. 22.00 o.p. *(0-671-89422-6,* Star Trek) Simon & Schuster.

—Federation. abr. ed. 1994. (Star Trek Ser.). audio 17.00 *(0-671-50575-0,* Simon & Schuster Audioworks) Simon & Schuster Audio.

—Federation. (Star Trek Ser.). 470p. pap. 4.98 o.p. *(0-7651-0507-1)* Smithmark Pubs., Inc.

Sargent, Pamela. A Fury Scorned. 2000. (Star Trek, The Next Generation Ser.: No. 43). E-Book 6.99 *(0-7434-2121-3,* Star Trek) Simon & Schuster.

Sargent, Pamela & Zebrowski, George. A Fury Scorned. 1996. (Star Trek, The Next Generation Ser.: No. 43). 288p. pap. 5.99 *(0-671-52703-7,* Star Trek) Simon & Schuster.

Sharee, Keith. Gulliver's Fugitives. (Star Trek, The Next Generation Ser.: No. 11). E-Book 6.99 *(0-7434-2091-8);* 1991. 256p. mass mkt. 5.50 *(0-671-74143-8)* Simon & Schuster. (Star Trek).

—Gulliver's Fugitives. (Star Trek Ser.: No. 11). 1999. audio 5.98 *(0-671-04522-9);* 1990. audio 9.95 *(0-671-72319-7)* Simon & Schuster Audio. (Simon & Schuster Audioworks).

Shatner, William. Preserver. (Star Trek Ser.). reprint ed. 2001. 448p. pap. 6.99 *(0-671-02126-5);* 2001. E-Book 23.95 *(0-7434-1955-3);* 2000. (Illus.). (J). E-Book 23.95 *(0-7434-1119-6)* Simon & Schuster. (Star Trek).

—Preserver. abr. ed. 2000. (Star Trek Ser.). audio 18.00 *(0-7435-0031-8,* Simon & Schuster Audioworks) Simon & Schuster Audio.

—Spectre. 1998. (Star Trek Ser.). 384p. mass mkt. 6.99 *(0-671-02053-6,* Pocket) Simon & Schuster.

—Spectre. abr. ed. 1998. (Star Trek Ser.: Vol. 2). audio 18.00 *(0-671-57998-3,* AF09R, Simon & Schuster Audioworks) Simon & Schuster Audio.

Shatner, William, et al. Avenger. (Star Trek Ser.). 1998. (Illus.). 416p. pap. 7.99 *(0-671-55131-0,* Star Trek); 1997. per. 6.99 *(0-671-01744-6,* Pocket); 1997. 384p. 23.00 o.s.i *(0-671-55132-9,* Star Trek) Simon & Schuster.

—Avenger. abr. ed. 1989. (Star Trek Ser.). audio 18.00 *(0-671-57524-4,* 395166, Simon & Schuster Audioworks) Simon & Schuster Audio.

—Dark Victory. (Star Trek Ser.). 320p. 1999. 23.00 o.s.i *(0-671-00882-X);* 2000. reprint ed. pap. 6.99 *(0-671-00884-6)* Simon & Schuster. (Star Trek).

—Preserver. 2000. (Star Trek Ser.). 384p. 23.95 o.s.i *(0-671-02125-7,* Star Trek) Simon & Schuster.

—The Return. (Star Trek Ser.). 1997. 400p. mass mkt. 6.99 *(0-671-52609-X,* Star Trek); 1996. 384p. 22.00 o.p. *(0-671-52610-3,* Atria) Simon & Schuster.

—The Return. abr. ed. 1996. (Star Trek Ser.). audio 18.00 o.s.i *(0-671-56848-5,* 393928, Simon & Schuster Audioworks) Simon & Schuster Audio.

—Spectre. 384p. 2002. E-Book 6.99 *(0-7434-5408-1);* 1998. (Illus.). 23.00 o.s.i *(0-671-00878-1);* 1999. reprint ed. pap. 6.50 *(0-671-00880-3)* Simon & Schuster. (Star Trek).

—Star Trek: The Return. l.t. ed. 1996. (Star Trek Ser.). 456p. 24.95 *(1-56895-359-3,* Wheeler Publishing, Inc.) Gale Group.

Sherman, Josepha & Shwartz, Susan. Vulcan's Heart. (Star Trek Ser.). 2000. per. 6.50 *(0-7434-1112-9);* 1999. 384p. 23.00 o.s.i *(0-671-01544-3);* 2000. 400p. reprint ed. pap. 6.50 *(0-671-01545-1)* Simon & Schuster. (Star Trek).

—Vulcan's Heart. abr. ed. 1999. (Star Trek Ser.). audio 18.00 *(0-671-04560-1,* Simon & Schuster Audioworks) Simon & Schuster Audio.

Slater, Robert. Dragon's Honor. 2000. (Star Trek, The Next Generation Ser.: No. 38). E-Book 6.99 *(0-7434-2141-8,* Star Trek) Simon & Schuster.

Smith, Dean & Rusch, Kristine K. Klingon. (Star Trek, The Next Generation Ser.). E-Book 6.99 *(0-7434-2077-2,* Star Trek) Simon & Schuster.

Smith, Dean Wesley. Invasion! No. 2: The Soldiers of Fear. (Star Trek, The Next Generation Ser.: No. 41). E-Book 6.99 *(0-7434-2119-1,* Star Trek) Simon & Schuster.

—Strange New Worlds IV. 2001. (Star Trek Ser.). reprint ed. E-Book 14.95 *(0-7434-2258-9,* Star Trek) Simon & Schuster.

—Vectors No. 2: Double Helix. (Star Trek, The Next Generation Ser.: No. 52). E-Book 6.99 *(0-7434-2132-9,* Star Trek) Simon & Schuster.

Smith, Dean Wesley & Rusch, Kristine K. Vectors No. 2: Double Helix. 1999. (Star Trek, The Next Generation: No. 52). (Illus.). 304p. pap. 6.50 *(0-671-03256-9,* Star Trek) Simon & Schuster.

Smith, Dean Wesley, et al. The Soldiers of Fear No. 2: Invasion! 1996. (Star Trek, The Next Generation Ser.: No. 41). 288p. (J). pap. 6.50 *(0-671-54174-9,* Star Trek) Simon & Schuster.

Somtow, S. P. Do Comets Dream? 2003. (Star Trek, The Next Generation Ser.). 288p. pap. 6.99 *(0-7434-1130-7,* Star Trek) Simon & Schuster.

Taylor, Jeri. Unification. (Star Trek, The Next Generation Ser.). E-Book 6.99 *(0-7434-2073-X);* 1991. 256p. mass mkt. 5.50 o.s.i *(0-671-77056-X)* Simon & Schuster. (Star Trek).

Thompson, W. R. Debtor's Planet. Ordover, John, ed. 1994. (Star Trek, The Next Generation Ser.: No. 30). 288p. (Orig.). mass mkt. 5.99 o.s.i *(0-671-88341-0,* Star Trek) Simon & Schuster.

—Infiltrator. 1996. (Star Trek, The Next Generation Ser.: No. 42). 288p. mass mkt. 5.99 *(0-671-56831-0,* Star Trek) Simon & Schuster.

The Valiant. 2000. (Star Trek, The Next Generation Ser.). E-Book 23.95 *(0-7434-0673-7,* Star Trek) Simon & Schuster.

Vornholt, John. Contamination. (Star Trek, The Next Generation Ser.: No. 16). E-Book 6.99 *(0-7434-2096-9,* Star Trek) Simon & Schuster.

—Contamination. Stern, David, ed. 1991. (Star Trek, The Next Generation Ser.: No. 16). 288p. mass mkt. 5.50 *(0-671-70561-X,* Star Trek) Simon & Schuster.

—Contamination. abr. ed. 1991. (Star Trek, The Next Generation Ser.: No. 16). audio 12.00 *(0-671-74045-8,* 326327, Simon & Schuster Audioworks) Simon & Schuster Audio.

—Dominion War: Behind Enemy Lines. 1998. (Star Trek, The Next Generation: Vol. 1). 269p. (J). pap. 6.50 *(0-671-02499-X,* Star Trek) Simon & Schuster.

—Dominion War: Tunnel Through the Stars. 3rd ed. 1998. (Star Trek, The Next Generation Ser.: Vol. 3). 288p. pap. 6.50 *(0-671-02500-7,* Star Trek) Simon & Schuster.

—The Dominion War No. 1: Behind Enemy Lines. 1999. (Star Trek, The Next Generation Ser.). E-Book 6.99 *(0-671-04104-5,* Star Trek) Simon & Schuster.

—The Dominion War No. 3: Tunnel Through the Stars. 1999. (Star Trek, The Next Generation Ser.). E-Book 6.99 *(0-671-04106-1,* Star Trek) Simon & Schuster.

—Double Helix: Quarantine. 1999. (Star Trek, The Next Generation Ser.: No. 54). (Illus.). 304p. pap. 6.99 *(0-671-03477-4,* Star Trek) Simon & Schuster.

—Gemworld. (Star Trek, The Next Generation Ser.). E-Book 6.99 *(0-7434-2142-6)*;No. 1. 2000. E-Book 6.99 *(0-7434-0677-X)*;No. 1. 2000. (Illus.). 288p. pap. 6.99 *(0-671-04270-X)*;No. 2. 2000. E-Book 6.99 *(0-7434-0678-8)*;No. 2. 2000. (Illus.). 272p. pap. 6.50 *(0-671-04271-8)* Simon & Schuster. (Star Trek).

—The Genesis Wave, Bk. 2. 2001. (Star Trek, The Next Generation Ser.). 288p. 23.95 *(0-7434-1181-1,* Star Trek) Simon & Schuster.

—Genesis Wave: Genesis Force, Bk. 4. 2003. (Star Trek, The Next Generation Ser.). 320p. 23.95 *(0-7434-6501-6,* Star Trek) Simon & Schuster.

—Masks. (Star Trek, The Next Generation Ser.: No. 7). E-Book 6.99 *(0-7434-2087-X);* 1991. mass mkt. 5.50 *(0-671-74139-X);* 1990. mass mkt. 4.50 o.s.i *(0-671-70878-3);* 1989. mass mkt. 3.95 o.s.i *(0-671-67980-5)* Simon & Schuster. (Star Trek).

—Rogue Saucer. 1996. (Star Trek, The Next Generation Ser.: No. 39). 288p. mass mkt. 5.99 *(0-671-54917-0,* Star Trek) Simon & Schuster.

—War Drums. (Star Trek, The Next Generation Ser.). E-Book 6.99 *(0-7434-2103-5,* Star Trek) Simon & Schuster.

—War Drums. Stern, Dave, ed. 1992. (Star Trek, The Next Generation Ser.: No. 23). 288p. mass mkt. 5.50 *(0-671-79236-9,* Star Trek) Simon & Schuster.

Weinstein, Howard. Exiles. Stern, David, ed. 1990. (Star Trek, The Next Generation Ser.: No. 14). 288p. (Orig.). mass mkt. 5.50 *(0-671-70560-1,* Star Trek) Simon & Schuster.

—Perchance to Dream. Stern, David, ed. 1991. (Star Trek, The Next Generation Ser.: No. 19). 288p. (Orig.). mass mkt. 5.50 *(0-671-70837-6,* Star Trek) Simon & Schuster.

—Power Hungry. (Star Trek, The Next Generation Ser.: No. 6). E-Book 6.99 *(0-7434-2086-1,* Star Trek) Simon & Schuster.

—Power Hungry. Stern, Dave, ed. 1991. (Star Trek, The Next Generation Ser.: No. 6). mass mkt. 5.50 *(0-671-74648-0,* Star Trek) Simon & Schuster.

Wright, Susan. Badlands. 1999. (Star Trek Ser.: Bk. 1). (Illus.). 304p. pap. 6.50 *(0-671-03957-1,* Star Trek) Simon & Schuster.

—The Badlands, No. 1. 2000. (Star Trek Ser.). E-Book 6.99 *(0-7434-0674-5,* Star Trek) Simon & Schuster.

—Sins of Commission. Ryan, Kevin, ed. 1994. (Star Trek, The Next Generation Ser.: No. 29). 288p. (Orig.). mass mkt. 5.50 *(0-671-79704-2,* Star Trek) Simon & Schuster.

### PICKETT, JOE (FICTITIOUS CHARACTER)—FICTION

Box, C. J. Open Season. 2002. 304p. reprint ed. mass mkt. 6.50 *(0-425-18546-X,* Prime Crime) Berkley Publishing Group.

—Open Season. 2002. lib. bdg. 28.95 *(1-58547-248-4,* Premier) Ctr. Point Large Print.

—Open Season. 2001. 304p. 23.95 *(0-399-14748-9)* Penguin Group (USA) Inc.

—Savage Run: A Joe Pickett Novel. 2003. 304p. mass mkt. 6.50 *(0-425-18924-4,* Prime Crime) Berkley Publishing Group.

—Savage Run: A Joe Pickett Novel. 2002. 288p. 23.95 *(0-399-14887-6)* Penguin Group (USA) Inc.

—Winterkill. 2004. 352p. mass mkt. 6.99 *(0-425-19595-3)* Berkley Publishing Group.

—Winterkill. abr. ed. 2004. (Joe Pickett Ser.). audio 12.99 *(1-59086-949-4,* 4551, Brilliance Audio Paperback Audiobooks); 2003. (Joe Pickett Series: Vol. 3). audio 24.95 *(1-59086-948-6,* 4550, Brilliance Audio); 2003. (Joe Pickett Series: Vol. 3). audio 32.95 *(1-59086-946-X,* 4548, Brilliance Audio Unabridged); 2003. (Joe Pickett Series: Vol. 3). audio 87.25 *(1-59086-947-8,* 4549, Unabridged Library Editions) Brilliance Audio.

—Winterkill. 2003. 239.50 *(0-399-19746-X)* Putnam Publishing Group, The.

—Winterkill: A Joe Pickett Novel. 2003. 384p. 23.95 *(0-399-15045-5)* Putnam Publishing Group, The.

### PICKETT, MEL (FICTITIOUS CHARACTER)—FICTION

Wright, Eric. Buried in Stone: A Mel Pickett Mystery. 1997. 256p. mass mkt. 7.99 *(0-7704-2741-3)* Bantam Bks.

—Buried in Stone: A Mel Pickett Mystery. 1996. 256p. 24.95 o.p. *(0-385-25518-7)* Doubleday Publishing.

—Buried in Stone: A Mel Pickett Mystery. 1998. (WWL Mystery Ser.). per. *(0-373-26286-8,* 1-26286-4, Worldwide Library) Harlequin Enterprises, Ltd.

—Buried in Stone: A Mel Pickett Mystery. 1996. 256p. 20.00 *(0-684-81304-1,* Scribner) Simon & Schuster.

### PIERCE, AMELIA (FICTITIOUS CHARACTER)—FICTION

Stryker, Dev. Deathright. 1995. 336p. 5.99 o.p. *(0-8125-2162-5,* Forge Bks.); 1992. 320p. 21.95 o.p. *(0-312-85386-6,* Tor Bks.) Doherty, Tom Assocs., LLC.

—A Wilderness of Mirrors. 2000. (Amelia Pierce Mysteries Ser.). 320p. 24.95 o.s.i *(0-312-86441-8,* Forge Bks.) Doherty, Tom Assocs., LLC.

### PIERCE, TYLER (FICTITIOUS CHARACTER)—FICTION

Smith, Mitchell. Sacrifice. 1997. 368p. 23.95 o.p. *(0-525-93978-4)* Dutton/Plume.

—Sacrifice. 1997. 432p. mass mkt. 6.99 o.s.i *(0-451-18475-0,* Signet Bks.) NAL.

—Sacrifice. abr. ed. 1997. audio 24.95 *(1-57511-022-9)* Publishing Mills, Inc., The.

### PIERCY, JOANNA (FICTITIOUS CHARACTER)—FICTION

Masters, Priscilla. And None Shall Sleep. l.t. ed. 1998. (Ulverscroft Large Print Ser.). 336p. 29.99 o.p. *(0-7089-3955-4,* Ulverscroft) Thorpe, F. A. Pubs. GBR. *Dist:* Ulverscroft Large Print Bks., Ltd., Ulverscroft Large Print Canada, Ltd.

—Embroidering Shrouds. 2002. (Joanna Piercy Mystery Ser.). 288p. pap. 9.95 *(0-7490-0587-4)* Allison & Busby, Ltd. GBR. *Dist:* International Publishers Marketing.

### PIGEON, ANNA (FICTITIOUS CHARACTER)—FICTION

Barr, Nevada. Blind Descent. l.t. ed. 1998. 25.95 o.p. *(1-56895-547-2,* Wheeler Publishing, Inc.) Gale Group.

—Blind Descent. 1999. (Anna Pigeon Mysteries Ser.). (Illus.). 384p. mass mkt. 7.99 *(0-380-72826-5,* Avon Bks.) Morrow/Avon.

—Blind Descent. 1998. 352p. (gr. 5 up). 22.95 o.p. *(0-399-14371-8,* G. P. Putnam's Sons) Penguin Group (USA) Inc.

—Blind Descent. 1999. audio compact disk 99.00; 1998. audio 83.00 *(0-7887-2038-4,* 95402E7) Recorded Bks., LLC.

—Blood Lure. 2002. 352p. reprint ed. mass mkt. 6.99 *(0-425-18375-0)* Berkley Publishing Group.

—Blood Lure. abr. ed. (Anna Pigeon Ser.). 2004. audio compact disk 16.99 *(1-59355-670-5,* 5289, Brilliance Audio on CD Value Priced); 2002. audio 12.99 *(1-58788-647-2,* 3012, Paperback Nova Audio Bks.); 2001. audio 44.25 *(1-58788-220-5,* 2481); 2001. audio 24.95 o.s.i *(1-58788-164-0,* 2423, Nova Audio Bks.); 2001. audio compact disk 57.25 *(1-58788-189-6,* 2448); 2001. audio compact disk 29.95 *(1-58788-165-9,* 2424, CD) Brilliance Audio.

—Blood Lure. l.t. ed. 2001. (Large Print Book Ser.). 417p. 29.95 *(1-58724-001-7,* Wheeler Publishing, Inc.) Gale Group.

—Blood Lure. 2001. 320p. 24.95 o.p. *(0-399-14702-0)* Penguin Group (USA) Inc.

—Blood Lure. unabr. ed. 2001. (Anna Pigeon Mystery Ser. : No. 9). audio 78.00 *(0-7887-5206-5,* 96471E7); audio 29.95 *(0-7887-4974-9);* audio 29.95 *(0-7887-4974-9);* audio compact disk 97.00 *(0-7887-7193-0)* Recorded Bks., LLC.

—Deep South. 2001. (Anna Pigeon Mysteries Ser.). 384p. mass mkt. 6.99 (*0-425-17895-1*) Berkley Publishing Group.
—Deep South. l.t. ed. 2000. 25.95 o.p. (*1-56895-867-6*, Wheeler Publishing, Inc.) Gale Group.
—Deep South. 2000. (Anna Pigeon Mysteries Ser.). 340p. 23.95 o.s.i (*0-399-14586-9*) Penguin Group (USA) Inc.
—Endangered Species. l.t. ed. 1997. 25.95 (*1-57490-108-7*, Beeler Large Print Bks.) Beeler, Thomas T. Publisher.
—Endangered Species. 1998. (Anna Pigeon Mysteries Ser.). 400p. mass mkt. 7.99 (*0-380-72583-5*, Avon Bks.) Morrow/Avon.
—Endangered Species, Set. abr. ed. 1997. 18.00 o.p. (*0-7871-1373-5*, 395114) NewStar Media, Inc.
—Endangered Species. 1997. 320p. 22.95 o.p. (*0-399-14246-0*, G. P. Putnam's Sons) Penguin Group (USA) Inc.
—Firestorm. l.t. ed. 1997. (Large Print Bks.). 24.95 o.p. (*1-56895-399-2*, Wheeler Publishing, Inc.) Gale Group.
—Firestorm. 1997. (Anna Pigeon Mysteries Ser.). 336p. reprint ed. mass mkt. 7.99 (*0-380-72582-7*, Avon Bks.) Morrow/Avon.
—Firestorm. 1996. 320p. 22.95 o.p. (*0-399-14126-X*, G. P. Putnam's Sons) Penguin Group (USA) Inc.
—Flashback. 2004. 416p. mass mkt. 7.99 (*0-425-19449-3*) Berkley Publishing Group.
—Flashback. 2004. 543p. pap. 13.95 (*1-4104-0172-3*); 2003. 32.95 (*1-58724-380-6*) Gale Group. (Wheeler Publishing, Inc.).
—Flashback. 2003. (Illus.). 400p. 24.95 (*0-399-14975-9*, Putnam & Grosset) Putnam Publishing Group, The.
—Flashback. audio 34.99 (*1-4025-3633-X*) Recorded Bks., LLC.
—High Country. 2004. 336p. 24.95 (*0-399-15144-3*) Putnam Publishing Group, The.
—Hunting Season. 2003. 352p. reprint ed. mass mkt. 6.99 (*0-425-18878-7*) Berkley Publishing Group.
—Hunting Season. abr. ed. (Anna Pigeon Ser.). 2004. audio compact disk 16.99 (*1-59355-696-9*, 5314, Brilliance Audio on CD Value Priced); 2003. audio 12.99 (*1-59086-005-5*, 3525, Brilliance Audio Paperback Audiobooks); 2002. audio 53.25 (*1-59086-004-7*, 3524, Library Edition); 2002. audio 24.95 o.p. (*1-59086-003-9*, 3523, Nova Audio Bks.); 2002. audio compact disk 29.95 (*1-59086-001-2*, 3521, CD); 2002. audio compact disk 69.25 (*1-59086-002-0*, 3522, CD Library Edition) Brilliance Audio.
—Hunting Season. l.t. ed. 2002. (Wheeler Large Print Book Ser.). 30.95 (*1-58724-181-1*, Wheeler Publishing, Inc.) Gale Group.
—Hunting Season. 2002. (Illus.). 320p. 24.95 o.s.i (*0-399-14846-9*); 249.50 o.p. (*0-399-19628-5*) Putnam Publishing Group, The.
—Hunting Season, 7 cass. 2002. audio 29.99 (*1-4025-0861-1*, 00974); audio 29.99 (*1-4025-0748-8*, 96913) Recorded Bks., LLC.
—Hunting Season. l.t. ed. 2003. (Paperback Bestsellers Ser.). 12.95 (*1-4104-0088-3*, Large Print Pr.) Thorndike Pr.
—Ill Wind. 2004. 320p. mass mkt. 6.99 (*0-425-19725-5*) Berkley Publishing Group.
—Ill Wind. l.t. ed. 1995. (Large Print Bks.). pap. 21.95 o.p. (*1-56895-252-X*, Wheeler Publishing, Inc.) Gale Group.
—Ill Wind. 1996. (Anna Pigeon Mysteries Ser.: No. 3). 320p. mass mkt. 7.99 (*0-380-72363-8*, Avon Bks.) Morrow/Avon.
—Ill Wind. abr. ed. 1995. 17.95 o.p. (*0-7871-0370-5*) NewStar Media, Inc.
—Ill Wind. 1995. 309p. 19.95 o.p. (*0-399-14015-8*, G. P. Putnam's Sons) Penguin Group (USA) Inc.
—Ill Wind. unabr. ed. 1999. (Anna Pigeon Mystery Ser. : No. 3). audio 62.00 (*0-7887-2932-2*, 95717E7) Recorded Bks., LLC.
—Liberty Falling. l.t. ed. 1999. (Wheeler Large Print Bks.). 26.95 (*1-56895-711-4*, Wheeler Publishing, Inc.) Gale Group.
—Liberty Falling. 2000. (Anna Pigeon Mysteries Ser.). (Illus.). 384p. mass mkt. 7.99 (*0-380-72827-3*, Avon Bks.) Morrow/Avon.
—Liberty Falling. 1999. (Anna Pigeon Mysteries Ser.). 321p. 23.95 o.s.i (*0-399-14459-5*) Penguin Group (USA) Inc.
—Liberty Falling. unabr. ed. 1999. (Anna Pigeon Mystery Ser. : No. 7). (Illus.). audio 83.00 (*0-7887-3465-2*, 95649E7) Recorded Bks., LLC.
—A Superior Death. 2003. 320p. mass mkt. 6.99 (*0-425-19471-X*) Berkley Publishing Group.
—A Superior Death. 2002. (Anna Pigeon Mysteries Ser.: No. 2). 384p. mass mkt. 7.50 o.s.i (*0-380-72362-X*, Avon Bks.) Morrow/Avon.
—A Superior Death. 1994. 303p. 19.95 o.s.i (*0-399-13916-8*, G. P. Putnam's Sons) Penguin Group (USA) Inc.
—A Superior Death. unabr. ed. 1998. (Anna Pigeon Mystery Ser. : No. 2). audio 72.00 (*0-7887-1896-7*, 95318E7) Recorded Bks., LLC.
—A Superior Death. l.t. ed. 1994. 431p. lib. bdg. 23.95 (*0-8161-7446-6*) Thorndike Pr.
—Track of the Cat. abr. ed. 2002. audio 25.00 (*1-59040-249-9*) Audio Literature.
—Track of the Cat. 2003. 272p. mass mkt. 6.99 (*0-425-19083-8*) Berkley Publishing Group.
—Track of the Cat. l.t. ed. 1998. pap. 23.95 o.p. (*1-56895-572-3*, Wheeler Publishing, Inc.) Gale Group.
—Track of the Cat. 2002. (Anna Pigeon Mysteries Ser.: No. 1). 320p. reprint ed. mass mkt. 6.99 o.s.i (*0-380-72164-3*, Avon Bks.) Morrow/Avon.
—Track of the Cat. 1993. 240p. 19.95 o.s.i (*0-399-13824-2*, G. P. Putnam's Sons) Penguin Group (USA) Inc.
—Track of the Cat. unabr. ed. 2000. (Anna Pigeon Mystery Ser. : No. 1). audio 51.00 (*0-7887-1778-2*, 95252E7) Recorded Bks., LLC.

**PIGEON, JOSIE (FICTITIOUS CHARACTER)—FICTION**

Wolzien, Valerie. Deck the Halls with Murder. (Josie Pigeon Mystery Ser.). 256p. 1998. mass mkt. 5.99 (*0-449-15036-4*); 1995. pap. 19.00 (*0-345-46621-7*) Ballantine Bks. (Fawcett).
—Murder in the Forecast. 2001. 272p. mass mkt. 6.99 (*0-449-00631-X*, Fawcett) Ballantine Bks.
—Murder in the Forecast. l.t. ed. 2002. 375p. pap. 25.95 (*0-7862-4718-5*) Thorndike Pr.
—Permit for Murder. 1997. (Josie Pigeon Mystery Ser.). 240p. mass mkt. 7.99 (*0-449-14960-9*, Fawcett) Ballantine Bks.
—Shore to Die. 1995. mass mkt. 5.50 o.s.i (*0-449-14958-7*, Fawcett) Ballantine Bks.
—This Old Murder. 2000. (Josie Pigeon Mystery Ser.). 288p. mass mkt. 6.50 (*0-449-00629-8*, Fawcett) Ballantine Bks.

**PIKE, JOE (FICTITIOUS CHARACTER)—FICTION**

Crais, Robert. The Devil's Cantina. 1999. 288p. 22.95 (*0-7868-6355-2*) Hyperion Pr.
—Free Fall. 1994. (Elvis Cole Mystery Ser.). mass mkt. 4.99 o.s.i (*0-553-56831-0*, Crimeline); 304p. mass mkt. 6.99 (*0-553-56509-5*) Bantam Bks.
—Indigo Slam. 2003. (Elvis Cole Mystery Ser.). 320p. mass mkt. 7.99 (*0-345-43564-8*, Ballantine Bks.) Ballantine Bks.
—Indigo Slam. unabr. ed. 1997. (Elvis Cole Mystery Ser.). audio 48.00 (*0-7366-3833-4*, 4553) Books on Tape, Inc.
—Indigo Slam. abr. ed. (Elvis Cole Mystery Ser.). 2000. audio 7.99 o.s.i (*1-58788-097-0*, 2352, Paperback Nova Audio Bks.); 1998. audio 7.99 o.s.i (*1-56740-252-6*, 2379, Nova Audio Bks.); 1997. audio 16.95 o.p. (*1-56100-977-6*, 1236, Nova Audio Bks.); 1997. audio 16.95 o.p.; 1997. audio 23.95 (*1-56100-752-8*, 144, Bookcassette); 1997. audio 57.25 (*1-56100-827-3*, 907, Unabridged Library Editions) Brilliance Audio.
—Indigo Slam. (Elvis Cole Mystery Ser.). 1999. 384p. mass mkt. 5.99 (*0-7868-8929-2*); 1997. 304p. 22.95 (*0-7868-6261-0*) Hyperion Pr.
—L. A. Requiem. 2000. (Elvis Cole Mystery Ser.). 416p. mass mkt. 6.99 (*0-345-43447-1*, Ballantine Bks.) Ballantine Bks.
—L. A. Requiem. l.t. ed. 2000. (Elvis Cole Mystery Ser.). 538p. 27.95 (*1-56895-881-1*, Wheeler Publishing, Inc.) Gale Group.
—L. A. Requiem, Set. abr. ed. 1999. (Elvis Cole Mystery Ser.). audio 25.00 Highsmith Inc.
—L. A. Requiem. abr. ed. 1999. (Elvis Cole Mystery Ser.). audio 25.00 (*0-553-52648-0*, RH Audio) Random Hse. Audio Publishing Group.
—Lullaby Town. (Elvis Cole Mystery Ser.). 1993. 352p. mass mkt. 6.99 (*0-553-29951-4*); 1992. 304p. 20.00 o.s.i (*0-553-08197-7*) Bantam Bks.
—The Monkey's Raincoat. (Elvis Cole Mystery Ser.). 1987. 208p. mass mkt. 2.95 o.s.i (*0-553-26336-6*); 1992. 224p. reprint ed. mass mkt. 7.50 (*0-553-27585-2*) Bantam Bks.
—Stalking the Angel. 1992. (Elvis Cole Mystery Ser.). 288p. mass mkt. 7.50 (*0-553-28644-7*) Bantam Bks.
—Sunset Express. unabr. ed. 1997. (Elvis Cole Mystery Ser.). audio 56.00 (*0-913369-89-6*, 4389) Books on Tape, Inc.
—Sunset Express. abr. ed. (Elvis Cole Mystery Ser.). 1997. audio 7.99 o.p. (*1-56740-166-X*, 707, Nova Audio Bks.); 1996. audio 16.95 o.p. (*1-56100-905-9*, 1066, Nova Audio Bks.); 1996. audio 57.25 o.p. (*1-56100-320-4*, 1065, Unabridged Library Editions); 1996. audio 23.95 o.p. (*1-56100-695-5*, 284, Bookcassette) Brilliance Audio.
—Sunset Express. (Elvis Cole Mystery Ser.). 1996. 288p. 21.95 o.p. (*0-7868-6096-0*); 2002. 416p. reprint ed. mass mkt. 6.99 (*0-7868-8915-2*) Hyperion Pr.
—Voodoo River. l.t. ed. 2002. (Elvis Cole Mystery Ser.). 499p. 29.95 (*0-7862-3404-0*) Gale Group.
—Voodoo River. abr. ed. 1995. (Elvis Cole Mystery Ser.). audio 17.00 (*1-56876-040-X*, 393047) Soundlines Entertainment, Inc.

**PINE, LEONARD (FICTITIOUS CHARACTER)—FICTION**

Lansdale, Joe R. Bad Chili. 1997. 288p. 22.00 o.p. (*0-89296-619-X*) Mysterious Pr.
—Bad Chili. 1998. 272p. mass mkt. 6.99 (*0-446-60602-2*); 1997. mass mkt. (*0-446-60421-6*) Warner Bks., Inc.
—Captains Outrageous. 2001. 336p. 24.45 o.p. (*0-89296-728-5*) Mysterious Pr.
—Captains Outrageous. 2003. 336p. pap. 12.95 (*0-446-67963-1*, Mysterious Pr. Paperback Bks.) Warner Bks., Inc.
—Mucho Mojo. 1994. 320p. 19.95 o.s.i (*0-89296-490-1*) Mysterious Pr.
—Mucho Mojo. 1995. 304p. mass mkt. 5.99 (*0-446-40187-0*) Warner Bks., Inc.
—Rumble Tumble. 1998. 244p. 22.00 o.p. (*0-89296-620-3*) Mysterious Pr.
—Rumble Tumble. 1999. 272p. mass mkt. 6.50 o.s.i (*0-446-60757-6*) Warner Bks., Inc.
—Savage Season. 1990. mass mkt. 4.50 o.s.i (*0-553-28563-7*) Bantam Bks.
—Savage Season. 1995. 192p. mass mkt. 5.50 o.p. (*0-446-40431-4*) Warner Bks., Inc.
—Savage Season. 1990. 200p. 25.00 o.p. (*0-929480-23-6*) Ziesing, Mark V.
—The Two-Bear Mambo. 1995. 273p. 19.95 o.s.i (*0-89296-491-X*) Mysterious Pr.
—The Two-Bear Mambo. 1996. 288p. mass mkt. 5.99 (*0-446-40188-9*) Warner Bks., Inc.

**PINK, MELINDA (FICTITIOUS CHARACTER)—FICTION**

Moffat, Gwen. Grizzly Trail. 1984. 208p. o.p. (*0-575-03503-X*) David & Charles Pubs.
—Grizzly Trail. l.t. ed. 1987. (Linford Mystery Library). 334p. pap. 17.99 o.p. (*0-7089-6357-9*, Linford) Thorpe, F. A. Pubs. GBR. *Dist:* Ulverscroft Large Print Bks., Ltd., Ulverscroft Large Print Canada, Ltd.
—Miss Pink at the Edge of the World. 1995. 208p. 19.50 (*0-7451-8667-X*, Black Dagger) BBC Audiobooks America.
—Miss Pink at the Edge of the World. 1993. (J). 6.95 o.p. (*0-684-14336-4*, Macmillan Reference USA) Gale Group.
—Miss Pink at the Edge of the World. l.t. ed. 1995. (Ulverscroft Large Print Ser.). 368p. 29.99 o.p. (*0-7089-3379-3*, Ulverscroft) Thorpe, F. A. Pubs. GBR. *Dist:* Ulverscroft Large Print Bks., Ltd., Ulverscroft Large Print Canada, Ltd.
—Over the Sea to Death. unabr. ed. 1996. audio 49.95 o.p. (*1-85903-099-8*, 30998) Magna Story Sound GBR. *Dist:* Ulverscroft Large Print Bks., Ltd.
—Over the Sea to Death. l.t. ed. 1994. (Ulverscroft Large Print Ser.). 368p. 29.99 o.p. (*0-7089-3137-5*, Ulverscroft) Thorpe, F. A. Pubs. GBR. *Dist:* Ulverscroft Large Print Bks., Ltd., Ulverscroft Large Print Canada, Ltd.
—Private Sins. l.t. ed. 2001. (Ulverscroft Large Print Ser.). 360p. 31.99 (*0-7089-4364-0*, Ulverscroft) Thorpe, F. A. Pubs. GBR. *Dist:* Ulverscroft Large Print Bks., Ltd., Ulverscroft Large Print Canada, Ltd.
—Rage. unabr. ed. 1998. audio 63.95 (*1-85903-147-1*) Magna Story Sound GBR. *Dist:* Ulverscroft Large Print Bks., Ltd.
—Rage. 1990. 208p. 16.95 o.p. (*0-312-04409-7*, Saint Martin's Minotaur) St. Martin's Pr.
—Rage. l.t. ed. 1993. (Ulverscroft Large Print Ser.). 400p. 29.99 o.p. (*0-7089-2901-X*, Ulverscroft) Thorpe, F. A. Pubs. GBR. *Dist:* Ulverscroft Large Print Bks., Ltd., Ulverscroft Large Print Canada, Ltd.
—Snare: A Miss Pink Mystery. l.t. ed. 2002. 292p. pap. 24.45 (*0-7862-3939-5*) Gale Group.
—Snare: A Miss Pink Mystery. 1988. 192p. 14.95 o.p. (*0-312-02284-0*, Saint Martin's Minotaur) St. Martin's Pr.
—Snare: A Miss Pink Mystery. l.t. ed. 1990. (Ulverscroft Large Print Ser.). 29.99 o.p. (*0-7089-2128-0*, Ulverscroft) Thorpe, F. A. Pubs. GBR. *Dist:* Ulverscroft Large Print Bks., Ltd., Ulverscroft Large Print Canada, Ltd.
—The Stone Hawk. 1989. 224p. 15.95 o.p. (*0-312-03434-2*, Saint Martin's Minotaur) St. Martin's Pr.
—Veronica's Sisters. l.t. ed. 1993. 21.95 o.p. (*0-7927-1801-1*); pap. 19.95 o.p. (*0-7927-1800-3*) BBC Audiobooks America.

**PINKERTON LADY (FICTITIOUS CHARACTER)—FICTION**

Roddy, Lee. Days of Deception. 1998. (Pinkerton Lady Chronicles Ser.: 1). 320p. (*1-56476-686-1*) Cook Communications Ministries.
—Days of Deception. l.t. ed. 2002. (Pinkerton Lady Chronicles: No. 1). 477p. pap. 16.95 (*1-4104-0018-2*, Walker Large Print) Gale Group.
—Days of Deception. l.t. ed. 2001. (Pinkerton Lady Chronicles Ser.). 477p. 23.95 (*0-7862-3186-6*) Thorndike Pr.
—Tomorrow's Promise. (Pinkerton Lady Chronicles Ser.: 3). 363p. pap. 10.99 (*1-56476-688-8*) Cook Communications Ministries.
—Tomorrow's Promise. l.t. ed. 2001. (Christian Mystery Ser.). 465p. 23.95 (*0-7862-3207-2*) Thorndike Pr.
—Yesterday's Shadows. (Pinkerton Lady Chronicles Ser.: 2). 320p. pap. 10.99 (*1-56476-635-7*); 335p. pap. 10.99 (*1-56476-687-X*) Cook Communications Ministries.
—Yesterday's Shadows. l.t. ed. 2002. (Pinkerton Lady Chronicles: No. 2). 470p. pap. 16.95 (*1-4104-0037-9*, Walker Large Print) Gale Group.
—Yesterday's Shadows. l.t. ed. 2001. (Pinkerton Lady Chronicles Ser.). 467p. 23.95 (*0-7862-3208-0*) Thorndike Pr.

**PIPER, MOLLY (FICTITIOUS CHARACTER)—FICTION**

Brooks, Patricia. But for the Grace. 2000. (Molly Piper Mysteries Ser.). 240p. mass mkt. 5.99 o.s.i (*0-440-22608-2*) Dell Publishing.
—Falling from Grace. 1998. (Molly Piper Mysteries Ser.). 256p. mass mkt. 5.99 o.s.i (*0-440-22607-4*) Dell Publishing.

**PITT, CHARLOTTE (FICTITIOUS CHARACTER)—FICTION**

Perry, Anne. Ashworth Hall. 1998. 384p. mass mkt. 7.50 (*0-449-00086-9*, Fawcett) Ballantine Bks.
—Bedford Square. 2000. 336p. mass mkt. 6.99 (*0-449-00582-8*, Ballantine Bks.); 1995. o.p. (*0-449-90633-7*, Fawcett) Ballantine Bks.
—Bedford Square. l.t. ed. 1999. (Basic Ser.). 571p. 30.95 (*0-7862-2018-X*) Thorndike Pr.
—Belgrave Square. 1993. 384p. mass mkt. 6.99 (*0-449-22227-6*, Fawcett) Ballantine Bks.
—Belgrave Square. 1994. 4.99 o.p. (*0-517-12853-5*) Random Hse. Value Publishing.
—Bethlehem Road. 1991. 320p. mass mkt. 5.99 o.p. (*0-449-45316-2*); mass mkt. 6.99 (*0-449-21914-3*) Ballantine Bks. (Fawcett).
—Bethlehem Road. l.t. ed. 2001. (Dales Large Print Ser.). 464p. pap. (*1-84262-093-2*) Dales Large Print Bks. GBR. *Dist:* Ulverscroft Large Print Canada, Ltd.
—Bethlehem Road. 1990. 17.95 o.p. (*0-312-04266-3*, Saint Martin's Minotaur) St. Martin's Pr.
—Bethlehem Road. l.t. ed. 1993. (Mystery Ser.). 592p. 29.99 o.p. (*0-7089-2939-7*, Ulverscroft) Thorpe, F. A. Pubs. GBR. *Dist:* Ulverscroft Large Print Bks., Ltd., Ulverscroft Large Print Canada, Ltd.
—Bluegate Fields. 1985. 288p. mass mkt. 5.99 o.p. (*0-449-45317-0*); mass mkt. 6.99 (*0-449-20766-8*) Ballantine Bks. (Fawcett).
—Bluegate Fields. l.t. ed. 2000. 398p. lib. bdg. 28.95 (*1-58547-017-1*) Ctr. Point Large Print.
—Bluegate Fields. l.t. ed. 2001. (Magna Large Print Ser.). 384p. (*0-7505-1709-3*) Magna Large Print Bks. GBR. *Dist:* Ulverscroft Large Print Canada, Ltd.
—Bluegate Fields. unabr. ed. 2002. audio 72.00 (*1-4025-3604-6*, Clipper Audio) Recorded Bks., LLC.
—Bluegate Fields. 1984. 320p. 13.95 o.p. (*0-312-08718-7*) St. Martin's Pr.
—Brunswick Gardens. 1999. 416p. mass mkt. 7.50 (*0-449-00318-3*, Fawcett) Ballantine Bks.
—Brunswick Gardens. (Charlotte & Thomas Pitt Novel Ser.). 2001. audio 9.99 (*0-375-41673-0*); Set. 1998. audio 18.00 o.s.i (*0-375-40177-6*) Random Hse. Audio Publishing Group. (RH Audio).
—Brunswick Gardens. l.t. ed. 1998. (Basic Ser.). 656p. 30.95 (*0-7862-1464-3*) Thorndike Pr.
—Callander Square. 1998. mass mkt. 3.99 o.s.i (*0-449-00461-9*); 1985. 256p. mass mkt. 6.99 (*0-449-20999-7*); 1981. mass mkt. 2.25 o.p. (*0-449-24365-6*) Ballantine Bks. (Fawcett).
—Callander Square. 1980. 10.00 o.p. (*0-312-11430-3*) St. Martin's Pr.
—Callander Square. l.t. ed. 1981. 447p. 12.00 o.p. (*0-7089-0718-0*, Ulverscroft) Thorpe, F. A. Pubs. GBR. *Dist:* Ulverscroft Large Print Bks., Ltd.
—Cardington Crescent. 1988. 304p. reprint ed. mass mkt. 6.99 (*0-449-21442-7*, Fawcett) Ballantine Bks.
—Cardington Crescent. l.t. ed. 2001. 375p. lib. bdg. 28.95 (*1-58547-015-5*) Ctr. Point Large Print.
—Cardington Crescent. unabr. ed. 1998. audio 83.95 (*1-85903-217-6*) Magna Story Sound GBR. *Dist:* Ulverscroft Large Print Bks., Ltd.
—Cardington Crescent. 1987. 304p. 15.95 o.p. (*0-312-00113-4*) St. Martin's Pr.
—The Cater Street Hangman. 1998. mass mkt. 3.99 o.s.i (*0-449-00460-0*); 1985. 288p. mass mkt. 6.99 (*0-449-20867-2*); 1980. mass mkt. 2.25 o.s.i (*0-449-24327-3*) Ballantine Bks. (Fawcett).
—The Cater Street Hangman. l.t. ed. 2000. 364p. lib. bdg. 27.95 (*1-58547-002-3*) Ctr. Point Large Print.
—The Cater Street Hangman. 1979. 8.95 o.p. (*0-312-12385-X*) St. Martin's Pr.
—Death in the Devil's Acre. 1987. 272p. mass mkt. 6.99 (*0-449-21095-2*, Fawcett) Ballantine Bks.

—Death in the Devil's Acre. l.t. ed. 2001. lib. bdg. 27.95 (*1-58547-016-3*) Ctr. Point Large Print.

—Death in the Devil's Acre. 1985. 288p. 14.95 o.p. (*0-312-18869-2*) St. Martin's Pr.

—Farriers' Lane. 1994. 432p. mass mkt. 7.50 (*0-449-21961-5*, Fawcett) Ballantine Bks.

—Half Moon Street. 2001. 320p. mass mkt. 6.99 (*0-449-00655-7*, Ballantine Bks.) Ballantine Bks.

—Half Moon Street. l.t. ed. 2000. 439p. 27.95 (*1-56895-857-9*, Wheeler Publishing, Inc.) Gale Group.

—Half Moon Street. abr. ed. 2000. (Charlotte & Thomas Pitt Novel Ser.). audio 18.00 (*0-553-52710-X*, RH Audio) Random Hse. Audio Publishing Group.

—Highgate Rise. 1992. 352p. mass mkt. 7.50 (*0-449-21959-3*, Fawcett) Ballantine Bks.

—Highgate Rise. l.t. ed. 1994. (Ulverscroft Ser.). 672p. 21.95 o.p. (*0-7089-3013-1*, Ulverscroft) Thorpe, F. A. Pubs. GBR. *Dist:* Ulverscroft Large Print Bks., Ltd., Ulverscroft Large Print Canada, Ltd.

—The Hyde Park Headsman. 1995. 352p. mass mkt. 7.50 (*0-449-22350-7*); 1994. 432p. 21.00 o.s.i (*0-449-90636-1*) Ballantine Bks. (Fawcett).

—Paragon Walk. 1986. 256p. mass mkt. 6.99 (*0-449-21168-1*); 1986. mass mkt. 5.99 (*0-449-45319-7*); 1982. mass mkt. 2.50 o.p. (*0-449-20110-4*); 1982. 224p. mass mkt. 2.50 o.p. (*0-449-24497-0*) Ballantine Bks. (Fawcett).

—Paragon Walk. l.t. ed. 2000. 308p. lib. bdg. 27.95 (*1-58547-005-8*) Ctr. Point Large Print.

—Paragon Walk. 1981. 224p. 9.95 o.p. (*0-312-59598-0*) St. Martin's Pr.

—Pentecost Alley. 1997. (Charlotte & Thomas Pitt Novel Ser.). 416p. mass mkt. 6.99 (*0-449-22566-6*, Fawcett) Ballantine Bks.

—Pentecost Alley. l.t. ed. 1996. (Cloak & Dagger Ser.). 708p. 27.95 (*0-7862-0812-0*) Thorndike Pr.

—Resurrection Row. 1986. 224p. mass mkt. 6.99 (*0-449-21067-7*, Fawcett) Ballantine Bks.

—Resurrection Row. l.t. ed. 2000. 312p. lib. bdg. 27.95 (*1-58547-009-0*) Ctr. Point Large Print.

—Resurrection Row. 1981. 224p. 9.95 o.p. (*0-312-67797-9*) St. Martin's Pr.

—Rutland Place. 1986. 224p. mass mkt. 6.99 (*0-449-21285-8*); 1986. 224p. mass mkt. 5.99 o.p. (*0-449-45318-9*); 1984. mass mkt. 2.50 o.p. (*0-449-20474-X*) Ballantine Bks. (Fawcett).

—Rutland Place. l.t. ed. 2000. 319p. lib. bdg. 27.95 (*1-58547-013-9*) Ctr. Point Large Print.

—Rutland Place. 224p. (*0-7278-5864-5*) Severn Hse. Pubs., Ltd.

—Rutland Place. 1983. 256p. 12.95 o.p. (*0-312-69621-3*) St. Martin's Pr.

—Seven Dials. 2004. 352p. mass mkt. 7.50 (*0-345-44008-0*); 2003. 352p. 25.95 (*0-345-44007-2*, Ballantine Bks.); 2003. E-Book 17.85 (*0-345-46352-8*, Ballantine Bks.) Ballantine Bks.

—Seven Dials. abr. ed. 2003. (Thomas & Charlotte Pitt Ser.: Vol. 23). audio 24.95 (*1-59086-499-9*, 4093, Nova Audio Bks.); audio compact disk 102.25 (*1-59086-501-4*, 4092) Brilliance Audio.

—Seven Dials. 2003. (Basic Ser.). 552p. 32.95 (*0-7862-5210-3*) Thorndike Pr.

—The Silence in Hanover Close. 1989. 352p. mass mkt. 7.50 (*0-449-21686-1*, Fawcett) Ballantine Bks.

—The Silence in Hanover Close. 1988. 384p. 17.95 o.p. (*0-312-01824-X*, Saint Martin's Minotaur) St. Martin's Pr.

—The Silence in Hanover Close. l.t. ed. 1990. (Mystery Ser.). 29.99 o.p. (*0-7089-2324-0*, Ulverscroft) Thorpe, F. A. Pubs. GBR. *Dist:* Ulverscroft Large Print Bks., Ltd., Ulverscroft Large Print Canada, Ltd.

—Southampton Row. 2003. 352p. mass mkt. 7.50 (*0-345-44004-8*); 2002. 336p. 25.00 (*0-345-44003-X*) Ballantine Bks. (Ballantine Bks.).

—Southampton Row. 2002. E-Book 20.00 (*1-4014-9974-0*) Barnes & Noble Digital.

—Southampton Row. abr. ed. (Thomas & Charlotte Pitt Ser.). 2005. audio compact disk 16.99 (*1-59355-704-3*, 5322, Brilliance Audio on CD Value Priced); 2003. audio 12.99 (*1-58788-918-8*, 3436, Brilliance Audio Paperback Audiobooks); 2002. audio 24.95 (*1-58788-915-3*, 3433, Nova Audio Bks.); 2002. audio compact disk 69.25 (*1-58788-917-X*, 3435, CD Library Edition); 2002. audio compact disk 29.95 (*1-58788-916-1*, 3434, CD); 2002. audio 34.95 (*1-58788-913-7*, 3431, Brilliance Audio Unabridged); 2002. audio 89.25 (*1-58788-914-5*, 3432, Unabridged Library Editions) Brilliance Audio.

—Southampton Row. unabr. ed. 2003. (Thomas & Charlotte Pitt Ser.). audio 19.99 (*1-59335-166-6*, 30262) Soulmate Audio Bks., Inc.

—Southampton Row. l.t. ed. 13.95 (*1-4104-0092-1*, Large Print Pr.); 2003. 571p. pap. 27.95 (*0-7862-4502-6*); 2002. 588p. 30.95 o.p. (*0-7862-4066-0*) Thorndike Pr.

—Traitor's Gate. 1996. 432p. mass mkt. 7.50 (*0-449-22439-2*, Fawcett) Ballantine Bks.

—The Whitechapel Conspiracy. unabr. ed. 2003. 10p. audio 84.95 (*0-7540-0858-4*, CAB 2280); audio compact disk 99.95 (*0-7540-5597-3*, CCD 288) BBC Audiobooks America.

—The Whitechapel Conspiracy. 2002. (Thomas & Charlotte Pitt Ser.). 352p. reprint ed. mass mkt. 6.99 (*0-449-00656-5*, Ballantine Bks.) Ballantine Bks.

—The Whitechapel Conspiracy. l.t. ed. 2001. 515p. 31.95 (*0-7838-9513-5*, Macmillan Reference USA) Gale Group.

—The Whitechapel Conspiracy. abr. ed. 2001. audio 25.95 (*0-553-52789-4*, RH Audio) Random Hse. Audio Publishing Group.

**PITT, DIRK (FICTITIOUS CHARACTER)—FICTION**

Cussler, Clive. Atlantis Found. 2001. (Dirk Pitt Adventure Ser.). 544p. mass mkt. 7.99 (*0-425-17717-3*); mass mkt. 7.99 (*0-425-18014-X*) Berkley Publishing Group.

—Atlantis Found. unabr. ed. 2000. (Dirk Pitt Adventure Ser.). audio 112.00 (*0-7366-4781-3*, 5126) Books on Tape, Inc.

—Atlantis Found. abr. ed. 1999. (Dirk Pitt Adventure Ser.). 534p. 26.95 o.s.i (*0-399-14588-5*) Penguin Group (USA) Inc.

—Atlantis Found. 2001. 26.95 o.s.i (*0-399-14911-2*); 1999. 24.95 incl. audio (*0-399-14607-5*); 1999. audio 49.95 (*0-399-14608-3*) Putnam Publishing Group, The.

—Atlantis Found. l.t. ed. 2000. (Dirk Pitt Adventure Ser.). 843p. 31.95 (*0-7862-2283-2*) Thorndike Pr.

—Clive Cussler: Floor Tide & Cyclops. 2001. (Dirk Pitt Adventure Ser.). 992p. 15.99 (*0-517-16277-6*) Random Hse., Inc.

—Cyclops. 1993. audio compact disk 120.00 (*0-7366-8282-1*); audio 96.00 (*0-7366-2567-4*, 3316) Books on Tape, Inc.

—Cyclops. unabr. ed. 1987. audio 0.00 o.p. (*1-56100-033-7*, 569, Unabridged Library Editions); audio 0.00 o.p. (*0-930435-38-9*, 387, Bookcassette) Brilliance Audio.

—Cyclops. l.t. ed. 1987. (Dirk Pitt Adventure Ser.). 733p. 20.95 o.p. (*0-8161-4201-7*, Macmillan Reference USA) Gale Group.

—Cyclops. 2001. (SPA.). 656p. (*84-01-46604-0*) Plaza & Janés Editories, S.A.

—Cyclops. 1997. (Dirk Pitt Adventure Ser.). mass mkt. 3.99 (*0-671-01130-8*, Pocket) Simon & Schuster.

—Cyclops. McCarthy, Paul, ed. (Dirk Pitt Adventure Ser.). 480p. 1989. mass mkt. 7.99 (*0-671-70464-8*); 1986. mass mkt. 4.95 o.s.i (*0-671-63184-5*) Simon & Schuster. (Pocket).

—Cyclops. 1986. (Dirk Pitt Adventure Ser.). 18.45 o.p. (*0-671-50374-X*, Simon & Schuster) Simon & Schuster.

—Cyclops. (Dirk Pitt Adventure Ser.). 1999. audio 9.98 (*0-671-04690-X*); 1990. audio 17.00 (*0-671-70300-5*) Simon & Schuster Audio. (Simon & Schuster Audioworks).

—Deep Six. 1992. audio compact disk 88.00 (*0-7366-5965-X*); 2001. audio compact disk 88.00; 1992. audio 72.00 (*0-7366-2275-6*, 3063) Books on Tape, Inc.

—Deep Six. unabr. ed. 1988. audio 73.25 o.p. (*1-56100-034-5*, 572, Unabridged Library Editions); audio 19.95 o.p. (*0-930435-39-7*, 390, Bookcassette) Brilliance Audio.

—Deep Six. McCarthy, Paul, ed. (Dirk Pitt Adventure Ser.). 480p. 1990. mass mkt. 7.99 (*0-671-70945-3*); 1987. mass mkt. 4.95 o.s.i (*0-671-64804-7*) Simon & Schuster. (Pocket).

—Deep Six. 1984. (Dirk Pitt Adventure Ser.). 432p. 18.45 o.p. (*0-671-50373-1*, Simon & Schuster) Simon & Schuster.

—Deep Six. 2001. audio 9.98 (*0-7435-0478-X*); 1991. audio 17.00 (*0-671-70301-3*); Set. 1999. audio (*0-671-57762-X*, 390640) Simon & Schuster Audio. (Simon & Schuster Audioworks).

—Dirk Pitt Revealed. 1998. (Dirk Pitt Adventure Ser.). (Illus.). 516p. pap. 7.99 (*0-671-02622-4*, Pocket) Simon & Schuster.

—Dragon. unabr. ed. 1990. (Dirk Pitt Adventure Ser.).Tr. of Dragon. audio 88.00 (*0-7366-1791-4*, 2628) Books on Tape, Inc.

—Dragon. l.t. ed. 1991. (Dirk Pitt Adventure Ser.).Tr. of Dragon. 654p. 24.95 (*0-8161-5096-6*, Macmillan Reference USA) Gale Group.

—Dragon. 1995. Tr. of Dragon. (SPA.). 720p. (*84-01-46603-2*) Plaza & Janés Editories, S.A.

—Dragon. 1990. (Dirk Pitt Adventure Ser.).Tr. of Dragon. 263.40 (*0-671-94486-X*); 21.95 o.p. (*0-671-62619-1*) Simon & Schuster. (Simon & Schuster).

—Dragon. McCarthy, Paul, ed. 1991. (Dirk Pitt Adventure Ser.).Tr. of Dragon. 352p. reprint ed. mass mkt. 7.99 (*0-671-74276-0*, Pocket) Simon & Schuster.

—Dragon. abr. ed. (Dirk Pitt Adventure Ser.).Tr. of Dragon. 1990. pap. 17.00 incl. audio (*0-671-70302-1*); Set. 1999. audio (*0-671-57763-8*, 390679) Simon & Schuster Audio. (Simon & Schuster Audioworks).

—Flood Tide. unabr. ed. 1998. (Dirk Pitt Adventure Ser.). audio 120.00 (*0-7366-4066-5*, 4577) Books on Tape, Inc.

—Flood Tide. 2003. 560p. mass mkt. 5.99 o.s.i (*0-7434-6730-2*, Pocket); 2002. 560p. mass mkt. 7.99 (*0-7434-5646-7*, Pocket); 1998. 560p. mass mkt. 7.99 (*0-671-00031-4*, Pocket); 1997. (Illus.). 512p. 26.00 o.s.i (*0-684-80298-8*, Simon & Schuster); 2002. 592p. reprint ed. pap. 16.00 (*0-7434-4210-5*, Pocket) Simon & Schuster.

—Flood Tide. abr. ed. 1997. (Dirk Pitt Adventure Ser.). audio 25.00 (*0-671-57719-0*, 495422, Simon & Schuster Audioworks) Simon & Schuster Audio.

—Flood Tide. l.t. ed. 1999. (Dirk Pitt Adventure Ser.). 914p. pap. 28.95 (*0-7862-1270-5*) Thorndike Pr.

—Iceberg. 1984. (Dirk Pitt Adventure Ser.). mass mkt. 3.95 o.s.i (*0-553-14641-6*) Bantam Bks.

—Iceberg. 2004. 352p. mass mkt. 7.99 (*0-425-19738-7*) Berkley Publishing Group.

—Iceberg. unabr. ed. 1992. (Dirk Pitt Adventure Ser.). audio 56.00 (*0-7366-2226-8*, 3016) Books on Tape, Inc.

—Iceberg. 1994. (Dirk Pitt Adventure Ser.). reprint ed. lib. bdg. 32.95 (*1-56849-270-7*) Buccaneer Bks., Inc.

—Iceberg. 2001. (SPA.). 376p. (*84-01-46609-1*) Plaza & Janés Editories, S.A.

—Iceberg. 1996. (Dirk Pitt Adventure Ser.). 256p. 24.00 (*0-684-82689-5*, Simon & Schuster) Simon & Schuster.

—Iceberg. McCarthy, Paul, ed. 1991. (Dirk Pitt Adventure Ser.). 304p. mass mkt. 7.99 o.s.i (*0-671-73777-5*, Pocket) Simon & Schuster.

—Iceberg. 1988. mass mkt. 4.95 o.s.i (*0-671-67041-7*); 1986. mass mkt. 4.50 o.s.i (*0-671-63255-8*); 1986. mass mkt. 3.95 o.s.i (*0-671-61850-4*) Simon & Schuster. (Pocket).

—Iceberg. abr. ed. 1996. (Dirk Pitt Adventure Ser.). 3p. audio 18.00 (*0-671-57376-4*, 394186, Simon & Schuster Audioworks) Simon & Schuster Audio.

—Iceberg. abr. ed. 2000. (Dirk Pitt Adventure Ser.). 192p. (YA). (gr. 7-12). per. 4.99 (*0-671-78626-1*, Simon Pulse) Simon & Schuster Children's Publishing.

—Inca Gold. unabr. ed. 1995. (Dirk Pitt Adventure Ser.). audio 120.00 (*0-7366-2896-7*, 3596) Books on Tape, Inc.

—Inca Gold. l.t. ed. (Dirk Pitt Adventure Ser.). 1995. 762p. lib. bdg. 18.95 o.p. (*0-8161-7444-X*); 1994. 850p. lib. bdg. 26.95 o.s.i (*0-8161-7443-1*) Gale Group. (Macmillan Reference USA).

—Inca Gold. McCarthy, Paul, ed. 1995. (Dirk Pitt Adventure Ser.). 592p. mass mkt. 7.99 (*0-671-51981-6*, Pocket) Simon & Schuster.

—Inca Gold. 1994. (Dirk Pitt Adventure Ser.). 537p. 24.00 (*0-671-68156-7*, Simon & Schuster) Simon & Schuster.

—Inca Gold. abr. ed. 1994. (Dirk Pitt Adventure Ser.). audio 23.00 (*0-671-88758-0*, 492041, Simon & Schuster Audioworks) Simon & Schuster Audio.

—Inca Gold. abr. ed. 1998. (Dirk Pitt Adventure Ser.). 400p. (YA). (gr. 5 up). mass mkt. 4.99 (*0-671-02056-0*, Simon Pulse) Simon & Schuster Children's Publishing.

—The Mediterranean Caper. 1984. (Dirk Pitt Adventure Ser.). mass mkt. 3.95 o.s.i (*0-553-23328-9*) Bantam Bks.

—The Mediterranean Caper. 2004. 336p. mass mkt. 7.99 (*0-425-19739-5*) Berkley Publishing Group.

—The Mediterranean Caper. unabr. ed. 1992. (Dirk Pitt Adventure Ser.). audio 48.00 (*0-7366-2257-8*, 3046) Books on Tape, Inc.

—The Mediterranean Caper. 1994. (Dirk Pitt Adventure Ser.). reprint ed. lib. bdg. 32.95 (*1-56849-271-5*) Buccaneer Bks., Inc.

—The Mediterranean Caper. l.t. ed. 2000. (Dirk Pitt Adventure Ser.). 327p. lib. bdg. 27.95 o.p. (*1-58547-014-7*) Ctr. Point Large Print.

—The Mediterranean Caper. 1996. (Dirk Pitt Adventure Ser.). 224p. 24.00 (*0-684-82690-9*, Simon & Schuster) Simon & Schuster.

—The Mediterranean Caper. McCarthy, Paul, ed. rev. ed. 1991. (Dirk Pitt Adventure Ser.). 256p. mass mkt. 7.99 o.s.i (*0-671-73778-3*, Pocket) Simon & Schuster.

—The Mediterranean Caper. abr. ed. 1996. (Dirk Pitt Adventure Ser.). audio 18.00 (*0-671-57377-2*, 394194, Simon & Schuster Audioworks) Simon & Schuster Audio.

—The Mediterranean Caper & Iceberg. 1995. (Dirk Pitt Adventure Ser.). 448p. 27.95 o.s.i (*0-684-82599-6*, Simon & Schuster) Simon & Schuster.

—Night Probe! (Dirk Pitt Adventure Ser.). 1991. mass mkt. 2.99 o.s.i (*0-553-19642-1*); 1984. 352p. mass mkt. 7.99 (*0-553-27740-5*); 1981. 352p. 13.95 o.p. (*0-553-05004-4*) Bantam Bks.

—Night Probe! unabr. ed. 1993. (Dirk Pitt Adventure Ser.). audio 72.00 (*0-7366-2343-4*, 3122) Books on Tape, Inc.

—Night Probe! 1982. (Dirk Pitt Adventure Ser.). 17.95 o.p. (*0-8161-3346-8*, Macmillan Reference USA) Gale Group.

—Pacific Vortex. 1984. (Dirk Pitt Adventure Ser.). 288p. mass mkt. 7.99 (*0-553-27632-8*) Bantam Bks.

—Pacific Vortex. (Dirk Pitt Adventure Ser.). (Illus.). 270p. 45.00 (*1-893205-27-4*); (*1-893205-28-2*) Cahill, James Publishing.

—Pacific Vortex. l.t. ed. 1985. (Dirk Pitt Adventure Ser.). 15.95 o.p. (*0-8161-3887-7*, Macmillan Reference USA) Gale Group.

—Pacific Vortex! unabr. ed. 1993. (Dirk Pitt Adventure Ser.). audio 48.00 (*0-7366-2484-8*, 3246) Books on Tape, Inc.

—Raise the Titanic! 1984. (Dirk Pitt Adventure Ser.). 384p. mass mkt. 4.50 o.s.i (*0-553-25896-6*) Bantam Bks.

—Raise the Titanic! McCarthy, Paul, ed. (Dirk Pitt Adventure Ser.). 352p. 1990. mass mkt. 7.99 o.s.i (*0-671-72519-X*); 1988. mass mkt. 4.95 (*0-671-66718-1*) Simon & Schuster. (Pocket).

—Raise the Titanic. 2004. 448p. mass mkt. 7.99 (*0-425-19452-3*) Berkley Publishing Group.

—Raise the Titanic. 1976. 8.95 o.p. (*0-670-58933-0*) Viking Penguin.

—Raise the Titanic! unabr. ed. 1991. (Dirk Pitt Adventure Ser.). audio 72.00 (*0-7366-2024-9*, 2839) Books on Tape, Inc.

—Raise the Titanic! 1994. (Dirk Pitt Adventure Ser.). reprint ed. lib. bdg. 32.95 (*1-56849-269-3*) Buccaneer Bks., Inc.

—Raise the Titanic! l.t. ed. 2000. (Dirk Pitt Adventure Ser.). 489p. lib. bdg. 28.95 o.p. (*1-58547-003-1*) Ctr. Point Large Print.

—The Red Horseman. abr. ed. 1999. (Dirk Pitt Adventure Ser.). audio 9.98 (*0-671-04413-3*, Simon & Schuster Audioworks) Simon & Schuster Audio.

—Sahara. unabr. ed. 1992. (Dirk Pitt Adventure Ser.). audio 104.00 (*0-7366-2264-0*, 3052) Books on Tape, Inc.

—Sahara. l.t. ed. 1993. (Dirk Pitt Adventure Ser.). 767p. lib. bdg. 18.95 o.s.i (*0-8161-5659-X*); 23.95 o.p. (*0-8161-5658-1*) Gale Group. (Macmillan Reference USA).

—Sahara. 5th ed. 1996. (SPA., Illus.). 656p. (*84-01-46601-6*) Plaza & Janés Editories, S.A.

—Sahara. (Dirk Pitt Adventure Ser.). 1995. 576p. mass mkt. 7.99 (*0-671-52110-1*, Pocket); 1992. (Illus.). 412p. 23.00 o.p. (*0-671-68155-9*, Simon & Schuster); 2002. 608p. reprint ed. pap. 16.00 (*0-7434-4211-3*, Pocket) Simon & Schuster.

—Sahara. McCarthy, Paul, ed. 1993. (Dirk Pitt Adventure Ser.). 576p. reprint ed. mass mkt. 6.99 o.s.i (*0-671-86731-8*, Pocket) Simon & Schuster.

—Sahara. abr. ed. (Dirk Pitt Adventure Ser.). 1999. audio (*0-671-57764-6*, 391506); 1992. audio 17.00 (*0-671-78400-5*) Simon & Schuster Audio. (Simon & Schuster Audioworks).

—Shock Wave. unabr. ed. 1996. (Dirk Pitt Adventure Ser.). audio 104.00 (*0-7366-3341-3*, 3990) Books on Tape, Inc.

—Shock Wave. l.t. ed. 1997. (Dirk Pitt Adventure Ser.). pap. 25.95 (*0-7838-1578-6*, Macmillan Reference USA) Gale Group.

—Shock Wave. (Dirk Pitt Adventure Ser.). 2002. 576p. pap. 16.00 (*0-7434-2679-7*, Pocket); 1996. 592p. mass mkt. 7.99 (*0-671-00030-6*, Pocket); 1996. 544p. 25.00 (*0-684-80297-X*, Simon & Schuster) Simon & Schuster.

—Shock Wave. abr. ed. 1996. (Dirk Pitt Adventure Ser.). audio 25.00 (*0-671-56762-4*, 493335, Simon & Schuster Audioworks) Simon & Schuster Audio.

—Shock Wave. 1998. (Dirk Pitt Adventure Ser.). (Illus.). 368p. (YA). mass mkt. 4.99 (*0-671-02055-2*, Simon Pulse) Simon & Schuster Children's Publishing.

—Shock Wave. l.t. ed. 1996. (Dirk Pitt Adventure Ser.). 757p. lib. bdg. 29.95 (*0-7838-1579-4*) Thorndike Pr.

—Treasure. unabr. ed. 1993. (Dirk Pitt Adventure Ser.). audio 96.00 (*0-7366-2450-3*, 3214) Books on Tape, Inc.

—Treasure. l.t. ed. 1988. (Dirk Pitt Adventure Ser.). 706p. 20.95 o.p. (*0-8161-4681-0*, Macmillan Reference USA) Gale Group.

—Treasure. McCarthy, Paul, ed. (Dirk Pitt Adventure Ser.). 1989. 544p. mass mkt. 7.99 (*0-671-70465-6*); 1988. 560p. bds. 4.95 o.s.i (*0-671-67113-8*) Simon & Schuster. (Pocket).

—Treasure. 1988. (Dirk Pitt Adventure Ser.). 400p. 18.95 o.p. (*0-671-62613-2*, Simon & Schuster) Simon & Schuster.

—Treasure. abr. ed. (Dirk Pitt Adventure Ser.). 1988. audio 17.00 (*0-671-66838-2*); 1988. audio 17.00 (*0-671-66863-3*); Set. 1999. audio (*0-671-57765-4*, 391801) Simon & Schuster Audio. (Simon & Schuster Audioworks).

—Trojan Odyssey: A Dirk Pitt Novel. 2003. (Dirk Pitt Adventure Ser.: No. 17). 496p. 27.95 (*0-399-15080-3*) Putnam Publishing Group, The.

—Valhalla Rising. 2001. audio 104.00 (*0-7366-7168-4*); audio compact disk 19.99. audio compact disk 128.00 (*0-7366-7561-2*); audio 104.00. audio compact disk 128.00 Books on Tape, Inc.

—Valhalla Rising. l.t. ed. 2002. (Basic Ser.). 805p. 32.95 (*0-7862-3813-5*) Gale Group.
—Valhalla Rising. 2002. audio compact disk (*0-14-180372-X*) Penguin Bks., Ltd.
—Valhalla Rising. 2001. (Illus.). 544p. 27.95 o.s.i (*0-399-14787-X*); 4p. audio 24.95 o.s.i (*0-399-14816-7*, Putnam Berkley Audio); 5p. audio compact disk 29.95 (*0-399-14817-5*, Putnam Berkley Audio); 12p. audio 49.95 o.s.i (*0-399-14818-3*, Putnam Berkley Audio) Penguin Group (USA) Inc.
—Valhalla Rising. l.t. ed. 2002. 832p. pap. 29.95 (*0-7862-3818-6*) Thorndike Pr.
—Valhalla Rising. abr. ed. 2001. audio (*0-14-180343-6*, Penguin AudioBooks) Viking Penguin.
—Vixen 03. 1976. (Dirk Pitt Adventure Ser.). 23.95 (*0-8488-0470-8*) Amereon, Ltd.
—Vixen 03. 1984. mass mkt. 4.50 o.s.i (*0-553-25487-1*);Vol. 3. 384p. mass mkt. 7.99 (*0-553-27390-6*) Bantam Bks.
—Vixen 03. unabr. ed. 1993. (Dirk Pitt Adventure Ser.). audio 64.00 (*0-7366-2364-7*, 1993) Books on Tape, Inc.
—Vixen 03. 1994. (Dirk Pitt Adventure Ser.). reprint ed. lib. bdg. 32.95 (*1-56849-272-3*) Buccaneer Bks., Inc.
—Vixen 03. l.t. ed. 2000. (Dirk Pitt Adventure Ser.). 583p. 28.95 (*0-7862-2492-4*, MML06400-171841); (*0-7540-1437-1*); (*0-7540-2329-X*) Thorndike Pr.
—Vixen 03. 1978. (Dirk Pitt Adventure Ser.). 9.95 o.p. (*0-670-74741-6*) Viking Penguin.

**PITT, THOMAS, INSPECTOR (FICTITIOUS CHARACTER)—FICTION**

Perry, Anne. Ashworth Hall. 1998. 384p. mass mkt. 7.50 (*0-449-00086-9*, Fawcett) Ballantine Bks.
—Bedford Square. 2000. 336p. mass mkt. 6.99 (*0-449-00582-8*, Ballantine Bks.); 1995. o.p. (*0-449-90633-7*, Fawcett) Ballantine Bks.
—Bedford Square. l.t. ed. 1999. (Basic Ser.). 571p. 30.95 (*0-7862-2018-X*) Thorndike Pr.
—Belgrave Square. 1993. 384p. mass mkt. 6.99 (*0-449-22227-6*, Fawcett) Ballantine Bks.
—Belgrave Square. 1994. 4.99 o.p. (*0-517-12853-5*) Random Hse. Value Publishing.
—Bethlehem Road. 1991. 320p. mass mkt. 5.99 o.p. (*0-449-45316-2*); mass mkt. 6.99 (*0-449-21914-3*) Ballantine Bks. (Fawcett).
—Bethlehem Road. l.t. ed. 2001. (Dales Large Print Ser.). 464p. pap. (*1-84262-093-2*) Dales Large Print Bks. GBR. *Dist:* Ulverscroft Large Print Canada, Ltd.
—Bethlehem Road. 1990. 17.95 o.p. (*0-312-04266-3*, Saint Martin's Minotaur) St. Martin's Pr.
—Bethlehem Road. l.t. ed. 1993. (Mystery Ser.). 592p. 29.99 o.p. (*0-7089-2939-7*, Ulverscroft) Thorpe, F. A. Pubs. GBR. *Dist:* Ulverscroft Large Print Bks., Ltd., Ulverscroft Large Print Canada, Ltd.
—Bluegate Fields. 1985. 288p. mass mkt. 6.99 (*0-449-20766-8*); mass mkt. 5.99 o.p. (*0-449-45317-0*) Ballantine Bks. (Fawcett).
—Bluegate Fields. l.t. ed. 2000. 398p. lib. bdg. 28.95 (*1-58547-017-1*) Ctr. Point Large Print.
—Bluegate Fields. l.t. ed. 2001. (Magna Large Print Ser.). 384p. (*0-7505-1709-3*) Magna Large Print Bks. GBR. *Dist:* Ulverscroft Large Print Canada, Ltd.
—Bluegate Fields. unabr. ed. 2002. audio 72.00 (*1-4025-3604-6*, Clipper Audio) Recorded Bks., LLC.
—Bluegate Fields. 1984. 320p. 13.95 o.p. (*0-312-08718-7*) St. Martin's Pr.
—Brunswick Gardens. 1999. 416p. mass mkt. 7.50 (*0-449-00318-3*, Fawcett) Ballantine Bks.
—Brunswick Gardens. (Charlotte & Thomas Pitt Novel Ser.). 2001. audio 9.99 (*0-375-41673-0*); Set. 1998. audio 18.00 o.s.i (*0-375-40177-6*) Random Hse. Audio Publishing Group. (RH Audio).
—Brunswick Gardens. l.t. ed. 1998. (Basic Ser.). 656p. 30.95 (*0-7862-1464-3*) Thorndike Pr.
—Callander Square. 1998. mass mkt. 3.99 o.s.i (*0-449-00461-9*); 1985. 256p. mass mkt. 6.99 (*0-449-20999-7*); 1981. mass mkt. 2.25 o.p. (*0-449-24365-6*) Ballantine Bks. (Fawcett).
—Callander Square. 1980. 10.00 o.p. (*0-312-11430-3*) St. Martin's Pr.
—Callander Square. l.t. ed. 1981. 447p. 12.00 o.p. (*0-7089-0718-0*, Ulverscroft) Thorpe, F. A. Pubs. GBR. *Dist:* Ulverscroft Large Print Bks., Ltd.
—Cardington Crescent. 1988. 304p. reprint ed. mass mkt. 6.99 (*0-449-21442-7*, Fawcett) Ballantine Bks.
—Cardington Crescent. l.t. ed. 2001. 375p. lib. bdg. 28.95 (*1-58547-015-5*) Ctr. Point Large Print.
—Cardington Crescent. unabr. ed. 1998. audio 83.95 (*1-85903-217-6*) Magna Story Sound GBR. *Dist:* Ulverscroft Large Print Bks., Ltd.
—Cardington Crescent. 1987. 304p. 15.95 o.p. (*0-312-00113-4*) St. Martin's Pr.
—The Cater Street Hangman. 1998. mass mkt. 3.99 o.s.i (*0-449-00460-0*); 1985. 288p. mass mkt. 6.99 (*0-449-20867-2*); 1980. mass mkt. 2.25 o.s.i (*0-449-24327-3*) Ballantine Bks. (Fawcett).
—The Cater Street Hangman. l.t. ed. 2000. 364p. lib. bdg. 27.95 (*1-58547-002-3*) Ctr. Point Large Print.
—The Cater Street Hangman. 1979. 8.95 o.p. (*0-312-12385-X*) St. Martin's Pr.
—Death in the Devil's Acre. 1987. 272p. mass mkt. 6.99 (*0-449-21095-2*, Fawcett) Ballantine Bks.
—Death in the Devil's Acre. l.t. ed. 2001. lib. bdg. 27.95 (*1-58547-016-3*) Ctr. Point Large Print.
—Death in the Devil's Acre. 1985. 288p. 14.95 o.p. (*0-312-18869-2*) St. Martin's Pr.
—Farriers' Lane. 1994. 432p. mass mkt. 7.50 (*0-449-21961-5*, Fawcett) Ballantine Bks.
—Half Moon Street. 2001. 320p. mass mkt. 6.99 (*0-449-00655-7*, Ballantine Bks.) Ballantine Bks.
—Half Moon Street. l.t. ed. 2000. 439p. 27.95 (*1-56895-857-9*, Wheeler Publishing, Inc.) Gale Group.
—Half Moon Street. abr. ed. 2000. (Charlotte & Thomas Pitt Novel Ser.). audio 18.00 (*0-553-52710-X*, RH Audio) Random Hse. Audio Publishing Group.
—Highgate Rise. 1992. 352p. mass mkt. 7.50 (*0-449-21959-3*, Fawcett) Ballantine Bks.
—Highgate Rise. l.t. ed. 1994. (Ulverscroft Ser.). 672p. 21.95 o.p. (*0-7089-3013-1*, Ulverscroft) Thorpe, F. A. Pubs. GBR. *Dist:* Ulverscroft Large Print Bks., Ltd., Ulverscroft Large Print Canada, Ltd.
—The Hyde Park Headsman. 1995. 352p. mass mkt. 7.50 (*0-449-22350-7*); 1994. 432p. 21.00 o.s.i (*0-449-90636-1*) Ballantine Bks. (Fawcett).
—Paragon Walk. 1986. 256p. mass mkt. 6.99 (*0-449-21168-1*); 1986. mass mkt. 5.99 (*0-449-45319-7*); 1982. mass mkt. 2.50 o.p. (*0-449-20110-4*); 1982. 224p. mass mkt. 2.50 o.p. (*0-449-24497-0*) Ballantine Bks. (Fawcett).
—Paragon Walk. l.t. ed. 2000. 308p. lib. bdg. 27.95 (*1-58547-005-8*) Ctr. Point Large Print.
—Paragon Walk. 1981. 224p. 9.95 o.p. (*0-312-59598-0*) St. Martin's Pr.
—Pentecost Alley. 1997. (Charlotte & Thomas Pitt Novel Ser.). 416p. mass mkt. 6.99 (*0-449-22566-6*, Fawcett) Ballantine Bks.
—Pentecost Alley. l.t. ed. 1996. (Cloak & Dagger Ser.). 708p. 27.95 (*0-7862-0812-0*) Thorndike Pr.
—Resurrection Row. 1986. 224p. mass mkt. 6.99 (*0-449-21067-7*, Fawcett) Ballantine Bks.
—Resurrection Row. l.t. ed. 2000. 312p. lib. bdg. 27.95 (*1-58547-009-0*) Ctr. Point Large Print.
—Resurrection Row. 1981. 224p. 9.95 o.p. (*0-312-67797-9*) St. Martin's Pr.
—Rutland Place. 1986. 224p. mass mkt. 6.99 (*0-449-21285-8*); 1986. 224p. mass mkt. 5.99 o.p. (*0-449-45318-9*); 1984. mass mkt. 2.50 o.p. (*0-449-20474-X*) Ballantine Bks. (Fawcett).
—Rutland Place. l.t. ed. 2000. 319p. lib. bdg. 27.95 (*1-58547-013-9*) Ctr. Point Large Print.
—Rutland Place. 224p. (*0-7278-5864-5*) Severn Hse. Pubs., Ltd.
—Rutland Place. 1983. 256p. 12.95 o.p. (*0-312-69621-3*) St. Martin's Pr.
—Seven Dials. 2004. 352p. mass mkt. 7.50 (*0-345-44008-0*); 2003. 352p. 25.95 (*0-345-44007-2*, Ballantine Bks.); 2003. E-Book 17.85 (*0-345-46352-8*, Ballantine Bks.) Ballantine Bks.
—Seven Dials. abr. ed. 2003. (Thomas & Charlotte Pitt Ser.: Vol. 23). audio 24.95 (*1-59086-499-9*, 4093, Nova Audio Bks.); audio compact disk 102.25 (*1-59086-501-4*, 4092) Brilliance Audio.
—Seven Dials. 2003. (Basic Ser.). 552p. 32.95 (*0-7862-5210-3*) Thorndike Pr.
—The Silence in Hanover Close. 1989. 352p. mass mkt. 7.50 (*0-449-21686-1*, Fawcett) Ballantine Bks.
—The Silence in Hanover Close. 1988. 384p. 17.95 o.p. (*0-312-01824-X*, Saint Martin's Minotaur) St. Martin's Pr.
—The Silence in Hanover Close. l.t. ed. 1990. (Mystery Ser.). 29.99 o.p. (*0-7089-2324-0*, Ulverscroft) Thorpe, F. A. Pubs. GBR. *Dist:* Ulverscroft Large Print Bks., Ltd., Ulverscroft Large Print Canada, Ltd.
—Southampton Row. 2003. 352p. mass mkt. 7.50 (*0-345-44004-8*); 2002. 336p. 25.00 (*0-345-44003-X*) Ballantine Bks. (Ballantine Bks.).
—Southampton Row. 2002. E-Book 20.00 (*1-4014-9974-0*) Barnes & Noble Digital.
—Southampton Row. abr. ed. (Thomas & Charlotte Pitt Ser.). 2005. audio compact disk 16.99 (*1-59355-704-3*, 5322, Brilliance Audio on CD Value Priced); 2003. audio 12.99 (*1-58788-918-8*, 3436, Brilliance Audio Paperback Audiobooks); 2002. audio 24.95 (*1-58788-915-3*, 3433, Nova Audio Bks.); 2002. audio compact disk 69.25 (*1-58788-917-X*, 3435, CD Library Edition); 2002. audio compact disk 29.95 (*1-58788-916-1*, 3434, CD); 2002. audio 89.25 (*1-58788-914-5*, 3432, Unabridged Library Editions); 2002. audio 34.95 (*1-58788-913-7*, 3431, Brilliance Audio Unabridged) Brilliance Audio.
—Southampton Row. unabr. ed. 2003. (Thomas & Charlotte Pitt Ser.). audio 19.99 (*1-59335-166-6*, 30262) Soulmate Audio Bks., Inc.
—Southampton Row. l.t. ed. 13.95 (*1-4104-0092-1*, Large Print Pr.); 2003. 571p. pap. 27.95 (*0-7862-4502-6*); 2002. 588p. 30.95 o.p. (*0-7862-4066-0*) Thorndike Pr.
—Traitor's Gate. 1996. 432p. mass mkt. 7.50 (*0-449-22439-2*, Fawcett) Ballantine Bks.
—The Whitechapel Conspiracy. unabr. ed. 2003. 10p. audio 84.95 (*0-7540-0858-4*, CAB 2280); audio compact disk 99.95 (*0-7540-5597-3*, CCD 288) BBC Audiobooks America.
—The Whitechapel Conspiracy. 2002. (Thomas & Charlotte Pitt Ser.). 352p. reprint ed. mass mkt. 6.99 (*0-449-00656-5*, Ballantine Bks.) Ballantine Bks.
—The Whitechapel Conspiracy. l.t. ed. 2001. 515p. 31.95 (*0-7838-9513-5*, Macmillan Reference USA) Gale Group.
—The Whitechapel Conspiracy. abr. ed. 2001. audio 25.95 (*0-553-52789-4*, RH Audio) Random Hse. Audio Publishing Group.

**PITTMAN, MRS. (FICTITIOUS CHARACTER)—FICTION**

Rinehart, Mary Roberts. The Case of Jennie Brice. 1997. 160p. mass mkt. 5.50 o.s.i (*1-57566-135-7*) Kensington Publishing Corp.

**PITTMORE, DARNELL (FICTITIOUS CHARACTER)—FICTION**

Strunk, Frank C. Throwback. 1997. 448p. mass mkt. 6.50 o.s.i (*0-06-101058-8*); 1996. 320p. mass mkt. 20.00 o.s.i (*0-06-101057-X*) Morrow/Avon. (HarperTorch).

**PLANT, MELROSE (FICTITIOUS CHARACTER)—FICTION**

Grimes, Martha. The Anodyne Necklace. 1990. 256p. reprint ed. mass mkt. 5.99 o.s.i (*0-440-10280-4*) Dell Publishing.
—The Anodyne Necklace. 1983. 252p. 15.95 o.p. (*0-316-32882-0*) Little Brown & Co.
—The Anodyne Necklace. 2004. 320p. mass mkt. 7.99 (*0-451-41089-0*, Onyx) NAL.
—The Anodyne Necklace. abr. ed. 1999. audio 9.98 (*0-671-04429-X*, Simon & Schuster Audioworks) Simon & Schuster Audio.
—The Anodyne Necklace. l.t. ed. 1983. 420p. reprint ed. 13.95 o.p. (*0-89621-486-9*) Thorndike Pr.
—The Case Has Altered: A Richard Jury Mystery. unabr. ed. 1998. audio 72.00 (*0-7366-4072-X*, 4581) Books on Tape, Inc.
—The Case Has Altered: A Richard Jury Mystery. l.t. ed. 1998. (Wheeler Large Print Book Ser.). 515p. 27.95 o.p. (*1-56895-546-4*, Wheeler Publishing, Inc.) Gale Group.
—The Case Has Altered: A Richard Jury Mystery. 1997. 384p. 24.00 o.s.i (*0-8050-5620-3*) Holt, Henry & Co.
—The Case Has Altered: A Richard Jury Mystery. 1998. 432p. mass mkt. 7.99 (*0-451-40868-3*, Onyx) NAL.
—The Case Has Altered: A Richard Jury Mystery. abr. ed. 1997. audio 24.00 (*0-671-57756-5*, 595585, Simon & Schuster Audioworks) Simon & Schuster Audio.
—The Deer Leap. 1986. 256p. mass mkt. 6.99 o.s.i (*0-440-11938-3*) Dell Publishing.
—The Deer Leap. 1985. 15.95 o.p. (*0-316-32886-3*) Little Brown & Co.
—The Dirty Duck. 1990. 256p. mass mkt. 6.99 o.s.i (*0-440-12050-0*) Dell Publishing.
—The Dirty Duck. 1984. 252p. 14.95 o.s.i (*0-316-32883-9*) Little Brown & Co.
—The Dirty Duck. abr. ed. 1993. (Inspector Richard Jury Ser.). audio 16.00 (*0-671-75989-2*, 390661, Simon & Schuster Audioworks) Simon & Schuster Audio.
—The Five Bells & Bladebone. 1988. 384p. mass mkt. 6.99 o.s.i (*0-440-20133-0*) Dell Publishing.
—The Five Bells & Bladebone. 1987. 15.95 o.p. (*0-316-32889-8*) Little Brown & Co.
—The Five Bells & Bladebone. 2002. 352p. reprint ed. mass mkt. 6.99 (*0-451-41038-6*, Onyx) NAL.
—The Grave Maurice: A Richard Jury Mystery. 2003. 400p. mass mkt. 7.99 (*0-451-41101-3*, Onyx) NAL.
—The Grave Maurice: A Richard Jury Mystery. l.t. ed. 2003. (Core Ser.). 574p. 31.95 (*0-7862-4929-3*) Thorndike Pr.
—The Grave Maurice: A Richard Jury Mystery. 2002. 432p. 25.95 o.s.i (*0-670-03045-7*) Viking Penguin.
—Help the Poor Struggler. 1986. 240p. mass mkt. 6.99 o.s.i (*0-440-13584-2*) Dell Publishing.
—Help the Poor Struggler. 1985. 288p. 15.95 o.p. (*0-316-32884-7*) Little Brown & Co.
—The Horse You Came in On. 1994. 384p. mass mkt. 7.99 (*0-345-38755-4*) Ballantine Bks.
—The Horse You Came in On. l.t. ed. 1993. 19.00 o.s.i (*0-679-74770-2*) Random Hse. Large Print.
—The Horse You Came in On. unabr. ed. 1994. audio 70.00 (*0-7887-0003-0*, 94142E7) Recorded Bks., LLC.
—The Horse You Came in On. abr. ed. 1993. (Inspector Richard Jury Ser.). audio 17.00 (*0-671-87223-0*, 390934, Simon & Schuster Audioworks) Simon & Schuster Audio.
—I Am the Only Running Footman. 1990. 320p. mass mkt. 5.99 o.s.i (*0-440-13924-4*) Dell Publishing.
—I Am the Only Running Footman. 1986. 15.95 o.s.i (*0-316-32887-1*) Little Brown & Co.
—I Am the Only Running Footman. 2001. 320p. mass mkt. 6.99 (*0-451-41002-5*, Onyx) NAL.
—I Am the Only Running Footman. 1992. 4.99 o.p. (*0-517-09217-4*) Random Hse. Value Publishing.
—Jerusalem Inn. 1990. 288p. reprint ed. mass mkt. 6.99 o.s.i (*0-440-14181-8*) Doubleday Publishing.
—Jerusalem Inn. 1984. 288p. 15.95 o.s.i (*0-316-32879-0*) Little Brown & Co.
—The Lamorna Wink: A Richard Jury Mystery. 2000. 432p. reprint ed. mass mkt. 6.99 (*0-451-40936-1*, Onyx) NAL.
—The Lamorna Wink: A Richard Jury Mystery. l.t. ed. 2000. (Basic Ser.). 515p. 29.95 (*0-7862-2324-3*) Thorndike Pr.
—The Lamorna Wink: A Richard Jury Mystery. 1999. 3384p. 22.95 o.s.i (*0-670-88870-2*, Viking) Viking Penguin.
—The Man with a Load of Mischief. 1990. 320p. mass mkt. 5.99 o.s.i (*0-440-15327-1*) Dell Publishing.
—The Man with a Load of Mischief. 1981. 255p. 15.95 o.s.i (*0-316-32880-4*) Little Brown & Co.
—The Man with a Load of Mischief. 2003. 288p. mass mkt. 6.99 (*0-451-41081-5*, Onyx) NAL.
—The Man with a Load of Mischief. abr. ed. 1992. audio 16.00 (*0-671-75960-4*, Simon & Schuster Audioworks) Simon & Schuster Audio.
—The Man with a Load of Mischief. l.t. ed. 1984. 455p. reprint ed. 13.95 o.p. (*0-89621-514-8*) Thorndike Pr.
—The Old Contemptibles. 1992. 304p. mass mkt. 6.99 (*0-345-37456-8*); 1991. mass mkt. 5.99 o.s.i (*0-345-37515-7*) Ballantine Bks.
—The Old Contemptibles. unabr. ed. 1991. audio 56.00 (*0-7366-1954-2*, 2775) Books on Tape, Inc.
—The Old Contemptibles. 1991. 22.95 o.s.i (*0-316-32898-7*); 19.95 o.s.i (*0-316-32894-4*) Little Brown & Co.
—The Old Contemptibles. l.t. ed. 1995. (Magna Large Print Ser.). 531p. o.p. (*0-7505-0835-3*) Magna Large Print Bks. GBR. *Dist:* Ulverscroft Large Print Canada, Ltd.
—The Old Contemptibles. abr. ed. 1999. audio 9.98 (*0-671-04500-8*); 1991. audio 15.95 (*0-671-73569-1*, 391301) Simon & Schuster Audio. (Simon & Schuster Audioworks).
—The Old Fox Deceiv'd. 1991. 304p. mass mkt. 5.99 o.s.i (*0-440-16747-7*) Dell Publishing.
—The Old Fox Deceiv'd. 1982. 288p. 16.95 o.p. (*0-316-32881-2*) Little Brown & Co.
—The Old Fox Deceiv'd. 2003. 320p. mass mkt. 7.99 (*0-451-41068-8*) NAL.
—The Old Fox Deceiv'd. 1999. pap. 9.98 (*0-671-04430-3*); 1992. audio 16.00 (*0-671-75991-4*, 391302) Simon & Schuster Audio. (Simon & Schuster Audioworks).
—The Old Silent. unabr. ed. 1990. audio 72.00 (*0-7366-1833-3*, 2668) Books on Tape, Inc.
—The Old Silent. 448p. 1993. mass mkt. 3.99 o.s.i (*0-440-21519-6*); 1990. mass mkt. 6.99 o.s.i (*0-440-20492-5*) Dell Publishing.
—The Old Silent. 1989. 296p. 18.95 o.p. (*0-316-32318-7*) Little Brown & Co.
—The Old Silent. 1992. 5.99 o.p. (*0-517-07973-9*) Random Hse. Value Publishing.
—The Old Silent. abr. ed. 1992. audio 16.00 (*0-671-73617-5*, Simon & Schuster Audioworks) Simon & Schuster Audio.
—Rainbow's End. 1996. 448p. mass mkt. 7.50 (*0-345-39426-7*) Ballantine Bks.
—Rainbow's End. unabr. ed. 1995. audio 60.00 (*0-7366-3138-0*, 3813) Books on Tape, Inc.
—Rainbow's End. l.t. ed. 1995. 22.00 o.s.i (*0-679-76228-0*) Random Hse. Large Print.
—Rainbow's End. abr. ed. 1995. (Inspector Richard Jury Ser.). audio 17.00 (*0-671-53450-5*, 392985, Simon & Schuster Audioworks) Simon & Schuster Audio.
—The Stargazey: A Richard Jury Mystery. unabr. ed. 1999. audio 64.00 (*0-7366-4463-6*, 4908) Books on Tape, Inc.
—The Stargazey: A Richard Jury Mystery. 1998. 384p. 25.00 o.s.i (*0-8050-5622-X*) Holt, Henry & Co.
—The Stargazey: A Richard Jury Mystery. 1999. 432p. reprint ed. mass mkt. 7.99 (*0-451-40897-7*, Onyx) NAL.
—The Stargazey: A Richard Jury Mystery. l.t. ed. (Thorndike/G. K. Hall Paperback Bestsellers Ser.). 2000. 647p. pap. 27.95 (*0-7862-1789-8*); 1999. 581p. 30.95 (*0-7862-1788-X*) Thorndike Pr.

**PLANTAINE FAMILY (FICTITIOUS CHARACTERS)—FICTION**

Mosco, Maisie. Between Two Worlds. 1984. 480p. pap. 3.95 o.p. (*0-553-23421-8*) Bantam Bks.

—The Price of Fame. 1994. 400p. mass mkt. 5.50 o.p. (*0-06-100625-4*, HarperTorch) Morrow/Avon.
—The Price of Fame. l.t. ed. 1986. (Charnwood Large Print Ser.). 464p. 15.45 o.p. (*0-7089-8346-4*, Charnwood) Thorpe, F. A. Pubs. GBR. *Dist:* Ulverscroft Large Print Bks., Ltd., Ulverscroft Large Print Canada, Ltd.
—A Sense of Place. 1994. 432p. mass mkt. 5.50 o.p. (*0-06-100624-6*, HarperTorch) Morrow/Avon.
—A Sense of Place. l.t. ed. 1985. (Charnwood Large Print Ser.). 512p. 13.95 o.p. (*0-7089-8279-4*, Charnwood) Thorpe, F. A. Pubs. GBR. *Dist:* Ulverscroft Large Print Bks., Ltd., Ulverscroft Large Print Canada, Ltd.

**PLATO, CHARLIE (FICTITIOUS CHARACTER)—FICTION**

Chittenden, Margaret. Dead Beat & Deadly, 1. (Charlie Plato Mysteries Ser.). 1999. 320p. mass mkt. 5.99 o.s.i (*1-57566-436-4*); 1998. 304p. 20.00 o.s.i (*1-57566-314-7*, Kensington Bks.) Kensington Publishing Corp.
—Dead Men Don't Dance. 1998. (Charlie Plato Mysteries Ser.: Vol. 2). 304p. mass mkt. 5.99 o.s.i (*1-57566-318-X*); 1997. 320p. pap. 18.95 o.p. (*1-57566-184-5*, Kensington Bks.) Kensington Publishing Corp.
—Don't Forget to Die. 2000. 320p. mass mkt. 5.99 o.s.i (*1-57566-566-2*); 1999. 293p. 20.00 o.s.i (*1-57566-435-6*) Kensington Publishing Corp.
—Dying to See You. 2001. (Charlie Plato Mysteries Ser.). 256p. mass mkt. 5.99 o.s.i (*1-57566-669-3*) Kensington Publishing Corp.
—Dying to See You: A Charlie Plato Mystery. 2000. (Charlie Plato Mysteries Ser.). 311p. 20.00 o.s.i (*1-57566-561-1*) Kensington Publishing Corp.
—Dying to Sing. 288p. 1997. (Charlie Plato Mysteries Ser.: Vol. 1). mass mkt. 5.50 o.s.i (*1-57566-189-6*); 1996. 18.95 o.s.i (*1-57566-052-0*) Kensington Publishing Corp.

**PLUM, MARVIA (FICTITIOUS CHARACTER)—FICTION**

Evanovich, Janet. High Five. unabr. ed. 1999. (Stephanie Plum Novel Ser.: No. 5). audio 58.00 (*0-7887-3664-7*) Recorded Bks., LLC.
—Hot Six. unabr. ed. 2001. audio compact disk 78.00 (*0-7887-6173-0*) Recorded Bks., LLC.
—Three Plums in One: One for the Money, Two for the Dough, Three to Get Deadly. 2001. 800p. 23.00 (*0-7432-1639-3*); E-Book 9.99 (*0-7432-1666-0*) Simon & Schuster. (Scribner).
Lupoff, Richard A. The Bessie Blue Killer: A Hobart Lindsey - Marvia Plum Mystery. 1994. 304p. 20.95 o.p. (*0-312-10425-1*, Saint Martin's Minotaur) St. Martin's Pr.
—The Classic Car Killer. 1992. 288p. (Orig.). mass mkt. 4.99 o.s.i (*0-553-29607-8*) Bantam Bks.
—The Comic Book Killer. 1989. mass mkt. 3.95 o.s.i (*0-553-27781-2*) Bantam Bks.
—The Cover Girl Killer: A Hobart Lindsey - Marvia Plum Mystery. 1995. 224p. 21.95 o.p. (*0-312-13455-X*, Saint Martin's Minotaur) St. Martin's Pr.
—The Radio Red Killer. 1997. (Marvia Plum Mystery Ser.). 268p. text 22.95 o.p. (*0-312-17181-1*, Saint Martin's Minotaur) St. Martin's Pr.
—The Sepia Siren Killer. 1994. (Hobart Lidsey-Mariva Plum Mystery Ser.). 304p. 20.95 o.p. (*0-312-11332-3*, Saint Martin's Minotaur) St. Martin's Pr.
—The Silver Chariot Killer. 1996. 192p. text 21.95 o.p. (*0-312-14736-8*, Saint Martin's Minotaur) St. Martin's Pr.

**PLUM, STEPHANIE (FICTITIOUS CHARACTER)—FICTION**

Evanovich, Janet. Four to Score. abr. ed. audio (*1-55927-963-X*); 1999. (Stephanie Plum Novel Ser.: No. 4). audio 17.95 (*1-55927-544-8*) Audio Renaissance.
—Four to Score. abr. ed. 2001. audio compact disk 11.99 (*1-57815-544-4*, 1111); audio 7.95 (*1-57815-263-1*) Media Bks., L. L. C.
—Four to Score. (Stephanie Plum Novel Ser.: No. 4). 2000. audio compact disk 89.00 (*0-7887-4749-5*, C1235E7); 1999. audio 66.00 (*0-7887-2593-9*, 95613E7) Recorded Bks., LLC.
—Four to Score. 1999. E-Book 23.95 o.s.i (*0-312-20762-X*); 1998. (Stephanie Plum Novel Ser.: No. 4). 304p. 24.95 (*0-312-18586-3*); 1999. (Stephanie Plum Novel Ser.: No. 4). 352p. reprint ed. mass mkt. 7.99 (*0-312-96697-0*, St. Martin's Paperbacks) St. Martin's Pr.
—Four to Score. abr. ed. 1998. (Stephanie Plum Novel Ser.: No. 4). audio 15.00 (*0-333-74772-0*) Ulverscroft Audio (U.S.A.).
—Hard Eight. unabr. ed. 2002. (Illus.). audio 36.95 (*1-55927-725-4*); audio compact disk 40.00 (*1-55927-724-6*) Audio Renaissance.
—Hard Eight. abr. ed. 2001. (Stephanie Plum Ser.: Vol. 7). audio 19.95 o.p. (*1-58788-531-X*, 2802, Nova Audio Bks.); audio compact disk 27.95 o.p. (*1-58788-532-8*, 2803, CD); audio compact disk 61.25 (*1-58788-533-6*, 2804, CD Library Edition); audio 29.95 (*1-58788-529-8*, 2800, Brilliance Audio Unabridged); audio 69.25 (*1-58788-530-1*, 2801, Unabridged Library Editions) Brilliance Audio.
—Hard Eight. l.t. ed. 2002. 432p. 25.95 (*0-375-43170-5*) Random Hse., Inc.
—Hard Eight. 2003. 352p. mass mkt. 7.99 (*0-312-98386-7*, St. Martin's Paperbacks); 2003. mass mkt. 7.99 (*0-312-98894-X*, St. Martin's Paperbacks); 2002. 320p. 25.95 (*0-312-26585-9*); 2002. mass mkt. 7.99 (*0-312-98451-0*, St. Martin's Paperbacks) St. Martin's Pr.
—High Five. abr. ed. audio (*1-55927-964-8*); 1999. (Stephanie Plum Novel Ser.: No. 5). audio 17.95 (*1-55927-545-6*) Audio Renaissance.
—High Five. abr. ed. 2001. audio (*0-333-76587-7*) Macmillan U.K. GBR. *Dist:* Macmillan Publishing Co., Inc.
—High Five. abr. ed. 2002. audio compact disk 11.99 (*1-57815-545-2*); 2001. audio 7.95 (*1-57815-264-X*) Media Bks., L. L. C.
—High Five. unabr. ed. (Stephanie Plum Novel Ser.: No. 5). 2000. audio compact disk 75.00 (*0-7887-4200-0*, C1129E7); 1999. audio 60.00 (*0-7887-3464-4*, 95857E7) Recorded Bks., LLC.
—High Five. (Stephanie Plum Novel Ser.: No. 5). 2000. 340p. mass mkt. 7.99 (*0-312-97134-6*, St. Martin's Paperbacks); 3rd ed. 1999. 292p. 24.95 (*0-312-20303-9*) St. Martin's Pr.
—High Five. l.t. ed. 1999. (Stephanie Plum Novel Ser.: No. 5). 419p. 30.95 (*0-7862-2107-0*) Thorndike Pr.
—Hot Six. abr. ed. audio (*1-55927-965-6*); 2000. (Stephanie Plum Novel Ser.: No. 6). audio 17.95 (*1-55927-605-3*) Audio Renaissance.
—Hot Six. l.t. ed. 2000. (Stephanie Plum Novel Ser.: No. 6). 350p. 31.95 (*0-7838-9083-4*, Macmillan Reference USA) Gale Group.
—Hot Six. abr. ed. 2001. audio (*0-333-78251-8*) Macmillan U.K. GBR. *Dist:* Macmillan Publishing Co., Inc.
—Hot Six. abr. ed. 2002. audio 7.95 (*1-57815-265-8*); audio compact disk 11.99 (*1-57815-546-0*, 1111) Media Bks., L. L. C.
—Hot Six. unabr. ed. 2000. (Stephanie Plum Novel Ser.: No. 6). audio 67.00 (*0-7887-4848-3*, 96103E7) Recorded Bks., LLC.
—Hot Six. 2001. (Stephanie Plum Novel Ser.: No. 6). 352p. mass mkt. 7.99 (*0-312-97627-5*, St. Martin's Paperbacks); 2000. (Stephanie Plum Novel Ser.: No. 6). x, 294p. 24.95 (*0-312-20540-6*); 2000. 0.01 (*0-312-26526-3*) St. Martin's Pr.
—Hot Six. l.t. ed. 2001. (Stephanie Plum Novel Ser.: No. 6). 350p. pap. 29.95 (*0-7838-9082-6*) Thorndike Pr.
—One for the Money. abr. ed. 2001. audio (*0-333-78015-9*) Macmillan U.K. GBR. *Dist:* Macmillan Publishing Co., Inc.
—One for the Money. 2002. (Stephanie Plum Novel Ser.: No. 1). 304p. mass mkt. 7.99 o.s.i (*0-06-100905-9*, HarperTorch) Morrow/Avon.
—One for the Money. unabr. ed. (Stephanie Plum Novel Ser.: No. 1). 1999. audio compact disk 66.00 (*0-7887-3406-7*, C1012E7); 1995. audio 51.00 (*0-7887-0449-4*, 94639E7) Recorded Bks., LLC.
—One for the Money. (Stephanie Plum Novel Ser.: No. 1). 2000. E-Book 20.00 (*0-684-86731-1*); 1994. 288p. 25.00 (*0-684-19639-5*) Simon & Schuster. (Scribner).
—One for the Money. abr. ed. (Stephanie Plum Novel Ser.: No. 1). 2000. audio compact disk 9.98 (*0-7435-1838-1*); 1996. audio 17.00 o.s.i (*0-671-56255-X*, 393338) Simon & Schuster Audio. (Simon & Schuster Audioworks).
—One for the Money. Date not set. pap. (*0-312-31635-6*); 2003. (Illus.). 352p. reprint ed. mass mkt. 7.99 (*0-312-99045-6*) St. Martin's Pr. (St. Martin's Paperbacks).
—One for the Money. l.t. ed. 1995. (Stephanie Plum Novel Ser.: No. 1). 333p. 23.95 (*0-7838-1186-1*) Thorndike Pr.
—Seven Up. l.t. ed. 2001. (Stephanie Plum Novel Ser.: Bk. 7). 400p. 24.95 (*0-375-43111-X*) Random Hse. Large Print.
—Seven Up. 2001. (Stephanie Plum Novel Ser.: Bk. 7). 309p. 24.95 (*0-312-26584-0*) St. Martin's Pr.
—Stephanie Plum. ARK. mass mkt. (*0-312-98534-7*, St. Martin's Paperbacks); Vol. 11. E-Book (*0-312-70499-2*) St. Martin's Pr.
—Three Plums in One: One for the Money, Two for the Dough, Three to Get Deadly, Set. abr. ed. 2001. audio compact disk 39.95 (*0-7435-0947-1*, Simon & Schuster Audioworks) Simon & Schuster Audio.
—Three to Get Deadly. l.t. ed. 1997. (Stephanie Plum Novel Ser.: No. 3). 25.95 o.p. (*1-56895-429-8*, Wheeler Publishing, Inc.) Gale Group.
—Three to Get Deadly. 2001. audio (*0-333-78011-6*) Macmillan U.K. GBR. *Dist:* Macmillan Publishing Co., Inc.
—Three to Get Deadly. unabr. ed. (Stephanie Plum Novel Ser.: No. 3). 2000. audio compact disk 89.00 (*0-7887-3964-6*, C1119E7); 1997. audio 60.00 (*0-7887-0927-5*, 95067E7) Recorded Bks., LLC.
—Three to Get Deadly. (Stephanie Plum Novel Ser.: No. 3). 1998. E-Book 24.00 (*0-684-86860-1*); 1997. 304p. 25.00 (*0-684-82265-2*); 1997. 24.00 o.s.i (*0-684-84466-4*) Simon & Schuster. (Scribner).
—Three to Get Deadly. abr. ed. (Stephanie Plum Novel Ser.: No. 3). 2000. audio 9.98 (*0-7435-1839-X*); 1994. audio 18.00 (*0-671-57520-1*, 394533) Simon & Schuster Audio. (Simon & Schuster Audioworks).
—Three to Get Deadly. 1998. (Stephanie Plum Novel Ser.: No. 3). 352p. reprint ed. mass mkt. 7.99 (*0-312-96609-1*, St. Martin's Paperbacks) St. Martin's Pr.
—To the Nines. l.t. ed. 2003. 416p. 27.95 (*0-375-43202-7*) Random Hse., Inc.
—To the Nines. Date not set. mass mkt. 7.99 (*0-312-99146-0*, St. Martin's Paperbacks); 2003. 320p. 25.95 (*0-312-26586-7*) St. Martin's Pr.
—Two for the Dough. l.t. ed. 1998. (Stephanie Plum Novel Ser.: No. 2). 25.95 (*1-57490-151-6*, Beeler Large Print Bks.) Beeler, Thomas T. Publisher.
—Two for the Dough. unabr. ed. (Stephanie Plum Novel Ser.: No. 2). 2000. audio 51.00 (*0-7887-0617-9*, 94788E7); 1999. audio compact disk 69.00 (*0-7887-3723-6*, C1080E7) Recorded Bks., LLC.
—Two for the Dough. (Stephanie Plum Novel Ser.: No. 2). 2000. E-Book 22.00 (*0-684-86853-9*, Scribner); 1996. 304p. 22.00 (*0-684-82592-9*, Scribner); 1996. 304p. 25.00 (*0-684-19638-7*, Scribner); 1996. 336p. reprint ed. mass mkt. 7.99 (*0-671-00179-5*, Pocket) Simon & Schuster.
—Two for the Dough. (Stephanie Plum Novel Ser.: No. 2). 1999. audio 9.98 (*0-671-04420-6*); Set. 1996. audio 17.00 (*0-671-56258-4*, 393428) Simon & Schuster Audio. (Simon & Schuster Audioworks).
—Visions of Sugar Plums. l.t. ed. 2002. 256p. 21.99 (*0-375-43188-8*) Random Hse. Large Print.
—Visions of Sugar Plums. 2003. 256p. mass mkt. 6.99 (*0-312-98634-3*, St. Martin's Paperbacks); 2002. 160p. 19.95 (*0-312-30632-6*) St. Martin's Pr.
Stephanie Plum. No. 10. pap. incl. audio (*1-55927-782-3*); No. 10. pap. incl. audio (*1-55927-783-1*); No. 10. audio (*1-55927-784-X*); No. 11. pap. incl. audio (*1-55927-785-8*); No. 11. pap. incl. audio (*1-55927-786-6*); No. 11. audio (*1-55927-787-4*) Audio Renaissance.
Stephanie Plum, 10 vols., Set. (*0-312-28991-X*) St. Martin's Pr.

**PLUMTREE, ALEX (FICTITIOUS CHARACTER)—FICTION**

Kaewert, Julie. Unbound. 1997. (Booklover's Mystery Ser.). 448p. mass mkt. 5.99 (*0-553-57715-8*, Crimeline) Bantam Bks.

**PLUNKETT, MARTIN (FICTITIOUS CHARACTER)—FICTION**

Ellroy, James. Killer on the Road. 1999. 272p. pap. 13.00 (*0-380-80896-X*, Perennial) HarperTrade.
—Killer on the Road. 1986. 288p. mass mkt. 5.99 (*0-380-89934-5*, Avon Bks.) Morrow/Avon.

**POE, JARED (FICTITIOUS CHARACTER)—FICTION**

Brite, Poppy Z. The Lazarus Heart. 1998. (Crow Ser.). 224p. pap. 13.00 (*0-06-105824-6*, HarperEntertainment) Morrow/Avon.

**POE, JOHN CHARLES (FICTITIOUS CHARACTER)—FICTION**

Peyser, Thomas. W. W. 2000. 124p. pap. 16.00 (*0-7388-2869-6*) Xlibris Corp.
Poe, Robert. The Black Cat. 1998. 278p. mass mkt. 6.99 (*0-8125-4932-5*, Tor Bks.); 1997. 384p. 23.95 (*0-312-86013-7*, Forge Bks.) Doherty, Tom Assocs., LLC.

**POIROT, HERCULE (FICTITIOUS CHARACTER)—FICTION**

Christie, Agatha. The A. B. C. Murders. 1991. (Hercule Poirot Mystery Ser.). 240p. mass mkt. 5.99 (*0-425-13024-X*); E-Book 5.99 (*0-425-17788-2*) Berkley Publishing Group.
—The A. B. C. Murders. l.t. ed. (Popular Author Ser.). 344p. 1989. 12.95 o.p. (*0-8161-4500-8*); 1988. lib. bdg. 20.95 o.p. (*0-8161-4459-1*) Gale Group. (Macmillan Reference USA).
—The A. B. C. Murders. 1985. (Agatha Christie Ser.). 256p. 12.95 (*0-396-08698-5*, G. P. Putnam's Sons) Penguin Putnam Bks. for Young Readers.
—The A. B. C. Murders. 1985. 240p. mass mkt. 3.50 o.s.i (*0-671-60063-X*); 1982. mass mkt. 2.95 o.s.i (*0-671-46477-9*) Simon & Schuster. (Pocket).
—The A. B. C. Murders. l.t. ed. 1980. (Ulverscroft Large Print Ser.). 345p. 12.00 o.p. (*0-7089-0590-0*, Ulverscroft) Thorpe, F. A. Pubs. GBR. *Dist:* Ulverscroft Large Print Bks., Ltd., Ulverscroft Large Print Canada, Ltd.
—The A. B. C. Murders. 1991. 12.04 (*0-606-12156-0*) Turtleback Bks.
—After the Funeral. 2000. (Hercule Poirot Mystery Ser.). 256p. mass mkt. 5.99 (*0-425-17390-9*) Berkley Publishing Group.
—After the Funeral. 1985. mass mkt. 3.50 o.s.i (*0-671-55695-9*); 1983. mass mkt. 2.95 o.s.i (*0-671-47287-9*) Simon & Schuster. (Pocket).
—Appointment with Death. 1987. 9.95 o.p. (*0-553-35062-5*) Bantam Bks.
—Appointment with Death. Pliner, Jayne, ed. 1988. (Hercule Poirot Mystery Ser.). 224p. mass mkt. 5.99 (*0-425-10858-9*) Berkley Publishing Group.
—Appointment with Death. 1986. mass mkt. 2.95 o.s.i (*0-425-09356-5*); 1984. mass mkt. 2.95 o.s.i (*0-425-06775-0*) Berkley Publishing Group.
—Appointment with Death. 1981. 192p. pap. 2.95 o.p. (*0-440-10246-4*) Dell Publishing.
—Appointment with Death. l.t. ed. 1993. 336p. pap. 12.95 o.p. (*0-8161-4530-X*); 1992. 296p. lib. bdg. 19.95 o.p. (*0-8161-4529-6*) Gale Group. (Macmillan Reference USA).
—Appointment with Death. 1996. 240p. 24.95 (*0-399-14136-7*); 1988. (YA). 14.95 (*0-396-09298-5*) Penguin Group (USA) Inc. (G. P. Putnam's Sons).
—Appointment with Death. l.t. ed. 1975. (Ulverscroft Large Print Ser.). 334p. 12.00 o.p. (*0-85456-366-0*, Ulverscroft) Thorpe, F. A. Pubs. GBR. *Dist:* Ulverscroft Large Print Bks., Ltd., Ulverscroft Large Print Canada, Ltd.
—Appointment with Death. 1988. 12.04 (*0-606-12169-2*) Turtleback Bks.
—The Big Four. 1986. mass mkt. 9.95 o.p. (*0-553-35041-2*) Bantam Bks.
—The Big Four. 1987. 208p. mass mkt. 5.99 (*0-425-09882-6*); 1986. mass mkt. 2.95 o.s.i (*0-425-09362-X*); 1984. mass mkt. 2.95 o.s.i (*0-425-06776-9*) Berkley Publishing Group.
—The Big Four. 1982. pap. 2.95 o.p. (*0-440-10562-5*) Dell Publishing.
—The Big Four. l.t. ed. (Agatha Christie Ser.). 280p. 1992. pap. 12.95 o.p. (*0-8161-4534-2*); 1991. 19.95 o.p. (*0-8161-4533-4*) Gale Group. (Macmillan Reference USA).
—The Big Four. l.t. ed. 1974. (Ulverscroft Large Print Ser.). 312p. 12.00 o.p. (*0-85456-283-4*, Ulverscroft) Thorpe, F. A. Pubs. GBR. *Dist:* Ulverscroft Large Print Bks., Ltd., Ulverscroft Large Print Canada, Ltd.
—Black Coffee. l.t. ed. 1999. 26.95 o.p. (*1-56895-625-8*, Wheeler Publishing, Inc.) Gale Group.
—Black Coffee. unabr. ed. 1998. (Hercule Poirot Mystery Ser.). 6p. audio 24.95 (*1-55935-281-7*, 696051) Soundelux Audio Publishing.
—Black Coffee. (Hercule Poirot Mystery Ser.). 1998. (Illus.). 221p. 22.95 o.p. (*0-312-19241-X*, Saint Martin's Minotaur); 3rd ed. 1999. 290p. mass mkt. 6.99 (*0-312-97007-2*, St. Martin's Paperbacks) St. Martin's Pr.
—Black Coffee. abr. ed. 1998. audio 24.35 (*0-00-105536-4*) Ulverscroft Audio (U.S.A.).
—Cards on the Table. mass mkt. 3.50 o.s.i (*0-425-12577-7*); 2001. E-Book 5.99 (*0-425-17790-4*); 1998. mass mkt. 3.99 o.s.i (*0-425-16924-3*); 1986. mass mkt. 2.95 o.s.i (*0-425-09317-4*); 1984. mass mkt. 2.95 o.s.i (*0-425-06778-5*) Berkley Publishing Group.
—Cards on the Table. 1980. pap. 2.95 o.p. (*0-440-11052-1*) Dell Publishing.
—Cards on the Table. 1987. (Agatha Christie Ser.). 14.95 (*0-396-09010-9*, G. P. Putnam's Sons) Penguin Putnam Bks. for Young Readers.
—Cards on the Table. 1984. (Hercule Poirot Mystery Ser.). 12.04 (*0-606-12211-7*) Turtleback Bks.
—The Cards on the Table. 1987. (Hercule Poirot Mystery Ser.). 224p. mass mkt. 5.99 (*0-425-10567-9*) Berkley Publishing Group.
—Cards on the Table. l.t. ed. 1983. 352p. 12.50 o.p. (*0-7089-1151-X*, Ulverscroft) Thorpe, F. A. Pubs. GBR. *Dist:* Ulverscroft Large Print Bks., Ltd.
—Cat among the Pigeons. 2000. (Hercule Poirot Mystery Ser.). 256p. mass mkt. 5.99 (*0-425-17547-2*) Berkley Publishing Group.
—Cat among the Pigeons. 1986. (Agatha Christie Ser.). 224p. 12.95 o.s.i (*0-396-08802-3*, G. P. Putnam's Sons) Penguin Putnam Bks. for Young Readers.
—Cat among the Pigeons. 1985. mass mkt. 3.50 o.s.i (*0-671-55700-9*); 1983. mass mkt. 2.95 o.s.i (*0-671-46766-2*) Simon & Schuster. (Pocket).
—Cat among the Pigeons. l.t. ed. 1983. 400p. 12.50 o.p. (*0-85456-771-2*, Ulverscroft) Thorpe, F. A. Pubs. GBR. *Dist:* Ulverscroft Large Print Bks., Ltd.
—Cat among the Pigeons. 1991. (Hercule Poirot Mystery Ser.). 12.04 (*0-606-12214-1*) Turtleback Bks.
—The Christmas Tragedy & Other Stories. unabr. ed. 1994. audio 5.99 (*0-88646-723-3*, PAC-7723) Durkin Hayes Publishing Ltd.
—The Clocks. unabr. ed. 1997. (Hercule Poirot Mystery Ser.). audio 69.95 o.p. (*0-7451-6814-0*, CAB 640) BBC Audiobooks America.

—The Clocks. 1988. (HC Collection). 9.95 o.s.i (*0-553-35071-4*) Bantam Bks.
—The Clocks. 2000. 272p. mass mkt. 5.99 (*0-425-17391-7*) Berkley Publishing Group.
—The Clocks. 1985. mass mkt. 3.50 o.s.i (*0-671-55822-6*); 1983. mass mkt. 2.95 o.s.i (*0-671-47296-8*) Simon & Schuster. (Pocket).
—The Clocks. l.t. ed. 1983. (Ulverscroft Large Print Ser.). 432p. o.p. (*0-85456-666-X*, Ulverscroft) Thorpe, F. A. Pubs. GBR. *Dist:* Ulverscroft Large Print Canada, Ltd.
—The Clocks. 1991. (Hercule Poirot Mystery Ser.). 12.04 (*0-606-12222-2*) Turtleback Bks.
—Curtain. 1976. 22.95 (*0-88411-386-8*) Amereon, Ltd.
—Curtain. 2000. (Hercule Poirot Mystery Ser.). 224p. mass mkt. 5.99 (*0-425-17374-7*) Berkley Publishing Group.
—Curtain. pap. 14.95 (*0-8161-4540-7*); 1992. 289p. lib. bdg. 19.95 o.p. (*0-8161-4539-3*) Gale Group. (Macmillan Reference USA).
—Curtain. 1995. 24.95 (*0-399-14016-6*, Philomel) Penguin Group (USA) Inc.
—Curtain. 1985. 288p. mass mkt. 4.99 o.p. (*0-671-54717-8*, Pocket) Simon & Schuster.
—Curtain. 1993. 12.04 (*0-606-12235-4*) Turtleback Bks.
—Dead Man's Folly. unabr. ed. 1997. audio 54.95 o.p. (*0-7451-6815-9*, CAB 314) BBC Audiobooks America.
—Dead Man's Folly. 2000. (Hercule Poirot Mystery Ser.). 240p. mass mkt. 5.99 (*0-425-17473-5*) Berkley Publishing Group.
—Dead Man's Folly. 1986. (Agatha Christie Ser.). 14.95 o.s.i (*0-396-08864-3*, G. P. Putnam's Sons) Penguin Putnam Bks. for Young Readers.
—Dead Man's Folly. 1990. 224p. mass mkt. 3.95 o.p. (*0-671-69484-7*); 1984. mass mkt. 3.50 o.s.i (*0-671-54318-0*); 1983. mass mkt. 2.95 o.s.i (*0-671-47317-4*) Simon & Schuster. (Pocket).
—Dead Man's Folly. 1988. audio 53.95 o.p. (*0-8161-9109-3*) Thorndike Pr.
—Dead Man's Folly. l.t. ed. 1983. 336p. 12.50 o.p. (*0-85456-772-0*, Ulverscroft) Thorpe, F. A. Pubs. GBR. *Dist:* Ulverscroft Large Print Bks., Ltd.
—Dead Man's Mirror. 1986. mass mkt. 2.95 o.s.i (*0-425-08765-4*); 1984. mass mkt. 2.95 o.s.i (*0-425-06779-3*) Berkley Publishing Group.
—Dead Man's Mirror. 1981. 192p. pap. 2.95 o.p. (*0-440-11699-6*) Dell Publishing.
—Dead Man's Mirror. abr. ed. 1990. 2p. audio 16.99 (*0-88646-203-7*, 7203) Durkin Hayes Publishing Ltd.
—Death in the Clouds. Orig. Title: Death in the Air. 2000. E-Book 5.99 (*0-425-17791-2*); 1998. mass mkt. 3.99 o.s.i (*0-425-16921-9*); 1987. 240p. mass mkt. 5.99 (*0-425-09914-8*) Berkley Publishing Group.
—Death in the Clouds. 1998. (Hercule Poirot Mystery Ser.). Orig. Title: Death in the Air. (Illus.). 256p. 24.95 (*0-399-14432-3*, G. P. Putnam's Sons) Penguin Group (USA) Inc.
—Death in the Clouds. l.t. ed. 1987. Orig. Title: Death in the Air. 16.95 (*0-7089-1738-0*, Ulverscroft) Thorpe, F. A. Pubs. GBR. *Dist:* Ulverscroft Large Print Bks., Ltd.
—Death in the Clouds. 2000. Orig. Title: Death in the Air. 12.04 (*0-606-20623-X*) Turtleback Bks.
—Death on the Nile. unabr. ed. 2001. audio 29.95 (*1-57270-203-6*, N61203u, Audio Editions Mystery Masters) Audio Partners Publishing Corp.
—Death on the Nile. abr. ed. 2003. (Agatha Christie Audio Mystery Ser.). (Illus.). audio 12.95 (*1-55927-905-2*) Audio Renaissance.
—Death on the Nile. unabr. ed. 1997. (Hercule Poirot Mystery Ser.). audio 69.95 (*0-7451-5839-0*, CAB 601) BBC Audiobooks America.
—Death on the Nile. 1987. mass mkt. o.s.i (*0-553-16787-1*) Bantam Bks.
—Death on the Nile. 2000. (Hercule Poirot Mystery Ser.). 320p. mass mkt. 5.99 (*0-425-17373-9*); (Illus.). 307p. reprint ed. pap. 12.00 o.s.i (*0-425-17441-7*) Berkley Publishing Group.
—Death on the Nile. 1985. (Agatha Christie Ser.). 12.95 o.s.i (*0-396-08573-3*, G. P. Putnam's Sons) Penguin Putnam Bks. for Young Readers.
—Death on the Nile. l.t. ed. 1983. 480p. 12.50 o.p. (*0-85456-671-6*, Ulverscroft) Thorpe, F. A. Pubs. GBR. *Dist:* Ulverscroft Large Print Bks., Ltd.
—Death on the Nile. 2001. 12.04 (*0-606-21143-8*); 1992. 12.04 (*0-606-12248-6*) Turtleback Bks.
—Death on the Nile: BBC. abr. ed. 1997. (Hercule Poirot Mystery Ser.). audio 16.99 o.s.i (*0-553-47811-7*, RH Audio) Random Hse. Audio Publishing Group.
—Double Sin & Other Stories. 1987. (HC Collection). 9.95 o.p. (*0-553-35057-9*) Bantam Bks.
—Double Sin & Other Stories. 1984. 224p. mass mkt. 5.99 o.s.i (*0-425-06781-5*) Berkley Publishing Group.
—Double Sin & Other Stories. 1977. pap. 1.95 o.p. (*0-440-12144-2*) Dell Publishing.
—Double Sin & Other Stories. l.t. ed. (Popular Author Ser.). 1991. 12.95 o.p. (*0-8161-4542-3*); 1990. 266p. lib. bdg. 19.95 o.p. (*0-8161-4541-5*) Gale Group. (Macmillan Reference USA).
—Double Sin & Other Stories. 1987. (Agatha Christie Ser.). 224p. 14.95 o.s.i (*0-396-09158-X*, G. P. Putnam's Sons) Penguin Putnam Bks. for Young Readers.
—Dumb Witness. 1986. (Hercule Poirot Mystery Ser.). 272p. mass mkt. 5.99 (*0-425-09854-0*) Berkley Publishing Group.
—Elephants Can Remember. 1984. (Agatha Christie Ser.). 224p. mass mkt. 5.99 (*0-425-06782-3*) Berkley Publishing Group.
—Elephants Can Remember. 1976. pap. 1.25 o.p. (*0-440-12329-1*) Dell Publishing.
—Elephants Can Remember. l.t. ed. (Agatha Christie Ser.). 1991. 291p. pap. 12.95 o.p. (*0-8161-4546-6*); 1990. 328p. lib. bdg. 19.95 o.p. (*0-8161-4545-8*); 1984. pap. 9.95 o.p. (*0-8161-3122-8*); 1973. reprint ed. lib. bdg. 9.95 o.p. (*0-8161-6086-4*) Gale Group. (Macmillan Reference USA).
—Elephants Can Remember. 1972. (Agatha Christie Ser.). 8.95 (*0-396-07769-2*, G. P. Putnam's Sons) Penguin Group (USA) Inc.
—Elephants Can Remember. 1992. 12.04 (*0-606-12274-5*) Turtleback Bks.
—Elephants Can Remember. l.t. ed. 2001. (Ulverscroft Large Print Ser.). 368p. 32.50 (*0-7089-2657-6*) Ulverscroft Large Print Bks., Ltd.
—Elephants Can Remember: A Hercule Poirot Mystery. unabr. ed. 1999. audio 49.95 (*0-7540-0334-5*, CAB1757) Chivers Audio Bks. GBR. *Dist:* BBC Audiobooks America.
—Evil under the Sun. unabr. ed. 1997. (Hercule Poirot Mystery Ser.). audio 54.95 (*0-7451-4014-9*, CAB 711) BBC Audiobooks America.
—Evil under the Sun. 1991. (Hercule Poirot Mystery Ser.). 208p. mass mkt. 5.99 (*0-425-12960-8*) Berkley Publishing Group.
—Evil under the Sun. l.t. ed. 291p. 1989. pap. 12.95 o.p. (*0-8161-4550-4*); 1988. lib. bdg. 20.95 o.p. (*0-8161-4549-0*) Gale Group. (Macmillan Reference USA).
—Evil under the Sun. 1985. 12.95 (*0-396-08701-9*) Putnam Publishing Group, The.
—Evil under the Sun. 1990. mass mkt. 3.95 o.s.i (*0-671-70612-8*); 1985. mass mkt. 3.50 o.p. (*0-671-60174-1*); 1983. mass mkt. 2.95 o.p. (*0-671-47427-8*) Simon & Schuster. (Pocket).
—Evil under the Sun. l.t. ed. 1971. (Ulverscroft Large Print Ser.). 362p. o.p. (*0-85456-042-4*, Ulverscroft) Thorpe, F. A. Pubs. GBR. *Dist:* Ulverscroft Large Print Canada, Ltd.
—Evil under the Sun. 1991. (Hercule Poirot Mystery Ser.). 12.04 (*0-606-12281-8*) Turtleback Bks.
—Five Little Pigs. 2000. E-Book 5.99 (*0-425-17787-4*); 1998. mass mkt. 3.99 o.s.i (*0-425-16923-5*); 1985. 224p. reprint ed. mass mkt. 5.99 (*0-425-09325-5*) Berkley Publishing Group.
—Five Little Pigs. l.t. ed. 1982. (Ulverscroft Large Print Ser.). 316p. (*0-7089-0814-4*, Ulverscroft) Thorpe, F. A. Pubs. GBR. *Dist:* Ulverscroft Large Print Canada, Ltd.
—Funerals Are Fatal. 224p. 21.95 o.s.i (*0-8488-2446-6*) Amereon, Ltd.
—Funerals Are Fatal. l.t. ed. pap. 14.95 (*0-8161-4552-0*); 1992. lib. bdg. 19.95 o.p. (*0-8161-4551-2*) Gale Group. (Macmillan Reference USA).
—Funerals Are Fatal. 1988. 14.95 (*0-396-09295-0*, G. P. Putnam's Sons) Penguin Group (USA) Inc.
—Funerals Are Fatal. 1990. 208p. 22.95 o.s.i (*0-399-13560-X*, G. P. Putnam's Sons) Penguin Putnam Bks. for Young Readers.
—Funerals Are Fatal. 1992. (Hercule Poirot Mystery Ser.). 12.04 (*0-606-12301-6*) Turtleback Bks.
—Hallowe'en Party. Set. unabr. ed. 1999. audio 54.95 (*0-7540-0377-9*, CAB1800) BBC Audiobooks America.
—Hallowe'en Party. 2000. E-Book 5.99 (*0-425-17789-0*); 1998. mass mkt. 3.99 o.s.i (*0-425-16922-7*); 1991. 240p. mass mkt. 5.99 (*0-425-12963-2*) Berkley Publishing Group.
—Hallowe'en Party. unabr. ed. 2000. (Hercule Poirot Mystery Ser.). audio compact disk 64.95 (*0-7540-5335-0*, CCD 026) Chivers Audio Bks. GBR. *Dist:* BBC Audiobooks America.
—Hallowe'en Party. 2003. (Hercule Poirot Investigates Ser.). E-Book 5.99 (*0-06-072146-4*, PerfectBound) HarperCollins General Bks. Group.
—Hallowe'en Party. 1987. (Agatha Christie Ser.). 14.95 o.s.i (*0-396-09012-5*, G. P. Putnam's Sons) Penguin Putnam Bks. for Young Readers.
—Hallowe'en Party. 1984. mass mkt. 3.50 o.s.i (*0-671-54203-6*); 1982. mass mkt. 2.95 o.s.i (*0-671-45935-X*); 1989. reprint ed. mass mkt. 4.99 o.p. (*0-671-70231-9*) Simon & Schuster. (Pocket).
—Hallowe'en Party. l.t. ed. 1987. (Ulverscroft Large Print Ser.). 400p. o.p. (*0-7089-1666-X*, Ulverscroft) Thorpe, F. A. Pubs. GBR. *Dist:* Ulverscroft Large Print Canada, Ltd.
—Hallowe'en Party. 1992. (Hercule Poirot Mystery Ser.). 12.04 (*0-606-12321-0*) Turtleback Bks.
—The Harlequin Tea Set & Other Stories. 1998. 224p. reprint ed. mass mkt. 5.99 (*0-425-16515-9*) Berkley Publishing Group.
—The Harlequin Tea Set & Other Stories. abr. ed. 2001. audio 24.95 (*1-56511-570-8*) HighBridge Co.
—The Harlequin Tea Set & Other Stories. 1997. 208p. 21.95 o.s.i (*0-399-14287-8*, G. P. Putnam's Sons) Penguin Group (USA) Inc.
—The Harlequin Tea Set & Other Stories. unabr. ed. 1998. audio 21.95 (*1-55935-260-4*) Soundelux Audio Publishing.
—Hercule Poirot's Casebook: Fifty Stories. 1998. 18.95 (*0-399-15021-8*); 1984. 18.95 (*0-396-08417-6*) Penguin Group (USA) Inc. (G. P. Putnam's Sons).
—Hercule Poirot's Early Cases. 22.95 (*0-88411-388-4*) Amereon, Ltd.
—Hercule Poirot's Early Cases. 1986. mass mkt. 9.95 o.p. (*0-553-35045-5*) Bantam Bks.
—Hercule Poirot's Early Cases. l.t. ed. 1979. (gr. 7-12). lib. bdg. 8.95 o.p. (*0-8161-6734-6*, Macmillan Reference USA) Gale Group.
—Hickory, Dickory, Death. 1987. (Agatha Christie Ser.). 224p. 14.95 o.s.i (*0-396-09160-1*, G. P. Putnam's Sons) Penguin Putnam Bks. for Young Readers.
—Hickory, Dickory, Death. 1989. mass mkt. 4.99 o.p. (*0-671-70263-7*, Pocket) Simon & Schuster.
—Hickory, Dickory, Death. l.t. ed. 1987. 352p. 14.95 o.p. (*0-7089-1637-6*, Ulverscroft) Thorpe, F. A. Pubs. GBR. *Dist:* Ulverscroft Large Print Bks., Ltd.
—Hickory, Dickory, Dock. 2000. (Hercule Poirot Mystery Ser.). 224p. mass mkt. 5.99 (*0-425-17546-4*) Berkley Publishing Group.
—A Holiday for Murder. 1983. mass mkt. 2.95 o.s.i (*0-553-24144-3*); 1962. 176p. mass mkt. 3.50 o.s.i (*0-553-26795-7*) Bantam Bks.
—The Hollow. 1986. 240p. mass mkt. 9.95 o.p. (*0-553-35050-1*) Bantam Bks.
—The Hollow. 1984. (Hercule Poirot Mystery Ser.). 272p. mass mkt. 5.99 (*0-425-06784-X*) Berkley Publishing Group.
—The Hollow. 1992. 304p. 24.95 (*0-399-13727-0*, G. P. Putnam's Sons) Penguin Group (USA) Inc.
—The Hollow. l.t. ed. 1974. (Ulverscroft Large Print Ser.). 431p. (*0-85456-301-6*, Ulverscroft) Thorpe, F. A. Pubs. GBR. *Dist:* Ulverscroft Large Print Canada, Ltd.
—The Hollow: A Hercule Poirot Mystery. l.t. ed. (Agatha Christie Ser.). 1992. 385p. pap. 12.95 o.p. (*0-8161-4556-3*); 1991. 370p. 19.95 o.p. (*0-8161-4555-5*) Gale Group. (Macmillan Reference USA).
—The Incredible Theft. unabr. ed. 1992. audio 4.99 (*0-88646-619-9*) Durkin Hayes Publishing Ltd.
—The Labors of Hercules. unabr. ed. 1995. audio 54.95 o.p. (*0-7451-5835-8*, CAB 134) BBC Audiobooks America.
—The Labors of Hercules. 1984. (Hercule Poirot Mystery Ser.). 272p. reprint ed. mass mkt. 5.99 (*0-425-06785-8*) Berkley Publishing Group.
—The Labors of Hercules. 1982. pap. 2.95 o.p. (*0-440-14620-8*) Dell Publishing.
—The Labors of Hercules, Vol. 111. unabr. ed. (Agatha Christie Mysteries Ser.). audio 16.99 Durkin Hayes Publishing Ltd.
—The Labors of Hercules. l.t. ed. 1993. 448p. 12.95 o.p. (*0-8161-4558-X*); 1992. 434p. lib. bdg. 20.95 o.p. (*0-8161-4557-1*) Gale Group. (Macmillan Reference USA).
—The Labors of Hercules. 1993. (Hercule Poirot Ser.). 224p. 24.95 (*0-399-13777-7*, G. P. Putnam's Sons) Penguin Group (USA) Inc.
—The Labors of Hercules. 1967. (Agatha Christie Ser.). 8.95 (*0-396-05578-8*, G. P. Putnam's Sons) Penguin Putnam Bks. for Young Readers.
—The Labors of Hercules. l.t. ed. 1978. (Ulverscroft Large Print Ser.). 344p. 32.50 o.p. (*0-7089-0119-0*, Ulverscroft) Thorpe, F. A. Pubs. GBR. *Dist:* Ulverscroft Large Print Bks., Ltd., Ulverscroft Large Print Canada, Ltd.
—Lord Edgware Dies. 1986. 256p. mass mkt. 5.99 (*0-425-09961-X*) Berkley Publishing Group.
—Lord Edgware Dies. l.t. ed. 1989. 380p. o.p. (*0-85456-479-9*, Ulverscroft) Thorpe, F. A. Pubs.
—The Love Detectives. unabr. ed. 1993. audio 4.99 (*0-88646-648-2*) Durkin Hayes Publishing Ltd.
—The Million Dollar Bond Robbery. unabr. ed. 1999. (Agatha Christie Ser.). audio 5.99 (*1-55204-602-8*, PAC-8602) Durkin Hayes Publishing Ltd.
—Mrs. McGinty's Dead. 1987. (HC Collection). 9.95 o.p. (*0-553-35059-5*) Bantam Bks.
—Mrs. McGinty's Dead. 1993. (Hercule Poirot Ser.). 304p. 24.95 (*0-399-13823-4*, G. P. Putnam's Sons) Penguin Group (USA) Inc.
—Mrs. McGinty's Dead. 1985. 240p. mass mkt. 3.50 o.s.i (*0-671-83440-1*); 1983. mass mkt. 2.95 o.s.i (*0-671-49806-1*) Simon & Schuster. (Pocket).
—Mrs. McGinty's Dead. l.t. ed. 1988. (Ulverscroft Large Print Ser.). 320p. 17.95 o.p. (*0-7089-1771-2*, Ulverscroft) Thorpe, F. A. Pubs. GBR. *Dist:* Ulverscroft Large Print Bks., Ltd., Ulverscroft Large Print Canada, Ltd.
—Mrs. McGinty's Dead. 1992. (Hercule Poirot Mystery Ser.). 12.04 (*0-606-12434-9*) Turtleback Bks.
—Mrs. McGinty's Dead: A Hecule Poirit Novel. 2000. (Hercule Poirot Mystery Ser.). 240p. mass mkt. 5.99 (*0-425-17545-6*) Berkley Publishing Group.
—Murder after Hours. 256p. 22.95 o.s.i (*0-8488-2447-4*) Amereon, Ltd.
—Murder after Hours. 1969. 224p. pap. 2.50 o.s.i (*0-440-15922-9*) Dell Publishing.
—Murder for Christmas. 1987. (Agatha Christie Ser.). 224p. 14.95 (*0-396-09161-X*, G. P. Putnam's Sons) Penguin Putnam Bks. for Young Readers.
—Murder for Christmas. l.t. ed. 1987. 400p. (*0-7089-1724-0*, Ulverscroft) Thorpe, F. A. Pubs.
—Murder in Mesopotamia. (Hercule Poirot Mystery Ser.). 1987. 272p. mass mkt. 5.99 (*0-425-10363-3*); 1986. mass mkt. 2.95 o.s.i (*0-425-09324-7*); 1984. mass mkt. 2.95 o.s.i (*0-425-06791-2*) Berkley Publishing Group.
—Murder in Mesopotamia. 1976. 192p. pap. 2.50 o.s.i (*0-440-15982-2*) Dell Publishing.
—Murder in Mesopotamia. l.t. ed. (G. K. Hall Large Print Book Ser.). 1992. 348p. 14.95 o.p. (*0-8161-4568-7*); 1991. 384p. 19.95 o.p. (*0-8161-4567-9*) Gale Group. (Macmillan Reference USA).
—Murder in Mesopotamia. l.t. ed. 1969. (Ulverscroft Large Print Ser.). 367p. 12.50 o.p. (*0-85456-667-8*, Ulverscroft) Thorpe, F. A. Pubs. GBR. *Dist:* Ulverscroft Large Print Bks., Ltd., Ulverscroft Large Print Canada, Ltd.
—Murder in Mesopotamia. 1984. 12.04 (*0-606-00965-5*) Turtleback Bks.
—Murder in Mesopotamia: BBC. abr. ed. 1997. (BBC Radio Presents Ser.). audio 18.00 o.s.i (*0-553-47846-X*, RH Audio) Random Hse. Audio Publishing Group.
—Murder in Retrospect. 1985. mass mkt. 9.95 o.p. (*0-553-35038-2*) Bantam Bks.
—Murder in Retrospect. mass mkt. 3.50 o.s.i (*0-425-12575-0*); 1984. mass mkt. 2.95 o.s.i (*0-425-06792-0*) Berkley Publishing Group.
—Murder in Retrospect. 1970. 192p. pap. 2.50 o.s.i (*0-440-16030-8*) Dell Publishing.
—Murder in the Mews. abr. ed. 1984. audio 16.99 (*0-88646-090-5*, TC-LFP 7020) Durkin Hayes Publishing Ltd.
—Murder in the Mews. l.t. ed. 1986. 416p. o.p. (*0-7089-1443-8*, Ulverscroft) Thorpe, F. A. Pubs.
—Murder in the Mews. 1984. 12.04 (*0-606-00967-1*) Turtleback Bks.
—Murder in the Mews & Other Stories. 1987. (Hercule Poirot Mystery Ser.). 256p. mass mkt. 5.99 (*0-425-10435-4*) Berkley Publishing Group.
—Murder in Three Acts. 1988. (HC Collection). 9.95 o.p. (*0-553-35069-2*) Bantam Bks.
—Murder in Three Acts. 1986. mass mkt. 2.95 o.s.i (*0-425-09041-8*); 1984. mass mkt. 2.95 o.s.i (*0-425-06793-9*) Berkley Publishing Group.
—Murder in Three Acts. l.t. ed. (Agatha Christie Ser.). 360p. 1990. pap. 12.95 o.p. (*0-8161-4570-9*); 1989. lib. bdg. 19.95 o.p. (*0-8161-4569-5*) Gale Group. (Macmillan Reference USA).
—Murder in Three Acts. 1986. (Agatha Christie Ser.). 14.95 o.s.i (*0-396-08866-X*, G. P. Putnam's Sons) Penguin Group (USA) Inc.
—The Murder of Roger Ackroyd. Date not set. 277p. 23.95 (*0-8488-2236-6*) Amereon, Ltd.
—The Murder of Roger Ackroyd, unabr. ed. 2000. (YA). (gr. 10 up). audio 35.95 (*1-55685-638-5*) Audio Bk. Contractors, Inc.
—The Murder of Roger Ackroyd. unabr. ed. 1995. audio 54.95 o.p. (*0-7451-5836-6*, CAB 199) BBC Audiobooks America.
—The Murder of Roger Ackroyd. 2000. (Hercule Poirot Mystery Ser.). 256p. reprint ed. pap. 12.00 (*0-425-17651-7*) Berkley Publishing Group.
—The Murder of Roger Ackroyd. l.t. ed. 1989. 12.95 o.p. (*0-8161-4499-0*); 1988. 376p. lib. bdg. 19.95 o.p. (*0-8161-4460-5*) Gale Group. (Macmillan Reference USA).
—The Murder of Roger Ackroyd. 1976. (Crime Fiction Ser). reprint ed. lib. bdg. 21.00 o.p. (*0-8240-2360-9*) Garland Publishing, Inc.
—The Murder of Roger Ackroyd. 1985. (Agatha Christie Ser.). 276p. 12.95 o.s.i (*0-396-08574-1*, G. P. Putnam's Sons) Penguin Putnam Bks. for Young Readers.
—The Murder of Roger Ackroyd. 1989. (Hercule Poirot Mystery Ser.). 256p. mass mkt. 4.99 o.p. (*0-671-70118-5*, Pocket) Simon & Schuster.
—The Murder of Roger Ackroyd. l.t. ed. 1972. (Ulverscroft Large Print Ser.). 414p. 12.00 o.p. (*0-85456-144-7*, Ulverscroft) Thorpe, F. A. Pubs. GBR. *Dist:* Ulverscroft Large Print Bks., Ltd., Ulverscroft Large Print Canada, Ltd.

—The Murder of Roger Ackroyd. 1991. (Hercule Poirot Mystery Ser.). 12.04 (*0-606-12438-1*) Turtleback Bks.

—The Murder of Roger Ackroyd: A Hercule Poirot Novel. 2000. (Hercule Poirot Mystery Ser.). 256p. mass mkt. 5.99 (*0-425-17389-5*) Berkley Publishing Group.

—Murder on the Links, unabr. ed. 1998. 35.95 incl. audio (*1-55685-504-4*) Audio Bk. Contractors, Inc.

—Murder on the Links. 1984. (Hercule Poirot Mystery Ser.). 240p. mass mkt. 5.99 (*0-425-06794-7*) Berkley Publishing Group.

—Murder on the Links. 1983. pap. 2.95 o.p. (*0-440-16102-9*) Dell Publishing.

—Murder on the Links. l.t. ed. (Popular Author Ser.). 1991. pap. 12.95 o.p. (*0-8161-4574-1*); 1990. 323p. lib. bdg. 19.95 o.p. (*0-8161-4573-3*) Gale Group. (Macmillan Reference USA).

—Murder on the Links. 1987. (Agatha Christie Ser.). 224p. 14.95 o.s.i (*0-396-09162-8*, G. P. Putnam's Sons) Penguin Putnam Bks. for Young Readers.

—Murder on the Links. l.t. ed. 1990. (Ulverscroft Large Print Ser.). 12.00 o.p. (*0-85456-516-7*, Ulverscroft) Thorpe, F. A. Pubs. GBR. *Dist:* Ulverscroft Large Print Bks., Ltd., Ulverscroft Large Print Canada, Ltd.

—Murder on the Links. 1984. 12.04 (*0-606-00970-1*) Turtleback Bks.

—Murder on the Orient Express. unabr. ed. 1996. audio 54.95 o.p. (*0-7451-6819-1*, CAB 315) BBC Audiobooks America.

—Murder on the Orient Express. 2000. (Hercule Poirot Mystery Ser.). 256p. mass mkt. 5.99 (*0-425-17375-5*) Berkley Publishing Group.

—Murder on the Orient Express. (Hercule Poirot Mystery Ser.). 19.95 (*0-399-13708-4*) Penguin Group (USA) Inc.

—Murder on the Orient Express. 1985. (Agatha Christie Ser.). 12.95 o.s.i (*0-396-08575-X*, G. P. Putnam's Sons) Penguin Putnam Bks. for Young Readers.

—Murder on the Orient Express. abr. ed. 1993. (BBC Radio Presents Ser.). audio 16.99 o.s.i (*0-553-47215-1*, 390218, RH Audio) Random Hse. Audio Publishing Group.

—Murder on the Orient Express. 1999. 295p. (*0-7621-0255-1*) Reader's Digest Assn., Inc., The.

—Murder on the Orient Express. 1984. 256p. mass mkt. 3.50 o.s.i (*0-671-52368-6*); 1982. mass mkt. 2.95 o.s.i (*0-671-46894-4*) Simon & Schuster. (Pocket).

—Murder on the Orient Express. l.t. ed. 1983. (Ulverscroft Large Print Ser.). 384p. 32.50 o.p. (*0-7089-0188-3*, Ulverscroft) Thorpe, F. A. Pubs. GBR. *Dist:* Ulverscroft Large Print Bks., Ltd., Ulverscroft Large Print Canada, Ltd.

—Murder on the Orient Express. 1991. (Hercule Poirot Mystery Ser.). 12.04 (*0-606-12439-X*) Turtleback Bks.

—Murder on the Orient Express: A Hercule Poirot Novel. 2000. (Hercule Poirot Ser.). 256p. pap. 12.00 (*0-425-17393-3*) Berkley Publishing Group.

—The Mysterious Affair at Styles. 22.95 (*0-88411-385-X*) Amereon, Ltd.

—The Mysterious Affair at Styles. 1995. audio 29.95 (*1-55685-373-4*) Audio Bk. Contractors, Inc.

—The Mysterious Affair at Styles. unabr. ed. 2004. audio compact disk 29.95 (*1-57270-297-4*); 1996. audio 22.95 (*1-57270-017-3*, N51017u, Audio Editions Mystery Masters) Audio Partners Publishing Corp.

—The Mysterious Affair at Styles. abr. ed. 2003. (Agatha Christie Audio Mystery Ser.). (Illus.). audio 12.95 (*1-55927-906-0*); audio 12.95 (*1-55927-906-0*) Audio Renaissance.

—The Mysterious Affair at Styles. 1992. 19.95 incl. audio (*1-882071-21-2*); 1998. audio 19.95 (*1-882071-59-X*, 023) B&B Audio, Inc.

—The Mysterious Affair at Styles. 1983. mass mkt. 2.95 o.s.i (*0-553-24093-5*); mass mkt. 3.50 o.s.i (*0-553-26547-4*); 192p. mass mkt. 3.50 o.s.i (*0-553-26587-3*) Bantam Bks.

—The Mysterious Affair at Styles. 1920. E-Book (*1-58734-006-2*) Bartleby.com.

—The Mysterious Affair at Styles. 1991. 208p. mass mkt. 5.99 (*0-425-12961-6*) Berkley Publishing Group.

—The Mysterious Affair at Styles. audio 26.95 (*1-885546-07-6*) Big Ben Audio, Inc.

—The Mysterious Affair at Styles. unabr. ed. 2000. audio compact disk 48.00 (*0-7861-9928-8*, z1362); 1996. audio 39.95 (*0-7861-0410-4*, 1362) Blackstone Audio Bks., Inc.

—The Mysterious Affair at Styles. unabr. collector's ed. 1996. audio 48.00 (*0-7366-3226-3*, 3887) Books on Tape, Inc.

—The Mysterious Affair at Styles. 1997. (Dover Mystery Classics Ser.). 160p. reprint ed. pap. text 2.00 (*0-486-29695-4*) Dover Pubns., Inc.

—The Mysterious Affair at Styles. E-Book 2.49 (*0-7574-0366-2*) Electric Umbrella Publishing.

—The Mysterious Affair at Styles. 1980. pap. 8.95 o.p. (*0-8161-3105-8*); 1976. lib. bdg. 10.95 o.p. (*0-8161-6343-X*); 1992. lib. bdg. 19.95 o.p. (*0-8161-4575-X*) Gale Group. (Macmillan Reference USA).

—The Mysterious Affair at Styles, unabr. ed. 1999. audio 39.95 Highsmith Inc.

—The Mysterious Affair at Styles. 2002. 208p. 94.99 (*1-4043-1778-3*); per. 89.99 (*1-4043-1779-1*) IndyPublish.com.

—The Mysterious Affair at Styles. E-Book 2.95 (*1-57799-806-5*); E-Book 2.95 (*1-57799-964-9*) Logos Research Systems, Inc.

—The Mysterious Affair at Styles. 2001. (Large Print Ser.). 310p. lib. bdg. 26.00 (*1-58287-654-1*); 205p. lib. bdg. 25.00 (*1-58287-171-X*) North Bks.

—The Mysterious Affair at Styles. 1985. (Agatha Christie Ser.). 236p. 12.95 o.s.i (*0-396-08703-5*, G. P. Putnam's Sons) Penguin Putnam Bks. for Young Readers.

—The Mysterious Affair at Styles. 1999. E-Book 8.99 incl. cd-rom (*1-891595-60-1*) Quiet Vision Publishing.

—The Mysterious Affair at Styles. 2003. (Illus.). 240p. pap. 9.95 (*0-8129-7010-1*, Modern Library) Random House Adult Trade Publishing Group.

—The Mysterious Affair at Styles. (Ebook Classic Ser.). E-Book 5.00 (*0-7410-0495-X*) SoftBook Pr.

—The Mysterious Affair at Styles. l.t. ed. 2001. (Ulverscroft Large Print Ser.). 32.50 o.p. (*0-7089-1955-3*) Ulverscroft Large Print Bks., Ltd.

—The Mysterious Affair at Styles. 2002. 188p. pap. 16.95 (*1-59224-889-6*); lib. bdg. 29.95 (*1-59224-888-8*) Wildside Pr.

—The Mysterious Affair at Styles & The Secret Adversary: An Agatha Christie Omnibus. 1998. 464p. pap. 12.95 (*0-7867-0434-9*, Carroll & Graf Pubs.) Avalon Publishing Group.

—The Mystery of the Blue Train. Date not set. lib. bdg. 20.95 (*0-8488-2138-6*) Amereon, Ltd.

—The Mystery of the Blue Train. 1987. (Hardcover Collection). 9.95 o.s.i (*0-553-35068-4*) Bantam Bks.

—The Mystery of the Blue Train. 1991. (Hercule Poirot Mystery Ser.). 288p. reprint ed. mass mkt. 5.99 (*0-425-13026-6*) Berkley Publishing Group.

—The Mystery of the Blue Train. l.t. ed. 1992. 391p. 13.95 o.p. (*0-8161-4580-6*); 1991. 350p. 19.95 o.p. (*0-8161-4579-2*) Gale Group. (Macmillan Reference USA).

—The Mystery of the Blue Train. abr. ed. 1993. (BBC Radio Presents Ser.). audio 18.00 o.s.i (*0-553-47181-3*, RH Audio) Random Hse. Audio Publishing Group.

—The Mystery of the Blue Train. 1989. 224p. mass mkt. 4.99 o.p. (*0-671-70264-5*); 1985. mass mkt. 3.50 o.s.i (*0-671-60637-9*) Simon & Schuster. (Pocket).

—The Mystery of the Blue Train. l.t. ed. 1976. 423p. 12.00 o.p. (*0-85456-438-1*, Ulverscroft) Thorpe, F. A. Pubs. GBR. *Dist:* Ulverscroft Large Print Bks., Ltd.

—The Mystery of the Blue Train. 1991. 12.04 (*0-606-12445-4*) Turtleback Bks.

—One, Two, Buckle My Shoe. 2000. E-Book 5.99 (*0-425-17792-0*); 1998. mass mkt. 3.99 o.s.i (*0-425-16925-1*) Berkley Publishing Group.

—One, Two, Buckle My Shoe. Cooper, Roger, ed. 1987. 256p. reprint ed. mass mkt. 5.99 (*0-425-10570-9*) Berkley Publishing Group.

—One, Two, Buckle My Shoe. l.t. ed. 1973. (Ulverscroft Large Print Ser.). 322p. 12.00 o.p. (*0-85456-185-4*, Ulverscroft) Thorpe, F. A. Pubs. GBR. *Dist:* Ulverscroft Large Print Bks., Ltd., Ulverscroft Large Print Canada, Ltd.

—One, Two, Buckle My Shoe. 1984. 12.04 (*0-606-00968-X*) Turtleback Bks.

—An Overdose of Death. 1972. mass mkt. 2.95 o.s.i (*0-440-16780-9*) Dell Publishing.

—The Patriotic Murders. 1986. mass mkt. 9.95 o.p. (*0-553-35042-0*) Bantam Bks.

—The Patriotic Murders. 1985. mass mkt. 2.95 o.s.i (*0-425-08900-2*); 1984. mass mkt. 2.95 o.s.i (*0-425-06797-1*) Berkley Publishing Group.

—The Patriotic Murders. l.t. ed. (Agatha Christie Ser.). 312p. 1990. 12.95 o.p. (*0-8161-4586-5*); 1989. lib. bdg. 20.95 (*0-8161-4585-7*) Gale Group. (Macmillan Reference USA).

—The Patriotic Murders. 1986. (Agatha Christie Ser.). 14.95 (*0-396-08868-6*, G. P. Putnam's Sons) Penguin Putnam Bks. for Young Readers.

—Peril at End House. 1991. (Hercule Poirot Mystery Ser.). 224p. mass mkt. 5.99 (*0-425-13025-8*) Berkley Publishing Group.

—Peril at End House. l.t. ed. (Popular Author Ser.). 281p. 1989. 13.95 o.p. (*0-8161-4588-1*); 1988. lib. bdg. 19.95 o.p. (*0-8161-4587-3*) Gale Group. (Macmillan Reference USA).

—Peril at End House. 1985. (Agatha Christie Ser.). 12.95 o.s.i (*0-396-08706-X*, G. P. Putnam's Sons) Penguin Putnam Bks. for Young Readers.

—Peril at End House. 1985. mass mkt. 3.50 o.s.i (*0-671-61120-8*); 1982. mass mkt. 2.95 o.s.i (*0-671-46538-4*) Simon & Schuster. (Pocket).

—Peril at End House. l.t. ed. 1978. (Ulverscroft Large Print Ser.). 327p. 12.00 (*0-7089-0153-0*, Ulverscroft) Thorpe, F. A. Pubs. GBR. *Dist:* Ulverscroft Large Print Bks., Ltd., Ulverscroft Large Print Canada, Ltd.

—Peril at End House. 1991. (Hercule Poirot Mystery Ser.). 12.04 (*0-606-12477-2*) Turtleback Bks.

—Poirot Investigates. 1983. mass mkt. 2.95 o.s.i (*0-553-23908-2*); 208p. mass mkt. 3.50 o.s.i (*0-553-27001-X*) Bantam Bks.

—Poirot Investigates. 2000. (Hercule Poirot Mystery Ser.). 256p. mass mkt. 5.99 (*0-425-17472-7*) Berkley Publishing Group.

—Poirot Investigates. unabr. ed. 1990. (Hercule Poirot Mystery Ser.). Set. audio 16.99 (*0-88646-168-5*, 7169); Vol. 2. audio 16.99 (*0-88646-237-1*) Durkin Hayes Publishing Ltd.

—Poirot Investigates. pap. 14.95 (*0-8161-4590-3*); 1992. 330p. lib. bdg. 19.95 o.p. (*0-8161-4589-X*) Gale Group. (Macmillan Reference USA).

—Poirot Investigates. l.t. ed. 2001. (Ulverscroft Large Print Ser.). 32.50 (*0-7089-2282-1*) Ulverscroft Large Print Bks., Ltd.

—Poirot Loses a Client. (Hercule Poirot Ser.). 1986. mass mkt. 2.95 o.s.i (*0-425-09038-8*); 1984. mass mkt. 2.95 o.s.i (*0-425-06799-8*) Berkley Publishing Group.

—Poirot Loses a Client. 1974. 224p. pap. 2.50 o.s.i (*0-440-16984-4*) Dell Publishing.

—Poirot Loses a Client. l.t. ed. (Agatha Christie Ser.). 420p. 1992. 14.95 o.p. (*0-8161-4592-X*); 1991. lib. bdg. 19.95 o.p. (*0-8161-4591-1*) Gale Group. (Macmillan Reference USA).

—Poirot Loses a Client. 1991. (Hercule Poirot Ser.). 336p. 22.95 (*0-399-13604-5*, G. P. Putnam's Sons) Penguin Group (USA) Inc.

—Poirot's Early Cases. l.t. ed. 2001. (Ulverscroft Large Print Ser.). 32.50 (*0-7089-2326-7*) Ulverscroft Large Print Bks., Ltd.

—The Regatta Mystery & Other Stories. 1986. 176p. mass mkt. 5.99 (*0-425-10041-3*) Berkley Publishing Group.

—The Regatta Mystery & Other Stories. 1976. mass mkt. 2.95 o.s.i (*0-440-17336-1*) Dell Publishing.

—The Regatta Mystery & Other Stories. l.t. ed. (Agatha Christie Ser.). 280p. 1990. 12.95 o.p. (*0-8161-4596-2*); 1989. 12.95 o.p. (*0-8161-4595-4*) Gale Group. (Macmillan Reference USA).

—The Regatta Mystery & Other Stories. 1986. (Agatha Christie Ser.). 229p. 12.95 o.s.i (*0-396-08805-8*, G. P. Putnam's Sons) Penguin Putnam Bks. for Young Readers.

—Sad Cypress. (Hercule Poirot Ser.). 1986. mass mkt. 2.95 o.s.i (*0-425-09328-X*); 1984. mass mkt. 2.95 o.s.i (*0-425-06801-3*) Berkley Publishing Group.

—Sad Cypress. 1970. 224p. pap. 2.50 o.s.i (*0-440-17552-6*) Dell Publishing.

—Sad Cypress. 1994. (Hercule Poirot Ser.). 320p. 24.95 (*0-399-13924-9*, G. P. Putnam's Sons) Penguin Group (USA) Inc.

—Sad Cypress. 1982. (Agatha Christie Ser.). 9.95 o.p. (*0-425-46801-1*, G. P. Putnam's Sons) Penguin Putnam Bks. for Young Readers.

—Sad Cypress. (Hercule Poirot Ser.). 9.95 o.s.i (*0-396-08112-6*) Putnam Publishing Group, The.

—Sad Cypress. abr. ed. 1993. (BBC Radio Presents Ser.). audio 16.99 o.s.i (*0-553-47132-5*, RH Audio) Random Hse. Audio Publishing Group.

—Sad Cypress. l.t. ed. 1965. (Ulverscroft Large Print Ser.). 384p. o.p. (*0-85456-690-2*, Ulverscroft) Thorpe, F. A. Pubs. GBR. *Dist:* Ulverscroft Large Print Canada, Ltd.

—Sad Cypress. 1984. (Hercule Poirot Mystery Ser.). 12.04 (*0-606-00971-X*) Turtleback Bks.

—Sad Cypress: A Hercule Poirot Mystery. unabr. ed. 1995. audio 54.95 o.p. (*0-7451-4186-2*, CAB 869) BBC Audiobooks America.

—Sad Cypress: A Hercule Poirot Novel. 1986. (Hercule Poirot Mystery Ser.). 240p. mass mkt. 5.99 (*0-425-09853-2*) Berkley Publishing Group.

—Taken at the Flood. (Agatha Christie Ser.). 1998. mass mkt. 3.99 o.s.i (*0-425-16927-8*); 1984. 256p. mass mkt. 5.99 (*0-425-06803-X*) Berkley Publishing Group.

—Taken at the Flood. l.t. ed. 1990. 386p. 12.00 o.p. (*0-85456-084-X*, Ulverscroft) Thorpe, F. A. Pubs. GBR. *Dist:* Ulverscroft Large Print Bks., Ltd.

—There Is a Tide. 1987. 9.95 o.s.i (*0-553-35066-8*) Bantam Bks.

—There Is a Tide. 1970. pap. 1.95 o.s.i (*0-440-18692-7*) Dell Publishing.

—There Is a Tide. l.t. ed. (Agatha Christie Ser.). 374p. 1992. pap. 12.95 o.p. (*0-8161-4604-7*); 1991. lib. bdg. 19.95 o.p. (*0-8161-4603-9*) Gale Group. (Macmillan Reference USA).

—There Is a Tide. 1988. 14.95 (*0-396-09299-3*, G. P. Putnam's Sons) Penguin Group (USA) Inc.

—Third Girl. 1991. (Agatha Christie Ser.). 400p. 12.95 o.p. (*0-8161-4608-X*, Macmillan Reference USA) Gale Group.

—Third Girl. 1990. (Hercule Poirot Ser.). 208p. 21.95 o.s.i (*0-399-13512-X*, G. P. Putnam's Sons) Penguin Putnam Bks. for Young Readers.

—Third Girl. 1984. mass mkt. 3.50 o.s.i (*0-671-54212-5*); 1982. mass mkt. 2.95 o.s.i (*0-671-46719-0*) Simon & Schuster. (Pocket).

—Third Girl. 1992. (Hercule Poirot Mystery Ser.). 12.04 (*0-606-12536-1*) Turtleback Bks.

—The Third Girl. 2000. (Hercule Poirot Mystery Ser.). 272p. mass mkt. 5.99 (*0-425-17471-9*) Berkley Publishing Group.

—Third Girl. l.t. ed. 1990. (Agatha Christie Ser.). 360p. lib. bdg. 13.95 o.p. (*0-8161-4607-1*, Macmillan Reference USA) Gale Group.

—Third Girl. l.t. ed. 1989. 406p. 12.00 o.p. (*0-85456-585-X*, Ulverscroft) Thorpe, F. A. Pubs. GBR. *Dist:* Ulverscroft Large Print Bks., Ltd.

—Third Girl: A Hercule Poirot Mystery. unabr. ed. 1997. audio 54.95 o.p. (*0-7451-5838-2*, CAB 105) BBC Audiobooks America.

—Thirteen at Dinner. 224p. 21.95 o.s.i (*0-8488-2445-8*) Amereon, Ltd.

—Thirteen at Dinner. 1985. mass mkt. 2.95 o.s.i (*0-425-08902-9*); 1984. mass mkt. 2.95 o.s.i (*0-425-06805-6*) Berkley Publishing Group.

—Thirteen at Dinner. 1969. 240p. pap. 2.50 o.s.i (*0-440-18742-7*) Dell Publishing.

—Thirteen at Dinner. l.t. ed. (Agatha Christie Ser.). 1990. 368p. 12.95 o.p. (*0-8161-4610-1*); 1989. 340p. lib. bdg. 19.95 o.p. (*0-8161-4609-8*) Gale Group. (Macmillan Reference USA).

—Thirteen at Dinner. 1986. (Agatha Christie Ser.). 255p. 12.95 (*0-396-08806-6*, G. P. Putnam's Sons) Penguin Putnam Bks. for Young Readers.

—Thirteen at Dinner. 1992. audio 15.95 o.s.i (*0-553-74533-6*); audio 18.00 o.s.i (*0-553-47109-0*) Random Hse. Audio Publishing Group. (RH Audio).

—Three Act Tragedy. 1986. (Hercule Poirot Mystery Ser.). 224p. mass mkt. 5.99 (*0-425-09180-5*) Berkley Publishing Group.

—Three Act Tragedy. l.t. ed. 1989. 351p. 12.00 o.p. (*0-85456-326-1*, Ulverscroft) Thorpe, F. A. Pubs. GBR. *Dist:* Ulverscroft Large Print Bks., Ltd.

—Three Act Tragedy. 1984. (Hercule Poirot Mystery Ser.). 12.04 (*0-606-12538-8*) Turtleback Bks.

—Three Blind Mice. abr. ed. 1990. audio 16.99 (*0-88646-172-3*, 7173) Durkin Hayes Publishing Ltd.

—Three Blind Mice & Other Stories. 1984. 224p. mass mkt. 5.99 o.s.i (*0-425-06806-4*) Berkley Publishing Group.

—Three Blind Mice & Other Stories. 1980. pap. 2.50 o.s.i (*0-440-15867-2*) Dell Publishing.

—Three Blind Mice & Other Stories. l.t. ed. (Popular Author Ser.). 338p. 1989. 10.95 o.p. (*0-8161-4462-1*); 1988. lib. bdg. 19.95 o.p. (*0-8161-4461-3*) Gale Group. (Macmillan Reference USA).

—Three Blind Mice & Other Stories. 1985. (Agatha Christie Ser.). 240p. 12.95 (*0-396-08707-8*, G. P. Putnam's Sons) Penguin Putnam Bks. for Young Readers.

—Three Blind Mice & Other Stories. 2001. 288p. reprint ed. mass mkt. 5.99 (*0-312-97976-2*, St. Martin's Paperbacks) St. Martin's Pr.

—The Under Dog & Other Stories. 1988. (HC Collection). mass mkt. 9.95 o.s.i (*0-553-35070-6*) Bantam Bks.

—The Under Dog & Other Stories. 1984. 208p. mass mkt. 5.99 (*0-425-06808-0*) Berkley Publishing Group.

—The Under Dog & Other Stories. 1969. 192p. pap. 2.25 o.s.i (*0-440-19228-5*) Dell Publishing.

—The Under Dog & Other Stories. l.t. ed. 1991. 320p. lib. bdg. 19.95 o.p. (*0-8161-4615-2*, Macmillan Reference USA) Gale Group.

**POLDARK, ROSS (FICTITIOUS CHARACTER)—FICTION**

Graham, Winston. The Angry Tide. unabr. ed. 1999. (Poldark Ser. ). Set audio 110.95; Vol. 7. audio 110.95 (*0-7540-0294-2*, CAB 1717) BBC Audiobooks America.

—The Angry Tide. 1979. mass mkt. 2.50 o.s.i (*0-345-28046-6*) Ballantine Bks.

—The Angry Tide. unabr. ed. 2000. (Poldark Ser.: Bk. 7). audio 89.95 Chivers Audio Bks. GBR. *Dist:* BBC Audiobooks America.

—The Angry Tide. 1978. 10.00 o.p. (*0-385-13682-X*) Doubleday Publishing.

—The Angry Tide. 1979. (Reader's Request Ser.). lib. bdg. 19.95 o.p. (*0-8161-6682-X*, Macmillan Reference USA) Gale Group.

—The Angry Tide: Cornwall - As the 18th Century Ebbs. 2002. (Poldark Saga Ser.: Vol. 7). (Illus.). 308p. mass mkt. 8.95 (*0-330-34500-1*) Pan Bks. Ltd. GBR. *Dist:* Trafalgar Square.

—Bella Poldark: A Novel of Cornwall, 1818-1820. 2002. (Poldark Saga). 530p. 24.95 (*0-333-98923-6*) Macmillan U.K. GBR. *Dist:* Trafalgar Square.

—Bella Poldark: A Novel of Cornwall, 1818-1820. 2003. xiii, 688p. pap. 8.95 (*0-330-49149-0*) Pan Bks. Ltd. GBR. *Dist:* Trafalgar Square.

—The Black Moon. 1978. (Poldark Ser.: No.5). mass mkt. 2.25 o.s.i (*0-345-27735-X*); 1977. mass mkt. 1.95 o.s.i (*0-345-26004-X*) Ballantine Bks.

—Black Moon, 2 vols. l.t. ed. 1979. (YA). (gr. 7-12). lib. bdg. 18.95 o.p. (*0-8161-6680-3*, Macmillan Reference USA) Gale Group.

—The Black Moon. unabr. ed. 1997. (Poldark Ser. : Vol. 5). audio 96.95 (*0-7451-6753-5*, CAB 1369) BBC Audiobooks America.

—The Black Moon. unabr. ed. 2000. (Poldark Ser.: Bk. 5). audio 79.95 Chivers Audio Bks. GBR. *Dist:* BBC Audiobooks America.

—The Black Moon: Cornwall 1794. 2002. (Poldark Saga Ser.: Vol. 5). (Illus.). 324p. mass mkt. 8.95 (*0-330-34498-6*) Pan Bks. Ltd. GBR. *Dist:* Trafalgar Square.

—Demelza. unabr. ed. 1995. (Poldark Ser. : Vol. 2). audio 96.95 (*0-7451-6469-2*, CAB 1086) BBC Audiobooks America.

—Demelza. 1977. mass mkt. 1.95 o.s.i (*0-345-26001-5*) Ballantine Bks.

—Demelza. unabr. ed. 2000. (Poldark Ser.: Bk. 2). audio 79.95 Chivers Audio Bks. GBR. *Dist:* BBC Audiobooks America.

—Demelza. 1979. (Reader's Request Ser.). lib. bdg. 17.95 o.p. (*0-8161-6677-3*, Macmillan Reference USA) Gale Group.

—Four Swans. 2002. (Poldark Saga Ser.: Vol. 6). (Illus.). 581p. mass mkt. 8.95 (*0-330-34499-4*) Pan Bks. Ltd. GBR. *Dist:* Trafalgar Square.

—The Four Swans. unabr. ed. 1998. (Poldark Ser. : Vol. 6). audio 110.95 (*0-7540-0124-5*, CAB1547) BBC Audiobooks America.

—The Four Swans. 1978. mass mkt. 2.25 o.s.i (*0-345-26005-8*) Ballantine Bks.

—The Four Swans. unabr. ed. 2000. (Poldark Ser.: Bk. 6). audio 89.95 Chivers Audio Bks. GBR. *Dist:* BBC Audiobooks America.

—The Four Swans. 1977. 8.95 o.p. (*0-385-12338-8*) Doubleday Publishing.

—The Four Swans. 1979. (Reader's Request Ser.). lib. bdg. 19.95 o.p. (*0-8161-6681-1*, Macmillan Reference USA) Gale Group.

—Jeremy Poldark. unabr. ed. 1996. (Poldark Ser. : Vol. 3). audio 69.95 (*0-7451-6612-1*, CAB1228) BBC Audiobooks America.

—Jeremy Poldark. 1977. mass mkt. 1.95 o.s.i (*0-345-26002-3*); No. 3. 1978. mass mkt. 2.25 o.s.i (*0-345-27733-3*) Ballantine Bks.

—Jeremy Poldark. unabr. ed. 2000. (Poldark Ser.: Bk. 3). audio 59.95 Chivers Audio Bks. GBR. *Dist:* BBC Audiobooks America.

—Jeremy Poldark. l.t. ed. 1979. (YA). (gr. 7-12). lib. bdg. 14.95 o.p. (*0-8161-6678-1*, Macmillan Reference USA) Gale Group.

—Loving Cup. 2002. (Poldark Saga Ser.: Vol. 10). (Illus.). 580p. mass mkt. 8.95 (*0-330-34503-6*) Pan Bks. Ltd. GBR. *Dist:* Trafalgar Square.

—Loving Cup: The Tenth Poldark Novel. 1985. 456p. 17.95 o.p. (*0-385-19834-5*) Doubleday Publishing.

—Miller's Dance. Date not set. lib. bdg. 22.95 (*0-8488-1016-3*) Amereon, Ltd.

—The Miller's Dance. 1983. (Poldark Ser.: No. 9). 384p. 15.95 o.p. (*0-385-18405-0*) Doubleday Publishing.

—The Miller's Dance. 2002. (Poldark Saga Ser.: Vol. 9). (Illus.). 496p. mass mkt. 8.95 (*0-330-34502-8*) Pan Bks. Ltd. GBR. *Dist:* Trafalgar Square.

—Ross Poldark. unabr. ed. 1992. (Poldark Ser. : Vol. 1). audio 84.95 (*0-7451-4035-1*, CAB 732) BBC Audiobooks America.

—Ross Poldark. (Poldark Ser.). 1978. mass mkt. 2.25 o.s.i (*0-345-27731-7*); 1977. mass mkt. 1.95 o.s.i (*0-345-25654-9*) Ballantine Bks.

—Ross Poldark. unabr. ed. 2000. (Poldark Ser.: Bk. 1). audio 69.95 Chivers Audio Bks. GBR. *Dist:* BBC Audiobooks America.

—Ross Poldark, 2 vols. l.t. ed. 1979. (Reader's Request Ser.). lib. bdg. 16.95 o.p. (*0-8161-6676-5*, Macmillan Reference USA) Gale Group.

—Stranger from the Sea. 22.95 (*0-8488-1017-1*) Amereon, Ltd.

—The Stranger from the Sea. unabr. ed. 2000. (Poldark Ser.: Vol. 8). audio 96.95 (*0-7540-0437-6*, CAB 1860) Chivers Audio Bks. GBR. *Dist:* BBC Audiobooks America.

—The Stranger from the Sea. 1982. 432p. 17.95 o.p. (*0-385-17967-7*) Doubleday Publishing.

—The Stranger from the Sea, Bk. 8. 2002. (Poldark Saga Ser.: Vol. 8). (Illus.). 304p. pap. 8.95 (*0-330-34501-X*) Pan Bks. Ltd. GBR. *Dist:* Trafalgar Square.

—The Twisted Sword: Cornwall - January 1815. 1991. (Poldark Novel Ser.). 512p. 21.95 o.p. (*0-88184-693-7*, Carroll & Graf Pubs.) Avalon Publishing Group.

—The Twisted Sword: Cornwall - January 1815, Bk. 11. 2002. (Poldark Saga Ser.: Vol. 11). (Illus.). 544p. pap. 8.95 (*0-330-31749-0*) Pan Bks. Ltd. GBR. *Dist:* Trafalgar Square.

—The Twisted Sword Pt. 1: Cornwall - January 1815. l.t. ed. 1995. (Charnwood Large Print Ser.). 496p. 29.99 o.p. (*0-7089-8822-9*, Charnwood) Thorpe, F. A. Pubs. GBR. *Dist:* Ulverscroft Large Print Bks., Ltd., Ulverscroft Large Print Canada, Ltd.

—The Twisted Sword Pt. 2: Cornwall - January 1815. l.t. ed. 1995. (Charnwood Large Print Ser.). 288p. 29.99 o.p. (*0-7089-8828-8*, Charnwood) Thorpe, F. A. Pubs. GBR. *Dist:* Ulverscroft Large Print Bks., Ltd., Ulverscroft Large Print Canada, Ltd.

—Warleggan. unabr. ed. 1996. (Poldark Ser. : Vol. 4). audio 96.95 (*0-7451-6691-1*, CAB1307) BBC Audiobooks America.

—Warleggan. 1978. (Poldark Ser.: No. 4). mass mkt. 2.25 o.s.i (*0-345-27734-1*); 1977. mass mkt. 1.95 o.s.i (*0-345-26003-1*) Ballantine Bks.

—Warleggan. unabr. ed. 2000. (Poldark Ser.: Bk. 4). audio 79.95 Chivers Audio Bks. GBR. *Dist:* BBC Audiobooks America.

—Warleggan, 2 vols. l.t. ed. 1979. (Reader's Request Ser.). lib. bdg. 17.95 o.p. (*0-8161-6679-X*, Macmillan Reference USA) Gale Group.

—Warleggan, Bk. 4. 2002. (Poldark Saga Ser.: Vol. 4). 471p. pap. 8.95 (*0-330-34496-X*) Pan Bks. Ltd. GBR. *Dist:* Trafalgar Square.

## POLLIFAX, EMILY (FICTITIOUS CHARACTER)—FICTION

Gilman, Dorothy. The Amazing Mrs. Pollifax. 1986. pap. 2.95 o.p. (*0-449-44215-2*); 1985. 176p. mass mkt. 6.50 (*0-449-20912-1*) Ballantine Bks. (Fawcett).

—The Amazing Mrs. Pollifax. 1970. 5.95 o.p. (*0-385-02907-1*) Doubleday Publishing.

—The Amazing Mrs. Pollifax. (Nightingale Ser.). 1983. 284p. pap. 9.95 o.p. (*0-8161-3371-9*); 1992. 286p. 17.95 o.p. (*0-8161-5355-8*) Gale Group. (Macmillan Reference USA).

—The Amazing Mrs. Pollifax. unabr. ed. 1989. (Mrs. Pollifax Mystery Ser.: Vol. 2). audio 44.00 (*1-55690-011-2*, 89740E7) Recorded Bks., LLC.

—The Elusive Mrs. Pollifax. 1987. 208p. mass mkt. 6.99 (*0-449-21523-7*); 1985. mass mkt. 2.95 o.s.i (*0-449-20855-9*) Ballantine Bks. (Fawcett).

—The Elusive Mrs. Pollifax. 1971. 8.95 o.p. (*0-385-09463-9*) Doubleday Publishing.

—The Elusive Mrs. Pollifax. (Nightingale Ser.). 1983. pap. 8.95 o.p. (*0-8161-3370-0*); 1993. 275p. 17.95 o.p. (*0-8161-5354-X*) Gale Group. (Macmillan Reference USA).

—The Elusive Mrs. Pollifax. unabr. ed. 1990. (Mrs. Pollifax Mystery Ser.: Vol. 3). audio 44.00 (*1-55690-162-3*, 90005E7) Recorded Bks., LLC.

—Mrs. Pollifax & the China Station. 1985. 224p. mass mkt. 6.99 (*0-449-20840-0*, Fawcett) Ballantine Bks.

—Mrs. Pollifax & the China Station. 1983. (Illus.). 192p. 12.95 o.p. (*0-385-14525-X*) Doubleday Publishing.

—Mrs. Pollifax & the Golden Triangle. 1989. 208p. mass mkt. 6.99 (*0-449-21515-6*, Fawcett) Ballantine Bks.

—Mrs. Pollifax & the Hong Kong Buddha. 1986. pap. 94.50 o.p. (*0-449-28189-2*); 224p. mass mkt. 6.99 (*0-449-20983-0*) Ballantine Bks. (Fawcett).

—Mrs. Pollifax & the Hong Kong Buddha. 1985. 192p. 14.95 o.p. (*0-385-19959-7*) Doubleday Publishing.

—Mrs. Pollifax & the Innocent Tourist. 1997. 224p. mass mkt. 6.99 (*0-449-18336-X*); 203p. 23.00 o.p. (*0-449-91137-3*) Ballantine Bks. (Fawcett).

—Mrs. Pollifax & the Lion Killer. 1996. 224p. mass mkt. 6.99 (*0-449-15004-6*, Fawcett) Ballantine Bks.

—Mrs. Pollifax & the Lion Killer. l.t. ed. 1996. 320p. 21.00 o.p. (*0-7838-1677-4*, Macmillan Reference USA) Gale Group.

—Mrs. Pollifax & the Lion Killer. l.t. ed. 1996. 320p. pap. 21.00 o.s.i (*0-679-75872-0*) Random Hse. Large Print.

—Mrs. Pollifax & the Second Thief. 1995. 208p. mass mkt. 6.99 (*0-449-14905-6*, Fawcett) Ballantine Bks.

—Mrs. Pollifax & the Second Thief. abr. ed. 1993. audio 16.95 o.p. (*1-56100-351-4*, 1328); audio 57.25 o.p. (*1-56100-161-9*, 954, Unabridged Library Editions); audio 21.95 o.p. (*1-56100-533-9*, 354, Bookcassette) Brilliance Audio.

—Mrs. Pollifax & the Second Thief. 1993. 208p. 20.00 o.s.i (*0-385-47109-2*) Doubleday Publishing.

—Mrs. Pollifax & the Second Thief. l.t. ed. 1994. 228p. lib. bdg. 16.95 o.p. (*0-8161-5918-1*); lib. bdg. 21.95 (*0-8161-5917-3*) Gale Group. (Macmillan Reference USA).

—Mrs. Pollifax & the Second Thief. abr. ed. 2000. audio 7.95 (*1-57815-020-5*, 1005, Media Bks. Audio Publishing) Media Bks., L. L. C.

—Mrs. Pollifax & the Second Thief. unabr. ed. 1993. (Mrs. Pollifax Mystery Ser.: Vol. 10). audio 44.00 (*1-55690-911-X*, 93407E7) Recorded Bks., LLC.

—Mrs. Pollifax & the Whirling Dervish. 1991. 224p. mass mkt. 6.99 (*0-449-14760-6*, Fawcett) Ballantine Bks.

—Mrs. Pollifax & the Whirling Dervish. l.t. ed. 1991. (General Ser.). 304p. 21.95 o.p. (*0-8161-5119-9*, Macmillan Reference USA) Gale Group.

—Mrs. Pollifax & the Whirling Dervish. 1991. audio 14.99 o.s.i (*0-553-45275-4*, RH Audio) Random Hse. Audio Publishing Group.

—Mrs. Pollifax, Innocent Tourist. l.t. ed. 1997. pap. 23.00 o.s.i (*0-679-77420-3*) Random Hse., Inc.

—Mrs. Pollifax on Safari. 1987. 224p. mass mkt. 6.99 (*0-449-21524-5*); 1985. mass mkt. 2.95 o.p. (*0-449-21011-1*) Ballantine Bks. (Fawcett).

—Mrs. Pollifax on Safari. 1977. 7.95 o.p. (*0-385-07506-5*) Doubleday Publishing.

—Mrs. Pollifax on Safari. 1977. lib. bdg. 10.95 o.p. (*0-8161-6490-8*, Macmillan Reference USA) Gale Group.

—Mrs. Pollifax Pursued. 1995. 198p. 20.00 o.p. (*0-449-90954-9*, Fawcett) Ballantine Bks.

—Mrs. Pollifax Pursued. l.t. ed. 1995. (Large Print Bks.). pap. 22.95 o.p. (*1-56895-088-8*, Wheeler Publishing, Inc.) Gale Group.

—Mrs. Pollifax Unveiled. 2001. E-Book 6.99 (*1-58945-767-6*) Adobe Systems, Inc.

—Mrs. Pollifax Unveiled. (Mrs. Pollifax Mystery Ser.). 2001. 224p. mass mkt. 6.99 (*0-449-00670-0*); 2001. E-Book 18.50 (*0-345-44307-1*, Ballantine Bks.); 2000. 208p. 23.00 (*0-345-43652-0*) Ballantine Bks.

—Mrs. Pollifax Unveiled. abr. ed. (Mrs. Pollifax Ser.). 2001. audio 7.99 o.s.i (*1-58788-081-4*, 2330, Paperback Nova Audio Bks.); 2000. audio 17.95 o.p. (*1-56740-876-1*, 1948, Nova Audio Bks.); 2000. audio 24.95 (*1-56740-480-4*, 1946, Brilliance Audio Unabridged); 2000. audio 44.25 (*1-56740-698-X*, 1947, Unabridged Library Editions) Brilliance Audio.

—Mrs. Pollifax Unveiled. l.t. ed. 2000. (Wheeler Large Print Book Ser.). 210p. 26.95 o.p. (*1-56895-826-9*, Wheeler Publishing, Inc.) Gale Group.

—Mrs. Pollifax Unveiled. 2000. (Mrs. Pollifax Mystery Ser.: Vol. 13). audio compact disk 48.00 (*0-7887-4901-3*, C1276E7); audio 37.00 (*0-7887-4308-2*, 96223E7) Recorded Bks., LLC.

—A Palm for Mrs. Pollifax. 1985. 192p. mass mkt. 6.50 (*0-449-20864-8*, Fawcett) Ballantine Bks.

—A Palm for Mrs. Pollifax. (Black Dagger Crime Ser.). 232p. 12.95 o.p. (*0-86220-742-8*) Chivers Pr. GBR. *Dist:* BBC Audiobooks America.

—A Palm for Mrs. Pollifax. 1973. 240p. 5.95 o.p. (*0-385-09134-6*) Doubleday Publishing.

—A Palm for Mrs. Pollifax. l.t. ed. 1994. 281p. lib. bdg. 14.95 o.p. (*0-8161-5353-1*, Macmillan Reference USA) Gale Group.

—The Unexpected Mrs. Pollifax. 1999. pap. 5.99 (*0-449-45854-7*); 1998. mass mkt. 0.00 (*0-449-45884-9*); 1986. pap. 2.95 o.p. (*0-449-44202-0*); 1985. 192p. mass mkt. 6.99 (*0-449-20828-1*) Ballantine Bks. (Fawcett).

—The Unexpected Mrs. Pollifax. 1991. 300p. reprint ed. lib. bdg. 22.95 (*0-89966-873-9*) Buccaneer Bks., Inc.

—The Unexpected Mrs. Pollifax. 1972. 216p. 6.95 o.p. (*0-385-05974-4*) Doubleday Publishing.

—The Unexpected Mrs. Pollifax. (Nightingale Paperbacks Ser.). 1984. 342p. pap. 9.95 o.p. (*0-8161-3368-9*); 1992. 400p. 18.95 o.p. (*0-8161-5352-3*) Gale Group. (Macmillan Reference USA).

—The Unexpected Mrs. Pollifax. unabr. ed. 2001. audio compact disk 78.00 (*0-7887-7162-0*, C1415); 1989. (Mrs. Pollifax Mystery Ser.: Vol. 1). audio 51.00 (*1-55690-537-8*, 89730E7) Recorded Bks., LLC.

Gilman, Dorothy. Mrs. Pollifax Pursued. 1995. 240p. mass mkt. 6.99 (*0-449-14956-0*, Fawcett) Ballantine Bks.

## POLO, NICK (FICTITIOUS CHARACTER)—FICTION

Keannealy, Jerry. Vintage Polo. 1993. 256p. 19.95 o.p. (*0-312-09932-0*, Saint Martin's Minotaur) St. Martin's Pr.

Kennealy, Jerry. All That Glitters: A Nick Polo Mystery. 1996. 240p. 21.95 o.p. (*0-312-15049-0*, Saint Martin's Minotaur) St. Martin's Pr.

—Beggar's Choice. 1994. 256p. 20.95 o.p. (*0-312-11478-8*, Saint Martin's Minotaur) St. Martin's Pr.

—Green with Envy: A Nick Polo Mystery. 1991. 240p. 17.95 o.p. (*0-312-06572-8*, Saint Martin's Minotaur) St. Martin's Pr.

—Polo, Anyone? 1988. 224p. 15.95 o.p. (*0-312-01491-0*, Saint Martin's Minotaur) St. Martin's Pr.

—Polo in the Rough. 1989. 14.95 o.p. (*0-312-02964-0*, Saint Martin's Minotaur) St. Martin's Pr.

—Polo Solo. 1988. pap. 2.95 o.p. (*0-312-91074-6*, St. Martin's Paperbacks); 1987. 192p. 13.95 o.p. (*0-312-00671-3*) St. Martin's Pr.

—Polo's Ponies. 1988. 176p. 14.95 o.p. (*0-312-02267-0*, Saint Martin's Minotaur) St. Martin's Pr.

—Polo's Wild Card. 1992. 1.99 o.p. (*0-517-08490-2*) Random Hse. Value Publishing.

—Polo's Wild Card. 1990. 15.95 o.p. (*0-312-04437-2*, Saint Martin's Minotaur) St. Martin's Pr.

—Special Delivery: A Case for Nick Polo. 1992. 224p. 17.95 o.p. (*0-312-08304-1*, Saint Martin's Minotaur) St. Martin's Pr.

## POLYCRATES, ROSCO (FICTITIOUS CHARACTER)—FICTION

Blanc, Nero. Corpus de Crossword. 2003. 320p. pap. 13.00 (*0-425-19021-8*, Prime Crime) Berkley Publishing Group.

—The Crossword Murder. 320p. 2000. mass mkt. 5.99 (*0-425-17701-7*); 1999. pap. 13.00 (*0-425-16977-4*, Prime Crime) Berkley Publishing Group.

—Two Down: A New Crossword Murder Mystery with Crosswords included. 2000. (Illus.). 304p. pap. 13.00 (*0-425-17510-3*, Prime Crime) Berkley Publishing Group.

## POND, MR. (FICTITIOUS CHARACTER)—FICTION

Chesterton, G. K. Paradoxes of Mister Pond. 1990. xiii, 126p. pap. 5.95 (*0-486-26185-9*) Dover Pubns., Inc.

## PONS, SOLAR (FICTITIOUS CHARACTER)—FICTION

Copper, Basil. The Dossier of Solar Pons. 1987. (Academy Book Ser.). 278p. pap. 7.95 (*0-89733-252-0*) Academy Chicago Pubs., Ltd.

—Exploits of Solar Pons. 1993. (Illus.). 256p. (C). 25.00 (*1-878252-11-9*); 45.00 (*1-878252-14-3*) Fedogan & Bremer.

—The Further Adventures of Solar Pons. 1987. (Academy Book Ser.). 256p. pap. 7.95 (*0-89733-273-3*) Academy Chicago Pubs., Ltd.

—The Recollections of Solar Pons. 1995. 25.00 (*1-878252-20-8*); 75.00 (*1-878252-21-6*) Fedogan & Bremer.

—The Secret Files of Solar Pons. 1979. (Solar Pons Ser.: No. 10). pap. 1.95 o.p. (*0-523-40656-8*, Pinnacle Bks.) Kensington Publishing Corp.

Derleth, August. The Final Adventures of Solar Pons. 1998. (August Derleth Library ). 240p. 28.00 (*1-55246-012-6*) Battered Silicon Dispatch Box, The.

—The Return of Solar Pons. 1975. (Solar Pons Ser.: No. 6). 288p. pap. 1.50 o.p. (*0-523-23650-6*, Pinnacle Bks.) Kensington Publishing Corp.

—Solar Pons: The Chronicles of Solar Pons, No. 1. 1973. 8.95 o.p. (*0-87054-005-X*, Mycroft & Moran) Arkham Hse. Pubs.

—The Solar Pons Omnibus Edition, 2 Vols., Set. Copper, Basil, ed. 1982. (Illus.). 39.95 o.p. (*0-87054-006-8*, Mycroft & Moran) Arkham Hse. Pubs.

## PONTOWSKI, MATT (FICTITIOUS CHARACTER)—FICTION

Herman, Richard, Jr. Dark Wing. 1994. 23.00 (*0-671-87306-7*, Simon & Schuster) Simon & Schuster.

Herman, Richard, Jr. Dark Wing. 1996. 512p. mass mkt. 6.99 (*0-671-53493-9*, Pocket) Simon & Schuster.

—Iron Gate. 1996. 432p. 22.50 o.p. (*0-684-81070-0*, Simon & Schuster) Simon & Schuster.

## POOLE, CHARLIE (FICTITIOUS CHARACTER)—FICTION

Westlake, Donald E. The Fugitive Pigeon. 1993. 208p. mass mkt. 4.99 o.s.i (*0-446-40132-3*) Warner Bks., Inc.

## POPEYE (FICTITIOUS CHARACTER)—FICTION

Grandinetti, Fred M. Popeye: An Illustrated History of E. C. Segar's Character in Print, Radio, Television & Film Appearances, 1929-1993. 1994. (Illus.). 288p. per. 35.00 (*0-89950-982-7*) McFarland & Co., Inc. Pubs.

London, Bobby. Mondo Popeye. 1988. 112p. (Orig.). pap. 5.95 o.p. (*0-312-02611-0*, Saint Martin's Griffin) St. Martin's Pr.

## PORTAL, ELLIS (FICTITIOUS CHARACTER)—FICTION

Aubert, Rosemary. The Feast of Stephen. 2001. 272p. mass mkt. 6.99 o.s.i (*0-425-17799-8*, Prime Crime) Berkley Publishing Group.

—The Feast of Stephen: An Ellis Portal Mystery. 1999. (Ellis Portal Mystery Ser.). 224p. 22.95 (*1-882593-27-8*) Bridge Works Publishing Co., Inc.

—The Ferryman Will Be There: An Ellis Portal Mystery. 2001. (Ellis Portal Mystery Ser.: Vol. 3). 264p. 22.95 (*1-882593-44-8*) Bridge Works Publishing Co., Inc.

—Free Reign. 1998. 304p. mass mkt. 6.99 o.s.i (*0-425-16427-6*) Berkley Publishing Group.

—Free Reign: A Suspense Novel. 1997. (Ellis Portal Mystery Ser.). 240p. 21.95 o.s.i (*1-882593-18-9*) Bridge Works Publishing Co., Inc.

—Leave Me by Dying: An Ellis Portal Mystery. 2003. (Ellis Portal Mystery Ser.). 280p. 23.95 (*1-882593-73-1*) Bridge Works Publishing Co., Inc.

PORTER, BEN (FICTITIOUS CHARACTER)—FICTION
Travis, Elizabeth. Under the Influence. 1992. (WWL Mystery Ser.: No. 92). per. (0-373-26092-X, 1-26092-6, Harlequin Bks.) Harlequin Enterprises, Ltd.
—Under the Influence. 1989. 16.95 o.p. (0-312-02994-2, Saint Martin's Minotaur) St. Martin's Pr.

PORTER, RACHEL (FICTITIOUS CHARACTER)—FICTION
Speart, Jessica. Bird Brained. l.t. ed. 2002. (Paperback Ser.). 502p. pap. 24.95 (0-7862-4979-X) Gale Group.
—Bird Brained. 1999. (Rachel Porter Mysteries Ser.). 288p. mass mkt. 5.99 (0-380-79290-7, Avon Bks.) Morrow/Avon.
—Coastal Disturbance. 2003. 304p. mass mkt. 6.99 (0-380-82062-5, Avon Bks.) Morrow/Avon.
—Gator Aide. 1997. (Rachel Porter Mysteries Ser.). 304p. mass mkt. 5.99 (0-380-79288-5, Avon Bks.) Morrow/Avon.
—Tortoise Soup. 1998. (Rachel Porter Mysteries Ser.). 304p. mass mkt. 5.99 (0-380-79289-3, Avon Bks.) Morrow/Avon.

PORTILLO, VICTOR (FICTITIOUS CHARACTER)—FICTION
Heffner, Cliff. Divine Justice. 1997. 318p. pap. 14.95 (0-9663214-0-5) Mastermind Publishing.

PORTUGAL, JOE (FICTITIOUS CHARACTER)—FICTION
Walpow, Nathan. The Cactus Club Killings. 1999. 288p. pap. 19.00 (0-440-61382-5, Dell Bks.); mass mkt. 5.99 o.s.i (0-440-23491-3) Dell Publishing.
—Death of an Orchid Lover. 2000. (Joe Portugal Mysteries Ser.). 320p. mass mkt. 5.99 o.s.i (0-440-23492-1) Bantam Dell Publishing Group.
—Death of an Orchid Lover. 2000. 320p. pap. 19.00 (0-440-61385-X, Dell Bks.) Dell Publishing.
—One Last Hit. 2003. 377p. pap. 14.95 (0-9724412-0-4) UglyTown.

POST, ED (FICTITIOUS CHARACTER)—FICTION
McClellan, Bill. Evidence of Murder. 1993. 352p. (Orig.). mass mkt. 6.99 (0-451-40347-9, Onyx) NAL.

POTAMOS, JOE (FICTITIOUS CHARACTER)—FICTION
Truman, Margaret. Murder in Georgetown. 1987. (Capital Crime Myteries Ser.). 336p. mass mkt. 7.50 (0-449-21332-3, Fawcett) Ballantine Bks.
—Murder in Georgetown. unabr. ed. 2000. audio 49.95 (0-7451-6334-3, CAB 404) Chivers Audio Bks. GBR. Dist: BBC Audiobooks America.
—Murder in Georgetown. l.t. ed. 1987. 359p. 10.95 o.p. (0-8161-4146-0, Macmillan Reference USA) Gale Group.
—Murder in Georgetown. 1986. 16.95 o.p. (0-87795-797-5, Morrow, William & Co.) Morrow/Avon.

POTEET, JORDAN (FICTITIOUS CHARACTER)—FICTION
Abbott, Jeff. Distant Blood. 1996. 352p. mass mkt. 6.99 (0-345-39470-4) Ballantine Bks.
—Do unto Others. 1994. (Southwest Mysteries Ser.). 256p. mass mkt. 6.99 (0-345-38948-4) Ballantine Bks.
—The Only Good Yankee. 1995. 256p. mass mkt. 6.50 (0-345-39438-0, Del Rey) Ballantine Bks.
—Promises of Home. 1996. 288p. mass mkt. 6.99 (0-345-39469-0) Ballantine Bks.
Lattany, Kristin Hunter. Do unto Others. E-Book 19.95 (1-58945-572-X) Adobe Systems, Inc.
—Do unto Others. E-Book 19.50 (0-345-44329-2, Ballantine Bks.) Ballantine Bks.

POTTER, ARTHUR (FICTITIOUS CHARACTER)—FICTION
Deaver, Jeffery. A Maiden's Grave. l.t. ed. 1996. 608p. lib. bdg. 25.95 o.p. (0-7838-1621-9, Macmillan Reference USA) Gale Group.
—A Maiden's Grave. 432p. 2001. mass mkt. 7.99 (0-451-20429-8); 1996. mass mkt. 7.99 o.s.i (0-451-18848-9); 1996. mass mkt. 6.99 o.s.i (0-451-19337-7) NAL. (Signet Bks.).
—A Maiden's Grave. 1995. 432p. 22.95 o.p. (0-670-86622-9, Viking); audio 16.95 o.p. (0-14-086210-2, Penguin AudioBooks) Viking Penguin.

POTTER, EUGENIA (FICTITIOUS CHARACTER)—FICTION
Pickard, Nancy. The Blue Corn Murders. 1999. (Eugenia Potter Mysteries Ser.). 356p. pap. (0-7540-3688-X) BBC Audiobooks America.
—The Blue Corn Murders. 1998. (Eugenia Potter Mysteries Ser.). 272p. 21.95 o.s.i (0-385-31224-5) Dell Publishing.
—The Blue Corn Murders. l.t. ed. 1999. (Eugenia Potter Mysteries Ser.). 353p. 28.95 (0-7838-8479-6, Macmillan Reference USA) Gale Group.
—The Secret Ingredient Murders. 2001. (Eugenia Potter Mysteries Ser.). 272p. 22.95 o.s.i (0-385-31227-X, Delacorte Pr.) Dell Publishing.
—The Twenty-Seven Ingredient Chili con Carne Murders. 1994. (Eugenia Potter Mysteries Ser.). 288p. mass mkt. 5.99 (0-440-21641-9) Dell Publishing.
Pickard, Nancy, contrib. by. The Blue Corn Murders. 1999. (Eugenia Potter Mysteries Ser.). (0-7540-3687-1) BBC Audiobooks America.
Pickard, Nancy & Pickard, Virginia. The Blue Corn Murders. 1999. (Eugenia Potter Mysteries Ser.). 304p. mass mkt. 5.99 (0-440-21765-2) Dell Publishing.
Rich, Virginia. The Baked Bean Supper Murders. 1984. mass mkt. 4.95 o.s.i (0-345-31252-X, Ballantine Bks.) Ballantine Bks.
—The Baked Bean Supper Murders. 1983. 12.95 o.p. (0-525-24185-X, Dutton) Dutton/Plume.
—The Baked Bean Supper Murders. l.t. ed. 1983. 499p. reprint ed. 14.95 o.p. (0-89621-487-7) Thorndike Pr.
—The Cooking School Murders. 1982. 168p. 11.95 o.p. (0-525-24110-8, 01160-350, Dutton) Dutton/Plume.
—The Cooking School Murders. l.t. ed. 1982. 384p. reprint ed. 10.95 o.p. (0-89621-399-4) Thorndike Pr.
—The Nantucket Diet Murders. (Eugenia Potter Mysteries Ser.). 1986. 288p. mass mkt. 6.99 (0-440-16264-5); 1985. 224p. 13.95 o.s.i (0-385-29386-0, Delacorte Pr.) Dell Publishing.
—The Nantucket Diet Murders. 1985. 13.95 o.p. (0-525-24233-3, Dutton) Dutton/Plume.

POTTER, FREDERICA (FICTITIOUS CHARACTER)—FICTION
Byatt, A. S. A Whistling Woman. 2004. 448p. pap. 15.00 (0-679-77690-7, Vintage) Knopf Publishing Group.
—A Whistling Woman. 2002. 448p. 26.00 (0-375-41534-3) Knopf, Alfred A. Inc.

POWDER, LEROY (FICTITIOUS CHARACTER)—FICTION
Lewin, Michael Z. Hard Line. 1984. 256p. mass mkt. 3.50 o.p. (0-06-080720-2, P 720) HarperCollins Pubs.
—Hard Line: A Lt. Leroy Powder Novel. 1996. (Lt. Leroy Powder Novel Ser.). 256p. reprint ed. pap. 10.00 (0-88150-346-0, Foul Play) Norton, W. W. & Co., Inc.
—Late Payments. 1986. 224p. 13.95 o.p. (0-688-04342-9, Morrow, William & Co.) Morrow/Avon.
—Late Payments. 1987. 224p. pap. 3.50 o.p. (0-14-009875-5, Penguin Bks.) Viking Penguin.
—Late Payments: A Lt. Leroy Powder Novel. 1996. (Lt. Leroy Powder Novel Ser.). 216p. reprint ed. pap. 10.00 (0-88150-347-9, Foul Play) Norton, W. W. & Co., Inc.
—Night Cover. 1995. (Lt. Leroy Powder Novel Ser.). 256p. reprint ed. pap. 10.00 o.p. (0-88150-345-2, Foul Play) Norton, W. W. & Co., Inc.
—Night Cover. 1976. 7.95 o.p. (0-394-49644-2, Knopf Bks. for Young Readers) Random Hse. Children's Bks.

POWELL, ERSKINE (FICTITIOUS CHARACTER)—FICTION
Thomas, Graham. Malice Downstream. 2002. 240p. mass mkt. 6.99 (0-449-00709-X) Ballantine Bks.
—Malice in Cornwall. 1998. (Erskine Powell Mysteries Ser.: Vol. 2). 240p. mass mkt. 6.50 (0-8041-1656-3, Ivy Bks.) Ballantine Bks.
—Malice in Cornwall. l.t. ed. 2000. (Ulverscroft Large Print Ser.). 312p. 31.99 (0-7089-4324-1, Ulverscroft) Thorpe, F. A. Pubs. GBR. Dist: Ulverscroft Large Print Bks., Ltd., Ulverscroft Large Print Canada, Ltd.
—Malice in London: An Erskine Powell Mystery. 2000. (Erskine Powell Mysteries Ser.). 240p. mass mkt. 6.50 (0-8041-1840-X, Fawcett) Ballantine Bks.
—Malice in the Highlands. 1998. (Erskine Powell Mysteries Ser.: Vol. 1). 240p. mass mkt. 6.50 (0-8041-1657-1, Ivy Bks.) Ballantine Bks.
—Malice on the Moors. 1999. 240p. mass mkt. 6.50 (0-8041-1839-6, Ivy Bks.) Ballantine Bks.
—Malice on the Moors. l.t. ed. 2001. (Ulverscroft Large Print Ser.). 288p. 32.50 (0-7089-4396-9, Ulverscroft) Thorpe, F. A. Pubs. GBR. Dist: Ulverscroft Large Print Bks., Ltd., Ulverscroft Large Print Canada, Ltd.

POWERS, AUSTIN (FICTITIOUS CHARACTER)—FICTION
Meyers, Mike & McCullers, Michael. Austin Powers: How to Be an International Man of Mystery. 1999. 112p. pap. 10.00 (0-425-17152-3) Berkley Publishing Group.
—Austin Powers: How to Be an International Man of Mystery. 1997. 160p. pap. 10.00 o.s.i (1-57297-317-X) Boulevard Bks.

POWERS, GEORGINA (FICTITIOUS CHARACTER)—FICTION
Danks, Denise. Baby Love. 2003. 245p. pap. (0-575-06843-4); 256p. mass mkt. (0-7528-4803-8) Orion Publishing Group, Ltd. GBR. Dist: Trafalgar Square.
—Better off Dead. 2002. 184p. pap. 7.95 (0-7528-4379-6) Trafalgar Square.
—Fame Grabber. 2003. 192p. mass mkt. 7.95 (0-7528-4398-2) Orion Publishing Group, Ltd. GBR. Dist: Trafalgar Square.
—Fame Grabber. 1992. 187p. 16.95 o.p. (0-312-08786-1, Saint Martin's Minotaur) St. Martin's Pr.
—Phreak. 2002. 240p. pap. 7.95 (0-7528-4377-X) Trafalgar Square.
—The Pizza House Crash. 2002. 260p. pap. 7.95 (0-7528-4378-8) Trafalgar Square.
—Wink a Hopeful Eye. 2003. 224p. mass mkt. 7.95 (0-7528-4397-4) Orion Publishing Group, Ltd. GBR. Dist: Trafalgar Square.
—Wink a Hopeful Eye. 1994. 224p. 19.95 o.p. (0-312-11355-2, Saint Martin's Minotaur) St. Martin's Pr.

POWERS, VIV (FICTITIOUS CHARACTER)—FICTION
Albright, Letha. Daredevil's Apprentice. 2002. (Viv Powers Mystery Ser.). 255p. pap. 12.95 (0-9705049-4-2) Avocet Pr., Inc.
—Tulsa Time. 2000. (Dark Oak Mysteries Ser.). 220p. pap. 11.95 (1-892343-12-6) Oak Tree Publishing.

POWERSCOURT, FRANCIS (FICTITIOUS CHARACTER)—FICTION
Dickinson, David. Death & the Jubilee. 2003. 352p. 24.00 (0-7867-1110-8, Carroll & Graf Pubs.) Avalon Publishing Group.
—Death of an Old Master. 2004. 272p. 24.00 (0-7867-1306-2, Carroll & Graf Pubs.) Avalon Publishing Group.
—Goodnight Sweet Prince. 2002. (Victorian Mystery Ser.). 320p. 24.00 (0-7867-0945-6, Carroll & Graf Pubs.) Avalon Publishing Group.

PRATT, TONY (FICTITIOUS CHARACTER)—FICTION
Lee, Bernie. Murder Without Reservation. 1991. 18.95 o.p. (1-55611-184-3) Fine, Donald I. Bks.
—Murder Without Reservation. 1992. (WWL Mystery Ser.: No. 96). mass mkt. (0-373-26096-2, 1-26096-7, Harlequin Bks.) Harlequin Enterprises, Ltd.

PREFECT, FORD (FICTITIOUS CHARACTER)—FICTION
Adams, Douglas. The Hitchhiker's Guide to the Galaxy. (Hitchhiker's Guide Ser.: No. 1). 224p. 1997. pap. 13.95 (0-345-41891-3); 1995. mass mkt. 7.50 (0-345-39180-2) Ballantine Bks.
—The Hitchhiker's Guide to the Galaxy. unabr. ed. 1994. (Hitchhiker's Guide Ser.). audio 30.00 (0-7366-2681-6, 3417) Books on Tape, Inc.
—The Hitchhiker's Guide to the Galaxy. 10th anniv. ed. 1989. (Hitchhiker's Guide Ser.: No. 1). 224p. reprint ed. 18.00 (0-517-54209-9) Crown Publishing Group.
—The Hitchhiker's Guide to the Galaxy. unabr. ed. 1993. (Hitchhiker's Guide Ser.). 24.95 o.p. (1-55800-273-1, 692228);Set. audio 99.95 o.p. (1-55800-758-X) NewStar Media, Inc.
—The Hitchhiker's Guide to the Galaxy. (Hitchhiker's Guide Ser.: No. 1). 1991. mass mkt. 5.99 (0-671-74606-5); 1990. mass mkt. 4.95 (0-671-70159-2); 1988. 224p. mass mkt. 4.50 (0-671-66496-4); 1983. mass mkt. 3.50 o.s.i (0-671-47709-9) Simon & Schuster. (Pocket).
—The Hitchhiker's Guide to the Galaxy. abr. ed. 1986. (Hitchhiker's Guide Ser.). audio 11.95 (0-671-62964-6, Simon & Schuster Audioworks) Simon & Schuster Audio.
—The Hitchhiker's Guide to the Galaxy. unabr. ed. 1994. (Hitchhiker's Guide Ser.). audio 65.00 o.p. (1-57042-126-9, 4-521269); audio compact disk 65.00 o.p. (1-57042-155-2) Time Warner AudioBooks.
—The Hitchhiker's Guide to the Galaxy. 1997. (Hitchhiker's Guide Ser.: No. 1). 19.00 (0-606-12336-9) Turtleback Bks.
—The Hitchhiker's Guide to the Galaxy: Live at the Almeida, Set. abr. ed. 1996. (Hitchhiker's Guide Ser.). 17.95 o.p. (0-7871-0896-0) NewStar Media, Inc.
—Life, the Universe & Everything. (Hitchhiker's Guide Ser.). 1997. pap. 11.00 o.s.i (0-345-41890-5); 1995. 240p. mass mkt. 7.50 (0-345-39182-9) Ballantine Bks.
—Life, the Universe & Everything. unabr. ed. 1993. (Hitchhiker's Guide Ser.). 24.95 o.p. (1-55800-292-8, 70180) NewStar Media, Inc.
—Life, the Universe & Everything. 1982. (Hitchhiker's Guide Ser.: No. 3). 3.99 o.p. (0-517-54874-7) Random Hse. Value Publishing.
—Life, the Universe & Everything. 1991. (Hitchhiker's Guide Ser.: No. 3). 240p. mass mkt. 5.99 (0-671-73967-0, Pocket) Simon & Schuster.
—Life, the Universe & Everything. 1982. (Hitchhiker's Guide Ser.: No. 3). (J). 12.04 (0-606-03137-5) Turtleback Bks.
—Life, the Universe & Everything. 1996. Bk. 2. E-Book (1-59019-736-4); Bk. 3. E-Book (1-59019-737-2) ipicturebooks, LLC.
—The More Than Complete Hitchhiker's Guide: Complete & Unabridged, 5 bks. in 1. deluxe unabr. ed. 1987. (Hitchhiker's Guide Ser.). 624p. 19.95 o.p. (0-681-40322-5) Borders Pr.
—The More Than Complete Hitchhiker's Guide: Complete & Unabridged. 1989. (Hitchhiker's Guide Ser.). 13.99 o.s.i (0-517-69311-9) Random Hse. Value Publishing.
—Mostly Harmless. (Hitchhiker's Guide Ser.: No. 5). 2000. 240p. mass mkt. 7.50 (0-345-41877-8); 1993. 288p. pap. 12.95 (0-345-37933-0) Ballantine Bks.
—Mostly Harmless. l.t. ed. 1996. (Isis Large Print Bks.). 272p. 24.95 (1-85695-333-5) ISIS Large Print Bks. GBR. Dist: Transaction Pubs.
—Mostly Harmless. unabr. ed. 1994. (Hitchhiker's Guide Ser.: Vol. 5). audio 24.95 o.p. (1-55800-568-4, Dove Audio) NewStar Media, Inc.
—The Original Hitchhiker Radio Scripts: 10th Anniversary Edition. Perkins, Geoffrey, ed. & intro. by. 1995. pap. 15.00 o.s.i (0-517-88384-8, Harmony) Crown Publishing Group.
—The Restaurant at the End of the Universe. (Hitchhiker's Guide Ser.: No. 2). 1997. pap. 11.00 o.s.i (0-345-41892-1); 1995. 256p. mass mkt. 7.50 (0-345-39181-0) Ballantine Bks.
—The Restaurant at the End of the Universe. 1982. (Hitchhiker's Guide Ser.: No. 2). 256p. 12.95 o.s.i (0-517-54535-7, Harmony) Crown Publishing Group.
—The Restaurant at the End of the Universe. abr. ed. (Hitchhiker's Guide Ser.). audio 15.95 o.p. (0-88646-102-2, 7115) Durkin Hayes Publishing Ltd.
—The Restaurant at the End of the Universe. unabr. ed. 1993. (Hitchhiker's Guide Ser.). 24.95 o.p. (1-55800-294-4, 692297) NewStar Media, Inc.
—The Restaurant at the End of the Universe. (Hitchhiker's Guide Ser.: No. 2). 1990. mass mkt. 5.99 (0-671-70160-6); 1988. 256p. mass mkt. 4.50 (0-671-66494-8); 1983. mass mkt. 3.50 o.s.i (0-671-49304-3) Simon & Schuster. (Pocket).
—So Long & Thanks for All the Fish. (Hitchhiker's Guide Ser.: No. 4). 1991. mass mkt. 6.99 (0-671-74553-0); 1988. 224p. mass mkt. 4.50 (0-671-66493-X) Simon & Schuster. (Pocket).
—So Long & Thanks for All the Fish. 1985. (Hitchhiker's Guide Ser.: No. 4). 12.09 o.p. (0-606-00985-X) Turtleback Bks.
—So Long, & Thanks for All the Fish. 1999. (Hitchhiker's Guide Ser.: No. 4). 224p. mass mkt. 6.99 (0-345-39183-7) Ballantine Bks.
—So Long & Thanks for All the Fish. abr. ed. 1985. (Hitchhiker's Guide Ser.). audio 15.95 o.p. (0-88646-144-8, 7145) Durkin Hayes Publishing Ltd.
—So Long & Thanks for All the Fish. unabr. ed. 1994. (Hitchhiker's Guide Ser.). 24.95 o.p. (1-55800-293-6) NewStar Media, Inc.
—The Ultimate Hitchhiker's Guide. (Hitchhiker's Guide Ser.). 1996. (Illus.). 832p. 14.99 (0-517-14925-7); 1999. 816p. 6.75 (0-517-12485-8) Random Hse. Value Publishing.
Adams, Douglas. The Hitchhiker's Guide to the Galaxy. Kahan, Bob, ed. 1997. (Hitchhiker's Guide Ser.: No. 1). (Illus.). 144p. pap. 14.95 (1-56389-271-5) DC Comics.

PRENTICE, JOY (FICTITIOUS CHARACTER)—FICTION
Black, Veronica. Last Seen Wearing. l.t. ed. 1993. (Dales Large Print Ser.). 278p. pap. 19.99 o.p. (1-85389-422-2) Dales Large Print Bks. GBR. Dist: Ulverscroft Large Print Bks., Ltd., Ulverscroft Large Print Canada, Ltd.
—Last Seen Wearing. 1991. 15.95 o.p. (0-312-05888-8) St. Martin's Pr.

PRESCOTT, AMY (FICTITIOUS CHARACTER)—FICTION
Hendricksen, Louise. Grave Secrets. 1994. (Dr. Amy Prescott Mystery Ser.). 288p. mass mkt. 3.99 o.s.i (0-8217-4737-1, Zebra Bks.) Kensington Publishing Corp.

PRESCOTT, CINDY (FICTITIOUS CHARACTER)—FICTION
Pine, Nicholas. School Spirit. 1995. (Terror Academy Ser.: No. 14). 192p. (Orig.). (YA). mass mkt. 3.99 o.s.i (0-425-14644-8) Berkley Publishing Group.
—Terror Academy, Box set. 1994. (Terror Academy Ser.). (YA). 14.00 o.s.i (0-425-14597-2) Berkley Publishing Group.

PRESCOTT, JAMIE (FICTITIOUS CHARACTER)—FICTION
Tadmor, Mariann. Murder at Machu Picchu: A Jamie Prescott Mystery. 2002. 272p. 31.99 (1-4010-5758-6); pap. 21.99 (1-4010-5757-8) Xlibris Corp.

**PRESLEY, ELVIS, 1935-1977—FICTION**

Buckley, William F., Jr. Elvis in the Morning. unabr. ed. 2001. audio 56.95 (*0-7861-2113-0*, P2874) Blackstone Audio Bks., Inc.

—Elvis in the Morning. 344p. 2001. (Illus.). 25.00 o.s.i (*0-15-100643-1*); 2002. reprint ed. pap. 14.00 (*0-15-600754-1*) Harcourt Trade Pubs.

Charters, Samuel B. Elvis Presley Calls His Mother after the Ed Sullivan Show. 1992. 128p. pap. 10.95 (*0-918273-98-6*) Coffee Hse. Pr.

DeMarco, Gordon. Elvis in Aspic. 1994. 224p. pap. 9.00 o.p. (*1-883303-11-7*, West Coast Crime) Blue Heron Publishing.

Dunn, Robert. Pink Cadillac. 2001. 375p. pap. 14.95 (*0-9708293-0-2*) Coral Pr.

Fox, Les & Fox, Sue. Return to Sender: The Secret Son of Elvis Presley. 1996. 350p. 21.95 (*0-9646986-0-9*) West Highland Publishing Co., Inc.

Graham, Robert & Baty, Keith. Elvis: The Novel. 1997. 222p. pap. 14.95 (*1-899344-19-5*) Do-Not Pr., The GBR. *Dist:* Dufour Editions, Inc.

Graham, Robert & Baty, Keith, contrib. by. Elvis: The Novel. 1984. pap. o.p. (*0-586-06162-2*) Flamingo GBR. *Dist:* Trafalgar Square.

Henderson, William M. Stark Raving Elvis. 1997. 272p. mass mkt. 6.99 o.s.i (*0-425-15935-3*) Berkley Publishing Group.

—Stark Raving Elvis. 1984. 224p. 14.95 o.p. (*0-525-24264-3*, 01451-440, Dutton) Dutton/Plume.

—Stark Raving Elvis. 1987. 224p. pap. 5.95 o.p. (*0-671-64081-X*, Fireside) Simon & Schuster.

Kalpakian, Laura. Graced Land. 2nd ed. 1997. 304p. reprint ed. pap. 14.95 (*0-936085-39-8*) Blue Heron Publishing.

—Graced Land. 1992. 18.95 o.p. (*0-8021-1474-1*) Grove/Atlantic, Inc.

Klein, Daniel. Kill Me Tender. 2000. 227p. 22.95 (*0-312-26187-X*, Saint Martin's Minotaur) St. Martin's Pr.

—Viva las Vengeance: A Murder Mystery Featuring Elvis Presley. 2003. 288p. 23.95 (*0-312-28806-9*, Saint Martin's Minotaur) St. Martin's Pr.

Klein, Daniel M. Kill Me Tender: A Murder Mystery Featuring Elvis Presley. E-Book 17.95 (*0-312-27583-8*) St. Martin's Pr.

Levinson, Robert S. The Elvis & Marilyn Affair. 1999. (Neil Gulliver & Steve Marriner Novels Ser.). 304p. 24.95 (*0-312-86968-1*, Forge Bks.) Doherty, Tom Assocs., LLC.

—The Elvis & Marilyn Affair: A Neil Gulliver & Stevie Marriner Novel. 2000. 340p. mass mkt. 6.99 (*0-8125-8432-5*, Forge Bks.) Doherty, Tom Assocs., LLC.

Sloan, Kay & Pierce, Constance, eds. Elvis Rising: Stories of the King. 1993. 176p. (Orig.). pap. 10.00 (*0-380-77216-7*, Avon Bks.) Morrow/Avon.

—Elvis Rising: Stories on the King. 1997. 262p. reprint ed. pap. text 7.00 o.p. (*0-7881-5120-7*) DIANE Publishing Co.

Womack, Jack. Elvissey: A Novel of Elvis Past & Elvis Future. 1997. 319p. reprint ed. pap. text 13.00 o.p. (*0-7881-5117-7*) DIANE Publishing Co.

—Elvissey: A Novel of Elvis Past & Elvis Future. 1992. pap. 12.95 o.p. (*0-312-85202-9*, Tor Bks.) Doherty, Tom Assocs., LLC.

—Elvissey: A Novel of Elvis Past & Elvis Future. 1997. 320p. reprint ed. pap. 13.50 (*0-8021-3495-5*, Grove Pr.) Grove/Atlantic, Inc.

**PRESTER, JACK (FICTITIOUS CHARACTER)—FICTION**

Dengler, Sandy. Death Valley. 1993. (Jack Prester Mysteries Ser.). 255p. pap. 9.99 o.p. (*0-8024-2176-8*) Moody Pr.

—A Model Murder. l.t. ed. 2002. 481p. 25.95 (*0-7862-4242-6*) Gale Group.

—A Model Murder. 1993. (Jack Prester Mysteries Ser.). pap. 9.99 o.p. (*0-8024-2177-6*) Moody Pr.

—Murder on the Mount. l.t. ed. 2002. 495p. pap. 14.95 (*1-4104-0005-0*, Walker Large Print) Gale Group.

—Murder on the Mount. 1994. (Jack Prester Mysteries Ser.). pap. 9.99 o.p. (*0-8024-2178-4*) Moody Pr.

—The Quick & the Dead. 1995. (Jack Prester Mysteries Ser.). pap. 9.99 o.p. (*0-8024-2179-2*) Moody Pr.

—The Quick & the Dead. l.t. ed. 1998. (Jack Prester Mysteries Ser.). 272p. 24.95 (*0-7862-1647-6*) Thorndike Pr.

**PRESTON, KIT (FICTITIOUS CHARACTER)—FICTION**

Coleridge, Nicholas. With Friends Like These. 1997. 384p. 24.95 (*0-312-17066-1*) St. Martin's Pr.

**PRESTON, MARK (FICTITIOUS CHARACTER)—FICTION**

Chambers, Peter. Dames Can Be Deadly. l.t. ed. 1993. (Dales Large Print Ser.). 291p. pap. 19.99 (*1-85389-427-3*) Dales Large Print Bks. GBR. *Dist:* Ulverscroft Large Print Bks., Ltd.

—The Lady Who Never Was. l.t. ed. 1995. (Linford Mystery Large Print Ser.). 272p. pap. 17.99 o.p. (*0-7089-7809-6*, Linford) Thorpe, F. A. Pubs. GBR. *Dist:* Ulverscroft Large Print Bks., Ltd., Ulverscroft Large Print Canada, Ltd.

—Lady, You're Killing Me. l.t. ed. 1994. (Linford Mystery Library). 304p. pap. 17.99 o.p. (*0-7089-7568-2*, Ulverscroft) Thorpe, F. A. Pubs. GBR. *Dist:* Ulverscroft Large Print Bks., Ltd., Ulverscroft Large Print Canada, Ltd.

—Somebody Has to Lose. l.t. ed. 1992. (Dales Mystery Ser.). 211p. pap. 19.99 o.p. (*1-85389-307-2*) Dales Large Print Bks. GBR. *Dist:* Ulverscroft Large Print Bks., Ltd.

—Speak Ill of the Dead. l.t. ed. 1993. (Linford Mystery Library). 368p. pap. 17.99 o.p. (*0-7089-7385-X*, Linford) Thorpe, F. A. Pubs. GBR. *Dist:* Ulverscroft Large Print Bks., Ltd., Ulverscroft Large Print Canada, Ltd.

—They Call It Murder. l.t. ed. 1993. (Linford Mystery Library). 288p. pap. 17.99 o.p. (*0-7089-7389-2*, Linford) Thorpe, F. A. Pubs. GBR. *Dist:* Ulverscroft Large Print Bks., Ltd., Ulverscroft Large Print Canada, Ltd.

**PRIAM, MARGARET (FICTITIOUS CHARACTER)—FICTION**

Christmas, Joyce. A Better Class of Murder: A Lady Margaret Priam/Betty Trenka Mystery. 2000. (Lady Margaret Priam Mysteries Ser.). 272p. mass mkt. 6.50 (*0-449-15013-5*, Fawcett) Ballantine Bks.

—A Better Class of Murder: A Lady Margaret Priam/Betty Trenka Mystery. l.t. ed. 2001. 264p. pap. 24.95 (*0-7838-9472-4*, Macmillan Reference USA) Gale Group.

—Dying Well. 2000. (Lady Margaret Priam Mysteries Ser.). 224p. mass mkt. 6.50 (*0-449-15011-9*, Fawcett) Ballantine Bks.

—Dying Well: A Lady Margaret Priam Mystery. l.t. ed. 2001. (G. K. Hall Paperback Ser.). 253p. pap. 24.95 (*0-7838-9438-4*, Macmillan Reference USA) Gale Group.

—A Fate Worse Than Death. 1990. 208p. mass mkt. 4.99 o.s.i (*0-449-14665-0*, Fawcett) Ballantine Bks.

—Forged in Blood. l.t. ed. 2002. 277p. (*0-7862-4829-7*) Thorndike Pr.

—Forged in Blood: A Lady Margaret Priam/Betty Trenka Mystery. 2002. 277p. (*0-7540-8849-9*) Thorndike Pr.

—Friend or Faux. 1991. mass mkt. 4.99 o.s.i (*0-449-14701-0*, Fawcett) Ballantine Bks.

—Going Out in Style. 1998. (Lady Margaret Priam Mysteries Ser.). 181p. mass mkt. 5.99 o.s.i (*0-449-15010-0*, Fawcett) Ballantine Bks.

—It's Her Funeral, No. 6. 1992. (Orig.). mass mkt. 3.99 o.s.i (*0-449-14702-9*, Fawcett) Ballantine Bks.

—Mourning Gloria. 1996. (Lady Margaret Priam Mysteries Ser.). 232p. mass mkt. 4.99 o.s.i (*0-449-14704-5*, Fawcett) Ballantine Bks.

—A Perfect Day for Dying. 1993. (Orig.). mass mkt. 4.99 o.s.i (*0-449-14703-7*, Fawcett) Ballantine Bks.

—Simply to Die For. 1989. 208p. mass mkt. 4.99 o.s.i (*0-449-14539-5*, Fawcett) Ballantine Bks.

—A Stunning Way to Die. 1990. (Lady Margaret Priam Mystery Ser.: No. 4). 192p. mass mkt. 4.99 o.s.i (*0-449-14666-9*, Fawcett) Ballantine Bks.

—A Stunning Way to Die. 1993. 192p. lib. bdg. 18.00 o.p. (*0-7278-4410-5*) Severn Hse. Pubs., Ltd.

—Suddenly in Her Sorbet. 1988. mass mkt. 5.99 o.s.i (*0-449-13311-7*, Fawcett) Ballantine Bks.

**PRICE, ROBIN (FICTITIOUS CHARACTER)—FICTION**

Morice, Anne. Dead on Cue. l.t. ed. 1986. (Nightingale Ser.). 291p. 11.95 o.p. (*0-8161-4118-5*, Macmillan Reference USA) Gale Group.

—Dead on Cue. 1985. 208p. 12.95 o.p. (*0-312-18519-7*) St. Martin's Pr.

—Death & the Dutiful Daughter. l.t. ed. 1986. (Nightingale Ser.). 288p. 10.95 o.p. (*0-8161-3866-4*, Macmillan Reference USA) Gale Group.

—Death in the Round. 1980. 192p. 8.95 o.p. (*0-312-18616-9*) St. Martin's Pr.

—Death in the Round. 1981. (Crime Monthly Ser.). 192p. pap. 2.95 o.p. (*0-14-005997-0*, Penguin Bks.) Viking Penguin.

—Death of a Wedding Guest. 1976. 7.95 o.p. (*0-312-18830-7*) St. Martin's Pr.

—Design for Dying. unabr. ed. 1991. (Audio Ser.). audio 39.95 (*0-7451-6174-X*, CAT 4070) BBC Audiobooks America.

—Design for Dying. 1988. 192p. 14.95 o.p. (*0-312-01759-6*, Saint Martin's Minotaur) St. Martin's Pr.

—Fatal Charm. l.t. ed. 1990. (Nightingale Ser.). 276p. pap. 13.95 o.p. (*0-8161-4925-9*, Macmillan Reference USA) Gale Group.

—Fatal Charm. 1989. 192p. 14.95 o.p. (*0-312-03338-9*, Saint Martin's Minotaur) St. Martin's Pr.

—Getting Away with Murder? l.t. ed. 1985. (Nightingale Ser.). 304p. 10.95 o.p. (*0-8161-3865-6*, Macmillan Reference USA) Gale Group.

—Getting Away with Murder? 1984. 11.95 o.p. (*0-312-32633-5*) St. Martin's Pr.

—Hollow Vengeance. 1982. 196p. 10.95 o.p. (*0-312-38834-9*) St. Martin's Pr.

—The Men in Her Death. 1981. 224p. 9.95 o.p. (*0-312-52939-2*) St. Martin's Pr.

—Murder by Proxy. 1978. 7.95 o.p. (*0-312-55292-0*) St. Martin's Pr.

—Murder in Outline. 1986. 176p. mass mkt. 2.95 o.s.i (*0-553-25647-5*) Bantam Bks.

—Murder in Outline. 1979. 8.95 o.p. (*0-312-55303-X*) St. Martin's Pr.

—Murder Post-Dated. 1986. 208p. mass mkt. 2.95 o.s.i (*0-553-25652-1*) Bantam Bks.

—Murder Post-Dated. l.t. ed. 1985. (Nightingale Ser.). 396p. pap. 11.95 o.p. (*0-8161-3769-2*, Macmillan Reference USA) Gale Group.

—Murder Post-Dated. 1984. 192p. 10.95 o.p. (*0-312-55321-8*) St. Martin's Pr.

—Nursery Tea & Poison, Vol. 1. 1975. 6.95 o.p. (*0-312-58030-4*) St. Martin's Pr.

—Planning for Murder. l.t. ed. 1991. (Nightingale Ser.). 267p. pap. 14.95 o.p. (*0-8161-5246-2*, Macmillan Reference USA) Gale Group.

—Planning for Murder. 1991. 15.95 o.p. (*0-312-04869-6*, Saint Martin's Minotaur) St. Martin's Pr.

—Publish & Be Killed. l.t. ed. 1988. (Nightingale Ser.). 294p. 12.95 o.p. (*0-8161-4394-3*, Macmillan Reference USA) Gale Group.

—Publish & Be Killed. 1986. 192p. 12.95 o.p. (*0-312-00178-9*) St. Martin's Pr.

—Scared to Death. 1986. mass mkt. 2.95 o.s.i (*0-553-25628-9*) Bantam Bks.

—Scared to Death. 1978. (General Ser.). lib. bdg. 10.95 o.p. (*0-8161-6584-X*, Macmillan Reference USA) Gale Group.

—Scared to Death. (Mystery Bookshelf Selection Ser.). 1978. pap. 2.95 o.p. (*0-312-70044-X*, Saint Martin's Griffin); 1977. 7.95 o.p. (*0-312-70043-1*) St. Martin's Pr.

—Sleep of Death. 1986. mass mkt. 2.95 o.s.i (*0-553-25877-X*) Bantam Bks.

—Sleep of Death. 1982. 176p. 10.95 o.p. (*0-312-72863-8*) St. Martin's Pr.

—Treble Exposure. l.t. ed. 1988. (Nightingale Ser.). 312p. 12.95 o.p. (*0-8161-4622-5*, Macmillan Reference USA) Gale Group.

—Treble Exposure. 1988. 192p. 13.95 o.p. (*0-312-01525-9*, Saint Martin's Minotaur) St. Martin's Pr.

**PRIESTER, SOLOMON (FICTITIOUS CHARACTER)—FICTION**

LeMone, Charles S. A Dance in the Street. 1993. 256p. (Orig.). mass mkt. 3.99 (*0-380-76713-9*, Avon Bks.) Morrow/Avon.

**PRINCIPAL, LAURA (FICTITIOUS CHARACTER)—FICTION**

Spring, Michelle. Every Breath You Take. 1999. (Laura Principal Mysteries Ser.). 256p. mass mkt. 5.99 (*0-345-43548-6*) Ballantine Bks.

—Every Breath You Take. 256p. 1995. mass mkt. 5.50 (*0-671-87092-0*, Pocket); 1994. 20.00 o.p. (*0-671-87091-2*, Atria) Simon & Schuster.

—Nights in White Satin: A Laura Principal Novel. 2000. 336p. mass mkt. 6.99 (*0-345-42494-8*, Fawcett); 1999. 288p. 23.00 o.s.i (*0-345-42493-X*) Ballantine Bks.

—Running for Shelter. 2000. (Laura Principal Mysteries Ser.). 256p. mass mkt. 6.50 (*0-345-43549-4*, Fawcett) Ballantine Bks.

—Running for Shelter: A Laura Principal Mystery. 1997. per. 5.99 (*0-671-87094-7*, Pocket); 1996. 288p. 21.00 o.p. (*0-671-87093-9*, Atria) Simon & Schuster.

—Standing in the Shadows. 1999. 336p. mass mkt. 5.99 (*0-345-42492-1*) Ballantine Bks.

—Standing in the Shadows. l.t. ed. 1999. (Ulverscroft Large Print Ser.). 464p. 31.99 o.p. (*0-7089-4053-6*, Ulverscroft) Thorpe, F. A. Pubs. GBR. *Dist:* Ulverscroft Large Print Bks., Ltd., Ulverscroft Large Print Canada, Ltd.

**PRINGLE, G. D. H. (FICTITIOUS CHARACTER)—FICTION**

Livingston, Nancy. Death in a Distant Land. l.t. ed. 1989. 15.95 o.p. (*0-7451-9454-0*, 252); pap. 14.95 o.p. (*1-55504-807-2*, 692) BBC Audiobooks America.

—Death in a Distant Land. 1989. 192p. 14.95 o.p. (*0-312-02565-3*, Saint Martin's Minotaur) St. Martin's Pr.

—Death in Close-Up. l.t. ed. 1990. 16.95 o.p. (*0-7451-9844-9*, C0325); pap. 15.95 o.p. (*0-7927-0303-0*) BBC Audiobooks America.

—Death in Close-Up. 1990. 15.95 o.p. (*0-312-04296-5*, Saint Martin's Minotaur) St. Martin's Pr.

—The Far Side of the Hill. 1988. 480p. 19.95 o.p. (*0-312-02207-7*) St. Martin's Pr.

—Fatality at Bath & Wells: A G. D. H. Pringle Mystery. 1986. 224p. 14.95 o.p. (*0-312-00004-9*) St. Martin's Pr.

—Incident at Parga. 1989. mass mkt. (*0-373-28001-7*, 1-28001-5, Harlequin Bks.) Harlequin Enterprises, Ltd.

—Incident at Parga. 1999. mass mkt. 2.95 (*0-312-91389-3*, St. Martin's Paperbacks); 1987. 224p. 15.95 o.p. (*0-312-01446-5*, Saint Martin's Minotaur) St. Martin's Pr.

—The Land of Our Dreams. 1989. 384p. 18.95 o.p. (*0-312-03374-5*) St. Martin's Pr.

—Mayhem in Parva. l.t. ed. 1992. 18.95 o.p. (*0-7451-8307-7*, AH0286); pap. 16.95 o.p. (*0-7927-0963-2*, AS0322) BBC Audiobooks America.

—Mayhem in Parva. 1991. 192p. 16.95 o.p. (*0-312-06410-1*, Saint Martin's Minotaur) St. Martin's Pr.

—Never Were Such Times. l.t. ed. 1992. (Magna Large Print Ser.). 763p. o.p. (*0-7505-0195-2*) Magna Large Print Bks. GBR. *Dist:* Ulverscroft Large Print Canada, Ltd.

—Never Were Such Times. 1991. 19.95 o.p. (*0-312-05902-7*) St. Martin's Pr.

—Quiet Murder. l.t. ed. 1993. 23.95 o.p. (*0-7927-1797-X*); pap. 21.95 o.p. (*0-7927-1796-1*) BBC Audiobooks America.

—Quiet Murder. 1995. 253p. per. (*0-373-26186-1*, 1-26186-6, Worldwide Library) Harlequin Enterprises, Ltd.

—Quiet Murder. l.t. ed. 1993. (Magna Large Print Ser.). 388p. o.p. (*0-7505-0582-6*) Magna Large Print Bks. GBR. *Dist:* Ulverscroft Large Print Canada, Ltd.

—Quiet Murder. 1993. 17.95 o.p. (*0-312-08878-7*, Saint Martin's Minotaur) St. Martin's Pr.

—The Trouble at Aquitaine. 1985. 192p. 12.95 o.p. (*0-312-81975-7*) St. Martin's Pr.

—Unwillingly to Vegas. l.t. ed. 1993. 21.95 o.p. (*0-7927-1488-1*); pap. 19.95 o.p. (*0-7927-1487-3*) BBC Audiobooks America.

—Unwillingly to Vegas. l.t. ed. 1993. (Magna Large Print Ser.). 354p. o.p. (*0-7505-0495-1*) Magna Large Print Bks. GBR. *Dist:* Ulverscroft Large Print Canada, Ltd.

—Unwillingly to Vegas. 1992. 192p. 16.95 o.p. (*0-312-08329-7*, Saint Martin's Minotaur) St. Martin's Pr.

**PRIOR, MATTHEW (FICTITIOUS CHARACTER)—FICTION**

Quogan, Anthony. The Fine Art of Murder. 1988. 216p. 15.95 o.p. (*0-312-02210-7*, Saint Martin's Minotaur) St. Martin's Pr.

**PRIZZI FAMILY (FICTITIOUS CHARACTERS)—FICTION**

Condon, Richard. Prizzi's Family. 1987. 320p. mass mkt. 4.50 o.s.i (*0-515-09106-5*, Jove) Berkley Publishing Group.

—Prizzi's Family. unabr. collector's ed. 1991. audio 40.00 (*0-7366-2009-5*, 2825) Books on Tape, Inc.

—Prizzi's Family. 1986. 17.95 o.p. (*0-399-13210-4*) Putnam Publishing Group, The.

—Prizzi's Glory. unabr. collector's ed. 1991. audio 48.00 (*0-7366-2076-1*, 2882) Books on Tape, Inc.

—Prizzi's Glory. 1988. 17.95 o.p. (*0-525-24689-4*, Dutton) Dutton/Plume.

—Prizzi's Glory. 1990. 368p. mass mkt. 4.95 o.p. (*0-451-16468-7*, NAL Bks.) NAL.

—Prizzi's Honor. 1986. 320p. mass mkt. 4.95 o.p. (*0-425-09507-X*) Berkley Publishing Group.

—Prizzi's Honor. unabr. collector's ed. 1985. audio 56.00 (*0-7366-0837-0*, 1788) Books on Tape, Inc.

—Prizzi's Honor, Set. abr. ed. 1987. audio 16.99 (*0-88646-193-6*, 7194) Durkin Hayes Publishing Ltd.

—Prizzi's Honor. 1982. 320p. 13.95 o.p. (*0-698-11143-5*) Putnam Publishing Group, The.

—Prizzi's Honor. l.t. ed. 1982. 480p. reprint ed. 14.95 o.p. (*0-89621-403-6*) Thorndike Pr.

—Prizzi's Money. 1995. 384p. mass mkt. 5.99 o.s.i (*0-7860-0167-4*) Kensington Publishing Corp.

**PROCTOR, ETHAN (FICTITIOUS CHARACTER)—FICTION**

Grant, Charles. Black Oak: Hunting Ground. 2000. (Black Oak Ser.: 4). 256p. mass mkt. 5.99 o.s.i (*0-451-45787-0*, ROC) NAL.

—Genesis. 1998. (Black Oak Ser.: Vol. 1). 272p. mass mkt. 5.99 o.s.i (*0-451-45677-7*, ROC) NAL.

—Winter Knight. 1999. (Black Oak Ser.: Vol. 3). 240p. (Orig.). mass mkt. 5.99 o.s.i (*0-451-45762-5*, ROC) NAL.

Grant, Charles L. The Hush of Dark Wings. 1999. (Black Oak Ser.: Vol. 2). 256p. mass mkt. 5.99 o.s.i (*0-451-45733-1*, ROC) NAL.

**PROFETT, JOHN (FICTITIOUS CHARACTER)—FICTION**

Baldwin, Stanley C. 1999. 1994. 220p. pap. 9.99 o.p. (*0-8308-1363-2*, 1363) InterVarsity Pr.

—1999. l.t. ed. 1999. (Christian Fiction Ser.). 336p. pap. 24.95 o.p. (*0-7862-1807-X*) Thorndike Pr.

**PROSPERO OF ARGYLLE (FICTITIOUS CHARACTER)—FICTION**

Willey, Elizabeth. The Price of Blood & Honor. 1997. 445p. pap. text 5.99 o.p. (*0-8125-5049-8*); 1996. 480p. 25.95 o.p. (*0-312-85784-5*) Doherty, Tom Assocs., LLC. (Tor Bks.).

—A Sorcerer & a Gentleman. 1995. 416p. 23.95 o.p. (*0-312-85783-7*); Vol. 1. 1996. (Sorcerer & a Gentleman Ser.: Vol. 1). mass mkt. 5.99 (*0-8125-5047-1*) Doherty, Tom Assocs., LLC. (Tor Bks.).

**PRY, PAUL (FICTITIOUS CHARACTER)—FICTION**

Gardner, Erle Stanley. The Adventures of Paul Pry. 1990. 304p. pap. 9.95 o.p. (*0-89296-976-8*) Mysterious Pr.

**PRYNNE, HESTER (FICTITIOUS CHARACTER)—FICTION**

Hawthorne, Nathaniel. Elements of Literature: The Scarlet Letter. 1989. pap. text, stu. ed. 15.33 (*0-03-023454-9*) Holt, Rinehart & Winston.
—The Scarlet Letter. 2000. 252p. E-Book 9.95 (*0-594-05375-7*) 1873 Pr.
—The Scarlet Letter. 1994. (Illustrated Classics Collection). 64p. pap. 4.95 (*0-7854-0722-7*, 40412); pap. 3.60 o.p. (*1-56103-500-9*) American Guidance Service, Inc.
—The Scarlet Letter. 1996. 90p. pap. 6.95 (*1-55783-243-9*) Applause Theatre Bk. Pubs.
—The Scarlet Letter. unabr. ed. 1994. audio 41.95 (*1-55685-341-6*) Audio Bk. Contractors, Inc.
—The Scarlet Letter. abr. ed. 2000. audio 15.95 (*0-88690-188-X*, F20014, Audio Editions Bks. on Cassette) Audio Partners Publishing Corp.
—The Scarlet Letter. 1997. (Cyber Classics Ser.). 246p. pap. 14.95 incl. disk (*1-55701-204-0*); 352p. pap. 19.95 (*1-55701-215-6*) BNI Pubns., Inc.
—The Scarlet Letter. 2001. 7.95 (*0-8010-1213-9*) Baker Bks.
—The Scarlet Letter. 1999. E-Book (*1-58734-022-4*) Bartleby.com.
—The Scarlet Letter. 1990. (Illus.). 3.75 o.s.i (*0-425-12024-4*, Classics Illustrated) Berkley Publishing Group.
—The Scarlet Letter. 1979. audio 33.95 (*0-7861-0559-3*); 1994. audio 49.95 (*0-7861-0876-2*, 1538) Blackstone Audio Bks., Inc.
—The Scarlet Letter. unabr. ed. audio 39.95 (*1-55686-104-4*, 104); 2001. audio compact disk 45.50 (*1-58116-194-8*) Books in Motion.
—The Scarlet Letter. unabr. collector's ed. 2000. audio 48.00 (*0-7366-5132-2*) Books on Tape, Inc.
—The Scarlet Letter. 2002. pap. 3.95 (*1-59109-017-2*) Booksurge, LLC.
—The Scarlet Letter. 1995. (Value Classics Ser.). 224p. 5.95 o.p. (*0-681-10360-4*) Borders Pr.
—The Scarlet Letter. unabr. ed. 2002. audio 29.95 (*1-59086-289-9*, 3875, Brilliance Audio Unabridged); 2001. audio compact disk 96.25 (*1-58788-611-1*, 2892, CD Unabridged Library Edition); 2001. audio compact disk 37.95 (*1-58788-610-3*, 2891, CD Unabridged); 1993. audio 57.25 (*1-56100-138-4*, 1027, Unabridged Library Editions); 1993. 8p. audio 17.95 o.p. (*1-56100-500-2*, 249, Bookcassette) Brilliance Audio.
—The Scarlet Letter. Martin, John S., ed. 1995. (Literary Texts Ser.). 260p. pap. (*1-55111-046-6*) Broadview Pr.
—The Scarlet Letter. 1984. 220p. lib. bdg. 25.95 o.p. (*0-89968-258-8*, Lightyear Pr.); 523p. reprint ed. lib. bdg. 25.95 (*0-89966-494-6*) Buccaneer Bks., Inc.
—The Scarlet Letter. 1997. (Cambridge Literature Ser.). audio 14.95 o.p. (*0-521-59799-4*); audio compact disk 18.95 o.p. (*0-521-59800-1*) Cambridge Univ. Pr.
—The Scarlet Letter. l.t. ed. 1997. 352p. pap. 19.95 (*1-58855-005-2*) Cyber Classics, Inc.
—The Scarlet Letter. 1988. (Illus.). 320p. pap. 2.50 o.p. (*0-440-37640-8*) Dell Publishing.
—The Scarlet Letter. 1994. (Thrift Editions Ser.). 192p. reprint ed. pap. 2.00 (*0-486-28048-9*) Dover Pubns., Inc.
—The Scarlet Letter. 1972. 3.95 o.p. (*0-460-01122-7*); 1957. 11.50 o.p. (*0-460-00122-1*) Dutton/Plume. (Dutton).
—The Scarlet Letter. 2002. (Illus.). 410p. (*0-9710756-1-1*) Everbind/Marco Bk. Co.
—The Scarlet Letter. audio 19.95 Filmic Archives.
—The Scarlet Letter. 2003. (Barnes & Noble Classics Ser.). 320p. pap. 3.95 (*1-59308-012-3*) Fine Communications.
—The Scarlet Letter. 1980. (Reader's Request Ser.). lib. bdg. 12.95 o.p. (*0-8161-3073-6*, Macmillan Reference USA) Gale Group.
—The Scarlet Letter. 1991. pap. text, stu. ed. 19.95 (*0-8224-9444-2*) Globe Fearon Educational Publishing.
—The Scarlet Letter. Warren, Austin, ed. 1947. 254p. (C). pap. text 27.50 (*0-03-009860-2*) Harcourt College Pubs.
—The Scarlet Letter. 1986. (Illus.). 256p. 22.95 o.s.i (*0-15-179568-1*) Harcourt Trade Pubs.
—The Scarlet Letter. abr. ed. 1984. audio 12.95 HarperTrade.
—The Scarlet Letter. unabr. ed. 1999. audio 49.95 Highsmith Inc.
—The Scarlet Letter. 1997. text 8.25 (*0-03-051497-5*); 1990. pap., tchr. ed., stu. ed. 24.00 (*0-15-348529-9*); 1990. pap., stu. ed. 11.25 (*0-15-348523-X*) Holt, Rinehart & Winston.
—The Scarlet Letter, 001. Levin, Harry, ed. 9999. (Riverside Library). 5.95 o.p. (*0-395-08128-9*) Houghton Mifflin Co.
—The Scarlet Letter. unabr. ed. 1980. audio 7.95; 1979. audio 29.00 Jimcin Recordings.
—The Scarlet Letter. 1990. 272p. pap. 7.50 o.p. (*0-679-72526-1*, Vintage) Knopf Publishing Group.
—The Scarlet Letter. 1992. (Everyman's Library). 304p. 17.00 (*0-679-41731-1*) Knopf, Alfred A. Inc.
—The Scarlet Letter. 1998. (Cloth Bound Pocket Ser.). 240p. 7.95 (*3-89508-457-3*, 521303) Konemann.
—The Scarlet Letter. 1993. audio 43.80 (*1-56544-005-6*, 350029) Literate Ear, Inc.
—The Scarlet Letter. E-Book 1.95 (*1-57799-932-0*) Logos Research Systems, Inc.
—The Scarlet Letter. (C). 5th ed. 1997. pap. text (*0-8013-3145-5*); Level 2. 2000. pap. 7.66 (*0-582-42176-4*) Longman Publishing Group.
—The Scarlet Letter. abr. ed. 2000. audio 7.95 (*1-57815-113-9*, 1075, Media Bks. Audio Publishing) Media Bks., L. L. C.
—The Scarlet Letter. 1970. pap. 1.50 (*0-06-080620-6*, HarperTorch) Morrow/Avon.
—The Scarlet Letter. (Signet Classics). 1999. 272p. mass mkt. 3.95 (*0-451-52608-2*, Signet Classics); 1997. pap. 2.95 (*0-89375-994-5*); 1977. mass mkt. 1.25 o.p. (*0-451-07499-8*, Signet Bks.); 1973. mass mkt. 0.95 o.p. (*0-451-05362-1*, Signet Bks.) NAL.
—The Scarlet Letter. Willard, Throp, ed. & intro. by. 1969. pap. NAL.
—The Scarlet Letter. 1959. mass mkt. 0.50 o.p. (*0-451-50008-3*, Signet Classics); mass mkt. 0.60 o.p. (*0-451-50650-2*, Signet Classics); mass mkt. 0.95 o.p. (*0-451-50910-2*, Signet Classics); mass mkt. 1.25 o.p. (*0-451-51067-4*, Signet Classics); mass mkt. 1.50 o.p. (*0-451-51188-3*, Signet Classics); mass mkt. 1.50 o.p. (*0-451-51232-4*, Signet Classics); 256p. mass mkt. 3.95 o.s.i (*0-451-52522-1*); mass mkt. 1.75 o.p. (*0-451-52350-4*); mass mkt. 1.50 o.p. (*0-451-51652-4*); mass mkt. 1.75 o.p. (*0-451-51431-9*, Signet Classics) NAL.
—The Scarlet Letter. abr. ed. 1994. (Classic Fiction Ser.). audio compact disk 15.98 (*962-634-013-4*, NA201312); 18p. audio 13.98 o.p. (*962-634-513-6*, NA201314) Naxos of America, Inc. (Naxos AudioBooks).
—The Scarlet Letter. abr. ed. 2002. audio compact disk 25.00 (*1-59007-135-2*); audio 25.00 (*1-59007-134-4*) New Millennium Entertainment. (New Millennium Audio).
—The Scarlet Letter. abr. ed. 1995. 29.95 o.p. (*0-7871-0119-2*); 19.95 o.p. (*0-7871-0118-4*, 693312) NewStar Media, Inc.
—The Scarlet Letter. l.t. ed. 1998. (Large Print Ser.). 430p. lib. bdg. 26.00 (*0-939495-57-0*); 220p. reprint ed. lib. bdg. 25.00 (*1-58287-067-5*) North Bks.
—The Scarlet Letter. unabr. ed. 2001. audio 38.95 NorthStar Audio Bks.
—The Scarlet Letter. Charvat, William et al, eds. 1963. (Centenary Edition of the Works of Nathaniel Hawthorne: Vol. 1). (Illus.). 292p. text 62.95 (*0-8142-0059-1*) Ohio State Univ. Pr.
—The Scarlet Letter. Harding, Brian, ed. & intro. by. 1990. (Oxford World's Classics Ser.). 352p. pap. 4.95 o.p. (*0-19-281753-1*) Oxford Univ. Pr., Inc.
—The Scarlet Letter. 1999. pap. 3.99 (*0-14-038239-9*) Penguin Group (USA) Inc.
—The Scarlet Letter. 1996. (Literary Classics). 284p. pap. 10.00 (*1-57392-047-9*) Prometheus Bks., Pubs.
—The Scarlet Letter. 2001. E-Book 2.95 (*1-58882-567-1*) PublishingOnline.
—The Scarlet Letter. annuals 2000. (Modern Library Classics). 304p. pap. 5.95 (*0-679-78338-5*, Modern Library) Random House Adult Trade Publishing Group.
—The Scarlet Letter. 1996. 6.99 o.s.i (*0-517-18062-6*) Random Hse. Value Publishing.
—The Scarlet Letter. 1950. pap. 3.95 o.p. (*0-394-30921-9*, T21) Random Hse., Inc.
—The Scarlet Letter. 1984. (Illus.). 256p. 12.95 o.p. (*0-89577-184-5*) Reader's Digest Assn., Inc., The.
—The Scarlet Letter, unabr. ed. 1999. audio 51.00 (*1-55690-459-2*, 81270E7) Recorded Bks., LLC.
—The Scarlet Letter. 1992. (Notable American Authors Ser.). reprint ed. lib. bdg. 75.00 (*0-7812-3038-1*) Reprint Services Corp.
—The Scarlet Letter. (Literary Classics Ser.). 1991. 208p. text 5.98 o.p. (*1-56138-036-9*, Courage Bks.); 1986. 192p. pap. 4.95 o.p. (*0-89471-474-0*); 1986. 192p. lib. bdg. 12.90 o.p. (*0-89471-475-9*) Running Pr. Bk. Pubs.
—The Scarlet Letter. 2004. 352p. mass mkt. 3.95 (*0-7434-8756-7*, Pocket); 1990. mass mkt. (*0-671-72467-3*, 45071, Washington Square Pr.); 1994. (Illus.). 352p. reprint ed. mass mkt. 4.99 (*0-671-51011-8*, Pocket) Simon & Schuster.
—The Scarlet Letter. (Ebook Classic Ser.). E-Book 5.00 (*0-7410-0475-5*) SoftBook Pr.
—The Scarlet Letter. unabr. ed. 2003. audio 19.99 (*1-59335-149-6*, 30245) Soulmate Audio Bks., Inc.
—The Scarlet Letter. abr. ed. 1979. (Mind's Eye Ser.). audio 14.95 o.p. (*0-88142-380-7*) Soundelux Audio Publishing.
—The Scarlet Letter. 1995. pap. 13.95 o.p. (*0-312-13846-6*) St. Martin's Pr.
—The Scarlet Letter. unabr. ed. 2002. audio compact disk 42.00 (*1-4001-0060-7*); audio compact disk 20.00 (*1-4001-5060-4*) Tantor Media, Inc.
—The Scarlet Letter. l.t. ed. 2002. (Perennial Bestsellers Ser.). 435p. 28.95 (*0-7862-4628-6*) Thorndike Pr.
—The Scarlet Letter. 2000. (Signature Classics Ser.). xiv, 298p. 24.95 (*1-58279-071-X*); (*1-58279-077-9*) Trident Pr. International.
—The Scarlet Letter. 1980. 10.00 (*0-606-00227-8*) Turtleback Bks.
—The Scarlet Letter. 320p. reprint ed. 1996. pap. 6.95 (*0-460-87785-2*); 1994. pap. text 6.95 o.p. (*0-460-87183-8*) Tuttle Publishing. (Everyman's Classic Library in Paperback).
—The Scarlet Letter. 2001. 185p. pap. 9.95 (*1-57002-158-9*) University Publishing Hse., Inc.
—The Scarlet Letter. 2002. 272p. pap. 6.00 (*0-14-243726-3*, Penguin Classics); 1983. 272p. (C). pap. 5.95 o.s.i (*0-14-039019-7*); 1995. audio 16.95 o.s.i (*0-14-086207-2*, Penguin AudioBooks) Viking Penguin.
—The Scarlet Letter. 2000. text 6.00 (*0-8220-7185-1*, Cliff Notes) Wiley, John & Sons, Inc.
—The Scarlet Letter. 1998. pap. 3.95 (*1-85326-568-3*); 1997. 224p. pap. 3.95 (*1-85326-029-0*, 0290WW) Wordsworth Editions, Ltd. GBR. *Dist:* Combined Publishing, Casemate Pubs. & Bk. Distributors, LLC.
—The Scarlet Letter: An Authoritative Text. Bradley, Sculley et al, eds. 2nd ed. 1978. (Critical Editions Ser.). 12.95 o.p. (*0-393-04495-5*) Norton, W. W. & Co., Inc.
—The Scarlet Letter: An Authoritative Text. Gross, Seymour L. et al, eds. 3rd ed. 1988. (Critical Editions Ser.). 480p. (C). pap. text (*0-393-95653-9*) Norton, W. W. & Co., Inc.
—The Scarlet Letter & Other Selected Tales. Harding, Brian, ed. & intro. by. 1998. (Oxford World's Classics Ser.). 352p. pap. 4.95 (*0-19-283371-5*) Oxford Univ. Pr., Inc.

Hawthorne, Nathaniel & Martin, John Stephen. The Scarlet Letter. 1998. E-Book 9.95 (*0-585-25257-2*) netLibrary, Inc.

**PSI-MAN (FICTITIOUS CHARACTER)—FICTION**

David, Peter. The Chaos Kid No. 4. 2000. (Psi-Man Ser.: Vol. 4). 192p. mass mkt. 5.99 o.s.i (*0-441-00745-7*) Ace Bks.
—Deathscape. 2000. (Psi-Man Ser.: No. 2). 192p. mass mkt. 5.99 o.s.i (*0-441-00710-4*) Ace Bks.
—Haven. 2000. (Psi-Man Ser.: Vol. 6). (Illus.). 192p. mass mkt. 5.99 o.s.i (*0-441-00764-3*) Ace Bks.
—Main Street D. O. A. 2000. (Psi-Man Ser.: Vol. 3). 192p. mass mkt. 5.99 o.s.i (*0-441-00717-1*) Ace Bks.
—Mind-Force Warrior. 2000. (Psi-Man Ser.: Vol. 1). (Illus.). 208p. mass mkt. 5.99 o.s.i (*0-441-00705-8*) Ace Bks.
—Psi-Man No. 3: Main Street D. O. A. 1991. 3.50 (*1-55773-492-5*, Diamond Bks.) Ace Bks.
—Psi-Man No. 5: Stalker. 2000. (Psi-Man Ser.: Vol. 5). 192p. mass mkt. 5.99 o.s.i (*0-441-00758-9*) Ace Bks.
—Psi-Man No. 6: Haven. 1992. 3.99 o.s.i (*1-55773-709-6*, Diamond Bks.) Ace Bks.

Peter, David. Psi-Man, No. 01. 1990. 3.50 o.p. (*1-55773-399-6*, Diamond Bks.) Berkley Publishing Group.
—Psi-Man No. 4: The Chaos Kid. 1991. 3.50 o.p. (*1-55773-540-9*, Diamond Bks.) Ace Bks.
—Psi-Man No. 5: Stalker. 1991. 3.99 (*1-55773-617-0*, Diamond Bks.) Ace Bks.

**PUG (FICTITIOUS CHARACTER)—FICTION**

Feist, Raymond E. Shadow of a Dark Queen. 1994. 22.00 o.p. (*0-688-12408-9*, Morrow, William & Co.) Morrow/Avon.
—Shards of a Broken Crown. (Serpentwar Saga: Vol. IV). 1999. 528p. mass mkt. 6.99 (*0-380-78983-3*, Eos); 1998. 432p. 24.00 (*0-380-97399-5*, Avon Bks.) Morrow/Avon.

**PUGH, E. J. (FICTITIOUS CHARACTER)—FICTION**

Cooper, Susan Rogers. A Crooked Little House. 1999. (E. J. Pugh Mysteries Ser.: No. 6). 352p. mass mkt. 5.99 o.s.i (*0-380-79469-1*, Avon Bks.) Morrow/Avon.
—Don't Drink the Water. 2000. (E. J. Pugh Mysteries Ser.). 192p. mass mkt. 5.99 o.s.i (*0-380-80533-2*, Avon Bks.) Morrow/Avon.
—Don't Drink the Water: An E. J. Pugh Mystery. l.t. ed. 2001. 192p. pap. 24.95 (*0-7838-9521-6*); 239p. (*0-7540-4631-1*); 239p. pap. (*0-7540-4632-X*) Gale Group. (Macmillan Reference USA).
—Hickory Dickory Stalk. 1996. (E. J. Pugh Mysteries Ser.). (Orig.). mass mkt. 5.50 o.s.i (*0-380-78155-7*, Avon Bks.) Morrow/Avon.
—Home Again, Home Again. 1997. (E. J. Pugh Mysteries Ser.). mass mkt. 5.99 o.s.i (*0-380-78156-5*, Avon Bks.) Morrow/Avon.
—Not in My Backyard. 1999. (E. J. Pugh Mysteries Ser.). 256p. mass mkt. 5.99 o.s.i (*0-380-80532-4*, Avon Bks.) Morrow/Avon.
—One, Two, What Did Daddy Do? 1996. (E. J. Pugh Mysteries Ser.). mass mkt. 5.50 o.s.i (*0-380-78417-3*, Avon Bks.) Morrow/Avon.
—One, Two, What Did Daddy Do? 1992. 224p. 17.95 o.p. (*0-312-08209-6*, Saint Martin's Minotaur) St. Martin's Pr.
—There Was a Little Girl. 1998. (E. J. Pugh Mysteries Ser.). 224p. mass mkt. 5.50 o.s.i (*0-380-79468-3*, Avon Bks.) Morrow/Avon.

**PULASKI, KATHERINE (FICTITIOUS CHARACTER)—FICTION**

Sharee, Keith. Gulliver's Fugitives. (Star Trek, The Next Generation Ser.: No. 11). E-Book 6.99 (*0-7434-2091-8*); 1991. 256p. mass mkt. 5.50 (*0-671-74143-8*) Simon & Schuster. (Star Trek).
—Gulliver's Fugitives. (Star Trek Ser.: No. 11). 1999. audio 5.98 (*0-671-04522-9*); 1990. audio 9.95 (*0-671-72319-7*) Simon & Schuster Audio. (Simon & Schuster Audioworks).

Smith, Dean Wesley & Rusch, Kristine K. Vectors No. 2: Double Helix. 1999. (Star Trek, The Next Generation: No. 52). (Illus.). 304p. pap. 6.50 (*0-671-03256-9*, Star Trek) Simon & Schuster.

**PURBRIGHT, WALTER, INSPECTOR (FICTITIOUS CHARACTER)—FICTION**

Watson, Colin. Charity Ends at Home. l.t. ed. 2003. (Dales Large Print Ser.). 272p. pap. 21.99 (*1-84262-160-2*) Dales Large Print Bks. GBR. *Dist:* Ulverscroft Large Print Bks., Ltd., Ulverscroft Large Print Canada, Ltd.
—Charity Ends at Home. 1983. (Murder Ink Mystery Ser.: No. 59). pap. 2.75 o.p. (*0-440-11187-0*) Dell Publishing.
—Coffin Scarcely Used. 1981. (Murder Ink Mystery Ser.: No. 29). pap. 2.25 o.p. (*0-440-11511-6*) Dell Publishing.
—Coffin Scarcely Used. unabr. ed. 1994. audio 54.95 (*1-85089-724-7*, 90093) ISIS Audio Bks. GBR. *Dist:* Ulverscroft Large Print Bks., Ltd.
—Hopjoy Was Here. 2002. (Crime ser.). 160p. 21.95 (*0-7540-8626-7*, Black Dagger) BBC Audiobooks America.
—Hopjoy Was Here. 1982. (Scene of the Crime Ser.: No. 53). pap. 2.50 o.p. (*0-440-13625-3*) Dell Publishing.
—It Shouldn't Happen to a Dog. 1977. (J). 7.95 o.p. (*0-399-11881-0*) Putnam Publishing Group, The.
—Just What the Doctor Ordered. 1982. (Murder Ink Mystery Ser.: No. 37). pap. 2.25 o.p. (*0-440-14242-3*) Dell Publishing.
—Just What the Doctor Ordered. 1983. (Crime Fiction 1950-1975 Ser.). 192p. lib. bdg. 5.00 o.p. (*0-8240-4952-7*) Garland Publishing, Inc.
—Lonelyheart 4122. 160p. pap. 5.95 o.p. (*0-89733-076-5*) Academy Chicago Pubs., Ltd.
—Lonelyheart 4122. (Black Dagger Crime Ser.). 1990. 18.50 o.p. (*0-86220-723-1*, Black Dagger); 18.95 o.p. (*0-7451-6429-3*); 1994. pap. 16.95 o.p. (*0-7451-6435-8*) BBC Audiobooks America.
—Plaster Sinners. 1981. (Crime Club Ser.). 192p. 10.95 o.p. (*0-385-17338-5*) Doubleday Publishing.
—Six Nuns & a Shotgun. 1983. (Murder Ink Mystery Ser.: No. 65). 192p. pap. 3.25 o.p. (*0-440-17871-1*) Dell Publishing.
—Whatever's Been Going on at Mumblesby? l.t. ed. 2002. (Dales Large Print Ser.). 272p. pap. 21.99 (*1-84262-161-0*) Dales Large Print Bks. GBR. *Dist:* Ulverscroft Large Print Bks., Ltd., Ulverscroft Large Print Canada, Ltd.
—Whatever's Been Going on at Mumblesby? 1983. (Crime Club Ser.). 192p. 11.95 o.p. (*0-385-18382-8*) Doubleday Publishing.

**PURDUE, THOMAS (FICTITIOUS CHARACTER)—FICTION**

Karp, Larry. The Music Box Murders. 2000. (WWL Mystery Ser.: Vol. 366). mass mkt. (*0-373-26366-X*, 1-26366-4, Worldwide Library) Harlequin Enterprises, Ltd.
—The Music Box Murders. 1999. 344p. 23.95 (*1-885173-58-X*) Write Way Publishing.
—Scamming the Birdman. 2000. 288p. 24.95 (*1-885173-84-9*) Write Way Publishing.

**PYATNITSKI, MAXIM ARTUROVICH (FICTITIOUS CHARACTER)—FICTION**

Moorcock, Michael. Byzantium Endures. 1981. (Illus.). 384p. 14.50 o.p. (*0-394-51972-8*) Random Hse., Inc.

Characters

**PUTTOCK, SIMON (FICTITIOUS CHARACTER)—FICTION**

Jecks, Michael. The Boy-Bishop's Glovemaker. 2001. (Medieval West Country Mysteries Ser.: Vol. 10). 320p. (J). mass mkt. 9.95 (*0-7472-6611-5*); 331p. 28.00 (*0-7472-7247-6*) Headline Bk. Publishing, Ltd. GBR. *Dist:* Trafalgar Square.

—The Devil's Acolyte. 2002. 416p. mass mkt. 9.95 (*0-7472-6725-1*); 320p. 28.00 (*0-7472-6920-3*) Headline Bk. Publishing, Ltd. GBR. *Dist:* Trafalgar Square.

—A Moorland Hanging. 1998. (Medieval West Country Mystery Ser.). 384p. mass mkt. 9.95 (*0-7472-5071-5*) Headline Bk. Publishing, Ltd. GBR. *Dist:* Trafalgar Square.

—Sticklepath Strangler. 2002. 366p. 28.00 (*0-7472-6919-X*) Headline Bk. Publishing, Ltd. GBR. *Dist:* Trafalgar Square.

—The Traitor of St. Giles. 2001. (Medieval West Country Mysteries Ser.: No. 9). 320p. (YA). mass mkt. 9.95 (*0-7472-6362-0*); 2000. 328p. 28.00 (*0-7472-7403-7*) Headline Bk. Publishing, Ltd. GBR. *Dist:* Trafalgar Square.

**PYM, HANNAH (FICTITIOUS CHARACTER)—FICTION**

Chesney, Marion. Beatrice Goes to Brighton. l.t. ed. 1993. (Travelling Matchmaker Ser.: Vol. 4). 252p. lib. bdg. 15.95 o.p. (*0-8161-5546-1*, Macmillan Reference USA) Gale Group.

—Beatrice Goes to Brighton. (Travelling Matchmaker Ser.: Vol. 4). 1992. mass mkt. 3.99 o.p. (*0-312-92794-0*, St. Martin's Paperbacks); 1991. 160p. 16.95 o.p. (*0-312-06302-4*) St. Martin's Pr.

—Belinda Goes to Bath. l.t. ed. 1992. (Travelling Matchmaker Ser.: Vol. 2). 232p. pap. 14.95 o.p. (*0-8161-5375-2*, Macmillan Reference USA) Gale Group.

—Belinda Goes to Bath. 1991. (Travelling Matchmaker Ser.: Vol. 2). 160p. mass mkt. 3.99 (*0-312-92642-1*, St. Martin's Paperbacks); 14.95 o.p. (*0-312-05382-7*) St. Martin's Pr.

—Deborah Goes to Dover. l.t. ed. 1993. (Travelling Matchmaker Ser.: Vol. 5). 254p. lib. bdg. 15.95 (*0-8161-5545-3*, Macmillan Reference USA) Gale Group.

—Deborah Goes to Dover. 1992. (Travelling Matchmaker Ser.: Vol. 5). mass mkt. 3.99 (*0-312-92902-1*, St. Martin's Paperbacks); 160p. 16.95 o.p. (*0-312-06952-9*) St. Martin's Pr.

—Emily Goes to Exeter. l.t. ed. 1992. (Travelling Matchmaker Ser.: Vol. 1). 245p. pap. 14.95 o.p. (*0-8161-5157-1*, Macmillan Reference USA) Gale Group.

—Emily Goes to Exeter. (Travelling Matchmaker Ser.: Vol. 1). 1991. 160p. mass mkt. 3.99 (*0-312-92582-4*, St. Martin's Paperbacks); 1990. 15.95 o.p. (*0-312-05078-X*) St. Martin's Pr.

—Penelope Goes to Portsmouth. l.t. ed. 1992. (Travelling Matchmaker Ser.: Vol. ). 247p. pap. 14.95 o.p. (*0-8161-5547-X*, Macmillan Reference USA) Gale Group.

—Penelope Goes to Portsmouth. (Travelling Matchmaker Ser.: Vol. 3). 1992. mass mkt. 3.99 (*0-312-92720-7*, St. Martin's Paperbacks); 1991. 15.95 o.p. (*0-312-05945-0*) St. Martin's Pr.

—Yvonne Goes to York. l.t. ed. 1993. (Travelling Matchmaker Ser.: Vol. 6). 264p. lib. bdg. 15.95 (*0-8161-5834-7*, Macmillan Reference USA) Gale Group.

—Yvonne Goes to York. 1992. (Travelling Matchmaker Ser.: Vol. 6). mass mkt. 3.99 (*0-312-92849-1*, St. Martin's Paperbacks); 160p. 16.95 o.p. (*0-312-07892-7*) St. Martin's Pr.

**PYNE, PARKER (FICTITIOUS CHARACTER)—FICTION**

Christie, Agatha. Mr. Parker Pyne, Detective. 1985. mass mkt. 2.95 o.s.i (*0-425-07999-6*); 1984. mass mkt. 2.95 o.s.i (*0-425-06788-2*) Berkley Publishing Group.

—Mr. Parker Pyne, Detective. l.t. ed. (Agatha Christie Ser.). 296p. 1990. pap. 13.95 (*0-8161-4564-4*); 1989. lib. bdg. 19.95 o.p. (*0-8161-4563-6*) Gale Group. (Macmillan Reference USA).

—Mr. Parker Pyne, Detective. 1986. (Agatha Christie Ser.). 14.95 o.s.i (*0-396-08865-1*, G. P. Putnam's Sons) Penguin Putnam Bks. for Young Readers.

—Parker Pyne Investigates. 1985. 208p. mass mkt. 5.99 o.s.i (*0-425-08770-0*) Berkley Publishing Group.

—Parker Pyne Investigates. l.t. ed. 1978. (Ulverscroft Large Print Ser.). 299p. 12.00 o.p. (*0-7089-0141-7*, Ulverscroft) Thorpe, F. A. Pubs. GBR. *Dist:* Ulverscroft Large Print Bks., Ltd., Ulverscroft Large Print Canada, Ltd.

—Parker Pyne Investigates. 1992. 12.04 (*0-606-12473-X*) Turtleback Bks.

—The Regatta Mystery & Other Stories. 1986. 176p. mass mkt. 5.99 (*0-425-10041-3*) Berkley Publishing Group.

—The Regatta Mystery & Other Stories. 1976. mass mkt. 2.95 o.s.i (*0-440-17336-1*) Dell Publishing.

—The Regatta Mystery & Other Stories. l.t. ed. (Agatha Christie Ser.). 280p. 1990. 12.95 o.p. (*0-8161-4596-2*); 1989. 12.95 o.p. (*0-8161-4595-4*) Gale Group. (Macmillan Reference USA).

—The Regatta Mystery & Other Stories. 1986. (Agatha Christie Ser.). 229p. 12.95 o.s.i (*0-396-08805-8*, G. P. Putnam's Sons) Penguin Putnam Bks. for Young Readers.

# Q

**Q (FICTITIOUS CHARACTER)—FICTION**

Bader, Hilary J. Borg: Experience the Collective. abr. ed. 1996. (Star Trek Ser.). audio compact disk 15.00 (*0-671-57502-3*, Simon & Schuster Audioworks) Simon & Schuster Audio.

Cox, Greg. The Q-Continuum No. 1: Q-Space. 1999. (Star Trek, The Next Generation Ser.: No. 47). E-Book 6.99 (*0-671-04101-0*, Star Trek) Simon & Schuster.

—The Q Continuum No. 2: Q-Zone. (Star Trek, The Next Generation Ser.: No. 48). (J). 1999. E-Book 6.99 (*0-671-04102-9*); 1998. 270p. mass mkt. 6.50 o.s.i (*0-671-01921-X*) Simon & Schuster. (Star Trek).

—Q-Space No. 1: The Q-Continuum. 1998. (Star Trek, The Next Generation Ser.: No. 47). 288p. (J). pap. 6.50 (*0-671-01915-5*, Star Trek) Simon & Schuster.

—Q-Strike No. 3: The Q Continuum. (Star Trek, The Next Generation Ser.: No. 49). 1999. E-Book 6.99 (*0-671-04103-7*); 1998. 272p. (J). mass mkt. 6.99 o.s.i (*0-671-01922-8*) Simon & Schuster. (Star Trek).

David, Peter. Q-in-Law. pap. text 7.50 (*0-8359-1105-5*) Globe Fearon Educational Publishing.

—Q-in-Law. 1999. (Star Trek, The Next Generation Ser.: No. 18). E-Book 6.99 (*0-671-04099-5*, Star Trek) Simon & Schuster.

—Q-in-Law. Stern, Dave, ed. 1991. (Star Trek, The Next Generation Ser.: No. 18). 272p. (J). mass mkt. 5.99 o.s.i (*0-671-73389-3*, Star Trek) Simon & Schuster.

—Q-in-Law. abr. ed. 1992. (Star Trek Ser.: No. 18). audio 12.00 (*0-671-75958-2*, Simon & Schuster Audioworks) Simon & Schuster Audio.

—Q-Squared. (Star Trek, The Next Generation Ser.). E-Book 6.99 (*0-7434-2065-9*); 1999. E-Book 6.99 (*0-671-04100-2*); 1995. 448p. (J). mass mkt. 6.50 o.s.i (*0-671-89151-0*) Simon & Schuster. (Star Trek).

—Q-Squared. Ryan, Kevin, ed. 1994. (Star Trek, The Next Generation Ser.). 448p. 22.00 o.p. (*0-671-89152-9*, Star Trek) Simon & Schuster.

—Q-Squared. abr. ed. 1994. (Star Trek Ser.). audio 17.00 (*0-671-89180-4*, Simon & Schuster Audioworks) Simon & Schuster Audio.

De Lancie, John. I, Q. 2003. (Star Trek Ser.). audio 9.95 (*0-7435-3256-2*); audio compact disk 9.95 (*0-7435-3275-9*) Simon & Schuster Audio. (Encore).

De Lancie, John & David, Peter. I, Q. (Star Trek Ser.). 2000. 256p. pap. 6.99 (*0-671-02444-2*); 1999. E-Book 23.00 (*0-7434-0079-8*); 1999. 256p. 22.95 o.s.i (*0-671-02443-4*); 1900. 252p. mass mkt. (*0-671-03581-9*) Simon & Schuster. (Star Trek).

—I, Q. abr. ed. 1999. (Star Trek Ser.). audio 18.00 (*0-671-04378-1*, Simon & Schuster Audioworks) Simon & Schuster Audio.

Friedman, Michael Jan. All Good Things. Ryan, Kevin, ed. 1995. (Star Trek, The Next Generation Ser.). (Illus.). 256p. mass mkt. 5.99 (*0-671-52148-9*, Star Trek) Simon & Schuster.

—All Good Things... (Star Trek, The Next Generation Ser.). E-Book 6.99 (*0-7434-2076-4*, Star Trek) Simon & Schuster.

—All Good Things. abr. ed. 1994. (Star Trek Ser.). audio 17.00 o.s.i (*0-671-89482-X*, Simon & Schuster Audioworks) Simon & Schuster Audio.

Gerrold, David. Encounter at Farpoint. (Star Trek, The Next Generation Ser.). E-Book 6.99 (*0-7434-2072-1*, Star Trek) Simon & Schuster.

—Encounter at Farpoint. Stern, Dave, ed. 1991. (Star Trek, The Next Generation Ser.). 192p. mass mkt. 5.99 (*0-671-74388-0*, Star Trek) Simon & Schuster.

—Encounter at Farpoint. 1987. (Star Trek, The Next Generation Ser.). mass mkt. 3.95 o.s.i (*0-671-65241-9*, Star Trek) Simon & Schuster.

**QUANTRILL, DOUGLAS (FICTITIOUS CHARACTER)—FICTION**

Radley, Sheila. Blood on the Happy Highway. l.t. ed. 1984. 384p. 16.95 o.p. (*0-7089-1316-4*, Ulverscroft) Thorpe, F. A. Pubs. GBR. *Dist:* Ulverscroft Large Print Bks., Ltd.

—The Chief Inspector's Daughter. 1987. (Mystery Ser.). 224p. mass mkt. 3.50 o.s.i (*0-553-26942-9*) Bantam Bks.

—The Chief Inspector's Daughter. 1982. (Nightingale Ser.). pap. 9.95 o.p. (*0-8161-3413-8*, Macmillan Reference USA) Gale Group.

—The Chief Inspector's Daughter. l.t. ed. 1982. (Ulverscroft Large Print Ser.). 432p. 29.99 o.p. (*0-7089-1033-5*, Ulverscroft) Thorpe, F. A. Pubs. GBR. *Dist:* Ulverscroft Large Print Bks., Ltd., Ulverscroft Large Print Canada, Ltd.

—Cross My Heart & Hope to Die: An Inspector Quantrill Mystery. 1992. (Quantrill Ser.: No. 8). 288p. text 19.00 (*0-684-19410-4*, Macmillan Reference USA) Gale Group.

—Cross My Heart & Hope to Die: An Inspector Quantrill Mystery. l.t. ed. 1998. (Ulverscroft Large Print Ser.). 416p. 29.99 o.p. (*0-7089-3956-2*, Ulverscroft) Thorpe, F. A. Pubs. GBR. *Dist:* Ulverscroft Large Print Bks., Ltd., Ulverscroft Large Print Canada, Ltd.

—Death in the Morning. 1987. 224p. reprint ed. mass mkt. 3.50 o.s.i (*0-553-26857-0*) Bantam Bks.

—Death in the Morning. 1980. pap. 3.50 o.p. (*0-440-11785-2*) Dell Publishing.

—Death in the Morning. 1981. (General Ser.). lib. bdg. 13.95 o.p. (*0-8161-3199-6*, Macmillan Reference USA) Gale Group.

—Fair Game. l.t. ed. 1999. (Ulverscroft Large Print Ser.). 416p. 31.99 o.p. (*0-7089-4028-5*, Ulverscroft) Thorpe, F. A. Pubs. GBR. *Dist:* Ulverscroft Large Print Bks., Ltd., Ulverscroft Large Print Canada, Ltd.

—Fate Worse Than Death. 1987. 208p. mass mkt. 2.95 o.s.i (*0-553-26538-5*) Bantam Bks.

—Fate Worse Than Death. 1986. 224p. 13.95 o.p. (*0-684-18582-2*, Macmillan Reference USA) Gale Group.

—Fate Worse Than Death. l.t. ed. 1986. (Mystery Ser.). 448p. 29.99 o.p. (*0-7089-1630-9*, Ulverscroft) Thorpe, F. A. Pubs. GBR. *Dist:* Ulverscroft Large Print Bks., Ltd., Ulverscroft Large Print Canada, Ltd.

—The Quiet Road to Death. 1984. 176p. 11.95 o.s.i (*0-684-18124-X*, Scribner) Simon & Schuster.

—The Quiet Road to Death. 1985. (Crime Monthly Ser.). 192p. pap. 3.95 o.p. (*0-14-007746-4*, Penguin Bks.) Viking Penguin.

—A Talent for Destruction. 1984. mass mkt. 2.50 o.s.i (*0-345-31250-3*) Ballantine Bks.

—A Talent for Destruction. 1982. 224p. 10.95 o.p. (*0-684-17663-7*, Scribner) Simon & Schuster.

—This Way Out. 1992. 2.99 o.p. (*0-517-08033-8*) Random Hse. Value Publishing.

—This Way Out. 1989. 256p. 16.95 o.s.i (*0-684-19125-3*, Scribner) Simon & Schuster.

—This Way Out. 1990. 224p. reprint ed. pap. 4.50 o.p. (*0-14-014453-6*, Penguin Bks.) Viking Penguin.

—Who Saw Him Die? 1988. 224p. mass mkt. 3.50 o.s.i (*0-553-27607-7*) Bantam Bks.

—Who Saw Him Die? 1988. (Inspector Douglas Quantrill Mystery Ser.). 224p. 14.95 o.s.i (*0-684-18883-X*, Scribner) Simon & Schuster.

**QUANTRILL, SNOHOMISH (FICTITIOUS CHARACTER)—FICTION**

Scarborough, Elizabeth Ann. The Godmother. (Orig.). 1995. 352p. mass mkt. 6.99 o.s.i (*0-441-00269-2*); 1994. 304p. 19.95 o.p. (*0-441-00096-7*) Ace Bks.

—The Godmother's Apprentice. 304p. 1996. mass mkt. 6.50 o.s.i (*0-441-00358-3*); 1995. 19.95 o.s.i (*0-441-00252-8*) Ace Bks.

—The Godmother's Web. 320p. 1998. 19.95 o.s.i (*0-441-00503-9*); 1999. reprint ed. mass mkt. 6.50 o.s.i (*0-441-00600-0*) Ace Bks.

**QUANTRILL, TED (FICTITIOUS CHARACTER)—FICTION**

Ing, Dean. Single Combat. (Orig.). 1993. 384p. mass mkt. 4.99 (*0-8125-1164-6*); 1983. 320p. pap. 2.95 o.s.i (*0-8125-4100-6*) Doherty, Tom Assocs., LLC. (Tor Bks.).

—Systemic Shock. 1986. mass mkt. 3.50 o.s.i (*0-441-79383-5*); 1981. mass mkt. 2.50 o.s.i (*0-441-79381-9*) Ace Bks.

—Systemic Shock. 1992. 320p. mass mkt. 4.99 o.p. (*0-8125-0038-5*, Tor Bks.) Doherty, Tom Assocs., LLC.

—Wild Country. (Orig.). 1993. 317p. mass mkt. 4.99 (*0-8125-1171-9*); 1985. 320p. mass mkt. 2.95 (*0-8125-4102-2*) Doherty, Tom Assocs., LLC. (Tor Bks.).

**QUARK (FICTITIOUS CHARACTER)—FICTION**

Carey, Diane L. What You Leave Behind. 1999. (Star Trek Deep Space Nine Ser.). 224p. pap. 6.50 (*0-671-03476-6*, Star Trek) Simon & Schuster.

David, Peter, et al. Wrath of the Prophets. 1997. (Star Trek Deep Space Nine Ser.: No. 20). 304p. pap. 5.99 (*0-671-53817-9*, Star Trek) Simon & Schuster.

Dillard, J. M., et al. Emissary; The Siege; Bloodletter; The Big Game; Betrayal, 5 bks. 1997. (Star Trek). pap. text 0.95 o.p. (*0-8359-1492-5*) Globe Fearon Educational Publishing.

Garland, Mark. Trial by Error. 1997. (Star Trek Deep Space Nine Ser.: No. 21). (Illus.). 304p. pap. 5.99 (*0-671-00251-1*, Star Trek) Simon & Schuster.

Graf, L. A. Caretaker. abr. ed. 1995. (Star Trek Voyager Ser.: No. 1). 17.00 o.s.i incl. audio (*0-671-52142-X*) Baen Bks.

—Caretaker. Ordover, John, ed. 1995. (Star Trek Voyager Ser.: No. 1). 288p. mass mkt. 5.99 Simon & Schuster.

Hugh, Dafydd ab. The Conquered No. 1: Rebels. 1999. (Star Trek Deep Space Nine Ser.: No. 24). 256p. pap. 6.50 o.s.i (*0-671-01140-5*, Star Trek) Simon & Schuster.

—Fallen Heroes. (Star Trek Deep Space Nine Ser.: No. 5). 1999. E-Book 6.50 (*0-671-04114-2*); 1994. E-Book 6.99 (*0-7434-1224-9*) Simon & Schuster. (Star Trek).

—Fallen Heroes. Ordover, John, ed. 1994. (Star Trek Deep Space Nine Ser.: No. 5). 288p. mass mkt. 5.50 (*0-671-88459-X*, Star Trek) Simon & Schuster.

—Fallen Heroes. abr. ed. 1994. (Star Trek Deep Space Nine Ser.: No. 5). audio 16.00 (*0-671-89182-0*, Simon & Schuster Audioworks) Simon & Schuster Audio.

—Fallen Heroes Star Trek Continuity. 1999. 12.99 (*0-671-02166-4*, Star Trek) Simon & Schuster.

—The Liberated No. 3: Rebels. 1999. (Resistance Trilogy Ser.: No. 26). 256p. mass mkt. 6.50 o.s.i (*0-671-01142-1*, Star Trek) Simon & Schuster.

—Rebels: The Conquered. (Star Trek Deep Space Nine Ser.: No. 24). E-Book 6.99 (*0-7434-2055-1*, Star Trek) Simon & Schuster.

Jeter, K. W. Warped. 1996. (Star Trek Deep Space Nine Ser.). 352p. mass mkt. 5.99 (*0-671-56781-0*, Star Trek) Simon & Schuster.

—Warped. Ryan, Kevin, ed. 1995. (Star Trek Deep Space Nine Ser.). 352p. 22.00 o.p. (*0-671-87252-4*, Star Trek) Simon & Schuster.

—Warped. abr. ed. (Star Trek Deep Space Nine Ser.). 1999. audio 9.98 (*0-671-04504-0*); 1995. 16.00 incl. audio (*0-671-52120-9*) Simon & Schuster Audio. (Simon & Schuster Audioworks).

Martin, Michael A. & Mangels, Andy. Mission Gamma: Cathedral. 2002. (Star Trek Deep Space Nine Ser.: Bk. 3). 432p. mass mkt. 6.99 (*0-7434-4564-3*, Star Trek) Simon & Schuster.

Quark. The Ferengi Rules of Acquisition. Ryan, Kevin, ed. 1995. (Star Trek Deep Space Nine Ser.). 96p. pap. 6.00 (*0-671-52936-6*, Star Trek) Simon & Schuster.

—Legends of the Ferengi. 1997. (Star Trek Deep Space Nine Ser.). (Illus.). 192p. pap. 12.00 (*0-671-00728-9*, Star Trek) Simon & Schuster.

—Legends of the Ferengi. abr. ed. 1997. (Star Trek Ser. ). audio 12.00 (*0-671-57901-0*, Simon & Schuster Audioworks) Simon & Schuster Audio.

Reeves-Stevens, Judith & Reeves-Stevens, Garfield. Millennium No. 1: The Fall of Terok Nor. 2000. (Star Trek Deep Space Nine Ser.). E-Book 6.99 (*0-7434-0679-6*); (Star Trek Deep Space Nine: Vol. 1). 464p. pap. 6.50 o.s.i (*0-671-02401-9*) Simon & Schuster. (Star Trek).

—Millennium No. 1: The Fall of Terok Nor. abr. ed. 2000. (Star Trek Ser. ). audio 18.00 (*0-7435-0010-5*, Simon & Schuster Audioworks) Simon & Schuster Audio.

Schofield, Sandy. The Big Game. 1994. (Star Trek Deep Space Nine Ser.: No. 4). E-Book 6.99 (*0-7434-1223-0*, Star Trek) Simon & Schuster.

—The Big Game. Ordover, John, ed. 1993. (Star Trek Deep Space Nine Ser.: No. 4). 288p. mass mkt. 5.50 (*0-671-88030-6*, Star Trek) Simon & Schuster.

Sheckley, Robert. Laertian Gamble. 1995. (Star Trek Deep Space Nine Ser.: No. 12). 288p. mass mkt. 5.99 (*0-671-88690-8*, Star Trek) Simon & Schuster.

Shimerman, Armin. The Merchant Prince. 2001. E-Book 23.95 (*1-58945-288-7*) Adobe Systems, Inc.

—The Merchant Prince. 2001. (Illus.). 368p. reprint ed. mass mkt. 6.99 (*0-671-03613-0*, Star Trek); Bk. 2. 2001. 320p. reprint ed. E-Book 6.99 (*0-7434-1748-8*, Star Trek); Bk. 3. 2003. 368p. mass mkt. 7.99 (*0-671-03594-0*, Pocket Star) Simon & Schuster.

Shimerman, Armin & George, David R., III. Star Trek Deep Space Nine: The 34th Rule. abr. ed. 1999. (Star Trek Deep Space Nine Ser.: No. 23). audio 16.85 (*0-671-03358-1*) Ulverscroft Audio (U.S.A.).

—The 34th Rule. 1999. (Star Trek Deep Space Nine Ser.: No. 23). 448p. pap. 6.50 (*0-671-00793-9*, Star Trek) Simon & Schuster.

—The 34th Rule. abr. ed. 1999. (Star Trek Ser. : No. 23). audio 18.00 (*0-671-04395-1*, Simon & Schuster Audioworks) Simon & Schuster Audio.

Shimerman, Armin & Scott, Michael. The Merchant Prince. 2000. 320p. 23.95 o.s.i (*0-671-03592-4*, Atria); Book 3. 2003. E-Book (*0-7434-8044-9*, Pocket) Simon & Schuster.

Smith, Dean Wesley. The Core. 2003. 256p. mass mkt. 6.99 (*0-7434-6398-6*, Pocket) Simon & Schuster.

Smith, Dean Wesley & Rusch, Kristine K. The Long Night. (Star Trek Deep Space Nine Ser.: No. 14). E-Book 6.99 (0-7434-2045-4); 1996. 288p. mass mkt. 5.99 (0-671-55165-5) Simon & Schuster. (Star Trek).

QUARRY (FICTITIOUS CHARACTER: COLLINS)—FICTION

Collins, Max Allan. The Broker's Wife. 1976. (Quarry Ser.). 1.50 o.p. (0-425-03187-X) Berkley Publishing Group.
—Primary Target. 1987. (Quarry Novel Ser.). 208p. 14.95 o.p. (0-88150-098-4) Countryman Pr.
—Quarry. 1985. (Quarry Ser.). 224p. pap. 4.95 o.p. (0-88150-057-7) Countryman Pr.
—Quarry's Cut. 1986. (Quarry Ser.). 224p. reprint ed. pap. 4.95 o.p. (0-88150-069-0) Countryman Pr.
—Quarry's Deal. 1986. (Quarry Ser.). 192p. reprint ed. pap. 4.95 o.p. (0-88150-068-2) Countryman Pr.
—Quarry's List. 1985. (Quarry Ser.). 192p. pap. 4.95 o.p. (0-88150-058-5) Countryman Pr.

QUASIMODO (FICTITIOUS CHARACTER)—FICTION

Cerasini, Marc A. The Hunchback of Notre Dame. 1995. (Bullseye Step into Classics Ser.). 9.09 o.p. (0-606-09442-3) Turtleback Bks.
Holland, Sharon. The Hunchback of Notre Dame. 1996. 96p. mass mkt. 3.50 o.p. (0-06-106434-3, HarperTorch) Morrow/Avon.
Hugo, Victor. The Hunchback of Notre-Dame. 1995. (Literary Classics Giant Ser.). 696p. text 8.98 o.p. (1-56138-602-2, Courage Bks.) Running Pr. Bk. Pubs.
—The Hunchback of Notre Dame. 1997. (Classics Illustrated Notes). pap. text 4.99 (1-57840-067-8) Acclaim Bks.
—The Hunchback of Notre Dame. 1976. 24.95 (0-8488-0534-8) Amereon, Ltd.
—The Hunchback of Notre Dame, Set. 1995. audio 71.95 (1-55685-390-4) Audio Bk. Contractors, Inc.
—The Hunchback of Notre Dame. 1981. mass mkt. 2.50 o.s.i (0-553-21224-9) Bantam Bks.
—The Hunchback of Notre Dame. Bair, Lowell, tr. 1981. 320p. mass mkt. 5.95 (0-553-21370-9, Bantam Classics) Bantam Bks.
—The Hunchback of Notre Dame. 1991. 3.95 (0-425-12667-6) Berkley Publishing Group.
—The Hunchback of Notre Dame. 1991. audio 73.95 (0-7861-0570-4); 1996. audio 85.95 (0-7861-0988-2, 1765) Blackstone Audio Bks., Inc.
—The Hunchback of Notre Dame. unabr. collector's ed. 1992. (J). audio 104.00 (0-7366-2281-0, 3068) Books on Tape, Inc.
—The Hunchback of Notre Dame. 1981. reprint ed. lib. bdg. 31.95 (0-89966-382-6) Buccaneer Bks., Inc.
—The Hunchback of Notre Dame. 1996. 458p. mass mkt. 3.99 (0-8125-6312-3, Tor Classics) Doherty, Tom Assocs., LLC.
—The Hunchback of Notre Dame. 1995. (Illus.). 96p. pap. text 1.00 (0-486-28564-2) Dover Pubns., Inc.
—The Hunchback of Notre Dame. abr. ed. audio 15.95 o.p. (0-88646-139-1, 7140); 1986. (YA). (gr. 7-9). audio 29.95 o.p. (0-88646-808-6, R 7140);Set. 1996. audio 9.99 (1-55204-005-4, 9005) Durkin Hayes Publishing Ltd.
—The Hunchback of Notre Dame. 1996. (Illus.). 584p. reprint ed. 17.95 (0-7868-6235-1) Hyperion Pr.
—The Hunchback of Notre Dame. 1986. (Illus.). (J). pap. 8.95 o.p. (0-86685-142-9) International Bk. Ctr., Inc.
—The Hunchback of Notre Dame. unabr. ed. 1991. audio 89.00 Jimcin Recordings.
—The Hunchback of Notre Dame. 1989. (English As a Second Language Bk.). pap. text 4.46 net. o.p. (0-582-53494-1, 74095) Longman Publishing Group.
—The Hunchback of Notre Dame. Cobb, Walter J., tr. 1965. 512p. mass mkt. 5.95 o.s.i (0-451-52222-2, Signet Classics) NAL.
—The Hunchback of Notre Dame. abr. ed. 1996. 37p. audio 13.98 (962-634-506-3, NA200614); 1994. audio compact disk 15.98 o.p. (962-634-006-1, NA200612) Naxos of America, Inc. (Naxos AudioBooks).
—The Hunchback of Notre Dame. abr. ed. 1996. (Ultimate Classics Ser.). 19.95 o.p. (0-7871-0526-0, 628385) NewStar Media, Inc.
—The Hunchback of Notre Dame. unabr. ed. 34.95 incl. audio Norton Pubs., Inc., Jeffrey /Audio-Forum.
—The Hunchback of Notre Dame. 1991. pap. 4.95 o.p. (0-8114-6827-5) Raintree Pubs.
—The Hunchback of Notre Dame. 1996. (Modern Library Ser.). 416p. 15.00 o.s.i (0-679-60255-0) Random Hse., Inc.
—The Hunchback of Notre Dame, unabr. ed. 1991. audio 128.00 (1-55690-241-7, 91224E7) Recorded Bks., LLC.
—The Hunchback of Notre Dame. 1989. 5.98 o.p. (0-86136-602-6) Smithmark Pubs., Inc.
—The Hunchback of Notre Dame. 1996. 9.60 o.p. (0-606-09443-1); 1956. 12.00 (0-606-00835-7) Turtleback Bks.
—The Hunchback of Notre Dame. 1998. (Classics Library). 448p. pap. 3.95 (1-85326-068-1, 0681WW) Wordsworth Editions, Ltd. GBR. Dist: Casemate Pubs. & Bk. Distributors, LLC.

QUATERMAIN, ALLAN (FICTITIOUS CHARACTER)—FICTION

Haggard, H. Rider. Allan Quatermain. E-Book 2.49 (1-58627-559-3) Electric Umbrella Publishing.
—Allan Quatermain & the Ice Gods. Reginald, R. & Menville, Douglas A., eds. 1976. (Supernatural & Occult Fiction Ser.). lib. bdg. 26.95 (0-405-08132-4) Ayer Co. Pubs., Inc.
—Allan Quatermain & the Ice Gods. 1999. 320p. pap. 7.95 (1-902058-11-9) Pulp Fictions GBR. Dist: 7 Hills Bk. Distributors.
—Allan Quatermain & the Ice Gods. 2002. (Wildside Fantasy Classics). 204p. pap. 15.99 (1-58715-708-X) Wildside Pr.
—Allan Quatermain, Being an Account of His Further Adventures & Discoveries in Company with Sir Henry Curtis, Bart., Commander John Good, R.N., & One Umslopogaas. Reginald, R. & Menville, Douglas A., eds. 1980. (Newcastle Forgotten Fantasy Library: Vol. 18). 278p. reprint ed. lib. bdg. 25.00 o.p. (0-89370-517-9) Millefleurs.
—Allan's Wife. 240p. 21.95 (0-8488-2607-8) Amereon, Ltd.
—Allan's Wife. 1980. (Forgotten Fantasy Library: Vol. 24). reprint ed. pap. 5.95 o.p. (0-87877-123-9, New Page Bks.) Career Pr., Inc.
—Allan's Wife. 2001. 128p. 23.99 (1-58827-532-9); per. 18.99 (1-58827-533-7) IndyPublish.com.
—Allan's Wife. 2002. 132p. per. 14.95 (1-58715-710-1) Wildside Pr.
—Allan's Wife: With Hunter Quatermain's Story, A Tale of Three Lions, & Long Odds. Reginald, R., ed. 1981. (Forgotten Fantasy Library: Vol. 24). 240p. lib. bdg. 27.00 o.p. (0-89370-523-3) Millefleurs.
—Ancient Allan. 1920. 298p. pap. 19.50 (1-58715-103-0) Wildside Pr.
—Black Heart & White Heart. unabr. ed. 1991. audio 21.95 o.p. (1-55656-096-6, DAB009) BBC Audiobooks America.
—Black Heart & White Heart. audio 16.95 o.p. (1-55656-057-5); 1997. pap. 16.95 o.p. incl. audio (1-55656-218-7) Dercum Audio.
—King Solomon's Mines. Date not set. reprint ed. lib. bdg. 20.95 (0-89190-703-3, American Reprint Co.) Amereon, Ltd.
—King Solomon's Mines. Kay, Marilyn, ed. abr. ed. 1987. pap. 12.95 incl. audio (1-882071-12-3, 014) B&B Audio, Inc.
—King Solomon's Mines. unabr. ed. 2000. audio compact disk 56.00 (0-7861-9882-6, z2575); audio 44.95 (0-7861-0610-7, 2575) Blackstone Audio Bks., Inc.
—King Solomon's Mines. unabr. collector's ed. 1984. (J). audio 48.00 (0-7366-0928-8, 1872) Books on Tape, Inc.
—King Solomon's Mines. 1976. reprint ed. lib. bdg. 19.95 (0-89968-513-7) Buccaneer Bks., Inc.
—King Solomon's Mines. l.t. ed. 1986. (Mainstream Ser.). (Illus.). xi, 317p. 15.95 o.p. (1-85089-063-3) ISIS Large Print Bks. GBR. Dist: Transaction Pubs.
—King Solomon's Mines. 1989. audio 35.00 Jimcin Recordings.
—King Solomon's Mines. l.t. ed. 1998. (Large Print Heritage Ser.). 365p. lib. bdg. 33.95 (1-58118-033-0, 22014) LRS.
—King Solomon's Mines. 1981. (English As a Second Language Bk.). pap. text 5.95 o.p. (0-582-53502-6, 74101) Longman Publishing Group.
—King Solomon's Mines. l.t. ed. (Large Print Ser.). 1992. 382p. lib. bdg. 26.00 (0-939495-49-X); 1998. 240p. reprint ed. lib. bdg. 25.00 (1-58287-044-6) North Bks.
—King Solomon's Mines. Butts, Dennis, ed. & intro. by. 1998. (Oxford World's Classics Ser.). (Illus.). 368p. pap. 9.95 (0-19-283485-1) Oxford Univ. Pr., Inc.
—King Solomon's Mines. Butts, Dennis, ed. 1990. (Oxford World's Classics Ser.). (Illus.). 366p. pap. 5.95 o.p. (0-19-282204-7) Oxford Univ. Pr., Inc.
—King Solomon's Mines. 1988. pap. 4.95 o.p. (0-19-581013-9) Oxford Univ. Pr., Inc.
—King Solomon's Mines. abr. l.t. ed. 1996. (Great Illustrated Classics Ser.: Vol. 54). (Illus.). 240p. (J). (gr. 3-7). 9.95 (0-86611-869-1) Playmore, Inc., Pubs.
—King Solomon's Mines, unabr. ed. 2001. audio 60.00 (1-55690-845-8, 93212E7) Recorded Bks., LLC.
—King Solomon's Mines. 1999. (Gateway Movie Classics Ser.). 382p. pap. 14.95 (0-89526-329-7, Gateway Editions) Regnery Publishing, Inc., An Eagle Publishing Co.
—King Solomon's Mines. 1998. (Children's Classics). 224p. pap. 3.95 (1-85326-105-X, 105XWW) Wordsworth Editions, Ltd. GBR. Dist: Advanced Global Distribution Services.
—She & Allan. reprint ed. lib. bdg. 25.95 (0-89190-706-8, Rivercity Pr.) Amereon, Ltd.
—She & Allan. 1978. (Del Rey Bk.). mass mkt. 1.95 o.s.i (0-345-27449-0) Ballantine Bks.
—She & Allan. 1975. (Forgotten Fantasy Library: Vol. 6). (Illus.). 302p. pap. 5.95 o.p. (0-87877-105-0, F-112, New Page Bks.) Career Pr., Inc.
—She & Allan. Reginald, R. & Menville, Douglas A., eds. 1980. (Forgotten Fantasy Library: Vol. 6). 303p. reprint ed. lib. bdg. 31.00 o.p. (0-89370-505-5) Millefleurs.
—She & Allan. 1999. 320p. pap. 7.95 (1-902058-05-4) Pulp Fictions GBR. Dist: 7 Hills Bk. Distributors.
—She & Allan. 2001. 408p. pap. 19.95 (1-58715-422-6) Wildside Pr.
—She, King Solomon's Mines & Allan Quartermain. 1951. 636p. pap. 12.95 (0-486-20643-2) Dover Pubns., Inc.

QUENTIN (FICTITIOUS CHARACTER)—FICTION

Lawhead, Stephen R. In the Hall of the Dragon King. (Dragon King Trilogy ). (YA). (gr. 7-12). 1990. pap. 9.99 o.p. (0-89107-563-1); Bk. 1. 1982. 348p. pap. 9.95 o.p. (0-89107-257-8) Crossway Bks.
—In the Hall of the Dragon King. 2003. (Illus.). 384p. pap. 6.95 (0-7459-4618-6) Lion Publishing PLC GBR. Dist: Trafalgar Square.
—In the Hall of the Dragon King. 1992. (Dragon King Trilogy : Bk. 1). (YA). pap. 6.50 (0-380-71629-1, Avon Bks.) Morrow/Avon.
—In the Hall of the Dragon King. 1996. (Dragon King Trilogy : Bk. 1). 352p. (YA). pap. 24.99 (0-310-20502-6) Zondervan.
—The Sword & the Flame. (Dragon King Trilogy : Bk. 3). (YA). (gr. 7-12). 1990. pap. 9.99 o.p. (0-89107-565-8); 1984. 348p. pap. 9.95 o.p. (0-89107-310-8) Crossway Bks.
—The Sword & the Flame. 2003. (Dragon King Saga: Bk. 3). (Illus.). 320p. (J). pap. 6.95 (0-7459-4619-4) Lion Publishing PLC GBR. Dist: Trafalgar Square.
—The Sword & the Flame. 1992. (Dragon King Trilogy : Bk. 3). 384p. (YA). mass mkt. 5.99 (0-380-71631-3, Avon Bks.) Morrow/Avon.
—The Sword & the Flame. 1996. (Dragon King Trilogy : Bk. 3). 320p. (YA). pap. 24.99 (0-310-20504-2) Zondervan.
—The Warlords of Nin. (Dragon King Saga: Bk. 2). (YA). (gr. 7-12). 1983. 488p. pap. 9.95 o.p. (0-89107-278-0); Bk. 2. 1990. pap. 9.99 o.p. (0-89107-564-X) Crossway Bks.
—The Warlords of Nin. 2003. (Illus.). 352p. pap. 6.95 (0-7459-4620-8) Lion Publishing PLC GBR. Dist: Trafalgar Square.
—The Warlords of Nin. 1992. (Dragon King Saga: Bk. 2). 416p. (YA). pap. 5.99 (0-380-71630-5, Avon Bks.) Morrow/Avon.
—The Warlords of Nin. 1996. (Dragon King Saga: Bk. 2). 400p. (YA). pap. 24.99 (0-310-20503-4) Zondervan.

QUI-GON JINN (FICTITIOUS CHARACTER)—FICTION

Brooks, Terry. Star Wars Episode I: The Phantom Menace. 2000. 352p. mass mkt. o.s.i (0-345-43975-9, Del Rey); 2000. 352p. mass mkt. 7.50 (0-345-43411-0, Del Rey); 1999. (0-345-43754-3); 1999. 324p. 25.00 (0-345-42765-3, Del Rey) Ballantine Bks.
—Star Wars Episode I: The Phantom Menace. abr. ed. 1999. (Star Wars Ser.). audio 19.95 (0-375-40635-2); audio compact disk 49.95 (0-375-40743-X); audio compact disk 24.95 (0-375-40637-9);Set. audio 39.95 (0-375-40655-7) Random Hse. Audio Publishing Group. (RH Audio).
—Star Wars Episode I: The Phantom Menace. 1999. (Star Wars Episode I Ser.). 13.55 (0-606-19372-3) Turtleback Bks.
Lucas, George. Star Wars: Episode I: The Phantom Menace Facsimile Script. 2000. (Star Wars Ser.). (Illus.). 144p. pap. 18.95 (0-345-43123-5, Del Rey) Ballantine Bks.
—Star Wars: Episode I: The Phantom Menace Illustrated Screenplay. 1999. (Star Wars Ser.). (Illus.). vii, 150p. (Orig.). pap. 14.95 (0-345-43110-3, Del Rey) Ballantine Bks.
Lucas, George, et al. Star Wars: Episode I: The Phantom Menace. 1999. (Star Wars Ser.). (Illus.). 112p. pap. 12.95 (1-56971-359-6) Dark Horse Comics.
Lucasfilm Ltd. Staff. Star Wars: Episode I: The Phantom Menace. 1999. pap. 1.94 o.s.i (0-375-80898-1, Random Hse. Bks. for Young Readers) Random Hse. Children's Bks.
—Star Wars: Episode I: The Phantom Menace. 1999. pap. 1.80 o.s.i (0-375-80897-3) Random Hse., Inc.
Rhino Records Staff, ed. Star Wars: Episode I: The Phantom Menace. 1999. (Star Wars Ser.). 24p. (J). 9.98 incl. audio compact disk. (J). 9.98 incl. audio compact disk. (Illus.). 5.98 incl. audio (1-56826-996-X, R4 75642); (Illus.). 5.98 incl. audio (1-56826-996-X, R4 75642) Rhino Entertainment.
Schultz, Mark, et al. Star Wars: Episode I: The Phantom Menace Adventures. 2000. (Star Wars Ser.). (Illus.). 112p. (YA). (gr. 5 up). pap. 12.95 (1-56971-443-6) Dark Horse Comics.
Whitman, John. Star Wars: Episode I: The Phantom Menace. 1999. (Star Wars Ser.). (Illus.). 344p. (YA). (gr. 3 up). 9.95 o.p. (0-8118-2315-6) Chronicle Bks. LLC.

QUILLER (FICTITIOUS CHARACTER: HALL)—FICTION

Hall, Adam. The Kobra Manifesto. 1986. 256p. (J). mass mkt. 3.50 o.s.i (0-515-08698-3, Jove) Berkley Publishing Group.
—The Kobra Manifesto. unabr. collector's ed. 1984. (Quiller Ser.). audio 48.00 (0-7366-0604-1, 1570) Books on Tape, Inc.
—The Kobra Manifesto. 1978. pap. 1.95 o.p. (0-440-14406-X) Dell Publishing.
—The Kobra Manifesto. 1977. lib. bdg. 13.50 o.p. (0-8161-6454-1, Macmillan Reference USA) Gale Group.
—The Kobra Manifesto. 1993. 352p. mass mkt. 4.50 o.p. (0-06-100532-0, HarperTorch) Morrow/Avon.
—The Mandarin Cypher. 1986. 240p. mass mkt. 3.50 o.s.i (0-515-08623-1, Jove) Berkley Publishing Group.
—The Mandarin Cypher. unabr. collector's ed. 1987. (Quiller Ser.). audio 48.00 (0-7366-1164-9, 2089) Books on Tape, Inc.
—The Mandarin Cypher. 1975. reprint ed. lib. bdg. 11.95 o.p. (0-8161-6333-2, Macmillan Reference USA) Gale Group.
—The Mandarin Cypher. 1993. 320p. mass mkt. 4.50 o.p. (0-06-100531-2, HarperTorch) Morrow/Avon.
—The Ninth Directive. 1988. mass mkt. 3.50 o.s.i (0-515-09498-6); 1979. o.s.i (0-515-05204-3) Berkley Publishing Group. (Jove).
—The Ninth Directive. 1993. 288p. mass mkt. 4.50 o.p. (0-06-100527-4, HarperTorch) Morrow/Avon.
—The Ninth Directive. 1972. mass mkt. 0.60 o.p. (0-451-03578-X); mass mkt. 0.75 o.p. (0-451-05243-9) NAL. (Signet Bks.).
—The Peking Target. 1988. mass mkt. 3.95 o.s.i (0-515-09680-6); 1983. 290p. 2.95 (0-86721-188-1) Berkley Publishing Group. (Jove).
—The Peking Target. 1994. (Quiller Ser.). 336p. mass mkt. 4.50 o.p. (0-06-100535-5, HarperTorch) Morrow/Avon.
—The Peking Target. 1982. 13.50 o.p. (0-87223-755-9) Playboy Enterprises, Inc.
—Quiller. mass mkt. 3.95 o.s.i (0-515-09152-9); 1985. 368p. mass mkt. 4.50 o.s.i (0-515-08415-8) Berkley Publishing Group. (Jove).
—Quiller Balalaika. 2003. 288p. 24.00 (0-7867-1265-1) Avalon Publishing Group.
—Quiller Bamboo. unabr. collector's ed. 1992. (Quiller Ser.). audio 56.00 (0-7366-2117-2, 2920) Books on Tape, Inc.
—Quiller Bamboo. 1992. 320p. mass mkt. 4.99 (0-380-71161-3, Avon Bks.); 1991. 288p. 20.00 o.p. (0-688-09696-4, Morrow, William & Co.) Morrow/Avon.
—Quiller Barracuda. unabr. collector's ed. 1991. (Quiller Ser.). audio 56.00 (0-7366-2023-0, 2838) Books on Tape, Inc.
—Quiller Barracuda. l.t. ed. 1992. 356p. 24.95 (1-85089-594-5) ISIS Large Print Bks. GBR. Dist: Transaction Pubs.
—Quiller Barracuda. 1991. 304p. mass mkt. 4.95 (0-380-70814-0, Avon Bks.); 1990. 18.95 o.p. (0-688-08784-1, Morrow, William & Co.) Morrow/Avon.
—Quiller KGB. 1989. 4.50 (1-55773-217-5, Diamond Bks.) Berkley Publishing Group.
—The Quiller Memorandum. 1986. 192p. mass mkt. 3.50 o.s.i (0-515-08503-0, Jove) Berkley Publishing Group.
—The Quiller Memorandum. 1994. lib. bdg. 24.95 (1-56849-396-7) Buccaneer Bks., Inc.
—The Quiller Memorandum. 2004. 224p. 24.95 (0-7653-0967-X); pap. 13.95 (0-7653-0968-8) Doherty, Tom Assocs., LLC. (Forge Bks.).
—The Quiller Memorandum. 1993. 288p. mass mkt. 4.50 o.p. (0-06-100526-6, HarperTorch) Morrow/Avon.
—The Quiller Memorandum. 2002. E-Book 5.99 (0-7953-0150-2) RosettaBooks.
—Quiller Meridian. unabr. collector's ed. 1994. (Quiller Ser.). audio 48.00 (0-7366-2641-7, 3379) Books on Tape, Inc.
—Quiller Meridian. 1994. 288p. mass mkt. 4.99 (0-380-71534-1, Avon Bks.); 1993. 287p. 22.00 o.p. (0-688-11797-X, Morrow, William & Co.) Morrow/Avon.
—Quiller Salamander. unabr. collector's ed. 1995. (Quiller Ser.). audio 48.00 (0-7366-2955-6, 3649) Books on Tape, Inc.
—Quiller Salamander. 1994. 272p. 23.00 (1-883402-40-9, Scribner) Simon & Schuster.

—Quiller Solitaire. unabr. collector's ed. 1992. (Quiller Ser.). audio 48.00 (*0-7366-2304-3*, 3087) Books on Tape, Inc.

—Quiller Solitaire. 288p. 1992. 20.00 o.p. (*0-688-10730-3*, Morrow, William & Co.); 1993. reprint ed. pap. 4.99 (*0-380-71921-5*, Avon Bks.) Morrow/Avon.

—Quiller's Run. 1988. mass mkt. 4.50 o.s.i (*0-515-09540-0*, Jove) Berkley Publishing Group.

—Quiller's Run. 1994. (Quiller Ser.: No. 12). 400p. mass mkt. 4.50 o.p. (*0-06-100537-1*, HarperTorch) Morrow/Avon.

—The Scorpion Signal. 1988. mass mkt. 3.95 o.s.i (*0-515-09645-8*); 1981. 288p. 2.95 (*0-87216-831-X*) Berkley Publishing Group. (Jove).

—The Scorpion Signal. unabr. collector's ed. 1982. (Quiller Ser.). audio 48.00 (*0-7366-0603-3*, 1569) Books on Tape, Inc.

—The Scorpion Signal. 1980. 10.00 o.p. (*0-385-12277-2*) Doubleday Publishing.

—The Scorpion Signal. 1993. (Quiller Ser.: No. 9). 79p. mass mkt. 4.50 o.p. (*0-06-100534-7*, HarperTorch) Morrow/Avon.

—The Sinkiang Executive. 1986. 240p. mass mkt. 3.50 o.s.i (*0-515-08678-9*, Jove) Berkley Publishing Group.

—The Sinkiang Executive. unabr. collector's ed. 1985. (Quiller Ser.). audio 48.00 (*0-7366-0605-X*, 1571) Books on Tape, Inc.

—The Sinkiang Executive. 1978. 7.95 o.p. (*0-385-12276-4*) Doubleday Publishing.

—The Sinkiang Executive. 1993. 352p. mass mkt. 4.50 o.p. (*0-06-100533-9*, HarperTorch) Morrow/Avon.

—The Striker Portfolio. 1988. mass mkt. 3.50 o.s.i (*0-515-09569-9*, Jove) Berkley Publishing Group.

—The Striker Portfolio. unabr. collector's ed. 1990. (Quiller Ser.). audio 42.00 (*0-7366-1804-X*, 2641) Books on Tape, Inc.

—The Striker Portfolio. 1993. 256p. mass mkt. 4.50 o.p. (*0-06-100528-2*, HarperTorch) Morrow/Avon.

—The Tango Briefing. 1986. 224p. mass mkt. 3.50 o.s.i (*0-515-08505-7*, Jove) Berkley Publishing Group.

—The Tango Briefing. unabr. collector's ed. 1990. (Quiller Ser.). audio 48.00 (*0-7366-1873-2*, 2704) Books on Tape, Inc.

—The Tango Briefing. 1993. 336p. mass mkt. 4.50 o.p. (*0-06-100530-4*, HarperTorch) Morrow/Avon.

—The Warsaw Document. 1988. mass mkt. 3.50 o.s.i (*0-515-09768-3*, Jove) Berkley Publishing Group.

—The Warsaw Document. unabr. collector's ed. 1990. (Quiller Ser.). audio 48.00 (*0-7366-1808-2*, 2645) Books on Tape, Inc.

—The Warsaw Document. 1993. 320p. mass mkt. 4.50 o.p. (*0-06-100529-0*, HarperTorch) Morrow/Avon.

**QUILLIAM, MEG (FICTITIOUS CHARACTER)—FICTION**

Bishop, Claudia. A Dash of Death. 1995. 240p. (Orig.). mass mkt. 5.99 (*0-425-14638-3*, Prime Crime) Berkley Publishing Group.

—Death Dines Out. 1997. (Hemlock Falls Mysteries Ser.). 256p. mass mkt. 5.99 (*0-425-16111-0*, Prime Crime) Berkley Publishing Group.

—Fried by Jury. 2003. (Hemlock Falls Mysteries Ser.: No. 10). 240p. (Orig.). mass mkt. 5.99 (*0-425-18994-5*, Prime Crime) Berkley Publishing Group.

—Marinade for Murder. 2000. (Hemlock Falls Mysteries Ser.). 256p. mass mkt. 5.99 (*0-425-17611-8*, Prime Crime) Berkley Publishing Group.

—Murder Well-Done. 1996. (Hemlock Falls Mysteries Ser.). 272p. mass mkt. 5.99 o.s.i (*0-425-15336-3*) Berkley Publishing Group.

—A Pinch of Poison. 1995. (Hemlock Falls Mysteries Ser.). 256p. mass mkt. 5.99 (*0-425-15104-2*) Berkley Publishing Group.

—A Steak in Murder. 1999. (Hemlock Falls Mysteries Ser.). 272p. mass mkt. 5.99 o.s.i (*0-425-16966-9*, Prime Crime) Berkley Publishing Group.

—A Taste for Murder. 1994. 240p. mass mkt. 5.99 (*0-425-14350-3*, Prime Crime) Berkley Publishing Group.

—A Touch of the Grape. 1998. (Hemlock Falls Mysteries Ser.). 256p. mass mkt. 5.99 (*0-425-16397-0*, Prime Crime) Berkley Publishing Group.

**QUILLIAM, SARAH (FICTITIOUS CHARACTER)—FICTION**

Bishop, Claudia. A Dash of Death. 1995. 240p. (Orig.). mass mkt. 5.99 (*0-425-14638-3*, Prime Crime) Berkley Publishing Group.

—Death Dines Out. 1997. (Hemlock Falls Mysteries Ser.). 256p. mass mkt. 5.99 (*0-425-16111-0*, Prime Crime) Berkley Publishing Group.

—Fried by Jury. 2003. (Hemlock Falls Mysteries Ser.: No. 10). 240p. (Orig.). mass mkt. 5.99 (*0-425-18994-5*, Prime Crime) Berkley Publishing Group.

—Marinade for Murder. 2000. (Hemlock Falls Mysteries Ser.). 256p. mass mkt. 5.99 (*0-425-17611-8*, Prime Crime) Berkley Publishing Group.

—Murder Well-Done. 1996. (Hemlock Falls Mysteries Ser.). 272p. mass mkt. 5.99 o.s.i (*0-425-15336-3*) Berkley Publishing Group.

—A Pinch of Poison. 1995. (Hemlock Falls Mysteries Ser.). 256p. mass mkt. 5.99 (*0-425-15104-2*) Berkley Publishing Group.

—A Steak in Murder. 1999. (Hemlock Falls Mysteries Ser.). 272p. mass mkt. 5.99 o.s.i (*0-425-16966-9*, Prime Crime) Berkley Publishing Group.

—A Taste for Murder. 1994. 240p. mass mkt. 5.99 (*0-425-14350-3*, Prime Crime) Berkley Publishing Group.

—A Touch of the Grape. 1998. (Hemlock Falls Mysteries Ser.). 256p. mass mkt. 5.99 (*0-425-16397-0*, Prime Crime) Berkley Publishing Group.

**QUINLAN, TAYLOR (FICTITIOUS CHARACTER)—FICTION**

Ferguson, Maggie. Crime of Passion. 1997. per. (*0-373-83333-4*, 1-83333-4); 1995. (Illus.). 251p. mass mkt. (*0-373-22347-1*) Harlequin Enterprises, Ltd. (Harlequin Bks.).

**QUINLIN, JEB (FICTITIOUS CHARACTER)—FICTION**

Swindle, Howard. Doin' Dirty. 2000. 292p. 22.95 (*0-312-20389-6*, Saint Martin's Minotaur) St. Martin's Pr.

**QUINN, DANIEL (FICTITIOUS CHARACTER)—FICTION**

Auster, Paul. City of Glass. 1987. (New York Trilogy). 210p. pap. 12.95 (*0-14-009731-7*, Penguin Bks.) Penguin Group (USA) Inc.

—City of Glass. 1985. (New York Trilogy Ser.). 208p. 30.00 o.p. (*0-940650-53-3*); 13.95 o.p. (*0-940650-52-5*) Sun & Moon Pr.

**QUINN, GARNER (FICTITIOUS CHARACTER)—FICTION**

Waterhouse, Jane. Dead Letter. 2000. 320p. mass mkt. 5.99 o.s.i (*0-425-17779-3*) Berkley Publishing Group.

—Dead Letter. l.t. ed. 2000. (Large Print Bks.). pap. 25.95 (*1-56895-953-2*, Wheeler Publishing, Inc.) Gale Group.

—Dead Letter. 1998. 304p. 23.95 o.p. (*0-399-14436-6*) Penguin Group (USA) Inc.

—Graven Images. 1997. 320p. mass mkt. 5.99 o.s.i (*0-425-15673-7*, Prime Crime) Berkley Publishing Group.

—Graven Images. 1995. 352p. 23.95 o.s.i (*0-399-14080-8*, G. P. Putnam's Sons) Penguin Group (USA) Inc.

—Shadow Walk. 1999. (Prime Crime Mysteries Ser.). 320p. reprint ed. mass mkt. 5.99 o.s.i (*0-425-16946-4*, Prime Crime) Berkley Publishing Group.

—Shadow Walk. 1997. 320p. 23.95 o.p. (*0-399-14305-X*, G. P. Putnam's Sons) Penguin Group (USA) Inc.

**QUINN, GRACE (FICTITIOUS CHARACTER)—FICTION**

Ridgway, Keith. The Long Falling. 1999. 306p. pap. 13.00 (*0-395-95782-6*); 1998. 320p. 22.00 o.p. (*0-395-90530-3*) Houghton Mifflin Co.

**QUINN, JASON (FICTITIOUS CHARACTER)—FICTION**

Fraser, Anthea. The Macbeth Prophecy. l.t. ed. 1997. 335p. pap. 21.95 (*0-7838-8101-0*, Macmillan Reference USA) Gale Group.

—The Macbeth Prophecy. 1995. 288p. 20.00 o.p. (*0-7278-4772-4*); 384p. 28.00 o.p. (*0-7278-7013-0*) Severn Hse. Pubs., Ltd.

**QUINN, JOHN (FICTITIOUS CHARACTER)—FICTION**

Hoag, Tami. Ashes to Ashes. unabr. ed. 2001. audio compact disk 119.95 (*0-7927-9992-5*, SLD 043); 2000. 12p. audio 96.95 (*0-7927-2365-1*, CSL 254) BBC Audiobooks America. (Chivers Sound Library).

—Ashes to Ashes. 1999. 496p. 24.95 o.s.i (*0-553-10633-3*); 2000. 592p. reprint ed. mass mkt. 7.99 (*0-553-57960-6*) Bantam Bks.

—Ashes to Ashes. l.t. ed. 2000. 12.95 (*1-56895-983-4*); 1999. 26.95 o.p. (*1-56895-713-0*) Gale Group. (Wheeler Publishing, Inc.).

—Ashes to Ashes. abr. ed. 1999. audio 25.00 Highsmith Inc.

—Ashes to Ashes. abr. ed. 2003. audio 14.95 (*0-7435-3294-5*, Encore); 2003. audio compact disk 14.95 (*0-7435-3295-3*, Encore); 1999. audio 25.00 (*0-671-58232-1*, 594124, Simon & Schuster Audioworks) Simon & Schuster Audio.

**QUINN, MARSHALL (FICTITIOUS CHARACTER)—FICTION**

Barrow, Adam. Blind Spot. 1997. 304p. 22.95 o.p. (*0-525-94186-X*) Dutton/Plume.

—Blind Spot. 1998. 416p. mass mkt. 5.99 o.s.i (*0-451-19187-0*, Signet Bks.) NAL.

**QUINN, RILEY (FICTITIOUS CHARACTER)—FICTION**

Furlong, Nicola. Teed Off! 399p. mass mkt. o.p. (*1-55197-091-0*) Picasso Pubns., Inc.

**QUINN, TERRY (FICTITIOUS CHARACTER)—FICTION**

Pelecanos, George P. Hell to Pay. abr. ed. 2003. audio 9.99 (*1-58788-961-7*, 3484, Brilliance Audio Paperback Audiobooks); 2002. audio 19.95 (*1-58788-960-9*, 3483, Nova Audio Bks.); 2002. audio 69.25 (*1-58788-959-5*, 3482, Unabridged Library Editions); 2002. audio 29.95 (*1-58788-958-7*, 3481, Brilliance Audio Unabridged) Brilliance Audio.

—Hell to Pay. 2002. E-Book 14.95 (*0-7595-8686-1*); 352p. 24.95 o.p. (*0-316-69506-8*) Little Brown & Co.

—Hell to Pay. unabr. ed. 2003. audio 19.99 (*1-59335-091-0*, 30183) Soulmate Audio Bks., Inc.

—Hell to Pay. l.t. ed. 2003. 536p. 30.45 (*0-7862-5615-X*) Thorndike Pr.

—Hell to Pay. 2003. 416p. mass mkt. 6.99 (*0-446-61132-8*) Warner Bks., Inc.

—Right As Rain. 2001. 336p. 24.95 (*0-316-69526-2*) Little Brown & Co.

—Right As Rain. l.t. ed. 2003. 525p. 30.45 (*0-7862-5609-5*) Thorndike Pr.

—Right As Rain. 2002. 384p. reprint ed. mass mkt. 6.99 (*0-446-61079-8*) Warner Bks., Inc.

**QUINTAGLIO (FICTITIOUS CHARACTERS)—FICTION**

Sawyer, Robert J. Far-Seer. 1992. mass mkt. 4.99 o.s.i (*0-441-22551-9*) Ace Bks.

—Foreigner. 1994. 304p. (Orig.). mass mkt. 4.99 o.s.i (*0-441-00017-7*) Ace Bks.

—Foreigner. Date not set. (Orig.). pap. (*0-7653-0972-6*, Tor Bks.) Doherty, Tom Assocs., LLC.

—Fossil Hunter. 1993. 304p. (Orig.). mass mkt. 4.99 o.s.i (*0-441-24884-5*) Ace Bks.

—Fossil Hunter. Date not set. (Orig.). pap. (*0-7653-0973-4*, Tor Bks.) Doherty, Tom Assocs., LLC.

**QUINTANA, ANTHONY (FICTITIOUS CHARACTER)—FICTION**

Parker, Barbara. Suspicion of Betrayal. 1999. 352p. 23.95 o.s.i (*0-525-94468-0*, Dutton Studio) Dutton/Plume.

—Suspicion of Betrayal. 2000. 432p. mass mkt. 6.99 (*0-451-19838-7*, Signet Bks.) NAL.

—Suspicion of Betrayal. l.t. ed. 1999. (Mystery Ser.). 568p. 29.95 (*0-7862-2000-7*) Thorndike Pr.

—Suspicion of Deceit. 1998. 368p. 23.95 o.p. (*0-525-94401-X*) Dutton/Plume.

—Suspicion of Deceit. 1999. 432p. reprint ed. mass mkt. 6.99 (*0-451-19549-3*, Signet Bks.) NAL.

—Suspicion of Deceit. unabr. ed. 1998. audio 78.00 (*0-7887-3572-1*, 95937E7) Recorded Bks., LLC.

—Suspicion of Deceit. l.t. ed. 1998. (Cloak & Dagger Ser.). 615p. 26.95 o.p. (*0-7862-1460-0*) Thorndike Pr.

—Suspicion of Guilt. 1995. 400p. 22.95 o.p. (*0-525-93769-2*, Dutton) Dutton/Plume.

—Suspicion of Guilt. l.t. ed. 1995. 26.95 (*1-56895-232-5*, Wheeler Publishing, Inc.) Gale Group.

—Suspicion of Guilt. 1996. 432p. mass mkt. 6.99 (*0-451-17703-7*, Signet Bks.) NAL.

—Suspicion of Guilt, unabr. ed. 1995. audio 91.00 (*0-7887-0353-6*, 94545E7) Recorded Bks., LLC.

—Suspicion of Innocence. 1994. 352p. 20.95 o.p. (*0-525-93744-7*); 20.95 (*0-525-93747-1*) Dutton/Plume. (Dutton).

—Suspicion of Innocence. 1994. 448p. mass mkt. 6.99 (*0-451-17340-6*, Signet Bks.) NAL.

—Suspicion of Innocence, unabr. ed. 1994. audio 85.00 (*0-7887-0024-3*, 94223E7) Recorded Bks., LLC.

—Suspicion of Innocence. 344p. 4.98 o.p. (*0-8317-4569-X*) Smithmark Pubs., Inc.

—Suspicion of Madness. 2003. (Illus.). 368p. 24.95 (*0-525-94681-0*) Dutton/Plume.

—Suspicion of Madness. 2003. 416p. mass mkt. 7.99 (*0-451-21089-1*, Signet Bks.) NAL.

—Suspicion of Madness. 2003. (Gail Connor & Anthony Quintana Novel Ser.). 597p. 30.95 (*0-7862-5422-X*) Thorndike Pr.

—Suspicion of Malice. 2000. 352p. 22.95 o.s.i (*0-525-94542-3*) Dutton/Plume.

—Suspicion of Malice. 2001. 432p. reprint ed. mass mkt. 6.99 (*0-451-20125-6*, Signet Bks.) NAL.

—Suspicion of Malice. l.t. ed. 2000. (Mystery Ser.). 565p. 29.95 (*0-7862-2655-2*) Thorndike Pr.

—Suspicion of Vengeance. 2001. 368p. 23.95 o.s.i (*0-525-94601-2*, Dutton) Dutton/Plume.

—Suspicion of Vengeance. l.t. ed. 2002. 30.95 (*0-7862-3751-1*) Gale Group.

—Suspicion of Vengeance. 2003. 448p. reprint ed. mass mkt. 7.50 (*0-451-20451-4*, Signet Bks.) NAL.

**QUIST, JULIAN (FICTITIOUS CHARACTER)—FICTION**

Pentecost, Hugh. Deadly Trap. l.t. ed. 1997. (Linford Mystery Library). 368p. pap. 17.99 o.p. (*0-7089-5170-8*, Ulverscroft) Thorpe, F. A. Pubs. GBR. *Dist:* Ulverscroft Large Print Bks., Ltd., Ulverscroft Large Print Canada, Ltd.

—Death Mask. 1983. (Nightingale Ser.). pap. 9.95 o.p. (*0-8161-3500-2*, Macmillan Reference USA) Gale Group.

—The Party Killer. l.t. ed. 1997. (Linford Mystery Library). 368p. pap. 17.99 o.p. (*0-7089-5099-X*, Linford) Thorpe, F. A. Pubs. GBR. *Dist:* Ulverscroft Large Print Bks., Ltd., Ulverscroft Large Print Canada, Ltd.

**QUY, IMOGEN (FICTITIOUS CHARACTER)—FICTION**

Paton Walsh, Jill. A Piece of Justice. pap. 15.95 (*0-312-29252-X*, Saint Martin's Griffin); 1995. 208p. 19.95 o.p. (*0-312-13145-3*, Saint Martin's Minotaur) St. Martin's Pr.

**QWILLERAN, JIM (FICTITIOUS CHARACTER)—FICTION**

Braun, Lilian Jackson. The Cat Who Ate Danish Modern. 1986. (Cat Who Ser.). 192p. mass mkt. 6.99 (*0-515-08712-2*, Jove) Berkley Publishing Group.

—The Cat Who Ate Danish Modern. 1989. (Black Dagger Crime Ser.). 200p. reprint ed. text 12.95 o.p. (*0-86220-755-X*) Chivers Pr. GBR. *Dist:* BBC Audiobooks America.

—The Cat Who Ate Danish Modern. l.t. ed. 1990. (Nightingale Ser.). 274p. 14.95 o.p. (*0-8161-4914-3*, Macmillan Reference USA) Gale Group.

—The Cat Who Ate Danish Modern. unabr. ed. 1990. (Cat Who Ser.). audio 35.00 (*1-55690-090-2*, 90081E7) Recorded Bks., LLC.

—The Cat Who Ate Danish Modern. 1986. 13.04 (*0-606-13246-5*) Turtleback Bks.

—The Cat Who Blew the Whistle. 1996. (Cat Who Ser.). 320p. mass mkt. 6.99 (*0-515-11824-9*, Jove) Berkley Publishing Group.

—The Cat Who Blew the Whistle. 1995. 240p. 21.95 o.p. (*0-399-13981-8*, G. P. Putnam's Sons) Penguin Group (USA) Inc.

—The Cat Who Blew the Whistle. l.t. ed. (Paperback Bestsellers Ser.). 270p. 1996. lib. bdg. 18.95 (*0-7838-1253-1*); 1995. lib. bdg. 24.95 (*0-7838-1252-3*) Thorndike Pr.

—The Cat Who Blew the Whistle. 1996. 13.04 (*0-606-12643-0*) Turtleback Bks.

—The Cat Who Brought down the House. 2003. 256p. mass mkt. 6.99 (*0-515-13655-7*, Jove) Berkley Publishing Group.

—The Cat Who Brought down the House. 2003. 240p. 23.95 (*0-399-14942-2*); audio 24.95 (*0-399-14993-7*, Putnam Berkley Audio) Putnam Publishing Group, The.

—The Cat Who Brought down the House. 2003. 299p. 32.95 (*0-7862-5036-4*); 2004. 304p. pap. 13.95 (*1-59413-011-6*, Large Print Pr.) Thorndike Pr.

—The Cat Who Came to Breakfast. 1995. (Cat Who Ser.). 272p. (J). pap. 6.99 (*0-515-11564-9*, Jove) Berkley Publishing Group.

—The Cat Who Came to Breakfast. l.t. ed. 296p. 1995. 17.95 o.p. (*0-8161-5935-1*); 1994. lib. bdg. 23.95 o.p. (*0-8161-5934-3*) Gale Group. (Macmillan Reference USA).

—The Cat Who Came to Breakfast. abr. ed. 1993. audio 16.95 o.p. (*1-55800-937-X*, 393255, Dove Audio) NewStar Media, Inc.

—The Cat Who Came to Breakfast. 1994. 240p. 19.95 o.p. (*0-399-13868-4*, G. P. Putnam's Sons) Penguin Group (USA) Inc.

—The Cat Who Came to Breakfast. 1995. 13.04 (*0-606-12644-9*) Turtleback Bks.

—The Cat Who Could Read Backwards. l.t. ed. 1991. 12.95 o.p. (*0-7927-0098-8*, C0139) BBC Audiobooks America.

—The Cat Who Could Read Backwards. 256p. 2003. pap. 10.00 (*0-425-19520-1*); 1986. mass mkt. 6.99 (*0-515-09017-4*, Jove) Berkley Publishing Group.

—The Cat Who Could Read Backwards. l.t. ed. 1997. (Large Print Book Ser.). 25.95 o.p. (*1-56895-470-0*, Wheeler Publishing, Inc.) Gale Group.

—The Cat Who Could Read Backwards. 1997. (Cat Who. . . Ser.). 240p. 19.95 o.p. (*0-399-14286-X*, G. P. Putnam's Sons) Penguin Group (USA) Inc.

—The Cat Who Could Read Backwards. unabr. ed. 1990. (Cat Who Ser.). audio 19.95 (*1-55690-091-0*, 90082) Recorded Bks., LLC.

—The Cat Who Had 14 Tales. 1988. (Cat Who Ser.). 256p. mass mkt. 6.99 (*0-515-09497-8*, Jove) Berkley Publishing Group.

—The Cat Who Had 14 Tales. l.t. ed. 1991. (Nightingale Ser.). 241p. 14.95 o.p. (*0-8161-4915-1*, Macmillan Reference USA) Gale Group.

—The Cat Who Had 14 Tales. unabr. ed. 2000. (Cat Who Ser.). (J). audio 35.00 (*0-7887-0312-9*, 94504E7) Recorded Bks., LLC.

—The Cat Who Had 14 Tales. 1988. 13.04 (*0-606-13247-3*) Turtleback Bks.

—The Cat Who Knew a Cardinal. 1992. (Cat Who Ser.). 288p. mass mkt. 6.99 (*0-515-10786-7*, Jove) Berkley Publishing Group.

—The Cat Who Knew a Cardinal. l.t. ed. 1992. (General Ser.). 316p. 18.95 (*0-8161-5279-9*); lib. bdg. 19.95 o.p. (*0-8161-5278-0*) Gale Group. (Macmillan Reference USA).

—The Cat Who Knew a Cardinal. abr. ed. 1993. 15.95 o.p. (*1-55800-444-0*, 390492) NewStar Media, Inc.
—The Cat Who Knew a Cardinal. 1991. (Cat Who Ser.). 240p. 16.95 o.p. (*0-399-13664-9*, G. P. Putnam's Sons) Penguin Group (USA) Inc.
—The Cat Who Knew a Cardinal. 1992. 13.04 (*0-606-12645-7*) Turtleback Bks.
—The Cat Who Knew a Cardinal; The Cat Who Moved a Mountain; The Cat Who Wasn't There. unabr. ed. 1993. audio 19.95 o.p. (*1-55800-782-2*) NewStar Media, Inc.
—The Cat Who Knew Shakespeare. 1988. (Cat Who Ser.). 256p. mass mkt. 6.99 (*0-515-09582-6*, Jove) Berkley Publishing Group.
—The Cat Who Knew Shakespeare. l.t. ed. 1989. 284p. 12.95 o.p. (*0-8161-4790-6*, Macmillan Reference USA) Gale Group.
—The Cat Who Knew Shakespeare. unabr. ed. 1991. (Cat Who Ser.). (YA). (gr. 10 up). audio 24.95 (*1-55690-092-9*, 91115E7) Recorded Bks., LLC.
—The Cat Who Knew Shakespeare. 1991. 13.04 (*0-606-13248-1*) Turtleback Bks.
—The Cat Who Lived High. 1991. (Cat Who Ser.). 304p. mass mkt. 6.99 (*0-515-10566-X*, Jove) Berkley Publishing Group.
—The Cat Who Lived High. l.t. ed. 1991. lib. bdg. 19.95 o.p. (*0-8161-5126-1*, Macmillan Reference USA) Gale Group.
—The Cat Who Lived High. 1990. 240p. 17.95 o.p. (*0-399-13554-5*, G. P. Putnam's Sons) Penguin Putnam Bks. for Young Readers.
—The Cat Who Lived High. unabr. ed. 1994. (Cat Who Ser.: No. 11). audio 32.95 (*1-55690-992-6*, 94131) Recorded Bks., LLC.
—The Cat Who Lived High. 1991. 13.04 (*0-606-12646-5*) Turtleback Bks.
—The Cat Who Moved a Mountain. 1992. (Cat Who Ser.). 272p. mass mkt. 6.99 (*0-515-10950-9*, Jove) Berkley Publishing Group.
—The Cat Who Moved a Mountain. l.t. ed. 1993. (General Ser.). 379p. 18.95 o.p. (*0-8161-5551-8*); 20.95 o.p. (*0-8161-5550-X*) Gale Group. (Macmillan Reference USA).
—The Cat Who Moved a Mountain. abr. ed. 1993. 15.95 o.p. (*1-55800-470-X*, 390493) NewStar Media, Inc.
—The Cat Who Moved a Mountain. 1992. (Cat Who Ser.). 240p. 18.95 o.p. (*0-399-13646-0*, G. P. Putnam's Sons) Penguin Group (USA) Inc.
—The Cat Who Moved a Mountain. 1992. 13.04 (*0-606-12647-3*) Turtleback Bks.
—The Cat Who Played Brahms. l.t. ed. 1990. 18.95 o.p. (*0-7927-0335-9*, C0029); pap. 16.95 o.p. (*0-7927-0345-6*) BBC Audiobooks America.
—The Cat Who Played Brahms. 1987. (Cat Who Ser.). 256p. mass mkt. 6.99 (*0-515-09050-6*, Jove) Berkley Publishing Group.
—The Cat Who Played Brahms. unabr. ed. 1992. (Cat Who Ser.). audio 24.95 (*1-55690-651-X*, 92133) Recorded Bks., LLC.
—The Cat Who Played Brahms. 1990. 13.04 (*0-606-13249-X*) Turtleback Bks.
—The Cat Who Played Post Office. 1987. (Cat Who Ser.). 272p. pap. 6.99 (*0-515-09320-3*, Jove) Berkley Publishing Group.
—The Cat Who Played Post Office. l.t. ed. 2000. (Wheeler Large Print Book Ser.). (Illus.). 230p. 27.95 o.p. (*1-56895-840-4*, Wheeler Publishing, Inc.) Gale Group.
—The Cat Who Played Post Office. unabr. ed. 2001. audio 24.95 (*0-7887-5432-7*); 2000. audio 24.95 (*1-55690-689-7*, 92343) Recorded Bks., LLC.
—The Cat Who Played Post Office. 1987. 13.04 (*0-606-13250-3*) Turtleback Bks.
—The Cat Who Robbed a Bank. 2001. (Cat Who Ser.). 304p. mass mkt. 6.99 (*0-515-12994-1*, Jove) Berkley Publishing Group.
—The Cat Who Robbed a Bank. l.t. ed. 2000. pap. 22.95 o.p. (*0-7838-8710-8*, Macmillan Reference USA) Gale Group.
—The Cat Who Robbed a Bank. 2000. (Cat Who Ser.). 256p. 23.95 o.p. (*0-399-14570-2*) Penguin Group (USA) Inc.
—The Cat Who Robbed a Bank, No. 2. abr. ed. 2000. (Cat Who Ser.: Vol. 22). 3p. 17.95 o.s.i (*0-399-14582-6*, Putnam Berkley Audio) Putnam Publishing Group, The.
—The Cat Who Robbed a Bank. l.t. ed. 2000. 400p. 23.95 (*0-375-40878-9*) Random Hse. Large Print.
—The Cat Who Robbed a Bank. unabr. ed. 1999. (Cat Who Ser.). audio 29.95 (*0-7887-4032-6*, 96010 ) Recorded Bks., LLC.
—The Cat Who Said Cheese. 1997. (Cat Who Ser.). 272p. reprint ed. pap. 6.99 (*0-515-12027-8*, Jove) Berkley Publishing Group.
—The Cat Who Said Cheese. l.t. ed. 1997. pap. 23.95 o.p. (*0-7838-1632-4*, Macmillan Reference USA) Gale Group.
—The Cat Who Said Cheese. abr. ed. 1996. 17.95 o.p. (*0-7871-0610-0*) NewStar Media, Inc.
—The Cat Who Said Cheese. 1996. (Cat Who Ser.). (*0-399-19300-6*); 256p. 22.95 o.p. (*0-399-14075-1*, G. P. Putnam's Sons) Penguin Group (USA) Inc.
—The Cat Who Said Cheese. l.t. ed. 1996. (Core Collection). 303p. 27.95 (*0-7838-1631-6*) Thorndike Pr.
—The Cat Who Said Cheese. 1997. 13.04 (*0-606-12648-1*) Turtleback Bks.
—The Cat Who Sang for the Birds. 1999. (Cat Who Ser.). (Illus.). 272p. reprint ed. mass mkt. 6.99 (*0-515-12463-X*, Jove) Berkley Publishing Group.
—The Cat Who Sang for the Birds. l.t. ed. 1998. 26.95 o.p. (*1-56895-555-3*, Wheeler Publishing, Inc.) Gale Group.
—The Cat Who Sang for the Birds. 1998. (Cat Who. . . Ser.). 256p. (YA). 22.95 o.p. (*0-399-14333-5*, G. P. Putnam's Sons);Set. 3p. (J). 17.95 o.s.i (*0-399-14350-5*, 395411, Putnam Berkley Audio) Penguin Group (USA) Inc.
—The Cat Who Sang for the Birds. unabr. ed. (Cat Who Ser.). 1999. audio compact disk 54.00 (*0-7887-3428-8*, C1034E7); 1998. audio 32.95 (*0-7887-1971-8*, 95358) Recorded Bks., LLC.
—The Cat Who Saw Red. 1986. (Cat Who Ser.). 256p. mass mkt. 6.99 (*0-515-09016-6*); mass mkt. 2.95 o.s.i (*0-515-08491-3*) Berkley Publishing Group. (Jove).
—The Cat Who Saw Red. l.t. ed. 1989. 13.95 o.p. (*0-8161-4388-9*, Macmillan Reference USA) Gale Group.
—The Cat Who Saw Red. unabr. ed. 1990. (Cat Who Ser.). (YA). (gr. 10 up). audio 35.00 (*1-55690-093-7*, 90083E7) Recorded Bks., LLC.
—The Cat Who Saw Red. 1986. 13.04 (*0-606-13251-1*) Turtleback Bks.
—The Cat Who Saw Stars. 2000. (Cat Who Ser.). 304p. reprint ed. mass mkt. 6.99 (*0-515-12739-6*, Jove) Berkley Publishing Group.
—The Cat Who Saw Stars. l.t. ed. 2000. 11.95 (*1-56895-980-X*); 1999. 27.95 (*1-56895-595-2*) Gale Group. (Wheeler Publishing, Inc.).
—The Cat Who Saw Stars. abr. ed. 1999. audio 17.95 Highsmith Inc.
—The Cat Who Saw Stars. 1999. (Cat Who. . . Ser.). 240p. 22.95 o.p. (*0-399-14431-5*); 17.95 o.p. (*0-399-14455-2*, 393651, Putnam Berkley Audio) Penguin Group (USA) Inc.
—The Cat Who Saw Stars. unabr. ed. 2001. (Cat Who Ser.: Vol. 21). audio compact disk 38.00 (*0-7887-3971-9*, C1090E7) Recorded Bks., LLC.
—The Cat Who Smelled a Rat. 2001. (Cat Who. . . Ser.). (Illus.). 256p. 23.95 o.s.i (*0-399-14665-2*, G. P. Putnam's Sons) Penguin Group (USA) Inc.
—The Cat Who Smelled a Rat. abr. ed. 2001. (Cat Who Ser.). audio 17.95 o.s.i (*0-399-14681-4*, Putnam Berkley Audio) Putnam Publishing Group, The.
—The Cat Who Smelled a Rat. unabr. ed. 2001. audio 29.95 (*0-7887-4977-3*, 964417); audio compact disk 48.00 Recorded Bks., LLC.
—The Cat Who Smelled a Rat. l.t. ed. 293p. 2002. pap. 29.95 (*0-7862-2823-7*); 2001. 32.95 (*0-7862-2822-9*) Thorndike Pr.
—The Cat Who Sniffed Glue. 1989. (Cat Who Ser.). 288p. mass mkt. 6.99 (*0-515-09954-6*, Jove) Berkley Publishing Group.
—The Cat Who Sniffed Glue. l.t. ed. 1990. (Nightingale Ser.). 312p. 13.95 o.p. (*0-8161-4864-3*, Macmillan Reference USA) Gale Group.
—The Cat Who Sniffed Glue. 1988. (Cat Who. . . Ser.). 192p. 14.95 o.p. (*0-399-13381-X*, G. P. Putnam's Sons) Penguin Putnam Bks. for Young Readers.
—The Cat Who Sniffed Glue. unabr. ed. 2000. audio 44.00 (*1-55690-837-7*, 93205E7) Recorded Bks., LLC.
—The Cat Who Sniffed Glue. 1989. 13.04 (*0-606-13252-X*) Turtleback Bks.
—The Cat Who Tailed a Thief. 1998. (Cat Who. . . Ser.). 272p. mass mkt. 6.99 (*0-515-12240-8*, Jove) Berkley Publishing Group.
—The Cat Who Tailed a Thief. l.t. ed. 1997. 293p. 27.95 o.p. (*0-7838-8046-4*, Macmillan Reference USA) Gale Group.
—The Cat Who Tailed a Thief. abr. ed. 1997. 17.95 o.p. (*0-7871-1352-2*, 394616) NewStar Media, Inc.
—The Cat Who Tailed a Thief. 1997. (Cat Who. . . Ser.). 256p. 22.95 o.p. (*0-399-14210-X*, G. P. Putnam's Sons) Penguin Group (USA) Inc.
—The Cat Who Tailed a Thief. l.t. ed. 1998. (Paperback Bestsellers Ser.). 293p. pap. 27.95 (*0-7838-8047-2*) Thorndike Pr.
—The Cat Who Tailed a Thief. 1998. 13.04 (*0-606-13253-8*) Turtleback Bks.
—The Cat Who Talked to Ghosts. 1990. (Cat Who Ser.). 288p. pap. 6.99 (*0-515-10265-2*, Jove) Berkley Publishing Group.
—The Cat Who Talked to Ghosts. l.t. ed. 1991. (General Ser.). 300p. 21.95 (*0-8161-5081-8*, Macmillan Reference USA) Gale Group.
—The Cat Who Talked to Ghosts. 1990. 224p. 15.95 o.p. (*0-399-13477-8*, G. P. Putnam's Sons) Penguin Putnam Bks. for Young Readers.
—The Cat Who Talked to Ghosts. unabr. ed. 1994. (Cat Who Ser.). audio 32.95 (*0-7887-0050-2*, 94249E7); audio 42.00 Recorded Bks., LLC.
—The Cat Who Talked to Ghosts. 1990. 13.04 (*0-606-13254-6*) Turtleback Bks.
—The Cat Who Talked Turkey. 2003. 288p. 23.95 (*0-399-15107-9*) Putnam Publishing Group, The.
—The Cat Who Turned on & Off. 1986. (Cat Who Ser.). 272p. mass mkt. 6.99 (*0-515-08794-7*, Jove) Berkley Publishing Group.
—The Cat Who Turned on & Off. l.t. ed. 1992. (Nightingale Ser.). 285p. 14.95 o.p. (*0-8161-4815-5*, Macmillan Reference USA) Gale Group.
—The Cat Who Turned on & Off. unabr. ed. 1991. (Cat Who Ser.). audio 44.00 (*1-55690-094-5*, 91402E7) Recorded Bks., LLC.
—The Cat Who Turned on & Off. 1986. 11.60 o.p. (*0-606-13255-4*) Turtleback Bks.
—The Cat Who Wasn't There. 1993. (Cat Who Ser.). 288p. mass mkt. 6.99 (*0-515-11127-9*, Jove) Berkley Publishing Group.
—The Cat Who Wasn't There. l.t. ed. 1993. (General Ser.). 367p. 17.95 o.p. (*0-8161-5694-8*); lib. bdg. 21.95 (*0-8161-5693-X*) Gale Group. (Macmillan Reference USA).
—The Cat Who Wasn't There. abr. ed. (Super Sound Buy, Dove Ser.). 1994. audio 8.99 o.p. (*0-7871-0071-4*, 390494, Dove Audio); 1993. 16.95 o.p. (*1-55800-667-2*) NewStar Media, Inc.
—The Cat Who Wasn't There. 1992. 240p. 18.95 o.p. (*0-399-13780-7*, G. P. Putnam's Sons) Penguin Group (USA) Inc.
—The Cat Who Wasn't There. 1993. 13.04 (*0-606-12649-X*) Turtleback Bks.
—The Cat Who Wasn't There; The Cat Who Blew the Whistle. abr. ed. 1999. audio 25.00 (*0-7871-1901-6*, Dove Audio) NewStar Media, Inc.
—The Cat Who Went into the Closet. 1994. (Cat Who Ser.). 288p. mass mkt. 6.99 (*0-515-11332-8*, Jove) Berkley Publishing Group.
—The Cat Who Went into the Closet. l.t. ed. 1993. 24.95 o.p. (*1-56895-050-0*, Wheeler Publishing, Inc.) Gale Group.
—The Cat Who Went into the Closet. abr. ed. 1993. (Jim Qwilleran Mystery Ser.). audio 16.95 o.p. (*1-55800-785-7*, 390495) NewStar Media, Inc.
—The Cat Who Went into the Closet. 1993. (Cat Who Ser.). 240p. 19.95 o.p. (*0-399-13830-7*, G. P. Putnam's Sons) Penguin Group (USA) Inc.
—The Cat Who Went into the Closet. 5.98 o.p. (*0-8317-5327-7*) Smithmark Pubs., Inc.
—The Cat Who Went into the Closet. 1994. 13.04 (*0-606-13256-2*) Turtleback Bks.
—The Cat Who Went Underground. 1989. (Cat Who Ser.). 288p. mass mkt. 6.99 (*0-515-10123-0*, Jove) Berkley Publishing Group.
—The Cat Who Went Underground. l.t. ed. 1990. (General Ser.). 324p. 19.95 o.p. (*0-8161-4941-0*, Macmillan Reference USA) Gale Group.
—The Cat Who Went Underground. 1989. (Cat Who. . . Ser.). 224p. 14.95 o.p. (*0-399-13431-X*, G. P. Putnam's Sons) Penguin Putnam Bks. for Young Readers.
—The Cat Who Went Underground. unabr. ed. 2000. (Cat Who Ser.). audio 32.95 (*1-55690-803-2*, 93112) Recorded Bks., LLC.
—The Cat Who Went Underground. 1989. 13.04 (*0-606-13257-0*) Turtleback Bks.
—The Cat Who Went up the Creek. 2002. 240p. 23.95 o.s.i (*0-399-14675-X*) Penguin Group (USA) Inc.
—The Cat Who Went up the Creek. abr. ed. 2002. audio 17.95 o.s.i (*0-399-14819-1*, Putnam Berkley Audio) Putnam Publishing Group, The.
—El Gato Que Leia del Reves. 1997. Tr. of Cat Who Could Read Backwards. (SPA.). 248p. 14.58 (*84-01-47431-0*) Plaza & Janés Editories, S.A. ESP. *Dist:* Distribooks, Inc., Lectorum Pubns., Inc.
—Lilian Jackson Braun: Three Complete Novels. 1998. 640p. 12.98 o.p. (*0-399-14364-5*); 1996. 12.98 o.p. (*0-399-14127-8*); 1994. 608p. 11.98 o.s.i (*0-399-13984-2*) Penguin Group (USA) Inc. (G. P. Putnam's Sons).
—The Private Life of the Cat Who... Tales of Koko & Yum Yum from the Journals of James Mackintosh Qwilleran. 2003. 144p. 10.95 (*0-399-15132-X*, Putnam & Grosset) Putnam Publishing Group, The.
—Short & Tall Tales: Moose County Legends Collected by James Mackintosh Quilleran. 2003. 192p. mass mkt. 6.50 (*0-515-13635-2*, Jove) Berkley Publishing Group.
—Three Complete Novels. 2002. 803p. 14.98 (*0-399-14813-2*) Penguin Group (USA) Inc.
—Three Complete Novels: The Cat Who Saw Red; The Cat Who Played Brahms; The Cat Who Played Post Office - Omnibus Edition. 1993. 608p. 12.98 o.s.i (*0-399-13885-4*, G. P. Putnam's Sons) Penguin Group (USA) Inc.
—Three Complete Novels: The Cat Who Talked to Ghosts; The Cat Who Knew a Cardinal; The Cat Who Lived High, 3 bks. in 1. 1997. 512p. 12.98 o.p. (*0-399-14258-4*, G. P. Putnam's Sons) Penguin Group (USA) Inc.
The Cat Who Could Read Backwards. 2002. audio 19.95 (*0-7887-5430-0*, 00144) Recorded Bks., LLC.
Feaster, Sharon A. The Cat Who . . . Companion: The Complete Guide to Lilian Jackson Braun's Beloved Cat Who . . . Mysteries. 1998. 336p. pap. 13.00 o.s.i (*0-425-16540-X*) Berkley Publishing Group.

## R

### RABB, JOSHUA (FICTITIOUS CHARACTER)—FICTION

Parrish, Richard. The Dividing Line. 1993. 368p. 20.00 o.p. (*0-525-93561-4*) Dutton/Plume.
—The Dividing Line. 1994. 432p. mass mkt. 5.99 o.s.i (*0-451-40430-0*, Onyx) NAL.
—Nothing but the Truth. 1995. (Joshua Rabb Ser.). 304p. 20.95 o.p. (*0-525-93852-4*, Dutton) Dutton/Plume.
—Nothing but the Truth. 1996. (Joshua Rabb Ser.). 352p. mass mkt. 5.99 o.s.i (*0-451-40538-2*, Onyx) NAL.
—Wind & Lies. 1999. pap. 22.95 (*0-525-93871-0*); 1997. 416p. mass mkt. 5.99 o.s.i (*0-451-40539-0*, Onyx) NAL.

### RABJOHNS, WILL (FICTITIOUS CHARACTER)—FICTION

Barker, Clive. Sacrament. 1996. 79p. 25.00 o.p. (*0-06-017949-X*) HarperCollins Pubs.
—Sacrament. 1997. 624p. mass mkt. 7.99 (*0-06-109199-5*, HarperTorch) Morrow/Avon.

### RACE, COLONEL JOHNNY (FICTITIOUS CHARACTER)—FICTION

Christie, Agatha. Cards on the Table. mass mkt. 3.50 o.s.i (*0-425-12577-7*); 2001. E-Book 5.99 (*0-425-17790-4*); 1998. mass mkt. 3.99 o.s.i (*0-425-16924-3*); 1986. mass mkt. 2.95 o.s.i (*0-425-09317-4*); 1984. mass mkt. 2.95 o.s.i (*0-425-06778-5*) Berkley Publishing Group.
—Cards on the Table. 1980. pap. 2.95 o.p. (*0-440-11052-1*) Dell Publishing.
—Cards on the Table. 1987. (Agatha Christie Ser.). 14.95 (*0-396-09010-9*, G. P. Putnam's Sons) Penguin Putnam Bks. for Young Readers.
—Cards on the Table. 1984. (Hercule Poirot Mystery Ser.). 12.04 (*0-606-12211-7*) Turtleback Bks.
—The Cards on the Table. 1987. (Hercule Poirot Mystery Ser.). 224p. mass mkt. 5.99 (*0-425-10567-9*) Berkley Publishing Group.
—Cards on the Table. l.t. ed. 1983. 352p. 12.50 o.p. (*0-7089-1151-X*, Ulverscroft) Thorpe, F. A. Pubs. GBR. *Dist:* Ulverscroft Large Print Bks., Ltd.
—The Man in the Brown Suit. unabr. ed. 1999. audio 35.95 (*1-55685-595-8*) Audio Bk. Contractors, Inc.
—The Man in the Brown Suit. 1984. (Agatha Christie Ser.). 240p. mass mkt. 5.99 o.s.i (*0-425-06786-6*) Berkley Publishing Group.
—The Man in the Brown Suit. 1970. 224p. pap. 2.50 o.s.i (*0-440-15230-5*) Dell Publishing.
—The Man in the Brown Suit. l.t. ed. 1984. (Ulverscroft Large Print Ser.). 416p. o.p. (*0-7089-1125-0*, Ulverscroft) Thorpe, F. A. Pubs. GBR. *Dist:* Ulverscroft Large Print Canada, Ltd.
—The Man in the Brown Suit. 1984. 12.04 (*0-606-00964-7*) Turtleback Bks.
—The Man in the Brown Suit. 1998. lib. bdg. 19.95 (*1-56723-032-6*) Yestermorrow, Inc.
—Remembered Death. l.t. ed. 368p. 1993. pap. 12.95 o.p. (*0-8161-4598-9*); 1992. lib. bdg. 19.95 o.p. (*0-8161-4597-0*) Gale Group. (Macmillan Reference USA).
—Remembered Death. 1984. mass mkt. 3.50 o.s.i (*0-671-54320-2*); 1982. mass mkt. 2.95 o.s.i (*0-671-46531-7*) Simon & Schuster. (Pocket).
—Sparkling Cyanide. unabr. ed. audio 54.95 o.p. (*0-7451-6820-5*, CAB 316) BBC Audiobooks America.
—Sparkling Cyanide. 1988. audio 53.95 o.p. (*0-8161-9106-9*) Thorndike Pr.
—Sparkling Cyanide. l.t. ed. 1978. (Ulverscroft Large Print Ser.). 12.00 o.p. (*0-7089-0223-5*, Ulverscroft) Thorpe, F. A. Pubs. GBR. *Dist:* Ulverscroft Large Print Bks., Ltd., Ulverscroft Large Print Canada, Ltd.
—Sparkling Cyanide. 1992. 12.04 (*0-606-12526-4*) Turtleback Bks.

### RADBURN, ADAM (FICTITIOUS CHARACTER)—FICTION

Longstreet, Roxanne. The Undead. 1993. 320p. mass mkt. 4.50 o.s.i (*0-8217-4068-7*, Zebra Bks.) Kensington Publishing Corp.
—The Undead. 2001. 320p. per. 20.95 (*0-595-17771-9*) iUniverse, Inc.

### RAFFERTY (FICTITIOUS CHARACTER)—FICTION

Duncan, W. Glenn. Rafferty: Cannon's Mouth. 1990. 176p. (Orig.). mass mkt. 3.95 o.s.i (*0-449-14551-4*, Fawcett) Ballantine Bks.

—Rafferty: Fatal Sisters. 1990. 192p. mass mkt. 3.95 o.s.i (*0-449-14552-2*, Fawcett) Ballantine Bks.
—Rafferty: Poor Dead Cricket. 1988. mass mkt. 3.50 o.s.i (*0-449-13325-7*, Fawcett) Ballantine Bks.
—Rafferty: Wrong Place, Wrong Time. 1989. 208p. mass mkt. 3.50 o.s.i (*0-449-14550-6*, Fawcett) Ballantine Bks.
—Rafferty Last Seen Alive. 1987. 208p. (Orig.). mass mkt. 2.95 o.s.i (*0-449-13223-4*, Fawcett) Ballantine Bks.
—Rafferty's Rules. 1987. (Orig.). mass mkt. 2.95 o.s.i (*0-449-13160-2*, Fawcett) Ballantine Bks.

**RAFFERTY, ALEXANDRA (FICTITIOUS CHARACTER)—FICTION**

Hall, James W. Body Language. abr. ed. 1999. audio 7.99 (*1-56740-310-7*, 1874, Paperback Nova Audio Bks.); 1998. audio 26.95 (*1-56740-073-6*, 1452, Bookcassette); 1998. 10p. audio 73.25 (*1-56740-602-5*, 1455, Unabridged Library Editions); Set. 1998. audio 17.95 o.p. (*1-56740-797-8*, 1453, Nova Audio Bks.) Brilliance Audio.
—Body Language. 1999. E-Book 24.95 o.s.i (*0-312-20761-1*); 1998. 352p. 24.95 (*0-312-19243-6*) St. Martin's Pr.
—Body Language. l.t. ed. 1998. (Americana Ser.). 527p. 28.95 (*0-7862-1686-7*) Thorndike Pr.

**RAFFERTY, JOSEPH (FICTITIOUS CHARACTER)—FICTION**

Evans, Geraldine. Dead Before Morning. 1995. (Mystery Ser.). 253p. per. (*0-373-26184-5*, 1-26184-1, Worldwide Library) Harlequin Enterprises, Ltd.
—Dead Before Morning. 1993. 222p. 17.95 o.p. (*0-312-08755-1*, Saint Martin's Minotaur) St. Martin's Pr.
—Down among the Dead Men. 1996. per. (*0-373-26208-6*, 1-26208-6, Worldwide Library) Harlequin Enterprises, Ltd.

**RAFFERTY, NEAL (FICTITIOUS CHARACTER)—FICTION**

Wiltz, Chris. A Diamond Before You Die. (Neal Rafferty Mystery Ser.). 208p. 1988. mass mkt. 3.95 o.s.i (*0-445-40536-8*); 1987. 15.95 o.p. (*0-89296-192-9*) Mysterious Pr.
—A Diamond Before You Die. l.t. ed. 1990. (Ulverscroft Large Print Ser.). 29.99 o.p. (*0-7089-2194-9*, Ulverscroft) Thorpe, F. A. Pubs. GBR. *Dist:* Ulverscroft Large Print Bks., Ltd., Ulverscroft Large Print Canada, Ltd.
—The Emerald Lizard: A Neal Rafferty Mystery. 1991. 224p. 17.95 o.p. (*0-525-24945-1*, Dutton) Dutton/Plume.
—The Killing Circle. l.t. ed. 1991. 8.95 o.p. (*0-7451-9395-1*, 1599); 1988. pap. 14.95 o.p. (*1-55504-628-2*, 333) BBC Audiobooks America.
—The Killing Circle. 1985. pap. 2.95 o.p. (*0-523-41933-3*, Pinnacle Bks.) Kensington Publishing Corp.

**RAFFLES (FICTITIOUS CHARACTER)—FICTION**

Hornung, E. W. The Amateur Cracksman. 1988. 289p. pap. 3.95 o.p. (*0-88184-359-8*, Carroll & Graf Pubs.) Avalon Publishing Group.
—The Amateur Cracksman. 1977. (Short Story Index Reprint Ser.). 19.95 (*0-8369-3150-5*) Ayer Co. Pubs., Inc.
—The Collected Raffles Stories. 1996. (Oxford Popular Fiction Ser.). (Illus.). 424p. pap. 11.95 o.p. (*0-19-282324-8*) Oxford Univ. Pr., Inc.
—The Complete Short Stories of Raffles: The Amateur Cracksman. 1984. 480p. 17.95 o.p. (*0-312-15849-1*) St. Martin's Pr.
—Raffles. E-Book 5.00 (*0-7410-1045-3*) SoftBook Pr.
—Raffles. 1976. (Crime Ser.). pap. 1.95 o.p. (*0-14-000063-1*, Penguin Bks.) Viking Penguin.
—Raffles: A Thief in the Night. 1976. 184p. 16.95 (*0-241-89358-5*) Boulevard Bks.
—Raffles: The Amateur Cracksman. l.t. ed. 1990. pap. 10.95 o.p. (*0-7927-0157-7*, C0154) BBC Audiobooks America.
—Raffles: The Amateur Cracksman. unabr. ed. 1992. audio 32.95 (*0-7861-0632-8*, 2122) Blackstone Audio Bks., Inc.
—Raffles: The Amateur Cracksman. unabr. collector's ed. 1989. audio 36.00 (*0-7366-3953-5*, 9199) Books on Tape, Inc.
—Raffles: The Amateur Cracksman. 1975. 154p. 16.95 (*0-241-89168-X*) Boulevard Bks.
—Raffles: The Amateur Cracksman. l.t. unabr. ed. 1991. 204p. 32.50 (*1-85089-468-X*, 89468X) ISIS Large Print Bks. GBR. *Dist:* Ulverscroft Large Print Bks., Ltd.
—Raffles: The Amateur Cracksman. 1976. (Illus.). x, 244p. pap. 5.95 o.p. (*0-8032-5836-4*, Bison Bks.) Univ. of Nebraska Pr.
—Raffles: The Amateur Cracksman. 2003. 240p. pap. 13.00 (*0-14-143933-5*, Penguin Classics) Viking Penguin.
—Raffles, the Amateur Cracksman. 1976. (Illus.). 268p. reprint ed. pap. 83.10 (*0-608-02671-9*, 206332400004) Bks. on Demand.
—Raffles, the Amateur Cracksman: The Complete Stories of E. W. Hornung. (Spies & Intrigues Ser.: No. 7). 478p. reprint ed. pap. 8.95 (*0-918172-20-9*) Leete's Island Bks.
Hornung, E. W. & Covell, Walter. Raffles: The Amateur Cracksman. unabr. ed. 1989. audio 26.00 Jimcin Recordings.

**RAFT, ANNIE (FICTITIOUS CHARACTER)—FICTION**

Ekman, Kerstin. Blackwater. 1999. pap. (*0-312-24519-X*) Picador.
—Blackwater. Tate, Joan, tr. 1996. 448p. pap. 15.00 (*0-312-15247-7*) Picador.

**RAHL, RICHARD (FICTITIOUS CHARACTER)—FICTION**

Goodkind, Terry. Faith of the Fallen. (Sword of Truth Ser.: Bk. 6). 2000. 512p. 27.95 (*0-312-86786-7*, NHC 0167); 2000. 512p. pap. 200.00 (*0-312-87521-5*); 2001. 800p. reprint ed. mass mkt. 7.99 (*0-8125-7639-X*) Doherty, Tom Assocs., LLC. (Tor Bks.).
—Naked Empire. abr. ed. (Sword of Truth Ser.: Bk. 8). 2005. audio 19.99 (*1-59086-306-2*, 3916, Brilliance Audio Paperback Audiobooks); 2003. audio 29.95 (*1-59086-305-4*, 3915, Bookcassette); 2003. audio compact disk 49.95 (*1-59086-303-8*, 3913, CD); 2003. audio 117.25 (*1-59086-302-X*, 3912, CD Unabridged Library Edition); 2003. audio 39.95 (*1-59086-301-1*, 3911, Brilliance Audio Unabridged); 2003. audio compact disk 142.25 (*1-59086-304-6*, 3914, Unabridged Library Editions) Brilliance Audio.
—Naked Empire. (Sword of Truth Ser.). 2004. 736p. mass mkt. 7.99 (*0-7653-4430-0*); 2003. (Illus.). 672p. 29.95 (*0-7653-0522-4*); 2003. (Illus.). 672p. 200.00 o.s.i (*0-7653-0733-2*) Doherty, Tom Assocs., LLC. (Tor Bks.).
—Soul of the Fire. unabr. ed. (Sword of Truth Ser.: Bk. 5). 2002. audio 39.95 (*1-59086-297-X*, 3883, Brilliance Audio Unabridged); 1999. 24p. audio 137.25 (*1-56740-632-7*, 1585, Unabridged Library Editions); 1999. audio 34.95 o.p. (*1-56740-403-0*, 1584, Bookcassette) Brilliance Audio.
—Soul of the Fire. (Sword of Truth Ser.: Bk. 5). 2000. 800p. mass mkt. 7.99 (*0-8125-5149-4*); 1999. 528p. 27.95 (*0-312-89054-0*) Doherty, Tom Assocs., LLC. (Tor Bks.).
—Soul of the Fire. unabr. ed. 2003. (Sword of Truth Ser.). audio 29.99 (*1-59335-118-6*, 30214) Soulmate Audio Bks., Inc.
—The Sword of Truth, 3 vols. 1998. (Sword of Truth Ser.). 23.97 o.s.i (*0-8125-7560-1*, Forge Bks.) Doherty, Tom Assocs., LLC.
—Temple of the Winds. (Sword of Truth Ser.: Bk. 4). 1999. 0.01 o.p. (*0-312-86406-X*); 1998. 832p. mass mkt. 7.99 (*0-8125-5148-6*); 1997. 416p. 29.95 (*0-312-89053-2*) Doherty, Tom Assocs., LLC. (Tor Bks.).
—Wizard's First Rule. unabr. ed. 1994. (Sword of Truth Ser.: Bk. 1). audio 35.95 (*1-56100-598-3*, 321, Bookcassette) Brilliance Audio.

**RAIN, JOHN (FICTITIOUS CHARACTER)—FICTION**

Eisler, Barry. Hard Rain. abr. ed. (John Rain Ser.). 2004. audio 12.99 (*1-59086-957-5*, 4559, Brilliance Audio Paperback Audiobooks); 2003. audio 24.95 (*1-59086-956-7*, 4558, Brilliance Audio); 2003. audio 32.95 (*1-59086-954-0*, 4556, Brilliance Audio Unabridged); 2003. audio 82.25 (*1-59086-955-9*, 4557, Unabridged Library Editions) Brilliance Audio.
—Hard Rain. 2003. 320p. text 24.95 (*0-399-15052-8*, Putnam & Grosset) Putnam Publishing Group, The.
—Rain Fall. 2003. 384p. reprint ed. mass mkt. 6.99 (*0-451-20915-X*, Signet Bks.) NAL.
—Rain Fall. 2002. 336p. 24.95 o.s.i (*0-399-14910-4*) Penguin Group (USA) Inc.

**RAINES, BEN (FICTITIOUS CHARACTER)—FICTION**

Johnstone, William W. Death in the Ashes. 1998. (Ashes Ser.: Vol. 11). 384p. mass mkt. 5.99 (*0-7860-0587-4*, Pinnacle Bks.); 1990. mass mkt. 3.95 o.s.i (*0-8217-2922-5*, Zebra Bks.) Kensington Publishing Corp.
—Slaughter in the Ashes. abr. ed. 1998. audio 16.95 (*1-882071-94-8*) B&B Audio, Inc.
—Slaughter in the Ashes, No. 23. 1997. (Slaughter in the Ashes Ser.: Vol. 23). 288p. mass mkt. 5.99 (*0-7860-0380-4*, Pinnacle Bks.) Kensington Publishing Corp.

**RAINES, HARRISON (FICTITIOUS CHARACTER)—FICTION**

Kilian, Michael. A Grave at Glorieta. 2004. 304p. mass mkt. 6.99 (*0-425-19531-7*) Berkley Publishing Group.
—A Grave at Glorieta: A Harrison Raines Civil War Mystery. 2003. 304p. 22.95 (*0-425-18829-9*, Prime Crime) Berkley Publishing Group.
—The Ironclad Alibi: A Harrison Raines Civil War Mystery. 2002. 320p. 22.95 o.s.i (*0-425-18325-4*, Prime Crime) Berkley Publishing Group.
—A Killing at Ball's Bluff: A Harrison Raines Civil War Mystery. 2001. (Harrison Raines Civil War Mysteries Ser.). 384p. 21.95 o.s.i (*0-425-17804-8*, Prime Crime) Berkley Publishing Group.
—Murder at Manassas: A Harrison Raines Civil War Mystery. 2000. (Harrison Raines Civil War Mysteries Ser.). 320p. mass mkt. 5.99 (*0-425-17743-2*); 306p. 21.95 o.s.i (*0-425-17233-3*) Berkley Publishing Group. (Prime Crime).

**RAINFINCH, ABE (FICTITIOUS CHARACTER)—FICTION**

Shaw, P. B. The Seraphim Kill: A Lt. Abe Rainfinch Mystery. 1994. 224p. 21.95 (*0-8027-3181-3*) Walker & Co.

**RAISIN, AGATHA (FICTITIOUS CHARACTER)—FICTION**

Beaton, M. C., pseud. Agatha Raisin & the Case of the Curious Curate. mass mkt. (*0-312-99061-8*, St. Martin's Paperbacks); 2003. 224p. 22.95 (*0-312-20768-9*, Saint Martin's Minotaur) St. Martin's Pr.
—Agatha Raisin & the Case of the Curious Curate. l.t. ed. 2003. (Mystery Ser.). 30.95 (*0-7862-5507-2*) Thorndike Pr.
—Agatha Raisin & the Day the Floods Came. l.t. ed. 2002. (Mystery Ser.). 341p. 30.95 (*0-7862-4679-0*) Gale Group.
—Agatha Raisin & the Day the Floods Came. E-Book 22.95 (*0-312-70710-X*); 2003. 240p. mass mkt. 6.50 (*0-312-98586-X*, St. Martin's Paperbacks); 2002. 224p. 22.95 (*0-312-20767-0*, Saint Martin's Minotaur) St. Martin's Pr.
—Agatha Raisin & the Deadly Dance. Date not set. (*0-312-30436-6*, Saint Martin's Minotaur); pap. (*0-312-30437-4*, Saint Martin's Griffin); mass mkt. (*0-312-98474-X*, St. Martin's Paperbacks); E-Book (*0-312-70375-9*) St. Martin's Pr.
—Agatha Raisin & the Fairies of Fryfam. 2001. 224p. mass mkt. 6.50 (*0-312-97626-7*, St. Martin's Paperbacks); 2000. 197p. 19.95 (*0-312-20496-5*, Saint Martin's Minotaur); 2000. E-Book 19.95 (*0-312-27420-3*) St. Martin's Pr.
—Agatha Raisin & the Fairies of Fryfam. l.t. ed. 2000. (Mystery Ser.). (Illus.). 283p. (J). 29.95 (*0-7862-2858-X*) Thorndike Pr.
—Agatha Raisin & the Haunted House. l.t. ed. 2003. 340p. 30.95 (*0-7862-6013-0*) Gale Group.
—Agatha Raisin & the Haunted House. Date not set. mass mkt. (*0-312-99482-6*, St. Martin's Paperbacks); E-Book (*0-312-71122-0*); 2003. 256p. 23.95 (*0-312-20769-7*) St. Martin's Pr.
—Agatha Raisin & the Love from Hell. l.t. ed. 2002. 366p. 30.95 (*0-7862-3862-3*) Gale Group.
—Agatha Raisin & the Love from Hell. 2003. 256p. mass mkt. 6.50 (*0-312-98318-2*, St. Martin's Paperbacks); 2001. 224p. 22.95 (*0-312-20766-2*, Saint Martin's Minotaur) St. Martin's Pr.
—Agatha Raisin & the Murderous Marriage. l.t. ed. 1997. (Large Print Book Ser.). pap. 22.95 (*1-56895-443-3*, Wheeler Publishing, Inc.) Gale Group.
—Agatha Raisin & the Murderous Marriage. (Agatha Raisin Mysteries Ser.). 1997. 224p. mass mkt. 6.50 (*0-312-96186-3*, St. Martin's Paperbacks); 1996. 208p. 20.95 (*0-312-14538-1*, Saint Martin's Minotaur) St. Martin's Pr.
—Agatha Raisin & the Perfect Paragon. Date not set. (*0-312-30448-X*, Saint Martin's Minotaur); pap. (*0-312-30449-8*, Saint Martin's Griffin); mass mkt. (*0-312-98479-0*, St. Martin's Paperbacks); E-Book (*0-312-70380-5*) St. Martin's Pr.
—Agatha Raisin & the Potted Gardener. 1995. 192p. mass mkt. 6.50 (*0-8041-1359-9*, Ivy Bks.) Ballantine Bks.
—Agatha Raisin & the Potted Gardener. l.t. ed. 1998. 204p. 21.95 o.p. (*0-7838-8392-7*, Macmillan Reference USA) Gale Group.
—Agatha Raisin & the Potted Gardener. 1994. 240p. 18.95 (*0-312-10927-X*, Saint Martin's Minotaur) St. Martin's Pr.
—Agatha Raisin & the Quiche of Death. 1993. 192p. mass mkt. 6.50 (*0-8041-1163-4*, Ivy Bks.) Ballantine Bks.
—Agatha Raisin & the Quiche of Death. unabr. collector's ed. 1999. audio 40.00 (*0-7366-4507-1*, 4940) Books on Tape, Inc.
—Agatha Raisin & the Quiche of Death. 1992. 208p. 17.95 o.p. (*0-312-08153-7*, Saint Martin's Minotaur) St. Martin's Pr.
—Agatha Raisin & the Terrible Tourist. l.t. ed. 1998. pap. 22.95 o.p. (*1-56895-574-X*, Wheeler Publishing, Inc.) Gale Group.
—Agatha Raisin & the Terrible Tourist. (Agatha Raisin Mysteries Ser.). 1997. 160p. 20.95 o.p. (*0-312-16761-X*, Saint Martin's Minotaur); 1958. E-Book 5.99 o.s.i (*0-312-20707-7*); 1998. 208p. reprint ed. mass mkt. 6.50 (*0-312-96566-4*, St. Martin's Paperbacks) St. Martin's Pr.
—Agatha Raisin & the Vicious Vet. 1994. 192p. mass mkt. 6.99 (*0-8041-1162-6*, Ivy Bks.) Ballantine Bks.
—Agatha Raisin & the Vicious Vet. 1999. audio compact disk 40.00 (*0-7366-8540-5*); audio 32.00 (*0-7366-4790-2*, 5137) Books on Tape, Inc.
—Agatha Raisin & the Vicious Vet. 1993. 208p. 17.95 o.p. (*0-312-09242-3*, Saint Martin's Minotaur) St. Martin's Pr.
—Agatha Raisin & the Vicious Vet. l.t. ed. 1998. (Paperback Ser.). 227p. pap. 24.95 (*0-7838-0368-0*) Thorndike Pr.
—Agatha Raisin & the Walkers of Dembley. 1996. (Agatha Raisin Ser.). 176p. mass mkt. 6.50 (*0-8041-1358-0*, Ivy Bks.) Ballantine Bks.
—Agatha Raisin & the Walkers of Dembley. 1995. 170p. 19.95 o.p. (*0-312-11738-8*, Saint Martin's Minotaur) St. Martin's Pr.
—Agatha Raisin & the Wellspring of Death. l.t. ed. 1999. (Large Print Book Ser.). pap. 23.95 (*1-56895-730-0*, Wheeler Publishing, Inc.) Gale Group.
—Agatha Raisin & the Wellspring of Death. (Dead Letter Mysteries Ser.). 1999. 256p. mass mkt. 6.50 (*0-312-96695-4*, St. Martin's Paperbacks); 1998. 272p. 21.95 o.p. (*0-312-18523-5*, Saint Martin's Minotaur) St. Martin's Pr.
—Agatha Raisin & the Witch of Wyckhadden. E-Book 21.95 (*0-312-26821-1*); 2000. 214p. mass mkt. 5.99 (*0-312-97369-1*, St. Martin's Paperbacks); 1999. 208p. 21.95 (*0-312-20494-9*, Saint Martin's Minotaur) St. Martin's Pr.
—Agatha Raisin & the Witch of Wyckhadden. l.t. ed. 2000. (Mystery Ser.). 288p. 28.95 (*0-7862-2418-5*) Thorndike Pr.
—Agatha Raisin & the Wizard of Evesham. pap. text (*0-312-20693-3*, Tor Bks.) Doherty, Tom Assocs., LLC.
—Agatha Raisin & the Wizard of Evesham. E-Book 20.95 (*0-312-26822-X*); 1999. 256p. mass mkt. 5.99 (*0-312-97062-5*, St. Martin's Paperbacks); 1999. (Agatha Raisin Mysteries Ser.: Vol. 8). 208p. 20.95 o.p. (*0-312-19822-1*, Saint Martin's Minotaur) St. Martin's Pr.
—Agatha Raisin & the Wizard of Evesham. l.t. ed. 2000. (Mystery Ser.). (Illus.). 272p. 28.95 (*0-7862-2417-7*) Thorndike Pr.

**RALSTON, DEB (FICTITIOUS CHARACTER)—FICTION**

Martin, Lee. Bird in a Cage. 1996. per. (*0-373-26225-6*, 1-26225-2, Worldwide Library) Harlequin Enterprises, Ltd.
—Bird in a Cage. 1995. 240p. 20.95 o.p. (*0-312-13028-7*, Saint Martin's Minotaur) St. Martin's Pr.
—A Conspiracy of Strangers. 1986. 208p. 13.95 o.p. (*0-312-16433-5*) St. Martin's Pr.
—The Day that Dusty Died. 1994. 304p. 20.95 o.p. (*0-312-09779-4*, Saint Martin's Minotaur) St. Martin's Pr.
—Death Warmed Over. 1991. mass mkt. (*0-373-26065-2*, Harlequin Bks.) Harlequin Enterprises, Ltd.
—Death Warmed Over. 1988. 224p. 15.95 o.p. (*0-312-02221-2*, Saint Martin's Minotaur) St. Martin's Pr.
—Deficit Ending. 1992. (Mystery Ser.: No. 101). mass mkt. (*0-373-26101-2*, Harlequin Bks.) Harlequin Enterprises, Ltd.
—Deficit Ending. 1990. 208p. 15.95 o.p. (*0-312-03813-5*, Saint Martin's Minotaur) St. Martin's Pr.
—Genealogy of Murder. 1997. (WWL Mystery Ser.: No. 239). per. (*0-373-26239-6*, 1-26239-3, Worldwide Library) Harlequin Enterprises, Ltd.
—Genealogy of Murder. 1996. 240p. 22.95 o.p. (*0-312-13975-6*, Saint Martin's Minotaur) St. Martin's Pr.
—Hacker. 1993. (WWL Mystery Ser.). per. (*0-373-26135-7*, 1-26135-3, Harlequin Bks.) Harlequin Enterprises, Ltd.
—Hacker: A Deb Ralston Mystery. 1992. 192p. 16.95 o.p. (*0-312-06990-1*, Saint Martin's Minotaur) St. Martin's Pr.
—Hal's Own Murder Case. 1991. mass mkt. (*0-373-26087-3*, Harlequin Bks.) Harlequin Enterprises, Ltd.
—Hal's Own Murder Case. 1989. 14.95 o.p. (*0-312-02925-X*, Saint Martin's Minotaur) St. Martin's Pr.
—Inherited Murder. 1994. (Deb Ralston Mystery Ser.). 304p. 19.95 o.p. (*0-312-11415-X*, Saint Martin's Minotaur) St. Martin's Pr.
—The Mensa Murders. 1993. mass mkt. (*0-373-26115-2*, 1-26115-5, Harlequin Bks.) Harlequin Enterprises, Ltd.
—The Mensa Murders. 1990. 192p. 15.95 o.p. (*0-312-05126-3*, Saint Martin's Minotaur) St. Martin's Pr.
—Murder at the Blue Owl. 1990. mass mkt. (*0-373-26054-7*, Harlequin Bks.) Harlequin Enterprises, Ltd.
—Murder at the Blue Owl. 1988. 208p. 14.95 o.p. (*0-312-01795-2*) St. Martin's Pr.
—Too Sane a Murder. 1984. 192p. 12.95 o.p. (*0-312-80901-8*) St. Martin's Pr.

**RAMADGE, GWENN (FICTITIOUS CHARACTER)—FICTION**

O'Donnell, Lillian. The Goddess Affair. 1997. mass mkt. 5.99 o.s.i (*0-449-28805-6*, Fawcett) Ballantine Bks.
—The Goddess Affair. l.t. ed. 1997. (Large Print Book Ser.). 25.95 o.p. (*1-56895-461-1*, Wheeler Publishing, Inc.) Gale Group.
—The Goddess Affair. 1996. 240p. 21.95 o.p. (*0-399-14183-9*, G. P. Putnam's Sons) Penguin Group (USA) Inc.
—The Raggedy Man. 1997. (Norah Mulcahaney Ser.). mass mkt. 5.99 o.s.i (*0-449-22428-7*, Fawcett) Ballantine Bks.
—The Raggedy Man. 1995. 240p. 19.95 o.p. (*0-399-14019-0*, G. P. Putnam's Sons) Penguin Group (USA) Inc.
—Used to Kill. 1994. mass mkt. 4.99 o.s.i (*0-449-22249-7*, Fawcett) Ballantine Bks.
—Used to Kill. 1993. 240p. 19.95 o.p. (*0-399-13782-3*, G. P. Putnam's Sons) Penguin Group (USA) Inc.
—A Wreath for the Bride. 1991. 224p. mass mkt. 4.99 o.s.i (*0-449-21867-8*, Fawcett) Ballantine Bks.
—A Wreath for the Bride. 1990. 240p. 18.95 o.p. (*0-399-13478-6*, G. P. Putnam's Sons) Penguin Putnam Bks. for Young Readers.
—A Wreath for the Bride. 1992. 2.99 o.p. (*0-517-07978-X*) Random Hse. Value Publishing.

**RAMAGE, NICHOLAS (FICTITIOUS CHARACTER)—FICTION**

Pope, Dudley. Ramage. unabr. ed. 1992. (Audio Bks.). audio 69.95 (*0-7451-6203-7*, CAB 682) BBC Audiobooks America.
—Ramage. 1991. 350p. reprint ed. lib. bdg. 26.95 (*0-89966-840-2*) Buccaneer Bks., Inc.
—Ramage. l.t. ed. 1992. (Windsor Ser.). 376p. 23.95 o.p. (*0-7451-7410-8*, Macmillan Reference USA) Gale Group.
—Ramage. 2000. (Lord Ramage Novels Ser.: No. 1). 319p. reprint ed. pap. 14.95 (*0-935526-76-5*) McBooks Pr., Inc.
—Ramage & the Dido. 2002. (Lord Ramage Novels Ser.: No. 18). (Illus.). 288p. pap. 15.95 (*1-59013-024-3*) McBooks Pr., Inc.
—Ramage & the Drumbeat. unabr. ed. 1994. audio 69.95 (*0-7451-4277-X*, CAB 960) BBC Audiobooks America.
—Ramage & the Drumbeat. 2000. (Lord Ramage Novels Ser.: No. 2). 287p. reprint ed. pap. 14.95 (*0-935526-77-3*) McBooks Pr., Inc.
—Ramage & the Freebooters. 2000. (Lord Ramage Novels Ser.: Vol. 3). 382p. reprint ed. pap. 15.95 (*0-935526-78-1*) McBooks Pr., Inc.
—Ramage & the Freebooters. 1969. 384p. (YA). (*0-297-17710-9*) Weidenfeld & Nicolson, Ltd. GBR. *Dist:* Trafalgar Square.
—Ramage & the Guillotine. 2000. (Lord Ramage Novels Ser.: Vol. 6). 288p. pap. 14.95 (*0-935526-81-1*) McBooks Pr., Inc.
—Ramage & the Guillotine. 1981. 256p. pap. 2.50 o.p. (*0-380-55491-7*, 55491-7, Avon Bks.) Morrow/Avon.
—Ramage & the Rebels. 2001. (Lord Ramage Novels Ser.: No. 9). (Illus.). 318p. pap. 15.95 (*0-935526-91-9*) McBooks Pr., Inc.
—Ramage & the Rebels. 1985. 286p. 13.95 o.p. (*0-8027-0842-0*) Walker & Co.
—Ramage & the Renegades Book #12. 2001. (Lord Ramage Novels Ser.: Vol. 12). 320p. pap. 15.95 (*1-59013-009-X*) McBooks Pr., Inc.
—Ramage & the Renegades Book #12. 1982. 288p. pap. 2.75 o.p. (*0-380-60137-0*, 60137-0, Avon Bks.) Morrow/Avon.
—Ramage & the Saracens. 2002. (Lord Ramage Novels: No. 17). (Illus.). 304p. pap. 15.95 (*1-59013-023-5*) McBooks Pr., Inc.
—Ramage at Trafalgar. 2002. (Lord Ramage Novels: 16). (Illus.). 256p. pap. 14.95 (*1-59013-022-7*) McBooks Pr., Inc.
—The Ramage Touch. 1984. 226p. 12.95 o.p. (*0-8027-0785-8*) Walker & Co.
—The Ramage Touch Book #10. 2001. (Lord Ramage Novels Ser.: Vol. 10). 272p. pap. 15.95 (*1-59013-007-3*) McBooks Pr., Inc.
—Ramage's Challenge. 2002. (Lord Ramage Novels Ser.: Vol. 14). (Illus.). 320p. pap. 15.95 (*1-59013-012-X*) McBooks Pr., Inc.
—Ramage's Devil. 2002. (Lord Ramage Novels Ser.: Vol. 13). (Illus.). 320p. pap. 15.95 (*1-59013-010-3*) McBooks Pr., Inc.
—Ramage's Diamond. 2001. (Lord Ramage Novels Ser.: Vol. 7). (Illus.). 332p. pap. 15.95 (*0-935526-89-7*) McBooks Pr., Inc.
—Ramage's Diamond. 1982. 288p. pap. 2.50 o.p. (*0-380-57828-X*, 57828-X, Avon Bks.) Morrow/Avon.
—Ramage's Mutiny. 2001. (Lord Ramage Novels Ser.: Vol. 8). (Illus.). 286p. pap. 14.95 (*0-935526-90-0*) McBooks Pr., Inc.
—Ramage's Prize. 2000. (Lord Ramage Novels Ser.: Vol. 5). (Illus.). 350p. pap. 15.95 (*0-935526-80-3*) McBooks Pr., Inc.
—Ramage's Prize. 1975. 344p. (J). 8.95 (*0-671-21860-3*, Simon & Schuster) Simon & Schuster.
—Ramage's Signal. 1984. 256p. 12.95 o.s.i (*0-8027-0811-0*) Walker & Co.
—Ramage's Signal Book #11. 2001. (Lord Ramage Novels Ser.: Vol. 11). 320p. pap. 15.95 (*1-59013-008-1*) McBooks Pr., Inc.

**RAMIREZ, CARMEN (FICTITIOUS CHARACTER)—FICTION**

Haddock, Lisa. Edited Out. 1994. (Carmen Ramirez Mystery Ser.: Vol. 1). 224p. pap. 9.95 (*1-56280-077-9*) Naiad Pr., Inc.
—Final Cut. 1995. (Carmen Ramirez Mystery Ser.: Vol. 2). 224p. pap. 10.95 o.p. (*1-56280-088-4*) Naiad Pr., Inc.

**RAMOS, LUCIA (FICTITIOUS CHARACTER)—FICTION**

Morell, Mary. Final Session. 1991. 224p. pap. 9.95 o.p. (*0-933216-78-5*) Spinsters Ink Bks.

**RAMOTSWE, PRECIOUS (FICTITIOUS CHARACTER)—FICTION**

Smith, Alexander McCall. The Full Cupboard of Life. 2004. 208p. 19.95 (*0-375-42218-8*, Pantheon) Knopf Publishing Group.
—The Full Cupboard of Life. l.t. ed. 2004. 352p. 21.95 (*0-375-43335-X*) Random Hse. Large Print.
—The Kalahari Typing School for Men. l.t. ed. 2003. lib. bdg. 29.95 (*1-58547-331-6*, Platinum) Ctr. Point Large Print.
—The Kalahari Typing School for Men. 192p. 2004. pap. 11.95 (*1-4000-3180-X*, Anchor); 2003. 19.95 (*0-375-42217-X*, Pantheon) Knopf Publishing Group.
—The Kalahari Typing School for Men. 2003. 192p. 32.95 (*0-676-97568-2*) Knopf, Alfred A. Inc.
—The Kalahari Typing School for Men. audio 24.99 (*1-4025-4178-3*); audio compact disk 29.99 (*1-4025-4706-4*); 2003. audio 24.99 Recorded Bks., LLC.
—Morality for Beautiful Girls. l.t. ed. 2003. lib. bdg. 29.95 (*1-58547-330-8*, Premier) Ctr. Point Large Print.
—Morality for Beautiful Girls. 2001. 236p. pap. 12.95 (*0-7486-6297-9*) Polygon GBR. *Dist:* Interlink Publishing Group, Inc.
—Morality for Beautiful Girls. 2002. 240p. pap. 11.95 (*1-4000-3136-2*) Random Hse., Inc.
—Morality for Beautiful Girls. audio compact disk 29.99 (*1-4025-4368-9*); 2003. audio 24.99 (*1-4025-4179-1*) Recorded Bks., LLC.
—The No. 1 Ladies' Detective Agency. l.t. ed. 2003. lib. bdg. 29.95 (*1-58547-328-6*, Platinum) Ctr. Point Large Print.
—The No. 1 Ladies' Detective Agency. 2003. 240p. pap. 11.95 (*1-4000-3477-9*, Anchor) Knopf Publishing Group.
—The No. 1 Ladies' Detective Agency. 2001. 202p. pap. 12.95 o.p. (*0-7486-6252-9*) Polygon GBR. *Dist:* AK Pr. Distribution.
—The No. 1 Ladies' Detective Agency. 2002. 240p. pap. 11.95 o.s.i (*1-4000-3134-6*, Knopf Bks. for Young Readers) Random Hse. Children's Bks.
—The No. 1 Ladies' Detective Agency. audio compact disk 29.99 (*1-4025-4535-5*); 2003. audio 24.99 (*1-4025-4180-5*) Recorded Bks., LLC.
—Tears of the Giraffe. 2001. 208p. 12.95 (*0-7486-6273-1*) Edinburgh Univ. Pr. GBR. *Dist:* Columbia Univ. Pr.
—Tears of the Giraffe. 2002. 240p. pap. 11.95 (*1-4000-3135-4*, Knopf Bks. for Young Readers) Random Hse. Children's Bks.
—Tears of the Giraffe. audio 24.99 (*1-4025-4177-5*); audio compact disk 29.99 (*1-4025-4705-6*); 2003. audio 24.99 Recorded Bks., LLC.

**RAMSAY, JULIAN (FICTITIOUS CHARACTER)—FICTION**

Wilson, A. N. A Bottle in the Smoke. 1991. 288p. pap. 8.95 o.p. (*0-14-013165-5*, Penguin Bks.) Penguin Group (USA) Inc.
—A Bottle in the Smoke. 1990. 288p. 18.95 o.p. (*0-670-83221-9*, Viking) Viking Penguin.
—Daughters of Albion. 1993. 304p. pap. 10.00 o.p. (*0-14-013166-3*, Penguin Bks.); pap. 10.00 o.p. (*0-14-017509-1*) Penguin Group (USA) Inc.
—Daughters of Albion. 1992. 304p. 21.00 o.p. (*0-670-83959-0*, Viking) Viking Penguin.
—Hearing Voices. 224p. 1997. pap. 12.00 (*0-393-31633-5*); 1996. 22.50 o.p. (*0-393-03875-0*) Norton, W. W. & Co., Inc.
—Incline Our Hearts. 1992. 2.99 o.p. (*0-517-08020-6*) Random Hse. Value Publishing.
—Incline Our Hearts. 256p. 1990. pap. 9.95 o.p. (*0-14-011337-1*, Penguin Bks.); 1989. 17.95 o.p. (*0-670-82358-9*) Viking Penguin.
—A Watch in the Night. 1998. 224p. pap. 12.00 (*0-393-31725-0*); 1996. 256p. 23.00 o.p. (*0-393-04042-9*) Norton, W. W. & Co., Inc.

**RAMSAY, STEPHEN (FICTITIOUS CHARACTER)—FICTION**

Cleeves, Ann. A Day in the Death of Dorothea Cassidy. 1992. mass mkt. 4.99 o.s.i (*0-449-14789-4*, Fawcett) Ballantine Bks.
—A Day in the Death of Dorothea Cassidy. l.t. ed. 1993. (Mystery Ser.). 384p. 29.99 o.p. (*0-7089-2965-6*, Ulverscroft) Thorpe, F. A. Pubs. GBR. *Dist:* Ulverscroft Large Print Bks., Ltd., Ulverscroft Large Print Canada, Ltd.
—The Healers. 1995. (Stephen Ramsay Mysteries Ser.). mass mkt. 5.99 o.s.i (*0-449-14944-7*, Fawcett) Ballantine Bks.
—Killjoy. 1995. (Orig.). mass mkt. 4.99 o.s.i (*0-449-14893-9*, Fawcett) Ballantine Bks.
—A Lesson in Dying. 1990. 176p. mass mkt. 4.99 o.s.i (*0-449-14677-4*, Fawcett) Ballantine Bks.
—A Lesson in Dying. l.t. ed. 1992. (Ulverscroft Large Print Ser.). 336p. 29.99 o.p. (*0-7089-2566-9*, Ulverscroft) Thorpe, F. A. Pubs. GBR. *Dist:* Ulverscroft Large Print Bks., Ltd., Ulverscroft Large Print Canada, Ltd.
—Murder in My Back Yard. unabr. ed. 2001. 8p. audio 69.95 (*1-86042-864-9*, 2-864-9) Soundings, Ltd. GBR. *Dist:* Ulverscroft Large Print Bks., Ltd.
—Murder in My Backyard. 1991. (Stephen Ramsay Mysteries Ser.). 256p. mass mkt. 4.99 o.s.i (*0-449-14720-7*, Fawcett) Ballantine Bks.

**RAMSEY, CURT (FICTITIOUS CHARACTER)—FICTION**

Hogan, Ray. The Crosshatch Men. 1997. 192p. reprint ed. mass mkt. 3.99 (*0-8439-4279-7*, Leisure Bks.) Dorchester Publishing Co., Inc.
—The Crosshatch Men. 1989. (Double D Western Ser.). pap. 12.95 o.s.i (*0-385-24752-4*) Doubleday Publishing.
—The Crosshatch Men. l.t. ed. 1992. (Nightingale Series Large Print Bks.). 245p. pap. 14.95 o.p. (*0-8161-5275-6*, Macmillan Reference USA) Gale Group.

**RAMSEY FAMILY (FICTITIOUS CHARACTERS)—FICTION**

Phillips, Michael R. Flight from Stonewycke. 1994. (Stonewycke Trilogy Ser.). 288p. mass mkt. 5.99 o.p. (*1-55661-453-5*) Bethany Hse. Pubs.
—Stranger at Stonewycke. 1995. (Stonewycke Legacy Ser.). 384p. mass mkt. 6.99 o.p. (*1-55661-581-7*) Bethany Hse. Pubs.
Phillips, Michael R. & Pella, Judith. Flight from Stonewycke. 1985. (Stonewycke Trilogy Ser.). 256p. pap. 8.99 o.p. (*0-87123-837-3*) Bethany Hse. Pubs.
—Flight from Stonewycke. 2002. (Stonewycke Trilogy: Bk. 2). 26.95 (*0-7862-4721-5*) Thorndike Pr.
—Heather Hills of Stonewycke. (Stonewycke Trilogy Ser.). (Orig.). 1993. 272p. mass mkt. 5.99 o.p. (*1-55661-373-3*); 1985. 256p. pap. 8.99 o.p. (*0-87123-803-9*) Bethany Hse. Pubs.
—Heather Hills of Stonewycke. l.t. ed. 2002. (Orig.). 25.95 (*0-7862-4724-X*) Thorndike Pr.
—The Lady of Stonewycke. 1986. (Stonewycke Trilogy Ser.: Vol. 3). 272p. pap. 8.99 o.p. (*0-87123-856-X*) Bethany Hse. Pubs.
—Shadows over Stonewycke. (Stonewycke Legacy Ser.: Bk. 2). (Orig.). 1995. 464p. mass mkt. 6.99 o.p. (*1-55661-632-5*); 1988. 400p. pap. 9.99 o.p. (*0-87123-901-9*) Bethany Hse. Pubs.
—The Stonewycke Legacy, Vols. 1-3. 1988. (Stonewycke Legacy Ser.: GIFT 1-3). pap. 29.99 o.p. (*1-55661-755-0*, 252755) Bethany Hse. Pubs.
—Stranger at Stonewycke. 1987. (Stonewycke Legacy Ser.). 352p. pap. 9.99 o.p. (*0-87123-900-0*) Bethany Hse. Pubs.
—Treasure of Stonewycke. (Stonewycke Legacy Ser.: Bk. 3). (Orig.). 1995. 464p. mass mkt. 6.99 o.p. (*1-55661-634-1*); 1988. 400p. pap. 9.99 o.p. (*0-87123-902-7*) Bethany Hse. Pubs.

**RAMSGILL, JAMIE (FICTITIOUS CHARACTER)—FICTION**

Bradberry, James. Eakins' Mistress: A Jamie Ramsgill Mystery. 1997. 169p. text 19.95 o.p. (*0-312-15518-2*, Saint Martin's Minotaur) St. Martin's Pr.
—Ruins of Civility. 1996. 256p. 21.95 o.p. (*0-312-14041-X*, Saint Martin's Minotaur) St. Martin's Pr.
—The Seventh Sacrament. 1994. 208p. 19.95 o.p. (*0-312-11059-6*, Saint Martin's Minotaur); Vol. 1. 1995. (Seventh Sacrament Ser.: Vol. 1). 209p. mass mkt. 4.99 (*0-312-95636-3*, St. Martin's Paperbacks) St. Martin's Pr.

**RAND, JOANNA (FICTITIOUS CHARACTER)—FICTION**

Koontz, Dean. The Key to Midnight. 1995. 432p. mass mkt. 7.99 (*0-425-14751-7*); 1990. 315p. 19.95 o.p. (*0-913165-51-4*) Berkley Publishing Group.
—The Key to Midnight. 1995. 14.04 (*0-606-15883-9*) Turtleback Bks.

**RAND AL'THOR (FICTITIOUS CHARACTER)—FICTION**

Jordan, Robert. Crossroads of Twilight. 2003. (Wheel of Time Ser.: Bk. 10). 864p. mass mkt. 7.99 (*0-8125-7133-9*); 672p. 200.00 o.s.i (*0-7653-0592-5*); (Illus.). 672p. 29.95 (*0-312-86459-0*) Doherty, Tom Assocs., LLC. (Tor Bks.).
—A Crown of Swords. unabr. ed. 1998. (Wheel of Time Ser.: Bk. 7). Pt. 1. audio 88.00 (*0-7366-4173-4*, 4673-A); Pt. 2. audio 88.00 (*0-7366-4174-2*, 4673-B) Books on Tape, Inc.
—A Crown of Swords. (Wheel of Time Ser.: Bk. 7). 1997. 880p. mass mkt. 7.99 (*0-8125-5028-5*); 1996. 684p. 29.95 (*0-312-85767-5*); 1996. 720p. 200.00 (*0-312-86133-8*) Doherty, Tom Assocs., LLC. (Tor Bks.).
—A Crown of Swords. abr. ed. 1996. (Wheel of Time Ser.: Bk. 7). audio 24.95 (*1-879371-96-0*) Publishing Mills, Inc., The.
—A Crown of Swords. 1997. (Wheel of Time Ser.: Bk. 7). (J). 14.04 (*0-606-13907-9*) Turtleback Bks.
—The Dragon Reborn. unabr. ed. 1997. (Wheel of Time Ser.: Bk. 3). Pt. 1. audio 72.00 (*0-7366-3601-3*, 4256-A); Pt. 2. audio 72.00 (*0-7366-3602-1*, 4256-B) Books on Tape, Inc.
—The Dragon Reborn. (Wheel of Time Ser.: Bk. 3). 2002. 624p. pap. 14.95 (*0-7653-0511-9*); 1992. 701p. mass mkt. 7.99 (*0-8125-1371-1*); 9th ed. 1991. (Illus.). 595p. 29.95 (*0-312-85248-7*) Doherty, Tom Assocs., LLC. (Tor Bks.).
—The Dragon Reborn. abr. ed. 1992. (Wheel of Time Ser.: Bk. 3). audio 15.95 (*1-879371-29-4*, 40120) Publishing Mills, Inc., The.
—The Dragon Reborn. 1992. (Wheel of Time Ser.: Bk. 3). 14.04 (*0-606-12076-9*) Turtleback Bks.
—The Eye of the World. unabr. ed. 1996. (Wheel of Time Ser.: Bk. 1). Pt. 1. audio 88.00 (*0-7366-3533-5*, 4179-A); Pt. 2. audio 80.00 (*0-7366-3534-3*, 4179-B) Books on Tape, Inc.
—The Eye of the World. (Wheel of Time Ser.: Bk. 1). 2000. 814p. mass mkt. 3.99 (*0-8125-7995-X*); 1990. 814p. mass mkt. 6.99 (*0-8125-1181-6*); 1990. 670p. pap. 14.95 (*0-8125-0048-2*); 1990. (Illus.). 670p. 27.95 (*0-312-85009-3*) Doherty, Tom Assocs., LLC. (Tor Bks.).
—The Eye of the World, abr. ed. 2000. (Wheel of Time Ser.: Bk. 1). 3p. audio 7.95 (*1-57815-132-5*, 1091, Media Bks. Audio Publishing) Media Bks., L. L. C.
—The Eye of the World. abr. ed. 1994. (Wheel of Time Ser.: Bk. 1). audio 16.95 (*1-879371-52-9*, 40020); 2001. audio compact disk 69.95 (*1-57511-098-9*); 1995. (Wheel of Time Ser.: Bk. 1). audio o.p. (*1-57511-003-2*, 70060) Publishing Mills, Inc., The.
—The Eye of the World. 1990. (Wheel of Time Ser.: Bk. 1). 13.04 (*0-606-12074-2*) Turtleback Bks.
—The Fires of Heaven. unabr. ed. 1997. (Wheel of Time Ser.: Bk. 5). Pt. 1. audio 104.00 (*0-7366-3765-6*, 4439-A); Pt. 2. audio 104.00 (*0-7366-3766-4*, 4439-B) Books on Tape, Inc.
—The Fires of Heaven. (Wheel of Time Ser.: Bk. 5). 1994. 989p. mass mkt. 7.99 (*0-8125-5030-7*); 5th ed. 1993. 702p. 29.95 (*0-312-85427-7*) Doherty, Tom Assocs., LLC. (Tor Bks.).
—The Fires of Heaven. abr. ed. 1993. (Wheel of Time Ser.: Bk. 5). audio 16.95 (*1-879371-65-0*) Publishing Mills, Inc., The.
—The Fires of Heaven. 1994. (Wheel of Time Ser.: Bk. 5). 14.04 (*0-606-12078-5*) Turtleback Bks.
—From the Two Rivers. 2002. (Eye of the World Ser.: Pt. 1). 360p. (J). reprint ed. mass mkt. 5.99 (*0-7653-4184-0*, Starscape) Doherty, Tom Assocs., LLC.
—The Great Hunt. unabr. ed. 1997. (Wheel of Time Ser.: Bk. 2). Pt. 1. audio 80.00 (*0-7366-3563-7*, 4208-A); Pt. 2. audio 64.00 Books on Tape, Inc.
—The Great Hunt. (Wheel of Time Ser.: Bk. 2). 1991. 705p. mass mkt. 7.99 (*0-8125-1772-5*); 1990. 600p. mass mkt. 14.95 (*0-8125-0971-4*); 1990. (Illus.). 600p. reprint ed. 27.95 (*0-312-85140-5*, NHC 0186) Doherty, Tom Assocs., LLC. (Tor Bks.).
—The Great Hunt, abr. ed. 2000. (Wheel of Time Ser.: Bk. 2). audio 7.95 (*1-57815-133-3*, 1092, Media Bks. Audio Publishing) Media Bks., L. L. C.
—The Great Hunt. abr. ed. 1994. (Wheel of Time Ser.: Bk. 2). 3p. audio 16.95 (*1-879371-53-7*, 40210) Publishing Mills, Inc., The.
—The Great Hunt. 1991. (Wheel of Time Ser.: Bk. 2). 14.04 (*0-606-12075-0*) Turtleback Bks.
—Lord of Chaos. unabr. ed. 1998. (Wheel of Time Ser.: Bk. 6). Pt. 1. audio 112.00 (*0-7366-4171-8*, 4672-A); Pt. 2. audio 120.00 (*0-7366-4172-6*, 4672-B) Books on Tape, Inc.
—Lord of Chaos. (Wheel of Time Ser.: Bk. 6). 1995. 1011p. mass mkt. 7.99 (*0-8125-1375-4*); 1994. 716p. 29.95 (*0-312-85428-5*); 1994. 704p. 200.00 (*0-312-85788-8*) Doherty, Tom Assocs., LLC. (Tor Bks.).

—Lord of Chaos. abr. ed. (Wheel of Time Ser.: Bk. 6). 1994. audio 16.95 (*1-879371-74-X*); 1995. audio o.p. (*1-57511-001-6*, 70050) Publishing Mills, Inc., The.
—Lord of Chaos. 1995. (Wheel of Time Ser.: Bk. 6). 14.04 (*0-606-12079-3*) Turtleback Bks.
—The Path of Daggers. unabr. ed. 1999. (Wheel of Time Ser.: Bk. 8). Pt. 1. audio 72.00 (*0-7366-4537-3*, 4801-A); Pt. 2. audio 64.00 (*0-7366-4538-1*, 4801-B) Books on Tape, Inc.
—The Path of Daggers. (Wheel of Time Ser.: Bk. 8). 1999. 685p. mass mkt. 7.99 (*0-8125-5029-3*); 1998. 604p. 27.95 (*0-312-85769-1*) Doherty, Tom Assocs., LLC. (Tor Bks.).
—The Path of Daggers. abr. ed. 1998. (Wheel of Time Ser.: Bk. 8). audio 39.95 (*1-57511-045-8*, 102534) Publishing Mills, Inc., The.
—The Shadow Rising. (Wheel of Time Ser.: Bk. 4). 1993. 1006p. mass mkt. 7.99 (*0-8125-1373-8*); 11th ed. 1992. 701p. 29.95 (*0-312-85431-5*, CPHC0627) Doherty, Tom Assocs., LLC. (Tor Bks.).
—The Shadow Rising. 1993. (Wheel of Time Ser.: Bk. 4). 14.04 (*0-606-12077-7*) Turtleback Bks.
—Snow: The Prologue to Winter's Heart. (Wheel of Time Ser.: Bk. 9). E-Book 5.00 (*1-930161-96-4*) Adobe Systems, Inc.
—Snow: The Prologue to Winter's Heart. 2000. (Wheel of Time Ser.: Bk. 9). E-Book 5.00 (*0-7432-1547-8*, Scribner) Simon & Schuster.
—Snow: The Prologue to Winter's Heart. (Wheel of Time Ser.: Bk. 9). E-Book 5.00 (*0-7410-0338-4*) SoftBook Pr.
—To the Blight. 2002. (Eye of the World Ser.: Bk. 1). (Illus.). 360p. reprint ed. mass mkt. 5.99 (*0-7653-4221-9*, Starscape) Doherty, Tom Assocs., LLC.
—Winter's Heart. 2002. mass mkt. 7.99 (*0-8125-4535-4*); 2001. (Wheel of Time Ser.: Bk. 9). (Illus.). 608p. 250.00 (*0-312-87775-7*); 2000. (Wheel of Time Ser.: Bk. 9). (Illus.). 668p. 29.95 (*0-312-86425-6*); 2002. (Wheel of Time Ser.: Bk. 9). 800p. reprint ed. mass mkt. 7.99 (*0-8125-7558-X*) Doherty, Tom Assocs., LLC. (Tor Bks.).

**RANDALL, CLAIRE (FICTITIOUS CHARACTER)—FICTION**

Lawrence, V. Public Enemy. 1996. 320p. mass mkt. 5.99 (*0-671-89561-3*, Pocket) Simon & Schuster.

**RANDALL, SUNNY (FICTITIOUS CHARACTER)—FICTION**

Parker, Robert B. Family Honor. 2000. (Sunny Randall Ser.). 338p. mass mkt. 7.50 (*0-425-17706-8*) Berkley Publishing Group.
—Family Honor. l.t. ed. (Wheeler Press Paperback Ser.). 2000. 10.95 (*1-56895-977-X*); 1999. 27.95 (*1-56895-788-2*) Gale Group. (Wheeler Publishing, Inc.).
—Family Honor, Set. abr. ed. 1999. audio 18.00 Highsmith Inc.
—Family Honor. 1999. audio 30.00 (*0-7871-2354-4*); audio compact disk 36.00 (*0-7871-2369-2*); audio 18.00 (*0-7871-2355-2*, Dove Audio); audio 30.00 NewStar Media, Inc.
—Family Honor. l.t. ed. 1999. (Sunny Randall Ser.). 322p. 22.95 o.p. (*0-399-14566-4*, G. P. Putnam's Sons) Penguin Group (USA) Inc.
—Perish Twice. 2001. 352p. reprint ed. mass mkt. 7.99 (*0-425-18215-0*) Berkley Publishing Group.
—Perish Twice. l.t. ed. (Wheeler Press Paperback Ser.). 2001. 12.95 (*1-56895-180-9*); 2000. 279p. 28.95 (*1-56895-992-3*) Gale Group. (Wheeler Publishing, Inc.).
—Perish Twice. 2000. 320p. 23.95 o.s.i (*0-399-14668-7*) Penguin Group (USA) Inc.
—Shrink Rap. 2003. 352p. mass mkt. 7.99 (*0-515-13620-4*, Jove) Berkley Publishing Group.
—Shrink Rap. unabr. ed. 2002. audio 29.95 (*1-59007-271-5*); audio compact disk 34.95 (*1-59007-272-3*) New Millennium Entertainment. (New Millennium Audio).
—Shrink Rap. 2002. 320p. 24.95 o.s.i (*0-399-14930-9*, Putnam & Grosset) Putnam Publishing Group, The.

**RANDOLPH, SNOOKY (FICTITIOUS CHARACTER)—FICTION**

Dank, Gloria. Friends till the End. 1989. 192p. mass mkt. 3.50 o.s.i (*0-553-28152-6*) Bantam Bks.
—Going out in Style. 1989. (Illus.). mass mkt. 3.95 o.s.i (*0-553-28346-4*) Bantam Bks.

**RANSOM, ELWIN (FICTITIOUS CHARACTER)—FICTION**

Lewis, C. S. Out of the Silent Planet. 2003. audio compact disk 19.95 (*0-7861-9367-0*); 2000. audio 32.95 (*0-7861-1814-8*, 2613); 2000. audio compact disk 49.99 (*0-7861-9808-7*, z2613) Blackstone Audio Bks., Inc.
—Out of the Silent Planet. unabr. collector's ed. 1983. audio 42.00 (*0-7366-0843-5*, 1794) Books on Tape, Inc.
—Out of the Silent Planet. 1991. reprint ed. lib. bdg. 21.95 (*1-56849-039-9*) Buccaneer Bks., Inc.
—Out of the Silent Planet. 2003. 160p. pap. 12.00 (*0-7432-3490-1*); 1996. 160p. 22.00 (*0-684-83364-6*); 1996. 160p. pap. 6.95 (*0-684-82380-2*); 1990. 174p. reprint ed. 45.00 (*0-02-570795-7*) Simon & Schuster. (Scribner).
—Out of the Silent Planet. l.t. ed. 1998. (Science Fiction Ser.). 247p. 24.95 (*0-7838-0411-3*) Thorndike Pr.
—Out of the Silent Planet. 1965. 13.00 (*0-606-01214-1*) Turtleback Bks.
—Out of the Silent Planet. (J). 18.95 o.p. (*0-8488-0563-1*); 1998. lib. bdg. 20.95 (*1-56723-071-7*) Yestermorrow, Inc.
—Perelandra. 1976. (J). 21.95 (*0-8488-0564-X*) Amereon, Ltd.
—Perelandra. unabr. collector's ed. 1983. audio 48.00 (*0-7366-0845-1*, 1796) Books on Tape, Inc.
—Perelandra. 2003. 192p. pap. 12.00 (*0-7432-3491-X*); 1996. (Scribner Classics Ser.). 192p. 22.00 (*0-684-83365-4*); 1996. (Space Trilogy Ser.: No. 2). 224p. pap. 6.95 (*0-684-82382-9*); 1987. (Space Trilogy Ser.: No. 2). 222p. pap. 5.95 o.s.i (*0-02-086950-9*); 1990. (Space Trilogy Ser.: No. 2). 222p. reprint ed. 40.00 (*0-02-570845-7*) Simon & Schuster. (Scribner).
—Perelandra. 1965. 13.00 (*0-606-00445-9*) Turtleback Bks.
—That Hideous Strength. unabr. collector's ed. 1984. audio 88.00 (*0-7366-0844-3*, 1795) Books on Tape, Inc.
—That Hideous Strength. 2003. 384p. pap. 13.00 (*0-7432-3492-8*, Scribner); 1996. 384p. 23.00 (*0-684-83367-0*, Scribner); 1987. 384p. pap. 5.95 o.s.i (*0-02-086960-6*, Scribner Paper Fiction); 1990. 382p. reprint ed. 60.00 (*0-02-571255-1*, Scribner) Simon & Schuster.
—That Hideous Strength. 1965. 13.00 (*0-606-05067-1*) Turtleback Bks.

**RANSOM, JEREMY (FICTITIOUS CHARACTER)—FICTION**

Hunter, Fred. Presence of Mind. 1998. (WWL Mystery Ser.). per. (*0-373-26282-5*, 1-26282-3, Worldwide Library) Harlequin Enterprises, Ltd.
—Presence of Mind. 1994. 19.95 (*0-8027-3245-3*) Walker & Co.
—Ransom at Sea. 2003. 272p. 23.95 (*0-312-30066-2*, Saint Martin's Minotaur) St. Martin's Pr.
—Ransom at the Opera. E-Book 22.95 (*0-312-27643-5*); 2000. 244p. 22.95 (*0-312-26257-4*, Saint Martin's Minotaur) St. Martin's Pr.
—Ransom for a Holiday. 1997. (Jeremy Ransom/Emily Charters Mysteries Ser.). 240p. 20.95 (*0-312-16976-0*, Saint Martin's Minotaur) St. Martin's Pr.
—Ransom for a Killing, 329. 1999. (WWL Mystery Ser.: Vol. 329). mass mkt. (*0-373-26329-5*, Worldwide Library) Harlequin Enterprises, Ltd.
—Ransom for a Killing. 1998. (Jeremy Ransom/Emily Charters Mysteries Ser.). 240p. 21.95 o.p. (*0-312-19323-8*, Saint Martin's Minotaur) St. Martin's Pr.
—Ransom for an Angel. 1996. mass mkt. (*0-373-26224-8*, 1-26224-5, Worldwide Library) Harlequin Enterprises, Ltd.
—Ransom for an Angel. 1995. 246p. 19.95 (*0-8027-3253-4*) Walker & Co.
—Ransom for Our Sins. 1997. per. (*0-373-26249-3*, 1-26249-2, Worldwide Library) Harlequin Enterprises, Ltd.
—Ransom for Our Sins. 1996. 238p. 22.95 (*0-8027-3284-4*) Walker & Co.
—Ransom Unpaid. 2000. (WWL Mystery Ser.: Vol. 365). mass mkt. (*0-373-26365-1*, 1-26365-6, Worldwide Library) Harlequin Enterprises, Ltd.
—Ransom Unpaid. 1999. 216p. 22.95 (*0-312-24233-6*, Saint Martin's Minotaur) St. Martin's Pr.
Smith, Barbara B., et al. 'Tis the Season for Murder: Christmas Crimes. 1998. mass mkt. (*0-373-26290-6*, 1-26290-6, Worldwide Library) Harlequin Enterprises, Ltd.

**RAPP, MITCH (FICTITIOUS CHARACTER)—FICTION**

Flynn, Vince. Separation of Power. l.t. ed. 2002. (Wheeler Large Print Book Ser.). 29.95 (*1-58724-196-X*, Wheeler Publishing, Inc.) Gale Group.
—Separation of Power. 2002. 368p. E-Book 25.00 (*0-7434-4922-3*, Atria); 2001. 368p. 25.00 (*0-671-04733-7*, Atria); 2001. 368p. 25.00 (*0-7434-4837-5*, Atria); 2002. (Illus.). 448p. reprint ed. mass mkt. 7.99 (*0-671-04734-5*, Pocket) Simon & Schuster.
—Separation of Power. abr. ed. 2001. audio 26.00 (*0-7435-0930-7*); audio compact disk 32.00 (*0-7435-0931-5*) Simon & Schuster Audio. (Simon & Schuster Audioworks).
—The Third Option. 2001. 368p. E-Book 9.99 (*0-7434-5158-9*, Atria); 2000. 368p. 24.95 (*0-671-04731-0*, Atria); 2001. (Illus.). 432p. reprint ed. mass mkt. 7.99 (*0-671-04732-9*, Pocket Star) Simon & Schuster.
—Transfer of Power. 2001. 416p. E-Book 9.99 (*0-7434-4924-X*, Atria); 1999. (Illus.). 395p. pap. 24.00 (*0-671-02319-5*, Atria); 2000. (Illus.). 592p. reprint ed. mass mkt. 7.99 (*0-671-02320-9*, Pocket Star) Simon & Schuster.
—Transfer of Power. 2003. audio 14.95 (*0-7435-3253-8*, Encore); 2003. audio compact disk 14.95 (*0-7435-3271-6*, Encore); 1999. (Illus.). 416p. audio 24.00 o.s.i (*0-671-04562-8*, Simon & Schuster Audioworks) Simon & Schuster Audio.
—Transfer of Power. l.t. ed. 2004. 751p. 29.95 (*0-7862-5872-1*) Thorndike Pr.

**RAVEN, JOHN (FICTITIOUS CHARACTER)—FICTION**

MacKenzie, Donald. Loose Cannon. l.t. ed. 1994. (Nightingale Mystery in Large Print Ser.). 269p. lib. bdg. 16.95 (*0-8161-5859-2*, Macmillan Reference USA) Gale Group.

**RAWLINGS, CLAIRE (FICTITIOUS CHARACTER)—FICTION**

Bugge, Carole. Who Killed Blanche Dubois? 1999. (Whodunnit Ser.). 256p. mass mkt. 5.99 o.s.i (*0-425-17195-7*, Prime Crime) Berkley Publishing Group.
—Who Killed Dorian Gray? 2000. (Claire Rawlings Mysteries Ser.). 48p. mass mkt. 5.99 o.s.i (*0-425-17553-7*) Berkley Publishing Group.
—Who Killed Mona Lisa? 2001. (Claire Rawlings Mysteries Ser.). 256p. mass mkt. 5.99 o.s.i (*0-425-17919-2*, Prime Crime) Berkley Publishing Group.

**RAWLINGS, MICKEY (FICTITIOUS CHARACTER)—FICTION**

Soos, Troy. Cincinnati Red Stalkings. 1999. 336p. mass mkt. 5.99 o.s.i (*1-57566-408-9*) Kensington Publishing Corp.
—Cincinnati Red Stalkings, unabr. ed. 1998. (Mickey Rawlings Baseball Ser.: Vol. 5). audio 52.00 (*0-7887-2478-9*, 95553E7) Recorded Bks., LLC.
—The Cincinnati Red Stalkings: A Mickey Rawlings Baseball Mystery. 1998. (Mickey Rawlings Baseball Mystery Ser.). 352p. 20.00 o.s.i (*1-57566-286-8*, Kensington Bks.) Kensington Publishing Corp.
—Hanging Curve. 2000. 352p. mass mkt. 5.99 (*1-57566-656-1*); 1999. 288p. 22.00 o.s.i (*1-57566-455-0*) Kensington Publishing Corp. (Kensington Bks.).
—Hanging Curve, unabr. ed. 1999. (Mickey Rawlings Baseball Ser.: Vol. 6). audio 60.00 (*0-7887-4057-1*, 96129E7) Recorded Bks., LLC.
—Hunting a Detroit Tiger. 352p. 1998. (Mickey Rawlings Baseball Mystery Ser.: Vol. 4). mass mkt. 5.99 o.s.i (*1-57566-291-4*); 1997. 18.95 o.s.i (*1-57566-150-0*) Kensington Publishing Corp.
—Hunting a Detroit Tiger, unabr. ed. 1999. (Mickey Rawlings Baseball Ser.: Vol. 4). audio 60.00 (*0-7887-0926-7*, 95066E7) Recorded Bks., LLC.
—Murder at Ebbets Field. 1996. mass mkt. 4.99 o.s.i (*1-57566-027-X*); 1995. 240p. mass mkt. 16.95 o.s.i (*0-8217-4889-0*) Kensington Publishing Corp.
—Murder at Ebbet's Field, unabr. ed. 1997. (Mickey Rawlings Baseball Ser.: Vol. 2). audio 51.00 (*0-7887-0817-1*, 94967E7) Recorded Bks., LLC.
—Murder at Fenway Park. 1995. 256p. mass mkt. 4.99 o.s.i (*0-8217-4909-9*, Zebra Bks.); 1994. mass mkt. 14.95 o.s.i (*0-8217-4518-2*) Kensington Publishing Corp.
—Murder at Fenway Park. unabr. ed. (Mickey Rawlings Baseball Ser.: Vol. 1). 1999. audio compact disk 58.00 (*0-7887-3418-0*, C1024E7); 1997. audio 51.00 (*0-7887-0874-0*, 95009E7) Recorded Bks., LLC.
—Murder at Fenway Park. l.t. ed. 1995. (Niagara Large Print Ser.). 277p. 29.50 o.p. (*0-7089-5813-3*, Ulverscroft) Thorpe, F. A. Pubs. GBR. *Dist:* Ulverscroft Large Print Bks., Ltd.
—Murder at Wrigley Field. (Mickey Rawlings Baseball Mystery Ser.). 304p. 1997. mass mkt. 5.50 o.s.i (*1-57566-155-1*); 1996. pap. 18.95 o.p. (*1-57566-023-7*) Kensington Publishing Corp.
—Murder at Wrigley Field, unabr. ed. 1998. (Mickey Rawlings Baseball Ser.: Vol. 3). audio 53.00 (*0-7887-2282-4*, 95533E7) Recorded Bks., LLC.

**RAWLINS, EASY (FICTITIOUS CHARACTER)—FICTION**

Mosley, Walter. Bad Boy Brawly Brown: An Easy Rawlins Mystery. abr. ed. 2002. (Easy Rawlins Mystery Ser.: Vol. 6). (Illus.). audio 17.95 (*1-55927-713-0*); audio 39.95 (*1-55927-714-9*); audio compact disk 42.00 o.s.i (*1-55927-715-7*) Audio Renaissance.
—Bad Boy Brawly Brown: An Easy Rawlins Mystery. unabr. ed. 2002. audio 54.00 (*0-7366-8649-5*); audio compact disk 63.00 (*0-7366-8650-9*) Books on Tape, Inc.
—Bad Boy Brawly Brown: An Easy Rawlins Mystery. l.t. ed. 2003. 426p. pap. 12.95 (*1-4104-0169-3*, Wheeler Publishing, Inc.) Gale Group.
—Bad Boy Brawly Brown: An Easy Rawlins Mystery. 2002. 320p. 24.95 (*0-316-07301-6*) Little Brown & Co.
—Bad Boy Brawly Brown: An Easy Rawlins Mystery. (Illus.). mass mkt. 0.00 (*0-671-88430-1*); 1900. pap. (*0-671-03839-7*) Simon & Schuster. (Pocket).
—Bad Boy Brawly Brown: An Easy Rawlins Mystery. l.t. ed. 2002. (Basic Ser.). 32.95 (*0-7862-4593-X*) Thorndike Pr.
—Bad Boy Brawly Brown: An Easy Rawlins Mystery. 2003. (Easy Rawlins Mystery Ser.). 360p. mass mkt. 7.50 (*0-446-61231-6*) Warner Bks., Inc.
—Black Betty. abr. ed. 1994. (Easy Rawlins Mystery Ser.: No. 4). 3p. audio 16.95 (*1-55927-290-2*, 390399) Audio Renaissance.
—Black Betty. unabr. ed. 1994. (Easy Rawlins Mystery Ser.). audio 56.00 (*0-7366-2853-3*, 3561) Books on Tape, Inc.
—Black Betty. 1994. (Easy Rawlins Mystery Ser.). 255p. 19.95 (*0-393-03644-8*) Norton, W. W. & Co., Inc.
—Black Betty. 368p. 1997. pap. 14.00 (*0-671-01983-X*, Pocket); 1995. (Illus.). mass mkt. 6.99 (*0-671-88427-1*, Pocket); 2002. reprint ed. pap. 14.00 (*0-7434-5178-3*, Washington Square Pr.) Simon & Schuster.
—Black Betty: Library Edition, Set. unabr. ed. 1994. audio 59.95 o.p. (*1-55927-302-X*) Audio Renaissance.
—Devil in a Blue Dress. abr. ed. 1993. (Easy Rawlins Mystery Ser.). audio 16.95 (*1-55927-238-4*, 390653) Audio Renaissance.
—Devil in a Blue Dress. unabr. ed. 1994. (Easy Rawlins Mystery Ser.). audio 36.00 (*0-7366-2810-X*, 3524) Books on Tape, Inc.
—Devil in a Blue Dress. 1990. (Easy Rawlins Mystery Ser.). 219p. 19.95 (*0-393-02854-2*) Norton, W. W. & Co., Inc.
—Devil in a Blue Dress. (Easy Rawlins Mystery Ser.). 1997. 240p. pap. 14.00 (*0-671-01982-1*); 2002. 272p. reprint ed. pap. 14.00 (*0-7434-5179-1*) Simon & Schuster. (Washington Square Pr.).
—Devil in a Blue Dress. Ryan, Kevin, ed. 1995. (Easy Rawlins Mystery Ser.). 240p. reprint ed. mass mkt. 6.99 (*0-671-51142-4*, Pocket) Simon & Schuster.
—Devil in a Blue Dress. Chelius, Jane, ed. 1991. 224p. reprint ed. mass mkt. 5.99 (*0-671-74050-4*, Pocket) Simon & Schuster.
—Devil in a Blue Dress: Library Edition, Set. unabr. ed. 1994. audio 39.95 o.p. (*1-55927-269-4*) Audio Renaissance.
—Gone Fishin' 1997. 208p. 22.00 o.p. (*1-57478-025-5*) Black Classic Pr.
—Gone Fishin', Set. abr. ed. 1997. (Easy Rawlins Mystery Ser.). 17.95 o.p. (*0-7871-1402-2*, 394867) NewStar Media, Inc.
—Gone Fishin' (Easy Rawlins Mystery Ser.). 1998. 272p. mass mkt. 6.50 (*0-671-01011-5*, Pocket); 1999. 256p. reprint ed. pap. 14.00 (*0-671-02746-8*, Washington Square Pr.) Simon & Schuster.
—Gone Fishin' l.t. ed. 1997. (Americana Ser.). 203p. 29.95 (*0-7862-1060-5*) Thorndike Pr.
—A Little Yellow Dog. unabr. ed. 1997. (Easy Rawlins Mystery Ser.). audio 48.00 (*0-7366-3732-X*, 4410) Books on Tape, Inc.
—A Little Yellow Dog. (Easy Rawlins Mystery Ser.). 1997. 336p. pap. 14.00 (*0-671-01986-4*, Washington Square Pr.); 1997. 336p. mass mkt. 6.50 (*0-671-88429-8*, Pocket); 2002. 384p. reprint ed. pap. 14.00 (*0-7434-5180-5*, Washington Square Pr.) Simon & Schuster.
—A Little Yellow Dog: An Easy Rawlins Mystery. abr. ed. 1996. (Easy Rawlins Mystery Ser.). audio 16.95 (*1-55927-374-7*, 394056) Audio Renaissance.
—A Little Yellow Dog: An Easy Rawlins Mystery. (Easy Rawlins Mystery Ser.). 1996. 300p. 23.00 (*0-393-03924-2*); 100.00 (*0-393-03978-1*) Norton, W. W. & Co., Inc.
—A Little Yellow Dog: An Easy Rawlins Mystery. l.t. ed. 1996. (Basic Ser.). 447p. 28.95 (*0-7862-0810-4*) Thorndike Pr.
—A Red Death. abr. ed. (Easy Rawlins Mystery Ser.). 1993. audio 16.95 (*1-55927-234-1*, 391455); Set. 1994. audio 59.95 o.p. (*1-55927-270-8*) Audio Renaissance.
—A Red Death. unabr. ed. 1994. audio 48.00 (*0-7366-2833-9*, 3541) Books on Tape, Inc.
—A Red Death. 1991. (Easy Rawlins Mystery Ser.). 284p. 19.95 (*0-393-02998-0*) Norton, W. W. & Co., Inc.
—A Red Death. 1997. (Easy Rawlins Mystery Ser.). 272p. pap. 14.00 (*0-671-01984-8*, Washington Square Pr.); pap. 3.99 (*0-671-01006-9*, Pocket) Simon & Schuster.
—A Red Death. Chelius, Jane, ed. 1992. (Easy Rawlins Mystery Ser.). 256p. reprint ed. mass mkt. 6.99 (*0-671-74989-7*, Pocket) Simon & Schuster.
—White Butterfly. abr. ed. 1993. (Easy Rawlins Mystery Ser.). audio 16.95 (*1-55927-224-4*, 391901) Audio Renaissance.
—White Butterfly. unabr. ed. 1994. (Easy Rawlins Mystery Ser.). audio 48.00 (*0-7366-2798-7*, 3513) Books on Tape, Inc.

—White Butterfly. 1992. (Easy Rawlins Mystery Ser.). 256p. 19.95 (*0-393-03366-X*) Norton, W. W. & Co., Inc.
—White Butterfly. (Easy Rawlins Mystery Ser.). 2002. 320p. pap. 14.00 (*0-7434-5177-5*); 1997. pap. 14.00 (*0-671-01985-6*) Simon & Schuster. (Washington Square Pr.).
—White Butterfly. Chelius, Jane, ed. 1993. (Easy Rawlins Mystery Ser.). 304p. reprint ed. mass mkt. 6.50 (*0-671-86787-3*, Pocket) Simon & Schuster.
—White Butterfly: Library Edition. unabr. ed. 1994. (Easy Rawlins Mystery Ser.). audio 59.95 o.p. (*1-55927-271-6*) Audio Renaissance.

**RAYBURN, JOANN (FICTITIOUS CHARACTER)—FICTION**

Larsen, Jodie. Deadly Company. 1996. 416p. mass mkt. 5.99 o.s.i (*0-451-40707-5*, Onyx) NAL.

**REACHER, JACK (FICTITIOUS CHARACTER)—FICTION**

Child, Lee. Die Trying. 1999. 448p. reprint ed. mass mkt. 7.99 (*0-515-12502-4*, Jove) Berkley Publishing Group.
—Die Trying. abr. ed. 1999. audio 7.99 (*1-56740-296-8*, 1855, Paperback Nova Audio Bks.); 1998. audio 28.95 (*1-56100-791-9*, 14, Bookcassette); 1998. audio 89.25 (*1-56740-570-3*, 864, Unabridged Library Editions); Set. 1998. audio 17.95 o.p. (*1-56740-766-8*, 445, Nova Audio Bks.) Brilliance Audio.
—Die Trying. 1998. 384p. 23.95 o.s.i (*0-399-14379-3*, G. P. Putnam's Sons) Penguin Group (USA) Inc.
—Echo Burning. l.t. ed. 2001. 510p. lib. bdg. 29.95 (*1-58547-135-6*) Ctr. Point Large Print.
—Echo Burning. 2001. (Illus.). 384p. 24.95 o.p. (*0-399-14726-8*) Penguin Group (USA) Inc.
—Killing Floor. 1998. 432p. mass mkt. 7.99 (*0-515-12344-7*, Jove) Berkley Publishing Group.
—Killing Floor. abr. ed. (Jack Reacher Ser.). 2004. audio compact disk 14.99 (*1-59355-558-X*, 5182, Brilliance Audio on CD Value Priced); 1997. audio 7.99 o.s.i (*1-56740-234-8*, 668, Paperback Nova Audio Bks.); 1997. audio 16.95 o.p. (*1-56100-969-5*, 1261, Nova Audio Bks.); 2004. audio 29.95 (*1-59355-557-1*, 5183, Brilliance Audio Unabridged); 1997. audio 27.95 (*1-56100-732-3*, 153, Bookcassette); 1997. audio 105.25 (*1-56100-806-0*, 918, Unabridged Library Editions) Brilliance Audio.
—Killing Floor. l.t. ed. 1998. pap. 23.95 (*1-56895-690-8*, Wheeler Publishing, Inc.) Gale Group.
—Killing Floor. 1997. 368p. 23.95 o.p. (*0-399-14253-3*, G. P. Putnam's Sons) Penguin Group (USA) Inc.
—Persuader: A Jack Reacher Novel. 2003. 352p. 24.95 (*0-385-33666-7*); E-Book 19.95 (*0-440-33386-5*) Dell Publishing. (Delacorte Pr.).
—Persuader: A Jack Reacher Novel. l.t. ed. 2003. (Jack Reacher Novel Ser.). 648p. 31.95 (*0-7862-5684-2*) Thorndike Pr.
—Running Blind. abr. ed. 2000. audio 24.95 o.p. (*1-56740-906-7*, 2100, Nova Audio Bks.); audio 32.95 (*1-56740-362-X*, 2099); audio 73.25 (*1-56740-729-3*, 2101, Unabridged Library Editions) Brilliance Audio.
—Running Blind. 2000. (Jack Reacher Ser.). 360p. 18.95 o.s.i (*0-399-14623-7*) Penguin Group (USA) Inc.
—Tripwire. 2000. 432p. mass mkt. 7.99 (*0-515-12863-5*, Jove) Berkley Publishing Group.
—Tripwire. abr. ed. 2000. audio 7.99 (*1-56740-979-2*, 2115, Paperback Nova Audio Bks.); 1999. audio 17.95 o.p. (*1-56740-834-6*, 1673, Nova Audio Bks.); 2004. audio 29.95 (*1-59355-560-1*, 5185, Brilliance Audio Unabridged); 1999. 14p. audio 89.25 (*1-56740-647-5*, 1672, Unabridged Library Editions); 1999. audio 28.95 (*1-56740-421-9*, 1671, Bookcassette) Brilliance Audio.
—Tripwire. l.t. ed. 2000. (Wheeler Softcover Ser.). pap. 25.95 (*1-56895-912-5*, Wheeler Publishing, Inc.) Gale Group.
—Tripwire, Set. abr. ed. 1999. audio 17.95 Highsmith Inc.
—Tripwire. 1999. 343p. 23.95 o.p. (*0-399-14467-6*, G. P. Putnam's Sons) Penguin Group (USA) Inc.
—Tripwire. unabr. ed. 2002. audio compact disk 104.95 (*1-84283-177-1*); 2000. 12p. audio 94.95 (*1-86042-691-3*, 26913) Soundings, Ltd. GBR. *Dist:* Ulverscroft Large Print Bks., Ltd.
—Without Fail. 2003. 416p. mass mkt. 7.99 (*0-515-13528-3*, Jove) Berkley Publishing Group.
—Without Fail. abr. ed. 2002. (Jack Reacher Ser.: Vol. 6). audio 24.95 o.p. (*1-59086-060-4*, 3613, Nova Audio Bks.); audio 32.95 (*1-59086-062-4*, 3611, Brilliance Audio Unabridged); audio 92.25 (*1-59086-063-2*, 3612, Unabridged Library Editions) Brilliance Audio.
—Without Fail. 2002. lib. bdg. 29.95 (*1-58547-258-1*, Platinum) Ctr. Point Large Print.
—Without Fail. 2002. 432p. 24.95 o.s.i (*0-399-14861-2*, Putnam & Grosset) Penguin Group (USA) Inc.
—Without Fail. 2003. (Jack Reacher Novel Ser.). E-Book 7.99 (*0-7865-4082-6*) Penguin Putnam, Inc E-Books.

**REBUS, INSPECTOR (FICTITIOUS CHARACTER)—FICTION**

Rankin, Ian. Black & Blue. unabr. ed. 1998. audio 80.00 (*0-7366-4176-9*, 4675) Books on Tape, Inc.
—Black & Blue. Date not set. E-Book (*0-312-70694-4*); 1999. (Black & Blue Ser.: Vol. 1). 352p. mass mkt. 6.99 (*0-312-96677-6*, St. Martin's Paperbacks); 1997. (Inspector Rebus Novel Ser.). 394p. 24.95 (*0-312-16783-0*, Saint Martin's Minotaur) St. Martin's Pr.
—Black & Blue: An Inspector Rebus Novel. l.t. ed. 1998. (Mystery Ser.). 623p. 28.95 (*0-7838-8443-5*) Thorndike Pr.
—The Black Book. E-Book 6.50 (*0-312-70693-6*); 2000. 352p. mass mkt. 7.50 (*0-312-97675-5*, St. Martin's Paperbacks) St. Martin's Pr.
—The Black Book: An Inspector Rebus Novel. unabr. ed. 1995. audio 59.95 (*0-7451-6514-1*, CAB 1130) Chivers Audio Bks. GBR. *Dist:* BBC Audiobooks America.
—The Black Book: An Inspector Rebus Novel. 1994. 288p. reprint ed. 21.00 (*1-883402-77-8*, Scribner) Simon & Schuster.
—Dead Souls. 2000. 448p. mass mkt. 6.99 (*0-312-97420-5*, St. Martin's Paperbacks); 1999. 320p. 24.95 o.p. (*0-312-20293-8*, Saint Martin's Minotaur) St. Martin's Pr.
—Death Is Not Enough. mass mkt. (*0-312-97628-3*, St. Martin's Paperbacks) St. Martin's Pr.
—Death Is Not the End: An Instpector Rebus Novella. 2000. 73p. 11.95 (*0-312-26142-X*, Saint Martin's Minotaur) St. Martin's Pr.
—The Falls. 2001. 399p. (*0-7528-2130-X*); pap. (*0-7528-3861-X*) Orion Publishing Group, Ltd. GBR. *Dist:* Trafalgar Square.
—The Falls. 2003. 496p. mass mkt. 7.50 (*0-312-98240-2*, St. Martin's Paperbacks); 2001. 400p. 24.95 (*0-312-20610-0*, Saint Martin's Minotaur) St. Martin's Pr.
—The Hanging Garden. unabr. ed. 1999. audio 64.00 Books on Tape, Inc.
—The Hanging Garden. E-Book 5.99 (*0-312-70698-7*); 1998. 352p. 24.95 o.p. (*0-312-19278-9*, Saint Martin's Minotaur); 1999. 384p. reprint ed. mass mkt. 6.99 (*0-312-96913-9*, St. Martin's Paperbacks) St. Martin's Pr.
—The Hanging Garden. l.t. ed. 1999. (Charnwood Large Print Ser.). 432p. 31.99 o.p. (*0-7089-9124-6*, Ulverscroft) Thorpe, F. A. Pubs. GBR. *Dist:* Ulverscroft Large Print Bks., Ltd., Ulverscroft Large Print Canada, Ltd.
—Hide & Seek. E-Book 6.50 (*0-312-70699-5*); 1997. 224p. mass mkt. 6.50 (*0-312-96397-1*, St. Martin's Paperbacks) St. Martin's Pr.
—Hide & Seek. l.t. ed. 1992. (General Ser.). 464p. 29.99 o.p. (*0-7089-2734-3*, Ulverscroft) Thorpe, F. A. Pubs. GBR. *Dist:* Ulverscroft Large Print Bks., Ltd., Ulverscroft Large Print Canada, Ltd.
—Hide & Seek: A John Rebus Mystery. 1994. 288p. reprint ed. 21.00 (*1-883402-74-3*, Scribner) Simon & Schuster.
—Knots & Crosses. 1987. (Crime Club Ser.). 192p. 12.95 o.s.i (*0-385-24307-3*) Doubleday Publishing.
—Knots & Crosses. 2002. E-Book 6.99 (*0-312-70721-5*); 1995. mass mkt. 7.50 o.s.i (*0-312-95673-8*, St. Martin's Paperbacks); 1995. pap. o.s.i (*0-312-95566-9*, St. Martin's Paperbacks) St. Martin's Pr.
—Let It Bleed. 1996. (Detective John Rebus Novels Ser.). 288p. 20.50 (*0-684-83055-8*, Simon & Schuster); 20.00 (*1-883402-76-X*, Scribner) Simon & Schuster.
—Let It Bleed. E-Book 6.50 (*0-312-70701-0*); 1998. 320p. mass mkt. 7.50 (*0-312-96665-2*, St. Martin's Paperbacks) St. Martin's Pr.
—Let It Bleed: An Inspector Rebus Novel. l.t. ed. 2000. (Mystery Ser.). 502p. 26.95 (*0-7862-2677-3*) Thorndike Pr.
—Mortal Causes. 1995. 21.50 (*1-883402-75-1*, Scribner) Simon & Schuster.
—Mortal Causes. E-Book 6.50 (*0-312-70702-9*); 3rd ed. 1997. 277p. mass mkt. 6.99 (*0-312-96094-8*, St. Martin's Paperbacks) St. Martin's Pr.
—Mortal Causes: A John Rebus Mystery. 1995. 288p. 22.00 o.p. (*0-684-81497-8*, Simon & Schuster) Simon & Schuster.
—Mortal Causes: An Inspector Rebus Novel. unabr. ed. 1996. audio 69.95 BBC Audiobooks America.
—The Question of Blood. unabr. ed. 2004. (Inspector Rebus Novel Ser.). audio 87.25 (*1-59086-490-5*, 4082, Brilliance Audio Unabridged Lib Ed) Brilliance Audio.
—The Question of Blood. 2004. (Inspector Rebus Novel Ser.). 416p. 22.95 (*0-316-09564-8*) Little Brown & Co.
—Resurrection Men. (Inspector Rebus Novel Ser.). 2004. 528p. mass mkt. 7.99 (*0-316-60849-1*); 2003. 448p. 19.95 (*0-316-76684-4*) Little Brown & Co.
—Resurrection Men. 2003. 28.95 (*0-7862-5204-9*) Thorndike Pr.
—Set in Darkness. E-Book 6.99 (*0-312-70703-7*, Tor Bks.) Doherty, Tom Assocs., LLC.
—Set in Darkness. l.t. ed. 2001. 583p. 29.95 (*0-7838-9406-6*, Macmillan Reference USA) Gale Group.
—Set in Darkness. 2000. 432p. 24.95 (*0-312-20609-7*, Saint Martin's Minotaur); 2001. reprint ed. mass mkt. 7.50 (*0-312-97789-1*, St. Martin's Paperbacks) St. Martin's Pr.
—Strip Jack. E-Book 6.50 (*0-312-70704-5*);Vol. 1. 1998. 272p. mass mkt. 6.99 (*0-312-96514-1*, St. Martin's Paperbacks) St. Martin's Pr.
—Strip Jack: An Inspector Rebus Novel. 1994. 272p. 20.95 o.p. (*0-312-10553-3*, Saint Martin's Minotaur) St. Martin's Pr.
—Tooth & Nail. E-Book 6.99 (*0-312-70705-3*); 1996. 304p. reprint ed. mass mkt. 7.50 (*0-312-95878-1*, St. Martin's Paperbacks) St. Martin's Pr.

Spencer, John B. Tooth & Nail. 1998. 184p. pap. 15.95 (*1-899344-31-4*) Do-Not Pr., The GBR. *Dist:* Dufour Editions, Inc.

**RED ORC (FICTITIOUS CHARACTER)—FICTION**

Farmer, Philip Jose. More Than Fire: A World of Tiers Novel. 1995. 320p. pap. 5.99 (*0-8125-1959-0*); 1993. 304p. 20.95 o.p. (*0-312-85280-0*) Doherty, Tom Assocs., LLC. (Tor Bks.).
—Red Orc's Rage. 1991. 18.95 o.p. (*0-312-85036-0*); 1992. 288p. reprint ed. mass mkt. 4.99 (*0-8125-0890-4*) Doherty, Tom Assocs., LLC. (Tor Bks.).

**REE, KILLASHANDRA (FICTITIOUS CHARACTER)—FICTION**

McCaffrey, Anne. Crystal Line. 1993. mass mkt. 5.99 o.s.i (*0-345-38425-3*); 320p. mass mkt. 6.99 (*0-345-38491-1*, Del Rey) Ballantine Bks.
—Crystal Line. abr. ed. 1993. 16.95 o.p. (*1-55800-732-6*) NewStar Media, Inc.
—Crystal Singer. 1982. mass mkt. 2.95 o.p. (*0-345-28598-0*, Del Rey) Ballantine Bks.
—Crystal Singer. 1993. (Super Sound Buy, Dove Ser.). 8.99 o.p. (*0-7871-0024-2*) Penguin Group (USA) Inc.
—Crystal Singer. 1982. 13.04 (*0-606-01372-5*) Turtleback Bks.
—The Crystal Singer. 1985. 320p. mass mkt. 6.99 (*0-345-32786-1*, Del Rey) Ballantine Bks.
—Crystal Singer. abr. ed. 1993. 15.95 o.p. (*1-55800-346-0*, 297027) NewStar Media, Inc.
—Killashandra. 1986. 384p. mass mkt. 7.50 (*0-345-31600-2*, Ballantine Bks.); 1986. mass mkt. 3.75 o.s.i (*0-345-33768-9*); 1985. 384p. 16.95 o.s.i (*0-345-31599-5*, Ballantine Bks.) Ballantine Bks.
—Killashandra. abr. ed. 1993. 15.95 o.p. (*1-55800-350-9*, 41400) NewStar Media, Inc.
—Killashandra. 1993. (Super Sound Buy, Dove Ser.). 8.99 o.p. (*0-7871-0023-4*) Penguin Group (USA) Inc.
—Killashandra. 1985. 303p. 25.00 (*0-89366-187-2*) Ultramarine Publishing Co., Inc.

**REECE, CAITLIN (FICTITIOUS CHARACTER)—FICTION**

Douglas, Lauren W. The Always Anonymous Beast. 1987. (Caitlin Reece Mysteries Ser.). 224p. pap. 8.95 o.p. (*0-941483-04-5*) Naiad Pr., Inc.
—The Daughters of Artemis. 1991. (Caitlin Reece Mystery Ser.). 240p. (Orig.). pap. 9.95 (*0-941483-95-9*) Naiad Pr., Inc.
—Goblin Market. 1993. (Caitlin Reece Mysteries Ser.: No. 5). 224p. pap. 10.95 (*1-56280-047-7*) Naiad Pr., Inc.
—Ninth Life. 1990. (Caitlin Reece Mysteries Ser.). 256p. pap. 9.95 (*0-941483-50-9*) Naiad Pr., Inc.
—A Rage of Maidens: Sixth Caitlin Reece Mystery. 1994. (Caitlin Reece Mysteries Ser.). 224p. pap. 10.95 (*1-56280-068-X*) Naiad Pr., Inc.
—A Tiger's Heart. 1992. (Caitlin Reece Mysteries Ser.: No. 4). 240p. pap. 9.95 (*1-56280-018-3*) Naiad Pr., Inc.

**REED, ANNABEL (FICTITIOUS CHARACTER)—FICTION**

*see Smith, Annabel (Fictitious Character)—Fiction*

**REED, EILEEN (FICTITIOUS CHARACTER)—FICTION**

Ramthun, Bonnie. Earthquake Games. 2001. 352p. mass mkt. 6.99 o.s.i (*0-515-13177-6*, Jove) Berkley Publishing Group.
—Earthquake Games. 2000. 304p. 24.95 o.s.i (*0-399-14666-0*) Penguin Group (USA) Inc.
—Ground Zero. 2000. 352p. reprint ed. mass mkt. 6.99 o.s.i (*0-425-17632-0*) Berkley Publishing Group.
—Ground Zero. 1999. 304p. 24.95 o.p. (*0-399-14509-5*, G. P. Putnam's Sons) Penguin Group (USA) Inc.
—The Thirteenth Skull. Teel, Barbara, ed. 2003. pap. 14.95 (*0-9662696-7-5*, 0966269675) Loveland Pr.

**REED, GARR (FICTITIOUS CHARACTER)—FICTION**

Dickson, Athol. Every Hidden Thing. 1998. (Garr Reed Mystery Ser.: Bk. 2). 352p. pap. 12.99 o.p. (*0-310-22002-5*) Zondervan.
—Whom Shall I Fear? A Garr Reed Mystery. 1996. (Garr Reed Mystery Ser.). 352p. pap. 10.99 (*0-310-20760-6*) Zondervan.

**REES, CLIO (FICTITIOUS CHARACTER)—FICTION**

Bannister, Jo. Gilgamesh. unabr. ed. 1998. audio 63.95 o.p. (*1-85903-013-0*) Magna Story Sound GBR. *Dist:* Ulverscroft Large Print Bks., Ltd.
—The Going down of the Sun. 1989. 12.95 o.s.i (*0-385-26451-8*) Doubleday Publishing.
—Striving with Gods. 1984. (Crime Club Ser.). 192p. 11.95 o.p. (*0-385-19482-X*) Doubleday Publishing.

**REESE, BEN (FICTITIOUS CHARACTER)—FICTION**

Wright, Sally S. Pride & Predator. 1999. (Ben Reese Mysteries Ser.). 336p. mass mkt. 6.50 (*0-345-42589-8*) Ballantine Bks.
—Pride & Predator, 3 vols. 2003. (Ben Reese Mysteries Ser.: Vol. 2). 350p. pap. 9.99 (*1-57673-084-0*, Multnomah Bks.) Multnomah Pubs., Inc.
—Pride & Predator. l.t. ed. 1999. (Christian Mystery Ser.). 507p. 24.95 (*0-7862-1801-0*) Thorndike Pr.
—Publish & Perish. 1999. 224p. mass mkt. 5.99 (*0-345-42588-X*) Ballantine Bks.
—Publish & Perish, 3 vols. 2003. (Ben Reese Mysteries Ser.: Vol. 1 ). 238p. pap. 9.99 (*1-57673-067-0*, Multnomah Bks.) Multnomah Pubs., Inc.
—Publish & Perish. l.t. ed. 1998. (Christian Mystery Ser.). 307p. 24.95 (*0-7862-1566-6*) Thorndike Pr.
—Pursuit & Persuasion. 2003. (Ben Reese Mysteries Ser.: Vol. 3). 364p. pap. 10.99 (*1-57673-416-1*, Multnomah Bks.) Multnomah Pubs., Inc.

**REGAN, FRANCIS X. (FICTITIOUS CHARACTER)—FICTION**

Love, William F. Bishop's Revenge: A Bishop Regan & Davey Goldman Myster. 1993. 276p. 20.00 o.p. (*1-55611-351-X*) Fine, Donald I. Bks.
—Bloody Ten. 1992. 19.95 o.p. (*1-55611-275-0*) Fine, Donald I. Bks.
—Bloody Ten. 1994. mass mkt. (*0-373-26140-3*, Harlequin Bks.) Harlequin Enterprises, Ltd.
—The Chartreuse Clue. 1990. 18.95 o.p. (*1-55611-211-4*) Fine, Donald I. Bks.
—The Chartreuse Clue. 1991. 352p. reprint ed. mass mkt. 5.50 o.p. (*0-451-40273-1*, Onyx) NAL.
—The Fundamentals of Murder. 1991. 18.95 o.p. (*1-55611-233-5*) Fine, Donald I. Bks.
—The Ruby-Red Clue. 1992. Orig. Title: The Fundamentals of Murder. 288p. mass mkt. 4.99 o.s.i (*0-451-40329-0*, Onyx) NAL.

**REID, SAVANNAH (FICTITIOUS CHARACTER)—FICTION**

McKevett, G. A. Bitter Sweets. 304p. 1997. mass mkt. 5.50 o.s.i (*1-57566-169-1*); 1996. 18.95 o.p. (*1-57566-032-6*) Kensington Publishing Corp.
—Cereal Killer. 2004. 304p. 22.00 (*0-7582-0458-2*, Kensington Bks.) Kensington Publishing Corp.
—Cooked Goose. 1999. 320p. mass mkt. 6.50 (*0-7582-0205-9*); 1999. 32p. mass mkt. 5.99 (*1-57566-479-8*); 1998. (Illus.). 304p. 20.00 o.s.i (*1-57566-359-7*) Kensington Publishing Corp.
—Death by Chocolate. 2003. mass mkt. 6.50 (*1-57566-728-2*, Kensington Bks.) Kensington Publishing Corp.
—Death by Chocolate: A Savannah Reid Mystery. 2003. 256p. 22.00 (*1-57566-712-6*) Kensington Publishing Corp.
—Death by Chocolate: A Savannah Reid Mystery. l.t. ed. 2003. (Paperback Ser.). 25.95 (*0-7862-5324-X*) Thorndike Pr.
—Just Desserts. (Savannah Reid Mystery Ser.). 1996. 320p. mass mkt. 4.99 o.s.i (*1-57566-037-7*); 1995. mass mkt. 16.95 o.s.i (*0-8217-4924-2*) Kensington Publishing Corp.
—Killer Calories. (Savannah Reid Mystery Ser.). 2000. 320p. mass mkt. 5.99 (*1-57566-521-2*, Kensington Bks.); 1998. 320p. mass mkt. 5.99 o.s.i (*1-57566-298-1*); 1997. 304p. 18.95 o.s.i (*1-57566-163-2*) Kensington Publishing Corp.
—Peaches & Screams. 2002. 34p. mass mkt. 6.50 (*1-57566-727-4*) Kensington Publishing Corp.
—Sour Grapes. 2001. (Savannah Reid Mystery Ser.). 288p. 22.00 o.s.i (*1-57566-632-4*) Kensington Publishing Corp.
—Sugar & Spite. (Savannah Reid Mystery Ser.). 2001. 34p. mass mkt. 5.99 (*1-57566-637-5*); 2000. 288p. 20.00 o.s.i (*1-57566-493-3*) Kensington Publishing Corp.
—Sugar & Spite. l.t. ed. 2003. (Savannah Reid Mystery Ser.). 397p. pap. 24.95 (*0-7862-5890-X*) Thorndike Pr.

**REILLY, CASSANDRA (FICTITIOUS CHARACTER)—FICTION**

Wilson, Barbara. Case of the Orphaned Bassoonists. 2000. (Cassandra Reilly Mysteries Ser.). (Illus.). 224p. pap. 12.95 (*1-58005-046-8*, Seal Pr.) Avalon Publishing Group.

—Gaudi Afternoon: A Cassandra Reilly Mystery. 172p. 2001. pap. 12.95 (*1-58005-056-5*); 1990. pap. 11.95 (*0-931188-89-X*) Avalon Publishing Group. (Seal Pr.).

—Trouble in Transylvania. 288p. 1993. 18.95 o.p. (*1-878067-34-6*); 3rd ed. 1994. pap. 10.95 (*1-878067-49-4*) Avalon Publishing Group. (Seal Pr.).

**REILLY, NINA (FICTITIOUS CHARACTER)—FICTION**

O'Shaughnessy, Perri. Acts of Malice. abr. ed. 1999. audio 17.95 o.p. (*1-56740-852-4*, 1759, Nova Audio Bks.); audio 73.25 (*1-56740-668-8*, 1758, Unabridged Library Editions); audio 26.95 (*1-56740-442-1*, 1757, Bookcassette) Brilliance Audio.

—Acts of Malice. 2000. 480p. mass mkt. 7.99 (*0-440-22581-7*) Dell Publishing.

—Acts of Malice. l.t. ed. 1999. 503p. 27.95 (*1-56895-766-1*, Wheeler Publishing, Inc.) Gale Group.

—Acts of Malice, Set. abr. ed. 1999. audio 17.95. audio 73.25 Highsmith Inc.

—Breach of Promise. abr. ed. 1999. audio 7.99 o.s.i (*1-56740-315-8*, 1870, Paperback Nova Audio Bks.); 1998. audio 17.95 o.p. (*1-56740-791-9*, 525, Nova Audio Bks.); 1998. audio 28.95 (*1-56740-066-3*, 361, Bookcassette); 1998. audio 89.25 (*1-56740-595-9*, 546, Unabridged Library Editions) Brilliance Audio.

—Breach of Promise. 1999. 560p. mass mkt. 7.99 (*0-440-22473-X*) Broadway Bks.

—Breach of Promise. l.t. ed. 1999. pap. 23.95 (*1-56895-808-0*, Wheeler Publishing, Inc.) Gale Group.

—Breach of Promise. unabr. ed. 1999. audio 89.25 Highsmith Inc.

—Invasion of Privacy. 1997. 544p. mass mkt. 7.99 (*0-440-22069-6*) Dell Publishing.

—Motion to Suppress. abr. ed. 1996. audio 7.99 o.s.i (*1-56740-116-3*, 1327, Paperback Nova Audio Bks.); 1995. audio 16.95 o.p. (*1-56100-423-5*, 1326, Nova Audio Bks.); 1995. audio 89.25 (*1-56100-260-7*, 950, Unabridged Library Editions); 1995. audio 25.95 o.s.i (*1-56100-635-1*, 184, Bookcassette) Brilliance Audio.

—Motion to Suppress. 1996. 480p. mass mkt. 7.99 (*0-440-22068-8*) Dell Publishing.

—Motion to Suppress. l.t. ed. 1999. pap. 24.95 (*1-56895-755-6*, Wheeler Publishing, Inc.) Gale Group.

—Move to Strike. abr. ed. (Nina Reilly Ser.). 2001. audio 12.99 (*1-58788-305-8*, 2681, Paperback Nova Audio Bks.); 2000. audio 24.95 o.p. (*1-56740-901-6*, 2087, Nova Audio Bks.); 2000. audio 32.95 (*1-56740-356-5*, 2086, Brilliance Audio Unabridged); 2000. audio 73.25 (*1-56740-723-4*, 2088, Unabridged Library Editions) Brilliance Audio.

—Move to Strike. 2001. 512p. reprint ed. mass mkt. 7.99 (*0-440-22582-5*) Dell Publishing.

—Move to Strike. l.t. ed. 2000. (Wheeler Large Print Book Ser.). 540p. 27.95 (*1-56895-988-5*, Wheeler Publishing, Inc.) Gale Group.

—Obstruction of Justice. abr. ed. 1998. audio 7.99 o.s.i (*1-56740-240-2*, 1333, Paperback Nova Audio Bks.); 1997. audio 16.95 o.p. (*1-56740-753-6*, 498, Nova Audio Bks.); 1997. audio 89.25 (*1-56740-553-3*, 969, Unabridged Library Editions); 1997. audio 25.95 (*1-56100-774-9*, 201, Bookcassette) Brilliance Audio.

—Obstruction of Justice. 1998. 512p. reprint ed. mass mkt. 7.99 (*0-440-22472-1*) Dell Publishing.

—Obstruction of Justice. 1997. 400p. 23.95 o.s.i (*0-385-31870-7*) Doubleday Publishing.

—Obstruction of Justice. l.t. ed. 2000. 27.95 (*1-56895-845-5*, Wheeler Publishing, Inc.) Gale Group.

—Obstruction of Justice. unabr. ed. 1999. audio 89.25 Highsmith Inc.

—Unfit to Practice. abr. ed. (Nina Reilly Ser.). 2003. audio 12.99 (*1-59086-105-1*, 3662, Brilliance Audio Paperback Audiobooks); 2002. audio 24.95 o.p. (*1-59086-104-3*, 3661, Nova Audio Bks.); 2002. audio 34.95 (*1-59086-102-7*, 3659, Brilliance Audio Unabridged); 2002. audio 87.25 (*1-59086-103-5*, 3660, Unabridged Library Editions); 2002. audio compact disk 40.95 (*1-59086-430-1*, 4022, CD Unabridged); 2002. audio compact disk 102.25 (*1-59086-431-X*, 4023, CD Unabridged Library Edition) Brilliance Audio.

—Unfit to Practice. 2003. 480p. mass mkt. 7.99 (*0-440-23606-1*); 2002. (Illus.). 432p. 24.95 (*0-385-33484-2*, Delacorte Pr.) Dell Publishing.

—Unfit to Practice. unabr. ed. 2003. (Nina Reilly Ser.). audio 19.99 (*1-59335-178-X*, 30274) Soulmate Audio Bks., Inc.

—Unfit to Practice. 2002. 30.95 (*0-7862-4855-6*) Thorndike Pr.

—Unlucky in Law. 2004. 416p. 25.00 (*0-385-33646-2*, Delacorte Pr.) Dell Publishing.

—Writ of Execution. abr. ed. (Nina Reilly Ser.). 2004. audio compact disk 16.99 (*1-59355-680-2*, 5298, Brilliance Audio on CD Value Priced); 2002. audio 12.99 (*1-58788-454-2*, 2724, Paperback Nova Audio Bks.); 2001. audio 24.95 o.p. (*1-58788-453-4*, 2723, Nova Audio Bks.); 2001. audio compact disk 29.95 (*1-58788-489-5*, 2787, CD); 2001. audio compact disk 69.25 (*1-58788-491-7*, 2790, CD Library Edition); 2001. audio 34.95 (*1-58788-451-8*, 2721, Brilliance Audio Unabridged); 2001. audio 87.25 (*1-58788-452-6*, 2722, Unabridged Library Editions) Brilliance Audio.

—Writ of Execution. unabr. ed. 2003. audio 19.99 (*1-59335-130-5*, 30226) Soulmate Audio Bks., Inc.

—Writ of Execution. l.t. ed. 2001. 665p. 29.95 o.p. (*0-7862-3511-X*) Thorndike Pr.

**REILLY, REGAN (FICTITIOUS CHARACTER)—FICTION**

Clark, Carol Higgins. Decked: A Regan Reilly Mystery. 1993. (Super Sound Buy, Dove Ser.). 8.99 o.p. (*1-55800-804-7*); audio 16.95 o.p. (*1-55800-575-7*, Dove Audio) NewStar Media, Inc.

—Decked: A Regan Reilly Mystery. 1999. 288p. mass mkt. 4.50 o.s.i (*0-446-60777-0*); 1993. 288p. mass mkt. 7.99 (*0-446-36470-3*); 1992. 230p. 17.95 (*0-446-51549-3*) Warner Bks., Inc.

—Fleeced: A Regan Reilly Mystery. 2001. E-Book 22.00 (*1-59061-270-1*) Adobe Systems, Inc.

—Fleeced: A Regan Reilly Mystery. (Regan Reilly Mystery Ser.). 2002. (Illus.). 368p. pap. 7.99 (*0-7434-1231-1*, Pocket); 2001. 272p. 22.00 (*0-7432-0581-2*, Scribner); 2001. E-Book 25.00 (*0-7432-1577-X*, Scribner); 2001. 320p. 22.00 (*0-7432-1661-X*, Scribner) Simon & Schuster.

—Fleeced: A Regan Reilly Mystery. 1999. 272p. 22.00 (*0-446-52292-9*) Warner Bks., Inc.

—Iced. 1996. o.s.i (*0-316-87854-5*) Little Brown & Co.

—Iced. unabr. ed. 1995. 29.95 o.p. (*0-7871-0575-9*);Set. audio 17.95 o.p. (*0-7871-0220-2*, 392963) NewStar Media, Inc.

—Iced. 1999. 320p. mass mkt. 4.50 (*0-446-60778-9*); 1996. 320p. mass mkt. 7.99 (*0-446-60198-5*); 1995. 272p. 28.00 (*0-446-51764-X*) Warner Bks., Inc.

—Jinxed: A Reagan Reilly Mystery. 2002. 272p. 23.00 (*0-7432-0582-0*); 272p. 23.00 (*0-7432-4625-X*); 352p. 23.00 (*0-7432-3519-3*) Simon & Schuster. (Scribner).

—Popped: A Regan Reilly Mystery. 2003. 288p. 23.00 (*0-7432-4937-2*); 400p. 24.00 (*0-7432-4749-3*) Simon & Schuster. (Scribner).

—Regan Reilly Mystery, No. 8. 2004. 272p. 23.00 (*0-7432-4275-0*, Scribner) Simon & Schuster.

—Snagged. l.t. ed. 1994. 22.95 o.p. (*0-7927-1915-8*); pap. 20.95 o.p. (*0-7927-1914-X*) BBC Audiobooks America.

—Snagged. abr. ed. 1993. (Regan Reilly Mystery Ser.). audio 16.95 o.p. (*1-55800-787-3*, 391606) NewStar Media, Inc.

—Snagged. 1994. 320p. mass mkt. 7.99 (*0-446-60076-8*); 1993. 227p. 28.00 (*0-446-51548-5*) Warner Bks., Inc.

—Twanged. abr. ed. 2000. audio compact disk 11.99 (*1-57815-517-7*, 1144 CD3, Media Bks. Audio Publishing) Media Bks., L. L. C.

—Twanged. abr. ed. 1997. audio 18.00 (*0-7871-1555-X*); audio 30.00 (*0-7871-1556-8*) NewStar Media, Inc. (Dove Audio).

—Twanged. l.t. ed. 1998. (Basic Ser.). 389p. 29.95 (*0-7862-1417-1*) Thorndike Pr.

—Twanged. abr. ed. 1998. (Regan Reilly Mysteries Ser.). audio 17.98 (*1-57042-612-0*, 395934 ) Time Warner AudioBooks.

—Twanged. 1999. 336p. mass mkt. 7.50 (*0-446-60536-0*); 1998. 272p. 28.00 (*0-446-51763-1*) Warner Bks., Inc.

**REITH, ADAM (FICTITIOUS CHARACTER)—FICTION**

Vance, Jack. City of the Chasch. 1979. (Science Fiction Ser.). mass mkt. 1.75 o.p. (*0-87997-461-3*, UE1461) DAW Bks., Inc.

—The Dirdir: Tschai, Planet of Adventure: 3. 1979. (Science Fiction Ser.). mass mkt. 1.75 o.p. (*0-87997-478-8*, UE1478) DAW Bks., Inc.

—The Dirdir: Tschai, Planet of Adventure: 3. 1983. 240p. lib. bdg. 15.95 o.p. (*0-934438-24-2*) Underwood Bks., Inc.

—Planet of Adventure. 1993. 541p. pap. 15.95 (*0-312-85488-9*, Orb Bks.) Doherty, Tom Assocs., LLC.

—Planet of Adventure: City of the Chasch; Servants of the Wankh the Dirdir; The Pnume. 1993. 24.95 o.p. (*0-312-85487-0*, Tor Bks.) Doherty, Tom Assocs., LLC.

—The Pnume. 1983. 224p. lib. bdg. 15.95 o.p. (*0-934438-57-9*) Underwood Bks., Inc.

—Servants of the Wankh: Tschai, Planet of Adventure, No. 2. 1979. (Science Fiction Ser.). mass mkt. 1.75 o.p. (*0-87997-467-2*, UE1467) DAW Bks., Inc.

**RELKIN (FICTITIOUS CHARACTER)—FICTION**

Rowley, Christopher B. Battle Dragon. 1995. (Basil Broketail Ser.). 416p. mass mkt. 5.99 o.s.i (*0-451-45343-3*, ROC) NAL.

—Bazil Broketail. 1992. (Bazil Broketail Ser.). 480p. mass mkt. 6.99 (*0-451-45206-2*, ROC) NAL.

—A Dragon at World's End. 1997. (Bazil Broketail Ser.). 416p. mass mkt. 6.99 o.s.i (*0-451-45546-0*, ROC) NAL.

—Dragon Ultimate. 1999. (Bazil Broketail Ser.). 384p. mass mkt. 6.99 o.s.i (*0-451-45548-7*, ROC) NAL.

—Dragons of Argonath. 1998. (Bazil Broketail Ser.: Vol. 6). 432p. mass mkt. 6.99 o.s.i (*0-451-45547-9*, ROC) NAL.

—Dragons of War. 1994. (Bazil Broketail Ser.). 496p. (Orig.). mass mkt. 6.99 o.s.i (*0-451-45342-5*, ROC) NAL.

—A Sword for a Dragon. 1993. (Bazil Broketail Ser.). 480p. (Orig.). mass mkt. 6.99 o.s.i (*0-451-45235-6*, ROC) NAL.

**REMO (FICTITIOUS CHARACTER)—FICTION**

Murphy, Warren. Acid Rock. 1989. (Destroyer Ser.: No. 13). mass mkt. 3.50 o.s.i (*1-55817-195-9*, Pinnacle Bks.) Kensington Publishing Corp.

—American Obsession. 1997. (Destroyer Ser.: No. 109). per. (*0-373-63224-X*, 1-63224-9, Worldwide Library) Harlequin Enterprises, Ltd.

—Assassin's Play-Off. 1989. (Destroyer Ser.: No. 20). mass mkt. 3.50 o.s.i (*1-55817-211-4*, Pinnacle Bks.) Kensington Publishing Corp.

—Bamboo Dragon. 1997. (Destroyer Ser.: No. 108). per. (*0-373-63223-1*, 1-63223-1, Worldwide Library) Harlequin Enterprises, Ltd.

—Bay City Blast. 1990. (Destroyer Ser.: No. 38). mass mkt. 3.50 o.s.i (*1-55817-443-5*, Pinnacle Bks.) Kensington Publishing Corp.

—Blue Smoke. 1989. (Destroyer Ser.: No. 78). mass mkt. 4.50 o.p. (*0-451-16219-6*, Signet Bks.) NAL.

—Bottom Line. 1990. (Destroyer Ser.: No. 37). mass mkt. 3.50 o.s.i (*1-55817-419-2*, Pinnacle Bks.) Kensington Publishing Corp.

—Brain Drain. 1989. (Destroyer Ser.: No. 22). (Orig.). mass mkt. 3.50 o.p. (*1-55817-247-5*, Pinnacle Bks.) Kensington Publishing Corp.

—Chained Reaction. 1990. (Destroyer Ser.: No. 34). mass mkt. 3.50 o.s.i (*1-55817-383-8*, Pinnacle Bks.) Kensington Publishing Corp.

—Child's Play. 1989. (Destroyer Ser.: No. 23). mass mkt. 3.50 o.s.i (*1-55817-258-0*, Pinnacle Bks.) Kensington Publishing Corp.

—Chinese Puzzle. (Destroyer Ser.: No. 3). (Orig.). 1988. mass mkt. 3.50 o.s.i (*1-55817-038-3*); 1984. 192p. pap. 2.95 o.p. (*0-523-42414-0*) Kensington Publishing Corp. (Pinnacle Bks.).

—The Color of Fear. 1995. (Destroyer Ser.: No. 99). per. (*0-373-63214-2*, 1-63214-0, Harlequin Bks.) Harlequin Enterprises, Ltd.

—Created, the Destroyer. 1988. (Destroyer Ser.: No. 1). mass mkt. 3.50 o.p. (*1-55817-036-7*, Pinnacle Bks.) Kensington Publishing Corp.

—Created, the Destroyer. 1986. (Destroyer Ser.: No. 1). pap. 2.50 o.p. (*0-380-70195-2*, Avon Bks.) Morrow/Avon.

—Dangerous Games. 1991. (Destroyer Ser.: No. 40). 192p. (Orig.). mass mkt. 3.50 o.s.i (*1-55817-468-0*, Pinnacle Bks.) Kensington Publishing Corp.

—Date with Death. 1984. (Destroyer Ser.: No. 57). 192p. pap. 2.50 o.p. (*0-523-41567-2*, Pinnacle Bks.) Kensington Publishing Corp.

—Deadly Seeds. 1989. (Destroyer Ser.: No. 21). (Orig.). mass mkt. 3.50 o.s.i (*1-55817-237-8*, Pinnacle Bks.) Kensington Publishing Corp.

—Death Check. 1988. (Destroyer Ser.: No. 2). mass mkt. 3.50 o.s.i (*1-55817-037-5*, Pinnacle Bks.) Kensington Publishing Corp.

—Death Sentence. 1990. (Destroyer Ser.: No. 80). mass mkt. 3.95 o.p. (*0-451-16471-7*, Signet Bks.) NAL.

—Death Therapy. 1988. (Destroyer Ser.: No. 6). mass mkt. 3.50 o.s.i (*1-55817-041-3*, Pinnacle Bks.) Kensington Publishing Corp.

—Dr. Quake. 1988. (Destroyer Ser.: No. 5). mass mkt. 3.50 o.s.i (*1-55817-040-5*, Pinnacle Bks.) Kensington Publishing Corp.

—Encounter Group. 1984. (Destroyer Ser.: No. 56). 192p. pap. 2.50 o.p. (*0-523-41566-4*, Pinnacle Bks.) Kensington Publishing Corp.

—Feast or Famine. 1997. (Destroyer Ser.: No. 107). per. (*0-373-63222-3*, 1-63222-3, Worldwide Library) Harlequin Enterprises, Ltd.

—The Final Death. 1990. (Destroyer Ser.: No. 29). mass mkt. 3.50 o.s.i (*1-55817-319-6*, Pinnacle Bks.) Kensington Publishing Corp.

—Firing Line. 1991. (Destroyer Ser.: No. 41). 192p. (Orig.). mass mkt. 3.50 o.s.i (*1-55817-483-4*, Pinnacle Bks.) Kensington Publishing Corp.

—Funny Money. 1989. (Destroyer Ser.: No. 18). mass mkt. 3.50 o.s.i (*1-55817-200-9*, Pinnacle Bks.) Kensington Publishing Corp.

—The Head Men. 1990. (Destroyer Ser.: No. 31). mass mkt. 3.50 o.s.i (*1-55817-343-9*, Pinnacle Bks.) Kensington Publishing Corp.

—High Priestess. 1999. (Destroyer Ser.: No. 95). pap. 4.50 (*0-451-17771-1*, Signet Bks.) NAL.

—Holy Terror. 1989. (Destroyer Ser.: No. 19). mass mkt. 3.50 o.s.i (*1-55817-210-6*, Pinnacle Bks.) Kensington Publishing Corp.

—In Enemy Hands. (Destroyer Ser.: No. 26). 1989. mass mkt. 3.50 o.s.i (*1-55817-285-8*); 1979. pap. 1.75 o.p. (*0-523-40902-8*) Kensington Publishing Corp. (Pinnacle Bks.).

—Infernal Revenue. 1994. (Destroyer Ser.: No. 96). mass mkt. (*0-373-63211-8*, 1-63211-6, Harlequin Bks.) Harlequin Enterprises, Ltd.

—Judgement Day. 1989. (Destroyer Ser.: No. 14). mass mkt. 3.50 o.s.i (*1-55817-196-7*) Kensington Publishing Corp.

—Killer Chromosomes. (Destroyer Ser.: No. 32). 1990. mass mkt. 3.50 o.s.i (*1-55817-355-2*); 1979. pap. 1.75 o.p. (*0-523-40908-7*) Kensington Publishing Corp. (Pinnacle Bks.).

—Killing Time. 1982. (Destroyer Ser.: No. 50). 208p. pap. 2.25 o.p. (*0-523-41560-5*, Pinnacle Bks.) Kensington Publishing Corp.

—King's Curse. (Destroyer Ser.: No. 24). 1989. mass mkt. 3.50 o.s.i (*1-55817-268-8*); 1980. pap. 1.95 o.p. (*0-523-41239-8*) Kensington Publishing Corp. (Pinnacle Bks.).

—Last Call. (Destroyer Ser.: No. 35). 1990. mass mkt. 3.50 o.p. (*1-55817-395-1*); 1980. pap. 1.95 o.p. (*0-523-41250-9*) Kensington Publishing Corp. (Pinnacle Bks.).

—Last Drop. 1983. (Destroyer Ser.: No. 54). 208p. pap. 2.50 o.p. (*0-523-41564-8*, Pinnacle Bks.) Kensington Publishing Corp.

—The Last Temple. 1989. (Destroyer Ser.: No. 27). mass mkt. 3.50 o.s.i (*1-55817-295-5*, Pinnacle Bks.) Kensington Publishing Corp.

—Last War Dance. 1989. (Destroyer Ser.: No. 17). mass mkt. 3.50 o.s.i (*1-55817-199-1*, Pinnacle Bks.) Kensington Publishing Corp.

—Mafia Fix. (Destroyer Ser.: No. 4). 1988. mass mkt. 3.50 o.s.i (*1-55817-039-1*); 1982. 192p. pap. 2.25 o.p. (*0-523-41758-6*) Kensington Publishing Corp. (Pinnacle Bks.).

—Missing Link. (Destroyer Ser.: No. 39). 1990. mass mkt. 3.50 o.s.i (*1-55817-457-5*); 1980. pap. 1.95 o.p. (*0-523-41254-1*) Kensington Publishing Corp. (Pinnacle Bks.).

—Mugger Blood. 1990. (Destroyer Ser.: No. 30). mass mkt. 3.50 o.s.i (*1-55817-328-5*, Pinnacle Bks.) Kensington Publishing Corp.

—Murder Ward. (Destroyer Ser.: No. 15). 1989. mass mkt. 3.50 o.s.i (*1-55817-197-5*); 1981. pap. 2.25 o.p. (*0-523-41768-3*) Kensington Publishing Corp. (Pinnacle Bks.).

—Never Say Die. 1998. (Destroyer Ser.: No. 110). per. (*0-373-63225-8*, 1-63225-6, Worldwide Library) Harlequin Enterprises, Ltd.

—Next of Kin. 1981. (Destroyer Ser.: No. 46). 192p. pap. 1.95 o.p. (*0-523-40720-3*, Pinnacle Bks.) Kensington Publishing Corp.

—Oil Slick. 1989. (Destroyer Ser.: No. 16). mass mkt. 3.50 o.s.i (*1-55817-198-3*, Pinnacle Bks.) Kensington Publishing Corp.

—Power Play. (Destroyer Ser.: No. 36). 1990. mass mkt. 3.50 o.s.i (*1-55817-406-0*); 1981. pap. 1.95 o.p. (*0-523-41251-7*) Kensington Publishing Corp. (Pinnacle Bks.).

—Profit Motive. 1982. (Destroyer Ser.: No. 48). 256p. pap. 2.75 o.p. (*0-523-41558-3*, Pinnacle Bks.) Kensington Publishing Corp.

—Prophet of Doom. 1998. (Destroyer Ser.: No. 111). per. (*0-373-63226-6*, 1-63226-4, Worldwide Library) Harlequin Enterprises, Ltd.

—Scorched Earth. 1996. (Destroyer Ser.: No. 105). per. (*0-373-63220-7*, 1-63220-7, Worldwide Library) Harlequin Enterprises, Ltd.

—Ship of Death. 1990. (Destroyer Ser.: No. 28). mass mkt. 3.50 o.s.i (*1-55817-310-2*, Pinnacle Bks.) Kensington Publishing Corp.

—Shock Value. 1983. (Destroyer Ser.: No. 51). 208p. pap. text 2.25 o.p. (*0-523-41561-3*, Pinnacle Bks.) Kensington Publishing Corp.

—Spoils of War. 1981. (Destroyer Ser.: No. 45). 192p. pap. 1.95 o.p. (*0-523-40719-X*, Pinnacle Bks.) Kensington Publishing Corp.

—Survival Course. 1990. (Destroyer Ser.: No. 82). mass mkt. 4.50 o.p. (*0-451-16736-8*, Signet Bks.) NAL.

—Sweet Dreams. (Destroyer Ser.: No. 25). 1989. mass mkt. 3.50 o.s.i (*1-55817-276-9*); 1979. pap. 1.75 o.p. (*0-523-40901-X*) Kensington Publishing Corp. (Pinnacle Bks.).

—Terror Squad. 1985. (Destroyer Ser.: No. 10). 192p. pap. 2.95 o.p. (*0-523-42415-9*, Pinnacle Bks.) Kensington Publishing Corp.

—Timber Lane. 1981. (Destroyer Ser.: No. 42). 192p. pap. 2.25 o.p. (*0-523-41767-5*, Pinnacle Bks.) Kensington Publishing Corp.

—Time Trial. 1983. (Destroyer Ser.: No. 53). 208p. pap. 2.50 o.p. (*0-523-41563-X*, Pinnacle Bks.) Kensington Publishing Corp.

—Voodoo Die. (Destroyer Ser.: No. 33). 1990. mass mkt. 3.50 o.s.i (*1-55817-370-6*); 1979. pap. 1.75 o.p. (*0-523-40909-5*) Kensington Publishing Corp. (Pinnacle Bks.).

—White Water. 1997. (Destroyer Ser.: No. 106). 352p. per. (*0-373-63221-5*, 1-63221-5, Worldwide Library) Harlequin Enterprises, Ltd.

Murphy, Warren & Sapir. Angry White Mailmen. 1996. (Destroyer Ser.: No. 104). per. (*0-373-63219-3*, 1-63219-9, Worldwide Library) Harlequin Enterprises, Ltd.

Murphy, Warren & Sapir, Richard. Angry White Mailmen. abr. ed. 2000. (Destroyer Ser.: No. 104). audio 7.99 (*1-55204-441-6*, GOL-3441) Durkin Hayes Publishing Ltd.

—Arms of Kali. 1984. (Destroyer Ser.: No. 59). mass mkt. 3.95 o.p. (*0-451-15569-6*, Signet Bks.) NAL.

—Bidding War. abr. ed. 2000. (Destroyer Ser.: Vol. 101). audio 7.99 (*1-55204-426-2*, GOL-3426) Durkin Hayes Publishing Ltd.

—Blood Ties. 1987. (Destroyer Ser.). mass mkt. 4.50 o.p. (*0-451-16813-5*); (Destroyer Ser.: No. 69). mass mkt. 3.95 o.p. (*0-451-14879-7*) NAL. (Signet Bks.).

—Brain Drain. 1985. (Destroyer Ser.: No. 22). 192p. (Orig.). pap. 2.95 o.p. (*0-523-42418-3*, Pinnacle Bks.) Kensington Publishing Corp.

—Coin of the Realm. 1989. (Destroyer Ser.: No. 77). 256p. (Orig.). mass mkt. 3.95 o.p. (*0-451-16057-6*, Signet Bks.) NAL.

—The Color of Fear. unabr. ed. 1999. (Destroyer Ser.: No. 99). audio 7.99 (*1-55204-417-3*, GOL-3417) Durkin Hayes Publishing Ltd.

—Deadly Genes. 1999. (Destroyer Ser.: No. 117). per. (*0-373-63232-0*, 1-63232-2, Worldwide Library) Harlequin Enterprises, Ltd.

—The Destroyer Collector's Edition. collector's ed. 2000. No. 2. audio 21.99 (*1-55204-923-X*, CGS-9923); No. 3. audio 21.99 (*1-55204-931-0*, CGS-9931) Durkin Hayes Publishing Ltd.

—Eleventh Hour. 1987. (Destroyer Ser.: No. 70). 224p. mass mkt. 3.50 o.p. (*0-451-15001-5*, Signet Bks.) NAL.

—The Empire Dreams. 1998. (Destroyer Ser.: No. 113). 352p. per. (*0-373-63228-2*, 1-63228-0, Worldwide Library) Harlequin Enterprises, Ltd.

—The End of the Game. 1985. (Destroyer Ser.: No. 60). mass mkt. 3.50 o.p. (*0-451-15265-4*, Signet Bks.) NAL.

—Engines of Destruction. 1996. (Destroyer Ser.: No. 103). per. (*0-373-63218-5*, 1-63218-1, Worldwide Library) Harlequin Enterprises, Ltd.

—Fade to Black. 2000. (Destroyer Ser.: No. 119). 348p. per. (*0-373-63234-7*, Harlequin Bks.) Harlequin Enterprises, Ltd.

—Failing Marks. 1999. (Destroyer Ser.: No. 114). per. (*0-373-63229-0*, Harlequin Bks.) Harlequin Enterprises, Ltd.

—Final Crusade. 1989. (Destroyer Ser.: No. 76). 224p. mass mkt. 4.50 o.p. (*0-451-15913-6*, Signet Bks.) NAL.

—The Final Reel. 1999. (Destroyer Ser.: No. 116). per. (*0-373-63231-2*, Worldwide Library) Harlequin Enterprises, Ltd.

—Fool's Gold. 1983. (Destroyer Ser.: No. 52). 256p. pap. 2.95 o.p. (*0-523-41562-1*, Pinnacle Bks.) Kensington Publishing Corp.

—High Priestess. abr. ed. 1999. (Destroyer Ser.: No. 95). audio 7.99 (*1-55204-393-2*, GOL-3393) Durkin Hayes Publishing Ltd.

—High Priestess. 1994. (Destroyer Ser.: No. 95). per. (*0-373-63210-X*, Harlequin Bks.) Harlequin Enterprises, Ltd.

—Identity Crisis. abr. ed. 1999. (Destroyer Ser.: No. 97). audio 7.99 (*1-55204-405-X*, GOL-3405) Durkin Hayes Publishing Ltd.

—Identity Crisis. 1994. (Destroyer Ser.: No. 97). per. (*0-373-63212-6*, 1-63212-4, Harlequin Bks.) Harlequin Enterprises, Ltd.

—Infernal Revenue. abr. ed. 1999. (Destroyer Ser.: No. 96). audio 7.99 (*1-55204-399-1*, GOL-3399) Durkin Hayes Publishing Ltd.

—Kill or Cure. 1988. (Destroyer Ser.: No. 11). (Orig.). mass mkt. 3.50 o.s.i (*1-55817-148-7*, Pinnacle Bks.) Kensington Publishing Corp.

—Killer Watts. 2000. (Destroyer Ser.: No. 118). mass mkt. (*0-373-63233-9*, 1-63233-0, Worldwide Library) Harlequin Enterprises, Ltd.

—The Last Alchemist. 1986. (Destroyer Ser.). mass mkt. 2.95 o.p. (*0-451-14221-7*); (Destroyer Ser.: No. 64). mass mkt. 3.50 o.p. (*0-451-15274-3*) NAL. (Signet Bks.).

—The Last Monarch. 2000. (Destroyer Ser.: No. 120). 352p. per. (*0-373-63235-5*, 1-63235-5, Worldwide Library) Harlequin Enterprises, Ltd.

—Last Rites. unabr. ed. 1999. (Destroyer Ser.: No. 100). audio 7.99 (*1-55204-423-8*, GOL-3423) Durkin Hayes Publishing Ltd.

—Line of Succession. 1988. (Destroyer Ser.: No. 73). 256p. mass mkt. 3.95 o.p. (*0-451-15396-0*, Signet Bks.) NAL.

—Look into My Eyes. 1987. (Destroyer Ser.: No. 67). mass mkt. 4.50 o.p. (*0-451-14646-8*, Signet Bks.) NAL.

—Lords of the Earth. 1985. (Destroyer Ser.: No. 61). mass mkt. 3.50 o.p. (*0-451-13560-1*, Signet Bks.) NAL.

—Lost Yesterday. 1986. (Destroyer Ser.: No. 65). 256p. mass mkt. 3.95 o.p. (*0-451-15735-4*, Signet Bks.) NAL.

—Master's Challenge. 1984. (Destroyer Ser.: No. 55). 256p. pap. 2.95 o.p. (*0-523-41565-6*, Pinnacle Bks.) Kensington Publishing Corp.

—Misfortune Teller. 1999. (Destroyer Ser.: No. 115). per. (*0-373-63230-4*, 1-63230-6, Harlequin Bks.) Harlequin Enterprises, Ltd.

—Mugger Blood. 1985. (Destroyer Ser.: No. 30). 192p. pap. 2.95 o.p. (*0-523-42419-1*, Pinnacle Bks.) Kensington Publishing Corp.

—Murder's Shield. 1988. (Destroyer Ser.: No. 9). (Orig.). mass mkt. 3.50 o.s.i (*1-55817-146-0*, Pinnacle Bks.) Kensington Publishing Corp.

—An Old-Fashioned War. 1987. (Destroyer Ser.: No. 68). mass mkt. 4.50 o.p. (*0-451-14776-6*, Signet Bks.) NAL.

—Rain of Terror. 1989. (Destroyer Ser.: No. 75). mass mkt. 3.95 o.p. (*0-451-15752-4*, Signet Bks.) NAL.

—Return Engagement. 1988. (Destroyer Ser.: No. 71). 256p. mass mkt. 3.95 o.p. (*0-451-15244-1*, Signet Bks.) NAL.

—Scorched Earth. abr. ed. 2000. (Destroyer Ser.: No. 105). audio 7.99 (*1-55204-446-7*, GOL-3446) Durkin Hayes Publishing Ltd.

—The Seventh Stone. 1985. (Destroyer Ser.). mass mkt. 2.95 o.p. (*0-451-13756-6*); (Destroyer Ser.: No. 62). mass mkt. 3.50 o.p. (*0-451-15571-8*) NAL. (Signet Bks.).

—Skull Duggery. 1991. (Destroyer Ser.: No. 83). 256p. mass mkt. 4.50 o.p. (*0-451-16905-0*, Signet Bks.) NAL.

—The Sky Is Falling. 1986. (Destroyer Ser.: No. 63). mass mkt. 3.95 o.p. (*0-451-15279-4*, Signet Bks.) NAL.

—Slave Safari. 1988. (Destroyer Ser.: No. 12). mass mkt. 3.50 o.s.i (*1-55817-149-5*, Pinnacle Bks.) Kensington Publishing Corp.

—Sole Survivor. 1988. (Destroyer Ser.: No. 72). mass mkt. 3.50 o.p. (*0-451-15359-6*, Signet Bks.) NAL.

—Sue Me. 1986. (Destroyer Ser.). mass mkt. 2.95 o.p. (*0-451-14556-9*); (Destroyer Ser.: No. 66). mass mkt. 3.50 o.p. (*0-451-15278-6*) NAL. (Signet Bks.).

—Summit Chase. 1988. (Destroyer Ser.: No. 8). (Orig.). mass mkt. 3.50 o.p. (*1-55817-145-2*, Pinnacle Bks.) Kensington Publishing Corp.

—Target of Opportunity. unabr. ed. 1999. (Destroyer Ser.: No. 98). audio 7.99 (*1-55204-411-4*, GOL-3411) Durkin Hayes Publishing Ltd.

—Target of Opportunity. 1994. (Destroyer Ser.: No. 98). mass mkt. (*0-373-63213-4*, 1-63213-2, Harlequin Bks.) Harlequin Enterprises, Ltd.

—Terror Squad. 1988. (Destroyer Ser.: No. 10). mass mkt. 3.50 o.s.i (*1-55817-147-9*, Pinnacle Bks.) Kensington Publishing Corp.

—Total Recall. 1984. (Destroyer Ser.: No. 58). pap. 2.50 o.p. (*0-523-41568-0*, Pinnacle Bks.) Kensington Publishing Corp.

—The Ultimate Death. 1992. (Destroyer Ser.: No. 88). 256p. (Orig.). mass mkt. 4.50 o.s.i (*0-451-17115-2*, Signet Bks.) NAL.

—Union Bust. 1988. (Destroyer Ser.: No. 7). (Orig.). mass mkt. 3.50 o.s.i (*1-55817-144-4*, Pinnacle Bks.) Kensington Publishing Corp.

—Unite & Conquer. 1996. (Destroyer Ser.: No. 102). 346p. per. (*0-373-63217-7*, 1-63217-3, Worldwide Library) Harlequin Enterprises, Ltd.

—Walking Wounded. 1988. (Destroyer Ser.: No. 74). mass mkt. 3.50 o.p. (*0-451-15600-5*, Signet Bks.) NAL.

—White Water. abr. ed. 2000. (Destroyer Ser.: No. 106). audio 7.99 (*1-55204-451-3*, GOL-3451) Durkin Hayes Publishing Ltd.

Murphy, Warren & Sapir, Richard, creators. Arabian Nightmare. 1991. (Destroyer Ser.: No. 86). 256p. mass mkt. 4.50 o.p. (*0-451-17060-1*, Signet Bks.) NAL.

—Bidding War. 1995. (Destroyer Ser.: No. 101). 347p. per. (*0-373-63216-9*, 1-63216-5, Worldwide Library) Harlequin Enterprises, Ltd.

—Blood Lust. 1991. (Destroyer Ser.: No. 85). (Illus.). 256p. mass mkt. 4.50 o.p. (*0-451-16990-5*, Signet Bks.) NAL.

—Last Rites. 1995. (Destroyer Ser.: No. 100). 349p. per. (*0-373-63215-0*, 1-63215-7, Harlequin Bks.) Harlequin Enterprises, Ltd.

Murphy, Warren & Sapir, Richard, eds. Hostile Takeover. 1990. (Destroyer Ser.: No. 81). 256p. mass mkt. 4.50 o.p. (*0-451-16601-9*, Signet Bks.) NAL.

Sapir, Richard. Mob Psychology. 1992. (Destroyer Ser.: No. 87). 256p. mass mkt. 4.50 o.p. (*0-451-17114-4*, Signet Bks.) NAL.

Sapir, Richard, ed. Cold Warrior. 1993. (Destroyer Ser.: No. 91). 256p. (Orig.). mass mkt. 4.50 o.p. (*0-451-17484-4*, Signet Bks.) NAL.

—Dark Horse. 1992. (Destroyer Ser.: No. 89). 256p. (Orig.). mass mkt. 4.50 o.s.i (*0-451-17116-0*, Signet Bks.) NAL.

—Feeding Frenzy. 1993. (Destroyer Ser.: No. 94). 256p. (Orig.). mass mkt. 4.50 o.p. (*0-451-17700-2*, Signet Bks.) NAL.

—Ghost in the Machine. 1992. (Destroyer Ser.: No. 90). 256p. mass mkt. 4.50 o.p. (*0-451-17326-0*, Signet Bks.) NAL.

—Ground Zero. 1991. (Destroyer Ser.: No. 84). 256p. (Orig.). mass mkt. 4.50 o.p. (*0-451-16934-4*, Signet Bks.) NAL.

—The Last Dragon. 1993. (Destroyer Ser.: No. 92). 256p. (Orig.). mass mkt. 4.50 o.s.i (*0-451-17558-1*, Signet Bks.) NAL.

—Shooting Schedule. 1990. (Destroyer Ser.: No. 79). 256p. mass mkt. 4.50 o.p. (*0-451-16358-3*, Signet Bks.) NAL.

—Terminal Transmission. 1993. (Destroyer Ser.: No. 93). 256p. (Orig.). mass mkt. 4.50 o.p. (*0-451-17668-5*, Signet Bks.) NAL.

Sapir, Richard & Murphy, Warren. Political Pressure. 2004. (Destroyer Ser.: No. 135). 352p. mass mkt. (*0-373-63250-9*, Gold Eagle) Harlequin Enterprises, Ltd.

**REMUS, UNCLE (FICTITIOUS CHARACTER)—FICTION**

Harris, Joel Chandler. Nights with Uncle Remus: Myths & Legends of the Old Plantation. Bickley, Bruce, ed. 2003. (Penguin Classics Ser.). 384p. pap. 14.00 (*0-14-243766-2*, Penguin Classics) Viking Penguin.

**RENARD, GIL (FICTITIOUS CHARACTER)—FICTION**

Abrahams, Peter. The Fan. l.t. ed. 1996. 352p. lib. bdg. 24.95 (*1-57490-062-5*, Beeler Large Print Bks.) Beeler, Thomas T. Publisher.

—The Fan, Set. abr. ed. 1995. audio 16.95 (*1-879371-93-6*, 392956) Publishing Mills, Inc., The.

—The Fan. 338p. pap. 5.98 o.p. (*0-7651-0362-1*) Smithmark Pubs., Inc.

—The Fan. abr. ed. 1995. audio 17.00 o.p. (*1-57042-237-0*, 4-522370) Time Warner AudioBooks.

—The Fan. 352p. 1996. mass mkt. 5.99 o.p. (*0-446-60314-7*); 1995. 22.95 o.s.i (*0-446-51860-3*) Warner Bks., Inc.

**RENKO, ARKADY (FICTITIOUS CHARACTER)—FICTION**

Smith, Martin Cruz. Gorky Park. 2000. mass mkt. 6.99 (*0-345-91704-9*); 1993. mass mkt. 5.99 o.s.i (*0-345-90112-6*); 1982. 448p. mass mkt. 7.99 (*0-345-29834-9*); 1981. mass mkt. 2.95 o.s.i (*0-345-30392-X*) Ballantine Bks.

—Gorky Park. l.t. ed. 1981. 18.95 o.p. (*0-8161-3295-X*, Macmillan Reference USA) Gale Group.

—Gorky Park. 1993. 4.99 o.p. (*0-517-10699-X*) Random Hse. Value Publishing.

—Havana Bay. 2001. (Illus.). 352p. mass mkt. 7.99 (*0-345-39045-8*, Ballantine Bks.) Ballantine Bks.

—Havana Bay. l.t. ed. pap. 25.95 o.p. (*0-7838-8547-4*, Macmillan Reference USA) Gale Group.

—Havana Bay. 1999. 416p. 24.95 o.s.i (*0-679-42662-0*) Random Hse., Inc.

—Polar Star. 2000. mass mkt. 6.99 (*0-345-91706-5*); 1993. mass mkt. 5.99 o.p. (*0-345-90113-4*); 1993. mass mkt. 3.99 o.p. (*0-345-38550-0*); 1990. 384p. mass mkt. 7.99 o.s.i (*0-345-36765-0*) Ballantine Bks.

—Polar Star. 1991. 4.99 o.p. (*0-517-06897-4*) Random Hse. Value Publishing.

—Red Square. 2000. mass mkt. 6.99 (*0-345-91707-3*) Ballantine Bks.

**RENNE (FICTITIOUS CHARACTER: PORTER)—FICTION**

Porter, Donald C. Ambush. 1984. (White Indian Ser.). 320p. mass mkt. 4.50 o.s.i (*0-553-25202-X*) Bantam Bks.

—Ambush. l.t. ed. 1993. (White Indian Ser.: Bk. VIII). 368p. lib. bdg. 22.95 (*0-8161-5846-0*, Macmillan Reference USA) Gale Group.

—Apache. 1987. (White Indian Ser.: No. 14). 332p. (Orig.). mass mkt. 4.99 o.s.i (*0-553-26206-8*) Bantam Bks.

—Cherokee. 1984. (White Indian Ser.: No. 10). 352p. (Orig.). mass mkt. 4.50 o.s.i (*0-553-24492-2*) Bantam Bks.

—Choctaw. 1985. (White Indian Ser.: No. 11). 352p. (Orig.). mass mkt. 4.50 o.s.i (*0-553-24950-9*) Bantam Bks.

—Fallen Timbers. 1990. (White Indian Ser.: No. 19). 368p. mass mkt. 4.50 o.s.i (*0-553-28474-6*) Bantam Bks.

—Father of Waters. 1989. (White Indian Ser.: No. 18). 320p. mass mkt. 4.99 o.s.i (*0-553-28285-9*) Bantam Bks.

—The Manitou: White Indian, Vol. 16. 1988. 272p. mass mkt. 4.50 o.s.i (*0-553-27264-0*) Bantam Bks.

—The Red Stick. 1994. (Red Stick Ser.: No. 26). 336p. mass mkt. 4.99 o.s.i (*0-553-56142-1*) Bantam Bks.

—The Renegade. 1984. (Colonization of America Ser.: No. 2). 384p. mass mkt. 4.50 o.s.i (*0-553-25020-5*) Bantam Bks.

—The Renegade. l.t. ed. 1983. 544p. lib. bdg. 19.95 o.p. (*0-8161-3447-2*, Macmillan Reference USA) Gale Group.

—Renno. 1985. 336p. (Orig.). mass mkt. 4.50 o.s.i (*0-553-25154-6*) Bantam Bks.

—The Sachem. 1984. 352p. mass mkt. 4.50 o.s.i (*0-553-24476-0*) Bantam Bks.

—The Sachem. l.t. ed. 1983. (Reader's Request Ser.). lib. bdg. 19.95 o.p. (*0-8161-3449-9*, Macmillan Reference USA) Gale Group.

—Sachem's Daughter. 1991. (White Indian Ser.: No. 21). 336p. mass mkt. 4.99 o.s.i (*0-553-29028-2*) Bantam Bks.

—Sachem's Son. 1990. (White Indian Ser.: No. 20). 352p. mass mkt. 4.50 o.s.i (*0-553-28805-9*) Bantam Bks.

—Seminole. 1986. (White Indian Ser.). 368p. mass mkt. 4.99 o.s.i (*0-553-25353-0*) Bantam Bks.

—Seneca. 1984. (White Indian Ser.: No. 9). 304p. mass mkt. 4.50 o.s.i (*0-553-23986-4*) Bantam Bks.

—Seneca. l.t. ed. 1994. (White Indian Ser.). 382p. lib. bdg. 22.95 (*0-8161-5847-9*, Macmillan Reference USA) Gale Group.

—Seneca Patriots. 1991. (White Indian Ser.: No. 22). 368p. mass mkt. 4.99 o.s.i (*0-553-29217-X*) Bantam Bks.

—Seneca Warrior. 1989. (Book of Justice Ser.: No. 1). 336p. mass mkt. 4.99 o.s.i (*0-553-27841-X*) Bantam Bks.

—The Spirit Knife. 1988. (White Indian Ser.: No. 15). 320p. mass mkt. 4.50 o.s.i (*0-553-27161-X*) Bantam Bks.

—War Chief. 1984. (Colonization of America Ser.). 384p. mass mkt. 4.50 o.s.i (*0-553-24751-4*) Bantam Bks.

—War Chief. l.t. ed. 1983. 528p. lib. bdg. 19.95 o.p. (*0-8161-3448-0*, Macmillan Reference USA) Gale Group.

—War Cry. 1983. 336p. mass mkt. 3.95 o.s.i (*0-553-25589-4*) Bantam Bks.

—War Cry. l.t. ed. 1984. (General Ser.). 15.95 o.p. (*0-8161-3452-9*, Macmillan Reference USA) Gale Group.

—War Drums. 1986. (White Indian Ser.: No. 13). 353p. (Orig.). mass mkt. 3.95 o.s.i (*0-553-25868-0*) Bantam Bks.

—White Indian. l.t. ed. 1983. 520p. lib. bdg. 19.95 o.p. (*0-8161-3446-4*, Macmillan Reference USA) Gale Group.

—The White Indian, No. 1. 1984. 416p. mass mkt. 4.99 o.s.i (*0-553-24650-X*) Bantam Bks.

—White Indian, Super Novel No. 1: Hawk's Journey. 1992. 352p. mass mkt. 5.50 o.s.i (*0-553-29218-8*) Bantam Bks.

**RENO, JIM (FICTITIOUS CHARACTER)—FICTION**

Morris, Gilbert. Boomtown, No. 4. 1992. (Reno Western Saga Ser.). 261p. pap. 7.99 o.p. (*0-8423-7789-1*) Tyndale Hse. Pubs.

—Lone Wolf. 1995. (Reno Western Saga Ser.: Vol. 6). 236p. pap. 7.99 o.p. (*0-8423-1997-2*) Tyndale Hse. Pubs.

—Reno. 1992. (Jim Reno Westerns Ser.: Vol. 1). 258p. pap. 7.99 o.p. (*0-8423-1058-4*) Tyndale Hse. Pubs.

—Ride the Wild River. 1992. (Jim Reno Westerns Ser.: No. 3). Orig. Title: The Runaway. 339p. pap. 7.99 o.p. (*0-8423-5795-5*) Tyndale Hse. Pubs.

—Rimrock. 1992. (Jim Reno Westerns Ser.: Vol. 2). 257p. pap. 7.99 o.p. (*0-8423-1059-2*) Tyndale Hse. Pubs.

—Valley Justice. 1995. (Reno Western Saga Ser.: Vol. 5). 256p. pap. 7.99 o.p. (*0-8423-7756-5*) Tyndale Hse. Pubs.

Names, Larry D. Boomtown. 1981. (Double D Western Ser.). 192p. 10.95 o.p. (*0-385-17429-2*) Doubleday Publishing.

—Boomtown. l.t. ed. 1983. 285p. reprint ed. 11.95 o.p. (*0-89621-429-X*) Thorndike Pr.

**RENZLER, MARK (FICTITIOUS CHARACTER)—FICTION**

Engleman, Paul. Left for Dead. 1996. 272p. 21.95 o.p. (*0-312-13534-3*, Saint Martin's Minotaur) St. Martin's Pr.

**REPAIRMAN JACK (FICTITIOUS CHARACTER)—FICTION**

Wilson, F. Paul. All the Rage. 2000. 383p. 25.95 (*0-312-86796-4*, Forge Bks.); 2001. 512p. reprint ed. mass mkt. 7.99 (*0-8125-6654-8*, Tor Bks.) Doherty, Tom Assocs., LLC.

—All the Rage. 2000. (Repairman Jack Ser.). 365p. 50.00 (*1-887368-29-9*) Gauntlet, Inc.

—Conspiracies. 2000. (Repairman Jack Ser.). 405p. mass mkt. 6.99 (*0-8125-6699-8*, Tor Bks.); 317p. 24.95 (*0-312-86797-2*, Forge Bks.) Doherty, Tom Assocs., LLC.
—Conspiracies. aut. ltd. ed. 1999. (Repairman Jack Ser.). 324p. 50.00 (*1-887368-20-5*) Gauntlet, Inc.
—Gateways: A Repairman Jack Novel. 2003. (Repairman Jack Ser.). 368p. 25.95 (*0-7653-0690-5*, Forge Bks.) Doherty, Tom Assocs., LLC.
—Gateways: A Repairman Jack Novel. 2003. 436p. 60.00 (*1-887368-67-1*) Gauntlett Pr.
—The Haunted Air: A Repairman Jack Novel. 2002. (Repairman Jack Ser.). 416p. 24.95 (*0-312-87868-0*, Tor Bks.) Doherty, Tom Assocs., LLC.
—The Haunted Air: A Repairman Jack Novel. 2002. (Repairman Jack Ser.). 50.00 (*1-887368-57-4*) Gauntlet, Inc.
—Hosts. aut. ltd. ed. 2001. (Repairman Jack Ser.). 360p. 50.00 (*1-887368-46-9*) Gauntlet, Inc.
—Legacies. 2000. 440p. mass mkt. 6.99 (*0-8125-7199-1*); 1998. 352p. 24.95 o.p. (*0-312-86414-0*) Doherty, Tom Assocs., LLC. (Forge Bks.).
—Repairman Jack No. 7. mass mkt. (*0-7653-4605-2*, Forge Bks.) Doherty, Tom Assocs., LLC.
—Repairman Jack No. 8. mass mkt. (*0-7653-4606-0*, Forge Bks.) Doherty, Tom Assocs., LLC.
—Sims. mass mkt. (*0-7653-4463-7*, Forge Bks.) Doherty, Tom Assocs., LLC.
—The Tomb. 1986. 410p. mass mkt. 5.99 o.s.i (*0-515-08876-5*, Jove); 1984. 416p. mass mkt. 3.95 o.s.i (*0-425-07295-9*) Berkley Publishing Group.
—The Tomb. 1998. (Repairman Jack Ser.). 448p. mass mkt. 7.99 (*0-8125-8037-0*, Tor Bks.) Doherty, Tom Assocs., LLC.
—The Tomb. 1984. 19.95 o.p. (*0-918372-11-9*); 41.00 o.p. (*0-918372-12-7*) Whispers Pr.
Wilson, Paul F. Repairman Jack, No. 8. (*0-7653-0691-3*, Forge Bks.) Doherty, Tom Assocs., LLC.

**RESNICK, CHARLIE (FICTITIOUS CHARACTER)—FICTION**

Harvey, John. Cold Light. 1994. 370p. 22.00 o.p. (*0-8050-2046-2*) Holt, Henry & Co.
—Cold Light. unabr. ed. 1997. audio 69.95 (*1-85695-970-8*, 950507) ISIS Audio Bks. GBR. *Dist:* Ulverscroft Large Print Bks., Ltd.
—Cold Light. unabr. ed. 2000. (Charlie Resnick Mystery Ser.: Vol. 6). audio 70.00 (*0-7887-0483-4*, 94676E7) Recorded Bks., LLC.
—Cold Light. unabr. ed. 2002. audio 89.95 (*0-7531-1482-8*) Soundings, Ltd. GBR. *Dist:* Ulverscroft Large Print Bks., Ltd.
—Cold Light. 1995. 370p. pap. text 4.99 (*0-312-95603-7*, St. Martin's Paperbacks) St. Martin's Pr.
—Cutting Edge. 1998. (Cutting Edge Ser.: Vol. 1). 288p. pap. 13.00 o.s.i (*0-8050-5497-9*, Owl Bks.) Holt, Henry & Co.
—Cutting Edge. 1992. 352p. mass mkt. 4.99 (*0-380-71615-1*, Avon Bks.) Morrow/Avon.
—Cutting Edge: A Charlie Resnick Mystery. 1991. 288p. 18.95 o.p. (*0-8050-1264-8*) Holt, Henry & Co.
—Easy Meat. 1997. 400p. pap. 11.00 o.s.i (*0-8050-5495-2*, Owl Bks.); 1996. 384p. 23.00 o.p. (*0-8050-4148-6*) Holt, Henry & Co.
—Easy Meat. unabr. ed. 1997. (Charlie Resnick Mystery Ser.: Vol. 8). audio 78.00 (*0-7887-0818-X*, 94968E7) Recorded Bks., LLC.
—Last Rites: A Novel. l.t. ed. 1999. (Core Ser.). 396p. 27.95 (*0-7838-8674-8*, Macmillan Reference USA) Gale Group.
—Last Rites: A Novel. 1999. (Charles Resnick Novels Ser.). 312p. 25.00 o.s.i (*0-8050-4150-8*) Holt, Henry & Co.
—Last Rites: A Novel. unabr. ed. 2000. audio 71.00 (*1-84197-042-5*, H1056E7, Clipper Audio) Recorded Bks., LLC.
—Living Proof. 1995. 283p. 22.50 o.p. (*0-8050-2045-4*) Holt, Henry & Co.
—Living Proof. unabr. ed. 1996. (Charlie Resnick Mystery Ser.: Vol. 7). audio 51.00 (*0-7887-0507-5*, 94700E7) Recorded Bks., LLC.
—Living Proof. 1996. mass mkt. 5.99 (*0-312-95863-3*, St. Martin's Paperbacks) St. Martin's Pr.
—Lonely Hearts. 288p. 1997. pap. 11.00 o.s.i (*0-8050-5494-4*, Owl Bks.); 1989. 16.95 o.p. (*0-8050-0982-5*) Holt, Henry & Co.
—Lonely Hearts. 1990. 320p. pap. 4.99 (*0-380-71006-4*, Avon Bks.) Morrow/Avon.
—Off Minor. 288p. 1998. pap. 11.00 o.s.i (*0-8050-5498-7*, Owl Bks.); 1992. 18.95 o.p. (*0-8050-1265-6*) Holt, Henry & Co.
—Off Minor. 1993. 288p. mass mkt. 4.99 (*0-380-72009-4*, Avon Bks.) Morrow/Avon.
—Rough Treatment. unabr. ed. 1992. 69.95 incl. audio (*0-7451-4062-9*) BBC Audiobooks America.
—Rough Treatment. 1997. 288p. pap. 11.00 o.s.i (*0-8050-5496-0*, Owl Bks.) Holt, Henry & Co.
—Rough Treatment. 1991. 304p. mass mkt. 3.99 (*0-380-71171-0*, Avon Bks.) Morrow/Avon.
—Rough Treatment: A Charlie Resnick Mystery. 1990. 288p. 17.95 o.p. (*0-8050-0983-3*) Holt, Henry & Co.
—Still Waters. unabr. ed. 2000. (Charlie Resnick Mystery Ser.: Vol. 9). audio 70.00 (*0-7887-3057-6*, 95751E7) Recorded Bks., LLC.
—Still Waters: A Crime Novel. 1997. 320p. 23.00 o.s.i (*0-8050-4149-4*) Holt, Henry & Co.
—Wasted Years. unabr. ed. 1998. audio 69.95 (*1-85695-764-0*, 951004) ISIS Audio Bks. GBR. *Dist:* Ulverscroft Large Print Bks., Ltd.
—Wasted Years. 1994. 352p. mass mkt. 4.99 (*0-380-72182-1*, Avon Bks.) Morrow/Avon.
—Wasted Years. unabr. ed. 1995. (Charlie Resnick Mystery Ser.: Vol. 5). audio. audio 70.00 (*0-7887-0450-8*, 94640E7) Recorded Bks., LLC.
—Wasted Years: A Charlie Resnick Mystery. 1993. 352p. 19.95 o.p. (*0-8050-2044-6*) Holt, Henry & Co.
—Wasted Years: A Crime Novel. 1999. 348p. pap. 13.00 o.s.i (*0-8050-5499-5*, Owl Bks.) Holt, Henry & Co.

**REUSCHEL, DEENA (FICTITIOUS CHARACTER)—FICTION**

Heckler, Jonellen. Circumstances Unknown. Grose, Bill, ed. 1993. 288p. 21.00 o.p. (*0-671-78056-5*, Atria); 1994. 336p. reprint ed. mass mkt. 5.99 (*0-671-78059-X*, Pocket) Simon & Schuster.

**REVILL, NICK (FICTITIOUS CHARACTER)—FICTION**

Gooden, Philip. Alms for Oblivion: A Shakespearean Murder Mystery. 2003. 288p. 24.00 (*0-7867-1142-6*, Carroll & Graf Pubs.) Avalon Publishing Group.
—Death of Kings: A Shakespearean Murder Mystery. 2001. 320p. pap. 12.95 (*0-7867-0875-1*, Carroll & Graf Pubs.) Avalon Publishing Group.
—Mask of Night: A Shakespearean Murder Mystery. 2004. 272p. 24.00 (*0-7867-1312-7*, Carroll & Graf Pubs.) Avalon Publishing Group.
—The Pale Companion: A Shakespearean Murder Mystery. 288p. 2002. 24.00 (*0-7867-1008-X*); 2003. reprint ed. 12.00 (*0-7867-1176-0*) Avalon Publishing Group. (Carroll & Graf Pubs.).

**REYMOND, STEPHANIE (FICTITIOUS CHARACTER)—FICTION**

Kaiser, R. J. Payback. 1998. 448p. mass mkt. (*1-55166-460-7*, 1-66460-6, Mira Bks.) Harlequin Enterprises, Ltd.

**REYNIER, CLAIRE (FICTITIOUS CHARACTER)—FICTION**

Van Gieson, Judith. Confidence Woman. l.t. ed. 2002. 315p. 27.95 (*0-7862-4217-5*) Gale Group.
—Confidence Woman. 2002. 272p. mass mkt. 5.99 (*0-451-20500-6*, Signet Bks.) NAL.
—Confidence Woman. 2002. (Claire Reynier Mysteries Ser.). 208p. 23.95 (*0-8263-2888-1*) Univ. of New Mexico Pr.
—Land of Burning Heat: A Claire Reynier Mystery. 2003. 272p. mass mkt. 5.99 (*0-451-20800-5*, Signet Bks.) NAL.
—Land of Burning Heat: A Claire Reynier Mystery. l.t. ed. 2003. (Senior Lifestyles Ser.). 28.95 (*0-7862-5470-X*) Thorndike Pr.
—Land of Burning Heat: A Claire Reynier Mystery. 2003. 264p. 24.95 (*0-8263-3172-6*) Univ. of New Mexico Pr.
—The Shadow of Venus. 2004. 272p. mass mkt. 5.99 (*0-451-21134-0*, Signet Bks.) NAL.
—The Stolen Blue: A Claire Reynier Mystery. 2000. (Claire Reynier Mysteries Ser.). 256p. mass mkt. 5.99 (*0-451-20001-2*, Signet Bks.) NAL.
—The Stolen Blue: A Claire Reynier Mystery. l.t. ed. 2001. (Senior Lifestyles Ser.). 320p. 28.95 (*0-7862-3586-1*) Thorndike Pr.
—The Stolen Blue: A Claire Reynier Mystery. 2000. 197p. 22.95 o.p. (*0-8263-2233-6*) Univ. of New Mexico Pr.
—Vanishing Point: A Claire Reynier Mystery. 2001. 272p. mass mkt. 5.99 (*0-451-20240-6*) NAL.
—Vanishing Point: A Claire Reynier Mystery. l.t. ed. 2001. (Senior Lifestyles Ser.). 293p. 28.95 (*0-7862-3587-X*) Thorndike Pr.
—Vanishing Point: A Claire Reynier Mystery. 2001. (Claire Reynier Mysteries Ser.). 216p. 24.95 (*0-8263-2383-9*) Univ. of New Mexico Pr.

**REYNOLDS, ALEX (FICTITIOUS CHARACTER)—FICTION**

Hunter, Fred. Capital Queers. (Alex Reynolds Mysteries Ser.). 2000. 232p. pap. 12.95 (*0-312-26301-5*, Saint Martin's Griffin); 1999. 224p. 23.95 o.p. (*0-312-20463-9*, Saint Martin's Minotaur) St. Martin's Pr.
—The Chicken Asylum. 2002. 256p. pap. 12.95 (*0-312-28710-0*, Saint Martin's Griffin); 2001. 272p. 23.95 (*0-312-27117-4*, Saint Martin's Minotaur) St. Martin's Pr.
—Federal Fag. (Alex Reynolds Mysteries Ser.). 272p. 1999. pap. 11.95 (*0-312-20649-6*, Saint Martin's Griffin); 1998. 22.95 o.p. (*0-312-18580-4*, Saint Martin's Minotaur) St. Martin's Pr.
—Government Gay. (Alex Reynolds Mysteries Ser.). 1998. 224p. pap. 11.95 (*0-312-18721-1*, Saint Martin's Griffin); 1997. 215p. text 21.95 o.p. (*0-312-15536-0*, Saint Martin's Minotaur) St. Martin's Pr.
—National Nancys. 240p. 2001. pap. 12.95 (*0-312-27699-0*, Saint Martin's Griffin); 2000. 22.95 (*0-312-25233-1*, Saint Martin's Minotaur) St. Martin's Pr.

**REYNOLDS, SAM (FICTITIOUS CHARACTER)—FICTION**

Hartman, Cherry. The Well-Heeled Murders. 1996. 224p. pap. 10.95 (*1-883523-10-9*) Spinsters Ink Bks.

**RHENFORD, LIAM (FICTITIOUS CHARACTER)—FICTION**

Hood, Daniel. Beggar's Banquet. 1997. 304p. reprint ed. mass mkt. 5.50 o.s.i (*0-441-00434-2*) Ace Bks.
—Fanuilh. 1994. 272p. (Orig.). mass mkt. 5.50 o.s.i (*0-441-00055-X*) Ace Bks.
—King's Cure. 2000. 320p. mass mkt. 5.99 o.s.i (*0-441-00789-9*) Ace Bks.
—Scales of Justice. 1998. (Return of the Dragon Fanuilh Ser.). 304p. mass mkt. 5.50 o.s.i (*0-441-00515-2*) Ace Bks.
—Wizard's Heir. 1995. 304p. (Orig.). mass mkt. 4.99 o.s.i (*0-441-00231-5*) Ace Bks.

**RHINEHEART, MICHAEL (FICTITIOUS CHARACTER)—FICTION**

Birkett, John. The Queen's Mare. 1990. 240p. pap. 3.50 (*0-380-75683-8*, Avon Bks.) Morrow/Avon.

**RHODENBARR, BERNIE (FICTITIOUS CHARACTER)—FICTION**

Block, Lawrence. The Burglar in the Closet. (Bernie Rhodenbarr Mystery Ser.: No. 2). audio 24.95 (*0-7861-1392-8*); 1997. audio 32.95 (*0-7861-1044-9*, 1816) Blackstone Audio Bks., Inc.
—The Burglar in the Closet. unabr. ed. 2000. (Bernie Rhodenbarr Mystery Ser.: Bk. 2). audio 54.95 (*0-7927-2209-4*, CSL 098) Chivers Audio Bks. GBR. *Dist:* BBC Audiobooks America.
—The Burglar in the Closet. 1995. (Bernie Rhodenbarr Mystery Ser.: No. 2). 256p. 21.95 o.p. (*0-525-93993-8*, Dutton) Dutton/Plume.
—The Burglar in the Closet. 1997. (Bernie Rhodenbarr Mystery Ser.: No. 2). 320p. mass mkt. 6.99 (*0-451-18074-7*, Signet Bks.) NAL.
—The Burglar in the Closet. 1978. (Bernie Rhodenbarr Mystery Ser.: No. 2). 6.95 o.p. (*0-394-42374-7*) Random Hse., Inc.
—The Burglar in the Closet. unabr. ed. 1998. (Bernie Rhodenbarr Mystery Ser.: No. 2). audio 35.00 (*0-7887-0854-6*, 95000E7 ) Recorded Bks., LLC.
—The Burglar in the Closet. 1986. (Bernie Rhodenbarr Mystery Ser.: No. 2). mass mkt. 3.50 o.s.i (*0-671-61704-4*, Pocket) Simon & Schuster.
—The Burglar in the Closet. l.t. ed. 1996. (Bernie Rhodenbarr Mystery Ser.: No. 2). 277p. 25.95 o.p. (*0-7862-0548-2*) Thorndike Pr.
—The Burglar in the Closet. abr. ed. 1995. (Bernie Rhodenbarr Mystery Ser.: No. 2). audio 16.95 o.s.i (*0-14-086198-X*, Penguin AudioBooks) Viking Penguin.
—The Burglar in the Library. 1997. (Bernie Rhodenbarr Mystery Ser.: No. 8). 320p. 23.95 o.p. (*0-525-94301-3*, Dutton) Dutton/Plume.
—The Burglar in the Library. 1998. (Bernie Rhodenbarr Mystery Ser.: No. 8). 368p. mass mkt. 6.99 (*0-451-40783-0*, Signet Bks.) NAL.
—The Burglar in the Library. l.t. ed. 1998. (Bernie Rhodenbarr Mystery Ser.: No. 8). 464p. 27.95 o.p. (*0-7862-1280-2*) Thorndike Pr.
—The Burglar in the Library. abr. ed. 1997. (Bernie Rhodenbarr Mystery Ser.: No. 8). 2p. audio 16.95 (*0-14-086582-9*, Penguin AudioBooks) Viking Penguin.
—The Burglar in the Rye. 1999. (Bernie Rhodenbarr Mystery Ser.: No. 9). 280p. 23.95 o.p. (*0-525-94500-8*, Dutton) Dutton/Plume.
—The Burglar in the Rye. 2000. (Bernie Rhodenbarr Mystery Ser.: No. 9). 320p. mass mkt. 6.99 (*0-451-19847-6*, Signet Bks.) NAL.
—The Burglar in the Rye. l.t. ed. 1999. (Bernie Rhodenbarr Mystery Ser.: No. 9). 440p. 30.95 (*0-7862-2136-4*) Thorndike Pr.
—The Burglar on the Prowl. l.t. ed. 2004. 416p. pap. 24.95 (*0-06-058979-5*, HarperLargePrint) HarperTrade.
—The Burglar on the Prowl. 2004. 320p. 24.95 (*0-06-019830-3*, Morrow, William & Co.) Morrow/Avon.
—The Burglar Who Dropped in on Elvis. unabr. ed. 1999. audio 5.99 (*1-55204-601-X*, PAC-8601) Durkin Hayes Publishing Ltd.
—The Burglar Who Liked to Quote Kipling. 1996. (Bernie Rhodenbarr Mystery Ser.: No. 3). 256p. 22.95 o.s.i (*0-525-94159-2*, Dutton) Dutton/Plume.
—The Burglar Who Liked to Quote Kipling. 1997. (Bernie Rhodenbarr Mystery Ser.: No. 3). 320p. mass mkt. 6.99 o.s.i (*0-451-18075-5*, Signet Bks.) NAL.
—The Burglar Who Liked to Quote Kipling. 1979. (Bernie Rhodenbarr Mystery Ser.: No. 3). 7.95 o.p. (*0-394-50417-8*) Random Hse., Inc.
—The Burglar Who Liked to Quote Kipling. 1998. (Bernie Rhodenbarr Mystery Ser.: No. 3). audio 44.00 (*0-7887-0810-4*, 94959E7 ) Recorded Bks., LLC.
—The Burglar Who Liked to Quote Kipling. 1986. (Bernie Rhodenbarr Mystery Ser.: No. 3). mass mkt. 3.50 o.s.i (*0-671-61831-8*, Pocket) Simon & Schuster.
—The Burglar Who Liked to Quote Kipling. abr. ed. 1996. (Bernie Rhodenbarr Mystery Ser.: No. 3). audio 16.95 o.s.i (*0-14-086345-1*, Penguin AudioBooks) Viking Penguin.
—The Burglar Who Painted Like Mondrian. 1998. (Bernie Rhodenbarr Mystery Ser.: No. 5). 224p. 23.95 o.p. (*0-525-94382-X*) Dutton/Plume.
—The Burglar Who Painted Like Mondrian. l.t. ed. 1999. (Bernie Rhodenbarr Mystery Ser.: No. 5). 27.95 (*1-56895-726-2*, Wheeler Publishing, Inc.) Gale Group.
—The Burglar Who Painted Like Mondrian. 1983. (Bernie Rhodenbarr Mystery Ser.: No. 5). 217p. 14.50 o.p. (*0-87795-517-4*, Morrow, William & Co.) Morrow/Avon.
—The Burglar Who Painted Like Mondrian. 1999. (Bernie Rhodenbarr Mystery Ser.: No. 5). 320p. reprint ed. mass mkt. 6.99 o.p. (*0-451-18076-3*, Signet Bks.) NAL.
—The Burglar Who Painted Like Mondrian. unabr. ed. 1993. (Bernie Rhodenbarr Mystery Ser.: No. 5). audio 46.00 (*0-7887-3214-5*, 95846E7) Recorded Bks., LLC.
—The Burglar Who Painted Like Mondrian. 1986. (Bernie Rhodenbarr Mystery Ser.: No. 5). mass mkt. 3.50 o.s.i (*0-671-49581-X*, Pocket) Simon & Schuster.
—The Burglar Who Painted Like Mondrian. abr. ed. 1998. (Bernie Rhodenbarr Mystery Ser.: No. 5). 2p. audio 17.95 o.p. (*0-14-086817-8*, Penguin AudioBooks) Viking Penguin.
—The Burglar Who Studied Spinoza. 1997. (Bernie Rhodenbarr Mystery Ser.: No. 4). 240p. 23.95 o.s.i (*0-525-94180-0*, Signet Bks.) Dutton/Plume.
—The Burglar Who Studied Spinoza. l.t. ed. 1998. (Bernie Rhodenbarr Mystery Ser.: No. 4). 26.95 (*1-56895-602-9*, Wheeler Publishing, Inc.) Gale Group.
—The Burglar Who Studied Spinoza. 1998. (Bernie Rhodenbarr Mystery Ser.: No. 4). 320p. mass mkt. 6.99 o.s.i (*0-451-19488-8*, Signet Bks.) NAL.
—The Burglar Who Studied Spinoza. 1981. (Bernie Rhodenbarr Mystery Ser.: No. 4). 8.95 o.p. (*0-394-51065-8*) Random Hse., Inc.
—The Burglar Who Studied Spinoza. unabr. ed. 1999. (Bernie Rhodenbarr Mystery Ser.: No. 4). audio 46.00 (*0-7887-1872-X*, 95294E7) Recorded Bks., LLC.
—The Burglar Who Studied Spinoza. 1986. (Bernie Rhodenbarr Mystery Ser.: No. 4). mass mkt. 3.50 o.s.i (*0-671-62485-7*, Pocket) Simon & Schuster.
—The Burglar Who Studied Spinoza. abr. ed. 1997. (Bernie Rhodenbarr Mystery Ser.: No. 4). audio 16.95. 3p. audio 16.95 o.p. (*0-14-086685-X*) Viking Penguin. (Penguin AudioBooks).
—The Burglar Who Thought He Was Bogart. unabr. ed. 1997. (Bernie Rhodenbarr Mystery Ser.: No. 7). audio 44.95 (*0-7861-1196-8*, 1957) Blackstone Audio Bks., Inc.
—The Burglar Who Thought He Was Bogart. 1996. (Bernie Rhodenbarr Mystery Ser.: No. 7). 384p. mass mkt. 6.99 o.s.i (*0-451-18634-6*, Onyx) NAL.
—The Burglar Who Thought He Was Bogart. unabr. ed. 1997. (Bernie Rhodenbarr Mystery Ser.: No. 7). audio 51.00 (*0-7887-0476-1*, 94669E7) Recorded Bks., LLC.
—The Burglar Who Thought He Was Bogart. abr. ed. 1995. (Bernie Rhodenbarr Mystery Ser.: No. 7). audio 16.95 o.s.i (*0-14-086190-4*, Penguin AudioBooks) Viking Penguin.
—The Burglar Who Traded Ted Williams. unabr. ed. 1997. (Bernie Rhodenbarr Mystery Ser.: No. 6). audio 44.95 (*0-7861-1166-6*, 1937) Blackstone Audio Bks., Inc.
—The Burglar Who Traded Ted Williams. 1994. (Bernie Rhodenbarr Mystery Ser.: No. 6). 272p. 19.95 o.p. (*0-525-93807-9*, Dutton) Dutton/Plume.
—The Burglar Who Traded Ted Williams. 1995. (Bernie Rhodenbarr Mystery Ser.: No. 6). 384p. mass mkt. 6.99 o.s.i (*0-451-18426-2*, Onyx) NAL.
—The Burglar Who Traded Ted Williams. abr. ed. 1994. (Bernie Rhodenbarr Mystery Ser.: No. 6). pap. 16.00 o.p. incl. audio (*0-453-00890-9*, 25024-31224) Penguin/HighBridge.
—The Burglar Who Traded Ted Williams. unabr. ed. 1994. (Bernie Rhodenbarr Mystery Ser.: No. 6). audio 51.00 (*0-7887-1302-7*, 95138E7) Recorded Bks., LLC.
—Burglars Can't Be Choosers. 1978. (Bernie Rhodenbarr Mystery Ser.: No. 1). pap. 1.75 o.s.i (*0-515-04584-5*, Jove) Berkley Publishing Group.

—Burglars Can't Be Choosers, unabr. ed. 1997. (Bernie Rhodenbarr Mystery Ser.: No. 1). audio 39.95 (*0-7861-1136-4*, 755302) Blackstone Audio Bks., Inc.

—Burglars Can't Be Choosers. 1995. (Bernie Rhodenbarr Mystery Ser.: No. 1). 256p. 19.95 o.p. (*0-525-93943-1*, Dutton) Dutton/Plume.

—Burglars Can't Be Choosers. 2004. 320p. mass mkt. 6.99 (*0-06-058255-3*, HarperTorch) Morrow/Avon.

—Burglars Can't Be Choosers. 1995. (Bernie Rhodenbarr Mystery Ser.: No. 1). 304p. mass mkt. 5.99 o.s.i (*0-451-18073-9*, Signet Bks.) NAL.

—Burglars Can't Be Choosers. abr. ed. 1995. (Bernie Rhodenbarr Mystery Ser.: No. 1). pap. 16.95 o.p. incl. audio (*0-453-00932-8*, 25024-39151) Penguin/HighBridge.

—Burglars Can't Be Choosers. 1977. (Bernie Rhodenbarr Mystery Ser.: No. 1). (Illus.). 6.95 o.p. (*0-394-41183-8*) Random Hse., Inc.

—Burglars Can't Be Choosers. unabr. ed. 1998. (Bernie Rhodenbarr Mystery Ser.: No. 1). audio 44.00 (*0-7887-1990-4*, 95377E7) Recorded Bks., LLC.

**RHODES, ANNE (FICTITIOUS CHARACTER)—FICTION**

Hauser, Thomas. The Hawthorne Group. 1993. 288p. mass mkt. 4.99 (*0-8125-1342-8*); 1991. 18.95 o.p. (*0-312-85161-8*) Doherty, Tom Assocs., LLC. (Tor Bks.).

**RHODES, CAROLINE (FICTITIOUS CHARACTER)—FICTION**

Welk, Mary V. A Deadly Little Christmas: A Caroline Rhodes Mystery. 1998. 262p. pap. 10.00 (*0-9665157-0-6*) Kleworks Publishing Co.

—Something Wicked in the Air: A Caroline Rhodes Mystery. 1999. 225p. pap. 10.00 (*0-9665157-1-4*) Kleworks Publishing Co.

—To Kill a King: A Caroline Rhodes Mystery. 2000. 248p. pap. 11.97 (*0-9665157-2-2*) Kleworks Publishing Co.

**RHODES, DAN (FICTITIOUS CHARACTER)—FICTION**

Crider, Bill. Booked for a Hanging. 1992. 224p. 17.95 o.p. (*0-312-08149-9*, Saint Martin's Minotaur) St. Martin's Pr.

—Cursed to Death. 1990. 176p. mass mkt. 3.95 o.s.i (*0-8041-0424-7*, Ivy Bks.) Ballantine Bks.

—Cursed to Death. 1988. 16.95 o.s.i (*0-8027-5698-0*) Walker & Co.

—Death by Accident. l.t. ed. 1998. (Large Print Book Ser.). pap. 23.95 (*1-56895-663-0*, Wheeler Publishing, Inc.) Gale Group.

—Death by Accident. 2000. (WWL Mystery Ser.: Vol. 343). 256p. per. (*0-373-26343-0*, Harlequin Bks.) Harlequin Enterprises, Ltd.

—Death by Accident. 1998. (Sheriff Dan Rhodes Mysteries Ser.). 288p. 22.95 o.p. (*0-312-18080-2*, Saint Martin's Minotaur) St. Martin's Pr.

—Death on the Move. 1990. mass mkt. 3.95 o.s.i (*0-8041-0425-5*, Ivy Bks.) Ballantine Bks.

—Death on the Move. 1989. 204p. 17.95 o.p. (*0-8027-5730-8*) Walker & Co.

—Evil at Root. 1992. 2.99 o.p. (*0-517-09041-4*) Random Hse. Value Publishing.

—Evil at Root. 1990. 15.95 o.p. (*0-312-04314-7*, Saint Martin's Minotaur) St. Martin's Pr.

—Evil at the Root. 1991. 192p. mass mkt. 3.95 o.s.i (*0-8041-0764-5*, Ivy Bks.) Ballantine Bks.

—A Ghost of a Chance. E-Book 23.95 (*0-312-27578-1*) St. Martin's Pr.

—Murder Most Fowl. 1994. 208p. 18.95 o.p. (*0-312-11387-0*, Saint Martin's Minotaur) St. Martin's Pr.

—A Romantic Way to Die: A Sheriff Dan Rhodes Mystery. 2001. 240p. 22.95 (*0-312-20907-X*) St. Martin's Pr.

—Shotgun Saturday Night. 1989. 176p. mass mkt. 3.95 o.s.i (*0-8041-0423-9*, Ivy Bks.) Ballantine Bks.

—Shotgun Saturday Night. 1987. 16.95 (*0-8027-5684-0*) Walker & Co.

—Too Late to Die. 1989. 192p. mass mkt. 3.95 o.s.i (*0-8041-0422-0*, Ivy Bks.) Ballantine Bks.

—Too Late to Die. 1986. 192p. 14.95 (*0-8027-5650-6*) Walker & Co.

—Winning Can Be Murder. 2000. (Sheriff Dan Rhodes Mysteries Ser.: Bk. 354). 256p. per. (*0-373-26354-6*, 1-26354-0, Worldwide Library) Harlequin Enterprises, Ltd.

—Winning Can Be Murder. 1996. 240p. 21.95 o.p. (*0-312-14072-X*, Saint Martin's Minotaur) St. Martin's Pr.

**RHODES, DUSTY (FICTITIOUS CHARACTER)—FICTION**

Thompson, Jim. A Swell-Looking Babe. 1986. 160p. reprint ed. pap. 3.95 o.p. (*0-916870-96-0*, Black Mask) Creative Arts Bk. Co.

—A Swell-Looking Babe. 1991. (Vintage Crime/Black Lizard Ser.). 160p. pap. 11.00 (*0-679-73311-6*, Vintage) Knopf Publishing Group.

**RHODES, EMMA (FICTITIOUS CHARACTER)—FICTION**

Smith, Cynthia. Impolite Society. 1997. 272p. mass mkt. 5.99 o.s.i (*0-425-15790-3*, Prime Crime) Berkley Publishing Group.

—Misleading Ladies. 1997. (Casebook of Emma Rhodes Ser.). 272p. mass mkt. 5.99 o.s.i (*0-425-16112-9*, Prime Crime) Berkley Publishing Group.

—Royals & Rogues. 1998. (Royals & Rogues Ser.: Vol. 4). 288p. mass mkt. 5.99 o.s.i (*0-425-16643-0*, Prime Crime) Berkley Publishing Group.

—Silver & Guilt. 1998. (Emma Rhodes Mysteries Ser.). 256p. mass mkt. 5.99 o.s.i (*0-425-16382-2*, Prime Crime) Berkley Publishing Group.

**RHODES, TRAVIS (FICTITIOUS CHARACTER)—FICTION**

Legg, John P. Blood in the Snow. 1993. 304p. mass mkt. 3.50 o.s.i (*0-8217-4136-5*, Zebra Bks.) Kensington Publishing Corp.

**RHOMANDI BROTHERS (FICTITIOUS CHARACTERS)—FICTION**

Fancher, Jane S. Ring of Destiny. 1999. (Dance of the Rings Ser.: No. 3). 720p. mass mkt. 6.99 (*0-88677-870-0*, D A W Fiction) DAW Bks., Inc.

—Ring of Intrigue. 1997. (Dance of the Rings Ser.: 2). 752p. mass mkt. 7.50 o.s.i (*0-88677-719-4*) DAW Bks., Inc.

—Ring of Lightning. 1995. (Dance of the Rings Ser.: Bk. 1). 576p. (Orig.). mass mkt. 7.99 o.s.i (*0-88677-653-8*) DAW Bks., Inc.

**RHYME, LINCOLN (FICTITIOUS CHARACTER)—FICTION**

Deaver, Jeffery. The Bone Collector: A Lincoln Rhyme Novel. unabr. ed. 1999. audio 64.00 (*0-7366-4133-5*, 4638) Books on Tape, Inc.

—The Bone Collector: A Lincoln Rhyme Novel. l.t. ed. 1998. (Large Print Bks.). pap. 23.95 o.p. (*1-56895-524-3*, Wheeler Publishing, Inc.) Gale Group.

—The Bone Collector: A Lincoln Rhyme Novel. 1998. 432p. mass mkt. 7.99 (*0-451-18845-4*, Signet Bks.); 1997. pap. 6.99 (*0-451-19394-6*) NAL.

—The Bone Collector: A Lincoln Rhyme Novel. 1997. 432p. 22.95 o.s.i (*0-670-86871-X*);Set. 2p. audio 16.95 (*0-14-086328-1*, Penguin AudioBooks) Viking Penguin.

—The Coffin Dancer: A Lincoln Rhyme Novel. E-Book 25.00 (*1-58945-266-6*) Adobe Systems, Inc.

—The Coffin Dancer: A Lincoln Rhyme Novel. unabr. ed. 1999. audio 72.00 (*0-7366-4603-5*, 4990) Books on Tape, Inc.

—The Coffin Dancer: A Lincoln Rhyme Novel. l.t. ed. 1998. 27.95 (*1-56895-698-3*, Wheeler Publishing, Inc.) Gale Group.

—The Coffin Dancer: A Lincoln Rhyme Novel. 1999. E-Book 25.00 (*0-684-86805-9*, Simon & Schuster); 1999. pap. 6.99 (*0-671-02606-2*, Pocket); 1998. 368p. 25.00 o.s.i (*0-684-85285-3*, Simon & Schuster); 1999. (Illus.). 560p. reprint ed. mass mkt. 7.99 (*0-671-02409-4*, Pocket) Simon & Schuster.

—The Coffin Dancer: A Lincoln Rhyme Novel. 2000. audio compact disk 15.99 (*0-7435-0548-4*); 1998. audio 25.00 (*0-671-04303-X*, 496096) Simon & Schuster Audio. (Simon & Schuster Audioworks).

—The Devil's Teardrop: A Novel of the Last Night of the Century. E-Book 25.00 (*1-930161-37-9*) Adobe Systems, Inc.

—The Devil's Teardrop: A Novel of the Last Night of the Century. l.t. ed. 1999. (Wheeler Large Print Bks.). 527p. 26.95 o.p. (*1-56895-804-8*, Wheeler Publishing, Inc.) Gale Group.

—The Devil's Teardrop: A Novel of the Last Night of the Century. 2000. E-Book 9.99 (*0-684-85659-X*, Simon & Schuster); 1999. 400p. mass mkt. 7.99 (*0-671-03712-9*, Pocket); 1999. 400p. 25.00 o.s.i (*0-684-85292-6*, Simon & Schuster); 2000. (Illus.). 480p. reprint ed. pap. 7.99 (*0-671-03844-3*, Pocket) Simon & Schuster.

—The Devil's Teardrop: A Novel of the Last Night of the Century. abr. ed. 1999. 352p. audio 24.00 (*0-671-04569-5*, Simon & Schuster Audioworks) Simon & Schuster Audio.

—The Empty Chair: A Lincoln Rhyme Novel. 2000. E-Book 25.00 (*0-7432-1165-0*, Simon & Schuster); 2000. (Illus.). 416p. 25.00 o.s.i (*0-684-85563-1*, Simon & Schuster); 2000. 416p. 25.00 (*0-7432-0162-0*, Simon & Schuster); 2000. 624p. 25.00 o.s.i (*0-7432-0424-7*, Simon & Schuster); 2001. (Illus.). 512p. reprint ed. mass mkt. 7.99 (*0-671-02601-1*, Pocket) Simon & Schuster.

—The Empty Chair: A Lincoln Rhyme Novel. abr. ed. 2000. audio 25.00 (*0-7435-0052-0*, Simon & Schuster Audioworks) Simon & Schuster Audio.

—Speaking in Tongues: A Novel. 2000. 336p. 25.00 o.s.i (*0-684-87126-2*, Simon & Schuster) Simon & Schuster.

—Speaking in Tongues: A Novel. 1999. 21.95 (*0-670-86073-5*, Viking) Viking Penguin.

—The Stone Monkey: A Lincoln Rhyme Novel. 2002. E-Book 25.00 (*1-59061-849-1*) Adobe Systems, Inc.

—The Stone Monkey: A Lincoln Rhyme Novel. 2002. mass mkt. 7.99 (*0-7434-6054-5*, Pocket); 2002. 432p. 25.00 (*0-7432-2199-0*, Simon & Schuster); 2002. E-Book 25.00 (*0-7432-2777-8*, Simon & Schuster); 2002. 640p. 25.00 (*0-7432-2876-6*, Simon & Schuster); 2002. 432p. 25.00 (*0-7432-3767-6*, Simon & Schuster); 2003. 576p. reprint ed. mass mkt. 7.99 (*0-7434-3780-2*, Pocket) Simon & Schuster.

—The Stone Monkey: A Lincoln Rhyme Novel. abr. ed. 2002. audio 26.00 (*0-7435-2064-5*); audio compact disk 30.00 (*0-7435-2065-3*) Simon & Schuster Audio. (Simon & Schuster Audioworks).

—The Stone Monkey: A Lincoln Rhyme Novel. l.t. ed. 2003. 13.95 (*1-4104-0096-4*); 657p. pap. 29.95 (*0-7862-4214-0*) Thorndike Pr.

—The Vanished Man: A Lincoln Rhyme Novel. 2004. (Illus.). 560p. mass mkt. 7.99 (*0-7434-3781-0*, Pocket); 2003. 416p. 25.00 (*0-7432-2200-8*, Simon & Schuster); 2003. E-Book 19.99 (*0-7432-4568-7*, Simon & Schuster); 2003. 416p. 25.00 (*0-7432-5131-8*, Simon & Schuster); 2003. 784p. 25.00 o.s.i (*0-7432-4646-2*, Simon & Schuster) Simon & Schuster.

—The Vanished Man: A Lincoln Rhyme Novel. abr. ed. 2003. audio compact disk 30.00 (*0-7435-2826-3*, Simon & Schuster Audioworks) Simon & Schuster Audio.

**RHYS, MADOC (FICTITIOUS CHARACTER)—FICTION**

Craig, Alisa, pseud. A Dismal Thing to Do. 1986. (Crime Club Ser.). 192p. 12.95 o.p. (*0-385-23263-2*) Doubleday Publishing.

—Murder Goes Mumming. 1989. 192p. mass mkt. 3.99 (*0-380-70335-1*, Avon Bks.) Morrow/Avon.

—A Pint of Murder. 1988. 192p. mass mkt. 3.99 (*0-380-70334-3*, Avon Bks.) Morrow/Avon.

—Trouble in the Brasses. 1989. 224p. mass mkt. 4.50 (*0-380-75539-4*, Avon Bks.) Morrow/Avon.

—The Wrong Rite. 1993. 288p. pap. 4.99 (*0-380-71043-9*, Avon Bks.); 1992. (Madoc & Janet Rhys Mystery Ser.: No. 5). 224p. 19.00 o.p. (*0-688-08643-8*, Morrow, William & Co.) Morrow/Avon.

**RICE, DALE (FICTITIOUS CHARACTER)—FICTION**

Sawyer, Robert J. Illegal Alien. 1997. 304p. 21.95 o.s.i (*0-441-00476-8*); 1999. 320p. reprint ed. mass mkt. 5.99 o.s.i (*0-441-00592-6*) Ace Bks.

**RICE, HARRY (FICTITIOUS CHARACTER)—FICTION**

Pedrazas, Allan. Angel's Cove: A Harry Rice Mystery. 1999. (WWL Mystery Ser.: No. 302). per. (*0-373-26302-3*, 1-26302-9, Worldwide Library) Harlequin Enterprises, Ltd.

—Angel's Cove: A Harry Rice Mystery. 1997. (Harry Rice Mystery Ser.). 272p. 21.95 (*0-312-16773-3*, Saint Martin's Minotaur) St. Martin's Pr.

—The Harry Chronicles: A Mystery. 1997. 256p. mass mkt. 4.99 o.p. (*0-06-104435-0*, HarperTorch) Morrow/Avon.

—The Harry Chronicles: A Mystery. 1995. 256p. 21.95 o.p. (*0-312-13506-8*, Saint Martin's Minotaur) St. Martin's Pr.

**RICE, MALINDA (FICTITIOUS CHARACTER)—FICTION**

Whitney, Phyllis A. Silverhill. 1981. 192p. pap. o.p. (*0-449-44782-0*); 1981. 192p. mass mkt. 5.99 o.s.i (*0-449-24094-0*); 1978. mass mkt. 1.75 o.s.i (*0-449-23592-0*) Ballantine Bks. (Fawcett).

—Silverhill, unabr. ed. 2000. audio 54.95 (*0-7540-0431-7*, CAB 1854) Chivers Audio Bks. GBR. *Dist:* BBC Audiobooks America.

—Silverhill. 1967. 6.95 o.p. (*0-385-03797-X*) Doubleday Publishing.

—Silverhill. l.t. ed. 1979. 12.00 o.p. (*0-7089-0340-1*, Ulverscroft) Thorpe, F. A. Pubs. GBR. *Dist:* Ulverscroft Large Print Bks., Ltd.

**RICE, PENELOPE "POPPY" (FICTITIOUS CHARACTER)—FICTION**

Smith, Mary-Ann Tirone. Love Her Madly. abr. ed. 2003. audio 9.99 (*1-59086-000-4*, 3520, Brilliance Audio Paperback Audiobooks); 2002. audio 19.95 o.p. (*1-58788-999-4*, 3519, Nova Audio Bks.); 2002. audio 29.95 (*1-58788-997-8*, 3517, Brilliance Audio Unabridged); 2002. audio 69.25 (*1-58788-998-6*, 3518, Unabridged Library Editions) Brilliance Audio.

—Love Her Madly. 2002. 320p. 25.00 (*0-8050-6648-9*) Holt, Henry & Co.

—Love Her Madly. 2004. 320p. mass mkt. 6.99 (*0-7860-1657-4*, Pinnacle Bks.) Kensington Publishing Corp.

**RICHARDS, NOAH (FICTITIOUS CHARACTER)—FICTION**

Morgan, Mary. Deeper Waters. E-Book 23.95 (*0-312-70683-9*); 2002. 304p. 23.95 (*0-312-29035-7*, Saint Martin's Minotaur) St. Martin's Pr.

—Willful Neglect. 1998. per. (*0-373-26297-3*, 1-26297-1, Mira Bks.) Harlequin Enterprises, Ltd.

—Willful Neglect. 1997. 256p. 22.95 o.p. (*0-312-15694-4*, Saint Martin's Minotaur) St. Martin's Pr.

**RICHARDS, SUZANNE (FICTITIOUS CHARACTER)—FICTION**

Brookes, Emma. Face Off. 1997. 256p. mass mkt. 5.99 (*0-312-96216-9*, St. Martin's Paperbacks) St. Martin's Pr.

**RICHARDSON, JESSALEA (FICTITIOUS CHARACTER)—FICTION**

Rich, Sue. Aim for the Heart. 1996. 304p. mass mkt. 5.99 (*0-671-89808-6*, Pocket) Simon & Schuster.

**RICHARDSON, RAY (FICTITIOUS CHARACTER)—FICTION**

Kerr, Philip. The Grid. l.t. ed. 1996. 578p. 25.95 o.p. (*0-7838-1654-5*, Macmillan Reference USA) Gale Group.

—The Grid. abr. ed. 1996. audio 12.98 (*1-57042-406-3*, 394054) Time Warner AudioBooks.

—The Grid. 1997. 464p. mass mkt. 6.99 (*0-446-60340-6*); 1996. 82p. 21.95 o.s.i (*0-446-52053-5*) Warner Bks., Inc.

Kerr, Philip. The Grid. unabr. ed. 1996. audio 72.00 (*0-7366-3468-1*, 4112) Books on Tape, Inc.

**RICHTER, MARTA (FICTITIOUS CHARACTER)—FICTION**

Scottoline, Lisa. Rough Justice. l.t. ed. 1998. (Large Print Book Ser.). 26.95 o.p. (*1-56895-521-9*, Wheeler Publishing, Inc.) Gale Group.

—Rough Justice. 1998. 480p. mass mkt. 7.99 (*0-06-109610-5*); 1997. 352p. 24.00 o.s.i (*0-06-018746-8*) HarperCollins Pubs.

—Rough Justice. abr. ed. 1997. audio 18.00 o.s.i (*0-694-51883-2*, 395445, HarperAudio) HarperTrade.

**RICIMER, PIET (FICTITIOUS CHARACTER)—FICTION**

Drake, David. Igniting the Reaches. (Igniting the Reaches Ser.: 1). (Orig.). 1995. 272p. mass mkt. 5.99 o.s.i (*0-441-00179-3*); 1994. 18.95 o.p. (*0-441-00026-6*) Ace Bks.

—Through the Breach. (Igniting the Reaches Ser.: 2). 336p. (Orig.). 1996. mass mkt. 5.99 o.s.i (*0-441-00326-5*); 1995. 19.95 o.p. (*0-441-00171-8*) Ace Bks.

**RIDDLE, HARRY (FICTITIOUS CHARACTER)—FICTION**

Rogers, Joel T. The Red Right Hand. 1983. 198p. reprint ed. pap. 3.50 o.p. (*0-88184-008-4*, Carroll & Graf Pubs.) Avalon Publishing Group.

Rogers, Joel Townsley. The Red Right Hand. 1997. 192p. mass mkt. 4.95 (*0-7867-0446-2*, Carroll & Graf Pubs.) Avalon Publishing Group.

**RIDGWAY, SCHUYLER (FICTITIOUS CHARACTER)—FICTION**

McClellan, Tierney. Closing Statement: A Schuyler Ridgway Mystery. 1995. 304p. (Orig.). mass mkt. 4.99 o.s.i (*0-451-18464-5*, Signet Bks.) NAL.

—Heir Condition. 1995. 256p. (Orig.). mass mkt. 5.50 o.s.i (*0-451-18144-1*, Signet Bks.) NAL.

—Killing in Real Estate. 1996. (Schuyler Ridgway Mystery Ser.). 256p. mass mkt. 5.50 o.s.i (*0-451-18765-2*) NAL.

—Two-Story Frame. 1997. (Schuyler Ridgway Mystery Ser.). 256p. mass mkt. 5.99 o.s.i (*0-451-19197-8*, Signet Bks.) NAL.

**RIDLEY, SAM (FICTITIOUS CHARACTER)—FICTION**

Niles, Chris. Run Time. 1999. 272p. reprint ed. mass mkt. 5.99 o.s.i (*0-425-17119-1*, Prime Crime) Berkley Publishing Group.

—Spike It. 1998. 272p. mass mkt. 5.99 o.s.i (*0-425-16565-5*, Prime Crime) Berkley Publishing Group.

**RIKARDON (FICTITIOUS CHARACTER)—FICTION**

Garrett, Randall. The River Wall. 1986. (Orig.). mass mkt. 3.95 o.s.i (*0-553-27671-9*, Spectra) Bantam Bks.

Garrett, Randall & Heydron, Vicki A. The Glass of Dyskornis. 1982. 144p. pap. 2.95 o.p. (*0-553-25230-5*) Bantam Bks.

—Return to Eddarta. 1985. (Gandalara Cycle Ser.: No. 6). 160p. pap. 2.75 o.p. (*0-553-24709-3*) Bantam Bks.

—The River Wall. 1986. 288p. (Orig.). mass mkt. 3.50 o.s.i (*0-553-25565-7*, Spectra) Bantam Bks.

—The Search for Ka. 1984. 192p. pap. 2.50 o.p. (*0-553-24120-6*) Bantam Bks.

—The Steel of Raithskar. 1981. 192p. pap. 2.75 o.p. (*0-553-24911-8*) Bantam Bks.

—The Well of Darkness. 1983. (Gandalara Cycle Ser.: No. 4). pap. 2.75 o.p. (*0-553-24505-8*) Bantam Bks.

**RIKER, WILLIAM THOMAS (FICTITIOUS CHARACTER)—FICTION**

Bischoff, David. Grounded. Stern, David, ed. 1993. (Star Trek, The Next Generation Ser.: No. 25). 288p. mass mkt. 5.50 (*0-671-79747-6*, Star Trek) Simon & Schuster.

Carey, Diane L. Day of Honor No. 1: Ancient Blood. 1997. (Star Trek, The Next Generation: Vol. 1). (Illus.). 304p. pap. 5.99 (*0-671-00238-4*, Star Trek) Simon & Schuster.

Cox, Greg. The Q-Continuum No. 1: Q-Space. 1999. (Star Trek, The Next Generation Ser.: No. 47). E-Book 6.99 (*0-671-04101-0*, Star Trek) Simon & Schuster.

—Q-Space No. 1: The Q-Continuum. 1998. (Star Trek, The Next Generation Ser.: No. 47). 288p. (J). pap. 6.50 (*0-671-01915-5*, Star Trek) Simon & Schuster.

David, Peter. Double or Nothing. 1999. (Star Trek, The Next Generation Ser.: Vol. 5). 277p. pap. 6.50 o.s.i (*0-671-03478-2*, Star Trek) Simon & Schuster.

—Imzadi. Stern, Dave, ed. (Star Trek, The Next Generation Ser.). 352p. 1998. mass mkt. 3.99 (*0-671-02610-0*); 1992. 20.00 (*0-671-79197-4*); 1993. reprint ed. mass mkt. 6.50 (*0-671-86729-6*) Simon & Schuster. (Star Trek).

—Imzadi. abr. ed. 1992. (Star Trek Ser.). audio 17.00 (*0-671-79198-2*, Simon & Schuster Audioworks) Simon & Schuster Audio.

—Imzadi II: Triangle. (Star Trek, The Next Generation Ser.). E-Book 6.99 (*0-7434-2071-3*); 1998. 384p. 23.00 o.s.i (*0-671-02532-5*); 1999. 400p. reprint ed. pap. 6.50 (*0-671-02538-4*) Simon & Schuster. (Star Trek).

—Imzadi II: Triangle. abr. ed. 1998. (Star Trek Ser.: Vol. 2). audio 18.00 (*0-671-04328-5*, Simon & Schuster Audioworks) Simon & Schuster Audio.

—Imzadi II: Triangle. abr. ed. 1999. (Star Trek Ser.). audio 15.00 (*0-671-03343-3*) Ulverscroft Audio (U.S.A.).

—A Rock & a Hard Place. (Star Trek, The Next Generation Ser.: No. 10). E-Book 6.99 (*0-7434-2090-X*, Star Trek) Simon & Schuster.

—A Rock & a Hard Place. Stern, Dave, ed. 1991. (Star Trek, The Next Generation Ser.: No. 10). 256p. mass mkt. 5.50 (*0-671-74142-X*, Star Trek) Simon & Schuster.

—A Rock & a Hard Place. 1990. (Star Trek, The Next Generation Ser.: No. 10). mass mkt. 3.95 o.s.i (*0-671-69364-6*, Star Trek) Simon & Schuster.

—Strike Zone. (Star Trek, The Next Generation Ser.: No. 5). 1991. mass mkt. 5.99 (*0-671-74647-2*); 1990. mass mkt. 4.50 o.s.i (*0-671-73516-0*) Simon & Schuster. (Star Trek).

—The Strike Zone. 1989. (Star Trek, The Next Generation Ser.: No. 5). E-Book 6.99 (*0-7434-1217-6*, Star Trek) Simon & Schuster.

Dillard, J. M. First Contact. abr. ed. 1996. (Star Trek Ser.: No. 8). audio 18.00 (*0-671-57391-8*, Simon & Schuster Audioworks) Simon & Schuster Audio.

—Generations. (Star Trek Ser.: No. 7). 1995. (Illus.). 304p. mass mkt. 5.99 (*0-671-53753-9*); 1994. 288p. 20.00 o.p. (*0-671-51742-2*) Simon & Schuster. (Star Trek).

—Generations. 1994. (Star Trek Ser.: No. 7). pap. 17.00 incl. audio (*0-671-51996-4*, Simon & Schuster Audioworks) Simon & Schuster Audio.

—Insurrection. abr. ed. (Star Trek Ser.: No. 9). 1998. audio 18.00 o.s.i (*0-671-58259-3*, 396208, Simon & Schuster Audioworks); 2003. audio 9.95 (*0-7435-3254-6*, Encore) Simon & Schuster Audio.

Dillard, J. M. & Berman, Rick. Insurrection. 1998. (Star Trek Ser.: No. 9). 304p. 22.00 o.s.i (*0-671-02447-7*, Star Trek) Simon & Schuster.

Durgin, Doranna. Tooth & Claw. 2001. (Star Trek, The Next Generation Ser.: Vol. 60). (Illus.). 272p. pap. 6.99 (*0-671-04211-4*, Star Trek) Simon & Schuster.

Forstchen, William R. The Forgotten War. (Star Trek, The Next Generation Ser.: No. 57). E-Book 6.99 (*0-7434-2138-8*); 1999. (Illus.). 304p. mass mkt. 6.50 o.s.i (*0-671-01159-6*) Simon & Schuster. (Star Trek).

Friedman, Michael Jan. All Good Things. 1994. (Star Trek Ser.). 256p. o.p. (*0-671-50014-7*, Atria) Simon & Schuster.

—The First Virtue No. 6: Double Helix. (Star Trek, The Next Generation Ser.: No. 56). E-Book 6.99 (*0-7434-2136-1*, Star Trek) Simon & Schuster.

—Requiem. 2000. (Star Trek, The Next Generation Ser.: No. 32). E-Book 6.99 (*0-7434-2115-9*, Star Trek) Simon & Schuster.

Friedman, Michael Jan & Ryan, Kevin. Requiem. 1994. (Star Trek, The Next Generation Ser.: No. 32). 288p. mass mkt. 5.50 (*0-671-79567-8*, Star Trek) Simon & Schuster.

Galanter, Dave & Brodeur, Greg. Foreign Foes. (Star Trek, The Next Generation Ser.: No. 31). E-Book 6.99 (*0-7434-2114-0*); 1994. 288p. mass mkt. 5.50 (*0-671-88414-X*) Simon & Schuster. (Star Trek).

Mancour, T. L. Spartacus. (Star Trek, The Next Generation Ser.: No. 20). E-Book 6.99 (*0-7434-2100-0*, Star Trek) Simon & Schuster.

—Spartacus. Stern, Dave, ed. 1992. (Star Trek, The Next Generation Ser.: No. 20). 288p. mass mkt. 5.50 (*0-671-76051-3*, Star Trek) Simon & Schuster.

Mitchell, V. E. Imbalance. (Star Trek, The Next Generation Ser.: No. 22). E-Book 6.99 (*0-7434-2102-7*, Star Trek) Simon & Schuster.

—Imbalance. Stern, Dave, ed. 1992. (Star Trek, The Next Generation Ser.: No. 22). 288p. mass mkt. 5.50 (*0-671-77571-5*, Star Trek) Simon & Schuster.

Peel, John. Death of Princes. 1996. (Star Trek, The Next Generation Ser.: No. 44). 304p. pap. 5.99 (*0-671-56808-6*, Star Trek) Simon & Schuster.

—Here There Be Dragons. Ryan, Kevin, ed. 1993. (Star Trek, The Next Generation Ser.: No. 28). 288p. (Orig.). mass mkt. 5.99 (*0-671-86571-4*, Star Trek) Simon & Schuster.

Shatner, William, et al. The Return. (Star Trek Ser.). 1997. 400p. mass mkt. 6.99 (*0-671-52609-X*, Star Trek); 1996. 384p. 22.00 o.p. (*0-671-52610-3*, Atria) Simon & Schuster.

—The Return. abr. ed. 1996. (Star Trek Ser.). audio 18.00 o.s.i (*0-671-56848-5*, 393928, Simon & Schuster Audioworks) Simon & Schuster Audio.

—Star Trek: The Return. l.t. ed. 1996. (Star Trek Ser.). 456p. 24.95 (*1-56895-359-3*, Wheeler Publishing, Inc.) Gale Group.

Smith, Dean Wesley. Invasion! No. 2: The Soldiers of Fear. (Star Trek, The Next Generation Ser.: No. 41). E-Book 6.99 (*0-7434-2119-1*, Star Trek) Simon & Schuster.

Smith, Dean Wesley, et al. The Soldiers of Fear No. 2: Invasion! 1996. (Star Trek, The Next Generation Ser.: No. 41). 288p. (J). pap. 6.50 (*0-671-54174-9*, Star Trek) Simon & Schuster.

Somtow, S. P. Do Comets Dream? 2003. (Star Trek, The Next Generation Ser.). 288p. pap. 6.99 (*0-7434-1130-7*, Star Trek) Simon & Schuster.

Thompson, W. R. Infiltrator. 1996. (Star Trek, The Next Generation Ser.: No. 42). 288p. mass mkt. 5.99 (*0-671-56831-0*, Star Trek) Simon & Schuster.

Vornholt, John. Double Helix: Quarantine. 1999. (Star Trek, The Next Generation Ser.: No. 54). (Illus.). 304p. pap. 6.99 (*0-671-03477-4*, Star Trek) Simon & Schuster.

—Gemworld, No. 2. 2000. (Star Trek, The Next Generation Ser.: No. 59). E-Book 6.99 (*0-7434-0678-8*); (Illus.). 272p. pap. 6.50 (*0-671-04271-8*) Simon & Schuster. (Star Trek).

—Rogue Saucer. 1996. (Star Trek, The Next Generation Ser.: No. 39). 288p. mass mkt. 5.99 (*0-671-54917-0*, Star Trek) Simon & Schuster.

Weinstein, Howard. Power Hungry. (Star Trek, The Next Generation Ser.: No. 6). E-Book 6.99 (*0-7434-2086-1*, Star Trek) Simon & Schuster.

—Power Hungry. Stern, Dave, ed. 1991. (Star Trek, The Next Generation Ser.: No. 6). mass mkt. 5.50 (*0-671-74648-0*, Star Trek) Simon & Schuster.

Wright, Susan. Badlands. 1999. (Star Trek Ser.: Bk. 1). (Illus.). 304p. pap. 6.50 (*0-671-03957-1*, Star Trek) Simon & Schuster.

—The Badlands, No. 1. 2000. (Star Trek Ser.). E-Book 6.99 (*0-7434-0674-5*, Star Trek) Simon & Schuster.

**RILEY, DAVE (FICTITIOUS CHARACTER)—FICTION**

Mayer, Bob. Cut-Out: A Novel. 1995. 256p. 19.95 o.p. (*0-89141-508-4*, Presidio Pr.) Ballantine Bks.

—Cut-Out: A Novel. 2002. 238p. reprint ed. 20.00 (*0-7567-5723-1*) DIANE Publishing Co.

—Dragon SIM-13: A Novel. 1992. 19.95 o.p. (*0-89141-415-0*, Presidio Pr.) Ballantine Bks.

—Eternity Base: A Dave Riley Novel. 1996. 320p. 21.95 o.p. (*0-89141-509-2*, Presidio Pr.) Ballantine Bks.

—Eyes of the Hammer. 1991. 19.95 o.p. (*0-89141-414-2*, Presidio Pr.) Ballantine Bks.

—Eyes of the Hammer. 1992. mass mkt. 4.99 (*0-312-92862-9*, St. Martin's Paperbacks) St. Martin's Pr.

—Eyes of the Hammer. 2001. E-Book 6.99 (*0-7592-4195-3*) ereads.com.

—Synbat: A Novel. 1993. 286p. 19.95 o.p. (*0-89141-416-9*, Presidio Pr.) Ballantine Bks.

—Z: A Dave Riley Novel. 1996. (Dave Riley Adventures Ser.: Vol. 6). 288p. 21.95 o.p. (*0-89141-510-6*, Presidio Pr.) Ballantine Bks.

**RINCEWIND THE WIZARD (FICTITIOUS CHARACTER)—FICTION**

Pratchett, Terry. The Colour of Magic. 2000. (Discworld Ser.). 240p. mass mkt. 6.99 (*0-06-102071-0*, Perennial) HarperTrade.

—Eric. 2002. 224p. mass mkt. 6.99 (*0-380-82121-4*) Morrow/Avon.

—Eric. 1995. (Discworld Ser.). 192p. mass mkt. 5.99 o.s.i (*0-451-45357-3*, Signet Bks.) NAL.

—Interesting Times. unabr. ed. 1997. (Discworld Ser.). audio 54.95 (*1-85695-814-0*, 950603) ISIS Audio Bks. GBR. *Dist:* Ulverscroft Large Print Bks., Ltd.

—Interesting Times. l.t. ed. (Discworld Ser.). 23.95 (*1-85695-254-1*) ISIS Large Print Bks. GBR. *Dist:* Transaction Pubs.

—Interesting Times. (Discworld Ser.). pap. o.s.i (*0-06-105341-4*, Eos); 1998. 400p. mass mkt. 6.99 (*0-06-105690-1*, HarperTorch); 1997. 288p. 22.00 o.p. (*0-06-105252-3*, Eos) Morrow/Avon.

—The Last Continent. 1999. (Illus.). 411p. mass mkt. (*0-552-14614-5*); 1998. 329p. o.s.i (*0-385-40989-3*) Bantam Bks. (Corgi).

—The Last Continent. 1999. (Discworld Ser.). 304p. 24.00 o.p. (*0-06-105048-2*) HarperCollins Pubs.

—The Last Continent. unabr. ed. 1999. (Discworld Ser.). audio 69.95 (*0-7531-0522-5*, 990203) ISIS Audio Bks. GBR. *Dist:* Ulverscroft Large Print Bks., Ltd.

—The Last Continent. 2000. (Discworld Ser.). 400p. mass mkt. 6.99 (*0-06-105907-2*, Eos) Morrow/Avon.

—The Light Fantastic. 1997. (Discworld Ser.). 284p. (YA). (gr. 9). mass mkt. 6.99 (*0-552-12848-1*) Bantam Bks.

—The Light Fantastic. 2000. (Discworld Ser.). (Illus.). 272p. mass mkt. 6.99 (*0-06-102070-2*, Perennial) HarperTrade.

—The Light Fantastic. unabr. ed. 1997. (Discworld Ser.). audio 54.95 (*1-85695-831-0*, 950508) ISIS Audio Bks. GBR. *Dist:* Ulverscroft Large Print Bks., Ltd.

—The Light Fantastic. l.t. ed. (Discworld Ser.). 24.95 (*1-85695-369-6*) ISIS Large Print Bks. GBR. *Dist:* Transaction Pubs.

—The Light Fantastic. 1988. (Discworld Ser.). 256p. mass mkt. 3.50 o.p. (*0-451-15297-2*, Signet Bks.); mass mkt. 5.99 o.s.i (*0-451-16241-2*, ROC) NAL.

—The Light Fantastic. 1987. (Discworld Ser.). 218p. 27.95 (*0-86140-203-0*) Smythe, Colin Ltd. GBR. *Dist:* Dufour Editions, Inc.

—The Light Fantastic. 1958. (Discworld Ser.). 240p. 14.95 o.p. (*0-312-48603-0*) St. Martin's Pr.

—Sourcery. 1989. (Discworld Ser.). 240p. mass mkt. 6.99 (*0-552-13107-5*) Bantam Bks.

—Sourcery. unabr. ed. 1997. (Discworld Ser.). audio 54.95 (*1-85695-862-0*, 950701) ISIS Audio Bks. GBR. *Dist:* Ulverscroft Large Print Bks., Ltd.

—Sourcery. 1989. (Discworld Ser.). 256p. mass mkt. 5.99 o.p. (*0-451-16233-1*, ROC) NAL.

**RINGWALD, CASSIE (FICTITIOUS CHARACTER)—FICTION**

Wooley, Marilyn. Jackpot Justice. E-Book 24.95 (*0-312-27384-3*); 2000. 352p. 24.95 (*0-312-25455-5*, Saint Martin's Minotaur) St. Martin's Pr.

**RIORDAN, MATT (FICTITIOUS CHARACTER)—FICTION**

Heubner, Fredrick. Methods of Execution: A Novel. 1994. 284p. 22.00 (*0-671-86724-5*, Simon & Schuster) Simon & Schuster.

Huebner, Frederick D. Methods of Execution. 1995. mass mkt. 5.99 o.s.i (*0-449-14939-0*, Fawcett) Ballantine Bks.

—Methods of Execution. unabr. ed. 1994. audio 56.00 (*0-7366-2882-7*, 3584) Books on Tape, Inc.

**RIORDANT, PAT (FICTITIOUS CHARACTER)—FICTION**

Gilligan, Roy. Poets Never Kill. 1991. (Pat Riordan Mystery Ser.). 200p. pap. 8.95 (*0-9626136-1-4*) Brendan Bks.

—Poets Never Kill. 1991. (Pat Riordan Mystery Ser.). 180p. (C). reprint ed. lib. bdg. 26.00 o.p. (*0-8095-4210-2*) Millefleurs.

**RIOS, HENRY (FICTITIOUS CHARACTER)—FICTION**

Nava, Michael. The Burning Plain. 1999. 432p. mass mkt. 5.99 o.s.i (*0-553-58085-X*) Bantam Bks.

—The Burning Plain. 1998. 240p. 23.95 o.p. (*0-399-14310-6*, G. P. Putnam's Sons) Penguin Group (USA) Inc.

—Death of Friends. 1996. 288p. 22.95 o.p. (*0-399-13977-X*, G. P. Putnam's Sons) Penguin Group (USA) Inc.

—The Death of Friends. 1998. 256p. reprint ed. mass mkt. 5.99 o.s.i (*0-553-57763-8*) Bantam Bks.

—Goldenboy. (Henry Rios Mystery Ser.). 2003. 216p. pap. 12.95 (*1-55583-829-4*, Alyson Bks.); 1988. 216p. 5.95 o.p. (*1-55583-141-9*); 1996. 224p. reprint ed. pap. 10.00 o.p. (*1-55583-366-7*); 1991. 215p. reprint ed. pap. 8.95 o.p. (*1-55583-130-3*) Alyson Pubns.

—The Hidden Law. 2003. (Henry Rios Mystery Ser.). 232p. pap. 12.95 (*1-55583-778-6*, Alyson Bks.) Alyson Pubns.

—The Hidden Law. 1994. (Los Angeles Mysteries Ser.). 192p. mass mkt. 4.99 o.s.i (*0-345-38406-7*) Ballantine Bks.

—The Hidden Law. 1992. 288p. 19.00 o.p. (*0-06-016783-1*) HarperTrade.

—How Town. 1991. (Los Angeles Mysteries Ser.). 240p. mass mkt. 4.99 o.s.i (*0-345-36987-4*) Ballantine Bks.

—How Town. 1990. 224p. 16.95 o.p. (*0-06-016207-4*) HarperTrade.

—Howtown. 2003. (Henry Rios Mystery Ser.). 232p. pap. 12.95 (*1-55583-779-4*, Advocate Bks.) Alyson Pubns.

—The Little Death. 165p. 1986. pap. 7.95 o.p. (*0-932870-96-1*); 1997. reprint ed. pap. 9.95 o.p. (*1-55583-388-8*); 3rd ed. 2001. (Illus.). pap. 11.95 (*1-55583-694-1*) Alyson Pubns.

—The Little Death: A Henry Rios Mystery. 2003. (Illus.). 168p. pap. 12.95 (*1-55583-830-8*, Alyson Bks.) Alyson Pubns.

—Rag & Bone: A Henry Rios Novel. 2002. 304p. pap. 14.00 (*0-425-18470-6*) Berkley Publishing Group.

—Rag & Bone: A Henry Rios Novel. 2001. 304p. 24.95 o.s.i (*0-399-14708-X*) Penguin Group (USA) Inc.

**RIPLEY, TOM (FICTITIOUS CHARACTER)—FICTION**

Highsmith, Patricia. The Boy Who Followed Ripley. 1993. (Mr. Ripley Ser.). 304p. pap. 12.00 (*0-679-74567-X*, Vintage) Knopf Publishing Group.

—The Boy Who Followed Ripley. 1985. (Mr. Ripley Ser.). 336p. pap. 3.95 o.p. (*0-14-005739-0*, Penguin Bks.) Viking Penguin.

—The Mysterious Mr. Ripley. 1985. (Crime Ser.). 656p. pap. 10.95 o.p. (*0-14-007196-2*, Penguin Bks.) Viking Penguin.

—Ripley under Ground. unabr. ed. 1993. (Mr. Ripley Ser.). audio 69.95 (*1-85088-853-1*, 91094) Eye in the Ear Inc.

—Ripley under Ground. l.t. ed. 1990. (Mr. Ripley Ser.). 416p. 19.95 (*1-85089-304-7*) ISIS Large Print Bks. GBR. *Dist:* Transaction Pubs.

—Ripley under Ground. 1992. (Mr. Ripley Ser.). 320p. pap. 12.95 (*0-679-74230-1*, Vintage) Knopf Publishing Group.

—Ripley under Water. unabr. ed. 2001. (Mr. Ripley Series). audio 69.95 (*1-85089-888-X*, 92061) ISIS Audio Bks. GBR. *Dist:* Ulverscroft Large Print Bks., Ltd.

—Ripley under Water. 1993. (Mr. Ripley Ser.). 320p. pap. 12.00 (*0-679-74809-1*, Vintage) Knopf Publishing Group.

—Ripley under Water. 1994. (Mr. Ripley Ser.). 4.99 o.p. (*0-517-11787-8*) Random Hse. Value Publishing.

—Ripley's Game. l.t. ed. 1991. (Mr. Ripley Ser.). 376p. 32.50 o.p. (*1-85089-423-X*) ISIS Large Print Bks. GBR. *Dist:* Ulverscroft Large Print Bks., Ltd.

—Ripley's Game. 1993. (Mr. Ripley Ser.). 288p. pap. 12.95 (*0-679-74568-8*, Vintage) Knopf Publishing Group.

—The Talented Mr. Ripley. unabr. ed. 2001. (Mr. Ripley Series). audio 69.95 (*1-85089-775-1*, 89102) ISIS Audio Bks. GBR. *Dist:* Ulverscroft Large Print Bks., Ltd.

—The Talented Mr. Ripley. l.t. ed. 1988. (Mr. Ripley Ser.). 392p. reprint ed. lib. bdg. 18.95 o.p. (*1-85089-184-2*) ISIS Large Print Bks. GBR. *Dist:* Transaction Pubs.

—The Talented Mr. Ripley. (Mr. Ripley Ser.). 304p. 1999. pap. 13.00 (*0-676-58972-3*); 1992. pap. 13.00 (*0-679-74229-8*) Knopf Publishing Group. (Vintage).

—The Talented Mr. Ripley, Set. unabr. ed. 1999. (Mr. Ripley Ser.). audio 39.95 (*0-375-40511-9*, RH Audio) Random Hse. Audio Publishing Group.

—The Talented Mr. Ripley. 2000. (Mr. Ripley Ser.). 287p. (*0-7621-8856-1*) Reader's Digest Assn., Inc., The.

—The Talented Mr. Ripley. 1982. (Mr. Ripley Ser.). 256p. pap. 4.95 o.p. (*0-14-004020-X*, Penguin Bks.) Viking Penguin.

—The Talented Mr. Ripley, Ripley Under Ground, Ripley's Game. 1999. (Mr. Ripley Ser.). 880p. 26.00 (*0-375-40792-8*) Knopf, Alfred A. Inc.

Minghella, Anthony. The Talented Mr. Ripley. 1999. (Mr. Ripley Ser.). 144p. 10.95 (*0-7868-8521-1*) Talk Miramax Bks.

Nagy, Phyllis. The Talented Mr. Ripley. 1999. (Mr. Ripley Ser.). 100p. pap. 10.95 (*0-413-73220-7*) Methuen Publishing Ltd. GBR. *Dist:* Consortium Bk. Sales & Distribution.

**RISK, DOCTOR (FICTITIOUS CHARACTER)—FICTION**

Berger, Bob. The Risk of Heaven. 1996. 352p. mass mkt. 4.99 o.s.i (*0-440-22052-1*) Dell Publishing.

—The Risk of Murder: A Dr. Risk Mystery. 1995. 288p. mass mkt. 4.99 o.s.i (*0-440-22051-3*) Dell Publishing.

**RITTENHOUSE, MEG (FICTITIOUS CHARACTER)—FICTION**

Michaels, Barbara, pseud. House of Many Shadows. 1978. pap. 1.75 o.s.i (*0-449-23720-6*, Fawcett) Ballantine Bks.

—House of Many Shadows. 1996. 304p. mass mkt. 7.50 o.s.i (*0-425-15189-1*) Berkley Publishing Group.

—House of Many Shadows. l.t. ed. 1981. 405p. o.p. (*0-7089-0666-4*, Ulverscroft) Thorpe, F. A. Pubs.

Characters

**RIVERS, JAMES (FICTITIOUS CHARACTER)—FICTION**

Herbert, James. Portent. 368p. 1997. mass mkt. 5.99 o.s.i (*0-06-105432-1*); 1996. 14.00 o.s.i (*0-06-105211-6*) Morrow/Avon. (Eos).

**ROBAK, DON (FICTITIOUS CHARACTER)—FICTION**

Hensley, Joe L. Killing in Gold. 1978. (Donald Robak Mysteries Ser.). 181p. pap. text 15.00 (*1-58715-036-0*) Wildside Pr.
—Outcasts. 1981. (Crime Club Ser.). 192p. 10.95 o.p. (*0-385-15820-3*) Doubleday Publishing.
—Outcasts. 1981. (Donald Robak Mysteries Ser.). 180p. pap. text 15.00 (*1-58715-041-7*) Wildside Pr.
—Rivertown Risk. 1977. (Donald Robak Mysteries Ser.). 187p. pap. text 15.00 (*1-58715-040-9*) Wildside Pr.
—Robak in Black: A Don Robak Mystery. 2001. 256p. 23.95 (*0-312-24109-7*) St. Martin's Pr.
—Robak's Witch: A Dan Robak Mystery. 1997. 256p. 21.95 o.p. (*0-312-15642-1*, Saint Martin's Minotaur) St. Martin's Pr.

**ROBERTS, AMANDA (FICTITIOUS CHARACTER)—FICTION**

Woods, Sherryl. Bank on It. 2000. 235p. 26.95 (*0-7351-0306-2*); pap. 16.95 (*0-7351-0307-0*) Replica Bks.
—Bank on It. 1993. 240p. mass mkt. 4.99 o.s.i (*0-446-36404-5*) Warner Bks., Inc.
—Body & Soul. 2000. 254p. 26.95 (*0-7351-0310-0*); pap. 16.95 (*0-7351-0311-9*) Replica Bks.
—Body & Soul. 1990. 19.00 o.p. (*0-7278-4111-4*) Severn Hse. Pubs., Ltd.
—Body & Soul. 1994. 256p. mass mkt. 5.50 o.s.i (*0-446-60155-1*, Mysterious Pr. Paperback Bks.); 1989. 3.95 (*0-445-20900-3*) Warner Bks., Inc.
—Deadly Obsession. 2000. 236p. 26.95 (*0-7351-0314-3*); pap. 16.95 (*0-7351-0315-1*) Replica Bks.
—Deadly Obsession. 1995. 256p. mass mkt. 5.50 (*0-446-60091-1*) Warner Bks., Inc.
—Hide & Seek. unabr. collector's ed. 1994. audio 36.00 (*0-7366-2778-2*, 3497) Books on Tape, Inc.
—Hide & Seek. 2000. 339p. 28.95 (*0-7351-0304-6*); pap. 18.95 (*0-7351-0305-4*) Replica Bks.
—Hide & Seek. 1993. 240p. mass mkt. 4.99 o.s.i (*0-446-36405-3*) Warner Bks., Inc.
—Reckless. 2000. 240p. 26.95 (*0-7351-0312-7*); 235p. pap. 16.95 (*0-7351-0313-5*) Replica Bks.
—Reckless. 1990. reprint ed. 18.00 o.p. (*0-7278-4048-7*) Severn Hse. Pubs., Ltd.
—Reckless. 1993. 240p. mass mkt. 4.99 o.s.i (*0-446-36549-1*); 1989. pap. 3.95 (*0-445-20819-8*) Warner Bks., Inc.
—Stolen Moments. 2000. 253p. 26.95 (*0-7351-0300-3*); pap. 16.95 (*0-7351-0301-1*) Replica Bks.
—Stolen Moments. 1991. reprint ed. 18.95 o.p. (*0-7278-4174-2*) Severn Hse. Pubs., Ltd.
—Stolen Moments. 1995. 256p. mass mkt. 5.99 o.s.i (*0-446-60163-2*); 1990. mass mkt. 4.95 (*0-445-21010-9*, Mysterious Pr. Paperback Bks.) Warner Bks., Inc.
—Ties That Bind. 2000. 255p. 16.95 (*0-7351-0309-7*); 26.95 (*0-7351-0308-9*) Replica Bks.
—Ties That Bind. 1991. 256p. reprint ed. 19.00 o.p. (*0-7278-4245-5*) Severn Hse. Pubs., Ltd.
—Ties That Bind. 1991. 256p. mass mkt. 4.99 (*0-446-36117-8*) Warner Bks., Inc.
—Wages of Sin. 1999. 254p. pap. 16.95 (*0-7351-0322-4*); reprint ed. 26.95 o.p. (*0-7351-0071-3*) Replica Bks.
—Wages of Sin. 1994. 272p. mass mkt. 5.50 (*0-446-60088-1*) Warner Bks., Inc.
—White Lightning. 2000. 316p. 28.95 (*0-7351-0302-X*); pap. 18.95 (*0-7351-0303-8*) Replica Bks.
—White Lightning. 1995. 320p. mass mkt. 5.99 o.p. (*0-446-60090-3*) Warner Bks., Inc.

**ROBERTS, MITCHELL (FICTITIOUS CHARACTER)—FICTION**

Dold, Gaylord. Samedi's Backpack: Mitch Robert's Mystery. 2001. 313p. 23.95 (*0-312-26643-X*, Saint Martin's Minotaur) St. Martin's Pr.

**ROBERTS, RALPH (FICTITIOUS CHARACTER)—FICTION**

King, Stephen. Insomnia. 1995. (SPA., Illus.). 610p. (*84-253-2703-2*) Grijalbo, Editorial.
—Insomnia. 1995. pap. 6.99 o.s.i (*0-451-18612-5*); (Illus.). 672p. mass mkt. 7.99 (*0-451-18496-3*, Signet Bks.) NAL.
—Insomnia. abr. unabr. ed. 1994. audio 79.95 (*0-453-00910-7*) Penguin/HighBridge.
—Insomnia. 788p. 7.98 o.p. (*0-8317-3612-7*) Smithmark Pubs., Inc.
—Insomnia. l.t. ed. 1995. (Core Collection). 951p. 31.95 (*0-7838-1183-7*) Thorndike Pr.
—Insomnia. 1995. 14.04 (*0-606-07708-1*) Turtleback Bks.
—Insomnia. 1994. (Illus.). 832p. 27.95 (*0-670-85503-0*, Viking) Viking Penguin.
—Insomnia. deluxe ed. 1994. (Illus.). 591p. 75.00 (*0-929480-37-6*) Ziesing, Mark V.

**ROBICHEAUX, DAVE (FICTITIOUS CHARACTER)—FICTION**

Burke, James Lee. Black Cherry Blues. l.t. ed. 1996. lib. bdg. 24.95 (*1-57490-070-6*, Beeler Large Print Bks.) Beeler, Thomas T. Publisher.
—Black Cherry Blues. 1989. 17.95 o.p. (*0-316-11699-8*) Little Brown & Co.
—Black Cherry Blues. 1990. 384p. reprint ed. mass mkt. 7.99 (*0-380-71204-0*, Avon Bks.) Morrow/Avon.
—Black Cherry Blues. unabr. ed. 2000. audio 78.00 (*1-55690-791-5*, 93106E7) Recorded Bks., LLC.
—Black Cherry Blues. abr. ed. 2001. audio 9.98 (*0-7435-2302-4*); 1991. audio 16.00 (*0-671-73610-8*); Set. 1998. audio 9.98 (*0-671-58255-0*, 390401) Simon & Schuster Audio. (Simon & Schuster Audioworks).
—Burning Angel. l.t. ed. 1995. 502p. 25.95 o.p. (*0-7838-1492-5*, Macmillan Reference USA) Gale Group.
—Burning Angel. 1995. 352p. 22.95 o.p. (*0-7868-6082-0*); 2002. 464p. reprint ed. mass mkt. 7.99 (*0-7868-8904-7*) Hyperion Pr.
—Burning Angel. unabr. ed. 2000. (Dave Robicheaux Ser.: Vol. 8). audio 85.00 (*0-7887-0345-5*, 94537E7) Recorded Bks., LLC.
—Burning Angel. 2001. audio 9.98 (*0-7435-2309-1*); 1998. audio 9.98 (*0-671-58254-2*); 1995. audio 17.00 (*0-671-52927-7*, 393120) Simon & Schuster Audio. (Simon & Schuster Audioworks).
—Burning Angel. deluxe ltd. num. ed. 1995. 340p. 125.00 o.s.i (*0-9631925-3-1*) Trice, B.E. Publishing.
—Cadillac Jukebox. l.t. ed. 1996. (Large Print Bks.). 27.95 o.p. (*1-56895-375-5*, Wheeler Publishing, Inc.) Gale Group.
—Cadillac Jukebox. 1996. 352p. 22.95 (*0-7868-6175-4*); 2002. 464p. reprint ed. mass mkt. 6.99 (*0-7868-8918-7*) Hyperion Pr.
—Cadillac Jukebox. unabr. ed. 1996. (Dave Robicheaux Ser.: Vol. 9). audio 83.00 (*0-7887-0725-6*, 94902E7) Recorded Bks., LLC.
—Cadillac Jukebox. abr. ed. 1998. audio 14.40 (*0-671-57732-8*, 908764); 1996. audio 18.00 (*0-671-57365-9*, 394156) Simon & Schuster Audio. (Simon & Schuster Audioworks).
—Cadillac Jukebox. deluxe ltd. num. ed. 1996. 303p. 150.00 (*0-9631925-5-8*) Trice, B.E. Publishing.
—Dixie City Jam. l.t. ed. 1994. 590p. lib. bdg. 22.95 o.p. (*0-8161-7488-1*, Macmillan Reference USA) Gale Group.
—Dixie City Jam. 1994. 352p. 22.95 (*0-7868-6019-7*); 2002. 512p. reprint ed. mass mkt. 7.99 (*0-7868-8900-4*) Hyperion Pr.
—Dixie City Jam. unabr. ed. 1994. audio. (Dave Robicheaux Ser.: Vol. 7). audio 85.00 (*0-7887-0060-X*, 94316E7) Recorded Bks., LLC.
—Dixie City Jam. 2001. audio 9.98 o.s.i (*0-7435-0476-3*); 1998. audio 9.98 (*0-671-58252-6*); 1994. audio 17.00 o.s.i (*0-671-88761-0*, 390665) Simon & Schuster Audio. (Simon & Schuster Audioworks).
—Heaven's Prisoners. l.t. ed. 1997. lib. bdg. 24.95 (*1-57490-086-2*, Beeler Large Print Bks.) Beeler, Thomas T. Publisher.
—Heaven's Prisoners. 1988. 17.95 o.p. (*0-8050-0665-6*) Holt, Henry & Co.
—Heaven's Prisoners. unabr. ed. 1996. (Dave Robicheaux Ser.: Vol. 2). audio 70.00 (*0-7887-0623-3*, 94797E7) Recorded Bks., LLC.
—Heaven's Prisoners. 288p. 1989. mass mkt. 5.99 o.s.i (*0-671-67629-6*); 1996. pap. 7.99 (*0-671-51741-4*) Simon & Schuster. (Pocket).
—Heaven's Prisoners. abr. ed. 1996. (Dave Robicheaux Mystery Ser.). 3p. audio 17.00 (*0-671-73608-6*, 392196, Simon & Schuster Audioworks) Simon & Schuster Audio.
—In the Electric Mist with Confederate Dead. unabr. collector's ed. 1995. audio 72.00 (*0-7366-2940-8*, 3636) Books on Tape, Inc.
—In the Electric Mist with Confederate Dead. l.t. ed. 1995. 483p. 23.95 o.p. (*0-8161-7487-3*, Macmillan Reference USA) Gale Group.
—In the Electric Mist with Confederate Dead. 1993. 352p. 19.95 o.p. (*1-56282-882-7*) Hyperion Pr.
—In the Electric Mist with Confederate Dead. 1994. 384p. reprint ed. mass mkt. 7.50 (*0-380-72121-X*, Avon Bks.) Morrow/Avon.
—In the Electric Mist with Confederate Dead. abr. ed. 1993. (Dave Robicheaux Mystery Ser.). 3p. audio 17.00 (*0-671-86816-0*, 390972, Simon & Schuster Audioworks) Simon & Schuster Audio.
—The Intruders. abr. ed. 1999. audio 9.98 (*0-671-04407-9*, Simon & Schuster Audioworks) Simon & Schuster Audio.
—Jolie Blon's Bounce. l.t. ed. 2002. (Wheeler Hardcover Ser.). 566p. 30.95 (*1-58724-273-7*, Wheeler Publishing, Inc.) Gale Group.
—Jolie Blon's Bounce. unabr. ed. 2002. audio 49.95 (*1-4025-2396-3*, RG088); audio compact disk 124.00 (*1-4025-2966-X*, C1855) Recorded Bks., LLC.
—Jolie Blon's Bounce. 2003. 480p. mass mkt. 7.99 (*0-7434-1144-7*, Pocket Star); 2003. E-Book (*0-7432-4462-1*, Simon & Schuster); 2002. 352p. 25.00 (*0-7432-0484-0*, Simon & Schuster); 2002. 48p. mass mkt. 7.99 (*0-7434-5599-1*, Pocket); 2002. 352p. 25.00 (*0-7432-3379-4*, Simon & Schuster) Simon & Schuster.
—Jolie Blon's Bounce. abr. ed. 2002. audio 26.00 (*0-7435-2463-2*); audio compact disk 30.00 (*0-7435-2460-8*); audio 45.00 (*0-7435-2594-9*); audio compact disk 49.95 (*0-7435-2595-7*) Simon & Schuster Audio. (Simon & Schuster Audioworks).
—Jolie Blon's Bounce. aut. ltd. num. ed. 2002. 349p. 150.00 (*1-890885-13-4*) Trice, B.E. Publishing.
—Last Car to Elysian Fields. 2003. 352p. 25.00 (*0-7432-4542-3*, Simon & Schuster) Simon & Schuster.
—A Morning for Flamingos. l.t. ed. 1998. 353p. 24.95 (*1-57490-155-9*, Beeler Large Print Bks.) Beeler, Thomas T. Publisher.
—A Morning for Flamingos. 1990. (Dave Robicheaux Ser.). 18.95 o.p. (*0-316-11721-8*) Little Brown & Co.
—A Morning for Flamingos. 1991. 384p. reprint ed. mass mkt. 7.50 (*0-380-71360-8*, Avon Bks.) Morrow/Avon.
—A Morning for Flamingos. unabr. ed. 1993. (Dave Robicheaux Ser.: Vol. 4). audio 75.00 (*1-55690-940-3*, 93436) Recorded Bks., LLC.
—A Morning for Flamingos. 1999. pap. 9.98 (*0-671-04408-7*); 1991. audio 16.00 (*0-671-73611-6*, 391205) Simon & Schuster Audio. (Simon & Schuster Audioworks).
—The Neon Rain: A Novel. 1987. 16.95 o.p. (*0-8050-0053-4*) Holt, Henry & Co.
—The Neon Rain: A Novel. l.t. ed. 1991. 377p. 21.95 (*1-85089-413-2*) ISIS Large Print Bks. GBR. *Dist:* Transaction Pubs.
—The Neon Rain: A Novel. 288p. reprint ed. 2002. (Illus.). pap. 14.00 (*0-7434-4920-7*); 1992. mass mkt. 6.99 (*0-671-75644-3*) Simon & Schuster. (Pocket).
—Purple Cane Road. l.t. ed. 2000. 512p. 24.95 (*0-375-43055-5*) Random Hse. Large Print.
—A Stained White Radiance. l.t. ed. 1993. (General Ser.). 465p. pap. 16.95 o.p. (*0-8161-5612-3*, Macmillan Reference USA) Gale Group.
—A Stained White Radiance. 1992. 384p. 19.95 o.p. (*1-56282-980-7*) Hyperion Pr.
—A Stained White Radiance. 1993. 384p. reprint ed. mass mkt. 7.50 (*0-380-72047-7*, Avon Bks.) Morrow/Avon.
—A Stained White Radiance. unabr. ed. 1994. (Dave Robicheaux Ser.: No. 5). audio 78.00 (*1-55690-999-3*, 94138E7) Recorded Bks., LLC.
—A Stained White Radiance. 1998. audio 9.98 (*0-671-58249-6*); 1995. audio 17.00 (*0-671-86817-9*, 394196) Simon & Schuster Audio. (Simon & Schuster Audioworks).
—Sunset Limited. 1999. (Dave Robicheaux Mysteries Ser.). 416p. mass mkt. 7.50 (*0-440-22398-9*) Dell Publishing.
—Sunset Limited, Set. abr. ed. 1999. audio 25.00 Highsmith Inc.
—Sunset Limited. (Dave Robicheaux Ser.: Vol. 10). 2001. audio compact disk 99.00 (*0-7887-3399-0*, C1005E7); 1998. audio 83.00 (*0-7887-2592-0*, 95498E7) Recorded Bks., LLC.
—Sunset Limited. abr. ed. 1998. (Dave Robicheaux Mystery Ser.). audio 25.00 (*0-671-58106-6*, 696022, Simon & Schuster Audioworks) Simon & Schuster Audio.
—Sunset Limited. l.t. ed. (Paperback Bestsellers Ser.). 429p. 1999. pap. 27.95 (*0-7838-0332-X*); 1998. 30.95 (*0-7838-0331-1*) Thorndike Pr.
—Sunset Limited. ltd. ed. 1998. 309p. 150.00 o.p. (*1-890885-03-7*) Trice, B.E. Publishing.

**ROBINSON, NAN (FICTITIOUS CHARACTER)—FICTION**

Cannon, Taffy. Class Reunions Are Murder. 9999. mass mkt. o.p. (*0-449-14951-X*); 1996. mass mkt. 5.50 o.s.i (*0-449-22389-2*) Ballantine Bks. (Fawcett).
—A Pocketful of Karma. 1993. 256p. 19.95 o.p. (*0-88184-906-5*, Carroll & Graf Pubs.) Avalon Publishing Group.
—A Pocketful of Karma. 1995. mass mkt. 5.50 o.s.i (*0-449-22388-4*, Fawcett) Ballantine Bks.
—Tangled Roots. 1995. 320p. 19.95 o.p. (*0-7867-0137-4*, Carroll & Graf Pubs.) Avalon Publishing Group.
—Tangled Roots. Date not set. mass mkt. (*0-449-14950-1*); 1995. mass mkt. 5.99 o.s.i (*0-449-22390-6*) Ballantine Bks. (Fawcett).

**ROBINSON, TRISH (FICTITIOUS CHARACTER)—FICTION**

Harper, Brian. Mortal Pursuit. 1997. 432p. mass mkt. 5.99 o.s.i (*0-451-18200-6*, Signet Bks.) NAL.

**ROCHE, MORGAN (FICTITIOUS CHARACTER)—FICTION**

Williams, Sean & Dix, Shane. A Dark Imbalance: Evergence. 2001. (Evergence Ser.: Vol. 3). 400p. mass mkt. 6.99 o.s.i (*0-441-00811-9*) Ace Bks.
—Evergence I: The Prodigal Sun. 1999. (Evergence Ser.: Vol. 1). 400p. mass mkt. 6.99 o.s.i (*0-441-00672-8*) Ace Bks.
—Evergence II: The Dying Light. 2000. (Evergence Ser.: Vol. 2). 432p. mass mkt. 6.99 o.s.i (*0-441-00742-2*) Ace Bks.

**ROCKFORD, JAMES (FICTITIOUS CHARACTER)—FICTION**

Kaminsky, Stuart M. Devil on My Doorstep. 1998. (Rockford Files: Vol. 2). 304p. 22.95 (*0-312-86444-2*, Forge Bks.) Doherty, Tom Assocs., LLC.
—The Green Bottle. unabr. ed. 1999. audio 69.95 (*0-7927-2300-7*, CSL189, Chivers Sound Library) BBC Audiobooks America.
—The Green Bottle. (Rockford Files: Vol. 1). 320p. 1996. 22.95 (*0-312-86229-6*); 1999. mass mkt. 5.99 (*0-8125-7105-3*) Doherty, Tom Assocs., LLC. (Forge Bks.).
—The Green Bottle. l.t. ed. 1998. (Americana Ser.). 437p. 28.95 (*0-7862-1521-6*) Thorndike Pr.
—The Rockford Files: Devil on My Doorstep. unabr. ed. 2000. audio 49.95 (*0-7927-2313-9*, CSL 202) Chivers Audio Bks. GBR. *Dist:* BBC Audiobooks America.

**ROCKY MOUNTAIN COMPANY (FICTITIOUS CHARACTERS)—FICTION**

Wheeler, Richard S. Fort Dance. 1991. (Rocky Mountain Company Ser.: No. 2). mass mkt. 3.99 o.s.i (*1-55817-558-X*, Pinnacle Bks.) Kensington Publishing Corp.
—The Rocky Mountain Company. l.t. ed. 2002. (Western Ser.). pap. 19.95 (*1-58724-255-9*, Wheeler Publishing, Inc.) Gale Group.
—The Rocky Mountain Company. 2002. 32p. mass mkt. 5.99 (*0-7860-1468-7*); 1991. mass mkt. 3.95 o.s.i (*1-55817-489-3*) Kensington Publishing Corp. (Pinnacle Bks.).
—The Rocky Mountain Company: Cheyenne Winter. 1992. mass mkt. 3.99 o.p. (*1-55817-599-7*, Pinnacle Bks.) Kensington Publishing Corp.
—The Rocky Mountain Company: Cheyenne Winter. l.t. ed. 2003. 26.95 (*0-7862-4656-1*) Thorndike Pr.

**RODE, JIMMY (FICTITIOUS CHARACTER)—FICTION**

King, Gary C., et al. Dead of Night: The True Story of a Serial Killer. 1997. (Onyx True Crime Ser.: Vol. 703). 360p. mass mkt. 6.99 o.s.i (*0-451-40703-2*, Onyx) NAL.

**RODENSKA, MIKE (FICTITIOUS CHARACTER)—FICTION**

MacDonald, John D. Slam the Big Door. 1987. 272p. mass mkt. 4.95 o.s.i (*0-449-13275-7*, Fawcett) Ballantine Bks.
—Slam the Big Door. 1987. 208p. 16.45 o.p. (*0-89296-190-2*) Mysterious Pr.
—Slam the Big Door. 1989. 3.99 o.p. (*0-517-00478-X*) Random Hse. Value Publishing.

**RODRIGUE, JOHN (FICTITIOUS CHARACTER)—FICTION**

Grissom, Ken. Big Fish. 1992. mass mkt. 3.99 o.p. (*0-312-92689-8*, St. Martin's Paperbacks) St. Martin's Pr.
—Drop-Off: A John Rodrigue Novel. 1989. mass mkt. 3.95 (*0-312-91617-5*, Tor Bks.) Doherty, Tom Assocs., LLC.
—Drop-Off: A John Rodrigue Novel. 1989. mass mkt. 3.95 (*0-312-91616-7*, St. Martin's Paperbacks); 1988. 224p. 15.95 o.p. (*0-312-02196-8*, Saint Martin's Minotaur) St. Martin's Pr.

**ROGER THE CHAPMAN (FICTITIOUS CHARACTER)—FICTION**

Sedley, Kate. Brothers of Glastonbury. 279p. text 29.95 (*0-7472-2087-5*); 1998. pap. 11.95 (*0-7472-5877-5*) Headline Bk. Publishing, Ltd. GBR. *Dist:* Trafalgar Square.
—Death & the Chapman. l.t. ed. 1992. (Mystery Ser.). 315p. 29.99 o.p. (*0-7505-0420-X*) Magna Large Print Bks. GBR. *Dist:* Ulverscroft Large Print Bks., Ltd., Ulverscroft Large Print Canada, Ltd.
—Death & the Chapman. 1994. 272p. mass mkt. 4.50 o.p. (*0-06-104319-2*, HarperTorch) Morrow/Avon.
—Death & the Chapman. 1991. 224p. 17.95 o.p. (*0-312-06945-6*, Saint Martin's Minotaur) St. Martin's Pr.
—Eve of Saint Hyacinth. 1996. 288p. 21.95 o.p. (*0-312-14331-1*, Saint Martin's Minotaur) St. Martin's Pr.
—The Hanged Man. unabr. ed. 2000. (Chapman Mystery Ser.). audio 54.95 (*0-7540-0241-1*, CAB 1664) Chivers Audio Bks. GBR. *Dist:* BBC Audiobooks America.
—The Holy Innocents, Set. unabr. ed. 1999. audio 69.95 (*0-7540-0330-2*, CAB1753) Chivers Audio Bks. GBR. *Dist:* BBC Audiobooks America.

—The Holy Innocents. 1996. 304p. mass mkt. 4.99 o.s.i (*0-06-104379-6*, HarperTorch) Morrow/Avon.
—The Holy Innocents. 1995. 21.00 o.p. (*0-312-11823-6*, Saint Martin's Minotaur) St. Martin's Pr.
—The Lammas Feast. (Roger the Chapman Medieval Mystery Ser.). 2002. 256p. 25.99 (*0-7278-5867-X*); 28.99 (*0-7278-7224-9*) Severn Hse. Pubs., Ltd.
—Nine Men Dancing. 2003. 224p. 26.99 (*0-7278-5977-3*) Severn Hse. Pubs., Ltd.
—The Plymouth Cloak. unabr. ed. 1998. audio 54.95 (*0-7540-0188-1*, CAB 1611) BBC Audiobooks America.
—The Plymouth Cloak. l.t. ed. 1994. (Magna Large Print Ser.). 317p. 29.99 o.p. (*0-7505-0614-8*) Magna Large Print Bks. GBR. *Dist:* Ulverscroft Large Print Bks., Ltd., Ulverscroft Large Print Canada, Ltd.
—The Plymouth Cloak. 1994. 224p. mass mkt. 4.50 o.p. (*0-06-104320-6*, HarperTorch) Morrow/Avon.
—The Plymouth Cloak. 1993. 192p. 16.95 o.p. (*0-312-08875-2*, Saint Martin's Minotaur) St. Martin's Pr.
—The Saint John's Fern: A Roger the Chapman Medieval Mystery. 1999. 246p. 29.95 o.s.i (*0-7472-7496-7*) Headline Bk. Publishing, Ltd. GBR. *Dist:* Trafalgar Square.
—The Saint John's Fern: A Roger the Chapman Medieval Mystery. Date not set. (*0-312-27883-7*); 2002. 256p. 23.95 (*0-312-27683-4*) St. Martin's Pr. (Saint Martin's Minotaur).
—The Weaver's Inheritance. 247p. 29.95 (*0-7472-2277-0*); 1999. pap. 11.95 (*0-7472-6128-8*) Headline Bk. Publishing, Ltd. GBR. *Dist:* Trafalgar Square.
—The Weaver's Inheritance. 2001. 256p. 23.95 (*0-312-27684-2*, Saint Martin's Minotaur) St. Martin's Pr.
—The Weaver's Tale. 1995. 224p. mass mkt. 4.50 o.p. (*0-06-104336-2*, HarperTorch) Morrow/Avon.
—The Weaver's Tale. 1994. 256p. 20.95 o.p. (*0-312-10474-X*, Saint Martin's Minotaur) St. Martin's Pr.
—The Wicked Winter. 1997. 282p. pap. 11.95 (*0-7472-5631-4*) Headline Bk. Publishing, Ltd. GBR. *Dist:* Trafalgar Square.
—The Wicked Winter. 2nd ed. 1999. 288p. 22.95 (*0-312-20625-9*, Saint Martin's Minotaur) St. Martin's Pr.

**ROGERS, BEN (FICTITIOUS CHARACTER)—FICTION**

Murano, Vincent. Dead File. 1996. mass mkt. 5.99 o.p. (*0-312-95692-4*, St. Martin's Paperbacks) St. Martin's Pr.

**ROGERS, BUCK (FICTITIOUS CHARACTER)—FICTION**

Caiden, Martin. Buck Rogers: Life in the Future. 1996. ix, 342p. pap. 5.99 (*0-7869-0527-1*) TSR, Inc.
Grubb, Jeff. Buck Rogers: Introduction to the 25th Century. 1993. (Illus.). 20.00 o.p. (*1-56076-636-0*) TSR, Inc.
Lupoff, Richard. Buck Rogers in the Twenty-Fifth Century. 1978. pap. 1.95 o.p. (*0-440-10843-8*) Dell Publishing.
Morrow, Gray & Lawrence, Jim. Buck Rogers in the Twenty-Fifth Century. 9999. (Illus.). 193p. pap. 12.95 o.p. (*0-8256-3221-8*) Ace Bks.
Outlet Book Company Staff. Buck Rogers. 1988. 7.99 o.s.i (*0-517-02767-4*) Random Hse. Value Publishing.
Steele, Addison. Buck Rogers: That Man on Beta, No. 2. 1979. pap. 1.95 o.p. (*0-440-10948-5*) Dell Publishing.
TSR Hobbies Staff. Buck Rogers Game Comic. No. 2. 1990. pap. 2.95 o.p. (*0-88038-938-9*); No. 3. 1990. pap. 2.95 o.p. (*0-88038-943-5*); No. 4. 1990. pap. 2.95 o.p. (*0-88038-948-6*); No. 7. 1991. pap. 2.95 o.p. (*0-88038-963-X*); No. 8. 1991. pap. 2.95 o.p. (*0-88038-968-0*); Pt. 2. 1991. pap. 2.95 o.p. (*0-88038-953-2*) TSR, Inc.
Williams, Lorraine D., ed. Buck Rogers: The First 60 Years in the 25th Century. 1988. (Buck Rogers Hardcover Collector's Volume Ser.). (Illus.). 368p. (J). 24.95 o.p. (*0-88038-604-5*) TSR, Inc.

**ROGERS, GEORGE (FICTITIOUS CHARACTER)—FICTION**

Ross, Jonathan. Murder! Murder! Burning Bright. 1997. 176p. text 20.95 o.p. (*0-312-15599-9*, Saint Martin's Minotaur) St. Martin's Pr.

**ROGERS, TOM (FICTITIOUS CHARACTER)—FICTION**

Ignatius, David. Agents of Innocence. 1988. 448p. mass mkt. 4.50 (*0-380-70593-1*, Avon Bks.) Morrow/Avon.
—Agents of Innocence. 1997. 448p. pap. 13.95 (*0-393-31738-2*); 1987. 17.95 o.p. (*0-393-02486-5*) Norton, W. W. & Co., Inc.
—Agents of Innocence. 1990. 3.99 o.p. (*0-517-05159-1*) Random Hse. Value Publishing.

**ROGUE WARRIOR (FICTITIOUS CHARACTER)—FICTION**

Marcinko, Richard. Designation Gold. 1997. (Rogue Warrior Ser.). mass mkt. 6.99 (*0-671-01743-8*, Pocket) Simon & Schuster.
—The Rogue Warrior: The Real Team. (Rogue Warrior Ser.). (Illus.). 1999. 256p. 23.00 o.s.i (*0-671-02464-7*, Atria); 2000. 288p. reprint ed. pap. 7.99 (*0-671-02465-5*, Pocket) Simon & Schuster.
—The Rogue Warrior: The Real Team. abr. ed. 1999. audio 18.00 (*0-671-04440-0*, 394298, Simon & Schuster Audioworks) Simon & Schuster Audio.
—Task Force Blue. 1997. (Rogue Warrior Ser.). (Illus.). 400p. mass mkt. 7.99 (*0-671-89672-5*, Pocket) Simon & Schuster.
Marcinko, Richard & Weisman, John. Designation Gold. (Rogue Warrior Ser.). 1998. 386p. pap. 6.99 (*0-671-89674-1*, Pocket); 1997. 368p. 24.00 (*0-671-89673-3*, Atria) Simon & Schuster.
—Designation Gold. 1998. audio 9.98 (*0-671-58142-2*, 394508); 1997. audio 18.00 (*0-671-57532-5*) Simon & Schuster Audio. (Simon & Schuster Audioworks).
—Detachment Bravo. 2001. 352p. 25.95 o.s.i (*0-671-00071-3*, Atria) Simon & Schuster.
—Echo Platoon. 2000. (Rogue Warrior Ser.). (Illus.). 368p. 24.95 o.s.i (*0-671-00070-5*, Atria) Simon & Schuster.
—Green Team. 1996. (Rogue Warrior Ser.). 448p. mass mkt. 6.99 (*0-671-79959-2*, Pocket) Simon & Schuster.
—Green Team. McCarthy, Paul, ed. 1995. (Rogue Warrior Ser.). 368p. 23.00 (*0-671-89671-7*, Atria) Simon & Schuster.
—Green Team. 1998. audio 9.98 (*0-671-58141-4*, 391487); 1996. audio 18.00 (*0-671-52117-9*) Simon & Schuster Audio. (Simon & Schuster Audioworks).
—Option Delta. (Rogue Warrior Ser.). (Illus.). 1999. 352p. 24.00 (*0-671-00068-3*, Atria); 2000. 432p. reprint ed. pap. 6.99 (*0-671-00073-X*, Pocket) Simon & Schuster.
—Option Delta. 2001. audio 9.98 (*0-7435-0865-3*); 1999. 352p. audio 18.00 (*0-671-04379-X*, 394179) Simon & Schuster Audio. (Simon & Schuster Audioworks).
—Red Cell. (Rogue Warrior Ser.: Vol. 2). 1998. 400p. mass mkt. 3.99 (*0-671-01977-5*, Pocket); 1994. 368p. 22.00 (*0-671-79956-8*, Atria) Simon & Schuster.
—Red Cell. Regan, Judith & McCarthy, Paul, eds. 1994. (Rogue Warrior Ser.: No. 2). (Illus.). 416p. reprint ed. mass mkt. 6.99 (*0-671-79957-6*, Pocket) Simon & Schuster.
—Red Cell. abr. ed. 1994. audio 17.00 (*0-671-88590-1*, Simon & Schuster Audioworks) Simon & Schuster Audio.
—Rogue Warrior. Regan, Judith & McCarthy, Paul, eds. (Rogue Warrior Ser.). 1993. (Illus.). 416p. mass mkt. 7.99 (*0-671-79593-7*, Pocket); 1992. 352p. 24.00 (*0-671-70390-0*, Atria) Simon & Schuster.
—Seal Force Alpha. abr. ed. 1998. audio 18.00 (*0-671-57993-2*, Simon & Schuster Audioworks) Simon & Schuster Audio.
—Task Force Blue. McCarthy, Paul, ed. 1996. (Rogue Warrior Ser.). 336p. 23.00 (*0-671-79958-4*, Atria) Simon & Schuster.
—Task Force Blue. abr. ed. 1996. (Rogue Warrior Ser.). audio 18.00 (*0-671-56260-6*, Simon & Schuster Audioworks) Simon & Schuster Audio.

**ROKE, DANIEL (FICTITIOUS CHARACTER)—FICTION**

Francis, Dick. Dead Cert; Nerve; For Kicks. 1996. mass mkt. 7.99 o.s.i (*0-449-28768-8*, Fawcett) Ballantine Bks.
—For Kicks. l.t. ed. 1994. 19.95 o.p. (*0-7927-1740-6*); 1994. pap. 18.95 o.p. (*0-7927-1739-2*); 1993. audio 54.95 o.p. (*0-7451-5950-8*) BBC Audiobooks America.
—For Kicks. 1987. 336p. mass mkt. 5.95 o.s.i (*0-449-21264-5*, Fawcett) Ballantine Bks.
—For Kicks. 304p. 2004. mass mkt. 6.99 (*0-425-19498-1*); 1998. mass mkt. 6.99 (*0-515-12386-2*, Jove) Berkley Publishing Group.
—For Kicks. unabr. ed. 1991. audio 56.00 (*0-7366-1918-6*, 2742) Books on Tape, Inc.
—For Kicks. 1984. mass mkt. 3.50 o.s.i (*0-671-53265-0*); 1982. mass mkt. 2.95 o.s.i (*0-671-45460-9*) Simon & Schuster. (Pocket).
—For Kicks. l.t. ed. 1973. o.p. (*0-85456-164-1*, Ulverscroft) Thorpe, F. A. Pubs.
—For Kicks. abr. ed. 1996. 2p. audio 16.95 o.s.i (*0-14-086222-6*) Viking Penguin.

**ROLAND (FICTITIOUS CHARACTER)—FICTION**

King, Stephen. The Dark Tower, 4 vols. 2003. 70.80 (*0-452-28495-3*, Plume) Dutton/Plume.
—The Dark Tower. 2003. 31.96 (*0-451-21124-3*, Signet Bks.) NAL.
—The Drawing of the Three. (Dark Tower Ser.: Bk. II). 1997. 416p. pap. 18.00 o.s.i (*0-452-27961-5*); 1989. (Illus.). 416p. pap. 16.95 o.s.i (*0-452-26214-3*); 2003. (Illus.). 432p. pap. 17.95 (*0-452-28470-8*) Dutton/Plume. (Plume).
—The Drawing of the Three. 1987. (Dark Tower Ser.: Bk. II). (Illus.). 399p. 35.00 o.p. (*0-937986-91-7*); pap. 100.00 o.p. (*0-937986-90-9*) Grant, Donald M. Pub., Inc.
—The Drawing of the Three. (Dark Tower Ser.: Bk. 2). 1990. 464p. mass mkt. 7.99 o.s.i (*0-451-16352-4*); 2003. 480p. mass mkt. 7.99 (*0-451-21085-9*) NAL. (Signet Bks.).
—The Drawing of the Three. rev. unabr. ed. 2003. (Dark Tower Ser.: Bk. II). audio compact disk 37.95 (*0-14-280038-4*) Penguin Group (USA) Inc.
—The Drawing of the Three. 2003. (Dark Tower Ser.: Bk. II). reprint ed. E-Book 7.99 (*0-7865-3750-7*) Penguin Putnam, Inc E-Books.
—The Drawing of the Three. abr. unabr. ed. 1989. (Dark Tower Ser.). audio 30.00 o.p. (*0-453-00643-4*, 25024-18082) Penguin/HighBridge.
—The Drawing of the Three. 1987. (Dark Tower Ser.: Bk. II). 14.04 (*0-606-00785-7*) Turtleback Bks.
—The Drawing of the Three. rev. ed. (Dark Tower Ser.: Bk. 2). 2003. (Illus.). 432p. 35.00 (*0-670-03255-7*); 1998. 8p. audio 35.95 (*0-14-086715-5*, Penguin AudioBooks) Viking Penguin.
—The Gunslinger. 1976. (Dark Tower Ser.: Bk. I). 21.95 (*0-8488-0780-4*) Amereon, Ltd.
—The Gunslinger. (Dark Tower Ser.: Bk. I). 1988. (Illus.). 224p. pap. 10.95 o.s.i (*0-452-26134-1*); 2003. (Illus.). 264p. pap. 15.95 (*0-452-28469-4*); Vol. 1. 1997. 224p. pap. 15.00 o.s.i (*0-452-27960-7*) Dutton/Plume. (Plume).
—The Gunslinger. 1982. (Dark Tower Ser.: Bk. I). (Illus.). 224p. 60.00 o.p. (*0-937986-51-8*); pap. 20.00 o.p. (*0-937986-50-X*) Grant, Donald M. Pub., Inc.
—The Gunslinger. 2003. 336p. mass mkt. 7.99 (*0-451-21084-0*, Signet Bks.); 1989. audio; 1989. (Illus.). 320p. reprint ed. mass mkt. 7.99 o.s.i (*0-451-16052-5*, Signet Bks.) NAL.
—The Gunslinger. exp. rev. unabr. ed. 2003. (Dark Tower Ser.: Bk. 1). 4p. audio 25.95 (*0-14-280036-8*) Penguin Group (USA) Inc.
—The Gunslinger. exp. rev. ed. 2003. (Dark Tower Ser.: Bk. 1). E-Book 7.99 (*0-7865-3721-3*) Penguin Putnam, Inc E-Books.
—The Gunslinger. abr. ed. 1988. (Dark Tower Ser.). audio 29.95 o.p. (*0-453-00636-1*, 1987) Penguin/HighBridge.
—The Gunslinger. unabr. ed. 2003. audio 58.00 (*1-4025-5859-7*, 97135); audio compact disk 58.00 (*1-4025-5944-5*, C2306); audio 34.95 (*1-4025-5860-0*, RG118) Recorded Bks., LLC.
—The Gunslinger. 1978. (Dark Tower Ser.: Bk. I). 20.05 (*0-606-04112-5*) Turtleback Bks.
—The Gunslinger. abr. ed. 1998. (Dark Tower Ser.: Bk. I). 4p. pap. 29.95 incl. audio (*0-14-086716-3*, Penguin AudioBooks) Viking Penguin.
—The Gunslinger. Whelan, Michael, tr. & illus. by. exp. rev. ed. 2003. (Dark Tower Ser.: Bk. 1). 256p. 25.00 (*0-670-03254-9*, Viking) Viking Penguin.
—The Gunslinger. exp. rev. unabr. ed. 2003. (Dark Tower Ser.: Bk. 1). 6p. audio compact disk 29.99 (*0-14-280037-6*, Penguin Bks.) Viking Penguin.
—The Waste Lands. (Dark Tower Ser.: Bk. III). 2003. (Illus.). 448p. pap. 17.95 (*0-452-28471-6*); 1997. 432p. pap. 17.95 o.s.i (*0-452-27962-3*); 1992. (Illus.). 432p. reprint ed. pap. 17.95 o.s.i (*0-452-26740-4*) Dutton/Plume. (Plume).
—The Waste Lands. 1991. (Dark Tower Ser.: Bk. III). (Illus.). 509p. 38.00 o.p. (*0-937986-17-8*); 2001. 30.00 (*1-880418-23-1*) Grant, Donald M. Pub., Inc.
—The Waste Lands. abr. unabr. ed. 1992. (Dark Tower Ser.: Bk. III). 34.95 o.p. incl. audio (*0-453-00770-8*, 51855-03495, NAL Bks.) HighBridge Co.
—The Waste Lands. (Dark Tower Ser.: No. 3). 2003. 608p. mass mkt. 7.99 (*0-451-21086-7*); 1993. (Illus.). 592p. mass mkt. 7.99 o.s.i (*0-451-17331-7*); 1992. pap. 5.99 o.s.i (*0-451-17475-5*) NAL. (Signet Bks.).
—The Waste Lands, Bk. 3. unabr. ed. 2003. (Dark Tower Ser.). 16p. audio compact disk 49.95 (*0-14-280039-2*) Penguin Group (USA) Inc.
—The Waste Lands. 2003. (Dark Tower Ser.: Bk. 3). E-Book 7.99 (*0-7865-3754-X*) Penguin Putnam, Inc E-Books.
—The Waste Lands. 1991. (Dark Tower Ser.: Bk. III). 14.04 (*0-606-02971-0*) Turtleback Bks.
—The Waste Lands. abr. unabr. ed. (Dark Tower Ser.: Vol. 3). 1998. 12p. audio 44.95 (*0-14-086717-1*, Penguin AudioBooks); 2003. (Illus.). 448p. reprint ed. 35.00 (*0-670-03256-5*) Viking Penguin.
—Wizard & Glass. (Dark Tower Ser.: Bk. IV). 2003. 720p. pap. 18.95 (*0-452-28472-4*, Plume); 1997. (Illus.). 688p. pap. 17.95 o.s.i (*0-452-27917-8*, Signet Bks.) Dutton/Plume.
—Wizard & Glass. 1997. (Dark Tower Ser.: Bk. IV). (Illus.). 792p. 45.00 (*1-880418-38-X*); 787 p. pap. o.p. (*1-880418-37-1*) Grant, Donald M. Pub., Inc.
—Wizard & Glass, Set. unabr. ed. 1999. audio 49.95 Highsmith Inc.
—Wizard & Glass. (Dark Tower Ser.: No. 4). 752p. 2003. mass mkt. 7.99 (*0-451-21087-5*); 1998. (Illus.). mass mkt. 7.99 o.s.i (*0-451-19486-1*) NAL. (Signet Bks.).
—Wizard & Glass. unabr. ed. 2003. (Dark Tower Ser.: Vol. 4). 23p. audio compact disk 59.95 (*0-14-280040-6*) Penguin Group (USA) Inc.
—Wizard & Glass. 2003. (Dark Tower Ser.: Bk. 4). E-Book 7.99 (*0-7865-3758-2*) Penguin Putnam, Inc E-Books.
—Wizard & Glass. 1998. (Dark Tower Ser.). 14.04 (*0-606-15772-7*) Turtleback Bks.
—Wizard & Glass. (Dark Tower Ser.). 2003. (Illus.). 704p. 40.00 (*0-670-03257-3*); 1997. 18p. audio 57.95 (*0-14-086688-4*, Penguin AudioBooks) Viking Penguin.
—Wolves of the Calla. 2003. (Dark Tower Ser.: Bk. 5). (Illus.). 736p. 35.00 (*1-880418-56-8*) Grant, Donald M. Pub., Inc.
—Wolves of the Calla. 2003. (Dark Tower Ser.: Bk. 5). E-Book 7.99 (*0-7432-5510-0*, Scribner) Simon & Schuster.

**ROLLISON, RICHARD (FICTITIOUS CHARACTER)—FICTION**

Creasey, John. A Bundle for the Toff. l.t. ed. (Atlantic Mystery Ser.). 1989. pap. 14.95 o.p. (*1-55504-766-1*, 28); 1993. audio 39.95 (*0-7451-5883-8*, CAT 4061) BBC Audiobooks America.
—Introducing the Toff. 1998. 19.50 o.p. (*0-7540-8508-2*, Black Dagger) BBC Audiobooks America.
—Kill the Toff. 10.00 National Assn. for Visually Handicapped.
—Salute the Toff. 1971. 143p. (*0-8027-5225-X*) Walker Publishing Co., Inc.
—Stars for the Toff. l.t. ed. 1997. (Nightingale Ser.). pap. 18.95 o.p. (*0-7838-1990-0*, Macmillan Reference USA) Gale Group.
—Stars for the Toff. 1968. (King Crime Ser.). 192p. (*0-340-02945-5*) St. Martin's Pr.
—The Toff & Old Harry. 1980. 192p. 1.95 o.s.i (*0-441-81524-3*) Ace Bks.
—The Toff & Old Harry. l.t. ed. 1991. pap. 16.95 o.p. (*0-7927-0518-1*, CS0137) BBC Audiobooks America.
—The Toff & Old Harry. 1970. 190p. (*0-8027-5217-9*) Walker Publishing Co., Inc.
—The Toff & the Deep Blue Sea. (Black Dagger Crime Ser.). 16.50 o.p. (*0-86220-785-1*, C1025, Black Dagger); 1993. 18.95 o.p. (*0-7451-6446-3*); 1993. audio 54.95 (*0-7451-2417-8*, CDA 018, Chivers Children's Audio Bks.) BBC Audiobooks America.
—The Toff & the Fallen Angels. 1970. (King Crime Ser.). 191p. (*0-340-10620-4*) St. Martin's Pr.
—The Toff & the Fallen Angels. 1983. 192p. pap. 2.95 o.p. (*0-8027-3004-3*) Walker & Co.
—The Toff & the Golden Boy. 1993. (Black Dagger Crime Ser.). 160p. 16.50 o.p. (*0-7451-8607-6*, Black Dagger) BBC Audiobooks America.
—The Toff & the Golden Boy. 1969. (King Crime Ser.). 158p. (J). (*0-340-10977-7*) St. Martin's Pr.
—The Toff & the Stolen Tresses. l.t. ed. 1998. 245p. (*0-7540-3124-1*) BBC Audiobooks America.
—The Toff & the Stolen Tresses. l.t. ed. 1998. (Nightingale Ser.). 268p. pap. 20.95 (*0-7838-8318-8*) Thorndike Pr.
—The Toff & the Terrified Taxman: The 55th Book of the Toff. 1973. 192p. (J). (*0-340-16487-5*) St. Martin's Pr.
—The Toff & the Terrified Taxman: The 55th Book of the Toff. 1973. 192p. (J). (*0-8027-5281-0*) Walker Publishing Co., Inc.
—The Toff & the Trip-Trip-Triplets. 1972. (King Crime Ser.). 190p. (J). (*0-340-15234-6*) St. Martin's Pr.
—The Toff & the Trip-Trip-Triplets. 1972. 190p. (J). (*0-8027-5264-0*) Walker Publishing Co., Inc.
—The Toff Goes to Market. l.t. ed. 1997. (Nightingale Ser.). 245p. lib. bdg. 17.95 o.p. (*0-7838-1991-9*, Macmillan Reference USA) Gale Group.
—The Toff on Board. 1973. 158p. (J). (*0-8027-5270-5*) Walker Publishing Co., Inc.
—Vote for the Toff. 1971. 189p. (J). (*0-8027-5236-5*) Walker Publishing Co., Inc.

**ROM (FICTITIOUS CHARACTER)—FICTION**

Quark. The Ferengi Rules of Acquisition. Ryan, Kevin, ed. 1995. (Star Trek Deep Space Nine Ser.). 96p. pap. 6.00 (*0-671-52936-6*, Star Trek) Simon & Schuster.
Shimerman, Armin & George, David R., III. Star Trek Deep Space Nine: The 34th Rule. abr. ed. 1999. (Star Trek Deep Space Nine Ser.: No. 23). audio 16.85 (*0-671-03358-1*) Ulverscroft Audio (U.S.A.).
—The 34th Rule. 1999. (Star Trek Deep Space Nine Ser.: No. 23). 448p. pap. 6.50 (*0-671-00793-9*, Star Trek) Simon & Schuster.
—The 34th Rule. abr. ed. 1999. (Star Trek Ser. : No. 23). audio 18.00 (*0-671-04395-1*, Simon & Schuster Audioworks) Simon & Schuster Audio.

**ROMAN, DAN (FICTITIOUS CHARACTER)—FICTION**

Mathis, Edward G. Another Path, Another Dragon. 1990. 256p. mass mkt. 3.95 o.s.i (*0-345-35901-1*) Ballantine Bks.
—Another Path, Another Dragon: A Dan Roman Mystery. 1988. 224p. 14.95 o.s.i (*0-684-18935-6*, Macmillan Reference USA) Gale Group.
—Dark Streaks & Empty Places. 1988. 289p. reprint ed. mass mkt. 3.95 o.s.i (*0-345-34305-0*) Ballantine Bks.
—Dark Streaks & Empty Places: A Dan Roman Mystery. 1986. 240p. 13.95 o.s.i (*0-684-18678-0*, Macmillan Reference USA) Gale Group.
—The Fifth Level: A Dan Roman Mystery. 1992. 256p. text 20.00 (*0-684-19386-8*, Macmillan Reference USA) Gale Group.
—Out of the Shadows: A Dan Roman Mystery. 1990. 224p. 17.95 o.s.i (*0-684-19038-9*, Macmillan Reference USA) Gale Group.

**ROME, MAGGIE (FICTITIOUS CHARACTER)—FICTION**

Kallen, Lucille. C. B. Greenfield: A Little Madness. 1987. mass mkt. 3.50 o.s.i (*0-345-31119-1*, Ballantine Bks.) Ballantine Bks.
—C. B. Greenfield: No Lady in the House. 1984. 208p. mass mkt. 3.95 o.s.i (*0-345-32396-3*) Ballantine Bks.
—C. B. Greenfield: No Lady in the House. 1982. 12.95 o.p. (*0-671-43240-0*, Simon & Schuster) Simon & Schuster.
—C. B. Greenfield: No Lady in the House. l.t. ed. 1982. 374p. reprint ed. 10.95 o.p. (*0-89621-365-X*) Thorndike Pr.
—C. B. Greenfield: The Piano Bird. 1985. 224p. mass mkt. 3.95 o.s.i (*0-345-31118-3*, Ballantine Bks.) Ballantine Bks.
—C. B. Greenfield: The Piano Bird. 1984. 175p. 13.95 o.p. (*0-394-53081-0*) Random Hse., Inc.
—C. B. Greenfield: The Tanglewood Murder. 1985. mass mkt. 3.95 o.s.i (*0-345-33143-5*) Ballantine Bks.
—Introducing C. B. Greenfield. 1985. 208p. mass mkt. 3.95 o.s.i (*0-345-33426-4*); 1984. mass mkt. 2.50 o.p. (*0-345-32159-6*) Ballantine Bks.
—Introducing C. B. Greenfield. l.t. ed. 1980. 363p. reprint ed. 11.95 o.p. (*0-89621-260-2*) Thorndike Pr.

**ROMERO, VAL (FICTITIOUS CHARACTER)—FICTION**

Flanders, Eric. Night Blood. 1993. 384p. mass mkt. 4.50 o.s.i (*0-8217-4063-6*, Zebra Bks.) Kensington Publishing Corp.

**ROOSEVELT, ELEANOR, 1884-1962—FICTION**

Roosevelt, Elliott. A First Class Murder. l.t. ed. 1992. (General Ser.). 339p. 20.95 o.p. (*0-8161-5317-5*); pap. 16.95 o.p. (*0-8161-5318-3*) Gale Group. (Macmillan Reference USA).
—A First Class Murder. 1993. 224p. reprint ed. pap. 4.99 (*0-380-71238-5*, Avon Bks.) Morrow/Avon.
—A First Class Murder. 1991. 17.95 o.p. (*0-312-05527-7*) St. Martin's Pr.
—The Hyde Park Murder. l.t. ed. 1986. (General Ser.). 390p. 16.95 o.p. (*0-8161-3991-1*, Macmillan Reference USA) Gale Group.
—The Hyde Park Murder. 1986. pap. 4.50 (*0-380-70058-1*, Avon Bks.) Morrow/Avon.
—The Hyde Park Murder. unabr. ed. 1986. (Eleanor Roosevelt Mystery Ser.: Vol. 2). audio 44.00 (*1-55690-243-3*, 86580E7) Recorded Bks., LLC.
—The Hyde Park Murder. 1985. 240p. 14.95 o.p. (*0-312-40160-4*) St. Martin's Pr.
—Murder & the First Lady. l.t. ed. 1985. (General Ser.). 14.95 o.p. (*0-8161-3785-4*, Macmillan Reference USA) Gale Group.
—Murder & the First Lady. 1985. (Eleanor Roosevelt Mystery Ser.). 240p. mass mkt. 4.99 (*0-380-69937-0*, Avon Bks.) Morrow/Avon.
—Murder & the First Lady, unabr. ed. 1986. (Eleanor Roosevelt Mystery Ser.: Vol. 1). audio 35.00 (*1-55690-357-X*, 86130E7) Recorded Bks., LLC.
—Murder & the First Lady. 1984. 208p. 12.95 o.p. (*0-312-55280-7*) St. Martin's Pr.
—Murder at Hobcaw Barony. l.t. ed. 1987. 379p. 17.95 o.p. (*0-8161-4195-9*, Macmillan Reference USA) Gale Group.
—Murder at Hobcaw Barony. 1987. (Eleanor Roosevelt Mystery Ser.). 224p. pap. 4.50 (*0-380-70021-2*, Avon Bks.) Morrow/Avon.
—Murder at Hobcaw Barony, unabr. ed. 1986. (Eleanor Roosevelt Mystery Ser.: Vol. 3). audio 51.00 (*1-55690-360-X*, 86680E7) Recorded Bks., LLC.
—Murder at Hobcaw Barony. 1986. (Eleanor Roosevelt Mystery Ser.). 240p. 15.95 o.p. (*0-312-55291-2*) St. Martin's Pr.
—Murder at Midnight: An Eleanor Roosevelt Mystery. (Eleanor Roosevelt Mystery Ser.). 1998. 240p. mass mkt. 5.99 (*0-312-96554-0*, St. Martin's Paperbacks); 1997. 224p. 20.95 o.p. (*0-312-15596-4*, Saint Martin's Minotaur) St. Martin's Pr.
—Murder at the Palace. l.t. unabr. ed. 1989. (General Ser.). 315p. 20.95 o.p. (*0-8161-4663-2*, Macmillan Reference USA) Gale Group.
—Murder at the Palace. 1989. pap. 4.99 (*0-380-70405-6*, Avon Bks.) Morrow/Avon.
—Murder at the Palace, unabr. ed. 1988. (Eleanor Roosevelt Mystery Ser.: Vol. 5). audio 44.00 (*1-55690-358-8*, 88882E7) Recorded Bks., LLC.
—Murder at the Palace. 1988. 240p. 15.95 o.p. (*0-312-01373-6*, Saint Martin's Minotaur) St. Martin's Pr.
—Murder at the President's Door. mass mkt. (*0-312-98275-5*, St. Martin's Paperbacks); E-Book 23.95 (*0-312-70355-4*); 2003. 240p. mass mkt. 6.50 (*0-312-98670-X*, St. Martin's Paperbacks) St. Martin's Pr.
—Murder in Georgetown. l.t. ed. 1999. (Illus.). pap. 23.95 (*1-56895-807-2*, Wheeler Publishing, Inc.) Gale Group.
—Murder in Georgetown. 2000. 240p. mass mkt. 5.99 (*0-312-97321-7*, St. Martin's Paperbacks); 1999. 230p. 23.95 o.p. (*0-312-24221-2*, Saint Martin's Minotaur) St. Martin's Pr.
—Murder in the Blue Room. l.t. ed. 1991. (General Ser.). 377p. 13.95 o.p. (*0-8161-5112-1*); lib. bdg. 21.95 (*0-8161-5100-8*) Gale Group. (Macmillan Reference USA).
—Murder in the Blue Room. 1992. 240p. pap. 4.99 (*0-380-71237-7*, Avon Bks.) Morrow/Avon.
—Murder in the Blue Room. 1990. 16.95 o.p. (*0-312-04354-6*, Saint Martin's Minotaur) St. Martin's Pr.
—Murder in the Chateau. l.t. ed. 1999. (Wheeler Large Print Bks.). pap. 23.95 o.p. (*1-56895-769-6*, Wheeler Publishing, Inc.) Gale Group.
—Murder in the Chateau. 1996. 276p. mass mkt. 5.99 (*0-312-96050-6*, St. Martin's Paperbacks); 192p. 19.95 o.p. (*0-312-14375-3*, Saint Martin's Minotaur) St. Martin's Pr.
—Murder in the East Room. l.t. ed. 2001. (Large Print Book Ser.). 246p. pap. 22.95 (*1-58724-020-3*, Wheeler Publishing, Inc.) Gale Group.
—Murder in the East Room. (Eleanor Roosevelt Mystery Ser.). 1995. 244p. mass mkt. 4.99 (*0-312-95410-7*, St. Martin's Paperbacks); 1993. 208p. 18.95 o.p. (*0-312-09878-2*, Saint Martin's Minotaur) St. Martin's Pr.
—Murder in the Executive Mansion. 1998. 256 p. (*0-7540-3423-2*) BBC Audiobooks America.
—Murder in the Executive Mansion. 1996. 242p. mass mkt. 5.99 (*0-312-95578-2*, St. Martin's Paperbacks); 1995. 208p. 19.95 o.p. (*0-312-13128-3*, Saint Martin's Minotaur) St. Martin's Pr.
—Murder in the Executive Mansion. l.t. ed. 1998. (Nightingale Ser.). 264p. pap. 21.95 (*0-7838-0284-6*) Thorndike Pr.
—Murder in the Lincoln Bedroom: An Eleanor Roosevelt Mystery. 2002. 240p. mass mkt. 6.50 (*0-312-97919-3*, St. Martin's Paperbacks); 2000. (Illus.). 228p. 22.95 (*0-312-26150-0*, Saint Martin's Minotaur) St. Martin's Pr.
—Murder in the Lincoln Bedroom: An Eleanor Roosevelt Mystery. l.t. ed. 2001. (Thorndike Americana Ser.). 279p. 30.95 (*0-7862-3049-5*); (*0-7540-4446-7*); (*0-7540-4447-5*) Thorndike Pr.
—Murder in the Map Room: An Eleanor Roosevelt Mystery. l.t. ed. (Large Print Bks.). 2001. pap. 24.95 o.p. (*1-58724-097-1*); 1998. pap. 22.95 o.p. (*1-56895-619-3*) Gale Group. (Wheeler Publishing, Inc.).
—Murder in the Map Room: An Eleanor Roosevelt Mystery. (Eleanor Roosevelt Mystery Ser.). 256p. 1999. mass mkt. 5.99 (*0-312-96764-0*, St. Martin's Paperbacks); 1998. 21.95 (*0-312-18168-X*) St. Martin's Pr.
—Murder in the Oval Office. l.t. ed. 1989. (General Ser.). 392p. 20.95 o.p. (*0-8161-4853-8*, Macmillan Reference USA) Gale Group.
—Murder in the Oval Office. 1990. pap. 4.99 (*0-380-70528-1*, Avon Bks.) Morrow/Avon.
—Murder in the Oval Office. 1991. 3.99 o.p. (*0-517-07815-5*) Random Hse. Value Publishing.
—Murder in the Oval Office, unabr. ed. 1989. (Eleanor Roosevelt Mystery Ser.: Vol. 7). audio 44.00 (*1-55690-365-0*, 89940E7) Recorded Bks., LLC.
—Murder in the Oval Office. 1989. 256p. 17.95 o.p. (*0-312-02259-X*) St. Martin's Pr.
—Murder in the Red Room. l.t. ed. 2000. (Wheeler Large Print Book Ser.). 263p. pap. 25.95 (*1-56895-901-X*, Wheeler Publishing, Inc.) Gale Group.
—Murder in the Red Room. 1994. (Eleanor Roosevelt Mystery Ser.). 256p. mass mkt. 4.99 (*0-380-72143-0*, Avon Bks.) Morrow/Avon.
—Murder in the Red Room. 1992. (Eleanor Roosevelt Mystery Ser.). 256p. 18.95 o.p. (*0-312-07637-1*, Saint Martin's Minotaur) St. Martin's Pr.
—Murder in the Rose Garden. l.t. ed. 1990. (Eleanor Roosevelt Mystery Ser.). 384p. reprint ed. pap. 11.95 o.s.i (*0-8161-5000-1*); lib. bdg. 20.95 o.p. (*0-8161-4998-4*) Gale Group. (Macmillan Reference USA).
—Murder in the Rose Garden. 1991. (Eleanor Roosevelt Mystery Ser.). reprint ed. pap. 4.95 (*0-380-70529-X*, Avon Bks.) Morrow/Avon.
—Murder in the Rose Garden. 1989. (Eleanor Roosevelt Mystery Ser.). 240p. 16.95 o.p. (*0-312-03406-7*) St. Martin's Pr.
—Murder in the West Wing. (Eleanor Roosevelt Mystery Ser.). 1993. mass mkt. 5.99 (*0-312-95144-2*, St. Martin's Paperbacks); 1992. 256p. 18.95 o.p. (*0-312-08144-8*, Saint Martin's Minotaur) St. Martin's Pr.
—A Royal Murder. l.t. ed. 1995. 284p. 22.95 o.p. (*1-56895-171-X*, Wheeler Publishing, Inc.) Gale Group.
—A Royal Murder. 1994. 240p. 19.95 o.p. (*0-312-10970-9*, Saint Martin's Minotaur) St. Martin's Pr.
—The White House Pantry Murder. l.t. ed. 1988. (General Ser.). 327p. 17.95 o.p. (*0-8161-4342-0*, Macmillan Reference USA) Gale Group.
—The White House Pantry Murder. 1988. (Eleanor Roosevelt Mystery Ser.). pap. 4.50 (*0-380-70404-8*, Avon Bks.) Morrow/Avon.
—The White House Pantry Murder, unabr. ed. 1988. (Eleanor Roosevelt Mystery Ser.: Vol. 4). audio 44.00 (*1-55690-561-0*, 88120E7) Recorded Bks., LLC.
—The White House Pantry Murder. 1987. (Eleanor Roosevelt Mystery Ser.). 224p. 15.95 o.p. (*0-312-00202-5*) St. Martin's Pr.

Roosevelt, Elliott & Harrington, William. Murder at the President's Door. l.t. ed. 2002. 30.95 (*0-7862-4093-8*) Gale Group.
—Murder at the President's Door. 2001. 240p. 23.95 (*0-312-27499-8*, Saint Martin's Minotaur) St. Martin's Pr.

Thorson, Pamela Kay. Camp David Diaries Vol. I: Eleanor Roosevelt 1942-1945, 11 vols. 2001. (Camp David Diaries: Vol. 1). 150p. pap. 19.95 (*0-931791-01-4*) Sterling-Miller Publishing Company, Inc.

**ROOSEVELT, THEODORE, 1858-1919—FICTION**

Alexander, Lawrence. The Strenuous Life. 1991. 304p. pap. 4.99 (*1-56129-236-2*) Knightsbridge Publishing.

Carr, Caleb. The Angel of Darkness. 1998. mass mkt. 7.99 o.s.i (*0-345-42514-6*); 768p. mass mkt. 7.99 (*0-345-42763-7*) Ballantine Bks.
—The Angel of Darkness. unabr. ed. 1998. audio 72.00 (*0-7366-4114-9*, 4619-A); audio 72.00 (*0-7366-4115-7*, 4619-B) Books on Tape, Inc.
—The Angel of Darkness. l.t. ed. 1999. pap. 25.95 o.p. (*0-7838-8242-4*, Macmillan Reference USA) Gale Group.
—The Angel of Darkness. abr. ed. 1997. audio 25.00 (*0-671-57748-4*, 595482, Simon & Schuster Audioworks) Simon & Schuster Audio.

Garfield, Brian. Manifest Destiny. 1989. 416p. 19.95 o.p. (*0-89296-382-4*) Mysterious Pr.
—Manifest Destiny. 1990. 416p. mass mkt. 5.95 o.p. (*0-445-40815-4*, Mysterious Pr. Paperback Bks.) Warner Bks., Inc.

Henry, Will. San Juan Hill. 1996. 368p. reprint ed. mass mkt. 4.99 (*0-8439-4045-X*, Leisure Bks.) Dorchester Publishing Co., Inc.

Jeffers, H. Paul. The Adventure of the Stalwart Companions. 1978. 7.95 o.p. (*0-06-012248-X*) HarperCollins Pubs.

Schorr, Mark. Bully! 1985. 192p. 12.95 o.p. (*0-312-10798-6*) St. Martin's Pr.

Vidal, Gore. Empire. 1988. 480p. mass mkt. 6.99 o.s.i (*0-345-35472-9*) Ballantine Bks.
—Empire. unabr. ed. 1993. (American Chronicles Ser.: Vol. 3). audio 112.00 (*0-7366-2471-6*, 3234) Books on Tape, Inc.
—Empire. 2000. (International Ser.). 496p. pap. 16.00 (*0-375-70874-X*, Vintage) Knopf Publishing Group.
—Empire. 1988. audio 16.00 o.s.i (*0-394-57079-0*); audio 14.95 o.p. Random Hse. Audio Publishing Group.
—Empire. 1989. 3.99 o.p. (*0-517-68969-3*) Random Hse. Value Publishing.
—Empire. ltd. ed. 1987. 512p. 100.00 o.p. (*0-394-56127-9*) Random Hse., Inc.

**ROPER, DOUGLAS (FICTITIOUS CHARACTER)—FICTION**

Hart, Roy. Blood Kin. 1991. 208p. 17.95 o.p. (*0-312-06909-X*, Saint Martin's Minotaur) St. Martin's Pr.
—Breach of Promise. 1990. 15.95 o.p. (*0-312-05393-2*, Saint Martin's Minotaur) St. Martin's Pr.
—A Deadly Schedule. 1996. (WWL Mystery Ser.). per. (*0-373-26205-1*, 1-26205-4, Worldwide Library) Harlequin Enterprises, Ltd.
—A Deadly Schedule. 1995. mass mkt. o.s.i (*0-7515-1034-3*) Little Brown & Co.
—A Deadly Schedule: An Inspector Roper Mystery. 1994. 224p. 19.95 o.p. (*0-312-10964-4*, Saint Martin's Minotaur) St. Martin's Pr.
—Final Appointment. 1993. 248p. 17.95 o.p. (*0-312-08777-2*, Saint Martin's Minotaur) St. Martin's Pr.
—A Fox in the Night. 1998. (WWL Mystery Ser.). per. (*0-373-26280-9*, 1-26280-7, Worldwide Library) Harlequin Enterprises, Ltd.
—A Fox in the Night. 1988. 224p. 15.95 o.p. (*0-312-02212-3*, Saint Martin's Minotaur) St. Martin's Pr.
—A Fox in the Night. l.t. ed. 1990. (Ulverscroft Large Print Ser.). 29.99 (*0-7089-2218-X*, Ulverscroft) Thorpe, F. A. Pubs. GBR. *Dist:* Ulverscroft Large Print Bks., Ltd., Ulverscroft Large Print Canada, Ltd.
—Remains to Be Seen. 1989. 15.95 o.p. (*0-312-02971-3*, Saint Martin's Minotaur) St. Martin's Pr.
—Remains to Be Seen. l.t. ed. 1991. (Ulverscroft Large Print Ser.). 29.99 (*0-7089-2535-9*, Ulverscroft) Thorpe, F. A. Pubs. GBR. *Dist:* Ulverscroft Large Print Bks., Ltd., Ulverscroft Large Print Canada, Ltd.
—Robbed Blind. 1998. (WWL Mystery Ser.: Vol. 289). per. (*0-373-26289-2*, 1-26289-8, Worldwide Library) Harlequin Enterprises, Ltd.
—Robbed Blind. 1990. 15.95 o.p. (*0-312-04414-3*, Saint Martin's Minotaur) St. Martin's Pr.
—Robbed Blind. l.t. ed. 1992. (Linford Mystery Library). 416p. 29.99 o.p. (*0-7089-2769-6*, Linford) Thorpe, F. A. Pubs. GBR. *Dist:* Ulverscroft Large Print Bks., Ltd., Ulverscroft Large Print Canada, Ltd.
—Seascape with Dead Figures. 1987. 192p. 13.95 o.p. (*0-312-01088-5*, Saint Martin's Minotaur) St. Martin's Pr.
—Seascape with Dead Figures. l.t. ed. 1989. (Ulverscroft Large Print Ser.). 29.99 o.p. (*0-7089-2105-1*, Ulverscroft) Thorpe, F. A. Pubs. GBR. *Dist:* Ulverscroft Large Print Bks., Ltd., Ulverscroft Large Print Canada, Ltd.
—Seascape with Dead Figures: A Detective Superintendent Roper Mystery. 1998. (WWL Mystery Ser.). per. (*0-373-26268-X*, 1-26268-2, Worldwide Library) Harlequin Enterprises, Ltd.

**ROPER, IAN (FICTITIOUS CHARACTER)—FICTION**

Bolitho, Janie. Dangerous Deceit. l.t. ed. 1997. (Dales Large Print Ser.). 288p. pap. 19.99 o.p. (*1-85389-731-0*) Dales Large Print Bks. GBR. *Dist:* Ulverscroft Large Print Bks., Ltd., Ulverscroft Large Print Canada, Ltd.
—Exposure of Evil. l.t. ed. 1999. (Magna Large Print Ser.). 384p. o.p. (*0-7505-1430-2*) Magna Large Print Bks. GBR. *Dist:* Ulverscroft Large Print Canada, Ltd.
—Kindness Can Kill. 1996. (Mystery Ser.). 252p. per. (*0-373-26193-4*, 1-26193-2, Worldwide Library) Harlequin Enterprises, Ltd.
—Kindness Can Kill: A Detective Chief Inspector Roper Mystery. 1993. 208p. 18.95 o.p. (*0-312-10488-X*, Saint Martin's Minotaur) St. Martin's Pr.
—Ripe for Revenge. 1996. per. (*0-373-26220-5*, 1-26220-3, Worldwide Library) Harlequin Enterprises, Ltd.
—Ripe for Revenge. 1995. 191p. 18.95 o.p. (*0-312-11881-3*, Saint Martin's Minotaur) St. Martin's Pr.
—Sequence of Shame. l.t. ed. 1998. (Dales Large Print Ser.). 304p. pap. o.p. (*1-85389-836-8*) Dales Large Print Bks. GBR. *Dist:* Ulverscroft Large Print Canada, Ltd.

**ROPER, TAGGART (FICTITIOUS CHARACTER)—FICTION**

Sanders, William. Blood Autumn. 1995. 272p. 21.00 o.p. (*0-312-11755-8*, Saint Martin's Minotaur) St. Martin's Pr.
—A Death on 66: A Taggart Roper Mystery. 1993. 256p. 20.95 o.p. (*0-312-10452-9*, Saint Martin's Minotaur) St. Martin's Pr.
—The Next Victim. 1993. 240p. 17.95 o.p. (*0-312-08861-2*, Saint Martin's Minotaur) St. Martin's Pr.

**ROSATO, BENEDETTA (FICTITIOUS CHARACTER)—FICTION**

Scottoline, Lisa. Courting Trouble. 2002. 320p. 25.95 (*0-06-018514-7*) HarperCollins Pubs.
—Courting Trouble. l.t. ed. 2002. 496p. 25.95 (*0-06-008193-7*, HarperLargePrint) HarperTrade.
—Courting Trouble. 2003. 432p. mass mkt. 7.99 (*0-06-103141-0*, HarperTorch) Morrow/Avon.
—Legal Tender. unabr. ed. 1997. audio 48.00 (*0-913369-42-X*, 4221) Books on Tape, Inc.
—Legal Tender. l.t. ed. 1997. (Large Print Bks.). pap. 24.95 (*1-56895-413-1*, Wheeler Publishing, Inc.) Gale Group.
—Legal Tender. 1997. 464p. mass mkt. 7.99 (*0-06-109412-9*); 1996. 304p. 23.00 o.p. (*0-06-017658-X*) HarperCollins Pubs.
—Legal Tender. abr. ed. 2000. audio 9.99 (*0-694-52328-3*); 1996. audio 18.00 o.s.i (*0-694-51737-2*, CPN 2594) HarperTrade. (HarperAudio).
—Mistaken Identity. unabr. ed. 2002. audio compact disk 49.95 (*0-7927-2766-5*, CMP 243); 2000. audio 110.95 (*0-7927-2354-6*, CSL 243) BBC Audiobooks America. (Chivers Sound Library).
—Mistaken Identity. 1999. 496p. 24.00 o.s.i (*0-06-018747-6*); 608p. mass mkt. 7.99 o.p. (*0-06-101419-2*) HarperCollins Pubs.
—Mistaken Identity. 2002. audio 9.99 (*0-06-009929-1*); 1999. audio 18.00 (*0-694-52110-8*, 394823) HarperTrade. (HarperAudio).
—Mistaken Identity, abr. ed. 1999. audio 18.00 Highsmith Inc.

Characters

—Mistaken Identity. 2000. 592p. mass mkt. 7.99 (*0-06-109611-3*, HarperTorch) Morrow/Avon.

—Mistaken Identity. l.t. ed. (Thorndike/G. K. Hall Paperback Bestsellers Ser.). 704p. 2000. pap. 27.95 (*0-7862-1976-9*); 1999. 30.95 (*0-7862-1975-0*) Thorndike Pr.

—Mistaken Identity. 2000. 13.55 (*0-606-17714-0*) Turtleback Bks.

**ROSE, MIKE (FICTITIOUS CHARACTER)—FICTION**

Ventura, Michael. The Death of Frank Sinatra: A Novel. 1996. 320p. 22.50 o.p. (*0-8050-3738-1*) Holt, Henry & Co.

—The Death of Frank Sinatra: A Novel. 1997. (Dead Letter Mysteries Ser.). 320p. mass mkt. 5.99 (*0-312-96474-9*, St. Martin's Paperbacks) St. Martin's Pr.

**ROSEN, NATE (FICTITIOUS CHARACTER)—FICTION**

Levitsky, Ronald. The Innocence That Kills. 1994. 254p. text 20.00 (*0-684-19707-3*, Macmillan Reference USA) Gale Group.

—The Wisdom of Serpents: A Nate Rosen Mystery. 1992. 256p. text 19.00 (*0-684-19411-2*, Scribner) Simon & Schuster.

**ROSS, BARRY (FICTITIOUS CHARACTER)—FICTION**

Livesay, Ann. Death in the Amazon. 1998. (Barry Ross International Mystery Ser.). 326p. pap. (*0-9662817-1-3*) Silver River Bks.

Livesay, Ann & Sutton, Myron D. The Isis Command: An Egyptian Mystery. 1998. (Barry Ross International Mystery Ser.: Vol. 1). 225p. pap., wbk. ed. (*0-9662817-0-5*) Silver River Bks.

**ROSS, CHIEF INSPECTOR (FICTITIOUS CHARACTER)—FICTION**

Grindle, Lucretia. So Little to Die For. Issacson, Dana, ed. 1994. 256p. (Orig.). mass mkt. 4.99 (*0-671-74846-7*, Pocket) Simon & Schuster.

**ROSS, DANIELLE (FICTITIOUS CHARACTER)—FICTION**

Morris, Gilbert. And Then There Were Two. l.t. ed. 2002. 431p. pap. 16.95 (*1-4104-0015-8*, Walker Large Print) Gale Group.

—And Then There Were Two. l.t. ed. 2001. (Dani Ross Mysteries Ser.). 463p. 24.95 o.p. (*0-7862-3088-6*) Thorndike Pr.

—The Danielle Ross Mystery, 3 vols., Set. 1990. (Danielle Ross Mystery Ser.). 992p. (gr. 10). pap. 27.00 o.p. (*0-8007-5454-9*) Revell, Fleming H. Co.

—Deadly Deception. 1991. (Danielle Ross Mystery Ser.: No. 3). 320p. (gr. 10). pap. 9.99 o.p. (*0-8007-5419-0*) Revell, Fleming H. Co.

—The End of Act Three. 2001. (Dani Ross Mysteries Ser.: Vol. 3). Orig. Title: The Final Curtain. 266p. reprint ed. pap. 12.99 (*1-58134-245-4*) Crossway Bks.

—The End of Act Three. l.t. ed. 2002. Orig. Title: The Final Curtain. 436p. pap. 16.95 (*1-4104-0032-8*, Walker Large Print) Gale Group.

—The End of Act Three. l.t. ed. 2001. Orig. Title: The Final Curtain. 423p. 24.95 (*0-7862-3406-7*) Thorndike Pr.

—The Final Curtain. 1991. (Danielle Ross Mystery Ser.). 320p. (gr. 10). pap. 9.99 o.p. (*0-8007-5411-5*) Revell, Fleming H. Co.

—Four of a Kind: A Dani Ross Mystery. 2001. (Dani Ross Mysteries Ser.: Vol. 4). 264p. reprint ed. pap. 12.99 (*1-58134-244-6*) Crossway Bks.

—Four of a Kind: A Dani Ross Mystery. l.t. ed. 2001. (Christian Mystery Ser.). 426p. 24.95 (*0-7862-3545-4*) Thorndike Pr.

—Guilt by Association. 1990. (Danielle Ross Mystery Ser.). 352p. (gr. 10). pap. 9.99 o.p. (*0-8007-5395-X*) Revell, Fleming H. Co.

—One by One. 2000. (Dani Ross Mysteries Ser.). Orig. Title: Guilt by Association. 286p. reprint ed. pap. 12.99 (*1-58134-192-X*) Crossway Bks.

—One by One. l.t. ed. 2002. Orig. Title: Guilt by Association. 490p. pap. 16.95 (*1-4104-0025-5*, Walker Large Print) Gale Group.

—One by One. l.t. ed. 2001. (Christian Mystery Ser.). Orig. Title: Guilt by Association. 467p. 24.95 (*0-7862-3087-8*) Thorndike Pr.

—The Quality of Mercy. 1993. (Danielle Ross Mystery Ser.). 312p. (gr. 10 up). pap. 9.99 o.p. (*0-8007-5474-3*) Revell, Fleming H. Co.

—Revenge at the Rodeo. 1993. (Danielle Ross Mystery Ser.). 320p. (gr. 10). pap. 9.99 o.p. (*0-8007-5457-3*) Revell, Fleming H. Co.

**ROSS, JACK (FICTITIOUS CHARACTER)—FICTION**

Schopen, Bernard. The Desert Look. 1990. 256p. 17.95 (*0-89296-354-9*) Mysterious Pr.

—The Desert Look. 1995. (Western Literature Ser.). 272p. pap. 18.00 (*0-87417-259-4*) Univ. of Nevada Pr.

—The Desert Look. 1991. mass mkt. 4.95 o.s.i (*0-446-40009-2*, Mysterious Pr. Paperback Bks.) Warner Bks., Inc.

—The Iris Deception. 1996. (Western Literature Ser.). 296p. pap. 18.00 (*0-87417-286-1*) Univ. of Nevada Pr.

**ROSS, JOHN (FICTITIOUS CHARACTER)—FICTION**

Brooks, Terry. Angel Fire East. 2000. 384p. mass mkt. 7.99 (*0-345-43525-7*, Del Rey) Ballantine Bks.

—Angel Fire East. unabr. ed. 1999. audio 80.00 (*0-7887-4052-0*, 96159E7, Clipper Audio) Recorded Bks., LLC.

—A Knight of the Word. E-Book 6.99 (*1-58945-521-5*) Adobe Systems, Inc.

—A Knight of the Word. 1999. mass mkt. (*0-345-42942-7*, Ballantine Bks.); 1999. (Trolltown Ser.: Vol. 2). 408p. mass mkt. 6.99 (*0-345-42464-6*); 1998. 25.95 o.s.i (*0-345-43005-0*) Ballantine Bks.

—A Knight of the Word. 2001. E-Book 6.99 (*0-345-44459-0*) Random Hse., Inc.

—A Knight of the Word. unabr. ed. 2000. audio 75.00 (*0-7887-2516-5*, 95589E7) Recorded Bks., LLC.

—Running with the Demon. 1998. (Trolltown Ser.: Vol. 1). 448p. mass mkt. 7.99 (*0-345-42258-9*); 1997. 432p. 5.99 o.s.i (*0-345-37962-4*) Ballantine Bks. (Del Rey).

—Running with the Demon. unabr. ed. 1998. audio 97.00 (*0-7887-2168-2*, 95464E7) Recorded Bks., LLC.

**ROSS, WILL (FICTITIOUS CHARACTER)—FICTION**

Moody, Gregory A. Perfect Circles. 1998. 400p. pap. 12.95 (*1-884737-44-7*) VeloPress.

**ROSTNIKOV, PORFIRY PETROVICH (FICTITIOUS CHARACTER)—FICTION**

Kaminsky, Stuart M. Black Knight in Red Square. 1989. (Inspector Porfiry Rostnikov Mystery Ser.). 224p. mass mkt. 5.99 o.s.i (*0-8041-0405-0*, Ivy Bks.) Ballantine Bks.

—Black Knight in Red Square. 1984. (Inspector Porfiry Rostnikov Mystery Ser.). 224p. 2.95 o.s.i (*0-441-06628-3*, Diamond Bks.) Berkley Publishing Group.

—Black Knight in Red Square. unabr. ed. 1993. (Inspector Porfiry Rostnikov Mystery Ser.: Vol. 2). audio 51.00 (*1-55690-943-8*, 93439E7) Recorded Bks., LLC.

—Blood & Rubles. 1996. (Inspector Porfiry Rostnikov Mystery Ser.). 261p. mass mkt. 5.99 o.s.i (*0-8041-1288-6*, Ivy Bks.); 272p. 21.00 o.s.i (*0-449-90949-2*, Fawcett) Ballantine Bks.

—Blood & Rubles. unabr. ed. 1997. audio 44.95 (*0-7861-1119-4*, 1880) Blackstone Audio Bks., Inc.

—Blood & Rubles. unabr. ed. 1997. audio 48.00 (*0-7366-3704-4*, 4388) Books on Tape, Inc.

—Blood & Rubles. l.t. ed. 1996. (Inspector Porfiry Rostnikov Mystery Ser.). 317p. 23.95 o.p. (*1-56895-329-1*, Wheeler Publishing, Inc.) Gale Group.

—Blood & Rubles. unabr. ed. 2000. (Inspector Porfiry Rostnikov Mystery Ser.). audio 60.00 (*0-7887-0511-3*, 94704E7) Recorded Bks., LLC.

—A Cold Red Sunrise. 1989. (Inspector Porfiry Rostnikov Mystery Ser.). mass mkt. 6.99 o.s.i (*0-8041-0428-X*, Ivy Bks.) Ballantine Bks.

—A Cold Red Sunrise. l.t. ed. 2000. 287p. lib. bdg. 27.95 (*1-58547-021-X*) Ctr. Point Large Print.

—A Cold Red Sunrise. 1988. (Inspector Porfiry Rostnikov Mystery Ser.). 224p. 16.95 o.s.i (*0-684-18905-4*, Macmillan Reference USA) Gale Group.

—A Cold Red Sunrise. unabr. ed. 1992. audio 49.00 (*1-55690-677-3*, 92330) Recorded Bks., LLC.

—Death of a Dissident. 1981. (Inspector Porfiry Rostnikov Mystery Ser.). 448p. 2.95 o.s.i (*0-441-14204-4*) Ace Bks.

—Death of a Dissident. 1989. (Inspector Porfiry Rostnikov Mystery Ser.). mass mkt. 5.50 o.s.i (*0-8041-0404-2*, Ivy Bks.) Ballantine Bks.

—Death of a Dissident. unabr. ed. 1993. (Inspector Porfiry Rostnikov Mystery Ser.: Vol. 1). audio 51.00 (*1-55690-898-9*, 93340E7) Recorded Bks., LLC.

—Death of a Russian Priest. (Inspector Porfiry Rostnikov Mystery Ser.). 1993. mass mkt. 5.99 o.s.i (*0-8041-0836-6*, Ivy Bks.); 1992. 256p. 18.00 o.s.i (*0-449-90724-4*, Fawcett) Ballantine Bks.

—Death of a Russian Priest. unabr. ed. 1995. (Inspector Porfiry Rostnikov Mystery Ser.: Vol. 8). audio 51.00 (*0-7887-0104-5*, 94345E7) Recorded Bks., LLC.

—The Dog Who Bit a Policeman. unabr. ed. 2000. audio 59.95 (*0-7927-2255-8*, CSL 144) Chivers Audio Bks. GBR. *Dist:* BBC Audiobooks America.

—The Dog Who Bit a Policeman. 2001. 288p. E-Book 14.95 (*0-7595-9371-X*); 2001. 288p. E-Book 14.95 (*0-7595-6335-7*); 2001. 288p. E-Book 14.95 (*0-7595-8341-2*); 1998. 275p. (gr. 8 up). 22.00 (*0-89296-667-X*) Mysterious Pr.

—The Dog Who Bit a Policeman. unabr. ed. 2000. (Inspector Porfiry Rostnikov Mystery Ser.: Vol. 12). audio 70.00 (*0-7887-2483-5*, 95558E7) Recorded Bks., LLC.

—The Dog Who Bit a Policeman. l.t. ed. 1999. (Mystery Ser.). 455p. 27.95 (*0-7862-1767-7*) Thorndike Pr.

—Fall of a Cosmonaut. l.t. ed. 2001. (Large Print Bks.). 348p. pap. 23.95 (*1-58724-114-5*, Wheeler Publishing, Inc.) Gale Group.

—Fall of a Cosmonaut. 2000. 288p. 24.95 (*0-89296-668-8*); 288p. E-Book 14.95 (*0-446-92256-0*); E-Book 14.95 (*0-446-93129-2*); 288p. E-Book 14.95 (*0-446-91365-0*); 288p. E-Book 14.95 (*0-446-92860-7*); (Illus.). E-Book 14.95 (*0-446-96089-6*) Mysterious Pr.

—Fall of a Cosmonaut. 2000. 288p. E-Book 14.95 (*0-446-92369-9*) Warner Bks., Inc.

—A Fine Red Rain. 1988. (Inspector Porfiry Rostnikov Mystery Ser.). 208p. mass mkt. 4.99 o.s.i (*0-8041-0279-1*, Ivy Bks.) Ballantine Bks.

—A Fine Red Rain. 1987. (Inspector Porfiry Rostnikov Mystery Ser.). 211p. 14.95 o.p. (*0-684-18666-7*, Macmillan Reference USA) Gale Group.

—A Fine Red Rain. unabr. ed. 1994. (Inspector Porfiry Rostnikov Mystery Ser.: Vol. 4). audio 51.00 (*1-55690-982-9*, 94121E7) Recorded Bks., LLC.

—A Fine Red Rain. 2000. (Inspector Porfiry Rostnikov Mystery Ser.). 224p. pap. 14.95 (*0-7432-1161-8*, Scribner) Simon & Schuster.

—Hard Currency. 1995. (Inspector Porfiry Rostnikov Mystery Ser.). mass mkt. 5.99 o.s.i (*0-8041-0837-4*, Ivy Bks.); 247p. 20.00 o.s.i (*0-449-90725-2*, Fawcett) Ballantine Bks.

—Hard Currency. unabr. ed. 1995. 9p. audio 44.95 (*0-7861-0822-3*, 893333) Blackstone Audio Bks., Inc.

—Hard Currency. unabr. ed. 1995. (Inspector Porfiry Rostnikov Mystery Ser.: Vol. 9). audio 60.00 (*0-7887-0412-5*, 94604E7) Recorded Bks., LLC.

—The Man Who Walked Like a Bear. unabr. ed. 1994. (Inspector Porfiry Rostnikov Mystery Ser.: Vol. 6). audio 44.00 (*0-7887-0049-9*, 94248E7) Recorded Bks., LLC.

—The Man Who Walked Like a Bear: An Inspector Porfiry Rostnikov Novel. 1991. (Inspector Porfiry Rostnikov Mystery Ser.). mass mkt. 4.95 o.s.i (*0-8041-0693-2*, Ivy Bks.) Ballantine Bks.

—Murder on the Trans-Siberian Express. l.t. ed. 2002. (Basic Ser.). 423p. 28.95 (*0-7862-3814-3*) Gale Group.

—Murder on the Trans-Siberian Express. 2001. 288p. 24.95 (*0-89296-747-1*) Mysterious Pr.

—Red Chameleon. 1989. (Inspector Porfiry Rostnikov Mystery Ser.). 208p. mass mkt. 4.99 o.s.i (*0-8041-0465-4*, Ivy Bks.) Ballantine Bks.

—Red Chameleon. 1986. (Inspector Porfiry Rostnikov Mystery Ser.). 240p. 3.50 o.s.i (*0-441-71086-7*, Diamond Bks.) Berkley Publishing Group.

—Red Chameleon. unabr. ed. 1992. (Inspector Porfiry Rostnikov Mystery Ser.: Vol. 3). audio 51.00 (*1-55690-725-7*, 92107E7) Recorded Bks., LLC.

—Red Chameleon. 1985. (Inspector Porfiry Rostnikov Mystery Ser.). 224p. 13.95 o.s.i (*0-684-18424-9*, Scribner) Simon & Schuster.

—Rostnikov's Vacation. 1992. (Inspector Porfiry Rostnikov Mystery Ser.). reprint ed. mass mkt. 5.99 o.s.i (*0-8041-0694-0*, Ivy Bks.) Ballantine Bks.

—Rostnikov's Vacation. unabr. ed. 1993. audio 51.00 (*1-55690-840-7*, 93208E7) Recorded Bks., LLC.

—Rostnikov's Vacation. 1991. (Inspector Porfiry Rostnikov Mystery Ser.). 244p. 19.95 o.s.i (*0-684-19022-2*, Scribner) Simon & Schuster.

—Tarnished Icons. 1997. (Inspector Porfiry Rostnikov Mystery Ser.). 277p. mass mkt. 6.99 o.s.i (*0-8041-1289-4*, Ivy Bks.) Ballantine Bks.

—Tarnished Icons. unabr. ed. 1997. (Inspector Porfiry Rostnikov Mystery Ser.: Vol. 11). audio 70.00 (*0-7887-0930-5*, 95070E7) Recorded Bks., LLC.

**ROTHMAN, RUBY (FICTITIOUS CHARACTER)—FICTION**

Kahn, Sharon. Don't Cry for Me, Hot Pastrami. 2002. (Ruby, the Rabbi's Wife Mystery Ser.). 240p. reprint ed. mass mkt. 5.99 (*0-425-18715-2*, Prime Crime) Berkley Publishing Group.

—Don't Cry for Me, Hot Pastrami: A Ruby, the Rabbi's Wife Mystery. 2001. 304p. 24.00 o.s.i (*0-684-87155-6*); E-Book 24.00 (*0-7432-1825-6*) Simon & Schuster. (Scribner).

—Don't Cry for Me, Hot Pastrami: A Ruby, the Rabbi's Wife Mystery. l.t. ed. 2001. (G.K. Hall Large Print Core Ser.). 339p. 27.95 o.p. (*0-7838-9679-4*) Thorndike Pr.

—Fax Me a Bagel: A Ruby the Rabbi's Wife Mystery. 2001. 272p. mass mkt. 5.99 (*0-425-18046-8*) Berkley Publishing Group.

—Fax Me a Bagel: A Ruby the Rabbi's Wife Mystery. 1998. (Ruby, the Rabbi's Wife Mysteries Ser.). 256p. 22.00 (*0-684-84737-X*); 22.00 (*0-684-85498-8*) Simon & Schuster. (Scribner).

—Never Nosh a Matzo Ball: A Ruby the Rabbi's Wife Mystery. 2000. 304p. 22.00 o.s.i (*0-684-84738-8*, Scribner) Simon & Schuster.

—Which Big Giver Stole the Chopped Liver? 2004. 272p. 24.00 (*0-7432-4357-9*, Scribner) Simon & Schuster.

**ROUNDTREE, TRUDY (FICTITIOUS CHARACTER)—FICTION**

Berry, Linda. Death & the Easter Bunny. 1999. (WWL Mystery Ser.: Vol. 326). per. (*0-373-26326-0*, Worldwide Library) Harlequin Enterprises, Ltd.

—Death & the Easter Bunny. 1998. 224p. 20.95 (*1-885173-44-X*) Write Way Publishing.

**ROURKE, JOHN THOMAS (FICTITIOUS CHARACTER)—FICTION**

Ahern, Jerry. War Mountain. 1993. (Survivalist Ser.: No. 25). 320p. mass mkt. 3.50 o.s.i (*0-8217-4100-4*, Zebra Bks.) Kensington Publishing Corp.

**RUBIO, VINCENT (FICTITIOUS CHARACTER)—FICTION**

Garcia, Eric. Anonymous Rex: A Detective Story. 2001. 336p. pap. 12.95 o.s.i (*0-425-17821-8*); 2003. 368p. reprint ed. mass mkt. 6.99 (*0-425-18888-4*, Prime Crime) Berkley Publishing Group.

—Anonymous Rex: A Detective Story. 2001. (GER.). 384p. pap. 19.00 o.s.i (*3-89480-087-9*) Prisma Verlag GmbH DEU. *Dist:* Random Hse. of Canada, Ltd.

—Anonymous Rex: A Detective Story, abr. ed. 2001. audio 24.95 (*1-57511-066-0*) Publishing Mills, Inc., The.

—Anonymous Rex: A Detective Story. 1999. 23.00 (*0-676-79523-4*); 384p. 23.00 o.s.i (*0-375-50326-9*) Random House Adult Trade Publishing Group. (Villard Bks.).

—Anonymous Rex: A Detective Story. 2002. (GER.). 384p. pap. 19.00 (*1-4000-3974-6*); 1999. (*0-375-75508-X*) Random Hse., Inc.

—Casual Rex: A Detective Story. 2001. E-Book 19.50 (*1-58945-782-X*) Adobe Systems, Inc.

—Casual Rex: A Detective Story. 2002. 352p. pap. 12.95 (*0-425-18339-4*) Berkley Publishing Group.

—Casual Rex: A Detective Story. abr. ed. 2001. audio 24.95 (*1-57511-088-1*) Publishing Mills, Inc., The.

—Casual Rex: A Detective Story. 2001. E-Book 19.50 (*0-375-50666-7*, Villard Bks.) Random House Adult Trade Publishing Group.

—Hot & Sweaty Rex: A Mystery. 2004. 352p. 24.95 (*0-375-50523-7*, Villard Bks.) Random House Adult Trade Publishing Group.

**RULE, KATHERINE (FICTITIOUS CHARACTER)—FICTION**

Woods, Stuart. Deep Lie. 1998. 432p. mass mkt. 7.99 (*0-06-104449-0*) HarperCollins Pubs.

—Deep Lie. 1987. pap. 6.50 (*0-380-70266-5*, Avon Bks.) Morrow/Avon.

—Deep Lie. 1986. 344p. 15.95 o.p. (*0-393-02272-2*) Norton, W. W. & Co., Inc.

—Deep Lie. l.t. ed. 1987. (Charnwood Large Print Ser.). 512p. 29.99 o.p. (*0-7089-8413-4*, Charnwood) Thorpe, F. A. Pubs. GBR. *Dist:* Ulverscroft Large Print Bks., Ltd., Ulverscroft Large Print Canada, Ltd.

**RUMPOLE, HORACE (FICTITIOUS CHARACTER)—FICTION**

Minds Eye Staff. Rumpole 2. 14.95 (*0-559-35014-7*) Penguin Group (USA) Inc.

Mortimer, John. The Best of Rumpole. 1994. (Rumpole Ser.). 288p. reprint ed. pap. 14.00 (*0-14-017684-5*, Penguin Bks.) Penguin Group (USA) Inc.

—The Best of Rumpole. 1993. (Rumpole Ser.). 288p. 21.00 o.p. (*0-670-84978-2*, Viking) Viking Penguin.

—A First Rumpole Omnibus. 1984. (Crime Monthly Ser.). 560p. pap. 18.00 (*0-14-006768-X*, Penguin Bks.) Penguin Group (USA) Inc.

—Rumpole a la Carte. l.t. ed. 1992. pap. 14.95 o.p. (*0-7927-1002-9*); 18.95 o.p. (*0-7927-1001-0*, E0023) BBC Audiobooks America.

—Rumpole a la Carte. unabr. ed. 1992. audio 49.95 (*0-7861-0351-5*, 1308) Blackstone Audio Bks., Inc.

—Rumpole a la Carte. unabr. ed. 1992. audio 4.99 (*0-88646-608-3*); Set. 1991. audio 16.99 (*0-88646-276-2*, LFP 7276) Durkin Hayes Publishing Ltd.

—Rumpole a la Carte. (Rumpole Ser.). 256p. 1993. pap. 10.00 o.p. (*0-14-017981-X*); 1991. reprint ed. pap. 12.00 (*0-14-015609-7*) Penguin Group (USA) Inc. (Penguin Bks.).

—Rumpole a la Carte. 1990. (Rumpole Ser.). 256p. 18.95 o.p. (*0-670-83284-7*) Viking Penguin.

—Rumpole & the Age of Miracles. l.t. ed. 1995. pap. 19.95 o.p. (*0-7838-1188-8*, Macmillan Reference USA) Gale Group.

—Rumpole & the Age of Miracles. 1989. (Rumpole Ser.). 240p. pap. 10.95 o.s.i (*0-14-013116-7*, Penguin Bks.) Penguin Group (USA) Inc.

—Rumpole & the Age of Miracles. 2001. audio compact disk 82.00 (*0-7887-5191-3*, C1348E7); 1988. audio 62.00 (*0-7887-3483-0*, 95892E7) Recorded Bks., LLC.

—Rumpole & the Age of Retirement. unabr. ed. 1994. audio 4.99 (*0-88646-700-4*) Durkin Hayes Publishing Ltd.

—Rumpole & the Angel of Death. unabr. ed. 1996. audio 49.95 (0-7861-0974-2, 1751) Blackstone Audio Bks., Inc.
—Rumpole & the Angel of Death. l.t. ed. 1996. 426p. lib. bdg. 22.95 o.p. (0-7838-1794-0, Macmillan Reference USA) Gale Group.
—Rumpole & the Angel of Death. 1997. 272p. reprint ed. pap. 9.95 o.s.i (0-14-026314-4) Penguin Group (USA) Inc.
—Rumpole & the Angel of Death. unabr. ed. 1996. (Rumpole of the Bailey Ser.: Vol. 7). audio 70.00 (0-7887-0514-8, 94708E7) Recorded Bks., LLC.
—Rumpole & the Angel of Death. 1996. 272p. 22.95 o.p. (0-670-86451-X); 2p. audio 16.95 (0-14-086197-1, Penguin AudioBooks) Viking Penguin.
—Rumpole & the Golden Thread. 2003. 8p. audio 69.95 (0-7540-0907-6, CAB 2329); 1993. pap. 16.95 o.p. (0-7927-1370-2); 1992. 18.95 o.p. (0-7927-1371-0); 2003. 8p. audio compact disk 79.95 (0-7540-5553-1, CCD 244) BBC Audiobooks America.
—Rumpole & the Golden Thread. unabr. ed. 1995. audio 49.95 (0-7861-0855-X, 1653) Blackstone Audio Bks., Inc.
—Rumpole & the Golden Thread. unabr. ed. 1991. (Rumpole of the Bailey Ser.: Vol. 5). audio 60.00 (1-55690-451-7, 91211E7) Recorded Bks., LLC.
—Rumpole & the Golden Thread. 1984. 256p. pap. 9.95 o.s.i (0-14-025014-X, Penguin Classics); pap. 5.95 o.p. (0-14-006331-5, Penguin Bks.) Viking Penguin.
—Rumpole & the Judge's Elbow. unabr. ed. 1992. audio 5.99 (0-88646-607-5, PAC-7607) Durkin Hayes Publishing Ltd.
—Rumpole & the Man of God. abr. ed. 1996. (Paperback Audio Ser.). audio 9.99 (0-88646-882-5, 7882) Durkin Hayes Publishing Ltd.
—Rumpole & the Primrose Path. 2003. (Rumpole Ser.). 224p. 24.95 (0-670-03146-1, Viking) Viking Penguin.
—Rumpole & the Primrose Path. 2003. audio 54.95 (0-7540-8356-X) Chivers Audio Bks. GBR. *Dist:* BBC Audiobooks America.
—Rumpole & the Younger Generation. 1995. 64p. pap. 0.95 o.p. (0-14-600006-4) Penguin Group (USA) Inc.
—Rumpole at the Bar. abr. ed. 1989. audio 16.99 (0-88646-238-X, LFP 7238) Durkin Hayes Publishing Ltd.
—The Rumpole Collection, 2 bks., Set. deluxe ed. 1992. (Rumpole Ser.). pap. 22.00 o.p. (0-14-095385-X, Penguin Bks.) Penguin Group (USA) Inc.
—Rumpole for the Defence. l.t. ed. 1994. pap. 16.95 o.p. (0-7927-1604-3); 1993. 18.95 o.p. (0-7927-1605-1) BBC Audiobooks America.
—Rumpole for the Defence. unabr. ed. 1991. audio 39.95 (0-7861-0236-5, 1206) Blackstone Audio Bks., Inc.
—Rumpole for the Defence. 1984. 192p. pap. 9.95 o.s.i (0-14-025013-1) Penguin Group (USA) Inc.
—Rumpole for the Defence. unabr. ed. 1991. (Rumpole of the Bailey Ser.: Vol. 4). audio 51.00 (1-55690-452-5, 91108E7) Recorded Bks., LLC.
—Rumpole for the Defence. 1984. (Crime Monthly Ser.). 192p. pap. 5.95 o.p. (0-14-006060-X, Penguin Bks.) Viking Penguin.
—Rumpole for the Prosecution. Set. unabr. ed. 1992. audio 16.99 (0-88646-283-5, 7283) Durkin Hayes Publishing Ltd.
—Rumpole of the Bailey. 17.95 (0-89190-275-9) Amereon, Ltd.
—Rumpole of the Bailey. l.t. ed. (Eagle Large Print Ser.). 1993. 19.95 o.p. (0-7927-1532-2); 1993. pap. o.p. (0-7927-1531-4); 2002. audio 49.95 (0-7540-5493-4, CCD 184, Chivers Sound Library); 2002. audio 54.95 (0-7540-0787-1, CAB 2209) BBC Audiobooks America.
—Rumpole of the Bailey. unabr. ed. 1991. audio 44.95 (0-7861-0255-1, 1223) Blackstone Audio Bks., Inc.
—Rumpole of the Bailey. abr. ed. 1983. audio 16.99 (0-88646-084-0, TC-LFP 7110) Durkin Hayes Publishing Ltd.
—Rumpole of the Bailey. unabr. ed. 1993. (Rumpole of the Bailey Ser.: Vol. 1). audio 51.00 (1-55690-920-9, 93416E7) Recorded Bks., LLC.
—Rumpole of the Bailey. 1980. (Rumpole Ser.). 208p. pap. 5.95 o.p. (0-14-004670-4, Penguin Bks.); pap. 9.95 o.s.i (0-14-025012-3) Viking Penguin.
—Rumpole on Trial. unabr. ed. 2002. audio 29.95 (1-57270-267-2) Audio Partners Publishing Corp.
—Rumpole on Trial. unabr. ed. 1995. audio 69.95 (0-7451-4289-3, CAB 972) BBC Audiobooks America.
—Rumpole on Trial. unabr. ed. 2000. 8p. audio compact disk 79.95 (0-7540-5361-X, CCD 052); audio 59.95 (0-7451-2841-6, CAB 972) Chivers Audio Bks. GBR. *Dist:* BBC Audiobooks America.
—Rumpole on Trial. 1993. (Rumpole Ser.). 256p. reprint ed. pap. 10.00 o.s.i (0-14-017510-5, Penguin Bks.) Penguin Group (USA) Inc.
—Rumpole on Trial. abr. ed. 1992. (Rumpole Ser.). 15.95 o.p. incl. audio (0-453-00794-5) Penguin/HighBridge.
—Rumpole on Trial. 1992. (Rumpole Ser.). 256p. 21.00 o.p. (0-670-84459-4, Viking) Viking Penguin.
—Rumpole Rests His Case. unabr. ed. 2002. audio 29.95 (1-57270-281-8, Audio Editions Bks. on Cassette) Audio Partners Publishing Corp.
—Rumpole Rests His Case. 2002. audio 54.95 (0-7540-0872-X, CAB 2294); audio compact disk 64.95 (0-7540-5532-9, CCD 223) BBC Audiobooks America. (Chivers Sound Library).
—Rumpole Rests His Case. 2002. 224p. 24.95 (0-670-03139-9, Viking) Viking Penguin.
—Rumpole Unabridged, Set. unabr. ed. lib. bdg. 29.99 incl. audio (1-55204-723-7, PAUB-024) Durkin Hayes Publishing Ltd.
—Rumpole's Last Case. unabr. ed. 1995. audio 44.95 (0-7861-0801-0, 1625) Blackstone Audio Bks., Inc.
—Rumpole's Last Case. abr. ed. 1988. audio 16.99 (0-88646-233-9, LFP 7233); 1993. audio 4.99 (0-88646-652-0) Durkin Hayes Publishing Ltd.
—Rumpole's Last Case. l.t. ed. 1988. (General Ser.). 393p. 18.95 o.p. (0-8161-4660-8, Macmillan Reference USA) Gale Group.
—Rumpole's Last Case. 140th ed. 1990. (Rumpole Ser.). 288p. pap. 10.95 o.s.i (0-14-012695-3, Penguin Bks.) Penguin Group (USA) Inc.
—Rumpole's Last Case. unabr. ed. 1994. (Rumpole of the Bailey Ser.: Vol. 6). audio 60.00 (0-7887-0057-X, 94256E7) Recorded Bks., LLC.
—Rumpole's Last Case. 1988. (Rumpole Ser.). 288p. pap. 3.95 o.p. (0-14-010447-X, Penguin Bks.) Viking Penguin.
—Rumpole's Return. 18.95 (0-89190-277-5) Amereon, Ltd.
—Rumpole's Return. unabr. ed. 2002. audio 39.95 (0-7540-0831-2, CAB 2253); audio compact disk 64.95 (0-7540-5513-2, CCD 204) Chivers Pr. GBR. *Dist:* BBC Audiobooks America.
—Rumpole's Return, Set. abr. ed. 1990. audio 16.99 (0-88646-162-6, 7163) Durkin Hayes Publishing Ltd.
—Rumpole's Return. unabr. ed. 1991. (Rumpole of the Bailey Ser.: Vol. 3). audio 35.00 (1-55690-453-3, 91102E7) Recorded Bks., LLC.
—Rumpole's Return. 1982. 160p. pap. 9.95 o.s.i (0-14-024698-3, Penguin Classics); pap. 6.00 o.p. (0-14-005571-1, Penguin Bks.) Viking Penguin.
—The Second Rumpole Omnibus: Rumpole & the Golden Thread, Rumpole for the Defence & Rumpole's Last Case. 1988. (Rumpole Ser.). 672p. pap. 16.95 (0-14-008958-6, Penguin Bks.) Penguin Group (USA) Inc.
—The Second Rumpole Omnibus: Rumpole & the Golden Thread, Rumpole for the Defence & Rumpole's Last Case. 1987. (Rumpole Ser.). 672p. 18.95 o.p. (0-670-81125-4) Viking Penguin.
—The Third Rumpole Omnibus: Rumpole a la Carte, Rumpole on Trial, Rumpole & the Angel of Death. 150th ed. 1998. (Rumpole Ser.). 752p. pap. 18.00 (0-14-025741-1, Penguin Bks.) Penguin Group (USA) Inc.
—The Trials of Rumpole. 20.95 (0-89190-276-7) Amereon, Ltd.
—The Trials of Rumpole. unabr. ed. 1993. audio 39.95 (0-7861-0422-8, 1374) Blackstone Audio Bks., Inc.
—The Trials of Rumpole. abr. ed. 1986. audio 16.99 (0-88646-118-9, TC-LFP 7118) Durkin Hayes Publishing Ltd.
—The Trials of Rumpole. unabr. ed. 1993. (Rumpole of the Bailey Ser.: Vol. 2). audio 51.00 (1-55690-825-3, 93126E7) Recorded Bks., LLC.
—The Trials of Rumpole. 1981. (Rumpole Ser.). 208p. pap. 6.00 o.p. (0-14-005162-7); pap. 9.95 o.s.i (0-14-024697-5) Viking Penguin. (Penguin Bks.).

**RUNE (FICTITIOUS CHARACTER)—FICTION**

Deaver, Jeffery. Hard News. 1992. 256p. mass mkt. 4.99 o.s.i (0-553-29622-1) Bantam Bks.
—Hard News. 1991. 320p. 15.00 o.s.i (0-385-42121-4) Doubleday Publishing.
—Hard News. l.t. ed. 2001. 438p. 29.95 (0-7862-3413-X) Thorndike Pr.

**RUSSELL, MARY (FICTITIOUS CHARACTER)—FICTION**

King, Laurie R. The Beekeeper's Apprentice. reprint ed. 2002. 384p. pap. 11.95 (0-553-38152-0); 1996. 448p. mass mkt. 6.99 (0-553-57165-6) Bantam Bks.
—The Beekeeper's Apprentice. abr. ed. 1996. 6p. audio 16.99 (0-88646-388-2, 7388) Durkin Hayes Publishing Ltd.
—The Beekeeper's Apprentice. l.t. ed. 1996. 574p. 24.95 (0-7838-1932-3, Macmillan Reference USA) Gale Group.
—The Beekeeper's Apprentice. unabr. ed. (Mary Russell Mystery Ser.: Vol. 1). 2001. audio compact disk 124.00; 1995. audio 85.00 (0-7887-0319-6, 94511E7) Recorded Bks., LLC.
—The Beekeeper's Apprentice. 1994. xvii, 347p. 23.95 (0-312-10423-5, Saint Martin's Minotaur) St. Martin's Pr.
—The Game. 2004. 384p. 23.95 (0-553-80194-5) Bantam Bks.
—Justice Hall. 2003. 464p. mass mkt. 6.99 (0-553-58111-2); 2002. 352p. 23.95 (0-553-11113-2) Bantam Bks.
—Justice Hall. l.t. ed. 2002. 625p. 30.95 (0-7862-3953-0) Thorndike Pr.
—A Letter of Mary. 1998. (Mary Russell Novels Ser.). 336p. reprint ed. mass mkt. 6.99 (0-553-57780-8) Bantam Bks.
—A Letter of Mary. abr. ed. 1997. audio 16.99 (0-88646-420-X, 7420) Durkin Hayes Publishing Ltd.
—A Letter of Mary. l.t. ed. 1997. (G. K. Hall Mystery Ser.). 384p. lib. bdg. 26.95 o.p. (0-7838-8067-7, Macmillan Reference USA) Gale Group.
—A Letter of Mary. unabr. ed. 1997. (Mary Russell Mystery Ser.: Vol. 3). audio 70.00 (0-7887-0649-7, 94826E7) Recorded Bks., LLC.
—A Letter of Mary. 1999. E-Book 23.95 (0-312-20728-X); 1996. viii, 276p. 23.95 (0-312-14670-1, Saint Martin's Minotaur) St. Martin's Pr.
—A Monstrous Regiment of Women. 1996. (Mary Russell Ser.: No. 2). 368p. mass mkt. 6.99 (0-553-57456-6, Crimeline) Bantam Bks.
—A Monstrous Regiment of Women. abr. ed. 1995. audio 16.99 (0-88646-390-4, 7390) Durkin Hayes Publishing Ltd.
—A Monstrous Regiment of Women. unabr. ed. 1996. (Mary Russell Mystery Ser.: Vol. 2). audio 78.00 (0-7887-0493-1, 94685E7) Recorded Bks., LLC.
—A Monstrous Regiment of Women. 1995. viii, 326p. 22.95 (0-312-13565-3, Saint Martin's Minotaur) St. Martin's Pr.
—The Moor. 1999. (Mary Russell Novels Ser.). 400p. (gr. 5 up). mass mkt. 6.99 (0-553-57952-5) Bantam Bks.
—The Moor. l.t. ed. 1998. (G. K. Hall Mystery Ser.). 419p. 27.95 (0-7838-0162-9, Macmillan Reference USA) Gale Group.
—The Moor. unabr. ed. 1998. (Mary Russell Mystery Ser.: Vol. 4). audio 75.00 (0-7887-1979-3, 95366E7 ) Recorded Bks., LLC.
—The Moor. 1999. E-Book 23.95 (0-312-20731-X); 1997. (Illus.). 307p. 23.95 o.p. (0-312-16934-5, Saint Martin's Minotaur) St. Martin's Pr.
—O Jerusalem. 2000. (Mary Russell Novels Ser.). 464p. mass mkt. 6.99 (0-553-58105-8) Bantam Bks.
—O Jerusalem. 1999. (Mary Russell Novels Ser.). (Illus.). 384p. 23.95 o.s.i (0-553-11093-4) Broadway Bks.
—O Jerusalem. unabr. ed. 1999. (Mary Russell Mystery Ser.: Vol. 5). audio 83.00 (0-7887-3746-5, 95781E7) Recorded Bks., LLC.

**RUTLEDGE, ALEX (FICTITIOUS CHARACTER)—FICTION**

Corcoran, Tom. Bone Island Mambo. 2002. 352p. mass mkt. 6.99 (0-312-98008-6, St. Martin's Paperbacks) St. Martin's Pr.
—Bone Island Mambo: An Alex Rutledge Mystery. 2001. E-Book 23.95 (1-58945-795-1) Adobe Systems, Inc.
—Bone Island Mambo: An Alex Rutledge Mystery. 2001. 278p. 23.95 (0-312-24281-6, Saint Martin's Minotaur) St. Martin's Pr.
—Gumbo Limbo. E-Book 23.95 (0-312-26833-5); 1999. 293p. 23.95 (0-312-24194-1, Saint Martin's Minotaur) St. Martin's Pr.
—Gumbo Limbo: An Alex Rutledge Mystery. 2000. 304p. mass mkt. 6.50 (0-312-97570-8, St. Martin's Paperbacks) St. Martin's Pr.
—The Mango Opera. 304p. 1999. mass mkt. 6.99 (0-312-96988-0, St. Martin's Paperbacks); Vol. 1. 1998. (Mango Opera Ser.: Vol. 1). 22.95 (0-312-18628-2, Saint Martin's Minotaur) St. Martin's Pr.
—Octopus Alibi: An Alex Rutledge Mystery. 2003. (Alex Rutledge Mystery Ser.). 304p. 24.95 (0-312-29127-2, Saint Martin's Minotaur) St. Martin's Pr.

**RUTLEDGE, IAN (FICTITIOUS CHARACTER)—FICTION**

Todd, Charles. A Fearsome Doubt: An Inspector Ian Rutledge Mystery. 2003. 384p. mass mkt. 6.99 (0-553-58317-4); 2002. 304p. 24.95 (0-553-80180-5); 2002. E-Book 19.99 (0-553-89709-8) Bantam Bks.
—Search the Dark. unabr. ed. 2001. audio compact disk 94.00 (1-84197-099-9, C1144E7); 1999. audio 79.00 (1-84197-039-5, H1039E7) Recorded Bks., LLC. (Clipper Audio).
—Search the Dark. E-Book 5.99 (0-312-26467-4); 1999. 336p. 24.95 o.p. (0-312-20000-5, Saint Martin's Minotaur) St. Martin's Pr.
—A Test of Wills. l.t. ed. 1998. 336p. mass mkt. 6.99 (0-553-57759-X) Bantam Bks.
—A Test of Wills. unabr. ed. 1999. audio compact disk 81.00 (1-84197-092-1, C1128E7, Clipper Audio); audio 71.00 (1-84197-006-9, H1006E7);Set. audio 71.00 Recorded Bks., LLC.
—A Test of Wills. 4th l.t. ed. 1996. 320p. 22.95 o.p. (0-312-14431-8, Saint Martin's Minotaur) St. Martin's Pr.
—A Test of Wills. l.t. ed. 1997. (Mystery Ser.). 416p. lib. bdg. 25.95 o.p. (0-7838-2023-2) Thorndike Pr.
—Watchers of Time: An Inspector Ian Rutledge Mystery. 2002. 448p. reprint ed. mass mkt. 6.99 (0-553-58316-6) Bantam Bks.
—Wings of Fire. unabr. ed. 1999. audio 71.00 (1-84197-023-9, H1023E7);Set. audio 71.00 Recorded Bks., LLC.
—Wings of Fire. 1999. (Wings of Fire Ser.: Vol. 1). 320p. mass mkt. 6.99 (0-312-96568-0, St. Martin's Paperbacks); 1999. E-Book 23.95 (0-312-20751-4); 1998. (Inspector Ian Rutledge Mysteries Ser.). 294p. (gr. 5 up). 23.95 (0-312-17064-5, Saint Martin's Minotaur) St. Martin's Pr.

**RYAN, ANTHONY (FICTITIOUS CHARACTER)—FICTION**

Dee, Ed. Bronx Angel. 1995. 304p. 21.95 o.p. (0-446-51774-7); 1996. 384p. reprint ed. mass mkt. 6.50 (0-446-60337-6) Warner Bks., Inc.
—Little Boy Blue. l.t. ed. 1997. (Wheeler Large Print Book Ser.). pap. 23.95 (1-56895-452-2, Wheeler Publishing, Inc.) Gale Group.
—Little Boy Blue. abr. ed. 2001. audio 7.95 (1-57815-217-8, Media Bks. Audio Publishing) Media Bks., L. L. C.
—Little Boy Blue. abr. ed. 1997. audio 12.98 (1-57042-475-6, 394925) Time Warner AudioBooks.
—Little Boy Blue. 1997. 272p. 22.50 o.p. (0-446-52038-1); 1998. 320p. reprint ed. mass mkt. 6.99 o.s.i (0-446-60522-0) Warner Bks., Inc.
—14 Peck Slip. 1994. 304p. 19.95 o.s.i (0-446-51770-4); 1995. 336p. reprint ed. mass mkt. 5.99 (0-446-60238-8) Warner Bks., Inc.
Dee, Edward. Nightbird. 2000. 352p. E-Book 4.95 (0-446-92362-1) Time Warner Bk. Group.
—Nightbird. 2001. 352p. E-Book 4.95 (0-446-96023-3); 2000. 352p. mass mkt. 6.99 (0-446-60913-7); 2000. E-Book 4.95 (0-446-91510-6); 1999. 304p. 23.95 (0-446-52039-X) Warner Bks., Inc.

**RYAN, BLACKIE (FICTITIOUS CHARACTER)—FICTION**

Andrew, Greeley. Blackie. 4th ed. mass mkt. (0-7653-4234-0, Forge Bks.) Doherty, Tom Assocs., LLC.
Greeley, Andrew M. The Bishop & the Beggar Girl of St. Germain: A Blackie Ryan Mystery. 2001. 304p. 24.95 (0-312-86874-X); 2002. 259p. reprint ed. mass mkt. 6.99 (0-8125-7597-0) Doherty, Tom Assocs., LLC. (Forge Bks.).
—The Bishop & the Missing L Train: A Blackie Ryan Mystery. 2002. lib. bdg. 27.95 (1-58547-254-9, Premier) Ctr. Point Large Print.
—The Bishop & the Missing L Train: A Blackie Ryan Mystery. E-Book 6.99 (0-312-70218-3, Tor Bks.); 2001. 304p. reprint ed. mass mkt. 6.99 (0-8125-7596-2, Forge Bks.); 2000. 288p. reprint ed. 24.95 o.p. (0-312-86875-8, NHC 0141, Forge Bks.) Doherty, Tom Assocs., LLC.
—The Bishop & the Three Kings: A Blackie Ryan Mystery. 1998. (Blackie Ryan Novels Ser.). (Illus.). 320p. mass mkt. 6.99 (0-425-16617-1) Berkley Publishing Group.
—The Bishop at Sea: A Blackie Ryan Mystery. 1997. (Blackie Ryan Novels Ser.). 304p. mass mkt. 6.99 (0-425-16080-7) Berkley Publishing Group.
—The Bishop at Sea: A Blackie Ryan Mystery. l.t. ed. 2000. (Americana Ser.). 407p. 27.95 (0-7862-2322-7) Thorndike Pr.
—The Bishop Goes to University, Vol. 4. 2003. (Blackie Ryan Ser.). 256p. 24.95 (0-7653-0333-7, Forge Bks.) Doherty, Tom Assocs., LLC.
—The Bishop in the West Wing: A Blackie Ryan Story. l.t. ed. 2003. lib. bdg. 28.95 (1-58547-280-8, Platinum) Ctr. Point Large Print.
—The Bishop in the West Wing: A Blackie Ryan Story. E-Book 24.95 (0-312-70724-X, Tor Bks.); 2002. (Illus.). 288p. 24.95 (0-312-86873-1, Forge Bks.); 2003. (Illus.). 320p. reprint ed. mass mkt. 6.99 (0-8125-7598-9, Forge Bks.) Doherty, Tom Assocs., LLC.
—Blackie. 5th ed. mass mkt. (0-7653-4235-9); Vol. 5. (0-7653-0334-5) Doherty, Tom Assocs., LLC. (Forge Bks.).
—Happy Are the Clean of Heart: A Blackie Ryan Novel. l.t. ed. 1987. 412p. 18.95 o.p. (0-8161-4278-5, Macmillan Reference USA) Gale Group.
—Happy Are the Clean of Heart: A Blackie Ryan Novel. 1988. mass mkt. 4.95 (0-446-35722-7) Warner Bks., Inc.
—Happy Are the Meek: A Blackie Ryan Novel. l.t. ed. 1986. (General Ser.). 373p. 16.95 o.p. (0-8161-4029-4, Macmillan Reference USA) Gale Group.
—Happy Are the Meek: A Blackie Ryan Novel. 1985. 288p. mass mkt. 3.95 (0-446-32706-9) Warner Bks., Inc.
—Happy Are the Merciful: A Blackie Ryan Novel. 1992. 336p. mass mkt. 6.99 o.s.i (0-515-10726-3, Jove) Berkley Publishing Group.

—Happy Are the Oppressed: A Blackie Ryan Novel. l.t. ed. 1997. lib. bdg. 24.95 (1-57490-083-8, Beeler Large Print Bks.) Beeler, Thomas T. Publisher.
—Happy Are the Oppressed: A Blackie Ryan Novel. 1996. (Illus.). 320p. mass mkt. 7.50 (0-515-11921-0, Jove) Berkley Publishing Group.
—Happy Are the Peace Makers: A Blackie Ryan Novel. l.t. ed. 1993. 24.95 o.p. (0-7927-1680-9); 22.95 o.p. (0-7927-1679-5) BBC Audiobooks America.
—Happy Are the Peace Makers: A Blackie Ryan Novel. 1993. 320p. mass mkt. 6.99 o.s.i (0-515-11075-2, Jove) Berkley Publishing Group.
—Happy Are the Poor in Spirit: A Blackie Ryan Novel. 1994. (Blackie Ryan Novels Ser.). (Illus.). 304p. mass mkt. 6.99 o.s.i (0-515-11502-9, Jove) Berkley Publishing Group.
—Happy Are the Poor in Spirit: A Blackie Ryan Novel. l.t. ed. 2000. (Americana Ser.). 392p. 28.95 (0-7862-2323-5) Thorndike Pr.
—Happy Are Those Who Mourn: A Blackie Ryan Novel. l.t. ed. 1996. (Large Print Ser.). 352p. lib. bdg. 23.95 (1-57490-038-2, Beeler Large Print Bks.) Beeler, Thomas T. Publisher.
—Happy Are Those Who Mourn: A Blackie Ryan Novel. 1995. (Illus.). 304p. mass mkt. 6.99 o.s.i (0-515-11761-7, Jove) Berkley Publishing Group.
—Happy Are Those Who Thirst for Justice: A Blackie Ryan Novel. l.t. ed. 1988. (General Ser.). 440p. 18.95 o.p. (0-8161-4488-5, Macmillan Reference USA) Gale Group.
—Happy Are Those Who Thirst for Justice: A Blackie Ryan Novel. 1987. 320p. 16.95 (0-89296-180-5) Mysterious Pr.
—Happy Are Those Who Thirst for Justice: A Blackie Ryan Novel. 1988. mass mkt. 4.50 (0-446-34946-1) Warner Bks., Inc.
—O' Malley. (Family Saga Ser.). 5th ed. 2004. 368p. mass mkt. 7.99 (0-7653-4238-3); 6th ed. mass mkt. (0-7653-4239-1) Doherty, Tom Assocs., LLC. (Forge Bks.).

### RYAN, FLIP (FICTITIOUS CHARACTER)—FICTION

Bickham, Jack M. Murder at Oklahoma. 1998. 288p. mass mkt. 5.99 o.s.i (0-425-16381-4, Prime Crime) Berkley Publishing Group.

### RYAN, JACK (FICTITIOUS CHARACTER)—FICTION

Clancy, Tom. The Bear & the Dragon. 2001. 1152p. reprint ed. mass mkt. 7.99 (0-425-18096-4) Berkley Publishing Group.
—The Bear & the Dragon. 2001. pap. text 28.99 (0-399-14916-3); 2000. 752p. 28.95 (0-399-14563-X) Penguin Group (USA) Inc.
—The Bear & the Dragon. abr. ed. 2000. audio 27.95 (0-375-41582-3); audio compact disk 31.95 (0-375-41583-1) Random Hse. Audio Publishing Group. (RH Audio).
—The Bear & the Dragon. l.t. ed. 1504p. 2001. pap. 15.95 (0-375-72810-4); 2000. 28.95 (0-375-43069-5) Random Hse. Large Print.
—The Cardinal of the Kremlin. 1989. 560p. mass mkt. 7.99 (0-425-11684-0) Berkley Publishing Group.
—The Cardinal of the Kremlin. unabr. ed. 1988. audio 112.00 (0-7366-1408-7, 2297-A) Books on Tape, Inc.
—The Cardinal of the Kremlin. 1988. 544p. 27.95 (0-399-13345-3, G. P. Putnam's Sons) Penguin Group (USA) Inc.
—The Cardinal of the Kremlin. abr. ed. 1988. audio 17.00 (0-671-66074-8, Simon & Schuster Audioworks) Simon & Schuster Audio.
—The Cardinal of the Kremlin. l.t. ed. 1991. 871p. lib. bdg. 25.95 (0-89621-232-7) Thorndike Pr.
—The Cardinal of the Kremlin. 1989. 13.09 o.p. (0-606-00979-5) Turtleback Bks.
—Clear & Present Danger. 704p. 1994. mass mkt. 7.50 o.s.i (0-425-14437-2); 1990. mass mkt. 7.99 (0-425-12212-3) Berkley Publishing Group.
—Clear & Present Danger, Pt. 1. unabr. ed. 1989. audio 80.00 (0-7366-1630-6, 2488-A) Books on Tape, Inc.
—Clear & Present Danger. unabr. ed. 1990. audio 162.55 (1-56100-055-8, 1144, Unabridged Library Editions); audio 38.95 (0-930435-61-3, 65, Bookcassette) Brilliance Audio.
—Clear & Present Danger. l.t. ed. 1990. (Magna Large Print Ser.). 1140p. o.p. (1-85057-853-2) Magna Large Print Bks. GBR. *Dist:* Ulverscroft Large Print Canada, Ltd.
—Clear & Present Danger. 1989. 544p. 27.95 (0-399-13440-9, G. P. Putnam's Sons) Penguin Putnam Bks. for Young Readers.
—Clear & Present Danger, Set. abr. ed. 1994. (Jack Ryan Adventure Ser.). 180p. audio 17.00 (0-671-89800-0, 390531, Simon & Schuster Audioworks) Simon & Schuster Audio.
—Clear & Present Danger. 1990. 13.09 o.p. (0-606-00980-9) Turtleback Bks.
—Debt of Honor. 1995. 1008p. mass mkt. 7.99 (0-425-14758-4) Berkley Publishing Group.
—Debt of Honor, Pt. 1. unabr. ed. 1994. audio 104.00 (0-7366-2862-2, 3569-A) Books on Tape, Inc.
—Debt of Honor. 1994. 640p. 25.95 o.s.i (0-399-13954-0); 150.00 (0-399-13960-5) Penguin Group (USA) Inc. (G. P. Putnam's Sons).
—Debt of Honor. abr. ed. 1999. audio compact disk 29.95 (0-375-40700-6); Set. 1994. audio 29.95; Set. 1994. audio 25.95 (0-679-43697-9, 692184) Random Hse. Audio Publishing Group. (RH Audio).
—Debt of Honor. 1995. 14.04 (0-606-17124-X) Turtleback Bks.
—Debt of Honor & Executive Orders, 2 vols. 1997. 15.98 o.s.i (0-425-16208-7) Berkley Publishing Group.
—Deuda de Honor. 1998. Orig. Title: Debt of Honor. (SPA.). 244p. (84-08-02191-5) GeoPlaneta, Editorial, S. A.
—Executive Orders. 1997. 1376p. mass mkt. 7.99 (0-425-15863-2); (YA). 7.50 (0-425-16057-2) Berkley Publishing Group.
—Executive Orders. unabr. ed. 1996. Pt. 1. audio 104.00 (0-7366-3513-0, 4152-A); Pt. 2. audio 104.00 (0-7366-3514-9, 4152-B); Pt. 3. audio 80.00 (0-7366-3515-7, 4152-C) Books on Tape, Inc.
—Executive Orders. 1996. 896p. 27.95 (0-399-14218-5); 752p. 150.00 (0-399-14219-3) Penguin Group (USA) Inc. (G. P. Putnam's Sons).
—Executive Orders, Set. abr. ed. 2000. audio 25.95 (0-375-43696-0); 1996. audio 26.95 (0-679-43696-0, 694152); 1996. audio compact disk 29.95 (0-679-45789-5) Random Hse. Audio Publishing Group. (RH Audio).
—Executive Orders. 1998. (YA). 7.98 o.p. (0-7651-0899-2) Smithmark Pubs., Inc.
—Executive Orders. l.t. ed. 1996. (Basic Ser.). 1437p. 30.95 (0-7862-0855-4) Thorndike Pr.
—Executive Orders. 1996. 14.04 (0-606-17126-6) Turtleback Bks.
—The Hunt for Red October. abr. ed. 1986. audio 16.95 (0-88690-092-1, A20006); 1993. audio 39.95 (0-945353-79-0, A90379u) Audio Partners Publishing Corp. (Audio Editions Bks. on Cassette).
—The Hunt for Red October. 1992. 480p. mass mkt. 7.99 (0-425-13351-6); 1990. 432p. mass mkt. 5.99 o.s.i (0-425-12027-9); 1985. mass mkt. 5.50 o.s.i (0-425-08383-7); 15th anniv. ed. 1999. 432p. pap. 13.95 (0-425-17290-2) Berkley Publishing Group.
—The Hunt for Red October. unabr. collector's ed. 1985. audio 96.00 (0-7366-0992-X, 1929) Books on Tape, Inc.
—The Hunt for Red October. unabr. ed. 1992. audio 25.95 o.p. (1-56100-473-1, 142, Bookcassette); audio 89.25 (1-56100-107-4, 1249, Unabridged Library Editions) Brilliance Audio.
—The Hunt for Red October. 1984. 388p. 26.95 (0-87021-285-0) Naval Institute Pr.
—The Hunt for Red October. unabr. ed. 1987. audio 91.00 (1-55690-242-5, 87600E7) Recorded Bks., LLC.
—The Hunt for Red October. l.t. ed. 1986. (Ulverscroft Large Print Ser.). 768p. 16.45 o.p. (0-7089-8312-X, Charnwood) Thorpe, F. A. Pubs. GBR. *Dist:* Ulverscroft Large Print Bks., Ltd., Ulverscroft Large Print Canada, Ltd.
—The Hunt for Red October. 1984. 14.04 (0-606-03908-2) Turtleback Bks.
—Ordenes Ejecutivas I. 3rd ed. 1998. (SPA., Illus.). 348p. (84-08-02448-5) GeoPlaneta, Editorial, S. A.
—Ordenes Ejecutivas II. 1998. (SPA., Illus.). 468p. (84-08-02449-3) GeoPlaneta, Editorial, S. A.
—Patriot Games. 1992. mass mkt. 6.99 o.s.i (0-425-13435-0); 1988. 512p. mass mkt. 7.99 (0-425-10972-0) Berkley Publishing Group.
—Patriot Games. unabr. ed. 1987. audio 120.00 (0-7366-1237-8, 2155) Books on Tape, Inc.
—Patriot Games. l.t. ed. 1988. (Large Print Bks.). 800p. 21.95 o.p. (0-8161-4382-X); 16.95 o.p. (0-8161-4383-8) Gale Group. (Macmillan Reference USA).
—Patriot Games. 1987. 416p. 27.95 (0-399-13241-4, G. P. Putnam's Sons) Penguin Group (USA) Inc.
—Patriot Games, Set. abr. ed. 1987. (Jack Ryan Adventure Ser.). audio 18.00 (0-394-29761-X, 391350, RH Audio) Random Hse. Audio Publishing Group.
—Patriot Games. 1992. 14.04 (0-606-00982-5) Turtleback Bks.
—Peligro Imminente. 6th ed. 1998. (Jet de Plaza & Janes Ser.: Vol. 150). Orig. Title: Clear & Present Danger. (SPA., Illus.). 617p. pap. 8.50 (84-01-49525-3) Plaza & Janés Editories, S.A. ESP. *Dist:* Lectorum Pubns., Inc.
—Red Rabbit. 2002. audio (0-7366-8887-0); audio 149.00 (0-7366-8884-6) Books on Tape, Inc.
—Red Rabbit. 2002. 640p. 28.95 (0-399-14870-1); (Illus.). 896p. 150.00 (0-399-14914-7) Penguin Group (USA) Inc.
—Red Rabbit. l.t. ed. 2002. 33.95 (0-7862-4064-4) Thorndike Pr.
—Red Rabbit. 2002. audio (0-14-180407-6) Viking Penguin.
—The Sum of All Fears. 928p. 1992. mass mkt. 7.99 o.s.i (0-425-13354-0); 2002. mass mkt. 7.99 (0-425-18422-6) Berkley Publishing Group.
—The Sum of All Fears, Pt. 1. unabr. ed. 1991. audio 112.00 (0-7366-2026-5, 2841-A) Books on Tape, Inc.
—The Sum of All Fears. 1991. 640p. 27.95 (0-399-13615-0); 100.00 o.p. (0-399-13631-2) Penguin Group (USA) Inc.
—The Sum of All Fears. abr. ed. 1991. (Jack Ryan Adventure Ser.). audio 24.00 (0-671-73806-2, 692319, Simon & Schuster Audioworks) Simon & Schuster Audio.
—The Sum of All Fears. l.t. ed. 1992. (Paperback Bestsellers Ser.). 1507p. pap. 20.95 (1-56054-947-5) Thorndike Pr.
—The Sum of All Fears. 1992. 14.04 (0-606-00978-7) Turtleback Bks.
—The Teeth of the Tiger. 2004. 496p. mass mkt. 7.99 (0-425-19740-9) Berkley Publishing Group.
—The Teeth of the Tiger. 2003. 448p. 27.95 (0-399-15079-X); 640p. 150.00 (0-399-15136-2) Putnam Publishing Group, The.
—The Teeth of the Tiger. l.t. ed. 2003. 32.95 (0-7862-5691-5) Thorndike Pr.
—The Teeth of the Tiger: Chapter Excerpt Booklets. 2003. (0-399-19783-4) Putnam Publishing Group, The.
—Three Complete Novels. 1994. 1456p. 14.98 o.s.i (0-399-13935-4) Penguin Group (USA) Inc.

### RYAN, MAGGIE (FICTITIOUS CHARACTER)—FICTION

Carlson, Pat M. Audition for Murder. 1985. 225p. pap. 2.75 o.p. (0-380-89538-2, Avon Bks.) Morrow/Avon.
—Bad Blood. 1991. 320p. 15.00 o.s.i (0-385-42122-2) Doubleday Publishing.
—Murder in the Dog Days. 1990. 256p. mass mkt. 4.50 o.s.i (0-553-27778-2) Bantam Bks.
—Murder Is Academic. 1985. pap. 2.95 o.p. (0-380-89738-5, Avon Bks.) Morrow/Avon.
—Murder Is Pathological. 1986. 192p. pap. 2.95 o.p. (0-380-75071-6, Avon Bks.) Morrow/Avon.
—Murder Misread. 1991. 256p. mass mkt. 4.50 o.s.i (0-553-29374-5) Bantam Bks.
—Murder Misread. 1990. 192p. 14.95 o.s.i (0-385-41642-3) Doubleday Publishing.
—Murder Unrenovated. 1990. 240p. mass mkt. 2.25 o.s.i (0-553-18522-5); 1987. mass mkt. 3.50 o.s.i (0-553-26989-5) Bantam Bks.
—Murder Unrenovated. 1999. (Mystery Ser.). 274p. pap. 19.95 (0-7862-2077-5, Five Star) Gale Group.
—Rehearsal for Murder. 1988. 224p. mass mkt. 3.50 o.s.i (0-553-27234-9) Bantam Bks.

### RYAN, MICHAEL (FICTITIOUS CHARACTER)—FICTION

Friedman, Philip. Reasonable Doubt. 1990. 448p. mass mkt. 7.99 (0-8041-0749-1, Ivy Bks.) Ballantine Bks.
—Reasonable Doubt. 1990. 19.95 o.s.i (1-55611-107-X) Fine, Donald I. Bks.

### RYAN, PEARL (FICTITIOUS CHARACTER)—FICTION

Harris, Jana. The Pearl of Ruby City. 1998. 368p. 23.95 (0-312-19315-7, Saint Martin's Minotaur) St. Martin's Pr.

### RYAN, SAMANTHA (FICTITIOUS CHARACTER)—FICTION

McCrery, Nigel. Silent Witness. pap. (0-312-30022-0, Saint Martin's Griffin); 2001. 324p. per. 15.95 (0-312-29197-3, Dunne, Thomas Bks.); 1998. 320p. 23.95 (0-312-18178-7, Saint Martin's Minotaur) St. Martin's Pr.
—Silent Witness. l.t. ed. 1999. (Charnwood Large Print Ser.). 344p. 31.99 o.p. (0-7089-9116-5, Ulverscroft) Thorpe, F. A. Pubs. GBR. *Dist:* Ulverscroft Large Print Bks., Ltd., Ulverscroft Large Print Canada, Ltd.
—The Spider's Web. 1999. 320p. 22.95 o.p. (0-312-20017-X, Saint Martin's Minotaur) St. Martin's Pr.
—Strange Screams of Death. l.t. ed. 2001. (Charnwood Large Print Ser.). 408p. 32.50 (0-7089-9191-2) Ulverscroft Large Print Bks., Ltd.

### RYLAND, GARTH (FICTITIOUS CHARACTER)—FICTION

Riggs, John R. Cold Hearts & Gentle People. 1994. 272p. 17.95 (1-56980-021-9) Barricade Bks., Inc.
—Dead Letter. 1992. 15.95 (0-942637-40-2) Barricade Bks., Inc.
—Dead Letter. 1994. 208p. mass mkt. 4.50 o.s.i (0-515-11280-1, Jove) Berkley Publishing Group.
—A Dragon Lives Forever. 1992. (Garth Ryland Mystery Ser.). 344p. 17.95 (0-942637-78-X) Barricade Bks., Inc.
—A Dragon Lives Forever. 1994. 224p. reprint ed. mass mkt. 4.50 o.p. (0-425-14301-5, Prime Crime) Berkley Publishing Group.
—Glory Hound. 1986. (Garth Ryland Mystery Ser.). 14.95 o.p. (0-934878-78-1, Dembner Bks.) Barricade Bks., Inc.
—Haunt of the Nightingale. (Garth Ryland Mystery Ser.). 224p. 15.95 o.p. (0-934878-97-8, Dembner Bks.) Barricade Bks., Inc.
—Haunt of the Nightingale. 1992. 192p. mass mkt. 3.99 o.s.i (0-515-10953-3, Jove) Berkley Publishing Group.
—He Who Waits: A Garth Ryland Mystery. 1997. (Garth Ryland Mystery Ser.). 288p. 17.95 (1-56980-096-0) Barricade Bks., Inc.
—Hunting Ground. 1992. mass mkt. 3.99 o.s.i (0-515-10829-4, Jove) Berkley Publishing Group.
—Killing Frost: A Garth Ryland Mystery. 1995. 304p. 17.95 (1-56980-053-7) Barricade Bks., Inc.
—The Last Laugh. l.t. ed. 1992. 19.95 o.p. (0-7927-1394-X); pap. 17.95 o.p. (0-7927-1393-1) BBC Audiobooks America.
—The Last Laugh. 1984. (Garth Ryland Mystery Ser.). 191p. 13.95 o.p. (0-934878-37-4, Dembner Bks.) Barricade Bks., Inc.
—The Last Laugh. 1993. 192p. mass mkt. 3.99 o.s.i (0-515-11134-1, Jove) Berkley Publishing Group.
—The Last Laugh. 1988. mass mkt. 2.95 (0-312-91131-9, St. Martin's Paperbacks) St. Martin's Pr.
—Let Sleeping Dogs Lie. 1986. (Garth Ryland Mystery Ser.). 14.95 o.p. (0-934878-67-6, Dembner Bks.) Barricade Bks., Inc.
—Let Sleeping Dogs Lie. 1993. mass mkt. 4.50 o.s.i (0-515-11211-9, Jove) Berkley Publishing Group.
—Let Sleeping Dogs Lie. 1988. mass mkt. 3.50 (0-312-91140-8, St. Martin's Paperbacks) St. Martin's Pr.
—The Lost Scout: A Garth Ryland Mystery. 1998. 352p. 17.95 (1-56980-121-5) Barricade Bks., Inc.
—One Man's Poison. 1991. (Garth Ryland Mystery Ser.). 17.95 o.p. (0-942637-31-3, Dembner Bks.) Barricade Bks., Inc.
—One Man's Poison, No. 4. 1993. 208p. mass mkt. 3.99 o.s.i (0-515-11078-7, Jove) Berkley Publishing Group.
—Snow on the Roses: A Garth Ryland Mystery. 1996. 272p. 17.95 (1-56980-072-3) Barricade Bks., Inc.
—Wolf in Sheep's Clothing. 1993. 192p. (Orig.). mass mkt. 3.99 o.s.i (0-515-11016-7, Jove) Berkley Publishing Group.
—Wolf in Sheep's Clothing: A Garth Ryland Mystery. 1989. 16.95 o.p. (0-942637-16-X, Dembner Bks.) Barricade Bks., Inc.

## S

### SAAVIK (FICTITIOUS CHARACTER)—FICTION

Clowes, Carolyn. The Pandora Principle. 1990. (Star Trek: No. 49). 288p. mass mkt. 4.99 (0-671-65815-8, Star Trek) Simon & Schuster.
McIntyre, Vonda N. The Search for Spock. 2000. (Star Trek Ser.: No. 3). E-Book 6.99 (0-7434-1968-5, Star Trek) Simon & Schuster.
Sherman, Josepha & Shwartz, Susan. Vulcan's Heart. (Star Trek Ser.). 2000. per. 6.50 (0-7434-1112-9); 1999. 384p. 23.00 o.s.i (0-671-01544-3); 2000. 400p. reprint ed. pap. 6.50 (0-671-01545-1) Simon & Schuster. (Star Trek).
—Vulcan's Heart. abr. ed. 1999. (Star Trek Ser.). audio 18.00 (0-671-04560-1, Simon & Schuster Audioworks) Simon & Schuster Audio.

### SABICH, RUSTY (FICTITIOUS CHARACTER)—FICTION

Turow, Scott. Presumed Innocent. 1989. audio 13.95 (1-55644-337-4, 9061) American Audio Prose Library, Inc.
—Presumed Innocent. unabr. collector's ed. 1988. audio 80.00 (0-7366-1336-6, 2239) Books on Tape, Inc.
—Presumed Innocent. 1987. 480p. 30.00 (0-374-23713-1); E-Book 4.95 (0-374-70109-1); E-Book 4.95 (0-374-70111-3); E-Book 4.95 (0-374-70117-2); E-Book 4.95 o.p. (0-374-70108-3) Farrar, Straus & Giroux.
—Presumed Innocent. l.t. ed. 1988. (General Ser.). 606p. 13.95 o.p. (0-8161-4470-2, Macmillan Reference USA) Gale Group.
—Presumed Innocent. 1999. (0-7621-0254-3) Reader's Digest Assn., Inc., The.
—Presumed Innocent. abr. ed. 1988. 17.00 incl. audio (0-671-65218-4, Simon & Schuster Audioworks) Simon & Schuster Audio.
—Presumed Innocent. reprint ed. 2000. 512p. pap. 14.95 (0-446-67644-6); 1989. 432p. mass mkt. 7.99 (0-446-35986-6) Warner Bks., Inc.

### SABINE (FICTITIOUS CHARACTER: BANTOCK)—FICTION

Bantock, Nick. Alexandria: In Which the Extraordinary Correspondence of Griffin & Sabine Unfolds. 19.95 o.s.i (0-8118-3699-1) Chronicle Bks. LLC.
—The Golden Mean: In Which the Extraordinary Correspondence of Griffin & Sabine Concludes. 1993. (Illus.). 48p. 17.95 (0-8118-0298-1) Chronicle Bks. LLC.

—The Golden Mean: In Which the Extraordinary Correspondence of Griffin & Sabine Concludes. unabr. ed. 1993. (Griffin & Sabine Trilogy). 40p. audio 10.95 (*1-879371-49-9*) Publishing Mills, Inc., The.
—Griffin & Sabine: An Extraordinary Address Book. 1994. (Illus.). 100p. 18.95 o.p. (*0-8118-0616-2*) Chronicle Bks. LLC.
—Griffin & Sabine: An Extraordinary Correspondence. (Illus.). 48p. 1991. 19.95 (*0-87701-788-3*); 10th anniv. ltd. ed. 2001. 19.95 o.p. (*0-8118-3200-7*) Chronicle Bks. LLC.
—Griffin & Sabine: An Extraordinary Correspondence. 1991. audio 10.95 (*1-879371-42-1*, 30000) Publishing Mills, Inc., The.
—Griffin & Sabine Art Cards. 1994. 13.95 o.p. (*0-8118-0729-0*) Chronicle Bks. LLC.
—The Griffin & Sabine Trilogy, 3 bks. 1994. (Illus.). 49.95 (*0-8118-0696-0*) Chronicle Bks. LLC.
—The Griffin & Sabine Trilogy. unabr. ed. 1994. 2p. audio 24.95 (*1-879371-58-8*, 70000) Publishing Mills, Inc., The.
—The Gryphon: In Which the Extraordinary Correspondence of Griffin & Sabine Is Rediscovered. 2001. 19.95 o.s.i (*0-8118-3384-4*); (Illus.). 56p. 19.95 (*0-8118-3162-0*) Chronicle Bks. LLC.
—Sabine's Notebook: In Which the Extraordinary Correspondence of Griffin & Sabine Continues. 1992. (Illus.). 48p. 17.95 (*0-8118-0180-2*) Chronicle Bks. LLC.
—Sabine's Notebook: In Which the Extraordinary Correspondence of Griffin & Sabine Continues. 1992. audio 10.95 (*1-879371-41-3*, 30010) Publishing Mills, Inc., The.
Bantock, Nick, illus. Alexandria: In Which the Extraordinary Correspondence of Griffin & Sabine Unfolds. 2002. 56p. 19.95 (*0-8118-3140-X*) Chronicle Bks. LLC.

**SACHS, AMELIA (FICTITIOUS CHARACTER)—FICTION**

Deaver, Jeffery. The Bone Collector: A Lincoln Rhyme Novel. unabr. ed. 1999. audio 64.00 (*0-7366-4133-5*, 4638) Books on Tape, Inc.
—The Bone Collector: A Lincoln Rhyme Novel. l.t. ed. 1998. (Large Print Bks.). pap. 23.95 o.p. (*1-56895-524-3*, Wheeler Publishing, Inc.) Gale Group.
—The Bone Collector: A Lincoln Rhyme Novel. 1998. 432p. mass mkt. 7.99 (*0-451-18845-4*, Signet Bks.); 1997. pap. 6.99 (*0-451-19394-6*) NAL.
—The Bone Collector: A Lincoln Rhyme Novel. 1997. 432p. 22.95 o.s.i (*0-670-86871-X*);Set. 2p. audio 16.95 (*0-14-086328-1*, Penguin AudioBooks) Viking Penguin.
—The Coffin Dancer: A Lincoln Rhyme Novel. E-Book 25.00 (*1-58945-266-6*) Adobe Systems, Inc.
—The Coffin Dancer: A Lincoln Rhyme Novel. unabr. ed. 1999. audio 72.00 (*0-7366-4603-5*, 4990) Books on Tape, Inc.
—The Coffin Dancer: A Lincoln Rhyme Novel. l.t. ed. 1998. 27.95 (*1-56895-698-3*, Wheeler Publishing, Inc.) Gale Group.
—The Coffin Dancer: A Lincoln Rhyme Novel. 1999. E-Book 25.00 (*0-684-86805-9*, Simon & Schuster); 1999. pap. 6.99 (*0-671-02606-2*, Pocket); 1998. 368p. 25.00 o.s.i (*0-684-85285-3*, Simon & Schuster); 1999. (Illus.). 560p. reprint ed. mass mkt. 7.99 (*0-671-02409-4*, Pocket) Simon & Schuster.
—The Coffin Dancer: A Lincoln Rhyme Novel. 2000. audio compact disk 15.99 (*0-7435-0548-4*); 1998. audio 25.00 (*0-671-04303-X*, 496096) Simon & Schuster Audio. (Simon & Schuster Audioworks).
—The Devil's Teardrop: A Novel of the Last Night of the Century. E-Book 25.00 (*1-930161-37-9*) Adobe Systems, Inc.
—The Devil's Teardrop: A Novel of the Last Night of the Century. l.t. ed. 2000. pap. 11.95 (*1-56895-982-6*); 1999. 527p. 26.95 o.p. (*1-56895-804-8*) Gale Group. (Wheeler Publishing, Inc.).
—The Devil's Teardrop: A Novel of the Last Night of the Century. 2000. E-Book 9.99 (*0-684-85659-X*, Simon & Schuster); 1999. 400p. mass mkt. 7.99 (*0-671-03712-9*, Pocket); 1999. 400p. 25.00 o.s.i (*0-684-85292-6*, Simon & Schuster); 2000. (Illus.). 480p. reprint ed. pap. 7.99 (*0-671-03844-3*, Pocket) Simon & Schuster.
—The Devil's Teardrop: A Novel of the Last Night of the Century. abr. ed. 1999. 352p. audio 24.00 (*0-671-04569-5*, Simon & Schuster Audioworks) Simon & Schuster Audio.
—The Devil's Teardrop: A Novel of the Last Night of the Century. l.t. ed. 2002. (Charnwood Large Print Ser.). 520p. 32.50 o.p. (*0-7089-9298-6*, Charnwood) Thorpe, F. A. Pubs. GBR. *Dist:* Ulverscroft Large Print Bks., Ltd., Ulverscroft Large Print Canada, Ltd.
—The Empty Chair: A Lincoln Rhyme Novel. 2000. E-Book 25.00 (*0-7432-1165-0*); (Illus.). 416p. 25.00 o.s.i (*0-684-85563-1*); 416p. 25.00 (*0-7432-0162-0*); 624p. 25.00 o.s.i (*0-7432-0424-7*) Simon & Schuster. (Simon & Schuster).
—The Empty Chair: A Lincoln Rhyme Novel. abr. ed. 2000. audio 25.00 (*0-7435-0052-0*, Simon & Schuster Audioworks) Simon & Schuster Audio.
—Speaking in Tongues: A Novel. 2000. 336p. 25.00 o.s.i (*0-684-87126-2*, Simon & Schuster) Simon & Schuster.
—Speaking in Tongues: A Novel. 1999. 21.95 (*0-670-86073-5*, Viking) Viking Penguin.
—The Stone Monkey: A Lincoln Rhyme Novel. 2003. 576p. reprint ed. mass mkt. 7.99 (*0-7434-3780-2*, Pocket) Simon & Schuster.
—The Vanished Man: A Lincoln Rhyme Novel. 2004. (Illus.). 560p. mass mkt. 7.99 (*0-7434-3781-0*, Pocket); 2003. 416p. 25.00 (*0-7432-2200-8*, Simon & Schuster); 2003. E-Book 19.99 (*0-7432-4568-7*, Simon & Schuster); 2003. 416p. 25.00 (*0-7432-5131-8*, Simon & Schuster); 2003. 784p. 25.00 o.s.i (*0-7432-4646-2*, Simon & Schuster) Simon & Schuster.
—The Vanished Man: A Lincoln Rhyme Novel. abr. ed. 2003. audio compact disk 30.00 (*0-7435-2826-3*, Simon & Schuster Audioworks) Simon & Schuster Audio.

**SACKETT FAMILY (FICTITIOUS CHARACTERS)—FICTION**

L'Amour, Louis. The Daybreakers. 1996. mass mkt. 4.99 (*0-553-85144-6*); 1984. mass mkt. 2.95 o.s.i (*0-553-25275-5*) Bantam Bks.
—The Daybreakers. 1979. (gr. 7-12). pap. 6.95 o.p. (*0-8161-6739-7*, Macmillan Reference USA) Gale Group.
—The Daybreakers. unabr. ed. 2000. (Sacketts Ser.). audio 25.95 (*0-553-50262-X*, RH Audio) Random Hse. Audio Publishing Group.
—The Daybreakers. l.t. ed. 1975. (Ulverscroft Large Print Ser.). 29.99 o.p. (*0-85456-381-4*, Ulverscroft) Thorpe, F. A. Pubs. GBR. *Dist:* Ulverscroft Large Print Bks., Ltd., Ulverscroft Large Print Canada, Ltd.
—The Daybreakers. 1960. 10.55 (*0-606-02082-9*) Turtleback Bks.
—The Daybreakers BK #5, No. 3. 1979. (Day Breakers Ser.: Vol. 3). 224p. mass mkt. 4.50 (*0-553-27674-3*) Bantam Bks.
—Galloway. 1984. mass mkt. 2.95 o.s.i (*0-553-24205-9*); 1970. 160p. mass mkt. 2.95 o.s.i (*0-553-25510-X*); 1970. 176p. mass mkt. 4.50 (*0-553-27675-1*) Bantam Bks.
—Galloway. l.t. ed. 1998. (Western Ser.). 247p. 25.95 (*0-7862-0872-4*) Thorndike Pr.
—Jubal Sackett. 1986. mass mkt. 3.95 o.s.i (*0-553-25673-4*); 368p. mass mkt. 5.50 (*0-553-27739-1*) Bantam Bks.
—Jubal Sackett. l.t. ed. 1986. (General Ser.). 448p. pap. 17.95 o.p. (*0-8161-3976-8*, Macmillan Reference USA) Gale Group.
—Jubal Sackett. unabr. ed. 2000. (Sacketts Ser.). audio 27.50 (*0-553-50248-4*, RH Audio) Random Hse. Audio Publishing Group.
—Jubal Sackett. 1986. 11.55 (*0-606-02260-0*) Turtleback Bks.
—Lando. (Sacketts Ser.). 1984. 160p. mass mkt. 2.95 o.s.i (*0-553-25504-5*); 1979. 176p. mass mkt. 4.50 (*0-553-27676-X*) Bantam Bks.
—The Lonely Men. 1984. mass mkt. 2.95 o.s.i (*0-553-25507-X*); 192p. mass mkt. 4.50 (*0-553-27677-8*) Bantam Bks.
—Lonely on the Mountain. 1999. mass mkt. (*0-553-20876-4*); 1996. mass mkt. 4.99 (*0-553-85153-5*); 1984. 208p. mass mkt. 4.50 (*0-553-27678-6*); 1984. 208p. mass mkt. 2.95 o.s.i (*0-553-25513-4*) Bantam Bks.
—Lonely on the Mountain. 1981. (General Ser.). lib. bdg. 11.95 o.p. (*0-8161-3247-X*, Macmillan Reference USA) Gale Group.
—Louis L'Amour: Sackett Boxed Set. 1999. 18.00 o.s.i (*0-553-66738-6*) Bantam Bks.
—Louis L'Amour: The Sackett Novels. 1997. mass mkt. 18.00 o.s.i (*0-553-94101-1*) Bantam Bks.
—Louis L'Amour: The Sackett Set. 1997. mass mkt. 29.94 o.s.i (*0-553-85156-X*) Bantam Bks.
—Louis L'Amour: The Sacketts. 1986. 14.75 o.p. (*0-553-32328-8*); Set. 1990. 17.50 (*0-553-60928-9*) Bantam Bks.
—Mojave Crossing. (Sacketts Ser.). 1979. 160p. mass mkt. 4.50 (*0-553-27680-8*); Vol. 16. 1985. 192p. mass mkt. 2.95 o.s.i (*0-553-25505-3*) Bantam Bks.
—Mustang Man. 1999. (*0-7540-3669-3*); 248 p. pap. (*0-7540-3670-7*) BBC Audiobooks America.
—Mustang Man. 1966. (Sacketts Ser.). 176p. mass mkt. 4.50 (*0-553-27681-6*); mass mkt. 2.95 o.s.i (*0-553-25509-6*) Bantam Bks.
—Mustang Man. unabr. ed. 2003. audio 25.95 (*0-7393-0452-6*, Listening Library) Random Hse. Audio Publishing Group.
—Mustang Man. l.t. ed. 1999. (Western Ser.). 248p. 26.95 (*0-7862-0873-2*) Thorndike Pr.
—Ride the Dark Trail. 1984. mass mkt. 2.95 o.s.i (*0-553-24212-1*); 1984. mass mkt. 2.95 o.s.i (*0-553-25512-6*); 1981. 176p. mass mkt. 4.50 (*0-553-27682-4*) Bantam Bks.
—Ride the River. 1999. mass mkt. (*0-553-23742-X*); No. 17. 1983. 192p. mass mkt. 4.50 (*0-553-27683-2*); Vol. 17. 1996. mass mkt. 4.99 (*0-553-85147-0*); Vol. 17. 1983. mass mkt. 2.95 o.s.i (*0-553-25274-7*) Bantam Bks.
—Ride the River. l.t. ed. 1984. (General Ser.). 304p. 12.95 o.p. (*0-8161-3658-0*); pap. 8.95 o.p. (*0-8161-3733-1*) Gale Group. (Macmillan Reference USA).
—Ride the River. unabr. ed. 2000. (Sacketts Ser.). audio 25.95 (*0-553-50251-4*, RH Audio) Random Hse. Audio Publishing Group.
—Sackett. 1996. mass mkt. 4.99 (*0-553-85138-1*); 1994. mass mkt. 4.99 (*0-553-85022-9*); 1984. (gr. 9-12). mass mkt. 2.95 o.s.i (*0-553-25276-3*); 1981. 160p. mass mkt. 4.50 (*0-553-27684-0*) Bantam Bks.
—Sackett. 1979. pap. 6.95 o.p. (*0-8161-6738-9*, Macmillan Reference USA) Gale Group.
—Sackett. 1961. 10.55 (*0-606-00580-3*) Turtleback Bks.
—The Sackett Brand. 160p. 1985. mass mkt. 2.95 o.s.i (*0-553-25506-1*); 1979. mass mkt. 4.50 (*0-553-27685-9*) Bantam Bks.
—The Sackett Novels of Louis L'Amour. 1982. 39.95 o.p. (*0-553-01379-3*) Bantam Bks.
—Sackett's Land. (Sacketts Ser.). 2003. E-Book 2.99 (*0-553-89973-2*); 1996. mass mkt. 4.99 (*0-553-85141-1*); 1984. 192p. mass mkt. 2.95 o.s.i (*0-553-25271-2*); 1980. 208p. mass mkt. 4.50 (*0-553-27686-7*) Bantam Bks.
—Sackett's Land. 1974. 6.95 o.p. (*0-8415-0342-7*, Dutton) Dutton/Plume.
—Sackett's Land. unabr. ed. 1999. audio 24.95 Highsmith Inc.
—Sackett's Land. l.t. ed. 1998. (Western Ser.). 264p. 25.95 (*0-7862-0871-6*) Thorndike Pr.
—Sackett's Land. 1975. 10.55 (*0-606-00582-X*) Turtleback Bks.
—The Sky-Liners. 1982. mass mkt. 2.95 o.s.i (*0-553-25511-8*); 1980. (Sacketts Ser.: Vol. 12). 208p. mass mkt. 4.50 (*0-553-27687-5*) Bantam Bks.
—To the Far Blue Mountains. 1999. mass mkt. (*0-553-12721-7*); 1999. mass mkt. (*0-553-24211-3*); 1984. 288p. mass mkt. 4.50 (*0-553-27688-3*) Bantam Bks.
—To the Far Blue Mountains. 1977. reprint ed. lib. bdg. 13.50 o.p. (*0-8161-6484-3*, Macmillan Reference USA) Gale Group.
—To the Far Blue Mountains. unabr. ed. 1999. audio 27.50 Highsmith Inc.
—To the Far Blue Mountains. 1976. (Sackett Titles Ser.). 10.55 (*0-606-02297-X*) Turtleback Bks.
—Treasure Mountain. 1984. mass mkt. 2.95 o.s.i (*0-553-24208-3*); 1984. 192p. mass mkt. 2.95 o.s.i (*0-553-25508-8*); 1979. 208p. mass mkt. 4.50 (*0-553-27689-1*) Bantam Bks.
—Treasure Mountain. unabr. ed. 2002. audio 25.95 (*0-553-71318-3*, RH Audio) Random Hse. Audio Publishing Group.
—The Warrior's Path. 1999. mass mkt. (*0-553-20786-5*); 1999. mass mkt. (*0-553-24201-6*); 1984. 240p. mass mkt. 2.95 o.s.i (*0-553-25273-9*); 1980. 240p. mass mkt. 4.50 (*0-553-27690-5*) Bantam Bks.
—The Warrior's Path. 1981. (General Ser.). lib. bdg. 13.95 o.p. (*0-8161-3145-7*, Macmillan Reference USA) Gale Group.
—The Warrior's Path, Set. unabr. ed. 1999. audio 27.50 Highsmith Inc.
—The Warrior's Path. unabr. ed. 1999. (Sacketts Ser.). audio 29.95 (*0-553-52627-8*, RH Audio) Random Hse. Audio Publishing Group.

**SAFFORD, BEN (FICTITIOUS CHARACTER)—FICTION**

Dominic, R. B. The Attending Physician. 1980. (Harper Novel of Suspense Ser.). o.p. (*0-06-011073-2*) HarperCollins Pubs.
—Unexpected Developments. 1983. 225p. 11.95 o.p. (*0-312-83278-8*) St. Martin's Pr.

**SAINT (FICTITIOUS CHARACTER)—FICTION**

Charteris, Leslie. Arrest the Saint. 1993. reprint ed. lib. bdg. 21.95 (*1-56849-129-8*) Buccaneer Bks., Inc.
—The Avenging Saint. 20.95 (*0-88411-267-5*) Amereon, Ltd.
—The First Saint Omnibus. 1990. 642p. reprint ed. pap. 10.95 o.p. (*1-55882-060-4*) International Polygonics, Ltd.
—Getaway. 1975. reprint ed. lib. bdg. 24.95 (*0-89190-388-7*, Rivercity Pr.) Amereon, Ltd.
—Getaway. 1994. reprint ed. lib. bdg. 29.95 (*1-56849-262-6*) Buccaneer Bks., Inc.
—Getaway. 1990. 250p. reprint ed. pap. 5.95 (*1-55882-084-1*) International Polygonics, Ltd.
—Knight Templar. 1989. 262p. reprint ed. pap. 5.95 o.p. (*1-55882-010-8*, Library of Crime Classics) International Polygonics, Ltd.
—The Saint: Alias the Saint. 1994. 192p. mass mkt. 3.95 o.p. (*0-7867-0099-8*, Carroll & Graf Pubs.) Avalon Publishing Group.
—The Saint: The Saint & Mr. Teal. 1995. 176p. mass mkt. 4.50 o.p. (*0-7867-0228-1*, Carroll & Graf Pubs.) Avalon Publishing Group.
—The Saint Abroad. 1993. reprint ed. lib. bdg. 21.95 (*1-56849-130-1*) Buccaneer Bks., Inc.
—The Saint & the Templar Treasure. 20.95 (*0-88411-266-7*) Amereon, Ltd.
—The Saint & the Templar Treasure. 1979. (Crime Club Ser.). 9.95 o.p. (*0-385-15097-0*) Doubleday Publishing.
—The Saint & the Templar Treasure. l.t. ed. 1986. lib. bdg. 17.50 o.p. (*0-7451-0387-1*, Macmillan Reference USA) Gale Group.
—The Saint Goes West. 18.95 (*0-89190-391-7*) Amereon, Ltd.
—The Saint in Europe. 1975. reprint ed. lib. bdg. 20.95 (*0-89190-387-9*, Rivercity Pr.) Amereon, Ltd.
—The Saint Meets His Match. 21.95 (*0-89190-343-7*) Amereon, Ltd.
—The Saint Overboard. 1993. reprint ed. lib. bdg. 20.95 (*1-56849-131-X*) Buccaneer Bks., Inc.
—The Saint Overboard. l.t. ed. 1976. (Ulverscroft Large Print Ser.). o.p. (*0-85456-430-6*, Ulverscroft) Thorpe, F. A. Pubs. GBR. *Dist:* Ulverscroft Large Print Canada, Ltd.
—Saint Sees It Through. 1976. 23.95 (*0-89190-389-5*) Amereon, Ltd.
—The Saint vs. Scotland Yard. 21.95 (*0-89190-390-9*) Amereon, Ltd.
—The Saint vs. Scotland Yard. 1993. reprint ed. lib. bdg. 17.95 (*1-56849-132-8*) Buccaneer Bks., Inc.

**SAINT, AUGUST (FICTITIOUS CHARACTER)—FICTION**

Arias-Misson, Alain. The Mind Crime of August Saint: A Novel. 1993. 420p. 22.95 (*0-932511-78-3*); pap. 11.95 (*0-932511-79-1*) Fiction Collective Two, Inc.

**SAINT-CYR, JEAN-LOUIS (FICTITIOUS CHARACTER)—FICTION**

Janes, J. Robert. Carousel. 1993. 20.00 o.p. (*1-55611-357-9*) Fine, Donald I. Bks.
—Carousel. 1999. (St-Cyr & Kohler Ser.). 288p. pap. 12.00 (*1-56947-175-4*) Soho Pr., Inc.
—Dollmaker. 2003. pap. 12.00 (*1-56947-346-3*); 2002. 258p. 23.00 (*1-56947-285-8*) Soho Pr., Inc.
—Mannequin. (St-Cyr & Kohler Ser.). 1999. 272p. pap. 12.00 (*1-56947-176-2*); 1998. 266p. 22.00 (*1-56947-129-0*) Soho Pr., Inc.
—Mayhem. 1999. 272p. pap. 12.00 (*1-56947-158-4*) Soho Pr., Inc.
—Mirage. 1992. 272p. 20.00 o.p. (*1-55611-340-4*) Fine, Donald I. Bks.
—Salamander. (Crime Ser.). 1999. 314p. pap. 12.00 (*1-56947-157-6*); 1998. 322p. 22.00 (*1-56947-119-3*) Soho Pr., Inc.
—Sandman. (St-Cyr & Kohler Ser.). 272p. 1998. pap. 12.00 (*1-56947-120-7*); 1997. 22.00 (*1-56947-106-1*) Soho Pr., Inc.
—Stonekiller. 1997. 261p. pap. 12.00 (*1-56947-107-X*); 22.00 o.p. (*1-56947-083-9*) Soho Pr., Inc.

**SAINT-GERMAIN (FICTITIOUS CHARACTER)—FICTION**

Yarbro, Chelsea Quinn. Better in the Dark. 1995. 412p. pap. 14.95 (*0-312-85978-3*, Orb Bks.); 1993. (Illus.). 416p. 23.95 o.p. (*0-312-85504-4*, Tor Bks.) Doherty, Tom Assocs., LLC.
—Blood Games. 1989. 480p. mass mkt. 4.95 (*0-8125-2801-8*, Tor Bks.) Doherty, Tom Assocs., LLC.
—Blood Games. 1980. mass mkt. 2.75 o.p. (*0-451-09405-0*, E9405, Signet Bks.) NAL.
—Blood Games. 1979. 458p. 11.95 o.p. (*0-312-08441-2*) St. Martin's Pr.
—Blood Games. 2004. 640p. mass mkt. 6.99 (*0-446-61379-7*) Warner Bks., Inc.
—Blood Roses: A Novel of Saint-Germain. 1999. 382p. pap. 15.95 (*0-312-87248-8*); 1998. E-Book 24.95 (*0-312-87173-2*); 1998. 384p. 24.95 (*0-312-86529-5*) Doherty, Tom Assocs., LLC. (Tor Bks.).
—Come Twilight: A Novel of Count Saint-Germain. (Illus.). 2000. 479p. 27.95 (*0-312-87330-1*); 2001. 480p. reprint ed. pap. 17.95 (*0-312-87371-9*) Doherty, Tom Assocs., LLC. (Tor Bks.).
—Communion Blood: A Saint-Germain Novel. 2000. 477p. pap. 16.95 (*0-312-86794-8*); 1999. 472p. 26.95 (*0-312-86793-X*) Doherty, Tom Assocs., LLC. (Tor Bks.).
—Darker Jewels. 398p. 1995. pap. 14.95 (*0-312-89031-1*, Orb Bks.); 1993. 19.95 (*0-312-85296-7*, Tor Bks.) Doherty, Tom Assocs., LLC.
—Hotel Transylvania. 1988. 320p. mass mkt. 3.95 (*0-8125-5850-2*, Tor Bks.) Doherty, Tom Assocs., LLC.
—Hotel Transylvania. 1979. mass mkt. 1.95 o.p. (*0-451-08461-6*, J8461, Signet Bks.) NAL.
—Hotel Transylvania. 1978. 279p. 8.95 o.p. (*0-312-39248-6*) St. Martin's Pr.
—Mansions of Darkness. 1997. 432p. pap. 15.95 (*0-312-86382-9*, Tor Bks.) Doherty, Tom Assocs., LLC.
—Out of the House of Life. 1994. 446p. pap. 15.95 (*0-312-89026-5*, Orb Bks.); Vol. 1. 1990. xi,446p. 19.95 (*0-312-93126-3*, Tor Bks.) Doherty, Tom Assocs., LLC.

Characters

—The Palace. 1988. 480p. mass mkt. 3.95 (*0-8125-2802-6*, Tor Bks.) Doherty, Tom Assocs., LLC.
—The Palace. 1979. mass mkt. 2.25 o.p. (*0-451-08949-9*, E8949, Signet Bks.) NAL.
—The Palace. 1978. 408p. 9.95 o.p. (*0-312-59474-7*) St. Martin's Pr.
—The Palace. 2003. 528p. reprint ed. mass mkt. 6.99 (*0-446-61099-2*) Warner Bks., Inc.
—Path of the Eclipse. 1989. mass mkt. 4.95 (*0-8125-2810-7*, Tor Bks.) Doherty, Tom Assocs., LLC.
—Path of the Eclipse. 1982. mass mkt. 3.50 o.p. (*0-451-11340-3*, AE1340, Signet Bks.) NAL.
—Path of the Eclipse. 1981. xi, 518p. 13.95 o.p. (*0-312-59802-5*) St. Martin's Pr.
—The St. Germain Chronicles. 1983. 256p. (Orig.). mass mkt. 2.95 o.s.i (*0-671-45903-1*, Pocket) Simon & Schuster.
—Tempting Fate. 1982. mass mkt. 3.95 o.p. (*0-451-11865-0*, AE1865, Signet Bks.) NAL.
—Tempting Fate. 1981. 662p. 17.95 o.p. (*0-312-79087-2*) St. Martin's Pr.
—Writ in Blood: A Novel of Saint-Germain. 1997. 544p. 26.95 o.p. (*0-312-86318-7*, Tor Bks.) Doherty, Tom Assocs., LLC.

### ST. IVES, PHILIP (FICTITIOUS CHARACTER)—FICTION

Thomas, Ross. The Brass Go-Between. 1993. 240p. mass mkt. 4.99 o.p. (*0-446-40175-7*) Warner Bks., Inc.
—No Questions Asked. 1993. 192p. mass mkt. 4.99 o.p. (*0-446-40180-3*, Mysterious Pr. Paperback Bks.) Warner Bks., Inc.
—The Procane Chronicle. 1993. 192p. mass mkt. 4.99 o.p. (*0-446-40177-3*) Warner Bks., Inc.

### SAINT JAMES, QUIN (FICTITIOUS CHARACTER)—FICTION

MacGregor, T. J. Blue Pearl. 1994. 384p. 21.95 (*0-7868-6061-8*) Hyperion Pr.
—Dark Fields. 9999. 4.95 o.p. (*0-345-22756-5*); 1986. mass mkt. 5.99 o.s.i (*0-345-33756-5*) Ballantine Bks.
—Death Flats. 1991. (Florida Mysteries Ser.). (Orig.). mass mkt. 4.99 o.s.i (*0-345-35768-X*) Ballantine Bks.
—Death Sweet. 1988. 384p. mass mkt. 4.99 o.s.i (*0-345-33753-0*) Ballantine Bks.
—Kill Flash. 1987. pap. 3.95 o.p. (*0-345-00751-4*); mass mkt. 4.99 o.s.i (*0-345-33754-9*) Ballantine Bks.
—Kin Dread. 1990. 320p. (Orig.). mass mkt. 4.95 o.s.i (*0-345-35766-3*) Ballantine Bks.
—Mistress of the Bones. 1995. 352p. 21.95 (*0-7868-6106-1*) Hyperion Pr.
—On Ice. 1989. mass mkt. 4.99 o.s.i (*0-345-35045-6*) Ballantine Bks.
—Spree. 1992. (Florida Mysteries Ser.). (Orig.). mass mkt. 4.99 o.s.i (*0-345-37346-4*) Ballantine Bks.
—Storm Surge. 1993. 336p. (YA). 19.95 o.p. (*1-56282-789-8*) Hyperion Pr.

### ST. JAMES, SIMON (FICTITIOUS CHARACTER)—FICTION

George, Elizabeth. La Justicia de los Inocentes. 1997. (SPA.). 640p. pap. 16.95 o.s.i (*0-553-06078-3*) Bantam Bks.

### ST. JOHN, DANNI (FICTITIOUS CHARACTER)—FICTION

Hoff, B. J. Masquerade. 1996. (Portraits Ser.: No. 1). 224p. pap. 8.99 o.p. (*1-55661-860-3*) Bethany Hse. Pubs.

### SAINT JOHN, DYLAN (FICTITIOUS CHARACTER)—FICTION

Funderburk, Robert. All the Days Were Summer, Vol. 2. 1997. (Dylan St John Ser.: Vol. 2). 208p. pap. 8.99 o.p. (*1-55661-615-5*) Bethany Hse. Pubs.
—The Fires of Autumn. l.t. ed. 1996. (Dylan St John Ser.: Vol. 1). 256p. pap. 8.99 o.p. (*1-55661-614-7*) Bethany Hse. Pubs.
—The Spring of Our Exile. 1999. (Dylan St John Ser.: Vol. 4). 224p. pap. 8.99 o.p. (*1-55661-617-1*) Bethany Hse. Pubs.
—Winter of Grace. 1998. (Dylan St John Ser.: Vol. 3). 224p. (YA). (gr. 10 up). pap. 8.99 o.p. (*1-55661-616-3*) Bethany Hse. Pubs.
—Winter of Grace. l.t. ed. 1999. (Thorndike Christian Mystery Ser.). 355p. pap. 22.95 (*0-7862-2067-8*, Macmillan Reference USA) Gale Group.

### ST. JOHN, JEREMIAH (FICTITIOUS CHARACTER)—FICTION

Babula, William. According to St. John. 2000. (Jeremiah St. John Detective Ser.: Vol. 2). 240p. pap. 12.95 (*1-58345-501-9*) Domhan Bks.
—St. John & the Seven Veils. 2000. (Jeremiah St. John Detective Ser.: Vol. 3). 208p. pap. 12.95 (*1-58345-506-X*) Domhan Bks.
—St. John's Baptism. 2000. (Jeremiah St. John Detective Ser.: Vol. 1). 260p. pap. 12.95 (*1-58345-496-9*) Domhan Bks.
—St. John's Bestiary. 2000. (Jeremiah St. John Detective Ser.: Vol. 4). 264p. pap. 12.95 (*1-58345-511-6*) Domhan Bks.
—St. John's Bestiary. 1994. 264p. 19.95 o.p. (*1-885173-01-6*) Write Way Publishing.

### ST. VIRE, NICHOLAS (FICTITIOUS CHARACTER)—FICTION

Harbaugh, Karen. The Vampire Viscount. 1995. (Regency Romance Ser.). 224p. mass mkt. 3.99 o.s.i (*0-451-18319-3*, Signet Bks.) NAL.

### SALTER, CHARLIE (FICTITIOUS CHARACTER)—FICTION

Wright, Eric. A Body Surrounded by Water. (Inspector Charlie Salter Mystery Ser.). 1987. 208p. 14.95 o.s.i (*0-684-18873-2*); 1992. 264p. pap. 14.95 o.p. (*0-8161-5319-1*) Gale Group. (Macmillan Reference USA).
—A Body Surrounded by Water. 1989. mass mkt. 3.95 o.p. (*0-451-16385-0*, Signet Bks.) NAL.
—Death by Degrees. 1995. 192p. reprint ed. mass mkt. 6.99 o.s.i (*0-7704-2601-8*) Bantam Bks.
—Death by Degrees. 1993. 192p. o.s.i (*0-385-25436-9*) Doubleday Canada, Ltd. CAN. *Dist:* Random Hse., Inc.
—Death by Degrees. 1993. 256p. 24.95 o.p. (*0-385-25433-4*) Doubleday Publishing.
—Death by Degrees. 1993. (Inspector Charlie Salter Mystery Ser.). 224p. 20.00 (*0-684-19648-4*, Macmillan Reference USA) Gale Group.
—Death by Degrees. 1995. (WWL Mystery Ser.). 251p. mass mkt. (*0-373-26169-1*, 1-26169-2, Harlequin Bks.) Harlequin Enterprises, Ltd.
—Death in the Old Country. l.t. ed. 1986. (Nightingale Ser.). 265p. 10.95 o.p. (*0-8161-3966-0*, Macmillan Reference USA) Gale Group.
—Death in the Old Country: An Inspector Charlie Salter Mystery. 1985. 192p. 12.95 o.s.i (*0-684-18384-6*, Macmillan Reference USA) Gale Group.
—Death in the Old Country: An Inspector Charlie Salter Mystery. 1986. 256p. mass mkt. 3.99 o.p. (*0-451-14450-3*, Signet Bks.) NAL.
—Final Cut: An Inspector Charlie Salter Novel. 1991. 256p. 22.50 o.s.i (*0-385-25289-7*) Doubleday Publishing.
—Final Cut: An Inspector Charlie Salter Novel. 1991. 256p. 18.95 o.s.i (*0-684-19300-0*, Macmillan Reference USA) Gale Group.
—Final Cut: An Inspector Charlie Salter Novel. 1992. (Inspector Charlie Salter Mystery Ser.). reprint ed. per. (*0-373-26107-1*, Harlequin Bks.) Harlequin Enterprises, Ltd.
—A Fine Italian Hand. l.t. ed. 1993. 21.95 o.p. (*0-7927-1564-0*); pap. 19.95 o.p. (*0-7927-1563-2*) BBC Audiobooks America.
—A Fine Italian Hand. 1993. 240p. mass mkt. 6.99 o.s.i (*0-7704-2569-0*) Bantam Bks.
—A Fine Italian Hand. 1992. 192p. 23.50 o.s.i (*0-385-25371-0*) Doubleday Publishing.
—A Fine Italian Hand. 1992. (Inspector Charlie Salter Mystery Ser.). 192p. text 20.00 (*0-684-19504-6*, Macmillan Reference USA) Gale Group.
—A Fine Italian Hand. 1994. mass mkt. (*0-373-26143-8*, Harlequin Bks.) Harlequin Enterprises, Ltd.
—The Last Hand: Charlie Salter Turns in His Badge. 2002. 256p. 23.95 (*0-312-28330-X*, Saint Martin's Minotaur) St. Martin's Pr.
—The Man Who Changed His Name. l.t. ed. 1987. (Nightingale Ser.). 288p. 11.95 o.p. (*0-8161-4285-8*, Macmillan Reference USA) Gale Group.
—The Man Who Changed His Name. 1987. 224p. mass mkt. 3.50 o.p. (*0-451-14930-0*, Signet Bks.) NAL.
—The Night the Gods Smiled. 1983. 192p. 12.95 o.s.i (*0-684-18009-X*, Macmillan Reference USA) Gale Group.
—The Night the Gods Smiled. 1985. mass mkt. 2.95 o.p. (*0-451-13409-5*, Signet Bks.) NAL.
—A Question of Murder. l.t. ed. 1992. 330p. pap. 14.95 o.p. (*0-8161-5372-8*, Macmillan Reference USA) Gale Group.
—A Question of Murder. 1989. mass mkt. (*0-373-26039-3*, Harlequin Bks.) Harlequin Enterprises, Ltd.
—A Question of Murder. 1988. 208p. 15.95 o.s.i (*0-684-19000-1*, Scribner) Simon & Schuster.
—A Sensitive Case. 1990. 224p. 22.95 o.s.i (*0-385-25250-1*) Doubleday Publishing.
—A Sensitive Case. 1991. (Inspector Charlie Salter Mystery Ser.). 224p. mass mkt. (*0-373-26083-0*, Harlequin Bks.) Harlequin Enterprises, Ltd.
—A Sensitive Case: A Charlie Salter Novel. l.t. ed. 1991. (Magna Large Print Ser.). 284p. (*0-7505-0119-7*) Magna Large Print Bks. GBR. *Dist:* Ulverscroft Large Print Canada, Ltd.
—A Sensitive Case: A Charlie Salter Novel. 1990. 224p. 17.95 o.s.i (*0-684-19132-6*, Scribner) Simon & Schuster.
—Smoke Detector. l.t. ed. 1985. (Nightingale Ser.). 286p. 10.95 o.p. (*0-8161-3900-8*, Macmillan Reference USA) Gale Group.
—Smoke Detector. 1986. mass mkt. 2.95 o.p. (*0-451-14123-7*, Signet Bks.) NAL.

### SAM (FICTITIOUS CHARACTER: WOOD)—FICTION

Wood, Ted. Corkscrew. 1987. (Reid Bennett Mystery Ser.). 240p. 14.95 o.p. (*0-684-18853-8*, Macmillan Reference USA) Gale Group.
—Corkscrew. 1989. 224p. reprint ed. mass mkt. (*0-373-26024-5*, Harlequin Bks.) Harlequin Enterprises, Ltd.
—Corkscrew. 2001. E-Book 6.99 (*0-7592-1043-8*); 1999. 188p. per. 19.95 (*1-58586-863-9*) ereads.com.
—Dead in the Water. 1984. 160p. mass mkt. 2.95 o.s.i (*0-7704-2006-0*) Bantam Bks.
—Flashback. l.t. ed. 1994. 21.95 o.p. (*0-7927-1819-4*); pap. 19.95 o.p. (*0-7927-1818-6*) BBC Audiobooks America.
—Flashback. 1992. 256p. text 20.00 (*0-684-19414-7*, Macmillan Reference USA) Gale Group.
—Flashback. 1994. (WWL Mystery Ser.). per. (*0-373-26137-3*, 1-26137-9, Harlequin Bks.) Harlequin Enterprises, Ltd.
—Fool's Gold. 1986. 192p. 13.95 o.s.i (*0-684-18568-7*, Macmillan Reference USA) Gale Group.
—Fool's Gold. 1988. 224p. reprint ed. mass mkt. (*0-373-26019-9*, Harlequin Bks.) Harlequin Enterprises, Ltd.
—Live Bait. 1986. (Mystery Ser.). 208p. mass mkt. 2.95 o.s.i (*0-553-25558-4*) Bantam Bks.
—Live Bait. 1985. 192p. 12.95 o.s.i (*0-684-18330-7*, Macmillan Reference USA) Gale Group.
—Live Bait. 2002. 174p. pap. 6.99 (*1-58586-855-8*); E-Book 6.99 (*1-58586-852-3*); E-Book 6.99 (*0-7592-1039-X*); E-Book 6.99 (*0-7592-0395-4*) ereads.com.
—Murder on Ice. 1985. 176p. mass mkt. 2.95 o.s.i (*0-7704-2049-4*) Bantam Bks.
—Murder on Ice. 1984. 160p. 12.95 o.s.i (*0-684-18134-7*, Macmillan Reference USA) Gale Group.
—On the Inside: A Reid Bennett Mystery. 1990. 256p. 18.95 o.s.i (*0-684-19090-7*, Macmillan Reference USA) Gale Group.
—On the Inside: A Reid Bennett Mystery. 1991. 224p. reprint ed. pap. (*0-373-26076-8*, Harlequin Bks.) Harlequin Enterprises, Ltd.
—Snowjob. 1995. (Mystery Ser.). 251p. per. (*0-373-26182-9*, 1-26182-5, Worldwide Library) Harlequin Enterprises, Ltd.
—Snowjob. 1993. 256p. 20.00 o.p. (*0-684-19563-1*, Scribner) Simon & Schuster.
—When the Killing Starts. 1990. mass mkt. (*0-373-26043-1*, Harlequin Bks.) Harlequin Enterprises, Ltd.
—When the Killing Starts. 1989. 224p. 16.95 o.s.i (*0-684-18331-5*, Scribner) Simon & Schuster.

### SAMMS, LANEY (FICTITIOUS CHARACTER)—FICTION

Schmidt, Carol. Cabin Fever. 1995. (Laney Samms Mysteries Ser.). 224p. pap. 10.95 (*1-56280-098-1*) Naiad Pr., Inc.
—Silverlake Heat. 1993. 224p. pap. 9.95 o.p. (*1-56280-031-0*) Naiad Pr., Inc.
—Sweet Cherry Wine. 1994. (Laney Samms Mysteries Ser.). 272p. pap. 9.95 (*1-56280-063-9*) Naiad Pr., Inc.

### SAMS, CHARLOTTE (FICTITIOUS CHARACTER)—FICTION

Glen, Alison. Showcase: A Charlotte Sams Mystery. 1992. 206p. 19.00 o.s.i (*0-671-74573-5*, Simon & Schuster) Simon & Schuster.
—Trunk Show. 1995. 238p. 20.00 (*0-671-79115-X*, Simon & Schuster) Simon & Schuster.

### SAMSON, ALBERT (FICTITIOUS CHARACTER)—FICTION

Lewin, Michael Z. And Baby Will Fall. l.t. ed. 1989. 304 p. pap. (*1-55504-755-6*) BBC Audiobooks America.
—And Baby Will Fall. 1990. mass mkt. (*0-373-26042-3*, Harlequin Bks.) Harlequin Enterprises, Ltd.
—And Baby Will Fall. 1988. 224p. 16.95 o.p. (*0-688-06880-4*, Morrow, William & Co.) Morrow/Avon.
—Ask the Right Question. 1979. 1.75 o.p. (*0-425-04027-5*) Berkley Publishing Group.
—Ask the Right Question. 1984. 192p. reprint ed. mass mkt. 3.50 o.p. (*0-06-080711-3*, P 711) HarperCollins Pubs.
—Ask the Right Question. 1991. mass mkt. 4.95 o.s.i (*0-446-40021-1*, Mysterious Pr. Paperback Bks.) Warner Bks., Inc.
—Called by a Panther. 1991. 17.95 o.p. (*0-89296-439-1*) Mysterious Pr.
—Called by a Panther. 1992. 272p. mass mkt. 4.99 o.s.i (*0-446-40159-5*) Warner Bks., Inc.
—The Enemies Within. 1979. mass mkt. 1.75 o.p. (*0-425-04029-1*) Berkley Publishing Group.
—Enemies Within. 1991. mass mkt. 4.95 o.s.i (*0-446-40024-6*, Mysterious Pr. Paperback Bks.) Warner Bks., Inc.
—The Enemies Within. 1984. 240p. reprint ed. mass mkt. 3.50 o.p. (*0-06-080712-1*, P 712, Perennial) HarperTrade.
—Missing Woman. 1982. mass mkt. 2.25 o.p. (*0-425-05391-1*) Berkley Publishing Group.
—Missing Woman. 1985. 224p. reprint ed. mass mkt. 3.50 o.p. (*0-06-080709-1*, P 709, Perennial) HarperTrade.
—Missing Woman. 1981. 224p. 10.95 o.p. (*0-394-50007-5*, Knopf Bks. for Young Readers) Random Hse. Children's Bks.
—Missing Woman. 1991. mass mkt. 4.99 (*0-446-40026-2*, Mysterious Pr. Paperback Bks.) Warner Bks., Inc.
—Out of Season. 1985. (Albert Samson Novel Ser.). 256p. reprint ed. mass mkt. 3.50 o.p. (*0-06-080774-1*, P 774, Perennial) HarperTrade.
—Out of Season. 1984. (Albert Samson, Private Eye Ser.). 256p. 12.95 o.p. (*0-688-03903-0*, Morrow, William & Co.) Morrow/Avon.
—Out of Season. 1991. mass mkt. 4.99 o.s.i (*0-446-40027-0*, Mysterious Pr. Paperback Bks.) Warner Bks., Inc.
—The Silent Salesman. 1981. mass mkt. 2.25 o.p. (*0-425-04031-3*) Berkley Publishing Group.
—The Silent Salesman. 1985. 272p. mass mkt. 3.50 o.p. (*0-06-080736-9*, P 736, Perennial) HarperTrade.
—The Silent Salesman. 1978. 7.95 o.p. (*0-394-40433-5*, Knopf Bks. for Young Readers) Random Hse. Children's Bks.
—The Silent Salesman. 1991. mass mkt. 4.99 o.s.i (*0-446-40025-4*, Mysterious Pr. Paperback Bks.) Warner Bks., Inc.
—Underdog. 1993. 272p. 18.95 (*0-89296-440-5*) Mysterious Pr.
—Underdog. 1995. 256p. mass mkt. 5.50 (*0-446-40436-5*, Mysterious Pr. Paperback Bks.) Warner Bks., Inc.
—Way We Die Now. 1991. mass mkt. 4.95 o.s.i (*0-446-40023-8*, Mysterious Pr. Paperback Bks.) Warner Bks., Inc.
—The Way We Die Now. 1979. 1.75 o.p. (*0-425-04028-3*) Berkley Publishing Group.
—The Way We Die Now. 1984. 224p. reprint ed. mass mkt. 3.50 o.p. (*0-06-080710-5*, P 710) HarperCollins Pubs.

### SAMSON, BERNARD (FICTITIOUS CHARACTER)—FICTION

Deighton, Len. Berlin Game. 1997. 344p. pap. 19.00 (*0-345-41834-4*); 1995. 352p. pap. 19.00 (*0-345-47177-6*); 1989. mass mkt. 4.95 o.p. (*0-345-01071-X*); 1984. 352p. mass mkt. 5.95 o.s.i (*0-345-31498-0*, Ballantine Bks.); 1984. mass mkt. 3.25 o.p. (*0-345-31756-4*) Ballantine Bks.
—Berlin Game. unabr. ed. 1999. audio 49.95 (*0-7861-1243-3*, 2151) Blackstone Audio Bks., Inc.
—Berlin Game. unabr. ed. 2000. (Game, Set, & Match Trilogy Ser.: Bk. 1). audio 59.95 (*0-7451-4085-8*, CAB 553) Chivers Audio Bks. GBR. *Dist:* BBC Audiobooks America.
—Berlin Game. l.t. ed. 1984. 16.95 o.p. (*0-8161-3685-8*, Macmillan Reference USA) Gale Group.
—Berlin Game. 1983. 289p. 15.95 o.s.i (*0-394-53407-7*) Knopf, Alfred A. Inc.
—Charity. unabr. ed. 2000. (Faith, Hope & Charity Trilogy: Bk. 3). audio 69.95 (*0-7540-0162-8*, CAB 1585) Chivers Audio Bks. GBR. *Dist:* BBC Audiobooks America.
—Charity. l.t. ed. 1997. (Large Print Book Ser.). 27.95 (*1-56895-436-0*, Wheeler Publishing, Inc.) Gale Group.
—Charity. 1996. 288p. 25.00 o.p. (*0-06-018728-X*) HarperCollins Pubs.
—Charity. 1997. 336p. mass mkt. 6.99 o.s.i (*0-06-109602-4*, HarperTorch) Morrow/Avon.
—Faith. 1994. 384p. 24.00 o.p. (*0-06-017622-9*) HarperTrade.
—Faith. 1995. 352p. mass mkt. 6.99 o.p. (*0-06-109419-6*, HarperTorch) Morrow/Avon.
—Hope. l.t. ed. 1996. (Bernard Samson Ser.). 27.95 (*1-56895-315-1*, Wheeler Publishing, Inc.) Gale Group.
—Hope. 1995. 320p. 24.00 o.p. (*0-06-017696-2*) HarperTrade.
—Hope. 1996. 320p. mass mkt. 6.99 o.s.i (*0-06-109555-9*, Eos) Morrow/Avon.
—London Match. 1997. pap. 12.95 o.p. (*0-345-41835-2*); 1989. mass mkt. 4.95 o.p. (*0-345-01073-6*); 1986. mass mkt. 5.95 o.s.i (*0-345-33268-7*); 1986. mass mkt. 3.50 o.s.i (*0-345-33293-8*) Ballantine Bks.
—London Match. unabr. ed. 1999. audio 62.95 (*0-7861-1284-0*, 2180) Blackstone Audio Bks., Inc.
—London Match. unabr. ed. 2000. (Game, Set, & Match Trilogy Ser.: Bk. 3). audio 69.95 (*0-7451-4003-3*, CAB 700) Chivers Audio Bks. GBR. *Dist:* BBC Audiobooks America.
—London Match. l.t. ed. 1987. 586p. 11.95 o.p. (*0-8161-4106-1*); 19.95 o.p. (*0-8161-4105-3*) Gale Group. (Macmillan Reference USA).

—Mexico Set. 1997. pap. 12.95 o.p. (0-345-41836-0); 1989. mass mkt. 4.95 o.p. (0-345-01072-8); 1985. 408p. mass mkt. 6.99 o.s.i (0-345-31499-9, Ballantine Bks.); 1985. mass mkt. 3.50 o.p. (0-345-32556-7) Ballantine Bks.

—Mexico Set, unabr. ed. 1998. audio 56.95 Blackstone Audio Bks., Inc.

—Mexico Set. unabr. ed. 2000. (Game, Set, & Match Trilogy Ser.: Bk. 2). audio 69.95 (0-7451-4086-6, CAB 621) Chivers Audio Bks. GBR. *Dist:* BBC Audiobooks America.

—Mexico Set. l.t. ed. 1985. (General Ser.). 528p. 17.95 o.p. (0-8161-3955-5); 9.95 o.p. (0-8161-3974-1) Gale Group. (Macmillan Reference USA).

—Mexico Set. Gottlieb, Robert, ed. 1985. 384p. 16.95 o.s.i (0-394-53525-1) Knopf, Alfred A. Inc.

—Spy Hook. 1997. pap. 12.00 o.p. (0-345-42016-0); 1989. 352p. mass mkt. 5.99 o.s.i (0-345-36520-8) Ballantine Bks.

—Spy Hook. 1990. 4.99 o.p. (0-517-05104-4) Random Hse. Value Publishing.

—Spy Line. 1997. pap. 12.00 o.p. (0-345-42017-9); 1990. 336p. reprint ed. mass mkt. 6.99 o.s.i (0-345-37006-6, Ballantine Bks.) Ballantine Bks.

—Spy Line. 2003. audio compact disk 24.95 (0-7861-8970-3); audio 49.95 (0-7861-2456-3); audio compact disk 64.00 (0-7861-9231-3) Blackstone Audio Bks., Inc.

—Spy Line. unabr. ed. 2000. (Hook, Line & Sinker Trilogy : Bk. 2). audio 59.95 (0-7451-4102-1, CAB 591) Chivers Audio Bks. GBR. *Dist:* BBC Audiobooks America.

—Spy Line. 1991. 4.99 o.p. (0-517-07906-2) Random Hse. Value Publishing.

—Spy Sinker. 1990. 374p. 21.95 o.p. (0-06-039118-9) HarperTrade.

—Spy Sinker. 1991. 448p. mass mkt. 5.99 o.s.i (0-06-109928-7, HarperTorch) Morrow/Avon.

—Spy Sinker. 1992. 4.99 o.p. (0-517-08061-3) Random Hse. Value Publishing.

**SAMSON, JAKE (FICTITIOUS CHARACTER)—FICTION**

Singer, Rochelle. Samson's Deal. 1983. 192p. 11.95 o.p. (0-312-69849-6) St. Martin's Pr.

Singer, Shelley. Free Draw: A Jake Samson Mystery. 1984. 192p. 12.95 o.p. (0-312-30366-1) St. Martin's Pr.

—Full House. 1988. (Jake Samson/Rosie Vicente Series). 224p. reprint ed. mass mkt. (0-373-26007-5, Harlequin Bks.) Harlequin Enterprises, Ltd.

—Full House: A Jake Samson Mystery. 1986. 208p. 13.95 o.p. (0-312-30973-2, 39-1127) St. Martin's Pr.

—Royal Flush: A Jake Samson & Rosie Vicente Mystery. 1999. 237p. pap. 12.95 (1-880284-33-2) Daniel, John & Co., Pubs.

—Spit in the Ocean. 1989. (Jake Samson/Rosie Vicente Series). 224p. reprint ed. mass mkt. (0-373-26026-1, Harlequin Bks.) Harlequin Enterprises, Ltd.

—Spit in the Ocean: A Jake Samson Mystery. 1987. 208p. 14.95 o.p. (0-312-00685-3, Saint Martin's Minotaur) St. Martin's Pr.

—Suicide King. 1989. per. (0-373-26040-7, Harlequin Bks.) Harlequin Enterprises, Ltd.

—Suicide King. 1988. 224p. 15.95 o.p. (0-312-02293-X, Saint Martin's Minotaur) St. Martin's Pr.

**SAMURAI CAT (FICTITIOUS CHARACTER)—FICTION**

Roe, JoAnn. Samurai Cat. 1992. (Illus.). 64p. pap. 6.95 (0-931551-07-2); lib. bdg. 11.95 (0-931551-08-0) Montevista Pr.

Rogers, Mark E. The Adventures of Samurai Cat. 1989. pap. 9.95 o.p. (0-312-85016-6); 1986. (Illus.). pap. 9.95 o.s.i (0-8125-5246-6); 1984. mass mkt. 8.95 o.s.i (0-8125-7681-0) Doherty, Tom Assocs., LLC. (Tor Bks.).

—More Adventures of Samurai Cat. 1986. 128p. (Orig.). pap. 9.95 o.p. (0-8125-5248-2, Tor Bks.) Doherty, Tom Assocs., LLC.

—Samurai Cat Goes to Hell. 1998. 320p. pap. 13.95 (0-312-86642-9, Tor Bks.) Doherty, Tom Assocs., LLC.

—Samurai Cat Goes to the Movies. 1994. 288p. pap. 10.95 o.p. (0-312-85744-6, Tor Bks.) Doherty, Tom Assocs., LLC.

—Samurai Cat in the Real World. 1989. (Illus.). 128p. (Orig.). pap. 12.95 (0-312-93198-0, Tor Bks.) Doherty, Tom Assocs., LLC.

—Sword of Samurai Cat. 1991. pap. 7.95 (0-312-85156-1, Tor Bks.) Doherty, Tom Assocs., LLC.

**SANDBERG FAMILY (FICTITIOUS CHARACTERS)—FICTION**

Mosco, Maisie. From the Bitter Land. 1985. 336p. pap. 3.95 o.p. (0-553-25086-8) Bantam Bks.

—Glittering Harvest: From the Bitter Land, No. 3. 1985. 352p. pap. 3.50 o.p. (0-553-20664-8) Bantam Bks.

—Scattered Seed. 1991. 608p. mass mkt. 4.95 o.p. (0-06-100185-6, HarperTorch) Morrow/Avon.

**SANDERS, ALEX (FICTITIOUS CHARACTER)—FICTION**

McKernan, Victoria. Crooked Island. 1994. 288p. 18.95 o.p. (0-88184-998-7, Carroll & Graf Pubs.) Avalon Publishing Group.

—Crooked Island. unabr. ed. 1994. audio 48.00 (0-7366-2860-6, 3567) Books on Tape, Inc.

—Osprey Reef. 1990. 224p. 17.95 o.p. (0-88184-635-X, Carroll & Graf Pubs.) Avalon Publishing Group.

—Point Deception. 1992. 288p. 19.95 o.p. (0-88184-798-4, Carroll & Graf Pubs.) Avalon Publishing Group.

**SANDERS, JOHN, INSPECTOR (FICTITIOUS CHARACTER)—FICTION**

Sale, Medora. Murder in a Good Cause. 1990. 224p. 18.95 o.s.i (0-684-19216-0) Macmillan Information.

—Murder in Focus. 1989. 288p. 17.95 o.s.i (0-684-19082-6, Macmillan Reference USA) Gale Group.

—Murder on the Run. unabr. ed. 1998. (Inspector John Sanders Mystery Ser.). audio 39.95 (1-55686-825-1) Books in Motion.

—Pursued by Shadows. 1992. (Inspector John Sanders Mystery Ser.). 256p. text 20.00 (0-684-19505-4, Scribner) Simon & Schuster.

—Shortcut to Santa Fe. 1994. 256p. 20.00 (0-684-19680-8, Scribner) Simon & Schuster.

—Sleep of the Innocent, unabr. ed. 1999. (Inspector John Sanders Mystery Ser.). audio 49.95 (1-55686-906-1) Books in Motion.

—Sleep of the Innocent. 1991. 256p. 18.95 o.s.i (0-684-19305-1, Scribner) Simon & Schuster.

**SANDERS, TOM (FICTITIOUS CHARACTER)—FICTION**

Crichton, Michael. Disclosure. 1997. pap. 12.00 o.s.i (0-345-41894-8); 1994. mass mkt. 6.99 o.s.i (0-345-39175-6); 1994. 512p. mass mkt. 7.99 (0-345-39105-5) Ballantine Bks.

—Disclosure. E-Book 7.95 (0-375-41219-0) Knopf, Alfred A. Inc.

—Disclosure. abr. ed. 1994. audio 22.50 o.s.i (0-679-43115-2, 491983, RH Audio) Random Hse. Audio Publishing Group.

—Disclosure. l.t. ed. 1994. pap. 23.00 o.s.i (0-679-75143-2) Random Hse. Large Print.

—Disclosure. 1994. 397p. 24.00 (0-679-41945-4) Random Hse., Inc.

**SANDILANDS, JOE (FICTITIOUS CHARACTER)—FICTION**

Cleverly, Barbara. The Last Kashmiri Rose: Murder & Mystery in the Final Days of the Raj. 2002. 288p. 24.00 (0-7867-1059-4, Carroll & Graf Pubs.) Avalon Publishing Group.

—The Last Kashmiri Rose: Murder & Mystery in the Final Days of the Raj. 2003. 320p. mass mkt. 6.99 (0-440-24156-1, Dell Bks.) Dell Publishing.

—The Last Kashmiri Rose: Murder & Mystery in the Final Days of the Raj. unabr. ed. 2002. audio 69.95 (1-84283-243-3) Soundings, Ltd. GBR. *Dist:* Ulverscroft Large Print Bks., Ltd.

—The Last Kashmiri Rose: Murder & Mystery in the Final Days of the Raj. l.t. ed. 2003. (Ulverscroft Large Print Ser.). 432p. 32.50 (0-7089-4935-5) Thorpe, F. A. Pubs. GBR. *Dist:* Ulverscroft Large Print Bks., Ltd.

—Ragtime in Simla. 2003. 288p. 24.00 (0-7867-1246-5, Carroll & Graf Pubs.) Avalon Publishing Group.

—Ragtime in Simla. unabr. ed. 2003. audio 69.95 (1-84283-461-4) Soundings, Ltd. GBR. *Dist:* Ulverscroft Large Print Bks., Ltd.

**SANDS, INSPECTOR (FICTITIOUS CHARACTER)—FICTION**

Millar, Margaret. The Iron Gates. 1987. 192p. reprint ed. pap. 4.95 o.p. (0-930330-67-6) International Polygonics, Ltd.

—The Iron Gates. 1974. pap. 0.95 o.p. (0-380-00015-6, 19158, Avon Bks.) Morrow/Avon.

—Wall of Eyes. 1986. 224p. pap. 4.95 (0-930330-42-0) International Polygonics, Ltd.

—Wall of Eyes. 1974. pap. 0.95 o.p. (0-380-00067-9, 19927, Avon Bks.) Morrow/Avon.

**SANSI, GEORGE (FICTITIOUS CHARACTER)—FICTION**

Mann, Paul. The Burning Ghats. (George Sansi Mystery Ser.). 1997. 336p. mass mkt. 5.99 o.s.i (0-8041-1550-8, Ivy Bks.); 1996. 368p. 23.00 o.s.i (0-449-90770-8, Fawcett) Ballantine Bks.

—The Ganja Coast. 1995. (George Sansi Mystery Ser.). mass mkt. 5.99 o.s.i (0-8041-1419-6, Ivy Bks.); 336p. 22.50 o.s.i (0-449-90769-4, Fawcett) Ballantine Bks.

—Season of the Monsoon. (George Sansi Mystery Ser.). 1994. mass mkt. 5.99 o.s.i (0-8041-1259-2, Ivy Bks.); 1993. 352p. 20.00 o.s.i (0-449-90768-6, Fawcett) Ballantine Bks.

**SANTANGELO, LUCKY (FICTITIOUS CHARACTER)—FICTION**

Collins, Jackie. Chances. 816p. 1981. 14.95 o.s.i (0-446-51237-0); 1991. reprint ed. mass mkt. 7.99 (0-446-35717-0) Warner Bks., Inc.

—Dangerous Kiss: A Lucky Santangelo Novel. l.t. ed. 2000. (Thorndike/G. K. Hall Paperback Bestsellers Ser.). 620p. pap. 28.95 (0-7838-8748-5, Macmillan Reference USA) Gale Group.

—Dangerous Kiss: A Lucky Santangelo Novel, Set. abr. ed. 1999. audio 25.00 Highsmith Inc.

—Dangerous Kiss: A Lucky Santangelo Novel. abr. ed. 2001. audio (0-333-78160-0) Macmillan U.K. GBR. *Dist:* Macmillan Publishing Co., Inc.

—Dangerous Kiss: A Lucky Santangelo Novel. unabr. ed. 2001. audio 94.00 (0-7887-4979-X, 96486L8) Recorded Bks., LLC.

—Dangerous Kiss: A Lucky Santangelo Novel. 2000. E-Book 25.00 (0-684-87371-0, Simon & Schuster); 1999. 528p. 25.00 (0-684-85030-3, Simon & Schuster); 2000. (Illus.). 592p. reprint ed. pap. 7.99 (0-671-02095-1, Pocket) Simon & Schuster.

—Dangerous Kiss: A Lucky Santangelo Novel. abr. ed. 1999. audio 25.00 (0-671-58199-6, Simon & Schuster Audioworks) Simon & Schuster Audio.

—Dangerous Kiss: A Lucky Santangelo Novel. l.t. ed. 1999. (Core Ser.). 620p. 31.95 (0-7838-8747-7) Thorndike Pr.

—Lady Boss. l.t. ed. 1991. (General Ser.). 760p. 16.95 o.p. (0-8161-5189-X); lib. bdg. 22.95 o.p. (0-8161-5193-8) Gale Group. (Macmillan Reference USA).

—Lady Boss. Peters, Sally, ed. 1992. mass mkt. 5.99 (0-671-79571-6, Pocket) Simon & Schuster.

—Lady Boss. 1990. 21.95 o.p. (0-671-61937-3); 21.95 (0-671-94826-1) Simon & Schuster. (Simon & Schuster).

—Lady Boss. Grose, Bill, ed. 1991. 640p. reprint ed. mass mkt. 7.99 (0-671-74418-6, Pocket) Simon & Schuster.

—Lady Boss. rev. ed. 1998. 640p. mass mkt. 7.99 (0-671-02347-0, Pocket) Simon & Schuster.

—Lucky. 1990. 608p. mass mkt. 5.95 o.s.i (0-671-63845-9); 1987. mass mkt. 6.99 (0-671-70419-2); 1986. 608p. mass mkt. 4.95 o.s.i (0-671-52496-8); 1998. 624p. mass mkt. 7.99 (0-671-02348-9) Simon & Schuster. (Pocket).

—Vendetta: Lucky's Revenge. l.t. ed. 1997. (Large Print Book Ser.). 28.95 (1-56895-435-2, Wheeler Publishing, Inc.) Gale Group.

—Vendetta: Lucky's Revenge. 1997. 544p. 25.00 o.p. (0-06-039209-6, ReganBooks); audio 25.00 o.p. (0-694-51809-3, CPN 4048, HarperAudio) HarperTrade.

—Vendetta: Lucky's Revenge. 1998. 5.98 o.p. (0-7651-0824-0) Smithmark Pubs., Inc.

**SANTOS, VICTORIA (FICTITIOUS CHARACTER)—FICTION**

Grippando, James M. The Informant. 1996. 368p. 23.00 o.p. (0-06-017693-8) HarperCollins Pubs.

—The Informant. 1997. 480p. mass mkt. 7.50 (0-06-101220-3, Avon Bks.) Morrow/Avon.

**SASSINAK (FICTITIOUS CHARACTER)—FICTION**

McCaffrey, Anne & Moon, Elizabeth. Sassinak. 2002. (Planet Pirate Ser.). 352p. pap. 6.99 (0-671-69863-X) Baen Bks.

McCaffrey, Anne & Nye, Jody L. The Death of Sleep. 1990. 384p. (Orig.). pap. 6.99 (0-671-69884-2) Baen Bks.

**SAVAGE, DOC (FICTITIOUS CHARACTER)—FICTION**

Farmer, Philip Jose. Doc Savage. 1981. 288p. (Orig.). 2.50 (0-87216-854-9) Berkley Publishing Group.

Murray, Will & Robeson, Kenneth. The Frightened Fish. 1992. 208p. mass mkt. 4.50 o.s.i (0-553-29748-1) Bantam Bks.

Robeson, Kenneth. Devils of the Deep. 1984. 240p. pap. 2.95 o.p. (0-553-24551-1) Bantam Bks.

—Doc Savage Omnibus. 1986. mass mkt. 3.95 o.s.i (0-553-25947-4); No. 8. 1989. mass mkt. 4.95 o.s.i (0-553-27861-4); No. 9. 1989. mass mkt. 4.95 o.s.i (0-553-28000-7); Vol. 2. 1986. mass mkt. 3.95 o.s.i (0-553-26207-6); Vol. 3. 1987. mass mkt. 3.95 o.s.i (0-553-26738-8, Spectra); Vol. 4. 1987. 336p. mass mkt. 3.95 o.s.i (0-553-26802-3); Vol. 5. 1988. mass mkt. 3.95 o.s.i (0-553-26996-8); Vol. 7. 1988. 384p. mass mkt. 4.95 o.s.i (0-553-27616-6); Vol. 10. 1989. mass mkt. 4.95 o.s.i (0-553-28325-1); Vol. 11. 1990. mass mkt. 4.95 o.s.i (0-553-28389-8); Vol. 12. 1990. mass mkt. 4.95 o.s.i (0-553-28510-6); Vol. 13. 1990. 464p. mass mkt. 4.95 o.s.i (0-553-28626-9, Spectra) Bantam Bks.

—The Forgotten Realm. 1993. 304p. mass mkt. 4.99 o.s.i (0-553-29555-1, Spectra) Bantam Bks.

—The Goblins-The Secret of the Su. 1985. (Doc Savage Ser.: No. 125). 224p. pap. 2.95 o.p. (0-553-24715-8) Bantam Bks.

—The Hate Genius, No. 94. 1979. pap. 1.75 o.p. (0-553-12780-2) Bantam Bks.

—Hell Below. 1980. (Doc Savage Ser.: Nos. 99 & 100). 208p. pap. 1.95 o.p. (0-553-14348-4) Bantam Bks.

—The Jade Ogre. 1992. 368p. mass mkt. 4.99 o.s.i (0-553-29553-5) Bantam Bks.

—Jiu San, No. 107. 1981. 208p. pap. text 1.95 o.p. (0-553-14901-6) Bantam Bks.

—The Man of Bronze. 1979. pap. 1.25 o.p. (0-553-15406-0) Bantam Bks.

—Monsters. Date not set. 144p. 18.95 (0-8488-2621-3) Amereon, Ltd.

—Mystery on Happy Bones. 1979. (Doc Savage Ser.: No. 96). pap. 1.75 o.p. (0-553-12885-X) Bantam Bks.

—The Red Spider, No. 95. 1979. pap. 1.75 o.p. (0-553-12787-X) Bantam Bks.

—Satan Black & Cargo Unknown. 1980. (Doc Savage Ser.: Nos. 97 & 98). 224p. pap. 1.95 o.p. (0-553-13421-3) Bantam Bks.

—They Died Twice, No. 105. 1981. (Doc Savage Ser.). 192p. pap. 1.95 o.p. (0-553-14916-4) Bantam Bks.

—The Whisker of Hercules No. 103. 1981. 208p. pap. 1.95 o.p. (0-553-14616-5) Bantam Bks.

—The Whistling Wraith. 1993. (Doc Savage Ser.). 288p. mass mkt. 4.99 o.s.i (0-553-29554-3) Bantam Bks.

—White Eyes. 1992. 336p. mass mkt. 4.99 o.s.i (0-553-29561-6) Bantam Bks.

**SAVAGE, GILBERT (FICTITIOUS CHARACTER)—FICTION**

Doherty, P. C. An Ancient Evil: The Knight's Tale of Mystery & Murder as He Goes on Pilgrimage from London to Canterbury. unabr. ed. 1998. audio 69.95 (1-85903-149-8) Magna Story Sound GBR. *Dist:* Ulverscroft Large Print Bks., Ltd.

—An Ancient Evil: The Knight's Tale of Mystery & Murder as He Goes on Pilgrimage from London to Canterbury. 1995. 248p. 21.00 o.p. (0-312-11740-X, Saint Martin's Minotaur) St. Martin's Pr.

—An Ancient Evil: The Knight's Tale of Mystery & Murder as He Goes on Pilgrimage from London to Canterbury. l.t. ed. 1995. (Ulverscroft Large Print Ser.). 432p. 29.99 o.p. (0-7089-3409-9, Ulverscroft) Thorpe, F. A. Pubs. GBR. *Dist:* Ulverscroft Large Print Bks., Ltd., Ulverscroft Large Print Canada, Ltd.

—Ghostly Murders: The Priest's Tale of Mystery & Murder as He Goes on Pilgrimage from London to Canterbury. 1998. 256p. 21.95 (0-312-19418-8, Saint Martin's Minotaur) St. Martin's Pr.

—Ghostly Murders: The Priest's Tale of Mystery & Murder as He Goes on Pilgrimage from London to Canterbury. l.t. ed. 1999. (Ulverscroft Large Print Ser.). 368p. 31.99 o.p. (0-7089-4059-5, Ulverscroft) Thorpe, F. A. Pubs. GBR. *Dist:* Ulverscroft Large Print Bks., Ltd., Ulverscroft Large Print Canada, Ltd.

—A Tapestry of Murders: The Lawyer's Tale of Mystery & Murder as He Goes on a Pilgrimage from London to Canterbury. unabr. ed. 1998. audio 69.95 (1-85903-165-X) Magna Story Sound GBR. *Dist:* Ulverscroft Large Print Bks., Ltd.

—A Tapestry of Murders: The Lawyer's Tale of Mystery & Murder as He Goes on a Pilgrimage from London to Canterbury. 1996. 256p. 21.95 (0-312-14052-5, Saint Martin's Minotaur) St. Martin's Pr.

—A Tapestry of Murders: The Lawyer's Tale of Mystery & Murder as He Goes on a Pilgrimage from London to Canterbury. l.t. ed. 1996. (Ulverscroft Large Print Ser.). 416p. 29.99 o.p. (0-7089-3446-3, Ulverscroft) Thorpe, F. A. Pubs. GBR. *Dist:* Ulverscroft Large Print Bks., Ltd., Ulverscroft Large Print Canada, Ltd.

—A Tournament of Murders: The Franklin's Tale of Mystery & Murder As He Goes on Pilgrimage from London to Canterbury. 1997. 256p. 21.95 (0-312-17048-3, Saint Martin's Minotaur) St. Martin's Pr.

—A Tournament of Murders: The Franklin's Tale of Mystery & Murder As He Goes on Pilgrimage from London to Canterbury. l.t. ed. 1998. (Ulverscroft Large Print Ser.). 384p. 29.99 o.p. (0-7089-3938-4, Ulverscroft) Thorpe, F. A. Pubs. GBR. *Dist:* Ulverscroft Large Print Bks., Ltd., Ulverscroft Large Print Canada, Ltd.

**SAVAGE, JACK (FICTITIOUS CHARACTER)—FICTION**

Higgins, Jack. Night Judgement at Sinos. 1997. 304p. mass mkt. 7.99 (0-425-16199-4) Berkley Publishing Group.

—Night Judgement at Sinos. 1982. mass mkt. 4.50 o.s.i (0-440-16263-7) Dell Publishing.

—Night Judgement at Sinos. l.t. ed. 1978. (Ulverscroft Large Print Ser.). 29.99 o.p. (0-7089-0149-2, Ulverscroft) Thorpe, F. A. Pubs. GBR. *Dist:* Ulverscroft Large Print Bks., Ltd., Ulverscroft Large Print Canada, Ltd.

**SAVICH, DILLON (FICTITIOUS CHARACTER)—FICTION**

Coulter, Catherine. Blindside. 2004. 368p. mass mkt. 7.99 (*0-515-13720-0*, Jove) Berkley Publishing Group.

—Blindside. 2003. 384p. 25.95 (*0-399-15056-0*) Putnam Publishing Group, The.

—Blindside. l.t. ed. 2004. 512p. pap. 13.95 (*1-59413-016-7*, Large Print Pr.); 2003. 495p. 32.95 (*0-7862-5625-7*) Thorndike Pr.

—Eleventh Hour: An FBI Thriller. 2002. 384p. 24.95 (*0-399-14877-9*) Putnam Publishing Group, The.

—Hemlock Bay. unabr. ed. 2001. audio 29.95 (*1-58788-498-4*, 2796, Brilliance Audio Unabridged); audio 69.25 (*1-58788-499-2*, 2797, CD Unabridged Library Edition); audio compact disk 96.25 (*1-58788-526-3*, 2799, CD Unabridged Library Edition); audio compact disk 37.95 (*1-58788-525-5*, 2798, CD Unabridged) Brilliance Audio.

—Hemlock Bay. 2001. 300p. 23.95 o.s.i (*0-399-14800-0*) Penguin Group (USA) Inc.

—Hemlock Bay. 2001. 432p. 24.95 o.p. (*0-399-14738-1*); audio 24.95 (*0-399-14822-1*, Putnam Berkley Audio); 4p. audio 25.95 o.p. (*0-399-14760-8*, Putnam Berkley Audio) Putnam Publishing Group, The.

—Hemlock Bay. l.t. ed. 2001. 496p. 24.95 (*0-375-43115-2*) Random Hse. Large Print.

**SAVILE, JUSTIN (FICTITIOUS CHARACTER)—FICTION**

Malone, Michael. Uncivil Seasons. 1988. 336p. pap. 3.95 o.p. (*0-440-19244-7*); 1983. 288p. 13.95 o.s.i (*0-385-29267-8*, Delacorte Pr.) Dell Publishing.

—Uncivil Seasons. Rosenman, Jane, ed. 1993. 320p. pap. 12.00 (*0-671-87528-0*, Pocket) Simon & Schuster.

—Uncivil Seasons. 1988. 336p. bds. 3.95 (*0-671-65838-7*, Pocket) Simon & Schuster.

—Uncivil Seasons. 2001. 368p. pap. 15.00 (*1-57071-755-9*, Sourcebooks Landmark) Sourcebooks, Inc.

**SAWYER, PETE (FICTITIOUS CHARACTER)—FICTION**

Albert, Marvin. Back in the Real World. 1986. mass mkt. 2.95 o.s.i (*0-449-12917-9*, Fawcett) Ballantine Bks.

—Bimbo Heaven. 1990. 240p. mass mkt. 3.95 o.s.i (*0-449-14623-5*, Fawcett) Ballantine Bks.

—Get off at Babylon. 1987. (Orig.). mass mkt. 2.95 o.s.i (*0-449-12918-7*, Fawcett) Ballantine Bks.

—The Last Smile. 1988. mass mkt. 3.50 o.s.i (*0-449-13162-9*, Fawcett) Ballantine Bks.

—Long Teeth. 1987. 288p. (Orig.). mass mkt. 2.95 o.s.i (*0-449-13161-0*, Fawcett) Ballantine Bks.

—The Midnight Sister, Vol. 6. 1989. 240p. (Orig.). mass mkt. 3.50 o.s.i (*0-449-13163-7*, Fawcett) Ballantine Bks.

—The Riviera Contract. 1992. mass mkt. 3.99 o.s.i (*0-449-14625-1*, Fawcett) Ballantine Bks.

—The Stone Angel. 1986. (Orig.). mass mkt. 2.95 o.s.i (*0-449-12919-5*, Fawcett) Ballantine Bks.

—Zig Zag Man. 1991. 240p. mass mkt. 4.95 o.s.i (*0-449-14624-3*, Fawcett) Ballantine Bks.

**SAWYER, TOM (FICTITIOUS CHARACTER)—FICTION**

The Adventures of Tom Sawyer. 2001. 8.97 (*0-673-58321-X*) Addison-Wesley Longman, Inc.

The Adventures of Tom Sawyer. 2001. E-Book 2.95 (*1-58853-036-1*) Sensory Publishing, Inc.

The Adventures of Tom Sawyer. abr. ed. Incl. Adventures of Tom Sawyer: Preface. audio Adventures of Tom Sawyer: The Cat & the Pain Killer. audio Set audio 10.95 Spoken Arts, Inc.

Fishkin, Shelley Fisher. The Stolen White Elephant & Other Detective Stories (1882, 1896, 1902) 1996. (Oxford Mark Twain Ser.). (Illus.). 714p. 25.00 o.p. (*0-19-510153-7*) Oxford Univ. Pr., Inc.

Fox, Liz. Tom & Huck. 1995. 64p. (J). (gr. 2-7). pap. 4.95 o.p. (*0-7868-4064-1*) Disney Pr.

Stewart, Stephen. Huck Finn & Tom Sawyer Collaboration: The Sequel to: Adventures of Huckleberry Finn. 2002. (Adventures of Huckleberry Finn Ser.). (Illus.). 289p. 26.95 (*0-9711335-0-6*) New Mill Publishing.

Twain, Mark. The Adventures of Tom Sawyer. Date not set. lib. bdg. 21.95 (*0-8488-1721-4*) Amereon, Ltd.

—The Adventures of Tom Sawyer. abr. ed. audio 10.95 (*0-89926-133-7*) Audio Bk. Co.

—The Adventures of Tom Sawyer. 2001. 7.95 (*0-8010-1217-1*) Baker Bks.

—The Adventures of Tom Sawyer. 274p. reprint ed. lib. bdg. 98.00 (*0-7222-0684-4*) Best Bks.

—The Adventures of Tom Sawyer. audio 26.95 (*1-885546-05-X*) Big Ben Audio, Inc.

—The Adventures of Tom Sawyer. unabr. ed. 1994. audio 44.95 (*0-7861-0849-5*, 1528) Blackstone Audio Bks., Inc.

—The Adventures of Tom Sawyer. unabr. ed. 2001. audio 29.95 (*0-7366-6797-0*); audio compact disk Books on Tape, Inc.

—The Adventures of Tom Sawyer. 2002. pap. 3.50 (*1-59109-030-X*) Booksurge, LLC.

—The Adventures of Tom Sawyer. 2000. 6.98 (*0-681-99538-6*, 50885589) Borders Pr.

—The Adventures of Tom Sawyer. unabr. ed. 2002. audio 29.95 (*1-59086-295-3*, 3881, Brilliance Audio Unabridged); 2001. audio compact disk 37.95 (*1-58788-602-2*, 2883, CD Unabridged); 2001. audio compact disk 96.25 (*1-58788-603-0*, 2884, CD Unabridged Library Edition); 1992. audio 57.25 (*1-56100-115-5*, 790, Unabridged Library Editions); 1992. audio 17.95 o.p. (*1-56100-481-2*, 27, Bookcassette) Brilliance Audio.

—The Adventures of Tom Sawyer. 1982. reprint ed. lib. bdg. 15.95 (*0-89967-046-6*, Harmony Raine & Co.) Buccaneer Bks., Inc.

—The Adventures of Tom Sawyer. reprint ed. lib. bdg. 48.00 (*0-7426-1052-7*); 2001. (Illus.). pap. text 28.00 (*0-7426-6052-4*) Classic Bks.

—The Adventures of Tom Sawyer. 1994. mass mkt. 2.50 (*1-55902-911-0*, Aerie); 1993. mass mkt. 2.50 (*1-55902-903-X*, Aerie); 1989. 235p. mass mkt. 3.99 (*0-8125-0420-8*, Tor Classics); 1988. mass mkt. 4.95 (*0-938819-91-7*, Aerie) Doherty, Tom Assocs., LLC.

—The Adventures of Tom Sawyer. 1998. (Thrift Editions Ser.). 192p. pap. 2.00 (*0-486-40077-8*) Dover Pubns., Inc.

—The Adventures of Tom Sawyer. abr. ed. 1986. (Read-Along Ser.). audio 29.99 (*0-88646-823-X*, LSR 7143) Durkin Hayes Publishing Ltd.

—The Adventures of Tom Sawyer. E-Book 1.79 (*1-929120-68-0*) Electric Umbrella Publishing.

—The Adventures of Tom Sawyer. audio 19.95 Filmic Archives.

—The Adventures of Tom Sawyer. (Illus.). 1942. 11.95 o.p. (*0-06-014465-3*); lib. bdg. 7.87 o.p. (*0-06-014427-0*) HarperTrade.

—The Adventures of Tom Sawyer, Set. abr. ed. 1999. audio 16.95 Highsmith Inc.

—The Adventures of Tom Sawyer. 1997. text 8.25 (*0-03-051507-6*) Holt, Rinehart & Winston.

—The Adventures of Tom Sawyer. 2001. 228p. 24.99 (*1-58827-454-3*); per. 19.99 (*1-58827-455-1*) IndyPublish.com.

—The Adventures of Tom Sawyer. 1999. 232p. pap. 9.95 o.p. (*1-930128-10-X*, JNMedia Bks.) JNMedia, Inc.

—The Adventures of Tom Sawyer. Sternach, Jerry, ed. l.t. ed. 2002. text 150.00 (*1-58702-056-4*) Johnston, Don Inc.

—The Adventures of Tom Sawyer. 1991. 256p. pap. 8.50 o.s.i (*0-679-73501-1*, Vintage) Knopf Publishing Group.

—The Adventures of Tom Sawyer. E-Book 2.95 (*1-57799-801-4*) Logos Research Systems, Inc.

—The Adventures of Tom Sawyer. (English As a Second Language Bk.). 1990. pap. text 4.62 net. (*0-582-53761-4*); Level 1. 2000. (Illus.). 32p. pap. 7.93 (*0-582-41923-9*) Longman Publishing Group.

—The Adventures of Tom Sawyer. E-Book 1.95 (*1-58515-202-1*) MesaView, Inc.

—The Adventures of Tom Sawyer. (Signet Classics). 1997. 240p. mass mkt. 4.95 (*0-451-52653-8*, Signet Classics); 1959. mass mkt. 0.60 o.p. (*0-451-50747-9*, Signet Classics); 1959. mass mkt. 0.75 o.p. (*0-451-50845-9*, Signet Classics); 1959. mass mkt. 1.50 o.p. (*0-451-51337-1*, Signet Classics); 1959. mass mkt. 1.75 o.p. (*0-451-51962-0*); 1959. mass mkt. 1.25 o.p. (*0-451-51165-4*, Signet Classics); 1959. mass mkt. 0.95 o.p. (*0-451-50978-1*, Signet Classics); 1959. mass mkt. 0.50 o.p. (*0-451-50002-4*, Signet Classics) NAL.

—The Adventures of Tom Sawyer. abr. ed. 2001. (Ultimate Classics Ser.). audio 18.00 (*1-931056-69-2*, New Millennium Audio) New Millennium Entertainment.

—The Adventures of Tom Sawyer. abr. ed. 1993. (Ultimate Classics Ser.). audio 16.95 o.p. (*1-55800-669-9*) NewStar Media, Inc.

—The Adventures of Tom Sawyer. l.t. ed. 2000. (Large Print Ser.). 350p. lib. bdg. 26.00 (*0-939495-10-4*); 215p. reprint ed. lib. bdg. 25.00 (*1-58287-117-5*) North Bks.

—The Adventures of Tom Sawyer. 2001. 'p. audio 38.95 NorthStar Audio Bks.

—The Adventures of Tom Sawyer. (Read-Along Ser.). 1994. pap. 34.95 incl. audio (*0-88432-962-3*, S23925); audio 34.95 o.p. Norton Pubs., Inc., Jeffrey /Audio-Forum.

—The Adventures of Tom Sawyer. 1998. (Illus.). 44p. pap. text 5.75 o.p. (*0-19-422878-9*) Oxford Univ. Pr., Inc.

—The Adventures of Tom Sawyer. Mitchell, Lee C., ed. & intro. by. 1998. (Oxford World's Classics Ser.). 296p. pap. 5.95 (*0-19-283389-8*) Oxford Univ. Pr., Inc.

—The Adventures of Tom Sawyer. Fishkin, Shelley Fisher, ed. 1997. (Oxford Mark Twain Ser.). (Illus.). 368p. text 22.00 o.p. (*0-19-511405-1*) Oxford Univ. Pr., Inc.

—The Adventures of Tom Sawyer. 1993. (Oxford World's Classics Ser.). 292p. (C). pap. 4.95 o.p. (*0-19-282837-1*); 2nd ed. (Illus.). 94p. pap. text 5.95 (*0-19-585333-4*) Oxford Univ. Pr., Inc.

—The Adventures of Tom Sawyer. 1995. (Classic, Ultimate, Dove Ser.). 29.95 o.p. (*0-7871-0231-8*) Penguin Group (USA) Inc.

—The Adventures of Tom Sawyer. (Illustrated Junior Library Ser.). 2000. 9.99 o.p. (*0-448-42427-4*, Grosset & Dunlap); 1994. (Illus.). 336p. (J). (gr. 4-7). 16.99 (*0-448-40560-1*, Grosset & Dunlap); 1950. 224p. pap. 1.95 o.p. (*0-14-030062-7*, Puffin Bks.) Penguin Putnam Bks. for Young Readers.

—The Adventures of Tom Sawyer. 2001. (Illus.). pap. (*1-57646-251-X*); 1999. 337p. E-Book 3.99 incl. audio compact disk (*1-57646-151-3*) Quiet Vision Publishing.

—The Adventures of Tom Sawyer. 1983. (Greenwich House Classic Library). (Illus.). 222p. 3.99 o.s.i (*0-517-39991-1*) Random Hse. Value Publishing.

—The Adventures of Tom Sawyer. 1988. (Works of Mark Twain). reprint ed. lib. bdg. 79.00 (*0-7812-1117-4*) Reprint Services Corp.

—The Adventures of Tom Sawyer. 1991. (Literary Classics Ser.). 162p. text 5.98 (*1-56138-023-7*, Courage Bks.) Running Pr. Bk. Pubs.

—The Adventures of Tom Sawyer. 1989. pap. 3.95 (*0-671-70137-1*, 44135, Washington Square Pr.); 2000. (Illus.). 320p. reprint ed. mass mkt. 4.99 (*0-7434-0635-4*, Pocket) Simon & Schuster.

—The Adventures of Tom Sawyer. abr. ed. 2000. audio 18.00 Simon & Schuster Audio.

—The Adventures of Tom Sawyer. unabr. ed. 2003. audio 19.99 (*1-59335-063-5*, 30148) Soulmate Audio Bks., Inc.

—The Adventures of Tom Sawyer. 1983. (Mark Twain Library: No. 1). (Illus.). 292p. text 45.00 (*0-520-04558-0*) Univ. of California Pr.

—The Adventures of Tom Sawyer. 1986. (Classics Ser.). 256p. 7.00 (*0-14-039083-9*); pap. o.s.i (*0-14-039048-0*) Viking Penguin. (Penguin Classics).

—The Adventures of Tom Sawyer. 2000. (New Millennium Library). 212p. pap. 11.95 (*1-58348-341-1*) iUniverse, Inc.

—The Adventures of Tom Sawyer. 1991. E-Book 5.98 (*0-585-23461-2*) netLibrary, Inc.

—The Adventures of Tom Sawyer: Tom Sawyer Abroad & Tom Sawyer Detective. Gerber, John C. et al, eds. 1979. (Iowa-California Edition of the Works of Mark Twain: No. 4). (Illus.). 736p. text 75.00 (*0-520-03353-1*) Univ. of California Pr.

—The Complete Tom Sawyer. 1996. (Illus.). 294p. 9.99 o.s.i (*0-517-15078-6*) Random Hse. Value Publishing.

—The Stolen White Elephant. 1882. 367p. (YA). reprint ed. pap. text 28.00 (*1-4047-4779-6*) Classic Textbooks.

—Tom Sawyer. 1994. (Illustrated Classics Collection: No. 1). 64p. pap. 3.60 o.p. (*1-56103-441-X*); pap. 4.95 (*0-7854-0671-9*, 40358) American Guidance Service, Inc.

—Tom Sawyer. 2000. (SPA.). per. 14.00 (*1-891355-13-9*); 2001. per. 15.50 (*1-58396-185-2*) Blue Unicorn Editions.

—Tom Sawyer. 1988. (Illustrated Childrens Classics Ser.). 3.99 o.s.i (*0-517-65590-X*, Crown) Crown Publishing Group.

—Tom Sawyer - Adventures with Injun Joe. abr. ed. 1971. audio 12.95 o.p. (*0-694-50122-0*, SWC 1165, HarperAudio) HarperTrade.

—Tom Sawyer Abroad. E-Book 1.49 (*1-929120-55-9*) Electric Umbrella Publishing.

—Tom Sawyer Abroad. E-Book 1.95 (*1-58515-206-4*) MesaView, Inc.

—Tom Sawyer Abroad. Fishkin, Shelley Fisher, ed. 1997. (Oxford Mark Twain Ser.). (Illus.). 304p. text 25.00 o.p. (*0-19-511414-0*) Oxford Univ. Pr., Inc.

—Tom Sawyer Abroad. 2001. pap. (*1-57646-252-8*); 1999. 141p. E-Book 3.99 incl. audio compact disk (*1-57646-152-1*) Quiet Vision Publishing.

—Tom Sawyer Abroad. 1999. pap. (*0-14-043383-X*) Viking Penguin.

—Tom Sawyer Abroad. Fishkin, Shelley Fisher, ed. 1996. (Oxford Mark Twain Ser.). (Illus.). 304p. 19.95 (*0-19-510148-0*) Oxford Univ. Pr., Inc.

—Tom Sawyer Abroad. rev. ed. 2000. 150p. per. 9.90 (*1-58396-057-0*) Blue Unicorn Editions.

—Tom Sawyer Abroad. 1988. (Works of Mark Twain). (Illus.). 452p. reprint ed. lib. bdg. 59.00 (*0-7812-1125-5*) Reprint Services Corp.

—Tom Sawyer Abroad & Tom Sawyer, Detective. 1981. (Mark Twain Library: No. 2). (Illus.). 207p. text 45.00 (*0-520-04560-2*); 160p. pap. text 13.95 (*0-520-04561-0*) Univ. of California Pr.

—Tom Sawyer & Friends. 1999. (Workhorse Library Ser.). E-Book 19.99 incl. cd-rom (*1-891595-40-7*) Quiet Vision Publishing.

—Tom Sawyer & Huckleberry Finn. 1972. reprint ed. 14.95 o.p. (*0-460-00976-1*); 2.95 o.p. (*0-460-01976-7*) Biblio Distribution.

—Tom Sawyer & Huckleberry Finn. 1991. (Everyman's Library). 608p. 20.00 (*0-679-40584-4*) Random Hse., Inc.

—Tom Sawyer & Huckleberry Finn. 1943. 448p. pap. 5.95 o.p. (*0-460-87111-0*, Everyman's Classic Library in Paperback) Tuttle Publishing.

—Tom Sawyer & Huckleberry Finn. 1998. (Wordsworth Collection). 400p. pap. 3.95 (*1-85326-011-8*, 0118WW) Wordsworth Editions, Ltd. GBR. *Dist:* Casemate Pubs. & Bk. Distributors, LLC.

—Tom Sawyer, Detective. 2000. per. 9.90 (*1-891355-63-5*); 2001. per. 15.50 (*1-58396-229-8*) Blue Unicorn Editions.

—Tom Sawyer, Detective. 1993. 78p. mass mkt. 2.50 (*0-8125-3035-7*, Tor Classics) Doherty, Tom Assocs., LLC.

—Tom Sawyer, Detective. E-Book 1.49 (*1-929120-74-5*) Electric Umbrella Publishing.

—Tom Sawyer, Detective. Exams Unlimited, Inc. Staff, ed. 2002. 90p. (C). reprint ed. cd-rom 5.95 (*1-59132-055-0*) Exams Unlimited, Inc.

—Tom Sawyer, Detective. E-Book 1.95 (*1-58515-207-2*) MesaView, Inc.

—Tom Sawyer, Detective. 2001. pap. (*1-57646-253-6*); 1999. 101p. E-Book 3.99 incl. audio compact disk (*1-57646-153-X*) Quiet Vision Publishing.

—Tom Sawyer, Detective. E-Book 3.00 (*0-7410-0460-7*) SoftBook Pr.

Twain, Mark & Mitchell, Lee Clark. The Adventures of Tom Sawyer. 1998. E-Book 5.20 (*0-585-35505-3*) netLibrary, Inc.

Twain, Mark & Nelson, Lee. Huck Finn & Tom Sawyer among the Indians. 2003. 268p. 18.95 (*1-55517-680-1*, 76801, Council Pr.) Cedar Fort, Inc./CFI Distribution.

**SAXON (ROBERTS: FICTITIOUS CHARACTER)—FICTION**

Roberts, Les. A Carrot for the Donkey: A Saxon Mystery. 1989. 256p. 16.95 o.p. (*0-312-02554-8*, Saint Martin's Minotaur) St. Martin's Pr.

—An Infinite Number of Monkeys. 1988. mass mkt. 2.95 o.p. (*0-312-91095-9*, St. Martin's Paperbacks); 1987. 176p. 12.95 o.p. (*0-312-00610-1*) St. Martin's Pr.

—The Lemon Chicken Jones. 1993. 288p. 20.95 o.p. (*0-312-10490-1*, Saint Martin's Minotaur) St. Martin's Pr.

—Not Enough Horses. 1988. 224p. mass mkt. 3.50 o.p. (*0-312-91225-0*, St. Martin's Paperbacks); 256p. 15.95 o.p. (*0-312-01485-6*, Saint Martin's Minotaur) St. Martin's Pr.

—Seeing the Elephant. 1992. 352p. 18.95 o.p. (*0-312-07081-0*, Saint Martin's Minotaur) St. Martin's Pr.

—Snake Oil. 1990. 17.95 o.p. (*0-312-04424-0*, Saint Martin's Minotaur) St. Martin's Pr.

**SAXON, ALAN (FICTITIOUS CHARACTER)—FICTION**

Miles, Keith. Bermuda Grass. 2002. 307p. 24.95 o.s.i (*1-59058-004-4*); pap. 14.95 (*1-59058-013-3*) Poisoned Pen Pr.

**SAYLER, CATHERINE (FICTITIOUS CHARACTER)—FICTION**

Grant, Linda. Blind Trust. 1991. (Catherine Sayler Mystery Ser.). mass mkt. 5.99 o.s.i (*0-8041-0791-2*, Ivy Bks.) Ballantine Bks.

—Blind Trust. 1990. 224p. 18.95 o.s.i (*0-684-19165-2*, Macmillan Reference USA) Gale Group.

—Lethal Genes. 1997. mass mkt. 5.99 o.s.i (*0-8041-1558-3*, Ivy Bks.) Ballantine Bks.

—Lethal Genes. 1996. 256p. 21.00 (*0-684-82653-4*, Scribner) Simon & Schuster.

—Love nor Money: An Inspector Catherine Sayler. 1992. (Northern California Mysteries Ser.). mass mkt. 4.50 o.s.i (*0-8041-0947-8*, Ivy Bks.) Ballantine Bks.

—Love nor Money: An Inspector Catherine Sayler. 1991. 288p. 19.95 o.s.i (*0-684-19379-5*, Macmillan Reference USA) Gale Group.

—Random Access Murder: The First Catherine Sayler Mystery. 1998. (Catherine Sayler Mystery Ser.: No. 1). 192p. reprint ed. mass mkt. 5.50 o.p. (*1-890768-09-X*, Intrigue Pr.) Corvus Publishing.

—Random Access Murder: The First Catherine Sayler Mystery. 1988. 192p. pap. 2.95 (*0-380-75534-3*, Avon Bks.) Morrow/Avon.

—Vampire Bytes: A Crime Novel with Catherine Sayler. 1999. mass mkt. 5.99 o.s.i (*0-8041-1862-0*, Ivy Bks.) Ballantine Bks.

—Vampire Bytes: A Crime Novel with Catherine Sayler. 1998. (Crime Novels Ser.). 288p. 22.00 (*0-684-82675-5*, Scribner) Simon & Schuster.

—A Woman's Place. 1995. (Catherine Sayler Mystery Ser.). mass mkt. 5.50 o.s.i (*0-8041-1327-0*, Ivy Bks.) Ballantine Bks.

—A Woman's Place. 1994. 288p. 20.00 o.p. (*0-684-19631-X*, Scribner) Simon & Schuster.

**SCANDAL (FICTITIOUS CHARACTER)—FICTION**

Farquhar, Michael. A Treasury of Royal Scandals: The Shocking True Stories of History's Wickedest, Weirdest, Most Wanton Kings, Queens, Tsars, Popes, & Emperors. 2001. (Illus.). 352p. pap. 13.00 (*0-14-028024-3*) Penguin Group (USA) Inc.

Wilner, Barry, et al. Villains: The Bad Boys (And Girls) of Sports. 2000. (Illus.). 160p. pap. 19.95 (*0-7407-1218-7*) Andrews McMeel Publishing.

**SCARLATTI, ELIZABETH WYCKMAN (FICTITIOUS CHARACTER)—FICTION**

Ludlum, Robert. The Scarlatti Inheritance. 1982. 368p. mass mkt. 7.99 (*0-553-27146-6*) Bantam Bks.

**SCARPETTA, KAY (FICTITIOUS CHARACTER)—FICTION**

Cornwell, Patricia. All That Remains. unabr. ed. 1996. 10p. audio 84.95 (*0-7451-6665-2*, CAB1281) BBC Audiobooks America.

—All That Remains. unabr. collector's ed. 1992. (Kay Scarpetta Mystery Ser.). audio 56.00 (*0-7366-2239-X*, 3029) Books on Tape, Inc.

—All That Remains. unabr. ed. 1992. audio 57.25 o.p. (*1-56100-102-3*, 604, Unabridged Library Editions); audio 22.95 o.p. (*1-56100-468-5*, 421, Bookcassette) Brilliance Audio.

—All That Remains. l.t. ed. 1992. (G. K. Hall Hardcover Ser.). 447p. 23.95 (*0-8161-5526-7*, Macmillan Reference USA) Gale Group.

—All That Remains. abr. ed. 1994. (Kay Scarpetta Mystery Ser.). audio 18.00 (*0-694-51471-3*, 390332, HarperAudio) HarperTrade.

—All That Remains. 1993. (Kay Scarpetta Mystery Ser.). 416p. mass mkt. 7.99 (*0-380-71833-2*, Avon Bks.) Morrow/Avon.

—All That Remains. unabr. ed. 1995. (Kay Scarpetta Mystery Ser. : Vol. 3). audio 78.00 (*0-7887-0168-1*, 94393E7) Recorded Bks., LLC.

—All That Remains. 1992. 416p. 26.00 (*0-684-19395-7*); 21.95 (*0-684-19515-1*) Simon & Schuster. (Scribner).

—Black Notice. 2000. 464p. mass mkt. 7.99 (*0-425-17540-5*) Berkley Publishing Group.

—Black Notice. unabr. ed. 1999. audio 72.00 (*0-7366-4581-0*, 4988) Books on Tape, Inc.

—Black Notice. l.t. ed. 1999. 25.95 o.p. (*0-7838-8688-8*, Macmillan Reference USA) Gale Group.

—Black Notice, Set. abr. ed. 1999. audio 24.95. audio 39.95 Highsmith Inc.

—Black Notice. abr. ed. 1999. 24.95 o.s.i (*0-399-14515-X*); 368p. 150.00 (*0-399-14522-2*, G. P. Putnam's Sons);Set. 5p. 39.95 o.s.i (*0-399-14516-8*, Putnam Berkley Audio) Penguin Group (USA) Inc.

—Black Notice. 2002. 25.95 o.s.i (*0-399-15031-5*); 1999. 415p. 25.95 o.p. (*0-399-14508-7*) Putnam Publishing Group, The.

—Black Notice. l.t. ed. 2000. 544p. pap. 13.95 (*0-375-70771-9*); 1999. 576p. 25.95 (*0-375-40845-2*) Random Hse. Large Print.

—Black Notice. unabr. ed. 2000. (Kay Scarpetta Mystery Ser. : Vol. 5). audio compact disk 112.00 (*0-7887-3975-1*, C1094E7); 1999. audio compact disk 112.00; 1999. (Kay Scarpetta Mystery Ser. : Vol. 5). audio 85.00 (*0-7887-3458-X*, 95881E7) Recorded Bks., LLC.

—Black Notice. 2000. 14.04 (*0-606-19510-6*) Turtleback Bks.

—Blow Fly: A Scarpetta Novel. l.t. ed. 2003. 674p. 32.95 (*0-7862-5690-7*) Gale Group.

—Blow Fly: A Scarpetta Novel. ltd. ed. 2003. 400p. (*0-399-15135-4*, G. P. Putnam's Sons) Penguin Putnam Bks. for Young Readers.

—Blow Fly: A Scarpetta Novel. 2003. E-Book 26.95 (*0-7865-4293-4*) Penguin Putnam, Inc E-Books.

—Blow Fly: A Scarpetta Novel. 2003. 480p. 26.95 (*0-399-15089-7*); audio 25.95 (*0-399-15117-6*, Putnam Berkley Audio); audio compact disk 29.95 (*0-399-15118-4*, Putnam Berkley Audio); 404.25 (*0-399-19755-9*); 508.05 (*0-399-19756-7*); audio 44.95 (*0-399-15119-2*, Putnam Berkley Audio) Putnam Publishing Group, The.

—The Body Farm. 1995. 368p. mass mkt. 7.99 (*0-425-14762-2*); 6.99 (*0-425-14863-7*, Prime Crime) Berkley Publishing Group.

—The Body Farm. unabr. ed. 1995. (Kay Scarpetta Mystery Ser.). audio 64.00 (*0-7366-3040-6*, 3722) Books on Tape, Inc.

—The Body Farm. 1994. 400p. 23.00 (*0-684-19597-6*); 403p. lib. bdg. 26.95 o.p. (*0-7838-1122-5*) Gale Group. (Macmillan Reference USA).

—The Body Farm. unabr. ed. 2002. audio 39.95 (*1-4025-2411-0*, RG096) Recorded Bks., LLC.

—The Body Farm. 1999. audio 9.98 (*0-671-04687-X*, Simon & Schuster Audioworks); 2002. audio 9.95 (*0-7435-2749-6*, Encore); Set. 1994. audio 17.00 o.p. (*0-671-86880-2*, 390161, Simon & Schuster Audioworks) Simon & Schuster Audio.

—The Body Farm. l.t. ed. 1996. (Paperback Bestsellers Ser.). pap. 20.95 (*0-7838-1123-3*) Thorndike Pr.

—Body of Evidence. unabr. ed. 1996. audio 69.95 (*0-7451-6580-X*, CAB1196) BBC Audiobooks America.

—Body of Evidence. unabr. collector's ed. 1991. (Kay Scarpetta Mystery Ser.). audio 56.00 (*0-7366-2001-X*, 2818) Books on Tape, Inc.

—Body of Evidence. unabr. ed. 1992. audio 22.95 o.p. (*1-56100-457-X*, 427); audio 57.25 o.p. (*1-56100-091-4*, 609) Brilliance Audio. (Bookcassette).

—Body of Evidence. 1991. 400p. 18.95 (*0-684-19240-3*); 1994. lib. bdg. 16.95 o.p. (*0-8161-5867-3*) Gale Group. (Macmillan Reference USA).

—Body of Evidence. abr. ed. 1995. audio 18.00 (*0-694-51592-2*, CPN 2267, HarperAudio) HarperTrade.

—Body of Evidence. 1992. (Kay Scarpetta Mystery Ser.). 416p. mass mkt. 6.99 (*0-380-71701-8*, Avon Bks.) Morrow/Avon.

—Body of Evidence. unabr. ed. 1994. audio 78.00 (*0-7887-0048-0*, 94247E7) Recorded Bks., LLC.

—Body of Evidence. Pocket Books Staff, ed. 1999. 416p. pap. 7.99 (*0-671-03856-7*, Pocket) Simon & Schuster.

—Body of Evidence. 1900. mass mkt. (*0-671-03880-X*, Pocket) Simon & Schuster.

—Body of Evidence. l.t. ed. 1994. (Mystery Ser.). lib. bdg. 26.95 (*0-8161-5866-5*) Thorndike Pr.

—Cause of Death. 1997. 368p. mass mkt. 7.99 (*0-425-15861-6*); 7.50 (*0-425-16198-6*) Berkley Publishing Group.

—Cause of Death. unabr. ed. 1996. audio 56.00 (*0-7366-3372-3*, 4022) Books on Tape, Inc.

—Cause of Death. l.t. ed. 1998. (Thorndike/G. K. Hall Paperback Bestsellers Ser.). 430p. pap. 25.95 o.p. (*0-7838-1793-2*, Macmillan Reference USA) Gale Group.

—Cause of Death. unabr. ed. 1999. audio 39.95 Highsmith Inc.

—Cause of Death. abr. unabr. ed. 2003. audio compact disk 49.95 (*1-59007-467-X*) New Millennium Entertainment.

—Cause of Death. 1996. 352p. 25.95 o.p. (*0-399-14146-4*); 340p. 150.00 (*0-399-14170-7*) Penguin Group (USA) Inc. (G. P. Putnam's Sons).

—Cause of Death. 25.95 o.s.i (*0-399-14482-X*) Putnam Publishing Group, The.

—Cause of Death. abr. ed. 1996. 23.50 o.s.i incl. audio (*0-679-44508-0*); audio compact disk 27.50 o.s.i (*0-679-45184-6*) Random Hse. Audio Publishing Group. (RH Audio).

—Cause of Death. unabr. ed. 2002. audio 24.99 (*1-4025-2893-0*, 02294); audio compact disk 34.99 (*1-4025-2894-9*, 00562) Recorded Bks., LLC.

—Cause of Death. 1998. 7.98 o.p. (*0-7651-1040-7*) Smithmark Pubs., Inc.

—Cause of Death. l.t. ed. 1996. (Core Collection). 407p. lib. bdg. 29.95 (*0-7838-1792-4*) Thorndike Pr.

—Cruel & Unusual. unabr. ed. 1996. audio 84.95 (*0-7451-4358-X*, CAB1041) BBC Audiobooks America.

—Cruel & Unusual. unabr. collector's ed. 1993. (Kay Scarpetta Mystery Ser.). audio 64.00 (*0-7366-2518-6*, 3273) Books on Tape, Inc.

—Cruel & Unusual. unabr. ed. 1993. audio 23.95 o.p. (*1-56100-506-1*, 76, Bookcassette); audio 73.25 o.p. (*1-56100-135-X*, 1164, Unabridged Library Editions) Brilliance Audio.

—Cruel & Unusual. 1993. 21.00 (*0-684-19599-2*); 448p. 23.00 (*0-684-19612-3*); 439p. 25.00 o.p. (*0-8161-5727-8*) Gale Group. (Macmillan Reference USA).

—Cruel & Unusual. abr. ed. 1993. (Kate Scarpetta Mystery Ser.). 3p. audio 18.00 (*1-55994-712-8*, 390583, HarperAudio) HarperTrade.

—Cruel & Unusual. 1994. 416p. mass mkt. 7.99 (*0-380-71834-0*, Avon Bks.) Morrow/Avon.

—Cruel & Unusual. unabr. ed. 2000. (Kay Scarpetta Mystery Ser. : No. 4). audio 70.00 (*1-55690-849-0*, 93217E7) Recorded Bks., LLC.

—Cruel & Unusual. 1993. 384p. 25.00 (*0-684-19530-5*, Scribner) Simon & Schuster.

—From Potter's Field. l.t. ed. 1996. 384p. mass mkt. 7.99 (*0-425-15409-2*) Berkley Publishing Group.

—From Potter's Field. unabr. ed. 1996. (Kay Scarpetta Mystery Ser.). audio 56.00 (*0-7366-3241-7*, 3900) Books on Tape, Inc.

—From Potter's Field. 1995. 29.50 (*0-684-81318-1*); 416p. 24.00 (*0-684-19598-4*, Scribner) Simon & Schuster.

—From Potter's Field. abr. ed. 1995. (Kay Scarpetta Mystery Ser.). audio 24.00 (*0-671-86881-0*, 493119, Simon & Schuster Audioworks) Simon & Schuster Audio.

—From Potter's Field. 1997. 7.98 o.p. (*0-7651-0544-6*) Smithmark Pubs., Inc.

—From Potter's Field. l.t. ed. (Thorndike/G. K. Hall Paperback Bestsellers Ser.). 434p. 1997. pap. 25.95 (*0-7838-1292-2*); 1995. 28.95 (*0-7838-1291-4*) Thorndike Pr.

—The Last Precinct. 2001. 480p. mass mkt. 7.99 (*0-425-18063-8*) Berkley Publishing Group.

—The Last Precinct. 2000. audio 39.95 Blackstone Audio Bks., Inc.

—The Last Precinct. ltd. ed. 2000. (Kay Scarpetta Ser.). 432p. 150.00 (*0-399-14639-3*) Penguin Group (USA) Inc.

—The Last Precinct. 2000. (Kay Scarpetta Ser.). 449p. 26.95 o.s.i (*0-399-14625-3*); E-Book 26.95 (*0-399-14756-X*); pap. 29.95 o.s.i incl. audio compact disk (*0-399-14682-2*, Putnam Berkley Audio); 4p. audio 24.95 o.s.i (*0-399-14637-7*, Putnam Berkley Audio); audio 44.95 o.s.i (*0-399-14636-9*, Putnam Berkley Audio) Putnam Publishing Group, The.

—The Last Precinct. l.t. ed. 2000. 736p. 26.95 (*0-375-43068-7*) Random Hse. Large Print.

—Patricia Cornwell: 3 Complete Novels: Postmortem; Body of Evidence; All That Remains. 1997. 832p. 14.98 (*0-7651-9112-1*) Smithmark Pubs., Inc.

—Point of Origin. l.t. ed. 1998. 542p. (*0-7540-2149-1*) BBC Audiobooks America.

—Point of Origin. 1999. 416p. reprint ed. mass mkt. 7.99 (*0-425-16986-3*) Berkley Publishing Group.

—Point of Origin, Set. abr. ed. 1999. audio 24.95. audio 39.95 Highsmith Inc.

—Point of Origin. 1998. 25.95 o.s.i (*0-399-14769-1*); 368p. 25.95 o.p. (*0-399-14394-7*, G. P. Putnam's Sons); 350p. 150.00 (*0-399-14412-9*, G. P. Putnam's Sons);Set. 24.95 o.p. (*0-399-14401-3*, 692891) Penguin Group (USA) Inc.

—Point of Origin. unabr. ed. 1998. (Kay Scarpetta Mystery Ser.). 39.95 incl. audio (*0-375-40353-1*, PC05M, RH Audio) Random Hse. Audio Publishing Group.

—Point of Origin. l.t. ed. (Paperback Bestsellers Ser.). 543p. 1999. pap. 28.95 (*0-7862-1478-3*); 1998. 31.95 (*0-7862-1477-5*) Thorndike Pr.

—Postmortem. unabr. ed. 1996. audio 69.95 (*0-7451-6482-X*, CAB 1098) BBC Audiobooks America.

—Postmortem. unabr. collector's ed. 1991. (Kay Scarpetta Mystery Ser.). audio 56.00 (*0-7366-2071-0*, 2879) Books on Tape, Inc.

—Postmortem. unabr. ed. 1993. 73.25 o.p. incl. audio (*1-56100-172-4*, 990, Unabridged Library Editions-);Set. audio 23.95 o.p. (*1-56100-545-2*, 217, Bookcassette) Brilliance Audio.

—Postmortem. 1999. (SPA.). pap. 14.95 (*970-05-0943-5*) Distribooks, Inc.

—Postmortem. l.t. ed. 1994. 441p. lib. bdg. 16.95 o.p. (*0-8161-5865-7*); lib. bdg. 23.95 o.p. (*0-8161-5864-9*) Gale Group. (Macmillan Reference USA).

—Postmortem. abr. ed. 1999. audio 18.00 (*0-694-52281-3*) HarperCollins Pubs.

—Postmortem, Set. abr. ed. 1992. audio 16.00 (*1-55994-528-1*, DCN 2268, HarperAudio) HarperTrade.

—Postmortem, Set. unabr. ed. 1999. audio 73.25 Highsmith Inc.

—Postmortem. 1991. 352p. pap. 6.49 (*0-380-71021-8*, Avon Bks.) Morrow/Avon.

—Postmortem. 2000. (Best Mysteries of All Time Ser.). 333p. (*0-7621-8859-6*) Reader's Digest Assn., Inc., The.

—Postmortem. unabr. ed. 1993. (Kay Scarpetta Mystery Ser. : Vol. 1). audio 70.00 (*1-55690-892-X*, 93334E7) Recorded Bks., LLC.

—Postmortem. 2004. 352p. mass mkt. 7.99 (*0-7434-7715-4*, Pocket); 1990. 293p. 21.00 o.s.i (*0-684-19141-5*, Scribner); 1998. 352p. mass mkt. 7.99 (*0-671-02361-6*, Pocket) Simon & Schuster.

—The Scarpetta Collection Vol. I: Postmortem & Body of Evidence. 2003. 640p. 26.95 (*0-7432-5580-1*, Scribner) Simon & Schuster.

—Scarpetta's Winter Table. 1998. (Illus.). 96p. 19.95 (*0-941711-42-0*) Penguin Group (USA) Inc.

—Unnatural Exposure. 1998. 384p. mass mkt. 7.99 (*0-425-16340-7*) Berkley Publishing Group.

—Unnatural Exposure. unabr. ed. 1997. (Kay Scarpetta Mystery Ser.). audio 56.00 (*0-913369-71-3*, 4323) Books on Tape, Inc.

—Unnatural Exposure, Set. unabr. ed. 1999. audio 34.95 Highsmith Inc.

—Unnatural Exposure. abr. unabr. ed. 2003. audio compact disk 49.95 (*1-59007-468-8*) New Millennium Entertainment.

—Unnatural Exposure. 25.95 (*0-399-14544-3*); 1997. 352p. 25.95 o.p. (*0-399-14285-1*, G. P. Putnam's Sons); 1997. 352p. 150.00 (*0-399-14295-9*, G. P. Putnam's Sons) Penguin Group (USA) Inc.

—Unnatural Exposure. l.t. ed. (Paperback Bestsellers Ser.). 415p. 1998. pap. 28.95 (*0-7838-8088-X*); 1997. lib. bdg. 30.95 (*0-7838-8087-1*) Thorndike Pr.

—Unnatural Exposure: A Novel, Set. abr. ed. 1997. (Kay Scarpetta Mystery Ser.). audio 24.00 o.s.i (*0-679-44509-9*, 495252, RH Audio) Random Hse. Audio Publishing Group.

Cornwell, Patricia & Brown, Marlene. Food to Die For: Secrets from Kay Scarpetta's Kitchen. 2001. (Illus.). 224p. 27.95 (*0-399-14799-3*) Penguin Group (USA) Inc.

**SCHAFER, WILL (FICTITIOUS CHARACTER)—FICTION**

Stout, David. The Dog Hermit. 1993. 320p. 18.95 o.p. (*0-89296-503-7*) Mysterious Pr.

—The Dog Hermit. 1995. 272p. mass mkt. 5.50 (*0-446-40406-3*, Mysterious Pr. Paperback Bks.) Warner Bks., Inc.

**SCHNEIDER, LENNY (FICTITIOUS CHARACTER)—FICTION**

Goldberg, Ed. Served Cold. 1997. 224p. mass mkt. 5.99 o.s.i (*0-425-15943-4*, Prime Crime) Berkley Publishing Group.

—Served Cold. 1994. 184p. pap. 9.00 (*1-883303-12-5*, West Coast Crime) Blue Heron Publishing.

**SCHOFIELD, SHANE (FICTITIOUS CHARACTER)—FICTION**

Reilly, Matthew. Area 7. E-Book 18.95 (*0-312-70417-8*); 2003. 512p. mass mkt. 6.99 (*0-312-98322-0*, St. Martin's Paperbacks); 2002. (Illus.). 400p. 24.95 (*0-312-26685-5*) St. Martin's Pr.

—Area 7. l.t. ed. 2002. (Adventure Ser.). 839p. 29.95 (*0-7862-4350-3*) Thorndike Pr.

—Ice Station. 2001. audio (*1-74030-109-9*, 500321) Bolinda Publishing Pty, Ltd.

—Ice Station. (Illus.). 2000. 544p. reprint ed. mass mkt. 6.99 (*0-312-97123-0*, St. Martin's Paperbacks); 2nd ed. 1999. 390p. 24.95 (*0-312-20551-1*) St. Martin's Pr.

—Ice Station. 2000. (GER.). 448p. (*3-548-25045-9*) Ullstein-Taschenbuch-Verlag DEU. *Dist:* International Bk. Import Service, Inc.

**SCHWARTZ, REBECCA (FICTITIOUS CHARACTER)—FICTION**

Smith, Julie. Dead in the Water. (Orig.). 1993. pap. 4.99 o.p. (*0-8041-9804-7*); 1991. mass mkt. 4.99 o.s.i (*0-8041-0855-2*) Ballantine Bks. (Ivy Bks.).

—Death Turns a Trick. 1993. pap. 3.99 o.p. (*0-8041-9805-5*); 1992. reprint ed. mass mkt. 5.99 o.s.i (*0-8041-0856-0*) Ballantine Bks. (Ivy Bks.).

—Mean Rooms: A Short Story Collection. 2000. (Five Star Mystery Ser.). 196p. 21.95 (*0-7862-2364-2*, Five Star) Gale Group.

—Other People's Skeletons. 1995. 240p. pap. 15.00 (*0-345-47164-4*); 1994. pap. 4.99 o.p. (*0-8041-9820-9*, Ivy Bks.); 1993. mass mkt. 5.99 o.s.i (*0-8041-1086-7*, Ivy Bks.) Ballantine Bks.

—Other People's Skeletons. 1999. (Mystery Ser.). 232p. 20.95 (*0-7862-1953-X*, Five Star) Gale Group.

—The Sourdough Wars. 1993. pap. 4.99 o.p. (*0-8041-9807-1*); 1992. mass mkt. 5.99 o.s.i (*0-8041-0929-X*) Ballantine Bks. (Ivy Bks.).

—Tourist Trap. 1993. pap. 4.99 o.p. (*0-8041-9806-3*); 1992. mass mkt. 5.99 o.s.i (*0-8041-0930-3*) Ballantine Bks. (Ivy Bks.).

—Tourist Trap. 1986. 240p. 15.45 o.p. (*0-89296-162-7*) Mysterious Pr.

—Tourist Trap. 1987. 240p. mass mkt. 3.95 o.s.i (*0-445-40640-2*, Mysterious Pr. Paperback Bks.) Warner Bks., Inc.

**SCOTT, LAURA (FICTITIOUS CHARACTER)—FICTION**

Curtis, Jack. Glory. 1988. 352p. 18.95 o.p. (*0-525-24668-1*, Dutton) Dutton/Plume.

—Glory. 1989. mass mkt. 4.50 o.s.i (*0-451-40133-6*, Onyx) NAL.

**SCOTT, LINDA (FICTITIOUS CHARACTER)—FICTION**

Buchanan, Bill. Virus: A Novel. 1997. 432p. mass mkt. 6.50 o.s.i (*0-515-12011-1*, Jove) Berkley Publishing Group.

—Virus: A Novel. 1998. 415p. pap. text 6.50 (*0-7881-5789-2*) DIANE Publishing Co.

**SCOTT, MONTGOMERY (FICTITIOUS CHARACTER)—FICTION**

Bonanno, Margaret W. Probe. Stern, Dave, ed. (Star Trek Ser.). 352p. 1992. 18.95 (*0-671-72420-7*); 1993. reprint ed. mass mkt. 5.99 (*0-671-79065-X*) Simon & Schuster. (Star Trek).

—Probe. abr. ed. 1992. (Star Trek Ser.: Vol. 2). audio 17.00 (*0-671-73727-9*, 297233, Simon & Schuster Audioworks) Simon & Schuster Audio.

Dillard, J. M. The Final Frontier. abr. ed. (Star Trek Ser.: No. 5). audio 7.95. 1990. audio 7.95 (*0-671-68507-4*, Simon & Schuster Audioworks) Simon & Schuster Audio.

—Star Trek 5: The Final Frontier. 1989. (Star Trek Ser.: No. 5). mass mkt. 4.50 (*0-671-68008-0*, Star Trek) Simon & Schuster.

—The Undiscovered Country. Stern, Dave, ed. 1992. (Star Trek Ser.: No. 6). 320p. mass mkt. 5.50 (*0-671-75883-7*, Pocket) Simon & Schuster.

—The Undiscovered Country. abr. ed. 1992. (Star Trek Ser.: No. 6). audio 11.00 (*0-671-75873-X*, Simon & Schuster Audioworks) Simon & Schuster Audio.

Ecklar, Julia. The Kobayashi Maru. 1989. (Star Trek: No. 47). mass mkt. 5.50 (*0-671-65817-4*, Star Trek) Simon & Schuster.

Characters

—The Kobayashi Maru. (Star Trek Ser.: No. 47). 1999. audio 5.98 (0-671-04486-9); 1990. audio 11.00 (0-671-70895-3) Simon & Schuster Audio. (Simon & Schuster Audioworks).

Fontana, D. C. Vulcan's Glory. 1991. (Star Trek: No. 44). mass mkt. 4.95 (0-671-74291-4, Star Trek) Simon & Schuster.

Ford, John M. How Much for Just the Planet?, No. 2. 1999. (Star Trek Ser.: No. 36). 256p. pap. 3.99 (0-671-03859-1, Star Trek) Simon & Schuster.

—Worlds Apart No. 2: How Much for Just the Planet? 2000. (Star Trek: No. 36). E-Book 6.99 (0-7434-1987-1, Star Trek) Simon & Schuster.

—Worlds Apart No. 2: How Much for Just the Planet? Stern, Dave, ed. 1990. (Star Trek: No. 36). mass mkt. 4.99 o.s.i (0-671-72214-X, Star Trek) Simon & Schuster.

Friedman, Michael Jan. Crossover. (Star Trek, The Next Generation Ser.). E-Book 6.99 (0-7434-2066-7); 1996. 320p. mass mkt. 5.99 (0-671-89676-8); 1995. 320p. 23.00 o.p. (0-671-89677-6) Simon & Schuster. (Star Trek).

—Crossover. abr. ed. 1995. (Star Trek Ser.). audio 17.00 o.s.i (0-671-53628-1, Simon & Schuster Audioworks) Simon & Schuster Audio.

—Faces of Fire. 2000. (Star Trek: No. 58). E-Book 6.99 (0-7434-2009-8, Star Trek) Simon & Schuster.

—Faces of Fire. Stern, Dave, ed. 1992. (Star Trek: No. 58). 320p. mass mkt. 5.50 (0-671-74992-7, Star Trek) Simon & Schuster.

—Faces of Fire. 1992. (Star Trek Ser.: No. 58). audio 16.00 o.s.i (0-671-77802-1, Simon & Schuster Audioworks) Simon & Schuster Audio.

—Legacy. 2000. (Star Trek: No. 56). E-Book 6.99 (0-7434-2007-1, Star Trek) Simon & Schuster.

—Legacy. Stern, Dave, ed. 1991. (Star Trek: No. 56). 256p. mass mkt. 4.95 (0-671-74468-2, Star Trek) Simon & Schuster.

—Relics. (Star Trek, The Next Generation Ser.). E-Book 6.99 (0-7434-2074-8, Star Trek) Simon & Schuster.

—Relics. Stern, Dave, ed. 1992. (Star Trek, The Next Generation Ser.). 256p. mass mkt. 5.50 (0-671-86476-9, Star Trek) Simon & Schuster.

—Relics. abr. ed. 1995. (Star Trek Ser.). audio 17.00 (0-671-86528-5, Simon & Schuster Audioworks) Simon & Schuster Audio.

Kramer-Rolls, Dana. Home Is the Hunter. 2000. (Star Trek: No. 52). E-Book 6.99 (0-7434-2003-9, Star Trek) Simon & Schuster.

—Home Is the Hunter. Stern, David, ed. 1990. (Star Trek: No. 52). 288p. mass mkt. 4.99 (0-671-66662-2, Star Trek) Simon & Schuster.

McIntyre, Vonda N. The Search for Spock. 2000. (Star Trek Ser.: No. 3). E-Book 6.99 (0-7434-1968-5); 1990. (Star Trek: No. 17). mass mkt. 5.50 (0-671-73133-5) Simon & Schuster. (Star Trek).

—The Wrath of Khan. (Star Trek: No. 7). 1991. mass mkt. 5.50 (0-671-74149-7); 1984. mass mkt. 2.95 o.s.i (0-671-55248-1) Simon & Schuster. (Star Trek).

Oltion, Jerry. Twilight's End. 1996. (Star Trek Ser.: No. 77). 288p. mass mkt. 5.99 (0-671-53873-X, Star Trek) Simon & Schuster.

—The Twilight's End. 2000. E-Book 6.99 (0-7434-2028-4, Star Trek) Simon & Schuster.

Peel, John. Where No Man Has Gone Before. 1986. (Star Trek Ser.). 96p. lib. bdg. 19.95 o.p. (0-8095-8019-5) Millefleurs.

Reeves-Stevens, Garfield. Memory Prime. 2000. (Star Trek: No. 42). E-Book 6.99 (0-7434-1993-6, Star Trek) Simon & Schuster.

Reeves-Stevens, Garfield & Reeves-Stevens, Judith. Memory Prime. 1991. (Star Trek: No. 42). 320p. mass mkt. 5.50 (0-671-74359-7, Star Trek) Simon & Schuster.

Roddenberry, Gene. The Motion Picture. 1979. (Star Trek: No. 1). E-Book 6.99 (0-7434-1208-7, Star Trek) Simon & Schuster.

—Star Trek: The Motion Picture. (Star Trek: No. 1). 1984. mass mkt. 2.95 o.s.i (0-671-54685-6); 1980. mass mkt. 2.95 o.s.i (0-671-83089-9) Simon & Schuster. (Star Trek).

Roddenberry, Gene, et al. Star Trek: The Motion Picture. 1979. (Star Trek: No. 1). 252 p. o.p. (0-671-25324-7, Simon & Schuster) Simon & Schuster.

Shatner, William, et al. Dark Victory. (Star Trek Ser.). 320p. 1999. 23.00 o.s.i (0-671-00882-X); 2000. reprint ed. pap. 6.99 (0-671-00884-6) Simon & Schuster. (Star Trek).

## SCOTT, NICKOLETTE (FICTITIOUS CHARACTER)—FICTION

Davis, Val. Track of the Scorpion. 1997. (Nicolette Scott Mystery Ser.). 336p. mass mkt. 5.50 o.s.i (0-553-57728-X) Bantam Bks.

—Track of the Scorpion. unabr. ed. 1997. audio 44.95 (0-7861-1176-3, 895507) Blackstone Audio Bks., Inc.

—Track of the Scorpion. 1996. 320p. 22.95 (0-312-14437-7) St. Martin's Pr.

—Wake of the Hornet. 2000. 304p. mass mkt. 5.99 o.s.i (0-553-57804-9) Bantam Bks.

## SCOTT, SHELL (FICTITIOUS CHARACTER)—FICTION

Prather, Richard S. The Amber Effect. 1987. 320p. (Orig.). 3.95 o.p. (0-8125-0775-4, Tor Bks.) Doherty, Tom Assocs., LLC.

—The Amber Effect. 2002. 220p. (Orig.). per. 15.95 (0-7592-4549-5) ereads.com.

—The Cheim Manuscripts. 1987. mass mkt. 3.50 (0-8125-0777-0, Tor Bks.) Doherty, Tom Assocs., LLC.

—The Kubla Khan Caper. 1988. 288p. pap. 3.50 o.p. (0-8125-0779-7, Tor Bks.) Doherty, Tom Assocs., LLC.

—Shellshock. 352p. 1988. mass mkt. 3.95 (0-8125-0783-5); 1987. 16.95 o.p. (0-312-93034-8) Doherty, Tom Assocs., LLC. (Tor Bks.).

—Sweet Ride. 1988. 256p. pap. 3.95 o.p. (0-8125-0785-1, Tor Bks.) Doherty, Tom Assocs., LLC.

—Take a Murder, Darling. 1988. 256p. pap. 3.50 o.p. (0-8125-0781-9, Tor Bks.) Doherty, Tom Assocs., LLC.

## SCOTT, STEVEN (FICTITIOUS CHARACTER)—FICTION

Francis, Dick. High Stakes. 1993. 272p. mass mkt. 6.99 (0-449-22114-8, Fawcett) Ballantine Bks.

—High Stakes. 2003. audio compact disk 19.95 (0-7861-9260-7); 2000. audio compact disk 40.00 (0-7861-9918-0, z1715); 1995. audio 32.95 (0-7861-0906-8, 1715) Blackstone Audio Bks., Inc.

—High Stakes. unabr. ed. 2000. audio 49.95 (0-7451-4047-5, CAB 744) Chivers Audio Bks. GBR. *Dist:* BBC Audiobooks America.

—High Stakes, abr. ed. 1980. audio 15.95 (0-88646-003-4, 390918) Durkin Hayes Publishing Ltd.

—High Stakes. 1990. mass mkt. 4.50 (0-671-70468-0); 1988. mass mkt. 3.95 (0-671-68077-3); 1985. mass mkt. 3.50 (0-671-55268-6); 1982. mass mkt. 2.95 o.s.i (0-671-46423-X) Simon & Schuster. (Pocket).

—High Stakes. l.t. ed. 1980. (Ulverscroft Large Print Ser.). 12.00 o.p. (0-7089-0412-2, Ulverscroft) Thorpe, F. A. Pubs. GBR. *Dist:* Ulverscroft Large Print Bks., Ltd., Ulverscroft Large Print Canada, Ltd.

## SCROOGE, EBENEZER (FICTITIOUS CHARACTER)—FICTION

Bueno de Mesquita, Bruce & Dickens, Charles. The Trial of Ebenezer Scrooge. 2001. 168p. 39.95 (0-8142-0888-6); pap. 23.95 (0-8142-5086-6) Ohio State Univ. Pr.

Dickens, Charles. The Annotated Christmas Carol. 1977. (Illus.). 15.00 o.s.i (0-517-52741-3) Crown Publishing Group.

—The Annotated Christmas Carol. 1984. (Illus.). mass mkt. 4.95 o.p. (0-380-01722-9, 34108-5, Avon Bks.) Morrow/Avon.

—The Annotated Christmas Carol. 2003. (Illus.). 288p. 29.95 (0-393-05158-7) Norton, W. W. & Co., Inc.

—The Annotated Christmas Carol. 1989. 5.99 o.s.i (0-517-68780-1) Random Hse. Value Publishing.

—A Christmas Carol. 1999. E-Book 7.95 incl. cd-rom (0-9669705-3-5) 23 Hse.

—A Christmas Carol. Date not set. pap. text (0-17-557046-9) Addison-Wesley Longman, Inc.

—A Christmas Carol. 1994. pap. text 39.50 (0-582-23664-9) Addison-Wesley Longman, Ltd. GBR. *Dist:* Trans-Atlantic Pubns., Inc.

—A Christmas Carol. 1994. (Illustrated Classics Collection). 64p. pap. 3.60 o.p. (1-56103-582-3); pap. 4.95 (0-7854-0747-2, 40494) American Guidance Service, Inc.

—A Christmas Carol. 1999. audio Art of Hearing, Inc.

—A Christmas Carol. 1989. (Illus.). 118p. 100.00 (0-933861-07-9) Berliner, Harold.

—A Christmas Carol. 2002. 12.32 (0-7587-7666-7) Book Wholesalers, Inc.

—A Christmas Carol. 1992. (Illus.). 144p. 6.95 o.p. (0-681-41606-8) Borders Pr.

—A Christmas Carol. 2000. audio 11.99 (0-660-17877-X); audio compact disk 15.95 (0-660-17878-8) Canadian Broadcasting Corp./Societe Radio-Canada CAN. *Dist:* Georgetown Terminal Warehouse.

—A Christmas Carol. audio 4.98 Covenant Communications, Inc.

—A Christmas Carol. 1982. (Illus.). o.p. (0-434-95857-3) David & Charles Pubs.

—A Christmas Carol. 1996. pap. 5.95 incl. audio Dover Pubns., Inc.

—A Christmas Carol. 1931. pap. 5.60 (0-87129-314-5, C23) Dramatic Publishing Co.

—A Christmas Carol. 1979. 15.50 o.p. (0-460-00239-2); 1972. 2.95 o.p. (0-460-01239-8) Dutton/Plume. (Dutton).

—A Christmas Carol. E-Book 2.49 (1-58744-953-6) Electric Umbrella Publishing.

—A Christmas Carol. 1993. 37p. pap. 5.00 (1-57514-211-2, 1150) Encore Performance Publishing.

—A Christmas Carol. (Focus on the Family Great Stories Ser.). 1999. (Illus.). 184p. pap. 7.99 o.p. (1-56179-746-4); 1997. 12.99 o.p. (1-56179-556-9) Focus on the Family Publishing.

—A Christmas Carol. audio 14.95 Halvorson Assocs.

—A Christmas Carol. 1996. 35.00 o.p. (0-15-100275-4) Harcourt Children's Bks.

—A Christmas Carol. 1995. pap. 20.00 (0-15-200952-3) Harcourt Trade Pubs.

—A Christmas Carol. 2003. audio 14.95 (1-84032-776-6) Hodder Headline Audiobooks GBR. *Dist:* Trafalgar Square.

—A Christmas Carol. 1997. (Illus.). text 8.25 (0-03-051492-4) Holt, Rinehart & Winston.

—A Christmas Carol. 2001. audio 12.95 Lodestone Catalog, The.

—A Christmas Carol. 1984. mass mkt. 2.75 o.p. (0-451-51869-1, Signet Classics) NAL.

—A Christmas Carol. audio 7.95 National Recording Co.

—A Christmas Carol. Green, Frank, ed. 1995. (Thornes Classic Novels Ser.). (Illus.). 221p. pap. 14.95 (0-7487-1832-X) Nelson Thornes GBR. *Dist:* Trans-Atlantic Pubns., Inc.

—A Christmas Carol. 1990. (Illus.). 144p. pap. 10.00 (0-14-007120-2, Penguin Bks.) Penguin Group (USA) Inc.

—A Christmas Carol. 1999. E-Book 3.99 incl. cd-rom (1-57646-075-4) Quiet Vision Publishing.

—A Christmas Carol. 2001. (Adventures in Old-Time Radio Ser.). audio 4.98. audio compact disk 4.98 Radio Spirits, Inc.

—A Christmas Carol. 1987. (Radiobook Ser.). audio 4.98 (0-929541-21-9) Radiola Co.

—A Christmas Carol. 1990. (Miniature Editions Ser.). (Illus.). 160p. text 4.95 o.p. (0-89471-854-1) Running Pr. Bk. Pubs.

—A Christmas Carol. (Illus.). 2003. 176p. mass mkt. 3.95 (0-7434-7737-5); 1997. 224p. mass mkt. 3.99 (0-671-52078-4) Simon & Schuster. (Pocket).

—A Christmas Carol. 1981. 240p. pap. 2.50 (0-671-44199-X, Simon Pulse) Simon & Schuster Children's Publishing.

—A Christmas Carol. 1987. (Illus.). 15.75 o.p. (0-8446-0078-4) Smith, Peter Pub., Inc.

—A Christmas Carol. 1979. (Illus.). 9.95 o.p. (0-312-13403-7) St. Martin's Pr.

—A Christmas Carol. 1991. 176p. pap. 4.95 o.p. (0-460-87097-1, Everyman's Classic Library in Paperback) Tuttle Publishing.

—A Christmas Carol. 1999. pap. 10.95 incl. audio (0-14-086224-2) Viking Penguin.

—A Christmas Carol. 1993. (Illus.). 168p. 35.00 o.p. (0-300-05843-8) Yale Univ. Pr.

—A Christmas Carol. Barbour Books Staff, ed. 1997. 99p. pap. text 0.99 o.p. (1-55748-963-7) Barbour Publishing, Inc.

—A Christmas Carol. ltd. ed. 1993. (Illus.). 116p. 685.00 (0-910457-28-X) Arion Pr.

—A Christmas Carol. abr. ed. audio 12.95 (0-89926-140-X, 828) Audio Bk. Co.

—A Christmas Carol. unabr. ed. 1999. audio 17.95 (1-57270-115-3, F21115u, Cover to Cover Classics) Audio Partners Publishing Corp.

—A Christmas Carol. unabr. ed. 1997. audio 18.95 o.p. (1-85549-922-3, C T C 125) BBC Audiobooks America.

—A Christmas Carol. 1986. (Bantam Classics Ser.). 112p. reprint ed. mass mkt. 3.95 (0-553-21244-3) Bantam Dell Publishing Group.

—A Christmas Carol. unabr. ed. 1989. audio 23.95 (0-7861-0069-9, 1065) Blackstone Audio Bks., Inc.

—A Christmas Carol. unabr. ed. 2001. audio 17.95 (0-7366-6763-6); audio 14.95 Books on Tape, Inc.

—A Christmas Carol. deluxe ed. 1976. 9.95 o.p. (0-385-12816-9) Doubleday Publishing.

—A Christmas Carol. 1991. (Thrift Editions Ser.). 80p. reprint ed. pap. 1.00 (0-486-26865-9) Dover Pubns., Inc.

—A Christmas Carol. abr. ed. audio 15.95 o.p. (0-88646-035-2, 7051) Durkin Hayes Publishing Ltd.

—A Christmas Carol. English, Martin & Warren, Bill, eds. unabr. ed. 1997. audio 12.00 (0-9662157-0-2) Grey Matter Productions.

—A Christmas Carol. unabr. ed. audio 14.95 Halvorson Assocs.

—A Christmas Carol, Set. unabr. ed. 1999. audio 23.95 Highsmith Inc.

—A Christmas Carol. unabr. ed. 1978. audio 7.95 Jimcin Recordings.

—A Christmas Carol. Sternach, Jerry, ed. l.t. ed. (Illus.). 2002. text 150.00 (1-58702-003-3); 2000. text 50.00 (1-58702-511-6) Johnston, Don Inc.

—A Christmas Carol. abr. ed. 1999. (Works of Charles Dickens). audio 13.98 (962-634-682-5, NA218214); audio compact disk 15.98 (962-634-182-3, NA218212) Naxos of America, Inc. (Naxos AudioBooks).

—A Christmas Carol. abr. ed. 1993. 16.95 o.p. (1-55800-700-8) NewStar Media, Inc.

—A Christmas Carol. unabr. ed. 2001. audio 29.95 NorthStar Audio Bks.

—A Christmas Carol. unabr. ed. 2000. audio compact disk 29.00 (0-7887-4480-1, C1182E7) Recorded Bks., LLC.

—A Christmas Carol. abr. ed. 2001. audio 34.95; Set. 1999. audio 34.95 Soundings, Ltd. GBR. *Dist:* Ulverscroft Large Print Bks., Ltd., ISIS Publishing.

—A Christmas Carol. abr. ed. audio 10.95 (0-8045-0728-7, SAC 728) Spoken Arts, Inc.

—A Christmas Carol. unabr. ed. 1993. (Audio Books Ser.). 26.95 o.p. incl. audio (1-85496-077-6) Thorndike Pr.

—A Christmas Carol. abr. ed. 1997. audio 16.95 (1-85998-048-1) Trafalgar Square.

—A Christmas Carol: A Facsimile Edition of the Autograph Manuscript in the Pierpont Morgan Library. 1993. (Illus.). 139p. (0-87598-098-8) Pierpont Morgan Library.

—A Christmas Carol: Adapted for Theater. 1993. (Illus.). 32p. (YA). (gr. 2-12). 14.95 (0-8362-4507-5) Andrews McMeel Publishing.

—A Christmas Carol: The Original Manuscript. 1971. (Illus.). 144p. reprint ed. pap. 8.95 (0-486-20980-6) Dover Pubns., Inc.

—A Christmas Carol: The Public Reading Version. Collins, Philip, ed. 1971. (Illus.). 232p. 20.00 (0-87104-228-2) New York Public Library.

—A Christmas Carol: The Radio Play. Williams, John, ed. abr. ed. 1992. audio 14.95 (0-9634652-1-X) Radio Theatre Productions - John L. Williams.

—A Christmas Carol & Other Christmas Stories. 1976. 21.95 (0-8488-0796-0) Amereon, Ltd.

—A Christmas Carol & Other Haunting Tales. 1998. (New York Public Library Collector's Edition Ser.). (Illus.). 416p. 18.50 o.s.i (0-385-48725-8) Doubleday Publishing.

—A Christmas Carol & Sketches of a Young Couple. rev. ed. 2001. 150p. per. 9.90 (1-58396-038-4) Blue Unicorn Editions.

—A Christmas Carol Christmas Book. 9999. 16.95 o.p. (0-316-41446-8) Little Brown & Co.

—A Christmas Carol Readalong. 1994. (Illustrated Classics Collection). 64p. (Orig.). pap. 13.50 o.p. incl. audio (1-56103-584-X); pap. 14.95 incl. audio (0-7854-0763-4, 40496) American Guidance Service, Inc.

Dickens, Charles, et al. A Christmas Carol & Other Victorian Fairy Tales. 1983. 368p. (Orig.). mass mkt. 2.95 o.s.i (0-553-21126-9, Bantam Classics) Bantam Bks.

Gilmore, Robert. Scrooge's Cryptic Carol: Visions of Energy, Time & Quantum Nature. 1996. (Illus.). 251p. text 22.00 (0-387-94800-7) Springer-Verlag New York, Inc.

Linney, Romulus. A Christmas Carol. 1996. per. 6.50 (0-8222-1539-X) Dramatists Play Service, Inc.

Okun, Milton, ed. Scrooge - The Musical. pap. 14.95 (0-89524-726-7) Cherry Lane Music Co.

Scarborough, Elizabeth Ann. Carol for Another Christmas. 1996. 208p. 18.00 o.s.i (0-441-00366-4) Ace Bks.

## SCUDDER, MATT (FICTITIOUS CHARACTER)—FICTION

Block, Lawrence. A Dance at the Slaughterhouse. abr. ed. 1991. (Matthew Scudder Mystery Ser.: No. 9). audio 17.95 o.p. (1-55994-503-6, CPN 2257, HarperAudio) HarperTrade.

—A Dance at the Slaughterhouse. (Matthew Scudder Mystery Ser.: No. 9). 2000. 304p. pap. 13.00 (0-380-81373-4, Avon Bks.); 1991. 304p. 19.00 o.p. (0-688-10349-9, Morrow, William & Co.); 1992. 384p. reprint ed. mass mkt. 7.50 (0-380-71374-8, Avon Bks.) Morrow/Avon.

—A Dance at the Slaughterhouse. l.t. ed. 2000. (Matthew Scudder Mystery Ser.: No. 9). 468p. 28.95 (0-7862-2983-7) Thorndike Pr.

—The Devil Knows You're Dead. (Matthew Scudder Mystery Ser.: No. 11). 1999. 288p. pap. 12.50 (0-380-80759-9, Avon Bks.); 1993. 316p. 20.00 o.p. (0-688-12192-6, Morrow, William & Co.); 1994. 384p. reprint ed. mass mkt. 7.50 (0-380-72023-X, Avon Bks.) Morrow/Avon.

—The Devil Knows You're Dead. l.t. ed. 2001. (Matthew Scudder Mystery Ser.: No. 11). 503p. 30.95 (0-7862-3109-2); (0-7540-1578-5); (0-7540-2440-7) Thorndike Pr.

—Eight Million Ways to Die. unabr. ed. 2000. (Matthew Scudder Mystery Ser.: No. 5). audio compact disk 94.95 (0-7927-9976-3, SLD 027, Chivers Sound Library) BBC Audiobooks America.

—Eight Million Ways to Die. 1986. (Matthew Scudder Mystery Ser.: No. 5). mass mkt. 3.50 o.s.i (0-515-08840-4); 1984. (Matthew Scudder Mystery Ser.: No. 5). 304p. mass mkt. 3.95 o.s.i (0-515-08090-X); 1983. mass mkt. 3.50 o.s.i (0-515-07537-X); 1983. mass mkt. 3.50 o.s.i (0-515-07257-5) Berkley Publishing Group. (Jove).

—Eight Million Ways to Die. l.t. ed. 2000. (Matthew Scudder Mystery Ser.: No. 5). 410p. pap. 24.95 (1-56895-939-7, Wheeler Publishing, Inc.) Gale Group.

—Eight Million Ways to Die. (Matthew Scudder Mystery Ser.: No. 5). 1982. 13.50 o.p. (*0-87795-405-4*, Morrow, William & Co.); 1993. 384p. reprint ed. mass mkt. 7.50 (*0-380-71573-2*, Avon Bks.) Morrow/Avon.
—Even the Wicked. (Matthew Scudder Mystery Ser.: No. 13). 1997. 328p. 23.00 (*0-688-14181-1*, Morrow, William & Co.); 1998. 400p. mass mkt. 7.50 (*0-380-72534-7*, Avon Bks.) Morrow/Avon.
—Everybody Dies. (Matthew Scudder Mystery Ser.: No. 14). 1999. 384p. mass mkt. 6.99 (*0-380-72535-5*, Avon Bks.); 1998. 336p. 25.00 o.p. (*0-688-14182-X*, Morrow, William & Co.) Morrow/Avon.
—Everybody Dies. l.t. ed. 1999. (Matthew Scudder Mystery Ser.: No. 14). 461p. 29.95 (*0-7862-1706-5*) Thorndike Pr.
—Hope to Die. l.t. ed. 2001. 480p. pap. 25.00 (*0-06-621400-9*) HarperCollins Pubs.
—Hope to Die. abr. ed. 2001. 32p. (ps-2). audio 25.95 (*0-694-52604-5*, HarperAudio) HarperTrade.
—Hope to Die. 2002. 400p. mass mkt. 7.99 (*0-06-103097-X*); 2001. 336p. 25.00 (*0-06-019832-X*) Morrow/Avon. (Morrow, William & Co.).
—In the Midst of Death. l.t. ed. 1991. (Matthew Scudder Mystery Ser.: No. 2). pap. 15.95 o.p. (*0-7927-0601-3*, AS0192); 17.95 o.p. (*0-7451-8095-7*, AH0156) BBC Audiobooks America.
—In the Midst of Death. 1989. (Matthew Scudder Mystery Ser.: No. 3). 192p. mass mkt. 3.50 o.s.i (*0-515-08684-3*); 1984. mass mkt. 2.95 o.s.i (*0-515-08098-5*); 1983. mass mkt. 2.95 o.s.i (*0-515-07430-6*); 1982. mass mkt. 2.75 o.s.i (*0-515-06731-8*) Berkley Publishing Group. (Jove).
—In the Midst of Death. 1976. (Matthew Scudder Mystery Ser.: No. 3). pap. 1.25 o.p. (*0-440-14037-4*) Dell Publishing.
—In the Midst of Death. 2002. E-Book 7.50 (*0-06-052094-9*); E-Book 7.50 (*0-06-052097-3*); E-Book 7.50 (*0-06-052098-1*); E-Book 7.50 (*0-06-052096-5*) HarperCollins General Bks. Group. (PerfectBound).
—In the Midst of Death. 1992. (Matthew Scudder Mystery Ser.: No. 3). 272p. mass mkt. 7.50 (*0-380-76362-1*, Avon Bks.) Morrow/Avon.
—A Long Line of Dead Men. (Matthew Scudder Mystery Ser.: No. 12). 1999. 304p. pap. 12.50 (*0-380-80604-5*, Avon Bks.); 1996. 368p. mass mkt. 7.50 (*0-380-72024-8*, Avon Bks.); 1994. 20.00 o.p. (*0-688-12193-4*, Morrow, William & Co.) Morrow/Avon.
—Out on the Cutting Edge. l.t. ed. 1995. (Matthew Scudder Mystery Ser.: No. 7). 330p. pap. 19.95 o.p. (*0-7838-1177-2*, Macmillan Reference USA) Gale Group.
—Out on the Cutting Edge. l.t. ed. 1995. (Magna Large Print Ser.). 348p. o.p. (*0-7505-0761-6*) Magna Large Print Bks. GBR. *Dist:* Ulverscroft Large Print Canada, Ltd.
—Out on the Cutting Edge. (Matthew Scudder Mystery Ser.: No. 7). 1989. 256p. 17.95 o.p. (*0-688-09069-9*, Morrow, William & Co.); 1990. 352p. reprint ed. mass mkt. 6.99 (*0-380-70993-7*, Avon Bks.) Morrow/Avon.
—The Sins of the Fathers. l.t. ed. 1990. (Matthew Scudder Mystery Ser.: No. 1). 17.95 o.p. (*0-7451-9866-X*, C0616); pap. 15.95 o.p. (*0-7927-0317-0*, C0810) BBC Audiobooks America.
—The Sins of the Fathers. mass mkt. 2.95 o.s.i (*0-515-08685-1*); 1988. (Matthew Scudder Mystery Ser.: No. 1). mass mkt. 3.50 o.s.i (*0-515-09831-0*); 1984. mass mkt. 2.95 o.s.i (*0-515-08157-4*); 1983. mass mkt. 2.95 o.s.i (*0-515-07516-7*); 1982. mass mkt. 2.75 o.s.i (*0-515-06729-6*) Berkley Publishing Group. (Jove).
—The Sins of the Fathers. 2002. E-Book 7.50 (*0-06-052105-8*); E-Book 7.50 (*0-06-052103-1*); E-Book 7.50 (*0-06-052104-X*); E-Book 7.50 (*0-06-052108-2*) HarperCollins General Bks. Group. (PerfectBound).
—A Stab in the Dark. 1989. (Matthew Scudder Mystery Ser.: No. 4). 192p. mass mkt. 3.50 o.s.i (*0-515-09885-X*); 1985. mass mkt. 2.95 o.s.i (*0-515-08635-5*); 1984. mass mkt. 2.95 o.s.i (*0-515-08158-2*); 1983. mass mkt. 2.95 o.s.i (*0-515-07399-7*); 1982. mass mkt. 2.75 o.s.i (*0-515-06717-2*) Berkley Publishing Group. (Jove).
—A Stab in the Dark. 2002. E-Book 7.50 (*0-06-052091-4*); E-Book 7.50 (*0-06-052093-0*); E-Book 7.50 (*0-06-052092-2*); E-Book 7.50 (*0-06-052090-6*) HarperCollins General Bks. Group. (PerfectBound).
—A Stab in the Dark. (Matthew Scudder Mystery Ser.: No. 4). 1981. 192p. 10.95 o.p. (*0-87795-340-6*, Morrow, William & Co.); 2002. 304p. reprint ed. mass mkt. 7.50 (*0-380-71574-0*, Avon Bks.) Morrow/Avon.
—A Ticket to the Boneyard. l.t. ed. (Matthew Scudder Mystery Ser.: No. 8). 1992. pap. 21.95 o.p. (*0-7927-1089-4*, CS0293); 1991. 23.95 o.p. (*0-7927-1088-6*, CH0221) BBC Audiobooks America.
—A Ticket to the Boneyard. l.t. ed. 1995. (Magna Large Print Ser.). 404p. (*0-7505-0911-2*) Magna Large Print Bks. GBR. *Dist:* Ulverscroft Large Print Canada, Ltd.
—A Ticket to the Boneyard. (Matthew Scudder Mystery Ser.: No. 8). 1990. 270p. 18.95 o.p. (*0-688-09070-2*, Morrow, William & Co.); 1991. 384p. reprint ed. mass mkt. 7.50 (*0-380-70994-5*, Avon Bks.) Morrow/Avon.
—Time to Murder & Create. 1984. (Matthew Scudder Mystery Ser.: No. 2). 192p. mass mkt. 3.50 o.s.i (*0-515-08159-0*, Jove) Berkley Publishing Group.
—Time to Murder & Create. l.t. ed. 1985. (Matthew Scudder Mystery Ser.: No. 2). 12.50 o.p. (*0-8166-0137-2*, Macmillan Reference USA) Gale Group.
—Time to Murder & Create. 1991. (Matthew Scudder Mystery Ser.: No. 2). 304p. mass mkt. 7.50 (*0-380-76365-6*, Avon Bks.) Morrow/Avon.
—A Walk among the Tombstones. l.t. ed. 1993. (Matthew Scudder Mystery Ser.: No. 10). 431p. lib. bdg. 22.95 (*0-8161-5759-6*, Macmillan Reference USA) Gale Group.
—A Walk among the Tombstones. (Matthew Scudder Mystery Ser.: No. 10). 2000. 304p. pap. 12.50 (*0-380-81118-9*, Avon Bks.); 1992. 309p. 17.00 o.p. (*0-688-10350-2*, Morrow, William & Co.); 1993. 384p. reprint ed. mass mkt. 7.50 (*0-380-71375-6*, Avon Bks.) Morrow/Avon.
—A Walk among the Tombstones. 4.98 o.p. (*0-8317-8575-6*) Smithmark Pubs., Inc.
—When the Sacred Ginmill Closes. (Matthew Scudder Mystery Ser.: No. 6). 1990. mass mkt. 4.99 o.s.i (*0-515-10278-4*, Jove); 1987. 272p. 3.95 o.s.i (*0-441-88097-5*, Diamond Bks.) Berkley Publishing Group.
—When the Sacred Ginmill Closes. l.t. ed. 1987. (Matthew Scudder Mystery Ser.: No. 6). 361p. lib. bdg. 20.95 o.p. (*0-8161-4244-0*, Macmillan Reference USA) Gale Group.
—When the Sacred Ginmill Closes. 2002. E-Book 7.50 (*0-06-052099-X*); E-Book 7.50 (*0-06-052102-3*); E-Book 7.50 (*0-06-052101-5*); E-Book 7.50 (*0-06-052100-7*) HarperCollins General Bks. Group. (PerfectBound).
—When the Sacred Ginmill Closes. (Matthew Scudder Mystery Ser.: No. 6). 1997. 384p. mass mkt. 7.50 (*0-380-72825-7*, Avon Bks.); 1986. 15.95 o.p. (*0-87795-774-6*, Morrow, William & Co.) Morrow/Avon.

**SCULLY, DANA (FICTITIOUS CHARACTER)—FICTION**

Anderson, Kevin J. Antibodies. 1998. (X-Files Ser.: Vol. 5). 288p. mass mkt. 6.50 (*0-06-105624-3*, HarperEntertainment) Morrow/Avon.
—Ground Zero. 1996. 304p. mass mkt. 6.50 o.s.i (*0-06-105677-4*, HarperEntertainment); 1995. 80p. 22.00 o.p. (*0-06-105223-X*, Eos); 1995. 304p. 50.00 o.p. (*0-06-105248-5*, Eos) Morrow/Avon.
—Ground Zero: TV Guide Edition. 1995. (X-Files Ser.). 176p. mass mkt. 5.99 (*0-06-105847-5*) HarperCollins Pubs.
—Ruins. 1996. (X-Files Ser.). 304p. mass mkt. 22.00 o.p. (*0-06-105247-7*) HarperCollins Pubs.
—Ruins. (X-Files Ser.: Vol. 4). 1997. 272p. mass mkt. 6.50 o.s.i (*0-06-105736-3*, HarperEntertainment); 1996. 304p. 50.00 o.s.i (*0-06-105273-6*, Eos) Morrow/Avon.
Grant, Charles L. Goblins. 1994. (X-Files Ser.: Vol. 1). 288p. mass mkt. 6.50 (*0-06-105414-3*, HarperEntertainment) Morrow/Avon.
Mezrich, Ben. Skin. l.t. ed. 1999. (Science Fiction Ser.). 336p. 26.95 (*0-7838-8778-7*) Thorndike Pr.

**SCULLY, SHANE (FICTITIOUS CHARACTER)—FICTION**

Cannell, Stephen J. Hollywood Tough: A Shane Scully Novel. 2004. 448p. mass mkt. 6.99 (*0-312-98942-3*, St. Martin's Paperbacks) St. Martin's Pr.
Cannell, Stephen J. The Tin Collectors. 2001. E-Book 24.95 (*0-312-27411-4*) St. Martin's Pr.
—The Tin Collectors. abr. ed. 2004. audio compact disk 16.99 (*1-59355-669-1*, 5288, Brilliance Audio on CD Value Priced); 2001. audio 12.99 (*1-58788-351-1*, 2959, Paperback Nova Audio Bks.); 2001. audio 24.95 (*1-58788-119-5*, 2368, Nova Audio Bks.); 2001. audio compact disk 57.25 (*1-58788-185-3*, 2458); 2001. audio compact disk 29.95 (*1-58788-166-7*, 2425, CD); 2001. audio 73.25 (*1-58788-118-7*, 2367); 2001. audio 32.95 (*1-58788-117-9*, 2366, Brilliance Audio Unabridged) Brilliance Audio.
—The Tin Collectors. l.t. ed. 2001. (Wheeler Large Print Book Ser.). viii, 467p. 29.95 o.p. (*1-58724-080-7*, Wheeler Publishing, Inc.) Gale Group.
—The Tin Collectors. E-Book 24.95 (*0-312-70062-8*); 2001. viii, 389p. 24.95 o.p. (*0-312-26959-5*); 2002. 384p. reprint ed. mass mkt. 6.99 (*0-312-97951-7*, St. Martin's Paperbacks) St. Martin's Pr.
—Vertical Coffin: A Shane Scully Novel. 2004. 400p. 24.95 (*0-312-30425-0*) St. Martin's Pr.
—The Viking Funeral. abr. ed. 2002. audio 19.95 o.p. (*1-59086-022-5*, 3562, Nova Audio Bks.) Brilliance Audio.
—The Viking Funeral. l.t. ed. 2002. (Wheeler Large Print Book Ser.). 27.95 (*1-58724-169-2*, Wheeler Publishing, Inc.) Gale Group.
—The Viking Funeral. E-Book 18.95 (*0-312-70409-7*); 2002. 384p. mass mkt. 6.99 (*0-312-98343-3*, St. Martin's Paperbacks); 2002. 400p. 24.95 (*0-312-26960-9*) St. Martin's Pr.

**SCURO, PETER (FICTITIOUS CHARACTER)—FICTION**

Sanders, Lawrence. The Seduction of Peter S. 1986. 400p. mass mkt. 4.95 o.s.i (*0-425-09314-X*); 1984. mass mkt. 4.95 o.s.i (*0-425-07317-3*); 1984. mass mkt. 3.95 o.s.i (*0-425-07019-0*); 1983. mass mkt. 3.50 o.s.i (*0-425-07000-X*); 1990. 400p. reprint ed. mass mkt. 7.50 (*0-425-12462-2*) Berkley Publishing Group.
—The Seduction of Peter S. 1983. 384p. 15.95 o.s.i (*0-399-12820-4*, G. P. Putnam's Sons) Penguin Putnam Bks. for Young Readers.

**SEACOURT, ALEX (FICTITIOUS CHARACTER)—FICTION**

Davis, Robert. The Doomsday Kiss. 1998. 450p. 24.95 (*1-890248-02-9*) Horizon Pr.
—The Plutonium Murders. 1997. 392p. pap. 24.95 (*1-890248-00-2*) Horizon Pr.

**SEAFORT, NICHOLAS (FICTITIOUS CHARACTER)—FICTION**

Feintuch, David. Challenger's Hope. 1995. (Seafort Saga Ser.). 416p. reprint ed. mass mkt. 6.99 (*0-446-60097-0*) Warner Bks., Inc.
—Children of Hope. 2001. 512p. 23.95 o.s.i (*0-441-00804-6*) Ace Bks.
—Fisherman's Hope. 1996. (Seafort Saga Ser.: Vol. 4). 496p. reprint ed. mass mkt. 6.99 (*0-446-60099-7*) Warner Bks., Inc.
—Midshipman's Hope. 1994. (Seafort Saga Ser.). 400p. reprint ed. mass mkt. 6.99 (*0-446-60096-2*) Warner Bks., Inc.
—Patriarch's Hope. 1999. 528p. 34.00 o.p. (*0-446-52458-1*) Warner Bks., Inc.
—The Patriarch's Hope. 2000. (Seafort Saga Ser.). 528p. mass mkt. 6.50 (*0-446-60846-7*) Warner Bks., Inc.
—Prisoner's Hope. 1995. (Seafort Saga Ser.). 528p. reprint ed. mass mkt. 6.99 (*0-446-60098-9*) Warner Bks., Inc.
—Voices of Hope. 1996. 544p. reprint ed. mass mkt. 6.99 (*0-446-60333-3*) Warner Bks., Inc.

**SEETON, MISS (FICTITIOUS CHARACTER)—FICTION**

Carvic, Heron. Miss Seeton Draws the Line. l.t. ed. 1991. pap. 10.95 o.p. (*0-7927-0097-X*, C0003) BBC Audiobooks America.
—Miss Seeton Draws the Line. 1988. mass mkt. 4.50 o.s.i (*0-425-11097-4*) Berkley Publishing Group.
—Miss Seeton Sings. l.t. ed. 1991. 19.95 o.p. (*0-7927-0690-0*, CH008); pap. 17.95 o.p. (*0-7927-0691-9*, CS0110) BBC Audiobooks America.
—Miss Seeton Sings. Fowler, Kathy, ed. 1988. 208p. reprint ed. mass mkt. 4.50 o.s.i (*0-425-10714-0*) Berkley Publishing Group.
—Odds on Miss Seeton. l.t. ed. 1991. 18.95 o.p. (*0-7927-0933-0*, CH0145); pap. 19.95 o.p. (*0-7927-0934-9*, CS0242) BBC Audiobooks America.
—Odds on Miss Seeton. 1989. mass mkt. 4.50 o.s.i (*0-425-11307-8*) Berkley Publishing Group.
—Odds on Miss Seeton. 1981. 279p. reprint ed. lib. bdg. 16.95 o.p. (*0-89966-307-9*) Buccaneer Bks., Inc.
—Odds on Miss Seeton. 1975. (Harper Novel of Suspense Ser.). 160p. 7.95 o.p. (*0-06-010654-9*) HarperCollins Pubs.
—Picture Miss Seeton. (Black Dagger Crime Ser.). 1993. 176p. 16.50 o.p. (*0-7451-8615-7*, Black Dagger); 1991. 12.95 o.p. (*0-7927-0041-4*, 476) BBC Audiobooks America.
—Picture Miss Seeton. 1988. (Heron Carvic's Miss Seeton Ser.). mass mkt. 4.50 o.s.i (*0-425-10929-1*) Berkley Publishing Group.
—Witch Miss Seeton. l.t. ed. 1990. pap. 16.95 o.p. (*0-7927-0428-2*, C0486); 18.95 o.p. (*0-7927-0427-4*, C0258) BBC Audiobooks America.
—Witch Miss Seeton. 1988. 192p. mass mkt. 4.50 o.s.i (*0-425-10713-2*) Berkley Publishing Group.
Charles, Hampton. Miss Seeton at the Helm. 1990. mass mkt. 3.99 o.s.i (*0-425-12264-6*) Berkley Publishing Group.
—Miss Seeton at the Helm. l.t. ed. 1998. (G. K. Hall Nightingale Ser.). pap. 18.95 o.p. (*0-8161-5926-2*, Macmillan Reference USA) Gale Group.
Crane, Hamilton. Bonjour, Miss Seeton. (Heron Carvic's Miss Seeton Ser.). 272p. 1997. 21.95 o.s.i (*0-425-15968-X*, Prime Crime); 1998. reprint ed. mass mkt. 5.99 o.s.i (*0-425-16534-5*) Berkley Publishing Group.
—Hands up, Miss Seeton. 1992. mass mkt. 5.50 o.s.i (*0-425-13132-7*) Berkley Publishing Group.
—Hands up, Miss Seeton. l.t. ed. 2001. (Heron Carvic's Miss Seeton Ser.). 335p. 28.95 (*0-7862-3544-6*); 351p. (*0-7540-4669-9*); 351p. (*0-7540-4670-2*) Thorndike Pr.
—Miss Seeton by Moonlight. 1992. mass mkt. 4.50 o.s.i (*0-425-13265-X*) Berkley Publishing Group.
—Miss Seeton by Moonlight. l.t. ed. 2000. (Mystery Ser.). 347p. 27.95 o.p. (*0-7862-2481-9*); (*0-7540-4140-9*); (*0-7540-4141-7*) Thorndike Pr.
—Miss Seeton Cracks the Case. 1991. mass mkt. 4.99 o.s.i (*0-425-12676-5*) Berkley Publishing Group.
—Miss Seeton Cracks the Case. l.t. ed. 1999. (Thorndike Mystery Ser.). o.p. (*0-7862-1766-9*, Macmillan Reference USA) Gale Group.
—Miss Seeton Goes to Bat. l.t. ed. 1999. (Mystery Ser.). 365p. 27.95 (*0-7862-2065-1*); (*0-7540-3898-X*); (*0-7540-3897-1*) Thorndike Pr.
—Miss Seeton Paints the Town. 1991. mass mkt. 4.99 o.s.i (*0-425-12848-2*) Berkley Publishing Group.
—Miss Seeton Paints the Town. l.t. ed. 2000. (Mystery Ser.). 352p. 27.95 (*0-7862-2339-1*) Thorndike Pr.
—Miss Seeton Rocks the Cradle. 1992. 208p. mass mkt. 4.99 o.s.i (*0-425-13400-8*) Berkley Publishing Group.
—Miss Seeton Rocks the Cradle. l.t. ed. 2000. (Mystery Ser.). 386p. 27.95 (*0-7862-2840-7*) Thorndike Pr.
—Miss Seeton Rules. 272p. 1995. mass mkt. 4.99 o.s.i (*0-425-15006-2*); 1994. 18.95 o.p. (*0-425-14354-6*) Berkley Publishing Group. (Prime Crime).
—Miss Seeton Undercover. 1994. 272p. mass mkt. 4.99 o.s.i (*0-425-14405-4*); 17.95 o.p. (*0-425-14137-3*) Berkley Publishing Group.
—Miss Seeton's Finest Hour. 1999. (Heron Carvic's Miss Seeton Ser.). 272p. mass mkt. 5.99 o.s.i (*0-425-17026-8*, Prime Crime) Berkley Publishing Group.
—Sold to Miss Seeton. 1996. mass mkt. 5.99 o.s.i (*0-425-15462-9*); 1995. 272p. 19.95 o.p. (*0-425-14936-6*, Prime Crime) Berkley Publishing Group.
—Sweet Miss Seeton. (Heron Carvic's Miss Seeton Ser.). 1996. 272p. 21.95 o.p. (*0-425-15471-8*); 1997. 256p. reprint ed. mass mkt. 5.99 o.s.i (*0-425-15962-0*) Berkley Publishing Group. (Prime Crime).
Crane, Hamilton & Carvic, Heron. Miss Seeton Goes to Bat. 1993. 208p. mass mkt. 4.99 o.s.i (*0-425-13576-4*) Berkley Publishing Group.

**SEFERIUS, CLAUDIA (FICTITIOUS CHARACTER)—FICTION**

Todd, Marilyn. Dream Boat. 2002. 256p. 26.99 (*0-7278-5818-1*) Severn Hse. Pubs., Ltd.
—Man Eater. 2002. 384p. mass mkt. 11.95 (*0-330-35407-8*) Pan Bks. Ltd. GBR. *Dist:* Trafalgar Square.
—Virgin Territory. l.t. unabr. ed. 1997. 351p. 32.50 o.p. (*0-7531-5529-X*, 15529X) ISIS Large Print Bks. GBR. *Dist:* Ulverscroft Large Print Bks., Ltd., Ulverscroft Large Print Canada, Ltd.
—Wolf Whistle. 2002. 356p. mass mkt. 11.95 (*0-330-37199-1*) Pan Bks. Ltd. GBR. *Dist:* Trafalgar Square.

**SEGALLA, NICHOLAS (FICTITIOUS CHARACTER)—FICTION**

Dukthas, Ann. In the Time of the Poisoned Queen. 1998. (Nicholas Segalla Time-Travel Mystery Ser.). 273p. 22.95 o.p. (*0-312-18030-6*, Saint Martin's Minotaur) St. Martin's Pr.
—The Prince Lost to Time. 1996. 229p. mass mkt. 5.99 (*0-312-95843-9*, St. Martin's Paperbacks); 1995. 240p. 21.95 o.p. (*0-312-13592-0*, Saint Martin's Minotaur) St. Martin's Pr.
—A Time for the Death of a King. 1995. 226p. mass mkt. 4.99 (*0-312-95613-4*, St. Martin's Paperbacks); 1994. viii, 226p. 19.95 o.p. (*0-312-11439-7*, Saint Martin's Minotaur) St. Martin's Pr.
—Time of Murder at Mayerling. 1996. 224p. text 20.95 o.p. (*0-312-14676-0*, Saint Martin's Minotaur) St. Martin's Pr.

**SELAR (FICTITIOUS CHARACTER)—FICTION**

David, Peter. Dark Allies. 1999. (Star Trek Ser.: No. 8). (Illus.). 288p. pap. 6.50 (*0-671-02080-3*, Star Trek) Simon & Schuster.
—Excalibur: Renaissance. 2000. (Star Trek Ser.: No. 10). 288p. pap. 6.99 (*0-671-04239-4*, Star Trek) Simon & Schuster.
—House of Cards; Into the Void; The Two-Front War; End Game. 1998. (Star Trek Ser.: Nos. 1-4). 704p. 15.00 (*0-671-01978-3*, Star Trek) Simon & Schuster.
—Into the Void. 1997. (Star Trek Ser.: No. 2). (Illus.). 176p. pap. 3.99 (*0-671-01396-3*, Star Trek) Simon & Schuster.
—Martyr. 1998. (Star Trek Ser.: No. 5). (Illus.). 288p. pap. 6.50 (*0-671-02036-6*, Star Trek) Simon & Schuster.
—The Two-Front War. 1997. (Star Trek Ser.: No. 3). 304p. per. 3.99 (*0-671-01397-1*, Star Trek) Simon & Schuster.

**SELDON, HARI (FICTITIOUS CHARACTER)—FICTION**

Asimov, Isaac. Foundation & Empire. 1986. (Foundation Ser.: Bk. 2). 304p. mass mkt. 5.95 o.s.i (*0-345-33628-3*); 1984. mass mkt. 2.95 o.s.i (*0-345-31799-8*); 1983. mass mkt. 2.75 o.s.i (*0-345-30900-6*) Ballantine Bks. (Del Rey).

—Foundation & Empire. 2004. 288p. 24.00 (*0-553-80372-7*, Spectra); 1991. 320p. mass mkt. 7.99 (*0-553-29337-0*) Bantam Bks.

—Foundation & Empire. 2002. audio 64.00 (*0-7366-8957-5*); 2002. audio compact disk 72.00 (*0-7366-9238-X*); 1979. audio 48.00 (*0-7366-0236-4*, 1232) Books on Tape, Inc.

—Foundation & Empire. 1963. 6.95 o.p. (*0-385-05045-3*) Doubleday Publishing.

—Foundation & Empire. unabr. ed. audio 12.95 o.p. (*0-89845-154-X*, SWC 1661, Caedmon) HarperTrade.

—Foundation & Empire. abr. ed. 1991. audio 14.95 o.s.i (*0-553-45261-4*, RH Audio) Random Hse. Audio Publishing Group.

—Foundation & Empire. 1991. 13.04 (*0-606-19274-3*) Turtleback Bks.

—Fundacion. 5th ed. 1998. (Jet de Plaza & Janes Ser.). (SPA.). pap. 9.50 (*84-01-49678-0*, JP9128) Plaza & Janés Editories, S.A. ESP. *Dist:* Lectorum Pubns., Inc.

—Fundacion. 2002. (SPA.). 264p. mass mkt. 6.95 (*1-4000-0082-3*) Random Hse., Inc.

—Fundacion. 1998. (SPA.). 15.55 (*0-606-21870-X*) Turtleback Bks.

—Fundacion e Imperio. 3rd ed. 1998. (Jet de Plaza & Janes Ser.). Orig. Title: Foundation & Empire. (SPA.). 336p. (*84-01-46332-7*) Plaza & Janés Editories, S.A.

—Fundacion e Imperio. 1994. Orig. Title: Foundation & Empire. (SPA.). 256p. 10.50 (*84-01-49652-7*) Plaza & Janés Editories, S.A. ESP. *Dist:* Astran, Inc.

Bear, Greg. Foundation & Chaos. (Second Foundation Trilogy : Vol. 2). 1999. 416p. mass mkt. 6.99 (*0-06-105640-5*); 1998. 352p. 24.00 o.s.i (*0-06-105242-6*) Morrow/Avon. (Eos).

Benford, Gregory. Foundation's Fear. 1998. (Second Foundation Trilogy : Vol. 2). 624p. mass mkt. 7.50 (*0-06-105638-3*); 1997. 400p. 23.00 o.p. (*0-06-105243-4*) Morrow/Avon. (Eos).

Brin, David. Foundation's Triumph. 2000. (Second Foundation Trilogy : Vol. 3). 400p. mass mkt. 7.50 (*0-06-105639-1*, Perennial) HarperTrade.

**SEREGE, LUJAN (FICTITIOUS CHARACTER)—FICTION**

Thornley, Diann. Dominion's Reach. 1999. (United Worlds Ser.: 3). (Illus.). 339p. pap. text 6.99 (*0-8125-5098-6*); 1997. 320p. 23.95 o.p. (*0-312-86286-5*) Doherty, Tom Assocs., LLC. (Tor Bks.).

—Echoes of Issel. 1996. 352p. 23.95 o.p. (*0-312-86087-0*); Vol. 2. 1997. (Saga of the Unified Worlds Ser.: Vol. 2). 349p. mass mkt. 5.99 (*0-8125-5097-8*) Doherty, Tom Assocs., LLC. (Tor Bks.).

—Ganwold's Child. 1996. (Saga of the Unified Worlds Ser.: Vol. 1). (Illus.). 349p. mass mkt. 5.99 (*0-8125-5095-1*); 1995. 352p. 22.95 o.p. (*0-312-85843-4*) Doherty, Tom Assocs., LLC. (Tor Bks.).

**SEREGIL OF RHIMINEE (FICTITIOUS CHARACTER)—FICTION**

Flewelling, Lynn. Luck in the Shadows. 1996. (Nightrunner Ser.: Bk. 1). 496p. mass mkt. 6.99 (*0-553-57542-2*) Bantam Bks.

—Stalking Darkness. 1997. (Nightrunner Ser.: No. 2). 512p. mass mkt. 6.99 (*0-553-57543-0*, Spectra) Bantam Bks.

—Traitor's Moon. 1999. (Nightrunner Ser.: No. 3). 560p. mass mkt. 6.99 (*0-553-57725-5*) Bantam Bks.

**SERRANO, HERIS (FICTITIOUS CHARACTER)—FICTION**

Moon, Elizabeth. Hunting Party. 1993. 384p. reprint ed. pap. 6.99 (*0-671-72176-3*) Baen Bks.

—Once a Hero. 416p. 1999. per. 1.99 (*0-671-57842-1*); 1997. 21.00 o.s.i (*0-671-87769-0*); 1998. reprint ed. mass mkt. 7.99 (*0-671-87871-9*) Baen Bks.

—Sporting Chance. 1994. 416p. reprint ed. pap. 7.99 (*0-671-87619-8*) Baen Bks.

—Winning Colors. 1995. 416p. reprint ed. pap. 6.99 (*0-671-87677-5*) Baen Bks.

**SEVEN OF NINE (FICTITIOUS CHARACTER)—FICTION**

Carey, Diane L. Equinox. 1999. (Star Trek Voyager Ser.). 272p. (J). pap. 6.99 (*0-671-04295-5*, Star Trek) Simon & Schuster.

Friedman, Michael Jan. The Television Episode: Day of Honor. 1997. (Star Trek Voyager). 224p. mass mkt. 5.99 (*0-671-01981-3*, Star Trek) Simon & Schuster.

Galanter, Dave & Brodeur, Greg. Battle Lines. 1999. (Star Trek Voyager Ser.: No. 18). 264p. mass mkt. 6.50 o.s.i (*0-671-00259-7*, Star Trek) Simon & Schuster.

Golden, Christie. Seven of Nine. 1998. (Star Trek Voyager Ser.: No. 16). 233p. mass mkt. 6.50 (*0-671-02491-4*, Star Trek) Simon & Schuster.

Kotani, Eric & Smith, Dean Wesley. Death of a Neutron Star. 1999. (Star Trek Voyager Ser.: No. 17). 263p. mass mkt. 6.50 o.s.i (*0-671-00425-5*, Star Trek) Simon & Schuster.

Roddenberry, Gene & Parker. Becoming Human: The Seven of Nine Saga. 1998. (Star Trek Scriptbooks: Vol. 2). (Illus.). 464p. pap. 16.00 (*0-671-03447-2*, Star Trek) Simon & Schuster.

Taylor, Jeri. Pathways. 1998. (Star Trek Voyager Ser.). (Illus.). 448p. 23.00 o.s.i (*0-671-00346-1*, Star Trek) Simon & Schuster.

**SEWELL, HITCHCOCK (FICTITIOUS CHARACTER)—FICTION**

Cockey, Tim. Backstabber. 2004. 368p. 23.95 (*0-7868-6713-2*) Hyperion Pr.

—Hearse of a Different Color. 2003. (*1-57490-536-8*, Beeler Large Print Bks.) Beeler, Thomas T. Publisher.

—Hearse of a Different Color. 2002. E-Book 5.95 (*0-7868-6955-0*); 2001. 318p. 23.95 (*0-7868-6571-7*); 2003. 416p. reprint ed. mass mkt. 7.99 (*0-7868-8963-2*) Hyperion Pr.

—The Hearse You Came in On. l.t. ed. 28.95 (*1-58724-216-8*, Wheeler Publishing, Inc.) Gale Group.

—The Hearse You Came in On. 2002. E-Book 5.95 (*0-7868-6961-5*); 2000. viii, 308p. 22.95 (*0-7868-6570-9*); 2003. 416p. reprint ed. mass mkt. 6.99 (*0-7868-8962-4*) Hyperion Pr.

—Murder in the Hearse Degree. 2003. 440p. 30.95 (*1-58724-428-4*) Gale Group.

—Murder in the Hearse Degree. 2004. mass mkt. 6.99 (*0-7868-8997-7*); 2003. 336p. 22.95 (*0-7868-6712-4*) Hyperion Pr.

**SHADE, RENE (FICTITIOUS CHARACTER)—FICTION**

Woodrell, Daniel. Muscle for the Wing: A Rene Shade Mystery. 1988. 16.95 o.p. (*0-8050-0788-1*) Holt, Henry & Co.

—Muscle for the Wing: A Rene Shade Mystery. 1990. 224p. mass mkt. 4.50 o.p. (*0-451-16569-1*, Signet Bks.) NAL.

—Muscle for the Wing: A Rene Shade Mystery. 1998. 224p. pap. 14.00 (*0-671-00137-X*, Pocket) Simon & Schuster.

—The Ones You Do. 1992. 224p. 19.95 o.p. (*0-8050-0972-8*) Holt, Henry & Co.

—The Ones You Do. 1993. 256p. mass mkt. 4.99 o.p. (*0-451-40385-1*, Onyx) NAL.

—The Ones You Do. 1998. 224p. pap. 17.95 (*0-671-00135-3*, Pocket) Simon & Schuster.

—Under the Bright Lights. 1986. o.p. (*0-03-008514-4*) Holt, Henry & Co.

—Under the Bright Lights. 1988. 192p. pap. 3.50 (*0-380-70456-0*, Avon Bks.) Morrow/Avon.

**SHADER, SUSAN (FICTITIOUS CHARACTER)—FICTION**

Glass, Joseph. Blood: A Susan Shader Novel. 2000. (Susan Shader Novels Ser.). 400p. 24.00 (*0-684-85963-7*, Simon & Schuster) Simon & Schuster.

—Eyes. 1999. mass mkt. 6.99 o.s.i (*0-449-00512-7*, Fawcett) Ballantine Bks.

**SHADOW (FICTITIOUS CHARACTER: LOGSTON)—FICTION**

Cox, J. Randolph. Man of Magic & Mystery: A Guide to the Work of Walter B. Gibson. 1989. (Illus.). 416p. 41.50 (*0-8108-2192-3*) Scarecrow Pr., Inc.

Eisgruber, Frank, Jr. Gangland's Doom: The Shadow of the Pulps. 1985. (Pulp & Dime Novel Studies: No. 1). (Illus.). 64p. reprint ed. 19.95 o.p. (*0-930261-71-2*); pap. 9.95 o.p. (*0-930261-74-7*) Millefleurs.

Logston, Anne. Shadow. 1991. mass mkt. 3.99 o.s.i (*0-441-75989-0*) Ace Bks.

—Shadow. 2002. pap. (*0-7592-2730-6*); E-Book (*0-7592-2726-8*); E-Book (*0-7592-2725-X*); E-Book (*0-7592-2727-6*) ereads.com.

—Shadow Dance. 1992. 224p. (Orig.). mass mkt. 4.99 o.s.i (*0-441-75990-4*) Ace Bks.

—Shadow Hunt. 1992. mass mkt. 4.50 o.s.i (*0-441-76007-4*) Ace Bks.

Shimeld, Thomas J. Walter B. Gibson & the Shadow. 2003. (Illus.). 152p. lib. bdg. 45.00 (*0-7864-1466-9*) McFarland & Co., Inc. Pubs.

**SHAKESPEARE, WILLIAM, 1564-1616—FICTION**

Berkman, Pamela Rafael. Her Infinite Variety: Stories of Shakespeare & the Women He Loved. 2001. 176p. pap. 12.00 (*0-7432-1255-X*, Touchstone) Simon & Schuster.

Burgess, Anthony. Nothing Like the Sun: A Story of Shakespeare's Love-Life. 1996. 240p. pap. 12.00 (*0-393-31507-X*) Norton, W. W. & Co., Inc.

Gordon, Alan. Thirteenth Night. 2000. (Illus.). 256p. mass mkt. 5.99 (*0-312-97684-4*, St. Martin's Paperbacks); 1998. 248p. 23.95 (*0-312-20035-8*, Saint Martin's Minotaur) St. Martin's Pr.

Hawke, Simon. Much Ado about Murder. E-Book 23.95 (*0-312-70933-1*, Tor Bks.); 2004. 240p. pap. 13.95 (*0-7653-0836-3*, Forge Bks.); 2002. 304p. 23.95 (*0-7653-0241-1*, Forge Bks.) Doherty, Tom Assocs., LLC.

—The Slaying of the Shrew. 2001. 255p. 23.95 (*0-312-87894-X*, Forge Bks.) Doherty, Tom Assocs., LLC.

Hoyt, Sarah A. All Night Awake. 2003. 368p. mass mkt. 6.50 (*0-441-01112-8*); 2002. 320p. 22.95 (*0-441-00973-5*) Ace Bks.

—Any Man So Daring. 2003. 336p. 23.95 (*0-441-01092-X*) Ace Bks.

Jong, Erica. Serenissima. unabr. ed. 1987. audio 17.95 o.p. (*0-930435-33-8*, 389); audio 57.25 o.p. (*1-56100-028-0*, 571) Brilliance Audio.

—Serenissima. 1988. 384p. mass mkt. 4.95 o.s.i (*0-440-20104-7*) Dell Publishing.

—Serenissima. 1987. 225p. 16.95 o.p. (*0-395-42922-6*) Houghton Mifflin Co.

—Serenissima. 1989. 3.99 o.p. (*0-517-68552-3*) Random Hse. Value Publishing.

Kaplow, Robert. Me & Orson Welles: A Novel. 2003. 278p. 18.50 (*1-931561-49-4*) MacAdam/Cage Publishing, Inc.

Nye, Robert. The Late Mr. Shakespeare. 1999. 400p. 25.95 (*1-55970-469-1*) Arcade Publishing, Inc.

—The Late Mr. Shakespeare. 2000. 416p. 13.95 (*0-14-028952-6*) Viking Penguin.

—Mrs. Shakespeare: The Complete Works. 2000. 324p. 23.95 (*1-55970-552-3*) Arcade Publishing, Inc.

O'Sullivan, Maurice J., Jr., ed. Shakespeare's Other Lives: An Anthology of Fictional Depictions of the Bard. 1995. text 35.00 (*0-89341-680-0*, Longwood Academic) Hollowbrook Publishing.

—Shakespeare's Other Lives: An Anthology of Fictional Depictions of the Bard. 1997. (Illus.). 231p. lib. bdg. 39.95 (*0-7864-0335-7*) McFarland & Co., Inc. Pubs.

Para, Robert. Shakespeare's Confession. 1996. 530p. pap. 19.95 (*1-889120-02-2*) StarsEnd Creations.

Robinson, Bruce. The Peculiar Memories of Thomas Penman. 1998. 256p. 29.95 (*0-7475-3614-7*) Chronicle Bks. LLC.

—The Peculiar Memories of Thomas Penman. 2000. 288p. pap. 13.00 (*0-06-095540-6*, Perennial) HarperTrade.

—The Peculiar Memories of Thomas Penman. 1999. 278p. 24.95 (*0-87951-914-2*) Overlook Pr., The.

Shirley, Edna I. As I Like It: A Tale of Shakespeare & His Associates. 1996. 196p. pap. 16.95 o.p. (*1-85756-295-X*) Janus Publishing Co. GBR. *Dist:* Paul & Co. Pubs. Consortium, Inc.

Simak, Clifford D. The Goblin Reservation. 1993. 192p. mass mkt. 3.95 (*0-88184-897-2*, Carroll & Graf Pubs.) Avalon Publishing Group.

—The Goblin Reservation. 1977. 1.25 o.s.i (*0-425-03399-6*) Berkley Publishing Group.

Tiffany, Grace. My Father Had a Daughter: Judith Shakespeare's Tale. 2003. 304p. 21.95 (*0-425-19003-X*) Berkley Publishing Group.

**SHALLOT, ROGER, SIR (FICTITIOUS CHARACTER)—FICTION**

Clynes, Michael, pseud. A Brood of Vipers: Being the Fourth Journal of Sir Roger Shallot Concerning Certain Wicked Conspiracies & Horrible Murders Perpetrated in the Reign of King Henry VIII. unabr. ed. 1998. audio 76.95 (*1-85903-164-1*) Magna Story Sound GBR. *Dist:* Ulverscroft Large Print Bks., Ltd.

—A Brood of Vipers: Being the Fourth Journal of Sir Roger Shallot Concerning Certain Wicked Conspiracies & Horrible Murders Perpetrated in the Reign of King Henry VIII. 1995. 256p. 21.95 o.p. (*0-312-13938-1*, Saint Martin's Minotaur) St. Martin's Pr.

—The Gallows Murders: Being the Fifth Journal of Sir Roger Shallot Concerning Certain Wicked Conspiracies & Horrible Murders Perpetrated in the Reign of King Henry VIII. 1996. 256p. text 21.95 o.p. (*0-312-14605-1*, Saint Martin's Minotaur) St. Martin's Pr.

—The Gallows Murders: Being the Fifth Journal of Sir Roger Shallot Concerning Certain Wicked Conspiracies & Horrible Murders Perpetrated in the Reign of King Henry VIII. l.t. ed. 1997. (Large Print Ser.). 448p. 29.99 (*0-7089-3789-6*, Ulverscroft) Thorpe, F. A. Pubs. GBR. *Dist:* Ulverscroft Large Print Bks., Ltd., Ulverscroft Large Print Canada, Ltd.

—The Grail Murders: Being the Third Journal of Sir Roger Shallot Concerning Certain Wicked Conspiracies & Horrible Murders Perpetrated in the Reign of King Henry the Eighth. unabr. ed. 1998. audio 76.95 (*1-85903-158-7*) Magna Story Sound GBR. *Dist:* Ulverscroft Large Print Bks., Ltd.

—The Grail Murders: Being the Third Journal of Sir Roger Shallot Concerning Certain Wicked Conspiracies & Horrible Murders Perpetrated in the Reign of King Henry the Eighth. 1994. 256p. reprint ed. 21.00 (*1-883402-49-2*, Scribner) Simon & Schuster.

—The Poisoned Chalice: Being the Second Journal of Sir Roger Shallot Concerning Wicked Conspiracies & Horrible Murders Perpetrated in the Reign of King Henry VIII. unabr. ed. 1998. audio 76.95 (*1-85903-137-4*) Magna Story Sound GBR. *Dist:* Ulverscroft Large Print Bks., Ltd.

—The Poisoned Chalice: Being the Second Journal of Sir Roger Shallot Concerning Wicked Conspiracies & Horrible Murders Perpetrated in the Reign of King Henry VIII. 1994. 288p. reprint ed. 20.00 (*1-883402-48-4*, Scribner) Simon & Schuster.

—The White Rose Murders: Being the First Journal of Sir Roger Shallot Concerning Wicked Conspiracies & Horrible Murders Perpetrated in the Reign of King Henry VIII. unabr. ed. 1998. audio 76.95 (*1-85903-113-7*) Magna Story Sound GBR. *Dist:* Ulverscroft Large Print Bks., Ltd.

—The White Rose Murders: Being the First Journal of Sir Roger Shallot Concerning Wicked Conspiracies & Horrible Murders Perpetrated in the Reign of King Henry VIII. l.t. ed. 1993. viii, 244p. 18.95 o.p. (*0-312-08920-1*, Saint Martin's Minotaur) St. Martin's Pr.

—The White Rose Murders: Being the First Journal of Sir Roger Shallot Concerning Wicked Conspiracies & Horrible Murders Perpetrated in the Reign of King Henry VIII. l.t. ed. 1995. (Ulverscroft Large Print Ser.). 464p. 29.99 o.p. (*0-7089-3218-5*, Ulverscroft) Thorpe, F. A. Pubs. GBR. *Dist:* Ulverscroft Large Print Bks., Ltd., Ulverscroft Large Print Canada, Ltd.

**SHANAHAN, DEETS (FICTITIOUS CHARACTER)—FICTION**

Tierney, Ronald. The Concrete Pillow. 1997. (Mystery Ser.). 256p. per. (*0-373-26230-2*, 1-26230-2, Worldwide Library) Harlequin Enterprises, Ltd.

—The Concrete Pillow. 1995. 230p. 21.00 o.p. (*0-312-11762-0*, Saint Martin's Minotaur) St. Martin's Pr.

—The Steel Web. l.t. ed. 1993. (General Ser.). 321p. pap. 17.95 (*0-8161-5458-9*, Macmillan Reference USA) Gale Group.

**SHAND, RUSSELL (FICTITIOUS CHARACTER)—FICTION**

Rinehart, Mary Roberts. The Wall. 1992. (Black Dagger Crime Ser.). 328p. reprint ed. 14.95 o.p. (*0-86220-831-9*) Chivers Pr. GBR. *Dist:* BBC Audiobooks America.

—The Wall. 1998. 352p. mass mkt. 5.99 (*1-57566-310-4*); 1989. 352p. mass mkt. 3.99 o.s.i (*0-8217-4017-2*, Zebra Bks.); 1989. mass mkt. 3.50 o.p. (*0-8217-2560-2*, Zebra Bks.) Kensington Publishing Corp.

**SHANDY, HELEN (FICTITIOUS CHARACTER)—FICTION**

MacLeod, Charlotte. The Corpse in Oozak's Pond. 1987. 224p. 15.45 o.p. (*0-89296-188-0*) Mysterious Pr.

—The Corpse in Oozak's Pond. 1989. 2.99 o.p. (*0-517-00184-5*) Random Hse. Value Publishing.

—The Corpse in Oozak's Pond. 1988. 203p. mass mkt. 5.99 o.p. (*0-445-40683-6*, Mysterious Pr. Paperback Bks.) Warner Bks., Inc.

—Curse of the Giant Hogweed. 1986. (Peter Shandy Ser.). 176p. pap. 3.50 (*0-380-70051-4*, Avon Bks.) Morrow/Avon.

—Exit the Milkman. l.t. ed. 1996. 22.95 o.p. (*1-56895-388-7*, Wheeler Publishing, Inc.) Gale Group.

—Exit the Milkman. 1996. 364p. 21.95 o.s.i (*0-89296-572-X*) Mysterious Pr.

—Exit the Milkman. 1997. 256p. mass mkt. 5.99 o.p. (*0-446-40398-9*) Warner Bks., Inc.

—Exit the Milkman. 2003. 320p. pap. 6.99 (*0-7434-4537-6*) ibooks, Inc.

—The Luck Runs Out. 1981. 192p. pap. 3.50 (*0-380-54171-8*, Avon Bks.) Morrow/Avon.

—An Owl Too Many. l.t. ed. 1991. (General Ser.). 355p. lib. bdg. 20.95 (*0-8161-5235-7*, Macmillan Reference USA) Gale Group.

—An Owl Too Many. 1991. 17.95 o.p. (*0-89296-431-6*) Mysterious Pr.

—An Owl Too Many. 1992. 240p. mass mkt. 4.99 o.p. (*0-446-40101-3*, Mysterious Pr. Paperback Bks.) Warner Bks., Inc.

—Rest You Merry. 1979. (General Ser.). lib. bdg. 13.50 o.p. (*0-8161-3000-0*, Macmillan Reference USA) Gale Group.

—Rest You Merry. 1980. 224p. reprint ed. mass mkt. 4.99 o.p. (*0-380-47530-8*, Avon Bks.) Morrow/Avon.

—Something in the Water. 1994. 272p. 18.95 o.s.i (*0-89296-430-8*) Mysterious Pr.

—Something in the Water. 1995. 240p. mass mkt. 5.50 o.p. (*0-446-40446-2*, Mysterious Pr. Paperback Bks.) Warner Bks., Inc.

—Something the Cat Dragged In. l.t. ed. 1984. (Nightingale Ser.). 10.95 o.p. (0-8161-3710-2, Macmillan Reference USA) Gale Group.
—Something the Cat Dragged In. 1984. 208p. mass mkt. 3.99 (0-380-69096-9, Avon Bks.) Morrow/Avon.
—Vane Pursuit: A Peter Shandy Mystery. l.t. ed. 1990. 368p. lib. bdg. 19.95 o.p. (0-8161-4850-3, Macmillan Reference USA) Gale Group.
—Vane Pursuit: A Peter Shandy Mystery. 1989. 15.95 o.p. (0-89296-369-7) Mysterious Pr.
—Vane Pursuit: A Peter Shandy Mystery. 1990. 224p. mass mkt. 5.50 o.p. (0-445-40780-8, Mysterious Pr. Paperback Bks.) Warner Bks., Inc.
—Wrack & Rune. 1983. 208p. mass mkt. 3.99 (0-380-61911-3, Avon Bks.) Morrow/Avon.
—Wrack & Rune. l.t. ed. 1982. 322p. reprint ed. 11.95 o.p. (0-89621-372-2) Thorndike Pr.

**SHANDY, PETER (FICTITIOUS CHARACTER)—FICTION**

MacLeod, Charlotte. The Corpse in Oozak's Pond. 1987. 224p. 15.45 o.p. (0-89296-188-0) Mysterious Pr.
—The Corpse in Oozak's Pond. 1989. 2.99 o.p. (0-517-00184-5) Random Hse. Value Publishing.
—The Corpse in Oozak's Pond. 1988. 203p. mass mkt. 5.99 o.p. (0-445-40683-6, Mysterious Pr. Paperback Bks.) Warner Bks., Inc.
—Curse of the Giant Hogweed. 1986. (Peter Shandy Ser.). 176p. pap. 3.50 (0-380-70051-4, Avon Bks.) Morrow/Avon.
—Exit the Milkman. l.t. ed. 1996. 22.95 o.p. (1-56895-388-7, Wheeler Publishing, Inc.) Gale Group.
—Exit the Milkman. 1996. 364p. 21.95 o.s.i (0-89296-572-X) Mysterious Pr.
—Exit the Milkman. 1997. 256p. mass mkt. 5.99 o.p. (0-446-40398-9) Warner Bks., Inc.
—Exit the Milkman. 2003. 320p. pap. 6.99 (0-7434-4537-6) ibooks, Inc.
—The Luck Runs Out. 1981. 192p. pap. 3.50 (0-380-54171-8, Avon Bks.) Morrow/Avon.
—An Owl Too Many. l.t. ed. 1991. (General Ser.). 355p. lib. bdg. 20.95 (0-8161-5235-7, Macmillan Reference USA) Gale Group.
—An Owl Too Many. 1991. 17.95 o.p. (0-89296-431-6) Mysterious Pr.
—An Owl Too Many. 1992. 240p. mass mkt. 4.99 o.p. (0-446-40101-3, Mysterious Pr. Paperback Bks.) Warner Bks., Inc.
—Rest You Merry. 1979. (General Ser.). lib. bdg. 13.50 o.p. (0-8161-3000-0, Macmillan Reference USA) Gale Group.
—Rest You Merry. 1980. 224p. reprint ed. mass mkt. 4.99 o.p. (0-380-47530-8, Avon Bks.) Morrow/Avon.
—Something in the Water. 1994. 272p. 18.95 o.s.i (0-89296-430-8) Mysterious Pr.
—Something in the Water. 1995. 240p. mass mkt. 5.50 o.p. (0-446-40446-2, Mysterious Pr. Paperback Bks.) Warner Bks., Inc.


—Something the Cat Dragged In. l.t. ed. 1984. (Nightingale Ser.). 10.95 o.p. (0-8161-3710-2, Macmillan Reference USA) Gale Group.
—Something the Cat Dragged In. 1984. 208p. mass mkt. 3.99 (0-380-69096-9, Avon Bks.) Morrow/Avon.
—Vane Pursuit: A Peter Shandy Mystery. l.t. ed. 1990. 368p. lib. bdg. 19.95 o.p. (0-8161-4850-3, Macmillan Reference USA) Gale Group.
—Vane Pursuit: A Peter Shandy Mystery. 1989. 15.95 o.p. (0-89296-369-7) Mysterious Pr.
—Vane Pursuit: A Peter Shandy Mystery. 1990. 224p. mass mkt. 5.50 o.p. (0-445-40780-8, Mysterious Pr. Paperback Bks.) Warner Bks., Inc.
—Wrack & Rune. 1983. 208p. mass mkt. 3.99 (0-380-61911-3, Avon Bks.) Morrow/Avon.
—Wrack & Rune. l.t. ed. 1982. 322p. reprint ed. 11.95 o.p. (0-89621-372-2) Thorndike Pr.


**SHANNON, LUCY (FICTITIOUS CHARACTER)—FICTION**

Belsky, R. G. Loverboy. 1998. mass mkt. 6.50 (0-380-79068-8); 1997. 313p. mass mkt. 23.00 (0-380-97439-8) Morrow/Avon. (Avon Bks.).

**SHAPIRO, DESIREE (FICTITIOUS CHARACTER)—FICTION**

Eichler, Selma. Murder Can Kill Your Social Life. 1994. (Desiree Shapiro Mystery Ser.). 256p. mass mkt. 5.99 (0-451-18139-5, Signet Bks.) NAL.
—Murder Can Kill Your Social Life. l.t. ed. 2001. 388p. 28.95 (0-7862-3473-3) Thorndike Pr.
—Murder Can Rain on Your Shower. 2003. 272p. mass mkt. 5.99 (0-451-20823-4) NAL.
—Murder Can Rain on Your Shower: A Desiree Shapiro Mystery. l.t. ed. 2003. (Mystery Ser.). 28.95 (0-7862-5566-8) Thorndike Pr.
—Murder Can Ruin Your Looks. 1995. (Desiree Shapiro Mystery Ser.: 2). 272p. (Orig.). mass mkt. 5.99 (0-451-18384-3, Signet Bks.) NAL.
—Murder Can Singe Your Old Flame. 1999. (Desiree Shapiro Mystery Ser.). 256p. mass mkt. 5.99 (0-451-19218-4, Signet Bks.) NAL.
—Murder Can Singe Your Old Flame: A Desiree Shapiro Mystery. l.t. ed. 2001. (Thorndike Mystery Ser.). 397p. 28.95 o.p. (0-7862-3191-2) Thorndike Pr.
—Murder Can Spoil Your Appetite. 2000. (Desiree Shapiro Mystery Ser.). 272p. mass mkt. 5.99 (0-451-19958-8, Signet Bks.) NAL.
—Murder Can Spook Your Cat: A Desiree Shapiro Mystery. 1998. (Desiree Shapiro Mystery Ser.). 272p. mass mkt. 5.99 (0-451-19217-6, Signet Bks.) NAL.
—Murder Can Stunt Your Growth. 1996. (Desiree Shapiro Mystery Ser.). 272p. mass mkt. 5.99 (0-451-18514-5, Signet Bks.) NAL.
—Murder Can Wreck a Reunion. 1997. (Desiree Shapiro Mystery Ser.). 272p. mass mkt. 5.99 (0-451-18521-8, Signet Bks.) NAL.

**SHAPIRO, FRANK (FICTITIOUS CHARACTER)—FICTION**

Bannister, Jo. A Bleeding of Innocents. 1999. 304p. (0-7540-3481-X); pap. (0-7540-3482-8) BBC Audiobooks America.
—A Bleeding of Innocents. 1997. (WWL Mystery Ser.: No. 241). per. (0-373-26241-8, 1-26241-9, Worldwide Library) Harlequin Enterprises, Ltd.
—A Bleeding of Innocents. unabr. ed. 1998. audio 69.95 (1-872672-97-3) Magna Story Sound GBR. *Dist:* Ulverscroft Large Print Bks., Ltd.
—A Bleeding of Innocents. 1993. 224p. 18.95 o.p. (0-312-09750-6, Saint Martin's Minotaur) St. Martin's Pr.
—A Bleeding of Innocents. l.t. ed. 1998. (General Ser.). 304p. pap. 24.95 (0-7862-1610-7) Thorndike Pr.
—Broken Lines. 2000. (Castlemere Mystery Ser.). 272p. per. (0-373-26338-4, Harlequin Bks.) Harlequin Enterprises, Ltd.
—Broken Lines. 1999. 304p. 22.95 (0-312-19842-6, Saint Martin's Minotaur) St. Martin's Pr.
—Broken Lines. l.t. ed. 1999. (General Ser.). 336p. pap. 23.95 (0-7862-1682-4) Thorndike Pr.
—Changelings. 2002. (WWL Mystery Ser.: No. 410). mass mkt. (0-373-26410-0, 1-26410-0, Worldwide Library) Harlequin Enterprises, Ltd.
—Changelings. 2000. 374p. (0-333-90189-4) Macmillan Pr.
—Changelings. l.t. ed. 2001. (Magna Large Print Ser.). 368p. (0-7505-1761-1) Magna Large Print Bks. GBR. *Dist:* Ulverscroft Large Print Canada, Ltd.
—Changelings. 2000. 384p. 23.95 (0-312-26567-0, Saint Martin's Minotaur) St. Martin's Pr.
—Charisma. 1997. per. (0-373-26253-1, 1-26253-4, Worldwide Library) Harlequin Enterprises, Ltd.
—Charisma. 1994. 208p. 18.95 o.p. (0-312-11252-1, Saint Martin's Minotaur) St. Martin's Pr.
—The Hireling's Tale. 1999. 316p. 23.95 (0-312-24400-2, Saint Martin's Minotaur) St. Martin's Pr.
—The Hireling's Tale. l.t. ed. 1999. (General Ser.). 352p. pap. 22.95 (0-7862-2163-1) Thorndike Pr.
—No Birds Sing. 1998. (WWL Mystery Ser.). per. (0-373-26283-3, 1-26283-1, Worldwide Library) Harlequin Enterprises, Ltd.
—No Birds Sing. 1996. 240p. 21.95 (0-312-14382-6, Saint Martin's Minotaur) St. Martin's Pr.
—No Birds Sing. l.t. ed. 1997. (Ulverscroft Large Print Ser.). 464p. 29.99 o.p. (0-7089-3732-2, Ulverscroft) Thorpe, F. A. Pubs. GBR. *Dist:* Ulverscroft Large Print Bks., Ltd., Ulverscroft Large Print Canada, Ltd.
—A Taste for Burning. 1997. (Castlemere Mystery Ser.). per. (0-373-26259-0, 1-26259-1, Worldwide Library) Harlequin Enterprises, Ltd.
—A Taste for Burning. 1995. 208p. 19.95 o.p. (0-312-13191-7, Saint Martin's Minotaur) St. Martin's Pr.

**SHARKEY, RAY (FICTITIOUS CHARACTER)—FICTION**

Campbell, Robert. Boneyards. Chelius, Jane, ed. 304p. 1992. 21.00 o.p. (0-671-70319-6, Atria); 1993. reprint ed. mass mkt. 5.50 (0-671-70320-X, Pocket) Simon & Schuster.

**SHARPE, RICHARD (FICTITIOUS CHARACTER)—FICTION**

Cornwell, Bernard. Sharpe's Battle: Richard Sharpe & the Battle of Fuentes de Onoro, May 1811. unabr. ed. 1996. (Richard Sharpe Adventure Ser.: No. 7). audio 84.95 (0-7451-6642-3, CAB 1258) BBC Audiobooks America.
—Sharpe's Battle: Richard Sharpe & the Battle of Fuentes de Onoro, May 1811. unabr. ed. 2000. (Richard Sharpe Adventure Ser.: No. 7). 12p. audio 56.95 (0-7861-1689-7, 2512) Blackstone Audio Bks., Inc.
—Sharpe's Battle: Richard Sharpe & the Battle of Fuentes de Onoro, May 1811. unabr. ed. 2000. (Richard Sharpe Adventure Ser.). audio 69.95 Chivers Audio Bks. GBR. *Dist:* BBC Audiobooks America.
—Sharpe's Battle: Richard Sharpe & the Battle of Fuentes de Onoro, May 1811. 1995. (Richard Sharpe Adventure Ser.: No. 7). 320p. 20.00 o.p. (0-06-017677-6) HarperTrade.
—Sharpe's Battle: Richard Sharpe & the Battle of Fuentes de Onoro, May 1811. 1996. (Richard Sharpe Adventure Ser.: No. 7). 432p. mass mkt. 6.50 o.s.i (0-06-109537-0, HarperTorch) Morrow/Avon.
—Sharpe's Battle: Richard Sharpe & the Battle of Fuentes de Onoro, May 1811. 1999. 18.05 (0-606-21712-6) Turtleback Bks.
—Sharpe's Battle: Spain 1811. 1999. (Richard Sharpe Adventure Ser.: No. 7). (Illus.). 368p. pap. 12.95 (0-06-093228-7, Perennial) HarperTrade.
—Sharpe's Company: Richard Sharpe & the Siege of Badajoz, January to April 1812. unabr. ed. 1994. (Richard Sharpe Adventure Ser.: No. 8). audio 69.95 (0-7451-4336-9, CAB 1019) BBC Audiobooks America.
—Sharpe's Company: Richard Sharpe & the Siege of Badajoz, January to April 1812. unabr. ed. 1995. (Richard Sharpe Adventure Ser.: No. 8). audio 49.95 (0-7861-0770-7, 1619) Blackstone Audio Bks., Inc.
—Sharpe's Company: Richard Sharpe & the Siege of Badajoz, January to April 1812. l.t. ed. 1988. (Richard Sharpe Adventure Ser.: No. 8). lib. bdg. 15.95 o.p. (1-85057-415-4, Macmillan Reference USA) Gale Group.
—Sharpe's Company: Richard Sharpe & the Siege of Badajoz, January to April 1812. 2001. (Richard Sharpe Adventure Ser.: No. 8). 288p. pap. 13.00 (0-14-029432-5) Penguin Group (USA) Inc.
—Sharpe's Company: Richard Sharpe & the Siege of Badajoz, January to April 1812. (Richard Sharpe Adventure Ser.: No. 8). 1990. 352p. pap. 4.95 o.p. (0-14-014443-9, Penguin Bks.); 1984. 288p. pap. 11.95 o.s.i (0-14-007023-0, Penguin Bks.); 1982. 288p. 14.95 o.p. (0-670-63942-7) Viking Penguin.
—Sharpe's Devil: Chile 1820. 1999. (Richard Sharpe Adventure Ser.). 336p. pap. 12.95 (0-06-093229-5, Perennial) HarperTrade.
—Sharpe's Devil: Richard Sharpe & the Emperor, 1820-1821. l.t. ed. 1993. pap. 17.95 o.p. (0-7927-1466-0); 1993. 19.95 o.p. (0-7927-1467-9); 1994. audio 69.95 (0-7451-4252-4, CAB 935) BBC Audiobooks America.
—Sharpe's Devil: Richard Sharpe & the Emperor, 1820-1821. unabr. ed. 1999. 5p. audio 49.95 (0-7861-1667-6, 2495) Blackstone Audio Bks., Inc.
—Sharpe's Devil: Richard Sharpe & the Emperor, 1820-1821. unabr. ed. 2000. audio 59.95 Chivers Audio Bks. GBR. *Dist:* BBC Audiobooks America.
—Sharpe's Devil: Richard Sharpe & the Emperor, 1820-1821. 1992. 256p. 20.00 o.p. (0-06-017977-5) HarperTrade.
—Sharpe's Devil: Richard Sharpe & the Emperor, 1820-1821. 1993. 368p. mass mkt. 6.50 o.s.i (0-06-109028-X, HarperTorch) Morrow/Avon.
—Sharpe's Devil: Richard Sharpe & the Emperor, 1820-1821. 1999. (Illus.). 18.05 (0-606-21713-4) Turtleback Bks.
—Sharpe's Eagle: Richard Sharpe & the Talavera Campaign, July 1809. 1982. (Richard Sharpe Adventure Ser.: No. 5). (Illus.). 352p. 3.25 o.s.i (0-441-76091-0) Ace Bks.
—Sharpe's Eagle: Richard Sharpe & the Talavera Campaign, July 1809, unabr. ed. 1993. (Richard Sharpe Adventure Ser.: No. 5). 69.95 incl. audio (0-7451-5879-X, CAB 429) BBC Audiobooks America.
—Sharpe's Eagle: Richard Sharpe & the Talavera Campaign, July 1809, unabr. ed. 1995. (Richard Sharpe Adventure Ser.: No. 5). 5p. audio 49.95 (0-7861-0662-X, 1564) Blackstone Audio Bks., Inc.
—Sharpe's Eagle: Richard Sharpe & the Talavera Campaign, July 1809. unabr. ed. 2000. (Richard Sharpe Adventure Ser.: No. 5). audio 42.00 Books on Tape, Inc.
—Sharpe's Eagle: Richard Sharpe & the Talavera Campaign, July 1809. 1991. (Richard Sharpe Adventure Ser.: No. 5). reprint ed. lib. bdg. 29.95 (1-56849-076-3) Buccaneer Bks., Inc.
—Sharpe's Eagle: Richard Sharpe & the Talavera Campaign, July 1809. 1989. (Richard Sharpe Adventure Ser.: No. 5). audio 64.95 o.p. (0-8161-9664-8) Thorndike Pr.
—Sharpe's Eagle: Richard Sharpe & the Talavera Campaign, July 1809. l.t. ed. 1983. (Richard Sharpe Adventure Ser.: No. 5). 480p. 29.99 o.p. (0-7089-0945-0, Ulverscroft) Thorpe, F. A. Pubs. GBR. *Dist:* Ulverscroft Large Print Bks., Ltd., Ulverscroft Large Print Canada, Ltd.
—Sharpe's Eagle: Richard Sharpe & the Talavera Campaign, July 1809. (Richard Sharpe Adventure Ser.: No. 5). 1987. 288p. pap. 10.95 o.s.i (0-14-009921-2, Penguin Bks.); 1981. 264p. 12.95 o.p. (0-670-63944-3) Viking Penguin.
—Sharpe's Enemy: Richard Sharpe & the Defense of Portugal, Christmas 1812. unabr. ed. 1995. (Richard Sharpe Adventure Ser.: No. 10). audio 84.95 (0-7451-6569-9, CAB 1185) BBC Audiobooks America.
—Sharpe's Enemy: Richard Sharpe & the Defense of Portugal, Christmas 1812, unabr. ed. 1996. (Richard Sharpe Adventure Ser.: No. 10). audio 56.95 (0-7861-0923-8, 1717) Blackstone Audio Bks., Inc.
—Sharpe's Enemy: Richard Sharpe & the Defense of Portugal, Christmas 1812. unabr. ed. 2000. (Richard Sharpe Adventure Ser.). audio 69.95 Chivers Audio Bks. GBR. *Dist:* BBC Audiobooks America.
—Sharpe's Enemy: Richard Sharpe & the Defense of Portugal, Christmas 1812. 2001. (Richard Sharpe Adventure Ser.: No. 10). 352p. pap. 12.00 (0-14-029434-1) Penguin Group (USA) Inc.
—Sharpe's Enemy: Richard Sharpe & the Defense of Portugal, Christmas 1812. (Richard Sharpe Adventure Ser.: No. 10). 1987. 352p. pap. 11.95 o.s.i (0-14-010430-5, Penguin Bks.); 1985. pap. 5.95 o.p. (0-14-007655-7, Penguin Bks.); 1984. 336p. 16.95 o.p. (0-670-63940-0) Viking Penguin.
—Sharpe's Fortress: Richard Sharpe & the Siege of Gawilghur, December 1803. 2002. 320p. pap. 12.95 (0-06-109863-9, Perennial) HarperTrade.
—Sharpe's Gold: Richard Sharpe & the Destruction of Almeida August, 1810. 1983. (Richard Sharpe Adventure Ser.: No. 6). 352p. 3.25 o.s.i (0-441-76089-9) Ace Bks.
—Sharpe's Gold: Richard Sharpe & the Destruction of Almeida August, 1810, unabr. ed. (Richard Sharpe Adventure Ser.: No. 6). 69.95 incl. audio (0-7451-5874-9, CAB 510) BBC Audiobooks America.
—Sharpe's Gold: Richard Sharpe & the Destruction of Almeida August, 1810. unabr. ed. 2001. audio compact disk 64.00 (0-7861-9745-5, z1594); 1995. (Richard Sharpe Adventure Ser.: No. 6). audio 44.95 (0-7861-0716-2, 1594) Blackstone Audio Bks., Inc.
—Sharpe's Gold: Richard Sharpe & the Destruction of Almeida August, 1810. unabr. ed. 2000. (Richard Sharpe Adventure Ser.). audio 59.95 Chivers Audio Bks. GBR. *Dist:* BBC Audiobooks America.
—Sharpe's Gold: Richard Sharpe & the Destruction of Almeida August, 1810. 2001. (Richard Sharpe Adventure Ser.: No. 6). 256p. pap. 12.00 (0-14-029431-7) Penguin Group (USA) Inc.
—Sharpe's Gold: Richard Sharpe & the Destruction of Almeida August, 1810. (Richard Sharpe Adventure Ser.: No. 6). 1987. 256p. pap. 3.50 o.p. (0-14-010028-8, Penguin Bks.); 1987. 288p. pap. 11.95 o.s.i (0-14-024305-4, Penguin Bks.); 1982. 252p. 13.95 o.p. (0-670-63943-5) Viking Penguin.
—Sharpe's Havoc: Richard Sharpe & the Campaign in Northern Portugal, Spring 1809. 2003. (Richard Sharpe Adventure Ser.). 320p. 25.95 (0-06-053046-4) HarperCollins Pubs.
—Sharpe's Havoc: Richard Sharpe & the Campaign in Northern Portugal, Spring 1809. 2004. 336p. pap. 12.95 (0-06-056670-1, Perennial) HarperTrade.
—Sharpe's Havoc: Richard Sharpe & the Campaign in Northern Portugal, Spring 1809. l.t. ed. 2003. (Sharpe Novels Ser.). 498p. 29.95 (0-7862-5601-X) Thorndike Pr.
—Sharpe's Honour: Richard Sharpe & the Vitoria Campaign, February to June, 1813, unabr. ed. 1996. (Richard Sharpe Adventure Ser.: No. 11). audio 56.95 (0-7861-0943-2, 1693) Blackstone Audio Bks., Inc.
—Sharpe's Honour: Richard Sharpe & the Vitoria Campaign, February to June, 1813. (Richard Sharpe Adventure Ser.: No. 11). 1990. 384p. pap. 11.95 o.s.i (0-14-014597-4); 1986. 360p. pap. 3.50 o.p. (0-14-008013-9) Viking Penguin. (Penguin Bks.).
—Sharpe's Prey: Richard Sharpe & the Expedition to Copenhagen, 1807. l.t. ed. 2002. 506p. 29.95 (0-7862-4121-7) Gale Group.
—Sharpe's Prey: Richard Sharpe & the Expedition to Copenhagen, 1807. 2002. E-Book 19.95 (0-06-050422-6); E-Book 19.95 (0-06-050421-8); E-Book 19.95 (0-06-050420-X); E-Book 19.95 (0-06-050423-4) HarperCollins General Bks. Group. (PerfectBound).
—Sharpe's Prey: Richard Sharpe & the Expedition to Copenhagen, 1807. 2002. (Illus.). 272p. 24.95 (0-06-000252-2) HarperCollins Pubs.
—Sharpe's Prey: Richard Sharpe & the Expedition to Copenhagen, 1807. 2003. 288p. pap. 12.95 (0-06-008453-7, Perennial) HarperTrade.
—Sharpe's Prey: Richard Sharpe & the Expedition to Copenhagen, 1807. unabr. ed. 2002. audio 84.00 (1-4025-1864-1) Recorded Bks., LLC.
—Sharpe's Regiment: Richard Sharpe & the Invasion of France, June to November 1913. unabr. ed. 1992. (Richard Sharpe Adventure Ser.). 84.95 incl. audio (0-7451-4073-4, CAB 770) BBC Audiobooks America.
—Sharpe's Regiment: Richard Sharpe & the Invasion of France, June to November 1913. unabr. ed. 1996. 12p. audio 56.95 (0-7861-0966-1, 1743) Blackstone Audio Bks., Inc.

—Sharpe's Regiment: Richard Sharpe & the Invasion of France, June to November 1913. unabr. ed. 2000. (Richard Sharpe Adventure Ser.). audio 69.95 Chivers Audio Bks. GBR. *Dist:* BBC Audiobooks America.

—Sharpe's Regiment: Richard Sharpe & the Invasion of France, June to November 1913. 1987. (Richard Sharpe Adventure Ser.: Vol. 8). 304p. pap. 11.95 o.s.i (*0-14-024306-2*, Penguin Bks.) Penguin Group (USA) Inc.

—Sharpe's Regiment: Richard Sharpe & the Invasion of France, June to November 1913. (Sharpe Ser.). 1987. 416p. pap. 3.95 o.p. (*0-14-009213-7*, Penguin Bks.); 1986. 304p. 16.95 o.p. (*0-670-81148-3*) Viking Penguin.

—Sharpe's Revenge: Richard Sharpe & the Peace of 1814. unabr. ed. 1996. 12p. audio 56.95 (*0-7861-1013-9*, 1791) Blackstone Audio Bks., Inc.

—Sharpe's Revenge: Richard Sharpe & the Peace of 1814. unabr. ed. (Richard Sharpe Adventure Ser.). 2000. audio 69.95; 1992. audio 84.95 (*0-7451-5875-7*, CAB 642) Chivers Audio Bks. GBR. *Dist:* BBC Audiobooks America.

—Sharpe's Revenge: Richard Sharpe & the Peace of 1814. 1989. (Sharpe Ser.). 352p. 17.95 o.p. (*0-670-80867-9*); No. 10. 1990. (Richard Sharpe Adventure Ser.: Vol. 10). 320p. pap. 11.95 o.s.i (*0-14-008472-X*, Penguin Bks.) Viking Penguin.

—Sharpe's Rifles: Richard Sharpe & the French Invasion of Galicia, January 1809. l.t. ed. 1990. (Richard Sharpe Adventure Ser.: No. 4). 479p. 29.99 o.p. (*1-85057-547-9*) Magna Large Print Bks. GBR. *Dist:* Ulverscroft Large Print Bks., Ltd., Ulverscroft Large Print Canada, Ltd.

—Sharpe's Rifles: Richard Sharpe & the French Invasion of Galicia, January 1809. 2001. (Richard Sharpe Adventure Ser.: No. 4). 304p. pap. 13.00 (*0-14-029429-5*) Penguin Group (USA) Inc.

—Sharpe's Rifles: Richard Sharpe & the French Invasion of Galicia, January 1809. (Richard Sharpe Adventure Ser.: No. 4). 304p. 1989. pap. 11.95 o.s.i (*0-14-011014-3*, Penguin Bks.); 1988. 17.95 o.p. (*0-670-82222-1*) Viking Penguin.

—Sharpe's Siege: Richard Sharpe & the Winter Campaign, 1814. unabr. ed. 1991. (Richard Sharpe Adventure Ser.). audio 84.95 (*0-7451-5877-3*, CAB 573) BBC Audiobooks America.

—Sharpe's Siege: Richard Sharpe & the Winter Campaign, 1814. unabr. ed. 1996. audio 56.95 (*0-7861-0993-9*, 1770); audio 56.95 Blackstone Audio Bks., Inc.

—Sharpe's Siege: Richard Sharpe & the Winter Campaign, 1814. unabr. collector's ed. 2001. audio 64.00 Books on Tape, Inc.

—Sharpe's Siege: Richard Sharpe & the Winter Campaign, 1814. unabr. ed. 2000. (Richard Sharpe Adventure Ser.). audio 69.95 Chivers Audio Bks. GBR. *Dist:* BBC Audiobooks America.

—Sharpe's Siege: Richard Sharpe & the Winter Campaign, 1814. l.t. ed. 1989. 444p. lib. bdg. 11.95 o.p. (*1-85057-378-6*, Macmillan Reference USA) Gale Group.

—Sharpe's Siege: Richard Sharpe & the Winter Campaign, 1814. 320p. 1987. (Sharpe Ser.). 17.95 o.p. (*0-670-80866-0*); No. 9. 1990. (Richard Sharpe Adventure Ser.: Vol. 9). pap. 11.95 o.s.i (*0-14-014442-0*, Penguin Bks.) Viking Penguin.

—Sharpe's Sword: Richard Sharpe & the Salamanca Campaign, June & July, 1812. unabr. ed. 1997. (Richard Sharpe Adventure Ser.: No. 9). audio 69.95 (*0-7451-6785-3*, CAB 1401) BBC Audiobooks America.

—Sharpe's Sword: Richard Sharpe & the Salamanca Campaign, June & July, 1812. unabr. ed. 1995. (Richard Sharpe Adventure Ser.: No. 9). audio 56.95 (*0-7861-0898-3*, 1670) Blackstone Audio Bks., Inc.

—Sharpe's Sword: Richard Sharpe & the Salamanca Campaign, June & July, 1812. unabr. ed. 2000. (Richard Sharpe Adventure Ser.: No. 9). 8p. audio compact disk 79.95 (*0-7540-5346-6*, CCD 037) Chivers Audio Bks. GBR. *Dist:* BBC Audiobooks America.

—Sharpe's Sword: Richard Sharpe & the Salamanca Campaign, June & July, 1812. l.t. ed. 1989. (Richard Sharpe Adventure Ser.: No. 9). lib. bdg. 11.95 o.p. (*1-85057-380-8*, Macmillan Reference USA) Gale Group.

—Sharpe's Sword: Richard Sharpe & the Salamanca Campaign, June & July, 1812. 2001. (Richard Sharpe Adventure Ser.: No. 9). 320p. pap. 12.00 (*0-14-029433-3*) Penguin Group (USA) Inc.

—Sharpe's Sword: Richard Sharpe & the Salamanca Campaign, June & July, 1812. (Richard Sharpe Adventure Ser.: No. 9). 1987. 320p. pap. 3.50 o.p. (*0-14-010264-7*, Penguin Bks.); 1987. 384p. pap. 12.00 o.s.i (*0-14-024304-6*, Penguin Bks.); 1984. 336p. pap. 5.95 o.p. (*0-14-007024-9*, Penguin Bks.); 1983. 324p. 15.75 o.p. (*0-670-63941-9*) Viking Penguin.

—Sharpe's Tiger: Richard Sharpe & the Siege of Seringapatam, 1799. 1997. (Richard Sharpe Adventure Ser.: No. 1). (Illus.). 303p. o.p. (*0-00-225010-1*) HarperSanFrancisco.

—Sharpe's Tiger: Richard Sharpe & the Siege of Seringapatam, 1799. 1999. (Richard Sharpe Adventure Ser.: No. 1). 400p. pap. 13.00 (*0-06-093230-9*, Perennial) HarperTrade.

—Sharpe's Tiger: Richard Sharpe & the Siege of Seringapatam, 1799. 1997. (Richard Sharpe Adventure Ser.: No. 1). 496p. mass mkt. 6.50 o.s.i (*0-06-101269-6*, HarperTorch) Morrow/Avon.

—Sharpe's Tiger: Richard Sharpe & the Siege of Seringapatam, 1799. 1999. (Richard Sharpe Adventures Ser.). (Illus.). 19.05 (*0-606-21714-2*) Turtleback Bks.

—Sharpe's Trafalgar: Richard Sharpe & the Battle of Trafalgar, 21 October 1805. unabr. ed. 2001. 10p. audio compact disk 94.95 (*0-7540-5400-4*, CCD091); audio 84.95 (*0-7540-0564-X*, CAB1987) Chivers Audio Bks. GBR. *Dist:* BBC Audiobooks America.

—Sharpe's Trafalgar: Richard Sharpe & the Battle of Trafalgar, 21 October 1805. 2001. (Illus.). 304p. 25.00 (*0-06-019425-1*); 19.95 (*0-06-621326-6*) HarperCollins Pubs.

—Sharpe's Trafalgar: Richard Sharpe & the Battle of Trafalgar, 21 October 1805. 2002. 320p. pap. 12.95 (*0-06-109862-0*, Perennial) HarperTrade.

—Sharpe's Trafalgar: Richard Sharpe & the Battle of Trafalgar, 21 October 1805. unabr. ed. 2001. audio 83.00 (*0-7887-7242-2*) Recorded Bks., LLC.

—Sharpe's Trafalgar: Richard Sharpe & the Battle of Trafalgar, 21 October 1805. l.t. ed. 2001. (Thorndike Press Large Print Adventure Ser.). (Illus.). 571p. 29.95 (*0-7862-3699-X*) Thorndike Pr.

—Sharpe's Triumph: Richard Sharpe & the Battle of Assaye, September 1803. unabr. ed. 2002. 10p. audio compact disk 94.95 (*0-7540-5474-8*, CCD 165); 1999. (Richard Sharpe Adventure Ser.: No. 2). audio 69.95 (*0-7540-0268-3*, CAB1691) BBC Audiobooks America.

—Sharpe's Triumph: Richard Sharpe & the Battle of Assaye, September 1803. unabr. ed. 2000. (Richard Sharpe Adventure Ser.: No. 2). audio compact disk 72.00 (*0-7861-9787-0*, z2701) Blackstone Audio Bks., Inc.

—Sharpe's Triumph: Richard Sharpe & the Battle of Assaye, September 1803. 1999. (Richard Sharpe Adventure Ser.: No. 2). 304p. 24.00 (*0-06-101270-X*) HarperCollins Pubs.

—Sharpe's Triumph: Richard Sharpe & the Battle of Assaye, September 1803. 2000. (Richard Sharpe Adventure Ser.: No. 2). 304p. pap. 13.00 (*0-06-095197-4*, Perennial) HarperTrade.

—Sharpe's Triumph: Richard Sharpe & the Battle of Assaye, September 1803. 2000. (Richard Sharpe Adventures Ser.). (Illus.). (J). 19.05 (*0-606-21715-0*) Turtleback Bks.

—Sharpe's Waterloo: Richard Sharpe & the Waterloo Campaign, 15 June to 18 June 1815. unabr. ed. 1992. (Richard Sharpe Adventure Ser.). audio 84.95 (*0-7451-5878-1*, CAB 671) BBC Audiobooks America.

—Sharpe's Waterloo: Richard Sharpe & the Waterloo Campaign, 15 June to 18 June 1815. unabr. ed. 2000. (Richard Sharpe Adventure Ser.). audio 69.95 Chivers Audio Bks. GBR. *Dist:* BBC Audiobooks America.

—Waterloo: Sharpe's Final Adventure. 1990. (Sharpe Ser.). 288p. 18.95 o.p. (*0-670-80868-7*) Viking Penguin.

—Waterloo No. 11: Sharpe's Final Adventure. unabr. ed. 1996. audio 69.95 Blackstone Audio Bks., Inc.

—Waterloo No. 11: Sharpe's Final Adventure. 1991. (Sharpe Ser.). 384p. pap. 11.95 o.s.i (*0-14-008473-8*, Penguin Bks.) Penguin Group (USA) Inc.

**SHARPLES, CLAIRE (FICTITIOUS CHARACTER)—FICTION**

Rothenberg, Rebecca. The Bulrush Murders: A Botanical Mystery. 1991. 240p. 18.95 o.p. (*0-88184-749-6*, Carroll & Graf Pubs.) Avalon Publishing Group.

—The Bulrush Murders: A Botanical Mystery. 1994. 256p. mass mkt. 5.99 o.s.i (*0-446-40404-7*) Warner Bks., Inc.

—The Dandelion Murders. 1994. 304p. 18.95 o.s.i (*0-89296-561-4*) Mysterious Pr.

—The Dandelion Murders. 1995. 272p. mass mkt. 5.50 (*0-446-40378-4*, Mysterious Pr. Paperback Bks.) Warner Bks., Inc.

—The Shy Tulip Murders. 1996. 336p. 21.95 o.s.i (*0-89296-607-6*) Mysterious Pr.

—The Shy Tulip Murders. 1997. 304p. mass mkt. 5.99 (*0-446-40462-4*, Mysterious Pr. Paperback Bks.) Warner Bks., Inc.

Rothenberg, Rebecca & Cannon, Taffy. The Tumbleweed Murders: A Claire Sharples Botanical Mystery. 2001. (Claire Sharples Botanical Mystery Ser.). (Illus.). 240p. pap. 12.95 (*1-880284-43-X*) Daniel, John & Co., Pubs.

**SHARTELLE, CLINTON (FICTITIOUS CHARACTER)—FICTION**

Thomas, Ross. The Seersucker Whipsaw. reprint ed. 1987. 304p. pap. 3.50 o.p. (*0-06-080849-7*, P 849); 1985. 256p. pap. 2.95 o.p. (*0-06-080728-8*, P728) HarperTrade. (Perennial).

—The Seersucker Whipsaw. 1992. 288p. mass mkt. 5.99 o.p. (*0-446-40169-2*, Mysterious Pr. Paperback Bks.) Warner Bks., Inc.

**SHAW, HANNAH (FICTITIOUS CHARACTER)—FICTION**

O'Connell, Jack. Wireless. 1993. 416p. 19.95 (*0-89296-546-0*) Mysterious Pr.

—Wireless. 1995. 416p. mass mkt. 5.99 (*0-446-40356-3*, Mysterious Pr. Paperback Bks.) Warner Bks., Inc.

**SHAW, MARTHA (FICTITIOUS CHARACTER)—FICTION**

Apodaca, Jennifer. Dating Can Be Murder. l.t. ed. 2003. (Samantha Shaw Mystery Ser.). 378p. 28.95 (*0-7862-5967-1*) Thorndike Pr.

**SHAW, SABINA (FICTITIOUS CHARACTER)—FICTION**

Schulenburg, Marnie. Murder off the Record. 1998. 304p. 23.95 o.p. (*1-885173-50-4*) Write Way Publishing.

**SHAW, SIMON (FICTITIOUS CHARACTER)—FICTION**

Shaber, Sarah R. The Fugitive King: A Professor Simon Shaw Mystery. 2002. (Illus.). 240p. 22.95 (*0-312-29046-2*, Saint Martin's Minotaur) St. Martin's Pr.

—Simon Said. (Simon Shaw Mysteries Ser.). 224p. 1998. pap. 5.99 (*0-312-96555-9*, St. Martin's Paperbacks); 1997. 20.95 o.p. (*0-312-15207-8*, Saint Martin's Minotaur) St. Martin's Pr.

—Snipe Hunt. 2000. (Professor Simon Shaw Mysteries Ser.). 288p. 23.95 (*0-312-25337-0*, Saint Martin's Minotaur) St. Martin's Pr.

—Snipe Hunt: A Professor Simon Shaw Mystery. E-Book 6.50 (*0-312-27376-2*); 2001. 304p. reprint ed. mass mkt. 6.50 (*0-312-97470-1*, 20-3260, St. Martin's Paperbacks) St. Martin's Pr.

**SHEA, HAROLD (FICTITIOUS CHARACTER)—FICTION**

de Camp, L. Sprague & Pratt, Fletcher. The Complete Compleat Enchanter. 1989. 544p. mass mkt. 5.99 (*0-671-69809-5*) Baen Bks.

Stasheff, Christopher. The Exotic Enchanter. 1995. 288p. pap. 5.99 (*0-671-87666-X*) Baen Bks.

**SHELBY, ELIZABETH PAULA (FICTITIOUS CHARACTER)—FICTION**

David, Peter. Double or Nothing. 1999. (Star Trek, The Next Generation Ser.: Vol. 5). 277p. pap. 6.50 o.s.i (*0-671-03478-2*, Star Trek) Simon & Schuster.

—End Game. 1997. (Star Trek Ser.: No. 4). (Illus.). 208p. pap. 3.99 (*0-671-01398-X*, Star Trek) Simon & Schuster.

—Excalibur: Requiem. 2000. (Star Trek Ser.: No. 9). 288p. pap. 6.99 (*0-671-04238-6*, Star Trek) Simon & Schuster.

—House of Cards; Into the Void; The Two-Front War; End Game. 1998. (Star Trek Ser.: Nos. 1-4). 704p. 15.00 (*0-671-01978-3*, Star Trek) Simon & Schuster.

—Into the Void. 1997. (Star Trek Ser.: No. 2). (Illus.). 176p. pap. 3.99 (*0-671-01396-3*, Star Trek) Simon & Schuster.

—Martyr. 1998. (Star Trek Ser.: No. 5). (Illus.). 288p. pap. 6.50 (*0-671-02036-6*, Star Trek) Simon & Schuster.

**SHEPERD, CHYNA (FICTITIOUS CHARACTER)—FICTION**

Koontz, Dean. Intensity. 1997. pap. text 7.99 (*0-345-91189-X*); 1997. pap. 12.95 o.p. (*0-345-41948-0*); 1996. 448p. mass mkt. 7.99 o.s.i (*0-345-38436-9*); 1996. mass mkt. 6.99 (*0-345-40514-5*) Ballantine Bks.

—Intensity. l.t. ed. 1996. 752p. 25.00 o.p. (*0-7838-1678-2*, Macmillan Reference USA) Gale Group.

—Intensity. deluxe ed. 1996. 25.00 o.s.i (*0-676-51387-5*) Random Hse., Inc.

**SHEPHERD, TRACY (FICTITIOUS CHARACTER)—FICTION**

Bell, James S. Circumstantial Evidence. 1997. 480p. pap. 13.99 o.p. (*0-8054-6359-3*) Broadman & Holman Pubs.

**SHERIDAN, ALEXANDER (FICTITIOUS CHARACTER)—FICTION**

Stuart, V. A. Battle for Lucknow: Sheridan 4. l.t. ed. 1995. (Ulverscroft Large Print Ser.). 480p. 29.99 o.p. (*0-7089-3383-1*, Ulverscroft) Thorpe, F. A. Pubs. GBR. *Dist:* Ulverscroft Large Print Bks., Ltd., Ulverscroft Large Print Canada, Ltd.

—Captain of Cavalry: Sheridan 1. l.t. ed. 1994. (Ulverscroft Large Print Ser.). 496p. 29.99 o.p. (*0-7089-3031-X*, Ulverscroft) Thorpe, F. A. Pubs. GBR. *Dist:* Ulverscroft Large Print Bks., Ltd., Ulverscroft Large Print Canada, Ltd.

—The Heroic Garrison. 2003. (Alexander Sheridan Novels: No. 5). 256p. pap. 13.95 (*1-59013-030-8*) McBooks Pr., Inc.

—The Heroic Garrison: Sheridan 5. l.t. ed. 1995. (Ulverscroft Large Print Ser.). 448p. 29.99 o.p. (*0-7089-3438-2*, Ulverscroft) Thorpe, F. A. Pubs. GBR. *Dist:* Ulverscroft Large Print Bks., Ltd., Ulverscroft Large Print Canada, Ltd.

—Massacre at Cawnpore. 1973. (Adventures of Alexander Sheridan Ser., No. 5). 224p. pap. 0.95 o.p. (*0-523-21254-2*, Pinnacle Bks.) Kensington Publishing Corp.

—Massacre at Cawnpore: Sheridan 3. l.t. ed. 1995. (Ulverscroft Large Print Ser.). 432p. 29.99 o.p. (*0-7089-3229-0*, Ulverscroft) Thorpe, F. A. Pubs. GBR. *Dist:* Ulverscroft Large Print Bks., Ltd., Ulverscroft Large Print Canada, Ltd.

—Mutiny in Meerut: Sheridan 2. l.t. ed. 1994. (Ulverscroft Large Print Ser.). 432p. 29.99 o.p. (*0-7089-3085-9*, Ulverscroft) Thorpe, F. A. Pubs. GBR. *Dist:* Ulverscroft Large Print Bks., Ltd., Ulverscroft Large Print Canada, Ltd.

—The Sepoy Mutiny Book #2: Alexander Sheridan Novels. 2001. (Alexander Sheridan Novels: No. 2). 256p. pap. 13.95 (*0-935526-99-4*) McBooks Pr., Inc.

—Victors & Lords Book #1: Alexander Sheridan Novels. 2001. (Alexander Sheridan Novels: No. 1). 272p. pap. 13.95 (*0-935526-98-6*) McBooks Pr., Inc.

**SHERIDAN, CHARLES, SIR (FICTITIOUS CHARACTER)—FICTION**

Paige, Robin. Death at Bishop's Keep: A Victorian Mystery. 1998. 304p. mass mkt. 6.50 (*0-425-16435-7*, Prime Crime) Berkley Publishing Group.

—Death at Bishop's Keep: A Victorian Mystery. 1994. pap. 4.99 (*0-380-77498-4*, Avon Bks.) Morrow/Avon.

—Death at Daisy's Folly. 1997. 288p. mass mkt. 6.50 (*0-425-15671-0*, Prime Crime) Berkley Publishing Group.

—Death at Dartmoor: A Victorian Mystery. 336p. 2003. mass mkt. 6.50 (*0-425-18909-0*, Prime Crime); 2002. 21.95 (*0-425-18342-4*) Berkley Publishing Group.

—Death at Devil's Bridge. 1998. (Prime Crime Mysteries Ser.). 288p. mass mkt. 6.50 (*0-425-16195-1*, Prime Crime) Berkley Publishing Group.

—Death at Epsom Downs. 2001. 304p. 21.95 o.s.i (*0-425-17807-2*, Prime Crime) Berkley Publishing Group.

—Death at Gallows Green. 1998. 288p. mass mkt. 6.50 (*0-425-16399-7*) Berkley Publishing Group.

—Death at Gallows Green. 1995. (Victorian Mystery Ser.). pap. 4.99 (*0-380-77499-2*, Avon Bks.) Morrow/Avon.

—Death at Glamis Castle. 352p. 2004. mass mkt. 6.50 (*0-425-19264-4*); 2003. 22.95 (*0-425-18847-7*, Prime Crime) Berkley Publishing Group.

—Death at Rottingdean. 1999. (Victorian Mystery Ser.). 304p. mass mkt. 6.50 (*0-425-16782-8*, Prime Crime) Berkley Publishing Group.

—Death at Whitechapel. 2000. (Victorian Mystery Ser.: Vol. 6). 288p. mass mkt. 6.50 (*0-425-17341-0*, Prime Crime) Berkley Publishing Group.

**SHERIDAN, DAN (FICTITIOUS CHARACTER)—FICTION**

Reed, Barry. The Indictment. 1995. 436p. mass mkt. 6.99 (*0-312-95416-6*, St. Martin's Paperbacks) St. Martin's Pr.

**SHERIDAN, T. S. W. (FICTITIOUS CHARACTER)—FICTION**

Wilcox, Stephen F. All the Dead Heroes. 1992. 224p. 18.95 o.p. (*0-312-06896-4*, Saint Martin's Minotaur) St. Martin's Pr.

—The Dry White Tear. 1989. 15.95 o.p. (*0-312-02909-8*, Saint Martin's Minotaur) St. Martin's Pr.

—The Green Mosaic. 1994. 272p. 20.95 o.p. (*0-312-11428-1*, Saint Martin's Minotaur) St. Martin's Pr.

—St. Lawrence Run. 1991. mass mkt. 3.95 o.p. (*0-312-92488-7*, St. Martin's Paperbacks); 1990. 16.95 o.p. (*0-312-04430-5*, Saint Martin's Minotaur) St. Martin's Pr.

**SHERLOCK, LACEY (FICTITIOUS CHARACTER)—FICTION**

Coulter, Catherine. Blindside. 2004. 368p. mass mkt. 7.99 (*0-515-13720-0*, Jove) Berkley Publishing Group.

—Blindside. 2003. 384p. 25.95 (*0-399-15056-0*) Putnam Publishing Group, The.

—Blindside. l.t. ed. 2004. 512p. pap. 13.95 (*1-59413-016-7*, Large Print Pr.); 2003. 495p. 32.95 (*0-7862-5625-7*) Thorndike Pr.

—Eleventh Hour: An FBI Thriller. 2002. 384p. 24.95 (*0-399-14877-9*) Putnam Publishing Group, The.

—Eleventh Hour: An FBI Thriller. l.t. ed. 2002. 576p. 26.95 (*0-375-43171-3*) Random Hse. Large Print.
—Hemlock Bay. unabr. ed. 2001. audio 29.95 (*1-58788-498-4*, 2796, Brilliance Audio Unabridged); audio 69.25 (*1-58788-499-2*, 2797, CD Unabridged Library Edition); audio compact disk 37.95 (*1-58788-525-5*, 2798, CD Unabridged); audio compact disk 96.25 (*1-58788-526-3*, 2799, CD Unabridged Library Edition) Brilliance Audio.
—Hemlock Bay. 2001. 300p. 23.95 o.s.i (*0-399-14800-0*) Penguin Group (USA) Inc.
—Hemlock Bay. 2001. 432p. 24.95 o.p. (*0-399-14738-1*); audio 24.95 (*0-399-14822-1*, Putnam Berkley Audio); 4p. audio 25.95 o.p. (*0-399-14760-8*, Putnam Berkley Audio) Putnam Publishing Group, The.
—Hemlock Bay. l.t. ed. 2001. 496p. 24.95 (*0-375-43115-2*) Random Hse. Large Print.

**SHERMAN, WINSTON MARLOWE (FICTITIOUS CHARACTER)—FICTION**

Lorens, M. K. Deception Island. 1990. 240p. mass mkt. 3.95 o.s.i (*0-553-28793-1*) Bantam Bks.
—Dreamland. 1993. 320p. mass mkt. 4.99 o.s.i (*0-553-29437-7*) Bantam Bks.
—Dreamland. 1992. 304p. 16.50 o.s.i (*0-385-42237-7*) Doubleday Publishing.
—Ropedancer's Fall. 1990. 288p. mass mkt. 3.95 o.s.i (*0-553-28312-X*) Bantam Bks.
—Sorrowheart. 1994. (Winston Marlowe Sherman Mystery Ser.). 416p. mass mkt. 4.99 o.s.i (*0-553-29441-5*) Bantam Bks.
—Sorrowheart: A Winston Marlowe Sherman Mystery. 1993. 384p. 17.00 o.s.i (*0-385-46781-8*) Doubleday Publishing.
—Sweet Narcissus. 1989. 288p. mass mkt. 3.95 o.s.i (*0-553-28005-8*) Bantam Bks.

**SHIGATA, MARK (FICTITIOUS CHARACTER)—FICTION**

Wingate, Anne. The Buzzards Must Also be Fed. 1992. 256p. mass mkt. 3.99 o.p. (*0-06-104099-1*, HarperTorch) Morrow/Avon.
—The Buzzards Must Also be Fed. 1991. 192p. 18.95 o.s.i (*0-8027-5773-1*) Walker & Co.
—Death by Deception. 1991. 208p. mass mkt. 3.95 o.p. (*0-06-100146-5*, Perennial) HarperTrade.
—Death by Deception. 1988. 192p. 17.95 o.p. (*0-8027-5714-6*) Walker & Co.
—Exception to Murder. pap. 2.98 o.p. (*0-8317-8133-5*) Smithmark Pubs., Inc.
—Exception to Murder. 1992. 192p. 19.95 (*0-8027-3203-8*) Walker & Co.
—The Eye of Anna. 1991. 208p. mass mkt. 3.95 o.p. (*0-06-100165-1*, HarperTorch) Morrow/Avon.
—The Eye of Anna. 1990. 192p. 17.95 o.p. (*0-8027-5749-9*) Walker & Co.
—Yakuza, Go Home! A Mark Shigata Mystery. 1993. 218p. 19.95 o.p. (*0-8027-3226-7*) Walker & Co.

**SHILLER, MIKE (FICTITIOUS CHARACTER)—FICTION**

Holleman, Jane. Killer Gorgeous. 1997. 256p. per. 5.99 (*0-671-00105-1*, Pocket) Simon & Schuster.

**SHILLING, GRACE (FICTITIOUS CHARACTER)—FICTION**

French, Nicci. Beneath the Skin. l.t. ed. 2000. (Illus.). 495p. (*0-7540-1478-9*, Macmillan Reference USA) Gale Group.
—Beneath the Skin. 2000. 368p. 24.95 (*0-89296-726-9*) Mysterious Pr.
—Beneath the Skin. l.t. ed. 2000. (G. K. Hall Core Ser.). (Illus.). 495p. 30.95 (*0-7838-9006-0*) Thorndike Pr.
—Beneath the Skin. abr. ed. 2001. 2p. audio (*0-14-180261-8*, Penguin AudioBooks) Viking Penguin.
—Beneath the Skin. 2001. 448p. reprint ed. mass mkt. 7.99 (*0-446-60978-1*) Warner Bks., Inc.

**SHIMURA, REI (FICTITIOUS CHARACTER)—FICTION**

Massey, Sujata. The Bride's Kimono. 2001. 320p. 25.00 (*0-06-019933-4*) HarperCollins Pubs.
—The Bride's Kimono. 2002. 400p. mass mkt. 6.99 (*0-06-103115-1*, Avon Bks.) Morrow/Avon.
—The Floating Girl. 2000. 304p. 24.00 (*0-06-019229-1*) HarperCollins Pubs.
—The Floating Girl. 2001. 384p. mass mkt. 6.99 (*0-06-109735-7*, Avon Bks.) Morrow/Avon.
—The Flower Master. 1999. 304p. 24.00 (*0-06-019228-3*) HarperCollins Pubs.
—The Flower Master. 2000. 400p. mass mkt. 6.99 (*0-06-109734-9*, HarperTorch) Morrow/Avon.
—The Flower Master. 2000. 13.04 (*0-606-21840-8*) Turtleback Bks.
—The Salaryman's Wife. 1997. 432p. mass mkt. 7.50 (*0-06-104443-1*, HarperTorch) Morrow/Avon.
—Salarymans Wife Arc. 2000. 368p. pap. 5.99 (*0-06-104384-2*) HarperCollins Pubs.
—Zen Attitude. 1998. 320p. mass mkt. 6.99 (*0-06-104444-X*, HarperTorch) Morrow/Avon.

**SHOCK, BEN (FICTITIOUS CHARACTER)—FICTION**

Bunn, T. Davis. The Amber Room. 1992. (Priceless Collection). 336p. pap. 9.99 o.p. (*1-55661-285-0*) Bethany Hse. Pubs.
—The Amber Room. l.t. ed. 2001. (Christian Mystery Ser.). 519p. 24.95 o.p. (*0-7862-3070-3*) Thorndike Pr.

**SHORE, JEMIMA (FICTITIOUS CHARACTER)—FICTION**

Fraser, Antonia. The Cavalier Case. l.t. ed. 1992. (Jemima Shore Mystery Ser.). pap. 14.95 o.p. (*0-7927-0818-0*); 18.95 o.p. (*0-7927-0817-2*, E0014); audio 69.95 (*0-7451-5967-2*, CAB 673) BBC Audiobooks America.
—The Cavalier Case. 1992. 256p. mass mkt. 4.99 o.s.i (*0-553-29544-6*) Bantam Bks.
—Cool Repentance: A Jemima Shore Mystery. unabr. ed. 1993. audio 54.95 (*0-7451-5964-8*, CSL 064) BBC Audiobooks America.
—Cool Repentance: A Jemima Shore Mystery. 1991. 240p. mass mkt. 4.50 o.s.i (*0-553-28072-4*) Bantam Bks.
—Cool Repentance: A Jemima Shore Mystery. unabr. collector's ed. 1988. audio 40.00 (*0-7366-1303-X*, 2210) Books on Tape, Inc.
—Cool Repentance: A Jemima Shore Mystery. 1983. 12.95 o.p. (*0-393-01625-0*); 1985. 224p. reprint ed. pap. 3.95 o.p. (*0-393-30264-4*) Norton, W. W. & Co., Inc.
—Jemima Shore at the Sunny Grave. l.t. ed. 1993. pap. 16.95 o.p. (*0-7927-1348-6*); 1992. 18.95 o.p. (*0-7927-1349-4*) BBC Audiobooks America.
—Oxford Blood: A Jemima Shore Mystery. l.t. ed. 1986. pap. 13.95 o.p. (*1-55504-037-3*); 1993. 54.95 incl. audio (*0-7451-5966-4*, CAB 204) BBC Audiobooks America.
—Oxford Blood: A Jemima Shore Mystery. 1989. 224p. mass mkt. 3.95 o.s.i (*0-553-28070-8*) Bantam Bks.
—Oxford Blood: A Jemima Shore Mystery. (Jemima Shore Mystery Ser.). 1998. 224p. pap. 10.00 (*0-393-31824-9*, Norton Paperbacks); 1985. 13.95 o.p. (*0-393-02229-3*) Norton, W. W. & Co., Inc.
—Oxford Blood: A Jemima Shore Mystery. 1987. audio 49.95 o.s.i (*0-8161-9661-3*) Thorndike Pr.
—Political Death: A Jemima Shore Mystery. unabr. ed. 1996. audio 54.95 (*0-7451-6583-4*, CAB1199) BBC Audiobooks America.
—Political Death: A Jemima Shore Mystery. 1997. 240p. mass mkt. 5.99 (*0-553-57203-2*, Crimeline) Bantam Bks.
—Political Death: A Jemima Shore Mystery. unabr. ed. 1994. audio 40.00 Books on Tape, Inc.
—Quiet as a Nun. l.t. ed. 1993. (J). (gr. 5 up). pap. 18.95 o.p. (*0-7927-1689-2*); 1993. (YA). (gr. 5 up). 20.95 o.p. (*0-7927-1690-6*); audio 54.95 (*0-7451-5971-0*, CAB 397) BBC Audiobooks America.
—Quiet as a Nun. 1991. 192p. mass mkt. 4.50 o.s.i (*0-553-28311-1*) Bantam Bks.
—Quiet as a Nun. unabr. collector's ed. 1984. audio 42.00 (*0-7366-0884-2*, 1828) Books on Tape, Inc.
—Quiet as a Nun. unabr. ed. 2000. (Jemima Shore Mystery Ser.: Bk. 1). audio 49.95 Chivers Audio Bks. GBR. *Dist:* BBC Audiobooks America.
—Quiet as a Nun. (Jemima Shore Mystery Ser.). 1998. 192p. pap. 10.00 (*0-393-31822-2*, Norton Paperbacks); 1982. pap. 3.95 o.p. (*0-393-30120-6*) Norton, W. W. & Co., Inc.
—Quiet as a Nun. 1977. 8.95 o.p. (*0-670-58556-4*) Viking Penguin.
—A Splash of Red: A Jemina Shore Mystery, unabr. ed. 1993. 54.95 incl. audio (*0-7451-5963-X*, CAB 101) BBC Audiobooks America.
—A Splash of Red: A Jemina Shore Mystery. 1990. 224p. mass mkt. 3.95 o.s.i (*0-553-28071-6*) Bantam Bks.
—A Splash of Red: A Jemina Shore Mystery. 1984. pap. 3.50 o.p. (*0-393-30213-X*); 1982. 12.95 o.p. (*0-393-01511-4*); 1998. 240p. pap. 10.00 (*0-393-31687-4*) Norton, W. W. & Co., Inc.
—A Splash of Red: A Jemina Shore Mystery. unabr. ed. 1985. audio 53.95 o.s.i (*0-8161-9823-3*) Thorndike Pr.
—The Wild Island: A Jemima Shore Mystery. l.t. ed. 1993. 20.95 o.p. (*0-7927-1486-5*); 1993. pap. 18.95 o.p. (*0-7927-1485-7*); 1992. 54.95 incl. audio (*0-7451-5968-0*, CAB 522) BBC Audiobooks America.
—The Wild Island: A Jemima Shore Mystery. 1991. 224p. mass mkt. 4.50 o.s.i (*0-553-29324-9*) Bantam Bks.
—The Wild Island: A Jemima Shore Mystery. unabr. collector's ed. 1986. audio 42.00 (*0-7366-0885-0*, 1829) Books on Tape, Inc.
—The Wild Island: A Jemima Shore Mystery. 1978. 8.95 o.p. (*0-393-08831-6*) Norton, W. W. & Co., Inc.
—Your Royal Hostage. l.t. ed. 1988. 13.95 o.p. (*1-55504-394-1*); Set. 1993. 54.95 incl. audio (*0-7451-5969-9*, CAB 261) BBC Audiobooks America.
—Your Royal Hostage. 1989. 272p. mass mkt. 3.95 o.s.i (*0-553-28019-8*) Bantam Bks.

**SHORE, MARLA (FICTITIOUS CHARACTER)—FICTION**

Cohen, Nancy J. Body Wave: A Bad Hair Day Mystery. 2002. (Bad Hair Day Mysteries Ser.: Vol. 4). 304p. 22.00 (*0-7582-0068-4*) Kensington Publishing Corp.
—Hair Raiser. (Bad Hair Day Mysteries Ser.). 2001. 288p. mass mkt. 5.99 o.s.i (*1-57566-688-X*); 2000. 34p. 20.00 o.s.i (*1-57566-622-7*) Kensington Publishing Corp.
—Murder by Manicure. (Bad Hair Day Mysteries Ser.). 2002. 34p. mass mkt. 5.99 (*1-57566-741-X*); 2001. 24p. 22.00 o.s.i (*1-57566-687-1*) Kensington Publishing Corp.
—Permed to Death. (Bad Hair Day Mysteries Ser.). 2000. 32p. mass mkt. 5.99 (*1-57566-624-3*); 1999. 293p. 20.00 o.s.i (*1-57566-482-8*, Kensington Bks.) Kensington Publishing Corp.

**SHORE, MATT (FICTITIOUS CHARACTER)—FICTION**

Francis, Dick. Rat Race. unabr. ed. 1993. audio 39.95 (*0-7451-5954-0*, CAB 020) BBC Audiobooks America.
—Rat Race. 1993. 256p. mass mkt. 6.99 (*0-449-22112-1*, Fawcett) Ballantine Bks.
—Rat Race. unabr. ed. 2000. audio 34.95 Chivers Audio Bks. GBR. *Dist:* BBC Audiobooks America.
—Rat Race. abr. ed. audio 15.95 o.p. (*1-55994-136-7*, CPN 2136, HarperAudio) HarperTrade.
—Rat Race. 1989. 224p. mass mkt. 4.50 (*0-671-70076-6*); 1988. mass mkt. 3.95 (*0-671-67643-1*); 1984. mass mkt. 3.50 (*0-671-53026-7*) Simon & Schuster. (Pocket).
—Rat Race. l.t. ed. 1974. 12.00 o.p. (*0-85456-256-7*, Ulverscroft) Thorpe, F. A. Pubs. GBR. *Dist:* Ulverscroft Large Print Bks., Ltd.

**SHUGAK, KATE (FICTITIOUS CHARACTER)—FICTION**

Stabenow, Dana. Blood Will Tell: A Kate Shugak Mystery. 1997. (Kate Shugak Mystery Ser.). 256p. mass mkt. 6.99 (*0-425-15798-9*) Berkley Publishing Group.
—Blood Will Tell: A Kate Shugak Mystery. 1996. (Kate Shugak Mystery Ser.). 256p. 21.95 o.p. (*0-399-14124-3*, G. P. Putnam's Sons) Penguin Group (USA) Inc.
—Breakup: A Kate Shugak Mystery. 1998. (Kate Shugak Mysteries Ser.). 256p. mass mkt. 6.99 (*0-425-16261-3*) Berkley Publishing Group.
—Breakup: A Kate Shugak Mystery. 1997. (Kate Shugak Mystery Ser.). 256p. 21.95 o.s.i (*0-399-14250-9*, G. P. Putnam's Sons) Penguin Group (USA) Inc.
—A Cold-Blooded Business: A Kate Shugak Mystery. 1995. (Kate Shugak Mystery Ser.). 240p. (Orig.). mass mkt. 6.99 (*0-425-15849-7*, Prime Crime) Berkley Publishing Group.
—Cold-Blooded Business: A Kate Shugak Mystery. 1994. (Kate Shugak Mysteries Ser.). 231p. (Orig.). 17.95 o.s.i (*0-425-14173-X*) Berkley Publishing Group.
—A Cold Day for Murder. unabr. ed. 1999. audio 24.95 (*0-7366-4423-7*, 4830) Books on Tape, Inc.
—A Cold Day for Murder: A Kate Shugak Mystery. l.t. ed. 2001. 189p. 26.95 (*1-57490-355-1*, Beeler Large Print Bks.) Beeler, Thomas T. Publisher.
—A Cold Day for Murder: A Kate Shugak Mystery. 1992. (Kate Shugak Mystery Ser.). 208p. mass mkt. 6.99 (*0-425-13301-X*) Berkley Publishing Group.
—Dead in the Water: A Kate Shugak Mystery. 1993. (Kate Shugak Mysteries Ser.). 224p. mass mkt. 6.99 (*0-425-13749-X*) Berkley Publishing Group.
—A Fatal Thaw. unabr. collector's ed. 1999. (Kate Shugak Mystery Ser.). audio 40.00 (*0-7366-4459-8*, 4904) Books on Tape, Inc.
—A Fatal Thaw: A Kate Shugak Mystery. 1993. (Kate Shugak Mystery Ser.). 208p. mass mkt. 6.99 (*0-425-13577-2*) Berkley Publishing Group.
—A Fine & Bitter Snow: A Kate Shugak Novel. 2002. 304p. 24.95 (*0-312-20548-1*, Saint Martin's Minotaur) St. Martin's Pr.
—A Grave Denied: A Kate Shugak Novel. 2003. 304p. 24.95 (*0-312-30681-4*, Saint Martin's Minotaur) St. Martin's Pr.
—Hunter's Moon. unabr. collector's ed. 1999. audio 40.00 (*0-7366-4635-3*, 5007) Books on Tape, Inc.
—Hunter's Moon: A Kate Shugak Mystery. 1999. (Prime Crime Mysteries Ser.). 256p. reprint ed. mass mkt. 6.99 (*0-425-17259-7*, Prime Crime) Berkley Publishing Group.
—Hunter's Moon: A Kate Shugak Mystery. 1999. (Kate Shugak Mystery Ser.). 260p. 23.95 o.s.i (*0-399-14468-4*) Penguin Group (USA) Inc.
—Killing Grounds. 1999. (Kate Shugak Mysteries Ser.). 256p. reprint ed. mass mkt. 6.99 (*0-425-16773-9*, Prime Crime) Berkley Publishing Group.
—Killing Grounds. 1999. 12.04 (*0-606-16389-1*) Turtleback Bks.
—The Killing Grounds: A Kate Shugak Mystery. 1998. (Kate Shugak Mystery Ser.). 273p. 22.95 o.p. (*0-399-14356-4*, G. P. Putnam's Sons) Penguin Group (USA) Inc.
—Midnight Come Again. l.t. ed. 2001. (Large Print Book Ser.). 351p. pap. 23.95 o.p. (*1-58724-031-9*, Wheeler Publishing, Inc.) Gale Group.
—Midnight Come Again. E-Book 23.95 (*0-312-27415-7*); 2001. 320p. reprint ed. mass mkt. 6.99 (*0-312-97876-6*, St. Martin's Paperbacks) St. Martin's Pr.
—Midnight Come Again: A Kate Shugak Novel. 2000. (Kate Shugak Mysteries Ser.). 291p. 23.95 o.p. (*0-312-20596-1*, Saint Martin's Minotaur) St. Martin's Pr.
—Play with Fire: A Kate Shugak Mystery. (Kate Shugak Mystery Ser.). 1996. 320p. mass mkt. 6.99 (*0-425-15254-5*); 1995. 288p. 19.95 o.p. (*0-425-14717-7*, Prime Crime) Berkley Publishing Group.
—The Singing of the Dead. 2001. E-Book 23.95 (*1-58945-791-9*) Adobe Systems, Inc.
—The Singing of the Dead. l.t. ed. 2001. (Illus.). 392p. 30.95 o.p. (*0-7838-9516-X*, Macmillan Reference USA) Gale Group.
—The Singing of the Dead. 2001. (Kate Shugak Mysteries Ser.: No. 11). (Illus.). 254p. 23.95 (*0-312-20957-6*, Saint Martin's Minotaur) St. Martin's Pr.

**SI CWAN (FICTITIOUS CHARACTER)—FICTION**

David, Peter. Dark Allies. 1999. (Star Trek Ser.: No. 8). (Illus.). 288p. pap. 6.50 (*0-671-02080-3*, Star Trek) Simon & Schuster.
—House of Cards. 1997. (Star Trek Ser.: No. 1). 168p. per. 3.99 o.s.i (*0-671-01395-5*, Star Trek) Simon & Schuster.
—House of Cards; Into the Void; The Two-Front War; End Game. 1998. (Star Trek Ser.: Nos. 1-4). 704p. 15.00 (*0-671-01978-3*, Star Trek) Simon & Schuster.
—House of Cards; Into the Void; The Two-Front War; End Game. abr. ed. 1997. (Star Trek Ser.: Nos. 1-4). audio 22.00 (*0-671-57625-9*, Simon & Schuster Audioworks) Simon & Schuster Audio.
—The Quiet Place. (Star Trek Ser.: No. 7). 288p. 2002. E-Book 6.99 (*0-7434-5574-6*); 1999. pap. 6.50 (*0-671-02079-X*) Simon & Schuster. (Star Trek).
—The Two-Front War. 1997. (Star Trek Ser.: No. 3). 304p. per. 3.99 (*0-671-01397-1*, Star Trek) Simon & Schuster.

**SIDDEN, JO BETH (FICTITIOUS CHARACTER)—FICTION**

Lanier, Virginia. Blind Bloodhound Justice: A Jo Beth Sidden Mystery. unabr. ed. 2000. (Bloodhound Ser.). audio 59.95 (*0-7927-2261-2*, CSL 150) Chivers Audio Bks. GBR. *Dist:* BBC Audiobooks America.
—Blind Bloodhound Justice: A Jo Beth Sidden Mystery. 1998. 288p. 24.00 o.s.i (*0-06-017547-8*) HarperCollins Pubs.
—Blind Bloodhound Justice: A Jo Beth Sidden Mystery. 1999. (Bloodhound Ser.). 352p. mass mkt. 6.99 (*0-06-109971-6*, HarperTorch) Morrow/Avon.
—A Bloodhound to Die For. 2003. 240p. 23.95 (*0-06-019388-3*) HarperCollins Pubs.
—A Bloodhound to Die For. 2004. 320p. mass mkt. 6.99 (*0-06-109840-X*, Avon Bks.) Morrow/Avon.
—A Brace of Bloodhounds. (Bloodhound Ser.). 1998. 448p. mass mkt. 6.50 (*0-06-101087-1*); 1997. 336p. 23.00 o.p. (*0-06-101089-8*) HarperCollins Pubs.
—Death in Bloodhound Red. 1996. (Bloodhound Ser.). 544p. mass mkt. 6.50 (*0-06-101025-1*, HarperTorch) Morrow/Avon.
—Death in Bloodhound Red. 1995. (Bloodhound Ser.). 462p. 19.95 (*1-56164-076-X*) Pineapple Pr., Inc.
—House on Bloodhound Lane. 1996. 352p. mass mkt. 20.00 o.p. (*0-06-101088-X*, HarperTorch) Morrow/Avon.
—The House on Bloodhound Lane. 1997. (Bloodhound Ser.). 384p. mass mkt. 5.99 (*0-06-101086-3*, HarperTorch) Morrow/Avon.
—Ten Little Bloodhounds: A Jo Beth Sidden Mystery, Set. unabr. ed. 1999. audio 69.95 (*0-7927-2335-X*, CSL 224, Chivers Sound Library) BBC Audiobooks America.
—Ten Little Bloodhounds: A Jo Beth Sidden Mystery. 1999. (Bloodhound Ser.). 288p. 24.00 (*0-06-017548-6*) HarperCollins Pubs.
—Ten Little Bloodhounds: A Jo Beth Sidden Mystery. 2000. (Bloodhound Ser.). 352p. mass mkt. 6.50 (*0-06-109066-2*, Avon Bks.) Morrow/Avon.

**SIDEL, ISAAC (FICTITIOUS CHARACTER)—FICTION**

Charyn, Jerome. El Bronx. l.t. ed. 1997. (Cloak & Dagger Ser.). 292p. 25.95 (*0-7862-1092-3*) Thorndike Pr.
—El Bronx. 1998. mass mkt. (*0-446-40538-8*, Mysterious Pr. Paperback Bks.); 1997. 256p. 21.50 o.p. (*0-89296-604-1*) Warner Bks., Inc.

—Citizen Sidel. 1999. 220p. 23.00 (*0-89296-605-X*) Mysterious Pr.
—The Education of Patrick Silver. 1977. 208p. pap. 2.75 o.p. (*0-380-01698-2*, 53603-X, Avon Bks.); 1976. 7.95 o.p. (*0-87795-142-X*, Morrow, William & Co.) Morrow/Avon.
—The Isaac Quartet: Blue Eyes; Marilyn the Wild; The Education of Patrick Silver; Secret Isaac. 2002. 548p. 35.00 (*1-56858-234-X*); reprint ed. pap. 17.95 (*1-56858-228-5*) Four Walls Eight Windows.
—Maria's Girls. 1993. 288p. mass mkt. 5.50 (*0-446-40046-7*, Mysterious Pr. Paperback Bks.) Warner Bks., Inc.
—Secret Isaac. 1984. 240p. pap. 2.75 o.p. (*0-380-47126-4*, 47126, Avon Bks.); 1978. 9.95 o.p. (*0-87795-196-9*, Morrow, William & Co.) Morrow/Avon.

**SIEGEL, ELLIE (FICTITIOUS CHARACTER)—FICTION**

Stewart, Edward. Mortal Grace. 1995. 560p. mass mkt. 6.50 o.s.i (*0-440-21697-4*) Dell Publishing.

**SIEGEL, PHOEBE (FICTITIOUS CHARACTER)—FICTION**

Prowell, Sandra West. By Evil Means. 1995. (Phoebe Siegel Mystery Ser.). 384p. mass mkt. 5.99 (*0-553-56966-X*) Bantam Bks.
—By Evil Means. 1993. 216p. 19.95 (*0-8027-1248-7*) Walker & Co.
—The Killing of Monday Brown. unabr. ed. 1994. audio 57.25 o.p. (*1-56100-207-0*, 919, Unabridged Library Editions); audio 21.95 o.p. (*1-56100-582-7*, 349, Bookcassette) Brilliance Audio.
—The Killing of Monday Brown: A Phoebe Siegel Mystery. 1996. 320p. mass mkt. 5.99 (*0-553-56969-4*) Bantam Bks.
—The Killing of Monday Brown: A Phoebe Siegel Mystery. 1994. 240p. 19.95 (*0-8027-3184-8*) Walker & Co.
—When Wallflowers Die. abr. ed. 1996. audio 16.95 o.p. (*1-56100-407-3*, 1406, Nova Audio Bks.); audio 7.99 o.p. (*1-56740-169-4*, 717, Paperback Nova Audio Bks.); audio 57.25 o.p. (*1-56100-239-9*, 1093, Unabridged Library Editions); audio 23.95 o.p. (*1-56100-614-9*, 313, Bookcassette) Brilliance Audio.
—When Wallflowers Die: A Phoebe Siegel Mystery. 1997. (Phoebe Siegel Mystery Ser.). 368p. mass mkt. 5.99 (*0-553-56970-8*, Crimeline) Bantam Bks.
—When Wallflowers Die: A Phoebe Siegel Mystery. 1996. 336p. 22.95 (*0-8027-3254-2*) Walker & Co.

**SIGISMONDO (FICTITIOUS CHARACTER)—FICTION**

Eyre, Elizabeth. Axe for an Abbot: An Italian Renaissance Whodunnit. 1996. 320p. 23.95 o.p. (*0-312-13925-X*, Saint Martin's Minotaur) St. Martin's Pr.
—Bravo for the Bride. 1995. 192p. 21.95 o.p. (*0-312-11756-6*, Saint Martin's Minotaur) St. Martin's Pr.
—Curtains for the Cardinal. 1994. 256p. mass mkt. 4.99 o.p. (*0-425-14126-8*) Berkley Publishing Group.
—Curtains for the Cardinal. 1993. vi, 260p. 19.95 (*0-15-123682-8*) Harcourt Trade Pubs.
—Curtains for the Cardinal. 26p. 3.98 o.p. (*0-8317-7438-X*) Smithmark Pubs., Inc.
—Death of the Duchess. 1993. 256p. mass mkt. 4.50 o.p. (*0-425-13902-6*) Berkley Publishing Group.
—Death of the Duchess. 1992. 19.95 (*0-15-124102-3*) Harcourt Trade Pubs.
—Dirge for a Doge. 1997. 320p. 23.95 o.p. (*0-312-15109-8*, Saint Martin's Minotaur) St. Martin's Pr.
—Poison for the Prince. 1994. viii, 309p. 19.95 (*0-15-172540-3*) Harcourt Trade Pubs.

**SILENCE, JOHN (FICTITIOUS CHARACTER)—FICTION**

Blackwood, Algernon. Complete John Silence Stories. Joshi, S. T., ed. & intro. by. 1998. (Illus.). 380p. reprint ed. pap. 9.95 (*0-486-29942-2*) Dover Pubns., Inc.

**SILVA, JOE (FICTITIOUS CHARACTER)—FICTION**

Oleksiw, Susan P. Double Take. 1994. (Chief Joe Silva Ser.). 256p. text 20.00 (*0-684-19656-5*, Macmillan Reference USA) Gale Group.
—Family Album. 1995. (Chief Joe Silva Ser.). 287p. 20.00 (*0-684-19731-6*, Scribner) Simon & Schuster.
—Murder in Mellingham. 1993. 288p. 20.00 o.p. (*0-684-19528-3*, Macmillan Reference USA) Gale Group.

**SILVER, MAUD (FICTITIOUS CHARACTER)—FICTION**

Wentworth, Patricia. The Alington Inheritance. 21.95 (*0-88411-730-8*) Amereon, Ltd.
—The Alington Inheritance. unabr. ed. 1992. audio 39.95 (*0-7861-0318-3*, 1279) Blackstone Audio Bks., Inc.
—The Alington Inheritance. 1992. 320p. reprint ed. pap. 8.00 o.p. (*0-06-092297-4*, Perennial) HarperTrade.
—The Alington Inheritance. 1990. 256p. (C). reprint ed. lib. bdg. 19.95 o.p. (*0-8095-9024-7*) Millefleurs.
—The Alington Inheritance. 1996. 272p. mass mkt. 4.99 o.p. (*0-06-104408-3*, HarperTorch) Morrow/Avon.
—The Alington Inheritance. l.t. ed. 1983. (Ulverscroft Large Print Ser.). 448p. 29.99 o.p. (*0-7089-1051-3*, Ulverscroft) Thorpe, F. A. Pubs. GBR. *Dist:* Ulverscroft Large Print Bks., Ltd., Ulverscroft Large Print Canada, Ltd.
—Anna, Where Are You? 21.95 (*0-88411-728-6*) Amereon, Ltd.
—Anna, Where Are You?, unabr. ed. 1992. audio 44.95 (*0-7861-0317-5*, 1278) Blackstone Audio Bks., Inc.
—Anna, Where Are You? (Miss Silver Mystery Ser.). 352p. 1992. pap. 8.00 o.p. (*0-06-092335-0*); 1991. reprint ed. pap. 5.95 o.p. (*0-06-081057-2*) HarperTrade. (Perennial).
—The Benevent Treasure. 1976. reprint ed. lib. bdg. 23.95 (*0-88411-731-6*) Amereon, Ltd.
—The Benevent Treasure. 1992. 224p. pap. 8.00 o.p. (*0-06-092336-9*); 1990. 256p. reprint ed. mass mkt. 4.95 o.p. (*0-06-081225-7*) HarperTrade. (Perennial).
—The Benevent Treasure. 1996. 288p. mass mkt. 4.99 o.s.i (*0-06-104406-7*, HarperTorch) Morrow/Avon.
—The Benevent Treasure. l.t. ed. 1982. 448p. 15.95 o.p. (*0-7089-0886-1*, Ulverscroft) Thorpe, F. A. Pubs. GBR. *Dist:* Ulverscroft Large Print Bks., Ltd.
—The Brading Collection. 22.95 (*0-88411-729-4*) Amereon, Ltd.
—The Brading Collection. 256p. 1992. pap. 8.00 o.p. (*0-06-092337-7*); 1990. reprint ed. mass mkt. 4.95 o.p. (*0-06-081226-5*) HarperTrade. (Perennial).
—The Brading Collection. l.t. ed. 1978. (Ulverscroft Large Print Ser.). 29.99 o.p. (*0-7089-0108-5*, Ulverscroft) Thorpe, F. A. Pubs. GBR. *Dist:* Ulverscroft Large Print Bks., Ltd., Ulverscroft Large Print Canada, Ltd.
—The Case Is Closed. 22.95 (*0-8488-0326-4*) Amereon, Ltd.
—The Case Is Closed. 1986. 256p. mass mkt. 3.99 o.s.i (*0-446-34471-0*) Warner Bks., Inc.
—The Case of William Smith. 24.95 (*0-88411-746-4*) Amereon, Ltd.
—The Case of William Smith. (Miss Silver Mystery Ser.). 352p. 1992. pap. 8.00 o.p. (*0-06-092340-7*); 1991. reprint ed. pap. 5.95 o.p. (*0-06-081058-0*) HarperTrade. (Perennial).
—The Catherine Wheel. 22.95 (*0-88411-747-2*) Amereon, Ltd.
—The Catherine Wheel. 1991. 352p. reprint ed. pap. 9.00 o.p. (*0-06-097441-9*, Perennial) HarperTrade.
—The Catherine Wheel. l.t. ed. 1977. (Ulverscroft Large Print Ser.). 12.00 o.p. (*0-85456-534-5*, Ulverscroft) Thorpe, F. A. Pubs. GBR. *Dist:* Ulverscroft Large Print Bks., Ltd., Ulverscroft Large Print Canada, Ltd.
—The Chinese Shawl. l.t. ed. 1992. (General Ser.). 305p. lib. bdg. 14.95 o.p. (*0-8161-5314-0*, Macmillan Reference USA) Gale Group.
—The Chinese Shawl. 1996. 272p. mass mkt. 4.99 o.p. (*0-06-104397-4*) HarperCollins Pubs.
—The Chinese Shawl. (Miss Silver Mystery Ser.). 256p. 1992. pap. 8.00 o.p. (*0-06-092339-3*); 1990. reprint ed. 5.95 o.p. (*0-06-081047-5*) HarperTrade. (Perennial).
—The Clock Strikes Twelve. 21.95 (*0-89190-923-0*) Amereon, Ltd.
—The Clock Strikes Twelve. 1996. 288p. mass mkt. 4.99 o.p. (*0-06-104400-8*) HarperCollins Pubs.
—The Clock Strikes Twelve. 1993. 256p. pap. 8.00 o.p. (*0-06-092408-X*, Perennial) HarperTrade.
—The Clock Strikes Twelve. l.t. ed. 1981. (Ulverscroft Large Print Ser.). 424p. o.p. (*0-7089-0604-4*, Ulverscroft) Thorpe, F. A. Pubs. GBR. *Dist:* Ulverscroft Large Print Canada, Ltd.
—The Clock Strikes Twelve. 1988. 295p. mass mkt. 3.95 o.s.i (*0-446-34905-4*) Warner Bks., Inc.
—Danger Point. l.t. ed. 1975. 12.00 o.p. (*0-85456-320-2*, Ulverscroft) Thorpe, F. A. Pubs. GBR. *Dist:* Ulverscroft Large Print Bks., Ltd.
—The Eternity Ring. 22.95 (*0-88411-748-0*) Amereon, Ltd.
—The Eternity Ring. 1991. 336p. reprint ed. pap. 9.00 o.p. (*0-06-097442-7*, Perennial) HarperTrade.
—The Fingerprint. 23.95 (*0-88411-727-8*) Amereon, Ltd.
—The Fingerprint. 1985. 240p. pap. 2.95 o.p. (*0-553-24986-X*) Bantam Bks.
—The Fingerprint. l.t. ed. 1990. (Ulverscroft Large Print Ser.). 29.99 o.p. (*0-7089-2265-1*, Ulverscroft) Thorpe, F. A. Pubs. GBR. *Dist:* Ulverscroft Large Print Bks., Ltd., Ulverscroft Large Print Canada, Ltd.
—The Fingerprint. 1988. 240p. mass mkt. 3.95 o.s.i (*0-446-34859-7*) Warner Bks., Inc.
—The Gazebo. 20.95 (*0-88411-725-1*) Amereon, Ltd.
—The Gazebo. (Miss Silver Mystery Ser.). 304p. 1992. pap. 8.00 o.p. (*0-06-092338-5*); 1990. reprint ed. 5.95 o.p. (*0-06-081048-3*) HarperTrade. (Perennial).
—The Gazebo. 1996. 288p. mass mkt. 4.99 o.p. (*0-06-104405-9*, HarperTorch) Morrow/Avon.
—The Girl in the Cellar. 20.95 (*0-89190-920-6*) Amereon, Ltd.
—The Girl in the Cellar. 1992. 192p. reprint ed. pap. 8.00 o.p. (*0-06-097445-1*, Perennial) HarperTrade.
—Grey Mask. 24.95 (*0-88411-726-X*) Amereon, Ltd.
—Grey Mask. 1996. 272p. mass mkt. 4.99 o.p. (*0-06-104398-2*) HarperCollins Pubs.
—Grey Mask. 1993. 224p. pap. 8.00 o.p. (*0-06-092364-4*, Perennial) HarperTrade.
—Grey Mask. l.t. ed. 1984. 432p. 12.50 o.p. (*0-7089-1221-4*, Ulverscroft) Thorpe, F. A. Pubs. GBR. *Dist:* Ulverscroft Large Print Bks., Ltd.
—Grey Mask. 1986. 256p. mass mkt. 3.95 o.s.i (*0-446-30135-3*) Warner Bks., Inc.
—The Ivory Dagger. 1976. reprint ed. lib. bdg. 21.95 (*0-88411-735-9*) Amereon, Ltd.
—The Ivory Dagger. 1981. 240p. mass mkt. 2.95 o.s.i (*0-553-25128-7*) Bantam Bks.
—The Ivory Dagger. 1992. 352p. reprint ed. pap. 8.00 o.p. (*0-06-092299-0*, Perennial) HarperTrade.
—The Ivory Dagger. 1996. 272p. mass mkt. 4.99 o.s.i (*0-06-104403-2*, HarperTorch) Morrow/Avon.
—The Ivory Dagger. l.t. ed. 1977. 12.00 o.p. (*0-85456-525-6*, Ulverscroft) Thorpe, F. A. Pubs. GBR. *Dist:* Ulverscroft Large Print Bks., Ltd.
—The Key. 1992. 224p. reprint ed. pap. 8.00 o.p. (*0-06-097446-X*, Perennial) HarperTrade.
—Ladies' Bane. 1976. reprint ed. lib. bdg. 21.95 (*0-88411-737-5*) Amereon, Ltd.
—Ladies' Bane. (Miss Silver Mystery Ser.). 1991. 368p. reprint ed. mass mkt. 5.95 o.p. (*0-06-081059-9*); 2nd ed. 1993. 336p. pap. 8.00 o.p. (*0-06-092361-X*) HarperTrade. (Perennial).
—Latter End. 25.95 (*0-89190-924-9*) Amereon, Ltd.
—Latter End. (Miss Silver Mystery Ser.). 272p. 1992. pap. 8.00 o.p. (*0-06-092334-2*); 1990. reprint ed. 5.95 o.p. (*0-06-081049-1*) HarperTrade. (Perennial).
—Latter End. l.t. ed. 1974. (Ulverscroft Large Print Ser.). 29.99 o.p. (*0-85456-252-4*, Ulverscroft) Thorpe, F. A. Pubs. GBR. *Dist:* Ulverscroft Large Print Bks., Ltd., Ulverscroft Large Print Canada, Ltd.
—The Listening Eye. 1976. reprint ed. lib. bdg. 23.95 (*0-88411-738-3*) Amereon, Ltd.
—The Listening Eye. 1985. mass mkt. 2.95 o.s.i (*0-553-24885-5*) Bantam Bks.
—The Listening Eye. l.t. ed. 1981. 405p. o.p. (*0-7089-0661-3*, Ulverscroft) Thorpe, F. A. Pubs.
—The Listening Eye. 1990. mass mkt. 4.50 (*0-446-34857-0*) Warner Bks., Inc.
—Lonesome Road. 1993. 320p. pap. 8.00 o.p. (*0-06-092406-3*, Perennial) HarperTrade.
—Lonesome Road. 1988. 208p. mass mkt. 3.50 o.s.i (*0-446-31466-8*) Warner Bks., Inc.
—Miss Silver Comes to Stay. 22.95 (*0-88411-749-9*) Amereon, Ltd.
—Miss Silver Comes to Stay. 1985. (Mystery Ser.). 208p. mass mkt. 2.95 o.s.i (*0-553-25362-X*) Bantam Bks.
—Miss Silver Comes to Stay. 320p. reprint ed. 1992. pap. 8.00 o.p. (*0-06-092300-8*); 1989. mass mkt. 3.95 o.p. (*0-06-080978-7*, P 978) HarperTrade. (Perennial).
—Miss Silver Comes to Stay. 1996. 288p. mass mkt. 4.99 o.p. (*0-06-104404-0*, HarperTorch) Morrow/Avon.
—Miss Silver Comes to Stay. l.t. ed. 1977. (Ulverscroft Large Print Ser.). 12.00 o.p. (*0-7089-0064-X*, Ulverscroft) Thorpe, F. A. Pubs. GBR. *Dist:* Ulverscroft Large Print Bks., Ltd., Ulverscroft Large Print Canada, Ltd.
—Miss Silver Deals with Death. 21.95 (*0-8488-1218-2*) Amereon, Ltd.
—Miss Silver Deals with Death. 1991. 336p. reprint ed. pap. 8.00 o.p. (*0-06-097443-5*, Perennial) HarperTrade.
—Out of the Past. 21.95 (*0-89190-922-2*) Amereon, Ltd.
—Out of the Past. (Miss Silver Mystery Ser.). 1991. 320p. reprint ed. mass mkt. 5.95 o.p. (*0-06-081060-2*); 2nd ed. 1993. 336p. pap. 8.00 o.p. (*0-06-092363-6*) HarperTrade. (Perennial).
—Out of the Past. l.t. ed. 1974. (Ulverscroft Large Print Ser.). 12.00 o.p. (*0-85456-235-4*, Ulverscroft) Thorpe, F. A. Pubs. GBR. *Dist:* Ulverscroft Large Print Bks., Ltd., Ulverscroft Large Print Canada, Ltd.
—Pilgrim's Rest. 25.95 (*0-88411-721-9*) Amereon, Ltd.
—Pilgrim's Rest. 1993. 256p. pap. 8.00 o.p. (*0-06-092407-1*, Perennial) HarperTrade.
—Pilgrim's Rest. 1996. 288p. mass mkt. 4.99 o.p. (*0-06-104402-4*, HarperTorch) Morrow/Avon.
—Pilgrim's Rest. l.t. ed. 1983. (Ulverscroft Large Print Ser.). 464p. 29.99 o.p. (*0-7089-0938-8*, Ulverscroft) Thorpe, F. A. Pubs. GBR. *Dist:* Ulverscroft Large Print Bks., Ltd., Ulverscroft Large Print Canada, Ltd.
—Pilgrim's Rest. 1988. 240p. mass mkt. 3.50 o.s.i (*0-446-31463-3*) Warner Bks., Inc.
—Poison in the Pen. 1976. reprint ed. lib. bdg. 23.95 (*0-88411-739-1*) Amereon, Ltd.
—Poison in the Pen. 1985. 208p. mass mkt. 2.95 o.s.i (*0-553-25067-1*) Bantam Bks.
—Poison in the Pen, unabr. ed. 1992. audio 39.95 (*0-7861-0320-5*, 752375) Blackstone Audio Bks., Inc.
—Poison in the Pen. l.t. ed. 1991. (Paperback Ser.). 315p. pap. 15.95 o.p. (*0-8161-5137-7*, Macmillan Reference USA) Gale Group.
—Poison in the Pen. 1992. 320p. reprint ed. pap. 8.00 o.p. (*0-06-092302-4*, Perennial) HarperTrade.
—Poison in the Pen. 1990. 352p. (C). reprint ed. lib. bdg. 20.00 o.p. (*0-8095-9025-5*) Millefleurs.
—Poison in the Pen. 1996. 79p. mass mkt. 4.99 o.p. (*0-06-104407-5*, HarperTorch) Morrow/Avon.
—She Came Back. 20.95 (*0-88411-744-8*) Amereon, Ltd.
—She Came Back. 1985. 208p. pap. 2.95 o.p. (*0-553-25173-2*) Bantam Bks.
—She Came Back, unabr. ed. 1993. audio 39.95 (*0-7861-0319-1*, 752406) Blackstone Audio Bks., Inc.
—She Came Back. 1996. 256p. mass mkt. 4.99 o.p. (*0-06-104399-0*) HarperCollins Pubs.
—She Came Back. 1992. 320p. reprint ed. pap. 8.00 o.p. (*0-06-092301-6*, Perennial) HarperTrade.
—The Silent Pool. 1980. reprint ed. lib. bdg. 20.95 (*0-88411-740-5*) Amereon, Ltd.
—The Silent Pool. (Miss Silver Mystery Ser.). 288p. 1992. pap. 8.00 o.p. (*0-06-092333-4*); 1990. reprint ed. 5.95 o.p. (*0-06-081050-5*) HarperTrade. (Perennial).
—The Silent Pool. l.t. ed. 1980. (Ulverscroft Large Print Ser.). 424p. 12.00 o.p. (*0-7089-0549-8*, Ulverscroft) Thorpe, F. A. Pubs. GBR. *Dist:* Ulverscroft Large Print Bks., Ltd., Ulverscroft Large Print Canada, Ltd.
—Spotlight. 22.95 (*0-88411-722-7*) Amereon, Ltd.
—Through the Wall. 22.95 (*0-88411-723-5*) Amereon, Ltd.
—Through the Wall. 1982. 240p. mass mkt. 2.95 o.s.i (*0-553-25255-0*) Bantam Bks.
—Through the Wall, unabr. ed. 1992. audio 44.95 (*0-7861-0321-3*, 892528) Blackstone Audio Bks., Inc.
—Through the Wall. reprint ed. 1992. 368p. pap. 8.00 o.p. (*0-06-092298-2*); 1989. 352p. mass mkt. 3.95 o.p. (*0-06-080979-5*, P979) HarperTrade. (Perennial).
—Through the Wall. l.t. ed. 1988. (Ulverscroft Large Print Ser.). 496p. 29.99 o.p. (*0-7089-1826-3*, Ulverscroft) Thorpe, F. A. Pubs. GBR. *Dist:* Ulverscroft Large Print Bks., Ltd., Ulverscroft Large Print Canada, Ltd.
—The Traveller Returns. 21.95 (*0-89190-921-4*) Amereon, Ltd.
—The Traveller Returns. l.t. ed. 1993. 21.95 o.p. (*0-7927-1638-8*); pap. 19.95 o.p. (*0-7927-1637-X*) BBC Audiobooks America.
—Vanishing Point. 1976. reprint ed. lib. bdg. 22.95 (*0-88411-742-1*) Amereon, Ltd.
—Vanishing Point. 1991. 368p. reprint ed. pap. 8.00 o.p. (*0-06-097444-3*, Perennial) HarperTrade.
—The Watersplash. 1976. reprint ed. lib. bdg. 22.95 (*0-88411-741-3*, 741) Amereon, Ltd.
—The Watersplash. 1994. reprint ed. lib. bdg. 32.95 (*1-56849-359-2*) Buccaneer Bks., Inc.
—The Watersplash. l.t. ed. 1976. o.p. (*0-85456-489-6*, Ulverscroft) Thorpe, F. A. Pubs.
—The Watersplash. 1989. 256p. mass mkt. 4.50 o.s.i (*0-446-35699-9*); 1987. mass mkt. 3.50 (*0-446-34448-6*) Warner Bks., Inc.
—Wicked Uncle. 22.95 (*0-88411-724-3*) Amereon, Ltd.
—Wicked Uncle. 1993. 288p. pap. 8.00 o.p. (*0-06-092362-8*, Perennial) HarperTrade.
—Wicked Uncle. 1996. 288p. mass mkt. 4.99 o.s.i (*0-06-104401-6*, HarperTorch) Morrow/Avon.
—Wicked Uncle. 1986. 272p. mass mkt. 3.99 o.s.i (*0-446-30083-7*) Warner Bks., Inc.

**SILVERHAND (FICTITIOUS CHARACTER)—FICTION**

Llywelyn, Morgan & Scott, Michael. Silverhand: The Arcana. (Arcana Ser.: Bk. I). 432p. 1995. 22.00 (*0-671-87652-X*); Bk. 1. 1996. pap. 5.99 (*0-671-87714-3*) Baen Bks.
—Silverlight: The Arcana, Bk. 2. 1997. (Arcana Ser.: Vol. 2). 432p. pap. 5.99 (*0-671-87790-9*) Baen Bks.
—Silverlight Bk. 2: The Arcana, 1996. 416p. 21.00 (*0-671-87728-3*) Baen Bks.

**SIMMONS, RACHEL (FICTITIOUS CHARACTER)—FICTION**

Rosenberg, Nancy Taylor. Abuse of Power. unabr. ed. 1997. audio 72.00 (*0-913369-73-X*, 4326) Books on Tape, Inc.
—Abuse of Power. 1997. 336p. 23.95 o.p. (*0-525-93768-4*) Dutton/Plume.
—Abuse of Power. l.t. ed. 1997. 448p. mass mkt. 7.99 (*0-451-18006-2*, Signet Bks.) NAL.
—Abuse of Power, unabr. ed. 1997. audio 78.00 (*0-7887-0916-X*, 94957E7) Recorded Bks., LLC.
—Abuse of Power. abr. ed. 1997. 3p. audio 16.95 o.s.i (*0-14-086507-1*, Penguin AudioBooks) Viking Penguin.

**SIMON, MARGO (FICTITIOUS CHARACTER)—FICTION**

Steinberg, Janice. The Dead Man & the Sea. 1997. 256p. mass mkt. 5.99 o.s.i (*0-425-16037-8*, Prime Crime) Berkley Publishing Group.
—Death Crosses the Border. 1995. 240p. mass mkt. 4.99 o.s.i (*0-425-15052-6*) Berkley Publishing Group.
—Death-Fires Dance. 1996. 272p. (Orig.). mass mkt. 5.99 o.s.i (*0-425-15551-X*, Prime Crime) Berkley Publishing Group.
—Death in a City of Mystics. 1998. (Prime Crime Mysteries Ser.). 288p. mass mkt. 5.99 o.s.i (*0-425-16615-5*, Prime Crime) Berkley Publishing Group.
—Death of a Postmodernist. 1995. 256p. (Orig.). mass mkt. 5.99 o.s.i (*0-425-14546-8*, Prime Crime) Berkley Publishing Group.

**SIMONS, BARBARA (FICTITIOUS CHARACTER)—FICTION**

Epstein, Carole. Perilous Friends. 1996. (Barbara Simons Mystery Ser.). 224p. 21.95 (*0-8027-3287-9*) Walker & Co.
—Perilous Relations: A Barbara Simons Mystery. 1997. (Barbara Simons Mystery Ser.). 276p. 22.95 (*0-8027-3309-3*) Walker & Co.

**SIMONS, ELLIE (FICTITIOUS CHARACTER)—FICTION**

Cannell, Dorothy. Bridesmaids Revisited: An Ellie Haskell Mystery. l.t. ed. 2000. (G. K. Hall Core Ser.). 342p. 30.95 (*0-7838-9272-1*, Macmillan Reference USA) Gale Group.
—Bridesmaids Revisited: An Ellie Haskell Mystery. 2001. (Ellie Haskell Mysteries Ser.). 256p. mass mkt. 5.99 (*0-14-100186-0*) Penguin Group (USA) Inc.
—Bridesmaids Revisited: An Ellie Haskell Mystery. 2000. (Ellie Haskell Mysteries Ser.). 256p. 22.95 o.s.i (*0-670-89205-X*, Viking) Viking Penguin.
—Down the Garden Path: A Pastoral Mystery. l.t. ed. 2002. 28.95 (*1-58547-218-2*, Premier) Ctr. Point Large Print.
—Femmes Fatal. 1994. 304p. mass mkt. 6.99 (*0-553-29684-1*) Bantam Bks.
—Femmes Fatal. l.t. ed. 1993. (General Ser.). 385p. 21.95 o.p. (*0-8161-5654-9*, Macmillan Reference USA) Gale Group.
—How to Murder the Man of Your Dreams. 1996. 304p. mass mkt. 6.99 (*0-553-57360-8*) Bantam Bks.
—How to Murder the Man of Your Dreams. l.t. ed. 1996. 428p. 23.95 o.p. (*0-7838-1493-3*, Macmillan Reference USA) Gale Group.
—How to Murder Your Mother-in-Law. 1995. 288p. mass mkt. 6.50 (*0-553-56951-1*); 1994. 272p. 19.95 o.s.i (*0-553-07493-8*) Bantam Bks.
—How to Murder Your Mother-in-Law. unabr. ed. 1994. audio 57.25 o.p. (*1-56100-178-3*, 904, Unabridged Library Editions); audio 21.95 o.p. (*1-56100-552-5*, 141, Bookcassette) Brilliance Audio.
—How to Murder Your Mother-in-Law. l.t. ed. 1994. 385p. lib. bdg. 23.95 (*0-8161-5930-0*, Macmillan Reference USA) Gale Group.
—The Importance of Being Ernestine. l.t. ed. 2002. (Wheeler Compass Ser.). 341p. 29.95 (*1-58724-327-X*, Wheeler Publishing, Inc.) Gale Group.
—The Importance of Being Ernestine. (Ellie Haskell Mysteries Ser.). 272p. 2003. 6.99 (*0-14-200284-4*); 2002. 23.95 (*0-670-03060-0*, Viking) Viking Penguin.
—Mum's the Word. 1991. 272p. mass mkt. 6.50 o.s.i (*0-553-28686-2*) Bantam Bks.
—Mum's the Word. l.t. ed. 2001. (Beeler Large Print Mystery Ser.). 324p. 26.95 (*1-57490-352-7*, Beeler Large Print Bks.) Beeler, Thomas T. Publisher.
—The Spring Cleaning Murders: An Ellie Haskell Mystery. l.t. ed. 1998. (Beeler Large Print Mystery Ser.). 26.95 (*1-57490-162-1*, Beeler Large Print Bks.) Beeler, Thomas T. Publisher.
—The Spring Cleaning Murders: An Ellie Haskell Mystery. 1999. (Ellie Haskell Mysteries Ser.). 288p. pap. 6.99 (*0-14-027615-7*) Penguin Group (USA) Inc.
—The Spring Cleaning Murders: An Ellie Haskell Mystery. 1998. (Ellie Haskell Mysteries Ser.). 256p. 21.95 o.p. (*0-670-87571-6*, Viking) Viking Penguin.
—The Thin Woman: An Epicurean Mystery. 1992. 304p. mass mkt. 6.99 (*0-553-29195-5*) Bantam Bks.
—The Thin Woman: An Epicurean Mystery. l.t. ed. 2000. 376p. lib. bdg. 28.95 (*1-58547-008-2*) Ctr. Point Large Print.
—The Thin Woman: An Epicurean Mystery. 1984. 288p. 13.95 o.p. (*0-312-80005-3*) St. Martin's Pr.
—The Thin Woman: An Epicurean Mystery. 1985. (Crime Monthly Ser.). 256p. pap. 4.50 o.p. (*0-14-007947-5*, Penguin Bks.) Viking Penguin.
—The Trouble with Harriet: An Ellie Haskell Mystery. l.t. ed. 2000. pap. 23.95 (*1-56895-833-1*, Wheeler Publishing, Inc.) Gale Group.
—The Trouble with Harriet: An Ellie Haskell Mystery. 2000. (Ellie Haskell Mysteries Ser.). 288p. pap. 5.99 (*0-14-029182-2*) Penguin Group (USA) Inc.
—The Trouble with Harriet: An Ellie Haskell Mystery. unabr. ed. (Ellie Haskell Mystery Ser.). 2001. audio compact disk 78.00 (*0-7887-5202-2*, C1359E7); 2000. audio 51.00 (*0-7887-4058-X*, 96087E7) Recorded Bks., LLC.
—The Trouble with Harriet: An Ellie Haskell Mystery. 1999. (Ellie Haskell Mysteries Ser.). 256p. 21.95 o.s.i (*0-670-88629-7*, Viking) Viking Penguin.
—The Widows' Club. 1989. 352p. mass mkt. 6.99 (*0-553-27794-4*) Bantam Bks.

**SIMPLE (FICTITIOUS CHARACTER)—FICTION**

Hughes, Langston. The Best of Simple. (Classics of Modern American Humor Ser.). (Illus.). reprint ed. 29.00 (*0-404-19936-4*) AMS Pr., Inc.
—The Best of Simple. 1990. pap. 6.95 o.p. (*0-8090-0039-3*, Hill & Wang) Farrar, Straus & Giroux.
—The Return of Simple. Harper, Akiba S., ed. 1995. 218p. pap. 20.00 (*0-8090-1582-X*); 1994. 256p. 20.00 o.s.i (*0-8090-8676-X*) Farrar, Straus & Giroux. (Hill & Wang).
—The Simple Omnibus. 22.95 (*0-88411-059-1*) Amereon, Ltd.
—Simple Stakes a Claim. Date not set. lib. bdg. 20.95 (*0-8488-2178-5*) Amereon, Ltd.
—Simple Takes a Wife. 22.95 (*0-88411-062-1*) Amereon, Ltd.
—Simple Takes a Wife. 1994. lib. bdg. 24.95 (*1-56849-398-3*) Buccaneer Bks., Inc.
—Simple's Uncle Sam. 20.95 (*0-88411-709-X*) Amereon, Ltd.
—Simple's Uncle Sam. (American Century Ser.). 1965. 180p. pap. 7.95 o.p. (*0-8090-0087-3*); 2000. xix, 180p. pap. 13.00 (*0-8090-8681-6*) Farrar, Straus & Giroux. (Hill & Wang).

**SIMPSON, TIM (FICTITIOUS CHARACTER)—FICTION**

Malcolm, John. A Back Room in Somers Town. 1986. 160p. mass mkt. 2.95 o.s.i (*0-345-33032-3*) Ballantine Bks.
—A Back Room in Somers Town. 1985. 160p. 12.95 o.s.i (*0-684-18301-3*, Macmillan Reference USA) Gale Group.
—A Deceptive Appearance. (Tim Simpson Mystery Ser.). 1992. 224p. text 20.00 o.s.i (*0-684-19508-9*); 1993. 318p. lib. bdg. 15.95 (*0-8161-5780-4*) Gale Group. (Macmillan Reference USA).
—The Godwin Sideboard. 1986. mass mkt. 2.95 o.s.i (*0-345-33371-3*) Ballantine Bks.
—The Godwin Sideboard. 1985. (Tim Simpson Mystery Ser.). 176p. 13.95 o.s.i (*0-684-18398-6*, Macmillan Reference USA) Gale Group.
—Gothic Pursuit. 1987. (Tim Simpson Mystery Ser.). 208p. 14.95 o.p. (*0-684-18833-3*, Macmillan Reference USA) Gale Group.
—The Gwen John Sculpture. 1987. mass mkt. 2.95 o.s.i (*0-345-33618-6*) Ballantine Bks.
—The Gwen John Sculpture. 1986. 208p. 13.95 o.p. (*0-684-18574-1*, Macmillan Reference USA) Gale Group.
—Hung Over. 1995. 240p. 19.95 o.p. (*0-312-13514-9*, Saint Martin's Minotaur) St. Martin's Pr.
—Into the Vortex, Vol. 1. 1997. (Into the Vortex Ser.: Vol. 1). 240p. 21.95 o.p. (*0-312-15555-7*, Saint Martin's Minotaur) St. Martin's Pr.
—Mortal Ruin. 1988. 208p. 15.95 o.s.i (*0-684-18958-5*, Macmillan Reference USA) Gale Group.
—Sheep, Goats & Soap: A Tim Simpson Mystery. l.t. ed. 1992. 275p. pap. 14.95 o.p. (*0-8161-5475-9*, Macmillan Reference USA) Gale Group.
—Sheep, Goats & Soap: A Tim Simpson Mystery. 1992. 224p. 19.95 o.s.i (*0-684-19384-1*, Scribner) Simon & Schuster.
—Simpson's Homer. 2002. (Tim Simpson Mystery Ser.). 239p. 25.95 (*0-7490-0586-6*) Allison & Busby, Ltd. GBR. *Dist:* International Publishers Marketing.
—Whistler in the Dark. 1988. mass mkt. 3.50 o.s.i (*0-345-34292-5*) Ballantine Bks.
—Whistler in the Dark. 1987. 160p. 14.95 o.p. (*0-684-18701-9*, Scribner) Simon & Schuster.
—The Wrong Impression: A Tim Simpson Mystery. 1990. 224p. 18.95 o.p. (*0-684-19252-7*, Scribner) Simon & Schuster.

**SIMPSON FAMILY (FICTITIOUS CHARACTERS)—FICTION**

Groening, Matt. Bart Simpson's Treehouse of Horror Heebie-Jeebie Hullabaloo. 1999. (Illus.). 144p. pap. 15.95 (*0-06-098762-6*, Perennial) HarperTrade.
—Big Book of Bart Simpson. 2002. (Illus.). 120p. pap. 12.95 (*0-06-008469-3*, Perennial) HarperTrade.

**SINCLAIR, ADAM (FICTITIOUS CHARACTER)—FICTION**

Kurtz, Katherine. The Adept. 1991. (Adept Ser.: No. 1). 336p. mass mkt. 6.99 (*0-441-00343-5*) Ace Bks.
—Death of an Adept. 1996. (Adept Ser.: No. 5). 464p. 21.95 o.s.i (*0-441-00367-2*) Ace Bks.
—The Lodge of the Lynx. 1993. (Adept Ser.: No. 2). 20.00 o.p. (*0-7278-4420-2*) Severn Hse. Pubs., Ltd.
—The Templar Treasure, 1993. (Adept Ser.: No. 3). 320p. mass mkt. 6.99 (*0-441-00345-1*) Ace Bks.
—The Templar Treasure. 1994. (Adept Ser.: No. 3). reprint ed. lib. bdg. 20.00 o.p. (*0-7278-4632-9*) Severn Hse. Pubs., Ltd.
Kurtz, Katherine & Harris, Deborah T. The Adept, Bk. I. 1992. (Adept Ser.: No. 1). 336p. reprint ed. 20.00 o.p. (*0-7278-4378-8*) Severn Hse. Pubs., Ltd.
—Dagger Magic. (Adept Ser.: No. 4). 1996. 384p. mass mkt. 6.99 (*0-441-00304-4*); 1995. 375p. 19.95 o.p. (*0-441-00149-1*) Ace Bks.
—Death of an Adept. 1997. (Adept Ser.: No. 5). 448p. mass mkt. 7.50 (*0-441-00484-9*) Ace Bks.
—The Lodge of the Lynx, Vol. 2. 1992. (Adept Ser.: No. 2). 432p. mass mkt. 6.99 (*0-441-00344-3*) Ace Bks.
—The Temple & the Stone. 1999. 560p. mass mkt. 6.99 (*0-446-60723-1*); 1998. 450p. 22.00 o.p. (*0-446-52260-0*) Warner Bks., Inc.

**SINCLAIR, CECILY (FICTITIOUS CHARACTER)—FICTION**

Kingsbury, Kate. Check-Out Time. 1995. 224p. (Orig.). mass mkt. 5.50 o.s.i (*0-425-14640-5*, Prime Crime) Berkley Publishing Group.
—Chivalry Is Dead. 1996. mass mkt. 5.50 o.s.i (*0-425-15515-3*) Berkley Publishing Group.
—Death with Reservations: A Pennyfoot Hotel Mystery. 1998. (Pennyfoot Hotel Mystery Ser.). 224p. mass mkt. 5.99 o.s.i (*0-425-16144-7*, Prime Crime) Berkley Publishing Group.
—Do Not Disturb. 1994. (Orig.). mass mkt. 4.99 o.s.i (*0-425-14914-5*); 208p. mass mkt. 4.50 o.s.i (*0-515-11282-8*) Berkley Publishing Group. (Jove).
—Dying Room Only. 1998. (Pennyfoot Hotel Mystery Ser.). 224p. mass mkt. 5.99 o.s.i (*0-425-16568-X*, Prime Crime) Berkley Publishing Group.
—Eat, Drink, & Be Buried. 1994. 208p. mass mkt. 4.50 o.p. (*0-425-14352-X*, Prime Crime) Berkley Publishing Group.
—Grounds for Murder. 1995. (Pennyfoot Hotel Mystery Ser.). 240p. (Orig.). mass mkt. 5.50 o.s.i (*0-425-14901-3*) Berkley Publishing Group.
—Maid to Murder, 1 vol. 1999. (Pennyfoot Hotel Mystery Ser.: Vol.12). 224p. mass mkt. 5.99 o.s.i (*0-425-16967-7*) Berkley Publishing Group.
—Pay the Piper. 1996. 224p. (Orig.). mass mkt. 5.50 o.s.i (*0-425-15231-6*) Berkley Publishing Group.
—Ring for Tomb Service: In Edwardian England Murder Rings a Bell. 1997. 240p. mass mkt. 5.99 o.s.i (*0-425-15857-8*, Prime Crime) Berkley Publishing Group.
—Room with a Clue. 1993. 208p. (Orig.). mass mkt. 3.99 o.s.i (*0-515-11188-0*, Jove) Berkley Publishing Group.
—A Room with a Clue. 1993. 208p. (Orig.). mass mkt. 5.50 o.s.i (*0-425-14326-0*) Berkley Publishing Group.
—Service for Two. 1994. 208p. (Orig.). mass mkt. 4.99 o.s.i (*0-425-14223-X*, Prime Crime) Berkley Publishing Group.

**SINCLAIR, EVANGELINE (FICTITIOUS CHARACTER)—FICTION**

Babson, Marian. Break a Leg, Darlings. l.t. ed. 1997. (G. K. Hall Nightingale Ser.). 300p. lib. bdg. 18.95 o.p. (*0-7838-8036-7*, Macmillan Reference USA) Gale Group.
—Break a Leg, Darlings. 1997. 183p. 20.95 o.p. (*0-312-15285-X*, Saint Martin's Minotaur) St. Martin's Pr.
—Encore Murder. l.t. ed. 1991. (Nightingale Ser.). 275p. pap. 14.95 o.p. (*0-8161-5139-3*, Macmillan Reference USA) Gale Group.
—Encore Murder. 1990. 15.95 o.p. (*0-312-04964-1*, Saint Martin's Minotaur) St. Martin's Pr.
—Reel Murder, unabr. ed. 1993. audio 39.95 (*0-7451-5753-X*, CAT 4025) BBC Audiobooks America.
—Reel Murder. 1988. mass mkt. 3.50 o.s.i (*0-553-27361-2*) Bantam Bks.
—Reel Murder. l.t. ed. 1988. (Nightingale Ser.). 307p. 12.95 o.p. (*0-8161-4492-3*, Macmillan Reference USA) Gale Group.
—Reel Murder. 1987. 192p. 12.95 o.p. (*0-312-00227-0*) St. Martin's Pr.
—Reel Murder. 1988. audio 35.95 o.p. (*0-8161-7780-5*) Thorndike Pr.
—Shadows in Their Blood. l.t. ed. 1994. 322p. lib. bdg. 16.95 (*0-8161-5952-1*, Macmillan Reference USA) Gale Group.
—Shadows in Their Blood. 1993. 192p. 16.95 o.p. (*0-312-09383-7*, Saint Martin's Minotaur) St. Martin's Pr.

**SINCLAIR, GAR (FICTITIOUS CHARACTER)—FICTION**

White, Teri. Thursday's Child. 1991. 18.95 o.s.i (*0-89296-255-0*) Mysterious Pr.
—Thursday's Child. 1992. 304p. mass mkt. 4.99 (*0-446-40092-0*, Mysterious Pr. Paperback Bks.) Warner Bks., Inc.

**SINCLAIR, JEFFREY (FICTITIOUS CHARACTER)—FICTION**

Bunn, T. Davis. The Amber Room. 1992. (Priceless Collection). 336p. pap. 9.99 o.p. (*1-55661-285-0*) Bethany Hse. Pubs.
—The Amber Room. l.t. ed. 2001. (Christian Mystery Ser.). 519p. 24.95 o.p. (*0-7862-3070-3*) Thorndike Pr.
—Florian's Gate. 1992. (Priceless Collection). 352p. (ps up). pap. 9.99 o.p. (*1-55661-244-3*) Bethany Hse. Pubs.
—Florian's Gate. l.t. ed. 2000. (Christian Mystery Ser.). 563p. 24.95 (*0-7862-2877-6*) Thorndike Pr.
—Winter Palace. 1993. (Priceless Collection: No. 3). 352p. pap. 9.99 o.p. (*1-55661-324-5*) Bethany Hse. Pubs.
—Winter Palace. 2001. audio 50.95 NorthStar Audio Bks.
—Winter Palace. l.t. ed. 2001. (Thorndike Christian Mystery Ser.). (Illus.). 512p. 24.95 (*0-7862-3179-3*) Thorndike Pr.

**SINCLAIR, MATTHEW (FICTITIOUS CHARACTER)—FICTION**

Fennelly, Tony. The Closet Hanging. 1987. (Matt Sinclair Ser.). 224p. 14.95 o.p. (*0-88184-306-7*); pap. 3.50 o.p. (*0-88184-393-8*) Avalon Publishing Group. (Carroll & Graf Pubs.).
—Murder with a Twist: The Glory Hole Murders & the Closet Hanging. 1991. 432p. pap. 4.95 o.p. (*0-88184-783-6*, Carroll & Graf Pubs.) Avalon Publishing Group.

**SIPOWICZ, ANDY (FICTITIOUS CHARACTER)—FICTION**

Collins, Max Allan. NYPD Blue Pt. 1: Blue Beginning. 1998. (Illus.). 48p. pap. 7.00 (*0-14-081644-5*); 1999. (Penguin Readers Ser.: Level 3). 1p. pap. 7.93 (*0-582-40170-4*) Longman Publishing Group.
—NYPD Blue Pt. I: Blue Blood. 1997. (NYPD Blues Ser.). 240p. mass mkt. 5.99 o.s.i (*0-451-18392-4*, Signet Bks.) NAL.

**SIRA THE SINGER (FICTITIOUS CHARACTER)—FICTION**

Marley, Louise. Receive the Gift. 1997. 304p. mass mkt. 5.99 o.s.i (*0-441-00486-5*) Ace Bks.
—Sing the Light. 1995. 304p. (Orig.). mass mkt. 5.50 o.s.i (*0-441-00272-2*) Ace Bks.
—Sing the Warmth. 1996. mass mkt. 5.99 o.s.i (*0-441-00386-9*) Ace Bks.

**SISCO, KAREN (FICTITIOUS CHARACTER)—FICTION**

Leonard, Elmore. Out of Sight. 1998. 304p. pap. 9.95 o.s.i (*0-385-33291-2*, 892924Q, Delta); 1997. 352p. mass mkt. 6.99 o.s.i (*0-440-21442-4*) Dell Publishing.
—Out of Sight. l.t. ed. 1996. 27.95 (*1-56895-385-2*, Wheeler Publishing, Inc.) Gale Group.
—Out of Sight: International Edition. 1997. mass mkt. 6.50 (*0-440-29553-X*) Dell Publishing.

**SISKO, BENJAMIN (FICTITIOUS CHARACTER)—FICTION**

Archer, Nathan. Valhalla. (Star Trek Deep Space Nine Ser.: No. 10). E-Book 6.99 (*0-7434-2041-1*, Star Trek) Simon & Schuster.
—Valhalla. Ordover, John, ed. 1995. (Star Trek Deep Space Nine Ser.: No. 10). 288p. mass mkt. 5.50 (*0-671-88115-9*, Star Trek) Simon & Schuster.
Barnes, Steve. Far Beyond the Stars. (Star Trek Deep Space Nine Ser.). E-Book 6.99 (*0-7434-2084-5*); 1998. 288p. pap. 6.50 (*0-671-02430-2*) Simon & Schuster. (Star Trek).
Betancourt, John. Devil in the Sky. (Star Trek Deep Space Nine Ser.: No. 11). E-Book 6.95 (*0-7434-2042-X*, Star Trek) Simon & Schuster.
Betancourt, John G. The Heart of the Warrior. 1996. (Star Trek Deep Space Nine Ser.: No. 17). 288p. pap. 5.99 (*0-671-00239-2*, Star Trek) Simon & Schuster.
The Captain's Table. 2000. (Star Trek, The Next Generation Ser.). E-Book 16.95 (*0-7434-0670-2*, Star Trek) Simon & Schuster.
Carey, Diane L. Dominion War: Call to Arms. 1998. (Star Trek Deep Space Nine: Vol. 2). 288p. pap. 6.50 (*0-671-02497-3*, Star Trek) Simon & Schuster.

—The Dominion War No. 2: Call to Arms. 1998. (Star Trek Deep Space Nine Ser.). E-Book 6.99 *(0-671-04105-3*, Star Trek) Simon & Schuster.

—The Dominion War No. 4: Sacrifice of Angels. 1999. (Star Trek Deep Space Nine Ser.). E-Book 6.99 *(0-671-04107-X*, Star Trek) Simon & Schuster.

—Dominion War No. 4: Sacrifice of Angels. 4th ed. 1998. (Star Trek Deep Space Nine: Vol. 4). 288p. pap. 6.50 *(0-671-02498-1*, Star Trek) Simon & Schuster.

—The Search. 1994. (Star Trek Deep Space Nine Ser.). 272p. mass mkt. 5.50 *(0-671-50604-8*, Star Trek) Simon & Schuster.

—Station Rage. 1995. (Star Trek Deep Space Nine Ser.: No. 13). 288p. mass mkt. 5.99 *(0-671-88561-8*, Star Trek) Simon & Schuster.

—Trials & Tribble-ations. 1996. (Star Trek Deep Space Nine Ser.). 144p. mass mkt. 3.99 *(0-671-00902-8*, Star Trek) Simon & Schuster.

—The Way of the Warrior. 1995. (Star Trek Deep Space Nine Ser.). 288p. mass mkt. 5.99 o.s.i *(0-671-56813-2*, Star Trek) Simon & Schuster.

—What You Leave Behind. 1999. (Star Trek Deep Space Nine Ser.). 224p. pap. 6.50 *(0-671-03476-6*, Star Trek) Simon & Schuster.

Carey, Diane L., et al. Invasion Omnibus: First Strike; The Soldiers of Fear; Time's Enemy; The Final Fury. 1998. (Star Trek Ser.). 960p. mass mkt. 14.00 *(0-671-02185-0*, Star Trek) Simon & Schuster.

Cox, Greg. Devil in the Sky. 1995. (Star Trek Deep Space Nine Ser.: No. 11). (Illus.). 288p. (J). mass mkt. 5.50 *(0-671-88114-0*, Star Trek) Simon & Schuster.

David, Peter. The Siege. 1993. (Star Trek Deep Space Nine Ser.: No. 2). E-Book 6.99 *(0-7434-1221-4)*; 288p. mass mkt. 5.50 *(0-671-87083-1)* Simon & Schuster. (Star Trek).

David, Peter, et al. Wrath of the Prophets. 1997. (Star Trek Deep Space Nine Ser.: No. 20). 304p. pap. 5.99 *(0-671-53817-9*, Star Trek) Simon & Schuster.

Dillard, J. M. Dark Victory. 1993. (Star Trek Deep Space Nine Ser.: No. 1). per. 5.50 *(0-671-78958-9*, Star Trek) Simon & Schuster.

—Dark Victory. Stern, Dave, ed. 1993. (Star Trek Deep Space Nine Ser.). 288p. mass mkt. 5.50 *(0-671-79858-8*, Star Trek) Simon & Schuster.

—Dark Victory. (Star Trek Deep Space Nine Ser.: No. 1). 1989. audio 17.00 *(0-671-79102-8)*; 1999. audio 18.00 *(0-671-04385-4)* Simon & Schuster Audio. (Simon & Schuster Audioworks).

—Emissary. 1993. (Star Trek Deep Space Nine Ser.: No. 1). E-Book 6.99 *(0-7434-1220-6*, Star Trek) Simon & Schuster.

Dillard, J. M., et al. Emissary; The Siege; Bloodletter; The Big Game; Betrayal, 5 bks. 1997. (Star Trek). pap. text 0.95 o.p. *(0-8359-1492-5)* Globe Fearon Educational Publishing.

Friedman, Michael Jan. Saratoga. 1996. (Star Trek Deep Space Nine Ser.: No. 18). 288p. mass mkt. 5.99 *(0-671-56897-3*, Star Trek) Simon & Schuster.

Friesner, Esther M. Warchild. (Star Trek Deep Space Nine Ser.: No. 7). E-Book 6.99 *(0-7434-2038-1*, Star Trek) Simon & Schuster.

—Warchild. Ordover, John, ed. 1994. (Star Trek Deep Space Nine Ser.: No. 7). 288p. mass mkt. 5.50 *(0-671-88116-7*, Star Trek) Simon & Schuster.

Garland, Mark. Trial by Error. 1997. (Star Trek Deep Space Nine Ser.: No. 21). (Illus.). 304p. pap. 5.99 *(0-671-00251-1*, Star Trek) Simon & Schuster.

Graf, L. A. Armageddon Sky: Day of Honor. Keenan, Randall, ed. 1997. (Star Trek, The Next Generation: Vol. 2). 304p. pap. 5.99 o.s.i *(0-671-00675-4*, Star Trek) Simon & Schuster.

—Invasion! No. 3: Time's Enemy. 1999. (Star Trek Deep Space Nine Ser.: No. 16). E-Book 6.99 *(0-671-04097-9*, Star Trek) Simon & Schuster.

—Time's Enemy: Invasion! 1996. (Star Trek Deep Space Nine Ser.: No. 16). 352p. (J). pap. 5.99 *(0-671-54150-1*, Star Trek) Simon & Schuster.

Graf, L. A., et al. The Captain's Table Omnibus. 2000. (Star Trek Ser.). 1152p. pap. 16.95 *(0-671-04052-9*, Star Trek) Simon & Schuster.

Hugh, Dafydd ab. The Conquered No. 1: Rebels. 1999. (Star Trek Deep Space Nine Ser.: No. 24). 256p. pap. 6.50 o.s.i *(0-671-01140-5*, Star Trek) Simon & Schuster.

—The Courageous. (Star Trek Deep Space Nine Ser.: No. 25). E-Book 6.99 *(0-7434-2056-X*, Star Trek) Simon & Schuster.

—The Courageous No. 2: Rebels. 1999. (Star Trek Deep Space Nine Ser.: No. 25). 256p. mass mkt. 6.50 o.s.i *(0-671-01141-3*, Star Trek) Simon & Schuster.

—Fallen Heroes. (Star Trek Deep Space Nine Ser.: No. 5). 1999. E-Book 6.50 *(0-671-04114-2)*; 1994. E-Book 6.99 *(0-7434-1224-9)* Simon & Schuster. (Star Trek).

—Fallen Heroes. Ordover, John, ed. 1994. (Star Trek Deep Space Nine Ser.: No. 5). 288p. mass mkt. 5.50 *(0-671-88459-X*, Star Trek) Simon & Schuster.

—Fallen Heroes. abr. ed. 1994. (Star Trek Deep Space Nine Ser.: No. 5). audio 16.00 *(0-671-89182-0*, Simon & Schuster Audioworks) Simon & Schuster Audio.

—Fallen Heroes Star Trek Continuity. 1999. 12.99 *(0-671-02166-4*, Star Trek) Simon & Schuster.

—The Liberated. (Star Trek Deep Space Nine Ser.: No. 26). E-Book 6.99 *(0-7434-2057-8*, Star Trek) Simon & Schuster.

—The Liberated No. 3: Rebels. 1999. (Resistance Trilogy Ser.: No. 26). 256p. mass mkt. 6.50 o.s.i *(0-671-01142-1*, Star Trek) Simon & Schuster.

—Rebels: The Conquered. (Star Trek Deep Space Nine Ser.: No. 24). E-Book 6.99 *(0-7434-2055-1*, Star Trek) Simon & Schuster.

—Vengeance. 1998. (Star Trek Deep Space Nine Ser.: No. 22). 304p. pap. 6.50 *(0-671-00468-9*, Star Trek) Simon & Schuster.

Jeter, K. W. Bloodletter. 1993. (Star Trek Deep Space Nine Ser.: No. 3). 288p. mass mkt. 5.50 *(0-671-87275-3*, Star Trek) Simon & Schuster.

—The Bloodletter. 1993. (Star Trek Deep Space Nine Ser.: No. 3). E-Book 6.99 *(0-7434-1222-2*, Star Trek) Simon & Schuster.

—Warped. 1996. (Star Trek Deep Space Nine Ser.). 352p. mass mkt. 5.99 *(0-671-56781-0*, Star Trek) Simon & Schuster.

—Warped. Ryan, Kevin, ed. 1995. (Star Trek Deep Space Nine Ser.). 352p. 22.00 o.p. *(0-671-87252-4*, Star Trek) Simon & Schuster.

—Warped. abr. ed. (Star Trek Deep Space Nine Ser.). 1999. audio 9.98 *(0-671-04504-0)*; 1995. 16.00 incl. audio *(0-671-52120-9)*; 1995. 16.00 incl. audio *(0-671-52120-9)* Simon & Schuster Audio. (Simon & Schuster Audioworks).

Martin, Michael A. & Mangels, Andy. Mission Gamma: Cathedral. 2002. (Star Trek Deep Space Nine Ser.: Bk. 3). 432p. mass mkt. 6.99 *(0-7434-4564-3*, Star Trek) Simon & Schuster.

Peel, John. Objective: Bajor. 1996. (Star Trek Deep Space Nine Ser.: No. 15). 288p. per. 5.99 *(0-671-56811-6*, Star Trek) Simon & Schuster.

Reeves-Stevens, Judith & Reeves-Stevens, Garfield. Inferno. 2000. (Star Trek Deep Space Nine Ser.). E-Book 6.99 *(0-7434-0681-8)*; (Star Trek Deep Space Nine: Vol. 3). (Illus.). 464p. pap. 6.50 *(0-671-02403-5)* Simon & Schuster. (Star Trek).

—Millennium No. 1: The Fall of Terok Nor. 2000. (Star Trek Deep Space Nine Ser.). E-Book 6.99 *(0-7434-0679-6)*; (Star Trek Deep Space Nine: Vol. 1). 464p. pap. 6.50 o.s.i *(0-671-02401-9)* Simon & Schuster. (Star Trek).

—Millennium No. 1: The Fall of Terok Nor. abr. ed. 2000. (Star Trek Ser. ). audio 18.00 *(0-7435-0010-5*, Simon & Schuster Audioworks) Simon & Schuster Audio.

—Millennium No. 2: The War of the Prophets. 2000. (Star Trek Deep Space Nine Ser.). E-Book 6.99 *(0-7434-0680-X*, Star Trek) Simon & Schuster.

—Millennium Vol. 2: The War of the Prophets. 2000. (Star Trek Deep Space Nine: Vol. 2). 432p. pap. 6.50 o.s.i *(0-671-02402-7*, Star Trek) Simon & Schuster.

Robinson, Andrew J. A Stitch in Time. (Star Trek Deep Space Nine Ser.: No. 27). E-Book 6.95 *(0-7434-2058-6)*; 2000. (Illus.). 432p. pap. 6.50 *(0-671-03885-0)* Simon & Schuster. (Star Trek).

Schofield, Sandy. The Big Game. 1994. (Star Trek Deep Space Nine Ser.: No. 4). E-Book 6.99 *(0-7434-1223-0*, Star Trek) Simon & Schuster.

—The Big Game. Ordover, John, ed. 1993. (Star Trek Deep Space Nine Ser.: No. 4). 288p. mass mkt. 5.50 *(0-671-88030-6*, Star Trek) Simon & Schuster.

Scott, Melissa. Proud Helios. Ordover, John, ed. 1995. (Star Trek Deep Space Nine Ser.: No. 9). 288p. mass mkt. 5.50 *(0-671-88390-9*, Star Trek) Simon & Schuster.

Sheckley, Robert. Laertian Gamble. 1995. (Star Trek Deep Space Nine Ser.: No. 12). 288p. mass mkt. 5.99 *(0-671-88690-8*, Star Trek) Simon & Schuster.

Shimerman, Armin. The Merchant Prince. 2001. E-Book 23.95 *(1-58945-288-7)* Adobe Systems, Inc.

—The Merchant Prince. 2001. (Illus.). 368p. reprint ed. mass mkt. 6.99 *(0-671-03613-0*, Star Trek); Bk. 2. 2001. 320p. reprint ed. E-Book 6.99 *(0-7434-1748-8*, Star Trek); Bk. 3. 2003. 368p. mass mkt. 7.99 *(0-671-03594-0*, Pocket Star) Simon & Schuster.

Shimerman, Armin & George, David R., III. Star Trek Deep Space Nine: The 34th Rule. abr. ed. 1999. (Star Trek Deep Space Nine Ser.: No. 23). audio 16.85 *(0-671-03358-1)* Ulverscroft Audio (U.S.A.).

—The 34th Rule. 1999. (Star Trek Deep Space Nine Ser.: No. 23). 448p. pap. 6.50 *(0-671-00793-9*, Star Trek) Simon & Schuster.

—The 34th Rule. abr. ed. 1999. (Star Trek Ser. : No. 23). audio 18.00 *(0-671-04395-1*, Simon & Schuster Audioworks) Simon & Schuster Audio.

Shimerman, Armin & Scott, Michael. The Merchant Prince. 2000. 320p. 23.95 o.s.i *(0-671-03592-4*, Atria); Book 3. 2003. E-Book *(0-7434-8044-9*, Pocket) Simon & Schuster.

Sisko, Benjamin. The Mist: Captain's Table. 1998. (Star Trek: Vol. 3). (Illus.). 288p. pap. 6.50 *(0-671-01471-4*, Star Trek) Simon & Schuster.

Smith, Dean Wesley. The Core. 2003. 256p. mass mkt. 6.99 *(0-7434-6398-6*, Pocket) Simon & Schuster.

Smith, Dean Wesley & Rusch, Kristine K. The Long Night. (Star Trek Deep Space Nine Ser.: No. 14). E-Book 6.99 *(0-7434-2045-4)*; 1996. 288p. mass mkt. 5.99 *(0-671-55165-5)* Simon & Schuster. (Star Trek).

A Stitch in Time. 2000. per. 6.50 *(0-7434-1111-0*, Pocket) Simon & Schuster.

Sutcliffe, Katherine. Fever. 2001. 416p. pap. 6.99 *(0-7434-1197-8)*; E-Book 6.99 *(0-7434-1774-7)* Simon & Schuster. (Pocket).

Tilton, Lois. Betrayal. Ryan, Kevin, ed. 1994. (Star Trek Deep Space Nine Ser.: No. 6). 288p. mass mkt. 5.50 *(0-671-88117-5*, Pocket) Simon & Schuster.

Vornholt, John. Antimatter. (Star Trek Deep Space Nine Ser.: No. 8). (Orig.). E-Book 6.95 *(0-7434-2039-X*, Star Trek) Simon & Schuster.

—Antimatter. Ordover, John, ed. 1994. (Star Trek Deep Space Nine Ser.: No. 8). 288p. (Orig.). mass mkt. 5.50 o.s.i *(0-671-88560-X*, Star Trek) Simon & Schuster.

Wright, Susan. Badlands. 1999. (Star Trek Ser.: Vol. 2). (Illus.). 288p. pap. 6.99 *(0-671-03958-X*, Star Trek) Simon & Schuster.

—The Badlands, No. 2. 2000. (Star Trek Ser.). E-Book 6.99 *(0-7434-0675-3*, Star Trek) Simon & Schuster.

—The Tempest. 1997. (Star Trek Deep Space Nine Ser.: No. 19). (Illus.). 304p. pap. 5.99 *(0-671-00227-9*, Star Trek) Simon & Schuster.

## SISKO, JAKE (FICTITIOUS CHARACTER)—FICTION

Reeves-Stevens, Judith & Reeves-Stevens, Garfield. Millennium No. 1: The Fall of Terok Nor. 2000. (Star Trek Deep Space Nine Ser.). E-Book 6.99 *(0-7434-0679-6)*; (Star Trek Deep Space Nine: Vol. 1). 464p. pap. 6.50 o.s.i *(0-671-02401-9)* Simon & Schuster. (Star Trek).

—Millennium No. 1: The Fall of Terok Nor. abr. ed. 2000. (Star Trek Ser. ). audio 18.00 *(0-7435-0010-5*, Simon & Schuster Audioworks) Simon & Schuster Audio.

## SIXSMITH, JOE (FICTITIOUS CHARACTER)—FICTION

Hill, Reginald. Blood Sympathy. 1996. (WWL Mystery Ser.). per. *(0-373-26210-8*, 1-26210-4, Worldwide Library) Harlequin Enterprises, Ltd.

—Blood Sympathy, Set. unabr. ed. 1998. audio 69.95 *(1-85903-203-6)* Magna Story Sound GBR. *Dist:* Ulverscroft Large Print Bks., Ltd.

—Blood Sympathy. 1994. 224p. 19.95 o.p. *(0-312-11249-1*, Saint Martin's Minotaur) St. Martin's Pr.

—Blood Sympathy. l.t. ed. 1995. (Ulverscroft Large Print Ser.). 464p. 29.99 o.p. *(0-7089-3368-8*, Ulverscroft) Thorpe, F. A. Pubs. GBR. *Dist:* Ulverscroft Large Print Bks., Ltd., Ulverscroft Large Print Canada, Ltd.

—Born Guilty. 1996. mass mkt. *(0-373-26226-4*, 1-26226-0, Worldwide Library) Harlequin Enterprises, Ltd.

—Born Guilty. unabr. ed. 1998. audio 69.95 *(1-85903-234-6)* Magna Story Sound GBR. *Dist:* Ulverscroft Large Print Bks., Ltd.

—Born Guilty. 1995. 240p. 20.95 o.p. *(0-312-13032-5*, Saint Martin's Minotaur) St. Martin's Pr.

—Born Guilty. l.t. ed. 1996. (Ulverscroft Large Print Ser.). 416p. 29.99 o.p. *(0-7089-3571-0*, Ulverscroft) Thorpe, F. A. Pubs. GBR. *Dist:* Ulverscroft Large Print Bks., Ltd., Ulverscroft Large Print Canada, Ltd.

—Killing the Lawyers. 1998. per. *(0-373-26298-1*, 1-26298-9, Mira Bks.) Harlequin Enterprises, Ltd.

—Killing the Lawyers. unabr. ed. 1998. audio 83.95 *(1-85903-235-4)* Magna Story Sound GBR. *Dist:* Ulverscroft Large Print Bks., Ltd.

—Killing the Lawyers. 1997. (Joe Sixsmith Mysteries Ser.). 336p. 23.95 o.p. *(0-312-16877-2*, Saint Martin's Minotaur) St. Martin's Pr.

—Singing the Sadness. 2001. (WWL Mystery Ser.: No. 371). 251p. mass mkt. *(0-373-26371-6*, 1-26371-4, Worldwide Library) Harlequin Enterprises, Ltd.

—Singing the Sadness. 2nd ed. 1999. 352p. 23.95 *(0-312-24238-7*, Saint Martin's Minotaur) St. Martin's Pr.

—Singing the Sadness. l.t. ed. 2000. (Charnwood Large Print Ser.). 392p. 31.99 *(0-7089-9143-2*, Ulverscroft) Thorpe, F. A. Pubs. GBR. *Dist:* Ulverscroft Large Print Bks., Ltd., Ulverscroft Large Print Canada, Ltd.

## SKEEN (FICTITIOUS CHARACTER)—FICTION

Clayton, Jo. Skeen's Leap. 1986. mass mkt. 3.50 o.p. *(0-88677-169-2)*; Bk. 1. 320p. mass mkt. 3.95 o.p. *(0-88677-304-0)* DAW Bks., Inc.

—Skeen's Return, Bk. 2. 1987. mass mkt. 3.50 o.p. *(0-88677-202-8)* DAW Bks., Inc.

—Skeen's Search, Bk. 3. 1987. (Bifrost Guardians Ser.). 304p. mass mkt. 3.50 o.p. *(0-88677-241-9)* DAW Bks., Inc.

## SKEEVE (FICTITIOUS CHARACTER)—FICTION

Asprin, Robert L. Another Fine Myth. 1986. 208p. mass mkt. 5.50 o.s.i *(0-441-02362-2)*; 1985. mass mkt. 2.95 o.s.i *(0-441-02361-4)*; 1984. mass mkt. 2.95 o.s.i *(0-441-02360-6)*; 1984. mass mkt. 2.75 o.s.i *(0-441-02359-2)* Ace Bks.

—Another Fine Myth. 1984. pap. 7.95 o.p. *(0-915442-54-X)* Donning Co. Pubs.

—Another Fine Myth. Freas, Polly & Freas, Kelly, eds. 1978. (Myth Adventures Ser.: No. 1). (Illus.). 12.95 o.p. *(0-89865-383-5)*; 35.00 o.p. *(0-89865-382-7)* Donning Co. Pubs. (Starblaze).

—Another Fine Myth. abr. ed. 1992. (Myth Ser.). audio 16.99 *(0-88646-329-7*, 7329) Durkin Hayes Publishing Ltd.

—Another Fine Myth. l.t. ed. 2001. 200p. 27.95 *(0-7838-9505-4)*; 256p. *(0-7540-4638-9)*; 256p. *(0-7540-4637-0)* Gale Group. (Macmillan Reference USA).

—Another Fine Myth. unabr. ed. 1997. audio 44.00 *(0-7887-0924-0*, 95064E7) Recorded Bks., LLC.

—Hit or Myth. 1985. mass mkt. 2.95 o.s.i *(0-441-33853-4)*; 176p. mass mkt. 5.50 o.s.i *(0-441-33851-8)*; mass mkt. 2.95 o.s.i *(0-441-33850-X)* Ace Bks.

—Hit or Myth. Reynolds, Kay, ed. 1983. (Myth Adventures Ser.: No. 4). (Illus.). 172p. pap. 7.95 o.p. *(0-89865-331-2)*; lib. bdg. 12.95 o.p. *(0-89865-339-8)* Donning Co. Pubs. (Starblaze).

—Little Myth Marker. 1987. (Myth Ser.). mass mkt. 5.99 o.s.i *(0-441-48499-9)* Ace Bks.

—Little Myth Marker. Reynolds, Kay, ed. 1985. (Myth Adventures Ser.). (Illus.). 172p. pap. 7.95 o.p. *(0-89865-413-0)*; lib. bdg. 12.95 o.p. *(0-89865-411-4)*; 35.00 o.p. *(0-89865-418-1)* Donning Co. Pubs. (Starblaze).

—M. Y. T. H. Inc. in Action. 1991. 256p. mass mkt. 5.99 o.s.i *(0-441-55282-X)* Ace Bks.

—M. Y. T. H. Inc. in Action. Hainer, Beverley B., ed. 1990. (Myth Adventures Ser.). (Illus.). 180p. pap. 8.95 o.p. *(0-89865-803-9*, Starblaze) Donning Co. Pubs.

—M. Y. T. H. Inc. in Action. 1989. pap. 7.95 o.p. *(0-89865-787-3)* Donning Co. Pubs.

—M. Y. T. H. Inc. in Action. Hainer, Beverley B., ed. ltd. ed. 1990. (Myth Adventures Ser.). (Illus.). 180p. 40.00 o.p. *(0-89865-788-1*, Starblaze) Donning Co. Pubs.

—M. Y. T. H. Inc. Link. 1988. (Myth Ser.: No. 7). 176p. (Orig.). mass mkt. 5.50 o.s.i *(0-441-55277-3)* Ace Bks.

—M. Y. T. H. Inc. Link. 1986. (Myth Adventures Ser.). (Illus.). 160p. (Orig.). pap. 7.95 o.p. *(0-89865-472-6)*; pap. 12.95 o.p. *(0-89865-471-8)*; pap. 35.00 o.p. *(0-89865-470-X)* Donning Co. Pubs. (Starblaze).

—Myth Adventures One. 2001. 16.00 *(1-892065-36-3)*; 30.00 *(1-892065-35-5)* Meisha Merlin Publishing, Inc.

—Myth Conceptions. (Myth Bks.). 1986. 224p. mass mkt. 5.99 o.s.i *(0-441-55521-7)*; 1985. mass mkt. 2.95 o.s.i *(0-441-55520-9)*; 1985. mass mkt. 2.95 o.s.i *(0-441-55519-5)* Ace Bks.

—Myth Conceptions. Freas, Polly & Freas, Kelly, eds. 1980. (Illus.). pap. 7.95 o.p. *(0-915442-94-9*, Starblaze) Donning Co. Pubs.

—Myth Conceptions. abr. ed. 1993. (Myth Ser.). audio 16.99 *(0-88646-330-0*, 7330) Durkin Hayes Publishing Ltd.

—Myth Conceptions. unabr. ed. 1998. (Myth Ser.: Vol. 2). audio 44.00 *(0-7887-1894-0*, 95316E7) Recorded Bks., LLC.

—Myth Conceptions. l.t. ed. 2001. 273p. 27.95 *(0-7838-9550-X)* Thorndike Pr.

—Myth Directions. (Myth Ser.). 1986. mass mkt. 5.99 o.s.i *(0-441-55529-2)*; 1985. mass mkt. 2.95 o.s.i *(0-441-55527-6)*; 1985. mass mkt. 2.95 o.s.i *(0-441-55525-X)* Ace Bks.

—Myth Directions. Stine, Hank, ed. 1982. (Myth Adventures Ser.: No. 3). (Illus.). 176p. pap. 7.95 o.p. *(0-89865-250-2*, Starblaze) Donning Co. Pubs.

—Myth Directions. abr. ed. 1993. (Myth Ser.: No. 3). audio 16.99 *(0-88646-331-9*, LFP 7331) Durkin Hayes Publishing Ltd.

—Myth Directions. l.t. ed. 2002. 261p. 27.95 *(0-7838-9551-8*, Macmillan Reference USA) Gale Group.

—Myth Directions. unabr. ed. 1998. (Myth Ser.: Vol. 3). audio 46.00 *(0-7887-2187-9*, 95483E7 ) Recorded Bks., LLC.

—M.Y.T.H. Inc. in Action. l.t. ed. 2003. 27.95 *(0-7838-9563-1)* Thorndike Pr.

—Myth-ing Persons. 1986. 176p. mass mkt. 5.50 o.s.i (*0-441-55276-5*) Ace Bks.
—Myth-ing Persons. Reynolds, Kay, ed. 1984. (Myth Adventures Ser.: No. 5). (Illus.). 170p. 12.95 o.p. (*0-89865-380-0*); pap. 7.95 o.p. (*0-89865-379-7*); 35.00 o.p. (*0-89865-381-9*) Donning Co. Pubs. (Starblaze).
—Myth-Nomers & Im-Pervections, No. 8. 1988. (Myth-Nomers & Im-Pervections Ser.: Vol. 8). mass mkt. 5.99 o.s.i (*0-441-55279-X*) Ace Bks.
—Myth-Nomers & Im-Pervections. Gray, Mary E., ed. 1987. (Myth Adventures Ser.). (Illus.). 180p. 12.95 o.p. (*0-89865-540-4*); pap. 7.95 o.p. (*0-89865-529-3*); 35.00 o.p. (*0-89865-530-7*) Donning Co. Pubs. (Starblaze).
—Myth-Nomers & Im-Pervections. 2003. (Science Fiction Ser.). 27.95 (*0-7838-9549-6*) Thorndike Pr.
—Sweet Myth-tery of Life. 1995. 240p. mass mkt. 5.99 o.s.i (*0-441-00194-7*) Ace Bks.
—Sweet Myth-tery of Life. 1994. (Illus.). 29.95 o.p. (*0-89865-891-8*); o.p. (*0-89865-892-6*) Donning Co. Pubs.
Asprin, Robert L. & Foglio, Phil. Myth Adventures One. Reynolds, Kay & Pini, Richard, eds. 1985. (Myth Adventures Ser.). (Illus.). 108p. pap. 12.95 o.p. (*0-89865-414-9*); 40.00 o.p. (*0-89865-419-X*) Donning Co. Pubs. (Starblaze).
Asprin, Robert L., et al. Myth Adventures Two. Pini, Richard, ed. 1986. (Myth Adventures Ser.). (Illus.). 110p. (Orig.). pap. 12.95 o.p. (*0-89865-473-4*); pap. 40.00 o.p. (*0-89865-474-2*) Donning Co. Pubs. (Starblaze).

**SKINNER, BOB (FICTITIOUS CHARACTER)—FICTION**

Jardine, Quintin. Gallery Whispers. 2001. 420p. mass mkt. 8.95 (*0-7472-5667-5*) Headline Bk. Publishing, Ltd. GBR. *Dist:* Trafalgar Square.
—Gallery Whispers. l.t. ed. 2001. (Ulverscroft Large Print Ser.). 480p. 31.99 (*0-7089-4360-8*, Ulverscroft) Thorpe, F. A. Pubs. GBR. *Dist:* Ulverscroft Large Print Bks., Ltd., Ulverscroft Large Print Canada, Ltd.
—Murmuring the Judges. 2001. 407p. mass mkt. 8.95 (*0-7472-5962-3*) Headline Bk. Publishing, Ltd. GBR. *Dist:* Trafalgar Square.
—Skinner's Festival. 2001. (J). mass mkt. 8.95 (*0-7472-4140-6*) Headline Bk. Publishing, Ltd. GBR. *Dist:* Trafalgar Square.
—Skinner's Festival. 1995. 310p. 21.95 o.p. (*0-312-11892-9*, Saint Martin's Minotaur) St. Martin's Pr.
—Skinner's Ghosts. l.t. ed. 1999. (Ulverscroft Large Print Ser.). 416p. 31.99 o.p. (*0-7089-4159-1*, Ulverscroft) Thorpe, F. A. Pubs. GBR. *Dist:* Ulverscroft Large Print Bks., Ltd., Ulverscroft Large Print Canada, Ltd.
—Skinner's Mission. 2001. 406p. mass mkt. 9.95 (*0-7472-5043-X*) Headline Bk. Publishing, Ltd. GBR. *Dist:* Trafalgar Square.
—Skinner's Mission. unabr. ed. 1999. audio 83.95 (*1-85903-291-5*) Magna Story Sound GBR. *Dist:* Ulverscroft Large Print Bks., Ltd.
—Skinner's Mission. l.t. ed. 1998. (Ulverscroft Large Print Ser.). 512p. 29.99 o.p. (*0-7089-3914-7*, Ulverscroft) Thorpe, F. A. Pubs. GBR. *Dist:* Ulverscroft Large Print Bks., Ltd., Ulverscroft Large Print Canada, Ltd.
—Skinner's Ordeal. 2001. 438p. mass mkt. 8.95 (*0-7472-5042-1*) Headline Bk. Publishing, Ltd. GBR. *Dist:* Trafalgar Square.
—Skinner's Ordeal. l.t. ed. 1997. (Ulverscroft Large Print Ser.). 720p. 29.99 (*0-7089-3826-4*, Ulverscroft) Thorpe, F. A. Pubs. GBR. *Dist:* Ulverscroft Large Print Bks., Ltd., Ulverscroft Large Print Canada, Ltd.
—Skinner's Round. 2001. 436p. mass mkt. 9.95 (*0-7472-5041-3*) Headline Bk. Publishing, Ltd. GBR. *Dist:* Trafalgar Square.
—Skinner's Round. 1996. 304p. 23.95 (*0-312-14737-6*, Saint Martin's Minotaur) St. Martin's Pr.
—Skinner's Rules. 2001. mass mkt. 8.95 (*0-7472-4139-2*) Headline Bk. Publishing, Ltd. GBR. *Dist:* Trafalgar Square.
—Skinner's Rules. 1994. 320p. 21.95 o.p. (*0-312-11066-9*, Saint Martin's Minotaur) St. Martin's Pr.
—Skinner's Trail. 1996. 320p. 22.95 o.p. (*0-312-14417-2*, Saint Martin's Minotaur) St. Martin's Pr.

**SKINNER FAMILY (FICTITIOUS CHARACTERS)—FICTION**

Bly, Stephen A. Hidden Treasure. 2000. (Skinners of Goldfield Ser.: Bk. 2). 250p. pap. 11.99 (*1-58134-199-7*) Crossway Bks.
Morris, Gilbert & Ferguson, J. Landon. Above the Clouds. 1999. (Chronicles of the Golden Frontier Ser.: Bk. 3). 319p. pap. 11.99 (*1-58134-108-3*) Crossway Bks.
—Riches Untold: Chronicles of the Golden Frontier. 1998. (Chronicles of the Golden Frontier Ser.: Vol. 1). 368p. pap. 11.99 o.p. (*1-58134-014-1*) Crossway Bks.
—The Silver Thread. 2000. (Chronicles of the Golden Frontier Ser.: Bk. 4). 316p. pap. 11.99 (*1-58134-212-8*) Crossway Bks.

**SKINNY (FICTITIOUS CHARACTER: COLBERT)—FICTION**

Colbert, James. All I Have Is Blue. unabr. ed. 1994. audio 51.00 (*0-7887-0033-2*, 94232E7) Recorded Bks., LLC.
—No Special Hurry. 1988. 192p. 16.95 o.p. (*0-395-47016-1*) Houghton Mifflin Co.
—No Special Hurry. 1989. 224p. pap. 3.95 o.p. (*0-14-012399-7*, Penguin Bks.) Viking Penguin.
—Skinny Man. unabr. ed. 1993. audio 44.00 (*1-55690-930-6*, 93426E7) Recorded Bks., LLC.
—Skinny Man. 1991. 224p. text 18.95 o.p. (*0-689-12098-2*, Scribner) Simon & Schuster.

**SKYE, BARNABY (FICTITIOUS CHARACTER)—FICTION**

Wheeler, Richard S. Bannack. 1989. (Skye's West Ser.: No. 2). 288p. mass mkt. 3.95 (*0-8125-1071-2*, Tor Bks.) Doherty, Tom Assocs., LLC.
—Bitterroot. 1991. mass mkt. 4.50 (*0-8125-1305-3*, Tor Bks.) Doherty, Tom Assocs., LLC.
—The Dark Passage. 2000. (Barnaby Skye Novels). 318p. mass mkt. 6.99 (*0-8125-4025-5*, Forge Bks.) Doherty, Tom Assocs., LLC.
—The Dark Passage: A Barnaby Skye Novel. 1998. 318p. 23.95 (*0-312-86526-0*, Forge Bks.) Doherty, Tom Assocs., LLC.
—The Deliverance. 2003. (Skye's West Ser.: Vol. 13). 320p. 24.95 (*0-312-87844-3*, Forge Bks.) Doherty, Tom Assocs., LLC.
—Downriver: A Barnaby Skye Novel, Vol. 12. 2001. 320p. 25.95 (*0-312-87845-1*, Forge Bks.) Doherty, Tom Assocs., LLC.
—Downriver: A Barnaby Skye Novel. l.t. ed. 2002. 429p. 28.95 (*0-7862-3968-9*) Thorndike Pr.
—Far Tribes. 1990. (Far Tribes Ser.: No. 3). 313p. mass mkt. 3.95 (*0-8125-1069-0*, Tor Bks.) Doherty, Tom Assocs., LLC.
—Going Home. 2000. 320p. 23.95 o.p. (*0-312-87310-7*, Forge Bks.) Doherty, Tom Assocs., LLC.
—Going Home: A Barnaby Skye Novel. l.t. ed. 2001. 19.95 o.p. (*1-58724-059-9*, Wheeler Publishing, Inc.) Gale Group.
—Rendezvous: A Barnaby Skye Novel. l.t. ed. 1998. (Western Ser.). 519p. 25.95 (*0-7862-1349-3*) Thorndike Pr.
—Rendezvous: A Skye's West Novel. 1998. (Skye's West Ser.). 340p. pap. 5.99 (*0-8125-6537-1*, Forge Bks.) Doherty, Tom Assocs., LLC.
—Rendezvous Skyes West. 1997. (Barnaby Skye Novels). 352p. 23.95 (*0-312-86319-5*, Forge Bks.) Doherty, Tom Assocs., LLC.
—Santa Fe. 1994. (Skye's West Ser.: Vol. 8). 345p. mass mkt. 5.99 (*0-8125-2144-7*, Forge Bks.) Doherty, Tom Assocs., LLC.
—Skye's West: Bannack. l.t. ed. 2000. (Western Ser.). 507p. 24.95 (*0-7862-2594-7*) Thorndike Pr.
—Sun River, Vol. 1. 1989. (Sun River Ser.: Vol. 1). mass mkt. 3.95 (*0-8125-1073-9*, Tor Bks.) Doherty, Tom Assocs., LLC.
—Sundance. 1992. (Skye's West Ser.: No. 6). 352p. (Orig.). mass mkt. 4.99 (*0-8125-1306-1*, Tor Bks.) Doherty, Tom Assocs., LLC.
—Wind River. 1993. 352p. (Orig.). pap. text 3.99 (*0-8125-2142-0*, Tor Bks.) Doherty, Tom Assocs., LLC.
—Yellowstone. 1990. (Skye's West Ser.: Vol. 4). mass mkt. 3.95 (*0-8125-0894-7*, Tor Bks.) Doherty, Tom Assocs., LLC.

**SKYWALKER, ANAKIN (FICTITIOUS CHARACTER)—FICTION**

Bear, Greg. Rogue Planet. 2000. (Star Wars Ser.). 352p. 26.00 (*0-345-43538-9*, Del Rey) Ballantine Bks.
—Rogue Planet. abr. ed. 2000. (Star Wars Ser.). audio 25.00 (*0-375-41563-7*); audio compact disk 29.95 (*0-375-41586-6*) Random Hse. Audio Publishing Group. (RH Audio).
Brooks, Terry. Star Wars Episode I: The Phantom Menace. 2000. 352p. mass mkt. o.s.i (*0-345-43975-9*, Del Rey); 2000. 352p. mass mkt. 7.50 (*0-345-43411-0*, Del Rey); 1999. (*0-345-43754-3*); 1999. 324p. 25.00 (*0-345-42765-3*, Del Rey) Ballantine Bks.
—Star Wars Episode I: The Phantom Menace. abr. ed. 1999. (Star Wars Ser.). audio 19.95 (*0-375-40635-2*); audio compact disk 49.95 (*0-375-40743-X*); audio compact disk 24.95 (*0-375-40637-9*);Set. audio 39.95 (*0-375-40655-7*) Random Hse. Audio Publishing Group. (RH Audio).
—Star Wars Episode I: The Phantom Menace. 1999. (Star Wars Episode I Ser.). 13.55 (*0-606-19372-3*) Turtleback Bks.
Lucas, George. Star Wars: Episode I: The Phantom Menace Facsimile Script. 2000. (Star Wars Ser.). (Illus.). 144p. pap. 18.95 (*0-345-43123-5*, Del Rey) Ballantine Bks.
—Star Wars: Episode I: The Phantom Menace Illustrated Screenplay. 1999. (Star Wars Ser.). (Illus.). vii, 150p. (Orig.). pap. 14.95 (*0-345-43110-3*, Del Rey) Ballantine Bks.
Lucas, George, et al. Star Wars: Episode I: The Phantom Menace. 1999. (Star Wars Ser.). (Illus.). 112p. pap. 12.95 (*1-56971-359-6*) Dark Horse Comics.
Lucasfilm Ltd. Staff. Star Wars: Episode I: The Phantom Menace. 1999. pap. 1.94 o.s.i (*0-375-80898-1*, Random Hse. Bks. for Young Readers) Random Hse. Children's Bks.
—Star Wars: Episode I: The Phantom Menace. 1999. pap. 1.80 o.s.i (*0-375-80897-3*) Random Hse., Inc.
Prima Publishing Staff. Star Wars Episode I: Racer. 2000. (Prima's Official Strategy Guides). (Illus.). 128p. pap. 14.99 o.s.i (*0-7615-2946-2*, Prima Lifestyles) Crown Publishing Group.
Rhino Records Staff, ed. Star Wars: Episode I: The Phantom Menace. 1999. (Star Wars Ser.). 24p. (J). 9.98 incl. audio compact disk. (Illus.). 5.98 incl. audio (*1-56826-996-X*, R4 75642); (Illus.). 5.98 incl. audio (*1-56826-996-X*, R4 75642) Rhino Entertainment.
Whitman, John. Star Wars: Episode I: The Phantom Menace. 1999. (Star Wars Ser.). (Illus.). 344p. (YA). (gr. 3 up). 9.95 o.p. (*0-8118-2315-6*) Chronicle Bks. LLC.

**SKYWALKER, LUKE (FICTITIOUS CHARACTER)—FICTION**

Allston, Aaron. Star Wars. 1999. (Star Wars Ser.). mass mkt. 5.99 (*0-553-58125-2*) Bantam Bks.
Anderson, Kevin J. Champions of the Force. 1994. (Star Wars: Vol. 3). 368p. mass mkt. 6.99 (*0-553-29802-X*) Bantam Bks.
—Champions of the Force. abr. ed. 1994. (star wars: Vol. 3). audio 16.99 (*0-553-47201-1*, RH Audio) Random Hse. Audio Publishing Group.
—Champions of the Force. 1994. (Star Wars: Vol. 3). 12.04 (*0-606-08204-2*) Turtleback Bks.
—Dark Apprentice. 1994. (Star Wars: Vol. 2). 368p. mass mkt. 6.99 (*0-553-29799-6*) Bantam Bks.
—Dark Apprentice. abr. ed. 1994. (star wars: Vol. 2). audio 16.99 (*0-553-47200-3*); audio 16.98 o.s.i (*0-553-74564-6*) Random Hse. Audio Publishing Group. (RH Audio).
—Dark Apprentice. 1994. (Star Wars: Vol. 2). 12.04 (*0-606-08203-4*) Turtleback Bks.
—Darksaber. 1996. (Star Wars Ser.). 464p. mass mkt. 6.99 (*0-553-57611-9*, Spectra); (YA). mass mkt. 10.95 o.s.i (*0-553-84011-8*) Bantam Bks.
—Darksaber. 1995. audio 16.98 o.s.i (*0-553-74672-3*); audio 16.99 (*0-553-47423-5*, 393257) Random Hse. Audio Publishing Group. (RH Audio).
—The Jedi Academy Trilogy Omnibus. abr. ed. 1997. (Star Wars Ser.). (gr. 5 up). 29.95 incl. audio (*0-553-47848-6*, RH Audio) Random Hse. Audio Publishing Group.
—Jedi Search. 1994. (Star Wars: Vol. 1). 384p. mass mkt. 6.99 (*0-553-29798-8*) Bantam Bks.
—Jedi Search. abr. ed. 1994. (star wars: Vol. 1). audio 16.98 o.s.i (*0-553-74512-3*); audio 16.99 (*0-553-47199-6*) Random Hse. Audio Publishing Group. (RH Audio).
—Jedi Search. 1994. (Star Wars: Vol. 1). 12.04 (*0-606-08202-6*) Turtleback Bks.
—Jedi Trilogy: Jedi Search; Dark Apprentice; Champions of the Force, 3 vols. 1997. (Star Wars). (YA). (gr. 5). 20.97 (*0-553-64839-X*) Bantam Bks.
Anderson, Kevin J., et al. Leviathan. Dark Horse Comics Staff, ed. 2000. (Star Wars Ser.). (Illus.). 96p. (YA). (gr. 5 up). pap. 11.95 (*1-56971-456-8*) Dark Horse Comics.
Austin, Terry, et al. Splinter of the Mind's Eye. 1996. (Star Wars Ser.). (Illus.). 112p. (YA). (gr. 5 up). pap. 14.95 (*1-56971-223-9*) Dark Horse Comics.
Baron, Mike, et al. Dark Force Rising. 1998. (Star Wars Ser.). (Illus.). 160p. (YA). (gr. 7 up). pap. 17.95 (*1-56971-269-7*) Dark Horse Comics.
Chiang, Doug. The Phantom Menace Portfolio, 20 vols. 1999. (Star Wars). 55.00 o.p. (*0-8118-2580-9*) Chronicle Bks. LLC.
Daley, Brian. The Empire Strikes Back: The National Public Radio Dramatization. 1995. (Star Wars Ser.). (Illus.). 320p. pap. 19.00 o.s.i (*0-345-39605-7*, Del Rey) Ballantine Bks.
—Return of the Jedi: The National Public Radio Dramatization. 1996. 208p. pap. 15.00 o.s.i (*0-345-40782-2*) Ballantine Bks.
—Star Wars: The National Public Radio Dramatization. 1994. (Star Wars Ser.). (Illus.). 352p. pap. 19.00 o.s.i (*0-345-39109-8*, Del Rey) Ballantine Bks.
Dark Horse Comics Staff, et al. Empires End. 1997. (Star Wars Ser.). (Illus.). 56p. (YA). (gr. 7 up). pap. 5.95 (*1-56971-306-5*) Dark Horse Comics.
—Shadows of the Empire. 1997. (Star Wars Ser.). (Illus.). 160p. (YA). (gr. 7 up). pap. 17.95 (*1-56971-183-6*) Dark Horse Comics.
Dorling Kindersley Publishing Staff. Star Wars: The Power of Myth. 2000. (Star Wars Ser.). (Illus.). 48p. (J). pap. 12.95 (*0-7894-5591-9*, D K Ink) Dorling Kindersley Publishing, Inc.
—Star Wars: The Power of Myth. l.t. ed. 2000. (Illus.). 48p. 11.55 o.p. (*0-7513-6679-X*) Thorpe, F. A. Pubs. GBR. *Dist:* Ulverscroft Large Print Bks., Ltd., Ulverscroft Large Print Canada, Ltd.
Foster, Alan Dean. Splinter of the Mind's Eye. 1994. mass mkt. 4.99 o.s.i (*0-345-90332-3*); 1986. 304p. mass mkt. 6.99 (*0-345-32023-9*); 1978. 7.95 o.p. (*0-345-27566-7*) Ballantine Bks. (Del Rey).
Gardner, J. J. The Empire Strikes Back. 1997. (Star Wars Ser.). (Illus.). (J). (gr. 5-7). mass mkt. 5.99 (*0-590-06656-0*) Scholastic, Inc.
—Star Wars Movie Story. 1997. (Star Wars Ser.). (J). (gr. 5-7). mass mkt. 5.99 (*0-590-06654-4*) Scholastic, Inc.
Glut, Donald F. The Empire Strikes Back. 1997. (Star Wars Ser.). pap. 5.99 (*0-345-91183-0*); 1995. (Star Wars Ser.). 224p. 16.00 o.s.i (*0-345-40078-X*); 1985. (Star Wars Ser.: Vol. 2). 224p. mass mkt. 5.99 (*0-345-32022-0*); 1980. mass mkt. 2.25 o.p. (*0-345-28392-9*) Ballantine Bks. (Del Rey).
Goodwin, Archie. The Empire Strikes Back: Classic Star Wars. 1995. (Star Wars Ser.). (Illus.). 104p. pap. 9.95 o.p. (*1-56971-088-0*) Dark Horse Comics.
Goodwin, Archie, et al. The Empire Strikes Back: Special Edition. 1997. (Star Wars Ser.). 104p. (J). (gr. 3 up). pap. 9.95 (*1-56971-234-4*) Dark Horse Comics.
—Return of the Jedi: Special Edition. 1997. (Star Wars Ser.). 104p. (YA). (gr. 3 up). pap. 9.95 (*1-56971-235-2*) Dark Horse Comics.
Hambly, Barbara. Children of the Jedi. 1996. (Star Wars Ser.). mass mkt. 10.95 o.s.i (*0-553-84008-8*); 432p. reprint ed. mass mkt. 6.99 (*0-553-57293-8*, Spectra) Bantam Bks.
—Children of the Jedi. 1995. audio 16.98 o.s.i (*0-553-74566-2*); audio 16.99 (*0-553-47195-3*) Random Hse. Audio Publishing Group. (RH Audio).
—Children of the Jedi. 1996. (Star Wars Ser.). 12.04 (*0-606-11887-X*) Turtleback Bks.
—Night Lily: The Lover's Tale. abr. ed. 1995. (Star Wars Ser.). audio compact disk 13.99 o.s.i (*0-553-45541-9*, , RH Audio) Random Hse. Audio Publishing Group.
—Nightlily: The Lover's Tale. abr. ed. 1995. (Star Wars Ser.). audio 12.00 o.p. (*0-553-45413-7*, RH Audio) Random Hse. Audio Publishing Group.
—Planet of Twilight. 1998. (Star Wars Ser.). 416p. reprint ed. mass mkt. 6.99 (*0-553-57517-1*) Bantam Bks.
—Planet of Twilight. abr. ed. 1997. (Star Wars Ser.). audio 16.99 (*0-553-47196-1*, RH Audio) Random Hse. Audio Publishing Group.
Hamill, Mark, et al. Star Wars: The Original Radio Drama. abr. unabr. ed. 1993. (Star Wars Ser.). audio 39.95 (*0-942110-99-4*, 692313); audio compact disk 64.95 (*1-56511-005-6*) HighBridge Co.
Jones, Bruce, et al. Star Wars: A New Hope. 1997. (Star Wars Ser.). 104p. (YA). (gr. 3 up). pap. 9.95 (*1-56971-213-1*) Dark Horse Comics.
—Star Wars Trilogy: A New Hope, Empire Strikes Back, Return of the Jedi. 2nd ed. 1997. (Star Wars Ser.). (Illus.). (J). (gr. 3 up). pap. 29.85 o.p. (*1-56971-257-3*) Dark Horse Comics.
Kahn, James. Return of the Jedi. (Star Wars Ser.). 1997. mass mkt. 5.99 (*0-345-91184-9*, Del Rey); 1995. 240p. 16.00 (*0-345-40079-8*, Del Rey); 1983. (Illus.). 224p. mass mkt. 5.95 o.p. (*0-345-30960-X*); 1983. 192p. mass mkt. 5.99 (*0-345-30767-4*, Del Rey) Ballantine Bks.
Kube-McDowell, Michael P. Before the Storm. 1996. (Star Wars: Bk. 1). 336p. mass mkt. 6.99 (*0-553-57273-3*, Spectra) Bantam Bks.
—Before the Storm. abr. ed. 1996. (Star Wars: Bk. 1). audio 16.99 (*0-553-47422-7*, 394259, RH Audio) Random Hse. Audio Publishing Group.
—Before the Storm. 1996. (Star Wars: Bk. 1). 12.04 (*0-606-11884-5*) Turtleback Bks.
—Shield of Lies. 1996. (Star Wars: Bk. 2). pap. 10.95 o.s.i (*0-553-84010-X*); 368p. mass mkt. 6.99 (*0-553-57277-6*, Spectra) Bantam Bks.
—Shield of Lies. abr. ed. 1996. (Star Wars: Bk. 2). audio 16.99 o.s.i (*0-553-47424-3*, 394260, RH Audio) Random Hse. Audio Publishing Group.
—Shield of Lies. 1996. (Star Wars: Bk. 2). 12.04 (*0-606-11885-3*) Turtleback Bks.
—Tyrant's Test. 1996. (Star Wars: Bk. 3). (Illus.). 400p. (gr. 5 up). mass mkt. 6.99 (*0-553-57275-X*, Spectra) Bantam Bks.
—Tyrant's Test. abr. ed. 1996. (Star Wars: Bk. 3). audio 16.99 (*0-553-47421-9*, 394598, RH Audio) Random Hse. Audio Publishing Group.
—Tyrant's Test. 1997. (Star Wars: Bk. 3). 12.04 (*0-606-11886-1*) Turtleback Bks.
Levy, Elizabeth, adapted by. Return of the Jedi. 1995. (Illus.). 64p. (J). (gr. 4-7). pap. 3.99 (*0-679-87205-1*) Random Hse., Inc.
Lucas, George. The Empire Strikes Back. 1994. 8.98 (*1-57042-172-2*) Warner Bks., Inc.
—The Empire Strikes Back: The Original Radio Drama. abr. unabr. ed. 1993. (Star Wars Ser.). audio 39.95 (*1-56511-000-5*, 492026); audio compact disk 59.95 (*1-56511-007-2*) HighBridge Co.
—Return of the Jedi. 1997. mass mkt. 5.99 o.s.i (*0-345-41356-3*, Del Rey) Ballantine Bks.

—Return of the Jedi. 1995. 8.98 (*1-57042-208-7*) Warner Bks., Inc.

—Return of the Jedi: The Original Radio Drama. abr. unabr. ed. 1996. (Star Wars Ser.). audio 25.95 (*1-56511-157-5*); audio compact disk 34.95 (*1-56511-158-3*) HighBridge Co.

—Star Wars: A New Hope. 1995. (Star Wars Ser.). 272p. 16.00 o.s.i (*0-345-40077-1*, Del Rey) Ballantine Bks.

—Star Wars: A New Hope. 1996. (YA). (gr. 7-12). audio 17.00 o.p. (*1-57042-248-6*) Time Warner AudioBooks.

—Star Wars: A New Hope. 1998. (Star Wars Manga Ser.: Bk. 4). (Illus.). 96p. (YA). (gr. 3 up). pap. 9.95 (*1-56971-365-0*); pap. 9.95 (*1-56971-364-2*); pap. 9.95 (*1-56971-362-6*) Dark Horse Comics.

—Star Wars: A New Hope, Script Facsimiles. deluxe ed. 1998. (Star Wars Ser.). (Illus.). 176p. pap. 18.95 (*0-345-42080-2*, Del Rey) Ballantine Bks.

—Star Wars: A New Hope: The Illustrated Screenplay. 1998. (Star Wars Trilogy Ser.). (Illus.). 208p. pap. 12.00 o.s.i (*0-345-42069-1*, Del Rey) Ballantine Bks.

—Star Wars Adventures. abr. ed. 1994. (Star Wars Ser.). audio 8.98 o.p. Time Warner AudioBooks.

Lucas, George. Star Wars Trilogy: Star Wars; The Empire Strikes Back; Return of the Jedi. unabr. ed. 1994. (Star Wars Ser.). audio 50.00 o.p. (*1-57042-157-9*, 4-521579); audio 75.00 o.p. (*1-57042-169-2*, 2-521579) Time Warner AudioBooks.

Lucas, George & Kasdan, Lawrence. Return of the Jedi. deluxe ed. 1998. (Star Wars Ser.). (Illus.). 144p. pap. 18.95 (*0-345-42082-9*, Ballantine Bks.) Ballantine Bks.

—Return of the Jedi: The Illustrated Screenplay. 1998. (Illus.). 208p. pap. 12.00 (*0-345-42079-9*, Del Rey) Ballantine Bks.

Lucas, George, et al. The Empire Strikes Back. deluxe ed. 1998. (Star Wars Ser.). (Illus.). 160p. pap. 18.95 o.s.i (*0-345-42081-0*, Del Rey) Ballantine Bks.

—Star Wars Trilogy: Star Wars; The Empire Strikes Back; Return of the Jedi. (Star Wars Ser.). 1997. mass mkt. 6.99 (*0-345-91126-1*); 1993. 480p. mass mkt. 7.99 (*0-345-38438-5*, Del Rey); 1987. 480p. pap. 12.95 (*0-345-34806-0*, Del Rey) Ballantine Bks.

—Star Wars Trilogy: Star Wars; The Empire Strikes Back; Return of the Jedi. 1987. (J). (gr. 3-7). 16.05 (*0-606-01231-1*) Turtleback Bks.

Lucasfilm Ltd. The Complete Trilogy Cassette Gift-Pack: Star Wars, The Empire Strikes Back, & Return of the Jedi. abr. ed. 1996. (Star Wars Ser.). audio 105.85 o.p. (*1-56511-173-7*) HighBridge Co.

Lucasfilm Ltd. Staff. The Last Command. unabr. ed. 1996. (Star Wars: Bk. 3). audio 104.00. audio Books on Tape, Inc.

—Star Wars. 1999. pap. 0.90 o.s.i (*0-375-80892-2*, Random Hse. Bks. for Young Readers) Random Hse. Children's Bks.

Luceno, James. Agents of Chaos II: Jedi Eclipse. 2000. (Star Wars Ser.: Bk. 5). 368p. mass mkt. 6.99 (*0-345-42859-5*, Ballantine Bks.) Ballantine Bks.

—Star Wars - Agents of Chaos II: Jedi Eclipse. abr. ed. 2000. audio 18.00 Random Hse. Audio Publishing Group.

Lund, Kristin. Inside the Worlds of Star Wars: Episode 1. Dorling Kindersley Publishing Staff, ed. l.t. ed. 2000. (Illus.). 48p. 21.45 o.p. (*0-7513-6222-0*) Thorpe, F. A. Pubs. GBR. *Dist:* Ulverscroft Large Print Bks., Ltd., Ulverscroft Large Print Canada, Ltd.

Manning, Russ & Goodwin, Archie. The Early Adventures. 1997. (Classic Star Wars Ser.). (Illus.). 240p. (J). (gr. 3 up). pap. 19.95 (*1-56971-178-X*) Dark Horse Comics.

Mason, Jane. Adventure in Beggar's Canyon. 1999. (Star Wars Ser.). (Illus.). 24p. (J). 2.29 o.s.i (*0-307-98879-1*, 98879, Golden Bks.) Random Hse. Children's Bks.

Mason, Jane & Ciccarelli, Gary. Adventure in Beggar's Canyon. 1999. (Star Wars Ser.). (Illus.). 24p. (J). 3.99 o.s.i (*0-307-16079-3*, 16079, Golden Bks.) Random Hse. Children's Bks.

McIntyre, Vonda N. The Crystal Star. 1994. audio 13.59 o.s.i (*0-553-70082-0*, RH Audio) Random Hse. Audio Publishing Group.

—Crystal Star. abr. ed. 1994. (Star Wars Ser.). audio 16.99 (*0-553-47194-5*, RH Audio) Random Hse. Audio Publishing Group.

—The Crystal Star. 1995. (Star Wars Ser.). 448p. reprint ed. mass mkt. 6.99 (*0-553-57174-5*) Bantam Bks.

Perry, Steve. Shadows of the Empire. 1997. (Star Wars Ser.). 416p. (gr. 5 up). mass mkt. 6.99 (*0-553-57413-2*, Spectra) Bantam Bks.

—Shadows of the Empire. abr. ed. 1996. (Star Wars Ser.). audio 16.99 (*0-553-47438-3*, 393956, RH Audio) Random Hse. Audio Publishing Group.

Perry, Steve, et al. Evolution: Shadows of the Empire. 2000. (Star Wars Ser.). (Illus.). 120p. (YA). (gr. 7 up). pap. 14.95 (*1-56971-441-X*) Dark Horse Comics.

Rusch, Kristine K. The New Rebellion. 1997. (Star Wars Ser.). 560p. mass mkt. 6.99 (*0-553-57414-0*, Spectra) Bantam Bks.

—The New Rebellion. 1997. (Star Wars Ser.). 12.04 (*0-606-11894-2*) Turtleback Bks.

—New Rebellion. abr. ed. 1996. (Star Wars Ser.). audio 16.99 (*0-553-47743-9*, RH Audio) Random Hse. Audio Publishing Group.

Salvatore, R. A. Star Wars: The New Jedi Order: Vector Prime. 1999. audio 18.00 Random Hse. Audio Publishing Group.

—Vector Prime. (Star Wars Ser.). 2003. E-Book 2.99 (*0-345-46740-X*, Ballantine Bks.); 2000. 416p. mass mkt. 7.50 (*0-345-42845-5*); 1999. 400p. 24.95 (*0-345-42844-7*) Ballantine Bks.

—Vector Prime. abr. ed. 1999. (Star Wars: Bk. 1). audio 18.00 (*0-375-40689-1*, RH Audio) Random Hse. Audio Publishing Group.

Stackpole, Michael A. Dark Tide: Onslaught. abr. ed. 2000. (Star Wars: Bk. 2). audio 18.00 (*0-375-40956-4*, RH Audio) Random Hse. Audio Publishing Group.

—Dark Tide I: Onslaught. 2000. (Star Wars Ser.: Bk. 2). 125.82 o.s.i (*0-345-43891-4*); 304p. mass mkt. 6.99 (*0-345-42854-4*, Del Rey) Ballantine Bks.

—Dark Tide II: Ruin. abr. ed. 2000. (Star Wars: Bk. 3). audio 18.00 (*0-375-40969-6*, RH Audio) Random Hse. Audio Publishing Group.

—I, Jedi. abr. ed. 1998. (Star Wars Ser.). audio 16.99 (*0-553-47948-2*, 391211, RH Audio) Random Hse. Audio Publishing Group.

—I, Jedi: Star Wars. 1999. (Star Wars Ser.). 608p. mass mkt. 6.99 (*0-553-57873-1*) Broadway Bks.

—Ruin: Dark Tide II. 2000. (Star Wars Ser.: No.3). 304p. mass mkt. 6.99 (*0-345-42856-0*) Ballantine Bks.

Stackpole, Michael A., et al. Star Wars X-Wing Rogue Squadron: Requiem for a Rogue. 1999. (Star Wars Ser.: Bk. 4). 112p. (YA). (gr. 5 up). pap. 12.95 (*1-56971-331-6*) Dark Horse Comics.

—The Union. 2000. (Star Wars Ser.). (Illus.). 96p. (J). (gr. 7 up). pap. 12.95 (*1-56971-464-9*) Dark Horse Comics.

Star Wars Trilogy: Star Wars; The Empire Strikes Back; Return of the Jedi, 3 vols. 1987. (Star Wars Ser.). pap. 8.65 o.p. (*0-345-32964-3*, Del Rey) Ballantine Bks.

Thomas, Jim K. Star Wars: Luke's Fate. 1996. (Step into Reading Step 3 Bks.). (J). (gr. 2-3). 10.14 (*0-606-11893-4*) Turtleback Bks.

Tyers, Kathy. Balance Point. 2000. (Star Wars Ser.: Bk. 6). 352p. 25.95 (*0-345-42857-9*, Del Rey) Ballantine Bks.

—Star Wars - The New Jedi Order: Balance Point. abr. ed. 2000. audio 18.00. audio 18.00 (*0-375-41624-2*) Random Hse. Audio Publishing Group. (RH Audio).

—The Truce at Bakura. 1994. (Star Wars Ser.). 352p. mass mkt. 6.99 (*0-553-56872-8*) Bantam Bks.

—The Truce at Bakura. 1993. audio 13.59 o.s.i (*0-553-70065-0*, RH Audio) Random Hse. Audio Publishing Group.

—The Truce at Bakura. 1994. (Star Wars Ser.). 11.09 o.p. (*0-606-08201-8*) Turtleback Bks.

Veitch, Tom. Dark Empire. 2nd ed. 1993. (Star Wars Ser.). (Illus.). 184p. (YA). (gr. 7 up). pap. 17.95 (*1-56971-073-2*) Dark Horse Comics.

—Dark Empire I. abr. ed. 1994. (Star Wars Ser.). audio 17.00 o.p. (*1-57042-083-1*, 4-520831) Time Warner AudioBooks.

—Dark Empire II. 1995. (Star Wars Ser.). (Illus.). 168p. (YA). (gr. 7 up). pap. 17.95 (*1-56971-119-4*) Dark Horse Comics.

—Dark Empire II. abr. ed. 1995. (Star Wars Ser.). audio 17.00 o.p. (*1-57042-309-1*, 4-523091) Time Warner AudioBooks.

—Star Wars: Dark Empire. abr. ed. 1997. (Star Wars Ser.). audio 16.95 (*1-56511-200-8*) HighBridge Co.

—Star Wars: Dark Empire II. abr. ed. 1997. (Star Wars Ser.). pap. 16.95 incl. audio (*1-56511-201-6*) HighBridge Co.

Veitch, Tom & Kennedy, Cam. Dark Empire: The Collected Edition. 1993. (Star Wars Ser.). (Illus.). pap. 16.95 o.p. (*1-878574-56-6*); 99.95 o.p. (*1-878574-57-4*) Dark Horse Comics.

Weinberg, Larry. The Empire Strikes Back: Classic Star Wars. 1995. (Star Wars Ser.). (Illus.). 54p. (J). (gr. 4-7). pap. 3.99 o.s.i (*0-679-87204-3*) Random Hse., Inc.

Whitman, John & Lucas, George. Star Wars. 1996. (Mighty Chronicles Ser.). (Illus.). 432p. (gr. 4-7). 9.95 o.s.i (*0-8118-1480-7*) Chronicle Bks. LLC.

Wolverton, Dave. The Courtship of Princess Leia. 1995. (Star Wars Ser.). 400p. mass mkt. 6.99 (*0-553-56937-6*) Bantam Bks.

—The Courtship of Princess Leia. abr. ed. 1994. (Star Wars Ser.). audio 16.99 (*0-553-47193-7*, RH Audio) Random Hse. Audio Publishing Group.

—The Courtship of Princess Leia. 1994. (Star Wars Ser.). 12.04 (*0-606-08199-2*) Turtleback Bks.

Zahn, Timothy. Dark Force Rising. (Star Wars: Bk. 2). 1993. 448p. mass mkt. 6.99 (*0-553-56071-9*); 1992. 368p. 18.50 o.s.i (*0-553-08574-3*); Vol. 2. 1992. 384p. 125.00 o.s.i (*0-553-08907-2*, Spectra) Bantam Bks.

—Dark Force Rising. unabr. ed. 1995. (Star Wars: Bk. 2). audio 96.00 Books on Tape, Inc.

—Dark Force Rising. abr. ed. 1992. (Star Wars: Bk. 2). audio 16.99 (*0-553-47055-8*, RH Audio) Random Hse. Audio Publishing Group.

—Heir to the Empire. (Star Wars: Bk. 1). 9999. pap. 9.90 o.s.i (*0-593-02481-8*); 1992. 432p. mass mkt. 6.99 (*0-553-29612-4*); 1991. 368p. 22.95 o.s.i (*0-553-07327-3*); 1991. 368p. 125.00 o.s.i (*0-553-07340-0*, Spectra) Bantam Bks.

—Heir to the Empire. unabr. ed. 1995. (Star Wars: Bk. 1). audio 88.00 Books on Tape, Inc.

—Heir to the Empire. abr. ed. 1991. (Star Wars: Bk. 1). audio 16.99 (*0-553-45296-7*, 391663, RH Audio) Random Hse. Audio Publishing Group.

—Heir to the Empire. 1993. (Star Wars: Bk. 1). 64.95 o.p. incl. audio (*0-7838-1100-4*); 64.95 o.p. incl. audio (*0-7838-1100-4*) Thorndike Pr.

—Heir to the Empire. 1991. (Star Wars: Bk. 1). 12.04 (*0-606-00751-2*) Turtleback Bks.

—The Last Command. (Star Wars: Bk. 3). 1994. 496p. mass mkt. 6.99 (*0-553-56492-7*, Spectra); 1993. 416p. 125.00 o.s.i (*0-553-09500-5*) Bantam Bks.

—The Last Command. abr. ed. 1993. (Star Wars: Bk. 3). audio 16.99 (*0-553-47157-0*, RH Audio) Random Hse. Audio Publishing Group.

—The Last Command. 1994. (Star Wars: Bk. 3). 12.04 (*0-606-08205-0*) Turtleback Bks.

—Specter of the Past. 1998. (Star Wars Hand of Thrawn Ser.: No. 1). 416p. (gr. 5 up). mass mkt. 6.99 (*0-553-29804-6*) Bantam Bks.

—Specter of the Past. abr. ed. 1997. (Star Wars Ser.: Vol. 1). (gr. 5 up). audio 16.99 (*0-553-47893-1*, RH Audio) Random Hse. Audio Publishing Group.

—Specter of the Past. l.t. ed. 1998. (Star Wars). 512p. 25.95 (*0-7838-8434-6*) Thorndike Pr.

—Star Wars. 1994. (Star Wars Ser.). pap. 17.95 o.s.i (*0-553-63485-2*) Bantam Bks.

—The Thrawn Trilogy. abr. ed. 2000. (Star Wars: Bk. 1,2,3). 29.95 incl. audio (*0-553-52699-5*);Set. (YA). 29.95 incl. audio Random Hse. Audio Publishing Group.

—Vision of the Future. 1999. (Star Wars Hand of Thrawn Ser.: No. 2). 720p. (gr. 5 up). mass mkt. 6.99 (*0-553-57879-0*) Bantam Bks.

—Vision of the Future. abr. ed. 1998. (Star Wars Ser.: Vol. 2). (gr. 5 up). audio 16.99 (*0-553-47921-0*, 392221, RH Audio) Random Hse. Audio Publishing Group.

Zahn, Timothy, et al. Heir to the Empire. 1996. (Star Wars Ser.). (Illus.). 160p. (YA). (gr. 7 up). pap. 19.95 (*1-56971-202-6*) Dark Horse Comics.

### SLADE, MAGGIE (FICTITIOUS CHARACTER)—FICTION

Cresswell, Jasmine. The Daughter. 1998. (Mira Bks.). 408p. per. (*1-55166-425-9*, 1-66425-9, Mira Bks.) Harlequin Enterprises, Ltd.

### SLAIGHT, RY (FICTITIOUS CHARACTER)—FICTION

Truscott, Lucian K., IV. Dress Gray. 1980. mass mkt. 2.75 o.p. (*0-449-24158-0*, Fawcett) Ballantine Bks.

—Dress Gray. 1979. 10.95 o.p. (*0-385-13475-4*) Doubleday Publishing.

—Dress Gray. 1997. 464p. mass mkt. 6.99 o.s.i (*0-451-19047-5*, Signet Bks.) NAL.

Truscott, Lucian K., Jr. Dress Gray. 1986. mass mkt. 3.95 o.s.i (*0-449-21163-0*, Fawcett) Ballantine Bks.

Truscott, Lucian K., IV. Full Dress Gray. abr. ed. 1998. audio 7.99 o.s.i (*1-56740-297-6*, 1801, Paperback Nova Audio Bks.); audio 26.95 (*1-56740-069-8*, 8, Bookcassette); audio 73.25 (*1-56740-598-3*, 848, Unabridged Library Editions);Set. audio 17.95 o.p. (*1-56740-794-3*, 441, Nova Audio Bks.) Brilliance Audio.

—Full Dress Gray, Pt. 2. 1998. (Full Dress Gray Ser.: Vol. 2). 320p. 25.00 (*0-688-15993-1*, Morrow, William & Co.) Morrow/Avon.

—Full Dress Gray. 1999. 464p. reprint ed. mass mkt. 6.99 o.s.i (*0-451-19933-2*) NAL.

### SLATE, SUE (FICTITIOUS CHARACTER)—FICTION

Lynch, Lee. Sue Slate, Private Eye. 1989. 176p. pap. 8.95 o.p. (*0-941483-52-5*) Naiad Pr., Inc.

### SLATER, JACK (FICTITIOUS CHARACTER)—FICTION

Odom, Mel. Headhunter. 1997. (Shadowrun Ser.: No. 27). 288p. mass mkt. 5.99 o.s.i (*0-451-45614-9*, Signet Bks.) NAL.

### SLEEPING BEAUTY (FICTITIOUS CHARACTER: ROQUELAURE)—FICTION

Rice, Anne. Beauty's Release. unabr. ed. 2004. audio (*0-06-057011-3*, HarperAudio) HarperTrade.

Roquelaure, A. N., pseud. Beauty's Punishment. 1999. (Sleeping Beauty Ser.: No. 2). 256p. pap. 12.95 (*0-452-28143-1*); 1984. 256p. pap. 12.95 o.s.i (*0-452-26662-9*, Plume); 1984. 14.95 o.p. (*0-525-24261-9*, Dutton); 1984. pap. 7.95 o.p. (*0-525-48092-7*, Plume); 1984. pap. 8.95 o.p. (*0-525-48458-2*, Plume) Dutton/Plume.

—Beauty's Punishment. 2004. audio 19.95 (*0-06-057009-1*) HarperCollins Pubs.

—Beauty's Punishment. 1999. (Sleeping Beauty Ser.: No. 2). pap. 5.99 (*0-451-17697-9*, Signet Bks.) NAL.

—Beauty's Punishment. abr. ed. 1994. audio 17.00 (*0-671-88656-8*, 390376, Simon & Schuster Audioworks) Simon & Schuster Audio.

—Beauty's Release. 1999. (Sleeping Beauty Ser.: No. 3). 256p. pap. 12.95 (*0-452-28145-8*); 1985. 15.95 o.p. (*0-525-24336-4*, Dutton); 1985. pap. 8.95 o.p. (*0-525-48168-0*, Plume); 1985. 256p. pap. 12.95 o.s.i (*0-452-26663-7*, Plume) Dutton/Plume.

—Beauty's Release. 1999. (Sleeping Beauty Ser.: No. 3). pap. 5.99 (*0-451-17696-0*, Signet Bks.) NAL.

—Beauty's Release. abr. ed. 1994. audio 17.00 (*0-671-88654-1*, 390377, Simon & Schuster Audioworks) Simon & Schuster Audio.

—The Claiming of Sleeping Beauty. 1999. (Sleeping Beauty Ser.: No. 1). 272p. pap. 14.00 (*0-452-28142-3*); 1985. (Sleeping Beauty Ser.: No. 1). 13.95 o.p. (*0-525-24219-8*, 0674-210, Dutton); 1983. pap. 8.95 o.p. (*0-525-48362-4*, Plume); 1983. 272p. pap. 12.95 o.s.i (*0-452-26656-4*, Plume); 1983. (Sleeping Beauty Ser.: No. 1). pap. 6.95 o.p. (*0-525-48054-4*, Dutton) Dutton/Plume.

—The Claiming of Sleeping Beauty. 1999. (Sleeping Beauty Ser.: No. 1). pap. 5.99 (*0-451-17698-7*, Signet Bks.) NAL.

—The Claiming of Sleeping Beauty. abr. ed. 1994. audio 17.00 (*0-671-88655-X*, 390522, Simon & Schuster Audioworks) Simon & Schuster Audio.

### SLIDER, BILL (FICTITIOUS CHARACTER)—FICTION

Harrod-Eagles, Cynthia. Blood Lines. 1996. 281p. o.s.i (*0-316-91420-7*) Little Brown & Co.

—Blood Lines. 1997. (Inspector Bill Slider Mysteries Ser.). mass mkt. 5.50 (*0-380-73052-9*, Avon Bks.) Morrow/Avon.

—Blood Lines. 1996. 281p. 20.50 o.p. (*0-684-80047-0*, Scribner) Simon & Schuster.

—Blood Sinister. l.t. ed. 2001. (Magna Large Print Ser.). 384p. (*0-7505-1599-6*) Magna Large Print Bks. GBR. *Dist:* Ulverscroft Large Print Canada, Ltd.

—Blood Sinister. E-Book 23.95 (*0-312-70251-5*); 2001. 308p. 23.95 (*0-312-27485-8*, Saint Martin's Minotaur) St. Martin's Pr.

—Dead End. 1996. 234p. mass mkt. o.s.i (*0-7515-1354-7*) Little Brown & Co.

—Dead End. unabr. ed. 2000. audio 79.95 (*1-86042-433-3*, 24333) Soundings, Ltd. GBR. *Dist:* Ulverscroft Large Print Bks., Ltd.

—Death to Go. l.t. ed. 1994. 413p. reprint ed. pap. 18.95 (*0-8161-5977-7*, Macmillan Reference USA) Gale Group.

—Death to Go. 1995. 288p. mass mkt. 4.99 o.s.i (*0-380-72346-8*, Avon Bks.) Morrow/Avon.

—Death to Go: An Inspector Bill Slider Mystery. 1994. 288p. 20.00 (*0-684-19650-6*, Macmillan Reference USA) Gale Group.

—Death Watch. 1994. 288p. mass mkt. 4.99 (*0-380-72065-5*, Avon Bks.) Morrow/Avon.

—Death Watch: An Inspector Bill Slider Mystery. 1993. 288p. 20.00 o.p. (*0-684-19519-4*, Macmillan Reference USA) Gale Group.

—Gone Tomorrow: A Bill Slider Mystery. 2001. 288p. (*0-316-85741-6*) Little Brown & Co.

—Gone Tomorrow: A Bill Slider Mystery. l.t. ed. 2002. (Magna Large Print Ser.). 496p. (*0-7505-1903-7*) Magna Large Print Bks. GBR. *Dist:* Ulverscroft Large Print Canada, Ltd.

—Gone Tomorrow: A Bill Slider Mystery. 2002. 368p. 24.95 (*0-312-30046-8*, Saint Martin's Minotaur) St. Martin's Pr.

—Grave Music. 1996. 256p. mass mkt. 5.50 o.s.i (*0-380-72636-X*, Avon Bks.) Morrow/Avon.

—Grave Music: An Inspector Bill Slider Mystery. l.t. ed. 1995. 370p. 23.95 o.p. (*0-7838-1469-0*, Macmillan Reference USA) Gale Group.

—Grave Music: An Inspector Bill Slider Mystery. 1995. 234p. 20.00 (*0-684-80046-2*, Scribner) Simon & Schuster.

—Killing Time. 1996. 313p. o.s.i (*0-316-88103-1*) Little Brown & Co.

—Killing Time. l.t. ed. 2000. (Magna Large Print Ser.). 464p. (*0-7505-1597-X*) Magna Large Print Bks. GBR. *Dist:* Ulverscroft Large Print Canada, Ltd.

—Killing Time: An Inspector Bill Slider Mystery. 1998. (Inspector Bill Slider Mysteries Ser.). 320p. 22.00 (*0-684-83776-5*, Scribner) Simon & Schuster.

—Killing Time Bk. 6: An Inspector Bill Slider Mystery. 1999. (Inspector Bill Slider Mysteries Ser.: No. 6). 288p. mass mkt. 5.99 (*0-380-73202-5*, Avon Bks.) Morrow/Avon.
—Necrochip. l.t. ed. 1994. (Magna Large Print Ser.). 462p. o.p. (*0-7505-0638-5*) Magna Large Print Bks. GBR. *Dist:* Ulverscroft Large Print Canada, Ltd.
—Orchestrated Death. 1993. 272p. mass mkt. 5.50 o.s.i (*0-380-71967-3*, Avon Bks.) Morrow/Avon.
—Orchestrated Death: A Mystery Introducing Inspector Bill Slider. 1992. 256p. text 19.95 (*0-684-19388-4*, Macmillan Reference USA) Gale Group.
—Shallow Grave. l.t. ed. 2001. (Magna Large Print Ser.). 464p. (*0-7505-1598-8*) Magna Large Print Bks. GBR. *Dist:* Ulverscroft Large Print Canada, Ltd.
—Shallow Grave. 1999. (Inspector Bill Slider Mysteries Ser.). 320p. 22.00 (*0-684-83777-3*, Scribner) Simon & Schuster.
—Shallow Grave. unabr. ed. 2000. audio 84.95 (*1-86042-521-6*, 25216) Soundings, Ltd. GBR. *Dist:* Ulverscroft Large Print Bks., Ltd.
—Shallow Grave. l.t. ed. 2000. (Mystery Ser.). 505p. 28.95 (*0-7862-2342-1*) Thorndike Pr.

**SLOAN, C. D. (FICTITIOUS CHARACTER)—FICTION**

Aird, Catherine. After Effects. l.t. ed. 1997. (G. K. Hall Nightingale Ser.). 206p. pap. 18.95 o.p. (*0-7838-1967-6*, Macmillan Reference USA) Gale Group.
—After Effects. 1996. (Detective Inspector C. D. Sloan Mystery). 208p. 20.95 (*0-312-14270-6*, Saint Martin's Minotaur) St. Martin's Pr.
—Amendment of Life: A Mystery. 2003. 240p. 22.95 (*0-312-29080-2*, Saint Martin's Minotaur) St. Martin's Pr.
—A Dead Liberty. Set. unabr. ed. 2001. (Inspector C. D. Sloan Mystery Ser.). audio 49.95 (*0-7451-5705-X*, CAB 234) Chivers Audio Bks. GBR. *Dist:* BBC Audiobooks America.
—A Dead Liberty. 1987. (Crime Club Ser.). 192p. 12.95 o.s.i (*0-385-23554-2*) Doubleday Publishing.
—A Dead Liberty. 1987. audio 49.95 o.p. (*0-8161-7688-4*) Thorndike Pr.
—A Dead Liberty. l.t. ed. 1987. 384p. 16.95 o.p. (*0-7089-1664-3*, Ulverscroft) Thorpe, F. A. Pubs. GBR. *Dist:* Ulverscroft Large Print Bks., Ltd.
—A Going Concern. l.t. ed. 1995. (G. K. Hall Nightingale Ser.). 235p. pap. 17.95 (*0-7838-1134-9*, Macmillan Reference USA) Gale Group.
—A Going Concern. 1994. 167p. 18.95 o.p. (*0-312-11423-0*, Saint Martin's Minotaur) St. Martin's Pr.
—Harm's Way. 1985. 192p. mass mkt. 2.95 o.s.i (*0-553-25191-0*) Bantam Bks.
—Harm's Way. 1984. (Crime Club Ser.). 192p. 11.95 o.p. (*0-385-19542-7*) Doubleday Publishing.
—Harm's Way. l.t. ed. 1985. (Ulverscroft Large Print Ser.). 384p. 12.50 o.p. (*0-7089-1359-8*, Ulverscroft) Thorpe, F. A. Pubs. GBR. *Dist:* Ulverscroft Large Print Bks., Ltd., Ulverscroft Large Print Canada, Ltd.
—Henrietta Who? 1981. mass mkt. 2.95 o.s.i (*0-553-25463-4*) Bantam Bks.
—Henrietta Who? l.t. ed. 2000. (G. K. Hall Nightingale Ser.). 247p. pap. 21.95 (*0-7838-9003-6*, Macmillan Reference USA) Gale Group.
—Henrietta Who? l.t. ed. 1979. (Ulverscroft Large Print Ser.). 299p. 12.00 o.p. (*0-7089-0352-5*, Ulverscroft) Thorpe, F. A. Pubs. GBR. *Dist:* Ulverscroft Large Print Bks., Ltd., Ulverscroft Large Print Canada, Ltd.
—His Burial Too. 1980. 208p. pap. 2.95 o.p. (*0-553-25441-3*) Bantam Bks.
—His Burial Too. l.t. ed. 1980. (Ulverscroft Large Print Ser.). 316p. 12.00 o.p. (*0-7089-0478-5*, Ulverscroft) Thorpe, F. A. Pubs. GBR. *Dist:* Ulverscroft Large Print Bks., Ltd., Ulverscroft Large Print Canada, Ltd.
—Injury Time: Featuring Inspector C. D. Sloan. unabr. ed. 1997. audio 16.99 (*0-88646-432-3*, 7432) Durkin Hayes Publishing Ltd.
—Injury Time: Featuring Inspector C. D. Sloan. l.t. ed. 1995. pap. 18.95 o.p. (*0-7838-1458-5*, Macmillan Reference USA) Gale Group.
—Injury Time: Featuring Inspector C. D. Sloan. 1995. 168p. 19.95 o.p. (*0-312-13095-3*, Saint Martin's Minotaur) St. Martin's Pr.
—Last Respects. 1984. 176p. mass mkt. 2.95 o.s.i (*0-553-25811-7*) Bantam Bks.
—Last Respects. 1982. (Crime Club Ser.). 192p. 11.95 o.p. (*0-385-18256-2*) Doubleday Publishing.
—Last Respects. l.t. ed. 1984. (Ulverscroft Large Print Ser.). 304p. 12.50 o.p. (*0-7089-1180-3*, Ulverscroft) Thorpe, F. A. Pubs. GBR. *Dist:* Ulverscroft Large Print Bks., Ltd., Ulverscroft Large Print Canada, Ltd.
—A Late Phoenix. l.t. ed. 1994. 18.95 o.p. (*0-7451-6427-7*) BBC Audiobooks America.
—A Late Phoenix. 1988. mass mkt. o.s.i (*0-552-12794-9*, Corgi); 1981. 176p. pap. 2.95 o.p. (*0-553-25442-1*) Bantam Bks.
—A Late Phoenix. 1988. audio 35.95 o.s.i (*0-8161-7797-X*) Thorndike Pr.
—A Most Contagious Game. 1994. 200p. 16.95 o.p. (*0-7451-8630-0*, Black Dagger) BBC Audiobooks America.
—Parting Breath. 1989. mass mkt. o.s.i (*0-552-13426-0*, Corgi); 1985. 176p. mass mkt. 2.95 o.s.i (*0-553-25414-6*); 1984. mass mkt. 2.75 o.s.i (*0-553-24601-1*) Bantam Bks.
—Parting Breath. unabr. ed. 2001. (Inspector C. D. Sloan Mystery Ser.). audio 49.95 (*0-7451-4344-X*) Chivers Audio Bks. GBR. *Dist:* BBC Audiobooks America.
—Parting Breath. l.t. ed. 2001. (Thorndike Mystery Ser.). 277p. pap. 23.95 (*0-7838-9431-7*) Thorndike Pr.
—Passing Strange. 1981. (Crime Club Ser.). 192p. 9.95 o.p. (*0-385-17271-0*) Doubleday Publishing.
—The Religious Body. unabr. ed. 2001. (Inspector C. D. Sloan Mystery Ser.). audio 34.95 (*0-7451-5709-2*, CSL 074) Chivers Audio Bks. GBR. *Dist:* BBC Audiobooks America.
—The Religious Body: The First C. D. Sloan Mystery. unabr. ed. 2000. (C. D. Sloan Mystery Ser.). audio 24.95 (*1-57270-149-8*, N41149u, Audio Editions Mystery Masters) Audio Partners Publishing Corp.
—The Religious Body: The First C. D. Sloan Mystery. l.t. ed. 1983. 288p. 12.50 o.p. (*0-7089-1038-6*, Ulverscroft) Thorpe, F. A. Pubs. GBR. *Dist:* Ulverscroft Large Print Bks., Ltd.
—The Religious Body: The First C.D. Sloan Mystery. 2000. 21.95 (*0-7540-8561-9*, Black Dagger) BBC Audiobooks America.
—The Religious Body: The First C.D. Sloan Mystery. 1980. 176p. pap. 2.95 o.p. (*0-553-24602-X*) Bantam Bks.
—Slight Mourning. 1989. mass mkt. o.s.i (*0-552-13427-9*, Corgi); 1982. 192p. mass mkt. 2.95 o.s.i (*0-553-25631-9*) Bantam Bks.
—Slight Mourning. l.t. ed. 1979. (Ulverscroft Large Print Ser.). 287p. o.p. (*0-7089-0271-5*, Ulverscroft) Thorpe, F. A. Pubs. GBR. *Dist:* Ulverscroft Large Print Canada, Ltd.
—Some Die Eloquent. 1981. 208p. pap. 2.95 o.p. (*0-553-25110-4*) Bantam Bks.
—Some Die Eloquent. 1980. (Crime Club Ser.). 10.95 o.p. (*0-385-15747-9*) Doubleday Publishing.
—Some Die Eloquent. l.t. ed. 1981. 328p. 12.00 o.p. (*0-7089-0631-1*, Ulverscroft) Thorpe, F. A. Pubs. GBR. *Dist:* Ulverscroft Large Print Bks., Ltd.
—The Stately Home Murder. 1980. 208p. pap. 2.75 o.p. (*0-553-24078-1*) Bantam Bks.
—Stiff News. 2000. audio compact disk 39.95; 1999. 222 p. (*0-7540-3643-X*) BBC Audiobooks America.
—Stiff News. 1998. 240p. 21.95 o.p. (*0-312-20023-4*, Saint Martin's Minotaur) St. Martin's Pr.
—Stiff News. l.t. ed. 1999. (Nightingale Ser.). 232p. pap. 21.95 (*0-7838-8477-X*) Thorndike Pr.

**SLOAN, CHARLEY (FICTITIOUS CHARACTER)—FICTION**

Coughlin, William Jeremiah. Death Penalty. l.t. ed. 1993. pap. 22.95 o.p. (*0-7927-1541-1*); 22.95 o.p. (*0-7927-1542-X*) BBC Audiobooks America.
—Death Penalty. 1992. 304p. 20.00 o.p. (*0-06-017701-2*) HarperTrade.
—Death Penalty. 1993. 432p. mass mkt. 5.99 o.s.i (*0-06-109053-0*, HarperTorch) Morrow/Avon.
—The Judgement. abr. l.t. ed. 1995. 352p. lib. bdg. 27.00 incl. audio (*1-57490-025-0*, Beeler Large Print Bks.) Beeler, Thomas T. Publisher.
—The Judgement. 1999. mass mkt. 223.68 (*0-312-96877-9*); 1997. 352p. 24.95 o.p. (*0-312-15558-1*) St. Martin's Pr.
—Shadow of a Doubt. l.t. ed. 1992. (General Ser.). 562p. 18.95 (*0-8161-5346-9*); lib. bdg. 21.95 (*0-8161-5345-0*) Gale Group. (Macmillan Reference USA).
—Shadow of a Doubt. 1993. 407p. mass mkt. 6.99 (*0-312-92745-2*, St. Martin's Paperbacks); 1991. 19.95 o.p. (*0-312-05961-2*) St. Martin's Pr.

Coughlin, William Jeremiah & Sorrells, Walter. Proof of Intent: A Charley Sloan Courtroom Thriller. 2002. 320p. 24.95 (*0-312-28066-1*) St. Martin's Pr.

**SLOAN, DUNCAN (FICTITIOUS CHARACTER)—FICTION**

Truluck, Bob. Saw Red. 2003. 230p. 30.00 (*0-939767-45-7*) McMillan, Dennis Pubns.
—Street Level. E-Book 22.95 (*0-312-27616-8*); 2000. 218p. 22.95 (*0-312-26626-X*, Saint Martin's Minotaur) St. Martin's Pr.

**SLOAN, POLLY (FICTITIOUS CHARACTER)—FICTION**

Gudger, S. I. Once upon a Murder. Gudger, S. I. & Allyson, Wendy, eds. 1995. 352p. (Orig.). pap. 6.95 (*0-9650224-7-1*) Ampersand Pr.

**SLOAN, SAM (FICTITIOUS CHARACTER)—FICTION**

Wise, Robert L. The Dead Detective: A Sam & Vera Sloan Mystery. 2002. 320p. pap. 13.99 (*0-7852-6696-8*) Nelson, Thomas Inc.
—Deleted! A Sam & Vera Sloan Mystery. 2003. xiii, 303p. pap. 12.99 (*0-7852-6697-6*) Nelson, Thomas Inc.
—The Empty Coffin: A Sam & Vera Sloan Mystery. 2001. 301p. pap. 12.99 (*0-7852-6687-9*) Nelson, Thomas Pubs.

**SLOAN, VERA (FICTITIOUS CHARACTER)—FICTION**

Wise, Robert L. The Dead Detective: A Sam & Vera Sloan Mystery. 2002. 320p. pap. 13.99 (*0-7852-6696-8*) Nelson, Thomas Inc.
—Deleted! A Sam & Vera Sloan Mystery. 2003. xiii, 303p. pap. 12.99 (*0-7852-6697-6*) Nelson, Thomas Inc.
—The Empty Coffin: A Sam & Vera Sloan Mystery. 2001. 301p. pap. 12.99 (*0-7852-6687-9*) Nelson, Thomas Pubs.

**SLOANE, SYDNEY (FICTITIOUS CHARACTER)—FICTION**

Lordon, Randye. East of Niece. 2001. (Sydney Sloane Mystery Ser.). 288p. 23.95 (*0-312-27114-X*, Saint Martin's Minotaur) St. Martin's Pr.
—Father Forgive Me. 1997. (Orig.). pap. 5.99 (*0-380-79165-X*, Avon Bks.) Morrow/Avon.
—Mother May I: A Sydney Sloane Mystery. 1998. pap. 5.99 o.p. (*0-380-79166-8*, Avon Bks.) Morrow/Avon.

**SLOCUM (FICTITIOUS CHARACTER)—FICTION**

Logan, Jake. Across the Rio Grande: John Slocum. 1987. (Slocum Ser.: Vol. 4). 208p. mass mkt. 2.75 o.s.i (*0-425-10025-1*) Berkley Publishing Group.
—Apache Sunrise: John Slocum. 1983. (Slocum Ser.: Vol. 54). 208p. mass mkt. 2.25 o.s.i (*0-425-06249-X*) Berkley Publishing Group.
—Bandit Gold: John Slocum. 1984. (Slocum Ser.: Vol. 65). 192p. mass mkt. 2.50 o.p. (*0-425-07018-2*) Berkley Publishing Group.
—The Blackmail Express: John Slocum. 1986. (Slocum Ser.: Vol. 91). 192p. mass mkt. 2.50 o.p. (*0-425-09088-4*) Berkley Publishing Group.
—Blood at the Crossing: John Slocum. 1988. (Slocum Ser.: Vol. 117). mass mkt. 2.95 o.p. (*0-425-11233-0*) Berkley Publishing Group.
—Blood in Kansas: John Slocum. 1998. (Jake Logan Ser.: Vol. 231). 192p. mass mkt. 4.99 o.s.i (*0-515-12291-2*, Jove) Berkley Publishing Group.
—Blood on the Brazos. 1998. (Jake Logan Ser.: Vol. 227). 192p. mass mkt. 4.99 o.s.i (*0-515-12229-7*, Jove) Berkley Publishing Group.
—Blood on the Rio Grande. 1996. (Slocum Ser.: No. 207). 192p. mass mkt. 4.99 o.s.i (*0-515-11860-5*, Jove) Berkley Publishing Group.
—Blood Trail: John Slocum. 1994. (Slocum Ser.: Vol. 186). 192p. (Orig.). mass mkt. 3.99 o.p. (*0-425-14341-4*) Berkley Publishing Group.
—Boomtown Showdown. 1995. (Slocum Ser.: Vol. 195). 192p. (Orig.). mass mkt. 3.99 o.p. (*0-425-14729-0*) Berkley Publishing Group.
—Cheyenne Bloodbath: John Slocum. 1986. (Slocum Ser.: Vol. 90). 192p. mass mkt. 2.50 o.p. (*0-425-08791-3*) Berkley Publishing Group.
—Colorado Killers: John Slocum. 1990. (Slocum Ser.: Vol. 134). mass mkt. 2.95 o.p. (*0-425-11971-8*) Berkley Publishing Group.
—Dancer's Trail. 2003. (Slocum Ser.: No. 295). 192p. mass mkt. 4.99 (*0-515-13598-4*, Jove) Berkley Publishing Group.
—Death Trap: John Slocum. 1989. (Slocum Ser.: Vol. 123). mass mkt. 2.95 o.p. (*0-425-11541-0*) Berkley Publishing Group.
—Death's Head Trail. 1992. (Slocum Ser.: Vol.161). 192p. (Orig.). mass mkt. 3.99 o.s.i (*0-425-13335-4*) Berkley Publishing Group.
—Final Draw: John Slocum. 1993. (Slocum Ser.: Vol. 172). 192p. (Orig.). mass mkt. 3.99 o.p. (*0-425-13707-4*) Berkley Publishing Group.
—Giant Slocum & the Carnahan Boys. 2002. (Slocum Ser.). 272p. mass mkt. 5.99 o.s.i (*0-515-13384-1*, Jove) Berkley Publishing Group.
—Gold Fever: John Slocum. 1989. (Slocum Ser.: Vol. 122). mass mkt. 2.95 o.p. (*0-425-11398-1*) Berkley Publishing Group.
—The Grandville Bank Heist: John Slocum. 1991. (Slocum Ser.: Vol. 153). mass mkt. 3.50 o.p. (*0-425-12971-3*) Berkley Publishing Group.
—Gunplay at Hobbs' Hole: John Slocum. 1985. (Slocum Ser.: Vol. 77). 192p. mass mkt. 2.50 o.p. (*0-425-07683-0*) Berkley Publishing Group.
—Hell's Fury: John Slocum. 1987. (Slocum Ser.: Vol. 101). 192p. (Orig.). mass mkt. 2.75 o.p. (*0-425-09896-6*) Berkley Publishing Group.
—High, Wide, & Deadly: John Slocum. 1987. (Slocum Ser.). 192p. (Orig.). mass mkt. 2.75 o.p. (*0-425-10016-2*) Berkley Publishing Group.
—The Horse Thief War: John Slocum. 1990. (Slocum Ser.: Vol. 143). mass mkt. 2.95 o.p. (*0-425-12445-2*) Berkley Publishing Group.
—Hot on the Trail, Vol. 279. 2002. (Slocum Ser.: 279). 192p. mass mkt. 4.99 o.s.i (*0-515-13295-0*, Jove) Berkley Publishing Group.
—Jailbreak Moon: John Slocum. (Slocum Ser.: Vol. 83). 1987. mass mkt. 2.75 o.p. (*0-425-10443-5*); 1985. 192p. mass mkt. 2.50 o.s.i (*0-425-08189-3*) Berkley Publishing Group.
—The Journey of Death: John Slocum. 1985. (Slocum Ser.: Vol. 78). 192p. mass mkt. 2.50 o.p. (*0-425-07753-5*) Berkley Publishing Group.
—The Lady Gambler. 1996. (Slocum Ser.: Vol. 205). 192p. mass mkt. 4.50 o.s.i (*0-515-11827-3*, Jove) Berkley Publishing Group.
—Louisiana Lovely: John Slocum. 1997. (Jake Logan Ser.: Vol. 224). 192p. mass mkt. 4.99 o.s.i (*0-515-12176-2*, Jove) Berkley Publishing Group.
—Mescalero Dawn: John Slocum. 1987. (Slocum Ser.: Vol. 85). 192p. mass mkt. 2.75 o.p. (*0-425-10444-3*) Berkley Publishing Group.
—Mexican Silver: John Slocum. 1989. (Slocum Ser.: Vol. 131). mass mkt. 2.95 o.s.i (*0-425-11838-X*) Berkley Publishing Group.
—Nebraska Burnout: John Slocum. 1983. (Slocum Ser.: Vol. 56). 208p. mass mkt. 2.25 o.p. (*0-425-06330-5*) Berkley Publishing Group.
—Nevada Gunmen: John Slocum. 1990. (Slocum Ser.: Vol. 142). mass mkt. 2.95 o.p. (*0-425-12354-5*) Berkley Publishing Group.
—A Noose for Slocum. 1990. (Slocum Ser.: Vol. 141). mass mkt. 2.95 o.p. (*0-425-12307-3*) Berkley Publishing Group.
—Pikes Peak Shoot-Out: John Slocum. 1994. (Slocum Ser.: Vol. 185). 192p. (Orig.). mass mkt. 3.99 o.p. (*0-425-14294-9*) Berkley Publishing Group.
—Prairie Fires: John Slocum. 1997. (Jake Logan Ser.: Vol. 225). 192p. mass mkt. 4.99 o.s.i (*0-515-12190-8*, Jove) Berkley Publishing Group.
—Railroad Baron: John Slocum. 1992. (Slocum Ser.: Vol. 157). mass mkt. 3.50 o.p. (*0-425-13187-4*) Berkley Publishing Group.
—Railroad to Hell, Vol. 269. 2001. (Slocum Ser.: Vol. 269). 192p. mass mkt. 4.99 o.s.i (*0-515-13102-4*, Jove) Berkley Publishing Group.
—The Rawhide Breed: John Slocum. 1989. (Slocum Ser.: Vol. 121). mass mkt. 2.95 o.p. (*0-425-11314-0*) Berkley Publishing Group.
—Rawhide Justice: John Slocum. 1986. (Slocum Ser.: Vol. 95). 192p. (Orig.). mass mkt. 2.50 o.p. (*0-425-09342-5*) Berkley Publishing Group.
—Revenge of the Gunfighter: John Slocum. 1990. (Slocum Ser.: Vol. 136). mass mkt. 2.95 o.s.i (*0-425-12054-6*) Berkley Publishing Group.
—Ride, Slocum, Ride. 1987. (Slocum Ser.). mass mkt. 2.95 o.p. (*0-425-10022-7*) Berkley Publishing Group.
—Ride to Vengeance: John Slocum. 1990. (Slocum Ser.: Vol. 135). mass mkt. 2.95 o.p. (*0-425-12010-4*) Berkley Publishing Group.
—River Chase: John Slocum. 1992. (Slocum Ser.: Vol. 158). mass mkt. 3.50 o.p. (*0-425-13214-5*) Berkley Publishing Group.
—San Angelo Shootout: John Slocum. 1992. (Slocum Ser.: Vol. 165). 192p. (Orig.). mass mkt. 3.99 o.p. (*0-425-13508-X*) Berkley Publishing Group.
—Seven Graves to Laredo: John Slocum. 1987. (Slocum Ser.: Vol. 97). 192p. mass mkt. 2.50 o.p. (*0-425-09479-0*) Berkley Publishing Group.
—Sheriff Slocum. 2000. (Slocum Giant Novel Ser.). 272p. mass mkt. 5.99 o.s.i (*0-515-12841-4*, Jove); 1993. (Slocum Ser.: Vol. 168). 192p. mass mkt. 3.99 o.p. (*0-425-13624-8*) Berkley Publishing Group.
—Shoot Out at Whiskey Springs. 2002. (Slocum Ser.: 278). 192p. mass mkt. 4.99 (*0-515-13280-2*, Jove) Berkley Publishing Group.
—Showdown at Drowning Creek: John Slocum. 1996. (Slocum Ser.: Vol. 203). 192p. (Orig.). mass mkt. 4.50 o.s.i (*0-515-11782-X*, Jove) Berkley Publishing Group.
—Showdown at Shiloh, Vol. 248. 1999. (Jake Logan Ser.: Vol. 248). 192p. mass mkt. 4.99 o.s.i (*0-515-12659-4*, Jove) Berkley Publishing Group.
—Showdown in Texas, Vol. 263. 2001. (Jake Logan Ser.: Vol. 263). 192p. mass mkt. 4.99 o.s.i (*0-515-13000-1*, Jove) Berkley Publishing Group.
—The Silver Stallion: John Slocum. 1995. (Slocum Ser.: Vol. 197). 192p. (Orig.). mass mkt. 3.99 o.s.i (*0-515-11654-8*, Jove) Berkley Publishing Group.
—Silver Town Showdown: John Slocum. 1992. (Slocum Ser.: Vol. 162). 192p. (Orig.). mass mkt. 3.99 o.p. (*0-425-13359-1*) Berkley Publishing Group.
—Sixgun Cemetery: John Slocum. 1987. (Slocum Ser.: Vol. 99). 100p. mass mkt. 2.75 o.p. (*0-425-09647-5*) Berkley Publishing Group.
—Sixgun Law: John Slocum. Colgan, Tom, ed. 1988. (Slocum Ser.: Vol. 113). mass mkt. 2.75 o.p. (*0-425-10850-3*) Berkley Publishing Group.
—Sixguns at Silverado: John Slocum. 1987. (Slocum Ser.: Vol. 107). mass mkt. 2.75 o.p. (*0-425-10347-1*) Berkley Publishing Group.
—Slocum & Doc Holliday. 1997. (Jake Logan Ser.: Vol. 221). 192p. mass mkt. 4.99 o.s.i (*0-515-12131-2*, Jove) Berkley Publishing Group.

—Slocum & Plain. 1991. (Slocum Ser.: Vol. 144). mass mkt. 2.95 o.p. (*0-425-12493-2*) Berkley Publishing Group.
—Slocum & Quantrill. 1994. (Slocum Ser.: Vol. 188). 192p. (Orig.). mass mkt. 3.99 o.p. (*0-425-14400-3*) Berkley Publishing Group.
—Slocum & the Abilene Swindle. 1988. (Slocum Ser.: Vol. 116). mass mkt. 2.95 o.p. (*0-425-10984-4*) Berkley Publishing Group.
—Slocum & the Apache Raiders. 1991. (Slocum Ser.: Vol. 147). mass mkt. 2.95 o.p. (*0-425-12659-5*) Berkley Publishing Group.
—Slocum & the Apache Ransom. 1996. (Slocum Ser.: Vol. 209). 192p. mass mkt. 4.99 o.s.i (*0-515-11894-X*, Jove) Berkley Publishing Group.
—Slocum & the Arizona Cowboys. 1987. (Slocum Ser.: Vol. 98). 192p. mass mkt. 2.75 o.p. (*0-425-09567-3*) Berkley Publishing Group.
—Slocum & the Arizona Kidnappers. 1988. (Slocum Ser.: Vol. 114). mass mkt. 2.95 o.p. (*0-425-10889-9*) Berkley Publishing Group.
—Slocum & the Avenging Gun, No. 79. 1985. (Slocum Ser.). 192p. mass mkt. 2.50 o.s.i (*0-425-07973-2*) Berkley Publishing Group.
—Slocum & the Aztec Priestess, No. 222. 1997. (Slocum Ser.). 192p. mass mkt. 4.99 o.s.i (*0-515-12143-6*, Jove) Berkley Publishing Group.
—Slocum & the Baroness. 1999. (Jake Logan Ser.: Vol. 238). 192p. mass mkt. 4.99 o.s.i (*0-515-12436-2*, Jove) Berkley Publishing Group.
—Slocum & the Big Three. 1999. (Jake Logan Ser.: Vol. 241). 192p. mass mkt. 4.99 o.s.i (*0-515-12484-2*, Jove) Berkley Publishing Group.
—Slocum & the Bitterroot Belle, No. 292. 2003. (Slocum Ser.). 192p. mass mkt. 4.99 (*0-515-13548-8*, Jove) Berkley Publishing Group.
—Slocum & the Blood Rage. 1988. (Slocum Ser.: Vol. 114). 192p. mass mkt. 2.75 o.p. (*0-425-10555-5*) Berkley Publishing Group.
—Slocum & the Bozeman Trail. (Slocum Ser.: Vol. 87). 1987. mass mkt. 2.75 o.p. (*0-425-10445-1*); 1986. 192p. mass mkt. 2.50 o.s.i (*0-425-08664-X*) Berkley Publishing Group.
—Slocum & the Buffalo Hunter. 1999. (Jake Logan Ser.: Vol. 243). 192p. mass mkt. 4.99 o.s.i (*0-515-12518-0*, Jove) Berkley Publishing Group.
—Slocum & the Buffalo Hunters. 1988. (Slocum Ser.: Vol. 118). mass mkt. 2.95 o.p. (*0-425-11056-7*) Berkley Publishing Group.
—Slocum & the Buffalo Soldiers. 1994. (Slocum Ser.: Vol. 179). 192p. (Orig.). mass mkt. 3.99 o.p. (*0-425-14050-4*) Berkley Publishing Group.
—Slocum & the Bushwhackers. 1992. (Slocum Ser.: Vol. 163). 192p. (Orig.). mass mkt. 3.99 o.p. (*0-425-13401-6*) Berkley Publishing Group.
—Slocum & the Cattle King. 1999. (Jake Logan Ser.: Vol. 246). 192p. mass mkt. 4.99 o.s.i (*0-515-12571-7*, Jove) Berkley Publishing Group.
—Slocum & the Cattle Queen. 1983. (Slocum Ser.: Vol. 57). 192p. mass mkt. 2.50 o.p. (*0-425-07182-0*) Berkley Publishing Group.
—Slocum & the Cattle War. 1990. (Slocum Ser.: Vol. 133). mass mkt. 2.95 o.p. (*0-425-11919-X*) Berkley Publishing Group.
—Slocum & the Cherokee Manhunt. 1987. (Slocum Ser.: Vol. 106). 192p. mass mkt. 2.75 o.p. (*0-425-10419-2*) Berkley Publishing Group.
—Slocum & the Circle Z Riders. 2003. (Slocum Ser.: No. 293). 192p. mass mkt. 4.99 (*0-515-13576-3*, Jove) Berkley Publishing Group.
—Slocum & the Claim Jumpers. 1987. (Slocum Ser.: Vol. 105). mass mkt. 2.75 o.p. (*0-425-10188-6*) Berkley Publishing Group.
—Slocum & the Colorado Riverboat, No. 219. 1997. (Jake Logan Ser.: Vol. 219). 192p. mass mkt. 4.99 o.s.i (*0-515-12081-2*, Jove) Berkley Publishing Group.
—Slocum & the Comanche Princess. 1999. (Jake Logan Ser.: Vol. 239). 192p. mass mkt. 4.99 o.s.i (*0-515-12449-4*, Jove) Berkley Publishing Group.
—Slocum & the Comanche Rescue. 1997. (Jake Logan Ser.: Vol. 223). 192p. mass mkt. 4.99 o.s.i (*0-515-12161-4*, Jove) Berkley Publishing Group.
—Slocum & the Comely Corpse. 1998. (Jake Logan Ser.: Vol. 230). 192p. mass mkt. 4.99 o.s.i (*0-515-12277-7*, Jove) Berkley Publishing Group.
—Slocum & the Cow Town Kill. 1994. (Slocum Ser.: Vol. 184). 192p. (Orig.). mass mkt. 3.99 o.s.i (*0-425-14255-8*) Berkley Publishing Group.
—Slocum & the Cracker Creek Killers. Colgan, Tom, ed. 1988. (Slocum Ser.: Vol. 110). 192p. (Orig.). mass mkt. 2.75 o.p. (*0-425-10635-7*) Berkley Publishing Group.
—Slocum & the Crooked Judge. 1989. (Slocum Ser.: Vol. 124). mass mkt. 2.95 o.p. (*0-425-11460-0*) Berkley Publishing Group.
—Slocum & the Dead Man's Spurs, Vol. 247. 1999. (Jake Logan Ser.: Vol. 247). 192p. mass mkt. 4.99 o.s.i (*0-515-12613-6*, Jove) Berkley Publishing Group.
—Slocum & the Deadly Damsel. 2003. (Slocum Ser.: No. 294). 192p. mass mkt. 4.99 (*0-515-13584-4*, Jove) Berkley Publishing Group.
—Slocum & the Deadly Feud. 1986. (Slocum Ser.: Vol. 94). 100p. mass mkt. 2.50 o.p. (*0-425-09212-7*) Berkley Publishing Group.
—Slocum & the Deadwood Treasure. 1991. (Slocum Ser.: Vol. 149). mass mkt. 2.95 o.p. (*0-425-12843-1*) Berkley Publishing Group.
—Slocum & the Death Council. 1991. (Slocum Ser.: Vol. 155). mass mkt. 3.50 o.s.i (*0-425-13081-9*) Berkley Publishing Group.
—Slocum & the Death Dealer. 1991. (Slocum Ser.: Vol. 145). mass mkt. 2.95 o.p. (*0-425-12558-0*) Berkley Publishing Group.
—Slocum & the Dirty Game. 1995. (Slocum Ser.: Vol. 202). 192p. (Orig.). mass mkt. 4.50 o.s.i (*0-515-11764-1*, Jove) Berkley Publishing Group.
—Slocum & the El Paso Blood Feud. 1987. (Slocum Ser.: Vol. 108). 192p. mass mkt. 2.75 o.p. (*0-425-10489-3*) Berkley Publishing Group.
—Slocum & the Fort Worth Ambush. 1994. (Slocum Ser.: Vol. 190). 192p. (Orig.). mass mkt. 3.99 o.s.i (*0-425-14496-8*) Berkley Publishing Group.
—Slocum & the Forty Thieves. 1993. (Slocum Ser.: Vol. 170). 192p. (Orig.). mass mkt. 3.99 o.p. (*0-425-13797-X*) Berkley Publishing Group.
—Slocum & the Frisco Killers. 1996. (Slocum Ser.: Vol. 212). 192p. mass mkt. 4.99 o.s.i (*0-515-11967-9*, Jove) Berkley Publishing Group.
—Slocum & the Gambler's Woman, Vol. 251. 2000. (Jake Logan Ser.: Vol. 251). 192p. mass mkt. 4.99 o.s.i (*0-515-12733-7*, Jove) Berkley Publishing Group.
—Slocum & the Gambler's Woman. abr. ed. 2000. (Jake Logan Ser.: Vol. 51). audio 16.95 (*1-890990-42-6*, 99042) Otis Audio, Inc.
—Slocum & the Ghost Rustlers. 192p. (Orig.). 1994. (Slocum Ser.: Vol. 189). mass mkt. 3.99 o.p. (*0-425-14462-3*); No. 283. 2002. mass mkt. 4.99 o.s.i (*0-515-13367-1*, Jove) Berkley Publishing Group.
—Slocum & the Gold-Mine Gamble. 1996. (Slocum Ser.: Vol. 208). 192p. mass mkt. 4.99 o.s.i (*0-515-11878-8*, Jove) Berkley Publishing Group.
—Slocum & the Gold Slaves. 1994. (Slocum Ser.: Vol. 187). 192p. mass mkt. 3.99 o.p. (*0-425-14363-5*) Berkley Publishing Group.
—Slocum & the Gravedigger. 2001. (Slocum Ser.: No. 275). 192p. mass mkt. 4.99 o.s.i (*0-515-13231-4*, Jove) Berkley Publishing Group.
—Slocum & the Great Diamond Hoax. 1998. (Jake Logan Ser.: Vol. 232). 192p. mass mkt. 4.99 o.s.i (*0-515-12301-3*, Jove) Berkley Publishing Group.
—Slocum & the Great Southern Hunt. 1996. (Slocum Ser.: Vol. 213). 192p. mass mkt. 4.99 o.s.i (*0-515-11983-0*, Jove) Berkley Publishing Group.
—Slocum & the Gun-Runners. 1984. (Slocum Ser.: Vol. 71). 192p. mass mkt. 2.50 o.p. (*0-425-07382-3*) Berkley Publishing Group.
—Slocum & the Gunfighter's Return. 1988. (Slocum Ser.: Vol. 120). mass mkt. 2.95 o.p. (*0-425-11265-9*) Berkley Publishing Group.
—Slocum & the Gunrunners, Vol. 252. 2000. (Jake Logan Ser.: Vol. 252). 187p. mass mkt. 4.99 o.s.i (*0-515-12754-X*, Jove) Berkley Publishing Group.
—Slocum & the Hanging Party. 1991. (Slocum Ser.: Vol. 152). mass mkt. 3.50 o.s.i (*0-425-12904-7*) Berkley Publishing Group.
—Slocum & the Hanging Tree. 1988. (Slocum Ser.: Vol. 115). mass mkt. 2.95 o.p. (*0-425-10935-6*) Berkley Publishing Group.
—Slocum & the Hatchet Men. 1984. (Slocum Ser.: Vol. 64). 192p. mass mkt. 2.50 o.p. (*0-425-07046-8*) Berkley Publishing Group.
—Slocum & the Horse Thieves. 1986. (Slocum Ser.: Vol.88). 192p. mass mkt. 2.50 o.p. (*0-425-08742-5*) Berkley Publishing Group.
—Slocum & the Idaho Breakout. 1989. (Slocum Ser.: Vol. 129). mass mkt. 2.95 o.p. (*0-425-11748-0*) Berkley Publishing Group.
—Slocum & the Indian Ghost. 1986. (Slocum Ser.: Vol. 96). 192p. mass mkt. 2.50 o.p. (*0-425-09395-6*) Berkley Publishing Group.
—Slocum & the Invaders. 1994. (Slocum Ser.: Vol. 182). 192p. mass mkt. 3.99 o.p. (*0-425-14182-9*) Berkley Publishing Group.
—Slocum & the Irish Lass. 1997. (Slocum Giant Novel Ser.). 256p. mass mkt. 5.99 o.s.i (*0-515-12155-X*, Jove) Berkley Publishing Group.
—Slocum & the Jersey Lily. 1999. (Jake Logan Ser.: Vol. 250). 192p. mass mkt. 4.99 o.s.i (*0-515-12706-X*, Jove) Berkley Publishing Group.
—Slocum & the Ketchem Gang. 1999. (Jake Logan Ser.: Vol. 249). 192p. mass mkt. 4.99 o.s.i (*0-515-12686-1*, Jove) Berkley Publishing Group.
—Slocum & the Lady from Abilene. 1999. (Jake Logan Ser.: Vol. 245). 192p. mass mkt. 4.99 o.s.i (*0-515-12555-5*, Jove) Berkley Publishing Group.
—Slocum & the Lady in Black. 2002. (Slocum Ser.: No. 282). 192p. mass mkt. 4.99 o.s.i (*0-515-13350-7*, Jove) Berkley Publishing Group.
—Slocum & the Lady in Blue. 1997. (Slocum Ser.: Vol. 217). 192p. mass mkt. 4.99 o.s.i (*0-515-12049-9*, Jove) Berkley Publishing Group.
—Slocum & the Lady 'Niners. 1995. (Slocum Ser.: Vol. 194). 192p. (Orig.). mass mkt. 3.99 o.s.i (*0-425-14684-7*) Berkley Publishing Group.
—Slocum & the Lakota Lady. 2001. (Jake Logan Ser.: Vol. 264). 192p. mass mkt. 4.99 o.s.i (*0-515-13017-6*, Jove) Berkley Publishing Group.
—Slocum & the Lakota Lady. 2001. (Jake Logan Ser.: No. 264). audio 16.95 (*1-890990-68-X*, 99068) Otis Audio, Inc.
—Slocum & the Laredo Showdown. 1987. (Slocum Ser.: Vol. 104). mass mkt. 2.75 o.p. (*0-425-10116-9*) Berkley Publishing Group.
—Slocum & the Last Gasp. 1998. (Jake Logan Ser.: Vol. 234). 192p. mass mkt. 4.99 o.s.i (*0-515-12355-2*, Jove) Berkley Publishing Group.
—Slocum & the Law. (Slocum Ser.). 1984. 224p. mass mkt. 2.50 o.p. (*0-425-07398-X*); 1983. mass mkt. 2.25 o.s.i (*0-425-06153-1*) Berkley Publishing Group.
—Slocum & the Live Oak Boys. 1999. (Jake Logan Ser.: Vol. 240). 192p. mass mkt. 4.99 o.s.i (*0-515-12467-2*, Jove) Berkley Publishing Group.
—Slocum & the Lone Star Feud. 1998. (Jake Logan Ser.: Vol. 233). 192p. mass mkt. 4.99 o.s.i (*0-515-12339-0*, Jove) Berkley Publishing Group.
—Slocum & the Long Wagon Train. 1986. (Slocum Ser.: Vol. 93). 192p. mass mkt. 2.50 o.p. (*0-425-09299-2*) Berkley Publishing Group.
—Slocum & the Lost Dutchman Mine. 1984. (Slocum Ser.: Vol. 61). 192p. mass mkt. 2.50 o.p. (*0-425-06744-0*) Berkley Publishing Group.
—Slocum & the Mad Major. 1982. (Slocum Ser.). 224p. 1.95 (*0-86721-217-9*) Berkley Publishing Group.
—Slocum & the Miner's Justice. 1998. (Jake Logan Ser.: Vol. 235). 192p. mass mkt. 4.99 o.s.i (*0-515-12371-4*, Jove) Berkley Publishing Group.
—Slocum & the Mountain of Gold. 1994. (Slocum Ser.: Vol. 183). 192p. (Orig.). mass mkt. 3.99 o.s.i (*0-425-14231-0*) Berkley Publishing Group.
—Slocum & the Nebraska Storm. 2000. (Jake Logan Ser.: Vol. 253). 185p. mass mkt. 4.99 o.s.i (*0-515-12769-8*, Jove) Berkley Publishing Group.
—Slocum & the Nightriders. 1993. (Slocum Ser.: Vol. 174). 192p. (Orig.). mass mkt. 3.99 o.p. (*0-425-13839-9*) Berkley Publishing Group.
—Slocum & the Noose of Hell. 1986. (Slocum Ser.: Vol. 89). 192p. mass mkt. 2.75 o.p. (*0-425-08773-5*) Berkley Publishing Group.
—Slocum & the Outlaw's Trail. 1989. (Slocum Ser.: Vol. 126). mass mkt. 2.95 o.p. (*0-425-11618-2*) Berkley Publishing Group.
—Slocum & the Phantom Gold. 1994. (Slocum Ser.: Vol. 180). 192p. (Orig.). mass mkt. 3.99 o.p. (*0-425-14100-4*) Berkley Publishing Group.
—Slocum & the Pirates, No. 196. 1995. (Slocum Ser.). 192p. (Orig.). mass mkt. 3.99 o.s.i (*0-515-11633-5*, Jove) Berkley Publishing Group.
—Slocum & the Plains Massacre. 1989. (Slocum Ser.: Vol. 128). mass mkt. 2.95 o.p. (*0-425-11693-X*) Berkley Publishing Group.
—Slocum & the Pomo Chief. 2000. (Jake Logan Ser.: Vol. 256). 192p. mass mkt. 4.99 o.s.i (*0-515-12838-4*, Jove) Berkley Publishing Group.
—Slocum & the Powder River Gamble. 1997. (Slocum Ser.: Vol. 218). 192p. mass mkt. 4.99 o.s.i (*0-515-12070-7*, Jove) Berkley Publishing Group.
—Slocum & the Preacher's Daughter. 1988. (Slocum Ser.). mass mkt. 2.95 o.p. (*0-425-11194-6*) Berkley Publishing Group.
—Slocum & the Real McCoy. 1998. (Jake Logan Ser.: Vol. 226). 192p. mass mkt. 4.99 o.s.i (*0-515-12208-4*, Jove) Berkley Publishing Group.
—Slocum & the Red River Renegade. Colgan, Tom, ed. 1988. (Slocum Ser.: Vol. 111). 192p. (Orig.). mass mkt. 2.75 o.p. (*0-425-10701-9*) Berkley Publishing Group.
—Slocum & the Scalplock Trail. 1998. (Jake Logan Ser.: Vol. 228). 192p. mass mkt. 4.99 o.s.i (*0-515-12243-2*, Jove) Berkley Publishing Group.
—Slocum & the Sharpshooter. 1992. (Slocum Ser.: Vol. 160). mass mkt. 3.50 o.p. (*0-425-13303-6*) Berkley Publishing Group.
—Slocum & the Shoshone Whiskey. 1995. (Slocum Ser.: Vol. 193). 192p. (Orig.). mass mkt. 3.99 o.p. (*0-425-14647-2*) Berkley Publishing Group.
—Slocum & the Silver Ranch Fight. 1986. (Slocum Ser.: Vol. 92). 100p. mass mkt. 2.50 o.p. (*0-425-09111-2*) Berkley Publishing Group.
—Slocum & the Spotted Horse. 1995. (Slocum Ser.: Vol. 198). 192p. (Orig.). mass mkt. 3.99 o.s.i (*0-515-11679-3*, Jove) Berkley Publishing Group.
—Slocum & the Stagecoach Bandits. 1991. (Slocum Ser.: Vol. 151). mass mkt. 3.50 o.p. (*0-425-12855-5*) Berkley Publishing Group.
—Slocum & the Texas Rose. 1998. (Jake Logan Ser.: Vol. 229). 192p. mass mkt. 4.99 o.s.i (*0-515-12264-5*, Jove) Berkley Publishing Group.
—Slocum & the Three Wives. 1999. (Slocum Giant Novel Ser.: Vol. 18). 288p. (Orig.). mass mkt. 5.99 o.s.i (*0-515-12569-5*, Jove) Berkley Publishing Group.
—Slocum & the Tin Star Swindle. 1993. (Slocum Ser.: Vol. 173). 192p. (Orig.). mass mkt. 3.99 o.p. (*0-425-13811-9*) Berkley Publishing Group.
—Slocum & the Tong Warriors. 1989. (Slocum Ser.: Vol. 125). mass mkt. 2.95 o.p. (*0-425-11589-5*) Berkley Publishing Group.
—Slocum & the Town Boss. 1997. (Slocum Ser.: Vol. 216). 192p. mass mkt. 4.99 o.s.i (*0-515-12030-8*, Jove) Berkley Publishing Group.
—Slocum & the Town Tamer. 1990. (Slocum Ser.: Vol. 140). mass mkt. 2.95 o.p. (*0-425-12221-2*) Berkley Publishing Group.
—Slocum & the Walapai War. 1996. (Slocum Ser.: Vol. 210). 192p. mass mkt. 4.99 o.s.i (*0-515-11924-5*, Jove) Berkley Publishing Group.
—Slocum & the Widow Kate. 1987. (Slocum Ser.: Vol. 3). 224p. mass mkt. 2.75 o.p. (*0-425-10024-3*) Berkley Publishing Group.
—Slocum & the Widow Maker. 2002. (Slocum Ser.: 281). 192p. mass mkt. 4.99 o.s.i (*0-515-13336-1*, Jove) Berkley Publishing Group.
—Slocum & the Wild Stallion Chase. 1987. (Slocum Ser.: Vol. 103). mass mkt. 2.75 o.p. (*0-425-09783-8*) Berkley Publishing Group.
—Slocum & the Wolf Hunt. 1998. (Jake Logan Ser.: Vol. 237). 192p. mass mkt. 4.99 o.s.i (*0-515-12413-3*, Jove) Berkley Publishing Group.
—Slocum & the Wyoming Frame-up. 1992. (Slocum Ser.: Vol. 164). 192p. (Orig.). mass mkt. 3.99 o.p. (*0-425-13472-5*) Berkley Publishing Group.
—Slocum & the Yellow Rose of Texas. 1999. (Jake Logan Ser.: Vol. 244). 192p. mass mkt. 4.99 o.s.i (*0-515-12532-6*, Jove) Berkley Publishing Group.
—Slocum at Dead Dog. 1997. (Slocum Ser.: Vol. 215). 192p. mass mkt. 4.99 o.s.i (*0-515-12015-4*, Jove) Berkley Publishing Group.
—Slocum at Dog Leg Creek. 1995. (Slocum Ser.: Vol. 199). 192p. (Orig.). mass mkt. 3.99 o.s.i (*0-515-11701-3*, Jove) Berkley Publishing Group.
—Slocum at Fort Desolation. 1991. (Slocum Ser.: Vol. 146). mass mkt. 2.95 o.p. (*0-425-12615-3*) Berkley Publishing Group.
—Slocum at Hell's Acre. 1998. (Jake Logan Ser.: Vol. 236). 192p. mass mkt. 4.99 o.s.i (*0-515-12391-9*, Jove) Berkley Publishing Group.
—Slocum at Outlaws' Haven. 1993. (Slocum Ser.: Vol. 176). mass mkt. 3.99 o.p. (*0-425-13951-4*) Berkley Publishing Group.
—Slocum at Scorpion Bend, Vol. 242. 1999. (Jake Logan Ser.: Vol. 242). 192p. mass mkt. 4.99 o.s.i (*0-515-12510-5*, Jove) Berkley Publishing Group.
—Slocum Busts Out. 1990. (Slocum Ser.). mass mkt. 3.50 o.s.i (*0-425-12270-0*) Berkley Publishing Group.
—Slocum Giant, the Gunman & the Greenhorn. 2003. (Slocum Ser.). 272p. mass mkt. 5.99 (*0-515-13639-5*, Jove) Berkley Publishing Group.
—Slocum in Deadwood. 1985. (Slocum Ser.: Vol. 69). 100p. mass mkt. 2.50 o.p. (*0-425-08382-9*) Berkley Publishing Group.
—Slocum in Paradise, No. 206. 1996. (Slocum Ser.: Vol. 206). 192p. (Orig.). mass mkt. 4.99 o.s.i (*0-515-11841-9*, Jove) Berkley Publishing Group.
—Slocum's Close Call, Vol. 254. 2000. (Jake Logan Ser.: Vol. 254). 192p. mass mkt. 4.99 o.s.i (*0-515-12789-2*, Jove) Berkley Publishing Group.
—Slocum's Command. 1983. (Slocum Ser.: Vol. 59). 192p. mass mkt. 2.25 o.p. (*0-425-06532-4*) Berkley Publishing Group.
—Slocum's Crime, No. 73. 1985. (Slocum Ser.: Vol. 73). 192p. mass mkt. 2.50 o.p. (*0-425-07460-9*) Berkley Publishing Group.
—Slocum's Deadly Game. 1987. (Slocum Ser.: Vol. 100). 192p. (Orig.). mass mkt. 2.75 o.s.i (*0-425-09712-9*) Berkley Publishing Group.
—Slocum's Debt. (Slocum Ser.: Vol. 132). 1989. mass mkt. 2.95 o.p. (*0-425-11882-7*); 1982. 224p. 1.95 (*0-86721-071-0*) Berkley Publishing Group.
—Slocum's Folly. 1996. (Slocum Ser.: Vol. 211). 192p. mass mkt. 4.99 o.s.i (*0-515-11940-7*, Jove) Berkley Publishing Group.
—Slocum's Fortune. 1991. (Slocum Ser.: Vol. 148). mass mkt. 2.95 o.p. (*0-425-12737-0*) Berkley Publishing Group.
—Slocum's Gold. 1987. (Slocum Ser.: Vol. 6). 192p. mass mkt. 2.75 o.p. (*0-425-10027-8*) Berkley Publishing Group.
—Slocum's Good Deed, No. 75. 1985. (Slocum Ser.: Vol.75). 192p. mass mkt. 2.50 o.p. (*0-425-07784-5*) Berkley Publishing Group.
—Slocum's Grubstake. 1996. (Slocum Ser.: Vol. 212). 272p. mass mkt. 5.50 o.s.i (*0-515-11955-5*, Jove) Berkley Publishing Group.
—Slocum's Hell. 1979. (Slocum Ser.: Vol. 19). 208p. 1.95 (*0-86721-023-0*) Berkley Publishing Group.
—Slocum's Inheritence. 1997. (Slocum Ser.: Vol. 220). 192p. mass mkt. 4.99 o.s.i (*0-515-12103-7*, Jove) Berkley Publishing Group.
—Slocum's Pride, No. 72. 1984. (Slocum Ser.: Vol. 72). 192p. mass mkt. 2.50 o.p. (*0-425-07567-2*) Berkley Publishing Group.

—Slocum's Raid. 1986. (Slocum Ser.: Vol. 32). 192p. mass mkt. 2.50 o.s.i (*0-425-07400-5*) Berkley Publishing Group.
—Slocum's Stampede, No. 76. 1985. (Slocum Ser.: Vol. 76). 192p. mass mkt. 2.50 o.p. (*0-425-07654-7*) Berkley Publishing Group.
—Slocum's Standoff. 1991. (Slocum Ser.: Vol. 154). mass mkt. 3.50 o.p. (*0-425-13037-1*) Berkley Publishing Group.
—Slocum's Winning Hand. 1984. (Slocum Ser.). 192p. mass mkt. 2.50 o.p. (*0-425-07494-3*) Berkley Publishing Group.
—Slow Death: John Slocum. 1989. (Slocum Ser.: Vol. 127). mass mkt. 2.95 o.p. (*0-425-11649-2*) Berkley Publishing Group.
—Stalker's Moon: John Slocum. 1989. (Slocum Ser.: Vol. 130). mass mkt. 2.95 o.p. (*0-425-11785-5*) Berkley Publishing Group.
—The Sunshine Basin War: John Slocum, No. 81. 1985. (Slocum Ser.: Vol. 81). 192p. mass mkt. 2.50 o.p. (*0-425-08087-0*) Berkley Publishing Group.
—Tequila Rose. 2003. (Slocum Ser.). 192p. mass mkt. 4.99 (*0-515-13640-9*, Jove) Berkley Publishing Group.
—Texas Trail Drive: John Slocum. 1990. (Slocum Ser.: Vol. 137). mass mkt. 2.95 o.p. (*0-425-12098-8*) Berkley Publishing Group.
—Timber King: John Slocum. 1992. (Slocum Ser.: Vol. 156). mass mkt. 3.50 o.p. (*0-425-13138-6*) Berkley Publishing Group.
—Tombstone Gold: John Slocum. 1992. (Slocum Ser.: Vol. 159). mass mkt. 3.50 o.p. (*0-425-13241-2*) Berkley Publishing Group.
—Trail of Death: John Slocum. 1991. (Slocum Ser.: Vol. 150). mass mkt. 3.50 o.p. (*0-425-12778-8*) Berkley Publishing Group.
—Two Coffins for Slocum. 2001. (Slocum Ser.: No. 273). 192p. mass mkt. 4.99 o.s.i (*0-515-13183-0*, Jove) Berkley Publishing Group.
—Vengeance Road: John Slocum. 1990. (Slocum Ser.: Vol. 139). mass mkt. 2.95 o.p. (*0-425-12174-7*) Berkley Publishing Group.
—Vigilante Justice: John Slocum. 1987. (Slocum Ser.: Vol. 82). 192p. mass mkt. 2.75 o.p. (*0-425-10442-7*) Berkley Publishing Group.
—The Wyoming Cattle War: John Slocum. 1990. (Slocum Ser.: Vol. 138). mass mkt. 2.95 o.p. (*0-425-12137-2*) Berkley Publishing Group.
Logan, Jake & Colgan, Tom. Slocum & the Gunfighter's Greed. 1988. (Slocum Ser.: Vol.112). 176p. reprint ed. mass mkt. 2.75 o.s.i (*0-425-10758-2*) Berkley Publishing Group.
Recknor, Ellen. Slocum. 2004. (Slocum Ser.). 192p. mass mkt. 4.99 (*0-515-13733-2*, Jove) Berkley Publishing Group.

**SLOCUM, JOHN (FICTITIOUS CHARACTER)—FICTION**

*see Slocum (Fictitious Character)—Fiction*

**SLOCUM, NINA (FICTITIOUS CHARACTER)—FICTION**

Crawford, Claudia. A Dangerous Gift. 1996. 352p. mass mkt. 5.50 o.s.i (*0-451-18537-4*, Signet Bks.) NAL.

**SMALL, DAVID (FICTITIOUS CHARACTER)—FICTION**

Kemelman, Harry. The Day the Rabbi Resigned. l.t. ed. 1993. (Large Print Mystery Ser.). 345p. 24.95 o.p. (*0-7927-1414-8*); pap. 19.95 o.p. (*0-7927-1413-X*) BBC Audiobooks America.
—The Day the Rabbi Resigned. 1992. mass mkt. 5.99 o.s.i (*0-449-21908-9*); 273p. 20.00 o.s.i (*0-449-90681-7*) Ballantine Bks. (Fawcett).
—The Day the Rabbi Resigned. 2004. 288p. mass mkt. 6.99 (*0-7434-7979-3*) ibooks, Inc.
—Friday the Rabbi Slept Late. 1993. pap. o.p. (*0-449-45127-5*); 1986. mass mkt. 5.99 o.s.i (*0-449-21180-0*) Ballantine Bks. (Fawcett).
—Friday the Rabbi Slept Late. 1964. 4.95 o.p. (*0-517-50691-2*, Crown) Crown Publishing Group.
—Friday the Rabbi Slept Late. l.t. ed. 1983. (General Ser.). 339p. lib. bdg. 13.95 o.p. (*0-8161-3537-1*, Macmillan Reference USA) Gale Group.
—Friday the Rabbi Slept Late. 2002. 208p. pap. 6.99 (*0-7434-3487-0*) ibooks, Inc.
—Monday the Rabbi Took Off. 1988. mass mkt. o.s.i (*0-449-20785-4*); 1986. 288p. mass mkt. 5.99 o.s.i (*0-449-21001-4*, Fawcett); 1981. mass mkt. 2.50 o.s.i (*0-449-23872-5*, Fawcett) Ballantine Bks.
—Monday the Rabbi Took Off. 1972. 316p. 5.95 o.p. (*0-399-10550-6*) Putnam Publishing Group, The.
—Monday the Rabbi Took Off. 2002. 368p. pap. 6.99 (*0-7434-5271-2*) ibooks, Inc.
—One Fine Day the Rabbi Bought a Cross. 1988. (Boston Mysteries Ser.). mass mkt. 5.99 o.s.i (*0-449-20687-4*, Fawcett) Ballantine Bks.
—One Fine Day the Rabbi Bought a Cross. l.t. ed. 1988. (Large Print Bks.). 353p. 18.95 o.p. (*0-8161-4347-1*, Macmillan Reference USA) Gale Group.
—One Fine Day the Rabbi Bought a Cross. 1987. 234p. 15.95 o.p. (*0-688-05631-8*, Morrow, William & Co.) Morrow/Avon.
—One Fine Day the Rabbi Bought a Cross. 1990. 3.99 o.p. (*0-517-05752-2*) Random Hse. Value Publishing.
—One Fine Day the Rabbi Bought a Cross. 2003. 320p. pap. 6.99 (*0-7434-7478-3*) ibooks, Inc.
—Rabbi Small, Bk. 2. 1924. o.s.i (*0-688-05617-2*, Morrow, William & Co.) Morrow/Avon.
—Saturday the Rabbi Went Hungry. 1987. 224p. mass mkt. 5.99 o.s.i (*0-449-21392-7*, Fawcett) Ballantine Bks.
—Saturday the Rabbi Went Hungry. 1988. 4.95 o.s.i (*0-517-01307-X*) Crown Publishing Group.
—Saturday the Rabbi Went Hungry. l.t. ed. 1983. 14.95 o.p. (*0-8161-3531-2*, Macmillan Reference USA) Gale Group.
—Someday the Rabbi Will Leave. 1986. 288p. mass mkt. 5.99 o.s.i (*0-449-20945-8*, Fawcett) Ballantine Bks.
—Someday the Rabbi Will Leave. 1985. 264p. 15.95 o.p. (*0-688-04174-4*, Morrow, William & Co.) Morrow/Avon.
—Someday the Rabbi Will Leave. 2003. 288p. pap. 6.99 (*0-7434-5911-3*) ibooks, Inc.
—Sunday the Rabbi Stayed Home. Date not set. mass mkt. (*0-449-20784-6*); 1985. 224p. mass mkt. 5.99 o.s.i (*0-449-21000-6*) Ballantine Bks. (Fawcett).
—Sunday the Rabbi Stayed Home. l.t. ed. 1977. (General Ser.). 420p. lib. bdg. 11.95 o.p. (*0-8161-6499-1*, Macmillan Reference USA) Gale Group.
—Sunday the Rabbi Stayed Home. 2002. (Rabbi Small Mystery Ser.). (Illus.). 304p. pap. 6.99 (*0-7434-5238-0*) ibooks, Inc.
—That Day the Rabbi Left Town. (Rabbi Small Mystery Ser.). 1997. 263p. mass mkt. 5.99 o.s.i (*0-449-22570-4*); 1996. 256p. 22.00 o.s.i (*0-449-91002-4*); 1996. 233p. lib. bdg. 22.95 (*1-57490-040-4*) Ballantine Bks. (Fawcett).
—Thursday the Rabbi Walked Out. 1986. mass mkt. 5.99 o.s.i (*0-449-21157-6*, Fawcett) Ballantine Bks.
—Thursday the Rabbi Walked Out. 2003. 256p. mass mkt. 6.99 (*0-7434-5860-5*) ibooks, Inc.
—Tuesday the Rabbi Saw Red. 1986. (Rabbi Ser.). mass mkt. 5.99 o.s.i (*0-449-21321-8*, Fawcett) Ballantine Bks.
—Tuesday the Rabbi Saw Red. 1974. (Adult Ser.). 508p. reprint ed. lib. bdg. 11.95 o.p. (*0-8161-6230-1*, Macmillan Reference USA) Gale Group.
—Tuesday the Rabbi Saw Red. 2003. 352p. pap. 6.99 (*0-7434-4534-1*) ibooks, Inc.
—Wednesday the Rabbi Got Wet. (Rabbi Ser.). 1986. mass mkt. 5.99 o.s.i (*0-449-21328-5*); 1983. mass mkt. 2.50 o.s.i (*0-449-20344-1*); 1981. mass mkt. 2.50 o.s.i (*0-449-23291-3*) Ballantine Bks. (Fawcett).
—Wednesday the Rabbi Got Wet. l.t. ed. 1977. (Winter Adult Ser.). 497p. reprint ed. lib. bdg. 13.50 o.p. (*0-8161-6413-4*, Macmillan Reference USA) Gale Group.
—Wednesday the Rabbi Got Wet. 2003. 336p. pap. 6.99 (*0-7434-5830-3*) ibooks, Inc.

**SMILEY, GEORGE (FICTITIOUS CHARACTER)—FICTION**

Le Carré, John. Call for the Dead. 1982. (George Smiley Novels Ser.). 160p. mass mkt. 3.95 o.s.i (*0-553-26623-3*) Bantam Bks.
—Call for the Dead. unabr. ed. 1991. (George Smiley Ser.). audio 32.95 (*0-7861-0235-7*, 1205) Blackstone Audio Bks., Inc.
—Call for the Dead. unabr. ed. 1982. (George Smiley Novels Ser.). audio 36.00 (*0-7366-0560-6*, 1532) Books on Tape, Inc.
—Call for the Dead. l.t. ed. 1988. (George Smiley Ser.). pap. 7.95 o.p. (*0-89621-193-2*, Macmillan Reference USA) Gale Group.
—Call for the Dead. abr. ed. 1999. audio 16.85 (*1-84032-113-X*) Hodder Headline Audiobooks GBR. *Dist:* Ulverscroft Large Print Bks., Ltd.
—Call for the Dead. 1989. 2.99 o.p. (*0-517-68434-9*) Random Hse. Value Publishing.
—Call for the Dead, unabr. ed. 1987. (George Smiley Novels Ser.). audio 26.00 (*1-55690-083-X*, 87810E7) Recorded Bks., LLC.
—Call for the Dead. 2002. 160p. pap. 13.00 (*0-7434-3167-7*, Scribner) Simon & Schuster.
—The Honourable Schoolboy: A Novel. 1985. (George Smiley Novels Ser.). 576p. mass mkt. 6.99 o.s.i (*0-553-27437-6*); mass mkt. 4.50 o.s.i (*0-553-25197-X*) Bantam Bks.
—The Honourable Schoolboy: A Novel. unabr. ed. 1991. audio 99.95 (*0-7861-0270-5*, 1236) Blackstone Audio Bks., Inc.
—The Honourable Schoolboy: A Novel. unabr. collector's ed. 1978. audio 120.00 (*0-7366-0112-0*, 1119) Books on Tape, Inc.
—The Honourable Schoolboy: A Novel. 1977. (General Ser.). lib. bdg. 18.95 o.p. (*0-8161-6539-4*, Macmillan Reference USA) Gale Group.
—The Honourable Schoolboy: A Novel. reprint ed. 2002. 608p. pap. 14.00 (*0-7434-5791-9*, Scribner); 2000. 688p. mass mkt. 7.99 (*0-671-04274-2*, Pocket) Simon & Schuster.
—John Le Carre: A New Collection of Three Complete Novels. 1996. 864p. 13.99 o.s.i (*0-517-15019-0*) Random Hse., Inc.
—John Le Carre: Three Complete Novels. 1995. 704p. 13.99 o.p. (*0-517-14697-5*); 1995. 12.99 o.s.i (*0-517-14899-4*); 1988. 9.99 o.s.i (*0-517-42284-0*) Random Hse. Value Publishing.
—The John Le Carre Value Collection, Set. abr. ed. 2000. audio 39.95 (*0-375-41589-0*, RH Audio) Random Hse. Audio Publishing Group.
—A Murder of Quality. 1990. (George Smiley Novels Ser.). 176p. mass mkt. 4.95 o.s.i (*0-553-26443-5*) Bantam Bks.
—A Murder of Quality. unabr. ed. 1991. (George Smiley Ser.). audio 32.95 (*0-7861-0272-1*, 1238) Blackstone Audio Bks., Inc.
—A Murder of Quality. unabr. ed. 1986. (George Smiley Novels Ser.). audio 36.00 (*0-7366-0456-1*, 1428) Books on Tape, Inc.
—A Murder of Quality. unabr. ed. 2000. (George Smiley Ser.: Bk. 2). audio 34.95 (*0-7451-4013-0*, CAB 710) Chivers Audio Bks. GBR. *Dist:* BBC Audiobooks America.
—A Murder of Quality. abr. ed. 1986. (George Smiley Novels Ser.). audio 15.95 (*0-88646-160-X*) Durkin Hayes Publishing Ltd.
—A Murder of Quality. abr. ed. 1999. (George Smiley Ser.). audio 16.85 (*1-84032-103-2*) Hodder Headline Audiobooks GBR. *Dist:* Ulverscroft Large Print Bks., Ltd.
—A Murder of Quality. 1968. mass mkt. 0.75 o.p. (*0-451-03667-0*); 1964. mass mkt. 0.50 o.p. (*0-451-02529-6*) NAL. (Signet Bks.).
—A Murder of Quality. 1989. 2.99 o.p. (*0-517-68437-3*) Random Hse. Value Publishing.
—A Murder of Quality, unabr. ed. 1990. (George Smiley Novels Ser.). audio 35.00 (*1-55690-361-8*, 90063E7) Recorded Bks., LLC.
—A Murder of Quality. 2002. 160p. pap. 13.00 (*0-7434-3168-5*, Scribner) Simon & Schuster.
—A Perfect Spy: A Novel. 2003. 608p. reprint ed. pap. 14.00 (*0-7434-5792-7*, Scribner) Simon & Schuster.
—The Secret Pilgrim. (George Smiley Ser.). 1997. pap. 12.00 o.s.i (*0-345-41832-8*); 1993. mass mkt. 3.99 o.p. (*0-345-38551-9*); 1992. 384p. mass mkt. 6.99 (*0-345-37476-2*); 1991. mass mkt. 6.99 o.s.i (*0-345-37528-9*) Ballantine Bks.
—The Secret Pilgrim, unabr. ed. 1992. (George Smiley Ser.). audio 62.95 (*0-7861-0325-6*, 1286) Blackstone Audio Bks., Inc.
—The Secret Pilgrim. unabr. collector's ed. 1992. (George Smiley Novels Ser.). audio 72.00 (*0-7366-2119-9*, 2922) Books on Tape, Inc.
—The Secret Pilgrim. unabr. ed. 2000. (George Smiley Ser.: Bk. 8). audio 69.95 (*0-7451-6467-6*, CAB 1084) Chivers Audio Bks. GBR. *Dist:* BBC Audiobooks America.
—The Secret Pilgrim. 1990. (George Smiley Novels Ser.). 27.50 (*0-394-58842-8*) Knopf, Alfred A. Inc.
—The Secret Pilgrim, unabr. ed. 1992. (George Smiley Novels Ser.). audio 85.00 (*1-55690-748-6*, 92114E7) Recorded Bks., LLC.
—Smiley's People: A Novel. (George Smiley Novels Ser.). 1991. mass mkt. 2.99 o.s.i (*0-553-19641-3*); 1985. 400p. mass mkt. 6.99 o.s.i (*0-553-26487-7*) Bantam Bks.
—Smiley's People: A Novel, unabr. ed. 1992. (George Smiley Ser.). audio 76.95 (*0-7861-0265-9*, 1232) Blackstone Audio Bks., Inc.
—Smiley's People: A Novel. unabr. ed. 1986. (George Smiley Novels Ser.). audio 96.00 (*0-7366-0967-9*, 1909) Books on Tape, Inc.
—Smiley's People: A Novel. unabr. ed. 2000. (George Smiley Ser.). 12p. audio 79.95 (*0-7451-6679-2*, CAB 1295) Chivers Audio Bks. GBR. *Dist:* BBC Audiobooks America.
—Smiley's People: A Novel. abr. ed. (George Smiley Novels Ser.). 1983. audio 15.95 o.p. (*0-88646-081-6*, TC-LFP 7106); (J). (gr. 7-9). 29.95 o.p. incl. audio Durkin Hayes Publishing Ltd.
—Smiley's People: A Novel. l.t. ed. 1981. (George Smiley Ser.). 632p. pap. 9.95 o.p. (*0-8161-3283-6*); lib. bdg. 16.95 o.p. (*0-8161-3090-6*) Gale Group. (Macmillan Reference USA).
—Smiley's People: A Novel. (George Smiley Ser.). 29.95 o.p. incl. audio Norton Pubs., Inc., Jeffrey /Audio-Forum.
—Smiley's People: A Novel. reprint ed. 2002. 416p. pap. 14.00 (*0-7434-5580-0*, Scribner); 2000. 448p. mass mkt. 7.99 (*0-671-04276-9*, Pocket) Simon & Schuster.
—Smiley's People Vol. 3: The Hunt for Karla, unabr. ed. 1999. (George Smiley Novels Ser.). audio 85.00 (*1-55690-482-7*, 90091E7) Recorded Bks., LLC.
—The Spy Who Came in from the Cold. (George Smiley Ser.). 1997. pap. 12.00 o.s.i (*0-345-41833-6*); 1992. 256p. mass mkt. 6.99 o.s.i (*0-345-37737-0*) Ballantine Bks.
—The Spy Who Came in from the Cold. 1984. (George Smiley Novels Ser.). mass mkt. 3.95 o.s.i (*0-553-23825-6*) Bantam Bks.
—The Spy Who Came in from the Cold. unabr. ed. 2000. (George Smiley Ser.: Bk. 3). audio 49.95 (*0-7451-6852-3*, CAB 500) Chivers Audio Bks. GBR. *Dist:* BBC Audiobooks America.
—The Spy Who Came in from the Cold, Set. abr. ed. 1986. (George Smiley Novels Ser.). audio 16.99 (*0-88646-121-9*, 391630) Durkin Hayes Publishing Ltd.
—The Spy Who Came in from the Cold, 2 vols., Set. l.t. ed. (George Smiley Novels Ser.). (YA). (gr. 10-12). reprint ed. 10.00 (*0-89064-058-0*) National Assn. for Visually Handicapped.
—The Spy Who Came in from the Cold. (George Smiley Ser.). audio 34.95. 1985. (YA). pap., stu. ed. 34.95 incl. audio (*0-88432-970-4*, S23911) Norton Pubs., Inc., Jeffrey /Audio-Forum.
—The Spy Who Came in from the Cold. 1978. (George Smiley Novels Ser.). 9.95 o.s.i (*0-698-10916-3*) Putnam Publishing Group, The.
—The Spy Who Came in from the Cold, unabr. ed. 1987. (George Smiley Novels Ser.). (ACE.). audio 32.95 (*1-55690-491-6*, RD805) Recorded Bks., LLC.
—The Spy Who Came in from the Cold. l.t. ed. 1976. (George Smiley Ser.). 12.00 o.p. (*0-85456-467-5*, Ulverscroft) Thorpe, F. A. Pubs. GBR. *Dist:* Ulverscroft Large Print Bks., Ltd., Ulverscroft Large Print Canada, Ltd.
—Tinker Tailor Soldier Spy. 1984. (George Smiley Novels Ser.). 384p. mass mkt. 6.99 o.s.i (*0-553-26778-7*) Bantam Bks.
—Tinker Tailor Soldier Spy. unabr. ed. 1991. (George Smiley Ser.). audio 62.95 (*0-7861-0278-0*, 1244) Blackstone Audio Bks., Inc.
—Tinker Tailor Soldier Spy. unabr. ed. 1984. (George Smiley Novels Ser.). audio 64.00 (*0-7366-0966-0*, 1908) Books on Tape, Inc.
—Tinker Tailor Soldier Spy. unabr. ed. 2000. (George Smiley Ser.: Bk. 5). audio 79.95 (*0-7451-6744-6*, CAB 1360) Chivers Audio Bks. GBR. *Dist:* BBC Audiobooks America.
—Tinker Tailor Soldier Spy. abr. ed. 1981. (George Smiley Novels Ser.). audio 16.99 o.p. (*0-88646-064-6*, TC-LFP 7082) Durkin Hayes Publishing Ltd.
—Tinker Tailor Soldier Spy. Date not set. (George Smiley Novels Ser.). 14.95 (*0-559-35018-X*) Putnam Publishing Group, The.
—Tinker Tailor Soldier Spy. reprint ed. 2002. 400p. pap. 14.00 (*0-7434-5790-0*, Scribner); 2000. 448p. per. 7.99 o.s.i (*0-671-04273-4*, Pocket) Simon & Schuster.
—Tinker, Tailor, Soldier, Spy Vol. 2: The Hunt for Karla, unabr. ed. 1988. (George Smiley Novels Ser.). audio 70.00 (*1-55690-516-5*, 88520E7) Recorded Bks., LLC.

**SMITH, ANNABEL (FICTITIOUS CHARACTER)—FICTION**

Truman, Margaret. Murder at Ford's Theatre. E-Book (*0-345-45870-2*); 2003. 384p. mass mkt. 7.50 (*0-449-00738-3*); 2002. 336p. 24.95 (*0-345-44489-2*, Ballantine Bks.) Ballantine Bks.
—Murder at Ford's Theatre. 2003. 540p. pap. 13.95 (*1-4104-0175-8*, Wheeler Publishing, Inc.) Gale Group.
—Murder at Ford's Theatre. 2003. (Basic Ser.). 30.95 (*0-7862-5038-0*) Thorndike Pr.
—Murder at the Kennedy Center. 1999. 6.99 (*0-449-45926-8*); 1990. 352p. mass mkt. 6.99 (*0-449-21208-4*) Ballantine Bks. (Fawcett).
—Murder at the Kennedy Center. 1993. audio. audio 48.00 (*1-56544-014-5*, 250029) Literate Ear, Inc.
—Murder at the Kennedy Center. 1991. 4.99 o.p. (*0-517-07459-1*) Random Hse. Value Publishing.
—Murder at the Kennedy Center, unabr. ed. 1990. audio 70.00 (*1-55690-363-4*, 90103E7) Recorded Bks., LLC.
—Murder at the Library of Congress. l.t. ed. 1999. pap. 25.00 o.p. (*0-7838-8706-X*, Macmillan Reference USA) Gale Group.
—Murder at the Library of Congress, abr. ed. 1999. audio 18.00 Highsmith Inc.
—Murder at the Library of Congress. abr. ed. 1999. audio 18.00 o.s.i (*0-375-40564-X*, RH Audio) Random Hse. Audio Publishing Group.
—Murder at the Library of Congress. l.t. ed. 1999. 384p. 25.00 o.s.i (*0-375-40865-7*) Random Hse. Large Print.
—Murder at the National Cathedral. 1999. 6.99 (*0-449-45928-4*); 1991. 336p. mass mkt. 6.99 (*0-449-21939-9*) Ballantine Bks. (Fawcett).
—Murder at the National Cathedral. abr. ed. 1990. (Capital Crime Ser.). audio 16.00 o.s.i (*0-394-58561-5*, RH Audio) Random Hse. Audio Publishing Group.

—Murder at the National Cathedral. 1993. 4.99 o.p. (*0-517-08679-4*); 5.99 o.p. (*0-517-10676-0*) Random Hse. Value Publishing.

—Murder at the National Gallery. 1997. mass mkt. 6.99 o.s.i (*0-449-22328-0*); 368p. mass mkt. 6.99 (*0-449-21938-0*) Ballantine Bks. (Fawcett).

—Murder at the National Gallery. l.t. ed. 1996. 486p. 23.00 o.p. (*0-7838-1687-1*, Macmillan Reference USA) Gale Group.

—Murder at the National Gallery. abr. ed. 1997. (Mac & Annabel Smith Mystery Ser.). audio 8.99 o.s.i (*0-679-46023-3*, 394047, RH Audio) Random Hse. Audio Publishing Group.

—Murder at the Watergate. 1999. (Capital Crime Myteries Ser.). 368p. mass mkt. 6.99 (*0-449-00194-6*, Fawcett) Ballantine Bks.

—Murder at the Watergate. l.t. ed. 1998. o.p. (*0-7838-0157-2*, Macmillan Reference USA) Gale Group.

—Murder in the House. 1998. (Capital Crime Myteries Ser.). 352p. mass mkt. 6.99 (*0-449-00172-5*, Fawcett) Ballantine Bks.

—Murder in the House, Set. abr. ed. 1997. (Mac & Annabel Smith Mystery Ser.). audio 18.00 o.s.i (*0-679-46009-8*, 395257, RH Audio) Random Hse. Audio Publishing Group.

—Murder in the House. l.t. ed. 1997. (Large Print Ser.). pap. 24.00 (*0-679-77435-1*) Random Hse. Large Print.

—Murder on the Potomac. 1995. (Capital Crime Myteries Ser.). 352p. reprint ed. mass mkt. 6.99 (*0-449-21937-2*, Fawcett) Ballantine Bks.

—Murder on the Potomac. 1994. audio 17.00 o.p. (*0-679-41235-2*) McKay, David Co., Inc.

—Murder on the Potomac. abr. ed. 1995. (Mac & Annabel Smith Mystery Ser.). audio 8.99 o.s.i (*0-679-44347-9*, 391231, RH Audio) Random Hse. Audio Publishing Group.

—Murder on the Potomac. l.t. ed. 1994. 404p. pap. 22.00 o.s.i (*0-679-75387-7*) Random Hse. Large Print.

—Murder on the Potomac, unabr. ed. 1994. audio 53.00 (*0-7887-3759-7*, 95957E7) Recorded Bks., LLC.

### SMITH, BILL (FICTITIOUS CHARACTER)—FICTION

Rozan, S. J. A Bitter Feast. 1998. 320p. 23.95 o.p. (*0-312-19259-2*, Saint Martin's Minotaur); 1999. 336p. reprint ed. mass mkt. 5.99 (*0-312-97011-0*, St. Martin's Paperbacks) St. Martin's Pr.

—A Bitter Feast. l.t. ed. 1999. (Mystery Ser.). 519p. 27.95 (*0-7862-1773-1*) Thorndike Pr.

—A Bitter Feast: A Bill Smith-Lydia Chin Mystery. unabr. ed. 1999. audio 69.95 (*0-7927-2280-9*, CSL169, Chivers Sound Library) BBC Audiobooks America.

—China Trade. 1994. 263 p. 20.95 o.p. (*0-312-11254-8*, Saint Martin's Minotaur); 1995. (Lydia Chin, Bill Smith Mystery Ser.: Vol. 1). 275p. reprint ed. mass mkt. 6.50 (*0-312-95590-1*, St. Martin's Paperbacks) St. Martin's Pr.

—Concourse: A Bill Smith-Lydia Chin Mystery. unabr. ed. 1998. audio 69.95 (*0-7927-2245-0*, CSL134, Chivers Sound Library) BBC Audiobooks America.

—Concourse: A Bill Smith-Lydia Chin Mystery. 1995. 288p. 21.95 o.p. (*0-312-13453-3*, Saint Martin's Minotaur); 3rd ed. 1996. (Lydia Chin, Bill Smith Mystery Ser.: Vol. 2). 291p. mass mkt. 6.50 (*0-312-95944-3*, St. Martin's Paperbacks) St. Martin's Pr.

—Mandarin Plaid. (Lydia Chin, Bill Smith Mystery Ser.: Vol. 3). 288p. 1996. 22.95 o.p. (*0-312-14674-4*, Saint Martin's Minotaur); Vol. 1. 1997. mass mkt. 6.50 (*0-312-96283-5*, St. Martin's Paperbacks) St. Martin's Pr.

—No Colder Place. 1998. (No Colder Place Ser.: Vol. 1). 304p. pap. 6.99 (*0-312-96664-4*, St. Martin's Paperbacks); 1997. (Lydia Chin, Bill Smith Mystery Ser.). 288p. 23.95 (*0-312-16811-X*, Saint Martin's Minotaur) St. Martin's Pr.

—No Colder Place. l.t. ed. 1997. (Cloak & Dagger Ser.). 473p. lib. bdg. 28.95 (*0-7862-1251-9*) Thorndike Pr.

—Reflecting the Sky. 2001. 312p. 24.95 (*0-312-24427-4*, Saint Martin's Minotaur); 2002. 384p. reprint ed. mass mkt. 6.50 (*0-312-98134-1*, St. Martin's Paperbacks) St. Martin's Pr.

—Stone Quarry. l.t. ed. 2003. 29.95 (*1-57490-532-5*) Beeler, Thomas T. Publisher.

—Stone Quarry. 2001. 336p. mass mkt. 6.50 (*0-312-97703-4*, St. Martin's Paperbacks); 1999. 288p. 23.95 o.p. (*0-312-20912-6*, Saint Martin's Minotaur) St. Martin's Pr.

—Winter & Night. E-Book 18.95 (*0-312-70434-8*); 2003. 400p. mass mkt. 6.99 (*0-312-98668-8*, St. Martin's Paperbacks); 2002. 304p. 24.95 (*0-312-24555-6*, Saint Martin's Minotaur) St. Martin's Pr.

### SMITH, BRAD (FICTITIOUS CHARACTER)—FICTION

Bickham, Jack M. Breakfast at Wimbledon. 1992. (Brad Smith Ser.: No. 4). 375p. mass mkt. 3.99 o.p. (*0-8125-1195-6*); 1991. 19.95 o.p. (*0-312-85144-8*) Doherty, Tom Assocs., LLC. (Tor Bks.).

—Breakfast at Wimbledon. 1991. 19.95 (*0-312-51195-7*) St. Martin's Pr.

—Overhead. 1993. (Brad Smith Ser.: No. 3). 352p. mass mkt. 4.50 o.p. (*0-8125-1194-8*); 1991. 18.95 o.p. (*0-312-85143-X*) Doherty, Tom Assocs., LLC. (Tor Bks.).

### SMITH, GRACE (FICTITIOUS CHARACTER)—FICTION

Evans, Liz. Barking! A Grace Smith Investigation. 311p. 28.00 (*0-7528-2540-2*); 2003. 320p. mass mkt. 7.95 (*0-7528-4793-7*); 2002. 312p. pap. 13.95 (*0-7528-2541-0*) Orion Publishing Group, Ltd. GBR. *Dist:* Trafalgar Square.

—Don't Mess with Mrs. In-Between. 2002. 406p. mass mkt. 7.95 (*0-7528-4297-8*) Trafalgar Square.

—JFK Is Missing. 2002. 345p. mass mkt. 7.95 (*0-7528-3696-X*) Orion Media.

—Who Killed Marilyn Monroe? 2002. 344p. mass mkt. 7.95 (*0-7528-3695-1*) Orion Media.

### SMITH, JILL (FICTITIOUS CHARACTER)—FICTION

Dunlap, Susan. As a Favor. 1991. 208p. mass mkt. 5.99 o.s.i (*0-440-20999-4*) Dell Publishing.

—As a Favor. 1984. 192p. 12.95 o.p. (*0-312-05594-3*) St. Martin's Pr.

—Cop Out. unabr. ed. 1997. audio 44.95 (*0-7861-1192-5*, 1949) Blackstone Audio Bks., Inc.

—Cop Out. 1998. (Jill Smith Mystery Ser.). 352p. mass mkt. 5.99 o.s.i (*0-440-22479-9*) Dell Publishing.

—Cop Out: A Jill Smith Mystery. 1997. 304p. 20.95 o.s.i (*0-385-31600-3*, Delacorte Pr.) Dell Publishing.

—Death & Taxes. l.t. ed. 1992. 24.95 o.p. (*0-7927-1329-X*); pap. 20.95 o.p. (*0-7927-1328-1*) BBC Audiobooks America.

—Death & Taxes. 1993. 288p. mass mkt. 5.50 o.s.i (*0-440-21406-8*) Dell Publishing.

—Diamond in the Buff. 1991. 192p. mass mkt. 5.50 o.s.i (*0-440-20788-6*) Dell Publishing.

—Diamond in the Buff. 1990. 176p. 14.95 o.p. (*0-312-03814-3*, Saint Martin's Minotaur) St. Martin's Pr.

—A Dinner to Die For. 1989. 240p. mass mkt. 5.99 o.s.i (*0-440-20495-X*) Dell Publishing.

—A Dinner to Die For. 1987. 224p. 15.95 o.p. (*0-312-01019-2*, Saint Martin's Minotaur) St. Martin's Pr.

—Karma. 1991. 240p. pap. 15.00 o.s.i (*0-440-61365-5*); mass mkt. 5.99 o.s.i (*0-440-20982-X*) Dell Publishing.

—Karma. 1991. reprint ed. 18.95 o.p. (*0-7278-4229-3*) Severn Hse. Pubs., Ltd.

—Not Exactly a Brahmin. 1991. 240p. mass mkt. 4.99 o.s.i (*0-440-20998-6*) Dell Publishing.

—Not Exactly a Brahmin. 1985. (Jill Smith Mystery Ser.). 192p. 12.95 o.p. (*0-312-57947-0*) St. Martin's Pr.

—Sudden Exposure. unabr. ed. 1998. audio 44.95 Blackstone Audio Bks., Inc.

—Sudden Exposure. 1997. 320p. pap. 19.00 o.s.i (*0-440-61350-7*); mass mkt. 5.50 o.s.i (*0-440-21563-3*) Dell Publishing.

—Sudden Exposure. abr. ed. 1996. (Jill Smith Mystery Ser.). audio 16.99 (*0-88646-408-0*, 7408) Durkin Hayes Publishing Ltd.

—Time Expired. l.t. ed. 1994. 24.95 o.p. (*0-7927-1779-1*); pap. 22.95 o.p. (*0-7927-1778-3*) BBC Audiobooks America.

—Time Expired. 1994. (Jill Smith Mystery Ser.). 304p. mass mkt. 5.99 o.s.i (*0-440-21683-4*) Dell Publishing.

—Too Close to the Edge. 1989. 224p. reprint ed. mass mkt. 5.50 o.s.i (*0-440-20356-2*) Dell Publishing.

—Too Close to the Edge. 1987. 240p. 14.95 o.p. (*0-312-00198-3*) St. Martin's Pr.

### SMITH, JOHN (FICTITIOUS CHARACTER)—FICTION

Alexie, Sherman. Indian Killer. 1996. 432p. 22.00 o.p. (*0-87113-652-X*, Atlantic Monthly Pr.) Grove/Atlantic, Inc.

—Indian Killer. 1998. 432p. reprint ed. pap. 14.95 (*0-446-67370-6*) Warner Bks., Inc.

Vachss, Andrew. Shella. 2001. E-Book 11.00 (*1-59061-227-2*) Adobe Systems, Inc.

—Shella. 1994. 240p. pap. 12.00 (*0-679-75681-7*, Vintage) Knopf Publishing Group.

### SMITH, JOHNNY (FICTITIOUS CHARACTER)—FICTION

King, Stephen. The Dead Zone. 1994. (Collectors' Editions Ser.). 416p. pap. 14.95 o.p. (*0-452-27329-3*, Plume) Dutton/Plume.

—The Dead Zone. l.t. ed. 1993. (General Ser.). 672p. lib. bdg. 23.95 o.p. (*0-8161-5668-9*, Macmillan Reference USA) Gale Group.

—The Dead Zone. 1983. mass mkt. 3.95 o.p. (*0-451-12666-1*); 1983. mass mkt. 4.50 o.p. (*0-451-13972-0*); 1983. mass mkt. 3.95 o.p. (*0-451-12792-7*); 1983. mass mkt. 4.50 o.p. (*0-451-15068-6*); 1980. mass mkt. 3.50 o.p. (*0-451-09338-0*); 1980. mass mkt. 3.95 o.p. (*0-451-11961-4*); 1980. 416p. reprint ed. mass mkt. 7.99 (*0-451-15575-0*) NAL. (Signet Bks.).

—The Dead Zone. l.t. ed. 1983. 656p. 13.95 o.p. (*0-7089-8157-7*, Charnwood) Thorpe, F. A. Pubs. GBR. *Dist:* Ulverscroft Large Print Bks., Ltd.

—The Dead Zone. 1979. 14.04 (*0-606-01917-0*) Turtleback Bks.

—The Dead Zone. 1979. 444p. text 35.00 (*0-670-26077-0*) Viking Penguin.

—La Zona Muerta. 13th ed. 1999. Tr. of Dead Zone. (SPA., Illus.). 456p. 14.95 (*84-01-49988-7*) Plaza & Janés Editories, S.A. ESP. *Dist:* Distribooks, Inc.

### SMITH, MAC (FICTITIOUS CHARACTER)—FICTION

Truman, Margaret. Murder at Ford's Theatre. E-Book (*0-345-45870-2*); 2003. 384p. mass mkt. 7.50 (*0-449-00738-3*); 2002. 336p. 24.95 (*0-345-44489-2*, Ballantine Bks.) Ballantine Bks.

—Murder at Ford's Theatre. 2003. 540p. pap. 13.95 (*1-4104-0175-8*, Wheeler Publishing, Inc.) Gale Group.

—Murder at Ford's Theatre. 2003. (Basic Ser.). 30.95 (*0-7862-5038-0*) Thorndike Pr.

—Murder at the Kennedy Center. 1999. 6.99 (*0-449-45926-8*); 1990. 352p. mass mkt. 6.99 (*0-449-21208-4*) Ballantine Bks. (Fawcett).

—Murder at the Kennedy Center. 1993. audio. audio 48.00 (*1-56544-014-5*, 250029) Literate Ear, Inc.

—Murder at the Kennedy Center. 1991. 4.99 o.p. (*0-517-07459-1*) Random Hse. Value Publishing.

—Murder at the Kennedy Center, unabr. ed. 1990. audio 70.00 (*1-55690-363-4*, 90103E7) Recorded Bks., LLC.

—Murder at the National Cathedral. 1999. 6.99 (*0-449-45928-4*); 1991. 336p. mass mkt. 6.99 (*0-449-21939-9*) Ballantine Bks. (Fawcett).

—Murder at the National Cathedral. abr. ed. 1990. (Capital Crime Ser.). audio 16.00 o.s.i (*0-394-58561-5*, RH Audio) Random Hse. Audio Publishing Group.

—Murder at the National Cathedral. 1993. 4.99 o.p. (*0-517-08679-4*); 5.99 o.p. (*0-517-10676-0*) Random Hse. Value Publishing.

—Murder at the National Gallery. 1997. mass mkt. 6.99 o.s.i (*0-449-22328-0*); 368p. mass mkt. 6.99 (*0-449-21938-0*) Ballantine Bks. (Fawcett).

—Murder at the National Gallery. l.t. ed. 1996. 486p. 23.00 o.p. (*0-7838-1687-1*, Macmillan Reference USA) Gale Group.

—Murder at the National Gallery. abr. ed. 1997. (Mac & Annabel Smith Mystery Ser.). audio 8.99 o.s.i (*0-679-46023-3*, 394047, RH Audio) Random Hse. Audio Publishing Group.

—Murder at the Pentagon. 1999. 6.99 (*0-449-45927-6*); 1994. mass mkt. 5.99 o.p. (*0-449-45334-0*); 1993. 336p. mass mkt. 6.99 (*0-449-21940-2*) Ballantine Bks. (Fawcett).

—Murder at the Pentagon. 1993. audio o.p. (*0-679-42642-6*); 1992. audio 16.00 o.p. (*0-394-58672-7*); Set. 1993. audio 8.99 o.s.i (*0-679-42348-6*) Random Hse. Audio Publishing Group. (RH Audio).

—Murder at the Pentagon. l.t. ed. 1992. 23.00 o.s.i (*0-679-41357-X*) Random Hse. Large Print.

—Murder at the Pentagon. 1994. 5.99 o.p. (*0-517-11744-4*) Random Hse. Value Publishing.

—Murder at the Watergate. 1999. (Capital Crime Myteries Ser.). 368p. mass mkt. 6.99 (*0-449-00194-6*, Fawcett) Ballantine Bks.

—Murder at the Watergate. l.t. ed. 1998. o.p. (*0-7838-0157-2*, Macmillan Reference USA) Gale Group.

—Murder in the House. 1998. (Capital Crime Myteries Ser.). 352p. mass mkt. 6.99 (*0-449-00172-5*, Fawcett) Ballantine Bks.

—Murder in the House, Set. abr. ed. 1997. (Mac & Annabel Smith Mystery Ser.). audio 18.00 o.s.i (*0-679-46009-8*, 395257, RH Audio) Random Hse. Audio Publishing Group.

—Murder in the House. l.t. ed. 1997. (Large Print Ser.). pap. 24.00 (*0-679-77435-1*) Random Hse. Large Print.

—Murder on the Potomac. 1995. (Capital Crime Myteries Ser.). 352p. reprint ed. mass mkt. 6.99 (*0-449-21937-2*, Fawcett) Ballantine Bks.

—Murder on the Potomac. 1994. audio 17.00 o.p. (*0-679-41235-2*) McKay, David Co., Inc.

—Murder on the Potomac. abr. ed. 1995. (Mac & Annabel Smith Mystery Ser.). audio 8.99 o.s.i (*0-679-44347-9*, 391231, RH Audio) Random Hse. Audio Publishing Group.

—Murder on the Potomac. l.t. ed. 1994. 404p. pap. 22.00 o.s.i (*0-679-75387-7*) Random Hse. Large Print.

—Murder on the Potomac, unabr. ed. 1994. audio 53.00 (*0-7887-3759-7*, 95957E7) Recorded Bks., LLC.

### SMITH, TRUMAN (FICTITIOUS CHARACTER)—FICTION

Crider, Bill. Dead on the Island. unabr. ed. 1995. audio 17.00 (*1-883268-19-2*) Spellbinders, Inc.

—Dead on the Island. 1991. 193p. 18.95 (*0-8027-5787-1*) Walker & Co.

—Gator Kill. Haywood, Richard, ed. unabr. ed. 1995. (Truman Smith Trilogy Ser.). audio 17.00 (*1-883268-27-3*) Spellbinders, Inc.

—Gator Kill: A Truman Smith. 1992. 202p. 18.95 (*0-8027-3213-5*) Walker & Co.

—Murder Takes a Break: A Truman Smith Mystery. 1997. (Truman Smith Mystery Ser.). 246p. 21.95 (*0-8027-3308-5*) Walker & Co.

—The Prairie Chicken Kill: A Truman Smith Mystery. 1996. (Truman Smith Mystery Ser.). 216p. 20.95 (*0-8027-3282-8*) Walker & Co.

—When Old Men Die. abr. ed. 1997. audio 17.00 (*1-883268-33-8*) Spellbinders, Inc.

—When Old Men Die. 1994. 192p. 19.95 (*0-8027-3195-3*) Walker & Co.

### SMITH, XENIA (FICTITIOUS CHARACTER)—FICTION

Meyers, Annette. The Big Killing. 1990. (Smith & Wetzon Ser.). 384p. mass mkt. 4.50 o.s.i (*0-553-28418-5*) Bantam Bks.

—The Big Killing. 1998. 270p. pap. 15.95 (*0-7351-0405-0*); reprint ed. lib. bdg. 29.95 (*0-7351-0035-7*) Replica Bks.

—Blood on the Street. 1993. (Smith & Wetzon Ser.). 400p. mass mkt. 4.99 o.s.i (*0-553-29731-7*) Bantam Bks.

—The Deadliest Option. 1992. (Smith & Wetzon Ser.). 416p. mass mkt. 4.99 o.s.i (*0-553-29530-6*) Bantam Bks.

—The Deadliest Option. 1998. 354p. pap. 15.95 (*0-7351-0404-2*); reprint ed. lib. bdg. 29.95 (*0-7351-0036-5*) Replica Bks.

—The Groaning Board: A Smith & Wetzon Mystery. 1998. 368p. mass mkt. 5.99 o.s.i (*0-553-56977-5*) Bantam Bks.

—The Groaning Board: A Smith & Wetzon Mystery. 1997. 336p. 21.95 o.s.i (*0-385-47654-X*) Doubleday Publishing.

—Murder: The Musical. 1994. (Smith & Wetzon Ser.). 496p. mass mkt. 5.50 o.s.i (*0-553-56785-3*) Bantam Bks.

—Murder: The Musical. 1998. 370p. pap. 15.95 (*0-7351-0403-4*); reprint ed. lib. bdg. 29.95 (*0-7351-0034-9*) Replica Bks.

—Tender Death. 1991. (Smith & Wetzon Ser.). 336p. mass mkt. 4.50 o.s.i (*0-553-28719-2*) Bantam Bks.

—Tender Death. 1998. 288p. pap. 15.95 (*0-7351-0406-9*); reprint ed. lib. bdg. 29.95 (*0-7351-0037-3*) Replica Bks.

—These Bones Were Made for Dancin' A Smith & Wetzon Mystery. 1996. 336p. reprint ed. mass mkt. 5.50 o.s.i (*0-553-56976-7*, Crimeline) Bantam Bks.

### SMITH, ZACHARIAH (FICTITIOUS CHARACTER)—FICTION

Thrasher, L. L. Cat's Paw, Incorporated. 1995. (Brown Bag Mystery Line Ser.). 616p. 3.00 o.p. (*0-933031-41-6*) Council Oak Bks.

—Dogsbody, Inc. 1999. 288p. 22.95 o.p. (*1-885173-65-2*) Write Way Publishing.

### SMOKE, BEN (FICTITIOUS CHARACTER)—FICTION

McBain, Ed, pseud. Where There's Smoke. 1977. mass mkt. 1.50 o.p. (*0-345-25463-5*) Ballantine Bks.

—Where There's Smoke. 1987. 192p. pap. 3.50 (*0-380-70372-6*, Avon Bks.) Morrow/Avon.

—Where There's Smoke. 1975. 6.95 o.p. (*0-394-49670-1*) Random Hse., Inc.

—Where There's Smoke. 1997. 224p. mass mkt. 5.99 (*0-446-60483-6*) Warner Bks., Inc.

### SNOPES FAMILY (FICTITIOUS CHARACTERS)—FICTION

Faulkner, William. Novels, 1957-1962: The Town; The Mansion; The Reivers. Polk, Noel, ed. 1999. (Library of America: Vol. 112). 1020p. 35.00 (*1-883011-69-8*) Library of America, The.

—Snopes: The Hamlet; The Town; The Mansion. 1994. (Modern Library Ser.). 1088p. 25.95 (*0-679-60092-2*) Random Hse., Inc.

### SNOW, CHRISTINE (FICTITIOUS CHARACTER)—FICTION

Anshaw, Carol. Seven Moves. 1996. 220p. tchr. ed. 21.95 o.p. (*0-395-69131-1*) Houghton Mifflin Co.

—Seven Moves. 1997. 240p. pap. 11.00 (*0-395-87756-3*, Mariner Bks.) Houghton Mifflin Co. Trade & Reference Div.

—Seven Moves. 1998. 242p. pap. o.s.i (*1-86049-436-6*) Virago Pr., Ltd. GBR. *Dist:* Little Brown & Co.

**SNOW, CHRISTOPHER (FICTITIOUS CHARACTER)—FICTION**

Koontz, Dean. Fear Nothing. 1998. 448p. mass mkt. 7.99 (*0-553-57975-4*); mass mkt. 7.99 (*0-553-84021-5*); 400p. 26.95 o.s.i (*0-553-10664-3*) Bantam Bks.

—Fear Nothing. l.t. ed. 1998. (Core Ser.). 577p. 29.95 o.p. (*0-7838-8358-7*, Macmillan Reference USA) Gale Group.

—Fear Nothing. unabr. ed. 1998. (Christopher Snow Stories Ser.). 12p. audio 39.95 (*0-553-47900-8*, 105583, RH Audio) Random Hse. Audio Publishing Group.

—Fear Nothing. 1998. 14.04 (*0-606-16374-3*) Turtleback Bks.

—Seize the Night. 1999. 480p. mass mkt. 7.99 o.s.i (*0-553-58229-1*); 480p. mass mkt. 7.99 (*0-553-58019-1*); mass mkt. 7.99 (*0-553-84020-7*) Bantam Bks.

—Seize the Night, unabr. ed. 1999. audio 39.95 Highsmith Inc.

—Seize the Night. unabr. ed. 1998. (Christopher Snow Stories Ser.). audio 39.95 (*0-553-47901-6*, 116030, RH Audio) Random Hse. Audio Publishing Group.

—Seize the Night. l.t. ed. (Paperback Bestsellers Ser.). 2000. 617p. pap. 27.95 (*0-7838-8529-6*); 1999. 605p. 30.95 (*0-7838-8528-8*) Thorndike Pr.

—Seize the Night. l.t. ed. 2000. (Charnwood Large Print Ser.). 616p. (*0-7089-9144-0*, Ulverscroft) Thorpe, F. A. Pubs. GBR. *Dist:* Ulverscroft Large Print Bks., Ltd., Ulverscroft Large Print Canada, Ltd.

—Seize the Night. 1999. 14.04 (*0-606-18001-X*) Turtleback Bks.

**SNOWDEN, REESY (FICTITIOUS CHARACTER)—FICTION**

Files, Lolita. Getting to the Good Part. 2000. 352p. pap. 13.95 (*0-446-67548-2*); 1999. 334p. 24.00 (*0-446-52420-4*) Warner Bks., Inc.

—Scenes from a Sistah. 1998. 288p. pap. 13.99 (*0-446-67442-7*); 1998. 320p. mass mkt. 6.50 (*0-446-60539-5*); 1997. 288p. 22.00 o.p. (*0-446-52100-0*) Warner Bks., Inc.

**SNOWMANE, LARISSA (FICTITIOUS CHARACTER)—FICTION**

Golden, Christie. Ravenloft: Dance of the Dead. 1992. 320p. (Orig.). pap. 4.95 o.p. (*1-56076-352-3*) Wizards of the Coast.

**SOCARIDES, ARISTOTLE PLATO (FICTITIOUS CHARACTER)—FICTION**

Kemprecos, Paul. Bluefin Blues: An Aristotle "Soc" Socarides Mystery. 1997. 224p. 20.95 o.p. (*0-312-16787-3*, Saint Martin's Minotaur) St. Martin's Pr.

—Cool Blue Tomb. 1991. 288p. mass mkt. 4.50 o.s.i (*0-553-28881-4*) Bantam Bks.

—Death in Deep Water. 1993. 336p. mass mkt. 4.99 o.s.i (*0-553-29735-X*) Bantam Bks.

—Death in Deep Water: An Aristotle "Soc" Socraides Mystery. 1992. 368p. 16.50 o.s.i (*0-385-42379-9*) Doubleday Publishing.

—A Feeding Frenzy. 1994. 336p. mass mkt. 4.99 o.s.i (*0-553-56774-8*) Bantam Bks.

—Mayflower Murder. 1996. 22.95 (*0-312-14852-6*, Saint Martin's Minotaur) St. Martin's Pr.

—Neptune's Eye. 1991. 320p. mass mkt. 4.50 o.s.i (*0-553-29353-2*) Bantam Bks.

**SOLANO, LUPE (FICTITIOUS CHARACTER)—FICTION**

Garcia-Aguilera, Carolina. Bitter Sugar. 2001. (Lupe Solano Mystery Ser.). 336p. 24.00 (*0-380-97781-8*, Morrow, William & Co.) Morrow/Avon.

—Bitter Sugar: A Lupe Solano Mystery. 2002. 336p. mass mkt. 6.50 (*0-380-80741-6*) Morrow/Avon.

—Bloody Secrets. 1999. 336p. reprint ed. mass mkt. 6.50 o.s.i (*0-425-16779-8*, Prime Crime) Berkley Publishing Group.

—Bloody Secrets. 1998. 274p. 23.95 o.p. (*0-399-14386-6*, G. P. Putnam's Sons) Penguin Group (USA) Inc.

—Bloody Shame: A Lupe Solano Mystery. 1998. 320p. mass mkt. 6.50 o.s.i (*0-425-16140-4*, Prime Crime) Berkley Publishing Group.

—Bloody Shame: A Lupe Solano Mystery. 1997. 288p. 22.95 o.p. (*0-399-14256-8*, G. P. Putnam's Sons) Penguin Group (USA) Inc.

—Bloody Waters: A Lupe Solano Mystery. 1997. (Lupo Solano Mystery Ser.). 304p. mass mkt. 5.99 o.s.i (*0-425-15670-2*, Prime Crime) Berkley Publishing Group.

—Bloody Waters: A Lupe Solano Mystery. 1996. 256p. 21.95 o.p. (*0-399-14157-X*, G. P. Putnam's Sons) Penguin Group (USA) Inc.

—Havana Heat: A Lupe Solano Mystery. 2001. 352p. mass mkt. 6.99 (*0-380-80740-8*, Avon Bks.) Morrow/Avon.

—A Miracle in Paradise. (Lupe Solano Mystery Ser.). 2000. 352p. mass mkt. 5.99 o.s.i (*0-380-80738-6*); 1999. viii, 277p. 23.00 (*0-380-97779-6*) Morrow/Avon. (Avon Bks.).

**SOLETA (FICTITIOUS CHARACTER)—FICTION**

David, Peter. Excalibur: Requiem. 2000. (Star Trek Ser.: No. 9). 288p. pap. 6.99 (*0-671-04238-6*, Star Trek) Simon & Schuster.

—Fire on High. 1998. (Star Trek Ser.: No. 6). 288p. pap. 6.50 (*0-671-02037-4*, Star Trek) Simon & Schuster.

—House of Cards. 1997. (Star Trek Ser.: No. 1). 168p. per. 3.99 o.s.i (*0-671-01395-5*, Star Trek) Simon & Schuster.

—House of Cards; Into the Void; The Two-Front War; End Game. 1998. (Star Trek Ser.: Nos. 1-4). 704p. 15.00 (*0-671-01978-3*, Star Trek) Simon & Schuster.

—The Quiet Place. (Star Trek Ser.: No. 7). 288p. 2002. E-Book 6.99 (*0-7434-5574-6*); 1999. pap. 6.50 (*0-671-02079-X*) Simon & Schuster. (Star Trek).

**SOLO, ANAKIN (FICTITIOUS CHARACTER)—FICTION**

Allen, Roger Macbride. Ambush at Corellia. 1995. (Star Wars: Bk. 1). 320p. mass mkt. 6.99 (*0-553-29803-8*, Spectra) Bantam Bks.

—Ambush at Corellia. abr. ed. 1995. (Star Wars: Bk. 1). audio 16.99 (*0-553-47202-X*, 392779, RH Audio) Random Hse. Audio Publishing Group.

—Ambush at Corellia. 1995. (Star Wars: Bk. 1). 12.04 (*0-606-08197-6*) Turtleback Bks.

—Assault at Selonia. 1995. (Star Wars: Bk. 2). 320p. mass mkt. 6.99 (*0-553-29805-4*, Spectra) Bantam Bks.

—Assault at Selonia. abr. ed. 1995. (Star Wars: Bk. 2). (J). (gr. k). audio 16.99 (*0-553-47203-8*, RH Audio) Random Hse. Audio Publishing Group.

—Assault at Selonia. 1995. (Star Wars: Bk. 2). 12.04 (*0-606-08198-4*) Turtleback Bks.

—The Corellian Trilogy Boxed Set: Ambush at Corellia; Assault at Selonia; Showdown at Centerpoint. 1997. (Star Wars). (YA). (gr. 5 up). mass mkt. 17.97 o.s.i (*0-553-94083-X*, Spectra) Bantam Bks.

—The Corellian Trilogy Boxed Set: Ambush at Corellia; Assault at Selonia; Showdown at Centerpoint. 1999. (Star Wars). (YA). (gr. 5 up). incl. audio Random Hse. Audio Publishing Group.

—Showdown at Centerpoint. 1995. (Star Wars: Bk. 3). 336p. mass mkt. 6.99 (*0-553-29806-2*, Spectra) Bantam Bks.

—Showdown at Centerpoint. abr. ed. 1995. (Star Wars: Bk. 3 ). audio 16.99 (*0-553-47204-6*, RH Audio) Random Hse. Audio Publishing Group.

—Showdown at Centerpoint. 1995. (Star Wars: Bk. 3). 11.09 o.p. (*0-606-09891-7*) Turtleback Bks.

Schultz, Mark, et al. Star Wars: Episode I: The Phantom Menace Adventures. 2000. (Star Wars Ser.). (Illus.). 112p. (YA). (gr. 5 up). pap. 12.95 (*1-56971-443-6*) Dark Horse Comics.

Stackpole, Michael A. Dark Tide: Onslaught. abr. ed. 2000. (Star Wars: Bk. 2). audio 18.00 (*0-375-40956-4*, RH Audio) Random Hse. Audio Publishing Group.

—Dark Tide I: Onslaught. 2000. (Star Wars Ser.: Bk. 2). 125.82 o.s.i (*0-345-43891-4*); 304p. mass mkt. 6.99 (*0-345-42854-4*, Del Rey) Ballantine Bks.

—Dark Tide II: Ruin. abr. ed. 2000. (Star Wars: Bk. 3). audio 18.00 (*0-375-40969-6*, RH Audio) Random Hse. Audio Publishing Group.

—Ruin: Dark Tide II. 2000. (Star Wars Ser.: No.3). 304p. mass mkt. 6.99 (*0-345-42856-0*) Ballantine Bks.

**SOLO, HAN (FICTITIOUS CHARACTER)—FICTION**

Alcala, Alfredo & Goodwin, Archie. Han Solo at Stars' End. 1997. (Classic Star Wars Ser.). 80p. (J). (gr. 3 up). pap. 6.95 (*1-56971-254-9*) Dark Horse Comics.

Allen, Roger Macbride. Ambush at Corellia. 1995. (Star Wars: Bk. 1). 320p. mass mkt. 6.99 (*0-553-29803-8*, Spectra) Bantam Bks.

—Ambush at Corellia. abr. ed. 1995. (Star Wars: Bk. 1). audio 16.99 (*0-553-47202-X*, 392779, RH Audio) Random Hse. Audio Publishing Group.

—Ambush at Corellia. 1995. (Star Wars: Bk. 1). 12.04 (*0-606-08197-6*) Turtleback Bks.

—Assault at Selonia. 1995. (Star Wars: Bk. 2). 320p. mass mkt. 6.99 (*0-553-29805-4*, Spectra) Bantam Bks.

—Assault at Selonia. abr. ed. 1995. (Star Wars: Bk. 2). (J). (gr. k). audio 16.99 (*0-553-47203-8*, RH Audio) Random Hse. Audio Publishing Group.

—Assault at Selonia. 1995. (Star Wars: Bk. 2). 12.04 (*0-606-08198-4*) Turtleback Bks.

—The Corellian Trilogy Boxed Set: Ambush at Corellia; Assault at Selonia; Showdown at Centerpoint. 1997. (Star Wars). (YA). (gr. 5 up). mass mkt. 17.97 o.s.i (*0-553-94083-X*, Spectra) Bantam Bks.

—The Corellian Trilogy Boxed Set: Ambush at Corellia; Assault at Selonia; Showdown at Centerpoint. 1999. (Star Wars). (YA). (gr. 5 up). incl. audio Random Hse. Audio Publishing Group.

—Showdown at Centerpoint. 1995. (Star Wars: Bk. 3). 336p. mass mkt. 6.99 (*0-553-29806-2*, Spectra) Bantam Bks.

—Showdown at Centerpoint. abr. ed. 1995. (Star Wars: Bk. 3 ). audio 16.99 (*0-553-47204-6*, RH Audio) Random Hse. Audio Publishing Group.

—Showdown at Centerpoint. 1995. (Star Wars: Bk. 3). 11.09 o.p. (*0-606-09891-7*) Turtleback Bks.

Allston, Aaron. Solo Command. 1999. (Star Wars: Bk. 7). 352p. mass mkt. 6.99 (*0-553-57900-2*) Bantam Bks.

—Solo Command, X-Wing 7. abr. ed. 1999. (Star Wars Ser.: Bk. 7). audio 18.00 (*0-553-52539-5*, RH Audio) Random Hse. Audio Publishing Group.

—Star Wars. 1999. (Star Wars Ser.). mass mkt. 5.99 (*0-553-58125-2*) Bantam Bks.

Anderson, Kevin J. Champions of the Force. 1994. (Star Wars: Vol. 3). 368p. mass mkt. 6.99 (*0-553-29802-X*) Bantam Bks.

—Champions of the Force. abr. ed. 1994. (star wars: Vol. 3). audio 16.99 (*0-553-47201-1*, RH Audio) Random Hse. Audio Publishing Group.

—Champions of the Force. 1994. (Star Wars: Vol. 3). 12.04 (*0-606-08204-2*) Turtleback Bks.

—Dark Apprentice. 1994. (Star Wars: Vol. 2). 368p. mass mkt. 6.99 (*0-553-29799-6*) Bantam Bks.

—Dark Apprentice. abr. ed. 1994. (star wars: Vol. 2). audio 16.99 (*0-553-47200-3*); audio 16.98 o.s.i (*0-553-74564-6*) Random Hse. Audio Publishing Group. (RH Audio).

—Dark Apprentice. 1994. (Star Wars: Vol. 2). 12.04 (*0-606-08203-4*) Turtleback Bks.

—Darksaber. 1996. (Star Wars Ser.). 464p. mass mkt. 6.99 (*0-553-57611-9*, Spectra); (YA). mass mkt. 10.95 o.s.i (*0-553-84011-8*) Bantam Bks.

—Darksaber. 1995. audio 16.98 o.s.i (*0-553-74672-3*); audio 16.99 (*0-553-47423-5*, 393257) Random Hse. Audio Publishing Group. (RH Audio).

—The Jedi Academy Trilogy Omnibus. abr. ed. 1997. (Star Wars Ser.). (gr. 5 up). 29.95 incl. audio (*0-553-47848-6*, RH Audio) Random Hse. Audio Publishing Group.

—Jedi Search. 1994. (Star Wars: Vol. 1). 384p. mass mkt. 6.99 (*0-553-29798-8*) Bantam Bks.

—Jedi Search. abr. ed. 1994. (star wars: Vol. 1). audio 16.98 o.s.i (*0-553-74512-3*); audio 16.99 (*0-553-47199-6*) Random Hse. Audio Publishing Group. (RH Audio).

—Jedi Search. 1994. (Star Wars: Vol. 1). 12.04 (*0-606-08202-6*) Turtleback Bks.

—Jedi Trilogy: Jedi Search; Dark Apprentice; Champions of the Force, 3 vols. 1997. (Star Wars). (YA). (gr. 5). 20.97 (*0-553-64839-X*) Bantam Bks.

Baron, Mike, et al. Dark Force Rising. 1998. (Star Wars Ser.). (Illus.). 160p. (YA). (gr. 7 up). pap. 17.95 (*1-56971-269-7*) Dark Horse Comics.

Chiang, Doug. The Phantom Menace Portfolio, 20 vols. 1999. (Star Wars). 55.00 o.p. (*0-8118-2580-9*) Chronicle Bks. LLC.

Crispin, A. C. The Hans Solo Omnibus. abr. ed. 2000. (Star Wars Ser.). (gr. 5 up). 29.95 incl. audio (*0-553-52700-2*, RH Audio) Random Hse. Audio Publishing Group.

—The Hutt Gambit. 1997. (Star Wars: Vol. 2). 368p. (gr. 5). mass mkt. 6.99 (*0-553-57416-7*, Spectra) Bantam Bks.

—The Hutt Gambit, Vol. 2. abr. ed. 1997. (Star Wars: Vol. 2 ). audio 16.99 (*0-553-47745-5*, 395234, RH Audio) Random Hse. Audio Publishing Group.

—The Paradise Snare. 1997. (Star Wars: Vol. 1). 336p. mass mkt. 6.99 (*0-553-57415-9*, Spectra) Bantam Bks.

—The Paradise Snare. abr. ed. 1997. (Star Wars: Vol. 1 ). audio 16.99 (*0-553-47744-7*, RH Audio) Random Hse. Audio Publishing Group.

—The Paradise Snare. 1997. (Star Wars: Vol. 1). 12.04 (*0-606-11896-9*) Turtleback Bks.

—Rebel Dawn. 1998. (Star Wars: Vol. 3). 400p. mass mkt. 6.99 (*0-553-57417-5*) Bantam Bks.

—Rebel Dawn. abr. ed. 1998. (Star Wars: Vol. 3). (gr. 5). audio 16.99 (*0-553-47746-3*, 395670, RH Audio) Random Hse. Audio Publishing Group.

Daley, Brian. The Empire Strikes Back: The National Public Radio Dramatization. 1995. (Star Wars Ser.). (Illus.). 320p. pap. 19.00 o.s.i (*0-345-39605-7*, Del Rey) Ballantine Bks.

—Han Solo Adventures. 1994. 566p. pap. 10.00; 1992. 576p. mass mkt. 6.99 (*0-345-37980-2*) Ballantine Bks.

—Han Solo & the Lost Legacy. (Star Wars Ser.: Bk. 3). (YA). (gr. 5 up). 1998. mass mkt. 5.99 (*0-345-91210-1*); 1986. 192p. mass mkt. 5.99 (*0-345-34514-2*) Ballantine Bks. (Del Rey).

—Han Solo at Stars' End. (Star Wars Ser.: Bk. 1). (YA). (gr. 5 up). 1997. mass mkt. 5.99 (*0-345-91208-X*); 1980. mass mkt. 5.99 o.s.i (*0-345-29664-8*) Ballantine Bks. (Del Rey).

—Han Solo's Revenge. (Star Wars Ser.: Bk. 2). (YA). (gr. 5 up). 1997. pap. 5.99 (*0-345-91209-8*); 1980. 208p. mass mkt. 5.99 o.s.i (*0-345-28840-8*); 1979. 8.95 o.s.i (*0-345-28475-5*) Ballantine Bks. (Del Rey).

—Return of the Jedi: The National Public Radio Dramatization. 1996. 208p. pap. 15.00 o.s.i (*0-345-40782-2*) Ballantine Bks.

—Star Wars: The National Public Radio Dramatization. 1994. (Star Wars Ser.). (Illus.). 352p. pap. 19.00 o.s.i (*0-345-39109-8*, Del Rey) Ballantine Bks.

Dark Horse Comics Staff, et al. Empires End. 1997. (Star Wars Ser.). (Illus.). 56p. (YA). (gr. 7 up). pap. 5.95 (*1-56971-306-5*) Dark Horse Comics.

—Shadows of the Empire. 1997. (Star Wars Ser.). (Illus.). 160p. (YA). (gr. 7 up). pap. 17.95 (*1-56971-183-6*) Dark Horse Comics.

Dorling Kindersley Publishing Staff. Star Wars: The Power of Myth. 2000. (Star Wars Ser.). (Illus.). 48p. (J). pap. 12.95 (*0-7894-5591-9*, D K Ink) Dorling Kindersley Publishing, Inc.

—Star Wars: The Power of Myth. l.t. ed. 2000. (Illus.). 48p. 11.55 o.p. (*0-7513-6679-X*) Thorpe, F. A. Pubs. GBR. *Dist:* Ulverscroft Large Print Bks., Ltd., Ulverscroft Large Print Canada, Ltd.

Gardner, J. J. The Empire Strikes Back. 1997. (Star Wars Ser.). (Illus.). (J). (gr. 5-7). mass mkt. 5.99 (*0-590-06656-0*) Scholastic, Inc.

—Star Wars Movie Story. 1997. (Star Wars Ser.). (J). (gr. 5-7). mass mkt. 5.99 (*0-590-06654-4*) Scholastic, Inc.

Glut, Donald F. The Empire Strikes Back. 1997. (Star Wars Ser.). pap. 5.99 (*0-345-91183-0*); 1995. (Star Wars Ser.). 224p. 16.00 o.s.i (*0-345-40078-X*); 1985. (Star Wars Ser.: Vol. 2). 224p. mass mkt. 5.99 (*0-345-32022-0*); 1980. mass mkt. 2.25 o.p. (*0-345-28392-9*) Ballantine Bks. (Del Rey).

Golden, Christopher. Shadows of the Empire. 1996. (Star Wars Ser.). (Illus.). 176p. (J). (gr. 4-7). pap. text 4.50 o.s.i (*0-440-41303-6*) Dell Publishing.

—Shadows of the Empire: A Junior Novelization. 1996. (Star Wars Ser.). 10.55 (*0-606-11835-7*) Turtleback Bks.

Goodwin, Archie. The Empire Strikes Back: Classic Star Wars. 1995. (Star Wars Ser.). (Illus.). 104p. pap. 9.95 o.p. (*1-56971-088-0*) Dark Horse Comics.

Goodwin, Archie, et al. The Empire Strikes Back: Special Edition. 1997. (Star Wars Ser.). 104p. (J). (gr. 3 up). pap. 9.95 (*1-56971-234-4*) Dark Horse Comics.

—Return of the Jedi: Special Edition. 1997. (Star Wars Ser.). 104p. (YA). (gr. 3 up). pap. 9.95 (*1-56971-235-2*) Dark Horse Comics.

Hambly, Barbara. Children of the Jedi. 1996. (Star Wars Ser.). mass mkt. 10.95 o.s.i (*0-553-84008-8*); 432p. reprint ed. mass mkt. 6.99 (*0-553-57293-8*, Spectra) Bantam Bks.

—Children of the Jedi. 1995. audio 16.98 o.s.i (*0-553-74566-2*); audio 16.99 (*0-553-47195-3*) Random Hse. Audio Publishing Group. (RH Audio).

—Children of the Jedi. 1996. (Star Wars Ser.). 12.04 (*0-606-11887-X*) Turtleback Bks.

—Night Lily: The Lover's Tale. abr. ed. 1995. (Star Wars Ser.). audio compact disk 13.99 o.s.i (*0-553-45541-9*, , RH Audio) Random Hse. Audio Publishing Group.

—Nightlily: The Lover's Tale. abr. ed. 1995. (Star Wars Ser.). audio 12.00 o.p. (*0-553-45413-7*, RH Audio) Random Hse. Audio Publishing Group.

—Planet of Twilight. 1998. (Star Wars Ser.). 416p. reprint ed. mass mkt. 6.99 (*0-553-57517-1*) Bantam Bks.

—Planet of Twilight. abr. ed. 1997. (Star Wars Ser.). audio 16.99 (*0-553-47196-1*, RH Audio) Random Hse. Audio Publishing Group.

Hamill, Mark, et al. Star Wars: The Original Radio Drama. abr. unabr. ed. 1993. (Star Wars Ser.). audio 39.95 (*0-942110-99-4*, 692313); audio compact disk 64.95 (*1-56511-005-6*) HighBridge Co.

Jones, Bruce, et al. Star Wars: A New Hope. 1997. (Star Wars Ser.). 104p. (YA). (gr. 3 up). pap. 9.95 (*1-56971-213-1*) Dark Horse Comics.

—Star Wars Trilogy: A New Hope, Empire Strikes Back, Return of the Jedi. 2nd ed. 1997. (Star Wars Ser.). (Illus.). (J). (gr. 3 up). pap. 29.85 o.p. (*1-56971-257-3*) Dark Horse Comics.

Kahn, James. Return of the Jedi. (Star Wars Ser.). 1997. mass mkt. 5.99 (*0-345-91184-9*, Del Rey); 1995. 240p. 16.00 (*0-345-40079-8*, Del Rey); 1983. (Illus.). 224p. mass mkt. 5.95 o.p. (*0-345-30960-X*); 1983. 192p. mass mkt. 5.99 (*0-345-30767-4*, Del Rey) Ballantine Bks.

Kube-McDowell, Michael P. Before the Storm. 1996. (Star Wars: Bk. 1). 336p. mass mkt. 6.99 (*0-553-57273-3*, Spectra) Bantam Bks.

—Before the Storm. abr. ed. 1996. (Star Wars: Bk. 1). audio 16.99 (*0-553-47422-7*, 394259, RH Audio) Random Hse. Audio Publishing Group.

—Before the Storm. 1996. (Star Wars: Bk. 1). 12.04 (*0-606-11884-5*) Turtleback Bks.

—Shield of Lies. 1996. (Star Wars: Bk. 2). pap. 10.95 o.s.i (*0-553-84010-X*); 368p. mass mkt. 6.99 (*0-553-57277-6*, Spectra) Bantam Bks.

—Shield of Lies. abr. ed. 1996. (Star Wars: Bk. 2). audio 16.99 o.s.i (*0-553-47424-3*, 394260, RH Audio) Random Hse. Audio Publishing Group.

—Shield of Lies. 1996. (Star Wars: Bk. 2). 12.04 (*0-606-11885-3*) Turtleback Bks.

Characters

—Tyrant's Test. 1996. (Star Wars: Bk. 3). (Illus.). 400p. (gr. 5 up) mass mkt. 6.99 (0-553-57275-X, Spectra) Bantam Bks.

—Tyrant's Test. abr. ed. 1996. (Star Wars: Bk. 3). audio 16.99 (0-553-47421-9, 394598, RH Audio) Random Hse. Audio Publishing Group.

—Tyrant's Test. 1997. (Star Wars: Bk. 3). 12.04 (0-606-11886-1) Turtleback Bks.

Levy, Elizabeth, adapted by. Return of the Jedi. 1995. (Illus.). 64p. (gr. 4-7). pap. 3.99 (0-679-87205-1) Random Hse., Inc.

Lucas, George. The Empire Strikes Back. 1994. 8.98 (1-57042-172-2) Warner Bks., Inc.

—The Empire Strikes Back: The Original Radio Drama. abr. unabr. ed. 1993. (Star Wars Ser.). audio 39.95 (1-56511-000-5, 492026); audio compact disk 59.95 (1-56511-007-2) HighBridge Co.

—Return of the Jedi. 1997. mass mkt. 5.99 o.s.i (0-345-41356-3, Del Rey) Ballantine Bks.

—Return of the Jedi. 1995. 8.98 (1-57042-208-7) Warner Bks., Inc.

—Return of the Jedi: The Original Radio Drama. abr. unabr. ed. 1996. (Star Wars Ser.). audio 25.95 (1-56511-157-5); audio compact disk 34.95 (1-56511-158-3) HighBridge Co.

—Star Wars: A New Hope. 1995. (Star Wars Ser.). 272p. 16.00 o.s.i (0-345-40077-1, Del Rey) Ballantine Bks.

—Star Wars: A New Hope. 1996. (YA). (gr. 7-12). audio 17.00 o.p. (1-57042-248-6) Time Warner AudioBooks.

—Star Wars: A New Hope. 1998. (Star Wars Manga Ser.: Bk. 4). (Illus.). 96p. (YA). (gr. 3 up). pap. 9.95 (1-56971-365-0); pap. 9.95 (1-56971-364-2); pap. 9.95 (1-56971-362-6) Dark Horse Comics.

—Star Wars: A New Hope, Script Facsimiles. deluxe ed. 1998. (Star Wars Ser.). (Illus.). 176p. pap. 18.95 (0-345-42080-2, Del Rey) Ballantine Bks.

—Star Wars: A New Hope: The Illustrated Screenplay. 1998. (Star Wars Ser.). (Illus.). 208p. pap. 12.00 o.s.i (0-345-42069-1, Del Rey) Ballantine Bks.

—Star Wars Adventures. abr. ed. 1994. (Star Wars Ser.). audio 8.98 o.p. Time Warner AudioBooks.

Lucas, George. Star Wars Trilogy: Star Wars; The Empire Strikes Back; Return of the Jedi. unabr. ed. 1994. (Star Wars Ser.). audio 50.00 o.p. (1-57042-157-9, 4-521579); audio 75.00 o.p. (1-57042-169-2, 2-521579) Time Warner AudioBooks.

Lucas, George & Kasdan, Lawrence. Return of the Jedi. deluxe ed. 1998. (Star Wars Ser.). (Illus.). 144p. pap. 18.95 (0-345-42082-9, Ballantine Bks.) Ballantine Bks.

—Return of the Jedi: The Illustrated Screenplay. 1998. (Illus.). 208p. pap. 12.00 (0-345-42079-9, Del Rey) Ballantine Bks.

Lucas, George, et al. The Empire Strikes Back. deluxe ed. 1998. (Star Wars Ser.). (Illus.). 160p. pap. 18.95 o.s.i (0-345-42081-0, Del Rey) Ballantine Bks.

—Star Wars Trilogy: Star Wars; The Empire Strikes Back; Return of the Jedi. (Star Wars Ser.). 1997. mass mkt. 6.99 (0-345-91126-1); 1993. 480p. mass mkt. 7.99 (0-345-38438-5, Del Rey); 1987. 480p. pap. 12.95 (0-345-34806-0, Del Rey) Ballantine Bks.

—Star Wars Trilogy: Star Wars; The Empire Strikes Back; Return of the Jedi. 1987. (J). (gr. 3-7). 16.05 (0-606-01231-1) Turtleback Bks.

Lucasfilm Ltd. The Complete Trilogy Cassette Gift-Pack: Star Wars, The Empire Strikes Back, & Return of the Jedi. abr. ed. 1996. (Star Wars Ser.). audio 105.85 o.p. (1-56511-173-7) HighBridge Co.

Lucasfilm Ltd. Staff. The Last Command. unabr. ed. 1996. (Star Wars: Bk. 3). audio 104.00. audio Books on Tape, Inc.

—Star Wars. 1999. pap. 0.90 o.s.i (0-375-80892-2, Random Hse. Bks. for Young Readers) Random Hse. Children's Bks.

Luceno, James. Agents of Chaos I: Hero's Trial. 2000. (Star Wars Ser.: No. 4). 368p. mass mkt. 6.99 (0-345-42860-9, Del Rey) Ballantine Bks.

—Agents of Chaos I: Hero's Trial. abr. ed. 2000. (Star Wars). 13.04 (0-606-19373-1) Turtleback Bks.

—Agents of Chaos II: Jedi Eclipse. 2000. (Star Wars Ser.: Bk. 5). 368p. mass mkt. 6.99 (0-345-42859-5, Ballantine Bks.) Ballantine Bks.

Lund, Kristin. Inside the Worlds of Star Wars: Episode I. Dorling Kindersley Publishing Staff, ed. l.t. ed. 2000. (Illus.). 48p. 21.45 o.p. (0-7513-6222-0) Thorpe, F. A. Pubs. GBR. Dist: Ulverscroft Large Print Bks., Ltd., Ulverscroft Large Print Canada, Ltd.

Manning, Russ & Goodwin, Archie. The Early Adventures. 1997. (Classic Star Wars Ser.). (Illus.). 240p. (J). (gr. 3 up). pap. 19.95 (1-56971-178-X) Dark Horse Comics.

McIntyre, Vonda N. The Crystal Star. 1994. audio 13.59 o.s.i (0-553-70082-0, RH Audio) Random Hse. Audio Publishing Group.

—Crystal Star. abr. ed. 1994. (Star Wars Ser.). audio 16.99 (0-553-47194-5, RH Audio) Random Hse. Audio Publishing Group.

—The Crystal Star. 1995. (Star Wars Ser.). 448p. reprint ed. mass mkt. 6.99 (0-553-57174-5) Bantam Bks.

Perry, Steve. Shadows of the Empire. 1997. (Star Wars Ser.). 416p. (gr. 5 up). mass mkt. 6.99 (0-553-57413-2, Spectra) Bantam Bks.

—Shadows of the Empire. abr. ed. 1996. (Star Wars Ser.). audio 16.99 (0-553-47438-3, 393956, RH Audio) Random Hse. Audio Publishing Group.

—Shadows of the Empire. 1996. (Star Wars Ser.). 12.04 (0-606-11895-0) Turtleback Bks.

Perry, Steve, et al. Evolution: Shadows of the Empire. 2000. (Star Wars Ser.). (Illus.). 120p. (YA). (gr. 7 up). pap. 14.95 (1-56971-441-X) Dark Horse Comics.

Rusch, Kristine K. The New Rebellion. 1997. (Star Wars Ser.). 560p. mass mkt. 6.99 (0-553-57414-0, Spectra) Bantam Bks.

—The New Rebellion. 1997. (Star Wars Ser.). 12.04 (0-606-11894-2) Turtleback Bks.

—New Rebellion. abr. ed. 1996. (Star Wars Ser.). audio 16.99 (0-553-47743-9, RH Audio) Random Hse. Audio Publishing Group.

Salvatore, R. A. Vector Prime. (Star Wars Ser.). 2003. E-Book 2.99 (0-345-46740-X, Ballantine Bks.); 2000. 416p. mass mkt. 7.50 (0-345-42845-5); 1999. 400p. 24.95 (0-345-42844-7) Ballantine Bks.

—Vector Prime. abr. ed. 1999. (Star Wars: Bk. 1). audio 18.00 (0-375-40689-1, RH Audio) Random Hse. Audio Publishing Group.

Stackpole, Michael A., et al. Blood & Honor. 1999. (Star Wars Ser.: Bk. 6). 96p. (YA). (gr. 5 up). pap. 12.95 (1-56971-387-1) Dark Horse Comics.

—Masquerade. 2000. (Star Wars Ser.: Bk. 7). 96p. (YA). (gr. 7 up). pap. 12.95 (1-56971-487-8) Dark Horse Comics.

Star Wars Trilogy: Star Wars; The Empire Strikes Back; Return of the Jedi, 3 vols. 1987. (Star Wars Ser.). pap. 8.65 o.p. (0-345-32964-3, Del Rey) Ballantine Bks.

Tyers, Kathy. Balance Point. 2000. (Star Wars Ser.: Bk. 6). 352p. 25.95 (0-345-42857-9, Del Rey) Ballantine Bks.

—Star Wars - The New Jedi Order: Balance Point. abr. ed. 2000. (Star Wars). audio 18.00 (0-375-41624-2, RH Audio) Random Hse. Audio Publishing Group.

—The Truce at Bakura. 1994. (Star Wars Ser.). 352p. mass mkt. 6.99 (0-553-56872-8) Bantam Bks.

—The Truce at Bakura. 1993. audio 13.59 o.s.i (0-553-70065-0, RH Audio) Random Hse. Audio Publishing Group.

—The Truce at Bakura. 1994. (Star Wars Ser.). 11.09 o.p. (0-606-08201-8) Turtleback Bks.

Veitch, Tom. Dark Empire. 2nd ed. 1993. (Star Wars). (Illus.). 184p. (YA). (gr. 7 up). pap. 17.95 (1-56971-073-2) Dark Horse Comics.

—Dark Empire I. abr. ed. 1994. (Star Wars). audio 17.00 o.p. (1-57042-083-1, 4-520831) Time Warner AudioBooks.

—Dark Empire II. 1995. (Star Wars). (Illus.). 168p. (YA). (gr. 7 up). pap. 17.95 (1-56971-119-4) Dark Horse Comics.

—Dark Empire II. abr. ed. 1995. (Star Wars). audio 17.00 o.p. (1-57042-309-1, 4-523091) Time Warner AudioBooks.

—Star Wars: Dark Empire. abr. ed. 1997. (Star Wars Ser.). audio 16.95 (1-56511-200-8) HighBridge Co.

—Star Wars: Dark Empire II. abr. ed. 1997. (Star Wars Ser.). pap. 16.95 incl. audio (1-56511-201-6) HighBridge Co.

Veitch, Tom & Kennedy, Cam. Dark Empire: The Collected Edition. 1997. (Star Wars). (Illus.). pap. 16.95 o.p. (1-878574-56-6); 99.95 o.p. (1-878574-57-4) Dark Horse Comics.

Weinberg, Larry. The Empire Strikes Back: Classic Star Wars. 1995. (Star Wars Ser.). (Illus.). 54p. (J). (gr. 4-7). pap. 3.99 (0-679-87204-3) Random Hse., Inc.

Whitman, John & Lucas, George. Star Wars. 1996. (Mighty Chronicles Ser.). (Illus.). 432p. (gr. 4-7). 9.95 o.s.i (0-8118-1480-7) Chronicle Bks. LLC.

Wolverton, Dave. The Courtship of Princess Leia. 1995. (Star Wars Ser.). 400p. mass mkt. 6.99 (0-553-56937-6) Bantam Bks.

—The Courtship of Princess Leia. abr. ed. 1994. (Star Wars Ser.). audio 16.99 (0-553-47193-7, RH Audio) Random Hse. Audio Publishing Group.

—The Courtship of Princess Leia. 1994. (Star Wars Ser.). 12.04 (0-606-08199-2) Turtleback Bks.

Zahn, Timothy. Dark Force Rising. (Star Wars: Bk. 2). 1993. 448p. mass mkt. 6.99 (0-553-56071-9); 1992. 368p. 18.50 o.s.i (0-553-08574-3); Vol. 2. 1992. 384p. 125.00 o.s.i (0-553-08907-2, Spectra) Bantam Bks.

—Dark Force Rising. unabr. ed. 1995. (Star Wars: Bk. 2). audio 96.00 Books on Tape, Inc.

—Dark Force Rising. abr. ed. 1992. (Star Wars: Bk. 2). audio 16.99 (0-553-47055-8, RH Audio) Random Hse. Audio Publishing Group.

—Heir to the Empire. (Star Wars: Bk. 1). 9999. pap. 9.90 o.s.i (0-593-02481-8); 1992. 432p. mass mkt. 6.99 (0-553-29612-4); 1991. 368p. 22.95 o.s.i (0-553-07327-3); 1991. 368p. 125.00 o.s.i (0-553-07340-0, Spectra) Bantam Bks.

—Heir to the Empire. unabr. ed. 1995. (Star Wars: Bk. 1). audio 88.00 Books on Tape, Inc.

—Heir to the Empire. abr. ed. 1991. (Star Wars: Bk. 1). audio 16.99 (0-553-45296-7, 391663, RH Audio) Random Hse. Audio Publishing Group.

—Heir to the Empire. 1993. (Star Wars: Bk. 1). 64.95 o.p. incl. audio (0-7838-1100-4) Thorndike Pr.

—Heir to the Empire. 1991. (Star Wars: Bk. 1). 12.04 (0-606-00751-2) Turtleback Bks.

—The Last Command. (Star Wars: Bk. 3). 1994. 496p. mass mkt. 6.99 (0-553-56492-7, Spectra); 1993. 416p. 125.00 o.s.i (0-553-09500-5) Bantam Bks.

—The Last Command. abr. ed. 1993. (Star Wars: Bk. 3). audio 16.99 (0-553-47157-0, RH Audio) Random Hse. Audio Publishing Group.

—The Last Command. 1994. (Star Wars: Bk. 3). 12.04 (0-606-08205-0) Turtleback Bks.

—Specter of the Past. 1998. (Star Wars Hand of Thrawn Ser.: No. 1). 416p. (gr. 5 up). mass mkt. 6.99 (0-553-29804-6) Bantam Bks.

—Specter of the Past. abr. ed. 1997. (Star Wars Ser.: Vol. 1). (gr. 5 up). audio 16.99 (0-553-47893-1, RH Audio) Random Hse. Audio Publishing Group.

—Specter of the Past. l.t. ed. 1998. (Star Wars Ser.). 512p. 25.95 (0-7838-8434-6) Thorndike Pr.

—Star Wars. 1994. (Star Wars Ser.). pap. 17.95 o.s.i (0-553-63485-2) Bantam Bks.

—The Thrawn Trilogy. abr. ed. 2000. (Star Wars: Bk. 1,2,3). 29.95 incl. audio (0-553-52699-5);Set. (YA). 29.95 incl. audio Random Hse. Audio Publishing Group.

—Vision of the Future. 1999. (Star Wars Hand of Thrawn Ser.: No. 2). 720p. (gr. 5 up). mass mkt. 6.99 (0-553-57879-0) Bantam Bks.

—Vision of the Future. abr. ed. 1998. (Star Wars Ser.: Vol. 2). (gr. 5 up). audio 16.99 (0-553-47921-0, 392221, RH Audio) Random Hse. Audio Publishing Group.

Zahn, Timothy, et al. Heir to the Empire. 1996. (Star Wars Ser.). (Illus.). 160p. (YA). (gr. 7 up). pap. 19.95 (1-56971-202-6) Dark Horse Comics.

## SOLO, JACEN (FICTITIOUS CHARACTER)—FICTION

Allen, Roger Macbride. Ambush at Corellia. 1995. (Star Wars: Bk. 1). 320p. mass mkt. 6.99 (0-553-29803-8, Spectra) Bantam Bks.

—Ambush at Corellia. abr. ed. 1995. (Star Wars: Bk. 1). audio 16.99 (0-553-47202-X, 392779, RH Audio) Random Hse. Audio Publishing Group.

—Ambush at Corellia. 1995. (Star Wars: Bk. 1). 12.04 (0-606-08197-6) Turtleback Bks.

—Assault at Selonia. 1995. (Star Wars: Bk. 2). 320p. mass mkt. 6.99 (0-553-29805-4, Spectra) Bantam Bks.

—Assault at Selonia. abr. ed. 1995. (Star Wars: Bk. 2). (J). (gr. k). audio 16.99 (0-553-47203-8, RH Audio) Random Hse. Audio Publishing Group.

—Assault at Selonia. 1995. (Star Wars: Bk. 2). 12.04 (0-606-08198-4) Turtleback Bks.

—The Corellian Trilogy Boxed Set: Ambush at Corellia; Assault at Selonia; Showdown at Centerpoint. 1997. (Star Wars). (YA). (gr. 5 up). mass mkt. 17.97 o.s.i (0-553-94083-X, Spectra) Bantam Bks.

—The Corellian Trilogy Boxed Set: Ambush at Corellia; Assault at Selonia; Showdown at Centerpoint. 1999. (Star Wars). (YA). (gr. 5 up). incl. audio Random Hse. Audio Publishing Group.

—Showdown at Centerpoint. 1995. (Star Wars: Bk. 3). 336p. mass mkt. 6.99 (0-553-29806-2, Spectra) Bantam Bks.

—Showdown at Centerpoint. abr. ed. 1995. (Star Wars: Bk. 3 ). audio 16.99 (0-553-47204-6, RH Audio) Random Hse. Audio Publishing Group.

—Showdown at Centerpoint. 1995. (Star Wars: Bk. 3). 11.09 o.p. (0-606-09891-7) Turtleback Bks.

Anderson, Kevin J. Champions of the Force. 1994. (Star Wars: Vol. 3). 368p. mass mkt. 6.99 (0-553-29802-X) Bantam Bks.

—Champions of the Force. abr. ed. 1994. (star wars: Vol. 3). audio 16.99 (0-553-47201-1, RH Audio) Random Hse. Audio Publishing Group.

—Champions of the Force. 1994. (Star Wars: Vol. 3). 12.04 (0-606-08204-2) Turtleback Bks.

—The Jedi Academy Trilogy Omnibus. abr. ed. 1997. (Star Wars Ser.). (gr. 5 up). 29.95 incl. audio (0-553-47848-6, RH Audio) Random Hse. Audio Publishing Group.

—Jedi Search. 1994. (Star Wars: Vol. 1). 384p. mass mkt. 6.99 (0-553-29798-8) Bantam Bks.

—Jedi Search. abr. ed. 1994. (star wars: Vol. 1). audio 16.98 o.s.i (0-553-74512-3); audio 16.99 (0-553-47199-6) Random Hse. Audio Publishing Group. (RH Audio)

—Jedi Search. 1994. (Star Wars: Vol. 1). 12.04 (0-606-08202-6) Turtleback Bks.

—Jedi Trilogy: Jedi Search; Dark Apprentice; Champions of the Force, 3 vols. 1997. (Star Wars). (YA). (gr. 5). 20.97 (0-553-64839-X) Bantam Bks.

Salvatore, R. A. Vector Prime. (Star Wars Ser.). 2003. E-Book 2.99 (0-345-46740-X, Ballantine Bks.); 2000. 416p. mass mkt. 7.50 (0-345-42845-5); 1999. 400p. 24.95 (0-345-42844-7) Ballantine Bks.

—Vector Prime. abr. ed. 1999. (Star Wars: Bk. 1). audio 18.00 (0-375-40689-1, RH Audio) Random Hse. Audio Publishing Group.

Stackpole, Michael A. Dark Tide: Onslaught. abr. ed. 2000. (Star Wars: Bk. 2). audio 18.00 (0-375-40956-4, RH Audio) Random Hse. Audio Publishing Group.

—Dark Tide I: Onslaught. 2000. (Star Wars Ser.: Bk. 2). 125.82 o.s.i (0-345-43891-4); 304p. mass mkt. 6.99 (0-345-42854-4, Del Rey) Ballantine Bks.

—Dark Tide II: Ruin. abr. ed. 2000. (Star Wars: Bk. 3). audio 18.00 (0-375-40969-6, RH Audio) Random Hse. Audio Publishing Group.

—Ruin: Dark Tide II. 2000. (Star Wars Ser.: No.3). 304p. mass mkt. 6.99 (0-345-42856-0) Ballantine Bks.

## SOLO, JAINA (FICTITIOUS CHARACTER)—FICTION

Allen, Roger Macbride. Ambush at Corellia. 1995. (Star Wars: Bk. 1). 320p. mass mkt. 6.99 (0-553-29803-8, Spectra) Bantam Bks.

—Ambush at Corellia. abr. ed. 1995. (Star Wars: Bk. 1). audio 16.99 (0-553-47202-X, 392779, RH Audio) Random Hse. Audio Publishing Group.

—Ambush at Corellia. 1995. (Star Wars: Bk. 1). 12.04 (0-606-08197-6) Turtleback Bks.

—Assault at Selonia. 1995. (Star Wars: Bk. 2). 320p. mass mkt. 6.99 (0-553-29805-4, Spectra) Bantam Bks.

—Assault at Selonia. abr. ed. 1995. (Star Wars: Bk. 2). (J). (gr. k). audio 16.99 (0-553-47203-8, RH Audio) Random Hse. Audio Publishing Group.

—Assault at Selonia. 1995. (Star Wars: Bk. 2). 12.04 (0-606-08198-4) Turtleback Bks.

—The Corellian Trilogy Boxed Set: Ambush at Corellia; Assault at Selonia; Showdown at Centerpoint. 1997. (Star Wars). (YA). (gr. 5 up). mass mkt. 17.97 o.s.i (0-553-94083-X, Spectra) Bantam Bks.

—The Corellian Trilogy Boxed Set: Ambush at Corellia; Assault at Selonia; Showdown at Centerpoint. 1999. (Star Wars). (YA). (gr. 5 up). incl. audio Random Hse. Audio Publishing Group.

—Showdown at Centerpoint. 1995. (Star Wars: Bk. 3). 336p. mass mkt. 6.99 (0-553-29806-2, Spectra) Bantam Bks.

—Showdown at Centerpoint. abr. ed. 1995. (Star Wars: Bk. 3 ). audio 16.99 (0-553-47204-6, RH Audio) Random Hse. Audio Publishing Group.

—Showdown at Centerpoint. 1995. (Star Wars: Bk. 3). 11.09 o.p. (0-606-09891-7) Turtleback Bks.

Anderson, Kevin J. Champions of the Force. 1994. (Star Wars: Vol. 3). 368p. mass mkt. 6.99 (0-553-29802-X) Bantam Bks.

—Champions of the Force. abr. ed. 1994. (star wars: Vol. 3). audio 16.99 (0-553-47201-1, RH Audio) Random Hse. Audio Publishing Group.

—Champions of the Force. 1994. (Star Wars: Vol. 3). 12.04 (0-606-08204-2) Turtleback Bks.

Stackpole, Michael A. Dark Tide: Onslaught. abr. ed. 2000. (Star Wars Ser.). audio 18.00 (0-375-40956-4, RH Audio) Random Hse. Audio Publishing Group.

—Dark Tide I: Onslaught. 2000. (Star Wars Ser.: Bk. 2). 125.82 o.s.i (0-345-43891-4); 304p. mass mkt. 6.99 (0-345-42854-4, Del Rey) Ballantine Bks.

—Dark Tide II: Ruin. abr. ed. 2000. (Star Wars: Bk. 3). audio 18.00 (0-375-40969-6, RH Audio) Random Hse. Audio Publishing Group.

—Ruin: Dark Tide II. 2000. (Star Wars Ser.: No.3). 304p. mass mkt. 6.99 (0-345-42856-0) Ballantine Bks.

## SOLOMON, BRETTA (FICTITIOUS CHARACTER)—FICTION

Harrison, Janis. Lilies That Fester. l.t. ed. 2002. (Mystery Ser.). 373p. 29.45 (0-7862-4401-1) Thorndike Pr.

—Lilies That Fester: A Gardening Mystery. 2001. 256p. 23.95 (0-312-28406-3, Saint Martin's Minotaur) St. Martin's Pr.

—Murder Sets Seed: A Gardening Mystery. 2001. 256p. mass mkt. 6.50 (0-312-97725-5, St. Martin's Paperbacks); 2000. 248p. 22.95 (0-312-20382-9, Saint Martin's Minotaur) St. Martin's Pr.

—Murder Sets Seed: A Gardening Mystery. l.t. ed. 2001. 347p. (0-7862-3351-6) Thorndike Pr.

—Roots of Murder. l.t. ed. 2002. (Mystery Ser.). 282p. 29.45 (0-7862-3914-X) Gale Group.

—Roots of Murder. 246p. 2000. mass mkt. 5.99 (0-312-97500-7, St. Martin's Paperbacks); 2nd ed. 1999. 21.95 (0-312-20304-7, Saint Martin's Minotaur) St. Martin's Pr.

**SOLOMON, JOHN (FICTITIOUS CHARACTER)—FICTION**

Blum, Bill. Prejudicial Error. 1995. 304p. 21.95 o.p. (*0-525-93905-9*, Dutton) Dutton/Plume.
—Prejudicial Error. 1996. 368p. mass mkt. 5.99 o.s.i (*0-451-18309-6*, Signet Bks.) NAL.

**SPACE, SAM (FICTITIOUS CHARACTER)—FICTION**

Nolan, William F. Look Out for Space. 1985. 192p. pap. 4.95 o.p. (*0-930330-20-X*) International Polygonics, Ltd.
—Space for Hire. 1985. 200p. reprint ed. pap. 4.95 o.p. (*0-930330-19-6*) International Polygonics, Ltd.
—3 for Space. 27.00 o.p. (*0-8095-4420-2*) Millefleurs.

**SPADE, SAM (FICTITIOUS CHARACTER)—FICTION**

Anobile, Richard J., ed. The Maltese Falcon. 1974. (Film Classics Library). (Illus.). 256p. mass mkt. 5.50 o.p. (*0-380-01485-8*, 19109-1, Avon Bks.) Morrow/Avon.
Bogart, Humphrey, et al. The Maltese Falcon. 1946. audio 7.95 National Recording Co.
Duff, Howard, et al. Sam Spade: The Kandy Tooth. unabr. ed. 1948. audio 7.95 National Recording Co.
Duff, Howard & Dunne, Steven. Sam Spade. vinyl bd. 10.95 incl. audio (*1-57816-077-4*, SP2401) Audio File, The.
Hammett, Dashiell. The Maltese Falcon. Date not set. 148p. 18.95 (*0-8488-2436-9*) Amereon, Ltd.
—The Maltese Falcon. 1983. (Illus.). 300p. 325.00 o.p. (*0-910457-01-8*) Arion Pr.
—The Maltese Falcon. abr. ed. audio 12.95 (*0-89926-141-8*, 829); audio 35.70 Audio Bk. Co.
—The Maltese Falcon. 1985. (Mystery Ser.). mass mkt. 9.95 o.p. (*0-553-06509-2*) Bantam Bks.
—The Maltese Falcon. unabr. ed. 1980. audio 42.00 (*0-7366-0263-1*, 1258) Books on Tape, Inc.
—The Maltese Falcon. unabr. ed. 1997. audio 54.95 Eye in the Ear Inc.
—The Maltese Falcon. (Illus.). 352p. reprint ed. 1987. pap. 9.95 o.p. (*0-86547-157-6*); 1982. 20.00 o.p. (*0-86547-156-8*) Farrar, Straus & Giroux. (North Point Pr.).
—The Maltese Falcon. unabr. ed. 1999. audio compact disk 71.95 (*0-7531-0700-7*, 107007); 1996. audio 54.95 (*1-85695-796-9*, 940305) ISIS Audio Bks. GBR. *Dist:* Ulverscroft Large Print Bks., Ltd.
—The Maltese Falcon. 1992. pap. 9.00 (*0-394-23903-2*); 1989. 224p. pap. 11.00 (*0-679-72264-5*) Knopf Publishing Group. (Vintage).
—The Maltese Falcon, Set. l.t. ed. (YA). (gr. 10 up). reprint ed. 10.00 (*0-89064-044-0*) National Assn. for Visually Handicapped.
—The Maltese Falcon. abr. ed. 1985. audio 16.00 o.s.i (*0-394-55047-1*, RH Audio) Random Hse. Audio Publishing Group.
—The Maltese Falcon. 1992. pap. 9.00 (*0-679-74094-5*); 1972. pap. 4.95 o.p. (*0-394-71772-4*) Random Hse., Inc.
—The Maltese Falcon. 1993. 284p. reprint ed. 35.00 o.p. (*1-883402-15-8*, Scribner) Simon & Schuster.
—The Maltese Falcon. abr. ed. 1982. (Radio Ser.). pap. 5.95 o.p. incl. audio (*0-88142-347-5*, 347); pap. 5.95 o.p. incl. audio (*0-88142-347-5*, 347) Soundelux Audio Publishing.
—The Maltese Falcon. 1989. (Vintage Crime Ser.). 16.05 (*0-606-12411-X*) Turtleback Bks.
Sam Spade. audio 24.98 Moonbeam Pubns., Inc.
Spier, William. Sam Spade, Detective. 1999. audio 19.98 Radio Spirits, Inc.

**SPARHAWK (FICTITIOUS CHARACTER)—FICTION**

Eddings, David. The Diamond Throne. (Elenium Ser.: Bk. 1). 1990. 448p. mass mkt. 6.99 (*0-345-36769-3*, Del Rey); 1989. mass mkt. 4.95 o.s.i (*0-345-36746-4*) Ballantine Bks.
—The Diamond Throne. 1991. 3.99 o.p. (*0-517-06776-5*) Random Hse. Value Publishing.
—The Diamond Throne. 1990. (Elenium: Bk. 1). 13.04 (*0-606-01249-4*) Turtleback Bks.
—Domes of Fire. 1993. (Tamuli Ser.: Bk. 1). (Illus.). 480p. mass mkt. 7.50 (*0-345-38327-3*); mass mkt. 5.99 o.s.i (*0-345-38390-7*) Ballantine Bks. (Del Rey).
—Domes of Fire. 1993. audio o.s.i (*0-679-43191-8*);Set. (Tamuli: Bk. 1). audio 8.99 o.s.i (*0-679-42954-9*, 390670) Random Hse. Audio Publishing Group. (RH Audio).
—The Hidden City. (Tamuli Ser.: Bk. 3). 1995. 512p. mass mkt. 6.99 (*0-345-39040-7*, Del Rey); 1994. mass mkt. 5.99 o.s.i (*0-345-39294-9*) Ballantine Bks.
—The Ruby Knight. 1991. (Elenium: Bk. 2). 384p. mass mkt. 6.99 (*0-345-37352-9*); mass mkt. 5.95 (*0-345-37240-9*) Ballantine Bks. (Del Rey).
—The Ruby Knight. 1992. 4.99 o.p. (*0-517-08367-1*) Random Hse. Value Publishing.
—The Ruby Knight. 1991. (Elenium: Bk. 2). 13.04 (*0-606-01250-8*) Turtleback Bks.
—The Sapphire Rose. 1992. (Elenium Ser.: Bk. 3). 512p. mass mkt. 6.99 (*0-345-37472-X*, Del Rey) Ballantine Bks.
—The Shining Ones. 1994. (Tamuli Ser.: Bk. 2). 480p. mass mkt. 7.99 (*0-345-38866-6*) Ballantine Bks.

**SPARROWHAWK (FICTITIOUS CHARACTER)—FICTION**

*see Ged (Fictitious Character)—Fiction*

**SPAULDING, DAVID (FICTITIOUS CHARACTER)—FICTION**

Ludlum, Robert. The Rhinemann Exchange. 1989. 464p. mass mkt. 3.99 o.s.i (*0-553-19952-8*); 448p. mass mkt. 7.99 (*0-553-28063-5*) Bantam Bks.
—The Rhinemann Exchange. 1991. 464p. reprint ed. lib. bdg. 31.95 (*0-89966-778-3*) Buccaneer Bks., Inc.
—The Rhinemann Exchange. 1975. 448p. mass mkt. 3.50 o.s.i (*0-440-15079-5*) Dell Publishing.
—The Rhinemann Exchange. 1974. 8.95 o.p. (*0-385-27476-9*) Doubleday Publishing.
—The Rhinemann Exchange. l.t. ed. 1983. (Charnwood Large Print Ser.). 672p. 29.99 o.p. (*0-7089-8100-3*, Ulverscroft) Thorpe, F. A. Pubs. GBR. *Dist:* Ulverscroft Large Print Bks., Ltd., Ulverscroft Large Print Canada, Ltd.

**SPEARMAN, HENRY (FICTITIOUS CHARACTER)—FICTION**

Jevons, Marshall. A Deadly Indifference. 1998. (Henry Spearman Mysteries Ser.). 179p. pap. text 14.95 (*0-691-05969-1*) Princeton Univ. Pr.
—The Fatal Equilibrium. 1985. 240p. 32.00 (*0-262-10032-0*) MIT Pr.
—Murder at the Margin: A Henry Spearman Mystery. 1993. 192p. text 47.50 o.p. (*0-691-03391-9*); pap. text 15.95 (*0-691-00098-0*) Princeton Univ. Pr.

**SPEED, DIANE (FICTITIOUS CHARACTER)—FICTION**

Gibbs, Tony. Shadow Queen. 1992. 336p. 17.95 o.p. (*0-89296-473-1*) Mysterious Pr.
—Shadow Queen. 1993. 336p. mass mkt. 4.99 (*0-446-40108-0*, Mysterious Pr. Paperback Bks.) Warner Bks., Inc.

**SPEETER, ALEX (FICTITIOUS CHARACTER)—FICTION**

Hautman, Pete. The Mortal Nuts. l.t. ed. 1996. 22.95 o.p. (*0-7838-1925-0*, Macmillan Reference USA) Gale Group.
—The Mortal Nuts. 1997. per. 5.99 (*0-671-00304-6*, Pocket); 1996. 288p. 21.00 o.p. (*0-684-81000-X*, Simon & Schuster) Simon & Schuster.

**SPENCER, JOAN (FICTITIOUS CHARACTER)—FICTION**

Frommer, Sara H. Buried in Quilts. 1996. (WWL Mystery Ser.). per. (*0-373-26204-3*, 1-26204-7, Worldwide Library) Harlequin Enterprises, Ltd.
—Buried in Quilts. 1994. (Joan Spencer Mystery Ser.). 224p. 19.95 o.p. (*0-312-11472-9*, Saint Martin's Minotaur) St. Martin's Pr.
—Murder & Sullivan: A Joan Spencer Mystery. 1998. (WWL Mystery Ser.). per. (*0-373-26285-X*, 1-26285-6, Worldwide Library) Harlequin Enterprises, Ltd.
—Murder & Sullivan: A Joan Spencer Mystery. 1997. 256p. 21.95 o.p. (*0-312-15595-6*, Saint Martin's Minotaur) St. Martin's Pr.
—Murder in C Major. 1988. 224p. reprint ed. spiral bd. (*0-373-26017-2*, Harlequin Bks.) Harlequin Enterprises, Ltd.
—Murder in C Major. 2000. (Missing Mysteries Ser.: Vol. 17). 183p. pap. 14.95 (*1-890208-31-0*) Poisoned Pen Pr.
—Murder in C Major. 1986. 240p. 14.95 o.p. (*0-312-55299-8*) St. Martin's Pr.
—Murder in C Major. l.t. ed. 2003. 331p. 24.95 (*0-7862-5987-6*) Thorndike Pr.
—The Vanishing Violinist. 2000. (WWL Mystery Ser.: No. 359). 256p. mass mkt. (*0-373-26359-7*, 1-26359-9, Worldwide Library) Harlequin Enterprises, Ltd.
—The Vanishing Violinist: A Joan Spencer Mystery. 2nd ed. 1999. 272p. 23.95 (*0-312-24104-6*, Saint Martin's Minotaur) St. Martin's Pr.
—Witness in Bishop Hill: A Joan Spencer Mystery. 2002. 256p. 23.95 (*0-312-30243-6*, Saint Martin's Minotaur) St. Martin's Pr.
Outlet Book Company Staff. Murder in C Major. 1987. 1.99 o.p. (*0-517-65735-X*) Random Hse. Value Publishing.

**SPENCER, LOU (FICTITIOUS CHARACTER)—FICTION**

Beale, Elaine. Murder in the Castro. 1997. 192p. pap. 10.95 (*0-934678-87-1*) New Victoria Pubs., Inc.

**SPENSER (FICTITIOUS CHARACTER: PARKER)—FICTION**

Parker, Robert B. Back Story. 2003. (Spencer Mystery Ser.). 304p. 24.95 (*0-399-14977-5*) Putnam Publishing Group, The.
—Bad Business. 2004. 320p. 24.95 (*0-399-15145-1*) Putnam Publishing Group, The.
—A Catskill Eagle. unabr. collector's ed. 1990. (Spenser Ser.). audio 40.00 (*0-7366-1676-4*, 2524) Books on Tape, Inc.
—A Catskill Eagle. 1986. (Spencer Mystery Ser.). 384p. mass mkt. 7.50 (*0-440-11132-3*) Dell Publishing.
—A Catskill Eagle. l.t. ed. 1985. (Spencer Mystery Ser.). 16.95 o.p. (*0-8161-3892-3*, Macmillan Reference USA) Gale Group.
—Ceremony. unabr. collector's ed. 1989. (Spenser Ser.). audio 30.00 (*0-7366-1628-4*, 2486) Books on Tape, Inc.
—Ceremony. 1992. (Spencer Mystery Ser.). 224p. mass mkt. 7.50 (*0-440-10993-0*) Dell Publishing.
—Ceremony. l.t. ed. 1985. (Nightingale-Lythway Ser.). 9.95 o.p. (*0-8161-3833-8*, Macmillan Reference USA) Gale Group.
—Chance. 1997. (Spenser Mystery Ser.). 336p. reprint ed. mass mkt. 7.99 (*0-425-15747-4*) Berkley Publishing Group.
—Chance. l.t. ed. 1996. (Spenser Mystery Ser.). 26.95 o.p. (*1-56895-335-6*, Wheeler Publishing, Inc.) Gale Group.
—Chance. unabr. ed. 1996. (Spenser Mystery Ser.). 24.95 o.p. (*0-7871-0712-3*, 693925) NewStar Media, Inc.
—Chance. 1996. 21.95 (*0-399-14688-1*); 1996. 320p. 21.95 o.p. (*0-399-14134-0*, G. P. Putnam's Sons); 2015. 100.00 (*0-399-14167-7*) Penguin Group (USA) Inc.
—Crimson Joy. unabr. collector's ed. 1990. (Spenser Ser.). audio 30.00 (*0-7366-1758-2*, 2597) Books on Tape, Inc.
—Crimson Joy. (Spencer Mystery Ser.). 1989. 304p. mass mkt. 7.99 (*0-440-20343-0*); 1988. 75.00 o.s.i (*0-385-29668-1*, Delacorte Pr.) Dell Publishing.
—Crimson Joy. abr. ed. 1988. (Spencer Mystery Ser.). audio 14.95 (*0-671-66617-7*, Simon & Schuster Audioworks) Simon & Schuster Audio.
—Double Deuce. 1993. (Spenser Mystery Ser.). 256p. mass mkt. 7.99 (*0-425-13793-7*) Berkley Publishing Group.
—Double Deuce. unabr. ed. 2000. (Spenser Mystery Ser.). audio (*1-56054-857-6*, SAB 053) Chivers Audio Bks. GBR. *Dist:* BBC Audiobooks America.
—Double Deuce. l.t. ed. 1993. (Spencer Mystery Ser.). 233p. pap. 17.95 o.p. (*0-8161-5597-6*); 20.95 o.p. (*0-8161-5596-8*) Gale Group. (Macmillan Reference USA).
—Double Deuce. unabr. ed. 2002. audio 25.00 (*1-59007-205-7*, New Millennium Audio) New Millennium Entertainment.
—Double Deuce. unabr. ed. 1993. (Spenser Mystery Ser.). 24.95 o.p. (*1-55800-473-4*, 492065) NewStar Media, Inc.
—Double Deuce. 1992. (Spenser Mystery Ser.). 224p. 19.95 o.s.i (*0-399-13721-1*); 100.00 o.p. (*0-399-13754-8*) Penguin Group (USA) Inc. (G. P. Putnam's Sons).
—Early Autumn. unabr. collector's ed. 1989. (Spenser Ser.). audio 30.00 (*0-7366-1589-X*, 2452) Books on Tape, Inc.
—Early Autumn. (Spencer Mystery Ser.). 1992. 224p. mass mkt. 2.99 o.s.i (*0-440-21387-8*); 1992. 224p. mass mkt. 7.99 (*0-440-12214-7*); 1981. 10.95 o.s.i (*0-440-02248-7*, Delacorte Pr.) Dell Publishing.
—The Early Spenser. 1989. pap. 13.95 o.s.i (*0-440-50196-2*) Dell Publishing.
—The Early Spenser - Three Complete Novels: The Godwulf Manuscript, God Save the Child, Mortal Stakes. 1989. 504p. 13.95 o.s.i (*0-385-29728-9*, Delacorte Pr.) Dell Publishing.
—God Save the Child. unabr. collector's ed. 1988. (Spenser Ser.). audio 36.00 (*0-7366-1381-1*, 2274) Books on Tape, Inc.
—God Save the Child. 1987. (Spencer Mystery Ser.). 208p. mass mkt. 7.99 (*0-440-12899-4*) Dell Publishing.
—God Save the Child. 1974. (Spenser Mystery Ser.). 192p. 5.95 o.p. (*0-395-19955-7*) Houghton Mifflin Co.
—God Save the Child. 1995. (Spenser Mystery Ser.). Random Hse., Inc.
—The Godwulf Manuscript. l.t. ed. 1994. (Spenser Mystery Ser.). pap. 18.95 o.p. (*0-7927-1883-6*); 19.95 o.p. (*0-7927-1884-4*) BBC Audiobooks America.
—The Godwulf Manuscript. 1978. (Spenser Mystery Ser.). 1.50 o.s.i (*0-425-03967-6*) Berkley Publishing Group.
—The Godwulf Manuscript. unabr. collector's ed. 1988. (Spenser Ser.). audio 36.00 (*0-7366-1353-6*, 2254) Books on Tape, Inc.
—The Godwulf Manuscript. 1994. (Spenser Mystery Ser.). 192p. reprint ed. lib. bdg. 29.95 (*1-56849-317-7*) Buccaneer Bks., Inc.
—The Godwulf Manuscript. 1992. (Spencer Mystery Ser.). 208p. mass mkt. 7.99 (*0-440-12961-3*) Dell Publishing.
—The Godwulf Manuscript. 1974. (Spenser Mystery Ser.). 5.95 o.p. (*0-395-18011-2*) Houghton Mifflin Co.
—The Godwulf Manuscript. 1995. (Spenser Mystery Ser.). Random Hse., Inc.
—Hugger Mugger. 2001. (Spenser Mystery Ser.: Bk. 27). 336p. reprint ed. mass mkt. 7.99 (*0-425-17955-9*) Berkley Publishing Group.
—Hugger Mugger. unabr. ed. 2000. audio 34.95 (*0-7366-4915-8*, 5222) Books on Tape, Inc.
—Hugger Mugger. l.t. ed. 2000. (Spenser Mystery Ser.). 309p. 27.95 (*1-56895-865-X*, Wheeler Publishing, Inc.) Gale Group.
—Hugger Mugger. 2000. (Spenser Mystery Ser.). 320p. 23.95 o.s.i (*0-399-14587-7*) Penguin Group (USA) Inc.
—Hugger Mugger. unabr. ed. 2000. (Spenser Mystery Ser.). audio 29.95 (*0-553-50246-8*); audio compact disk 34.99 (*0-553-45673-3*);Set. audio 29.95 Random Hse. Audio Publishing Group.
—Hush Money. 2000. (Spenser Mystery Ser.). 336p. pap. 7.99 (*0-425-17401-8*) Berkley Publishing Group.
—Hush Money. l.t. ed. 1999. (Spenser Mystery Ser.). 27.95 (*1-56895-739-4*, Wheeler Publishing, Inc.) Gale Group.
—Hush Money. unabr. ed. 2002. audio 34.95 (*1-59007-206-5*, New Millennium Audio) New Millennium Entertainment.
—Hush Money. abr. ed. 1999. (Spenser Mystery Ser.). audio 18.00 (*0-7871-1898-2*, 394162); audio 30.00 (*0-7871-1870-2*, 890100) NewStar Media, Inc.
—Hush Money. 1999. (Spenser Mystery Ser.). 336p. 22.95 o.p. (*0-399-14458-7*) Penguin Group (USA) Inc.
—Hush Money. 2000. 13.55 (*0-606-20394-X*); 13.55 (*0-606-20098-3*) Turtleback Bks.
—The Judas Goat. (Spenser Mystery Ser.). 20.95 (*0-89190-371-2*) Amereon, Ltd.
—The Judas Goat. 1979. (Spenser Mystery Ser.). 1.95 o.p. (*0-425-04204-9*) Berkley Publishing Group.
—The Judas Goat. unabr. collector's ed. 1989. (Spenser Ser.). audio 36.00 (*0-7366-1571-7*, 2438) Books on Tape, Inc.
—The Judas Goat. 1992. (Spencer Mystery Ser.). 208p. mass mkt. 7.99 (*0-440-14196-6*) Dell Publishing.
—The Judas Goat, 001. 1978. (Spenser Mystery Ser.). 7.95 o.p. (*0-395-26682-3*) Houghton Mifflin Co.
—Looking for Rachel Wallace. unabr. collector's ed. 1989. (Spenser Ser.). audio 36.00 (*0-7366-1597-0*, 2458) Books on Tape, Inc.
—Looking for Rachel Wallace. (Spencer Mystery Ser.). 1987. 224p. mass mkt. 7.50 (*0-440-15316-6*); 1980. 10.95 o.s.i (*0-440-04764-1*, Delacorte Pr.) Dell Publishing.
—Mortal Stakes. unabr. collector's ed. 1989. (Spenser Ser.). audio 36.00 (*0-7366-1530-X*, 2400) Books on Tape, Inc.
—Mortal Stakes. 1994. (Spenser Mystery Ser.). reprint ed. lib. bdg. 32.95 (*1-56849-316-9*) Buccaneer Bks., Inc.
—Mortal Stakes. 1987. (Spencer Mystery Ser.). 336p. mass mkt. 7.50 (*0-440-15758-7*) Dell Publishing.
—Mortal Stakes, 001. 1975. (Spenser Mystery Ser.). 192p. 6.95 o.p. (*0-395-21969-8*) Houghton Mifflin Co.
—Mortal Stakes. 2002. (Best Mysteries of All Time Ser.). 288p. (*0-7621-8875-8*, Impress) Scriptorium Pr., The.
—A New Collection of Three Complete Spencer Novel. 1996. 13.99 o.s.i (*0-517-14891-9*) Random Hse. Value Publishing.
—Pale Kings & Princes. unabr. collector's ed. 1990. (Spenser Ser.). audio 30.00 (*0-7366-1772-8*, 2611) Books on Tape, Inc.
—Pale Kings & Princes. (Spencer Mystery Ser.). 1993. 320p. mass mkt. 3.99 o.s.i (*0-440-21584-6*); 1987. 288p. 75.00 o.s.i (*0-385-29568-5*, Delacorte Pr.); 1988. 320p. reprint ed. mass mkt. 7.99 (*0-440-20004-0*) Dell Publishing.
—Pale Kings & Princes. abr. ed. 1988. (Spencer Mystery Ser.). 14.95 incl. audio (*0-671-66073-X*, Simon & Schuster Audioworks) Simon & Schuster Audio.
—Paper Doll. 1994. (Spenser Mystery Ser.). 288p. mass mkt. 7.99 (*0-425-14155-1*) Berkley Publishing Group.
—Paper Doll. unabr. ed. 1993. (Spenser Ser.). audio 36.00 (*0-7366-2636-0*, 3375) Books on Tape, Inc.
—Paper Doll. unabr. ed. 2000. (Spenser Mystery Ser.). audio (*0-7862-9942-8*, SAB 072) Chivers Audio Bks. GBR. *Dist:* BBC Audiobooks America.
—Paper Doll. unabr. ed. 2002. audio 25.00 (*1-59007-207-3*, New Millennium Audio) New Millennium Entertainment.
—Paper Doll. unabr. ed. 1993. (Spenser Mystery Ser.). 24.95 o.p. (*1-55800-707-5*, 592092) NewStar Media, Inc.
—Paper Doll. 1993. (Spenser Mystery Ser.). 224p. 19.95 o.p. (*0-399-13818-8*, G. P. Putnam's Sons) Penguin Group (USA) Inc.
—Paper Doll. (Spencer Mystery Ser.). 5.98 o.p. (*0-8317-5332-3*) Smithmark Pubs., Inc.



 

—Pastime. 1992. (Spenser Mystery Ser.). 352p. reprint ed. mass mkt. 7.99 (*0-425-13293-5*) Berkley Publishing Group.

—Pastime. unabr. ed. 2000. (Spenser Mystery Ser.). audio 49.95 (*1-56054-910-6*, SAB 035) Chivers Audio Bks. GBR. *Dist:* BBC Audiobooks America.

—Pastime. l.t. ed. 1992. (Spencer Mystery Ser.). 269p. lib. bdg. 20.95 o.p. (*0-8161-5347-7*, Macmillan Reference USA) Gale Group.

—Pastime. unabr. ed. 2002. audio 25.00 (*1-59007-208-1*, New Millennium Audio) New Millennium Entertainment.

—Pastime. abr. ed. 1993. (Spencer Mystery Ser.). 15.95 o.p. (*1-55800-272-3*, 41180); audio 8.99 o.p. (*1-55800-902-7*, Dove Audio); 24.95 o.p. (*1-55800-433-5*, 692282) NewStar Media, Inc.

—Pastime. (Select Sound, Dove Ser.). 1995. pap. 4.99 o.p. (*0-7871-0305-5*); 1991. 224p. 19.95 o.s.i (*0-399-13628-2*, G. P. Putnam's Sons); 1991. 100.00 o.p. (*0-399-13630-4*) Penguin Group (USA) Inc.

—Pastime. 1992. (Spencer Mystery Ser.). 5.99 o.p. (*0-517-09584-X*) Random Hse. Value Publishing.

—Playmates. 1990. (Spenser Mystery Ser.). 288p. mass mkt. 7.99 (*0-425-12001-5*) Berkley Publishing Group.

—Playmates. unabr. collector's ed. 1990. (Spenser Ser.). audio 30.00 (*0-7366-1774-4*, 2613) Books on Tape, Inc.

—Playmates. 1989. (Spencer Mystery Ser.). 17.95 o.p. (*0-399-13425-5*, G. P. Putnam's Sons) Penguin Putnam Bks. for Young Readers.

—Playmates. abr. ed. 1989. (Spencer Mystery Ser.). audio 14.95 (*0-671-67832-9*, Simon & Schuster Audioworks) Simon & Schuster Audio.

—Potshot. l.t. ed. 2001. 359p. (*0-7540-9075-2*); (*0-7540-1661-7*) BBC Audiobooks America.

—Potshot. 2002. 352p. reprint ed. mass mkt. 7.99 (*0-425-18288-6*) Berkley Publishing Group.

—Potshot. 2001. (Spenser Ser.). 294p. 23.95 o.p. (*0-399-14710-1*) Penguin Group (USA) Inc.

—Potshot. l.t. ed. (Paperback Bestsellers Ser.). 2002. 359p. pap. 29.95 (*0-7862-3237-4*); 2001. 407p. 32.95 (*0-7862-3232-3*) Thorndike Pr.

—Potshot: A Spencer Novel. unabr. ed. 2001. audio 25.95 (*0-553-50282-4*); audio compact disk 29.95 (*0-553-71247-0*) Random Hse. Audio Publishing Group. (RH Audio).

—Promised Land. 1978. (Spenser Mystery Ser.). 1.75 o.p. (*0-425-03614-6*) Berkley Publishing Group.

—Promised Land. unabr. collector's ed. 1989. (Spenser Ser.). audio 36.00 (*0-7366-1551-2*, 2420) Books on Tape, Inc.

—Promised Land. 1992. (Spencer Mystery Ser.). 224p. mass mkt. 7.50 (*0-440-17197-0*) Dell Publishing.

—Promised Land. 2002. E-Book 6.99 (*0-7953-0732-2*) RosettaBooks.

—A Savage Place. unabr. collector's ed. 1989. (Spenser Ser.). audio 30.00 (*0-7366-1621-7*, 2481) Books on Tape, Inc.

—A Savage Place. (Spencer Mystery Ser.). 1982. 192p. mass mkt. 6.99 (*0-440-18095-3*); 1981. 6.99 (*0-440-08094-0*); 1981. 14.95 o.s.i (*0-385-28951-0*, Delacorte Pr.) Dell Publishing.

—A Savage Place. l.t. ed. 1982. (Spenser Mystery Ser.). 264p. reprint ed. 12.95 o.p. (*0-89621-343-9*) Thorndike Pr.

—Small Vices. 1998. (Spenser Mystery Ser.). 352p. mass mkt. 7.99 (*0-425-16248-6*) Berkley Publishing Group.

—Small Vices. l.t. ed. 1997. (Spenser Mystery Ser.). 25.95 o.p. (*1-56895-466-2*, Wheeler Publishing, Inc.) Gale Group.

—Small Vices. unabr. ed. 2002. audio 34.95 (*1-59007-210-3*, New Millennium Audio) New Millennium Entertainment.

—Small Vices. unabr. ed. 1997. (Spenser Mysteries Ser.). 29.95 o.p. (*0-7871-1133-3*, 754969) NewStar Media, Inc.

—Small Vices. 1997. (Spenser Mystery Ser.). 320p. (J). 21.95 o.p. (*0-399-14244-4*, G. P. Putnam's Sons) Penguin Group (USA) Inc.

—Spenser's Boston. 1994. (Illus.). 208p. 22.50 o.p. (*1-883402-50-6*, Scribner) Simon & Schuster.

—Stardust, Set. unabr. ed. 1995. (Spenser Mystery Ser.). audio 54.95 (*1-56054-968-8*, SAB 012, Sterling Audio Bks.) BBC Audiobooks America.

—Stardust. 1991. (Spenser Mystery Ser.). 304p. mass mkt. 7.99 (*0-425-12723-0*) Berkley Publishing Group.

—Stardust. unabr. collector's ed. 1990. (Spenser Ser.). audio 36.00 (*0-7366-1840-6*, 2673) Books on Tape, Inc.

—Stardust. 1990. (Spencer Mystery Ser.). 224p. 18.95 o.s.i (*0-399-13537-5*); 75.00 o.p. (*0-399-13514-6*) Penguin Putnam Bks. for Young Readers. (G. P. Putnam's Sons).

—Stardust. 1992. (Spencer Mystery Ser.). 4.99 o.p. (*0-517-08606-9*) Random Hse. Value Publishing.

—Stardust. abr. ed. 1990. (Spencer Mystery Ser.). audio 14.95 (*0-671-70481-8*, Simon & Schuster Audioworks) Simon & Schuster Audio.

—Sudden Mischief. l.t. ed. 1998. (Spenser Mystery Ser.). 27.95 (*1-56895-569-3*, Wheeler Publishing, Inc.) Gale Group.

—Sudden Mischief. unabr. ed. 2002. audio 25.00 (*1-59007-211-1*, New Millennium Audio) New Millennium Entertainment.

—Sudden Mischief. unabr. ed. 1998. (Spenser Mystery Ser.). audio 25.00 (*0-7871-1675-0*, 695658, Dove Audio) NewStar Media, Inc.

—Sudden Mischief. 1998. 22.95 o.s.i (*0-399-14696-2*); 304p. 22.95 o.p. incl. audio (*0-399-14370-X*, G. P. Putnam's Sons); 304p. 22.95 o.p. incl. audio (*0-399-14370-X*, G. P. Putnam's Sons) Penguin Group (USA) Inc.

—Taming a Seahorse. unabr. collector's ed. 1990. (Spenser Ser.). audio 30.00 (*0-7366-1750-7*, 2589) Books on Tape, Inc.

—Taming a Seahorse. 1987. (Spencer Mystery Ser.). 320p. mass mkt. 7.99 (*0-440-18841-5*) Dell Publishing.

—Taming a Seahorse. l.t. ed. 1987. (Spencer Mystery Ser.). 362p. 18.95 o.p. (*0-8161-4166-5*, Macmillan Reference USA) Gale Group.

—Thin Air. 1996. (Spenser Mystery Ser.). 304p. reprint ed. mass mkt. 7.99 (*0-425-15290-1*) Berkley Publishing Group.

—Thin Air. l.t. ed. 1995. (Spencer Mystery Ser.). 26.95 o.p. (*1-56895-212-0*, Wheeler Publishing, Inc.) Gale Group.

—Thin Air. unabr. ed. 2002. audio 25.00 (*1-59007-212-X*, New Millennium Audio) New Millennium Entertainment.

—Thin Air. unabr. ed. 1995. (Spenser Mystery Ser.). 24.95 o.p. (*0-7871-0277-6*, 692871) NewStar Media, Inc.

—Thin Air. (*0-399-19276-X*); 1995. 293p. 21.95 o.p. (*0-399-14020-4*, G. P. Putnam's Sons); 1995. 125.00 o.p. (*0-399-14063-8*, G. P. Putnam's Sons) Penguin Group (USA) Inc.

—Three Complete Novels, 3 vols. Incl. God Save the Child. 1995. Godwulf Manuscript. 1995. Mortal Stakes. 192p. 1975. 6.95 o.p. (*0-395-21969-8*); 560p. 1995. 13.99 o.s.i (*0-517-14802-1*) Random Hse., Inc.

—Valediction. unabr. collector's ed. 1989. (Spenser Ser.). audio 30.00 (*0-7366-1670-5*, 2519) Books on Tape, Inc.

—Valediction. (Spencer Mystery Ser.). 1992. 288p. mass mkt. 7.50 (*0-440-19246-3*); 1984. 240p. 12.95 o.s.i (*0-385-29330-5*, Delacorte Pr.) Dell Publishing.

—Valediction. 1985. (Spencer Mystery Ser.). mass mkt. 3.50 o.s.i (*0-440-19247-1*) Doubleday Publishing.

—Valediction. l.t. ed. 1984. (Spencer Mystery Ser.). 14.95 o.p. (*0-8161-3702-1*, Macmillan Reference USA) Gale Group.

—Walking Shadow. 1995. (Spenser Mystery Ser.). 304p. mass mkt. 7.99 (*0-425-14774-6*) Berkley Publishing Group.

—Walking Shadow. unabr. ed. 1995. (Spenser Ser.). audio 48.00 (*0-7366-2924-6*, 3622) Books on Tape, Inc.

—Walking Shadow. l.t. ed. 1994. (Spencer Mystery Ser.). 25.95 o.p. (*1-56895-106-X*, Wheeler Publishing, Inc.) Gale Group.

—Walking Shadow. abr. ed. 2002. audio 25.00 (*1-59007-213-8*, New Millennium Audio) New Millennium Entertainment.

—Walking Shadow. abr. ed. 1993. (Spencer Mystery Ser.). audio 24.95 o.p. (*1-55800-999-X*, Dove Audio) NewStar Media, Inc.

—Walking Shadow. 1994. (Spenser Mystery Ser.). 224p. 19.95 o.p. (*0-399-13920-6*); 100.00 o.p. (*0-399-13961-3*) Penguin Group (USA) Inc. (G. P. Putnam's Sons).

—The Widening Gyre. unabr. collector's ed. 1989. (Spenser Ser.). audio 30.00 (*0-7366-1655-1*, 2506) Books on Tape, Inc.

—The Widening Gyre. (Spencer Mystery Ser.). 192p. 1992. mass mkt. 7.99 (*0-440-19535-7*); 1983. 13.95 o.p. (*0-385-29220-1*, Delacorte Pr.) Dell Publishing.

—Widow's Walk. 2003. 336p. mass mkt. 7.99 (*0-425-18904-X*) Berkley Publishing Group.

—Widow's Walk. 2002. 320p. 24.95 o.s.i (*0-399-14845-0*) Putnam Publishing Group, The.

—Widow's Walk. unabr. ed. 2002. audio 25.95 (*0-553-52903-X*); audio compact disk 29.95 (*0-553-71471-6*) Random Hse. Audio Publishing Group.

—Widow's Walk. l.t. ed. 2003. 343p. pap. 13.95 (*1-4104-0099-9*, Large Print Pr.) Thorndike Pr.

—Widow's Walk: A Spenser Novel. 2003. (Paperback Bestsellers Ser.). pap. 13.95 (*0-7862-4216-7*) Thorndike Pr.

—Wilderness. l.t. ed. 1994. 19.95 o.p. (*0-7927-1726-0*); pap. 18.95 o.p. (*0-7927-1725-2*) BBC Audiobooks America.

—Wilderness. 1980. 256p. mass mkt. 7.99 (*0-440-19328-1*); 1979. 8.95 o.s.i (*0-440-09328-7*, Delacorte Pr.) Dell Publishing.

Parker, Robert B. & Cohen, Stan. Sudden Mischief. 1999. (Spenser Mystery Ser.). 306p. reprint ed. pap. 7.99 (*0-425-16828-X*) Berkley Publishing Group.

**SPIDER (FICTITIOUS CHARACTER)—FICTION**

Sampson, Robert. Spider. 1987. 250p. 32.95 o.p. (*0-87972-397-1*); pap. 16.95 o.p. (*0-87972-398-X*) Univ. of Wisconsin Pr. (Popular Pr.).

**SPIDER-MAN (FICTITIOUS CHARACTER)—FICTION**

Askegren, Pierce & Fingeroth, Danny. Sabotage: Doom's Day, Bk. 2. 1997. (Spider-Man & Iron Man Ser.). (J). mass mkt. 5.99 o.s.i (*1-57297-235-1*) Boulevard Bks.

Barrett, Neal. Lizard's Rage. 1997. (Spider-Man Super Thriller Ser.: No.8). 144p. per. 4.99 (*0-671-00798-X*, Pocket) Simon & Schuster.

Bendis, Brian Michael. Ultimate Spider-Man. (Illus.). 2002. 144p. pap. 17.95 (*0-7851-0879-3*); Vol. 3. 2003. 304p. (J). 29.99 (*0-7851-1156-5*) Marvel Enterprises.

—Ultimate Spider-Man, Vol. 4. Youngquist, Jeff, ed. 2004. (Spider-Man Ser.). (Illus.). 304p. 29.99 (*0-7851-1249-9*) Marvel Enterprises.

—Ultimate Spider-Man, 8 vols., Vol. 8. 2004. (Ultimate Spider-man Ser.). (Illus.). 152p. (J). pap. 14.99 (*0-7851-1250-2*) Marvel Enterprises.

—Ultimate Spider-Man: Learning Curve. (Illus.). 2002. 352p. 34.95 (*0-7851-0898-X*); 2001. 192p. pap. 14.95 (*0-7851-0820-3*) Marvel Enterprises.

Busiek, Kurt. Untold Tales of Spider-Man. 1997. 176p. pap. text 16.95 (*0-7851-0263-9*) Marvel Enterprises.

Busiek, Kurt & Archer, Nathan. Spider-Man: Goblin Moon. 1999. (Spider-Man Ser.). (Illus.). 304p. 24.95 o.s.i (*0-399-14512-5*, G. P. Putnam's Sons) Penguin Group (USA) Inc.

Castro, Adam-Troy. Spider-Man: The Gathering of the Sinister Six. 1999. (Spider-Man Ser.). 320p. (Orig.). mass mkt. 6.99 o.s.i (*0-425-16774-7*) Berkley Publishing Group.

—Spider-Man Bk. 2: The Revenge of the Sinister Six. 2000. mass mkt. 6.99 (*0-425-17337-2*) Berkley Publishing Group.

Conway, Gerry. Spider-Man: Death of Gwen Stacy. 1999. 112p. pap. text 14.95 (*0-7851-0716-9*) Marvel Enterprises.

—Spider-Man: Parallel Lives. 1990. (Illus.). 64p. 9.95 o.p. (*0-87135-573-6*) Marvel Enterprises.

—Spider-Man Clone Genesis. 1995. (Illus.). 192p. pap. 16.95 (*0-7851-0134-9*) Marvel Enterprises.

Conway, Gerry, et al. Spider-Man: Fear Itself. 1992. 64p. 12.95 o.p. (*0-87135-752-6*) Marvel Enterprises.

Coyote, Ivan. Close to Spider Man. 2000. (Illus.). 93p. pap. 11.95 (*1-55152-086-9*) Arsenal Pulp Pr., Ltd. CAN. *Dist:* Consortium Bk. Sales & Distribution.

David, Peter. Spider-Man. novel ed. 2002. 320p. mass mkt. 6.99 (*0-345-45005-1*, Ballantine Bks.) Ballantine Bks.

David, Peter, et al. The Death of Jean DeWolff. 1990. (Spider-Man Ser.). (Illus.). 96p. pap. 10.95 o.p. (*0-87135-704-6*) Marvel Enterprises.

DeCandido, Keith R. A. & Nieto, Jose R. Venom's Wrath. 1998. (Spider-Man Ser.). 352p. (YA). mass mkt. 6.99 o.s.i (*0-425-16574-4*) Boulevard Bks.

DeFalco, Tom. X-Men: Spider-Man Past. 1998. (X-Men Ser.: Vol. 1). 304p. mass mkt. 6.99 o.s.i (*0-425-16452-7*) Berkley Publishing Group.

—X-Men & Spider-Man's Future. 1998. (X-Men Ser.: Vol. 3). (Illus.). 304p. mass mkt. 6.99 o.p. (*0-425-16500-0*) Berkley Publishing Group.

DeFalco, Tom & Castro, Adam-Troy. Time's Arrow: The Present. 1998. (X-Men Ser.: Bk. II). 304p. mass mkt. 6.99 o.s.i (*0-425-16415-2*) Berkley Publishing Group.

DeFalco, Tom & Stern, Roger. Spider-Man: Origin of Hobgoblin. 1992. (Illus.). 160p. pap. 14.95 (*0-87135-917-0*) Marvel Enterprises.

DeFalco, Tom, et al. Spider-Man: Saga of the Alien Costume. 1988. (Illus.). 192p. pap. 9.95 o.p. (*0-87135-396-2*) Marvel Enterprises.

Delrio, Martin. Global Terror. 1997. (Spider-Man Super Thriller Ser.: No. 3). 176p. mass mkt. 4.99 (*0-671-00799-8*, Pocket) Simon & Schuster.

—Spider Man: Eye of the Storm. 1996. 224p. mass mkt. 4.99 (*0-671-56851-5*, Pocket) Simon & Schuster.

Dematteis, J. M. Batman/Spider-Man. 1997. (Illus.). 48p. pap. 4.95 (*1-56389-308-8*) DC Comics.

—Spider-Man: The Lost Years. 1996. (Illus.). 96p. pap. text 9.95 (*0-7851-0202-7*) Marvel Enterprises.

DeMatteis, J. M., et al. Spider-Man: Soul of the Hunter. 1992. 48p. 5.95 o.p. (*0-87135-942-1*) Marvel Enterprises.

Demattwis, J. M., et al. Spider-Man Legends Vol. 1: Kraven's Last Hunt. 1990. (Illus.). 160p. pap. 15.95 (*0-87135-691-0*) Marvel Enterprises.

Dezago, Todd. Spider-Man: Revelations. 1997. (Illus.). 112p. pap. text 14.95 (*0-7851-0560-3*) Marvel Enterprises.

Dezago, Todd, et al. Spider-Man: Identity Crisis. 1998. (Marvel's Finest' Collection). (Illus.). 208p. 19.95 (*0-7851-0663-4*) Marvel Enterprises.

Ditko, Steve, et al. Spider-Man: Unmasked. 1997. (Illus.). 64p. pap. 5.95 (*0-7851-0288-4*) Marvel Enterprises.

Duane. Spider Man Lizard. 1999. pap. 5.98 (*0-671-04419-2*, Simon & Schuster Audioworks) Simon & Schuster Audio.

Duane, Diane. The Lizard Sanction. (Spider-Man Ser.). (J). 1996. 304p. mass mkt. 6.50 o.s.i (*1-57297-148-7*); 1995. 352p. 19.95 o.p. (*0-399-14105-7*) Boulevard Bks.

—The Octopus Agenda. 1997. (Spider-Man Ser.). 272p. mass mkt. 6.50 o.s.i (*1-57297-279-3*) Boulevard Bks.

—Spider-Man: The Venom Factor. 1998. (Spider-Man Ser.). (Illus.). 343p. (J). mass mkt. 6.99 o.s.i (*0-425-16978-2*) Berkley Publishing Group.

—Spider-Man: The Venom Factor. 1994. (Illus.). 352p. 19.95 o.p. (*0-399-14002-6*, G. P. Putnam's Sons) Penguin Group (USA) Inc.

—Spiderman: The Octopus Agenda. 1996. (Spider-Man Ser.). (Illus.). 352p. 21.95 o.p. (*0-399-14211-8*, G. P. Putnam's Sons) Penguin Group (USA) Inc.

—The Venom Factor. 1995. (Spider-Man Ser.). 352p. (YA). mass mkt. 6.50 o.s.i (*1-57297-038-3*) Boulevard Bks.

Fein, Eric & Askegren, Pierce. Wreckage. 1997. (Spider-Man & Fantastic Four Ser.: No. 3). 272p. (YA). mass mkt. 6.50 o.s.i (*1-57297-311-0*) Boulevard Bks.

Frank Miller's Spider-Man. 1994. 208p. 50.00 o.p. (*0-7851-0054-7*) Marvel Enterprises.

Gardner, Craig S. Spider-Man: Wanted Dead or Alive. 1999. (Spider-Man Ser.). 320p. reprint ed. mass mkt. 6.99 o.p. (*0-425-16930-8*) Berkley Publishing Group.

—Spider-Man: Wanted Dead or Alive. 1998. (Spider-Man Ser.). (Illus.). 352p. 23.95 o.p. (*0-399-14385-8*, G. P. Putnam's Sons) Penguin Group (USA) Inc.

Ghost Rider - Spider-Man: Spirits of Venom. 1993. 96p. 9.95 o.p. (*0-87135-984-7*) Marvel Enterprises.

Johnson, Harold. Spider Man - Marvel Team-Up. 2000. (Marvel Super Heroes Ser.). 64p. pap. 9.95 (*0-7869-1668-0*) Wizards of the Coast.

Knowledge Adventures Staff. Spider-Man Cartoon Maker. 1995. 16.00 net. (*1-56997-144-7*) Knowledge Adventure, Inc.

Larsen, Eric. Spider-Man: Revenge of the Sinister Six. 1994. (Spider-Man Ser.). (Illus.). 128p. pap. 15.95 o.p. (*0-7851-0047-4*) Marvel Enterprises.

Lee, Stan. The Amazing Spider-Man. 1992. 128p. mass mkt. 3.99 (*0-8125-1019-4*, Tor Bks.) Doherty, Tom Assocs., LLC.

—The Amazing Spider-Man. 1987. (Marvel Masterworks Ser.: Vol. 1). (Illus.). 224p. 34.95 o.p. (*0-87135-305-9*) Marvel Enterprises.

—The Essential Spider-Man. (Illus.). 528p. Vol. I. 1997. pap. 12.95 (*0-7851-0286-8*); Vol. 2. 1998. pap. 12.99 (*0-7851-0299-X*); Vol. III. 1998. pap. 12.95 (*0-7851-0658-8*); Vol. IV. 2000. pap. 14.95 (*0-7851-0760-6*) Marvel Enterprises.

—Greatest Spider-Man & Daredevil Team-Ups. 1996. (Illus.). 176p. pap. text 16.95 (*0-7851-0223-X*) Marvel Enterprises.

—Spider-Man. (Illus.). 2002. (Masterworks Ser.: Vol. 1). 224p. 49.95 (*0-7851-0864-5*); 1999. (Marvel Masterworks Ser.: Vol. 1). 240p. 34.95 o.p. (*0-7851-0703-7*); 1994. (Masterworks Ser.). 256p. 34.95 (*0-7851-0051-2*) Marvel Enterprises.

—Spider-Man: Sensational. 1988. 80p. 6.95 (*0-87135-514-0*) Marvel Enterprises.

—Spider-Man: The Movie. 2002. 112p. pap. 12.95 (*0-7851-0903-X*) Marvel Enterprises.

—Spider-Man Greatest Villians. 1995. (Illus.). 176p. pap. 15.95 (*0-7851-0136-5*) Marvel Enterprises.

—Spider-Man vs. Doctor Octopus. 1999. (From the House of Ideas Ser.). (Illus.). 176p. pap. 17.95 (*0-7851-0742-8*, From the Hse. of Ideas) Marvel Enterprises.

—Spider-Man Wedding. 1991. 144p. pap. 12.95 o.p. (*0-87135-770-4*) Marvel Enterprises.

—Spider-Man's Greatest Team-Ups. 1996. (Illus.). 176p. pap. text 16.95 (*0-7851-0203-5*) Marvel Enterprises.

—Spider-Man's Strangest Adventures. 1996. (Illus.). 176p. pap. text 16.95 o.p. (*0-7851-0221-3*) Marvel Enterprises.

—Ultimate Spider-Man. 1996. (Spiderman Ser.). (Illus.). 347p. mass mkt. 6.99 o.s.i (*0-425-17000-4*) Berkley Publishing Group.

—The Ultimate Spiderman. 1994. (Spiderman Ser.). 352p. (Orig.). pap. 12.00 o.s.i (*0-425-14610-3*) Berkley Publishing Group.

—The Very Best of Spider-Man. 1994. (Illus.). 176p. pap. 16.95 (*0-7851-0045-8*) Marvel Enterprises.

Lee, Stan & Busiek, Kurt, eds. The Untold Tales of Spider Man. 1997. (Spiderman Ser.). 320p. (J). pap. 13.00 (*1-57297-294-7*) Boulevard Bks.

Lee, Stan & Ditko, Steve. The Amazing Spider-Man. 1989. (Marvel Masterworks Ser.: Vol. 10). 264p. 34.95 (*0-87135-596-5*) Marvel Enterprises.

—Spider-Man. 1988. (Marvel Masterworks Ser.: Vol. 5). 232p. 34.95 (*0-87135-480-2*) Marvel Enterprises.

—Spider-Man: Masterworks. 1992. (Illus.). 144p. pap. 12.95 (*0-87135-902-2*) Marvel Enterprises.

Lee, Stan & Shooter, Jim. Spider-Man: The Wedding. 2002. (Illus.). 144p. pap. 15.95 (*0-7851-0904-8*) Marvel Enterprises.

Lee, Stan, et al. Spider-Man. 1991. (Marvel Masterworks Ser.: Vol. 16). 244p. 34.95 o.s.i (*0-87135-730-5*) Marvel Enterprises.

Marvel Entertainment Staff. Spider Man 99. 1998. 13.95 o.p. (*0-7893-0206-3*) Universe Publishing.

Matthews, Brett. Spider-Man Legends Vol. 4: Spider-Man & Wolverine. 2004. (Illus.). 128p. (YA). pap. 13.99 (*0-7851-1297-9*) Marvel Enterprises.

McCay, Bill. Plague of Perfection. 1996. (Spider-Man Super Thriller Ser.: No. 2). 144p. mass mkt. 4.99 (*0-671-00320-8*, Pocket) Simon & Schuster.

McDonnell, David. Starlog Movie Magic Presents: Spiderman. 2002. pap. 6.99 (*0-88013-048-2*) Profile Entertainment, Inc.

McFarlane, Todd. Spider-Man: Torment. 1992. (Spider-man Ser.). (Illus.). 128p. pap. 15.95 (*0-87135-805-0*) Marvel Enterprises.

Michelinie, David. Spider-Man: Maximum Carnage. 1994. (Illus.). 336p. 24.95 (*0-7851-0038-5*) Marvel Enterprises.

—Spider-Man: The Return of Sinister Six. 1994. (Spider-Man Ser.). (Illus.). 144p. pap. 15.95 (*0-7851-0043-1*) Marvel Enterprises.

—Spider-Man: Venom Returns. 1993. (Illus.). 112p. pap. 12.95 o.p. (*0-87135-966-9*) Marvel Enterprises.

—Spider-Man vs. Doctor Doom. 1995. (Illus.). 64p. pap. 5.95 (*0-7851-0110-1*) Marvel Enterprises.

Michelinie, David & McFarlane, Todd. Spider-Man vs. Venom. 1992. 112p. pap. 12.95 (*0-87135-616-3*) Marvel Enterprises.

Michelinie, David & Smith, Dean W. Carnage in New York. 1995. (Spider-Man Ser.). 336p. (YA). mass mkt. 5.99 o.s.i (*1-57297-019-7*) Boulevard Bks.

Michelinie, David, et al. Spider-Man: Cosmic Adventures. 1993. (Illus.). 192p. pap. 19.95 o.p. (*0-87135-963-4*) Marvel Enterprises.

—Spider-Man: The Assassin Nation Plot. 1992. (Illus.). 144p. pap. 14.95 o.p. (*0-87135-889-1*) Marvel Enterprises.

Milgrom, Al. Spider-Man: Round Robin. 1994. (Illus.). 144p. pap. 15.95 o.p. (*0-7851-0027-X*) Marvel Enterprises.

Olmesdahl, B. & Brown, S. Marvel Super Dice: Spider Man. 1998. 8.95 o.p. (*0-7869-1226-X*) TSR, Inc.

Owsley, Jim, et al. Wolverine vs. Spider-Man. 1990. 64p. 5.95 o.p. (*0-87135-645-7*) Marvel Enterprises.

Putney, Susan & Wrightson, Berni. Spider-Man: Hooky. 1986. 64p. 6.95 o.p. (*0-87135-154-4*) Marvel Enterprises.

Romita, John S., et al. Spider-Man vs. Green Goblin. 1995. (Illus.). 176p. pap. 15.95 (*0-7851-0139-X*) Marvel Enterprises.

Running Press Staff. Spider-Man: The Postcard Book. 1995. 64p. text 8.95 o.p. (*1-56138-648-0*) Running Pr. Bk. Pubs.

Smith, Dean W. Spider-Man: Emerald Mystery. 2000. (Spider-Man Ser.). 224p. mass mkt. 6.99 o.s.i (*0-425-17037-3*) Berkley Publishing Group.

Smith, Dean Wesley. The Goblin's Revenge, No. 2. 1996. (Spider-Man Ser.). 224p. (YA). mass mkt. 5.99 o.s.i (*1-57297-172-X*) Boulevard Bks.

Spider-Man. 1992. (Marvel Masterworks Ser.: Vol. 22). 256p. 34.95 (*0-87135-914-6*) Marvel Enterprises.

Spider-Man. 2002. (J). per. o.p. (*1-57657-786-4*); per. o.p. (*1-57657-785-6*) Paradise Pr., Inc.

Spider-Man - Punisher - Sabretooth: Designer Genes. 64p. 8.95 o.p. (*0-87135-977-4*) Marvel Enterprises.

Spider-Man Unmasked. 1997. pap. text 5.95 (*0-7851-0275-2*) Marvel Enterprises.

Spiderman: Magic Eye. 1996. (Illus.). 32p. 14.95 (*0-8362-1332-7*) Andrews McMeel Publishing.

Stern, Roger. Spider Man: The Secret Story. 1985. 11.95 o.p. (*0-516-02414-0*, Children's Pr.) Scholastic Library Publishing.

Stern, Roger, et al. Spider-Man: Nothing Stops the Juggernaut. 1989. 48p. 4.95 o.p. (*0-87135-572-8*) Marvel Enterprises.

Stockbridge, Grant. The Spider 46 the Man Who Ruled in Hell. 1998. (Spider). (Illus.). 96p. reprint ed. per. 10.00 o.p. (*1-891729-03-9*, S-46) Pulp Adventures, Inc.

Straczynski, J. Michael. The Best of Spider-Man, Vol. 1. 2003. 336p. 34.95 (*0-7851-0900-5*) Marvel Enterprises.

Straczynski, J. Michael & Avery, Fiona. Amazing Spider-Man: Unintended Consequences, 5 vols., Vol. 5. 2003. (Amazing Spider-man Ser.). (Illus.). 144p. (YA). (gr. 6 up). pap. 12.99 (*0-7851-1098-4*) Marvel Enterprises.

Straczynski, J. Michael, et al. The Amazing Spiderman: Coming Home. 2001. (Illus.). 144p. pap. 15.95 (*0-7851-0806-8*) Marvel Enterprises.

Thomas, Roy. Spider-Man: X Men Team-Ups. 1996. (Illus.). 176p. pap. 16.95 (*0-7851-0200-0*) Marvel Enterprises.

Wells, Zeb. Peter Parker: Senseless Violence, 5 vols. 2003. (Spider-Man Ser.: Vol. 5). (Illus.). 160p. (YA). (gr. 7 up). pap. 14.99 (*0-7851-1171-9*) Marvel Enterprises.

Xyz Distributors Staff. Spider-Man: Lights, Camera, Danger! with Sound Stix. 1996. (Spider Man Ser.). pap. text 12.95 o.p. (*1-879332-45-0*) Futech Interactive Products, Inc.

Yomtov, Nel. Spider-Man Adventures, No. 01. 1995. (Illus.). 112p. pap. o.p. (*0-7851-0104-7*) Marvel Enterprises.

## SPOCK (FICTITIOUS CHARACTER)—FICTION

Black Fire. 2000. E-Book 6.99 (*0-7434-1959-6*, Star Trek) Simon & Schuster.

Blish, James. Spock Must Die! 1985. (Star Trek Ser.). 128p. mass mkt. 5.50 o.s.i (*0-553-24634-8*) Bantam Bks.

Bonanno, Margaret W. Dwellers in the Crucible. 1991. (Star Trek: No. 25). 320p. mass mkt. 4.95 (*0-671-74147-0*, Star Trek) Simon & Schuster.

—Probe. Stern, Dave, ed. (Star Trek Ser.). 352p. 1992. 18.95 (*0-671-72420-7*); 1993. reprint ed. mass mkt. 5.99 (*0-671-79065-X*) Simon & Schuster. (Star Trek).

—Probe. abr. ed. 1992. (Star Trek Ser.: Vol. 2). audio 17.00 (*0-671-73727-9*, 297233, Simon & Schuster Audioworks) Simon & Schuster Audio.

—Strangers from the Sky. 1990. (Star Trek Ser.). mass mkt. 5.99 (*0-671-73481-4*, Star Trek) Simon & Schuster.

—Strangers from the Sky. abr. ed. (Star Trek Ser.). 1990. audio 11.00; 1987. audio 11.00 (*0-671-64718-0*, Simon & Schuster Audioworks) Simon & Schuster Audio.

Carey, Diane L. Battlestations! (Star Trek: No. 31). 2000. E-Book 6.99 (*0-7434-1982-0*); 1999. 288p. pap. 3.99 (*0-671-03858-3*) Simon & Schuster. (Star Trek).

—Challenger No. 6: New Earth. 2000. (Star Trek: No. 94). 416p. pap. 6.99 (*0-671-04298-X*, Star Trek) Simon & Schuster.

—Double Helix No. 3: Red Sector. 1999. (Star Trek, The Next Generation Ser.: No. 53). (Illus.). 336p. mass mkt. 6.50 (*0-671-03257-7*, Star Trek) Simon & Schuster.

—Dreadnought! 2000. (Star Trek: No. 29). E-Book 6.99 (*0-7434-1980-4*, Star Trek) Simon & Schuster.

—Fortunes of War No. 2: Battlestations! (Star Trek: No. 31). 1991. mass mkt. 4.99 (*0-671-74025-3*); 1989. mass mkt. 4.50 o.s.i (*0-671-70183-5*) Simon & Schuster. (Star Trek).

Carey, Diane L. & Smith, Dean Wesley. Belle Terre No. 2: New Earth. 2000. (Star Trek: No. 90). (Illus.). 288p. pap. 6.50 (*0-671-04297-1*, Star Trek) Simon & Schuster.

—New Earth No. 2: Belle Terre. 2000. (Star Trek: No. 90). mass mkt. 6.50 (*0-7434-1115-3*, Star Trek) Simon & Schuster.

Carter, Carmen. Dreams of the Raven. (Star Trek: No. 34). 2000. E-Book 6.99 (*0-7434-1985-5*); 1991. mass mkt. 5.50 o.s.i (*0-671-74356-2*) Simon & Schuster. (Star Trek).

Clowes, Carolyn. The Pandora Principle. (Star Trek: No. 49). 2000. E-Book 6.99 (*0-7434-2000-4*); 1990. 288p. mass mkt. 4.99 (*0-671-65815-8*) Simon & Schuster. (Star Trek).

Cogswell, Theodore. Spock, Messiah! 1993. (Star Trek Ser.). 192p. mass mkt. 4.99 o.s.i (*0-553-24674-7*) Bantam Bks.

Cooper, Sonni. Black Fire. 1986. (Star Trek Ser.: No. 8). pap. 1.95 o.s.i (*0-440-82036-7*) Dell Publishing.

—Black Fire. (Star Trek: No. 8). 1989. mass mkt. 4.50 o.s.i (*0-671-70548-2*); 1986. per. 3.50 (*0-671-62747-3*); 1985. mass mkt. 3.50 o.s.i (*0-671-61758-3*); 1983. mass mkt. 2.95 o.s.i (*0-671-83632-3*) Simon & Schuster. (Star Trek).

Correy, Lee, pseud. The Abode of Life. (Star Trek: No. 6). 1989. mass mkt. 4.99 o.s.i (*0-671-70596-2*, Star Trek); 1986. mass mkt. 3.50 o.s.i (*0-671-62746-5*, Star Trek); 1984. 11.80 o.p. (*0-671-90086-2*, Pocket); 1983. mass mkt. 2.95 o.s.i (*0-671-47719-6*, Star Trek) Simon & Schuster.

Crispin, A. C. Sarek. Ryan, Kevin, ed. (Star Trek Ser.). 1999. E-Book 6.99 (*0-671-04112-6*); 1995. 416p. (J). mass mkt. 5.99 (*0-671-79562-7*) Simon & Schuster. (Star Trek).

—Sarek. (Star Trek Ser.). 1994. 448p. 22.00 o.p. (*0-671-79561-9*); 2000. 416p. pap. 3.99 (*0-7434-0374-6*) Simon & Schuster. (Star Trek).

—Sarek. abr. ed. (Star Trek Ser.). 1999. audio 9.98 (*0-671-04480-X*); 1996. audio 17.00 (*0-671-88591-X*) Simon & Schuster Audio. (Simon & Schuster Audioworks).

—Time for Yesterday. 2000. E-Book 6.99 (*0-7434-1990-1*); 1999. (Star Trek Ser.: No. 39). 320p. pap. 3.99 (*0-671-03857-5*); 1989. (Star Trek: No. 39). 288p. mass mkt. 5.50 (*0-671-70094-4*) Simon & Schuster. (Star Trek).

—Time for Yesterday. abr. ed. 1989. (Star Trek Ser.: No. 39). audio 11.00 (*0-671-67017-4*, Simon & Schuster Audioworks) Simon & Schuster Audio.

—Yesterday's Son. (Star Trek: No. 11). 2000. E-Book 6.99 (*0-7434-1962-6*); 1999. 192p. pap. 3.99 (*0-671-03851-6*); 1990. 192p. mass mkt. 4.50 o.s.i (*0-671-72449-5*) Simon & Schuster. (Star Trek).

Culbreath, Myrna & Culbreath, Marshak. Triangle. 2000. (Star Trek: No. 9). E-Book 6.99 (*0-7434-1960-X*, Star Trek) Simon & Schuster.

David, Peter. The Captain's Daughter. 2000. (Star Trek: No. 76). E-Book 6.99 (*0-7434-2027-6*, Star Trek) Simon & Schuster.

—House of Cards. 1997. (Star Trek Ser.: No. 1). 168p. per. 3.99 o.s.i (*0-671-01395-5*, Star Trek) Simon & Schuster.

—The Rift. Stern, Dave, ed. 1991. (Star Trek: No. 57). 288p. mass mkt. 4.99 (*0-671-74796-7*, Star Trek) Simon & Schuster.

David, Peter, et al. Disinherited. 1992. (Star Trek: No. 59). 272p. mass mkt. 4.99 (*0-671-77958-3*, Star Trek) Simon & Schuster.

—The Disinherited. (Star Trek: No. 59). E-Book 6.99 (*0-7434-2010-1*, Star Trek) Simon & Schuster.

DeWeese, Gene. Chain of Attack. (Star Trek: No. 32). 2000. E-Book 6.99 (*0-7434-1983-9*); 1988. 256p. mass mkt. 5.50 (*0-671-66658-4*) Simon & Schuster. (Star Trek).

—Renegade. 2000. (Star Trek: No. 55). E-Book 6.99 (*0-7434-2006-3*, Star Trek) Simon & Schuster.

—Renegade. Stern, Dave, ed. 1991. (Star Trek: No. 55). 256p. mass mkt. 4.95 (*0-671-65814-X*, Star Trek) Simon & Schuster.

Dillard, J. M. Demons. (Star Trek: No. 30). 2000. E-Book 6.99 (*0-7434-1981-2*); 1990. mass mkt. 4.50 (*0-671-70877-5*) Simon & Schuster. (Star Trek).

—The Final Frontier. abr. ed. (Star Trek Ser.: No. 5). audio 7.95. 1990. audio 7.95 (*0-671-68507-4*, Simon & Schuster Audioworks) Simon & Schuster Audio.

—The Lost Years. 1989. (Star Trek Ser.). (Illus.). 320p. 17.95 o.p. (*0-671-68293-8*, Star Trek) Simon & Schuster.

—The Lost Years. Stern, David, ed. 1990. (Star Trek). 448p. reprint ed. mass mkt. 5.99 (*0-671-70795-7*, Star Trek) Simon & Schuster.

—The Lost Years. abr. ed. 1989. (Star Trek Ser.: Vol. 2). audio 15.95 o.s.i (*0-671-68632-1*, Simon & Schuster Audioworks) Simon & Schuster Audio.

—Mindshadow. (Star Trek: No. 27). 2000. E-Book 6.99 (*0-7434-1978-2*); 1989. 256p. mass mkt. 5.50 (*0-671-70420-6*) Simon & Schuster. (Star Trek).

—Star Trek 5: The Final Frontier. 1989. (Star Trek Ser.: No. 5). mass mkt. 4.50 (*0-671-68008-0*, Star Trek) Simon & Schuster.

—The Undiscovered Country. Stern, Dave, ed. 1992. (Star Trek Ser.: No. 6). 320p. mass mkt. 5.50 (*0-671-75883-7*, Pocket) Simon & Schuster.

—The Undiscovered Country. abr. ed. 1992. (Star Trek Ser.: No. 6). audio 11.00 (*0-671-75873-X*, Simon & Schuster Audioworks) Simon & Schuster Audio.

Duane, Diane. Doctor's Orders. (Star Trek: No. 50). 2000. E-Book 6.99 (*0-7434-2001-2*); 1990. 288p. mass mkt. 5.50 (*0-671-66189-2*) Simon & Schuster. (Star Trek).

—Spock's World. (Star Trek Ser.). 1989. 400p. mass mkt. 6.50 (*0-671-66773-4*); 1988. pap. 16.95 o.p. (*0-671-66851-X*); 2000. 400p. pap. 3.99 (*0-7434-0371-1*) Simon & Schuster. (Star Trek).

—Spock's World. abr. ed. 1989. (Star Trek Ser.). audio 16.00 (*0-671-67917-1*, Simon & Schuster Audioworks) Simon & Schuster Audio.

—The Wounded Sky. (Star Trek: No. 13). 2000. E-Book 6.99 (*0-7434-1964-2*); 1991. 224p. mass mkt. 5.50 o.s.i (*0-671-74352-X*) Simon & Schuster. (Star Trek).

Dwellers in the Crucible. 2000. E-Book 6.99 (*0-7434-1976-6*, Star Trek) Simon & Schuster.

Fantasimulations Associates Staff. Triangle. 1985. (Star Trek Ser.: No. 9). 92p. (Orig.). pap. 12.00 o.p. (*0-931787-25-4*) FASA Corp.

Flinn, Denny Martin. Fearful Summons. 1995. (Star Trek: No. 74). 288p. mass mkt. 5.50 (*0-671-89007-7*, Star Trek) Simon & Schuster.

—The Fearful Summons. 2000. (Star Trek: No. 74). E-Book 6.99 (*0-7434-2025-X*, Star Trek) Simon & Schuster.

Fontana, D. C. Vulcan's Glory. 2000. (Star Trek Ser.). E-Book 6.99 (*0-7434-1995-2*); 1991. (Star Trek: No. 44). mass mkt. 4.95 (*0-671-74291-4*) Simon & Schuster. (Star Trek).

Ford, John M. How Much for Just the Planet?, No. 2. 1999. (Star Trek Ser.: No. 36). 256p. pap. 3.99 (*0-671-03859-1*, Star Trek) Simon & Schuster.

—Worlds Apart No. 2: How Much for Just the Planet? 2000. (Star Trek: No. 36). E-Book 6.99 (*0-7434-1987-1*, Star Trek) Simon & Schuster.

—Worlds Apart No. 2: How Much for Just the Planet? Stern, Dave, ed. 1990. (Star Trek: No. 36). mass mkt. 4.99 o.s.i (*0-671-72214-X*, Star Trek) Simon & Schuster.

Foster, Alan Dean. Star Trek Log One. 1975. (Star Trek Ser.). reprint ed. lib. bdg. 22.95 (*0-88411-081-8*) Amereon, Ltd.

—Star Trek Logs One, Two & Three. 1992. (Star Trek Ser.). mass mkt. 4.99 o.s.i (*0-345-38247-1*, Del Rey) Ballantine Bks.

—Star Trek Logs Seven, Eight & Nine. 1993. (Star Trek Ser.). mass mkt. 5.99 o.s.i (*0-345-38561-6*, Del Rey) Ballantine Bks.

Friedman, Michael Jan. Crossover. (Star Trek, The Next Generation Ser.). E-Book 6.99 (*0-7434-2066-7*); 1996. 320p. mass mkt. 5.99 (*0-671-89676-8*); 1995. 320p. 23.00 o.p. (*0-671-89677-6*) Simon & Schuster. (Star Trek).

—Crossover. abr. ed. 1995. (Star Trek Ser.). audio 17.00 o.s.i (*0-671-53628-1*, Simon & Schuster Audioworks) Simon & Schuster Audio.

—Enterprise No. 3: My Brother's Keeper. 1999. (Star Trek My Brother's Keeper Ser.: No. 87). 288p. pap. 6.50 (*0-671-01920-1*, Star Trek) Simon & Schuster.

—Faces of Fire. 2000. (Star Trek: No. 58). E-Book 6.99 (*0-7434-2009-8*, Star Trek) Simon & Schuster.

—Faces of Fire. Stern, Dave, ed. 1992. (Star Trek: No. 58). 320p. mass mkt. 5.50 (*0-671-74992-7*, Star Trek) Simon & Schuster.

—Faces of Fire. 1992. (Star Trek Ser.: No. 58). audio 16.00 o.s.i (*0-671-77802-1*, Simon & Schuster Audioworks) Simon & Schuster Audio.

—Legacy. 2000. (Star Trek: No. 56). E-Book 6.99 (*0-7434-2007-1*, Star Trek) Simon & Schuster.

—Legacy. Stern, Dave, ed. 1991. (Star Trek: No. 56). 256p. mass mkt. 4.95 (*0-671-74468-2*, Star Trek) Simon & Schuster.

—Star Trek: Modala Imperative. Kahan, Bob, ed. 1992. (Star Trek Ser.). (Illus.). 208p. pap. 19.95 (*1-56389-040-2*) DC Comics.

Golden, Christie. Last Roundup. 2003. (Star Trek). 352p. pap. 6.99 (*0-7434-4910-X*, Star Trek) Simon & Schuster.

Graf, L. A. Death Count. 2000. (Star Trek: No. 62). E-Book 6.99 (*0-7434-2013-6*, Star Trek) Simon & Schuster.

—Death Count. Stern, Dave, ed. 1992. (Star Trek Ser.: No. 62). 288p. mass mkt. 4.99 (*0-671-79322-5*, Star Trek) Simon & Schuster.

—Ice Trap. 2000. (Star Trek: No. 60). E-Book 6.99 (*0-7434-2011-X*, Star Trek) Simon & Schuster.

Graf, L. A. & Ecklar, Julia. Ice Trap. Stern, Dave, ed. 1992. (Star Trek: No. 60). 288p. mass mkt. 4.99 (*0-671-78068-9*, Star Trek) Simon & Schuster.

Gunn, James & Sturgeon, Theodore. The Joy Machine. 1996. (Star Trek: No. 80). 288p. pap. 5.99 (*0-671-00221-X*, Star Trek) Simon & Schuster.

Hambly, Barbara. Ghost-Walker. (Star Trek: No. 53). 2000. E-Book 6.99 (*0-7434-2004-7*); 1991. 13p. mass mkt. 4.95 o.s.i (*0-671-64398-3*) Simon & Schuster. (Star Trek).

—Ishmael. (Star Trek: No. 23). 2000. E-Book 6.99 (*0-7434-1974-X*); 1991. 256p. mass mkt. 5.50 (*0-671-74355-4*); 1990. mass mkt. 4.50 o.s.i (*0-671-73587-X*) Simon & Schuster. (Star Trek).

Hawke, Simon. The Patrian Transgression. 1994. (Star Trek: No. 69). 288p. mass mkt. 5.50 (*0-671-88044-6*, Star Trek) Simon & Schuster.

The Joy Machine. 2000. No. 80. E-Book 6.99 (*0-7434-2031-4*, Star Trek) Simon & Schuster.

Kagan, Janet. Uhura's Song. (Star Trek: No. 21). 384p. 1987. mass mkt. 5.50 (*0-671-65227-3*); 1985. mass mkt. 3.50 o.s.i (*0-671-54730-5*); 2000. pap. 3.99 (*0-7434-0373-8*) Simon & Schuster. (Star Trek).

—Uhura's Song. 1985. (Star Trek Ser.: No. 21). 373p. 20.00 o.p. (*0-89366-169-4*) Ultramarine Publishing Co., Inc.

Kramer-Rolls, Dana. Home Is the Hunter. 2000. (Star Trek: No. 52). E-Book 6.99 (*0-7434-2003-9*, Star Trek) Simon & Schuster.

Larson, Majliss. Pawns & Symbols. 2000. (Star Trek: No. 26). E-Book 6.99 (*0-7434-1977-4*, Star Trek) Simon & Schuster.

Lorrah, Jean. The Vulcan Academy Murders. (Star Trek: No. 20). 2000. E-Book 6.99 (*0-7434-1971-5*); 1991. mass mkt. 4.95 (*0-671-74283-3*); 1990. mass mkt. 4.50 o.s.i (*0-671-72367-7*) Simon & Schuster. (Star Trek).

Marshak, Sondra & Culbreath, Myrna. The Prometheus Design. (Star Trek: No. 5). 1990. mass mkt. 5.50 (*0-671-72366-9*); 1982. mass mkt. 2.50 o.s.i (*0-671-83398-7*); 1982. E-Book 6.99 (*0-7434-1212-5*) Simon & Schuster. (Star Trek).

—Triangle. (Star Trek: No. 9). 1991. mass mkt. 5.50 (*0-671-74351-1*); 1986. per. 3.50 (*0-671-62748-1*); 1985. mass mkt. 3.50 o.s.i (*0-671-60548-8*); 1983. mass mkt. 2.95 o.s.i (*0-671-49298-5*) Simon & Schuster. (Star Trek).

McIntyre, Vonda N. Enterprise: The First Adventure. (Star Trek Ser.). 1990. mass mkt. 5.99 (*0-671-73032-0*); 1988. 320p. mass mkt. 4.50 o.s.i (*0-671-65912-X*) Simon & Schuster. (Star Trek).

—Enterprise: The First Adventure. 1988. (Star Trek Ser.). audio 11.00 (*0-671-62951-4*, Simon & Schuster Audioworks) Simon & Schuster Audio.

—The Entropy Effect. (Star Trek: No. 2). 1990. mass mkt. 5.50 (*0-671-72416-9*); 1986. pap. 3.50 (*0-671-62743-0*); 1985. mass mkt. 3.50 o.s.i (*0-671-62229-3*); 1983. 224p. mass mkt. 2.95 o.s.i (*0-671-49300-0*); 1981. E-Book 6.99 (*0-7434-1209-5*); 1981. mass mkt. 2.50 o.s.i (*0-671-83692-7*) Simon & Schuster. (Star Trek).

—The Entropy Effect. abr. ed. 1988. (Star Trek: No. 2). audio 11.00 (*0-671-66864-1*, Simon & Schuster Audioworks) Simon & Schuster Audio.

—The Search for Spock. 1990. (Star Trek: No. 17). mass mkt. 5.50 (*0-671-73133-5*, Star Trek) Simon & Schuster.

—The Wrath of Khan. (Star Trek: No. 7). 1991. mass mkt. 5.50 (*0-671-74149-7*); 1984. mass mkt. 2.95 o.s.i (*0-671-55248-1*) Simon & Schuster. (Star Trek).

McIntyre, Vonda N., et al. Star Trek Boxed Set: The Entropy Effect; The Covenant of the Crown; Yesterday's Son; The IDIC Epidemic. 1991. (Star Trek: Nos. 2, 4, 11, 38). pap. 18.00 (*0-671-96368-6*, Pocket) Simon & Schuster.

Milan, Victor. From the Depths. (Star Trek: No. 66). 2000. E-Book 6.99 (*0-7434-2017-9*); 1993. 288p. mass mkt. 5.50 (*0-671-86911-6*) Simon & Schuster. (Star Trek).

Mitchell, V. E. Enemy Unseen. Stern, David, ed. 1990. (Star Trek: No. 51). 288p. mass mkt. 4.99 (*0-671-68403-5*, Star Trek) Simon & Schuster.

—Windows on a Lost World. Stern, Dave, ed. 1993. (Star Trek: No. 65). 288p. mass mkt. 5.99 (*0-671-79512-0*, Star Trek) Simon & Schuster.

—Windows on a Lost World. abr. ed. 1993. (Star Trek Ser.: No. 65). audio 17.00 (*0-671-86962-0*, 391662, Simon & Schuster Audioworks) Simon & Schuster Audio.

Murdock, M. S. Web of the Romulans. 2000. E-Book 6.99 (*0-7434-1961-8*); 1989. (Star Trek: No. 10). mass mkt. 5.50 o.s.i (*0-671-70093-6*) Simon & Schuster. (Star Trek).

Nelson, Majiliss. Pawns & Symbols. 1988. (Star Trek: No. 26). 288p. (Orig.). mass mkt. 5.50 o.s.i (*0-671-66497-2*, Star Trek) Simon & Schuster.

Oltion, Jerry. Mudd in Your Eye. (Star Trek: No. 81). 2000. E-Book 6.99 (*0-7434-2032-2*); 1997. 304p. pap. 5.99 (*0-671-00260-0*) Simon & Schuster. (Star Trek).

Pasotti, Robert, et al. Vulcan's Forge. 1997. (Star Trek Ser.). 352p. 23.00 o.s.i (*0-671-00926-5*, Star Trek) Simon & Schuster.

The Patrian Transgression. 2000. (Star Trek Ser.: No. 69). E-Book 6.99 (*0-7434-2020-9*, Star Trek) Simon & Schuster.

Paul, Barbara. The Three-Minute Universe. 1991. (Star Trek: No. 41). mass mkt. 4.95 o.s.i (*0-671-74358-9*, Star Trek) Simon & Schuster.

Peel, John. Where No Man Has Gone Before. 1986. (Star Trek Ser.). 96p. lib. bdg. 19.95 o.p. (*0-8095-8019-5*) Millefleurs.

Reeves-Stevens, Garfield. Memory Prime. 2000. (Star Trek: No. 42). E-Book 6.99 (*0-7434-1993-6*, Star Trek) Simon & Schuster.

Reeves-Stevens, Garfield & Reeves-Stevens, Judith. Memory Prime. 1991. (Star Trek: No. 42). 320p. mass mkt. 5.50 (*0-671-74359-7*, Star Trek) Simon & Schuster.

Reeves-Stevens, Judith. Prime Directive. abr. ed. 2001. (Star Trek Ser.). audio 9.98 (*0-671-04465-6*, Simon & Schuster Audioworks) Simon & Schuster Audio.

Reeves-Stevens, Judith & Reeves-Stevens, Garfield. Prime Directive. Stern, David, ed. 1990. (Star Trek Ser.). 416p. 18.95 (*0-671-70772-8*, Star Trek) Simon & Schuster.

—Prime Directive. Stern, Dave, ed. 1991. (Star Trek Ser.). 416p. reprint ed. mass mkt. 5.99 (*0-671-74466-6*, Star Trek) Simon & Schuster.

—Prime Directive. abr. ed. 1990. (Star Trek Ser.). audio 15.95 (*0-671-72631-5*, Simon & Schuster Audioworks) Simon & Schuster Audio.

The Rift. 2000. E-Book 6.99 (*0-7434-2008-X*, Star Trek) Simon & Schuster.

Roddenberry, Gene. The Motion Picture. 1979. (Star Trek: No. 1). E-Book 6.99 (*0-7434-1208-7*, Star Trek) Simon & Schuster.

—Star Trek: The Motion Picture. (Star Trek: No. 1). 1984. mass mkt. 2.95 o.s.i (*0-671-54685-6*); 1980. mass mkt. 2.95 o.s.i (*0-671-83089-9*) Simon & Schuster. (Star Trek).

Roddenberry, Gene, et al. Star Trek: The Motion Picture. 1979. (Star Trek: No. 1). 252 p. o.p. (*0-671-25324-7*, Simon & Schuster) Simon & Schuster.

Rotsler, William. Distress Call. Barish, Wendy, ed. 1982. (Star Trek Ser.). (Illus.). (Orig.). (J). (gr. 3-7). pap. 2.85 o.s.i (*0-671-46389-6*, Simon & Schuster Children's Publishing) Simon & Schuster Children's Publishing.

Rusch, Kristine K. & Smith, Dean Wesley. Thin Air, No. 5. 2000. (Star Trek Ser.: No. 93). 256p. pap. 6.50 (*0-671-78577-X*, Star Trek) Simon & Schuster.

Sargent, Pamela & Zebrowski, George. Garth of Izar. 2003. (Star Trek). 288p. pap. 6.99 (*0-7434-0641-9*, Star Trek) Simon & Schuster.

—Heart of the Sun. 1997. (Star Trek Ser.: No. 83). 304p. per. 5.99 (*0-671-00237-6*, Star Trek) Simon & Schuster.

Shatner, William. Ashes of Eden. Ryan, Kevin, ed. 1995. (Star Trek Ser.). 320p. 23.00 o.p. (*0-671-52035-0*, Star Trek) Simon & Schuster.

—Preserver. (Star Trek Ser.). reprint ed. 2001. 448p. pap. 6.99 (*0-671-02126-5*); 2001. E-Book 23.95 (*0-7434-1955-3*); 2000. (Illus.). (J). E-Book 23.95 (*0-7434-1119-6*) Simon & Schuster. (Star Trek).

—Preserver. abr. ed. 2000. (Star Trek Ser.). audio 18.00 (*0-7435-0031-8*, Simon & Schuster Audioworks) Simon & Schuster Audio.

Shatner, William, et al. Ashes of Eden. 1996. (Star Trek Ser.). 320p. mass mkt. 6.99 (*0-671-52036-9*, Star Trek) Simon & Schuster.

—Ashes of Eden. abr. ed. 1995. (Star Trek Ser.). audio 18.00 o.s.i (*0-671-52892-0*, 392990, Simon & Schuster Audioworks) Simon & Schuster Audio.

—Avenger. (Star Trek Ser.). 1998. (Illus.). 416p. pap. 7.99 (*0-671-55131-0*, Star Trek); 1997. per. 6.99 (*0-671-01744-6*, Pocket); 1997. 384p. 23.00 o.s.i (*0-671-55132-9*, Star Trek) Simon & Schuster.

—Avenger. abr. ed. 1989. (Star Trek Ser.). audio 18.00 (*0-671-57524-4*, 395166, Simon & Schuster Audioworks) Simon & Schuster Audio.

—Dark Victory. (Star Trek Ser.). 320p. 1999. 23.00 o.s.i (*0-671-00882-X*); 2000. reprint ed. pap. 6.99 (*0-671-00884-6*) Simon & Schuster. (Star Trek).

—Preserver. 2000. (Star Trek Ser.). 384p. 23.95 o.s.i (*0-671-02125-7*, Star Trek) Simon & Schuster.

—The Return. (Star Trek Ser.). 1997. 400p. mass mkt. 6.99 (*0-671-52609-X*, Star Trek); 1996. 384p. 22.00 o.p. (*0-671-52610-3*, Atria) Simon & Schuster.

—The Return. abr. ed. 1996. (Star Trek Ser.). audio 18.00 o.s.i (*0-671-56848-5*, 393928, Simon & Schuster Audioworks) Simon & Schuster Audio.

—Star Trek: The Ashes of Eden. 2001. (Star Trek Ser.). (Illus.). 94p. pap. 14.95 (*1-56389-235-9*) DC Comics.

—Star Trek: The Return. l.t. ed. 1996. (Star Trek Ser.). 456p. 24.95 (*1-56895-359-3*, Wheeler Publishing, Inc.) Gale Group.

Sherman, Josepha & Shwartz, Susan. Vulcan's Forge. 1998. (Star Trek Ser.). 288p. pap. 6.50 (*0-671-00927-3*, Star Trek) Simon & Schuster.

—Vulcan's Forge. abr. ed. 1995. (Star Trek Ser.: Vol. 2). audio 18.00 (*0-671-57621-6*, Simon & Schuster Audioworks) Simon & Schuster Audio.

—Vulcan's Heart. (Star Trek Ser.). 2000. per. 6.50 (*0-7434-1112-9*); 1999. 384p. 23.00 o.s.i (*0-671-01544-3*); 2000. 400p. reprint ed. pap. 6.50 (*0-671-01545-1*) Simon & Schuster. (Star Trek).

—Vulcan's Heart. abr. ed. 1999. (Star Trek Ser.). audio 18.00 (*0-671-04560-1*, Simon & Schuster Audioworks) Simon & Schuster Audio.

Sky, Kathleen. Death's Angel. 1995. (Star Trek Ser.). 224p. mass mkt. 4.99 o.s.i (*0-553-24983-5*, Spectra) Bantam Bks.

—Vulcan. 1998. (Star Trek Ser.). 192p. mass mkt. 5.50 o.s.i (*0-553-24633-X*, Spectra) Bantam Bks.

Smith, Dean W., et al. Rings of Tautee, No. 078. 1996. (Star Trek Ser.: No. 78). 256p. pap. 5.99 (*0-671-00171-X*, Star Trek) Simon & Schuster.

Smith, Dean Wesldy. The Rings of Tautee. 2000. E-Book 6.99 (*0-7434-2029-2*, Star Trek) Simon & Schuster.

Snodgrass, Melinda. The Tears of the Singers. 2000. (Star Trek: No. 19). E-Book 6.99 (*0-7434-1970-7*, Star Trek) Simon & Schuster.

Snodgrass, Melinda M. Tears of the Singers. 1989. (Star Trek: No. 19). mass mkt. 5.50 (*0-671-69654-8*, Star Trek) Simon & Schuster.

Taylor, Jeri. Unification. (Star Trek, The Next Generation Ser.). E-Book 6.99 (*0-7434-2073-X*); 1991. 256p. mass mkt. 5.50 o.s.i (*0-671-77056-X*) Simon & Schuster. (Star Trek).

Van Hise, Della. Killing Time. (Star Trek: No. 24). 2000. E-Book 6.99 (*0-7434-1975-8*); 1989. mass mkt. 4.99 (*0-671-70597-0*) Simon & Schuster. (Star Trek).

Vardeman, Robert E. The Klingon Gambit. (Star Trek: No. 3). 1990. mass mkt. 4.50 (*0-671-70767-1*); 1987. mass mkt. 3.95 o.s.i (*0-671-66342-9*); 1986. per. 3.50 (*0-671-62744-9*); 1985. mass mkt. 3.50 o.s.i (*0-671-62231-5*); 1983. mass mkt. 2.95 o.s.i (*0-671-47720-X*); 1981. E-Book 6.99 (*0-7434-1210-9*) Simon & Schuster. (Star Trek).

Vornholt, John. Mind Meld. 1997. (Star Trek Ser.: No. 82). 304p. per. 5.99 o.s.i (*0-671-00258-9*, Star Trek) Simon & Schuster.

—Sanctuary. 2000. (Star Trek: No. 61). E-Book 6.99 (*0-7434-2012-8*, Star Trek) Simon & Schuster.

—Sanctuary. Stern, Dave, ed. 1992. (Star Trek Ser.: No. 61). 288p. mass mkt. 4.99 (*0-671-76994-4*, Star Trek) Simon & Schuster.

Weinstein, Howard. The Covenant of the Crown. (Star Trek: No. 4). 1989. mass mkt. 4.50 (*0-671-70078-2*); 1988. mass mkt. 3.95 o.s.i (*0-671-67072-7*); 1983. 192p. mass mkt. 2.95 o.s.i (*0-671-49297-7*); 1981. E-Book 6.99 (*0-7434-1211-7*) Simon & Schuster. (Star Trek).

—Deep Domain. (Star Trek: No. 33). 2000. E-Book 6.99 (*0-7434-1984-7*); 1989. mass mkt. 5.50 (*0-671-70549-0*); 1988. 288p. mass mkt. 3.95 o.s.i (*0-671-67077-8*) Simon & Schuster. (Star Trek).

Weinstein, Howard, et al. Star Trek: Revisitations. Kahan, Bob, ed. 1996. (Star Trek Ser.). (Illus.). 176p. pap. 19.95 (*1-56389-223-5*) DC Comics.

Windows on a Lost World. 2000. (Star Trek Ser.: No. 65). E-Book 6.99 (*0-7434-2016-0*, Star Trek) Simon & Schuster.

**SPRAGGUE, MICHAEL (FICTITIOUS CHARACTER)—FICTION**

Barnes, Linda. Bitter Finish. 1985. 208p. mass mkt. 4.95 o.s.i (*0-449-20690-4*, Fawcett) Ballantine Bks.

—Bitter Finish. l.t. ed. 2000. 263p. lib. bdg. 28.95 (*1-58547-031-7*) Ctr. Point Large Print.

—Bitter Finish. 1994. 272p. mass mkt. 5.99 o.s.i (*0-440-21606-0*) Dell Publishing.

—Bitter Finish. 1983. 192p. 11.95 o.p. (*0-312-08236-3*) St. Martin's Pr.

—Blood Will Have Blood. 1986. 192p. mass mkt. 5.99 o.s.i (*0-449-20901-6*, Fawcett) Ballantine Bks.

—Blood Will Have Blood. 1985. 192p. pap. 2.25 o.p. (*0-380-79368-7*, 79368, Avon Bks.) Morrow/Avon.

—Cities of the Dead. l.t. ed. 1991. 8.95 o.p. (*0-7451-9581-4*, 5059); pap. 10.95 o.p. (*0-7927-0009-0*, 4616) BBC Audiobooks America.

—Cities of the Dead. 1987. mass mkt. 4.99 o.s.i (*0-449-21188-6*, Fawcett) Ballantine Bks.

—Cities of the Dead. 1996. 272p. mass mkt. 5.99 o.s.i (*0-440-22095-5*) Dell Publishing.

—Cities of the Dead. 1985. 224p. 14.95 o.p. (*0-312-13940-3*) St. Martin's Pr.

—Dead Heat. 1985. 256p. mass mkt. 4.99 o.s.i (*0-449-20689-0*, Fawcett) Ballantine Bks.

—Dead Heat. 1995. 288p. mass mkt. 5.99 o.s.i (*0-440-21862-4*) Dell Publishing.

—Dead Heat. 1984. 224p. 11.95 o.p. (*0-312-18498-0*) St. Martin's Pr.

**SPRING, PENNY (FICTITIOUS CHARACTER)—FICTION**

Arnold, Margot, pseud. The Cape Cod Caper. 1982. (Murder Mystery Ser.). 192p. 2.50 (*0-86721-206-3*, Jove) Berkley Publishing Group.

—The Cape Cod Caper. 1988. (Penny Spring & Sir Toby Glendower Mystery Ser.). 192p. pap. 7.95 (*0-88150-116-6*, Foul Play) Norton, W. W. & Co., Inc.

—The Cape Cod Conundrum. (Penny Spring & Sir Toby Glendower Mystery Ser.). 224p. 1992. text 20.00 o.p. (*0-88150-244-8*); 1994. reprint ed. pap. 7.95 (*0-88150-293-6*) Norton, W. W. & Co., Inc. (Foul Play).

—The Catacomb Conspiracy. 1992. (Penny Spring & Sir Toby Glendower Mystery Ser.). 260p. 18.95 o.p. (*0-88150-208-1*) Countryman Pr.

—The Catacomb Conspiracy. 1993. (Penny Spring & Sir Toby Glendower Mystery Ser.). 240p. pap. 7.95 (*0-88150-255-3*, Foul Play) Norton, W. W. & Co., Inc.

—Death of a Voodoo Doll. 1989. 220p. reprint ed. pap. 7.95 (*0-88150-132-8*, Foul Play) Norton, W. W. & Co., Inc.

—Death on the Dragon's Tongue. 1982. 224p. 2.50 (*0-86721-150-4*, Jove) Berkley Publishing Group.

—Death on the Dragon's Tongue. 1990. (Penny Spring & Sir Toby Glendower Mystery Ser.). 224p. reprint ed. pap. 7.95 (*0-88150-158-1*, Foul Play) Norton, W. W. & Co., Inc.

—Dirge for a Dorset Druid. (Penny Spring & Sir Toby Glendower Mystery Ser.). 240p. 1995. pap. 7.95 (*0-88150-334-7*); 1993. 20.00 (*0-88150-266-9*) Norton, W. W. & Co., Inc. (Foul Play).

—Exit Actors, Dying. 1982. 176p. 2.50 (*0-86721-181-4*, Jove) Berkley Publishing Group.

—Exit Actors, Dying. 1988. (Penny Spring & Sir Toby Glendower Mystery Ser.). 176p. reprint ed. pap. 7.95 (*0-88150-115-8*, Foul Play) Norton, W. W. & Co., Inc.

—Lament for a Lady Laird. 1982. 224p. 2.50 (*0-86721-132-6*, Jove) Berkley Publishing Group.

—Lament for a Lady Laird. 1990. (Penny Spring & Sir Toby Glendower Mystery Ser.). 224p. reprint ed. pap. 7.95 (*0-88150-159-X*, Foul Play) Norton, W. W. & Co., Inc.

—The Menehune Murders. 1989. (Penny Spring & Sir Toby Glendower Mystery Ser.). 240p. 17.95 o.p. (*0-88150-149-2*) Countryman Pr.

—The Menehune Murders. 1991. (Penny Spring & Sir Toby Glendower Mystery Ser.). 260p. pap. 7.95 (*0-88150-196-4*, Foul Play) Norton, W. W. & Co., Inc.

—The Midas Murders. 1995. (Penny Spring & Sir Toby Glendower Mystery Ser.). 224p. 20.00 (*0-88150-340-1*, Foul Play) Norton, W. W. & Co., Inc.

—The Midas Murders: A Penny Spring & Sir Toby Glendower Mystery. 1997. (Penny Spring & Sir Toby Glendower Mystery Ser.). 224p. pap. 7.95 (*0-88150-394-0*) Norton, W. W. & Co., Inc.

—Toby's Folly. 1990. 256p. 18.95 o.p. (*0-88150-177-8*) Countryman Pr.

—Toby's Folly. 1992. (Penny Spring & Sir Toby Glendower Mystery Ser.). 256p. pap. 7.95 (*0-88150-228-6*, Foul Play) Norton, W. W. & Co., Inc.

—Zadok's Treasure. 1982. 192p. 2.50 (*0-86721-228-4*, Jove) Berkley Publishing Group.

—Zadok's Treasure. 1989. (Penny Spring & Sir Toby Glendower Mystery Ser.). 192p. reprint ed. pap. 7.95 (*0-88150-133-6*, Foul Play) Norton, W. W. & Co., Inc.

**SPRINGER, JULIA (FICTITIOUS CHARACTER)—FICTION**

Ross, Ann B. Miss Julia Hits the Road. 2003. 9p. 89.95 (*0-7927-2873-4*); 7p. 59.95 (*0-7927-2872-6*) BBC Audiobooks America.

—Miss Julia Hits the Road. unabr. ed. 2003. audio 34.95 (*0-06-053225-4*, HarperAudio) HarperTrade.

—Miss Julia Hits the Road. 2004. 352p. pap. 14.00 (*0-14-200404-9*) Penguin Group (USA) Inc.

—Miss Julia Hits the Road. l.t. ed. 2003. (Basic Ser.). 30.95 (*0-7862-5497-1*) Thorndike Pr.

—Miss Julia Hits the Road. 2003. 320p. 24.95 (*0-670-03207-7*, Viking) Viking Penguin.

—Miss Julia Speaks Her Mind: A Novel. 2000. 288p. pap. 13.00 (*0-688-17775-1*); 1999. 273p. 23.00 (*0-688-16788-8*, Morrow, William & Co.) Morrow/Avon.

—Miss Julia Speaks Her Mind: A Novel. l.t. ed. 1999. (Thorndike Senior Lifestyle Ser.). 393p. 27.95 (*0-7862-2255-7*) Thorndike Pr.

—Miss Julia Takes Over. 2002. 336p. reprint ed. pap. 14.00 (*0-14-200089-2*) Penguin Group (USA) Inc.

—Miss Julia Takes Over. l.t. ed. 2001. (Thorndike Press Large Print Senior Lifestyles Ser.). 482p. 28.95 (*0-7862-3515-2*) Thorndike Pr.

—Miss Julia Takes Over. 2001. 352p. 24.95 o.s.i (*0-670-91026-0*, Viking) Viking Penguin.

—Miss Julia Throws a Wedding. 2003. 336p. pap. 14.00 (*0-14-200271-2*) Penguin Group (USA) Inc.

—Miss Julia Throws a Wedding. l.t. ed. 2002. (Basic Ser.). 453p. 28.95 o.p. (*0-7862-4561-1*) Thorndike Pr.

—Miss Julia Throws a Wedding. 2002. 304p. text 24.95 (*0-670-03105-4*, Viking) Viking Penguin.

**SPROWLS, DOLLY MADISON (FICTITIOUS CHARACTER)—FICTION**

Corwin, C. R. The Cross Kisses Back: A Morgue Mama Mystery. 2003. 327p. 24.95 o.s.i (*1-59058-074-5*) Poisoned Pen Pr.

**SQUIRES, LEE (FICTITIOUS CHARACTER)—FICTION**

Andreae, Christine. Grizzly: A Mystery. 1996. (WWL Mystery Ser.). per. (*0-373-26202-7*, 1-26202-1, Worldwide Library) Harlequin Enterprises, Ltd.

—Grizzly: A Mystery. pap. 15.95 (*0-312-29259-7*, Saint Martin's Griffin); 1994. 288p. 19.95 o.p. (*0-312-11433-8*, Saint Martin's Minotaur) St. Martin's Pr.

—A Small Target. 1998. (WWL Mystery Ser.). per. (*0-373-26264-7*, 1-26264-1, Worldwide Library) Harlequin Enterprises, Ltd.

—A Small Target, Vol. 1. 1996. 272p. 21.95 o.p. (*0-312-14543-8*, Saint Martin's Minotaur) St. Martin's Pr.

—Trail of Murder. 1995. (Mystery Ser.). 253p. per. (*0-373-26183-7*, 1-26183-3, Worldwide Library) Harlequin Enterprises, Ltd.

—Trail of Murder. 1992. 256p. 17.95 o.p. (*0-312-08327-0*, Saint Martin's Minotaur) St. Martin's Pr.

**STAGNORO, DANTE (FICTITIOUS CHARACTER)—FICTION**

Gores, Joe. Menaced Assassin. 1994. 336p. 19.95 o.s.i (*0-89296-542-8*) Mysterious Pr.

—Menaced Assassin. 1995. 384p. mass mkt. 5.50 (*0-446-40390-3*) Warner Bks., Inc.

**STAINLESS STEEL RAT (FICTITIOUS CHARACTER)—FICTION**

*see Digriz, James Bolivar (Fictitious Character)—Fiction*

**STAINTON, ALEC (FICTITIOUS CHARACTER)—FICTION**

Murray, Stephen. Fatal Opinions. 1992. 256p. 18.95 o.p. (*0-312-08193-6*, Saint Martin's Minotaur) St. Martin's Pr.

**STANISLASKI FAMILY (FICTITIOUS CHARACTERS)—FICTION**

Roberts, Nora. Convincing Alex. 1994. mass mkt. (*0-373-09872-3*, 5-09872-8, Silhouette) Harlequin Enterprises, Ltd.
—Falling for Rachel. 1993. per. (*0-373-09810-3*, 5-09810-8, Silhouette) Harlequin Enterprises, Ltd.
—Luring a Lady. l.t. ed. 1994. (Silhouette Special Edition Ser.). 17.95 o.p. (*0-373-58894-1*) BBC Audiobooks America.
—Luring a Lady. 1991. (Silhouette Special Edition Ser.: No. 709). mass mkt. (*0-373-09709-3*, Harlequin Bks.) Harlequin Enterprises, Ltd.
—The Stanislaski Brothers: Two Complete Novels. 2000. (Illus.). 448p. mass mkt. (*0-373-48422-4*, Harlequin Bks.) Harlequin Enterprises, Ltd.
—The Stanislaski Sisters, 2 bks. in 1. 1997. mass mkt. (*0-373-20134-6*, 1-20134-2, Harlequin Bks.) Harlequin Enterprises, Ltd.
—Taming Natasha. l.t. ed. 1992. (Special Edition Ser.). pap. 15.95 o.p. (*0-373-58577-2*) BBC Audiobooks America.
—Taming Natasha. 1990. (Silhouette Special Edition Ser.: No. 583). pap. (*0-373-09583-X*, Silhouette) Harlequin Enterprises, Ltd.
—Waiting for Nick. 1997. (Silhouette Special Edition Ser.: Vol. 1088). (Illus.). 244p. mass mkt. (*0-373-24088-0*, 1-24088-6, Silhouette) Harlequin Enterprises, Ltd.
—Waiting for Nick. l.t. ed. 1999. (Silhouette Romance Ser.). 218p. 21.95 (*0-373-59651-0*) Silhouette Bks. GBR. *Dist:* Thorndike Pr.

**STANTON, GREY (FICTITIOUS CHARACTER)—FICTION**

Brandon, Jay. Deadbolt. 1985. mass mkt. 2.95 o.s.i (*0-553-25184-8*) Bantam Bks.
—Deadbolt. 1999. (Mystery Ser.). 213p. 19.95 (*0-7862-1815-0*, Five Star) Gale Group.
—Deadbolt. Isaacson, Dana, ed. 1992. 288p. reprint ed. mass mkt. 4.99 (*0-671-70887-2*, Pocket) Simon & Schuster.

**STAPLETON, JACK (FICTITIOUS CHARACTER)—FICTION**

Cook, Robin. Contagion. 1996. 496p. reprint ed. pap. 7.99 (*0-425-15594-3*) Berkley Publishing Group.
—Contagion. 1996. 384p. 24.95 o.p. (*0-399-14106-5*, G. P. Putnam's Sons) Penguin Group (USA) Inc.

**STAPLETON FAMILY (FICTITIOUS CHARACTER)—FICTION**

Fleming, Thomas J. Promises to Keep. 1978. 10.00 o.p. (*0-385-13555-6*) Doubleday Publishing.
—Promises to Keep. 1980. 400p. pap. 2.50 o.s.i (*0-446-91192-5*) Warner Bks., Inc.
—Remember the Morning. 1998. 544p. mass mkt. 6.99 (*0-8125-0849-1*); 1997. 384p. 24.95 o.p. (*0-312-86308-X*) Doherty, Tom Assocs., LLC. (Forge Bks.).
—Remember the Morning. 1999. 24.95 (*0-312-87100-7*) St. Martin's Pr.
—The Spoils of War. 1986. 640p. mass mkt. 4.50 (*0-380-70065-4*, Avon Bks.) Morrow/Avon.
—The Spoils of War. 1985. 528p. 18.95 o.p. (*0-399-12968-5*, G. P. Putnam's Sons) Penguin Putnam Bks. for Young Readers.
—The Wages of Fame. 1999. 688p. mass mkt. 6.99 (*0-8125-7182-7*); 1998. 461p. 26.95 (*0-312-86309-8*) Doherty, Tom Assocs., LLC. (Forge Bks.).

**STAR, JADE (FICTITIOUS CHARACTER)—FICTION**

Coulter, Catherine. Midnight Star. 1986. mass mkt. 4.50 o.p. (*0-451-15379-0*, Signet Bks.) NAL.

**STARBRANCH, HARRY (FICTITIOUS CHARACTER)—FICTION**

Bean, Gregory. A Death in Victory: A Harry Starbranch Mystery. 1997. 323p. 24.95 o.p. (*0-312-15512-3*, Saint Martin's Minotaur) St. Martin's Pr.
—Grave Victory. 1998. (Harry Starbranch Mysteries Ser.). 336p. 23.95 (*0-312-18590-1*, Saint Martin's Minotaur) St. Martin's Pr.
—Long Shadows in Victory: A Harry Starbranch Mystery. (Dead Letter Mysteries Ser.). 1997. 336p. mass mkt. 5.99 (*0-312-96217-7*, St. Martin's Paperbacks); 1996. 352p. 23.95 o.p. (*0-312-14348-6*, Saint Martin's Minotaur) St. Martin's Pr.
—No Comfort in Victory: A Sheriff Harry Starbranch Mystery. 353p. 1996. mass mkt. 5.99 o.p. (*0-312-95877-3*, St. Martin's Paperbacks); 1995. 23.95 o.p. (*0-312-13133-X*, Saint Martin's Minotaur) St. Martin's Pr.

**STARBUCK, JESSICA (FICTITIOUS CHARACTER)—FICTION**

Ellis, Wesley. The Chicago Showdown. 1993. (Lone Star Ser.: No. 126). 192p. (Orig.). mass mkt. 3.99 o.s.i (*0-515-11044-2*, Jove) Berkley Publishing Group.
—Lone Star & a Comstock Crossfire, No. 78. 1989. mass mkt. 2.95 o.s.i (*0-515-09925-2*, Jove) Berkley Publishing Group.
—Lone Star & a Saloon Called Hell. 1994. (Lone Star Ser.: No. 143). 192p. (Orig.). mass mkt. 3.99 o.s.i (*0-515-11408-1*, Jove) Berkley Publishing Group.
—Lone Star & Deep Water Princess. 1992. (Lone Star Ser.: No. 116). 192p. mass mkt. 3.50 o.s.i (*0-515-10833-2*, Jove) Berkley Publishing Group.
—Lone Star & Hickok's Ghost. 1988. mass mkt. 2.95 o.s.i (*0-515-09586-9*, Jove) Berkley Publishing Group.
—Lone Star & the Alaskan Guns. 1985. (Lone Star Ser.: No. 40). 192p. mass mkt. 2.50 o.s.i (*0-515-08423-9*, Jove) Berkley Publishing Group.
—Lone Star & the Alaskan Renegades No. 104. 1991. mass mkt. 2.95 o.s.i (*0-515-10592-9*, Jove) Berkley Publishing Group.
—Lone Star & the Amarillo Rifles, No. 29. 1985. 192p. mass mkt. 2.50 o.s.i (*0-515-08082-9*, Jove) Berkley Publishing Group.
—Lone Star & the Apache Revenge, No. 21. 1984. 192p. mass mkt. 2.50 o.s.i (*0-515-07533-7*, Jove) Berkley Publishing Group.
—Lone Star & the Apache Warrior. 1985. (Lone Star Ser.: No. 37). 192p. mass mkt. 2.50 o.s.i (*0-515-08344-5*, Jove) Berkley Publishing Group.
—Lone Star & the Arizona Gunmen. 1990. (Lone Star Ser.: No. 91). mass mkt. 2.95 o.s.i (*0-515-10271-7*, Jove) Berkley Publishing Group.
—Lone Star & the Arizona Stranger. 1989. (Lone Star Ser.: No. 87). mass mkt. 2.95 o.s.i (*0-515-10174-5*, Jove) Berkley Publishing Group.
—Lone Star & the Aztec Treasure. 1992. (Lone Star Ser.: No. 123). 192p. mass mkt. 3.99 o.s.i (*0-515-10981-9*, Jove) Berkley Publishing Group.
—Lone Star & the Babary Killers, No. 80. 1989. mass mkt. 2.95 o.s.i (*0-515-09986-4*, Jove) Berkley Publishing Group.
—Lone Star & the Badlands War, No. 16. 1984. 192p. mass mkt. 2.50 o.s.i (*0-515-08199-X*, Jove) Berkley Publishing Group.
—Lone Star & the Bank Robbers. 1990. (Lone Star Ser.: No. 99). mass mkt. 2.95 o.s.i (*0-515-10446-9*, Jove) Berkley Publishing Group.
—Lone Star & the Bellwether Kid. 1993. (Lone Star Ser.: No. 133). 192p. (Orig.). mass mkt. 3.99 o.s.i (*0-515-11195-3*, Jove) Berkley Publishing Group.
—Lone Star & the Biggest Gun in the West. 1985. (Lone Star Ser.: No. 36). 192p. mass mkt. 2.50 o.s.i (*0-515-08332-1*, Jove) Berkley Publishing Group.
—Lone Star & the Black Bandana Gang. 1992. (Lone Star Ser.: No. 117). mass mkt. 3.50 o.s.i (*0-515-10850-2*, Jove) Berkley Publishing Group.
—Lone Star & the Bogus Banker. 1995. (Lone Star Ser.: No. 152). 192p. (Orig.). mass mkt. 3.99 o.s.i (*0-515-11592-4*, Jove) Berkley Publishing Group.
—Lone Star & the Border Bandits, No. 3. 1983. 192p. mass mkt. 2.50 o.s.i (*0-515-07540-X*, Jove) Berkley Publishing Group.
—Lone Star & the Bounty Hunters. 1990. (Lone Star Ser.: No. 97). mass mkt. 2.95 o.s.i (*0-515-10402-7*, Jove) Berkley Publishing Group.
—Lone Star & the Brutus Gang. 1993. (Lone Star Ser.: No. 127). 192p. (Orig.). mass mkt. 3.99 o.s.i (*0-515-11062-0*, Jove) Berkley Publishing Group.
—Lone Star & the Buccaneers. 1992. (Lone Star Ser.: No. 122). 192p. (Orig.). mass mkt. 3.99 o.s.i (*0-515-10956-8*, Jove) Berkley Publishing Group.
—Lone Star & the Buffalo Hunters. 1985. (Lone Star Ser.: No. 35). 192p. mass mkt. 2.50 o.s.i (*0-515-08233-3*, Jove) Berkley Publishing Group.
—Lone Star & the California Gold. 1991. (Lone Star Ser.: No. 105). mass mkt. 2.95 o.s.i (*0-515-10571-6*, Jove) Berkley Publishing Group.
—Lone Star & the California Oil War. 1985. (Lone Star Ser.: No. 39). 192p. mass mkt. 2.50 o.s.i (*0-515-08397-6*, Jove) Berkley Publishing Group.
—Lone Star & the Cheyenne Showdown. 1990. (Lone Star Ser.: No. 100). 192p. mass mkt. 3.50 o.s.i (*0-515-10473-6*, Jove) Berkley Publishing Group.
—Lone Star & the Cheyenne Trackdown, No. 67. 1988. mass mkt. 2.75 o.s.i (*0-515-09492-7*, Jove) Berkley Publishing Group.
—Lone Star & the Colorado Ambush. 1990. (Lone Star Ser.: No. 98). mass mkt. 2.95 o.s.i (*0-515-10427-2*, Jove) Berkley Publishing Group.
—Lone Star & the Comancheros, No. 69. 1988. mass mkt. 2.75 o.s.i (*0-515-09549-4*, Jove) Berkley Publishing Group.
—Lone Star & the Con Man's Ransom, No. 52. 1986. 192p. mass mkt. 2.75 o.s.i (*0-515-08797-1*, Jove) Berkley Publishing Group.
—Lone Star & the Deadly Stranger No. 71. 1988. mass mkt. 2.95 o.s.i (*0-515-09648-2*, Jove) Berkley Publishing Group.
—Lone Star & the Deadly Vigilantes No. 111. 1991. mass mkt. 3.50 o.s.i (*0-515-10709-3*, Jove) Berkley Publishing Group.
—Lone Star & the Deadly Vixens. 1994. (Lone Star Ser.: No. 142). 192p. (Orig.). mass mkt. 3.99 o.s.i (*0-515-11376-X*, Jove) Berkley Publishing Group.
—Lone Star & the Death Chase. 1994. (Lone Star Ser.: No. 138). 192p. (Orig.). mass mkt. 3.99 o.s.i (*0-515-11314-X*, Jove) Berkley Publishing Group.
—Lone Star & the Death Merchants No. 77. 1989. mass mkt. 2.95 o.s.i (*0-515-09876-0*, Jove) Berkley Publishing Group.
—Lone Star & the Death Mine, No. 136. 1993. 192p. (Orig.). mass mkt. 3.99 o.s.i (*0-515-11256-9*, Jove) Berkley Publishing Group.
—Lone Star & the Death Train, No. 57. 1987. 192p. mass mkt. 2.75 o.s.i (*0-515-08960-5*, Jove) Berkley Publishing Group.
—Lone Star & the Denver Madam, No. 13. 1985. 192p. mass mkt. 2.50 o.s.i (*0-515-08219-8*, Jove) Berkley Publishing Group.
—Lone Star & the Devil Worshipers No. 96. 1990. mass mkt. 2.95 o.s.i (*0-515-10386-1*, Jove) Berkley Publishing Group.
—Lone Star & the Devil's Playground No. 106. 1991. mass mkt. 2.95 o.s.i (*0-515-10598-8*, Jove) Berkley Publishing Group.
—Lone Star & the Diamond Swindlers, No. 85. 1989. mass mkt. 2.95 o.s.i (*0-515-10131-1*, Jove) Berkley Publishing Group.
—Lone Star & the Galvanized Yankees. 1995. (Lone Star Ser.: No. 150). 192p. (Orig.). mass mkt. 3.99 o.s.i (*0-515-11552-5*, Jove) Berkley Publishing Group.
—Lone Star & the Gamble of Death. 1990. (Lone Star Ser.: No. 89). mass mkt. 2.95 o.s.i (*0-515-10213-X*, Jove) Berkley Publishing Group.
—Lone Star & the Gemstone Robbers, Vol. 102. 1991. mass mkt. 2.95 o.s.i (*0-515-10513-9*, Jove) Berkley Publishing Group.
—Lone Star & the Ghost Dancers No. 112. 1991. mass mkt. 3.50 o.s.i (*0-515-10734-4*, Jove) Berkley Publishing Group.
—Lone Star & the Ghost Pirates, No. 18. 1984. 192p. mass mkt. 2.50 o.s.i (*0-515-08095-0*, Jove) Berkley Publishing Group.
—Lone Star & the Ghost Ship Pirates No. 130. 1993. 192p. (Orig.). mass mkt. 3.99 o.s.i (*0-515-11120-1*, Jove) Berkley Publishing Group.
—Lone Star & the Gold Mine. 1993. (Lone Star Ser.: No 128). 192p. (Orig.). mass mkt. 3.99 o.s.i (*0-515-11083-3*, Jove) Berkley Publishing Group.
—Lone Star & the Gold Mine War. 1985. (Lone Star Ser.: No. 38). 192p. mass mkt. 2.50 o.s.i (*0-515-08368-2*, Jove) Berkley Publishing Group.
—Lone Star & the Gold Raiders, No. 12. 1984. 192p. mass mkt. 2.50 o.s.i (*0-515-08162-0*, Jove) Berkley Publishing Group.
—Lone Star & the Golden Mesa, No. 33. 1985. 192p. mass mkt. 2.50 o.s.i (*0-515-08191-4*, Jove) Berkley Publishing Group.
—Lone Star & the Great Pilgrim Heist. 1993. (Lone Star Ser.: No. 134). mass mkt. 3.99 o.s.i (*0-515-11217-8*, Jove) Berkley Publishing Group.
—Lone Star & the Gulf Pirates, No. 49. 1986. 192p. mass mkt. 2.75 o.s.i (*0-515-08676-2*, Jove) Berkley Publishing Group.
—Lone Star & the Gunpowder Cure, No. 47. 1986. 192p. mass mkt. 2.50 o.s.i (*0-515-08608-8*, Jove) Berkley Publishing Group.
—Lone Star & the Gunrunners. 1992. (Lone Star Ser.: No. 121). 192p. (Orig.). mass mkt. 3.99 o.s.i (*0-515-10930-4*, Jove) Berkley Publishing Group.
—Lone Star & the Hangrope Heritage, No. 23. 1984. 192p. mass mkt. 2.50 o.s.i (*0-515-07734-8*, Jove) Berkley Publishing Group.
—Lone Star & the Hardrock Payoff, No. 9. 1984. 192p. mass mkt. 2.50 o.s.i (*0-515-08260-0*, Jove) Berkley Publishing Group.
—Lone Star & the Hellbound Pilgrims. 1992. (Lone Star Ser.: No. 113). 192p. mass mkt. 3.50 o.s.i (*0-515-10754-9*, Jove) Berkley Publishing Group.
—Lone Star & the Horse Thieves, No. 115. 1992. mass mkt. 3.50 o.s.i (*0-515-10809-X*, Jove) Berkley Publishing Group.
—Lone Star & the Indian Gold. 1990. (Lone Star Ser.: No. 94). mass mkt. 2.95 o.s.i (*0-515-10335-7*, Jove) Berkley Publishing Group.
—Lone Star & the Indian Rebellion, No. 50. 1986. 192p. mass mkt. 2.75 o.s.i (*0-515-08716-5*, Jove) Berkley Publishing Group.
—Lone Star & the James Gang's Loot, No. 65. 1988. 192p. mass mkt. 2.75 o.s.i (*0-515-09379-3*, Jove) Berkley Publishing Group.
—Lone Star & the Kansas Wolves, No. 4. 1983. 192p. mass mkt. 2.50 o.s.i (*0-515-07419-5*, Jove) Berkley Publishing Group.
—Lone Star & the Land Barons, No. 48. 1986. 192p. mass mkt. 2.50 o.s.i (*0-515-08649-5*, Jove) Berkley Publishing Group.
—Lone Star & the Land Grabbers, No. 6. 1984. 192p. mass mkt. 2.50 o.s.i (*0-515-08258-9*, Jove) Berkley Publishing Group.
—Lone Star & the Lost Gold Mine, No. 68. 1988. mass mkt. 2.75 o.s.i (*0-515-09522-2*, Jove) Berkley Publishing Group.
—Lone Star & the Medicine Lodge Shoot-Out, No. 79. 1989. mass mkt. 2.95 o.s.i (*0-515-09960-0*, Jove) Berkley Publishing Group.
—Lone Star & the Mescalero Outlaws, No. 28. 1984. 192p. mass mkt. 2.50 o.s.i (*0-515-08055-1*, Jove) Berkley Publishing Group.
—Lone Star & the Mexican Muskets. 1992. (Lone Star Ser.: No. 119). 192p. (Orig.). mass mkt. 3.50 o.s.i (*0-515-10881-2*, Jove) Berkley Publishing Group.
—Lone Star & the Mexican Standoff, No. 15. 1984. 192p. mass mkt. 2.50 o.s.i (*0-515-07887-5*, Jove) Berkley Publishing Group.
—Lone Star & the Mission War, No. 46. 1986. 192p. mass mkt. 2.50 o.s.i (*0-515-08581-2*, Jove) Berkley Publishing Group.
—Lone Star & the Montana Land Grab, No. 64. 1987. mass mkt. 2.75 o.s.i (*0-515-09328-9*, Jove) Berkley Publishing Group.
—Lone Star & the Montana Marauders. 1994. (Lone Star Ser.: No. 140). 192p. (Orig.). mass mkt. 3.99 o.s.i (*0-515-11357-3*, Jove) Berkley Publishing Group.
—Lone Star & the Montana Troubles, No. 24. 1984. 192p. (Orig.). mass mkt. 2.50 o.s.i (*0-515-07748-8*, Jove) Berkley Publishing Group.
—Lone Star & the Moon Trail Feud, No. 32. 1985. 192p. mass mkt. 2.50 o.s.i (*0-515-08174-4*, Jove) Berkley Publishing Group.
—Lone Star & the Mountain Man, No. 25. 1984. 192p. mass mkt. 2.50 o.s.i (*0-515-07880-8*, Jove) Berkley Publishing Group.
—Lone Star & the Mountain of Fire. 1995. (Lone Star Ser.: No. 153). 192p. (Orig.). mass mkt. 3.99 o.s.i (*0-515-11613-0*, Jove) Berkley Publishing Group.
—Lone Star & the Mountain of Gold No. 84. 1989. mass mkt. 2.95 o.s.i (*0-515-10108-7*, Jove) Berkley Publishing Group.
—Lone Star & the Nevada Bloodbath. 1988. (Lone Star Ser.: No. 73). mass mkt. 2.95 o.s.i (*0-515-09708-X*, Jove) Berkley Publishing Group.
—Lone Star & the Nevada Gold. 1994. (Lone Star Ser.: No. 147). 192p. (Orig.). mass mkt. 3.99 o.s.i (*0-515-11494-4*, Jove) Berkley Publishing Group.
—Lone Star & the Nevada Mustangs, No. 51. 1986. 192p. mass mkt. 2.75 o.s.i (*0-515-08755-6*, Jove) Berkley Publishing Group.
—Lone Star & the Oklahoma Ambush No. 103. 1991. mass mkt. 2.95 o.s.i (*0-515-10527-9*, Jove) Berkley Publishing Group.
—Lone Star & the Oklahoma Rustlers No. 110. 1991. mass mkt. 3.50 o.s.i (*0-515-10690-9*, Jove) Berkley Publishing Group.
—Lone Star & the Opium Rustlers, No. 2. 1983. 192p. mass mkt. 2.50 o.s.i (*0-515-07520-5*, Jove) Berkley Publishing Group.
—Lone Star & the Oregon Rail Sabotage, No. 45. 1986. 192p. mass mkt. 2.50 o.s.i (*0-515-08570-7*, Jove) Berkley Publishing Group.
—Lone Star & the Outlaw Posse, No. 60. 1987. 192p. mass mkt. 2.75 o.s.i (*0-515-09114-6*, Jove) Berkley Publishing Group.
—Lone Star & the Phantom Gunmen, No. 63. 1987. mass mkt. 2.75 o.s.i (*0-515-09257-6*, Jove) Berkley Publishing Group.
—Lone Star & the Railroad Killers. 1990. (Lone Star Ser.: No. 95). mass mkt. 2.95 o.s.i (*0-515-10353-5*, Jove) Berkley Publishing Group.
—Lone Star & the Railroad War, No. 14. 1984. 192p. mass mkt. 2.50 o.s.i (*0-515-07888-3*, Jove) Berkley Publishing Group.
—Lone Star & the Redemption Massacre, No. 137. 1994. 192p. (Orig.). mass mkt. 3.99 o.s.i (*0-515-11284-4*, Jove) Berkley Publishing Group.
—Lone Star & the Renegade Comanches, No. 10. 1983. 192p. mass mkt. 2.25 o.s.i (*0-515-06235-9*, Jove) Berkley Publishing Group.
—Lone Star & the Renegade Rancher. 1990. (Lone Star Ser.: No. 92). mass mkt. 2.95 o.s.i (*0-515-10287-3*, Jove) Berkley Publishing Group.
—Lone Star & the Rio Grande Bandits, No. 34. 1985. 192p. mass mkt. 2.50 o.s.i (*0-515-08255-4*, Jove) Berkley Publishing Group.
—Lone Star & the Ripper. 1990. (Lone Star Ser.: No. 93). mass mkt. 2.95 o.s.i (*0-515-10309-8*, Jove) Berkley Publishing Group.
—Lone Star & the River of No Return. 1993. (Lone Star Ser.: No. 135). mass mkt. 3.99 o.s.i (*0-515-11239-9*, Jove) Berkley Publishing Group.
—Lone Star & the River Pirates. 1991. (Lone Star Ser.: No. 107). mass mkt. 3.50 o.s.i (*0-515-10614-3*, Jove) Berkley Publishing Group.
—Lone Star & the River Queen. 1994. (Lone Star Ser.: No. 145). 192p. mass mkt. 3.99 o.s.i (*0-515-11455-3*, Jove) Berkley Publishing Group.
—Lone Star & the Riverboat. 1984. (Gamblers Ser.: No. 27). 192p. mass mkt. 2.50 o.s.i (*0-515-07916-2*, Jove) Berkley Publishing Group.
—Lone Star & the Rogue Grizzlies, No. 81. 1989. mass mkt. 2.95 o.s.i (*0-515-10016-1*, Jove) Berkley Publishing Group.
—Lone Star & the Rustler's Ambush, No. 58. 1987. 192p. (Orig.). mass mkt. 2.75 o.s.i (*0-515-09008-5*, Jove) Berkley Publishing Group.
—Lone Star & the San Antonio Rais, No. 17. 1983. 192p. mass mkt. 2.50 o.s.i (*0-515-07353-9*, Jove) Berkley Publishing Group.
—Lone Star & the San Diego Bonanza No. 129. 1993. 192p. (Orig.). mass mkt. 3.99 o.s.i (*0-515-11104-X*, Jove) Berkley Publishing Group.

—Lone Star & the Santa Fe Showdown. 1992. (Lone Star Ser.: No. 120). 192p. (Orig.). mass mkt. 3.99 o.s.i (*0-515-10902-9*, Jove) Berkley Publishing Group.
—Lone Star & the School for Outlaws. 1985. (Lone Star Ser.: No. 30). mass mkt. 2.50 o.s.i (*0-515-08110-8*, Jove) Berkley Publishing Group.
—Lone Star & the Scorpion. 1995. 192p. mass mkt. 3.99 o.s.i (*0-515-11570-3*, Jove) Berkley Publishing Group.
—Lone Star & the Shadow Catcher. 1989. (Lone Star Ser.: No. 88). mass mkt. 2.95 o.s.i (*0-515-10194-X*, Jove) Berkley Publishing Group.
—Lone Star & the Showdowners, No. 8. 1983. 192p. mass mkt. 2.50 o.s.i (*0-515-07521-3*, Jove) Berkley Publishing Group.
—Lone Star & the Sierra Sabotage. 1991. (Lone Star Ser.: No. 101). mass mkt. 2.95 o.s.i (*0-515-10495-7*, Jove) Berkley Publishing Group.
—Lone Star & the Sierra Swindlers, No. 55. 1987. mass mkt. 2.75 o.s.i (*0-515-08908-7*, Jove) Berkley Publishing Group.
—Lone Star & the Silver Bandits No. 72. 1988. mass mkt. 2.95 o.s.i (*0-515-09683-0*, Jove) Berkley Publishing Group.
—Lone Star & the Sky Warriors, No. 61. 1987. mass mkt. 2.75 o.s.i (*0-515-09170-7*, Jove) Berkley Publishing Group.
—Lone Star & the Slaughter Showdown. 1994. (Lone Star Ser.: No. 139). 192p. (Orig.). mass mkt. 3.99 o.s.i (*0-515-11339-5*, Jove) Berkley Publishing Group.
—Lone Star & the Stagecoach War, No. 53. 1987. 192p. mass mkt. 2.75 o.s.i (*0-515-08839-0*, Jove) Berkley Publishing Group.
—Lone Star & the Steel Rail No. 132. 1993. (Lone Star Ser.: No. 132). 192p. (Orig.). mass mkt. 3.99 o.s.i (*0-515-11167-8*, Jove) Berkley Publishing Group.
—Lone Star & the Stockyard Showdown, No. 26. 1984. 192p. mass mkt. 2.50 o.s.i (*0-515-07920-0*, Jove) Berkley Publishing Group.
—Lone Star & the Suicide Spread, No. 75. 1988. mass mkt. 2.95 o.s.i (*0-515-09808-6*, Jove) Berkley Publishing Group.
—Lone Star & the Temperance Army. 1995. (Lone Star Ser.: No. 149). 192p. (Orig.). mass mkt. 3.99 o.s.i (*0-515-11529-0*, Jove) Berkley Publishing Group.
—Lone Star & the Texas Gambler, No. 22. 1984. 192p. mass mkt. 2.50 o.s.i (*0-515-07628-7*, Jove) Berkley Publishing Group.
—Lone Star & the Texas Killers, No. 86. 1989. mass mkt. 2.95 o.s.i (*0-515-10155-9*, Jove) Berkley Publishing Group.
—Lone Star & the Texas Rangers No. 76. 1988. mass mkt. 2.95 o.s.i (*0-515-09848-5*, Jove) Berkley Publishing Group.
—Lone Star & the Texas Tornado. 1994. (Lone Star Ser.: No. 148). 192p. mass mkt. 3.99 o.s.i (*0-515-11506-1*, Jove) Berkley Publishing Group.
—Lone Star & the Timber Pirates, No. 5. 1983. 192p. mass mkt. 2.50 o.s.i (*0-515-07415-2*, Jove) Berkley Publishing Group.
—Lone Star & the Timberland Terror, No. 43. 1986. 192p. mass mkt. 2.50 o.s.i (*0-515-08496-4*, Jove) Berkley Publishing Group.
—Lone Star & the Tombstone Gamble, No. 42. 1986. 192p. mass mkt. 2.50 o.s.i (*0-515-08462-X*, Jove) Berkley Publishing Group.
—Lone Star & the Tong's Revenge, No. 59. 1987. mass mkt. 2.75 o.s.i (*0-515-09057-3*, Jove) Berkley Publishing Group.
—Lone Star & the Trail of Blood. 1994. (Lone Star Ser.: No. 141). 192p. (Orig.). mass mkt. 3.99 o.s.i (*0-515-11392-1*, Jove) Berkley Publishing Group.
—Lone Star & the Trail of Murder No. 124. 1992. 192p. (Orig.). mass mkt. 3.99 o.s.i (*0-515-10998-3*, Jove) Berkley Publishing Group.
—Lone Star & the Trail to Abilene. 1992. (Lone Star Ser.: No. 114). 192p. mass mkt. 3.50 o.s.i (*0-515-10791-3*, Jove) Berkley Publishing Group.
—Lone Star & the Utah Kid, No. 5. 1982. 192p. mass mkt. 2.25 o.s.i (*0-515-06230-8*, Jove) Berkley Publishing Group.
—Lone Star & the Warpath No. 83. 1989. mass mkt. 2.95 o.s.i (*0-515-10062-5*, Jove) Berkley Publishing Group.
—Lone Star & the White River Curse, No. 41. 1986. 192p. mass mkt. 2.50 o.s.i (*0-515-08446-8*, Jove) Berkley Publishing Group.
—Lone Star & the Wolf Pack No. 125. 1993. 192p. (Orig.). mass mkt. 3.99 o.s.i (*0-515-11019-1*, Jove) Berkley Publishing Group.
—Lone Star & the Yuma Prison Break No. 109. 1991. mass mkt. 3.50 o.s.i (*0-515-10670-4*, Jove) Berkley Publishing Group.
—Lone Star in a Range War, No. 62. 1987. 192p. mass mkt. 2.75 o.s.i (*0-515-09216-9*, Jove) Berkley Publishing Group.
—Lone Star in Cripple Creek. 1990. (Lone Star Ser.: No. 90). mass mkt. 2.95 o.s.i (*0-515-10242-3*, Jove) Berkley Publishing Group.
—Lone Star in Hell's Canyon, No. 82. 1989. mass mkt. 2.95 o.s.i (*0-515-10036-6*, Jove) Berkley Publishing Group.
—Lone Star in the Big Horn Mountains, No. 56. 1987. 192p. mass mkt. 2.75 o.s.i (*0-515-08935-4*, Jove) Berkley Publishing Group.
—Lone Star in the Big Thicket. 1988. (Lone Star Ser.: No. 74). mass mkt. 2.95 o.s.i (*0-515-09759-4*, Jove) Berkley Publishing Group.
—Lone Star in the Cherokee Strip, No. 44. 1986. 192p. mass mkt. 2.50 o.s.i (*0-515-08515-4*, Jove) Berkley Publishing Group.
—Lone Star in the Choctaw Nation, No. 108. 1991. mass mkt. 3.50 o.s.i (*0-515-10650-X*, Jove) Berkley Publishing Group.
—Lone Star in the Sierra Diablos, No. 144. 1994. (Lone Star Ser.). 192p. (Orig.). mass mkt. 3.99 o.s.i (*0-515-11436-7*, Jove) Berkley Publishing Group.
—Lone Star in the Timberlands. 1992. (Lone Star Ser.: No. 118). mass mkt. 3.50 o.s.i (*0-515-10866-9*, Jove) Berkley Publishing Group.
—Lone Star on Outlaw Mountain, No. 11. 1984. 192p. mass mkt. 2.50 o.s.i (*0-515-08198-1*, Jove) Berkley Publishing Group.
—Lone Star on the Devil's Trail, No. 20. 1984. 192p. mass mkt. 2.50 o.s.i (*0-515-07436-5*, Jove) Berkley Publishing Group.
—Lone Star on the Hangman's Tale. 1993. (Lone Star Ser.: No. 131). 192p. (Orig.). mass mkt. 3.99 o.s.i (*0-515-11137-6*, Jove) Berkley Publishing Group.
—Lone Star on the Owlhoot Trail, No. 19. 1984. 192p. mass mkt. 2.50 o.s.i (*0-515-07409-8*, Jove) Berkley Publishing Group.
—Lone Star on the Treasure River, No. 31. 1985. 192p. mass mkt. 2.50 o.s.i (*0-515-08043-8*, Jove) Berkley Publishing Group.
—Lone Star On Treachery Trail. 1986. (Lone Star Ser.: No. 1). 192p. mass mkt. 3.99 o.s.i (*0-515-08708-4*, Jove) Berkley Publishing Group.

## STARBUCK, NATHANIEL (FICTITIOUS CHARACTER)—FICTION

Cornwell, Bernard. Copperhead. unabr. ed. 2001. audio 88.00 (*0-7366-6013-5*) Books on Tape, Inc.
—Copperhead. 1994. (Starbuck Chronicles Ser.: Vol. 2). (Illus.). 352p. 15.95 o.p. (*0-06-017766-7*) HarperTrade.
—Copperhead. unabr. ed. 2001. audio 94.95 (*1-85695-915-5*, 950801) ISIS Audio Bks. GBR. *Dist:* Ulverscroft Large Print Bks., Ltd.
—Copperhead. 1995. 448p. mass mkt. 6.99 o.s.i (*0-06-109196-0*, HarperTorch) Morrow/Avon.
—Copperhead. unabr. ed. 1994. (Starbuck Chronicles Ser.: Vol. 2). audio 91.00 (*0-7887-3496-2*, 95778E7) Recorded Bks., LLC.
—Rebel. 2001. audio compact disk 104.00 (*0-7861-9785-4*, z2704); audio 76.25 (*0-7861-1932-2*, 2704) Blackstone Audio Bks., Inc.
—Rebel. unabr. ed. 2001. (Starbuck Chronicles Ser.: Vol. 1). audio 88.00 (*0-7366-8384-4*) Books on Tape, Inc.
—Rebel. (Nathaniel Starbuck Chronicles ). 2001. 416p. pap. 13.95 (*0-06-093461-1*, Perennial); 1993. 320p. 20.00 o.p. (*0-06-017713-6*) HarperTrade.
—Rebel. unabr. ed. 2001. audio 94.95 (*1-85695-914-7*, 960506); audio compact disk 99.95 (*0-7531-1083-0*, 110830) ISIS Audio Bks. GBR. *Dist:* Ulverscroft Large Print Bks., Ltd.
—Rebel. 1994. (Starbuck Chronicles Ser.: Vol. 1). 512p. mass mkt. 6.99 (*0-06-109187-1*, HarperTorch) Morrow/Avon.
—Rebel, unabr. ed. 1993. (Starbuck Chronicles Ser.: Vol. 1). audio 91.00 (*0-7887-3129-7*, 95779E7) Recorded Bks., LLC.

## STARBUCK, SHAWN (FICTITIOUS CHARACTER)—FICTION

Hogan, Ray. Bounty Hunter's Moon. l.t. ed. 2000. (Western Ser.). 201p. 22.95 (*0-7862-2421-5*); (*0-7540-4098-4*); (*0-7540-4097-6*) Thorndike Pr.
—A Bullet for Mr. Texas. 1979. mass mkt. 1.95 o.p. (*0-451-08563-9*, J8563); 1971. mass mkt. 0.60 o.p. (*0-451-04583-1*) NAL. (Signet Bks.).
—A Bullet for Mr. Texas. l.t. ed. 1999. (G. K. Hall Western Ser.). 176p. 25.95 (*0-7838-8613-6*) Thorndike Pr.
—Day of the Hangman. l.t. ed. 2000. (G. K. Hall Western Ser.). 187p. 24.95 (*0-7838-9023-0*, Macmillan Reference USA) Gale Group.
—Deputy of Violence. 1971. mass mkt. 0.60 o.p. (*0-451-04522-X*, Signet Bks.) NAL.
—Deputy of Violence. l.t. ed. 1999. (Western Ser.). 203p. 25.95 (*0-7838-0438-5*) Thorndike Pr.
—The Devil's Gunhand. 1980. 272p. mass mkt. 1.95 o.p. (*0-451-09355-0*, J9355); 1972. mass mkt. 0.75 o.p. (*0-451-05248-X*) NAL. (Signet Bks.).
—The Devil's Gunhand. l.t. ed. 2000. (Western Ser.). 204p. 23.95 (*0-7862-2980-2*) Thorndike Pr.
—The Guns of Stingaree. l.t. ed. 2001. (Thorndike Western Ser.). 211p. 25.95 (*0-7862-3140-8*, Macmillan Reference USA) Gale Group.
—The Guns of Stingaree. 1973. mass mkt. 0.75 o.p. (*0-451-05430-X*, Signet Bks.) NAL.
—The Guns of Stingaree. l.t. ed. 2001. 211p. (*0-7540-4441-6*); (*0-7540-4442-4*) Thorndike Pr.
—The Outlawed. l.t. ed. 1996. (G. K. Hall Western Ser.). 205p. 21.95 (*0-7838-1908-0*, Macmillan Reference USA) Gale Group.
—The Rimrocker. (Rimrocker Ser.). 1978. mass mkt. 1.75 o.p. (*0-451-07888-8*, E7888); 1970. mass mkt. 0.60 o.p. (*0-451-04198-4*) NAL. (Signet Bks.).
—Three Cross. 1970. mass mkt. 0.60 o.p. (*0-451-04396-0*, Signet Bks.) NAL.
—Three Cross. l.t. ed. 2000. (*0-7540-4032-1*); 2000. (*0-7540-4031-3*); 1999. 240p. 23.95 o.p. (*0-7862-2278-6*) Thorndike Pr.
—Three Cross & Deputy of Violence. 1978. (Orig.). mass mkt. 1.75 o.p. (*0-451-08127-7*); mass mkt. 1.95 o.p. (*0-451-09501-4*); mass mkt. 2.50 o.p. (*0-451-11604-6*, AE1604) NAL. (Signet Bks.).

## STARGARD, CONRAD (FICTITIOUS CHARACTER)—FICTION

Frankowski, Leo A. The Cross-Time Engineer. 1998. pap. 5.99 (*0-345-91439-2*, Del Rey) Ballantine Bks.
—The Cross-Time Engineer Bk. 1: In the Adventure of Conrad Stargard. (Orig.). 1989. pap. 3.95 o.p. (*0-345-00991-6*); 1986. 272p. mass mkt. 5.99 o.s.i (*0-345-32762-4*) Ballantine Bks. (Del Rey).
—The Flying Warlord. 1998. pap. 5.99 (*0-345-91442-2*); 1989. 240p. mass mkt. 5.99 o.s.i (*0-345-32765-9*) Ballantine Bks. (Del Rey).
—The High-Tech Knight. 1998. pap. 5.99 (*0-345-91440-6*); 1989. mass mkt. 5.99 o.s.i (*0-345-32763-2*) Ballantine Bks. (Del Rey).
—Lord Conrad's Lady, Vol. 5. 1990. mass mkt. 5.99 o.s.i (*0-345-36849-5*, Del Rey) Ballantine Bks.
—The Radiant Warrior. 1998. pap. 5.99 (*0-345-91441-4*); 1989. (Adventures of Conrad Stargard Ser.: Bk. 3). 288p. mass mkt. 5.99 o.s.i (*0-345-32764-0*) Ballantine Bks. (Del Rey).

## STARHAWK (FICTITIOUS CHARACTER: HAMBLY)—FICTION

Hambly, Barbara. The Dark Hand of Magic. 1990. 320p. mass mkt. 5.99 o.s.i (*0-345-35807-4*, Del Rey) Ballantine Bks.
—The Ladies of Mandrigyn. 1997. pap. 12.00 (*0-345-42059-4*); 1984. 320p. mass mkt. 5.99 o.s.i (*0-345-30919-7*, Del Rey) Ballantine Bks.
—The Witches of Wenshar. (Orig.). 1997. pap. 12.00 (*0-345-42060-8*); 1987. 352p. mass mkt. 5.99 o.s.i (*0-345-32934-1*, Del Rey) Ballantine Bks.

## STARK, EARL (FICTITIOUS CHARACTER)—FICTION

Reasoner, James. Stark's Justice: A Judge Earl Stark Western. l.t. ed. 1994. 21.95 o.p. (*1-56895-153-1*, Wheeler Publishing, Inc.) Gale Group.
—Stark's Justice: A Judge Earl Stark Western. 1994. 224p. mass mkt. 3.99 (*0-671-87140-4*, Pocket) Simon & Schuster.

## STARK, JOANNA (FICTITIOUS CHARACTER)—FICTION

Muller, Marcia. The Cavalier in White. l.t. ed. 1990. 19.95 o.p. (*0-7927-0633-1*, C0594); pap. 17.95 o.p. (*0-7927-0634-X*) BBC Audiobooks America.
—The Cavalier in White. 1993. per. (*0-373-83304-0*, 1-83304-5); 1988. 224p. reprint ed. pap. (*0-373-26008-3*) Harlequin Enterprises, Ltd. (Harlequin Bks.).
—The Cavalier in White. 1986. 256p. 15.95 o.p. (*0-312-12539-9*) St. Martin's Pr.
—Dark Star. l.t. ed. 2000. 218p. 27.95 (*1-57490-327-6*, Beeler Large Print Bks.) Beeler, Thomas T. Publisher.
—Dark Star. 1993. per. (*0-373-83308-3*, 1-83308-6); 1990. 224p. mass mkt. (*0-373-26058-X*) Harlequin Enterprises, Ltd. (Harlequin Bks.).
—Dark Star. 1989. 15.95 o.p. (*0-312-02897-0*, Saint Martin's Minotaur) St. Martin's Pr.
—There Hangs the Knife. 1993. per. (*0-373-83307-5*, 1-83307-8); 1989. mass mkt. (*0-373-26034-2*) Harlequin Enterprises, Ltd. (Harlequin Bks.).
—There Hangs the Knife. 1990. 2.99 o.p. (*0-517-05927-4*) Random Hse. Value Publishing.
—There Hangs the Knife. 1988. 240p. 15.95 o.p. (*0-312-01833-9*, Saint Martin's Minotaur) St. Martin's Pr.

## STARKEY, CAROL (FICTITIOUS CHARACTER)—FICTION

Crais, Robert. Demolition Angel. 2001. 400p. mass mkt. 6.99 (*0-345-43448-X*, Ballantine Bks.) Ballantine Bks.
—Demolition Angel. l.t. ed. 2000. (Wheeler Large Print Book Ser.). 474p. 29.95 (*1-56895-921-4*, Wheeler Publishing, Inc.) Gale Group.
—Demolition Angel. abr. ed. 2000. audio 25.95 (*0-553-52738-X*); audio compact disk 29.95 (*0-553-71208-X*) Random Hse. Audio Publishing Group. (RH Audio).

## STARKEY, DAN (FICTITIOUS CHARACTER)—FICTION

Bateman, Colin. Cycle of Violence. 1997. pap. 12.95 (*1-55970-378-4*); 1996. 256p. 21.95 (*1-55970-349-0*) Arcade Publishing, Inc.
—Divorcing Jack. 1996. 288p. pap. 11.95 (*1-55970-359-8*); 1995. 272p. 19.95 (*1-55970-310-5*) Arcade Publishing, Inc.
—Of Wee Sweetie Mice & Men. 1997. 326p. 23.95 (*1-55970-376-8*) Arcade Publishing, Inc.

## STEELE, KATHERINE, LADY (FICTITIOUS CHARACTER)—FICTION

Boucher, Rita. The Devil's Due. 1996. 224p. mass mkt. 4.99 o.s.i (*0-451-18751-2*, Signet Bks.) NAL.

## STEELE, KATY (FICTITIOUS CHARACTER)—FICTION

Morris, Alan & Morris, Gilbert. Imperial Intrigue. 1996. (Katy Steele Adventures Ser.: Vol. 2). 275p. pap. 8.99 o.p. (*0-8423-2040-7*) Tyndale Hse. Pubs.
—Tracks of Deceit. l.t. ed. 1998. (Christian Fiction Ser.). 357p. 24.95 (*0-7862-1412-0*) Thorndike Pr.
—Tracks of Deceit. 1996. (Katy Steele Adventures Ser.: No. 1). 256p. pap. 8.99 o.p. (*0-8423-2039-3*) Tyndale Hse. Pubs.

## STEELE, RAYFORD (FICTITIOUS CHARACTER)—FICTION

LaHaye, Tim. Apollyon: The Destroyer Is Unleashed. 2002. (Left Behind Ser.: No. 5). E-Book 14.99 (*0-8423-7157-5*) Tyndale Hse. Pubs.
—The Indwelling: The Beast Takes Possession. E-Book 14.99 (*0-8423-7168-0*) Tyndale Hse. Pubs.
—The Mark: The Beast Rules the World. E-Book 14.99 (*0-8423-7180-X*) Tyndale Hse. Pubs.
—Nicolae: The Rise of Antichrist. 2002. (Left Behind Ser.: No. 3). E-Book 14.99 (*0-8423-7137-0*) Tyndale Hse. Pubs.
—Soul Harvest: The World Takes Sides. 2002. (Left Behind Ser.: No. 4). E-Book 14.99 (*0-8423-7148-6*) Tyndale Hse. Pubs.
—Tribulation Force: The Continuing Drama of Those Left Behind. 2002. No. 2. E-Book 14.99 (*0-8423-6157-X*) Tyndale Hse. Pubs.

LaHaye, Tim & Jenkins, Jerry B. Apollyon: The Destroyer Is Unleashed. (Left Behind Ser.: Bk. 5). 2000. audio compact disk 89.00 (*0-7887-4770-3*, C1236E7); 2000. audio 70.00 (*0-7887-4050-4*, 95870E7); Vol. 5. 2001. audio 29.95 (*0-7887-5127-1*); Vol. 5. 2001. audio compact disk 39.95 (*0-7887-5136-0*) Recorded Bks., LLC.
—Apollyon: The Destroyer Is Unleashed. 2000. (Left Behind Ser.: Bk. 5). (SPA.). pap. 9.99 (*0-7899-0655-4*) Spanish Hse. Distributors.
—Apollyon: The Destroyer Is Unleashed. l.t. ed. 2001. (Left Behind Ser.: Bk. 5). 480p. 30.95 (*0-7862-2907-1*) Thorndike Pr.
—Apollyon: The Destroyer Is Unleashed. (Left Behind Ser.: Bk. 5). 2000. audio compact disk 19.99 (*0-8423-4334-2*, Tyndale Audio); 2000. 416p. pap. 14.99 (*0-8423-2926-9*); 1999. 416p. 22.99 (*0-8423-2916-1*); 1999. audio compact disk 15.99 (*0-8423-1933-6*); 2002. 480p. pap. 19.99 (*0-8423-6554-0*) Tyndale Hse. Pubs.
—Armageddon: The Cosmic Battle of the Ages. l.t. ed. 2003. 516p. 31.95 (*0-7862-5640-0*) Thorndike Pr.
—Armageddon: The Cosmic Battle of the Ages. 2003. (Left Behind Ser.). (Illus.). 432p. pap. 14.99 (*0-8423-3236-7*); E-Book 24.99 (*0-8423-8557-6*); (Left Behind Ser.: Vol. 11). (Illus.). 432p. 24.99 (*0-8423-3234-0*); (Left Behind Ser.: Bk. 11). E-Book 24.99 (*0-8423-8575-4*); (Left Behind Ser.). (Illus.). xvi, 395p. pap. 19.99 (*0-8423-6560-5*) Tyndale Hse. Pubs.
—Asesinos. 1999. (Left Behind Ser.: Bk. 6). Tr. of Assassins. (SPA.). pap. 9.99 (*0-7899-0725-9*) Spanish Hse. Distributors.
—Asesinos: Mision: Jerusalen, Blanco: el Anticristo. l.t. ed. 2003. (Left Behind Series - Translation: Assassins Ser.). (SPA.). 543p. 28.95 (*0-7862-5883-7*) Thorndike Pr.
—Assassins: Assignment: Jerusalem, Target: Antichrist. (Left Behind Ser.: Bk. 6). 2000. audio compact disk 97.00 (*0-7887-4900-5*, C1275E7); 2000. audio 77.00 (*0-7887-4400-3*, 95871E7); Vol. 6. 2001. audio 29.95 (*0-7887-5128-X*); Vol. 6. 2001. audio compact disk 39.95 (*0-7887-5137-9*) Recorded Bks., LLC.
—Assassins: Assignment: Jerusalem, Target: Antichrist. l.t. ed. 2001. (Left Behind Ser.: Bk. 6). 509p. 30.95 (*0-7862-2906-3*) Thorndike Pr.
—Assassins: Assignment: Jerusalem, Target: Antichrist. (Left Behind Ser.: Bk. 6). 2000. 448p. pap. 14.99 (*0-8423-2927-7*); 1999. 448p. 22.99 (*0-8423-2920-X*); 1999. audio compact disk 19.99 (*0-8423-3682-6*); 1999. 180p. audio compact disk 15.99 (*0-8423-1934-4*); 2002. 512p. pap. 19.99 (*0-8423-6555-9*) Tyndale Hse. Pubs.
—El Comando Tribulacion. 2000. (Left Behind Ser.: Bk. 2). Tr. of Tribulation Force. (SPA.). pap. 9.99 (*0-7899-0374-1*, 497476) Editorial Unilit.

—El Comando Tribulacion. l.t. ed. 2003. (Left Behind Ser.).Tr. of Tribulation Force. 28.95 (*0-7862-5030-5*) Thorndike Pr.

—Cosecha de Almas. 2000. (Left Behind Ser.: Bk. 4). Tr. of Soul Harvest. (SPA.). pap. 9.99 (*0-7899-0577-9*) Spanish Hse. Distributors.

—Dejados Atras. 2000. (Left Behind Ser.: Bk. 1). Tr. of Left Behind. (SPA.). pap. 8.99 (*0-7899-0373-3*, 497475) Editorial Unilit.

—Dejados Atras. 2002. (Spanish Language Ser.).Tr. of Left Behind. (SPA.). 609p. 28.95 (*0-7862-4895-5*) Thorndike Pr.

—Desecration: Antichrist Takes the Throne. l.t. ed. 2002. 535p. 30.95 (*0-7862-3861-5*) Gale Group.

—Desecration: Antichrist Takes the Throne. 2001. (Left Behind Ser.: Bk. 9). 432p. 24.99 (*0-8423-3226-X*); E-Book 24.99 (*0-8423-7067-6*) Tyndale Hse. Pubs.

—The Indwelling: The Beast Takes Possession. (Left Behind Ser.: Bk. 7). 2001. audio compact disk 89.00 (*0-7887-5156-5*, C1319E7); 2000. audio 76.00 (*0-7887-4670-7*, 96381E7); Vol. 7. 2001. audio 29.95 (*0-7887-5129-8*); Vol. 7. 2001. audio compact disk 39.95 (*0-7887-5138-7*) Recorded Bks., LLC.

—The Indwelling: The Beast Takes Possession. l.t. ed. 2001. (Left Behind Ser.: Bk. 7). 477p. 30.95 (*0-7862-2904-7*) Thorndike Pr.

—The Indwelling: The Beast Takes Possession. (Left Behind Ser.: Bk. 7). 2001. 416p. pap. 14.99 (*0-8423-2929-3*); 2000. 416p. 22.99 (*0-8423-2928-5*); 2000. audio compact disk 19.99 (*0-8423-3966-3*); 2000. 180p. audio compact disk 15.99 (*0-8423-1935-2*, Tyndale Audio); 2002. 464p. pap. 19.99 (*0-8423-6556-7*) Tyndale Hse. Pubs.

—Left Behind: A Novel of the Earth's Last Days. unabr. ed. 1998. (Left Behind Ser.: Bk. 1). audio 64.95 (*1-55686-868-5*) Books in Motion.

—Left Behind: A Novel of the Earth's Last Days. unabr. ed. (Left Behind Ser.: Bk. 1). 2000. audio 34.95 (*0-7887-4972-2*); 2000. audio 34.95 (*0-7887-4972-2*); 1999. audio compact disk 91.00 (*0-7887-3438-5*, C1044E7); 1998. audio 70.00 (*0-7887-2494-0*, 95569E7) Recorded Bks., LLC.

—Left Behind: A Novel of the Earth's Last Days. l.t. ed. 2000. (Left Behind Ser.: Bk. 1). 575p. 29.95 (*0-7862-2468-1*) Thorndike Pr.

—Left Behind: A Novel of the Earth's Last Days. (Left Behind Ser.: Bk. 1). 2000. 352p. mass mkt. 7.99 o.p. (*0-8423-4270-2*); 1996. 320p. pap. 14.99 (*0-8423-2912-9*); 1995. 320p. 22.99 (*0-8423-2911-0*); 2000. audio compact disk 19.99 (*0-8423-4323-7*, Tyndale Audio); 1995. audio compact disk 15.99 (*0-8423-1675-2*); 2001. 560p. pap. 19.99 (*0-8423-5420-4*) Tyndale Hse. Pubs.

—Left Behind: An Experience in Sound & Drama. 1999. (Left Behind Ser.: Bk. 1). audio compact disk 19.99 (*0-8423-5181-7*); audio compact disk 19.99 (*0-8423-5146-9*) Tyndale Hse. Pubs.

—Left Behind Vol. 1: Graphic Novel, 5 vols. 2001. (Left Behind Ser.: Bk. 1). (Illus.). 48p. pap. 5.99 (*0-8423-5502-2*) Tyndale Hse. Pubs.

—Left Behind Vol. 2: Graphic Novel, 5 vols. 2001. (Left Behind Ser.: Bk. 1). (Illus.). 48p. pap. 5.99 (*0-8423-5503-0*) Tyndale Hse. Pubs.

—Left Behind Vol. 3: Graphic Novel, 5 vols. 2002. (Left Behind Ser.: Bk. 1). (Illus.). 48p. pap. 5.99 (*0-8423-5504-9*) Tyndale Hse. Pubs.

—Left Behind Vol. 4: Graphic Novel, 5 vols. 2002. (Left Behind Ser.: Bk. 1). (Illus.). 48p. pap. 5.99 (*0-8423-5505-7*) Tyndale Hse. Pubs.

—Left Behind Vol. 5: Graphic Novel, 5 vols. 2002. (Left Behind Graphic Novel Ser.: Bk. 1). (Illus.). 48p. pap. 5.99 (*0-8423-5506-5*) Tyndale Hse. Pubs.

—Left Behind Collection, Vol 1-6. gif. ed. 2000. (Left Behind Ser.). pap. 77.99 o.p. (*0-8423-1523-3*) Tyndale Hse. Pubs.

—The Left Behind Collection I, Vol. 14. 2001. (Left Behind Ser.). pap. 55.96 (*0-8423-5745-9*) Tyndale Hse. Pubs.

—The Left Behind Collection II Boxed Set, Vol. 58. 2001. (Left Behind Ser.). pap. 55.96 (*0-8423-5746-7*) Tyndale Hse. Pubs.

—La Marca. 2001. (Left Behind Ser.: Bk. 8). Tr. of Mark. (SPA.). pap. 9.99 (*0-7899-0909-X*) Spanish Hse. Distributors.

—The Mark: The Beast Rules the World. l.t. ed. 2001. (Left Behind Ser.: Bk. 8). 389p. 30.95 (*0-7862-3223-4*) Thorndike Pr.

—The Mark: The Beast Rules the World. (Left Behind Ser.: Bk. 8). 2001. 380p. pap. 14.99 (*0-8423-3228-6*); 2000. 400p. 22.99 (*0-8423-3225-1*); 2002. 464p. pap. 19.99 (*0-8423-6557-5*) Tyndale Hse. Pubs.

—Nicolae: The Rise of Antichrist. unabr. ed. 1999. (Left Behind Ser.: Bk. 3). audio 64.95 (*1-55686-889-8*) Books in Motion.

—Nicolae: The Rise of Antichrist. 2000. (Left Behind Ser.: Bk. 3). (SPA.). pap. 9.99 (*0-7899-0457-8*) Editorial Unilit.

—Nicolae: The Rise of Antichrist. unabr. ed. (Left Behind Ser.: Bk. 3). 2000. audio compact disk 97.00 (*0-7887-4638-3*, C1213E7); 1997. audio 72.00 (*0-7887-3478-4*, 95694E7) Recorded Bks., LLC.

—Nicolae: The Rise of Antichrist. (Left Behind Ser.: Bk. 3). 2000. audio compact disk 19.99 (*0-8423-4355-5*, Tyndale Audio); 1998. 432p. pap. 14.99 (*0-8423-2924-2*, 910666Q); 1997. 432p. 22.99 (*0-8423-2914-5*); 1997. audio compact disk 15.99 (*0-8423-1788-0*); 2002. 512p. pap. 19.99 (*0-8423-6552-4*) Tyndale Hse. Pubs.

—El Poseido. 2000. (Left Behind Ser.: Bk. 7). Tr. of Indwelling. (SPA.). pap. 9.99 (*0-7899-0755-0*) Editorial Unilit.

—The Remnant: On the Brink of Armageddon, Vol. 10. 2002. (Left Behind Ser.: No. 10). audio compact disk 39.95 (*1-4025-1819-6*, 00322); audio 29.95 (*1-4025-1860-9*, 01384) Recorded Bks., LLC.

—The Remnant: On the Brink of Armageddon. 2002. (Left Behind Ser.: Bk. 10). audio compact disk 19.99 (*0-8423-3233-2*, Tyndale Audio); 432p. 24.99 (*0-8423-3227-8*) Tyndale Hse. Pubs.

—El Sacrilegio: El Anticristo Toma el Trono. (Left Behind Ser.: No. 9). Tr. of Desecration: Antichrist Takes the Throne. (SPA.). pap. (*0-7899-0985-5*) Editorial Unilit.

—Soul Harvest: The World Takes Sides. (Left Behind Ser.: Bk. 4). 2000. audio compact disk 89.00 (*0-7887-4902-1*, C1277E7); 1999. audio 70.00 (*0-7887-3896-8*, 95693E7); Vol. 4. 2001. audio 29.95 (*0-7887-5126-3*); Vol. 4. 2001. audio compact disk 39.95 (*0-7887-5135-2*) Recorded Bks., LLC.

—Soul Harvest: The World Takes Sides. l.t. ed. 2000. (Left Behind Ser.: Bk. 4). 517p. 29.95 (*0-7862-2905-5*) Thorndike Pr.

—Soul Harvest: The World Takes Sides. (Left Behind Ser.: Bk. 4). 2000. audio compact disk 19.99 (*0-8423-4333-4*, Tyndale Audio); 1999. 448p. pap. 14.99 (*0-8423-2925-0*); 1998. 448p. 22.99 (*0-8423-2915-3*); 1998. audio compact disk 15.99 (*0-8423-5175-2*); 2002. 512p. pap. 19.99 (*0-8423-6553-2*) Tyndale Hse. Pubs.

—Tribulation Force: An Experience in Sound & Drama. 1999. (Left Behind Ser.: Bk. 2). audio compact disk 19.99 (*0-8423-3583-8*) Tyndale Hse. Pubs.

—Tribulation Force: The Continuing Drama of Those Left Behind. unabr. ed. 1996. (Left Behind Ser.: Bk. 2). audio 70.00 (*0-7887-3124-6*, 95692E7) Recorded Bks., LLC.

—Tribulation Force: The Continuing Drama of Those Left Behind. l.t. ed. 2000. (Left Behind Ser.: Bk. 2). 552p. 29.95 (*0-7862-2471-1*) Thorndike Pr.

—Tribulation Force: The Continuing Drama of Those Left Behind. (Left Behind Ser.: Bk. 2). 1996. 450p. pap. 14.99 (*0-8423-2921-8*); 1996. 450p. 22.99 (*0-8423-2913-7*); 2002. 528p. pap. 19.99 (*0-8423-6551-6*) Tyndale Hse. Pubs.

—Tribulation Force Vol. 1: Graphic Novel. 2002. (Left Behind Ser.: Bk. 2). (Illus.). 48p. pap. 5.99 (*0-8423-5759-9*) Tyndale Hse. Pubs.

—Tribulation Force Vol. 2: Graphic Novel. 2002. (Left Behind Ser.: Bk. 2). (Illus.). 48p. pap. 5.99 (*0-8423-5760-2*) Tyndale Hse. Pubs.

**STEFANOS, NICK (FICTITIOUS CHARACTER)—FICTION**

Pelecanos, George P. The Big Blowdown. 1999. 320p. pap. 14.95 (*0-312-24291-3*, Saint Martin's Griffin); 1996. 304p. 24.95 o.p. (*0-312-14284-6*) St. Martin's Pr.

—Down by the River Where the Dead Men Go. 1998. 240p. pap. text o.p. (*1-85242-529-6*) Serpent's Tail Ltd.

—Down by the River Where the Dead Men Go. 1999. 216p. pap. 13.00 (*1-85242-716-7*) Serpent's Tail Ltd. GBR. *Dist:* Consortium Bk. Sales & Distribution.

—Down by the River Where the Dead Men Go. 1995. 240p. 20.95 o.p. (*0-312-13056-2*, Saint Martin's Minotaur) St. Martin's Pr.

—A Firing Offense. 1999. 224p. pap. 13.00 (*1-85242-715-9*); 1998. 216p. pap. text 12.99 o.p. (*1-85242-563-6*) Serpent's Tail Ltd. GBR. *Dist:* Consortium Bk. Sales & Distribution.

—A Firing Offense. 1992. 224p. 17.95 o.p. (*0-312-06970-7*, Saint Martin's Minotaur) St. Martin's Pr.

—Nick's Trip. 1998. 276p. pap. o.p. (*1-85242-562-8*) Serpent's Tail Ltd.

—Nick's Trip. 1999. 288p. pap. 13.00 (*1-85242-714-0*) Serpent's Tail Ltd. GBR. *Dist:* Consortium Bk. Sales & Distribution.

—Nick's Trip. 1993. 276p. 18.95 o.p. (*0-312-08862-0*, Saint Martin's Minotaur) St. Martin's Pr.

—Shame the Devil. 2000. 304p. 24.95 (*0-316-69523-8*) Little Brown & Co.

—The Sweet Forever. 1999. 384p. mass mkt. 6.99 (*0-440-23493-X*) Dell Publishing.

—The Sweet Forever. 1998. 304p. (gr. 8). 23.95 (*0-316-69109-7*) Little Brown & Co.

**STEFANOVICH, JOHN (FICTITIOUS CHARACTER)—FICTION**

Patterson, James. The Midnight Club. 1993. pap. 5.99 o.p. (*0-8041-9803-9*); 1990. 256p. mass mkt. 5.99 o.s.i (*0-8041-0597-9*) Ballantine Bks. (Ivy Bks.).

—The Midnight Club. l.t. ed. 1999. (Large Print Book Ser.). pap. 24.95 o.p. (*1-56895-716-5*, Wheeler Publishing, Inc.) Gale Group.

—The Midnight Club. 1989. 320p. 17.95 o.p. (*0-316-69363-4*) Little Brown & Co.

—The Midnight Club. 1999. 368p. reprint ed. mass mkt. 7.99 (*0-446-60638-3*) Warner Bks., Inc.

**STELLA THE STARGAZER (FICTITIOUS CHARACTER)—FICTION**

Jorgensen, Christine T. Curl up & Die. 1998. (WWL Mystery Ser.). per. (*0-373-26266-3*, 1-26266-6, Worldwide Library) Harlequin Enterprises, Ltd.

—Curl up & Die: A Stella the Stargazer Mystery. 1997. (Stella the Stargazer Mystery Ser.). 224p. 21.95 (*0-8027-3288-7*) Walker & Co.

—Dead on Her Feet. 2000. (Stella the Stargazer Mystery Ser.). 253p. per. (*0-373-26344-9*, Harlequin Bks.) Harlequin Enterprises, Ltd.

—Dead on Her Feet. 1999. (Stella the Stargazer Mystery Ser.). 256p. 23.95 (*0-8027-3334-4*) Walker & Co.

—Death of a Dustbunny. 1999. (WWL Mystery Ser.: Bk. 308). per. (*0-373-26308-2*, 1-26308-6, Harlequin Bks.) Harlequin Enterprises, Ltd.

—Death of a Dustbunny. l.t. ed. 1998. (Stella the Stargazer Mystery Ser.). 246p. 22.95 (*0-8027-3315-8*) Walker & Co.

—A Love to Die For. 1997. (Mystery Ser.). 256p. per. (*0-373-26231-0*, 1-262310, Worldwide Library) Harlequin Enterprises, Ltd.

—A Love to Die For. 1994. 214p. 19.95 (*0-8027-3188-0*) Walker & Co.

—You Bet Your Life. 1997. 48p. per. (*0-373-26245-0*, 1-26245-0, Worldwide Library) Harlequin Enterprises, Ltd.

—You Bet Your Life: A Stella the Stargazer Mystery. 1995. 224p. 19.95 (*0-8027-3265-8*) Walker & Co.

**STEN (FICTITIOUS CHARACTER: COLE)—FICTION**

Cole, Allan. Sten. 1982. mass mkt. 2.50 o.s.i (*0-345-28503-4*) Ballantine Bks.

Cole, Allan & Bunch, Chris. The Court of a Thousand Suns. 1985. 288p. (Orig.). mass mkt. 4.99 o.s.i (*0-345-31681-9*, Ballantine Bks.) Ballantine Bks.

—Fleet of the Damned. 1988. 352p. mass mkt. 4.99 o.s.i (*0-345-33172-9*, Del Rey) Ballantine Bks.

—The Return of the Emperor. 1990. (Sten Adventure Ser.: No. 6). mass mkt. 5.99 o.s.i (*0-345-36130-X*, Del Rey) Ballantine Bks.

—Revenge of the Damned. 1989. mass mkt. 5.99 o.s.i (*0-345-33173-7*, Del Rey) Ballantine Bks.

—Sten. 1988. pap. o.p. (*0-345-00692-5*); 1984. mass mkt. 5.99 o.s.i (*0-345-32460-9*) Ballantine Bks. (Del Rey).

—Vortex. 1992. mass mkt. 4.99 o.s.i (*0-345-37151-8*, Ballantine Bks.) Ballantine Bks.

—The Wolf Worlds. 1984. 304p. mass mkt. 5.99 o.s.i (*0-345-31229-5*, Ballantine Bks.) Ballantine Bks.

**STERN, ALEJANDRO 'SANDY' (FICTITIOUS CHARACTER)—FICTION**

Turow, Scott. The Burden of Proof. 1990. audio 8.95 American Audio Prose Library, Inc.

—The Burden of Proof. unabr. collector's ed. 1990. audio 96.00 (*0-7366-1786-8*, 2623) Books on Tape, Inc.

—The Burden of Proof. 1990. 640p. 30.00 (*0-374-11734-9*); 367.20 o.p. (*0-374-11735-7*); 640p. E-Book 9.95 o.p. (*0-374-70091-5*); E-Book 22.95 (*0-374-70093-1*); E-Book 22.92 (*0-374-70092-3*) Farrar, Straus & Giroux.

—The Burden of Proof. l.t. ed. 1991. (General Ser.). 690p. 14.95 o.p. (*0-8161-5125-3*); 14.95 o.p. (*0-8161-5132-6*) Gale Group. (Macmillan Reference USA).

—The Burden of Proof. abr. ed. 1990. audio 17.00 (*0-671-70743-4*, Simon & Schuster Audioworks) Simon & Schuster Audio.

—The Burden of Proof. reprint ed. 2000. 608p. pap. 14.95 (*0-446-67712-4*); 1991. 576p. mass mkt. 7.99 (*0-446-36058-9*) Warner Bks., Inc.

—Presumed Innocent. 1989. audio 13.95 (*1-55644-337-4*, 9061) American Audio Prose Library, Inc.

—Presumed Innocent. unabr. collector's ed. 1988. audio 80.00 (*0-7366-1336-6*, 2239) Books on Tape, Inc.

—Presumed Innocent. 1987. 480p. 30.00 (*0-374-23713-1*); E-Book 4.95 (*0-374-70111-3*); E-Book 4.95 (*0-374-70117-2*); E-Book 4.95 (*0-374-70109-1*); E-Book 4.95 o.p. (*0-374-70108-3*) Farrar, Straus & Giroux.

—Presumed Innocent. l.t. ed. 1988. (General Ser.). 606p. 13.95 o.p. (*0-8161-4470-2*, Macmillan Reference USA) Gale Group.

—Presumed Innocent. 1999. (*0-7621-0254-3*) Reader's Digest Assn., Inc., The.

—Presumed Innocent. abr. ed. 1988. 17.00 incl. audio (*0-671-65218-4*, Simon & Schuster Audioworks) Simon & Schuster Audio.

—Presumed Innocent. reprint ed. 2000. 512p. pap. 14.95 (*0-446-67644-6*); 1989. 432p. mass mkt. 7.99 (*0-446-35986-6*) Warner Bks., Inc.

**STEVENS, DELTA 'STORM' (FICTITIOUS CHARACTER)—FICTION**

Silva, Linda K. Storm Rising: A Delta Stevens Mystery. 2000. 241p. pap. 12.00 (*1-883061-27-X*) Rising Tide Pr.

—Tropical Storm. 1996. 245p. pap. 11.99 (*1-883061-14-8*) Rising Tide Pr.

**STEVENS, TED (FICTITIOUS CHARACTER)—FICTION**

Crump, David. Conflict of Interest: A Novel about Trial Lawyers, Greed, Passion, Power, Revenge...& Justice. 1997. 288p. (Orig.). pap. 14.95 (*0-89407-122-X*, 122X) Strawberry Hill Pr.

Lewis, Terry. Conflict of Interest. 1998. 352p. mass mkt. 5.99 o.s.i (*0-7860-0539-4*, Pinnacle Bks.) Kensington Publishing Corp.

—Conflict of Interest. 1997. 328p. 18.95 (*1-56164-132-4*) Pineapple Pr., Inc.

**STEWART, BLAINE (FICTITIOUS CHARACTER)—FICTION**

Zukowski, Sharon. Dancing in the Dark. 1994. (Mystery Ser.). mass mkt. (*0-373-26148-9*, 1-26148-6, Harlequin Bks.) Harlequin Enterprises, Ltd.

—Dancing in the Dark. 1992. 224p. 17.95 o.p. (*0-312-08174-X*, Saint Martin's Minotaur) St. Martin's Pr.

—The Hour of the Knife. 1993. (Mystery Ser.). mass mkt. (*0-373-26123-3*, 1-26123-9, Harlequin Bks.) Harlequin Enterprises, Ltd.

—The Hour of the Knife. 1991. 208p. 17.95 o.p. (*0-312-06372-5*, Saint Martin's Minotaur) St. Martin's Pr.

—Jungleland. 1999. pap. 22.95 (*0-525-93917-2*); 1997. 384p. mass mkt. 5.99 o.s.i (*0-451-19253-2*, Signet Bks.) NAL.

—Leap of Faith. 240p. pap. 3.98 o.p. (*0-7651-0402-4*) Smithmark Pubs., Inc.

—Leap of Faith: A Blaine Stewart Mystery. 1994. (Blaine Stewart Mystery Ser.). 256p. 18.95 o.p. (*0-525-93897-4*, Dutton) Dutton/Plume.

—Leap of Faith: A Blaine Stewart Mystery. 1995. (Blaine Stewart Mystery Ser.). 256p. mass mkt. 4.99 o.s.i (*0-451-18273-1*, Signet Bks.) NAL.

—Prelude to Death: A Blaine Stewart Mystery. 1996. (Blaine Stewart Mystery Ser.). 256p. 20.95 o.p. (*0-525-94079-0*, Dutton) Dutton/Plume.

—Prelude to Death: A Blaine Stewart Mystery. 1997. (Blaine Stewart Mystery Ser.). 272p. mass mkt. 5.50 o.s.i (*0-451-18272-3*) NAL.

**STEWART, JOHN (FICTITIOUS CHARACTER)—FICTION**

Ridley, John. Stray Dogs. 2003. (Illus.). 176p. pap. 11.95 (*0-345-41346-6*) Ballantine Bks.

**STEWART, KELLEN (FICTITIOUS CHARACTER)—FICTION**

Scott, Manda. Hen's Teeth. 1999. 352p. mass mkt. 5.50 (*0-553-57967-3*) Bantam Bks.

—Night Mares. 1999. 320p. mass mkt. 5.50 (*0-553-57968-1*) Bantam Bks.

—Stronger Than Death. 2000. 304p. mass mkt. 5.50 (*0-553-57969-X*) Bantam Bks.

**STEWART, LINDA (FICTITIOUS CHARACTER)—FICTION**

Borgenicht, Miriam. No Duress. 1992. (WWL Mystery Ser.). per. (*0-373-26105-5*, 1-26105-6, Harlequin Bks.) Harlequin Enterprises, Ltd.

—No Duress. 1991. 192p. 15.95 o.p. (*0-312-05934-5*, Saint Martin's Minotaur) St. Martin's Pr.

Borthwick, J. S. Dolly Is Dead. 324p. 1996. mass mkt. 6.50 (*0-312-95675-4*, St. Martin's Paperbacks); 1995. 22.95 o.p. (*0-312-13052-X*, Saint Martin's Minotaur) St. Martin's Pr.

**STEWART, TEAL (FICTITIOUS CHARACTER)—FICTION**

Lamb, J. Dayne. A Question of Preference: A Teal Stewart Mystery. 1995. mass mkt. 4.99 o.s.i (*0-8217-5099-2*); 1994. 304p. mass mkt. 16.95 o.s.i (*0-8217-4631-6*) Kensington Publishing Corp.

—Questionable Behavior. 1993. 288p. mass mkt. 3.99 o.s.i (*0-8217-4333-3*, Zebra Bks.) Kensington Publishing Corp.

—Unquestioned Loyalty: A Teal Stewart Mystery. 1996. 352p. mass mkt. 4.99 o.s.i (*1-57566-054-7*); 1995. mass mkt. 16.95 o.s.i (*0-8217-5090-9*) Kensington Publishing Corp.

**STILLWATER, MARTIN (FICTITIOUS CHARACTER)—FICTION**

Koontz, Dean. Mr. Murder. 1994. 496p. mass mkt. 7.99 (*0-425-14442-9*) Berkley Publishing Group.

—Mr. Murder. 1993. 416p. 23.95 o.p. (*0-399-13874-9*, G. P. Putnam's Sons); (Illus.). (J). 150.00 o.p. (*0-399-13899-4*, Puffin Bks.) Penguin Group (USA) Inc.

**STOCK, JOAN (FICTITIOUS CHARACTER)—FICTION**

Tourney, Leonard. The Bartholomew Fair Murders. 1987. 256p. reprint ed. mass mkt. 4.99 o.s.i (*0-345-34370-0*) Ballantine Bks.

—The Bartholomew Fair Murders. 1986. 240p. 14.95 o.p. (*0-312-06710-0*) St. Martin's Pr.

—Familiar Spirits. 1989. 240p. mass mkt. 3.50 o.s.i (*0-345-34372-7*) Ballantine Bks.

—Familiar Spirits. 1984. 224p. 13.95 o.p. (*0-312-28025-4*) St. Martin's Pr.

—Frobisher's Savage. 1994. 304p. 20.95 o.p. (*0-312-11437-0*, Saint Martin's Minotaur) St. Martin's Pr.

—Knaves Templar. 1992. mass mkt. 3.99 o.s.i (*0-345-37335-9*) Ballantine Bks.

—Knaves Templar. 1991. 17.95 o.p. (*0-312-04961-7*, Saint Martin's Minotaur) St. Martin's Pr.

—Low Treason. 1989. mass mkt. 3.50 o.s.i (*0-345-34368-9*) Ballantine Bks.

—Low Treason. 1983. 228p. 12.95 o.p. (*0-525-24153-1*, 01258-370, Dutton) Dutton/Plume.

—Old Saxon Blood. 1989. 288p. mass mkt. 4.95 o.s.i (*0-345-35765-5*) Ballantine Bks.

—Old Saxon Blood. 1988. 240p. 15.95 o.p. (*0-312-01799-5*, Saint Martin's Minotaur) St. Martin's Pr.

—The Player's Boy Is Dead. 1988. mass mkt. 4.99 o.s.i (*0-345-34371-9*) Ballantine Bks.

—The Player's Boy Is Dead. 1980. 208p. o.p. (*0-06-014341-X*) HarperCollins Pubs.

—Witness of Bones. 1993. reprint ed. mass mkt. 4.99 o.s.i (*0-345-38319-2*) Ballantine Bks.

—Witness of Bones. 1992. 256p. 18.95 o.p. (*0-312-08339-4*, Saint Martin's Minotaur) St. Martin's Pr.

**STOCK, MATTHEW (FICTITIOUS CHARACTER)—FICTION**

Tourney, Leonard. The Bartholomew Fair Murders. 1987. 256p. reprint ed. mass mkt. 4.99 o.s.i (*0-345-34370-0*) Ballantine Bks.

—The Bartholomew Fair Murders. 1986. 240p. 14.95 o.p. (*0-312-06710-0*) St. Martin's Pr.

—Familiar Spirits. 1989. 240p. mass mkt. 3.50 o.s.i (*0-345-34372-7*) Ballantine Bks.

—Familiar Spirits. 1984. 224p. 13.95 o.p. (*0-312-28025-4*) St. Martin's Pr.

—Frobisher's Savage. 1994. 304p. 20.95 o.p. (*0-312-11437-0*, Saint Martin's Minotaur) St. Martin's Pr.

—Knaves Templar. 1992. mass mkt. 3.99 o.s.i (*0-345-37335-9*) Ballantine Bks.

—Knaves Templar. 1991. 17.95 o.p. (*0-312-04961-7*, Saint Martin's Minotaur) St. Martin's Pr.

—Low Treason. 1989. mass mkt. 3.50 o.s.i (*0-345-34368-9*) Ballantine Bks.

—Low Treason. 1983. 228p. 12.95 o.p. (*0-525-24153-1*, 01258-370, Dutton) Dutton/Plume.

—Old Saxon Blood. 1989. 288p. mass mkt. 4.95 o.s.i (*0-345-35765-5*) Ballantine Bks.

—Old Saxon Blood. 1988. 240p. 15.95 o.p. (*0-312-01799-5*, Saint Martin's Minotaur) St. Martin's Pr.

—The Player's Boy Is Dead. 1988. mass mkt. 4.99 o.s.i (*0-345-34371-9*) Ballantine Bks.

—The Player's Boy Is Dead. 1980. 208p. o.p. (*0-06-014341-X*) HarperCollins Pubs.

—Witness of Bones. 1993. reprint ed. mass mkt. 4.99 o.s.i (*0-345-38319-2*) Ballantine Bks.

—Witness of Bones. 1992. 256p. 18.95 o.p. (*0-312-08339-4*, Saint Martin's Minotaur) St. Martin's Pr.

**STONE, DETECTIVE SERGEANT (FICTITIOUS CHARACTER)—FICTION**

Mason, Sarah J. Corpse in the Kitchen. 1993. 224p. (Orig.). mass mkt. 4.50 o.p. (*0-425-14006-7*) Berkley Publishing Group.

—Dying Breath. 1994. 240p. (Orig.). mass mkt. 4.50 o.p. (*0-425-14245-0*, Prime Crime) Berkley Publishing Group.

—Frozen Stiff. 1993. 224p. (Orig.). mass mkt. 4.50 o.p. (*0-425-13837-2*) Berkley Publishing Group.

—Murder in the Maze. 1993. 224p. mass mkt. 4.99 o.s.i (*0-425-13795-3*) Berkley Publishing Group.

—Murder in the Maze. l.t. ed. 1999. (Linford Mystery Large Print Ser.). 448p. pap. 18.99 (*0-7089-5561-4*, Linford) Thorpe, F. A. Pubs. GBR. *Dist:* Ulverscroft Large Print Bks., Ltd., Ulverscroft Large Print Canada, Ltd.

—Seeing Is Deceiving. 1997. 208p. mass mkt. 5.99 o.s.i (*0-425-15901-9*, Prime Crime) Berkley Publishing Group.

—Seeing Is Deceiving. l.t. ed. 2000. (Linford Mystery Large Print Ser.). 384p. pap. 18.99 (*0-7089-5673-4*, Linford) Thorpe, F. A. Pubs. GBR. *Dist:* Ulverscroft Large Print Bks., Ltd., Ulverscroft Large Print Canada, Ltd.

—Sew Easy to Kill. 1996. 208p. mass mkt. 5.99 o.s.i (*0-425-15310-X*) Berkley Publishing Group.

—Sew Easy to Kill. l.t. ed. 2000. (Linford Mystery Large Print Ser.). 392p. pap. 18.99 o.p. (*0-7089-5656-4*, Linford) Thorpe, F. A. Pubs. GBR. *Dist:* Ulverscroft Large Print Bks., Ltd., Ulverscroft Large Print Canada, Ltd.

**STONE, HAZEL (FICTITIOUS CHARACTER)—FICTION**

Heinlein, Robert A. The Cat Who Walks Through Walls. 1988. 400p. mass mkt. 7.99 (*0-441-09499-6*) Ace Bks.

—The Cat Who Walks Through Walls. 1986. 400p. 3.95 o.s.i (*0-425-09332-8*) Berkley Publishing Group.

—The Cat Who Walks Through Walls. 1985. 75.00 o.p. (*0-399-13116-7*); 384p. 17.95 o.s.i (*0-399-13103-5*) Putnam Publishing Group, The.

—The Cat Who Walks Through Walls. unabr. ed. 1999. audio 91.00 (*0-7887-2940-3*, 95721E7) Recorded Bks., LLC.

—The Moon Is a Harsh Mistress. 1987. mass mkt. 5.99 o.s.i (*0-441-53699-9*) Ace Bks.

—The Moon Is a Harsh Mistress. 1985. 304p. 3.50 o.s.i (*0-425-08899-5*) Berkley Publishing Group.

—The Moon Is a Harsh Mistress. 2000. audio compact disk 96.00 (*0-7861-9885-0*, z2566); audio 69.95 (*0-7861-1764-8*, 2566) Blackstone Audio Bks., Inc.

—The Moon Is a Harsh Mistress. 1997. 384p. pap. 14.95 (*0-312-86355-1*, Orb Bks.); 1996. 382p. 24.95 (*0-312-86176-1*, Tor Bks.) Doherty, Tom Assocs., LLC.

—The Moon Is a Harsh Mistress. 1989. 288p. 22.95 o.p. (*0-450-50280-5*) Hodder & Stoughton, Ltd. GBR. *Dist:* Lubrecht & Cramer, Ltd., Trafalgar Square.

—The Moon Is a Harsh Mistress. 1966. 9.95 o.p. (*0-399-10556-5*) Putnam Publishing Group, The.

—The Moon Is a Harsh Mistress. unabr. ed. 1998. audio 93.00 (*0-7887-1987-4*, 95374 E7) Recorded Bks., LLC.

—The Rolling Stones. 1985. 256p. mass mkt. 6.99 (*0-345-32451-X*, Del Rey); 1982. mass mkt. 2.25 o.s.i (*0-345-30332-6*); 1978. mass mkt. 1.75 o.s.i (*0-345-27581-0*); 1977. mass mkt. 1.50 o.s.i (*0-345-26067-8*, Del Rey) Ballantine Bks.

**STONE, JESSE (FICTITIOUS CHARACTER)—FICTION**

Parker, Robert B. Death in Paradise. 2002. 304p. reprint ed. mass mkt. 7.99 (*0-425-18706-3*) Berkley Publishing Group.

—Death in Paradise. l.t. ed. 2002. 382p. 31.95 (*0-7862-3850-X*) Gale Group.

—Death in Paradise. unabr. ed. 2001. (Jesse Stone Ser.: Vol. 3). audio 29.95 (*1-59007-071-2*, New Millennium Audio) New Millennium Entertainment.

—Death in Paradise. 2001. 320p. 23.95 o.s.i (*0-399-14779-9*) Penguin Group (USA) Inc.

—Death in Paradise. unabr. ed. 2002. audio 29.95 (*1-4025-0732-1*, 96890) Recorded Bks., LLC.

—Death in Paradise. l.t. ed. 13.95 (*1-4104-0054-9*, Large Print Pr.); 2003. pap. 13.95 (*0-7862-3851-8*) Thorndike Pr.

—Night Passage. 336p. 2001. mass mkt. 7.99 (*0-425-18396-3*); 1998. reprint ed. mass mkt. 7.50 o.s.i (*0-515-12349-8*, Jove) Berkley Publishing Group.

—Night Passage. l.t. ed. 1998. (Large Print Book Ser.). 26.95 o.p. (*1-56895-530-8*, Wheeler Publishing, Inc.) Gale Group.

—Night Passage. 1997. 21.95 o.s.i (*0-399-14694-6*); 320p. 21.95 o.p. (*0-399-14304-1*, G. P. Putnam's Sons) Penguin Group (USA) Inc.

—Stone Cold: A Jesse Stone Novel. 2003. 336p. 24.95 (*0-399-15087-0*, Putnam & Grosset) Putnam Publishing Group, The.

—Stone Cold: A Jesse Stone Novel. l.t. ed. 2003. 323p. 32.95 (*0-7862-6079-3*, Large Print Pr.) Thorndike Pr.

—Trouble in Paradise. 1999. (Jesse Stone Ser.). 320p. reprint ed. mass mkt. 7.99 (*0-515-12649-7*, Jove) Berkley Publishing Group.

—Trouble in Paradise. l.t. ed. 1998. 27.95 (*1-56895-681-9*, Wheeler Publishing, Inc.) Gale Group.

—Trouble in Paradise. 1998. 336p. 22.95 o.p. (*0-399-14433-1*, G. P. Putnam's Sons) Penguin Group (USA) Inc.

—Trouble in Paradise. l.t. ed. 2000. (Charnwood Large Print Ser.). 304p. (*0-7089-9137-8*, Ulverscroft) Thorpe, F. A. Pubs. GBR. *Dist:* Ulverscroft Large Print Bks., Ltd., Ulverscroft Large Print Canada, Ltd.

**STONE, LUCY (FICTITIOUS CHARACTER)—FICTION**

Meier, Leslie. Back to School Murder: A Lucy Stone Mystery. (Lucy Stone Mysteries Ser.). 1998. 272p. mass mkt. 5.99 (*1-57566-330-9*); 1997. 256p. 18.95 o.s.i (*1-57566-216-7*) Kensington Publishing Corp.

—Birthday Party Murder: A Lucy Stone Mystery. 2003. mass mkt. 6.50 (*1-57566-833-5*); 2002. 288p. 22.00 (*1-57566-832-7*, Kensington Bks.) Kensington Publishing Corp.

—Christmas Cookie Murder, Vol. 1. 1999. (Lucy Stone Mysteries Ser.). 256p. (J). pap. 20.00 o.s.i (*1-57566-476-3*) Kensington Publishing Corp.

—Father's Day Murder. 2004. 256p. mass mkt. 6.50 (*1-57566-835-1*, Kensington Bks.) Kensington Publishing Corp.

—Father's Day Murder. l.t. ed. 2003. (Lucy Stone Mystery Ser.). 307p. 28.95 (*0-7862-5617-6*) Thorndike Pr.

—Mail-Order Murder. 1999. pap. 5.95 (*0-14-015832-4*, Viking) Viking Penguin.

—Mail-Order Murder: A Christmas Mystery. 1991. 192p. 18.95 o.p. (*0-670-84111-0*, Viking) Viking Penguin.

—Mail Order Murders. 1993. 256p. mass mkt. 4.99 o.s.i (*0-440-21452-1*) Dell Publishing.

—Mistletoe Murder. 1998. Orig. Title: Mail-Order Murder. 224p. mass mkt. 6.50 (*0-7582-0337-3*); mass mkt. 5.99 o.s.i (*1-57566-370-8*, Kensington Bks.) Kensington Publishing Corp.

—Tippy Toe Murder. (Lucy Stone Mysteries Ser.). 1999. 352p. mass mkt. 5.99 (*1-57566-392-9*); 1996. 256p. mass mkt. 4.99 o.s.i (*1-57566-099-7*) Kensington Publishing Corp.

—Tippy Toe Murder. 1994. 240p. 18.95 o.p. (*0-670-84791-7*, Viking) Viking Penguin.

—Tippy-Toe Murder: A Lucy Stone Mystery. 2003. (Paperback Ser.). lib. bdg. 24.95 (*0-7862-5025-9*) Thorndike Pr.

—Trick or Treat Murder. (Lucy Stone Mysteries Ser.). 256p. 1997. mass mkt. 5.99 (*1-57566-219-1*); 1996. 18.95 o.s.i (*1-57566-093-8*, Kensington Bks.) Kensington Publishing Corp.

—Turkey Day Murder. (Lucy Stone Mystery Ser.). 2001. 256p. mass mkt. 5.99 (*1-57566-685-5*); 2000. (Illus.). 24p. 20.00 o.s.i (*1-57566-605-7*, Kensington Bks.) Kensington Publishing Corp.

—Turkey Day Murder. l.t. ed. 2002. (Mystery Ser.). 318p. 28.95 (*0-7862-4727-4*) Thorndike Pr.

—Valentine Murder. (Lucy Stone Mysteries Ser.). 2000. 272p. mass mkt. 5.99 (*1-57566-499-2*); 1999. 248p. 20.00 o.s.i (*1-57566-390-2*) Kensington Publishing Corp.

—Wedding Day Murder. 2002. 256p. mass mkt. 6.50 (*1-57566-734-7*); 2001. 24p. 22.00 o.s.i (*1-57566-652-9*, Kensington Bks.) Kensington Publishing Corp.

—Wedding Day Murder. l.t. ed. 2003. (Lucy Stone Mystery Ser.). 391p. 24.95 (*0-7862-5597-8*) Thorndike Pr.

**STONE, LUNA (FICTITIOUS CHARACTER)—FICTION**

Betts, Doris. The Sharp Teeth of Love. 1998. 352p. pap. 12.00 (*0-684-84475-3*, Touchstone) Simon & Schuster.

**STONE, MICHAEL (FICTITIOUS CHARACTER)—FICTION**

Jacobs, Jonnie. Murder among Friends. 2001. 352p. mass mkt. 5.99 (*0-7582-0098-6*); 1996. 352p. mass mkt. 5.99 o.s.i (*1-57566-089-X*, Kensington Bks.); 1995. 304p. mass mkt. 16.95 o.s.i (*0-8217-5030-5*) Kensington Publishing Corp.

—Murder among Neighbors. 304p. 1995. mass mkt. 5.99 (*1-57566-275-2*); 1995. mass mkt. 4.99 o.s.i (*0-8217-5039-9*); 1994. mass mkt. 16.95 o.p. (*0-8217-4680-4*, Zebra Bks.) Kensington Publishing Corp.

—Murder among Strangers. 2000. (Kate Austen Mystery Ser.). 378p. 20.00 o.s.i (*1-57566-540-9*) Kensington Publishing Corp.

Salter, Anna. Fault Lines. 1998. E-Book 22.00 (*0-671-03696-3*, Atria); 1998. 272p. 22.00 (*0-671-00312-7*, Atria); 1999. 368p. reprint ed. mass mkt. 6.99 o.s.i (*0-671-00313-5*, Pocket Star); Vol. 2. Date not set. (*0-671-02352-7*, Atria) Simon & Schuster.

—Shiny Water. 1998. 320p. per. 6.50 (*0-671-00311-9*, Pocket Star); 1997. 272p. 23.00 (*0-671-00310-0*, Atria) Simon & Schuster.

**STONE, NATHAN (FICTITIOUS CHARACTER)—FICTION**

Compton, Ralph. Autumn of the Gun. 1996. 432p. mass mkt. 5.99 (*0-451-19045-9*, Signet Bks.) NAL.

—Border Empire. 1997. (Border Empire Ser.). 352p. mass mkt. 5.99 (*0-451-19209-5*, Signet Bks.) NAL.

—The Dawn of Fury. 1995. 496p. mass mkt. 5.99 (*0-451-18631-1*, Signet Bks.) NAL.

—The Dawn of Fury. abr. ed. 2000. (Gun Ser.). audio 24.95 (*1-890990-39-6*, 99039) Otis Audio, Inc.

—The Killing Season. 1996. 448p. mass mkt. 5.99 (*0-451-18787-3*, Signet Bks.) NAL.

—The Killing Season. abr. ed. 2000. (Gun Ser.). audio 24.95 (*1-890990-47-7*) Otis Audio, Inc.

**STONE, NICK (FICTITIOUS CHARACTER)—FICTION**

McNab, Andy. Crisis Four. 2001. 416p. reprint ed. mass mkt. 6.99 (*0-345-42808-0*, Ballantine Bks.) Ballantine Bks.

—Crisis Four. 2001. 416p. mass mkt. (*0-7704-2866-5*, Random Hse. Bks. for Young Readers) Random Hse. Children's Bks.

—Firewall. 2001. 384p. mass mkt. 7.99 (*0-7434-3515-X*, Pocket); 24.95 (*0-7434-0626-5*, Atria) Simon & Schuster.

—The Last Light. 2003. 464p. mass mkt. 7.50 (*0-7434-0629-X*, Pocket) Simon & Schuster.

—Liberation Day. 2003. 368p. 25.00 (*0-7434-0630-3*); 25.00 (*0-7434-7717-0*) Simon & Schuster. (Atria).

—Liberation Day: A Nick Stone Mission. 400p. 2004. mass mkt. 7.99 (*0-7434-0631-1*); 2003. mass mkt. 7.99 (*0-7434-7437-6*) Simon & Schuster. (Pocket).

—Remote Control. unabr. ed. 1998. audio 96.95 (*0-7540-0175-X*, CAB 1598) BBC Audiobooks America.

—Remote Control. 2000. 384p. mass mkt. 6.99 (*0-345-42806-4*, One World/Ballantine) Ballantine Bks.

—Remote Control. abr. ed. 1999. audio 26.95 (*0-7871-1916-4*, Dove Audio) NewStar Media, Inc.

**STONER, BELL (FICTITIOUS CHARACTER)—FICTION**

Tell, Dorothy. The Hallelujah Murders. 1991. (Poppy Dillworth Mystery Ser.). 176p. pap. 8.95 (*0-941483-88-6*) Naiad Pr., Inc.

—Murder at Red Rook Ranch. 1990. 224p. pap. 8.95 (*0-941483-80-0*) Naiad Pr., Inc.

—Wilderness Trek. 1990. 160p. pap. 8.95 o.p. (*0-941483-60-6*) Naiad Pr., Inc.

**STONER, HARRY (FICTITIOUS CHARACTER)—FICTION**

Valin, Jonathan. Day of Wrath. 1994. 320p. mass mkt. 4.99 o.s.i (*0-440-21041-0*) Dell Publishing.

—Day of Wrath. 1983. (Harry Stoner Mystery Ser.). 256p. pap. 3.50 (*0-380-63917-3*, Avon Bks.) Morrow/Avon.

—Dead Letter. 1994. 320p. mass mkt. 4.99 o.s.i (*0-440-21038-0*) Dell Publishing.

—Dead Letter. 1983. (Harry Stoner Mystery Ser.). 224p. pap. 3.50 (*0-380-61366-2*, Avon Bks.) Morrow/Avon.

—Extenuating Circumstances. 1989. 15.95 o.s.i (*0-440-50110-5*, Delacorte Pr.); 1989. 240p. 15.95 o.s.i (*0-385-29683-5*, Delacorte Pr.); 1990. 256p. reprint ed. mass mkt. 3.95 o.s.i (*0-440-20630-8*) Dell Publishing.

—Final Notice. 1994. 320p. mass mkt. 4.99 o.s.i (*0-440-21032-1*) Dell Publishing.

—Final Notice. 1982. (Harry Stoner Mystery Ser.). 192p. pap. 3.50 (*0-380-57893-X*, Avon Bks.) Morrow/Avon.

—Fire Lake. 1989. 272p. (YA). reprint ed. mass mkt. 4.99 o.s.i (*0-440-20145-4*) Dell Publishing.

—Fire Lake: A Harry Stoner Novel. 1987. 264p. 14.95 o.s.i (*0-385-29589-8*, Delacorte Pr.) Dell Publishing.

—Life's Work. 1987. 256p. reprint ed. mass mkt. 4.99 o.s.i (*0-440-14790-5*) Dell Publishing.

—Life's Work: A Harry Stoner Novel. 1986. 240p. 14.95 o.s.i (*0-385-29503-0*, Delacorte Pr.) Dell Publishing.

—The Lime Pit. 1994. 320p. mass mkt. 4.99 o.s.i (*0-440-21029-1*) Dell Publishing.

—The Lime Pit. 1983. (Harry Stoner Mystery Ser.). 208p. pap. 3.50 (*0-380-55442-9*, Avon Bks.) Morrow/Avon.

—The Music Lovers: A Harry Stoner Mystery. 1994. 304p. mass mkt. 4.99 o.s.i (*0-440-21686-9*) Dell Publishing.

—Natural Causes. 1994. 384p. mass mkt. 4.99 o.s.i (*0-440-21035-6*) Dell Publishing.

—Natural Causes. 1984. (Harry Stoner Mystery Ser.). 304p. pap. 2.95 o.p. (*0-380-68247-8*, 68247, Avon Bks.) Morrow/Avon.

—Second Chance: A Harry Stoner Mystery. 288p. 1992. mass mkt. 4.99 o.s.i (*0-440-21222-7*); 1991. 18.00 o.s.i (*0-385-29912-5*, Delacorte Pr.) Dell Publishing.

**STORME, WYATT (FICTITIOUS CHARACTER)—FICTION**

Ripley, W. L. Dreamsicle. unabr. ed. 1993. 57.25 o.p. incl. audio (*1-56100-149-X*, 1189, Unabridged Library Editions); audio 21.95 o.p. (*1-56100-516-9*, 341, Bookcassette) Brilliance Audio.

—Dreamsicle. 1993. 267p. 19.95 o.p. (*0-316-74726-2*) Little Brown & Co.

—Electric Country Roulette: A Wyatt Storme Mystery. 1996. 88p. 25.00 o.p. (*0-8050-3792-6*) Holt, Henry & Co.

—Storme Front. 1995. 340p. 22.50 o.p. (*0-8050-3601-6*) Holt, Henry & Co.

**STORMS, SERGE (FICTITIOUS CHARACTER)—FICTION**

Dorsey, Tim. Cadillac Beach. 2004. 352p. 24.95 (*0-06-052046-9*, Morrow, William & Co.) Morrow/Avon.

—Florida Roadkill. 2000. 384p. mass mkt. 6.99 (*0-380-73233-5*, HarperTorch); 1999. 273p. 24.00 o.p. (*0-688-16782-9*, Morrow, William & Co.) Morrow/Avon.

—Hammerhead Ranch Motel. 2001. 384p. mass mkt. 6.99 (*0-380-73234-3*, HarperTorch); 2000. 304p. 24.00 (*0-688-16783-7*, Morrow, William & Co.) Morrow/Avon.
—The Stingray Shuffle. 2004. 400p. mass mkt. 7.50 (*0-06-055693-5*, HarperTorch); 2003. 320p. 24.95 (*0-06-052045-0*, Morrow, William & Co.) Morrow/Avon.
—The Stingray Shuffle. l.t. ed. 2003. 517p. 28.95 (*0-7862-5643-5*) Thorndike Pr.
—Triggerfish Twist. 2003. 400p. mass mkt. 6.99 (*0-06-103155-0*, HarperTorch); 2002. 320p. 24.95 (*0-06-018571-6*, Morrow, William & Co.) Morrow/Avon.

**STORR, NICK (FICTITIOUS CHARACTER)—FICTION**

Daniel, Mark. The Devil to Pay. l.t. ed. 1995. 391p. pap. 20.95 o.p. (*0-7838-1351-1*, Macmillan Reference USA) Gale Group.
—The Devil to Pay. 1993. 260p. 19.95 o.p. (*0-316-17265-0*) Little Brown & Co.
—The Devil to Pay. l.t. ed. 1995. (Magna Large Print Ser.). 442p. o.p. (*0-7505-0773-X*) Magna Large Print Bks. GBR. *Dist:* Ulverscroft Large Print Canada, Ltd.
—The Devil to Pay. 1995. 256p. mass mkt. 4.99 (*0-380-72328-X*, Avon Bks.) Morrow/Avon.

**STOWE, BEECHER (FICTITIOUS CHARACTER)—FICTION**

Brady, James. Further Lane. 1999. E-Book 6.50 o.s.i (*0-312-20716-6*); 1998. (Further Lane Ser.: Vol. 1). 304p. pap. 6.50 (*0-312-96598-2*, St. Martin's Paperbacks); 1997. 224p. 22.95 (*0-312-15533-6*) St. Martin's Pr.

**STRACHEY, DONALD (FICTITIOUS CHARACTER)—FICTION**

Stevenson, Richard. Chain of Fools. 1996. 208p. 20.95 o.p. (*0-312-14563-2*, Saint Martin's Minotaur) St. Martin's Pr.
—Chain of Fools: A Donald Strachey Mystery. 1997. (Donald Strachey Mystery Ser.). 192p. pap. 11.95 (*0-312-16796-2*, Saint Martin's Griffin) St. Martin's Pr.
—Death Trick. 190p. reprint ed. 1983. pap. 6.95 o.p. (*0-932870-27-9*); 2nd ed. 1996. pap. 9.95 o.p. (*1-55583-387-X*) Alyson Pubns.
—Death Trick. 1981. 224p. 10.95 o.p. (*0-312-18876-5*) St. Martin's Pr.
—Death Trick: A Murder Mystery. 2003. 199p. pap. 15.95 (*1-56023-470-9*, Southern Tier Editions) Haworth Pr., Inc., The.
—Ice Blues. 1987. 224p. mass mkt. 3.95 o.p. (*0-14-009403-2*, Penguin Bks.) Viking Penguin.
—Ice Blues: A Donald Strachey Mystery. 1995. 224p. pap. 8.95 (*0-312-13517-3*, Saint Martin's Griffin); 1986. 256p. 15.95 o.p. (*0-312-40379-8*) St. Martin's Pr.
—On the Other Hand, Death. 1995. 216p. 8.95 (*0-312-11871-6*, Saint Martin's Griffin) St. Martin's Pr.
—On the Other Hand, Death. 1985. (Crime Monthly Ser.). 224p. pap. 3.95 o.p. (*0-14-008319-7*, Penguin Bks.) Viking Penguin.
—On the Other Hand, Death: A Donald Strachey Mystery. 1984. 224p. 12.95 o.p. (*0-312-58458-X*) St. Martin's Pr.
—A Shock to the System: A Donald Strachey Mystery. 192p. 1996. pap. 9.95 (*0-312-14732-5*, Saint Martin's Griffin); 1995. 19.95 o.p. (*0-312-13610-2*, Saint Martin's Minotaur) St. Martin's Pr.
—Strachey's Folly. (Donald Strachey Mystery Ser.). 1999. 224p. pap. 11.95 (*0-312-24328-6*, Saint Martin's Griffin); 1998. 216p. 22.95 o.p. (*0-312-18669-X*, Saint Martin's Minotaur) St. Martin's Pr.
—Third Man Out: A Donald Strachey Mystery. pap. 15.95 (*0-312-30214-2*, Saint Martin's Griffin); 1993. pap. 8.95 (*0-312-08906-6*, Saint Martin's Griffin); 1992. 224p. 17.95 o.p. (*0-312-07110-8*, Saint Martin's Minotaur) St. Martin's Pr.
—Tongue Tied: A Donald Strachey Mystery. 2003. 224p. 22.95 (*0-312-30974-0*, Saint Martin's Minotaur) St. Martin's Pr.

**STRAIT, JAKE (FICTITIOUS CHARACTER)—FICTION**

Rich, Frank. Avenging Angel. 1993. mass mkt. (*0-373-63607-5*, 1-63607-5, Harlequin Bks.) Harlequin Enterprises, Ltd.

**STRANAHAN, MICK (FICTITIOUS CHARACTER)—FICTION**

Hiaasen, Carl. Skin Tight. 1990. (Florida Mysteries Ser.). 384p. mass mkt. 6.99 o.s.i (*0-449-21941-0*, Fawcett) Ballantine Bks.
—Skin Tight. l.t. ed. 1996. (G. K. Hall Mystery Ser.). 599p. 24.95 o.p. (*0-7838-1648-0*, Macmillan Reference USA) Gale Group.
—Skin Tight. 1989. 320p. 18.95 o.p. (*0-399-13489-1*, G. P. Putnam's Sons) Penguin Putnam Bks. for Young Readers.

**STRANGE, DEREK (FICTITIOUS CHARACTER)—FICTION**

Pelecanos, George P. Hard Revolution. 2004. 384p. 24.95 (*0-316-60897-1*) Little Brown & Co.
—Hard Revolution. abr. ed. 2004. audio 25.98 (*1-58621-600-7*); audio compact disk 31.98 (*1-58621-601-5*) Time Warner AudioBooks.
—Hell to Pay. abr. ed. 2003. audio 9.99 (*1-58788-961-7*, 3484, Brilliance Audio Paperback Audiobooks); 2002. audio 19.95 (*1-58788-960-9*, 3483, Nova Audio Bks.); 2002. audio 29.95 (*1-58788-958-7*, 3481, Brilliance Audio Unabridged); 2002. audio 69.25 (*1-58788-959-5*, 3482, Unabridged Library Editions) Brilliance Audio.
—Hell to Pay. 2002. E-Book 14.95 (*0-7595-8686-1*); 352p. 24.95 o.p. (*0-316-69506-8*) Little Brown & Co.
—Hell to Pay. unabr. ed. 2003. audio 19.99 (*1-59335-091-0*, 30183) Soulmate Audio Bks., Inc.
—Hell to Pay. l.t. ed. 2003. 536p. 30.45 (*0-7862-5615-X*) Thorndike Pr.
—Hell to Pay. 2003. 416p. mass mkt. 6.99 (*0-446-61132-8*) Warner Bks., Inc.
—Right As Rain. 2001. 336p. 24.95 (*0-316-69526-2*) Little Brown & Co.
—Right As Rain. l.t. ed. 2003. 525p. 30.45 (*0-7862-5609-5*) Thorndike Pr.
—Right As Rain. 2002. 384p. reprint ed. mass mkt. 6.99 (*0-446-61079-8*) Warner Bks., Inc.

**STRANGE, SYLVIA (FICTITIOUS CHARACTER)—FICTION**

Lovett, Sarah. Acquired Motives: A Novel. 1997. mass mkt. 5.99 o.s.i (*0-8041-1298-3*, Ivy Bks.) Ballantine Bks.
—Acquired Motives: A Novel. aut. ed. 1996. 22.95 o.s.i (*0-676-51776-5*, Villard Bks.) Random House Adult Trade Publishing Group.
—Acquired Motives: A Novel. 2003. (Illus.). 368p. pap. 6.99 (*0-7434-6335-8*, Pocket) Simon & Schuster.
—Dangerous Attachments. 1996. 344p. mass mkt. 5.99 o.s.i (*0-8041-1297-5*, Ivy Bks.) Ballantine Bks.
—Dangerous Attachments: A Dr. Sylvia Strange Novel. 2003. 400p. pap. 6.99 (*0-7434-6334-X*, Pocket) Simon & Schuster.
—Dante's Inferno. 2001. (Dr. Sylvia Strange Novels Ser.: No. 4). 320p. 24.00 (*0-684-85598-4*, Simon & Schuster) Simon & Schuster.
—Dark Alchemy. 2003. 304p. 24.00 (*0-684-85599-2*, Simon & Schuster) Simon & Schuster.
—A Desperate Silence: A Novel. 1998. mass mkt. 5.99 o.s.i (*0-8041-1299-1*, Ivy Bks.) Ballantine Bks.
—A Desperate Silence: A Novel. l.t. ed. 1998. 24.95 (*1-57490-152-4*) Beeler, Thomas T. Publisher.
—A Desperate Silence: A Novel. 2003. (Illus.). 400p. pap. 7.50 (*0-7434-6336-6*, Pocket) Simon & Schuster.

**STRATTON, JOHN (FICTITIOUS CHARACTER)—FICTION**

Menos, Dennis. A Test of Allegiance. 1997. vii, 252p. pap. 15.00 (*0-9660404-0-6*) Vergina Pr.

**STRAUSS, DAVID (FICTITIOUS CHARACTER)—FICTION**

Patterson, James. The Jericho Commandment & See How They Run. 1981. mass mkt. 2.50 o.s.i (*0-345-29241-3*) Ballantine Bks.
—See How They Run. l.t. ed. 1997. 26.95 o.p. (*1-56895-480-8*, Wheeler Publishing, Inc.) Gale Group.
—See How They Run. 1997. mass mkt. (*0-316-69382-0*) Little Brown & Co.
—See How They Run. 1997. 336p. reprint ed. mass mkt. 7.99 (*0-446-60392-9*) Warner Bks., Inc.

**STRAWBERRY SHORTCAKE (FICTITIOUS CHARACTER)—FICTION**

Artists, Si, illus. Hello, Strawberry Shortcake! 2003. (Strawberry Shortcake Ser.). 14p. bds. 6.99 (*0-448-43208-0*, Grosset & Dunlap) Penguin Putnam Bks. for Young Readers.
Bolson, Sarah. Strawberry Shortcake. 2003. mass mkt. 122.76 (*0-448-42800-8*, Grosset & Dunlap) Penguin Putnam Bks. for Young Readers.
Bryant, Megan E. The Berry Big Storm. 2003. (All Aboard Reading Station Stop Ser.). (Illus.). 32p. 13.89 (*0-448-43157-2*); (J). mass mkt. 3.99 (*0-448-43135-1*) Penguin Putnam Bks. for Young Readers. (Grosset & Dunlap).
—Strawberry Shortcake's Snow Day. 2003. (Strawberry Shortcake Ser.). (Illus.). 24p. text 4.99 (*0-448-43206-4*, Grosset & Dunlap) Penguin Putnam Bks. for Young Readers.
Fontes, Justine. Meet Strawberry Shortcake. 2003. (Strawberry Shortcake Ser.). (Illus.). 32p. (J). mass mkt. 3.99 (*0-448-43132-7*, Grosset & Dunlap) Penguin Putnam Bks. for Young Readers.
—Where Are Custard & Pupcake? 2003. (Strawberry Shortcake Ser.). (Illus.). 16p. (J). mass mkt. 5.99 (*0-448-43133-5*, Grosset & Dunlap) Penguin Putnam Bks. for Young Readers.
Glassman, Jackie. The Berry Best Friends' Picnic. 2003. (All Aboard Reading Station Stop Ser.). (Illus.). 32p. 13.89 (*0-448-43156-4*); (J). mass mkt. 3.99 (*0-448-43134-3*) Penguin Putnam Bks. for Young Readers. (Grosset & Dunlap).
Koeppel, Ruth. Strawberry Shortcake Plays Soccer. 2003. (Strawberry Shortcake Ser.). (Illus.). 32p. (J). 3.49 (*0-448-43207-2*, Grosset & Dunlap) Penguin Putnam Bks. for Young Readers.
Lindenberger, Jan & Bowles, Jennifer. More Strawberry Shortcake: An Unauthorized Handbook & Price Guide. 1999. (Books for Collectors Ser.). (Illus.). 160p. 16.95 (*0-7643-0762-2*) Schiffer Publishing, Ltd.
SI Artists, illus. It's a Strawberry World. 2003. (Sticker Stories Ser.). 16p. mass mkt. 4.99 (*0-448-43136-X*, Grosset & Dunlap) Penguin Putnam Bks. for Young Readers.
—What's Growing Strawberry Shortcake? 2003. (Sticker Stories Ser.). 16p. mass mkt. 4.99 (*0-448-43137-8*, Grosset & Dunlap) Penguin Putnam Bks. for Young Readers.
Stephens, Monique. Apple Dumplin's Day. 2003. (Strawberry Shortcake Ser.). (Illus.). 14p. bds. 6.99 (*0-448-43192-0*, Grosset & Dunlap) Penguin Putnam Bks. for Young Readers.
—The Strawberry Shortcake Berrylicious Bake Off: A Scratch-and-Sniff Story. 2003. (Strawberry Shortcake Ser.). (Illus.). 16p. mass mkt. 4.99 (*0-448-43186-6*, Grosset & Dunlap) Penguin Putnam Bks. for Young Readers.
—Strawberry Shortcake's Berry Merry Christmas. 2003. (Strawberry Shortcake Ser.). (Illus.). 32p. (J). 9.99 (*0-448-43200-5*, Grosset & Dunlap) Penguin Putnam Bks. for Young Readers.
Stephens, Monique Z. Spring for Strawberry Shortcake. Yee, Josie, tr. & illus. by. 2004. (Strawberry Shortcake Ser.). 32p. (J). mass mkt. 3.49 (*0-448-43373-7*, Grosset & Dunlap) Penguin Putnam Bks. for Young Readers.
—Strawberry Shortcake & the Friendship Party. 2003. (Strawberry Shortcake Ser.). (Illus.). 24p. (J). mass mkt. 4.99 (*0-448-43222-6*, Grosset & Dunlap) Penguin Putnam Bks. for Young Readers.
Strawberry Shortcake Goes Camping. 2004. (Strawberry Shortcake Ser.). (Illus.). 12p. 4.99 (*0-448-43506-3*, Grosset & Dunlap) Penguin Putnam Bks. for Young Readers.
What's Baking Strawberry Shortcake. 2004. (Strawberry Shortcake Ser.). (Illus.). 12p. 5.99 (*0-448-43532-2*, Grosset & Dunlap) Penguin Putnam Bks. for Young Readers.

**STREET, JASON (FICTITIOUS CHARACTER)—FICTION**

Smith, Jerry. Deadman's Throttle. 1998. (Jason Street Mysteries Ser.). 191p. pap. 12.95 (*1-884313-13-2*, DT) Whitehorse Pr.

**STREET, JIMMY (FICTITIOUS CHARACTER)—FICTION**

Tanger, Woody. Blood Games. 1977. 284p. pap. 13.95 (*0-8283-2022-5*) Branden Bks.

**STREETER (FICTITIOUS CHARACTER: STONE)—FICTION**

Stone, Michael. A Long Reach. 1998. (Streeter Mystery Ser.). 240p. pap. 5.99 o.s.i (*0-14-024703-3*) Penguin Group (USA) Inc.
—A Long Reach. l.t. ed. 1997. (Niagara Large Print Ser.). 320p. 29.50 o.p. (*0-7089-5875-3*, Ulverscroft) Thorpe, F. A. Pubs. GBR. *Dist:* Ulverscroft Large Print Bks., Ltd.
—A Long Reach. 1997. (Streeter Mystery Ser.). 240p. 20.95 o.s.i (*0-670-86166-9*) Viking Penguin.
—The Low End of Nowhere: A Streeter Mystery. 1997. (Viking Mystery Suspense Ser.). 240p. pap. 5.95 o.s.i (*0-14-024694-0*) Penguin Group (USA) Inc.
—The Low End of Nowhere: A Streeter Mystery. l.t. ed. 1997. (Niagara Large Print Ser.). 290p. 29.50 o.p. (*0-7089-5863-X*, Linford) Thorpe, F. A. Pubs. GBR. *Dist:* Ulverscroft Large Print Bks., Ltd.
—The Low End of Nowhere: A Streeter Mystery. 1996. (Streeter Mystery Ser.). 240p. 20.95 o.p. (*0-670-86154-5*) Viking Penguin.
—Token of Remorse. 1998. (Streeter Mystery Ser.). 256p. 22.95 o.p. (*0-670-87774-3*) Viking Penguin.
—Token of Remorse: A Streeter Mystery. 1999. (Streeter Mystery Ser.). 256p. pap. 5.99 (*0-14-027546-0*, Puffin Bks.) Penguin Group (USA) Inc.
—Totally Dead. 2000. (Streeter Mystery Ser.). 240p. pap. 5.99 o.s.i (*0-14-028598-9*, Penguin Bks.) Penguin Group (USA) Inc.
—Totally Dead. 1999. (Streeter Mystery Ser.). 256p. 22.95 o.s.i (*0-670-88208-9*, Viking) Viking Penguin.

**STREUSEL, ROB (FICTITIOUS CHARACTER)—FICTION**

Smith, Ronald L. Murder in the Skin Trade. 1993. 276p. (Orig.). pap. 4.99 (*1-56171-220-5*) SPI Bks.

**STRICKLAND, DAVE (FICTITIOUS CHARACTER)—FICTION**

Davis, Thomas D. Murdered Sleep: A Dave Strickland Mystery. 1994. 264p. 21.95 o.p. (*0-8027-3177-5*) Walker & Co.
—Suffer Little Children. 1991. 208p. 19.95 o.p. (*0-8027-3205-4*) Walker & Co.

**STROHEM, SABINE (FICTITIOUS CHARACTER: BANTOCK)—FICTION**

*see Sabine (Fictitious Character: Bantock)—Fiction*

**STRUMMAR, SETH (FICTITIOUS CHARACTER)—FICTION**

Fackler, Elizabeth. Badlands. 1996. 352p. 23.95 o.p. (*0-312-86230-X*, Forge Bks.) Doherty, Tom Assocs., LLC.
—Breaking Even. 448p. 1998. 25.95 o.p. (*0-312-85911-2*); 2001. reprint ed. pap. 17.95 (*0-312-87509-6*) Doherty, Tom Assocs., LLC. (Forge Bks.).
—Road from Betrayal: An Evans Novel of the West. 1994. 238p. 18.95 o.p. (*0-87131-734-6*) Evans, M. & Co., Inc.

**STRYKER, JACK (FICTITIOUS CHARACTER)—FICTION**

Gosling, Paula. Backlash. 1989. 12.95 o.s.i (*0-385-24995-0*) Doubleday Publishing.
—Backlash. 1991. reprint ed. mass mkt. (*0-373-26082-2*, Harlequin Bks.) Harlequin Enterprises, Ltd.
—Hoodwink. 1988. (Crime Club Ser.). 192p. 12.95 o.s.i (*0-385-24333-2*) Doubleday Publishing.
—Hoodwink. l.t. ed. 1990. (Ulverscroft Large Print Ser.). 29.99 o.p. (*0-7089-2209-0*, Ulverscroft) Thorpe, F. A. Pubs. GBR. *Dist:* Ulverscroft Large Print Bks., Ltd., Ulverscroft Large Print Canada, Ltd.

**STUART, JANE (FICTITIOUS CHARACTER)—FICTION**

Marshall, Evan. Hanging Hannah. (Jane Stuart & Winky Mystery Ser.). 2001. 32p. mass mkt. 5.99 (*1-57566-663-4*); 2000. (Illus.). 307p. 20.00 o.s.i (*1-57566-550-6*) Kensington Publishing Corp. (Kensington Bks.).
—Icing Ivy: A Jan Stuart & Winky Mystery. 2002. (Jane Stuart & Winky Mystery Ser.). (Illus.). 304p. 22.00 (*0-7582-0224-5*) Kensington Publishing Corp.
—Missing Marlene. (Jane Stuart & Winky Mystery Ser.). 2000. 336p. mass mkt. 5.99 (*1-57566-555-7*, Kensington Bks.); 1999. 309p. 20.00 o.s.i (*1-57566-420-8*) Kensington Publishing Corp.
—Stabbing Stephanie. (Jane Stuart & Winky Mystery Ser.). 2002. 352p. mass mkt. 5.99 (*1-57566-729-0*); 2001. 34p. 22.00 o.s.i (*1-57566-657-X*) Kensington Publishing Corp.
—Toasting Tina. 2003. 304p. 22.00 (*0-7582-0226-1*, Kensington Bks.) Kensington Publishing Corp.

**STUART, MATTHEW (FICTITIOUS CHARACTER)—FICTION**

Caunitz, William J. Pigtown. 352p. 2002. mass mkt. 6.99 (*0-7860-1484-9*); 1996. mass mkt. 6.99 o.s.i (*0-7860-0293-X*, Pinnacle Bks.) Kensington Publishing Corp.

**STUBBS, HERMAN 'FATTY' (FICTITIOUS CHARACTER)—FICTION**

Lovisi, Gary. Hellbent on Homicide. 1997. (Bloodlines Ser.). 140p. pap. 14.95 (*1-899344-18-7*) Do-Not Pr., The GBR. *Dist:* Dufour Editions, Inc.

**STURGIS, MILO (FICTITIOUS CHARACTER)—FICTION**

Kellerman, Jonathan. Bad Love. 2003. 512p. mass mkt. 7.99 (*0-345-46072-3*, Ballantine Bks.) Ballantine Bks.
—Bad Love. 1994. 496p. mass mkt. 6.99 o.s.i (*0-553-18118-1*); 512p. mass mkt. 7.99 o.s.i (*0-553-56870-1*); 27.50 o.s.i (*0-553-09636-2*) Bantam Bks.
—Bad Love. unabr. ed. 1994. audio 64.00 Books on Tape, Inc.
—Bad Love. l.t. ed. 2001. 386p. 31.95 (*0-7838-9456-2*, Macmillan Reference USA) Gale Group.
—Bad Love. 1994. audio 13.59 o.s.i (*0-553-70076-6*, RH Audio) Random Hse. Audio Publishing Group.
—Billy Straight. 1999. 448p. mass mkt. 7.99 (*0-345-41386-5*) Ballantine Bks.
—Billy Straight. 1998. pap. 25.95 o.p. (*0-7838-0268-4*, Macmillan Reference USA) Gale Group.
—Billy Straight: A Novel. l.t. ed. 1998. 663p. pap. 25.95 (*0-375-70422-1*) Random Hse. Large Print.
—Billy Straight: A Novel. 1998. 467p. 25.95 o.s.i (*0-679-45959-6*) Random Hse., Inc.
—Blood Test. 2003. 320p. mass mkt. 7.99 (*0-345-46661-6*, Ballantine Bks.) Ballantine Bks.
—Blood Test. 1995. (Alex Delaware Novel Ser.). 320p. mass mkt. 7.99 o.s.i (*0-553-56963-5*) Bantam Bks.
—Blood Test. 2000. audio compact disk 64.00 (*0-7366-8058-6*); 2000. audio 56.00 (*0-7366-5642-1*); 2001. audio 29.95 (*0-7366-5718-5*) Books on Tape, Inc.
—Blood Test. l.t. ed. 2002. (Famous Authors Ser.). 405p. 29.95 (*0-7862-3753-8*) Gale Group.
—Blood Test. 1987. mass mkt. 4.50 o.p. (*0-451-15434-7*, Signet Bks.); mass mkt. 4.50 o.p. (*0-451-14737-5*, Signet Bks.); 352p. mass mkt. 5.99 o.p. (*0-451-15929-2*, Signet Bks.); mass mkt. 5.99 o.s.i (*0-451-17802-5*) NAL.

—Blood Test. abr. ed. 2002. audio 9.99 o.s.i (0-553-75609-5, RH Audio) Random Hse. Audio Publishing Group.

—Blood Test. 1986. 258p. bds. 14.95 o.s.i (0-689-11634-9, Scribner) Simon & Schuster.

—The Clinic. 2003. 496p. mass mkt. 7.99 (0-345-46074-X, Ballantine Bks.) Ballantine Bks.

—The Clinic. 1997. (Alex Delaware Novel Ser.). 496p. mass mkt. 7.99 o.s.i (0-553-57230-X); mass mkt. 6.99 (0-553-84009-6) Bantam Bks.

—The Clinic. l.t. ed. 1998. (Thorndike/G. K. Hall Paperback Bestsellers Ser.). 600p. pap. 28.95 (0-7862-0983-6) Thorndike Pr.

—A Cold Heart. 2003. 432p. mass mkt. 7.99 (0-345-45256-9); 400p. 26.95 (0-345-45255-0, Ballantine Bks.); E-Book 18.85 (0-345-46365-X, Ballantine Bks.) Ballantine Bks.

—Dr. Death. l.t. ed. 2000. 592p. 26.95 (0-375-43079-2) Random Hse. Large Print.

—Flesh & Blood. abr. ed. 2001. audio 25.95 (0-375-41940-3); audio compact disk 29.95 (0-375-41941-1); audio 39.95 (0-375-41942-X) Random Hse. Audio Publishing Group. (RH Audio).

—Flesh & Blood. l.t. ed. 2001. 592p. 26.95 (0-375-43129-2) Random Hse. Large Print.

—Flesh & Blood. 2001. E-Book 21.95 (1-58836-141-1) Random Hse., Inc.

—Monster. 2000. 416p. mass mkt. (0-345-44172-9); mass mkt. 7.99 (0-345-41387-3, Ballantine Bks.) Ballantine Bks.

—Monster. l.t. ed. 512p. 2000. pap. 14.95 (0-375-72794-9); 1999. 25.95 (0-375-40868-1) Random Hse. Large Print.

—The Murder Book. 2003. 544p. mass mkt. 7.99 (0-345-41390-3); 2002. 416p. 26.95 (0-345-45253-4); 2002. E-Book 18.95 (0-345-45864-8) Ballantine Bks. (Ballantine Bks.).

—The Murder Book. l.t. ed. 2002. 672p. 28.95 (0-375-43173-X) Random Hse. Large Print.

—Over the Edge. 1988. 448p. mass mkt. 5.99 o.p. (0-451-15219-0); mass mkt. 7.99 o.s.i (0-451-17801-7) NAL. (Signet Bks.).

—Over the Edge. 1987. 384p. bds. 17.95 o.s.i (0-689-11635-7, Scribner) Simon & Schuster.

—Private Eyes. 2003. 560p. mass mkt. 7.99 (0-345-46070-7, Ballantine Bks.) Ballantine Bks.

—Private Eyes. 1992. (Alex Delaware Novel Ser.). 560p. mass mkt. 7.99 o.s.i (0-553-29950-6); pap. 5.50 (0-553-18085-1) Bantam Bks.

—Private Eyes. l.t. ed. 1992. 720p. 25.00 o.s.i (0-385-42283-0, Bantam Large Type) Bantam Doubleday Dell Large Print Group, Inc.

—Private Eyes. 1992. audio 12.79 o.s.i (0-553-70022-7, RH Audio); 2004. audio compact disk 14.99 (0-7393-1223-5, RH Audio Price-Less); 1999. audio 9.99 o.s.i (0-553-70201-7, RH Audio) Random Hse. Audio Publishing Group.

—Self-Defense. 1995. 528p. mass mkt. 6.99 o.s.i (0-553-84002-9); (Illus.). reprint ed. mass mkt. 7.99 o.s.i (0-553-57220-2) Bantam Bks.

—Self-Defense. l.t. ed. 1995. (Large Print Bks.). 556p. 26.95 o.p. (1-56895-206-6, Wheeler Publishing, Inc.) Gale Group.

—Self-Defense. 2002. (Illus.). 528p. mass mkt. 7.99 (0-345-45883-4) Random Hse., Inc.

—Survival of the Fittest. l.t. ed. 1998. 621p. (0-7540-2083-5) BBC Audiobooks America.

—Survival of the Fittest. 1998. (Alex Delaware Novel Ser.). 544p. mass mkt. 7.99 o.s.i (0-553-57232-6) Bantam Bks.

—Survival of the Fittest. 2002. (Illus.). 544p. mass mkt. 7.99 (0-345-45884-2) Random Hse., Inc.

—Survival of the Fittest. l.t. ed. (Paperback Bestsellers Ser.). 667p. 1999. 27.95 o.p. (0-7862-1283-7); 1998. 30.95 (0-7862-1282-9) Thorndike Pr.

—Time Bomb. 2003. 496p. mass mkt. 7.99 (0-345-46069-3, Ballantine Bks.) Ballantine Bks.

—Time Bomb. 1991. (Alex Delaware Novel Ser.). 496p. mass mkt. 7.99 o.s.i (0-553-29170-X); 480p. mass mkt. 5.95 o.s.i (0-553-18041-X) Bantam Bks.

### SUCCORSO, NICK (FICTITIOUS CHARACTER)—FICTION

Stephens, Reed, pseud. The Gap into Conflict: The Real Story. (Gap Ser.: No. 1). 1992. 272p. mass mkt. 7.50 (0-553-29509-8); 1991. 224p. 6.00 o.s.i (0-553-08049-0) Bantam Bks.

—The Gap into Madness: Chaos & Order. 1995. (Gap Ser.: No. 4). 688p. mass mkt. 6.99 (0-553-57253-9) Bantam Bks.

—The Gap into Power: A Dark & Hungry God Arises. 1993. (Gap Ser.: No. 3). 528p. mass mkt. 7.50 (0-553-56260-6) Bantam Bks.

—The Gap into Vision: Forbidden Knowledge. (Gap Ser.: No. 2). 1992. 480p. mass mkt. 7.50 (0-553-29760-0); 1991. 416p. 125.00 o.s.i (0-553-07387-7) Bantam Bks.

Stephens, Reed, pseud & Donaldson, Stephen R. The Gap into Ruin: This Day All Gods Die. 1997. (Gap Ser.: No. 5). 704p. mass mkt. 6.99 (0-553-57328-4) Bantam Bks.

### SUENO, GEORGE (FICTITIOUS CHARACTER)—FICTION

Limon, Martin. Buddha's Money. 1999. 416p. mass mkt. 5.99 o.s.i (0-553-57610-0) Bantam Bks.

—Jade Lady Burning. 1994. 224p. pap. 13.00 (1-56947-020-0); 1992. 226p. 19.95 (0-939149-71-0) Soho Pr., Inc.

### SUGHRUE, C. W. (FICTITIOUS CHARACTER)—FICTION

Crumley, James. Bordersnakes. 1997. 288p. mass mkt. 6.50 (0-446-60448-8); 1996. 336p. 22.00 o.p. (0-89296-573-8) Warner Bks., Inc.

—Dancing Bear. unabr. ed. 1997. audio 48.00 (0-7366-3819-9, 4487) Books on Tape, Inc.

—Dancing Bear. 1984. (Vintage Contemporaries Ser.). 240p. pap. 13.00 (0-394-72576-X, Vintage) Knopf Publishing Group.

—Dancing Bear. 1983. 256p. 12.95 o.p. (0-394-52195-1) Random Hse., Inc.

—The Last Good Kiss. 1992. audio 13.95 (1-55644-375-7, 12021) American Audio Prose Library, Inc.

—The Last Good Kiss. 1988. (Vintage Contemporaries Ser.). 256p. pap. 11.95 (0-394-75989-3, Vintage) Knopf Publishing Group.

—The Last Good Kiss. 1978. 8.95 o.p. (0-394-41946-4) Random Hse., Inc.

—The Last Good Kiss. 1983. mass mkt. 3.50 o.s.i (0-671-49889-4, Pocket) Simon & Schuster.

—The Mexican Tree Duck. unabr. ed. 1997. audio 48.00 (0-7366-3820-2, 4488) Books on Tape, Inc.

—The Mexican Tree Duck. 1993. 256p. 19.95 (0-89296-391-3) Mysterious Pr.

—The Mexican Tree Duck. 1994. 272p. mass mkt. 5.99 (0-446-40407-1); 2001. 256p. reprint ed. pap. 11.95 (0-446-67791-4) Warner Bks., Inc.

—The Wrong Case. 1985. (Vintage Contemporaries Ser.). 288p. pap. 12.00 (0-394-73558-7) Random Hse., Inc.

### SULLIVAN, DAVID (FICTITIOUS CHARACTER)—FICTION

Deitz, Tom. Darkthunder's Way. 1989. pap. 3.95 (0-380-75508-4, Avon Bks.) Morrow/Avon.

—Dreamseeker's Road. 2000. 20.00 (0-380-97254-9); 1996. 368p. mass mkt. 5.99 (0-380-77484-4, Avon Bks.); 1995. 356p. 20.00 o.p. (0-688-14155-2, Morrow, William & Co.) Morrow/Avon.

—Fireshaper's Doom. 1987. 320p. pap. 3.95 (0-380-75329-4, Avon Bks.) Morrow/Avon.

—Ghostcountry's Wrath. 1995. 400p. (Orig.). mass mkt. 5.50 o.p. (0-380-76838-0, Avon Bks.) Morrow/Avon.

—Landslayer's Law. 1997. 304p. mass mkt. 5.99 (0-380-78649-4, Avon Bks.) Morrow/Avon.

—Stoneskin's Revenge. 1991. 320p. pap. 3.95 (0-380-76063-0, Avon Bks.) Morrow/Avon.

—Sunshaker's War. 1990. 368p. mass mkt. 3.95 (0-380-76062-2, Avon Bks.) Morrow/Avon.

—Warstalker's Track. 1999. 384p. mass mkt. 6.50 o.s.i (0-380-78650-8, Eos) Morrow/Avon.

—Windmaster's Bane. 1986. (Orig.). pap. 4.99 (0-380-75029-5, Avon Bks.) Morrow/Avon.

### SULLIVAN, LIZ (FICTITIOUS CHARACTER)—FICTION

Roberts, Lora. Murder Bone by Bone. 1997. (Liz Sullivan Mysteries Ser.). mass mkt. 5.50 o.s.i (0-449-14946-3, Fawcett) Ballantine Bks.

—Murder Crops Up. 1998. (Liz Sullivan Mysteries Ser.). 240p. mass mkt. 5.99 o.s.i (0-449-15048-8, Fawcett) Ballantine Bks.

—Murder Follows Money. 2000. (Liz Sullivan Mysteries Ser.). 240p. mass mkt. 6.50 o.s.i (0-449-00539-9, Fawcett) Ballantine Bks.

—Murder Follows Money. l.t. ed. 2001. 262p. pap. 24.95 (0-7838-9591-7, Macmillan Reference USA) Gale Group.

—Murder in a Nice Neighborhood. 1994. (Liz Sullivan Mysteries Ser.). (Orig.). mass mkt. 4.99 o.s.i (0-449-14891-2, Fawcett) Ballantine Bks.

—Murder in the Marketplace. 1995. mass mkt. 5.50 o.s.i (0-449-14890-4, Fawcett) Ballantine Bks.

—Murder Mile High. 1996. (Liz Sullivan Mysteries Ser.). mass mkt. 5.50 o.s.i (0-449-14947-1, Fawcett) Ballantine Bks.

### SULLIVAN, RITA ANGELA (FICTITIOUS CHARACTER)—FICTION

Sanders, Lawrence. Sullivan's Sting. 1991. 368p. mass mkt. 7.99 (0-425-12845-8); 1990. 384p. 19.95 o.s.i (0-399-13542-1) Berkley Publishing Group.

—Sullivan's Sting. l.t. ed. 1991. (General Ser.). 428p. 18.95 (0-8161-5088-5); lib. bdg. 22.95 o.p. (0-8161-5087-7) Gale Group. (Macmillan Reference USA).

### SULU, HIKARU (FICTITIOUS CHARACTER)—FICTION

David, Peter. The Captain's Daughter. (Star Trek: No. 76). 2000. E-Book 6.99 (0-7434-2027-6); 1995. 288p. mass mkt. 5.99 o.s.i (0-671-52047-4) Simon & Schuster. (Star Trek).

Duane, Diane. Doctor's Orders. (Star Trek: No. 50). 2000. E-Book 6.99 (0-7434-2001-2); 1990. 288p. mass mkt. 5.50 (0-671-66189-2) Simon & Schuster. (Star Trek).

—The Wounded Sky. (Star Trek: No. 13). 2000. E-Book 6.99 (0-7434-1964-2); 1991. 224p. mass mkt. 5.50 o.s.i (0-671-74352-X) Simon & Schuster. (Star Trek).

Ecklar, Julia. The Kobayashi Maru. 1989. (Star Trek: No. 47). mass mkt. 5.50 (0-671-65817-4, Star Trek) Simon & Schuster.

—The Kobayashi Maru. (Star Trek Ser.: No. 47). 1999. audio 5.98 (0-671-04486-9); 1990. audio 11.00 (0-671-70895-3) Simon & Schuster Audio. (Simon & Schuster Audioworks).

Flinn, Denny Martin. Fearful Summons. 1995. (Star Trek: No. 74). 288p. mass mkt. 5.50 (0-671-89007-7, Star Trek) Simon & Schuster.

—The Fearful Summons. 2000. (Star Trek: No. 74). E-Book 6.99 (0-7434-2025-X, Star Trek) Simon & Schuster.

Graf, L. A. Death Count. 2000. (Star Trek: No. 62). E-Book 6.99 (0-7434-2013-6, Star Trek) Simon & Schuster.

—Death Count. Stern, Dave, ed. 1992. (Star Trek Ser.: No. 62). 288p. mass mkt. 4.99 (0-671-79322-5, Star Trek) Simon & Schuster.

—Envoy: A Captain Sulu Adventure. 1997. (Star Trek Ser.). audio 12.00 (0-671-52141-1); audio compact disk 16.00 (0-671-52286-8) Simon & Schuster Audio. (Simon & Schuster Audioworks).

—Firestorm. (Star Trek: No. 68). 2000. E-Book 6.99 (0-7434-2019-5); 1994. 288p. mass mkt. 5.50 (0-671-86588-9) Simon & Schuster. (Star Trek).

—New Earth No. 3: Rough Trails. 2000. (Star Trek: No. 91). reprint ed. E-Book 6.50 (0-7434-1117-X, Star Trek) Simon & Schuster.

—New Earth No. 33: Rough Trails. 2000. (Star Trek: No. 91). 400p. pap. 6.50 (0-671-03600-9, Star Trek) Simon & Schuster.

—Traitor Winds. 2000. (Star Trek: No. 70). E-Book 6.99 (0-7434-2021-7, Star Trek) Simon & Schuster.

—Traitor Winds. Ryan, Kevin, ed. 1994. (Star Trek Ser.: No. 70). 288p. mass mkt. 5.50 (0-671-86913-2, Star Trek) Simon & Schuster.

Kirk, James T. & Sulu, Hikaru. War Dragons No. 1: The Captain Table. 1998. (Star Trek: Vol. 1). 288p. pap. 6.50 (0-671-01463-3, Star Trek) Simon & Schuster.

Kramer-Rolls, Dana. Home Is the Hunter. 2000. (Star Trek: No. 52). E-Book 6.99 (0-7434-2003-9, Star Trek) Simon & Schuster.

—Home Is the Hunter. Stern, David, ed. 1990. (Star Trek: No. 52). 288p. mass mkt. 4.99 (0-671-66662-2, Star Trek) Simon & Schuster.

Mangels, Andy & Martin, Michael A. Lost Era: Sundered. 2003. (Star Trek Ser.). 416p. mass mkt. 6.99 (0-7434-6401-X, Star Trek) Simon & Schuster.

McIntyre, Vonda N. The Search for Spock. 2000. (Star Trek Ser.: No. 3). E-Book 6.99 (0-7434-1968-5, Star Trek) Simon & Schuster.

Mitchell, V. E. Enemy Unseen. Stern, David, ed. 1990. (Star Trek: No. 51). 288p. mass mkt. 4.99 (0-671-68403-5, Star Trek) Simon & Schuster.

Molloy, J. J. & David, Peter. Cacophony. abr. ed. 1994. (Star Trek Ser.). audio 12.00 (0-671-89483-8); audio compact disk 16.00 (0-671-89484-6) Simon & Schuster Audio. (Simon & Schuster Audioworks).

Reynolds, Mack. Mission to Horatius. 1999. (Star Trek Ser.). (Illus.). 208p. 16.00 o.s.i (0-671-02812-X, Atria) Simon & Schuster.

—Well Meet Again. unabr. ed. 1999. (Star Trek Ser.). audio 39.95 (0-671-04380-3, Simon & Schuster Audioworks) Simon & Schuster Audio.

Shatner, William, et al. Ashes of Eden. abr. ed. 1995. (Star Trek Ser.). audio 18.00 o.s.i (0-671-52892-0, 392990, Simon & Schuster Audioworks) Simon & Schuster Audio.

Stern, Dave. Transformations: A Captain Sulu Adventure. abr. ed. 1994. (Star Trek Ser.). audio 12.00 (0-671-86438-6); (J). audio compact disk 16.00 (0-671-88624-X) Simon & Schuster Audio. (Simon & Schuster Audioworks).

Weinstein, Howard. Star Trek: Tests of Courage. Kahan, Bob, ed. 1994. (Star Trek Ser.). (Illus.). 160p. pap. 17.95 (1-56389-151-4) DC Comics.

### SUMMER, MAGGIE (FICTITIOUS CHARACTER)—FICTION

Wait, Lea. Shadows at the Fair: An Antique Print Mystery. (Illus.). 272p. 2003. mass mkt. 6.99 (0-7434-5620-3, Pocket); 2002. 24.00 (0-7432-2553-8, Scribner) Simon & Schuster.

—Shadows at the Fair: An Antique Print Mystery. 2003. (Americana Ser.). 28.95 (0-7862-5003-8) Thorndike Pr.

—Shadows on the Coast of Maine: An Antique Print Mystery. unabr. ed. 2003. audio 49.95 (0-7861-2513-6); audio compact disk 14.95 (0-7861-9144-9); audio compact disk 24.95 (0-7861-8909-6) Blackstone Audio Bks., Inc.

—Shadows on the Coast of Maine: An Antique Print Mystery. 2004. 272p. mass mkt. 6.99 (0-7434-5621-1, Pocket); 2003. 288p. 24.00 (0-7432-2554-6, Scribner) Simon & Schuster.

—Shadows on the Ivy: An Antique Print Mystery. 256p. Date not set. mass mkt. (0-7434-7559-3, Pocket); 2005. (0-7432-4951-8, Scribner); 2005. mass mkt. 5.99 (0-7434-7558-5, Pocket); 2004. 24.00 (0-7432-4950-X, Scribner) Simon & Schuster.

### SUN WOLF (FICTITIOUS CHARACTER: HAMBLY)—FICTION

Hambly, Barbara. The Dark Hand of Magic. 1990. 320p. mass mkt. 5.99 o.s.i (0-345-35807-4, Del Rey) Ballantine Bks.

—The Ladies of Mandrigyn. 1997. pap. 12.00 (0-345-42059-4); 1984. 320p. mass mkt. 5.99 o.s.i (0-345-30919-7, Del Rey) Ballantine Bks.

—The Witches of Wenshar. (Orig.). 1997. pap. 12.00 (0-345-42060-8); 1987. 352p. mass mkt. 5.99 o.s.i (0-345-32934-1, Del Rey) Ballantine Bks.

### SUNSET WARRIOR (FICTITIOUS CHARACTER)—FICTION

Van Lustbader, Eric. Beneath an Opal Moon. 272p. 1995. pap. 19.00 (0-345-46686-1); 1990. mass mkt. 6.99 (0-449-21649-7) Ballantine Bks. (Fawcett).

—Beneath an Opal Moon. 1983. 2.75 o.p. (0-425-07040-9); 1982. 2.50 o.s.i (0-425-05080-7) Berkley Publishing Group.

—Beneath an Opal Moon. 1980. (Double D Science Fiction Ser.). 10.95 o.p. (0-385-14892-5) Doubleday Publishing.

—Dai-San. 256p. 1995. pap. 19.00 (0-345-46675-6); 1989. (Sunset Warrior Cycle Ser.: Bk. 3). mass mkt. 6.99 (0-449-21648-9) Ballantine Bks. (Fawcett).

—Dai-San. 1984. 272p. 3.50 o.p. (0-425-09971-7); 1984. 2.95 o.s.i (0-425-07141-3); 1982. 2.75 o.s.i (0-425-06194-9); 1981. 2.50 o.s.i (0-425-04454-8) Berkley Publishing Group.

—Dai-San. 1978. 9.95 o.p. (0-385-12987-4) Doubleday Publishing.

—Dai-San. 1991. 21.95 o.p. (0-7278-4129-7) Severn Hse. Pubs., Ltd.

—Shallows of Night. 272p. 1995. pap. 19.00 (0-345-46680-2); 1989. mass mkt. 6.99 (0-449-21647-0) Ballantine Bks. (Fawcett).

—Shallows of Night. 1986. 3.50 o.p. (0-425-09964-4); 1983. 2.75 o.s.i (0-425-06550-2); 1980. 2.50 o.s.i (0-425-04453-X); 1979. pap. o.s.i (0-515-04715-5, Jove) Berkley Publishing Group.

—Shallows of Night. 1978. 7.95 o.p. (0-385-12968-8) Doubleday Publishing.

—Shallows of Night. 1991. reprint ed. 18.95 o.p. (0-7278-4133-5) Severn Hse. Pubs., Ltd.

—The Sunset Warrior. 256p. 1995. pap. 19.00 (0-345-46678-0); 1989. mass mkt. 6.99 (0-449-21646-2) Ballantine Bks. (Fawcett).

—The Sunset Warrior. 1986. 3.50 o.s.i (0-425-09786-2); 1985. 2.95 o.s.i (0-425-08265-2); 1983. 2.75 o.s.i (0-425-06169-8); 1980. 2.50 o.s.i (0-425-04452-1); 1978. 1.50 o.s.i (0-515-04714-7, Jove) Berkley Publishing Group.

—The Sunset Warrior. 1977. 6.95 o.p. (0-385-12967-X) Doubleday Publishing.

—The Sunset Warrior. 1990. reprint ed. 19.00 o.p. (0-7278-4073-8) Severn Hse. Pubs., Ltd.

### SUNDAY, GIDEON (FICTITIOUS CHARACTER)—FICTION

Fenn, Lionel. Agnes Day. 1987. 256p. (Orig.). pap. 2.95 o.p. (0-8125-3789-0, Tor Bks.) Doherty, Tom Assocs., LLC.

—Blood River Down. 1986. 320p. (Orig.). pap. 2.95 o.p. (0-8125-3785-8, Tor Bks.) Doherty, Tom Assocs., LLC.

—Web of Defeat. 1987. 288p. (Orig.). mass mkt. 2.95 (0-8125-3787-4, Tor Bks.) Doherty, Tom Assocs., LLC.

### SUNSTAR, JANDER (FICTITIOUS CHARACTER)—FICTION

Golden, Christie. Ravenloft: Vampire of the Mists. 1999. 341p. (Orig.). pap. 5.99 o.p. (1-56076-155-5) Wizards of the Coast.

### SUPERMAN (FICTITIOUS CHARACTER)—FICTION

Beck, Jackson, frwd. Superman on Radio, abr. collector's ed. (Smithsonian Historical Performances Ser.). 60p. (J). 1997. pap. 24.98 incl. audio (1-57019-036-4, 5010); 1998. (Illus.). pap. 39.98 incl. audio compact disk (1-57019-037-2, 5011) Radio Spirits, Inc.

Bifulco, Michael J. Superman on Television: Tenth Anniversary Edition. 10th anniv. rev. ed. 1998. (Illus.). 240p. pap. 24.95 (0-9619596-3-0) Bifulco, Michael.

Byrne, John. Superman: The Earth Steelers. O'Neil, Dennis, ed. 1995. (Superman Ser.). (Illus.). 48p. pap. 3.95 o.p. (1-56389-067-4) DC Comics.

Chaykin, Howard. Superman: Distant Fires. 1998. (Illus.). 64p. pap. text 5.95 o.p. (*1-56389-289-8*) DC Comics.
Chaykin, Howard & Tischman, David. Son of Superman. 2000. (Illus.). 95p. pap. 14.95 (*1-56389-596-X*) DC Comics.
Cherryh, C. J. Lois & Clark: A Superman Novel. 288p. 1997. pap. 12.00 o.s.i (*0-7615-1169-5*); 1996. 20.00 o.p. (*0-7615-0482-6*) Crown Publishing Group. (Prima Lifestyles).
Collyer, Bud. Superman with Batman & Robin on Radio, collector's ed. 1997. (Smithsonian Historical Performances Ser.). 60p. pap. 12.49 incl. audio (*1-57019-086-0*, 5012); 19.99 incl. audio compact disk (*1-57019-087-9*, 5013) Radio Spirits, Inc.
Comics, D.C. & Siegel, Jerry. The Action Comics Archives. 1998. (Superman Ser.: Vol. 1). (Illus.). 240p. 49.95 (*1-56389-335-5*) DC Comics.
Daniels, Les. Superman: The Golden Age. 1998. (J). 0.01 o.p. (*0-8118-2219-2*) Chronicle Bks. LLC.
DC Comics Staff. Superman: Bizarro's World. Kahan, Bob, ed. 1996. (Illus.). 128p. pap. 9.95 (*1-56389-260-X*) DC Comics.
—Superman: The Wedding & Beyond. 1998. (Illus.). 192p. pap. 14.95 (*1-56389-392-4*) DC Comics.
—Superman Collector's Set, 6 vols. 1996. (Illus.). pap. 11.70 (*1-56389-283-9*) DC Comics.
—Superman Lives. 1993. 17.00 (*1-57042-024-6*) Warner Bks., Inc.
Dini, Paul. Batman & Superman Adventures: World's Finest. 1997. (Illus.). 64p. pap. 6.95 (*1-56389-386-X*) DC Comics.
—Superman: Adventures of the Man of Steel. 1998. (Illus.). 144p. pap. 7.95 (*1-56389-429-7*) DC Comics.
—Superman: Peace on Earth. 1998. (Superman Ser.). (Illus.). 64p. pap. 9.95 (*1-56389-464-5*) DC Comics.
—Superman: Peace on Earth. 1999. (Illus.). 60p. reprint ed. pap. 14.00 (*0-7567-5574-3*) DIANE Publishing Co.
Dooley, Dennis & Engle, Gary, eds. Superman at Fifty! The Persistence. 1987. (Illus.). 192p. 16.95 (*0-940601-00-1*) Octavia Pr.
Friedman, M. J. Deadly Games: The New Adventures of Superman. 1996. (Lois & Clark Ser.: No. 3). 144p. mass mkt. 4.99 o.p. (*0-06-101063-4*, HarperTorch) Morrow/Avon.
—Exile: The New Adventures of Superman. 1996. (Lois & Clark Ser.: Vol. 2). 176p. mass mkt. 4.99 o.p. (*0-06-101062-6*, HarperTorch) Morrow/Avon.
—The New Adventures of Superman. 1996. (Lois & Clark Ser.: No. 1). 144p. (J). mass mkt. 4.99 o.p. (*0-06-101061-8*) HarperCollins Pubs.
Friedman, Michael Jan. Superman Lives! 1999. 224p. mass mkt. 6.50 (*0-446-60652-9*, Aspect) Warner Bks., Inc.
—Superman's First Flight. 2000. (Hello Reader! Ser.). 10.14 (*0-606-18609-3*) Turtleback Bks.
Friedman, Michael Jan & Motter, Dean, illus. Superman's First Flight. 2000. (Hello Reader! Ser.). 32p. (J). (gr. 1-3). mass mkt. 3.99 (*0-439-09550-6*) Scholastic, Inc.
Gold, M. & Kahan, Bob, eds. The Greatest Superman Stories Ever Told. 1991. (DC Comics Ser.). (Illus.). 336p. pap. 15.95 o.p. (*0-930289-39-0*) DC Comics.
Golden Books Staff. Superman Man of Steel. 1997. 12p. pap. 1.79 o.s.i (*0-307-08467-1*, Golden Bks.) Random Hse. Children's Bks.
Jergens, Dan. Superman: Exile. 1998. (Illus.). 304p. pap. 14.95 (*1-56389-438-6*) DC Comics.
Jurgens, Dan. Superman: The Doomsday Wars. 1999. (Illus.). 142p. pap. 12.95 (*1-56389-562-5*) DC Comics.
—Superman Doomsday: Hunter - Prey. Kahan, Bob, ed. 1995. (Superman Ser.). (Illus.). 160p. pap. 14.95 (*1-56389-201-4*) DC Comics.
Jurgens, Dan, et al. Superman: Lois & Clark. Kahan, Bob, ed. 1994. (Illus.). 192p. mass mkt. 9.95 (*1-56389-128-X*) DC Comics.
Kahan, Bob, ed. Superman: Eradication!: The Origin of the Eradicator. 1995. (Superman Ser.). (Illus.). 160p. pap. 12.95 (*1-56389-193-X*) DC Comics.
—Superman: Krisis of the Krimson Kryptonite. 1996. (Superman Ser.). (Illus.). 176p. pap. 12.95 o.p. (*1-56389-275-8*) DC Comics.
—Superman: The Death of Clark Kent. 1997. (Superman Ser.). (Illus.). 320p. pap. 19.95 (*1-56389-323-1*) DC Comics.
—Superman - Batman: Elseworlds. 1996. (Illus.). 224p. pap. 14.95 (*1-56389-263-4*) DC Comics.
—Superman Transformed! 1998. (Illus.). 208p. pap. 12.95 (*1-56389-406-8*) DC Comics.
Kesel, Karl, et al, eds. Superman vs. the Revenge Squad! 1999. 144p. pap. 12.95 (*1-56389-487-4*) DC Comics.
Loeb, Jeph. No Limits. 2000. (Superman Ser.). (Illus.). 208p. pap. 14.95 (*1-56389-699-0*) DC Comics.
—Superman for All Seasons. (Illus.). 2000. 208p. pap. 14.95 (*1-56389-529-3*); 1999. 206p. 24.95 (*1-56389-528-5*) DC Comics.
Moore, John. Superman: The Dark Side. 1999. (Illus.). 160p. pap. 12.95 (*1-56389-526-9*) DC Comics.
Morrison, Grant. JLA: American Dreams. 1998. (Illus.). 112p. pap. 7.95 (*1-56389-394-0*) DC Comics.
—JLA: New World Order. 1997. (Illus.). 96p. pap. 5.95 (*1-56389-369-X*) DC Comics.
Nolan, Graham & Dixon, Chuck. Superman: The Oddyssey. 2000. (Prestige Bk.). 48p. pap. (*1-56389-774-1*) DC Comics.
Pasko, Marvin. The Superman Story, 1987. (Superman Story Ser.: Vol. 1). 160p. (gr. 4-7). pap. text 3.99 (*0-8125-7742-6*, Tor Bks.) Doherty, Tom Assocs., LLC.
Schoenstein, Ralph. Superman & Son. 1995. (Illus.). 156p. pap. 14.95 (*0-8135-2194-7*) Rutgers Univ. Pr.
Schwartz, Alvin. An Unlikely Prophet: Revelations on the Path Without Form. 1998. 242p. 45.00 (*0-9659521-0-X*) Divina.
Siegel, Jerry. Superman: The Dailies. 1998. 560p. 75.00 (*1-56389-471-8*) DC Comics.
—Superman: The Sunday Classics. 1998. (Illus.). 192p. 60.00 o.p. (*1-56389-472-6*) DC Comics.
—Superman: The Sunday Classics, 1939-1943. 1999. (Illus.). 192p. pap. 19.95 (*1-56389-463-7*) DC Comics.
—Superman Vol. 1: The Dailies 1939-1940. 1999. (Superman: The Dailies Ser.). (Illus.). 176p. pap. 14.95 (*1-56389-460-2*) DC Comics.
—Superman Vol. 2: The Dailies 1940-1941. 1999. (Superman: The Dailies Ser.). (Illus.). 176p. 14.95 (*1-56389-461-0*) DC Comics.
—Superman Vol. 3: The Dailies 1941-1942. 1999. (Superman: The Dailies Ser.). (Illus.). 176p. pap. 14.95 (*1-56389-462-9*) DC Comics.
—Superman Archives. 1994. (Superman Archives Ser.: Vol. 4). (Illus.). 224p. 49.95 (*1-56389-107-7*) DC Comics.
—Superman Archives, Vol. 1. Waid, Mark & Bruning, Richard, eds. 1989. (Superman Archives Ser.: Vol. 1). (Illus.). 272p. 49.95 (*0-930289-47-1*) DC Comics.
—Superman Archives, Vol. 2. Crane, Dale, ed. 1990. (Superman Archives Ser.: Vol. 2). (Illus.). 272p. 39.95 (*0-930289-76-5*) DC Comics.
—Superman Archives, Vol. 3. Gold, M. & Hill, M., eds. 1991. (Superman Archives Ser.: Vol. 3). (Illus.). 272p. 39.95 (*1-56389-002-X*) DC Comics.
—Superman in the Sixties. 1999. (Illus.). 240p. pap. 19.95 (*1-56389-522-6*) DC Comics.
Siegel, Jerry & Shuster, Joe. Action Comics Archives. 1998. (Superman Ser.: Vol. 2). (Illus.). 224p. 49.95 (*1-56389-426-2*) DC Comics.
Stern, Roger. The Death & Life of Superman. 1994. 544p. mass mkt. 5.99 o.s.i (*0-553-56930-9*) Bantam Bks.
—The Death & Life of Superman. 4.98 o.p. (*0-8317-7733-8*) Smithmark Pubs., Inc.
—Superman: A Nation Divided. 1998. (Prestige Bk.). (Illus.). 48p. pap. 4.95 (*1-56389-441-6*) DC Comics.
Superman - Batman: Alternate Destinies. 1996. (Illus.). 232p. pap. 14.95 (*1-56389-272-3*) DC Comics.
Superman in the Fifties. 2002. (Illus.). 192p. pap. 14.95 (*1-56389-826-8*) DC Comics.
Thomas, Roy. Superman: War of the Worlds. 1998. (Prestige Bk.). (Illus.). 63p. pap. 5.95 (*1-56389-396-7*) DC Comics.
Veitch, Tom. Superman: At Earth's End. Carlin, ed. 1995. (Illus.). 48p. pap. 4.95 o.p. (*1-56389-243-X*) DC Comics.
Waid, Mark. Superman in Action Comics: Featuring the Complete Covers of the First 25 Years. 1993. (Tiny Folios Ser.). (Illus.). 320p. (J). pap. 11.95 (*1-55859-595-3*) Abbeville Pr., Inc.
Waid, Mark, intro. The Silver Age of Superman: The Greatest Covers of Action Comics from the '50s to the '70s. 1995. (Illus.). 144p. 9.98 (*0-89660-055-6*, Artabras) Abbeville Pr., Inc.
Wessel, Craig. Superman: The New Superman Adventures Official Strategy Guide. Brady Games Staff, ed. 1999. (Brady Games Ser.). (Illus.). 112p. pap. 11.99 o.p. (*1-56686-863-7*) Brady Publishing.

**SUSSMAN, ANDY (FICTITIOUS CHARACTER)—FICTION**

Katz, Michael J. The Big Freeze. 1991. 256p. 21.95 o.p. (*0-399-13558-8*, G. P. Putnam's Sons) Penguin Group (USA) Inc.
—Last Dance in Redondo Beach. 1989. 256p. 17.95 o.p. (*0-399-13445-X*, G. P. Putnam's Sons) Penguin Putnam Bks. for Young Readers.
—Last Dance in Redondo Beach. 1990. 288p. bds. 3.95 (*0-671-67913-9*, Pocket) Simon & Schuster.
—Murder off the Glass. 1987. 16.95 o.p. (*0-8027-5667-0*) Walker & Co.

**SUSSOCK, RAY (FICTITIOUS CHARACTER)—FICTION**

Turnbull, Peter. Long Day Monday. 1994. per. (*0-373-26160-8*, 1-26160-1, Harlequin Bks.) Harlequin Enterprises, Ltd.
—Long Day Monday. l.t. ed. 1994. (Ulverscroft Large Print Ser.). 320p. 29.99 o.p. (*0-7089-3175-8*, Ulverscroft) Thorpe, F. A. Pubs. GBR. *Dist:* Ulverscroft Large Print Bks., Ltd., Ulverscroft Large Print Canada, Ltd.

**SUTCLIFFE, EVELYN (FICTITIOUS CHARACTER)—FICTION**

Robinson, Leah Ruth. Blood Run. 1999. 352p. mass mkt. 6.99 (*0-380-79113-7*, Avon Bks.) Morrow/Avon.
—Blood Run. 1989. mass mkt. 4.50 o.p. (*0-451-40143-3*, Onyx); 1988. 17.95 o.p. (*0-453-00611-6*) NAL.
—Unnatural Causes. 1999. 384p. 24.00 (*0-380-97459-2*, Avon Bks.) Morrow/Avon.
Robinson, Leah Ruth, photos by. First Cut. 1997. 368p. mass mkt. 24.00 o.p. (*0-380-97458-4*); 1998. reprint ed. mass mkt. 6.99 (*0-380-79124-2*) Morrow/Avon. (Avon Bks.).

**SUTCLIFFE, SUPERINTENDENT (FICTITIOUS CHARACTER)—FICTION**

Barnard, Robert. Political Suicide. 1987. 224p. mass mkt. 3.50 o.s.i (*0-440-16946-1*) Dell Publishing.
—Political Suicide. l.t. ed. 1987. (Nightingale Ser.). 304p. 12.95 o.p. (*0-8161-4221-1*, Macmillan Reference USA) Gale Group.
—Political Suicide. 1995. 224p. pap. 7.95 (*0-88150-326-6*, Foul Play) Norton, W. W. & Co., Inc.
—Political Suicide. 1986. 192p. 13.95 o.s.i (*0-684-18625-X*, Scribner) Simon & Schuster.

**SVENSDOTTER, ESTHER "STAR" (FICTITIOUS CHARACTER)—FICTION**

Stabenow, Dana. A Handful of Stars. 1991. 224p. mass mkt. 4.50 o.s.i (*0-441-31615-8*) Ace Bks.
—Red Planet. 1995. 240p. (Orig.). mass mkt. 5.50 o.s.i (*0-441-00135-1*) Ace Bks.
—Second Star. 1991. 208p. mass mkt. 4.50 o.s.i (*0-441-75722-7*) Ace Bks.

**SVENSON, MIKE (FICTITIOUS CHARACTER)—FICTION**

Sandstrom, Eve K. Homicide Report. 1998. 368p. mass mkt. 5.99 o.s.i (*0-451-19034-3*, Onyx) NAL.
—The Smoking Gun: A Nell Matthews Mystery. 2000. (Neil Matthews Mysteries Ser.). 240p. mass mkt. 5.99 o.s.i (*0-451-19976-6*, Signet Bks.) NAL.
—The Smoking Gun: A Nell Matthews Mystery. l.t. ed. 2000. (Mystery Ser.). 365p. 26.95 (*0-7862-2977-2*) Thorndike Pr.
—Violence Beat. 1997. 384p. mass mkt. 5.99 o.s.i (*0-451-19033-5*, Signet Bks.) NAL.

**SWAGGER, BOB LEE (FICTITIOUS CHARACTER)—FICTION**

Hunter, Stephen. Black Light. 1997. 528p. mass mkt. 7.99 (*0-440-22313-X*) Dell Publishing.
—Black Light. unabr. ed. 1996. audio 23.95 o.s.i (*0-553-47748-X*, RH Audio) Random Hse. Audio Publishing Group.
—The Point of Impact. 1993. 592p. mass mkt. 7.99 (*0-553-56351-3*) Bantam Bks.
—The Point of Impact. 1993. audio 12.79 o.s.i (*0-553-70063-4*, RH Audio) Random Hse. Audio Publishing Group.
—Point of Impact. abr. ed. 1999. audio 9.99 o.s.i (*0-553-70193-2*, RH Audio) Random Hse. Audio Publishing Group.
—Time to Hunt. 1999. 608p. mass mkt. 7.99 (*0-440-22645-7*) Dell Publishing.

**SWAIN, BERT (FICTITIOUS CHARACTER)—FICTION**

Nathan, Paul. Count Your Enemies: A Bert Swain Mystery. 2000. (Bert Swain Mystery Ser.). per. (*0-373-26348-1*, Harlequin Bks.) Harlequin Enterprises, Ltd.
—Count Your Enemies: A Bert Swain Mystery. 1997. (Bert Swain Mystery Ser.). 224p. 21.95 (*0-8027-3296-8*) Walker & Co.
—No Good Deed. 1995. (Bert Swain Mystery Ser.). 202p. 24.00 (*1-877946-56-7*) Permanent Pr., The.
—Protocol for Murder. 1994. (Bert Swain Mystery Ser.). 176p. 24.00 (*1-877946-46-X*); pap. 16.00 (*1-877946-64-8*) Permanent Pr., The.

**SWANN, CASSANDRA (FICTITIOUS CHARACTER)—FICTION**

Moody, Susan. Death Takes a Hand. 1995. 240p. mass mkt. 4.99 o.s.i (*0-425-14639-1*, Prime Crime) Berkley Publishing Group.
—Death Takes a Hand. 1994. 288p. 20.00 (*1-883402-00-X*, Scribner) Simon & Schuster.
—Doubled in Spades. l.t. ed. 1997. pap. 23.95 o.p. (*1-56895-494-8*, Wheeler Publishing, Inc.) Gale Group.
—Doubled in Spades. 1997. 313p. 21.50 (*0-684-80259-7*, Scribner) Simon & Schuster.
—Dummy Hand. l.t. ed. 1999. (Ulverscroft Large Print Ser.). 368p. 31.99 o.p. (*0-7089-4088-9*, Ulverscroft) Thorpe, F. A. Pubs. GBR. *Dist:* Ulverscroft Large Print Bks., Ltd., Ulverscroft Large Print Canada, Ltd.
—Grand Slam. 1996. 272p. mass mkt. 5.99 o.s.i (*0-425-15229-4*, Prime Crime) Berkley Publishing Group.
—Grand Slam. unabr. ed. 1998. audio 83.95 (*1-85903-229-X*) Magna Story Sound GBR. *Dist:* Ulverscroft Large Print Bks., Ltd.
—Grand Slam. 1995. 310p. 20.50 (*1-883402-32-8*, Scribner) Simon & Schuster.
—King of Hearts: A Cassandra Swann Bridge Mystery. 1997. 304p. reprint ed. mass mkt. 5.99 o.s.i (*0-425-15725-3*, Prime Crime) Berkley Publishing Group.
—King of Hearts: A Cassandra Swann Bridge Mystery. unabr. ed. 1998. audio 76.95 (*1-85903-230-3*) Magna Story Sound GBR. *Dist:* Ulverscroft Large Print Bks., Ltd.
—King of Hearts: A Cassandra Swann Bridge Mystery. 1996. 320p. 21.00 o.s.i (*0-684-80258-9*, Scribner) Simon & Schuster.
—Takeout Double, Set. unabr. ed. 1998. audio 69.95 (*1-85903-204-4*) Magna Story Sound GBR. *Dist:* Ulverscroft Large Print Bks., Ltd.

**SWANN, JACKIE (FICTITIOUS CHARACTER)—FICTION**

Cantrell, Lisa W. Boneman. 256p. 1995. mass mkt. 4.99 (*0-8125-1970-1*); 1992. 18.95 o.p. (*0-312-85307-6*) Doherty, Tom Assocs., LLC. (Tor Bks.).

**SWEENEY, BILL (FICTITIOUS CHARACTER)—FICTION**

Brown, Fredric. The Screaming Mimi. 1989. 166p. mass mkt. 3.50 o.p. (*0-88184-449-7*, Carroll & Graf Pubs.) Avalon Publishing Group.

**SWEENEY, PARIS (FICTITIOUS CHARACTER)—FICTION**

Howard, Linda. Now You See Her. 1998. 336p. 23.00 o.s.i (*0-671-56882-5*, Atria); 1999. 368p. reprint ed. mass mkt. 7.99 (*0-671-03405-7*, Pocket) Simon & Schuster.
—Now You See Her. abr. ed. 1998. 18.00 (*0-671-58261-5*, Simon & Schuster Audioworks) Simon & Schuster Audio.
—Now You See Her. l.t. ed. 1999. (Paperback Bestsellers Ser.). 456p. pap. 27.95 (*0-7862-1728-6*); 28.95 o.p. (*0-7862-1727-8*) Thorndike Pr.

**SWEET, DEE (FICTITIOUS CHARACTER)—FICTION**

Saxton, Lisa. Caught in a Rundown. 1997. 287p. 20.50 (*0-684-82967-3*, Scribner) Simon & Schuster.

**SWENSEN, HANNAH (FICTITIOUS CHARACTER)—FICTION**

Fluke, Joanne. The Blueberry Muffin Murder. 2003. 34p. mass mkt. 6.50 (*1-57566-722-3*); 2002. 336p. 22.00 o.s.i (*1-57566-707-X*) Kensington Publishing Corp.
—Chocolate Chip Cookie Murder. 2001. 336p. mass mkt. 6.50 (*0-7582-0230-X*); 2001. 336p. mass mkt. 5.99 o.s.i (*1-57566-650-2*, Kensington Bks.); 2000. 312p. 20.00 o.s.i (*1-57566-524-7*) Kensington Publishing Corp.
—Fudge Cupcake Murder. 2004. 256p. 22.00 (*0-7582-0152-4*, Kensington Bks.) Kensington Publishing Corp.
—Strawberry Shortcake Murder. 2002. 32p. mass mkt. 6.50 (*1-57566-721-5*); 2001. 34p. 22.00 o.s.i (*1-57566-644-8*) Kensington Publishing Corp.

**SWIFT, BOBBY (FICTITIOUS CHARACTER)—FICTION**

Kimball, Michael. Undone. 1997. 416p. mass mkt. 5.99 (*0-380-78670-2*); 1996. 352p. 23.00 o.p. (*0-380-97305-7*) Morrow/Avon. (Avon Bks.).

**SWIFT, LOREN (FICTITIOUS CHARACTER)—FICTION**

Hornig, Doug. Deep Dive. l.t. ed. 1989. (General Ser.). 373p. lib. bdg. 18.95 o.p. (*0-8161-4690-X*, Macmillan Reference USA) Gale Group.
—Deep Dive. 1988. 15.45 o.p. (*0-89296-257-7*) Mysterious Pr.
—Deep Dive. 1989. mass mkt. 4.50 (*0-445-40788-3*, Mysterious Pr. Paperback Bks.) Warner Bks., Inc.

**SWINBROOKE, KATHRYN (FICTITIOUS CHARACTER)—FICTION**

Grace, C. L. The Book of Shadows. 1996. 208p. 20.95 (*0-312-14287-0*, Saint Martin's Minotaur) St. Martin's Pr.
—The Eye of God. 1994. 208p. 18.95 o.p. (*0-312-10978-4*, Saint Martin's Minotaur) St. Martin's Pr.
—A Feast of Poisons: A Kathryn Swinbrooke Mystery. 2004. 256p. 23.95 (*0-312-31014-5*, Saint Martin's Minotaur) St. Martin's Pr.
—A Maze of Murders: A Medieval Mystery Featuring Kathryn Swinbrooke. 2003. 256p. 23.95 (*0-312-29016-0*, Saint Martin's Minotaur) St. Martin's Pr.
—The Merchant of Death. 1995. 182p. (YA). 19.95 (*0-312-13124-0*, Saint Martin's Minotaur) St. Martin's Pr.
—Saintly Murders: A Medieval Mystery. 2001. 256p. 23.95 (*0-312-26993-5*, Saint Martin's Minotaur) St. Martin's Pr.

—A Shrine of Murders. 1993. 208p. 17.95 o.p. (*0-312-09388-8*, Saint Martin's Minotaur) St. Martin's Pr.

**SYLVESTER, BEN (FICTITIOUS CHARACTER)—FICTION**

Badke, William B. Avenger, Vol. 3. 2003. (Ben Sylvester Mystery Ser.: Vol. 3). 250p. pap. 9.99 (*1-57673-031-X*, Multnomah Bks.) Multnomah Pubs., Inc.

—Saluso's Game. 1996. (Ben Sylvester Mystery Ser.). 260p. pap. 9.99 o.p. (*0-88070-866-2*, Multnomah Bks.) Multnomah Pubs., Inc.

—Saluso's Game. l.t. ed. 2000. (Christian Mystery Ser.). 317p. 23.95 (*0-7862-2524-6*) Thorndike Pr.

—The Search, Vol. 1. 1995. (Ben Sylvester Mystery Ser.: No. 1). 256p. pap. 9.99 o.p. (*0-88070-719-4*) Multnomah Pubs., Inc.

—The Search. l.t. ed. 1999. (Christian Mystery Ser.). 248p. 22.95 o.p. (*0-7862-1967-X*) Thorndike Pr.

**SYLVESTER, WILLIAM (FICTITIOUS CHARACTER)—FICTION**

Keating, H. R. F. The Rich Detective. l.t. ed. 1994. (Magna Large Print Ser.). 349p. o.p. (*0-7505-0623-7*) Magna Large Print Bks. GBR. *Dist:* Ulverscroft Large Print Canada, Ltd.

—The Rich Detective. 1993. 256p. 18.95 (*0-89296-506-1*) Mysterious Pr.

—The Rich Detective. 1994. 256p. mass mkt. 5.50 (*0-446-40382-2*, Mysterious Pr. Paperback Bks.) Warner Bks., Inc.

# T

**TACKETT, DEL (FICTITIOUS CHARACTER)—FICTION**

Nofziger, Lyn. Tackett. 2000. 214p. pap. text 10.95 (*0-915463-85-7*); 1998. 19.95 (*0-915463-80-6*) Jameson Bks., Inc.

—Tackett. 1993. 192p. 16.95 (*0-89526-495-1*) Regnery Publishing, Inc., An Eagle Publishing Co.

—Tackett & the Indian. 1998. (Tackett Ser.: Vol. 4). 208p. 19.95 (*0-915463-75-X*, Frontier Library, The) Jameson Bks., Inc.

—Tackett & the Saloon Keeper. 1998. 19.95 (*0-915463-82-2*) Jameson Bks., Inc.

—Tackett & the Saloon Keeper. 1994. (Tackett Trilogy Ser.: Vol. 3). 233p. 16.95 (*0-89526-480-3*) Regnery Publishing, Inc., An Eagle Publishing Co.

—Tackett & the Teacher. 1998. (Ground Source Chronicles Ser.). pap. 19.95 (*0-915463-81-4*) Jameson Bks., Inc.

—Tackett & the Teacher. 1994. 192p. 16.95 (*0-89526-488-9*) Regnery Publishing, Inc., An Eagle Publishing Co.

**TAGGERT FAMILY (FICTITIOUS CHARACTERS)—FICTION**

Deveraux, Jude. An Angel for Emily. l.t. ed. 1998. (Thorndike/G. K. Hall Paperback Bestsellers Ser.). 336p. 20.00 (*0-7838-0186-6*, Macmillan Reference USA) Gale Group.

—An Angel for Emily. 1998. 320p. pap. 7.99 (*0-671-00359-3*); mass mkt. 6.99 (*0-671-02044-7*) Simon & Schuster. (Pocket).

—An Angel for Emily. l.t. ed. 1998. (Core Ser.). 336p. 30.95 (*0-7838-0185-8*) Thorndike Pr.

—The Black Lyon. (Star-Romance Ser.). 1997. 339p. 23.95 o.p. (*0-7862-0951-8*, Five Star); 1987. 429p. 19.95 o.p. (*0-8161-4177-0*, Macmillan Reference USA) Gale Group.

—The Black Lyon. 2000. 352p. pap. 12.50 (*0-380-81206-1*); 1980. 288p. mass mkt. 7.99 (*0-380-75911-X*) Morrow/Avon. (Avon Bks.).

—The Black Lyon. 1991. reprint ed. 18.95 o.p. (*0-7278-4049-5*) Severn Hse. Pubs., Ltd.

—The Blessing. l.t. ed. 1999. 27.95 (*1-56895-629-0*, Wheeler Publishing, Inc.) Gale Group.

—The Blessing. 1999. 336p. pap. 7.99 (*0-671-89109-X*, Pocket Star); 1998. 320p. 20.00 o.s.i (*0-671-89108-1*, Atria) Simon & Schuster.

—The Blessing. abr. ed. 1998. audio 18.00 (*0-671-04330-7*, 496023, Simon & Schuster Audioworks) Simon & Schuster Audio.

—The Invitation. l.t. ed. 524p. reprint ed. 1995. lib. bdg. 16.95 o.p. (*0-8161-5663-8*); 1994. lib. bdg. 24.95 o.p. (*0-8161-5662-X*) Gale Group. (Macmillan Reference USA).

—The Invitation. Marrow, Linda, ed. 1994. 384p. reprint ed. mass mkt. 7.99 (*0-671-74458-5*, Pocket) Simon & Schuster.

—The Raider. l.t. ed. 1988. 395p. 17.95 o.p. (*0-8161-4371-4*, Macmillan Reference USA) Gale Group.

—The Raider. 1990. mass mkt. 4.95 (*0-671-70681-0*); 1991. 320p. reprint ed. mass mkt. 7.99 (*0-671-74381-3*) Simon & Schuster. (Pocket).

—Remembrance. l.t. ed. 1995. 601p. 25.95 o.p. (*0-7838-1171-3*); pap. 19.95 o.p. (*0-7838-1172-1*) Gale Group. (Macmillan Reference USA).

—Remembrance. 432p. 1997. pap. 7.99 (*0-671-02357-8*); 1995. (Illus.). mass mkt. 6.99 o.s.i (*0-671-74460-7*) Simon & Schuster. (Pocket).

—Remembrance. Marrow, Linda, ed. 1994. 416p. 22.00 o.p. (*0-671-74459-3*, Atria) Simon & Schuster.

—Remembrance. 2002. audio 9.95 (*0-7435-2757-7*, Encore); 1999. audio 9.98 (*0-671-04608-X*, Simon & Schuster Audioworks); 1995. audio 17.01 (*0-671-87224-9*, 391465, Simon & Schuster Audioworks) Simon & Schuster Audio.

—Sweet Liar. l.t. ed. 1993. (General Ser.). 586p. pap. 18.95 o.p. (*0-8161-5623-9*); 23.95 o.p. (*0-8161-5622-0*) Gale Group. (Macmillan Reference USA).

—Sweet Liar. Marrow, Linda, ed. 1993. 448p. mass mkt. 7.99 (*0-671-68974-6*, Pocket); 1992. 384p. 22.00 (*0-671-68973-8*, Atria) Simon & Schuster.

—Sweet Liar. abr. ed. 1999. (Angel Ser.). audio 9.98 o.s.i (*0-671-04417-6*, Simon & Schuster Audioworks) Simon & Schuster Audio.

—Sweet Liar. Marrow, Linda, ed. abr. ed. 1992. 384p. pap. 17.00 incl. audio (*0-671-79190-7*, Simon & Schuster Audioworks) Simon & Schuster Audio.

—Twin of Fire. l.t. ed. 1992. 432p. pap. 17.95 (*0-8161-5340-X*, Macmillan Reference USA) Gale Group.

—Twin of Fire. Marrow, Linda, ed. 1991. 384p. mass mkt. 7.99 (*0-671-73979-4*, Pocket) Simon & Schuster.

—Twin of Fire. 1990. mass mkt. 4.95 (*0-671-72299-9*); 1989. mass mkt. 4.50 (*0-671-68091-9*); 1985. mass mkt. 3.95 (*0-671-50050-3*) Simon & Schuster. (Pocket).

—Twin of Fire & Twin of Ice. 1997. 592p. 12.00 (*0-671-01689-X*, Atria) Simon & Schuster.

—Twin of Ice. l.t. ed. 1992. (General Ser.). 406p. pap. 17.95 (*0-8161-5333-7*, Macmillan Reference USA) Gale Group.

—Twin of Ice. Marrow, Linda, ed. 1991. 384p. mass mkt. 7.99 (*0-671-73971-9*, Pocket) Simon & Schuster.

—Twin of Ice. 1990. mass mkt. 4.95 (*0-671-72646-3*); 1989. mass mkt. 4.50 (*0-671-68769-7*); 1985. mass mkt. 3.95 (*0-671-50049-X*) Simon & Schuster. (Pocket).

Kane, Andrea, et al. A Gift of Love. 1996. 464p. mass mkt. 7.99 (*0-671-53661-3*, Pocket) Simon & Schuster.

McNaught, Judith, et al. A Gift of Love. abr. ed. 1995. 496p. 20.00 o.p. (*0-671-53662-1*, Atria) Simon & Schuster.

—A Holiday of Love. Marrow, Linda & Tolley, Carolyn, eds. 1994. 384p. mass mkt. 6.99 o.s.i (*0-671-50252-2*, Pocket) Simon & Schuster.

**TALLCHIEF FAMILY (FICTITIOUS CHARACTERS)—FICTION**

London, Cait. The Cowboy & the Cradle: The Tallchiefs. 1996. (Silhouette Desire Ser.). 184p. per. (*0-373-76006-X*, 1-76006-5, Silhouette) Harlequin Enterprises, Ltd.

—The Groom Candidate. 1997. (Illus.). 186p. per. (*0-373-76093-0*, 1-76093-3, Silhouette) Harlequin Enterprises, Ltd.

—The Seduction of Fiona Tallchief. 1998. per. (*0-373-76135-X*, 1-76135-2, Silhouette) Harlequin Enterprises, Ltd.

—Tallchief: The Homecoming. 2000. (Silhouette Desire Ser.: Vol. 1310). 186p. mass mkt. (*0-373-76310-7*, 1-76310-1, Silhouette) Harlequin Enterprises, Ltd.

—Tallchief for Keeps. 1997. 304p. mass mkt. (*0-373-48337-6*, 1-48337-9, Harlequin Bks.) Harlequin Enterprises, Ltd.

—Tallchief's Bride. 1996. (Silhouette Desire Ser.). 186p. per. (*0-373-76021-3*, 1-76021-4, Silhouette) Harlequin Enterprises, Ltd.

**TALON FAMILY (FICTITIOUS CHARACTERS)—FICTION**

L'Amour, Louis. The Man from the Broken Hills. 1999. mass mkt. (*0-553-22648-7*); 1982. mass mkt. 2.95 o.s.i (*0-553-24956-8*); 1975. 224p. mass mkt. 2.95 o.s.i (*0-553-25514-2*); 1996. 224p. reprint ed. mass mkt. 4.50 (*0-553-27679-4*) Bantam Bks.

—The Man from the Broken Hills. 1976. (Adult Ser.). reprint ed. lib. bdg. 10.95 o.p. (*0-8161-6375-8*, Macmillan Reference USA) Gale Group.

—Milo Talon. 1999. mass mkt. (*0-553-20270-7*); 1987. 9.95 o.s.i (*0-553-06296-4*); 1981. 224p. reprint ed. mass mkt. 4.50 (*0-553-24763-8*) Bantam Bks.

—Milo Talon. 1981. (General Ser.). lib. bdg. 13.50 o.p. (*0-8161-3311-5*, Macmillan Reference USA) Gale Group.

—Rivers West. 1993. 160p. (Orig.). mass mkt. 4.50 (*0-553-25436-7*) Bantam Bks.

—Rivers West. 1989. 208p. (Orig.). pap. 17.95 o.p. (*0-525-24576-6*, Dutton) Dutton/Plume.

**TALTOS, VLAD (FICTITIOUS CHARACTER)—FICTION**

Brust, Steven. Athyra. 1993. 256p. mass mkt. 5.99 o.s.i (*0-441-03342-3*) Ace Bks.

—The Book of Jhereg. 1999. 480p. pap. 16.00 (*0-441-00615-9*) Ace Bks.

—The Book of Taltos. 2002. 400p. pap. 14.00 (*0-441-00894-1*); 1988. mass mkt. 5.99 o.s.i (*0-441-18200-3*) Ace Bks.

—Dragon. 288p. 1999. mass mkt. 6.99 (*0-8125-8916-5*); 1998. 22.95 (*0-312-86692-5*) Doherty, Tom Assocs., LLC. (Tor Bks.).

—Issola. 2001. 256p. 23.95 (*0-312-85927-9*, Tor Bks.) Doherty, Tom Assocs., LLC.

—Jhereg. 1987. 256p. mass mkt. 5.99 o.s.i (*0-441-38554-0*); 1985. mass mkt. 2.95 o.s.i (*0-441-38553-2*); 1984. mass mkt. 2.75 o.s.i (*0-441-38552-4*); 1983. mass mkt. 2.50 o.s.i (*0-441-38551-6*) Ace Bks.

—Orca. 1996. 304p. (Orig.). mass mkt. 6.50 o.s.i (*0-441-00196-3*) Ace Bks.

—The Phoenix Guards. 1990. mass mkt. 4.99 o.s.i (*0-441-66225-0*) Ace Bks.

—Teckla. 1987. 224p. mass mkt. 5.99 o.s.i (*0-441-79977-9*) Ace Bks.

—Yendi. 1984. mass mkt. 2.95 o.s.i (*0-441-94457-4*); mass mkt. 2.75 o.s.i (*0-441-94456-6*) Ace Bks.

—Yendi. 1987. 224p. pap. 2.95 o.s.i (*0-441-94459-0*, Diamond Bks.) Berkley Publishing Group.

**TAMAR, HILARY (FICTITIOUS CHARACTER)—FICTION**

Caudwell, Sarah L. The Shortest Way to Hades. 1995. 320p. mass mkt. 6.50 (*0-440-21233-2*) Dell Publishing.

—The Shortest Way to Hades. (Crime, Penguin Ser.). 2015. 208p. pap. 3.50 o.p. (*0-14-008488-6*); 1986. pap. 3.50 o.p. (*0-14-009401-6*) Penguin Group (USA) Inc.

—The Shortest Way to Hades. 1985. 208p. 12.95 o.s.i (*0-684-18292-0*, Scribner) Simon & Schuster.

—The Shortest Way to Hades. 1989. 208p. pap. 5.95 o.p. (*0-14-012874-3*, Penguin Bks.) Viking Penguin.

—The Sibyl in Her Grave. 2000. (Illus.). 304p. 23.95 o.s.i (*0-385-29934-6*, Delacorte Pr.) Dell Publishing.

—The Sirens Sang of Murder. l.t. ed. 1991. 17.95 o.p. (*0-7451-8046-9*, AH096); pap. 15.95 o.p. (*0-7927-0503-3*, AS0132) BBC Audiobooks America.

—The Sirens Sang of Murder. 1990. 288p. mass mkt. 5.99 (*0-440-20745-2*) Dell Publishing.

—Thus Was Adonis Murdered. 1994. 320p. mass mkt. 5.99 (*0-440-21231-6*) Dell Publishing.

—Thus Was Adonis Murdered. 1982. 256p. pap. 5.95 o.p. (*0-14-006310-2*, Penguin Bks.) Viking Penguin.

**TANAKA, KEN (FICTITIOUS CHARACTER)—FICTION**

Furutani, Dale. Death in Little Tokyo. unabr. collector's ed. 1999. (Ken Tanaka Ser. ). audio 32.00 (*0-7366-4414-8*, 4875) Books on Tape, Inc.

—Death in Little Tokyo. 1996. 256p. 21.95 o.p. (*0-312-14580-2*, Saint Martin's Minotaur); Vol. 1. 1997. (Death in Little Tokyo Ser.: Vol. 1). 224p. mass mkt. 5.99 o.p. (*0-312-96323-8*, St. Martin's Paperbacks) St. Martin's Pr.

—The Toyotomi Blades, Vol. 1. 1998. (Toyotomi Blades Ser.: Vol. 1). 240p. mass mkt. 5.99 (*0-312-96667-9*, St. Martin's Paperbacks) St. Martin's Pr.

—The Toyotomi Blades: A Ken Tanaka Mystery. 1997. (Ken Tanaka Mystery Ser.). 224p. 21.95 (*0-312-17050-5*, Saint Martin's Minotaur) St. Martin's Pr.

**TANARI (FICTITIOUS CHARACTER)—FICTION**

Garrett, Randall. The River Wall. 1986. (Orig.). mass mkt. 3.95 o.s.i (*0-553-27671-9*, Spectra) Bantam Bks.

Garrett, Randall & Heydron, Vicki A. The Glass of Dyskornis. 1982. 144p. pap. 2.95 o.p. (*0-553-25230-5*) Bantam Bks.

—Return to Eddarta. 1985. (Gandalara Cycle Ser.: No. 6). 160p. pap. 2.75 o.p. (*0-553-24709-3*) Bantam Bks.

—The River Wall. 1986. 288p. (Orig.). mass mkt. 3.50 o.s.i (*0-553-25565-7*, Spectra) Bantam Bks.

—The Search for Ka. 1984. 192p. pap. 2.50 o.p. (*0-553-24120-6*) Bantam Bks.

—The Steel of Raithskar. 1981. 192p. pap. 2.75 o.p. (*0-553-24911-8*) Bantam Bks.

—The Well of Darkness. 1983. (Gandalara Cycle Ser.: No. 4). pap. 2.75 o.p. (*0-553-24505-8*) Bantam Bks.

**TANNER, ALEX (FICTITIOUS CHARACTER)—FICTION**

Donald, Anabel. The Glass Ceiling. l.t. ed. 1995. pap. 20.95 o.p. (*0-7838-1522-0*, Macmillan Reference USA) Gale Group.

—The Glass Ceiling. 1995. 217p. 20.95 o.p. (*0-312-13501-7*, Saint Martin's Minotaur) St. Martin's Pr.

—In at the Deep End. l.t. ed. 1995. 332p. pap. 20.95 o.p. (*0-7838-1244-2*, Macmillan Reference USA) Gale Group.

—In at the Deep End. 1994. 224p. 19.95 o.p. (*0-312-11290-4*, Saint Martin's Minotaur) St. Martin's Pr.

—An Uncommon Murder. 1993. 217p. 17.95 o.p. (*0-312-08917-1*, Saint Martin's Minotaur) St. Martin's Pr.

Two for Tanner. 2000. pap. 5.95 (*0-7540-3658-8*) BBC Audiobooks America.

**TANNER, ELI (FICTITIOUS CHARACTER)—FICTION**

Scott, Leonard B. Solemn Duty. 1998. 5.99 (*0-345-39186-1*); 1997. 320p. mass mkt. 5.99 (*0-345-41997-9*) Ballantine Bks.

**TANNER, EVAN (FICTITIOUS CHARACTER)—FICTION**

Block, Lawrence. The Canceled Czech. 1986. 192p. mass mkt. 2.95 o.s.i (*0-515-08689-4*, Jove) Berkley Publishing Group.

—Here Comes a Hero. 1986. 176p. mass mkt. 2.95 o.s.i (*0-515-08686-X*); 1985. mass mkt. 2.95 o.s.i (*0-515-08420-4*) Berkley Publishing Group. (Jove).

—Me Tanner, You Jane. 1986. mass mkt. 2.95 o.s.i (*0-515-08516-2*, Jove) Berkley Publishing Group.

—The Scoreless Thai: An Evan Tanner Novel. 2000. 160p. reprint ed. 30.00 (*1-892284-99-5*) Subterranean Pr.

—Tanner on Ice. 1998. (Evan Tanner Mystery Ser.). 256p. 23.95 o.p. (*0-525-94421-4*) Dutton/Plume.

—Tanner on Ice. l.t. ed. 1999. 26.95 (*1-56895-701-7*, Wheeler Publishing, Inc.) Gale Group.

—Tanner on Ice. 1999. (Evan Tanner Mysteries Ser.). 320p. reprint ed. mass mkt. 6.99 o.s.i (*0-451-19410-1*, Signet Bks.) NAL.

—Tanner's Tiger. 1986. mass mkt. 2.95 o.s.i (*0-515-08687-8*); 1985. 192p. mass mkt. 2.95 o.s.i (*0-515-08328-3*) Berkley Publishing Group. (Jove).

—Tanner's Tiger. l.t. ed. 2002. 276p. lib. bdg. 27.95 (*1-58547-172-0*) Ctr. Point Large Print.

—Tanner's Twelve Swingers. unabr. ed. 2000. (Evan Tanner Mysteries Ser: Vol. 3). audio 39.95 (*0-7927-2360-0*, CSL 249, Chivers Sound Library) BBC Audiobooks America.

—Tanner's Twelve Swingers. 1985. 192p. mass mkt. 2.95 o.s.i (*0-515-08106-X*, Jove) Berkley Publishing Group.

—Tanner's Twelve Swingers. l.t. ed. 2001. lib. bdg. 26.95 (*1-58547-130-5*) Ctr. Point Large Print.

—Tanner's Twelve Swingers. 1999. (Evan Tanner Mysteries Ser.). 272p. mass mkt. 5.99 (*0-451-19833-6*, Signet Bks.) NAL.

—The Thief Who Couldn't Sleep. unabr. ed. 1999. (Evan Tanner Mysteries Ser). 5p. audio 54.95 (*0-7927-2321-X*, CSL 210, Chivers Sound Library) BBC Audiobooks America.

—The Thief Who Couldn't Sleep. 1985. 208p. mass mkt. 2.95 o.s.i (*0-515-08636-3*); 1984. mass mkt. 2.95 o.s.i (*0-515-08311-9*); 1984. mass mkt. 2.95 o.s.i (*0-515-07870-0*) Berkley Publishing Group. (Jove).

—The Thief Who Couldn't Sleep. l.t. ed. 2001. 239p. lib. bdg. 26.95 (*1-58547-129-1*); 248p. (*1-74030-501-9*) Ctr. Point Large Print.

—The Thief Who Couldn't Sleep. 1998. (Evan Tanner Mysteries Ser.). 256p. mass mkt. 5.99 o.s.i (*0-451-19403-9*, Signet Bks.) NAL.

—Two for Tanner. 1986. 192p. mass mkt. 2.95 o.s.i (*0-515-08688-6*); 1985. mass mkt. 2.95 o.s.i (*0-515-08187-6*) Berkley Publishing Group. (Jove).

**TANNER, JOHN MARSHALL (FICTITIOUS CHARACTER)—FICTION**

Greenleaf, Stephen. Beyond Blame. 1986. pap. o.s.i (*0-345-00733-6*); mass mkt. 4.99 o.s.i (*0-345-33670-4*) Ballantine Bks.

—Blood Type: The New John Marshall Tanner Mystery. 1993. 304p. mass mkt. 4.99 o.s.i (*0-553-56106-5*) Bantam Bks.

—Blood Type: The New John Marshall Tanner Mystery. 1992. 304p. 20.00 o.p. (*0-688-11268-4*, Morrow, William & Co.) Morrow/Avon.

—Book Case: A John Marshall Tanner Mystery. 1991. 352p. mass mkt. 4.99 o.s.i (*0-553-29061-4*) Bantam Bks.

—Book Case: A John Marshall Tanner Mystery. 1991. 19.95 o.p. (*0-688-07669-6*, Morrow, William & Co.) Morrow/Avon.

—Death Bed. 1982. mass mkt. 2.50 o.s.i (*0-345-30189-7*) Ballantine Bks.

—Death Bed. 1991. 304p. mass mkt. 4.99 o.s.i (*0-553-29348-6*) Bantam Bks.

—Death Bed. 1980. 320p. 10.95 o.p. (*0-385-27139-5*) Doubleday Publishing.

—Death Bed. 1980. 306p. (J). o.p. (*0-8037-1701-6*, Dial Bks. for Young Readers) Penguin Putnam Bks. for Young Readers.

—The Death Bed. 1985. mass mkt. 2.95 o.s.i (*0-345-32742-X*) Ballantine Bks.

—Ellipsis: A John Marshall Tanner Novel. 2001. E-Book 24.00 (*1-58945-174-0*) Adobe Systems, Inc.

—Ellipsis: A John Marshall Tanner Novel. 2000. (John Marshall Tanner Mysteries Ser.). 272p. 24.00 o.s.i (*0-684-84955-0*); E-Book 24.00 (*0-7432-1075-1*) Simon & Schuster. (Scribner).

—False Conception: A John Marshall Tanner Novel. (John Marshall Tanner Mysteries Ser.). 1997. 336p. pap. 5.99 (*0-671-00794-7*, Pocket); 1994. 320p. 22.00 (*1-883402-87-5*, Scribner) Simon & Schuster.
—Fatal Obsession. 1985. mass mkt. 2.95 o.s.i (*0-345-33287-3*); 1984. mass mkt. 2.50 o.s.i (*0-345-31485-9*) Ballantine Bks.
—Fatal Obsession. 1991. 256p. mass mkt. 4.99 o.s.i (*0-553-29350-8*) Bantam Bks.
—Fatal Obsession. 1983. 264p. 14.95 o.p. (*0-385-27886-1*) Doubleday Publishing.
—Flesh Wounds: A John Marshall Tanner Mystery. (John Marshall Tanner Mysteries Ser.). 1997. 288p. per. 5.99 (*0-671-00795-5*, Pocket); 1996. 318p. 22.00 (*0-684-81583-4*, Scribner) Simon & Schuster.
—Grave Error. 1982. 240p. mass mkt. 2.50 o.s.i (*0-345-30188-9*) Ballantine Bks.
—Grave Error. 1991. 272p. mass mkt. 4.99 o.s.i (*0-553-29347-8*) Bantam Bks.
—Grave Error. 1985. 8.95 o.p. (*0-385-27058-5*) Doubleday Publishing.
—Past Tense. 1997. (John Marshall Tanner Mysteries Ser.). 352p. 22.00 (*0-684-83249-6*, Scribner) Simon & Schuster.
—Southern Cross: A John Marshall Tanner Novel. 1995. 320p. mass mkt. 4.99 o.s.i (*0-553-56817-5*) Bantam Bks.
—Southern Cross: A John Marshall Tanner Novel. 1993. 320p. 20.00 o.p. (*0-688-12772-X*, Morrow, William & Co.) Morrow/Avon.
—State's Evidence. 1985. 288p. mass mkt. 2.95 o.s.i (*0-345-32534-6*); 1983. mass mkt. 2.50 o.s.i (*0-345-30869-7*) Ballantine Bks.
—State's Evidence. 1991. 320p. mass mkt. 4.99 o.s.i (*0-553-29349-4*) Bantam Bks.
—State's Evidence. 1982. 320p. 15.95 o.p. (*0-385-27236-7*) Doubleday Publishing.
—Strawberry Sunday: A John Marshall Tanner Novel, 2000. audio 44.95 (*0-7861-1574-2*, P2403) Blackstone Audio Bks., Inc.
—Strawberry Sunday: A John Marshall Tanner Novel. 1999. 288p. 23.00 o.p. (*0-684-84954-2*, Scribner) Simon & Schuster.
—Strawberry Sunday: A John Marshall Tanner Novel. l.t. ed. 1999. (Americana Ser.). 439p. 27.95 (*0-7862-1951-3*) Thorndike Pr.
—Toll Call. 1988. mass mkt. 4.99 o.s.i (*0-345-35349-8*) Ballantine Bks.

**TARZAN (FICTITIOUS CHARACTER)—FICTION**

Burroughs, Edgar Rice. The Beasts of Tarzan. 2000. 252p. E-Book 3.95 (*0-594-05518-0*) 1873 Pr.
—The Beasts of Tarzan. 1985. (Tarzan Ser.: No. 3). 160p. mass mkt. 4.99 o.s.i (*0-345-32433-1*, Del Rey); 1980. mass mkt. 1.95 o.p. (*0-345-29513-7*); 1979. mass mkt. 1.75 o.p. (*0-345-28324-4*); 1977. mass mkt. 1.50 o.p. (*0-345-25832-0*); 1975. mass mkt. 1.25 o.p. (*0-345-24161-4*) Ballantine Bks.
—The Beasts of Tarzan. rev. ed. 2000. 200p. per. 9.90 (*1-58396-013-9*) Blue Unicorn Editions.
—The Beasts of Tarzan, Bk. 3. unabr. ed. 1993. audio 39.95 (*1-55686-480-9*, 480) Books in Motion.
—The Beasts of Tarzan. E-Book 3.49 (*1-929120-13-3*) Electric Umbrella Publishing.
—The Beasts of Tarzan. 2002. 192p. 24.99 (*1-58827-834-4*); per. 19.99 (*1-58827-835-2*) IndyPublish.com.
—The Beasts of Tarzan. (Tarzan Ser.: No. 3). E-Book 1.95 (*1-57799-821-9*) Logos Research Systems, Inc.
—The Beasts of Tarzan. 1999. E-Book 1.95 (*1-58515-077-0*) MesaView, Inc.
—The Beasts of Tarzan. 2003. (Quiet Vision Classic Ser.). (Illus.). 210p. text 24.99 (*1-57646-658-2*); 2003. (Quiet Vision Classic Ser.). (Illus.). 210p. pap. 12.99 (*1-57646-641-8*); 2000. (Tarzan Ser.: Vol. 3). 144p. pap. 9.99 (*1-57646-236-6*); 2000. (Tarzan Ser.: Vol. 3). 144p. lib. bdg. 27.99 (*1-57646-474-1*); 2000. (Tarzan Ser.: Vol. 3). 270p. pap. 17.99 (*1-57646-475-X*); 2000. (Tarzan Ser.: Vol. 3). 270p. lib. bdg. 29.99 (*1-57646-476-8*) Quiet Vision Publishing.
—The Beasts of Tarzan. E-Book 5.00 (*0-7410-0833-5*) SoftBook Pr.
—The Beasts of Tarzan. 2002. 240p. lib. bdg. 29.95 (*1-58715-621-0*) Wildside Pr.
—The Golden Age of Tarzan 1939-42. Horn, Maurice, ed. ltd. ed. 1977. (Illus.). 200.00 o.p. (*0-87754-055-1*) Chelsea Hse. Pubs.
—The Jungle Tales of Tarzan. E-Book 3.95 (*0-594-06141-5*) 1873 Pr.
—The Jungle Tales of Tarzan. 1980. mass mkt. 1.95 o.p. (*0-345-29478-5*); 1975. mass mkt. 1.25 o.p. (*0-345-24164-9*); No. 6. 1986. 192p. mass mkt. 3.95 o.s.i (*0-345-34413-8*, Del Rey) Ballantine Bks.
—The Jungle Tales of Tarzan. l.t. ed. 2000. 350p. per. 15.50 (*1-58396-103-8*); 2001. 200p. per. 9.90 (*1-58396-007-4*) Blue Unicorn Editions.
—The Jungle Tales of Tarzan. E-Book 3.49 (*1-929120-18-4*) Electric Umbrella Publishing.
—The Jungle Tales of Tarzan. 2002. 184p. 93.99 (*1-4043-1154-8*); per. 89.99 (*1-4043-1155-6*) IndyPublish.com.
—The Jungle Tales of Tarzan. (Tarzan Ser.: No. 6). E-Book 1.95 (*1-57799-824-3*) Logos Research Systems, Inc.
—The Jungle Tales of Tarzan. 1999. E-Book 1.95 (*1-58515-079-7*) MesaView, Inc.
—The Jungle Tales of Tarzan. 2003. (Quiet Vision Classic Ser.). (Illus.). text 24.99 (*1-57646-661-2*); 2003. (Quiet Vision Classic Ser.). (Illus.). pap. 12.99 (*1-57646-646-9*); 2000. (Tarzan Ser.: Vol. 6). 140p. pap. 9.99 (*1-57646-237-4*); 2000. (Tarzan Ser.: Vol. 6). 140p. lib. bdg. 27.99 (*1-57646-483-0*); 1999. (Tarzan Ser.: Vol. 6). 344p. E-Book 3.99 o.p. incl. cd-rom (*1-891595-58-X*); 2000. (Tarzan Ser.: Vol. 6). 298p. pap. 19.99 (*1-57646-484-9*); 2000. (Tarzan Ser.: Vol. 6). 298p. lib. bdg. 31.99 (*1-57646-485-7*) Quiet Vision Publishing.
—The Jungle Tales of Tarzan. 2nd ed. 2002. 256p. lib. bdg. 29.95 (*1-59224-958-2*) Wildside Pr.
—The Return of Tarzan. Date not set. 221p. 21.95 (*0-8488-2223-4*) Amereon, Ltd.
—The Return of Tarzan. 1984. (Tarzan Ser.: Vol. 2). 224p. mass mkt. 5.99 (*0-345-31575-8*, Ballantine Bks.) Ballantine Bks.
—The Return of Tarzan. unabr. ed. 2000. audio 44.95 (*0-7861-1728-1*, 2531) Blackstone Audio Bks., Inc.
—The Return of Tarzan. rev. ed. 2000. 300p. per. 9.90 (*1-58396-021-X*) Blue Unicorn Editions.
—The Return of Tarzan, Bk. 2. unabr. ed. 1993. audio 39.95 (*1-55686-479-5*, 479) Books in Motion.
—The Return of Tarzan. E-Book 1.49 (*1-929120-22-2*) Electric Umbrella Publishing.
—The Return of Tarzan. (Tarzan Ser.: No. 2). E-Book 2.95 (*1-57799-820-0*) Logos Research Systems, Inc.
—The Return of Tarzan. 1999. E-Book 1.95 (*1-58515-080-0*) MesaView, Inc.
—The Return of Tarzan. (Tarzan Ser.: Vol. 2). 2000. 178p. pap. 9.99 (*1-57646-244-7*); 2000. 178p. lib. bdg. 29.99 (*1-57646-471-7*); 1999. 443p. E-Book 3.99 o.p. incl. cd-rom (*1-891595-54-7*); 2000. 370p. pap. 24.99 (*1-57646-472-5*); 2000. 370p. lib. bdg. 34.99 (*1-57646-473-3*) Quiet Vision Publishing.
—The Son of Tarzan. 2000. 252p. pap. 9.95 (*0-594-04535-5*); E-Book 3.95 (*0-594-04538-X*) 1873 Pr.
—The Son of Tarzan. 1986. (Tarzan Ser.: No. 4). 222p. mass mkt. 4.99 o.s.i (*0-345-33556-2*, Del Rey) Ballantine Bks.
—The Son of Tarzan. rev. ed. 2000. 300p. per. 9.90 (*1-58396-022-8*) Blue Unicorn Editions.
—The Son of Tarzan, Bk. 4. unabr. ed. 1993. audio 49.95 (*1-55686-481-7*, 481) Books in Motion.
—The Son of Tarzan. E-Book 1.49 (*1-929120-23-0*) Electric Umbrella Publishing.
—The Son of Tarzan. (Tarzan Ser.: No. 4). E-Book 1.95 (*1-57799-822-7*) Logos Research Systems, Inc.
—The Son of Tarzan. 1999. E-Book 1.95 (*1-58515-081-9*) MesaView, Inc.
—The Son of Tarzan. 2000. (Tarzan Ser.: Vol. 4). 184p. pap. 9.99 (*1-57646-245-5*); 154p. lib. bdg. 28.99 (*1-57646-477-6*); 388p. pap. 24.99 (*1-57646-478-4*); 388p. lib. bdg. 35.99 (*1-57646-479-2*) Quiet Vision Publishing.
—The Son of Tarzan. unabr. ed. 2002. audio compact disk 42.00 (*1-4001-0056-9*); audio compact disk 20.00 (*1-4001-5056-6*) Tantor Media, Inc.
—The Son of Tarzan. 1998. lib. bdg. 27.95 (*1-56723-026-1*) Yestermorrow, Inc.
—Tarzan: Jungle Stories. unabr. ed. 1995. audio 39.95 (*1-55686-591-0*) Books in Motion.
—Tarzan & the Ant Men. (Tarzan Ser.). 1980. mass mkt. 1.95 o.p. (*0-345-28997-8*); 1979. mass mkt. 1.75 o.p. (*0-345-27984-0*); 1976. mass mkt. 1.25 o.p. (*0-345-24169-X*); 1969. mass mkt. 0.50 o.p. (*0-345-21752-7*); No. 10. 1985. 190p. mass mkt. 3.99 o.s.i (*0-345-32393-9*, Del Rey) Ballantine Bks.
—Tarzan & the Castaways. 1987. mass mkt. 2.50 o.s.i (*0-345-35255-6*); 1985. mass mkt. 2.25 o.s.i (*0-345-33433-7*); 1979. mass mkt. 1.95 o.p. (*0-345-28615-4*); 1977. mass mkt. 1.75 o.p. (*0-345-25964-5*) Ballantine Bks.
—Tarzan & the Castaways. 1975. (Illus.). reprint ed. 14.95 o.p. (*0-940724-10-3*) Hunt, Paul.
—Tarzan & the City of Gold. (Tarzan Ser.). 1980. mass mkt. 1.75 o.p. (*0-345-28035-0*); 1975. mass mkt. 1.25 o.p. (*0-345-24486-9*); No. 16. 1980. mass mkt. 3.95 o.s.i (*0-345-28987-0*, Del Rey) Ballantine Bks.
—Tarzan & the Forbidden City. 1980. 176p. mass mkt. 4.50 o.s.i (*0-345-29106-9*, Del Rey); 1977. mass mkt. 1.75 o.p. (*0-345-25960-2*); 1975. mass mkt. 1.25 o.p. (*0-345-24976-3*) Ballantine Bks.
—Tarzan & the Foreign Legion. 1987. mass mkt. 3.99 o.s.i (*0-345-34750-1*, Del Rey); 1984. mass mkt. 2.25 o.p. (*0-345-32454-4*); 1980. mass mkt. 1.95 o.p. (*0-345-28981-1*); 1977. mass mkt. 1.75 o.p. (*0-345-25962-9*); 1975. mass mkt. 1.25 o.p. (*0-345-24978-X*) Ballantine Bks.
—Tarzan & the Golden Lion. (Tarzan Ser.). 1980. mass mkt. 1.95 o.p. (*0-345-28998-6*); 1978. mass mkt. 1.75 o.p. (*0-345-27983-2*); 1976. mass mkt. 1.25 o.p. (*0-345-24168-1*); No. 9. 1986. 192p. mass mkt. 3.99 o.s.i (*0-345-34237-2*, Del Rey) Ballantine Bks.
—Tarzan & the Jewels of Opar. 2000. 252p. pap. 9.95 (*0-594-04520-7*); E-Book 3.95 (*0-594-04523-1*) 1873 Pr.
—Tarzan & the Jewels of Opar. 1998. mass mkt. 5.99 (*0-345-91423-6*, Del Rey); 1980. mass mkt. 1.95 o.p. (*0-345-28917-X*); 1978. mass mkt. 1.75 o.p. (*0-345-27728-7*); 1977. mass mkt. 1.50 o.p. (*0-345-27277-3*); 1975. mass mkt. 1.25 o.p. (*0-345-24163-0*); No. 5. 1984. 158p. mass mkt. 5.99 o.s.i (*0-345-32161-8*, Del Rey) Ballantine Bks.
—Tarzan & the Jewels of Opar. 2000. 200p. per. 9.90 (*1-58396-010-4*); 2001. 350p. per. 15.50 (*1-58396-105-4*) Blue Unicorn Editions.
—Tarzan & the Jewels of Opar, Bk. 5. unabr. ed. 1994. audio 39.95 (*1-55686-495-7*) Books in Motion.
—Tarzan & the Jewels of Opar. E-Book 3.49 (*1-929120-20-6*) Electric Umbrella Publishing.
—Tarzan & the Jewels of Opar. (Tarzan Ser.: No. 5). E-Book 1.95 (*1-57799-823-5*) Logos Research Systems, Inc.
—Tarzan & the Jewels of Opar. 1999. E-Book 1.95 (*1-58515-084-3*) MesaView, Inc.
—Tarzan & the Jewels of Opar. 2003. (Illus.). 196p. text 24.99 (*1-57646-660-4*); 2003. (Illus.). 196p. pap. 12.99 (*1-57646-644-2*); 2000. (Tarzan Ser.: Vol. 5). 146p. pap. 9.99 (*1-57646-247-1*); 2000. (Tarzan Ser.: Vol. 5). 146p. lib. bdg. 27.99 (*1-57646-480-6*); 1999. (Tarzan Ser.: Vol. 5). 333p. E-Book 3.99 o.p. incl. cd-rom (*1-891595-57-1*); 2000. (Tarzan Ser.: Vol. 5). 280p. pap. 19.99 (*1-57646-481-4*); 2000. (Tarzan Ser.: Vol. 5). 280p. lib. bdg. 30.99 (*1-57646-482-2*) Quiet Vision Publishing.
—Tarzan & the Jewels of Opar. E-Book 5.00 (*0-7410-0800-9*) SoftBook Pr.
—Tarzan & the Jewels of Opar. 2002. 248p. lib. bdg. 29.95 (*1-59224-959-0*) Wildside Pr.
—Tarzan & the Leopard Men. 1986. (Tarzan Ser.: Vol. 18). mass mkt. 4.99 o.s.i (*0-345-33828-6*, Del Rey); 1979. mass mkt. 1.95 o.p. (*0-345-28687-1*); 1978. mass mkt. 1.75 o.p. (*0-345-27804-6*); 1975. mass mkt. 1.25 o.p. (*0-345-24488-5*) Ballantine Bks.
—Tarzan & the Lion Men. (Tarzan Ser.). 1978. mass mkt. 1.75 o.p. (*0-345-28008-3*); 1975. mass mkt. 1.25 o.p. (*0-345-24487-7*); No. 17. 1980. 192p. mass mkt. 2.95 o.s.i (*0-345-28988-9*, Del Rey) Ballantine Bks.
—Tarzan & the Lost Empire, No. 12. 1985. 190p. mass mkt. 3.95 o.s.i (*0-345-32957-0*, Del Rey) Ballantine Bks.
—Tarzan & the Madman No. 23. 1987. mass mkt. 3.95 o.s.i (*0-345-35037-5*, Del Rey); 1977. mass mkt. 1.75 o.s.i (*0-345-25963-7*) Ballantine Bks.
—Tarzan & the Madman No. 23. 1975. (Illus.). reprint ed. 60.00 o.p. (*0-940724-11-1*) Hunt, Paul.
—Tarzan & the Tarzan Twins. 1982. (Illus.). 14.95 o.p. (*0-940724-12-X*) Hunt, Paul.
—Tarzan at the Earth's Core. (Pellucidar Ser.). 1985. 256p. mass mkt. 2.75 o.s.i (*0-441-79858-6*); 1982. mass mkt. 2.25 o.s.i (*0-441-79856-X*) Ace Bks.
—Tarzan at the Earth's Core. 1986. 192p. mass mkt. 3.95 o.s.i (*0-345-32822-1*, Del Rey); 1981. mass mkt. 1.95 o.p. (*0-345-29663-X*); 1975. mass mkt. 1.25 o.p. (*0-345-24483-4*); 1974. mass mkt. 0.95 o.p. (*0-345-21907-4*) Ballantine Bks.
—Tarzan at the Earth's Core. 1982. (Illus.). 75.00 o.p. (*0-940724-13-8*) Hunt, Paul.
—The Tarzan Collection, 3 vols. rev. ed. 2000. 1200p. per. 35.00 (*1-58396-009-0*) Blue Unicorn Editions.
—The Tarzan Collection. 1999. E-Book 8.99 incl. cd-rom (*1-57646-061-4*) Quiet Vision Publishing.
—Tarzan, Lion Man & Leopard Man. 1999. mass mkt. (*0-345-41754-2*, Del Rey) Ballantine Bks.
—Tarzan, Lord of the Jungle. 1980. mass mkt. 1.95 o.p. (*0-345-28986-2*); 1978. mass mkt. 1.75 o.p. (*0-345-27985-9*); No. 11. 1984. 190p. mass mkt. 4.99 o.s.i (*0-345-32455-2*, Del Rey) Ballantine Bks.
—Tarzan of the Apes. 22.95 (*0-8488-1257-3*) Amereon, Ltd.
—Tarzan of the Apes. 1984. (Tarzan Ser.: Vol. 1). (Illus.). 288p. mass mkt. 6.99 (*0-345-31977-X*, Del Rey); 1983. mass mkt. 2.50 o.p. (*0-345-31531-6*); 1979. mass mkt. 1.95 o.p. (*0-345-28377-5*); 1976. mass mkt. 1.50 o.p. (*0-345-25830-4*); 1975. mass mkt. 1.25 o.p. (*0-345-24159-2*) Ballantine Bks.
—Tarzan of the Apes. 2003. 220p. per. 17.95 (*1-58509-250-9*, 509) Book Tree, The.
—Tarzan of the Apes. 2002. pap. 4.95 (*1-59109-026-1*) Booksurge, LLC.
—Tarzan of the Apes. 1999. (Tarzan of the Apes Ser.). 352p. mass mkt. 4.99 (*0-8125-7238-6*, Tor Bks.) Doherty, Tom Assocs., LLC.
—Tarzan of the Apes. E-Book 3.49 (*1-929120-09-5*) Electric Umbrella Publishing.
—Tarzan of the Apes. E-Book 2.95 (*1-57799-819-7*) Logos Research Systems, Inc.
—Tarzan of the Apes. 1990. 228p. (YA). mass mkt. 4.95 (*0-451-52423-3*, Signet Classics) NAL.
—Tarzan of the Apes. 2003. (Quiet Vision Classic Ser.). 256p. text 24.99 (*1-57646-656-6*); 2003. (Quiet Vision Classic Ser.). 256p. pap. 12.99 (*1-57646-636-1*); 2000. (Tarzan Ser.: Vol. 1). 186p. pap. 9.99 (*1-57646-246-3*); 2000. (Tarzan Ser.: Vol. 1). 186p. lib. bdg. 30.99 (*1-57646-468-7*); 1999. (Tarzan Ser.: Vol. 1). 483p. E-Book 3.99 o.p. incl. cd-rom (*1-891595-53-9*) Quiet Vision Publishing.
—Tarzan of the Apes. 2003. (Modern Library Classics). 288p. pap. 8.95 (*0-8129-6706-2*, Modern Library) Random House Adult Trade Publishing Group.
—Tarzan of the Apes. 1998. 672p. 9.99 o.s.i (*0-517-18907-0*); 1988. xvi, 848p. 7.99 o.s.i (*0-517-65957-3*) Random Hse. Value Publishing.
—Tarzan of the Apes. 2001. 266p. E-Book 4.00 (*1-929670-93-1*) Renaissance E Bks.
—Tarzan of the Apes. E-Book 5.00 (*0-7410-0432-1*) SoftBook Pr.
—Tarzan of the Apes. 1963. 12.04 (*0-606-14346-7*) Turtleback Bks.
—Tarzan of the Apes. 2001. 184p. pap. 11.95 (*1-57002-146-5*) University Publishing Hse., Inc.
—Tarzan of the Apes. 1990. (Penguin Twentieth-Century Classics Ser.). 320p. 8.95 (*0-14-018464-3*, Penguin Classics) Viking Penguin.
—Tarzan of the Apes. 2002. 324p. lib. bdg. 29.95 (*1-58715-617-2*) Wildside Pr.
—Tarzan of the Apes. 1982. (Step into Classics Ser.). (Illus.). 96p. (J). (gr. 2-7). pap. 3.99 o.s.i (*0-394-85089-0*, Random Hse. Bks. for Young Readers) Random Hse. Children's Bks.
—Tarzan of the Apes, unabr. ed. 1999. (YA). (gr. 5 up). audio 41.95 (*1-55685-633-4*) Audio Bk. Contractors, Inc.
—Tarzan of the Apes. abr. ed. 1999. audio 16.95 (*1-882071-43-3*) B&B Audio, Inc.
—Tarzan of the Apes. unabr. ed. 1995. 9p. audio 44.95 (*0-7861-0673-5*, 1575) Blackstone Audio Bks., Inc.
—Tarzan of the Apes. l.t. ed. 2001. 350p. per. 15.50 (*1-58396-106-2*); 2000. 300p. per. 9.90 (*1-58396-011-2*) Blue Unicorn Editions.
—Tarzan of the Apes, Bk. 1. unabr. ed. 1993. audio 49.95 (*1-55686-477-9*, 477) Books in Motion.
—Tarzan of the Apes. unabr. collector's ed. 1993. (YA). (gr. 8 up). audio 48.00 (*0-7366-2596-8*, 3341) Books on Tape, Inc.
—Tarzan of the Apes. 1976. reprint ed. lib. bdg. 25.95 (*0-89966-046-0*) Buccaneer Bks., Inc.
—Tarzan of the Apes. 1997. (Thrift Editions Ser.). 224p. reprint ed. pap. text 2.00 (*0-486-29570-2*) Dover Pubns., Inc.
—Tarzan of the Apes. l.t. ed. 901p. pap. 70.02 (*0-7583-2517-7*); 327p. pap. 27.50 (*0-7583-2513-4*); 732p. pap. 51.89 (*0-7583-2516-9*); 569p. pap. 42.24 (*0-7583-2515-0*); 260p. pap. 23.72 (*0-7583-2512-6*); 1293p. pap. 90.00 (*0-7583-2519-3*); 1108p. pap. 80.22 (*0-7583-2518-5*); 901p. lib. bdg. 82.02 (*0-7583-2509-6*); 1293p. lib. bdg. 102.00 (*0-7583-2511-8*); 447p. lib. bdg. 40.20 (*0-7583-2506-1*); 327p. lib. bdg. 33.50 (*0-7583-2505-3*); 569p. lib. bdg. 48.24 (*0-7583-2507-X*); 1108p. lib. bdg. 92.22 (*0-7583-2510-X*); 732p. lib. bdg. 57.89 (*0-7583-2508-8*); 260p. lib. bdg. 29.72 (*0-7583-2504-5*) Huge Print Pr.
—Tarzan of the Apes. unabr. ed. 1989. (YA). (gr. 6-10). audio 39.00 Jimcin Recordings.
—Tarzan of the Apes. abr. ed. (Ultimate Classics Ser.). 1994. audio 29.95 o.p. (*0-7871-0063-3*, Dove Audio); 1993. 16.95 o.p. (*1-55800-757-1*, 391741) NewStar Media, Inc.
—Tarzan of the Apes. l.t. ed. 2003. (Large Print Ser.). lib. bdg. 26.00 (*1-58287-701-7*) North Bks.
—Tarzan of the Apes. l.t. ed. 2003. 304p. E-Book 2.99 (*1-932681-40-X*) NuVision Pubns.
—Tarzan of the Apes. l.t. ed. 2000. (Tarzan Ser.: Vol. 1). 378p. pap. 24.99 (*1-57646-469-5*); lib. bdg. 35.99 (*1-57646-470-9*) Quiet Vision Publishing.
—Tarzan of the Apes. l.t. ed. 1994. 381p. lib. bdg. 21.95 (*0-7838-1160-8*) Thorndike Pr.
—Tarzan the Invincible. 1987. 192p. mass mkt. 3.99 o.s.i (*0-345-35163-0*, Del Rey); 1980. mass mkt. 1.95 o.p. (*0-345-28989-7*); 1978. mass mkt. 1.25 o.p. (*0-345-24484-2*); 1978. mass mkt. 1.75 o.p. (*0-345-28055-5*); 1974. mass mkt. 0.95 o.p. (*0-345-21908-2*) Ballantine Bks.
—Tarzan the Magnificent. 1980. 200p. mass mkt. 3.95 o.s.i (*0-345-28980-3*, Del Rey); 1977. mass mkt. 1.75 o.p. (*0-345-25961-0*); 1975. mass mkt. 1.25 o.p. (*0-345-24977-1*) Ballantine Bks.

—Tarzan the Terrible. 1979. mass mkt. 1.95 o.p. (*0-345-28745-2*); 1978. mass mkt. 1.75 o.p. (*0-345-27982-4*); 1969. mass mkt. 0.50 o.p. (*0-345-21750-0*); No. 8. 1985. 190p. mass mkt. 3.99 o.s.i (*0-345-32392-0*, Del Rey) Ballantine Bks.

—Tarzan the Terrible. 2001. per. (*1-58396-255-7*); 2000. per. 9.90 (*1-58396-093-7*); 2001. per. 15.50 (*1-58396-179-8*); 2001. per. (*1-58396-256-5*) Blue Unicorn Editions.

—Tarzan the Terrible. E-Book 2.49 (*0-7574-0327-1*) Electric Umbrella Publishing.

—Tarzan the Terrible. 2003. (Illus.). 266p. text 24.99 (*1-57646-663-9*); 2003. (Illus.). 266p. pap. 12.99 (*1-57646-648-5*); 2000. (Tarzan Ser.: Vol. 8). 186p. pap. 9.99 (*1-57646-249-8*); 2000. (Tarzan Ser.: Vol. 8). 186p. lib. bdg. 30.99 (*1-57646-489-X*); 2000. (Tarzan Ser.: Vol. 8). 388p. lib. bdg. 34.99 (*1-57646-491-1*) Quiet Vision Publishing.

—Tarzan the Terrible. 2002. 284p. lib. bdg. 29.95 (*1-59224-960-4*) Wildside Pr.

—Tarzan the Triumphant. 1987. mass mkt. 2.50 o.s.i (*0-345-35274-2*); 1978. mass mkt. 1.75 o.p. (*0-345-28054-7*) Ballantine Bks.

—Tarzan the Untamed. 1979. mass mkt. 1.95 o.p. (*0-345-28868-8*); 1978. mass mkt. 1.75 o.p. (*0-345-27697-3*); 1971. mass mkt. 0.50 o.p. (*0-345-21749-7*); No. 7. 1984. 254p. mass mkt. 4.99 o.s.i (*0-345-32391-2*, Del Rey) Ballantine Bks.

—Tarzan the Untamed. 2000. 300p. per. 9.90 (*1-58396-012-0*); 2001. per. 15.50 (*1-58396-107-0*) Blue Unicorn Editions.

—Tarzan the Untamed. 1999. 96p. (YA). (gr. 7 up). pap. 11.95 (*1-56971-418-5*) Dark Horse Comics.

—Tarzan the Untamed. E-Book 1.49 (*1-929120-24-9*) Electric Umbrella Publishing.

—Tarzan the Untamed. (Tarzan Ser.: No. 7). E-Book 1.95 (*1-57799-825-1*) Logos Research Systems, Inc.

—Tarzan the Untamed. 2003. (Illus.). 294p. text 24.99 (*1-57646-662-0*); 2003. (Illus.). 294p. pap. 12.99 (*1-57646-647-7*); 2000. (Tarzan Ser.: Vol. 7). 206p. pap. 9.99 (*1-57646-248-X*); 2000. (Tarzan Ser.: Vol. 7). 206p. lib. bdg. 31.99 (*1-57646-486-5*); 1999. (Tarzan Ser.: Vol. 7). 510p. E-Book 3.99 o.p. incl. cd-rom (*1-891595-59-8*); 2000. (Tarzan Ser.: Vol. 7). 434p. pap. 29.99 (*1-57646-487-3*); 2000. (Tarzan Ser.: Vol. 7). 434p. lib. bdg. 38.99 (*1-57646-488-1*) Quiet Vision Publishing.

—Tarzan the Untamed. 2002. 236p. lib. bdg. 29.95 (*1-58715-311-4*) Wildside Pr.

—Tarzan Triumphant: And Tarzan & the City of Gold. 1997. (Tarzan Ser.). mass mkt. 6.99 o.s.i (*0-345-41641-4*, Del Rey) Ballantine Bks.

—Tarzan 2 in 1: Tarzan & the Golden Lion & Tarzan & the Ant Men, Vols. 9 and10. 1997. (Access to History Ser.). 426p. mass mkt. 5.99 o.s.i (*0-345-41348-2*, Del Rey) Ballantine Bks.

—Tarzan 2 in 1: Tarzan & the Jewels of Opar & Jungle Tales of Tarzan. 1996. (Tarzan Ser.). 340p. mass mkt. 5.99 o.s.i (*0-345-40831-4*) Ballantine Bks.

—Tarzan 2 in 1: Tarzan, Lord of the Jungle & Tarzan & the Lost Empire. 1997. (Tarzan the Classics Ser.). 406p. mass mkt. 5.99 o.s.i (*0-345-41347-4*, Del Rey) Ballantine Bks.

—Tarzan 2 in 1: Tarzan the Untamed & Tarzan the Terrible, Vol. 7 & 8. 1997. mass mkt. 5.99 o.s.i (*0-345-40832-2*, Del Rey) Ballantine Bks.

—Tarzan 2-in-1: The Beasts of Tarzan/The Son of Tarzan, 2 vols. in 1, Vols. 3-4. 1996. (Tarzan the Classics Ser.). 384p. mass mkt. 6.99 (*0-345-40830-6*, Del Rey) Ballantine Bks.

—Tarzan 3 in 1. 1996. mass mkt. o.s.i (*0-345-40647-8*) Ballantine Bks.

—Tarzan's Quest. 1999. mass mkt. (*0-345-41755-0*, Del Rey); 1977. mass mkt. 1.75 o.p. (*0-345-25959-9*) Ballantine Bks.

—Tarzan's Quest No. 19. 1980. 178p. mass mkt. 4.99 o.s.i (*0-345-29562-5*, Del Rey) Ballantine Bks.

Burroughs, Edgar Rice & Lansdale, Joe R. Tarzan: The Lost Adventures. 1997. (Tarzan Ser.). 272p. mass mkt. 5.99 o.s.i (*0-345-41273-7*, Del Rey) Ballantine Bks.

—Tarzan: The Lost Adventures. ltd. ed. 1996. (Illus.). 208p. (YA). (gr. 7 up). pap. 19.95 (*1-56971-083-X*) Dark Horse Comics.

—Terminator: The Tempest. ltd. ed. 1996. (Illus.). 208p. (YA). (gr. 7 up). 99.95 o.p. (*1-56971-128-3*) Dark Horse Comics.

Burroughs, Edgar Rice, et al. Tarzan: Le Monstre. 1998. (Illus.). 160p. (YA). (gr. 9 up). pap. 16.95 (*1-56971-296-4*) Dark Horse Comics.

—Tarzan of the Apes. 1999. 104p. (YA). (gr. 7 up). pap. 12.95 (*1-56971-416-9*) Dark Horse Comics.

Echenique, Alfredo Bryce. La Amigdalitis de Tarzan. 2000. (SPA.). 319p. pap. 15.95 (*968-19-0562-8*) Aguilar Editorial MEX. *Dist:* Lectorum Pubns., Inc., Santillana USA Publishing Co., Inc.

Farmer, Philip Jose. The Dark Heart of Time: A Tarzan Novel. 1999. 512p. mass mkt. 6.99 o.s.i (*0-345-42463-8*, Del Rey) Ballantine Bks.

Foster, Hal. Tarzan, 1931-1933, Vol. 1. 1997. (Tarzan Ser.: Vol. 1). (Illus.). 128p. pap. 5.00 o.p. (*1-56163-178-7*, Flying Buttress Classics Library The) NBM Publishing Co.

—Tarzan, 1933-1935, Vol. 2. 1997. (Job Bank Ser.). (Illus.). 128p. pap. 5.00 o.p. (*1-56163-186-8*, Flying Buttress Classics Library The) NBM Publishing Co.

Foster, Harold. Tarzan in Color, Vol. 1. Blackbeard, Bill, ed. 1992. 64p. text 35.00 o.p. (*1-56163-049-7*) NBM Publishing Co.

—Tarzan in Color (1932-1933), Vol. 2. Blackbeard, Bill, ed. 1993. (Tarzan in Color (1932-1933) Ser.: Vol. 2). 64p. 9.95 o.p. (*1-56163-063-2*, Flying Buttress Classics Library The) NBM Publishing Co.

—Tarzan in Color (1933-1934), Vol. 3. Blackbeard, Bill, ed. 1993. 64p. 35.00 o.p. (*1-56163-067-5*) NBM Publishing Co.

—Tarzan in Color (1934-1935), Vol. 4. Blackbeard, Bill, ed. 1993. (Illus.). 64p. 35.00 o.p. (*1-56163-082-9*) NBM Publishing Co.

—Tarzan in Color (1935-1936), Vol. 5. Blackbeard, Bill, ed. 1993. (Tarzan Ser.: Vol. 5). (Illus.). 64p. 9.95 o.p. (*1-56163-083-7*, Flying Buttress Classics Library The) NBM Publishing Co.

Foster, Harold & Hogarth, Burne. Tarzan in Color (1936-1937), Vol. 6. Blackbeard, Bill, ed. 1994. (Tarzan Ser.: Vol. 6). 64p. 9.95 o.p. (*1-56163-092-6*, Flying Buttress Classics Library The) NBM Publishing Co.

Hogarth, Burne. Tarzan in Color (1937-1938), Vol. 7. Blackbeard, Bill, ed. 1994. (Tarzan Ser.: Vol. 7). 64p. 9.95 o.p. (*1-56163-093-4*, Flying Buttress Classics Library The) NBM Publishing Co.

—Tarzan, 1938-1939, Vol. 8. 1994. (Tarzan, 1938-1939 Ser.: Vol. 8). 64p. 9.95 o.p. (*1-56163-105-1*, Flying Buttress Classics Library The) NBM Publishing Co.

—Tarzan, 1939-1940, Vol. 9. 1994. (Tarzan Ser.: Vol. 9). 64p. 9.95 o.p. (*1-56163-106-X*, Flying Buttress Classics Library The) NBM Publishing Co.

—Tarzan, 1940-1941, Vol. 10. 1995. (Tarzan, 1940-1941 Ser.: Vol. 1). 64p. 9.95 o.p. (*1-56163-120-5*, Flying Buttress Classics Library The) NBM Publishing Co.

—Tarzan, 1941-1942, Vol. 11. 1995. (Tarzan Ser.: Vol. 11). 64p. 25.00 o.p. (*1-56163-121-3*, Flying Buttress Classics Library The) NBM Publishing Co.

—Tarzan, 1942-1943, Vol. 12. 1995. (Tarzan Ser.: Vol. 12). 64p. 25.00 o.p. (*1-56163-126-4*, Flying Buttress Classics Library The) NBM Publishing Co.

—Tarzan, 1943-1944, Vol. 13. 1995. (Tarzan Ser.: Vol. 13). 64p. 25.00 o.p. (*1-56163-134-5*, Flying Buttress Classics Library The) NBM Publishing Co.

—Tarzan, 1944-1945, Vol. 14. 1996. (Tarzan Ser.: Vol. 14). 64p. 25.00 o.p. (*1-56163-135-3*) NBM Publishing Co.

—Tarzan, 1945-1946, Vol. 15. 1996. (Tarzan Ser.: Vol. 15). 64p. 25.00 o.p. (*1-56163-136-1*, Flying Buttress Classics Library The) NBM Publishing Co.

—Tarzan, 1947-1948, Vol. 16. 1996. (Tarzan (1947-1948) Ser.: Vol. 16). (Illus.). 64p. 25.00 o.p. (*1-56163-163-9*, Flying Buttress Classics Library The) NBM Publishing Co.

—Tarzan, 1948-1949, Vol. 17. 1996. (Tarzan Ser.: Vol. 17). (Illus.). 64p. 25.00 o.p. (*1-56163-164-7*, Flying Buttress Classics Library The) NBM Publishing Co.

—Tarzan (1949-1950), Vol. 18. 1996. (Tarzan Ser.). (Illus.). 64p. 25.00 o.p. (*1-56163-165-5*, Flying Buttress Classics Library The) NBM Publishing Co.

Hogarth, Burne, et al. The Jungle Tales of Tarzan. 1976. 35 p. o.p. (*0-8230-2576-4*) Watson-Guptill Pubns., Inc.

Johnson, Lamont. Tarzan, collector's ed. 1997. 64p. pap. 59.98 o.p. incl. audio (*1-57019-239-1*, 4203) Radio Spirits, Inc.

Metacom Staff, prod. Tarzan: Nostalgia Radio Six-Pack. 1998. audio 9.98 o.p. (*0-7672-0000-4*) MediaBay Audio Publishing.

Moreira, Reuben. Tarzan (1946-1947), Vol. 15B. 1996. (Illus.). 72p. 24.95 o.p. (*1-56163-155-8*) NBM Publishing Co.

Salvatore, R. A. Tarzan: The Epic Adventures. 1997. 280p. mass mkt. 5.99 o.s.i (*0-345-41295-8*, Del Rey) Ballantine Bks.

Simonson, Walter & Burroughs, Edgar Rice. Tarzan vs. Predator at the Earth's Core. 1997. 104p. (YA). (gr. 7 up). pap. 12.95 (*1-56971-231-X*) Dark Horse Comics.

Weissmuller, Johnny, Jr., contrib. by. Tarzan. unabr. ed. 1993. audio 19.95 (*1-55935-118-7*) Soundelux Audio Publishing.

**TATE, GERRY (FICTITIOUS CHARACTER)—FICTION**

Babson, Marian. Cover-up Story. 1991. 208p. mass mkt. 3.99 o.s.i (*0-553-29330-3*) Bantam Bks.

—Cover-up Story. l.t. ed. 1991. (Nightingale Ser.). 264p. pap. 14.95 o.p. (*0-8161-4926-7*, Macmillan Reference USA) Gale Group.

—Cover-up Story. 2003. 224p. mass mkt. 6.50 (*0-312-98822-2*, St. Martin's Paperbacks); 1988. 192p. 14.95 o.p. (*0-312-02180-1*, Saint Martin's Minotaur) St. Martin's Pr.

—In the Teeth of Adversity. 1992. 208p. mass mkt. 4.99 o.s.i (*0-553-29131-9*) Bantam Bks.

—In the Teeth of Adversity. l.t. ed. 1992. (Nightingale Ser.). 250p. 14.95 o.p. (*0-8161-5259-4*, Macmillan Reference USA) Gale Group.

—In the Teeth of Adversity. 2003. 176p. mass mkt. 6.50 (*0-312-99103-7*, St. Martin's Paperbacks); 1990. 14.95 o.p. (*0-312-04332-5*, Saint Martin's Minotaur) St. Martin's Pr.

—Murder at the Cat Show. 1990. 192p. reprint ed. mass mkt. 3.95 o.s.i (*0-553-28590-4*) Bantam Bks.

—Murder at the Cat Show. l.t. ed. 1992. (Nightingale Ser.). 264p. 14.95 o.p. (*0-8161-5258-6*, Macmillan Reference USA) Gale Group.

—Murder at the Cat Show. pap. 15.95 (*0-312-31278-4*, Saint Martin's Griffin); 2003. 192p. mass mkt. 5.99 (*0-312-98974-1*, St. Martin's Paperbacks); 1989. 14.95 o.p. (*0-312-02954-3*, Saint Martin's Minotaur) St. Martin's Pr.

—Tourists Are for Trapping. 1991. 192p. mass mkt. 3.99 o.s.i (*0-553-29031-2*) Bantam Bks.

—Tourists Are for Trapping. 1992. 2.99 o.p. (*0-517-09060-0*) Random Hse. Value Publishing.

—Tourists Are for Trapping. 2003. 208p. mass mkt. 5.99 (*0-312-99099-5*, St. Martin's Paperbacks); 1989. 192p. 14.95 o.p. (*0-312-03444-X*, Saint Martin's Minotaur) St. Martin's Pr.

**TATE, SHELBY KAY (FICTITIOUS CHARACTER)—FICTION**

Shankman, Sarah. I Still Miss My Man, but My Aim Is Getting Better. 1997. 288p. pap. 5.99 (*0-671-89750-0*, Pocket); 1996. 272p. 21.00 o.p. (*0-671-89751-9*, Atria) Simon & Schuster.

**TATUM TWINS (FICTITIOUS CHARACTERS)—FICTION**

McCafferty, Barbara Taylor. Double Cross. (Bert & Nan Tatum Mystery Ser.). 2000. 256p. mass mkt. 5.99 o.s.i (*1-57566-511-5*); 1998. 240p. 20.00 o.s.i (*1-57566-338-4*) Kensington Publishing Corp.

—Double Dealer. 2000. (Bert & Nan Tatum Mystery Ser.). 250p. 20.00 o.s.i (*1-57566-507-7*, Kensington Bks.) Kensington Publishing Corp.

—Double Exposure. annuals 1998. (Bert & Nan Tatum Mystery Ser.). 320p. mass mkt. 5.99 o.s.i (*1-57566-343-0*) Kensington Publishing Corp.

—Double Murder. 1996. 288p. 18.95 o.s.i (*1-57566-084-9*, Kensington Bks.) Kensington Publishing Corp.

McCafferty, Barbara Taylor & Herald, Beverly Taylor. Double Date. (Partners in Crime Ser.). 2002. 288p. mass mkt. 5.99 (*1-57566-732-0*); 2001. 256p. 22.00 o.s.i (*1-57566-639-1*) Kensington Publishing Corp.

—Double Date. l.t. ed. 2001. 336p. 28.95 (*0-7862-3326-5*) Thorndike Pr.

—Double Dealer. 2000. 272p. mass mkt. 5.99 o.s.i (*1-57566-642-1*) Kensington Publishing Corp.

—Double Dealer. l.t. ed. 2000. (Mystery Ser.). 352p. 26.95 (*0-7862-2835-0*) Thorndike Pr.

—Double Exposure. annuals 1997. (Bert & Nan Tatum Mystery Ser.). 288p. 18.95 o.s.i (*1-57566-207-8*) Kensington Publishing Corp.

—Double Murder. 1997. (Bert & Nan Tatum Mystery Ser.). 288p. mass mkt. 5.50 (*1-57566-212-4*) Kensington Publishing Corp.

**TAVERNER, MILOS (FICTITIOUS CHARACTER)—FICTION**

Stephens, Reed, pseud. The Gap into Power: A Dark & Hungry God Arises. 1993. (Gap Ser.: No. 3). 528p. mass mkt. 7.50 (*0-553-56260-6*) Bantam Bks.

**TAYLOR, DOV (FICTITIOUS CHARACTER)—FICTION**

Rosenbaum, David. Zaddik. 2002. 448p. pap. 14.95 (*1-931229-20-1*) Invisible Cities Pr.

—Zaddik. 1993. 448p. 19.95 (*0-89296-540-1*) Mysterious Pr.

—Zaddik. 1994. 464p. mass mkt. 5.99 o.s.i (*0-446-40322-9*) Warner Bks., Inc.

**TAYLOR, EASY (FICTITIOUS CHARACTER)—FICTION**

Keller, Roland. Pardee Holler: An Easy Taylor Mystery. 1996. (Easy Taylor Mystery Ser.). 256p. (Orig.). pap. 8.95 (*0-9651928-0-6*) PKA Pubns.

**TAYLOR, FRED (FICTITIOUS CHARACTER)—FICTION**

Kilmer, Nicholas. Dirty Linen. 1999. (Fred Taylor Mystery Ser.). 256p. 25.00 o.s.i (*0-8050-5034-5*) Holt, Henry & Co.

—Dirty Linen. 2001. 218p. pap. 14.95 o.s.i (*1-890208-53-1*) Poisoned Pen Pr.

—Harmony in Flesh & Black. 1995. 261p. 21.00 o.p. (*0-8050-3663-6*) Holt, Henry & Co.

—Harmony in Flesh & Black. 1996. 272p. mass mkt. 4.99 o.p. (*0-06-104425-3*, HarperTorch) Morrow/Avon.

—Man with a Squirrel. unabr. ed. 1997. audio 44.95 (*0-7861-1226-3*, 1969) Blackstone Audio Bks., Inc.

—Man with a Squirrel. 1996. 88p. 22.50 o.p. (*0-8050-3666-0*) Holt, Henry & Co.

—Man with a Squirrel, Vol. 22. 2000. (Missing Mysteries Ser.: Vol. 22). 231p. pap. 14.95 o.s.i (*1-890208-39-6*) Poisoned Pen Pr.

—O Sacred Head. 1997. 288p. 23.00 o.p. (*0-8050-5033-7*) Holt, Henry & Co.

—O Sacred Head, Vol. 24. 2000. (Missing Mysteries Ser.: Vol. 24). pap. 14.95 (*1-890208-48-5*) Poisoned Pen Pr.

**TAYLOR, HOLLAND (FICTITIOUS CHARACTER)—FICTION**

Housewright, David. Dearly Departed: A Holland Taylor Mystery. 1999. (Holland Taylor Mystery Ser.). 224p. text 23.95 o.p. (*0-393-04771-7*) Norton, W. W. & Co., Inc.

—Penance. 1997. (Holland Taylor Mystery Ser.). 304p. mass mkt. 6.50 o.s.i (*0-425-15942-6*, Prime Crime) Berkley Publishing Group.

—Penance. 1995. (Holland Taylor Mystery Ser.). 296p. 21.00 (*0-88150-341-X*, Foul Play) Norton, W. W. & Co., Inc.

—Practice to Deceive. 2000. (Holland Taylor Mystery Ser.). 275p. mass mkt. 5.99 o.s.i (*0-425-17312-7*) Berkley Publishing Group.

—Practice to Deceive. unabr. ed. 1998. audio 44.95 (*0-7861-1421-5*, 2297) Blackstone Audio Bks., Inc.

—Practice to Deceive: A Holland Taylor Mystery. 1997. (Holland Taylor Mystery Ser.). 256p. 22.00 (*0-88150-404-1*, Foul Play) Norton, W. W. & Co., Inc.

**TAYLOR, JACK (FICTITIOUS CHARACTER)—FICTION**

Bruen, Ken. The Guards: A Novel. 304p. 2004. pap. 12.95 (*0-312-32027-2*, Saint Martin's Griffin); 2003. 23.95 (*0-312-30355-6*, Saint Martin's Minotaur) St. Martin's Pr.

—The Killing of the Tinkers. Date not set. (*0-312-30357-2*); 2004. 256p. 22.95 (*0-312-30411-0*) St. Martin's Pr. (Saint Martin's Minotaur).

**TAYLOR, MARILYN (FICTITIOUS CHARACTER)—FICTION**

Sanders, Lawrence. Stolen Blessings. l.t. ed. 1992. pap. 14.95 o.p. (*0-7927-0558-0*); 1991. 17.95 o.p. (*0-7927-0557-2*, E0001) BBC Audiobooks America.

—Stolen Blessings. 1989. 320p. mass mkt. 7.50 o.s.i (*0-425-11872-X*) Berkley Publishing Group.

**TAYLOR, SANGAMON (FICTITIOUS CHARACTER)—FICTION**

Stephenson, Neal. Zodiac: The Eco-Thriller. 1995. 320p. mass mkt. 7.50 (*0-553-57386-1*, Spectra) Bantam Bks.

—Zodiac: The Eco-Thriller. 1988. 300p. pap. 7.95 o.p. (*0-87113-181-1*, Atlantic Monthly Pr.) Grove/Atlantic, Inc.

**TEAGARDEN, AURORA ROE (FICTITIOUS CHARACTER)—FICTION**

Harris, Charlaine. A Bone to Pick. 1993. (WWL Mystery Ser.). per. (*0-373-26136-5*, 1-26136-1, Harlequin Bks.) Harlequin Enterprises, Ltd.

—A Bone to Pick. 1992. 168p. 18.95 o.s.i (*0-8027-1245-2*) Walker & Co.

—Dead over Heels. 1997. per. (*0-373-26260-4*, 1-26260-9, Worldwide Library) Harlequin Enterprises, Ltd.

—Dead over Heels. 1996. 208p. 20.50 o.p. (*0-684-80429-8*, Scribner) Simon & Schuster.

—A Fool & His Honey. 2001. (WWL Mystery Ser.: No. 384). 253p. mass mkt. (*0-373-26384-8*, 1-26384-7, Worldwide Library) Harlequin Enterprises, Ltd.

—A Fool & His Honey. 1999. 224p. 22.95 (*0-312-20306-3*, Saint Martin's Minotaur) St. Martin's Pr.

—A Fool & His Honey. l.t. ed. 2000. (Mystery Ser.). 304p. 28.95 (*0-7862-2467-3*) Thorndike Pr.

—The Julius House. 1996. per. (*0-373-26217-5*, 1-26217-9, Worldwide Library) Harlequin Enterprises, Ltd.

—The Julius House. 1995. 221p. 20.00 (*0-684-19640-9*, Scribner) Simon & Schuster.

—Last Scene Alive. l.t. ed. 2002. (Wheeler Hardcover Ser.). 320p. 28.95 (*1-58724-364-4*, Wheeler Publishing, Inc.) Gale Group.

—Last Scene Alive. 2003. (WWL Mystery Ser.: No. 476). 256p. mass mkt. (*0-373-26476-3*, Worldwide Library) Harlequin Enterprises, Ltd.

—Last Scene Alive. 2002. (Aurora Teagarden Mystery Ser.). 224p. 22.95 (*0-312-26246-9*, Saint Martin's Minotaur) St. Martin's Pr.

—Poppy Done to Death: An Aurora Teagarden Mystery. 2003. 240p. 22.95 o.s.i (*0-312-27764-4*, Saint Martin's Minotaur) St. Martin's Pr.

—Real Murders. l.t. ed. 1991. 17.95 o.p. (*0-7451-8204-6*, AH0240) BBC Audiobooks America.

—Real Murders. 1992. mass mkt. (*0-373-26104-7*, 1-26104-9, Harlequin Bks.) Harlequin Enterprises, Ltd.
—Real Murders. 1990. 192p. 18.95 o.s.i (*0-8027-5769-3*) Walker & Co.
—Three Bedrooms, One Corpse. 1995. per. (*0-373-26177-2*, Harlequin Bks.) Harlequin Enterprises, Ltd.
—Three Bedrooms, One Corpse. 2001. 224p. pap. 14.95 o.p. (*0-7432-2891-X*); 1994. 256p. 20.00 (*0-684-19643-3*) Simon & Schuster. (Scribner).

**TEAGUE, KATE (FICTITIOUS CHARACTER)—FICTION**

Hornsby, Wendy. Half a Mind. 304p. 1991. mass mkt. 3.99 o.p. (*0-451-40245-6*, Onyx); 1990. 16.95 o.p. (*0-453-00710-4*) NAL.
—No Harm. 1989. (WWL Mystery Ser.: No. 30). mass mkt. (*0-373-26030-X*, Harlequin Bks.) Harlequin Enterprises, Ltd.

**TEAGUE, SYDNEY (FICTITIOUS CHARACTER)—FICTION**

Grant, Anne U. Multiple Listing. 1998. (Sydney Teague Mysteries Ser.: Vol. 1). 336p. mass mkt. 5.99 o.s.i (*0-440-22551-5*) Dell Publishing.

**TEMPLAR, SIMON (FICTITIOUS CHARACTER)—FICTION**

*see Saint (Fictitious Character)—Fiction*

**TENNISON, JANE (FICTITIOUS CHARACTER)—FICTION**

La Plante, Lynda. Prime Suspect. 1993. 272p. mass mkt. 4.99 o.s.i (*0-440-21494-7*); No. 2. 1993. 272p. mass mkt. 4.99 o.s.i (*0-440-21495-5*); No. 3. 1994. 320p. mass mkt. 4.99 o.s.i (*0-440-21496-3*) Dell Publishing.

**THACKERAY, CONSTABLE (FICTITIOUS CHARACTER)—FICTION**

Hitt, Jack, et al. Perfect Murder: Five Great Mystery Writers Create the Perfect Crime, Set. abr. ed. 1992. audio 16.99 (*0-88646-317-3*, 7317) Durkin Hayes Publishing Ltd.
Lovesey, Peter. Abracadaver. 1994. 224p. 16.95 o.p. (*0-7451-8645-9*, Black Dagger); 1996. audio 54.95 (*0-7451-6110-3*, CAB294) BBC Audiobooks America.
—Abracadaver. 1989. 256p. reprint ed. pap. 4.50 o.p. (*0-06-081000-9*, Perennial) HarperTrade.
—Abracadaver. 1981. 224p. pap. 3.95 o.p. (*0-14-005803-6*, Penguin Bks.) Viking Penguin.
—Bertie & the Seven Bodies. 1991. (Audio Books Ser.). audio 53.95 o.p. (*0-8161-9247-2*) Thorndike Pr.
—Bertie & the Tin Man, from the Detective Memoirs of King Edward the Seventh. unabr. ed. 1990. audio 54.95 (*0-7451-6113-8*) BBC Audiobooks America.
—The Bloodhounds. unabr. ed. 1999. audio 84.95 (*1-86042-283-7*, 22837) Soundings, Ltd. GBR. *Dist:* Ulverscroft Large Print Bks., Ltd.
—A Case of Spirits. l.t. ed. 2002. (General Ser.). 280p. pap. 24.95 (*0-7862-4224-8*) Thorndike Pr.
—A Case of Spirits. 1977. (Crime Ser.). 192p. pap. 3.95 o.p. (*0-14-004333-0*, Penguin Bks.) Viking Penguin.
—The Detective Wore Silk Drawers. 1988. audio 35.95 o.p. (*0-8161-9452-1*) Thorndike Pr.
—The Detective Wore Silk Drawers. 1980. (Crime Monthly Ser.). pap. 3.95 o.p. (*0-14-005558-4*, Penguin Bks.) Viking Penguin.
—The Detective Wore Silk Drawers: A Sergeant Cribb Adventure. unabr. ed. 1995. audio 39.95 (*0-7451-6112-X*, CAB 338) BBC Audiobooks America.
—The Detective Wore Silk Drawers: A Sergeant Cribb Mystery. 1989. 208p. reprint ed. pap. 4.50 o.p. (*0-06-080999-X*, Perennial) HarperTrade.
—The Detective Wore Silk Drawers: A Sergeant Cribb Mystery. l.t. ed. 2000. (General Ser.). 268p. pap. 23.95 (*0-7862-2426-6*) Thorndike Pr.
—Invitation to a Dynamite Party. 1981. 176p. pap. 3.95 o.p. (*0-14-004029-3*, Penguin Bks.) Viking Penguin.
—Mad Hatter's Holiday. 1990. 256p. reprint ed. pap. 4.50 o.p. (*0-06-081022-X*, Perennial) HarperTrade.
—Mad Hatter's Holiday. 1990. 256p. (C). reprint ed. lib. bdg. 20.00 o.p. (*0-8095-9022-0*) Millefleurs.
—Mad Hatter's Holiday. l.t. ed. 2001. 246p. pap. 25.95 (*0-7862-3498-9*); 259p. (*0-7540-4593-5*); 259p. (*0-7540-4594-3*) Thorndike Pr.
—Mad Hatter's Holiday. 1981. 192p. pap. 3.95 o.p. (*0-14-005804-4*, Penguin Bks.) Viking Penguin.
—Rough Cider. unabr. ed. 2001. audio 54.95 (*1-85089-785-9*, 88022) ISIS Audio Bks. GBR. *Dist:* Ulverscroft Large Print Bks., Ltd.
—Rough Cider. l.t. ed. 1987. (Mainstream Ser.). 242p. reprint ed. 15.95 o.p. (*1-85089-149-4*) ISIS Large Print Bks. GBR. *Dist:* Transaction Pubs.
—Rough Cider. 1987. 224p. 15.95 (*0-89296-194-5*) Mysterious Pr.
—Rough Cider. 2001. 206p. pap. 13.00 (*1-56947-228-9*) Soho Pr., Inc.
—Rough Cider. 1988. mass mkt. 3.95 (*0-445-40545-7*, Mysterious Pr. Paperback Bks.) Warner Bks., Inc.
—Swing, Swing Together. 1976. 21.95 (*0-89190-093-4*) Amereon, Ltd.
—Swing, Swing Together. 1990. 352p. (C). reprint ed. lib. bdg. 20.00 o.p. (*0-8095-9023-9*) Millefleurs.
—Swing, Swing Together. 1978. (Crime Ser.). pap. 3.95 o.p. (*0-14-004618-6*, Penguin Bks.) Viking Penguin.
—Swing, Swing Together: A Sergeant Cribb Mystery. 1990. 352p. reprint ed. pap. 4.50 o.p. (*0-06-081023-8*, Perennial) HarperTrade.
—Swing, Swing Together: A Sergeant Cribb Mystery. 2002. (General Ser.). 24.95 (*0-7862-4408-9*) Thorndike Pr.
—Waxwork. l.t. ed. 1978. 12.95 o.p. (*0-8161-6651-X*, Macmillan Reference USA) Gale Group.
—Waxwork. 1978. 7.95 o.p. (*0-394-50066-0*, Pantheon) Knopf Publishing Group.
—Waxwork. 1980. (Crime Monthly Ser.). pap. 3.95 o.p. (*0-14-004887-1*, Penguin Bks.) Viking Penguin.
—Wobble to Death. l.t. ed. 1999. (General Ser.). 272p. pap. 23.95 (*0-7862-1868-1*) Thorndike Pr.
—Wobble to Death. 1980. pap. 3.95 o.p. (*0-14-005557-6*, Penguin Bks.) Viking Penguin.

**THACKERAY, MICHAEL (FICTITIOUS CHARACTER)—FICTION**

Hall, Patricia. The Dead of Winter. 1996. (Yorkshire Mystery Ser.). 21.95 o.p. (*0-312-15148-9*, Saint Martin's Minotaur) St. Martin's Pr.
—Dead on Arrival. l.t. ed. 2000. (Dales Large Print Ser.). 400p. pap. (*1-84262-012-6*) Dales Large Print Bks. GBR. *Dist:* Ulverscroft Large Print Canada, Ltd.
—Dead on Arrival. 2001. (Yorkshire Mystery Ser.). 224p. 22.95 (*0-312-26572-7*, Saint Martin's Minotaur) St. Martin's Pr.
—Death by Election. l.t. ed. 1994. (Dales Large Print Ser.). 418p. pap. o.p. (*1-85389-519-9*) Dales Large Print Bks. GBR. *Dist:* Ulverscroft Large Print Canada, Ltd.
—Death by Election. 1994. (Yorkshire Mystery Ser.). 256p. 20.95 o.p. (*0-312-11461-3*, Saint Martin's Minotaur) St. Martin's Pr.
—Deep Freeze. l.t. ed. 2002. (Magna Large Print Ser.). 416p. (*0-7505-1880-4*) Magna Large Print Bks. GBR. *Dist:* Ulverscroft Large Print Canada, Ltd.
—Deep Freeze. unabr. ed. 2002. (Yorkshire Mystery Ser.). audio 69.95 (*1-84283-190-9*) Soundings, Ltd. GBR. *Dist:* Ulverscroft Large Print Bks., Ltd.
—Deep Freeze: A Yorkshire Mystery. 2003. (Yorkshire Mystery Ser.). 272p. 23.95 (*0-312-28212-5*, Saint Martin's Minotaur) St. Martin's Pr.
—Dying Fall. l.t. ed. 1995. (Dales Large Print Ser.). 432p. pap. o.p. (*1-85389-561-X*) Dales Large Print Bks. GBR. *Dist:* Ulverscroft Large Print Canada, Ltd.
—Dying Fall. 1996. 248p. mass mkt. o.s.i (*0-7515-1204-4*) Little Brown & Co.
—Dying Fall. 1995. (Yorkshire Mystery Ser.). 248p. 21.95 o.p. (*0-312-13477-0*, Saint Martin's Minotaur) St. Martin's Pr.
—The Italian Girl. 2000. 208p. 21.95 (*0-312-26489-5*, Saint Martin's Minotaur) St. Martin's Pr.
—Perils of the Night. 1998. (Yorkshire Mystery Ser.). 224p. 22.95 (*0-312-19996-1*, Saint Martin's Minotaur) St. Martin's Pr.
—Skeleton at the Feast. l.t. ed. 2001. (Magna Large Print Ser.). 368p. (*0-7505-1728-X*) Magna Large Print Bks. GBR. *Dist:* Ulverscroft Large Print Canada, Ltd.
—Skeleton at the Feast. 2002. (Yorkshire Mystery Ser.). 256p. 23.95 (*0-312-28208-7*, Saint Martin's Minotaur) St. Martin's Pr.

**THANET, LUKE (FICTITIOUS CHARACTER)—FICTION**

Simpson, Dorothy. Close Her Eyes. 1990. 208p. mass mkt. 2.25 o.s.i (*0-553-18518-7*); mass mkt. 4.50 o.s.i (*0-553-29826-7*) Bantam Bks.
—Close Her Eyes. 1984. 224p. 12.95 o.p. (*0-684-18197-5*, Macmillan Reference USA) Gale Group.
—Close Her Eyes. l.t. ed. 1986. 448p. 15.95 o.p. (*0-7089-1450-0*, Ulverscroft) Thorpe, F. A. Pubs. GBR. *Dist:* Ulverscroft Large Print Bks., Ltd.
—A Day for Dying. l.t. ed. 1996. (G. K. Hall Mystery Ser.). 339p. 24.95 o.p. (*0-7838-1930-7*, Macmillan Reference USA) Gale Group.
—A Day for Dying. 1996. 280p. mass mkt. o.s.i (*0-7515-1377-6*) Little Brown & Co.
—A Day for Dying. 1996. 288p. 21.00 (*0-684-81568-0*, Scribner) Simon & Schuster.
—Dead by Morning. 1990. 256p. mass mkt. 3.95 o.s.i (*0-553-28606-4*) Bantam Bks.
—Dead by Morning. 1989. 224p. 16.95 o.s.i (*0-684-19123-7*, Macmillan Reference USA) Gale Group.
—Dead by Morning. l.t. ed. 1990. (Ulverscroft Large Print Ser.). 29.99 o.p. (*0-7089-2342-9*, Ulverscroft) Thorpe, F. A. Pubs. GBR. *Dist:* Ulverscroft Large Print Bks., Ltd., Ulverscroft Large Print Canada, Ltd.
—Dead on Arrival. 1989. 224p. mass mkt. 3.50 o.s.i (*0-553-27000-1*) Bantam Bks.
—Dead on Arrival. 1987. 208p. 14.95 o.p. (*0-684-18732-9*, Macmillan Reference USA) Gale Group.
—Dead on Arrival. l.t. ed. 1987. 400p. 14.95 o.p. (*0-7089-1716-X*, Ulverscroft) Thorpe, F. A. Pubs. GBR. *Dist:* Ulverscroft Large Print Bks., Ltd.
—Dead on Arrival. 1995. mass mkt. o.s.i (*0-7515-1411-X*) Virago Pr., Ltd.
—Doomed to Die. 1992. 288p. mass mkt. 4.50 o.s.i (*0-553-29694-9*) Bantam Bks.
—Doomed to Die. 1991. 288p. 19.95 o.s.i (*0-684-19381-7*, Macmillan Reference USA) Gale Group.
—Element of Doubt. 1989. 224p. mass mkt. 3.50 o.s.i (*0-553-28175-5*) Bantam Bks.
—Element of Doubt. 1988. 256p. 14.95 o.s.i (*0-684-18885-6*, Macmillan Reference USA) Gale Group.
—Element of Doubt. l.t. ed. 1989. 469p. 17.95 o.p. (*0-7089-1949-9*, Ulverscroft) Thorpe, F. A. Pubs. GBR. *Dist:* Ulverscroft Large Print Bks., Ltd.
—Last Seen Alive: A Luke Thanet Mystery. 1986. 224p. mass mkt. 3.95 o.s.i (*0-553-27773-1*) Bantam Bks.
—Last Seen Alive: A Luke Thanet Mystery. 1985. (Luke Thanet Mystery Ser.). 224p. 13.95 (*0-684-18435-4*, Macmillan Reference USA) Gale Group.
—Last Seen Alive: A Luke Thanet Mystery. l.t. ed. 1986. (Ulverscroft Large Print Ser.). 416p. 29.99 o.p. (*0-7089-1508-6*, Ulverscroft) Thorpe, F. A. Pubs. GBR. *Dist:* Ulverscroft Large Print Bks., Ltd., Ulverscroft Large Print Canada, Ltd.
—The Night She Died. 1985. (Mystery Ser.). 208p. mass mkt. 3.50 o.s.i (*0-553-27772-3*) Bantam Bks.
—The Night She Died. 1981. 192p. 9.95 o.s.i (*0-684-16869-3*); 1982. pap. 9.95 o.p. (*0-8161-3329-8*) Gale Group. (Macmillan Reference USA).
—The Night She Died. 1998. (Missing Mysteries Ser.: Vol. 4). 206p. reprint ed. pap. 8.95 (*1-890208-06-X*) Poisoned Pen Pr.
—No Laughing Matter. 1993. (Inspector Luke Thanet Ser.). 256p. 20.00 o.p. (*0-684-19626-3*, Macmillan Reference USA) Gale Group.
—Once Too Often. 1998. (Inspector Luke Thanet Ser.). 224p. 20.50 o.s.i (*0-684-84578-4*); 223p. 21.00 (*0-684-84912-7*) Simon & Schuster. (Scribner).
—Puppet for a Corpse: A Luke Thanet Mystery. 1985. 224p. mass mkt. 4.50 o.s.i (*0-553-27774-X*) Bantam Bks.
—Puppet for a Corpse: A Luke Thanet Mystery. 1983. 192p. 11.95 o.s.i (*0-684-17909-1*, Scribner) Simon & Schuster.
—Puppet for a Corpse: A Luke Thanet Mystery. l.t. ed. 1984. (Ulverscroft Large Print Ser.). 384p. 12.50 o.p. (*0-7089-1206-0*, Ulverscroft) Thorpe, F. A. Pubs. GBR. *Dist:* Ulverscroft Large Print Bks., Ltd., Ulverscroft Large Print Canada, Ltd.
—Six Feet Under. 176p. 1989. mass mkt. 2.25 o.s.i (*0-553-18506-3*); 1985. mass mkt. 3.95 o.s.i (*0-553-25192-9*) Bantam Bks.
—Six Feet Under. 1982. 192p. 10.95 o.p. (*0-684-17665-3*, Scribner) Simon & Schuster.
—Six Feet Under. l.t. ed. 1983. 352p. 15.95 o.p. (*0-7089-1047-5*, Ulverscroft) Thorpe, F. A. Pubs. GBR. *Dist:* Ulverscroft Large Print Bks., Ltd.
—Suspicious Death: A Luke Thanet Mystery. 1990. 240p. mass mkt. 3.95 o.s.i (*0-553-28459-2*) Bantam Bks.
—Suspicious Death: A Luke Thanet Mystery. 1988. 272p. 16.95 o.s.i (*0-684-19026-5*, Scribner) Simon & Schuster.
—Suspicious Death: A Luke Thanet Mystery. l.t. ed. 1990. (Ulverscroft Large Print Ser.). 29.99 o.p. (*0-7089-2246-5*, Ulverscroft) Thorpe, F. A. Pubs. GBR. *Dist:* Ulverscroft Large Print Bks., Ltd., Ulverscroft Large Print Canada, Ltd.
—Wake the Dead. 1993. 272p. mass mkt. 4.99 o.s.i (*0-553-56252-5*) Bantam Bks.
—Wake the Dead. 1992. (Inspector Luke Thanet Ser.). 256p. text 19.00 (*0-684-19507-0*, Scribner) Simon & Schuster.

**THATCH, KELSEY (FICTITIOUS CHARACTER)—FICTION**

Brandon, Jay. Defiance County. 1997. 288p. pap. 6.99 (*0-671-53655-9*, Pocket); 1996. 384p. 23.00 o.p. (*0-671-53654-0*, Atria) Simon & Schuster.

**THATCHER, JOHN PUTNAM (FICTITIOUS CHARACTER)—FICTION**

Lathen, Emma. Accounting for Murder. 1995. pap. 7.00 (*0-684-80103-5*); pap. 7.00 (*0-684-80245-7*) Simon & Schuster. (Scribner).
—Accounting for Murder: A John Putnam Thatcher Mystery. 1995. 192p. per. 7.00 o.p. (*1-57283-000-X*, Scribner); 1987. mass mkt. 3.50 (*0-671-64550-1*, Pocket) Simon & Schuster.
—Banking on Death: A John Putnam Thatcher Mystery. 1993. 168p. reprint ed. pap. 6.95 o.s.i (*1-883402-06-9*, Scribner) Simon & Schuster.
—Brewing up a Storm. l.t. ed. 1998. 368p. mass mkt. 5.99 o.s.i (*0-06-104434-2*, HarperTorch) Morrow/Avon.
—Brewing up a Storm. l.t. ed. 1996. (John Thatcher Mystery Ser.). 272p. 21.95 o.p. (*0-312-14554-3*, Saint Martin's Minotaur) St. Martin's Pr.
—By Hook or by Crook. l.t. ed. 1993. (Nightingale Ser.). 313p. lib. bdg. 15.95 o.p. (*0-8161-5707-3*, Macmillan Reference USA) Gale Group.
—Come to Dust. 1997. (Black Dagger Crime Ser.). 256p. 18.50 o.p. (*0-7451-8940-7*, Black Dagger) BBC Audiobooks America.
—Double, Double Oil & Trouble. 1983. mass mkt. 2.95 o.s.i (*0-671-49990-4*, Pocket); 1978. 8.95 o.s.i (*0-671-24215-6*, Simon & Schuster) Simon & Schuster.
—East Is East. 1994. 336p. mass mkt. 5.99 o.s.i (*0-06-104296-X*) HarperCollins Children's Bk. Group.
—East Is East. 1994. 79p. mass mkt. 5.99 o.p. (*0-06-104297-8*, HarperTorch) Morrow/Avon.
—East Is East: A John Putnam Thatcher Mystery. 1991. 224p. 19.00 o.p. (*0-671-73707-4*, Simon & Schuster) Simon & Schuster.
—Going for the Gold. 1981. (General Ser.). lib. bdg. 12.95 o.p. (*0-8161-3200-3*, Macmillan Reference USA) Gale Group.
—Going for the Gold. 1981. 12.95 o.p. (*0-671-41407-0*, Simon & Schuster) Simon & Schuster.
—Green Grow the Dollars. 1982. (General Ser.). lib. bdg. 14.95 o.p. (*0-8161-3397-2*, Macmillan Reference USA) Gale Group.
—Green Grow the Dollars. 1984. mass mkt. 3.95 o.s.i (*0-671-52767-3*, Pocket); 1983. mass mkt. 2.95 o.s.i (*0-671-45049-2*, Pocket); 1982. 12.95 o.p. (*0-671-44130-2*, Simon & Schuster) Simon & Schuster.
—The Longer the Thread. l.t. ed. 1984. (Nightingale Ser.). 328p. pap. 9.95 o.p. (*0-8161-3668-8*, Macmillan Reference USA) Gale Group.
—The Longer the Thread. 1988. 192p. mass mkt. 3.50 (*0-671-65053-X*, Pocket) Simon & Schuster.
—Murder Against the Grain. 1987. 192p. mass mkt. 3.95 o.s.i (*0-671-63973-0*, Pocket) Simon & Schuster.
—Murder Makes the Wheels Go 'Round. Barzun, Jacques & Taylor, W. H., eds. 1983. (Crime Fiction 1950-1975 Ser.). 183p. lib. bdg. 18.00 o.p. (*0-8240-4985-3*) Garland Publishing, Inc.
—Murder Makes the Wheels Go 'Round. 1987. 192p. mass mkt. 3.50 o.s.i (*0-671-45528-1*, Pocket) Simon & Schuster.
—Murder to Go. 1983. mass mkt. 2.95 o.s.i (*0-671-45529-X*, Pocket) Simon & Schuster.
—Murder Without Icing. l.t. ed. 1989. lib. bdg. 22.95 o.p. (*0-7451-7186-9*, Macmillan Reference USA) Gale Group.
—Murder Without Icing. 1983. mass mkt. 2.95 o.s.i (*0-671-49202-0*, Pocket); 1972. 5.95 o.s.i (*0-671-21207-9*, Simon & Schuster) Simon & Schuster.
—Pick-Up Sticks. 1984. 240p. mass mkt. 2.95 o.s.i (*0-671-50997-7*, Pocket) Simon & Schuster.
—A Place for Murder. 1983. mass mkt. 2.95 o.s.i (*0-671-47760-9*, Pocket) Simon & Schuster.
—Right on the Money: A John Putman Thatcher Mystery. 1995. (John Putnam Thatcher Mystery Ser.). 288p. mass mkt. 4.99 o.s.i (*0-06-104295-1*, HarperTorch) Morrow/Avon.
—Right on the Money: A John Putman Thatcher Mystery. 1993. 256p. 20.00 o.p. (*0-671-73708-2*, Simon & Schuster) Simon & Schuster.
—A Shark out of Water. 1998. (John Putnam Thatcher Mystery Ser.). 336p. reprint ed. mass mkt. 5.99 o.s.i (*0-06-104460-1*, HarperTorch) Morrow/Avon.
—A Shark Out of Water: A John Putnam Thatcher Mystery. 1997. 293p. 22.95 (*0-312-17018-1*, Saint Martin's Minotaur) St. Martin's Pr.
—A Shark Out of Water: A John Thatcher Mystery. l.t. ed. 1997. (G. K. Hall Mystery Ser.). 372p. 25.95 o.p. (*0-7838-8357-9*, Macmillan Reference USA) Gale Group.
—Something in the Air. 1989. 256p. mass mkt. 3.95 o.s.i (*0-671-68356-X*, Pocket); 1988. 240p. 16.95 o.p. (*0-671-66599-5*, Simon & Schuster) Simon & Schuster.
—Stitch in Time. 1983. mass mkt. 2.95 o.s.i (*0-671-45526-5*, Pocket) Simon & Schuster.
—Sweet & Low. 1983. mass mkt. 2.95 o.s.i (*0-671-45527-3*, Pocket); 1974. 6.95 o.s.i (*0-671-21785-2*, Simon & Schuster) Simon & Schuster.

**THERMOPYLE, ANGUS (FICTITIOUS CHARACTER)—FICTION**

Stephens, Reed, pseud. The Gap into Conflict: The Real Story. (Gap Ser.: No. 1). 1992. 272p. mass mkt. 7.50 (*0-553-29509-8*); 1991. 224p. 6.00 o.s.i (*0-553-08049-0*) Bantam Bks.
—The Gap into Madness: Chaos & Order. 1995. (Gap Ser.: No. 4). 688p. mass mkt. 6.99 (*0-553-57253-9*) Bantam Bks.
—The Gap into Power: A Dark & Hungry God Arises. 1993. (Gap Ser.: No. 3). 528p. mass mkt. 7.50 (*0-553-56260-6*) Bantam Bks.
—The Gap into Vision: Forbidden Knowledge. (Gap Ser.: No. 2). 1992. 480p. mass mkt. 7.50 (*0-553-29760-0*); 1991. 416p. 125.00 o.s.i (*0-553-07387-7*) Bantam Bks.

Stephens, Reed, pseud & Donaldson, Stephen R. The Gap into Ruin: This Day All Gods Die. 1997. (Gap Ser.: No. 5). 704p. mass mkt. 6.99 (*0-553-57328-4*) Bantam Bks.

**THOMAS, BIGGER (FICTITIOUS CHARACTER)—FICTION**

Wright, Richard A. Native Son. Date not set. 371p. 26.95 (*0-8488-2577-2*) Amereon, Ltd.
—Native Son. 1997. 594p. 49.95 (*1-56849-694-X*) Buccaneer Bks., Inc.
—Native Son. audio 19.95 Filmic Archives.
—Native Son. abr. ed. 1989. 432p. pap. 7.95 (*0-06-080977-9*) HarperCollins Pubs.
—Native Son. (Perennial Classics Ser.). 2004. 528p. pap. 13.00 (*0-06-092980-4*, Perennial); 1986. 398p. mass mkt. 4.95 o.p. (*0-06-080855-1*, P 855, Perennial); 1942. mass mkt. 3.95 o.p. (*0-06-083055-7*, P 3055, Perennial); 1998. audio 18.00 (*0-89845-916-8*, 393493, HarperAudio); 1993. 624p. reprint ed. pap. 7.00 o.p. (*0-06-081249-4*, P 977, Perennial); 1969. reprint ed. 24.95 o.p. (*0-06-014762-8*) HarperTrade.
—Native Son. unabr. ed. 1998. audio 102.00 audio 102.00 (*0-7887-2112-7*, 95437E7) Recorded Bks., LLC.
—Native Son. l.t. ed. 1993. 619p. lib. bdg. 22.95 (*0-8161-5787-1*) Thorndike Pr.

**THOMAS, HANS (FICTITIOUS CHARACTER)—FICTION**

Gaarder, Jostein. The Solitaire Mystery. 1997. 368p. reprint ed. 6.99 (*0-425-16047-5*) Berkley Publishing Group.
—The Solitaire Mystery. 2003. pap. (*0-374-52943-4*); 1996. 356p. 22.00 o.p. (*0-374-26651-4*) Farrar, Straus & Giroux.
—The Solitaire Mystery: A Novel about Family & Destiny. 1997. 336p. reprint ed. pap. 14.00 (*0-425-15999-X*) Berkley Publishing Group.

**THOMAS, LENORE (FICTITIOUS CHARACTER)—FICTION**

O'Connell, Jack. Box Nine. 1992. 272p. 17.95 o.p. (*0-89296-472-3*) Mysterious Pr.
—Box Nine. 1993. 336p. mass mkt. 4.99 (*0-446-40100-5*, Mysterious Pr. Paperback Bks.) Warner Bks., Inc.

**THOMAS, MAURA (FICTITIOUS CHARACTER)—FICTION**

Fluke, Joanne. Deadly Memories. 1995. 352p. mass mkt. 4.50 o.s.i (*0-8217-4841-6*, Zebra Bks.) Kensington Publishing Corp.

**THOMPSON, DAN, REVEREND (FICTITIOUS CHARACTER)—FICTION**

Feldmeyer, Dean. Pitchfork Hollow. Chelius, Jane, ed. 1995. 256p. (Orig.). mass mkt. 5.50 (*0-671-76983-9*, Pocket) Simon & Schuster.
—Viper Quarry. 1994. 256p. mass mkt. 4.99 (*0-671-76982-0*, Pocket) Simon & Schuster.

**THONGOR (FICTITIOUS CHARACTER)—FICTION**

Carter, Lin. Thongor Against the Gods. 1967. pap. 1.75 o.s.i (*0-446-94178-6*) Warner Bks., Inc.
—Thongor & the Wizard of Lemuria. 1976. 1.25 o.s.i (*0-425-03435-6*) Berkley Publishing Group.
—Thongor at the End of Time. 1968. pap. 1.75 o.s.i (*0-446-94332-0*) Warner Bks., Inc.
—Thongor Fights the Pirates of Takakus. 1976. 1.25 o.s.i (*0-425-03147-0*) Berkley Publishing Group.
—Thongor in the City of Magicians. 1968. pap. 1.75 o.s.i (*0-446-94208-1*) Warner Bks., Inc.

**THORN (FICTITIOUS CHARACTER)—FICTION**

Hall, James W. Blackwater Sound. abr. ed. 2002. audio 12.99 (*1-58788-895-5*, 3414, Nova Audio Bks.); audio 24.95 o.p. (*1-58788-894-7*, 3413, Nova Audio Bks.); audio 78.25 (*1-58788-893-9*, 3412, Unabridged Library Editions); audio 32.95 (*1-58788-892-0*, 3411, Brilliance Audio Unabridged) Brilliance Audio.
—Blackwater Sound. l.t. ed. 2002. lib. bdg. 29.95 (*1-58547-168-2*) Ctr. Point Large Print.
—Blackwater Sound. unabr. ed. 2003. audio 19.99 (*1-59335-180-1*, 30276) Soulmate Audio Bks., Inc.
—Blackwater Sound. E-Book 24.95 (*0-312-70384-8*); 2002. 368p. mass mkt. 6.99 (*0-312-98628-9*, St. Martin's Paperbacks); 2002. (Illus.). 352p. 24.95 (*0-312-20384-5*) St. Martin's Pr.
—Buzz Cut. 1997. 464p. mass mkt. 7.50 (*0-440-21782-2*) Dell Publishing.
—Buzz Cut. abr. ed. 1999. audio 9.99 o.s.i (*0-553-70207-6*, RH Audio) Random Hse. Audio Publishing Group.
—Buzz Cut. unabr. ed. 1999. audio compact disk 99.00 (*0-7887-3413-X*, C1019E7); 1996. audio 85.00 (*0-7887-0628-4*, 94802E7) Recorded Bks., LLC.
—Gone Wild. 1996. 464p. mass mkt. 7.50 (*0-440-21781-4*) Dell Publishing.
—Gone Wild. l.t. ed. 1995. 607p. 25.95 o.p. (*0-7838-1368-6*, Macmillan Reference USA) Gale Group.
—Gone Wild, unabr. ed. 1995. audio 85.00 (*0-7887-0264-5*, 94473E7) Recorded Bks., LLC.
—Hard Aground. 1994. 464p. mass mkt. 7.50 (*0-440-21357-6*) Dell Publishing.
—Hard Aground. l.t. ed. 1993. 89.95 o.p. incl. audio (*0-7838-1113-6*, Macmillan Reference USA) Gale Group.
—Mean High Tide. 1995. 448p. mass mkt. 7.50 (*0-440-21355-X*) Dell Publishing.
—Mean High Tide. l.t. ed. 1994. 545p. lib. bdg. 23.95 (*0-8161-7441-5*, Macmillan Reference USA) Gale Group.
—Mean High Tide. abr. ed. 1999. audio 9.99 o.s.i (*0-553-70191-6*, RH Audio) Random Hse. Audio Publishing Group.
—Mean High Tide, unabr. ed. 1994. audio 78.00 (*0-7887-0026-X*, 94225E7) Recorded Bks., LLC.
—Mean High Tide. 372p. 4.98 o.p. (*0-8317-5431-1*) Smithmark Pubs., Inc.
—Off the Chart. 2003. (Illus.). audio compact disk 30.00 (*1-55927-825-0*); pap. 25.95 incl. audio (*1-55927-883-8*) Audio Renaissance.
—Off the Chart. 2003. 8p. 69.95 (*0-7927-2890-4*); 10p. pap. 94.95 (*0-7927-2891-2*) BBC Audiobooks America.
—Off the Chart. E-Book 20.95 (*0-312-71013-5*); 2003. 352p. 24.95 (*0-312-27178-6*, Saint Martin's Minotaur) St. Martin's Pr.
—Off the Chart. l.t. ed. 2003. 586p. 30.95 (*0-7862-5796-2*, Large Print Pr.) Thorndike Pr.
—Red Sky at Night. l.t. ed. 2001. 384p. lib. bdg. 28.95 (*1-58547-117-8*) Ctr. Point Large Print.
—Red Sky at Night. 1998. 400p. reprint ed. mass mkt. 6.99 (*0-440-22574-4*) Doubleday Publishing.
—Red Sky at Night, unabr. ed. 1997. audio 75.00 (*0-7887-1294-2*, 95128E7) Recorded Bks., LLC.
—Tropical Freeze. l.t. ed. 2003. lib. bdg. 28.95 (*1-58547-288-3*, Premier) Ctr. Point Large Print.
—Tropical Freeze. 1999. 446p. pap. 9.00 (*0-393-31895-8*); 1989. 18.95 o.p. (*0-393-02694-9*) Norton, W. W. & Co., Inc.
—Tropical Freeze. 1991. 320p. mass mkt. 6.50 o.p. (*0-446-36062-7*) Warner Bks., Inc.
—Under Cover of Daylight. 1997. 352p. pap. 9.95 o.s.i (*0-385-31867-7*, Delta) Dell Publishing.
—Under Cover of Daylight. l.t. ed. 2001. (Large Print Book Ser.). 358p. 26.95 (*1-58724-028-9*, Wheeler Publishing, Inc.) Gale Group.
—Under Cover of Daylight. 2001. 272p. pap. 10.00 (*0-393-32125-8*); 1987. 16.95 o.p. (*0-393-02484-9*) Norton, W. W. & Co., Inc.
—Under Cover of Daylight. 1988. 384p. mass mkt. 6.50 o.s.i (*0-446-35231-4*) Warner Bks., Inc.

**THORN, PETER (FICTITIOUS CHARACTER)—FICTION**

Bond, Larry. Day of Wrath. unabr. ed. 1998. audio 96.00 (*0-7366-4187-4*, 4685) Books on Tape, Inc.
—Day of Wrath. abr. ed. 1998. 5p. audio 25.00 (*0-671-58224-0*, 495728, Simon & Schuster Audioworks) Simon & Schuster Audio.
—Day of Wrath. l.t. ed. 1999. (Mystery Ser.). 725p. 30.95 o.p. (*0-7862-1616-6*) Thorndike Pr.
—Day of Wrath. 1999. 528p. mass mkt. 7.99 (*0-446-60705-3*); 1998. 496p. 25.00 (*0-446-51677-5*) Warner Bks., Inc.
—The Enemy Within. abr. ed. audio. 1999. audio 12.98 (*0-671-04632-2*, Simon & Schuster Audioworks-);Set. 1996. 192p. pap. 23.00 incl. audio (*0-671-57054-4*, 493929, Simon & Schuster Audioworks) Simon & Schuster Audio.
—The Enemy Within. 1997. 528p. mass mkt. 7.99 (*0-446-60385-6*); 1996. 496p. 32.00 (*0-446-51676-7*) Warner Bks., Inc.
Bond, Larry & Larkin, Patrick. The Enemy Within. unabr. ed. 1996. audio 104.00 (*0-7366-3388-X*, 4038) Books on Tape, Inc.

**THORNDYKE, DOCTOR (FICTITIOUS CHARACTER)—FICTION**

Freeman, R. Austin. The Red Thumb Mark. 1986. 305p. mass mkt. 3.95 o.p. (*0-88184-240-0*, Carroll & Graf Pubs.) Avalon Publishing Group.
—The Red Thumb Mark. 1986. 320p. reprint ed. pap. 6.95 (*0-486-25210-8*) Dover Pubns., Inc.
—The Red Thumb Mark. 2001. 230p. pap. 9.95 (*0-7551-0374-2*) House of Stratus, Inc. GBR. *Dist:* Midpoint Trade Bks., Inc.

**THORNE, HOLLY (FICTITIOUS CHARACTER)—FICTION**

Koontz, Dean. Cold Fire. 1991. 432p. mass mkt. 7.99 (*0-425-13071-1*) Berkley Publishing Group.
—Cold Fire. 1991. 14.04 (*0-606-00937-X*) Turtleback Bks.

**THORNE, IRIS (FICTITIOUS CHARACTER)—FICTION**

Pugh, Dianne G. Fast Friends. 1997. 320p. 22.00 (*0-671-51912-3*, Atria) Simon & Schuster.
—Foolproof. 1998. (Iris Thorne Mystery Ser.). 344p. 23.00 (*0-671-01424-2*, Atria) Simon & Schuster.
—Slow Squeeze: An Iris Thorne Mystery. 1995. 288p. mass mkt. 5.99 (*0-671-77844-7*, Pocket) Simon & Schuster.

**THORNHILL, RICHARD (FICTITIOUS CHARACTER)—FICTION**

Taylor, Andrew. An Air That Kills. 1995. 266p. 19.95 o.p. (*0-312-11739-6*, Saint Martin's Minotaur) St. Martin's Pr.
—The Lover of the Grave. 1997. 309p. 22.95 o.p. (*0-312-15573-5*, Saint Martin's Minotaur) St. Martin's Pr.
—The Mortal Sickness. 1996. 304p. 22.95 o.p. (*0-312-14371-0*, Saint Martin's Minotaur) St. Martin's Pr.
—The Suffocating Night. l.t. ed. 2000. (Ulverscroft Large Print Ser.). 392p. 31.99 (*0-7089-4188-5*, Ulverscroft) Thorpe, F. A. Pubs. GBR. *Dist:* Ulverscroft Large Print Bks., Ltd., Ulverscroft Large Print Canada, Ltd.

**THORNTON, JUDITH (FICTITIOUS CHARACTER)—FICTION**

Benke, Patricia D. False Witness. 1996. mass mkt. 5.99 (*0-380-78184-0*, Avon Bks.) Morrow/Avon.

**THORNTON FAMILY (FICTITIOUS CHARACTERS)—FICTION**

Michaels, Fern. Kentucky Rich. abr. ed. (Kentucky Ser.: Vol. 1). 2002. audio 9.99 (*1-58788-486-0*, 2781, Paperback Nova Audio Bks.); 2001. audio 19.95 o.p. (*1-58788-238-8*, 2499, Nova Audio Bks.); 2001. audio 32.95 (*1-58788-236-1*, 2497, Brilliance Audio Unabridged) Brilliance Audio.
—Kentucky Rich. l.t. ed. 2002. 13.95 (*1-56895-195-7*); 2001. 425p. 31.95 (*1-58724-105-6*) Gale Group. (Wheeler Publishing, Inc.).
—Kentucky Rich. 2002. 48p. mass mkt. 7.99 (*0-8217-7234-1*); 2001. 336p. 24.00 o.s.i (*1-57566-761-4*, Kensington Bks.) Kensington Publishing Corp.
—Kentucky Rich. unabr. ed. 2003. (Kentucky Ser.). audio 19.99 (*1-59335-019-8*, 30101) Soulmate Audio Bks., Inc.
—Vegas Heat. abr. ed. 1997. (Vegas Ser.). audio 7.99 o.p. (*1-56740-236-4*, 715, Paperback Nova Audio Bks.); audio 16.95 o.p. (*1-56100-973-3*, 1399, Nova Audio Bks.); 15p. audio 89.25 o.p. (*1-56100-810-9*, 1086, Unabridged Library Editions); audio 29.95 o.p. (*1-56100-735-8*, 308, Bookcassette) Brilliance Audio.
—Vegas Heat. 1997. 480p. mass mkt. 6.99 o.s.i (*0-8217-5758-X*); 400p. 25.00 o.s.i (*1-57566-138-1*) Kensington Publishing Corp.
—Vegas Rich. abr. ed. (Vegas Ser.). 1997. audio 7.99 o.p. (*1-56740-183-X*, 714, Paperback Nova Audio Bks.); 1996. audio 16.95 o.p. (*1-56100-914-8*, 1400, Nova Audio Bks.); 1996. audio 29.95 o.p. (*1-56100-706-4*, 307, Bookcassette); 1996. audio 121.25 o.p. (*1-56100-331-X*, 1087, Unabridged Library Editions) Brilliance Audio.
—Vegas Rich, Vol. 1. l.t. ed. 1996. 26.95 o.p. (*1-56895-370-4*, Wheeler Publishing, Inc.) Gale Group.
—Vegas Rich. 2001. 54p. mass mkt. 7.50 (*0-8217-7206-6*); 1997. 544p. mass mkt. 6.99 o.s.i (*0-8217-5594-3*); 1996. 512p. 25.00 o.s.i (*1-57566-057-1*) Kensington Publishing Corp.
—Vegas Sunrise. abr. ed. (Vegas Ser.). 1998. audio 7.99 o.s.i (*1-56740-259-3*, 1402, Paperback Nova Audio Bks.); 1997. audio 16.95 o.p. (*1-56100-995-4*, 514, Nova Audio Bks.); 1999. audio 17.95 o.p. (*1-56740-844-3*, 1727, Bookcassette); 1997. audio 89.25 (*1-56100-844-3*, 1088, Unabridged Library Editions); 1997. audio 25.95 (*1-56100-769-2*, 309, Bookcassette) Brilliance Audio.
—Vegas Sunrise. l.t. ed. 1998. 28.95 (*1-56895-571-5*, Wheeler Publishing, Inc.) Gale Group.
—Vegas Sunrise. 1998. 48p. mass mkt. 7.50 o.s.i (*0-8217-7208-2*); 1998. 480p. mass mkt. 6.99 o.s.i (*0-8217-5983-3*); 1997. 384p. 25.00 o.s.i (*1-57566-214-0*) Kensington Publishing Corp.

**THORPE, CALVIN (FICTITIOUS CHARACTER)—FICTION**

Ferrigno, Robert. Dead Silent. l.t. ed. 1998. 320p. mass mkt. 6.99 o.s.i (*0-425-16149-8*) Berkley Publishing Group.
—Dead Silent. 1996. 320p. 24.95 o.p. (*0-399-14148-0*, G. P. Putnam's Sons) Penguin Group (USA) Inc.

**THORSSEN, ALIX (FICTITIOUS CHARACTER)—FICTION**

McClendon, Lise. Blue Wolf: An Alix Thorssen Mystery. 2001. 240p. 24.95 (*0-8027-3352-2*) Walker & Co.
—The Bluejay Shaman. 1996. (Mystery Ser.). per. (*0-373-26213-2*, Worldwide Library) Harlequin Enterprises, Ltd.
—Nordic Nights. 1999. (Alix Thorssen Mysteries Ser.). 292p. 23.95 (*0-8027-3340-9*) Walker & Co.
—Painted Truth: An Alix Thorssen Mystery. 1996. per. (*0-373-26222-1*, 1-26222-9, Worldwide Library) Harlequin Enterprises, Ltd.
—Painted Truth: An Alix Thorssen Mystery. 1995. 252p. 22.95 (*0-8027-3271-2*) Walker & Co.

**THREE MUSKETEERS (FICTITIOUS CHARACTERS)—FICTION**

Dumas, Alexandre. Aerie Three Musketeers. 1995. mass mkt. 4.99 (*1-55902-919-6*, Aerie) Doherty, Tom Assocs., LLC.
—Louise de la Valliere. 1994. reprint ed. lib. bdg. 37.95 (*1-56849-274-X*) Buccaneer Bks., Inc.
—Louise de la Valliere. 2002. 492p. 22.99 (*1-4043-1446-6*); per. 17.99 (*1-4043-1447-4*) IndyPublish.com.
—Louise de la Valliere. Coward, David, ed. & intro. by. (Oxford World's Classics Ser.). 1998. 768p. pap. 15.95 (*0-19-283465-7*); 1995. 764p. pap. 14.95 o.p. (*0-19-282389-2*) Oxford Univ. Pr., Inc.
—The Man in the Iron Mask. 1976. 27.95 (*0-8488-1293-X*) Amereon, Ltd.
—The Man in the Iron Mask. 1994. (Illustrated Classics Collection). 64'p. pap. 4.95 (*0-7854-0750-2*, 40503) American Guidance Service, Inc.
—The Man in the Iron Mask. unabr. ed. 1994. Pt. 1. audio 69.95 (*0-7861-0487-2*, 1439-A); Pt. 2. audio 62.95 (*0-7861-0641-7*, 1439-B) Blackstone Audio Bks., Inc.
—The Man in the Iron Mask. unabr. collector's ed. 1985. (J). audio 48.00 (*0-7366-3904-7*, 895784) Books on Tape, Inc.
—The Man in the Iron Mask. unabr. ed. 1999. (Bookcassette Classic Collection). 16p. audio 66.25 (*1-56740-680-7*, 1818, Unabridged Library Editions) Brilliance Audio.
—The Man in the Iron Mask. 1976. lib. bdg. 35.95 (*0-89968-146-8*, Lightyear Pr.) Buccaneer Bks., Inc.
—The Man in the Iron Mask. 1998. 574p. pap. text 4.99 (*0-8125-6499-5*, Tor Classics) Doherty, Tom Assocs., LLC.
—The Man in the Iron Mask. 2002. 504p. 29.99 (*1-4043-1632-9*); per. 24.99 (*1-4043-1633-7*) IndyPublish.com.
—The Man in the Iron Mask. abr. ed. 1985. audio 42.00 Jimcin Recordings.
—The Man in the Iron Mask. rev. ed. 1998. (Signet Regency Romance Ser.: Vol. 9700). 496p. mass mkt. 6.99 (*0-451-19700-3*, Signet Bks.) NAL.
—The Man in the Iron Mask. Rogers, Jacqueline, tr. rev. ed. 1992. 496p. mass mkt. 6.95 (*0-451-52564-7*, Signet Classics) NAL.
—The Man in the Iron Mask. abr. ed. (Works of Alexandre Dumas). 1996. audio 13.98 (*962-634-569-1*, NA206914); 1995. audio compact disk 15.98 (*962-634-069-X*, NA206912) Naxos of America, Inc. (Naxos AudioBooks).
—The Man in the Iron Mask. abr. ed. 1994. (Classic, Ultimate, Dove Ser.). audio 19.95 o.p. (*0-7871-0155-9*, 693103) NewStar Media, Inc.
—The Man in the Iron Mask. Coward, David, ed. & intro. by. 1998. (Oxford World's Classics Ser.). 656p. pap. 13.95 (*0-19-283842-3*) Oxford Univ. Pr., Inc.
—The Man in the Iron Mask. 1992. (Oxford World's Classics Ser.). 654p. pap. 11.95 o.p. (*0-19-282752-9*) Oxford Univ. Pr., Inc.
—The Man in the Iron Mask. 2003. (Penguin Classics Ser.). 496p. pap. 13.00 (*0-14-043924-2*) Penguin Group (USA) Inc.
—The Man in the Iron Mask. 1998. (Gateway Movie Classics Ser.). 448p. pap. 14.95 o.p. (*0-89526-348-3*, Gateway Editions) Regnery Publishing, Inc., An Eagle Publishing Co.
—The Man in the Iron Mask. abr. ed. 1998. audio 17.95 (*1-55935-267-1*) Soundelux Audio Publishing.
—The Man in the Iron Mask. 2000. (Signature Classics Ser.). 456p. 24.95 (*1-58279-067-1*); (*1-58279-073-6*) Trident Pr. International.
—Ten Years Later. abr. ed. 1996. 19.95 o.p. (*0-7871-0501-5*, 693547) NewStar Media, Inc.
—The Three Musketeers. 1997. (Classics Illustrated Study Guides). (Illus.). mass mkt. 4.99 (*1-57840-029-5*) Acclaim Bks.
—The Three Musketeers. 1976. 29.95 (*0-8488-1295-6*) Amereon, Ltd.
—The Three Musketeers, unabr. ed. 1997. audio 77.95 (*1-55685-477-3*, 477-3) Audio Bk. Contractors, Inc.
—The Three Musketeers. 1977. 1.75 o.p. (*0-515-03492-4*, V3492, Jove) Berkley Publishing Group.
—The Three Musketeers. 1977. reprint ed. 14.95 o.p. (*0-460-00081-0*) Biblio Distribution.
—The Three Musketeers. unabr. ed. 1990. Pt. 1. audio 69.95 (*0-7861-0577-1*, 2067-A); Pt. 2. audio 62.95 (*0-7861-0578-X*, 2067-B) Blackstone Audio Bks., Inc.
—The Three Musketeers, Pt. A. unabr. collector's ed. 1991. (J). audio 80.00 (*0-7366-3957-8*, 9209-A) Books on Tape, Inc.
—The Three Musketeers. unabr. ed. 1998. (Bookcassette Classic Collection). audio 22.95 (*1-56740-053-1*, 12, Bookcassette); audio 66.25 (*1-56740-582-7*, 1074, Unabridged Library Editions) Brilliance Audio.
—The Three Musketeers. adapted ed. 1976. per. 6.50 (*0-8222-1140-8*) Dramatists Play Service, Inc.

—The Three Musketeers. abr. ed. (Read-Along Ser.). 1994. pap. 29.99 incl. audio (*0-88646-845-0*, LSR 7208); Set. 1987. audio 16.99 (*0-88646-208-8*, 7208) Durkin Hayes Publishing Ltd.

—The Three Musketeers. abr. ed. audio 8.98 o.p. (*0-89845-115-9*, CPN 1692, HarperAudio) HarperTrade.

—The Three Musketeers, Set. abr. ed. 1999. audio 16.95 Highsmith Inc.

—The Three Musketeers. unabr. ed. 1991. (YA). (gr. 9-12). audio 104.00 Jimcin Recordings.

—The Three Musketeers. 1999. (Everyman's Library Children's Classics). (Illus.). 720p. (gr. 8-12). 17.95 (*0-375-40657-3*) Knopf, Alfred A. Inc.

—The Three Musketeers. E-Book 2.95 (*1-57799-942-8*) Logos Research Systems, Inc.

—The Three Musketeers. abr. ed. 2000. audio 7.95 (*1-57815-126-0*, 1088, Media Bks. Audio Publishing) Media Bks., L. L. C.

—The Three Musketeers. E-Book 1.95 (*1-58515-020-7*) MesaView, Inc.

—The Three Musketeers. abr. ed. 1999. (Adventure Theatre Ser.). audio 16.95 (*1-56994-520-9*, 345344, Monterey SoundWorks) Monterey Media, Inc.

—The Three Musketeers. 1993. 648p. mass mkt. 6.95 o.s.i (*0-451-52594-9*, Signet Classics) NAL.

—The Three Musketeers. audio 7.95 National Recording Co.

—The Three Musketeers. abr. ed. 1996. (Works of Alexandre Dumas). audio compact disk 19.98 (*962-634-089-4*, NA308912); audio 17.98 (*962-634-589-6*, NA308914) Naxos of America, Inc. (Naxos AudioBooks).

—The Three Musketeers. abr. ed. 1993. (Ultimate Classics Ser.). audio 19.95 o.p. (*1-55800-788-1*, 692322) NewStar Media, Inc.

—The Three Musketeers. Coward, David, ed. & intro. by. 1999. (Oxford World's Classics Ser.). 704p. pap. 8.95 (*0-19-283575-0*) Oxford Univ. Pr., Inc.

—The Three Musketeers. 1987. (Classics for Young Readers Ser.). 400p. pap. 4.99 o.p. (*0-14-035054-3*, Puffin Bks.) Penguin Putnam Bks. for Young Readers.

—The Three Musketeers. 1998. (Gateway Movie Classics Ser.). 416p. pap. 14.95 o.p. (*0-89526-349-1*, Gateway Editions) Regnery Publishing, Inc., An Eagle Publishing Co.

—The Three Musketeers. 1999. (Signature Classics Ser.). (Illus.). 776p. 24.95 (*1-58279-035-3*); 29.95 (*1-58279-047-7*) Trident Pr. International.

—The Three Musketeers. 1984. (Bantam Classics Ser.). 12.00 (*0-606-02468-9*) Turtleback Bks.

—The Three Musketeers. Sudley, Lord, tr. from FRE. 1982. (Penguin Classics Ser.). 720p. 11.00 (*0-14-044025-9*, Penguin Classics) Viking Penguin.

—The Three Musketeers. abr. ed. 1996. (Classic Ser.). audio 10.95 o.s.i (*0-14-086348-6*, Penguin AudioBooks) Viking Penguin.

—The Three Musketeers. 1997. (Classics Ser.). 576p. pap. 3.95 (*1-85326-040-1*, j0401WW) Wordsworth Editions, Ltd. GBR. *Dist:* Combined Publishing.

—Les Trois Mousquetaires. unabr. ed. 1999. (World Classics Ser.). (FRE.). pap. 7.95 (*2-87714-198-5*) Bookking International FRA. *Dist:* Distribooks, Inc.

—Les Trois Mousquetaires. 1962. (FRE.). 115.00 (*0-8288-3443-1*, F60650); 1962. (FRE.). 1800p. 95.00 (*0-7859-1098-0*, 2070101800); 1935. pap. 11.90 o.p.; Tome I. 1973. (FRE.). 448p. pap. 11.95 (*0-7859-1771-3*, 2070365263); Tome II. 1973. (FRE.). 448p. pap. 11.95 (*0-7859-1772-1*, 2070365271) French & European Pubns., Inc.

—Les Trois Mousquetaires. 2001. (FRE., Illus.). 168p. (C). pap. 11.25 (*0-8442-1229-6*, VF1229-6) McGraw-Hill/Contemporary.

—Les Trois Mousquetaires. (FRE.). pap. 12.95 (*2-266-08579-4*) Presses Pocket FRA. *Dist:* Distribooks, Inc.

—Les Trois Mousquetaires. deluxe ed. (Pleiade Ser.). (FRE.). 82.95 (*2-07-010180-0*) Schoenhof's Foreign Bks., Inc.

—Twenty Years After. 1999. pap. 4.99 o.p. (*1-57840-192-5*) Acclaim Bks.

—Twenty Years After. 1976. 28.95 (*0-8488-1296-4*) Amereon, Ltd.

—Twenty Years After. 1979. reprint ed. 14.95 o.p. (*0-460-00175-2*) Biblio Distribution.

—Twenty Years After. unabr. ed. 1999. Pt. 1. audio 76.95 (*0-7861-1308-1*, 2218-A); Pt. 2. audio 62.95 Blackstone Audio Bks., Inc.

—Twenty Years After. 1981. 467p. reprint ed. lib. bdg. 31.95 (*0-89968-229-4*, Lightyear Pr.) Buccaneer Bks., Inc.

—Twenty Years After. 2001. 508p. per. 29.95 (*1-58963-225-7*) International Law & Taxation Pubs.

—Twenty Years After. E-Book 1.95 (*1-58515-021-5*); E-Book 1.95 (*1-58515-019-3*) MesaView, Inc.

—Twenty Years After. (Oxford World's Classics Ser.). 1998. (Illus.). 880p. pap. 15.95 (*0-19-283843-1*); 1993. 872p. (C). pap. 13.95 o.p. (*0-19-283074-0*) Oxford Univ. Pr., Inc.

—Le Vicomte de Bragelonne. Coward, David, ed. & intro. by. (Oxford World's Classics Ser.). 768p. 1998. pap. 15.95 (*0-19-283463-0*); 1995. pap. 14.95 o.p. (*0-19-282390-6*) Oxford Univ. Pr., Inc.

—Vingt Ans Apres. Samaran, Charles, ed. 1989. (Class. Garnier Ser.). pap. 20.95 (*0-7859-3150-3*, 2253050520) French & European Pubns., Inc.

—Vingt Ans Apres, 2 tomes. 1935. pap. 11.90 o.p.; Tome I. 1975. (FRE.). 544p. pap. 11.95 (*0-7859-1803-5*, 2070366820); Tome II. 1975. (FRE.). 544p. pap. 12.95 (*0-7859-1804-3*, 2070366839) French & European Pubns., Inc.

—Vingt Ans Apres. (FRE.). pap. 23.95 (*2-07-040478-1*) Gallimard, Editions FRA. *Dist:* Distribooks, Inc.

—Vingt Ans Apres, 2 vols. 1975. (Folio Ser.: Nos. 682 & 683). 1. pap. 7.95 o.p. (*2-07-036682-0*); 2. pap. 9.95 o.p. (*2-07-036683-9*) Schoenhof's Foreign Bks., Inc.

Dumas, Alexandre & Page, Michael. The Man in the Iron Mask. unabr. ed. 1999. (Bookcassette Classic Collection). audio 22.95 (*1-56740-454-5*, 1816, Bookcassette) Brilliance Audio.

Dumas, Alexandre & Rizvi, S. N. The Three Musketeers. 1997. 156p. pap. 20.00 (*81-209-0218-1*) Pitambar Publishing IND. *Dist:* State Mutual Bk. & Periodical Service, Ltd.

Loughery, David. The Three Musketeers: The Screenplay. 2000. pap. 19.95 o.p. (*1-929750-05-6*) Harvest Moon Publishing.

**TIBALDI, JIMMY (FICTITIOUS CHARACTER)—FICTION**

Westermann, John. High Crimes. McCarthy, Paul, ed. 1989. 256p. mass mkt. 5.99 (*0-671-67968-6*, Pocket) Simon & Schuster.

—High Crimes. 2001. 208p. pap. 12.00 (*1-56947-244-0*); 1988. 234p. 15.95 (*0-939149-15-X*) Soho Pr., Inc.

**TIBBETT, EMMY (FICTITIOUS CHARACTER)—FICTION**

Moyes, Patricia. Angel Death. 1982. (Henry Tibbett Mystery Ser.). 240p. pap. 5.95 o.s.i (*0-8050-0505-6*, Owl Bks.) Holt, Henry & Co.

—Black Girl, White Girl. l.t. ed. 1991. (Henry Tibbett Mystery Ser.). 326p. lib. bdg. 19.95 o.p. (*0-8161-5011-7*, Macmillan Reference USA) Gale Group.

—Black Girl, White Girl. (Henry Tibbett Mystery Ser.). 224p. 1990. pap. 5.95 o.s.i (*0-8050-1149-8*, Owl Bks.); 1989. 15.95 o.p. (*0-8050-1148-X*) Holt, Henry & Co.

—Dead Men Don't Ski. 1984. (Henry Tibbett Mystery Ser.). 288p. pap. 5.95 o.s.i (*0-8050-0705-9*, Owl Bks.) Holt, Henry & Co.

—Death & the Dutch Uncle. 1983. (Henry Tibbett Mystery Ser.). 256p. pap. 5.95 o.s.i (*0-8050-0506-4*, Owl Bks.) Holt, Henry & Co.

—Death on the Agenda. 1984. (Henry Tibbett Mystery Ser.). 192p. pap. 5.95 o.s.i (*0-8050-0507-2*, Owl Bks.) Holt, Henry & Co.

—Down among the Dead Men. 1986. (Henry Tibbett Mystery Ser.). 240p. pap. 5.95 o.s.i (*0-8050-0117-4*, Owl Bks.) Holt, Henry & Co.

—Falling Star. 1982. (Henry Tibbett Mystery Ser.). 256p. (Orig.). pap. 5.95 o.s.i (*0-8050-0755-5*, Owl Bks.) Holt, Henry & Co.

—Murder Fantastical. 1984. (Henry Tibbett Mystery Ser.). 256p. pap. 5.95 o.s.i (*0-8050-0504-8*, Owl Bks.) Holt, Henry & Co.

—Season of Snows & Sins. 1988. (Henry Tibbett Mystery Ser.). 224p. pap. 6.95 o.s.i (*0-8050-0849-7*, Owl Bks.) Holt, Henry & Co.

**TIBBETT, HENRY (FICTITIOUS CHARACTER)—FICTION**

Moyes, Patricia. Angel Death. 1982. (Henry Tibbett Mystery Ser.). 240p. pap. 5.95 o.s.i (*0-8050-0505-6*, Owl Bks.) Holt, Henry & Co.

—Angel Death. l.t. ed. 1982. (Henry Tibbett Mystery Ser.). 457p. 12.50 o.p. (*0-7089-0746-6*, Ulverscroft) Thorpe, F. A. Pubs. GBR. *Dist:* Ulverscroft Large Print Bks., Ltd., Ulverscroft Large Print Canada, Ltd.

—Black Girl, White Girl. unabr. ed. 1993. (Henry Tibbett Mystery Ser.). audio 36.00 (*0-7366-2327-2*, 3107) Books on Tape, Inc.

—Black Girl, White Girl. l.t. ed. 1991. (Henry Tibbett Mystery Ser.). 326p. lib. bdg. 19.95 o.p. (*0-8161-5011-7*, Macmillan Reference USA) Gale Group.

—Black Girl, White Girl. (Henry Tibbett Mystery Ser.). 224p. 1990. pap. 5.95 o.s.i (*0-8050-1149-8*, Owl Bks.); 1989. 15.95 o.p. (*0-8050-1148-X*) Holt, Henry & Co.

—Black Widower. unabr. ed. 1992. (Henry Tibbett Mystery Ser.). audio 42.00 (*0-7366-2272-1*, 3060) Books on Tape, Inc.

—Black Widower. 1985. (Henry Tibbett Mystery Ser.). 224p. pap. 5.95 o.s.i (*0-8050-0243-X*, Owl Bks.) Holt, Henry & Co.

—Black Widower. 1977. (Henry Tibbett Mystery Ser.). 224p. pap. 2.95 o.p. (*0-14-004334-9*, Penguin Bks.) Viking Penguin.

—The Coconut Killings. 1985. pap. o.p. (*0-03-005608-X*, Owl Bks.); 1985. 224p. pap. 5.95 o.s.i (*0-8050-0754-7*, Owl Bks.); 1977. o.p. (*0-03-018481-9*) Holt, Henry & Co.

—The Coconut Killings. 1979. (Henry Tibbett Mystery Ser.). pap. 1.95 o.p. (*0-14-004593-7*, Penguin Bks.) Viking Penguin.

—The Curious Affair of the Third Dog. unabr. ed. 1993. (Henry Tibbett Mystery Ser.). audio 44.95 (*0-7861-0428-7*, 1380) Blackstone Audio Bks., Inc.

—The Curious Affair of the Third Dog. 1986. (Henry Tibbett Mystery Ser.). 224p. pap. 5.95 o.s.i (*0-8050-0503-X*); pap. o.p. (*0-03-009534-4*) Holt, Henry & Co. (Owl Bks.).

—The Curious Affair of the Third Dog. 1976. (Henry Tibbett Mystery Ser.). 208p. pap. 1.95 o.p. (*0-14-004027-7*, Penguin Bks.) Viking Penguin.

—Dead Men Don't Ski. 1984. (Henry Tibbett Mystery Ser.). 288p. pap. 5.95 o.s.i (*0-8050-0705-9*, Owl Bks.) Holt, Henry & Co.

—Dead Men Don't Ski. l.t. ed. 1983. (Ulverscroft Large Print Ser.). 496p. 29.99 o.p. (*0-7089-1006-8*, Ulverscroft) Thorpe, F. A. Pubs. GBR. *Dist:* Ulverscroft Large Print Bks., Ltd., Ulverscroft Large Print Canada, Ltd.

—Death & the Dutch Uncle. 1983. (Henry Tibbett Mystery Ser.). 256p. pap. 5.95 o.s.i (*0-8050-0506-4*, Owl Bks.) Holt, Henry & Co.

—Death on the Agenda. 1984. (Henry Tibbett Mystery Ser.). 192p. pap. 5.95 o.s.i (*0-8050-0507-2*, Owl Bks.) Holt, Henry & Co.

—Down among the Dead Men. (Henry Tibbett Mystery Ser.). 18.50 o.p. (*0-86220-823-8*, BD022, Black Dagger); 1994. 18.95 o.p. (*0-7451-6461-7*) BBC Audiobooks America.

—Down among the Dead Men. 1982. (Henry Tibbett Mystery Ser.). 240p. pap. 2.50 o.p. (*0-440-11627-9*) Dell Publishing.

—Down among the Dead Men. 1986. (Henry Tibbett Mystery Ser.). 240p. pap. 5.95 o.s.i (*0-8050-0117-4*, Owl Bks.) Holt, Henry & Co.

—Falling Star. 1982. (Henry Tibbett Mystery Ser.). (Orig.). 256p. pap. 5.95 o.s.i (*0-8050-0755-5*); pap. o.p. (*0-03-059784-6*) Holt, Henry & Co. (Owl Bks.).

—Johnny under Ground. (Henry Tibbett Mystery Ser.). 18.50 o.p. (*0-86220-789-4*, C1029, Black Dagger); 1993. 18.95 o.p. (*0-7451-6441-2*); 1996. audio 54.95 (*0-7451-2414-3*, CDA015) BBC Audiobooks America.

—Johnny under Ground. 1983. (Henry Tibbett Mystery Ser.). pap. 2.95 o.p. (*0-440-14211-3*) Dell Publishing.

—Johnny under Ground. Barzun, Jacques & Taylor, W. H., eds. 1983. (Henry Tibbett Mystery Ser.). 253p. lib. bdg. 18.00 o.p. (*0-8240-4987-X*) Garland Publishing, Inc.

—Johnny under Ground: An Inspector Henry Tibbett Mystery. 1987. (Henry Tibbett Mystery Ser.). 256p. pap. 5.95 o.s.i (*0-8050-0270-7*, Owl Bks.) Holt, Henry & Co.

—Many Deadly Returns. unabr. ed. 1994. (Henry Tibbett Mystery Ser.). audio 49.95 (*0-7861-0433-3*, 1385) Blackstone Audio Bks., Inc.

—Many Deadly Returns. 1981. (Henry Tibbett Mystery Ser.). pap. 2.25 o.p. (*0-440-16172-X*) Dell Publishing.

—Many Deadly Returns: An Inspector Henry Tibbett Mystery. 1987. (Henry Tibbett Mystery Ser.). 256p. pap. 5.95 o.s.i (*0-8050-0598-6*, Owl Bks.) Holt, Henry & Co.

—Murder a la Mode. 1983. (Henry Tibbett Mystery Ser.). 224p. pap. 5.95 o.s.i (*0-8050-0706-7*, Owl Bks.) Holt, Henry & Co.

—Murder Fantastical. (Henry Tibbett Mystery Ser.). 189p. 12.95 o.p. (*0-86220-722-3*) Chivers Pr. GBR. *Dist:* BBC Audiobooks America.

—Murder Fantastical. 1984. (Henry Tibbett Mystery Ser.). 256p. pap. 5.95 o.s.i (*0-8050-0504-8*, Owl Bks.) Holt, Henry & Co.

—Night Ferry to Death. (Henry Tibbett Mystery Ser.). 192p. 1986. pap. 5.95 o.s.i (*0-8050-0116-6*, Owl Bks.); 1985. o.p. (*0-03-004477-4*) Holt, Henry & Co.

—Night Ferry to Death. l.t. ed. 1987. (Henry Tibbett Mystery Ser.). 336p. 29.99 o.p. (*0-7089-1615-5*, Ulverscroft) Thorpe, F. A. Pubs. GBR. *Dist:* Ulverscroft Large Print Bks., Ltd., Ulverscroft Large Print Canada, Ltd.

—Season of Snows & Sins. (Henry Tibbett Mystery Ser.). 1988. 224p. pap. 6.95 o.s.i (*0-8050-0849-7*); 1983. pap. o.p. (*0-03-063542-X*) Holt, Henry & Co. (Owl Bks.).

—A Six-Letter Word for Death. 1985. (Henry Tibbett Mystery Ser.). 256p. pap. 5.95 o.s.i (*0-8050-0244-8*, Owl Bks.) Holt, Henry & Co.

—A Six-Letter Word for Death. l.t. ed. 1984. (Henry Tibbett Mystery Ser.). 432p. 29.99 o.p. (*0-7089-1163-3*, Ulverscroft) Thorpe, F. A. Pubs. GBR. *Dist:* Ulverscroft Large Print Bks., Ltd., Ulverscroft Large Print Canada, Ltd.

—To Kill a Coconut. l.t. ed. 1981. (Ulverscroft Large Print Ser.). 336p. 29.99 o.p. (*0-7089-0632-X*, Ulverscroft) Thorpe, F. A. Pubs. GBR. *Dist:* Ulverscroft Large Print Bks., Ltd., Ulverscroft Large Print Canada, Ltd.

—Twice in a Blue Moon. (Henry Tibbett Mystery Ser.). 1994. pap. 5.95 o.s.i (*0-8050-2948-6*, Owl Bks.); 1993. 192p. 19.95 o.p. (*0-8050-2823-4*) Holt, Henry & Co.

—Who Is Simon Warwick? (Henry Tibbett Mystery Ser.). 1982. 176p. pap. 5.95 o.s.i (*0-8050-0719-9*, Owl Bks.); 1982. pap. o.p. (*0-03-059783-8*, Owl Bks.); 1979. 180p. o.p. (*0-03-044726-7*) Holt, Henry & Co.

**TIBBS, VIRGIL (FICTITIOUS CHARACTER)—FICTION**

Ball, John. The Cool Cottontail. 1985. 176p. (Orig.). mass mkt. 3.50 o.p. (*0-06-080734-2*, P734, Perennial) HarperTrade.

—The Eyes of Buddha: A Virgil Tibbs Mystery. 1985. 256p. reprint ed. mass mkt. 3.50 o.p. (*0-06-080751-2*, P751, Perennial) HarperTrade.

—Five Pieces of Jade. l.t. ed. 1983. (Ulverscroft Large Print Ser.). 352p. 29.99 o.p. (*0-7089-0997-3*, Ulverscroft) Thorpe, F. A. Pubs. GBR. *Dist:* Ulverscroft Large Print Bks., Ltd., Ulverscroft Large Print Canada, Ltd.

—In the Heat of the Night. 1992. (Mystery Scene Bk.). 208p. mass mkt. 4.50 (*0-88184-887-5*, Carroll & Graf Pubs.) Avalon Publishing Group.

—In the Heat of the Night. 1992. 158p. reprint ed. lib. bdg. 14.95 (*0-89966-916-6*) Buccaneer Bks., Inc.

—In the Heat of the Night. 1985. 256p. pap. 4.50 o.p. (*0-06-080735-0*, P735, Perennial) HarperTrade.

—Then Came Violence. 1980. (Crime Club Ser.). 8.95 o.p. (*0-385-15726-6*) Doubleday Publishing.

—Then Came Violence. l.t. ed. 1982. (Ulverscroft Large Print Ser.). 352p. 29.99 o.p. (*0-7089-0870-5*, Ulverscroft) Thorpe, F. A. Pubs. GBR. *Dist:* Ulverscroft Large Print Bks., Ltd., Ulverscroft Large Print Canada, Ltd.

—Then Came Violence: A Virgil Tibbs Mystery. 1988. 208p. reprint ed. mass mkt. 3.95 o.p. (*0-06-080883-7*, P-883, Perennial) HarperTrade.

**TICHY, IJON (FICTITIOUS CHARACTER)—FICTION**

Lem, Stanislaw. Peace On Earth. 1994. 240p. 19.95 o.s.i (*0-15-171554-8*) Harcourt Trade Pubs.

**TIDEWATER, JORDAN (FICTITIOUS CHARACTER)—FICTION**

Stokes, Naomi M. The Tree People. 1996. 520p. pap. text 6.99 (*0-8125-3510-3*); Bk. 2. 1995. 384p. 22.95 o.p. (*0-312-85633-4*); No. 3. 2000. 23.95 (*0-312-86109-5*) Doherty, Tom Assocs., LLC. (Forge Bks.).

**TIMBERLAKE, ABIGAIL (FICTITIOUS CHARACTER)—FICTION**

Myers, Tamar. Baroque & Desperate. 1999. (Den of Antiquity Ser.). 256p. mass mkt. 6.99 (*0-380-80225-2*, Avon Bks.) Morrow/Avon.

—Estate of Mind. 1999. 320p. mass mkt. 6.50 (*0-380-80227-9*, Avon Bks.) Morrow/Avon.

—Guilt by Association. 1996. (Den of Antiquity Ser.). 256p. mass mkt. 6.50 (*0-380-78237-5*, Avon Bks.) Morrow/Avon.

—Larceny & Old Lace. 1996. (Den of Antiquity Ser.). 224p. (Orig.). mass mkt. 6.99 (*0-380-78239-1*, Avon Bks.) Morrow/Avon.

—Ming & I. 1997. (Den of Antiquity Ser.). 256p. mass mkt. 6.99 (*0-380-79255-9*, Avon Bks.) Morrow/Avon.

—So Faux, So Good. 1998. (Den of Antiquity Ser.). 256p. mass mkt. 6.50 (*0-380-79254-0*, Avon Bks.) Morrow/Avon.

**TINTIN (FICTITIOUS CHARACTER)—FICTION**

Tuten, Frederic. Tintin in the New World: A Romance. 1996. 240p. 12.00 o.s.i (*1-57322-529-0*, Riverhead Trade (Paperbacks)) Berkley Publishing Group.

—Tintin in the New World: A Romance. 1993. 22.00 o.p. (*0-688-12314-7*, Morrow, William & Co.) Morrow/Avon.

**TITUS, NICKY (FICTITIOUS CHARACTER)—FICTION**

Sandstrom, Eve K. Death Down Home. 1990. 256p. 18.95 o.s.i (*0-684-19244-6*, Macmillan Reference USA) Gale Group.

—Death down Home. 1993. per. (*0-373-26125-X*, 1-26125-4, Harlequin Bks.) Harlequin Enterprises, Ltd.

—The Devil down Home. 1991. (Sam & Nicky Titus Mystery Ser.: No. 2). 256p. 19.95 o.s.i (*0-684-19268-3*, Macmillan Reference USA) Gale Group.

—The Devil down Home. 1994. per. (*0-373-26139-X*, Harlequin Bks.) Harlequin Enterprises, Ltd.

—Down Home Heifer Heist. 1994. per. (*0-373-26153-5*, 1-26153-6, Harlequin Bks.) Harlequin Enterprises, Ltd.

—Down Home Heifer Heist: A Sam & Nicky Titus Mystery. 1993. 256p. 20.00 o.p. (*0-684-19428-7*, Macmillan Reference USA) Gale Group.

**TITUS, SAM (FICTITIOUS CHARACTER)—FICTION**

Sandstrom, Eve K. Death Down Home. 1990. 256p. 18.95 o.s.i (*0-684-19244-6*, Macmillan Reference USA) Gale Group.

—Death down Home. 1993. per. (*0-373-26125-X*, 1-26125-4, Harlequin Bks.) Harlequin Enterprises, Ltd.

—The Devil down Home. 1991. (Sam & Nicky Titus Mystery Ser.: No. 2). 256p. 19.95 o.s.i (*0-684-19268-3*, Macmillan Reference USA) Gale Group.

—The Devil down Home. 1994. per. (*0-373-26139-X*, Harlequin Bks.) Harlequin Enterprises, Ltd.

—Down Home Heifer Heist. 1994. per. (*0-373-26153-5*, 1-26153-6, Harlequin Bks.) Harlequin Enterprises, Ltd.

—Down Home Heifer Heist: A Sam & Nicky Titus Mystery. 1993. 256p. 20.00 o.p. (*0-684-19428-7*, Macmillan Reference USA) Gale Group.

**TOBIN, MITCH (FICTITIOUS CHARACTER)—FICTION**

Coe, Tucker. A Jade in Aries. 2001. (Mystery Ser.). 203p. 23.95 (*0-7862-3015-0*, Five Star) Gale Group.

—Murder among Children. 2000. (Five Star Mystery Ser.). 194p. 22.95 (*0-7862-2893-8*, Five Star) Gale Group.

—Wax Apple: A Mitchell Tobin Mystery. l.t. ed. 2000. (Mystery Ser.). 208p. 23.95 (*0-7862-3004-5*, Five Star) Gale Group.

Gale Group Staff, contrib. by. Don't Lie to Me. l.t. ed. 2001. (Five Star Mystery Ser.). 200p. 24.95 (*0-7862-3011-8*) Thorndike Pr.

**TODD, CHARLES (FICTITIOUS CHARACTER)—FICTION**

Francis, Dick. In the Frame. 1993. 272p. mass mkt. 6.99 (*0-449-22116-4*, Fawcett) Ballantine Bks.

—In the Frame. unabr. ed. 1996. audio 39.95 (*0-7861-1021-X*, 1799) Blackstone Audio Bks., Inc.

—In the Frame. l.t. ed. 1994. 327p. lib. bdg. 22.95 o.p. (*0-8161-5783-9*, Macmillan Reference USA) Gale Group.

—In the Frame. unabr. ed. 1990. audio 44.00 (*1-55690-253-0*, 90026E7) Recorded Bks., LLC.

—In the Frame. 1989. 208p. mass mkt. 4.50 (*0-671-69648-3*); 1988. mass mkt. 3.95 (*0-671-67429-3*); 1987. mass mkt. 3.50 (*0-671-55658-4*); 1984. mass mkt. 3.50 (*0-671-50754-0*); 1982. mass mkt. 2.95 o.s.i (*0-671-45461-7*) Simon & Schuster. (Pocket).

—In the Frame. l.t. ed. 1977. (Ulverscroft Large Print Ser.). 12.00 o.p. (*0-7089-0060-7*, Ulverscroft) Thorpe, F. A. Pubs. GBR. *Dist:* Ulverscroft Large Print Bks., Ltd., Ulverscroft Large Print Canada, Ltd.

**TOFF, THE (FICTITIOUS CHARACTER)—FICTION**

*see Rollison, Richard (Fictitious Character)—Fiction*

**TOLLIVER, BEN (FICTITIOUS CHARACTER)—FICTION**

Harvey, James N. By Reason of Insanity. 1991. 346p. pap. 5.99 o.p. (*0-312-92533-6*, St. Martin's Paperbacks); 1990. 18.95 o.p. (*0-312-04295-7*) St. Martin's Pr.

—Dead Game. 1997. 304p. text 24.95 o.p. (*0-312-15100-4*) St. Martin's Pr.

—Flesh & Blood: A Lt. Ben Tolliver Thriller. 1996. 408p. mass mkt. 6.50 o.p. (*0-312-95318-6*, St. Martin's Paperbacks); 1994. 384p. 22.95 o.p. (*0-312-10985-7*) St. Martin's Pr.

—Mental Case. 1997. 346p. mass mkt. 6.99 (*0-312-95995-8*, St. Martin's Paperbacks); 1996. 352p. 23.95 o.p. (*0-312-14014-2*) St. Martin's Pr.

—Painted Ladies. 1992. 375p. mass mkt. 5.99 (*0-312-92895-5*, St. Martin's Paperbacks); 448p. 19.95 o.p. (*0-312-07056-X*) St. Martin's Pr.

**TONNEMAN, PIETER (FICTITIOUS CHARACTER)—FICTION**

Meyers, Maan. The Dutchman. 1993. mass mkt. 5.50 o.s.i (*0-553-56285-1*) Bantam Bks.

—The Dutchman. 1992. 18.50 o.s.i (*0-385-42603-8*) Doubleday Publishing.

—The Dutchman's Dilemma. 1996. 304p. mass mkt. 5.99 o.s.i (*0-553-57201-6*, Crimeline) Bantam Bks.

—The House on Mulberry Street. 1997. 352p. reprint ed. mass mkt. 5.99 o.s.i (*0-553-57212-1*, Crimeline) Bantam Bks.

—The House on Mulberry Street. 2000. 312p. 27.95 (*0-7351-0433-6*); pap. 17.95 (*0-7351-0434-4*) Replica Bks.

—The Kingsbridge Plot. 1994. (Dutchman Historical Ser.). 432p. mass mkt. 4.99 o.s.i (*0-553-56380-7*) Bantam Bks.

—The Lucifer Contract: A Civil War Thriller. 1999. 320p. reprint ed. mass mkt. 6.50 o.s.i (*0-553-57199-0*) Bantam Bks.

**TOOLE, SANTIAGO (FICTITIOUS CHARACTER)—FICTION**

Wheeler, Richard S. Deuces & Ladies Wild. 1991. 208p. mass mkt. 1.96 o.s.i (*0-449-14710-X*, Fawcett) Ballantine Bks.

—The Fate. 1992. mass mkt. 4.99 o.s.i (*0-449-14784-3*, Fawcett) Ballantine Bks.

—The Final Tally. 1990. 208p. mass mkt. 3.99 o.s.i (*0-449-14709-6*, Fawcett) Ballantine Bks.

—Incident at Fort Keogh. 192p. 2000. mass mkt. 3.99 o.s.i (*0-345-44048-X*, Ballantine Bks.); 1990. mass mkt. 2.95 o.s.i (*0-345-36555-0*) Ballantine Bks.

**TORRANCE, JACK (FICTITIOUS CHARACTER)—FICTION**

King, Stephen. The Shining. 1990. 464p. 35.00 (*0-385-12167-9*) Doubleday Publishing.

—The Shining. 1991. (Stephen King Collectors Editions Ser.). (Illus.). 432p. pap. 14.95 o.p. (*0-452-26722-6*, Plume) Dutton/Plume.

—The Shining. 1997. 464p. mass mkt. 7.50 o.s.i (*0-451-19388-1*); 1978. mass mkt. 4.50 o.p. (*0-451-15032-5*); 1978. 464p. reprint ed. mass mkt. 7.99 o.s.i (*0-451-16091-6*) NAL. (Signet Bks.).

—The Shining. reprint ed. 2002. 528p. pap. 14.00 (*0-7434-3749-7*); 2001. 704p. pap. 7.99 (*0-7434-2442-5*) Simon & Schuster. (Pocket).

—The Shining. l.t. ed. 1993. 656p. lib. bdg. 23.95 (*0-8161-5685-9*) Thorndike Pr.

—The Shining. 1977. 14.04 (*0-606-01215-X*) Turtleback Bks.

**TORRES, B'ELANNA (FICTITIOUS CHARACTER)—FICTION**

Carey, Diane L., et al. Day of Honor Omnibus: Ancient Blood; Armageddon Sky; Her Klingon Soul; Treaty's Law; Day of Honor; Honor Bound. 1999. (Star Trek Ser.). (Illus.). 1104p. pap. 16.00 (*0-671-02813-8*, Pocket) Simon & Schuster.

Cox, Greg. The Black Shore. 1997. (Star Trek Voyager Ser.: No. 13). (Illus.). 288p. mass mkt. 5.99 (*0-671-56061-1*, Star Trek) Simon & Schuster.

Friedman, Michael Jan. Day of Honor No. 3: Her Klingon Soul. 1997. (Star Trek Voyager: Vol. 3). (Illus.). 304p. mass mkt. 5.99 (*0-671-00240-6*, Star Trek) Simon & Schuster.

—The Television Episode: Day of Honor. 1997. (Star Trek Voyager). 224p. mass mkt. 5.99 (*0-671-01981-3*, Star Trek) Simon & Schuster.

Galanter, Dave & Brodeur, Greg. Battle Lines. 1999. (Star Trek Voyager Ser.: No. 18). 264p. mass mkt. 6.50 o.s.i (*0-671-00259-7*, Star Trek) Simon & Schuster.

Hugh, Dafydd ab. The Final Fury No. 4: Invasion! 1996. (Star Trek Voyager Ser.: No. 9). 320p. (J). mass mkt. 6.50 (*0-671-54181-1*, Star Trek) Simon & Schuster.

—Invasion! No. 4: The Final Fury. 1999. (Star Trek Voyager Ser.: No. 9). E-Book 6.99 (*0-671-04098-7*, Star Trek) Simon & Schuster.

Taylor, Jeri. Pathways. (Star Trek Voyager Ser.: Vol. 2). 1999. 528p. pap. 6.50 o.s.i (*0-671-02626-7*); 1998. (Illus.). 448p. 23.00 o.s.i (*0-671-00346-1*) Simon & Schuster. (Star Trek).

—Pathways. abr. ed. 1998. (Star Trek Voyager Ser.: Vol. 2). 24.00 incl. audio (*0-671-58230-5*, Simon & Schuster Audioworks) Simon & Schuster Audio.

—Pathways. 1999. (Star Trek Voyager Ser.). 12.55 (*0-606-19503-3*) Turtleback Bks.

—Star Trek Voyager: Pathways. abr. ed. 1999. (Star Trek Voyager Ser.). audio 24.35 (*0-671-01115-4*) Ulverscroft Audio (U.S.A.).

Vornholt, John. Double Helix: Quarantine. 1999. (Star Trek, The Next Generation Ser.: No. 54). (Illus.). 304p. pap. 6.99 (*0-671-03477-4*, Star Trek) Simon & Schuster.

Wright, Susan. Violations. 1995. (Star Trek Voyager Ser.: No. 4). 288p. mass mkt. 5.99 (*0-671-52046-6*, Star Trek) Simon & Schuster.

**TOWNSEND, KEITH (FICTITIOUS CHARACTER)—FICTION**

Archer, Jeffrey. The Fourth Estate. l.t. ed. 1997. (Thorndike/G. K. Hall Paperback Bestsellers Ser.). 793p. pap. 26.95 (*0-7838-1913-7*, Macmillan Reference USA) Gale Group.

—The Fourth Estate. 1996. 528p. o.p. (*0-06-017521-4*); 560p. 26.00 o.p. (*0-06-017518-4*) HarperCollins Pubs.

—The Fourth Estate. 1997. 752p. mass mkt. 7.99 (*0-06-109203-7*, HarperTorch) Morrow/Avon.

—The Fourth Estate. l.t. ed. 1996. (Core Ser.). 793p. 30.95 (*0-7838-1912-9*) Thorndike Pr.

**TOWNSEND, MARK (FICTITIOUS CHARACTER)—FICTION**

Reynolds, Brad. Cruel Sanctuary. 1999. (Father Mark Townsend Mystery Ser.: No. 3). 352p. mass mkt. 5.99 (*0-380-79843-3*, Avon Bks.) Morrow/Avon.

—A Ritual Death: A Father Mark Townsend Mystery. 1997. (Father Mark Townsend Mystery Ser.). (Orig.). mass mkt. 5.50 (*0-380-78401-7*, Avon Bks.) Morrow/Avon.

—The Story Knife. 1996. (Father Mark Townsend Mystery Ser.). mass mkt. 5.99 (*0-380-78400-9*, Avon Bks.) Morrow/Avon.

**TOWNSEND, SUSAN (FICTITIOUS CHARACTER)—FICTION**

Rendell, Ruth. The Secret House of Death. reprint ed. lib. bdg. 21.95 (*0-88411-144-X*) Amereon, Ltd.

—The Secret House of Death. 1987. 240p. mass mkt. 5.99 o.s.i (*0-345-34950-4*) Ballantine Bks.

**TOZZI, MIKE (FICTITIOUS CHARACTER)—FICTION**

Bruno, Anthony. Bad Apple. 1995. 336p. mass mkt. 4.99 o.s.i (*0-440-21121-2*) Dell Publishing.

—Bad Blood. 1990. 288p. reprint ed. mass mkt. 4.99 o.s.i (*0-440-20705-3*) Dell Publishing.

—Bad Blood. 1989. 256p. 19.95 o.p. (*0-399-13432-8*, G. P. Putnam's Sons) Penguin Putnam Bks. for Young Readers.

—Bad Business. 1992. 304p. mass mkt. 4.99 o.s.i (*0-440-21120-4*) Dell Publishing.

—Bad Guys. 1992. 288p. mass mkt. 4.99 o.s.i (*0-440-21363-0*) Dell Publishing.

—Bad Guys. 1988. 256p. 17.95 o.p. (*0-399-13340-2*) Putnam Publishing Group, The.

—Bad Luck. 1991. 288p. mass mkt. 4.99 o.s.i (*0-440-20924-2*) Dell Publishing.

—Bad Moon. 1993. 336p. mass mkt. 4.99 o.s.i (*0-440-21559-5*) Dell Publishing.

**TRACY, DICK (FICTITIOUS CHARACTER)—FICTION**

Collins, Max Allan. Dick Tracy. 1990. mass mkt. o.s.i (*0-553-16962-9*); 272p. mass mkt. 4.95 o.s.i (*0-553-28528-9*) Bantam Bks.

—Dick Tracy: Tracy's Wartime Memories. 1986. (U. S. Classics Ser.). (Illus.). 64p. pap. 5.95 (*0-912277-32-7*) Pierce, Ken Bks.

—Dick Tracy & Nightmare Machine. 1991. (Illus.). 124p. mass mkt. 3.50 (*0-8125-1344-4*, Tor Bks.) Doherty, Tom Assocs., LLC.

—Dick Tracy Casebook: Favorite Adventures, 1931-1990. 1990. pap. 15.95 o.p. (*0-312-04462-3*, Saint Martin's Griffin) St. Martin's Pr.

—Dick Tracy Goes to War. 1991. 256p. mass mkt. 4.95 o.s.i (*0-553-28890-3*) Bantam Bks.

—Dick Tracy Meets Angel Top, No. 1. 1990. mass mkt. 3.50 o.p. (*0-425-12743-5*) Berkley Publishing Group.

—Dick Tracy Meets His Match. 1992. 256p. mass mkt. 4.99 o.s.i (*0-553-28891-1*) Bantam Bks.

—Dick Tracy Meets the Punks, No. 2. 1990. mass mkt. 3.50 o.p. (*0-425-12744-3*) Berkley Publishing Group.

Collins, Max Allan & Locher, Dick, compiled by. Dick Tracy Casebook. 1990. (Illus.). 224p. (Orig.). 0.01 o.p. (*0-312-04461-5*) St. Martin's Pr.

Greenberg, Martin H., ed. Dick Tracy: The Secret Files. 1990. mass mkt. 4.95 o.p. (*0-8125-1010-0*, Tor Bks.) Doherty, Tom Assocs., LLC.

Locher, Dick, ed. Dick Tracy's Fiendish Foes: A Sixtieth Anniversary Celebration. 1991. (Illus.). 288p. (Orig.). pap. 18.95 o.p. (*0-312-06338-5*, Saint Martin's Griffin) St. Martin's Pr.

Meader, Jay. Dick Tracy the Official Biography. 1990. 22p. pap. 16.95 o.p. (*0-452-26544-4*, Plume) Dutton/Plume.

**TRAKOS, NIKKI (FICTITIOUS CHARACTER)—FICTION**

Horansky, Ruby. Dead Ahead. 1992. 240p. mass mkt. 4.99 (*0-380-71653-4*, Avon Bks.) Morrow/Avon.

—Dead Ahead: A Mystery Introducing Nikki Trakos. 1990. 256p. 17.95 o.s.i (*0-684-19229-2*, Macmillan Reference USA) Gale Group.

—Dead Center: A Nikki Trakos Mystery. 1994. 224p. 20.00 o.p. (*0-684-19606-9*, Macmillan Reference USA) Gale Group.

**TRAMWELL, PRIMROSE (FICTITIOUS CHARACTER)—FICTION**

Cannell, Dorothy. The Widows' Club. 1989. 352p. mass mkt. 6.99 (*0-553-27794-4*) Bantam Bks.

**TRANSFORMERS (FICTITIOUS CHARACTERS)—FICTION**

Ciencin, Scott. Transformers. 2003. (Transformer Ser.). Bk. 1. 336p. mass mkt. 6.99 (*0-7434-5898-2*); Bk. 2. 320p. mass mkt. 6.99 (*0-7434-7442-2*) ibooks, Inc.

Furman, Simon. Transformers: Legacy of Unicron. 2003. (Illus.). 136p. pap. 19.95 (*1-84023-578-0*) Titan Bks. Ltd. GBR. *Dist:* Client Distribution Services.

Marvel. Transformers Battle Continues. 1985. (Transformers Collected Comics Ser.). 2.95 o.s.i (*0-517-56056-9*, Crown) Crown Publishing Group.

Transformers Universe. 1987. 128p. pap. 5.95 o.p. (*0-87135-296-6*) Marvel Enterprises.

**TRASK, GINNY (FICTITIOUS CHARACTER)—FICTION**

Wallingford, Lee. Clear-Cut Murder: A Frank Carver - Ginny Trask Mystery. 1995. (WWL Mystery Ser.). mass mkt. (*0-373-26165-9*, 1-26165-0, Harlequin Bks.) Harlequin Enterprises, Ltd.

—Clear-Cut Murder: A Frank Carver - Ginny Trask Mystery. 1993. 212p. 19.95 o.s.i (*0-8027-3231-3*) Walker & Co.

—Cold Tracks. 1993. (Mystery Ser.). mass mkt. (*0-373-26114-4*, 1-26114-8, Harlequin Bks.) Harlequin Enterprises, Ltd.

—Cold Tracks. 1991. 192p. 18.95 (*0-8027-5783-9*) Walker & Co.

**TRAVELER, MORONI (FICTITIOUS CHARACTER)—FICTION**

Irvine, Robert. The Angels' Share. Isaacson, Dana, ed. 1990. 224p. reprint ed. bds. 3.95 (*0-671-69494-4*, Pocket) Simon & Schuster.

—The Angels' Share. 1989. 15.95 o.p. (*0-312-02862-8*, Saint Martin's Minotaur) St. Martin's Pr.

—Baptism for the Dead. 1990. 256p. mass mkt. 3.95 (*0-671-69495-2*, Pocket) Simon & Schuster.

—Called Home. 1991. 17.95 o.p. (*0-312-05829-2*, Saint Martin's Minotaur) St. Martin's Pr.

—Gone to Glory. Isaacson, Dana, ed. 1991. 224p. reprint ed. mass mkt. 3.95 (*0-671-72799-0*, Pocket) Simon & Schuster.

—Gone to Glory. 1990. 16.95 o.p. (*0-312-04321-X*, Saint Martin's Minotaur) St. Martin's Pr.

—The Great Reminder. 1993. 224p. 17.95 o.p. (*0-312-09302-0*, Saint Martin's Minotaur) St. Martin's Pr.

—The Hosanna Shout. 1994. 240p. 19.95 o.p. (*0-312-11418-4*, Saint Martin's Minotaur) St. Martin's Pr.

—Pillar of Fire: A Moroni Traveler Mystery. 1995. 272p. 21.95 o.p. (*0-312-13588-2*, Saint Martin's Minotaur) St. Martin's Pr.

—The Spoken Word. 1992. 224p. 17.95 o.p. (*0-312-07841-2*, Saint Martin's Minotaur) St. Martin's Pr.

**TRAVERS, FENWICK (FICTITIOUS CHARACTER)—FICTION**

Saunders, Raymond M. Fenwick Travers & the Forbidden Kingdom: An Entertainment. 352p. 1995. pap. 9.95 o.p. (*0-89141-587-4*); 1994. 21.95 o.p. (*0-89141-480-0*) Ballantine Bks. (Presidio Pr.).

—Fenwick Travers & the Panama Canal: An Entertainment. 336p. 1996. pap. 12.95 o.p. (*0-89141-607-2*); 1995. (Illus.). 21.95 o.p. (*0-89141-481-9*) Ballantine Bks. (Presidio Pr.).

—Fenwick Travers & the Years of Empire: An Entertainment. 1995. 368p. pap. 9.95 o.p. (*0-89141-571-8*); 1993. 400p. 21.95 o.p. (*0-89141-479-7*) Ballantine Bks. (Presidio Pr.).

**TRAVERS, MOLLY (FICTITIOUS CHARACTER)—FICTION**

Goldstein, Lisa. Walking the Labyrinth. 256p. 1998. pap. 12.95 (*0-312-85968-6*, Forge Bks.); 1996. 21.95 o.p. (*0-312-86175-3*, Tor Bks.) Doherty, Tom Assocs., LLC.

**TRAVERS, NICK (FICTITIOUS CHARACTER)—FICTION**

Atkins, Ace. Dark End of the Street. abr. ed. 2002. audio 18.95 (*0-06-052695-5*, HarperAudio) HarperTrade.

—Dark End of the Street. 2004. 416p. mass mkt. 7.50 (*0-06-000461-4*, HarperTorch); 2002. 336p. 23.95 (*0-06-000460-6*, Morrow, William & Co.) Morrow/Avon.

Atkins, P. W. Crossroad Blues. (Nick Travers Mysteries Ser.). 2000. 256p. mass mkt. 5.99 (*0-312-97192-3*, St. Martin's Paperbacks); 1998. 226p. 21.95 o.p. (*0-312-19254-1*, Saint Martin's Minotaur) St. Martin's Pr.

**TRAVERS, TORY (FICTITIOUS CHARACTER)—FICTION**

Schumacher, Aileen. Affirmative Reaction. 2000. (Tory Travers/David Alvarez Mysteries Ser.: Bk. 355). 256p. mass mkt. (*0-373-26355-4*, 1-26355-7, Worldwide Library) Harlequin Enterprises, Ltd.

—Affirmative Reaction. 1999. (Travers/Alvarez Mystery Ser.: No. 4). 310p. 24.95 o.p. (*1-885173-69-5*) Write Way Publishing.

—Engineered for Murder. 1996. 293p. 21.95 o.p. (*1-885173-17-2*); mass mkt. 5.95 o.p. (*1-885173-43-1*) Write Way Publishing.

—Framework for Death. 1998. (Tory Travers/David Alvarez Mysteries Ser.). 360p. 23.95 o.p. (*1-885173-55-5*) Write Way Publishing.

**TRAVIS, BARRIE (FICTITIOUS CHARACTER)—FICTION**

Brown, Sandra. Exclusive, Set. unabr. ed. 1999. audio 49.95 Highsmith Inc.

—Exclusive, Set. abr. ed. 1996. 17.95 o.p. (*0-7871-0880-4*, 394140); 49.95 o.p. (*0-7871-0881-2*, 104018) NewStar Media, Inc.

—Exclusive. l.t. ed. 1996. (Basic Ser.). 688p. 28.95 (*0-7862-0698-5*) Thorndike Pr.

—Exclusive. 1996. 464p. 22.95 o.s.i (0-446-51978-2); 1997. 496p. reprint ed. mass mkt. 7.99 (0-446-60423-2) Warner Bks., Inc.

**TRAVIS, MELANIE (FICTITIOUS CHARACTER)—FICTION**

Berenson, Laurien. Best in Show. l.t. ed. 2003. 400p. 28.95 (0-7862-6002-5) Gale Group.

—Best in Show: A Melanie Travis Mystery. 2003. 288p. 22.00 (1-57566-783-5) Kensington Publishing Corp.

—Dog Eat Dog: A Melanie Travis Mystery. (Melanie Travis Mystery Ser.). 1997. 336p. mass mkt. 5.99 (1-57566-227-2); 1996. 352p. 18.95 o.s.i (1-57566-103-9) Kensington Publishing Corp.

—Hair of the Dog: A Melanie Travis Mystery. (Melanie Travis Mystery Ser.). 1998. 336p. mass mkt. 5.99 (1-57566-356-2); 1997. 320p. 18.95 o.s.i (1-57566-222-1) Kensington Publishing Corp.

—Hot Dog: A Melanie Travis Mystery. l.t. ed. 2003. (Paperback Ser.). lib. bdg. 24.95 (0-7862-5224-3) Thorndike Pr.

—Hush Puppy. (Melanie Travis Mystery Ser.). 2000. 32p. mass mkt. 5.99 (1-57566-600-6); 1999. 304p. 20.00 o.s.i (1-57566-469-0, Kensington Bks.) Kensington Publishing Corp.

—Once Bitten. 2002. 32p. mass mkt. 6.50 (0-7582-0182-6); 2001. 288p. 22.00 o.s.i (1-57566-677-4) Kensington Publishing Corp.

—Once Bitten. l.t. ed. 2003. (Melanie Travis Mystery Ser.). 415p. pap. 25.95 (0-7862-5810-1) Thorndike Pr.

—A Pedigree to Die For: A Melanie Travis Mystery. l.t. ed. 1995. 347p. pap. 20.95 o.p. (0-7838-1446-1, Macmillan Reference USA) Gale Group.

—A Pedigree to Die For: A Melanie Travis Mystery, 1. 1998. mass mkt. 5.99 (1-57566-374-0); 1997. 288p. pap. 9.95 o.s.i (1-57566-125-X); 1996. 288p. mass mkt. 4.99 o.s.i (1-57566-003-2); 1996. mass mkt. 4.99 o.p. (0-8217-5227-8); 1995. 304p. mass mkt. 16.95 o.p. (0-8217-4827-0, Zebra Bks.) Kensington Publishing Corp.

—Underdog: A Melanie Travis Mystery. 1996. 336p. mass mkt. 4.99 o.s.i (1-57566-108-X); 320p. 18.95 o.s.i (1-57566-011-3); mass mkt. 16.95 o.s.i (0-8217-5224-3) Kensington Publishing Corp.

—Unleashed. 2000. (Melanie Travis Mystery Ser.). 34p. 20.00 o.s.i (1-57566-596-4) Kensington Publishing Corp.

—Watchdog. (Melanie Travis Mystery Ser.). 1999. 320p. mass mkt. 5.99 (1-57566-472-0, Kensington Bks.); 1998. 314p. (J). (gr. 10 up). 20.00 o.s.i (1-57566-350-3) Kensington Publishing Corp.

**TRAVIS, ROSEMARY (FICTITIOUS CHARACTER)—FICTION**

Dibdin, Michael. The Dying of the Light: A Mystery. 1995. 160p. pap. 11.00 (0-679-75310-9, Vintage) Knopf Publishing Group.

**TRAVIS, SHEILA (FICTITIOUS CHARACTER)—FICTION**

Sprinkle, Patricia H. Deadly Secrets on the St. Johns. 1995. 320p. mass mkt. 4.99 o.s.i (0-553-56857-4, Crimeline) Bantam Bks.

—Death of a Dunwoody Matron. 1994. 304p. mass mkt. 4.99 o.s.i (0-553-29887-9) Bantam Bks.

—Death of a Dunwoody Matron. 1993. 272p. 17.00 o.s.i (0-385-42485-X) Doubleday Publishing.

—Murder at Markham. 1992. (Sheila Travis Mystery Ser.). reprint ed. per. (0-373-26108-X, Harlequin Bks.) Harlequin Enterprises, Ltd.

—Murder at Markham. 1988. 208p. 15.95 o.p. (0-312-02257-3, Saint Martin's Minotaur) St. Martin's Pr.

—The Murder in Charleston Manner. 1990. 17.95 o.p. (0-312-04355-4, Saint Martin's Minotaur) St. Martin's Pr.

—Murder in the Charleston Manner. 1993. (Mystery Ser.). per. (0-373-26119-5, 1-26119-7, Harlequin Bks.) Harlequin Enterprises, Ltd.

—Murder on Peachtree Street. 1993. (Mystery Ser.). mass mkt. (0-373-26131-4, 1-26131-2, Harlequin Bks.) Harlequin Enterprises, Ltd.

—Murder on Peachtree Street. 1991. 17.95 o.p. (0-312-05476-9, Saint Martin's Minotaur) St. Martin's Pr.

—A Mystery Bred in Buckhead. 1994. 288p. mass mkt. 4.99 o.s.i (0-553-56897-3) Bantam Bks.

—Somebody's Dead in Snellville. 1993. (WWL Mystery Ser.). mass mkt. (0-373-26149-7, 1-26149-4, Harlequin Bks.) Harlequin Enterprises, Ltd.

—Somebody's Dead in Snellville. 1992. 256p. 18.95 o.p. (0-312-07809-9, Saint Martin's Minotaur) St. Martin's Pr.

**TREASURE, MARK (FICTITIOUS CHARACTER)—FICTION**

Williams, David. Advertise for Treasure: A Mark Treasure Novel. 1984. 256p. 12.95 o.p. (0-312-00724-8) St. Martin's Pr.

—Copper, Gold & Treasure: A Mark Treasure Novel. 1982. 210p. 9.95 o.p. (0-312-16967-1) St. Martin's Pr.

—Divided Treasure. 1988. (Mark Treasure Mystery Ser.). 224p. 15.95 o.p. (0-312-01422-8, Saint Martin's Minotaur) St. Martin's Pr.

—Holy Treasure! l.t. ed. 1991. (Lythway Ser.). 304p. 23.95 (0-7451-1264-1, Macmillan Reference USA) Gale Group.

—Holy Treasure! 1989. 224p. 15.95 o.p. (0-312-03362-1, Saint Martin's Minotaur) St. Martin's Pr.

—Murder in Advent. l.t. ed. 2002. (Magna Large Print Ser.). 304p. 32.50 (0-7505-1871-5) Magna Large Print Bks. GBR. *Dist:* Ulverscroft Large Print Bks., Ltd., Ulverscroft Large Print Canada, Ltd.

—Murder in Advent. 1987. 192p. pap. 2.95 o.p. (0-380-70257-6, Avon Bks.) Morrow/Avon.

—Murder in Advent. 1986. 224p. 14.95 o.p. (0-312-55297-1) St. Martin's Pr.

—Prescription for Murder. 1991. 15.95 o.p. (0-312-05009-7, Saint Martin's Minotaur) St. Martin's Pr.

—Treasure by Degrees. l.t. ed. 1990. 280p. 20.95 (0-7451-1134-3, Macmillan Reference USA) Gale Group.

—Treasure by Degrees. 1984. reprint ed. pap. 3.95 o.s.i (0-89296-093-0) Mysterious Pr.

—Treasure by Degrees. 1977. 7.95 o.p. (0-312-81643-X) St. Martin's Pr.

—Treasure by Post. l.t. ed. 1992. pap. 16.95 o.p. (0-7927-1161-0) BBC Audiobooks America.

—Treasure by Post: A Mark Treasure Mystery. l.t. ed. 1992. 18.95 o.p. (0-7451-8409-X) BBC Audiobooks America.

—Treasure by Post: A Mark Treasure Mystery. 1992. mass mkt. 4.99 (0-00-647253-2) HarperCollins Pubs. Ltd. GBR. *Dist:* HarperCollins Pubs.

—Treasure by Post: A Mark Treasure Mystery. 1992. 192p. 16.95 o.p. (0-312-07101-9, Saint Martin's Minotaur) St. Martin's Pr.

—Treasure in Oxford: A Mark Treasure Mystery. 1988. 224p. 15.95 o.p. (0-312-02662-5, Saint Martin's Minotaur) St. Martin's Pr.

—Treasure in Roubles: A Mark Treasure Mystery. l.t. ed. 1987. pap. 13.95 o.p. (1-55504-358-5) BBC Audiobooks America.

—Treasure in Roubles: A Mark Treasure Mystery. 1988. 224p. pap. 2.95 (0-380-70546-X, Avon Bks.) Morrow/Avon.

—Treasure in Roubles: A Mark Treasure Mystery. 1987. 208p. 14.95 o.p. (0-312-00697-7) St. Martin's Pr.

—Treasure Preserved: A Mark Treasure Novel. 1987. 224p. pap. 2.95 o.p. (0-380-70256-8, Avon Bks.) Morrow/Avon.

—Treasure Preserved: A Mark Treasure Novel. 1983. 224p. 10.95 o.p. (0-312-81647-2) St. Martin's Pr.

—Treasure up in Smoke. 2003. 200p. 21.95 (0-7540-8638-0, Black Dagger) BBC Audiobooks America.

—Treasure up in Smoke. 1978. 7.95 o.p. (0-312-81648-0) St. Martin's Pr.

—Wedding Treasure. l.t. ed. 1986. pap. 13.95 o.p. (1-55504-041-1) BBC Audiobooks America.

—Wedding Treasure. 1987. 224p. pap. 2.95 o.p. (0-380-70258-4, Avon Bks.) Morrow/Avon.

—Wedding Treasure. 1985. 240p. 10.95 o.p. (0-312-86002-1) St. Martin's Pr.

**TREGALLES, JOHN (FICTITIOUS CHARACTER)—FICTION**

Smith, Frank. Stone Dead. 1999. (WWL Mystery Ser.: No. 20). per. (0-373-26320-1, 1-26320-1, Worldwide Library) Harlequin Enterprises, Ltd.

—Stone Dead. 1998. 192p. 20.95 o.p. (0-312-18186-8, Saint Martin's Minotaur) St. Martin's Pr.

—Stone Dead. l.t. ed. 1998. (Mystery Ser.). 373p. 26.95 (0-7862-1664-6) Thorndike Pr.

**TREGAR, JANE (FICTITIOUS CHARACTER)—FICTION**

Godfrey, Ellen. Murder Behind Locked Doors. 1988. 336p. 17.95 o.p. (0-312-02258-1, Saint Martin's Minotaur) St. Martin's Pr.

**TREGARDE, DIANA (FICTITIOUS CHARACTER)—FICTION**

Lackey, Mercedes. Burning Water. 1992. 314p. pap. text 6.99 (0-8125-2485-3, Tor Bks.) Doherty, Tom Assocs., LLC.

—Children of the Night. 1992. 313p. pap. text 6.99 (0-8125-2272-9); 1990. mass mkt. 3.95 o.s.i (0-8125-2112-9) Doherty, Tom Assocs., LLC. (Tor Bks.).

—Jinx High. 1991. 314p. (Orig.). pap. text 4.99 o.s.i (0-8125-2114-5, Tor Bks.) Doherty, Tom Assocs., LLC.

**TREGARTH, JESSICA (FICTITIOUS CHARACTER)—FICTION**

Peters, Elizabeth, pseud. The Camelot Caper. unabr. ed. 1995. audio 39.95 (0-7861-0908-4, 1713) Blackstone Audio Bks., Inc.

—The Camelot Caper. 1990. 320p. mass mkt. 5.99 (0-8125-1241-3, Tor Bks.) Doherty, Tom Assocs., LLC.

—The Camelot Caper. l.t. ed. 1991. 352p. pap. 19.95 o.p. (0-8161-5165-2, Macmillan Reference USA) Gale Group.

—The Camelot Caper. 2001. 352p. mass mkt. 6.99 (0-380-73113-4, Avon Bks.) Morrow/Avon.

—The Camelot Caper. 1996. 320p. reprint ed. 24.00 (0-7278-4936-0) Severn Hse. Pubs., Ltd.

**TREGARTH, SIMON (FICTITIOUS CHARACTER)—FICTION**

Norton, Andre. The Gates of Witch World. 2001. (Witch World). (Illus.). 464p. 27.95 (0-7653-0050-8, Tor Bks.) Doherty, Tom Assocs., LLC.

—Web of the Witch World. 1986. (Witch World Ser.: 2). mass mkt. 3.50 o.s.i (0-441-87879-2) Ace Bks.

—Witch World. 1986. 288p. mass mkt. 3.50 o.s.i (0-441-89708-8); 1984. mass mkt. 2.50 o.s.i (0-441-89707-X); 1982. mass mkt. 2.50 o.s.i (0-441-89706-1); No. 3. 1981. mass mkt. 3.50 o.s.i (0-441-94255-5) Ace Bks.

—Witch World Omnibus, No. 2. Date not set. (0-7653-0052-4, Tor Bks.) Doherty, Tom Assocs., LLC.

**TREHERN, KERARA (FICTITIOUS CHARACTER)—FICTION**

Norton, Andre. Echoes in Time. 2000. (Time Traders Adventure Ser.). 320p. mass mkt. 5.99 (0-8125-5274-1, Tor Bks.) Doherty, Tom Assocs., LLC.

—The Time Traders. 1987. 224p. mass mkt. 3.99 o.s.i (0-441-81255-4); 1984. mass mkt. 2.50 o.s.i (0-441-81254-6); 1980. mass mkt. 1.95 o.s.i (0-441-81253-8) Ace Bks.

—The Time Traders. 2000. 384p. (J). 24.00 (0-671-31952-3) Baen Bks.

—The Time Traders. 1979. lib. bdg. 9.95 o.p. (0-8398-2421-1, Macmillan Reference USA) Gale Group.

Norton, Andre & Griffin, P. M. Fire Hand. 1995. 288p. mass mkt. 4.99 (0-8125-1984-1); 1994. 224p. 19.95 o.p. (0-312-85313-0) Doherty, Tom Assocs., LLC. (Tor Bks.).

Norton, Andre & Smith, Sherwood. Echoes in Time. 1999. (Time Traders Adventure Ser.). 319p. 23.95 (0-312-85921-X, Tor Bks.) Doherty, Tom Assocs., LLC.

**TRELAINE, LUCY MACALPIN (FICTITIOUS CHARACTER)—FICTION**

Mathes, Charles. The Girl with the Phony Name. 1997. 48p. per. (0-373-26246-9, 1-26246-8, Worldwide Library) Harlequin Enterprises, Ltd.

—The Girl with the Phony Name. 17.95 (0-312-33170-3); 1992. 256p. 17.95 o.p. (0-312-08198-7, Saint Martin's Minotaur) St. Martin's Pr.

**TRELOAR, GABE (FICTITIOUS CHARACTER)—FICTION**

Roberts, John Maddox. Desperate Highways. 1997. 304p. 23.95 o.p. (0-312-17176-5, Saint Martin's Minotaur) St. Martin's Pr.

—Ghosts of Saigon. 1996. 288p. 21.95 o.p. (0-312-14345-1, Saint Martin's Minotaur) St. Martin's Pr.

—A Typical American Town. 1994. 256p. 20.95 o.p. (0-312-11359-5, Saint Martin's Minotaur) St. Martin's Pr.

—A Typical American Town. l.t. ed. 1996. (Ulverscroft Large Print Ser.). 480p. 29.99 o.p. (0-7089-3507-9, Ulverscroft) Thorpe, F. A. Pubs. GBR. *Dist:* Ulverscroft Large Print Bks., Ltd., Ulverscroft Large Print Canada, Ltd.

**TRENKA, BETTY (FICTITIOUS CHARACTER)—FICTION**

Christmas, Joyce. A Better Class of Murder: A Lady Margaret Priam/Betty Trenka Mystery. 2000. (Lady Margaret Priam Mysteries Ser.). 272p. mass mkt. 6.50 (0-449-15013-5, Fawcett) Ballantine Bks.

—A Better Class of Murder: A Lady Margaret Priam/Betty Trenka Mystery. l.t. ed. 2001. 264p. pap. 24.95 (0-7838-9472-4, Macmillan Reference USA) Gale Group.

—Death at Face Value. 1995. (Betty Trenka Mystery Ser.). (Orig.). mass mkt. 4.99 o.s.i (0-449-14801-7, Fawcett) Ballantine Bks.

—Down-Sized to Death. 1997. (Betty Trenka Mystery Ser.). 199p. mass mkt. 5.99 o.s.i (0-449-14802-5, Fawcett) Ballantine Bks.

—Forged in Blood. l.t. ed. 2002. 277p. (0-7862-4829-7) Thorndike Pr.

—Forged in Blood: A Lady Margaret Priam/Betty Trenka Mystery. 2002. 277p. (0-7540-8849-9) Thorndike Pr.

—Mood to Murder. 1999. (Betty Trenka Mystery Ser.). mass mkt. 5.99 o.s.i (0-449-15012-7) Ballantine Bks.

—This Business Is Murder. 1993. (Betty Trenka Mystery Ser.). mass mkt. 4.50 o.s.i (0-449-14800-9, Fawcett) Ballantine Bks.

**TRENT, NIGEL (FICTITIOUS CHARACTER)—FICTION**

Coram, Robert. Kill the Angels. 1996. 352p. mass mkt. 5.99 o.s.i (0-451-40340-1, Onyx) NAL.

**TRETHEWAY, ALBERT (FICTITIOUS CHARACTER)—FICTION**

Eddenden, A. E. A Good Year for Murder. (Tretheway Ser.). 2000. 178p. pap. 12.00 (0-89733-476-0); 1988. 184p. 18.95 o.p. (0-89733-284-9) Academy Chicago Pubs., Ltd.

—Murder at the Movies. 1996. 159p. 20.00 (0-89733-428-0) Academy Chicago Pubs., Ltd.

—Murder on the Thirteenth. 1992. 168p. 20.00 (0-89733-380-2) Academy Chicago Pubs., Ltd.

**TRETHOWAN, PERRY, SUPERINTENDENT (FICTITIOUS CHARACTER)—FICTION**

Barnard, Robert. Bodies. unabr. ed. 2001. audio 34.95 (0-7451-5775-0, CAT 4026) Chivers Audio Bks. GBR. *Dist:* BBC Audiobooks America.

—Bodies. 1988. 224p. mass mkt. 3.50 o.s.i (0-440-20007-5) Dell Publishing.

—Bodies. 1986. 224p. 13.95 o.p. (0-684-18729-9, Macmillan Reference USA) Gale Group.

—Bodies. 1988. audio 35.95 o.s.i (0-8161-7781-3) Thorndike Pr.

—The Case of the Missing Bronte. 1984. 192p. mass mkt. 2.95 o.s.i (0-440-11108-0) Dell Publishing.

—The Case of the Missing Bronte. 1983. 192p. 11.95 o.s.i (0-684-17910-5); 1984. 248p. 8.95 o.p. (0-8161-3590-8) Gale Group. (Macmillan Reference USA).

—The Case of the Missing Bronte. 1994. (Crime Ser.). 192p. reprint ed. pap. 5.95 o.p. (0-14-023785-2, Penguin Bks.) Penguin Group (USA) Inc.

—The Cherry Blossom Corpse. 1988. 256p. mass mkt. 3.50 o.s.i (0-440-20178-0) Dell Publishing.

—The Cherry Blossom Corpse. 1996. (Crime Ser.). 256p. pap. 5.95 o.p. (0-14-023789-5, Penguin Bks.) Penguin Group (USA) Inc.

—The Cherry Blossom Corpse. 1987. 14.95 o.p. (0-684-18825-2, Scribner) Simon & Schuster.

—Death & the Princess, Vol. 66. 1983. 192p. mass mkt. 3.25 o.s.i (0-440-12153-1) Dell Publishing.

—Death & the Princess. 1982. 192p. 10.95 o.s.i (0-684-17759-5); 1985. (Nightingale Ser.: No. 2). pap. 9.95 o.p. (0-8161-3520-7) Gale Group. (Macmillan Reference USA).

—Death by Sheer Torture. 1995. (Crime Ser.). 192p. pap. 5.95 o.p. (0-14-023787-9, Penguin Bks.) Penguin Group (USA) Inc.

—Sheer Torture. unabr. ed. 1998. audio 69.95 o.p. (1-872672-22-1) Magna Story Sound GBR. *Dist:* Ulverscroft Large Print Bks., Ltd.

**TREVAYNE, ANDREW (FICTITIOUS CHARACTER)—FICTION**

Ludlum, Robert. Trevayne. 480p. 1992. mass mkt. 3.99 o.s.i (0-553-19955-2); 1989. mass mkt. 7.99 (0-553-28179-8) Bantam Bks.

**TREVELLYAN, NICK (FICTITIOUS CHARACTER)—FICTION**

Kelly, Susan B. Hope Against Hope. 1991. 256p. 19.95 o.s.i (0-684-19387-6, Macmillan Reference USA) Gale Group.

—Hope Against Hope. 1993. per. (0-373-26118-7, 1-26118-9, Harlequin Bks.) Harlequin Enterprises, Ltd.

—Hope Against Hope. l.t. ed. 1991. (Magna Large Print Ser.). 345p. o.p. (0-7505-0163-4) Magna Large Print Bks. GBR. *Dist:* Ulverscroft Large Print Canada, Ltd.

—Hope Will Answer: An Inspector Nick Trevellyan - Alison Hope Mystery. 1993. 256p. 20.00 o.p. (0-684-19523-2, Macmillan Reference USA) Gale Group.

—Hope Will Answer: An Inspector Nick Trevellyan - Alison Hope Mystery. l.t. ed. 1994. (Magna Large Print Ser.). 428p. 29.99 o.p. (0-7505-0594-X) Magna Large Print Bks. GBR. *Dist:* Ulverscroft Large Print Bks., Ltd., Ulverscroft Large Print Canada, Ltd.

—Kids' Stuff. 1994. 256p. 20.00 (0-684-19649-2, Macmillan Reference USA) Gale Group.

—Time of Hope. 1994. (WWL Mystery Ser.). mass mkt. (0-373-26141-1, 1-26141-1, Harlequin Bks.) Harlequin Enterprises, Ltd.

—Time of Hope. 1992. 224p. 20.00 o.s.i (0-684-19423-6, Scribner) Simon & Schuster.

—A Time of Hope. l.t. ed. 1993. (Magna Large Print Ser.). 346p. 29.99 o.p. (0-7505-0487-0) Magna Large Print Bks. GBR. *Dist:* Ulverscroft Large Print Bks., Ltd., Ulverscroft Large Print Canada, Ltd.

**TREVELYAN, ROSE (FICTITIOUS CHARACTER)—FICTION**

Bolitho, Janie. Framed in Cornwall. 2001. 192p. pap. 10.95 (0-7490-0590-4) Allison & Busby, Ltd. GBR. *Dist:* International Publishers Marketing.

—Framed in Cornwall. l.t. ed. 1999. (Dales Large Print Ser.). 368p. pap. o.p. (1-85389-932-1) Dales Large Print Bks. GBR. *Dist:* Ulverscroft Large Print Canada, Ltd.

—Killed in Cornwall: A Rose Trevelyan Mystery. 2002. 206p. 24.95 (0-7490-0508-4) Allison & Busby, Ltd. GBR. *Dist:* International Publishers Marketing.

—Snapped in Cornwall. 2000. 208p. mass mkt. 9.95 (0-7490-0469-X, London Hse.) Allison & Busby, Ltd. GBR. *Dist:* International Publishers Marketing.

**TREVOR, HANNAH (FICTITIOUS CHARACTER)—FICTION**

Lawrence, Margaret. Blood Red Roses: A Novel of Historical Suspense. 1998. 416p. mass mkt. 6.50 (*0-380-78880-2*); 1997. 368p. 23.00 (*0-380-97352-9*) Morrow/Avon. (Avon Bks.).
—The Burning Bride. 400p. 1999. mass mkt. 6.99 (*0-380-79612-0*); 1998. 23.00 (*0-380-97620-X*) Morrow/Avon. (Avon Bks.).
—Hearts & Bones. 1997. 352p. mass mkt. 6.50 (*0-380-78879-9*); 1996. 304p. 23.00 (*0-380-97351-0*) Morrow/Avon. (Avon Bks.).

**TREWLEY, DETECTIVE SUPERINTENDENT (FICTITIOUS CHARACTER)—FICTION**

Mason, Sarah J. Corpse in the Kitchen. 1993. 224p. (Orig.). mass mkt. 4.50 o.p. (*0-425-14006-7*) Berkley Publishing Group.
—Dying Breath. 1994. 240p. (Orig.). mass mkt. 4.50 o.p. (*0-425-14245-0*, Prime Crime) Berkley Publishing Group.
—Frozen Stiff. 1993. 224p. (Orig.). mass mkt. 4.50 o.p. (*0-425-13837-2*) Berkley Publishing Group.
—Murder in the Maze. 1993. 224p. mass mkt. 4.99 o.s.i (*0-425-13795-3*) Berkley Publishing Group.
—Murder in the Maze. l.t. ed. 1999. (Linford Mystery Large Print Ser.). 448p. pap. 18.99 (*0-7089-5561-4*, Linford) Thorpe, F. A. Pubs. GBR. *Dist:* Ulverscroft Large Print Bks., Ltd., Ulverscroft Large Print Canada, Ltd.
—Seeing Is Deceiving. 1997. 208p. mass mkt. 5.99 o.s.i (*0-425-15901-9*, Prime Crime) Berkley Publishing Group.
—Seeing Is Deceiving. l.t. ed. 2000. (Linford Mystery Large Print Ser.). 384p. pap. 18.99 (*0-7089-5673-4*, Linford) Thorpe, F. A. Pubs. GBR. *Dist:* Ulverscroft Large Print Bks., Ltd., Ulverscroft Large Print Canada, Ltd.
—Sew Easy to Kill. 1996. 208p. mass mkt. 5.99 o.s.i (*0-425-15310-X*) Berkley Publishing Group.
—Sew Easy to Kill. l.t. ed. 2000. (Linford Mystery Large Print Ser.). 392p. pap. 18.99 (*0-7089-5656-4*, Linford) Thorpe, F. A. Pubs. GBR. *Dist:* Ulverscroft Large Print Bks., Ltd., Ulverscroft Large Print Canada, Ltd.

**TRIBBLE, AMY (FICTITIOUS CHARACTER)—FICTION**

Chesney, Marion. Animating Maria. l.t. ed. 1991. (School for Manners Ser.: Vol. 5). 232p. pap. 14.95 o.p. (*0-8161-5099-0*, Macmillan Reference USA) Gale Group.
—Animating Maria. 1990. (School for Manners Ser.: Vol. 5). pap. 3.95 o.p. (*0-312-92343-0*, St. Martin's Paperbacks); 160p. 14.95 o.p. (*0-312-03820-8*) St. Martin's Pr.
—Enlightening Delilah. l.t. ed. 1991. (School for Manners Ser.: Vol. 3). 248p. 14.95 o.p. (*0-8161-4950-X*, Macmillan Reference USA) Gale Group.
—Enlightening Delilah. 1990. 2.99 o.p. (*0-517-05815-4*) Random Hse. Value Publishing.
—Enlightening Delilah. (School for Manners Ser.: Vol. 3). 1990. mass mkt. 3.50 (*0-312-92157-8*, St. Martin's Paperbacks); 1989. 14.95 o.p. (*0-312-02912-8*) St. Martin's Pr.
—Finessing Clarissa. l.t. ed. 1991. (School for Manners Ser.: Vol. 4). 243p. lib. bdg. 14.95 o.p. (*0-8161-5013-3*, Macmillan Reference USA) Gale Group.
—Finessing Clarissa. (School for Manners Ser.: Vol. 4). 1990. pap. 3.95 o.p. (*0-312-92283-3*, St. Martin's Paperbacks); 1989. 160p. 14.95 o.p. (*0-312-03341-9*) St. Martin's Pr.
—Marrying Harriet. l.t. ed. 1992. (School for Manners Ser.: Vol. 6). 252p. pap. 15.95 (*0-8161-5158-X*, Macmillan Reference USA) Gale Group.
—Marrying Harriet. (School for Manners Ser.: Vol. 6). 1991. pap. 3.95 o.p. (*0-312-92420-8*, St. Martin's Paperbacks); 1990. 14.95 o.p. (*0-312-04276-0*) St. Martin's Pr.
—Perfecting Fiona. l.t. ed. 1990. (School for Manners Ser.: Vol. 2). 244p. 14.95 o.p. (*0-8161-4869-4*, Macmillan Reference USA) Gale Group.
—Perfecting Fiona. 1990. 2.99 o.p. (*0-517-05822-7*) Random Hse. Value Publishing.
—Perfecting Fiona. (School for Manners Ser.: Vol. 2). 1990. pap. 3.50 o.p. (*0-312-92059-8*, St. Martin's Paperbacks); 1989. 176p. 14.95 o.p. (*0-312-02577-7*) St. Martin's Pr.
—Refining Felicity. l.t. ed. 1989. (School for Manners Ser.: Vol. 1). 248p. 13.95 o.p. (*0-8161-4797-3*, Macmillan Reference USA) Gale Group.
—Refining Felicity. (School for Manners Ser.: Vol. 1). 1989. pap. 3.50 o.p. (*0-312-91585-3*, St. Martin's Paperbacks); 1988. 176p. 14.95 o.p. (*0-312-02288-3*) St. Martin's Pr.

**TRIBBLE, EFFY (FICTITIOUS CHARACTER)—FICTION**

Chesney, Marion. Animating Maria. l.t. ed. 1991. (School for Manners Ser.: Vol. 5). 232p. pap. 14.95 o.p. (*0-8161-5099-0*, Macmillan Reference USA) Gale Group.
—Animating Maria. 1990. (School for Manners Ser.: Vol. 5). pap. 3.95 o.p. (*0-312-92343-0*, St. Martin's Paperbacks); 160p. 14.95 o.p. (*0-312-03820-8*) St. Martin's Pr.
—Enlightening Delilah. l.t. ed. 1991. (School for Manners Ser.: Vol. 3). 248p. 14.95 o.p. (*0-8161-4950-X*, Macmillan Reference USA) Gale Group.
—Enlightening Delilah. 1990. 2.99 o.p. (*0-517-05815-4*) Random Hse. Value Publishing.
—Enlightening Delilah. (School for Manners Ser.: Vol. 3). 1990. mass mkt. 3.50 (*0-312-92157-8*, St. Martin's Paperbacks); 1989. 14.95 o.p. (*0-312-02912-8*) St. Martin's Pr.
—Finessing Clarissa. l.t. ed. 1991. (School for Manners Ser.: Vol. 4). 243p. lib. bdg. 14.95 o.p. (*0-8161-5013-3*, Macmillan Reference USA) Gale Group.
—Finessing Clarissa. (School for Manners Ser.: Vol. 4). 1990. pap. 3.95 o.p. (*0-312-92283-3*, St. Martin's Paperbacks); 1989. 160p. 14.95 o.p. (*0-312-03341-9*) St. Martin's Pr.
—Marrying Harriet. l.t. ed. 1992. (School for Manners Ser.: Vol. 6). 252p. pap. 15.95 (*0-8161-5158-X*, Macmillan Reference USA) Gale Group.
—Marrying Harriet. (School for Manners Ser.: Vol. 6). 1991. pap. 3.95 o.p. (*0-312-92420-8*, St. Martin's Paperbacks); 1990. 14.95 o.p. (*0-312-04276-0*) St. Martin's Pr.
—Perfecting Fiona. l.t. ed. 1990. (School for Manners Ser.: Vol. 2). 244p. 14.95 o.p. (*0-8161-4869-4*, Macmillan Reference USA) Gale Group.
—Perfecting Fiona. 1990. 2.99 o.p. (*0-517-05822-7*) Random Hse. Value Publishing.
—Perfecting Fiona. (School for Manners Ser.: Vol. 2). 1990. pap. 3.50 o.p. (*0-312-92059-8*, St. Martin's Paperbacks); 1989. 176p. 14.95 o.p. (*0-312-02577-7*) St. Martin's Pr.
—Refining Felicity. l.t. ed. 1989. (School for Manners Ser.: Vol. 1). 248p. 13.95 o.p. (*0-8161-4797-3*, Macmillan Reference USA) Gale Group.
—Refining Felicity. (School for Manners Ser.: Vol. 1). 1989. pap. 3.50 o.p. (*0-312-91585-3*, St. Martin's Paperbacks); 1988. 176p. 14.95 o.p. (*0-312-02288-3*) St. Martin's Pr.

**TRIPPER, LEE (FICTITIOUS CHARACTER)—FICTION**

Maxwell, Thomas. The Suspense Is Killing Me. 1990. 272p. 19.95 o.p. (*0-89296-167-8*) Mysterious Pr.
—The Suspense Is Killing Me. 1991. 272p. mass mkt. 4.99 (*0-446-40042-4*, Mysterious Pr. Paperback Bks.) Warner Bks., Inc.

**TROI, DEANNA (FICTITIOUS CHARACTER)—FICTION**

Betancourt, John Gregory. Infection Vol. 1: Double Helix. 1999. (Star Trek, The Next Generation Ser.: No. 51). (Illus.). 256p. pap. 6.50 (*0-671-03255-0*, Star Trek) Simon & Schuster.
Carey, Diane L. Ghost Ship. (Star Trek, The Next Generation Ser.: No. 1). 1991. mass mkt. 5.50 (*0-671-74608-1*); 1990. mass mkt. 4.50 o.s.i (*0-671-73515-2*); 1988. E-Book 6.99 (*0-7434-1213-3*) Simon & Schuster. (Star Trek).
David, Peter. Imzadi. Stern, Dave, ed. (Star Trek, The Next Generation Ser.). 352p. 1998. mass mkt. 3.99 (*0-671-02610-0*); 1992. 20.00 (*0-671-79197-4*); 1993. reprint ed. mass mkt. 6.50 (*0-671-86729-6*) Simon & Schuster. (Star Trek).
—Imzadi. abr. ed. 1992. (Star Trek Ser.). audio 17.00 (*0-671-79198-2*, Simon & Schuster Audioworks) Simon & Schuster Audio.
—Imzadi II: Triangle. (Star Trek, The Next Generation Ser.). E-Book 6.99 (*0-7434-2071-3*); 1998. 384p. 23.00 o.s.i (*0-671-02532-5*); 1999. 400p. reprint ed. pap. 6.50 (*0-671-02538-4*) Simon & Schuster. (Star Trek).
—Imzadi II: Triangle. abr. ed. 1998. (Star Trek Ser.: Vol. 2). audio 18.00 (*0-671-04328-5*, Simon & Schuster Audioworks) Simon & Schuster Audio.
—Imzadi II: Triangle. abr. ed. 1999. (Star Trek Ser.). audio 15.00 (*0-671-03343-3*) Ulverscroft Audio (U.S.A.).
Dillard, J. M. Insurrection. abr. ed. (Star Trek Ser.: No. 9). 1998. audio 18.00 o.s.i (*0-671-58259-3*, 396208, Simon & Schuster Audioworks); 2003. audio 9.95 (*0-7435-3254-6*, Encore) Simon & Schuster Audio.
Dillard, J. M. & O'Malley, Kathleen. Possession. 1996. (Star Trek, The Next Generation Ser.: No. 40). 288p. mass mkt. 5.99 (*0-671-86485-8*, Star Trek) Simon & Schuster.
Duane, Diane. Dark Mirror. 1993. (Star Trek, The Next Generation Ser.). 352p. 22.00 o.p. (*0-671-79377-2*, Star Trek) Simon & Schuster.
—Dark Mirror. Ryan, Kevin, ed. 1994. (Star Trek, The Next Generation Ser.). 352p. reprint ed. mass mkt. 5.99 (*0-671-79438-8*, Star Trek) Simon & Schuster.
—Dark Mirror. abr. ed. 1996. (Star Trek Ser.). audio 17.00 (*0-671-87974-X*, Simon & Schuster Audioworks) Simon & Schuster Audio.
Friedman, Michael Jan. Stargazer: Three, Bk. 3. 2003. (Star Trek, The Next Generation Ser.). 288p. mass mkt. 6.99 (*0-7434-4852-9*, Star Trek) Simon & Schuster.
Friesner, Esther M. To Storm Heaven. 1997. (Star Trek, The Next Generation Ser.: No. 46). (Illus.). 304p. pap. 5.99 (*0-671-56838-8*, Star Trek) Simon & Schuster.
Galanter, Dave & Brodeur, Greg. Foreign Foes. (Star Trek, The Next Generation Ser.: No. 31). E-Book 6.99 (*0-7434-2114-0*); 1994. 288p. mass mkt. 5.50 (*0-671-88414-X*) Simon & Schuster. (Star Trek).
Hamilton, Laurell K. Nightshade. Stern, Dave, ed. 1992. (Star Trek, The Next Generation Ser.: No. 24). 288p. mass mkt. 5.50 (*0-671-79566-X*, Star Trek) Simon & Schuster.
McCay, W. A. Chains of Command. (Star Trek, The Next Generation Ser.: No. 21). E-Book 6.99 (*0-7434-2101-9*, Star Trek) Simon & Schuster.
McCay, W. A. & Flood, E. L. Chains of Command. Stern, David, ed. 1992. (Star Trek, The Next Generation Ser.: No. 21). 288p. mass mkt. 5.50 (*0-671-74264-7*, Star Trek) Simon & Schuster.
Neason, Rebecca. Guises of the Mind. Ryan, Kevin, ed. 1993. (Star Trek, The Next Generation Ser.: No. 27). 288p. (Orig.). mass mkt. 5.50 (*0-671-79831-6*, Star Trek) Simon & Schuster.
Peel, John. Death of Princes. 1996. (Star Trek, The Next Generation Ser.: No. 44). 304p. pap. 5.99 (*0-671-56808-6*, Star Trek) Simon & Schuster.
Sargent, Pamela & Zebrowski, George. A Fury Scorned. 1996. (Star Trek, The Next Generation Ser.: No. 43). 288p. pap. 5.99 (*0-671-52703-7*, Star Trek) Simon & Schuster.
Sharee, Keith. Gulliver's Fugitives. (Star Trek, The Next Generation Ser.: No. 11). E-Book 6.99 (*0-7434-2091-8*); 1991. 256p. mass mkt. 5.50 (*0-671-74143-8*) Simon & Schuster. (Star Trek).
—Gulliver's Fugitives. (Star Trek Ser.: No. 11). 1999. audio 5.98 (*0-671-04522-9*); 1990. audio 9.95 (*0-671-72319-7*) Simon & Schuster Audio. (Simon & Schuster Audioworks).
Somtow, S. P. Do Comets Dream? 2003. (Star Trek, The Next Generation Ser.). 288p. pap. 6.99 (*0-7434-1130-7*, Star Trek) Simon & Schuster.
Vornholt, John. Contamination. (Star Trek, The Next Generation Ser.: No. 16). E-Book 6.99 (*0-7434-2096-9*, Star Trek) Simon & Schuster.
—Contamination. Stern, David, ed. 1991. (Star Trek, The Next Generation Ser.: No. 16). 288p. mass mkt. 5.50 (*0-671-70561-X*, Star Trek) Simon & Schuster.
—Contamination. abr. ed. 1991. (Star Trek, The Next Generation Ser.: No. 16). audio 12.00 (*0-671-74045-8*, 326327, Simon & Schuster Audioworks) Simon & Schuster Audio.
—Gemworld, No. 2. 2000. (Star Trek, The Next Generation Ser.: No. 59). E-Book 6.99 (*0-7434-0678-8*); (Illus.). 272p. pap. 6.50 (*0-671-04271-8*) Simon & Schuster. (Star Trek).
—Genesis Wave: Genesis Force, Bk. 4. 2003. (Star Trek, The Next Generation Ser.). 320p. 23.95 (*0-7434-6501-6*, Star Trek) Simon & Schuster.
—War Drums. (Star Trek, The Next Generation Ser.). E-Book 6.99 (*0-7434-2103-5*, Star Trek) Simon & Schuster.
—War Drums. Stern, Dave, ed. 1992. (Star Trek, The Next Generation Ser.: No. 23). 288p. mass mkt. 5.50 (*0-671-79236-9*, Star Trek) Simon & Schuster.

**TROTTER, TILLY (FICTITIOUS CHARACTER)—FICTION**

Cookson, Catherine. Tilly Trotter. l.t. ed. 1981. o.p. (*0-7089-0698-2*, Ulverscroft) Thorpe, F. A. Pubs.
—Tilly Trotter. 2000. 1097p. pap. 13.95 (*0-552-14683-8*); 1997. 398p. mass mkt. 10.95 (*0-552-11737-4*) Transworld Publishers Ltd. GBR. *Dist:* Trafalgar Square.
—Tilly Trotter Wed. 1982. mass mkt. 3.50 o.s.i (*0-671-42605-2*, Pocket) Simon & Schuster.
—Tilly Trotter Wed. l.t. ed. 1982. o.p. (*0-7089-0824-1*, Ulverscroft) Thorpe, F. A. Pubs.
—Tilly Trotter Wed. 1989. 352p. mass mkt. 10.95 (*0-552-11960-1*) Transworld Publishers Ltd. GBR. *Dist:* Trafalgar Square.
—Tilly Trotter Widowed. l.t. ed. 1983. 544p. o.p. (*0-7089-0915-9*, Ulverscroft) Thorpe, F. A. Pubs.
—Tilly Trotter Widowed. 1997. 352p. mass mkt. 10.95 (*0-552-12200-9*) Transworld Publishers Ltd. GBR. *Dist:* Trafalgar Square.

**TROWBRIDGE, DAVID (FICTITIOUS CHARACTER)—FICTION**

Voien, Steven. Black Leopard. 1997. 287p. 23.00 o.s.i (*0-679-44702-4*) Random Hse., Inc.

**TROY, BILL (FICTITIOUS CHARACTER)—FICTION**

Slesar, Henry. Murder at Heartbreak Hospital. 247p. reprint ed. 2000. pap. 14.00 (*0-89733-486-8*); 1998. 21.00 (*0-89733-463-9*) Academy Chicago Pubs., Ltd.

**TROY, FREDERICK (FICTITIOUS CHARACTER)—FICTION**

Lawton, John. Black Out. unabr. ed. 2002. audio compact disk 99.95 (*0-7531-1570-0*) ISIS Audio Bks. GBR. *Dist:* Ulverscroft Large Print Bks., Ltd.
—Black Out. 1996. 352p. pap. 11.95 o.s.i (*0-14-024081-0*, Penguin Bks.) Penguin Group (USA) Inc.
—Black Out. 2002. 432p. 6.99 (*0-14-200276-3*); 1995. 352p. 22.95 o.p. (*0-670-85767-X*, Viking) Viking Penguin.

**TRUE, STARKY (FICTITIOUS CHARACTER)—FICTION**

Kammen, Robert. Outside the Law. 1995. 160p. mass mkt. 4.50 o.s.i (*0-8217-5078-X*) Kensington Publishing Corp.

**TRUETT, ELIZABETH (FICTITIOUS CHARACTER)—FICTION**

Brandon, Jay. Tripwire. 1987. 250p. mass mkt. 3.50 o.s.i (*0-553-26279-3*) Bantam Bks.
—Tripwire. Isaacson, Dana, ed. 1992. 320p. mass mkt. 4.99 (*0-671-70888-0*, Pocket) Simon & Schuster.

**TRUMBULL, VICTORIA (FICTITIOUS CHARACTER)—FICTION**

Riggs, Cynthia. The Cemetery Yew. 2003. 208p. 22.95 (*0-312-32126-0*) St. Martin's Pr.
—The Cemetery Yew. l.t. ed. 2003. (Martha's Vineyard Mystery Ser.). 377p. 28.95 (*0-7862-5929-9*) Thorndike Pr.
—The Cranefly Orchid Murders. 2004. 272p. mass mkt. 5.99 (*0-451-20961-3*, Signet Bks.) NAL.
—The Cranefly Orchid Murders. E-Book 23.95 (*0-312-70620-0*); 2002. 272p. 23.95 (*0-312-30145-6*, Saint Martin's Minotaur) St. Martin's Pr.
—The Cranefly Orchid Murders. l.t. ed. 2002. (Senior Lifestyles Ser.). 398p. 28.95 (*0-7862-4544-1*) Thorndike Pr.
—Deadly Nightshade. 2003. 272p. mass mkt. 5.99 (*0-451-20816-1*, Signet Bks.) NAL.
—Deadly Nightshade. 2001. ix, 276p. 23.95 (*0-312-27252-9*, Saint Martin's Minotaur) St. Martin's Pr.
—Deadly Nightshade. l.t. ed. 2001. (Thorndike Press Large Print Senior Lifestyles Ser.). 437p. 28.95 (*0-7862-3754-6*) Thorndike Pr.

**TRUMPER, CHARLIE (FICTITIOUS CHARACTER)—FICTION**

Archer, Jeffrey. As the Crow Flies. 1991. 608p. 275.40 o.p. (*0-06-017915-5*) HarperCollins Pubs.
—As the Crow Flies. 1991. 22.95 o.p. (*0-06-017914-7*); 608p. pap. 24.95 o.p. (*0-06-017916-3*) HarperTrade.
—As the Crow Flies. 1992. 800p. mass mkt. 7.99 (*0-06-109934-1*, HarperTorch) Morrow/Avon.
—As the Crow Flies. 1992. 5.99 o.p. (*0-517-09222-0*); 5.99 o.p. (*0-517-09221-2*) Random Hse. Value Publishing.

**TRUMPINGTON, PHILIP (FICTITIOUS CHARACTER)—FICTION**

Doherty, P. C. An Ancient Evil: The Knight's Tale of Mystery & Murder as He Goes on Pilgrimage from London to Canterbury. unabr. ed. 1998. audio 69.95 (*1-85903-149-8*) Magna Story Sound GBR. *Dist:* Ulverscroft Large Print Bks., Ltd.
—An Ancient Evil: The Knight's Tale of Mystery & Murder as He Goes on Pilgrimage from London to Canterbury. 1995. 248p. 21.00 o.p. (*0-312-11740-X*, Saint Martin's Minotaur) St. Martin's Pr.
—An Ancient Evil: The Knight's Tale of Mystery & Murder as He Goes on Pilgrimage from London to Canterbury. l.t. ed. 1995. (Ulverscroft Large Print Ser.). 432p. 29.99 o.p. (*0-7089-3409-9*, Ulverscroft) Thorpe, F. A. Pubs. GBR. *Dist:* Ulverscroft Large Print Bks., Ltd., Ulverscroft Large Print Canada, Ltd.
—Ghostly Murders: The Priest's Tale of Mystery & Murder as He Goes on Pilgrimage from London to Canterbury. 1998. 256p. 21.95 (*0-312-19418-8*, Saint Martin's Minotaur) St. Martin's Pr.
—Ghostly Murders: The Priest's Tale of Mystery & Murder as He Goes on Pilgrimage from London to Canterbury. l.t. ed. 1999. (Ulverscroft Large Print Ser.). 368p. 31.99 o.p. (*0-7089-4059-5*, Ulverscroft) Thorpe, F. A. Pubs. GBR. *Dist:* Ulverscroft Large Print Bks., Ltd., Ulverscroft Large Print Canada, Ltd.
—A Tapestry of Murders: The Lawyer's Tale of Mystery & Murder as He Goes on a Pilgrimage from London to Canterbury. unabr. ed. 1998. audio 69.95 (*1-85903-165-X*) Magna Story Sound GBR. *Dist:* Ulverscroft Large Print Bks., Ltd.
—A Tapestry of Murders: The Lawyer's Tale of Mystery & Murder as He Goes on a Pilgrimage from London to Canterbury. 1996. 256p. 21.95 (*0-312-14052-5*, Saint Martin's Minotaur) St. Martin's Pr.
—A Tapestry of Murders: The Lawyer's Tale of Mystery & Murder as He Goes on a Pilgrimage from London to Canterbury. l.t. ed. 1996. (Ulverscroft Large Print Ser.). 416p. 29.99 o.p. (*0-7089-*

*3446-3*, Ulverscroft) Thorpe, F. A. Pubs. GBR. *Dist:* Ulverscroft Large Print Bks., Ltd., Ulverscroft Large Print Canada, Ltd.
—A Tournament of Murders: The Franklin's Tale of Mystery & Murder As He Goes on Pilgrimage from London to Canterbury. 1997. 256p. 21.95 (*0-312-17048-3*, Saint Martin's Minotaur) St. Martin's Pr.
—A Tournament of Murders: The Franklin's Tale of Mystery & Murder As He Goes on Pilgrimage from London to Canterbury. l.t. ed. 1998. (Ulverscroft Large Print Ser.). 384p. 29.99 o.p. (*0-7089-3938-4*, Ulverscroft) Thorpe, F. A. Pubs. GBR. *Dist:* Ulverscroft Large Print Bks., Ltd., Ulverscroft Large Print Canada, Ltd.

**TRYON, GLYNIS (FICTITIOUS CHARACTER)—FICTION**

Monfredo, Miriam G. Blackwater Spirits. 1996. 368p. reprint ed. mass mkt. 6.99 o.s.i (*0-425-15266-9*) Berkley Publishing Group.
—Blackwater Spirits. 1995. vii, 328p. 21.95 o.p. (*0-312-11754-X*, Saint Martin's Minotaur) St. Martin's Pr.
—Must the Maiden Die? 1999. (Seneca Falls Historical Mysteries Ser.: No. 6). 384p. 21.95 o.s.i (*0-425-16699-6*, Prime Crime) Berkley Publishing Group.
—Must the Maiden Die: A Seneca Falls Historical Mystery. 2000. (Seneca Falls Historical Mysteries Ser.). 384p. mass mkt. 6.99 o.s.i (*0-425-17610-X*) Berkley Publishing Group.
—North Star Conspiracy. 1993. 256p. 21.95 o.p. (*0-312-09355-1*, Saint Martin's Minotaur) St. Martin's Pr.
—The North Star Conspiracy. 1995. 368p. mass mkt. 6.99 (*0-425-14720-7*, Prime Crime) Berkley Publishing Group.
—Seneca Falls Inheritance. 1994. 304p. mass mkt. 6.99 (*0-425-14465-8*, Prime Crime) Berkley Publishing Group.
—Seneca Falls Inheritance. 1992. 320p. 19.95 o.p. (*0-312-07082-9*, Saint Martin's Minotaur) St. Martin's Pr.
—Sisters of Cain. 2001. 384p. reprint ed. mass mkt. 6.99 (*0-425-18092-1*, Prime Crime) Berkley Publishing Group.
—Sisters of Cain: A Seneca Falls Civil War Mystery. 2000. (Illus.). 384p. 21.95 o.s.i (*0-425-17672-X*, Prime Crime) Berkley Publishing Group.
—The Stalking Horse. 1999. (Historical Mystery Ser.: Vol. 5). 352p. reprint ed. mass mkt. 6.99 o.s.i (*0-425-16695-3*, Prime Crime) Berkley Publishing Group.
—The Stalking Horse: A Seneca Falls Historical Mystery. 1998. (Glynis Tryon Historical Mysteries Ser.). 352p. 21.95 o.s.i (*0-425-15783-0*, Prime Crime) Berkley Publishing Group.
—Through a Gold Eagle: A Glynis Tryon Mystery. 1997. 384p. mass mkt. 6.50 o.s.i (*0-425-15898-5*); 1996. 400p. 21.95 o.p. (*0-425-15318-5*) Berkley Publishing Group. (Prime Crime).

**TSIA (FICTITIOUS CHARACTER)—FICTION**

Harper, Tara K. Cat Scratch Fever. 1994. 352p. mass mkt. 6.99 o.s.i (*0-345-38051-7*, Del Rey) Ballantine Bks.
—Cataract. 1995. mass mkt. 5.99 o.s.i (*0-345-38052-5*, Del Rey) Ballantine Bks.

**TUCKER, FLAP (FICTITIOUS CHARACTER)—FICTION**

DePoy, Phillip. Dancing Made Easy. 1999. (Flap Tucker Mysteries Ser.). 304p. mass mkt. 5.99 o.s.i (*0-440-22618-X*) Dell Publishing.
—Dead Easy. 2000. (Flap Tucker Mysteries Ser.). 288p. mass mkt. 5.99 o.s.i (*0-440-23643-6*) Dell Publishing.
—Easy. 1997. (Flap Tucker Mysteries Ser.). 288p. mass mkt. 5.99 o.s.i (*0-440-22494-2*) Dell Publishing.
—Easy: A Flap Tucker Mystery. 1999. E-Book 5.99 (*0-440-33375-X*) Random Hse., Inc.
—Easy as One, Two, Three: A Flap Tucker Mystery. 1999. (Flap Tucker Mysteries Ser.: Bk. 3). 288p. mass mkt. 5.99 o.s.i (*0-440-22617-1*) Dell Publishing.
—Easy as One, Two, Three: A Flap Tucker Mystery. 1999. E-Book 5.99 (*0-440-33381-4*) Random Hse., Inc.
—Too Easy. 1998. (Flap Tucker Mysteries Ser.). 288p. mass mkt. 5.99 o.s.i (*0-440-22495-0*) Dell Publishing.

**TUDOR, BESS (FICTITIOUS CHARACTER)—FICTION**

Harper, Karen. The Poyson Garden: An Elizabethan Mystery. l.t. ed. 1999. (*1-57490-191-5*, Beeler Large Print Bks.) Beeler, Thomas T. Publisher.
—The Poyson Garden: An Elizabethan Mystery. (Elizabeth I Mysteries Ser.). 320p. 2000. mass mkt. 6.99 (*0-440-22592-2*); 1999. 21.95 o.s.i (*0-385-33283-1*, Delacorte Pr.) Dell Publishing.
—The Queene's Cure: An Elizabeth I Mystery. 2003. 368p. mass mkt. 6.99 (*0-440-23595-2*); 2002. (Illus.). 288p. 23.95 (*0-385-33478-8*) Dell Publishing.

**TULL, RICHARD (FICTITIOUS CHARACTER)—FICTION**

Amis, Martin. The Information. unabr. ed. 1998. audio 88.00 (*0-7366-4163-7*, 4666) Books on Tape, Inc.
—The Information. ltd. ed. 1995. 150.00 o.s.i (*0-517-70155-3*, Harmony) Crown Publishing Group.
—The Information. 1996. 384p. pap. 14.00 (*0-679-73573-9*, Vintage) Knopf Publishing Group.
—The Information. audio o.p. National Humanities Ctr.

**TUNET, TORREY (FICTITIOUS CHARACTER)—FICTION**

Deere, Dicey. The Irish Cairn Murder. 2002. 256p. 23.95 (*0-312-27519-6*, Saint Martin's Minotaur) St. Martin's Pr.
—The Irish Cottage Murder. (Torrey Tunet Mysteries Ser.). 2000. 295p. mass mkt. 6.50 (*0-312-97131-1*, St. Martin's Paperbacks); 1999. 240p. 22.95 (*0-312-20552-X*, Saint Martin's Minotaur) St. Martin's Pr.
—The Irish Manor House Murder. l.t. ed. 2000. (G. K. Hall Core Ser.). 296p. 27.95 (*0-7838-9283-7*, Macmillan Reference USA) Gale Group.
—The Irish Manor House Murder. 2001. 288p. mass mkt. 6.99 (*0-312-97645-3*, St. Martin's Paperbacks) St. Martin's Pr.
—The Irish Manor House Murder: A Torrey Tunet Mystery. 2000. 260p. 23.95 (*0-312-20606-2*, Saint Martin's Minotaur) St. Martin's Pr.

**TURNBUCKLE, HENRY (FICTITIOUS CHARACTER)—FICTION**

Nevins, Francis M. & Greenberg, Martin H., eds. The Adventures of Henry Turnbuckle: Detective Comedies by Jack Ritchie. 1987. (Mystery Makers Ser.). 386p. 31.95 (*0-8093-1397-9*) Southern Illinois Univ. Pr.

**TURNER, NICHOLAS (FICTITIOUS CHARACTER)—FICTION**

Leigh, Robert. The Turner Journals. 1996. 288p. 22.95 (*0-8027-3260-7*) Walker & Co.

**TURNER, PAUL (FICTITIOUS CHARACTER)—FICTION**

Zubro, Mark Richard. Another Dead Teenager. 1995. 194p. 19.95 o.p. (*0-312-13024-4*, Saint Martin's Minotaur) St. Martin's Pr.
—Dead Egotistical Morons: A Paul Turner Mystery. 2003. 288p. 23.95 (*0-312-26682-0*) St. Martin's Pr.
—Drop Dead. (Paul Turner Mystery Ser.). 2000. 256p. pap. 12.95 (*0-312-26314-7*, Saint Martin's Griffin); 1999. 245p. 22.95 (*0-312-20532-5*, Saint Martin's Minotaur) St. Martin's Pr.
—Political Poison: A Paul Turner Mystery. (Paul Turner Mystery Ser.). 1994. 208p. pap. 11.95 (*0-312-11044-8*, Saint Martin's Griffin); 1993. 192p. 10.99 o.p. (*0-312-09364-0*, Saint Martin's Minotaur) St. Martin's Pr.
—Sex & Murder.Com. 2001. (Paul Turner Mystery Ser.). 294p. 23.95 (*0-312-26683-9*, Saint Martin's Minotaur) St. Martin's Pr.
—Sorry Now? 1991. 208p. 11.99 o.p. (*0-312-06470-5*, Saint Martin's Minotaur); 3rd ed. 1992. 192p. pap. 10.95 (*0-312-08299-1*, Saint Martin's Griffin) St. Martin's Pr.
—The Truth Can Get You Killed. (Stonewall Inn Editions Ser.). 224p. 1998. pap. 11.95 (*0-312-18765-3*, Saint Martin's Griffin); 1997. 21.95 (*0-312-15679-0*, Saint Martin's Minotaur) St. Martin's Pr.

**TURNER, SAM (FICTITIOUS CHARACTER)—FICTION**

Baker, John. Poet in the Gutter. 1996. 240p. 21.95 o.p. (*0-312-14393-1*, Saint Martin's Minotaur) St. Martin's Pr.

**TURNER, SAMANTHA (FICTITIOUS CHARACTER)—FICTION**

Landreth, Marsha. A Clinic for Murder. 1993. (Dr. Sam Turner Mystery Ser.). 212p. 19.95 o.s.i (*0-8027-3241-0*) Walker & Co.
—The Holiday Murders. l.t. ed. 1999. (Paperback Ser.). 328p. 24.95 (*0-7838-8827-9*) Thorndike Pr.
—The Holiday Murders. 1992. 243p. 19.95 o.s.i (*0-8027-1246-0*) Walker & Co.
—Vial Murders. 1994. (Doctor Samantha Turner Mystery Ser.). 224p. 19.95 (*0-8027-3199-6*) Walker & Co.

**TUVOK (FICTITIOUS CHARACTER)—FICTION**

Betancourt, John G. Incident at Arbuk. 1995. (Star Trek Voyager Ser.: No. 5). 224p. mass mkt. 5.99 o.s.i (*0-671-52048-2*, Star Trek) Simon & Schuster.
Carey, Diane L. Flashback. 1996. (Star Trek Voyager Ser.). 288p. per. 5.99 (*0-671-00383-6*, Star Trek) Simon & Schuster.
Friedman, Michael Jan. The First Virtue No. 6: Double Helix. 1999. (Star Trek, The Next Generation: No. 56). 271p. pap. 6.50 o.s.i (*0-671-03258-5*, Star Trek) Simon & Schuster.
Garland, Mark A. & McGraw, Charles G. Ghost of a Chance. 1996. (Star Trek Voyager Ser.: No. 7). 288p. pap. 5.99 (*0-671-56798-5*, Star Trek) Simon & Schuster.
Golden, Christie. Homecoming. 2003. (Star Trek Voyager Ser.). 288p. mass mkt. 6.99 (*0-7434-6754-X*);Bk. 1. E-Book 5.99 (*0-7434-7563-1*) Simon & Schuster. (Star Trek).
Hugh, Dafydd ab. The Final Fury No. 4: Invasion! 1996. (Star Trek Voyager Ser.: No. 9). 320p. (J). mass mkt. 6.50 (*0-671-54181-1*, Star Trek) Simon & Schuster.
—Invasion! No. 4: The Final Fury. 1999. (Star Trek Voyager Ser.: No. 9). E-Book 6.99 (*0-671-04098-7*, Star Trek) Simon & Schuster.
Lewitt, S. N. Cybersong. 1996. (Star Trek Voyager Ser.: No. 8). 288p. mass mkt. 5.99 (*0-671-56783-7*, Star Trek) Simon & Schuster.
Taylor, Jeri. Mosaic. (Star Trek Voyager Ser.). 320p. 1997. pap. 5.99 (*0-671-56312-2*); 1996. 22.00 (*0-671-56311-4*) Simon & Schuster. (Star Trek).
—Mosaic. abr. ed. 1996. (Star Trek Ser.). audio 18.00 (*0-671-57400-0*, Simon & Schuster Audioworks) Simon & Schuster Audio.
Vornholt, John. Double Helix: Quarantine. 1999. (Star Trek, The Next Generation Ser.: No. 54). (Illus.). 304p. pap. 6.99 (*0-671-03477-4*, Star Trek) Simon & Schuster.

**TWAIN, MARK, 1835-1910—FICTION**

Hauser, Thomas. Harder Than It Looks: The Final Recollections of Mark Twain. 1998. 208p. 19.95 o.p. (*0-8038-9432-5*) Publishers Group West.
—Mark Twain Remembers. 1999. 208p. 20.00 (*1-56980-154-1*) Barricade Bks., Inc.
Heck, Peter J. A Connecticut Yankee in Criminal Court. 1997. (Mark Twain Mystery Ser.). 320p. mass mkt. 5.99 o.s.i (*0-425-16034-3*, Prime Crime) Berkley Publishing Group.
—A Connecticut Yankee in Criminal Court: A Mark Twain Mystery. 1996. (Mark Twain Mystery Ser.). 320p. 21.95 o.p. (*0-425-15470-X*); viii, 311p. pap. o.p. (*0-425-15474-2*) Berkley Publishing Group. (Prime Crime).
—Death on the Mississippi. 1996. (Mark Twain Mystery Ser.). (Illus.). x, 290p. mass mkt. 5.99 o.s.i (*0-425-15512-9*) Berkley Publishing Group.
—Death on the Mississippi: A Mark Twain Mystery. 1995. (Mark Twain Mystery Ser.). 304p. 21.95 o.p. (*0-425-14938-2*); pap. 10.00 o.p. (*0-425-14939-0*) Berkley Publishing Group. (Prime Crime).
—Guilty Abroad. 1999. (Mark Twain Mystery Ser.). 320p. mass mkt. 6.50 o.s.i (*0-425-17122-1*) Berkley Publishing Group.
—The Prince & the Prosecutor. (Mark Twain Mystery Ser.: No. 3). 336p. 1998. mass mkt. 5.99 o.s.i (*0-425-16567-1*); 1997. 21.95 o.s.i (*0-425-15970-1*) Berkley Publishing Group. (Prime Crime).
Twain, Mark. The $30,000 Bequest. 2000. pap. 7.99 (*1-930142-44-7*); 1999. 14.99 (*1-930142-45-5*) Write Together Publishing.
—The $30,000 Bequest & Other Stories. E-Book 2.49 (*1-929120-45-1*) Electric Umbrella Publishing.

**TWEETY PIE (FICTITIOUS CHARACTER)—FICTION**

Heller, Sarah E. Around the World in Tweety Time: Tattoo Storybook. 2000. (Illus.). 24p. (J). (ps-3). mass mkt. 5.99 (*0-439-20282-5*) Scholastic, Inc.
—Tweety's High Flying Adventures. 2000. (Illus.). 32p. (J). (ps-3). mass mkt. 3.50 (*0-439-20281-7*) Scholastic, Inc.

**TYGART, MARY 'IKE' (FICTITIOUS CHARACTER)—FICTION**

Whitney, Polly. Until Death. 1996. per. (*0-373-26219-1*, 1-26219-5, Worldwide Library) Harlequin Enterprises, Ltd.
—Until Death. 1994. 320p. 21.95 o.p. (*0-312-11089-8*, Saint Martin's Minotaur) St. Martin's Pr.
—Until It Hurts. 1998. (Worldwide Library Mysteries: Vol. 272). per. (*0-373-26272-8*, 0-26272-5, Worldwide Library) Harlequin Enterprises, Ltd.
—Until It Hurts: An Ike & Abby Mystery. 1997. 304p. 22.95 (*0-312-15237-X*, Saint Martin's Minotaur) St. Martin's Pr.
—Until the End of Time. 1997. per. (*0-373-26233-7*, 1-26233-6, Worldwide Library) Harlequin Enterprises, Ltd.
—Until the End of Time. 1995. 272p. 21.95 o.p. (*0-312-13199-2*, Saint Martin's Minotaur) St. Martin's Pr.

**TYLER, WENDY (FICTITIOUS CHARACTER)—FICTION**

Yorke, Margaret. Act of Violence. 1997. 282p. o.s.i (*0-316-88254-2*) Little Brown & Co.
—Act of Violence. 1998. 288p. 22.95 o.p. (*0-312-18522-7*, Saint Martin's Minotaur) St. Martin's Pr.
—Act of Violence. 1998. 282p. mass mkt. o.s.i (*0-7515-2024-1*) Warner Futura GBR. *Dist:* Little Brown & Co.

**TYRONE, JAMES (FICTITIOUS CHARACTER)—FICTION**

Francis, Dick. Forfeit. unabr. ed. 1993. audio 54.95 o.p. (*0-7451-5951-6*) BBC Audiobooks America.
—Forfeit. 1987. mass mkt. 5.95 o.s.i (*0-449-21272-6*, Fawcett) Ballantine Bks.
—Forfeit. 1999. 256p. pap. 6.99 (*0-515-12445-1*, Jove) Berkley Publishing Group.
—Forfeit. unabr. ed. 1991. audio 48.00 (*0-7366-1885-6*, 2714) Books on Tape, Inc.
—Forfeit. l.t. ed. 1994. 22.95 (*0-8161-5781-2*, Macmillan Reference USA) Gale Group.
—Forfeit. 1969. (Harper Novel of Suspense Ser.). 6.95 o.p. (*0-06-011328-6*) HarperCollins Pubs.
—Forfeit. 1985. mass mkt. 3.50 (*0-671-54692-9*, Pocket) Simon & Schuster.
—Forfeit. l.t. ed. 1979. (Ulverscroft Large Print Ser.). 12.00 o.p. (*0-7089-0373-8*, Ulverscroft) Thorpe, F. A. Pubs. GBR. *Dist:* Ulverscroft Large Print Bks., Ltd., Ulverscroft Large Print Canada, Ltd.

**TYSON, BEN (FICTITIOUS CHARACTER)—FICTION**

DeMille, Nelson. Word of Honor. l.t. ed. 1986. (Special Editions Ser.). 930p. 21.95 o.p. (*0-8161-4082-0*); 13.95 o.p. (*0-8161-4083-9*) Gale Group. (Macmillan Reference USA).
—Word of Honor. abr. ed. 1990. audio 15.95 o.s.i (*0-394-58378-7*, RH Audio) Random Hse. Audio Publishing Group.
—Word of Honor. 1985. 448p. 17.00 o.s.i (*0-446-51280-X*); 1998. 880p. reprint ed. pap. 14.00 (*0-446-67482-6*); 1987. 752p. reprint ed. mass mkt. 7.99 (*0-446-30158-2*) Warner Bks., Inc.



## U

**UBU (FICTITIOUS CHARACTER)—FICTION**

Taylor, Jane. Ubu & the Truth Commision: The Play. 1998. (Illus.). 92p. pap. 69.95 (*1-919713-16-6*, University Pr. for West Africa) International Scholars Pubns.

**UHURA, NYOTA (FICTITIOUS CHARACTER)—FICTION**

David, Peter, et al. Disinherited. 1992. (Star Trek: No. 59). 272p. mass mkt. 4.99 (*0-671-77958-3*, Star Trek) Simon & Schuster.
—The Disinherited. (Star Trek: No. 59). E-Book 6.99 (*0-7434-2010-1*, Star Trek) Simon & Schuster.
Dillard, J. M. The Final Frontier. abr. ed. (Star Trek Ser.: No. 5). audio 7.95. 1990. audio 7.95 (*0-671-68507-4*, Simon & Schuster Audioworks) Simon & Schuster Audio.
—Star Trek 5: The Final Frontier. 1989. (Star Trek Ser.: No. 5). mass mkt. 4.50 (*0-671-68008-0*, Star Trek) Simon & Schuster.
—The Undiscovered Country. Stern, Dave, ed. 1992. (Star Trek Ser.: No. 6). 320p. mass mkt. 5.50 (*0-671-75883-7*, Pocket) Simon & Schuster.
—The Undiscovered Country. abr. ed. 1992. (Star Trek Ser.: No. 6). audio 11.00 (*0-671-75873-X*, Simon & Schuster Audioworks) Simon & Schuster Audio.
Graf, L. A. Death Count. 2000. (Star Trek: No. 62). E-Book 6.99 (*0-7434-2013-6*, Star Trek) Simon & Schuster.
—Death Count. Stern, Dave, ed. 1992. (Star Trek Ser.: No. 62). 288p. mass mkt. 4.99 (*0-671-79322-5*, Star Trek) Simon & Schuster.
—Firestorm. (Star Trek: No. 68). 2000. E-Book 6.99 (*0-7434-2019-5*); 1994. 288p. mass mkt. 5.50 (*0-671-86588-9*) Simon & Schuster. (Star Trek).
—Ice Trap. 2000. (Star Trek: No. 60). E-Book 6.99 (*0-7434-2011-X*, Star Trek) Simon & Schuster.
—New Earth No. 3: Rough Trails. 2000. (Star Trek: No. 91). reprint ed. E-Book 6.50 (*0-7434-1117-X*, Star Trek) Simon & Schuster.
—New Earth No. 33: Rough Trails. 2000. (Star Trek: No. 91). 400p. pap. 6.50 (*0-671-03600-9*, Star Trek) Simon & Schuster.
—Traitor Winds. 2000. (Star Trek: No. 70). E-Book 6.99 (*0-7434-2021-7*, Star Trek) Simon & Schuster.
—Traitor Winds. Ryan, Kevin, ed. 1994. (Star Trek Ser.: No. 70). 288p. mass mkt. 5.50 (*0-671-86913-2*, Star Trek) Simon & Schuster.
Graf, L. A. & Ecklar, Julia. Ice Trap. Stern, Dave, ed. 1992. (Star Trek: No. 60). 288p. mass mkt. 4.99 (*0-671-78068-9*, Star Trek) Simon & Schuster.
Kagan, Janet. Uhura's Song. (Star Trek: No. 21). 384p. 1987. mass mkt. 5.50 (*0-671-65227-3*); 1985. mass mkt. 3.50 o.s.i (*0-671-54730-5*); 2000. pap. 3.99 (*0-7434-0373-8*) Simon & Schuster. (Star Trek).
—Uhura's Song. 1985. (Star Trek Ser.: No. 21). 373p. 20.00 o.p. (*0-89366-169-4*) Ultramarine Publishing Co., Inc.
McIntyre, Vonda N. The Search for Spock. 2000. (Star Trek Ser.: No. 3). E-Book 6.99 (*0-7434-1968-5*); 1990. (Star Trek: No. 17). mass mkt. 5.50 (*0-671-73133-5*) Simon & Schuster. (Star Trek).
—The Wrath of Khan. (Star Trek: No. 7). 1991. mass mkt. 5.50 (*0-671-74149-7*); 1984. mass mkt. 2.95 o.s.i (*0-671-55248-1*) Simon & Schuster. (Star Trek).

Peel, John. Where No Man Has Gone Before. 1986. (Star Trek Ser.). 96p. lib. bdg. 19.95 o.p. (*0-8095-8019-5*) Millefleurs.

Roddenberry, Gene. The Motion Picture. 1979. (Star Trek: No. 1). E-Book 6.99 (*0-7434-1208-7*, Star Trek) Simon & Schuster.

—Star Trek: The Motion Picture. (Star Trek: No. 1). 1984. mass mkt. 2.95 o.s.i (*0-671-54685-6*); 1980. mass mkt. 2.95 o.s.i (*0-671-83089-9*) Simon & Schuster. (Star Trek).

Roddenberry, Gene, et al. Star Trek: The Motion Picture. 1979. (Star Trek: No. 1). 252 p. o.p. (*0-671-25324-7*, Simon & Schuster) Simon & Schuster.

Sherman, Josepha & Shwartz, Susan. Vulcan's Heart. (Star Trek Ser.). 2000. per. 6.50 (*0-7434-1112-9*); 1999. 384p. 23.00 o.s.i (*0-671-01544-3*); 2000. 400p. reprint ed. pap. 6.50 (*0-671-01545-1*) Simon & Schuster. (Star Trek).

—Vulcan's Heart. abr. ed. 1999. (Star Trek Ser.). audio 18.00 (*0-671-04560-1*, Simon & Schuster Audioworks) Simon & Schuster Audio.

Snodgrass, Melinda. The Tears of the Singers. 2000. (Star Trek: No. 19). E-Book 6.99 (*0-7434-1970-7*, Star Trek) Simon & Schuster.

Snodgrass, Melinda M. Tears of the Singers. 1989. (Star Trek: No. 19). mass mkt. 5.50 (*0-671-69654-8*, Star Trek) Simon & Schuster.

### UNDERHILL, FREDDY (FICTITIOUS CHARACTER)—FICTION

Ellroy, James. Clandestine. 1999. 336p. pap. 12.95 (*0-380-80529-4*); 1982. 352p. mass mkt. 5.99 (*0-380-81141-3*) Morrow/Avon. (Avon Bks.).

### UNDERHILL, TIM (FICTITIOUS CHARACTER)—FICTION

Straub, Peter. Koko. 1988. 19.95 o.p. (*0-525-24660-6*, Dutton) Dutton/Plume.

—Koko. 1989. 608p. mass mkt. 7.99 (*0-451-16214-5*, 001, Signet Bks.) NAL.

—Koko. 1990. 4.99 o.p. (*0-517-05233-4*) Random Hse. Value Publishing.

—Koko. 1999. pap. 9.98 (*0-671-04461-3*); 1988. audio 14.95 (*0-671-65239-7*) Simon & Schuster Audio. (Simon & Schuster Audioworks).

—Lost Boy Lost Girl: A Novel. 2003. 304p. 24.95 (*1-4000-6092-3*) Random Hse., Inc.

—The Throat. 1993. 688p. 24.00 o.p. (*0-525-93503-7*) Dutton/Plume.

—The Throat. 1994. 704p. mass mkt. 7.99 (*0-451-17918-8*, Signet Bks.) NAL.

—The Throat. abr. ed. 1993. audio 25.00 (*0-671-72591-2*, 692323, Simon & Schuster Audioworks) Simon & Schuster Audio.

### UNDERWOOD, TONI (FICTITIOUS CHARACTER)—FICTION

Davidson, Diane. Deadly Butterfly: A Toni Underwood Mystery. 2001. 224p. pap. 12.00 (*1-883061-34-2*) Rising Tide Pr.

—Deadly Gamble: A Toni Underwood Mystery. 1997. 211p. pap. 11.99 (*1-883061-12-1*) Rising Tide Pr.

—Deadly Rendezvous: A Toni Underwood Mystery. 1994. 191p. pap. 9.99 (*1-883061-02-4*) Rising Tide Pr.

### UPSHAW, DANNY (FICTITIOUS CHARACTER)—FICTION

Ellroy, James. The Big Nowhere. 1988. 416p. 17.95 o.s.i (*0-89296-283-6*) Mysterious Pr.

—The Big Nowhere. 1989. 60.00 (*0-89366-239-9*) Ultramarine Publishing Co., Inc.

—The Big Nowhere. 1998. 416p. pap. 13.95 (*0-446-67437-0*); 1990. mass mkt. 4.95 (*0-445-77285-9*); 1989. 496p. mass mkt. 6.99 (*0-445-40832-4*) Warner Bks., Inc.

### URSULA, SISTER (FICTITIOUS CHARACTER)—FICTION

Boucher, Anthony. Nine Times Nine. 1986. 254p. pap. 4.95 o.p. (*0-930330-37-4*) International Polygonics, Ltd.

—Rocket to the Morgue. 1988. 176p. pap. 4.95 (*0-930330-82-X*) International Polygonics, Ltd.

## V

### VADER, DARTH (FICTITIOUS CHARACTER)—FICTION

*see Skywalker, Anakin (Fictitious Character)—Fiction*

### VAIL, MARTIN (FICTITIOUS CHARACTER)—FICTION

Diehl, William. Primal Fear. 1998. pap. 6.99 (*0-345-91452-X*); 1995. mass mkt. 6.99 o.p. (*0-345-90885-6*); 1995. mass mkt. 6.99 o.p. (*0-345-90644-6*); 1994. 432p. mass mkt. 7.99 (*0-345-38877-1*, Ballantine Bks.); 1993. mass mkt. 6.99 (*0-345-38391-5*) Ballantine Bks.

—Primal Fear. unabr. ed. 1993. audio 25.95 o.p. (*1-56100-490-1*, 220, Bookcassette);Set. audio 89.25 o.p. (*1-56100-124-4*, 993) Brilliance Audio.

—Primal Fear. 1994. audio 8.99 o.s.i (*0-679-43414-3*); 1993. audio 18.00 o.s.i (*0-679-42014-2*, 391398); Set. 1999. audio 8.99 o.s.i (*0-375-40574-7*) Random Hse. Audio Publishing Group. (RH Audio).

—Reign in Hell. 1998. 480p. mass mkt. 7.99 (*0-345-39506-9*, Ballantine Bks.) Ballantine Bks.

—Show of Evil. 1998. pap. 6.99 (*0-345-91453-8*); 1996. 416p. mass mkt. 7.99 (*0-345-37536-X*, Ballantine Bks.); 1995. mass mkt. 6.99 (*0-345-40133-6*) Ballantine Bks.

—Show of Evil. abr. ed. 1995. audio 17.00 o.s.i (*0-679-44304-5*, RH Audio) Random Hse. Audio Publishing Group.

### VALADAN, WARHORSE OF ESDRAGON (FICTITIOUS CHARACTER)—FICTION

Dexter, Susan. The Prince of Ill Luck. 1994. (Wizards of Fantasy Promotion Ser.: Bk. 1). (Orig.). mass mkt. 4.99 o.s.i (*0-345-38065-7*, Del Rey) Ballantine Bks.

—The True Knight Bk. 3: The Warhorse of Esdragon. 1995. mass mkt. 5.99 o.s.i (*0-345-39345-7*, Del Rey) Ballantine Bks.

—The Wind Witch. 1994. mass mkt. 5.99 o.s.i (*0-345-38770-8*, Del Rey) Ballantine Bks.

### VALENTINE, AMANDA (FICTITIOUS CHARACTER)—FICTION

Beecham, Rose. Fair Play: An Amanda Valentine Mystery. 1995. (Amanda Valentine Mysteries Ser.: Vol. 3). 256p. pap. 10.95 o.p. (*1-56280-081-7*) Naiad Pr., Inc.

—Introducing Amanda Valentine. 1992. (Amanda Valentine Mystery Ser.: No. 1). 256p. pap. 10.95 o.p. (*1-56280-021-3*) Naiad Pr., Inc.

—Second Guess: Second Amanda Valentine Mystery. 1994. (Amanda Valentine Mysteries Ser.: Vol. 2). 208p. pap. 9.95 o.p. (*1-56280-069-8*) Naiad Pr., Inc.

### VALENTINE, CLAUDIA (FICTITIOUS CHARACTER)—FICTION

Day, Marele. The Case of the Chinese Boxes. 1993. 192p. pap. 9.95 o.p. (*0-04-442277-6*) Allen & Unwin Pty., Ltd. AUS. *Dist:* Independent Pubs. Group.

—The Disappearances of Madalena Grimaldi: A Claudia Valentine Mystery. abr. ed. 1996. 224p. 19.95 (*0-8027-3277-1*) Walker & Co.

—The Last Tango of Delores Delgado. 1993. 192p. pap. 9.95 o.p. (*1-86373-323-X*) Allen & Unwin Pty., Ltd. AUS. *Dist:* Independent Pubs. Group.

—The Life & Crimes of Harry Lavender. 1993. 176p. pap. 9.95 o.p. (*1-86373-394-9*) Allen & Unwin Pty., Ltd. AUS. *Dist:* Independent Pubs. Group.

—The Life & Crimes of Harry Lavender. l.t. ed. 1997. (Bolinda Large Print Ser.). 24.95 o.p. (*1-86340-566-6*) Beeler, Thomas T. Publisher.

### VALENTINE, DAN (FICTITIOUS CHARACTER)—FICTION

Aldyne, Nathan. The Canary. 1986. (Orig.). mass mkt. 3.50 o.s.i (*0-345-33167-2*) Ballantine Bks.

—Canary: A Daniel Valentine & Clarisse Lovelace Mystery. 1999. 188p. (Orig.). reprint ed. pap. 10.00 o.p. (*1-55583-443-4*, Alyson Bks.) Alyson Pubns.

—Cobalt. 1998. (Daniel Valentine & Clarisse Lovelace Mystery Ser.: Vol. 2). 200p. pap. 10.00 o.p. (*1-55583-441-8*) Alyson Pubns.

—Cobalt. 1985. 208p. mass mkt. 2.95 o.s.i (*0-345-32705-5*) Ballantine Bks.

—Cobalt. 1982. 224p. pap. 2.75 o.p. (*0-380-81117-0*, 81117-0, Avon Bks.) Morrow/Avon.

—Cobalt. 1982. 168p. 9.95 o.p. (*0-312-14515-2*) St. Martin's Pr.

—Slate: A Daniel Valentine & Clarissa Lovelace Mystery. 1999. 234p. reprint ed. pap. 10.00 (*1-55583-442-6*) Alyson Pubns.

—Slate: A Daniel Valentine & Clarissa Walker Mystery. 1985. 192p. mass mkt. 3.50 o.s.i (*0-345-31366-6*, Ballantine Bks.) Ballantine Bks.

—Slate: A Daniel Valentine & Clarissa Walker Mystery. 1984. 12.95 o.p. (*0-394-53697-5*, Villard Bks.) Random House Adult Trade Publishing Group.

—Vermilion. 1997. 220p. pap. 10.95 o.p. (*1-55583-434-5*) Alyson Pubns.

—Vermilion. 1980. pap. 2.25 o.p. (*0-380-76596-9*, 81570-2, Avon Bks.) Morrow/Avon.

### VALENTINE, TONY (FICTITIOUS CHARACTER)—FICTION

Swain, James. Funny Money: A Tony Valentine Novel. 2003. 336p. mass mkt. 6.99 (*0-345-46344-7*, Ballantine Bks.) Ballantine Bks.

—Funny Money: A Tony Valentine Novel. 2003. 352p. mass mkt. 6.99 (*0-7434-3687-3*, Pocket); 2002. 304p. 24.00 (*0-7434-3686-5*, Atria); 2002. 304p. E-Book 23.95 (*0-7434-3988-0*, Atria) Simon & Schuster.

—Grift Sense. 2003. 336p. mass mkt. 6.99 (*0-345-46383-8*, Ballantine Bks.) Ballantine Bks.

—Grift Sense. 2001. 320p. 23.95 o.s.i (*0-7434-0622-2*, Atria); 2002. (Illus.). 416p. reprint ed. pap. 6.99 (*0-7434-0623-0*, Pocket) Simon & Schuster.

—Sucker Bet. 2004. 336p. mass mkt. 6.99 (*0-345-46323-4*, Fawcett); 2003. 320p. 19.95 (*0-345-46175-4*, Ballantine Bks.) Ballantine Bks.

—Sucker Bet. 2004. 24.00 (*0-7434-3688-1*, Atria) Simon & Schuster.

### VALJEAN, JEAN (FICTITIOUS CHARACTER)—FICTION

Hugo, Victor. Les Miserables. abr. ed. audio 62.95Pt. 1. 1996. audio 99.95 (*0-7861-0534-8*, 1810-A);Pt. 2. 1996. audio 85.95 (*0-7861-0535-6*, 1810-B);Pt. 3. audio 83.95 Blackstone Audio Bks., Inc.

—Les Miserables. unabr. collector's ed. 1993. (J). audio 72.00 (*0-7366-2339-6*, 116013) Books on Tape, Inc.

—Les Miserables. abr. ed. 2000. audio 7.95 (*1-57815-117-1*, 1079, Media Bks. Audio Publishing) Media Bks., L. L. C.

—Les Miserables. audio 23.85 National Recording Co.

—Les Miserables. abr. ed. 1996. audio 22.98 (*962-634-605-1*, NA410514); audio compact disk 26.98 (*962-634-105-X*, NA410512) Naxos of America, Inc. (Naxos AudioBooks).

—Les Miserables. abr. ed. 1993. audio 16.95 o.p. (*1-55800-036-4*, Dove Audio); Set. 1998. audio compact disk 29.95; Set. 1995. 29.95 o.p. (*0-7871-0289-X*) NewStar Media, Inc.

—Les Miserables. Fahnestock, Lee & MacAfee, Norman, trs. abr. ed. (Classics on Cassette). 1998. audio compact disk 34.95 (*0-453-00966-2*); 1992. 23.95 incl. audio (*0-453-00785-6*, 693468) Penguin/HighBridge.

—Les Miserables. 1987. (Radiola 3-CMR 5). audio 16.95 (*0-929541-48-0*); audio 4.98 (*0-929541-22-7*) Radiola Co.

—Les Miserables. abr. ed. 1998. audio 22.95 (*1-55935-273-6*) Soundelux Audio Publishing.

—Les Miserables. audio Spoken Arts, Inc.

—Les Miserables. abr. ed. 1997. (Penguin Classics Ser.). 4p. (J). pap. 18.95 o.p. incl. audio (*0-14-086261-7*); pap. 18.95 o.p. incl. audio (*0-14-086261-7*) Viking Penguin. (Penguin AudioBooks).

—Les Miserables: Parts I & II. abr. ed. 1989. audio 120.00 Jimcin Recordings.

Hugo, Victor & Dawson, Michael. Les Miserables. adapted collector's ed. 1998. (Smithsonian Historical Performances Ser.). 29p. (Illus.). pap. 24.98 incl. audio compact disk (*1-57019-066-6*, 4035); pap. 9.99 incl. audio (*1-57019-065-8*, 4034) Radio Spirits, Inc.

### VALLANCE, ANTHONY (FICTITIOUS CHARACTER)—FICTION

Pantziarka, Pan. A Tangled Web. 1997. (Crime & Passion Ser.). 243p. mass mkt. 5.95 (*0-7535-0156-2*) Virgin Bks. GBR. *Dist:* London Bridge.

### VALMONT, EUGENE (FICTITIOUS CHARACTER)—FICTION

Barr, Robert. The Triumphs of Eugene Valmont. 1985. 192p. reprint ed. pap. 5.95 o.p. (*0-486-24894-1*) Dover Pubns., Inc.

—The Triumphs of Eugene Valmont. 1997. (Oxford Popular Fiction Ser.). 246p. pap. 9.95 o.p. (*0-19-283248-4*) Oxford Univ. Pr., Inc.

### VAN ALSTYNE, RUSS (FICTITIOUS CHARACTER)—FICTION

Spencer-Fleming, Julia. A Fountain Filled with Blood. E-Book 23.95 (*0-312-71002-X*); 2004. mass mkt. 6.99 (*0-312-99543-1*, St. Martin's Paperbacks); 2003. 304p. 23.95 (*0-312-30410-2*, Saint Martin's Minotaur) St. Martin's Pr.

—In the Bleak Midwinter. E-Book 17.95 (*0-312-70446-1*); 2003. 384p. mass mkt. 6.99 (*0-312-98676-9*, St. Martin's Paperbacks); 2002. 272p. 23.95 (*0-312-28847-6*, Saint Martin's Minotaur) St. Martin's Pr.

—Out of the Deep I Cry. 2004. 304p. 23.95 (*0-312-31262-8*) St. Martin's Pr.

### VANCE, PHILO (FICTITIOUS CHARACTER)—FICTION

Van Dine, S. S. The Benson Murder Case. reprint ed. lib. bdg. 24.95 (*0-89190-511-1*, Rivercity Pr.) Amereon, Ltd.

—The Benson Murder Case. 1983. 256p. pap. 3.95 o.s.i (*0-684-17976-8*, Macmillan Reference USA) Gale Group.

—The Bishop Murder Case. reprint ed. lib. bdg. 25.95 (*0-89190-512-X*, Rivercity Pr.) Amereon, Ltd.

—The Bishop Murder Case. 1983. 256p. pap. 3.95 o.s.i (*0-684-17977-6*, Macmillan Reference USA) Gale Group.

—The Bishop Murder Case. l.t. ed. 1984. (Philo Vance Mystery Ser.). 453p. reprint ed. 14.95 o.p. (*0-89621-501-6*) Thorndike Pr.

—The Canary Murder Case. reprint ed. lib. bdg. 25.95 (*0-89190-513-8*, Rivercity Pr.) Amereon, Ltd.

—The Canary Murder Case. 1979. pap. 2.25 o.s.i (*0-684-16404-3*, Macmillan Reference USA) Gale Group.

—The Casino Murder Case. 1985. 312p. pap. 3.95 o.p. (*0-684-18503-2*, Macmillan Reference USA) Gale Group.

—The Dragon Murder Case: A Philo Vance Mystery. 1994. 336p. 35.00 (*1-883402-21-2*, Scribner) Simon & Schuster.

—Gracie Allen Murder Case: A Philo Vance Story. 21.95 (*0-8488-0850-9*) Amereon, Ltd.

—Gracie Allen Murder Case: A Philo Vance Story. 1994. 336p. reprint ed. pap. 6.95 (*1-883402-09-3*, Scribner) Simon & Schuster.

—The Greene Murder Case. reprint ed. lib. bdg. 27.95 (*0-89190-514-6*, Rivercity Pr.) Amereon, Ltd.

—The Greene Murder Case. 1980. pap. 2.95 o.s.i (*0-684-16734-4*, Scribner Paper Fiction) Simon & Schuster.

—The Kennel Murder Case: A Philo Vance Mystery. 1984. 312p. pap. 3.95 o.s.i (*0-684-18248-3*, Macmillan Reference USA) Gale Group.

—The Kidnap Murder Case: A Philo Vance Story. 1994. 320p. reprint ed. pap. 7.95 o.s.i (*1-883402-93-X*, Scribner) Simon & Schuster.

—The Scarab Murder Case. 1984. (Philo Vance Mystery Ser.). pap. 4.50 o.s.i (*0-684-18159-2*, Scribner Paper Fiction) Simon & Schuster.

—The Winter Murder Case: A Philo Vance Story. 1993. 196p. pap. 6.95 o.s.i (*1-883402-08-5*, Scribner) Simon & Schuster.

### VANDER, BOBBIE (FICTITIOUS CHARACTER)—FICTION

Sanders, Lawrence. Love Songs. 1989. 400p. mass mkt. 7.50 (*0-425-11273-X*) Berkley Publishing Group.

### VAN DER LYN, DINAH (FICTITIOUS CHARACTER)—FICTION

Peters, Elizabeth, pseud. The Dead Sea Cipher. unabr. ed. 1998. audio compact disk 29.95 (*0-7861-1458-4*); audio 44.95 (*0-7861-1357-X*, 2266) Blackstone Audio Bks., Inc.

—The Dead Sea Cipher. l.t. ed. 2000. 303p. lib. bdg. 25.95 (*1-58547-039-2*) Ctr. Point Large Print.

—The Dead Sea Cipher. 1988. 216p. mass mkt. 4.99 (*0-8125-0756-8*, Tor Bks.) Doherty, Tom Assocs., LLC.

—The Dead Sea Cipher, Set. unabr. ed. 1999. audio 44.95 Highsmith Inc.

—The Dead Sea Cipher. 2001. 384p. mass mkt. 6.99 (*0-380-73114-2*, Avon Bks.) Morrow/Avon.

### VAN DER VALK, ARLETTE (FICTITIOUS CHARACTER)—FICTION

Freeling, Nicolas. Arlette. 1982. pap. 2.95 o.p. (*0-394-75260-0*, Pantheon) Knopf Publishing Group.

—Aupres de Ma Blonde. 1979. pap. 2.95 o.p. (*0-394-74550-7*, Vintage) Knopf Publishing Group.

—Because of the Cats. 2000. 190p. pap. (*1-900850-36-2*) Arcadia Bks.

—Because of the Cats. l.t. ed. 1987. pap. 13.95 o.p. (*1-55504-040-3*) BBC Audiobooks America.

—Because of the Cats. 1975. (Crime Ser.). 192p. pap. 3.95 o.p. (*0-14-002282-1*, Penguin Bks.) Viking Penguin.

—Criminal Conversation. 2001. 218p. pap. 9.95 (*1-84232-842-5*) House of Stratus, Inc. GBR. *Dist:* Midpoint Trade Bks., Inc.

—Criminal Conversation. 1981. (Inspector Van der Valk Suspense Novel Ser.). 213p. pap. 2.50 o.p. (*0-394-74692-9*, V-692) Random Hse., Inc.

—Criminal Convictions: Errant Essays on Perpetrators of Literary License. 1994. 176p. 22.95 (*0-87923-973-5*) Godine, David R. Pub.

—Double - Barrel. 1981. (Inspector Van der Valk Suspense Novel Ser.). 224p. pap. 2.50 o.p. (*0-394-74693-7*, V-693) Random Hse., Inc.

—Double - Barrel. 1975. 208p. pap. 1.95 o.p. (*0-14-002585-5*, Penguin Bks.) Viking Penguin.

—Gun Before Butter. 2001. 216p. pap. 9.95 (*1-84232-838-7*) House of Stratus, Inc. GBR. *Dist:* Midpoint Trade Bks., Inc.

—The King of the Rainy Country. 2001. 167p. pap. 9.95 (*1-84232-843-3*) House of Stratus, Inc. GBR. *Dist:* Midpoint Trade Bks., Inc.

—The King of the Rainy Country. 1975. (Crime Ser.). 160p. pap. 3.95 o.p. (*0-14-002853-6*, Penguin Bks.) Viking Penguin.

—Love in Amsterdam. 1990. 190p. pap. 3.95 o.p. (*0-88184-613-9*, Carroll & Graf Pubs.) Avalon Publishing Group.

—Love in Amsterdam. 2001. 196p. pap. 9.95 (*1-84232-839-5*) House of Stratus, Inc. GBR. *Dist:* Midpoint Trade Bks., Inc.

—Love in Amsterdam. 1975. (Crime Ser.). 192p. pap. 3.95 o.p. (*0-14-002281-3*, Penguin Bks.) Viking Penguin.

—The Lovely Ladies. 1981. (Inspector Van der Valk Suspense Novel Ser.). pap. 3.95 o.p. (*0-394-74694-5*, V-694) Random Hse., Inc.

—The Lovely Ladies. 1989. 288p. pap. 3.95 o.p. (*0-14-011367-3*, Penguin Bks.) Viking Penguin.

—Sand Castles. l.t. ed. 1990. 17.95 o.p. (*0-7451-9898-8*, C0626); pap. 15.95 o.p. (*0-7927-0358-8*, C0820) BBC Audiobooks America.
—Sand Castles. 2001. 210p. pap. 9.95 (*1-84232-864-6*) House of Stratus, Inc. GBR. *Dist:* Midpoint Trade Bks., Inc.
—Sand Castles. 1990. 17.95 (*0-89296-372-7*) Mysterious Pr.
—Sand Castles. 1991. mass mkt. 4.95 o.s.i (*0-445-40925-8*) Warner Bks., Inc.
—Strike Out Where Not Applicable. 2001. 206p. pap. 9.95 (*1-84232-845-X*) House of Stratus, Inc. GBR. *Dist:* Midpoint Trade Bks., Inc.
—Strike Out Where Not Applicable. 1985. (Crime Ser.). 176p. pap. 3.95 o.p. (*0-14-003009-3*, Penguin Bks.) Viking Penguin.
—The Widow. 2001. 280p. pap. 9.95 (*1-84232-850-6*) House of Stratus, Inc. GBR. *Dist:* Midpoint Trade Bks., Inc.
—The Widow. 1980. 256p. pap. 3.95 o.p. (*0-394-74467-5*, Vintage); 1979. 8.95 o.p. (*0-394-50336-8*, Pantheon) Knopf Publishing Group.

**VAN DER VALK, PIET (FICTITIOUS CHARACTER)—FICTION**

Freeling, Nicolas. Arlette. 1982. pap. 2.95 o.p. (*0-394-75260-0*, Pantheon) Knopf Publishing Group.
—Aupres de Ma Blonde. 1979. pap. 2.95 o.p. (*0-394-74550-7*, Vintage) Knopf Publishing Group.
—Because of the Cats. 2000. 190p. pap. (*1-900850-36-2*) Arcadia Bks.
—Because of the Cats. l.t. ed. 1987. pap. 13.95 o.p. (*1-55504-040-3*) BBC Audiobooks America.
—Because of the Cats. 1975. (Crime Ser.). 192p. pap. 3.95 o.p. (*0-14-002282-1*, Penguin Bks.) Viking Penguin.
—Criminal Conversation. 2001. 218p. pap. 9.95 (*1-84232-842-5*) House of Stratus, Inc. GBR. *Dist:* Midpoint Trade Bks., Inc.
—Criminal Conversation. 1981. (Inspector Van der Valk Suspense Novel Ser.). 213p. pap. 2.50 o.p. (*0-394-74692-9*, V-692) Random Hse., Inc.
—Criminal Convictions: Errant Essays on Perpetrators of Literary License. 1994. 176p. 22.95 (*0-87923-973-5*) Godine, David R. Pub.
—Double - Barrel. 1981. (Inspector Van der Valk Suspense Novel Ser.). 224p. pap. 2.50 o.p. (*0-394-74693-7*, V-693) Random Hse., Inc.
—Double - Barrel. 1975. 208p. pap. 1.95 o.p. (*0-14-002585-5*, Penguin Bks.) Viking Penguin.
—Gun Before Butter. 2001. 216p. pap. 9.95 (*1-84232-838-7*) House of Stratus, Inc. GBR. *Dist:* Midpoint Trade Bks., Inc.
—The King of the Rainy Country. 2001. 167p. pap. 9.95 (*1-84232-843-3*) House of Stratus, Inc. GBR. *Dist:* Midpoint Trade Bks., Inc.
—The King of the Rainy Country. 1975. (Crime Ser.). 160p. pap. 3.95 o.p. (*0-14-002853-6*, Penguin Bks.) Viking Penguin.
—Love in Amsterdam. 1990. 190p. pap. 3.95 o.p. (*0-88184-613-9*, Carroll & Graf Pubs.) Avalon Publishing Group.
—Love in Amsterdam. 2001. 196p. pap. 9.95 (*1-84232-839-5*) House of Stratus, Inc. GBR. *Dist:* Midpoint Trade Bks., Inc.
—Love in Amsterdam. 1975. (Crime Ser.). 192p. pap. 3.95 o.p. (*0-14-002281-3*, Penguin Bks.) Viking Penguin.
—The Lovely Ladies. 1981. (Inspector Van der Valk Suspense Novel Ser.). pap. 3.95 o.p. (*0-394-74694-5*, V-694) Random Hse., Inc.
—The Lovely Ladies. 1989. 288p. pap. 3.95 o.p. (*0-14-011367-3*, Penguin Bks.) Viking Penguin.
—Sand Castles. l.t. ed. 1990. 17.95 o.p. (*0-7451-9898-8*, C0626); pap. 15.95 o.p. (*0-7927-0358-8*, C0820) BBC Audiobooks America.
—Sand Castles. 2001. 210p. pap. 9.95 (*1-84232-864-6*) House of Stratus, Inc. GBR. *Dist:* Midpoint Trade Bks., Inc.
—Sand Castles. 1990. 17.95 (*0-89296-372-7*) Mysterious Pr.
—Sand Castles. 1991. mass mkt. 4.95 o.s.i (*0-445-40925-8*) Warner Bks., Inc.
—Strike Out Where Not Applicable. 2001. 206p. pap. 9.95 (*1-84232-845-X*) House of Stratus, Inc. GBR. *Dist:* Midpoint Trade Bks., Inc.
—Strike Out Where Not Applicable. 1985. (Crime Ser.). 176p. pap. 3.95 o.p. (*0-14-003009-3*, Penguin Bks.) Viking Penguin.
—The Widow. 2001. 280p. pap. 9.95 (*1-84232-850-6*) House of Stratus, Inc. GBR. *Dist:* Midpoint Trade Bks., Inc.
—The Widow. 1980. 256p. pap. 3.95 o.p. (*0-394-74467-5*, Vintage); 1979. 8.95 o.p. (*0-394-50336-8*, Pantheon) Knopf Publishing Group.

**VANE, HARRIET (FICTITIOUS CHARACTER)—FICTION**

Paton Walsh, Jill. A Presumption of Death. E-Book 24.95 (*0-312-70987-0*) St. Martin's Pr.
Paton Walsh, Jill & Sayers, Dorothy L. A Presumption of Death. unabr. ed. 2003. (Lord Peter Wimsey Mystery Ser.). audio 29.95 (*1-57270-322-9*); audio compact disk 34.95 (*1-57270-323-7*) Audio Partners Publishing Corp. (Audio Editions Mystery Masters).
—A Presumption of Death. 2003. audio 69.95 (*0-7540-8309-8*); audio compact disk 79.95 (*0-7540-8752-2*) Chivers Audio Bks. GBR. *Dist:* BBC Audiobooks America.
—A Presumption of Death. l.t. ed. 2003. (New Lord Peter Wimsey/Harriet Vane Mystery Ser.). 449p. 28.95 (*0-7862-5561-7*) Thorndike Pr.
Sayers, Dorothy L. Busman's Honeymoon. unabr. ed. 2002. audio 34.95 (*1-57270-317-2*) Audio Partners Publishing Corp.
—Busman's Honeymoon. l.t. ed. (Lord Peter Wimsey Mystery Ser.). 1993. pap. 17.95 o.p. (*0-7927-1366-4*); 1992. 21.95 o.p. (*0-7927-1367-2*) BBC Audiobooks America.
—Busman's Honeymoon. unabr. ed. 2000. (Lord Peter Wimsey Mysteries Ser.: Bk. 13). audio 69.95 (*0-7451-4313-X*, CAB 996) Chivers Audio Bks. GBR. *Dist:* BBC Audiobooks America.
—Busman's Honeymoon. 1981. (Lord Peter Wimsey Mystery Ser.). lib. bdg. 16.95 o.p. (*0-8161-3041-8*, Macmillan Reference USA) Gale Group.
—Busman's Honeymoon. 1960. (Lord Peter Wimsey Mystery Ser.). 12.95 o.p. (*0-06-013765-7*) HarperCollins Pubs.
—Busman's Honeymoon. (Lord Peter Wimsey Mystery Ser.). 1986. 17.95 o.p. (*0-06-055021-X*); 1986. pap. 6.00 o.p. (*0-06-080823-3*, Perennial); 1993. 400p. reprint ed. pap. 8.00 o.p. (*0-06-092393-8*, Perennial) HarperTrade.
—Busman's Honeymoon. (Lord Peter Wimsey Mystery Ser.). 1995. 416p. mass mkt. 6.99 (*0-06-104351-6*, HarperTorch); 1978. pap. 2.75 o.p. (*0-380-01076-3*, 62489-3, Avon Bks.) Morrow/Avon.
—Gaudy Night. unabr. ed. 1993. (Lord Peter Wimsey Mysteries Ser.: Bk. 12). audio 79.95 (*0-7451-4106-4*, CAB 789) Chivers Audio Bks. GBR. *Dist:* BBC Audiobooks America.
—Gaudy Night. abr. ed. 1996. (Lord Peter Wimsey Mystery Ser.). audio 16.99 (*0-88646-284-3*, 7284) Durkin Hayes Publishing Ltd.
—Gaudy Night. l.t. ed. 1981. (Lord Peter Wimsey Mystery Ser.). lib. bdg. 18.95 o.p. (*0-8161-3040-X*, Macmillan Reference USA) Gale Group.
—Gaudy Night. (Lord Peter Wimsey Mystery Ser.). 1986. 17.95 o.p. (*0-06-055022-8*); 1986. pap. 6.50 o.p. (*0-06-080824-1*); 1993. 480p. reprint ed. pap. 9.00 o.p. (*0-06-092392-X*, Perennial); 1987. 464p. reprint ed. pap. 5.50 o.p. (*0-06-080907-8*, P-907, Perennial) HarperTrade.
—Gaudy Night. (Lord Peter Wimsey Mystery Ser.). 1995. 512p. mass mkt. 6.99 (*0-06-104349-4*, HarperTorch); 1976. pap. 3.50 o.p. (*0-380-01207-3*, 65037, Avon Bks.) Morrow/Avon.
—A Presumption of Death. Date not set. mass mkt. (*0-312-99138-X*, St. Martin's Paperbacks) St. Martin's Pr.
Sayers, Dorothy L. & Paton Walsh, Jill. A Presumption of Death. 2003. (Lord Peter Wimsey Mystery Ser.). 384p. 24.95 (*0-312-29100-0*, Saint Martin's Minotaur) St. Martin's Pr.
—Thrones, Dominations. unabr. ed. 2001. (Lord Peter Wimsey Mystery Ser.). audio 34.95 (*1-57270-129-3*, N81129u, Audio Editions Mystery Masters) Audio Partners Publishing Corp.
—Thrones, Dominations. unabr. ed. 1998. (Lord Peter Wimsey Mysteries Ser.: Bk. 15). audio 59.95 (*0-7540-0203-9*, CAB 1626) Chivers Audio Bks. GBR. *Dist:* BBC Audiobooks America.
Sayers, Dorothy L. & Walsh, J. P. Thrones, Dominations. unabr. collector's ed. 1999. (Lord Peter Wimsey Mystery Ser.). audio 56.00 (*0-7366-4299-4*, 4791) Books on Tape, Inc.
Sayers, Dorothy L., et al. Thrones, Dominations. 1999. 322p. mass mkt. 6.50 (*0-312-96830-2*, St. Martin's Paperbacks); 1998. 312p. (gr. 5-6). 23.95 o.p. (*0-312-18196-5*, Saint Martin's Minotaur) St. Martin's Pr.
—Thrones, Dominations. l.t. ed. 1998. (Lord Peter Wimsey Mystery Ser.). 439p. 29.95 (*0-7838-8438-9*) Thorndike Pr.

**VAN VOREEN, LEIGH (FICTITIOUS CHARACTER)—FICTION**

Andrews, V. C. Web of Dreams. unabr. ed. 1991. audio 80.00 (*0-7366-1908-9*, 2734) Books on Tape, Inc.
—Web of Dreams. l.t. ed. 1991. (General Ser.). 581p. pap. 17.95 (*0-8161-5039-7*); lib. bdg. 20.95 o.p. (*0-8161-5038-9*) Gale Group. (Macmillan Reference USA).
—Web of Dreams. Marrow, Linda, ed. 1990. (Casteel Saga Ser.). 432p. mass mkt. 7.99 (*0-671-72949-7*, Pocket) Simon & Schuster.
—Web of Dreams. 1990. 19.95 o.p. (*0-671-70057-X*, Atria) Simon & Schuster.
—Web of Dreams. 1990. (Casteel Saga Ser.). (J). 14.04 (*0-606-04418-3*) Turtleback Bks.

**VAN WINKLE, RIP (FICTITIOUS CHARACTER)—FICTION**

Irving, Washington. Rip Van Winkle. 1976. 17.95 (*0-8488-1382-0*) Amereon, Ltd.
—Rip Van Winkle. 2002. (Read-Along Radio Dramas Ser.). ring bd. 38.00 (*1-878298-38-0*) Balance Publishing Co.
—Rip Van Winkle. l.t. ed. 2000. (Illus.). 110p. text 14.95 (*1-883789-40-0*) Black Dome Pr. Corp.
—Rip Van Winkle. 1983. 73p. reprint ed. lib. bdg. 16.95 (*0-89966-411-3*) Buccaneer Bks., Inc.
—Rip Van Winkle & Other Selected Stories. 1993. 209p. pap. text 2.99 (*0-8125-2332-6*, Tor Classics) Doherty, Tom Assocs., LLC.
—Rip Van Winkle & Other Stories. 2001. per. 9.90 (*1-891355-92-9*) Blue Unicorn Editions.
—Rip Van Winkle & Other Stories. unabr. collector's ed. 1993. (YA). audio 30.00 (*0-7366-2352-3*, 3129) Books on Tape, Inc.
—Rip Van Winkle & Other Stories. 1994. mass mkt. 2.50 (*1-55902-909-9*); 1993. mass mkt. 2.50 (*1-55902-901-3*) Doherty, Tom Assocs., LLC. (Aerie).
—Rip Van Winkle & Other Stories. l.t. ed. 2001. (G. K. Hall Perennial Bestsellers Ser. ). 280p. 27.95 (*0-7838-9376-0*) Thorndike Pr.
—Rip Van Winkle & the Legend of Sleepy Hollow. 2002. pap. 3.95 (*1-59109-079-2*) Booksurge, LLC.
—Rip Van Winkle & the Legend of Sleepy Hollow. 2002. pap. text 5.95 (*0-19-424337-0*) Oxford Univ. Pr., Inc.
—Rip Van Winkle & the Legend of Sleepy Hollow. 1995. 96p. pap. 0.95 o.p. (*0-14-600071-4*) Penguin Group (USA) Inc.
—Rip Van Winkle & the Legend of Sleepy Hollow. 1987. (Radiobook Ser.). audio 4.98 (*0-929541-25-1*) Radiola Co.
—Rip Van Winkle & the Legend of Sleepy Hollow. (Illus.). 152p. 1974. (J). 9.95 o.p. (*0-912882-09-3*); 2nd ed. 1980. 19.95 (*0-912882-42-5*) Sleepy Hollow Pr.
—Rip Van Winkle & the Legend of Sleepy Hollow. 1980. (Facsimile Classics Ser.). xi, 218 p. o.p. (*0-8317-7410-X*) Smithmark Pubs., Inc.
—Rip Van Winkle & the Legend of Sleepy Hollow. 1998. (Children's Library). (J). pap. 3.95 (*1-85326-169-6*, 1696WW) Wordsworth Editions, Ltd. GBR. *Dist:* Casemate Pubs. & Bk. Distributors, LLC.

**VAN ZAND, PETER (FICTITIOUS CHARACTER)—FICTION**

Goshgarian, Gary. Stone Circle. 1997. 296p. 24.95 o.p. (*1-55611-533-4*) Fine, Donald I. Bks.

**VAN ZANDT, MAGGIE (FICTITIOUS CHARACTER)—FICTION**

Gross, Ken. Full Blown Rage. (Maggie Van Zandt Novels Ser.). 288p. 1996. mass mkt. 5.99 (*0-8125-5024-2*); 1995. 21.00 o.p. (*0-312-85757-8*) Doherty, Tom Assocs., LLC. (Forge Bks.).

**VARADAY, FRAN (FICTITIOUS CHARACTER)—FICTION**

Granger, Ann. Asking for Trouble. l.t. ed. 1998. (General Ser.). 360p. pap. 24.95 (*0-7862-1394-9*) Thorndike Pr.

**VARNEY, HALLY (FICTITIOUS CHARACTER)—FICTION**

Jamison, Ellen. Stone Dead. 1993. 352p. mass mkt. 4.50 o.s.i (*0-8217-4265-5*, Zebra Bks.) Kensington Publishing Corp.

**VAUGHAN (FICTITIOUS CHARACTER: O'DONOHOE)—FICTION**

O'Donohoe, Nick. The Healing of Crossroads. 1996. 336p. mass mkt. 5.99 o.s.i (*0-441-00391-5*) Ace Bks.
—The Magic & the Healing. 1994. 352p. (Orig.). mass mkt. 4.99 o.s.i (*0-441-00053-3*) Ace Bks.
—Under the Healing Sun. 1995. 352p. (Orig.). mass mkt. 4.99 o.s.i (*0-441-00180-7*) Ace Bks.

**VAUGHAN, ROBIN (FICTITIOUS CHARACTER)—FICTION**

Banks, Carolyn. Death by Dressage. 1993. mass mkt. 5.50 o.s.i (*0-449-14843-2*, Fawcett) Ballantine Bks.
—Death on the Diagonal. 1996. mass mkt. 4.99 o.s.i (*0-449-14968-4*, Fawcett) Ballantine Bks.
—Groomed for Death. 1994. 192p. mass mkt. 6.50 o.s.i (*0-449-14913-7*, Fawcett) Ballantine Bks.
—A Horse to Die For. 1996. 182p. mass mkt. 5.50 o.s.i (*0-449-14969-2*, Fawcett) Ballantine Bks.
—Murder Well-Bred. 1995. mass mkt. 5.50 o.s.i (*0-449-14914-5*, Fawcett) Ballantine Bks.

**VENTANA, RONNIE (FICTITIOUS CHARACTER)—FICTION**

White, Gloria. Charged with Guilt. 1995. 336p. mass mkt. 5.50 o.s.i (*0-440-22049-1*) Dell Publishing.
—Money to Burn. 1993. 320p. mass mkt. 4.99 o.s.i (*0-440-21612-5*, Dell Bks.) Dell Publishing.
—Money to Burn. unabr. ed. 1993. (Ronnie Ventana Mystery Ser.). audio 36.00 (*0-9624010-6-4*, 752466) Reader's Chair, Inc., The.
—Murder on the Run. 1991. 288p. mass mkt. 5.50 o.s.i (*0-440-20983-8*) Dell Publishing.
—Murder on the Run. unabr. ed. 1993. (Ronnie Ventana Mystery Ser.). audio 30.00 (*0-9624010-4-8*) Reader's Chair, Inc., The.
—Murder on the Run. 1992. 304p. 20.00 o.p. (*0-7278-4317-6*) Severn Hse. Pubs., Ltd.
—Sunset & Santiago. 1997. 320p. mass mkt. 5.50 o.s.i (*0-440-22326-1*) Dell Publishing.

**VENTURA, ACE (FICTITIOUS CHARACTER)—FICTION**

Cerasini, Marc. Ace Ventura 2: When Nature Calls. 1995. 128p. pap. 3.99 o.s.i (*0-679-87497-6*); (Illus.). pap. 3.99 o.s.i (*0-679-87870-X*) Random Hse., Inc.
Oedekerk, Steve. Ace Ventura: When Nature Calls. 1996. pap. 4.99 (*0-590-74151-9*) Scholastic, Inc.
Random House Staff. Ace Ventura: Pet Detective Activity Book. 1995. pap. 35.28 o.s.i (*0-679-87605-7*) Random Hse., Inc.

**VERDEAN, GILLIAN (FICTITIOUS CHARACTER)—FICTION**

Gibbs, Tony. Dead Run. 1989. mass mkt. 3.50 o.s.i (*0-8041-0420-4*, Ivy Bks.) Ballantine Bks.
—Landfall: A Novel. 1992. 256p. 20.00 o.p. (*0-688-11102-5*, Morrow, William & Co.) Morrow/Avon.
—Running Fix. 1990. 18.95 o.s.i (*0-394-57580-6*) Random Hse., Inc.

**VERDI, KATE (FICTITIOUS CHARACTER)—FICTION**

Kimball, Stephen. Death Duty. 1996. 320p. 24.95 o.s.i (*0-525-94230-0*) Dutton/Plume.
—Death Duty. 1998. 400p. mass mkt. 5.99 o.s.i (*0-451-19107-2*, Signet Bks.) NAL.

**VERGIL MAGUS (FICTITIOUS CHARACTER)—FICTION**

Davidson, Avram. The Phoenix & the Mirror. 1983. 288p. mass mkt. 2.50 o.s.i (*0-441-66156-4*) Ace Bks.

**VERINDER, RACHEL (FICTITIOUS CHARACTER)—FICTION**

Collins, Wilkie. The Moonstone. (World Digital Library). 2002. E-Book 3.95 (*0-594-08173-4*); 2000. 252p. E-Book 9.95 (*0-594-04118-X*) 1873 Pr.
—The Moonstone. 1965. (Airmont Classics Ser.). (gr. 10 up). mass mkt. 2.95 o.p. (*0-8049-0076-0*, CL-76) Airmont Publishing Co., Inc.
—The Moonstone. 1976. reprint ed. lib. bdg. 29.95 (*0-89190-241-4*, Rivercity Pr.) Amereon, Ltd.
—The Moonstone. unabr. ed. 1998. audio 71.95 (*1-55685-553-2*) Audio Bk. Contractors, Inc.
—The Moonstone. unabr. ed. audio 104.95 o.p. (*1-85549-919-3*, CTC 052) BBC Audiobooks America.
—The Moonstone. 1982. 464p. mass mkt. 4.50 o.s.i (*0-553-21156-0*, Bantam Classics) Bantam Bks.
—The Moonstone. unabr. ed. 1986. Pt. 1. audio 56.95 (*0-7861-0553-4*, 2047-A); Pt. 2. audio 49.95 (*0-7861-0554-2*, 2047-B) Blackstone Audio Bks., Inc.
—The Moonstone, Pt. 1. unabr. collector's ed. 1984. audio 64.00 (*0-7366-3896-2*, 9127-A) Books on Tape, Inc.
—The Moonstone. Farmer, Steve, ed. 1999. 720p. pap. (*1-55111-243-4*) Broadview Pr.
—The Moonstone. 1990. reprint ed. lib. bdg. 25.95 (*0-89968-498-X*) Buccaneer Bks., Inc.
—The Moonstone. 1999. (Works of Wilkie Collins: Vol. 7). reprint ed. 602p. lib. bdg. 98.00 (*1-58201-028-5*);Pt. 1. 580p. lib. bdg. 98.00 (*1-58201-027-7*) Classic Bks.
—The Moonstone. 1988. audio 87.95 Cover to Cover Cassettes, Ltd.
—The Moonstone. 2002. (Thrift Editions Ser.). 400p. pap. 3.50 (*0-486-42451-0*) Dover Pubns., Inc.
—The Moonstone. 1972. 5.95 o.p. (*0-460-01979-1*, Dutton) Dutton/Plume.
—The Moonstone. abr. ed. 10.00 o.p. (*0-06-010820-7*) HarperCollins Pubs.
—The Moonstone. l.t. ed. 1992. (Isis Large Print Bks.). 605p. 27.95 (*1-85089-543-0*) ISIS Large Print Bks. GBR. *Dist:* Transaction Pubs., Ulverscroft Large Print Canada, Ltd.
—The Moonstone. 2002. 528p. 23.99 (*1-4043-1934-4*); per. 18.99 (*1-4043-1935-2*) IndyPublish.com.
—The Moonstone. 1989. audio 89.00 Jimcin Recordings.
—The Moonstone. 1992. (Everyman's Library: Vol. 122). 480p. 17.00 (*0-679-41722-2*) Knopf, Alfred A. Inc.
—The Moonstone, Level 6. 2000. pap. 7.66 (*0-582-41822-4*) Longman Publishing Group.
—The Moonstone. 2002. 512p. mass mkt. 6.95 (*0-451-52829-8*); 1984. mass mkt. 3.25 o.p. (*0-451-52031-9*, Signet Classics); 1984. mass mkt. 3.50 o.p. (*0-451-52167-6*); 1984. mass mkt. 2.95 o.p. (*0-451-51837-3*, Signet Classics); 1984. 480p. mass mkt. 6.95 o.s.i (*0-451-52394-6*, Signet Classics) NAL.

—The Moonstone. abr. ed. 1995. audio 17.98 (*962-634-527-6*, NA302714); audio compact disk 19.98 (*962-634-027-4*, NA302712) Naxos of America, Inc. (Naxos AudioBooks).
—The Moonstone. 1998. 570p. reprint ed. lib. bdg. 25.00 (*1-58287-094-2*) North Bks.
—The Moonstone. 1999. (Oxford World's Classics Ser.). 576p. 16.50 o.p. (*0-19-210028-9*) Oxford Univ. Pr., Inc.
—The Moonstone. Trodd, Anthea, ed. & intro. by. 1998. (Oxford World's Classics Ser.). 572p. pap. 6.95 o.p. (*0-19-283471-1*) Oxford Univ. Pr., Inc.
—The Moonstone. Trodd, Anthea, ed. 1982. (Oxford World's Classics Ser.). 572p. pap. 6.95 o.p. (*0-19-281579-2*) Oxford Univ. Pr., Inc.
—The Moonstone. Sutherland, John, ed. 2nd ed. 2000. (Oxford World's Classics Ser.). 560p. pap. 6.95 (*0-19-283338-3*) Oxford Univ. Pr., Inc.
—The Moonstone. 1987. (Regents Illustrated Classics Ser.). 62p. (gr. 7-12). pap. text o.p. (*0-13-600677-9*, 20420) Prentice Hall, ESL Dept.
—The Moonstone. 2001. (Modern Library Classics). 528p. pap. 6.95 (*0-375-75785-6*, Modern Library) Random House Adult Trade Publishing Group.
—The Moonstone. 2002. (Best Mysteries of All Time Ser.). 557p. (*0-7621-8873-1*, IM Pr.) Reader's Digest Assn., Inc., The.
—The Moonstone. unabr. ed. 1989. audio 112.00 (*1-55690-348-0*, 89300E7) Recorded Bks., LLC.
—The Moonstone. E-Book 5.00 (*0-7410-1426-2*) SoftBook Pr.
—The Moonstone. 1984. 13.00 (*0-606-01905-7*) Turtleback Bks.
—The Moonstone. 1999. (Penguin Classics Ser.). 528p. 8.00 (*0-14-043408-9*) Viking Penguin.
—The Moonstone. Stewart, J. I., ed. & intro. by. 1966. (Penguin Classics Ser.). 528p. pap. 6.95 o.s.i (*0-14-043014-8*, Penguin Classics) Viking Penguin.
—The Moonstone. abr. ed. 1995. (Classics on Audio Ser.). 4p. pap. 23.95 o.s.i incl. audio (*0-14-086089-4*); pap. 23.95 o.s.i incl. audio (*0-14-086089-4*) Viking Penguin. (Penguin AudioBooks).
—The Moonstone. 2002. 436p. 39.95 (*1-59224-786-5*) Wildside Pr.
—The Moonstone. 1997. (Classics Ser.). 464p. pap. 3.95 (*1-85326-044-4*, 0444WW) Wordsworth Editions, Ltd. GBR. *Dist:* Combined Publishing.
Collins, Wilkie & Farmer, Steve. The Moonstone. 1999. E-Book 9.95 (*0-585-27957-8*) netLibrary, Inc.
Collins, Wilkie & Sutherland, John. The Moonstone. 1999. E-Book 7.30 (*0-585-36165-7*) netLibrary, Inc.

**VERMEILLE, CHARLES (FICTITIOUS CHARACTER)—FICTION**

Fiechter, J. J. A Masterpiece of Revenge: A Novel. 1998. 192p. 21.95 (*1-55970-430-6*) Arcade Publishing, Inc.

**VERNET, VICTOIRE, MME. (FICTITIOUS CHARACTER)—FICTION**

Fawcett, Quinn. Death Wears a Crown: A Mme. Vernet Investigation. 1993. 224p. (Orig.). mass mkt. 4.99 (*0-380-76542-X*, Avon Bks.) Morrow/Avon.
—Napoleon Must Die: A Mme. Vernet Investigation. 1993. 256p. (Orig.). mass mkt. 4.99 (*0-380-76541-1*, Avon Bks.) Morrow/Avon.

**VERNON, ANNE (FICTITIOUS CHARACTER)—FICTION**

Scholefield, Alan. Burn Out. 1995. 346p. 22.95 o.p. (*0-312-13035-X*, Saint Martin's Minotaur) St. Martin's Pr.

**VICENTE, ROSIE (FICTITIOUS CHARACTER)—FICTION**

Singer, Shelley. Free Draw: A Jake Samson Mystery. 1984. 192p. 12.95 o.p. (*0-312-30366-1*) St. Martin's Pr.
—Full House. 1988. (Jake Samson/Rosie Vicente Series). 224p. reprint ed. mass mkt. (*0-373-26007-5*, Harlequin Bks.) Harlequin Enterprises, Ltd.
—Full House: A Jake Samson Mystery. 1986. 208p. 13.95 o.p. (*0-312-30973-2*, 39-1127) St. Martin's Pr.
—Royal Flush: A Jake Samson & Rosie Vicente Mystery. 1999. 237p. pap. 12.95 (*1-880284-33-2*) Daniel, John & Co., Pubs.
—Spit in the Ocean: A Jake Samson Mystery. 1987. 208p. 14.95 o.p. (*0-312-00685-3*, Saint Martin's Minotaur) St. Martin's Pr.
—Suicide King. 1989. per. (*0-373-26040-7*, Harlequin Bks.) Harlequin Enterprises, Ltd.
—Suicide King. 1988. 224p. 15.95 o.p. (*0-312-02293-X*, Saint Martin's Minotaur) St. Martin's Pr.

**VICKERS, LISSA (FICTITIOUS CHARACTER)—FICTION**

Little, Constance & Little, Gwenyth. The Black Gloves. Schantz, Tom & Schantz, Enid, eds. 1998. (Classic Mystery Ser.). 192p. reprint ed. pap. 14.00 (*0-915230-20-8*) Rue Morgue Pr.

**VICKERY, FRED (FICTITIOUS CHARACTER)—FICTION**

Lewis, Sherry. No Place for Death. 1996. 256p. mass mkt. 5.99 o.s.i (*0-425-15383-5*, Prime Crime) Berkley Publishing Group.
—No Place for Secrets. 1995. 256p. (Orig.). mass mkt. 4.99 o.s.i (*0-425-14835-1*, Prime Crime) Berkley Publishing Group.
—No Place for Sin. 1997. (Fred Vickery Novel Ser.). 256p. mass mkt. 5.99 o.s.i (*0-425-16113-7*, Prime Crime) Berkley Publishing Group.
—No Place for Tears. 1997. (Senior Sleuth Fred Vickery Ser.). 256p. (Orig.). mass mkt. 5.99 o.s.i (*0-425-15626-5*, Prime Crime) Berkley Publishing Group.
—No Place Like Home. 1996. 256p. (Orig.). mass mkt. 5.50 o.s.i (*0-425-15185-9*) Berkley Publishing Group.

**VICTOR, EMMA (FICTITIOUS CHARACTER)—FICTION**

Wings, Mary. She Came by the Book. (Mistery Ser.). 272p. 1996. 21.95 o.p. (*0-425-15147-6*, Prime Crime); 1996. pap. 10.00 o.p. (*0-425-15144-1*); 1997. reprint ed. mass mkt. 5.99 o.s.i (*0-425-15697-4*, Prime Crime) Berkley Publishing Group.
—She Came in a Flash. 2001. (Emma Victor Mystery Ser.: Vol. 2). 234p. pap. 11.95 o.p. (*1-55583-548-1*) Alyson Pubns.
—She Came in a Flash. 1990. 24p. pap. 10.00 o.p. (*0-452-26384-0*, Plume) Dutton/Plume.
—She Came in a Flash. 1989. 208p. 17.95 o.p. (*0-453-00648-5*) NAL.
—She Came in Drag. 1999. (Emma Victor Mysteries Ser.). 352p. mass mkt. 6.50 o.s.i (*0-425-16935-9*) Berkley Publishing Group.
—She Came to the Castro. (Emma Victor Mysteries Ser.). 272p. 1998. mass mkt. 5.99 o.s.i (*0-425-16222-2*); 1997. 21.95 o.s.i (*0-425-15629-X*) Berkley Publishing Group. (Prime Crime).
—She Came Too Late. 1987. (WomanSleuth Mystery Ser.). 208p. reprint ed. 20.95 o.p. (*0-89594-244-5*); pap. 7.95 o.p. (*0-89594-243-7*) Crossing Pr., Inc., The.
—She Came Too Late: An Emma Victor Mystery. 2000. (Emma Victor Mysteries Ser.: No. 1). 263p. reprint ed. pap. 10.95 o.p. (*1-55583-547-3*, Alyson Bks.) Alyson Pubns.

**VICTORIA, QUEEN OF GREAT BRITAIN, 1819-1901—FICTION**

Anthony, Evelyn. Victoria. l.t. ed. 1994. pap. 20.95 o.p. (*0-7927-1606-X*); 1993. 22.95 o.p. (*0-7927-1607-8*) BBC Audiobooks America.
Continental Historical Society Staff. Queen Victoria's "Alice in Wonderland" 2nd ed. Orig. Title: Queen Victoria's Secret Diaries. (Illus.). 1990. (Queen Victoria's Secret Diaries Ser.: Vol. 1). 476p. (C). pap. text 16.95 (*0-9609900-3-8*); 1984. 290p. pap. 9.95 (*0-9609900-1-1*) Continental Historical Society.
Harrod-Eagles, Cynthia. I, Victoria. 1995. 432p. 24.95 o.p. (*0-312-13516-5*) St. Martin's Pr.
Plaidy, Jean. Victoria in the Wings. 1992. reprint ed. mass mkt. 4.99 o.s.i (*0-449-22025-7*, Fawcett) Ballantine Bks.
—Victoria in the Wings. 1990. 352p. 19.95 o.p. (*0-399-13539-1*, G. P. Putnam's Sons) Penguin Putnam Bks. for Young Readers.
—Victoria in the Wings. l.t. ed. 1974. (Shadows of the Crown Ser.). 29.99 o.p. (*0-85456-598-1*, Ulverscroft) Thorpe, F. A. Pubs. GBR. *Dist:* Ulverscroft Large Print Bks., Ltd., Ulverscroft Large Print Canada, Ltd.
—Victoria Victorious. 1987. 560p. reprint ed. mass mkt. 4.95 o.s.i (*0-449-21251-3*, Fawcett) Ballantine Bks.
—Victoria Victorious. 1986. 560p. 17.95 o.p. (*0-399-13102-7*) Putnam Publishing Group, The.

**VIERLING, FRANCESCA (FICTITIOUS CHARACTER)—FICTION**

Viets, Elaine. Back Stab: A Francesca Vierling Mystery. 1997. (Francesca Vierling Mystery Ser.). 320p. mass mkt. 5.99 o.s.i (*0-440-22431-4*) Dell Publishing.
—Doc in the Box: A Francesca Vierling Mystery. 2000. (Francesca Vierling Mystery Ser.). 256p. mass mkt. 5.99 o.s.i (*0-440-23620-7*) Bantam Dell Publishing Group.
—The Pink Flamingo Murders: A Francesca Vierling Mystery. 1999. 272p. mass mkt. 5.99 o.s.i (*0-440-22445-4*) Dell Publishing.
—The Pink Flamingo Murders: A Francesca Vierling Mystery. 1999. 272p. pap. 19.00 (*0-440-61351-5*) Random Hse., Inc.
—Rubout: A Francesca Vierling Mystery. 1998. (Francesca Vierling Mystery Ser.). 320p. mass mkt. 5.99 o.s.i (*0-440-22444-6*) Dell Publishing.
—Rubout: A Francesca Vierling Mystery. 1998. 320p. pap. 19.00 (*0-440-61348-5*) Random Hse., Inc.

**VIRDON, MERCY (FICTITIOUS CHARACTER)—FICTION**

Weber, Ronald. The Aluminum Hatch: A Michigan Mystery. 1999. (WWL Mystery Ser.: Vol. 324). 256p. pap. (*0-373-26324-4*, Worldwide Library) Harlequin Enterprises, Ltd.
—The Aluminum Hatch: A Michigan Mystery. 1998. 216p. 19.95 o.p. (*1-885173-48-2*) Write Way Publishing.
—Catch & Keep. 2000. 248p. 23.95 (*1-885173-25-3*) Write Way Publishing.

**VOLGER, DEENA (FICTITIOUS CHARACTER)—FICTION**

Krich, Rochelle Majer. Till Death Do Us Part. 1992. 304p. mass mkt. 4.99 (*0-380-76533-0*, Avon Bks.) Morrow/Avon.

**VOINOV, TOLEA (FICTITIOUS CHARACTER)—FICTION**

Manea, Norman. The Black Envelope. 2004. Tr. of Plicul Negru. pap. (*0-374-52947-7*) Farrar, Straus & Giroux.
—The Black Envelope. Camiller, Patrick, tr. 1995. Tr. of Plicul Negru. (ENG & RUM.). 336p. 25.00 o.p. (*0-374-11397-1*) Farrar, Straus & Giroux.
—The Black Envelope. Camiller, Patrick, tr. 1996. Tr. of Plicul Negru. 329p. pap. 16.95 (*0-8101-1377-5*, Hydra Bks.) Northwestern Univ. Pr.

**VON REISDEN, ALEXANDER, BARON (FICTITIOUS CHARACTER)—FICTION**

Smith, Sarah. The Vanished Child. 1997. 432p. pap. 23.00 (*0-345-41805-0*); 1996. mass mkt. 5.99 (*0-345-90947-X*); 1993. 304p. mass mkt. 7.50 (*0-345-38164-5*) Ballantine Bks.

**VOORT, CONRAD (FICTITIOUS CHARACTER)—FICTION**

Black, Ethan. All the Dead Were Strangers. 2001. 464p. 24.00 (*0-345-43900-7*, Ballantine Bks.) Ballantine Bks.
—All the Dead Were Strangers. l.t. ed. 2002. (Americana Ser.). 648p. 30.95 (*0-7862-3766-X*) Gale Group.
—All the Dead Were Strangers. 2003. (Illus.). 480p. mass mkt. 7.50 (*0-7434-7104-0*, Pocket) Simon & Schuster.
—Dead for Life. 2003. 320p. 24.00 (*0-7432-4400-1*, Simon & Schuster) Simon & Schuster.
—Irresistible. 2001. 384p. mass mkt. 6.99 (*0-345-43348-3*, Ballantine Bks.) Ballantine Bks.
—Irresistible. 2000. audio 25.00 (*0-7871-2358-7*, Dove Audio) NewStar Media, Inc.

**VORKOSIGAN, MILES (FICTITIOUS CHARACTER)—FICTION**

Bujold, Lois McMaster. Barrayar. 1991. 400p. per. 5.99 (*0-671-72083-X*) Baen Bks.
—Barrayar. unabr. ed. 1997. (Vorkosigan Ser.: Vol. 2). audio 54.00 (*1-885585-01-2*) Reader's Chair, Inc., The.
—Borders of Infinity. 320p. 1999. mass mkt. 1.99 (*0-671-57829-4*); 1989. pap. 3.95 o.s.i (*0-671-69841-9*); 1991. reprint ed. pap. 6.99 (*0-671-72093-7*) Baen Bks.
—Borders of Infinity: 3 Miles Vorkosigan Adventures. unabr. ed. 2000. audio 54.00 (*1-885585-06-3*, 90017) Reader's Chair, Inc., The.
—Brothers in Arms. 2001. 352p. pap. 5.99 (*0-671-69799-4*) Baen Bks.
—Cetaganda. 1996. 352p. mass mkt. 7.99 (*0-671-87744-5*); 1995. 320p. 21.00 (*0-671-87701-1*) Baen Bks.
—Cetaganda. unabr. ed. 1999. (Vorkosigan Ser.: Vol. 5). audio 48.00 (*1-885585-04-7*) Reader's Chair, Inc., The.
—Cetaganda. 1996. 12.04 (*0-606-17118-5*) Turtleback Bks.
—Cordelia's Honor. (Hugo Winners Ser.). 1999. 608p. mass mkt. 7.99 (*0-671-57828-6*); 1996. 496p. pap. 15.00 (*0-671-87749-6*) Baen Bks.
—Diplomatic Immunity. 2003. 384p. pap. 7.99 (*0-7434-3612-1*) Baen Bks.
—Ethan of Athos. 2002. 256p. reprint ed. pap. 5.99 (*0-671-65604-X*) Baen Bks.
—Ethan of Athos. Lewis, Suford, ed. 2003. 23.00 (*1-886778-39-6*) New England Science Fiction Assn., Inc.
—Falling Free. 1999. (Nebula Award Stories Ser.). 320p. reprint ed. pap. 6.99 (*0-671-57812-X*) Baen Bks.
—Komarr. 1999. (Miles Vorkosigan Adventure Ser.). 384p. reprint ed. pap. 6.99 (*0-671-57808-1*) Baen Bks.
—Komarr: A Miles Vorkosigan Adventure. 1998. (Miles Vorkosigan Adventure Ser.). 320p. 22.00 (*0-671-87877-8*) Baen Bks.
—Memory. (Miles Vorkosigan Adventure Ser.). 480p. 1997. mass mkt. 7.99 (*0-671-87845-X*); 1996. 22.00 (*0-671-87743-7*) Baen Bks.
—Mirror Dance. 1995. 592p. pap. 7.99 (*0-671-87646-5*); 1994. 400p. 21.00 o.s.i (*0-671-72210-7*) Baen Bks.
—Shards of Honor. 1991. mass mkt. 5.99 o.s.i (*0-671-72087-2*); 1986. pap. 2.95 o.s.i (*0-671-65574-4*) Baen Bks.
—Shards of Honor. unabr. ed. 1996. (Vorkosigan Ser.: Vol. 1). audio 42.00 (*1-885585-00-4*) Reader's Chair, Inc., The.
—The Vor Game. 2002. 352p. reprint ed. pap. 6.99 (*0-671-72014-7*) Baen Bks.
—The Vor Game. unabr. ed. 1998. (Vorkosigan Ser.: Vol. 4). audio 54.00 (*1-885585-03-9*) Reader's Chair, Inc., The.
—The Warrior's Apprentice. 1991. 320p. mass mkt. 6.99 (*0-671-72066-X*) Baen Bks.
—The Warrior's Apprentice. unabr. ed. 1997. (Vorkosigan Ser.: Vol. 3). audio 54.00 (*1-885585-02-0*) Reader's Chair, Inc., The.
—Young Miles. 592p. 2002. pap. 17.00 (*0-671-87782-8*); 1997. bds. 22.00 o.s.i (*0-671-87787-9*) Baen Bks.
Bujold, Lois McMaster & Baen, James P. Young Miles. 2003. (Illus.). 848p. mass mkt. 7.99 (*0-7434-3616-4*) Baen Bks.

**VOUTE, J. M. (FICTITIOUS CHARACTER)—FICTION**

Elsink, Henk. Murder by Fax. 1992. 241p. pap. 7.95 (*1-881164-52-7*) Intercontinental Publishing, Inc.

**VRYCE, DAMIEN (FICTITIOUS CHARACTER)—FICTION**

Friedman, C. S. Black Sun Rising. (Daw Book Collectors Ser.: Bk. I). 1992. 592p. mass mkt. 7.99 (*0-88677-527-2*); 1991. 496p. 18.95 o.p. (*0-88677-485-3*) DAW Bks., Inc.
—Crown of Shadows. 1996. (Daw Book Collectors Ser.: 3). 528p. mass mkt. 7.99 (*0-88677-717-8*) DAW Bks., Inc.
—Crown of Shadows: The Final Volume of the Coldfire Trilogy. 1995. (Coldfire Trilogy Ser.: Vol. 3). 448p. 21.95 o.p. (*0-88677-664-3*) DAW Bks., Inc.
—When True Night Falls. (Coldfire Trilogy Ser.: Bk. II). 1993. 592p. 22.00 o.p. (*0-88677-569-8*); Vol. 2. 1994. 624p. mass mkt. 7.99 (*0-88677-615-5*) DAW Bks., Inc.

## W

**WADE, NYLA (FICTITIOUS CHARACTER)—FICTION**

McConnell, Vicki P. The Burnton Widows: A Nyla Wade Mystery. 1984. (Nyla Wade Mystery Ser.). (Illus.). 240p. pap. 7.95 o.p. (*0-930044-52-5*) Naiad Pr., Inc.
—Double Daughter. 1988. 216p. pap. 8.95 o.p. (*0-941483-26-6*) Naiad Pr., Inc.
—Mrs. Porter's Letter. 1982. (Nyla Wade Ser.). 224p. pap. 7.95 o.p. (*0-930044-29-0*) Naiad Pr., Inc.

**WAGER, GABRIEL (FICTITIOUS CHARACTER)—FICTION**

Burns, Rex. The Alvarez Journal. 1975. (Harper Novel of Suspense Ser.). 208p. 8.95 o.p. (*0-06-010576-3*) HarperCollins Pubs.
—The Alvarez Journal. 1991. (Crime Monthly Ser.). 288p. reprint ed. pap. 5.95 o.p. (*0-14-015788-3*, Penguin Bks.) Penguin Group (USA) Inc.
—Angle of Attack. 1979. (Harper Novel of Suspense Ser.). o.p. (*0-06-010523-2*) HarperCollins Pubs.
—The Avenging Angel: A Gabe Wager Mystery. (Crime Monthly Ser.). 1984. 24p. pap. 3.95 o.p. (*0-14-007104-0*, Penguin Bks.); 1983. 240p. 12.50 o.p. (*0-670-14317-0*) Viking Penguin.
—Blood Line. 1995. 204p. 19.95 (*0-8027-3256-9*) Walker & Co.
—Endangered Species. 1993. 288p. 19.00 o.p. (*0-670-84601-5*, Viking) Viking Penguin.
—The Farnsworth Score. 1978. 1.75 o.p. (*0-425-03749-5*) Berkley Publishing Group.
—The Farnsworth Score. 1977. (Harper Novel of Suspense Ser.). o.p. (*0-06-010573-9*) HarperCollins Pubs.
—The Farnsworth Score. 1993. (Crime Ser.). 208p. pap. 5.95 o.p. (*0-14-016949-0*, Penguin Bks.) Penguin Group (USA) Inc.
—Ground Money. 1987. 256p. mass mkt. 3.95 o.p. (*0-14-008515-7*, Penguin Bks.); 1986. 187p. 15.95 o.p. (*0-670-80904-7*) Viking Penguin.
—The Killing Zone. 1989. 272p. pap. 3.95 o.p. (*0-14-010532-8*, Penguin Bks.); 1988. 261p. 17.95 o.p. (*0-670-81955-7*) Viking Penguin.
—The Leaning Land: A Gabe Wager Mystery. 1997. (Gabe Wagner Mystery Ser.). 246p. 22.95 o.p. (*0-8027-3306-9*) Walker & Co.
—Speak for the Dead. 1978. (Harper Novel of Suspense Ser.). 8.95 o.p. (*0-06-010526-7*) HarperCollins Pubs.
—Strip Search. (Crime Monthly Ser.). 1985. 272p. pap. 3.95 o.p. (*0-14-007747-2*, Penguin Bks.); 1984. 300p. 13.95 o.p. (*0-670-67905-4*) Viking Penguin.

**WAGNER, LAUREN (FICTITIOUS CHARACTER)—FICTION**

Pike, Christopher, pseud. The Season of Passage. 1993. 438p. pap. text 6.99 (*0-8125-1048-8*); 1992. 336p. 18.95 o.p. (*0-312-85115-4*) Doherty, Tom Assocs., LLC. (Tor Bks.).

**WALES, JOSEY (FICTITIOUS CHARACTER)—FICTION**

Carter, Forrest. Gone to Texas. 1976. 20.95 (*0-8488-0954-8*) Amereon, Ltd.

—Gone to Texas. 1975. 9.95 o.s.i (*0-440-04565-7*, Delacorte Pr.) Dell Publishing.

—Gone to Texas. l.t. ed. 1979. 278p. 12.00 o.p. (*0-7089-0417-3*, Ulverscroft) Thorpe, F. A. Pubs. GBR. *Dist:* Ulverscroft Large Print Bks., Ltd.

—Josey Wales: Two Westerns by Forrest Carter. 1989. 419p. reprint ed. pap. 15.95 (*0-8263-1168-7*) Univ. of New Mexico Pr.

—Vengeance Trail of Josey Wales. Date not set. 22.95 (*0-8488-2647-7*) Amereon, Ltd.

Roberts, C. New Mexico. 1989. (Illus.). 220p. pap. 16.95 (*0-8263-1145-8*) Univ. of New Mexico Pr.

**WALKER, AMOS (FICTITIOUS CHARACTER)—FICTION**

Estleman, Loren D. Angel Eyes. abr. ed. 2001. audio (*1-58807-602-4*); 2000. audio 25.00 (*1-58807-045-X*) Americana Publishing, Inc.

—Angel Eyes. 1986. mass mkt. 3.95 o.s.i (*0-449-21134-7*, Fawcett) Ballantine Bks.

—Angel Eyes. unabr. ed. 1986. (Amos Walker Ser.). audio 19.95 o.p. (*0-930435-19-2*, 369, Bookcassette); audio 57.25 o.p. (*1-56100-014-0*, 551) Brilliance Audio.

—Angel Eyes. 1981. 11.95 o.p. (*0-395-31558-1*) Houghton Mifflin Co.

—Angel Eyes. 1984. 256p. pap. 2.75 o.p. (*0-523-42185-0*, Pinnacle Bks.) Kensington Publishing Corp.

—Angel Eyes. 2000. (Amos Walker Mysteries Ser.). 256p. reprint ed. pap. 14.00 (*0-671-03900-8*) ibooks, Inc.

—Downriver. 1989. mass mkt. 3.95 o.s.i (*0-449-21623-3*, Fawcett) Ballantine Bks.

—Downriver, 001. 1988. 192p. 15.95 o.p. (*0-395-41073-8*) Houghton Mifflin Co.

—Every Brilliant Eye. 1987. mass mkt. 4.95 o.s.i (*0-449-21137-1*, Fawcett) Ballantine Bks.

—Every Brilliant Eye. unabr. ed. 1986. (Amos Walker Ser.). audio 19.95 o.p. (*0-930435-26-5*, 378, Bookcassette) Brilliance Audio.

—Every Brilliant Eye. Howe, J. C., ed. unabr. ed. 1986. (Amos Walker Ser.). audio 57.25 o.p. (*1-56100-021-3*, 560) Brilliance Audio.

—Every Brilliant Eye, 001. 1986. 264p. 15.95 o.p. (*0-395-39428-7*) Houghton Mifflin Co.

—Every Brilliant Eye. 2001. (Amos Walker Mysteries Ser.). 304p. pap. 14.00 (*0-7434-1325-3*) ibooks, Inc.

—General Murders: Ten Amos Walker Mysteries. 1989. 192p. mass mkt. 3.95 o.s.i (*0-449-21696-9*, Fawcett) Ballantine Bks.

—General Murders: Ten Amos Walker Mysteries, 001. 1988. 256p. 16.95 o.p. (*0-395-41071-1*) Houghton Mifflin Co.

—General Murders: Ten Amos Walker Mysteries. l.t. ed. 1992. (Ulverscroft Large Print Ser.). 432p. 29.99 o.p. (*0-7089-2622-3*, Ulverscroft) Thorpe, F. A. Pubs. GBR. *Dist:* Ulverscroft Large Print Bks., Ltd., Ulverscroft Large Print Canada, Ltd.

—The Glass Highway. 1987. mass mkt. 3.95 o.s.i (*0-449-21136-3*, Fawcett) Ballantine Bks.

—The Glass Highway. unabr. ed. 1986. (Amos Walker Ser.). audio 57.25 o.p. (*1-56100-019-1*, 561) Brilliance Audio.

—The Glass Highway, 001. 1983. (Amos Walker Mysteries Ser.). 179p. 13.95 o.p. (*0-395-34636-3*) Houghton Mifflin Co.

—The Glass Highway. 1984. 224p. pap. 2.95 o.p. (*0-523-42263-6*, Pinnacle Bks.) Kensington Publishing Corp.

—The Glass Highway. E-Book 9.99 (*1-58824-389-3*); 2000. 240p. pap. 14.00 (*0-7434-0729-6*) ibooks, Inc.

—The Hours of the Virgin. abr. ed. 1999. (Amos Walker Ser.). audio 17.95 o.p. (*1-56740-847-8*, 1743, Nova Audio Bks.); 7p. audio 24.95 (*1-56740-437-5*, 1741, Bookcassette); audio 57.25 (*1-56740-663-7*, 1742, Unabridged Library Editions) Brilliance Audio.

—The Hours of the Virgin. 1999. (Amos Walker Mysteries Ser.). 288p. 23.00 (*0-89296-683-1*) Mysterious Pr.

—The Hours of the Virgin. 2000. 336p. (gr. 8 up). mass mkt. 6.99 (*0-446-60868-8*) Warner Bks., Inc.

—Lady Yesterday. 1988. 224p. mass mkt. 3.95 o.s.i (*0-449-21467-2*, Fawcett) Ballantine Bks.

—Lady Yesterday, 001. 1987. 15.95 o.p. (*0-395-41072-X*) Houghton Mifflin Co.

—Lady Yesterday. 1990. 2.99 o.p. (*0-517-02954-5*) Random Hse. Value Publishing.

—Lady Yesterday. 2002. (Amos Walker Mysteries Ser.). 240p. pap. 6.99 (*0-7434-3495-1*) ibooks, Inc.

—The Midnight Man. 1987. mass mkt. 4.95 o.s.i (*0-449-21135-5*, Fawcett) Ballantine Bks.

—The Midnight Man. unabr. ed. 1986. (Amos Walker Ser.). audio 19.95 o.p. (*0-930435-18-4*, 370); audio 57.25 o.p. (*1-56100-013-2*, 552) Brilliance Audio.

—The Midnight Man, 001. 1982. 230p. 12.95 o.p. (*0-395-32204-9*) Houghton Mifflin Co.

—The Midnight Man. 1984. (Amos Walker Mysteries Ser.). 256p. pap. 2.95 o.p. (*0-523-42186-9*, Pinnacle Bks.) Kensington Publishing Corp.

—The Midnight Man. 2000. (Amos Walker Mysteries Ser.). 288p. pap. 14.00 (*0-7434-0002-X*) ibooks, Inc.

—Motor City Blue. 1986. mass mkt. 4.95 o.s.i (*0-449-21133-9*, Fawcett) Ballantine Bks.

—Motor City Blue, 001. 1980. 9.95 o.p. (*0-395-29447-9*) Houghton Mifflin Co.

—Never Street. abr. ed. (Amos Walker Mysteries Ser.). 1998. audio 7.99 o.p. (*1-56740-245-3*, 684, Paperback Nova Audio Bks.); 1997. audio 16.95 o.p. (*1-56100-934-2*, 1311, Nova Audio Bks.); 1997. audio 57.25 o.p. (*1-56100-823-0*, 961, Unabridged Library Editions); 1997. audio 23.95 o.p. (*1-56100-748-X*, 192, Bookcassette) Brilliance Audio.

—Never Street. l.t. ed. 1999. (Magna Large Print Ser.). 432p. (*0-7505-1448-5*) Magna Large Print Bks. GBR. *Dist:* Ulverscroft Large Print Canada, Ltd.

—Never Street. 1998. mass mkt. (*0-446-40483-7*, Mysterious Pr. Paperback Bks.); 1998. 352p. mass mkt. 6.99 (*0-446-60596-4*); 1997. 352p. 23.00 o.p. (*0-89296-633-5*) Warner Bks., Inc.

—Peeper. l.t. ed. 1991. 17.95 o.p. (*0-7451-8203-8*, AH0239); pap. 15.95 o.p. (*0-7927-0751-6*, AS0275) BBC Audiobooks America.

—Peeper. 1990. 224p. reprint ed. mass mkt. 4.99 o.s.i (*0-553-28605-6*) Bantam Bks.

—Poison Blonde: An Amos Walker Novel. 2003. (Amos Walker Ser.). 272p. 24.95 (*0-7653-0447-3*, Forge Bks.) Doherty, Tom Assocs., LLC.

—Silent Thunder. 1990. 224p. mass mkt. 4.95 o.s.i (*0-449-21854-6*, Fawcett) Ballantine Bks.

—Silent Thunder. l.t. ed. 1990. (Large Print Bks.). 286p. lib. bdg. 18.95 o.p. (*0-8161-4976-3*, Macmillan Reference USA) Gale Group.

—Silent Thunder, 001. 1989. 224p. 16.95 o.p. (*0-395-41074-6*) Houghton Mifflin Co.

—Silent Thunder. 2003. 240p. mass mkt. 6.99 (*0-7434-7480-5*) ibooks, Inc.

—Sinister Heights. abr. ed. 2003. (Amos Walker Mysteries Ser.: Vol. 15). audio 9.99 (*1-58788-977-3*, 3493, Brilliance Audio Paperback Audiobooks); 2002. (Amos Walker Ser.). audio 19.95 o.p. (*1-58788-976-5*, 3492, Nova Audio Bks.); 2002. (Amos Walker Ser.). audio 27.95 (*1-58788-974-9*, 3490, Brilliance Audio Unabridged); 2002. (Amos Walker Ser.). audio 57.25 (*1-58788-975-7*, 3491, Unabridged Library Editions) Brilliance Audio.

—Sinister Heights. 2002. lib. bdg. 29.95 (*1-58547-223-9*, Premier) Ctr. Point Large Print.

—Sinister Heights. 2002. 272p. 24.95 (*0-89296-738-2*) Mysterious Pr.

—A Smile on the Face of the Tiger. l.t. ed. 2001. (Large Print Book Ser.). 311p. 28.95 (*1-58724-024-6*, Wheeler Publishing, Inc.) Gale Group.

—A Smile on the Face of the Tiger. 2000. 304p. E-Book 14.95 (*0-446-92250-1*); E-Book 14.95 (*0-446-93125-X*); 304p. E-Book 14.95 (*0-446-92366-4*); 304p. 24.95 o.p. (*0-89296-706-4*) Mysterious Pr.

—A Smile on the Face of the Tiger. 2000. 304p. E-Book 14.95 (*0-446-91368-5*); E-Book 14.95 (*0-446-96087-X*); E-Book 14.95 (*0-446-92858-5*) Warner Bks., Inc.

—Sugartown. l.t. ed. 1985. lib. bdg. 16.95 o.p. (*0-89340-931-6*, 159) BBC Audiobooks America.

—Sugartown. l.t. ed. 1985. mass mkt. 4.99 o.s.i (*0-449-20998-9*, Fawcett) Ballantine Bks.

—Sugartown. unabr. ed. 1986. (Amos Walker Ser.). audio 15.95 o.p. (*0-930435-25-7*, 380, Bookcassette); audio 57.25 o.p. (*1-56100-020-5*, 562) Brilliance Audio.

—Sugartown. 1984. 220p. 13.95 o.p. (*0-395-36449-3*) Houghton Mifflin Co.

—Sugartown. 1984. 220p. 25.00 (*0-89366-256-9*) Ultramarine Publishing Co., Inc.

—Sugartown. E-Book 9.99 (*1-58824-394-X*); 2001. 256p. pap. 14.00 (*0-7434-1293-1*) ibooks, Inc.

—Sweet Women Lie. 1991. mass mkt. 4.99 o.s.i (*0-449-21944-5*, Fawcett) Ballantine Bks.

—Sweet Women Lie. 1990. (Amos Walker Mysteries Ser.). 208p. 18.95 o.p. (*0-395-53767-3*) Houghton Mifflin Co.

—The Witchfinder. abr. ed. (Amos Walker Mysteries Ser.). 1999. audio 7.99 o.s.i (*1-56740-292-5*, 1753, Paperback Nova Audio Bks.); 1998. audio 24.95 (*1-56740-052-3*, 7, Bookcassette); 1998. audio 57.25 (*1-56740-581-9*, 1101, Unabridged Library Editions); Set. 1998. audio 17.95 o.p. (*1-56740-778-1*, 440, Nova Audio Bks.) Brilliance Audio.

—The Witchfinder. 1998. (Amos Walker Mysteries Ser.). 320p. 23.00 o.p. (*0-89296-663-7*) Mysterious Pr.

—The Witchfinder. l.t. ed. 1998. (Cloak & Dagger Ser.). 408p. 27.95 (*0-7862-1509-7*) Thorndike Pr.

—The Witchfinder. l.t. ed. 2000. (Ulverscroft Large Print Ser.). 416p. 31.99 (*0-7089-4252-0*, Ulverscroft) Thorpe, F. A. Pubs. GBR. *Dist:* Ulverscroft Large Print Bks., Ltd., Ulverscroft Large Print Canada, Ltd.

—The Witchfinder. 1999. E-Book 4.95 (*0-446-92328-1*) Time Warner Bk. Group.

—The Witchfinder. 1999. 320p. mass mkt. 6.50 (*0-446-60760-6*); E-Book 4.95 (*0-446-91300-6*) Warner Bks., Inc.

**WALKER, CALICO JACK (FICTITIOUS CHARACTER)—FICTION**

Bishop, Paul. Sand Against the Tide. 1992. 307p. mass mkt. 4.99 o.p. (*0-8125-0918-8*); 1990. 12.99 o.p. (*0-312-93158-1*) Doherty, Tom Assocs., LLC. (Tor Bks.).

**WALKER, CAMELLIA (FICTITIOUS CHARACTER)—FICTION**

Spizer, Joyce. The Cop Was White As Snow. 1998. (Harbour Pointe Mysteries Ser.). 298p. pap. 10.95 (*1-881164-83-7*) Intercontinental Publishing, Inc.

**WALKER, KIRSTEN (FICTITIOUS CHARACTER)—FICTION**

Ludwig, Dale. Blood Secrets. 1993. 304p. mass mkt. 4.50 o.s.i (*1-55817-695-0*) Kensington Publishing Corp.

**WALKINSHAW, TOM (FICTITIOUS CHARACTER)—FICTION**

Mitcheltree, Tom. Dataman. 1998. 240p. 22.95 o.p. (*1-885173-52-0*) Write Way Publishing.

**WALLANDER, KURT (FICTITIOUS CHARACTER)—FICTION**

Mankell, Henning. The Dogs of Riga. 2004. 336p. pap. 13.00 (*1-4000-3152-4*, Vintage) Knopf Publishing Group.

—The Dogs of Riga: A Kurt Wallander Mystery. Thompson, Laurie, tr. from SWE. 2003. 336p. pap. 24.95 (*1-56584-787-3*) New Pr., The.

—Faceless Killers. 2003. (Illus.). 279p. pap. 17.95 (*1-86046-756-3*) Harvill Pr., The GBR. *Dist:* Trafalgar Square.

—Faceless Killers: A Kurt Wallander Mystery. 2003. 288p. pap. 13.00 (*1-4000-3157-5*, Vintage) Knopf Publishing Group.

—Faceless Killers: A Kurt Wallander Mystery. Murray, Steven T., tr. (Kurt Wallander Mystery Ser.). 288p. 2000. pap. 14.95 (*1-56584-605-2*); 1997. text 23.00 (*1-56584-341-X*) New Pr., The.

—The Fifth Woman: A Kurt Wallander Mystery. Murray, Steven T., tr. from SWE. 2000. (Kurt Wallander Mystery Ser.). 392p. 24.95 (*1-56584-547-1*) New Pr., The.

—Firewall: A Kurt Wallander Mystery. Segerberg, Ebba, tr. from SWE. 2002. 416p. 25.95 (*1-56584-767-9*) New Pr., The.

—One Step Behind: A Kurt Wallander Mystery. 2003. 448p. pap. 13.00 (*1-4000-3151-6*, Vintage) Knopf Publishing Group.

—One Step Behind: A Kurt Wallander Mystery. Segerberg, Ebba, tr. from SWE. 2001. 416p. text 24.95 (*1-56584-652-4*) New Pr., The.

—Sidetracked: A Kurt Wallander Mystery. Murray, Steven T., tr. from SWE. 2003. (Vintage Crime/Black Lizard Ser.). (Illus.). 432p. reprint ed. pap. 13.00 (*1-4000-3156-7*, Vintage) Knopf Publishing Group.

—Sidetracked: A Kurt Wallander Mystery. Murray, Steven T., tr. (Kurt Wallander Mystery Ser.). 352p. 2000. pap. 14.95 (*1-56584-611-7*); 1999. text 25.00 (*1-56584-507-2*) New Pr., The.

—The White Lioness. Thompson, Laurie, tr. from SWE. 2003. (Kurt Wallander Mystery Ser.). Orig. Title: Den Vita Lejoninnan. (Illus.). 448p. reprint ed. pap. 13.00 (*1-4000-3155-9*, Vintage) Knopf Publishing Group.

—The White Lioness. Thompson, Laurie, tr. from SWE. 1998. (Kurt Wallander Mystery Ser.). Orig. Title: Den Vita Lejoninnan. 942p. 25.00 (*1-56584-424-6*) New Pr., The.

**WALSH, JACK (FICTITIOUS CHARACTER)—FICTION**

Abel, Kenneth. Bait. 1995. 384p. mass mkt. 4.99 o.s.i (*0-440-21720-2*) Dell Publishing.

—Bait. l.t. ed. 1994. 411p. lib. bdg. 23.95 (*0-8161-7436-9*, Macmillan Reference USA) Gale Group.

**WALSH, JACKIE (FICTITIOUS CHARACTER: CLEARY)—FICTION**

Cleary, Melissa. And Your Little Dog, Too. 1998. (Dog Lover's Mysteries Ser.). 208p. mass mkt. 5.99 o.s.i (*0-425-16242-7*, Prime Crime) Berkley Publishing Group.

—Dead & Buried. 1994. 208p. (Orig.). mass mkt. 4.99 o.s.i (*0-425-14547-6*, Prime Crime) Berkley Publishing Group.

—Dog Collar Crime. 1993. 192p. (Orig.). 3.99 o.s.i (*1-55773-896-3*, Diamond Bks.) Ace Bks.

—A Dog Collar Crime. 1994. (Orig.). mass mkt. 4.99 o.s.i (*0-425-14857-2*, Prime Crime) Berkley Publishing Group.

—First Pedigree Murder: A Dog Lover's Mystery. 1994. 208p. (Orig.). mass mkt. 4.99 o.s.i (*0-425-14299-X*, Prime Crime) Berkley Publishing Group.

—Hounded to Death. 1993. 192p. mass mkt. 4.99 o.s.i (*0-425-14324-4*) Berkley Publishing Group.

—The Maltese Puppy. 1995. 256p. (Orig.). mass mkt. 4.99 o.s.i (*0-425-14721-5*, Prime Crime) Berkley Publishing Group.

—A Murder Most Beastly. 1996. 208p. (Orig.). mass mkt. 4.99 o.s.i (*0-425-15139-5*) Berkley Publishing Group.

—Old Dogs. 1997. (Dog Lover's Mysteries Ser.). 224p. mass mkt. 5.99 o.s.i (*0-425-15858-6*, Prime Crime) Berkley Publishing Group.

—Skull & Dog Bones. 1994. (Orig.). mass mkt. 4.99 o.s.i (*0-425-14541-7*); 208p. mass mkt. 4.50 o.s.i (*0-515-11279-8*, Jove) Berkley Publishing Group.

—Tail of Two Murders. 1993. 192p. (Orig.). mass mkt. 4.99 o.s.i (*0-425-15809-8*, Prime Crime) Berkley Publishing Group.

Cleary, Melissa & Jove Publications Staff. Hounded to Death. 1993. (Dog Lover's Mysteries Ser.). 184p. mass mkt. 3.99 o.s.i (*0-515-11190-2*, Jove) Berkley Publishing Group.

Minear, Lola F. In the Dog House: A Collection of Short Stories. 1981. 47p. 6.95 o.p. (*0-533-04878-8*) Vantage Pr., Inc.

**WALSH, SIDNEY (FICTITIOUS CHARACTER)—FICTION**

Hunt, Richard. Dead Man's Shoes. 1999. 224p. 25.00 (*0-7278-2255-1*) Severn Hse. Pubs., Ltd.

—Deadlocked. 1995. 192p. 19.95 o.p. (*0-312-13461-4*, Saint Martin's Minotaur) St. Martin's Pr.

—Death of a Merry Widow. Set. unabr. ed. 1998. audio 69.95 o.p. (*1-85903-048-3*) Magna Story Sound GBR. *Dist:* Ulverscroft Large Print Bks., Ltd.

—Death of a Merry Widow. 1994. 191p. 18.95 o.p. (*0-312-11773-6*, Saint Martin's Minotaur) St. Martin's Pr.

—The Man Trap. l.t. ed. 1998. (Dales Large Print Ser.). 336p. pap. 19.99 o.p. (*1-85389-866-X*) Dales Large Print Bks. GBR. *Dist:* Ulverscroft Large Print Bks., Ltd., Ulverscroft Large Print Canada, Ltd.

—Murder Benign. l.t. ed. 1997. (Dales Large Print Ser.). 305p. pap. 19.99 (*1-85389-721-3*) Dales Large Print Bks. GBR. *Dist:* Ulverscroft Large Print Bks., Ltd.

—Murder Benign. 1996. 192p. 20.95 o.p. (*0-312-14684-1*, Saint Martin's Minotaur) St. Martin's Pr.

**WANAWAKE, PENNY (FICTITIOUS CHARACTER)—FICTION**

Moody, Susan. Penny Black. 1986. 272p. mass mkt. 2.95 o.s.i (*0-449-12864-4*, Fawcett) Ballantine Bks.

—Penny Black. 1997. (Missing Mysteries Ser.: Vol. 1). pap. 7.95 (*1-890208-01-9*) Poisoned Pen Pr.

—Penny Black. l.t. ed. 1985. (Ulverscroft Large Print Ser.). 464p. 29.99 o.p. (*0-7089-1391-1*, Ulverscroft) Thorpe, F. A. Pubs. GBR. *Dist:* Ulverscroft Large Print Bks., Ltd., Ulverscroft Large Print Canada, Ltd.

—Penny Dreadful. 1986. mass mkt. 2.95 o.s.i (*0-449-12865-2*, Fawcett) Ballantine Bks.

—Penny Dreadful. unabr. ed. 2000. (Penny Wanawake Mystery Ser.). audio 59.95 (*0-7451-4183-8*, CAB 866) Chivers Audio Bks. GBR. *Dist:* BBC Audiobooks America.

—Penny Dreadful. l.t. ed. 1987. (Ulverscroft Large Print Ser.). 432p. 29.99 o.p. (*0-7089-1603-1*, Ulverscroft) Thorpe, F. A. Pubs. GBR. *Dist:* Ulverscroft Large Print Bks., Ltd., Ulverscroft Large Print Canada, Ltd.

—Penny Pinching. 1989. 240p. mass mkt. 3.50 o.s.i (*0-449-13237-4*, Fawcett) Ballantine Bks.

—Penny Pinching. l.t. ed. 1991. (Ulverscroft Large Print Ser.). 29.99 o.p. (*0-7089-2374-7*, Ulverscroft) Thorpe, F. A. Pubs. GBR. *Dist:* Ulverscroft Large Print Bks., Ltd., Ulverscroft Large Print Canada, Ltd.

—Penny Post. 1986. mass mkt. 2.95 o.s.i (*0-449-12866-0*, Fawcett) Ballantine Bks.

—Penny Post. l.t. ed. 1987. (Ulverscroft Large Print Ser.). 416p. 29.99 o.p. (*0-7089-1703-8*, Ulverscroft) Thorpe, F. A. Pubs. GBR. *Dist:* Ulverscroft Large Print Bks., Ltd., Ulverscroft Large Print Canada, Ltd.

—Penny Royal. 1987. 304p. mass mkt. 2.95 o.s.i (*0-449-12867-9*, Fawcett) Ballantine Bks.

—Penny Royal. l.t. ed. 1988. (Ulverscroft Large Print Ser.). 464p. 29.99 o.p. (*0-7089-1763-1*, Ulverscroft) Thorpe, F. A. Pubs. GBR. *Dist:* Ulverscroft Large Print Bks., Ltd., Ulverscroft Large Print Canada, Ltd.

—Penny Saving. unabr. ed. 2000. (Penny Wanawake Mystery Ser.). audio 59.95 (*0-7451-4007-6*, CAB 704) Chivers Audio Bks. GBR. *Dist:* BBC Audiobooks America.

—Penny Saving. l.t. ed. 1993. (Mystery Ser.). 464p. 29.99 o.p. (*0-7089-2938-9*, Ulverscroft) Thorpe, F. A. Pubs. GBR. *Dist:* Ulverscroft Large Print Bks., Ltd., Ulverscroft Large Print Canada, Ltd.

—Penny Wise. unabr. ed. 1992. (Penny Wanawake Mysteries Ser.). 69.95 incl. audio (*0-7451-4066-1*, CAB 763) BBC Audiobooks America.

—Penny Wise, No. 5. 1989. mass mkt. 3.50 o.s.i (*0-449-13236-6*, Fawcett) Ballantine Bks.

**WARD, EMERSON (FICTITIOUS CHARACTER)—FICTION**

Sherer, Michael W. A Forever Death. l.t. ed. 2001. (Mystery Ser.). 277p. 23.95 (*0-7862-3016-9*, Five Star) Gale Group.

**WARD, ERIC (FICTITIOUS CHARACTER)—FICTION**

Lewis, Roy. A Kind of Transaction: An Eric Ward Novel. l.t. ed. 1993. 296p. 15.95 o.p. (*0-7451-1679-5*, Macmillan Reference USA) Gale Group.

—The Nightwalker. 2002. (Eric Ward Mysteries Ser.). 187p. 25.95 (*0-7490-0591-2*) Allison & Busby, Ltd. GBR. *Dist:* International Publishers Marketing.

Lewis, Roy H. A Blurred Reality. 1985. 192p. 12.95 o.p. (*0-312-08725-X*) St. Martin's Pr.

—Dwell in Danger. 1982. 192p. 10.95 o.p. (*0-312-22286-6*) St. Martin's Pr.

—Once Dying, Twice Dead. l.t. ed. 1985. 12.95 o.p. (*0-8166-0110-0*, Macmillan Reference USA) Gale Group.

—Once Dying, Twice Dead. 1984. 192p. 10.95 o.p. (*0-312-58476-8*) St. Martin's Pr.

—Premium on Death: An Eric Ward Novel. 1987. 208p. 13.95 o.p. (*0-312-00019-7*) St. Martin's Pr.

—The Salamander Chill. l.t. ed. 1991. 8.95 o.p. (*0-7451-9504-0*, 73); pap. 10.95 o.p. (*1-55504-903-6*, 359) BBC Audiobooks America.

—The Salamander Chill. 1988. 192p. 14.95 o.p. (*0-312-02637-4*, Saint Martin's Minotaur) St. Martin's Pr.

**WARDEN, JESSE (FICTITIOUS CHARACTER)—FICTION**

Woods, Stuart. Heat. 1994. 320p. 138.00 o.p. (*0-06-017623-7*, HarperCollins); 23.00 o.p. (*0-06-017776-4*) HarperTrade.

—Heat. 1995. 384p. mass mkt. 7.99 (*0-06-109358-0*, HarperTorch) Morrow/Avon.

**WAREEN, WYATT (FICTITIOUS CHARACTER)—FICTION**

Disher, Garry. Kickback. (Orig.). 1994. 200p. pap. 5.95 o.p. (*1-86373-591-7*); 1993. 192p. pap. 9.95 o.p. (*1-86373-107-5*) Allen & Unwin Pty., Ltd. AUS. *Dist:* Independent Pubs. Group.

—Paydirt. (Orig.). 1994. 176p. mass mkt. 5.95 (*1-86373-581-X*); 1993. 173p. pap. 9.95 o.p. (*1-86373-197-0*) Allen & Unwin Pty., Ltd. AUS. *Dist:* Independent Pubs. Group.

**WAREHAM, LIZ (FICTITIOUS CHARACTER)—FICTION**

Brennan, Carol. Full Commission: A Liz Wareham Mystery. 1993. 224p. 18.95 o.p. (*0-88184-911-1*, Carroll & Graf Pubs.) Avalon Publishing Group.

—Full Commission: A Liz Wareham Mystery. 1994. 256p. mass mkt. 4.50 o.s.i (*0-425-14467-4*, Prime Crime) Berkley Publishing Group.

**WARNER, WILLIAM (FICTITIOUS CHARACTER)—FICTION**

Sylvester, Martin. Rough Red. l.t. ed. 1991. (Ulverscroft Large Print Ser.). 29.99 o.p. (*0-7089-2354-2*, Ulverscroft) Thorpe, F. A. Pubs. GBR. *Dist:* Ulverscroft Large Print Bks., Ltd., Ulverscroft Large Print Canada, Ltd.

**WARREN, PENELOPE (FICTITIOUS CHARACTER)—FICTION**

Allen, Garrison. Baseball Cat. (Big Mike Mystery Ser.: Vol. 4). 1998. 336p. mass mkt. 5.99 (*1-57566-309-0*); 1997. 304p. 18.95 o.s.i (*1-57566-183-7*) Kensington Publishing Corp.

—Desert Cat. 1994. 304p. mass mkt. 3.99 o.s.i (*0-8217-4503-4*, Zebra Bks.) Kensington Publishing Corp.

—Dinosaur Cat. (Big Mike Mystery Ser.). 336p. 1999. mass mkt. 5.99 o.s.i (*1-57566-426-7*); 1998. (J). 20.00 o.s.i (*1-57566-304-X*, Kensington Bks.) Kensington Publishing Corp.

—Movie Cat. 1999. (Big Mike Mystery Ser.). 304p. 20.00 o.s.i (*1-57566-413-5*) Kensington Publishing Corp.

—Royal Cat: A Big Mike Mystery. 1996. (Big Mike Mystery Ser.: Vol. 2). 304p. mass mkt. 4.99 o.s.i (*1-57566-045-8*); 1995. mass mkt. 16.95 o.s.i (*0-8217-4957-9*, Zebra Bks.) Kensington Publishing Corp.

—Stable Cat. 304p. 1997. mass mkt. 5.50 o.s.i (*1-57566-188-8*); 1996. pap. 18.95 o.p. (*1-57566-042-3*) Kensington Publishing Corp.

**WARSHAWSKI, V. I. (FICTITIOUS CHARACTER)—FICTION**

Clark, Mary Higgins, et al. Great Mysteries, Great Writers. abr. ed. 1994. audio 24.95 o.p. (*0-7871-0047-1*, 692220, Dove Audio) NewStar Media, Inc.

Dunlop, Susan, et al. Crime's Leading Ladies. unabr. ed. 1995. 3p. audio 16.99 (*0-88646-376-9*, 390575) Durkin Hayes Publishing Ltd.

Paretsky, Sara. At the Old Swimming Hole. abr. ed. 1999. audio 5.99 Durkin Hayes Publishing Ltd.

—Bitter Medicine. 1988. 272p. mass mkt. 6.99 o.s.i (*0-345-34722-6*) Ballantine Bks.

—Bitter Medicine. 1993. audio compact disk 56.00 (*0-7366-7125-0*); audio 48.00 (*0-7366-2417-1*, 3184) Books on Tape, Inc.

—Bitter Medicine. 1999. 352p. mass mkt. 7.50 (*0-440-23476-X*) Dell Publishing.

—Bitter Medicine. l.t. ed. 1989. 352p. 19.95 o.p. (*0-8161-4467-2*, Macmillan Reference USA) Gale Group.

—Bitter Medicine. 1987. 320p. 17.95 o.p. (*0-688-06448-5*, Morrow, William & Co.) Morrow/Avon.

—Bitter Medicine. unabr. ed. 2000. audio 58.00 (*1-55690-695-1*, 92428) Recorded Bks., LLC.

—Blacklist. abr. ed. (V. I. Warshawski Ser.). 2004. audio 12.99 (*1-58788-871-8*, 3384, Brilliance Audio Paperback Audiobooks); 2003. audio 24.95 (*1-58788-868-8*, 3381, Brilliance Audio Unabridged); 2003. audio 34.95 (*1-58788-866-1*, 3379, Brilliance Audio Unabridged); 2003. audio 97.25 (*1-58788-867-X*, 3380, Brilliance Audio Unabridged Lib Ed); 2003. audio compact disk 40.95 (*1-58788-869-6*, 3382, Brilliance Audio on CD Unabridged); 2003. audio compact disk 117.25 (*1-58788-870-X*, 3383, Brilliance Audio on CD Unabridged Lib Ed) Brilliance Audio.

—Blacklist. 2003. (V. I. Warshawski Novel Ser.). 448p. 24.95 (*0-399-15085-4*) Putnam Publishing Group, The.

—Blood Shot. unabr. ed. 1993. (V. I. Warshawski Ser.). audio 56.00 (*0-7366-2328-0*, 3108) Books on Tape, Inc.

—Blood Shot. 1989. (V.I. Warshawski Novels Ser.). 384p. mass mkt. 7.99 (*0-440-20420-8*) Dell Publishing.

—Blood Shot. l.t. ed. 1989. (General Ser.). 20.95 o.p. (*0-8161-4775-2*, Macmillan Reference USA) Gale Group.

—Blood Shot. abr. ed. 1990. audio 14.95 o.s.i (*0-553-45215-0*, RH Audio) Random Hse. Audio Publishing Group.

—Blood Shot. unabr. ed. 1993. (V. I. Warshawski Mystery Ser.: Vol. 1). audio 70.00 (*1-55690-899-7*, 93341E7) Recorded Bks., LLC.

—Burn Marks. unabr. ed. 1992. (V. I. Warshawski Ser.). audio 64.00 (*0-7366-2168-7*, 2967) Books on Tape, Inc.

—Burn Marks. 1991. (V.I. Warshawski Novels Ser.). 416p. mass mkt. 7.99 (*0-440-20845-9*) Dell Publishing.

—Burn Marks. l.t. ed. 1990. (Large Print Bks.). 533p. lib. bdg. 21.95 o.p. (*0-8161-5004-4*, Macmillan Reference USA) Gale Group.

—Burn Marks. abr. ed. 1990. audio 14.95 o.s.i (*0-553-45208-8*, RH Audio) Random Hse. Audio Publishing Group.

—Deadlock. abr. ed. 2001. audio 25.00 (*1-59040-109-3*, Phoenix Audio) American International Publishing Group.

—Deadlock. l.t. ed. 1985. lib. bdg. 13.95 o.p. (*0-89340-898-0*, 842) BBC Audiobooks America.

—Deadlock. 1984. 272p. mass mkt. 5.95 o.s.i (*0-345-31954-0*) Ballantine Bks.

—Deadlock. unabr. collector's ed. 1993. (V. I. Warshawski Ser.). audio 48.00 (*0-7366-2382-5*, 3153) Books on Tape, Inc.

—Deadlock. unabr. ed. 1985. audio 14.95 o.p. (*0-930435-02-8*, 364); audio 57.25 o.p. (*1-56100-001-9*, 549, Unabridged Library Editions) Brilliance Audio.

—Deadlock. 1992. (V.I. Warshawski Novels Ser.). 320p. mass mkt. 6.99 (*0-440-21332-0*) Dell Publishing.

—Deadlock. 1984. 264p. 14.95 o.p. (*0-385-27933-7*) Doubleday Publishing.

—Deadlock. l.t. ed. 1993. (General Ser.). 271p. pap. 18.95 o.p. (*0-8161-5562-3*); lib. bdg. 20.95 o.p. (*0-8161-5561-5*) Gale Group. (Macmillan Reference USA).

—Guardian Angel. unabr. ed. 1992. (V. I. Warshawski Ser.). audio 72.00 (*0-7366-2203-9*, 2998) Books on Tape, Inc.

—Guardian Angel. 1993. 432p. mass mkt. 7.99 (*0-440-21399-1*) Dell Publishing.

—Guardian Angel. l.t. ed. 1992. (General Ser.). 544p. 18.95 o.p. (*0-8161-5542-9*); lib. bdg. 21.95 o.p. (*0-8161-5541-0*) Gale Group. (Macmillan Reference USA).

—Guardian Angel. 1992. audio 15.95 o.s.i (*0-553-74558-1*); audio 16.99 o.s.i (*0-553-47035-3*) Random Hse. Audio Publishing Group. (RH Audio).

—Guardian Angel. 1993. 5.99 o.p. (*0-517-10926-3*) Random Hse. Value Publishing.

—Guardian Angel. unabr. ed. 1992. (V. I. Warshawski Mystery Ser.: Vol. 7). audio 85.00 (*1-55690-669-2*, 92233E7) Recorded Bks., LLC.

—Guardian Angel. 1992. (Audio Books Ser.). 69.95 o.p. incl. audio (*0-7838-8000-6*) Thorndike Pr.

—Guardian Angel: International Edition. 1992. 432p. mass mkt. 5.50 o.s.i (*0-440-29522-X*) Dell Publishing.

—Hard Time. (V.I. Warshawski Novels Ser.). 2000. 512p. mass mkt. 7.99 (*0-440-22470-5*, Delta); 1999. 400p. 24.95 (*0-385-31363-2*, Delacorte Pr.) Dell Publishing.

—Hard Time. l.t. ed. 1999. pap. 24.95 o.p. (*0-7838-8696-9*, Macmillan Reference USA) Gale Group.

—Hard Time, Set. abr. ed. 1999. audio 25.00 Highsmith Inc.

—Hard Time. abr. ed. 1999. audio 25.00 (*0-7871-2013-8*); audio compact disk 50.00 (*0-7871-2371-4*); audio 36.00 (*0-7871-2012-X*) NewStar Media, Inc. (Dove Audio).

—Hard Time. l.t. ed. 2000. 656p. pap. 13.95 (*0-375-70780-8*) Random Hse. Large Print.

—Hard Time. 2000. 13.04 (*0-606-18985-8*) Turtleback Bks.

—Indemnity Only. 1985. 224p. mass mkt. 4.95 o.s.i (*0-345-33634-8*); 1983. mass mkt. 2.50 o.s.i (*0-345-30684-8*) Ballantine Bks.

—Indemnity Only. unabr. ed. 1992. (V. I. Warshawski Ser.). audio 48.00 (*0-7366-2282-9*, 3069) Books on Tape, Inc.

—Indemnity Only. 1991. (V.I. Warshawski Novels Ser.). 336p. mass mkt. 6.99 (*0-440-21069-0*) Dell Publishing.

—Indemnity Only. 1982. 14.95 o.p. (*0-385-27213-8*) Doubleday Publishing.

—Indemnity Only. (Nightingale Ser.). 1982. pap. 9.95 o.p. (*0-8161-3439-1*); 1992. 381p. lib. bdg. 20.95 (*0-8161-5455-4*) Gale Group. (Macmillan Reference USA).

—Indemnity Only. abr. ed. 1991. audio 15.99 o.s.i (*0-553-45271-1*, RH Audio) Random Hse. Audio Publishing Group.

—Indemnity Only. l.t. ed. 1992. (Novels Ser.). 381p. pap. 20.95 (*0-8161-5456-2*) Thorndike Pr.

—Killing Orders. l.t. ed. 1986. lib. bdg. 17.95 o.p. (*1-55504-024-1*) BBC Audiobooks America.

—Killing Orders. 1988. pap. o.p. (*0-345-00730-1*); 1986. 288p. mass mkt. 5.95 o.s.i (*0-345-32777-2*) Ballantine Bks.

—Killing Orders. unabr. collector's ed. 1993. (V. I. Warshawski Ser.). audio 48.00 (*0-7366-2391-4*, 3162) Books on Tape, Inc.

—Killing Orders. 1993. 352p. mass mkt. 7.99 (*0-440-21528-5*, Dell Bks.) Dell Publishing.

—Sara Paretsky, 3 vols., Set. 1992. pap. 14.85 o.s.i (*0-440-36046-3*) Dell Publishing.

—Sara Paretsky: Three Complete Novels. 1995. 704p. 13.99 o.s.i (*0-517-14801-3*) Random Hse., Inc.

—The Sara Paretsky Value Collection: Indemnity Only, Blood Shots, & Burn Marks. abr. ed. 2000. audio 29.95 (*0-553-52724-X*, RH Audio) Random Hse. Audio Publishing Group.

—Settled Score. abr. ed. 1998. audio 4.99 (*0-88646-964-3*, 7964) Durkin Hayes Publishing Ltd.

—Skin Deep & Other Stories. unabr. ed. 1994. (V. I. Warshawski Mystery Ser.). audio 16.99 (*0-88646-373-4*, 391592) Durkin Hayes Publishing Ltd.

—Strung Out. unabr. ed. 1997. audio 4.99 (*0-88646-940-6*, 7940) Durkin Hayes Publishing Ltd.

—Three-Dot Po. unabr. ed. 1994. audio 8.95 o.p. (*1-879371-80-4*, 30030) Publishing Mills, Inc., The.

—Total Recall. 2002. 544p. mass mkt. 7.99 (*0-440-22471-3*) Dell Publishing.

—Total Recall. l.t. ed. 2001. 25.95 (*0-375-43136-5*) Random Hse. Large Print.

—Tunnel Vision. unabr. ed. 1994. (V. I. Warshawski Ser.). audio 80.00 (*0-7366-2842-8*, 3550) Books on Tape, Inc.

—Tunnel Vision. (V.I. Warshawski Novels Ser.). 1995. 480p. mass mkt. 7.50 (*0-440-21752-0*); 1995. E-Book 6.99 (*0-440-33393-8*); 1994. 736p. 26.95 o.s.i (*0-385-31307-1*, Delacorte Pr.) Dell Publishing.

—Tunnel Vision. l.t. ed. 1994. (Large Print Bks.). pap. 22.95 o.p. (*1-56895-084-5*, Wheeler Publishing, Inc.) Gale Group.

—Tunnel Vision. abr. ed. 1993. (V.I. Warshawski Novels Ser.). audio 24.95 o.p. (*1-55800-975-2*, 692333) NewStar Media, Inc.

—Windy City Blues. unabr. ed. 1996. (V. I. Warshawski Ser.). audio 48.00 (*0-7366-3243-3*, 3902) Books on Tape, Inc.

—Windy City Blues. 1996. (V.I. Warshawski Novels Ser.). 352p. mass mkt. 7.99 (*0-440-21873-X*) Dell Publishing.

—Windy City Blues. 1996. pap. 6.99 (*0-440-29546-7*) Doubleday Publishing.

—Windy City Blues. unabr. ed. 1995. (V. I. Warshawski Mystery Ser.). 24.95 o.p. (*0-7871-0478-7*, 693248) NewStar Media, Inc.

—Windy City Blues. l.t. ed. 1996. (Paperback Bestsellers Ser.). 336p. pap. 24.95 (*0-7838-1562-X*); 26.95 (*0-7838-1561-1*) Thorndike Pr.

—A Woman's Eye. 1992. 464p. reprint ed. mass mkt. 6.99 (*0-440-21335-5*) Dell Publishing.

—A Woman's Eye. 1993. 5.99 o.p. (*0-517-11187-X*) Random Hse. Value Publishing.

—Women on the Case: 26 Original Stories by the Best Women Crime Writers of Our Times. 1997. 464p. mass mkt. 7.50 (*0-440-22325-3*) Dell Publishing.

Paretsky, Sara, ed. Beastly Tales. 1995. (Select Sound, Dove Ser.). 4.99 o.p. (*0-7871-0326-8*); 4.99 o.p. (*0-7871-0311-X*) Penguin Group (USA) Inc.

—Beastly Tales. 1989. 17.95 o.p. (*0-922066-14-0*) Wynwood.

Paretsky, Sara, intro. A Woman's Eye. l.t. ed. 1992. (General Ser.). 569p. lib. bdg. 21.95 o.p. (*0-8161-5457-0*, Macmillan Reference USA) Gale Group.

Paretsky, Sara & McCrumb, Sharyn. Lily & the Sockeyes & Happiness Is a Dead Poet. unabr. ed. 1994. audio 4.99 (*0-88646-725-X*) Durkin Hayes Publishing Ltd.

**WATERMAN, LEO (FICTITIOUS CHARACTER)—FICTION**

Ford, G. M. The Bum's Rush. 1998. (Leo Waterman Mysteries Ser.). 320p. mass mkt. 5.99 (*0-380-72763-3*, Avon Bks.) Morrow/Avon.

—The Bum's Rush. 1997. (Leo Waterman Mysteries Ser.). 246p. 22.95 (*0-8027-3299-2*) Walker & Co.

—Cast in Stone. 1997. (Leo Waterman Mysteries Ser.). 304p. mass mkt. 5.99 (*0-380-72762-5*, Avon Bks.) Morrow/Avon.

—Cast in Stone. 1996. (Leo Waterman Mysteries Ser.). 288p. 21.95 (*0-8027-3267-4*) Walker & Co.

—The Deader the Better. (Leo Waterman Mysteries Ser.). 352p. 2000. 22.00 (*0-380-97723-0*); 2001. reprint ed. mass mkt. 6.99 (*0-380-80420-4*, Avon Bks.) Morrow/Avon.

—The Last Ditch. (Leo Waterman Mysteries Ser.). 2000. 320p. mass mkt. 5.99 (*0-380-79369-5*); 1999. 288p. 22.00 (*0-380-97557-2*) Morrow/Avon. (Avon Bks.).

—Slow Burn. (Leo Waterman Mysteries Ser.). 1999. 304p. mass mkt. 5.99 (*0-380-79367-9*); 1998. 288p. 20.00 (*0-380-97556-4*) Morrow/Avon. (Avon Bks.).

—Who in Hell Is Wanda Fuca? 1996. (Leo Waterman Mysteries Ser.). 320p. mass mkt. 5.99 (*0-380-72761-7*, Avon Bks.) Morrow/Avon.

—Who in Hell Is Wanda Fuca? 1995. 244p. 21.95 (*0-8027-3255-0*) Walker & Co.

**WATERS, STANLEY (FICTITIOUS CHARACTER)—FICTION**

Scott, Willard. Murder under Blue Skies: A Stanley Waters Mystery. 1998. 208p. (YA). 23.95 o.p. (*0-525-94324-2*) Dutton/Plume.

**WATKINS, MERRILY (FICTITIOUS CHARACTER)—FICTION**

Rickman, Phil. A Crown of Lights. 2002. 566p. pap. 7.95 (*0-330-48450-8*) Pan Bks. Ltd. GBR. *Dist:* Trafalgar Square.

—The Cure of Souls. 2003. 496p. pap. 7.95 (*0-330-48756-6*) Pan Bks. Ltd. GBR. *Dist:* Trafalgar Square.

—The Cure of Souls. 2002. (Illus.). 485p. 28.00 (*0-333-90623-3*) Trafalgar Square.

—The Lamp of the Wicked. 2003. 356p. 19.95 (*0-333-90805-8*) Macmillan U.K. GBR. *Dist:* Trafalgar Square.

—Midwinter of the Spirit. 2001. 539p. pap. 7.95 (*0-330-37401-X*) Pan Bks. Ltd. GBR. *Dist:* Trafalgar Square.

—The Wine of Angels. 2001. 631p. pap. 7.95 (*0-330-34268-1*) Pan Bks. Ltd. GBR. *Dist:* Trafalgar Square.

**WATSON, EDGAR J. (FICTITIOUS CHARACTER)—FICTION**

Matthiessen, Peter. Killing Mister Watson. 1991. 384p. pap. 14.00 (*0-679-73405-8*, Vintage) Knopf Publishing Group.

—Killing Mister Watson. 1992. 3.99 o.p. (*0-517-08671-9*) Random Hse. Value Publishing.

**WATSON, JOHN H. (FICTITIOUS CHARACTER)—FICTION**

Berger, Arthur A. Durkheim Is Dead! Sherlock Holmes Is Introduced to Social Theory. 2003. 200p. pap. 24.95 (*0-7591-0298-8*) AltaMira Pr.

Berger, Arthur Asa. Durkheim Is Dead! A Sherlock Holmes Mystery of Social Theory. 2003. (Illus.). 272p. 19.95 (*0-7591-0300-3*); 200p. pap. 70.00 o.s.i (*0-7591-0299-6*) AltaMira Pr.

Boucher, Anthony. The New Adventures of Sherlock Holmes, Vol. 5. abr. ed. 1994. (New Adventures of Sherlock Holmes Gift Edition Ser.: Vol. 5). 25.00 o.s.i incl. audio (*0-671-50143-7*, Simon & Schuster Audioworks) Simon & Schuster Audio.

—The New Adventures of Sherlock Holmes Vol. 1: The Unfortunate Tobacconist & the Paradol Chamber. abr. ed. 1999. (New Adventures of Sherlock Holmes Ser.: Vol. 1). audio (*0-671-04341-2*, Simon & Schuster Audioworks) Simon & Schuster Audio.

—The New Adventures of Sherlock Holmes Vol. 2: The Viennese Strangler & the Notorious Canary Trainer. abr. ed. 1999. audio (*0-671-04342-0*, Simon & Schuster Audioworks) Simon & Schuster Audio.

—The New Adventures of Sherlock Holmes Vol. 3: The April Fool's Day Adventure & the Strange Adventure of the Uneasy Chair. abr. ed. 1999. audio (*0-671-04343-9*, Simon & Schuster Audioworks) Simon & Schuster Audio.

—The New Adventures of Sherlock Holmes Vol. 4: The Strange Case of the Demon Barber & the Mystery of the Headless Monk. abr. ed. 1999. audio (*0-671-04344-7*, Simon & Schuster Audioworks) Simon & Schuster Audio.

—The New Adventures of Sherlock Holmes Vol. 5: The Amateur Mendicant Society & the Case of the Vanishing White Elephant. abr. ed. 1999. (New Adventures of Sherlock Holmes Ser.: Vol. 5). audio (*0-671-04346-3*, Simon & Schuster Audioworks) Simon & Schuster Audio.

—The New Adventures of Sherlock Holmes Vol. 6: The Case of the Limping Ghost & the Girl with the Gazelle. abr. ed. 1999. audio 5.98 (*0-671-04340-4*, Simon & Schuster Audioworks); 1998. audio 5.98 Simon & Schuster Audio.

—The New Adventures of Sherlock Holmes Vol. 7: The Case of the Out of Date Murder & the Waltz of Death. abr. ed. 1999. (New Adventures of Sherlock Holmes Ser.: Vol. 7). audio (*0-671-04347-1*, Simon & Schuster Audioworks) Simon & Schuster Audio.

—The New Adventures of Sherlock Holmes Vol. 8: Colonel Warburton's Madness. abr. ed. 1999. (New Adventures of Sherlock Holmes Ser.: Vol. 8). audio (*0-671-04348-X*, Simon & Schuster Audioworks) Simon & Schuster Audio.

—The New Adventures of Sherlock Holmes Vol. 9: A Scandal in Bohemia & the Second Generation. 1999. (New Adventures of Sherlock Holmes Ser.: Vol. 9). audio (*0-671-04349-8*, Simon & Schuster Audioworks) Simon & Schuster Audio.

—The New Adventures of Sherlock Holmes Vol. 10: In Flanders Fields & the Eyes of Mr. Leyton. abr. ed. 1999. (New Adventures of Sherlock Holmes Ser.: Vol. 10). audio (*0-671-04350-1*, Simon & Schuster Audioworks) Simon & Schuster Audio.

—The New Adventures of Sherlock Holmes Vol. 11: The Tell Tale Pigeon Feathers & the Indiscretion of Mr. Edwards. abr. ed. 1999. audio (*0-671-04351-X*, Simon & Schuster Audioworks) Simon & Schuster Audio.

—The New Adventures of Sherlock Holmes Vol. 11: The Tell Tale Pigeon Feathers & The Indiscretion of Mr. Edwards. abr. ed. 1991. audio 9.95 (*0-671-69083-3*, Simon & Schuster Audioworks) Simon & Schuster Audio.

—The New Adventures of Sherlock Holmes Vol. 12: The Problem of Thor Bridge & the Double Zero. 1999. audio (*0-671-04352-8*, Simon & Schuster Audioworks) Simon & Schuster Audio.

—The New Adventures of Sherlock Holmes Vol. 13: Murder in the Casbah & the Tankerville Club. abr. ed. 1999. (New Adventures of Sherlock Holmes Ser.: Vol. 13). audio (*0-671-04353-6*, Simon & Schuster Audioworks) Simon & Schuster Audio.

—The New Adventures of Sherlock Holmes Vol. 14: The Strange Case of the Murderer in Wax & the Man with the Twisted Lip. abr. ed. 1999. audio (*0-671-04354-4*, Simon & Schuster Audioworks) Simon & Schuster Audio.

—The New Adventures of Sherlock Holmes Vol. 15: The Guileless Gypsy & the Camberville Poisoners. abr. ed. 1999. (New Adventures of Sherlock Holmes Ser.: Vol. 15). audio (*0-671-04355-2*, Simon & Schuster Audioworks) Simon & Schuster Audio.

—The New Adventures of Sherlock Holmes Vol. 16: The Terrifying Cats & the Submarine Club. abr. ed. 1999. (New Adventures of Sherlock Holmes Ser.: Vol. 16). audio (*0-671-04356-0*, Simon & Schuster Audioworks) Simon & Schuster Audio.

—The New Adventures of Sherlock Holmes Vol. 17: The Living Doll & the Disappearing Scientists. abr. ed. 1999. audio (*0-671-04357-9*, Simon & Schuster Audioworks) Simon & Schuster Audio.

—The New Adventures of Sherlock Holmes Vol. 18: The Adventure of the Speckled Band & the Purloined Ruby. abr. ed. 1999. audio (*0-671-04358-7*, Simon & Schuster Audioworks) Simon & Schuster Audio.

—The New Adventures of Sherlock Holmes Vol. 19: The Book of Tobit & Murder Beyond the Mountains. abr. ed. 1999. audio (*0-671-04359-5*, Simon & Schuster Audioworks) Simon & Schuster Audio.

—The New Adventures of Sherlock Holmes Vol. 20: The Manor House Case & the Adventure of the Stuttering Ghost. abr. ed. 1999. audio (*0-671-04360-9*, Simon & Schuster Audioworks) Simon & Schuster Audio.

—The New Adventures of Sherlock Holmes Vol. 21: The Great Gandolfo & the Adventure of the Original Hamlet. abr. ed. 1999. audio (*0-671-04361-7*, Simon & Schuster Audioworks) Simon & Schuster Audio.

—The New Adventures of Sherlock Holmes Vol. 22: Murder by Moonlight & the Singular Affair of the Coptic Compass. 1999. (New Adventures of Sherlock Holmes Ser.). audio (*0-671-04362-5*, Simon & Schuster Audioworks) Simon & Schuster Audio.

—The New Adventures of Sherlock Holmes Vol. 23: The Gunpowder Plot & the Babbling Butler. abr. ed. 1999. audio (*0-671-04363-3*, Simon & Schuster Audioworks) Simon & Schuster Audio.

—The New Adventures of Sherlock Holmes Vol. 24: The Accidental Murderess & the Adventure of the Blarney Stone. abr. ed. 1999. (New Adventures of Sherlock Holmes Ser.). audio (*0-671-04364-1*, Simon & Schuster Audioworks) Simon & Schuster Audio.

—The New Adventures of Sherlock Holmes Vol. 25: The Night Before Christmas & the Darlington Substitution. abr. ed. 1999. (New Adventures of Sherlock Holmes Ser.). audio (*0-671-04365-X*, Simon & Schuster Audioworks) Simon & Schuster Audio.

—The New Adventures of Sherlock Holmes Vol. 26: The Haunting of Sherlock Holmes & the Baconian Cipher. abr. ed. 1999. audio (*0-671-04366-8*, Simon & Schuster Audioworks) Simon & Schuster Audio.

Boucher, Anthony & Green, Denis. The New Adventures of Sherlock Holmes. abr. ed. 1990. (Sherlock Holmes Ser.). audio 25.00 o.s.i (*0-671-72702-8*); 1993. (Sherlock Holmes Ser.). audio 25.00 o.s.i (*0-671-87587-6*); 2001. audio 49.95 (*0-7435-2045-9*); Set. 1992. (New Adventures of Sherlock Holmes Gift Edition Ser.: Vol. 3). audio 25.00 o.s.i (*0-671-79367-5*); Vol. 5-18. 1991. (New Adventures of Sherlock Holmes Ser.: Vol. 2). audio 25.00 o.s.i (*0-671-74750-9*); Vol. 10. 1990. audio 9.95 (*0-671-69082-5*) Simon & Schuster Audio. (Simon & Schuster Audioworks).

—The New Adventures of Sherlock Holmes Vol. 1: The Unfortunate Tobacconist & The Paradol Chamber. abr. ed. 1988. 9.95 incl. audio (*0-671-66076-4*, Simon & Schuster Audioworks) Simon & Schuster Audio.

—The New Adventures of Sherlock Holmes Vol. 3: The April Fool's Day Adventure & The Strange Adventure of the Uneasy Easy Chair. abr. ed. 1989. 9.95 incl. audio (*0-671-67785-3*, Simon & Schuster Audioworks) Simon & Schuster Audio.

—The New Adventures of Sherlock Holmes Vol. 4: The Strange Case of the Demon Barber & The Mystery of the Headless Monk. abr. ed. 1989. 9.95 incl. audio (*0-671-68088-9*, Simon & Schuster Audioworks) Simon & Schuster Audio.

—The New Adventures of Sherlock Holmes Vol. 5: The Amateur Mendicant Society & The Case of the Vanishing White Elephant. abr. ed. 1990. audio 9.95 (*0-671-68423-X*, Simon & Schuster Audioworks) Simon & Schuster Audio.

—The New Adventures of Sherlock Holmes Vol. 6: Eight Classic Radio Mysteries. gif. ed. 1995. (New Adventures of Sherlock Holmes Gift Edition Ser.: Vol. 6). audio 25.00 o.s.i (*0-671-53703-2*, Simon & Schuster Audioworks) Simon & Schuster Audio.

—The New Adventures of Sherlock Holmes Vol. 6: The Case of the Limping Ghost & The Girl with the Gazelle. abr. ed. 1989. audio 9.95 (*0-671-68772-7*, Simon & Schuster Audioworks) Simon & Schuster Audio.

—The New Adventures of Sherlock Holmes Vol. 7: The Case of the Out of Date Murder & The Waltz of Death. abr. ed. 1990. audio 9.95 (*0-671-68773-5*, Simon & Schuster Audioworks) Simon & Schuster Audio.

—The New Adventures of Sherlock Holmes Vol. 8: Colonel Warburton's Madness & The Iron Box. abr. ed. 1990. (New Adventures of Sherlock Holmes Ser.: Vol. 8). 60p. audio 9.95 (*0-671-68774-3*, Simon & Schuster Audioworks) Simon & Schuster Audio.

—The New Adventures of Sherlock Holmes Vol. 9: A Scandal in Bohemia & The Second Generation. abr. ed. 1990. audio 9.95 (*0-671-69081-7*, Simon & Schuster Audioworks) Simon & Schuster Audio.

—The New Adventures of Sherlock Holmes Vol. 12: The Problem of Thor Bridge & The Double Zero. abr. ed. 1991. audio 9.95 (*0-671-70744-2*, 326340, Simon & Schuster Audioworks) Simon & Schuster Audio.

—The New Adventures of Sherlock Holmes Vol. 14: The Strange Case of the Murderer in Wax & The Man with the Twisted Lip. abr. ed. 1991. audio 9.95 (*0-671-70746-9*, Simon & Schuster Audioworks) Simon & Schuster Audio.

—The New Adventures of Sherlock Holmes Vol. 20: The Manor House Case & The Adventure of the Stuttering Ghost. abr. ed. 1993. audio 11.00 (*0-671-79411-6*, Simon & Schuster Audioworks) Simon & Schuster Audio.

Boucher, Anthony & Greene, Denis. The New Adventures of Sherlock Holmes Slip Case, Vols. 1-13. unabr. ed. audio 129.35 Simon & Schuster Audio.

Dare, M. P. The Shadow of the Rat: A Sherlock Holmes Adventure. 1999. 162p. pap. (*1-899562-71-0*) Ash-Tree Pr.

Davies, David Stuart. The Shadow of the Rat: A Sherlock Holmes Adventure. 1999. 162p. (*1-899562-70-2*, Calabash Pr.) Ash-Tree Pr.

Douglas, Carole Nelson. Good Morning, Irene. (Irene Adler Adventure Ser.). 1992. (Illus.). 374p. mass mkt. 4.99 (*0-8125-0949-8*); 1991. 19.95 o.p. (*0-312-93211-1*) Doherty, Tom Assocs., LLC. (Tor Bks.).

—Good Morning, Irene. unabr. ed. 1999. audio 80.00 (*0-7887-2487-8*, 95562E7) Recorded Bks., LLC.

—Good Night, Mr. Holmes. 1991. 408p. mass mkt. 4.99 o.s.i (*0-8125-1430-0*); 1990. 18.95 o.p. (*0-312-93210-3*) Doherty, Tom Assocs., LLC. (Tor Bks.).

—Good Night, Mr. Holmes. unabr. ed. 1998. audio 78.00 (*0-7887-2489-4*, 95564E7) Recorded Bks., LLC.

—Irene at Large. 1993. (Irene Adler Adventure Ser.). 395p. mass mkt. 5.99 (*0-8125-1702-4*, Tor Bks.) Doherty, Tom Assocs., LLC.

—Irene at Large. unabr. ed. 2000. audio 91.00 (*0-7887-2492-4*, 95567E7) Recorded Bks., LLC.

—Irene's Last Waltz. 1994. (Irene Adler Adventure Ser.). 480p. mass mkt. 4.99 (*0-8125-1703-2*); 22.95 o.p. (*0-312-85224-X*) Doherty, Tom Assocs., LLC. (Forge Bks.).

—Irene's Last Waltz. unabr. ed. 2000. audio 97.00 (*0-7887-2493-2*, 95568E7) Recorded Bks., LLC.

Downing, Noel. Doctor Watson & the Invisible Man. 1992. 200p. 25.00 (*0-86025-275-2*) Henry, Ian Pubns. GBR. *Dist:* Empire Publishing Service.

Doyle, Arthur Conan. The Case of Mr. George Edalji. reprint ed. lib. bdg. 98.00 (*0-7426-2716-0*); 2001. pap. text 28.00 (*0-7426-7716-8*) Classic Bks.

—My Life with Sherlock Holmes: Conversations in Baker Street. Hamilton, J. R., ed. 1970. (Illus.). 5.75 o.p. (*0-7195-1837-7*) Transatlantic Arts, Inc.

—The Valley of Fear. 1976. 17.95 (*0-8488-1288-3*) Amereon, Ltd.

—The Valley of Fear. unabr. ed. 2003. (YA). (gr. 10 up). audio 29.95 (*1-55685-676-8*, ) Audio Bk. Contractors, Inc.

—The Valley of Fear. l.t. ed. 1990. pap. 16.95 o.p. (*0-7927-0475-4*, C0775) BBC Audiobooks America.

—The Valley of Fear. 1987. 176p. mass mkt. 2.50 o.p. (*0-425-10330-7*); 1986. mass mkt. 2.50 o.s.i (*0-425-09580-0*); 1984. mass mkt. 2.50 o.s.i (*0-425-07140-5*); 1981. mass mkt. 2.25 o.s.i (*0-425-05221-4*); 1980. mass mkt. 1.95 o.s.i (*0-425-04911-6*); 1979. mass mkt. 1.75 o.s.i (*0-425-04537-4*); 1978. mass mkt. 1.50 o.s.i (*0-425-03981-1*); 1976. mass mkt. 1.25 o.s.i (*0-425-03136-5*) Berkley Publishing Group.

—The Valley of Fear. unabr. ed. 1991. audio 39.95 (*0-7861-0612-3*, 2102) Blackstone Audio Bks., Inc.

—The Valley of Fear. unabr. collector's ed. 1991. audio 36.00 (*0-7366-2030-3*, 2844) Books on Tape, Inc.

—The Valley of Fear. 1988. lib. bdg. 16.95 (*0-89966-232-3*) Buccaneer Bks., Inc.

—The Valley of Fear. 1977. 7.95 o.p. (*0-385-12284-5*) Doubleday Publishing.

—The Valley of Fear. unabr. ed. 1991. audio 16.99 (*0-88646-296-7*, 7296) Durkin Hayes Publishing Ltd.

—The Valley of Fear, Set. unabr. ed. 1999. audio 39.95 Highsmith Inc.

—The Valley of Fear. 2001. iv, 200p. pap. 8.95 (*0-7551-0645-8*) House of Stratus, Inc. GBR. *Dist:* Midpoint Trade Bks., Inc.

—The Valley of Fear. unabr. ed. 1991. (YA). (gr. 9-12). audio 29.00 Jimcin Recordings.

—The Valley of Fear. Edwards, Owen D., ed. 1993. (Oxford Sherlock Holmes Ser.). 292p. (C). 13.95 o.p. (*0-19-212314-9*, 8951) Oxford Univ. Pr., Inc.

—The Valley of Fear. Edwards, Owen D., ed. & intro. by. 1995. (Oxford World's Classics Ser.). 292p. reprint ed. pap. 6.95 o.p. (*0-19-282382-5*) Oxford Univ. Pr., Inc.

—The Valley of Fear. 1991. (Classic Crime Ser.). 192p. pap. 6.00 o.p. (*0-14-005710-2*, Penguin Bks.) Penguin Group (USA) Inc.

—The Valley of Fear. collector's ed. 2002. (Illus.). im. lthr. 38.85 (*1-4115-1255-3*); pap. 19.95 (*1-4115-0524-7*); 25.95 (*1-4115-0890-4*); pap. 17.95 (*1-4115-0320-1*) Polyglot Pr., Inc.

—The Valley of Fear. 1999. 256p. E-Book 3.99 incl. cd-rom (*1-57646-184-X*) Quiet Vision Publishing.

—The Valley of Fear. abr. ed. 1999. (BBC Radio Presents Ser.). audio 18.00 o.s.i (*0-553-52622-7*, RH Audio) Random Hse. Audio Publishing Group.

—The Valley of Fear. unabr. ed. 1986. (Sherlock Holmes Mystery Ser.). audio 35.00 (*1-55690-539-4*, 86250E7) Recorded Bks., LLC.

—The Valley of Fear. unabr. ed. 2002. audio compact disk 33.00 (*1-4001-0040-2*); audio compact disk 20.00 (*1-4001-5040-X*) Tantor Media, Inc.

—The Valley of Fear. l.t. ed. 1978. (Ulverscroft Large Print Ser.). 29.99 o.p. (*0-7089-0086-0*, Ulverscroft) Thorpe, F. A. Pubs. GBR. *Dist:* Ulverscroft Large Print Bks., Ltd., Ulverscroft Large Print Canada, Ltd.

Doyle, Arthur Conan & Reyburn, Stanley. The Valley of Fear. Landes, William-Alan, ed. 1998. 55p. pap. 10.00 (*0-88734-742-8*) Players Pr., Inc.

Estleman, Loren D. Sherlock Holmes vs. Dracula or, The Adventure of the Sanguinary Count. 2000. 224p. pap. 14.00 (*0-7434-0714-8*) ibooks, Inc.

Green, Denis & Boucher, Anthony. The New Adventures of Sherlock Holmes Vol. 2: The Viennese Strangler & The Notorious Canary Trainer. abr. ed. 1988. 9.95 incl. audio (*0-671-66433-6*, Simon & Schuster Audioworks) Simon & Schuster Audio.

Greenberg, Martin H., et al, eds. Holmes for the Holidays. 304p. 1996. 21.95 o.s.i (*0-425-15473-4*); 1998. reprint ed. pap. 13.00 o.s.i (*0-425-16754-2*) Berkley Publishing Group. (Prime Crime).

—More Holmes for the Holidays. 1999. 272p. 21.95 o.s.i (*0-425-17033-0*, Prime Crime) Berkley Publishing Group.

Greenberg, Martin H. & Rossel-Waugh, Carol-Lynn, eds. The New Adventures of Sherlock Holmes. 1987. (Illus.). 18.95 o.p. (*0-88184-344-X*, Carroll & Graf Pubs.) Avalon Publishing Group.

Greenberg, Martin H. & Waugh, Carol-Lynn Rossel, eds. The New Adventures of Sherlock Holmes. 1999. (Illus.). 344p. pap. 13.95 (*0-7867-0698-8*, Carroll & Graf Pubs.) Avalon Publishing Group.

Gregson, J. M. Sherlock Holmes & the Frightened Golfer. 1999. (Sherlock Holmes... Ser.). (*0-947533-68-0*) Breese Bks., Ltd.

—Sherlock Holmes & the Frightened Golfer. 2000. (Sherlock Holmes Ser.). 176p. pap. 12.95 (*0-947533-63-X*) Breese Bks., Ltd. GBR. *Dist:* Midpoint Trade Bks., Inc.

Hall, John. Sherlock Holmes & the Boulevard Assassin. 1998. 174p. pap. 14.95 (*0-947533-52-4*) Breese Bks., Ltd. GBR. *Dist:* Midpoint Trade Bks., Inc.

—Sherlock Holmes & the Disgraced Inspector. 1998. 140p. pap. 14.95 (*0-947533-88-5*) Breese Bks., Ltd. GBR. *Dist:* Midpoint Trade Bks., Inc.

—Sherlock Holmes & the Disgraced Inspector. l.t. ed. 2000. (Linford Mystery Large Print Ser.). 248p. pap. 18.99 (*0-7089-5783-8*, Linford) Thorpe, F. A. Pubs. GBR. *Dist:* Ulverscroft Large Print Bks., Ltd., Ulverscroft Large Print Canada, Ltd.

—Sherlock Holmes & the Telephone Murder Mystery. 1998. 189p. pap. 14.95 (*0-947533-47-8*) Breese Bks., Ltd. GBR. *Dist:* Midpoint Trade Bks., Inc.

Hall, John, ed. The Abominable Wife & Other Unrecorded Cases of Mr. Sherlock Holmes. 1998. 114p. pap. (*1-899562-61-3*, Calabash Pr.) Ash-Tree Pr.

Janda, Anita. The Secret Diary of Dr. Watson. 2001. 280p. 27.95 (*0-7490-0570-X*) Allison & Busby, Ltd. GBR. *Dist:* International Publishers Marketing.

King, Stephen, et al. The New Adventures of Sherlock Holmes. Greenberg, Martin H. & Rossel Waugh, Carol-Lynn, eds. 1988. (Illus.). 344p. pap. 11.95 o.p. (*0-88184-435-7*, Carroll & Graf Pubs.) Avalon Publishing Group.

Meyer, Nicholas. The West End Horror. 1982. mass mkt. 2.50 o.s.i (*0-345-30592-2*) Ballantine Bks.

—The West End Horror: From the Memoirs of John H. Watson. 1994. 224p. pap. 10.95 (*0-393-31153-8*) Norton, W. W. & Co., Inc.

Mitchelson, Austin & Utechin, Nicholas. Sherlock Holmes & the Hellbirds. 1995. 35.00 (*0-86025-284-1*) Players Pr., Inc.

Naslund, Sena Jeter. Sherlock in Love: A Novel. 2001. 240p. pap. 13.00 (*0-688-17844-8*, Perennial) HarperTrade.

Rathbone, Basil & Bruce, Nigel. The New Adventures of Sherlock Holmes. 1998. Vol. 1 24.98 incl. audio; Vol. 2 24.98 incl. audio; Vol. 3 24.98 incl. audio; Vol. 4. 24.98 incl. audio; Vol. 5. 24.98 incl. audio; Vol. 6. 24.98 incl. audio Radio Spirits, Inc.

Worcester, Wayne. The Jewel of Covent Garden. 2000. 336p. mass mkt. 5.99 o.s.i (*0-451-20195-7*) NAL.

**WATSON, LUCIUS (FICTITIOUS CHARACTER)—FICTION**

Matthiessen, Peter. Lost Man's River. 1998. 560p. pap. 15.00 (*0-679-73564-X*) Random Hse., Inc.

**WAYLES, LUCY (FICTITIOUS CHARACTER)—FICTION**

Adamson, Lydia. Beware Butcher Bird. 1997. (Birdwatcher Mystery Ser.). 256p. mass mkt. 5.99 o.s.i (*0-451-19121-8*, Signet Bks.) NAL.
—Beware the Laughing Gull. 1998. (Lucy Wayles Mysteries Ser.: Vol. 3). 256p. mass mkt. 5.99 o.s.i (*0-451-19598-1*, Signet Bks.) NAL.
—Beware the Tufted Duck: A Lucy Wayles Mystery. 1996. (Birdwatcher Mystery Ser.). 224p. mass mkt. 5.50 o.s.i (*0-451-19024-6*, Signet Bks.) NAL.

**WAYNEST, JENNY (FICTITIOUS CHARACTER)—FICTION**

Hambly, Barbara. Dragonsbane. (Wizards of Fantasy Promotion Ser.). (Orig.). 1987. 352p. mass mkt. 6.99 (*0-345-34939-3*); 1985. mass mkt. 3.50 o.p. (*0-345-31572-3*) Ballantine Bks. (Del Rey).
—Dragonshadow. 2000. 320p. mass mkt. 6.99 (*0-345-42188-4*); 1999. 304p. 24.00 o.s.i (*0-345-42187-6*) Ballantine Bks. (Del Rey).
—Knight of the Demon Queen. 2000. 352p. mass mkt. 6.99 (*0-345-42190-6*, Del Rey) Ballantine Bks.

**WEARIE, EAMON (FICTITIOUS CHARACTER)—FICTION**

McGrady, Sean. Dead Letter. Chelius, Jane, ed. 1992. 240p. (Orig.). mass mkt. 4.99 (*0-671-74267-1*, Pocket) Simon & Schuster.
—Town Without a Zip. 1997. (Eamon Wearie Mystery Ser.). 288p. pap. 5.99 (*0-671-86942-6*, Pocket) Simon & Schuster.

**WEATHERBY, ARTIE (FICTITIOUS CHARACTER)—FICTION**

Miller, J. M. The Big Lie: A Weatherby Mystery. 1994. pap. 10.99 (*0-8407-6357-3*) Nelson, Thomas Inc.

**WEATHERFORD, BIGGIE (FICTITIOUS CHARACTER)—FICTION**

Bell, Nancy. Biggie & the Fricasseed Fat. 1998. 224p. 20.95 o.p. (*0-312-19238-X*, Saint Martin's Minotaur) St. Martin's Pr.
—Biggie & the Mangled Mortician. (Dead Letter Mysteries Ser.). 1998. 208p. mass mkt. 5.99 (*0-312-96491-9*, St. Martin's Paperbacks); 1997. 201p. text 20.95 o.p. (*0-312-15477-1*, Saint Martin's Minotaur) St. Martin's Pr.
—Biggie & the Mangled Mortician. l.t. ed. 2000. (Thorndike Senior Lifestyle Ser.). (Illus.). 288p. 27.95 (*0-7862-2562-9*) Thorndike Pr.
—Biggie & the Meddlesome Mailman. 1999. 214p. 22.95 (*0-312-20880-4*, Saint Martin's Minotaur) St. Martin's Pr.
—Biggie & the Meddlesome Mailman. l.t. ed. 2000. (Mystery Ser.). 274p. 28.95 (*0-7862-2552-1*) Thorndike Pr.
—Biggie & the Poisoned Politician. (Dead Letter Mysteries Ser.). 1997. 192p. mass mkt. 5.50 (*0-312-96219-3*, St. Martin's Paperbacks); 1996. 208p. text 21.95 o.p. (*0-312-14285-4*, Saint Martin's Minotaur) St. Martin's Pr.
—Biggie & the Poisoned Politician. l.t. ed. 2000. (Thorndike Senior Lifestyle Ser.). 253p. 28.95 o.p. (*0-7862-2550-5*) Thorndike Pr.
—Biggie & the Quincy Ghost. 2001. 224p. 22.95 (*0-312-26560-3*, Saint Martin's Minotaur) St. Martin's Pr.
—Biggie & the Quincy Ghost. l.t. ed. 2002. (Mystery Ser.). 254p. 30.45 (*0-7862-3842-9*) Thorndike Pr.

**WEATHERFORD, J. R. (FICTITIOUS CHARACTER)—FICTION**

Bell, Nancy. Biggie & the Fricasseed Fat. 1998. 224p. 20.95 o.p. (*0-312-19238-X*, Saint Martin's Minotaur) St. Martin's Pr.
—Biggie & the Mangled Mortician. (Dead Letter Mysteries Ser.). 1998. 208p. mass mkt. 5.99 (*0-312-96491-9*, St. Martin's Paperbacks); 1997. 201p. text 20.95 o.p. (*0-312-15477-1*, Saint Martin's Minotaur) St. Martin's Pr.
—Biggie & the Mangled Mortician. l.t. ed. 2000. (Thorndike Senior Lifestyle Ser.). (Illus.). 288p. 27.95 (*0-7862-2562-9*) Thorndike Pr.
—Biggie & the Meddlesome Mailman. 1999. 214p. 22.95 (*0-312-20880-4*, Saint Martin's Minotaur) St. Martin's Pr.
—Biggie & the Meddlesome Mailman. l.t. ed. 2000. (Mystery Ser.). 274p. 28.95 (*0-7862-2552-1*) Thorndike Pr.
—Biggie & the Poisoned Politician. (Dead Letter Mysteries Ser.). 1997. 192p. mass mkt. 5.50 (*0-312-96219-3*, St. Martin's Paperbacks); 1996. 208p. text 21.95 o.p. (*0-312-14285-4*, Saint Martin's Minotaur) St. Martin's Pr.
—Biggie & the Poisoned Politician. l.t. ed. 2000. (Thorndike Senior Lifestyle Ser.). 253p. 28.95 o.p. (*0-7862-2550-5*) Thorndike Pr.
—Biggie & the Quincy Ghost. 2001. 224p. 22.95 (*0-312-26560-3*, Saint Martin's Minotaur) St. Martin's Pr.
—Biggie & the Quincy Ghost. l.t. ed. 2002. (Mystery Ser.). 254p. 30.45 (*0-7862-3842-9*) Thorndike Pr.

**WEBB, DAVID (FICTITIOUS CHARACTER)—FICTION**

Fraser, Anthea. The April Rainers. 1990. 14.95 o.s.i (*0-385-41088-3*) Doubleday Publishing.
—Death Speaks Softly. 1987. (Crime Club Ser.). 192p. 12.95 o.s.i (*0-385-24147-X*) Doubleday Publishing.
—Death Speaks Softly. l.t. ed. 1988. 336p. (*0-7089-1846-8*, Ulverscroft) Thorpe, F. A. Pubs.
—The Gospel Makers. 1994. 224p. 14.99 (*0-00-232490-3*) HarperSanFrancisco.
—The Gospel Makers. 1996. 208p. 20.95 o.p. (*0-312-13979-9*, Saint Martin's Minotaur) St. Martin's Pr.
—Home Through the Dark. 2000. 21.95 (*0-7540-8575-9*, Black Dagger) BBC Audiobooks America.
—Home Through the Dark. l.t. ed. 2002. (Dales Large Print Ser.). 304p. pap. 21.99 o.p. (*1-84262-204-8*) Dales Large Print Bks. GBR. *Dist:* Ulverscroft Large Print Bks., Ltd., Ulverscroft Large Print Canada, Ltd.
—Home Through the Dark. 1977. (General Ser.). lib. bdg. 10.95 o.p. (*0-8161-6442-8*, Macmillan Reference USA) Gale Group.
—I'll Sing You Two-O Vol. 1: An Inspector Webb Mystery. 1996. 192p. 20.95 o.p. (*0-312-14623-X*, Saint Martin's Minotaur) St. Martin's Pr.
—A Necessary End. 1986. 192p. 13.95 o.s.i (*0-8027-5641-7*) Walker & Co.
—The Nine Bright Shiners. 1988. (Crime Club Ser.). 192p. pap. 12.95 o.s.i (*0-385-24323-5*) Doubleday Publishing.
—The Nine Bright Shiners. l.t. ed. 1990. (Ulverscroft Large Print Ser.). 29.99 o.p. (*0-7089-2173-6*, Ulverscroft) Thorpe, F. A. Pubs. GBR. *Dist:* Ulverscroft Large Print Bks., Ltd., Ulverscroft Large Print Canada, Ltd.
—One Is One & All Alone. 1998. 192p. 20.95 (*0-312-19309-2*, Saint Martin's Minotaur) St. Martin's Pr.
—Pretty Maids All in a Row. l.t. ed. 2001. (Dales Large Print Ser.). 272p. pap. 21.99 (*1-84262-075-4*) Dales Large Print Bks. GBR. *Dist:* Ulverscroft Large Print Bks., Ltd., Ulverscroft Large Print Canada, Ltd.
—Pretty Maids All in a Row. 1987. (Crime Club Ser.). 192p. 12.95 o.s.i (*0-385-23798-7*) Doubleday Publishing.
—Pretty Maids All in a Row. l.t. ed. 1987. (Ulverscroft Large Print Ser.). 336p. o.p. (*0-7089-1624-4*, Ulverscroft) Thorpe, F. A. Pubs. GBR. *Dist:* Ulverscroft Large Print Canada, Ltd.
—The Seven Stars. 1997. 224p. 20.95 o.p. (*0-312-15650-2*, Saint Martin's Minotaur) St. Martin's Pr.
—A Shroud for Delilah. 1986. (Crime Club Ser.). 192p. 12.95 o.p. (*0-385-23543-7*) Doubleday Publishing.
—A Shroud for Delilah. l.t. ed. 1985. 368p. 15.95 o.p. (*0-7089-1377-6*, Ulverscroft) Thorpe, F. A. Pubs. GBR. *Dist:* Ulverscroft Large Print Bks., Ltd.
—Six Proud Walkers. 1989. (Crime Club Ser.). 12.95 o.s.i (*0-385-24615-3*) Doubleday Publishing.
—Six Proud Walkers. l.t. ed. 1989. (Ulverscroft Large Print Ser.). 29.99 o.p. (*0-7089-2181-7*, Ulverscroft) Thorpe, F. A. Pubs. GBR. *Dist:* Ulverscroft Large Print Bks., Ltd., Ulverscroft Large Print Canada, Ltd.
—Symbols at Your Door. 1991. 192p. 15.00 o.s.i (*0-385-41685-7*) Doubleday Publishing.
—The Ten Commandments. unabr. ed. 1998. audio 49.95 (*0-7540-0172-5*, CAB 1595) Chivers Audio Bks. GBR. *Dist:* BBC Audiobooks America.
—The Ten Commandments. 2000. (DCI Webb Mysteries Ser.). 190p. 22.95 (*0-312-20915-0*); 192p. text 20.95 (*0-312-18672-X*) St. Martin's Pr. (Saint Martin's Minotaur).
—The Ten Commandments. l.t. ed. 2000. 279p. (*0-7540-4070-4*); (*0-7540-4071-2*) Thorndike Pr.
—Three, Three, the Rivals. 1992. 13.99 (*0-00-232380-X*) HarperSanFrancisco.
—Three, Three, the Rivals. 1995. 188p. 18.95 o.p. (*0-312-11902-X*, Saint Martin's Minotaur) St. Martin's Pr.
—Three, Three, the Rivals. l.t. ed. 1993. (Mystery Ser.). 368p. 29.99 o.p. (*0-7089-2984-2*, Ulverscroft) Thorpe, F. A. Pubs. GBR. *Dist:* Ulverscroft Large Print Bks., Ltd., Ulverscroft Large Print Canada, Ltd.

**WEBER, JON (FICTITIOUS CHARACTER)—FICTION**

Maier, Paul L. A Skeleton in God Closet. 1996. 360p. mass mkt. 5.99 (*0-7852-7537-1*) Nelson, Thomas Inc.

**WEINSTEIN, JOSHUA (FICTITIOUS CHARACTER)—FICTION**

Parker, T. Jefferson. The Triggerman's Dance. 1996. 352p. 21.95 (*0-7868-6142-8*); 2003. 576p. reprint ed. mass mkt. 6.99 (*0-7868-8917-9*) Hyperion Pr.

**WEISS, SCOTT (FICTITIOUS CHARACTER)—FICTION**

Klavan, Andrew. Dynamite Road. Date not set. mass mkt. (*0-7653-4694-X*); 2003. 320p. 25.95 (*0-7653-0785-5*) Doherty, Tom Assocs., LLC. (Forge Bks.).

**WELFORD, KAREN (FICTITIOUS CHARACTER)—FICTION**

Maclean, Charles. The Silence. 1997. 336p. mass mkt. 5.99 o.s.i (*0-06-101233-5*) HarperCollins Pubs.

**WELLESLEY BROTHERS (FICTITIOUS CHARACTERS)—FICTION**

Kidder, Jane. Mail-Order Temptress. 1992. 384p. mass mkt. 4.25 o.s.i (*0-8217-3863-1*, Zebra Bks.) Kensington Publishing Corp.
—Passion's Bargain. 1994. 416p. mass mkt. 4.50 o.s.i (*0-8217-4539-5*) Kensington Publishing Corp.
—Passion's Captive. 1993. 416p. mass mkt. 4.50 o.s.i (*0-8217-4341-4*, Zebra Bks.) Kensington Publishing Corp.
—Passion's Fever. 1991. mass mkt. 4.25 o.s.i (*0-8217-3646-9*, Zebra Bks.) Kensington Publishing Corp.
—Passion's Gift. 1995. 384p. mass mkt. 4.99 o.s.i (*0-8217-4865-3*) Kensington Publishing Corp.
—Passion's Kiss. 1996. 384p. mass mkt. 4.99 o.s.i (*0-8217-5317-7*) Kensington Publishing Corp.
—Passion's Song. 1993. 384p. mass mkt. 4.25 o.s.i (*0-8217-4174-8*, Zebra Bks.) Kensington Publishing Corp.

**WELLS, KATHERINE (FICTITIOUS CHARACTER)—FICTION**

Allison, Margaret. Indiscretion. 1996. 336p. mass mkt. 5.99 (*0-671-56328-9*, Pocket) Simon & Schuster.

**WELLS BROTHERS (FICTITIOUS CHARACTERS)—FICTION**

Adams, Andy. The Ranch on the Beaver. 1997. (Illus.). 313p. pap. 12.95 (*0-8032-5930-1*, Bison Bks.) Univ. of Nebraska Pr.
—Wells Brothers: The Young Cattle Kings. 1997. (Illus.). 370p. pap. 12.95 (*0-8032-5929-8*, Bison Bks.) Univ. of Nebraska Pr.

**WENTWORTH, BEA (FICTITIOUS CHARACTER)—FICTION**

Forrest, Richard. A Child's Garden of Death. 1982. (Scene of the Crime Ser.: No. 44). pap. 2.25 o.p. (*0-440-11325-3*) Dell Publishing.
—A Child's Garden of Death. 1977. pap. 1.50 o.p. (*0-671-80924-5*, Pocket) Simon & Schuster.
—The Death at Yew Corner. 1984. 176p. pap. 2.95 o.p. (*0-440-11782-8*) Dell Publishing.
—The Death at Yew Corner. 1981. (Rinehart Suspense Novel Ser.). 228p. o.p. (*0-03-053386-4*) Holt, Henry & Co.
—The Death in the Willows. 1979. (Rinehart Suspense Novel Ser.). 228p. o.p. (*0-03-049296-3*) Holt, Henry & Co.
—Death on the Mississippi. 1989. 224p. 15.95 o.p. (*0-312-03323-0*, Saint Martin's Minotaur) St. Martin's Pr.
—Death Through the Looking Glass. 1979. pap. 1.75 o.s.i (*0-671-82157-1*, Pocket) Simon & Schuster.
—Death under the Lilacs. 1985. 208p. 13.95 o.p. (*0-312-18878-1*) St. Martin's Pr.
—Pied Piper of Death: A Lyon & Bea Wentworth Mystery. 1997. 240p. 21.95 o.p. (*0-312-15292-2*, Saint Martin's Minotaur) St. Martin's Pr.

**WENTWORTH, LYON (FICTITIOUS CHARACTER)—FICTION**

Forrest, Richard. A Child's Garden of Death. 1982. (Scene of the Crime Ser.: No. 44). pap. 2.25 o.p. (*0-440-11325-3*) Dell Publishing.
—A Child's Garden of Death. 1977. pap. 1.50 o.p. (*0-671-80924-5*, Pocket) Simon & Schuster.
—The Death at Yew Corner. 1984. 176p. pap. 2.95 o.p. (*0-440-11782-8*) Dell Publishing.
—The Death at Yew Corner. 1981. (Rinehart Suspense Novel Ser.). 228p. o.p. (*0-03-053386-4*) Holt, Henry & Co.
—The Death in the Willows. 1979. (Rinehart Suspense Novel Ser.). 228p. o.p. (*0-03-049296-3*) Holt, Henry & Co.
—Death on the Mississippi. 1989. 224p. 15.95 o.p. (*0-312-03323-0*, Saint Martin's Minotaur) St. Martin's Pr.
—Death Through the Looking Glass. 1979. pap. 1.75 o.s.i (*0-671-82157-1*, Pocket) Simon & Schuster.
—Death under the Lilacs. 1985. 208p. 13.95 o.p. (*0-312-18878-1*) St. Martin's Pr.
—Pied Piper of Death: A Lyon & Bea Wentworth Mystery. 1997. 240p. 21.95 o.p. (*0-312-15292-2*, Saint Martin's Minotaur) St. Martin's Pr.

**WESCOTT SISTERS (FICTITIOUS CHARACTERS)—FICTION**

Kihlstrom, April. An Honorable Rogue. 1997. 224p. mass mkt. 4.99 o.s.i (*0-451-18817-9*, Signet Bks.) NAL.
—The Wicked Groom. 1996. (Regency Romance Ser.). 224p. mass mkt. 4.99 o.s.i (*0-451-18750-4*, Signet Bks.) NAL.
—Widowed Bride. 1996. 224p. mass mkt. 5.50 o.s.i (*0-451-18816-0*, Signet Bks.) NAL.

**WEST, DELILAH (FICTITIOUS CHARACTER)—FICTION**

O'Callaghan, Maxine. Death Is Forever. l.t. ed. 1999. (Five Star Mystery Ser.). 205p. 19.95 o.p. (*0-7862-1729-4*, Five Star) Gale Group.
—Down for the Count: A Delilah West Novel. 1998. (WWL Mystery Ser.: No. 294). per. (*0-373-26294-9*, 0-26294-9, Worldwide Library) Harlequin Enterprises, Ltd.
—Down for the Count: A Delilah West Novel. 1997. (Delilah West Mystery Ser.: Vol. 60). 240p. 20.95 (*0-312-16820-9*, Saint Martin's Minotaur) St. Martin's Pr.
—Down for the Count: A Delilah West Novel. l.t. ed. 1998. (Mystery Ser.). 307p. 26.95 (*0-7838-8404-4*) Thorndike Pr.
—Hit & Run. 1991. pap. 3.95 o.p. (*0-312-92440-2*, St. Martin's Paperbacks); 1989. 192p. 14.95 o.p. (*0-312-02584-X*, Saint Martin's Minotaur) St. Martin's Pr.
—Set-Up: A Delilah West Mystery. 1994. mass mkt. (*0-373-26144-6*, Harlequin Bks.) Harlequin Enterprises, Ltd.
—Set-Up: A Delilah West Mystery. 1991. 208p. 18.95 o.p. (*0-312-06462-4*, Saint Martin's Minotaur) St. Martin's Pr.
—Trade-Off. 1996. (Mystery Ser.). per. (*0-373-26191-8*, 1-26191-6, Worldwide Library) Harlequin Enterprises, Ltd.
—Trade-Off. 1994. 224p. 19.95 o.p. (*0-312-11081-2*, Saint Martin's Minotaur) St. Martin's Pr.

**WEST, HELEN (FICTITIOUS CHARACTER)—FICTION**

Fyfield, Frances. A Clear Conscience. unabr. ed. 1995. audio 69.95 (*0-7451-6547-8*, CAB 1163) BBC Audiobooks America.
—A Clear Conscience. 1996. (Helen West Mystery Ser.). mass mkt. 5.99 o.s.i (*0-345-38508-X*) Ballantine Bks.
—A Clear Conscience. unabr. ed. 2000. (West & Bailey Mystery Ser.). audio 59.95 Chivers Audio Bks. GBR. *Dist:* BBC Audiobooks America.
—A Clear Conscience. deluxe ed. 1995. 20.00 (*0-676-50224-5*, Pantheon) Knopf Publishing Group.
—A Clear Conscience. 2001. 272p. mass mkt. 6.99 (*0-14-028251-3*) Penguin Group (USA) Inc.
—A Clear Conscience. 1995. o.p. (*0-676-50194-X*) Random Hse., Inc.
—Deep Sleep. unabr. ed. 1996. (Prosecutor Helen West Mysteries Ser.). audio 54.95 (*0-7451-4144-7*, CAB827) BBC Audiobooks America.
—Deep Sleep. Chelius, Jane, ed. 240p. 1993. mass mkt. 4.99 o.p. (*0-671-73547-0*, Pocket); 1992. 18.00 o.p. (*0-671-73546-2*, Atria) Simon & Schuster.
—Not That Kind of Place. 1990. 224p. 17.95 o.p. (*0-671-67666-0*, Atria) Simon & Schuster.
—Not That Kind of Place. Chelius, Jane, ed. 1991. 256p. reprint ed. mass mkt. 5.50 (*0-671-73945-X*, Pocket) Simon & Schuster.
—A Question of Guilt. unabr. ed. 1993. (Prosecutor Helen West Mysteries Ser.). audio 69.95 (*0-7451-5972-9*, CAB 602) BBC Audiobooks America.
—A Question of Guilt. unabr. ed. 2000. (West & Bailey Mystery Ser.). audio 59.95 Chivers Audio Bks. GBR. *Dist:* BBC Audiobooks America.
—A Question of Guilt. 1990. 288p. mass mkt. 4.99 (*0-671-67665-2*, Pocket); 1989. 16.95 o.p. (*0-671-67664-4*, Atria) Simon & Schuster.
—A Question of Guilt. 1991. (Audio Books Ser.). audio 69.95 o.p. (*0-8161-9227-8*) Thorndike Pr.
—Shadow Play. l.t. ed. 1994. 22.95 o.p. (*0-7927-1828-3*); pap. 20.95 o.p. (*0-7927-1827-5*); audio 69.95 (*0-7451-4232-X*, CAB 915) BBC Audiobooks America.
—Shadow Play. 1994. mass mkt. 5.99 o.s.i (*0-345-38507-1*) Ballantine Bks.
—Shadow Play. unabr. ed. 2000. (West & Bailey Mystery Ser.). audio 59.95 Chivers Audio Bks. GBR. *Dist:* BBC Audiobooks America.
—Shadow Play. 1999. 288p. pap. 5.99 (*0-14-028683-7*, Penguin Bks.) Penguin Group (USA) Inc.
—Trial by Fire. l.t. ed. 1992. 18.95 o.p. (*0-7927-1200-5*); pap. 16.95 o.p. (*0-7927-1174-2*); 69.95 incl. audio (*0-7451-4025-4*, CAB 722) BBC Audiobooks America.
—Trial by Fire. unabr. ed. 2000. (West & Bailey Mystery Ser.). audio 59.95 Chivers Audio Bks. GBR. *Dist:* BBC Audiobooks America.
—Without Consent. unabr. ed. 1997. (West & Bailey Mystery Ser.). audio 59.95 (*0-7451-6799-3*, CAB 1415) Chivers Audio Bks. GBR. *Dist:* BBC Audiobooks America.
—Without Consent. 1998. 272p. mass mkt. 5.99 (*0-14-027477-4*) Penguin Group (USA) Inc.
—Without Consent. l.t. ed. 1998. (Mystery Ser.). 325p. 26.95 (*0-7838-8437-0*) Thorndike Pr.
—Without Consent. 1997. (Helen West Mystery Ser.). 224p. 21.95 o.p. (*0-670-87682-8*) Viking Penguin.

**WEST, MOLLY (FICTITIOUS CHARACTER)—FICTION**

Westfall, Patricia T. Fowl Play. 1998. (Worldwide Library Mysteries: Vol. 273). per. (*0-373-26273-6*, 0-26273-3, Worldwide Library) Harlequin Enterprises, Ltd.

—Fowl Play. 1996. 208p. 21.95 (*0-312-14604-3*, Saint Martin's Minotaur) St. Martin's Pr.

—Mother of the Bride. 1999. (WWL Mystery Ser.: No. 312). per. (*0-373-26312-0*, 1-26312-8, Worldwide Library) Harlequin Enterprises, Ltd.

—Mother of the Bride. pap. 15.95 (*0-312-30103-0*, Saint Martin's Griffin);Vol. 1. 1998. 224p. 21.95 (*0-312-18631-2*, Saint Martin's Minotaur) St. Martin's Pr.

**WEST, ROGER, INSPECTOR (FICTITIOUS CHARACTER)—FICTION**

Creasey, John. A Beauty for Inspector West. 1998. 192p. 19.50 o.p. (*0-7540-8516-3*, Black Dagger) BBC Audiobooks America.

—The Case Against Paul Raeburn: An Inspector West Mystery. 1987. 192p. reprint ed. mass mkt. 3.95 o.p. (*0-06-080892-6*, P/892, Perennial) HarperTrade.

—The Creepers: An Inspector West Mystery. 1987. 224p. reprint ed. mass mkt. 3.95 o.p. (*0-06-080889-6*, P/889, Perennial) HarperTrade.

—Death of a Postman: An Inspector West Mystery. 1987. 192p. reprint ed. mass mkt. 3.95 o.p. (*0-06-080890-X*, P/890, Perennial) HarperTrade.

—The Figure in the Dusk: An Inspector West Mystery. 1987. 224p. reprint ed. mass mkt. 3.95 o.p. (*0-06-080891-8*, P/891, Perennial) HarperTrade.

—Find Inspector West. l.t. ed. 1990. pap. 15.95 o.p. (*0-7927-0323-5*, C0798) BBC Audiobooks America.

—Holiday for Inspector West. l.t. ed. 1976. 328p. 12.00 o.p. (*0-85456-490-X*, Ulverscroft) Thorpe, F. A. Pubs. GBR. *Dist:* Ulverscroft Large Print Bks., Ltd.

—Inspector West Alone. unabr. collector's ed. 1984. audio 56.00 (*0-7366-0343-3*, 1329) Books on Tape, Inc.

—Inspector West Cries Wolf. unabr. ed. 1990. audio 54.95 (*0-7451-5884-6*, CAT 4058) BBC Audiobooks America.

—Inspector West Cries Wolf. (Black Dagger Crime Ser.). 192p. 12.95 o.p. (*0-86220-738-X*) Chivers Pr. GBR. *Dist:* BBC Audiobooks America.

—Inspector West Cries Wolf. l.t. ed. 2003. lib. bdg. 24.45 (*0-7862-5212-X*) Thorndike Pr.

—Two for Inspector West. l.t. ed. 1979. 330p. 12.00 o.p. (*0-7089-0270-7*, Ulverscroft) Thorpe, F. A. Pubs. GBR. *Dist:* Ulverscroft Large Print Bks., Ltd.

**WESTBOROUGH, THEOCRITUS LUCIUS (FICTITIOUS CHARACTER)—FICTION**

Clason, Clyde B. The Man from Tibet. 1998. 224p. pap. 14.00 (*0-915230-17-8*) Rue Morgue Pr.

**WESTCOTT, SAM (FICTITIOUS CHARACTER)—FICTION**

Chappell, Helen. Dead Duck. 1997. (Sam & Hollis Mystery Ser.). mass mkt. 5.50 o.s.i (*0-449-15001-1*, Fawcett) Ballantine Bks.

—Dead Duck. l.t. ed. 2000. (Beeler Large Print Mystery Ser.). 231p. 25.95 (*1-57490-320-9*, Beeler Large Print Bks.) Beeler, Thomas T. Publisher.

—Ghost of a Chance. l.t. ed. 1999. (Beeler Large Print Mystery Ser.). 25.95 (*1-57490-202-4*, Beeler Large Print Bks.) Beeler, Thomas T. Publisher.

—Ghost of a Chance. 1998. (Sam & Hollis Mystery Ser.: No. 3). 256p. mass mkt. 5.99 o.s.i (*0-440-22567-1*) Doubleday Publishing.

—Giving up the Ghost. l.t. ed. 2001. (Beeler Large Print Mystery Ser.). 188p. 25.95 (*1-57490-350-0*, Beeler Large Print Bks.) Beeler, Thomas T. Publisher.

—Giving up the Ghost: A Sam & Hollis Mystery. 1999. (Sam & Hollis Mystery Ser.). 256p. mass mkt. 5.99 o.s.i (*0-440-22575-2*) Dell Publishing.

—Slow Dancing with the Angel of Death. 1996. mass mkt. 5.50 o.s.i (*0-449-14983-8*, Fawcett) Ballantine Bks.

**WESTLAKE, PEYTON (FICTITIOUS CHARACTER)—FICTION**

*see Darkman (Fictitious Character)—Fiction*

**WESTON, CARLY (FICTITIOUS CHARACTER)—FICTION**

Warren, Pat. Nowhere to Run. 1993. 320p. mass mkt. 4.50 o.s.i (*0-8217-4132-2*, Zebra Bks.) Kensington Publishing Corp.

**WESTPHAL, CONNER (FICTITIOUS CHARACTER)—FICTION**

Warner, Penny. Blind Side: A Connor Westphal Mystery. 2001. (Perseverance Press Mystery Ser.: No. 6). 213p. pap. 12.95 (*1-880284-42-1*, Perseverance Pr.) Daniel, John & Co., Pubs.

—Dead Body Language. 1997. (Connor Westphal Mystery Ser.). 288p. mass mkt. 5.50 o.s.i (*0-553-57586-4*, Crimeline) Bantam Bks.

—A Quiet Undertaking. 2000. 272p. mass mkt. 5.50 o.s.i (*0-553-57965-7*) Bantam Bks.

—Right to Remain Silent. 1998. 288p. mass mkt. 5.50 o.s.i (*0-553-57962-2*, Crimeline) Bantam Bks.

—Sign of Foul Play: A Connor Westphal Mystery. 1997. (Connor Westphal Mystery Ser.). 288p. mass mkt. 5.50 o.s.i (*0-553-57587-2*, Crimeline) Bantam Bks.

—Silence Is Golden: A Connor Westphal Mystery. 2003. 216p. pap. 13.95 (*1-880284-66-9*) Daniel, John & Co., Pubs.

**WETZON, LESLIE (FICTITIOUS CHARACTER)—FICTION**

Meyers, Annette. The Big Killing. 1990. (Smith & Wetzon Ser.). 384p. mass mkt. 4.50 o.s.i (*0-553-28418-5*) Bantam Bks.

—The Big Killing. 1998. 270p. pap. 15.95 (*0-7351-0405-0*); reprint ed. lib. bdg. 29.95 (*0-7351-0035-7*) Replica Bks.

—Blood on the Street. 1993. (Smith & Wetzon Ser.). 400p. mass mkt. 4.99 o.s.i (*0-553-29731-7*) Bantam Bks.

—The Deadliest Option. 1992. (Smith & Wetzon Ser.). 416p. mass mkt. 4.99 o.s.i (*0-553-29530-6*) Bantam Bks.

—The Deadliest Option. 1998. 354p. pap. 15.95 (*0-7351-0404-2*); reprint ed. lib. bdg. 29.95 (*0-7351-0036-5*) Replica Bks.

—The Groaning Board: A Smith & Wetzon Mystery. 1998. 368p. mass mkt. 5.99 o.s.i (*0-553-56977-5*) Bantam Bks.

—The Groaning Board: A Smith & Wetzon Mystery. 1997. 336p. 21.95 o.s.i (*0-385-47654-X*) Doubleday Publishing.

—Murder: The Musical. 1994. (Smith & Wetzon Ser.). 496p. mass mkt. 5.50 o.s.i (*0-553-56785-3*) Bantam Bks.

—Murder: The Musical. 1998. 370p. pap. 15.95 (*0-7351-0403-4*); reprint ed. lib. bdg. 29.95 (*0-7351-0034-9*) Replica Bks.

—Tender Death. 1991. (Smith & Wetzon Ser.). 336p. mass mkt. 4.50 o.s.i (*0-553-28719-2*) Bantam Bks.

—Tender Death. 1998. 288p. pap. 15.95 (*0-7351-0406-9*); reprint ed. lib. bdg. 29.95 (*0-7351-0037-3*) Replica Bks.

—These Bones Were Made for Dancin' A Smith & Wetzon Mystery. 1996. 336p. reprint ed. mass mkt. 5.50 o.s.i (*0-553-56976-7*, Crimeline) Bantam Bks.

**WEXFORD, INSPECTOR (FICTITIOUS CHARACTER)—FICTION**

Rendell, Ruth. The Babes in the Wood. unabr. ed. 2004. audio 34.95 (*1-57270-310-5*); audio compact disk 37.95 (*1-57270-331-8*) Audio Partners Publishing Corp.

—The Babes in the Wood. 2003. 336p. 25.00 (*1-4000-4930-X*, Crown) Crown Publishing Group.

—Barker VC. 1997. (Chief Inspector Wexford Novel Ser.). (Illus.). 320p. 29.95 o.s.i (*0-385-25682-5*) Doubleday Publishing.

—The Best Man to Die. reprint ed. lib. bdg. 20.95 (*0-89190-887-0*, American Reprint Co.) Amereon, Ltd.

—The Best Man to Die. 1987. 208p. mass mkt. 6.99 (*0-345-34530-4*) Ballantine Bks.

—The Best Man to Die, unabr. ed. 1991. (Inspector Reginald Wexford Mystery Novel Ser.: Vol. 4). audio 42.00 (*1-55690-050-3*, 91124K8) Recorded Bks., LLC.

—Death Notes. (Chief Inspector Wexford Ser.). 1986. 224p. mass mkt. 6.99 (*0-345-34198-8*); 1982. mass mkt. 2.50 o.p. (*0-345-30272-9*) Ballantine Bks.

—Death Notes. l.t. ed. 1982. (General Ser.). 352p. lib. bdg. 13.95 o.p. (*0-8161-3335-2*, Macmillan Reference USA) Gale Group.

—Death Notes. 1981. 207p. 9.95 o.p. (*0-394-52078-5*, Pantheon) Knopf Publishing Group.

—From Doon with Death. abr. ed. 1996. audio 24.95 (*0-7451-2835-1*) BBC Audiobooks America.

—From Doon with Death. (Chief Inspector Wexford Ser.). 1988. 208p. mass mkt. 6.99 (*0-345-34817-6*); 1985. mass mkt. 2.95 o.s.i (*0-345-32414-5*); 1980. mass mkt. 1.95 o.p. (*0-345-29287-1*); 1975. mass mkt. 1.25 o.p. (*0-345-24799-X*) Ballantine Bks.

—From Doon with Death. unabr. ed. 2000. (Inspector Reginald Wexford Mystery Novel Ser.: Bk. 1). audio 34.95 (*0-7451-4202-8*, CAB 885) Chivers Audio Bks. GBR. *Dist:* BBC Audiobooks America.

—A Guilty Thing Surprised. Date not set. 174p. 19.95 (*0-8488-2381-8*) Amereon, Ltd.

—A Guilty Thing Surprised. 1987. (Chief Inspector Wexford Mysteries Ser.). 208p. mass mkt. 6.99 (*0-345-34811-7*) Ballantine Bks.

—A Guilty Thing Surprised. unabr. ed. 2000. (Inspector Reginald Wexford Mystery Novel Ser.: Bk. 5). audio 49.95 (*0-7451-4399-7*, CAB 1083) Chivers Audio Bks. GBR. *Dist:* BBC Audiobooks America.

—Harm Done. 1999. audio compact disk 96.00 (*0-7366-6297-9*); 1999. audio 80.00 (*0-7366-4794-5*, 5142); 2001. audio compact disk 96.00; 2000. audio 34.95 (*0-7366-4699-X*) Books on Tape, Inc.

—Harm Done. l.t. ed. 1999. (Inspector Reginald Wexford Mystery Novel Ser.). 26.95 o.p. (*1-56895-805-6*, Wheeler Publishing, Inc.) Gale Group.

—Harm Done, unabr. ed. 1999. (Inspector Reginald Wexford Mystery Novel Ser.: Vol. 18). audio 91.00 (*0-7887-4033-4*, 96151E7) Recorded Bks., LLC.

—Harm Done: A New Inspector Wexford Mystery. 2000. (Inspector Reginald Wexford Mystery Novel Ser.). 368p. pap. 12.00 (*0-375-72484-2*, Vintage) Knopf Publishing Group.

—Kissing the Gunner's Daughter. 1997. (Inspector Reginald Wexford Mystery Novel Ser.). 368p. mass mkt. 6.99 (*0-7704-2515-1*) Bantam Bks.

—Kissing the Gunner's Daughter. unabr. collector's ed. 1993. (Inspector Reginald Wexford Mystery Novel Ser.). audio 72.00 (*0-7366-2337-X*, 3116) Books on Tape, Inc.

—Kissing the Gunner's Daughter. unabr. ed. 1995. (Inspector Reginald Wexford Mystery Novel Ser.: Bk. 16). audio 69.95 (*0-7451-4150-1*, CAB 833) Chivers Audio Bks. GBR. *Dist:* BBC Audiobooks America.

—Kissing the Gunner's Daughter. l.t. ed. 2000. (Inspector Reginald Wexford Mystery Novel Ser.). 480p. lib. bdg. 29.95 (*1-58547-050-3*) Ctr. Point Large Print.

—Kissing the Gunner's Daughter, Set. abr. ed. 1992. (Inspector Reginald Wexford Mystery Novel Ser.). audio 16.99 (*0-88646-313-0*, 7313) Durkin Hayes Publishing Ltd.

—Kissing the Gunner's Daughter. 1992. (Inspector Reginald Wexford Mystery Novel Ser.). 378p. 19.95 o.p. (*0-89296-390-5*) Mysterious Pr.

—Kissing the Gunner's Daughter, unabr. ed. 1992. (Inspector Reginald Wexford Mystery Novel Ser.: Vol. 15). audio 85.00 (*1-55690-790-7*, 92424K8) Recorded Bks., LLC.

—Kissing the Gunner's Daughter. 1993. (Inspector Reginald Wexford Mystery Novel Ser.). 384p. mass mkt. 6.99 (*0-446-40334-2*) Warner Bks., Inc.

—Murder Being Once Done. 1998. (Wexford Mystery Ser.). 21.95 (*0-89190-372-0*) Amereon, Ltd.

—Murder Being Once Done. 1995. (Wexford Mystery Ser.). audio 29.95 (*0-7451-2826-2*) BBC Audiobooks America.

—Murder Being Once Done. 1999. (Wexford Mystery Ser.). 224p. pap. 11.00 (*0-679-70488-4*); pap. 11.00 (*0-375-70488-4*) Knopf Publishing Group. (Vintage).

—Murder Being Once Done, abr. ed. 1999. (Chief Inspector Wexford Novel Ser.). audio 18.00 o.s.i (*0-375-40710-3*, 396742, RH Audio) Random Hse. Audio Publishing Group.

—Murder Being Once Done. 1992. pap. o.p. (*0-09-174313-3*) Random Hse. of Canada, Ltd.

—A New Lease of Death. 1998. audio 29.95 (*0-7540-7517-6*) BBC Audiobooks America.

—A New Lease of Death. unabr. ed. 2000. (Inspector Reginald Wexford Mystery Novel Ser.: Bk. 2). audio 49.95 (*0-7451-6758-6*, CAB 1374) Chivers Audio Bks. GBR. *Dist:* BBC Audiobooks America.

—A New Lease of Death. Barzun, Jacques & Taqylor, W. H., eds. 1982. 214p. lib. bdg. 18.00 o.p. (*0-8240-4998-5*) Garland Publishing, Inc.

—No More Dying Then. 21.95 (*0-89190-373-9*) Amereon, Ltd.

—No More Dying Then. 1999. 224p. pap. 11.00 (*0-679-70489-2*); pap. 12.00 (*0-375-70489-2*) Knopf Publishing Group. (Vintage).

—Put on by Cunning. unabr. ed. 2000. (Inspector Reginald Wexford Mystery Novel Ser.: Bk. 12). audio 49.95 (*0-7451-6597-4*, CAB 1213) Chivers Audio Bks. GBR. *Dist:* BBC Audiobooks America.

—Put on by Cunning. 1992. 208p. mass mkt. o.p. (*0-09-927730-1*) Random Hse. of Canada, Ltd. CAN. *Dist:* Random Hse., Inc.

—Road Rage. 1998. (Chief Inspector Wexford Novel Ser.). 400p. mass mkt. 6.99 (*0-440-22602-3*); mass mkt. 5.99 (*0-440-29558-0*) Dell Publishing.

—Road Rage. l.t. ed. 1997. (Chief Inspector Wexford Novel Ser.). pap. 25.00 o.p. (*0-7838-8243-2*, Macmillan Reference USA) Gale Group.

—Road Rage, unabr. ed. 1998. (Inspector Reginald Wexford Mystery Novel Ser.: Vol. 17). audio 85.00 (*0-7887-1867-3*, 95289K8) Recorded Bks., LLC.

—Road Rage: An Inspector Wexford Novel. 1997. 384p. 29.95 o.s.i (*0-385-25681-7*) Bantam Bks.

—Shake Hands Forever. 1980. 208p. mass mkt. 3.50 o.s.i (*0-553-25970-9*) Bantam Bks.

—Shake Hands Forever. 2000. (Crime - Black Lizard Ser.). 192p. pap. 11.00 (*0-375-70495-7*, Vintage) Knopf Publishing Group.

—Simisola. 1997. (Inspector Reginald Wexford Mystery Novel Ser.). 336p. mass mkt. 6.50 (*0-7704-2714-6*) Bantam Bks.

—Simisola. unabr. ed. 1996. (Inspector Reginald Wexford Mystery Novel Ser.). audio 64.00 (*0-7366-3263-8*, 3920) Books on Tape, Inc.

—Simisola. abr. ed. (Inspector Reginald Wexford Mystery Novel Ser.). 1996. audio 7.99 o.p. (*1-56740-134-1*, 424, Paperback Nova Audio Bks.); 1995. audio 16.95 o.p. (*1-56100-408-1*, 1369, Nova Audio Bks.); 1995. audio 73.25 o.p. (*1-56100-240-2*, 1045, Unabridged Library Editions); 1995. audio 23.95 o.p. (*1-56100-615-7*, 1044, Bookcassette) Brilliance Audio.

—Simisola. unabr. ed. 2000. (Inspector Reginald Wexford Mystery Novel Ser.: Bk. 17). audio 69.95 (*0-7451-6515-X*, CAB 1131) Chivers Audio Bks. GBR. *Dist:* BBC Audiobooks America.

—Simisola. 1996. (Chief Inspector Wexford Novel Ser.). 384p. mass mkt. 6.99 (*0-440-22202-8*) Dell Publishing.

—Simisola. l.t. ed. 1995. (Inspector Reginald Wexford Mystery Novel Ser.). 512p. 22.00 o.p. (*0-7838-1588-3*, Macmillan Reference USA) Gale Group.

—Simisola. l.t. ed. 1995. (Inspector Reginald Wexford Mystery Novel Ser.). 488p. 22.00 o.s.i (*0-679-76502-6*) Random Hse. Large Print.

—Sins of the Fathers. 1985. mass mkt. 2.95 o.p. (*0-345-32740-3*); 1980. mass mkt. 1.95 o.p. (*0-345-29283-9*); 1976. mass mkt. 1.25 o.p. (*0-345-24862-7*) Ballantine Bks.

—Sins of the Fathers. 1994. reprint ed. lib. bdg. 29.95 (*1-56849-322-3*) Buccaneer Bks., Inc.

—A Sleeping Life. lib. bdg. 19.95 (*0-8488-2019-3*) Amereon, Ltd.

—A Sleeping Life. 1998. (Chief Inspector Wexford Mysteries Ser.). audio 29.95 (*0-7540-7523-0*) BBC Audiobooks America.

—A Sleeping Life. 1986. 192p. mass mkt. 3.50 o.s.i (*0-553-25969-5*) Bantam Bks.

—A Sleeping Life. unabr. ed. 2000. (Inspector Reginald Wexford Mystery Novel Ser.: Bk. 10). audio 49.95 (*0-7540-0036-2*, CAB 1459) Chivers Audio Bks. GBR. *Dist:* BBC Audiobooks America.

—A Sleeping Life. 1978. 180p. 7.95 o.p. (*0-385-13224-7*) Doubleday Publishing.

—A Sleeping Life. 1979. (General Ser.). 344p. lib. bdg. 11.95 o.p. (*0-8161-6711-7*, Macmillan Reference USA) Gale Group.

—A Sleeping Life. 2000. (Crime - Black Lizard Ser.). 192p. pap. 11.00 (*0-375-70493-0*, Vintage) Knopf Publishing Group.

—Some Lie & Some Die. lib. bdg. 20.95 (*0-8488-2020-7*) Amereon, Ltd.

—Some Lie & Some Die. 1999. (Vintage Crime/Black Lizard Ser.). (Illus.). 192p. pap. 11.00 (*0-375-70490-6*, Vintage) Knopf Publishing Group.

—Speaker of Mandarin. lib. bdg. 21.95 (*0-8488-2016-9*) Amereon, Ltd.

—Speaker of Mandarin. 1999. 11p. audio 29.95 (*0-7451-2820-3*) BBC Audiobooks America.

—Speaker of Mandarin. 1984. (Chief Inspector Wexford Ser.). 224p. mass mkt. 5.99 o.s.i (*0-345-30274-5*) Ballantine Bks.

—Speaker of Mandarin. unabr. ed. 2000. (Inspector Reginald Wexford Mystery Novel Ser.: Bk. 13). audio 49.95 (*0-7451-6239-8*, CAB 108) Chivers Audio Bks. GBR. *Dist:* BBC Audiobooks America.

—Speaker of Mandarin. 1983. 223p. 12.95 o.s.i (*0-394-52272-9*, Pantheon) Knopf Publishing Group.

—An Unkindness of Ravens. 1986. 352p. mass mkt. 6.99 (*0-345-32746-2*) Ballantine Bks.

—An Unkindness of Ravens. unabr. ed. 2000. (Inspector Reginald Wexford Mystery Novel Ser.: Bk. 14). audio 49.95 (*0-7451-6232-0*, CAB 151) Chivers Audio Bks. GBR. *Dist:* BBC Audiobooks America.

—An Unkindness of Ravens. 1992. mass mkt. o.p. (*0-09-174862-3*) Random Hse. of Canada, Ltd.

—An Unkindness of Ravens, unabr. ed. 1990. (Inspector Reginald Wexford Mystery Novel Ser.: Vol. 13). audio 51.00 (*1-55690-538-6*, 90021E7) Recorded Bks., LLC.

—The Veiled One. 1989. (Inspector Reginald Wexford Mystery Novel Ser.). 320p. mass mkt. 6.99 (*0-345-35994-1*) Ballantine Bks.

—The Veiled One. unabr. ed. 2000. (Inspector Reginald Wexford Mystery Novel Ser.: Bk. 15). audio 59.95 (*0-7451-6241-X*, CAB 385) Chivers Audio Bks. GBR. *Dist:* BBC Audiobooks America.

—The Veiled One. l.t. ed. 1989. (Inspector Reginald Wexford Mystery Novel Ser.). 450p. lib. bdg. 19.95 o.p. (*0-8161-4804-X*, Macmillan Reference USA) Gale Group.

—The Veiled One. 1990. 4.99 o.p. (*0-517-05108-7*) Random Hse. Value Publishing.

—The Veiled One, unabr. ed. 1990. (Inspector Reginald Wexford Mystery Novel Ser.: Vol. 14). audio 67.00 (*1-55690-541-6*, 90069K8) Recorded Bks., LLC.

—The Veiled One. 1989. (Inspector Reginald Wexford Mystery Novel Ser.). audio 69.95 o.s.i (*0-8161-9387-8*, 90069) Thorndike Pr.

—Wolf to the Slaughter. 1987. 224p. mass mkt. 6.99 (*0-345-34520-7*); 1983. mass mkt. 2.25 o.p. (*0-345-31744-0*); 1980. mass mkt. 1.95 o.p. (*0-345-29284-7*); 1976. mass mkt. 1.25 o.p. (*0-345-24817-1*) Ballantine Bks.

—Wolf to the Slaughter. unabr. ed. 2000. (Inspector Reginald Wexford Mystery Novel Ser.: Bk. 3). audio 49.95 (*0-7451-6242-8*, CAB 541) Chivers Audio Bks. GBR. *Dist:* BBC Audiobooks America.

**WHALBY, STEPHEN (FICTITIOUS CHARACTER)—FICTION**

Rendell, Ruth. Master of the Moor. 1986. 256p. mass mkt. 6.99 (*0-345-34147-3*); 1983. mass mkt. 2.95 o.p. (*0-345-30273-7*) Ballantine Bks.

—Master of the Moor. l.t. ed. 1982. (General Ser.). 367p. lib. bdg. 13.95 o.p. (*0-8161-3437-5*, Macmillan Reference USA) Gale Group.

**WHALE, JAMES (FICTITIOUS CHARACTER)—FICTION**

Bram, Christopher. The Father of Frankenstein. 288p. 1996. pap. 12.95 (*0-452-27337-4*, Plume); 1995. 19.95 o.s.i (*0-525-93913-X*) Dutton/Plume.

**WHEATLEY, CHAS (FICTITIOUS CHARACTER)—FICTION**

Richman, Phyllis C. The Butter Did It. unabr. ed. 1998. audio 49.95 (*0-7861-1293-X*, 2197) Blackstone Audio Bks., Inc.

—The Butter Did It: A Gastronomic Tale of Love & Murder. 1997. 320p. 23.00 o.s.i (*0-06-018370-5*) HarperCollins Pubs.

—The Butter Did It: A Gastronomic Tale of Love & Murder. 1998. (Chas Wheatley Mysteries Ser.). 384p. mass mkt. 6.99 (*0-06-109625-3*, HarperTorch) Morrow/Avon.

—The Butter Did It: A Gastronomic Tale of Love & Murder. l.t. ed. 1997. (Cloak & Dagger Ser.). 459p. 25.95 o.p. (*0-7862-1183-0*) Thorndike Pr.

—Murder on the Gravy Train. 1999. viii, 243p. 23.00 (*0-06-018390-X*) HarperCollins Pubs.

—Murder on the Gravy Train. 2000. 336p. mass mkt. 6.50 (*0-06-109783-7*, Avon Bks.) Morrow/Avon.

—Murder on the Gravy Train. l.t. ed. 1999. (Mystery Ser.). 416p. 29.95 (*0-7862-2208-5*) Thorndike Pr.

—Who's Afraid of Virginia Ham. 2002. 352p. mass mkt. 6.99 (*0-06-109782-9*, Avon Bks.) Morrow/Avon.

**WHEELER, EPHRAIM (FICTITIOUS CHARACTER)—FICTION**

Beasley, David. Chocolate for the Poor: A Story of Rape in 1805. 1996. 280p. pap. 11.95 (*0-915317-04-4*) Davus Publishing.

**WHELAN, MURRAY (FICTITIOUS CHARACTER)—FICTION**

Maloney, Shane. The Big Ask: A Murray Whelan Mystery. 2001. 304p. pap. 23.95 (*1-55970-560-4*) Arcade Publishing, Inc.

—The Brush-Off: A Murray Whelan Mystery. 2001. 320p. reprint ed. pap. 13.95 (*1-55970-582-5*) Arcade Publishing, Inc.

—The Brush-Off: A Murray Whelan Novel. 2001. 320p. 14.05 (*1-84195-204-4*) Canongate Bks. GBR. *Dist:* Grove/Atlantic, Inc.

—The Brush-Off: An Arcade Mystery. 1998. 320p. 23.95 (*1-55970-440-3*) Arcade Publishing, Inc.

—Nice Try: A Murray Whelan Mystery. (Murray Whelan Mystery Ser.). 2000. 259p. 24.95 (*1-55970-513-2*); 2001. 272p. reprint ed. pap. 12.95 (*1-55970-600-7*) Arcade Publishing, Inc.

—Stiff. 1999. (Murray Whelan Thrillers Ser.). 227p. 23.95 (*1-55970-481-0*) Arcade Publishing, Inc.

—Stiff: A Murray Whelan Mystery. 2001. 240p. reprint ed. pap. 12.95 (*1-55970-599-X*) Arcade Publishing, Inc.

**WHELAN, PAUL (FICTITIOUS CHARACTER)—FICTION**

Raleigh, Michael. A Body in Belmont Harbor. 1993. 277p. 17.95 o.p. (*0-312-08707-1*, Saint Martin's Minotaur) St. Martin's Pr.

—A Body in Belmont Harbor. 2000. (Paul Whelan Mystery Ser.). 292p. pap. 15.95 (*0-595-09340-X*) iUniverse, Inc.

—Death in Uptown. 2000. (Paul Whelan Mystery Ser.). 256p. pap. 14.95 (*0-595-09341-8*) iUniverse, Inc.

—Death in Uptown: A Paul Whelan Mystery. 1991. 17.95 o.p. (*0-312-05849-7*, Saint Martin's Minotaur) St. Martin's Pr.

—Killer on Argyle Street. 2000. (Paul Whelan Mystery Ser.). 256p. pap. 14.95 (*0-595-09343-4*) iUniverse, Inc.

—Killer on Argyle Street: A Chicago Mystery Featuring Paul Whelan. 1995. 298p. 21.95 o.p. (*0-312-13532-7*, Saint Martin's Minotaur) St. Martin's Pr.

—The Maxwell Street Blues. 1994. 280p. 20.95 o.p. (*0-312-11394-3*, Saint Martin's Minotaur) St. Martin's Pr.

—The Maxwell Street Blues. 2000. (Paul Whelan Mystery Ser.). 288p. pap. 15.95 (*0-595-09342-6*) iUniverse, Inc.

—The Riverview Murders. 1997. 213p. 21.95 o.p. (*0-312-15641-3*, Saint Martin's Minotaur) St. Martin's Pr.

**WHISTLER (FICTITIOUS CHARACTER: CAMPBELL)—FICTION**

Campbell, Robert. Alice in La-La Land. 1999. 232p. pap. 17.95 (*1-58444-024-4*) Disc-Us Bks., Inc.

—Alice in La-La Land. Chelius, Jane, ed. 1990. mass mkt. 4.95 (*0-671-73343-5*, Pocket) Simon & Schuster.

—Alice in La-La Land. 1987. 256p. 16.45 o.p. (*0-671-64483-1*, Simon & Schuster) Simon & Schuster.

—In La-La Land We Trust. 2000. E-Book 19.95 incl. cd-rom (*1-58444-076-7*); 1999. 230p. pap. 17.95 (*1-58444-051-1*) Disc-Us Bks., Inc.

—In La-La Land We Trust. 1986. 15.45 o.p. (*0-89296-170-8*) Mysterious Pr.

—In La-La Land We Trust. 1987. mass mkt. 4.95 o.p. (*0-445-40596-1*, Mysterious Pr. Paperback Bks.) Warner Bks., Inc.

—The La-La Land Quartet: Contains 4 Titles- Alice in La-La Land, in La-La Land We Trust, Sweet La-La Land, & Wizard of La-La Land. 2000. E-Book 24.95 incl. cd-rom (*1-58444-083-X*) Disc-Us Bks., Inc.

—Sweet La-La Land. 2000. E-Book 16.95 incl. cd-rom (*1-58444-075-9*); 1999. 232p. pap. 17.95 (*1-58444-050-3*) Disc-Us Bks., Inc.

—Sweet La-La Land. 1990. 18.95 o.p. (*0-671-64484-X*, Simon & Schuster) Simon & Schuster.

—Sweet La-La Land. Chelius, Jane, ed. 1991. 320p. reprint ed. mass mkt. 4.99 (*0-671-73236-6*, Pocket) Simon & Schuster.

—The Wizard of La-La Land. 1999. 244p. pap. 17.95 (*1-58444-052-X*) Disc-Us Bks., Inc.

—The Wizard of La-La Land. Chelius, Jane, ed. 1995. 288p. 20.00 o.p. (*0-671-70321-8*, Atria) Simon & Schuster.

**WHISTLER, NICHOLAS (FICTITIOUS CHARACTER)—FICTION**

Davidson, Lionel. The Night of Wenceslas. (Black Dagger Crime Ser.). 16.50 o.p. (*0-86220-725-8*, C0853, Black Dagger) BBC Audiobooks America.

—The Night of Wenceslas. 1982. 224p. pap. 2.95 o.p. (*0-06-080595-1*, P595) HarperCollins Pubs.

—The Night of Wenceslas. 1996. 313p. pap. text 6.99 o.p. (*0-312-95876-5*, St. Martin's Paperbacks) St. Martin's Pr.

—The Night of Wenceslas. 1977. pap. 1.95 o.p. (*0-14-001758-5*, Penguin Bks.) Viking Penguin.

**WHITE, BLANCHE (FICTITIOUS CHARACTER)—FICTION**

Neely, Barbara. Blanche among the Talented Tenth. 1995. 240p. pap. 5.99 (*0-14-025036-0*, Penguin Bks.) Penguin Group (USA) Inc.

—Blanche among the Talented Tenth. 1994. 240p. 19.95 o.p. (*0-312-11248-3*, Saint Martin's Minotaur) St. Martin's Pr.

—Blanche Cleans Up. 1999. 352p. mass mkt. 6.99 (*0-14-027747-1*) Penguin Group (USA) Inc.

—Blanche Cleans Up. 1998. 288p. 19.95 o.p. (*0-670-87626-7*) Viking Penguin.

—Blanche on the Lam. 1993. (Crime Ser.). 224p. pap. 5.99 (*0-14-017439-7*, Penguin Bks.) Penguin Group (USA) Inc.

—Blanche on the Lam. 1991. 192p. 16.95 o.p. (*0-312-06908-1*, Saint Martin's Minotaur) St. Martin's Pr.

—Blanche Passes Go. 2000. 272p. 22.95 o.s.i (*0-670-89165-7*, Viking) Viking Penguin.

**WHITE, CARRIE (FICTITIOUS CHARACTER)—FICTION**

King, Stephen. Carrie. 1990. 192p. 32.50 (*0-385-08695-4*) Doubleday Publishing.

—Carrie. 1991. (Stephen King Collectors Editions Ser.). 176p. pap. 12.95 o.p. (*0-452-26719-6*, Plume) Dutton/Plume.

—Carrie. 1992. (SPA.). 288p. pap. 3.95 (*1-56780-057-2*) La Costa Pr., Inc.

—Carrie. 1975. mass mkt. 3.95 o.p. (*0-451-15071-6*); 256p. reprint ed. mass mkt. 7.99 o.s.i (*0-451-15744-3*) NAL. (Signet Bks.).

—Carrie. 1999. (SPA., Illus.). 288p. (*84-01-49966-6*) Plaza & Janés Editories, S.A.

—Carrie. (SPA.). 288p. 12.95 (*84-01-49888-0*) Plaza & Janés Editories, S.A. ESP. *Dist:* Distribooks, Inc.

—Carrie. 2002. 272p. pap. 7.99 (*0-671-03972-5*); 2000. 208p. pap. 12.95 (*0-671-03973-3*) Simon & Schuster. (Pocket).

—Carrie. 1975. 14.04 (*0-606-00823-3*) Turtleback Bks.

**WHITE, LILY (FICTITIOUS CHARACTER)—FICTION**

Isaacs, Susan. Lily White. 1996. 480p. 25.00 o.p. (*0-06-017607-5*) HarperCollins Pubs.

—Lily White. l.t. ed. 1997. 656p. mass mkt. 7.99 (*0-06-109309-2*, HarperTorch) Morrow/Avon.

—Lily White. l.t. ed. (Paperback Bestsellers Ser.). 738p. 1997. pap. 27.95 (*0-7862-0829-5*); 1996. 28.95 o.p. (*0-7862-0828-7*) Thorndike Pr.

**WHITEFIELD, JANE (FICTITIOUS CHARACTER)—FICTION**

Perry, Thomas. Blood Money. l.t. ed. 2000. (Large Print Book Ser.). 513p. pap. 26.95 (*1-56895-925-7*, Wheeler Publishing, Inc.) Gale Group.

—Blood Money. 2000. audio 30.00 (*0-7871-2284-X*) NewStar Media, Inc.

—Blood Money: A Novel. 1999. (Illus.). 368p. 24.95 o.s.i (*0-679-45304-0*) Random Hse., Inc.

—Dance for the Dead. 1997. (Jane Whitefield Novels Ser.). 416p. mass mkt. 6.99 (*0-8041-1425-0*, Ivy Bks.) Ballantine Bks.

—Dance for the Dead. l.t. ed. 1996. 416p. lib. bdg. 24.95 (*1-57490-065-X*, Beeler Large Print Bks.) Beeler, Thomas T. Publisher.

—Dance for the Dead, Set. abr. ed. 1998. (Jane Whitefield Mystery Ser.). audio 8.99 o.s.i (*0-375-40298-5*, 393900, RH Audio) Random Hse. Audio Publishing Group.

—Dance for the Dead. l.t. ed. 1997. (Charnwood Large Print Ser.). 464p. 34.50 o.p. (*0-7089-8938-1*, Ulverscroft) Thorpe, F. A. Pubs. GBR. *Dist:* Ulverscroft Large Print Bks., Ltd., Ulverscroft Large Print Canada, Ltd.

—Dance for the Dead: A Jane Whitefield Novel. abr. ed. 1996. audio 18.00 o.s.i (*0-679-45169-2*, 393900, RH Audio) Random Hse. Audio Publishing Group.

—The Face-Changers. 1999. (Jane Whitefield Novels Ser.). 432p. mass mkt. 7.50 (*0-8041-1540-0*, Ivy Bks.) Ballantine Bks.

—The Face-Changers. l.t. ed. 1998. (Americana Ser.). 640p. 28.95 (*0-7862-1611-5*) Thorndike Pr.

—The Face-Changers: A Novel. aut. ed. 1998. 372p. 24.00 o.s.i (*0-676-57765-2*) Random Hse., Inc.

—Shadow Woman. 1998. (Jane Whitefield Novels Ser.). 432p. mass mkt. 6.99 (*0-8041-1539-7*, Ivy Bks.) Ballantine Bks.

—Shadow Woman. l.t. ed. 1997. (Large Print Book Ser.). pap. 24.95 (*1-56895-513-8*, Wheeler Publishing, Inc.) Gale Group.

—Shadow Woman. l.t. ed. 1999. (Charnwood Large Print Ser.). 480p. 31.99 (*0-7089-9098-3*, Ulverscroft) Thorpe, F. A. Pubs. GBR. *Dist:* Ulverscroft Large Print Bks., Ltd., Ulverscroft Large Print Canada, Ltd.

—Vanishing Act. 1997. mass mkt. 2.99 o.s.i (*0-8041-1648-2*); 1996. 368p. mass mkt. 6.99 (*0-8041-1387-4*) Ballantine Bks. (Ivy Bks.).

—Vanishing Act. l.t. ed. 1995. (Large Print Bks.). pap. 22.95 (*1-56895-234-1*, Wheeler Publishing, Inc.) Gale Group.

**WHITEHEAD, ANN (FICTITIOUS CHARACTER)—FICTION**

Knode, Helen. The Ticket Out. 352p. 2004. pap. 13.00 (*0-15-602905-7*, Harvest Bks.); 2003. 24.00 (*0-15-100184-7*) Harcourt Trade Pubs.

**WHITEOAK FAMILY (FICTITIOUS CHARACTERS)—FICTION**

De La Roche, Mazo. The Building of Jalna. unabr. ed. 1993. 69.95 incl. audio (*0-7451-6246-0*); 1990. audio 64.95 o.s.i (*0-8161-9513-7*) BBC Audiobooks America.

—The Building of Jalna. 1976. 288p. mass mkt. 1.50 o.s.i (*0-449-23071-6*, Fawcett) Ballantine Bks.

—The Building of Jalna. 1944. (Jalna Ser.). 8.95 o.p. (*0-316-17996-5*) Little Brown & Co.

—The Building of Jalna. l.t. ed. 1972. (Whiteoak Chronicles Ser.). 16.95 o.p. (*0-85456-673-2*, Ulverscroft) Thorpe, F. A. Pubs. GBR. *Dist:* Ulverscroft Large Print Bks., Ltd.

—Centenary at Jalna. l.t. ed. 1973. (Whiteoak Chronicles Ser.). 12.00 o.p. (*0-85456-688-0*, Ulverscroft) Thorpe, F. A. Pubs. GBR. *Dist:* Ulverscroft Large Print Bks., Ltd.

—Finch's Fortune. 1976. mass mkt. 1.50 o.s.i (*0-449-23053-8*, Fawcett) Ballantine Bks.

—Finch's Fortune. l.t. ed. 1973. (Whiteoak Chronicles Ser.). 12.00 o.p. (*0-85456-681-3*, Ulverscroft) Thorpe, F. A. Pubs. GBR. *Dist:* Ulverscroft Large Print Bks., Ltd.

—Jalna. 1979. mass mkt. 1.95 o.s.i (*0-449-24118-1*, Fawcett); 1976. mass mkt. 1.50 o.s.i (*0-449-23138-0*) Ballantine Bks.

—Jalna. l.t. ed. 2002. 400p. pap. 21.99 (*0-7531-6462-0*) ISIS Large Print Bks. GBR. *Dist:* Ulverscroft Large Print Bks., Ltd., Ulverscroft Large Print Canada, Ltd.

—Jalna. l.t. ed. 2001. 400p. 32.50 (*0-7531-6461-2*); 1973. 29.99 o.p. (*0-85456-679-1*, Ulverscroft) Thorpe, F. A. Pubs. GBR. *Dist:* Ulverscroft Large Print Bks., Ltd., Ulverscroft Large Print Canada, Ltd.

—Mary Wakefield. unabr. ed. 1991. (Audio Bks.). audio 69.95 (*0-7451-6244-4*) BBC Audiobooks America.

—Mary Wakefield. 1976. mass mkt. 1.50 o.s.i (*0-449-23057-0*, Fawcett) Ballantine Bks.

—Mary Wakefield. l.t. ed. 1973. (Whiteoak Chronicles Ser.). 12.00 o.p. (*0-85456-675-9*, Ulverscroft) Thorpe, F. A. Pubs. GBR. *Dist:* Ulverscroft Large Print Bks., Ltd., Ulverscroft Large Print Canada, Ltd.

—The Master of Jalna. (Jalna Ser.). 1979. mass mkt. 1.95 o.s.i (*0-449-23932-2*, Fawcett); 1975. mass mkt. 1.50 o.s.i (*0-449-22797-9*) Ballantine Bks.

—The Master of Jalna. l.t. ed. 1973. (Whiteoak Chronicles Ser.). 29.99 o.p. (*0-85456-682-1*, Ulverscroft) Thorpe, F. A. Pubs. GBR. *Dist:* Ulverscroft Large Print Bks., Ltd., Ulverscroft Large Print Canada, Ltd.

—Morning at Jalna. unabr. ed. 1991. (Audio Bks.). audio 69.95 (*0-7451-6245-2*) BBC Audiobooks America.

—Morning at Jalna. (Jalna Ser.). 1978. mass mkt. 1.75 o.s.i (*0-449-23712-5*, Fawcett); 1975. mass mkt. 1.25 o.s.i (*0-449-22411-2*) Ballantine Bks.

—Morning at Jalna. 1960. (Jalna Ser.). 8.95 o.p. (*0-316-18003-3*) Little Brown & Co.

—Morning at Jalna. l.t. ed. 1972. (Whiteoak Chronicles Ser.). 29.99 o.p. (*0-85456-674-0*, Ulverscroft) Thorpe, F. A. Pubs. GBR. *Dist:* Ulverscroft Large Print Bks., Ltd., Ulverscroft Large Print Canada, Ltd.

—Renny's Daughter. 1975. 304p. mass mkt. 1.50 o.s.i (*0-449-22550-X*, Q2550, Fawcett) Ballantine Bks.

—Renny's Daughter. l.t. ed. 1973. (Whiteoak Chronicles Ser.). 29.99 o.p. (*0-85456-686-4*, Ulverscroft) Thorpe, F. A. Pubs. GBR. *Dist:* Ulverscroft Large Print Bks., Ltd., Ulverscroft Large Print Canada, Ltd.

—Return to Jalna. 1977. (Jalna Ser.). mass mkt. 1.75 o.s.i (*0-449-23386-3*, Fawcett) Ballantine Bks.

—Return to Jalna. l.t. ed. 1973. (Whiteoak Chronicles Ser.). 12.00 o.p. (*0-85456-685-6*, Ulverscroft) Thorpe, F. A. Pubs. GBR. *Dist:* Ulverscroft Large Print Bks., Ltd.

—Variable Winds at Jalna. l.t. ed. 1973. (Whiteoak Chronicles Ser.). 12.00 o.p. (*0-85456-687-2*, Ulverscroft) Thorpe, F. A. Pubs. GBR. *Dist:* Ulverscroft Large Print Bks., Ltd.

—Wakefield's Course. 1977. (Jalna Ser.). mass mkt. 1.95 o.s.i (*0-449-23431-2*, Fawcett) Ballantine Bks.

—Wakefield's Course. l.t. ed. 1973. (Whiteoak Chronicles Ser.). o.p. (*0-85456-684-8*, Ulverscroft) Thorpe, F. A. Pubs.

—Whiteoak Brothers. 1978. (Jalna Ser.). mass mkt. 1.75 o.s.i (*0-449-23643-9*, Fawcett) Ballantine Bks.

—The Whiteoak Brothers. l.t. ed. 1973. (Whiteoak Chronicles Ser.). 29.99 o.p. (*0-85456-678-3*, Ulverscroft) Thorpe, F. A. Pubs. GBR. *Dist:* Ulverscroft Large Print Bks., Ltd., Ulverscroft Large Print Canada, Ltd.

—Whiteoak Harvest. 1978. (Jalna Ser.). mass mkt. 1.75 o.s.i (*0-449-23521-1*, Fawcett) Ballantine Bks.

—Whiteoak Harvest. 1936. (Jalna Ser.). 7.95 o.p. (*0-316-18013-0*) Little Brown & Co.

—Whiteoak Harvest. l.t. ed. 1973. (Whiteoak Chronicles Ser.). 12.00 o.p. (*0-85456-683-X*, Ulverscroft) Thorpe, F. A. Pubs. GBR. *Dist:* Ulverscroft Large Print Bks., Ltd.

—Whiteoak Heritage. 1979. mass mkt. 1.95 o.s.i (*0-449-22214-4*, Fawcett) Ballantine Bks.

—Whiteoak Heritage. 1940. (Jalna Ser.). 8.95 o.p. (*0-316-18012-2*) Little Brown & Co.

—Whiteoak Heritage. l.t. ed. 1973. (Whiteoak Chronicles Ser.). o.p. (*0-85456-677-5*, Ulverscroft) Thorpe, F. A. Pubs.

—Whiteoaks of Jalna. (Jalna Ser.). 1980. mass mkt. 2.25 o.s.i (*0-449-23510-6*, Fawcett); 1975. mass mkt. 1.50 o.s.i (*0-449-22764-2*) Ballantine Bks.

**WHITLAW, KAREN (FICTITIOUS CHARACTER)—FICTION**

Howard, Linda. Kill & Tell. l.t. ed. 1998. pap. 23.95 o.p. (*1-56895-554-5*, Wheeler Publishing, Inc.) Gale Group.

—Kill & Tell. 1998. 320p. mass mkt. 7.99 (*0-671-56883-3*, Pocket) Simon & Schuster.

**WIGGIN, ENDER (FICTITIOUS CHARACTER)—FICTION**

*see Ender (Fictitious Character)—Fiction*

**WILCOX, CARL (FICTITIOUS CHARACTER)—FICTION**

Adams, Harold. The Barbed Wire Noose. l.t. ed. 1991. pap. 10.95 o.p. (*0-7927-0073-2*, C0125) BBC Audiobooks America.

—The Barbed Wire Noose. 192p. 1988. pap. 3.95 o.p. (*0-445-40727-1*); 1987. 15.45 (*0-89296-250-X*) Mysterious Pr.

—The Ditched Blonde. (Carl Wilcox Mystery Ser.). 168p. 1998. pap. 7.95 (*0-8027-7555-1*); 1995. 19.95 (*0-8027-3263-1*) Walker & Co.

—The Fourth Widow. 208p. 1987. pap. 3.50 o.p. (*0-445-40581-3*); 1986. 15.95 (*0-89296-231-3*) Mysterious Pr.

—Hatchet Job: A Carl Wilcox Mystery. 1996. (Carl Wilcox Mystery Ser.). 176p. 19.95 (*0-8027-3286-0*) Walker & Co.

—The Ice Pick Artist: A Carl Wilcox Mystery. 1997. (Carl Wilcox Mystery Ser.). 240p. 21.95 (*0-8027-3310-7*) Walker & Co.
—Lead, So I Can Follow. (Carl Wilcox Mystery Ser.). 2000. 224p. pap. 8.95 (*0-8027-7596-9*); 1999. 219p. 22.95 (*0-8027-3336-0*) Walker & Co.
—The Man Who Met the Train. (Carl Wilcox Mystery Ser.: No. 7). 240p. 1989. pap. 3.95 o.p. (*0-445-40810-3*); 1988. 15.95 (*0-89296-251-8*) Mysterious Pr.
—The Man Who Missed the Party. l.t. ed. 1992. 18.95 o.p. (*0-7451-8330-1*); pap. 16.95 o.p. (*0-7927-1017-7*) BBC Audiobooks America.
—The Man Who Missed the Party. 1990. 192p. mass mkt. 4.95 o.s.i (*0-445-40885-5*, Mysterious Pr. Paperback Bks.) Warner Bks., Inc.
—The Man Who Missed the Party: A Carol Wilcox Mystery. 1989. 192p. 16.95 (*0-89296-252-6*) Mysterious Pr.
—The Man Who Was Taller Than God. 1998. (Carl Wilcox Mystery Ser.). 156p. (gr. 8). pap. 7.95 (*0-8027-7554-3*) Walker & Co.
—The Man Who Was Taller Than God: A Carl Wilcox Mystery. 1992. (Carl Wilcox Mystery Ser.). 156p. 18.95 (*0-8027-1239-8*) Walker & Co.
—The Missing Moon. 1983. 256p. mass mkt. 2.50 o.s.i (*0-441-53401-5*) Ace Bks.
—The Missing Moon. l.t. ed. 1991. 17.95 o.p. (*0-7451-9761-2*, C0076); 1990. pap. 15.95 o.p. (*0-7927-0216-6*, C0224) BBC Audiobooks America.
—The Missing Moon. 1988. 256p. mass mkt. 3.95 o.s.i (*0-445-40629-1*, Mysterious Pr. Paperback Bks.) Warner Bks., Inc.
—Murder. 1981. 256p. 2.50 o.s.i (*0-441-54706-0*) Ace Bks.
—Murder. l.t. ed. 1991. pap. 8.95 o.p. (*1-55504-839-0*, 102); 1989. 16.95 o.p. (*0-7451-9459-1*, 340) BBC Audiobooks America.
—Murder. 1988. 224p. mass mkt. 3.95 o.s.i (*0-445-40627-5*, Mysterious Pr. Paperback Bks.) Warner Bks., Inc.
—The Naked Liar. 1986. 15.95 o.p. (*0-89296-126-0*) Mysterious Pr.
—The Naked Liar. 1986. mass mkt. 3.95 o.s.i (*0-445-40126-5*, Mysterious Pr. Paperback Bks.) Warner Bks., Inc.
—No Badge, No Gun. (Carl Wilcox Mystery Ser.). 1999. 212p. pap. 7.95 (*0-8027-7575-6*); 1998. (Illus.). 208p. 22.95 (*0-8027-3321-2*) Walker & Co.
—Paint the Town Red. 1988. 208p. 3.95 o.p. (*0-445-40631-3*) Mysterious Pr.
—A Perfectly Proper Murder: A Carl Wilcox Mystery. 1993. 18.95 (*0-8027-3237-2*) Walker & Co.
—A Way with Widows. l.t. ed. 1995. (Nightingale Ser.). 219p. pap. 17.95 (*0-7838-1144-6*, Macmillan Reference USA) Gale Group.
—A Way with Widows. (Carl Wilcox Mystery Ser.). 1999. 156p. pap. 7.95 (*0-8027-7574-8*); 1994. 142p. 18.95 (*0-8027-3190-2*) Walker & Co.
—When Rich Men Die. 1987. 240p. 16.95 o.s.i (*0-385-24005-8*) Doubleday Publishing.
—When Rich Men Die. l.t. ed. 1988. (Mainstream Ser.). 377p. reprint ed. lib. bdg. 19.95 o.p. (*1-55736-085-5*) ISIS Large Print Bks. GBR. *Dist:* Transaction Pubs.
—When Rich Men Die. 1988. 256p. pap. 3.50 (*0-380-70539-7*, Avon Bks.) Morrow/Avon.

**WILDE, CAT (FICTITIOUS CHARACTER)—FICTION**

Ruryk, Jean. Chicken Little Was Right. 1994. 208p. 18.95 o.p. (*0-312-10952-0*, Saint Martin's Minotaur) St. Martin's Pr.
—Next Week Will Be Better. 1998. (Cat Wilde Mystery Ser.). 256p. 21.95 (*0-312-18144-2*, Saint Martin's Minotaur) St. Martin's Pr.
—Next Week Will Be Better: A Cat Wilde Mystery. 1999. (WWL Mystery Ser.: Vol. 333). 256p. per. (*0-373-26333-3*, Harlequin Bks.) Harlequin Enterprises, Ltd.
—Whatever Happened to Jennifer Steele? A Cat Wilde Mystery. 1996. 208p. 20.95 (*0-312-14067-3*, Saint Martin's Minotaur) St. Martin's Pr.

**WILDER, JOE (FICTITIOUS CHARACTER)—FICTION**

Phillips, T. J. Woman in the Dark. 1997. (Joe Wilder Mysteries Ser.). 208p. reprint ed. mass mkt. 5.99 o.s.i (*0-425-16110-2*, Prime Crime) Berkley Publishing Group.
—Woman in the Dark: A Joe Wilder Mystery. 1997. (Joe Wilder Mysteries Ser.). 288p. 21.95 o.p. (*0-425-15312-6*, Prime Crime) Berkley Publishing Group.

**WILDER, JONATHAN (FICTITIOUS CHARACTER)—FICTION**

Sipherd, Ray. The Audubon Quartet. 1999. (WWL Mystery Ser.: No. 311). per. (*0-373-26311-2*, 1-26311-0, Worldwide Library) Harlequin Enterprises, Ltd.
—Audubon Quartet, Vol. 1. 1998. (Jonathan Wilder Mysteries Ser.). 272p. 22.95 o.p. (*0-312-18536-7*, Saint Martin's Minotaur) St. Martin's Pr.
—Dance of the Scarecrows. 1998. (WWL Mystery Ser.: Vol. 287). per. (*0-373-26287-6*, 1-26287-2, Worldwide Library) Harlequin Enterprises, Ltd.
—Dance of the Scarecrows. 1996. 256p. 21.95 o.p. (*0-312-14306-0*, Saint Martin's Minotaur) St. Martin's Pr.

**WILDER, TOM (FICTITIOUS CHARACTER)—FICTION**

Froshcer, Jonathan. The Woodstock Murders: (Or Happiness Is a Naked Policeman) 1998. 228p. pap. 23.95 (*0-87951-858-8*, Elephant's Eye) Overlook Pr., The.

**WILDER, MARY (FICTITIOUS CHARACTER)—FICTION**

Lind, Judi. Veil of Fear. 1995. (Harlequin Intrigue Ser.). (Illus.). 248p. per. (*0-373-22310-2*, 1-22310-6, Harlequin Bks.) Harlequin Enterprises, Ltd.

**WILL, ELIZABETH (FICTITIOUS CHARACTER)—FICTION**

Yeager, Dorian. Murder Will Out. 1994. (Elizabeth Will Mystery Ser.). 208p. 18.95 o.p. (*0-312-11388-9*, Saint Martin's Minotaur) St. Martin's Pr.
—Summer Will End. 1996. (Elizabeth Will Mystery Ser.). 182p. text 20.95 o.p. (*0-312-14743-0*, Saint Martin's Minotaur) St. Martin's Pr.

**WILLETT, WOLF (FICTITIOUS CHARACTER)—FICTION**

Woods, Stuart. Santa Fe Rules. 1992. 320p. 20.00 o.p. (*0-06-017963-5*) HarperTrade.
—Santa Fe Rules. 1993. 368p. mass mkt. 7.99 (*0-06-109089-1*, HarperTorch) Morrow/Avon.

**WILLIAM OF BASKERVILLE (FICTITIOUS CHARACTER)—FICTION**

Eco, Umberto. The Name of the Rose. abr. ed. 1995. audio 24.95 (*1-55927-361-5*, 693211) Audio Renaissance.
—The Name of the Rose. unabr. ed. 1996. audio 112.00 (*0-7366-3259-X*, 3916) Books on Tape, Inc.
—The Name of the Rose. 1994. reprint ed. lib. bdg. 29.95 (*1-56849-544-7*) Buccaneer Bks., Inc.
—The Name of the Rose. l.t. ed. 1984. 9.95 o.p. (*0-8161-3695-5*, Macmillan Reference USA) Gale Group.
—The Name of the Rose. Weaver, William, tr. l.t. ed. 1984. (General Ser.). 16.95 o.p. (*0-8161-3663-7*, Macmillan Reference USA) Gale Group.
—The Name of the Rose. 1995. pap. 10.95 (*0-15-600370-8*) Harcourt Trade Pubs.
—The Name of the Rose. Weaver, William, tr. 1995. 29.95 (*0-15-100213-4*); 1994. (Illus.). 552p. pap. 15.00 (*0-15-600131-4*, Harvest Bks.); 1983. 512p. 35.00 (*0-15-144647-4*) Harcourt Trade Pubs.
—The Name of the Rose. 640p. 1988. mass mkt. 6.99 (*0-446-35720-0*); 4th ed. 1986. mass mkt. 4.95 (*0-446-34410-9*) Warner Bks., Inc.

**WILLIAMS, CALEB (FICTITIOUS CHARACTER)—FICTION**

Godwin, William. Caleb Williams. McCracken, David, ed. (Oxford World's Classics Ser.). 1982. (Illus.). 384p. pap. o.p. (*0-19-281621-7*); 1970. 9.95 o.p. (*0-19-255331-3*) Oxford Univ. Pr., Inc.
—Caleb Williams. Hindle, Maurice, ed. & intro. by. 1988. (Classics Ser.). 448p. pap. 14.00 (*0-14-043256-6*, Penguin Classics) Viking Penguin.

**WILLIAMS, CATHERINE (FICTITIOUS CHARACTER)—FICTION**

Lewis, Stephen. The Blind in Darkness. 2000. (Mystery of Colonial Times Ser.). 272p. mass mkt. 5.99 o.s.i (*0-425-17466-2*, Prime Crime) Berkley Publishing Group.
—The Dumb Shall Sing: A Mystery of Colonial Times. 1999. 272p. mass mkt. 5.99 o.s.i (*0-425-16997-9*, Prime Crime) Berkley Publishing Group.

**WILLIAMS, RACE (FICTITIOUS CHARACTER)—FICTION**

Daly, Carroll J. The Adventures of Race Williams. 1989. 352p. 9.95 (*0-89296-959-8*) Mysterious Pr.

**WILLIAMS, TERRY (FICTITIOUS CHARACTER)—FICTION**

Strong, Tony. The Death Pit. 2000. 448p. mass mkt. 6.50 (*0-440-22623-6*) Dell Publishing.
—The Death Pit. 2000. 448p. mass mkt. o.s.i (*0-7704-2861-4*) Seal Bks. CAN. *Dist:* Random Hse. of Canada, Ltd.
—The Poison Tree. 1998. 400p. pap. 23.00 (*0-440-61402-3*); mass mkt. 6.50 o.s.i (*0-440-22498-5*) Dell Publishing.
—The Poison Tree. 1998. 400p. mass mkt. o.s.i (*0-7704-2793-6*) Seal Bks. CAN. *Dist:* Random Hse. of Canada, Ltd.

**WILLIAMSON, LUKE (FICTITIOUS CHARACTER)—FICTION**

Brewer, James D. No Bottom: A Masey Baldridge/Luke Williamson Mystery. 1994. 256p. 19.95 o.p. (*0-8027-3178-3*) Walker & Co.
—No Escape. 1998. (Masey Baldridge/Luke Williamson Mystery Ser.). 264p. 22.95 (*0-8027-3318-2*) Walker & Co.
—No Justice: A Masey Baldridge/Luke Williamson Mystery. 1996. (Masey Baldridge/Luke Williamson Mystery Ser.). 232p. 21.95 (*0-8027-3283-6*) Walker & Co.
—No Remorse: A Masey Baldridge/Luke Williamson Mystery. 1997. (Luke Williamson/Masey Baldridge Mystery Ser.). 224p. 22.95 (*0-8027-3302-6*) Walker & Co.
—No Virtue: A Masey Baldridge/Luke Williamson Mystery. 1995. (Masey Baldridge/Luke Williamson Mystery Ser.). 232p. (YA). 20.95 (*0-8027-3259-3*) Walker & Co.

**WILLMARTH, RUTH (FICTITIOUS CHARACTER)—FICTION**

Wright, Nancy M. Harvest of Bones: A Vermont Mystery. 1999. 256p. per. (*0-373-26325-2*, Worldwide Library) Harlequin Enterprises, Ltd.
—Harvest of Bones: A Vermont Mystery. 1998. 304p. 23.95 (*0-312-19280-0*, Saint Martin's Minotaur) St. Martin's Pr.
—Mad Season: A Mystery. 1998. (WWL Mystery Ser.). per. (*0-373-26270-1*, 1-26270-8, Worldwide Library) Harlequin Enterprises, Ltd.
—Mad Season: A Mystery. 1996. (Mad Season Ser.: Vol. 1). 208p. 20.95 o.p. (*0-312-14819-4*, Saint Martin's Minotaur) St. Martin's Pr.
—Poison Apples. 2000. 322p. 24.95 (*0-312-26220-5*, Saint Martin's Minotaur) St. Martin's Pr.
—Stolen Honey. 2003. (WWL Mystery Ser.: No. 453). 272p. mass mkt. (*0-373-26453-4*, Worldwide Library) Harlequin Enterprises, Ltd.
—Stolen Honey. 2002. 256p. 23.95 (*0-312-26245-0*, Saint Martin's Minotaur) St. Martin's Pr.
—Stolen Honey. l.t. ed. 2003. 465p. pap. 24.95 (*0-7862-5681-8*) Thorndike Pr.

**WILLOWS, JACK (FICTITIOUS CHARACTER)—FICTION**

Gough, Laurence. Death on a No. 8 Hook. 2001. (Willows & Parker Mystery Ser.). 232p. mass mkt. 7.95 (*0-7710-3533-0*) McClelland & Stewart/Tundra Bks.
—Funny Money. 264p. 2002. mass mkt. 6.95 (*0-7710-3544-6*); 2000. 23.95 o.s.i (*0-7710-3401-6*) McClelland & Stewart/Tundra Bks.
—The Goldfish Bowl. 2001. (Willows & Parker Mystery Ser.). 216p. mass mkt. 7.95 (*0-7710-3532-2*) McClelland & Stewart/Tundra Bks.
—The Goldfish Bowl. 1988. 192p. 13.95 o.p. (*0-312-01434-1*, Saint Martin's Minotaur) St. Martin's Pr.
—The Goldfish Bowl. 1990. 192p. pap. 3.95 o.p. (*0-14-011596-X*, Penguin Bks.) Viking Penguin.
—Heartbreaker. 1996. (Willows & Parker Mystery Ser.). 272p. mass mkt. 5.99 (*0-7710-3447-4*) McClelland & Stewart/Tundra Bks.
—Heartbreaker: A Willows & Parker Mystery. 1996. 272p. 22.95 o.p. (*0-7710-3438-5*) McClelland & Stewart/Tundra Bks.
—Hot Shots. 2002. 224p. mass mkt. 6.95 (*0-7710-3545-4*) McClelland & Stewart/Tundra Bks.
—Hot Shots. 1991. (Crime Monthly Ser.). 192p. pap. 4.95 o.p. (*0-14-015488-4*, Penguin Bks.) Penguin Group (USA) Inc.
—Hot Shots. 1990. 192p. 16.95 o.p. (*0-670-83014-3*) Viking Penguin.
—Karaoke Rap. 1998. (Willows & Parker Mystery Ser.). 368p. 20.95 o.p. (*0-7710-3403-2*) McClelland & Stewart/Tundra Bks.
—Killers. 1995. 256p. pap. 8.95 o.p. (*0-575-05782-3*) Gollancz, Victor GBR. *Dist:* Trafalgar Square.
—Killers. 1993. o.p. (*0-7710-3439-3*) McClelland & Stewart/Tundra Bks.
—Memory Lane. 1997. (Willows & Parker Mystery Ser.). 304p. mass mkt. 5.95 (*0-7710-3404-0*) McClelland & Stewart/Tundra Bks.
—Memory Lane: A Willows & Parker Mystery. 1997. 296p. 24.95 o.p. (*0-7710-3437-7*) McClelland & Stewart/Tundra Bks.
—Serious Crimes. 2002. 256p. mass mkt. 6.95 (*0-7710-3546-2*) McClelland & Stewart/Tundra Bks.
—Serious Crimes. 1999. pap. (*0-670-83675-3*) Viking Penguin.
—Shutterbug. 1999. (Willows & Parker Mystery Ser.). 288p. mass mkt. 7.95 (*0-7710-3429-6*) McClelland & Stewart/Tundra Bks.
—Shutterbug: A Willows & Parker Mystery. 1998. (Willows & Parker Mystery Ser.: Bk. 11). 288p. 20.95 o.p. (*0-7710-3531-4*) McClelland & Stewart/Tundra Bks.
—Silent Knives. 1988. 192p. 13.95 o.p. (*0-312-01747-2*, Saint Martin's Minotaur) St. Martin's Pr.
—Silent Knives. 1990. 192p. pap. 3.95 o.p. (*0-14-012189-7*, Penguin Bks.) Viking Penguin.

**WILLUM, PERSIS (FICTITIOUS CHARACTER)—FICTION**

Watson, Clarissa. The Bishop in the Back Seat. 1986. 256p. mass mkt. 2.95 o.s.i (*0-345-33084-6*) Ballantine Bks.
—The Bishop in the Back Seat. 1979. 9.95 o.p. (*0-689-11012-X*, Scribner) Simon & Schuster.
—The Fourth Stage of Gainsborough Brown. 1986. 224p. mass mkt. 2.95 o.s.i (*0-345-33531-7*) Ballantine Bks.
—The Fourth Stage of Gainsborough Brown. 1977. 7.95 o.p. (*0-679-50667-5*) McKay, David Co., Inc.
—The Fourth Stage of Gainsborough Brown. 1978. (Crime Ser.). pap. 1.95 o.p. (*0-14-004789-1*, Penguin Bks.) Viking Penguin.
—Last Plane from Nice. 1988. (Persis Willum Mystery Ser.). 224p. 16.95 o.s.i (*0-689-11835-X*, Scribner) Simon & Schuster.
—Runaway. l.t. ed. 1989. (Atlantic Mystery Ser.). pap. 14.95 o.p. (*1-55504-739-4*, 838) BBC Audiobooks America.
—Runaway. 1986. 208p. mass mkt. 2.95 o.s.i (*0-345-33114-1*) Ballantine Bks.
—Runaway. 1985. 250p. 12.95 o.p. (*0-689-11521-0*, Scribner) Simon & Schuster.
—Somebody Killed the Messenger. 1988. 224p. 16.95 o.s.i (*0-689-11963-1*, Scribner) Simon & Schuster.

**WILSON, ANGELA (FICTITIOUS CHARACTER)—FICTION**

Cook, Robin. Fatal Cure. abr. ed. 1994. audio 24.95 (*1-55927-263-5*, 692199) Audio Renaissance.
—Fatal Cure. 1995. 464p. mass mkt. 7.99 (*0-425-14563-8*) Berkley Publishing Group.
—Fatal Cure. unabr. ed. 1994. audio 96.00 (*0-7366-2774-X*, 3493) Books on Tape, Inc.
—Fatal Cure. l.t. ed. 618p. 1995. lib. bdg. 17.95 o.p. (*0-8161-5943-2*); 1994. lib. bdg. 22.95 o.p. (*0-8161-5942-4*) Gale Group. (Macmillan Reference USA).
—Fatal Cure. 1994. 432p. 22.95 o.p. (*0-399-13879-X*, G. P. Putnam's Sons) Penguin Group (USA) Inc.
—Fatal Cure: Library Edition. unabr. ed. 1994. audio 119.95 (*1-55927-279-1*) Audio Renaissance.

**WILSON, FRANCESCA (FICTITIOUS CHARACTER)—FICTION**

Neel, Janet. Death among the Dons. l.t. ed. 1994. 369p. lib. bdg. 21.95 (*0-8161-7439-3*, Macmillan Reference USA) Gale Group.
—Death among the Dons. 1995. (Illus.). 272p. (J). mass mkt. 5.50 (*0-671-89952-X*, Pocket) Simon & Schuster.
—Death among the Dons. 1993. 240p. 19.95 o.p. (*0-312-10450-2*, Saint Martin's Minotaur) St. Martin's Pr.
—Death of a Partner. l.t. ed. 1996. 384p. pap. 20.95 (*0-7838-1641-3*, Macmillan Reference USA) Gale Group.
—Death of a Partner. Chelius, Jane, ed. 1994. 256p. reprint ed. mass mkt. 4.99 (*0-671-74839-4*, Pocket) Simon & Schuster.
—Death of a Partner. 1991. 16.95 o.p. (*0-312-05411-4*, Saint Martin's Minotaur) St. Martin's Pr.
—Death on Site. l.t. ed. 1996. 363p. pap. 20.95 o.p. (*0-7838-1640-5*, Macmillan Reference USA) Gale Group.
—Death on Site. Chelius, Jane, ed. 1993. 288p. reprint ed. mass mkt. 4.99 (*0-671-73581-0*, Pocket) Simon & Schuster.
—Death on Site. 1990. 256p. 16.95 o.p. (*0-312-04298-1*, Saint Martin's Minotaur) St. Martin's Pr.
—Death's Bright Angel. Chelius, Jane, ed. 1991. 288p. reprint ed. mass mkt. 4.99 (*0-671-73579-9*, Pocket) Simon & Schuster.
—Death's Bright Angel. 1988. 224p. 15.95 o.p. (*0-312-02568-8*, Saint Martin's Minotaur) St. Martin's Pr.
—Death's Bright Angel. l.t. ed. 1998. (General Ser.). 365p. pap. 23.95 (*0-7862-1289-6*) Thorndike Pr.
—O Gentle Death. 2001. 240p. 22.95 (*0-312-28052-1*, Saint Martin's Minotaur) St. Martin's Pr.
—A Timely Death. l.t. ed. 1997. 382p. pap. 21.95 (*0-7838-8140-1*, Macmillan Reference USA) Gale Group.
—A Timely Death. 1996. 219p. text 21.95 o.p. (*0-312-15223-X*, Saint Martin's Minotaur) St. Martin's Pr.
—To Die for: A Mystery. 1999. 240p. 21.95 o.p. (*0-312-20598-8*, Saint Martin's Minotaur) St. Martin's Pr.

**WIMSEY, PETER, LORD (FICTITIOUS CHARACTER)—FICTION**

Paton Walsh, Jill. A Presumption of Death. E-Book 24.95 (*0-312-70987-0*) St. Martin's Pr.
Paton Walsh, Jill & Sayers, Dorothy L. A Presumption of Death. unabr. ed. 2003. (Lord Peter Wimsey Mystery Ser.). audio 29.95 (*1-57270-322-9*); audio compact disk 34.95 (*1-57270-323-7*) Audio Partners Publishing Corp. (Audio Editions Mystery Masters).
—A Presumption of Death. 2003. audio 69.95 (*0-7540-8309-8*); audio compact disk 79.95 (*0-7540-8752-2*) Chivers Audio Bks. GBR. *Dist:* BBC Audiobooks America.

—A Presumption of Death. l.t. ed. 2003. (New Lord Peter Wimsey/Harriet Vane Mystery Ser.). 449p. 28.95 (*0-7862-5561-7*) Thorndike Pr.

Sayers, Dorothy L. Busman's Honeymoon. unabr. ed. 2002. audio 34.95 (*1-57270-317-2*) Audio Partners Publishing Corp.

—Busman's Honeymoon. l.t. ed. (Lord Peter Wimsey Mystery Ser.). 1993. pap. 17.95 o.p. (*0-7927-1366-4*); 1992. 21.95 o.p. (*0-7927-1367-2*) BBC Audiobooks America.

—Busman's Honeymoon. unabr. ed. 2000. (Lord Peter Wimsey Mysteries Ser.: Bk. 13). audio 69.95 (*0-7451-4313-X*, CAB 996) Chivers Audio Bks. GBR. *Dist:* BBC Audiobooks America.

—Busman's Honeymoon. 1981. (Lord Peter Wimsey Mystery Ser.). lib. bdg. 16.95 o.p. (*0-8161-3041-8*, Macmillan Reference USA) Gale Group.

—Busman's Honeymoon. 1960. (Lord Peter Wimsey Mystery Ser.). 12.95 o.p. (*0-06-013765-7*) HarperCollins Pubs.

—Busman's Honeymoon. (Lord Peter Wimsey Mystery Ser.). 1986. 17.95 o.p. (*0-06-055021-X*); 1986. pap. 6.00 o.p. (*0-06-080823-3*, Perennial); 1993. 400p. reprint ed. pap. 8.00 o.p. (*0-06-092393-8*, Perennial) HarperTrade.

—Busman's Honeymoon. (Lord Peter Wimsey Mystery Ser.). 1995. 416p. mass mkt. 6.99 (*0-06-104351-6*, HarperTorch); 1978. pap. 2.75 o.p. (*0-380-01076-3*, 62489-3, Avon Bks.) Morrow/Avon.

—Clouds of Witness. l.t. ed. 1993. (Lord Peter Wimsey Mystery Ser.). 21.95 o.p. (*0-7927-1435-0*); pap. o.p. (*0-7927-1434-2*) BBC Audiobooks America.

—Clouds of Witness. unabr. ed. 2000. (Lord Peter Wimsey Mysteries Ser.: Bk. 2). audio 59.95 (*0-7451-4008-4*, CAB 705) Chivers Audio Bks. GBR. *Dist:* BBC Audiobooks America.

—Clouds of Witness, Set. abr. ed. 1992. (Lord Peter Wimsey Mystery Ser.). 30p. audio 16.99 (*0-88646-310-6*, 390538) Durkin Hayes Publishing Ltd.

—Clouds of Witness. l.t. ed. 1979. (Lord Peter Wimsey Mystery Ser.). (YA). lib. bdg. 15.95 o.p. (*0-8161-6721-4*, Macmillan Reference USA) Gale Group.

—Clouds of Witness. 1987. (Lord Peter Wimsey Mystery Ser.). 288p. 17.95 o.p. (*0-06-055035-X*); pap. 6.50 o.p. (*0-06-080835-7*, PL835, Perennial) HarperTrade.

—Clouds of Witness. (Lord Peter Wimsey Mystery Ser.). 1995. 288p. mass mkt. 5.99 (*0-06-104353-2*, HarperTorch); 1976. 224p. pap. 2.75 o.p. (*0-380-01107-7*, 64394-4, Avon Bks.) Morrow/Avon.

—Clouds of Witness. 1973. mass mkt. 1.25 o.p. (*0-451-05594-2*); 1969. mass mkt. 0.75 o.p. (*0-451-03970-X*) NAL. (Signet Bks.).

—Dorothy L. Sayers: Four Complete Lord Peter Wimsey Novels. 1990. 752p. reprint ed. 9.99 o.s.i (*0-517-39575-4*) Random Hse. Value Publishing.

—Dorothy L. Sayers: On the Case with Lord Peter Wimsey: Three Complete Novels. 1992. 576p. reprint ed. 6.99 o.s.i (*0-517-07243-2*) Random Hse. Value Publishing.

—Dorothy L. Sayers: The Complete Stories. 2002. 816p. pap. 17.95 (*0-06-008461-8*, Perennial) HarperTrade.

—Dorothy L. Sayers: Three Complete Lord Peter Wimsey Novels. 1992. 586p. 7.99 o.s.i (*0-517-07777-9*) Random Hse. Value Publishing.

—The Five Red Herrings. 1994. (Lord Peter Wimsey Mystery Ser.). reprint ed. lib. bdg. 32.95 (*1-56849-332-0*) Buccaneer Bks., Inc.

—The Five Red Herrings. unabr. ed. 2000. (Lord Peter Wimsey Mysteries Ser.: Bk. 7). audio 69.95 (*0-7451-6259-2*, CAB 607) Chivers Audio Bks. GBR. *Dist:* BBC Audiobooks America.

—The Five Red Herrings. l.t. ed. (Lord Peter Wimsey Mystery Ser.). 1991. pap. 15.95 o.p. (*0-8161-5225-X*); 1980. 525p. lib. bdg. 15.95 o.p. (*0-8161-3044-2*) Gale Group. (Macmillan Reference USA).

—The Five Red Herrings. (Lord Peter Wimsey Mystery Ser.). 1995. 368p. mass mkt. 6.99 (*0-06-104363-X*); 1958. o.p. (*0-06-013775-4*) HarperCollins Pubs.

—The Five Red Herrings. (Lord Peter Wimsey Mystery Ser.). 1993. 320p. pap. 8.00 o.p. (*0-06-092387-3*); 1986. pap. 6.00 o.p. (*0-06-080830-6*) HarperTrade. (Perennial).

—The Five Red Herrings. 1976. (Lord Peter Wimsey Mystery Ser.). pap. 2.75 o.p. (*0-380-01187-5*, 62109-6, Avon Bks.) Morrow/Avon.

—The Five Red Herrings. 1974. mass mkt. 0.95 o.p. (*0-451-05887-9*); mass mkt. 0.75 o.p. (*0-451-03346-9*) NAL. (Signet Bks.).

—Four Classic Dorothy L. Sayers Mysteries: Strong Poison; Have His Carcase; Gaudy Night; Busman's Honeymoon, 4 vols. 1990. 1504p. reprint ed. pap. 22.95 o.p. (*0-06-081051-3*, Perennial) HarperTrade.

—Gaudy Night. unabr. ed. 1993. (Lord Peter Wimsey Mysteries Ser.: Bk. 12). audio 79.95 (*0-7451-4106-4*, CAB 789) Chivers Audio Bks. GBR. *Dist:* BBC Audiobooks America.

—Gaudy Night. abr. ed. 1996. (Lord Peter Wimsey Mystery Ser.). audio 16.99 (*0-88646-284-3*, 7284) Durkin Hayes Publishing Ltd.

—Gaudy Night. l.t. ed. 1981. (Lord Peter Wimsey Mystery Ser.). lib. bdg. 18.95 o.p. (*0-8161-3040-X*, Macmillan Reference USA) Gale Group.

—Gaudy Night. (Lord Peter Wimsey Mystery Ser.). 1986. 17.95 o.p. (*0-06-055022-8*); 1986. pap. 6.50 o.p. (*0-06-080824-1*); 1993. 480p. reprint ed. pap. 9.00 o.p. (*0-06-092392-X*, Perennial); 1987. 464p. reprint ed. pap. 5.50 o.p. (*0-06-080907-8*, P-907, Perennial) HarperTrade.

—Gaudy Night. (Lord Peter Wimsey Mystery Ser.). 1995. 512p. mass mkt. 6.99 (*0-06-104349-4*, HarperTorch); 1976. pap. 3.50 o.p. (*0-380-01207-3*, 65037, Avon Bks.) Morrow/Avon.

—Hangman's Holiday. unabr. ed. 1993. (Lord Peter Wimsey Mystery Ser.). audio 39.95 (*0-7861-0405-8*, 752397) Blackstone Audio Bks., Inc.

—Hangman's Holiday. 1979. (Lord Peter Wimsey Mystery Ser.). (gr. 7-12). lib. bdg. 12.95 o.p. (*0-8161-6783-4*, Macmillan Reference USA) Gale Group.

—Hangman's Holiday. (Lord Peter Wimsey Mystery Ser.). 1987. 288p. 21.95 o.p. (*0-06-055033-3*); 1987. 288p. pap. 6.00 o.p. (*0-06-080837-3*, P837, Perennial); 1993. 368p. reprint ed. pap. 13.00 (*0-06-092396-2*, Perennial) HarperTrade.

—Hangman's Holiday. 1979. (Lord Peter Wimsey Mystery Ser.). pap. 2.50 o.p. (*0-380-01240-5*, 60048-X, Avon Bks.) Morrow/Avon.

—Have His Carcase. l.t. ed. 1993. (Lord Peter Wimsey Mystery Ser.). 24.95 o.p. (*0-7927-1589-6*); pap. 22.95 o.p. (*0-7927-1588-8*) BBC Audiobooks America.

—Have His Carcase. unabr. ed. 2000. (Lord Peter Wimsey Mystery Ser.). 12p. audio compact disk 110.95 (*0-7540-5367-9*, CCD 058); (Lord Peter Wimsey Mysteries Ser.: Bk. 8). audio 79.95 (*0-7540-0355-8*, CAB 1778) Chivers Audio Bks. GBR. *Dist:* BBC Audiobooks America.

—Have His Carcase, Set. abr. ed. 1990. (Lord Peter Wimsey Mystery Ser.). 29p. audio 16.99 (*0-88646-270-3*, 390905) Durkin Hayes Publishing Ltd.

—Have His Carcase. l.t. ed. 1980. (Lord Peter Wimsey Mystery Ser.). 17.95 o.p. (*0-8161-3043-4*, Macmillan Reference USA) Gale Group.

—Have His Carcase. 1959. (Lord Peter Wimsey Mystery Ser.). 12.95 o.p. (*0-06-013785-1*) HarperCollins Pubs.

—Have His Carcase. (Lord Peter Wimsey Mystery Ser.). 1987. 416p. pap. 5.50 o.p. (*0-06-080909-4*, P-909); 1986. pap. 6.50 o.p. (*0-06-080827-6*); 1993. 448p. reprint ed. pap. 8.00 o.p. (*0-06-092391-1*) HarperTrade. (Perennial).

—Have His Carcase. (Lord Peter Wimsey Mystery Ser.). 1995. 448p. mass mkt. 7.99 (*0-06-104352-4*, HarperTorch); 1976. pap. 2.75 o.p. (*0-380-00939-0*, 58305-4, Avon Bks.) Morrow/Avon.

—In the Teeth of the Evidence: And Other Mysteries. 1997. (Lord Peter Wimsey Mysteries Ser.). audio 34.95 (*0-7540-7504-4*) BBC Audiobooks America.

—In the Teeth of the Evidence: And Other Mysteries. 1987. 320p. 17.95 o.p. (*0-06-055031-7*); 1987. 320p. pap. 6.00 o.p. (*0-06-080838-1*, P838, Perennial); 2001. 352p. reprint ed. pap. 13.00 (*0-06-092397-0*, Perennial) HarperTrade.

—In the Teeth of the Evidence: And Other Mysteries. (Lord Peter Wimsey Mystery Ser.). 1995. 272p. mass mkt. 5.99 (*0-06-104356-7*, HarperTorch); 1976. pap. 2.50 o.p. (*0-380-01280-4*, 62943-7, Avon Bks.) Morrow/Avon.

—In the Teeth of the Evidence: And Other Mysteries. 1974. mass mkt. 0.75 o.p. (*0-451-03321-3*); mass mkt. 0.95 o.p. (*0-451-05885-2*) NAL. (Signet Bks.).

—Lord Peter: A Collection of All the Lord Peter Wimsey Stories. (Lord Peter Wimsey Mystery Ser.). 31.95 (*0-8488-1153-4*) Amereon, Ltd.

—Lord Peter: A Collection of All the Lord Peter Wimsey Stories. 1995. (Lord Peter Wimsey Mystery Ser.). 496p. mass mkt. 5.99 o.s.i (*0-06-104361-3*) HarperCollins Pubs.

—Lord Peter: A Collection of All the Lord Peter Wimsey Stories. Sandoe, James, ed. 1972. (Lord Peter Wimsey Mystery Ser.). o.p. (*0-06-013788-6*) HarperCollins Pubs.

—Lord Peter: A Collection of All the Lord Peter Wimsey Stories. 1986. (Lord Peter Wimsey Mystery Ser.). 512p. 18.95 o.p. (*0-06-055039-2*); 496p. pap. 16.00 (*0-06-091380-0*, Perennial) HarperTrade.

—Lord Peter: A Collection of All the Lord Peter Wimsey Stories. Sandoe, James, ed. 1991. (Lord Peter Wimsey Mystery Ser.). 501p. reprint ed. lib. bdg. 27.00 o.p. (*0-8095-9129-4*) Millefleurs.

—Lord Peter: A Collection of All the Lord Peter Wimsey Stories. 1976. (Lord Peter Wimsey Mystery Ser.). mass mkt. 6.95 o.p. (*0-380-01694-X*, 59683-0, Avon Bks.) Morrow/Avon.

—Lord Peter Views the Body. (Lord Peter Wimsey Mystery Ser.). 1986. pap. 6.50 o.p. (*0-06-080839-X*); 1993. 336p. reprint ed. pap. 8.00 o.p. (*0-06-092395-4*) HarperTrade. (Perennial).

—Lord Peter Views the Body. (Lord Peter Wimsey Mystery Ser.). 1995. 320p. mass mkt. 5.99 o.s.i (*0-06-104359-1*, HarperTorch); 1976. pap. 2.50 o.p. (*0-380-00946-3*, 63503-8, Avon Bks.) Morrow/Avon.

—Murder Must Advertise. unabr. ed. audio 29.95 (*1-57270-300-8*) Audio Partners Publishing Corp.

—Murder Must Advertise. unabr. ed. 1997. (Lord Peter Wimsey Mystery Ser.). audio 56.95 (*0-7861-1165-8*, 1936) Blackstone Audio Bks., Inc.

—Murder Must Advertise. unabr. ed. 2000. (Lord Peter Wimsey Mysteries Ser.: Bk. 10). audio 69.95 (*0-7451-6862-0*, CAB 331) Chivers Audio Bks. GBR. *Dist:* BBC Audiobooks America.

—Murder Must Advertise. l.t. ed. 1980. (Lord Peter Wimsey Mystery Ser.). 508p. lib. bdg. 15.95 o.p. (*0-8161-3045-0*, Macmillan Reference USA) Gale Group.

—Murder Must Advertise. (Lord Peter Wimsey Mystery Ser.). 352p. 1993. pap. 8.00 o.p. (*0-06-092388-1*, Perennial); 1986. 17.95 o.p. (*0-06-055024-4*); 1986. pap. 6.50 o.p. (*0-06-080825-X*, P825, Perennial) HarperTrade.

—Murder Must Advertise. (Lord Peter Wimsey Mystery Ser.). 1995. 368p. mass mkt. 6.99 (*0-06-104355-9*, HarperTorch); 1985. pap. 2.25 o.p. (*0-380-00916-1*, 60913-4, Avon Bks.) Morrow/Avon.

—Murder Must Advertise. 1974. mass mkt. 0.95 o.p. (*0-451-06170-5*); 1968. mass mkt. 0.75 o.p. (*0-451-03369-8*) NAL. (Signet Bks.).

—Murder Must Advertise. unabr. ed. 1997. (Lord Peter Wimsey Mystery Ser.). audio 78.00 (*0-7887-1289-6*, 95145E7) Recorded Bks., LLC.

—The Nine Tailors. Date not set. (Lord Peter Wimsey Mystery Ser.). 320p. 24.95 (*0-8488-2388-5*) Amereon, Ltd.

—The Nine Tailors. l.t. ed. 1981. (Lord Peter Wimsey Mystery Ser.). lib. bdg. 15.95 o.p. (*0-8161-3036-1*, Macmillan Reference USA) Gale Group.

—The Nine Tailors. (Lord Peter Wimsey Mystery Ser.). 1989. 331p. 15.95 o.s.i (*0-15-165897-8*); 1966. 420p. pap. 12.00 (*0-15-665899-2*, Harvest Bks.) Harcourt Trade Pubs.

—A Presumption of Death. Date not set. mass mkt. (*0-312-99138-X*, St. Martin's Paperbacks) St. Martin's Pr.

—Striding Folly. unabr. ed. 1994. (Lord Peter Wimsey Mystery Ser.). audio 24.95 (*0-7451-4265-6*, CAB 948) BBC Audiobooks America.

—Striding Folly. (Lord Peter Wimsey Mystery Ser.). text 34.95 (*0-450-54973-9*) Hodder & Stoughton, Ltd. GBR. *Dist:* Lubrecht & Cramer, Ltd., Trafalgar Square.

—Strong Poison. (Lord Peter Wimsey Mystery Ser.). 20.95 (*0-8488-1154-2*) Amereon, Ltd.

—Strong Poison. unabr. ed. 2001. (Lord Peter Wimsey Mystery Ser.). audio 29.95 (*1-57270-124-2*, N61124u, Audio Editions Mystery Masters) Audio Partners Publishing Corp.

—Strong Poison. unabr. ed. 2000. (Lord Peter Wimsey Mysteries Ser.: Bk. 6). audio 49.95 (*0-7451-6258-4*, CAB 400) Chivers Audio Bks. GBR. *Dist:* BBC Audiobooks America.

—Strong Poison, Set. abr. ed. 1990. (Lord Peter Wimsey Mystery Ser.). audio 16.99 (*0-88646-257-6*, 391702) Durkin Hayes Publishing Ltd.

—Strong Poison. l.t. ed. 1980. (Lord Peter Wimsey Mystery Ser.). 450p. lib. bdg. 15.95 o.p. (*0-8161-3042-6*, Macmillan Reference USA) Gale Group.

—Strong Poison. 1976. (Lord Peter Wimsey Mystery Ser.). reprint ed. lib. bdg. 21.00 o.p. (*0-8240-2392-7*) Garland Publishing, Inc.

—Strong Poison. (Lord Peter Wimsey Mystery Ser.). 1987. 256p. 17.95 o.p. (*0-06-055025-2*); 1987. pap. 6.00 o.p. (*0-06-080826-8*, Perennial); 1993. 256p. reprint ed. pap. 8.00 o.p. (*0-06-092390-3*, Perennial); 1987. 240p. reprint ed. pap. 4.95 o.p. (*0-06-080908-6*, P-908, Perennial) HarperTrade.

—Strong Poison. (Lord Peter Wimsey Mystery Ser.). 1995. 272p. mass mkt. 6.99 (*0-06-104350-8*, HarperTorch); 1978. pap. 2.75 o.p. (*0-380-01567-6*, 69401-8, Avon Bks.) Morrow/Avon.

—Strong Poison. 1974. mass mkt. 0.60 o.p. (*0-451-03264-0*); mass mkt. 0.75 o.p. (*0-451-05748-1*) NAL. (Signet Bks.).

—Strong Poison. 2001. (Best Mysteries of All Time Ser.). 320p. (*0-7621-8865-0*, IM Pr.) Reader's Digest Assn., Inc., The.

—Unnatural Death. unabr. ed. 2001. (Lord Peter Wimsey Mystery Ser.). audio 29.95 (*1-57270-144-7*, N61144u, Audio Editions Mystery Masters) Audio Partners Publishing Corp.

—Unnatural Death. l.t. ed. 1992. (Lord Peter Wimsey Mystery Ser.). pap. 17.95 o.p. (*0-7927-1264-1*); 20.95 o.p. (*0-7927-1265-X*, E0039) BBC Audiobooks America.

—Unnatural Death. unabr. ed. 2000. (Lord Peter Wimsey Mysteries Ser.: Bk. 3). audio 49.95 (*0-7451-6262-2*, CAB 496) Chivers Audio Bks. GBR. *Dist:* BBC Audiobooks America.

—Unnatural Death. 1979. (Lord Peter Wimsey Mystery Ser.). lib. bdg. 15.95 o.p. (*0-8161-6723-0*, Macmillan Reference USA) Gale Group.

—Unnatural Death. 1956. (Lord Peter Wimsey Mystery Ser.). 12.95 o.p. (*0-06-013800-9*) HarperCollins Pubs.

—Unnatural Death. (Lord Peter Wimsey Mystery Ser.). 1993. 256p. pap. 8.00 o.p. (*0-06-092386-5*, Perennial); 1987. 288p. 17.95 o.p. (*0-06-055032-5*) HarperTrade.

—Unnatural Death. (Lord Peter Wimsey Mystery Ser.). 1995. 288p. mass mkt. 6.99 (*0-06-104358-3*, HarperTorch); 1978. pap. 2.50 o.p. (*0-380-00794-0*, 68353-9, Avon Bks.) Morrow/Avon.

—The Unpleasantness at the Bellona Club. (Lord Peter Wimsey Mystery Ser.). 256p. 22.95 o.s.i (*0-8488-2463-6*) Amereon, Ltd.

—The Unpleasantness at the Bellona Club. unabr. ed. 2000. (Lord Peter Wimsey Mysteries Ser.: Bk. 5 ). audio 49.95 (*0-7451-6261-4*, CAB 448) Chivers Audio Bks. GBR. *Dist:* BBC Audiobooks America.

—The Unpleasantness at the Bellona Club. l.t. ed. 1979. (Lord Peter Wimsey Mystery Ser.). (YA). lib. bdg. 14.95 o.p. (*0-8161-6724-9*, Macmillan Reference USA) Gale Group.

—The Unpleasantness at the Bellona Club. 1957. (Lord Peter Wimsey Mystery Ser.). 12.95 o.p. (*0-06-013805-X*) HarperCollins Pubs.

—The Unpleasantness at the Bellona Club. (Lord Peter Wimsey Mystery Ser.). 1993. 240p. pap. 8.00 o.p. (*0-06-092389-X*, Perennial); 1987. 352p. 17.95 o.p. (*0-06-055026-0*); 1987. 192p. reprint ed. pap. 6.00 o.p. (*0-06-080828-4*, P-828, Perennial) HarperTrade.

—The Unpleasantness at the Bellona Club. 1995. 256p. mass mkt. 6.99 (*0-06-104354-0*, HarperTorch); 1978. pap. 2.50 o.p. (*0-380-01597-8*, 67132-8, Avon Bks.) Morrow/Avon.

—Whose Body?, unabr. ed. 1998. (Lord Peter Wimsey Mystery Ser.). audio 29.95 (*1-55685-503-6*) Audio Bk. Contractors, Inc.

—Whose Body?, unabr. ed. 2001. (Lord Peter Wimsey Mystery Ser.). audio 22.95 (*1-57270-018-1*, N51018u, Audio Editions Bks. on Cassette) Audio Partners Publishing Corp.

—Whose Body? unabr. ed. (Lord Peter Wimsey Mystery Ser.). 2000. audio compact disk 48.00 (*0-7861-9940-7*, z2391); 1999. audio 39.95 (*0-7861-1561-0*, 2391) Blackstone Audio Bks., Inc.

—Whose Body? 1979. (Lord Peter Wimsey Mystery Ser.). lib. bdg. 12.95 o.p. (*0-8161-6722-2*, Macmillan Reference USA) Gale Group.

—Whose Body? (Lord Peter Wimsey Mystery Ser.). 1993. 176p. pap. 9.00 o.p. (*0-06-092385-7*, Perennial); 1987. 256p. 17.95 o.p. (*0-06-055036-8*); 1987. 256p. pap. 5.50 o.p. (*0-06-080829-2*, P829, Perennial) HarperTrade.

—Whose Body? (Lord Peter Wimsey Mystery Ser.). 1995. 224p. mass mkt. 6.99 (*0-06-104357-5*, HarperTorch); 1978. pap. 2.50 o.p. (*0-380-00897-1*, 69781-5, Avon Bks.) Morrow/Avon.

Sayers, Dorothy L. & Paton Walsh, Jill. A Presumption of Death. 2003. (Lord Peter Wimsey Mystery Ser.). 384p. 24.95 (*0-312-29100-0*, Saint Martin's Minotaur) St. Martin's Pr.

—Thrones, Dominations. unabr. ed. 2001. (Lord Peter Wimsey Mystery Ser.). audio 34.95 (*1-57270-129-3*, N81129u, Audio Editions Mystery Masters) Audio Partners Publishing Corp.

—Thrones, Dominations. unabr. ed. 1998. (Lord Peter Wimsey Mysteries Ser.: Bk. 15). audio 59.95 (*0-7540-0203-9*, CAB 1626) Chivers Audio Bks. GBR. *Dist:* BBC Audiobooks America.

Sayers, Dorothy L. & Walsh, J. P. Thrones, Dominations. unabr. collector's ed. 1999. (Lord Peter Wimsey Mystery Ser.). audio 56.00 (*0-7366-4299-4*, 4791) Books on Tape, Inc.

Sayers, Dorothy L., et al. Thrones, Dominations. 1999. 322p. mass mkt. 6.50 (*0-312-96830-2*, St. Martin's Paperbacks); 1998. 312p. (gr. 5-6). 23.95 o.p. (*0-312-18196-5*, Saint Martin's Minotaur) St. Martin's Pr.

—Thrones, Dominations. l.t. ed. 1998. (Lord Peter Wimsey Mystery Ser.). 439p. 29.95 (*0-7838-8438-9*) Thorndike Pr.

### WINDER, JOE (FICTITIOUS CHARACTER)—FICTION

Hiaasen, Carl. Native Tongue. 1992. (Florida Mysteries Ser.). 416p. mass mkt. 7.50 o.s.i (*0-449-22118-0*, Fawcett) Ballantine Bks.

—Native Tongue. l.t. ed. 1996. (Large Print Bks.). pap. 21.95 o.p. (*1-56895-344-5*, Wheeler Publishing, Inc.) Gale Group.

—Native Tongue, Set. abr. ed. 1991. audio 16.00 o.s.i (*0-394-58966-1*, 391249, RH Audio) Random Hse. Audio Publishing Group.

—Native Tongue. 1993. 4.99 o.p. (*0-517-10755-4*) Random Hse. Value Publishing.

—Native Tongue. unabr. ed. 1992. audio 91.00 (*1-55690-761-3*, 92421E7) Recorded Bks., LLC.

—Native Tongue. 2003. mass mkt. 7.99 (*0-446-61320-7*) Warner Bks., Inc.

**WINDROSE, ANTRYG (FICTITIOUS CHARACTER)—FICTION**

Hambly, Barbara. Dog Wizard. 1992. (Windrose Chronicles Ser.: Bk. 3). 448p. mass mkt. 5.99 o.s.i (*0-345-37714-1*, Del Rey) Ballantine Bks.
—The Silent Tower. 1986. 384p. mass mkt. 5.99 o.s.i (*0-345-33764-6*, Del Rey) Ballantine Bks.
—The Silicon Mage. 1988. 352p. mass mkt. 5.99 o.s.i (*0-345-33763-8*, Del Rey) Ballantine Bks.

**WINE, MOSES (FICTITIOUS CHARACTER)—FICTION**

Simon, Roger L. The Big Fix. 1924. o.s.i (*1-55710-050-0*, Morrow, William & Co.) Morrow/Avon.
—The Big Fix. 1978. pap. 1.95 o.p. (*0-671-82010-9*, Pocket) Simon & Schuster.
—The Big Fix. 1986. 208p. mass mkt. 3.50 o.s.i (*0-446-30043-8*) Warner Bks., Inc.
—The Big Fix. E-Book 11.95 (*1-58824-010-X*); 2000. (Illus.). 192p. reprint ed. pap. 14.00 (*0-671-03906-7*) ibooks, Inc.
—California Roll. 1986. 208p. mass mkt. 3.50 o.s.i (*0-446-32965-7*) Warner Bks., Inc.
—Dead Meet. 1988. 160p. reprint ed. pap. 4.95 o.p. (*0-88739-095-1*, Black Mask) Creative Arts Bk. Co.
—The Lost Coast. 1997. 79p. 22.50 o.p. (*0-06-017707-1*) HarperTrade.
—The Lost Coast. 272p. 2003. mass mkt. 6.99 (*0-7434-5913-X*); 2000. reprint ed. pap. 14.00 (*0-671-03904-0*) ibooks, Inc.
—The Lost Coast: The New Moses Wine Novel. E-Book 11.95 (*1-58824-011-8*) ibooks, Inc.
—Peking Duck. 1987. 256p. mass mkt. 3.95 (*0-446-34932-1*) Warner Bks., Inc.
—Peking Duck. 2002. E-Book 9.99 (*1-58824-340-0*); 2000. 304p. pap. 14.00 (*0-7434-0716-4*) ibooks, Inc.
—Raising the Dead: A Moses Wine Mystery. 1989. 240p. mass mkt. 4.95 (*0-446-34822-8*) Warner Bks., Inc.
—The Straight Man. 1987. 240p. mass mkt. 3.95 (*0-446-34389-7*) Warner Bks., Inc.
—Wild Turkey: A Moses Wine Mystery. 1986. 240p. mass mkt. 3.50 o.s.i (*0-446-30044-6*) Warner Bks., Inc.
—Wild Turkey: A Moses Wine Mystery. E-Book 11.95 (*1-58824-039-8*); 2000. 208p. pap. 14.00 (*0-7434-0012-7*) ibooks, Inc.

**WING, ISADORA (FICTITIOUS CHARACTER)—FICTION**

Jong, Erica. Fear of Flying. 1995. 368p. pap. 13.95 o.p. (*0-452-27479-6*); 1975. pap. 4.95 o.p. (*0-452-25106-0*, Z5106) Dutton/Plume. (Plume).
—Fear of Flying. 1990. audio 15.95; audio 15.95 o.p. (*1-55994-163-4*, CPN 2149) HarperTrade. (Harper-Audio).
—Fear of Flying. 1973. 320p. o.p. (*0-03-010731-8*) Holt, Henry & Co.
—Fear of Flying. 2003. 448p. mass mkt. 7.99 (*0-451-20994-X*, Signet Bks.); 1995. 336p. mass mkt. 7.99 o.s.i (*0-451-18556-0*, Signet Bks.); 1974. mass mkt. 3.50 o.p. (*0-451-11329-2*, Signet Bks.); 1974. mass mkt. 2.95 o.p. (*0-451-09715-7*, Signet Bks.); 1974. mass mkt. 2.50 o.p. (*0-451-08677-5*, Signet Bks.); 1974. mass mkt. 2.25 o.p. (*0-451-07970-1*, Signet Bks.); 1974. mass mkt. 1.95 o.p. (*0-451-06139-X*, Signet Bks.); 1974. 336p. mass mkt. 5.99 o.p. (*0-451-15851-2*, Signet Bks.); 1974. mass mkt. 3.95 o.p. (*0-451-13139-8*, Signet Bks.); 30th anniv. ed. 2003. 480p. pap. 14.00 (*0-451-20943-5*) NAL.
—Fear of Flying. 2003. 224p. pap. 13.95 (*0-393-32492-3*) Norton, W. W. & Co., Inc.
—Fear of Flying & Poems. abr. ed. audio 10.95 (*0-8045-1140-3*, SAC 1140) Spoken Arts, Inc.
—How to Save Your Own Life. 1995. 320p. pap. 11.95 o.p. (*0-452-27454-0*, Plume) Dutton/Plume.
—How to Save Your Own Life. 1977. 8.95 o.p. (*0-03-017726-X*) Holt, Henry & Co.
—How to Save Your Own Life. 1986. mass mkt. 4.50 o.p. (*0-451-14834-7*); 1986. 320p. mass mkt. 5.95 o.p. (*0-451-15948-9*); 1978. mass mkt. 3.95 o.p. (*0-451-13148-7*); 1978. mass mkt. 2.50 o.p. (*0-451-07959-0*) NAL. (Signet Bks.).
—Parachutes & Kisses. 1985. 688p. mass mkt. 5.95 o.p. (*0-451-13877-5*, Signet Bks.); 1985. mass mkt. 2.95 o.p. (*0-451-15160-7*, Signet Bks.); 1984. 405p. 16.95 o.p. (*0-453-00466-0*) NAL.

**WING, JAMES (FICTITIOUS CHARACTER)—FICTION**

MacDonald, John D. A Flash of Green. 1984. (Travis McGee Novel Ser.). 336p. mass mkt. 6.99 (*0-449-12692-7*, Fawcett) Ballantine Bks.
—A Flash of Green. 1962. 5.50 o.p. (*0-671-26183-5*) Simon & Schuster.

**WINGATE, CALEDONIA (FICTITIOUS CHARACTER)—FICTION**

Sawyer, Corinne Holt. The Geezer Factory Murders. 1997. 263p. mass mkt. 5.99 o.s.i (*0-449-22532-1*, Fawcett) Ballantine Bks.
—The Geezer Factory Murders. 1996. (Benbow/Wingate Mystery Ser.). 240p. 21.95 o.s.i (*1-55611-497-4*, Dutton) Fine, Donald I. Bks.
—Ho-Ho Homicide. 1996. mass mkt. 5.99 o.s.i (*0-449-22409-0*, Fawcett) Ballantine Bks.
—Ho-Ho Homicide. 1995. (Benbow/Wingate Mystery Ser.). 256p. 20.95 o.s.i (*1-55611-459-1*) Fine, Donald I. Bks.
—The J. Alfred Prufrock Murders. 1989. 256p. mass mkt. 4.99 o.s.i (*0-449-21743-4*, Fawcett) Ballantine Bks.
—The J. Alfred Prufrock Murders. 1988. (Benbow/Wingate Mystery Ser.). 17.95 o.s.i (*1-55611-081-2*) Fine, Donald I. Bks.
—Murder by Owl Light. 1994. mass mkt. 4.99 o.s.i (*0-449-22171-7*) Ballantine Bks.
—Murder by Owl Light. 1992. (Benbow/Wingate Mystery Ser.). 240p. 19.00 o.p. (*1-55611-332-3*) Fine, Donald I. Bks.
—Murder Has No Calories. 1995. mass mkt. 5.99 o.s.i (*0-449-22338-8*, Fawcett) Ballantine Bks.
—Murder Has No Calories. 1994. (Benbow/Wingate Mystery Ser.). 224p. 19.95 o.p. (*1-55611-412-5*) Fine, Donald I. Bks.
—Murder in Gray & White. 1989. (Benbow/Wingate Mystery Ser.). 17.95 o.p. (*1-55611-153-3*) Fine, Donald I. Bks.
—Murder in Grey & White. 1991. 272p. mass mkt. 3.95 o.s.i (*0-449-21965-8*, Fawcett) Ballantine Bks.
—Murder Ole! 1998. 260p. mass mkt. 5.99 o.s.i (*0-449-00034-6*, Fawcett) Ballantine Bks.
—Murder Ole! 1997. (Benbow/Wingate Mystery Ser.). 272p. 22.95 (*1-55611-514-8*) Fine, Donald I. Bks.
—The Peanut Butter Murders. 1994. mass mkt. 4.99 o.s.i (*0-449-22172-5*) Ballantine Bks.
—The Peanut Butter Murders. 1993. (Benbow/Wingate Mystery Ser.). 233p. 18.95 o.p. (*1-55611-350-1*) Fine, Donald I. Bks.

**WINN ADAMI, KAI (FICTITIOUS CHARACTER)—FICTION**

David, Peter, et al. Wrath of the Prophets. 1997. (Star Trek Deep Space Nine Ser.: No. 20). 304p. pap. 5.99 (*0-671-53817-9*, Star Trek) Simon & Schuster.
Hugh, Dafydd ab. The Conquered No. 1: Rebels. 1999. (Star Trek Deep Space Nine Ser.: No. 24). 256p. pap. 6.50 o.s.i (*0-671-01140-5*, Star Trek) Simon & Schuster.
—The Courageous No. 2: Rebels. 1999. (Star Trek Deep Space Nine Ser.: No. 25). 256p. mass mkt. 6.50 o.s.i (*0-671-01141-3*, Star Trek) Simon & Schuster.
—The Liberated No. 3: Rebels. 1999. (Resistance Trilogy Ser.: No. 26). 256p. mass mkt. 6.50 o.s.i (*0-671-01142-1*, Star Trek) Simon & Schuster.
—Rebels: The Conquered. (Star Trek Deep Space Nine Ser.: No. 24). E-Book 6.99 (*0-7434-2055-1*, Star Trek) Simon & Schuster.
Peel, John. Objective: Bajor. 1996. (Star Trek Deep Space Nine Ser.: No. 15). 288p. per. 5.99 (*0-671-56811-6*, Star Trek) Simon & Schuster.
Reeves-Stevens, Judith & Reeves-Stevens, Garfield. Millennium No. 2: The War of the Prophets. 2000. (Star Trek Deep Space Nine Ser.). E-Book 6.99 (*0-7434-0680-X*, Star Trek) Simon & Schuster.
—Millennium Vol. 2: The War of the Prophets. 2000. (Star Trek Deep Space Nine: Vol. 2). 432p. pap. 6.50 o.s.i (*0-671-02402-7*, Star Trek) Simon & Schuster.

**WINSLOW, LAURA (FICTITIOUS CHARACTER)—FICTION**

Cole, David. Butterfly Lost. 2000. 384p. mass mkt. 5.99 (*0-06-101394-3*) HarperCollins Pubs.
—The Killing Maze. 2001. 336p. mass mkt. 6.50 (*0-06-101395-1*, Avon Bks.) Morrow/Avon.
—Scorpion Rain. 2002. 304p. mass mkt. 6.50 (*0-380-81971-6*, Avon Bks.) Morrow/Avon.
—Stalking Moon. 2002. 304p. mass mkt. 6.50 (*0-380-81970-8*, Avon Bks.) Morrow/Avon.

**WINSLOW, LIBBY (FICTITIOUS CHARACTER)—FICTION**

Van Wormer, Laura. Jury Duty. 1996. 364p. 24.00 o.s.i (*0-517-70065-4*); 1995. o.s.i (*0-517-70674-1*) Crown Publishing Group.
—Jury Duty. 1996. 410p. mass mkt. (*1-55166-169-1*, 1-66169-3, Mira Bks.) Harlequin Enterprises, Ltd.

**WINSLOW, STEVE (FICTITIOUS CHARACTER)—FICTION**

Hailey, J. P. The Anonymous Client. 1993. 320p. mass mkt. 4.99 (*0-8125-1388-6*, Tor Bks.) Doherty, Tom Assocs., LLC.
—The Anonymous Client. 1989. 300p. 16.95 o.p. (*1-55611-124-X*) Fine, Donald I. Bks.
—The Baxter Trust. 1988. 256p. 17.95 o.p. (*1-55611-090-1*) Fine, Donald I. Bks.
—The Baxter Trust. 1999. 240p. per. 15.95 (*0-7592-4105-8*) ereads.com.
—The Naked Typist. 1990. 18.95 o.p. (*1-55611-175-4*) Fine, Donald I. Bks.
—The Underground Man. 1994. (C). mass mkt. 4.99 (*0-8125-5011-0*, Forge Bks.) Doherty, Tom Assocs., LLC.
—The Underground Man. 1990. (Steve Winslow Courtroom Drama Ser.). 18.95 o.p. (*1-55611-215-7*) Fine, Donald I. Bks.
—The Wrong Gun. 1992. 288p. 20.95 o.p. (*1-55611-333-1*) Fine, Donald I. Bks.

**WINSLOW FAMILY (FICTITIOUS CHARACTERS)—FICTION**

Morris, Gilbert. The Amazon Quest. 2001. (House of Winslow Ser.: Vol. 28). 320p. pap. 11.99 (*0-7642-2117-5*) Bethany Hse. Pubs.
—The Beloved Enemy. 2003. (House of Winslow Ser.). 320p. pap. 11.99 (*0-7642-2704-1*) Bethany Hse. Pubs.
—The Captive Bride. 1987. (House of Winslow Ser.: Bk. 2). 240p. (Orig.). pap. 11.99 (*0-87123-978-7*) Bethany Hse. Pubs.
—The Crossed Sabres. 1993. (House of Winslow Ser.: No. 13). 320p. pap. 11.99 (*1-55661-309-1*) Bethany Hse. Pubs.
—The Dixie Widow. 1991. (House of Winslow Ser.: Bk. 9). 320p. pap. 11.99 (*1-55661-115-3*) Bethany Hse. Pubs.
—The Fiery Ring. 2002. (House of Winslow Ser.: Bk. 28). (Illus.). 320p. pap. 11.99 (*0-7642-2622-3*) Bethany Hse. Pubs.
—The Final Adversary. 1992. (House of Winslow Ser.: Bk. 12). 304p. pap. 11.99 (*1-55661-261-3*) Bethany Hse. Pubs.
—Flying Cavalier. 1999. (House of Winslow Ser.: Vol. 23). 320p. pap. 11.99 (*0-7642-2115-9*) Bethany Hse. Pubs.
—The Gallant Outlaw. 1994. (House of Winslow Ser.: No. 15). 288p. pap. 11.99 o.s.i (*1-55661-311-3*) Bethany Hse. Pubs.
—The Gentle Rebel. 1988. (House of Winslow Ser.: Vol. 4). 288p. pap. 11.99 (*1-55661-006-8*) Bethany Hse. Pubs.
—The Glorious Prodigal. 2000. (House of Winslow Ser.: Vol. 24). (Illus.). 320p. (J). pap. 11.99 (*0-7642-2116-7*) Bethany Hse. Pubs.
—The Holy Warrior. 1989. (House of Winslow Ser.: Vol. 6). 288p. pap. 11.99 (*1-55661-054-8*) Bethany Hse. Pubs.
—The Honorable Imposter. 1987. (House of Winslow Ser.: No. 1). 336p. pap. 11.99 (*0-87123-933-7*) Bethany Hse. Pubs.
—The Honorable Imposter. l.t. ed. 1993. (General Ser.). 464p. lib. bdg. 20.95 o.p. (*0-8161-5672-7*, Macmillan Reference USA) Gale Group.
—The Indentured Heart. 1988. (House of Winslow Ser.: Vol. 3). 288p. pap. 11.99 (*1-55661-003-3*) Bethany Hse. Pubs.
—The Iron Lady. 1996. (House of Winslow Ser.: Vol. 19). 320p. pap. 11.99 (*1-55661-687-2*) Bethany Hse. Pubs.
—The Iron Lady. l.t. ed. 1997. (Inspirational Ser.). 522p. lib. bdg. 23.95 (*0-7838-8221-1*, Macmillan Reference USA) Gale Group.
—Jeweled Spur. 1994. (House of Winslow Ser.: Vol. 16). 304p. pap. 11.99 (*1-55661-392-X*) Bethany Hse. Pubs.
—The Last Confederate. 1990. (House of Winslow Ser.: Vol. 8). 336p. pap. 11.99 (*1-55661-109-9*) Bethany Hse. Pubs.
—Pilgrim Song. 2003. (House of Winslow Ser.). 320p. pap. 11.99 (*0-7642-2638-X*) Bethany Hse. Pubs.
—The Reluctant Bridegroom. 1990. (House of Winslow Ser.: Vol. 7). 304p. pap. 11.99 (*1-55661-069-6*) Bethany Hse. Pubs.
—The Rough Rider, Vol. 18. 1995. (House of Winslow Ser.: Vol. 18). 304p. pap. 11.99 (*1-55661-394-6*) Bethany Hse. Pubs.
—The Rough Rider. l.t. ed. 1996. 458p. lib. bdg. 22.95 (*0-7838-1853-X*, Macmillan Reference USA) Gale Group.
—The Saintly Buccaneer. 1989. (House of Winslow Ser.: Vol. 5). 304p. pap. 11.99 (*1-55661-048-3*) Bethany Hse. Pubs.
—The Shadow Portrait. 1998. (House of Winslow Ser.: Vol. 21). 320p. pap. 11.99 (*1-55661-689-9*) Bethany Hse. Pubs.
—The Silver Star, Vol. 20. 1997. (House of Winslow Ser.: Vol. 20). 336p. pap. 11.99 (*1-55661-688-0*) Bethany Hse. Pubs.
—The Union Belle. 1992. (House of Winslow Ser.: No. 11). 336p. pap. 11.99 (*1-55661-186-2*) Bethany Hse. Pubs.
—The Valiant Gunman. 1993. (House of Winslow Ser.: Bk. 14). 320p. pap. 11.99 (*1-55661-310-5*) Bethany Hse. Pubs.
—White Hunter. 1999. (House of Winslow Ser.: Vol. 22). (Illus.). 320p. pap. 11.99 (*1-55661-909-X*) Bethany Hse. Pubs.
—Wounded Yankee. 1991. (House of Winslow Ser.: Bk. 10). 304p. pap. 11.99 (*1-55661-116-1*) Bethany Hse. Pubs.
—The Yukon Queen. 1995. (House of Winslow Ser.: Bk. 17). 288p. (J). pap. 11.99 (*1-55661-393-8*) Bethany Hse. Pubs.
Morris, Lynn & Morris, Gilbert. Driven with the Wind. 2002. (Five Star Christian Fiction Ser.). 376p. 24.95 (*0-7862-4790-8*, Five Star) Gale Group.

**WINSTON, ALEX (FICTITIOUS CHARACTER)—FICTION**

Myers, Tim. Innkeeping with Murder. 2001. 208p. mass mkt. 5.99 (*0-425-18002-6*, Prime Crime) Berkley Publishing Group.
—Reservations for Murder. 2002. 192p. mass mkt. 5.99 (*0-425-18525-7*) Berkley Publishing Group.
—Room for Murder. 2003. 192p. mass mkt. 5.99 (*0-425-19310-1*, Prime Crime) Berkley Publishing Group.

**WINSTON, STONEY (FICTITIOUS CHARACTER)—FICTION**

Stinson, Jim. Double Exposure. 1988. (Illus.). 160p. mass mkt. 3.50 o.s.i (*0-553-26665-9*) Bantam Bks.
—Double Exposure. 1986. (Stoney Winston Mystery Ser.). 224p. 13.95 o.s.i (*0-684-18458-3*, Macmillan Reference USA) Gale Group.
—Low Angles: A Stoney Winston Mystery. 1986. 240p. 13.95 o.s.i (*0-684-18626-8*, Macmillan Reference USA) Gale Group.
—Truck Shot: A Stoney Winston Mystery. 1989. 256p. 17.95 o.p. (*0-684-18876-7*, Scribner) Simon & Schuster.
—TV Safe. 1991. 256p. 19.95 o.p. (*0-684-19225-X*, Scribner) Simon & Schuster.

**WINTER, DANIEL (FICTITIOUS CHARACTER)—FICTION**

Telushkin, Joseph. An Eye for an Eye. 1992. 288p. mass mkt. 4.99 o.s.i (*0-553-29620-5*) Bantam Bks.
—An Eye for an Eye. 1991. 272p. 15.00 o.s.i (*0-385-42116-8*) Doubleday Publishing.

**WINTER, HOLLY (FICTITIOUS CHARACTER)—FICTION**

Conant, Susan. Animal Appetite: A Dog Lover's Mystery. 1998. (Dog Lover's Mysteries Ser.). 304p. reprint ed. mass mkt. 5.99 o.s.i (*0-553-57186-9*, Crimeline) Bantam Bks.
—Animal Appetite: A Dog Lover's Mystery. 1997. 288p. 21.95 o.s.i (*0-385-47725-2*) Doubleday Publishing.
—The Barker Street Regulars: A Dog Lover's Mystery. 1999. (Dog Lover's Mysteries Ser.). 288p. mass mkt. 6.99 (*0-553-57655-0*) Bantam Bks.
—The Barker Street Regulars: A Dog Lover's Mystery. l.t. ed. 1998. (Large Print Book Ser.). pap. 23.95 (*1-56895-609-6*, Wheeler Publishing, Inc.) Gale Group.
—Bite of Death. 1991. 4.50 (*1-55773-490-9*) Ace Bks.
—Bite of Death. 1994. mass mkt. 5.99 o.s.i (*0-425-14542-5*) Berkley Publishing Group.
—Black Ribbon: A Dog Lover's Mystery. 1995. (Dog Lover's Mysteries Ser.). 288p. reprint ed. mass mkt. 5.99 o.s.i (*0-553-29875-5*, Crimeline) Bantam Bks.
—Bloodlines. 1993. (Dog Lover's Mysteries Ser.). 272p. mass mkt. 5.99 (*0-553-29886-0*) Bantam Bks.
—Bride & Groom. 2004. 272p. 22.95 (*0-425-19412-4*) Berkley Publishing Group.
—Creature Discomforts. 2001. (Dog Lover's Mysteries Ser.). 224p. mass mkt. 6.99 (*0-553-58059-0*, Spectra) Bantam Bks.
—Creature Discomforts: A Dog Lover's Mystery. l.t. ed. 2001. (Beeler Large Print Mystery Ser.). 228p. 25.95 (*1-57490-360-8*, Beeler Large Print Bks.) Beeler, Thomas T. Publisher.
—Creature Discomforts: A Dog Lover's Mystery. 2000. 256p. 22.95 o.s.i (*0-385-49446-7*) Doubleday Publishing.
—Dead & Doggone. 2003. (Mystery Ser.). 27.95 (*1-57490-466-3*) Beeler, Thomas T. Publisher.
—Dead & Doggone. 1990. mass mkt. 5.99 o.s.i (*0-425-14429-1*, Prime Crime) Berkley Publishing Group.
—Evil Breeding. 2000. (Dog Lover's Mysteries Ser.). 224p. reprint ed. mass mkt. 6.99 (*0-553-58052-3*) Bantam Bks.
—Gone to the Dogs: A Dog Lover's Mystery. 1992. (Dog Lover's Mysteries Ser.). 272p. mass mkt. 5.99 (*0-553-29734-1*) Bantam Bks.
—Gone to the Dogs: A Dog Lover's Mystery. l.t. ed. 2003. (Mystery Ser.). 27.95 (*1-57490-488-4*, Beeler Large Print Bks.) Beeler, Thomas T. Publisher.
—Gone to the Dogs: A Dog Lover's Mystery. 1992. 224p. 16.50 o.s.i (*0-385-42378-0*) Doubleday Publishing.
—New Leash on Death. 1990. 4.50 (*1-55773-385-6*) Berkley Publishing Group.
—A New Leash on Death. 1994. 192p. mass mkt. 5.99 (*0-425-14622-7*) Berkley Publishing Group.
—Paws Before Dying. 1991. 4.50 (*1-55773-550-6*) Ace Bks.
—Paws Before Dying. 1991. mass mkt. 5.99 o.s.i (*0-425-14430-5*) Berkley Publishing Group.

Characters

—Ruffly Speaking: A Dog Lover's Mystery. 1994. (Dog Lover's Mysteries Ser.). 304p. mass mkt. 6.99 (*0-553-29484-9*) Bantam Bks.

—Stud Rites: A Dog Lover's Mystery. 1997. (Dog Lover's Mysteries Ser.). 272p. mass mkt. 5.99 o.s.i (*0-553-57300-4*, Crimeline) Bantam Bks.

—The Wicked Flea. 304p. 2002. 22.95 (*0-425-18334-3*); 2003. reprint ed. mass mkt. 6.99 (*0-425-18885-X*) Berkley Publishing Group. (Prime Crime).

**WINTER, PETER (FICTITIOUS CHARACTER)—FICTION**

Deighton, Len. Winter. 1997. pap. 14.00 o.p. (*0-345-42018-7*) Ballantine Bks.

—Winter. l.t. ed. 1988. (General Ser.). 816p. 21.95 o.p. (*0-8161-4659-4*, Macmillan Reference USA) Gale Group.

—Winter. 1989. 5.99 o.p. (*0-517-69931-1*) Random Hse. Value Publishing.

—Winter: A Novel of a Berlin Family. 1988. 544p. mass mkt. 6.99 o.s.i (*0-345-35931-3*) Ballantine Bks.

**WINTER, SIMON (FICTITIOUS CHARACTER)—FICTION**

Katzenbach, John. The Shadow Man. 1996. mass mkt. 6.99 o.s.i (*0-345-38630-2*); 1995. 480p. 22.00 o.p. (*0-345-38629-9*) Ballantine Bks.

—The Shadow Man. l.t. ed. 1995. 655p. 24.95 o.p. (*0-7838-1357-0*, Macmillan Reference USA) Gale Group.

**WIRE, BARB (FICTITIOUS CHARACTER)—FICTION**

Arcudi, John, et al. Barb Wire. unabr. ed. 1996. (Illus.). 96p. (Orig.). pap. 8.95 (*1-56971-139-9*) Dark Horse Comics.

**WITHERALL, LEONIDAS (FICTITIOUS CHARACTER)—FICTION**

Taylor, Phoebe Atwood. Cold Steal. 23.95 (*0-8488-1200-X*) Amereon, Ltd.

—Cold Steal. 1993. (Leonidas Witherall Mystery Ser.). 288p. pap. 6.00 o.p. (*0-88150-269-3*, Foul Play) Norton, W. W. & Co., Inc.

—The Cut Direct. 1993. (Leonidas Witherall Mystery Ser.). 288p. pap. 6.00 (*0-88150-270-7*, Foul Play) Norton, W. W. & Co., Inc.

—Dead Ernest. 1992. (Leonidas Witherall Mystery Ser.). 240p. pap. 6.50 (*0-88150-242-1*, Foul Play) Norton, W. W. & Co., Inc.

—File for Record. 1987. (Leonidas Witherall Mystery Ser.). 287p. reprint ed. pap. 7.95 (*0-88150-101-8*, Foul Play) Norton, W. W. & Co., Inc.

—The Iron Clew. 1992. (Leonidas Witherall Mystery Ser.). 216p. pap. 6.00 (*0-88150-241-3*, Foul Play) Norton, W. W. & Co., Inc.

Tilton, Alice. Beginning with a Bash. 1987. (Leonidas Witherall Mystery Ser.). 288p. reprint ed. pap. 5.95 o.p. (*0-88150-100-X*) Countryman Pr.

**WITHERS, HILDEGARDE (FICTITIOUS CHARACTER)—FICTION**

Palmer, Stuart. A Murder on the Blackboard. 1988. (Mystery Ser.). 224p. mass mkt. 3.50 o.s.i (*0-553-26796-5*) Bantam Bks.

—Murder on the Blackboard. 1992. 186p. reprint ed. pap. 5.95 (*1-55882-124-4*, Library of Crime Classics) International Polygonics, Ltd.

—Murder on Wheels. 1992. 307p. pap. 6.95 o.p. (*1-55882-113-9*) International Polygonics, Ltd.

—The Penguin Pool Murder. 1987. 224p. mass mkt. 2.95 o.s.i (*0-553-26334-X*) Bantam Bks.

—The Penguin Pool Murder. 1990. 182p. reprint ed. pap. 7.95 (*1-55882-076-0*) International Polygonics, Ltd.

Palmer, Stuart & Rice, Craig. People vs. Withers & Malone. 1990. 254p. reprint ed. pap. 7.95 o.p. (*1-55882-077-9*) International Polygonics, Ltd.

**WITHERSPOON, GERALD (FICTITIOUS CHARACTER)—FICTION**

Brightwell, Emily. The Ghost & Mrs. Jeffries. 1993. (Victorian Mystery Ser.). mass mkt. 5.50 o.s.i (*0-425-13949-2*) Berkley Publishing Group.

—The Ghost & Mrs. Jeffries. l.t. ed. 1999. (Paperback Ser.). 279p. pap. 24.95 (*0-7838-8602-0*) Thorndike Pr.

—The Inspector & Mrs. Jeffries. 1993. (Victorian Mystery Ser.). 192p. mass mkt. 5.99 (*0-425-13622-1*) Berkley Publishing Group.

—The Inspector & Mrs. Jeffries. l.t. ed. 1999. (Paperback Ser.). 256p. pap. 23.95 (*0-7838-0417-2*) Thorndike Pr.

—Mrs. Jeffries & the Missing Alibi. 1996. (Victorian Mystery Ser.). 240p. mass mkt. 5.99 o.s.i (*0-425-15256-1*) Berkley Publishing Group.

—Mrs. Jeffries Dusts for Clues. 1993. (Victorian Mystery Ser.). 192p. mass mkt. 5.50 o.s.i (*0-425-13704-X*) Berkley Publishing Group.

—Mrs. Jeffries Dusts for Clues. 1999. (G. K. Hall Paperback Ser.). 253p. pap. 23.95 (*0-7838-8721-3*, Macmillan Reference USA) Gale Group.

—Mrs. Jeffries on the Ball. l.t. ed. 1995. (Nightingale Ser.). 282p. reprint ed. pap. 18.95 o.p. (*0-7838-1284-1*, Macmillan Reference USA) Gale Group.

—Mrs. Jeffries on the Ball: A Victorian Mystery. 1994. (Victorian Mystery Ser.). 208p. mass mkt. 5.99 o.s.i (*0-425-14491-7*, Prime Crime) Berkley Publishing Group.

—Mrs. Jeffries on the Trail. 1995. (Victorian Mystery Ser.). 240p. mass mkt. 5.50 o.s.i (*0-425-14691-X*, Prime Crime) Berkley Publishing Group.

—Mrs. Jeffries Plays the Cook. 1995. (Victorian Mystery Ser.). 240p. mass mkt. 5.50 o.s.i (*0-425-15053-4*) Berkley Publishing Group.

—Mrs. Jeffries Questions the Answer. 1997. (Victorian Mystery Ser.). 240p. mass mkt. 5.99 o.s.i (*0-425-16093-9*, Prime Crime) Berkley Publishing Group.

—Mrs. Jeffries Questions the Answer. l.t. ed. 2000. (G. K. Hall Paperback Ser.). 287p. pap. 23.95 (*0-7838-9266-7*, Macmillan Reference USA) Gale Group.

—Mrs. Jeffries Reveals Her Art. 1998. (Victorian Mystery Ser.). 240p. mass mkt. 5.99 o.s.i (*0-425-16243-5*, Prime Crime) Berkley Publishing Group.

—Mrs. Jeffries Reveals Her Art. l.t. ed. 2000. (G. K. Hall Paperback Ser.). 272p. pap. 23.95 (*0-7838-9104-0*, Macmillan Reference USA) Gale Group.

—Mrs. Jeffries Rocks the Boat. 1999. (Victorian Mystery Ser.: Vol. 12). 208p. mass mkt. 5.99 o.s.i (*0-425-16934-0*) Berkley Publishing Group.

—Mrs. Jeffries Rocks the Boat. l.t. ed. 2002. pap. 24.95 (*0-7862-4463-1*) Thorndike Pr.

—Mrs. Jeffries Stands Corrected. 1996. (Victorian Mystery Ser.). 224p. mass mkt. 5.99 o.s.i (*0-425-15580-3*, Prime Crime) Berkley Publishing Group.

—Mrs. Jeffries Takes Stock. 1994. (Victorian Mystery Ser.). 208p. mass mkt. 4.99 o.s.i (*0-425-14282-5*, Prime Crime) Berkley Publishing Group.

—Mrs. Jeffries Takes Stock. l.t. ed. 2000. (Paperback Ser.). 261p. pap. 23.95 (*0-7838-9157-1*) Thorndike Pr.

—Mrs. Jeffries Takes the Cake. 1998. (Victorian Mystery Ser.). 240p. mass mkt. 5.99 o.s.i (*0-425-16569-8*, Prime Crime) Berkley Publishing Group.

—Mrs. Jeffries Takes the Cake. l.t. ed. 1999. (Paperback Ser.). 282p. pap. 24.95 (*0-7838-8798-1*, Macmillan Reference USA) Gale Group.

—Mrs. Jeffries Takes the Stage. 1997. (Victorian Mystery Ser.). 240p. mass mkt. 5.99 o.s.i (*0-425-15724-5*, Prime Crime) Berkley Publishing Group.

—Mrs. Jeffries Takes the Stage. l.t. ed. 2000. (G. K. Hall Paperback Ser.). 280p. pap. 23.95 (*0-7838-9035-4*, Macmillan Reference USA) Gale Group.

**WOHL, PETER (FICTITIOUS CHARACTER)—FICTION**

Griffin, W. E. B. Special Operations: A Badge of Honor Novel. 1989. (Badge of Honor Ser.). (Illus.). 368p. mass mkt. 7.99 (*0-515-10148-6*, Jove) Berkley Publishing Group.

—Special Operations: A Badge of Honor Novel. unabr. collector's ed. 1993. audio 64.00 (*0-7366-2492-9*, 3251) Books on Tape, Inc.

**WOLFE, HANNAH (FICTITIOUS CHARACTER)—FICTION**

Dunant, Sarah. Birth Marks. unabr. ed. 1993. (Hannah Wolfe Mysteries Ser.). audio 69.95 (*0-7451-4034-3*, CAB 731) BBC Audiobooks America.

—Birth Marks. 1992. 240p. 17.00 o.s.i (*0-385-42318-7*) Doubleday Publishing.

—Birth Marks. l.t. ed. 1992. (Magna Large Print Ser.). 373p. o.p. (*0-7505-0270-3*) Magna Large Print Bks. GBR. *Dist:* Ulverscroft Large Print Canada, Ltd.

—Fatlands. unabr. ed. 1994. (Hannah Wolfe Mysteries Ser.). audio 54.95 (*0-7451-4297-4*, CAB 980) BBC Audiobooks America.

—Fatlands: A Hannah Wolfe Mystery. 1994. 256p. reprint ed. pap. 21.00 (*1-883402-82-4*, Scribner) Simon & Schuster.

—Under My Skin: A Hannah Wolfe Novel. 1995. 288p. 20.00 (*0-684-81521-4*, Scribner) Simon & Schuster.

**WOLFE, NERO (FICTITIOUS CHARACTER)—FICTION**

Allingham, Margery, et al. Canine Crimes. Mason, Cynthia, ed. 1993. 240p. (Orig.). mass mkt. 4.50 o.s.i (*0-515-11250-X*, Jove) Berkley Publishing Group.

Goldsborough, Robert. The Bloodied Ivy. 1989. 208p. mass mkt. 4.99 o.s.i (*0-553-27816-9*) Bantam Bks.

—Death on a Deadline. 1988. mass mkt. 4.95 o.s.i (*0-553-27024-9*) Bantam Bks.

—Fade to Black. 1991. 256p. mass mkt. 4.99 o.s.i (*0-553-29264-1*) Bantam Bks.

—The Last Coincidence. 1990. 224p. mass mkt. 4.50 o.s.i (*0-553-28616-1*) Bantam Bks.

—The Missing Chapter. 1993. 240p. 19.95 o.s.i (*0-553-07241-2*) Bantam Bks.

—The Missing Chapter: A Nero Wolfe Mystery. 1994. 272p. mass mkt. 4.99 o.s.i (*0-553-56874-4*) Bantam Bks.

—Murder in E Minor. 1987. 224p. (Orig.). mass mkt. 3.50 o.s.i (*0-553-26120-7*); mass mkt. 3.95 o.s.i (*0-553-27938-6*) Bantam Bks.

—Silver Spire. 1993. (Crime Line Ser.). 256p. mass mkt. 4.99 o.s.i (*0-553-56387-4*) Bantam Bks.

Stout, Rex. And Be a Villain. 1994. 256p. mass mkt. 5.99 (*0-553-23931-7*) Bantam Bks.

—And Four to Go. 1992. 240p. mass mkt. 5.99 (*0-553-24985-1*) Bantam Bks.

—And Four to Go. unabr. collector's ed. 1997. (Nero Wolfe Ser.). audio 42.00 (*0-7366-4059-2*, 4570) Books on Tape, Inc.

—And Four to Go. 1958. 2.95 o.p. (*0-670-12285-8*) Viking Penguin.

—Before Midnight. 1995. 224p. pap. 15.00 (*0-553-76304-0*); 1981. 160p. pap. 2.25 o.p. (*0-553-14797-8*) Bantam Bks.

—Before Midnight. unabr. collector's ed. 1995. (Nero Wolfe Ser.). audio 36.00 (*0-7366-3166-6*, 3836) Books on Tape, Inc.

—Before Midnight. l.t. ed. 1994. 267p. lib. bdg. 15.95 o.p. (*0-8161-5985-8*, Macmillan Reference USA) Gale Group.

—Before Midnight. 1955. 2.75 o.p. (*0-670-15525-X*) Viking Penguin.

—Bitter End: A Nero Wolfe Mystery. unabr. ed. 1997. audio 4.99 (*0-88646-941-4*, 7941) Durkin Hayes Publishing Ltd.

—The Black Mountain. unabr. ed. 2001. (Nero Wolfe Mystery Ser.). audio 29.95 (*1-57270-039-4*, N61039u, Audio Editions Bks. on Cassette) Audio Partners Publishing Corp.

—The Black Mountain. 1988. 224p. mass mkt. 3.50 o.s.i (*0-553-27291-8*) Bantam Bks.

—The Black Mountain. unabr. collector's ed. 1995. (Nero Wolfe Ser.). audio 42.00 (*0-7366-3167-4*, 3837) Books on Tape, Inc.

—The Black Mountain. 1954. 2.75 o.p. (*0-670-17258-8*) Viking Penguin.

—Black Orchids. 1992. 208p. mass mkt. 5.99 (*0-553-25719-6*) Bantam Bks.

—Black Orchids. unabr. collector's ed. 1994. (Nero Wolfe Ser.). audio 42.00 (*0-7366-2797-9*, 3512) Books on Tape, Inc.

—Black Orchids. abr. ed. 1996. (Paperback Audio Ser.). audio 9.99 (*0-88646-889-2*, 7889) Durkin Hayes Publishing Ltd.

—Black Orchids. 1982. (Reader's Request Ser.). lib. bdg. 13.95 o.p. (*0-8161-3289-5*, Macmillan Reference USA) Gale Group.

—Champagne for One: A Nero Wolfe Mystery. 1995. 224p. mass mkt. 5.99 (*0-553-24438-8*); 1980. 160p. pap. 1.95 o.p. (*0-553-13657-7*) Bantam Bks.

—Champagne for One: A Nero Wolfe Mystery. unabr. collector's ed. 1996. (Nero Wolfe Ser.). audio 36.00 (*0-7366-3345-6*, 3995) Books on Tape, Inc.

—Champagne for One: A Nero Wolfe Mystery. abr. ed. 1998. (Nero Wolfe Mysteries Ser.). audio 16.99 (*0-88646-456-0*, 7456) Durkin Hayes Publishing Ltd.

—Champagne for One: A Nero Wolfe Mystery. l.t. ed. 1987. (Nightingale Ser.). 302p. 11.95 o.p. (*0-8161-4282-3*, Macmillan Reference USA) Gale Group.

—The Cop-Killer: A Nero Wolfe Mystery. unabr. ed. 1994. audio 4.99 (*0-88646-705-5*) Durkin Hayes Publishing Ltd.

—Curtains for Three. 240p. 1995. pap. 15.00 (*0-553-76294-X*); 1994. mass mkt. 4.99 (*0-553-24498-1*) Bantam Bks.

—Curtains for Three. unabr. collector's ed. 1997. (Nero Wolfe Ser.). audio 42.00 (*0-7366-3747-8*, 4422) Books on Tape, Inc.

—Death of a Doxy. unabr. collector's ed. 1998. (Nero Wolfe Ser.). audio 36.00 (*0-7366-4044-4*, 4543) Books on Tape, Inc.

—Death of a Doxy. l.t. ed. 1996. (Nightingale Ser.). 208p. pap. 17.95 o.p. (*0-7838-1573-5*, Macmillan Reference USA) Gale Group.

—Death of a Doxy. 1966. 3.75 o.p. (*0-670-26126-2*) Viking Penguin.

—Death of a Dude: A Nero Wolfe Novel. 1990. 160p. pap. 3.95 o.s.i (*0-553-27422-8*); Vol. 1. 1994. (Death of a Dude Ser.: Vol. 1). 208p. mass mkt. 4.99 (*0-553-24730-1*) Bantam Bks.

—Death of a Dude: A Nero Wolfe Novel, Set. unabr. ed. 1994. audio 32.95 (*0-7861-0793-6*, 1533) Blackstone Audio Bks., Inc.

—Death of a Dude: A Nero Wolfe Novel. l.t. ed. 1999. (Mystery Ser.). 271p. 27.95 (*0-7862-1904-1*) Thorndike Pr.

—Death Times Three. 1995. 254p. pap. 15.00 (*0-553-76305-9*); 1994. 256p. mass mkt. 4.99 o.s.i (*0-553-27828-2*); 1991. mass mkt. 2.99 o.s.i (*0-553-19646-4*); 1985. 240p. mass mkt. 3.50 (*0-553-25425-1*) Bantam Bks.

—Death Times Three, Set. unabr. ed. 1995. audio 32.95 (*0-7861-0701-4*, 1578) Blackstone Audio Bks., Inc.

—The Doorbell Rang. 1992. 192p. mass mkt. 5.99 (*0-553-23721-7*) Bantam Bks.

—The Doorbell Rang. audio 19.95 (*0-7861-1394-4*); 1994. audio 23.95 (*0-7861-0775-8*, 1503) Blackstone Audio Bks., Inc.

—The Doorbell Rang. abr. ed. (Nero Wolfe Mystery Ser.). 2000. audio 19.99 (*0-88646-561-3*, DHA-6561); 1997. audio (*0-88646-443-9*, 7443) Durkin Hayes Publishing Ltd.

—The Doorbell Rang. l.t. ed. 1985. (Nightingale Ser.). 227p. 9.95 o.p. (*0-8161-3795-1*, Macmillan Reference USA) Gale Group.

—The Doorbell Rang. 2000. (Best Mysteries of All Time Ser.). 207p. (*0-7621-8857-X*) Reader's Digest Assn., Inc., The.

—The Doorbell Rang. 1968. 9.95 o.p. (*0-670-28021-6*, LT4); 1965. 3.50 o.p. (*0-670-27993-5*) Viking Penguin.

—Eeny Meeny Murder Mo: A Nero Wolfe Mystery. abr. ed. 1999. (Nero Wolfe Ser.). audio 5.99 o.p. Brilliance Audio.

—Eeny Meeny Murder Mo: A Nero Wolfe Mystery. unabr. ed. 1999. audio 5.99 (*0-88646-992-9*, PAC-7992) Durkin Hayes Publishing Ltd.

—A Family Affair. 1993. 208p. mass mkt. 4.99 o.s.i (*0-553-24122-2*) Bantam Bks.

—A Family Affair. l.t. ed. 1978. lib. bdg. 9.95 o.p. (*0-8161-6561-0*, Macmillan Reference USA) Gale Group.

—A Family Affair. 1975. 152p. 9.95 o.p. (*0-670-30611-8*) Viking Penguin.

—The Father Hunt. 208p. 1995. pap. 15.00 (*0-553-76297-4*); Vol. 1. 1991. mass mkt. 3.95 (*0-553-24728-X*) Bantam Bks.

—The Father Hunt. 1983. (Nightingale Ser.). 240p. pap. 9.95 o.p. (*0-8161-3548-7*, Macmillan Reference USA) Gale Group.

—The Father Hunt. 1968. 4.50 o.p. (*0-670-30945-1*) Viking Penguin.

—Fer-de-Lance. Date not set. 304p. 23.95 (*0-8488-2403-2*) Amereon, Ltd.

—Fer-de-Lance. unabr. ed. 1997. (Nero Wolfe Mystery Ser.). audio 29.95 (*1-57270-035-1*, N61035u, Audio Editions Mystery Masters) Audio Partners Publishing Corp.

—Fer-de-Lance. 1997. 304p. mass mkt. 5.99 (*0-553-27819-3*); 1992. pap. 2.50 o.s.i (*0-553-23033-6*); 1984. mass mkt. 2.95 o.s.i (*0-553-24918-5*) Bantam Bks.

—Fer-de-Lance. unabr. collector's ed. 1994. (Nero Wolfe Ser.). audio 48.00 (*0-7366-2621-2*, 3361) Books on Tape, Inc.

—Fer-de-Lance. 1994. 320p. reprint ed. 35.00 (*1-883402-17-4*, Scribner) Simon & Schuster.

—The Final Deduction: A Nero Wolfe Novel. 1999. 261p. (*0-7540-3706-1*) BBC Audiobooks America.

—The Final Deduction: A Nero Wolfe Novel. 1992. 144p. mass mkt. 4.99 (*0-553-25254-2*) Bantam Bks.

—The Final Deduction: A Nero Wolfe Novel. unabr. collector's ed. 1996. (Nero Wolfe Ser.). audio 36.00 (*0-7366-3413-4*, 4059) Books on Tape, Inc.

—The Final Deduction: A Nero Wolfe Novel. l.t. ed. 1999. (Mystery Ser.). 261p. 26.95 (*0-7862-1771-5*) Thorndike Pr.

—Five of a Kind: The Third Nero Wolfe Omnibus. 1980. (Short Story Index Reprint Ser.). reprint ed. 37.95 (*0-8369-4136-5*) Ayer Co. Pubs., Inc.

—Frame-up for Murder. unabr. ed. 1997. audio 4.99 (*0-88646-931-7*, 7931) Durkin Hayes Publishing Ltd.

—Gambit. 1985. 160p. mass mkt. 2.95 o.s.i (*0-553-25172-4*) Bantam Bks.

—Gambit. unabr. collector's ed. 1996. (Nero Wolfe Ser.). audio 36.00 (*0-7366-3415-0*, 4061) Books on Tape, Inc.

—Gambit. l.t. ed. 1997. (Nightingale Ser.). 18.95 o.p. (*0-7838-1571-9*, Macmillan Reference USA) Gale Group.

—Gambit. 1962. 3.50 o.p. (*0-670-33376-X*) Viking Penguin.

—The Golden Spiders. unabr. ed. 1997. (Nero Wolfe Mystery Ser.). audio 29.95 (*1-57270-038-6*, N61038u, Audio Editions Mystery Masters) Audio Partners Publishing Corp.

—The Golden Spiders. 1984. 160p. pap. 2.50 o.p. (*0-553-23995-3*) Bantam Bks.

—The Golden Spiders. unabr. collector's ed. 1995. (Nero Wolfe Ser.). audio 42.00 (*0-7366-3132-1*, 3807) Books on Tape, Inc.

—The Golden Spiders. l.t. ed. 1996. (Nightingale Ser.). pap. 17.95 (*0-7838-1572-7*, Macmillan Reference USA) Gale Group.

—The Golden Spiders. 1953. 2.50 o.p. (*0-670-34452-4*) Viking Penguin.

—The Hand in the Glove. 1992. 256p. mass mkt. 4.99 o.s.i (*0-553-22857-9*) Bantam Bks.

—Hand in the Glove. l.t. ed. 1986. (Nightingale Ser.). 384p. 10.95 o.p. (*0-8161-3964-4*, Macmillan Reference USA) Gale Group.

—Her Forbidden Knight. 256p. 2000. mass mkt. 5.95 (*0-7867-0729-1*); 1997. mass mkt. 4.95 o.p. (*0-7867-0444-6*) Avalon Publishing Group. (Carroll & Graf Pubs.).

—Her Forbidden Knight. 1998. 256p. 24.00 o.p. (*0-7278-5369-4*) Severn Hse. Pubs., Ltd.

—Homicide Trinity. 1993. 224p. mass mkt. 5.99 (*0-553-23446-3*) Bantam Bks.

—Homicide Trinity. unabr. collector's ed. 1999. (Nero Wolfe Ser.). audio 64.00 (*0-7366-4062-2*, 4573) Books on Tape, Inc.
—Homicide Trinity. 1962. 2.95 o.p. (*0-670-37758-9*) Viking Penguin.
—If Death Ever Slept. unabr. ed. 2002. (Nero Wolfe Mystery Ser.). audio 24.95 (*1-57270-252-4*, Audio Editions Bks. on Cassette) Audio Partners Publishing Corp.
—If Death Ever Slept. 208p. 1995. pap. 15.00 (*0-553-76296-6*); 1992. mass mkt. 4.99 (*0-553-23649-0*) Bantam Bks.
—If Death Ever Slept. unabr. collector's ed. 1996. (Nero Wolfe Ser.). audio 42.00 (*0-7366-3323-5*, 3975) Books on Tape, Inc.
—If Death Ever Slept. abr. l.t. ed. 1989. 274p. 13.95 o.p. (*0-8161-4794-9*, Macmillan Reference USA) Gale Group.
—In the Best of Families. 1995. 272p. mass mkt. 5.99 (*0-553-27776-6*); 1988. 256p. mass mkt. 3.50 (*0-553-27733-2*); 1980. pap. 2.50 o.p. (*0-553-24375-6*) Bantam Bks.
—In the Best of Families. l.t. ed. 1991. (Nightingale Series Large Print Bks.). 322p. pap. 13.95 o.p. (*0-8161-5203-9*, Macmillan Reference USA) Gale Group.
—Invitation to Murder. unabr. ed. 1996. (Paperback Audio Ser.). audio 9.99 (*0-88646-883-3*, 7883) Durkin Hayes Publishing Ltd.
—Justice Ends at Home & Other Stories. 1977. 8.95 o.p. (*0-670-41105-1*) Viking Penguin.
—The League of Frightened Men. unabr. ed. 1999. (Nero Wolfe Mystery Ser.). audio 29.95 (*1-57270-037-8*, N61037u) Audio Partners Publishing Corp.
—The League of Frightened Men. 320p. 1995. pap. 19.00 (*0-553-76298-2*); 1992. mass mkt. 4.99 (*0-553-25933-4*) Bantam Bks.
—The League of Frightened Men. 1979. 1.75 o.p. (*0-515-05116-0*, Jove) Berkley Publishing Group.
—The League of Frightened Men. unabr. collector's ed. 1994. (Nero Wolfe Ser.). audio 56.00 (*0-7366-2631-X*, 3370) Books on Tape, Inc.
—The League of Frightened Men. abr. ed. 1996. audio 16.99 (*0-88646-418-8*) Durkin Hayes Publishing Ltd.
—The League of Frightened Men. 1981. (Reader's Request Ser.). lib. bdg. 14.50 o.p. (*0-8161-3225-9*, Macmillan Reference USA) Gale Group.
—Might As Well Be Dead. 1980. 160p. pap. 1.95 o.p. (*0-553-14447-2*) Bantam Bks.
—Might as Well Be Dead. 1995. 224p. pap. 15.00 (*0-553-76303-2*) Bantam Bks.
—Might As Well Be Dead, Vol. 1. 1992. 224p. mass mkt. 4.99 (*0-553-24729-8*) Bantam Bks.
—Might As Well Be Dead. unabr. collector's ed. 1996. (Nero Wolfe Ser.). audio 42.00 (*0-7366-3225-5*, 3886) Books on Tape, Inc.
—Might As Well Be Dead. l.t. ed. 1997. (Nightingale Ser.). 262p. lib. bdg. 18.95 (*0-7838-1570-0*) Thorndike Pr.
—More Deaths Than One: A Nero Wolfe Mystery. l.t. ed. 1993. (Nightingale Ser.). 304p. reprint ed. pap. 16.95 o.p. (*0-8161-5757-X*, Macmillan Reference USA) Gale Group.
—The Mother Hunt. 1993. 224p. mass mkt. 5.99 (*0-553-24737-9*) Bantam Bks.
—The Mother Hunt. unabr. collector's ed. 1996. (Nero Wolfe Ser.). audio 36.00 (*0-7366-3523-8*, 4160) Books on Tape, Inc.
—The Mother Hunt. 1963. 3.50 o.p. (*0-670-49015-6*) Viking Penguin.
—The Mountain Cat Murders. 1993. 272p. mass mkt. 4.99 o.s.i (*0-553-25879-6*); 1982. 176p. pap. 2.50 o.p. (*0-553-20826-8*) Bantam Bks.
—Murder by the Book. 1995. 256p. pap. 19.00 (*0-553-76311-3*); 1985. mass mkt. 2.95 o.s.i (*0-553-24884-7*) Bantam Bks.
—Murder by the Book. unabr. collector's ed. 1995. (Nero Wolfe Ser.). audio 48.00 (*0-7366-3103-8*, 3779) Books on Tape, Inc.
—Murder by the Book. l.t. ed. 1996. 301p. 21.95 o.p. (*0-7838-1568-9*, Macmillan Reference USA) Gale Group.
—Murder by the Book. 1951. 2.50 o.p. (*0-670-49547-6*) Viking Penguin.
—Nero Wolfe: And Be a Villain. l.t. ed. 1988. 19.95 o.p. (*1-55504-643-6*); pap. 17.95 o.p. (*1-55504-644-4*) BBC Audiobooks America.
—Nero Wolfe Omnibus. lib. bdg. 26.95 (*0-8488-1893-8*) Amereon, Ltd.
—Not Quite Dead Enough. 1992. 208p. mass mkt. 5.99 (*0-553-26109-6*) Bantam Bks.
—Not Quite Dead Enough. unabr. collector's ed. 1994. (Nero Wolfe Ser.). audio 36.00 (*0-7366-2828-2*, 3536) Books on Tape, Inc.
—Not Quite Dead Enough. 1994. reprint ed. lib. bdg. 27.95 (*1-56849-341-X*) Buccaneer Bks., Inc.
—Not Quite Dead Enough. unabr. ed. 1994. audio 4.99 (*0-88646-727-6*) Durkin Hayes Publishing Ltd.
—An Officer & a Lady & Other Stories. 2000. 192p. mass mkt. 5.95 (*0-7867-0764-X*, Carroll & Graf Pubs.) Avalon Publishing Group.
—Over My Dead Body. 20.95 (*0-89190-341-0*) Amereon, Ltd.
—Over My Dead Body. unabr. ed. 2001. (Nero Wolfe Mystery Ser.). audio 29.95 (*1-57270-062-9*, N61062u, Audio Editions Bks. on Cassette) Audio Partners Publishing Corp.
—Over My Dead Body. 1993. (Crime Line Ser.). 272p. mass mkt. 5.99 (*0-553-23116-2*) Bantam Bks.
—Over My Dead Body. unabr. collector's ed. 1994. (Nero Wolfe Ser.). audio 48.00 (*0-7366-2747-2*, 3472) Books on Tape, Inc.
—Over My Dead Body. l.t. ed. 1982. lib. bdg. 13.95 o.p. (*0-8161-3288-7*, Macmillan Reference USA) Gale Group.
—Please Pass the Guilt. 1995. 176p. pap. 15.00 (*0-553-76308-3*); 1993. 192p. mass mkt. 4.99 (*0-553-23854-X*) Bantam Bks.
—Please Pass the Guilt. unabr. collector's ed. 1999. (Nero Wolfe Ser.). audio 32.00 (*0-7366-4456-3*, 4901) Books on Tape, Inc.
—Please Pass the Guilt. 1979. pap. 10.95 o.p. (*0-8161-6737-0*, Macmillan Reference USA) Gale Group.
—Plot It Yourself. unabr. ed. 2002. audio 24.95 (*1-57270-301-6*) Audio Partners Publishing Corp.
—Plot It Yourself. 1989. pap. 3.50 o.s.i (*0-553-27849-5*); 1985. 176p. mass mkt. 4.99 o.s.i (*0-553-25363-8*) Bantam Bks.
—Plot It Yourself. unabr. collector's ed. 1996. (Nero Wolfe Ser.). audio 36.00 (*0-7366-3354-5*, 4005) Books on Tape, Inc.
—Plot It Yourself. l.t. ed. 1984. (Nightingale Ser.). 248p. 8.95 o.p. (*0-8161-3547-9*, Macmillan Reference USA) Gale Group.
—Plot It Yourself. 1959. 2.95 o.p. (*0-670-56144-4*) Viking Penguin.
—The President Vanishes. 1982. 272p. pap. 2.50 o.p. (*0-553-22665-7*) Bantam Bks.
—Prisoner's Base. unabr. ed. 2001. (Nero Wolfe Mystery Ser.). audio 29.95 (*1-57270-191-9*, N61191u, Audio Editions Mystery Masters) Audio Partners Publishing Corp.
—Prisoner's Base. 1992. 224p. mass mkt. 5.99 (*0-553-24269-5*) Bantam Bks.
—Prisoner's Base. unabr. collector's ed. 1995. (Nero Wolfe Ser.). audio 42.00 (*0-7366-3137-2*, 3812) Books on Tape, Inc.
—Prisoner's Base. 1952. 2.50 o.p. (*0-670-57839-8*) Viking Penguin.
—A Prize for Princes. 1994. 256p. mass mkt. 4.95 o.p. (*0-7867-0104-8*, Carroll & Graf Pubs.) Avalon Publishing Group.
—A Prize for Princes. 1999. 312p. 26.00 (*0-7278-2277-2*) Severn Hse. Pubs., Ltd.
—The Red Box. unabr. ed. 1997. audio 29.95 (*1-57270-053-X*, N61053u, Audio Editions Bks. on Cassette) Audio Partners Publishing Corp.
—The Red Box. 1992. (Crime Line Ser.). 272p. mass mkt. 4.99 o.s.i (*0-553-24919-3*) Bantam Bks.
—The Red Box. 1979. 1.75 o.s.i (*0-515-05117-9*, Jove) Berkley Publishing Group.
—The Red Box. unabr. collector's ed. 1994. (Nero Wolfe Ser.). audio 48.00 (*0-7366-2697-2*, 3431) Books on Tape, Inc.
—The Red Box. abr. ed. 1995. audio 16.99 (*0-88646-377-7*, LFP 7377) Durkin Hayes Publishing Ltd.
—The Red Box. 1981. (Reader's Request Ser.). lib. bdg. 13.50 o.p. (*0-8161-3223-2*, Macmillan Reference USA) Gale Group.
—A Right to Die? 1991. 208p. mass mkt. 5.99 (*0-553-24032-3*) Bantam Bks.
—A Right to Die? l.t. ed. 1996. (G. K. Hall Mystery Ser.). 224p. lib. bdg. 21.95 o.p. (*0-7838-1569-7*, Macmillan Reference USA) Gale Group.
—A Right to Die. unabr. collector's ed. 1997. (Nero Wolfe Ser.). audio 36.00 (*0-7366-3531-9*, 4170) Books on Tape, Inc.
—Royal Flush. 1965. 3.95 o.p. (*0-670-60934-X*) Viking Penguin.
—The Rubber Band. unabr. ed. 1997. (Nero Wolfe Mystery Ser.). audio 29.95 (*1-57270-052-1*, N61052u, Audio Editions Mystery Masters) Audio Partners Publishing Corp.
—The Rubber Band. 1995. 208p. pap. 15.00 (*0-553-76309-1*); 1982. 192p. mass mkt. 2.95 (*0-553-25550-9*) Bantam Bks.
—The Rubber Band. 1979. 1.75 o.s.i (*0-515-04867-4*, Jove) Berkley Publishing Group.
—The Rubber Band. unabr. collector's ed. 1994. (Nero Wolfe Ser.). audio 48.00 (*0-7366-2695-6*, 3429) Books on Tape, Inc.
—The Rubber Band. 1981. (Reader's Request Ser.). lib. bdg. 12.95 o.p. (*0-8161-3224-0*, Macmillan Reference USA) Gale Group.
—The Second Confession. unabr. ed. 2000. (Nero Wolfe Mystery Ser.). audio 29.95 (*1-57270-132-3*, N61132u, Audio Editions Mystery Masters) Audio Partners Publishing Corp.
—The Second Confession. 1995. 256p. mass mkt. 5.99 (*0-553-24594-5*) Bantam Bks.
—The Second Confession. unabr. collector's ed. 1995. (Nero Wolfe Ser.). audio 48.00 (*0-7366-3070-8*, 3752) Books on Tape, Inc.
—The Second Confession. l.t. ed. 1992. (Nightingale Series Large Print Bks.). 311p. pap. 15.95 (*0-8161-5202-0*, Macmillan Reference USA) Gale Group.
—The Silent Speaker. 1994. (Crime Line Ser.). 288p. mass mkt. 5.99 (*0-553-23497-8*) Bantam Bks.
—The Silent Speaker. unabr. collector's ed. 1994. (Nero Wolfe Ser.). audio 48.00 (*0-7366-2837-1*, 3545) Books on Tape, Inc.
—The Silent Speaker. l.t. ed. 2002. 350p. 29.45 (*0-7862-4195-0*) Thorndike Pr.
—Some Buried Caesar. 20.95 (*0-89190-340-2*) Amereon, Ltd.
—Some Buried Caesar. 1990. (Nero Wolfe Ser.). 288p. mass mkt. 5.99 (*0-553-25464-2*) Bantam Bks.
—Some Buried Caesar. 1982. (Reader's Request Ser.). 13.95 o.p. (*0-8161-3286-0*, Macmillan Reference USA) Gale Group.
—Some Buried Caeser. 1979. 1.75 o.s.i (*0-515-05118-7*, Jove) Berkley Publishing Group.
—The Sound of Murder. 1986. (Mystery Ser.). 192p. pap. 2.95 o.p. (*0-553-26148-7*) Bantam Bks.
—The Sound of Murder. 1979. 1.75 o.s.i (*0-515-05281-7*, Jove) Berkley Publishing Group.
—Target Practice. 1998. 320p. mass mkt. 5.95 (*0-7867-0496-9*, Carroll & Graf Pubs.) Avalon Publishing Group.
—Target Practice. l.t. ed. 1998. (Mystery Ser.). 424p. 28.95 (*0-7838-0178-5*) Thorndike Pr.
—This Won't Kill You. unabr. ed. 1998. audio 5.99 (*0-88646-865-5*, PAC-7865) Durkin Hayes Publishing Ltd.
—Three Aces. 1971. 8.95 o.p. (*0-670-70622-1*) Viking Penguin.
—Three at Wolfe's Door. 1995. 240p. mass mkt. 5.99 (*0-553-23803-5*, Crimeline) Bantam Bks.
—Three at Wolfe's Door. unabr. collector's ed. 1997. (Nero Wolfe Ser.). audio 48.00 (*0-7366-4060-6*, 4571) Books on Tape, Inc.
—Three Doors to Death. 1995. 240p. mass mkt. 5.99 (*0-553-25127-9*) Bantam Bks.
—Three for the Chair. 1985. 240p. mass mkt. 5.99 (*0-553-24813-8*) Bantam Bks.
—Three for the Chair. unabr. collector's ed. 1997. (Nero Wolfe Ser.). audio 42.00 (*0-7366-3750-8*, 4425) Books on Tape, Inc.
—Three for the Chair. 1957. 2.95 o.p. (*0-670-70779-1*) Viking Penguin.
—Three Men Out. 1991. 224p. mass mkt. 3.99 o.s.i (*0-553-24547-3*) Bantam Bks.
—Three Men Out. l.t. ed. 1990. (Nightingale Ser.). 296p. lib. bdg. 13.95 o.p. (*0-8161-4793-0*, Macmillan Reference USA) Gale Group.
—Three Men Out. 1954. 2.50 o.p. (*0-670-70846-1*) Viking Penguin.
—Three Trumps. 1973. 6.95 o.p. (*0-670-71031-8*) Viking Penguin.
—Three Witnesses. 1981. 224p. mass mkt. 5.99 (*0-553-24959-2*) Bantam Bks.
—Three Witnesses. unabr. collector's ed. 1997. (Nero Wolfe Ser.). audio 42.00 (*0-7366-3751-6*, 4426) Books on Tape, Inc.
—Three Witnesses. 1956. 2.75 o.p. (*0-670-71080-6*) Viking Penguin.
—Too Many Clients. 1955. 192p. mass mkt. 2.95 o.s.i (*0-553-25423-5*) Bantam Bks.
—Too Many Clients. unabr. collector's ed. 1996. (Nero Wolfe Ser.). audio 36.00 (*0-7366-3400-2*, 4047) Books on Tape, Inc.
—Too Many Clients. 1983. (Nightingale Ser.). 241p. pap. 9.95 o.p. (*0-8161-3549-5*, Macmillan Reference USA) Gale Group.
—Too Many Clients. 1960. 2.95 o.p. (*0-670-72010-0*) Viking Penguin.
—Too Many Cooks. 1995. 208p. pap. 15.00 (*0-553-76306-7*); 1988. 256p. mass mkt. 3.50 (*0-553-27290-X*) Bantam Bks.
—Too Many Cooks, Set. unabr. ed. 1995. 5p. audio 39.95 (*0-7861-0660-3*, 1561) Blackstone Audio Bks., Inc.
—Too Many Cooks. 2000. audio compact disk 56.00 (*0-7366-8053-5*); audio 48.00 (*0-7366-5462-3*, 5333) Books on Tape, Inc.
—Too Many Cooks. l.t. ed. 1985. (Nightingale Ser.). 397p. 10.95 o.p. (*0-8161-3868-0*, Macmillan Reference USA) Gale Group.
—Too Many Cooks. 1976. (Crime Fiction Ser.). reprint ed. lib. bdg. 21.00 o.p. (*0-8240-2394-3*) Garland Publishing, Inc.
—Too Many Women: A Nero Wolfe Mystery. unabr. ed. 1999. audio 29.95 (*1-57270-104-8*, N61104u, Audio Editions Mystery Masters) Audio Partners Publishing Corp.
—Too Many Women: A Nero Wolfe Mystery. l.t. ed. 1999. 355p. (*0-7540-3882-3*); pap. (*0-7540-3883-1*) BBC Audiobooks America.
—Too Many Women: A Nero Wolfe Mystery. unabr. collector's ed. 1995. (Nero Wolfe Ser.). audio 48.00 (*0-7366-3045-7*, 3727) Books on Tape, Inc.
—Too Many Women: A Nero Wolfe Mystery. l.t. ed. 1999. (Mystery Ser.). 355p. 26.95 o.p. (*0-7862-2049-X*) Thorndike Pr.
—Trio for Blunt Instruments. 1979. pap. 1.75 o.p. (*0-553-13232-6*) Bantam Bks.
—Trio for Blunt Instruments. unabr. collector's ed. 1997. (Nero Wolfe Ser.). audio 48.00 (*0-7366-4061-4*, 4572) Books on Tape, Inc.
—Triple Jeopardy. 1995. 192p. pap. 15.00 (*0-553-76307-5*); 1993. 256p. mass mkt. 4.99 (*0-553-23591-5*) Bantam Bks.
—Triple Jeopardy. 1952. 2.50 o.p. (*0-670-73109-9*) Viking Penguin.
—Trouble in Triplicate. unabr. collector's ed. 1996. (Nero Wolfe Ser.). audio 48.00 (*0-7366-3268-9*, 3925) Books on Tape, Inc.
—Trouble in Triplicate. 1949. 2.50 o.p. (*0-670-73241-9*) Viking Penguin.
—Under the Andes. 1994. 290p. mass mkt. 4.95 (*0-7867-0179-X*, Carroll & Graf Pubs.) Avalon Publishing Group.
—Under the Andes. unabr. ed. 1997. audio 49.95 (*0-7861-1187-9*, 1947) Blackstone Audio Bks., Inc.
—Under the Andes. E-Book 2.95 (*1-57799-901-0*) Logos Research Systems, Inc.
—Under the Andes. 1985. 15.95 o.p. (*0-89296-119-8*) Mysterious Pr.
—Under the Andes. 1986. 312p. reprint ed. mass mkt. 3.50 (*0-445-40507-4*, Mysterious Pr. Paperback Bks.) Warner Bks., Inc.
—Where There's a Will. unabr. ed. 1999. (Nero Wolfe Mystery Ser.). audio 29.95 (*1-57270-096-3*, N61096u, Audio Editions Mystery Masters) Audio Partners Publishing Corp.
—Where There's a Will. l.t. ed. (Nero Wolfe Mystery Ser.). 1992. pap. 20.95 o.p. (*0-7927-1138-6*, CS0304); 1991. 22.95 o.p. (*0-7927-1137-8*, CH0233) BBC Audiobooks America.
—Where There's a Will. 256p. 1995. pap. 15.00 (*0-553-76301-6*); 1992. mass mkt. 4.99 (*0-553-29591-8*) Bantam Bks.
—Where There's a Will. unabr. collector's ed. 1994. (Nero Wolfe Ser.). audio 42.00 (*0-7366-2766-9*, 3487) Books on Tape, Inc.
—Where There's a Will. 1982. (Reader's Request Ser.). 13.95 o.p. (*0-8161-3287-9*, Macmillan Reference USA) Gale Group.
—Where There's a Will. 1941. pap. 1.50 o.p. (*0-380-01620-6*, 39529, Avon Bks.) Morrow/Avon.
Stout, Rex, contrib. by. Death of a Dude: A Nero Wolfe Novel. 1999. (*0-7540-3797-5*); (*0-7540-3798-3*) BBC Audiobooks America.
—The Final Deduction: A Nero Wolfe Novel. (*0-7540-3705-3*) BBC Audiobooks America.

**WOMEN'S MURDER CLUB (FICTITIOUS CHARACTERS)—FICTION**

Patterson, James. 1st to Die. unabr. ed. 2001. audio 35.95 (*0-7366-6199-9*); audio compact disk 54.98 Books on Tape, Inc.
—1st to Die. 2001. 432p. 26.95 o.p. (*0-316-66600-9*) Little Brown & Co.
—1st to Die. l.t. ed. 2001. 464p. 32.95 (*0-7862-3291-9*); pap. 29.95 (*0-7862-3292-7*); (*0-7540-1631-5*); (*0-7540-2486-5*) Thorndike Pr.
—1st to Die. abr. ed. 2001. audio 29.98 (*1-58621-057-2*); audio 25.98 (*1-58621-053-X*); audio 39.98 (*1-58621-056-4*); audio 49.98 (*1-58621-059-9*) Time Warner AudioBooks.
—1st to Die. 2001. E-Book 4.95 (*0-7595-8434-6*) Time Warner Bk. Group.
—1st to Die. 2001. 432p. pap. 16.00 (*0-446-67842-2*); 2002. 488p. reprint ed. mass mkt. 7.99 (*0-446-61003-8*) Warner Bks., Inc.
—1st to Die. 2001. E-Book 4.95 (*0-7595-6427-2*) ereads.com.
—2nd Chance. 2002. 400p. pap. 16.00 (*0-446-67876-7*) Warner Bks., Inc.
Patterson, James & Gross, Andrew. 2nd Chance. 2002. 400p. 26.95 o.p. (*0-316-69320-0*); 512p. 26.95 o.p. (*0-316-69597-1*) Little Brown & Co.
—2nd Chance. abr. ed. 2002. audio 25.98 (*1-58621-232-X*); audio 29.98 (*1-58621-233-8*); audio 32.98 (*1-58621-234-6*); audio 39.98 (*1-58621-235-4*) Time Warner AudioBooks.
—2nd Chance. 2003. 432p. reprint ed. mass mkt. 7.99 (*0-446-61279-0*) Warner Bks., Inc.
—3rd Degree. 2004. 352p. 26.95 (*0-316-60357-0*); 400p. 27.95 (*0-316-74386-0*) Little Brown & Co.
—3rd Degree. unabr. ed. 2004. audio 26.98 (*1-58621-598-1*); audio compact disk 31.98 (*1-58621-599-X*) Time Warner AudioBooks.
—3rd Degree. 2004. pap. 16.00 (*0-446-69258-1*) Warner Bks., Inc.

**WONDER WOMAN (FICTITIOUS CHARACTER)—FICTION**

Beatty, Scott. Wonder Woman: The Ultimate Guide to the Amazon Princess. 2003. 144p. (J). 24.99 (*0-7894-9616-X*) Dorling Kindersley Publishing, Inc.
Byrne, John. Wonder Woman: Gods & Goddesses. 320p. 1998. pap. 12.95 o.p. (*0-7615-1713-8*); 1997. 20.00 o.p. (*0-7615-0483-4*) Crown Publishing Group. (Prima Lifestyles).

—Wonder Woman: Lifelines. Kahan, Bob, ed. 1998. (Illus.). 160p. pap. 9.95 (*1-56389-403-3*) DC Comics.

—Wonder Woman: Second Genesis. Kahan, Bob, ed. 1997. (Illus.). 128p. pap. 9.95 (*1-56389-318-5*) DC Comics.

Chronicle Books Staff. Wonder Woman Notecards. 1998. 13.95 (*0-8118-2196-X*) Chronicle Bks. LLC.

Daniels, Les. Wonder Woman: The Complete History. Incl. (Illus.). 80p. 40.00 (*0-8118-3123-X*); (Illus.). 206p. 2000. 29.95 (*0-8118-2913-8*) Chronicle Bks. LLC.

Greenberg, Martin H. The Further Adventures of Wonder Woman. 1993. 352p. mass mkt. 5.99 o.s.i (*0-553-28624-2*, Spectra) Bantam Bks.

Jimenez, Phil & Jimenez/Lanning/Moore/Badeaux. Wonder Woman: Paradise Found. 2003. 192p. pap. 14.95 (*1-56389-956-6*) DC Comics.

Lay, Carol. Wonder Woman: Mythos. 2003. (Justice League of America Ser.: Vol. 2). 320p. mass mkt. 6.99 (*0-7434-1711-9*, Star Trek) Simon & Schuster.

Lords, Bill. Wonder Woman: The Contest. Kahan, Bob, ed. 1995. (Illus.). 120p. pap. 9.95 (*1-56389-194-8*) DC Comics.

Marston, William Moulton. Wonder Woman Archives. 2000. (Archive Editions Ser.: Vol. 2). (Illus.). 240p. 49.95 (*1-56389-594-3*) DC Comics.

—Wonder Woman Archives. Kahan, Bob, ed. 1998. (Wonder Woman Archives Ser.: Vol. 1). (Illus.). 240p. 49.95 (*1-56389-402-5*) DC Comics.

—Wonder Woman Archives, Vol. 4. 2004. 204p. 49.95 (*1-4012-0145-8*) DC Comics.

Messner-Loebs, William F. Wonder Woman: Amazonia. Kupperberg, Paul, ed. 1998. (Illus.). 48p. pap. 7.95 (*1-56389-301-0*) DC Comics.

—Wonder Woman: The Challenge of Artemis. 1996. (Illus.). 192p. pap. 9.95 o.p. (*1-56389-264-2*) DC Comics.

Morrison, Grant. JLA: American Dreams. 1998. (Illus.). 112p. pap. 7.95 (*1-56389-394-0*) DC Comics.

—JLA: New World Order. 1997. (Illus.). 96p. pap. 5.95 (*1-56389-369-X*) DC Comics.

Robbins, Trina. Wonder Woman: The Once & Future Story. 1998. (Illus.). 48p. pap. 4.95 (*1-56389-373-8*) DC Comics.

Rucka, Greg & Jones, Grawbadger. Wonder Woman: The Hiketeia. 2003. 96p. pap. 17.95 (*1-56389-914-0*) DC Comics.

Wonder Woman. 2000. 29.95 o.s.i (*0-8118-3135-3*); 29.95 o.s.i (*0-8118-3111-6*) Chronicle Bks. LLC.

### WOO, APRIL (FICTITIOUS CHARACTER)—FICTION

Glass, Leslie. Burning Time. 1995. (April Woo Suspense Novels Ser.). 464p. mass mkt. 7.50 (*0-553-56172-3*) Bantam Bks.

—Hanging Time. 1996. (April Woo Suspense Novels Ser.). 448p. mass mkt. 7.50 (*0-553-57191-5*) Bantam Bks.

—Judging Time. 1998. (April Woo Suspense Novels Ser.). 320p. 24.95 o.p. (*0-525-94404-4*) Dutton/Plume.

—Judging Time. 1999. (April Woo Suspense Novels Ser.). 400p. mass mkt. 6.99 (*0-451-19550-7*, Signet Bks.) NAL.

—Loving Time. 1997. (April Woo Suspense Novels Ser.). 432p. reprint ed. mass mkt. 6.99 (*0-553-57209-1*) Bantam Bks.

—Stealing Time. 2000. audio 25.00 (*1-58807-055-7*); 2003. audio (*1-58807-611-3*) Americana Publishing, Inc.

—Stealing Time. unabr. ed. 2000. (April Woo Mystery Ser.). audio 69.95 (*0-7927-2384-8*, CSL273, Chivers Sound Library) BBC Audiobooks America.

—Stealing Time. 1999. (April Woo Suspense Novels Ser.). 320p. 24.95 o.p. (*0-525-94460-5*) Dutton/Plume.

—Stealing Time. 2000. (April Woo Suspense Novels Ser.). 400p. reprint ed. mass mkt. 6.99 (*0-451-19965-0*, Signet Bks.) NAL.

—Tracking Time. l.t. ed. 2001. (Wheeler Large Print Book Ser.). 437p. 28.95 (*1-58724-108-0*, Wheeler Publishing, Inc.) Gale Group.

—Tracking Time: An April Woo Suspense Novel. 2000. (April Woo Suspense Novels Ser.). 336p. 23.95 o.s.i (*0-525-94469-9*) Dutton/Plume.

### WOODEND, CHARLIE (FICTITIOUS CHARACTER)—FICTION

Spencer, Sally. A Death Left Hanging. 2003. 256p. 25.99 (*0-7278-5930-7*) Severn Hse. Pubs., Ltd.

—Death of a Cave Dweller. l.t. ed. 2001. (Magna Large Print Ser.). 336p. (*0-7505-1704-2*) Magna Large Print Bks. GBR. *Dist:* Ulverscroft Large Print Canada, Ltd.

—Death of a Cave Dweller. 256p. 26.00 (*0-7278-5543-3*) Severn Hse. Pubs., Ltd.

—Death of an Innocent. 2002. 256p. 25.99 (*0-7278-5708-8*); 28.99 (*0-7278-7237-0*) Severn Hse. Pubs., Ltd.

—Murder at Swann's Lake. l.t. ed. 2000. (Dales Large Print Ser.). 400p. pap. 20.99 o.p. (*1-84137-001-0*) Magna Large Print Bks. GBR. *Dist:* Ulverscroft Large Print Bks., Ltd.

—Murder at Swann's Lake. 1999. 224p. 25.00 (*0-7278-2285-3*) Severn Hse. Pubs., Ltd.

—The Red Herring. 28.99 (*0-7278-7185-4*); 2002. 252p. 25.99 (*0-7278-5707-X*) Severn Hse. Pubs., Ltd.

—The Salton Killings. l.t. ed. 1999. (Dales Large Print Ser.). 336p. pap. 20.99 o.p. (*1-85389-924-0*) Dales Large Print Bks. GBR. *Dist:* Ulverscroft Large Print Bks., Ltd., Ulverscroft Large Print Canada, Ltd.

—The Salton Killings. 1998. 224p. 24.00 (*0-7278-5344-9*) Severn Hse. Pubs., Ltd.

### WOODHOUSE, EMMA (FICTITIOUS CHARACTER)—FICTION

Aiken, Joan. Jane Fairfax: Jane Austen's Emma, Through Another's Eyes. unabr. ed. 1997. audio 69.95 (*1-85695-527-3*, 93067) ISIS Audio Bks. GBR. *Dist:* Ulverscroft Large Print Bks., Ltd.

—Jane Fairfax: Jane Austen's Emma, Through Another's Eyes. 1997. 256p. reprint ed. pap. 12.95 (*0-312-15707-X*, Saint Martin's Griffin) St. Martin's Pr.

Aiken, Joan & Austen, Jane. Jane Fairfax: Jane Austen's Emma, Through Another's Eyes. 1991. 18.95 o.p. (*0-312-05884-5*) St. Martin's Pr.

Austen, Jane. Emma. 2002. (World Digital Library). E-Book 3.95 (*0-594-08158-0*) 1873 Pr.

—Emma. 1997. (Modern Library Ser.). E-Book 4.95 (*1-931208-08-5*) Adobe Systems, Inc.

—Emma. 1966. (Airmont Classics Ser.). mass mkt. 2.95 o.p. (*0-8049-0102-3*, CL-102) Airmont Publishing Co., Inc.

—Emma. Date not set. 232p. 21.95 (*0-8488-2522-5*) Amereon, Ltd.

—Emma, Set. unabr. ed. 1986. audio 65.95 (*1-55685-005-0*) Audio Bk. Contractors, Inc.

—Emma. unabr. ed. 1998. audio 39.95 (*1-57270-071-8*, F91071u, Cover to Cover Classics) Audio Partners Publishing Corp.

—Emma. unabr. ed. audio 84.95 o.p. (*1-85549-913-4*, CTC 056) BBC Audiobooks America.

—Emma. l.t. ed. 1999. 630p. pap. 24.95 (*1-55701-279-2*) BNI Pubns., Inc.

—Emma. 1984. mass mkt. 1.95 o.s.i (*0-553-21159-5*, Bantam Classics); 432p. mass mkt. 4.95 (*0-553-21273-7*) Bantam Bks.

—Emma. abr. ed. 1996. audio 26.95 (*1-885546-10-6*) Big Ben Audio, Inc.

—Emma. 2000. audio 76.95 (*0-7861-1842-3*, P2641); 1983. audio 85.95 (*0-7861-0526-7*, 2025) Blackstone Audio Bks., Inc.

—Emma. 2002. audio compact disk 120.00 (*0-7366-8766-1*); 1983. audio 104.00 (*0-7366-3894-6*, 134507) Books on Tape, Inc.

—Emma. unabr. ed. 1996. (Bookcassette Classic Collection). audio 19.95 o.p. (*1-56100-721-8*, 101, Bookcassette) Brilliance Audio.

—Emma. 1986. lib. bdg. 19.95 (*0-89966-242-0*) Buccaneer Bks., Inc.

—Emma. unabr. ed. 1998. audio 79.95 (*0-7451-7365-9*, SAB 140) Chivers Audio Bks. GBR. *Dist:* BBC Audiobooks America.

—Emma, 3 Vols. (Collected Works of Jane Austen). reprint ed. lib. bdg. 294.00 (*0-7426-2073-5*); 2001. pap. text 84.00 (*0-7426-7073-2*) Classic Bks.

—Emma. audio 69.95 Cover to Cover Cassettes, Ltd.

—Emma. l.t. ed. 1999. 630p. pap. 24.95 (*1-58855-018-4*) Cyber Classics, Inc.

—Emma. unabr. ed. 1999. 384p. pap. text 2.50 (*0-486-40648-2*) Dover Pubns., Inc.

—Emma. abr. ed. audio 15.95 o.p. (*0-88646-023-9*, 7033); 1996. audio 9.99 (*1-55204-002-X*, 9002); 1986. audio 29.95 o.p. (*0-88646-792-6*, R 7033) Durkin Hayes Publishing Ltd.

—Emma. 1956. 10.50 o.p. (*0-460-00024-1*, Dutton) Dutton/Plume.

—Emma. E-Book 2.49 (*1-58744-220-5*) Electric Umbrella Publishing.

—Emma. 1998. (SPA.). 416p. (*84-320-3877-6*) GeoPlaneta, Editorial, S. A.

—Emma. audio. 2000. 624p. pap. 22.00 (*0-06-095693-3*, HarperCollins) HarperTrade.

—Emma. abr. ed. 1996. (Classics Ser.). audio 16.95 (*1-56511-170-2*) HighBridge Co.

—Emma, Set. unabr. ed. 1999. audio 85.95 Highsmith Inc.

—Emma. 2003. audio 14.95 (*1-84032-771-5*) Hodder Headline Audiobooks GBR. *Dist:* Trafalgar Square.

—Emma. Trilling, Lionel, ed. 1972. (C). pap. 16.36 (*0-395-05115-0*) Houghton Mifflin Co.

—Emma. l.t. ed. 436p. pap. 33.67 (*0-7583-0810-8*); 555p. pap. 41.61 (*0-7583-0811-6*); 865p. pap. 68.70 (*0-7583-0813-2*); 1063p. pap. 79.19 (*0-7583-0814-0*); 254p. pap. 23.38 (*0-7583-0808-6*); 1233p. pap. 88.84 (*0-7583-0815-9*); 319p. pap. 27.06 (*0-7583-0809-4*); 708p. pap. 51.13 (*0-7583-0812-4*); 1233p. lib. bdg. 100.84 (*0-7583-0807-8*); 865p. lib. bdg. 81.13 (*0-7583-0805-1*); 555p. lib. bdg. 47.61 (*0-7583-0803-5*); 1063p. lib. bdg. 91.19 (*0-7583-0806-X*); 254p. lib. bdg. 29.38 (*0-7583-0800-0*); 319p. lib. bdg. 33.06 (*0-7583-0801-9*); 436p. lib. bdg. 39.67 (*0-7583-0802-7*); 708p. lib. bdg. 57.13 (*0-7583-0804-3*) Huge Print Pr.

—Emma. 1996. (Illus.). 464p. reprint ed. pap. 9.95 (*0-7868-8183-6*) Hyperion Pr.

—Emma. unabr. ed. 1984. audio 69.00 Jimcin Recordings.

—Emma. 1991. (Everyman's Library). 484p. (*1-85715-036-8*, Everyman's Library) Knopf Publishing Group.

—Emma. 1999. (Cloth Bound Pocket Ser.). 7.95 (*3-8290-0827-9*, 520519) Konemann.

—Emma. E-Book 2.95 (*1-57799-980-0*); E-Book 2.95 (*1-57799-846-4*) Logos Research Systems, Inc.

—Emma. Cheetham, Paul, ed. 1984. (Study Texts Ser.). pap. text 4.29 (*0-582-33153-6*, 72058) Longman Publishing Group.

—Emma. E-Book 1.95 (*1-58515-171-8*) MesaView, Inc.

—Emma. (Signet Classics). 1996. 416p. mass mkt. 4.95 (*0-451-52627-9*, Signet Classics); 1968. mass mkt. 0.75 o.p. (*0-451-50388-0*, Signet Classics); 1968. mass mkt. 0.50 o.p. (*0-451-50216-7*, Signet Classics); 1964. 400p. mass mkt. 4.95 o.p. (*0-451-52306-7*, Signet Classics); 1964. mass mkt. 2.25 o.p. (*0-451-51941-8*); 1964. mass mkt. 1.95 o.p. (*0-451-51524-2*, Signet Classics); 1964. mass mkt. 1.75 o.p. (*0-451-51357-6*, Signet Classics); 1964. mass mkt. 1.25 o.p. (*0-451-50798-3*, Signet Classics); 1964. mass mkt. 0.95 o.p. (*0-451-50705-3*, Signet Classics); 1943. mass mkt. 1.50 o.p. (*0-451-51010-0*, Signet Classics) NAL.

—Emma. abr. ed. 1996. (Works of Jane Austen). audio 17.98 (*962-634-595-0*, NA309514); audio compact disk 19.98 (*962-634-095-9*, NA309512) Naxos of America, Inc. (Naxos AudioBooks).

—Emma. abr. ed. 1996. (Ultimate Classics Ser.). audio 19.95 o.p. (*0-7871-1068-X*) NewStar Media, Inc.

—Emma. l.t. ed. reprint ed. 1997. 610p. lib. bdg. 26.00 (*0-939495-08-2*); 1998. 478p. lib. bdg. 25.00 (*1-58287-025-X*) North Bks.

—Emma. abr. ed. audio 22.95 Norton Pubs., Inc., Jeffrey /Audio-Forum.

—Emma. Parrish, Stephen M., ed. (Critical Editions Ser.). 430p. (C). 1972. pap. o.p. (*0-393-09667-X*); 2nd ed. 1993. pap. text o.p. (*0-393-96014-5*) Norton, W. W. & Co., Inc.

—Emma. 1999. (Oxford World's Classics Ser.). 464p. 13.00 o.p. (*0-19-210030-0*) Oxford Univ. Pr., Inc.

—Emma. Kinsley, James, ed. (Oxford World's Classics Ser.). 1998. 488p. pap. 6.95 o.p. (*0-19-283357-X*); 1990. 482p. pap. 4.50 o.p. (*0-19-282756-1*) Oxford Univ. Pr., Inc.

—Emma. Kinsley, James & Lodge, David, eds. 1980. (Oxford World's Classics Ser.). pap. 2.50 o.p. (*0-19-281504-0*) Oxford Univ. Pr., Inc.

—Emma. Pinch, Adela, ed. 2nd ed. 2003. (Oxford World's Classics Ser.). 672p. pap. 6.95 (*0-19-280237-2*) Oxford Univ. Pr., Inc.

—Emma. Kinsley, James, ed. 2nd ed. 1995. (Oxford World's Classics Ser.). 484p. pap. 4.95 o.p. (*0-19-282432-5*) Oxford Univ. Pr., Inc.

—Emma, Vol. IV. Chapman, R. W., ed. 3rd ed. 1988. (Illus.). 536p. reprint ed. 20.00 (*0-19-254704-6*) Oxford Univ. Pr., Inc.

—Emma. collector's ed. 2002. (Illus.). im. lthr. 38.85 (*1-931927-22-7*); pap. 19.95 (*1-931927-23-5*); 25.95 (*1-931927-21-9*); pap. 17.95 (*1-931927-14-6*) Polyglot Pr., Inc.

—Emma. (Jane Austen Works). 2000. 364p. lib. bdg. 41.99 (*1-57646-332-X*); 2000. 364p. pap. 19.99 o.p. (*1-57646-261-7*); 1999. 200p. E-Book 3.99 incl. audio compact disk (*1-57646-144-0*); 2000. 646p. pap. 39.99 (*1-57646-333-8*); 2000. 646p. lib. bdg. 49.99 (*1-57646-334-6*) Quiet Vision Publishing.

—Emma. (Modern Library Classics). 2001. 384p. pap. 7.95 (*0-375-75742-2*); 2001. E-Book 4.95 (*0-679-64108-4*); 1995. 14.95 o.s.i (*0-679-60193-7*) Random House Adult Trade Publishing Group. (Modern Library).

—Emma. abr. ed. 1994. (BBC Radio Presents Ser.). audio 22.00 o.s.i (*0-553-47291-7*, RH Audio) Random Hse. Audio Publishing Group.

—Emma. 1988. (Zodiac Press Ser.). 520p. o.p. (*0-7011-1232-8*) Random Hse. of Canada, Ltd. CAN. *Dist:* Random Hse., Inc.

—Emma. 2002. (SPA.). 600p. mass mkt. 9.95 (*1-4000-0083-1*); 1997. 13.00 o.s.i (*0-679-60257-7*); 1991. 560p. 18.00 (*0-679-40581-X*); 1989. o.s.i (*1-85381-096-7*) Random Hse., Inc.

—Emma. 1994. (World's Best Reading Ser.). 391p. (*0-89577-582-4*) Reader's Digest Assn., Inc., The.

—Emma. unabr. ed. 1987. audio 97.00 (*1-55690-165-8*, 87350E7) Recorded Bks., LLC.

—Emma. 2000. E-Book 2.95 incl. cd-rom (*1-58853-011-6*) Sensory Publishing, Inc.

—Emma. E-Book 5.00 (*0-7410-0560-3*) SoftBook Pr.

—Emma. unabr. ed. 2003. audio 19.99 (*1-59335-041-4*, 30126) Soulmate Audio Bks., Inc.

—Emma. audio 14.95 o.p. (*0-88142-367-X*, 367) Soundelux Audio Publishing.

—Emma. l.t. ed. 1985. (Charnwood Large Print Ser.). 547p. 29.99 (*0-7089-8258-1*, Charnwood) Thorpe, F. A. Pubs. GBR. *Dist:* Ulverscroft Large Print Bks., Ltd., Ulverscroft Large Print Canada, Ltd.

—Emma. Daleski, H. M., ed. 2003. 9.95 (*1-59264-004-4*); 510p. pap. 9.95 (*1-59264-003-6*) Toby Pr.

—Emma. 2000. (Signature Classics Ser.). 459p. 24.95 (*1-58279-090-6*); lib. bdg. 29.95 (*1-58279-081-7*) Trident Pr. International.

—Emma. 1997. 19.00 (*0-606-17578-4*); 1980. 11.00 (*0-606-03147-2*) Turtleback Bks.

—Emma. 1994. 464p. pap. 3.95 o.p. (*0-460-87467-5*); 1964. 432p. pap. 5.95 o.p. (*0-460-15024-3*) Tuttle Publishing. (Everyman's Classic Library in Paperback).

—Emma. 2000. 9.00 (*81-85944-76-8*) UBS Pubs. Distributions, Ltd. IND. *Dist:* South Asia Bks.

—Emma. (Classics Ser.). 2003. 512p. pap. 8.00 (*0-14-143958-0*, Penguin Classics); 1997. 448p. 7.95 (*0-14-043415-1*); 1971. 4.50 o.p. (*0-460-01024-7*) Viking Penguin.

—Emma. Blythe, Ronald, ed. 1966. (English Library). 480p. pap. 6.95 o.s.i (*0-14-043010-5*, Penguin Classics) Viking Penguin.

—Emma. abr. ed. 1995. (Classics on Audio Ser.). 4p. audio 23.95 o.s.i (*0-14-086106-8*, Penguin AudioBooks) Viking Penguin.

—Emma. 1999. E-Book 5.99 (*0-8220-7063-4*); E-Book 5.99 (*0-8220-7063-4*) Wiley, John & Sons, Inc. (Cliff Notes).

—Emma. 1997. (Classics Library). 384p. pap. 3.95 (*1-85326-028-2*, 0282WW) Wordsworth Editions, Ltd. GBR. *Dist:* Casemate Pubs. & Bk. Distributors, LLC.

—Emma: Critical Edition. Parrish, Stephen M., ed. 3rd ed. 2000. (Critical Editions Ser.). (Illus.). ix, 449p. pap. 11.00 (*0-393-97284-4*) Norton, W. W. & Co., Inc.

—Emma, Northanger Abbey & Persuasion, Vol. 2. 1976. pap. 8.95 o.p. (*0-394-71892-5*, V-892) Random Hse., Inc.

Austen, Jane, et al. Emma. 1998. E-Book 7.30 (*0-585-36169-X*) netLibrary, Inc.

Tennant, Emma. Emma in Love: Jane Austen's Emma Continued. 229p. 1997. pap. 11.00 o.p. (*1-85702-663-2*); 1996. pap. (*1-85702-527-X*) Fourth Estate, Ltd. GBR. *Dist:* Trafalgar Square.

### WOODRUFF, BERNARD (FICTITIOUS CHARACTER)—FICTION

Dank, Gloria. Friends till the End. 1989. 192p. mass mkt. 3.50 o.s.i (*0-553-28152-6*) Bantam Bks.

—Going out in Style. 1989. (Illus.). mass mkt. 3.95 o.s.i (*0-553-28346-4*) Bantam Bks.

### WOOSTER, BERTIE (FICTITIOUS CHARACTER)—FICTION

Eckhardt, Jason C. & Cannon, P. H. Scream for Jeeves: A Parody. 1994. (Illus.). 86p. 20.00 (*0-940884-61-5*); pap. 7.50 (*0-940884-60-7*) Necronomicon Pr.

Parkinson, C. Northcote. Jeeves: A Gentleman's Personal Gentleman. 1981. 191p. 8.95 o.p. (*0-312-44144-4*) St. Martin's Pr.

Wodehouse, P. G. Aunts Aren't Gentlemen. unabr. ed. 2000. (Wooster & Jeeves Comedy Ser.). audio 34.95 (*0-7451-4098-X*, CAB 786) Chivers Audio Bks. GBR. *Dist:* BBC Audiobooks America.

—Bertie Wooster Sees It Through. 18.95 (*0-8488-0671-9*) Amereon, Ltd.

—Bertie Wooster Sees It Through. 2000. 240p. pap. 13.00 (*0-7432-0361-5*, Touchstone) Simon & Schuster.

—Carry On, Jeeves! 19.95 (*0-89190-296-1*) Amereon, Ltd.

—Carry On, Jeeves! unabr. ed. 2000. audio compact disk 48.00 (*0-7861-9949-0*, z2442) Blackstone Audio Bks., Inc.

—Carry On, Jeeves! 1990. reprint ed. lib. bdg. 15.95 (*0-89968-559-5*) Buccaneer Bks., Inc.

—Carry On, Jeeves! 2003. 17.95 (*1-58567-392-7*) Overlook Pr., The.

—Carry On, Jeeves! 240p. 2000. 7.95 (*0-14-028408-7*); 1975. pap. 8.95 o.s.i (*0-14-001174-9*, Penguin Bks.) Viking Penguin.

—Carry on, Jeeves! 8 Complete Stories. unabr. ed. 1999. audio 22.95 (*1-57270-109-9*, C41109u, Audio Editions Bks. on Cassette) Audio Partners Publishing Corp.

—The Cat-Nappers. unabr. ed. 2001. audio compact disk 19.95; 2000. audio compact disk 32.00 (*0-7861-6897-8*, z1783); 1996. audio 23.95 (*0-7861-1006-6*, 1783); 1996. audio 23.95 (*0-7861-1393-6*, 1783) Blackstone Audio Bks., Inc.

—The Cat-Nappers. reprint ed. 1990. 240p. pap. 11.00 o.p. (*0-06-097250-5*); 1985. 192p. mass mkt. 3.95 o.p. (*0-06-080769-5*, P 769) HarperTrade. (Perennial).

—The Cat-Nappers. 1975. 192p. 7.95 o.s.i (*0-671-21972-3*, Simon & Schuster) Simon & Schuster.

—The Code of the Woosters. reprint ed. lib. bdg. 21.95 (*0-89190-291-0*, Rivercity Pr.) Amereon, Ltd.

—The Code of the Woosters. unabr. ed. 2000. (Wooster & Jeeves Comedy Ser.). audio 49.95 (*0-7451-6372-6*, CAB 497) Chivers Audio Bks. GBR. *Dist:* BBC Audiobooks America.
—The Code of the Woosters. 1975. 240p. mass mkt. 9.00 (*0-394-72028-8*, Vintage) Knopf Publishing Group.
—The Code of the Woosters. unabr. ed. 1997. (Wodehouse's Bertie & Jeeves Ser.). audio 22.95 (*1-58081-060-8*, CTA60) L. A. Theatre Works.
—The Code of the Woosters. 2000. (Collector's Wodehouse Ser.). 224p. 17.95 (*1-58567-057-X*) Overlook Pr., The.
—The Code of the Woosters. unabr. ed. 1989. audio 51.00 (*1-55690-109-7*, 89600E7) Recorded Bks., LLC.
—Enter Jeeves: 15 Early Stories. 1997. 288p. reprint ed. pap. 8.95 (*0-486-29717-9*) Dover Pubns., Inc.
—How Right You Are, Jeeves. reprint ed. lib. bdg. 21.95 (*0-89190-293-7*, Rivercity Pr.) Amereon, Ltd.
—How Right You Are, Jeeves. 1990. reprint ed. lib. bdg. 17.95 (*0-89968-560-9*) Buccaneer Bks., Inc.
—How Right You Are, Jeeves. 1985. 192p. reprint ed. pap. 3.95 o.p. (*0-06-080770-9*, P 770, Perennial) HarperTrade.
—How Right You Are, Jeeves. 2000. 208p. pap. 12.00 (*0-7432-0359-3*, Touchstone); 1960. 3.50 o.p. (*0-671-32460-8*, Simon & Schuster) Simon & Schuster.
—How Right You Are, Jeeves: A Jeeves & Bertie Novel. 1990. 205p. reprint ed. pap. 11.00 o.p. (*0-06-096499-5*, Perennial) HarperTrade.
—The Inimitable Jeeves. 21.95 (*0-8488-0676-X*) Amereon, Ltd.
—The Inimitable Jeeves. unabr. ed. 2000. audio 29.95 (*1-57270-150-1*, C61150u, Audio Editions Bks. on Cassette) Audio Partners Publishing Corp.
—The Inimitable Jeeves. unabr. ed. 2000. audio 27.95 (*0-7861-1775-3*); audio 39.95 (*0-7861-1740-0*, 2545); audio compact disk 48.00 (*0-7861-9903-2*, z2545) Blackstone Audio Bks., Inc.
—The Inimitable Jeeves. unabr. ed. 2000. (Wooster & Jeeves Comedy Ser.). audio 49.95 (*0-7451-6373-4*, CSL 061) Chivers Audio Bks. GBR. *Dist:* BBC Audiobooks America.
—The Inimitable Jeeves. 2000. 240p. pap. 7.95 (*0-14-028412-5*) Penguin Group (USA) Inc.
—The Inimitable Jeeves. unabr. ed. 2000. audio 27.95 Penton Overseas, Inc.
—The Inimitable Jeeves. 1975. 224p. pap. 8.95 o.s.i (*0-14-000933-7*, Penguin Bks.) Viking Penguin.
—Jeeves & the Feudal Spirit: A Jeeves & Bertie Novel. 19.95 (*0-8488-0673-5*) Amereon, Ltd.
—Jeeves & the Feudal Spirit: A Jeeves & Bertie Novel. 1996. audio 29.95 (*0-7451-2847-5*) BBC Audiobooks America.
—Jeeves & the Feudal Spirit: A Jeeves & Bertie Novel. unabr. ed. 1996. audio 39.95 (*0-7861-0916-5*, 1723) Blackstone Audio Bks., Inc.
—Jeeves & the Feudal Spirit: A Jeeves & Bertie Novel. 1990. 246p. pap. 10.00 o.p. (*0-06-096500-2*); 1983. 176p. mass mkt. 3.95 o.p. (*0-06-080666-4*, P666) HarperTrade. (Perennial).
—Jeeves & the Feudal Spirit: A Jeeves & Bertie Novel. 2002. (Illus.). 231p. 16.95 (*1-58567-229-7*) Overlook Pr., The.
—Jeeves & the Tie That Binds. 20.95 (*0-8488-0674-3*) Amereon, Ltd.
—Jeeves & the Tie That Binds. audio 24.95 (*0-7861-1398-7*); 1992. audio 32.95 (*0-7861-0291-8*, 1255) Blackstone Audio Bks., Inc.
—Jeeves & the Tie That Binds. 1983. 192p. mass mkt. 3.95 o.p. (*0-06-080667-2*, P667); 1990. 79p. reprint ed. pap. 10.00 o.p. (*0-06-097283-1*) HarperTrade. (Perennial).
—Jeeves & the Tie That Binds, Set. unabr. ed. 1999. audio 32.95 Highsmith Inc.
—Jeeves & the Tie That Binds. 1971. 5.95 o.s.i (*0-671-21038-6*, Simon & Schuster) Simon & Schuster.
—Jeeves in the Morning. unabr. ed. 2000. audio compact disk 69.99 (*0-7861-9941-5*, z1740); 1996. audio 39.95 (*0-7861-0963-7*, 1740) Blackstone Audio Bks., Inc.
—Jeeves in the Morning. 1983. reprint ed. pap. 3.95 o.p. (*0-06-080658-3*, P 658, Perennial) HarperTrade.
—Jeeves in the Offing. 2002. 16.95 (*1-58567-325-0*) Penguin Group (USA) Inc.
—Jeeves in the Offing. 1984. audio 53.95 o.p. (*0-8161-9784-9*) Thorndike Pr.
—Life with Jeeves. 1983. 560p. pap. 15.95 (*0-14-005902-4*, Penguin Bks.) Penguin Group (USA) Inc.
—Mating Season. 22.95 (*0-8488-0677-8*) Amereon, Ltd.
—The Mating Season. unabr. ed. 1995. audio 44.95 (*0-7861-0761-8*, 1610) Blackstone Audio Bks., Inc.
—The Mating Season. 1989. 224p. reprint ed. pap. 10.00 o.p. (*0-06-097248-3*, Perennial) HarperTrade.
—P. G. Wodehouse: Five Complete Novels. annuals 1995. (Avenel Readers Library). 688p. 12.99 o.s.i (*0-517-40538-5*) Random Hse. Value Publishing.
—The Return of Jeeves. 21.95 (*0-8488-0332-9*) Amereon, Ltd.
—The Return of Jeeves. 1985. 240p. reprint ed. pap. 3.95 o.p. (*0-06-080768-7*, P 768, Perennial) HarperTrade.
—The Return of Jeeves. mass mkt. 0.50 o.p. (*0-451-02843-0*, Signet Bks.) NAL.
—The Return of Jeeves: A Jeeves & Bertie Novel. 1990. 231p. reprint ed. pap. 11.00 o.p. (*0-06-096502-9*, Perennial) HarperTrade.
—Right Ho, Jeeves. 22.95 (*0-8488-0680-8*) Amereon, Ltd.
—Right Ho, Jeeves. 1999. audio 29.95 (*0-7451-2814-9*) BBC Audiobooks America.
—Right Ho, Jeeves. unabr. ed. 1992. audio 44.95 (*0-7861-0363-9*, 1320) Blackstone Audio Bks., Inc.
—Right Ho, Jeeves. unabr. ed. 2000. (Wooster & Jeeves Comedy Ser.). audio 49.95 (*0-7451-6371-8*, CAB 414) Chivers Audio Bks. GBR. *Dist:* BBC Audiobooks America.
—Right Ho, Jeeves. 2000. (Collector's Wodehouse Ser.). 224p. 17.95 (*1-58567-058-8*) Overlook Pr., The.
—Right Ho, Jeeves. 2000. 272p. pap. 7.95 (*0-14-028409-5*) Penguin Group (USA) Inc.
—Right Ho, Jeeves, unabr. ed. 1988. audio 44.00 (*1-55690-444-4*, 88070E7) Recorded Bks., LLC.
—Right Ho, Jeeves. 2001. 2p. audio (*0-14-180315-0*, Penguin AudioBooks); 1975. 256p. pap. 9.95 o.s.i (*0-14-000934-5*, Penguin Bks.) Viking Penguin.
—Stiff Upper Lip, Jeeves. 20.95 (*0-8488-0682-4*) Amereon, Ltd.
—Stiff Upper Lip, Jeeves. unabr. ed. 1991. audio 39.95 (*0-7861-0279-9*, 1245) Blackstone Audio Bks., Inc.
—Stiff Upper Lip, Jeeves. unabr. ed. 2000. (Wooster & Jeeves Comedy Ser.). audio 49.95 (*0-7451-4043-2*, CAB 740) Chivers Audio Bks. GBR. *Dist:* BBC Audiobooks America.
—Stiff Upper Lip, Jeeves. 192p. 1983. mass mkt. 3.95 o.p. (*0-06-080668-0*, P668); 1990. reprint ed. pap. 10.00 o.p. (*0-06-097284-X*) HarperTrade. (Perennial).
—Stiff Upper Lip, Jeeves. mass mkt. 0.50 o.p. (*0-451-02841-4*, Signet Bks.) NAL.
—Stiff Upper Lip, Jeeves. 2000. 224p. pap. 12.00 (*0-7432-0360-7*, Touchstone); (Illus.). 24.00 (*0-7432-0410-7*, Simon & Schuster) Simon & Schuster.
—Thank You, Jeeves. reprint ed. lib. bdg. 23.95 (*0-89190-294-5*, Rivercity Pr.) Amereon, Ltd.
—Thank You, Jeeves. unabr. ed. 1989. audio 39.95 (*0-7861-0174-1*, 1155) Blackstone Audio Bks., Inc.
—Thank You, Jeeves. 1983. 480p. mass mkt. 3.95 o.p. (*0-06-080657-5*) HarperCollins Pubs.
—Thank You, Jeeves. 1989. 288p. reprint ed. pap. 10.00 o.p. (*0-06-097249-1*, Perennial) HarperTrade.
—Thank You, Jeeves. unabr. ed. 1998. audio 19.95 (*1-58081-119-1*, TPT117) L. A. Theatre Works.
—Thank You, Jeeves. 2003. 288p. 17.95 (*1-58567-434-6*) Overlook Pr., The.
—Thank You, Jeeves, unabr. ed. 1984. audio 35.00 (*1-55690-509-2*, 84130E7) Recorded Bks., LLC.
—Very Good, Jeeves. 1998. (Bertie Wooster & Jeeves Ser.). audio 34.95 (*0-7540-7524-9*) BBC Audiobooks America.
—Very Good, Jeeves. 1975. (ACE.). 256p. pap. 8.95 o.s.i (*0-14-001173-0*, Penguin Bks.) Viking Penguin.
—Very Good, Jeeves! 2000. 288p. 7.95 (*0-14-028410-9*) Viking Penguin.
—Very Good, Jeeves. reprint ed. lib. bdg. 22.95 (*0-89190-295-3*, Rivercity Pr.) Amereon, Ltd.
—Very Good, Jeeves. unabr. ed. 1992. audio 44.95 (*0-7861-0310-8*, 1272) Blackstone Audio Bks., Inc.
—Very Good, Jeeves. 1990. reprint ed. lib. bdg. 18.95 (*0-89968-561-7*) Buccaneer Bks., Inc.
—The World of Jeeves. 672p. 1988. 25.00 o.p. (*0-06-015968-5*); 1989. reprint ed. pap. 18.00 o.s.i (*0-06-097244-0*, Perennial) HarperTrade.

Wodehouse, P. G., et al. Jeeves & the Feudal Spirit: A Jeeves & Bertie Novel. 1991. (BBC Humor Ser.). audio 14.95 Minds Eye.

**WORF (FICTITIOUS CHARACTER)—FICTION**

Betancourt, John G. The Heart of the Warrior. 1996. (Star Trek Deep Space Nine Ser.: No. 17). 288p. pap. 5.99 (*0-671-00239-2*, Star Trek) Simon & Schuster.
Carey, Diane L. Day of Honor No. 1: Ancient Blood. 1997. (Star Trek, The Next Generation: Vol. 1). (Illus.). 304p. pap. 5.99 (*0-671-00238-4*, Star Trek) Simon & Schuster.
—The Way of the Warrior. 1995. (Star Trek Deep Space Nine Ser.). 288p. mass mkt. 5.99 o.s.i (*0-671-56813-2*, Star Trek) Simon & Schuster.
Carey, Diane L., et al. Day of Honor Omnibus: Ancient Blood; Armageddon Sky; Her Klingon Soul; Treaty's Law; Day of Honor; Honor Bound. 1999. (Star Trek Ser.). (Illus.). 1104p. pap. 16.00 (*0-671-02813-8*, Pocket) Simon & Schuster.
David, Peter. Imzadi II: Triangle. (Star Trek, The Next Generation Ser.). E-Book 6.99 (*0-7434-2071-3*); 1998. 384p. 23.00 o.s.i (*0-671-02532-5*); 1999. 400p. reprint ed. pap. 6.50 (*0-671-02538-4*) Simon & Schuster. (Star Trek).
—Imzadi II: Triangle. abr. ed. 1998. (Star Trek Ser.: Vol. 2). audio 18.00 (*0-671-04328-5*, Simon & Schuster Audioworks) Simon & Schuster Audio.
—Imzadi II: Triangle. abr. ed. 1999. (Star Trek Ser.). audio 15.00 (*0-671-03343-3*) Ulverscroft Audio (U.S.A.).
DeCandido, Keith R. A. Diplomatic Implausibility. 2001. (Star Trek, The Next Generation Ser.: Vol. 61). 272p. pap. 6.99 (*0-671-78554-0*, Star Trek) Simon & Schuster.
Dillard, J. M. Insurrection. abr. ed. (Star Trek Ser.: No. 9). 1998. audio 18.00 o.s.i (*0-671-58259-3*, 396208, Simon & Schuster Audioworks); 2003. audio 9.95 (*0-7435-3254-6*, Encore) Simon & Schuster Audio.
Dillard, J. M. & Berman, Rick. Insurrection. 1998. (Star Trek Ser.: No. 9). 304p. 22.00 o.s.i (*0-671-02447-7*, Star Trek) Simon & Schuster.
Dillard, J. M. & O'Malley, Kathleen. Possession. 1996. (Star Trek, The Next Generation Ser.: No. 40). 288p. mass mkt. 5.99 (*0-671-86485-8*, Star Trek) Simon & Schuster.
Duane, Diane. Intellivore. 1997. (Star Trek, The Next Generation Ser.: No. 45). 272p. mass mkt. 6.50 o.s.i (*0-671-56832-9*, Star Trek) Simon & Schuster.
Durgin, Doranna. Tooth & Claw. 2001. (Star Trek, The Next Generation Ser.: Vol. 60). (Illus.). 272p. pap. 6.99 (*0-671-04211-4*, Star Trek) Simon & Schuster.
Friedman, Michael Jan. All Good Things. 1994. (Star Trek Ser.). 256p. o.p. (*0-671-50014-7*, Atria) Simon & Schuster.
—A Call to Darkness. (Star Trek, The Next Generation Ser.: No. 9). E-Book 6.99 (*0-7434-2089-6*); 1991. mass mkt. 5.50 (*0-671-74141-1*); 1989. 304p. mass mkt. 3.95 o.s.i (*0-671-68708-5*) Simon & Schuster. (Star Trek).
—Kahless. (Star Trek, The Next Generation Ser.). 1997. (Illus.). 336p. mass mkt. 5.99 (*0-671-00887-0*); 1996. 320p. 23.00 (*0-671-54779-8*) Simon & Schuster. (Star Trek).
—Kahless, Set. 1996. (Star Trek Ser.). audio 18.00 o.s.i (*0-671-57068-4*, 394072, Simon & Schuster Audioworks) Simon & Schuster Audio.
—Planet X. (Star Trek, The Next Generation Ser.). E-Book 6.99 (*0-7434-2070-5*); 1998. (Illus.). 288p. mass mkt. 6.99 (*0-671-01916-3*) Simon & Schuster. (Star Trek).
—Stargazer: Three, Bk. 3. 2003. (Star Trek, The Next Generation Ser.). 288p. mass mkt. 6.99 (*0-7434-4852-9*, Star Trek) Simon & Schuster.
Galanter, Dave & Brodeur, Greg. Foreign Foes. (Star Trek, The Next Generation Ser.: No. 31). E-Book 6.99 (*0-7434-2114-0*); 1994. 288p. mass mkt. 5.50 (*0-671-88414-X*) Simon & Schuster. (Star Trek).
Graf, L. A. Armageddon Sky: Day of Honor. Keenan, Randall, ed. 1997. (Star Trek, The Next Generation: Vol. 2). 304p. pap. 5.99 o.s.i (*0-671-00675-4*, Star Trek) Simon & Schuster.
Hamilton, Laurell K. Nightshade. Stern, Dave, ed. 1992. (Star Trek, The Next Generation Ser.: No. 24). 288p. mass mkt. 5.50 (*0-671-79566-X*, Star Trek) Simon & Schuster.
Hugh, Dafydd ab. Vengeance. 1998. (Star Trek Deep Space Nine Ser.: No. 22). 304p. pap. 6.50 (*0-671-00468-9*, Star Trek) Simon & Schuster.
Peel, John. Death of Princes. 1996. (Star Trek, The Next Generation Ser.: No. 44). 304p. pap. 5.99 (*0-671-56808-6*, Star Trek) Simon & Schuster.
—Here There Be Dragons. Ryan, Kevin, ed. 1993. (Star Trek, The Next Generation Ser.: No. 28). 288p. (Orig.). mass mkt. 5.99 (*0-671-86571-4*, Star Trek) Simon & Schuster.
Smith, Dean & Rusch, Kristine K. Klingon. (Star Trek, The Next Generation Ser.). E-Book 6.99 (*0-7434-2077-2*, Star Trek) Simon & Schuster.
Thompson, W. R. Debtor's Planet. Ordover, John, ed. 1994. (Star Trek, The Next Generation Ser.: No. 30). 288p. (Orig.). mass mkt. 5.99 o.s.i (*0-671-88341-0*, Star Trek) Simon & Schuster.
—Infiltrator. 1996. (Star Trek, The Next Generation Ser.: No. 42). 288p. mass mkt. 5.99 (*0-671-56831-0*, Star Trek) Simon & Schuster.
Vornholt, John. Contamination. (Star Trek, The Next Generation Ser.: No. 16). E-Book 6.99 (*0-7434-2096-9*, Star Trek) Simon & Schuster.
—Contamination. Stern, David, ed. 1991. (Star Trek, The Next Generation Ser.: No. 16). 288p. mass mkt. 5.50 (*0-671-70561-X*, Star Trek) Simon & Schuster.
—Contamination. abr. ed. 1991. (Star Trek, The Next Generation Ser.: No. 16). audio 12.00 (*0-671-74045-8*, 326327, Simon & Schuster Audioworks) Simon & Schuster Audio.
—Rogue Saucer. 1996. (Star Trek, The Next Generation Ser.: No. 39). 288p. mass mkt. 5.99 (*0-671-54917-0*, Star Trek) Simon & Schuster.
—War Drums. (Star Trek, The Next Generation Ser.). E-Book 6.99 (*0-7434-2103-5*, Star Trek) Simon & Schuster.
—War Drums. Stern, Dave, ed. 1992. (Star Trek, The Next Generation Ser.: No. 23). 288p. mass mkt. 5.50 (*0-671-79236-9*, Star Trek) Simon & Schuster.
Wright, Susan. Dark Passions, 2001. (Star Trek Ser.: Bk. 1). 256p. pap. 6.99 (*0-671-78785-3*, Star Trek) Simon & Schuster.
—Sins of Commission. Ryan, Kevin, ed. 1994. (Star Trek, The Next Generation Ser.: No. 29). 288p. (Orig.). mass mkt. 5.50 (*0-671-79704-2*, Star Trek) Simon & Schuster.
—The Tempest. 1997. (Star Trek Deep Space Nine Ser.: No. 19). (Illus.). 304p. pap. 5.99 (*0-671-00227-9*, Star Trek) Simon & Schuster.

**WORRELL, ERNEST P. (FICTITIOUS CHARACTER)—FICTION**

Worrell, Ernest P. Ask Ernest! What, When, Where, Why, Who Cares. 1993. 128p. (Orig.). pap. 7.95 o.p. (*1-55853-247-1*) Rutledge Hill Pr.

**WORTHING, MATILDA (FICTITIOUS CHARACTER)—FICTION**

Drummond, John K. Thy Sting, Oh Death: A Matilda Worthing Mystery. 1985. 240p. 14.95 o.p. (*0-312-80419-9*) St. Martin's Pr.
—'Tis the Season to Be Dying: A Matilda Worthing Mystery. 1988. 336p. 16.95 o.p. (*0-312-01901-7*, Saint Martin's Minotaur) St. Martin's Pr.

**WREN, PORTER (FICTITIOUS CHARACTER)—FICTION**

Harrison, Colin. Manhattan Nocturne. 1997. o.s.i (*0-517-70696-2*); 1996. 384p. 5.99 o.s.i (*0-517-58492-1*) Crown Publishing Group.
—Manhattan Nocturne. 1997. 416p. mass mkt. 6.99 o.s.i (*0-440-22433-0*) Dell Publishing.
—Manhattan Nocturne. unabr. ed. 1996. 24.95 o.p. (*0-7871-1115-5*) NewStar Media, Inc.
—Manhattan Nocturne. 2004. 416p. mass mkt. 6.99 (*0-312-99303-X*, St. Martin's Paperbacks) St. Martin's Pr.

**WREN, SUSAN (FICTITIOUS CHARACTER)—FICTION**

Weir, Charlene. A Cold Christmas. 2002. (WWL Mystery Ser.: No. 439). 256p. mass mkt. (*0-373-26439-9*, Worldwide Library) Harlequin Enterprises, Ltd.
—A Cold Christmas. 2001. 272p. 23.95 (*0-312-26931-5*, Saint Martin's Minotaur) St. Martin's Pr.
—Consider the Crows. 1995. (WWL Mystery Ser.). 251p. per. (*0-373-26172-1*, 1-26172-6, Harlequin Bks.) Harlequin Enterprises, Ltd.
—Consider the Crows. 1993. 272p. 19.95 o.p. (*0-312-09772-7*, Saint Martin's Minotaur) St. Martin's Pr.
—Family Practice. 1997. (Susan Wren Mystery Ser.). 301p. per. (*0-373-26236-1*, 0-26236-0, Worldwide Library) Harlequin Enterprises, Ltd.
—Family Practice. 1995. 320p. 22.95 (*0-312-13492-4*, Saint Martin's Minotaur) St. Martin's Pr.
—Murder Take Two. pap. 16.95 o.p. (*0-312-30029-8*, Saint Martin's Griffin); pap. 15.95 (*0-312-29193-0*, Saint Martin's Griffin); 1998. 336p. 23.95 (*0-312-18136-1*, Saint Martin's Minotaur) St. Martin's Pr.
—Up in Smoke. pap. (*0-312-31021-8*); mass mkt. (*0-312-98758-7*) St. Martin's Pr. (St. Martin's Paperbacks).
—Up in Smoke: A Case for Kansas Police Chief Susan Wren. 2003. 272p. 23.95 (*0-312-31020-X*, Saint Martin's Minotaur) St. Martin's Pr.
—The Winter Widow. 1993. per. (*0-373-26128-4*, 1-26128-8, Harlequin Bks.) Harlequin Enterprises, Ltd.
—The Winter Widow. 1992. 256p. 18.95 o.p. (*0-312-07009-8*, Saint Martin's Minotaur) St. Martin's Pr.

**WRIGHT, BETH (FICTITIOUS CHARACTER)—FICTION**

Blackstock, Terri. Presumption of Guilt. l.t. ed. 1999. (Christian Mystery Ser.). 453p. 25.95 (*0-7862-1959-9*) Thorndike Pr.
—Presumption of Guilt. 1997. (Sun Coast Chronicles Ser.). 304p. pap. 12.99 (*0-310-20018-0*); audio 14.99 (*0-310-21085-2*) Zondervan.

**WRIGHT, JESSICA (FICTITIOUS CHARACTER)—FICTION**

Van Wormer, Laura. Talk, abr. ed. 1998. audio 7.99 (*1-55204-150-6*) Durkin Hayes Publishing Ltd.
—Talk. 1999. 403p. mass mkt. (*1-55166-514-X*, 1-66514-0); 1998. 378p. (*1-55166-317-1*, 1-6637-8) Harlequin Enterprises, Ltd. (Mira Bks.).

**WU, ARTIE (FICTITIOUS CHARACTER)—FICTION**

Thomas, Ross. Chinaman's Chance. 1979. pap. 2.25 o.p. (*0-380-41517-8*, 41517-8, Avon Bks.) Morrow/Avon.
—Chinaman's Chance, unabr. ed. 1985. (Durant & Wu Ser.). audio 60.00 (*1-55690-100-3*, 85450E7) Recorded Bks., LLC.

—Chinaman's Chance. 1978. 9.95 o.p. (*0-671-24070-6*, Simon & Schuster) Simon & Schuster.
—Chinaman's Chance. 1988. 352p. mass mkt. 5.99 o.s.i (*0-445-40725-5*) Warner Bks., Inc.
—Out on the Rim. E-Book 13.95 (*0-312-70961-7*) Holtzbrinck Pubs.
—Out on the Rim. 1987. 320p. 17.95 o.p. (*0-89296-212-7*) Mysterious Pr.
—Out on the Rim, unabr. ed. 1988. (Durant & Wu Ser.). audio 70.00 (*1-55690-399-5*, 88883E7) Recorded Bks., LLC.
—Out on the Rim. 2003. 336p. reprint ed. pap. 13.95 (*0-312-29059-4*, Saint Martin's Griffin) St. Martin's Pr.
—Out on the Rim. 1988. 336p. mass mkt. 5.99 o.s.i (*0-445-40693-3*) Warner Bks., Inc.
—Voodoo, Ltd. l.t. ed. 1993. (General Ser.). 367p. lib. bdg. 21.95 (*0-8161-5679-4*, Macmillan Reference USA) Gale Group.
—Voodoo, Ltd. 1992. 288p. 19.95 (*0-89296-451-0*) Mysterious Pr.
—Voodoo, Ltd., unabr. ed. 1993. (Durant & Wu Ser.). audio 51.00 (*1-55690-785-0*, 93105E7) Recorded Bks., LLC.
—Voodoo, Ltd. 1993. 320p. mass mkt. 5.99 (*0-446-40030-0*, Mysterious Pr. Paperback Bks.) Warner Bks., Inc.

**WUNTVOR (FICTITIOUS CHARACTER)—FICTION**

Gardner, Craig S. A Difficulty with Dwarves. 1987. 192p. (Orig.). mass mkt. 5.99 (*0-441-14779-8*) Ace Bks.
—A Disagreement with Death. 1989. 192p. mass mkt. 5.99 (*0-441-14924-3*) Ace Bks.
—An Excess of Enchantments. 1988. 192p. mass mkt. 5.99 (*0-441-22363-X*) Ace Bks.
—A Malady of Magicks. 1986. 240p. mass mkt. 5.99 o.s.i (*0-441-51662-9*) Ace Bks.
—A Multitude of Monsters. 1986. 208p. mass mkt. 5.99 o.s.i (*0-441-54523-8*) Ace Bks.
—A Night in the Netherhells. 1987. 192p. mass mkt. 5.99 o.s.i (*0-441-02314-2*) Ace Bks.

**WYATT (FICTITIOUS CHARACTER)—FICTION**

Disher, Garry. The Fallout: A Wyatt Novel. 1997. 209p. (Orig.). pap. 5.95 (*1-86448-330-X*) Allen & Unwin Pty., Ltd. AUS. *Dist:* Independent Pubs. Group.
—Port Vila Blues: A Wyatt Novel. 1996. 232p. (Orig.). pap. 6.95 (*1-86448-025-4*) Allen & Unwin Pty., Ltd. AUS. *Dist:* Independent Pubs. Group.

**WYATT, JOLIE (FICTITIOUS CHARACTER)—FICTION**

Smith, Barbara B. Dust Devils of the Purple Sage. 1997. per. (*0-373-26234-5*, 1-26234-4, Worldwide Library) Harlequin Enterprises, Ltd.
—Dust Devils of the Purple Sage. 1995. 256p. 21.95 o.p. (*0-312-13476-2*, Saint Martin's Minotaur) St. Martin's Pr.
—Writers of the Purple Sage. 1996. (Mystery Ser.). per. (*0-373-26214-0*, Worldwide Library) Harlequin Enterprises, Ltd.
—Writers of the Purple Sage. 1994. 304p. 20.95 o.p. (*0-312-11352-8*, Saint Martin's Minotaur) St. Martin's Pr.
Smith, Barbara B., et al. 'Tis the Season for Murder: Christmas Crimes. 1998. mass mkt. (*0-373-26290-6*, 1-26290-6, Worldwide Library) Harlequin Enterprises, Ltd.

**WYC, WINSTON (FICTITIOUS CHARACTER)—FICTION**

Johnston, Brian. Dutch Treat Murders. 1991. mass mkt. 3.99 o.s.i (*1-55817-570-9*, Pinnacle Bks.) Kensington Publishing Corp.
—The Gift Horse Murders: A Wynston Wyc Mystery. 1992. 288p. mass mkt. 3.99 o.s.i (*1-55817-652-7*, Pinnacle Bks.) Kensington Publishing Corp.
—Good Luck Murders. 1991. mass mkt. 3.95 o.s.i (*1-55817-479-6*, Pinnacle Bks.) Kensington Publishing Corp.
—With Mallets Aforethought: A Winston Wyc Mystery. 1995. 256p. 20.50 (*1-883402-44-1*, Scribner) Simon & Schuster.

**WYCLIFFE, CHARLES (FICTITIOUS CHARACTER)—FICTION**

Burley, W. J. Wycliffe & Death in Stanley Street. l.t. ed. 1997. (Magna Large Print Ser.). 295p. 29.99 o.p. (*0-7505-1143-5*) Magna Large Print Bks. GBR. *Dist:* Ulverscroft Large Print Bks., Ltd., Ulverscroft Large Print Canada, Ltd.
—Wycliffe & Death in Stanley Street. 2003. 220p. mass mkt. 7.95 (*0-7528-4969-7*) Orion Publishing Group, Ltd. GBR. *Dist:* Trafalgar Square.
—Wycliffe & the Beales. 1984. (Crime Club Ser.). 192p. 11.95 o.p. (*0-385-19189-8*) Doubleday Publishing.
—Wycliffe & the Beales. 1987. 192p. pap. 2.95 o.p. (*0-380-70329-7*, Avon Bks.) Morrow/Avon.
—Wycliffe & the Cycle of Death. 1991. 192p. 15.00 o.s.i (*0-385-41800-0*) Doubleday Publishing.
—Wycliffe & the Cycle of Death. l.t. ed. 1991. (Magna Large Print Ser.). 309p. o.p. (*0-7505-0038-7*) Magna Large Print Bks. GBR. *Dist:* Ulverscroft Large Print Canada, Ltd.
—Wycliffe & the Cycle of Death. 2000. pap. 8.95 (*0-552-14109-7*) Transworld Publishers Ltd. GBR. *Dist:* Trafalgar Square.
—Wycliffe & the Dead Flautist. l.t. ed. 1992. (Magna Large Print Ser.). 303p. 29.99 o.p. (*0-7505-0196-0*) Magna Large Print Bks. GBR. *Dist:* Ulverscroft Large Print Bks., Ltd., Ulverscroft Large Print Canada, Ltd.
—Wycliffe & the Dead Flautist. unabr. ed. 1999. audio 49.95 Soundings, Ltd. GBR. *Dist:* Ulverscroft Large Print Bks., Ltd.
—Wycliffe & the Dead Flautist. 1992. 192p. 16.95 o.p. (*0-312-07129-9*, Saint Martin's Minotaur) St. Martin's Pr.
—Wycliffe & the Dead Flautist. 2000. pap. 8.95 (*0-552-14264-6*) Transworld Publishers Ltd. GBR. *Dist:* Trafalgar Square.
—Wycliffe & the Dunes Mystery. 1995. mass mkt. o.s.i (*0-552-14221-2*, Corgi) Bantam Bks.
—Wycliffe & the Dunes Mystery. l.t. ed. 1994. (Magna Large Print Ser.). 299p. o.p. (*0-7505-0629-6*) Magna Large Print Bks. GBR. *Dist:* Ulverscroft Large Print Canada, Ltd.
—Wycliffe & the Dunes Mystery. 1994. 192p. 18.95 o.p. (*0-312-11100-2*, Saint Martin's Minotaur) St. Martin's Pr.
—Wycliffe & the Four Jacks. 1994. mass mkt. 5.99 o.s.i (*0-552-14267-0*) Bantam Bks.
—Wycliffe & the Four Jacks. 1986. (Crime Club Ser.). 192p. 12.95 o.p. (*0-385-23262-4*) Doubleday Publishing.
—Wycliffe & the Four Jacks. 1987. 192p. pap. 2.95 o.p. (*0-380-70328-9*, Avon Bks.) Morrow/Avon.
—Wycliffe & the Guilt Edged Alibi. 1994. mass mkt. o.s.i (*0-552-14115-1*, Corgi) Bantam Bks.
—Wycliffe & the House of Death. 1995. 192p. 19.95 o.p. (*0-312-14080-0*, Saint Martin's Minotaur) St. Martin's Pr.
—Wycliffe & the House of Fear. l.t. ed. 1996. (Magna Large Print Ser.). 327p. o.p. (*0-7505-1006-4*) Magna Large Print Bks. GBR. *Dist:* Ulverscroft Large Print Canada, Ltd.
—Wycliffe & the Last Rites. l.t. ed. 1993. (Magna Large Print Ser.). 337p. o.p. (*0-7505-0492-7*) Magna Large Print Bks. GBR. *Dist:* Ulverscroft Large Print Canada, Ltd.
—Wycliffe & the Last Rites. 1993. 192p. 17.95 o.p. (*0-312-09946-0*, Saint Martin's Minotaur) St. Martin's Pr.
—Wycliffe & the Last Rites. 2000. 219p. pap. 8.95 (*0-552-14265-4*) Transworld Publishers Ltd. GBR. *Dist:* Trafalgar Square.
—Wycliffe & the Pea Green Boat. 1998. 208p. mass mkt. 4.99 o.s.i (*0-552-12804-X*) Bantam Bks.
—Wycliffe & the Quiet Virgin. 1986. (Crime Club Ser.). 192p. 12.95 o.p. (*0-385-23549-6*) Doubleday Publishing.
—Wycliffe & the Quiet Virgin. 1988. 176p. mass mkt. 2.95 (*0-380-70510-9*, Avon Bks.) Morrow/Avon.
—Wycliffe & the Quiet Virgin. 1989. 192p. mass mkt. 8.95 o.s.i (*0-552-13435-X*) Transworld Publishers Ltd. GBR. *Dist:* Trafalgar Square.
—Wycliffe & the Redhead. 1999. (Illus.). 255p. mass mkt. (*0-552-14661-7*, Corgi) Bantam Bks.
—Wycliffe & the Redhead. l.t. ed. 1999. (Magna Large Print Ser.). 320p. o.p. (*0-7505-1373-X*) Magna Large Print Bks. GBR. *Dist:* Ulverscroft Large Print Canada, Ltd.
—Wycliffe & the Redhead. 1998. 192p. 20.95 (*0-312-19374-2*, Saint Martin's Minotaur) St. Martin's Pr.
—Wycliffe & the Scapegoat. 1988. mass mkt. o.s.i (*0-552-12806-6*) Corgi Bks. Ltd.
—Wycliffe & the Scapegoat. l.t. ed. 2001. (Dales Large Print Ser.). 256p. pap. (*1-84262-055-X*) Dales Large Print Bks. GBR. *Dist:* Ulverscroft Large Print Canada, Ltd.
—Wycliffe & the Scapegoat. 1979. (Crime Club Ser.). 9.95 o.p. (*0-385-15126-8*) Doubleday Publishing.
—Wycliffe & the Scapegoat. 1987. 160p. pap. 2.95 o.p. (*0-380-70330-0*, Avon Bks.) Morrow/Avon.
—Wycliffe & the Scapegoat. 1998. 208p. mass mkt. 8.95 o.p. (*0-552-14266-2*) Transworld Publishers Ltd. GBR. *Dist:* Trafalgar Square.
—Wycliffe & the Schoolgirls. 1987. mass mkt. 3.95 o.s.i (*0-552-12805-8*) Bantam Bks.
—Wycliffe & the Schoolgirls. l.t. ed. 1989. 277p. lib. bdg. 11.95 o.p. (*1-85057-477-4*, Macmillan Reference USA) Gale Group.
—Wycliffe & the Schoolgirls. 1984. (British Mystery Ser.). 175p. reprint ed. pap. 2.95 o.p. (*0-8027-3064-7*) Walker & Co.
—Wycliffe & the Tangled Web. 2000. pap. 8.95 (*0-552-14268-9*) Transworld Publishers Ltd. GBR. *Dist:* Trafalgar Square.
—Wycliffe & the Three-Toed Pussy. 1997. 18.50 o.p. (*0-7451-8702-1*, Black Dagger) BBC Audiobooks America.
—Wycliffe & the Three-Toed Pussy. l.t. ed. 1996. (Magna Large Print Ser.). 320p. 29.99 o.p. (*0-7505-0963-5*) Magna Large Print Bks. GBR. *Dist:* Ulverscroft Large Print Bks., Ltd., Ulverscroft Large Print Canada, Ltd.
—Wycliffe & Winsor Blue. 1987. (Crime Club Ser.). 192p. 12.95 o.s.i (*0-385-24311-1*) Doubleday Publishing.
—Wycliffe in Paul's Court. 1980. (Crime Club Ser.). 192p. 10.95 o.p. (*0-385-17208-7*) Doubleday Publishing.
—Wycliffe in Paul's Court. 2003. 192p. mass mkt. 7.95 (*0-7528-4932-8*) Orion Publishing Group, Ltd. GBR. *Dist:* Trafalgar Square.
—Wycliffe in Paul's Court. 1981. 192p. pap. 3.95 o.p. (*0-14-005917-2*, Penguin Bks.) Viking Penguin.
—Wycliffe's Wild Goose Chase. 1982. (Crime Club Ser.). 192p. 11.95 o.p. (*0-385-18254-6*) Doubleday Publishing.
—Wycliffe's Wild Goose Chase. 2000. (J). pap. 8.95 (*0-552-14269-7*) Transworld Publishers Ltd. GBR. *Dist:* Trafalgar Square.

**WYLIE, EVA (FICTITIOUS CHARACTER)—FICTION**

Cody, Liza. Bucket Nut. 1993. 240p. 18.50 o.s.i (*0-385-46776-1*) Doubleday Publishing.
—Bucket Nut. l.t. unabr. ed. 1998. 24.95 (*0-7531-5173-1*, 151731) ISIS Large Print Bks. GBR. *Dist:* ISIS Publishing.
—Bucket Nut. 1995. 224p. mass mkt. 5.50 o.p. (*0-446-40459-4*) Warner Bks., Inc.
—Monkey Wrench. 1995. 256p. 18.95 o.s.i (*0-89296-600-9*) Mysterious Pr.
—Monkey Wrench. 1996. 240p. mass mkt. 5.99 o.p. (*0-446-40457-8*) Warner Bks., Inc.
—Muscle Bound. 1997. 288p. 22.00 o.p. (*0-89296-601-7*) Mysterious Pr.

## X

**X, MR. (FICTITIOUS CHARACTER)—FICTION**

Hernandez, Gilbert & Hernandez, Jaime. The Return of Mr. X. Motter, Dean, ed. deluxe ltd. ed. 1987. (Limited-Signed Edition Ser.: No. 5). (Illus.). 114p. 34.95 (*0-936211-03-2*) Graphitti Designs.
Hernandez, Gilbert, et al. The Return of Mr. X. 1987. mass mkt. 8.95 (*0-446-38698-7*) Warner Bks., Inc.

**X-MEN (FICTITIOUS CHARACTERS)—FICTION**

Austen, Chuck. Uncanny X-Men: Holy War, 3 vols. 2003. (Uncanny X-men Ser.). (Illus.). 192p. (YA). pap. 17.99 (*0-7851-1133-6*) Marvel Enterprises.
Bendis, Brian Michael. Ultimate X-Men: Blockbuster, 7 vols. 2004. (Ultimate X-men Ser.). (Illus.). 144p. (J). pap. 12.99 (*0-7851-1219-7*) Marvel Enterprises.
Busiek, Kurt. Alterniverse Visions: The X-Men. 1996. (Illus.). 144p. pap. text 15.95 o.p. (*0-7851-0194-2*) Marvel Enterprises.
Byers, Richard L. Soul Killer. 1999. (X-Men Ser.). 320p. (J). mass mkt. 6.99 o.s.i (*0-425-16737-2*) Berkley Publishing Group.
Byrne, John. X-Men: The Coming of Bishop. 1995. (Illus.). 96p. pap. 12.95 (*0-7851-0099-7*) Marvel Enterprises.
Clarement, Chris. Enter the Phoenix, No. 2. 1996. (X-Men, Enter the Phoenix Ser.: Vol. 2). mass mkt. 3.99 (*0-8125-4325-4*, Tor Bks.) Doherty, Tom Assocs., LLC.
Clarement, Chris, et al. X-Men: Days of Future Present. 1991. (Illus.). 160p. pap. 14.95 o.p. (*0-87135-739-9*) Marvel Enterprises.
Claremont, Chris. Essential X-Men. (Illus.). 528p. Vol. II. 1997. pap. 14.95 (*0-7851-0298-1*); Vol. III. 1998. pap. 12.95 (*0-7851-0661-8*) Marvel Enterprises.
—Mutant Genesis. 2002. (X-Men Legends Ser.: Vol. 1). (Illus.). 176p. (YA). (gr. 7 up). pap. 17.95 (*0-7851-0895-5*) Marvel Enterprises.
—X-Men: Annuals. 1996. (Illus.). 208p. pap. text 19.95 o.p. (*0-7851-0195-0*) Marvel Enterprises.
—X-Men: Crossroads. 1998. (Finest Ser.). (Illus.). 128p. pap. 15.95 (*0-7851-0662-6*) Marvel Enterprises.
—X-Men: God Loves, Man Kills Bookshelf Edition. 1994. (X-Men Ser.). (Illus.). 64p. pap. 6.95 (*0-7851-0039-3*) Marvel Enterprises.
—X-Men: Inferno. 1996. (Illus.). 208p. pap. text 19.95 (*0-7851-0222-1*) Marvel Enterprises.
—X-Men: Mutations. 1996. (Illus.). 176p. pap. text 19.95 (*0-7851-0197-7*) Marvel Enterprises.
—X-Men: Savage Land. 1991. (Spiderman Ser.). (Illus.). 9.95 o.p. (*0-87135-552-3*) Marvel Enterprises.
—X-Men Visionaries: Chris Claremont, Vol. 1. 1998. (Illus.). 240p. pap. text 24.95 (*0-7851-0598-0*) Marvel Enterprises.
—X-Men vs. the Avengers. 1993. (Illus.). pap. 12.95 o.p. (*0-87135-967-7*) Marvel Enterprises.
—X-Treme X-Men: God Loves, Man Kills, 6 vols. 2003. (X-Treme X-men Ser.: Vol. 5). (Illus.). 216p. (YA). pap. 19.99 (*0-7851-1254-5*) Marvel Enterprises.
Claremont, Chris & Anderson, Brent Eric. X-Men: God Loves, Man Kills. 1982. 64p. 9.95 o.p. (*0-939766-22-1*) Marvel Enterprises.
Claremont, Chris & Golden, Michael. X-Men: Savage Land. 2002. (Illus.). 96p. pap. 9.95 (*0-7851-0891-2*) Marvel Enterprises.
Claremont, Chris & Simonson, Louise. X-Men: X-Tinction Agenda. 1992. (Marvel Comics Ser.). (Illus.). 224p. pap. 24.95 (*0-87135-922-7*) Marvel Enterprises.
Claremont, Chris & Simonson, Walter. X-Men Legends: Art Adams Book I, 3 vols. 2003. (X-Men Legends Ser.). (Illus.). 272p. (YA). pap. 24.99 (*0-7851-1049-6*) Marvel Enterprises.
Claremont, Chris & Thomas, Roy. Greatest Battles of the X-Men. 1994. (Illus.). 176p. pap. 15.95 (*0-7851-0042-3*) Marvel Enterprises.
Claremont, Chris, et al. The All-New, All-Different X-Men: Masterworks, Vol. 1. 1993. (Illus.). 122p. 12.95 (*0-87135-988-X*) Marvel Enterprises.
—Essential X-Men, Vol. I. 1997. (Illus.). 528p. pap. 14.95 (*0-7851-0256-6*) Marvel Enterprises.
—Fantastic Four vs. the X-Men. 1990. (Illus.). 96p. pap. 9.95 o.p. (*0-87135-650-3*) Marvel Enterprises.
—X-Men: Days of Future Past. 1989. (Comics Ser.). (Illus.). 48p. 15.95 (*0-87135-582-5*) Marvel Enterprises.
—X-Men: Mutant Genesis. 1995. (Illus.). 160p. pap. 15.95 o.p. (*0-7851-0137-3*) Marvel Enterprises.
—X-Men: Savage Land. 1988. 80p. pap. 9.95 o.p. (*0-87135-338-5*) Marvel Enterprises.
—X-Men: The Asgardian Wars. 1988. 228p. pap. 15.95 o.p. (*0-87135-434-9*) Marvel Enterprises.
—X-Men Vol. 2: The Dark Phoenix Saga. 1984. (Spiderman Ser.). (Illus.). 192p. pap. 15.95 (*0-7851-1147-6*) Marvel Enterprises.
Claremount, Chris. X-Men: Mutant Massacre. 1996. (Illus.). 256p. pap. text 24.95 (*0-7851-0224-8*) Marvel Enterprises.
Clarmont, Chris, et al. X-Men. 1989. (Marvel Masterworks Ser.: Vol. 11). 169p. 29.95 (*0-87135-597-3*) Marvel Enterprises.
Cox, Greg. Friend or Foe? X-Men & the Avengers. 2000. (Gamma Quest Trilogy Ser.: Vol. 3). 288p. (J). mass mkt. 6.99 o.s.i (*0-425-17038-1*) Berkley Publishing Group.
—Lost & Found: X-Men & the Avengers, Vol. 1. 1999. (Gamma Quest Trilogy Ser.: Vol. 1). (Illus.). 288p. (J). mass mkt. 6.99 o.s.i (*0-425-16973-1*) Berkley Publishing Group.
—Search & Rescue: X-Men & the Avengers, Vol. 2. 1999. (Gamma Quest Trilogy Ser.: Vol. 2). 288p. (J). mass mkt. 6.99 o.s.i (*0-425-16989-8*) Berkley Publishing Group.
Davis, Alan. Clandestine vs. the X-Men. 1997. (Illus.). 240p. pap. text 24.95 (*0-7851-0557-3*) Marvel Enterprises.
DeFalco, Tom. X-Men: Spider-Man Past. 1998. (X-Men Ser.: Vol. 1). 304p. mass mkt. 6.99 o.s.i (*0-425-16452-7*) Berkley Publishing Group.
DeFalco, Tom & Castro, Adam-Troy. Time's Arrow: The Present. 1998. (X-Men Ser.: Bk. II). 304p. mass mkt. 6.99 o.s.i (*0-425-16415-2*) Berkley Publishing Group.
Duane, Diane. Empire's End. 1998. (X-Men Ser.). (Illus.). 352p. reprint ed. mass mkt. 6.99 o.s.i (*0-425-16448-9*) Berkley Publishing Group.
—X-Men: Empire's End. 1997. (X-Men Ser.). (Illus.). 352p. 23.95 o.p. (*0-399-14334-3*, G. P. Putnam's Sons) Penguin Group (USA) Inc.
Fingeroth, Danny. X-Men Cartoon Adaption Pryde of the X-Men. 1990. 64p. 10.95 o.p. (*0-87135-694-5*) Marvel Enterprises.
Friedman, Michael Jan. Planet X. (Star Trek, The Next Generation Ser.). E-Book 6.99 (*0-7434-2070-5*); 1998. (Illus.). 288p. mass mkt. 6.99 (*0-671-01916-3*) Simon & Schuster. (Star Trek).
—X-Men: Shadows of the Past. (X-Men Ser.). 336p. 2004. mass mkt. 6.99 (*0-7434-8650-1*); 2000. mass mkt. 24.95 (*0-7434-0018-6*) ibooks, Inc.
Golden, Christopher. Codename Wolverine. 2000. (X-Men Ser.). (Illus.). 336p. (J). reprint ed. mass mkt. 6.99 (*0-425-17111-6*) Berkley Publishing Group.
—Mutant Empire: Salvation. 1997. (X-Men: Mutant Empire Ser.: Vol. 3). (Illus.). 276p. reprint ed. mass mkt. 6.99 o.p. (*0-425-16640-6*) Berkley Publishing Group.
—Salvation, Vol. 3. 1997. (X-Men: Mutant Empire Bk.: No. 3). 288p. (J). mass mkt. 5.99 o.s.i (*1-57297-247-5*) Boulevard Bks.
—Sanctuary No. 2, No. 1. 1996. (X-Men: Mutant Empire Bk.: Vol. 2). (YA). mass mkt. 6.99 o.p. (*1-57297-180-0*) Boulevard Bks.
—Siege, No. 1. 1996. (X-Men: Mutant Empire Bk.: Vol. 1). 352p. (YA). mass mkt. 6.50 o.s.i (*1-57297-114-2*) Boulevard Bks.

—X Men: Codename Wolverine. 1998. (X-Men Ser.). (Illus.). 304p. 24.95 o.p. (0-399-14450-1) Penguin Group (USA) Inc.
Hama, Larry. X-Men: The Origin of Generation X. 1996. (Illus.). 336p. pap. text 24.95 (0-7851-0196-9) Marvel Enterprises.
Hill, Simon. X-Men: Children of the Atom. 1998. 96p. pap. 12.99 o.p. (0-7615-0784-1, Prima Games) Random Hse. Information Group.
Kavanagh, et al. X-Men "Spotlight - Starjammers" 1990. 48p. Vol. 1. 4.50 o.p. (0-87135-658-9); Vol. 2. 4.50 o.p. (0-87135-659-7) Marvel Enterprises.
Lee, Stan. Essential Uncanny X-Men. 1999. (X-Men Ser.). (Illus.). 528p. pap. 14.95 o.p. (0-7851-0730-4, Essential Series, The) Marvel Enterprises.
—Uncanny X-Men Masterworks. 1993. (Illus.). pap. 12.95 o.p. (0-87135-964-2) Marvel Enterprises.
—The X-Men. 1998. (Masterworks Collection). (Illus.). 240p. 29.95 (0-7851-0664-2) Marvel Enterprises.
—X-Men, Vol. 3. 1994. (Masterworks Ser.). (Illus.). 224p. pap. 34.95 (0-7851-0052-0) Marvel Enterprises.
—X-Men: Legends. 2000. (X-Men Ser.). (Illus.). 272p. pap. 12.00 (0-425-17082-9) Berkley Publishing Group.
Lee, Stan, ed. The Ultimate X-Men. 1996. (X-Men Ser.). 320p. (YA). pap. 14.00 o.s.i (1-57297-217-3) Boulevard Bks.
Lee, Stan & Kirby, Jack. Marvel Masterworks: The X-Men. 1987. (Marvel Masterworks Ser.: Vol. 3). (Illus.). 232p. (YA). 34.95 (0-87135-308-3) Marvel Enterprises.
—X-Men. 1988. (Marvel Masterworks Ser.: Vol. 7). 232p. 34.95 (0-87135-482-9) Marvel Enterprises.
Lobdell, Scott. The Ultimate Astonishing X-Men. 1995. (Illus.). 96p. pap. 8.95 o.p. (0-7851-0127-6) Marvel Enterprises.
—X-Men: The Adventures of Cyclops & Phoenix. 1996. (Illus.). 96p. pap. text 12.95 (0-7851-0171-3) Marvel Enterprises.
—X-Men: Twilight of the Age of Apocalypse. 1996. 128p. pap. 8.95 (0-7851-0181-0) Marvel Enterprises.
Lobdell, Scott, et al. Wild C. A. T.s/X-Men Trade Paperback. 1998. (Illus.). 184p. pap. 19.95 (1-58240-022-9) Image Comics.
Loeb, Jeph. X-Men: Dawn of the Age Apocalypse. 1996. (Illus.). 96p. pap. 8.95 (0-7851-0180-2) Marvel Enterprises.
Lyons, Steve. X-Men: The Legacy Quest Trilogy, Book 3. 2003. (X-Men Ser.). 272p. mass mkt. 6.99 (0-7434-7519-4) ibooks, Inc.
—X-Men Bk. 1: The Legacy Quest Trilogy. 2002. (X-Men Ser.). 272p. pap. 14.00 (0-7434-4468-X) ibooks, Inc.
—X-Men Bk. 2: The Legacy Quest Trilogy. 2002. (X-Men Ser.). (Illus.). 272p. pap. 14.00 (0-7434-5243-7) ibooks, Inc.
—X-Men Bk. 3: The Legacy Quest Trilogy. 2002. (X-Men Ser.). (Illus.). 272p. pap. 14.00 (0-7434-5266-6) ibooks, Inc.
Macchio, Ralph. X-Men Adventures. (Illus.). 96p. Vol. 2. 1994. pap. 4.95 (0-7851-0028-8); Vol. III. 1994. pap. 5.95 o.p. (0-7851-0044-X); Vol. 4. 1995. pap. 4.95 o.p. (0-7851-0113-6) Marvel Enterprises.
Mackie, Howard. X-Men: Logan. 1996. (Illus.). 48p. pap. text 5.95 o.p. (0-7851-0172-1) Marvel Enterprises.
Mantell, Paul & Hart, Avery. The Brood. 1994. (X-Men Digest Novels Ser.). (Illus.). 112p. (Orig.). (J). (gr. 2 up). pap. 3.50 o.s.i (0-679-86568-3, Random Hse. Bks. for Young Readers) Random Hse. Children's Bks.
Marvel Comics Staff. X-Men, No. 3. 1996. (X-Men: The Brood Saga Ser.: Vol. 1). mass mkt. 3.99 (0-8125-4405-6, Tor Bks.) Doherty, Tom Assocs., LLC.
Marvel Entertainment Staff. The Uncanny X-Men. 1990. 128p. mass mkt. 3.99 (0-8125-1021-6, Tor Bks.) Doherty, Tom Assocs., LLC.
Marvel Staff, ed. Marvel Encyclopedia Vol. 2: X-Men. 2003. (Illus.). 240p. (YA). 29.99 (0-7851-1199-9) Marvel Enterprises.
Morrison, Grant. New X-Men, 2 vols. 2003. (New X-men Ser.). (Illus.). 288p. (YA). 29.99 (0-7851-1118-2) Marvel Enterprises.
—New X-Men: Assault on Weapon Plus, 5 vols. 2003. (New X-men Ser.). (Illus.). 168p. (YA). pap. 14.99 (0-7851-1119-0) Marvel Enterprises.
Nicieza, Fabian. The Ultimate Amazing X-Men. 1995. (Illus.). 96p. pap. 8.95 o.p. (0-7851-0126-8) Marvel Enterprises.
—X-Men: Fatal Attractions. 1994. (X-Men Ser.). (Illus.). 256p. pap. 24.95 (0-7851-0065-2) Marvel Enterprises.
—X-Men: Legion Quest. 1996. (Illus.). 112p. pap. 8.95 (0-7851-0179-9) Marvel Enterprises.
—X-Men Visionaries: The Art of Andy & Adam Kubert. 1996. (X-Men Visionaries Ser.). (Illus.). 96p. pap. text 8.95 (0-7851-0178-0) Marvel Enterprises.
Nicieza, Fabian, et al. X-Cutioner's Song. 1994. (X-Men Ser.). (Illus.). 272p. pap. 24.95 (0-7851-0025-3) Marvel Enterprises.
—X-Men - Avengers: Bloodties. 1995. (Illus.). 128p. pap. 15.95 (0-7851-0103-9) Marvel Enterprises.
Nocenti, Ann. X-Men: Prisoner X. 1998. (X-Men Ser.). (Illus.). 304p. mass mkt. 6.99 o.s.i (0-425-16493-4) Berkley Publishing Group.
Ostrander, John. X-Men vs. the Brood: Day of Wrath. 1997. (Illus.). 176p. pap. text 16.95 o.p. (0-7851-0558-1) Marvel Enterprises.
Redman, Rich. Age of Apocalypse. 2000. (X-Men Ser.). 64p. pap. 9.95 (0-7869-1664-8) Wizards of the Coast.
—X-Men: Resurrection of Cyclops. 2000. (Marvel Super Heroes Adventures Ser.). pap. 4.95 (0-7869-1665-6) Wizards of the Coast.
Roman, Steven A. X-Men/Red Skull: The Chaos Engine Trilogy, Book 3. 2003. 384p. mass mkt. 6.99 (0-7434-7958-0) ibooks, Inc.
Romita, John S., et al. X-Men: From the Ashes. 1990. (Illus.). 226p. pap. 19.95 (0-87135-615-5) Marvel Enterprises.
Running Press Staff. X-Men Postcard Book. 1995. (Illus.). 64p. text 8.95 o.p. (1-56138-584-0) Running Pr. Bk. Pubs.
Rusch, Kristine K. & Smith, Dean W. X-Men. 2000. 256p. mass mkt. 6.99 (0-345-44095-1, Del Rey) Ballantine Bks.
Rusch, Kristine K. & Smith, Dean Wesley. X-Men. novel ed. 2003. E-Book 6.99 (0-345-46490-7) Ballantine Bks.
Shahar, Eluki B. Smoke & Mirrors. 1997. (X-Men Ser.). 352p. (J). mass mkt. 6.50 o.s.i (1-57297-291-2) Boulevard Bks.
Smeds, Dave. X-Men: Law of the Jungle. 1998. (X-Men Ser.). 304p. mass mkt. 6.99 o.s.i (0-425-16486-1) Berkley Publishing Group.
—X-Men Law of the Jungle. 1998. (X-Men Ser.). mass mkt. 6.99 (1-57297-321-8) Boulevard Bks.
Smith, Dean W. The Jewels of Cyttorak. 1997. (X-Men Ser.). 304p. (J). mass mkt. 6.50 o.p. (1-57297-329-3) Boulevard Bks.
Thomas, Roy. X-Men Visionaries: The Neal Adams Collection. 1996. (Illus.). 160p. pap. 15.95 (0-7851-0198-5) Marvel Enterprises.
Torres, J. Marvel Mangaverse: X-Men Ronin, 4 vols., Vol. 4. 2003. (Marvel Mangaverse Ser.). (Illus.). 128p. (YA). (gr. 7 up). pap. 13.99 (0-7851-1115-8) Marvel Enterprises.
TSR Inc. Staff. X-Men: Who Goes There? 1998. 48p. pap. 8.95 o.p. (0-7869-1229-4) Wizards of the Coast.
—X-Men Roster. 1998. (Marvel Super Heroes Dice Game Ser.). 143p. (J). pap. 17.95 (0-7869-1228-6) Wizards of the Coast.
van Hise, James. X-Men Files. 1986. 96p. lib. bdg. 19.95 o.p. (0-8095-8086-1) Millefleurs.
X-Men - Ghost Rider: Brood Trouble in the Big Easy. 1993. 64p. 6.95 o.p. (0-87135-974-X) Marvel Enterprises.
The X-Men Adventures. 1993. 96p. 4.95 o.p. (0-7851-0006-7) Marvel Enterprises.
X-Men Index, No. 1. 1987. 48p. 2.95 o.p. (0-87135-216-8) Marvel Enterprises.
Yaco, Linc. Science of the X-Men. 2000. (Illus.). 288p. 22.95 (0-7434-0020-8) ibooks, Inc.
Yaco, Linc & Haber, Karen. Science of the X-Men. 2001. (Illus.). 288p. pap. 14.00 (0-7434-3478-1) ibooks, Inc.

**XENA (FICTITIOUS CHARACTER)—FICTION**

Cox, Greg. Battle on! An Unauthorized, Irreverent Look at Xena, Warrior Princess. 1998. 256p. pap. 11.95 o.s.i (0-451-45731-5, ROC) NAL.
Emerson, Ru. Empty Throne. 1999. (Xena, Warrior Princess Ser.). 231p. (J). mass mkt. 5.99 o.s.i (0-425-17062-4) Berkley Publishing Group.
—The Empty Throne. 1996. (Xena, Warrior Princess Ser.). 240p. mass mkt. 5.99 o.s.i (1-57297-200-9) Boulevard Bks.
—How the Quest Was Won. 2000. (Xena, Warrior Princess Ser.). 288p. mass mkt. 5.99 o.s.i (0-441-00674-4) Ace Bks.
—The Huntress & the Sphinx. 1997. (Xena, Warrior Princess Ser.: No. 2). 240p. mass mkt. 5.99 o.s.i (1-57297-215-7) Boulevard Bks.
—The Thief of Hermes. 1997. (Xena, Warrior Princess Ser.). mass mkt. 5.99 o.s.i (1-57297-232-7); mass mkt. 5.99 (1-57207-237-7) Boulevard Bks.
—Xena: The Huntress & the Sphinx. 1997. (Xena, Warrior Princess Ser.: No. 2). mass mkt. 5.99 o.s.i (0-425-16721-6) Berkley Publishing Group.
—Xena: The Thief of Hermes. 1998. (Xena Ser.). 240p. mass mkt. 5.99 o.s.i (0-425-16800-X) Berkley Publishing Group.
—Xena, Warrior Princess: Go Quest Young Man, 3, Vol. 1. 1999. (Xena, Warrior Princess Ser.). 288p. mass mkt. 5.99 o.s.i (0-441-00637-X) Ace Bks.
Harper, Ashley. The Xena Warrior Princess Internet Guide. 1999. 50p. pap. 10.00 o.p. (1-883573-22-X, Lightning Rod Limited) Windstorm Creative Ltd.
HarperPrism Staff, ed. Xena Warrior Princess: The Xena Scrolls. 1998. (Xena, Warrior Princess Ser.). 1p. pap. 13.00 o.p. (0-06-107507-8) HarperCollins Pubs.
Howard, Stella. Prophecy of Darkness. 1997. (Xena, Warrior Princess Ser.). 224p. (YA). mass mkt. 5.99 o.s.i (1-57297-249-1) Boulevard Bks.
Kreski, Chris. Life Lessons from Xena, Warrior Princess: A Guide to Happiness, Success & Body Armor. 1998. (Illus.). 112p. pap. 9.95 o.p. (0-8362-6767-2) Andrews McMeel Publishing.
Perry, S. D. Xena Warrior Princess Prophecy. 1998. (Xena, Warrior Princess Ser.). (Illus.). mass mkt. 5.99 o.s.i (0-425-17084-5) Berkley Publishing Group.
Prima Publishing Staff & Odom, Mel. Xena: Warrior Princess. 1999. (Prima's Official Strategy Guides). (Illus.). 104p. pap. 12.99 o.s.i (0-7615-2349-9, Prima Lifestyles) Crown Publishing Group.
Sherman, Josepha. Xena: All I Need to Know I Learned from the Warrior Princess. 1998. (Illus.). 144p. pap. 15.95 (0-671-02389-6, Pocket) Simon & Schuster.
van Hise, James. Hercules & Xena: The Unofficial Companion. 1998. (Illus.). 272p. pap. 15.95 o.p. (1-58063-001-4, Renaissance Bks.) St. Martin's Pr.
Wagner, John, et al. Blood & Shadows. 2001. (Xena Ser.). 96p. (YA). (gr. 5 up). pap. 11.95 (1-56971-521-1) Dark Horse Comics.
Weisbrot, Robert. Xena, Warrior Princess: The Official Guide to the Xenaverse. 1998. (Illus.). 240p. pap. 14.00 (0-385-49136-0) Doubleday Publishing.

# Y

**YABLONSKY, ALVIN (FICTITIOUS CHARACTER)—FICTION**

Trigoboff, Joseph. The Bone Orchard. l.t. ed. 1992. 20.95 o.p. (0-7927-1167-X); pap. 18.95 o.p. (0-7927-1166-1) BBC Audiobooks America.
—The Bone Orchard. 1991. 256p. mass mkt. 4.50 o.p. (0-451-17014-8, Signet Bks.) NAL.
—The Bone Orchard. 1990. 192p. 18.95 o.p. (0-8027-5758-8) Walker & Co.
—The Shooting Gallery: A Detective Yablonsky Mystery. 320p. 2004. pap. 14.95 (1-59228-143-5); 2002. 19.95 (1-58574-547-2) Globe Pequot Pr., The. (Lyons Pr.).

**YABLONSKY, BUBBLES (FICTITIOUS CHARACTER)—FICTION**

Strohmeyer, Sarah. Bubbles Ablaze: A Mystery. 2003. 256p. 23.95 (0-525-94738-8, Dutton) Dutton/Plume.
—Bubbles in Trouble. 2002. 288p. 22.95 o.s.i (0-525-94649-7, Dutton) Dutton/Plume.
—Bubbles Unbound. 2001. (Illus.). 288p. 22.95 o.s.i (0-525-94580-6, Dutton) Dutton/Plume.
—Bubbles Unbound. 2002. 352p. reprint ed. mass mkt. 6.99 (0-451-20544-8) NAL.

**YAMA (FICTITIOUS CHARACTER)—FICTION**

McAuley, Paul J. Ancients of Days. 2000. (Confluence Trilogy Ser.: Vol. 2). 416p. mass mkt. 6.99 o.s.i (0-380-79297-4, Eos) Morrow/Avon.
—Ancients of Days: The Second Book of Confluence. 1999. 400p. 16.00 o.p. (0-380-97516-5, Eos) Morrow/Avon.
—Child of the River, No. 1. 1999. 336p. mass mkt. 6.99 (0-380-79296-6, Eos) Morrow/Avon.
—Child of the River: The First Book of Confluence. 1998. 320p. 14.00 (0-380-97515-7, Eos) Morrow/Avon.
—A Shrine of Stars: The Third Book of Confluence. 2000. (Confluence Trilogy Ser.). 384p. 18.00 (0-380-97517-3, Avon Bks.) Morrow/Avon.

**YANCY, KATE (FICTITIOUS CHARACTER)—FICTION**

Adams, Deborah. All the Blood Relations. 1996. mass mkt. 5.50 o.s.i (0-345-40378-9) Ballantine Bks.
—All the Crazy Winters. 1992. (Holiday Mysteries Ser.). mass mkt. 5.50 o.s.i (0-345-37076-7, Ballantine Bks.) Ballantine Bks.
—All the Dark Disguises. 1993. mass mkt. 4.99 o.s.i (0-345-37765-6) Ballantine Bks.
—All the Deadly Beloved. 1995. mass mkt. 5.99 (0-345-39222-1); 240p. pap. 15.00 (0-345-47170-9) Ballantine Bks.
—All the Great Pretenders. 1991. (Orig.). mass mkt. 5.99 o.s.i (0-345-37075-9, Ballantine Bks.) Ballantine Bks.
—All the Hungry Mothers. 1994. (Southern Mysteries Ser.). mass mkt. 4.99 o.s.i (0-345-38552-7) Ballantine Bks.
—All the Hungry Mothers. 1999. 192p. pap. 14.95 (1-57072-122-X); reprint ed. 24.95 (1-57072-106-8) Overmountain Pr. (Silver Dagger Mysteries).

**YAR, TASHA (FICTITIOUS CHARACTER)—FICTION**

Betancourt, John Gregory. Infection Vol. 1: Double Helix. 1999. (Star Trek, The Next Generation Ser.: No. 51). (Illus.). 256p. pap. 6.50 (0-671-03255-0, Star Trek) Simon & Schuster.
Carter, Carmen. The Children of Hamlin. Stern, Dave, ed. 1990. (Star Trek, The Next Generation Ser.: No. 3). mass mkt. 5.50 o.s.i (0-671-73555-1, Star Trek) Simon & Schuster.
—The Children of Hamlin. 1989. (Star Trek, The Next Generation Ser.: No. 3). E-Book 6.99 (0-7434-1215-X, Star Trek) Simon & Schuster.
Friedman, Michael Jan. All Good Things. 1994. (Star Trek Ser.). 256p. o.p. (0-671-50014-7, Atria) Simon & Schuster.
Lorrah, Jean. Survivors. Stern, Dave, ed. 1991. (Star Trek, The Next Generation Ser.: No. 4). 256p. mass mkt. 5.50 (0-671-74290-6, Star Trek) Simon & Schuster.
—Survivors. 1989. (Star Trek, The Next Generation Ser.: No. 4). E-Book 6.99 (0-7434-1216-8, Star Trek) Simon & Schuster.

**YARBROUGH, MACLAREN (FICTITIOUS CHARACTER)—FICTION**

Sprinkle, Patricia. But Why Shoot the Magistrate? l.t. ed. 1999. (Christian Mystery Ser.). 456p. 23.95 (0-7862-2060-0) Thorndike Pr.
—But Why Shoot the Magistrate? 1998. (MacLaren Yarbrough Mysteries Ser.: Vol. 2). 320p. pap. 9.99 (0-310-21324-X) Zondervan.
—When Did We Lose Harriet? l.t. ed. 1998. (Christian Mystery Ser.). 440p. 22.95 o.p. (0-7862-1472-4) Thorndike Pr.
—When Did We Lose Harriet? 1997. (MacLaren Yarbrough Mysteries Ser.). 304p. pap. 19.99 (0-310-21294-4) Zondervan.
—Who Invited the Dead Man? l.t. ed. 2002. pap. 23.95 (1-58724-349-0, Wheeler Publishing, Inc.) Gale Group.
—Who Invited the Dead Man? 2002. 272p. mass mkt. 5.99 (0-451-20659-2) NAL.
—Who Let That Killer in the House? 2003. 272p. mass mkt. 5.99 (0-451-21019-0, Signet Bks.) NAL.

**YATES, GIL (FICTITIOUS CHARACTER)—FICTION**

Boyle, Alistair. Bluebeard's Last Stand: A Gil Yates Private Investigator Novel. 1998. (Gil Yates Private Investigator Ser.). 155p. 20.00 (1-888310-45-6) Knoll, Allen A. Pubs.
—The Con: A Gil Yates Private Investigator Novel. 1996. 222p. 19.95 (0-9627297-9-5) Knoll, Allen A. Pubs.
—The Missing Link: A Gil Yates Private Investigator Novel. 1995. 224p. 19.95 (0-9627297-3-6) Knoll, Allen A. Pubs.
—Ship Shapely: A Gil Yates Private Investigator Novel. 1999. 228p. 20.00 (1-888310-99-5) Knoll, Allen A. Pubs.
—The Unholy Ghost: A Gil Yates Private Investigator Novel. 2003. (Gil Yates Private Investigator Ser.: 7). 271p. 23.00 (1-888310-67-7) Knoll, Allen A. Pubs.
—The Unlucky Seven: A Gil Yates Private Investigator Novel. 1997. 176p. 20.00 (1-888310-77-4) Knoll, Allen A. Pubs.
—What Now, King Lear? A Gil Yates Private Investigator Novel. 2001. (Gil Yates Private Investigator Ser.: Vol. 6). 247p. 22.00 (1-888310-85-5) Knoll, Allen A. Pubs.

**YEADINGS, MIKE (FICTITIOUS CHARACTER)—FICTION**

Curzon, Clare. All Unwary. (0-7540-3467-4); 1999. 340p. pap. (0-7540-3468-2) BBC Audiobooks America.
—All Unwary. 1998. (Thames Valley Mystery Ser.). 256p. 21.95 o.p. (0-312-18037-3, Saint Martin's Minotaur) St. Martin's Pr.
—All Unwary. l.t. ed. 1999. (General Ser.). 352p. pap. 23.95 (0-7862-1544-5) Thorndike Pr.
—The Blue-Eyed Boy. 1991. 192p. 14.95 o.s.i (0-385-41668-7) Doubleday Publishing.
—The Blue-Eyed Boy. l.t. ed. 1992. (Ulverscroft Large Print Ser.). 416p. 29.99 o.p. (0-7089-2585-5, Ulverscroft) Thorpe, F. A. Pubs. GBR. *Dist:* Ulverscroft Large Print Bks., Ltd., Ulverscroft Large Print Canada, Ltd.
—Cat's Cradle. 1994. (WWL Mystery Ser.). per. (0-373-26151-9, 1-26151-0, Harlequin Bks.) Harlequin Enterprises, Ltd.
—Cat's Cradle. 1992. 224p. 17.95 o.p. (0-312-07664-9, Saint Martin's Minotaur) St. Martin's Pr.
—Close Quarters: A Thames Valley Mystery. l.t. ed. 1997. 357p. lib. bdg. 21.95 (0-7838-8214-9, Macmillan Reference USA) Gale Group.
—Close Quarters: A Thames Valley Mystery. l.t. ed. 1998. 256p. per. (0-373-26292-2, 1-26292-2, Worldwide Library) Harlequin Enterprises, Ltd.

Characters

—Close Quarters: A Thames Valley Mystery. l.t. ed. 1996. 192p. 20.95 (*0-312-15079-2*, Saint Martin's Minotaur) St. Martin's Pr.
—Cold Hands. 218p. 26.00 o.p. (*0-7278-5462-3*) Severn Hse. Pubs., Ltd.
—Cold Hands. l.t. ed. 2001. (Ulverscroft Large Print Ser.). 376p. 31.99 (*0-7089-4329-2*) Thorpe, F. A. Pubs. GBR. *Dist:* Ulverscroft Large Print Bks., Ltd., Ulverscroft Large Print Canada, Ltd.
—Cold Hands: A Mike Yeadings Mystery. 2001. 256p. 22.95 (*0-312-20464-7*, Saint Martin's Minotaur) St. Martin's Pr.
—Death Prone. 1995. (Mystery Ser.). 251p. per. (*0-373-26189-6*, 1-26189-0, Worldwide Library) Harlequin Enterprises, Ltd.
—Death Prone. 1994. 224p. 19.95 o.p. (*0-312-10453-7*, Saint Martin's Minotaur) St. Martin's Pr.
—Don't Leave Me. 2003. 256p. mass mkt. (*0-373-26469-0*) Harlequin Enterprises, Ltd.
—Don't Leave Me. 2001. 256p. (*0-7278-5718-5*) Severn Hse. Pubs., Ltd.
—Don't Leave Me: A Superintendent Mike Yeadings Mystery. 2002. 224p. 22.95 (*0-312-28678-3*, Saint Martin's Minotaur) St. Martin's Pr.
—First Wife, Twice Removed. 1995. (WWL Mystery Ser.). per. (*0-373-26168-3*, 1-26168-4, Harlequin Bks.) Harlequin Enterprises, Ltd.
—First Wife, Twice Removed. 1993. (Thames Valley Mystery Ser.). 224p. 17.95 o.p. (*0-312-09289-X*, Saint Martin's Minotaur) St. Martin's Pr.
—Guilty Knowledge. 2000. 256p. 23.95 (*0-312-26169-1*, Saint Martin's Minotaur) St. Martin's Pr.
—Nice People. 1995. 246p. 20.95 o.p. (*0-312-13132-1*, Saint Martin's Minotaur) St. Martin's Pr.
—Past Mischief. 1997. per. (*0-373-26256-6*, 1-26256-7, Worldwide Library) Harlequin Enterprises, Ltd.
—Past Mischief. 1995. 280p. mass mkt. o.s.i (*0-7515-1301-6*) Little Brown & Co.
—Past Mischief. 1996. 224p. text 21.95 o.p. (*0-312-14388-5*, Saint Martin's Minotaur) St. Martin's Pr.
—Three-Core Lead. 1990. 14.95 o.s.i (*0-385-41139-1*) Doubleday Publishing.
—Three-Core Lead. l.t. ed. 1992. (Lythway Ser.). 308p. 15.95 o.p. (*0-7451-1615-9*, Macmillan Reference USA) Gale Group.
—Trojan Hearse. l.t. ed. 1986. lib. bdg. 14.95 o.p. (*0-7451-0318-9*, Macmillan Reference USA) Gale Group.

### YEARMAN, DOLLY (FICTITIOUS CHARACTER)—FICTION

Rendell, Ruth. The Killing Doll. 1985. 288p. mass mkt. 4.95 o.s.i (*0-345-31199-X*) Ballantine Bks.
—The Killing Doll. l.t. ed. 1984. (General Ser.). 354p. 15.95 o.p. (*0-8161-3720-X*, Macmillan Reference USA) Gale Group.
—The Killing Doll. 1984. 258p. 12.95 o.s.i (*0-394-53097-7*, Pantheon) Knopf Publishing Group.

### YODER, MAGDALENA (FICTITIOUS CHARACTER)—FICTION

Myers, Tamar. Between a Wok & a Hard Place. 1998. (Magdalena Yoda Ser.: Vol. 5). 272p. mass mkt. 5.99 (*0-451-19230-3*, Signet Bks.) NAL.
—Between a Wok & a Hard Place. l.t. ed. 2002. (Mystery Ser.). 373p. 29.45 (*0-7862-4640-5*) Thorndike Pr.
—The Crepes of Wrath: A Pennsylvania Dutch Mystery with Recipes. 2001. (Pennsylvania Dutch Mystery with Recipes Ser.). 240p. 19.99 o.s.i (*0-451-20225-2*) NAL.
—The Crepes of Wrath: A Pennsylvania Dutch Mystery with Recipes. l.t. ed. 2001. 415p. 28.95 (*0-7862-3673-6*) Thorndike Pr.
—Custard's Last Stand. 2004. 240p. mass mkt. 5.99 (*0-451-20848-X*, Signet Bks.) NAL.
—Custard's Last Stand: A Pennsylvania Dutch Mystery with Recipes. 2003. 240p. 19.95 (*0-451-20782-3*) NAL.
—Eat, Drink & Be Wary: A Pennsylvania Dutch Mystery with Recipes. 1998. (PennDutch Mysteries Ser.). 272p. mass mkt. 5.99 (*0-451-19231-1*, Signet Bks.) NAL.
—Eat, Drink, & Be Wary: A Pennsylvania Dutch Mystery with Recipes. l.t. ed. 2001. 384p. 28.95 o.p. (*0-7862-3455-5*) Thorndike Pr.
—Hand That Rocks the Ladle. 2000. (Pennsylvania Dutch Mystery with Recipes Ser.). 272p. mass mkt. 5.99 (*0-451-19755-0*, Signet Bks.) NAL.
—Just Plain Pickled. 1997. 272p. mass mkt. 5.99 (*0-451-19293-1*, Signet Bks.) NAL.
—No Use Dying over Spilled Milk: A Pennsylvania-Dutch Mystery with Recipes. 1996. 272p. 20.95 o.p. (*0-525-94099-5*, Dutton) Dutton/Plume.
—No Use Dying over Spilled Milk: A Pennsylvania-Dutch Mystery with Recipes. 1997. 272p. mass mkt. 5.99 (*0-451-18854-3*, Signet Bks.) NAL.
—Parsley, Sage, Rosemary & Crime. 1996. (PennDutch Inn Mystery Ser.). 272p. mass mkt. 5.99 (*0-451-18297-9*, Signet Bks.) NAL.
—Play It Again Spam. 1999. (Pennsylvania Dutch Mystery with Recipes Ser.). 272p. mass mkt. 5.99 (*0-451-19754-2*, Signet Bks.) NAL.
—Thou Shalt Not Grill. 2004. 240p. 19.95 (*0-451-21113-8*) NAL.
—Too Many Crooks Spoil the Broth. 1995. (PennDutch Inn Mystery Ser.). 256p. mass mkt. 5.99 (*0-451-18296-0*, Signet Bks.) NAL.
—Too Many Crooks Spoil the Broth: A Pennsylvania-Dutch Mystery with Recipes. 1993. 256p. 17.00 o.s.i (*0-385-47139-4*) Doubleday Publishing.

### YORK, ALAN (FICTITIOUS CHARACTER)—FICTION

Francis, Dick. Dead Cert. 1987. mass mkt. 6.99 o.s.i (*0-449-21263-7*, Fawcett) Ballantine Bks.
—Dead Cert. 288p. 2004. mass mkt. 6.99 (*0-425-19497-3*); 2000. mass mkt. 6.99 (*0-515-12726-4*, Jove) Berkley Publishing Group.
—Dead Cert. unabr. ed. 1994. audio 48.00 (*0-7366-2721-9*, 3451) Books on Tape, Inc.
—Dead Cert. unabr. ed. 2000. audio 49.95 (*0-7451-6828-0*, CAB 437) Chivers Audio Bks. GBR. *Dist:* BBC Audiobooks America.
—Dead Cert. l.t. ed. 1994. 365p. 22.95 (*0-8161-5784-7*, Macmillan Reference USA) Gale Group.
—Dead Cert. Barzun, Jacques & Taylor, W. H., eds. 1983. (Crime Fiction 1950-1975 Ser.). 220p. lib. bdg. 18.00 o.p. (*0-8240-4991-8*) Garland Publishing, Inc.
—Dead Cert. 1990. audio 15.95; audio 16.00 o.s.i (*1-55994-142-1*, CPN 2139) HarperTrade. (Harper-Audio).
—Dead Cert; Nerve; For Kicks. 1996. mass mkt. 7.99 o.s.i (*0-449-28768-8*, Fawcett) Ballantine Bks.

### YOUNGER, CECIL (FICTITIOUS CHARACTER)—FICTION

Straley, John. The Angels Will Not Care. 2000. 256p. mass mkt. 5.99 (*0-553-58064-7*); 1998. 240p. 22.95 o.s.i (*0-553-10642-2*) Bantam Bks.
—Cold Water Burning. 2001. 224p. mass mkt. 6.50 (*0-553-58076-0*); 208p. 23.95 o.s.i (*0-553-10643-0*) Bantam Bks.
—Curious Eat Themselves: An Alaskan Mystery. 1993. 264p. 19.95 (*0-939149-94-X*) Soho Pr., Inc.
—The Curious Eat Themselves: An Alaskan Mystery. 1995. 240p. mass mkt. 5.99 (*0-553-56805-1*, Crimeline) Bantam Bks.
—The Music of What Happens. 1997. 272p. mass mkt. 5.99 (*0-553-57205-9*, Crimeline) Bantam Bks.
—The Woman Who Married a Bear: An Alaskan Mystery. 1994. 240p. mass mkt. 5.99 o.s.i (*0-451-40421-1*, Signet Bks.) NAL.
—The Woman Who Married a Bear: An Alaskan Mystery. 1992. 240p. 19.95 o.p. (*0-939149-64-8*) Soho Pr., Inc.

### YUM YUM (FICTITIOUS CHARACTER: BRAUN)—FICTION

Braun, Lilian Jackson. The Cat Who Ate Danish Modern. 1986. (Cat Who Ser.). 192p. mass mkt. 6.99 (*0-515-08712-2*, Jove) Berkley Publishing Group.
—The Cat Who Ate Danish Modern. 1989. (Black Dagger Crime Ser.). 200p. reprint ed. text 12.95 o.p. (*0-86220-755-X*) Chivers Pr. GBR. *Dist:* BBC Audiobooks America.
—The Cat Who Ate Danish Modern. l.t. ed. 1990. (Nightingale Ser.). 274p. 14.95 o.p. (*0-8161-4914-3*, Macmillan Reference USA) Gale Group.
—The Cat Who Ate Danish Modern. unabr. ed. 1990. (Cat Who Ser.). audio 35.00 (*1-55690-090-2*, 90081E7) Recorded Bks., LLC.
—The Cat Who Ate Danish Modern. 1986. 13.04 (*0-606-13246-5*) Turtleback Bks.
—The Cat Who Blew the Whistle. 1996. (Cat Who Ser.). 320p. mass mkt. 6.99 (*0-515-11824-9*, Jove) Berkley Publishing Group.
—The Cat Who Blew the Whistle. abr. ed. 1995. (J). audio 17.95 o.p. (*0-7871-0229-6*, 393238) NewStar Media, Inc.
—The Cat Who Blew the Whistle. 1995. 240p. 21.95 o.p. (*0-399-13981-8*, G. P. Putnam's Sons) Penguin Group (USA) Inc.
—The Cat Who Blew the Whistle. l.t. ed. (Paperback Bestsellers Ser.). 270p. 1996. lib. bdg. 18.95 (*0-7838-1253-1*); 1995. lib. bdg. 24.95 (*0-7838-1252-3*) Thorndike Pr.
—The Cat Who Blew the Whistle. 1996. 13.04 (*0-606-12643-0*) Turtleback Bks.
—The Cat Who Brought down the House. 2003. 256p. mass mkt. 6.99 (*0-515-13655-7*, Jove) Berkley Publishing Group.
—The Cat Who Brought down the House. 2003. 240p. 23.95 (*0-399-14942-2*); audio 24.95 (*0-399-14993-7*, Putnam Berkley Audio) Putnam Publishing Group, The.
—The Cat Who Brought down the House. 2003. 299p. 32.95 (*0-7862-5036-4*); 2004. 304p. pap. 13.95 (*1-59413-011-6*, Large Print Pr.) Thorndike Pr.
—The Cat Who Came to Breakfast. 1995. (Cat Who Ser.). 272p. (J). pap. 6.99 (*0-515-11564-9*, Jove) Berkley Publishing Group.
—The Cat Who Came to Breakfast. l.t. ed. 296p. 1995. 17.95 o.p. (*0-8161-5935-1*); 1994. lib. bdg. 23.95 o.p. (*0-8161-5934-3*) Gale Group. (Macmillan Reference USA).
—The Cat Who Came to Breakfast. abr. ed. 1993. audio 16.95 o.p. (*1-55800-937-X*, 393255, Dove Audio) NewStar Media, Inc.
—The Cat Who Came to Breakfast. 1994. 240p. 19.95 o.p. (*0-399-13868-4*, G. P. Putnam's Sons) Penguin Group (USA) Inc.
—The Cat Who Came to Breakfast. 1995. 13.04 (*0-606-12644-9*) Turtleback Bks.
—The Cat Who Had 14 Tales. 1988. (Cat Who Ser.). 256p. mass mkt. 6.99 (*0-515-09497-8*, Jove) Berkley Publishing Group.
—The Cat Who Had 14 Tales. l.t. ed. 1991. (Nightingale Ser.). 241p. 14.95 o.p. (*0-8161-4915-1*, Macmillan Reference USA) Gale Group.
—The Cat Who Had 14 Tales. unabr. ed. 2000. (Cat Who Ser.). (J). audio 35.00 (*0-7887-0312-9*, 94504E7) Recorded Bks., LLC.
—The Cat Who Had 14 Tales. 1988. 13.04 (*0-606-13247-3*) Turtleback Bks.
—The Cat Who Knew a Cardinal. 1992. (Cat Who Ser.). 288p. mass mkt. 6.99 (*0-515-10786-7*, Jove) Berkley Publishing Group.
—The Cat Who Knew a Cardinal. l.t. ed. 1992. (General Ser.). 316p. 18.95 (*0-8161-5279-9*); lib. bdg. 19.95 o.p. (*0-8161-5278-0*) Gale Group. (Macmillan Reference USA).
—The Cat Who Knew a Cardinal. abr. ed. 1993. 15.95 o.p. (*1-55800-444-0*, 390492) NewStar Media, Inc.
—The Cat Who Knew a Cardinal. 1991. (Cat Who Ser.). 240p. 16.95 o.p. (*0-399-13664-9*, G. P. Putnam's Sons) Penguin Group (USA) Inc.
—The Cat Who Knew a Cardinal. 1992. 13.04 (*0-606-12645-7*) Turtleback Bks.
—The Cat Who Knew a Cardinal; The Cat Who Moved a Mountain; The Cat Who Wasn't There. unabr. ed. 1993. audio 19.95 o.p. (*1-55800-782-2*) NewStar Media, Inc.
—The Cat Who Knew Shakespeare. 1988. (Cat Who Ser.). 256p. mass mkt. 6.99 (*0-515-09582-6*, Jove) Berkley Publishing Group.
—The Cat Who Knew Shakespeare. l.t. ed. 1989. 284p. 12.95 o.p. (*0-8161-4790-6*, Macmillan Reference USA) Gale Group.
—The Cat Who Knew Shakespeare. unabr. ed. 1991. (Cat Who Ser.). (YA). (gr. 10 up). audio 24.95 (*1-55690-092-9*, 91115E7) Recorded Bks., LLC.
—The Cat Who Knew Shakespeare. 1991. 13.04 (*0-606-13248-1*) Turtleback Bks.
—The Cat Who Lived High. 1991. (Cat Who Ser.). 304p. mass mkt. 6.99 (*0-515-10566-X*, Jove) Berkley Publishing Group.
—The Cat Who Lived High. l.t. ed. 1991. lib. bdg. 19.95 o.p. (*0-8161-5126-1*, Macmillan Reference USA) Gale Group.
—The Cat Who Lived High. 1990. 240p. 17.95 o.p. (*0-399-13554-5*, G. P. Putnam's Sons) Penguin Putnam Bks. for Young Readers.
—The Cat Who Lived High. unabr. ed. 1994. (Cat Who Ser.: No. 11). audio 32.95 (*1-55690-992-6*, 94131) Recorded Bks., LLC.
—The Cat Who Lived High. 1991. 13.04 (*0-606-12646-5*) Turtleback Bks.
—The Cat Who Moved a Mountain. 1992. (Cat Who Ser.). 272p. mass mkt. 6.99 (*0-515-10950-9*, Jove) Berkley Publishing Group.
—The Cat Who Moved a Mountain. l.t. ed. 1993. (General Ser.). 379p. 18.95 o.p. (*0-8161-5551-8*); 20.95 o.p. (*0-8161-5550-X*) Gale Group. (Macmillan Reference USA).
—The Cat Who Moved a Mountain. abr. ed. 1993. 15.95 o.p. (*1-55800-470-X*, 390493) NewStar Media, Inc.
—The Cat Who Moved a Mountain. 1992. (Cat Who Ser.). 240p. 18.95 o.p. (*0-399-13646-0*, G. P. Putnam's Sons) Penguin Group (USA) Inc.
—The Cat Who Moved a Mountain. 1992. 13.04 (*0-606-12647-3*) Turtleback Bks.
—The Cat Who Played Brahms. l.t. ed. 1990. 18.95 o.p. (*0-7927-0335-9*, C0029); pap. 16.95 o.p. (*0-7927-0345-6*) BBC Audiobooks America.
—The Cat Who Played Brahms. 1987. (Cat Who Ser.). 256p. mass mkt. 6.99 (*0-515-09050-6*, Jove) Berkley Publishing Group.
—The Cat Who Played Brahms. unabr. ed. 1992. (Cat Who Ser.). audio 24.95 (*1-55690-651-X*, 92133) Recorded Bks., LLC.
—The Cat Who Played Brahms. 1990. 13.04 (*0-606-13249-X*) Turtleback Bks.
—The Cat Who Played Post Office. 1987. (Cat Who Ser.). 272p. pap. 6.99 (*0-515-09320-3*, Jove) Berkley Publishing Group.
—The Cat Who Played Post Office. l.t. ed. 2000. (Wheeler Large Print Book Ser.). (Illus.). 230p. 27.95 o.p. (*1-56895-840-4*, Wheeler Publishing, Inc.) Gale Group.
—The Cat Who Played Post Office. unabr. ed. 2001. audio 24.95 (*0-7887-5432-7*); 2000. audio 24.95 (*1-55690-689-7*, 92343) Recorded Bks., LLC.
—The Cat Who Played Post Office. 1987. 13.04 (*0-606-13250-3*) Turtleback Bks.
—The Cat Who Robbed a Bank. 2001. (Cat Who Ser.). 304p. mass mkt. 6.99 (*0-515-12994-1*, Jove) Berkley Publishing Group.
—The Cat Who Robbed a Bank. l.t. ed. 2000. pap. 22.95 o.p. (*0-7838-8710-8*, Macmillan Reference USA) Gale Group.
—The Cat Who Robbed a Bank. 2000. (Cat Who Ser.). 256p. 23.95 o.p. (*0-399-14570-2*) Penguin Group (USA) Inc.
—The Cat Who Robbed a Bank, No. 2. abr. ed. 2000. (Cat Who Ser.: Vol. 22). 3p. 17.95 o.s.i (*0-399-14582-6*, Putnam Berkley Audio) Putnam Publishing Group, The.
—The Cat Who Robbed a Bank. l.t. ed. 2000. 400p. 23.95 (*0-375-40878-9*) Random Hse. Large Print.
—The Cat Who Robbed a Bank. unabr. ed. 1999. (Cat Who Ser.). audio 29.95 (*0-7887-4032-6*, 96010 ) Recorded Bks., LLC.
—The Cat Who Said Cheese. 1997. (Cat Who Ser.). 272p. reprint ed. pap. 6.99 (*0-515-12027-8*, Jove) Berkley Publishing Group.
—The Cat Who Said Cheese. l.t. ed. 1997. pap. 23.95 o.p. (*0-7838-1632-4*, Macmillan Reference USA) Gale Group.
—The Cat Who Said Cheese. abr. ed. 1996. 17.95 o.p. (*0-7871-0610-0*) NewStar Media, Inc.
—The Cat Who Said Cheese. 1996. (Cat Who Ser.). (*0-399-19300-6*); 256p. 22.95 o.p. (*0-399-14075-1*, G. P. Putnam's Sons) Penguin Group (USA) Inc.
—The Cat Who Said Cheese. l.t. ed. 1996. (Core Collection). 303p. 27.95 (*0-7838-1631-6*) Thorndike Pr.
—The Cat Who Said Cheese. 1997. 13.04 (*0-606-12648-1*) Turtleback Bks.
—The Cat Who Sang for the Birds. 1999. (Cat Who Ser.). (Illus.). 272p. reprint ed. mass mkt. 6.99 (*0-515-12463-X*, Jove) Berkley Publishing Group.
—The Cat Who Sang for the Birds. l.t. ed. 1998. 26.95 o.p. (*1-56895-555-3*, Wheeler Publishing, Inc.) Gale Group.
—The Cat Who Sang for the Birds. 1998. (Cat Who. . . Ser.). 256p. (YA). 22.95 o.p. (*0-399-14333-5*, G. P. Putnam's Sons);Set. 3p. (J). 17.95 o.s.i (*0-399-14350-5*, 395411, Putnam Berkley Audio) Penguin Group (USA) Inc.
—The Cat Who Sang for the Birds. unabr. ed. (Cat Who Ser.). 1999. audio compact disk 54.00 (*0-7887-3428-8*, C1034E7); 1998. audio 32.95 (*0-7887-1971-8*, 95358) Recorded Bks., LLC.
—The Cat Who Saw Red. 1986. (Cat Who Ser.). 256p. mass mkt. 6.99 (*0-515-09016-6*); mass mkt. 2.95 o.s.i (*0-515-08491-3*) Berkley Publishing Group. (Jove).
—The Cat Who Saw Red. l.t. ed. 1989. 13.95 o.p. (*0-8161-4388-9*, Macmillan Reference USA) Gale Group.
—The Cat Who Saw Red. unabr. ed. 1990. (Cat Who Ser.). (YA). (gr. 10 up). audio 35.00 (*1-55690-093-7*, 90083E7) Recorded Bks., LLC.
—The Cat Who Saw Red. 1986. 13.04 (*0-606-13251-1*) Turtleback Bks.
—The Cat Who Saw Stars. 2000. (Cat Who Ser.). 304p. reprint ed. mass mkt. 6.99 (*0-515-12739-6*, Jove) Berkley Publishing Group.
—The Cat Who Saw Stars. l.t. ed. 2000. 11.95 (*1-56895-980-X*); 1999. 27.95 (*1-56895-595-2*) Gale Group. (Wheeler Publishing, Inc.).
—The Cat Who Saw Stars, abr. ed. 1999. audio 17.95 Highsmith Inc.
—The Cat Who Saw Stars. 1999. (Cat Who. . . Ser.). 240p. 22.95 o.p. (*0-399-14431-5*); 17.95 o.p. (*0-399-14455-2*, 393651, Putnam Berkley Audio) Penguin Group (USA) Inc.
—The Cat Who Saw Stars. unabr. ed. (Cat Who Ser.: Vol. 21). 2001. audio compact disk 38.00 (*0-7887-3971-9*, C1090E7); 1999. audio 32.95 (*0-7887-2913-6*, 95706 ) Recorded Bks., LLC.
—The Cat Who Smelled a Rat. 2002. (Cat Who Ser.). 304p. reprint ed. mass mkt. 6.99 (*0-515-13226-8*, Jove) Berkley Publishing Group.
—The Cat Who Smelled a Rat. 2001. (Cat Who. . . Ser.). (Illus.). 256p. 23.95 o.s.i (*0-399-14665-2*, G. P. Putnam's Sons) Penguin Group (USA) Inc.
—The Cat Who Smelled a Rat. abr. ed. 2001. (Cat Who Ser.). audio 17.95 o.s.i (*0-399-14681-4*, Putnam Berkley Audio) Putnam Publishing Group, The.
—The Cat Who Smelled a Rat. unabr. ed. 2001. audio 29.95 (*0-7887-4977-3*, 964417); audio compact disk 48.00 Recorded Bks., LLC.
—The Cat Who Smelled a Rat. l.t. ed. 293p. 2002. pap. 29.95 (*0-7862-2823-7*); 2001. 32.95 (*0-7862-2822-9*) Thorndike Pr.
—The Cat Who Sniffed Glue. 1989. (Cat Who Ser.). 288p. mass mkt. 6.99 (*0-515-09954-6*, Jove) Berkley Publishing Group.
—The Cat Who Sniffed Glue. l.t. ed. 1990. (Nightingale Ser.). 312p. 13.95 o.p. (*0-8161-4864-3*, Macmillan Reference USA) Gale Group.

—The Cat Who Sniffed Glue. 1988. (Cat Who. . . Ser.). 192p. 14.95 o.p. (*0-399-13381-X*, G. P. Putnam's Sons) Penguin Putnam Bks. for Young Readers.
—The Cat Who Sniffed Glue. unabr. ed. 2000. audio 44.00 (*1-55690-837-7*, 93205E7) Recorded Bks., LLC.
—The Cat Who Sniffed Glue. 1989. 13.04 (*0-606-13252-X*) Turtleback Bks.
—The Cat Who Tailed a Thief. 1998. (Cat Who. . . Ser.). 272p. mass mkt. 6.99 (*0-515-12240-8*, Jove) Berkley Publishing Group.
—The Cat Who Tailed a Thief. l.t. ed. 1997. 293p. 27.95 o.p. (*0-7838-8046-4*, Macmillan Reference USA) Gale Group.
—The Cat Who Tailed a Thief. abr. ed. 1997. 17.95 o.p. (*0-7871-1352-2*, 394616) NewStar Media, Inc.
—The Cat Who Tailed a Thief. 1997. (Cat Who. . . Ser.). 256p. 22.95 o.p. (*0-399-14210-X*, G. P. Putnam's Sons) Penguin Group (USA) Inc.
—The Cat Who Tailed a Thief. l.t. ed. 1998. (Paperback Bestsellers Ser.). 293p. pap. 27.95 (*0-7838-8047-2*) Thorndike Pr.
—The Cat Who Tailed a Thief. 1998. 13.04 (*0-606-13253-8*) Turtleback Bks.
—The Cat Who Talked to Ghosts. 1990. (Cat Who Ser.). 288p. pap. 6.99 (*0-515-10265-2*, Jove) Berkley Publishing Group.
—The Cat Who Talked to Ghosts. l.t. ed. 1991. (General Ser.). 300p. 21.95 (*0-8161-5081-8*, Macmillan Reference USA) Gale Group.
—The Cat Who Talked to Ghosts. 1990. 224p. 15.95 o.p. (*0-399-13477-8*, G. P. Putnam's Sons) Penguin Putnam Bks. for Young Readers.
—The Cat Who Talked to Ghosts. unabr. ed. 1994. (Cat Who Ser.). audio 32.95 (*0-7887-0050-2*, 94249E7) Recorded Bks., LLC.
—The Cat Who Talked to Ghosts. 1990. 13.04 (*0-606-13254-6*) Turtleback Bks.
—The Cat Who Talked Turkey. 2003. 288p. 23.95 (*0-399-15107-9*) Putnam Publishing Group, The.
—The Cat Who Turned on & Off. 1986. (Cat Who Ser.). 272p. mass mkt. 6.99 (*0-515-08794-7*, Jove) Berkley Publishing Group.
—The Cat Who Turned on & Off. l.t. ed. 1992. (Nightingale Ser.). 285p. 14.95 o.p. (*0-8161-4815-5*, Macmillan Reference USA) Gale Group.
—The Cat Who Turned on & Off. unabr. ed. 1991. (Cat Who Ser.). audio 44.00 (*1-55690-094-5*, 91402E7) Recorded Bks., LLC.
—The Cat Who Turned on & Off. 1986. 11.60 o.p. (*0-606-13255-4*) Turtleback Bks.
—The Cat Who Wasn't There. 1993. (Cat Who Ser.). 288p. mass mkt. 6.99 (*0-515-11127-9*, Jove) Berkley Publishing Group.
—The Cat Who Wasn't There. l.t. ed. 1993. (General Ser.). 367p. 17.95 o.p. (*0-8161-5694-8*); lib. bdg. 21.95 (*0-8161-5693-X*) Gale Group. (Macmillan Reference USA).
—The Cat Who Wasn't There. abr. ed. (Super Sound Buy, Dove Ser.). 1994. audio 8.99 o.p. (*0-7871-0071-4*, 390494, Dove Audio); 1993. 16.95 o.p. (*1-55800-667-2*) NewStar Media, Inc.
—The Cat Who Wasn't There. 1992. 240p. 18.95 o.p. (*0-399-13780-7*, G. P. Putnam's Sons) Penguin Group (USA) Inc.
—The Cat Who Wasn't There. 1993. 13.04 (*0-606-12649-X*) Turtleback Bks.
—The Cat Who Wasn't There; The Cat Who Blew the Whistle. abr. ed. 1999. audio 25.00 (*0-7871-1901-6*, Dove Audio) NewStar Media, Inc.
—The Cat Who Went into the Closet. 1994. (Cat Who Ser.). 288p. mass mkt. 6.99 (*0-515-11332-8*, Jove) Berkley Publishing Group.
—The Cat Who Went into the Closet. l.t. ed. 1993. 24.95 o.p. (*1-56895-050-0*, Wheeler Publishing, Inc.) Gale Group.
—The Cat Who Went into the Closet. abr. ed. 1993. (Jim Qwilleran Mystery Ser.). audio 16.95 o.p. (*1-55800-785-7*, 390495) NewStar Media, Inc.
—The Cat Who Went into the Closet. 1993. (Cat Who Ser.). 240p. 19.95 o.p. (*0-399-13830-7*, G. P. Putnam's Sons) Penguin Group (USA) Inc.
—The Cat Who Went into the Closet. 5.98 o.p. (*0-8317-5327-7*) Smithmark Pubs., Inc.
—The Cat Who Went into the Closet. 1994. 13.04 (*0-606-13256-2*) Turtleback Bks.
—The Cat Who Went Underground. 1989. (Cat Who Ser.). 288p. mass mkt. 6.99 (*0-515-10123-0*, Jove) Berkley Publishing Group.
—The Cat Who Went Underground. l.t. ed. 1990. (General Ser.). 324p. 19.95 o.p. (*0-8161-4941-0*, Macmillan Reference USA) Gale Group.
—The Cat Who Went Underground. 1989. (Cat Who. . . Ser.). 224p. 14.95 o.p. (*0-399-13431-X*, G. P. Putnam's Sons) Penguin Putnam Bks. for Young Readers.
—The Cat Who Went Underground. unabr. ed. 2000. (Cat Who Ser.). audio 32.95 (*1-55690-803-2*, 93112) Recorded Bks., LLC.
—The Cat Who Went Underground. 1989. 13.04 (*0-606-13257-0*) Turtleback Bks.
—The Cat Who Went up the Creek. 2002. 240p. 23.95 o.s.i (*0-399-14675-X*) Penguin Group (USA) Inc.
—The Cat Who Went up the Creek. abr. ed. 2002. audio 17.95 o.s.i (*0-399-14819-1*, Putnam Berkley Audio) Putnam Publishing Group, The.
—The Private Life of the Cat Who... Tales of Koko & Yum Yum from the Journal of James Macintosh Quilleran. l.t. ed. 2003. 109p. 32.95 (*0-7862-5692-3*) Thorndike Pr.
—The Private Life of the Cat Who... Tales of Koko & Yum Yum from the Journals of James Mackintosh Qwilleran. 2003. 144p. 10.95 (*0-399-15132-X*, Putnam & Grosset) Putnam Publishing Group, The.
—Three Complete Novels. 2002. 803p. 14.98 (*0-399-14813-2*) Penguin Group (USA) Inc.

## Z

### ZARKON, LORD OF THE UNKNOWN (FICTITIOUS CHARACTER)—FICTION

Carter, Lin. Invisible Death. 1975. 173p. 25.00 (*0-385-08768-3*) Ultramarine Publishing Co., Inc.
—Invisible Death. 1999. (Zarkon, Lord of the Unknown Ser.). 192p. pap. 14.00 (*1-58715-058-1*) Wildside Pr.
—Nemesis of Evil. 1999. (Zarkon, Lord of the Unknown Ser.: Vol. 1). 219p. pap. 14.00 (*1-58715-057-3*) Wildside Pr.

### ZEN, AURELIO (FICTITIOUS CHARACTER)—FICTION

Dibdin, Michael. And Then You Die. (Aurelio Zen Mystery Ser.). 192p. 2003. pap. 12.00 (*0-375-71925-3*, Vintage); 2002. 21.00 (*0-375-42188-2*, Pantheon) Knopf Publishing Group.
—Blood Rain. unabr. ed. 2000. (Aurelio Zen Mystery Ser.). 8p. audio 69.95 (*0-7540-0463-5*, CAB 1886, Sterling Audio Bks.) BBC Audiobooks America.
—Blood Rain. unabr. ed. 2002. 8p. audio compact disk 79.95 (*0-7540-5543-4*, CCD 234) Chivers Audio Bks. GBR. *Dist:* BBC Audiobooks America.
—Blood Rain. 2001. (Aurelio Zen Mystery Ser.). 288p. pap. 12.00 (*0-375-70830-8*, Vintage) Knopf Publishing Group.
—Blood Rain: An Aurelio Zen Mystery. 2000. (Aurelio Zen Mystery Ser.: Vol. 7). 288p. 23.00 o.s.i (*0-375-40915-7*, Pantheon) Knopf Publishing Group.
—Cabal. 2000. (Aurelio Zen Mystery Ser.). 256p. pap. 12.00 (*0-375-70770-0*, Vintage) Knopf Publishing Group.
—Cosi Fan Tutti. 1996. 332p. o.p. (*0-571-17920-7*) Faber & Faber Ltd.
—Cosi Fan Tutti: An Aurelio Zen Mystery. 1998. 256p. pap. 12.00 (*0-679-77911-6*, Vintage) Knopf Publishing Group.
—Cosi Fan Tutti: An Aurelio Zen Mystery. l.t. ed. 1997. (Cloak & Dagger Ser.). 423p. 25.95 (*0-7862-1244-6*) Thorndike Pr.
—Dead Lagoon: An Aurelio Zen Mystery. 1996. 320p. pap. 13.00 (*0-679-75311-7*) Random Hse., Inc.
—A Long Finish: An Aurelio Zen Mystery. 2000. (Aurelio Zen Mystery Ser.). 272p. pap. 12.00 (*0-375-70401-9*, Vintage) Knopf Publishing Group.
—A Long Finish: An Aurelio Zen Mystery. l.t. ed. 1999. (Mystery Ser.). 408p. 27.95 (*0-7862-1762-6*) Thorndike Pr.
—Medusa: An Aurelio Zen Mystery. 2004. 288p. (*0-385-66035-9*) Doubleday Canada, Ltd. CAN. *Dist:* Random Hse., Inc.
—Medusa: An Aurelio Zen Mystery. 2004. 272p. 23.00 (*0-375-42269-2*, Pantheon) Knopf Publishing Group.
—Ratking. 1991. 320p. mass mkt. 4.99 o.s.i (*0-553-28237-9*) Bantam Bks.
—Ratking. 1991. (Portway Ser.). 376p. 21.95 (*0-7451-7247-4*, Macmillan Reference USA) Gale Group.
—Ratking. 1997. 272p. pap. 12.00 (*0-679-76854-8*, Vintage) Knopf Publishing Group.
—Vendetta. 1993. 304p. mass mkt. 4.99 o.s.i (*0-553-29639-6*) Bantam Bks.
—Vendetta: An Aurelio Zen Mystery. 1998. (Aurelio Zen Mystery Ser.). 272p. pap. 12.00 (*0-679-76853-X*, Vintage) Knopf Publishing Group.

### ZERO, NINA (FICTITIOUS CHARACTER)—FICTION

Eversz, Robert M. Burning Garbo: A Nina Zero Novel. 2003. 288p. 23.00 (*0-7432-5013-3*); E-Book (*0-7432-5356-6*) Simon & Schuster. (Simon & Schuster).
—Killing Paparazzi. 320p. 2002. (Illus.). 23.95 (*0-312-28902-2*, Saint Martin's Minotaur); 2003. reprint ed. pap. 13.95 (*0-312-30999-6*, Saint Martin's Griffin) St. Martin's Pr.
—Shooting Elvis. 224p. 1996. pap. 21.00 o.p. (*0-8021-1582-9*); 1997. reprint ed. pap. 12.00 (*0-8021-3501-3*) Grove/Atlantic, Inc. (Grove Pr.).

### ZHONG, FONG, INSPECTOR (FICTITIOUS CHARACTER)—FICTION

Rotenberg, David. The Lake Ching Murders: A Mystery of Fire & Ice. 2002. 208p. 22.95 (*0-312-27671-0*, Saint Martin's Minotaur) St. Martin's Pr.
—The Shanghai Murders. 1998. 320p. o.p. (*0-312-18661-4*); 24.95 o.p. (*0-312-18175-2*, 853565) St. Martin's Pr. (Saint Martin's Minotaur).

### ZIGGY (FICTITIOUS CHARACTER)—FICTION

Benzle, Robin C. The Ziggy Cookbook: Great Food from Mom's Diner. 1993. (Illus.). 254p. (Orig.). pap. 16.00 (*0-9629398-2-X*) VanTine Publishing Co.
Campbell, Andrea. Bringing up Ziggy. 1999. (Illus.). 206p. pap. 21.95 (*1-58063-085-5*, Renaissance Bks.) St. Martin's Pr.
Wilson, Tom. A Day in the Life of Ziggy. 1993. (Ziggy Collection Ser.). (Illus.). 104p. pap. 6.95 (*0-8362-1713-6*) Andrews McMeel Publishing.
—Encore! Encore! A Collection of Ziggy Favorites. 1980. (Ziggy Collection Ser.). (Illus.). 160p. pap. 8.95 (*0-8362-1151-0*) Andrews McMeel Publishing.
—The First 25 Years Are the Hardest! A 25 Year Retrospective of Ziggy Favorites. 1996. (Ziggy Collection Ser.). (Illus.). 160p. pap. 12.95 (*0-8362-1033-6*) Andrews McMeel Publishing.
—Get Ziggy with It: A Ziggy Collection. 2000. (Illus.). 128p. pap. 9.95 (*0-7407-0459-1*) Andrews McMeel Publishing.
—It's a Ziggy World. 1975. (J). mass mkt. 1.75 o.p. (*0-451-11968-1*, AE1968, Signet Bks.) NAL.
—Look Out World . . . Here I Come! Ziggy's Down-to-Earth Humor: A Look at the Environment & Ourselves. 1991. (Ziggy Collection Ser.). (Illus.). 104p. (Orig.). pap. 5.95 (*0-8362-1872-8*) Andrews McMeel Publishing.
—My Life as a Cartoon. 1995. (Ziggy Collection Ser.). (Illus.). 104p. pap. 6.95 (*0-8362-1786-1*) Andrews McMeel Publishing.
—Promises to Myself: Ziggy's Thirty-Day Ledger of I Owe Me's. 1975. (Alligator Bks.). pap. 2.50 o.p. (*0-8362-0643-6*) Andrews McMeel Publishing.
—The Z Files. 1997. (Ziggy Collection Ser.). (Illus.). 128p. (Orig.). pap. 8.95 (*0-8362-3681-5*) Andrews McMeel Publishing.
—Ziggy... A Rumor in His Own Time. 1992. (Illus.). 104p. pap. 6.95 (*0-8362-1887-6*) Andrews McMeel Publishing.
—Ziggy & Friends. 1982. (Ziggy Collection Ser.). (Illus.). 104p. pap. 3.95 (*0-8362-1136-7*) Andrews McMeel Publishing.
—Ziggy & Friends. 1983. (J). mass mkt. 1.95 o.p. (*0-451-12248-8*, Signet Bks.) NAL.
—A Ziggy Christmas. 1987. 48p. (gr. 4 up). 4.95 o.p. (*0-8362-1161-8*) Andrews McMeel Publishing.
—Ziggy Faces Life. 1981. (Ziggy Collection Ser.). (Illus.). 104p. pap. 4.95 (*0-8362-1167-7*) Andrews McMeel Publishing.
—Ziggy Faces Life. 1982. mass mkt. 1.75 o.p. (*0-451-11428-0*, AE1428, Signet Bks.) NAL.
—Ziggy Faces Life . . . Again! 1982. mass mkt. 1.95 o.p. (*0-451-11790-5*, AJ1790, Signet Bks.) NAL.
—Ziggy in the Fast Lane. 1987. (Ziggy Collection Ser.). (Illus.). 256p. (Orig.). pap. 4.95 (*0-8362-2089-7*) Andrews McMeel Publishing.
—Ziggy in the Rough. 1985. 104p. (Orig.). pap. 5.95 o.p. (*0-8362-2076-5*) Andrews McMeel Publishing.
—Ziggy Love Notes. 1979. (Illus.). 2.50 o.p. (*0-8362-1909-0*) Andrews McMeel Publishing.
—Ziggy on the Outside Looking In. 1990. (Ziggy Collection Ser.). (Illus.). 104p. (Orig.). pap. 5.95 (*0-8362-1811-6*) Andrews McMeel Publishing.
—Ziggy Thinking of You Notebook. 1979. (Illus.). 2.50 o.p. (*0-8362-1910-4*) Andrews McMeel Publishing.
—The Ziggy Treasury. (Ziggy Collection Ser.). (Illus.). 1980. 160p. pap. 8.95 (*0-8362-0738-6*); 1977. 12.95 o.p. (*0-8362-0737-8*) Andrews McMeel Publishing.
—Ziggy Weighs In. 1984. mass mkt. 1.95 o.p. (*0-451-13175-4*, Signet Bks.) NAL.
—Ziggy's Big Little Book. 1983. (Ziggy Collection Ser.). (Illus.). 256p. pap. 3.95 (*0-8362-1990-2*) Andrews McMeel Publishing.
—Ziggy's Divine Comedy. 1998. (Ziggy Collection Ser.). (Illus.). 128p. pap. 8.95 (*0-8362-6826-1*) Andrews McMeel Publishing.
—Ziggy's Door Openers. 1980. 20p. (gr. 4 up). pap. 4.95 o.p. (*0-8362-1914-7*) Andrews McMeel Publishing.
—Ziggy's Fleeting Thoughts Notebook. 1979. (Illus.). 2.50 o.p. (*0-8362-1912-0*) Andrews McMeel Publishing.
—Ziggy's Follies. 1988. (Ziggy Collection Ser.). (Illus.). 104p. pap. 5.95 (*0-8362-1827-2*) Andrews McMeel Publishing.
—Ziggy's for You with Love. 1982. 24p. (gr. 4 up). 3.95 o.p. (*0-8362-1189-8*) Andrews McMeel Publishing.
—Ziggy's Funday Sunnies. 1983. (Illus.). 80p. pap. 6.95 o.p. (*0-8362-1215-0*) Andrews McMeel Publishing.
—Ziggy's Ins & Outs. 1985. mass mkt. 1.95 o.p. (*0-451-13537-7*, Signet Bks.) NAL.
—Ziggy's Little Book of Friendship. 1998. (Cartoon Bks.). (Illus.). 80p. 4.95 (*0-8362-6606-4*) Andrews McMeel Publishing.
—Ziggy's Little Book of Heart Thoughts To Cheer You. 1998. (Cartoon Bks.). (Illus.). 80p. 4.95 (*0-8362-6607-2*) Andrews McMeel Publishing.
—Ziggy's Little Wish Book for Someone Special. 1997. (Cartoon Bks.). (Illus.). 80p. 4.95 (*0-8362-3679-3*) Andrews McMeel Publishing.
—Ziggy's Little Wish Book for Your Birthday. 1997. (Cartoon Bks.). (Illus.). 80p. 4.95 (*0-8362-3680-7*) Andrews McMeel Publishing.
—Ziggy's Place. 1985. (Ziggy Collection Ser.). (Illus.). 256p. pap. 4.95 (*0-8362-7961-1*) Andrews McMeel Publishing.
—Ziggy's School of Hard Knocks. 1989. (Ziggy Collection Ser.). (Illus.). 104p. pap. 5.95 (*0-8362-1839-6*) Andrews McMeel Publishing.
—Ziggy's Ship Comes In. 1984. 128p. mass mkt. 1.95 o.p. (*0-451-12884-2*, Signet Bks.) NAL.
—Ziggy's Star Performances. 1989. (Ziggy Collection Ser.). (Illus.). 152p. (Orig.). pap. 8.95 (*0-8362-1859-0*) Andrews McMeel Publishing.
—Ziggy's Ups & Downs. 1986. (Ziggy Collection Ser.). (Illus.). 256p. pap. 4.95 (*0-8362-2078-1*) Andrews McMeel Publishing.
—Ziggy's Ups & Downs. 1985. mass mkt. 1.95 o.p. (*0-451-13875-9*, Signet Bks.) NAL.
—1-800-Ziggy. 1994. (Ziggy Collection Ser.). (Illus.). 104p. pap. 6.95 (*0-8362-1749-7*) Andrews McMeel Publishing.

### ZINDEL, FANNY (FICTITIOUS CHARACTER)—FICTION

Stevens, Serita & Moore, Rayanne. Bagels for Tea. 2002. 212p. pap. 10.95 (*0-7599-0374-3*); 2nd ed. 2000. (Fanny Zendel Mystery Ser.: Vol. 2). E-Book 6.00 (*1-58200-506-0*) Hard Shell Word Factory.
—Bagels for Tea. 1993. 272p. 18.95 o.p. (*0-312-09348-9*, Saint Martin's Minotaur) St. Martin's Pr.
—Red Sea, Dead Sea. l.t. ed. 1993. (General Ser.). 348p. lib. bdg. 19.95 o.p. (*0-8161-5442-2*, Macmillan Reference USA) Gale Group.
—Red Sea, Dead Sea. 2002. 176p. pap. 10.95 (*0-7599-0373-5*); 2000. (Fanny Zendel Mystery Ser.: Vol. 1). 235p. E-Book 5.50 (*1-58200-505-2*); 2000. (Fanny Zendel Mystery Ser.: Vol.1). E-Book 5.50 (*1-58200-327-0*) Hard Shell Word Factory.
—Red Sea, Dead Sea. 1991. 224p. 17.95 o.p. (*0-312-06451-9*, Saint Martin's Minotaur) St. Martin's Pr.

### ZONDI, MICKEY (FICTITIOUS CHARACTER)—FICTION

McClure, James. The Artful Egg. l.t. ed. 1986. 19.95 o.p. (*1-55504-011-X*, 247) BBC Audiobooks America.
—The Artful Egg. 1985. 283p. 13.95 o.p. (*0-394-53472-7*, Pantheon) Knopf Publishing Group.
—The Artful Egg. 1986. 5.95 (*0-07-544541-7*) McGraw-Hill Cos., The.
—The Blood of an Englishman. 1981. 288p. 11.00 o.p. (*0-06-013046-6*) HarperCollins Pubs.
—The Blood of an Englishman. l.t. ed. 1982. (Ulverscroft Large Print Ser.). 498p. 29.99 o.p. (*0-7089-0744-X*, Ulverscroft) Thorpe, F. A. Pubs. GBR. *Dist:* Ulverscroft Large Print Bks., Ltd., Ulverscroft Large Print Canada, Ltd.
—The Caterpillar Cop. 1973. (Harper Novel of Suspense Ser.). 240p. 7.95 o.p. (*0-06-012897-6*) HarperCollins Pubs.
—The Caterpillar Cop. 1982. reprint ed. pap. 2.95 o.s.i (*0-394-71058-4*, Pantheon) Knopf Publishing Group.
—Four & Twenty Virgins. l.t. ed. 1990. (Magna Large Print Ser.). 258p. o.p. (*1-85057-723-4*) Magna Large Print Bks. GBR. *Dist:* Ulverscroft Large Print Canada, Ltd.
—The Gooseberry Fool. 1974. (Novel of Suspense Ser.). 224p. 7.95 o.p. (*0-06-012898-4*) HarperCollins Pubs.
—Imago. 1988. 16.95 o.p. (*0-89296-273-9*) Mysterious Pr.
—Imago. 1989. mass mkt. 4.50 o.s.i (*0-445-40729-8*, Mysterious Pr. Paperback Bks.) Warner Bks., Inc.
—Rogue Eagle. 1976. 256p. 8.95 o.p. (*0-06-012949-2*) HarperCollins Pubs.
—Snake. 1976. (Harper Novel of Suspense Ser.). 224p. o.p. (*0-06-012884-4*) HarperCollins Pubs.
—The Song Dog. l.t. ed. 1992. (General Ser.). 408p. 20.95 o.p. (*0-8161-5344-2*, Macmillan Reference USA) Gale Group.
—The Song Dog. 1991. 17.95 (*0-89296-274-7*) Mysterious Pr.
—The Song Dog. 1992. 304p. mass mkt. 4.99 o.s.i (*0-446-40186-2*, Mysterious Pr. Paperback Bks.) Warner Bks., Inc.

—The Steam Pig. 1972. (Harper Novel of Suspense Ser.). 256p. 7.95 o.p. (0-06-012896-8) HarperCollins Pubs.

—The Steam Pig. l.t. ed. 1990. (Magna Large Print Ser.). 373p. o.p. (1-85057-635-1) Magna Large Print Bks. GBR. *Dist:* Ulverscroft Large Print Canada, Ltd.

—The Sunday Hangman. 1977. (Harper Novel of Suspense Ser.). o.p. (0-06-012859-3) HarperCollins Pubs.

**ZORRO (FICTITIOUS CHARACTER)—FICTION**

Arguedas, Jose M. El Zorro de Arriba y el Zorro de Abajo. Fell, Eve M., ed. 1990. (Latin American Series - Coleccion Archivos). (SPA.). 472p. (C). reprint ed. 34.95 o.p. (84-00-07023-2) Univ. of Pittsburgh Pr.

Bergantino, David. Zorro & the Dragon Riders. 1999. (Zorro Ser.). 224p. mass mkt. 5.99 (0-8125-6768-4, Forge Bks.) Doherty, Tom Assocs., LLC.

Boland, Janice. El Zorro. Torres, Raquel, tr. 1996. (Books for Young Learners).Tr. of Fox. (SPA., Illus.). 8p. (J). (gr. k-2). pap. text 5.00 (1-57274-037-X, A2920) Owen, Richard C. Pubs., Inc.

Curtis, Sandra. Zorro Unmasked: The Official History. 1998. (Illus.). 320p. pap. 14.95 o.p. (0-7868-8285-9) Hyperion Pr.

Dunster, Mark. Zorro. 1995. 17p. (Orig.). pap. 4.00 (0-89642-262-3) Linden Pubs.

Lauria, Frank. The Mask of Zorro. 1998. 176p. (J). (gr. 4-7). pap. 4.50 (0-671-51967-0, Aladdin) Simon & Schuster Children's Publishing.

Luceno, James. Zorro. 1998. 224p. pap. 6.50 (0-671-51989-1, Pocket) Simon & Schuster.

Marshall, Edward. Zorro y Sus Amigos. 1996. (Libro Puffin Facil-de-Leer Ser.).Tr. of Fox & His Friends. 8.70 o.p. (0-606-10538-7) Turtleback Bks.

—Zorro y Sus Amigos: Fox & His Friends. Fiol, Maria A., tr. 1996. Tr. of Fox & His Friends. (SPA., Illus.). 56p. (J). (gr. 1-4). pap. 3.99 o.s.i (0-14-038020-5, Puffin Bks.) Penguin Putnam Bks. for Young Readers.

McCulley, Johnston. The Mark of Z: The Original Zorro. 1976. reprint ed. lib. bdg. 24.95 (0-89190-999-0, Rivercity Pr.) Amereon, Ltd.

—The Mark of Zorro. 1990. reprint ed. lib. bdg. 25.95 (0-89968-541-2) Buccaneer Bks., Inc.

—The Mark of Zorro. 1998. 288p. mass mkt. 4.99 (0-8125-4007-7, Tor Bks.) Doherty, Tom Assocs., LLC.

—The Mark of Zorro. 1998. 11.04 (0-606-13597-9) Turtleback Bks.

—The Mark of Zorro. 2003. pap. text (0-8095-3070-8); 2002. 24.95 (1-59224-060-7) Wildside Pr.

—Zorro Vol. 1: The Masters Edition Volume One, 5 vols. 2000. (Illus.). 128p. per. 15.00 (1-891729-20-9, Z-1) Pulp Adventures, Inc.

—Zorro & the Pirate Raiders. 1986. 176p. pap. 2.50 o.p. (0-553-24670-4) Bantam Bks.

—Zorro Rides Again. 1986. (Starfire Ser.). 160p. pap. 2.50 o.p. (0-553-24671-2) Bantam Bks.

McGregor, Don. Zorro: The Lady Wears Red. 1999. (Illus.). 96p. 12.95 (1-58240-061-X) Image Comics.

Preisler, Jerome. Zorro & the Jaguar Warriors. 1998. 224p. mass mkt. 4.99 (0-8125-6767-6, Forge Bks.) Doherty, Tom Assocs., LLC.

—Zorro & the Jaguar Warriors. 1998. (J). 11.04 (0-606-13946-X) Turtleback Bks.

—Zorro & the Shadow Riders. 1998. 12.04 (0-606-13947-8) Turtleback Bks.

—Zorro & the Witch's Curse. 3rd ed. 2000. (Zorro Ser.: No. 3). 216p. mass mkt. 5.99 (0-8125-6769-2, Forge Bks.) Doherty, Tom Assocs., LLC.

Sechan, Olivier. El Zorro. 1996. (SPA.). 168p. 12.95 (84-372-2191-9) Santillana USA Publishing Co., Inc.

Toth, Alex. Zorro No. 2: The Complete Classic Adventures by Alex Toth. 1998. (Illus.). 120p. pap. 15.95 (1-58240-027-X) Image Comics.

Whitman, John. The Mask of Zorro. 1998. (Mighty Chronicles Ser.). (Illus.). 320p. (J). (gr. 3-7). 9.95 o.p. (0-8118-2036-X) Chronicle Bks. LLC.

**ZUCKERMAN, NATHAN (FICTITIOUS CHARACTER)—FICTION**

Roth, Philip. The Anatomy Lesson. 1984. 240p. mass mkt. 4.95 o.s.i (0-449-20614-9, Fawcett) Ballantine Bks.

—The Anatomy Lesson. 1983. 291p. 14.95 o.p. (0-374-10491-3); 60.00 o.s.i (0-374-10492-1) Farrar, Straus & Giroux.

—The Anatomy Lesson. 1996. 304p. pap. 13.00 (0-679-74902-0) Random Hse., Inc.

—The Ghost Writer. 1982. 224p. mass mkt. 4.95 o.s.i (0-449-20009-4); 1980. mass mkt. 2.95 o.p. (0-449-24322-2) Ballantine Bks. (Fawcett).

—The Ghost Writer. 1979. 180p. 8.95 o.p. (0-374-16189-5) Farrar, Straus & Giroux.

—The Ghost Writer. 1980. lib. bdg. 10.95 o.p. (0-8161-3069-8, Macmillan Reference USA) Gale Group.

—The Ghost Writer. 1995. 192p. pap. 12.00 (0-679-74898-9, Vintage) Knopf Publishing Group.

—The Prague Orgy. 1952. o.p. (0-374-23679-8) Farrar, Straus & Giroux.

—The Prague Orgy. 1996. 96p. pap. 10.00 (0-679-74903-9) Knopf, Alfred A. Inc.

—Zuckerman Bound: A Trilogy & Epilogue. 1986. 480p. mass mkt. 5.95 o.s.i (0-449-21090-1, Fawcett) Ballantine Bks.

—Zuckerman Bound: A Trilogy & Epilogue. 1985. 800p. 22.50 o.s.i (0-374-29943-9); 784p. pap. 9.95 o.p. (0-374-51899-8) Farrar, Straus & Giroux.

—Zuckerman Bound: A Trilogy & Epilogue. abr. ed. 1988. audio 14.00 o.s.i (0-694-50958-2, SWC 1768, HarperAudio) HarperTrade.

—Zuckerman Unbound. 1982. mass mkt. 3.50 o.s.i (0-449-24521-7, Fawcett) Ballantine Bks.

—Zuckerman Unbound. 1981. 225p. 10.95 o.p. (0-374-29945-5); 50.00 o.p. (0-374-29946-3) Farrar, Straus & Giroux.

—Zuckerman Unbound. l.t. ed. 1981. lib. bdg. 13.95 o.p. (0-8161-3291-7, Macmillan Reference USA) Gale Group.

—Zuckerman Unbound. 1995. 240p. pap. 13.00 (0-679-74899-7, Vintage) Knopf Publishing Group.

**ZUKAS, HELMA (FICTITIOUS CHARACTER)—FICTION**

Dereske, Jo. Final Notice, Bk. 3. 1998. (Miss Zukas Mystery Ser.). 240p. mass mkt. 5.99 (0-380-78245-6, Avon Bks.) Morrow/Avon.

—Miss Zukas & Stroke of Death. 1995. (Miss Zukas Mystery Ser.: No. 3). 224p. mass mkt. 6.50 (0-380-77033-4, Avon Bks.) Morrow/Avon.

—Miss Zukas & the Island Murders. 1995. (Miss Zukas Mystery Ser.). 224p. (Orig.). mass mkt. 5.99 (0-380-77031-8, Avon Bks.) Morrow/Avon.

—Miss Zukas & the Library Murders. l.t. ed. 2003. (Mystery Ser.). (Orig.). 27.95 (1-57490-511-2) Beeler, Thomas T. Publisher.

—Miss Zukas & the Library Murders. 1994. (Miss Zukas Mystery Ser.). 224p. (Orig.). mass mkt. 5.99 (0-380-77030-X, Avon Bks.) Morrow/Avon.

—Miss Zukas & the Raven's Dance. 1996. (Miss Zukas Mystery Ser.). 256p. mass mkt. 5.99 (0-380-78243-X, Avon Bks.) Morrow/Avon.

—Miss Zukas in Death's Shadow. 1999. 224p. mass mkt. 5.99 (0-380-80472-7, Avon Bks.) Morrow/Avon.

—Miss Zukas Shelves the Evidence. l.t. ed. 2002. (Paperback Ser.). 310p. pap. 25.95 (0-7838-9734-0) Gale Group.

—Miss Zukas Shelves the Evidence. 2001. (Miss Zukas Mystery Ser.). 256p. mass mkt. 5.99 (0-380-80474-3, Avon Bks.) Morrow/Avon.

—Out of Circulation. 1997. (Miss Zukas Mystery Ser.). mass mkt. 5.99 (0-380-78244-8, Avon Bks.) Morrow/Avon.

# ETHNIC GROUPS

## A

**AFRO-AMERICANS—FICTION**

Adams, Jenoyne. Resurrecting Mingus. 2002. 256p. reprint ed. pap. 13.00 (0-671-78781-0, Free Pr.) Simon & Schuster.

—Resurrecting Mingus: A Novel. 2001. 256p. 23.00 (0-684-87352-4, Free Pr.) Simon & Schuster.

Alcorn, Randy. Dominion. 2003. 612p. pap. 14.99 (1-57673-661-X, Multnomah Bks.); 2003. audio 24.99 (1-57673-682-2); 1986. 612p. pap. 14.99 o.p. (0-88070-939-1, Multnomah Bks.) Multnomah Pubs., Inc.

Alcott, Louisa May. Louisa May Alcott on Race, Sex, & Slavery. Elbert, Sarah, ed. & intro. by. 1997. (Illus.). 160p. text 42.50 (1-55553-308-6); pap. text 17.95 (1-55553-307-8) Northeastern Univ. Pr.

Alef, Daniel. Pale Truth. 2000. (California Chronicles: Vol. 1). (Illus.). 588p. 27.00 (0-9700174-1-3) Maxit Publishing, Inc.

—Pale Truth: The California Chronicles. 2001. 588p. E-Book 8.95 (0-9700174-7-2);Vol. 1. E-Book 12.00 (0-9700174-8-0) Maxit Publishing, Inc.

Alers, Rochelle. Careless Whispers. 1994. 189p. pap. 8.95 (1-885478-00-3) Genesis Pr., Inc.

—Gentle Yearning. 1998. (Indigo Love Stories Ser.). 213p. pap. 10.95 (1-885478-24-0) Genesis Pr., Inc.

—Hideaway. 1995. (Arabesque Ser.). mass mkt. 5.99 (1-58314-179-0); 224p. mass mkt. 0.46 o.s.i (0-8217-0135-5, Zebra Bks.) Kensington Publishing Corp.

—My Love's Keeper. 2001. pap. 11.95 (1-58345-970-7) Domhan Bks.

—Reckless Surrender. 1997. 206p. pap. 6.95 o.p. (1-885478-17-8); 3rd ed. 2000. 254p. reprint ed. pap. 8.95 (1-58571-053-9, Indigo) Genesis Pr., Inc.

Alers, Rochelle, et al. Della's House of Style. 2000. 343p. mass mkt. 6.99 (0-312-97497-3, St. Martin's Paperbacks) St. Martin's Pr.

—Island Bliss. 2002. 320p. mass mkt. 6.50 (0-312-97893-6, St. Martin's Paperbacks) St. Martin's Pr.

Alexander, Truman H. Loot. 1977. (Black Heritage Library Collection). reprint ed. 21.95 (0-8369-9015-3) Ayer Co. Pubs., Inc.

Allegra, Donna. Witness to the League of Blond Hip-Hop Dancers: A Novella & Short Stories. 2000. 306p. pap. 12.95 o.p. (1-55583-550-3, Alyson Bks.) Alyson Pubns.

Allen, Jeffrey Renard. Rails under My Back. 2001. (Illus.). 576p. reprint ed. pap. 14.00 (0-15-601415-7, Harvest Bks.) Harcourt Trade Pubs.

Allen, Preston L. Churchboys & Other Sinners. 2003. (Illus.). 152p. 15.95 (0-932112-44-7) Carolina Wren Pr.

Allen, Stephanie. A Place Between Stations: Stories. 2003. 184p. pap. 19.95 (0-8262-1444-4) Univ. of Missouri Pr.

Andrews, William L., ed. & intro. Three African-American Novels. 2003. 368p. mass mkt. 6.95 (0-451-52870-0, Signet Classics) NAL.

Angelique & Dixon, Nia. Indigo after Dark, Vol. I. 2001. (Illus.). 166p. pap. 10.95 (1-58571-050-4, Indigo) Genesis Pr., Inc.

Ansa, Tina McElroy. The Hand I Fan With. unabr. ed. 1997. audio 96.00 (0-7366-3660-9, 4334) Books on Tape, Inc.

—The Hand I Fan With. 1997. 496p. pap. 14.00 (0-385-47601-9) Doubleday Publishing.

—The Hand I Fan With, Set. abr. ed. 1996. 360p. audio 23.95 o.s.i (0-553-47804-4, 694513, RH Audio) Random Hse. Audio Publishing Group.

—Sidekick S03 Avon Trade, 24 Copies. 2003. pap. 326.25 (0-06-057067-9, Perennial) HarperTrade.

—Ugly Ways. 1993. 277p. 19.95 o.s.i (0-15-192553-4) Harcourt Trade Pubs.

Anthony, Sterling. Cookie Cutter. 2000. 336p. pap. 14.00 (0-345-43568-0, One World/Ballantine) Ballantine Bks.

Apollo. Concrete Candy: Stories. 1996. 144p. pap. 15.00 (0-385-47780-5) Doubleday Publishing.

Ashton, Warren T. Hatchie, the Guardian Slave. 1977. (Black Heritage Library Collection). reprint ed. 22.95 (0-8369-8976-7) Ayer Co. Pubs., Inc.

Askew, Rilla. Fire in Beulah. 2001. 352p. 25.95 o.p. (0-670-88843-5, Viking) Viking Penguin.

Attaway, William. Blood on the Forge. 1987. (Voices of Resistance Ser.). 320p. reprint ed. pap. 14.00 o.s.i (0-85345-722-0) Monthly Review Pr.

Austin, Doris J. & Simmons, Martin, eds. Streetlights: Illuminating Tales of the Urban Black Experience. 1996. 544p. (Orig.). pap. 14.95 o.p. (0-14-017471-0) Penguin Group (USA) Inc.

Bacon, Eugenia J. Lyddy. 1977. (Black Heritage Library Collection). reprint ed. 22.95 (0-8369-8958-9) Ayer Co. Pubs., Inc.

Bacon, Eugenia J. & MacKethan, Lucinda H. Lyddy: A Tale of the Old South. 1998. (Illus.). iix, 287p. pap. 17.00 (0-8203-1967-8) Univ. of Georgia Pr.

Bailey-Williams, Nicole. A Little Piece of Sky. 2002. 176p. reprint ed. pap. 9.95 (0-7679-1216-0, Harlem Moon) Broadway Bks.

Baisden, Michael. Men Cry in the Dark. 1999. (Illus.). 305p. pap. 13.95 (0-9643675-1-3) Legacy Publishing.

—Men Cry in the Dark. 352p. 2002. E-Book 6.99 (0-7432-2286-5, Simon & Schuster); 2001. mass mkt. 6.99 (0-7432-1802-7, Touchstone) Simon & Schuster.

Baisden, Michael, ed. Men Cry in the Dark. 1997. 305p. 22.95 (0-9643675-0-5) Legacy Publishing.

Baker, Calvin. Naming the New World. 1999. E-Book 9.95 (0-312-20732-8); 1997. 128p. 18.95 o.p. (0-312-15178-0) St. Martin's Pr.

Baldwin, James. Another Country. 1992. 448p. pap. 14.00 (0-679-74471-1, Vintage) Knopf Publishing Group.

—Go Tell It on the Mountain. 2000. 240p. pap. 12.95 (0-385-33457-5); 1985. 224p. mass mkt. 6.99 (0-440-33007-6, Laurel) Dell Publishing.

—Go Tell It on the Mountain. 1953. 256p. 13.95 o.p. (0-385-27053-4) Doubleday Publishing.

—Go Tell It on the Mountain. 1995. (Modern Library Ser.). 320p. 14.95 (0-679-60154-6, Modern Library) Random House Adult Trade Publishing Group.

—Go Tell It on the Mountain. 1985. 13.04 (0-606-01584-1) Turtleback Bks.

—Going to Meet the Man. 1985. 7.95 o.p. (0-385-27466-1) Doubleday Publishing.

—Going to Meet the Man: Stories. 1995. 256p. pap. 11.95 (0-679-76179-9, Vintage) Knopf Publishing Group.

—If Beale Street Could Talk. l.t. ed. 1996. (Perennial Bestsellers Ser.). 229p. 23.95 (0-7838-1817-3) Thorndike Pr.

Baldwin, Lydia W. A Yankee School-Teacher in Virginia. 1977. (Black Heritage Library Collection). reprint ed. 22.95 (0-8369-8959-7) Ayer Co. Pubs., Inc.

Baldwin, William P. The Fennel Family Papers. 1996. 304p. tchr. ed. 19.95 o.p. (1-56512-069-8, 72069) Algonquin Bks. of Chapel Hill.

Ball, John. The Cool Cottontail. 1985. 176p. (Orig.). mass mkt. 3.50 o.p. (0-06-080734-2, P734, Perennial) HarperTrade.

—The Eyes of Buddha: A Virgil Tibbs Mystery. 1985. 256p. reprint ed. mass mkt. 3.50 o.p. (0-06-080751-2, P751, Perennial) HarperTrade.

—Five Pieces of Jade. l.t. ed. 1983. (Ulverscroft Large Print Ser.). 352p. 29.99 o.p. (0-7089-0997-3, Ulverscroft) Thorpe, F. A. Pubs. GBR. *Dist:* Ulverscroft Large Print Bks., Ltd., Ulverscroft Large Print Canada, Ltd.

—In the Heat of the Night. 1992. (Mystery Scene Bk.). 208p. mass mkt. 4.50 (0-88184-887-5, Carroll & Graf Pubs.) Avalon Publishing Group.

—In the Heat of the Night. 1992. 158p. reprint ed. lib. bdg. 14.95 (0-89966-916-6) Buccaneer Bks., Inc.

—In the Heat of the Night. 1985. 256p. pap. 4.50 o.p. (0-06-080735-0, P735, Perennial) HarperTrade.

—Then Came Violence. 1980. (Crime Club Ser.). 8.95 o.p. (0-385-15726-6) Doubleday Publishing.

—Then Came Violence. l.t. ed. 1982. (Ulverscroft Large Print Ser.). 352p. 29.99 o.p. (0-7089-0870-5, Ulverscroft) Thorpe, F. A. Pubs. GBR. *Dist:* Ulverscroft Large Print Bks., Ltd., Ulverscroft Large Print Canada, Ltd.

—Then Came Violence: A Virgil Tibbs Mystery. 1988. 208p. reprint ed. mass mkt. 3.95 o.p. (0-06-080883-7, P-883, Perennial) HarperTrade.

Ballard, Allen B. Where I'm Bound. 2000. (Illus.). 320p. 24.00 o.s.i (0-684-87031-2, Simon & Schuster) Simon & Schuster.

—Where I'm Bound: A Novel. 2001. 320p. reprint ed. pap. 14.00 (0-684-87032-0, Simon & Schuster) Simon & Schuster.

Bambara, Toni Cade. Gorilla, My Love. 1992. (Vintage Contemporaries Ser.). 192p. pap. 11.00 (0-679-73898-3, Vintage) Knopf Publishing Group.

—Gorilla, My Love. 1972. 8.95 o.p. (0-394-48201-8) Random Hse., Inc.

—The Salt Eaters. (Vintage Contemporaries Ser.). 304p. 1992. pap. 13.00 (0-679-74076-7); 1981. pap. 8.00 o.p. (0-394-75050-0) Knopf Publishing Group. (Vintage).

—The Salt Eaters. 1980. 9.95 o.p. (0-394-50712-6) Random Hse., Inc.

—Those Bones Are Not My Child. 2000. (Illus.). 688p. pap. 16.00 (0-679-77408-4, Vintage) Knopf Publishing Group.

Bandele, Asha. Daughter: A Novel. 2003. 272p. 23.00 (0-7432-1184-7, Scribner) Simon & Schuster.

Banks, Leslie E. Soul Food, Vol. 3. 2003. (Soul Food Ser.). 256p. mass mkt. 6.99 (0-7434-6292-0, Pocket Star) Simon & Schuster.

—Soul Food: For Better, for Worse. 2002. (Soul Food Ser.). 272p. mass mkt. 6.99 (0-7434-5739-0, Pocket) Simon & Schuster.

Barnes, Judith. Salthill: A Novel. 2003. 384p. pap. 13.95 (0-312-32015-9, Saint Martin's Griffin); 2002. 368p. 24.95 (0-312-29018-7) St. Martin's Pr.

Barre, Richard. The Star. 2002. 48p. 17.95 (1-59266-008-8); 43p. 85.00 (1-59266-009-6); 43p. 125.00 (1-59266-010-X) Capra Pr.

Bates, Karen Grigsby. Plain Brown Wrapper: An Alex Powell Novel. 2001. 336p. pap. 13.00 (0-380-80890-0, Avon Bks.) Morrow/Avon.

Baxt, George. A Queer Kind of Death. 1998. 300p. pap. 10.00 o.p. (1-55583-448-5) Alyson Pubns.

—A Queer Kind of Death: A Pharoah Love Mystery. 1986. (Library of Crime Classics). pap. 4.95 o.p. (0-930330-46-3) International Polygonics, Ltd.

—A Queer Kind of Death: A Pharoah Love Mystery. 1979. pap. 4.95 o.p. (0-312-66022-7, Saint Martin's Griffin) St. Martin's Pr.

—A Queer Kind of Love: A Pharoah Love Mystery. 1994. 288p. 20.00 (1-883402-01-8, Scribner) Simon & Schuster.

—A Queer Kind of Love: A Pharoah Love Mystery. pap. (0-312-29217-1); 1995. pap. 8.95 (0-312-13152-6) St. Martin's Pr. (Saint Martin's Griffin).

—A Queer Kind of Umbrella: A Pharoah Love Mystery. 1995. 240p. 20.50 (0-684-81496-X, Simon & Schuster); 21.00 (1-883402-35-2, Scribner) Simon & Schuster.

—Topsy & Evil. 1987. 232p. reprint ed. pap. 4.95 o.p. (0-930330-66-8) International Polygonics, Ltd.

Beatty, Paul. Tuff: A Novel. 2000. reprint ed. pap. 13.00 o.p. (0-375-70124-9, Anchor) Knopf Publishing Group.

—The White Boy Shuffle. 1997. 240p. pap. 13.00 o.s.i (0-8050-5351-4, Owl Bks.) Holt, Henry & Co.

—The White Boy Shuffle. 1996. 223p. tchr. ed. 19.95 o.p. (0-395-74280-3) Houghton Mifflin Co.

—The White Boy Shuffle. 2001. 240p. pap. 13.00 (0-312-28019-X) Picador.

Beckham, Barry. Runner Mack. 1984. (Howard University Press Library of Contemporary Literature). 213p. pap. 14.95 (0-88258-116-3) Howard Univ. Pr.

Bell, Derrick A. Gospel Choirs: Psalms of Survival in an Alien Land Called Home. 240p. 1997. pap. 13.00 (*0-465-02413-0*); 1996. 23.00 o.p. (*0-465-02412-2*) Basic Bks.

Bell, Madison Smartt. Ten Indians. 1997. 272p. pap. 12.95 o.s.i (*0-14-026846-4*) Penguin Group (USA) Inc.

Belle Scott: Or, Liberty Overthrown. 1977. (Black Heritage Library Collection). 22.95 (*0-8369-8724-1*) Ayer Co. Pubs., Inc.

Bennett, Oscar H. The Colored Garden. 2000. 264p. pap. 12.50 (*0-9659701-9-1*); (Illus.). pap. text (*0-9659701-7-5*) Laughing Owl Publishing, Inc.

Benson, Angela. The Nicest Guy in America. l.t. ed. 1998. (Romance Ser.). 384p. 25.95 (*0-7862-1461-9*) Thorndike Pr.

Benson, Chris. Special Interest. 2003. 288p. pap. 12.95 (*0-345-45727-7*) Ballantine Bks.

—Special Interest. 2001. 300p. pap. 15.95 (*0-88378-230-8*) Third World Press.

Benson, Christopher. Special Interest. 2001. 300p. 24.95 (*0-88378-227-8*) Third World Press.

Berry, Bertice. The Haunting of Hip Hop: A Novel. 2002. 240p. pap. 12.00 (*0-7679-1212-8*) Broadway Bks.

—Redemption Song: A Novel. 2001. 192p. pap. 10.95 (*0-345-43885-X*, One World/Ballantine) Ballantine Bks.

Berry, Faith, ed. A Scholar's Conscience: Selected Writings of J. Saunders Redding, 1942-1977. 1992. 248p. pap. text 19.95 (*0-8131-0806-3*) Univ. Pr. of Kentucky.

Berry, Venise. All of Me: A Voluptuous Tale. 2001. 288p. reprint ed. pap. 13.95 (*0-451-20262-7*) NAL.

—Colored Sugar Water. 2002. 256p. 23.95 o.s.i (*0-525-94471-0*, Dutton) Dutton/Plume.

—Colored Sugar Water. 2003. 272p. reprint ed. pap. 13.95 (*0-451-20775-0*) NAL.

Berry, Venise T. All of Me: A Voluptuous Tale. 2000. 288p. 23.95 o.s.i (*0-525-94463-X*, Dutton) Dutton/Plume.

Biggs, Undra E. Backfield in Motion. Cadet, Guichard, ed. 2002. 288p. pap. 15.00 (*0-9718191-3-0*) La Caille Nous Publishing Co.

—When You Look at Me. Cadet, Guichard & Salcedo, Judy, eds. 2004. 252p. pap. 15.00 (*0-9647635-6-7*) La Caille Nous Publishing Co.

Bikis, Gwendolyn. Your Loving Arms. 2002. 247p. (C). 27.95 (*1-56023-220-X*); pap. 17.95 (*1-56023-221-8*) Haworth Pr., Inc., The. (Alice Street Editions).

Black, Jim. River Season: A Novel. 2003. 208p. 23.95 (*0-670-03227-1*, Viking) Viking Penguin.

Blackman, Marci. Po Man's Child: A Novel. 1999. 240p. pap. 12.95 (*0-916397-59-9*) Manic D Pr.

Blair, Emma. Moonlit Eyes. 2001. 416p. pap. (*0-316-85585-5*); lib. bdg. (*0-316-85578-2*) Little Brown & Co.

—Moonlit Eyes. l.t. ed. 2002. (Charnwood Large Print Ser.). 536p. 32.50 o.p. (*0-7089-9326-5*, Charnwood) Thorpe, F. A. Pubs. GBR. *Dist:* Ulverscroft Large Print Bks., Ltd., Ulverscroft Large Print Canada, Ltd.

Bland, Eleanor Taylor. Dead Time. 2001. (Marti MacAlister Ser.). 224p. mass mkt. 6.50 (*0-312-97719-0*, St. Martin's Paperbacks) St. Martin's Pr.

—Fatal Remains. 2003. 288p. 23.95 (*0-312-30097-2*, Saint Martin's Minotaur) St. Martin's Pr.

—See No Evil. (Marti MacAlister Ser.). 288p. 1999. mass mkt. 5.99 (*0-312-96818-3*, St. Martin's Paperbacks); 1998. 22.95 o.p. (*0-312-16910-8*, Saint Martin's Minotaur) St. Martin's Pr.

—See No Evil. l.t. ed. 1998. (Core Ser.). 392p. 29.95 (*0-7838-0112-2*) Thorndike Pr.

—Tell No Tales: A Marti MacAlister Mystery. l.t. ed. 1999. (Wheeler Large Print Book Ser.). 352p. pap. 23.95 (*1-56895-756-4*, Wheeler Publishing, Inc.) Gale Group.

—Tell No Tales: A Marti MacAlister Mystery. (Marti MacAlister Ser.). 2000. 288p. mass mkt. 5.99 (*0-312-97113-3*, St. Martin's Paperbacks); 1999. vii, 264p. 22.95 o.p. (*0-312-20067-6*, Saint Martin's Minotaur) St. Martin's Pr.

—Whispers in the Dark. l.t. ed. 2002. 28.95 o.p. (*1-58724-187-0*, Wheeler Publishing, Inc.) Gale Group.

—Whispers in the Dark: A Marti MacAlister Mystery. 2002. 256p. pap. 12.95 (*0-312-30733-0*, Saint Martin's Griffin) St. Martin's Pr.

—Windy City Dying: A Marti MacAlister Mystery. 320p. 2003. pap. 13.95 (*0-312-32048-5*, Saint Martin's Griffin); 2002. 24.95 (*0-312-30098-0*, Saint Martin's Minotaur) St. Martin's Pr.

Bland, Eleanor Taylor, ed. Shades of Black: Crime & Mystery Stories by African-American Authors. 2004. 368p. 23.95 (*0-425-19402-7*, Prime Crime) Berkley Publishing Group.

Bloodline. unabr. collector's ed. Incl. Just Like a Tree. audio Long Day in November. audio Sky in Gray. audio Three Men. audio 1982. Set audio 42.00 (*0-7366-0515-0*, 1489) Books on Tape, Inc.

Blue, Montana & Morena, Coco. Indigo after Dark, Vol. III. 2001. (Illus.). 166p. pap. 10.95 (*1-58571-052-0*, Indigo) Genesis Pr., Inc.

Bluest Eye. 1970. 16.95 o.s.i (*0-8050-1116-1*) Holt, Henry & Co.

Bonner, Sherwood. Dialect Tales. 1977. (Black Heritage Library Collection). reprint ed. 23.95 (*0-8369-8998-8*) Ayer Co. Pubs., Inc.

—Dialect Tales & Other Stories. Frank, William L., ed. 1991. 164p. pap. 26.95 (*0-8084-0427-X*) Rowman & Littlefield Pubs., Inc.

—Suwanee River Tales. 1977. (Black Heritage Library Collection). (Illus.). reprint ed. 30.95 (*0-8369-8999-6*) Ayer Co. Pubs., Inc.

Bontemps, Arna. Black Thunder: Gabriel's Revolt: Virginia, 1800. 1992. 254p. pap. 19.00 (*0-8070-6337-1*) Beacon Pr.

Bontemps, Arna, ed. Black Thunder. 1968. pap. 14.95 o.p. (*0-8070-6429-7*) Beacon Pr.

Booker, T. Gotta Be Down. 2001. pap. 20.23 (*0-7596-0994-2*) 1stBooks Library.

Bowen, Michele Andrea. Church Folk. 2001. 368p. 21.95 o.p. (*0-446-52799-8*) Warner Bks., Inc.

—Second Sunday. 2003. 336p. 22.95 (*0-446-53033-6*, Walk Worthy Pr.) Warner Bks., Inc.

Boyd, Randy. Uprising: The Suspense Thriller. 1998. 335p. pap. 11.95 (*0-9665333-7-2*, 966-001) West Beach Bks.

Boyle, Virginia F. Devil Tales. 1977. (Black Heritage Library Collection). (Illus.). reprint ed. 23.95 (*0-8369-9001-3*) Ayer Co. Pubs., Inc.

Brackett, Leigh. Follow the Free Wind. 1980. 224p. pap. 1.75 o.s.i (*0-345-29008-9*) Ballantine Bks.

—Follow the Free Wind. l.t. ed. 2002. 284p. lib. bdg. 28.95 (*1-58547-174-7*) Ctr. Point Large Print.

Bracy, Ihsan. Ibo Landing: A Offering of Short Stories by Ihsan Bracy. 1998. (Illus.). 170p. pap. 12.95 (*1-887276-10-6*) Cool Grove Publishing, Inc.

—Ibo Landing: An Offering of Short Stories by Ihsan Bracy. 1998. (Illus.). 154p. 22.95 (*1-887276-11-4*) Cool Grove Publishing, Inc.

Bradley, David. South Street. 1988. 16.25 o.p. (*0-8446-6323-9*) Smith, Peter Pub., Inc.

Bradley, Mary E. Douglass Farm. Cousin Alice, ed. 1977. (Black Heritage Library Collection). reprint ed. 23.95 (*0-8369-8960-0*) Ayer Co. Pubs., Inc.

Bradley, Robert L. Stories about the Black Experience: The Lord Will Make a Way, Set 2. 2001. 73p. (C). pap. 8.75 (*0-9702912-0-5*) Bradley, Robert L.

Brandon, Jay. Angel of Death. 1999. 383p. mass mkt. 6.99 (*0-8125-4043-3*, Forge Bks.) Doherty, Tom Assocs., LLC.

Brashler, William. The Bingo Long Traveling All-Stars & Motor Kings. 1976. mass mkt. 1.50 o.p. (*0-451-06833-5*, W6833, Signet Bks.) NAL.

—The Bingo Long Traveling All-Stars & Motor Kings. 1993. (Illus.). 280p. pap. text 16.95 (*0-252-06287-6*) Univ. of Illinois Pr.

Breaux, Magdalene. The Family Curse. 2000. 244p. pap. 15.00 (*0-9701709-0-4*) Breaux Bks., LLC.

Bridgforth, Sharon. Bull-Jean Stories. 1998. 111p. pap. 12.00 (*0-9656659-1-7*) RedBone Pr.

Briscoe, Connie. Big Girls Don't Cry. 1999. 416p. mass mkt. 6.99 (*0-449-00564-X*, Fawcett); 1998. mass mkt. 6.99 (*0-449-00258-6*, Fawcett); 1998. mass mkt. o.s.i (*0-8041-1520-6*, Ivy Bks.); 1997. 384p. pap. 14.00 (*0-345-41362-8*) Ballantine Bks.

—Big Girls Don't Cry. l.t. ed. 1996. 25.95 o.p. (*1-56895-346-1*, Wheeler Publishing, Inc.) Gale Group.

—Big Girls Don't Cry. 1996. 384p. 23.00 o.s.i (*0-06-017277-0*); 207.00 o.p. (*0-06-017473-0*) HarperCollins Pubs.

—A Long Way from Home. 1999. 368p. 25.00 (*0-06-017278-9*) HarperCollins Pubs.

—A Long Way from Home. 2000. 416p. mass mkt. 7.50 (*0-06-103021-X*, Avon Bks.) Morrow/Avon.

—A Long Way from Home. 2000. 13.04 (*0-606-22863-2*) Turtleback Bks.

—P. G. County. 2003. 336p. pap. 13.95 (*0-345-44413-2*, One World/Ballantine) Ballantine Bks.

—P. G. County. 2002. 336p. 24.95 (*0-385-50161-7*) Doubleday Publishing.

—P. G. County. l.t. ed. 2003. (Basic Ser.). 469p. 29.95 (*0-7862-4931-5*) Thorndike Pr.

Brodber, Erna. Louisiana: A Novel. 1997. 168p. (Orig.). pap. 17.00 (*1-57806-031-1*) Univ. Pr. of Mississippi.

Brookhouse, Christopher. Passing Game. 2000. 160p. 19.95 (*0-9665798-2-8*) Safe Harbor Bks.

Brooks, Eva O'Nay. Angie Lou's Avenues to Circle U. 2000. (Illus.). 120p. pap. 8.95 (*0-9703045-0-1*) JMT Pubns.

Brown, Cecil. The Life & Loves of Mr. Jive Ass Nigger. 1996. 256p. reprint ed. pap. 12.00 o.p. (*0-88001-517-9*) HarperCollins Pubs.

Brown, Charlotte H. Mammy: An Appeal to the Heart of the South; &, The Correct Thing to Do—to Say—to Wear. 1995. (African American Women Writers, 1910-1940 Ser.). 149p. 25.00 (*0-8161-1632-6*, Macmillan Reference USA) Gale Group.

Brown, John G. The Wrecked, Blessed Body of Shelton Lafleur. l.t. ed. 1997. (Paperback Ser.). 361p. pap. 21.95 (*0-7838-8198-3*, Macmillan Reference USA) Gale Group.

—The Wrecked, Blessed Body of Shelton Lafleur. 1996. 256p. 21.95 o.p. (*0-395-72988-2*) Houghton Mifflin Co.

—The Wrecked, Blessed Body of Shelton Lafleur. 1997. pap. 12.00 (*0-380-72965-2*, Avon Bks.) Morrow/Avon.

Brown, Linda Beatrice. Crossing over Jordan. 1995. 320p. 22.00 o.p. (*0-345-37857-1*) Ballantine Bks.

Brown, Lloyd L. Iron City. 1994. (Library of Black Literature). 288p. text 45.00 (*1-55553-205-5*) Northeastern Univ. Pr.

Brown, Parry. Sittin' in the Front Pew: A Novel. 2002. 256p. pap. 13.95 (*0-375-75705-8*, Villard Bks.) Random House Adult Trade Publishing Group.

Brown, Parry A. The Shirt Off His Back. 1998. 244p. pap. 14.95 (*0-9666503-0-1*) ShanKrys Publishing, Inc.

—The Shirt off His Back. E-Book 11.00 (*1-58945-615-7*) Adobe Systems, Inc.

—The Shirt off His Back. 2001. E-Book 11.00 (*0-375-50654-3*) Random Hse., Inc.

—The Shirt off His Back: A Novel. 2001. 256p. pap. 13.95 (*0-375-75659-0*, Villard Bks.) Random House Adult Trade Publishing Group.

Brown, Richard E. & Brown, Beverly A. The Rose Engagement. exp. ed. 1996. 205p. (Orig.). (C). pap. text 12.00 (*0-9654000-2-6*) Kent Information Services, Inc.

Brown, Rosellen. Civil Wars. 1994. 544p. mass mkt. 5.99 o.s.i (*0-440-21695-8*) Dell Publishing.

—Civil Wars. 1985. (Contemporary American Fiction Ser.). 432p. pap. 9.95 o.p. (*0-14-007783-9*, Penguin Bks.) Viking Penguin.

Brown, Wesley. Darktown Strutters: A Novel. 1994. 225p. (C). pap. text 11.95 (*0-943433-11-8*) Cane Hill Pr.

—Darktown Strutters: A Novel. 2000. 240p. pap. 18.95 (*1-55849-270-4*) Univ. of Massachusetts Pr.

Brown, William Wells. Clotel. 2003. 320p. pap. 11.00 (*0-14-243772-7*, Penguin Classics) Viking Penguin.

—Clotel or the President's Daughter. 2001. pap. 12.95 o.s.i (*0-8065-2184-8*, Citadel Pr.) Kensington Publishing Corp.

Browne, Martha G. Autobiography of a Female Slave. 1970. 401p. reprint ed. 45.00 o.s.i (*0-8371-2194-9*, GRS&) Greenwood Publishing Group, Inc.

—Autobiography of a Female Slave. 1991. (American Biography Ser.). 401p. reprint ed. lib. bdg. 89.00 (*0-7812-8046-X*) Reprint Services Corp.

Bruce, Andasia K. Uncle Tom's Cabin of To-Day. 1977. (Black Heritage Library Collection). reprint ed. 18.95 (*0-8369-9161-3*) Ayer Co. Pubs., Inc.

Bryant, Henry E. Tar Heel Tales. 1977. (Black Heritage Library Collection). reprint ed. 23.95 (*0-8369-9162-1*) Ayer Co. Pubs., Inc.

Bryant, Jerold M. Single Man Screaming. 1999. 224p. pap. 14.95 (*0-9669595-1-5*, S M S Marketing & Publishing); 1997. 24.95 (*0-9669595-0-7*) SMS Cos., Inc.

Bryant, Niobia. Three Times a Lady. 2001. (Arabesque Ser.). 320p. mass mkt. 5.99 (*1-58314-165-0*, Arabesque) BET Bks.

Buffa, D. W. The Legacy. l.t. ed. 2002. (Americana Ser.). 656p. 29.95 (*0-7862-4655-3*) Thorndike Pr.

—The Legacy. 2004. 480p. mass mkt. 8.00 (*0-446-61013-5*); 2003. 496p. mass mkt. 7.99 (*0-446-61368-1*); 2002. 448p. 25.95 (*0-446-52738-6*) Warner Bks., Inc.

Buford, G. Dan. Separate but Equal, , Jasma, Ricardy & Morton, Randolph B., eds. 2003. (Politics of Black Love Novel Ser.: Vol. 2). 288p. pap. 15.00 (*0-9718191-4-9*) La Caille Nous Publishing Co.

Bullard, Linda M. Shades of Justice. 1999. 352p. reprint ed. mass mkt. 6.99 o.s.i (*0-451-19768-2*, Signet Bks.) NAL.

Bundy, Dolores & Riley, Cole. Indigo after Dark, Vol. II. 2001. (Illus.). pap. 10.95 (*1-58571-051-2*, Indigo) Genesis Pr., Inc.

Bunkley, Anita Richmond. Balancing Act. 1997. 352p. 23.95 o.p. (*0-525-94010-3*) Dutton/Plume.

—Balancing Act. 1998. 400p. mass mkt. 6.99 o.s.i (*0-451-18483-1*, Signet Bks.) NAL.

—Starlight Passage. 1996. (Illus.). 368p. 23.95 o.p. (*0-525-94009-X*, Dutton) Dutton/Plume.

Bunkley, Anita Richmond, et al. Girlfriends. 1999. 368p. mass mkt. 6.99 (*0-06-101369-2*, Harper-Torch) Morrow/Avon.

Burke, James Lee. Half of Paradise. Date not set. lib. bdg. 24.95 (*0-8488-1778-8*) Amereon, Ltd.

—Half of Paradise. 1998. 469p. mass mkt. 6.50 (*0-7868-8946-2*); 1995. 288p. pap. 10.95 (*0-7868-8117-8*) Hyperion Pr.

—Half of Paradise. l.t. ed. 2001. 482p. 29.95 (*0-7862-3398-2*); 487p. (*0-7540-9079-5*); 487p. (*0-7540-1683-8*) Thorndike Pr.

Burks, Cris. SilkyDreamGirl. 2002. (Illus.). 304p. pap. 12.95 (*0-7679-1295-0*) Broadway Bks.

Burton, Rainelle. The Root Worker. 2001. 208p. 25.95 (*1-58567-140-1*) Overlook Pr., The.

—The Root Worker. 2002. 208p. reprint ed. pap. 13.00 (*0-14-200085-X*) Viking Penguin.

Butler, Octavia E. Parable of the Sower. 1993. 299p. 19.95 o.p. (*0-941423-99-9*) Four Walls Eight Windows.

—Parable of the Sower. 1993. 352p. 19.95 (*1-888363-25-8*) Seven Stories Pr.

—Parable of the Sower. 2000. 20.00 (*0-606-19220-4*) Turtleback Bks.

—Parable of the Sower. 2000. 352p. reprint ed. pap. 13.95 (*0-446-67550-4*) Warner Bks., Inc.

—Parable of the Talents. 1998. 365p. 24.95 (*1-888363-81-9*) Seven Stories Pr.

—Parable of the Talents. 2000. 20.00 (*0-606-21854-8*) Turtleback Bks.

—Parable of the Talents. 2000. 464p. pap. 13.95 (*0-446-67578-4*) Warner Bks., Inc.

—Wild Seed. 2001. 320p. pap. 13.95 o.s.i (*0-446-67697-7*) Warner Bks., Inc.

Butler, Octavia E., contrib. by. Parable of the Talents. 1998. Seven Stories Pr.

Butler, Octavia E. & Butler, Cctavia E. Parable of the Sower. 1995. 304p. reprint ed. mass mkt. 6.99 (*0-446-60197-7*) Warner Bks., Inc.

Butler, Tajuana. The Night Before Thirty: A Novel. 2003. 240p. 19.95 (*1-4000-6020-6*, Villard Bks.) Random House Adult Trade Publishing Group.

—Sorority Sisters: A Novel. 1998. 301p. 17.00 (*0-9659254-3-9*) Lavelle Publishing.

—Sorority Sisters: A Novel. 2001. 240p. pap. 12.95 (*0-375-75758-9*, Villard Bks.) Random House Adult Trade Publishing Group.

Byrd, Adrianne. All I've Ever Wanted. 2001. (Arabesque Ser.). 256p. mass mkt. 5.99 (*1-58314-137-5*) BET Bks.

—I Promise. 1999. mass mkt. 4.99 (*1-58314-019-0*) BET Bks.

Cain, George. Blueschild Baby. 1987. 180p. reprint ed. pap. 7.50 o.p. (*0-88001-133-5*) HarperCollins Pubs.

—Blueschild Baby. 1994. pap. o.p. (*0-88001-349-4*, Ecco) HarperTrade.

Caldwell, Erskine. The Black & White Stories of Erskine Caldwell. McIver, Ray, ed. 1984. 189p. 14.95 o.p. (*0-931948-63-0*) Peachtree Pubs., Ltd.

—Terre Tragique. 1986. (FRE.). 224p. pap. 10.95 (*0-7859-2049-8*, 2070377733) French & European Pubns., Inc.

—Trouble in July. 1977. (Illus.). 160p. 25.00 (*0-88322-025-3*) Beehive Pr., The.

—Trouble in July. 1975. mass mkt. 1.25 o.p. (*0-451-06527-1*, Y6527); 1970. mass mkt. 0.50 o.p. (*0-451-02616-0*); 1970. mass mkt. 0.75 o.p. (*0-451-04331-6*); 1970. mass mkt. 0.35 o.p. (*0-451-01608-4*); 1970. mass mkt. 0.25 o.p. (*0-451-00567-8*) NAL. (Signet Bks.).

—Trouble in July. 1999. (Brown Thrasher Bks.). xxiii, 241p. pap. 14.95 (*0-8203-2105-2*) Univ. of Georgia Pr.

Campbell, Bebe Moore. Brothers & Sisters. 2000. 480p. pap. 13.95 (*0-425-17267-8*); 1995. 560p. mass mkt. 7.99 (*0-425-14940-4*) Berkley Publishing Group.

—Brothers & Sisters. l.t. ed. 1995. (Large Print Bks.). 26.95 o.p. (*1-56895-211-2*, Wheeler Publishing, Inc.) Gale Group.

—Brothers & Sisters. 476p. pap. 22.95 o.p. (*0-7651-0630-2*) Smithmark Pubs., Inc.

—Brothers & Sisters. 1995. 14.04 (*0-606-19295-6*) Turtleback Bks.

—Brothers & Sisters. 1997. 4.98 (*0-681-56088-6*) Waldenbooks, Inc.

—Singing in the Comeback Choir. 1999. 400p. reprint ed. mass mkt. 7.99 (*0-425-16662-7*) Berkley Publishing Group.

—Singing in the Comeback Choir. l.t. ed. 1998. (Large Print Book Ser.). 27.95 (*1-56895-613-4*, Wheeler Publishing, Inc.) Gale Group.

—Singing in the Comeback Choir. 1998. 320p. 24.95 o.p. (*0-399-14298-3*, G. P. Putnam's Sons) Penguin Group (USA) Inc.

—Singing in the Comeback Choir. 1999. 13.55 (*0-606-19302-2*) Turtleback Bks.

—What You Owe Me. 2001. 400p. 25.95 o.p. (*0-399-14784-5*) Penguin Group (USA) Inc.

—What You Owe Me. 2002. (African American Ser.). 915p. 29.95 (*0-7862-3875-5*) Thorndike Pr.

—Your Blues Ain't Like Mine. 1995. 448p. mass mkt. 7.50 o.s.i (*0-345-40112-3*); 1993. 352p. pap. 14.00 (*0-345-38395-8*, One World/Ballantine) Ballantine Bks.

—Your Blues Ain't Like Mine. l.t. ed. 1995. (Large Print Bks.). 24.95 o.p. (*1-56895-221-X*, Wheeler Publishing, Inc.) Gale Group.

—Your Blues Ain't Like Mine. 1992. 352p. 23.95 o.p. (*0-399-13746-7*) Penguin Group (USA) Inc.

Cantor, Jay. Great Neck: A Novel. 720p. 2004. pap. 15.00 (*0-375-71339-5*); 2003. 27.95 (*0-375-41394-4*) Knopf, Alfred A. Inc.

Carbado, Devon W., et al, eds. Black Like Us: A Century of Lesbian, Gay & Bisexual African American Fiction. 2002. 575p. pap. 24.95 (*1-57344-108-2*) Cleis Pr.

Carey, Robert D. & Furbay, John H. Freedom Ships: The Spectacular Epic of African Americans Who Dared to Find Their Freedom Long Before Emancipation. 1999. (Illus.). 358p. (Orig.). pap. 14.95 (*0-9669613-0-7*, 101) Af-Am Links Pr.

Carlysle, Viveca. Temptation. 2001. (Arabesque Ser.). 256p. mass mkt. 5.99 (*1-58314-170-7*) BET Bks.

Carroll, Lee. Victim of the Game. 2003. E-Book 12.95 incl. cd-rom (*1-58444-030-9*); 1999. 432p. pap. 19.95 (*1-58444-069-4*) Disc-Us Bks., Inc.

Carter, Charlotte. Coq Au Vin. 1999. (Nanette Hayes Mystery Ser.). 200p. 22.00 o.s.i (*0-89296-678-5*) Mysterious Pr.

—Coq Au Vin. 2000. (Nanette Hayes Mysteries Ser.). 224p. mass mkt. 6.50 (*0-446-60787-8*) Warner Bks., Inc.

—Drumsticks. 2000. (Nanette Hayes Mystery Ser.). 208p. 22.95 (*0-89296-679-3*) Mysterious Pr.

—Rhode Island Red. (Mask Noir Ser.). 1998. 176p. pap. (*1-85242-591-1*); Vol. 1. 1997. 250p. (*1-85242-564-4*) Serpent's Tail Ltd.

—Rhode Island Red. 1999. (Nanette Hayes Mysteries Ser.). 224p. mass mkt. 5.99 (*0-446-60664-2*) Warner Bks., Inc.

—Walking Bones. 2002. 192p. pap. 14.00 (*1-85242-680-2*) Serpent's Tail Ltd. GBR. *Dist:* Consortium Bk. Sales & Distribution.

Carter, Lee. Carry Me Home. 1995. 12.99 o.p. (*0-7852-7858-3*) Nelson, Thomas Inc.

Carter, Reon & Laudat, Reon. Picture Perfect. 2000. 281p. pap. 8.95 (*1-58571-004-0*, Indigo) Genesis Pr., Inc.

Carter, Stephen L. The Emperor of Ocean Park: A Novel. 2003. 672p. reprint ed. pap. 14.00 (*0-375-71292-5*, Vintage) Knopf Publishing Group.

—The Emperor of Ocean Park: A Novel. 2002. 672p. 26.95 (*0-375-41363-4*) Knopf, Alfred A. Inc.

—The Emperor of Ocean Park: A Novel. l.t. ed. 2002. 1152p. 26.95 (*0-375-43165-9*) Random Hse. Large Print.

Carter, Vincent O. Such Sweet Thunder: A Novel. 2003. (Illus.). 560p. 25.95 (*1-58642-058-5*) Steerforth Pr.

Cary, Lorene. Pride: A Novel. 1999. 336p. pap. 14.00 (*0-385-48183-7*) Doubleday Publishing.

Caulton, Sonia. No More Love Making. Wallace, Gary, ed. 2001. 358p. pap. 16.00 (*0-9655545-2-X*) SistahGirl Publishing Co.

Charters, Samuel B. Louisiana Black. 1986. 224p. 18.95 o.p. (*0-7145-2855-2*) Boyars, Marion Pubs., Inc.

Charyn, Jerome. The Seventh Babe. 1984. 352p. pap. 2.95 o.p. (*0-380-51540-7*, 51540, Avon Bks.); 1979. 9.95 o.p. (*0-87795-220-5*, Morrow, William & Co.) Morrow/Avon.

—The Seventh Babe. 1996. 352p. (C). 46.00 (*0-87805-898-2*); pap. 16.95 (*0-87805-882-6*) Univ. Pr. of Mississippi.

Chase-Riboud, Barbara. Sally Hemings: A Novel. 1994. 416p. reprint ed. pap. 12.00 o.s.i (*0-345-38971-9*) Ballantine Bks.

—Sally Hemings: A Novel. 1992. 300p. reprint ed. lib. bdg. 37.95 (*0-89966-915-8*) Buccaneer Bks., Inc.

—Sally Hemings: A Novel. 1980. 416p. mass mkt. 4.95 (*0-380-48686-5*, Avon Bks.) Morrow/Avon.

—Sally Hemings: A Novel. 2000. 368p. pap. 14.95 (*0-312-24704-4*, Saint Martin's Griffin) St. Martin's Pr.

—Sally Hemings: A Novel. 1979. 12.95 o.p. (*0-670-61605-2*) Viking Penguin.

Cheatham, Tony M. Father's Footsteps. Morton, Randolph B. & Cadet, Guichard, eds. 2002. 300p. pap. 15.00 (*0-9718191-1-4*) La Caille Nous Publishing Co.

Chesnutt, Charles Waddell. The Conjure Woman. 1988. reprint ed. lib. bdg. 59.00 (*0-7812-0047-4*) Reprint Services Corp.

—The Conjure Woman. reprint ed. 45.00 (*0-403-07386-3*) Scholarly Pr., Inc.

—The Conjure Woman. 1969. (Ann Arbor Paperbacks Ser.). (Illus.). 256p. (C). pap. text 14.95 (*0-472-06156-9*, 06156) Univ. of Michigan Pr.

—The Conjure Woman. 2000. (Classics Ser.). 304p. 10.95 (*0-14-118502-3*, Penguin Classics) Viking Penguin.

—The Conjure Woman & Other Conjure Tales. 1993. 216p. pap. 15.95 (*0-8223-1387-1*); text 54.95 (*0-8223-1378-2*) Duke Univ. Pr.

—The House Behind the Cedars. 2002. 196p. 94.99 (*1-4043-0866-0*); per. 89.99 (*1-4043-0867-9*) IndyPublish.com.

—The House Behind the Cedars. Jackson Fossett, Judith, ed. 2003. 256p. pap. 12.95 (*0-8129-6616-3*, Modern Library) Random House Adult Trade Publishing Group.

—The House Behind the Cedars. l.t. ed. 1999. 440p. text 29.95 (*1-56000-494-0*) Transaction Pubs.

—The House Behind the Cedars. 2000. xxi, 294p. pap. 11.95 (*0-8203-2194-X*) Univ. of Georgia Pr.

—The House Behind the Cedars. Gibson, Donald, ed. & intro. by. 1993. (Twentieth Century Classics Ser.). 336p. 12.95 (*0-14-018685-9*, Penguin Classics) Viking Penguin.

—The Marrow of Tradition. reprint ed. 42.50 (*0-404-00014-2*) AMS Pr., Inc.

—The Marrow of Tradition. 1976. 25.95 (*0-8488-0962-9*) Amereon, Ltd.

—The Marrow of Tradition. 1977. (Black Heritage Library Collection). 17.95 (*0-8369-8539-7*) Ayer Co. Pubs., Inc.

—The Marrow of Tradition. 1986. (Muckrakers Ser.). reprint ed. pap. 6.95 o.p. (*0-89197-836-4*); lib. bdg. 13.00 o.p. (*0-8398-0260-9*) Irvington Pubs.

—The Marrow of Tradition. 2001. 352p. 12.95 (*0-375-75690-6*, Modern Library) Random House Adult Trade Publishing Group.

—The Marrow of Tradition. l.t. ed. 1999. 310p. text 29.95 (*1-56000-493-2*) Transaction Pubs.

—The Marrow of Tradition. 2nd ed. 1969. (Ann Arbor Paperbacks Ser.). (Illus.). 352p. (C). pap. text 14.95 (*0-472-06147-X*, 06147) Univ. of Michigan Pr.

—The Marrow of Tradition. Sundquist, Eric J., ed. & intro. by. 1993. (Penguin Twentieth-Century Classics Ser.). 400p. pap. 13.95 (*0-14-018686-7*, Penguin Classics) Viking Penguin.

—The Marrow of Tradition: American Negro. 1968. (His History & Literature Ser.: No. 2). reprint ed. 17.95 (*0-405-01855-X*) Ayer Co. Pubs., Inc.

Chesnutt, Charles Waddell & Andrews, William L. The House Behind the Cedars. 1988. (Brown Thrasher Bks.). 312p. reprint ed. pap. 14.95 o.s.i (*0-8203-1021-2*) Univ. of Georgia Pr.

Chesnutt, Charles Waddell & McWilliams, Dean. The Quarry. 1999. 288p. text 42.50 o.p. (*0-691-05995-0*); pap. text 18.95 (*0-691-05996-9*) Princeton Univ. Pr.

Childers, James S. In the Deep South: A Novel about a White Man & a Black Man. 1988. (Library of Alabama Classics). (Illus.). 304p. reprint ed. pap. 16.50 o.p. (*0-8173-0387-1*) Univ. of Alabama Pr.

Christopher Murray, Victoria. Temptation. 1997. 279p. pap. 12.95 o.p. (*1-881524-14-0*) Milligan Bks.

Church, J. W. Deep in Piney Woods. 1977. (Black Heritage Library Collection). (Illus.). reprint ed. 19.95 (*0-8369-9018-8*) Ayer Co. Pubs., Inc.

Clair, Maxine. October Suite: A Novel. 2002. E-Book 19.00 (*1-59061-867-X*) Adobe Systems, Inc.

—October Suite: A Novel. 2002. 352p. pap. 12.95 (*0-375-76095-4*) Random House Adult Trade Publishing Group.

—October Suite: A Novel. 2001. E-Book 19.00 (*1-58836-059-8*) Random Hse., Inc.

—October Suite: A Novel. l.t. ed. 2002. (African American Ser.). 563p. 28.95 (*0-7862-4094-6*) Thorndike Pr.

—Rattlebone. 1994. 224p. 19.00 o.p. (*0-374-24716-1*) Farrar, Straus & Giroux.

—Rattlebone. 1995. 224p. 10.95 (*0-14-024825-0*) Viking Penguin.

Clark, Beverly. A Love to Cherish. 1999. 287p. mass mkt. 8.95 (*1-885478-84-4*, Indigo) Genesis Pr., Inc.

—Yesterday Is Gone. 1997. 293p. mass mkt. 10.95 (*1-885478-12-7*, Indigo) Genesis Pr., Inc.

Clark, Stephen J. Southern Latitudes. 2002. 272p. mass mkt. 6.50 o.s.i (*0-425-18637-7*, Prime Crime) Berkley Publishing Group.

Clarke, Breena. River, Cross My Heart. 2000. 272p. mass mkt. 7.50 (*0-316-89816-3*) Hyperion Pr.

—River, Cross My Heart. 2000. 288p. E-Book 6.95 (*0-7595-8007-3*); 2000. 288p. E-Book 6.95 (*0-7595-0007-X*); 1999. 288p. 23.00 o.p. (*0-316-89999-2*); 1999. 256p. pap. 14.95 (*0-316-89998-4*) Little Brown & Co.

—River, Cross My Heart. 1999. 224p. 23.00 (*0-316-14423-1*) Little Brown Children's Bks.

—River, Cross My Heart. l.t. ed. 2000. (Thorndike General Ser.). 341p. pap. 28.95 (*0-7862-2432-0*); 30.95 (*0-7862-2431-2*) Thorndike Pr.

—River, Cross My Heart. 1999. 20.50 (*0-606-19030-9*) Turtleback Bks.

—River, Cross My Heart. 2000. 288p. E-Book 6.95 (*0-7595-9007-9*) Warner Bks., Inc.

Clarke, John Henrik, ed. American Negro Short Stories. 1966. (American Century Ser.). 374p. pap. 10.95 o.p. (*0-374-52141-7*, Hill & Wang) Farrar, Straus & Giroux.

—Black American Short Stories. rev. ed. 1993. (American Century Ser.). 448p. pap. 15.00 (*0-374-52354-1*, Hill & Wang) Farrar, Straus & Giroux.

Cleage, Pearl. I Wish I Had a Red Dress. l.t. ed. 2001. (Hardcover Ser.). 340p. 30.95 (*1-58724-062-9*, Wheeler Publishing, Inc.) Gale Group.

—I Wish I Had a Red Dress. 2001. 336p. 24.00 (*0-380-97733-8*, Morrow, William & Co.) Morrow/Avon.

—What Looks Like Crazy on an Ordinary Day. unabr. ed. 2001. audio 54.95 (*0-7927-2439-9*, CSL 328, Chivers Sound Library) BBC Audiobooks America.

—What Looks Like Crazy on an Ordinary Day. 256p. 1998. pap. 13.00 (*0-380-79487-X*, Avon Bks.); 1997. 20.00 (*0-380-97584-X*, Morrow, William & Co.) Morrow/Avon.

—What Looks Like Crazy on an Ordinary Day. l.t. ed. (Americana Ser.). 416p. 2000. pap. 26.95 (*0-7862-1760-X*); 1999. 29.95 (*0-7862-1759-6*) Thorndike Pr.

Close, Ellis. The Best Defense. 1999. 432p. mass mkt. 6.99 o.s.i (*0-06-093087-X*); 1998. 272p. 24.00 (*0-06-017496-X*) HarperCollins Pubs.

Cobb, William. A Walk Through Fire: A Novel. 1992. 544p. 22.00 o.p. (*0-688-11366-4*, Morrow, William & Co.) Morrow/Avon.

Coleman, Evelyn. What a Woman's Gotta Do. 1999. 400p. mass mkt. 6.99 (*0-440-23500-6*) Dell Publishing.

—What a Woman's Gotta Do. 1998. 320p. 23.00 (*0-684-83175-9*, Simon & Schuster) Simon & Schuster.

Coleman, Wanda. Mambo Hips & Make Believe. ltd. ed. 1999. 250p. 35.00 o.p. (*1-57423-096-4*, Black Sparrow Pr.) Godine, David R. Pub.

—Mambo Hips & Make Believe: A Novel. 1999. 403p. 25.00 o.p. (*1-57423-095-6*, Black Sparrow Pr.) Godine, David R. Pub.

—Mambo Hips & Make Believe: A Novel. 1999. 403p. pap. 16.00 (*1-57423-094-8*) HarperCollins Pubs.

—A War of Eyes & Other Stories. 1988. 246p. 20.00 o.p. (*0-87685-737-3*, Black Sparrow Pr.) Godine, David R. Pub.

—A War of Eyes & Other Stories. 246p. 1989. pap. 15.00 (*0-87685-735-7*); 1988. 20.00 (*0-87685-736-5*) HarperCollins Pubs.

Collins, Jane S. Free at Last. 1977. (Black Heritage Library Collection). reprint ed. 25.95 (*0-8369-8962-7*) Ayer Co. Pubs., Inc.

Colter, Cyrus. The Amoralists & Other Tales: Collected Stories. 1988. (Contemporary Fiction Ser.). 288p. 19.95 o.p. (*0-938410-67-9*, Thunder's Mouth Pr.) Avalon Publishing Group.

—The Beach Umbrella & Other Stories. 1996. 283p. pap. 18.00 o.p. (*0-8101-5050-6*) Northwestern Univ. Pr.

—A Chocolate Soldier. 1988. (Contemporary Fiction Ser.). 350p. (C). 19.95 o.p. (*0-938410-42-3*); pap. 9.95 o.p. (*0-938410-49-0*) Avalon Publishing Group. (Thunder's Mouth Pr.).

—A Chocolate Soldier. 1995. 278p. pap. 18.00 o.p. (*0-8101-5038-7*) Northwestern Univ. Pr.

—City of Light: A Novel. 1993. 352p. 22.95 o.p. (*1-56025-059-3*); pap. 12.95 o.p. (*1-56025-061-5*) Avalon Publishing Group. (Thunder's Mouth Pr.).

—City of Light: A Novel. 1998. 432p. pap. 22.00 (*0-8101-5080-8*, TriQuarterly Bks.) Northwestern Univ. Pr.

Connelly-Craig, Dawn. The Rest of Our Lives. 2001. 370p. pap. 15.00 (*0-9650970-4-8*); 2000. (*0-9650970-5-6*) Waverly Hse. Publishing Co.

Cooper, Clarence, Jr. Black. 1997. 320p. pap. 12.00 o.p. (*0-393-31541-X*) Norton, W. W. & Co., Inc.

Cooper, J. California. The Future Has a Past. pap. (*0-385-72883-2*) Knopf Publishing Group.

—The Future Has a Past: Stories. 2001. 288p. pap. 13.00 (*0-385-49681-8*, Knopf Bks. for Young Readers) Random Hse. Children's Bks.

—Homemade Love. 1988. 192p. pap. 9.95 o.p. (*0-312-01039-7*, Saint Martin's Griffin); 1986. 160p. 12.95 o.p. (*0-312-38895-0*) St. Martin's Pr.

—In Search of Satisfaction. 1994. 21.95 o.s.i (*0-385-46785-0*); 1995. 368p. reprint ed. pap. 13.00 (*0-385-46786-9*) Doubleday Publishing.

—The Matter Is Life. 240p. 1992. pap. 12.00 (*0-385-41174-X*); 1991. 18.00 o.s.i (*0-385-41173-1*) Doubleday Publishing.

—A Piece of Mine: A New Short Story Collection. 1991. 144p. (Orig.). reprint ed. pap. 10.50 (*0-385-42087-0*) Doubleday Publishing.

—Some Love, Some Pain, Sometime. 1995. 288p. 22.95 o.s.i (*0-385-46787-7*) Doubleday Publishing.

—Some Soul to Keep. 1998. 224p. pap. 11.95 (*0-312-19337-8*, Saint Martin's Griffin); 1988. 224p. pap. 10.95 o.p. (*0-312-02285-9*, Saint Martin's Griffin); 1987. 192p. 14.95 o.p. (*0-312-00684-5*) St. Martin's Pr.

—The Wake of the Wind: A Novel. 384p. 1999. pap. 13.95 (*0-385-48705-3*); 1998. 22.95 o.s.i (*0-385-48704-5*) Doubleday Publishing.

Copeland, Sheila. A Chocolate Affair. 288p. mass mkt. 6.99 (*1-58314-441-2*, Arabesque); 2001. 240p. pap. 15.00 (*1-58314-234-7*, Sepia) BET Bks.

—Chocolate Star. 1997. 384p. 23.95 (*0-312-15493-3*) St. Martin's Pr.

Corbin, Steven. Fragments That Remain. 1995. 318p. pap. 9.95 o.p. (*1-55583-274-1*); 1993. 280p. 19.95 o.p. (*1-55583-218-0*) Alyson Pubns.

Craft, Francine. Star Crossed. 2000. (Arabesque Ser.). 336p. mass mkt. 5.99 (*1-58314-099-9*) BET Bks.

Crafts, Hannah. The Bondwoman's Narrative. l.t. ed. 2002. (African American Ser.). 29.95 (*0-7862-4471-2*) Thorndike Pr.

—The Bondwoman's Narrative. Gates, Henry Louis, Jr., ed. 2002. (Illus.). 416p. 24.95 (*0-446-53008-5*) Warner Bks., Inc.

—The Bondwoman's Narrative. Gates, Henry Louis, Jr., ed. & intro. by. fac. ed. 2003. (Illus.). 384p. 50.00 (*0-446-53173-1*) Warner Bks., Inc.

—The Bondwoman's Narrative. Gates, Henry Louis, Jr., ed. 2003. 464p. reprint ed. pap. 14.95 (*0-446-69029-5*) Warner Bks., Inc.

Crayton, Spurgeon E. Screams of Protest. 1982. (Illus.). 10.00 (*0-8315-0188-X*) Speller, Robert & Sons, Pubs., Inc.

Criswell, Robert. Uncle Tom's Cabin Contrasted with Buckingham Hall, the Planter's Home. reprint ed. 32.50 (*0-404-00254-4*) AMS Pr., Inc.

Crooks, Paul. Ancestors. 2002. (Illus.). 296p. pap. 12.95 (*1-901969-07-X*) BlackAmber Bks. GBR. *Dist:* SPD-Small Pr. Distribution.

—Ancestors. l.t. ed. 2003. (Ulverscroft Large Print Ser.). 456p. 32.50 (*0-7089-4791-3*) Thorpe, F. A. Pubs. GBR. *Dist:* Ulverscroft Large Print Bks., Ltd., Ulverscroft Large Print Canada, Ltd.

Crouch, Stanley. Don't the Moon Look Lonesome? A Novel in Blues & Swing. 2000. 560p. 26.95 o.s.i (*0-375-40932-7*, Pantheon) Knopf Publishing Group.

Cruz, Ricardo C. Straight Outta Compton. 1992. 121p. 18.95 (*0-932511-60-0*); pap. 10.95 (*0-932511-61-9*) Fiction Collective Two, Inc.

Cuthbert, Margaret. The Silent Cradle. 1999. 496p. mass mkt. 6.99 (*0-671-01514-1*, Pocket); 1998. 368p. 23.00 o.s.i (*0-671-01513-3*, Atria) Simon & Schuster.

—The Silent Cradle. abr. ed. 1998. audio 18.00 (*0-671-58064-7*, 393598, Simon & Schuster Audioworks) Simon & Schuster Audio.

—The Silent Cradle. abr. ed. 1999. audio 16.85 (*0-671-01116-2*) Ulverscroft Audio (U.S.A.).

D'Aguiar, Fred. Feeding the Ghosts. 1999. 240p. o.p. (*0-88001-623-X*, Ecco) HarperTrade.

Dande, Leon. Blue Blood. 1977. (Black Heritage Library Collection). reprint ed. 40.95 (*0-8369-8965-1*) Ayer Co. Pubs., Inc.

Darden, Christopher A. L. A. Justice. 2002. 464p. reprint ed. mass mkt. 6.99 o.s.i (*0-451-20541-3*, Signet Bks.) NAL.

Darden, Christopher A. & Lochte, Dick. L. A. Justice. 2001. 448p. 25.95 o.p. (*0-446-52327-5*) Warner Bks., Inc.

—The Last Defense. 2002. 368p. 24.95 (*0-451-20732-7*) NAL.

—The Trials of Nikki Hill. 2001. 496p. mass mkt. 7.50 o.s.i (*0-446-60798-3*); 1999. 448p. 25.00 (*0-446-52326-7*) Warner Bks., Inc.

Dash, Julie. Daughters of the Dust: The Making of an African American Woman's Film. 320p. 1999. pap. 13.95 o.s.i (*0-452-27607-1*, Plume); 1997. 24.95 o.p. (*0-525-94109-6*) Dutton/Plume.

Daugharty, Janice. Whistle: A Novel. 1998. 224p. 22.00 (*0-06-017551-6*) HarperSanFrancisco.

Daugherty, Tracy. Axeman's Jazz: A Novel. 2003. 240p. 22.50 (*0-87074-481-X*) Southern Methodist Univ. Pr.

David, Nicholas. Notes by the Piano: A Hip-Hop Novel. 2003. 167p. pap. 20.99 o.p. (*0-7388-2935-8*); E-Book 8.00 o.p. (*0-7388-7113-3*) Xlibris Corp.

Davis, Kathleen Legeia. Serpentina: A Novel. 2003. (Illus.). 323p. 18.50 (*0-9715402-1-7*, 410-707-6686) Barnhardt & Ashe Publishing, Inc.

Davis, Thulani. 1959. 1992. 295p. 18.95 o.p. (*0-8021-1230-7*) Grove/Atlantic, Inc.

—1959: A Novel. 1993. 304p. pap. 11.00 o.p. (*0-06-097529-6*, Perennial) HarperTrade.

De Forest, John W. The Bloody Chasm. 1977. (Black Heritage Library Collection). reprint ed. 29.95 (*0-8369-8979-1*) Ayer Co. Pubs., Inc.

—The Bloody Chasm. 1988. (Collected Works of John W. De Forest). reprint ed. lib. bdg. 79.00 (*0-7812-1164-6*) Reprint Services Corp.

—The Bloody Chasm. reprint ed. 69.00 (*0-403-04572-X*) Somerset Pubs., Inc.

DeBerry, Virginia. Trying to Sleep in the Bed You Made. 1996. 384p. 24.95 (*0-312-15233-7*) St. Martin's Pr.

DeLoach, Nora L. Mama Pursues Murderous Shadows. 2000. 192p. mass mkt. 5.99 (*0-553-57722-0*) Bantam Bks.

Dennis, Denise & Willmarth, Susan. Black History for Beginners. 4th ed. 1984. (Illus.). 192p. pap. 9.95 (*0-86316-068-9*) Writers & Readers Publishing, Inc.

Detter, Thomas. Nellie Brown: Or the Jealous Wife, with Other Sketches. 1996. (Blacks in the American West Ser.). 122p. (C). text 35.00 (*0-8032-1704-8*) Univ. of Nebraska Pr.

Devoto, Pat Cunningham. Out of the Night That Covers Me. l.t. ed. 2001. 434p. 28.95 (*1-58724-095-5*, Wheeler Publishing, Inc.) Gale Group.

—Out of the Night That Covers Me. 2001. 448p. pap. 13.95 (*0-446-67802-3*); 432p. 23.95 o.p. (*0-446-52751-3*) Warner Bks., Inc.

Dickey, Eric Jerome. Between Lovers. 2002. 400p. mass mkt. 7.50 (*0-451-20467-0*, Signet Bks.) NAL.
—Between Lovers: A Novel. 2001. 320p. 23.95 o.p. (*0-525-94603-9*, Dutton) Dutton/Plume.
—Between Lovers: A Novel. l.t. ed. 2002. 28.95 (*1-58724-172-2*, Wheeler Publishing, Inc.) Gale Group.
—Cheaters. 1999. 224p. 24.95 o.s.i (*0-525-94386-2*) Dutton/Plume.
—Cheaters. 2001. 368p. pap. 13.95 (*0-451-20300-3*); 2000. 448p. mass mkt. 7.50 (*0-451-19407-1*, Signet Bks.) NAL.
—Friends & Lovers. 1997. 416p. 23.95 (*0-525-94127-4*) Dutton/Plume.
—Liar's Game. 2000. 336p. 23.95 o.s.i (*0-525-94483-4*) Dutton/Plume.
—Liar's Game. l.t. ed. 2000. (Wheeler Large Print Book Ser.). 28.95 (*1-56895-986-9*, Wheeler Publishing, Inc.) Gale Group.
—Liar's Game. 2001. 400p. reprint ed. mass mkt. 7.50 (*0-451-20134-5*, Signet Bks.) NAL.
—Milk in My Coffee. 1998. 304p. 23.95 o.s.i (*0-525-94385-4*, Dutton Children's Bks.) Dutton/Plume.
—Milk in My Coffee. 1999. 384p. reprint ed. mass mkt. 7.50 (*0-451-19406-3*, Signet Bks.) NAL.
—Naughty or Nice. 2003. 176p. 17.95 (*0-525-94776-0*, Dutton) Dutton/Plume.
—The Other Woman: A Novel. 2003. 304p. 23.95 (*0-525-94724-8*, Dutton) Dutton/Plume.
—Thieves' Paradise. l.t. ed. 2002. (African American Ser.). 645p. 29.95 (*0-7862-4768-1*) Thorndike Pr.
Dickinson, Anna E. What Answer? 1977. (Black Heritage Library Collection). reprint ed. 22.95 (*0-8369-9004-8*) Ayer Co. Pubs., Inc.
—What Answer? 2003. (Classics in Black Studies). 316p. pap. 18.00 (*1-59102-050-6*, Humanity Bks.) Prometheus Bks., Pubs.
Dixon, Collen. Simon Says: A Novel of Intrigue, Betrayal... And Murder. 2003. 336p. pap. 12.95 (*0-8129-6881-6*, Villard Bks.) Random House Adult Trade Publishing Group.
Dooley, James H. Dem Good Ole Times. 1977. (Black Heritage Library Collection). (Illus.). reprint ed. 19.95 (*0-8369-9166-4*) Ayer Co. Pubs., Inc.
Douglass, Frederick, et al. Three Classic African-American Novels. Andrews, William L., ed. 1990. 368p. mass mkt. 6.99 (*0-451-62788-1*, Mentor) NAL.
Dry, Richard. Leaving: A Novel. 2003. 464p. pap. 14.95 (*0-312-30287-8*, Saint Martin's Griffin); 2002. 448p. 24.95 (*0-312-28331-8*) St. Martin's Pr.
Du Bois, W. E. B. Dark Princess: A Romance. 1995. (Banner Bks.). 312p. 48.00 (*0-87805-764-1*); 311p. pap. 20.00 (*0-87805-765-X*) Univ. Pr. of Mississippi.
Dunbar, Gloria. Dangling on a String. 2001. 192p. pap. 11.95 (*1-56315-234-7*) SterlingHouse Pubs., Inc.
Dunbar, Paul Laurence. Folks from Dixie. 2000. 252p. E-Book 3.95 (*0-594-04683-1*) 1873 Pr.
—Folks from Dixie. 1977. (Short Story Index Reprint Ser.). 18.95 (*0-8369-3218-8*); (Illus.). 17.95 (*0-8369-8699-7*) Ayer Co. Pubs., Inc.
—Folks from Dixie. reprint ed. pap. 75.00 (*1-4047-3526-7*) Classic Textbooks.
—Folks from Dixie. 1969. (Illus.). reprint ed. 18.75 o.p. (*0-8371-1098-X*) Greenwood Publishing Group, Inc.
—Folks from Dixie. (Illus.). 263p. reprint ed. pap. text 6.95 o.p. (*0-89197-761-9*); lib. bdg. 12.50 o.p. (*0-8290-2367-4*) Irvington Pubs.
—Heart of Happy Hollow. (Short Story Index Reprint Ser.). (C). reprint ed. 1991. pap. 29.95 (*0-88143-127-3*); 1977. 43.95 (*0-8369-3318-4*) Ayer Co. Pubs., Inc.
—Heart of Happy Hollow. reprint ed. 35.00 o.p. (*0-8371-1811-5*, DUH&) Greenwood Publishing Group, Inc.
—The Love of Landry. E-Book 3.95 (*0-594-04001-9*) 1873 Pr.
—The Love of Landry. (Black Heritage Library Collection). reprint ed. 1991. pap. text 24.95 (*0-88143-126-5*); 1977. 37.95 (*0-8369-8559-1*) Ayer Co. Pubs., Inc.
—The Love of Landry. 200p. reprint ed. 1986. lib. bdg. 12.25 o.p. (*0-8398-0372-9*); 1984. pap. 1.95 o.p. (*0-8290-1564-7*) Irvington Pubs.
—The Love of Landry. 1992. (Notable American Authors Ser.). reprint ed. lib. bdg. 75.00 (*0-7812-2712-7*) Reprint Services Corp.
—The Sport of the Gods. (American Negro). 262p. (C). reprint ed. 1991. pap. 27.95 (*0-88143-136-2*); 1978. 38.95 (*0-405-01859-2*) Ayer Co. Pubs., Inc.
—The Sport of the Gods. 1999. (Signet Classics). 176p. mass mkt. 5.95 (*0-451-52755-0*) NAL.
—The Sport of the Gods. 1992. (Notable American Authors Ser.). reprint ed. lib. bdg. 75.00 (*0-7812-2714-3*) Reprint Services Corp.
—The Strength of Gideon & Other Stories. reprint ed. 1991. pap. (*0-88143-137-0*); 1974. (Illus.). (C). 38.95 (*0-405-01860-6*) Ayer Co. Pubs., Inc.
Durham, David Anthony. Gabriel's Story. pap. (*0-385-72869-7*) Knopf Publishing Group.
—Gabriel's Story. 2002. 304p. pap. 13.00 (*0-385-72033-5*, Knopf Bks. for Young Readers) Random Hse. Children's Bks.
—Gabriel's Story. l.t. ed. 2002. (African American Ser.). 451p. 29.95 (*0-7862-4430-5*) Thorndike Pr.
—A Walk Through Darkness. l.t. ed. 2002. 28.95 (*1-58724-242-7*, Wheeler Publishing, Inc.) Gale Group.
—A Walk Through Darkness. 2003. 304p. reprint ed. pap. 13.00 (*0-385-72036-X*, Anchor) Knopf Publishing Group.
—A Walk Through Darkness: A Novel. 2002. 304p. 23.95 (*0-385-49925-6*) Doubleday Publishing.
Eakins, Patricia. The Marvelous Adventures of Pierre Baptiste. 1999. 264p. 20.00 (*0-8147-2209-1*) New York Univ. Pr.
Edwards, Grace F. Do or Die: A Mali Anderson Mystery. 2000. (Mali Anderson Mystery Ser.). 272p. 22.95 o.s.i (*0-385-49248-0*) Doubleday Publishing.
—If I Should Die. 1998. (Mali Anderson Mystery Ser.). 320p. reprint ed. mass mkt. 6.50 (*0-553-57631-3*) Bantam Bks.
—If I Should Die. 1997. 272p. 21.95 o.s.i (*0-385-48523-9*) Doubleday Publishing.
—No Time to Die. 2000. (Mali Anderson Mystery Ser.). 240p. mass mkt. 5.99 (*0-553-57956-8*) Bantam Bks.
—No Time to Die. 1999. 272p. 22.95 o.s.i (*0-385-49247-2*) Doubleday Publishing.
—A Toast Before Dying. 1999. 304p. mass mkt. 5.99 (*0-553-57953-3*) Bantam Bks.
—The Viaduct. 2003. 272p. 22.95 (*0-385-50200-1*) Doubleday Publishing.
Edwards, Louis. N: A Romantic Mystery. 240p. 1998. pap. 12.95 o.s.i (*0-452-27788-4*, Plume); 1997. 22.95 o.p. (*0-525-94182-7*) Dutton/Plume.
—Oscar Wilde Discovers America. 2003. 304p. 24.00 (*0-7432-3689-0*, Scribner) Simon & Schuster.
Eidson, Thomas. All God's Children. 1997. 320p. 23.95 o.p. (*0-525-94235-1*) Dutton/Plume.
—All God's Children. 1998. 400p. mass mkt. 5.99 o.s.i (*0-451-19081-5*, Signet Bks.) NAL.
Elam, Patricia. Breathing Room. 2001. (Illus.). 352p. 24.95 (*0-671-02842-1*, Atria) Simon & Schuster.
Ellis, Jamellah. That Faith, That Trust, That Love: A Novel. 2003. (Strivers Row Ser.). 352p. pap. 12.95 (*0-8129-6656-2*, Villard Bks.) Random House Adult Trade Publishing Group.
Ellison, Ralph. Flying Home: And Other Stories. Callahan, John F., ed. 1998. 224p. pap. 12.00 (*0-679-77661-3*, Vintage) Knopf Publishing Group.
—Invisible Man. Bloom, Harold, ed. 1999. (Bloom's Reviews Comprehensive Research & Study Guides). 72p. pap. 4.95 (*0-7910-4131-X*) Chelsea Hse. Pubs.
—Invisible Man. 2nd ed. 1995. 608p. pap. 12.95 (*0-679-73276-4*, Vintage) Knopf Publishing Group.
—Invisible Man. 1968. mass mkt. 0.50 o.p. (*0-451-01030-2*); mass mkt. 0.75 o.p. (*0-451-01823-0*); mass mkt. 0.95 o.p. (*0-451-02722-1*); mass mkt. 1.25 o.p. (*0-451-03814-2*) NAL. (Signet Bks.).
—Invisible Man. 2002. 448p. 23.00 (*0-375-50791-4*); 1994. 624p. 19.95 (*0-679-60139-2*); 1992. 6.95 o.s.i (*0-394-60803-8*); 1992. 17.50 o.s.i (*0-679-60015-9*); 1989. 508p. pap. 11.00 o.p. (*0-679-72313-7*); 1982. 19.95 o.s.i (*0-394-52549-3*); 1972. pap. 5.95 o.p. (*0-394-71715-5*); 1963. 3.95 o.s.i (*0-394-60338-9*) Random Hse., Inc.
—Invisible Man. 1980. 18.05 (*0-606-01617-1*) Turtleback Bks.
—Invisible Man: A Novel. abr. unabr. ed. 1999. audio 39.95 (*0-375-40717-0*, N150, RH Audio) Random Hse. Audio Publishing Group.
—Juneteenth: A Novel. 2000. (International Ser.). 400p. pap. 14.00 (*0-375-70754-9*, Vintage) Knopf Publishing Group.
—Juneteenth: A Novel. Callahan, John F., ed. 1999. xxiii, 368p. 25.00 o.s.i (*0-394-46457-5*) Random Hse., Inc.
Elmore, Ronn. Mercy, Mercy Me. 2003. 304p. 22.95 (*0-446-52984-2*, Walk Worthy Pr.) Warner Bks., Inc.
Emery, Lynn. Gotta Get Next to You. 2001. 384p. mass mkt. 6.50 (*0-380-81304-1*) Morrow/Avon.
Erickson, Steve. Arc'D X: A Novel. 1996. 304p. pap. 14.00 o.p. (*0-8050-4882-0*, Owl Bks.) Holt, Henry & Co.
Esdaile, Leslie. Love Notes. 2001. (Arabesque Ser.). 288p. mass mkt. 5.99 (*1-58314-185-5*) BET Bks.
Esdaile, Leslie, et al. The Sistahood of Shopaholics. 2003. 320p. pap. 13.95 (*0-312-32188-0*, Saint Martin's Griffin) St. Martin's Pr.
Estleman, Loren D. Stress: A Novel of Detroit. 1996. 82p. 21.95 (*0-89296-553-3*) Mysterious Pr.
—Stress: A Novel of Detroit. 1999. E-Book 4.95 (*0-446-92340-0*) Time Warner Bk. Group.
—Stress: A Novel of Detroit. 1999. E-Book 4.95 (*0-446-91299-9*); 1997. 256p. reprint ed. mass mkt. 5.99 o.p. (*0-446-40367-9*) Warner Bks., Inc.
Evans, Max. Faraway Blue. 2000. 304p. mass mkt. 6.99 (*0-8125-7076-6*); 1998. (Illus.). 303p. 22.95 (*0-312-86749-2*) Doherty, Tom Assocs., LLC. (Forge Bks.).
Everett, Percival. God's Country. 2nd ed. 2003. 240p. pap. 14.00 (*0-8070-8363-1*) Beacon Pr.
Eyes of Faith. 2000. 464p. pap. 15.00 (*0-9667938-2-X*) 7-Fold Publishing.
Farley, Christopher John. My Favorite War: A Novel. 1996. 220p. 20.00 o.p. (*0-374-21696-7*) Farrar, Straus & Giroux.
—My Favorite War: A Novel. 1998. pap. 13.00 o.p. (*0-88001-590-X*) HarperCollins Pubs.
Faulkner, William. Intruder in the Dust. Polk, Noel, ed. 1987. (William Faulkner Manuscripts). 752p. text 90.00 (*0-8240-6838-6*) Garland Publishing, Inc.
—Intruder in the Dust. 1991. (Vintage International Ser.). 256p. pap. 10.95 (*0-679-73651-4*, Vintage) Knopf Publishing Group.
—Intruder in the Dust. 1967. (C). pap. text 6.50 net. (*0-07-553662-5*) McGraw-Hill Cos., The.
—Intruder in the Dust. mass mkt. 0.35 o.p. (*0-451-01511-8*); mass mkt. 0.35 o.p. (*0-451-01253-4*); mass mkt. 0.50 o.p. (*0-451-01848-6*); mass mkt. 0.25 o.p. (*0-451-00743-3*) NAL. (Signet Bks.).
—Intruder in the Dust. (Modern Library College Editions Ser.). 1972. (C). pap. 8.00 o.p. (*0-394-71792-9*, T88); 1964. 3.95 o.s.i (*0-394-60351-6*); 1948. 13.95 o.s.i (*0-394-43074-3*) Random Hse., Inc.
—Intruder in the Dust. 1948. 16.05 (*0-606-02910-9*) Turtleback Bks.
—The Unvanquished. 1991. (Vintage International Ser.). 272p. pap. 12.95 (*0-679-73652-2*, Vintage) Knopf Publishing Group.
Fauset, Jessie Redmon. The Chinaberry Tree: A Novel of American Life. reprint ed. 29.50 (*0-404-00256-0*) AMS Pr., Inc.
—The Chinaberry Tree: A Novel of American Life. 36.95 (*0-405-18503-0*) Ayer Co. Pubs., Inc.
—The Chinaberry Tree: A Novel of American Life. 1995. (African American Women Writers, 1910-1940 Ser.). 341p. 25.00 o.s.i (*0-8161-1627-X*, Macmillan Reference USA) Gale Group.
—The Chinaberry Tree: A Novel of American Life. 1969. 341p. reprint ed. 60.00 o.s.i (*0-8371-1919-7*, FAC&) Greenwood Publishing Group, Inc.
—The Chinaberry Tree & Selected Writings. 1994. (Library of Black Literature). 384p. reprint ed. pap. text 17.95 (*1-55553-207-1*) Northeastern Univ. Pr.
—Comedy, American Style. reprint ed. 29.50 (*0-404-00257-9*) AMS Pr., Inc.
—Comedy, American Style. 1969. reprint ed. o.p. (*0-8371-1992-8*, FAA&) Greenwood Publishing Group, Inc.
—Plum Bun: A Novel Without a Moral. 1990. (Black Women Writers Ser.). 416p. pap. 17.00 o.p. (*0-8070-0909-1*) Beacon Pr.
—There Is Confusion. reprint ed. 23.50 (*0-404-11386-9*) AMS Pr., Inc.
—There Is Confusion. 1989. (Library of Black Literature). 304p. reprint ed. pap. text 17.95 (*1-55553-066-4*) Northeastern Univ. Pr.
Files, Lolita. Blind Ambitions. 288p. 2000. 23.00 o.s.i (*0-684-87144-0*); 2001. reprint ed. pap. 13.00 (*0-684-87145-9*) Simon & Schuster. (Simon & Schuster).
—Child of God: A Novel. 2001. 320p. 23.00 (*0-684-84143-6*, Simon & Schuster) Simon & Schuster.
—Getting to the Good Part. 2000. 352p. pap. 13.95 (*0-446-67548-2*); 1999. 334p. 24.00 (*0-446-52420-4*) Warner Bks., Inc.
—Scenes from a Sistah. 1998. 288p. pap. 13.99 (*0-446-67442-7*); 1998. 320p. mass mkt. 6.50 (*0-446-60539-5*); 1997. 288p. 22.00 o.p. (*0-446-52100-0*) Warner Bks., Inc.
Finney, Nikky. Heartwood. 1997. (New Books for New Readers: Vol. 10). 80p. pap. text 5.95 (*0-8131-0910-8*) Univ. Pr. of Kentucky.
Fisher, Rudolph. The Walls of Jericho. 1994. (Ann Arbor Paperbacks Ser.). (Illus.). 300p. reprint ed. (C). text 39.50 o.p. (*0-472-09565-X*, 09565); pap. 19.95 (*0-472-06565-3*, 06565) Univ. of Michigan Pr.
Flander, Scott. Four to Midnight. 2004. 368p. mass mkt. 7.50 (*0-06-103170-4*, Avon Bks.) Morrow/Avon.
Fleming, Robert, ed. Intimacy: Erotic Tales of Love, Lust, & Marriage by Black Men. 2004. 288p. pap. 14.00 (*0-452-28474-0*, Plume) Dutton/Plume.
Flowers, Arthur R. Another Good Loving Blues. 1994. 224p. pap. 15.00 o.s.i (*0-345-38103-3*) Ballantine Bks.
—Another Good Loving Blues. 1993. 224p. 20.00 o.p. (*0-670-84821-2*, Viking) Viking Penguin.
Ford, Bette. After Dark. 1997. (Arabesque Ser.). 316p. mass mkt. 5.99 (*1-58314-175-8*) Kensington Publishing Corp.
Forrest, Leon. The Bloodworth Orphans. 2001. 383p. pap. 18.00 (*0-226-25722-3*) Univ. of Chicago Pr.
—Divine Days. 1995. 1144p. pap. 18.00 (*0-393-31221-6*); 1993. 135p. 32.00 o.p. (*0-393-03612-X*) Norton, W. W. & Co., Inc.
—Meteor in the Madhouse. 2001. xxiv, 273p. 26.95 (*0-8101-5114-6*) Northwestern Univ. Pr.
—There Is a Tree More Ancient Than Eden. 2001. 213p. pap. 13.00 (*0-226-25721-5*) Univ. of Chicago Pr.
Forstchen, William R. We Look Like Men of War. 192p. 2001. 21.95 (*0-7653-0114-8*); 2003. reprint ed. pap. 12.95 (*0-7653-0115-6*) Doherty, Tom Assocs., LLC. (Forge Bks.).
Forster, Gwynne. Against the Wind. 1999. (Love Spectrum Romance Ser.). 257p. pap. text 8.95 (*1-885478-90-9*) Genesis Pr., Inc.
—Blues from down Deep. 2004. 304p. pap. 14.00 (*0-7582-0010-2*, Kensington Bks.) Kensington Publishing Corp.
—Ecstacy. 1997. (Arabesque Ser.). 377p. mass mkt. 5.99 (*1-58314-177-4*) Kensington Publishing Corp.
—Wedding Bells. 1999. mass mkt. 4.99 o.s.i (*1-58314-016-6*) BET Bks.
—When Twlight Comes. 2003. 34p. pap. 15.00 (*0-7582-0009-9*) Kensington Publishing Corp.
Fortune, Gwendoline Y. Family Lines: A Novel. 2003. 288p. 23.00 (*1-58980-146-6*) Pelican Publishing Co., Inc.
—Growing up Nigger Rich. 2002. 256p. 22.00 (*1-56554-963-5*) Pelican Publishing Co., Inc.
Foster, Sharon Ewell. Passing by Samaria. 2003. 566p. pap. 16.95 (*1-4104-0157-X*, Walker Large Print) Gale Group.
—Passing by Samaria. 2003. 384p. pap. 12.99 (*1-57673-615-6*, Alabaster) Multnomah Pubs., Inc.
—Passing by Samaria. l.t. ed. 2003. 566p. 26.95 (*0-7862-5572-2*) Thorndike Pr.
—Riding Through Shadows. 2003. 350p. pap. 11.99 (*1-57673-807-8*) Multnomah Pubs., Inc.
Fox, Paula. A Servant's Tale. 1982. 336p. 16.50 o.p. (*0-86547-164-9*, North Point Pr.) Farrar, Straus & Giroux.
—A Servant's Tale. 2001. (Norton Paperback Fiction Ser.). 336p. pap. 13.00 (*0-393-32285-8*) Norton, W. W. & Co., Inc.
—A Servant's Tale. 1986. (Contemporary American Fiction Ser.). 336p. pap. 6.95 o.p. (*0-14-008386-3*, Penguin Bks.) Viking Penguin.
Francis, Suzette. Rules for a Pretty Woman. 2003. 320p. pap. 13.95 (*0-06-053542-3*, Avon Bks.) Morrow/Avon.
Frank, Waldo. Holiday. 2003. 240p. pap. text 16.95 (*0-252-07133-6*) Univ. of Illinois Pr.
Frisby, Mister Mann. Blinking Red Light. 2004. 320p. pap. 13.00 (*1-59448-019-2*, Riverhead Trade (Paperbacks)) Berkley Publishing Group.
Fuller, Jack. The Best of Jackson Payne. 2000. 336p. 25.00 (*0-375-40535-6*) Knopf, Alfred A. Inc.
—The Best of Jackson Payne: Novel. 2001. (Phoenix Fiction Ser.). 321p. pap. 15.00 (*0-226-26868-3*) Univ. of Chicago Pr.
Fuller, M. W. The Georgians. 1977. (Black Heritage Library Collection). reprint ed. 24.95 (*0-8369-9021-8*) Ayer Co. Pubs., Inc.
Fullilove, Eric James. Blowback. 2001. 304p. 24.00 (*0-06-621250-2*, Amistad Pr.) HarperTrade.
Fullilove, Maggie S. & Spencer, Mary E. Who Was Responsible?, Vol. 9. 1996. (Who Was Responsible? & Stories Ser.: Vol. 9). 462p. 25.00 (*0-8161-1630-X*, Macmillan Reference USA) Gale Group.
Fulton, Al. Alpomegans. 1997. xv, 334p. 21.95 (*0-9658573-0-1*) Acirfa Pubs.
Gaines, Ernest J. The Autobiography of Miss Jane Pittman. 1982. (Illus.). 272p. mass mkt. 6.50 (*0-553-26357-9*) Bantam Bks.
—The Autobiography of Miss Jane Pittman. 1987. 255p. 16.95 o.s.i (*0-385-24017-1*); 1971. 12.95 o.p. (*0-385-27009-7*) Doubleday Publishing.
—The Autobiography of Miss Jane Pittman. 1972. (Illus.). 13.55 (*0-88103-562-9*) Econo-Clad Bks.
—The Autobiography of Miss Jane Pittman. 1977. (Adult Ser.). reprint ed. lib. bdg. 10.95 o.p. (*0-8161-6010-4*, Macmillan Reference USA) Gale Group.
—The Autobiography of Miss Jane Pittman. 1972. 12.04 (*0-606-02213-9*) Turtleback Bks.
—Bloodline: Five Stories. 1997. 256p. pap. 12.00 (*0-679-78165-X*, Vintage) Knopf Publishing Group.
—A Gathering of Old Men. 1984. 224p. pap. 8.00 o.p. (*0-394-72591-3*, Vintage) Knopf Publishing Group.
—A Gathering of Old Men. 224p. 1992. pap. 11.00 (*0-679-73890-8*); 1983. 23.00 o.s.i (*0-394-51468-8*) Knopf, Alfred A. Inc.
—A Gathering of Old Men. 1992. 17.05 (*0-606-01027-0*) Turtleback Bks.
—In My Father's House. l.t. ed. 1993. 12.50 o.p. (*0-8161-6648-X*, Macmillan Reference USA) Gale Group.
—In My Father's House. 1978. 13.95 o.s.i (*0-394-47938-6*) Knopf, Alfred A. Inc.
—In My Father's House. 1983. 224p. reprint ed. pap. 6.95 o.p. (*0-393-30124-9*) Norton, W. W. & Co., Inc.

Ethnic Groups

—In My Father's House. 1992. (Vintage Contemporaries Ser.). 224p. pap. 11.95 (*0-679-72791-4*) Random Hse., Inc.

—Of Love & Dust. 1994. 288p. pap. 12.95 (*0-679-75248-X*, Vintage) Knopf Publishing Group.

—Of Love & Dust. 1979. reprint ed. pap. 8.95 o.p. (*0-393-00914-9*) Norton, W. W. & Co., Inc.

Gale, Barbara. The Ambassador's Vow. 2002. (Silhouette Special Edition Ser.). mass mkt. (*0-373-24500-9*, Silhouette) Harlequin Enterprises, Ltd.

Garland, Ardella. Details at Ten. E-Book 21.00 (*1-58945-169-4*) Adobe Systems, Inc.

—Details at Ten: A Georgia Barnett Mystery. 2000. 208p. 21.00 o.s.i (*0-684-87375-3*, Simon & Schuster) Simon & Schuster.

Garland, Ardella & Joe, Yolanda. Details at Ten. 2002. (Illus.). 272p. reprint ed. mass mkt. 6.99 (*0-7434-1480-2*, Pocket) Simon & Schuster.

Gates, Henry Louis, Jr., ed. Three Classic African-American Novels. 1990. (Vintage Bks.). 768p. pap. 16.00 (*0-679-72742-6*, Vintage) Knopf Publishing Group.

Gauthier, LaFlorya. Whispers in the Sand. 1994. 160p. pap. 10.95 o.p. (*1-885478-09-7*) Genesis Pr., Inc.

Gayle, Roberta. Something Old, Something New. 1999. mass mkt. 4.99 (*1-58314-018-2*) BET Bks.

George, Nelson. Night Work. 2003. 256p. pap. 12.00 (*0-7432-3551-7*, Touchstone) Simon & Schuster.

—Urban Romance. 1998. mass mkt. 5.99 (*0-345-42685-1*) Ballantine Bks.

—Urban Romance. 1994. 286p. reprint ed. pap. 12.98 (*1-879360-36-5*) Noble Pr., Inc., The.

—Urban Romance: A Novel of New York in the '80s. 1994. 288p. 24.95 o.p. (*0-399-13865-X*, G. P. Putnam's Sons) Penguin Group (USA) Inc.

Gilmore, Monique. The Grass Ain't Greener. l.t. ed. 1996. 320p. mass mkt. 4.99 o.s.i (*0-7860-0318-9*, Pinnacle Bks.) Kensington Publishing Corp.

—The Grass Ain't Greener. l.t. ed. 1999. (Romance Ser.). 360p. 27.95 (*0-7838-8508-3*) Thorndike Pr.

—Soul Deep. 1997. 256p. mass mkt. 4.99 o.s.i (*0-7860-0395-2*, Pinnacle Bks.) Kensington Publishing Corp.

Giusto, Layle. Wind Across Kylarmi. 1993. 416p. pap. 5.95 (*0-9633851-2-7*) Iami Bks.

Glasrud, Bruce A. & Champion, Laurie, eds. The African American West: A Century of Short Stories. 2000. xi, 463p. 29.95 (*0-87081-559-8*) Univ. Pr. of Colorado.

Glenn, Maurice W. Exposed: An African-American Novel of Ideas. 3rd rev. ed. 1998. 434p. pap. 19.00 (*0-9661744-0-2*) Concentric Pubns.

Godwin, Rebecca T. Keeper of the House. 288p. 1994. 19.95 o.p. (*0-312-11405-2*); 1995. reprint ed. pap. 13.95 (*0-312-13529-7*, NPB 0331, Saint Martin's Griffin) St. Martin's Pr.

Goff, H. N. Other Fools & Their Doings. 1977. (Black Heritage Library Collection). reprint ed. 21.95 (*0-8369-9009-9*) Ayer Co. Pubs., Inc.

Goines, Donald. Daddy Cool. 1997. (Old School Bks.). 142p. pap. 12.00 (*0-393-31664-5*) Norton, W. W. & Co., Inc.

Goldblatt, Mark. Africa Speaks. 2002. 176p. 24.00 (*1-57962-037-X*) Permanent Pr., The.

Golden, Marita. The Edge of Heaven. 1999. 272p. pap. 12.95 (*0-345-43172-3*) Ballantine Bks.

—The Edge of Heaven. 1997. 256p. 22.95 o.s.i (*0-385-41507-9*) Doubleday Publishing.

—Long Distance Life. 1999. mass mkt. 6.99 (*0-345-36711-1*); 1992. 336p. pap. 19.00 o.s.i (*0-345-37616-1*) Ballantine Bks.

—Long Distance Life. 1989. 336p. 18.95 o.s.i (*0-385-19455-2*) Doubleday Publishing.

—Long Distance Life. l.t. ed. 1990. (Large Print Bks.). 373p. lib. bdg. 19.95 o.p. (*0-8161-5005-2*, Macmillan Reference USA) Gale Group.

Goldsborough, Edmund K. Ole Mars An' Ole Miss. 1977. (Black Heritage Library Collection). reprint ed. 22.95 (*0-8369-8968-6*) Ayer Co. Pubs., Inc.

Gomez, Jewelle. Don't Explain: Short Fiction. 1998. 168p. pap. 10.95 (*1-56341-094-X*); lib. bdg. 22.95 (*1-56341-095-8*) Firebrand Bks.

—The Gilda Stories. 1991. 256p. pap. 12.95 (*0-932379-94-X*); lib. bdg. 24.95 (*0-932379-95-8*) Firebrand Bks.

Gonzales, Ambrose E. The Captain. 1977. (Black Heritage Library Collection). reprint ed. 22.95 (*0-8369-8969-4*) Ayer Co. Pubs., Inc.

Gordon, Gus, illus. Simon & the Aliens. 1999. (*0-7608-3293-5*) Sundance Publishing.

Gordon, Howard. The African in Me. 1993. 176p. 19.95 (*0-8076-1296-0*) Braziller, George Inc.

Gordon-Love, Sharel E. When He Calls. Cadet, Guichard, ed. 2002. 256p. pap. 15.00 (*0-9647635-9-1*) La Caille Nous Publishing Co.

Goss, Clay & Goss, Linda, eds. Jump up & Say! A Collection of Black Storytelling. 1995. 320p. 25.00 (*0-684-81090-5*, Simon & Schuster); pap. 13.00 o.s.i (*0-684-81001-8*, Touchstone) Simon & Schuster.

Gover, Robert. One Hundred Dollar Misunderstanding. 2000. 288p. pap. 14.95 (*0-88739-327-6*) Creative Arts Bk. Co.

—One Hundred Dollar Misunderstanding. 1981. 256p. reprint ed. pap. 2.95 o.p. (*0-394-17764-9*, B448) Grove/Atlantic, Inc.

Grant, John W. Out of the Darkness. 1977. (Black Heritage Library Collection). reprint ed. 22.95 (*0-8369-9023-4*) Ayer Co. Pubs., Inc.

Grau, Shirley A. Keepers of the House. 1976. pap. 1.50 o.s.i (*0-449-23031-7*, Fawcett) Ballantine Bks.

—Keepers of the House. 1985. (Southern Writers Ser.). mass mkt. 4.50 (*0-380-70047-6*, Avon Bks.) Morrow/Avon.

—Keepers of the House. 1964. 11.95 o.s.i (*0-394-43182-0*, Knopf Bks. for Young Readers) Random Hse. Children's Bks.

—Keepers of the House: A Novel. 1995. (Voices of the South Ser.). 328p. (C). pap. 16.95 o.p. (*0-8071-2031-6*) Louisiana State Univ. Pr.

Grau, Shirley Ann. The Keepers of the House. 2003. 320p. pap. 13.00 (*1-4000-3074-9*, Vintage) Knopf Publishing Group.

Gray, Etha. Odyssey of Courage. 2001. 298p. 14.95 (*1-879940-07-8*) Concepts 'N' Publishing.

Green, Carmen. Atlanta Live. 2003. 288p. pap. 15.00 (*1-58314-293-2*) BET Bks.

Greene, Gloria & Johnson, Doris. Love Unveiled. 1994. (Indigo Love Stories Ser.). 178p. pap. 10.95 (*1-885478-08-9*) Genesis Pr., Inc.

Greer, Ben. Slammer. 2002. (Voices of the South Ser.). 280p. pap. 16.95 (*0-8071-2789-2*) Louisiana State Univ. Pr.

—Slammer. 1985. pap. 1.75 o.p. (*0-380-01845-4*, 36418, Avon Bks.) Morrow/Avon.

—Slammer. 1975. 8.95 o.p. (*0-689-10649-1*, Atheneum) Simon & Schuster Children's Publishing.

Greer, Robert. The Devil's Backbone. 1998. 368p. 22.00 o.p. (*0-89296-653-X*) Mysterious Pr.

—The Devil's Backbone. 1999. (C J Floyd Mystery Ser.). 320p. mass mkt. 6.99 (*0-446-60711-8*) Warner Bks., Inc.

—The Devil's Hatband. 1996. 82p. 21.95 o.p. (*0-89296-634-3*) Mysterious Pr.

—The Devil's Hatband. 1997. 304p. reprint ed. mass mkt. 5.99 (*0-446-40485-3*) Warner Bks., Inc.

—The Devil's Red Nickel. 1997. 368p. 22.00 o.p. (*0-89296-652-1*) Mysterious Pr.

—The Devil's Red Nickel. 1998. (C J Floyd Mystery Ser.). 352p. mass mkt. 5.99 (*0-446-60592-1*); mass mkt. 5.99 (*0-446-40529-9*, Mysterious Pr. Paperback Bks.) Warner Bks., Inc.

Gregory, Garland. New Breed. 2001. 180p. pap. 14.00 (*0-9659789-1-5*) Southwest Publishing.

Griffin, Bettye. From This Day Forward. 2002. 288p. mass mkt. 6.99 (*1-58314-275-4*) BET Bks.

—Love Affair. 2001. (Arabesque Ser.). 288p. mass mkt. 5.99 (*1-58314-138-3*) BET Bks.

Griffith, Mattie. Autobiography of a Female Slave. 1998. 408p. 48.00 (*1-57806-046-X*); pap. 18.00 (*1-57806-047-8*) Univ. Pr. of Mississippi. (A Banner Bk.).

Grimes, Terris M. Blood Will Tell. 1997. 272p. mass mkt. 5.50 o.s.i (*0-451-40696-6*, Onyx) NAL.

—Somebody Else's Child. 1996. 272p. mass mkt. 5.99 o.s.i (*0-451-18672-9*, Signet Bks.) NAL.

Grooms, Anthony. Bombingham. 2002. 320p. pap. 13.95 (*0-345-45293-3*) Random Hse., Inc.

—Bombingham. 2001. 320p. 24.00 (*0-7432-0558-8*, Free Pr.) Simon & Schuster.

Grosvenor, Linda Dominique. Like Boogie on Tuesday. 2002. 448p. pap. 15.00 (*1-58314-260-6*, Sepia) BET Bks.

—Like Boogie on Tuesday. unabr. ed. 2000. 355p. pap. 14.95 o.p. (*0-9700102-1-4*) Sadorian Pubns.

Grosvenor, Shelia. Like Boogie on Tuesday. 2003. 448p. mass mkt. 6.99 (*1-58314-442-0*, Arabesque) BET Bks.

Groth, Alexander J. Progress & Chaos. 1983. (ENG.). 242p. (C). reprint ed. pap. text 13.50 o.p. (*0-89874-677-9*) Krieger Publishing Co.

Guidry, Jacqueline. The Year the Colored Sisters Came to Town. 256p. 2003. pap. 15.00 (*1-56649-256-4*); 2001. 25.00 (*1-56649-200-9*) Welcome Rain Pubs.

Gunn, Gay G. Everlastin' Love. 1994. 220p. pap. 10.95 (*1-885478-02-X*) Genesis Pr., Inc.

Gunter, Archibald C. Bob Covington: A Novel. 1977. (Black Heritage Library Collection). reprint ed. 30.95 (*0-8369-9074-9*) Ayer Co. Pubs., Inc.

Gurley-Highgate, Hilda. Sapphire's Grave: A Novel. 2002. 256p. 23.95 (*0-385-50323-7*) Doubleday Publishing.

Hailstock, Shirley. Mirror Image. 1998. (Arabesque Ser.). mass mkt. 5.99 (*1-58314-178-2*) Kensington Publishing Corp.

Hains, Thornton J. The Black Barque. 1977. (Black Heritage Library Collection). (Illus.). reprint ed. 26.95 (*0-8369-8941-4*) Ayer Co. Pubs., Inc.

Hairston, Alex. Love Don't Come Easy. 2004. 304p. mass mkt. 6.99 (*1-58314-454-4*, Kensington Bks.) Kensington Publishing Corp.

Haley, Alex. A Different Kind of Christmas. 2000. 112p. 7.99 (*0-517-16269-5*) Random Hse. Value Publishing.

Haley, Alex & Stevens, David. Mama Flora's Family. 1999. 464p. mass mkt. 6.99 (*0-440-23543-X*); (Illus.). 462p. pap. 23.00 (*0-440-61409-0*, Delta) Dell Publishing.

—Mama Flora's Family. 1998. 400p. 25.00 o.s.i (*0-684-83471-5*, Scribner) Simon & Schuster.

Hall, Asa Z. Stanton White. 1977. (Black Heritage Library Collection). reprint ed. 22.95 (*0-8369-9024-2*) Ayer Co. Pubs., Inc.

Hall, Rachel Howzell. A Quiet Storm: A Novel. 2002. 256p. pap. 13.00 (*0-7432-2616-X*, Touchstone) Simon & Schuster.

Hambly, Barbara. Die upon a Kiss. 2002. 480p. mass mkt. 5.99 (*0-553-58165-1*) Bantam Bks.

—Die upon a Kiss. l.t. ed. 2003. 608p. 25.95 (*0-375-43266-3*) Random Hse. Large Print.

—A Free Man of Color. 1998. 432p. reprint ed. mass mkt. 6.99 (*0-553-57526-0*) Bantam Bks.

—Sold down the River. 2001. 432p. reprint ed. mass mkt. 6.99 (*0-553-57529-5*) Bantam Bks.

—Wet Grave. 2003. 384p. mass mkt. 6.50 (*0-553-58159-7*); 2002. (Illus.). 304p. 23.95 (*0-553-10935-9*) Bantam Bks.

—Wet Grave. l.t. ed. 2003. 486p. 25.95 (*0-375-43274-4*, Random House Large Print) Random Hse. Large Print.

Hampton, Robin L. & Gunn, Gay G. Breeze. 1997. mass mkt. 4.99 o.s.i (*0-345-42225-2*) Random Hse., Inc.

Handler, David. The Cold Blue Blood. 2002. 320p. mass mkt. 6.50 (*0-312-98610-6*, St. Martin's Paperbacks); 2001. 304p. 23.95 (*0-312-28003-3*, Saint Martin's Minotaur) St. Martin's Pr.

—The Hot Pink Farmhouse. Date not set. mass mkt. (*0-312-98579-7*, St. Martin's Paperbacks); E-Book 17.95 (*0-312-70893-9*); 2002. 336p. 23.95 (*0-312-28015-7*, Saint Martin's Minotaur) St. Martin's Pr.

Hardwick, Gary. Supreme Justice: A Novel of Suspense. 1999. 368p. 24.00 (*0-688-16513-3*, Morrow, William & Co.) Morrow/Avon.

Hardy, James E. Back 2 Back: An Anthology Featuring the Best-Sellers: B-Boy Blues & 2nd Time Around, 2 vols., Set. 1997. 530p. reprint ed. 22.95 o.p. (*1-55583-420-5*) Alyson Pubns.

—If Only for One Nite. 1998. 208p. pap. 12.95 (*1-55583-467-1*); 1997. 185p. 17.95 (*1-55583-373-X*) Alyson Pubns.

Hardy, James Earl. Love the One You're With. 2002. 272p. 22.95 (*0-06-621248-0*, Amistad Pr.) HarperTrade.

Harper, Frances E. W. Minnie's Sacrifice, Sowing & Reaping, Trial & Triumph: Three Rediscovered Novels. Harper, Frances E. W., ed. 2000. (Black Women Writers Ser.). 304p. pap. 14.00 (*0-8070-6233-2*) Beacon Pr.

Harper, Frances Ellen Watkins. Iola Leroy. (Black Women Writers Ser.). 320p. 1999. pap. 14.00 (*0-8070-6519-6*); 1987. reprint ed. pap. 13.00 o.p. (*0-8070-6317-7*) Beacon Pr.

—Iola Leroy: Or, Shadows Uplifted. 2nd ed. reprint ed. 42.50 (*0-404-00169-6*) AMS Pr., Inc.

—Iola Leroy: Or, Shadows Uplifted. (Schomburg Library of Nineteenth-Century Black Women Writers). 336p. reprint ed. 1990. pap. text 16.95 (*0-19-506324-4*); 1988. text 39.95 o.s.i (*0-19-505240-4*) Oxford Univ. Pr., Inc.

—Minnie's Sacrifice, Sowing & Reaping, Trial & Triumph: Three Rediscovered Novels. Foster, Frances Smith, ed. 336p. 1996. (C). pap. 12.95 o.p. (*0-8070-8333-X*); 1994. 22.00 o.p. (*0-8070-8332-1*) Beacon Pr.

Harper, Frances Ellen Watkins, et al. The African-American Novel in the Age of Reaction: Three Classics. Andrews, William L., ed. & intro. by. 1992. 592p. (Orig.). mass mkt. 5.99 o.s.i (*0-451-62849-7*, Mentor) NAL.

Harris, E. Lynn. Abide with Me. 1999. (Abide with Me Ser.: Vol. 3). 368p. 24.95 (*0-385-48657-X*) Doubleday Publishing.

—Abide with Me. 2000. 368p. pap. 13.00 (*0-385-48658-8*, Knopf Bks. for Young Readers) Random Hse. Children's Bks.

—Abide with Me. 2003. (African American Ser.). 535p. 29.95 (*0-7862-5062-3*) Thorndike Pr.

—And This Too Shall Pass. 1996. 320p. 23.95 o.s.i (*0-385-48030-X*) Doubleday Publishing.

—And This Too Shall Pass: A Novel. 1997. 368p. pap. 12.95 (*0-385-48031-8*, Knopf Bks. for Young Readers) Random Hse. Children's Bks.

—Any Way the Wind Blows. 2001. 352p. 19.95 (*0-385-49505-6*, Talese, Nan A.) Doubleday Publishing.

—Any Way the Wind Blows. abr. unabr. ed. 2001. audio 24.95 (*0-553-52829-7*, RH Audio) Random Hse. Audio Publishing Group.

—If This World Were Mine. 1998. 336p. pap. 13.00 (*0-385-48656-1*, Knopf Bks. for Young Readers) Random Hse. Children's Bks.

—If This World Were Mine. l.t. ed. 2003. 525p. 29.95 (*0-7862-5895-0*) Thorndike Pr.

—Not a Day Goes By. 2000. 288p. 19.95 (*0-385-49824-1*) Doubleday Publishing.

—Not a Day Goes By. pap. (*0-385-72885-9*) Knopf Publishing Group.

—Not a Day Goes By. 2001. 304p. reprint ed. mass mkt. 6.99 (*0-385-49825-X*, Knopf Bks. for Young Readers) Random Hse. Children's Bks.

—Not a Day Goes By. l.t. ed. 347p. 2002. 28.95 (*0-7862-3042-8*); 2001. 31.95 (*0-7862-3041-X*) Thorndike Pr.

Harris, Joel Chandler. Little Union Scout. 1977. (Black Heritage Library Collection). (Illus.). reprint ed. 20.95 (*0-8369-9075-7*) Ayer Co. Pubs., Inc.

—Mingo & Other Sketches in Black & White. 1977. (Black Heritage Library Collection). 18.95 (*0-8369-8696-2*); 24.95 (*0-8369-3395-8*) Ayer Co. Pubs., Inc.

—Mingo & Other Sketches in Black & White. 273p. reprint ed. pap. text 7.50 (*0-8290-5206-2*); lib. bdg. 15.50 (*0-8290-0764-4*) Irvington Pubs.

—Mingo & Other Sketches in Black & White. 1992. (Notable American Authors Ser.). reprint ed. lib. bdg. 75.00 (*0-7812-3017-9*) Reprint Services Corp.

—Nights with Uncle Remus: Myths & Legends of the Old Plantation. Bickley, Bruce, ed. 2003. (Penguin Classics Ser.). 384p. pap. 14.00 (*0-14-243766-2*, Penguin Classics) Viking Penguin.

Harris, Langston O. This Magic Moment. 1992. (Illus.). 469p. pap. 10.00 (*0-9631730-1-4*) DRL Bks.

Harris, Toni Staton. By Chance or Choice. 2002. xii, 220p. pap. 14.95 (*0-9710695-0-6*) Epiphany Publishing Hse. LLC.

Hatch, John. Mississippi Swamp. 2001. (New Africa Chronicles Ser.: Vol. 1). (Illus.). 360p. 27.98 (*0-9706854-0-8*) 2ndsightbooks.com.

Hawkins, Odie. Ghetto Sketches. 2001. 300p. reprint ed. mass mkt. 8.50 (*1-892343-19-3*, Oak Tree Pr.) Oak Tree Publishing.

Hayes, Hunter. A Pair Like No Otha' A Novel. 2002. 384p. pap. 13.95 (*0-380-81485-4*, Avon Bks.) Morrow/Avon.

—Shoe's on the Otha' Foot. 2000. 320p. mass mkt. 6.99 (*0-06-101466-4*, HarperTorch) Morrow/Avon.

—Shoe's on the Otha' Foot. Green, Brandi C., ed. 1999. 240p. pap. 12.95 (*0-9666435-7-7*) Stone Edge Pr.

Haynes, David. All American Dream Dolls. 1999. (Harvest Book Ser.). 288p. pap. 12.00 (*0-15-600572-7*, Harvest Bks.) Harcourt Trade Pubs.

—All American Dream Dolls. 1997. 288p. 21.95 (*1-57131-015-0*) Milkweed Editions.

—Heathens. 1996. (Minnesota Voices Project Ser.: No. 72). 182p. 21.95 (*0-89823-166-3*) New Rivers Pr.

—Live at Five. 1997. (Harvest Book Ser.). 288p. (C). pap. 12.00 (*0-15-600503-4*, Harvest Bks.) Harcourt Trade Pubs.

—Live at Five. 1996. 280p. 21.95 (*1-57131-009-6*) Milkweed Editions.

—Somebody Else's Mama. 1996. (Harvest American Writing Ser.). 360p. (C). pap. 13.00 (*0-15-600408-9*, Harvest Bks.) Harcourt Trade Pubs.

—Somebody Else's Mama. 1995. 352p. 21.95 (*1-57131-003-7*) Milkweed Editions.

Haynes, Melinda Rucker. Mother of Pearl. l.t. ed. 2000. (Thorndike/G. K. Hall Paperback Bestsellers Ser.). 760p. 30.00 (*0-7862-2182-8*, Macmillan Reference USA) Gale Group.

—Mother of Pearl. 1999. 445p. 23.95 (*0-7868-6485-0*); 448p. 23.95 (*0-7868-6627-6*) Hyperion Pr.

—Mother of Pearl. reprint ed. 2001. 512p. pap. 7.99 (*0-7434-3103-0*, Pocket); 2000. 496p. pap. 13.95 (*0-671-77467-0*, Washington Square Pr.) Simon & Schuster.

—Mother of Pearl. l.t. ed. 1999. (Basic Ser.). 760p. 31.95 (*0-7862-2181-X*) Thorndike Pr.

—Mother of Pearl. 2000. 20.00 (*0-606-19128-3*) Turtleback Bks.

Haywood, Gar Anthony. All the Lucky Ones Are Dead. 2000. 272p. mass mkt. 5.99 o.s.i (*0-425-17778-5*) Berkley Publishing Group.

—All the Lucky Ones Are Dead. 2000. 12.04 (*0-606-20097-5*) Turtleback Bks.

—All the Lucky Ones Are Dead: An Aaron Gunner Mystery. 2000. 240p. 23.95 o.s.i (*0-399-14540-0*, G. P. Putnam's Sons) Penguin Group (USA) Inc.

—Fear of the Dark. 1988. 192p. 13.95 o.p. (*0-312-01796-0*, Saint Martin's Minotaur) St. Martin's Pr.

—Fear of the Dark. 1990. 192p. pap. 3.95 o.p. (*0-14-013153-1*, Penguin Bks.) Viking Penguin.

—It's Not a Pretty Sight: An Aaron Gunner Mystery. 1998. 256p. mass mkt. 5.99 o.s.i (*0-425-16196-X*, Prime Crime) Berkley Publishing Group.

—It's Not a Pretty Sight: An Aaron Gunner Mystery. 1996. 240p. 22.95 o.p. (*0-399-14132-4*, G. P. Putnam's Sons) Penguin Group (USA) Inc.

—Not Long for This World. 1991. (Crime Monthly Ser.). 272p. pap. 4.95 o.p. (*0-14-015265-2*, Penguin Bks.) Penguin Group (USA) Inc.

—Not Long for This World. 1990. 17.95 o.p. (*0-312-04398-8*, Saint Martin's Minotaur) St. Martin's Pr.

—When Last Seen Alive. 1999. 256p. mass mkt. 5.99 o.s.i (*0-425-17027-6*) Berkley Publishing Group.

—When Last Seen Alive. 1997. 240p. 22.95 o.p. (*0-399-14303-3*, G. P. Putnam's Sons) Penguin Group (USA) Inc.
—You Can Die Trying. 1993. 224p. 17.95 o.p. (*0-312-09425-6*, Saint Martin's Minotaur) St. Martin's Pr.
—You Can Die Trying: An Aaron Gunner Mystery. 1994. (Crime Ser.). 224p. reprint ed. pap. 5.95 o.p. (*0-14-023946-4*, Penguin Bks.) Penguin Group (USA) Inc.
Hedden, Worth Tuttle. The Other Room. 2002. 274p. pap. 14.95 (*0-9624878-1-3*, 0-9624878-1-3) Paperback Rack Bks.
Hemphill, Paul. Nobody's Hero: A Novel. 2002. 336p. 25.95 (*1-57966-029-0*) River City Publishing.
Henderson, Walter. Death by Suicidal Means. 1994. 227p. 19.95 (*0-9638086-0-5*); pap. 8.95 (*0-9638086-1-3*) Inheritance Pr., Inc.
Hendricks, Carl. Rootin' for the Crusher. 1998. 258p. pap. 12.95 (*1-881524-17-5*) Milligan Bks.
Henley, John A. The Buchmans: A Novel. l.t. ed. 2001. (Five Star Western Ser.). 248p. 22.95 (*0-7862-2385-5*, Five Star) Gale Group.
Heyward, Du Bose & Heyward, Dorothy. Porgy. 1980. (American Drama Ser.). Dell Publishing.
Heyward, DuBose. Porgy. Date not set. reprint ed. lib. bdg. 20.95 (*0-89190-684-3*, American Reprint Co.) Amereon, Ltd.
—Porgy. 1991. 196p. reprint ed. lib. bdg. 18.95 (*0-89966-768-6*) Buccaneer Bks., Inc.
—Porgy. 2nd ed. (Illus.). 192p. reprint ed. pap. 20.00 o.p. (*0-937684-22-8*, P23.H1587PO) Tradd Street Pr.
—Porgy. 2001. (Banner Bks.). 208p. reprint ed. pap. 18.00 (*1-57806-356-6*) Univ. Pr. of Mississippi.
Heyward, Dubose & Heyward, Dorothy. Porgy: A Gullah Version. Geraty, Virginia M., tr. & intro. by. 1990. 129p. pap. 8.95 (*0-941711-11-0*) Wyrick & Co.
Hiatt, James M. The Test of Loyalty. 1977. (Black Heritage Library Collection). reprint ed. 21.95 (*0-8369-9027-7*) Ayer Co. Pubs., Inc.
Hill, Donna. If I Could. 2000. 256p. pap. 12.00 o.s.i (*1-57566-597-2*) Kensington Publishing Corp.
—Pieces of a Dreams. 1999. mass mkt. 4.99 (*1-58314-020-4*) BET Bks.
—Private Affair. 2000. (Arabesque Ser.). 384p. mass mkt. 5.99 (*1-58314-158-8*) BET Bks.
—Rhythms. mass mkt. (*0-312-98024-8*, St. Martin's Paperbacks); 2001. 352p. 23.95 (*0-312-27299-5*) St. Martin's Pr.
—Rhythms: A Novel. 2002. 336p. pap. 12.95 (*0-312-30069-7*, Saint Martin's Griffin) St. Martin's Pr.
—Through the Fire. 2001. (Arabesque Ser.). 352p. mass mkt. 5.99 (*1-58314-130-8*) BET Bks.
Hill, Donna & Ray, Francis. Rockin' Around That Christmas Tree. 2003. 160p. 14.95 (*0-312-32195-3*) St. Martin's Pr.
Hill, Ernest. Cry Me a River. 2004. 304p. pap. 15.00 (*0-7582-0277-6*, Kensington Bks.); 2003. 24.00 (*0-7582-0276-8*) Kensington Publishing Corp.
—A Life for a Life. 1998. 240p. 23.00 (*0-684-82278-4*, Simon & Schuster) Simon & Schuster.
Hill, Mars. The Moaner's Bench. 1998. 384p. o.s.i (*0-06-019102-3*, HarperFlamingo) HarperCollins Pubs. Canada, Ltd.
—The Moaner's Bench: A Novel. 1999. 384p. pap. 14.00 (*0-06-093058-6*, Perennial) HarperTrade.
Hilmon, Darrious. Five Dimes: A Novel. 2003. 256p. pap. 12.95 (*0-451-20869-2*) NAL.
Hime, James. The Night of the Dance: A Novel. 2003. 320p. 24.95 (*0-312-31322-5*, Saint Martin's Minotaur) St. Martin's Pr.
Himes, Chester B. All Shot up. 1973. 160p. reprint ed. 7.95 o.p. (*0-911860-29-0*) Chatham Bookseller.
—All Shot Up. 2nd ed. 1996. 170p. reprint ed. pap. 12.95 (*1-56025-103-4*, Thunder's Mouth Pr.) Avalon Publishing Group.
—The Big Gold Dream. 2nd ed. 1996. 156p. reprint ed. pap. 12.95 (*1-56025-104-2*, Thunder's Mouth Pr.) Avalon Publishing Group.
—The Big Gold Dream. 1973. 160p. reprint ed. 7.95 o.p. (*0-911860-30-4*) Chatham Bookseller.
—Blind Man with a Pistol. 1989. (Vintage Crime Ser.). 192p. pap. 11.00 (*0-394-75998-2*, Vintage) Knopf Publishing Group.
—The Collected Stories of Chester Himes. 2002. 15.95 (*1-56025-311-8*); 1991. 440p. 24.95 o.p. (*1-56025-020-8*, Thunder's Mouth Pr.) Avalon Publishing Group.
—Collected Stories of Chester Himes. 2000. 448p. pap. text 15.95 (*1-56025-268-5*, Thunder's Mouth Pr.) Avalon Publishing Group.
—The Collected Stories of Chester Himes. 2000. 448p. reprint ed. pap. 15.95 (*1-56025-021-6*, Thunder's Mouth Pr.) Avalon Publishing Group.
—Cotton Comes to Harlem. 1994. (Illus.). lib. bdg. 11.95 (*1-56849-422-X*) Buccaneer Bks., Inc.
—Cotton Comes to Harlem. 1975. reprint ed. 8.95 o.p. (*0-911860-55-X*) Chatham Bookseller.
—Cotton Comes to Harlem. 1988. (Crime Ser.). (Illus.). 160p. pap. 11.00 (*0-394-75999-0*, Vintage) Knopf Publishing Group.
—The Crazy Kill. 1973. 160p. reprint ed. 7.95 o.p. (*0-911860-32-0*) Chatham Bookseller.
—The Crazy Kill. 160p. 1995. pap. 25.00 o.s.i (*0-8052-8217-3*, Schocken); 1989. pap. 11.00 (*0-679-72572-5*, Vintage) Knopf Publishing Group.
—End of a Primitive. 1997. 220p. pap. 12.00 (*0-393-31540-1*) Norton, W. W. & Co., Inc.
—For Love of Imabelle. 1973. 192p. reprint ed. 7.95 o.p. (*0-911860-33-9*) Chatham Bookseller.
—The Heat's On. 1975. 220p. reprint ed. 17.00 (*0-911860-57-6*) Chatham Bookseller.
—The Heat's On. 1988. (Vintage Crime Ser.). 176p. pap. 15.00 (*0-394-75997-4*, Vintage) Knopf Publishing Group.
—If He Hollers Let Him Go: A Novel. 1995. 203p. pap. 12.95 (*1-56025-097-6*, Thunder's Mouth Pr.) Avalon Publishing Group.
—A Rage in Harlem. 1989. (Vintage Crime Ser.). Orig. Title: For Love of Imabelle. 160p. pap. 10.00 (*0-679-72040-5*, Vintage) Knopf Publishing Group.
—The Real Cool Killers. 1973. 160p. reprint ed. 7.95 o.p. (*0-911860-36-3*) Chatham Bookseller.
—The Real Cool Killers. 1988. (Vintage Crime Ser.). 160p. pap. 10.95 (*0-679-72039-1*, Pantheon) Knopf Publishing Group.
—Run Man Run. 1995. 192p. pap. 8.95 (*0-7867-0209-5*, Carroll & Graf Pubs.) Avalon Publishing Group.
—Run Man Run. 1975. 192p. reprint ed. 8.50 o.p. (*0-911860-56-8*) Chatham Bookseller.
—Yesterday Will Make You Cry: A Novel. (Old School Bks.). 1999. 364p. pap. 13.00 (*0-393-31829-X*, Norton Paperbacks); 1998. 320p. 25.00 (*0-393-04577-3*) Norton, W. W. & Co., Inc.
Hobson, Anne. In Old Alabama: Being the Chronicles of Miss Mouse, the Little Black Merchant. 1977. (Short Story Index Reprint Ser.). reprint ed. 25.95 (*0-8369-4246-9*) Ayer Co. Pubs., Inc.
Hoffman, Roy. Almost Family. 1983. 256p. 14.95 o.p. (*0-385-27664-8*) Doubleday Publishing.
—Almost Family. 2000. (Deep South Book Ser.). 248p. pap. 16.95 (*0-8173-1031-2*) Univ. of Alabama Pr.
Hollyday, Thomas. Slave Graves. 2003. 284p. pap. 12.95 (*0-9741287-0-8*); E-Book 12.95 (*0-9741287-1-6*) Happy Bird Corp.
Holman, John. Squabble & Other Stories. 1990. 144p. 18.45 (*0-89919-935-6*) Houghton Mifflin Co.
Holmes, Jean E. Bound Fo' Glory. 1996. (Weldon Oaks Ser.: Pt. 5). pap. 4.97 o.p. (*0-8163-1275-3*) Pacific Pr. Publishing Assn.
Hoover, Jerald LeVon. He Was My Hero Too. 2002. 5.99 (*1-886433-78-X*) A & B Distributors & Pubs. Group.
Hopkins, Pauline E. Contending Forces: A Romance Illustrative of Negro Life in the North & South. 1991. (Schomburg Library of Nineteenth-Century Black Women Writers). (Illus.). 464p. reprint ed. pap. 18.95 (*0-19-506785-1*) Oxford Univ. Pr., Inc.
—Contending Forces: A Romance Illustrative of Negro Life North & South. (Illus.). reprint ed. 29.50 (*0-404-00173-4*) AMS Pr., Inc.
—Contending Forces: A Romance Illustrative of Negro Life North & South. 1988. (Schomburg Library of Nineteenth-Century Black Women Writers). 450p. text 37.50 (*0-19-505258-7*) Oxford Univ. Pr., Inc.
—The Magazine Novels of Pauline Hopkins Including Hagar's Daughter, & Of One Blood. 1988. (Schomburg Library of Nineteenth-Century Black Women Writers). (Illus.). 672p. text 52.00 (*0-19-505248-X*) Oxford Univ. Pr., Inc.
Hopkinson, Nalo, ed. Mojo: Conjure Stories. 2003. 352p. pap. 13.95 (*0-446-67929-1*, Aspect) Warner Bks., Inc.
How I Come by This Cryin' Song. Date not set. (Illus.). 25.95 (*0-312-19899-X*) St. Martin's Pr.
Howard, Tracie & Carter, Danita. Revenge Is Best Served Cold. 2001. 304p. pap. 12.95 (*0-451-20475-1*, Signet Bks.) NAL.
—Talk of the Town. 2002. 304p. pap. 12.95 (*0-451-20703-3*) NAL.
Howell, Harry D., Sr. Strange Negro Stories of the Old Deep South. 1977. (Short Story Index Reprint Ser.). 30.95 (*0-8369-3555-1*) Ayer Co. Pubs., Inc.
Hudson, Helen. Criminal Trespass. 1985. 256p. 17.95 o.p. (*0-399-13055-1*, G. P. Putnam's Sons) Penguin Putnam Bks. for Young Readers.
—Criminal Trespass. 1986. (Contemporary American Fiction Ser.). pap. 6.95 o.p. (*0-14-008494-0*, Penguin Bks.) Viking Penguin.
Hudson-Smith, Linda. Desperate Deceptions. 2001. (Arabesque Ser.). 288p. mass mkt. 5.99 (*1-58314-141-3*) BET Bks.
Hughes, Langston. The Best of Simple. (Classics of Modern American Humor Ser.). (Illus.). reprint ed. 29.00 (*0-404-19936-4*) AMS Pr., Inc.
—The Best of Simple. 1990. pap. 6.95 o.p. (*0-8090-0039-3*, Hill & Wang) Farrar, Straus & Giroux.
—Not Without Laughter. 1976. 23.95 (*0-8488-1055-4*) Amereon, Ltd.
—Not Without Laughter. xiv, 224p. pap. 12.95 (*0-86241-768-6*) Payback Pr. GBR. *Dist:* AK Pr. Distribution.
—Not Without Laughter. 1995. 17.05 (*0-606-16259-3*) Turtleback Bks.
—The Return of Simple. Harper, Akiba S., ed. 1995. 218p. pap. 20.00 (*0-8090-1582-X*); 1994. 256p. 20.00 o.s.i (*0-8090-8676-X*) Farrar, Straus & Giroux. (Hill & Wang).
—Short Stories of Langston Hughes. Harper, Akiba S., ed. 1996. 299p. 25.00 o.s.i (*0-8090-8658-1*, Hill & Wang) Farrar, Straus & Giroux.
—The Simple Omnibus. 22.95 (*0-88411-059-1*) Amereon, Ltd.
—Simple Stakes a Claim. Date not set. lib. bdg. 20.95 (*0-8488-2178-5*) Amereon, Ltd.
—Simple Takes a Wife. 22.95 (*0-88411-062-1*) Amereon, Ltd.
—Simple Takes a Wife. 1994. lib. bdg. 24.95 (*1-56849-398-3*) Buccaneer Bks., Inc.
—Simple's Uncle Sam. 20.95 (*0-88411-709-X*) Amereon, Ltd.
—Simple's Uncle Sam. (American Century Ser.). 1965. 180p. pap. 7.95 o.p. (*0-8090-0087-3*); 2000. xix, 180p. pap. 13.00 (*0-8090-8681-6*) Farrar, Straus & Giroux. (Hill & Wang).
—Something in Common & Other Stories. 1963. (American Century Ser.). 236p. (Orig.). pap. 7.95 o.p. (*0-8090-0057-1*, Hill & Wang) Farrar, Straus & Giroux.
—The Ways of White Folks. (Vintage Bks.). 1990. 272p. pap. 12.00 (*0-679-72817-1*); 1971. pap. 6.95 o.p. (*0-394-71304-4*) Knopf Publishing Group. (Vintage).
—The Ways of White Folks. 1934. 10.00 o.p. (*0-394-45116-3*, Knopf Bks. for Young Readers) Random Hse. Children's Bks.
Hughes, Langston, ed. The Best Short Stories by Negro Writers. 1969. 19.95 (*0-316-38032-6*); 512p. pap. 15.95 (*0-316-38031-8*) Little Brown & Co.
Hunter, Stephen. Pale Horse Coming. 2003. 608p. pap. 7.99 (*0-671-03546-0*, Pocket); 2001. 496p. 25.00 (*0-684-86361-8*, Simon & Schuster); 2002. 624p. mass mkt. 7.99 (*0-7434-4382-9*, Pocket) Simon & Schuster.
—Pale Horse Coming. l.t. ed. 825p. 2003. 13.95 (*0-7862-3949-2*); 2002. 28.95 (*0-7862-3950-6*) Thorndike Pr.
Hunter, Travis E. The Hearts of Men: A Novel. 2001. 288p. pap. 13.95 (*0-375-75709-0*, Villard Bks.) Random House Adult Trade Publishing Group.
—Married but Still Looking: A Novel. 2003. 272p. pap. 11.95 (*0-8129-6838-7*); 2002. 256p. 21.95 (*0-375-50569-5*) Random House Adult Trade Publishing Group. (Villard Bks.).
—Trouble Man: A Novel. 2003. (Strivers Row Ser.). 240p. 22.95 (*0-375-50895-3*, Villard Bks.) Random House Adult Trade Publishing Group.
Hurston, Zora Neale. The Complete Stories. 1996. 336p. pap. 14.00 (*0-06-092171-4*, Perennial); 1995. 256p. 25.00 o.p. (*0-06-016732-7*) HarperTrade.
—Jonah's Gourd Vine. 1990. 240p. pap. 13.95 (*0-06-091651-6*, Perennial) HarperTrade.
—Jonah's Gourd Vine. 766th l.t. ed. 1998. (Perennial Bestsellers Ser.). 280p. 25.95 o.p. (*0-7838-0255-2*) Thorndike Pr.
—Novels & Stories: Jonah's Gourd Vine; Their Eyes Were Watching God; Moses, Man of the Mountain; Seraph on the Suwanee, Vol. I. Wall, Cheryl A., ed. 1995. (Novels & Stories Ser.: Vol. 74). 1041p. 35.00 (*0-940450-83-6*) Library of America, The.
—Spunk: Three Tales by Zora Neale Hurston. 1997. 128p. pap. 10.95 (*1-56924-743-9*, Marlowe & Co.) Avalon Publishing Group.
—Their Eyes Were Watching God. 1995. reprint ed. lib. bdg. 24.95 (*1-56849-625-7*) Buccaneer Bks., Inc.
—Their Eyes Were Watching God. 1970. reprint ed. lib. bdg. 35.00 o.p. (*0-8371-1885-9*, HUE&, Greenwood Pr.) Greenwood Publishing Group, Inc.
—Their Eyes Were Watching God. 2000. (Illus.). 256p. 22.00 (*0-06-019949-0*); 1990. (C). pap. 7.66 (*0-06-502371-4*) HarperCollins Pubs.
—Their Eyes Were Watching God. 1994. 224p. pap. 13.50 (*0-06-091650-8*, Perennial) HarperTrade.
—Their Eyes Were Watching God. 1990. 286p. (C). reprint ed. lib. bdg. 35.00 o.p. (*0-8095-9019-0*) Millefleurs.
—Their Eyes Were Watching God. 1999. 11.95 (*1-56137-809-7*) Novel Units, Inc.
—Their Eyes Were Watching God. l.t. ed. 1996. 261p. lib. bdg. 24.95 (*0-7838-1884-X*) Thorndike Pr.
—Their Eyes Were Watching God. 1990. 19.55 (*0-606-04401-9*) Turtleback Bks.
—Their Eyes Were Watching God. 1991. (Illus.). 288p. 26.95 (*0-252-01778-1*) Univ. of Illinois Pr.
Icilyn, Sonia. Infatuation. 2001. (Arabesque Ser.). 288p. mass mkt. 5.99 (*1-58314-217-7*) BET Bks.
Iles, Greg. The Quiet Game. l.t. ed. 2000. (G. K. Hall Core Ser.). 720p. 30.95 (*0-7838-9299-3*, Macmillan Reference USA) Gale Group.
Jackson, Brenda. One Special Moment. 2001. (Arabesque Ser.). 304p. mass mkt. 5.99 (*1-58314-227-4*) BET Bks.
—Perfect Timing. 2004. 304p. mass mkt. 6.99 (*0-7582-0029-3*, Kensington Bks.); 2003. 304p. pap. 15.00 (*0-7582-0011-0*); 2002. 34p. 24.00 o.s.i (*1-57566-921-8*, Kensington Bks.) Kensington Publishing Corp.
—The Savvy Sistahs. Date not set. (*0-312-31511-2*); 2003. 320p. pap. 13.95 o.s.i (*0-312-31512-0*, Saint Martin's Griffin) St. Martin's Pr.
Jackson, Brian Keith. The Queen of Harlem. l.t. ed. 2002. (African Amercan Ser.). 454p. 28.95 (*0-7862-4581-6*) Thorndike Pr.
—The Queen of Harlem: A Novel. 2003. 256p. pap. 12.95 (*0-7679-0839-2*, Harlem Moon) Broadway Bks.
—The Queen of Harlem: A Novel. 2002. 256p. 22.95 (*0-385-50295-8*) Doubleday Publishing.
—Walking Through Mirrors. 1999. 272p. pap. 14.00 (*0-671-56894-9*, Washington Square Pr.); 1998. 258p. 23.00 (*0-671-56893-0*, Atria) Simon & Schuster.
—Walking Through Mirrors. 1999. 20.05 (*0-606-19129-1*) Turtleback Bks.
Jackson, Bruce. Growing up Free in America. 1998. 144p. pap. 11.95 (*0-916397-48-3*) Manic D Pr.
Jackson, Edwardo. Ever After: A Novel. 2002. 384p. pap. 13.95 (*0-375-75773-2*); 2001. E-Book 18.00 (*1-58836-072-5*) Random House Adult Trade Publishing Group. (Villard Bks.).
—Ever After: A Novel. 1999. 300p. pap. 13.95 o.p. (*1-58348-545-7*) iUniverse, Inc.
—Neva Hafta: A Novel. 368p. 2003. pap. 13.95 (*0-375-75774-0*); 2002. 22.95 (*0-375-50637-3*, Villard Bks.) Random House Adult Trade Publishing Group.
Jackson, James D. Wrong Perception. 1999. (Illus.). 189p. pap. 13.00 o.p. (*1-57197-180-7*) Pentland Pr., Inc.
Jackson, Monica. A Magical Moment. 1999. 256p. mass mkt. 4.99 (*1-58314-021-2*) BET Bks.
Jackson-Opoku, Sandra. The River Where Blood Is Born. 1998. (Ballantine Reader's Circle Ser.). 432p. pap. 12.95 (*0-345-42476-X*) Ballantine Bks.
Jackson, Sheneska. Blessings. 2003. mass mkt. 6.99 (*0-7434-8246-8*); 1999. 400p. pap. 13.00 (*0-684-85312-4*); 1998. 400p. 23.00 (*0-684-85035-4*) Simon & Schuster. (Simon & Schuster).
Jakes, T. D. Cover Girls. 2003. 256p. 22.95 (*0-446-52906-0*); pap. 14.00 (*0-446-69139-9*) Warner Bks., Inc. (Warner Faith).
James, Breggie. Sister Secrets. 1997. 432p. (Orig.). pap. 12.95 (*0-9659042-0-2*) BeeJay Enterprises.
James, Darius. Negrophobia: An Urban Parable. 1993. 192p. pap. 8.95 (*0-312-09350-0*, Saint Martin's Griffin) St. Martin's Pr.
Jarrett, Norma L. Sunday Brunch. 1999. 238p. pap. 15.95 (*0-9671923-5-8*) Jarrett, Norma L.
Jasper, Kenji. Dark: A Novel. 2001. 256p. pap. 12.95 (*0-7679-0707-8*) Broadway Bks.
Jefferson, Roland S. The School on 103rd Street. 1997. (Old School Bks.). 192p. pap. 11.00 (*0-393-31662-9*) Norton, W. W. & Co., Inc.
Joe, Yolanda. Bebe's by Golly Wow! 1999. 352p. mass mkt. 6.50 (*0-440-23525-1*) Dell Publishing.
—The Hatwearer's Lesson. l.t. ed. 2003. lib. bdg. 28.95 (*1-58547-339-1*, Platinum) Ctr. Point Large Print.
—The Hatwearer's Lesson. 2003. 288p. 23.95 (*0-525-94716-7*) Dutton/Plume.
—My Fine Lady. 2004. 288p. 23.95 (*0-525-94808-2*, Dutton) Dutton/Plume.
Johnson, Amelia A. Clarence & Corrine: Or God's Way. 1988. (Schomburg Library of Nineteenth-Century Black Women Writers). (Illus.). 240p. text 39.95 (*0-19-505264-1*) Oxford Univ. Pr., Inc.
—The Hazeley Family. 1988. (Schomburg Library of Nineteenth-Century Black Women Writers). 240p. text 37.50 (*0-19-505257-9*) Oxford Univ. Pr., Inc.
Johnson, Charles. Dreamer: A Novel. 240p. 1999. pap. 12.00 (*0-684-85443-0*); 1998. 23.00 (*0-684-81224-X*) Simon & Schuster. (Scribner).
—Dreamer: A Novel. abr. ed. 1998. audio 25.00 (*0-671-58240-2*, Simon & Schuster Audioworks) Simon & Schuster Audio.
—Oxherding Tale. 1995. 224p. pap. 12.95 o.s.i (*0-452-27503-2*, Plume) Dutton/Plume.
—Oxherding Tale. 1984. 192p. pap. 9.95 o.p. (*0-8021-5051-9*, Grove Pr.) Grove/Atlantic, Inc.
—Oxherding Tale. 1982. 192p. 15.00 o.p. (*0-253-16607-1*) Indiana Univ. Pr.
—The Sorcerer's Apprentice: Tales & Conjurations. 1994. 192p. pap. 11.95 o.p. (*0-452-27237-8*, Plume) Dutton/Plume.
—The Sorcerer's Apprentice: Tales & Conjurations. 1987. 192p. pap. 8.95 o.p. (*0-14-009865-8*, Penguin Bks.) Viking Penguin.
Johnson, Charles R. Middle Passage: A Novel. 1991. (Contemporary Fiction Ser.). 224p. reprint ed. pap. 11.95 o.s.i (*0-452-26638-6*, Plume) Dutton/Plume.
—Middle Passage: A Novel. 1990. 160p. 17.95 (*0-689-11968-2*, Scribner) Simon & Schuster.

Johnson-Coleman, Lorraine. Just Plain Folks: Original Tales of Living, Loving, & Learning, as Told by a Perfectly Ordinary, Quite Commonly Sensible & Absolutely Awe-Inspiring Colored Woman. 2000. 256p. pap. 12.95 (*0-316-46007-9*, Back Bay) Little Brown & Co.

—Just Plain Folks: Original Tales of Living, Loving, Longing & Learning, As Told by a Perfectly Ordinary, Quite Commonly Sensible & Absolutely Awe-Inspiring Colored Woman. 1998. 256p. 22.00 o.p. (*0-316-46084-2*) Little Brown & Co.

—Just Plain Folks: Original Tales of Living, Loving, Longing & Learning as Told by a Perfectly Ordinary, Quite Commonly Sensible & Absolutely Awe-Inspiring Colored Woman. 2001. 192p. E-Book 9.95 (*0-446-91468-1*) Little Brown & Co.

—Just Plain Folks: Original Tales of Living, Loving, Longing, & Learning as Told by a Perfectly Ordinary, Quite Commonly Sensible & Absolutely Awe-Inspiring Colored Woman. 2001. 192p. E-Book 9.95 (*0-446-92360-5*) Warner Bks., Inc.

Johnson, Fenton. Tales of Darkest America. 1977. (Black Heritage Library Collection). reprint ed. 12.95 (*0-8369-8926-0*) Ayer Co. Pubs., Inc.

Johnson, Freddie Lee, III. Bittersweet. 384p. 2003. pap. 13.95 (*0-345-44597-X*); 2002. 23.95 o.s.i (*0-345-44596-1*) Ballantine Bks. (One World/Ballantine).

—A Man Finds His Way. 2003. 352p. 23.95 (*0-345-44598-8*, One World/Ballantine) Ballantine Bks.

Johnson, Guy. Standing at the Scratch Line. 2001. E-Book 11.95 (*1-58945-866-4*) Adobe Systems, Inc.

—Standing at the Scratch Line. 2001. E-Book 11.95 (*0-375-50656-X*) Random Hse., Inc.

—Standing at the Scratch Line: A Novel. 2001. 576p. pap. 14.95 o.s.i (*0-375-75667-1*, Villard Bks.) Random House Adult Trade Publishing Group.

—Standing at the Scratch Line: A Novel. 1998. 432p. 24.95 o.s.i (*0-375-50158-4*) Random Hse. Information Group.

Johnson-Hodge, Margaret. Butterscotch Blues. 2000. 295p. 23.95 o.p. (*0-312-26484-4*); E-Book 6.50 (*0-312-27429-7*) St. Martin's Pr.

—Butterscotch Blues: A Novel. 2001. 320p. mass mkt. 6.50 (*0-312-97630-5*, St. Martin's Paperbacks) St. Martin's Pr.

—Some Sunday. 2003. 320p. mass mkt. 6.99 (*0-7582-0026-9*, Kensington Bks.); 2002. 32p. pap. 15.00 (*0-7582-0003-X*); 2001. 32p. 24.00 o.s.i (*1-57566-916-1*, Dafina) Kensington Publishing Corp.

—Some Sunday. l.t. ed. 2002. (African American Ser.). 562p. 29.95 (*0-7862-3870-4*) Thorndike Pr.

—True Lies. 2002. 320p. 24.00 (*1-57566-917-X*, Dafina) Kensington Publishing Corp.

Johnson, James Weldon. The Autobiography of an Ex-Colored Man. 2000. 252p. E-Book 9.95 (*0-594-06491-0*) 1873 Pr.

—The Autobiography of an Ex-Colored Man. unabr. ed. 1995. (Thrift Editions Ser.). 112p. pap. 1.50 (*0-486-28512-X*) Dover Pubns., Inc.

—The Autobiography of an Ex-Colored Man. 1991. (American Century Ser.). 214p. pap. 10.00 (*0-8090-0032-6*, Hill & Wang) Farrar, Straus & Giroux.

—The Autobiography of an Ex-Colored Man. 1989. 256p. pap. 11.00 (*0-679-72753-1*, Vintage) Knopf Publishing Group.

—The Autobiography of an Ex-Colored Man. 1933. 11.95 o.s.i (*0-394-41582-5*) Knopf, Alfred A. Inc.

—The Autobiography of an Ex-Colored Man. Morrow/Avon.

—The Autobiography of an Ex-Colored Man. 1948. mass mkt. 0.35 o.p. (*0-451-60029-0*, Signet Bks.) NAL.

—The Autobiography of an Ex-Colored Man. 1999. (Critical Editions Ser.). pap. 10.95 (*0-393-97286-0*, Norton Paperbacks) Norton, W. W. & Co., Inc.

—The Autobiography of an Ex-Colored Man. 1990. pap. 5.95 o.p. (*0-14-043333-3*, Penguin Classics) Viking Penguin.

—The Autobiography of an Ex-Colored Man. Andrews, William L., ed. & intro. by. 1990. (Twentieth Century Classics Ser.). 192p. pap. 9.95 (*0-14-018402-3*, Penguin Classics) Viking Penguin.

—The Autobiography of an Ex-Colored Man. 1996. (X Press Black Classics Ser.). 183p. pap. 9.95 (*1-874509-31-X*) X Pr., The GBR. *Dist:* LPC Group.

Johnson, Jasmine. Mr Soon Come. 2003. 240p. pap. 10.95 (*1-902934-15-6*) X Pr., The GBR. *Dist:* National Bk. Network.

Johnson, Mat. Drop. 2000. 288p. pap. 23.95 (*1-58234-104-4*) Bloomsbury Publishing.

Johnson, R. M. The Harris Men. 336p. 1999. 23.00 o.s.i (*0-684-84470-2*); 2000. reprint ed. pap. 12.95 (*0-7434-0059-3*) Simon & Schuster. (Simon & Schuster).

Johnson, Shawne. Eden, Ohio. 2004. 288p. 23.95 (*0-525-94810-4*, Dutton) Dutton/Plume.

—Getting Our Breath Back: A Novel. 2002. 224p. 22.95 o.s.i (*0-525-94654-3*, Dutton) Dutton/Plume.

Jones, Callie Adams. Soul of a Black Woman. 2002. 130p. pap. (*1-55369-219-5*) Trafford Publishing.

Jones, Edward P. The Known World. unabr. ed. 2003. audio 39.95 (*0-06-056943-3*) HarperCollins Pubs.

—The Known World. 2003. 400p. 24.95 (*0-06-055754-0*, Amistad Pr.) HarperTrade.

—Lost in the City: Stories. 2003. 256p. pap. 12.95 (*0-06-056628-0*, Amistad Pr.) HarperTrade.

Jones, Gayl. Corregidora. 1987. (Bluestreak Ser.). 192p. reprint ed. pap. 11.00 (*0-8070-6315-0*) Beacon Pr.

—Corregidora. 1975. 6.95 o.p. (*0-394-49323-0*) Random Hse., Inc.

—The Healing. 1999. (Blue Streak). 296p. pap. 12.00 (*0-8070-6325-8*) Beacon Pr.

—The Healing. Atwan, Helene, ed. 1998. 336p. 23.00 o.p. (*0-8070-6314-2*) Beacon Pr.

—The Healing. l.t. ed. 1998. (Americana Ser.). 488p. 28.95 (*0-7862-1504-6*) Thorndike Pr.

—Mosquito. Atwan, Helene, ed. (Bluestreak Ser.). 2000. 624p. pap. 18.00 (*0-8070-8347-X*); 1999. 616p. 28.50 o.p. (*0-8070-8346-1*) Beacon Pr.

—Mosquito. unabr. collector's ed. 1999. Pt. 1. audio 64.00 (*0-7366-4830-5*, 5176-A); Pt. 2. audio 72.00 (*0-7366-4899-2*, 5176-B) Books on Tape, Inc.

—The White Rat. 1991. (Library of Black Literature). 200p. reprint ed. pap. text 12.95 o.p. (*1-55553-100-8*) Northeastern Univ. Pr.

—The White Rat. 1977. 7.95 o.p. (*0-394-49939-5*) Random Hse., Inc.

Jones, Jack P. Hamhocks, Turnip Greens & Blackeyed Peas: The Novel. 1999. 240p. 24.95 (*0-9666721-5-1*) GoldenIsle Pubs., Inc.

Jones, Patricia. Red on a Rose: A Novel. 2001. 352p. (Orig.). pap. 14.00 (*0-380-81730-6*, Avon Bks.) Morrow/Avon.

Jones, Solomon. Pipe Dream: A Novel. 2001. 368p. pap. 13.95 (*0-375-75660-4*, Villard Bks.) Random House Adult Trade Publishing Group.

Jones, Tayari. Leaving Atlanta. 272p. 2003. pap. 13.95 (*0-446-69089-9*); 2002. 23.95 (*0-446-52830-7*) Warner Bks., Inc.

Kalam, Murad. Night Journey. 2003. (Illus.). 320p. 23.00 (*0-7432-4418-4*, Simon & Schuster) Simon & Schuster.

Karlin, Wayne. The Wished-For Country. 2002. (Illus.). 340p. pap. 16.95 (*1-880684-89-6*) Curbstone Pr.

Kay, Terry. The Runaway. abr. ed. 1998. audio 7.99 o.s.i (*1-56740-265-8*, 1564); 1997. audio 17.95 o.p. (*1-56740-754-4*, 504, Nova Audio Bks.); 1997. audio 25.95 o.p. (*1-56100-775-7*, 243, Bookcassette); 1997. audio 89.25 o.p. (*1-56740-554-1*, 1021, Unabridged Library Editions) Brilliance Audio.

—The Runaway. 1997. 448p. 24.00 o.p. (*0-688-15033-0*, Morrow, William & Co.); 1998. 496p. reprint ed. pap. 6.99 (*0-380-72904-0*, Avon Bks.) Morrow/Avon.

Kaye, Mavis. Who Killed Tiffany Jones? A Novel. 2002. 208p. 22.95 (*0-06-621333-9*) HarperCollins Pubs.

Keene, John. Annotations. 1995. (Paperbook Ser.: Vol. 809). 96p. (Orig.). pap. 8.95 (*0-8112-1304-8*, NDP809) New Directions Publishing Corp.

Kelley, Norman. The Big Mango. 2000. (Illus.). 270p. pap. 14.95 (*1-888451-10-6*) Akashic Bks.

—Black Heat. 228p. 1997. 22.00 o.p. (*1-887276-02-5*); 1996. (Illus.). pap. 12.95 (*1-887276-03-3*) Cool Grove Publishing, Inc. (Coolgrove Pr.).

—The Black Heat. 2002. 320p. mass mkt. 6.99 (*0-06-095994-0*, Avon Bks.) Morrow/Avon.

—Black Heat: A Nina Halligan Mystery. 2001. 320p. 23.00 (*0-06-018542-2*) HarperTrade.

—A Phat Death: A Nina Halligan Mystery. 2003. 260p. pap. 14.95 (*1-888451-48-3*) Akashic Bks.

Kemper, Marjorie. Until That Good Day: A Novel. 2003. 320p. 24.95 (*0-312-29079-9*) St. Martin's Pr.

Kenan, Randall. A Visitation of Spirits. 1990. 272p. pap. 12.95 o.s.i (*0-385-41505-2*) Doubleday Publishing.

—A Visitation of Spirits. 1989. 272p. 17.95 o.p. (*0-8021-1118-1*) Grove/Atlantic, Inc.

Kensington. African American Sam. 2000. (*1-57566-822-X*) Kensington Publishing Corp.

Kidd, Sue Monk. The Secret Life of Bees: A Novel. 2002. 320p. 24.95 (*0-670-89460-5*, Viking) Viking Penguin.

Kimball, Philip. Liar's Moon: A Long Story. 1999. (Marian Wood Book Ser.). 304p. 23.00 o.s.i (*0-8050-6148-7*) Holt, Henry & Co.

—Liar's Moon: A Novel. 2000. 304p. pap. 12.95 o.s.i (*0-452-28183-0*, Plume) Dutton/Plume.

Kincaid, Jamaica. Jupiter. 2004. (Illus.). (*0-374-18056-3*) Farrar, Straus & Giroux.

—My Favorite Tool. 2005. (*0-374-21694-0*) Farrar, Straus & Giroux.

King-Gamble, Marcia. Illusions of Love. 2000. (Arabesque Ser.). 288p. mass mkt. 5.99 (*1-58314-104-9*) BET Bks.

—A Reason to Love. 2001. (Arabesque Ser.). 288p. mass mkt. 5.99 (*1-58314-133-2*) BET Bks.

Kitt, Sandra. Close Encounters. l.t. ed. 2000. (G. K. Hall Core Ser.). 432p. 27.95 (*0-7838-9271-3*, Macmillan Reference USA) Gale Group.

—Close Encounters. 2000. 368p. mass mkt. 6.99 (*0-451-20048-9*, Signet Bks.) NAL.

—Family Affairs. l.t. ed. 2003. (Large Print Ser.). 29.95 (*1-57490-470-1*, Beeler Large Print Bks.) Beeler, Thomas T. Publisher.

—Family Affairs. 1999. (Signet Book Ser.). 368p. mass mkt. 6.99 (*0-451-19185-4*, Signet Bks.) NAL.

—Significant Others. 1996. 400p. mass mkt. 6.99 (*0-451-18824-1*, Signet Bks.) NAL.

—Suddenly. 2001. (Arabesque Ser.). 288p. mass mkt. 5.99 (*1-58314-202-9*) BET Bks.

Klavan, Andrew. Hunting down Amanda. 1999. 369p. 25.00 (*0-688-16895-7*, Morrow, William & Co.) Morrow/Avon.

Komo, Dolores. Clio Browne: Private Investigator. 1988. (WomanSleuth Mystery Ser.). 200p. pap. 6.95 o.p. (*0-89594-320-4*); lib. bdg. 22.95 o.p. (*0-89594-321-2*) Crossing Pr., Inc., The.

La Fleur, Geralyn Marie. C. E. O. Chief Executive Oreo. 2002. pap. 14.95 (*0-9719749-1-8*) Milligan Bks.

Ladd, Florence. Sarah's Psalm. 1996. 320p. 22.50 (*0-684-80410-7*, Scribner) Simon & Schuster.

Lamar, Jake. If 6 Were 9: A Militant Mystery. 2001. 240p. 19.95 o.s.i (*0-609-60537-2*) Crown Publishing Group.

Lambright, Evelyn Slim. The Justus Girls. 2001. 368p. 24.00 (*0-06-018476-0*) HarperCollins Pubs.

Larence, Anna. Give & Take. (Arabesque Ser.). 2000. 288p. mass mkt. 5.99 (*1-58314-111-1*); 1999. mass mkt. 4.99 (*1-58314-017-4*) BET Bks.

Larsen, Nella. The Complete Fiction of Nella Larsen: Passing, Quicksand & Three Stories. 2001. 304p. pap. 13.00 (*0-385-72100-5*, Knopf Bks. for Young Readers) Random Hse. Children's Bks.

—Passing. 1970. (American Negro: His History & Literature, Ser. No. 3). reprint ed. 27.95 (*0-405-01930-0*) Ayer Co. Pubs., Inc.

—Passing. 1969. 215p. reprint ed. 57.95 (*0-8371-1541-8*, LAP&, Greenwood Pr.) Greenwood Publishing Group, Inc.

—Passing. 2002. (Modern Library Classics). 304p. pap. 9.95 (*0-375-75813-5*, Modern Library) Random House Adult Trade Publishing Group.

—Passing. 2003. 160p. pap. 10.00 (*0-14-243727-1*, Penguin Classics) Viking Penguin.

—Passing. Davis, Thadious, ed. & intro. by. 1997. (Penguin Twentieth-Century Classics Ser.). 160p. pap. 10.00 o.s.i (*0-14-118025-0*) Viking Penguin.

—Quicksand. 1970. 310p. reprint ed. 60.95 (*0-8371-1127-7*, LAQ&, Greenwood Pr.) Greenwood Publishing Group, Inc.

—Quicksand & Passing. McDowell, Deborah, ed. 1986. (American Women Writers Ser.). 300p. (C). text 35.00 o.p. (*0-8135-1169-0*); pap. text 10.00 (*0-8135-1170-4*) Rutgers Univ. Pr.

Larson, Charles R., ed. & intro. An Intimation of Things Distant: The Collected Fiction of Nella Larsen. 1992. 336p. pap. 10.95 o.s.i (*0-385-42149-4*) Doubleday Publishing.

Larson, Charles R. & Golden, Marita. An Intimation of Things Distant: The Collected Fiction of Nella Larsen. 1999. pap. 18.95 (*0-385-50016-5*) Doubleday Publishing.

Lattany, Kristin Hunter. Breaking Away. 2003. 304p. 23.95 (*0-345-44249-0*, Ballantine Bks.) Ballantine Bks.

—Kinfolks. 1997. 304p. pap. 10.95 (*0-345-41720-8*); 1996. 320p. 23.00 o.p. (*0-345-40706-7*) Ballantine Bks.

Le Beau, Sinclair. Your Precious Love. 2001. (Indigo Love Stories Ser.). 290p. mass mkt. 8.95 (*1-58571-042-3*, Indigo) Genesis Pr., Inc.

LeBeau, Sinclair. Glory of Love. 1997. 191p. mass mkt. 10.95 (*1-885478-19-4*, Indigo) Genesis Pr., Inc.

Lee, Helen E. Water Marked. 1999. 320p. 24.00 o.s.i (*0-684-83843-5*, Scribner) Simon & Schuster.

Lee, Helen Elaine. Water Marked: A Novel. 2001. 320p. reprint ed. pap. 13.00 (*0-684-86573-4*, Scribner) Simon & Schuster.

Lee, Rochunda. Love at Last. 2001. (Arabesque Ser.). 320p. mass mkt. 5.99 (*1-58314-211-8*) BET Bks.

Lent, Jeffrey. In the Fall. 2000. 560p. 25.00 o.p. (*0-87113-765-8*, Atlantic Monthly Pr.) Grove/Atlantic, Inc.

—In the Fall. 2000. pap. (*0-375-72589-X*, Vintage) Knopf Publishing Group.

—In the Fall. l.t. ed. 2000. (Americana Ser.). 967p. 28.95 (*0-7862-2783-4*) Thorndike Pr.

—In the Fall: A Novel. 2001. 528p. reprint ed. pap. 14.95 (*0-375-70745-X*, Vintage) Knopf Publishing Group.

Leonard, Elmore. Jackie Brown. 1997. 352p. mass mkt. 6.50 o.s.i (*0-440-22606-6*) Dell Publishing.

—Rum Punch. 1998. 304p. pap. 9.95 o.s.i (*0-385-33280-7*, Dell Bks.) Dell Publishing.

Lester, Julius. Do Lord Remember Me. 1985. 224p. 13.95 o.p. (*0-03-071534-2*) Holt, Henry & Co.

—Do Lord Remember Me. 1986. mass mkt. 5.95 o.s.i (*0-671-60707-3*, Pocket) Simon & Schuster.

—Do Lord Remember Me. Date not set. pap. (*0-312-28556-6*, Saint Martin's Griffin) St. Martin's Pr.

Lewis, W. H. In the Arms of Our Elders. 1995. 170p. pap. 10.95 (*0-932112-35-8*) Carolina Wren Pr.

Lincoln, Christine. Sap Rising: Stories. 2002. 176p. pap. 11.00 (*0-375-72777-9*) Random Hse., Inc.

Lintner, Grace. Bond & Free. 1977. (Black Heritage Library Collection). reprint ed. 22.95 (*0-8369-9014-5*) Ayer Co. Pubs., Inc.

Litman, Robert B. Allergy Shots. 1993. 254p. (Orig.). pap. text 9.95 (*0-918921-04-X*) Ivy League Pr., Inc.

Little, Benilde. Acting Out. 2004. 288p. pap. 13.00 (*0-684-85481-3*, Free Pr.) Simon & Schuster.

—Acting Out. l.t. ed. 2003. 345p. 28.95 (*0-7862-5896-9*) Thorndike Pr.

—Acting Out: A Novel. 2003. 288p. 23.00 (*0-684-85480-5*, Free Pr.) Simon & Schuster.

—Good Hair. 1996. 240p. 22.00 (*0-684-80176-0*, Simon & Schuster) Simon & Schuster.

—Good Hair: A Novel. 2003. 240p. pap. 12.00 (*0-684-83557-6*, Free Pr.) Simon & Schuster.

—The Itch: A Novel. 1998. (Illus.). 288p. 23.00 o.s.i (*0-684-83834-6*, Simon & Schuster) Simon & Schuster.

Love, Monifa A. Freedom in The Dismal. 1998. 191p. 20.00 (*0-917635-26-4*); pap. 10.00 (*0-917635-27-2*) Plover Pr.

Lovell, Glenville. Too Beautiful to Die. 2004. 320p. mass mkt. 6.99 (*0-425-19702-6*) Berkley Publishing Group.

—Too Beautiful to Die. 2003. 304p. 23.95 (*0-399-15048-X*) Putnam Publishing Group, The.

Ludlow, Susie Nickens. Carry Me Back: A Family & National History of Slavery & Freedom. Tennant, Roberta, ed. 2000. 288p. pap. 17.95 (*0-9679879-0-3*) Honocan Pr.

Luntta, Karl. Know It by Heart. 2003. 256p. pap. 15.95 (*1-880684-95-0*) Curbstone Pr.

Maguire, Elizabeth. Thinner, Blonder, Whiter. 2004. 336p. pap. 14.00 (*0-7867-1299-6*); 2002. 320p. 25.00 (*0-7867-1019-5*) Avalon Publishing Group. (Carroll & Graf Pubs.).

Major, Clarence. Dirty Bird Blues. 1996. 224p. 22.95 o.p. (*1-56279-083-8*) Mercury Hse.

Major, Clarence, ed. Calling the Wind: Twentieth Century African-American Short Stories. 1993. 528p. 30.00 o.p. (*0-06-018337-3*); 368th ed. 656p. pap. 19.95 (*0-06-098201-2*) HarperTrade. (Perennial).

Major, Devorah. Brown Glass Windows. 2002. 194p. pap. 15.95 (*1-880684-87-X*) Curbstone Pr.

Major, Marcus. A Family Affair. 2003. 304p. 24.95 (*0-525-94768-X*, Dutton) Dutton/Plume.

—Four Guys & Trouble. 2001. 272p. 23.95 o.p. (*0-525-94568-7*, Dutton) Dutton/Plume.

—Four Guys & Trouble. 2002. 384p. mass mkt. 6.99 (*0-451-41017-3*, Onyx) NAL.

—Good Peoples: A Novel. 2000. 272p. 22.95 o.s.i (*0-525-94535-0*, Dutton) Dutton/Plume.

—A Man Most Worthy. 2003. 288p. 23.95 (*0-525-94685-3*, Dutton) Dutton/Plume.

—A Man Most Worthy. 2004. 336p. pap. 13.95 (*0-451-21107-3*) NAL.

Mallette, Gloria. Shades of Jade: A Novel. 2001. 272p. pap. 13.95 (*0-375-75743-0*); E-Book 12.50 (*0-375-50663-2*) Random House Adult Trade Publishing Group. (Villard Bks.).

Malloy, Max Alexander. Black Maids Pass Our Mops to Ms. Ann: Breaking the Shackles of Racial Servitude. 2000. 368p. E-Book 8.00 (*0-7388-7517-1*) Xlibris Corp.

Malone, Michael. Time's Witness: A Justin & Cuddy Novel. 2002. 576p. pap. 15.00 (*1-57071-754-0*, Sourcebooks Landmark) Sourcebooks, Inc.

Manning, Kate. Whitegirl. 416p. 2003. pap. 13.95 (*0-385-33721-3*); 2002. 23.95 (*0-385-33287-4*, Delacorte Pr.) Dell Publishing.

Mansaray, Alasan. A Haunting Heritage: An African Saga in America. 1994. 320p. 21.95 (*0-9639497-5-6*) Sahara Publishing.

Mansbach, Adam. Shackling Water. 2002. 240p. 22.95 (*0-385-50205-2*) Doubleday Publishing.

—Shackling Water. 2003. 240p. reprint ed. pap. 12.00 (*1-4000-3159-1*, Anchor) Knopf Publishing Group.

Manuel, Melissa A. No Crystal Stair, Vol. I. Wren, Dawn, ed. 2000. (*0-9702879-0-9*) Manuel, Melissa.

Marshall, Paule. The Fisher King: A Novel. l.t. ed. 2001. 256p. lib. bdg. 27.95 (*1-58547-074-0*) Ctr. Point Large Print.

—The Fisher King: A Novel. 224p. 2000. 23.00 o.s.i (*0-684-87283-8*); 2001. reprint ed. pap. 12.00 (*0-684-86970-5*) Simon & Schuster. (Scribner).

Martin-Arnold, Edwina. Eve's Prescription. 2001. (Indigo Love Stories Ser.). 333p. pap. 8.95 (*1-58571-049-0*, Indigo) Genesis Pr., Inc.

Martin, Lee. Quakertown: A Novel. 2002. 304p. pap. 14.00 (*0-452-28336-1*, Plume); 2001. (Illus.). 320p. 23.95 o.p. (*0-525-94583-0*) Dutton/Plume.

Mason, J. D. And on the Eighth Day She Rested. 2001. 244p. pap. 14.95 (*0-9700102-8-1*) Sadorian Pubns.

—And on the Eighth Day She Rested: A Novel. 2003. 288p. pap. 13.95 (*0-312-30989-9*, Saint Martin's Griffin) St. Martin's Pr.

Matson, Henrietta. The Mississippi Schoolmaster. 1977. (Black Heritage Library Collection). reprint ed. 25.95 (*0-8369-9035-8*) Ayer Co. Pubs., Inc.

Matthews, Kimberly T. Promise You Won't Tell Nobody. 1998. 126p. pap. 10.00 o.p. (*1-56411-202-0*) Conquering Bks.

—Promise You Won't Tell Nobody. 2nd rev. ed. 1998. 130p. pap. 11.00 (*0-9667609-0-5*) Kissed Pubns.

Matthews, Steve & Wilson, Mark, contrib. by. Brain-in-a-Box. 1999. (Illus.). (*0-7608-3284-6*) Sundance Publishing.

Maund, Alfred. The Big Boxcar. 1999. (Radical Novel Reconsidered Ser.). 216p. pap. text 15.95 (*0-252-06754-1*) Univ. of Illinois Pr.

Mayfield, Julian. The Hit & the Long Night. 1989. (Library of Black Literature). 310p. reprint ed. pap. text 17.95 (*1-55553-065-6*) Northeastern Univ. Pr.

Mayhew, Dianne. Stolen Moments. 2000. (Arabesque Ser.). 256p. mass mkt. 5.99 (*1-58314-119-7*) BET Bks.

Mayo, William S. Kaloolah: or Journeyings to the Djebel Kumri: An Autobiography of Jonathan Romer. 1977. (Black Heritage Library Collection). reprint ed. 43.95 (*0-8369-9059-5*) Ayer Co. Pubs., Inc.

McBride, James. Miracle at St. Anna. l.t. ed. 2003. 345p. 29.95 (*1-58724-473-X*, Wheeler Publishing, Inc.) Gale Group.

—Miracle at St. Anna: A Novel. 2002. 64p. audio 25.95 (*0-06-009318-8*); 64p. audio compact disk 29.95 (*0-06-009319-6*); 128p. audio 34.95 (*0-06-009320-X*) HarperTrade. (Caedmon).

—Miracle at St. Anna: A Novel. 2002. 228p. 24.95 o.s.i (*1-57322-212-7*, Riverhead Bks. (Hardcovers)) Putnam Publishing Group, The.

McCaig, Donald. Jacob's Ladder. abr. ed. 1998. pap. 24.95 o.p. incl. audio (*1-55927-508-1*, JM77D) Audio Renaissance.

—Jacob's Ladder: A Story of Virginia During the War. 1998. 525p. 25.95 o.p. (*0-393-04629-X*) Norton, W. W. & Co., Inc.

—Jacob's Ladder: A Story of Virginia During the War. 1999. 528p. 15.00 (*0-14-028265-3*) Viking Penguin.

McCann, Timmothy B. Emotions. l.t. ed. 2002. 442p. 29.95 (*0-7862-4278-7*) Gale Group.

—Emotions. 2003. 272p. pap. 15.00 (*1-57566-760-6*) Kensington Publishing Corp.

—Until... 1999. 272p. pap. 12.00 (*0-380-80579-0*, Avon Bks.) Morrow/Avon.

McCann, Timothy B. Emotions. 2002. 272p. 24.00 (*1-57566-785-1*) Kensington Publishing Corp.

McCarthy, Susan Carol. Lay That Trumpet in Our Hands. 288p. 2003. pap. 12.95 (*0-553-38103-2*); 2002. 23.95 (*0-553-80169-4*) Bantam Bks.

McClain-Watson, Teresa. Plenty Good Room. 1997. (Discoveries Ser.: No. 1). 272p. pap. 14.00 (*0-940242-74-5*) Fjord Pr.

McCracken, Susan Nyswonger. For the Blessings of a Friend. 2001. 284p. pap. 15.00 (*0-944350-55-0*) Friends United Pr.

McEachin, James. Tell Me a Tale. 1996. 224p. 18.95 o.s.i (*0-89141-584-X*, Presidio Pr.) Ballantine Bks.

McFadden, Bernice L. Loving Donovan. 2003. (Illus.). 256p. 23.95 (*0-525-94706-X*) Dutton/Plume.

—Loving Donovan. l.t. ed. 2003. 351p. 28.95 (*0-7862-5630-3*) Thorndike Pr.

—Sugar. 240p. 2000. 22.95 (*0-525-94531-8*, Dutton); 2001. reprint ed. pap. 13.00 (*0-452-28220-9*, Plume) Dutton/Plume.

—Sugar. l.t. ed. 2002. (African American Ser.). 386p. 28.95 (*0-7862-3871-2*) Thorndike Pr.

—Sugar. 2001. 19.05 (*0-606-20932-8*) Turtleback Bks.

—This Bitter Earth. 2002. 288p. pap. 13.00 (*0-452-28381-7*, Plume); 23.95 o.s.i (*0-525-94636-5*, Dutton) Dutton/Plume.

—This Bitter Earth. l.t. ed. 2002. (African American Ser.). 420p. 29.95 (*0-7862-3882-8*) Thorndike Pr.

—The Warmest December. l.t. ed. 2001. 208p. 29.95 (*0-7862-3439-3*) Thorndike Pr.

McGirt, James E. The Triumphs of Ephraim. 1977. (Black Heritage Library Collection). reprint ed. 22.95 (*0-8369-9031-5*) Ayer Co. Pubs., Inc.

McGlothin, Victor. What's a Woman to Do? 2003. 352p. 19.95 (*0-312-28687-2*) St. Martin's Pr.

McIntosh, Maria J. Two Pictures. 1977. (Black Heritage Library Collection). reprint ed. 28.95 (*0-8369-9032-3*) Ayer Co. Pubs., Inc.

McKay, Claude. Gingertown. 1977. (Short Story Index Reprint Ser.). reprint ed. 30.95 (*0-8369-4113-6*) Ayer Co. Pubs., Inc.

McKinney-Whetstone, Diane. Leaving Cecil Street. 2004. 320p. 24.95 (*0-688-16385-8*, Morrow, William & Co.) Morrow/Avon.

—Tumbling. 1996. 288p. 24.00 (*0-688-14487-X*, Morrow, William & Co.) Morrow/Avon.

—Tumbling. 1997. 352p. pap. 12.00 (*0-684-83724-2*, Touchstone) Simon & Schuster.

McKnight, Reginald. He Sleeps. 2001. 224p. 23.00 o.s.i (*0-8050-4828-6*) Holt, Henry & Co.

—He Sleeps: A Novel. 2002. 224p. pap. 13.00 (*0-312-42104-4*) Picador.

—The Kind of Light That Shines on Texas. 1993. pap. 9.95 o.p. (*0-316-56059-6*); 1992. 18.95 o.p. (*0-316-56056-1*) Little Brown & Co.

—The Kind of Light That Shines on Texas: Stories. 1997. 208p. reprint ed. pap. 12.95 (*0-87074-414-3*) Southern Methodist Univ. Pr.

—Moustapha's Eclipse. 1989. 144p. reprint ed. pap. o.p. (*0-88001-179-3*, Ecco) HarperTrade.

—Moustapha's Eclipse. 1988. (Drue Heinz Literature Prize Ser.). 160p. text 22.50 o.p. (*0-8229-3589-9*) Univ. of Pittsburgh Pr.

McLarin, Kim. Taming It Down: A Novel. 1998. 320p. 24.00 (*0-688-15516-2*, Morrow, William & Co.) Morrow/Avon.

McMillan, Ann. Civil Blood: A Civil War Mystery. l.t. ed. 2001. (Thorndike Press Large Print Americana Ser.). (Illus.). 447p. 28.95 o.p. (*0-7862-3614-0*) Gale Group.

—Civil Blood: A Civil War Mystery. 2003. 320p. mass mkt. 6.99 (*0-14-200124-4*) Penguin Group (USA) Inc.

—Civil Blood: A Civil War Mystery. 2001. (Illus.). 224p. 22.95 o.p. (*0-670-89997-6*, Viking) Viking Penguin.

—Dead March: A Civil War Mystery. 1998. 224p. 21.95 o.p. (*0-670-88147-3*) Viking Penguin.

McMillan, Rosalyn. Blue Collar Blues, Set. abr. ed. 1998. audio 18.00 (*0-7871-1793-5*, 396117, Dove Audio) NewStar Media, Inc.

—Blue Collar Blues. 2001. 416p. E-Book 4.95 (*0-446-92303-6*); 2000. 400p. mass mkt. 7.50 (*0-446-60764-9*); 1999. E-Book 4.95 (*0-446-91291-3*); 1998. 352p. 30.00 o.p. (*0-446-52243-0*) Warner Bks., Inc.

—The Flip Side of Sin. 2000. 352p. 24.00 o.s.i (*0-684-86287-5*, Simon & Schuster); 2001. 432p. reprint ed. pap. 6.99 (*0-671-03435-9*, Pocket) Simon & Schuster.

—Knowing. 2001. 416p. E-Book 4.95 (*0-446-92304-4*); 1997. E-Book 4.95 (*0-446-91290-5*); 1996. 416p. 19.95 o.p. (*0-446-51866-2*); 1997. 416p. reprint ed. mass mkt. 7.50 (*0-446-60376-7*) Warner Bks., Inc.

—One Better. 2001. 384p. E-Book 4.95 (*0-446-92307-9*) Time Warner Bk. Group.

—One Better. 1999. E-Book 4.95 (*0-446-91289-1*); 1998. 400p. mass mkt. 7.99 (*0-446-60599-9*); 1997. 416p. 22.00 o.p. (*0-446-52242-2*) Warner Bks., Inc.

—This Side of Eternity: A Novel. 2001. 320p. 24.00 o.s.i (*0-684-86288-3*, Free Pr.) Simon & Schuster.

McMillan, Terry. A Day Late & a Dollar Short. 2004. 464p. pap. 14.00 (*0-451-21108-1*); 2002. 480p. reprint ed. mass mkt. 7.99 (*0-451-20494-8*, Signet Bks.) NAL.

—A Day Late & a Dollar Short. l.t. ed. 661p. 2002. 29.95 (*0-7862-3350-8*); 2001. 32.95 (*0-7862-3349-4*) Thorndike Pr.

—A Day Late & a Dollar Short. Date not set. (*0-670-78287-4*, Viking); 2001. (Illus.). 448p. 25.95 o.s.i (*0-670-89676-4*); 2000. 23.95 (*0-670-86042-5*, Viking) Viking Penguin.

—Disappearing Acts. l.t. ed. 1993. 24.95 o.p. (*1-56895-033-0*, Wheeler Publishing, Inc.) Gale Group.

—Disappearing Acts. 2002. 448p. mass mkt. 7.99 (*0-451-20563-4*, Signet Bks.) NAL.

—Disappearing Acts. abr. ed. 1993. 2p. pap. 16.00 incl. audio (*0-453-00843-7*) Penguin/HighBridge.

—Disappearing Acts. Miller, Nancy, ed. 2000. 400p. pap. 14.95 (*0-7434-2270-8*, Washington Square Pr.) Simon & Schuster.

—Disappearing Acts. Rosenman, Jane, ed. 1993. 384p. mass mkt. 7.99 (*0-671-87200-1*, Pocket); 1990. 400p. reprint ed. pap. (*0-671-70843-0*, Washington Square Pr.) Simon & Schuster.

—Disappearing Acts. 1989. 448p. 26.95 (*0-670-82461-5*) Viking Penguin.

—How Stella Got Her Groove Back. l.t. ed. 1996. (Large Print Bks.). 28.95 (*1-56895-355-0*, Wheeler Publishing, Inc.) Gale Group.

—How Stella Got Her Groove Back. 448p. 2004. pap. 14.00 (*0-451-20914-1*); 1998. mass mkt. 7.99 o.s.i (*0-451-19741-0*, Signet Bks.); 1997. mass mkt. 7.99 (*0-451-19200-1*, Signet Bks.) NAL.

—The Interruption of Everything. 2003. 400p. 25.95 (*0-670-03144-5*) Viking Penguin.

—Mama. l.t. ed. 1994. 23.95 o.p. (*0-7927-1777-5*); pap. 21.95 o.p. (*0-7927-1776-7*) BBC Audiobooks America.

—Mama. 1987. 272p. 16.95 o.p. (*0-395-39974-2*) Houghton Mifflin Co.

—Mama. abr. ed. 1994. audio 16.00 (*0-453-00865-8*) Penguin/HighBridge.

—Mama. 1989. pap. (*0-671-70362-5*); 1988. pap. 6.95 (*0-671-67883-3*) Simon & Schuster. (Washington Square Pr.).

—Waiting to Exhale. l.t. ed. 1993. (General Ser.). 600p. pap. 17.95 (*0-8161-5618-2*); lib. bdg. 23.95 o.p. (*0-8161-5617-4*) Gale Group. (Macmillan Reference USA).

—Waiting to Exhale. 1996. 155p. per. 20.97 (*0-671-85153-5*); 1993. 416p. mass mkt. 6.50 (*0-671-86417-3*); 1992. 264.00 o.p. (*0-670-77972-5*); 1995. 416p. reprint ed. mass mkt. 7.99 (*0-671-53745-8*) Simon & Schuster. (Pocket).

—Waiting to Exhale. Rosenman, Jane, ed. 1994. 416p. reprint ed. pap. 14.00 (*0-671-50148-8*, Washington Square Pr.) Simon & Schuster.

—Waiting to Exhale. 1992. 416p. 22.95 (*0-670-83980-9*, Viking) Viking Penguin.

McMillan, Terry, ed. Breaking Ice: An Anthology of Contemporary African-American Fiction. 1990. 560p. 18.00 (*0-14-011697-4*); 30.00 o.p. (*0-670-82562-X*) Viking Penguin.

McPherson, James A. Elbow Room: Stories. 1986. (Black History Titles Ser.). 288p. mass mkt. 7.99 (*0-449-21357-9*, Fawcett) Ballantine Bks.

—Elbow Room: Stories. 1987. (Scribner Signature Edition Ser.). 256p. pap. 10.00 o.p. (*0-684-18822-8*, Macmillan Reference USA) Gale Group.

—Elbow Room: Stories. 1977. o.p. (*0-316-56328-5*) Little Brown & Co.

McPherson, James Alan. Hue & Cry. 2001. 304p. pap. 14.00 (*0-06-093647-9*, Ecco) HarperTrade.

Meadows, Lee E. Silent Conspiracy. 2002. (Lincoln Keller Mystery Ser.). pap. 16.95 (*1-928623-06-9*) Proctor Pubns.

—Silent Conspiracy: A Lincoln Keller Mystery. 1997. 270p. 24.95 o.p. (*1-882792-38-6*) Proctor Pubns.

—Silent Suspicion: A Lincoln Keller Mystery. 2000. (Lincoln Keller Mystery Ser.). 437p. 24.95 (*1-882792-93-9*) Proctor Pubns.

Means, Eldred K. Black Fortune. 1977. (Black Heritage Library Collection). reprint ed. 27.95 (*0-8369-9110-9*) Ayer Co. Pubs., Inc.

—Further E. K. Means. 1977. (Black Heritage Library Collection). (Illus.). reprint ed. 31.95 (*0-8369-9111-7*) Ayer Co. Pubs., Inc.

—More E. K. Means. 1977. (Black Heritage Library Collection). (Illus.). reprint ed. 32.95 (*0-8369-9112-5*) Ayer Co. Pubs., Inc.

Meriwether, Louise. Daddy Was a Number Runner. 2002. (Contemporary Classics by Women Ser.). 240p. pap. 16.95 (*1-55861-442-7*) Feminist Pr. at The City Univ. of New York.

Merrill, Henry A. Alexander Gifford, or, Vi'let's Boy: A Story of Negro Life. 1977. (Black Heritage Library Collection). reprint ed. 31.95 (*0-8369-9036-6*) Ayer Co. Pubs., Inc.

Micheaux, Oscar. The Conquest: The Story of a Negro Pioneer. 1977. (Black Heritage Library Collection). 30.95 (*0-8369-8632-6*) Ayer Co. Pubs., Inc.

—The Homesteader: A Novel. 1994. (Illus.). 533p. pap. 12.95 (*0-8032-8208-7*, Bison Bks.) Univ. of Nebraska Pr.

—The Wind from Nowhere. 1977. (Black Heritage Library Collection). reprint ed. 35.95 (*0-8369-9109-5*) Ayer Co. Pubs., Inc.

Mickelbury, Penny. One Must Wait. 1998. 256p. 22.00 (*0-684-83741-2*, Simon & Schuster) Simon & Schuster.

—One Must Wait. 1999. 304p. mass mkt. 6.50 (*0-312-97186-9*, St. Martin's Paperbacks) St. Martin's Pr.

—Paradise Interrupted. 2001. 288p. 23.00 (*0-684-85991-2*, Simon & Schuster) Simon & Schuster.

—The Step Between. 240p. 2002. pap. 17.95 (*0-7432-4636-5*); 2000. 22.00 (*0-684-85990-4*) Simon & Schuster. (Simon & Schuster).

—Where to Choose. 1999. 256p. 22.00 (*0-684-83742-0*, Simon & Schuster) Simon & Schuster.

—Where to Choose. 2001. 240p. reprint ed. mass mkt. 6.50 (*0-312-97708-5*, 20-3261, St. Martin's Paperbacks) St. Martin's Pr.

Miller, Brenda Rhodes. The Laying on of Hands. 2004. 256p. pap. 12.95 (*0-7679-1556-9*) Broadway Bks.

Miller, Denene & Chiles, Nick. Love Don't Live Here Anymore. 2003. 320p. reprint ed. pap. 13.95 (*0-451-20778-5*) NAL.

Millner, Denene & Chiles, Nick. Love Don't Live Here Anymore. 2002. 324p. 23.95 o.s.i (*0-525-94641-1*, Dutton) Dutton/Plume.

Mitchell, Kathryn. Proud & Angry Dust. 2001. 233p. 24.95 o.p. (*0-87081-608-X*) Univ. Pr. of Colorado.

Mitchell, Sharon. Near Perfect. 2001. 336p. 23.95 o.s.i (*0-525-94621-7*, Dutton) Dutton/Plume.

—Near Perfect. 2002. 352p. reprint ed. mass mkt. 6.99 o.s.i (*0-451-20689-4*, Signet Bks.) NAL.

—Near Perfect. l.t. ed. 2002. (African American Ser.). 572p. 29.95 (*0-7862-3865-8*) Thorndike Pr.

—Nothing but the Rent. 1999. 352p. mass mkt. 6.99 (*0-451-19260-5*, Signet Bks.) NAL.

—Sheer Necessity. 1999. 304p. 23.95 o.p. (*0-525-94523-7*) Dutton/Plume.

—Sheer Necessity. 2000. 352p. reprint ed. mass mkt. 6.99 o.s.i (*0-451-19947-2*, Signet Bks.) NAL.

—Sheer Necessity. 2000. 13.04 (*0-606-19634-X*) Turtleback Bks.

Monroe, Mary. God Don't Like Ugly. 2000. 352p. pap. 15.00 (*1-57566-607-3*) Kensington Publishing Corp.

—God Still Don't Like Ugly. 2004. pap. 15.00 (*0-7582-0343-8*); 2003. 320p. 24.00 (*1-57566-912-9*, Kensington Bks.) Kensington Publishing Corp.

—The Upper Room. 1986. 304p. mass mkt. 3.95 o.s.i (*0-345-32913-9*) Ballantine Bks.

—The Upper Room. 2002. 32p. pap. 15.00 (*0-7582-0023-4*); 2001. 352p. 24.00 o.s.i (*1-57566-910-2*); 2001. 15.00 (*0-7582-0000-5*, Dafina) Kensington Publishing Corp.

—The Upper Room. 1985. 272p. 14.95 o.p. (*0-312-83402-0*) St. Martin's Pr.

—The Upper Room. 2002. (African American Ser.). 28.95 (*0-7862-4864-5*) Thorndike Pr.

Monteilh, Marissa. May December Souls. Jones, Nicole, ed. 2000. 287p. pap. 13.95 (*0-9704141-0-2*) 4D Publishing.

—May December Souls: A Novel. 2002. 288p. pap. 13.95 (*0-06-000732-X*, Avon Bks.) Morrow/Avon.

Montemarano, Nicholas. A Fine Place. 226p. 2002. 21.95 (*1-893956-21-0*); 2003. reprint ed. pap. 14.00 (*1-893956-43-1*) Context Bks.

Montgomery, Selena. Rules of Engagement. 2001. (Arabesque Ser.). 352p. mass mkt. 5.99 (*1-58314-224-X*) BET Bks.

Moody, Bill. The Sound of the Trumpet: An Evan Horne Mystery. 1998. (Evan Horne Mysteries Ser.: Vol. 3). 304p. mass mkt. 5.99 o.s.i (*0-440-22194-3*) Dell Publishing.

—The Sound of the Trumpet: An Evan Horne Mystery. 1997. (Evan Horne Mysteries Ser.). 240p. 21.95 (*0-8027-3291-7*) Walker & Co.

Moore, Christopher & Johnson, Pamela. Santa & Pete: A Novel of Christmas Present & Past. 1998. (Illus.). 176p. 14.95 (*0-684-85495-3*, Simon & Schuster) Simon & Schuster.

Moore, Lisa C., ed. Does Your Mama Know? An Anthology of Black Lesbian Coming Out Stories. 1997. 314p. (Orig.). pap. 19.95 (*0-9656659-0-9*) RedBone Pr.

Moore, Stephanie Perry. A Lova' Like No Otha' l.t. ed. 2003. 300p. 28.95 (*0-7862-5941-8*) Gale Group.

—A Lova' Like No Otha' 2003. 256p. pap. 13.95 (*0-446-67967-4*, Walk Worthy Pr.) Warner Bks., Inc.

Moore, Yanier Blak. Triple Take: A Novel. 2003. (Strivers Row Ser.). 240p. pap. 12.95 (*0-375-76066-0*, Villard Bks.) Random House Adult Trade Publishing Group.

Morris, Monique W. Too Beautiful for Words. 288p. 2002. pap. 11.95 (*0-06-093594-4*); 2001. 24.00 (*0-06-621105-0*) HarperTrade. (Amistad Pr.).

Morris, Robert. The Faithful Slave. 1977. (Black Heritage Library Collection). (Illus.). reprint ed. 17.95 (*0-8369-9039-0*) Ayer Co. Pubs., Inc.

Morrison, Mary B. Somebody's Gotta Be on Top. 2004. 24.00 (*0-7582-0724-7*) Kensington Publishing Corp.

Morrison, Toni. Beloved. 2002. (SPA., Illus.). 445p. pap. 12.50 (*84-406-5695-5*, EB9055) B Ediciones S.A. ESP. *Dist:* Lectorum Pubns., Inc.

—Beloved. unabr. ed. 2000. audio 39.95 Blackstone Audio Bks., Inc.

—Beloved. Bloom, Harold, ed. 1999. (Modern Critical Interpretations Ser.). 223p. 34.95 (*0-7910-5132-3*) Chelsea Hse. Pubs.

—Beloved. 1996. (*0-452-26897-4*, Plume); 1988. pap. 9.95 o.p. (*0-452-25230-X*, Plume); 1988. (Illus.). 288p. pap. 12.95 (*0-452-26446-4*); 1998. 512p. reprint ed. pap. 12.95 (*0-452-28062-1*) Dutton/Plume.

—Beloved. l.t. ed. 1998. pap. 16.95 o.p. (*0-7838-0262-5*); 1991. lib. bdg. 10.95 o.p. (*0-89621-207-6*) Gale Group. (Macmillan Reference USA).

—Beloved. 2004. 288p. pap. 13.00 (*1-4000-3341-1*, Vintage) Knopf Publishing Group.

—Beloved. 1987. 275p. 27.50 (*0-394-53597-9*); 1998. 16.95 o.s.i (*0-375-40562-3*); 1998. 322p. 16.95 (*0-375-40273-X*) Knopf, Alfred A. Inc.

—Beloved. 1997. (C). pap. text (*0-8013-3148-X*) Longman Publishing Group.

—Beloved. 1991. 352p. mass mkt. 5.95 o.p. (*0-451-16139-4*); 1991. mass mkt. 5.99 (*0-451-15659-5*); 1988. pap. 8.95 o.p. (*0-452-26136-8*) NAL.

—Beloved. 2000. (Penguin Great Books of the 20th Century Ser.). (Illus.). 272p. pap. 14.95 (*0-14-028340-4*) Penguin Group (USA) Inc.

—Beloved. abr. ed. 1998. audio 18.00 o.s.i (*0-375-40432-5*, 395999); audio 39.95 (*0-375-40487-2*, 104512) Random Hse. Audio Publishing Group. (RH Audio).

—Beloved. l.t. ed. 1998. 379p. pap. 19.95 (*0-375-70414-0*) Random Hse. Large Print.

—Beloved. 1989. 4.99 o.p. (*0-517-01209-X*); 4.99 o.p. (*0-517-01744-X*) Random Hse. Value Publishing.

—Beloved. 1987. 19.00 (*0-606-04046-3*) Turtleback Bks.

—Beloved. abr. ed. 1999. audio 16.85 (*1-85686-751-X*) Ulverscroft Audio (U.S.A.).

—The Bluest Eye. Bloom, Harold, ed. 1999. (Bloom's Notes Ser.). viii, 270p. 34.95 (*0-7910-5191-9*) Chelsea Hse. Pubs.

—The Bluest Eye. 224p. 2000. pap. 12.95 (*0-452-28219-5*, Plume); 1994. pap. 12.95 (*0-452-27305-6*) Dutton/Plume.
—The Bluest Eye. 1993. 224p. 24.00 o.s.i (*0-679-43373-2*) Knopf, Alfred A. Inc.
—The Bluest Eye. 1994. mass mkt. 5.99 o.s.i (*0-451-18367-3*) NAL.
—The Bluest Eye. abr. ed. 2000. audio 18.00 (*0-375-41652-8*); 2000. audio compact disk 22.95 (*0-375-41653-6*); Set. 1994. audio 17.00 o.s.i (*0-679-43474-7*, 390426) Random Hse. Audio Publishing Group. (RH Audio).
—The Bluest Eye. 1993. (Oprah's Book Club Ser.). 224p. 15.00 (*0-375-41155-0*) Random Hse., Inc.
—The Bluest Eye. 2001. audio compact disk 58.00 (*0-7887-5158-1*, C1321E7); 1970. audio 53.00 (*0-7887-4354-6*, 96306K8) Recorded Bks., LLC. (Griot Audio).
—The Bluest Eye. 1991. mass mkt. 5.50 (*0-671-74292-2*, Pocket); 1984. 160p. pap. 3.95 (*0-671-53146-8*, Washington Square Pr.) Simon & Schuster.
—The Bluest Eye. l.t. ed. 1999. (Core Ser.). 253p. 29.95 (*0-7838-8815-5*) Thorndike Pr.
—The Bluest Eye. 1994. 215p. 19.00 (*0-606-06940-2*) Turtleback Bks.
—Jazz. 1993. (Contemporary Fiction Ser.). 240p. pap. 12.95 (*0-452-26965-2*, Plume) Dutton/Plume.
—Jazz. l.t. ed. 1993. (General Ser.). 312p. lib. bdg. 22.95 (*0-8161-5624-7*, Macmillan Reference USA) Gale Group.
—Jazz. 2004. 240p. pap. 13.00 (*1-4000-7621-8*, Vintage) Knopf Publishing Group.
—Jazz. 1992. o.s.i (*0-394-22282-2*) Knopf, Alfred A. Inc.
—Jazz. 1992. 240p. 26.95 (*0-679-41167-4*) McKay, David Co., Inc.
—Jazz. 1993. pap. 5.99 (*0-451-17780-0*, Signet Bks.) NAL.
—Jazz. 1993. 19.04 (*0-606-19196-8*) Turtleback Bks.
—Love. 2003. 208p. 25.00 (*0-375-40944-0*) Knopf, Alfred A. Inc.
—Love. l.t. ed. 2003. 320p. 25.95 (*0-375-43233-7*) Random Hse. Large Print.
—Paradise. 1999. 340p. pap. 13.95 (*0-452-28039-7*, Plume) Dutton/Plume.
—Paradise. l.t. ed. 1998. 26.95 o.p. (*0-7838-8336-6*, Macmillan Reference USA) Gale Group.
—Paradise. 1997. 320p. 25.00 (*0-679-43374-0*) Knopf, Alfred A. Inc.
—Paradise. enl. l.t. ed. 1997. 453p. pap. 25.00 (*0-375-70217-2*) Random Hse. Large Print.
—Paradise. 1999. 20.00 (*0-606-15852-9*) Turtleback Bks.
—Song of Solomon. l.t. ed. 1994. 24.95 o.p. (*0-7927-1936-0*); pap. 22.95 o.p. (*0-7927-1935-2*) BBC Audiobooks America.
—Song of Solomon. 1995. reprint ed. lib. bdg. 24.95 (*1-56849-632-X*) Buccaneer Bks., Inc.
—Song of Solomon. 1987. pap. 8.95 o.p. (*0-452-25244-X*, Plume); 352p. pap. 14.00 (*0-452-26011-6*) Dutton/Plume.
—Song of Solomon. 2004. 352p. pap. 14.00 (*1-4000-3342-X*, Vintage) Knopf Publishing Group.
—Song of Solomon. 1995. (Everyman's Library). 362p. 20.00 (*0-679-44504-8*) Knopf, Alfred A. Inc.
—Song of Solomon. 1993. pap. 5.99 o.s.i (*0-451-18237-5*, Signet Bks.); 1978. mass mkt. 4.50 o.p. (*0-451-15261-1*); 1978. 352p. mass mkt. 5.99 o.p. (*0-451-15828-8*, Signet Bks.); 1978. 352p. mass mkt. 3.95 o.p. (*0-451-12933-4*, AE2933, Signet Bks.); 1978. mass mkt. 2.50 o.p. (*0-451-08340-7*, Signet Bks.); 1978. mass mkt. 2.95 o.p. (*0-451-11446-9*, Signet Bks.); 1978. mass mkt. 2.75 o.p. (*0-451-09443-3*, Signet Bks.); 1978. mass mkt. 3.50 o.p. (*0-451-12315-8*, Signet Bks.) NAL.
—Song of Solomon. 1977. 352p. 27.50 (*0-394-49784-8*) Random Hse. Value Publishing.
—Song of Solomon. (SparkNotes Literature Study Guides). 64-96p. pap., stu. ed. 4.95 (*1-58663-826-2*) Spark Publishing Group.
—Song of Solomon. 1987. (Plume Contemporary Fiction Ser.). 19.00 (*0-606-05092-2*) Turtleback Bks.
—Song of Solomon: Modern Critical Interpretations. Bloom, Harold, ed. 1999. (Bloom's Notes Ser.). 176p. 34.95 (*0-7910-5193-5*) Chelsea Hse. Pubs.
—Song of Solomon/Beloved/Jazz, 3, Set. 1998. 37.85 o.s.i (*0-452-15562-2*) Dutton/Plume.
—Sula. Bloom, Harold, ed. 1999. (Modern Critical Interpretations Ser.). 176p. 34.95 (*0-7910-5194-3*) Chelsea Hse. Pubs.
—Sula. 1987. pap. 7.95 o.p. (*0-452-25227-X*, Plume); 1987. 192p. pap. 13.00 (*0-452-26349-2*); 1987. 176p. pap. 6.95 o.p. (*0-452-26010-8*, Z5476, Plume); 1982. pap. 5.95 o.p. (*0-452-25333-0*, Plume); 1982. pap. 5.95 o.p. (*0-452-25476-0*, Plume) Dutton/Plume.
—Sula. 2004. 192p. pap. 13.00 (*1-4000-3343-8*, Vintage) Knopf Publishing Group.
—Sula. 192p. 2002. 15.00 (*0-375-41535-1*); 1973. 26.00 (*0-394-48044-9*) Knopf, Alfred A. Inc.
—Sula. 2002. 192p. pap. 13.00 (*0-452-28386-8*); 1993. mass mkt. 5.99 o.s.i (*0-451-18240-5*, Signet Bks.) NAL.
—Sula. l.t. ed. 2002. (Basic Ser.). 214p. 30.95 (*0-7862-4653-7*) Thorndike Pr.
—Tar Baby. 1987. pap. 8.95 o.p. (*0-452-25258-X*); 1987. 320p. pap. 12.95 (*0-452-26479-0*); 1987. 352p. pap. 7.95 o.p. (*0-452-26012-4*, Z5326); 1982. pap. 6.95 o.p. (*0-452-25326-8*) Dutton/Plume. (Plume).
—Tar Baby. 2004. 320p. pap. 13.00 (*1-4000-3344-6*, Vintage) Knopf Publishing Group.
—Tar Baby. 1981. 320p. 26.95 (*0-394-42329-1*) Knopf, Alfred A. Inc.
—Tar Baby. 1993. pap. 5.99 o.s.i (*0-451-18238-3*); 1983. 320p. mass mkt. 4.50 o.p. (*0-451-15260-3*); 1983. 272p. mass mkt. 5.99 o.p. (*0-451-16639-6*); 1983. mass mkt. 3.95 o.p. (*0-451-12224-0*) NAL. (Signet Bks.).
—Tar Baby. 1983. 19.00 (*0-606-01962-6*) Turtleback Bks.
—Toni Morrison: Paradise/Beloved/Song of Solomon, 3 vols. 1999. 39.85 (*0-452-15640-8*, Plume) Dutton/Plume.
Mosley, Walter. Always Outnumbered, Always Outgunned. abr. ed. 1997. (Easy Rawlins Mystery Ser.). 25.00 o.p. (*0-7871-1646-7*, 695538) NewStar Media, Inc.
—Always Outnumbered, Always Outgunned. 1997. 224p. 23.00 (*0-393-04539-0*) Norton, W. W. & Co., Inc.
—Always Outnumbered, Always Outgunned. 1998. 208p. pap. 14.00 (*0-671-01499-4*, Washington Square Pr.) Simon & Schuster.
—Always Outnumbered, Always Outgunned. l.t. ed. 1998. (Basic Ser.). 360p. 30.95 (*0-7862-1268-3*) Thorndike Pr.
—Bad Boy Brawly Brown: An Easy Rawlins Mystery. 2002. 320p. 24.95 (*0-316-07301-6*) Little Brown & Co.
—Bad Boy Brawly Brown: An Easy Rawlins Mystery. (Illus.). mass mkt. 0.00 (*0-671-88430-1*); 1900. pap. (*0-671-03839-7*) Simon & Schuster. (Pocket).
—Black Betty. abr. ed. 1994. (Easy Rawlins Mystery Ser.: No. 4). 3p. audio 16.95 (*1-55927-290-2*, 390399) Audio Renaissance.
—Black Betty. unabr. ed. 1994. (Easy Rawlins Mystery Ser.). audio 56.00 (*0-7366-2853-3*, 3561) Books on Tape, Inc.
—Black Betty. 1994. (Easy Rawlins Mystery Ser.). 255p. 19.95 (*0-393-03644-8*) Norton, W. W. & Co., Inc.
—Black Betty. 368p. 1997. pap. 14.00 (*0-671-01983-X*, Pocket); 1995. (Illus.). mass mkt. 6.99 (*0-671-88427-1*, Pocket); 2002. reprint ed. pap. 14.00 (*0-7434-5178-3*, Washington Square Pr.) Simon & Schuster.
—Black Betty: Library Edition, Set. unabr. ed. 1994. audio 59.95 o.p. (*1-55927-302-X*) Audio Renaissance.
—Devil in a Blue Dress. abr. ed. 1993. (Easy Rawlins Mystery Ser.). audio 16.95 (*1-55927-238-4*, 390653) Audio Renaissance.
—Devil in a Blue Dress. unabr. ed. 1994. (Easy Rawlins Mystery Ser.). audio 36.00 (*0-7366-2810-X*, 3524) Books on Tape, Inc.
—Devil in a Blue Dress. 1990. (Easy Rawlins Mystery Ser.). 219p. 19.95 (*0-393-02854-2*) Norton, W. W. & Co., Inc.
—Devil in a Blue Dress. (Easy Rawlins Mystery Ser.). 1997. 240p. pap. 14.00 (*0-671-01982-1*); 2002. 272p. reprint ed. pap. 14.00 (*0-7434-5179-1*) Simon & Schuster. (Washington Square Pr.).
—Devil in a Blue Dress. Ryan, Kevin, ed. 1995. (Easy Rawlins Mystery Ser.). 240p. reprint ed. mass mkt. 6.99 (*0-671-51142-4*, Pocket) Simon & Schuster.
—Devil in a Blue Dress. Chelius, Jane, ed. 1991. 224p. reprint ed. mass mkt. 5.99 (*0-671-74050-4*, Pocket) Simon & Schuster.
—Devil in a Blue Dress: Library Edition, Set. unabr. ed. 1994. audio 39.95 o.p. (*1-55927-269-4*) Audio Renaissance.
—Fearless Jones. l.t. ed. 2001. (Hardcover Ser.). 322p. 31.95 (*1-58724-050-5*, Wheeler Publishing, Inc.) Gale Group.
—Fearless Jones. Pietsch, Michael, ed. 2001. 320p. 24.95 o.p. (*0-316-59238-2*) Little Brown & Co.
—Gone Fishin' 1997. 208p. 22.00 o.p. (*1-57478-025-5*) Black Classic Pr.
—Gone Fishin', Set. abr. ed. 1997. (Easy Rawlins Mystery Ser.). 17.95 o.p. (*0-7871-1402-2*, 394867) NewStar Media, Inc.
—Gone Fishin' (Easy Rawlins Mystery Ser.). 1998. 272p. mass mkt. 6.50 (*0-671-01011-5*, Pocket); 1999. 256p. reprint ed. pap. 14.00 (*0-671-02746-8*, Washington Square Pr.) Simon & Schuster.
—Gone Fishin' l.t. ed. 1997. (Americana Ser.). 203p. 29.95 (*0-7862-1060-5*) Thorndike Pr.
—A Little Yellow Dog. unabr. ed. 1997. (Easy Rawlins Mystery Ser.). audio 48.00 (*0-7366-3732-X*, 4410) Books on Tape, Inc.
—A Little Yellow Dog. (Easy Rawlins Mystery Ser.). 1997. 336p. pap. 14.00 (*0-671-01986-4*, Washington Square Pr.); 1997. 336p. mass mkt. 6.50 (*0-671-88429-8*, Pocket); 2002. 384p. reprint ed. pap. 14.00 (*0-7434-5180-5*, Washington Square Pr.) Simon & Schuster.
—A Little Yellow Dog: An Easy Rawlins Mystery. abr. ed. 1996. (Easy Rawlins Mystery Ser.). audio 16.95 (*1-55927-374-7*, 394056) Audio Renaissance.
—A Little Yellow Dog: An Easy Rawlins Mystery. (Easy Rawlins Mystery Ser.). 1996. 300p. 23.00 (*0-393-03924-2*); 100.00 (*0-393-03978-1*) Norton, W. W. & Co., Inc.
—A Little Yellow Dog: An Easy Rawlins Mystery. l.t. ed. 1996. (Basic Ser.). 447p. 28.95 (*0-7862-0810-4*) Thorndike Pr.
—A Red Death. abr. ed. (Easy Rawlins Mystery Ser.). 1993. audio 16.95 (*1-55927-234-1*, 391455); Set. 1994. audio 59.95 o.p. (*1-55927-270-8*) Audio Renaissance.
—A Red Death. unabr. ed. 1994. audio 48.00 (*0-7366-2833-9*, 3541) Books on Tape, Inc.
—A Red Death. 1991. (Easy Rawlins Mystery Ser.). 284p. 19.95 (*0-393-02998-0*) Norton, W. W. & Co., Inc.
—A Red Death. 1997. (Easy Rawlins Mystery Ser.). 272p. pap. 14.00 (*0-671-01984-8*, Washington Square Pr.); pap. 3.99 (*0-671-01006-9*, Pocket) Simon & Schuster.
—A Red Death. Chelius, Jane, ed. 1992. (Easy Rawlins Mystery Ser.). 256p. reprint ed. mass mkt. 6.99 (*0-671-74989-7*, Pocket) Simon & Schuster.
—Walkin' the Dog. l.t. ed. 2000. (Core Ser.). 301p. 31.95 (*0-7838-8961-5*, Macmillan Reference USA) Gale Group.
—Walkin' the Dog. 2000. 288p. pap. 13.95 (*0-316-88171-6*, Back Bay); 2000. 14.95 (*0-316-57054-0*); 1999. 272p. 24.95 o.p. (*0-316-96620-7*) Little Brown & Co.
—Walkin' the Dog. l.t. ed. 2001. (G. K. Hall Paperback Ser.). 301p. pap. 29.95 (*0-7838-8962-3*) Thorndike Pr.
—White Butterfly. abr. ed. 1993. (Easy Rawlins Mystery Ser.). audio 16.95 (*1-55927-224-4*, 391901) Audio Renaissance.
—White Butterfly. unabr. ed. 1994. (Easy Rawlins Mystery Ser.). audio 48.00 (*0-7366-2798-7*, 3513) Books on Tape, Inc.
—White Butterfly. 1992. (Easy Rawlins Mystery Ser.). 256p. 19.95 (*0-393-03366-X*) Norton, W. W. & Co., Inc.
—White Butterfly. (Easy Rawlins Mystery Ser.). 2002. 320p. pap. 14.00 (*0-7434-5177-5*); 1997. pap. 14.00 (*0-671-01985-6*) Simon & Schuster. (Washington Square Pr.).
—White Butterfly. Chelius, Jane, ed. 1993. (Easy Rawlins Mystery Ser.). 304p. reprint ed. mass mkt. 6.50 (*0-671-86787-3*, Pocket) Simon & Schuster.
—White Butterfly: Library Edition. unabr. ed. 1994. (Easy Rawlins Mystery Ser.). audio 59.95 o.p. (*1-55927-271-6*) Audio Renaissance.
Mowry, Jess. Rats in the Trees. 1993. 176p. pap. 9.00 o.p. (*0-14-017873-2*, Penguin Bks.) Penguin Group (USA) Inc.
Murphy, Edward F. The Tenth Man. 1977. (Black Heritage Library Collection). reprint ed. 29.95 (*0-8369-9114-1*) Ayer Co. Pubs., Inc.
Murray, Albert. The Spyglass Tree. 1992. pap. 15.00 (*0-679-73085-0*, Vintage); 1991. 207p. 21.00 o.s.i (*0-394-58887-8*, Pantheon) Knopf Publishing Group.
Murray, J. J. Renee & Jay. 2002. 288p. mass mkt. 6.99 (*1-57566-864-5*); 2001. 34p. 23.00 o.s.i (*1-57566-862-9*) Kensington Publishing Corp.
Murray, Victoria Christopher. Joy. l.t. ed. 2002. (African American Ser.). 643p. 29.95 (*0-7862-3864-X*) Thorndike Pr.
—Joy. 2002. 400p. pap. 13.95 (*0-446-67944-5*); 2001. 384p. 23.95 o.p. (*0-446-52875-7*) Warner Bks., Inc. (Walk Worthy Pr.).
—Temptation. 2003. (African American Ser.). 28.95 (*0-7862-5072-0*) Thorndike Pr.
—Temptation. 2001. 400p. pap. 13.95 (*0-446-67783-3*); 2000. 368p. 19.95 o.p. (*0-446-52792-0*); 2000. 368p. E-Book 14.95 (*0-446-91364-2*); 2000. E-Book 14.95 (*0-446-93136-5*); 2000. 368p. E-Book 14.95 (*0-446-92263-3*); 2000. 368p. E-Book 14.95 (*0-446-92372-9*); 2000. E-Book 14.95 (*0-446-92864-X*); 2000. 368p. E-Book 14.95 (*0-446-96092-6*) Warner Bks., Inc.
Napoleon, Landon J. ZigZag. 1999. 273p. 24.00 o.s.i (*0-8050-6048-0*) Holt, Henry & Co.
Naylor, Gloria. Mama Day. l.t. ed. 1989. 496p. 19.95 o.p. (*0-8161-4692-6*, Macmillan Reference USA) Gale Group.
—Mama Day. 1988. 320p. 17.95 (*0-89919-716-7*) Houghton Mifflin Co.
—Mama Day. 1989. (Vintage Contemporaries Ser.). 336p. pap. 13.95 (*0-679-72181-9*, Vintage) Knopf Publishing Group.
—The Men of Brewster Place. 1999. 192p. pap. 11.95 (*0-7868-8405-3*) Disney Pr.
—The Men of Brewster Place. l.t. ed. 1999. 26.95 (*1-56895-712-2*, Wheeler Publishing, Inc.) Gale Group.
—The Men of Brewster Place. 1998. 173p. 22.95 (*0-7868-6421-4*) Hyperion Pr.
—Short Story, Vol. 2. 1997. (Short Story Ser.: Vol. 2). 592p. pap. 14.95 (*0-316-59923-9*) Little Brown & Co.
Naylor, Gloria, ed. Children of the Night: The Best Short Stories by Black Writers, 1967 to the Present. 1996. 592p. 24.95 o.p. (*0-316-59926-3*) Little Brown & Co.
Nearing, Scott. Free Born: An Unpublishable Novel. 1977. (Black Heritage Library Collection). reprint ed. 25.95 (*0-8369-9115-X*) Ayer Co. Pubs., Inc.
Neely, Barbara. Blanche among the Talented Tenth. 1995. 240p. pap. 5.99 (*0-14-025036-0*, Penguin Bks.) Penguin Group (USA) Inc.
—Blanche among the Talented Tenth. 1994. 240p. 19.95 o.p. (*0-312-11248-3*, Saint Martin's Minotaur) St. Martin's Pr.
—Blanche Cleans Up. 1999. 352p. mass mkt. 6.99 (*0-14-027747-1*) Penguin Group (USA) Inc.
—Blanche Cleans Up. 1998. 288p. 19.95 o.p. (*0-670-87626-7*) Viking Penguin.
—Blanche on the Lam. 1993. (Crime Ser.). 224p. pap. 5.99 (*0-14-017439-7*, Penguin Bks.) Penguin Group (USA) Inc.
—Blanche on the Lam. 1991. 192p. 16.95 o.p. (*0-312-06908-1*, Saint Martin's Minotaur) St. Martin's Pr.
—Blanche Passes Go. 2001. 288p. 5.99 (*0-14-100197-6*); 2000. 272p. 22.95 o.s.i (*0-670-89165-7*, Viking) Viking Penguin.
Neihart, Ben. Rough Amusements: The True Story of A'Lelia Walker, Patroness of the Harlem Renaissance's Down-Low Culture: An Urban Historical. 2003. 160p. 21.95 (*1-58234-285-7*) Bloomsbury Publishing.
Nelscott, Kris. A Dangerous Road. 2001. 336p. mass mkt. 6.50 (*0-312-97643-7*, St. Martin's Paperbacks); 2000. 325p. 24.95 (*0-312-26264-7*, Saint Martin's Minotaur) St. Martin's Pr.
—Smoke-Filled Rooms: Smokey Dalton Novel. 2001. 320p. 24.95 (*0-312-26265-5*, Saint Martin's Minotaur) St. Martin's Pr.
—Stone Cribs. E-Book 18.95 (*0-312-71111-5*); 2004. 320p. 24.95 (*0-312-28784-4*, Saint Martin's Minotaur) St. Martin's Pr.
—Thin Walls: A Smokey Dalton Novel. 2004. 400p. pap. 13.95 (*0-312-32044-2*, Saint Martin's Griffin) St. Martin's Pr.
Nelson, Jill. Sexual Healing. 2003. 318p. 23.95 (*0-9724562-0-1*) Agate Publishing, Incorporated.
Newberry, Sandra. September's Autumn. 2001. pap. 12.00 (*0-8059-5023-0*) Dorrance Publishing Co., Inc.
Newton, Gaye. Past Presence. 2000. 288p. pap. 14.95 (*0-9700849-0-0*) Galibren Written Treasures, LLC.
Nicholls, Josephine H. Bayou Triste: A Story of Louisiana. 1977. (Black Heritage Library Collection). reprint ed. 26.95 (*0-8369-9040-4*) Ayer Co. Pubs., Inc.
Nova, Curie. The Sight of the Lord. 2000. 224p. pap. 14.95 (*0-88739-273-3*) Creative Arts Bk. Co.
Nunez, Elizabeth. Beyond the Limbo Silence. 1998. 320p. 24.00 o.p. (*1-58005-017-4*); pap. 12.00 (*1-58005-013-1*) Avalon Publishing Group. (Seal Pr.).
—Beyond the Limbo Silence. 2003. 336p. pap. 13.95 (*0-345-45108-2*, One World/Ballantine) Ballantine Bks.
Oates, Joyce Carol. I Lock My Door upon Myself. 1991. 112p. pap. 9.95 o.p. (*0-452-26708-0*, Plume) Dutton/Plume.
—I Lock My Door upon Myself. 1990. (Fiction on Art Ser.). 108p. pap. 15.95 o.s.i (*0-88001-260-9*, Ecco) HarperTrade.
Okpewho, Isidore. Call Me by My Rightful Name. 2004. (*1-59221-191-7*); pap. (*1-59221-190-9*) Africa World Pr.
Olsen, Austin. Apache Ambush. 2000. 384p. mass mkt. 5.99 (*0-7860-1148-3*, Pinnacle Bks.) Kensington Publishing Corp.
Olsen, Theodore V. Track the Man Down. l.t. ed. 1993. (Nightingale Ser.). pap. 15.95 o.p. (*0-8161-5722-7*, Macmillan Reference USA) Gale Group.
Olshan, Joseph. In Clara's Hands. 2003. 305p. 26.00 (*0-7475-5497-8*); 2002. 320p. pap. 12.00 (*0-7475-5704-7*) Bloomsbury Publishing, Ltd. GBR. *Dist:* Trafalgar Square.
O'Nan, Stewart. Everyday People. 2001. 295p. 24.00 o.p. (*0-8021-1681-7*) Grove/Atlantic, Inc.
Oseye, Ebele. Let the Lion Eat Straw. 2004. 192p. 19.95 (*0-06-072420-X*, Amistad Pr.) HarperTrade.
Our World: or The Slave-Holder's Daughter. 1977. (Black Heritage Library Collection). 33.95 (*0-8369-8771-3*) Ayer Co. Pubs., Inc.
Ovington, Mary W. Hazel. 1977. (Black Heritage Library Collection). (Illus.). reprint ed. 23.95 (*0-8369-9117-6*) Ayer Co. Pubs., Inc.
—The Shadow. 1977. (Black Heritage Library Collection). reprint ed. 31.95 (*0-8369-9118-4*) Ayer Co. Pubs., Inc.

Owens, Michael E. A Key Lost in Time: The Return of the Past. 1998. 233p. pap. 13.95 (*0-9665404-0-9*) SAL Productions.

Packer, George. Central Square. 1998. 304p. 24.95 (*1-55597-277-2*) Graywolf Pr.

Packer, Z. Z. Drinking Coffee Elsewhere. 2004. 304p. pap. 14.00 (*1-57322-378-6*, Riverhead Trade (Paperbacks)) Berkley Publishing Group.

—Drinking Coffee Elsewhere: Stories. abr. ed. 2003. audio compact disk 32.95 (*1-56511-759-X*); audio 32.95 (*1-56511-758-1*) HighBridge Co.

—Drinking Coffee Elsewhere: Stories. 2003. 224p. 24.95 (*1-57322-234-8*, Riverhead Bks. (Hardcovers)) Putnam Publishing Group, The.

Pagan, Margaret D. More Than a Slave: The Life of Katherine Ferguson. 2003. 202p. 7.99 (*0-8024-3481-9*) Moody Pr.

Page, Thomas Nelson. The Land of the Spirit. E-Book 3.95 (*0-594-05630-6*) 1873 Pr.

—The Land of the Spirit. 1999. (Notable American Authors Ser.). reprint ed. lib. bdg. 125.00 (*0-7812-4713-6*) Reprint Services Corp.

Palfrey, Evelyn. Dangerous Dilemmas. 2001. 272p. pap. 12.95 (*0-671-04222-X*, Atria) Simon & Schuster.

Parker, Gwendolyn M. These Same Long Bones. 1995. 272p. pap. 10.95 o.p. (*0-452-27428-1*, Plume) Dutton/Plume.

—These Same Long Bones. 1994. 260p. 21.95 o.s.i (*0-395-67172-8*) Houghton Mifflin Co.

Parks, Suzan-Lori. Getting Mother's Body: A Novel. 2004. 288p. pap. 12.95 (*0-8129-6800-X*, Random Hse. Trade Paperbacks) Random House Adult Trade Publishing Group.

—Getting Mother's Body: A Novel. 2003. 272p. 23.95 (*1-4000-6022-2*) Random Hse., Inc.

Parrish, P. J. Dark of the Moon. 2000. 432p. mass mkt. 6.99 (*0-7860-1054-1*, Pinnacle Bks.); 1999. (Illus.). 384p. 23.00 o.s.i (*1-57566-394-5*) Kensington Publishing Corp.

Pate, Alexs D. Losing Absalom. 1995. 320p. mass mkt. 7.50 o.s.i (*0-425-15013-5*) Berkley Publishing Group.

—Losing Absalom. 1994. 220p. 5.00 (*1-56689-017-9*) Coffee Hse. Pr.

—The Multicultiboho Sideshow, Vol. 1. 1999. 241p. 23.00 (*0-380-97678-1*, Avon Bks.) Morrow/Avon.

Peacock, Nancy. Home Across the Road. 2001. 256p. pap. 12.95 (*0-553-38102-4*) Bantam Bks.

—Home Across the Road. 1999. 249p. 18.95 (*1-56352-509-7*) Longstreet Pr., Inc.

Pearson, Emily C. Cousin Franck's Household: Or Scenes in the Old Dominion, by Pochanontas. 1977. (Black Heritage Library Collection). reprint ed. 28.95 (*0-8369-9041-2*) Ayer Co. Pubs., Inc.

—The Poor White: or The Rebel Conscript. 1977. (Illus.). 326p. reprint ed. 28.95 (*0-8369-9042-0*) Ayer Co. Pubs., Inc.

Peck, Dale. Now It's Time to Say Goodbye: A Novel. 1998. 480p. 25.00 o.p. (*0-374-22271-1*) Farrar, Straus & Giroux.

—Now It's Time to Say Goodbye: A Novel. 1999. 464p. pap. 15.95 (*0-688-16841-8*, Quill) HarperTrade.

—Now It's Time to Say Goodbye Readers Guide. stu. ed. (*0-374-96122-0*) Farrar, Straus & Giroux.

Pelecanos, George P. Hard Revolution. 2004. 384p. 24.95 (*0-316-60897-1*) Little Brown & Co.

—Hard Revolution. abr. ed. 2004. audio 25.98 (*1-58621-600-7*); audio compact disk 31.98 (*1-58621-601-5*) Time Warner AudioBooks.

—Right As Rain. 2001. 336p. 24.95 (*0-316-69526-2*) Little Brown & Co.

—Right As Rain. l.t. ed. 2003. 525p. 30.45 (*0-7862-5609-5*) Thorndike Pr.

—Right As Rain. 2002. 384p. reprint ed. mass mkt. 6.99 (*0-446-61079-8*) Warner Bks., Inc.

Peltier-Draine, Elsaida. What's up Girlfriend? 1994. (Illus.). 170p. 19.00 (*0-9643320-1-9*); 163p. pap. 13.00 (*0-9643320-0-0*); 245p. 19.00 (*0-9643320-2-7*) Zenon Pubn. Co.

Pemberton, Caroline H. Stephen the Black. 1977. (Black Heritage Library Collection). reprint ed. 28.95 (*0-8369-9044-7*) Ayer Co. Pubs., Inc.

Penley, Gary. Jubal. 2003. 272p. 23.00 (*1-58980-129-6*) Pelican Publishing Co., Inc.

Perrin, Kayla. Again, My Love. 1999. 286p. mass mkt. 5.99 (*0-345-43255-X*) Ballantine Bks.

—Again, My Love. 1998. (Indigo Love Stories Ser.). 212p. pap. 10.95 (*1-885478-23-2*) Genesis Pr., Inc.

—The Sisters of the Theta Phi Kappa: A Novel. 2002. 352p. pap. 12.95 (*0-312-30521-4*, Saint Martin's Griffin) St. Martin's Pr.

—The Sisters of Theta Phi Kappa. 2001. 352p. 24.95 o.s.i (*0-312-28290-7*) St. Martin's Pr.

Perry, Irene Egerton. Light in the Basement, Bks. 1-3. aut. ltd. num. ed. 2001. 762p. per. 24.95 (*0-9652655-0-1*) C.E. Publishing Group.

Perry, Margaret, ed. The Short Fiction of Rudolph Fisher, 107. 1987. (Contributions in Afro-American & African Studies Ser.: No. 107). 242p. 67.95 (*0-313-21348-8*, FPF, Greenwood Pr.) Greenwood Publishing Group, Inc.

Perry, Phyllis A. Stigmata. 1998. 224p. 21.95 (*0-7868-6408-7*) Hyperion Pr.

Perry, Richard. Montgomery's Children. 1985. pap. 7.95 o.p. (*0-452-25674-7*, Plume) Dutton/Plume.

—Montgomery's Children. 1984. 288p. 12.95 o.p. (*0-15-162124-1*) Harcourt Trade Pubs.

—No Other Tale to Tell: A Novel. 1994. 313p. 25.00 o.p. (*0-688-11595-0*, Morrow, William & Co.) Morrow/Avon.

Pete, Eric E. Real for Me. 2000. 214p. pap. 14.95 (*0-9704995-2-3*) E-fect Publishing.

—Someone's in the Kitchen. 2002. 243p. pap. 15.00 (*0-9704995-1-5*) E-fect Publishing.

Peterkin, Julia. Black April. 24.95 (*0-89190-527-8*) Amereon, Ltd.

—Black April. 1998. 328p. reprint ed. pap. 15.95 (*0-8203-1953-8*) Univ. of Georgia Pr.

—Green Thursday. 1998. 200p. reprint ed. pap. 15.95 (*0-8203-1955-4*) Univ. of Georgia Pr.

Peterson, Brian. Move over, Girl. 1998. 316p. pap. 12.00 (*0-9664587-0-2*) Chance22 Publishing.

Petry, Ann. Miss Muriel & Other Stories. 1989. (Black Women Writers Ser.). 305p. pap. 12.95 o.p. (*0-8070-8311-9*) Beacon Pr.

—Miss Muriel & Other Stories. 1999. 304p. pap. 13.00 o.s.i (*0-618-00709-1*) Houghton Mifflin Co.

Pharr, Robert Deane. The Book of Numbers. 2001. (Virginia Bookshelf). 382p. reprint ed. pap. 18.95 (*0-8139-2046-9*) Univ. Pr. of Virginia.

Phillips, Caryl. Crossing the River. 1995. 256p. pap. 13.00 (*0-679-75794-5*, Vintage) Knopf Publishing Group.

Phillips, Debra. The High Price of a Good Man: A Novel. 2003. 288p. pap. 12.95 (*0-312-30525-7*, Saint Martin's Griffin) St. Martin's Pr.

Phillips, Delores. The Darkest Child: A Novel. 2004. 388p. 26.00 (*1-56947-345-5*) Soho Pr., Inc.

Phillips, Gary. High Hand. 2000. 32p. reprint ed. 22.00 o.s.i (*1-57566-616-2*, Dafina) Kensington Publishing Corp.

—High Hand: A Martha Chainey Mystery. 2001. 34p. mass mkt. 5.99 o.s.i (*1-57566-684-7*) Kensington Publishing Corp.

—Only the Wicked. 2000. 342p. 24.95 (*1-885173-64-4*) Write Way Publishing.

—Shooter's Point. 2002. 34p. mass mkt. 5.99 (*1-57566-745-2*); 2001. 24p. 22.00 (*1-57566-682-0*) Kensington Publishing Corp.

Phillips, Patricia A. June in Winter. 2003. 304p. mass mkt. 6.99 (*0-7582-0375-6*) Kensington Publishing Corp.

Pickens, William. The Vengeance of the Gods & Three Other Stories of Real American Color Line Life. reprint ed. 24.50 (*0-404-11376-1*) AMS Pr., Inc.

Pierce, Donna. A Secret of Color. l.t. ed. 1999. E-Book 14.99 incl. cd-rom (*1-929077-19-X*, Books OnScreen) PageFree Publishing, Inc.

Pike, Mary H. Ida May: A Story of Things Actual & Possible, by Mary Langdon. 1977. (Black Heritage Library Collection). reprint ed. 39.95 (*0-8369-9171-0*) Ayer Co. Pubs., Inc.

Pilgrim, Millie W. All Kneel down & Pray. 1998. 186p. pap. 10.95 (*0-9613184-3-0*) H&M Enterprises.

Pinckney, Darryl. High Cotton. 1992. 320p. 21.00 o.s.i (*0-374-16998-5*) Farrar, Straus & Giroux.

Pinson, William W. In White & Black: A Story. 1977. (Black Heritage Library Collection). reprint ed. 32.95 (*0-8369-9047-1*) Ayer Co. Pubs., Inc.

Pitts, Gertrude & Scott, Anne. George Sampson Brite. 1996. (African American Women Writers, 1910-1940 Ser.). xxix, 243p. 25.00 (*0-8161-1634-2*, Macmillan Reference USA) Gale Group.

Poitier-Henderson, Beverly. Nana. 2001. 136p. pap. 10.95 o.p. (*0-595-17730-1*, Writers Club Pr.) iUniverse, Inc.

Polite, Carlene H. The Flagellants. 1988. (Black Women Writers Ser.). 256p. reprint ed. pap. 7.95 o.p. (*0-8070-6321-5*, BP 752) Beacon Pr.

—The Flagellants. Alien, Pierre, tr. 1999. 214p. pap. 18.00 (*0-374-52656-7*) Farrar, Straus & Giroux.

—The Flagellants. 1967. 5.95 o.p. (*0-374-15601-8*) Farrar, Straus & Giroux.

Poole, Daaimah S. Yo Yo Love. 2003. 304p. mass mkt. 6.99 (*0-7582-0239-3*, Kensington Bks.); 2002. 66p. pap. 15.00 (*0-7582-0238-5*); 2002. 34p. 24.00 o.s.i (*0-7582-0237-7*) Kensington Publishing Corp.

—Yo Yo Love. Armstrong, Jenice S., ed. 2000. 240p. pap. 12.95 (*0-9676028-1-5*) Oshun Publishing Co., Inc.

Pope, Patricia. Colored Waiting Room. 2002. 422p. pap. (*1-55369-136-9*) Trafford Publishing.

Porter, Connie Rose. Imani All Mine. 2000. (Illus.). 208p. pap. 12.00 (*0-618-05678-5*); 1999. 212p. tchr. ed. 23.00 o.p. (*0-395-83808-8*) Houghton Mifflin Co.

—Imani All Mine. 2000. 18.05 (*0-606-19008-2*) Turtleback Bks.

Porter, Linn B. A Black Adonis. 1977. (Black Heritage Library Collection). reprint ed. 30.95 (*0-8369-9060-9*) Ayer Co. Pubs., Inc.

Postell, Catherine. On Toplecote Bayou. 1977. (Black Heritage Library Collection). reprint ed. 15.95 (*0-8369-9048-X*) Ayer Co. Pubs., Inc.

Powell, Jacqueline. Anyone Who Has a Heart. 2003. 352p. 23.95 (*0-446-53174-X*) Warner Bks., Inc.

—Someone to Catch My Drift. 2003. 448p. pap. 14.95 (*0-446-69033-3*) Warner Bks., Inc.

Powers, Richard. The Time of Our Singing. 2003. E-Book 15.00 o.p. (*0-374-70465-1*); 2003. 640p. 27.00 (*0-374-27782-6*); 2003. E-Book 15.00 (*0-374-70463-5*); 2002. E-Book (*0-374-70467-8*) Farrar, Straus & Giroux.

Preston, Fayrene. In the Heat of the Night. 1992. (Loveswept Ser.: No. 573). 192p. mass mkt. 2.79 o.s.i (*0-553-44172-8*) Bantam Bks.

Preston, Margaret J. Aunt Dorothy: An Old Virginia Plantation Story. 1977. (Black Heritage Library Collection). (Illus.). reprint ed. 15.95 (*0-8369-9050-1*) Ayer Co. Pubs., Inc.

Price, Charles F. Freedom's Altar. 1999. (Salem Selections Ser.). (Illus.). 291p. 19.95 (*0-89587-177-7*) Blair, John F. Pub.

—Where the Water-Dogs Laughed: Or the Sacred Dream of the Great Bear. 2003. 24.95 (*1-932158-50-2*) High Country Pubs., Ltd.

Price, Hugh B. & Walker, Blair S. Up Jumped the Devil. 1997. 292p. 22.00 o.s.i (*0-380-97420-7*, Avon Bks.) Morrow/Avon.

Price, Richard. Clockers. 2001. 608p. pap. 14.95 (*0-06-093498-0*, Perennial) HarperTrade.

—Freedomland. 1999. 736p. mass mkt. 7.99 (*0-440-22644-9*) Dell Publishing.

Price-Thompson, Tracy. Black Coffee: A Novel. 2002. 336p. pap. 12.95 (*0-375-75777-5*, Villard Bks.) Random House Adult Trade Publishing Group.

Proctor, George W. Walks Without a Soul. 1990. 14.95 o.s.i (*0-385-24470-3*) Doubleday Publishing.

Ptah, Heru. A Hip-Hop Story. 2003. 416p. pap. 13.95 (*0-7434-8323-5*, MTV) Simon & Schuster.

Quinn, Peter. Banished Children of Eve. 1995. 624p. pap. 14.00 (*0-14-023003-3*, Penguin Bks.) Penguin Group (USA) Inc.

—Banished Children of Eve. 1994. 624p. 22.95 o.p. (*0-670-85076-4*, Viking) Viking Penguin.

Quinones Miller, Karen E. Satin Doll. 2002. 320p. pap. 13.00 (*0-7432-1434-X*, Simon & Schuster) Simon & Schuster.

—Satin Doll: A Novel. 2000. 288p. pap. 12.95 (*0-9676028-0-7*) Oshun Publishing Co., Inc.

—Satin Doll: A Novel. 2001. 320p. 21.00 (*0-7432-1433-1*, Simon & Schuster) Simon & Schuster.

Rainey, John C. The Thang That Ate My Grandaddy's Dog. 1997. 368p. 18.95 o.p. (*1-56164-130-8*) Pineapple Pr., Inc.

Randall, Alice. The Wind Done Gone. 2001. (Illus.). 224p. 22.00 (*0-618-10450-X*); 210p. 23.00 (*0-618-13309-7*) Houghton Mifflin Co.

—The Wind Done Gone: A Novel. 2002. (Illus.). 224p. pap. 12.00 (*0-618-21906-4*, Mariner Bks.) Houghton Mifflin Co. Trade & Reference Div.

Rawles, Nancy. Love Like Gumbo. 1997. (Discoveries Ser.: No. 2). 272p. pap. 14.00 (*0-940242-75-3*) Fjord Pr.

Ray, Francis. Heart of the Falcon. 1998. (Arabesque Ser.). mass mkt. 5.99 (*1-58314-182-0*) Kensington Publishing Corp.

—Only Hers. 1996. (Arabesque Ser.). mass mkt. 5.99 (*1-58314-181-2*) Kensington Publishing Corp.

—Somebody's Knockin' at My Door: A Novel. 2003. 368p. pap. 13.95 (*0-312-30734-9*, Saint Martin's Griffin) St. Martin's Pr.

Raymond, Walter M. Rebels of the New South. 1977. (Black Heritage Library Collection). (Illus.). reprint ed. 19.95 (*0-8369-9055-2*) Ayer Co. Pubs., Inc.

Read, Opie & Pixley, Frank. The Carpetbagger: A Novel. 1977. (Black Heritage Library Collection). reprint ed. 27.95 (*0-8369-9056-0*) Ayer Co. Pubs., Inc.

Redding, J. Saunders. A Scholar's Conscience: Selected Writings of J. Saunders Redding. Berry, Faith, ed. 1992. 248p. 39.95 o.p. (*0-8131-1770-4*) Univ. Pr. of Kentucky.

Redmon, Jessie R. F. & Fauset, Jessie Redmon. Comedy, American Style, Vol. 4. 1995. (Comedy, American Style Ser.: Vol. 4). 327p. 25.00 (*0-8161-1628-8*, Macmillan Reference USA) Gale Group.

Reed, Ishmael. Flight to Canada. 1989. 180p. pap. 11.00 (*0-689-70733-9*) Central Bureau voor Schimmelcultures NLD. *Dist:* Lubrecht & Cramer, Ltd.

—Flight to Canada. 1977. pap. 2.75 o.p. (*0-380-01798-9*, 52019, Avon Bks.) Morrow/Avon.

—Flight to Canada. 1998. 192p. pap. 11.00 (*0-684-84750-7*, Scribner) Simon & Schuster.

Reeves, Adrienne Ellis, et al. Truly. 2001. (Arabesque Ser.). 352p. mass mkt. 5.99 (*1-58314-196-0*) BET Bks.

Reid, Maryann. Sex & the Single Sister: Five Novellas. 2001. 240p. 23.95 (*0-312-27498-X*) St. Martin's Pr.

—Use Me or Lose Me: A Novel of Love, Sex, & Drama. 2003. 320p. 23.95 (*0-312-31437-X*) St. Martin's Pr.

Render, Sylvia L., ed. The Short Fiction of Charles W. Chesnutt. 1981. 428p. (C). 15.00 o.p. (*0-88258-012-4*) Howard Univ. Pr.

Revoyr, Nina. The Necessary Hunger. 1997. 368p. 22.50 (*0-684-83234-8*, Simon & Schuster) Simon & Schuster.

—The Necessary Hunger. 1998. 368p. pap. 14.95 (*0-312-18142-6*, Saint Martin's Griffin) St. Martin's Pr.

Reynolds, April. Knee-Deep in Wonder: A Novel. 2003. 320p. 23.00 (*0-8050-7346-9*, Metropolitan Bks.) Holt, Henry & Co.

Rice, Patty. Reinventing the Woman: A Novel. 2001. 368p. 23.00 o.s.i (*0-684-85341-8*, Simon & Schuster) Simon & Schuster.

Richardson, Brenda L. Chesapeake Song. 371p. 1999. pap. 19.95 (*1-56743-040-6*); 1994. pap. 10.95 (*1-56743-063-5*) HarperTrade. (Amistad Pr.).

—Chesapeake Song. 1996. 480p. mass mkt. 5.99 o.s.i (*0-7860-0304-9*, Pinnacle Bks.) Kensington Publishing Corp.

Richardson, Patricia. A Place for Ida. 2003. 197p. pap. 19.95 (*1-59286-480-5*) PublishAmerica, Inc.

Ridley, John. A Conversation with the Mann. 448p. 2003. pap. 14.95 (*0-446-69075-9*); 2002. 24.95 (*0-446-52836-6*) Warner Bks., Inc.

Riehl, Gene. Quantico Rules: A Novel. 2003. 304p. 24.95 (*0-312-31051-X*) St. Martin's Pr.

Riley, Len. Harlem. 1998. (Berkeley Signature Edition Ser.). 304p. mass mkt. 6.99 o.s.i (*0-425-16343-1*) Berkley Publishing Group.

—Harlem. 1997. 384p. 21.95 o.s.i (*0-385-48508-5*) Doubleday Publishing.

Riley, Mildred E. Love Always. 1997. 191p. pap. 10.95 (*1-885478-15-1*) Genesis Pr., Inc.

Rives, Hallie E. Smoking Flax. 1977. (Black Heritage Library Collection). reprint ed. 26.95 (*0-8369-9057-9*) Ayer Co. Pubs., Inc.

Ro, Ronin. Street Sweeper. 2000. (Illus.). 156p. pap. 16.98 incl. audio compact disk (*1-930306-00-8*) Syndicate Media Group, The.

Roberts, Clifford. Run Lee Run. 2001. 192p. pap. 20.99 (*1-4010-2560-9*); text 30.99 (*1-4010-2559-5*) Xlibris Corp.

Robertson, Florence H. Shadow Land: Stories of the South. 1977. (Black Heritage Library Collection). reprint ed. 19.95 (*0-8369-9077-3*) Ayer Co. Pubs., Inc.

Robinson, C. Kelly. Between Brothers: A Novel. 2001. 384p. pap. 13.95 (*0-375-75772-4*); 256p. pap. 13.95 (*0-676-90055-0*) Random House Adult Trade Publishing Group. (Villard Bks.).

—The Perfect Blend. 2004. 288p. pap. 13.95 (*0-451-21036-0*) NAL.

Robinson, Chet Kelly. No More Mr. Nice Guy: A Love Story. 2002. 288p. pap. 13.95 (*0-375-76047-4*, Villard Bks.) Random House Adult Trade Publishing Group.

Robotham, Rosemarie. Zachary's Wings. 288p. mass mkt. 6.99 (*0-7434-8255-7*); 1999. pap. 12.00 (*0-684-85736-7*); 1998. 22.00 (*0-684-84726-4*) Simon & Schuster. (Scribner).

Roby, Kimberla Lawson. Behind Closed Doors. 1997. 244p. reprint ed. pap. 12.00 (*1-57478-005-0*) Black Classic Pr.

—Behind Closed Doors. 1997. x, 250p. pap. 12.00 (*0-9653470-4-4*) Lenox Pr.

—Casting the First Stone. 2000. x, 300p. 22.00 o.s.i (*1-57566-489-5*, Kensington Bks.); 2001. 32p. reprint ed. pap. 14.00 (*1-57566-633-2*) Kensington Publishing Corp.

—Here & Now. 288p. 2000. pap. 13.00 o.s.i (*1-57566-494-1*, Dafina); 1998. 22.00 o.s.i (*1-57566-336-8*) Kensington Publishing Corp.

—It's a Thin Line. 2002. 352p. pap. 15.00 (*1-57566-744-4*); 2001. 288p. 23.00 (*1-57566-629-4*) Kensington Publishing Corp.

—It's a Thin Line. l.t. ed. 2003. (African American Ser.). 28.95 (*0-7862-5235-9*) Thorndike Pr.

—A Taste of Reality. 2004. 320p. pap. 13.95 (*0-06-050567-2*, Avon Bks.) Morrow/Avon.

—A Taste of Reality. l.t. ed. 2004. 473p. 29.95 (*0-7862-6192-7*) Thorndike Pr.

—Too Much of a Good Thing. 2004. 288p. 23.95 (*0-06-056849-6*, Morrow, William & Co.) Morrow/Avon.

Rose, Odessa. Water in a Broken Glass. 2000. pap. 15.00 (*0-9647635-7-5*) La Caille Nous Publishing Co.

Rosen, Roger & Sevastiades, Patra McSharry, eds. Celebration: Visions & Voices of the African Diaspora. 1994. (Icarus World Issues Ser.). (Illus.). pap. 8.95 (*0-8239-1809-2*, IPCELE); lib. bdg. 16.95 (*0-8239-1808-4*, ICCELE) Rosen Publishing Group, Inc., The.

Ross, Fran. Oreo. 1974. 10.95 o.p. (*0-914870-00-9*) Greyfalcon Hse.

—Oreo. 2000. (Library of Black Literature). 212p. pap. 16.95 (*1-55553-464-3*) Northeastern Univ. Pr.

Ross, L. M. The Long Blue Moan. 2002. 300p. pap. 13.95 (*1-55583-621-6*) Alyson Pubns.

Roth, Philip. The Human Stain. tchr. ed. 234.00 o.p. (*0-618-06598-9*); 2000. 368p. tchr. ed. 26.00 (*0-618-05945-8*) Houghton Mifflin Co.

—The Human Stain. 2001. (International Ser.). 384p. pap. 14.95 (*0-375-72634-9*, Vintage) Knopf Publishing Group.

—The Human Stain. l.t. ed. 2000. (Basic Ser.). 614p. 27.95 (*0-7862-2964-0*) Thorndike Pr.

Rush, Caroline E. North & South: Slavery - Its Contrasts. 1977. (Black Heritage Library Collection). 28.95 (*0-8369-8757-8*) Ayer Co. Pubs., Inc.

Rush, Norman. Mortals. 2004. (Illus.). 736p. pap. 15.95 (*0-679-73711-1*, Vintage) Knopf Publishing Group.

—Mortals. 2003. (Illus.). 736p. 26.95 (*0-679-40622-0*) Knopf, Alfred A. Inc.

Russell, Charlie L. The Worthy Ones: A Novel. 2002. (Illus.). 221p. 15.95 (*0-932693-11-3*) Jukebox Pr.

Rutkoff, Peter M. Shadow Ball: A Novel of Baseball & Chicago. 2001. 232p. per. 24.95 (*0-7864-0981-9*) McFarland & Co., Inc. Pubs.

Rutland, Eva. No Crystal Stair. 2003. 368p. pap. (*1-55166-662-6*); 2000. 480p. per. (*1-55166-519-0*, 1-66519-9) Harlequin Enterprises, Ltd. (Mira Bks.).

Ryan, Marah E. A Flower of France: A Story of Old Louisiana. 1977. (Black Heritage Library Collection). reprint ed. 29.95 (*0-8369-9078-1*) Ayer Co. Pubs., Inc.

Sallis, James. Black Hornet. 1994. 208p. 18.95 o.p. (*0-7867-0118-8*, Carroll & Graf Pubs.) Avalon Publishing Group.

—Black Hornet. 1996. (New Orleans Mystery Ser.: No. 3). 192p. mass mkt. 5.50 (*0-380-72515-0*, Avon Bks.) Morrow/Avon.

—Bluebottle. (Lew Griffin Mysteries Ser.). 161p. 2000. pap. 8.95 (*0-8027-7595-0*); 1999. (Illus.). pap. 22.95 (*0-8027-3323-9*) Walker & Co.

—Eye of the Cricket. 2000. (Lew Griffin Mysteries Ser.). 196p. reprint ed. pap. 8.95 (*0-8027-7581-0*) Walker & Co.

—Eye of the Cricket: A Lew Griffin Mystery. 1997. (Lew Griffin Mysteries Ser.). 204p. 21.95 (*0-8027-3313-1*) Walker & Co.

—The Long-Legged Fly. 1992. 208p. 17.95 o.p. (*0-88184-810-7*, Carroll & Graf Pubs.) Avalon Publishing Group.

—The Long-Legged Fly. 1994. 192p. mass mkt. 4.99 (*0-380-72242-9*, Avon Bks.) Morrow/Avon.

—The Long-Legged Fly. 183p. pap. 15.00 (*1-901982-41-6*) No Exit Pr. GBR. *Dist:* Trafalgar Square.

—Moth. 1993. 208p. 18.95 o.p. (*0-88184-945-6*, Carroll & Graf Pubs.) Avalon Publishing Group.

—Moth. 1995. (Lew Griffin Ser.). reprint ed. pap. 4.99 o.p. (*0-380-72377-8*, Avon Bks.) Morrow/Avon.

Sanders, Dori. Clover. 1999. 196p. 17.95 (*0-945575-26-2*, 71526) Algonquin Bks. of Chapel Hill.

—Clover. 1991. 192p. pap. 11.95 (*0-449-90624-8*, Fawcett) Ballantine Bks.

—Clover. l.t. ed. 1990. (General Ser.). 224p. lib. bdg. 18.95 o.p. (*0-8161-5048-6*, Macmillan Reference USA) Gale Group.

—Her Own Place. 1994. 256p. reprint ed. pap. 11.95 (*0-449-90875-5*, Fawcett) Ballantine Bks.

—Her Own Place. l.t. ed. 1993. (Large Print Bks.). 249p. lib. bdg. 20.95 o.p. (*0-8161-5754-5*, Macmillan Reference USA) Gale Group.

—Her Own Place. unabr. ed. 1998. audio 44.00 (*0-7887-0404-4*, 94837E7) Recorded Bks., LLC.

—Her Own Place: A Novel. 1999. 252p. tchr. ed. 16.95 (*1-56512-027-2*, 72027) Algonquin Bks. of Chapel Hill.

Sanders, Marcella. Love by Design. 1999. 236p. mass mkt. 4.99 (*1-58314-022-0*) BET Bks.

—Shadow of Love. 2001. (Arabesque Ser.). 336p. mass mkt. 5.99 (*1-58314-166-9*) BET Bks.

Sanford, John B. The People from Heaven. 1995. (Radical Novel Reconsidered Ser.). 264p. pap. text 14.95 (*0-252-06491-7*) Univ. of Illinois Pr.

Santangello, Elena. Hang My Head & Cry. 2001. 322p. 24.95 (*0-312-26939-0*, Saint Martin's Minotaur) St. Martin's Pr.

Sapphire. Push: A Novel. 1997. 192p. pap. 11.95 (*0-679-76675-8*, Vintage) Knopf Publishing Group.

Savoy, Deidre. Once & Again. 2001. (Arabesque Ser.). 304p. mass mkt. 5.99 (*1-58314-169-3*) BET Bks.

Sawyer, David J. My Great-Grandfather Was Stonewall Jackson: The Story of a Negro Boy Growing up in the Segregated South. 1994. (Illus.). 288p. pap. 14.00 (*0-9635159-1-8*) Publishing Concepts.

—My Great-Grandfather Was Stonewall Jackson Vol. 1: The Story of a Negro Boy Growing up in the Segregated South. Evans, Paul, ed. 2nd rev. ed. 1994. (Illus.). 304p. reprint ed. pap. 16.00 (*0-9634206-1-5*) Jonathan Publishing Co.

—My Great-Grandfather Was Stonewall Jackson Vol. 2: Stonewalling in the Shadow of a Legend. Evans, Paul, ed. rev. ed. 1994. 317p. (Orig.). reprint ed. pap. 16.00 (*0-9634206-9-0*) Jonathan Publishing Co.

Schuster, Melanie. Lucky in Love. 2002. 320p. mass mkt. 5.99 (*1-58314-362-9*) BET Bks.

Schuyler, George S. Black Empire. Hill, Robert A. & Rasmussen, R. Kent, eds. 1993. (Library of Black Literature). 368p. reprint ed. text 45.00 (*1-55553-114-8*) Northeastern Univ. Pr.

—Black No More: A Novel. 1999. (Modern Library Ser.). 208p. pap. 13.95 (*0-375-75380-X*) Random Hse., Inc.

—Black No More: Being an Account of the Strange & Wonderful Workings of Science in the Land of the Free, A. D. 1933-1940. 1969. reprint ed. o.p. (*0-8371-1028-9*, SCB&) Greenwood Publishing Group, Inc.

—Black No More: Being an Account of the Strange & Wonderful Workings of Science in the Land of the Free, A. D. 1933-1940. 1989. (Library of Black Literature). 222p. reprint ed. pap. text 14.95 (*1-55553-063-X*) Northeastern Univ. Pr.

—Black No More: Being an Account of the Strange & Wonderful Workings of Science in the Land of the Free, A. D. 1933-1940. 2003. 192p. pap. (*1-874509-63-8*) X Pr., The.

Scott, Sophfronia. All I Need to Get By. 2004. 320p. pap. 13.95 (*0-312-31856-1*, Saint Martin's Griffin) St. Martin's Pr.

Selby, Hubert, Jr. The Willow Tree. 1998. 288p. 22.95 (*0-7145-3024-7*) Boyars, Marion Pubs., Inc.

Shades of Black. rev. ed. 1999. reprint ed. pap. 14.00 (*0-9667938-1-1*) 7-Fold Publishing.

Shange, Ntozake. Betsey Brown. 2001. pap., tchr.'s training gde. ed. (*0-312-28190-0*, Saint Martin's Griffin) St. Martin's Pr.

—Betsey Brown. 1995. 17.05 (*0-606-22697-4*) Turtleback Bks.

—Liliane: Resurrection of the Daughter. 1995. 304p. pap. 12.00 (*0-312-13559-9*) Picador.

—Liliane: Resurrection of the Daughter. 1994. 224p. 18.95 o.p. (*0-312-11310-2*) St. Martin's Pr.

—Sassafrass, Cypress & Indigo. 2nd ed. 1996. 240p. pap. 13.00 (*0-312-14091-6*) Picador.

Shaw, Frederick Douglas, Jr. Fast Black. 2000. 212p. pap. 13.95 (*1-881524-75-2*) Milligan Bks.

Sherman, Charlotte W. Killing Color. 1992. 120p. 19.95 (*0-934971-18-8*); pap. 9.95 (*0-934971-17-X*) Calyx Bks.

—One Dark Body: A Novel. 1993. 224p. 20.00 o.p. (*0-06-016924-9*) HarperTrade.

Shockley, Ann A. Say Jesus & Come to Me. 1985. 288p. pap. 2.95 o.p. (*0-380-79657-0*, 79657-0, Avon Bks.) Morrow/Avon.

—Say Jesus & Come to Me. 1987. 288p. reprint ed. pap. 8.95 o.p. (*0-930044-98-3*) Naiad Pr., Inc.

Simanga, Michael. In the Shadow of the Son. 1999. 261p. 24.95 (*0-88378-206-5*); 1998. 24.95 o.p. (*0-88378-207-3*) Third World Press.

Simmons, Herbert. Corner Boy. 1996. (Old School Bks.). 256p. pap. 11.00 o.p. (*0-393-31465-0*, Norton Paperbacks) Norton, W. W. & Co., Inc.

—Man Walking on Eggshells. 1997. (Old School Bks.). 221p. pap. 11.00 (*0-393-31618-1*) Norton, W. W. & Co., Inc.

Simone, Nea A. Reaching Back. 2002. 272p. pap. 15.00 (*1-58314-317-3*, Sepia) BET Bks.

Sims, Janice, et al. A Very Special Love. 2000. (Arabesque Ser.). 320p. mass mkt. 5.99 (*1-58314-106-5*) BET Bks.

Sinclair, April. Coffee Will Make You Black: A Novel. 1995. 256p. pap. 12.00 (*0-380-72459-6*, Perennial) HarperTrade.

—Coffee Will Make You Black: A Novel. 1994. 256p. 19.95 o.p. (*1-56282-796-0*) Hyperion Pr.

—Coffee Will Make You Black: A Novel. 1995. 18.05 (*0-606-12860-3*) Turtleback Bks.

—I Left My Back Door Open. 1999. 290p. 22.95 (*0-7868-6229-7*) Hyperion Pr.

—I Left My Back Door Open: A Novel. 2000. 304p. pap. 13.00 (*0-380-73280-7*) Morrow/Avon.

Singleton, Elyse. This Side of the Sky. 2003. 336p. pap. 14.00 (*0-425-19312-8*); 2002. 304p. 24.95 o.s.i (*0-399-14920-1*) Putnam Publishing Group, The. (BlueHen Bks.).

Sister Souljah. The Coldest Winter Ever: A Novel. (Ann Rule's Crime Files Ser.). 1999. 352p. 23.00 o.s.i (*0-671-02578-3*, Atria); 2001. (Illus.). 320p. reprint ed. pap. 13.95 (*0-7434-2681-9*, Washington Square Pr.); 2000. 432p. reprint ed. mass mkt. 7.99 (*0-671-02536-8*, Pocket) Simon & Schuster.

Skinner, Robert E. Cat-Eyed Trouble. 1999. 256p. mass mkt. 5.99 o.s.i (*1-57566-381-3*); 1998. 288p. 19.95 o.s.i (*1-57566-250-7*) Kensington Publishing Corp.

—Daddy's Gone A-Hunting: A Wesley Farrell Novel. 1999. 256p. 22.00 o.s.i (*1-57566-376-7*) Kensington Publishing Corp.

—Daddy's Gone A-Hunting: A Wesley Farrell Novel. 2000. (Illus.). 306p. 23.95 (*1-890208-17-5*) Poisoned Pen Pr.

—Pale Shadow: A Wesley Farrell Novel. 2003. 226p. pap. 14.95 o.s.i (*1-890208-87-6*) Poisoned Pen Pr.

—Skin Deep, Blood Red. 1998. 256p. mass mkt. 5.99 o.s.i (*1-57566-254-X*); 1997. 288p. 19.95 o.s.i (*1-57566-092-X*, Kensington Bks.) Kensington Publishing Corp.

Slim, Iceberg. Doom Fox. 1998. 256p. pap. 12.00 (*0-8021-3588-9*, Grove Pr.) Grove/Atlantic, Inc.

—Doom Fox. viii, 260p. pap. 11.95 (*0-86241-762-7*) Payback Pr. GBR. *Dist:* AK Pr. Distribution.

—Mama Black Widow. 1988. (Orig.). pap. 3.25 o.p. (*0-87067-828-0*) Holloway Hse. Publishing Co.

—Mama Black Widow. 1998. 288p. (Orig.). pap. 13.95 (*0-393-31765-X*) Norton, W. W. & Co., Inc.

—Mama Black Widow. vii, 237p. (Orig.). pap. 12.99 (*0-86241-632-9*) Payback Pr. GBR. *Dist:* AK Pr. Distribution.

Slim, Iceberg, et al. Mama Black Widow: Becks Tragic Tale of a Tragic Black Ghetto Homosexual. 1996. 320p. mass mkt. 6.99 (*0-87067-975-9*, BH975-9) Holloway Hse. Publishing Co.

Smith, Andrea. Friday Nights at Honeybee's. 2003. 320p. 22.95 (*0-385-33428-1*, Dial Bks.) Dell Publishing.

Smith, Debra White. To Rome with Love. 2001. (Seven Sisters Ser.: No. 4). 298p. pap. 10.99 (*0-7369-0660-6*) Harvest Hse. Pubs.

Smith, Eunice Y. A Trumpet Sounds. 1985. (Illus.). 272p. (C). 14.95 o.p. (*0-88208-198-5*) Chicago Review Pr., Inc.

Smith, Faye M. Flight of the Blackbird. 1996. 348p. 22.50 (*0-684-82971-1*, Scribner) Simon & Schuster.

—The Flight of the Blackbird. 1997. 464p. reprint ed. mass mkt. 6.50 (*0-446-60561-1*) Warner Bks., Inc.

Smith, Horane. The Lynching Stream. 2003. 187p. pap. 19.95 (*1-59286-614-X*) PublishAmerica, Inc.

Smith, Julie. Louisiana Bigshot. (Talba Wallis Ser.). 2003. 320p. mass mkt. 6.99 (*0-7653-4380-0*, Tor Bks.); 2002. 304p. 24.95 (*0-7653-0059-1*, Forge Bks.) Doherty, Tom Assocs., LLC.

—Louisiana Hotshot. 2001. 335p. 24.95 (*0-7653-0058-3*, Forge Bks.) Doherty, Tom Assocs., LLC.

Smith, Lillian. Strange Fruit. 1994. lib. bdg. 24.95 (*1-56849-420-3*) Buccaneer Bks., Inc.

—Strange Fruit. 1992. 384p. pap. 13.00 (*0-15-685636-0*, Harvest Bks.); 1948. 371p. 12.95 o.s.i (*0-15-185769-5*) Harcourt Trade Pubs.

—Strange Fruit. 1968. mass mkt. 0.50 o.p. (*0-451-01953-9*); mass mkt. 0.75 o.p. (*0-451-02677-2*); mass mkt. 0.25 o.p. (*0-451-00665-8*); mass mkt. 0.95 o.p. (*0-451-03508-9*); mass mkt. 0.35 o.p. (*0-451-01074-4*) NAL. (Signet Bks.).

—Strange Fruit. 1985. (Brown Thrasher Bks.). 392p. reprint ed. pap. 11.95 o.p. (*0-8203-0779-3*) Univ. of Georgia Pr.

Smith, Mary B. Ring Around the Moon. 1998. 288p. 24.00 (*0-688-15987-7*, Morrow, William & Co.) Morrow/Avon.

Smith, Vern. The Jones Men. 1998. (Old School Bks.). 224p. pap. 12.00 o.p. (*0-393-31707-2*) Norton, W. W. & Co., Inc.

Snoe, Eboni. Emerald's Fire. 2001. (Arabesque Ser.). 288p. mass mkt. 5.99 (*1-58314-203-7*) BET Bks.

—The Passion Ruby. 2000. 320p. mass mkt. 5.99 (*1-58314-207-X*) BET Bks.

Soos, Troy. Hanging Curve. 2000. 352p. mass mkt. 5.99 (*1-57566-656-1*); 1999. 288p. 22.00 o.s.i (*1-57566-455-0*) Kensington Publishing Corp. (Kensington Bks.).

—Hanging Curve, unabr. ed. 1999. (Mickey Rawlings Baseball Ser.: Vol. 6). audio 60.00 (*0-7887-4057-1*, 96129E7) Recorded Bks., LLC.

Southgate, Martha. The Fall of Rome. 224p. 2003. mass mkt. 6.99 (*0-7434-8256-5*); 2002. 23.00 (*0-684-86500-9*); 2003. reprint ed. pap. 12.00 (*0-7432-2721-2*) Simon & Schuster. (Scribner).

Spencer, Camika C. When All Hell Breaks Loose. pap. 12.00 (*0-9662578-0-4*) Akimac Publishing.

—When All Hell Breaks Loose. 1999. (*0-375-75509-8*) Random Hse. Value Publishing.

—When All Hell Breaks Loose. 2000. 256p. pap. 12.95 (*0-312-26793-2*, Saint Martin's Griffin) St. Martin's Pr.

Spirit Ran Free: At the Awakening Dawn of America. 2000. 294p. 26.95 (*1-57479-036-6*) ForGen Productions.

Sport, Kathryn M. & Hitchcock, Bert, eds. De Remnant Truth: The Tales of Jake Mitchell & Robert Wilton Burton. 1991. 256p. pap. text 19.95 (*0-8173-0515-7*) Univ. of Alabama Pr.

Stadler, Quandra P., ed. Out of Our Lives: A Selection of Contemporary Black Fiction. 1981. 324p. pap. 12.95 (*0-88258-095-7*) Howard Univ. Pr.

Stafford, Tim. The Stamp of Glory: A Novel of the Abolitionist Movement. 2000. (River of Freedom Ser.). 380p. 14.99 (*0-7852-6905-3*) Nelson, Thomas Pubs.

Staten, Lawanda M. How to Kill Your Willie Lynch. 1998. (Illus.). 128p. (Orig.). pap. 11.00 (*0-9664722-0-9*) Staten, LaWanda M.

Steen, Fred. Bluesman. 1998. 190p. pap. 16.95 (*1-85756-353-0*) Janus Publishing Co. GBR. *Dist:* Independent Pubs. Group, Paul & Co. Pubs. Consortium, Inc.

Stein, Michael. The Lynching Tree. 2000. 196p. 24.00 (*1-57962-070-1*) Permanent Pr., The.

Stephens, Nathan. A Different Breed of Brother. 2000. 290p. per. 12.95 (*0-9700572-0-2*) Stephens Publishing Co.

Stockton, Frank Richard. Amos Kilbright: His Adscititious Experiences; with Other Stories. 1977. (Black Heritage Library Collection). reprint ed. 22.95 (*0-8369-9067-6*) Ayer Co. Pubs., Inc.

Stoller, Paul. Jaguar: A Story of Africans in America. 1999. 213p. pap. 15.00 (*0-226-77528-3*); lib. bdg. 35.00 (*0-226-77527-5*) Univ. of Chicago Pr.

Stowe, Harriet Beecher. Three Novels: Uncle Tom's Cabin; The Minister's Wooing; Oldtown Folks. Sklar, Kathryn K., ed. 1982. 1478p. 45.00 (*0-940450-01-1*) Library of America, The.

—Uncle Sam's Emancipation. 1977. (Black Heritage Library Collection). 24.95 (*0-8369-8719-5*) Ayer Co. Pubs., Inc.

—Uncle Sam's Emancipation. 9.00 o.p. (*0-403-00147-1*) Scholarly Pr., Inc.

—Uncle Tom's Cabin. 1991. (Vintage Books - the Library of America). 560p. pap. 11.50 o.s.i (*0-679-72537-7*, Vintage) Knopf Publishing Group.

—Uncle Tom's Cabin. 1994. (Library of Liberal Arts). 315p. (C). pap. text 12.40 o.p. (*0-02-379631-6*, Macmillan College) Prentice Hall PTR.

Stowe, Harriet Beecher & Sklar, Kathryn Kish. Three Novels: Uncle Tom's Cabin; The Minister's Wooing; Oldtown Folks. 1982. E-Book 45.00 (*0-585-20223-0*) netLibrary, Inc.

Straight, Susan. Aquaboogie: A Novel in Stories. 1990. (Illus.). 196p. pap. 12.95 (*0-915943-59-X*) Milkweed Editions.

—I Been in Sorrow's Kitchen & Licked Out All the Pots. 1993. 368p. pap. 13.00 (*0-385-47012-6*) Doubleday Publishing.

—I Been in Sorrow's Kitchen & Licked Out All the Pots. 1992. 384p. 19.95 o.p. (*1-56282-963-7*) Hyperion Pr.

Stuart, Ruth M. George Washington Jones: A Christmas Gift That Went A-Begging. 1977. (Black Heritage Library Collection). (Illus.). reprint ed. 19.95 (*0-8369-9068-4*) Ayer Co. Pubs., Inc.

Subdued Southern Nobility: A Southern Ideal, by One of the Nobility. 1977. (Black Heritage Library Collection). reprint ed. 32.95 (*0-8369-9070-6*) Ayer Co. Pubs., Inc.

Swindle, Renee. Please Please Please. 2000. 336p. mass mkt. 6.99 (*0-440-22376-8*) Dell Publishing.

Tademy, Lalita. Cane River: A Novel. l.t. ed. (Americana Ser.). (Illus.). 2002. 645p. pap. 13.95 (*0-7862-3373-7*); 2001. 672p. 31.95 (*0-7862-3372-9*) Thorndike Pr.

—Cane River: A Novel. (Oprah's Book Club Selection Ser.). 2002. (Illus.). 560p. pap. 13.95 (*0-446-67845-7*); 2001. 432p. 24.95 o.p. (*0-446-53052-2*); 2001. 432p. E-Book 14.95 (*0-7595-8245-9*); 2001. 432p. E-Book 14.95 (*0-7595-0239-0*); 2001. 432p. E-Book 14.95 (*0-7595-6239-3*); 2001. 432p. E-Book 14.95 (*0-7595-9271-3*); 2001. 432p. E-Book 14.95 (*0-7595-4242-2*); 2001. (Illus.). 432p. 24.95 o.p. (*0-446-52732-7*) Warner Bks., Inc.

Taylor, Carol. Brown Sugar Vol. 2: Great One Night Stands. 2003. 400p. pap. 14.00 (*0-7434-4244-X*, Washington Square Pr.) Simon & Schuster.

—Brown Sugar 3: A Collection of Erotic Black Fiction. 2004. 384p. pap. 15.00 (*0-7434-6686-1*, Washington Square Pr.) Simon & Schuster.

Taylor, Carol, ed. Brown Sugar: A Collection of Erotic Black Fiction. 2001. 256p. pap. 14.00 (*0-452-28224-1*, Plume) Dutton/Plume.

Taylor, Mel. The Mitt Man. 1999. 352p. 24.00 (*0-688-16094-8*, Morrow, William & Co.) Morrow/Avon.

Tervalon, Jervey. All the Trouble You Need. 2002. 224p. 24.00 (*0-7434-2238-4*, Atria) Simon & Schuster.

—All the Trouble You Need: A Novel. 2003. 224p. reprint ed. pap. 13.00 (*0-7434-2239-2*, Washington Square Pr.) Simon & Schuster.

—Dead above Ground. 2001. (Illus.). 240p. pap. 12.95 (*0-671-03469-3*, Washington Square Pr.); 2000. 272p. 23.95 o.s.i (*0-671-03468-5*, Atria) Simon & Schuster.

—Lita. 224p. 2004. pap. 13.00 (*0-7434-4885-5*, Washington Square Pr.); 2003. 24.00 (*0-7434-4884-7*, Atria) Simon & Schuster.

—Understand This. 1995. 272p. pap. 19.00 o.s.i (*0-385-47824-0*) Knopf, Alfred A. Inc.

Tessler, Stephanie G. & Enderle, Judith. Elizabeth Jones: Emergency. 1984. (Bayshore Medical Center Ser.). 160p. 12.95 o.s.i (*0-8027-6538-6*) Walker & Co.

Thelwell, Michael. Duties, Pleasures, & Conflicts: Essays in Struggle. 1987. 266p. pap. 20.95 (*0-87023-523-0*) Univ. of Massachusetts Pr.

Thomas-Graham, Pamela. Blue Blood. (Ivy League Mysteries Ser.). 1999. 288p. 23.00 (*0-684-84527-X*, Simon & Schuster); 2000. 320p. reprint ed. pap. 6.99 (*0-671-01671-7*, Pocket) Simon & Schuster.

—A Darker Shade of Crimson: An Ivy League Mystery. (Ivy League Mysteries Ser.). 1999. (Illus.). 416p. pap. 6.99 (*0-671-01670-9*, Pocket); 1998. 288p. 23.00 (*0-684-84526-1*, Simon & Schuster) Simon & Schuster.

Thomas, Jacquelin. Love's Miracle. 2000. (Arabesque Ser.). 288p. mass mkt. 5.99 (*1-58314-126-X*) BET Bks.

—Singsation. 352p. 2003. pap. 13.95 (*0-446-67886-4*, Walk Worthy Pr.); 2001. 21.95 o.p. (*0-446-52798-X*); 2001. E-Book 14.95 (*0-7595-9273-X*); 2001. E-Book 14.95 (*0-7595-8247-5*); 2001. E-Book 14.95 (*0-7595-0241-2*); 2001. E-Book 14.95 (*0-7595-6241-5*); 2001. E-Book 14.95 (*0-7595-4244-9*) Warner Bks., Inc.

Thomas, Jacqueline. Undeniably Yours. 2001. (Arabesque Ser.). 288p. mass mkt. 5.99 (*1-58314-131-6*) BET Bks.

Thomas, Joyce Carol. House of Light: A Novel. 2001. 273p. 22.95 (*0-7868-6606-3*) Hyperion Pr.

Thomas, Trisha R. Nappily Ever After. 2001. E-Book 11.00 (*1-59061-593-X*) Adobe Systems, Inc.

—Nappily Ever After: A Novel. 2001. 320p. pap. 12.00 (*0-609-80898-2*, Three Rivers Pr.); 2000. (Illus.). 288p. 22.00 o.s.i (*0-609-60583-6*, Crown) Crown Publishing Group.

—Roadrunner: A Novel. 2003. 288p. pap. 12.00 (*1-4000-4791-9*) Crown Publishing Group.

—Roadrunner: A Novel. 2002. 288p. 22.95 (*0-609-60584-4*, Compass American Guides, Inc.) Fodor's Travel Pubns.

—Would I Lie to You? A Novel. 2004. (Illus.). 304p. 22.00 (*1-4000-4874-5*, Crown) Crown Publishing Group.

Thomas, Wanda Y. Subtle Secrets. 2001. (Indigo Love Stories Ser.). 379p. pap. 8.95 (*1-58571-041-5*, Indigo) Genesis Pr., Inc.

—Truly Inseparable. 330p. 1999. pap. 8.95 (*1-885478-99-2*); 1998. 15.95 (*1-885478-54-2*) Genesis Pr., Inc.

Thompson, Albert. The Fire Within: The Poetic Lyrical Voice of a Black Man. 2000. 120p. pap. 20.99 (*0-7388-2133-0*); E-Book 8.00 (*0-7388-8740-4*) Xlibris Corp.

Thompson, Maxine E. No Pockets in a Shroud. 2nd ed. 2000. 242p. pap. 13.95 (*0-9647576-1-3*) Black Butterfly Pr.

Thurman, Wallace. The Blacker the Berry. reprint ed. 27.50 (*0-404-00217-X*) AMS Pr., Inc.

—The Blacker the Berry. 1978. (American Negro). reprint ed. 34.06 (*0-405-01897-5*) Ayer Co. Pubs., Inc.

—The Blacker the Berry. 1996. 224p. pap. 12.00 (*0-684-81580-X*, Touchstone) Simon & Schuster.

—The Blacker the Berry. 1996. (X Press Black Classics Ser.). 215p. pap. 9.95 (*1-874509-13-1*) X Pr., The GBR. *Dist:* LPC Group.

—Infants of the Spring. reprint ed. 29.50 (*0-404-11418-0*) AMS Pr., Inc.

—Infants of the Spring. 1977. (Black Heritage Library Collection). reprint ed. 28.95 (*0-8369-9129-X*) Ayer Co. Pubs., Inc.

—Infants of the Spring. 1992. (Library of Black Literature). 284p. pap. text 15.95 (*1-55553-128-8*) Northeastern Univ. Pr.

—Infants of the Spring. 1999. (Harlem Renaissance Ser.: Vol. 2). xii, 175p. pap. 11.95 o.s.i (*0-375-75232-3*) Random Hse., Inc.

—Infants of the Spring. 2003. (Black Classics Ser.). 186p. pap. (*1-874509-61-1*) X Pr., The GBR. *Dist:* National Bk. Network.

—Infants of the Spring. A Novel. 1979. (Lost American Fiction Ser.). 314p. reprint ed. 13.95 o.p. (*0-8093-0864-9*) Southern Illinois Univ. Pr.

Tomlinson, Dar. A Risk of Rain. 2000. (Love Spectrum Romance Ser.). 428p. pap. 8.95 (*1-58571-025-3*, 909-103, Love Spectrum) Genesis Pr., Inc.

Toomer, Jean. Cane. 2000. 252p. E-Book 9.95 (*0-594-06102-4*) 1873 Pr.

—Cane. 2000. (Illus.). (*0-910457-41-7*) Arion Pr.

—Cane. 1993. 144p. (C). pap. 9.95 (*0-87140-151-7*); 1975. 116p. 7.95 o.p. (*0-87140-611-X*); 1975. 116p. pap. 5.95 o.p. (*0-87140-104-5*) Liveright Publishing Corp.

—Cane. Turner, Darwin T., ed. 1987. (Critical Editions Ser.). 320p. (C). pap. text (*0-393-95600-8*) Norton, W. W. & Co., Inc.

—Cane. 1994. 182p. 12.50 o.s.i (*0-679-60109-0*) Random Hse., Inc.

—Cane. 1990. 28.00 (*0-8446-6367-0*) Smith, Peter Pub., Inc.

Toomer, Jean & Hutchinson, George B. Cane. 1999. (Penguin Twentieth-Century Classics Ser.). 160p. pap. 7.95 (*0-14-118132-X*) Viking Penguin.

Tracy, Roger S. The White Man's Burden: A Satirical Forecast. 1977. (Black Heritage Library Collection). reprint ed. 25.95 (*0-8369-9130-3*) Ayer Co. Pubs., Inc.

Tramble, Nichelle D. The Dying Ground: A Hip-Hop Noir Novel. E-Book 11.00 (*1-58945-588-6*) Adobe Systems, Inc.

—The Dying Ground: A Hip-Hop Noir Novel. 2001. 336p. pap. 13.95 (*0-375-75653-1*, Villard Bks.) Random House Adult Trade Publishing Group.

—The Last King: A Maceo Redfield Novel. 2004. 336p. pap. 13.95 (*0-375-75882-8*) Random Hse., Inc.

Travis, Dempsey J. They Heard a Thousand Thunders. 1999. 166p. 19.75 (*0-941484-28-9*) Urban Research Pr., Inc.

Trice, Dawn T. Only Twice I've Wished for Heaven. l.t. ed. 1997. (Wheeler Large Print Book Ser.). 24.95 (*1-56895-468-9*, Wheeler Publishing, Inc.) Gale Group.

Trice, Dawn Turner. Only Twice I've Wished for Heaven. 1997. 304p. 23.00 o.s.i (*0-517-70428-5*) Random Hse. Value Publishing.

—Only Twice I've Wished for Heaven. 1998. 18.05 (*0-606-19398-7*) Turtleback Bks.

—Only Twice I've Wished for Heaven: A Novel. 1998. 320p. pap. 12.00 (*0-385-49123-9*) Doubleday Publishing.

Trobaugh, Augusta. River Jordan. 2004. 272p. 23.95 (*0-525-94755-8*, Dutton) Dutton/Plume.

Troubaugh, Augusta. Swan Place. 2004. 304p. pap. 13.00 (*0-452-28414-7*, Plume) Dutton/Plume.

Troutt, David Dante. The Monkey Suit: And Other Short Fiction on African Americans & Justice. 328p. 1999. pap. text 14.95 (*1-56584-524-2*); 1998. text 24.00 (*1-56584-326-6*) New Pr., The.

Turner, Vernon Kitabo. The Secret of Freedom. 1994. 112p. pap. 8.95 (*1-878901-69-9*) Hampton Roads Publishing Co., Inc.

Twain, Mark. Pudd'nhead Wilson. 1997. (Classics Illustrated Notes). (Illus.). pap. text 4.99 (*1-57840-065-1*) Acclaim Bks.

—Pudd'nhead Wilson. 1966. (Airmont Classics Ser.). (Illus.). mass mkt. 2.50 (*0-8049-0124-4*, CL-124) Airmont Publishing Co., Inc.

—Pudd'nhead Wilson. 20.95 (*0-89190-348-8*) Amereon, Ltd.

—Pudd'nhead Wilson. 1984. (Bantam Classics Ser.). 160p. mass mkt. 4.95 (*0-553-21158-7*, Bantam Classics) Bantam Bks.

—Pudd'nhead Wilson. unabr. ed. 1997. audio 39.95 (*1-86015-428-X*) Beeler, Thomas T. Publisher.

—Pudd'nhead Wilson. unabr. ed. 1982. audio 32.95 (*0-7861-0556-9*, 2049) Blackstone Audio Bks., Inc.

—Pudd'nhead Wilson. unabr. collector's ed. 1982. audio 36.00 (*0-7366-3870-9*, 9078) Books on Tape, Inc.

—Pudd'nhead Wilson. 1987. 172p. reprint ed. lib. bdg. 19.95 (*0-89966-577-2*) Buccaneer Bks., Inc.

—Pudd'nhead Wilson. 1999. (Thrift Editions Ser.). 96p. pap. text 1.50 (*0-486-40885-X*) Dover Pubns., Inc.

—Pudd'nhead Wilson. 1989. audio 24.00; 1982. audio 24.00 Jimcin Recordings.

—Pudd'nhead Wilson. E-Book 1.95 (*1-58515-204-8*) MesaView, Inc.

—Pudd'nhead Wilson. 1964. mass mkt. 1.50 o.p. (*0-451-51229-4*); 176p. mass mkt. 4.95 (*0-451-52374-1*); mass mkt. 0.50 o.p. (*0-451-50184-5*); mass mkt. 1.25 o.p. (*0-451-51083-6*); mass mkt. 0.60 o.p. (*0-451-50703-7*); mass mkt. 0.75 o.p. (*0-451-50840-8*) NAL. (Signet Classics).

—Pudd'nhead Wilson. l.t. ed. 2001. 269p. 26.00 (*1-58287-635-5*) North Bks.

—Pudd'nhead Wilson, unabr. ed. 1999. audio 46.00 (*1-55690-687-0*, 92342E7) Recorded Bks., LLC.

—Pudd'nhead Wilson. 1989. (Works of Samuel Clemens). reprint ed. lib. bdg. 79.00 (*0-7812-1119-0*) Reprint Services Corp.

—Pudd'nhead Wilson. 9999. pap. 1.95 o.s.i (*0-590-03437-5*) Scholastic, Inc.

—Pudd'nhead Wilson. 1998. 940p. 22.00 (*0-684-81908-2*, Simon & Schuster) Simon & Schuster.

—Pudd'nhead Wilson. l.t. ed. 2000. (Perennial Bestsellers Ser.). 237p. 27.95 (*0-7838-9147-4*) Thorndike Pr.

—Pudd'nhead Wilson. Bradbury, Malcolm, ed. & intro. by. 1969. (English Library). 320p. 10.00 (*0-14-043040-7*, Penguin Classics) Viking Penguin.

—Pudd'nhead Wilson. (Classics Library). pap. 3.95 (*1-85326-572-1*, 5721WW) Wordsworth Editions, Ltd. GBR. *Dist:* Combined Publishing.

—Pudd'nhead Wilson & Other Tales. Gooder, R. D., ed. 1992. (Oxford World's Classics Ser.). 312p. pap. 7.95 o.p. (*0-19-281806-6*) Oxford Univ. Pr., Inc.

—Pudd'nhead Wilson & Other Tales: Those Extraordinary Twins, The Man that Corrupted Hadleyburg. Gooder, R. D., ed. 1999. (Oxford World's Classics Ser.). 320p. pap. 8.95 (*0-19-283730-3*) Oxford Univ. Pr., Inc.

—Pudd'nhead Wilson & Those Extraordinary Twins. Berger, Sidney E., ed. 1981. (Critical Editions Ser.). (Illus.). 384p. 22.50 o.p. (*0-393-01337-5*); (C). pap. text 9.00 (*0-393-95027-1*) Norton, W. W. & Co., Inc.

—Pudd'nhead Wilson & Those Extraordinary Twins. 2002. (Modern Library Classics). (Illus.). 288p. pap. 9.95 (*0-8129-6622-8*) Random House Adult Trade Publishing Group.

Tyler, Charles W. The K.K.K: The Black Heritage Library Collection. 1977. (Black Heritage Library Collection). reprint ed. 28.95 (*0-8369-9072-2*) Ayer Co. Pubs., Inc.

Tyner, Marilyn. Everything to Gain. 2001. (Arabesque Ser.). 256p. mass mkt. 5.99 (*1-58314-128-6*) BET Bks.

—Secrets of the Heart. 2000. (Arabesque Ser.). 256p. mass mkt. 5.99 (*1-58314-105-7*) BET Bks.

Tyree, Omar R. College Boy. 3rd rev. ed. 2002. 256p. pap. 12.00 (*0-9710397-2-0*) Mars Productions.

—An Interview with a Loverboy: The Prequel to Just Say No! 2001. (*0-7432-2465-5*, Simon & Schuster) Simon & Schuster.

—Leslie. 400p. 2002. (Illus.). 21.00 (*0-7432-2866-9*); 2003. reprint ed. pap. 13.00 (*0-7432-2870-7*) Simon & Schuster. (Simon & Schuster).

—One Crazy-A** Night. 2003. pap. 12.00 (*0-9710397-3-9*) Mars Productions.

—Single Mom: A Novel. (Illus.). 400p. 1999. pap. 13.00 (*0-684-85593-3*); 1998. 24.00 (*0-684-85592-5*) Simon & Schuster. (Simon & Schuster).

—Sweet St. Louis. mass mkt. 6.99 (*0-7434-8242-5*, Pocket); 2000. 368p. pap. 14.00 (*0-684-85611-5*, Simon & Schuster); 1999. (Illus.). 368p. 24.00 (*0-684-85610-7*, Simon & Schuster) Simon & Schuster.

Urban Griot Staff. College Boy. 2003. 384p. mass mkt. 6.99 (*0-7434-8273-5*, Simon & Schuster) Simon & Schuster.

Urban Griot Staff, et al. The Underground: A Hardcore Novel. Chanel, Lisa & Penrice, Ronda Rasha, eds. 3rd ed. 2001. (Urban Groit Ser.). 400p. pap. 12.95 (*0-9710397-0-4*) Mars Productions.

Van Dyke, Henry Jackson. Dead Piano. 1971. 182p. 5.95 o.p. (*0-374-13550-9*) Farrar, Straus & Giroux.

—Dead Piano. 1997. (Old School Bks.). 200p. pap. 10.00 (*0-393-31542-8*) Norton, W. W. & Co., Inc.

Van Peebles, Melvin. Panther. 1995. 230p. pap. 10.95 o.p. (*1-56025-096-8*, Thunder's Mouth Pr.) Avalon Publishing Group.

Van Vechten, Carl. Nigger Heaven. 1973. reprint ed. 20.50 (*0-374-98069-1*) Farrar, Straus & Giroux.

—Nigger Heaven. 2000. 336p. pap. 17.95 (*0-252-06860-2*) Univ. of Illinois Pr.

Vernon, Olympia. Eden. 288p. 2004. pap. 12.00 (*0-8021-4040-8*); 2003. 23.00 (*0-8021-1728-7*) Grove/Atlantic, Inc. (Grove Pr.).

Victor, Metta V. Maum Guinea, & Her Plantation "Children": or Holiday-Week on a Louisiana Estate: A Slave Romance. 1977. (Black Heritage Library Collection). reprint ed. 25.95 (*0-8369-9087-0*) Ayer Co. Pubs., Inc.

Victory. 1977. (Black Heritage Library Collection-Prize Ser.). reprint ed. 29.95 (*0-8369-9051-X*) Ayer Co. Pubs., Inc.

Victory. pap. text 10.00 o.p. (*1-882821-14-9*) DPK Pubns.

Victory. 2004. Vol. 2. mass mkt. (*0-8125-6168-6*); Vol. 3. mass mkt. (*0-8125-6169-4*) Doherty, Tom Assocs., LLC. (Forge Bks.).

Wade, Brent. Company Man. 1993. 240p. pap. 10.95 o.s.i (*0-385-42563-5*) Doubleday Publishing.

—Company Man: A Novel. 1992. 240p. 18.95 o.p. (*0-945575-73-4*) Algonquin Bks. of Chapel Hill.

Walker. Love & Trouble. 2004. 156p. pap. 12.00 (*0-15-602863-8*) Harcourt Trade Pubs.

Walker, Alice. Alice Walker Banned: The Banned Works. 1996. 105p. 10.95 (*1-879960-47-8*) Aunt Lute Bks.

—Alice Walker Boxed Set-Fiction: The Third Life of Grange Copeland, You Can't Keep a Good Woman Down & In Love & Trouble, Set. 1985. 565p. pap. 12.95 (*0-15-694101-5*, Harvest Bks.) Harcourt Trade Pubs.

—The Color Purple. l.t. ed. 1986. (General Ser.). 266p. 16.95 o.p. (*0-8161-4141-X*, Macmillan Reference USA) Gale Group.

—The Color Purple. Bernard, Andre, ed. 2003. 300p. pap. 14.00 (*0-15-602835-2*, Harvest Bks.) Harcourt Trade Pubs.

—The Color Purple. 1982. 245p. 15.95 o.s.i (*0-15-119153-0*); 10th anniv. ed. 1992. (Illus.). 304p. 24.00 (*0-15-119154-9*) Harcourt Trade Pubs.

—The Color Purple. Rubenstein, Julie, ed. 1990. 304p. mass mkt. 7.99 o.s.i (*0-671-72779-6*, Pocket) Simon & Schuster.

—The Color Purple. 1988. 251p. pap. (*0-671-66878-1*, Washington Square Pr.); 1985. mass mkt. 3.95 (*0-671-61702-8*, Pocket) Simon & Schuster.

—Everyday Use. 1994. (Women Writers: Text & Contexts Ser.). vi, 229p. (C). 30.00 o.p. (*0-8135-2075-4*); pap. text 14.00 (*0-8135-2076-2*) Rutgers Univ. Pr.

—In Love & Trouble: Stories of Black Women. 1973. 6.50 o.p. (*0-15-144405-6*); 1974. (Harvest Book Ser.: Vol. 277). 156p. reprint ed. pap. 10.00 (*0-15-644450-X*, HB277, Harvest Bks.) Harcourt Trade Pubs.

—Meridian. l.t. ed. 1987. 299p. reprint ed. lib. bdg. 19.95 o.p. (*1-55736-019-7*) Bantam Doubleday Dell Large Print Group, Inc.

—Meridian. Bernard, Andre, ed. 2003. 264p. pap. 13.00 (*0-15-602834-4*, Harvest Bks.) Harcourt Trade Pubs.

—Meridian. 1976. 256p. 18.95 o.p. (*0-15-159265-9*) Harcourt Trade Pubs.

—Meridian. Rubenstein, Julie, ed. 1990. 224p. mass mkt. 6.99 (*0-671-72701-X*, Pocket) Simon & Schuster.

—Meridian. 1989. 224p. mass mkt. 4.50 (*0-671-68765-4*, Pocket); 1983. 228p. mass mkt. 3.95 (*0-671-47256-9*, Pocket); 1981. mass mkt. 2.75 o.p. (*0-671-43750-X*, Washington Square Pr.) Simon & Schuster.

—Possessing the Secret of Joy. l.t. ed. 1996. 252p. 24.95 o.p. (*1-56895-351-8*, Wheeler Publishing, Inc.) Gale Group.

—Possessing the Secret of Joy. 1992. 304p. 25.00 (*0-15-173152-7*) Harcourt Trade Pubs.

—Possessing the Secret of Joy. 1997. (Illus.). 304p. pap. 14.00 (*0-671-78945-7*, Washington Square Pr.) Simon & Schuster.

—Possessing the Secret of Joy. Grose, Bill, ed. 1993. 304p. reprint ed. mass mkt. 7.99 (*0-671-78942-2*, Pocket) Simon & Schuster.

—Possessing the Secret of Joy. unabr. ed. 1992. pap. 25.00 incl. audio (*0-671-79306-3*, 592128, Simon & Schuster Audioworks) Simon & Schuster Audio.

—The Temple of My Familiar. 1989. 416p. 19.95 (*0-15-188533-8*) Harcourt Trade Pubs.

—The Temple of My Familiar. 1997. (Illus.). 432p. pap. 14.00 (*0-671-00376-3*, Washington Square Pr.) Simon & Schuster.

—The Third Life of Grange Copeland. Bernard, Andre, ed. 2003. 328p. pap. 14.00 (*0-15-602836-0*, Harvest Bks.) Harcourt Trade Pubs.

—The Way Forward Is with a Broken Heart. 2001. (Ballantine Reader's Circle Ser.). 240p. reprint ed. pap. 14.00 (*0-345-40795-4*, Ballantine Bks.) Ballantine Bks.

—The Way Forward Is with a Broken Heart. l.t. ed. 2001. (Women's Fiction Ser.). 224p. 29.95 (*0-7862-3355-9*) Thorndike Pr.

Walker, Blair S. Don't Believe Your Lying Eyes: A Darryl Billups Mystery. 2002. 240p. 22.95 (*0-345-44682-8*) Ballantine Bks.

—Hidden in Plain View: A Darryl Billups Mystery. 2000. (Darryl Billups Ser.). 240p. mass mkt. 5.99 o.s.i (*0-380-79026-2*, Avon Bks.) Morrow/Avon.

—Up Jumped the Devil. abr. ed. 2001. audio 12.99 (*1-57815-210-0*, Media Bks. Audio Publishing) Media Bks., L. L. C.

—Up Jumped the Devil. 1999. 272p. mass mkt. 5.99 o.s.i (*0-380-79025-4*, Avon Bks.) Morrow/Avon.

—Up Jumped the Devil, Set. abr. ed. 1997. audio 24.95 (*1-57511-027-X*) Publishing Mills, Inc., The.

Walker, Margaret. Jubilee. 1983. 432p. mass mkt. 6.99 o.s.i (*0-553-27383-3*, Bantam Classics) Bantam Bks.

—Jubilee. 1999. 512p. pap. 8.95 (*0-395-92495-2*); 1966. 15.95 o.p. (*0-395-08288-9*) Houghton Mifflin Co.

—Jubilee. 1967. 11.60 o.p. (*0-606-01623-6*) Turtleback Bks.

Walker, Margie, et al. Season's Greetings. 1998. (Arabesque Ser.). mass mkt. 5.99 (*1-58314-184-7*) Kensington Publishing Corp.

Walker, Persia. Harlem Redux. 2003. 352p. reprint ed. pap. 12.95 (*0-451-20874-9*) NAL.

—Harlem Redux. 2002. 320p. 23.00 (*0-7432-2497-3*, Simon & Schuster) Simon & Schuster.

—Harlem Redux. 2000. 319p. pap. 16.95 o.p. (*0-595-12921-8*) iUniverse, Inc.

Wallace, Irving. The Man. l.t. ed. 1977. (Ulverscroft Large Print Ser.). 29.99 o.p. (*0-85456-558-2*, Ulverscroft) Thorpe, F. A. Pubs. GBR. *Dist:* Ulverscroft Large Print Bks., Ltd., Ulverscroft Large Print Canada, Ltd.

—The Man. E-Book 16.00 (*1-58824-007-X*) ibooks, Inc.

Walworth, Jeanette H. On the Winning Side: A Southern Story of Ante-Bellum Times. 1977. (Black Heritage Library Collection). reprint ed. 28.95 (*0-8369-9088-9*) Ayer Co. Pubs., Inc.

—Without Blemish: Today's Problem. 1977. (Black Heritage Library Collection). reprint ed. 32.95 (*0-8369-9089-7*) Ayer Co. Pubs., Inc.

Ward, Elizabeth S. & Ward, Herbert D. A Lost Hero. 1977. (Black Heritage Library Collection). (Illus.). reprint ed. 16.95 (*0-8369-9090-0*) Ayer Co. Pubs., Inc.

Ward-Rainey, Tracia. Painted Smiles, Vol. 1. 1997. 136p. pap. 12.00 (*0-9659118-0-2*) Akili Publishing.

Wartofsky, Victor. Meeting the Pieman. 2001. 320p. reprint ed. pap. 12.95 (*0-88739-282-2*) Creative Arts Bk. Co.

Washington, Geno. Blood Brothers, 1. 1999. 311p. pap. text 12.95 (*1-899344-44-6*) Dufour Editions, Inc.

Weber, Carl. Baby Momma Drama. 2004. 328p. pap. 15.00 (*0-7582-0013-7*, Kensington Bks.); 2003. 320p. 24.00 (*1-57566-908-0*) Kensington Publishing Corp.

—Baby Momma Drama. l.t. ed. 2003. (African American Ser.). 29.95 (*0-7862-5423-8*) Thorndike Pr.

—Lookin' for Luv. 2001. 416p. mass mkt. 6.99 (*0-7582-0118-4*); 2000. 34p. pap. 14.00 (*1-57566-695-2*) Kensington Publishing Corp.

—Player Haters. 2004. 320p. 24.00 (*1-57566-909-9*, Kensington Bks.) Kensington Publishing Corp.

Wesley, Valerie Wilson. Ain't Nobody's Business If I Do. 2000. 384p. mass mkt. 6.99 (*0-380-80304-6*); 1999. 323p. 24.00 (*0-380-97703-6*) Morrow/Avon. (Avon Bks.).

—Always True to You in My Own Fashion. abr. ed. 2002. audio 25.95 (*0-06-051352-7*, HarperAudio) HarperTrade.

—Always True to You in My Own Fashion. 320p. 2003. pap. 13.95 (*0-06-054942-4*, Avon Bks.); 2002. 23.95 (*0-06-018883-9*, Morrow, William & Co.) Morrow/Avon.

—The Devil Riding. l.t. ed. 2001. (Softcover Ser.). 240p. pap. 23.95 o.p. (*1-58724-084-X*, Wheeler Publishing, Inc.) Gale Group.

—The Devil Riding. 2000. 208p. 23.95 o.s.i (*0-399-14617-2*) Penguin Group (USA) Inc.

—Devil's Gonna Get Him. 1996. (Tamara Hayle Mystery Ser.: Vol. 2). 288p. mass mkt. 6.99 (*0-380-72492-8*, Avon Bks.) Morrow/Avon.

—Devil's Gonna Get Him. 1995. 212p. 19.95 o.p. (*0-399-14027-1*, G. P. Putnam's Sons) Penguin Group (USA) Inc.

—Easier to Kill. l.t. ed. 1999. pap. 23.95 o.p. (*1-56895-704-1*, Wheeler Publishing, Inc.) Gale Group.

—Easier to Kill. 1999. (Tamara Hayle Mystery Ser.). 304p. mass mkt. 6.99 (*0-380-72910-5*, Avon Bks.) Morrow/Avon.

—Easier to Kill. 1998. (Tamara Hayle Mystery Ser.: Vol. 5). 193p. 23.95 o.p. (*0-399-14445-5*) Penguin Group (USA) Inc.

—The Hiding Place. 1998. (Tamara Hayle Mystery Ser.). 288p. mass mkt. 6.99 (*0-380-72909-1*, Avon Bks.) Morrow/Avon.

—No Hiding Place. unabr. ed. 1998. audio 40.00 (*0-7366-4214-5*, 4712) Books on Tape, Inc.

—No Hiding Place: A Tamara Hayle Mystery. 1997. 207p. 21.95 o.s.i (*0-399-14318-1*, G. P. Putnam's Sons) Penguin Group (USA) Inc.

—When Death Comes Stealin. 1995. (Tamara Hayle Mystery Ser.: Vol. 1). 320p. reprint ed. mass mkt. 6.99 (*0-380-72491-X*, Avon Bks.) Morrow/Avon.

—When Death Comes Stealing. 1994. 224p. 19.95 o.p. (*0-399-13949-4*, G. P. Putnam's Sons) Penguin Group (USA) Inc.

—Where Evil Sleeps. unabr. ed. 1998. audio 40.00 (*0-7366-4120-3*, 4624) Books on Tape, Inc.

—Where Evil Sleeps. 1997. 288p. mass mkt. 6.50 (*0-380-72908-3*, Avon Bks.) Morrow/Avon.

—Where Evil Sleeps. 1996. 224p. 21.95 o.p. (*0-399-14145-6*, G. P. Putnam's Sons) Penguin Group (USA) Inc.

West, Chassie. Killer Riches: A Leigh Ann Warren Mystery. 2001. 304p. mass mkt. 6.50 (*0-06-104391-5*, Avon Bks.) Morrow/Avon.

West, Dorothy. Living Is Easy. 1970. (American Negro). reprint ed. 45.95 (*0-405-01942-4*) Ayer Co. Pubs., Inc.

—Living Is Easy. 1982. 376p. (C). reprint ed. pap. 14.95 o.p. (*0-912670-97-5*) Feminist Pr. at The City Univ. of New York.

—The Wedding. 1995. 20.00 o.s.i (*0-385-47143-2*); 200.00 o.s.i (*0-385-47915-8*) Doubleday Publishing.

—The Wedding. 1996. 256p. pap. 12.00 (*0-385-47144-0*, Knopf Bks. for Young Readers) Random Hse. Children's Bks.

Wetzler, Barbara B. Pathway to Life Achievement. 2002. 216p. pap. (*1-55369-481-3*) Trafford Publishing.

Whack, Rita Coburn. Meant to Be: A Novel. 2002. 320p. pap. 11.95 (*0-375-75809-7*, Villard Bks.) Random House Adult Trade Publishing Group.

White, Franklin. Cup of Love: A Novel. 2001. 320p. pap. 13.00 (*0-684-86565-3*, Simon & Schuster) Simon & Schuster.

White, Walter. Flight. 1998. (Voices of the South Ser.). 304p. pap. 14.95 (*0-8071-2280-7*) Louisiana State Univ. Pr.

Whitehead, Colson. The Intuitionist: A Novel. 1998. 272p. 19.95 o.s.i (*0-385-49299-5*) Doubleday Publishing.

—John Henry Days: A Novel. 2002. 400p. pap. 14.00 (*0-385-49820-9*, Knopf Bks. for Young Readers) Random Hse. Children's Bks.

Whiteside, Kim L. Destiny's Song. 2000. 288p. mass mkt. 5.99 (*1-58314-173-1*) BET Bks.

Whitfield, Van. Guys in Suits. 2002. 272p. pap. 12.95 (*0-385-49847-0*, Anchor) Knopf Publishing Group.

—Something's Wrong with Your Scale! 1999. 304p. 22.95 (*0-385-48935-8*) Doubleday Publishing.

Whyte, Anthony J. Ghetto Falsehoods. 2001. 244p. pap. 19.95 (*1-58721-772-4*) 1stBooks Library.

Wideman, John Edgar. All Stories Are True. 1993. pap. 12.00 o.s.i (*0-679-73752-9*, Vintage) Knopf Publishing Group.

—Damballah. 1998. (Illus.). 205p. pap. 14.00 (*0-395-89797-1*) Houghton Mifflin Co.

—Damballah. 1988. pap. 11.00 o.s.i (*0-679-72028-6*, Vintage) Knopf Publishing Group.

—Damballah. 1988. 6.95 (*0-07-541813-4*) McGraw-Hill Cos., The.

—Damballah. 1981. pap. 2.95 o.p. (*0-380-78519-6*, 78519-6, Avon Bks.) Morrow/Avon.

—Hiding Place. 1998. 158p. pap. 12.00 (*0-395-89798-X*, Mariner Bks.) Houghton Mifflin Co. Trade & Reference Div.

—Hiding Place. 1988. pap. 10.00 o.s.i (*0-679-72027-8*, Vintage) Knopf Publishing Group.

—Hiding Place. 1981. pap. 2.95 o.p. (*0-380-78501-3*, 78501-3, Avon Bks.) Morrow/Avon.

—The Homewood Books. 1992. 536p. text 24.95 (*0-8229-3831-6*) Univ. of Pittsburgh Pr.

—Identities: Three Novels: A Glance Away, Hurry Home, The Lynchers. 1994. pap. 14.95 o.p. (*0-8050-3592-3*, Owl Bks.) Holt, Henry & Co.

—Philadelphia Fire. 1990. 240p. 18.95 o.p. (*0-8050-1266-4*) Holt, Henry & Co.

—Philadelphia Fire. 1991. (Vintage Contemporaries Ser.). 208p. pap. 12.00 o.s.i (*0-679-73650-6*, Vintage) Knopf Publishing Group.

—Reuben. 1987. 16.95 o.p. (*0-8050-0375-4*) Holt, Henry & Co.

—Reuben. 1988. 224p. pap. 7.95 o.p. (*0-14-010595-6*, Penguin Bks.) Viking Penguin.

—Sent for You Yesterday. 1998. 208p. pap. 14.00 (*0-395-87729-6*) Houghton Mifflin Co.

—Sent for You Yesterday. 1988. pap. 11.00 o.s.i (*0-679-72029-4*, Vintage) Knopf Publishing Group.

—Sent for You Yesterday. 1983. 208p. pap. 3.50 o.p. (*0-380-82644-5*, 82644-5, Avon Bks.) Morrow/Avon.

—Two Cities: A Love Story. 1998. 256p. tchr. ed. 24.00 (*0-395-85730-9*) Houghton Mifflin Co.

—Two Cities: A Love Story. 1999. 256p. pap. 13.00 (*0-618-00185-9*, Mariner Bks.) Houghton Mifflin Co. Trade & Reference Div.

Wiley, George E. Southern Plantation Stories & Sketches. 1977. (Black Heritage Library Collection). (Illus.). reprint ed. 18.95 (*0-8369-8836-1*) Ayer Co. Pubs., Inc.

Wilkinson, Crystal E. Water Street. 2002. 192p. 24.95 (*1-902881-59-1*) Toby Pr.

Willard, Tom. Buffalo Soldiers: A Novel. unabr. collector's ed. 1997. (Black Sabre Chronicles). audio 48.00 (*0-7366-3555-6*, 4200) Books on Tape, Inc.

—Buffalo Soldiers: A Novel. 1996. (Black Sabre Chronicles Ser.: Bk. 1). 336p. 22.95 o.p. (*0-312-86041-2*, Forge Bks.) Doherty, Tom Assocs., LLC.

—Buffalo Soldiers: A Novel. l.t. ed. 1997. (West-Hall Ser.). 441p. lib. bdg. 21.95 (*0-7838-1943-9*, Macmillan Reference USA) Gale Group.

—Buffalo Soldiers: A Novel. 1997. 12.04 (*0-606-20473-3*) Turtleback Bks.

—Buffalo Soliders. l.t. ed. 1997. (Black Sabre Chronicles Ser.: Vol. 1). 336p. mass mkt. 5.99 (*0-8125-5105-2*, Forge Bks.) Doherty, Tom Assocs., LLC.

—Sable Doughboys. 1996. (Black Sabre Chronicles: Bk. 2). 319p. 22.95 o.p. (*0-312-86040-4*, Forge Bks.) Doherty, Tom Assocs., LLC.

—Sable Doughboys. 1998. 12.04 (*0-606-19669-2*) Turtleback Bks.

—The Sable Doughboys. unabr. collector's ed. 1997. audio 48.00 (*0-7366-3672-2*, 4349) Books on Tape, Inc.

—The Stone Ponies. 320p. 2001. (Black Sabre Chronicles Ser.). mass mkt. 6.99 (*0-8125-6478-2*); 2000. (Black Sabre Chronicles Ser.: No. 4). 24.95 o.p. (*0-312-85763-2*) Doherty, Tom Assocs., LLC. (Forge Bks.).

—Sword of Valor. 2003. (Black Sabre Chronicles Ser.). (Illus.). 384p. 24.95 (*0-312-87385-9*, Tor Bks.) Doherty, Tom Assocs., LLC.

—Wings of Honor. 1998. (Black Sabre Chronicles Ser.: Vol. 3). (Illus.). 320p. 23.95 (*0-312-86967-3*, Forge Bks.); 1997. 299.40 o.s.i (*0-312-86053-6*, Tor Bks.); Bk. 3. 2000. (Black Sabre Chronicles Ser.: Vol. 3). 352p. mass mkt. 6.99 (*0-8125-6477-4*, Forge Bks.) Doherty, Tom Assocs., LLC.

Williams, Dennis A. Crossover: A Novel. 1992. 320p. 21.00 o.p. (*0-671-72640-4*) Summit Bks.

Williams, John A. The Angry Ones. 1996. 192p. pap. 11.00 o.p. (*0-393-31464-2*) Norton, W. W. & Co., Inc.

—Captain Blackman. 1988. (Classic Reprint Ser.). 336p. reprint ed. pap. 10.95 o.s.i (*0-938410-68-7*, Thunder's Mouth Pr.) Avalon Publishing Group.

—Captain Blackman. 2000. (Black Art Movement Ser.). ix, 264p. pap. 15.95 (*1-56689-096-9*) Coffee Hse. Pr.

—Click Song. 1987. (Contemporary Fiction Ser.). 430p. reprint ed. pap. 10.95 (*0-938410-43-1*, Thunder's Mouth Pr.) Avalon Publishing Group.

—Click Song. 1982. 13.95 o.p. (*0-395-31841-6*) Houghton Mifflin Co.

—Clifford's Blues. 1999. 272p. pap. 14.95 (*1-56689-080-2*) Coffee Hse. Pr.

—The Man Who Cried I Am. 1985. 400p. reprint ed. pap. 12.95 (*0-938410-24-5*, Thunder's Mouth Pr.) Avalon Publishing Group.

—The Man Who Cried I Am. 1967. 7.50 o.p. (*0-316-94143-3*) Little Brown & Co.

—Sons of Darkness, Sons of Light: A Novel of Some Probability. 1999. (Library of Black Literature). 279p. pap. text 16.95 (*1-55553-396-5*) Northeastern Univ. Pr.

Williams, Lori Aurelia. When Kambia Elaine Flew in from Neptune. l.t. ed. 2001. 369p. 22.95 (*0-7862-3657-4*) Thorndike Pr.

Williams, Sherley A. Dessa Rose. 1987. mass mkt. 6.50 o.s.i (*0-425-10337-4*) Berkley Publishing Group.

—Dessa Rose. abr. ed. 2000. audio 7.95 (*1-57815-148-1*, 1107, Media Bks. Audio Publishing) Media Bks., L. L. C.

—Dessa Rose: A Novel. 1999. 240p. pap. 13.00 (*0-688-16643-1*, Quill) HarperTrade.

—Dessa Rose: A Riveting Story of the South During Slavery. 1986. 256p. 15.95 o.p. (*0-688-05113-8*, Morrow, William & Co.) Morrow/Avon.

Williams, Shirley A. Dessa Rose. abr. ed. 1993. audio 15.95 o.p. (*1-55800-001-1*, 40000, Dove Audio) NewStar Media, Inc.

Williams, Vincent. Temples. 2000. 224p. 19.95 (*0-9647635-5-9*) La Caille Nous Publishing Co.

Williamson, Denise. The Dark Sun Rises: A Novel. 1999. (Roots of Faith Ser.: Bk. 1). 448p. pap. 12.99 (*1-55661-882-4*) Bethany Hse. Pubs.

—When Stars Begin to Fall. 2000. (Roots of Faith Ser.: Vol. 2). 448p. pap. 12.99 (*1-55661-883-2*) Bethany Hse. Pubs.

Wilson-Harris, Crystal. Good Intentions. 2001. (Arabesque Ser.). 256p. mass mkt. 5.99 (*1-58314-154-5*) BET Bks.

Wilson, P. B. Night Comes Swiftly. 1997. 350p. (Orig.). pap. 9.99 o.p. (*1-56507-718-0*) Harvest Hse. Pubs.

Wimberley, Darryl. A Rock & a Hard Place. 1999. 260p. 22.95 o.p. (*0-312-20504-X*, Saint Martin's Minotaur) St. Martin's Pr.

Winer, Andrew. The Color Midnight Made. 2003. 288p. pap. 13.00 (*0-7434-3992-9*, Washington Square Pr.); 2002. 272p. 24.00 (*0-7434-3990-2*, Atria) Simon & Schuster.

Winters, Angela. Dangerous Memories. 2002. 256p. mass mkt. 6.99 (*1-58314-334-3*) Kensington Publishing Corp.

—Know by Heart. 2001. (Arabesque Ser.). 256p. mass mkt. 5.99 (*1-58314-215-0*) BET Bks.

—Sudden Love. 1999. 288p. mass mkt. 4.99 (*1-58314-023-9*) BET Bks.

Wise, John S. The Lion's Skin: A Historical Novel & a Novel History. 1977. (Black Heritage Library Collection). reprint ed. 35.95 (*0-8369-9073-0*) Ayer Co. Pubs., Inc.

Woods, Paula L. Inner City Blues: A Charlotte Justice Novel. 1999. 316p. 23.95 (*0-393-04680-X*) Norton, W. W. & Co., Inc.

—Stormy Weather. 304p. 2003. mass mkt. 6.99 (*0-449-00724-3*, One World/Ballantine); 2002. pap. 14.00 (*0-345-44908-8*, Ballantine Bks.) Ballantine Bks.

—Stormy Weather: A Charlotte Justice Novel. 2001. 320p. 24.95 (*0-393-02021-5*) Norton, W. W. & Co., Inc.

Woods, Stuart. Chiefs. 1982. pap. 3.95 o.p. (*0-553-24080-3*) Bantam Bks.

—Chiefs. 1999. 432p. mass mkt. 7.99 (*0-380-70347-5*, Avon Bks.) Morrow/Avon.

—Chiefs. 1981. 14.95 o.s.i (*0-393-01461-4*) Norton, W. W. & Co., Inc.

—Chiefs. l.t. ed. 2001. (Thorndike Basic Ser.). 701p. 30.95 (*0-7862-3150-5*) Thorndike Pr.

Wren, M. K. Neely Jones: The Medusa Pool. 1999. 313p. 24.95 (*0-312-24223-9*, Saint Martin's Minotaur) St. Martin's Pr.

Wright, Bill. Sunday You Learn How to Box. 2000. 224p. pap. 12.00 (*0-684-85795-2*, Touchstone) Simon & Schuster.

Wright, Charles. Absolutely Nothing to Get Alarmed About: The Complete Novels of Charles Wright. 1993. 624p. pap. 13.00 o.p. (*0-06-096958-X*, Perennial) HarperTrade.

—The Wig. 2003. (NEA Heritage & Preservation Ser.: Vol. 2). 192p. pap. 14.95 (*1-56279-127-3*) Mercury Hse.

Wright, Courtni. New Beginning. 2000. (Arabesque Ser.). 256p. mass mkt. 5.99 (*1-58314-189-8*) BET Bks.

Wright, Richard. Eight Men. 1987. (Classic Reprint Ser.). 272p. reprint ed. pap. 12.95 o.p. (*0-938410-39-3*, Thunder's Mouth Pr.) Avalon Publishing Group.

—Eight Men. 1969. pap. 1.50 o.s.i (*0-515-02034-6*, V2034, Jove) Berkley Publishing Group.

—Eight Men. 1996. 272p. pap. 13.00 (*0-06-097681-0*, Perennial) HarperTrade.

—The Outsider. 2003. 672p. pap. 13.95 (*0-06-053925-9*, Perennial) HarperTrade.

—Uncle Tom's Children. 1993. (Perennial Library). 336p. reprint ed. pap. 7.00 (*0-06-081251-6*, P 988, Perennial) HarperTrade.

Wright, Richard A. Native Son. Date not set. 371p. 26.95 (*0-8488-2577-2*) Amereon, Ltd.

—Native Son. 1997. 594p. 49.95 (*1-56849-694-X*) Buccaneer Bks., Inc.

—Native Son. audio 19.95 Filmic Archives.

—Native Son. abr. ed. 1989. 432p. pap. 7.95 (*0-06-080977-9*) HarperCollins Pubs.

—Native Son. (Perennial Classics Ser.). 2004. 528p. pap. 13.00 (*0-06-092980-4*, Perennial); 1986. 398p. mass mkt. 4.95 o.p. (*0-06-080855-1*, P 855, Perennial); 1942. mass mkt. 3.95 o.p. (*0-06-083055-7*, P 3055, Perennial); 2003. 432p. pap. 12.95 (*0-06-053348-X*, Perennial); 1998. audio 18.00 (*0-89845-916-8*, 393493, HarperAudio); 1993. 624p. reprint ed. pap. 7.00 o.p. (*0-06-081249-4*, P 977, Perennial); 1969. reprint ed. 24.95 o.p. (*0-06-014762-8*) HarperTrade.

—Native Son. mass mkt. 0.35 o.p. (*0-451-00794-8*, Signet Bks.); mass mkt. 0.75 o.p. (*0-451-02598-9*, Signet Bks.); mass mkt. 0.75 o.p. (*0-451-50081-4*, Signet Classics) NAL.

—Native Son. 1989. 4.99 o.p. (*0-517-01227-8*) Random Hse. Value Publishing.

—Native Son. unabr. ed. 1998. audio 102.00 audio 102.00 (*0-7887-2112-7*, 95437E7) Recorded Bks., LLC.

—Native Son. l.t. ed. 1993. 619p. lib. bdg. 22.95 (*0-8161-5787-1*) Thorndike Pr.

—Untitled Richard A. Wright. 2003. (Perennial Classics Ser.). pap. 303.20 (*0-06-057379-1*, Perennial) HarperTrade.

Wright, Sarah E. This Child's Gonna Live. 1986. 304p. (C). reprint ed. pap. 10.95 o.p. (*0-935312-67-6*); 2nd ed. 2002. 320p. pap. 15.95 (*1-55861-397-8*) Feminist Pr. at The City Univ. of New York.

Wright, Zara. Black & White Tangled Threads. reprint ed. 45.00 (*0-404-11378-8*) AMS Pr., Inc.

Yarbrough, Camille. Watch Hour. 2015. 14.95 (*0-399-22614-1*, G. P. Putnam's Sons) Penguin Group (USA) Inc.

Youmans, Marly. The Wolf Pit. 2001. 352p. 24.00 o.p. (*0-374-29195-0*) Farrar, Straus & Giroux.

—The Wolf Pit. 2003. 352p. pap. 14.00 (*0-15-602714-3*, Harvest Bks.) Harcourt Trade Pubs.

Young, L. M. Michael's Journal Bk. 1: Being the Journals of Michael Cooke Holt, 1917-1925. 2001. 148p. pap. 17.95 (*0-7596-4694-5*) 1stBooks Library.

Young, Margaret Blair & Gray, Darius. The Last Mile of the Way, 3. 2003. (Standing on the Promises Ser.: 3). xvi, 448p. 21.95 (*1-57008-904-3*, 5730) Deseret Bk. Co.

Young, Margaret Blair & Gray, Darius Aidan. One More River to Cross. 2000. (Standing on the Promises Ser.: Vol. 1). xxiii, 337p. 19.95 (*1-57345-629-2*, Bookcraft, Inc.) Deseret Bk. Co.

Youngblood, Shay. Soul Kiss. 1998. 224p. 13.00 (*1-57322-658-0*, Riverhead Trade (Paperbacks)) Berkley Publishing Group.

—Soul Kiss. 1997. 224p. 21.00 o.s.i (*1-57322-063-9*, Riverhead Bks. (Hardcovers)) Putnam Publishing Group, The.

## AMISH—FICTION

Bender, Carrie. Beechwood Acres: Joy's Journal #2. 2003. pap. 7.95 (*1-930353-57-X*) Masthof Pr.

—Birch Hollow Schoolmarm. 1999. (Dora's Diary Ser.: Bk. 1). (Illus.). 192p. pap. 8.99 (*0-8361-9095-5*) Herald Pr.

—Birch Hollow Schoolmarm. l.t. ed. 2002. (Christian Fiction Ser.). 189p. 27.95 (*0-7862-4584-0*) Thorndike Pr.

—Birch Hollow Schoolmarm. 1999. E-Book 8.99 (*0-585-32381-X*) netLibrary, Inc.

—A Fruitful Vine. 1996. (Miriam's Journal Ser.: Vol. 1). 192p. pap. 8.99 (*0-8361-3613-6*) Herald Pr.

—A Fruitful Vine. 1993. E-Book 7.99 (*0-585-28248-X*) netLibrary, Inc.

—A Fruitful Vine Bk. 1: Miriam's Journal. 2002. (Five Star Christian Fiction Ser.). (Illus.). 187p. 24.95 (*0-7862-4425-9*, Five Star) Gale Group.

—Tall Cedars Homestead: Joy's Journal #1. 2002. pap. 7.95 (*1-930353-56-1*) Masthof Pr.

—A Treasured Friendship. 1996. (Miriam's Journal Ser.: Vol. 4). 160p. (gr. 8-12). pap. 8.99 (*0-8361-9033-5*) Herald Pr.

—Woodland Dell's Secret. 2002. (Whispering Brook Ser.: Bk. 5). (Illus.). 176p. pap. 8.99 (*0-8361-9169-2*) Herald Pr.

Borntrager, Mary Christner. Andy. l.t. ed. 2002. 161p. 25.95 (*0-7862-4029-6*) Gale Group.

—Andy. 1993. E-Book 7.99 (*0-585-26279-9*) netLibrary, Inc.

—Annie. l.t. ed. 2000. (Christian Fiction Ser.). (Illus.). 173p. 23.95 o.p. (*0-7862-2379-0*) Thorndike Pr.

—Annie. 1997. E-Book 7.99 (*0-585-26280-2*) netLibrary, Inc.

—Daniel. l.t. ed. 2000. (Christian Fiction Ser.). 191p. 23.95 (*0-7862-2859-8*) Thorndike Pr.

—Daniel. 1991. E-Book 7.99 (*0-585-16205-0*) netLibrary, Inc.

—Ellie. l.t. ed. 2001. (Christian Fiction Ser.). 208p. 23.95 (*0-7862-3383-4*) Thorndike Pr.

—Ellie. 1988. E-Book 7.99 (*0-585-18195-0*) netLibrary, Inc.

—Rebecca. l.t. ed. 2001. (Thorndike Christian Fiction Ser.). 245p. 24.95 (*0-7862-3252-8*) Thorndike Pr.

Delffs, Dudley J. The Judas Tree. 1999. (Father Grif Mystery Ser.: Vol. 2). 320p. pap. 10.99 o.p. (*0-7642-2087-X*) Bethany Hse. Pubs.

—The Judas Tree. l.t. ed. 2002. 557p. 25.95 (*0-7862-4245-0*) Gale Group.

Gaus, P. L. Blood of the Prodigal: An Ohio Amish Mystery. 1999. (Ohio Amish Mysteries Ser.). 230p. pap. 12.95 (*0-8214-1277-9*); 24.95 (*0-8214-1276-0*) Ohio Univ. Pr.

—Broken English: An Ohio Amish Mystery. 2000. (Ohio Amish Mysteries Ser.). 205p. 24.95 (*0-8214-1325-2*); pap. 12.95 (*0-8214-1326-0*) Ohio Univ. Pr. (Ohio Univ. Ctr. for International Studies).

—Cast a Blue Shadow: An Ohio Amish Mystery. 2003. (Ohio Amish Mysteries Ser.). 24.95 (*0-8214-1529-8*); pap. 12.95 (*0-8214-1530-1*) Ohio Univ. Pr.

—Clouds Without Rain: An Ohio Amish Mystery. 2001. (Ohio Amish Mysteries Ser.). vii, 196p. 24.95 (*0-8214-1379-1*); pap. 12.95 (*0-8214-1380-5*) Ohio Univ. Pr.

Harper, Karen. Down to the Bone. 2004. mass mkt. (*0-7783-2115-0*); 2000. 408p. mass mkt. (*1-55166-589-1*, 1-66589-2) Harlequin Enterprises, Ltd. (Mira Bks.).

Hoag, Tami. Sarah's Sin. 1992. 256p. mass mkt. 7.50 (*0-553-56050-6*); 1991. (Loveswept Ser.: No. 480). 192p. mass mkt. 2.75 o.s.i (*0-553-44145-0*) Bantam Bks.

—Sarah's Sin. l.t. ed. 2000. 254p. lib. bdg. 25.95 o.p. (*1-58547-034-1*) Ctr. Point Large Print.

Lewis, Beverly. The Covenant. 2002. (Abram's Daughters Ser.: No. 1). 320p. 16.99 (*0-7642-2717-3*); 320p. pap. 12.99 (*0-7642-2330-5*); pap. 16.99 (*0-7642-2719-X*); 400p. pap. 16.99 (*0-7642-2718-1*) Bethany Hse. Pubs.

—The Crossroad. 1999. 320p. pap. 12.99 (*0-7642-2212-0*); 320p. text 15.99 o.p. (*0-7642-2239-2*); 1p. audio 15.99 o.p. (*0-7642-2238-4*); 352p. pap. 16.99 o.p. (*0-7642-2240-6*) Bethany Hse. Pubs.

—The Crossroad. l.t. ed. 2000. 369p. 25.95 (*0-7862-2712-5*) Thorndike Pr.

—October Song: Lancaster County is Cloaked in Autumn Splendor, & a Reunion is in the Air... abr. ed. 2001. pap. 15.99 (*0-7642-2589-8*) Bethany Hse. Pubs.

—October Song: Lancaster County is Cloaked in Autumn Splendor, & a Reunion is in the Air... l.t. ed. 2002. 317p. 28.95 (*0-7862-4028-8*) Gale Group.

—The Postcard. 1999. 1p. audio 15.99 o.p. (*0-7642-2223-6*); 320p. pap. 12.99 (*0-7642-2211-2*) Bethany Hse. Pubs.

—Postcard. l.t. ed. 1999. 384p. pap. 16.99 o.p. (*0-7642-2225-2*) Bethany Hse. Pubs.

—The Postcard. l.t. ed. 2000. (Christian Romance Ser.). 408p. 25.95 (*0-7862-2713-3*) Thorndike Pr.

—The Reckoning. (Heritage of Lancaster County Ser.). 288p. 2000. pap. 6.99 (*0-7642-2475-1*); 1998. pap. 12.99 (*1-55661-868-9*) Bethany Hse. Pubs.

—The Reckoning. l.t. ed. 1999. (Christian Fiction Ser.). 383p. 25.95 (*0-7862-1691-3*) Thorndike Pr.

—The Redemption of Sarah Cain. 2000. (Heritage of Lancaster County Ser.). 320p. 16.99 (*0-7642-2388-7*); 320p. pap. 12.99 (*0-7642-2329-1*); 1p. pap. 15.99 o.p. (*0-7642-2389-5*); 384p. pap. 15.99 o.p. (*0-7642-2390-9*) Bethany Hse. Pubs.

—The Redemption of Sarah Cain. l.t. ed. 2001. (Thorndike Press Large Print Christian Romance Ser.). 384p. 25.95 (*0-7862-3113-0*) Thorndike Pr.

Myers, Tamar. No Use Dying over Spilled Milk: A Pennsylvania-Dutch Mystery with Recipes. 1996. 272p. 20.95 o.p. (*0-525-94099-5*, Dutton) Dutton/Plume.

—No Use Dying over Spilled Milk: A Pennsylvania-Dutch Mystery with Recipes. 1997. 272p. mass mkt. 5.99 (*0-451-18854-3*, Signet Bks.) NAL.

Picoult, Jodi. Plain Truth. 2000. 416p. 24.95 (*0-671-77612-6*, Atria); 2001. (Illus.). 432p. reprint ed. pap. 14.00 (*0-671-77613-4*, Washington Square Pr.) Simon & Schuster.

Stutzman, Ervin R. Tobias of the Amish: A True Story of Tangled Strands in Faith, Family & Community. 2001. 352p. (Illus.). pap. 15.99 (*0-8361-9170-6*); 22.99 (*0-8361-9190-0*) Herald Pr.

Wojtasik, Ted. No Strange Fire. 1996. 400p. (Orig.). pap. 14.99 (*0-8361-9041-6*) Herald Pr.

—No Strange Fire. 1996. (Orig.). E-Book 14.99 (*0-585-18192-6*) netLibrary, Inc.

Yoder Miller, Evie. Eyes at the Window. 2003. 22.95 (*1-56148-405-9*) Good Bks.

**ASIAN AMERICANS—FICTION**

Chan, David Marshall. Goblin Fruit. 2003. 226p. 21.95 (*1-893956-32-6*) Context Bks.

Chang, Diana. The Frontiers of Love. E-Book 12.95 (*0-295-98003-6*); 1993. 246p. pap. 14.95 (*0-295-97326-9*) Univ. of Washington Pr.

Cunningham, E. V., pseud. The Case of the Angry Actress. 1984. 192p. pap. 2.95 o.p. (*0-440-11093-9*) Dell Publishing.

—The Case of the Kidnapped Angel. 192p. 1983. (Masao Masuto Mystery Ser.: No. 5). pap. 2.95 o.p. (*0-440-11224-9*); 1982. 12.95 o.s.i (*0-385-28118-8*, Delacorte Pr.) Dell Publishing.

—The Case of the Kidnapped Angel. l.t. ed. 1983. 216p. pap. 7.95 o.p. (*0-8161-3471-5*, Macmillan Reference USA) Gale Group.

—The Case of the Murdered MacKenzie. l.t. ed. 1985. (Nightingale Ser.). 386p. 9.95 o.p. (*0-8161-3771-4*, Macmillan Reference USA) Gale Group.

—The Case of the One-Penny Orange. l.t. ed. 1982. (Nightingale Ser.). lib. bdg. 11.95 o.p. (*0-8161-3334-4*, Macmillan Reference USA) Gale Group.

—The Case of the One-Penny Orange. 1982. (Masao Masuto Mystery Ser.). 176p. pap. o.p. (*0-03-059858-3*, Owl Bks.) Holt, Henry & Co.

—The Case of the Poisoned Eclairs. 1980. pap. 2.25 o.p. (*0-440-11256-7*) Dell Publishing.

—The Case of the Poisoned Eclairs. 1982. (Nightingale Ser.). pap. 9.95 o.p. (*0-8161-3333-6*, Macmillan Reference USA) Gale Group.

—The Case of the Poisoned Eclairs. 1979. o.p. (*0-03-044721-6*) Holt, Henry & Co.

—The Case of the Russian Diplomat. 1979. 1.75 o.s.i (*0-515-04881-X*, 04881-X, Jove) Berkley Publishing Group.

—The Case of the Russian Diplomat. (Masao Masuto Mystery Ser.). 1982. 176p. pap. o.p. (*0-03-059857-5*, Owl Bks.); 1978. o.p. (*0-03-022456-X*) Holt, Henry & Co.

—The Case of the Sliding Pool. 1983. pap. 2.95 o.p. (*0-440-12092-6*); 1981. 10.95 o.s.i (*0-440-01114-0*, Delacorte Pr.) Dell Publishing.

—The Case of the Sliding Pool. 1982. (Nightingale Ser.). pap. 9.95 o.p. (*0-8161-3348-4*, Macmillan Reference USA) Gale Group.

Esaki-Smith, Anna. Meeting Luciano. 1999. 252p. tchr. ed. 18.95 (*1-56512-215-1*, 72215) Algonquin Bks. of Chapel Hill.

—Meeting Luciano. 2000. 272p. pap. 12.00 (*0-345-43682-2*, Ballantine Bks.) Ballantine Bks.

Glass, Leslie. Burning Time. 1995. (April Woo Suspense Novels Ser.). 464p. mass mkt. 7.50 (*0-553-56172-3*) Bantam Bks.

—Hanging Time. 1996. (April Woo Suspense Novels Ser.). 448p. mass mkt. 7.50 (*0-553-57191-5*) Bantam Bks.

—Judging Time. 1998. (April Woo Suspense Novels Ser.). 320p. 24.95 o.p. (*0-525-94404-4*) Dutton/Plume.

—Judging Time. 1999. (April Woo Suspense Novels Ser.). 400p. mass mkt. 6.99 (*0-451-19550-7*, Signet Bks.) NAL.

—Loving Time. 1997. (April Woo Suspense Novels Ser.). 432p. reprint ed. mass mkt. 6.99 (*0-553-57209-1*) Bantam Bks.

—Stealing Time. 1999. (April Woo Suspense Novels Ser.). 320p. 24.95 o.p. (*0-525-94460-5*) Dutton/Plume.

—Stealing Time. 2000. (April Woo Suspense Novels Ser.). 400p. reprint ed. mass mkt. 6.99 (*0-451-19965-0*, Signet Bks.) NAL.

Hagedorn, Jessica. Charlie Chan Is Dead. 2004. 592p. pap. 18.00 (*0-14-200390-5*) Penguin Group (USA) Inc.

Huo, T. C. Land of Smiles: A Novel. 224p. 2000. 12.95 o.s.i (*0-452-28185-7*, Plume); 1999. 23.95 (*0-525-94281-5*, Dutton) Dutton/Plume.

Jen, Gish. Who's Irish? 2000. (Contemporaries Ser.). 224p. pap. 12.00 (*0-375-70592-9*, Vintage) Knopf Publishing Group.

—Who's Irish? Stories. 1999. 224p. 22.00 (*0-375-40621-2*) Knopf, Alfred A. Inc.

Kim, Nancy. Chinhominey's Secret: A Novel. 1999. 240p. 22.95 (*1-882593-28-6*) Bridge Works Publishing Co., Inc.

Law-Yone, Wendy. The Coffin Tree. 1988. (Asian Voices Ser.). 208p. reprint ed. pap. 8.95 o.p. (*0-8070-8301-1*, BP 781) Beacon Pr.

—The Coffin Tree. 1983. 195p. 12.95 o.s.i (*0-394-52957-X*) Knopf, Alfred A. Inc.

—The Coffin Tree. 2003. 208p. pap. 15.95 (*0-8101-5141-3*, TriQuarterly Bks.) Northwestern Univ. Pr.

Lee, Don. Yellow: Stories. 2002. 256p. pap. 13.95 (*0-393-32308-0*); 2001. 192p. 22.95 (*0-393-02562-4*) Norton, W. W. & Co., Inc.

Leong, Russell Charles. Phoenix Eyes & Other Stories. 2000. (Scott & Laurie Oki Series in Asian American Studies). 172p. 35.00 (*0-295-97944-5*); pap. 16.95 (*0-295-97945-3*) Univ. of Washington Pr.

Massey, Sujata. The Floating Girl. 2000. 304p. 24.00 (*0-06-019229-1*) HarperCollins Pubs.

—The Floating Girl. 2001. 384p. mass mkt. 6.99 (*0-06-109735-7*, Avon Bks.) Morrow/Avon.

—The Flower Master. 1999. 304p. 24.00 (*0-06-019228-3*) HarperCollins Pubs.

—The Flower Master. 2000. 400p. mass mkt. 6.99 (*0-06-109734-9*, HarperTorch) Morrow/Avon.

—The Flower Master. 2000. 13.04 (*0-606-21840-8*) Turtleback Bks.

—The Salaryman's Wife. 1997. 432p. mass mkt. 7.50 (*0-06-104443-1*, HarperTorch) Morrow/Avon.

—Salarymans Wife Arc. 2000. 368p. pap. 5.99 (*0-06-104384-2*) HarperCollins Pubs.

—Zen Attitude. 1998. 320p. mass mkt. 6.99 (*0-06-104444-X*, HarperTorch) Morrow/Avon.

McFerrin, Linda W. Namako: Sea Cucumber. 1998. 256p. (YA). pap. 14.95 (*1-56689-075-6*) Coffee Hse. Pr.

Nakamura, Hiroshi. Treadmill: A Documentary Novel. 1996. 220p. pap. 16.95 (*0-88962-595-6*) Mosaic Pr.

Ong, Han. Fixer Chao. 2001. 377p. 25.00 (*0-374-15575-5*) Farrar, Straus & Giroux.

—Fixer Chao. 2002. 384p. pap. 14.00 (*0-312-42053-6*) Picador.

Ozeki, Ruth L. My Year of Meats. 1999. 384p. 14.00 (*0-14-028046-4*); 1998. 432p. 23.95 o.p. (*0-670-87904-5*, Viking) Viking Penguin.

Pak, Ty. Moonbay: Short Stories by Ty Pak. 1999. 214p. pap. 12.00 (*0-9667458-1-7*) Woodhouse.

Revoyr, Nina. The Necessary Hunger. 1997. 368p. 22.50 (*0-684-83234-8*, Simon & Schuster) Simon & Schuster.

Rizzuto, R. Why She Left Us: A Novel. 2000. 304p. pap. 13.00 (*0-06-093182-5*, Perennial) HarperTrade.

Rizzuto, Rahna Reiko. Why She Left Us: A Novel. 1999. 304p. 24.00 o.s.i (*0-06-019370-0*) HarperCollins Pubs.

Shepard, Karen. An Empire of Women. 2002. 272p. pap. 12.95 (*0-425-18456-0*) Berkley Publishing Group.

—An Empire of Women. l.t. ed. 2001. (Hardcover Ser.). 281p. 29.95 (*1-58724-077-7*, Wheeler Publishing, Inc.) Gale Group.

—An Empire of Women. 2000. 320p. 24.95 o.s.i (*0-399-14667-9*) Penguin Group (USA) Inc.

Sunga, David I. Mariko Tan & the Mystery of the Missing Money. E-Book (*1-84045-026-6*) Online Originals.

Tan, Amy. The Kitchen God's Wife. 1996. mass mkt. 6.99 (*0-8041-9897-7*); 1992. 544p. mass mkt. 7.99 (*0-8041-0753-X*) Ballantine Bks. (Ivy Bks.).

—The Kitchen God's Wife. 1993. 432p. pap. 13.00 (*0-679-74808-3*, Vintage) Knopf Publishing Group.

—The Kitchen God's Wife. unabr. ed. 1993. audio 39.95 o.p. (*0-7871-0018-8*, Dove Audio); 39.95 o.p. (*1-55800-434-3*, 133134);Set. 15.95 o.p. (*1-55800-266-9*, 391032) NewStar Media, Inc.

—The Kitchen God's Wife. 1991. 320p. 22.95 o.p. (*0-399-13578-2*) Putnam Publishing Group, The.

—The Kitchen God's Wife. 1992. 14.04 (*0-606-01177-3*) Turtleback Bks.

Thomson, Maynard F. Dreams of Gold. 2001. 464p. E-Book 4.95 (*0-7595-4631-2*); 2001. 464p. E-Book 4.95 (*0-7595-6629-1*); 2001. 464p. E-Book 4.95 (*0-7595-8638-1*); 2001. 464p. E-Book 4.95 (*0-7595-9699-9*); 2001. 464p. E-Book 4.95 (*0-7595-0628-0*); 2000. 464p. mass mkt. 6.99 (*0-446-60775-4*); 1999. 452p. 22.00 o.p. (*0-446-52445-X*) Warner Bks., Inc.

Watanna, Onoto. A Half Caste & Other Writings. Moser, Linda Trinh & Rooney, Elizabeth, eds. 2003. (Asian American Experience Ser.). 208p. text 34.95 (*0-252-02782-5*); pap. text 16.95 (*0-252-07094-1*) Univ. of Illinois Pr.

Yamanaka, Lois-Ann. Heads by Harry. 1999. 336p. 24.00 o.p. (*0-374-16850-4*) Farrar, Straus & Giroux.

—Heads by Harry. 2000. 320p. pap. 13.00 (*0-380-73316-1*) Morrow/Avon.

Yoshikawa, Mako. One Hundred & One Ways. 2000. 288p. pap. 12.95 (*0-553-37969-0*, Spectra) Bantam Bks.

# B

**BLACKS—FICTION**

Antoni, Robert. Blessed Is the Fruit. 1997. 399p. 25.00 o.p. (*0-8050-4925-8*) Holt, Henry & Co.

Beyala, Calixthe. Loukoum: The Little Prince of Belleville. 1995. (African Writers Ser.). 177p. pap. 10.95 (*0-435-90968-1*) Heinemann.

Colter, Cyrus. City of Light: A Novel. 1993. 352p. 22.95 o.p. (*1-56025-059-3*); pap. 12.95 o.p. (*1-56025-061-5*) Avalon Publishing Group. (Thunder's Mouth Pr.).

—City of Light: A Novel. 1998. 432p. pap. 22.00 (*0-8101-5080-8*, TriQuarterly Bks.) Northwestern Univ. Pr.

Dadie, Bernard B. An African in Paris. Hatch, Karen C., tr. from FRE. 1994. Tr. of Negre a Paris. 184p. text 32.50 (*0-252-02040-5*); 136p. pap. text 16.95 (*0-252-06407-0*) Univ. of Illinois Pr.

De Duras, Claire. Ourika: An English Translation. Fowles, John, tr. from FRE. & frwd. by. 1994. (MLA Texts & Translations Ser.: No. 3b). xxxiii, 47p. (Orig.). pap. 7.95 (*0-87352-780-1*, P003P) Modern Language Assn. of America.

—Ourika: The Original French Text. DeJean, Joan, ed. & intro. by. Waller, Margaret, intro. 1994. (MLA Texts & Translations Ser.: No. 3a). (FRE.). xxviii, 45p. (Orig.). pap. 6.95 (*0-87352-779-8*, Q003P) Modern Language Assn. of America.

De Duras, Madame. Ourika: Madame de Duras. Little, Roger, ed. 2nd rev. ed. 1998. (Exeter French Texts). (FRE., Illus.). 136p. pap. 25.95 (*0-85989-573-4*) Univ. of Exeter Pr. GBR. *Dist:* Brown, David Bk. Co.

Durfort, Claire de. Ourika. Fowles, John, tr. ltd. ed. 1977. 110.00 o.p. (*0-935072-01-2*) Taylor, W. Thomas Inc.

Fraser, George MacDonald. Black Ajax. 256p. 1999. pap. 12.95 (*0-7867-0618-X*); 1998. 23.00 o.p. (*0-7867-0553-1*) Avalon Publishing Group. (Carroll & Graf Pubs.).

Greenhall, Ken. Lenoir. (GER.). (*3-612-27475-9*) Econ-Verlag GmbH DEU. *Dist:* International Bk. Import Service, Inc.

—Lenoir. 1999. 246p. pap. o.p. (*1-58195-013-6*); 1998. 272p. 24.00 o.p. (*0-944072-93-3*) Steerforth Pr. (Zoland Bks., Inc.).

Hill, Reginald. Blood Sympathy. 1996. (WWL Mystery Ser.). per. (*0-373-26210-8*, 1-26210-4, Worldwide Library) Harlequin Enterprises, Ltd.

—Blood Sympathy, Set. unabr. ed. 1998. audio 69.95 (*1-85903-203-6*) Magna Story Sound GBR. *Dist:* Ulverscroft Large Print Bks., Ltd.

—Blood Sympathy. 1994. 224p. 19.95 o.p. (*0-312-11249-1*, Saint Martin's Minotaur) St. Martin's Pr.

—Blood Sympathy. l.t. ed. 1995. (Ulverscroft Large Print Ser.). 464p. 29.99 o.p. (*0-7089-3368-8*, Ulverscroft) Thorpe, F. A. Pubs. GBR. *Dist:* Ulverscroft Large Print Bks., Ltd., Ulverscroft Large Print Canada, Ltd.

—Born Guilty. 1996. mass mkt. (*0-373-26226-4*, 1-26226-0, Worldwide Library) Harlequin Enterprises, Ltd.

—Born Guilty. unabr. ed. 1998. audio 69.95 (*1-85903-234-6*) Magna Story Sound GBR. *Dist:* Ulverscroft Large Print Bks., Ltd.

—Born Guilty. 1995. 240p. 20.95 o.p. (*0-312-13032-5*, Saint Martin's Minotaur) St. Martin's Pr.

—Born Guilty. l.t. ed. 1996. (Ulverscroft Large Print Ser.). 416p. 29.99 o.p. (*0-7089-3571-0*, Ulverscroft) Thorpe, F. A. Pubs. GBR. *Dist:* Ulverscroft Large Print Bks., Ltd., Ulverscroft Large Print Canada, Ltd.

—Killing the Lawyers. 1998. per. (*0-373-26298-1*, 1-26298-9, Mira Bks.) Harlequin Enterprises, Ltd.

—Killing the Lawyers. unabr. ed. 1998. audio 83.95 (*1-85903-235-4*) Magna Story Sound GBR. *Dist:* Ulverscroft Large Print Bks., Ltd.

—Killing the Lawyers. 1997. (Joe Sixsmith Mysteries Ser.). 336p. 23.95 o.p. (*0-312-16877-2*, Saint Martin's Minotaur) St. Martin's Pr.

—Singing the Sadness. 2001. (WWL Mystery Ser.: No. 371). 251p. mass mkt. (*0-373-26371-6*, 1-26371-4, Worldwide Library) Harlequin Enterprises, Ltd.

—Singing the Sadness. 2nd ed. 1999. 352p. 23.95 (*0-312-24238-7*, Saint Martin's Minotaur) St. Martin's Pr.

—Singing the Sadness. l.t. ed. 2000. (Charnwood Large Print Ser.). 392p. 31.99 (*0-7089-9143-2*, Ulverscroft) Thorpe, F. A. Pubs. GBR. *Dist:* Ulverscroft Large Print Bks., Ltd., Ulverscroft Large Print Canada, Ltd.

Hopkinson, Nalo, ed. Mojo: Conjure Stories. 2003. 352p. pap. 13.95 (*0-446-67929-1*, Aspect) Warner Bks., Inc.

Lansens, Lori. Rush Home Road. 2002. 400p. 23.95 o.p. (*0-316-06902-7*) Little Brown & Co.

Magagula, Modison Salayedvwa, et al. The Rainbow Flute: A Collection of Short Stories Translated from Indigenous Languages to Reflect the Spectrum of Black Experience in Southern Africa. 1997. (Illus.). (*0-7960-1098-6*) Shuter & Shooter.

Magona, Sindiwe. Mother to Mother. (Bluestreak Ser.). 216p. 2000. pap. 13.00 (*0-8070-0949-0*); 1999. 20.00 o.p. (*0-8070-0948-2*) Beacon Pr.

Magona, Sindiwe, et al, contrib. by. Mother to Mother. 1998. 210p. 22.00 (*0-86486-433-7*) Interlink Publishing Group, Inc.

Mda, Zakes. Ways of Dying. 1995. (Southern African Writing Ser.). 192p. (Orig.). pap. 10.95 o.p. (*0-19-571106-8*) Oxford Univ. Pr., Inc.

—Ways of Dying. 2002. 216p. (Orig.). pap. 13.00 (*0-312-42091-9*) Picador.

Parks, Tim. Judge Savage. 2003. 456p. 22.95 (*1-55970-691-0*) Arcade Publishing, Inc.

Phillips, Caryl. The Final Passage. 1985. 208p. o.p. (*0-571-13437-8*) Faber & Faber Ltd.

—The Final Passage. 1985. 208p. pap. 8.95 o.p. (*0-571-13438-6*) Faber & Faber, Inc.

—The Final Passage. 1995. 208p. pap. 15.00 (*0-679-75931-X*, Vintage) Knopf Publishing Group.

—The Final Passage. 1990. 208p. pap. 7.95 o.p. (*0-14-012796-8*, Penguin Bks.) Viking Penguin.

Phillips, Mike. Image to Die For: A Sam Dean Mystery. 1997. 239p. 22.95 o.p. (*0-312-15147-0*, Saint Martin's Minotaur) St. Martin's Pr.

—The Late Candidate. 1991. 320p. mass mkt. 3.99 o.s.i (*0-440-20942-0*) Dell Publishing.

—The Late Candidate. 1990. 256p. 17.95 o.p. (*0-312-04866-1*, Saint Martin's Minotaur) St. Martin's Pr.

—Point of Darkness: A Sam Dean Mystery. 1995. 310p. 21.95 o.p. (0-312-11875-9, Saint Martin's Minotaur) St. Martin's Pr.
Price, Richard & Price, Sally. Enigma Variations. (Illus.). 176p. 1995. (C). 18.95 (0-674-25726-X); 1997. reprint ed. 12.95 (0-674-25728-6) Harvard Univ. Pr.
Reed, Ishmael. The Freelance Pallbearers. 1975. 155p. reprint ed. 7.50 o.p. (0-911860-46-0) Chatham Bookseller.
—The Freelance Pallbearers. 1977. pap. 1.75 o.p. (0-380-00987-0, 32649-3, Avon Bks.) Morrow/Avon.
Slaughter, Carolyn. The Black Englishman. 2004. (0-374-11399-8) Farrar, Straus & Giroux.
Zobel, Joseph. Black Shack Alley. Warner, Keith Q., tr. from FRE. Orig. Title: La Rue Cases-Negres. (Illus.). 184p. reprint ed. 1991. 25.00 o.s.i (0-914478-67-2); 1980. pap. 14.50 (0-914478-68-0) Rienner, Lynne Pubs., Inc. (Three Continents).

# C

## CHINESE AMERICANS—FICTION

Buck, Pearl S. Kinfolk. 3rd ed. 1996. (Oriental Novels of Pearl S. Buck Ser.). 418p. reprint ed. pap. 11.95 (1-55921-156-3) Moyer Bell.
Burrows, Geraldine. Chinatown Mission. 2002. (Five Star First Edition Women's Fiction Ser.). 381p. 25.95 (0-7862-3613-2, Five Star) Gale Group.
Chun, Pam. The Money Dragon. 352p. 2003. pap. 14.00 (1-57071-867-9); 2002. (Illus.). 24.00 (1-57071-866-0) Sourcebooks, Inc. (Sourcebooks Landmark).
Glass, Leslie. Tracking Time. l.t. ed. 2001. (Wheeler Large Print Book Ser.). 437p. 28.95 (1-58724-108-0, Wheeler Publishing, Inc.) Gale Group.
Keltner, Kim Wong. The Dim Sum of All Things. 2004. 352p. pap. 13.95 (0-06-056075-4, Avon Bks.) Morrow/Avon.
Lee, Gus. No Physical Evidence. 1998. 400p. 24.95 o.s.i (0-449-91139-X, Fawcett) Ballantine Bks.
—No Physical Evidence: A Courtroom Novel. 2000. 384p. mass mkt. 6.99 o.s.i (0-8041-1779-9, Ivy Bks.) Ballantine Bks.
Lee, Y. C. The Flower Drum Song. 2002. 272p. 14.00 (0-14-200218-6) Viking Penguin.
Long, Jean Yee. Educated Lady. 2001. (Illus.). 324p. pap. 16.00 o.p. (0-7388-2289-2) Xlibris Corp.
Louie, David Wong. The Barbarians Are Coming. 2001. 384p. reprint ed. pap. 12.95 (0-425-17828-5) Berkley Publishing Group.
—The Barbarians Are Coming. 2000. 336p. 23.95 o.s.i (0-399-14603-2, Wood, Marian Bks.) Penguin Group (USA) Inc.
Lu, Alvin. The Hell Screens: A Novel. 2000. 196p. 24.00 (1-56858-167-X, No Exit Pr.) Four Walls Eight Windows.
Ng, Mei. Eating Chinese Food Naked. 1998. 256p. mass mkt. 14.00 (0-671-01145-6, Scribner) Simon & Schuster.
—Eating Chinese Food Naked. l.t. ed. 1998. (Core Ser.). 344p. 26.95 (0-7838-0240-4) Thorndike Pr.
—Eating Chinese Food Naked: A Novel. 1998. 224p. 20.50 (0-684-81416-1, Scribner) Simon & Schuster.
Payne, David. Confessions of a Taoist on Wall Street. 1996. pap. 15.00 o.s.i (0-345-41038-6); 1985. 864p. mass mkt. 5.99 o.s.i (0-345-32696-2) Ballantine Bks.
—Confessions of a Taoist on Wall Street: A Chinese American Romance, 001. 1984. 17.95 o.p. (0-395-35562-1) Houghton Mifflin Co.
Rozan, S. J. A Bitter Feast. 1998. 320p. 23.95 o.p. (0-312-19259-2, Saint Martin's Minotaur); 1999. 336p. reprint ed. mass mkt. 5.99 (0-312-97011-0, St. Martin's Paperbacks) St. Martin's Pr.
—A Bitter Feast. l.t. ed. 1999. (Mystery Ser.). 519p. 27.95 (0-7862-1773-1) Thorndike Pr.
—A Bitter Feast: A Bill Smith-Lydia Chin Mystery. unabr. ed. 1999. audio 69.95 (0-7927-2280-9, CSL169, Chivers Sound Library) BBC Audiobooks America.
—China Trade. 1994. 263 p. 20.95 o.p. (0-312-11254-8, Saint Martin's Minotaur); 1995. (Lydia Chin, Bill Smith Mystery Ser.: Vol. 1). 275p. reprint ed. mass mkt. 6.50 (0-312-95590-1, St. Martin's Paperbacks) St. Martin's Pr.
—Concourse: A Bill Smith-Lydia Chin Mystery. unabr. ed. 1998. audio 69.95 (0-7927-2245-0, CSL134, Chivers Sound Library) BBC Audiobooks America.
—Concourse: A Bill Smith-Lydia Chin Mystery. 1995. 288p. 21.95 o.p. (0-312-13453-3, Saint Martin's Minotaur); 3rd ed. 1996. (Lydia Chin, Bill Smith Mystery Ser.: Vol. 2). 291p. mass mkt. 6.50 (0-312-95944-3, St. Martin's Paperbacks) St. Martin's Pr.
—Mandarin Plaid. (Lydia Chin, Bill Smith Mystery Ser.: Vol. 3). 288p. 1996. 22.95 o.p. (0-312-14674-4, Saint Martin's Minotaur); Vol. 1. 1997. mass mkt. 6.50 (0-312-96283-5, St. Martin's Paperbacks) St. Martin's Pr.
—No Colder Place. 1998. (No Colder Place Ser.: Vol. 1). 304p. pap. 6.99 (0-312-96664-4, St. Martin's Paperbacks); 1997. (Lydia Chin, Bill Smith Mystery Ser.). 288p. 23.95 (0-312-16811-X, Saint Martin's Minotaur) St. Martin's Pr.
—No Colder Place. l.t. ed. 1997. (Cloak & Dagger Ser.). 473p. lib. bdg. 28.95 (0-7862-1251-9) Thorndike Pr.
—Stone Quarry. 1999. 288p. 23.95 o.p. (0-312-20912-6, Saint Martin's Minotaur) St. Martin's Pr.
Sheridan, Juanita. The Chinese Shop. Schantz, Tom & Schantz, Enid, eds. 2000. 155p. pap. 14.00 (0-915230-32-1) Rue Morgue Pr.
Tan, Amy. The Bonesetter's Daughter. 2003. 400p. pap. 14.95 (0-345-45737-4, Ballantine Bks.); 2002. 416p. mass mkt. o.s.i (0-345-45571-1); 2002. 416p. reprint ed. mass mkt. 7.99 (0-8041-1498-6, Ballantine Bks.) Ballantine Bks.
—The Bonesetter's Daughter. 2001. 400p. 25.95 o.s.i (0-399-14643-1); 150.00 (0-399-14685-7) Penguin Group (USA) Inc.
—The Bonesetter's Daughter. l.t. ed. 567p. 2002. pap. 29.95 (0-7862-2951-9); 2001. 32.95 (0-7862-2952-7); 2001. (0-7540-2453-9); 2001. (0-7540-1594-7) Thorndike Pr.
—The Joy Luck Club. 1996. mass mkt. 6.99 (0-8041-9896-9); 1990. 352p. mass mkt. 7.99 (0-8041-0630-4); 1989. mass mkt. 4.95 o.s.i (0-8041-0642-8) Ballantine Bks. (Ivy Bks.).
—The Joy Luck Club. Andrews, Richard, ed. 1995. (Cambridge Literature Ser.). (Illus.). 336p. pap. text 11.95 (0-521-48562-2) Cambridge Univ. Pr.
—The Joy Luck Club. (Modern Critical Interpretations Ser.). 176p. pap. 19.95 (0-7910-7117-0) Chelsea Hse. Pubs.
—The Joy Luck Club. 1991. (Vintage Contemporaries Ser.). (Illus.). 288p. pap. 12.95 (0-679-72768-X, Vintage) Knopf Publishing Group.
—The Joy Luck Club. 1989. 288p. 24.95 (0-399-13420-4) Penguin Group (USA) Inc.
—The Joy Luck Club. 2003. E-Book 8.99 (0-7953-1076-5) RosettaBooks.
—The Joy Luck Club. 1990. 14.04 (0-606-01172-2) Turtleback Bks.
—The Joy Luck Club & The Kitchen God's Wife. 1992. 15.98 o.s.i (0-8041-1052-2, Ivy Bks.) Ballantine Bks.
Telemaque, Eleanor. It's Crazy to Stay Chinese in Minnesota: Chasing Bingo Tang. 2000. 104p. E-Book 8.00 (0-7388-8567-3) Xlibris Corp.
Tsiang, H. T. And China Has Hands. Cheung, Floyd, ed. 2003. (Asian-American Heritage Collection). 133p. per. 14.95 (1-931336-02-4) Ironweed Pr., Inc.

## CREOLES—FICTION

Agualusa, Jose Eduardo. Creole Nation. 2002. 288p. pap. 16.00 (1-900850-61-3) Arcadia Bks. GBR. *Dist:* Consortium Bk. Sales & Distribution.
Cable, George W. Old Creole Days. E-Book 3.95 (0-594-04343-3) 1873 Pr.
—Old Creole Days, Set, Pts. 1 & 2. 1977. (Black Heritage Library Collection). 27.95 (0-8369-8530-3) Ayer Co. Pubs., Inc.
—Old Creole Days. 1883. 300p. (YA). reprint ed. pap. text 28.00 (1-4047-1132-5) Classic Textbooks.
—Old Creole Days. 1972. reprint ed. lib. bdg. 9.00 o.p. (0-8422-8184-3) Irvington Pubs.
—Old Creole Days. 1989. mass mkt. 3.95 o.p. (0-451-52349-0, Signet Classics) NAL.
—Old Creole Days. 1990. (Pelican Pouch Ser.). 312p. (YA). (gr. 10-12). reprint ed. pap. 6.99 (0-88289-780-2) Pelican Publishing Co., Inc.
—Old Creole Days. 1990. (Works of George Washington Cable). reprint ed. lib. bdg. 79.00 (0-7812-1132-8) Reprint Services Corp.
—Old Creole Days. 1974. reprint ed. 10.00 (0-403-03056-0) Somerset Pubs., Inc.
Cable, George Washington. The Grandissimes. 2001. (Illus.). 528p. pap. 7.99 (1-56554-901-5) Pelican Publishing Co., Inc.
Leblance, Whitney J. Blues in the Wind. 2002. 330p. 23.95 (0-913515-47-7) River City Publishing.
Martin, Gilbert E. Passe Pour Blanc: Creole Secrets. 2001. 197p. (1-55212-736-2) Trafford Publishing.
Rawles, Nancy. Crawfish Dreams. 2004. 368p. pap. 13.00 (0-385-72213-3, Anchor) Knopf Publishing Group.
—Crawfish Dreams: A Novel. 2003. 368p. 21.95 (0-385-50418-7) Doubleday Publishing.

## CUBAN AMERICANS—FICTION

Abella, Alex. The Killing of the Saints. 1993. (Crime Ser.). 320p. pap. 5.95 o.p. (0-14-017419-2, Penguin Bks.) Penguin Group (USA) Inc.
Abreu-Felippe, Nicolas. Miami en Brumas. 2000. (Coleccion Caniqui).Tr. of Miami in Fog. (SPA.). 205p. pap. 16.00 (0-89729-919-1) Ediciones Universal.
Bell, Christine. The Perez Family: A Novel. 1991. 256p. reprint ed. pap. 11.00 o.p. (0-06-097401-X, Perennial) HarperTrade.
—The Perez Family: A Novel. 1990. 19.95 o.p. (0-393-02798-8) Norton, W. W. & Co., Inc.
Bertematti, Richard. Project Death: A Tito Rico Mystery. 1997. (Tito Rico Mystery Ser.). 200p. 22.95 o.p. (1-55885-193-3) Arte Publico Pr.
Brackenbury, Rosalind. Seas Outside the Reef: A Novel. 2000. 222p. pap. 14.95 (1-880284-41-3) Daniel, John & Co., Pubs.
Curtis, James R. Shango. 1996. 197p. (Orig.). pap. 11.95 (1-55885-096-1) Arte Publico Pr.
Engle, Margarita M. Singing to Cuba. 1993. (Illus.). 164p. (C). pap. 9.50 o.p. (1-55885-070-8) Arte Publico Pr.
Fernandez, Roberto G. Holy Radishes. 1995. 298p. 17.95 (1-55885-075-9); pap. 9.95 (1-55885-076-7) Arte Publico Pr.
—Raining Backwards. 224p. 1988. pap. 11.95 o.p. (0-934770-79-4); 2nd ed. 1998. pap. 11.95 (1-55885-223-9) Arte Publico Pr.
Fraxedas, J. Joaquin. The Lonely Crossing of Juan Cabrera. 1994. 192p. pap. 9.95 (0-312-11022-7, Saint Martin's Griffin); 1994. (SPA.). 192p. pap. 8.95 o.p. (0-312-11082-0, Saint Martin's Griffin); 1993. 176p. 18.95 o.p. (0-312-08897-3) St. Martin's Pr.
—La Travesia Solitaria de Juan Cabrera. 1993. 18.95 o.p. (0-312-09066-8) St. Martin's Pr.
Garcia-Aguilera, Carolina. Bloody Secrets. 1999. 336p. reprint ed. mass mkt. 6.50 o.s.i (0-425-16779-8, Prime Crime) Berkley Publishing Group.
—Bloody Secrets. 1998. 274p. 23.95 o.p. (0-399-14386-6, G. P. Putnam's Sons) Penguin Group (USA) Inc.
—Bloody Shame: A Lupe Solano Mystery. 1998. 320p. mass mkt. 6.50 o.s.i (0-425-16140-4, Prime Crime) Berkley Publishing Group.
—Bloody Shame: A Lupe Solano Mystery. 1997. 288p. 22.95 o.p. (0-399-14256-8, G. P. Putnam's Sons) Penguin Group (USA) Inc.
—Bloody Waters: A Lupe Solano Mystery. 1997. (Lupo Solano Mystery Ser.). 304p. mass mkt. 5.99 o.s.i (0-425-15670-2, Prime Crime) Berkley Publishing Group.
—Bloody Waters: A Lupe Solano Mystery. 1996. 256p. 21.95 o.p. (0-399-14157-X, G. P. Putnam's Sons) Penguin Group (USA) Inc.
—A Miracle in Paradise. (Lupe Solano Mystery Ser.). 2000. 352p. mass mkt. 5.99 o.s.i (0-380-80738-6); 1999. viii, 277p. 23.00 (0-380-97779-6) Morrow/Avon. (Avon Bks.).
—One Hot Summer. 2002. 288p. (gr. 5 up). 23.95 (0-06-000980-2, Rayo) HarperTrade.
Garcia, Cristina. The Aguero Sisters. 1998. 103.60 o.s.i (0-345-91389-2); 103.60 o.s.i (0-345-91390-6); 336p. pap. 14.00 (0-345-40651-6, Ballantine Bks.) Ballantine Bks.
—Dreaming in Cuban. 1999. pap. (0-345-91367-1, Ballantine Bks.); 1993. (SPA.). 256p. pap. 14.00 (0-345-38143-2, One World/Ballantine) Ballantine Bks.
—Dreaming in Cuban. 1992. 20.00 o.s.i (0-679-40883-5) Knopf, Alfred A. Inc.
—Las Hermanas Aguero: Una Novela. 1997. (SPA.). 320p. pap. 13.95 (0-679-78145-5, RH9081, Vintage) Knopf Publishing Group.
—Sonar en Cubano. 1994. (SPA.). 336p. pap. 12.95 (0-345-39139-X, RH9018, Ballantine Bks.) Ballantine Bks.
Gonzalez, Luis. Spirits of the Revolution, 3 Vols., Vol. 1. 1998. 892p. 26.00 (0-9663058-0-9) Colonnade Bks.
Granger, Bill. The New York Yanquis. 1995. 288p. 21.95 (1-55970-289-3) Arcade Publishing, Inc.
Hanlon, Julia. The Wedding Wager. 2000. 352p. mass mkt. 5.99 o.s.i (0-8217-6524-8, Zebra Bks.) Kensington Publishing Corp.
Hijuelos, Oscar. The Empress of the Splendid Season. 1999. 352p. mass mkt. 7.99 (0-06-101418-4) HarperCollins Pubs.
—The Empress of the Splendid Season. 1999. 352p. o.s.i (0-06-017570-2, HarperFlamingo) HarperCollins Pubs. Canada, Ltd.
—The Empress of the Splendid Season. 2000. 352p. pap. 13.00 (0-06-092870-0, Perennial) HarperTrade.
—The Fourteen Sisters of Emilio Montez O'Brien. 1993. 484p. 22.00 o.p. (0-374-15815-0) Farrar, Straus & Giroux.
—The Fourteen Sisters of Emilio Montez O'Brien. 2004. 496p. pap. 15.00 (0-06-097594-6, Perennial) HarperTrade.
—The Fourteen Sisters of Emilio Montez O'Brien. 1994. 544p. mass mkt. 5.99 o.p. (0-06-100759-5, HarperTorch) Morrow/Avon.
—The Fourteen Sisters of Emilio Montez O'Brien & The Mambo Kings Play Songs of Love. 1993. 29.95 o.p. (1-55800-793-8) NewStar Media, Inc.
—The Mambo Kings Play Songs of Love. 1989. 384p. 18.95 o.s.i (0-374-20125-0) Farrar, Straus & Giroux.
—The Mambo Kings Play Songs of Love. (Perennial Classics Ser.). 2004. 464p. pap. 14.00 (0-06-095545-7); 1994. 416p. pap. 13.00 (0-06-097327-7); 1992. 416p. reprint ed. pap. 12.00 o.p. (0-06-097451-6) HarperTrade. (Perennial).
—Our House in the Last World. 1991. 236p. reprint ed. pap. 12.00 o.p. (0-89255-165-8); 1989. 236p. reprint ed. 18.95 (0-89255-069-4); 2nd ed. 2002. 256p. pap. 13.00 (0-89255-283-2) Persea Bks., Inc.
—Our House in the Last World. Rosenman, Jane, ed. 1990. 256p. pap. (0-671-72722-2, Washington Square Pr.) Simon & Schuster.
—Our House in the Last World. 1984. reprint ed. pap. 3.95 (0-671-50785-0, Washington Square Pr.) Simon & Schuster.
—Los Reyes del Mambo Tocan Canciones de Amor. 1996. (SPA.). 560p. pap. 14.00 (0-06-095214-8, HC12648, Perennial) HarperTrade.
Hood, Mary. Familiar Heat. 1995. 416p. 25.00 o.s.i (0-394-58658-1) Knopf, Alfred A. Inc.
—Familiar Heat. 1996. 464p. pap. 19.99 (0-446-67274-2) Warner Bks., Inc.
Leuci, Robert. Snitch. 1998. (Snitch Ser.: Vol. 1). 352p. pap. 6.99 (0-312-96510-9, St. Martin's Paperbacks); 1997. 384p. 24.95 (0-312-14739-2) St. Martin's Pr.
McKinney, Mel. Where There's Smoke. 1999. 224p. 22.95 (0-312-20623-2) St. Martin's Pr.
Menendez, Ana. In Cuba I Was a German Shepherd. 2001. 229p. 23.00 o.p. (0-8021-1688-4); 2002. 240p. reprint ed. pap. 12.00 (0-8021-3887-X) Grove/Atlantic, Inc. (Grove Pr.).
Mestre-Reed, Ernesto, tr. The Second Death of Unica Aveyano: A Novel. 2004. 272p. pap. 13.00 (1-4000-3316-0, Vintage) Knopf Publishing Group.
Munoz, Elias M. Brand New Memory. 1998. 224p. pap. 12.95 (1-55885-227-1) Arte Publico Pr.
Novas, Himilce. Mangos, Bananas & Coconuts: A Cuban Love Story. 1996. 168p. 9.95 (1-55885-092-9) Arte Publico Pr.
Obejas, Achy. Days of Awe. 2002. 400p. pap. 14.00 (0-345-44154-0, Ballantine Bks.) Ballantine Bks.
—Days of Awe. l.t. ed. 2002. (Women's Fiction Ser.). 657p. 28.95 (0-7862-3847-X) Gale Group.
Puig Zaldivar, Raquel, et al. Women Don't Need to Write. 1998. 352p. pap. 13.95 (1-55885-257-3) Arte Publico Pr.
Sayles, John. Los Gusanos. 1999. (SPA.). 536p. (84-8306-223-2) Debate, Editorial.
—Los Gusanos. (SPA.). 536p. 30.95 (84-8306-224-0, DB11247) Debate, Editorial ESP. *Dist:* Lectorum Pubns., Inc.
—Los Gusanos. 480p. 1992. pap. 12.00 o.p. (0-06-092159-5, Perennial); 1991. 22.95 o.p. (0-06-016653-3) HarperTrade.
—Los Gusanos. 1992. 4.99 o.p. (0-517-09228-X) Random Hse. Value Publishing.
Suarez, Virgil. Going Under. 1996. 159p. 18.95 (1-55885-159-3) Arte Publico Pr.
—Havana Thursdays. 1995. 250p. 19.95 (1-55885-143-7) Arte Publico Pr.
—Latin Jazz. 2002. (Voices of the South Ser.). 304p. pap. 16.95 (0-8071-2790-6) Louisiana State Univ. Pr.
—Latin Jazz. 1989. 290p. 18.95 o.p. (0-688-08475-3, Morrow, William & Co.) Morrow/Avon.
—Latin Jazz. 1990. pap. 9.95 o.p. (0-671-70535-0, Fireside) Simon & Schuster.
Veciana-Suarez, Ana. The Chin Kiss King. 1998. 320p. pap. 12.95 o.s.i (0-452-28009-5, Plume) Dutton/Plume.
—The Chin Kiss King. 1997. 496p. 24.00 o.p. (0-374-12130-3) Farrar, Straus & Giroux.
Williams, Lee. Author of Destiny: (Also Known As the Ochoa Case) 2002. (Illus.). 224p. pap. 14.95 (0-942979-98-2); lib. bdg. 26.00 (0-942979-99-0) Livingston Pr.
Yglesias, Jose. The Truth about Them. 1999. (Pioneer Ser.). 272p. pap. 12.95 (1-55885-273-5) Arte Publico Pr.
—A Wake in Ybor City. 1998. (Pioneer Ser.). 212p. pap. 14.95 (1-55885-248-4) Arte Publico Pr.
—A Wake in Ybor City. 1981. 31.95 (0-405-13172-0) Ayer Co. Pubs., Inc.

# D

## DOMINICAN AMERICANS—FICTION

Alvarez, Julia. En el Nombre de Salome. 2002. Tr. of In the Name of Salome. (SPA.). 384p. pap. 14.00 (0-375-72690-X, Vintage) Knopf Publishing Group.
—How the Garcia Girls Lost Their Accents. 1999. 308p. (YA). (ps up). 17.95 (0-945575-57-2, 71557) Algonquin Bks. of Chapel Hill.
—How the Garcia Girls Lost Their Accents. 1992. (Contemporary Fiction Ser.). (Illus.). 304p. pap. 14.00 (0-452-26806-0) Dutton/Plume.
—How the Garcia Girls Lost Their Accents. 1997. (C). pap. text o.p. (0-8013-3147-1) Longman Publishing Group.

—In the Name of Salome. 2000. 357p. tchr. ed. 23.95 (*1-56512-276-3*, 72276) Algonquin Bks. of Chapel Hill.
—Yo! 1999. 350p. tchr. ed. 18.95 (*1-56512-157-0*, 72157) Algonquin Bks. of Chapel Hill.
—Yo! 1999. (SPA.). 416p. pap. 16.95 (*0-452-28140-7*); 1997. 320p. pap. 14.00 (*0-452-27918-6*, Plume) Dutton/Plume.
—Yo! l.t. ed. 2003. (Spanish Language Ser.). (SPA.). 28.95 (*0-7862-5190-5*) Thorndike Pr.
—Yo! 1997. 19.00 (*0-606-22212-X*) Turtleback Bks.
Benedict, Helen. Bad Angel. 304p. 1997. pap. 12.95 o.p. (*0-452-27586-5*, Plume); 1996. 22.95 o.p. (*0-525-94100-2*, Dutton) Dutton/Plume.
Diaz, Junot. Drown. 1997. 224p. reprint ed. pap. 13.00 (*1-57322-606-8*, Riverhead Trade (Paperbacks)) Berkley Publishing Group.
—Drown. 1996. 208p. 21.95 o.s.i (*1-57322-041-8*, Riverhead Bks. (Hardcovers)) Putnam Publishing Group, The.
Perez, Loida Maritza. Geographies of Home. 2000. 336p. 12.95 (*0-14-025371-8*); 1999. 288p. 23.95 o.p. (*0-670-86889-2*) Viking Penguin.
Rosario, Nelly. El Canto de Agua: A Novel. 2003. (SPA.). 272p. pap. 12.00 (*1-4000-3004-8*, Vintage) Knopf Publishing Group.

## E

### ESKIMOS—FICTION

Beirne, Gerard. The Eskimo in the Net: A Novel. 2003. 388p. pap. 14.95 (*0-7145-3093-X*) Boyars, Marion Pubs., Inc.
De Laguna, Frederica. Fog on the Mountain. 1997. pap. text 14.95 (*0-9651157-2-0*) Kachemak Country Pubns.
Haile, Sarah V. Maniilaq: Eskimo Prophet. 2002. 270p. pap. 16.95 (*1-55517-670-4*, Bonneville Bks.) Cedar Fort, Inc./CFI Distribution.
Houston, James. Spirit Wrestler. 1980. 320p. 12.50 o.p. (*0-15-184755-X*) Harcourt Trade Pubs.
—Spirit Wrestler. 1981. 288p. pap. 2.75 o.p. (*0-380-56911-6*, 56911-6, Avon Bks.) Morrow/Avon.
—The Spirit Wrestler. 1997. (Illus.). 320p. pap. 19.99 (*0-7710-4206-X*) McClelland & Stewart/Tundra Bks.
—Spirit Wrestler. l.t. ed. 1982. (Ulverscroft Large Print Ser.). 480p. 29.99 o.p. (*0-7089-0768-7*, Ulverscroft) Thorpe, F. A. Pubs. GBR. *Dist:* Ulverscroft Large Print Bks., Ltd., Ulverscroft Large Print Canada, Ltd.
—The White Dawn. 1972. (YA). (gr. 10). mass mkt. 1.50 o.p. (*0-451-07853-5*, W7853, Signet Bks.) NAL.
—The White Dawn: An Eskimo Saga. 1971. (J). 8.50 o.p. (*0-15-196115-8*) Harcourt Children's Bks.
Houston, James R. The White Dawn: An Eskimo Saga. 1989. (Harvest Book Ser.). (Illus.). 288p. pap. 10.00 (*0-15-696256-X*, Harvest Bks.) Harcourt Trade Pubs.
Houston, John. The White Dawn: An Eskimo Saga. 1984. 15.25 o.p. (*0-8446-6123-6*) Smith, Peter Pub., Inc.
Jones, Stan. White Sky, Black Ice: An Alaskan Mystery. 1999. 264p. 22.00 (*1-56947-152-5*) Soho Pr., Inc.
Lane, Christopher. A Deadly Quiet. 2001. (Inupiat Eskimo Mysteries Ser.). 352p. mass mkt. 6.50 (*0-380-81626-1*, Avon Bks.) Morrow/Avon.
—The Elements of a Kill. 1998. 416p. mass mkt. 5.99 (*0-380-79870-0*, Avon Bks.) Morrow/Avon.
—The Season of Death: An Inupiat Eskimo Mystery. 1999. 352p. mass mkt. 5.99 (*0-380-79872-7*, Avon Bks.) Morrow/Avon.
—A Shroud of Midnight Sun. 2000. (Inupiat Eskimo Mysteries Ser.). 352p. mass mkt. 5.99 (*0-380-79873-5*, Avon Bks.) Morrow/Avon.
—Silent as the Hunter. 2001. (Inupiat Eskimo Mysteries Ser.). 352p. mass mkt. 6.50 (*0-380-81625-3*, Avon Bks.) Morrow/Avon.
Murie, Margaret E. Island Between. 1977. (Illus.). 228p. 9.95 (*0-912006-04-8*) Univ. of Alaska Pr.
—Island Between. 1977. E-Book 9.95 (*0-585-18622-7*) netLibrary, Inc.
Rodahl, Kaare. Akiviak. 1979. 9.95 o.p. (*0-393-01181-X*) Norton, W. W. & Co., Inc.
Tourney, Leonard. Frobisher's Savage. 1994. 304p. 20.95 o.p. (*0-312-11437-0*, Saint Martin's Minotaur) St. Martin's Pr.

## F

### FRENCH-CANADIANS—FICTION

Godbout, Jacques. Knife on the Table. 1976. mass mkt. o.p. (*0-7710-9230-X*) McClelland & Stewart CAN. *Dist:* Random Hse. of Canada, Ltd.
Patterson, Kevin. Country of Cold: Stories. 2004. 272p. pap. 13.00 (*0-385-72217-6*, Anchor) Knopf Publishing Group.
Roy, Gabrielle. The Road Past Altamont. 1996. (New Canadian Library). 160p. mass mkt. 6.95 (*0-7710-9856-1*) McClelland & Stewart/Tundra Bks.
—The Road Past Altamont. Marshall, Joyce, tr. 1993. 147p. pap. 7.95 (*0-8032-8948-0*, Bison Bks.) Univ. of Nebraska Pr.
—Windflower. 1991. (New Canadian Library). 176p. mass mkt. 5.95 (*0-7710-9879-0*) McClelland & Stewart/Tundra Bks.

## H

### HISPANIC AMERICANS—FICTION

Alico, Stella H. Maria, Mota & the Grandmother: A Novel. Ware, Laura, ed. 1993. (Illus.). 128p. (YA). (gr. 6-10). pap. 12.95 (*0-86534-190-7*) Sunstone Pr.
Allende, Isabel. Daughter of Fortune. 2001. 464p. mass mkt. 7.99 (*0-380-82101-X*) HarperCollins Pubs.
—Daughter of Fortune. Peden, Margaret Sayers, tr. from SPA. 1999. (Oprah's Book Club Ser.). (Illus.). 416p. 26.00 (*0-06-019491-X*) HarperCollins Pubs.
—Daughter of Fortune. Peden, Margaret Sayers, tr. from SPA. 2000. 416p. pap. 14.00 (*0-06-093275-9*, Perennial) HarperTrade.
—Daughter of Fortune. 2000. 20.05 (*0-606-20501-2*) Turtleback Bks.
—The Infinite Plan: A Novel. Peden, Margaret Sayers, tr. from ENG. 1993. 384p. 23.00 o.p. (*0-06-017016-6*) HarperTrade.
Ambert, Alba. Porque Hay Silencio. 1998. (Pioneer Ser.).Tr. of Perfect Silence. (SPA.). 208p. pap. 11.95 (*1-55885-250-6*) Arte Publico Pr.
Ambert, Alba N. A Perfect Silence. 1995. 199p. 9.95 (*1-55885-125-9*) Arte Publico Pr.
Augenbraum, Harold & Stavans, Ilan, eds. Growing up Latino: Memoirs & Stories. 1993. 384p. pap. 15.00 (*0-395-66124-2*) Houghton Mifflin Co.
Bethancourt, T. Ernesto. New York City Too Far. 12.95 o.p. (*0-8234-0256-8*) Holiday Hse., Inc.
Braithwaite, Kent. The Wonderland Murders. 2000. 324p. pap. 14.95 (*1-891929-33-X*) Four Seasons Pubs.
Carlson, Lori M. Reyes: Three Kings' Day. 1998. (Illus.). (J). o.p. (*0-525-67569-8*, Dutton Children's Bks.) Penguin Putnam Bks. for Young Readers.
Carlstrom, Nancy White. Barney Is Best. 1994. (Illus.). 32p. (J). (ps-3). lib. bdg. 14.89 o.p. (*0-06-022876-8*); 15.00 o.p. (*0-06-022875-X*) HarperCollins Children's Bk. Group.
Castillo, Ana. Peel My Love Like an Onion. 1999. 240p. 23.95 o.s.i (*0-385-49676-1*) Doubleday Publishing.
—Peel My Love Like an Onion: A Novel. 2000. 240p. reprint ed. pap. 12.00 (*0-385-49677-X*) Doubleday Publishing.
Chacon, Daniel. And the Shadows Took Him. 2005. pap. (*0-7434-6639-X*, Washington Square Pr.); 2004. 336p. 24.00 (*0-7434-6638-1*, Atria) Simon & Schuster.
Christopher, Matt. Centerfield Ballhawk. (Peach Street Mudders Story Ser.). (Illus.). (J). 1994. 59p. (ps-3). pap. 4.50 (*0-316-14272-7*); 1992. 64p. (gr. 2-4). 13.95 o.p. (*0-316-14079-1*) Little Brown & Co.
—Centerfield Ballhawk. 1992. (Springboard Bks.). 10.65 (*0-606-06270-X*) Turtleback Bks.
Cofer, Judith Ortiz. The Year of Our Revolution. 1998. 128p. (gr. 5-9). 16.95 (*1-55885-224-7*) Arte Publico Pr.
Colon-Vila, Lillian & Collier-Morales, Roberta. Salsa! 1998. (SPA., Illus.). 32p. (J). (ps-2). 14.95 (*1-55885-220-4*, Piñata Books) Arte Publico Pr.
Cooper, Cecilia Romero. Stolen Love. 2002. 256p. mass mkt. 4.99 o.s.i (*0-7860-1335-4*, Encanto) Kensington Publishing Corp.
Corpi, Lucha. Black Widow's Wardrobe. 1999. (Gloria Damasco Detective Ser.). 193p. pap. 12.95 o.p. (*1-55885-288-3*) Arte Publico Pr.
—Cactus Blood: A Mystery Novel. 1995. 249p. 9.50 o.p. (*1-55885-134-8*) Arte Publico Pr.
—Eulogy for a Brown Angel: A Mystery Novel. 2002. 208p. pap. 12.95 (*1-55885-356-1*); 1992. 200p. 9.00 (*1-55885-050-3*) Arte Publico Pr.
Cruz, Angie. Soledad. 240p. 2001. 23.00 (*0-7432-1201-0*); 2002. reprint ed. pap. 13.00 (*0-7432-1202-9*) Simon & Schuster. (Simon & Schuster).
De Anda, Diane. The Ice Dove & Other Stories. 1997. (Illus.). 64p. (YA). (gr. 3-7). pap. 7.95 (*1-55885-189-5*, Piñata Books) Arte Publico Pr.
Diamond, Diana. The Babysitter. 2002. 368p. mass mkt. 6.99 (*0-312-98364-6*, St. Martin's Paperbacks); 2001. 313p. 23.95 (*0-312-28047-5*) St. Martin's Pr.
—The Babysitter. l.t. ed. 2001. 592p. 28.95 (*0-7862-3637-X*) Thorndike Pr.
Diaz Valcarcel, Emilio. Hot Soles in Harlem. Miller, Yvette E., ed. Fayen, Tanya T., tr. from SPA. 1993. (Discoveries Ser.). 175p. pap. 16.95 (*0-935480-61-7*) Latin American Literary Review Pr.
Dorros, Arthur. Isla. 1995. Orig. Title: The Island. (SPA., Illus.). 48p. (J). (ps-1). 16.99 (*0-525-45149-8*, Dutton Children's Bks.) Penguin Putnam Bks. for Young Readers.
Duarte, Stella P. Fragile Night. 1997. 160p. (Orig.). pap. 13.00 (*0-927534-71-1*) Bilingual Pr./Editorial Bilingue.
Forte-Escamilla, Kleya. The Storyteller with Nike Airs & Other Barrio Stories. 1994. 208p. (Orig.). pap. 8.95 (*1-879960-34-6*) Aunt Lute Bks.
Gallegos, Sally. Stone Horses. 1996. 272p. 16.95 (*0-8263-1666-2*) Univ. of New Mexico Pr.
Garcia, Lionel G. The Day They Took My Uncle & Other Short Stories. 2001. x, 234p. 22.50 (*0-87565-235-2*) Texas Christian Univ. Pr.
Garcia, Ricardo L. Coal Camp Days: A Boy's Remembrance. 2001. (Illus.). viii, 278p. 24.95 (*0-8263-2304-9*); pap. (*0-8263-2305-7*) Univ. of New Mexico Pr.
Gershator, David & Gershator, Phillis. Bread Is for Eating, ERS. (Illus.). 1998. 32p. pap. 6.95 (*0-8050-5798-6*); 1995. (J). 15.95 (*0-8050-3173-1*) Holt, Henry & Co. (Holt, Henry & Co. Bks. For Young Readers).
Hawxhurst, Joan C. Antonia Novello: U. S. Surgeon General. (Hispanic Heritage Ser.: 4). (Illus.). 32p. (gr. 2-4). 1995. pap. 7.95 o.p. (*1-56294-862-8*); 1993. (J). 19.90 o.p. (*1-56294-299-9*) Millbrook Pr., Inc.
Hurwitz, Johanna. Class President. 1990. (Illus.). 96p. (J). (gr. 2 up). 15.99 (*0-688-09114-8*) HarperCollins Children's Bk. Group.
—Class President. 1991. 96p. (J). (gr. 4-7). reprint ed. pap. 4.50 (*0-590-44064-0*, Scholastic Paperbacks) Scholastic, Inc.
—Class President. 1991. 10.65 (*0-606-04895-2*) Turtleback Bks.
Jaime-Becerra, M. Every Night Is Ladies' Night: Stories. 2004. 304p. 23.95 (*0-06-055962-4*, Rayo) HarperTrade.
Kanellos, Nicolás., ed. Short Fiction by Hispanic Writers of the United States. 1993. 256p. pap. 15.95 (*1-55885-044-9*) Arte Publico Pr.
Keats, Ezra Jack. Dreams. 2000. (Illus.). 40p. (J). (ps-3). pap. 6.99 (*0-14-056744-5*, Puffin Bks.) Penguin Putnam Bks. for Young Readers.
Kleven, Elisa. Hooray, a Pinata! 1996. (Illus.). 32p. (J). (ps-3). 16.99 (*0-525-45605-8*, Dutton Children's Bks.) Penguin Putnam Bks. for Young Readers.
—Viva!... Una Pinata! 1996. (SPA., Illus.). 32p. (J). (gr. 2-4). 15.99 o.p. (*0-525-45606-6*) Penguin Putnam Bks. for Young Readers.
Lachtman, Ofelia Dumas. Pepita Talks Twice. 1995. Tr. of Pepita Habla dos Veces. (ENG & SPA., Illus.). 32p. (J). (ps-3). 14.95 (*1-55885-077-5*, APP77, Piñata Books) Arte Publico Pr.
Lopez, Jack. Snapping Lines: Stories. 2001. (Camino del Sol). 133p. 36.00 (*0-8165-2075-5*); pap. 16.95 (*0-8165-2076-3*) Univ. of Arizona Pr.
Manrique, Jaime. Latin Moon in Manhattan. 1992. 224p. 17.95 o.p. (*0-312-07100-0*) St. Martin's Pr.
—Latin Moon in Manhattan: A Novel. 2003. 212p. pap. 15.95 (*0-299-18754-3*) Univ. of Wisconsin Pr.
Marzollo, Jean. Best Friends Club. 1990. (Thirty-Nine Kids on the Block Ser.: No. 4). (J). pap. 2.50 o.p. (*0-590-42726-1*) Scholastic, Inc.
Medearis, Angela Shelf. The Adventures of Sugar & Junior. 1995. (Illus.). 32p. (J). (ps-3). 15.95 (*0-8234-1182-6*) Holiday Hse., Inc.
Medina, C. C. A Little Love. 2000. 368p. 18.95 (*0-446-52448-4*) Warner Bks., Inc.
Muller, Marcia. The Legend of the Slain Soldiers: An Elena Oliverez Mystery. 1987. 224p. mass mkt. 3.50 o.p. (*0-451-15050-3*, Signet Bks.) NAL.
—The Legend of the Slain Soldiers: An Elena Oliverez Mystery. 1985. 181p. 13.95 o.p. (*0-8027-5617-4*) Walker & Co.
—The Legend of the Slain Soldiers: An Elena Oliverez Mystery. 1996. 192p. mass mkt. 5.99 (*0-446-40421-7*) Warner Bks., Inc.
—The Tree of Death. 1987. mass mkt. 3.50 o.p. (*0-451-14749-9*, Signet Bks.) NAL.
—The Tree of Death. 1983. (Mysteries Ser.). 192p. 12.95 o.s.i (*0-8027-5576-3*) Walker & Co.
—The Tree of Death. 1996. 208p. mass mkt. 5.99 o.s.i (*0-446-40420-9*) Warner Bks., Inc.
Muller, Marcia & Pronzini, Bill. Beyond the Grave. 240p. 1999. mass mkt. 5.95 (*0-7867-0650-3*); 1991. mass mkt. 3.95 o.p. (*0-88184-731-3*) Avalon Publishing Group. (Carroll & Graf Pubs.).
—Beyond the Grave. l.t. ed. 2001. 388p. pap. 24.95 (*0-7838-9537-2*, Macmillan Reference USA) Gale Group.
—Beyond the Grave. 1986. 224p. 15.95 o.p. (*0-8027-5651-4*) Walker & Co.
Olivas, Daniel A. Assumption & Other Stories. 2003. 136p. pap. text 11.00 (*1-931010-19-6*) Bilingual Pr./Editorial Bilingue.
Poey, Delia & Suarez, Virgil, eds. Iguana Dreams: New Latino Fiction. 1992. 320p. 25.00 o.p. (*0-06-055329-4*); 400p. pap. 17.95 (*0-06-096917-2*) HarperTrade. (Perennial).
—Iguana Dreams: New Latino Fiction. 1994. 400p. lib. bdg. 39.00 o.p. (*0-8095-9142-1*) Millefleurs.
Quesada, Roberto. The Big Banana. Krochmal, Walter, tr. 1999. 304p. pap. 12.95 (*1-55885-255-7*) Arte Publico Pr.
Quintana, Leroy V. La Promesa & Other Stories. 2002. (Chicana & Chicano Visions of the Americas Ser.: Vol. 1). 192p. 24.95 (*0-8061-3449-6*) Univ. of Oklahoma Pr.
Rios, Lara. Winner Take All. 2002. 256p. mass mkt. 4.99 o.s.i (*0-7860-1374-5*, Encanto) Kensington Publishing Corp.
Rivera, Beatriz. Midnight Sandwiches at the Mariposa Express. 1997. 118p. pap. 11.95 (*1-55885-216-6*) Arte Publico Pr.
Rodriguez, Luis. The Republic of East L. A. Stories. 2002. 256p. 23.95 (*0-06-621263-4*) HarperCollins Pubs.
—The Republic of East L. A. Stories. 2003. 256p. pap. 12.95 (*0-06-093686-X*, Rayo) HarperTrade.
Romero, Leo. Rita & Los Angeles. 1994. 144p. (Orig.). pap. 13.00 (*0-927534-44-4*) Bilingual Pr./Editorial Bilingue.
Ruiz, Joseph J. Little Juan Learns a Lesson: A Story for Children. Adelo, Samuel, tr. 1997. (ENG & SPA., Illus.). 64p. (J). (ps-3). pap. 8.95 (*0-86534-267-9*) Sunstone Pr.
Shea, Pegi Deitz. New Moon. 1996. (Illus.). 32p. (J). (ps-k). 14.95 (*1-56397-410-X*) Boyds Mills Pr.
Skinner, Jose. Flight & Other Stories. 2001. (Western Literature Ser.). (Illus.). ix, 186p. pap. 15.00 (*0-87417-359-0*) Univ. of Nevada Pr.
Slate, Joseph. The Secret Stars. (Illus.). (J). 2003. 5.95 (*0-7614-5152-8*); 1998. 32p. 15.95 (*0-7614-5027-0*) Cavendish, Marshall Corp. (Cavendish Children's Bks.).
Smith, Michael. Sanctuary Stories. 1996. 242p. (Orig.). pap. 16.00 (*0-927534-50-9*) Bilingual Pr./Editorial Bilingue.
Soto, Gary. Crazy Weekend. 2002. 160p. (YA). (gr. 4-9). pap. 8.95 (*0-89255-286-7*) Persea Bks., Inc.
—Crazy Weekend. 160p. (J). (gr. 4-6). 1995. mass mkt. 3.50 o.p. (*0-590-47076-0*); 1994. pap. 13.95 (*0-590-47814-1*) Scholastic, Inc.
Soto, Gary & Fondo de Cultura Staff. Tomando Partido. 1996. (SPA.). (YA). 9.95 (*968-16-5023-9*, FC239) Fondo de Cultura Economica MEX. *Dist:* Continental Bk. Co., Inc., Lectorum Pubns., Inc.
Steinbeck, John. Tortilla Flat. mass mkt. 0.25 o.p. (*0-451-00599-6*); mass mkt. 0.25 o.p. (*0-451-01380-8*); mass mkt. 0.35 o.p. (*0-451-01737-4*); mass mkt. 0.60 o.p. (*0-451-02189-4*); mass mkt. 0.25 o.p. (*0-451-00816-2*) NAL. (Signet Bks.).
—Tortilla Flat. (Fiction Ser.). 1977. 224p. pap. 8.00 (*0-14-004240-7*, Penguin Bks.); 1963. pap. 2.25 o.p. (*0-670-00134-1*) Penguin Group (USA) Inc.
—Tortilla Flat. l.t. ed. 1994. 226p. reprint ed. lib. bdg. 21.95 (*0-8161-5901-7*) Thorndike Pr.
—Tortilla Flat. 1986. 13.00 (*0-606-00987-6*) Turtleback Bks.
—Tortilla Flat. (Great Books of the 20th Century Ser.). 1997. 192p. 10.00 (*0-14-018740-5*, Penguin Classics); 1935. 16.95 o.s.i (*0-670-72109-3*) Viking Penguin.
Suarez, Virgil. Welcome to the Oasis & Other Stories. 1992. 128p. pap. 9.50 o.p. (*1-55885-043-0*) Arte Publico Pr.
Suzanne, Kathleen. Rocky Mountain Romance. 1999. (Tango 2 Ser.). 240p. pap. 8.95 (*1-885478-80-1*) Genesis Pr., Inc.
Tarbox, Todd. Maria. 1993. (J). pap. 6.60 (*0-8442-7218-3*) McGraw-Hill/Contemporary.
Tello, Jerry. Abuelo y los Tres Osos. 1997. Tr. of Grandfather & the Three Bears. (SPA.). (J). (ps-3). pap. 3.99 (*0-590-04320-X*, 691722Q) Scholastic, Inc.
Valdes-Rodriguez, Alisa. El Club Social de las Chicas Temerarias. 2003. Tr. of Dirty Girls Social Club. (SPA.). 304p. pap. 13.95 (*0-312-31812-X*, Saint Martin's Griffin) St. Martin's Pr.
—The Dirty Girls Social Club. abr. ed. 2003. (Illus.). audio 24.95 (*1-55927-877-3*); audio compact disk 30.00 (*1-55927-875-7*) Audio Renaissance.
—The Dirty Girls Social Club. 2003. 7p. pap. 59.95 (*0-7927-2892-0*); 8p. pap. 79.95 (*0-7927-2893-9*) BBC Audiobooks America.
—The Dirty Girls Social Club. Date not set. pap. (*0-312-31382-9*, St. Martin's Paperbacks); E-Book 10.45 (*0-312-71024-0*); 2003. 304p. 24.95 (*0-312-31381-0*) St. Martin's Pr.
Venegas, Daniel. Las Aventuras de Don Chipote, O, Cuando los Pericos Mamen. Kanellos, Nicolás., ed. 2nd ed. 1998. (ENG & SPA., Illus.). 170p. pap. 12.95 (*1-55885-252-2*) Arte Publico Pr.
Villatoro, Marcos M. Minos: A Romilia Chacon Mystery. 2003. 320p. 24.95 (*1-932112-13-8*) Justin, Charles & Co. Pubs.

Wishnia, K. J. A. The Glass Factory: A Filomena Buscarsela Mystery. 2000. (Filomena Buscarsela Mysteries Ser.). 224p. 23.95 o.s.i (*0-525-94545-8*, Dutton) Dutton/Plume.

—The Glass Factory: A Filomena Buscarsela Mystery. 2001. 256p. reprint ed. mass mkt. 5.99 o.s.i (*0-451-19751-8*, Signet Bks.) NAL.

—The Glass Factory: A Filomena Buscarsela Mystery. l.t. ed. 2000. (Mystery Ser.). 375p. 27.95 (*0-7862-2841-5*) Thorndike Pr.

—Red House: A Filomena Buscarsela Mystery. 2001. 288p. 23.95 (*0-312-28182-X*, Saint Martin's Minotaur) St. Martin's Pr.

—Soft Money. 1999. (Filomena Se La Busca Misteriosamente Ser.). 226p. 23.95 o.p. (*0-525-94501-6*) Dutton/Plume.

Ybarra, Ricardo M. Brotherhood of Dolphins. 1997. 160p. pap. 12.95 (*1-55885-215-8*) Arte Publico Pr.

Zeplin, Zeno. Secrets of Silver Valley. 1985. 89p. pap. 7.95 o.p. (*0-9615760-1-4*); 2nd ed. 1987. (Illus.). 130p. (J). 16.95 (*0-9615760-4-9*); 2nd ed. 1987. (Illus.). 130p. (J). pap. 9.95 (*0-9615760-5-7*) Nel-Mar Publishing.

Zesch, Scott. Alamo Heights. 1999. 322p. 24.50 (*0-87565-194-1*) Texas Christian Univ. Pr.

# I

## INDIAN WOMEN—CANADA—FICTION

Hogan, Linda. Solar Storms. 1997. 352p. pap. 13.00 (*0-684-82539-2*); 1995. 320p. 22.00 o.p. (*0-684-81227-4*); 1994. 21.00 o.s.i (*0-689-12190-3*) Simon & Schuster. (Scribner).

Oke, Janette. Drums of Change: The Story of Running Fawn. 1996. (Women of the West Ser.). 240p. text 15.99 o.p. (*1-55661-818-2*); 240p. pap. 10.99 (*1-55661-812-3*); 352p. pap. 12.99 o.p. (*1-55661-817-4*) Bethany Hse. Pubs.

—Drums of Change: The Story of Running Fawn. l.t. ed. 1996. 318p. lib. bdg. 23.95 o.p. (*0-7838-1822-X*, Macmillan Reference USA) Gale Group.

## INDIAN WOMEN—NORTH AMERICA—FICTION

Alcala, Kathleen. The Flower in the Skull: A Novel. 1998. 182p. 22.95 o.p. (*0-8118-1916-7*) Chronicle Bks. LLC.

—The Flower in the Skull: A Novel. 1999. 192p. pap. 13.00 (*0-15-600634-0*, Harvest Bks.) Harcourt Trade Pubs.

Bailey, Larry. San Poil Chronicle. 1998. 640p. pap. 28.99 (*0-7388-0050-3*); text 38.99 (*0-7388-0049-X*) Xlibris Corp.

Bell, Betty L. Faces in the Moon. (American Indian Literature & Critical Studies Ser.: Vol. 9). 1995. 200p. pap. 14.95 (*0-8061-2774-0*); 1994. 192p. 19.95 o.p. (*0-8061-2601-9*) Univ. of Oklahoma Pr.

Bittner, Rosanne. Mystic Dreamers. 2000. 384p. mass mkt. 6.99 (*0-8125-6540-1*, Tor Bks.); 1999. (Mystic Dreamers Ser.: Vol. 1). (Illus.). 288p. 23.95 (*0-312-86511-2*, Forge Bks.) Doherty, Tom Assocs., LLC.

Callahan, S. Alice. Wynema: A Child of the Forest. Ruoff, A. LaVonne, ed. & intro. by. 1997. (Illus.). 120p. text 30.00 (*0-8032-1460-X*); pap. text 19.95 (*0-8032-6378-3*, Bison Bks.) Univ. of Nebraska Pr.

Dorris, Michael. Yellow Raft in Blue Water. 2003. pap., tchr. ed. (*0-312-42271-7*) Picador.

Feagans, Carolyn T. In the Shadow of the Blue Ridge, Vol. 1. 1998. 389p. pap. 9.95 (*1-890306-10-X*) Warwick Hse. Publishing.

Glancy, Diane. Stone Heart. 2004. 156p. pap. 11.95 (*1-58567-514-8*) Overlook Pr., The.

Hager, Jean. Ravenmocker. 1992. 272p. 17.95 (*0-89296-493-6*) Mysterious Pr.

—Ravenmocker. 1994. 256p. reprint ed. mass mkt. 5.99 o.s.i (*0-446-40107-2*) Warner Bks., Inc.

—The Redbird's Cry. l.t. ed. 1994. 357p. pap. 18.95 (*0-8161-7402-4*, Macmillan Reference USA) Gale Group.

—The Redbird's Cry. 1994. 288p. 18.95 (*0-89296-494-4*) Mysterious Pr.

—The Redbird's Cry. 1995. 256p. reprint ed. mass mkt. 5.50 (*0-446-40106-4*) Warner Bks., Inc.

—Seven Black Stones. 1995. (Molly Bearpaw Ser.). 304p. 18.95 o.s.i (*0-89296-565-7*) Mysterious Pr.

—Seven Black Stones. 1996. 256p. reprint ed. mass mkt. 5.99 (*0-446-40386-5*) Warner Bks., Inc.

—The Spirit Caller. 1997. 272p. 21.50 o.p. (*0-89296-640-8*) Mysterious Pr.

—The Spirit Caller. 1998. mass mkt. (*0-446-40488-8*, Mysterious Pr. Paperback Bks.); 320p. mass mkt. 6.99 (*0-446-60595-6*) Warner Bks., Inc.

Hale, Janet C. Women on the Run. 1999. 192p. 16.95 (*0-89301-217-3*) Univ. of Idaho Pr.

Hauptman, William. Storm Season. 2001. (Southwestern Writers Collection). (Illus.). 318p. (C). pap. 21.95 (*0-292-73453-0*) Univ. of Texas Pr.

—The Storm Season. 1993. 336p. mass mkt. 5.99 o.s.i (*0-553-56386-6*) Bantam Bks.

Hazen-Hammond, Susan. Spider Woman's Web: Traditional Native American Tales about Women's Power. 1999. (Illus.). 256p. pap. 14.00 (*0-399-52546-7*, Perigee Bks.) Berkley Publishing Group.

Hecht, Daniel. Land of Echoes: A Cree Black Novel. 2004. 400p. 24.95 (*1-58234-393-4*) Bloomsbury Publishing.

Johnston, Terry C. Ride the Moon Down: The Plainsmen. 1999. 592p. mass mkt. 6.99 (*0-553-57282-2*) Bantam Bks.

Matthews, Patricia & Matthews, Clayton. The Scent of Fear. 1992. 320p. 18.95 o.p. (*0-7278-4350-8*) Severn Hse. Pubs., Ltd.

—The Sound of Murder. 1994. 20.00 o.p. (*0-7278-4594-2*) Severn Hse. Pubs., Ltd.

—Taste of Evil. 1993. 256p. lib. bdg. 20.00 o.p. (*0-7278-4505-5*) Severn Hse. Pubs., Ltd.

—Touch of Terror. 1995. 256p. 20.00 (*0-7278-4746-5*) Severn Hse. Pubs., Ltd.

—Vision of Death. 1993. 256p. lib. bdg. 19.00 (*0-7278-4397-4*) Severn Hse. Pubs., Ltd.

Mitchell, Kirk. Sky Woman Falling. 2003. 352p. 22.95 (*0-425-19191-5*, Prime Crime) Berkley Publishing Group.

Pettigrew, Dawn Karima. The Way We Make Sense: A Novel. 2002. 136p. pap. 11.95 (*1-879960-66-4*) Aunt Lute Bks.

Silko, Leslie Marmon. Yellow Woman. 1993. (Woman Writers: Text & Contexts Ser.). 220p. (C). text 35.00 (*0-8135-2004-5*); pap. text 14.00 (*0-8135-2005-3*) Rutgers Univ. Pr.

Tabor, Doe. Do Drums Beat There? 2000. 239p. pap. 10.95 (*1-892281-09-0*) New Victoria Pubs., Inc.

Thurlo, Aimee & Thurlo, David. Bad Medicine. 384p. 1998. mass mkt. 6.99 (*0-8125-6458-8*); 1997. 23.95 (*0-312-86328-4*) Doherty, Tom Assocs., LLC. (Forge Bks.).

—Blackening Song. (Ella Clah Novel Ser.). 1997. 429p. mass mkt. 5.99 (*0-8125-6756-0*); 1995. 384p. 14.99 o.p. (*0-312-85652-0*); 2001. 384p. reprint ed. pap. 14.95 (*0-7653-0256-X*) Doherty, Tom Assocs., LLC. (Forge Bks.).

—Death Walker: An Ella Clah Novel. (Ella Clah Novel Ser.). 1997. 338p. mass mkt. 6.99 (*0-8125-6758-7*); 1996. 352p. 23.95 o.p. (*0-312-85651-2*); 2003. 384p. reprint ed. pap. 14.95 (*0-7653-0651-4*) Doherty, Tom Assocs., LLC. (Forge Bks.).

—Enemy Way. (Ella Clah Novel Ser.: No. 4). 1999. 352p. mass mkt. 6.99 (*0-8125-6459-6*); 1998. 350p. 23.95 (*0-312-85520-6*) Doherty, Tom Assocs., LLC. (Forge Bks.).

—Shooting Chant: An Ella Clah Novel. 2000. 349p. 23.95 (*0-312-87061-2*, Forge Bks.) Doherty, Tom Assocs., LLC.

Tooley, S. D. Nothing Else Matters. 2000. (Sam Casey Mystery Ser.). 288p. 22.95 (*0-9666021-2-9*) Full Moon Publishing.

—When the Dead Speak. 2000. (Sam Casey Mystery Ser.). 304p. pap. 6.50 (*0-9666021-3-7*) Full Moon Publishing.

—When the Dead Speak. Roerden, Chris, ed. 1999. (Sam Casey Mystery Ser.). 304p. 21.95 (*0-9666021-0-2*) Full Moon Publishing.

Trainor, J. F. Corona Blue. 1995. mass mkt. 4.99 o.s.i (*0-8217-5134-4*); 1994. 357p. mass mkt. 16.95 o.s.i (*0-8217-4739-8*, Zebra Bks.) Kensington Publishing Corp.

## INDIANS OF CENTRAL AMERICA—FICTION

Brazaitis, Mark. The River of Lost Voices: Stories from Guatemala. 1998. (Iowa Short Fiction Award Ser.). 202p. pap. 16.95 (*0-87745-642-9*) Univ. of Iowa Pr.

Lee, Rachel. When I Wake. l.t. ed. 2000. (Wheeler Large Print Book Ser.). 416p. pap. 25.95 (*1-56895-996-6*, Wheeler Publishing, Inc.) Gale Group.

—When I Wake. 2000. 400p. E-Book 4.95 (*0-7595-0019-3*); 400p. E-Book 4.95 (*0-7595-9031-1*); 400p. E-Book 4.95 (*0-7595-4019-5*); 400p. E-Book 4.95 (*0-7595-8020-0*); 384p. reprint ed. mass mkt. 6.99 (*0-446-60655-3*, Warner Romance) Warner Bks., Inc.

Lundin, Steve. A Ruin of Feathers. 1992. pap. text (*0-920661-23-8*) TSAR Pubns.

Peters, Daniel. Tikal: A Novel about the Maya. 1983. 422p. 16.95 o.s.i (*0-394-53278-3*) Random Hse., Inc.

## INDIANS OF MEXICO—FICTION

Daniel, A. B. Incas Bk. 2: The Gold of Cuzco. 2002. 384p. pap. 14.00 (*0-7434-3275-4*, Touchstone) Simon & Schuster.

Gonzalez, Francisco Rojas. The Medicine Man. Rudder, Robert S. & Ajona, Gloria, trs. from SPA. 2000. 120p. pap. 13.95 (*1-891270-07-9*) Latin American Literary Review Pr.

Janvier, Thomas A. The Aztec Treasure House. 2000. 252p. pap. 9.95 (*0-594-01032-2*); E-Book 3.95 (*0-594-02493-5*) 1873 Pr.

—The Aztec Treasure-House. 1985. (Illus.). reprint ed. lib. bdg. 16.50 o.p. (*0-8398-0952-2*) Irvington Pubs.

Jennings, Gary. Aztec. 1995. lib. bdg. 49.95 (*1-56849-410-6*) Buccaneer Bks., Inc.

—Aztec. 1997. 1038p. mass mkt. 7.99 (*0-8125-2146-3*, Tor Bks.) Doherty, Tom Assocs., LLC.

—Aztec Autumn. 1998. 468p. mass mkt. 6.99 (*0-8125-9096-1*, Tor Bks.); 1997. 378p. mass mkt. 295.48 (*0-8125-3948-6*, Forge Bks.); 1997. 384p. 24.95 o.p. (*0-312-86250-4*, Forge Bks.) Doherty, Tom Assocs., LLC.

—Aztec Autumn. abr. ed. 1997. 25.00 o.p. (*0-7871-1459-6*) NewStar Media, Inc.

—Aztec Autumn. 1999. 6.99 (*0-312-87131-7*) St. Martin's Pr.

—Azteca. Correa, Maria de los Angeles, tr. 2003. (SPA.). 872p. 34.95 (*84-08-04841-4*) Editorial Planeta, S. A. ESP. *Dist:* Giron Bks.

—Azteca. 1999. (SPA.). 880p. pap. (*84-08-03362-X*) GeoPlaneta, Editorial, S. A.

—Azteca. 2001. (SPA.). 880p. 18.98 (*84-08-03998-9*, PT13487); 1998. pap. (*84-08-01207-X*) GeoPlaneta, Editorial, S. A. ESP. *Dist:* Continental Bk. Co., Inc., Lectorum Pubns., Inc., Planeta Publishing Corp.

—Azteca. 1995. (SPA.). pap. 10.00 o.s.i (*968-406-032-7*) Planeta Publishing Corp.

Morrissey, Tom. Yucatan Deep. 2002. 368p. pap. 12.99 (*0-310-23959-1*) Zondervan.

Sands, Marella. Serpent & Storm. 352p. 2001. mass mkt. 6.99 (*0-8125-7765-5*, Tor Bks.); No. 2. 1999. (Sky Knife Ser.: Vol. 2). (Illus.). 24.95 (*0-312-86127-3*, Forge Bks.) Doherty, Tom Assocs., LLC.

—Sky Knife. 2000. 304p. mass mkt. 6.99 (*0-8125-7764-7*, Tor Bks.); 1997. 288p. 22.95 (*0-312-86126-5*, Forge Bks.) Doherty, Tom Assocs., LLC.

Silko, Leslie Marmon. Almanac of the Dead: A Novel. 1992. (Contemporay American Fiction Ser.). 784p. reprint ed. pap. 16.00 (*0-14-017319-6*, Penguin Bks.) Penguin Group (USA) Inc.

—Almanac of the Dead: A Novel. 1991. 25.00 o.p. (*0-671-66608-8*, Simon & Schuster) Simon & Schuster.

Villarreal, Rosa Martha. Chronicles of Air & Dreams. 1999. (Illus.). 235p. 22.00 (*0-9662299-2-4*) Archer Bks.

## INDIANS OF NORTH AMERICA—FICTION

Abbott, Kate. Mystery at Echo Cliffs. 1994. (Illus.). 184p. (J). (gr. 4-7). pap. 11.95 (*1-878610-37-6*) Red Crane Bks., Inc.

Abreu Gomez, Emilio. Canek, History & Legend of a Maya Hero. Davila, Mario L. & Wilson, Carter, trs. from SPA. 1979. 45.00 o.p. (*0-520-03148-2*) Univ. of California Pr.

Ackerman, Ned. The Spirit Horse. 1998. 167p. (J). (gr. 5-9). pap. 15.95 (*0-590-39650-1*) Scholastic, Inc.

Adler, C. S. A Tribe for Lexi. 1991. 160p. (J). (gr. 3-7). lib. bdg. 13.95 o.p. (*0-02-700361-2*, Simon & Schuster Children's Publishing) Simon & Schuster Children's Publishing.

Albright, Letha. Daredevil's Apprentice. 2002. (Viv Powers Mystery Ser.). 255p. pap. 12.95 (*0-9705049-4-2*) Avocet Pr., Inc.

Alexie, Sherman. Indian Killer. 1996. 432p. 22.00 o.p. (*0-87113-652-X*, Atlantic Monthly Pr.) Grove/Atlantic, Inc.

—Indian Killer. 1998. 432p. reprint ed. pap. 14.95 (*0-446-67370-6*) Warner Bks., Inc.

—The Lone Ranger & Tonto Fistfight in Heaven. 2001. E-Book 7.95 (*1-4014-0042-6*); E-Book 7.95 (*1-4014-0043-4*); E-Book 7.95 (*1-4014-0044-2*) Barnes & Noble Digital.

—The Lone Ranger & Tonto Fistfight in Heaven. 1993. 223p. 21.00 o.p. (*0-87113-548-5*, Atlantic Monthly Pr.) Grove/Atlantic, Inc.

—The Lone Ranger & Tonto Fistfight in Heaven. 1994. 240p. pap. 13.00 (*0-06-097624-1*, Perennial) HarperTrade.

—Reservation Blues. 1996. 320p. reprint ed. pap. 13.99 (*0-446-67235-1*) Warner Bks., Inc.

—Reservation Blues: A Novel. 1995. 306p. 21.00 o.p. (*0-87113-594-9*, Atlantic Monthly Pr.) Grove/Atlantic, Inc.

—The Toughest Indian in the World. 2000. 238p. 24.00 o.p. (*0-87113-801-8*, Atlantic Monthly Pr.); 2001. 256p. reprint ed. pap. 12.00 (*0-8021-3800-4*, Grove Pr.) Grove/Atlantic, Inc.

Allen, Paula Gunn. The Song of the Turtle Vol. 2: American Indian Literature, 1974-1994. 1996. 352p. 25.00 o.p. (*0-345-37525-4*, One World/Ballantine) Ballantine Bks.

—The Woman Who Owned the Shadows. 1983. (Orig.). 217p. lib. bdg. 19.95 o.s.i (*1-879960-19-2*); 225p. pap. 10.95 (*1-879960-18-4*) Aunt Lute Bks.

Allen, Paula Gunn & Anderson, Carolyn Dunn. Hozho? Walking in Beauty: Native American Stories of Inspiration, Humor, & Life. 2001. 256p. pap. 16.95 (*0-7373-0585-1*, Contemporary Bks.) McGraw-Hill Trade.

Altsheler, Joseph A. The Horsemen of the Plains. E-Book 3.95 (*0-594-01833-1*) 1873 Pr.

—The Horsemen of the Plains. 1976. reprint ed. lib. bdg. 27.95 (*0-88411-946-7*) Amereon, Ltd.

—The Last of the Chiefs. 2000. 252p. E-Book 3.95 (*0-594-01834-X*) 1873 Pr.

Anderson, Leone C. Sean's War. 1998. (Illus.). 192p. (J). (gr. 3-9). 16.95 (*0-9638819-4-9*); pap. 10.95 (*0-9638819-5-7*) ShadowPlay Pr.

Anthony, Piers & Gilliam, Richard, eds. Tales from the Great Turtle. 1995. 500p. pap. text 5.99 (*0-8125-3490-5*); 1994. 396 p. (YA). 22.95 o.p. (*0-312-85628-8*) Doherty, Tom Assocs., LLC. (Tor Bks.).

Appel, Allen. Twice upon a Time. 1988. (Pastmaster Ser.). 345p. 18.95 o.p. (*0-88184-384-9*, Carroll & Graf Pubs.) Avalon Publishing Group.

Armer, Laura A. Waterless Mountain. 1993. (Illus.). 240p. (J). (gr. 3-5). 16.00 o.s.i (*0-679-84502-X*, Knopf Bks. for Young Readers) Random Hse. Children's Bks.

Assiniwi, Bernard. The Beothuk Saga. Grady, Wayne, tr. from FRE. (Illus.). 352p. 2001. pap. (*0-7710-0799-X*); 2000. (*0-7710-0798-1*) McClelland & Stewart/Tundra Bks.

Austin, Mary H. The Basket Woman. 1969. reprint ed. 37.50 (*0-404-00429-6*) AMS Pr., Inc.

—The Basket Woman. 1998. (Collected Works of Mary Hunter Austin). 222p. reprint ed. lib. bdg. 88.00 (*1-58201-512-0*) Classic Bks.

—The Basket Woman: A Book of Indian Tales. 1999. (Western Literature Ser.). 136p. (gr. 3-7). reprint ed. pap. 17.00 (*0-87417-336-1*) Univ. of Nevada Pr.

—Stories from the Country of Lost Borders. Pryse, Marjorie, ed. 1987. (American Women Writers Ser.). 267p. text 40.00 (*0-8135-1217-4*); pap. text 16.00 (*0-8135-1218-2*) Rutgers Univ. Pr.

Awiakta, Marilou. Rising Fawn & the Fire Mystery. Easson, Roger R., ed. 1984. (Illus.). 48p. (J). (gr. 5 up). pap. 11.95 (*0-918518-29-6*); lib. bdg. 9.95 o.p. (*0-918518-35-0*) Bell Buckle Pr.

Baer, Judy. More Than Friends. 1992. (Cedar River Daydreams Ser.: No. 18). 128p. (YA). (gr. 7-10). mass mkt. 4.99 o.p. (*1-55661-298-2*) Bethany Hse. Pubs.

Bagdon, Paul. Scrapper John: Rendezvous at Skull Mountain. 1992. 128p. (Orig.). (J). pap. 3.50 (*0-380-76418-0*, Avon Bks.) Morrow/Avon.

Baker, Betty. Little Runner of the Longhouse. 1962. (I Can Read Bks.). (Illus.). 64p. (J). (gr. k-3). lib. bdg. 15.89 (*0-06-020341-2*) HarperCollins Children's Bk. Group.

Baker, Madeline. Lakota Love Song. 2002. (Signet Historical Romance Ser.). 352p. mass mkt. 5.99 (*0-451-20498-0*) NAL.

—Lakota Love Song. l.t. ed. 2002. (Thorndike Romance Ser.). 508p. 29.95 (*0-7862-4275-2*) Thorndike Pr.

Baker, Olaf. Where the Buffaloes Begin. (Illus.). 48p. (J). 1989. (ps-4). 14.95 o.s.i (*0-670-82760-6*, Viking Children's Bks.); 1981. (gr. 2-5). 10.95 o.p. (*0-7232-6195-4*, Warne, Frederick) Penguin Putnam Bks. for Young Readers.

Balch, Glenn. Horse of Two Colors. 1969. (Illus.). (J). (gr. 3-9). 7.95 o.p. (*0-690-40360-7*) HarperCollins Children's Bk. Group.

Ballantyne, R. M. The Norsemen in the West. E-Book 3.95 (*0-594-02074-3*) 1873 Pr.

Banks, Lynne Reid. La Llave Magica. 1996. (SPA., Illus.). 224p. (J). (gr. 4-7). 8.95 (*84-241-3266-1*, EV1769) Everest de Ediciones y Distribucion, S.L. ESP. *Dist:* Lectorum Pubns., Inc.

—The Return of the Indian. l.t. ed. 1995. (Indian in the Cupboard Ser.: No. 2). (Illus.). 196p. (J). (gr. 4-7). reprint ed. lib. bdg. 16.95 o.p. (*1-885885-11-3*, Cornerstone Bks.) Pages, Inc.

Barak, Anthony J. The Mongrel: A Story of Logan Fontenelle of the Omaha Indians. 2000. 156p. pap. 10.95 (*0-595-01087-3*) iUniverse, Inc.

Bartlett, Mary D., ed. The New Native American Novel: Works in Progress. 1986. (Illus.). 140p. 22.50 o.p. (*0-8263-0849-X*) Univ. of New Mexico Pr.

Bauer, Marion Dane. Tangled Butterfly, 001. 1980. 162p. (YA). (gr. 6 up). 12.95 o.p. (*0-395-29110-0*, Clarion Bks.) Houghton Mifflin Co. Trade & Reference Div.

Baylor, Byrd. Before You Came This Way. 1969. (Illus.). (J). (gr. 1-5). 8.95 o.p. (*0-525-26312-8*, Dutton) Dutton/Plume.

—Yes Is Better Than No. 1991. (Illus.). 242p. reprint ed. 18.95 o.s.i (*0-918080-59-2*); pap. 9.95 o.p. (*0-918080-53-3*) Treasure Chest Bks.

Beatty, Patricia. Wait for Me, Watch for Me, Eula Bee. 1990. (Illus.). 224p. (J). (gr. 7 up). reprint ed. pap. 5.95 (*0-688-10077-5*, Harper Trophy) HarperCollins Children's Bk. Group.

—Wait for Me, Watch for Me, Eula Bee. 1978. (J). (gr. 7-9). 12.50 o.p. (*0-688-22151-3*, Morrow, William & Co.) Morrow/Avon.

Bechko, Peggy A. Cloud Dancer. 2000. (Five Star Romance Ser.). 278p. 26.95 (*0-7862-2332-4*, Five Star) Gale Group.

Bedford, Denton R. Tsali. 1972. (Illus.). 256p. pap. 15.00 (*0-913436-24-0*) Indian Historian Pr., Inc.

Begaye, Lisa S. Building a Bridge. 1993. (Illus.). 32p. (J). (ps-3). lib. bdg. 14.95 o.p. (*0-87358-557-7*) Northland Publishing.

Ethnic Groups

Belanger, Sean Pierre. Modoc Sundance: A Novel. 2002. (Illus.). 224p. pap. 13.00 (*1-59209-001-X*) USA Bks.
—Savage Mountain: A Novel. 2002. 194p. pap. 13.00 (*1-59209-002-8*) USA Bks.
Bell, Betty L. Faces in the Moon. (American Indian Literature & Critical Studies Ser.: Vol. 9). 1995. 200p. pap. 14.95 (*0-8061-2774-0*); 1994. 192p. 19.95 o.p. (*0-8061-2601-9*) Univ. of Oklahoma Pr.
Bell, Clare. People of the Sky. 1989. 384p. 18.95 o.p. (*0-312-93131-X*, Tor Bks.) Doherty, Tom Assocs., LLC.
Belvins, Win. Stories from an Indian Country. Date not set. pap. (*0-7653-0031-1*, Forge Bks.) Doherty, Tom Assocs., LLC.
Benchley, Nathaniel. Only Earth & Sky Last Forever. 1974. (Trophy Bk.). 204p. (YA). (gr. 7 up). pap. 4.95 o.s.i (*0-06-440049-2*, Harper Trophy) HarperCollins Children's Bk. Group.
—Running Owl the Hunter. 1979. (I Can Read Bks.). (Illus.). 64p. (J). (ps-2). lib. bdg. 11.89 o.p. (*0-06-020454-0*) HarperCollins Children's Bk. Group.
Bendix, Jane. Chaco: The Anasazi Mystery. 1996. (Illus.). 125p. (J). (gr. 4-12). pap. 9.95 (*0-89992-142-6*) Council for Indian Education.
—Mi'Ca: Buffalo Hunter. 1992. (Illus.). 188p. (J). (gr. 4-12). 9.95 (*0-89992-131-0*) Council for Indian Education.
Bennett, James. Dakota Dream. 1994. 144p. (YA). (gr. 7-9). pap. 14.95 o.p. (*0-590-46680-1*) Scholastic, Inc.
Berdine, William C. My Granddaddy Was a Ramblin' Man. 1997. 264p. 20.00 o.p. (*0-9631802-3-1*) Berdine Publishing Co.
Berger, Thomas. Little Big Man. 30.95 (*0-8488-0429-5*) Amereon, Ltd.
—Little Big Man. 1982. mass mkt. 3.75 o.s.i (*0-449-20026-4*); 1981. 448p. mass mkt. 3.50 o.s.i (*0-449-23854-7*) Ballantine Bks. (Fawcett).
—Little Big Man. 1985. 448p. mass mkt. 5.95 o.s.i (*0-440-34976-1*, Laurel) Dell Publishing.
—Little Big Man, unabr. collector's ed. 1988. audio 96.00 (*0-7366-2706-5*, 3439) Books on Tape, Inc.
—Little Big Man. 1979. 10.95 o.s.i (*0-385-28606-6*, Delacorte Pr.) Dell Publishing.
—Little Big Man. 25th ed. 1989. 480p. pap. 15.95 (*0-385-29829-3*, Delta) Dell Publishing.
—The Return of Little Big Man: A Novel. 448p. 2000. pap. 13.95 (*0-316-09117-0*, Back Bay); 1999. (YA). (gr. 8 up). 25.00 o.p. (*0-316-09844-2*) Little Brown & Co.
—The Return of Little Big Man: A Novel. l.t. ed. 1999. (Core Ser.). 695p. 30.95 (*0-7838-8600-4*) Thorndike Pr.
Bergon, Frank. Shoshone Mike. 1987. 288p. 17.95 o.p. (*0-670-81563-2*) Viking Penguin.
Bergquist, J. Gordon. Minnetaka Indian Boy. 1985. (Illus.). 150p. (Orig.). pap. text 9.75 (*0-9615483-0-4*) Bergquist Publishing.
Bibee, John. The Mystery of the Vanishing Cave, Bk. 5. 1996. (Home School Detectives Ser.: Vol. 5). (Illus.). 127p. (J). (gr. 4-7). pap. 5.00 (*0-8308-1915-0*, 1915) InterVarsity Pr.
Biggar, Joan R. Danger at Half-Moon Lake. 1991. (Adventure Quest Ser.). (Illus.). 143p. (J). (gr. 5-8). pap. 4.99 o.s.i (*0-570-04194-5*, 56-1653) Concordia Publishing Hse.
Bittner, Rosanne. Into the Wilderness: The Long Hunters. (Westerward America! Ser.). 288p. 2003. mass mkt. 6.99 (*0-7653-4022-4*); 2nd ed. 2002. 23.95 (*0-7653-0066-4*, CPB0701) Doherty, Tom Assocs., LLC. (Forge Bks.).
—Mystic Visions, Bk. 2. 2000. (Mystic Dreamers Ser.: Vol. 2). (Illus.). 320p. 23.95 o.s.i (*0-312-86512-0*, Forge Bks.) Doherty, Tom Assocs., LLC.
—Mystic Warriors. 2001. 352p. 24.95 (*0-312-86513-9*, Forge Bks.); 2002. reprint ed. mass mkt. 6.99 (*0-8125-6543-6*, Tor Bks.) Doherty, Tom Assocs., LLC.
Black, Elizabeth. Buffalo Spirits. 2003. 350p. 23.95 (*1-58654-032-7*) Story Line Pr.
Black, Michelle. An Uncommon Enemy. (Illus.). 400p. pap. 6.99 (*0-7653-4065-8*); 2001. 416p. 26.95 (*0-7653-0103-2*) Doherty, Tom Assocs., LLC. (Forge Bks.).
Blades, Ann. A Boy of Tache. 1995. (Illus.). 32p. (J). (gr. 3-7). pap. 5.95 (*0-88776-350-2*) Tundra Bks. of Northern New York.
—A Boy of Tache. 1995. 13.15 o.p. (*0-606-08703-6*) Turtleback Bks.
Blair, L. E. The Ghost of Eagle Mountain. 1994. (Girl Talk Ser.: Bk. 6). (Illus.). 128p. (J). (ps-3). pap. 2.95 o.s.i (*0-307-22006-0*, Golden Bks.) Random Hse. Children's Bks.
Blake, Michael. The Holy Road: A Novel. 2001. 352p. 24.95 o.s.i (*0-679-44866-7*, Villard Bks.) Random House Adult Trade Publishing Group.
—Marching to Valhalla: A Novel of Custer's Last Days. l.t. ed. 1997. 304p. pap. 19.00 (*0-449-00044-3*, Fawcett) Ballantine Bks.
—Marching to Valhalla: A Novel of Custer's Last Days. 2002. 261p. 24.95 (*0-9724753-3-8*) Hrymfaxe.
—Marching to Valhalla: A Novel of Custer's Last Days. l.t. ed. 1997. (G. K. Hall Western Ser.). 403p. 25.95 (*0-7838-8091-X*) Thorndike Pr.
Blake, Robert J. Yudonsi: A Tale from the Canyons. 1999. (Illus.). 32p. (J). (ps-3). 15.99 o.p. (*0-399-23320-2*, Philomel) Penguin Putnam Bks. for Young Readers.
Blatchford, Claire. Shawna's Bit of Blue Sky. 2nd ed. 1992. (Hippy Ser.). (Illus.). 24p. (Orig.). (J). (ps). pap. text 3.00 o.p. (*1-56134-164-9*, McGraw-Hill/Dushkin) McGraw-Hill Higher Education.
Blevins, Wade. And Then the Feather Fell. 1996. (Cherokee Indian Legend Ser.: No. 1). (Illus.). 35p. (J). pap. 2.95 o.p. (*1-56763-097-9*) Ozark Publishing.
—Atagahi's Gift. 51p. (J). (gr. 4-7). 1996. (Cherokee Indian Legend Ser.: Vol. 6). (Illus.). lib. bdg. 17.25 (*1-56763-135-5*); 1995. pap. text 2.95 o.p. (*1-56763-136-3*) Ozark Publishing.
—Legend of Little Deer. 1993. (Cherokee Indian Legend Ser.: Vol. No. 3). (Illus.). 49p. (J). (gr. 2 up). pap. 6.00 o.p. (*1-56763-074-X*); lib. bdg. 17.25 (*1-56763-073-1*) Ozark Publishing.
—Path of Destiny. 1993. (Cherokee Indian Legends Ser.: Vol. No. 2). (Illus.). 49p. (J). (gr. 2 up). pap. 6.00 o.p. (*1-56763-072-3*) Ozark Publishing.
—Se-lu's Song. 1996. (Cherokee Indian Legend Ser.: Vol. 7). (Illus.). 53p. (J). lib. bdg. 17.25 (*1-56763-133-9*) Ozark Publishing.
Blevins, Win. Ravenshadow. 2000. 423p. mass mkt. 6.99 (*0-8125-9017-1*); 1999. 448p. 25.95 (*0-312-86565-1*) Doherty, Tom Assocs., LLC. (Forge Bks.).
—The Rock Child. 1999. 464p. pap. 6.99 (*0-8125-4472-2*); 1997. 416p. 24.95 (*0-312-86400-0*) Doherty, Tom Assocs., LLC. (Forge Bks.).
Blevins, Winfred. Stone Song. 1996. (Illus.). 544p. pap. 6.99 (*0-8125-3369-0*); 1995. 400p. 23.95 o.p. (*0-312-85567-2*) Doherty, Tom Assocs., LLC. (Forge Bks.).
BlueWolf, James Don & Lupe, Nathan S. Grandpa Says... Stories for a Seventh Generation. 2000. ix, 67p. 12.95 (*1-887400-24-9*) Earthen Vessel Production, Inc.
Boegeheld, Betty D. A Horse Called Starfire. 1998. (Bank Street Reader Collection). (Illus.). 48p. (J). (gr. 2-4). lib. bdg. 21.26 (*0-8368-1763-X*) Stevens, Gareth Inc.
Boegehold, Betty D. A Horse Called Starfire. 1990. 48p. (J). 9.99 o.s.i (*0-553-05861-4*) Bantam Bks.
—Horse Called Starfire, Level 3. 1990. 48p. (J). pap. 4.50 o.s.i (*0-553-34853-1*) Bantam Bks.
Booky, Albert R. Apache Shadows: A Novel. 1986. 144p. pap. 10.95 (*0-86534-084-6*) Sunstone Pr.
Bowering, George. Shoot! 1995. 304p. 22.95 o.p. (*0-312-14045-2*) St. Martin's Pr.
Bowman, Doug. West to Comanche County. 2001. 304p. mass mkt. 5.99 (*0-8125-4046-8*, Forge Bks.) Doherty, Tom Assocs., LLC.
Boyce, George A. Neither Red nor White: And Other Indian Stories. Muth, Marcia, ed. 1996. (Illus.). 128p. (J). pap. 12.95 (*0-86534-237-7*) Sunstone Pr.
Boyle, Patton L. Screaming Hawk: Flying Eagle's Training of a Mystic Warrior, a Narrative. 1994. 135p. pap. 12.95 (*0-88268-159-1*) Station Hill Pr.
—Screaming Hawk Returns: Flying Eagle Teaches the Mystic Warrior. 1995. 135p. pap. text 9.95 (*0-88268-192-3*) Station Hill Pr.
Brand, Max. Farewell, Thunder Moon. l.t. ed. 1998. (Sagebrush Large Print Westerns Ser.). 18.95 (*1-57490-123-0*) Beeler, Thomas T. Publisher.
—Farewell, Thunder Moon. 1996. 84p. (C). text 40.00 (*0-8032-1267-4*) Univ. of Nebraska Pr.
—Red Wind & Thunder Moon. 1999. 256p. pap. 5.50 (*0-8439-4630-X*, Leisure Bks.) Dorchester Publishing Co., Inc.
—Red Wind & Thunder Moon. 1996. 166p. (C). text 40.00 (*0-8032-1268-2*) Univ. of Nebraska Pr.
—Thunder Moon & Red Wind. l.t. ed. 1997. (Sagebrush Large Print Westerns Ser.). lib. bdg. 20.95 (*1-57490-096-X*) Beeler, Thomas T. Publisher.
—War Party. 1982. 224p. reprint ed. 16.00 (*0-8376-0460-5*) Bentley Pubs.
Brashear, Charles. Comeuppance at Kicking Horse Casino: And Other Stories. 2000. (Native American Literature Ser.: No. 10). 200p. (C). pap. 15.00 (*0-935626-51-4*) Univ. of California, American Indian Studies Ctr.
—Killing Cynthia Ann. 1999. 216p. 21.50 (*0-87565-209-3*) Texas Christian Univ. Pr.
Brouwer, Sigmund. Sun Dance. 2000. (Sam Keaton Ser.: Vol. 3). 304p. pap. 10.99 (*0-7642-2367-4*) Bethany Hse. Pubs.
—Sun Dance. 1995. (Illus.). 312p. pap. 9.99 o.p. (*1-56476-427-3*, 6-3427) Cook Communications Ministries.
Brown, Dee. Creek Mary's Blood. 1983. 496p. mass mkt. 4.95 o.s.i (*0-671-50709-5*, Pocket) Simon & Schuster.
Brown, Margaret Wise. David's Little Indian. 1992. 48p. (J). (ps-3). pap. 3.25 o.s.i (*0-440-40587-4*) Dell Publishing.
—David's Little Indian. 1992. (Illus.). 48p. (J). (gr. k-4). reprint ed. 11.95 o.s.i (*1-56282-209-8*) Hyperion Bks. for Children.
Brown, Sandra. Hawk O'Toole's Hostage. l.t. ed. 1997. 26.95 (*1-56895-425-5*, Wheeler Publishing, Inc.) Gale Group.
Bruchac, Joseph. Children of the Longhouse. (Illus.). 160p. (J). (gr. 3-7). 1998. pap. 5.99 (*0-14-038504-5*, Puffin Bks.); 1996. 14.89 o.s.i (*0-8037-1794-6*, Dial Bks. for Young Readers); 1996. 14.99 o.p. (*0-8037-1793-8*, Dial Bks. for Young Readers) Penguin Putnam Bks. for Young Readers.
—Dawn Land. 336p. 1995. pap. 12.95 (*1-55591-215-X*); 1993. 19.95 (*1-55591-134-X*) Fulcrum Publishing.
—Dawn Land. 1995. 19.00 (*0-606-12673-2*); 19.00 (*0-606-22699-0*) Turtleback Bks.
—Dog People: Native Dog Stories. 1995. (Kids Ser.). (Illus.). 64p. (J). (gr. 4-7). 14.95 (*1-55591-228-1*) Fulcrum Publishing.
—Foot of the Mountain: And Other Stories. 2003. 188p. pap. 13.95 (*0-930100-62-X*) Holy Cow! Pr.
—Fox Song. (Illus.). 32p. (J). (ps-3). 1997. pap. 5.95 o.s.i (*0-698-11561-9*, PaperStar); 1993. 14.95 o.p. (*0-399-22346-0*, Philomel) Penguin Putnam Bks. for Young Readers.
—Long River: A Novel. 1995. 312p. 19.95 (*1-55591-213-3*) Fulcrum Publishing.
—Turtle Meat & Other Stories. 1992. (Orig.). 144p. 18.95 o.p. (*0-930100-48-4*); 119p. pap. 12.95 (*0-930100-49-2*) Holy Cow! Pr.
—The Waters Between: A Novel of the Dawn Land. 1998. 310p. pap. 14.95 (*1-58465-015-X*); text 26.00 o.p. (*0-87451-881-4*) Univ. Pr. of New England. (Hardscrabble Bks.).
Bryers, Paul. The Prayer of the Bone. 2000. 256p. pap. 13.95 (*1-58234-075-7*); 1999. 23.95 (*1-58234-022-6*) Bloomsbury Publishing.
Bryson, Jamie S. The War Canoe. 1990. 198p. (J). pap. 9.95 o.p. (*0-88240-368-0*, Alaska Northwest Bks.) Graphic Arts Ctr. Publishing Co.
Buchanan, William J. One Last Time. 1992. (Orig.). (YA). pap. 2.99 (*0-380-76152-1*, Avon Bks.) Morrow/Avon.
Bulla, Clyde Robert & Syson, Michael. Conquista! 1978. (Illus.). (J). (gr. 2-5). lib. bdg. 12.89 (*0-690-03871-2*) HarperCollins Children's Bk. Group.
Bunting, Eve. Cheyenne Again. (Illus.). 32p. (J). (ps-3). 2002. pap. 5.95 (*0-618-19465-7*); 1995. 16.00 (*0-395-70364-6*) Houghton Mifflin Co. Trade & Reference Div. (Clarion Bks.).
Burchardt, Bill. The Lighthorsemen. 1981. (Double D Western Ser.). 192p. 9.95 o.s.i (*0-385-17148-X*) Doubleday Publishing.
Burks, Brian. Walks Alone. (YA). (gr. 6 up). 2000. 144p. pap. 6.00 (*0-15-202472-7*, Harcourt Paperbacks); 1998. 128p. 16.00 (*0-15-201612-0*) Harcourt Children's Bks.
—Walks Alone. 2000. 12.05 (*0-606-20336-2*) Turtleback Bks.
Burleson, Frank. Devil Dance. 1997. (Apache Wars Ser.). 352p. mass mkt. 5.99 o.s.i (*0-451-18731-8*, Signet Bks.) NAL.
Burrill, Richard. River of Sorrows: Life History of the Maidu-Nisenan Indians. 1988. (Illus.). 219p. pap. 8.95 (*0-87961-187-1*); (YA). (gr. 8-12). 14.95 o.p. (*0-87961-186-3*) Naturegraph Pubs., Inc.
Bushey, Jeanne. A Sled Dog for Moshi. 1994. (Illus.). 40p. (J). (gr. k-3). 14.95 o.p. (*1-56282-631-X*); (gr. 3-7). lib. bdg. 15.49 (*1-56282-632-8*) Hyperion Bks. for Children.
Butler, Robert Olen. Countrymen of Bones. 1985. 256p. mass mkt. 2.95 o.s.i (*0-345-32118-9*) Ballantine Bks.
—Countrymen of Bones. 1994. 25.00 o.p. (*0-8050-3202-9*); 224p. pap. 11.00 o.s.i (*0-8050-3142-1*, Owl Bks.) Holt, Henry & Co.
Callahan, John. Kincaid. 2001. 187p. (*0-7838-9417-1*, Macmillan Reference USA) Gale Group.
Callen, Paulette. Charity. 1998. 320p. reprint ed. mass mkt. 6.99 o.s.i (*0-425-16516-7*) Berkley Publishing Group.
—Charity. 1997. 308p. 21.50 (*0-684-82942-8*, Simon & Schuster) Simon & Schuster.
Cameron, Anne. Child of Her People. 1987. 204p. pap. 10.95 o.p. (*0-933216-28-9*) Spinsters Ink Bks.
—Daughters of Copper Woman. 4th exp. ed. 2002. 156p. pap. (*1-55017-245-X*) Harbour Publishing Co., Ltd.
Cameron, Lou. The Spirit Horses. 1976. mass mkt. 1.25 o.p. (*0-345-24915-1*) Ballantine Bks.
—The Spirit Horses. 1986. 192p. 2.50 o.s.i (*0-441-77809-7*, Diamond Bks.) Berkley Publishing Group.
—The Spirit Horses. l.t. ed. 2000. (Western Ser.). 291p. 20.95 (*0-7862-2424-X*) Thorndike Pr.
Cameron, Meg. Savage Spirit. 1985. (Dawn of Love Ser.: No. 3). (YA). (gr. 7 up). pap. (*0-671-55155-8*, Simon Pulse) Simon & Schuster Children's Publishing.
Cannon, A. E. Shadow Brothers. 1990. 192p. (J). 14.95 o.s.i (*0-385-29982-6*) Doubleday Publishing.
Canty, Kevin. Nine Below Zero. 2000. (Contemporaries Ser.). 384p. pap. 13.00 (*0-375-70799-9*, Vintage) Knopf Publishing Group.
Carpenter, Frances. Pocahontas & Her World. 1966. (Illus.). (J). (gr. 5-9). lib. bdg. 5.69 o.p. (*0-394-91513-5*, Knopf Bks. for Young Readers) Random Hse. Children's Bks.
Carr, A. A. Eye Killers: A Novel. 1996. (American Indian Literature & Critical Studies Ser.: Vol. 13). 352p. (C). pap. 17.95 o.p. (*0-8061-2854-2*, 2854); 1995. (American Indian Literature & Critical Studies Ser.: Vol. 13). 352p. 24.95 (*0-8061-2707-4*); 1995. E-Book 19.95 (*0-8061-7239-8*) Univ. of Oklahoma Pr.
Carroll, Jeffrey. Climbing to the Sun, 001. 1979. 128p. (J). (gr. 6 up). 6.95 o.p. (*0-395-28898-3*, Clarion Bks.) Houghton Mifflin Co. Trade & Reference Div.
Carter, Alden R. Dogwolf. 272p. (gr. 7 up). 1996. (YA). mass mkt. 4.50 (*0-590-46742-5*); 1994. (J). pap. 13.95 (*0-590-46741-7*) Scholastic, Inc.
Carter, Forrest. The Education of Little Tree. 1986. 216p. reprint ed. lib. bdg. 25.95 (*0-89966-536-5*) Buccaneer Bks., Inc.
—The Education of Little Tree. 1976. (J). 9.95 o.s.i (*0-440-02319-X*, Delacorte Pr.) Dell Publishing.
—The Education of Little Tree. l.t. ed. 1992. (General Ser.). 327p. pap. 16.95 (*0-8161-5497-X*); lib. bdg. 20.95 o.p. (*0-8161-5496-1*) Gale Group. (Macmillan Reference USA).
—The Education of Little Tree. (Zia Bks.). 216p. 1990. (J). reprint ed. pap. 12.95 (*0-8263-0879-1*); 1990. (gr. 10-12). reprint ed. 19.95 (*0-8263-1233-0*); 25th anniv. ed. 2001. 21.95 (*0-8263-2808-3*); 25th anniv. ed. 2001. pap. 13.95 (*0-8263-2809-1*) Univ. of New Mexico Pr.
Castle, Vernon H. Tecumtha & the Story of the American Indian. 2003. (Illus.). 512p. pap. (*1-882897-67-6*) Lost Coast Pr.
Chacon, Michelle N. & Strete, Craig K. How the Indians Bought the Farm. 1996. (Illus.). 32p. (J). (gr. k up). 15.00 o.p. (*0-688-14130-7*, Greenwillow Bks.) HarperCollins Children's Bk. Group.
Champlin, Tim. A Trail to Wounded Knee: A Western Story. l.t. ed. 2001. (Five Star Western Ser.). 232p. 23.95 (*0-7862-2401-0*, Five Star) Gale Group.
—A Trail to Wounded Knee: A Western Story. 2002. 320p. 24.95 (*0-7862-2402-9*) Thorndike Pr.
Chandonnet, Ann. Chief Stephen's Parky. 2nd ed. 1993. (Council for Indian Education Ser.). (Illus.). 80p. (J). (gr. 4-7). reprint ed. pap. 7.95 o.p. (*1-879373-39-4*) Rinehart, Roberts Pubs.
Chanin, Michael. Grandfather Four Winds & Rising Moon. 1994. (Illus.). 32p. (J). (ps-4). 14.95 (*0-915811-47-2*, Starseed Pr.) Kramer, H.J. Inc.
Chappell, Henry C. The Callings. 2002. (Illus.). 224p. 24.95 (*0-89672-494-8*) Texas Tech Univ. Pr.
Charbonneau, Eileen. Rachel Lemoyne. (Women of the West Novels Ser.). 320p. 1999. pap. 5.99 (*0-8125-7114-2*); 1998. (YA). (gr. 8 up). 22.95 o.p. (*0-312-86448-5*) Doherty, Tom Assocs., LLC. (Forge Bks.).
Chavez Ballejos, Gilberto & Witt, Shirley H. El Indio Jesus: A Novel. 2000. (Politics & International Relations of Southeast Asia Ser.: Vol. 35). x, 257p. 29.95 (*0-8061-3230-2*) Univ. of Oklahoma Pr.
Chavez Ballejos, Gilberto & Witt, Shirley Hill. El Indio Jesus: A Novel. 2002. pap. 17.95 (*0-8061-3376-7*) Univ. of Oklahoma Pr.
Cheshire, Gifford Paul. Thunder on the Mountain. l.t. ed. 2001. 245p. pap. 22.95 (*0-7838-9568-2*) Thorndike Pr.
Chester, William L. Kioga of the Wilderness. 1976. mass mkt. 1.50 o.p. (*0-87997-253-X*) DAW Bks., Inc.
—Kioga of the Wilderness. 1990. (Hardcover Collection: Vol. 3). 19.95 o.p. (*1-55742-046-7*) Millefleurs.
Chew, Ruth. Last Chance for Magic. 1996. (J). (gr. 4-7). mass mkt. 2.99 (*0-590-60210-1*) Scholastic, Inc.
—Magic of the Black Mirror. 1990. 128p. (J). (gr. 4-7). mass mkt. 2.99 (*0-590-43186-2*) Scholastic, Inc.
Chiaventone, Frederick J. Moon of Bitter Cold. 2003. 400p. mass mkt. 6.99 (*0-7653-4657-5*); pap. (*0-7653-0240-3*) Doherty, Tom Assocs., LLC. (Forge Bks.).
—Moon of the Bitter Cold. 2002. (Illus.). 400p. 26.95 (*0-7653-0093-1*, Forge Bks.) Doherty, Tom Assocs., LLC.
Chief Buffalo Child & Long, Sylvester. Long Lance. 1995. 320p. lib. bdg. 45.00 o.p. (*0-87805-829-X*) Univ. Pr. of Mississippi.
Child, Lydia M. Hobomok: A Tale of Early Times. 1972. reprint ed. 16.50 o.p. (*0-8422-8185-1*) Irvington Pubs.
Child, Lydia Maria. Hobomok & Other Writings on Indians. Karcher, Carolyn L., ed. 1986. (American Women Writers Ser.). 350p. (C). pap. 15.00 (*0-8135-1164-X*); text 40.00 (*0-8135-1163-1*) Rutgers Univ. Pr.

Ethnic Groups

Childers, Bob, contrib. by. Home Beyond the Mountains. 1997. (1-890795-00-3) Revelation I Publishing.

Chimera, Donna. WolfStar. 1997. (Illus.). 17.95 (0-9656422-8-3) WolfStar Pr.

Chong, Kevin. Baroque-a-Nova. 2002. 224p. 23.95 o.s.i (0-399-14825-6) Penguin Group (USA) Inc.

Christofferson, April. Clinical Trial. 2000. 333p. 24.95 o.p. (0-312-86899-5); 2001. 464p. reprint ed. mass mkt. 7.99 (0-8125-7468-0) Doherty, Tom Assocs., LLC. (Forge Bks.).

Clancy, Diane. The Man Who Heard the Land. 2001. (Native Voices Ser.). 185p. 19.95 (0-87351-417-3) Minnesota Historical Society Pr.

Clarke, Richard. The Oldest Treachery. l.t. ed. 1994. 18.95 o.p. (0-7927-1836-4); pap. 16.95 o.p. (0-7927-1835-6) BBC Audiobooks America.

Clayton, Paol. Calling Crow Nation. 1997. 320p. (Orig.). mass mkt. 5.99 o.s.i (0-425-15604-4) Berkley Publishing Group.

Clayton, Paul. Flight of the Crow. 2001. E-Book 6.99 (0-7592-0865-4) ereads.com.

—The Flight of the Crow. 1996. 304p. (Orig.). mass mkt. 5.50 o.s.i (0-515-11803-6, Jove) Berkley Publishing Group.

—Flight of the Crow. 2nd rev. ed. 1998. 234p. pap. 9.95 (1-57502-059-9, PO2391) Morris Publishing.

Clymer, E. The Spider, the Cave & the Pottery Bowl. 1989. 80p. (J). (gr. k-6). pap. 2.75 o.s.i (0-440-40166-6, Yearling) Random Hse. Children's Bks.

Coates, Belle. Mak, 001. 1981. (J). (gr. 5 up). 8.95 o.p. (0-395-31603-0) Houghton Mifflin Co.

Cockrell, Amanda. The Rain Child. 2001. (Horse Catchers Trilogy Ser.: Vol. 3). 336p. mass mkt. 6.50 (0-380-79551-5, Avon Bks.) Morrow/Avon.

Coel, Margaret. The Dream Stalker. 1997. 256p. 21.95 o.s.i (0-425-15967-1); 1998. 272p. reprint ed. mass mkt. 6.50 (0-425-16533-7) Berkley Publishing Group. (Prime Crime).

—The Dream Stalker. unabr. ed. 1999. (O'Malley Mystery Ser.). audio 39.95 (1-55686-873-1) Books in Motion.

—The Eagle Catcher. 1996. (Arapaho Indian Mysteries Ser.). 256p. mass mkt. 6.50 (0-425-15463-7) Berkley Publishing Group.

—The Eagle Catcher. 16th l.t. ed. 2002. 248p. lib. bdg. 28.95 (1-58547-159-3) Ctr. Point Large Print.

—The Eagle Catcher. 1995. (Arapaho Indian Mysteries Ser.). 224p. 22.50 (0-87081-367-6) Univ. Pr. of Colorado.

—The Eagle Catcher. 1995. E-Book 22.50 (0-585-02336-0) netLibrary, Inc.

—The Ghost Walker. 256p. 1996. 21.95 o.p. (0-425-15468-8); 1997. reprint ed. mass mkt. 6.50 (0-425-15961-2) Berkley Publishing Group. (Prime Crime).

—The Ghost Walker. unabr. ed. 1999. (O'Malley Mystery Ser.). audio 39.95 (1-55686-865-0) Books in Motion.

—The Lost Bird. 2000. 304p. mass mkt. 6.50 (0-425-17030-6) Berkley Publishing Group.

—The Lost Bird. l.t. ed. 2000. (G. K. Hall Core Ser.). 332p. 28.95 (0-7838-8958-5, Macmillan Reference USA) Gale Group.

—The Lost Bird: A Mystery. 1999. 304p. 21.95 o.s.i (0-425-17059-4, Prime Crime) Berkley Publishing Group.

—The Spirit Woman. 2000. 272p. 21.95 o.s.i (0-425-17597-9); 2001. 304p. reprint ed. mass mkt. 6.50 (0-425-18090-5, Prime Crime) Berkley Publishing Group.

—The Spirit Woman. l.t. ed. 2001. 294p. lib. bdg. 28.95 (1-58547-063-5) Ctr. Point Large Print.

—The Story Teller. 1998. (Wind River Arapaho Ser.). 256p. 21.95 o.s.i (0-425-16538-8, Prime Crime) Berkley Publishing Group.

—The Story Teller. unabr. ed. 1999. (O'Malley Mystery Ser.). audio 49.95 (1-55686-891-X) Books in Motion.

Cogan, Priscilla. Compass of the Heart: A Novel of Discovery. 1998. 352p. (J). (gr. 4). 23.00 (0-684-84764-7, Simon & Schuster) Simon & Schuster.

Coldsmith, Dan. Fort de Chastaigne. l.t. ed. 1993. (Nightingale Ser.). 237p. lib. bdg. 15.95 o.p. (0-8161-5773-1, Macmillan Reference USA) Gale Group.

Coldsmith, Don. Bride of the Morning Star. 1991. 192p. 15.00 o.s.i (0-385-26303-1) Doubleday Publishing.

—Child of the Dead. 1995. 256p. 21.95 o.s.i (0-385-47029-0) Doubleday Publishing.

—Daughter of the Eagle, No. 6. 1988. (Spanish Bit Saga: Bk. 6). 208p. mass mkt. 4.50 o.s.i (0-553-27209-8) Bantam Bks.

—Daughter of the Eagle, Vol. 4. Date not set. (Spanish Bit Ser.). (0-312-87621-1, Forge Bks.) Doherty, Tom Assocs., LLC.

—Daughter of the Eagle. 1984. 178p. 11.95 (0-385-18092-6) Doubleday Publishing.

—Don Coldsmith: Three Complete Novels. 1995. 6.99 o.s.i (0-517-12333-9) Random Hse. Value Publishing.

—The Elk-Dog Heritage. 2002. (Spanish Bit Ser.). 224p. 22.95 (0-312-87618-1, Forge Bks.) Doherty, Tom Assocs., LLC.

—The Flower in the Mountains. 1988. (Double D Western Ser.). 12.95 o.s.i (0-385-24231-X) Doubleday Publishing.

—Follow the Wind, Vol. 2. Date not set. (Spanish Bit Ser.). (0-312-87619-X, Forge Bks.) Doherty, Tom Assocs., LLC.

—Follow the Wind. 1983. 11.95 (0-385-17502-7) Doubleday Publishing.

—Fort de Chastaigne. 1991. (Spanish Bit Saga: No. 16). 256p. mass mkt. 4.50 o.s.i (0-553-29419-9) Bantam Bks.

—Kenzas: A Novel. 1997. o.s.i (0-553-29474-1) Bantam Bks.

—The Lost Band. 2001. (Spanish Bit Saga Ser.: Bk. 26). 336p. mass mkt. 5.99 (0-553-29473-3) Bantam Bks.

—Medicine Hat: A Novel. 1997. (Spanish Bit Saga of the Plains Indians Ser.: Vol. 25). vi, 266p. 22.95 (0-8061-2959-X) Univ. of Oklahoma Pr.

—The Medicine Knife. 1988. (Double D Western Ser.). 192p. pap. 15.00 (0-385-23521-6) Broadway Bks.

—Moon of Thunder. 1985. 179p. 11.95 (0-385-18923-0) Doubleday Publishing.

—Pale Star. 1986. 12.95 (0-385-23227-6) Doubleday Publishing.

—Quest for the White Bull. 1990. (Spanish Bit Saga Ser.: Bk. 17). 192p. 14.95 o.s.i (0-385-26301-5) Doubleday Publishing.

—Raven Mocker. 2002. (Spanish Bit Saga: Bk. 2). 272p. reprint ed. mass mkt. 6.50 (0-553-29472-5) Bantam Bks.

—Raven Mocker. 2001. 253p. 22.95 (0-8061-3316-3) Univ. of Oklahoma Pr.

—Return of the Spanish, No. 18. 1992. 240p. mass mkt. 4.50 o.s.i (0-553-29681-7) Bantam Bks.

—Return of the Spanish. 1991. (Spanish Bit Saga Ser.: Bk. 18). 192p. 15.00 o.s.i (0-385-26302-3) Doubleday Publishing.

—Return to the River. 1987. (Double D Western Ser.). 192p. 12.95 o.s.i (0-385-23520-8) Doubleday Publishing.

—River of Swans. 1986. (Spanish Bit Saga Ser.: Bk. 10). 192p. 12.95 o.s.i (0-385-23228-4) Doubleday Publishing.

—The Sacred Hills. 1985. 179p. 12.95 (0-385-18924-9) Doubleday Publishing.

—Song of the Rock, Vol. 15. 1989. 12.95 o.s.i (0-385-24575-0) Doubleday Publishing.

—Spanish Bit Saga: Fort de Chastaigne, Vol. 16. 1990. 192p. 14.95 o.s.i (0-385-24576-9) Doubleday Publishing.

—Tallgrass. 1998. 576p. reprint ed. mass mkt. 6.50 o.s.i (0-553-57776-X) Bantam Bks.

—Trail from Taos. 1989. (Double D Western Ser.). o.s.i (0-385-24232-8) Doubleday Publishing.

—Walks in the Sun. 1993. 256p. pap. 19.00 (0-553-76285-0, Domain) Bantam Bks.

Cole, Judd. Blood on the Arrows. 2000. (Cheyenne Giant Ser.). 368p. mass mkt. 5.50 (0-8439-4734-9, Leisure Bks.) Dorchester Publishing Co., Inc.

Collette, Rondi. The Meadow Dancers. 2001. 250p. pap. 14.95 (0-9705031-0-5) Hawthorne Pubs.

Comfort, Will L. Apache. 1976. reprint ed. lib. bdg. 23.95 (0-89190-851-X, Rivercity Pr.) Amereon, Ltd.

—Apache. 1980. lib. bdg. 11.95 o.p. (0-8398-2678-8, Macmillan Reference USA) Gale Group.

—Apache. 1986. 274p. reprint ed. pap. 11.95 o.p. (0-8032-6319-8, Bison Bks.) Univ. of Nebraska Pr.

Cone, Molly. Number Four, 001. 1972. (Illus.). 160p. (J). (gr. 5-9). 6.95 o.p. (0-395-13889-2) Houghton Mifflin Co.

Conley, Robert J. Cherokee Dragon: A Novel of the Real People. 2000. ix, 289p. 23.95 (0-312-20884-7) St. Martin's Pr.

—Cherokee Dragon: A Novel of the Real People. 2001. ix, 289p. pap. 14.95 (0-8061-3370-8) Univ. of Oklahoma Pr.

—The Dark Island. 1996. (Cherokee Ser.: 6). 224p. mass mkt. 4.99 o.s.i (0-553-56033-6) Bantam Bks.

—The Dark Island. l.t. ed. 2003. lib. bdg. 28.95 (1-58547-256-5, Western) Ctr. Point Large Print.

—The Dark Island. 2000. (Real People Ser.: Vol. 6). (Illus.). 181p. pap. 11.95 (0-8061-3277-9) Univ. of Oklahoma Pr.

—The Long Way Home. 1994. (Real People Ser.: Bk. 5). 17.50 o.s.i (0-385-42621-6) Doubleday Publishing.

—The Long Way Home. 2000. (Real People Ser.: Vol. 5). (Illus.). 182p. pap. 11.95 (0-8061-3276-0) Univ. of Oklahoma Pr.

—The Peace Chief: A Novel of the Real People. 1999. E-Book 25.95 (0-312-24616-1); 1998. 336p. 25.95 (0-312-19314-9) St. Martin's Pr.

—The Peace Chief: A Novel of the Real People. 2001. 339p. pap. 17.95 (0-8061-3368-6) Univ. of Oklahoma Pr.

—Sequoyah: A Novel of the Real People. 2002. 240p. 22.95 (0-312-28134-X) St. Martin's Pr.

—Spanish Jack. 2001. 240p. 22.95 (0-312-26231-0) St. Martin's Pr.

—War Woman: A Novel of the Real People. 1998. 368p. pap. 15.95 (0-312-19361-0, Saint Martin's Griffin); 1997. 384p. 25.95 o.p. (0-312-17058-0) St. Martin's Pr.

—War Woman: A Novel of the Real People. 2001. 357p. pap. 17.95 (0-8061-3369-4) Univ. of Oklahoma Pr.

Cook-Lynn, Elizabeth. Aurelia: A Crow Creek Trilogy. 1999. 416p. 27.50 (0-87081-539-3) Univ. Pr. of Colorado.

—Aurelia: A Crow Creek Trilogy. 2002. 462p. pap. 16.95 (0-87081-685-3) Univ. of Oklahoma Pr.

—Aurelia: A Crow Creek Trilogy. 1999. E-Book 27.50 (0-585-34185-0) netLibrary, Inc.

—The Power of Horses & Other Stories. 1990. 160p. 17.95 o.p. (1-55970-050-5) Arcade Publishing, Inc.

Cook, Will. Apache Ambush. 2000. 192p. 19.00 (0-7540-8076-5, Gunsmoke) BBC Audiobooks America.

—The Wranglers. 1999. 241 p. (0-7540-3540-9); (0-7540-3539-5) BBC Audiobooks America.

—The Wranglers. l.t. ed. 1999. (Nightingale Ser.). 248p. pap. 21.95 (0-7838-0356-7) Thorndike Pr.

Cooke, John B. Hoop of the Nation. 1986. (Snowblind Moon Ser.: No. II). mass mkt. 3.95 (0-8125-8152-0, Tor Bks.) Doherty, Tom Assocs., LLC.

—The Snowblind Moon: A Novel of the West. 1985. 687p. 18.45 o.p. (0-671-45089-1, Simon & Schuster) Simon & Schuster.

—Snowblind Moon I: Between the Worlds. 1986. (Snowblind Moon Ser.: No. 1). 384p. reprint ed. mass mkt. 3.95 (0-8125-8150-4, Tor Bks.) Doherty, Tom Assocs., LLC.

Cooks, John B. The Pipe Carriers. 1986. (Snowblind Moon Ser.: No. III). 384p. (Orig.). mass mkt. 3.95 (0-8125-8154-7, Tor Bks.) Doherty, Tom Assocs., LLC.

Coontz, Otto. Isle of the Shapeshifters, 001. 1983. 224p. (J). (gr. 5). 6.95 o.p. (0-395-34552-9) Houghton Mifflin Co.

Cooper, Amy J. Dream Quest: Stories from Spirit Bay. 1988. (Illus.). 128p. (J). (gr. 3-7). 7.95 o.p. (0-920303-86-2); pap. 5.95 o.p. (0-920303-84-6) Annick Pr., Ltd. CAN. *Dist:* Firefly Bks., Ltd.

Cooper, James Fenimore. Aerie's The Last of the Mohicans. 1995. mass mkt. 3.99 (1-55902-920-X, Aerie) Doherty, Tom Assocs., LLC.

—The Deerslayer. 1964. (YA). (gr. 6 up). pap. 2.95 o.p. (0-8049-0031-0, CL31) Airmont Publishing Co., Inc.

—The Deerslayer. Date not set. 410p. 27.95 (0-8488-2517-9) Amereon, Ltd.

—The Deerslayer. 1991. (States & Their Symbols Ser.). 528p. (gr. 9-12). mass mkt. 5.95 (0-553-21085-8, Bantam Classics) Bantam Bks.

—The Deerslayer. unabr. collector's ed. 1983. Pt. A. (J). audio 64.00 (0-7366-3981-0, 9529A); Pt. B. audio 64.00 (0-7366-3982-9, 9529-B) Books on Tape, Inc.

—The Deerslayer. 1984. 517p. lib. bdg. 27.95 o.p. (0-89966-490-3); 1976. lib. bdg. 21.95 (0-89968-162-X, Lightyear Pr.) Buccaneer Bks., Inc.

—The Deerslayer. 1841. 572p. (YA). reprint ed. pap. text 34.00 (1-4047-2387-0) Classic Textbooks.

—The Deerslayer. l.t. ed. 298p. lib. bdg. 32.00 (0-7583-3384-6) Huge Print Pr.

—The Deerslayer. 1963. 544p. (J). (gr. 7). mass mkt. 5.95 (0-451-52484-5, CE1645); mass mkt. 2.95 o.p. (0-451-51645-1) NAL. (Signet Classics).

—The Deerslayer. Peck, Daniel H., ed. 2000. (Oxford World's Classics Ser.). (Illus.). 592p. pap. 10.95 (0-19-283725-7) Oxford Univ. Pr., Inc.

—The Deerslayer. 1993. (Oxford World's Classics Ser.). (Illus.). 588p. pap. 7.95 o.p. (0-19-282811-8) Oxford Univ. Pr., Inc.

—The Deerslayer. 1990. (Works of James Fenimore Cooper). reprint ed. lib. bdg. 79.00 (0-7812-2387-3) Reprint Services Corp.

—The Deerslayer. Pease, Donald, ed. & intro. by. 1996. (Classics Ser.). 576p. pap. 10.95 (0-14-039061-8, Penguin Classics) Viking Penguin.

—The Deerslayer. 1998. (Classics Library). pap. 3.95 (1-85326-552-7, 5527WW) Wordsworth Editions, Ltd. GBR. *Dist:* Combined Publishing.

—The Deerslayer, or the First Warpath. 1990. (Scribner Illustrated Classics Ser.). (Illus.). 480p. (YA). (gr. 7 up). 27.00 (0-684-19224-1, Atheneum) Simon & Schuster Children's Publishing.

—The Deerslayer, or the First Warpath. 1987. 12.00 (0-606-00553-6) Turtleback Bks.

—The Deerslayer or the First Warpath. Schachterle, Lance, ed. & intro. by. 1987. (Writings of James Fenimore Cooper Ser.). 682p. (C). pap. text 19.95 (0-87395-790-3); text 59.50 (0-87395-361-4) State Univ. of New York Pr.

—The Deerslayer, or the First Warpath. deluxe ed. 1990. (Illustrated Classics Ser.). (Illus.). 480p. (YA). 75.00 o.s.i (0-684-19234-9, Atheneum) Simon & Schuster Children's Publishing.

—Oak Openings. 2002. 388p. 97.99 (1-4043-2232-9); per. 92.99 (1-4043-2233-7) IndyPublish.com.

—Oak Openings. 1984. 520p. reprint ed. 40.00 (0-938190-33-4) North Atlantic Bks.

—Prairie. Date not set. 411p. 27.95 (0-8488-2546-2) Amereon, Ltd.

—The Prairie. unabr. ed. 1995. audio 76.95 (0-7861-0911-4, 1705) Blackstone Audio Bks., Inc.

—The Prairie. 1976. lib. bdg. 28.95 (0-89968-160-3, Lightyear Pr.) Buccaneer Bks., Inc.

—The Prairie, Set. unabr. ed. 1999. audio 76.95 Highsmith Inc.

—The Prairie. 1970. mass mkt. 0.60 o.p. (0-451-50223-X); 1970. mass mkt. 0.75 o.p. (0-451-50519-0); 1964. mass mkt. 2.95 o.p. (0-451-51511-0); 1964. mass mkt. 3.95 o.p. (0-451-51780-6); 1964. mass mkt. 1.75 o.p. (0-451-51202-2); 1964. mass mkt. 1.50 o.p. (0-451-50987-0); 1964. mass mkt. 1.25 o.p. (0-451-50794-0); 1964. mass mkt. 0.95 o.p. (0-451-50623-5) NAL. (Signet Classics).

—The Prairie. Ringe, Donald A., ed. (Oxford World's Classics Ser.). 2000. 432p. pap. 11.95 (0-19-283766-4); 1992. 418p. pap. 8.95 o.p. (0-19-282824-X) Oxford Univ. Pr., Inc.

—The Prairie. 1990. (Works of James Fenimore Cooper). reprint ed. lib. bdg. 79.00 (0-7812-2375-X) Reprint Services Corp.

—The Prairie. Elliott, James P., ed. 1985. 566p. (C). pap. text 19.95 (0-87395-672-9) State Univ. of New York Pr.

—The Prairie. Elliott, James P., ed. & intro. by. 1985. 566p. (C). text 21.50 (0-87395-363-0) State Univ. of New York Pr.

—The Prairie. Nevius, Blake, ed. & intro. by. 1987. (Classics Ser.). 416p. pap. 13.00 (0-14-039026-X, Penguin Classics) Viking Penguin.

—The Wept of Wish-Ton-Wish, 2 vols. in 1. (BCL Ser. I). reprint ed. 42.50 (0-404-01715-0) AMS Pr., Inc.

—The Wept of Wish-Ton-Wish. 1990. (Works of James Fenimore Cooper). reprint ed. lib. bdg. 79.00 (0-7812-2378-4) Reprint Services Corp.

—The Wept of Wish-Ton-Wish, 2 vols. in 1. 1971. reprint ed. 39.00 (0-403-00432-2) Scholarly Pr., Inc.

Cooper, Virgil R. Virg-1 Promised Land. per. 4.99 (0-9668804-4-7) A-bar-V Publishing.

—Virg-2 A Helping Hand. per. 4.99 (0-9668804-3-9) A-bar-V Publishing.

—Virg-3 'A New Threat' Honest Rustlers. 2000. 224p. per. 4.99 (0-9668804-2-0) A-bar-V Publishing.

Coren, Alan. Arthur's Last Stand. 1979. (Illus.). (J). (gr. 4-6). o.p. (0-316-15742-2) Little Brown & Co.

Cornelissen, Cornelia. Soft Rain: A Story of the Cherokee Trail of Tears. 1998. 128p. (gr. 3-7). text 14.95 o.s.i (0-385-32253-4, Dell Books for Young Readers) Random Hse. Children's Bks.

Cornelius, Kay. Twin Willows. 1996. pap. 7.99 (0-345-40356-8, Ballantine Bks.) Ballantine Bks.

—Twin Willows. 1999. 384p. mass mkt. 5.99 o.s.i (0-06-101376-5, HarperTorch) Morrow/Avon.

Courlander, Harold. Journey of the Grey Fox People. 2002. 256p. pap. 17.95 (0-8263-2814-8) Univ. of New Mexico Pr.

Cowley, Joy. Big Moon Tortilla. 2003. (Illus.). 32p. (J). (gr. 1-4). 14.95 (1-56397-601-3) Boyds Mills Pr.

Crabbe, Richard Edward. The Empire of Shadows. 2003. 384p. 24.95 (0-312-20614-3) St. Martin's Pr.

Cramer, Rebecca. Mission to Sonora. 1998. 298p. pap. 10.95 (1-881542-50-5) Book World, Inc.

—View from Frog Mountain. Date not set. 10.95 (1-881542-63-7) Book World, Inc.

Crompton, Anne E. The Ice Trail. 1980. 128p. (J). (gr. 3-7). 9.50 o.p. (0-416-30691-8, NO. 0191) Routledge.

Culleton, Beatrice. Spirit of the White Bison. 1989. (Illus.). 64p. (J). (gr. 4-7). reprint ed. pap. 5.95 (0-913990-64-7) Book Publishing Co., The.

Cullum, Ridgwell. The Watchers of the Plains. 2000. 252p. E-Book 3.95 (0-594-02077-8) 1873 Pr.

Cunningham, Chet. Battle Cry, No. 9. 1989. (Pony Soldiers Ser.: No. 9). 176p. pap. 2.75 (0-8439-2729-1) Dorchester Publishing Co., Inc.

—Battle Cry. l.t. ed. 2001. 169p. 23.95 (0-7862-3381-8); 224p. (0-7540-4601-X); 224p. (0-7540-4602-8) Thorndike Pr.

—Sioux Showdown, No. 5. 1988. (Pony Soldiers Ser.: No. 5). 192p. pap. 2.75 (0-8439-2620-1) Dorchester Publishing Co., Inc.

—Sioux Showdown. l.t. ed. 2002. (Thorndike Western Ser.). 272p. 24.95 (0-7862-3816-X) Gale Group.

—Sioux Slaughter: Pony Soldiers. l.t. ed. 1998. (Western Ser.). 245p. 20.95 (0-7862-1643-3) Thorndike Pr.

Curry, Jane Louise. Dark Shade. 1998. 168p. (YA). (gr. 7-12). 16.00 (0-689-81812-2, 870382, McElderry, Margaret K.) Simon & Schuster Children's Publishing.

Dakota, Wes. Under Two Heavens. 1991. (Illus.). 240p. pap. 14.95 (0-933025-22-X) Blue Bird Publishing.

Dalgliesh, Alice. Coraje de Sarah Noble. 2001. (SPA.). 80p. (YA). (gr. 4-7). (84-279-3462-9, NG5918) Noguer y Caralt Editores, S. A. ESP. *Dist:* Lectorum Pubns., Inc.

—The Courage of Sarah Noble. 1986. (Illus.). 60p. (J). (gr. 1-5). reprint ed. pap. 4.95 o.s.i (*0-689-71057-7*, Aladdin) Simon & Schuster Children's Publishing.

Dalton, Dori. The Shamrock & the Feather: A Novel. 2002. 403p. pap. 28.95 (*1-890109-39-8*, Cross Time) Crossquarter Publishing Group.

Daniel, Tony. Warpath. 1993. 320p. (YA). 19.95 o.p. (*0-312-85282-7*, Tor Bks.) Doherty, Tom Assocs., LLC.

Davis, Deborah. The Secret of the Seal. 1994. (Illus.). 64p. (J). (gr. 2 up). pap. 3.99 o.s.i (*0-679-86566-7*, Random Hse. Bks. for Young Readers) Random Hse. Children's Bks.

De Coteau Orie, Sandra. Did You Hear Wind Sing Your Name? An Oneida Song of Spring. 1996. (Illus.). 32p. (J). (ps-3). pap. 6.95 (*0-8027-7485-7*) Walker & Co.

DeCalves, Don A., et al. The Narrative of Don Alonso DeCalves, John Van Delure & Capt. James Vanleason. 1996. 17.95 (*0-87770-582-8*); pap. 12.95 (*0-87770-583-6*) Ye Galleon Pr.

Deitz, Tom. Above the Lower Sky. 2000. 23.00 (*0-380-97244-1*); 1996. mass mkt. 5.99 (*0-380-77483-6*, Avon Bks.); 1994. 23.00 (*0-688-13716-4*, Avon Bks.) Morrow/Avon.

—The Demons in the Green. 1996. 432p. (Orig.). mass mkt. 5.99 (*0-380-78271-5*, Avon Bks.) Morrow/Avon.

DeJarnett, Don Patrick. I Cry But I Shed No Tears. 2000. 136p. pap. 17.95 (*1-56167-587-3*) American Literary Pr., Inc.

Dellin, Genell. Cherokee Warriors. 2003. 384p. mass mkt. 5.99 (*0-06-000147-X*, Avon Bks.) Morrow/Avon.

Dewdney, Selwyn. The Hungry Time. 1980. (Kids of Canada Ser.). (Illus.). 32p. (J). (gr. k-3). bds. 12.95 (*0-88862-261-9*) Lorimer, James & Co. CAN. *Dist:* Formac Distributing, Ltd.

Doane, Michael. Bullet Heart. 1995. 448p. mass mkt. 6.99 o.s.i (*0-425-15099-2*) Berkley Publishing Group.

Doner, Kim. Buffalo Dreams. 1999. (Illus.). 40p. (YA). (gr. 2-7). 16.95 (*1-55868-475-1*); pap. 9.95 (*1-55868-476-X*) Graphic Arts Ctr. Publishing Co. (West Winds Pr.).

Dorame, Anthony. Peril at Thunder Ridge. 1993. (Illus.). 128p. (YA). (gr. 7-12). pap. 9.95 o.p. (*1-878610-26-0*) Red Crane Bks., Inc.

Dorris, Michael. A Yellow Raft in Blue Water. 1987. 356p. 16.95 o.p. (*0-8050-0045-3*) Holt, Henry & Co.

—A Yellow Raft in Blue Water. 2001. pap., stu. ed., wbk. ed. (*1-56137-934-4*) Novel Units, Inc.

—A Yellow Raft in Blue Water. 1988. 384p. reprint ed. pap. 14.00 o.p. (*0-446-38787-8*) Warner Bks., Inc.

—A Yellow Raft in Blue Water: A Novel. 2003. 384p. pap. 14.00 (*0-312-42185-0*) Picador.

Doss, James D. The Night Visitor. 2000. (Shaman Mysteries Ser.). 384p. reprint ed. mass mkt. 6.99 (*0-380-80393-3*, Avon Bks.) Morrow/Avon.

—The Night Visitor: A Shaman Mystery. 1999. 400p. 23.00 (*0-380-97721-4*, Avon Bks.) Morrow/Avon.

—The Shaman Laughs. 1995. 272p. 21.95 o.p. (*0-312-13601-3*, Saint Martin's Minotaur) St. Martin's Pr.

—Shaman Laughs. 1997. (Shaman Mysteries Ser.). 352p. mass mkt. 6.99 (*0-380-72690-4*, Avon Bks.) Morrow/Avon.

—The Shaman Sings. 1994. 272p. 3000.00 o.p. (*0-312-10547-9*, Saint Martin's Minotaur) St. Martin's Pr.

—Shaman Sings. 1995. (Shaman Mysteries Ser.). 256p. mass mkt. 6.99 (*0-380-72496-0*, Avon Bks.) Morrow/Avon.

—The Shaman's Bones. 1997. 288p. 22.00 (*0-380-97424-X*, Avon Bks.) Morrow/Avon.

—The Shaman's Game. (Shaman Mysteries Ser.). 1999. 352p. mass mkt. 6.50 (*0-380-79030-0*); 1998. 384p. 22.00 (*0-380-97425-8*) Morrow/Avon. (Avon Bks.).

—The Shaman's Mistake. 1998. (Shaman Mysteries Ser.). 352p. mass mkt. 6.99 (*0-380-79029-7*, Avon Bks.) Morrow/Avon.

—White Shell Woman: A Charlie Moon Mystery. 2002. 304p. 23.95 (*0-06-019932-6*, Morrow, William & Co.) Morrow/Avon.

Dowd, John. Ring of Tall Trees. 1992. 128p. (J). (gr. 3-7). (*0-920417-15-9*) Raincoast Bk. Distribution.

Dreamwalker, Richard. Four Winds Returning: A Novel. 1996. 190p. (Orig.). pap. (*1-887786-10-4*) Sky & Sage Bks.

Dreher, Sarah. Gray Magic. 1987. (Stoner McTavish Mystery Ser.). 282p. (Orig.). pap. 9.95 (*0-934678-11-1*) New Victoria Pubs., Inc.

Driving Hawk Sneve, Virginia. Grandpa Was a Cowboy & an Indian & Other Stories. 2000. (Illus.). 116p. pap. 11.95 (*0-8032-9300-3*, Bison Bks.); text 19.95 (*0-8032-4274-3*) Univ. of Nebraska Pr.

Ducornet, Rikki. The Fan-Maker's Inquisition: A Novel of the Marquis de Sade. 2000. 240p. pap. 14.00 (*0-345-44104-4*, Ballantine Bks.) Ballantine Bks.

—The Fan-Maker's Inquisition: A Novel of the Marquis de Sade. 1999. 224p. 22.00 o.s.i (*0-8050-5926-1*) Holt, Henry & Co.

Dumont, Julia L. Tecumseh & Other Stories of the Ohio River Valley. Parker, Sandra, ed. & intro. by. 2001. 195p. 49.95 (*0-87972-823-X*, Popular Pr.) Univ. of Wisconsin Pr.

Durrant, Lynda. The Beaded Moccasins: The Story of Mary Campbell. 1998. 192p. (J). (gr. 4-6). tchr. ed. 15.00 (*0-395-85398-2*, Clarion Bks.) Houghton Mifflin Co. Trade & Reference Div.

—The Beaded Moccasins: The Story of Mary Campbell. 2000. (Illus.). 192p. (gr. 4-7). pap. text 4.99 (*0-440-41591-8*, Yearling) Random Hse. Children's Bks.

Dye, Kitty. Maconaquah's Story: The Saga of Frances Slocum. 1996. (Illus.). 110p. pap. 8.95 (*0-9642058-2-3*) InChem Publishing Div.

—Maconaquah's Story: The Saga of Frances Slocum. 2nd rev. ed. 2000. (Illus.). 172p. pap. 17.95 (*0-9702501-0-X*) LeClere Publishing Co.

Eagle, Kathleen. The Night Remembers. 1997. 368p. 16.00 o.p. (*0-380-97521-1*, Avon Bks.) Morrow/Avon.

—What the Heart Knows. l.t. ed. 1999. 26.95 (*1-56895-798-X*, Wheeler Publishing, Inc.) Gale Group.

—What the Heart Knows. 384p. 2000. mass mkt. 6.99 (*0-380-80309-7*); 1999. 22.00 (*0-380-97705-2*) Morrow/Avon. (Avon Bks.).

Eagle Walking Turtle. Full Moon Stories. 1997. (Illus.). 47p. (J). (gr. 3-7). lib. bdg. 16.49 (*0-7868-2175-2*) Hyperion Bks. for Children.

—Keepers of the Fire: Journey to the Tree of Life Based on Black Elk's Vision. 1986. (Illus.). 128p. (Orig.). pap. 19.95 o.p. (*0-939680-30-0*, Bear & Co.) Bear & Co.

Eastlake, William. The Bronc People. 1991. 254p. pap. 11.00 o.p. (*0-9627387-5-1*) Bamberger Bks.

—The Bronc People. 1975. (Zia Bks.). 263p. reprint ed. pap. 8.95 o.p. (*0-8263-0379-X*) Univ. of New Mexico Pr.

—Go in Beauty. 1991. 279p. pap. 11.00 o.p. (*0-9627387-3-5*) Bamberger Bks.

—Go in Beauty. 1980. (Zia Bks.). 286p. pap. 8.95 o.p. (*0-8263-0538-5*) Univ. of New Mexico Pr.

—Lyric of the Circle Heart: The Bowman Family Trilogy. rev. ed. 1996. 518p. pap. 14.95 (*1-56478-136-4*) Dalkey Archive Pr.

—Portrait of an Artist with Twenty-Six Horses. 1991. 221p. pap. 11.00 o.p. (*0-9627387-4-3*) Bamberger Bks.

—Portrait of an Artist with Twenty-Six Horses. 1980. (Zia Bks.). 230p. reprint ed. pap. 8.95 o.p. (*0-8263-0558-X*) Univ. of New Mexico Pr.

Eastman, Charles A. Old Indian Days. E-Book 2.49 (*1-58744-179-9*) Electric Umbrella Publishing.

—Old Indian Days. E-Book 5.00 (*0-7410-0787-8*) SoftBook Pr.

—Old Indian Days. 1991. (Illus.). 279p. reprint ed. pap. 9.95 (*0-8032-6718-5*, Bison Bks.) Univ. of Nebraska Pr.

Edmonds, Walter D. In the Hands of the Senecas. 1995. (New York Classics Ser.). 214p. pap. 15.95 (*0-8156-0326-6*) Syracuse Univ. Pr.

Edson, J. T. Texas Warrior. 1997. mass mkt. 5.50 (*0-440-22396-2*); 240p. mass mkt. 5.50 o.s.i (*0-440-22399-7*) Dell Publishing.

Edwards, Cassie. Embers. 1999. (Love Spell Ser.). 448p. mass mkt. 5.99 (*0-8439-4546-X*, Leisure Bks.) Dorchester Publishing Co., Inc.

—Fires. 1999. 400p. mass mkt. 5.99 (*0-8439-4551-6*, Leisure Bks.) Dorchester Publishing Co., Inc.

—Grace. 2000. (Savage Ser.). 400p. mass mkt. 5.99 (*0-8439-4666-0*, Leisure Bks.) Dorchester Publishing Co., Inc.

—Heat. 1998. (Savage Ser.). 400p. mass mkt. 5.99 (*0-8439-4349-1*, Leisure Bks.) Dorchester Publishing Co., Inc.

—Joy. 1999. (Savage Ser.). 400p. mass mkt. 5.99 (*0-8439-4480-3*, Leisure Bks.) Dorchester Publishing Co., Inc.

—Longings. 1997. (Savage Ser.). 400p. mass mkt. 5.99 (*0-8439-4176-6*, Leisure Bks.) Dorchester Publishing Co., Inc.

—Mists. 1998. (Savage Ser.). 448p. (Orig.). reprint ed. mass mkt. 5.99 (*0-8439-4535-4*, Leisure Bks.) Dorchester Publishing Co., Inc.

—Passions. 1998. (Savage Ser.). 448p. reprint ed. mass mkt. 5.99 (*0-8439-4534-6*, Leisure Bks.) Dorchester Publishing Co., Inc.

—Savage Bliss. 1991. mass mkt. 4.99 o.s.i (*0-515-10860-X*, Jove); 1990. 4.50 (*1-55773-285-X*, Diamond Bks.) Berkley Publishing Group.

—Savage Bliss. 1996. 336p. reprint ed. pap. 5.50 (*0-505-52150-4*) Dorchester Publishing Co., Inc.

—Savage Bliss. 1996. E-Book 9.95 (*0-585-29825-4*) netLibrary, Inc.

—Savage Dance. 1991. mass mkt. 4.95 o.s.i (*0-515-10579-1*, Jove) Berkley Publishing Group.

—Savage Dance. 1997. 320p. reprint ed. mass mkt. 5.99 (*0-505-52242-X*, Love Spell) Dorchester Publishing Co., Inc.

—Savage Dance. 1997. E-Book 9.95 (*0-585-28593-4*) netLibrary, Inc.

—Savage Destiny. 2003. 384p. mass mkt. 6.99 (*0-8439-5051-X*) Dorchester Publishing Co., Inc.

—Savage Destiny. 2003. (Basic Ser.). 389p. 28.95 (*0-7862-5394-0*) Thorndike Pr.

—Savage Dream. 1991. mass mkt. 4.99 o.s.i (*0-515-10822-7*, Jove) Berkley Publishing Group.

—Savage Dream. 2002. 320p. reprint ed. mass mkt. 5.99 (*0-505-52161-X*, Love Spell) Dorchester Publishing Co., Inc.

—Savage Dream. l.t. ed. 2003. (Savage Ser.). 545p. 29.95 (*0-7862-5881-0*) Thorndike Pr.

—Savage Dream. 1997. E-Book 9.95 (*0-585-29167-5*) netLibrary, Inc.

—Savage Eden. 1991. mass mkt. 4.99 o.s.i (*0-515-10823-5*, Jove) Berkley Publishing Group.

—Savage Eden. (Savage Ser.). 336p. reprint ed. 1998. mass mkt. 5.99 (*0-505-52316-7*); 1996. pap. 5.50 (*0-505-52097-4*) Dorchester Publishing Co., Inc. (Love Spell).

—Savage Eden. 1996. E-Book 9.95 (*0-585-28448-2*) netLibrary, Inc.

—Savage Embers. 448p. 1995. pap. 5.99 (*0-8439-4009-3*); 1994. pap. 4.99 (*0-8439-3568-5*) Dorchester Publishing Co., Inc.

—Savage Embers. 1994. E-Book 9.95 (*0-585-29223-X*) netLibrary, Inc.

—Savage Grace. l.t. ed. 2002. (Wheeler Romance Ser.). 521p. 27.95 (*1-58724-333-4*, Wheeler Publishing, Inc.) Gale Group.

—Savage Heart. 1997. 384p. mass mkt. 3.99 o.s.i (*0-8217-7305-4*); 1997. 384p. mass mkt. 5.99 o.s.i (*0-8217-5635-4*, Zebra Bks.); 1985. mass mkt. 4.50 o.s.i (*0-8217-3890-9*); 1985. mass mkt. 3.95 o.p. (*0-8217-1582-8*, Zebra Bks.) Kensington Publishing Corp.

—Savage Heart. 1998. E-Book 9.95 (*0-585-28452-0*) netLibrary, Inc.

—Savage Illusion. 448p. 2003. mass mkt. 5.99 (*0-8439-3837-4*); 1993. pap. 4.99 (*0-8439-3480-8*) Dorchester Publishing Co., Inc.

—Savage Illusion. 1995. E-Book 9.95 (*0-585-30683-4*) netLibrary, Inc.

—Savage Innocence. 1997. 448p. mass mkt. 3.99 o.s.i (*0-8217-7307-0*); 1997. 448p. mass mkt. 5.99 o.s.i (*0-8217-5578-1*, Zebra Bks.); 1984. mass mkt. 3.75 o.p. (*0-8217-1486-4*) Kensington Publishing Corp.

—Savage Longings. 1997. E-Book 9.95 (*0-585-29622-7*) netLibrary, Inc.

—Savage Mists. 448p. (Orig.). 1995. pap. 5.99 (*0-8439-3979-6*); 1992. pap. 4.99 (*0-8439-3304-6*) Dorchester Publishing Co., Inc.

—Savage Obsession. l.t. ed. 2002. 28.95 o.p. (*0-7862-4049-0*) Gale Group.

—Savage Obsession. 1997. 432p. mass mkt. 3.99 o.s.i (*0-8217-7308-9*); 1985. mass mkt. 4.50 o.s.i (*0-8217-3199-8*); 1985. mass mkt. 3.95 o.p. (*0-8217-1638-7*, Zebra Bks.); 1983. mass mkt. 3.50 o.p. (*0-8217-1269-1*, Zebra Bks.); 1997. 432p. reprint ed. mass mkt. 5.99 o.s.i (*0-8217-5554-4*, Zebra Bks.) Kensington Publishing Corp.

—Savage Paradise. 1997. 48p. mass mkt. 3.99 o.s.i (*0-8217-7304-6*); 1997. 480p. mass mkt. 5.99 o.s.i (*0-8217-5637-0*, Zebra Bks.); 1987. 480p. mass mkt. 3.95 o.p. (*0-8217-1985-8*, Zebra Bks.) Kensington Publishing Corp.

—Savage Passions. 1996. 448p. pap. 5.99 (*0-8439-3902-8*) Dorchester Publishing Co., Inc.

—Savage Persuasion. (Savage Ser.). 448p. (Orig.). 1995. mass mkt. 5.99 (*0-8439-4010-7*, Leisure Bks.); 1993. pap. 4.99 (*0-8439-3543-X*); 1991. pap. 4.95 (*0-8439-3140-X*) Dorchester Publishing Co., Inc.

—Savage Pride. 1995. (Savage Ser.). 448p. pap. 5.99 (*0-8439-3732-7*) Dorchester Publishing Co., Inc.

—Savage Pride. 1995. E-Book 9.95 (*0-585-30568-4*) netLibrary, Inc.

—Savage Promise. (Savage Ser.). 448p. 1995. mass mkt. 5.99 (*0-8439-3978-8*); 1992. pap. 4.99 (*0-8439-3226-0*) Dorchester Publishing Co., Inc.

—Savage Promise. 1992. E-Book 9.95 (*0-585-30572-2*) netLibrary, Inc.

—Savage Secrets. 1995. 448p. pap. 5.99 (*0-8439-3823-4*) Dorchester Publishing Co., Inc.

—Savage Shadows. 1999. 400p. pap. 5.99 (*0-505-52355-8*, Love Spell); 1996. 448p. pap. 5.99 (*0-8439-4051-4*, Leisure Bks.) Dorchester Publishing Co., Inc.

—Savage Shadows. 1999. E-Book 9.95 (*0-585-33251-7*) netLibrary, Inc.

—Savage Spirit. 1994. (Savage Ser.). 448p. pap. 5.99 (*0-8439-3639-8*) Dorchester Publishing Co., Inc.

—Savage Spirit. 1994. E-Book 9.95 (*0-585-28314-1*) netLibrary, Inc.

—Savage Splendor. 1991. mass mkt. 4.99 o.s.i (*0-515-10825-1*, Jove) Berkley Publishing Group.

—Savage Splendor. (Savage Ser.). 336p. reprint ed. 1998. mass mkt. 5.50 (*0-505-52317-5*); 1996. pap. 5.50 (*0-505-52112-1*) Dorchester Publishing Co., Inc. (Love Spell).

—Savage Sunrise. 448p. (Orig.). 1995. pap. 5.99 (*0-8439-4008-5*); 1993. pap. 4.99 (*0-8439-3387-9*) Dorchester Publishing Co., Inc.

—Savage Surrender. 1991. mass mkt. 4.99 o.s.i (*0-515-10821-9*, Jove) Berkley Publishing Group.

—Savage Surrender. (Savage Ser.). 352p. reprint ed. 1998. mass mkt. 5.99 (*0-505-52315-9*); 1996. pap. 5.50 (*0-505-52093-1*) Dorchester Publishing Co., Inc. (Love Spell).

—Savage Surrender. 1996. E-Book 9.95 (*0-585-28449-0*) netLibrary, Inc.

—Savage Torment. 1997. 384p. mass mkt. 3.99 o.s.i (*0-8217-7306-2*); 1986. mass mkt. 3.95 o.p. (*0-8217-1739-1*); 1982. mass mkt. 4.50 o.s.i (*0-8217-3885-2*); No. 3. 1997. 384p. mass mkt. 5.99 o.s.i (*0-8217-5581-1*, Zebra Bks.) Kensington Publishing Corp.

—Savage Whispers. 1991. (Savage Ser.: Bk. 4). mass mkt. 4.99 o.s.i (*0-515-10824-3*, Jove) Berkley Publishing Group.

—Savage Whispers. 320p. reprint ed. 2000. mass mkt. 5.99 (*0-505-52381-7*); 1996. pap. 5.50 (*0-505-52142-3*) Dorchester Publishing Co., Inc. (Love Spell).

—Savage Whispers. 1996. E-Book 9.95 (*0-585-30269-3*) netLibrary, Inc.

—Savage Wonder. 1998. E-Book 9.95 (*0-585-28973-5*) netLibrary, Inc.

—Silver Wing. 1999. (Topaz Historical Romance Ser.). 352p. mass mkt. 6.99 (*0-451-40843-8*, Topaz) NAL.

—Sun Hawk. 2000. 384p. mass mkt. 6.99 o.s.i (*0-451-20014-4*, Signet Bks.) NAL.

—Sunrise. 1998. (Savage Ser.). 448p. (Orig.). reprint ed. mass mkt. 5.99 (*0-8439-4536-2*, Leisure Bks.) Dorchester Publishing Co., Inc.

—Tears. 1997. (Savage Ser.). 400p. mass mkt. 5.99 (*0-8439-4281-9*, Leisure Bks.) Dorchester Publishing Co., Inc.

—Wonder. 1998. (Savage Ser.). 400p. mass mkt. 5.99 (*0-8439-4414-5*, Leisure Bks.) Dorchester Publishing Co., Inc.

Eickhoff, Randy Lee. Then Came Christmas. 2003. 160p. 12.95 (*0-7653-0142-3*, Forge Bks.) Doherty, Tom Assocs., LLC.

Eisenstadt, Melvin M. Navajo Afterglow. 2000. 270p. pap. 15.95 (*0-88739-271-7*) Creative Arts Bk. Co.

Elder, Gary. Tending the Dream. 1998. 115p. pap. 9.95 (*0-931896-17-7*) Cove View Pr.

Ell, Flynn J. Dakota Scouts. 1992. 192p. 18.95 (*0-8027-4130-4*) Walker & Co.

Ellison, Suzanne P. The Last Warrior. 1997. (J). (gr. 7-10). 140p. pap. 6.95 (*0-87358-679-4*); 240p. lib. bdg. 12.95 o.p. (*0-87358-678-6*) Northland Publishing. (Rising Moon Bks. for Young Readers).

Elwood, Roger. Nightmare at Skull Junction. 1992. (Bartlett Brothers Ser.). 128p. (J). (gr. 3-9). pap. 5.99 o.p. (*0-8499-3361-7*) W Publishing Group.

Epstein, Anne M. Good Stones, 001. 1977. (Illus.). 274p. (J). (gr. 5-9). 6.95 o.p. (*0-395-25154-0*) Houghton Mifflin Co.

Erdrich, Louise. The Antelope Wife: A Novel, unabr. ed. 1999. audio 48.00 (*0-7366-4277-3*, 4775) Books on Tape, Inc.

—The Antelope Wife: A Novel. 1999. 240p. text 24.00 (*0-7881-6505-4*) DIANE Publishing Co.

—The Antelope Wife: A Novel. l.t. ed. 1998. 27.95 (*1-56895-614-2*, Wheeler Publishing, Inc.) Gale Group.

—The Antelope Wife: A Novel. 1998. 256p. o.s.i (*0-06-018726-3*, HarperFlamingo) HarperCollins Pubs. Canada, Ltd.

—The Antelope Wife: A Novel. 1999. 256p. pap. 13.00 (*0-06-093007-1*, Perennial); 1998. audio 25.00 (*0-694-51922-7*, 695743, Caedmon) HarperTrade.

—The Bingo Palace. l.t. ed. 1994. 25.95 o.p. (*1-56895-073-X*, Wheeler Publishing, Inc.) Gale Group.

—The Bingo Palace. 288p. 1995. pap. 78.00 o.p. (*0-06-092614-7*); 1994. 207.00 o.p. (*0-06-017102-2*) HarperCollins Pubs.

—The Bingo Palace. 288p. 1995. pap. 13.00 (*0-06-092585-X*, Perennial); 1994. 23.00 o.p. (*0-06-017080-8*) HarperTrade.

—The Last Report on the Miracles at Little No Horse: A Novel. 2001. 368p. 26.00 (*0-06-018727-1*); E-Book 19.95 (*0-06-000563-7*) HarperCollins Pubs.

—The Last Report on the Miracles at Little No Horse: A Novel. l.t. ed. 2001. 677p. 29.95 (*0-7862-3520-9*) Thorndike Pr.

—Love Medicine. 288p. 1989. pap. 11.00 o.s.i (*0-553-34423-4*); 1987. mass mkt. 4.50 o.s.i (*0-553-26808-2*) Bantam Bks.

—Love Medicine. l.t. ed. 1986. (General Ser.). 360p. 17.95 o.p. (*0-8161-3957-1*, Macmillan Reference USA) Gale Group.

—Love Medicine. 1993. 288p. pap. 10.00 o.p. (*0-06-097581-4*); 304p. pap. 72.00 o.p. (*0-06-097571-7*); 384p. pap. 14.00 (*0-06-097554-7*) HarperTrade. (Perennial).

—Love Medicine. 1984. 88p. 19.95 o.p. (*0-8050-1716-X*); 1984. 288p. 13.95 o.p. (*0-03-070611-4*); 1993. 352p. 24.00 o.p. (*0-8050-2798-X*) Holt, Henry & Co.

Estes, Allison. Legend of the Zuni Stallion. 1996. (Short Stirrup Club Ser.: No. 7). 144p. (J). (gr. 3-7). pap. 3.99 (*0-671-00101-9*, Aladdin) Simon & Schuster Children's Publishing.

Evans, Max. Bluefeather Fellini. Vol. 1. 1994. 432p. mass mkt. 5.99 o.s.i (*0-553-56539-7*); Vol. II. 1995. 480p. mass mkt. 5.99 o.s.i (*0-553-56540-0*) Bantam Bks.

—Bluefeather Fellini. 1993. 304p. 24.95 (*0-87081-307-2*) Univ. Pr. of Colorado.

—Bluefeather Fellini. 1993. E-Book 22.50 (*0-585-00425-0*) netLibrary, Inc.

—Bluefeather Fellini in the Sacred Realm. 1994. 368p. 24.95 (*0-87081-345-5*) Univ. Pr. of Colorado.

—Bluefeather Fellini in the Sacred Realm. 1994. E-Book 22.50 (*0-585-02059-0*) netLibrary, Inc.

—Faraway Blue. 2000. 304p. mass mkt. 6.99 (*0-8125-7076-6*); 1998. (Illus.). 303p. 22.95 (*0-312-86749-2*) Doherty, Tom Assocs., LLC. (Forge Bks.).

Evans, Shirlee. Tree Tall & the Horse Race. 1986. (Tree Tall Ser.: Vol. 2). (Illus.). 136p. (Orig.). (J). (gr. 3-8). pap. 3.95 o.p. (*0-8361-3414-1*) Herald Pr.

—Tree Tall & the Whiteskins. 1985. (Illus.). 112p. (YA). (gr. 9 up). pap. 3.95 o.p. (*0-8361-3402-8*) Herald Pr.

—Tree Tall to the Rescue. 1987. (Tree Tall Ser.: Vol. 3). (Illus.). 144p. (Orig.). (J). (gr. 4-9). pap. 4.50 o.p. (*0-8361-3444-3*) Herald Pr.

Everett, Percival. Watershed. 2nd ed. 2003. 224p. pap. 14.00 (*0-8070-8361-5*) Beacon Pr.

—Watershed. 1996. 202p. 22.95 (*1-55597-237-3*) Graywolf Pr.

Ewell, Alice M. & Scheick, William J. Alice Maude Ewell's Atlantic Monthly Fiction, 1892-1905: Facsimile Reproductions. 1997. (Scholars' Facsimiles & Reprints Ser.). 136p. 50.00 (*0-8201-1503-7*) Scholars' Facsimiles & Reprints.

Faber, Gail & Lasagna, Michele. Pasquala: The Story of a California Indian Girl. 1990. (Whispers Ser.). (Illus.). 95p. (J). (gr. 4-8). 12.95 (*0-936480-07-6*) Magpie Pubns.

Fall, Thomas. The Ordeal of Running Standing. 1993. 312p. 15.95 (*0-8061-2571-3*) Univ. of Oklahoma Pr.

—The Ordeal of Running Standing. 1993. E-Book 15.95 (*0-585-10056-X*) netLibrary, Inc.

Farraday, Tess. Blue Rain. 1999. (Magical Love Ser.). 286p. mass mkt. 5.99 o.s.i (*0-515-12652-7*, Jove) Berkley Publishing Group.

Faucher, Elizabeth. White Fang II: Myths of the White Wolf. 1994. 184p. (YA). mass mkt. 3.50 (*0-590-48611-X*) Scholastic, Inc.

Feagans, Carolyn T. In the Shadow of the Blue Ridge, Vol. 1. 1998. 389p. pap. 9.95 (*1-890306-10-X*) Warwick Hse. Publishing.

Feldman, Ron & McPherson, M. Zigzag Canyon: The Legend of Gold Gulch. 1994. 288p. pap. 14.95 (*0-86534-212-1*) Sunstone Pr.

Fergus, Charles. Shadow Catcher. 320p. 1993. pap. 12.00 (*0-939149-91-5*); 1991. text 19.95 o.p. (*0-939149-55-9*) Soho Pr., Inc.

Fisher, Clay Henry Will. Red Blizzard. l.t. ed. 1994. 20.95 o.p. (*0-7927-1811-9*); pap. 18.95 o.p. (*0-7927-1810-0*) BBC Audiobooks America.

Fo, Dario. Johan Padan & the Discovery of the Americas. Jenkins, Ron, tr. from ITA. 2001. (Illus.). xii, 131p. pap. 15.00 (*0-8021-3777-6*, Grove Pr.) Grove/Atlantic, Inc.

Forman, James. The Life & Death of Yellow Bird, RS. 1973. 224p. (J). (gr. 7 up). 13.95 o.s.i (*0-374-34408-6*, Farrar, Straus & Giroux (BYR)) Farrar, Straus & Giroux.

Fox, Zachary Alan. All Fall Down. 1997. 480p. mass mkt. 5.99 o.s.i (*0-7860-0450-9*, Pinnacle Bks.); 384p. 22.00 o.p. (*1-57566-139-X*, Kensington Bks.) Kensington Publishing Corp.

Franklin, Kristine L. The Shepherd Boy - El Nino Pastor. Ada, Alma Flor, tr. 1994. (Illus.). 32p. (J). (ps-1). (ENG & SPA.). 14.95 (*0-689-31809-X*); (SPA.). 14.95 (*0-689-31918-5*) Simon & Schuster Children's Publishing. (Atheneum).

Fraser, George MacDonald. Flashman & the Redskins. unabr. ed. 1995. (Flashman Ser.). audio 96.00 (*0-7366-3007-4*, 3693) Books on Tape, Inc.

—Flashman & the Redskins. 1983. (Flashman Ser.). 480p. pap. 14.00 (*0-452-26487-1*); 480p. pap. 8.95 o.p. (*0-452-26066-3*); pap. 7.95 o.p. (*0-452-25431-0*) Dutton/Plume. (Plume).

—Flashman & the Redskins. l.t. ed. 1983. (Charnwood Large Print Ser.). 708p. 29.99 o.p. (*0-7089-8127-5*, Ulverscroft) Thorpe, F. A. Pubs. GBR. *Dist:* Ulverscroft Large Print Bks., Ltd., Ulverscroft Large Print Canada, Ltd.

French, Michael. The Throwing Season. 1980. (YA). (gr. 9-12). 8.95 o.s.i (*0-440-08600-0*, Delacorte Pr.) Dell Publishing.

Friskey, Margaret. Indian Two Feet & His Eagle Feather. 1967. (Indian Two Feet Ser.). (Illus.). 64p. (J). (gr. k-3). lib. bdg. 15.93 o.p. (*0-516-03503-7*, Children's Pr.) Scholastic Library Publishing.

—Indian Two Feet & the ABC Moose Hunt. 1977. (Indian Two Feet Ser.). (Illus.). 32p. (J). (gr. k-2). lib. bdg. 15.00 o.p. (*0-516-03500-2*, Children's Pr.) Scholastic Library Publishing.

—Indian Two Feet & the Wolf Cubs. 1971. (Illus.). 64p. (J). (gr. k-3). lib. bdg. 15.93 o.p. (*0-516-03506-1*, Children's Pr.) Scholastic Library Publishing.

—Indian Two Feet Rides Alone. 1980. (Indian Two Feet Ser.). (Illus.). 32p. (J). (gr. k-3). lib. bdg. 15.00 o.p. (*0-516-03523-1*, Children's Pr.) Scholastic Library Publishing.

Fugate, Clara T. From Massacre to Matriarch: Six Weeks in the Life of Fanny Scott. Calvera, Elizabeth C., ed. Socarras-Roufagalas, Gilda, tr. 1989. (Tales of the Virginia Wilderness Ser.: No. 2). (ENG & SPA., Illus.). 98p. (Orig.). pap. 8.95 (*0-936015-08-X*) Pocahontas Pr., Inc.

Full Moon Stories. 1997. (Illus.). 48p. (J). (gr. 3-7). 15.95 (*0-7868-0225-1*) Hyperion Bks. for Children.

Fuller, Iola. Loon Feather. 1967. 468p. pap. 14.00 (*0-15-653200-X*, Harvest Bks.); 1940. 9.50 o.p. (*0-15-153201-X*) Harcourt Trade Pubs.

Furgerson, Celesta. Sculptured in Twilight. 1999. 202p. pap. 12.00 (*0-9679875-0-4*) River Bend Pr., Inc.

Ganesan, Indira. The Journey. 2001. (Bluestreak Ser.). 176p. pap. 13.00 (*0-8070-8353-4*) Beacon Pr.

Gansworth, Eric. Indian Summers. 1998. (Native American Ser.). 220p. pap. 21.95 (*0-87013-479-5*) Michigan State Univ. Pr.

Garaway, Margaret Kahn. Ashkii & His Grandfather. 1989. (Illus.). 33p. (J). (gr. k-6). 5.95 o.p. (*0-918080-41-X*, 20974) Treasure Chest Bks.

Garcia y Robertson, Rodrigo. American Woman. 2001. 352p. pap. 15.95 (*0-312-87629-7*, Forge Bks.) Doherty, Tom Assocs., LLC.

Garcia y Robertson, Rodrigo, et al. American Woman. 1998. 352p. 24.95 (*0-312-86146-X*, Forge Bks.) Doherty, Tom Assocs., LLC.

Garing, Ward C. Legacy: The Treaty of Little Big Horn. Baker, Linda, ed. 2000. 320p. pap. 17.95 (*1-891571-06-0*) Easy Break, First Time Publishing.

Gaskin, Carol. The Legend of Hiawatha, Vol. 2. 1986. 80p. (Orig.). (J). pap. 2.50 o.s.i (*0-553-15450-8*) Bantam Bks.

Gates, Viola R. Journey to Center Place. 1998. (Illus.). 32p. (gr. 4-7). pap. 10.95 (*1-57098-061-6*) Rinehart, Roberts Pubs.

Gear. Thin Moon Cold Mist. 1996. mass mkt. 167.76 (*0-8125-6332-8*) Doherty, Tom Assocs., LLC.

Gear, Kathleen O'Neal. This Widowed Land. 1994. 436p. pap. text 5.99 (*0-8125-8307-8*); 1993. 384p. 4.50 o.p. (*0-312-85464-1*) Doherty, Tom Assocs., LLC. (Tor Bks.).

Gear, Kathleen O'Neal & Gear, W. Michael. Bone Walker. 2002. (Illus.). 352p. 26.95 (*0-312-87742-0*, Forge Bks.) Doherty, Tom Assocs., LLC.

—People of the Fire. 1991. mass mkt. 4.95 o.s.i (*0-8125-0739-8*, Tor Bks.) Doherty, Tom Assocs., LLC.

—People of the Lakes. 1994. 608p. 24.95 o.p. (*0-312-85722-5*, Forge Bks.) Doherty, Tom Assocs., LLC.

—People of the Lightning. (First North Americans Ser.). 1996. 587p. mass mkt. 7.99 (*0-8125-1556-0*, Tor Bks.); 1995. 480p. 16.25 o.p. (*0-312-85852-3*, Forge Bks.) Doherty, Tom Assocs., LLC.

—People of the Lightning. 1996. 13.04 (*0-606-11733-4*) Turtleback Bks.

—People of the Masks. 1999. mass mkt. 125.82 (*0-8125-7624-1*); 1999. (Illus.). 552p. mass mkt. 6.99 (*0-8125-1561-7*, Tor Bks.); 1998. (Illus.). 416p. 25.95 (*0-312-85857-4*, Forge Bks.) Doherty, Tom Assocs., LLC.

—People of the Mist. (First North Americans Ser.). 1998. (Illus.). 553p. mass mkt. 7.99 (*0-8125-1560-9*, Tor Bks.); 1997. 480p. 26.95 o.p. (*0-312-85854-X*, Forge Bks.) Doherty, Tom Assocs., LLC.

—People of the Mist. l.t. ed. 1998. (Western Ser.). 679p. 26.95 (*0-7838-0251-X*) Thorndike Pr.

—People of the Owl: A Novel of Prehistoric North America. 2003. (First North Americans Ser.). (Illus.). 560p. 25.95 (*0-312-87741-2*, Forge Bks.) Doherty, Tom Assocs., LLC.

—People of the River. 1992. 384p. 21.95 o.p. (*0-312-85235-5*, Tor Bks.) Doherty, Tom Assocs., LLC.

—People of the Silence. (First North Americans Ser.). 1997. 650p. mass mkt. 7.99 (*0-8125-1559-5*, Tor Bks.); 1996. 448p. 25.95 o.p. (*0-312-85853-1*, Forge Bks.) Doherty, Tom Assocs., LLC.

—People of the Silence, Set. 1996. audio 19.95 o.p. (*1-55935-235-3*) Soundelux Audio Publishing.

—The Summoning God. (Illus.). 366p. pap. 15.95 (*0-312-87639-4*, Forge Bks.); 2000. (Anasazia Mysteries Ser.: Vol. 2). (Illus.). 352p. 25.95 (*0-312-86532-5*, Forge Bks.); 2001. (Anasazi Ser.). 576p. reprint ed. mass mkt. 7.99 (*0-8125-4034-4*, Tor Bks.) Doherty, Tom Assocs., LLC.

—The Visitant. (Anasazia Mysteries Ser.: Vol. 1). (Illus.). 2000. 501p. mass mkt. 6.99 (*0-8125-4033-6*, Tor Bks.); 1999. 364p. 19.95 (*0-312-86531-7*, Forge Bks.) Doherty, Tom Assocs., LLC.

Gear, W. Michael. People of the Sea, Vol. 1. 1958. 425p. 22.95 o.p. (*0-312-93122-0*, Tor Bks.) Doherty, Tom Assocs., LLC.

Gear, W. Michael & Gear, Kathleen O'Neal. People of the River. 1993. (First North Americans Ser.). 526p. mass mkt. 7.99 (*0-8125-0743-6*, Tor Bks.) Doherty, Tom Assocs., LLC.

—People of the Sea. (First North Americans Ser.). 1994. 560p. mass mkt. 6.99 (*0-8125-0745-2*); 1993. 432p. 22.95 o.p. (*0-312-85648-2*) Doherty, Tom Assocs., LLC. (Tor Bks.).

—People of the Wolf. 1992. (First North Americans Ser.). 435p. mass mkt. 7.99 (*0-8125-2133-1*, Tor Bks.) Doherty, Tom Assocs., LLC.

Gentry, Christine. Mesozoic Murder. 2003. 300p. 24.95 o.s.i (*1-59058-048-6*); 500p. pap. 22.95 o.s.i (*1-59058-086-9*) Poisoned Pen Pr.

Gentry, Georgina. Warrior's Honor. 2002. (Five Star Romance Ser.). (Illus.). 340p. 26.95 (*0-7862-3920-4*, Five Star) Gale Group.

—Warrior's Honor. 2000. mass mkt. 3.99 (*0-8217-7728-9*); 32p. mass mkt. 5.99 o.s.i (*0-8217-6726-7*) Kensington Publishing Corp.

George, Jean Craighead. La Tierra Que Habla.Tr. of Talking Earth. (SPA.). 136p. (J). 9.95 (*84-204-3699-2*) Santillana USA Publishing Co., Inc.

—Water Sky. (Trophy Bk.). (Illus.). 224p. (gr. 6 up). 1989. (J). pap. 5.99 (*0-06-440202-9*, Harper Trophy); 1987. (YA). 16.89 (*0-06-022199-2*) HarperCollins Children's Bk. Group.

Gessner. Brother to the Navajo. 1979. (J). 8.95 o.p. (*0-525-66659-1*) NAL.

—To See a Witch. 1978. (J). 6.95 o.p. (*0-525-66589-7*) NAL.

Gessner, Lynne. Navajo Slave. 1978. (J). (gr. 6). mass mkt. 1.50 o.p. (*0-451-08128-5*, W8128, Signet Bks.) NAL.

Giambastiani, Kurt R. A. The Year the Cloud Fell. 2001. (Illus.). 352p. mass mkt. 6.99 o.s.i (*0-451-45821-4*, Onyx) NAL.

Giencke, Jill. Fatal Facts. 1992. 192p. 18.95 o.s.i (*0-8034-8976-5*, Avalon Bks.) Bouregy, Thomas & Co., Inc.

Gill, Shelley R. Mammoth Magic. 4th ed. 1986. (Illus.). 36p. (J). (gr. 4-7). pap. 8.95 (*0-934007-01-2*) Paws IV Publishing.

Gilman, Dorothy. Girl in Buckskin. 1990. 144p. (YA). (gr. 7-12). mass mkt. 3.99 o.s.i (*0-449-70380-0*, Fawcett) Ballantine Bks.

Girion, Barbara. Indian Summer. 1993. 192p. (J). (gr. 4-7). mass mkt. 2.95 o.p. (*0-590-42637-0*) Scholastic, Inc.

Glancy, Diane. Trigger Dance. 1990. 250p. 18.95 (*0-932511-35-X*) Fiction Collective Two, Inc.

—The Voice That Was in Travel: Stories. 1999. (American Indian Literature & Critical Studies Ser.: Vol. 33). x, 116p. 19.95 (*0-8061-3157-8*) Univ. of Oklahoma Pr.

—The Voice That Was in Travel: Stories. 1999. E-Book 19.95 (*0-585-11326-2*) netLibrary, Inc.

Glancy, Diane H. Monkey Secret. 1995. 116p. 24.00 (*0-8101-5016-6*) Northwestern Univ. Pr.

—Pushing the Bear: A Novel of the Trail of Tears. 1996. 320p. 22.00 (*0-15-100225-8*); 2nd ed. 1998. 256p. pap. 13.00 (*0-15-600544-1*, Harvest Bks.) Harcourt Trade Pubs.

—Pushing the Bear: A Novel of the Trail of Tears, unabr. ed. 1999. audio 53.00 (*0-7887-0850-3*, 94996E7) Recorded Bks., LLC.

—Trigger Dance. 1990. 250p. pap. 11.95 (*0-932511-36-8*) Fiction Collective Two, Inc.

Glasco, Michael. Angels in Tesuque: A Novel. 1995. 160p. 24.95 (*0-86534-103-6*); pap. 14.95 (*0-86534-071-4*) Sunstone Pr.

Goble, Paul. Death of the Iron Horse. (Illus.). 32p. (J). (gr. k-3). 1987. lib. bdg. 14.95 o.s.i (*0-02-737830-6*, Atheneum/Richard Jackson Bks.); 1993. reprint ed. pap. 5.99 (*0-689-71686-9*, Aladdin) Simon & Schuster Children's Publishing.

—Death of the Iron Horse. 1993. (J). 12.14 (*0-606-02590-1*) Turtleback Bks.

—Dream Wolf. (Picture Bks.). (Illus.). 32p. (J). 1997. (gr. k-3). pap. 6.99 (*0-689-81506-9*, Aladdin); 2nd ed. 1990. (gr. 2 up). 14.95 o.s.i (*0-02-736585-9*, Atheneum/Richard Jackson Bks.) Simon & Schuster Children's Publishing.

—La Nina Que Amaba los Caballos Salvajes. Kohen, Clarita, tr. 1998. (SPA., Illus.). 32p. (J). (gr. k-3). pap. 6.99 (*0-689-81455-0*, SS4305, Aladdin) Simon & Schuster Children's Publishing.

Goingback, Owl. Breed. 2002. 352p. mass mkt. 6.99 o.s.i (*0-451-20567-7*) NAL.

—Crota: A Novel. 1996. 304p. 21.95 o.s.i (*1-55611-480-X*) Fine, Donald I. Bks.

Goldsmith, Don. The Lost Band: A Novel. 2000. (Spanish Bit Ser.). viii, 260p. 22.95 (*0-8061-3226-4*) Univ. of Oklahoma Pr.

Goodweather, Hartley, pseud. Dreadful Water Work 1. 2004. 256p. mass mkt. 6.99 (*0-7434-6396-X*, Pocket) Simon & Schuster.

—DreadfulWater Shows Up: A Novel. 2003. 272p. 24.00 (*0-7432-4392-7*, Scribner) Simon & Schuster.

Gordon, Caroline. Green Centuries. 1972. reprint ed. 23.50 o.p. (*0-8154-0398-4*) Cooper Square Pubs., Inc.

—Green Centuries. 1992. (Cumberland & Westmorland Antiquarian & Ar Ser.). 489p. reprint ed. pap. 14.95 (*1-879941-05-8*, Sanders, J. S. & Co., Inc.) Dee, Ivan R. Pub.

Gorman, Ed. Hawk Moon. 1996. 256p. 21.95 o.p. (*0-312-13980-2*, Saint Martin's Minotaur) St. Martin's Pr.

Gotcher, J. C. Shadow Warrior: A Novel of the Old West. 2003. (Illus.). 256p. 22.95 (*1-59228-122-2*, Lyons Pr.) Globe Pequot Pr., The.

Graham, Heather. Captive. l.t. ed. 2000. (Large Print Book Ser.). 580p. 28.95 (*1-56895-889-7*, Wheeler Publishing, Inc.) Gale Group.

—Captive. 1996. 464p. mass mkt. 6.99 o.s.i (*0-451-40687-7*, Topaz) NAL.

Grammer, Maurine. The Navajo Brothers & the Stolen Herd. 2004. (Illus.). 120p. (J). (gr. 4-7). pap. 9.95 (*1-878610-23-6*) Red Crane Bks., Inc.

Grandy, Walter T., Jr. & Schick, L. H., eds. Maximum Entropy & Bayesian Methods: Laramie, Wyoming, 1990. 1991. (C). text 166.50 (*0-7923-1140-X*) Kluwer Academic Pubs.

Grant, Joan. Scarlet Feather. 1990. 290p. pap. 10.95 (*0-89804-148-1*) Ariel Pr.

—Scarlet Feather. 1980. 25.95 (*0-405-11789-2*) Ayer Co. Pubs., Inc.

—Scarlet Feather. 1975. mass mkt. 1.50 o.p. (*0-380-00380-5*, 24877, Avon Bks.) Morrow/Avon.

Grant, Joan M. & Layers, Ralph. Redskin Morning, & Other Stories. 1980. 21.95 (*0-405-11787-6*) Ayer Co. Pubs., Inc.

Gray, Muriel. The Trickster. 1997. 480p. mass mkt. 6.99 o.s.i (*0-312-96100-6*, St. Martin's Paperbacks) St. Martin's Pr.

Gray, Patsey. Barefoot a One Thousand Miles. 1984. 11.95 o.p. (*0-8027-6528-9*) Walker & Co.

Green, Timothy. Twilight Boy. 1998. 127p. (J). (gr. 7 up). pap. 6.95 o.p. (*0-87358-640-9*); lib. bdg. 12.95 o.p. (*0-87358-670-0*) Northland Publishing. (Rising Moon Bks. for Young Readers).

—Twilight Boy. 1998. 13.00 (*0-606-16641-6*) Turtleback Bks.

Gregg, Andy. Cannibal Lake: A Thriller. 2003. 214p. 25.95 (*1-59414-059-6*, Five Star) Gale Group.

Gregor, Elmer Russel. Jim Mason, Scout. 2000. 252p. pap. 9.95 (*0-594-00759-3*); E-Book 3.95 (*0-594-02297-5*) 1873 Pr.

Grey, Zane. Greatest Indian Stories. l.t. ed. 1988. lib. bdg. 18.95 o.p. (*1-55504-731-9*); pap. 16.95 o.p. (*1-55504-707-6*) BBC Audiobooks America.

—The Last Trail. 1976. reprint ed. lib. bdg. 22.95 (*0-89190-754-8*) Amereon, Ltd.

—The Last Trail. 1993. reprint ed. lib. bdg. 18.95 (*1-56849-203-0*) Buccaneer Bks., Inc.

—The Last Trail. 1994. 288p. mass mkt. 4.99 (*0-8125-3467-0*, Forge Bks.) Doherty, Tom Assocs., LLC.

—The Last Trail. 256p. 1988. pap. 2.95 (*0-8439-2636-8*); 1986. pap. 2.75 o.p. (*0-8439-2347-4*); 1981. pap. 2.25 o.s.i (*0-505-51761-2*) Dorchester Publishing Co., Inc.

—The Last Trail. 1993. 304p. mass mkt. 3.99 o.p. (*0-06-100583-5*, HarperTorch) Morrow/Avon.

—The Vanishing American. 1976. 24.95 (*0-8488-1030-9*) Amereon, Ltd.

—The Vanishing American. l.t. ed. 1984. (General Ser.). 16.95 o.p. (*0-8161-3502-9*, Macmillan Reference USA) Gale Group.

—The Vanishing American. 1991. 336p. mass mkt. 3.99 o.p. (*0-06-100295-X*, HarperTorch) Morrow/Avon.

—The Vanishing American. 1984. mass mkt. 3.50 (*0-671-55696-7*); 1983. mass mkt. 2.95 o.s.i (*0-671-47724-2*) Simon & Schuster. (Pocket).

—The Vanishing American. l.t. ed. 2000. (*1-56000-439-8*) Transaction Pubs.

Griese, Arnold A. At the Mouth of the Luckiest River. 1973. (Illus.). 80p. (J). (gr. 3-5). lib. bdg. 12.89 o.p. (*0-690-10787-0*) HarperCollins Children's Bk. Group.

—The Way of Our People. 2003. (Illus.). 96p. (J). pap. 9.95 (*1-56397-648-X*) Boyds Mills Pr.

—The Way of Our People. 1975. (Illus.). 90p. (J). (gr. 4-7). lib. bdg. 12.89 o.p. (*0-690-00707-8*) HarperCollins Children's Bk. Group.

Grinnell, George B. The Punishment of the Stingy & Other Indian Stories. 1982. (Illus.). reprint ed. xx, 265p. 27.50 o.p. (*0-8032-2113-4*); 265p. pap. 9.95 o.p. (*0-8032-7008-9*) Univ. of Nebraska Pr. (Bison Bks.).

Grove, Fred. Warrior Road. l.t. ed. 2001. 252p. 20.95 (*1-57490-330-6*, Sagebrush Large Print Westerns) Beeler, Thomas T. Publisher.

—The Years of Fear. 2002. 241p. pap. 13.95 (*1-4104-0069-7*, Five Star Trade); 24.95 (*0-7862-3272-2*) Gale Group.

Hager, Jean. Masked Dancers. 1998. 288p. 23.00 o.p. (*0-89296-641-6*) Mysterious Pr.

—The Redbird's Cry. l.t. ed. 1994. 357p. pap. 18.95 (*0-8161-7402-4*, Macmillan Reference USA) Gale Group.

—The Redbird's Cry. 1994. 288p. 18.95 (*0-89296-494-4*) Mysterious Pr.

—The Redbird's Cry. 1995. 256p. reprint ed. mass mkt. 5.50 (*0-446-40106-4*) Warner Bks., Inc.

—The Spirit Caller. 1997. 272p. 21.50 o.p. (*0-89296-640-8*) Mysterious Pr.

—The Spirit Caller. 1998. mass mkt. (*0-446-40488-8*, Mysterious Pr. Paperback Bks.); 320p. mass mkt. 6.99 (*0-446-60595-6*) Warner Bks., Inc.

Hale, Deborah. Whitefeather's Woman. 2001. (Harlequin Historicals Ser.: No. 581). 304p. mass mkt. (*0-373-29181-7*, Harlequin Bks.) Harlequin Enterprises, Ltd.

Hale, Janet C. The Jailing of Cecelia Capture. 1985. 15.95 o.p. (*0-394-54327-0*) Random Hse., Inc.

—The Owl's Song. 1995. 192p. pap. 11.00 o.p. (*0-06-097642-X*, Perennial) HarperTrade.

—The Owl's Song. 1990. 160p. (J). (gr. 5 up). mass mkt. 2.95 o.s.i (*0-553-28829-6*, Starfire) Random Hse. Children's Bks.

—Women on the Run. 1999. 192p. 16.95 (*0-89301-217-3*) Univ. of Idaho Pr.

Hale, Janet Campbell. Jailing of Cecelia Capture. 1987. 208p. reprint ed. pap. 15.95 (*0-8263-1003-6*) Univ. of New Mexico Pr.

Hall, Brian. I Should Be Extremely Happy in Your Company. 2003. 432p. pap. 14.00 (*0-14-200371-9*) Penguin Group (USA) Inc.

—I Should Be Extremely Happy in Your Company. l.t. ed. 2003. 682p. 29.95 (*0-7862-5577-3*) Thorndike Pr.

Haller, Danita R. Not Just Any Ring. 1982. (Illus.). 48p. (J). (gr. 1-5). 9.95 o.p. (*0-394-85082-3*, Knopf Bks. for Young Readers) Random Hse. Children's Bks.

Hamilton, Steve. Winter of the Wolf Moon. E-Book 6.50 (*0-312-27360-6*); 2001. 320p. reprint ed. mass mkt. 6.50 (*0-312-97475-2*, 20-3320, St. Martin's Paperbacks) St. Martin's Pr.

—Winter of the Wolf Moon: An Alex McKnight Mystery. 2000. (Alex McKnight Mysteries Ser.). 274p. 23.95 (*0-312-25295-1*, Saint Martin's Minotaur) St. Martin's Pr.

Hanson, Jack. Blood Trail. 2000. (Wildgun Ser.: Vol. 4). 192p. mass mkt. 5.99 o.s.i (*0-515-12870-8*, Jove) Berkley Publishing Group.

—Hostile Country. 2000. (Wildgun Ser.: Vol. 3). 208p. mass mkt. 5.99 o.s.i (*0-515-12788-4*, Jove) Berkley Publishing Group.

—Oregon Trail. 8th ed. 2003. (Wildgun Ser.). 224p. mass mkt. 5.99 (*0-515-13470-8*, Jove) Berkley Publishing Group.

—Vengeance Trail. 2000. (Wildgun Ser.: Vol. 2). 192p. mass mkt. 5.99 o.s.i (*0-515-12732-9*, Jove) Berkley Publishing Group.

—Wildgun. 1999. (Wildgun Ser.: Vol. 1). 288p. mass mkt. 5.99 o.s.i (*0-515-12656-X*, Jove) Berkley Publishing Group.

Hardie, Wallace. Dog Warrior Down: (Kanaizomita Ahtomina Kitaiinz) 2001. 344p. pap. 23.95 (*0-7596-5469-7*) 1stBooks Library.

Harjo, Joy. The Good-Luck Cat. 2000. (Illus.). 32p. (J). (gr. 1-4). 16.00 (*0-15-232197-7*) Harcourt Children's Bks.

Harper, Karen. Black Orchid. l.t. ed. 1997. lib. bdg. 25.95 (*1-57490-099-4*, Beeler Large Print Bks.) Beeler, Thomas T. Publisher.

—Black Orchid. 1996. 384p. mass mkt. 5.99 o.s.i (*0-451-18866-7*, Signet Bks.) NAL.

Harrington, M. R. The Iroquois Trail: Dickon among the Onondagas & Senecas. 1991. (Illus.). 215p. (YA). reprint ed. pap. text 9.95 (*0-8135-0480-5*) Rutgers Univ. Pr.

Harris, Christie. Raven's Cry. 1992. (Illus.). 196p. pap. 19.95 (*0-295-97221-1*) Univ. of Washington Pr.

Harrison, Sue. Brother Wind: A Novel. 1994. 494p. 22.00 o.p. (*0-688-12888-2*, Morrow, William & Co.) Morrow/Avon.

—Cry of the Wind. 2000. (Storyteller Trilogy Ser.: Vol. 2). 512p. mass mkt. 6.99 (*0-380-72604-1*, Avon Bks.) Morrow/Avon.

—Cry of the Wind: Book Two of the Storyteller Trilogy. 1998. (Storyteller Trilogy Ser.: Bk. 2). 464p. 24.00 (*0-380-97371-5*, Avon Bks.) Morrow/Avon.

—Mother Earth, Father Sky. 1995. audio 24.95 (*0-939643-66-9*, NorthWord) Creative Publishing international, Inc.

—Mother Earth, Father Sky. 1991. 416p. mass mkt. 7.99 (*0-380-71592-9*, Avon Bks.) Morrow/Avon.

—Song of the River. 1998. 608p. mass mkt. 6.99 (*0-380-72603-3*); 1997. (Bright & Early Bks.: Vol. 1). 496p. mass mkt. 24.00 (*0-380-97370-7*) Morrow/Avon. (Avon Bks.).

Harte, Holly. Apache Destiny. 2001. 368p. mass mkt. 5.50 (*0-8439-4930-9*, Leisure Bks.) Dorchester Publishing Co., Inc.

Haseley, Dennis. The Scared One. 1983. (Illus.). 32p. (J). (gr. 1-5). 10.95 o.p. (*0-7232-6185-7*, Warne, Frederick) Penguin Putnam Bks. for Young Readers.

Haseloff, Cynthia. The Chains of Sarai Stone. 1998. 224p. reprint ed. pap. 4.50 (*0-8439-4381-5*, Leisure Bks.) Dorchester Publishing Co., Inc.

—The Chains of Sarai Stone. l.t. ed. 1996. (Western Ser.). 322p. 20.95 (*0-7862-0804-X*) Thorndike Pr.

—Man Without Medicine. 1999. 240p. mass mkt. 4.50 (*0-8439-4581-8*, Leisure Bks.) Dorchester Publishing Co., Inc.

—Man Without Medicine. l.t. ed. 1999. 20.00 o.p. (*0-7838-1675-8*, Macmillan Reference USA) Gale Group.

—Man Without Medicine. 1999. E-Book 9.95 (*0-585-28583-7*) netLibrary, Inc.

—Man Without Medicine: A Western Story. l.t. ed. 1997. (Western Ser.). 309p. lib. bdg. 21.95 (*0-7862-1192-X*) Thorndike Pr.

—Satanta's Woman. 1998. (Western Ser.). 284p. 19.95 (*0-7862-1335-3*); 18.95 o.p. (*0-7862-1319-1*) Gale Group. (Five Star).

—Satanta's Woman Vol. 1: A Western Story. l.t. ed. 1999. (G. K. Hall Western Ser.). 360p. 22.95 (*0-7838-8400-1*) Thorndike Pr.

Hassler, Jon. Jemmy. 1988. 160p. (J). (gr. 7-12). mass mkt. 5.50 (*0-449-70302-9*, Fawcett) Ballantine Bks.

—Jemmy. 1980. 180p. (J). (gr. 7 up). 10.95 o.s.i (*0-689-50130-7*, McElderry, Margaret K.) Simon & Schuster Children's Publishing.

Hathaway, Robin. The Doctor Digs a Grave. 272p. 1998. 22.95 (*0-312-18568-5*, Saint Martin's Minotaur); Vol. 1. 2nd ed. 1999. mass mkt. 5.99 (*0-312-96703-9*, St. Martin's Paperbacks) St. Martin's Pr.

Hausman, Gerald. Stargazer. 1989. (Stargazer Trilogy Ser.: Bk. 1). 219p. (Orig.). pap. 9.95 (*0-914955-03-9*) Lotus Pr.

—Tunkashila: From the Birth of Turtle Island to the Blood of Wounded Knee. 1993. (Illus.). 272p. 22.95 o.p. (*0-312-09928-2*) St. Martin's Pr.

—Turtle Dream. 1989. (Illus.). 128p. pap. 11.95 (*0-933553-06-4*) Mariposa Printing & Publishing, Inc.

Haussler, Stuart. Territorial Justice. 2000. 388p. pap. 22.99 (*0-7388-1845-3*); text 32.99 (*0-7388-1844-5*) Xlibris Corp.

Haynes, Richard T. The Thong Tree. 1990. (Illus.). 64p. (J). (gr. 3-7). 11.95 (*0-929146-02-6*) Voyageur Publishing Co.

Headapohl, Betty R. Whispers in the Wind. 1996. 158p. pap. 9.99 (*0-88092-297-4*) Royal Fireworks Publishing Co.

Hebert, Ernest. The Old American: A Novel. l.t. ed. 2001. (Thorndike Americana Ser.). 496p. 28.95 (*0-7862-3182-3*) Thorndike Pr.

—The Old American: A Novel. 2000. (Hardscrabble Books). 304p. text 26.95 (*1-58465-073-7*, Hardscrabble Bks.) Univ. Pr. of New England.

Heffron, Dorris. Nice Fire & Some Moonpennies. 1972. (J). (gr. 6-9). 0.98 o.p. (*0-689-30029-8*, Atheneum) Simon & Schuster Children's Publishing.

Henry, Gordon. The Light People: A Novel. 2003. x, 226p. 19.95 (*0-87013-664-X*) Michigan State Univ. Pr.

Henry, Will. Brass Command. l.t. ed. 1999. (Paperback Ser.). 264p. pap. 22.95 o.p. (*0-7838-8532-6*) Thorndike Pr.

—No Survivors. 1991. 352p. mass mkt. 3.99 o.s.i (*0-553-23698-9*) Bantam Bks.

—No Survivors. l.t. ed. 2002. lib. bdg. 28.95 (*1-58547-250-6*, Western) Ctr. Point Large Print.

—No Survivors. 1996. (Illus.). 345p. pap. 12.00 (*0-8032-7282-0*, Bison Bks.) Univ. of Nebraska Pr.

Hernandez, Irene B. Heartbeat - Drumbeat. 1992. 134p. (YA). (ps up). pap. text 9.50 (*1-55885-052-X*) Arte Publico Pr.

Highwater, Jamake. The Ceremony of Innocence. 1985. (Charlotte Zolotow Bk.). 192p. (YA). (gr. 7 up). lib. bdg. 12.89 o.p. (*0-06-022302-2*) HarperCollins Children's Bk. Group.

—Eyes of Darkness. 1985. 192p. (J). (gr. 6 up). 13.00 o.p. (*0-688-41993-3*) HarperCollins Children's Bk. Group.

—Legend Days. 1984. (Charlotte Zolotow Bk.). 160p. (YA). (gr. 7 up). 12.95 (*0-06-022303-0*) HarperCollins Children's Bk. Group.

—Moonsong Lullaby. 1981. (Illus.). 32p. (J). (ps-3). 14.95 o.p. (*0-688-00427-X*) HarperCollins Children's Bk. Group.

Highway, Tomson. The Kiss of the Fur Queen. 1999. 320p. pap. (*0-385-25880-1*) Doubleday Canada, Ltd. CAN. *Dist:* Random Hse., Inc.

—The Kiss of the Fur Queen. 2000. (American Indian Literature & Critical Studies Ser.: Vol. 34). 320p. 24.95 (*0-8061-3236-1*) Univ. of Oklahoma Pr.

Hill, Morgan. Lost Patrol. 2003. (Lost Patrol Ser.). 272p. pap. 5.99 (*1-59052-050-5*) Multnomah Pubs., Inc.

Hillerman, Tony. The Blessing Way. unabr. ed. 1993. audio 36.00 (*0-7366-2510-0*, 3266) Books on Tape, Inc.

—The Blessing Way. l.t. ed. 1992. (General Ser.). 304p. pap. 17.95 o.p. (*0-8161-5431-7*); lib. bdg. 20.95 o.p. (*0-8161-5430-9*) Gale Group. (Macmillan Reference USA).

—The Blessing Way. (Harper Novel of Suspense Ser.). 1970. 10.00 o.p. (*0-06-011896-2*); 1990. 304p. reprint ed. mass mkt. 6.99 (*0-06-100001-9*) HarperCollins Pubs.

—The Blessing Way. abr. ed. 1995. (Joe Leaphorn Mystery Ser.). 3p. audio 18.00 (*1-55994-160-X*, 394151, HarperAudio) HarperTrade.

—The Blessing Way. 1993. audio. audio 39.80 (*1-56544-006-4*, 250020) Literate Ear, Inc.

—The Blessing Way. 1978. (gr. 7 up). pap. 2.95 o.p. (*0-380-39941-5*, Avon Bks.) Morrow/Avon.

—The Blessing Way. unabr. ed. 1990. (Joe Leaphorn Mystery Ser.: Vol. 1). audio 44.00 (*1-55690-058-9*, 90080E7) Recorded Bks., LLC.

—The Blessing Way. 1990. 12.55 (*0-606-16174-0*) Turtleback Bks.

—Coyote Waits. unabr. ed. 1990. audio 42.00 (*0-7366-1788-4*, 2625) Books on Tape, Inc.

—Coyote Waits. 1990. 292p. 75.00 o.p. (*0-06-016422-0*); 1990. 292p. 19.95 o.p. (*0-06-016370-4*); 1995. 3p. audio 18.00 o.s.i (*1-55994-198-7*, 390569, HarperAudio); 1990. pap. 19.95 o.p. (*0-06-016423-9*) HarperTrade.

—Coyote Waits. 1992. 368p. mass mkt. 6.99 (*0-06-109932-5*, HarperTorch) Morrow/Avon.

—Coyote Waits. 1990. audio 10.00 New Letters on Air.

—Coyote Waits. 1990. (J). 13.04 (*0-606-01125-0*) Turtleback Bks.

—Dance Hall of the Dead. abr. ed. 1986. audio 15.95 (*0-88690-127-8*, N20024, Audio Editions Bks. on Cassette) Audio Partners Publishing Corp.

—Dance Hall of the Dead. unabr. ed. 1994. audio 36.00 (*0-7366-2610-7*, 3352) Books on Tape, Inc.

—Dance Hall of the Dead. 1997. lib. bdg. 37.95 (*1-56849-695-8*) Buccaneer Bks., Inc.

—Dance Hall of the Dead. 2004. 224p. pap. 11.95 (*0-06-056374-5*); 1990. 272p. reprint ed. mass mkt. 6.99 (*0-06-100002-7*) HarperTrade. (Perennial).

—Dance Hall of the Dead. 1993. audio. audio 37.20 (*1-56544-025-0*, 250021) Literate Ear, Inc.

—Dance Hall of the Dead. 1982. (YA). (gr. 9 up). mass mkt. 2.95 o.p. (*0-380-00217-5*, 60093-5, Avon Bks.) Morrow/Avon.

—Dance Hall of the Dead. unabr. ed. 1991. (Joe Leaphorn Mystery Ser.: Vol. 2). (YA). (gr. 10). audio 44.00 (*1-55690-134-8*, 91122E7) Recorded Bks., LLC.

—Dance Hall of the Dead. l.t. ed. (Paperback Bestsellers Ser.). 239p. 1994. pap. 20.95 (*0-8161-5433-3*); 1993. lib. bdg. 25.95 (*0-8161-5432-5*) Thorndike Pr.

—Dance Hall of the Dead. 1990. 12.55 (*0-606-16124-4*) Turtleback Bks.

—The Dark Wind. unabr. ed. 1994. audio 42.00 (*0-7366-2689-1*, 3424) Books on Tape, Inc.

—The Dark Wind. 1982. 224p. o.p. (*0-06-014936-1*) HarperCollins Pubs.

—The Dark Wind. 1990. 320p. reprint ed. mass mkt. 6.99 (*0-06-100003-5*, Perennial); Set. 1993. audio 18.00 (*1-55994-774-8*, CPN 4032, HarperAudio) HarperTrade.

—The Dark Wind. 1993. audio. audio 39.80 Literate Ear, Inc.

—The Dark Wind. 1992. 79p. mass mkt. 5.99 o.p. (*0-06-100491-X*, HarperTorch); 1983. 224p. pap. 3.50 o.p. (*0-380-63321-3*, Avon Bks.) Morrow/Avon.

—The Dark Wind. unabr. ed. 1990. (Jim Chee Mystery Ser.: Vol. 2). (YA). (gr. 10 up). audio 51.00 (*1-55690-136-4*, 91101E7) Recorded Bks., LLC.

—The Fallen Man. unabr. ed. 1997. audio 42.00 (*0-913369-37-3*, 4211) Books on Tape, Inc.

—The Fallen Man. 1996. 304p. 24.00 o.p. (*0-06-017773-X*) HarperCollins Pubs.

—The Fallen Man, Set. abr. ed. 1996. (Joe Leaphorn Mystery Ser.). audio 25.00 (*1-55994-978-3*, 694496, HarperAudio) HarperTrade.

—The Fallen Man. 1997. 320p. mass mkt. 6.99 (*0-06-109288-6*, HarperTorch) Morrow/Avon.

—The Fallen Man. unabr. ed. 1997. (Jim Chee Mystery Ser.: Vol. 9). audio 51.00 (*0-7887-0907-0*, 94961E7) Recorded Bks., LLC.

—The Fallen Man. 1998. 5.98 o.p. (*0-7651-0823-2*) Smithmark Pubs., Inc.

—The First Eagle. 1998. 224p. 25.00 (*0-00-224569-8*); 288p. 25.00 o.s.i (*0-06-017581-8*); 25.00 o.s.i (*0-06-099536-X*) HarperCollins Pubs.

—The First Eagle. unabr. ed. 1998. audio 34.95 (*0-694-52051-9*, 896038);Set. audio 25.00 (*0-694-52011-X*, 696034) HarperTrade. (HarperAudio).

—The First Eagle. 1999. 336p. mass mkt. 6.99 (*0-06-109785-3*, HarperTorch) Morrow/Avon.

—The First Eagle. unabr. ed. (Joe Leaphorn Mystery Ser.). 1999. audio compact disk 58.00 (*0-7887-3445-8*, C1051E7); 1998. audio 56.00 (*0-7887-2160-7*, 95456E7) Recorded Bks., LLC.

—The First Eagle. l.t. ed. (Paperback Bestsellers Ser.). 360p. 1999. pap. 28.95 o.p. (*0-7862-1625-5*); 1998. 30.95 (*0-7862-1624-7*) Thorndike Pr.

—The First Eagle. 1999. 13.04 (*0-606-16536-3*) Turtleback Bks.

—The Ghostway. unabr. ed. 1994. audio 42.00 (*0-7366-2748-0*, 3473) Books on Tape, Inc.

—The Ghostway. 1985. 224p. 13.95 o.p. (*0-06-015396-2*); 1992. 3p. audio 18.00 (*1-55994-606-7*, CPN 2301, HarperAudio) HarperTrade.

—The Ghostway. 1993. audio. audio 47.20 (*1-56544-040-4*, 250033) Literate Ear, Inc.

—The Ghostway. 1992. 320p. mass mkt. 6.99 (*0-06-100345-X*, HarperTorch); 1986. 208p. mass mkt. 4.95 (*0-380-70024-7*, Avon Bks.) Morrow/Avon.

—The Ghostway. unabr. ed. 1990. (Jim Chee Mystery Ser.: Vol. 3). audio 44.00 (*1-55690-194-1*, 90098E7) Recorded Bks., LLC.

—The Ghostway. 1984. (J). 12.55 (*0-606-01124-2*) Turtleback Bks.

—Hunting Badger. 1999. 288p. 26.00 (*0-00-224550-7*); 26.00 (*0-06-019289-5*) HarperCollins Pubs.

—Hunting Badger. l.t. ed. 1999. 256p. pap. 26.00 (*0-06-095564-3*, HarperLargePrint); 2000. audio compact disk 29.95 (*0-694-52287-2*, HarperAudio); Set. 2000. 30p. audio 25.00 (*0-694-52057-8*, HarperAudio) HarperTrade.

—Hunting Badger. 2001. 352p. mass mkt. 7.50 (*0-06-109786-1*, HarperTorch) Morrow/Avon.

—Hunting Badger. unabr. ed. 1999. (Joe Leaphorn Mystery Ser.). audio 29.95 (*0-7887-3894-1*, 96076 ) Recorded Bks., LLC.

—The Jim Chee Mysteries: Three Classic Hillerman Mysteries Featuring Officer Jim Chee: The Dark Wind, People of Darkness & The Ghostway. 1990. 576p. 26.00 (*0-06-016478-6*) HarperTrade.

—The Jim Chee Mysteries: Three Classic Hillerman Mysteries Featuring Officer Jim Chee: The Dark Wind, People of Darkness & The Ghostway. 1993. 576p. 13.99 o.s.i (*0-517-09281-6*) Random Hse. Value Publishing.

—The Joe Leaphorn Mysteries: Three Classic Hillerman Mysteries Featuring Lt. Joe Leaphorn: The Blessing Way, Dance Hall of the Dead, Listening Woman. 1989. 448p. 19.00 o.p. (*0-06-016174-4*) HarperTrade.

—Listening Woman. unabr. ed. 1994. audio 36.00 (*0-7366-2671-9*, 3408) Books on Tape, Inc.

—Listening Woman. l.t. ed. (General Ser.). 303p. 1994. pap. 18.95 o.p. (*0-8161-5435-X*); 1993. lib. bdg. 22.95 (*0-8161-5434-1*) Gale Group. (Macmillan Reference USA).

—Listening Woman. 1993. audio. audio 44.20 (*1-56544-036-6*, 250022) Literate Ear, Inc.

—Listening Woman. 1990. 336p. mass mkt. 6.99 (*0-06-100029-9*, HarperTorch); 1979. pap. 3.95 (*0-380-43554-3*, Avon Bks.) Morrow/Avon.

—Listening Woman. unabr. ed. 1990. (Joe Leaphorn Mystery Ser.: Vol. 3). audio 44.00 (*1-55690-310-3*, 90073E7) Recorded Bks., LLC.

—People of Darkness. unabr. ed. 1994. audio 36.00 (*0-7366-2725-1*, 3455) Books on Tape, Inc.

—People of Darkness. 1988. 196p. reprint ed. mass mkt. 4.95 o.p. (*0-06-080950-7*, P 950, Perennial) HarperTrade.

—People of Darkness. 1993. audio 44.20 (*1-56544-037-4*, 250034); audio Literate Ear, Inc.

—People of Darkness. 1991. 304p. mass mkt. 6.99 (*0-06-109915-5*, HarperTorch); 1983. 192p. pap. 2.95 o.p. (*0-380-57778-X*, Avon Bks.) Morrow/Avon.

—People of Darkness. unabr. ed. 1990. (Jim Chee Mystery Ser.: Vol. 1). audio 44.00 (*1-55690-405-3*, 90087E7) Recorded Bks., LLC.

—Sacred Clowns. unabr. ed. 1994. audio 48.00 (*0-7366-2645-X*, 3382) Books on Tape, Inc.

—Sacred Clowns. 1994. 368p. mass mkt. 6.99 (*0-06-109260-6*) HarperCollins Pubs.

—Sacred Clowns. 1993. 304p. 100.00 o.p. (*0-06-016830-7*); 304p. 23.00 o.p. (*0-06-016767-X*); audio 17.00 (*1-55994-549-4*, 391505, HarperAudio) HarperTrade.

—Sacred Clowns. unabr. ed. 1993. (Jim Chee Mystery Ser.: Vol. 8). audio 51.00 (*1-55690-910-1*, 93406E7) Recorded Bks., LLC.

—Sacred Clowns. 1994. 13.04 (*0-606-16175-9*) Turtleback Bks.

—Sacred Clowns: A Novel. 2003. 320p. pap. 11.95 (*0-06-053805-8*, Perennial) HarperTrade.

—The Sinister Pig. 2003. (*0-06-601944-3*) HarperCollins Pubs.

—The Sinister Pig. 2003. 240p. 25.95 (*0-06-019443-X*, HarperCollins); E-Book 19.95 (*0-06-055860-1*, HarperCollins); 320p. pap. 25.95 (*0-06-054543-7*, HarperLargePrint) HarperTrade.

—The Sinister Pig. 2004. mass mkt. (*0-06-109878-7*, HarperTorch) Morrow/Avon.

—Skinwalkers. unabr. ed. 1994. audio 36.00 (*0-7366-2795-2*, 3510) Books on Tape, Inc.

—Skinwalkers. 1990. 320p. mass mkt. 6.99 (*0-06-100017-5*); 1987. mass mkt. 4.95 o.p. (*0-06-080893-4*, P/893) HarperCollins Pubs.

—Skinwalkers. 1990. audio 15.95; 1987. 224p. 19.95 o.p. (*0-06-015695-3*); 1991. audio 18.00 (*1-55994-166-9*, CPN 2152, HarperAudio) HarperTrade.

—Skinwalkers. 1993. audio 39.80 (*1-56544-007-2*, 250032); audio Literate Ear, Inc.

—Skinwalkers. unabr. ed. 1990. (Jim Chee Mystery Ser.: Vol. 4). audio 44.00 (*1-55690-480-0*, 90074E7) Recorded Bks., LLC.

—Skinwalkers. 1987. 13.04 (*0-606-03655-5*) Turtleback Bks.

—Talking God. unabr. ed. 1989. audio 42.00 (*0-7366-1656-X*, 2507) Books on Tape, Inc.

—Talking God. 2003. E-Book 6.99 (*0-06-054725-1*) HarperCollins Pubs.

—Talking God. 1991. 368p. mass mkt. 6.99 (*0-06-109918-X*, Perennial); 1989. 17.95 o.p. (*0-06-016118-3*) HarperTrade.

—Talking God. 1989. 13.04 (*0-606-04823-5*) Turtleback Bks.

—A Thief of Time. unabr. ed. 1994. audio 36.00 (*0-7366-2841-X*, 3549) Books on Tape, Inc.

—A Thief of Time. l.t. ed. 1990. 14.95 o.p. (*0-8161-5061-3*); 1989. 344p. 18.95 o.p. (*0-8161-4699-3*) Gale Group. (Macmillan Reference USA).

—A Thief of Time. 2002. E-Book 6.99 (*0-06-054713-8*); E-Book (*0-06-054720-0*) HarperCollins Pubs.

—A Thief of Time. 1988. 224p. 15.45 o.p. (*0-06-015938-3*); 2002. 176p. audio 9.99 (*0-06-008296-8*, HarperAudio); Set. 1995. audio 18.00 (*0-89845-794-7*, 391761, HarperAudio) HarperTrade.

—A Thief of Time. 1990. 352p. reprint ed. mass mkt. 6.99 (*0-06-100004-3*, HarperTorch) Morrow/Avon.

—A Thief of Time. 1989. 13.04 (*0-606-04346-2*) Turtleback Bks.

—The Wailing Wind. 2002. (Illus.). 240p. 25.95 (*0-06-019444-8*); E-Book 19.95 (*0-06-054703-0*); E-Book (*0-06-054708-1*) HarperCollins Pubs.

—The Wailing Wind. l.t. ed. 2002. 320p. pap. 25.95 (*0-06-009388-9*, HarperLargePrint) HarperTrade.

—The Wailing Wind. 2003. 368p. mass mkt. 7.99 (*0-06-109879-5*, HarperTorch) Morrow/Avon.

Hillerman, Tony, reader. Talking God, . abr. ed. 1995. audio 18.00 (*0-89845-956-7*, CPN 2122, HarperAudio) HarperTrade.

Hirsh, M. E. Dreaming Back. 1996. (WWL Mystery Ser.). per. (*0-373-26195-0*, 1-26195-7, Worldwide Library) Harlequin Enterprises, Ltd.

—Dreaming Back. 1993. 320p. 19.95 o.p. (*0-312-09789-1*, Saint Martin's Minotaur) St. Martin's Pr.

Hobbs, William. Beardance. 1995. 208p. (J). (gr. 5 up). reprint ed. pap. 5.99 (*0-380-72317-4*, Harper Trophy) HarperCollins Children's Bk. Group.

—Beardance. 1993. 192p. (YA). (gr. 5-9). 17.00 (*0-689-31867-7*, Atheneum) Simon & Schuster Children's Publishing.

—Beardance. 1995. 11.00 (*0-606-07155-5*) Turtleback Bks.

Hobson, Geary. The Last of the Ofos. 2000. (Hypatia Book Ser.: Vol. 39). 114p. pap. 13.95 (*0-8165-1959-5*) Univ. of Arizona Pr.

Hoff, Syd. Little Chief. 1961. (I Can Read Bks.). (Illus.). 64p. (J). (ps-3). lib. bdg. 13.89 o.p. (*0-06-022501-7*) HarperCollins Children's Bk. Group.

Hogan, Linda. Power. (Norton Paperback Fiction Ser.). 1999. 248p. pap. 13.00 (*0-393-31968-7*, Norton Paperbacks); 1998. 192p. 23.00 (*0-393-04636-2*) Norton, W. W. & Co., Inc.

Hogan, Ray. The Doomsday Marshal & the Comancheros. 2001. 192p. mass mkt. 4.50 (*0-8439-4824-8*, Leisure Bks.) Dorchester Publishing Co., Inc.

—The Doomsday Marshal & the Comancheros. 1989. 14.95 o.s.i (*0-385-26296-5*) Doubleday Publishing.

Hoge, Harry. Jajadeh: Mountain Spirit. 1999. 483p. pap. 24.99 (*0-7388-0515-7*); text 34.99 (*0-7388-0514-9*) Xlibris Corp.

Holdstock, Pauline. The Burial Ground. 1991. 98p. pap. 8.95 (*0-921586-25-6*) New Star Bks., Ltd. CAN. *Dist:* General Distribution Services, Inc.

Holmas, Stig. Apache Pass. Born, Anne, tr. from NOR. (Chiracuhua Apache Ser.). (Illus.). (gr. 7 up). 1996. 128p. (YA). 15.95 (*1-57140-010-9*); 1955. 48p. pap. 9.95 (*1-57140-011-7*) Rinehart, Roberts Pubs.

—Fire Wagons. Born, Anne, tr. from NOR. 1996. (Chiricahua Apache Ser.). (Illus.). 128p. (YA). (gr. 7 up). 15.95 o.p. (*1-57140-016-8*); pap. 9.95 o.p. (*1-57140-017-6*) Rinehart, Roberts Pubs.

—Son-of-Thunder. Born, Anne, tr. from NOR. (Chiricahua Apache Series / Stig Holmas Ser.: Vol. 1). (Illus.). (gr. 7-12). 2000. 139p. 10.95 (*0-943173-87-6*); 1999. 32p. pap. 16.95 (*0-943173-88-4*) Rinehart, Roberts Pubs.

Holmes, L. P. Apache Desert. l.t. ed. 2000. 151p. 19.00 (*0-7540-8100-1*) BBC Audiobooks America.

—Apache Desert. l.t. ed. 2001. 267p. 23.95 o.p. (*0-7862-3610-8*); 285p. (*0-7540-4718-0*); 285p. (*0-7540-4719-9*) Thorndike Pr.

Holmes, Mary Z. Thunder Foot. 1992. (History's Children Ser.). (Illus.). 48p. (J). (gr. 4-5). lib. bdg. 21.36 o.p. (*0-8114-3500-8*) Raintree Pubs.

Hotze, Sollace. A Circle Unbroken. (YA). (gr. 7 up). 1991. 208p. pap. 7.95 (*0-395-59702-1*); 1988. 224p. 14.95 o.p. (*0-89919-733-7*) Houghton Mifflin Co. Trade & Reference Div. (Clarion Bks.).

Houston, James. Drifting Snow. 1992. (J). 16.99 (*0-7710-4283-3*) McClelland & Stewart/Tundra Bks.

—Drifting Snow: An Arctic Search. 1992. (Illus.). 160p. (YA). (gr. 5 up). lib. bdg. 13.95 o.s.i (*0-689-50563-9*, McElderry, Margaret K.) Simon & Schuster Children's Publishing.

—The Falcon Bow: An Arctic Legend. 1986. 96p. (J). (gr. 3-7). lib. bdg. 13.95 o.s.i (*0-689-50411-X*, McElderry, Margaret K.) Simon & Schuster Children's Publishing.

—Ghost Paddle: A Northwest Coast Indian Tale. 1972. (Illus.). 64p. (J). (gr. 2-6). 5.50 o.p. (*0-15-230760-5*) Harcourt Children's Bks.

—River Runners: A Tale of Hardship & Bravery. 1979. (Illus.). 160p. (J). (gr. 7 up). 11.95 o.s.i (*0-689-50151-X*, McElderry, Margaret K.) Simon & Schuster Children's Publishing.

—Running West. 1996. pap. 14.00 o.p. (*1-57566-044-X*); 1992. (Illus.). 380p. mass mkt. 4.99 o.s.i (*0-8217-3505-5*, Zebra Bks.) Kensington Publishing Corp.

—Running West. 1990. mass mkt. 5.95 (*0-7710-4268-X*); 1989. o.p. (*0-7710-4262-0*) McClelland & Stewart/Tundra Bks.

Houston, James R. Akavak: An Inuit-Eskimo Legend. 1990. (Illus.). 80p. (YA). (gr. 4-7). pap. 9.00 o.s.i (*0-15-201731-3*, Harcourt Paperbacks) Harcourt Children's Bks.

—Drifting Snow: An Arctic Search. 1994. 160p. (J). pap. 3.99 o.p. (*0-14-036530-3*, Puffin Bks.) Penguin Putnam Bks. for Young Readers.

—The Falcon Bow: An Arctic Legend. 1992. (Illus.). 96p. (YA). (gr. 5 up). pap. 3.99 o.p. (*0-14-036078-6*, Puffin Bks.) Penguin Putnam Bks. for Young Readers.

—River Runners: A Tale of Hardship & Bravery. 1992. 160p. (J). (gr. 5 up). pap. 4.50 o.s.i (*0-14-036093-X*, Puffin Bks.) Penguin Putnam Bks. for Young Readers.

Howe, James, adapted by. Dances with Wolves: The Children's Picture Book. 2004. (Illus.). 64p. (YA). (gr. 2 up). 14.95 (*1-55704-104-0*) Newmarket Pr.

Howe, LeAnne. Shell Shaker. 2001. 228p. 11.95 (*1-879960-61-3*); pap. 11.95 (*1-879960-62-1*) Aunt Lute Bks.

Hoyt, Edwin P. The Last Stand: A Novel about George Armstrong Custer & the Indians of the Plains. 320p. 1998. pap. 14.95 (*0-312-86501-5*); 1995. 22.95 o.p. (*0-312-85533-8*) Doherty, Tom Assocs., LLC. (Forge Bks.).

Hubert, Cam. Dreamspeaker. 1981. pap. 3.50 (*0-380-56622-2*, Avon Bks.) Morrow/Avon.

Hudson, Jan. Sweetgrass. 1989. 160p. (J). (gr. 3-7). 13.95 o.p. (*0-399-21721-5*, Philomel) Penguin Putnam Bks. for Young Readers.

—Sweetgrass. 1991. 160p. (YA). (gr. 7-9). pap. 3.99 (*0-590-43486-1*) Scholastic, Inc.

Hudson, Joyce Rockwood. Apalachee. 416p. 2002. pap. 18.95 (*0-8203-2402-7*); 2000. 27.95 (*0-8203-2190-7*) Univ. of Georgia Pr.

Huebner, Andrew. American by Blood. E-Book 23.00 (*1-58945-121-X*) Adobe Systems, Inc.

—American by Blood. 256p. 2001. pap. 13.00 (*0-684-85771-5*); 2000. (Illus.). 23.00 (*0-684-85770-7*) Simon & Schuster. (Simon & Schuster).

Huebner, Kenneth H. & Andrew. American by Blood. 2000. 256p. 23.00 (*0-684-87358-3*, Simon & Schuster) Simon & Schuster.

Humphreys, J. R. Maya Red. 1989. 254p. (Orig.). (C). pap. 9.95 (*0-943433-01-0*) Cane Hill Pr.

Hunt, Angela Elwell. Rehoboth. 1997. (Keepers of the Ring Ser.: No. 4). 356p. pap. 11.99 o.p. (*0-8423-2015-6*) Tyndale Hse. Pubs.

Hunter, Sara H. The Unbreakable Code. 1996. (Illus.). 32p. (J). (gr. 1-3). lib. bdg. 15.95 (*0-87358-638-7*, Rising Moon Bks. for Young Readers) Northland Publishing.

Hurmence, Belinda. Dixie in the Big Pasture. 1994. (J). (gr. 4 up). 13.95 o.s.i (*0-395-52002-9*) Clarion IND. *Dist:* Houghton Mifflin Co.

Irvine, Alexander C. A Scattering of Jades. E-Book 25.95 (*0-312-70730-4*); 2002. 448p. 25.95 (*0-7653-0116-4*) Doherty, Tom Assocs., LLC. (Tor Bks.).

Irwin, Hadley. Fettered for Life. 2004. 432p. (YA). (gr. 7 up). reprint ed. pap. 18.95 (*1-55861-148-7*) Feminist Pr. at The City Univ. of New York.

—We Are Mesquakie, We Are One. 1980. 128p. (YA). (gr. 5 up). 10.95 o.s.i (*0-912670-85-1*) Feminist Pr. at The City Univ. of New York.

Jackson, Helen H. Ramona: Wyeth Edition. 1939. (Illus.). (YA). (gr. 6 up). reprint ed. 17.95 o.s.i (*0-316-45467-2*) Little Brown & Co.

Jackson, Hunt H. Ramona. 2002. 400p. mass mkt. 5.95 (*0-451-52842-5*) NAL.

Jackson, Kent, ed. Manuscript Found: The Complete Original "Spaulding Manuscript" 1997. 18.95 (*1-57008-297-9*, Bookcraft, Inc.) Deseret Bk. Co.

Jacobs, Shannon K. Boy Who Loved Morning. 1993. (J). (ps-3). 15.95 o.p. (*0-316-45556-3*) Little Brown & Co.

James, J. Alison. Sing for a Gentle Rain. 1990. 224p. (YA). (gr. 7 up). lib. bdg. 14.95 o.p. (*0-689-31561-9*, Atheneum) Simon & Schuster Children's Publishing.

Jaskoski, H. CliffsNotes TM House Made of Dawn. 1999. E-Book 5.99 (*0-8220-7093-6*, Cliff Notes) Wiley, John & Sons, Inc.

Jerkins, Terri Wood. On Wings & Prayers: Living with Diabetes One Sugar at a Time. 2001. (Illus.). 368p. pap. 13.95 (*1-880292-64-5*) LangMarc Publishing.

Jerman, Jerry. Phantom of Pueblo, No. 3. 1995. (Journeys of Jessie Land Ser.). 132p. (J). pap. 5.99 o.p. (*1-56476-466-4*, 6-3466) Cook Communications Ministries.

Johnsgard, Paul. Prairie Children: Mountain Dreams. 1985. (Illus.). 96p. 7.95 o.p. (*0-939644-12-6*) Media Publishing.

Johnson, Annabel & Johnson, Edgar. Gamebuster. 1990. (Illus.). 192p. (J). (gr. 7 up). 14.95 o.p. (*0-525-65033-4*, Dutton Children's Bks.) Penguin Putnam Bks. for Young Readers.

Johnson, Dorothy M. All the Buffalo Returning. 1996. 248p. (J). pap. 11.00 (*0-8032-7590-0*, Bison Bks.) Univ. of Nebraska Pr.

—Buffalo Woman. l.t. ed. 1997. (G. K. Hall Western Ser.). 309p. 23.95 (*0-7838-8235-1*) Thorndike Pr.

—Buffalo Woman. 1995. 248p. pap. 12.95 (*0-8032-7583-8*, Bison Bks.) Univ. of Nebraska Pr.

Johnson, E. Pauline. The Moccasin Maker. 1987. 272p. reprint ed. pap. 84.40 (*0-608-00729-3*, 206150500009) Bks. on Demand.

—The Moccasin Maker. 1987. 267p. reprint ed. pap. 12.95 o.p. (*0-8165-0910-7*) Univ. of Arizona Pr.

Johnson, E. Pauline, et al. The Moccasin Maker. 1998. (Illus.). 272p. pap. 12.95 (*0-8061-3079-2*) Univ. of Oklahoma Pr.

Johnson, Wayne. Don't Think Twice. 1999. 304p. 23.00 o.s.i (*0-609-60460-0*, Harmony) Crown Publishing Group.

—Don't Think Twice. 2000. 304p. reprint ed. pap. 12.95 (*0-7434-0632-X*, Pocket) Simon & Schuster.

Johnston, Basil. Ojibway Heritage. 1990. (Illus.). 171p. reprint ed. pap. 11.95 (*0-8032-7572-2*, Bison Bks.) Univ. of Nebraska Pr.

—Ojibway Tales. 1993. Orig. Title: Moose Meat & Wild Rice. 188p. reprint ed. pap. 13.95 (*0-8032-7578-1*, Bison Bks.) Univ. of Nebraska Pr.

Johnston, Basil H. Ojibway Ceremonies. 1987. 192p. pap. 16.99 (*0-7710-4445-3*) McClelland & Stewart/Tundra Bks.

—Ojibway Ceremonies. 1990. (Illus.). 188p. reprint ed. pap. 13.95 (*0-8032-7573-0*, Bison Bks.) Univ. of Nebraska Pr.

—Ojibway Heritage. 1976. (Illus.). 171p. 20.50 o.p. (*0-231-04168-3*) Columbia Univ. Pr.

Johnston, Terry C. Borderlords. 1986. 528p. mass mkt. 6.99 (*0-553-26224-6*) Bantam Bks.

—Borderlords. 1985. (Frontier Library). 500p. 19.95 (*0-915463-11-3*, Frontier Library, The) Jameson Bks., Inc.

—A Cold Day in Hell. 1996. (Plainsmen Ser.: Vol. 11). 512p. mass mkt. 7.50 (*0-553-29976-X*) Bantam Bks.

—Lay the Mountains Low, No. 2. 2000. (Plainsmen Ser.: Vol. 15). (Illus.). xxii, 495p. 24.95 (*0-312-26189-6*) St. Martin's Pr.

—Lay the Mountains Low: The Flight of the Nez Perce from Idaho & the Battle of the Big Hole, August 9-10, 1877. mass mkt. o.p. (*0-312-97547-3*, St. Martin's Paperbacks) St. Martin's Pr.

—Red Cloud's Revenge: Showdown on the Northern Plains, 1867. 1991. (Plainsmen Ser.). (Illus.). 400p. reprint ed. mass mkt. 6.99 (*0-312-92733-9*, St. Martin's Paperbacks) St. Martin's Pr.

—Shadow Riders: The Southern Plains Uprising, 1873. 2001. (Plainsmen Ser.: Bk. 6). (Illus.). 400p. mass mkt. 6.99 (*0-312-92597-2*, St. Martin's Paperbacks) St. Martin's Pr.

—Turn the Stars Upside Down: The Last Days & Tragic Death of Crazy Horse. 2001. (Plainsmen Ser.: Bk. 16). (Illus.). 384p. 24.95 (*0-312-27757-1*) St. Martin's Pr.

Jones, Dorothy M. Tatiana. 2001. 377p. (Orig.). pap. 12.00 (*0-940055-51-1*) Vanessapress.

Jones, Douglas C. A Creek Called Wounded Knee. 1984. pap. 7.95 (*0-684-18257-2*, Macmillan Reference USA) Gale Group.

—A Creek Called Wounded Knee. 1996. 288p. mass mkt. 5.99 o.p. (*0-06-101029-4*, HarperTorch) Morrow/Avon.

—A Creek Called Wounded Knee. 1979. pap. 2.50 o.s.i (*0-446-91121-6*) Warner Bks., Inc.

Jones, Robert F. Tie My Bones to Her Back. l.t. ed. 1996. 256p. 23.00 o.p. (*0-374-27759-1*) Farrar, Straus & Giroux.

—Tie My Bones to Her Back. l.t. ed. 1997. (Western Ser.). 380p. 24.95 (*0-7838-1986-2*) Thorndike Pr.

Jones, Stephen Graham. All the Beautiful Sinners. 2003. 354p. 23.95 (*1-59071-008-8*) Rugged Land.

—The Bird Is Gone: A Manifesto. 2003. 175p. pap. 13.95 (*1-57366-109-0*) Fiction Collective Two, Inc.

—The Fast Red Road—A Plainsong. 2000. 326p. pap. 13.95 (*1-57366-088-4*) Fiction Collective Two, Inc.

Joseph, James. Shadow of the Serpent: A Coyote Moon Story. 1997. 423p. pap. 14.95 (*1-879418-80-0*) Audenreed Pr.

Joynes, Monty. Dead Water Rites. 2000. (Booker Ser.: Vol. 4). (Illus.). 288p. pap. 13.95 (*1-57174-190-9*) Hampton Roads Publishing Co., Inc.

—Save the Good Seed: A Novel. 1999. (Booker Ser.: Vol. 3). 288p. pap. 12.95 (*1-57174-130-5*) Hampton Roads Publishing Co., Inc.

Kammer, Robert, et al. Soldiers Falling into Camp: The Battles at the Rosebud & the Little Big Horn. 1992. 240p. 19.95 o.p. (*1-879915-04-9*) Alexander & Fraser, Inc.

Katz, Welwyn W. False Face. 1990. 208p. (J). (gr. k up). mass mkt. 3.50 o.s.i (*0-440-20676-6*, Laurel Leaf) Random Hse. Children's Bks.

—False Face. 1988. 208p. (J). (gr. 5-9). lib. bdg. 14.95 o.s.i (*0-689-50456-X*, McElderry, Margaret K.) Simon & Schuster Children's Publishing.

Kay, Karen. Night Thunder's Bride. 1999. (Blackfoot Warrior Ser.). 384p. mass mkt. 5.99 (*0-380-80339-9*, Avon Bks.) Morrow/Avon.

Keehn, Sally M. Moon of Two Dark Horses. 1995. 224p. (J). (gr. 4-7). 16.95 o.p. (*0-399-22783-0*, Philomel) Penguin Putnam Bks. for Young Readers.

Kegley, Mary B. Free in Chains. 2002. 266p. pap. 9.50 (*0-9641315-1-X*) Kegley Bks.

Kellerman, Faye. Moon Music. l.t. ed. 1998. (Large Print Bks.). 621p. 27.95 (*1-56895-672-X*, Wheeler Publishing, Inc.) Gale Group.

—Moon Music. 1999. 512p. pap. 7.50 (*0-380-72626-2*); 1998. 424p. 25.50 (*0-688-14369-5*, Morrow, William & Co.) Morrow/Avon.

Kelton, Elmer. Badger Boy. E-Book 23.95 (*1-58945-577-0*) Adobe Systems, Inc.

—Badger Boy. pap. text 23.95 (*0-312-70067-9*, Tor Bks.); 2002. mass mkt. 5.99 (*0-8125-7750-7*, Forge Bks.); 2001. 272p. 23.95 (*0-312-87319-0*, Forge Bks.) Doherty, Tom Assocs., LLC.

—Buffalo Wagons. 1984. 2.25 o.s.i (*0-441-08395-1*) Ace Bks.

—Buffalo Wagons. 1988. 256p. mass mkt. 2.75 o.s.i (*0-515-09499-4*, Jove) Berkley Publishing Group.

—Buffalo Wagons. 1997. 218p. pap. 5.99 (*0-8125-5120-6*, Forge Bks.) Doherty, Tom Assocs., LLC.

—Buffalo Wagons. l.t. ed. 2001. (Thorndike Western Ser.). 317p. 25.95 (*0-7862-3156-4*) Thorndike Pr.

—Buffalo Wagons. 1997. 12.04 (*0-606-19647-1*) Turtleback Bks.

—The Way of the Coyote. 2001. 288p. 23.95 (*0-312-87318-2*, Forge Bks.) Doherty, Tom Assocs., LLC.

Kenny, Maurice. Tortured Skins & Other Fictions. 2000. (Native American Ser.). 280p. pap. 22.95 (*0-87013-531-7*) Michigan State Univ. Pr.

Kershen, L. Michael. Why Buffalo Roam. 1992. (Illus.). 32p. (J). (gr. 2 up). 15.00 (*0-88045-043-6*) Stemmer Hse. Pubs., Inc.

Kesey, Ken. The Sea Lion: A Story of the Sea Cliff People. (Illus.). (J). 1995. 48p. pap. 4.99 o.p. (*0-14-054950-1*, Puffin Bks.); 1991. 480p. (gr. 2 up). 14.95 o.s.i (*0-670-83916-7*, Viking Children's Bks.) Penguin Putnam Bks. for Young Readers.

Kilpatrick, Terrence. Swimming Man Burning: A Rip-Roaring Novel of the American West. 1993. (Western Literature Ser.). 248p. reprint ed. pap. 18.00 (*0-87417-219-5*) Univ. of Nevada Pr.

Kimball, Philip. Liar's Moon: A Long Story. 1999. (Marian Wood Book Ser.). 304p. 23.00 o.s.i (*0-8050-6148-7*) Holt, Henry & Co.

—Liar's Moon: A Novel. 2000. 304p. pap. 12.95 o.s.i (*0-452-28183-0*, Plume) Dutton/Plume.

King, Kathleen. Cricket Sings: A Novel of Pre-Columbian Cahokia. 1983. x, 162p. 15.95 o.p. (*0-8214-0704-X*); pap. 12.95 (*0-8214-0705-8*) Ohio Univ. Pr.

King, Thomas. Green Grass, Running Water. 1994. 480p. pap. 12.95 (*0-553-37368-4*) Bantam Bks.

—Green Grass, Running Water. 1998. (Between the Covers Collection). audio (*0-86492-244-2*) Goose Lane Editions.

—Green Grass, Running Water. 1993. (Marc Jaffe Bk.). 352p. 21.95 o.s.i (*0-395-62304-9*) Houghton Mifflin Co.

Kinsella, W. P. Dance Me Outside: More Tales from the Ermineskin Reserve. 1986. 158p. 14.95 o.p. (*0-87923-583-7*) Godine, David R. Pub.

—The Fencepost Chronicles. 1987. 192p. 16.95 o.p. (*0-395-44646-5*); pap. 7.95 o.p. (*0-395-45393-3*) Houghton Mifflin Co.

—The Moccasin Telegraph & Other Indian Tales. 1985. (Penguin Short Fiction). 208p. pap. 10.00 o.p. (*0-14-008363-4*, Penguin Bks.) Viking Penguin.

Kirkpatrick, Jane. Love to Water My Soul, 3 vols. 2003. (Dreamcatcher Ser.: Vol. 2). 368p. pap. 12.99 (*0-88070-938-3*, Multnomah Bks.) Multnomah Pubs., Inc.

Kittleman, Laurence R. Canyons Beyond the Sky. 1985. 228p. (J). (gr. 5-8). 13.95 o.s.i (0-689-31138-9, Atheneum) Simon & Schuster Children's Publishing.

Knudson, R. R. Fox Running. 1977. 128p. pap. 2.50 (0-380-00930-7, 60286-5, Avon Bks.) Morrow/Avon.

Kohler, Vincent. Raven's Widows. 1997. 256p. text 22.95 o.p. (0-312-14714-7, Saint Martin's Minotaur) St. Martin's Pr.

Kramer, Remi. Legend of LoneStar Bear Bk. 3: Mystery of the Walking Cactus. 1994. (Illus.). 80p. (Orig.). (J). (gr. 2-8). reprint ed. bds. 13.00 (0-945887-15-9) Northwind Pr.

Krantz, Hazel. Walks in Beauty. 1997. 192p. (YA). pap. 6.95 (0-87358-671-9); (J). (gr. 7 up). lib. bdg. 12.95 (0-87358-667-0) Northland Publishing. (Rising Moon Bks. for Young Readers).

Krensky, Stephen. Children of the Wind & Water. 1994. 32p. (J). (ps-3). pap. 4.95 (0-590-46963-0) Scholastic, Inc.

Kroll, Virginia L. The Seasons & Someone. 1994. (Illus.). 32p. (J). (ps-3). 15.00 (0-15-271233-X) Harcourt Trade Pubs.

Krueger, William Kent. Iron Lake: A Cork O'Connor Mystery. 1999. (Illus.). 464p. mass mkt. 6.99 (0-671-01697-0, Pocket Star); 1998. E-Book 23.00 (0-671-03690-4, Atria); 1998. (Cork O'Connor Mysteries Ser.: Vol. 1). 320p. 23.00 (0-671-01696-2, Atria) Simon & Schuster.

—Iron Lake: A Cork O'Connor Mystery. l.t. ed. 2001. 584p. 29.95 (0-7862-3174-2) Thorndike Pr.

Krupat, Arnold. Woodsmen: or Thoreau & the Indians: A Novel. 1994. (American Indian Literature & Critical Studies Ser.: Vol. 11). 140p. reprint ed. pap. 10.95 (0-8061-2671-X) Univ. of Oklahoma Pr.

Kudlinski, Kathleen V. Night Bird: A Story of the Seminole Indians. (Once upon America Ser.). (Illus.). 64p. (J). (gr. 2-6). 1995. pap. 3.99 o.s.i (0-14-034353-9, Puffin Bks.); 1993. 12.99 o.s.i (0-670-83157-3, Viking Children's Bks.) Penguin Putnam Bks. for Young Readers.

Kusugak, Michael Arvaarluk. Northern Lights: The Soccer Trails. 1993. (Illus.). 24p. (J). (ps-2). pap. 6.95 (1-55037-338-2); lib. bdg. 16.95 (1-55037-339-0) Annick Pr., Ltd. CAN. Dist: Firefly Bks., Ltd.

—Northern Lights: The Soccer Trails. ed. 1994. (J). (gr. 2). spiral bd. (0-616-01694-8) Canadian National Institute for the Blind/Institut National Canadien pour les Aveugles.

La Farge, Oliver. Yellow Sun, Bright Sky: The Indian Country Stories of Oliver La Farge. Caffey, David L., ed. 1988. 212p. 22.50 o.p. (0-8263-1101-6); pap. 12.95 o.p. (0-8263-1033-8) Univ. of New Mexico Pr.

Lackey, Mercedes. Sacred Ground. 1995. 375p. mass mkt. 5.99 (0-8125-1965-5); 1994. 384p. 22.95 o.p. (0-312-85281-9) Doherty, Tom Assocs., LLC. (Tor Bks.).

Lacy, Al. Silent Abduction. 1999. (Christian Fiction Ser.). 320p. 23.95 o.p. (0-7862-1747-2, Five Star) Gale Group.

Lacy, Al & Lacy, JoAnna. No Place for Fear, 8 vols. 2003. (Hannah of Fort Bridger Ser.: Vol. 3). 322p. pap. 10.99 (1-57673-083-2, Multnomah Fiction) Multnomah Pubs., Inc.

LaDuke, Winona. Last Standing Woman. 304p. 1999. pap. 14.95 (0-89658-452-6); 1997. 22.95 (0-89658-278-7) Voyageur Pr., Inc.

LaFavor, Carole. Along the Journey River. 1996. 192p. pap. 10.95 (1-56341-070-2); lib. bdg. 22.95 (1-56341-071-0) Firebrand Bks.

—Evil Dead Center: A Mystery. 1997. 224p. pap. 11.95 (1-56341-088-5); 216p. lib. bdg. 24.95 (1-56341-089-3) Firebrand Bks.

Lafferty, R. A. Okla Hannali. 1991. 240p. pap. 12.95 (0-8061-2349-4) Univ. of Oklahoma Pr.

Laird, Brian A. To Bury the Dead. 1997. 176p. 20.95 o.p. (0-312-15224-8, Saint Martin's Minotaur) St. Martin's Pr.

Lambert, Page. Shifting Stars. 1997. 384p. 23.95 (0-312-86324-1, Forge Bks.) Doherty, Tom Assocs., LLC.

L'Amour, Louis. Last of the Breed. 1987. mass mkt. 3.95 o.s.i (0-553-26499-0); (Illus.). 384p. mass mkt. 5.50 (0-553-28042-2) Bantam Bks.

—Last of the Breed. l.t. ed. 1987. (Magna Large Print Ser.). o.p. (1-85057-125-2) Magna Large Print Bks. GBR. Dist: Ulverscroft Large Print Canada, Ltd.

—Last of the Breed. 1987. (J). 11.55 (0-606-03599-0) Turtleback Bks.

Lampman, Evelyn S. Rattlesnake Cave. 1974. (Illus.). (J). (gr. 4-7). 7.95 o.p. (0-689-30429-3, McElderry, Margaret K.) Simon & Schuster Children's Publishing.

—Squaw Man's Son. 1978. 192p. (J). (gr. 5-9). 7.95 o.p. (0-689-50102-1, McElderry, Margaret K.) Simon & Schuster Children's Publishing.

—Year of Small Shadow. 1971. 190p. (J). (gr. 5-7). 5.95 o.p. (0-15-299815-2) Harcourt Children's Bks.

Larsen, Deborah. The White: A Novel. 2002. 240p. 22.00 (0-375-41359-6) Knopf, Alfred A. Inc.

Lassie Danger at Echo Cliffs, No. 5. 1996. 144p. (J). mass mkt. 5.99 (0-7814-0274-3) Cook Communications Ministries.

Latterman, Terry. Little Joe, a Hopi Indian Boy, Learns a Hopi Indian Secret. Hawkins, Mary E., ed. 1985. (Illus.). 32p. (J). (gr. 4-12). 12.95 (0-934739-01-3) Pussywillow Publishing Hse.

Layman, Carol Spurlock. Isaac McCoy & the American Indians. 2002. 445p. 30.95 (0-7596-8973-3); pap. 20.95 (0-7596-8972-5) 1stBooks Library.

Le May, Alan. The Searchers. 1985. 352p. mass mkt. 3.50 o.s.i (0-425-07968-6) Berkley Publishing Group.

—The Searchers. l.t. ed. 2001. lib. bdg. 25.95 (1-58547-080-5) Ctr. Point Large Print.

—The Searchers. 1978. lib. bdg. 9.95 o.p. (0-8398-2464-5, Macmillan Reference USA) Gale Group.

Leech, Jay & Spencer, Zane. Bright Fawn & Me. 1979. (Illus.). (J). (ps-3). 12.95 o.p. (0-690-03937-9) HarperCollins Children's Bk. Group.

Leppard, Lois Gladys. Mandie & the Dangerous Imposter. 1994. (Mandie Bks.: No. 23). 176p. (J). (gr. 4-7). pap. 4.99 (1-55661-459-4) Bethany Hse. Pubs.

Leppart, Jerry. Headwaters. 1998. 256p. pap. 14.95 (1-880090-66-X) Galde Pr., Inc.

—Pest Control. 2000. 224p. pap. 14.95 (1-880090-95-3) Galde Pr., Inc.

Lesley, Craig. River Song. 1989. 352p. 18.95 o.p. (0-395-43083-6) Houghton Mifflin Co.

—Storm Raiders. 2001. 352p. pap. 13.00 (0-312-26398-8) Picador.

—Storm Riders. 2001. pap. (0-312-27745-8); 2000. 352p. 24.00 o.s.i (0-312-24554-8) Picador.

—Winterkill. 1984. 306p. 14.95 o.p. (0-395-35485-4) Houghton Mifflin Co.

—Winterkill. 1996. 336p. pap. 14.00 (0-312-15244-2) Picador.

Lesley, Craig, ed. Talking Leaves: Contemporary Native American Short Stories. 1991. 416p. reprint ed. pap. 14.95 (0-385-31272-5, Delta) Dell Publishing.

Levin, Betty. Brother Moose. 1990. (J). (gr. 5 up). 12.95 o.p. (0-688-09266-7, Greenwillow Bks.) HarperCollins Children's Bk. Group.

Levitsky, Ronald. Stone Boy: A Nate Rosen Mystery. 1993. 224p. 20.00 o.p. (0-684-19554-2, Scribner) Simon & Schuster.

Lewis, Alfred H. Apaches of New York. 1977. (Short Story Index Reprint Ser.). reprint ed. 25.95 (0-8369-4088-1) Ayer Co. Pubs., Inc.

Lewis, Janet. Invasion. 1998. (Illus.). 248p. pap. 21.95 (0-87013-495-7) Michigan State Univ. Pr.

—Invasion: A Narrative of Events Concerning the Johnston Family of St. Mary's. 1964. 356p. 15.00 o.p. (0-8040-0166-9); pap. 9.00 o.p. (0-8040-0167-7) Swallow Pr.

Liloia, C. Tony. The Appaloosa Kid. 2000. 276p. pap. 21.99 (0-7388-1865-8); text 31.99 (0-7388-1864-X) Xlibris Corp.

Linzer, Anna. Ghost Dancing. 1998. 192p. 21.00 o.s.i (0-312-19548-6) Picador.

Lipsyte, Robert. The Chief. (Trophy Bk.). 240p. (gr. 7 up). 1995. (J). pap. 5.99 (0-06-447097-0); 1993. (YA). 15.00 o.p. (0-06-021064-8); 1993. (YA). lib. bdg. 14.89 o.p. (0-06-021068-0) HarperCollins Children's Bk. Group.

—Chief. 1995. 11.00 (0-606-07362-0) Turtleback Bks.

Littlesugar, Amy. The Spinner's Daughter. 1994. (Illus.). 40p. (J). (gr. 1-4). lib. bdg. 14.95 (0-945912-22-6) Pippin Pr.

Livelsberger, D. W. Cheyenne Vengeance. 2000. E-Book 9.95 incl. cd-rom (1-58338-317-4); E-Book 3.95 (1-58338-309-3); E-Book 3.95 (1-58338-313-1) CrossroadsPub.com.

London, David. Sun Dancer. 1996. 320p. 23.00 o.p. (0-684-81458-7, Simon & Schuster) Simon & Schuster.

London, David, contrib. by. Sun Dancer. 1998. 320p. pap. 14.95 (0-8032-7978-7, Bison Bks.) Univ. of Nebraska Pr.

Long, Sylvester. Long Lance. 1995. (Banner Bks.). 320p. pap. 16.95 (0-87805-830-3) Univ. Pr. of Mississippi.

Lopez, Barry. Crow & Weasel. (Illus.). 64p. (J). 1990. (ps-3). 16.95 o.s.i (0-86547-439-7, North Point Pr.); RS. 1998. (gr. 4-7). pap. 8.95 (0-374-41613-3, Sunburst) Farrar, Straus & Giroux.

—Crow & Weasel. 1993. 80p. pap. 96.00 o.p. (0-06-097563-6); (Illus.). pap. 12.00 o.p. (0-06-097528-8) HarperTrade. (Perennial).

Louis, Adrian C. Skins. 2002. 320p. reprint ed. pap. 18.00 (0-944024-44-0) Ellis Pr., The.

—Wild Indians & Other Creatures. 1997. (Western Literature Ser.). 200p. reprint ed. pap. 18.00 (0-87417-303-5); 21.00 (0-87417-279-9) Univ. of Nevada Pr.

Lucas, Janice. Long Sun. 1994. 266p. 22.00 o.p. (1-56947-013-8) Soho Pr., Inc.

Lucas, Walter. Blood on the Plains. l.t. ed. 2001. (Wheeler Large Print Book Ser.). 19.95 o.p. (1-58724-134-X, Wheeler Publishing, Inc.) Gale Group.

Ludlum, Robert. The Road to Omaha. 1993. 608p. mass mkt. 7.99 (0-553-56044-1) Bantam Bks.

Luenn, Nancy. Nessa's Fish. (Aladdin Picture Bks.). 32p. (J). (gr. k-3). 1997. pap. 5.99 (0-689-81465-8, Aladdin); 1990. (Illus.). 15.00 (0-689-31477-9, Atheneum) Simon & Schuster Children's Publishing.

—Nessa's Story - El Cuento de Nessa. Ada, Alma Flor, tr. 1994. (ENG & SPA., Illus.). 32p. (J). (gr. k-3). 14.95 (0-689-31782-4); 14.95 (0-689-31919-3) Simon & Schuster Children's Publishing. (Atheneum).

—La Pesca de Nessa. Ada, Alma Flor, tr. (SPA., Illus.). 32p. (J). (gr. k-3). 1997. pap. 6.99 o.s.i (0-689-81467-4, SS7475, Aladdin); 1994. 15.95 (0-689-31977-0, SS0508, Atheneum) Simon & Schuster Children's Publishing.

Lyon, George Ella. Dreamplace. (Illus.). 32p. (J). (ps-2). 1998. mass mkt. 6.95 (0-531-07101-4); 1993. mass mkt. 16.99 o.p. (0-531-08616-X); 1993. pap. 15.95 (0-531-05466-7) Scholastic, Inc. (Orchard Bks.).

MacGregor, Rob. Prophecy Rock. 1998. 208p. (YA). (gr. 7-12). reprint ed. mass mkt. 4.50 o.s.i (0-440-22738-0, Laurel Leaf) Random Hse. Children's Bks.

—Prophecy Rock. 1995. 208p. (YA). (gr. 7-12). mass mkt. 16.00 o.s.i (0-689-80056-8, Simon & Schuster Children's Publishing) Simon & Schuster Children's Publishing.

Maddison, Lauren. Deceptions: A Connor Hawthorne Mystery. 1999. (Connor Hawthorne Mysteries Ser.). 424p. pap. 14.95 (1-55583-490-6) Alyson Pubns.

Magorian, James. Keeper of Fire. 1984. (Indian Culture Ser.). (Illus.). 78p. (Orig.). (J). (gr. 4-12). pap. 6.95 (0-89992-088-8) Council for Indian Education.

Major, Charles. Bears of Blue River. reprint ed. lib. bdg. 23.95 (0-88411-094-X) Amereon, Ltd.

Major, Clarence. Painted Turtle: Woman with Guitar. 1996. (Sun & Moon Classics Ser.: No. 73). 64p. pap. 11.95 o.p. (1-55713-085-X); 1988. (New American Fiction Ser.: No. 13). 14.95 o.p. (1-55713-002-7) Sun & Moon Pr.

Major, Kevin. Blood Red Ochre. 1990. 160p. (J). (gr. k up). mass mkt. 3.25 o.s.i (0-440-20730-4, Laurel Leaf) Random Hse. Children's Bks.

Malcolm, Jahnna N. Spirit of the West. 1997. (Treasured Horses Ser.: No. 1). (Illus.). (J). (gr. 3-7). mass mkt. 4.50 (0-590-06866-0) Scholastic, Inc.

Manfred, Frederick. Scarlet Plume. 1983. xviii, 365p. reprint ed. pap. 12.95 o.p. (0-8032-8120-X, Bison Bks.) Univ. of Nebraska Pr.

Manning, Jason. Last Chance. 2003. (Untitled Yonder Man Ser.). 336p. mass mkt. 5.99 (0-312-98204-6, St. Martin's Paperbacks) St. Martin's Pr.

—The Long Hunters. 2002. 320p. mass mkt. 5.99 o.s.i (0-451-20723-8, Signet Bks.) NAL.

Maracle, Lee. Daughters are Forever. 2001. 208p. pap. (1-55192-410-2, Polestar Book Pubs.) Raincoast Bk. Distribution.

—Ravensong. 1994. 208p. pap. (0-88974-044-5, Press Gang Pubs.) Raincoast Bk. Distribution.

—Sundogs. 1992. 224p. pap. 10.95 o.p. (0-919441-41-6) Theytus Bks., Ltd. CAN. Dist: Orca Bk. Pubs.

Marshall, Joseph. The Dance House: Stories from Rosebud. 1998. (Literature Ser.). (Illus.). 248p. pap. 13.95 (1-878610-66-X) Red Crane Bks., Inc.

Marshall, Joseph, III. Winter of the Holy Iron. 1994. (Literature Ser.). (Illus.). 304p. 19.95 (1-878610-44-9) Red Crane Bks., Inc.

Martin, LaJoyce. The Broken Bow. 1996. 192p. (Orig.). pap. 9.99 (1-56722-139-4, 1567221394) Word Aflame Pr.

Martin, Larry J. Sounding Drum. 1999. 345p. 23.00 o.s.i (1-57566-368-6) Kensington Publishing Corp.

Matcheck, Diane. The Sacrifice, RS. 1998. 208p. (J). (gr. 7-12). 16.00 o.p. (0-374-36378-1, Farrar, Straus & Giroux (BYR)) Farrar, Straus & Giroux.

Matheson, David. Red Thunder. 2001. 316p. pap. 16.00 (0-9647212-3-6) Media Weavers LLC.

Matthews, Greg. Heart of the Country. 1986. 17.95 o.p. (0-393-02289-7) Norton, W. W. & Co., Inc.

May, Karl. Winnetou. Shaw, Michael, tr. 1977. 13.95 o.p. (0-8264-0174-0) Continuum International Publishing Group, Inc.

—Winnetou. 1998. (Collected Works of Karl May). 762p. reprint ed. pap. 19.95 (0-8264-1092-8) Continuum International Publishing Group, Inc.

May, Karl F. Winnetou. Koblick, David, tr. from GER. & abr. by. abr. ed. 1999. 256p. pap. 16.95 (0-87422-179-X) Washington State Univ. Pr.

May, Karl Friedrich. Winnetou. E-Book 15.25 (0-87422-231-1) Washington State Univ. Pr.

May, Karl Friedrich & Koblick, David. Winnetou. 1999. E-Book 16.95 (0-585-07976-5) netLibrary, Inc.

May, Richard J. The Killing Frost. 2001. 184p. per. 12.99 (1-58827-060-2); E-Book 6.50 (1-58827-061-0) IndyPublish.com.

Mayne, William. Drift. 1986. 168p. (J). (gr. 4-6). 14.95 o.p. (0-385-29446-8, Delacorte Pr.); 1990. 176p. (YA). reprint ed. pap. 3.25 o.s.i (0-440-40381-2) Dell Publishing.

Mayo, Gretchen W. Earthmaker's Tales: North American Indian Stories about Earth Happenings. 1989. (Illus.). 96p. (J). (gr. 5 up). 12.95 (0-8027-6839-3); lib. bdg. 13.85 (0-8027-6840-7) Walker & Co.

McCall, Dan. Messenger Bird. (Harvest Book Ser.). 1994. 228p. pap. 15.00 (0-15-600042-3); 1993. 192p. 19.95 o.s.i (0-15-159284-5) Harcourt Trade Pubs.

McCarthy, Cathy. The Hollow. 2000. 270p. pap. 14.95 (1-58749-019-6); 1999. E-Book 4.75 incl. disk (1-928670-37-7); 1999. E-Book 4.75 (1-928670-38-5) Awe-Struck E-Bks.

McCarthy, Cormac. Blood Meridian: Or the Evening Redness in the West. 2001. 368p. 19.95 (0-679-64104-1, Modern Library) Random House Adult Trade Publishing Group.

—Blood Meridian or the Evening Redness in the West. 1986. 337p. reprint ed. pap. 9.50 o.p. (0-88001-092-4) HarperCollins Pubs.

—Blood Meridian or the Evening Redness in the West. 1992. 352p. pap. 14.00 (0-679-72875-9, Vintage) Knopf Publishing Group.

—Blood Meridian or the Evening Redness in the West. 1985. 327p. 17.95 o.p. (0-394-54482-X) Random Hse., Inc.

—Blood Meridian or the Evening Redness in the West. 1994. 26.50 (0-8446-6793-5) Smith, Peter Pub., Inc.

McClain, Florence W. & Wagner, Mcclain. Visions of Murder. 1995. 336p. pap. 5.99 (1-56718-452-9) Llewellyn Pubns.

McDonald, Kay L. Beyond the Vision. 2000. (First Edition Romance Ser.). 361p. 25.95 (0-7862-2304-9, Five Star) Gale Group.

—The Vision Is Fulfilled. 1984. 384p. mass mkt. 3.50 o.p. (0-451-12901-6, Signet Bks.) NAL.

—The Vision is Fulfilled. 2000. 364p. pap. 21.95 (0-595-16086-7, Backinprint.com) iUniverse, Inc.

—The Vision Is Fulfilled. l.t. ed. 2000. (Romance Ser.). 619p. 26.95 (0-7862-3018-5) Thorndike Pr.

McElrath, William N. Indian Treasure on Rockhouse Creek. 1984. (J). (gr. 5-8). pap. 5.95 o.p. (0-8054-4517-X, 4245-17) Broadman & Holman Pubs.

McGahan, Jerry. A Condor Brings the Sun: A Novel. 1996. 276p. 25.00 o.p. (0-87156-354-1) Sierra Club Bks.

McGraw, Eloise Jarvis. The Moccasin Trail. 1986. (Puffin Newbery Library). 256p. (J). (gr. 4-7). pap. 5.99 (0-14-032170-5, Puffin Bks.) Penguin Putnam Bks. for Young Readers.

McGuinn, Doug. The Apple Indians: A Novel. 2000. 315p. 19.95 (1-887905-46-4) Parkway Pubs., Inc.

McMurtry, Larry. Comanche Moon. 2000. (Lonesome Dove Ser.: No. 2). 720p. pap. 16.00 (0-684-85755-3, Simon & Schuster); 1998. (Lonesome Dove Ser.: No. 2). 816p. pap. 7.99 (0-671-02064-1, Pocket); 1998. mass mkt. 6.99 (0-671-02049-8, Pocket); 1997. (Lonesome Dove Ser.: No. 2). 752p. 28.50 (0-684-80754-8, Simon & Schuster) Simon & Schuster.

—Comanche Moon. l.t. ed. 1999. (Paperback Bestsellers Ser.: No. 2). 921p. pap. 28.95 (0-7862-1392-2) Thorndike Pr.

—Comanche Moon. 1998. 14.04 (0-606-16182-1) Turtleback Bks.

—Dead Man's Walk. unabr. ed. 1996. audio 80.00 (0-7366-3211-5, 3874) Books on Tape, Inc.

—Dead Man's Walk. l.t. ed. (Lonesome Dove Ser.: No. 1). 1999. 800p. 27.95 o.p. (0-7838-1510-7); 1996. pap. 25.95 o.p. (0-7838-1511-5) Gale Group. (Macmillan Reference USA).

—Dead Man's Walk. (Lonesome Dove Ser.: No. 1). 2000. 464p. pap. 15.00 (0-684-85754-5, Simon & Schuster); 1995. 480p. 26.00 (0-684-80753-X, Simon & Schuster); 1996. 528p. pap. 7.99 (0-671-00116-7, Pocket) Simon & Schuster.

—Dead Man's Walk. unabr. ed. 1995. (Lonesome Dove Ser.: No. 1). audio 45.00 (0-671-55169-8, 113285, Simon & Schuster Audioworks) Simon & Schuster Audio.

—Dead Man's Walk. l.t. ed. 1998. (Lonesome Dove Ser.: No. 1). 5.98 o.p. (0-7651-0771-6) Smithmark Pubs., Inc.

—Dead Man's Walk. 2000. 21.05 (0-606-20274-9) Turtleback Bks.

McNichols, Charles L. Crazy Weather. 1967. viii, 195p. pap. 3.95 o.p. (0-8032-5132-7); 1994. 195p. reprint ed. pap. 7.95 o.p. (0-8032-8219-2) Univ. of Nebraska Pr. (Bison Bks.).

—Crazy Weather. 1978. (J). (gr. 7 up). reprint ed. 6.95 o.p. (0-670-24558-5) Viking Penguin.

McNickle, D'Arcy. Hawk Is Hungry. 1992. (Sun Tracks: Vol. 22). 180p. (Orig.). pap. 17.95 (0-8165-1331-7) Univ. of Arizona Pr.

—The Hawk Is Hungry & Other Stories. Hans, Birgit, ed. 1992. (Sun Tracks: Vol. 22). 180p. lib. bdg. 33.95 (*0-8165-1326-0*) Univ. of Arizona Pr.

—Runner in the Sun. 1987. (Zia Book Ser.). (Illus.). 249p. (J). (gr. 2 up). reprint ed. pap. 15.95 (*0-8263-0974-7*) Univ. of New Mexico Pr.

—Wind from an Enemy Sky. 1988. 268p. reprint ed. pap. 12.95 (*0-8263-1100-8*) Univ. of New Mexico Pr.

Mead, Alice. Crossing the Starlight Bridge. 128p. (J). (gr. 4-7). 1995. pap. 4.50 (*0-689-80105-X*, Aladdin); 1994. lib. bdg. 15.00 (*0-02-765950-X*, Simon & Schuster Children's Publishing) Simon & Schuster Children's Publishing.

—Crossing the Starlight Bridge. 1995. 10.00 (*0-606-07403-1*) Turtleback Bks.

Means, Florence C. Our Cup Is Broken, 001. 1969. (Illus.). (J). (gr. 7 up). 6.95 o.p. (*0-395-06937-8*) Houghton Mifflin Co.

Medawar, Mardi Oakley. The Fort Larned Incident. 2000. (Tay-Bodal Mystery Ser.). 270p. 23.95 (*0-312-20878-2*, Saint Martin's Minotaur) St. Martin's Pr.

—The Ft. Larned Incident. E-Book 23.95 (*0-312-27592-7*) St. Martin's Pr.

—Murder at Medicine Lodge. 1999. (Tay-Bodal Mystery Ser.). 272p. 23.95 o.p. (*0-312-19925-2*, Saint Martin's Minotaur) St. Martin's Pr.

—Witch of the Palo Duro. 1997. (Tay-Bodal Mystery Ser.). 224p. 21.95 (*0-312-17065-3*, Saint Martin's Minotaur) St. Martin's Pr.

Mercier, Ron. Dance the River Whale. 1999. 256p. pap. 13.95 (*0-9668527-0-2*) Deerbridge Bks.

Meyers, Harold B. Reservations. 1999. 287p. 24.95 (*0-87081-524-5*) Univ. Pr. of Colorado.

Micheaux, Oscar. The Conquest: The Story of a Negro Pioneer. 1994. (Illus.). 332p. pap. text 15.00 (*0-8032-8209-5*, Bison Bks.) Univ. of Nebraska Pr.

—The Conquest: The Story of a Negro Pioneer. 1994. E-Book 9.95 (*0-585-26635-2*) netLibrary, Inc.

Miles, Miska. Annie & the Old One. (Illus.). 44p. (J). 1972. (ps-3). 16.95 (*0-316-57117-2*, Joy Street Bks.); 1985. (gr. 1-3). reprint ed. pap. 7.99 (*0-316-57120-2*) Little Brown & Co.

—Annie & the Old One. 1971. (J). 14.10 (*0-606-03336-X*) Turtleback Bks.

Miller, Montzalee. My Grandmother's Cookie Jar. 1989. (Storybook Special Ser.). (Illus.). 32p. (J). (gr. 1-4). 9.95 o.p. (*0-8431-1587-4*, Price Stern Sloan) Penguin Putnam Bks. for Young Readers.

Miller, Richard. Coyote: An Indian Casino Blues. 2001. (Illus.). viii, 293p. pap. 19.50 (*0-9658423-1-2*); vi, 297p. 27.50 (*0-9658423-3-9*) Dada Foundation Imprints, LLC.

Mills, Anita. Comanche Rose. 1996. 384p. mass mkt. 5.99 o.s.i (*0-451-40554-4*, Topaz) NAL.

Minshull, Evelyn W. The Cornhusk Doll. 1987. (Illus.). 72p. (J). (ps). 14.95 o.p. (*0-8361-3431-1*) Herald Pr.

Mitchell, Kirk. Ancient Ones. 2002. 400p. mass mkt. 6.50 (*0-553-57920-7*) Bantam Bks.

—Ancient Ones. l.t. ed. 2004. 336p. 25.95 (*0-375-43247-7*) Random Hse. Large Print.

—Cry Dance. 2000. (Illus.). 368p. mass mkt. 6.50 (*0-553-57914-2*) Bantam Bks.

—Cry Dance. l.t. ed. 2003. 560p. 25.95 (*0-375-43265-5*) Random Hse. Large Print.

—The Cry Dance: A Novel of Suspense. 1999. 368p. 23.95 o.s.i (*0-553-10810-7*) Bantam Bks.

—Sky Woman Falling. 2003. 352p. 22.95 (*0-425-19191-5*, Prime Crime) Berkley Publishing Group.

—Spirit Sickness. 2001. 400p. reprint ed. mass mkt. 6.50 (*0-553-57917-7*) Bantam Bks.

—Spirit Sickness. l.t. ed. 2003. 592p. 25.95 (*0-375-43246-9*) Random Hse. Large Print.

Momaday, N. Scott. The Ancient Child: A Novel. 1989. 336p. 18.95 o.s.i (*0-385-27972-8*) Doubleday Publishing.

—The Ancient Child: A Novel. 1990. 336p. reprint ed. pap. 13.95 (*0-06-097345-5*, Perennial) Harper-Trade.

—House Made of Dawn. 1999. o.s.i (*0-06-093211-2*); 1977. pap. 4.95 o.p. (*0-06-080421-1*) HarperCollins Pubs.

—House Made of Dawn. (Perennial Classics Ser.). 1999. 208p. pap. 13.00 (*0-06-093194-9*); 1989. 224p. reprint ed. pap. 13.00 o.p. (*0-06-091633-8*) HarperTrade. (Perennial).

—House Made of Dawn. 1994. 192p. lib. bdg. 35.00 o.p. (*0-8095-9141-3*) Millefleurs.

—House Made of Dawn. 1969. mass mkt. 1.50 o.p. (*0-451-06611-1*); mass mkt. 0.95 o.p. (*0-451-04065-1*); mass mkt. 1.25 o.p. (*0-451-05680-9*) NAL. (Signet Bks.).

—House Made of Dawn. 1999. 19.05 (*0-606-21890-4*) Turtleback Bks.

—House Made of Dawn. 1996. (Momaday Collection). 212p. 35.00 (*0-8165-1705-3*) Univ. of Arizona Pr.

—Owl in the Cedar Tree. 1992. (Illus.). 116p. (J). (gr. 4-7). reprint ed. pap. 9.95 (*0-8032-8184-6*) Univ. of Nebraska Pr.

Montgomery, Ramsey. Grave Robbers. 1990. (Choose Your Own Adventure Ser.: No. 103). 128p. (J). (gr. 4-8). pap. 2.95 o.s.i (*0-553-28554-8*) Bantam Bks.

Montgomery, Raymond A. The Indian Trail. 1983. (Choose Your Own Adventure Ser.: No. 8). (J). (gr. 2-4). pap. 2.25 o.s.i (*0-553-15496-6*, Skylark) Random Hse. Children's Bks.

Moore, Brian. Black Robe. 1991. mass mkt. 4.99 o.p. (*0-449-45066-X*, Fawcett); 1986. mass mkt. 5.99 o.s.i (*0-449-20947-4*) Ballantine Bks.

—Black Robe. 1997. 256p. pap. 14.00 (*0-452-27865-1*, Plume); 1985. 15.95 o.p. (*0-525-24311-9*, Dutton) Dutton/Plume.

—Black Robe. 1995. 80p. pap. 10.00 o.p. (*0-586-08615-3*) HarperCollins Pubs. Ltd. GBR. *Dist:* HarperCollins Pubs.

Moore, Christopher. Coyote Blue. 1994. 303p. 21.00 (*0-671-88188-4*, Simon & Schuster) Simon & Schuster.

Moore, Lonnie W. & Moore, Iola. A Cherokee Spirit: The Saga of Oroville Annie & White Wolf. 1999. (Illus.). 45p. pap. 15.95 (*0-9661244-2-1*) I & L Publishing.

Moore, Ruth N. Mystery of the Lost Heirloom. 1985. (Sara & Sam Mysteries Ser.: Vol. 3). (Illus.). 152p. (J). (gr. 6-9). pap. 6.99 o.p. (*0-8361-3408-7*) Herald Pr.

—Peace Treaty. 1977. (Christian Peace Shelf Ser.). (Illus.). 154p. (J). (gr. 3-10). text 4.95 o.p. (*0-8361-1804-9*) Herald Pr.

Moreillon, Judi. Sing down the Rain. 1997. (Illus.). 32p. (J). (ps-3). 14.95 (*1-885772-07-6*) Kiva Publishing, Inc.

Morgan, Mary. Deeper Waters. E-Book 23.95 (*0-312-70683-9*); 2002. 304p. 23.95 (*0-312-29035-7*, Saint Martin's Minotaur) St. Martin's Pr.

Morgan, Speer. The Whipping Boy. 1994. 326p. 21.95 o.p. (*0-395-67725-4*) Houghton Mifflin Co.

Morris, Alan. Between Earth & Sky. 1998. (Guardians of the North Ser.: Vol. 4). 288p. pap. 9.99 o.p. (*1-55661-695-3*) Bethany Hse. Pubs.

—Between Earth & Sky. l.t. ed. 1999. (Christian Fiction Ser.). 448p. 25.95 (*0-7862-1692-1*) Thorndike Pr.

—Bright Sword of Justice. 1997. (Guardians of the North Ser.: Vol. 3). 256p. pap. 9.99 o.p. (*1-55661-694-5*) Bethany Hse. Pubs.

—Bright Sword of Justice. l.t. ed. 1998. (Guardians of the North Ser.: Vol. 3). 376p. 24.95 (*0-7862-1470-8*) Thorndike Pr.

—Wings of Healing. 1999. (Guardians of the North Ser.: Vol. 5). 272p. pap. 9.99 (*1-55661-696-1*) Bethany Hse. Pubs.

—Wings of Healing. l.t. ed. 2000. (Christian Fiction Ser.). 408p. 24.95 (*0-7862-2378-2*) Thorndike Pr.

Morris, Gilbert. The Crossed Sabres. 1993. (House of Winslow Ser.: No. 13). 320p. pap. 11.99 (*1-55661-309-1*) Bethany Hse. Pubs.

—Lone Wolf. 1995. (Reno Western Saga Ser.: Vol. 6). 236p. pap. 7.99 o.p. (*0-8423-1997-2*) Tyndale Hse. Pubs.

—The Rustlers of Panther Gap. 1994. (Ozark Adventures Ser.: Vol. 2). 144p. (J). (gr. 3-7). pap. 3.99 o.p. (*0-8423-4393-8*) Tyndale Hse. Pubs.

Morris, Irvin. From the Glittering World: A Navajo Story. 272p. 2000. pap. text 14.95 (*0-8061-3242-6*); 1997. (American Indian Literature & Critical Studies Ser.: No. 22). (Illus.). 24.95 o.p. (*0-8061-2895-X*) Univ. of Oklahoma Pr.

—From the Glittering World: A Navajo Story. 1997. E-Book 24.95 (*0-585-15428-7*) netLibrary, Inc.

Moss, Robert. Fire Along the Sky. 1992. 352p. 19.95 o.p. (*0-312-07011-X*) St. Martin's Pr.

Mount, Guy. Coyote's Big Penis & Other Stories. 1989. 80p. per. 5.95 (*0-9604462-5-7*) Sweetlight Bks.

Mukherjee, Bharati. Wife. 1992. reprint ed. mass mkt. 5.99 o.s.i (*0-449-22098-2*, Fawcett) Ballantine Bks.

—Wife, 001. 1975. 224p. 7.95 o.p. (*0-395-20439-9*) Houghton Mifflin Co.

—Wife. 1987. 224p. pap. 6.95 o.p. (*0-14-009300-1*, Penguin Bks.) Viking Penguin.

Muller, Marcia. Listen to the Silence. l.t. ed. 2000. (Wheeler Large Print Book Ser.). 328p. 28.95 o.p. (*1-56895-908-7*, Wheeler Publishing, Inc.) Gale Group.

Munch, Theodore W. & Winthrop, Robert D. Thunder on Forbidden Mountain. 1976. (J). (gr. 5-9). 6.95 o.p. (*0-664-32588-2*) Westminster John Knox Pr.

Munn, Vella. Blackfeet Season. 2000. 376p. mass mkt. 5.99 (*0-8125-7065-0*, Tor Bks.); 1999. (Illus.). 400p. 25.95 (*0-312-86734-4*, Forge Bks.) Doherty, Tom Assocs., LLC.

—Cheyenne Summer. 2002. 384p. mass mkt. 6.99 (*0-8125-7018-9*); 2001. 366p. 24.95 (*0-312-86948-7*) Doherty, Tom Assocs., LLC. (Forge Bks.).

—Seminole Song. 1997. 352p. 23.95 (*0-312-85896-5*, Forge Bks.) Doherty, Tom Assocs., LLC.

—The Seminole Song. 1998. 306p. mass mkt. 5.99 (*0-8125-3883-8*, Forge Bks.) Doherty, Tom Assocs., LLC.

—Spirit of the Eagle. 1996. 352p. 23.95 o.p. (*0-312-86096-X*, Forge Bks.) Doherty, Tom Assocs., LLC.

—The Wind Warrior. 350p. 1999. pap. 6.99 (*0-8125-3876-5*); 1998. 23.95 o.p. (*0-312-86446-9*) Doherty, Tom Assocs., LLC. (Forge Bks.).

Munroe, Kirk. At War with Pontiac. 2000. 252p. pap. 9.95 (*0-594-01771-8*); E-Book 3.95 (*0-594-02683-0*) 1873 Pr.

Murphy, Barbara B. Eagles in Their Flight. 1994. 192p. (J). (gr. 6 up). 14.95 o.s.i (*0-385-32035-3*, Delacorte Pr.) Dell Publishing.

—Fly Like an Eagle. 1995. 192p. (J). mass mkt. 3.99 o.s.i (*0-440-21948-5*) Dell Publishing.

Murphy, Garth. The Indian Lover. 2002. (Illus.). 448p. 26.00 (*0-7432-1943-0*, Simon & Schuster) Simon & Schuster.

Murray, Earl P. Blue Savage. 1985. 192p. 14.95 o.p. (*0-8027-4048-0*) Walker & Co.

My Name Is Lion. 11.95 o.p. (*0-8234-0179-0*) Holiday Hse., Inc.

Myers, Bill. Ancients. 1998. (Forbidden Doors Ser.: Vol .10). 160p. mass mkt. 4.99 o.p. (*0-8423-5971-0*) Tyndale Hse. Pubs.

Naylor, Phyllis Reynolds. To Walk the Sky Path. 1992. 144p. (gr. 4-7). pap. text 4.50 o.s.i (*0-440-40636-6*, Yearling) Random Hse. Children's Bks.

Neihardt, John G. The End of the Dream & Other Stories. 1991. 115p. text 25.00 (*0-8032-3326-4*) Univ. of Nebraska Pr.

—Indian Tales & Others. 1988. reprint ed. vi, 306p. 28.50 o.p. (*0-8032-3318-3*); 306p. pap. text 22.00 (*0-8032-8358-X*, Bison Bks.) Univ. of Nebraska Pr.

Neilson, Helen P. What the Cow Said to the Calf: Native American Historical Biography. 1993. 200p. (C). pap. text 17.95 o.p. (*1-880222-15-9*) Red Apple Publishing.

Nelson, Roger. The Shaman's Destiny. Date not set. 188p. E-Book 16.95 incl. cd-rom (*0-9704237-1-3*) Nelson Publishing Co.

Niswander, Adam. The Charm: A Southwestern Supernatural Thriller. 1993. 288p. lib. bdg. 21.95 (*0-9626148-1-5*) Integra Pr.

Nofziger, Lyn. Tackett. 2000. 214p. pap. text 10.95 (*0-915463-85-7*); 1998. 19.95 (*0-915463-80-6*) Jameson Bks., Inc.

—Tackett. 1993. 192p. 16.95 (*0-89526-495-1*) Regnery Publishing, Inc., An Eagle Publishing Co.

—Tackett & the Indian. 1998. (Tackett Ser.: Vol. 4). 208p. 19.95 (*0-915463-75-X*, Frontier Library, The) Jameson Bks., Inc.

Noon, Jack. The Big Fish of Barston Falls. 1995. (Illus.). 289p. (C). 24.00 (*0-9642213-2-2*) Moose Country Pr.

Norman, Howard. The Northern Lights. 2001. 240p. pap. 13.00 (*0-312-28337-7*) Picador.

—The Northern Lights. 1988. 240p. pap. (*0-671-65877-8*, Washington Square Pr.) Simon & Schuster.

—The Northern Lights. 1987. 224p. 17.45 o.p. (*0-671-53231-6*) Summit Bks.

O'Brien, Dan. The Contract Surgeon. 1999. 324p. 24.95 (*1-55821-932-3*, Lyons Pr.) Globe Pequot Pr., The.

—The Contract Surgeon. 2001. (Illus.). 224p. pap. 12.00 (*0-618-08783-4*, Mariner Bks.) Houghton Mifflin Co. Trade & Reference Div.

O'Dell, Scott. La Isla de los Deilfines Azules. 1997. (SPA., Illus.). 176p. (J). (gr. 4-7). 17.90 (*84-279-3108-5*, NG0956) Noguer y Caralt Editores, S. A. ESP. *Dist:* Lectorum Pubns., Inc.

—Island of the Blue Dolphins. l.t. ed. 1987. 161p. (J). (gr. 2-6). reprint ed. lib. bdg. 14.95 o.s.i (*1-55736-002-2*) Bantam Doubleday Dell Large Print Group, Inc.

—Sing down the Moon. l.t. ed. 1989. 176p. (YA). (gr. 9-12). reprint ed. lib. bdg. 16.95 o.s.i (*1-55736-142-8*, Cornerstone Bks.) Pages, Inc.

—Thunder Rolling in the Mountains. 1993. 144p. (J). (gr. 7 up). pap. text 5.50 (*0-440-40879-2*) Dell Publishing.

—Zia. 1998. 208p. (gr. 4-7). mass mkt. 2.99 o.s.i (*0-440-22817-4*, Yearling) Random Hse. Children's Bks.

O'Dell, Scott & Hall, Elizabeth. Thunder Rolling in the Mountains. 1992. (Illus.). 144p. (YA). (gr. 7-7). 17.00 (*0-395-59966-0*) Houghton Mifflin Co.

—Thunder Rolling in the Mountains. Set. unabr. ed. 1997. (J). (gr. 4). pap. 48.70 incl. audio (*0-7887-2196-8*, 40267) Recorded Bks., LLC.

Odenbach, Ginny & Osborn, Linda. Feather. Yarnaught, Paula, ed. 1995. (Illus.). 88p. (Orig.). (J). (gr. 3-8). pap. 4.50 (*1-885101-14-7*) Writers Pr., Inc.

Oke, Janette. Drums of Change: The Story of Running Fawn. 1996. (Women of the West Ser.). 240p. text 15.99 o.p. (*1-55661-818-2*); 240p. pap. 10.99 (*1-55661-812-3*); 352p. pap. 12.99 o.p. (*1-55661-817-4*) Bethany Hse. Pubs.

—Drums of Change: The Story of Running Fawn. l.t. ed. 1996. 318p. lib. bdg. 23.95 o.p. (*0-7838-1822-X*, Macmillan Reference USA) Gale Group.

O'Keefe, Dennis. Dixon's Edge: A Western Novel. 2001. 308p. pap. 15.00 (*0-9702160-0-9*) Parintel Bks.

Oliver, Louis L. Caught in a Willow Net. 1983. (American Indian Poetry Ser.). 88p. 5.00 (*0-912678-57-7*, Greenfield Review Pr.) Greenfield Review Literary Ctr., Inc.

Olsen, Theodore V. The Stalking Moon. 1997. 256p. reprint ed. mass mkt. 4.50 (*0-8439-4180-4*, Leisure Bks.) Dorchester Publishing Co., Inc.

—The Stalking Moon. l.t. ed. 2000. (G. K. Hall Nightingale Ser.). 234p. pap. 21.95 (*0-7838-9174-1*, Macmillan Reference USA) Gale Group.

Olson, Helen K. The Secret of Spirit Mountain. 1980. (YA). (gr. 7-11). 8.95 o.p. (*0-396-07856-7*, G. P. Putnam's Sons) Penguin Putnam Bks. for Young Readers.

O'Reilly, Jackson, pseud. Cheyenne Raiders. l.t. ed. 2001. (G.K. Hall Large Print Western Ser.). 392p. 25.95 (*0-7838-9538-0*, Macmillan Reference USA) Gale Group.

Organick, Avrum B. Blessings. 1999. iii, 250p. pap. 13.50 (*0-9671068-0-X*); 2nd ed. 2000. 270p. 22.95 (*0-9671068-2-6*); 2nd rev. ed. 2000. 270p. pap. 14.50 (*0-9671068-1-8*) Red Lake Pr.

Ortiz, Simon J. Men on the Moon: Collected Short Stories. 1999. (Sun Tracks). 216p. pap. 18.95 (*0-8165-1930-7*); 35.00 (*0-8165-1929-3*) Univ. of Arizona Pr.

Ovecka, Janice. Cave of Falling Water. 1992. (Illus.). (J). pap. 10.95 (*0-933050-98-4*) New England Pr., Inc., The.

Owens, Louis. Dark River: A Novel. 1999. (American Indian Literature & Critical Studies Ser.: Vol. 30). 296p. 23.95 (*0-8061-3115-2*); E-Book 23.95 (*0-8061-7202-9*) Univ. of Oklahoma Pr.

—Wolfsong: A Novel. 1995. (American Indian Literature & Critical Studies Ser.: Vol. 17). 256p. pap. 12.95 (*0-8061-2737-6*) Univ. of Oklahoma Pr.

—Wolfsong: A Novel. 1991. (Illus.). 256p. pap. 12.95 o.p. (*0-931122-66-X*) West End Pr.

Packard, Mary. Little Star. 1995. (J). pap. 12.95 (*0-590-54425-X*) Scholastic, Inc.

Page, Jake. The Stolen Gods. (Southwest Mysteries Ser.). 1994. 272p. mass mkt. 4.99 o.s.i (*0-345-37929-2*); 1993. 256p. 19.00 o.s.i (*0-345-37928-4*) Ballantine Bks.

—The Stolen Gods. 2002. 260p. pap. 13.95 (*0-8263-2860-1*) Univ. of New Mexico Pr.

Paige, Harry W. Johnny Stands. 1982. 160p. (J). (gr. 5-9). 8.95 o.p. (*0-7232-6213-6*, Warne, Frederick) Penguin Putnam Bks. for Young Readers.

Paine, Lauran. Apache Trail. l.t. ed. 2000. (G. K. Hall Paperback Ser.). 228p. pap. 23.95 (*0-7838-8928-3*, Macmillan Reference USA) Gale Group.

—The Long Years. l.t. ed. 2001. 248p. 24.95 (*0-7862-3395-8*); 275p. (*0-7540-4599-4*); 275p. (*0-7540-4600-1*) Thorndike Pr.

—Spirit Meadow. 1987. 192p. 15.95 o.p. (*0-8027-0970-2*) Walker & Co.

—Trail of the Sioux. l.t. ed. 2001. 155p. 21.95 (*1-57490-345-4*, Sagebrush Large Print Westerns) Beeler, Thomas T. Publisher.

Panagopoulos, Janie Lynn. Little Ship under Full Sail. 1997. 146p. (J). 15.95 (*0-938682-46-6*) River Road Pubns., Inc.

Parks, Mary A. The Circle Leads Home. 1998. (Women's West Ser.: Vol. 3). 224p. 22.50 o.p. (*0-87081-488-5*) Univ. Pr. of Colorado.

Parrish, Richard. The Dividing Line. 1993. 368p. 20.00 o.p. (*0-525-93561-4*) Dutton/Plume.

—The Dividing Line. 1994. 432p. mass mkt. 5.99 o.s.i (*0-451-40430-0*, Onyx) NAL.

Pascal, Francine, creator. The Twin's Big Pow-Wow. 1993. (Sweet Valley Kids Ser.: No. 44). 80p. (J). (gr. 1-3). pap. 2.99 o.s.i (*0-553-48098-7*) Bantam Bks.

Patten, Lewis B. Bones of the Buffalo. l.t. ed. 2000. (*0-7540-4023-2*); 2000. (*0-7540-4024-0*); 1999. 256p. 21.95 (*0-7862-2275-1*) Thorndike Pr.

—Cheyenne Drums. 1984. 2.25 o.s.i (*0-441-10369-3*) Ace Bks.

—Cheyenne Drums. 1986. 176p. 2.50 o.s.i (*0-441-10370-7*, Diamond Bks.) Berkley Publishing Group.

—Cheyenne Drums. l.t. ed. 1999. (Nightingale Ser.). 200p. pap. 20.95 (*0-7838-8651-9*) Thorndike Pr.

Patterson, Rosemary I. Return of the Canoe Societies: A History of the First Nations' Coastal Tribes of B. C. 2000. 168p. pap. 20.99 (*0-7388-1201-3*); text 30.99 (*0-7388-1200-5*) Xlibris Corp.

Paulsen, Gary. Canyons. 1990. 11.55 (*0-606-04884-7*) Turtleback Bks.

—The Night the White Deer Died. 1990. 112p. (J). 13.95 o.s.i (*0-385-30154-5*, Delacorte Pr.) Dell Publishing.

—The Night the White Deer Died. 1991. 112p. (YA). (gr. 7 up). mass mkt. 4.50 (*0-440-21092-5*, Yearling) Random Hse. Children's Bks.

Peck, Robert Newton. Fawn. 1975. (J). (gr. 7 up). 14.95 o.s.i (*0-316-69652-8*) Little Brown & Co.

Pelham, Howard. Judas Guns. 1990. 192p. 18.95 o.p. (*0-8027-4104-5*) Walker & Co.

Pellett, Franklin. Black Hawk's White Dilemma. 2002. 180p. pap. 10.95 (*0-87714-253-X*); 2000. E-Book 6.95 (*0-87714-518-0*) Denlingers Pubs., Ltd.

Penney, Grace Jackson. Moki. 1997. 160p. (gr. 3-7). pap. 4.99 o.s.i (*0-14-038430-8*) Penguin Putnam Bks. for Young Readers.
Perrine, Mary. Nannabah's Friend. 1989. (Illus.). 32p. (J). (gr. k-3). pap. 5.95 (*0-395-52020-7*) Houghton Mifflin Co.
Perry, Thomas. Blood Money. l.t. ed. 2000. (Large Print Book Ser.). 513p. pap. 26.95 (*1-56895-925-7*, Wheeler Publishing, Inc.) Gale Group.
—Blood Money. 2000. audio 30.00 (*0-7871-2284-X*) NewStar Media, Inc.
—Blood Money: A Novel. 1999. (Illus.). 368p. 24.95 o.s.i (*0-679-45304-0*) Random Hse., Inc.
—Dance for the Dead. 1997. (Jane Whitefield Novels Ser.). 416p. mass mkt. 6.99 (*0-8041-1425-0*, Ivy Bks.) Ballantine Bks.
—Dance for the Dead. l.t. ed. 1996. 416p. lib. bdg. 24.95 (*1-57490-065-X*, Beeler Large Print Bks.) Beeler, Thomas T. Publisher.
—Dance for the Dead, Set. abr. ed. 1998. (Jane Whitefield Mystery Ser.). audio 8.99 o.s.i (*0-375-40298-5*, 393900, RH Audio) Random Hse. Audio Publishing Group.
—Dance for the Dead. l.t. ed. 1997. (Charnwood Large Print Ser.). 464p. 34.50 o.p. (*0-7089-8938-1*, Ulverscroft) Thorpe, F. A. Pubs. GBR. *Dist:* Ulverscroft Large Print Bks., Ltd., Ulverscroft Large Print Canada, Ltd.
—Dance for the Dead: A Jane Whitefield Novel. abr. ed. 1996. audio 18.00 o.s.i (*0-679-45169-2*, 393900, RH Audio) Random Hse. Audio Publishing Group.
—The Face-Changers. 1999. (Jane Whitefield Novels Ser.). 432p. mass mkt. 7.50 (*0-8041-1540-0*, Ivy Bks.) Ballantine Bks.
—The Face-Changers. l.t. ed. 1998. (Americana Ser.). 640p. 28.95 (*0-7862-1611-5*) Thorndike Pr.
—The Face-Changers: A Novel. aut. ed. 1998. 372p. 24.00 o.s.i (*0-676-57765-2*) Random Hse., Inc.
—Shadow Woman. 1998. (Jane Whitefield Novels Ser.). 432p. mass mkt. 6.99 (*0-8041-1539-7*, Ivy Bks.) Ballantine Bks.
—Shadow Woman. l.t. ed. 1997. (Large Print Book Ser.). pap. 24.95 (*1-56895-513-8*, Wheeler Publishing, Inc.) Gale Group.
—Shadow Woman. l.t. ed. 1999. (Charnwood Large Print Ser.). 480p. 31.99 (*0-7089-9098-3*, Ulverscroft) Thorpe, F. A. Pubs. GBR. *Dist:* Ulverscroft Large Print Bks., Ltd., Ulverscroft Large Print Canada, Ltd.
—Vanishing Act. 1997. mass mkt. 2.99 o.s.i (*0-8041-1648-2*); 1996. 368p. mass mkt. 6.99 (*0-8041-1387-4*) Ballantine Bks. (Ivy Bks.).
—Vanishing Act. l.t. ed. 1995. (Large Print Bks.). pap. 22.95 (*1-56895-234-1*, Wheeler Publishing, Inc.) Gale Group.
Peters, Dory J. The Warriors' Code. 2002. 138p. pap. 12.95 (*1-55517-613-5*) Cedar Fort, Inc./CFI Distribution.
Peyer, Bernd C., ed. The Singing Spirit: Early Short Stories by North American Indians. 1991. (Sun Tracks). 175p. reprint ed. pap. 13.95 (*0-8165-1220-5*) Univ. of Arizona Pr.
Pfaff, Eugene E., Jr. & Causey, Michael. Uwharrie. 1993. 256p. 19.95 (*0-936389-30-3*) Tudor Pubs., Inc.
Pirone, James & Sweeney, Paula. Jake Montana: A Matter of Destiny. 1993. 124p. (YA). lib. bdg. 15.00 o.p. (*0-88092-073-4*) Royal Fireworks Publishing Co.
Pitts, Paul. The Shadowman's Way. 1992. 128p. (Orig.). (J). (gr. 5). pap. 3.99 (*0-380-76210-2*, Avon Bks.) Morrow/Avon.
Plante, David. The Country. 1981. 9.95 o.p. (*0-689-11189-4*, Scribner) Simon & Schuster.
—The Francoeur Novels: The Family, The Country, The Woods. 1983. 592p. pap. 10.95 o.p. (*0-525-48067-6*, Obelisk) NAL.
Plumlee, Harry J. Shadow of the Wolf: An Apache Tale. 1997. 216p. 21.95 (*0-8061-2905-0*) Univ. of Oklahoma Pr.
Pomerantz, Charlotte. Timothy Tall Feather. 1986. (Illus.). 32p. (J). (gr. k-3). lib. bdg. 12.93 o.p. (*0-688-04247-3*, Greenwillow Bks.) HarperCollins Children's Bk. Group.
Porter, Donald C. Ambush. 1984. (White Indian Ser.). 320p. mass mkt. 4.50 o.s.i (*0-553-25202-X*) Bantam Bks.
—Ambush. l.t. ed. 1993. (White Indian Ser.: Bk. VIII). 368p. lib. bdg. 22.95 (*0-8161-5846-0*, Macmillan Reference USA) Gale Group.
—Apache. 1987. (White Indian Ser.: No. 14). 332p. (Orig.). mass mkt. 4.99 o.s.i (*0-553-26206-8*) Bantam Bks.
—Cherokee. 1984. (White Indian Ser.: No. 10). 352p. (Orig.). mass mkt. 4.50 o.s.i (*0-553-24492-2*) Bantam Bks.
—Choctaw. 1985. (White Indian Ser.: No. 11). 352p. (Orig.). mass mkt. 4.50 o.s.i (*0-553-24950-9*) Bantam Bks.
—Fallen Timbers. 1990. (White Indian Ser.: No. 19). 368p. mass mkt. 4.50 o.s.i (*0-553-28474-6*) Bantam Bks.
—The Manitou: White Indian, Vol. 16. 1988. 272p. mass mkt. 4.50 o.s.i (*0-553-27264-0*) Bantam Bks.
—The Red Stick. 1994. (Red Stick Ser.: No. 26). 336p. mass mkt. 4.99 o.s.i (*0-553-56142-1*) Bantam Bks.
—The Renegade. 1984. (Colonization of America Ser.: No. 2). 384p. mass mkt. 4.50 o.s.i (*0-553-25020-5*) Bantam Bks.
—The Renegade. l.t. ed. 1983. 544p. lib. bdg. 19.95 o.p. (*0-8161-3447-2*, Macmillan Reference USA) Gale Group.
—Renno. 1985. 336p. (Orig.). mass mkt. 4.50 o.s.i (*0-553-25154-6*) Bantam Bks.
—The Sachem. 1984. 352p. mass mkt. 4.50 o.s.i (*0-553-24476-0*) Bantam Bks.
—The Sachem. l.t. ed. 1983. (Reader's Request Ser.). lib. bdg. 19.95 o.p. (*0-8161-3449-9*, Macmillan Reference USA) Gale Group.
—Sachem's Daughter. 1991. (White Indian Ser.: No. 21). 336p. mass mkt. 4.99 o.s.i (*0-553-29028-2*) Bantam Bks.
—Sachem's Son. 1990. (White Indian Ser.: No. 20). 352p. mass mkt. 4.50 o.s.i (*0-553-28805-9*) Bantam Bks.
—Seminole. 1986. (White Indian Ser.). 368p. mass mkt. 4.99 o.s.i (*0-553-25353-0*) Bantam Bks.
—Seneca. 1984. (White Indian Ser.: No. 9). 304p. mass mkt. 4.50 o.s.i (*0-553-23986-4*) Bantam Bks.
—Seneca. l.t. ed. 1994. (White Indian Ser.). 382p. lib. bdg. 22.95 (*0-8161-5847-9*, Macmillan Reference USA) Gale Group.
—Seneca Patriots. 1991. (White Indian Ser.: No. 22). 368p. mass mkt. 4.99 o.s.i (*0-553-29217-X*) Bantam Bks.
—Seneca Warrior. 1989. (Book of Justice Ser.: No. 1). 336p. mass mkt. 4.99 o.s.i (*0-553-27841-X*) Bantam Bks.
—The Spirit Knife. 1988. (White Indian Ser.: No. 15). 320p. mass mkt. 4.50 o.s.i (*0-553-27161-X*) Bantam Bks.
—War Chief. 1984. (Colonization of America Ser.). 384p. mass mkt. 4.50 o.s.i (*0-553-24751-4*) Bantam Bks.
—War Chief. l.t. ed. 1983. 528p. lib. bdg. 19.95 o.p. (*0-8161-3448-0*, Macmillan Reference USA) Gale Group.
—War Cry. 1983. 336p. mass mkt. 3.95 o.s.i (*0-553-25589-4*) Bantam Bks.
—War Cry. l.t. ed. 1984. (General Ser.). 15.95 o.p. (*0-8161-3452-9*, Macmillan Reference USA) Gale Group.
—War Drums. 1986. (White Indian Ser.: No. 13). 353p. (Orig.). mass mkt. 3.95 o.s.i (*0-553-25868-0*) Bantam Bks.
—White Indian. l.t. ed. 1983. 520p. lib. bdg. 19.95 o.p. (*0-8161-3446-4*, Macmillan Reference USA) Gale Group.
—The White Indian, No. 1. 1984. 416p. mass mkt. 4.99 o.s.i (*0-553-24650-X*) Bantam Bks.
—White Indian, Super Novel No. 1: Hawk's Journey. 1992. 352p. mass mkt. 5.50 o.s.i (*0-553-29218-8*) Bantam Bks.
Power, Susan. The Grass Dancer. 352p. 1995. mass mkt. 6.99 (*0-425-14962-5*); 1997. reprint ed. pap. 13.00 o.s.i (*0-425-15953-1*) Berkley Publishing Group.
—The Grass Dancer. l.t. ed. 1995. 23.95 o.p. (*1-56895-215-5*, Wheeler Publishing, Inc.) Gale Group.
—The Grass Dancer. 1994. 300p. 22.95 o.p. (*0-399-13911-7*, G. P. Putnam's Sons) Penguin Group (USA) Inc.
—The Grass Dancer. 1995. 13.04 (*0-606-16268-2*) Turtleback Bks.
—Roofwalker. 2002. 224p. 20.00 (*1-57131-039-8*) Milkweed Editions.
Preston, Douglas J. & Child, Lincoln. Thunderhead. 1999. 496p. 32.00 (*0-446-52337-2*); 2000. 560p. reprint ed. mass mkt. 7.50 (*0-446-60837-8*) Warner Bks., Inc.
Pruitt, Robert G., Jr. Rivers of Stone: A Story of Adventure & Mineral Exploration in the American Southwest. 2002. (First Fiction Ser.). (Illus.). 160p. pap. 14.95 (*0-86534-347-0*) Sunstone Pr.
Prusski, Jeffrey. Bring Back the Deer. 1988. (Illus.). 32p. (J). (ps-3). 13.95 (*0-15-200418-1*, Gulliver Bks.) Harcourt Children's Bks.
Querry, Ronald B. Bad Medicine. 1999. 336p. reprint ed. pap. 10.95 (*0-553-37799-X*) Bantam Bks.
Querry, Ronald B., ed. Growing Old at Willie Nelson's Picnic & Other Sketches of Life in the Southwest. 1983. (Illus.). 292p. (Orig.). 18.50 o.p. (*0-89096-164-6*) Texas A&M Univ. Pr.
Raczek, Linda T. The Night the Grandfathers Danced. 1995. (Illus.). 32p. (J). (gr. k-3). lib. bdg. 14.95 o.p. (*0-87358-610-7*) Northland Publishing.
Rafferty, Carin. Touch of Lightning. 1996. (Dreamspun Ser.). 384p. mass mkt. 5.50 o.s.i (*0-451-40613-3*, Topaz) NAL.
Rain, Mary Summer. The Seventh Mesa: A Novel. 1997. 272p. reprint ed. pap. 12.95 (*1-57174-061-9*) Hampton Roads Publishing Co., Inc.
Rain, Mary Summer, ed. The Seventh Mesa: A Novel. 1994. 272p. text 19.95 (*1-57174-012-0*) Hampton Roads Publishing Co., Inc.
Reasoner, J. L. Cossack Three Ponies. 1997. 288p. (Orig.). mass mkt. 5.99 o.s.i (*0-425-15666-4*) Berkley Publishing Group.
Reavis, Cheryl. The Captive Heart. 2000. (Harlequin Historicals Ser.: Vol. 512). 296p. pap. (*0-373-29112-4*, Harlequin Bks.) Harlequin Enterprises, Ltd.
Reed, Nat. Thunderbird Gold. 1997. 154p. (J). (gr. 4-7). pap. 6.49 (*0-89084-919-6*, 103325) Jones, Bob Univ. Pr.
Reynolds, Marjorie. The Civil Wars of Jonah Moran. 2001. 336p. reprint ed. pap. 13.95 o.s.i (*0-425-17834-X*) Berkley Publishing Group.
Ricciuti, Edward R. The Menominee. 1997. (Native American People Ser.: Set V). (Illus.). 32p. (J). (gr. 3-6). lib. bdg. 29.27 (*0-86625-603-2*) Rourke Publishing, LLC.
Richardson, Jean. The Courage Seed. 1993. (Illus.). 76p. (J). (gr. 4-5). 14.95 (*0-89015-902-5*) Eakin Pr.
Richter, Conrad. A Country of Strangers. 1966. (Illus.). (YA). (gr. 7 up). 9.95 o.s.i (*0-394-42065-9*, Knopf Bks. for Young Readers) Random Hse. Children's Bks.
Riddle, Paxton. The Education of Ruby Loonfoot. (Five Star First Edition Women's Fiction Ser.). 2002. 340p. 25.95 (*0-7862-4437-2*, Five Star); 2003. 351p. pap. 13.95 (*1-4104-0133-2*, Five Star Trade) Gale Group.
—The Education of Ruby Loonfoot. l.t. ed. 2003. (Core Ser.). 28.95 (*0-7862-5496-3*) Thorndike Pr.
Riefe, Barbara. For Love of Two Eagles. 1995. 384p. 22.95 o.p. (*0-312-85703-9*, Forge Bks.) Doherty, Tom Assocs., LLC.
—For the Love of Two Eagles. 1996. 416p. mass mkt. 5.99 (*0-8125-3660-6*, Forge Bks.) Doherty, Tom Assocs., LLC.
Rinaldi, Ann. My Heart Is on the Ground: The Diary of Nannie Little Rose, a Sioux Girl, Carlisle Indian School, Pennsylvania, 1880. 1999. (Dear America Ser.). (Illus.). 197p. (J). (gr. 4-9). pap. 10.95 (*0-590-14922-9*) Scholastic, Inc.
Ringstad, Muriel. Eye of the Changer: A Northwest Indian Tale. 1984. (Illus.). 96p. (Orig.). (YA). (gr. 7 up). pap. 9.95 (*0-88240-251-X*, Alaska Northwest Bks.) Graphic Arts Ctr. Publishing Co.
Roarke, Mike. Blood River: The War for the Northwest Territory. 1995. mass mkt. 4.99 (*0-312-95420-4*, St. Martin's Paperbacks) St. Martin's Pr.
Robbennolt, Roger. Tales of Tony Great Turtle. 1994. (Illus.). 159p. pap. 9.95 (*0-939516-27-6*, Forest of Peace Publishing) Ave Maria Pr.
Robbins, Judith Redman. Moonfire. 2000. 384p. mass mkt. 6.99 o.s.i (*0-451-20192-2*, Signet Bks.) NAL.
Robinson, Eden. Monkey Beach. 2000. 384p. 24.00 (*0-618-10168-3*) Houghton Mifflin Co.
—Monkey Beach. 2000. 384p. (*0-676-97075-3*) Knopf, Alfred A. Inc.
Robinson, Margaret A. A Woman of Her Tribe. 1991. 160p. (YA). (gr. 7-12). mass mkt. 4.50 o.s.i (*0-449-70405-X*, Fawcett) Ballantine Bks.
—A Woman of Her Tribe. 1990. 144p. (YA). (gr. 7 up). mass mkt. 13.95 (*0-684-19223-3*, Atheneum) Simon & Schuster Children's Publishing.
Robinson, Marileta. Mr. Goat's Bad Good Idea: Three Stories. 1979. (J). (gr. 1-4). 11.50 (*0-690-03862-3*) HarperCollins Children's Bk. Group.
Robson, Lucia St Clair. Ghost Warrior: Lozen of the Apaches. 2nd ed. 2002. 496p. 27.95 (*0-312-87186-4*, CPHC0689, Forge Bks.) Doherty, Tom Assocs., LLC.
—Walk in My Soul. 1987. 608p. mass mkt. 5.99 o.s.i (*0-345-34701-3*); 1985. 656p. pap. 29.00 (*0-345-30789-5*) Ballantine Bks.
Rockwood, Joyce. To Spoil the Sun. ERS. 1994. (YA). (gr. 7 up). pap. 7.95 o.p. (*0-8050-3465-X*); 1976. (J). (gr. k-3). 12.95 o.p. (*0-8050-0293-6*) Holt, Henry & Co. (Holt, Henry & Co. Bks. For Young Readers).
—To Spoil the Sun. 1987. (Brown Thrasher Bks.). 180p. reprint ed. pap. 11.95 o.p. (*0-8203-0910-9*) Univ. of Georgia Pr.
Roesch, E. P. Ashana. 1991. mass mkt. 5.99 o.s.i (*0-345-37298-0*) Ballantine Bks.
Rogers, Gayle. Nakoa's Woman. 1975. pap. 2.25 o.s.i (*0-440-17568-2*) Dell Publishing.
—Nakoa's Woman. l.t. ed. 2000. (G. K. Hall Romance Ser.). 501p. 27.95 (*0-7838-9263-2*, Macmillan Reference USA) Gale Group.
Roop, Peter. The Buffalo Jump. 1996. (Illus.). 32p. (J). (gr. 1-3). lib. bdg. 14.95 (*0-87358-616-6*, Rising Moon Bks. for Young Readers) Northland Publishing.
Root, Eldon, ed. A Star for Benny Peeples. 1999. (Illus.). 383 p. pap. 9.95 (*1-929117-01-9*) BlueOak Publishing.
Root, Phyllis. The Listening Silence. 1992. (Illus.). 128p. (J). (gr. 3-7). 14.00 o.p. (*0-06-025092-5*) HarperCollins Children's Bk. Group.
Rosen, Kenneth H., intro. The Man to Send Rain Clouds: Contemporary Stories by American Indians. 1992. 192p. reprint ed. 12.95 (*0-14-017317-X*) Viking Penguin.
Ross, David W. Beyond the Stars. 1991. 528p. mass mkt. 5.95 (*0-380-71471-X*, Avon Bks.) Morrow/Avon.
—Beyond the Stars. 1990. 19.95 o.p. (*0-671-70314-5*, Simon & Schuster) Simon & Schuster.
Ross, Val Gene. Secret Treasures of the Superstition Mountains. 2001. ix, 409p. (*1-55517-538-4*, Bonneville Bks.) Cedar Fort, Inc./CFI Distribution.
Rumbaut, Hendle. Dove Dream. 1994. (J). 13.95 o.p. (*0-395-68393-9*) Houghton Mifflin Co.
RunningWolf, Michael B. & Smith, Patricia Clark. On the Trail of Elder Brother: Glous'gap Stories of the Micmac Indians. 2000. (Illus.). xii, 142p. (YA). (gr. 5 up). 17.95 (*0-89255-248-4*) Persea Bks., Inc.
Ryan, Nan. Written in the Stars. 1992. 448p. mass mkt. 4.99 o.s.i (*0-440-21072-0*) Dell Publishing.
—Written in the Stars. 2003. 448p. mass mkt. 5.99 (*0-505-52510-0*, Love Spell) Dorchester Publishing Co., Inc.
Sabbeleu. Witch or Prophet? 1997. (Illus.). 100p. 20.00 (*0-9653990-1-X*) Whispering Willows, Ltd., Co.
Sala, Sharon. Legend. 1998. 352p. mass mkt. 6.99 (*0-06-108701-7*, HarperTorch) Morrow/Avon.
Salisbury, Luke. The Cleveland Indian: The Legend of King Saturday. 1992. 288p. (Orig.). pap. 24.95 (*0-912292-95-4*) Smith, The.
—Cleveland Indian: The Legend of King Saturday. 1995. 288p. (Orig.). pap. 14.95 (*1-882986-14-8*) Smith, The.
Salter, Robert B. Chamisa Dreams: A Novel. 1994. 160p. pap. 12.95 (*0-86534-220-2*) Sunstone Pr.
Sanchez, Joseph P. The Aztec Chronicles: The True History of Christopher Columbus, as Narrated by Quilaztli of Texcoco. 1995. pap. 9.95 (*0-89229-030-7*) TQS Pubns., Eclectic Chicano Literature.
Sanchez, Thomas. Rabbit Boss. 1974. mass mkt. 1.95 o.s.i (*0-345-23847-8*) Ballantine Bks.
—Rabbit Boss. 1989. (Vintage Contemporaries Ser.). 544p. pap. 16.00 (*0-679-72621-7*, Vintage) Knopf Publishing Group.
Sanders, William. Smoke. 2000. 216p. pap. 16.00 o.p. (*0-7388-3034-8*) Xlibris Corp.
Sanderson, William E. Nez Perce Buffalo Horse. 1972. (Illus.). (YA). (gr. 8-10). 4.95 o.p. (*0-87004-212-2*) Caxton Pr.
Sandoz, Mari. The Story Catcher. 1986. (Illus.). 175p. (YA). (gr. 7 up). pap. 8.95 (*0-8032-9163-9*, Bison Bks.) Univ. of Nebraska Pr.
Sarabande, William. Beyond the Sea of Ice. 1987. (First Americans Saga Ser.: Vol. 1). 384p. mass mkt. 7.50 (*0-553-26889-9*) Bantam Bks.
—Corridor of Storms, Bk. 2. 1988. (First Americans Saga Ser.: Vol. 2). 432p. mass mkt. 7.50 (*0-553-27159-8*) Bantam Bks.
—The Edge of the World, No. 7. 1993. (First Americans Saga Ser.: Vol. 7). 480p. mass mkt. 7.50 (*0-553-56028-X*) Bantam Bks.
—The Face of the Rising Sun. 1996. (First Americans Saga Ser.: No. 9). 496p. mass mkt. 6.99 (*0-553-56030-1*) Bantam Bks.
—Forbidden Land: A Novel of the First Americans. 1989. (First Americans Saga Ser.: Vol. 3). 448p. mass mkt. 7.50 (*0-553-28206-9*) Bantam Bks.
—The Sacred Stones: A Novel of the First Americans. 1991. (First Americans Saga Ser.: No. 5). 608p. mass mkt. 6.99 (*0-553-29105-X*) Bantam Bks.
—The Shadow of the Watching Star: The First Americans, Bk. 8. 1995. (First Americans Saga Ser.: Vol. 8). 512p. mass mkt. 6.99 (*0-553-56029-8*) Bantam Bks.
—Spirit Moon. 2000. (First Americans Saga Ser.: Vol. 11). 640p. mass mkt. 6.99 (*0-553-57909-6*) Bantam Bks.
—Thunder in the Sky. 1992. (First Americans Saga Ser.: No. 6). 464p. mass mkt. 6.99 (*0-553-29106-8*) Bantam Bks.
—Walkers of the Wind. 1990. (First Americans Saga Ser.: No. IV). 448p. mass mkt. 7.50 (*0-553-28579-3*) Bantam Bks.
Sargent, Pamela. Climb the Wind. 1999. 512p. mass mkt. 6.99 o.s.i (*0-06-105808-4*) HarperCollins Pubs.
—Climb the Wind. 1999. 448p. 25.00 o.s.i (*0-06-105029-6*, Eos) Morrow/Avon.
Sarris, Greg. Watermelon Nights. 1998. 432p. (J). 24.95 (*0-7868-6110-X*) Hyperion Pr.
Savage, Douglas. Highpockets. 1998. 176p. reprint ed. mass mkt. 3.99 (*0-8439-4400-5*, Leisure Bks.) Dorchester Publishing Co., Inc.
—Highpockets: An Evans Novel of the West. 1994. (Evans Novel of the West Ser.). 168p. 18.95 (*0-87131-757-5*) Evans, M. & Co., Inc.
Savage, Les, Jr. Fire Dance at Spider Rock. 2000. 240p. mass mkt. 4.50 (*0-8439-4696-2*, Leisure Bks.) Dorchester Publishing Co., Inc.
—Fire Dance at Spider Rock. 2000. E-Book 9.95 (*0-585-32712-2*) netLibrary, Inc.
Schalesky, Marlo M. Freedom's Shadow. 2001. 333p. pap. 10.99 (*1-58134-266-7*) Crossway Bks.
Schick, Eleanor. My Navajo Sister. 1996. (Illus.). 32p. (J). (ps-3). 16.00 (*0-689-80529-2*, Simon & Schuster Children's Publishing) Simon & Schuster Children's Publishing.



 

—Navajo Wedding Day: A Dine Marriage Ceremony. 1999. (Accelerated Reader Bks. ). (Illus.). 40p. (J). (gr. k-3). 15.95 (*0-7614-5031-9*, Cavendish Children's Bks.) Cavendish, Marshall Corp.

Schober, Annette R. The Book of One Tree. 1992. 96p. (Orig.). pap. 9.95 o.p. (*0-87358-539-9*) Northland Publishing.

Schraff, Anne. As the Eagle Goes. rev. ed. 1999. (Standing Tall Mysteries Ser.). 48p. (YA). (gr. 4 up). pap. 3.95 (*1-58659-086-3*) Artesian Pr.

—As the Eagle Goes. Hagerty, Carol, ed. 1995. (Standing Tall Mystery Ser.). (Illus.). 49p. (J). (gr. 5-9). pap. text 4.95 o.p. (*1-56254-150-1*, SP1501) Saddleback Publishing, Inc.

—As the Eagle Goes. 1995. (Standing Tall Mystery Ser.). 11.10 (*0-606-11059-3*) Turtleback Bks.

Schultz, James W. With the Indians in the Rockies. 1984. (J. W. Schultz Reprint Ser.). pap. (*0-8253-0319-2*) Beaufort Bks., Inc.

—With the Indians in the Rockies. 1984. (J. W. Schultz Reprint Ser.). 15.95 o.s.i (*0-8253-0324-9*) Confluence Pr., Inc.

Schurfranz, Vivian. Cassie, No. 14. 1985. 368p. (Orig.). (J). (gr. 7 up). pap. 2.95 o.p. (*0-590-33688-6*) Scholastic, Inc.

Seals, David. The Powwow Highway. 1990. (Contemporary Fiction Ser.). 30p. pap. 13.00 o.s.i (*0-452-26377-8*, Plume) Dutton/Plume.

—Sweet Medicine. 1994. 256p. pap. 10.00 o.s.i (*0-517-88188-8*) Crown Publishing Group.

—Thunder Nation. 1996. (7 Council Fires of Sweet Medicine Ser.: Vol. 3). 750p. 26.00 (*1-887786-13-9*) Sky & Sage Bks.

Searcy, Margaret Z. The Charm of the Bear Claw Necklace. 1990. (Illus.). 80p. (J). reprint ed. (gr. 3-7). 13.95 (*0-88289-821-3*); (gr. 5-7). pap. 7.95 o.s.i (*0-88289-777-2*) Pelican Publishing Co., Inc.

—The Charm of the Bear Claw Necklace: A Story of Stone Age Southeastern Indians. 1981. (Illus.). 80p. (J). (gr. 4-5). 9.95 o.s.i (*0-8173-0060-0*) Univ. of Alabama Pr.

—Ikwa of the Mound-Builder Indians. 1989. (Illus.). 80p. (J). (gr. 3-7). reprint ed. 13.95 o.p. (*0-88289-762-4*) Pelican Publishing Co., Inc.

—Wolf Dog of the Woodland Indians. 1982. (Illus.). 100p. (J). (gr. 4-8). 9.95 o.p. (*0-8173-0091-0*) Univ. of Alabama Pr.

Sears, Vickie. Simple Songs. 1990. 168p. (Orig.). pap. 8.95 (*0-932379-81-8*); lib. bdg. 18.95 (*0-932379-82-6*) Firebrand Bks.

Sedgwick, Catharine Maria. Hope Leslie. Kelley, Mary, ed. 1987. (American Women Writers Ser.). 365p. text 40.00 (*0-8135-1221-2*); pap. text 15.00 (*0-8135-1222-0*) Rutgers Univ. Pr.

—Hope Leslie: Or, Early Times in the Massachusetts. 1972. reprint ed. lib. bdg. 29.50 o.p. (*0-8422-8107-X*) Irvington Pubs.

—Hope Leslie: Or Early Times in the Massachusetts. reprint ed. 20.00 o.p. (*0-403-02083-2*) Somerset Pubs., Inc.

Sedgwick, Catharine Maria & Karcher, Carolyn L. Hope Leslie. 1998. (Classics Ser.). 448p. pap. 13.95 (*0-14-043676-6*, Penguin Classics) Viking Penguin.

Seno, William J. Enemies: A Saga of the Great Lakes Wilderness. 1993. 240p. pap. 12.95 (*1-879483-10-6*) Prairie Oak Pr., Inc.

Service, Pamela F. Vision Quest. 1990. 128p. mass mkt. 3.99 o.s.i (*0-449-70372-X*, Fawcett) Ballantine Bks.

—Vision Quest. 1989. 160p. (J). (gr. 3-7). lib. bdg. 13.95 o.s.i (*0-689-31498-1*, Atheneum) Simon & Schuster Children's Publishing.

Shaw, Janet Beeler. Kirsten Learns a Lesson: A School Story. Thieme, Jeanne, ed. 1986. (American Girls Collection: Bk. 2). (Illus.). 80p. (J). (gr. 2 up). pap. 5.95 (*0-937295-10-8*, American Girl) Pleasant Co. Pubns.

Shayne, Maggie. Badlands Bad Boy. 1997. 249p. per. (*0-373-07809-9*, 1-07809-6, Silhouette) Harlequin Enterprises, Ltd.

—Badlands Bad Boy. l.t. ed. 2000. (Silhouette Romance Ser.). 22.95 (*0-373-59697-9*) Silhouette Bks. GBR. *Dist:* Thorndike Pr.

Shearer, Tony. The Praying Flute: Song of the Earth Mother. 1991. (Illus.). 128p. reprint ed. pap. 8.95 o.p. (*0-939680-91-2*, Bear & Co.) Bear & Co.

Shefelman, Janice J. Spirit of Iron. 1997. 136p. (J). pap. 6.95 (*0-89015-889-4*) Eakin Pr.

—Spirit of Iron. Eakin, Edwin M., ed. 1987. (Mina Jordan Ser.: No. 3). (Illus.). 136p. (J). (gr. 4-7). pap. 5.95 o.p. (*0-89015-624-7*); 13.95 (*0-89015-636-0*) Eakin Pr.

—Young Wolf's First Hunt. 1995. (Step into Reading Step 3 Bks.). (Illus.). 48p. (J). (ps-3). pap. 3.99 o.s.i (*0-679-86364-8*, Random Hse. Bks. for Young Readers) Random Hse. Children's Bks.

Sheldon, Dyan. Under the Moon. 1994. (Illus.). 32p. (J). (ps-3). 15.99 o.s.i (*0-8037-1670-2*, Dial Bks. for Young Readers) Penguin Putnam Bks. for Young Readers.

Shelton, Kathleen. Bana: Slave - Soldier - Comanche War Chief. l.t. ed. 2000. 256p. 14.95 (*1-893566-09-9*) Kisco Pubns.

Shirreffs, Gordon D. Apache Butte. l.t. ed. 1989. (Linford Western Library). 186p. pap. 17.99 o.p. (*0-7089-6719-1*, Linford) Thorpe, F. A. Pubs. GBR. *Dist:* Ulverscroft Large Print Bks., Ltd., Ulverscroft Large Print Canada, Ltd.

Shrake, Edwin. Blessed McGill: A Novel. 2nd rev. ed. 1997. (Southwestern Writers Collection). 246p. pap. 15.95 o.p. (*0-292-77724-8*) Univ. of Texas Pr.

—The Borderland: A Novel of Texas. 2001. 432p. pap. 14.95 (*0-7868-8493-2*); 2000. 416p. 24.95 (*0-7868-6579-2*) Hyperion Pr.

Shuler, Linda L. She Who Remembers. 1988. 432p. 18.95 o.p. (*0-87795-892-0*, Morrow, William & Co.) Morrow/Avon.

—She Who Remembers. 1989. 512p. mass mkt. 7.99 (*0-451-16053-3*, Signet Bks.) NAL.

Shuler, Linda Lay. She Who Remembers. 2003. 496p. pap. 10.00 (*0-451-21144-8*) NAL.

Shura, Mary Francis. Jessica, No. 6. 1984. 368p. (YA). (gr. 7 up). pap. 2.95 o.p. (*0-590-33242-2*) Scholastic, Inc.

Silko, Leslie Marmon. Almanac of the Dead: A Novel. 1992. (Contemporary American Fiction Ser.). 784p. reprint ed. pap. 16.00 (*0-14-017319-6*, Penguin Bks.) Penguin Group (USA) Inc.

—Almanac of the Dead: A Novel. 1991. 25.00 o.p. (*0-671-66608-8*, Simon & Schuster) Simon & Schuster.

—Gardens in the Dunes. 1999. 480p. 25.00 (*0-684-81154-5*, Simon & Schuster) Simon & Schuster.

—Gardens in the Dunes: A Novel. 2000. 480p. pap. 14.00 (*0-684-86332-4*, Simon & Schuster) Simon & Schuster.

Silver, Alfred. Red River Story. 1990. 576p. mass mkt. 5.95 o.p. (*0-345-36562-3*) Ballantine Bks.

—The Red River Story. 1988. pap. 8.95 o.s.i (*0-345-32692-X*) Ballantine Bks.

Simpson, Marcia. Crow in Stolen Colors. 2000. 264p. 24.95 (*1-890208-36-1*) Poisoned Pen Pr.

Singer, A. L. Davy Crockett & the Pirates at Cave-In Rock. 1991. (Disney's American Frontier Ser.: Bk. 3). (Illus.). 80p. (J). (gr. 1-4). lib. bdg. 12.89 o.s.i (*1-56282-002-8*); pap. 3.50 (*1-56282-003-6*) Disney Pr.

Skarie, Heidi. Red Willow's Quest. 2000. (Illus.). ix, 261p. pap. 14.95 (*1-888604-10-7*) SunShine Pr. Pubns., Inc.

Skimin, Robert. The River & the Horsemen: A Novel of the Little Bighorn. 2001. (Illus.). 370p. reprint ed. pap. 15.00 (*1-928746-15-2*) Herodias.

Slater, Susan. The Pumpkin Seed Massacre. Ellison, Lee, ed. 1999. (Ben Pecos Mysteries Ser.: Vol. 1). 240p. 22.95 o.p. (*1-890768-17-0*, Intrigue Pr.) Corvus Publishing.

—Yellow Lies: A Ben Pecos Mystery. 2000. (Ben Pecos Mysteries Ser.). 297p. 22.95 (*1-890768-26-X*, Intrigue Pr.) Corvus Publishing.

Slipperjack, Ruby. Weesquachak & the Lost Ones. 2000. 203p. (C). pap. 15.95 (*0-919441-88-2*) Theytus Bks., Ltd. CAN. *Dist:* Orca Bk. Pubs.

Smith, A. Tanner. Anasazi & the Viking: A Novel. 1992. (Illus.). 144p. pap. 10.95 (*0-86534-152-4*) Sunstone Pr.

Smith, Lawrence R. The Map of Who We Are: A Novel. 1997. (American Indian Literature & Critical Studies: Vol. 24). (Illus.). 320p. 24.95 (*0-8061-2956-5*) Univ. of Oklahoma Pr.

—The Map of Who We Are: A Novel. 1997. E-Book 24.95 (*0-585-19667-2*) netLibrary, Inc.

Smith, Martin Cruz. Nightwing. 1977. 10.95 o.p. (*0-393-08783-2*) Norton, W. W. & Co., Inc.

—Stallion Gate. l.t. ed. 1987. 374p. 18.95 o.p. (*0-8161-4249-1*, Macmillan Reference USA) Gale Group.

—Stallion Gate. 1986. 336p. 17.95 o.s.i (*0-394-53006-3*) Random Hse., Inc.

Smith, T. H. Cry to the Night Wind. 1988. (J). (gr. 5-9). pap. 4.95 o.p. (*0-14-031931-X*, Puffin Bks.) Penguin Putnam Bks. for Young Readers.

Sneve, Virginia Driving Hawk. The Chichi Hoohoo Bogeyman. 1993. (Illus.). 63p. (J). (gr. 4-7). pap. 6.95 o.p. (*0-8032-9219-8*, Bison Bks.) Univ. of Nebraska Pr.

—High Elk's Treasure. 2002. (EMC Masterpiece Series Access Editions). (Illus.). xxv, 110p. (J). 9.95 (*0-8219-2414-1*, 35370) EMC/Paradigm Publishing.

—High Elk's Treasure. 1995. (Illus.). 96p. (J). (gr. 4-7). tchr. ed. 15.95 (*0-8234-0212-6*) Holiday Hse., Inc.

—When Thunders Spoke. 1993. (Illus.). 95p. (J). (gr. 4-7). pap. 9.95 (*0-8032-9220-1*, Bison Bks.) Univ. of Nebraska Pr.

Somtow, S. P. The Vampire's Beautiful Daughter. 1997. (Vampire's Beautiful Daughter Ser.: Vol. 2). (Illus.). 128p. (J). (gr. 7 up). 17.00 (*0-689-31968-1*, Atheneum) Simon & Schuster Children's Publishing.

Spalding-Stacy, Joanne. Black Eagle of the Nimapu. 1994. (J). pap. 9.95 o.p. (*0-87770-540-2*) Ye Galleon Pr.

Spanbauer, Tom. The Man Who Fell in Love with the Moon: A Novel. 2000. 368p. pap. 13.00 (*0-8021-3663-X*); 1991. 355p. 21.95 o.p. (*0-87113-468-3*) Grove/Atlantic, Inc.

—The Man Who Fell in Love with the Moon: A Novel. 1992. 368p. pap. 14.00 (*0-06-097497-4*, Perennial) HarperTrade.

Speare, Elizabeth George. Calico Captive. 1973. 288p. (gr. 4-7). pap. text 4.99 o.s.i (*0-440-41156-4*, Yearling) Random Hse. Children's Bks.

—El Signo del Castor. 1996. (SPA.). 144p. (YA). (gr. 5-8). 7.95 (*84-279-3188-3*, NG2978) Noguer y Caralt Editores, S. A. ESP. *Dist:* Lectorum Pubns., Inc.

Speerstra, Karen. The Earthshapers. 1980. (Illus.). 80p. (Orig.). lib. bdg. 13.95 o.p. (*0-87961-108-1*); pap. 5.95 (*0-87961-109-X*) Naturegraph Pubs., Inc.

Spence, Peggy. The Day of the Ogre Kachinas. 1999. (Council for Indian Education Ser.). (Illus.). 40p. (gr. 2-4). 4.95 (*1-57098-002-0*) Rinehart, Roberts Pubs.

Spinka, Penina K. Picture Maker. 2002. (Illus.). 480p. 24.95 o.s.i (*0-525-94624-1*, Dutton) Dutton/Plume.

Spinka, Penina Keen. Dream Weaver. 2003. (Illus.). 464p. 26.95 (*0-525-94684-5*, Dutton) Dutton/Plume.

—Dream Weaver. 2004. 512p. mass mkt. 7.99 (*0-451-41111-0*, Onyx) NAL.

—White Hare's Horses. 1992. 174p. mass mkt. 3.99 o.s.i (*0-449-70407-6*, Fawcett) Ballantine Bks.

Spinka, Penina Keen, ed. White Hare's Horses. 1991. 160p. (J). (gr. 5-9). lib. bdg. 13.95 o.s.i (*0-689-31654-2*, Atheneum) Simon & Schuster Children's Publishing.

Stahl, Hilda. Hannah & the Special 4th of July. 1992. (Best Friends Ser.: Vol. 4). 160p. (J). (gr. 4-7). pap. 4.99 o.p. (*0-89107-660-3*) Crossway Bks.

—No Friends for Hannah. 1992. (Best Friends Ser.: Vol. 8). 160p. (J). (gr. 4-7). pap. 4.99 o.p. (*0-89107-684-0*) Crossway Bks.

Stainer, M. L. The Lyon's Pride. unabr. ed. 1998. (Lyon Saga Ser.: Bk. 3). (Illus.). 163p. (YA). (gr. 5-9). pap. 6.95 (*0-9646904-9-7*); lib. bdg. 9.95 (*0-9646904-8-9*) Chicken Soup Pr., Inc.

Staley, Ida Jean. Turtle Medicine. 1999. E-Book 4.95 (*1-930364-03-2*, Bookmice) McGraw Publishing, Inc.

Stan-Padilla, Viento. Dream Feather. 1987. (Illus.). 60p. (J). (gr. 2 up). reprint ed. pap. 11.95 (*0-913990-57-4*) Book Publishing Co., The.

—Dream Feather. 1980. (Illus.). 64p. (J). (gr. 3 up). 8.95 o.s.i (*0-89742-035-7*) Celestial Arts Publishing Co.

Stauffacher, Sue. S'gana: The Black Whale. 1992. 224p. (YA). (gr. 7 up). 15.95 (*0-88240-396-6*, Alaska Northwest Bks.) Graphic Arts Ctr. Publishing Co.

Steele, Allen. Chronospace. 2001. 336p. 22.95 o.s.i (*0-441-00832-1*) Ace Bks.

—Chronospace. 2003. E-Book 6.99 (*0-7865-3390-0*) Penguin Putnam, Inc E-Books.

Steele, William O. The Man with the Silver Eyes. 1976. (J). (gr. 5 up). 5.95 o.p. (*0-15-251720-0*) Harcourt Children's Bks.

—The War Party. 1978. (J). (gr. k-3). 4.95 o.p. (*0-15-294789-2*) Harcourt Children's Bks.

Stein, Garth. Raven Stole the Moon. 1998. 336p. 22.00 (*0-671-00459-X*, Atria) Simon & Schuster.

—Raven Stole the Moon: A Novel. 1998. (*0-16-710045-9*) Pocket Bks.

Steiner, Barbara. Ghost Cave. 1990. 144p. (J). (gr. 3-7). 13.95 o.s.i (*0-15-230752-4*) Harcourt Trade Pubs.

—Ghost Cave. Ashby, Ruth, ed. 1993. 144p. (J). (gr. 3-6). reprint ed. pap. 2.99 (*0-671-74785-1*, Aladdin) Simon & Schuster Children's Publishing.

—Whale Brother. (Illus.). (J). (ps-3). 1995. 32p. pap. 6.95 (*0-8027-7460-1*); 1988. 28p. 12.95 (*0-8027-6804-0*); 1988. lib. bdg. 13.85 o.p. (*0-8027-6805-9*) Walker & Co.

—Whale Brother. 1998. E-Book (*1-59019-115-3*); 1988. E-Book (*1-58824-251-X*) ipicturebooks, LLC.

Stevenson, Melody. The Life Stone of Singing Bird: A Novel. 1996. 176p. 19.95 o.p. (*0-571-19886-4*) Faber & Faber, Inc.

Stewart, Elizabeth J. On the Long Trail Home. 1994. (Illus.). 112p. (J). (gr. 4-6). tchr. ed. 15.00 (*0-395-68361-0*, Clarion Bks.) Houghton Mifflin Co. Trade & Reference Div.

Stewart, Frank. River Rising: A Cherokee Odyssey. 1998. (Illus.). 798p. 34.95 (*0-9663853-0-6*) Wohali Pr.

Stokes, Naomi M. Listening Ones. 1997. 416p. 25.95 (*0-312-86108-7*, Forge Bks.) Doherty, Tom Assocs., LLC.

—The Listening Ones. 1999. 493p. mass mkt. 6.99 (*0-8125-4295-9*, Tor Bks.) Doherty, Tom Assocs., LLC.

Stone, Gerald Eugene Nathan. Rockhand Lizzie. 1999. 177p. pap. 12.95 (*0-9640513-6-2*) Tattersall Publishing.

Straley, John. The Woman Who Married a Bear: An Alaskan Mystery. 1994. 240p. mass mkt. 5.99 o.s.i (*0-451-40421-1*, Signet Bks.) NAL.

—The Woman Who Married a Bear: An Alaskan Mystery. 1992. 240p. 19.95 o.p. (*0-939149-64-8*) Soho Pr., Inc.

Strete, Craig K. Death Chants. 1988. (Science Fiction Ser.). 192p. 12.95 o.p. (*0-385-23353-1*) Doubleday Publishing.

Strete, Craig K. & Chacon, Michelle N. How the Indians Bought the Farm. 1924. (Illus.). 32p. (J). lib. bdg. o.s.i (*0-688-14131-5*, Greenwillow Bks.) HarperCollins Children's Bk. Group.

Strigenz, Geri K., illus. Thunder Foot. 1992. (History's Children Ser.). 48p. (J). (gr. 4-5). pap. o.p. (*0-8114-6425-3*) Raintree Pubs.

Stroud, Virginia A. A Walk to the Great Mystery. 1995. (Illus.). 32p. (J). 14.99 o.s.i (*0-8037-1636-2*); 14.89 o.s.i (*0-8037-1637-0*) Penguin Putnam Bks. for Young Readers. (Dial Bks. for Young Readers).

Sullivan, Mark T. Ghost Dance. 1999. 352p. 24.00 o.s.i (*0-380-97429-0*, Avon Bks.) Morrow/Avon.

—The Purification Ceremony. 1998. mass mkt. 6.99 o.s.i (*0-380-79042-4*); 1997. 335p. 24.00 o.s.i (*0-380-97428-2*) Morrow/Avon. (Avon Bks.).

Sutton, Margaret. The Spirit of Fog Island. 1976. (Judy Bolton Mystery Ser.). reprint ed. lib. bdg. 21.95 (*0-88411-713-8*) Amereon, Ltd.

Swanson, Steven. Brad Benson & the Secret Weapon. (Pennypinchers Ser.). 127p. (J). (gr. 5-10). pap. 2.95 o.p. (*0-89191-821-3*) Cook Communications Ministries.

Swayne, Zoa L. Do Them No Harm! Lewis & Clark among the Nez Perce. Bates, Carol Ann Goodrich, ed. 2003. (Illus.). 350p. pap. 16.95 (*0-87004-427-3*) Caxton Pr.

Tatsch, J. H. Coal Deposits: Origin, Evolution, & Present Characteristics. 1980. (Illus.). 590p. 156.00 o.p. (*0-912890-13-4*) Tatsch Assocs.

Tayler, Mark A. Chaco: A Novel. 1993. 288p. pap. 14.95 (*0-86534-203-2*) Sunstone Pr.

Taylor, Janelle. Chase the Wind. 1994. mass mkt. 14.95 o.s.i (*0-8217-4553-0*) Kensington Publishing Corp.

—Destiny Mine. l.t. ed. 1995. 448p. lib. bdg. 21.95 o.p. (*0-7838-1208-6*, Macmillan Reference USA) Gale Group.

—Destiny Mine. 1995. 352p. mass mkt. 18.95 o.s.i (*0-8217-4824-6*) Kensington Publishing Corp.

—Lakota Winds. 1999. mass mkt. 3.99 (*0-8217-7737-8*, Zebra Bks.); 1999. 352p. mass mkt. 6.99 o.s.i (*0-8217-6199-4*); 1997. 320p. 23.00 o.s.i (*1-57566-264-7*, Kensington Bks.) Kensington Publishing Corp.

—A New Collection of Three Complete Novels: Bittersweet Ecstasy, Forever Ecstasy & Savage Conguest. 1994. 13.99 o.s.i (*0-517-12205-7*) Random Hse. Value Publishing.

—Savage Ecstasy. l.t. ed. 2000. (G. K. Hall Romance Ser.). 600p. 27.95 (*0-7838-9306-X*, Macmillan Reference USA) Gale Group.

—Savage Ecstasy. 1996. 528p. mass mkt. 5.99 o.s.i (*0-8217-5453-X*); 1991. mass mkt. 4.95 o.s.i (*0-8217-3496-2*, Zebra Bks.); 1982. mass mkt. 4.50 o.p. (*0-8217-3306-0*, Zebra Bks.); 1982. mass mkt. 3.50 o.p. (*0-89083-824-0*, Zebra Bks.); 1982. mass mkt. 3.95 o.p. (*0-8217-2671-4*, Zebra Bks.) Kensington Publishing Corp.

Teague, Wells. Theo, the Indian Fighter. Eakin, Edwin M., ed. 1987. (Illus.). 112p. (J). (gr. 4-5). 8.95 (*0-89015-614-X*) Eakin Pr.

Thayer, Cynthia. Strong for Potatoes. 1997. 248p. 22.95 o.p. (*0-312-18187-6*); 1999. 256p. reprint ed. pap. 12.95 (*0-312-20027-7*, NPB 0336, Saint Martin's Griffin) St. Martin's Pr.

Thom, James A. The Red Heart. 1997. 448p. 25.00 o.p. (*0-345-39004-0*) Ballantine Bks.

Thom, James Alexander. The Red Heart. 1998. 544p. mass mkt. 7.50 (*0-345-36471-6*, Ballantine Bks.) Ballantine Bks.

Thom, James Alexander & Thom, Dark Rain. Warrior Woman: The Exceptional Life Story of Nonhelma, Shawnee Indian Woman Chief. 2003. 464p. 25.95 (*0-345-44554-6*, Ballantine Bks.) Ballantine Bks.

Thompson, Peggy. Song of the Wild Violets. 1993. (Illus.). 36p. (J). (gr. 2 up). pap. 5.95 (*0-913990-37-X*) Book Publishing Co., The.

Thon, Melanie Rae. Sweet Hearts. 2001. (Illus.). 256p. tchr. ed. 23.00 (*0-395-78589-8*, Mariner Bks.) Houghton Mifflin Co. Trade & Reference Div.

Thornton, Lawrence. Ghost Woman. 1992. 288p. 19.95 o.p. (*0-395-61592-5*) Houghton Mifflin Co.

—Ghost Woman. 1999. (California Fiction Ser.). (Illus.). 302p. pap. 15.95 (*0-520-22068-4*) Univ. of California Pr.

Thurlo, Aimee & Thurlo, David. Changing Woman. E-Book 24.95 (*0-312-70549-2*, Tor Bks.); 2nd ed. 2002. 384p. 24.95 (*0-312-87059-0*, CPHC0654, Forge Bks.) Doherty, Tom Assocs., LLC.

—Death Walker: An Ella Clah Novel. (Ella Clah Novel Ser.). 1997. 338p. mass mkt. 6.99 (*0-8125-6758-7*); 1996. 352p. 23.95 o.p. (*0-312-85651-2*); 2003. 384p. reprint ed. pap. 14.95 (*0-7653-0651-4*) Doherty, Tom Assocs., LLC. (Forge Bks.).

Thurlo, David & Thurlo, Aimee. Second Sunrise: A Lee Nez Novel. 2002. (Lee Nez Novel Ser.). 336p. 24.95 (0-7653-0441-4, Forge Bks.) Doherty, Tom Assocs., LLC.

Tinus, Arline W. Young Goat's Discovery. 1994. (Illus.). 32p. (J). (ps-3). 13.95 o.p. (1-878610-38-4) Red Crane Bks., Inc.

Tolbert, Frank X. The Staked Plain: A Novel. 1987. (Southwest Life & Letters Ser.). 292p. reprint ed. 22.50 (0-87074-252-3); pap. 10.95 (0-87074-253-1) Southern Methodist Univ. Pr.

Trafzer, Clifford E., ed. Earth Song, Sky Spirit: Short Stories of the Contemporary Native American Experience. 1997. 512p. pap. 12.76 (0-385-46960-8) Doubleday Publishing.

Traven, B. The Bridge in the Jungle. 2002. Tr. of Brucke in Dschungel. 255p. pap. 14.90 (1-56663-063-0, Elephant Paperbacks) Dee, Ivan R. Pub.

Tremblay, William. The June Rise: The Apocryphal Letters of Joseph Antoine Janis. 2001. 256p. 22.95 (1-55591-452-7) Fulcrum Publishing.

—The June Rise: The Apocryphal Letters of Joseph Antoine Janis. 1994. 225p. pap. 19.95 o.p. (0-87421-176-X) Utah State Univ. Pr.

Tremblay, William & Janis, Joseph Antoine. The June Rise: The Apocryphal Letters of Joseph Antoine Janis. 1994. E-Book 5.00 (0-585-03266-1) netLibrary, Inc.

Treuer, David. The Hiawatha. 1999. 320p. 24.00 o.p. (0-312-20313-6) Picador.

—Little. 1995. 224p. 22.95 o.s.i (1-55597-231-4) Graywolf Pr.

—Little. 1996. 272p. pap. 12.00 (0-312-15164-0) Picador.

Truett, John H. To Die in Dinetah: A Novel. 1994. 256p. pap. 14.95 (0-86534-225-3) Sunstone Pr.

Turner, Vickery. The Testimony of Daniel Pagels: A Novel. 1992. 352p. 22.95 o.p. (0-684-19366-3, Scribner) Simon & Schuster.

Turrill, David A. Michilimackinac: A Tale of the Straits. (Orig.). 1989. (Illus.). 490p. pap. 12.95 (0-923568-04-2); 2nd ed. 2003. pap. (0-923568-48-4) Wilderness Adventure Bks.

Twain, Mark & Nelson, Lee. Huck Finn & Tom Sawyer among the Indians. 2003. 268p. 18.95 (1-55517-680-1, 76801, Council Pr.) Cedar Fort, Inc./CFI Distribution.

Udall, Brady. The Miracle Life of Edgar Mint: A Novel. 2002. 432p. pap. 14.00 (0-375-71918-0, Vintage) Knopf Publishing Group.

—The Miracle Life of Edgar Mint: A Novel. 2001. 384p. 24.95 (0-393-02036-3) Norton, W. W. & Co., Inc.

Ude, Wayne. Becoming Coyote. 1979. 165p. 13.95 o.s.i (0-89924-023-2); pap. 12.95 (0-89924-031-3) Lynx Hse. Pr.

Urrea, Luis Alberto. Six Kinds of Sky: A Collection of Short Fiction. 2002. 160p. pap. 12.95 (0-938317-63-6) Cinco Puntos Pr.

Ury, Allen B. & Random House Staff. Fangs! 1997. (Illus.). pap. 2.99 o.s.i (0-679-88372-X) Random Hse. Value Publishing.

Vallo, Lawrence. Tales of a Pueblo Boy: A Memoir. 2nd ed. 1987. (Illus.). 48p. (J). (gr. 6-9). pap. 5.95 (0-86534-089-7) Sunstone Pr.

Van der Veer, Judy. Higher Than the Arrow. 1975. (J). (gr. 4-6). pap. 1.50 o.p. (0-380-00194-2, 44859-9, Avon Bks.) Morrow/Avon.

Velie, Alan R., ed. & intro. The Lightning Within: An Anthology of Contemporary American Indian Fiction. 1991. 164p. text 30.00 o.p. (0-8032-4659-5) Univ. of Nebraska Pr.

Vestal, Stanley. Happy Hunting Grounds. 1975. (Illus.). 228p. 13.95 o.p. (0-8061-1141-0); pap. 5.95 o.p. (0-8061-1543-2) Univ. of Oklahoma Pr.

Vick, Helen H. Tag Against Time. 1955. (Illus.). (gr. 7 up). 188p. pap. 15.95 (1-57140-006-0); 128p. pap. 9.95 (1-57140-007-9) Rinehart, Roberts Pubs.

—Walker of Time. (Illus.). (gr. 7-12). 1999. 212p. 9.95 (0-943173-80-9); 1955. 139p. pap. 15.95 (0-943173-84-1) Rinehart, Roberts Pubs.

—Walker's Journey Home. (Illus.). (Orig.). (gr. 7 up). 2000. 96p. 9.95 (1-57140-001-X); 1995. 192p. (YA). 14.95 (1-57140-000-1) Rinehart, Roberts Pubs.

Vizenor, Gerald. Wordarrows: Native States of Literary Sovereignty. 2003. 178p. pap. text 16.00 (0-8032-9629-0) Univ. of Nebraska Pr.

Vizenor, Gerald, contrib. by. Hiroshima Bugi: Atomu 57. 2003. (Native Storiers Ser.). 224p. 26.95 (0-8032-4673-0) Univ. of Nebraska Pr.

Vizenor, Gerald R. Earthdivers: Tribal Narratives on Mixed Descent. 1981. (Illus.). 203p. (C). 16.95 (0-8166-1048-7) Univ. of Minnesota Pr.

—The Heirs of Columbus. 1991. 189p. lib. bdg. 22.95 o.p. (0-8195-5241-0); per. 17.95 (0-8195-6249-1) Wesleyan Univ. Pr.

—Wordarrows: Indians & Whites in the New Fur Trade. 1978. xiv, 164p. (C). reprint ed. pap. 14.95 (0-8166-0862-8) Univ. of Minnesota Pr.

Vizenor, Gerald Robert. Chancers: A Novel. 2001. pap. (0-8061-3388-0); 2000. (American Indian Literature & Critical Studies: Vol. 36). 159p. 19.95 (0-8061-3266-3); 2000. E-Book 19.95 (0-8061-7185-5) Univ. of Oklahoma Pr.

Vollmann, William T. Argall. 2002. (Illus.). 768p. 18.00 (0-14-200150-3) Viking Penguin.

—Argall: The True Story of Pocahontas & Captain John Smith. 2001. (Seven Dreams Ser.: Vol. 3). (Illus.). 736p. 40.00 o.s.i (0-670-91030-9, Viking) Viking Penguin.

Von Ahnen, Katherine. Heart of Naosaqua. 1999. (Council for Indian Education Ser.). (Illus.). 160p. (gr. 4-7). pap. 9.95 (1-57098-010-1) Rinehart, Roberts Pubs.

Wagamese, Richard. A Quality of Light. 1997. 288p. pap. 18.95 o.s.i (0-385-25606-X) Doubleday Publishing.

Wakeland, Marcia A. The Big Fish: An Alaskan Fairy Tale. 1996. (Illus.). 32p. (J). (ps-4). pap. 7.95 (0-9635083-2-6) Misty Mountain Publishing Co.

Waldo, Anna Lee. Sacajawea. 1984. 1424p. mass mkt. 8.99 (0-380-84293-9, Avon Bks.) Morrow/Avon.

Waldorf, Mary. Thousand Camps, 001. 1982. (J). (gr. 5-9). 8.95 o.p. (0-395-31866-1) Houghton Mifflin Co.

Walker, Christina. The Naked Shield. 2000. E-Book 4.95 (1-930364-34-2, Bookmice) McGraw Publishing, Inc.

Walker, Robert W. Cold Edge. 2001. 336p. mass mkt. 6.99 o.s.i (0-515-12970-4, Jove) Berkley Publishing Group.

—Cutting Edge. 1997. 432p. mass mkt. 6.99 o.s.i (0-515-12012-X, Jove) Berkley Publishing Group.

Walsh, M. M. B. Grass Heart. 2001. 170p. 22.95 (0-8263-2338-3) Univ. of New Mexico Pr.

Walters, Anna. Ghost Singer. 1988. 236p. pap. 15.95 o.p. (0-87358-472-4) Northland Publishing.

Walters, Anna L. The Sun Is Not Merciful: Short Stories. 1985. 136p. lib. bdg. 18.95 (0-932379-11-7); pap. 8.95 (0-932379-10-9) Firebrand Bks.

Walters, Anna Lee. Ghost Singer: A Novel. 1994. 248p. pap. 17.95 (0-8263-1545-3) Univ. of New Mexico Pr.

Warren, Patricia N. One Is the Sun. 1991. 512p. pap. 12.95 o.s.i (0-345-37042-2) Ballantine Bks.

Watkins, Sherrin. Green Snake Ceremony. 1995. (Greyfeather Ser.). (Illus.). 408p. (J). (ps-5). 17.95 (0-933031-89-0) Council Oak Bks.

—White Bead Ceremony. 1995. (Greyfeather Ser.). (Illus.). 512p. (J). (gr. 1-5). 16.95 (0-933031-92-0) Council Oak Bks.

Weaver, Will. Red Earth, White Earth. 1986. 352p. 17.45 o.p. (0-671-61977-2, Simon & Schuster) Simon & Schuster.

Weil, Ann. Bzzzz. 1995. (Science Fiction Ser.). 80p. (gr. 5-9). pap. text 3.41 (0-8114-9322-9) Raintree Pubs.

Weinberg, Karen. A Cherokee Passage. 1996. (WM Kids Ser.). 158p. (J). pap. 12.95 (0-942597-47-8, WM Kids) White Mane Publishing Co., Inc.

Weisman, Joan. The Storyteller. 1993. (Illus.). 32p. (J). 15.95 o.p. (0-8478-1742-3) Rizzoli International Pubns., Inc.

Welch, James. Fools Crow. 1987. (Contemporary American Fiction Ser.). 400p. pap. 13.95 (0-14-008937-3, Penguin Bks.) Penguin Group (USA) Inc.

—Fools Crow. 1986. 400p. 18.95 o.p. (0-670-81121-1) Viking Penguin.

—The Heartsong of Charging Elk. pap. (0-385-72880-8) Knopf Publishing Group.

—The Heartsong of Charging Elk: A Novel. 2001. 448p. pap. 14.95 (0-385-49675-3, Knopf Bks. for Young Readers) Random Hse. Children's Bks.

—The Indian Lawyer. 1990. 19.95 o.p. (0-393-02896-8) Norton, W. W. & Co., Inc.

—Winter in the Blood. 1975. reprint ed. lib. bdg. 8.95 o.p. (0-8161-6299-9, Macmillan Reference USA) Gale Group.

—Winter in the Blood. 1981. 256p. pap. o.p. (0-06-080537-4) HarperCollins Pubs.

—Winter in the Blood. 1986. (Contemporary American Fiction Ser.). 192p. pap. 14.00 (0-14-008644-7, Penguin Bks.) Penguin Group (USA) Inc.

Welsch, Roger. Touching the Fire: Buffalo Dancers, the Sky Bundle & Other Tales. 1993. 304p. pap. 10.00 o.s.i (0-449-90869-0, Fawcett) Ballantine Bks.

—Touching the Fire: Buffalo Dancers, the Sky Bundle & Other Tales. 1997. (Illus.). 272p. pap. 12.00 (0-8032-9798-X, Bison Bks.) Univ. of Nebraska Pr.

West, Jessamyn. The Massacre at Fall Creek. 1976. 320p. mass mkt. 1.95 o.s.i (0-449-22771-5, C2771, Fawcett) Ballantine Bks.

—The Massacre at Fall Creek. unabr. ed. 1980. audio 72.00 (0-7366-0255-0, 1250) Books on Tape, Inc.

—The Massacre at Fall Creek. 1986. 384p. pap. 12.00 (0-15-657681-3, Harvest Bks.); 1975. 14.95 o.s.i (0-15-157820-6) Harcourt Trade Pubs.

—The Massacre at Fall Creek. 1987. 18.50 o.p. (0-8446-6274-7) Smith, Peter Pub., Inc.

Wheeler, Bernelda. Where Did You Get Your Moccasins? 1992. (Illus.). 24p. (J). (gr. k-2). pap. 6.00 (1-895411-50-5) Peguis Pubs., Ltd.

Wheeler, Richard. Richard Lamb. 1988. mass mkt. 2.95 o.s.i (0-345-35628-4) Ballantine Bks.

Wheeler, Richard S. The Dark Passage. 2000. (Barnaby Skye Novels). 318p. mass mkt. 6.99 (0-8125-4025-5, Forge Bks.) Doherty, Tom Assocs., LLC.

—The Dark Passage: A Barnaby Skye Novel. 1998. 318p. 23.95 (0-312-86526-0, Forge Bks.) Doherty, Tom Assocs., LLC.

—Dodging Red Cloud. l.t. ed. 1989. (Nightingale Ser.). 311p. 13.95 o.p. (0-8161-4657-8, Macmillan Reference USA) Gale Group.

—Dodging Red Cloud. 1987. (Evans Novel of the West Ser.). 202p. 14.51 o.p. (0-87131-526-2) Holt, Henry & Co.

—Richard Lamb. 1987. 16.95 o.p. (0-8027-4076-6) Walker & Co.

Whelan, Gloria. The Indian School. (Illus.). 96p. (J). (gr. 2-5). 1996. lib. bdg. 13.89 o.p. (0-06-027078-0); 1996. 13.95 o.p. (0-06-027077-2); 1997. reprint ed. pap. 4.25 (0-06-442056-6, Harper Trophy) HarperCollins Children's Bk. Group.

—Next Spring an Oriole. 1987. (Stepping Stone Bks.). (Illus.). 64p. (J). (ps-3). 6.99 o.s.i (0-394-99125-7); pap. 3.99 (0-394-89125-2) Random Hse. Children's Bks. (Random Hse. Bks. for Young Readers).

—Next Spring an Oriole. 1987. (Stepping Stone Bks.). (J). 10.14 (0-606-03037-9) Turtleback Bks.

—Night of the Full Moon. 1993. (Illus.). 64p. (J). (gr. 2-4). 15.00 o.s.i (0-679-84464-3, Knopf Bks. for Young Readers) Random Hse. Children's Bks.

—The Shadow of the Wolf. 1997. 80p. (J). (gr. 2-5). lib. bdg. 11.99 o.s.i (0-679-98108-X); (Illus.). (gr. 1-4). lib. bdg. 3.99 (0-679-88108-5) Random Hse., Inc.

Wheller, Richard S. Dodging Red Cloud. 1988. mass mkt. 2.95 o.s.i (0-345-35665-9) Ballantine Bks.

Whipple, Dan. Click: A Novel. 2001. 258p. 35.00 (0-87081-632-2) Univ. Pr. of Colorado.

White Deer of Autumn Staff. Ceremony-In the Circle of Life. 1983. (Heritage Bks.). (Illus.). 32p. (J). (gr. 3-6). reprint ed. lib. bdg. 14.65 o.p. (0-940742-24-1) Raintree Pubs.

Whitefeather, Willy. Willy Whitefeather's River Book for Kids. 1995. (Willy Whitefeather's Ser.). (Illus.). 153p. (gr. 1 up). pap. 11.95 (0-943173-94-9) Rinehart, Roberts Pubs.

Whitney, Phyllis A. Secret of the Haunted Mesa. 1975. 144p. (J). (gr. 6 up). 5.75 o.p. (0-664-32568-8) Westminster John Knox Pr.

Whitson, Stephanie G. Red Bird: A Novel. 1997. (Prairie Winds Ser.: 3). 288p. pap. 10.99 (0-7852-7484-7) Nelson, Thomas Pubs.

—Soaring Eagle. 1996. (Prairie Winds Ser.: Bk. 2). 312p. pap. 10.99 (0-7852-7617-3) Nelson, Thomas Pubs.

—Walks the Fire: A Novel. 1994. (Prairie Winds Ser.: Bk. 1). 301p. pap. 9.99 (0-7852-7981-4) Nelson, Thomas Pubs.

Whitson, Stephanie Grace. Edge of Wilderness. 2001. (Dakota Moons Ser.: Bk. 2). xxi, 288p. pap. 12.99 (0-7852-6823-5) Nelson, Thomas Pubs.

—Heart of the Sandhills. 2002. 288p. pap. 13.99 (0-7852-6824-3) Nelson, Thomas Inc.

Wiebe, Rudy. The Temptations of Big Bear. 1996. 408p. (J). mass mkt. 7.95 (0-7710-3454-7) McClelland & Stewart/Tundra Bks.

—The Temptations of Big Bear. 2000. (Illus.). 423p. pap. 16.95 (0-8040-1029-3) Swallow Pr.

Wilkinson, Daniel Marion. Not Between Brothers: An Epic Novel of Texas. (Celestial Arts Ser.). 680p. 2003. pap. 15.95 (0-9651879-3-4); 1996. (Illus.). 27.95 (0-9651879-0-X) Boaz Publishing Co.

Wilkinson, David Marion. Not Between Brothers: An Epic Novel of Texas. 1999. 656p. reprint ed. mass mkt. 6.99 o.s.i (0-451-19686-4, Signet Bks.) NAL.

Wilkinson, Marion David. Oblivion's Alter: A Novel of Courage. 2002. (Illus.). 384p. pap. 14.00 (0-451-20546-4) NAL.

Williams, Barbara. The Secret Name. 1972. (Illus.). 123p. (J). (gr. 3-7). 6.50 o.p. (0-15-272227-0) Harcourt Children's Bks.

Williams, Jeanne. New Medicine. rev. ed. 1994. (Illus.). 168p. (J). 8.95 (0-937460-90-7); pap. 9.95 (0-937460-93-1) Hendrick-Long Publishing Co.

Williamson, Larry. Tallapoosa. 2001. 256p. pap. 17.95 (1-58838-039-4) NewSouth, Inc.

Willman, Marianne. Pieces of Sky. 2000. 408p. mass mkt. (1-55166-564-6); 1993. per. (0-373-28795-X, 1-28795-2); 1986. 400p. per. (0-373-97022-6) Harlequin Enterprises, Ltd. (Harlequin Bks.).

Wilson, Tom. Black Wolf. 1995. 432p. mass mkt. 5.99 o.s.i (0-451-40607-9, Signet Bks.) NAL.

Windle, Jeanette. Mystery at Death Canyon. 2002. (Parker Twins Ser.: No. 4). 176p. (J). (gr. 3-8). pap. 5.99 (0-8254-4148-X) Kregel Pubns.

—Mystery at Death Canyon. 1996. (Twin Pursuits Ser.: No. 1). 128p. pap. 4.99 o.p. (0-88070-904-9, Multnomah Bks.) Multnomah Pubs., Inc.

Wisler, G. Clifton. Lakota. 1989. (Novel of the West Ser.). 180p. 14.95 o.p. (0-87131-563-7) Evans, M. & Co., Inc.

—Winter of the Wolf. 1981. (J). (gr. 6 up). 10.95 o.p. (0-525-66716-4, Dutton Children's Bks.) Penguin Putnam Bks. for Young Readers.

—The Wolf's Tooth. 1987. 128p. (J). (gr. 5-9). 12.95 o.p. (0-525-67197-8, Dutton Children's Bks.) Penguin Putnam Bks. for Young Readers.

Wolfe, Swain. The Lake Dreams the Sky: A Love Story. 1999. 352p. pap. 13.00 o.s.i (0-06-092993-6, Perennial); 1998. 320p. 23.00 o.s.i (0-06-017412-9, HarperCollins) HarperTrade.

—The Parrot Trainer. (Illus.). mass mkt. (0-312-98793-5, St. Martin's Paperbacks); 2003. 288p. 24.95 (0-312-31091-9) St. Martin's Pr.

Wood, Nancy. The Girl Who Loved Coyotes: Stories of the Southwest. 1995. (Illus.). 48p. (J). (gr. k up). lib. bdg. 15.93 o.p. (0-688-13982-5, Morrow, William & Co.) Morrow/Avon.

—Shamans Daughter. 1981. mass mkt. 3.25 o.s.i (0-440-17863-0) Dell Publishing.

—Thunderwoman. 1999. (Illus.). 304p. (YA). 19.95 o.p. (0-525-45498-5) Penguin Putnam Bks. for Young Readers.

Woodall, Bobby R. Clearwater. 2001. 250p. per. 15.95 (0-9707093-9-0) McGraw Publishing, Inc.

—Clearwater. 2002. 276p. per. 16.95 (0-7443-0335-4) SynergEbks.

Woodruff, Joan L. Neighbors. 1993. 160p. pap. 11.95 (0-943219-08-6) 3rd Woman Pr.

Wooley, Marilyn. Jackpot Justice. E-Book 24.95 (0-312-27384-3); 2000. 352p. 24.95 (0-312-25455-5, Saint Martin's Minotaur) St. Martin's Pr.

Worcester, Donald E. Lone Hunter & the Cheyennes. 1985. (Chaparral Bks.). (Illus.). 78p. (J). (gr. 4 up). reprint ed. 10.95 (0-87565-018-X) Texas Christian Univ. Pr.

—Lone Hunter's Gray Pony. 1985. (Chaparral Bks.). (Illus.). 70p. (J). (gr. 4 up). 10.95 (0-87565-001-5) Texas Christian Univ. Pr.

—War Pony. 1984. (Chaparral Bks.). (Illus.). 96p. (J). (gr. 4 up). reprint ed. 10.95 (0-912646-85-3) Texas Christian Univ. Pr.

Worcester, Donald Emmet. Man on Two Ponies. 2001. 272p. mass mkt. 4.50 (0-8439-4832-9, Leisure Bks.) Dorchester Publishing Co., Inc.

Wosmek, Frances. A Brown Bird Singing. 1986. (Illus.). 160p. (YA). (gr. 5-10). 11.95 o.p. (0-688-06251-2) HarperCollins Children's Bk. Group.

—A Brown Bird Singing. 1993. (Illus.). 128p. (J). (gr. 5 up). pap. 4.95 o.p. (0-688-04596-0, Morrow, William & Co.) Morrow/Avon.

Wunderli, Stephen. The Blue Between the Clouds. ERS. 1996. (J). (gr. 4-7). pap. 5.95 o.p. (0-8050-4819-7); 1992. 80p. (YA). (gr. 5 up). 13.95 o.p. (0-8050-1772-0) Holt, Henry & Co. (Holt, Henry & Co. Bks. For Young Readers).

Wyman, Margaret. Mission: The Birth of California, the Death of a Nation. Orton, Jerry, ed. 2002. 316p. per. 16.95 (1-931857-00-8) Idyllwild Publishing Co.

Yarbro, Chelsea Quinn. Ogilvie, Tallant & Moon. 1976. (Red Mask Mystery Ser.). (Illus.). 214p. 6.95 o.p. (0-399-11630-3) Putnam Publishing Group, The.

Yockey, R. Paul. Peace Out. Ashby, Ruth, ed. 1992. (New Kids on the Block Ser.). 144p. (J). pap. 3.50 (0-671-73943-3, Simon Pulse) Simon & Schuster Children's Publishing.

Yoder, James. Lucy of the Trail of Tears: Survivor of the Trail - Oklahoma Seminry Girl, & Andrews Wichita Bride. 2000. 347p. E-Book 8.00 (0-7388-8428-6) Xlibris Corp.

Yolen, Jane. Sky Dogs. 1995. (Illus.). 32p. (J). (ps-3). pap. 5.00 (0-15-200776-8, Voyager Bks./Libros Viajeros) Harcourt Children's Bks.

—Sky Dogs. 1990. (Illus.). 32p. (J). (ps-3). 15.95 o.s.i (0-15-275480-6); 100.00 o.p. (0-15-275481-4) Harcourt Trade Pubs.

—Sky Dogs. 1995. (J). 10.20 o.p. (0-606-08171-2) Turtleback Bks.

Yorgason, Blaine M. To Soar with the Eagle. 1993. 280p. o.p. (0-87579-745-8) Deseret Bk. Co.

Yorgason, Blaine M. & Yorgason, Brenton G. Seeker of the Gentle Heart. 1982. 156p. 7.95 o.p. (0-88494-456-5, Bookcraft, Inc.) Deseret Bk. Co.

Young Bear, Ray A. Black Eagle Child: The Facepaint Narratives. 1992. (Singular Lives Ser.). (Illus.). 281p. 25.95 (0-87745-356-X) Univ. of Iowa Pr.

—Remnants of the First Earth. 1996. 23.00 o.p. (0-8021-1581-0); 1998. reprint ed. pap. 12.00 (0-8021-3552-8) Grove/Atlantic, Inc. (Grove Pr.).

Youseyah, You. When Hopi Children Were Bad: A Monster Story. 1989. (Illus.). 41p. (Orig.). (J). (gr. 4-7). pap. 46.95 (0-940113-20-1) Sierra Oaks Publishing Co.

Zimmer, Michael. Cottonwood Station. l.t. ed. 1994. 19.95 o.p. (0-8161-5920-3, Macmillan Reference USA) Gale Group.

—Cottonwood Station. 1994. 224p. mass mkt. 3.99 o.p. (0-06-100794-3, HarperTorch) Morrow/Avon.

—Cottonwood Station. 1993. 182p. 19.95 o.p. (0-8027-1273-8) Walker & Co.

**INDIANS OF SOUTH AMERICA—FICTION**

Gallegos, Rómulo. Canaima. Tello, Jaime, tr. 1986. (Illus.). 360p. reprint ed. 22.95 o.p. (*0-8061-9928-8*); pap. 11.95 (*0-8061-2119-X*) Univ. of Oklahoma Pr.

—Canaima. Minguet, Charles, ed. 1991. (Coleccion Archivos). (SPA.). 513p. 34.95 o.p. (*84-00-07120-4*) Univ. of Pittsburgh Pr.

Lieberman, Herbert. The Climate of Hell. 1978. 9.95 o.s.i (*0-671-24363-2*, Simon & Schuster) Simon & Schuster.

Matthiessen, Peter. At Play in the Fields of the Lord. 1991. 384p. pap. 14.00 (*0-679-73741-3*); 1987. pap. 10.95 o.p. (*0-394-75083-7*) Knopf Publishing Group. (Vintage).

—At Play in the Fields of the Lord. 1967. mass mkt. 1.25 o.p. (*0-451-03057-5*, Signet Bks.) NAL.

—At Play in the Fields of the Lord. unabr. ed. 1999. audio 91.00 (*1-55690-701-X*, 92414E7) Recorded Bks., LLC.

—At Play in the Fields of the Lord. 1992. 26.75 (*0-8446-6636-X*) Smith, Peter Pub., Inc.

Matto de Turner, Clorinda. Birds Without a Nest: A Novel. 1996. (Texas Pan American Ser.). 205p. pap. 15.95 (*0-292-75195-8*) Univ. of Texas Pr.

—Birds Without a Nest: A Novel. Hudson, J. G., tr. 1996. (Texas Pan American Ser.). 205p. 30.00 o.p. (*0-292-75194-X*) Univ. of Texas Pr.

Mueller, Marnie. Green Fires: Assault on Eden: A Novel of the Ecuadorian Rainforest. 1999. 318p. pap. 13.95 (*1-880684-59-4*) Curbstone Pr.

Pallamary, Matthew J. Land Without Evil. unabr. ed. 2000. (Illus.). 358p. 23.95 (*0-912880-09-0*) Charles Publishing Co.

Scorza, Manuel. Garabombo, the Invisible. Aldaz, Ana-Marie, tr. 1994. (American University Studies: Ser. XXII, Vol. 22). Tr. of Historia de Garabombo el Invisible. (ENG & SPA.). XIX, 230p. (C). text 51.95 (*0-8204-2157-X*) Lang, Peter Publishing, Inc.

Upton, Peter. Green Hill Far Away. 1978. mass mkt. 2.25 o.s.i (*0-345-27208-0*) Ballantine Bks.

**INUIT—FICTION**

Gloliorte, John I. An Inuk Boy Becomes a Hunter. 1999. (Illus.). 102p. (YA). (gr. 5-8). reprint ed. pap. text 15.00 (*0-7881-6562-3*) DIANE Publishing Co.

Lane, Christopher. The Elements of a Kill. 1998. 416p. mass mkt. 5.99 (*0-380-79870-0*, Avon Bks.) Morrow/Avon.

—The Season of Death: An Inupiat Eskimo Mystery. 1999. 352p. mass mkt. 5.99 (*0-380-79872-7*, Avon Bks.) Morrow/Avon.

—A Shroud of Midnight Sun. 2000. (Inupiat Eskimo Mysteries Ser.). 352p. mass mkt. 5.99 (*0-380-79873-5*, Avon Bks.) Morrow/Avon.

—Silent as the Hunter. 2001. (Inupiat Eskimo Mysteries Ser.). 352p. mass mkt. 6.50 (*0-380-81625-3*, Avon Bks.) Morrow/Avon.

Spinka, Penina Keen. Dream Weaver. 2003. (Illus.). 464p. 26.95 (*0-525-94684-5*, Dutton) Dutton/Plume.

—Dream Weaver. 2004. 512p. mass mkt. 7.99 (*0-451-41111-0*, Onyx) NAL.

Young, Scott. Murder in a Cold Climate. 1989. mass mkt. o.s.i (*0-449-21746-9*) Ballantine Bks.

—Murder in a Cold Climate. (Crime Ser.). 1990. 240p. pap. 4.50 o.p. (*0-14-012336-9*, Penguin Bks.); 1989. 256p. 16.95 o.p. (*0-670-82889-0*) Viking Penguin.

—The Shaman's Knife. 1994. (Crime Ser.). 288p. pap. 5.95 o.p. (*0-14-014353-X*, Penguin Bks.) Penguin Group (USA) Inc.

—The Shaman's Knife. 1993. 288p. 20.00 o.p. (*0-670-83555-2*, Viking) Viking Penguin.

**IRISH AMERICANS—FICTION**

Alcorn, Alfred. The Long Run of Myles Mayberry. 1999. (Illus.). 240p. pap. 13.00 o.p. (*1-58195-001-2*, Zoland Bks., Inc.) Steerforth Pr.

Bens, Jeff W. Albert, Himself. 2001. 200p. pap. 14.00 (*1-883285-22-4*) Delphinium Bks., Inc.

Binchy, Maeve. Firefly Summer. 1989. 672p. mass mkt. 7.99 (*0-440-20419-4*, 2765753); 1988. 608p. 19.95 o.s.i (*0-440-50017-6*, Delacorte Pr.) Dell Publishing.

—Firefly Summer. l.t. ed. 1989. (General Ser.). 1056p. 21.95 o.p. (*0-8161-4750-7*, Macmillan Reference USA) Gale Group.

Block, Lawrence. Everybody Dies. (Matthew Scudder Mystery Ser.: No. 14). 1999. 384p. mass mkt. 6.99 (*0-380-72535-5*, Avon Bks.); 1998. 336p. 25.00 o.p. (*0-688-14182-X*, Morrow, William & Co.) Morrow/Avon.

—Everybody Dies. Set. abr. ed. 1998. (Matthew Scudder Mystery Ser.: No. 14). audio 25.00 (*0-7871-1800-1*, 694543, Dove Audio) NewStar Media, Inc.

—Everybody Dies. unabr. ed. 1999. (Matthew Scudder Mystery Ser.: No. 14). audio 70.00 (*0-7887-2484-3*, 95559E7) Recorded Bks., LLC.

—Everybody Dies. l.t. ed. 1999. (Matthew Scudder Mystery Ser.: No. 14). 461p. 29.95 (*0-7862-1706-5*) Thorndike Pr.

Bradley, Nancy. The Connemara Connection. 2002. 300p. pap. (*1-55369-531-3*) Trafford Publishing.

Brady, Catherine. The End of the Class War. 1999. 230p. 27.95 (*0-934971-67-6*); 270p. pap. 13.95 (*0-934971-66-8*) Calyx Bks.

Breslin, Jimmy. Table Money. l.t. ed. 1987. 707p. 19.95 o.p. (*0-8161-4260-2*, Macmillan Reference USA) Gale Group.

—Table Money. 1986. 434p. 17.95 (*0-89919-312-9*) Houghton Mifflin Co.

—Table Money. 1990. 4.99 o.p. (*0-517-02971-5*) Random Hse. Value Publishing.

—Table Money. 1987. 608p. mass mkt. 4.95 o.p. (*0-14-010046-6*, Penguin Bks.) Viking Penguin.

—World Without End, Amen. 1976. pap. 1.75 o.p. (*0-380-01628-1*, 19042, Avon Bks.) Morrow/Avon.

—World Without End, Amen. 1987. 384p. pap. 4.95 o.p. (*0-14-010364-3*, Penguin Bks.); 1973. 6.95 o.p. (*0-670-79020-6*) Viking Penguin.

Brodine, Virginia W. Seed of the Fire. 1996. 310p. 18.95 (*0-7178-0721-5*); pap. 9.95 (*0-7178-0722-3*) International Publishers Co., Inc.

Callaghan, Mary R. Emigrant Dreams. 1996. 298p. pap. 12.95 (*1-85371-620-0*) Poolbeg Pr. IRL. *Dist:* Dufour Editions, Inc.

—I Met a Man Who Was Not There. 1997. 280p. 24.95 o.p. (*0-7145-3019-0*) Boyars, Marion Pubs., Inc.

Carey, Lisa. The Mermaids Singing. 2001. 288p. pap. 13.00 (*0-380-81559-1*, Perennial) HarperTrade.

—The Mermaids Singing. 1998. 257p. (YA). 22.00 (*0-380-97674-9*, Avon Bks.) Morrow/Avon.

—Mermaids Singing. 1999. 352p. (gr. 8 up). mass mkt. 6.99 (*0-380-79960-X*, Avon Bks.) Morrow/Avon.

Casey, Daniel J. & Rhodes, Robert E., eds. Modern Irish-American Fiction: A Reader. 1989. (Irish Studies). 336p. text 45.00 (*0-8156-2462-X*); pap. text 19.95 (*0-8156-0234-0*) Syracuse Univ. Pr.

Clark, Mary Higgins. The Lottery Winner. E-Book 9.95 (*1-930161-64-6*) Adobe Systems, Inc.

—The Lottery Winner. 1997. reprint ed. lib. bdg. 32.95 (*1-56849-588-9*) Buccaneer Bks., Inc.

—The Lottery Winner. 1995. 304p. mass mkt. 7.99 (*0-671-86717-2*, Pocket); 1994. 26.00 o.s.i (*0-684-80222-8*, Simon & Schuster); 1994. (Illus.). 256p. 22.00 (*0-671-86716-4*, Simon & Schuster) Simon & Schuster.

—The Lottery Winner. abr. ed. 1994. (Willy & Alvirah Mystery Ser.). audio 22.00 (*0-671-50136-4*, 592256, Simon & Schuster Audioworks) Simon & Schuster Audio.

—The Lottery Winner. 265p. pap. 5.98 o.p. (*0-7651-0558-6*) Smithmark Pubs., Inc.

Conway, Cyril Francis. While the Banshee Cried. unabr. ed. 1999. 518p. pap. 25.95 (*0-9674415-0-1*, 2502) Emerald Isle Pubs., Inc.

Curran, Mary Doyle. The Parish & the Hill. (Contemporary Classics by Women Ser.). 2002. 280p. pap. 15.95 (*1-55861-396-X*); 1986. 272p. reprint ed. pap. 12.95 o.p. (*0-935312-58-7*) Feminist Pr. at The City Univ. of New York.

Dalton, Dori. The Shamrock & the Feather: A Novel. 2002. 403p. pap. 28.95 (*1-890109-39-8*, Cross Time) Crossquarter Publishing Group.

Deasy, Mary. The Hour of Spring. 1976. (Irish Americans Ser.). reprint ed. 33.95 (*0-405-09330-6*) Ayer Co. Pubs., Inc.

Dee, Ed. The Con Man's Daughter. 2003. 304p. 23.95 (*0-89296-794-3*) Mysterious Pr.

DeMille, Nelson. Cathedral. 1982. 576p. mass mkt. 5.95 o.s.i (*0-440-11620-1*); 1981. 13.95 o.s.i (*0-440-01140-X*, Delacorte Pr.) Dell Publishing.

—Cathedral, Set. abr. ed. 1998. audio 8.99 o.s.i (*0-375-40296-9*, RH Audio) Random Hse. Audio Publishing Group.

—Cathedral. l.t. ed. 1982. (Charnwood Large Print Ser.). 720p. 29.99 o.p. (*0-7089-8079-1*, Charnwood) Thorpe, F. A. Pubs. GBR. *Dist:* Ulverscroft Large Print Bks., Ltd., Ulverscroft Large Print Canada, Ltd.

—Cathedral. 2001. 575p. E-Book 6.95 (*0-7595-8261-0*); 2001. 575p. E-Book 6.95 (*0-7595-0255-2*); 2001. 575p. E-Book 6.95 (*0-7595-6255-5*); 2001. 575p. E-Book 6.95 (*0-7595-4258-9*); 2001. 575p. E-Book 6.95 (*0-7595-9288-8*); 1990. 576p. reprint ed. mass mkt. 7.99 (*0-446-35857-6*) Warner Bks., Inc.

Dinneen, Joseph. Ward Eight. 1976. (Irish Americans Ser.). reprint ed. 29.95 (*0-405-09331-4*) Ayer Co. Pubs., Inc.

Donnelly, Gabrielle. The Girl in the Photograph. 1999. 288p. reprint ed. pap. 12.95 o.s.i (*0-425-17058-6*) Berkley Publishing Group.

—The Girl in the Photograph. 1998. 288p. 23.95 o.p. (*0-399-14417-X*, G. P. Putnam's Sons) Penguin Group (USA) Inc.

Dorris, Michael. Cloud Chamber: A Novel. 1998. pap. (*0-684-00606-5*, Scribner Paper Fiction); 1998. 320p. pap. 13.00 (*0-684-83535-5*, Scribner); 1997. 320p. 23.50 (*0-684-81567-2*, Scribner) Simon & Schuster.

—Cloud Chamber: A Novel. 1998. 18.05 (*0-606-12660-0*) Turtleback Bks.

Dunphy, Jack. John Fury: A Novel in Four Parts. 1976. (Irish Americans Ser.). reprint ed. 25.95 (*0-405-09333-0*) Ayer Co. Pubs., Inc.

—The Murderous McLaughlins. 1988. 256p. text 16.95 o.p. (*0-07-018316-3*) McGraw-Hill Cos., The.

Eisenstadt, Jill. From Rockaway. 1987. 224p. 15.95 o.s.i (*0-394-55970-3*) Knopf, Alfred A. Inc.

Fanning, Charles, ed. The Exiles of Erin: Nineteenth-Century Irish-American Fiction. 1988. (American Irish Studies Ser.: Vol. 1). 300p. text 34.50 o.p. (*0-268-00919-8*) Univ. of Notre Dame Pr.

Farrell, James T. Chicago Stories. Fanning, Charles, ed. 1998. (Prairie State Bks.). 245p. pap. 17.95 (*0-252-01981-4*) Univ. of Illinois Pr.

—Father & Son. 1976. (Irish Americans Ser.). reprint ed. 42.95 (*0-405-09335-7*) Ayer Co. Pubs., Inc.

—Studs Lonigan. Date not set. lib. bdg. 38.95 (*0-8488-1974-8*) Amereon, Ltd.

—Studs Lonigan. 1979. pap. 2.75 o.p. (*0-380-00934-X*, 59758-6, Avon Bks.) Morrow/Avon.

—Studs Lonigan. 1993. (Prairie State Bks.). 912p. pap. 21.95 (*0-252-06282-5*); text 49.95 o.p. (*0-252-02062-6*) Univ. of Illinois Pr.

—Studs Lonigan: A Trilogy. 2004. (Library of America: Vol. 148). 1024p. 35.00 (*1-931082-55-3*) Library of America, The.

—Young Lonigan. 2003. 224p. mass mkt. 7.95 (*0-451-52913-8*, Signet Classics) NAL.

—Young Lonigan. 2003. 224p. pap. 13.00 (*0-14-218007-6*, Penguin Classics) Viking Penguin.

Fink, John. Painted Leaves. 1995. 266p. 22.95 o.p. (*0-312-13137-2*, Saint Martin's Minotaur) St. Martin's Pr.

Fleming, Thomas J. All Good Men. 1976. (Irish Americans Ser.). reprint ed. 34.95 (*0-405-09336-5*) Ayer Co. Pubs., Inc.

—Hours of Gladness: A Novel of the Irish in America. 1999. 304p. 24.95 (*0-312-86781-6*, Forge Bks.) Doherty, Tom Assocs., LLC.

Fredrickson, Michael. Witness for the Dead. 2001. 384p. 25.95 (*0-312-87447-2*, Forge Bks.); 2002. reprint ed. mass mkt. 7.99 (*0-8125-6528-2*, Tor Bks.) Doherty, Tom Assocs., LLC.

Goran, Lester. Outlaws of the Purple Cow & Other Stories. 1999. 358p. pap. 35.00 (*0-87338-639-6*) Kent State Univ. Pr.

—She Loved Me Once: And Other Stories. 1997. 306p. (gr. 11-12). 26.00 (*0-87338-576-4*) Kent State Univ. Pr.

—Tales from the Irish Club: A Collection of Short Stories. 1996. 144p. (Orig.). (gr. 9-12). pap. 12.00 (*0-87338-539-X*) Kent State Univ. Pr.

Gordon, Mary. The Other Side. l.t. ed. 1994. 24.95 o.p. (*1-56895-072-1*, Wheeler Publishing, Inc.) Gale Group.

—The Other Side. 1990. (Contemporary American Fiction Ser.). 400p. pap. 15.00 (*0-14-014408-0*, Penguin Bks.) Penguin Group (USA) Inc.

—The Other Side. 1992. 4.99 o.p. (*0-517-08006-0*) Random Hse. Value Publishing.

—The Other Side. 1989. 400p. 19.95 o.p. (*0-670-82566-2*) Viking Penguin.

Graham, Brendan. Element of Fire. 2001. 356p. (*0-00-225977-X*) HarperCollins Pubs.

Graham, Heather. Night of the Blackbird. 2001. 384p. mass mkt. (*1-55166-812-2*, Mira Bks.) Harlequin Enterprises, Ltd.

—Night of the Blackbird. l.t. ed. 2002. (Americana Ser.). 566p. 31.95 (*0-7862-3976-X*) Thorndike Pr.

Greeley, Andrew M. A Christmas Wedding. l.t. ed. 2001. lib. bdg. 27.95 (*1-58547-158-5*) Ctr. Point Large Print.

—A Christmas Wedding. 2000. 349p. 24.95 (*0-312-87224-0*); 2001. 512p. reprint ed. mass mkt. 7.99 (*0-8125-6667-X*) Doherty, Tom Assocs., LLC. (Forge Bks.).

—Irish Eyes: A Nuala Anne McGrail Novel. 2000. 320p. 24.95 (*0-312-86570-8*); 2001. 352p. reprint ed. mass mkt. 6.99 (*0-8125-9024-4*) Doherty, Tom Assocs., LLC. (Forge Bks.).

—Irish Eyes: A Nuala Anne McGrail Novel. l.t. ed. 2001. 525p. 29.95 (*0-7862-3091-6*); (*0-7540-1621-8*) Thorndike Pr.

—Irish Gold: A Nuala Anne McGrail Novel. (Nuala Anne McGrail Novel Ser.). 1995. 493p. pap. 7.99 (*0-8125-5076-5*); 1994. 336p. 14.29 o.p. (*0-312-85813-2*) Doherty, Tom Assocs., LLC. (Forge Bks.).

—Irish Gold: A Nuala Anne McGrail Novel. abr. ed. 1994. 17.95 o.p. (*0-7871-0332-2*, 390987) NewStar Media, Inc.

—Irish Lace: A Nuala Anne McGrail Novel. (Nuala Anne McGrail Novel Ser.). 1997. 345p. pap. 6.99 (*0-8125-5077-3*, Tor Bks.); 1996. 304p. 23.95 o.p. (*0-312-86234-2*, Forge Bks.) Doherty, Tom Assocs., LLC.

—Irish Lace: A Nuala Anne McGrail Novel. abr. ed. 1996. 17.95 o.p. (*0-7871-1022-1*, 394462) NewStar Media, Inc.

—Irish Lace: A Nuala Anne McGrail Novel. 1998. 4.98 o.p. (*0-7651-1156-X*) Smithmark Pubs., Inc.

—Irish Love: A Nuala Anne McGrail Novel. 2001. 304p. 24.95 (*0-312-87187-2*); 2002. 368p. reprint ed. mass mkt. 6.99 (*0-8125-7606-3*) Doherty, Tom Assocs., LLC. (Forge Bks.).

—Irish Love: A Nuala Anne McGrail Novel. l.t. ed. 2001. (Wheeler Large Print Book Ser.). 386p. 29.95 o.p. (*1-58724-058-0*, Wheeler Publishing, Inc.) Gale Group.

—Irish Stew: A Nuala Anne McGrail Novel. 2002. 304p. 25.95 (*0-312-87188-0*, Forge Bks.) Doherty, Tom Assocs., LLC.

—Irish Stew: A Nuala Anne McGrail Novel. l.t. ed. 2003. 25.95 (*1-58724-413-6*, Wheeler Publishing, Inc.) Gale Group.

—Irish Whiskey: A Nuala Anne McGrail Novel. 1998. (Nuala Anne McGrail Novel Ser.). 309p. pap. 6.99 (*0-8125-7770-1*, Tor Bks.); 304p. 23.95 o.p. (*0-312-85596-6*, Forge Bks.) Doherty, Tom Assocs., LLC.

—Irish Whiskey: A Nuala Anne McGrail Novel. l.t. ed. 2000. (Basic Ser.). 549p. 28.95 (*0-7862-2930-6*) Thorndike Pr.

—A Midwinter's Tale. 1999. 448p. mass mkt. 6.99 (*0-8125-9025-2*); No. 1. 1998. (Midwinter's Tale Ser.: Vol. 1). 383p. 24.95 (*0-312-86571-6*) Doherty, Tom Assocs., LLC. (Forge Bks.).

—A Midwinter's Tale. l.t. ed. 2000. 542p. 26.95 (*1-56895-949-4*, Wheeler Publishing, Inc.) Gale Group.

—Second Spring: A Love Story. 2003. 8p. 69.95 (*0-7927-2874-2*); 10p. 94.95 (*0-7927-2875-0*) BBC Audiobooks America.

—Second Spring: A Love Story. 2003. (O'Malley Ser.: Bk. 5). (Illus.). 352p. 24.95 (*0-7653-0236-5*, Forge Bks.) Doherty, Tom Assocs., LLC.

—Second Spring: A Love Story. l.t. ed. 2003. (Americana Ser.). 29.95 (*0-7862-5402-5*) Thorndike Pr.

—September Song. l.t. ed. 2002. 392p. lib. bdg. 29.95 (*1-58547-163-1*) Ctr. Point Large Print.

—September Song. 2001. 272p. 24.95 (*0-312-87225-9*, Forge Bks.) Doherty, Tom Assocs., LLC.

—Star Bright! A Christmas Story. l.t. ed. 1998. 19.95 (*1-57490-166-4*) Beeler, Thomas T. Publisher.

—Star Bright! A Christmas Story. 1997. 127p. 13.95 (*0-312-86387-X*); 128p. 111.60 o.s.i (*0-312-86500-7*) Doherty, Tom Assocs., LLC. (Forge Bks.).

—Star Bright! A Christmas Story. 1999. 13.95 (*0-312-87116-3*) St. Martin's Pr.

—Younger Than Springtime. 1999. 348p. 24.95 (*0-312-86572-4*); 2000. 469p. reprint ed. mass mkt. 6.99 (*0-8125-9026-0*) Doherty, Tom Assocs., LLC. (Forge Bks.).

Griffin, Frank James. Till the Tide Comes In. 2003. (*0-945582-90-0*) Down The Shore Publishing.

Grimes, Tom. A Stone of the Heart. 1990. 131p. 15.95 (*0-941423-40-9*) Four Walls Eight Windows.

—A Stone of the Heart: A Novel. 1997. 144p. reprint ed. pap. 12.95 (*0-87074-418-6*) Southern Methodist Univ. Pr.

Hamill, Denis. Fork in the Road. 496p. 2000. 24.95 o.s.i (*0-671-01673-3*, Atria); 2001. (Illus.). reprint ed. pap. 14.95 (*0-671-01674-1*, Washington Square Pr.) Simon & Schuster.

Hanson, Jacquelyn. Susan's Quest. 1998. (Illus.). 280p. pap. 5.95 (*0-9637265-2-8*, 9802); 268p. (*0-9637265-7-9*) Glenhaven Pr.

Harrington, Jonathan. The Death of Cousin Rose. 2000. mass mkt. (*0-373-26347-3*, Worldwide Library) Harlequin Enterprises, Ltd.

—The Death of Cousin Rose. 1996. (Danny O'Flaherty Mysteries Ser.). 215p. 19.95 o.p. (*1-885173-06-7*) Write Way Publishing.

—The Second Sorrowful Mystery. 2000. (Danny O'Flaherty Mysteries Ser.). 256p. mass mkt. (*0-373-26358-9*, 1-26358-1, Worldwide Library) Harlequin Enterprises, Ltd.

—The Second Sorrowful Mystery. 1999. 240p. 21.95 (*1-885173-37-7*) Write Way Publishing.

Hatcher, Robin Lee. In His Arms. l.t. ed. 2000. 312p. 26.95 (*1-57490-279-2*, Beeler Large Print Bks.) Beeler, Thomas T. Publisher.

—In His Arms. 1998. 432p. mass mkt. 6.99 o.s.i (*0-06-108689-4*) HarperCollins Pubs.

—In His Arms. 2001. (Coming to America Bk.). 304p. pap. 10.99 (*0-310-23120-5*) Zondervan.

Helprin, Mark. Winter's Tale. (Harvest Book Ser.). 688p. 1995. pap. 17.00 (*0-15-600194-2*, Harvest Bks.); 1983. 35.00 (*0-15-197203-6*) Harcourt Trade Pubs.

—Winter's Tale. 1985. 704p. mass mkt. 4.95 o.s.i (*0-671-62118-1*); 1984. mass mkt. 4.50 o.s.i (*0-671-50987-X*) Simon & Schuster. (Pocket).

—Winter's Tale. Rosenman, Jane, ed. 1990. 704p. reprint ed. pap. (*0-671-72707-9*, Washington Square Pr.) Simon & Schuster.

Hijuelos, Oscar. The Fourteen Sisters of Emilio Montez O'Brien. 1993. 484p. 22.00 o.p. (*0-374-15815-0*) Farrar, Straus & Giroux.

—The Fourteen Sisters of Emilio Montez O'Brien. 2004. 496p. pap. 15.00 (*0-06-097594-6*, Perennial) HarperTrade.

—The Fourteen Sisters of Emilio Montez O'Brien. 1994. 544p. mass mkt. 5.99 o.p. (*0-06-100759-5*, HarperTorch) Morrow/Avon.

—The Fourteen Sisters of Emilio Montez O'Brien. abr. ed. 1993. audio 24.95 o.p. (*1-55800-790-3*); Set. 1994. audio 12.99 o.p. (*0-7871-0129-X*) NewStar Media, Inc.

Hoff, B. J. Ashes & Lace, Vol. 2. 1999. (Song of Erin Ser.). 432p. pap. 8.99 o.p. (*0-8423-1479-2*) Tyndale Hse. Pubs.

—Dawn of the Golden Promise. 1994. (Emerald Ballad Ser.: Bk. 5). 400p. pap. 11.99 o.p. (*1-55661-114-5*) Bethany Hse. Pubs.

—Dawn of the Golden Promise. l.t. ed. 2002. 707p. 28.95 (*0-7862-3578-0*) Gale Group.

—An Emerald Ballad, Bks. 1-5. 1994. (Emerald Ballad Ser.). 59.99 o.p. (*1-55661-794-1*, 252794) Bethany Hse. Pubs.

—An Emerald Ballad 1-3 Giftset. 1992. (Emerald Ballad Ser.). (YA). 29.99 o.p. (*1-55661-771-2*) Bethany Hse. Pubs.

—Heart of the Lonely Exile. 1991. (Emerald Ballad Ser.: Bk. 2). 384p. pap. 11.99 o.p. (*1-55661-111-0*) Bethany Hse. Pubs.

—Heart of the Lonely Exile. l.t. ed. 2002. (Emerald Ballad Ser.: No. 2). 715p. pap. 17.95 (*1-4104-0020-4*, Walker Large Print) Gale Group.

—Heart of the Lonely Exile. l.t. ed. 2001. (Christian Fiction Ser.). 716p. 27.95 (*0-7862-3577-2*) Thorndike Pr.

—Land of a Thousand Dreams. 1992. (Emerald Ballad Ser.: Bk. 3). 400p. pap. 11.99 o.p. (*1-55661-112-9*) Bethany Hse. Pubs.

—Land of a Thousand Dreams. l.t. ed. 2002. (Emerald Ballad Ser.: No. 3). 672p. pap. 17.95 (*1-4104-0024-7*, Walker Large Print) Gale Group.

—Land of a Thousand Dreams. l.t. ed. 2001. 672p. 27.95 (*0-7862-3576-4*) Thorndike Pr.

—Song of the Silent Harp. 1991. (Emerald Ballad Ser.: Vol. 1). 416p. (ps-3). pap. 11.99 o.p. (*1-55661-110-2*) Bethany Hse. Pubs.

—Song of the Silent Harp. l.t. ed. 2002. (Emerald Ballad Ser.: No. 1). 715p. pap. 17.95 (*1-4104-0030-1*, Walker Large Print) Gale Group.

—Song of the Silent Harp. l.t. ed. 2000. (Christian Fiction Ser.). 709p. 26.95 (*0-7862-2880-6*) Thorndike Pr.

—Sons of an Ancient Glory. 1993. (Emerald Ballad Ser.: Vol. 4). 400p. pap. 11.99 o.p. (*1-55661-113-7*) Bethany Hse. Pubs.

—Sons of an Ancient Glory. l.t. ed. 2002. 698p. 28.95 (*0-7862-3575-6*) Gale Group.

Hruby, Andes. The Trouble with Catherine. 2002. 288p. 23.95 o.s.i (*0-525-94640-3*, Dutton) Dutton/Plume.

Hynes, James. The Wild Colonial Boy. 1990. 384p. 18.95 o.s.i (*0-689-12089-3*, Scribner) Simon & Schuster.

—The Wild Colonial Boy. Rosenman, Jane, ed. 1992. 368p. reprint ed. pap. (*0-671-74186-1*, Washington Square Pr.) Simon & Schuster.

Jewett, Sarah Orne. The Irish Short Stories of Sarah Orne Jewett. Morgan, Jack & Renza, Louis A., eds. 1996. (Illus.). 192p. (C). 24.95 (*0-8093-2039-8*) Southern Illinois Univ. Pr.

Kiely, Benedict. Nothing Happens in Carmincross. 1987. 280p. pap. 10.95 o.p. (*0-87923-725-2*); 1985. 288p. 16.95 o.p. (*0-87923-585-3*) Godine, David R. Pub.

Lasky, Kathryn. Prank. 1986. (J). (gr. 6 up). mass mkt. 2.75 o.s.i (*0-440-97144-6*, Laurel Leaf) Random Hse. Children's Bks.

Lescroart, John. Dead Irish. l.t. ed. 2001. 359p. 28.95 (*1-57490-358-6*, Beeler Large Print Bks.) Beeler, Thomas T. Publisher.

Lewis, Janet. Invasion. 1998. (Illus.). 248p. pap. 21.95 (*0-87013-495-7*) Michigan State Univ. Pr.

—Invasion: A Narrative of Events Concerning the Johnston Family of St. Mary's. 1964. 356p. 15.00 o.p. (*0-8040-0166-9*); pap. 9.00 o.p. (*0-8040-0167-7*) Swallow Pr.

The Long Journey Home. 2000. (Illus.). 180p. pap. 16.95 (*1-930897-01-4*) Wings Pubs., LLC.

Lordan, Beth. But Come Ye Back: A Novel. 2004. 288p. 23.95 (*0-06-053036-7*, Morrow, William & Co.) Morrow/Avon.

Maher, Mary. The Devil's Card. 1992. 288p. 18.95 o.p. (*0-312-07715-7*, Saint Martin's Minotaur) St. Martin's Pr.

Mallon, James. Magazine. 2000. 278p. 22.95 o.p. (*1-57197-181-5*) Pentland Pr., Inc.

Marzollo, Jean. Halfway down Paddy Lane. 1981. 176p. (J). (gr. 6 up). 9.95 o.p. (*0-8037-3329-1*, Dial Bks. for Young Readers) Penguin Putnam Bks. for Young Readers.

McCann, Colum. Fishing the Sloe-Black River: Stories. 1997. 208p. pap. 12.00 o.s.i (*0-8050-4107-9*, Owl Bks.); 1996. 196p. 22.00 o.s.i (*0-8050-4106-0*, Metropolitan Bks.) Holt, Henry & Co.

—Fishing the Sloe-Black River: Stories. 2004. 208p. pap. 12.00 (*0-312-42338-1*) Picador.

McDermott, Alice. At Weddings & Wakes. 1998. 224p. pap. 12.95 (*0-385-31985-1*, Delacorte Pr.); 1993. 320p. mass mkt. 6.50 o.s.i (*0-440-21523-4*) Dell Publishing.

—At Weddings & Wakes. 1992. 213p. 19.00 o.p. (*0-374-10674-6*) Farrar, Straus & Giroux.

—At Weddings & Wakes. l.t. ed. 1993. (General Ser.). 320p. 20.95 (*0-8161-5570-4*); lib. bdg. 16.95 o.p. (*0-8161-5571-2*) Gale Group. (Macmillan Reference USA).

—At Weddings & Wakes. abr. ed. 1993. audio 8.99 o.p. (*1-55800-829-2*); 16.95 o.p. (*1-55800-693-1*) NewStar Media, Inc.

—Charming Billy. 1999. 256p. pap. 12.95 (*0-385-33334-X*, Delta) Dell Publishing.

—Charming Billy. 1997. 280p. 22.00 (*0-374-12080-3*); (*0-374-91390-0*) Farrar, Straus & Giroux.

—Charming Billy. l.t. ed. 1998. 26.95 (*1-56895-685-1*, Wheeler Publishing, Inc.) Gale Group.

McSorley, Edward. Our Own Kind. 1976. (Irish Americans Ser.). reprint ed. 26.95 (*0-405-09350-0*) Ayer Co. Pubs., Inc.

Mitchell, Kirk. Fredericksburg: A Novel of the Irish at Marye's Heights. 1996. 384p. 23.95 o.p. (*0-312-13974-8*) St. Martin's Pr.

—Fredericksburg: A Novel of the Irish at Marye's Heights. 2003. 384p. mass mkt. 7.99 (*0-7434-5827-3*) ibooks, Inc.

Moore, Ann. Leaving Ireland. 2002. 400p. (Orig.). pap. 13.95 (*0-451-20707-6*) NAL.

—Leaving Ireland. 2003. (Women's Fiction Ser.). (Orig.). 28.95 (*0-7862-5191-3*) Thorndike Pr.

Moran, Thomas. The World I Made for Her. 1999. 288p. reprint ed. 12.00 (*1-57322-731-5*, Riverhead Trade (Paperbacks)) Berkley Publishing Group.

—The World I Made for Her. 1998. 267p. 23.95 o.p. (*1-57322-084-1*, Riverhead Bks. (Hardcovers)) Putnam Publishing Group, The.

Moreton, Cole. Hungry for Home: Leaving the Blaskets: A Journey from the Edge of Ireland. 2000. 288p. reprint ed. pap. 24.00 (*0-7567-5614-6*) DIANE Publishing Co.

—Hungry for Home: Leaving the Blaskets: A Journey from the Edge of Ireland. 2000. (Illus.). 288p. 23.95 o.s.i (*0-670-89207-6*, Viking) Viking Penguin.

Myles, Eileen. Cool for You. 2000. 196p. pap. 14.00 (*1-887128-59-X*) Soft Skull Pr., Inc.

Nielsen, Elizabeth. Sweet Geraniums & Soda Bread, Too. 1999. 262p. 19.95 (*1-58141-033-6*) Rivercross Publishing, Inc.

O'Hagan, Christine. Benediction at the Savoia. 1992. 21.95 o.s.i (*0-15-111810-8*) Harcourt Trade Pubs.

O'Neal, Charles. Three Wishes for Jamie. 1976. 22.95 (*0-8488-0184-9*) Amereon, Ltd.

—Three Wishes for Jamie. 1991. 256p. reprint ed. pap. 5.95 (*1-56129-066-1*) Knightsbridge Publishing.

—Three Wishes for Jamie. 1980. 256p. reprint ed. 26.00 (*0-933256-08-6*); pap. text 16.00 (*0-933256-09-4*) Second Chance Pr.

O'Sullivan, Bill. Precious Blood. 1992. 202p. 18.95 o.p. (*0-939149-67-2*) Soho Pr., Inc.

Parry, Owen. Bold Sons of Erin: A Novel of Suspense. 2003. 352p. 24.95 (*0-06-051390-X*, Morrow, William & Co.) Morrow/Avon.

Pratt, James Michael. The Lighthouse Keeper. l.t. ed. 2000. (Wheeler Large Print Book Ser.). 277p. 28.95 (*1-56895-896-X*, Wheeler Publishing, Inc.) Gale Group.

—The Lighthouse Keeper. 2000. ix, 257p. 23.95 o.s.i (*0-312-24113-5*); 2001. 336p. reprint ed. mass mkt. 6.99 o.s.i (*0-312-97469-8*, 20-3283, St. Martin's Paperbacks) St. Martin's Pr.

Quinn, Peter. Banished Children of Eve. 1995. 624p. pap. 14.00 (*0-14-023003-3*, Penguin Bks.) Penguin Group (USA) Inc.

—Banished Children of Eve. 1994. 624p. 22.95 o.p. (*0-670-85076-4*, Viking) Viking Penguin.

Raleigh, Michael. In the Castle of the Flynns. 2003. 368p. pap. 14.00 (*0-425-19036-6*) Berkley Publishing Group.

Richards, Emilie. Whiskey Island. 2000. 512p. mass mkt. (*1-55166-570-0*, 1-66570-2, Mira Bks.) Harlequin Enterprises, Ltd.

Roberts, Les. Irish Sports Pages. mass mkt. (*0-312-98380-8*, St. Martin's Paperbacks); 2002. 304p. 23.95 (*0-312-28661-9*, Saint Martin's Minotaur) St. Martin's Pr.

Roberts, Nora. Irish Hearts: Irish Thoroughbred & Irish Rose, 2 bks. in 1. 2000. 512p. mass mkt. (*0-373-48400-3*, Harlequin Bks.) Harlequin Enterprises, Ltd.

—Irish Hearts: Irish Thoroughbred & Irish Rose. l.t. ed. 568p. 2001. pap. 28.95 (*0-7862-2967-5*); 2000. 30.95 (*0-7862-2966-7*) Thorndike Pr.

—Irish Rebel. 2002. 256p. mass mkt. (*0-373-23993-9*, Harlequin Bks.); 2000. (Silhouette Special Edition Ser.: Bk. 1328). 250p. per. (*0-373-24328-6*, 1-24328-6, Silhouette) Harlequin Enterprises, Ltd.

—Irish Rebel. l.t. ed. 2000. (Americana Ser.). 295p. 30.95 (*0-7862-2968-3*) Thorndike Pr.

Rossi, Angnes. Fancy. 2000. (Illus.). 304p. 23.95 o.s.i (*0-525-94365-X*) Dutton/Plume.

Ryan, Mary. Hope. mass mkt. (*0-312-98744-7*, St. Martin's Paperbacks) St. Martin's Pr.

—Hope: A Novel. 2003. 480p. 27.95 (*0-312-30970-8*) St. Martin's Pr.

Shenley, Paul. A Bit of Irish Earth. 1996. 158p. pap. 9.99 (*0-88092-179-X*, 179X) Royal Fireworks Publishing Co.

Skinner, Margaret. Old Jim Canaan. 1990. 288p. 18.95 o.p. (*0-945575-37-8*) Algonquin Bks. of Chapel Hill.

Smith, Betty. Maggie-Now. l.t. ed. 1982. 18.95 o.p. (*0-8161-3303-4*, Macmillan Reference USA) Gale Group.

—Maggie-Now. 1966. pap. 2.25 o.p. (*0-06-080098-4*, P98, Perennial) HarperTrade.

Snell, Gordon, ed. Thicker Than Water: Coming-of-Age Stories by Irish & Irish American Writers. 2001. 256p. (YA). (gr. 7 up). 17.95 o.s.i (*0-385-32571-1*, Random Hse. Bks. for Young Readers) Random Hse. Children's Bks.

Stephens, Michael. The Brooklyn Book of the Dead. 1994. 228p. 19.95 o.p. (*1-56478-037-6*) Dalkey Archive Pr.

Sullivan, Paul. The Unforgiving Land. Kemnitz, Myrna, ed. 1996. 220p. (YA). pap. 9.99 (*0-88092-256-7*) Royal Fireworks Publishing Co.

Sylvester, Harry. Moon Gaffney. 1976. (Irish Americans Ser.). reprint ed. 26.95 (*0-405-09359-4*) Ayer Co. Pubs., Inc.

Thorp, A. D. Volunteers for Glory. 1999. 560p. (Orig.). pap. 18.95 (*1-56167-477-X*) American Literary Pr., Inc.

Tobin, Greg. Conclave. 2002. 453p. mass mkt. 7.99 (*0-8125-7921-6*, Tor Bks.); 2001. 432p. 25.95 (*0-312-87352-2*, Forge Bks.) Doherty, Tom Assocs., LLC.

Trocheck, Kathy Hogan. Irish Eyes. 2000. (Callahan Garrity Mystery Ser.). 304p. 24.00 (*0-06-019421-9*) HarperCollins Pubs.

—Irish Eyes. 2001. (Callahan Garrity Mystery Ser.). 320p. mass mkt. 5.99 (*0-06-109869-8*, Avon Bks.) Morrow/Avon.

—Irish Eyes. l.t. ed. 2000. (Mystery Ser.). 473p. 28.95 (*0-7862-2837-7*) Thorndike Pr.

Watkins, Paul. The Promise of Light, Set. l.t. ed. 1993. (Studio Ser.). 64.95 o.p. incl. audio (*0-7862-9998-3*, Macmillan Reference USA) Gale Group.

**ITALIAN AMERICANS—FICTION**

Appollo, Annette. The Last One Home. 2000. 400p. mass mkt. 6.99 o.s.i (*0-06-109721-7*); 1999. 288p. 24.00 o.s.i (*0-06-019208-9*) HarperCollins Pubs.

—The Last One Home. l.t. ed. 1999. (Thorndike Senior Lifestyle Ser.). 464p. pap. 26.95 (*0-7862-2069-4*) Thorndike Pr.

Ardizzone, Tony. In the Garden of Papa Santuzzu. 2000. 352p. pap. 14.00 (*0-312-26341-4*); 1999. 368p. 24.00 o.p. (*0-312-20307-1*) Picador.

Barolini, Helen. More Italian Hours & Other Stories. 2001. (VIA Folios Ser.: Vol. 28). 176p. (C). per. (*1-884419-48-8*, VIA Folios) Bordighera, Inc.

—Umbertina. 1983. audio 13.95 (*1-55644-064-2*, 3021) American Audio Prose Library, Inc.

—Umbertina. 1989. 432p. (C). reprint ed. pap. 12.95 (*0-88143-107-9*) Ayer Co. Pubs., Inc.

—Umbertina. 1985. 448p. pap. 2.75 o.p. (*0-553-13817-0*) Bantam Bks.

Barolini, Helena. Umbertina. 1998. 464p. 35.00 (*1-55861-204-1*); pap. 18.95 (*1-55861-205-X*) Feminist Pr. at The City Univ. of New York.

Bartone, Elisa. Peppe the Lamplighter. 1993. (Illus.). 32p. (J). (ps-3). 16.95 (*0-688-10268-9*); lib. bdg. 16.89 (*0-688-10269-7*) HarperCollins Children's Bk. Group.

—Peppe the Lamplighter. 1997. (Illus.). 32p. (J). (gr. k-3). pap. 5.99 (*0-688-15469-7*, Morrow, William & Co.) Morrow/Avon.

Bunting, Eve. A Picnic in October. 1999. (Illus.). 32p. (J). (gr. k-5). 16.00 (*0-15-201656-2*) Harcourt Children's Bks.

Carcaterra, Lorenzo. Gangster. l.t. ed. 2001. 583p. 30.95 (*0-7838-9499-6*, Macmillan Reference USA) Gale Group.

Ciresi, Rita. Pink Slip. 1999. 416p. pap. 12.95 (*0-385-32363-8*, Delta) Dell Publishing.

—Sometimes I Dream in Italian. 2001. 224p. pap. 12.95 (*0-385-33494-X*, Delta) Dell Publishing.

—Sometimes I Dream in Italian. l.t. ed. 2001. (Basic Ser.). 320p. 28.95 (*0-7862-3080-0*) Thorndike Pr.

Collins, Jackie. Chances. abr. ed. 1991. audio 15.95 (*0-671-73807-0*); Pt. 2. 1995. audio 15.95 (*0-671-75510-2*) Simon & Schuster Audio. (Simon & Schuster Audioworks).

—Chances. 816p. 1981. 14.95 o.s.i (*0-446-51237-0*); 1991. reprint ed. mass mkt. 7.99 (*0-446-35717-0*) Warner Bks., Inc.

—Dangerous Kiss: A Lucky Santangelo Novel. l.t. ed. 2000. (Thorndike/G. K. Hall Paperback Bestsellers Ser.). 620p. pap. 28.95 (*0-7838-8748-5*, Macmillan Reference USA) Gale Group.

—Dangerous Kiss: A Lucky Santangelo Novel. 2000. E-Book 25.00 (*0-684-87371-0*, Simon & Schuster); 1999. 528p. 25.00 (*0-684-85030-3*, Simon & Schuster); 2000. (Illus.). 592p. reprint ed. pap. 7.99 (*0-671-02095-1*, Pocket) Simon & Schuster.

—Dangerous Kiss: A Lucky Santangelo Novel. l.t. ed. 1999. (Core Ser.). 620p. 31.95 (*0-7838-8747-7*) Thorndike Pr.

—Lady Boss. l.t. ed. 1991. (General Ser.). 760p. 16.95 o.p. (*0-8161-5189-X*); lib. bdg. 22.95 o.p. (*0-8161-5193-8*) Gale Group. (Macmillan Reference USA).

—Lady Boss. Peters, Sally, ed. 1992. mass mkt. 5.99 (*0-671-79571-6*, Pocket) Simon & Schuster.

—Lady Boss. 1990. 21.95 o.p. (*0-671-61937-3*); 21.95 (*0-671-94826-1*) Simon & Schuster. (Simon & Schuster).

—Lady Boss. Grose, Bill, ed. 1991. 640p. reprint ed. mass mkt. 7.99 (*0-671-74418-6*, Pocket) Simon & Schuster.

—Lady Boss. rev. ed. 1998. 640p. mass mkt. 7.99 (*0-671-02347-0*, Pocket) Simon & Schuster.

—Lady Boss. abr. ed. 1990. audio 15.95 (*0-671-73710-4*, Simon & Schuster Audioworks) Simon & Schuster Audio.

—Lucky. 1990. 608p. mass mkt. 5.95 o.s.i (*0-671-63845-9*); 1987. mass mkt. 6.99 (*0-671-70419-2*); 1986. 608p. mass mkt. 4.95 o.s.i (*0-671-52496-8*); 1998. 624p. mass mkt. 7.99 (*0-671-02348-9*) Simon & Schuster. (Pocket).

—Lucky. abr. ed. 1991. audio 15.95 (*0-671-73808-9*, Simon & Schuster Audioworks) Simon & Schuster Audio.

—Vendetta: Lucky's Revenge. l.t. ed. 1997. (Large Print Book Ser.). 28.95 (*1-56895-435-2*, Wheeler Publishing, Inc.) Gale Group.

—Vendetta: Lucky's Revenge. 1997. 544p. 25.00 o.p. (*0-06-039209-6*, ReganBooks); audio 25.00 o.p. (*0-694-51809-3*, CPN 4048, HarperAudio) HarperTrade.

—Vendetta: Lucky's Revenge. 1998. 5.98 o.p. (*0-7651-0824-0*) Smithmark Pubs., Inc.

Condon, Richard. Prizzi's Family. 1987. 320p. mass mkt. 4.50 o.s.i (*0-515-09106-5*, Jove) Berkley Publishing Group.

—Prizzi's Family. unabr. collector's ed. 1991. audio 40.00 (*0-7366-2009-5*, 2825) Books on Tape, Inc.

—Prizzi's Family. 1986. 17.95 o.p. (*0-399-13210-4*) Putnam Publishing Group, The.

—Prizzi's Glory. unabr. collector's ed. 1991. audio 48.00 (*0-7366-2076-1*, 2882) Books on Tape, Inc.

—Prizzi's Glory. 1988. 17.95 o.p. (*0-525-24689-4*, Dutton) Dutton/Plume.

—Prizzi's Glory. 1990. 368p. mass mkt. 4.95 o.p. (*0-451-16468-7*, NAL Bks.) NAL.

—Prizzi's Honor. 1986. 320p. mass mkt. 4.95 o.p. (*0-425-09507-X*) Berkley Publishing Group.

—Prizzi's Honor. unabr. collector's ed. 1985. audio 56.00 (*0-7366-0837-0*, 1788) Books on Tape, Inc.

—Prizzi's Honor, Set. abr. ed. 1987. audio 16.99 (*0-88646-193-6*, 7194) Durkin Hayes Publishing Ltd.

—Prizzi's Honor. 1982. 320p. 13.95 o.p. (*0-698-11143-5*) Putnam Publishing Group, The.

—Prizzi's Honor. l.t. ed. 1982. 480p. reprint ed. 14.95 o.p. (*0-89621-403-6*) Thorndike Pr.

—Prizzi's Money. 1995. 384p. mass mkt. 5.99 o.s.i (*0-7860-0167-4*) Kensington Publishing Corp.

Crespi, Camilla T. The Trouble with a Bad Fit. 1996. 272p. 21.00 o.p. (*0-06-017661-X*) HarperCollins Pubs.

—The Trouble with a Bad Fit. 1997. 320p. mass mkt. 4.99 (*0-06-109408-0*, HarperTorch) Morrow/Avon.

—The Trouble with a Hot Summer: A Simona Griffo Mystery. 1997. 320p. 23.00 o.p. (*0-06-017662-8*) HarperCollins Pubs.

—The Trouble with a Hot Summer: A Simona Griffo Mystery. mass mkt. o.s.i (*0-06-109409-9*); 1998. 368p. mass mkt. 5.99 o.s.i (*0-06-104464-4*) Morrow/Avon. (HarperTorch).

—The Trouble with a Small Raise. 1991. 288p. mass mkt. 3.95 o.s.i (*0-8217-3274-9*, Zebra Bks.) Kensington Publishing Corp.

—The Trouble with Going Home. 1996. 224p. mass mkt. 4.99 o.s.i (*0-06-109153-7*) HarperCollins Pubs.

—The Trouble with Going Home. 1994. 288p. 20.00 o.p. (*0-06-017725-X*) HarperTrade.

—The Trouble with Moonlighting. 1991. 224p. mass mkt. 3.95 o.s.i (*0-8217-3452-0*, Zebra Bks.) Kensington Publishing Corp.

—The Trouble with Thin Ice. 1994. 288p. 18.00 o.p. (*0-06-017726-8*) HarperTrade.

—The Trouble with Thin Ice. 1994. 304p. mass mkt. 4.50 o.p. (*0-06-109154-5*, HarperTorch) Morrow/Avon.

—The Trouble with Too Much Sun. 1992. (Simona Griffo Mystery Ser.). mass mkt. 3.99 o.s.i (*0-8217-3776-7*, Zebra Bks.) Kensington Publishing Corp.

Criscuolo, Joseph A. Roses for Mama: An Italian-American Saga. 2001. ii, 326p. (*0-9709175-0-3*) Culter, Robert Bks.

Criswell, Millie. The Trouble with Mary. l.t. ed. 2001. 325p. 26.95 (*1-57490-342-X*) Beeler, Thomas T. Publisher.

Cusumano, Camille. The Last Cannoli: A Novel: A Sicilian American Family Comes of Age Through the Ancient Power of Storytelling. 1999. (Illus.). 237p. per. (*1-881901-20-3*) LEGAS.

De Rosa, Tina. Paper Fish. (Contemporary Classics by Women Ser.). 176p. 2003. pap. 15.95 (*1-55861-439-7*); 1996. lib. bdg. 20.00 (*1-55861-146-0*); 1996. pap. 9.95 o.p. (*1-55861-145-2*) Feminist Pr. at The City Univ. of New York.

Di Donato, Pietro. Christ in Concrete. 1977. pap. 1.95 o.p. (*0-671-81183-5*, Pocket) Simon & Schuster.

—Christ in Concrete: A Novel. 1993. 256p. mass mkt. 6.95 (*0-451-52575-2*, Signet Classics) NAL.

Dionetti, Michelle V. Coal Mine Peaches. 1991. (Illus.). 32p. (J). (ps-2). 14.95 o.p. (*0-531-05948-0*); mass mkt. 14.99 o.p. (*0-531-08548-1*) Scholastic, Inc. (Orchard Bks.).

Fast, Howard. The Establishment, 001. 1979. 11.95 o.p. (*0-395-28160-1*) Houghton Mifflin Co.

—The Immigrants, 001. 1977. 12.95 o.p. (*0-395-25699-2*) Houghton Mifflin Co.

—The Second Generation, 001. 1978. 10.95 o.p. (*0-395-26683-1*) Houghton Mifflin Co.

Fusco, John. Paradise Salvage. 384p. 2004. pap. 15.95 (*1-58567-382-X*); 2002. 26.95 (*1-58567-209-2*) Overlook Pr., The.

Giardina, Anthony. Recent History. 2001. E-Book 19.50 (*1-58945-783-8*) Adobe Systems, Inc.

—Recent History. 2002. 272p. pap. 13.95 (*0-375-75938-7*) Random House Adult Trade Publishing Group.

—Recent History: A Novel. 2001. E-Book 19.50 (*0-375-50694-2*) Random Hse., Inc.

Giles, Janice Holt. Act of Contrition. 2001. 240p. 25.00 (*0-8131-2172-8*) Univ. Pr. of Kentucky.

Gross, Virginia T. It's Only Goodbye: An Immigrant Story. 1992. (Once upon America Ser.). (Illus.). 64p. (J). (gr. 2-6). pap. 3.99 o.s.i (*0-14-034409-8*, Puffin Bks.) Penguin Putnam Bks. for Young Readers.

Hendin, Josephine Gattuso. The Right Thing to Do. 1999. 240p. pap. 13.95 (*1-55861-220-3*) Feminist Pr. at The City Univ. of New York.

—The Right Thing to Do. 1988. 256p. 16.95 o.p. (*0-87923-639-6*) Godine, David R. Pub.

Hoff, B. J. Cadence. l.t. ed. 2004. 375p. pap. 15.95 (*1-59415-017-6*, Walker Large Print) Gale Group.

—Cadence. 2003. 264p. pap. 12.99 (*0-8499-4390-6*) W Publishing Group.

Kriegel, Mark. Bless Me, Father. 1996. 352p. reprint ed. mass mkt. 6.99 o.s.i (*0-425-15574-9*) Berkley Publishing Group.

Labozzetta, Marisa. Stay with Me, Lella. 1999. (Prose Ser.: Vol. 54). 172p. pap. 13.00 (*1-55071-076-1*) Guernica Editions, Inc.

Lamb, Wally. I Know This Much Is True. l.t. ed. 1998. 949 p. 29.95 (*1-57490-164-8*) Beeler, Thomas T. Publisher.

—I Know This Much Is True. 2003. 912p. mass mkt. 7.99 (*0-06-109764-0*); 2000. (*0-06-039280-0*); 1998. 912p. pap. 16.00 o.s.i (*0-06-109812-4*) HarperCollins Pubs.

—I Know This Much Is True. 1999. 912p. pap. 16.00 (*0-06-098756-1*, ReganBooks); 1998. 912p. 27.50 (*0-06-039162-6*, ReganBooks); 1998. audio 25.00 (*0-694-51940-5*, 695741, HarperAudio) HarperTrade.

—I Know This Much Is True. unabr. ed. 1999. audio 177.00 (*0-7887-2491-6*, 95566E7) Recorded Bks., LLC.

Lancelotta, Victoria. Far: A Novel. 2003. 224p. text 24.00 (*1-58243-114-0*, Counterpoint Pr.) Basic Bks.

Larzar, John. La Strada. White, Bradford, ed. unabr. ed. 1999. 312p. 21.75 (*0-9620016-1-9*) Great Lakes Publishing Co.

Lasky, Kathryn. Hope in My Heart. 2003. (My America Ser.). 112p. (J). mass mkt. 4.99 (*0-439-44962-6*) Scholastic, Inc.

Lee, Wendi. Crazy Like a Fox: An Angela Matelli Mystery. 2002. 240p. 22.95 (*0-312-26139-X*, Saint Martin's Minotaur) St. Martin's Pr.

Lentricchia, Frank. The Music of the Inferno. (Suny Series, Italian/American Culture Ser.). 220p. (C). 2000. pap. text 20.95 (*0-7914-4348-5*); 1999. text 21.50 (*0-7914-4347-7*) State Univ. of New York Pr.

Malyszko, Bill. The Godfather. 2001. 88p. pap. 9.99 (*0-582-43188-3*) Longman Publishing Group.

Martinelli, Robin A. Poppy's Plate Full of Smiles. 1995. pap. 7.95 o.p. (*1-880218-22-4*) Marketing Directions, Inc.

Mays, Lucinda. The Other Shore. 1979. (J). (gr. 5-10). 8.95 o.p. (*0-689-30717-9*, Atheneum) Simon & Schuster Children's Publishing.

Merullo, Roland. In Revere, in Those Days: A Novel. 2002. 320p. 22.00 (*0-609-61032-5*) Crown Publishing Group.

—In Revere, in Those Days: A Novel. 2003. 320p. pap. 13.00 (*0-375-71405-7*, Vintage) Knopf Publishing Group.

—In Revere, in Those Days: A Novel. 2002. (Americana Ser.). 28.95 (*0-7862-4823-8*) Thorndike Pr.

—Revere Beach Boulevard: A Novel. 336p. 1999. (Revere Beach Trilogy Ser.: Vol. 1). pap. 13.00 o.s.i (*0-8050-6006-5*, Owl Bks.); 1998. (Book One of the Revere Beach Trilogy Ser.). 23.00 o.s.i (*0-8050-6005-7*) Holt, Henry & Co.

Messina, Calogero. St. Giordano: A Sicilian Martyr in Nagasaki. 2002. 160p. pap. (*1-881901-27-0*) LEGAS.

Milton, Terry. And the Devil Makes Three: An Italian Saga. 2000. 385p. pap. 22.99 (*0-7388-1181-5*); text 32.99 (*0-7388-1180-7*) Xlibris Corp.

Monardo, Anna. The Courtyard of Dreams. 1993. 21.50 o.s.i (*0-385-42606-2*) Doubleday Publishing.

Montemarano, Nicholas. A Fine Place. 226p. 2002. 21.95 (*1-893956-21-0*); 2003. reprint ed. pap. 14.00 (*1-893956-43-1*) Context Bks.

Papaleo, Joseph. Italian Stories. 2003. 295p. pap. 13.95 (*1-56478-306-5*) Dalkey Archive Pr.

Parini, Jay. The Patch Boys. l.t. ed. 1987. pap. 17.95 o.p. (*1-55504-458-1*) BBC Audiobooks America.

—The Patch Boys. 1988. pap. 8.95 o.s.i (*0-8050-0770-9*, Owl Bks.); 1986. 15.95 o.p. (*0-8050-0047-X*) Holt, Henry & Co.

—Patch Boys. l.t. ed. 1987. 19.95 o.p. (*1-55504-298-8*) BBC Audiobooks America.

Passen, Lisa. Uncle's New Suit, ERS. 1992. (Illus.). 32p. (J). (gr. 1-3). 14.95 o.p. (*0-8050-1652-X*, Holt, Henry & Co. Bks. For Young Readers) Holt, Henry & Co.

Pease, R. Book & Page: A Cape Cod Novel. 1997. 185p. per. 12.95 (*1-889455-02-4*) Flagg Mountain Pr.

Perona, Tony. Second Advent: A Novel. 2002. (Five Star First Edition Mystery Ser.). 285p. 24.95 (*0-7862-4327-9*, Five Star) Gale Group.

Puzo, Mario. The Fortunate Pilgrim. 1998. 304p. pap. 13.95 (*0-449-00358-2*); 1982. mass mkt. 2.50 o.s.i (*0-449-23456-8*) Ballantine Bks. (Fawcett).

—The Fortunate Pilgrim. 1985. 256p. mass mkt. 3.95 o.s.i (*0-553-24859-6*) Bantam Bks.

—The Fortunate Pilgrim. abr. ed. 1998. audio 7.99 o.p. (*1-56740-239-9*, 651, Paperback Nova Audio Bks.); 1997. audio 16.95 o.p. (*1-56100-986-5*, 1201, Nova Audio Bks.); 1997. audio 23.95 o.p. (*1-56100-760-9*, 113, Bookcassette); 1997. audio 73.25 o.p. (*1-56100-835-4*, 841, Unabridged Library Editions) Brilliance Audio.

—The Fortunate Pilgrim. abr. ed. 2000. audio 7.95 (*1-57815-171-6*, 1114, Media Bks. Audio Publishing) Media Bks., L. L. C.

—The Fortunate Pilgrim. 1997. 304p. 23.00 o.s.i (*0-679-45778-X*) Random Hse., Inc.

—The Godfather. abr. ed. 1998. audio 24.95 (*1-882071-84-0*) B&B Audio, Inc.

—The Godfather. 1977. mass mkt. 2.25 o.p. (*0-449-23408-8*, Fawcett) Ballantine Bks.

—The Godfather. unabr. collector's ed. 1993. audio 88.00 (*0-7366-2386-8*, 3157) Books on Tape, Inc.

—The Godfather. unabr. ed. 1986. audio 23.95 o.p. (*0-930435-21-4*, 122, Bookcassette); audio 89.25 (*1-56100-016-7*, 1220, Unabridged Library Editions) Brilliance Audio.

—The Godfather. l.t. ed. 1985. (Special Editions Ser.). 688p. 19.95 o.p. (*0-8161-3875-3*, Macmillan Reference USA) Gale Group.

—The Godfather. 2002. 9.99 (*0-451-20844-7*); 2002. 464p. pap. 14.00 (*0-451-20576-6*); 1983. mass mkt. 1.95 o.p. (*0-451-12891-5*, Signet Bks.); 1983. mass mkt. 4.50 o.p. (*0-451-14506-2*, Signet Bks.); 1983. 448p. mass mkt. 7.99 (*0-451-16771-6*, Signet Bks.); 1983. mass mkt. 4.95 o.p. (*0-451-15736-2*, Signet Bks.); 1983. mass mkt. 3.95 o.p. (*0-451-13644-6*, Signet Bks.); 1978. mass mkt. 2.50 o.p. (*0-451-08508-6*, Signet Bks.); 1978. mass mkt. 2.95 o.p. (*0-451-09438-7*, Signet Bks.); 1978. mass mkt. 3.50 o.p. (*0-451-12580-0*, Signet Bks.); 1978. mass mkt. 2.75 o.p. (*0-451-08970-7*, Signet Bks.) NAL.

—The Godfather. 1969. 448p. 24.95 (*0-399-10342-2*, G. P. Putnam's Sons) Penguin Group (USA) Inc.

—The Godfather. l.t. ed. 1986. (Charnwood Large Print Ser.). 752p. 29.99 o.p. (*0-7089-8351-0*, Charnwood) Thorpe, F. A. Pubs. GBR. *Dist:* Ulverscroft Large Print Bks., Ltd., Ulverscroft Large Print Canada, Ltd.

—The Godfather Papers & Other Confessions. 1972. 224p. 6.95 o.p. (*0-399-10935-8*) Putnam Publishing Group, The.

Puzo, Mario & Sinatra, Nancy. The Godfather Pack: The Godfather & Frank Sinatra: An American Legend. abr. unabr. ed. 2001. audio 34.95 (*0-929071-26-3*) B&B Audio, Inc.

Rimanelli, Giose. Benedetta in Guysterland, No. 22. 1993. 300p. pap. 13.00 (*0-920717-88-8*) Guernica Editions, Inc.

Rimo Publications Staff, et al. Sepia Tones (7 Short Stories) 2nd ed. 1986. pap. 12.00 (*0-918680-32-8*) Griffon Hse. Pubns.

Scottoline, Lisa. The Vendetta Defense. 2001. 403p. E-Book 19.95 (*0-06-621323-1*); 400p. 25.00 (*0-06-018507-4*) HarperCollins Pubs.

Smith, D. L. The Miracles of Santo Fico. 2003. 28.95 (*0-7862-5243-X*) Thorndike Pr.

—The Miracles of Santo Fico. 368p. 2004. pap. 16.00 (*0-446-69036-8*); 2003. 22.95 (*0-446-53103-0*) Warner Bks., Inc.

Stansberry, Domenic. Exit Paradise. 1992. 146p. (Orig.). pap. 10.00 (*0-89924-081-X*) Lynx Hse. Pr.

—The Last Days of Il Duce. 1998. 168p. 22.00 (*1-57962-004-3*) Permanent Pr., The.

Stoehr, Shelley. Wannabe. 1997. 176p. (YA). (gr. 9 up). 15.95 o.s.i (*0-385-32223-2*, Dell Books for Young Readers) Random Hse. Children's Bks.

Trigiani, Adriana. Big Cherry Holler: A Big Stone Gap Novel. 2002. 320p. pap. 13.95 (*0-345-44584-8*, Ballantine Bks.) Ballantine Bks.

—Big Cherry Holler: A Big Stone Gap Novel. l.t. ed. 2001. 29.95 (*1-58724-141-2*, Wheeler Publishing, Inc.) Gale Group.

—Big Cherry Holler: A Big Stone Gap Novel. 2001. E-Book 19.95 (*1-58836-010-5*); 288p. 24.95 (*0-375-50617-9*) Random Hse., Inc.

—Lucia, Lucia: A Novel. 2004. 288p. pap. 13.95 (*0-8129-6779-8*) Ballantine Bks.

—Lucia, Lucia: A Novel. 2003. 272p. 24.95 (*1-4000-6005-2*) Random Hse., Inc.

—Lucia, Lucia: A Novel. l.t. ed. 2003. 440p. 31.95 (*0-7862-5863-2*, Large Print Pr.) Thorndike Pr.

Varni, Steven. The Inland Sea. 2001. 288p. pap. 13.00 (*0-06-095934-7*, Perennial) HarperTrade.

—The Inland Sea. 2000. 269p. 22.00 (*0-688-16906-6*, Morrow, William & Co.) Morrow/Avon.

Wachtel, Chuck. The Gates: A Novel. 1994. 416p. 23.95 o.p. (*0-670-83886-1*, Viking) Viking Penguin.

Woodruff, Elvira. The Orphan of Ellis Island: A Time Travel Adventure. (J). 2000. pap. 4.50 (*0-590-48246-7*); 1997. 160p. (gr. 4-7). pap. 15.95 (*0-590-48245-9*) Scholastic, Inc.

Zucker, David. Uncle Carmello. 1993. (Illus.). 32p. (J). (gr. k-4). lib. bdg. 14.95 (*0-02-793760-7*, Simon & Schuster Children's Publishing) Simon & Schuster Children's Publishing.

## J

### JAPANESE—FICTION

Curzon, Clare. All Unwary. (*0-7540-3467-4*); 1999. 340p. pap. (*0-7540-3468-2*) BBC Audiobooks America.

—All Unwary. 1998. (Thames Valley Mystery Ser.). 256p. 21.95 o.p. (*0-312-18037-3*, Saint Martin's Minotaur) St. Martin's Pr.

—All Unwary. l.t. ed. 1999. (General Ser.). 352p. pap. 23.95 (*0-7862-1544-5*) Thorndike Pr.

Kyle, Kristin. The Last Warrior. 1999. (Fanfare Ser.). 384p. mass mkt. 5.99 o.s.i (*0-553-57963-0*) Bantam Bks.

Natsume, Soseki. I Am a Cat: Three Volumes in One. Ito, Aiko & Wilson, Graeme, trs. from JPN. 2001. 696p. reprint ed. pap. 19.95 (*0-8048-3265-X*) Tuttle Publishing.

Sakamoto, Kerri. The Electrical Field. 2000. 320p. pap. text 13.00 (*0-393-32048-0*, Norton Paperbacks); 1999. 305p. 23.95 o.p. (*0-393-04692-3*) Norton, W. W. & Co., Inc.

Schlossstein, Steven. Yakuza: The Japanese Godfather. 1990. 320p. 19.95 (*0-9627060-1-9*) Stratford Bks.

Togawa, Masako. A Kiss of Fire. 1989. 224p. mass mkt. 3.50 o.s.i (*0-345-35580-6*) Ballantine Bks.

Yamashita, Karen T. Brazil-Maru. 1992. 248p. 19.95 (*1-56689-000-4*) Coffee Hse. Pr.

### JAPANESE AMERICANS—FICTION

Cliffs Notes Staff. Snow Falling on Cedars. 2000. (CliffsNotes Ser.). 96p. pap. 5.99 (*0-7645-8567-3*, Cliff Notes) Wiley, John & Sons, Inc.

Colbert, Curt. Sayonaraville. 2003. 14.95 (*0-9724412-1-2*) UglyTown.

Creel, Ann Howard. The Magic of Ordinary Days. l.t. ed. 2001. 27.95 o.p. (*0-7862-3741-4*) Thorndike Pr.

—The Magic of Ordinary Days. 288p. 2002. 13.00 (*0-14-200090-6*); 2001. 24.95 o.p. (*0-670-91027-9*, Viking) Viking Penguin.

Eisler, Barry. Hard Rain. abr. ed. (John Rain Ser.). 2004. audio 12.99 (*1-59086-957-5*, 4559, Brilliance Audio Paperback Audiobooks); 2003. audio 24.95 (*1-59086-956-7*, 4558, Brilliance Audio); 2003. audio 32.95 (*1-59086-954-0*, 4556, Brilliance Audio Unabridged); 2003. audio 82.25 (*1-59086-955-9*, 4557, Unabridged Library Editions) Brilliance Audio.

—Hard Rain. 2003. 320p. text 24.95 (*0-399-15052-8*, Putnam & Grosset) Putnam Publishing Group, The.

—Rain Fall. 2003. 384p. reprint ed. mass mkt. 6.99 (*0-451-20915-X*, Signet Bks.) NAL.

—Rain Fall. 2002. 336p. 24.95 o.s.i (*0-399-14910-4*) Penguin Group (USA) Inc.

Furutani, Dale. Death in Little Tokyo. unabr. collector's ed. 1999. (Ken Tanaka Ser. ). audio 32.00 (*0-7366-4414-8*, 4875) Books on Tape, Inc.

—Death in Little Tokyo. 1996. 256p. 21.95 o.p. (*0-312-14580-2*, Saint Martin's Minotaur); Vol. 1. 1997. (Death in Little Tokyo Ser.: Vol. 1). 224p. mass mkt. 5.99 o.p. (*0-312-96323-8*, St. Martin's Paperbacks) St. Martin's Pr.

—The Toyotomi Blades, Vol. 1. 1998. (Toyotomi Blades Ser.: Vol. 1). 240p. mass mkt. 5.99 (*0-312-96667-9*, St. Martin's Paperbacks) St. Martin's Pr.

—The Toyotomi Blades: A Ken Tanaka Mystery. 1997. (Ken Tanaka Mystery Ser.). 224p. 21.95 (*0-312-17050-5*, Saint Martin's Minotaur) St. Martin's Pr.

Guterson, David. Snow Falling on Cedars. 1999. 352p. 20.00 o.s.i (*0-15-100443-9*, Harvest Bks.); 1994. 100.00 o.s.i (*0-15-100242-8*); 1994. 368p. 21.95 (*0-15-100100-6*) Harcourt Trade Pubs.

—Snow Falling on Cedars. 1998. 512p. pap. 14.00 (*0-676-57609-5*); 1995. 480p. pap. 14.00 (*0-679-76402-X*) Knopf Publishing Group. (Vintage).

—Snow Falling on Cedars, Level 6. 2000. pap. 7.93 (*0-582-41928-X*) Longman Publishing Group.

—Snow Falling on Cedars. 1995. (Vintage Contemporaries Ser.). 20.05 (*0-606-12140-4*) Turtleback Bks.

Hara, Marie. Bananaheart & Other Stories. 1994. (Bamboo Ridge Ser.: Nos. 61-62). 172p. pap. 8.00 (*0-910043-33-7*); pap. incl. audio. audio 8.00 (*0-910043-34-5*) Bamboo Ridge Pr.

Iida, Deborah. Middle Son: A Novel. 1996. 228p. tchr. ed. 18.95 (*1-56512-119-8*, 72119) Algonquin Bks. of Chapel Hill.

—Middle Son: A Novel. 224p. 2000. pap. 12.95 (*0-425-17443-3*); 1998. mass mkt. 6.99 o.s.i (*0-425-16151-X*) Berkley Publishing Group.

Lee, Chang-Rae. A Gesture Life. 2000. 368p. pap. 14.00 (*1-57322-828-1*, Riverhead Trade (Paperbacks)) Berkley Publishing Group.

—A Gesture Life. 1999. 356p. 23.95 o.s.i (*1-57322-146-5*, Riverhead Bks. (Hardcovers)) Putnam Publishing Group, The.

Massey, Sujata. The Bride's Kimono. 2001. 320p. 25.00 (*0-06-019933-4*) HarperCollins Pubs.

—The Bride's Kimono. 2002. 400p. mass mkt. 6.99 (*0-06-103115-1*, Avon Bks.) Morrow/Avon.

Miyakawa, Edward. Tule Lake. 2002. 342p. per. (*1-55369-844-4*) Trafford Publishing.

Moore, Harker. A Cruel Season for Dying. 2003. 336p. 24.95 (*0-89296-774-9*) Mysterious Pr.

—A Cruel Season for Dying. 2004. mass mkt. (*0-446-61373-8*) Warner Bks., Inc.

Mueller, Marnie. The Climate of the Country: A Novel. 1999. 308p. 24.95 (*1-880684-58-6*); 1994. 318p. 19.95 (*1-880684-16-0*) Curbstone Pr.

Murayama, Milton. All I'm Asking for Is My Body. 1988. (Kolowalu Bks.). 120p. reprint ed. pap. 9.95 (*0-8248-1172-0*, Kolowalu Bk.) Univ. of Hawaii Pr.

—Plantation Boy. 1998. 180p. 24.95 (*0-8248-1965-9*); pap. 14.95 (*0-8248-2007-X*) Univ. of Hawaii Pr.

Otsuka, Julie. When the Emperor Was Divine: A Novel. 2003. 160p. pap. 9.95 (*0-385-72181-1*) Doubleday Publishing.

—When the Emperor Was Divine: A Novel. 2002. 160p. 18.00 (*0-375-41429-0*) Knopf, Alfred A. Inc.

—When the Emperor Was Divine: A Novel. l.t. ed. 2003. 256p. 20.00 (*0-375-43278-7*) Random Hse. Large Print.

Pella, Judith. Toward the Sunrise. 2003. (Daughters of Fortune Ser.). 720p. pap. 16.99 (*0-7642-2845-5*) Bethany Hse. Pubs.

Power, Nani. Crawling at Night. 2001. 234p. 24.00 o.p. (*0-87113-784-4*, Atlantic Monthly Pr.); 2002. 240p. reprint ed. pap. 13.00 (*0-8021-3884-5*, Grove Pr.) Grove/Atlantic, Inc.

Shallit, Barney. Song of Anger: Tales of Tule Lake. 2001. (Michi Nishiura & Walter Weglyn Multicultural Publication Ser.). (Illus.). xvii, 121p. pap. (*0-930046-15-3*) California State Univ. Fullerton, Ctr. for Oral & Public History.

Shimoda, Todd A. The Fourth Treasure. 2002. (Illus.). 368p. 24.95 (*0-385-50352-0*, Talese, Nan A.) Doubleday Publishing.

Shimoda, Todd A. & Shimoda, L. J. C. The Fourth Treasure. 2002. (Illus.). 349p. E-Book 22.50 (*0-385-50561-2*, Talese, Nan A.) Doubleday Publishing.

Tatlock, Ann. All the Way Home: A Friendship That Once Bridged Two Cultural Will It Survive The Span of Time. 2002. 448p. pap. 12.99 (*0-7642-2663-0*) Bethany Hse. Pubs.

Trobaugh, Augusta. Sophie & the Rising Sun. 2002. 224p. pap. 13.00 (*0-452-28349-3*, Plume); 2001. 208p. 22.95 o.s.i (*0-525-94627-6*, Dutton) Dutton/Plume.

—Sophie & the Rising Sun. l.t. ed. 2002. (Women's Fiction Ser.). 291p. 28.95 (*0-7862-4052-0*) Gale Group.

Uchida, Yoshiko. Picture Bride. 1987. 200p. 14.95 o.p. (*0-87358-429-5*) Northland Publishing.

—Picture Bride. 1988. 224p. 20.85 o.p. (*0-671-92720-5*); pap. 6.95 o.p. (*0-671-66874-9*) Simon & Schuster. (Fireside).

—Picture Bride. E-Book 12.95 (*0-295-97998-4*); 2003. 222p. reprint ed. pap. 14.95 (*0-295-97616-0*) Univ. of Washington Pr.

Yamamoto, Hisaye. Seventeen Syllables & Other Stories. (C). 1998. 150p. pap. 14.00 (*0-8135-2607-8*); 2001. xxiii, 178p. pap. text 16.00 (*0-8135-2953-0*) Rutgers Univ. Pr.

Yamanaka, Lois A. Wild Meat & the Bully Burgers. 1997. (Harvest American Writing Ser.). 288p. pap. 12.00 (*0-15-600483-6*, Harvest Bks.) Harcourt Trade Pubs.

Yamanaka, Lois-Ann. Wild Meat & the Bully Burgers. 1996. 240p. 20.00 o.p. (*0-374-29020-2*) Farrar, Straus & Giroux.

Zeldis, Chayym. The Geisha's Granddaughter. 288p. 2004. pap. 13.95 (*1-4104-0194-4*, Five Star Trade); 2003. 26.95 (*0-7862-5112-3*, Five Star) Gale Group.

**JEWS—FICTION**

Aaron, Chester. Gideon. 1982. 192p. (YA). (gr. 7 up). lib. bdg. 11.89 (*0-397-31993-2*) HarperCollins Children's Bk. Group.

Abraham, Pearl. Giving America. 1998. 309p. 22.95 o.p. (*1-57322-121-X*, Riverhead Bks. (Hardcovers)) Putnam Publishing Group, The.

—The Romance Reader. 1996. 304p. pap. 13.00 (*1-57322-548-7*, Riverhead Trade (Paperbacks)) Berkley Publishing Group.

—The Romance Reader. 1995. 304p. 21.95 o.s.i (*1-57322-015-9*, Riverhead Bks. (Hardcovers)) Putnam Publishing Group, The.

Abrahams, Lionel. Celibacy of Felix Greenspan. 1993. 181p. reprint ed. 21.95 (*0-89733-396-9*) Academy Chicago Pubs., Ltd.

Abse, Dannie. The Strange Case of Dr. Simmonds & Dr. Glas. 2003. 208p. 23.00 (*0-7867-1201-5*, Carroll & Graf Pubs.) Avalon Publishing Group.

Ackerman, Karen. The Night Crossing. 1994. (Illus.). 64p. (J). (gr. 2-5). 14.00 o.s.i (*0-679-83169-X*, Knopf Bks. for Young Readers) Random Hse. Children's Bks.

—The Night Crossing. 1995. (Illus.). 64p. (gr. 4-7). pap. 4.50 (*0-679-87040-7*) Random Hse., Inc.

Adahan, Miriam. Awareness. 1994. 24.95 (*0-87306-668-5*) Feldheim, Philipp Inc.

Adahan, Miriam, contrib. by. Awareness. 1994. pap. 20.95 (*0-87306-671-5*) Feldheim, Philipp Inc.

Adler, David A. The House on the Roof. 1984. (Illus.). 32p. (J). (ps-4). 10.95 o.p. (*0-930494-34-2*) Kar-Ben Publishing.

—Malke's Secret Recipe: A Chanukah Story from Chelm. 1989. (J). (ps-3). 10.95 o.p. (*0-930494-88-1*); (Illus.). 32p. pap. 4.95 o.p. (*0-930494-89-X*) Kar-Ben Publishing.

—The Number on My Grandfather's Arm. 1987. (Illus.). 28p. (J). (ps-3). 10.95 (*0-8074-0328-8*, 103641) UAHC Pr.

Adler, Jacob. Laugh, Jew, Laugh. London, Abraham, tr. 1977. (Short Story Index Reprint Ser.). 19.95 (*0-8369-3427-X*) Ayer Co. Pubs., Inc.

The Adventures of Jeremy Levy. 1981. 11.95 (*0-87306-319-8*) Feldheim, Philipp Inc.

Agel, Jerome & Boe, Eugene. Deliverance in Shanghai. 1983. 362p. 14.95 o.p. (*0-934878-32-3*, Dembner Bks.) Barricade Bks., Inc.

Alder, David A. The Children of Chelm. 1979. (Story Bks.). (Illus.). (J). (gr. 1-5). pap. 5.00 (*0-88482-773-9*) Hebrew Publishing Co.

Aleichem, Sholem. Hanukah Money. Shulevitz, Uri, tr. from YID. & illus. by. 1978. 32p. (J). (gr. k-3). lib. bdg. 12.88 o.p. (*0-688-84120-1*, Greenwillow Bks.) HarperCollins Children's Bk. Group.

—Hanukah Money. Shulevitz, Uri & Shub, Elizabeth, trs. 1991. (Illus.). 32p. (J). (ps up). reprint ed. pap. 3.95 o.p. (*0-688-10993-4*, Morrow, William & Co.) Morrow/Avon.

—Tevye the Dairyman & the Railroad Stories. 1996. (Library of Yiddish Classics). 352p. pap. 15.00 (*0-8052-1069-5*, Schocken) Knopf Publishing Group.

—Tevye the Dairyman & the Railroad Stories. Wisse, Ruth R., ed. Halkin, Hillel, tr. from YID. & intro. by. 1987. 352p. 19.95 o.p. (*0-8052-4026-8*, Schocken) Knopf Publishing Group.

Ames, Jonathan. I Pass Like Night. 1989. 160p. 15.95 o.p. (*0-688-07804-4*, Morrow, William & Co.) Morrow/Avon.

—I Pass Like Night. 1993. 2.99 o.p. (*0-517-10862-3*) Random Hse. Value Publishing.

—I Pass Like Night. 1999. (Contemporary Classics Ser.). 176p. pap. 12.00 (*0-671-03426-X*, Washington Square Pr.) Simon & Schuster.

Amichai, Yehuda. The World Is a Room, & Other Stories. 1984. 197p. 9.95 o.p. (*0-8276-0234-0*) Jewish Pubn. Society.

Angell, Judie. One-Way to Ansonia. 1985. 192p. (J). (gr. 6-8). 11.95 o.s.i (*0-02-705860-3*, Simon & Schuster Children's Publishing) Simon & Schuster Children's Publishing.

Antler, Joyce, ed. America & I: Short Stories by American Jewish Women Writers. 1991. 368p. pap. 22.50 (*0-8070-3607-2*) Beacon Pr.

Antler, Joyce, intro. America & I: Short Stories by American Jewish Women Writers. 1990. 356p. 19.95 o.p. (*0-8070-3604-8*) Beacon Pr.

Appel, Allan. Club Revelation: A Novel. 2001. 220p. pap. 14.95 (*1-56689-118-3*) Coffee Hse. Pr.

Appel, Allen. High Holiday Sutra. 1997. 192p. (Orig.). pap. 13.95 (*1-56689-065-9*) Coffee Hse. Pr.

Appelfeld, Aharon. The Retreat. Bilu, Dalya, tr. from HEB. 1998. 164p. pap. 13.00 o.s.i (*0-8052-1096-2*, Schocken) Knopf Publishing Group.

—Unto the Soul. Green, Jeffery M., tr. 1998. pap. 13.00 o.s.i (*0-8052-1097-0*, Schocken) Knopf Publishing Group.

Aron, Paul. Ben: The Alien Bird. Aron, Paul & Auswaks, Alex, trs. from DAN. 1999. 248p. 19.95 (*965-229-183-8*) Gefen Publishing Hse., Ltd ISR. *Dist:* Gefen Bks.

Aronin, Ben. The Secret of the Sabbath Fish. 1979. (Illus.). (J). (gr. k-4). 9.95 o.p. (*0-8276-0110-7*) Jewish Pubn. Society.

Ararat, Y. B. The Rabbi & the Priest. 1988. 224p. 12.95 o.p. (*0-944070-02-7*) Targum Pr., Inc.

Arrick, Fran. Chernowitz. 1983. 192p. (YA). mass mkt. 5.99 (*0-451-16253-6*) NAL.

Arthur, Kay. Israel, My Beloved. 2001. 448p. 12.99 (*0-7369-0370-4*); 1997. 450p. pap. 12.99 o.p. (*1-56507-624-9*); 1996. 450p. 17.99 o.p. (*1-56507-403-3*) Harvest Hse. Pubs.

Asch, Sholem. Kiddush Ha-Shem: An Epic of 1648. Learsi, Rufus, tr. 1975. (Modern Jewish Experience Ser.). reprint ed. 23.95 (*0-405-06691-0*) Ayer Co. Pubs., Inc.

—Tales of My People. Levin, Meyer, tr. 1977. (Short Story Index Reprint Ser.). 25.95 (*0-8369-3609-4*) Ayer Co. Pubs., Inc.

Ascher, Carol. The Flood. 1987. 22.95 o.p. (*0-89594-227-5*); pap. 8.95 o.p. (*0-89594-256-9*) Crossing Pr., Inc., The.

—The Flood: A Novel. 1996. 184p. reprint ed. pap. 11.95 (*1-880684-43-8*) Curbstone Pr.

Atzmon, Gilad. A Guide to the Perplexed. Simpson, Philip, tr. from HEB. 2003. 160p. pap. 14.00 (*1-85242-826-0*) Serpent's Tail Ltd. GBR. *Dist:* Consortium Bk. Sales & Distribution.

Bar Am, Meir. The Parnas. Van Handel, Esther, tr. 1986. 10.95 o.p. (*0-87306-393-7*); pap. 6.95 (*0-87306-400-3*) Feldheim, Philipp Inc.

Barkhordar-Nahai, Gina. Cry of the Peacock, an Excerpt. 1991. o.s.i (*0-517-58475-1*) Crown Publishing Group.

—Moonlight on the Avenue of Faith. 2000. 400p. reprint ed. pap. 13.95 (*0-671-04283-1*, Washington Square Pr.) Simon & Schuster.

Baron, Devorah. "The First Day" & Other Stories. 2001. (Illus.). xxv, 236p. pap. 16.95 (*0-520-08538-8*) Univ. of California Pr.

—The First Day & Other Stories. Seidman, Naomi & Kronfeld, Chana, eds. & trs. by. from HEB. 2001. (Illus.). xxv, 236p. text 40.00 (*0-520-08536-1*) Univ. of California Pr.

Barragan, Nina. Losers & Keepers in Argentina. 2001. (Jewish Latin America Ser.). (Illus.). (*0-8263-2221-2*) Univ. of New Mexico Pr.

—Losers & Keepers in Argentina: A Work of Fiction. 2001. (Jewish Latin America Ser.). xv, 254p. pap. 19.95 (*0-8263-2222-0*) Univ. of New Mexico Pr.

Batterman, Lee C. Two Cents & a Milk Bottle. 1997. (Illus.). 272p. (J). (ps-3). 15.95 (*1-881283-17-8*) Alef Design Group.

Becker, Jurek. Jacob the Liar. 1997. pap. 12.95 o.p. (*1-55970-374-1*) Arcade Publishing, Inc.

—Jacob the Liar. Vennewitz, Leila, tr. from GER. 1996. (Illus.). 256p. 21.95 (*1-55970-315-6*) Arcade Publishing, Inc.

—Jacob the Liar. Vennewitz, Leila, tr. from GER. 1997. 256p. pap. 11.95 o.s.i (*0-452-27903-8*, Plume) Dutton/Plume.

—Jacob the Liar. Kornfeld, Melvin, tr. 1975. (Helen & Kurt Wolff Bk.). 256p. 7.95 o.p. (*0-15-145975-4*) Harcourt Trade Pubs.

—Jacob the Liar. 1990. 19.95 o.p. (*0-8052-4097-7*, Schocken) Knopf Publishing Group.

Be'er, Haim. The Pure Element of Time. Harshav, Barbara, tr. from HEB. 2003. (Tauber Institute for the Study of European Jewry Ser.). 304p. text 26.00 (*1-58465-277-2*) Univ. Pr. of New England.

Beim, Norman. Hymie & the Angel. 1999. 198p. pap. 12.95 (*0-931231-09-4*) Newconcept Pr., Inc.

Bellow, Saul, ed. Great Jewish Short Stories. 1985. 416p. (Orig.). mass mkt. 6.99 o.s.i (*0-440-33122-6*, Laurel) Dell Publishing.

Benjamin, Alan. Hanukkah Chubby Board Book. 1993. (Chubby Board Bks.). (Illus.). 16p. (J). (ps up). pap. 3.95 (*0-671-87069-6*, Little Simon) Simon & Schuster Children's Publishing.

—Hanukkah with Three Dreidels. 1997. (Chubby Board Bks.). (Illus.). (J). (ps-k). bds. 6.99 (*0-689-80911-5*, Little Simon) Simon & Schuster Children's Publishing.

Bergman, Andrew. Sleepless Nights. 1994. 224p. 19.95 o.p. (*1-55611-400-1*) Fine, Donald I. Bks.

Berkewicz, Ulla. Angels Are Black & White. Willson, A. Leslie, tr. from GER. 1997. 300p. 39.95 (*1-57113-112-4*) Camden Hse.

Berliner, Janet. Children of the Dusk, Bk. 3. 1997. (Madagascar Manifesto Ser.). 447p. mass mkt. 5.99 (*1-56504-932-2*, Borealis) White Wolf Publishing, Inc.

Berliner, Janet & Guthridge, George. Child of the Journey. 1996. (Child of the Journey Ser.: Bk. II). 471p. pap. 5.99 (*1-56504-942-X*, Borealis) White Wolf Publishing, Inc.

—Child of the Light. 1996. (Madagascar Manifesto Ser.: Bk. 1). (Illus.). 440p. (Orig.). pap. 5.99 (*1-56504-931-4*, 12100, Borealis) White Wolf Publishing, Inc.

Berman, Hannah. Melutovna: A Novel. 1975. (Modern Jewish Experience Ser.). reprint ed. 33.95 (*0-405-06694-5*) Ayer Co. Pubs., Inc.

Berman, Sabina. Bubbeh. Labinger, Andrea G., tr. from SPA. 1998. (Discoveries Ser.). 96p. pap. 12.95 (*0-935480-93-5*) Latin American Literary Review Pr.

Bermant, Chaim. Dancing Bear. 1985. 256p. 13.95 o.p. (*0-312-18211-2*) St. Martin's Pr.

—The House of Women. 1983. 304p. 12.95 o.p. (*0-312-39306-7*) St. Martin's Pr.

Betancourt, Lin. Grandfathers & Demons. 2000. (Rabbi Adam Trilogy Ser.: Bk. 1). (Illus.). 108p. pap. 20.99 (*0-7388-2886-6*) Xlibris Corp.

Bianchini, Angela. The Edge of Europe. Jeannet, Angela M. & Castronuovo, David, trs. from ITA. 2000. (European Women Writers Ser.). 145p. pap. 15.00 (*0-8032-6171-3*, Bison Bks.); text 50.00 (*0-8032-1308-5*) Univ. of Nebraska Pr.

Birmingham, Stephen. The Auerbach Will. 1985. 416p. 16.95 o.p. (*0-316-09646-6*) Little Brown & Co.

Bishop, Claire Huchet. Twenty & Ten. 1978. (Illus.). 80p. (J). (ps-3). pap. 4.99 (*0-14-031076-2*, Puffin Bks.) Penguin Putnam Bks. for Young Readers.

—Twenty & Ten. 76p. (J). (gr. 3-5). pap. 4.99 (*0-8072-1418-3*, Listening Library) Random Hse. Audio Publishing Group.

—Twenty & Ten. 1984. (Illus.). (J). (gr. 5-9). 18.75 (*0-8446-6168-6*) Smith, Peter Pub., Inc.

—Twenty & Ten. 1952. (Illus.). (J). (gr. 4-6). 6.50 o.p. (*0-670-73407-1*) Viking Penguin.

Black, Cara. Murder in the Marais. 1999. (Aimee Leduc Investigation Ser.). 354p. 22.00 (*1-56947-159-2*) Soho Pr., Inc.

—Murder in the Marais: An Aimee Leduc Investigation. 2000. (Illus.). 360p. pap. 13.00 (*1-56947-212-2*) Soho Pr., Inc.

Black, David. An Impossible Life. 1998. 200p. pap. 18.95 (*1-55921-222-5*) Moyer Bell.

—Impossible Life: A False Family History. 1996. 224p. 22.95 (*1-882206-13-4*) Argonaut Pr.

Blackman, Murray. A Guide to Jewish Themes in American Fiction, 1940-1980. 1981. 271p. lib. bdg. 19.00 o.p. (*0-8108-1380-7*) Scarecrow Pr., Inc.

Blanc, Esther S. Berchick. 1989. (Illus.). 32p. (J). (gr. k-5). 14.95 (*0-912078-81-2*) Volcano Pr.

Blos, Joan W. Brooklyn Doesn't Rhyme. (Illus.). 96p. (gr. 3-7). 2000. pap. 4.50 (*0-689-83557-4*, Aladdin); 1994. (J). 16.00 o.s.i (*0-684-19694-8*, Atheneum) Simon & Schuster Children's Publishing.

Blue, Rose. Cold Rain on the Water. 1979. (J). (gr. 7 up). text 7.95 o.p. (*0-07-006168-8*) McGraw-Hill Cos., The.

Blume, Judy. Starring Sally J. Freedman As Herself. l.t. ed. 1988. 368p. (J). (gr. 4-7). 14.95 o.p. (*0-8161-4448-6*, Macmillan Reference USA) Gale Group.

—Starring Sally J. Freedman As Herself. 1982. 296p. (J). (gr. 4-7). 17.00 (*0-02-711070-2*, Atheneum/Richard Jackson Bks.) Simon & Schuster Children's Publishing.

Bottome, Phyllis. The Mortal Storm: A Novel. 1998. xxv, 357p. pap. 18.95 (*0-8101-1471-2*) Northwestern Univ. Pr.

Brady, John. Kaddish in Dublin. 2002. (Matt Minogue Mystery Ser.). 253p. pap. 14.95 (*1-58642-042-9*) Steerforth Pr.

Brodkey, Harold. Women & Angels. 1985. (Author's Workshop Ser.). 176p. 25.00 (*0-8276-0250-2*) Jewish Pubn. Society.

Brooker, Barbara. The Rise & Fall of a Jewish American Princess. 2000. 632p. E-Book 8.00 (*0-7388-9228-9*) Xlibris Corp.

Brookner, Anita. Family & Friends. l.t. ed. 1986. (General Ser.). 272p. 15.95 o.p. (*0-8161-4061-8*, Macmillan Reference USA) Gale Group.

—Family & Friends. 1998. 192p. pap. 12.00 (*0-679-78164-1*, Vintage) Knopf Publishing Group.

—Family & Friends. 1987. 1.99 o.p. (*0-517-64896-2*) Random Hse. Value Publishing.

—Family & Friends. 1986. pap. 6.95 o.s.i (*0-671-62575-6*, Pocket) Simon & Schuster.

Brooks, Jerome. Make Me a Hero. 1980. 176p. (J). (gr. 5-9). 9.95 o.p. (*0-525-34475-6*, 0966-290, Dutton) Dutton/Plume.

Brownstein, Gabriel. The Curious Case of Benjamin Button, Apt. 3W. 2003. 224p. pap. 13.95 (*0-393-32478-8*); 2002. 192p. 23.95 (*0-393-05151-X*) Norton, W. W. & Co., Inc.

Buck, Pearl S. Peony. 1996. pap. 18.00 (*0-7892-5111-6*) Abbeville Pr., Inc.

—Peony. expurg. ed. 2004. (Oriental Novels of Peal S. Buck Ser.). 336p. (C). pap. 12.95 (*1-55921-338-8*) Acorn Alliance.

—Peony. 1990. (Illus.). 340p. reprint ed. pap. 11.95 o.p. (*0-930395-12-3*) Biblio Pr., the Jewish Women's Pub.

—Peony. 338p. 1990. pap. 11.95 (*0-8197-0593-4*); 1990. lib. bdg. 24.95 o.p. (*0-8197-0592-6*); 1996. (Illus.). reprint ed. lib. bdg. 24.95 o.p. (*0-8197-0617-5*) Bloch Publishing Co.

—Peony. 1996. 320p. reprint ed. pap. 11.95 (*1-55921-168-7*) Moyer Bell.

Bukiet, Melvin J. Stories of an Imaginary Childhood. 1992. 197p. 29.95 o.p. (*0-8101-1006-7*); pap. 16.00 o.p. (*0-8101-1031-8*) Northwestern Univ. Pr.

—While the Messiah Tarries: Stories. 1995. 197p. 20.00 (*0-15-100083-2*) Harcourt Trade Pubs.

Bukiet, Melvin Jules. Neurotica: Jewish Writers on Sex. 2000. 380p. pap. 19.00 (*0-7679-0650-0*) Broadway Bks.

—Stories of an Imaginary Childhood. 2002. (Library of American Fiction). 201p. pap. 17.95 (*0-299-18074-3*) Univ. of Wisconsin Pr.

Bukiet, Melvin Jules, ed. Neurotica: Jewish Writers on Sex. 1999. 352p. 26.95 o.p. (*0-393-04808-X*) Norton, W. W. & Co., Inc.

Burstein, Chaya M. The Mystery of the Coins. 1988. (Illus.). 160p. (Orig.). (J). (gr. 4-6). pap. text 9.95 o.p. (*0-8074-0350-4*, 123000) UAHC Pr.

—Rifka Bangs the Teakettle. 1970. (Illus.). (J). (gr. 4-6). 4.95 o.p. (*0-15-266944-2*) Harcourt Children's Bks.

Cahan, Abraham. The Rise of David Levinsky. 2002. 464p. pap. 8.95 (*0-486-42517-7*) Dover Pubns., Inc.

—The Rise of David Levinsky. 2001. (Paperback Classics Ser.). 560p. pap. 13.95 (*0-375-75798-8*, Modern Library) Random House Adult Trade Publishing Group.

—The White Terror & Red. 2000. 252p. E-Book 3.95 (*0-594-05960-7*) 1873 Pr.

—The White Terror & the Red: A Novel of Revolutionary Russia. 1975. (Modern Jewish Experience Ser.). reprint ed. 37.95 (*0-405-06699-6*) Ayer Co. Pubs., Inc.

—Yekl & the Imported Bridegroom & Other Stories of the New York Ghetto. 1970. 240p. pap. 6.95 (*0-486-22427-9*) Dover Pubns., Inc.

—Yekl & the Imported Bridegroom & Other Stories of the New York Ghetto. 1990. 17.75 (*0-8446-0048-2*) Smith, Peter Pub., Inc.

Canin, Ethan. Carry Me Across the Water: A Novel. 2001. E-Book 19.00 (*1-58945-887-7*) Adobe Systems, Inc.

—Carry Me Across the Water: A Novel. 2002. 240p. pap. 12.95 (*0-375-75993-X*); 2001. E-Book 19.00 (*1-58836-007-5*) Random Hse., Inc.

Cantor, Jay. Great Neck: A Novel. 2003. 720p. 27.95 (*0-375-41394-4*) Knopf, Alfred A. Inc.

Caseley, Judith. When Grandpa Came to Stay. 1986. (Illus.). 32p. (J). (gr. k-2). lib. bdg. 12.93 o.p. (*0-688-06129-X*, Greenwillow Bks.) HarperCollins Children's Bk. Group.

Chaikin, Miriam. Friends Forever. 1988. (Charlotte Zolotow Bk.). (Illus.). 128p. (J). (gr. 3-6). lib. bdg. 11.89 o.p. (*0-06-021204-7*) HarperCollins Children's Bk. Group.

—Getting Even. 1982. (Charlotte Zolotow Bk.). (Illus.). 128p. (J). (gr. 3-7). lib. bdg. 12.89 o.p. (*0-06-021165-2*) HarperCollins Children's Bk. Group.

—How Yossi Beat the Evil Urge. 1983. (Charlotte Zolotow Bk.). (Illus.). 64p. (J). (gr. 3-5). lib. bdg. 11.89 o.p. (*0-06-021185-7*) HarperCollins Children's Bk. Group.

—I Should Worry, I Should Care. 1979. (Illus.). (J). (gr. 3-6). lib. bdg. 11.89 o.p. (*0-06-021175-X*) HarperCollins Children's Bk. Group.

—Lower! Higher! You're a Liar! 1984. (Charlotte Zolotow Bk.). (Illus.). 160p. (J). (gr. 3-7). 12.95 (*0-06-021186-5*) HarperCollins Children's Bk. Group.

—Yossi Asks the Angels for Help. 1985. (Charlotte Zolotow Bk.). (Illus.). 64p. (J). (gr. 3-5). 11.95 (*0-06-021195-4*) HarperCollins Children's Bk. Group.

—Yossi Tries to Help God. 1987. (Charlotte Zolotow Bk.). (Illus.). 80p. (J). (gr. 3-5). 11.95 (0-06-021197-0); lib. bdg. 11.89 o.p. (0-06-021198-9) HarperCollins Children's Bk. Group.

Charchat, Isaac. A Constant Reminder. 1984. 460p. 20.00 o.p. (0-88400-109-1, Shengold Bks.) Schreiber Publishing, Inc.

Chefitz, Mitchell. The Seventh Telling. E-Book 24.95 (0-312-70058-X) St. Martin's Pr.

—The Seventh Telling: A Novel. 2002. (Illus.). 432p. pap. 14.95 (0-312-28922-7, Saint Martin's Griffin) St. Martin's Pr.

—Seventh Telling: The Kabbalah of Moshe Katan. 2001. (Illus.). viii, 422p. 24.95 (0-312-26645-6) St. Martin's Pr.

—The Thirty-Third Hour: A Novel. 2002. 320p. 24.95 (0-312-27758-X, Saint Martin's Minotaur); 2003. 288p. reprint ed. pap. 13.95 (0-312-30323-8, Saint Martin's Griffin) St. Martin's Pr.

Cheuse, Alan. The Grandmother's Club. 1985. 15.95 o.p. (0-918222-67-2) Applewood Bks.

—The Grandmother's Club. 1986. 326p. 18.95 o.p. (0-87905-253-8) Smith, Gibbs Pub.

—The Grandmother's Club. 1994. 348p. reprint ed. pap. 10.95 (0-87074-374-0) Southern Methodist Univ. Pr.

—The Grandmother's Club. 1988. 336p. pap. 6.95 o.p. (0-14-010484-4, Penguin Bks.) Viking Penguin.

Clayton, John J. Radiance: Ten Stories. 1998. 256p. 24.95 (0-8142-0779-0, CLARAD); 203p. pap. 16.95 (0-8142-0780-4, CLARAX) Ohio State Univ. Pr.

Clifford, Eth. The Remembering Box. ALC Staff, ed. 1992. (Illus.). 64p. (J). (gr. 4-7). pap. 4.95 (0-688-11777-5, Harper Trophy) HarperCollins Children's Bk. Group.

—The Remembering Box, 001. 1985. (Illus.). 80p. (J). (gr. 4-6). tchr. ed. 16.00 (0-395-38476-1) Houghton Mifflin Co.

Cohen. Queen for a Day. 1981. 12.95 o.p. (0-688-00437-7) HarperCollins Children's Bk. Group.

Cohen, Barbara. Benny. 1977. (J). (gr. 3-7). 7.25 o.p. (0-688-41804-X) HarperCollins Children's Bk. Group.

—The Carp in the Bathtub. 1987. (Illus.). 32p. (J). (gr. k-5). pap. 5.95 (0-930494-67-9) Kar-Ben Publishing.

—The Christmas Revolution. 1993. 176p. (J). pap. 3.50 o.s.i (0-440-40871-7) Dell Publishing.

—The Christmas Revolution. 1987. (Illus.). 96p. (J). (gr. 3-6). 15.00 o.p. (0-688-06806-5) HarperCollins Children's Bk. Group.

—First Fast. 1987. (Illus.). 32p. (J). (gr. 4-7). 8.95 (0-8074-0354-7, 101066) UAHC Pr.

—Here Come the Purim Players! 1984. (Illus.). 32p. (J). (gr. 1-4). 12.00 o.p. (0-688-02106-9) HarperCollins Children's Bk. Group.

—Here Come the Purim Players! 1998. (Illus.). (J). (ps-3). 12.95 (0-8074-0645-7, 101251) UAHC Pr.

—King of the Seventh Grade. 1982. (J). (gr. 4 up). 15.00 o.p. (0-688-01302-3) HarperCollins Children's Bk. Group.

—People Like Us. 1989. 144p. (YA). mass mkt. 2.95 o.s.i (0-553-27445-7, Starfire) Random Hse. Children's Bks.

Cohen, Matt. The Spanish Doctor. 1985. 352p. 16.95 o.p. (0-8253-0227-7) Beaufort Bks., Inc.

Cohen, Paula Marantz. Jane Austen in Boca. l.t. ed. 2003. (Thorndike Press Large Print Women's Fiction Ser.). 388p. 28.95 (0-7862-4973-0) Thorndike Pr.

Cohen, Sholem. Yitzy & the G. O. L. E. M. 1992. (Yitz Berg from Pittsburgh Ser.). 128p. (J). (gr. 4-8). pap. text 6.95 o.p. (0-922613-50-8) Hachai Publishing.

Collins, Alan. Jacob's Ladder. 1989. 160p. (YA). (gr. 7 up). 13.95 o.p. (0-525-67272-9, Dutton Children's Bks.) Penguin Putnam Bks. for Young Readers.

Cooper, Armin A. Tribes: A Novel. 2001. pap. 16.95 (0-595-18046-9) iUniverse, Inc.

Cushnir, Howard. The Secret Spinner: Tales of Rav Gedalia. 1985. (Illus.). 48p. (J). (gr. 2-5). pap. 5.95 o.p. (0-930494-47-4) Kar-Ben Publishing.

Daley, Robert. The Innocents Within. 2001. 480p. mass mkt. 7.50 (0-449-00415-5, Ballantine Bks.) Ballantine Bks.

—The Innocents Within. 2001. 13.55 (0-606-20497-0) Turtleback Bks.

—The Innocents Within: A Novel. 1999. 448p. 25.95 o.s.i (0-375-50178-9, Villard Bks.) Random House Adult Trade Publishing Group.

Dann, Jack, ed. Wandering Stars: An Anthology of Jewish Fantasy & Science Fiction. 1974. 252p. 8.95 o.p. (0-06-010944-0) HarperCollins Pubs.

—Wandering Stars: An Anthology of Jewish Fantasy & Science Fiction. 1998. 272p. reprint ed. pap. 16.95 (1-58023-005-9) Jewish Lights Publishing.

David, Esther. The Walled City. 2002. (Library of Modern Jewish Literature). 204p. pap. 19.95 (0-8156-0750-4) Syracuse Univ. Pr.

Davis, Jerry Lee. Twin City. 2000. 300p. pap. 14.95 o.p. (1-928704-13-1, Authorlink Pr.) Authorlink.

Delbanco, Nicholas. What Remains. 2000. 208p. 24.95 o.p. (0-446-52416-6); E-Book 14.95 (0-7595-4037-3); E-Book 14.95 (0-7595-0037-1); E-Book 14.95 (0-7595-8038-3) Warner Bks., Inc.

Derman, Martha. The Friendstone. 1981. 160p. (J). (gr. 4-7). 8.95 o.p. (0-8037-2472-1); 8.44 o.p. (0-8037-2480-2) Penguin Putnam Bks. for Young Readers. (Dial Bks. for Young Readers).

Desai, Anita. Baumgartner's Bombay. 2000. (Illus.). 240p. pap. 13.00 (0-618-05680-7) Houghton Mifflin Co.

—Baumgartner's Bombay. 1989. 18.95 o.s.i (0-394-57229-7) Knopf, Alfred A. Inc.

—Baumgartner's Bombay. 1990. 240p. pap. 11.95 o.p. (0-14-011474-2, Viking); pap. 9.00 o.p. (0-14-013176-0, Penguin Bks.) Viking Penguin.

Devori's Day. 1992. (Brookville Chessed Committee Ser.: Vol. II). pap. 7.99 (0-89906-137-0) Mesorah Pubns., Ltd.

Diamant, Anita. Good Harbor: A Novel. l.t. ed. 2001. 31.95 (1-58724-140-4, Wheeler Publishing, Inc.) Gale Group.

—Good Harbor: A Novel. 256p. 2002. E-Book (0-7432-2976-2); 2001. 25.00 (0-7432-2532-5); 2002. reprint ed. pap. 13.00 (0-7432-2572-4) Simon & Schuster. (Scribner).

Dickson, Athol. They Shall See God: A Novel. 2002. (Moving Fiction Ser.). 464p. pap. 11.99 (0-8423-5292-9) Tyndale Hse. Pubs.

Dillon, Eilis. Children of Bach. 1992. 176p. (J). (gr. 5-8). 14.95 o.p. (0-684-19440-6, Atheneum) Simon & Schuster Children's Publishing.

Dolin, Simon. The Will to Survive: A Historical Novel. 1995. 18.95 o.p. (0-533-11502-7) Vantage Pr., Inc.

Double Trouble. 1992. (Brookville Chese Committee Ser. - Tamar Bks.: Vol. III). pap. 7.99 (0-89906-138-9) Mesorah Pubns., Ltd.

Douglas, Kirk. Dance with the Devil. l.t. ed. 1994. 554p. lib. bdg. 23.95 o.p. (0-8161-7464-4, Macmillan Reference USA) Gale Group.

—Dance with the Devil. abr. ed. 1993. 15.95 o.p. (1-55800-406-8) NewStar Media, Inc.

—Dance with the Devil. 1992. 3.99 o.p. (0-517-08346-9) Random Hse. Value Publishing.

—Dance with the Devil. 1991. 384p. mass mkt. 5.99 o.s.i (0-446-36191-7) Warner Bks., Inc.

DuCharme, Dede Fox. The Treasure in the Tiny Blue Tin. 1998. (Chaparral Books for Young Readers). 144p. (J). (gr. 5-8). pap. 11.95 (0-87565-180-1) Texas Christian Univ. Pr.

Dunn, J. R. Days of Cain. 1997. 336p. 23.00 o.p. (0-380-97433-9, Avon Bks.) Morrow/Avon.

—Days of Cain. 1998. 9.09 o.p. (0-606-13319-4) Turtleback Bks.

—The Days of Cain. 1998. mass mkt. 6.50 (0-380-79049-1, Eos); 1997. pap. 13.00 o.p. (0-380-79280-X, Avon Bks.) Morrow/Avon.

Dykewoman, Elana. Beyond the Pale. 1997. 404p. pap. (0-88974-074-7, Press Gang Pubs.) Raincoast Bk. Distribution.

Eberstadt, Fernanda. The Furies: A Novel. 2003. 464p. 26.00 (0-375-41256-5) Knopf, Alfred A. Inc.

Edelman, Gwen. War Story: A Novel. 2002. 176p. pap. 13.00 (1-57322-939-3, Riverhead Trade (Paperbacks)) Berkley Publishing Group.

—War Story: A Novel. l.t. ed. 2001. (Large Print Book Ser.). 150p. 26.95 (1-58724-146-3, Wheeler Publishing, Inc.) Gale Group.

—War Story: A Novel. 2001. 224p. 21.95 o.p. (1-57322-189-9, Riverhead Bks. (Hardcovers)) Putnam Publishing Group, The.

Edwards, Michelle. A Baker's Portrait. 1991. (Illus.). 32p. (J). (gr. k up). lib. bdg. 13.88 o.p. (0-688-09713-8) HarperCollins Children's Bk. Group.

—Bakers Portrait. 1991. 13.95 o.p. (0-688-09712-X, Morrow, William & Co.) Morrow/Avon.

—Misha the Minstrel. 2004. (Illus.). 21p. (J). (gr. 3-7). 8.95 (0-930100-19-0) Holy Cow! Pr.

—Papa's Latkes. 2001. (Illus.). (J). 15.99 (0-7636-0779-7) Candlewick Pr.

Ehrlich, Yosef. Shabbath. 1999. 102p. 24.95 (0-8156-0590-0) Syracuse Univ. Pr.

Elberg, Yehuda, tr. from YID. Ship of the Hunted. 1997. (Library of Modern Jewish Literature). 400p. reprint ed. 28.95 (0-8156-0449-1) Syracuse Univ. Pr.

Elias, Miriam L. All Because of Raizy. 1990. 11.95 o.p. (0-87306-535-2) Feldheim, Philipp Inc.

—Goodbye, My Friends. 1989. (J). (gr. 6-9). 10.95 o.p. (0-87306-491-7) Feldheim, Philipp Inc.

Eliot, George. Daniel Deronda. (Writings of George Eliot Ser.: Vol. 15). reprint ed. Pt. 1. 1999. 400p. lib. bdg. 88.00 (1-58201-082-X); Pt. 2. 2001. 400p. pap. text 28.00 (0-7426-5083-9); Pt. 2. 1999. 400p. lib. bdg. 88.00 (1-58201-083-8); Pt. 3. 2001. 400p. pap. text 28.00 (0-7426-5084-7); Pt. 3. 1999. 88.00 (1-58201-084-6); Pt.1. 2001. 400p. pap. text 28.00 (0-7426-5082-0) Classic Bks.

—Daniel Deronda. 1999. (Everyman Paperback Classics Ser.). xxxi, 842p. pap. (0-460-87686-4, Everyman Paperbacks) Dent, J. M. & Sons (Canada), Ltd.

—Daniel Deronda. 2000. 928p. 23.00 (0-375-41123-2) Knopf, Alfred A. Inc.

—Daniel Deronda. 1979. mass mkt. 3.50 o.p. (0-451-51204-9, CE1204, Signet Classics) NAL.

—Daniel Deronda. Handley, Graham, ed. & intro. by. 1998. (Oxford World's Classics Ser.). 758p. pap. 9.95 (0-19-283481-9) Oxford Univ. Pr., Inc.

—Daniel Deronda. Handley, Graham, ed. (Oxford World's Classics Ser.). 1988. 758p. pap. 7.95 o.p. (0-19-281787-6); 1985. (Illus.). 792p. text 145.00 o.p. (0-19-812557-7) Oxford Univ. Pr., Inc.

—Daniel Deronda. 2002. (Modern Library Classics). 832p. pap. 9.95 (0-375-76013-X) Random Hse., Inc.

—Daniel Deronda. Hardy, Barbara, ed. 1967. (English Library). 912p. pap. 7.95 o.p. (0-14-043020-2, Penguin Classics) Viking Penguin.

—Daniel Deronda. Cave, Terence, ed. & intro. by. abr. ed. 1996. (Penguin Classics Ser.). 848p. 9.95 (0-14-043427-5, Penguin Classics) Viking Penguin.

—Daniel Deronda. 1998. (Classics Library). pap. 3.95 (1-85326-176-9, 1769WW) Wordsworth Editions, Ltd. GBR. *Dist:* Combined Publishing.

Elkin, Stanley. The Rabbi of Lud. 2001. (American Literature Ser.). 277p. pap. 12.95 (1-56478-270-0) Dalkey Archive Pr.

—The Rabbi of Lud. 1989. 256p. pap. 8.95 o.s.i (0-684-19013-3, Scribner Paper Fiction); 1987. 222p. 17.95 o.s.i (0-684-18902-X, Scribner) Simon & Schuster.

Ellis, Julie. Trespassing Hearts. 1992. 384p. 21.95 o.s.i (0-399-13738-6, G. P. Putnam's Sons) Penguin Group (USA) Inc.

Elman, Richard. Tar Beach. 1991. (New American Fiction Ser.: No. 23). 280p. (Orig.). pap. 12.95 o.p. (1-55713-117-1) Sun & Moon Pr.

Ely, Stanley E. Perfect Mondays. E-Book 9.95 (1-891305-87-5); 2002. 271p. pap. 15.95 (1-891305-62-X) Painted Leaf Pr.

Englander, Nathan. For the Relief of Unbearable Urges: Stories. 2000. 224p. pap. 12.00 (0-375-70443-4, Vintage) Knopf Publishing Group.

—For the Relief of Unbearable Urges: Stories. aut. ed. 1999. 22.00 (0-676-54953-5) Knopf, Alfred A. Inc.

Epstein, Joseph. Fabulous Small Jews: Stories. 2003. 352p. tchr. ed. 24.00 (0-395-94402-3) Houghton Mifflin Co.

—Fabulous Small Jews: Stories. 2004. 352p. pap. 13.00 (0-618-44658-3, Mariner Bks.) Houghton Mifflin Co. Trade & Reference Div.

Epstein, Leslie. Goldkorn Tales. 1986. 256p. pap. 8.95 o.p. (0-452-25822-7, Plume); 252p. 16.95 o.p. (0-525-24286-4, Dutton) Dutton/Plume.

—Goldkorn Tales: Three Novellas. 1998. 264p. reprint ed. pap. 12.95 (0-87074-435-6) Southern Methodist Univ. Pr.

—Ice Fire Water. 2000. (Leib Goldkorn Cocktail Ser.). 272p. reprint ed. pap. 13.95 (0-393-32090-1) Norton, W. W. & Co., Inc.

—Ice Fire Water: A Leib Goldkorn Cocktail. 1999. 288p. text 23.95 (0-393-04804-7) Norton, W. W. & Co., Inc.

—King of the Jews. unabr. ed. 1997. audio 56.95 (0-7861-1178-X, 1924) Blackstone Audio Bks., Inc.

—King of the Jews. 1986. 352p. pap. 7.95 o.p. (0-452-25823-5, Plume) Dutton/Plume.

—King of the Jews. 1985. pap. 2.50 o.p. (0-380-48074-3, 48074-3, Avon Bks.) Morrow/Avon.

—King of the Jews. 1993. 352p. pap. 17.95 (0-393-30959-2) Norton, W. W. & Co., Inc.

—King of the Jews. 2003. pap. 15.00 (1-59051-079-8, Handsel Bks.) Other Pr., LLC.

Epstein, Lesly. King of the Jews. 1989. pap. 8.95 o.p. (0-671-69003-5) Summit Bks.

Eskinazi, Salamon. The Reluctant Messiah. 2002. ix, 354p. pap. 30.00 (0-7657-6168-8) Aronson, Jason Pubs.

Espinosa, Maria. Incognito: Journey of a Secret Jew. 2002. 190p. (C). pap. 17.95 (0-930324-79-X) Wings Pr.

—Longing. 1995. 298p. pap. 9.95 (1-55885-145-3) Arte Publico Pr.

Esquivel, Laura. The Law of Love. 1997. Tr. of Ley del Amor. (Illus.). 288p. pap. 18.95 (0-609-80127-9) Random Hse. Value Publishing.

Eve, Nomi. The Family Orchard: A Novel. 2001. (Illus.). 336p. reprint ed. pap. 13.00 (0-375-72457-5, Vintage) Knopf Publishing Group.

—The Family Orchard: A Novel. l.t. ed. 2001. (Women's Fiction Ser.). (Illus.). 499p. 28.95 (0-7862-3303-6) Thorndike Pr.

Everdenn, Margery. The Dream Keeper. 1985. (Illus.). 160p. (J). (gr. 6 up). 11.95 o.p. (0-688-04638-X) HarperCollins Children's Bk. Group.

Fass, David E. The Shofar That Lost Its Voice. 1982. (Illus.). 48p. (J). (gr. 4-7). 7.95 (0-8074-0168-4, 103500) UAHC Pr.

Fast, Howard. My Glorious Brothers. 23.95 (0-89190-579-0) Amereon, Ltd.

—My Glorious Brothers. 1977. (Illus.). pap. 7.95 o.s.i (0-88482-758-5) Hebrew Publishing Co.

—My Glorious Brothers. 2003. 288p. pap. 12.95 (0-7434-8003-1) ibooks, Inc.

—The Outsider. 1985. 320p. mass mkt. 3.95 o.s.i (0-440-16778-7) Dell Publishing.

—The Outsider. l.t. ed. 1984. (Special Editions Ser.). 17.95 o.p. (0-8161-3760-9, Macmillan Reference USA) Gale Group.

—The Outsider, 001. 1984. 311p. 15.95 o.p. (0-395-36101-X) Houghton Mifflin Co.

Feierstein, Ricardo. Mestizo: A Novel. 2000. (Jewish Latin America Ser.). (Illus.). 352p. 45.00 (0-8263-2115-1); pap. 19.95 (0-8263-2116-X) Univ. of New Mexico Pr.

Feinstein, Elaine. The Border. 1990. 122p. reprint ed. pap. 9.95 (0-7145-2900-1) Boyars, Marion Pubs., Inc.

—The Border. 1985. 10.95 o.p. (0-312-09269-5) St. Martin's Pr.

Feldman, Eve B. Seymour, the Formerly Fearful. 1990. 160p. (J). (gr. 3-6). 13.95 o.p. (0-02-734371-5, Simon & Schuster Children's Publishing) Simon & Schuster Children's Publishing.

Felman, Jyl Lynn. Hot Chicken Wings. 1992. 176p. pap. 9.95 (1-879960-21-4); 145p. text 18.95 o.s.i (1-879960-23-0) Aunt Lute Bks.

Ferber, Edna. Fanny Herself. 1975. (Modern Jewish Experience Ser.). (Illus.). reprint ed. 31.95 (0-405-06708-9) Ayer Co. Pubs., Inc.

Fiedler, Jean. The Year the World Was Out of Step with Jancy Fried. 1981. 156p. (J). 9.95 o.p. (0-15-299818-7) Harcourt Children's Bks.

Fink, Ida. A Scrap of Time: And Other Stories. Prose, Francine & Levine, Madeline, trs. from POL. 1995. (Jewish Lives Ser.). 174p. pap. 16.00 (0-8101-1259-0) Northwestern Univ. Pr.

Finkelstein, Chaim. Cheery Bim Band No. 3: March to the Music. 1993. 176p. (J). (gr. 5-6). 13.95 (1-56062-218-0, CJR140H) CIS Communications, Inc.

Finklestein, Barbara. Summer Long-a-Coming. 2000. E-Book 16.95 incl. cd-rom (1-58444-039-2) Disc-Us Bks., Inc.

Fisher, Leonard Everett, illus. The Spotted Pony: A Collection of Hanukkah Stories. 1992. 72p. (J). (gr. 4-7). tchr. ed. 15.95 (0-8234-0936-8) Holiday Hse., Inc.

Fishtein, Oscar. I'll Sell You a Million Jews. 1995. 272p. 19.95 (0-8158-0517-9) Christopher Publishing Hse.

Frankel, Ellen & Levine, Sarah. Tell It Like It Is: Tough Choices for Today's Teens. 1995. (YA). 16.95 o.p. (0-88125-522-X) Ktav Publishing Hse., Inc.

Freed, Lynn. The Bungalow. 1999. 240p. reprint ed. pap. 14.00 (1-885266-76-6) Story Line Pr.

—The Bungalow: A Novel. 1993. 237p. 21.00 (0-671-75587-0, Simon & Schuster) Simon & Schuster.

—Home Ground. 1986. 273p. (0-434-27170-5, Butterworth-Heinemann) Elsevier Science & Technology Bks.

—Home Ground. 2nd ed. 1999. 288p. reprint ed. pap. 14.00 (1-885266-71-5) Story Line Pr.

—Home Ground. 1986. 16.45 o.p. (0-671-61965-9) Summit Bks.

—Home Ground. 1987. 288p. pap. 7.95 o.p. (0-14-008948-9, Penguin Bks.) Viking Penguin.

Freilich, Alicia. Claper. 1998. xiv, 182p. 39.95 (0-8263-1854-1); pap. 17.95 (0-8263-1855-X) Univ. of New Mexico Pr.

Friedman, Bruce Jay. Stern. 2001. 192p. pap. 12.00 (0-8021-3750-4) Grove/Atlantic, Inc.

—Stern. mass mkt. 0.60 o.p. (0-451-02349-8, Signet Bks.) NAL.

Friedman, Carl. The Gray Lover: And Other Stories. Ringold, Jeanette K., tr. from DUT. 1988. 176p. 22.00 (0-89255-232-8) Persea Bks., Inc.

Friedman, Sashi. The Living Letters. 1996. (Illus.). (J). (gr. 1). 12.00 (0-8266-0369-6, Merkos L'Inyonei Chinuch) Kehot Pubn. Society.

Friedmann, Thomas. Hero-Azriel. 1979. 98p. pap. 6.00 o.p. (0-916288-07-2) Micah Pubns.

Fruchter, Yaakov. The Best of Olomeinu: Stories for All Year Round, Bk. 1. Scherman, Nosson, ed. 1981. (ArtScroll Youth Ser.). (Illus.). 160p. (YA). (gr. 5-12). 10.95 o.p. (0-89906-750-6) Mesorah Pubns., Ltd.

Fulford, Margaret & Sharp, Aaron J. The Leafy Hepaticae of Mexico: One Hundred & Twenty-Seven Years After C. M. Gottsche. 1990. (Memoirs Ser.: No. 63). 86p. pap. text 13.00 (0-89327-361-9) New York Botanical Garden, The.

Furst, Peter. Don Quixote in Exile. 1996. (Jewish Lives Ser.). 210p. (C). 64.00 (0-8101-1447-X); pap. 21.00 (0-8101-1448-8) Northwestern Univ. Pr.

Gabay, Taity. Bonjour Bijoux. 1992. 350p. pap. text (0-9632052-0-X) Cliffrose Pubns.

Gallant, Janet. My Brother's Bar Mitzvah. 1990. (Illus.). 32p. (J). (ps-3). 8.95 (0-929371-20-8); pap. 4.95 o.p. (0-929371-21-6) Kar-Ben Publishing.

Gallanter, Marty. A Little Lower Than the Angels. 1999. E-Book 9.99 (1-929429-05-3); E-Book 11.99 (1-929429-13-4); E-Book 9.99 o.p. (1-929429-14-2) Dead End Street, LLC.

—A Little Lower Than the Angels. Mrazovich, Christine & Rutledge, John P., eds. rev. ed. 2000. 398p. pap. 14.99 (*1-929429-51-7*) Dead End Street, LLC.

Gantz, David. Davey's Hanukkah Golem. 1991. (Illus.). 32p. (J). (gr. k-3). 14.95 o.p. (*0-8276-0380-0*) Jewish Pubn. Society.

Ganz, Yaffa. Savta Simcha & the Cinnamon Tree. 1983. (Illus.). (J). (gr. 6-10). 14.95 (*0-87306-354-6*) Feldheim, Philipp Inc.

—Savta Simcha & the Incredible Shabbes Bag. 1980. (Illus.). (J). (gr. 1-5). 14.95 (*0-87306-187-X*) Feldheim, Philipp Inc.

—The Terrible Wonderful Day. 1986. (Illus.). 11.95 (*0-87306-423-2*) Feldheim, Philipp Inc.

—The Travels & Tales of Dr. Emanuel J. Mitzva. 2003. (J). 14.95 (*1-58330-581-5*) Feldheim Pubs.

Gee, Maurice. Live Bodies. 1998. 264p. (*0-14-027380-8*) Penguin Bks. Canada, Ltd.

Gellhorn, Martha. Point of No Return. 1995. 333p. pap. 12.00 (*0-8032-7051-8*) Univ. of Nebraska Pr.

Gellin, William. Strangers No More. 1986. 192p. 11.95 o.p. (*0-88400-121-0*, Shengold Bks.) Schreiber Publishing, Inc.

Gellman, Ellie. Justin's Hebrew Name. 1988. (Illus.). 32p. (J). (gr. k-3). pap. 4.95 o.p. (*0-930494-78-4*) Kar-Ben Publishing.

—Shai's Shabbat Walk. 1985. (Illus.). 12p. (J). (ps). bds. 4.95 o.p. (*0-930494-49-0*) Kar-Ben Publishing.

—Tamar's Sukkah. 1988. (Illus.). 32p. (J). (ps-2). pap. 4.95 o.p. (*0-930494-79-2*) Kar-Ben Publishing.

Geras, Adele. Golden Windows: And Other Stories of Jerusalem. 1993. (Willa Perlman Bks.). 160p. (J). (gr. 3-7). 14.95 o.p. (*0-06-022941-1*); lib. bdg. 13.89 o.p. (*0-06-022942-X*) HarperCollins Children's Bk. Group.

—Voyage. 1983. 12.95 o.s.i (*0-689-30955-4*, Atheneum) Simon & Schuster Children's Publishing.

Gerber, Merrill J. Handsome As Anything. 1992. 176p. (YA). pap. 2.95 o.p. (*0-590-43020-3*, Scholastic Paperbacks) Scholastic, Inc.

Gerber, Merrill Joan. Also Known as Sadzia! The Belly Dancer! 1987. 192p. (YA). (gr. 7 up). lib. bdg. 12.89 o.p. (*0-06-022163-1*) HarperCollins Children's Bk. Group.

—Anna in the Afterlife: A Novel. 2001. (Library of Modern Jewish Literature). 130p. pap. 22.95 (*0-8156-0699-0*) Syracuse Univ. Pr.

Gerchunoff, Alberto. Jewish Gauchos of the Pampas. de Pereda, Prudencio, tr. from SPA. 1998. (Jewish Latin America Ser.). xxx, 149p. pap. 18.95 (*0-8263-1767-7*) Univ. of New Mexico Pr.

Gilbert, Peter. Laughter in a Dark Wood. 2002. 224p. pap. 13.95 (*1-899235-12-4*) Lewis, Dewi Publishing GBR. *Dist:* Consortium Bk. Sales & Distribution.

Gille, Elisabeth. Shadows of a Childhood: A Novel of War & Friendship. Coverdale, Linda, tr. 1999. (Illus.). 144p. pap. text 12.95 (*1-56584-528-5*) New Pr., The.

Gille, Elisabeth. Shadows of a Childhood: A Novel of War & Friendship. Coverdale, Linda, tr. from FRE. 1998. 144p. text 23.00 (*1-56584-388-6*) New Pr., The.

Ginsburg, Marvell. The Tattooed Torah. 1994. (Illus.). 32p. (J). (gr. 4-7). 11.95 (*0-8074-0252-4*, 104030) UAHC Pr.

Glenn, Mel. Squeeze Play. 1989. 12.95 o.p. (*0-89919-859-7*) Houghton Mifflin Co.

Gold, Margery. Happy Hanukkah: A Look & Find Book. 1996. (Look-Look Bks.). (Illus.). 24p. (J). (ps-3). pap. 3.29 o.s.i (*0-307-12887-3*, Golden Bks.) Random Hse. Children's Bks.

Gold, Michael. Jews Without Money. 1996. 320p. pap. 11.95 (*0-7867-0370-9*, Carroll & Graf Pubs.) Avalon Publishing Group.

—Jews Without Money. l.t. ed. 1996. 475p. text 27.95 (*1-56000-543-2*) ISIS Large Print Bks. GBR. *Dist:* Transaction Pubs.

—Jews Without Money. pap. o.p. (*0-87140-129-0*) Liveright Publishing Corp.

—Jews Without Money. 1981. pap. 0.95 o.p. (*0-380-01309-6*, 29520-2, Avon Bks.) Morrow/Avon.

Goldberg, Myla. Bee Season. pap. (*0-385-72882-4*) Knopf Publishing Group.

—Bee Season, 7 cass. 2002. audio 29.99 (*1-4025-0217-6*, 00624) Recorded Bks., LLC.

—Bee Season: A Novel. 2000. E-Book 18.50 (*1-58945-543-6*) Adobe Systems, Inc.

—Bee Season: A Novel. 2001. E-Book 18.50 (*0-385-50209-5*); 2000. 288p. 22.95 o.s.i (*0-385-49879-9*) Doubleday Publishing.

—Bee Season: A Novel. 2001. 288p. reprint ed. pap. 13.00 (*0-385-49880-2*, Knopf Bks. for Young Readers) Random Hse. Children's Bks.

—Bee Season: A Novel. l.t. ed. 2000. (Americana Ser.). (Illus.). 494p. pap. 28.95 (*0-7862-2544-0*) Thorndike Pr.

Goldin, Barbara Diamond. The Magician's Visit: A Passover Tale. 1995. 10.19 o.p. (*0-606-07827-4*) Turtleback Bks.

—Night Lights: A Sukkot Story. 1995. (Illus.). 32p. (J). (ps-3). 15.00 o.s.i (*0-15-200536-6*, Gulliver Bks.) Harcourt Children's Bks.

—Night Lights: A Sukkot Story. 2002. (Illus.). (J). (ps-3). 2.00 (*0-8074-0803-4*) UAHC Pr.

Goldreich, Gloria. Ten Traditional Jewish Children's Stories. 1996. (Illus.). 48p. (J). (gr. 1-4). 16.95 (*0-943706-69-6*) Pitspopany Pr.

—That Year of Our War. l.t. ed. 1994. pap. 21.95 (*1-56895-081-0*, Wheeler Publishing, Inc.) Gale Group.

—That Year of Our War. 1994. 356p. 22.95 o.p. (*0-316-31943-0*) Little Brown & Co.

Goldshlag-Cooks, Roberta. Gittel & the Bell. 1987. (Illus.). (J). (gr. k-4). 8.95 o.p. (*0-930494-68-7*) Kar-Ben Publishing.

Goldsmith, Andrea. The Prosperous Thief. 2002. 291p. (*1-86508-756-4*) Allen & Unwin Pty., Ltd.

Goldsmith, Milton. Rabbi & Priest. 2000. 252p. E-Book 3.95 (*0-594-03353-5*) 1873 Pr.

Goldstein, Rebecca. Mazel. 1996. 368p. pap. 12.95 o.s.i (*0-14-023905-7*, Penguin Bks.) Penguin Group (USA) Inc.

—Mazel. 2002. (Library of American Fiction). 368p. pap. 19.95 (*0-299-18124-3*) Univ. of Wisconsin Pr.

—Mazel. 1995. 368p. 23.95 o.s.i (*0-670-85648-7*, Viking) Viking Penguin.

Goliger, Gabriella. Song of Ascent. 2001. 177p. pap. (*1-55192-374-2*) Raincoast Bk. Distribution.

Goodman, Allegra. Kaaterskill Falls. 1999. 336p. pap. 13.95 (*0-385-32390-5*, Delta) Dell Publishing.

—Kaaterskill Falls. l.t. ed. 1999. (Americana Ser.). 576p. 29.95 (*0-7862-1863-0*) Thorndike Pr.

Goran, Lester. Outlaws of the Purple Cow & Other Stories. 1999. 358p. pap. 35.00 (*0-87338-639-6*) Kent State Univ. Pr.

Gordon, Noah. The Last Jew. 2000. 348p. 24.95 (*0-312-26504-2*) St. Martin's Pr.

Granit, Arthur. I Am from Brownsville. 1985. (Illus.). 271p. 16.95 (*0-8022-2456-3*) Philosophical Library, Inc.

Grant, Linda. Still Here. 2001. 320p. (*0-316-85995-8*); pap. (*0-316-85993-1*) Little Brown & Co.

—Still Here. l.t. ed. 2003. (Charnwood Large Print Ser.). 480p. 32.50 (*0-7089-9421-0*) Thorpe, F. A. Pubs. GBR. *Dist:* Ulverscroft Large Print Bks., Ltd., Ulverscroft Large Print Canada, Ltd.

—When I Lived in Modern Times. 2001. (Illus.). 288p. 23.95 o.s.i (*0-525-94594-6*) Dutton/Plume.

—When I Lived in Modern Times. l.t. ed. 2001. (Women's Fiction Ser.). 399p. 28.95 (*0-7862-3396-6*) Thorndike Pr.

Graubart, Philip. Planet of the Jews. 1999. 206p. pap. 13.95 (*0-88739-186-9*) Creative Arts Bk. Co.

Gray, Elmer L. Furious & Free. 1984. (J). (gr. 10 up). 7.95 o.p. (*0-8054-7320-3*) Broadman & Holman Pubs.

Greenberg, Joanne. The King's Persons. 1985. 288p. pap. o.p. (*0-03-005623-3*, Owl Bks.) Holt, Henry & Co.

Greene, Jacqueline Dembar. Out of Many Waters. (J). (gr. 5 up). 1993. 208p. pap. 8.95 (*0-8027-7401-6*); 1988. 16.95 (*0-8027-6811-3*) Walker & Co.

Grekova, I. Svezho Predanie: Roman. 1995. (RUS.). 216p. (Orig.). pap. 12.00 o.s.i (*1-55779-084-1*) Hermitage Pubs.

Gross, Sukey S. Passport to Russia. 1989. (Girls of Riukah Gross Academy Ser.). (Illus.). 158p. (J). (gr. 5-8). 13.95 (*0-935063-59-5*, CJR108H); pap. 10.95 (*0-935063-60-9*, CJR108S) CIS Communications, Inc.

Grynberg, Henryk. The Jewish War & the Victory. Lourie, Richard & Wieniewska, Celina, trs. from POL. 2001. (Jewish Lives Ser.). 152p. text 49.95 (*0-8101-1901-3*) Northwestern Univ. Pr.

—The Jewish War & the Victory. Wieniewska, Celina & Lourie, Richard, trs. from POL. 2001. (Jewish Lives Ser.). 152p. reprint ed. pap. 15.95 (*0-8101-1785-1*) Northwestern Univ. Pr.

Gurewich, David. Travels with Duvinsky & Cline. 1987. 16.95 o.p. (*0-670-81621-3*) Viking Penguin.

Guttmann, B. J. Magdalene. 1996. 231 p. (*1-85863-742-2*) Minerva Pr. GBR. *Dist:* Unity Distribution.

Haber, Leo. The Red Heifer: A Novel. 2001. (New York City History & Culture Ser.). x, 289p. 24.95 (*0-8156-0692-3*) Syracuse Univ. Pr.

Halevi, Z'ev ben Shimon. The Annointed: A Kabbalistic Novel. 2001. (Illus.). 256p. pap. 16.95 (*1-57863-228-5*, Red Wheel) Red Wheel/Weiser.

Halpern, Chaiky. The House on Kyverdale Road. 1995. 16.95 (*0-87306-737-1*); pap. 12.95 (*0-87306-738-X*) Feldheim, Philipp Inc.

Halter, Marek. The Book of Abraham. Blair, Lowell, tr. 1987. 704p. mass mkt. 4.95 o.s.i (*0-440-10841-1*) Dell Publishing.

—The Book of Abraham. Blair, Lowell, tr. 1986. 768p. o.p. (*0-03-071887-2*) Holt, Henry & Co.

—The Book of Abraham. 2003. 600p. pap. (*1-59264-039-7*) Toby Pr.

Hamill, Pete. Snow in August. 2001. 17.95 (*1-56511-626-7*) HighBridge Co.

—Snow in August. 1997. 304p. 23.95 o.p. (*0-316-34094-4*) Little Brown & Co.

—Snow in August. l.t. ed. (Thorndike/G. K. Hall Paperback Bestsellers Ser.). 507p. 1998. pap. 25.95 o.p. (*0-7862-1222-5*); 1997. 28.95 (*0-7862-1221-7*) Thorndike Pr.

—Snow in August. 1999. 20.05 (*0-606-20074-6*) Turtleback Bks.

—Snow in August. reprint ed. 1999. 384p. pap. 14.00 (*0-446-67525-3*); 1998. 400p. mass mkt. 7.99 (*0-446-60625-1*) Warner Bks., Inc.

Hanauer, Cathi. My Sister's Bones. 1997. 272p. pap. 14.95 (*0-385-31704-2*) Doubleday Publishing.

Handler, Daniel. Watch Your Mouth. 2000. 232p. 23.95 (*0-312-20940-1*) St. Martin's Pr.

Harris, Rosemary. Summers of the Wild Rose. 1988. 188p. (YA). 11.95 o.p. (*0-571-14702-X*) Faber & Faber, Inc.

Hart, Jan S. Hanna, the Immigrant. Roberts, Melissa, ed. 1991. (Illus.). 114p. (J). (gr. 6-8). 12.95 o.p. (*0-89015-805-3*) Eakin Pr.

Harvey, Brett. Immigrant Girl: Becky of Eldridge Street. 1987. (Illus.). 40p. (J). (ps-3). tchr. ed. 15.95 o.p. (*0-8234-0638-5*) Holiday Hse., Inc.

Hautzig, Esther. Riches. (J). 1994. 48p. (gr. 4-7). pap. 3.95 o.p. (*0-06-440550-8*); 1992. (Illus.). 32p. (gr. 3 up). lib. bdg. 13.89 o.p. (*0-06-022260-3*) HarperCollins Children's Bk. Group.

Hautzig, Esther, tr. from YID. The Seven Good Years & Other Stories of I. L. Peretz. 1984. (Illus.). 96p. (J). (gr. 3-6). 10.95 o.p. (*0-8276-0244-8*) Jewish Pubn. Society.

Head, Constance. Isaiah: The Prophet Prince. 1988. 384p. (Orig.). (J). (ps-6). pap. 4.50 o.p. (*0-8423-1751-1*) Tyndale Hse. Pubs.

Heller, Joseph. Good As Gold. 1979. (gr. 12). pap. 2.95 o.s.i (*0-671-82388-4*, Pocket) Simon & Schuster.

Helmreich, Helaine. The Chimney Tree. 2003. 506p. 19.95 (*1-59264-031-1*) Toby Pr.

—The Chimney Tree. 2000. 296p. 24.95 (*0-87081-562-8*) Univ. Pr. of Colorado.

Herman, Ben. The Rhapsody in Blue of Mickey Klein. 1981. 144p. (J). (gr. 7 up). 8.95 o.p. (*0-916144-68-2*) Stemmer Hse. Pubs., Inc.

Herman, Charlotte. The House of Walenska Street. annuals 1998. (Puffin Chapters Ser.). (Illus.). 96p. (J). (gr. 2-5). pap. 3.99 o.p. (*0-14-130129-5*, Puffin Bks.) Penguin Putnam Bks. for Young Readers.

—What Happened to Heather Hopkowitz? 1985. 192p. (J). (gr. 3-6). 10.75 o.p. (*0-525-42455-5*, 01044-310, Dutton) Dutton/Plume.

—What Happened to Heather Hopkowitz? 1994. 186p. (J). (gr. 4 up). pap. 9.95 (*0-8276-0520-X*) Jewish Pubn. Society.

Herzl, Theodor. Old New Land. Kornberg, Jacques, ed. Levensohn, Lotta, tr. from GER. 1997. Tr. of Altneuland. (Illus.). 325p. (C). reprint ed. pap. text 18.95 (*1-55876-160-8*) Wiener, Markus Pubs., Inc.

—Old New Land. Sarna, Jonathan D., ed. 2nd ed. 1987. (Masterworks of Modern Jewish Writings).Tr. of Altneuland. (Illus.). 220p. (C). reprint ed. 19.95 o.p. (*0-910129-64-9*); pap. 16.95 o.p. (*0-910129-61-4*) Wiener, Markus Pubs., Inc.

Hest, Amy. Fancy Aunt Jess. 1990. (Illus.). (J). lib. bdg. 12.88 o.p. (*0-688-08097-9*, Morrow, William & Co.) Morrow/Avon.

—The Private Notebook of Katie Roberts, Age 11. 1996. (Illus.). 80p. (J). (gr. 4-7). bds. 4.99 o.s.i (*1-56402-859-3*) Candlewick Pr.

—When Jessie Came Across the Sea. (Illus.). 40p. 2003. bds. 6.99 (*0-7636-1274-X*); 1997. (J). (gr. 1-7). 16.99 (*0-7636-0094-6*) Candlewick Pr.

Heym, Stefan. Queen Against Defoe & Other Stories. 1974. (Illus.). 128p. 6.95 o.p. (*0-88208-041-5*, Hill, Lawrence Bks.) Chicago Review Pr., Inc.

Heymsfeld, Carla. The Matzah Ball Fairy. 1996. (Illus.). 32p. (J). (ps-3). 12.95 (*0-8074-0600-7*, 101070) UAHC Pr.

Hirsh, Marilyn. Joseph Who Loved the Sabbath. 1988. (Illus.). 32p. (J). (ps-3). pap. 4.99 o.s.i (*0-14-050670-5*, Puffin Bks.) Penguin Putnam Bks. for Young Readers.

—Where Is Yonkele? 1988. 32p. (J). (ps-1). pap. 6.95 o.p. (*0-8276-0294-4*) Jewish Pubn. Society.

Hoban, Russell. Pilgermann. 1986. mass mkt. 2.95 o.s.i (*0-671-61893-8*, Pocket) Simon & Schuster.

—Pilgermann. 1983. 13.50 o.p. (*0-671-45968-6*) Summit Bks.

Hoffman, Allen. Big League Dreams. 1997. (Small Worlds Ser.). 296p. 24.95 (*0-7892-0191-7*) Abbeville Pr., Inc.

—Kagan's Superfecta & Other Stories. 304p. 2000. pap. 15.95 (*0-7892-0686-2*); 1983. 12.95 o.p. (*0-89659-234-0*); 1983. pap. 100.00 o.p. (*0-89659-271-5*) Abbeville Pr., Inc.

—Small Worlds: A Novel. 1996. (Small Worlds Ser.). 280p. 24.95 (*0-7892-0129-1*) Abbeville Pr., Inc.

—Two for the Devil. 256p. (J). 2000. pap. 12.95 (*0-7892-0641-2*); 1998. (Illus.). 24.95 (*0-7892-0397-9*) Abbeville Pr., Inc. (Abbeville Kids).

Hoffman, Roy. Almost Family. 1983. 256p. 14.95 o.p. (*0-385-27664-8*) Doubleday Publishing.

—Almost Family. 2000. (Deep South Book Ser.). 248p. pap. 16.95 (*0-8173-1031-2*) Univ. of Alabama Pr.

Hoffmann, Yoel. Katschen & The Book of Joseph. Kriss, David et al, trs. from HEB. 1998. 160p. 17.95 (*0-8112-1373-0*); 1999. 161p. reprint ed. pap. 11.95 (*0-8112-1405-2*, NDP875) New Directions Publishing Corp.

Holland, Isabelle. Crazy in Love. 1988. (Orig.). mass mkt. 2.95 o.p. (*0-449-70189-1*, Fawcett) Ballantine Bks.

Holmes, Mary Z. Dear Dad. 1992. (History's Children Ser.). (Illus.). 48p. (J). (gr. 4-5). pap. o.p. (*0-8114-6428-8*); lib. bdg. 21.36 o.p. (*0-8114-3503-2*) Raintree Pubs.

Horn, Dara. In the Image. 2003. 288p. (Illus.). 24.95 (*0-393-05106-4*); pap. 13.95 (*0-393-32526-1*) Norton, W. W. & Co., Inc.

Howe, Irving & Greenberg, Eliezer. A Treasury of Yiddish Stories. 1954. 6.95 o.p. (*0-670-72740-7*) Viking Penguin.

Howe, Irving & Greenberg, Eliezer, eds. A Treasury of Yiddish Stories. rev. ed. 1990. 688p. reprint ed. pap. 19.95 o.s.i (*0-14-014419-6*, Penguin Bks.) Penguin Group (USA) Inc.

—A Treasury of Yiddish Stories. rev. ed. 1989. 688p. 29.95 o.p. (*0-670-83037-2*) Viking Penguin.

Hubner, Carol K. The Haunted Shul. 1979. (Judaica Youth Ser.). (Illus.). (J). (gr. 3-8). 7.95 o.p. (*0-910818-14-2*) Judaica Pr., Inc., The.

—The Tattered Tallis. 1979. (Judaica Youth Ser.). (Illus.). 128p. (J). (gr. 3-8). 5.95 o.p. (*0-910818-19-3*) Judaica Pr., Inc., The.

—The Twisted Menorah & Other Devora Doresh Mysteries. 1981. 7.95 o.p. (*0-910818-41-X*); pap. 9.95 (*0-910818-42-8*) Judaica Pr., Inc., The.

—The Whispering Mezuzah. 1979. (Judaica Youth Ser.). (Illus.). (J). (gr. 3-9). 6.95 o.p. (*0-910818-18-5*) Judaica Pr., Inc., The.

Hull, Eleanor. Summer People. 1984. 11.95 o.s.i (*0-689-31037-4*, Atheneum) Simon & Schuster Children's Publishing.

Humphreys, Helen. Leaving Earth. 1998. 224p. 22.00 o.s.i (*0-8050-5957-1*, Metropolitan Bks.) Holt, Henry & Co.

—Leaving Earth. 2000. 256p. pap. 13.00 (*0-312-25500-4*) Picador.

Hurwitz, Johanna. Faraway Summer. 1998. (Illus.). 160p. (J). (gr. 3-7). 14.95 (*0-688-15334-8*) HarperCollins Children's Bk. Group.

—Once I Was a Plum Tree. ALC Staff, ed. 1992. (Illus.). 160p. (J). (gr. 4-7). pap. 4.95 o.s.i (*0-688-11848-8*, Harper Trophy) HarperCollins Children's Bk. Group.

—Once I Was a Plum Tree. 1980. (Illus.). 160p. (J). (gr. 4-6). lib. bdg. 12.93 o.p. (*0-688-32223-9*, Morrow, William & Co.) Morrow/Avon.

—The Rabbi's Girls. 1982. Orig. Title: The Diddakoi. (Illus.). 192p. (J). (gr. 4-6). 15.00 o.p. (*0-688-01089-X*, Morrow, William & Co.) Morrow/Avon.

—The Rabbi's Girls. 1989. Orig. Title: The Diddakoi. (Illus.). 160p. (J). (gr. 3-7). pap. 4.99 o.p. (*0-14-032951-X*, Puffin Bks.) Penguin Putnam Bks. for Young Readers.

Hyde, Catherine R. Funerals for Horses. 1997. (Emerging Writers Ser.). 256p. 19.95 (*0-9653524-3-9*) Russian Hill Pr.

Isaacs, Susan. Lily White. 1996. 480p. 25.00 o.p. (*0-06-017607-5*) HarperCollins Pubs.

—Lily White. l.t. ed. 1997. 656p. mass mkt. 7.99 (*0-06-109309-2*, HarperTorch) Morrow/Avon.

—Lily White. l.t. ed. (Paperback Bestsellers Ser.). 738p. 1997. pap. 27.95 (*0-7862-0829-5*); 1996. 28.95 o.p. (*0-7862-0828-7*) Thorndike Pr.

—Red, White & Blue. unabr. ed. 1999. audio 83.95 (*0-7861-1519-X*, 2369) Blackstone Audio Bks., Inc.

—Red, White & Blue. 1998. 416p. 25.00 o.s.i (*0-06-017608-3*) HarperCollins Pubs.

—Red, White & Blue. abr. ed. 1998. audio 25.00 (*0-694-51982-0*, 696054, HarperAudio) HarperTrade.

—Red, White & Blue. abr. ed. 1999. audio 25.00 Highsmith Inc.

—Red, White & Blue. l.t. ed. (Thorndike/G. K. Hall Paperback Bestsellers Ser.). 749p. 2000. pap. 27.95 (*0-7862-1742-1*); 1999. 30.95 (*0-7862-1741-3*) Thorndike Pr.

—Red, White & Blue: A Novel. 1999. 592p. mass mkt. 6.99 (*0-06-109310-6*, HarperTorch) Morrow/Avon.

Isler, Alan. Op. Non Cit: Four Tales. 1997. 215p. (*0-224-04386-2*) Cape, Jonathan Ltd. GBR. *Dist:* National Geographic Society, Trafalgar Square.

Issaroff, Penina. Kindergarten Carousel. 1993. (Illus.). (J). (ps). bds. 12.95 (*0-943706-12-2*) Pitspopany Pr.

Jacobs, Chana R. Elimelech Wakes Up. 1993. (Illus.). 32p. (J). (ps-3). 9.95 (*0-922613-54-0*); pap. 6.95 (*0-922613-55-9*) Hachai Publishing.

Jaffe, Daniel M. The Limits of Pleasure: A Novel. 2001. 172p. pap. 14.95 (*1-56023-373-7*); lib. bdg. 24.95 (*1-56023-372-9*) Haworth Pr., Inc., The. (Harrington Park Pr.).

Jagendorf, Zvi. Wolfy & the Strudelbakers. 2002. 192p. pap. 13.95 (*1-899235-38-8*) Lewis, Dewi Publishing GBR. *Dist:* Consortium Bk. Sales & Distribution.

Jones, Dennis. Winter Palace. 1988. 352p. 17.95 (*0-316-47295-6*) Little Brown & Co.

Jules, Jacqueline. Once upon a Shabbos. 1998. (Illus.). 32p. (J). (ps-2). pap. 6.95 (*1-58013-021-6*); 15.95 (*1-58013-020-8*) Kar-Ben Publishing.

Justus, James H., intro. Wilderness: A Tale of the Civil War. 2001. (Tennesseana Editions Ser.). (Illus.). xxii, 310p. reprint ed. pap. 19.50 (*1-57233-134-8*) Univ. of Tennessee Pr.

Kadish, Rachel. From a Sealed Room. 2000. 368p. pap. 13.95 (*0-425-17641-X*) Berkley Publishing Group.

—From a Sealed Room. 1998. 320p. 25.95 o.s.i (*0-399-14300-9*, G. P. Putnam's Sons) Penguin Group (USA) Inc.

Kahn, Sharon. Don't Cry for Me, Hot Pastrami. 2002. (Ruby, the Rabbi's Wife Mystery Ser.). 240p. reprint ed. mass mkt. 5.99 (*0-425-18715-2*, Prime Crime) Berkley Publishing Group.

—Don't Cry for Me, Hot Pastrami: A Ruby, the Rabbi's Wife Mystery. 2001. 304p. 24.00 o.s.i (*0-684-87155-6*); E-Book 24.00 (*0-7432-1825-6*) Simon & Schuster. (Scribner).

—Don't Cry for Me, Hot Pastrami: A Ruby, the Rabbi's Wife Mystery. l.t. ed. 2001. (G.K. Hall Large Print Core Ser.). 339p. 27.95 o.p. (*0-7838-9679-4*) Thorndike Pr.

—Fax Me a Bagel: A Ruby the Rabbi's Wife Mystery. 2001. 272p. mass mkt. 5.99 (*0-425-18046-8*) Berkley Publishing Group.

—Fax Me a Bagel: A Ruby the Rabbi's Wife Mystery. 1998. (Ruby, the Rabbi's Wife Mysteries Ser.). 256p. 22.00 (*0-684-84737-X*); 22.00 (*0-684-85498-8*) Simon & Schuster. (Scribner).

—Never Nosh a Matzo Ball: A Ruby the Rabbi's Wife Mystery. 2000. 304p. 22.00 o.s.i (*0-684-84738-8*, Scribner) Simon & Schuster.

Kalechofsky, Roberta. A Boy, a Chicken & the Lion of Judah: How Ari Became a Vegetarian. 1995. (Illus.). 45p. (J). (gr. 2-5). pap. 8.00 (*0-916288-39-0*) Micah Pubns.

—K'Tia, a Savior of the Jewish People. 1995. 234p. pap. 15.00 (*0-916288-41-2*) Micah Pubns.

Kane, Andrew. Rabbi, Rabbi. 1995. 306p. 22.95 o.p. (*0-312-11879-1*) St. Martin's Pr.

Kantor, Herman I. The Merchant of Groski: And Other Tales My Great Great Grandfather Might Tell About Life in a Ghetto of Russia in the Time of the Czars. 1993. 176p. (Orig.). 18.95 (*1-56474-034-X*); pap. 9.95 (*1-56474-035-8*) Fithian Pr.

Kantor, Herman I. & Larson, Eric. The Bear & the Baby: Still More Tales My Great-Great Grandfather Might Tell about Life in a Ghetto of Russia in the Time of the Czars. 1995. (Illus.). 192p. (Orig.). pap. 9.95 (*1-56474-118-4*); 18.95 (*1-56474-117-6*) Fithian Pr.

—The Matzo Mitzvah: Even More Tales My Great-Great-Grandfather Might Tell about Life in a Ghetto of Russia in the Time of the Czars. 1996. (Illus.). 192p. 18.95 (*1-56474-179-6*); 144p. pap. 9.95 (*1-56474-178-8*) Fithian Pr.

—The Miraculous Milk Cow: More Tales My Great, Great Grandfather Might Tell about Life in a Ghetto in Russia in the Time of the Czars. 1994. (Illus.). 176p. (Orig.). 18.95 (*1-56474-094-3*); pap. 9.95 (*1-56474-095-1*) Fithian Pr.

Karlins, Mark. Salmon Moon. 1993. (Illus.). (J). pap. 14.00 (*0-671-73624-8*, Simon & Schuster Children's Publishing) Simon & Schuster Children's Publishing.

Kasdan, Sara. So It Was Just a Simple Wedding. Date not set. 249p. pap. 14.95 (*1-57090-083-3*) aBOOKS Distributing.

Katchor, Ben. The Jew of New York: A Historical Romance. 1998. (Illus.). 104p. 20.00 o.s.i (*0-375-40104-0*) Random Hse., Inc.

Kaufman, Joseph. A Good, Protected Life. 1992. 166p. 19.95 o.s.i (*0-8027-1212-6*) Walker & Co.

Kaufman, Stephen. Does Anyone Here Know the Way to Thirteen?, 001. 1985. 157p. (YA). (gr. 5 up). 11.95 o.p. (*0-395-35974-0*) Houghton Mifflin Co.

Kay, Terry. Shadow Song. l.t. ed. 1994. (Wheeler Large Print Book Ser.). 473p. 25.95 (*1-56895-157-4*, Wheeler Publishing, Inc.) Gale Group.

—Shadow Song. Rosenman, Jane, ed. 1994. 400p. 20.00 o.p. (*0-671-89261-4*, Atria) Simon & Schuster.

—Shadow Song. Ng, Donna, ed. 1995. 400p. reprint ed. pap. 14.00 (*0-671-89260-6*, Washington Square Pr.) Simon & Schuster.

—Shadow Song. 388p. pap. 4.98 o.s.i (*0-7651-0607-8*) Smithmark Pubs., Inc.

Kaye-Kantrowitz, Melanie. My Jewish Face & Other Stories. 1990. 256p. (Orig.). lib. bdg. 19.95 (*0-933216-72-6*); pap. 9.95 (*0-933216-71-8*) Aunt Lute Bks.

Kaye, Marilyn. Mindy Wise. 1993. 144p. (J). (gr. 5). pap. 3.50 (*0-380-71879-0*, Avon Bks.) Morrow/Avon.

Kelly, Myra. Little Aliens. 1975. (Modern Jewish Experience Ser.). (Illus.). reprint ed. 26.95 (*0-405-06719-4*) Ayer Co. Pubs., Inc.

Kemelman, Harry. The Day the Rabbi Resigned. l.t. ed. 1993. (Large Print Mystery Ser.). 345p. 24.95 o.p. (*0-7927-1414-8*); pap. 19.95 o.p. (*0-7927-1413-X*) BBC Audiobooks America.

—The Day the Rabbi Resigned. 1992. mass mkt. 5.99 o.s.i (*0-449-21908-9*); 273p. 20.00 o.s.i (*0-449-90681-7*) Ballantine Bks. (Fawcett).

—The Day the Rabbi Resigned. 2004. 288p. mass mkt. 6.99 (*0-7434-7979-3*) ibooks, Inc.

—Friday the Rabbi Slept Late. 1993. pap. o.p. (*0-449-45127-5*); 1986. mass mkt. 5.99 o.s.i (*0-449-21180-0*) Ballantine Bks. (Fawcett).

—Friday the Rabbi Slept Late. l.t. ed. 1983. (General Ser.). 339p. lib. bdg. 13.95 o.p. (*0-8161-3537-1*, Macmillan Reference USA) Gale Group.

—Monday the Rabbi Took Off. 1988. mass mkt. o.s.i (*0-449-20785-4*); 1986. 288p. mass mkt. 5.99 o.s.i (*0-449-21001-4*, Fawcett); 1981. mass mkt. 2.50 o.s.i (*0-449-23872-5*, Fawcett) Ballantine Bks.

—Monday the Rabbi Took Off. 1972. 316p. 5.95 o.p. (*0-399-10550-6*) Putnam Publishing Group, The.

—Monday the Rabbi Took Off. 2002. 368p. pap. 6.99 (*0-7434-5271-2*) ibooks, Inc.

—One Fine Day the Rabbi Bought a Cross. 1988. (Boston Mysteries Ser.). mass mkt. 5.99 o.s.i (*0-449-20687-4*, Fawcett) Ballantine Bks.

—One Fine Day the Rabbi Bought a Cross. l.t. ed. 1988. (Large Print Bks.). 353p. 18.95 o.p. (*0-8161-4347-1*, Macmillan Reference USA) Gale Group.

—One Fine Day the Rabbi Bought a Cross. 1987. 234p. 15.95 o.p. (*0-688-05631-8*, Morrow, William & Co.) Morrow/Avon.

—One Fine Day the Rabbi Bought a Cross. 1990. 3.99 o.p. (*0-517-05752-2*) Random Hse. Value Publishing.

—One Fine Day the Rabbi Bought a Cross. 2003. 320p. pap. 6.99 (*0-7434-7478-3*) ibooks, Inc.

—Saturday the Rabbi Went Hungry. 1987. 224p. mass mkt. 5.99 o.s.i (*0-449-21392-7*, Fawcett) Ballantine Bks.

—Saturday the Rabbi Went Hungry. 1988. 4.95 o.s.i (*0-517-01307-X*) Crown Publishing Group.

—Saturday the Rabbi Went Hungry. l.t. ed. 1983. 14.95 o.p. (*0-8161-3531-2*, Macmillan Reference USA) Gale Group.

—Someday the Rabbi Will Leave. 1986. 288p. mass mkt. 5.99 o.s.i (*0-449-20945-8*, Fawcett) Ballantine Bks.

—Someday the Rabbi Will Leave. 1985. 264p. 15.95 o.p. (*0-688-04174-4*, Morrow, William & Co.) Morrow/Avon.

—Someday the Rabbi Will Leave. 2003. 288p. pap. 6.99 (*0-7434-5911-3*) ibooks, Inc.

—Sunday the Rabbi Stayed Home. Date not set. mass mkt. (*0-449-20784-6*); 1985. 224p. mass mkt. 5.99 o.s.i (*0-449-21000-6*) Ballantine Bks. (Fawcett).

—Sunday the Rabbi Stayed Home. l.t. ed. 1977. (General Ser.). 420p. lib. bdg. 11.95 o.p. (*0-8161-6499-1*, Macmillan Reference USA) Gale Group.

—Sunday the Rabbi Stayed Home. 2002. (Rabbi Small Mystery Ser.). (Illus.). 304p. pap. 6.99 (*0-7434-5238-0*) ibooks, Inc.

—That Day the Rabbi Left Town. (Rabbi Small Mystery Ser.). 1997. 263p. mass mkt. 5.99 o.s.i (*0-449-22570-4*); 1996. 256p. 22.00 o.s.i (*0-449-91002-4*); 1996. 233p. lib. bdg. 22.95 (*1-57490-040-4*) Ballantine Bks. (Fawcett).

—Thursday the Rabbi Walked Out. 1986. mass mkt. 5.99 o.s.i (*0-449-21157-6*, Fawcett) Ballantine Bks.

—Thursday the Rabbi Walked Out. 2003. 256p. mass mkt. 6.99 (*0-7434-5860-5*) ibooks, Inc.

—Tuesday the Rabbi Saw Red. 1986. (Rabbi Ser.). mass mkt. 5.99 o.s.i (*0-449-21321-8*, Fawcett) Ballantine Bks.

—Tuesday the Rabbi Saw Red. 1974. (Adult Ser.). 508p. reprint ed. lib. bdg. 11.95 o.p. (*0-8161-6230-1*, Macmillan Reference USA) Gale Group.

—Tuesday the Rabbi Saw Red. 2003. 352p. pap. 6.99 (*0-7434-4534-1*) ibooks, Inc.

—Wednesday the Rabbi Got Wet. 1986. (Rabbi Ser.). mass mkt. 5.99 o.s.i (*0-449-21328-5*, Fawcett) Ballantine Bks.

Kertes, Joseph & Perko, Peter. The Gift. 1995. (Illus.). 48p. (J). (gr. 1 up). text 12.95 (*0-88899-235-1*) Groundwood Bks. CAN. *Dist:* Publishers Group West.

Kertesz, Imre. Kaddish for a Child Not Born. Wilson, Christopher C. & Wilson, Katharina M., trs. from HUN. 1999. 95p. pap. 14.95 (*0-8101-1161-6*, Hydra Bks.) Northwestern Univ. Pr.

—Kaddish for a Child Not Born. Wilson, Christopher C. & Wilson, Katharine M., trs. 1997. 95p. 24.95 (*0-8101-1176-4*, Hydra Bks.) Northwestern Univ. Pr.

Kessler, Raizy. A Tale of Two Wagons & Other Chanuka Stories. 1994. 171p. (J). (gr. 5-9). 13.95 (*1-56062-287-3*, CYT103H) CIS Communications, Inc.

Kirchheimer, Gloria DeVidas. Goodbye, Evil Eye. 2000. xvii, 150p. 21.95 (*0-8419-1404-4*) Holmes & Meier Pubs., Inc.

Kirshenbaum, Binnie. An Almost Perfect Moment: A Novel. 2004. 288p. 23.95 (*0-06-052086-8*, Ecco) HarperTrade.

—Hester among the Ruins: A Novel. 2002. 288p. 24.95 (*0-393-04152-2*) Norton, W. W. & Co., Inc.

—Pure Poetry. 208p. 2002. pap. 14.95 (*0-7432-4182-7*); 2000. 22.00 o.s.i (*0-684-86471-1*) Simon & Schuster. (Simon & Schuster).

Klein, A. M. The Second Scroll. Popham, Elizabeth A. & Pollock, Zailig, eds. 1999. (Illus.). 594p. text (*0-8020-4478-6*) Univ. of Toronto Pr.

Kluger, Steve. Last Days of Summer. 1998. 348p. 21.00 (*0-380-97645-5*, Avon Bks.) Morrow/Avon.

—Last Days of Summer. 1999. 18.05 (*0-606-19266-2*) Turtleback Bks.

—The Last Days of Summer. 1999. 368p. reprint ed. pap. 13.00 (*0-380-79763-1*, Avon Bks.) Morrow/Avon.

Kohler, Sheila. Children of Pithiviers. 2001. 224p. 22.00 (*1-58195-032-2*, Zoland Bks., Inc.) Steerforth Pr.

Konecky, Edith. Allegra Maud Goldman. 1990. (Illus.). 160p. pap. 12.95 o.p. (*1-55861-022-7*); 2nd ed. 2001. 187p. pap. 14.95 (*1-55861-281-5*) Feminist Pr. at The City Univ. of New York.

—Allegra Maud Goldman. 1976. 160p. 7.95 o.p. (*0-06-012452-0*) HarperCollins Pubs.

—Allegra Maud Goldman. 1987. (Gems of American Jewish Literature Ser.). 150p. pap. 7.95 o.p. (*0-8276-0282-0*) Jewish Pubn. Society.

Kornblatt, Joyce R. The Reason for Wings. 1999. (Library of Modern Jewish Literature). 233p. 24.95 (*0-8156-0578-1*) Syracuse Univ. Pr.

Kosman, Miriam. Red Blue & Yellow Yarn: A Tale of Forgiveness. 1996. (Illus.). 32p. (J). (ps-1). 9.95 (*0-922613-78-8*) Hachai Publishing.

Koss, Amy Goldman. How I Saved Hanukkah. 1998. (Illus.). 96p. (J). (gr. 2-5). 15.99 (*0-8037-2241-9*, Dial Bks. for Young Readers) Penguin Putnam Bks. for Young Readers.

Kossoff, David. A Small Town Is a World. 1979. 8.95 o.p. (*0-312-72985-5*) St. Martin's Pr.

Kotlowitz, Robert. His Master's Voice. 1992. 21.00 o.s.i (*0-679-40868-1*) Knopf, Alfred A. Inc.

Kranzler, Gershon. The Broken Bracelet. 1967. 218p. (YA). reprint ed. 12.00 (*0-8266-0367-X*, Merkos L'Inyonei Chinuch) Kehot Pubn. Society.

Kress, Camille. Tot Shabbat. 1997. (Illus.). 6p. (J). (ps-k). bds. 5.95 (*0-8074-0607-4*, 102005) UAHC Pr.

Krich, Rochelle Majer. Blues in the Night. 352p. 2003. mass mkt. 6.99 (*0-449-00726-X*); 2002. 23.95 (*0-345-44971-1*, Ballantine Bks.) Ballantine Bks.

—Blues in the Night. 2003. (Women's Fiction Ser.). 29.95 (*0-7862-5188-3*) Thorndike Pr.

—Shadows of Sin. 2001. (Jessie Drake Mysteries Ser.). 352p. 25.00 (*0-380-97770-2*, Morrow, William & Co.) Morrow/Avon.

Krulik, Nancy E. Penny & the Four Questions. 1993. (Read with Me Ser.). (Illus.). 32p. (J). (ps-3). mass mkt. 3.25 (*0-590-46339-X*) Scholastic, Inc.

Kushner, Donn. Uncle Jacob's Ghost Story, ERS. 1986. 144p. (J). (gr. 4-9). o.p. (*0-03-006502-X*, Holt, Henry & Co. Bks. For Young Readers) Holt, Henry & Co.

Lakin, Patricia. Don't Forget. 1994. (Illus.). 32p. (J). 14.00 o.p. (*0-688-12075-X*); lib. bdg. 13.93 (*0-688-12076-8*) Morrow/Avon. (Morrow, William & Co.).

Langer, Adam. Crossing California. 2004. 24.95 (*1-57322-274-7*, Riverhead Bks. (Hardcovers)) Putnam Publishing Group, The.

Langley, Lee. Distant Music. 2003. 322p. 22.00 (*1-57131-040-1*) Milkweed Editions.

Lasky, Kathryn. The Night Journey. 1986. (J). 12.95 o.p. (*0-670-80935-7*, Viking Children's Bks.); (Illus.). 160p. (gr. 4-7). pap. 5.99 (*0-14-032048-2*, Puffin Bks.) Penguin Putnam Bks. for Young Readers.

—The Night Journey. 2002. (YA). (gr. 6 up). 20.25 (*0-8446-7210-6*) Smith, Peter Pub., Inc.

—Pageant. 1988. 240p. (J). (gr. k-12). mass mkt. 3.95 o.s.i (*0-440-20161-6*, Laurel Leaf) Random Hse. Children's Bks.

—Pageant. 1986. 240p. (YA). (gr. 7 up). lib. bdg. 14.95 o.p. (*0-02-751720-9*, Simon & Schuster Children's Publishing) Simon & Schuster Children's Publishing.

Lazar, Zachary. Aaron, Approximately. 1998. 352p. 22.00 o.p. (*0-06-039211-8*, ReganBooks) HarperTrade.

—Aaron, Approximately. 1999. 352p. pap. 13.50 (*0-380-73213-0*, Avon Bks.) Morrow/Avon.

Lazewnik, Libby. Shira's New Start. 1988. (J). (gr. 6-9). 12.95 o.p. (*0-87306-471-2*) Feldheim, Philipp Inc.

—Shira's Summer. 1988. (YA). (gr. 6-9). 12.95 o.p. (*0-87306-467-4*) Feldheim, Philipp Inc.

Leader, R. L. Faithful Soldiers. 1989. (J). (gr. 7 up). 12.95 o.p. (*0-944070-12-4*) Targum Pr., Inc.

Leavitt, June. The Flight to Seven Swan Bay. 1985. 10.95 o.p. (*0-87306-381-3*); pap. 8.95 o.p. (*0-87306-387-2*) Feldheim, Philipp Inc.

Lehmann, Marcus & Zucker, Pearl. Akiva: The Story of Rabbi Akiva & His Times. 2003. 22.95 (*1-58330-602-1*) Feldheim Pubs.

Lehrman, Robert. Juggling. 1988. 2.50 o.p. (*0-425-11128-8*) Berkley Publishing Group.

—Juggling. 1982. 256p. (YA). (gr. 7 up). lib. bdg. 13.89 o.p. (*0-06-023819-4*) HarperCollins Children's Bk. Group.

Lelchuk, Alan. On Home Ground. 1987. (Illus.). 80p. (YA). (gr. 4-7). 9.95 o.s.i (*0-15-200560-9*, Gulliver Bks.) Harcourt Children's Bks.

Lemmons, Thom. Jabez: A Novel. l.t. ed. 2002. (Wheeler Large Print Book Ser.). 27.95 (*1-58724-182-X*, Wheeler Publishing, Inc.) Gale Group.

—Jabez: A Novel. unabr. ed. 2001. audio 16.99 (*0-553-71305-1*, RH Audio) Random Hse. Audio Publishing Group.

Lenard-Cook, Lisa. Dissonance: A Novel. 2003. 186p. 21.95 (*0-8263-3090-8*) Univ. of New Mexico Pr.

Lentin, Ronit. Night Train to Mother. 1990. 220p. (Orig.). reprint ed. 24.95 o.p. (*0-939416-32-8*); pap. 9.95 o.p. (*0-939416-33-6*) Cleis Pr.

—Songs on the Death of Children. 1997. 220p. pap. 13.95 (*1-85371-625-1*) Poolbeg Pr. IRL. *Dist:* Dufour Editions, Inc.

Lerman, Rhoda. God's Ear: A Novel. 1988. 320p. 19.95 o.s.i (*0-8050-0413-0*) Holt, Henry & Co.

—God's Ear: A Novel. 1996. (Library of Modern Jewish Literature). 309p. reprint ed. pap. 17.95 (*0-8156-0427-0*, LEGEP) Syracuse Univ. Pr.

Levi, Primo. If Not Now, When? Weaver, William, tr. 1985. 384p. 15.45 o.p. (*0-671-49336-1*) Summit Bks.

—If Not Now, When? Weaver, William, tr. (Twentieth Century Classics Ser.). 352p. 1995. pap. 13.95 (*0-14-018893-2*, Penguin Classics); 1986. pap. 11.00 o.p. (*0-14-008492-4*, Penguin Bks.) Viking Penguin.

Leviant, Curt. Diary of an Adulterous Woman: A Novel. 2000. (Library of Modern Jewish Literature). 389p. 29.95 (*0-8156-0670-2*) Syracuse Univ. Pr.

—The Man Who Thought He Was Messiah. 1990. 226p. 9.95 (*0-8276-0371-1*) Jewish Pubn. Society.

—The Yemenite Girl: A Novel. 1978. pap. 1.95 o.p. (*0-380-41293-4*, Avon Bks.) Morrow/Avon.

—The Yemenite Girl: A Novel. 1999. (Library of Modern Jewish Literature). 192p. pap. text 17.95 (*0-8156-0619-2*) Syracuse Univ. Pr.

Levin, Jane W. Star of Danger. 1966. (Illus.). (J). (gr. 7 up). 5.50 o.p. (*0-15-279380-1*) Harcourt Children's Bks.

Levin, Meyer. Citizens: A Novel. reprint ed. 39.00 (*0-404-58447-0*) AMS Pr., Inc.

Levine, Arthur. All the Lights in the Night. 1997. (Illus.). 32p. (J). (gr. k-3). pap. 4.95 (*0-688-15592-8*, Morrow, William & Co.) Morrow/Avon.

Levine, Arthur A. All the Lights in the Night. 1991. (Illus.). 32p. (J). (ps-3). 16.00 o.p. (*0-688-10107-0*); lib. bdg. 15.93 o.p. (*0-688-10108-9*) Morrow/Avon. (Morrow, William & Co.).

Levinson, Nancy S. Sweet Notes, Sour Notes. 1993. (Illus.). 64p. (J). (gr. 2-5). 12.99 o.p. (*0-525-67379-2*) NAL.

Levinson, Riki. DinnieAbbieSister-r-r! 1987. (Illus.). 96p. (J). (gr. 1-3). 11.95 o.s.i (*0-02-757380-X*, Simon & Schuster Children's Publishing) Simon & Schuster Children's Publishing.

—Soon, Annala. 1993. (Illus.). 32p. (J). (ps-2). mass mkt. 15.95 o.p. (*0-531-05494-2*); mass mkt. 16.99 o.p. (*0-531-08644-5*) Scholastic, Inc. (Orchard Bks.).

Levitin, Sonia. Escape from Egypt. 1996. 272p. (YA). (gr. 7 up). pap. 5.99 o.p. (*0-14-037537-6*, Puffin Bks.) Penguin Putnam Bks. for Young Readers.

—Escape from Egypt: A Novel. 1994. (YA). (gr. 7 up). 16.95 o.p. (*0-316-52273-2*) Little Brown & Co.

—Escape from Egypt: A Novel. 1996. 12.04 (*0-606-08678-1*) Turtleback Bks.

—Silver Days. 192p. 1989. (YA). (gr. 5 up). lib. bdg. 16.00 o.s.i (*0-689-31563-5*, Atheneum); 1992. (J). (gr. 4-7). reprint ed. pap. 4.99 (*0-689-71570-6*, Aladdin) Simon & Schuster Children's Publishing.

—A Sound to Remember. 1979. (Illus.). (J). (ps-3). 6.95 o.p. (*0-15-277248-0*) Harcourt Children's Bks.

Lewald, Fanny. Prinz Louis Ferdinand. Rogols-Siegel, Linda, tr. from GER. 1989. (Studies in German Thought & History: Vol. 6). 507p. lib. bdg. 119.95 (*0-88946-357-3*) Mellen, Edwin Pr., The.

Lewisohn, Ludwig. The Island Within. 1975. (Modern Jewish Experience Ser.). reprint ed. 33.95 (*0-405-06730-5*) Ayer Co. Pubs., Inc.

—The Island Within. 1979. (Jewish Legacy Ser.). reprint ed. pap. 5.95 o.p. (*0-87441-318-4*) Behrman Hse., Inc.

Licht, Fred. Shelter the Pilgrim. 1993. (Short Stories Ser.). 48p. (YA). (gr. 4 up). lib. bdg. 18.60 (*0-88682-307-2*, Creative Education) Creative Co., The.

Lind, Jakov. Soul of Wood. 1986. pap. 6.95 o.p. (*0-8090-1526-9*, Hill & Wang) Farrar, Straus & Giroux.
Lipman, Elinor. The Inn at Lake Devine. 1999. 272p. pap. 13.00 (*0-375-70485-X*, Vintage) Knopf Publishing Group.
—The Inn at Lake Devine. 1998. 23.00 (*0-676-54572-6*) Random Hse., Inc.
—The Inn at Lake Devine: A Novel. 1998. 272p. 23.95 o.s.i (*0-679-45693-7*) Random Hse., Inc.
Lipshitz, Arye. We Built Jerusalem: Tales of Pioneering Days. Louvish, Misha, tr. 1985. 176p. 14.95 (*0-8453-4787-X*, Cornwall Bks.) Associated Univ. Presses.
Liss, David. The Coffee Trader: A Novel. 2004. 416p. pap. 14.95 (*0-375-76090-3*) Ballantine Bks.
—The Coffee Trader: A Novel. 2003. 400p. 24.95 (*0-375-50854-6*) Random Hse., Inc.
—A Conspiracy of Paper. E-Book 19.95 (*1-58945-562-2*) Adobe Systems, Inc.
—A Conspiracy of Paper. 2001. (Reader's Circle Ser.). 464p. pap. 14.95 (*0-8041-1912-0*, Ballantine Bks.) Ballantine Bks.
—A Conspiracy of Paper. 2000. E-Book 19.95 (*0-375-50504-0*) Random Hse., Inc.
—A Conspiracy of Paper. l.t. ed. 2000. (Basic Ser.). 781p. pap. 28.95 (*0-7862-2665-X*) Thorndike Pr.
Loeb, Evelyn. Dreidelcat. 1997. (Charming Petites Ser.). (Illus.). 64p. (ps-3). 4.95 (*0-88088-819-9*) Peter Pauper Pr. Inc.
Lourie, Richard. Zero Gravity. 1987. 16.95 (*0-15-199984-8*) Harcourt Trade Pubs.
Lowry, Lois. Quien Cuenta las Estrellas. 1997. (SPA.). 184p. (J). 9.95 o.p. (*84-239-7124-4*) Elliot's Bks.
Luban, Marianne. The Samaritan Treasure. 1990. 226p. pap. 9.95 (*0-918273-79-X*) Coffee Hse. Pr.
Lustiger, Gila. The Inventory. Morrison, Rebecca, tr. from GER. 2001. 294p. 24.95 (*1-55970-549-3*) Arcade Publishing, Inc.
Magun, Carol. Circling Eden: A Novel of Israel in Stories. 1995. 200p. 19.95 (*0-89733-412-4*) Academy Chicago Pubs., Ltd.
Malamud, Bernard. The Fixer. 1966. 352p. 17.50 o.p. (*0-374-15572-0*) Farrar, Straus & Giroux.
Mamet, David. Passover. 1995. (Illus.). 64p. 14.95 (*0-312-13141-0*) St. Martin's Pr.
Manus, Willard. The Pigskin Rabbi. 1999. 304p. 23.00 (*1-891369-07-5*) Breakaway Bks.
Marcus, Shmuel M. Chicken Kiev. 2002. 12p. 14.00 (*1-880880-70-9*) Israeli Trading Co.
Margolin, Miriam. Little Stories for Little Children. 1986. (Illus.). 32p. (J). (gr. k-3). reprint ed. 11.95 o.p. (*0-918825-53-9*) Moyer Bell.
Markham, Marion M. Starlight & Candles: The Joys of the Sabbath. 1995. (Illus.). 40p. (J). (ps-3). pap. 15.00 (*0-689-80274-9*, Simon & Schuster Children's Publishing) Simon & Schuster Children's Publishing.
Markish, David. Jesters. Bouis, Antonina W., tr. 1988. 19.95 o.p. (*0-8050-0444-0*) Holt, Henry & Co.
Markus, Julia. Uncle, 001. 1978. (Literary Fellowship Award Novel Ser.). 7.95 o.p. (*0-395-27098-7*) Houghton Mifflin Co.
Marvin, Isabel R. Bridge to Freedom. 148p. (YA). 1997. pap. text 9.95 (*0-8276-0640-0*); 1991. (gr. 5-9). 14.95 o.p. (*0-8276-0377-0*) Jewish Pubn. Society.
Matas, Carol. The Birth of Israel. 1997. 144p. (J). (gr. 7 up). per. 15.00 (*0-689-80349-4*, Simon & Schuster Children's Publishing) Simon & Schuster Children's Publishing.
Mathias, Bernard. The Caretakers. Henry, Freeman G., tr. from FRE. 1988. 231p. 17.95 o.p. (*0-670-82127-6*) Viking Penguin.
Matlin, David. How the Night Is Divided: A Novel. 1993. 201p. 20.00 (*0-929701-33-X*) McPherson & Co.
McDonnell, Janet. Sharing Hanukkah. 1993. (Circle the Year with Holidays Ser.). (Illus.). 32p. (J). lib. bdg. 19.00 o.p. (*0-516-00685-1*, Children's Pr.) Scholastic Library Publishing.
Meier, Marcie. A Fitting Bar Mitzvah. 1996. (Illus.). 24p. (YA). (ps-3). pap. text 12.95 (*965-229-127-7*) Gefen Publishing Hse., Ltd ISR. *Dist:* Gefen Bks.
Meir Bar-Am. The Fateful Mission. 1986. 180p. 10.95 o.p. (*0-87306-420-8*) Feldheim, Philipp Inc.
Meir, Mira. Alina: A Russian Girl Comes to Israel. Shapiro, Zeva, tr. from HEB. 1982. (Illus.). 48p. (J). (gr. 2-4). 9.95 o.p. (*0-8276-0208-1*) Jewish Pubn. Society.
Michelson, Richard. Grandpa's Gamble. 1999. (Accelerated Reader Bks. ). (Illus.). 32p. (J). (ps up). 15.95 (*0-7614-5034-3*, Cavendish Children's Bks.) Cavendish, Marshall Corp.
Michener, James A. Source. 1982. mass mkt. 3.95 o.p. (*0-449-23859-8*, Fawcett) Ballantine Bks.
—Source. 1965. 45.00 o.s.i (*0-394-44630-5*) Random Hse., Inc.
Miklowitz, Gloria D. The Love Bombers. 1980. 160p. (J). (gr. 7 up). pap. 8.95 o.s.i (*0-385-28545-0*, Delacorte Pr.) Dell Publishing.
—Masada: The Last Fortress. 1999. 198p. (J). (gr. 4-7). 16.00 (*0-8028-5165-7*); pap. 7.00 (*0-8028-5168-1*) Eerdmans, William B. Publishing Co. (Eerdmans Bks For Young Readers).
Miller, Arthur. Focus. 1984. (Library of Contemporary Americana). 224p. reprint ed. pap. 7.95 o.p. (*0-87795-649-9*, Morrow, William & Co.) Morrow/Avon.
—Focus. 1978. pap. 3.95 o.p. (*0-14-004584-8*, Penguin Bks.); 2001. 240p. 13.00 (*0-14-200042-6*) Viking Penguin.
Miller, Deborah & Ostrove, Karen. Fins & Scales: A Kosher Tale. 2004. (Israel Ser.). (Illus.). 32p. (J). (gr. 1-3). pap. 4.95 (*0-929371-25-9*) Kar-Ben Publishing.
Miller, Deborah U. Poppy Seeds, Too: A Twisted Tale for Shabbat. 1982. (Illus.). 48p. (J). (ps-3). pap. 4.95 o.p. (*0-930494-17-2*) Kar-Ben Publishing.
Miller, Risa. Welcome to Heavenly Heights: A Novel. 2003. 256p. 23.95 (*0-312-30180-4*) St. Martin's Pr.
Millman, M. C. Juggling Act. 2003. 224p. (J). 17.95 (*0-910818-28-2*) Judaica Pr., Inc., The.
Milofsky, David. Eternal People. 1998. 320p. 22.50 (*0-87081-502-4*) Univ. Pr. of Colorado.
Mindel, Nissan. The Call of the Shofar. 1971. (Illus.). 64p. (YA). reprint ed. 11.00 (*0-8266-0345-9*, Merkos L'Inyonei Chinuch) Kehot Pubn. Society.
Mirsky, Mark. The Secret Table. 1975. 167p. 15.95 (*0-914590-10-3*) Fiction Collective Two, Inc.
Mirvis, Tova. The Ladies Auxiliary. 2000. (Ballantine Reader's Circle Ser.). 336p. pap. 14.00 (*0-345-44126-5*, Ballantine Bks.) Ballantine Bks.
—The Ladies Auxiliary. 1999. 352p. 23.95 (*0-393-04814-4*) Norton, W. W. & Co., Inc.
—The Ladies Auxiliary. 2000. 20.05 (*0-606-19737-0*) Turtleback Bks.
Mondry, Adele. A Shtetl on the Bug River. 1979. 11.95 o.p. (*0-87068-657-7*) Ktav Publishing Hse., Inc.
Mor, Noam. ARC: The Cleavage of Ghosts. 2002. 280p. pap. 14.95 (*1-881471-79-9*) Spuyten Duyvil.
Moran, Thomas. The Man in the Box. 272p. 1998. 12.00 (*1-57322-649-1*); 1997. 21.95 o.p. (*1-57322-060-4*) Putnam Publishing Group, The. (Riverhead Bks. (Hardcovers)).
Morris, Gilbert. Jacob's Way. 2001. 416p. pap. 12.99 (*0-310-22696-1*) Zondervan.
Morton, Leah, pseud & Morton, Leah. I Am a Woman & a Jew. 1986. (Masterworks of Modern Jewish Writings). (Illus.). 372p. (C). reprint ed. pap. 9.95 (*0-910129-56-8*) Wiener, Markus Pubs., Inc.
Moss, Marissa. In America. 1994. (Illus.). 32p. (J). 14.99 o.s.i (*0-525-45152-8*, Dutton Children's Bks.) Penguin Putnam Bks. for Young Readers.
Mossanen, Dora Levy. Harem: A Novel. 2002. 384p. pap. 14.00 (*0-7432-3021-3*, Touchstone) Simon & Schuster.
Muchnik, Michael. Leah & Leibel's Lighthouse. 1984. (Illus.). 48p. (J). reprint ed. 7.00 (*0-8266-0355-6*, Merkos L'Inyonei Chinuch) Kehot Pubn. Society.
—The Scribe Who Lived in a Tree. 1984. (Illus.). 48p. (J). reprint ed. 7.00 (*0-8266-0351-3*, Merkos L'Inyonei Chinuch) Kehot Pubn. Society.
Muchnik, Michoel. The Cuckoo Clock Castle of Shir. 1980. (Illus.). (J). (ps-3). 8.95 (*0-8197-0476-8*) Bloch Publishing Co.
Murdoch, Iris. Something Special: A Story. 2000. (Illus.). 55p. 15.95 (*0-393-05007-6*) Norton, W. W. & Co., Inc.
—Something Special: A Story. 1999. (Illus.). 48p. o.p. (*0-7011-6918-4*) Random Hse. of Canada, Ltd. CAN. *Dist:* Random Hse., Inc.
Nachman of Breslov. The Fixer. Mykoff, Moshe, ed. 1996. (Illus.). 52p. (J). (gr. 1-4). 8.00 (*0-930213-64-5*) Breslov Research Institute.
Nadelson, Scott. Saving Stanley: The Brickman Stories. 2003. pap. 12.95 (*0-9716915-2-5*) Hawthorne Bks. & Literary Arts, Inc.
Nahai, Gina B. Cry of the Peacock. 2000. 352p. reprint ed. pap. 13.95 (*0-7434-0337-1*, Washington Square Pr.) Simon & Schuster.
—Moonlight on the Avenue of Faith. 1999. 384p. 24.00 o.s.i (*0-15-100388-2*) Harcourt Trade Pubs.
Nattel, Lilian. The River Midnight: A Novel. 1999. 416p. pap. 14.00 (*0-684-85304-3*); (Illus.). 25.00 o.s.i (*0-684-85303-5*) Simon & Schuster. (Scribner).
—The Singing Fire. 2004. 352p. (*0-676-97600-X*) Knopf Canada CAN. *Dist:* Random Hse. of Canada, Ltd., Random Hse., Inc.
Neugeboren, Jay. Before My Life Began. 1985. 18.45 o.p. (*0-671-54372-5*, Simon & Schuster) Simon & Schuster.
Neville, Emily C. Berries Goodman. 1975. (Trophy Bk.). (J). (gr. 5-9). pap. 3.95 o.p. (*0-06-440072-7*, Harper Trophy) HarperCollins Children's Bk. Group.
Newman, Leslea. In Every Laugh a Tear. 256p. (Orig.). 1992. pap. 9.95 o.p. (*0-934678-46-4*); 2nd ed. 1998. pap. 11.95 (*0-934678-92-8*) New Victoria Pubs., Inc.
Nichols, Anne. Abie's Irish Rose. 1975. (Modern Jewish Experience Ser.). reprint ed. 30.95 (*0-405-06736-4*) Ayer Co. Pubs., Inc.
Norfolk, Lawrence. In the Shape of a Boar. 2001. 336p. 25.00 o.p. (*0-8021-1701-5*) Grove/Atlantic, Inc.
Norman, Howard. The Museum Guard. 1998. 310p. 24.00 o.p. (*0-374-21649-5*); 1994. E-Book 13.00 (*0-374-70237-3*); 1994. E-Book 13.00 (*0-374-70236-5*); 1994. E-Book 13.00 (*0-374-70234-9*); 1994. E-Book 13.00 o.p. (*0-374-70235-7*) Farrar, Straus & Giroux.
—The Museum Guard. 1999. pap. (*0-312-24716-8*); 320p. pap. 14.00 (*0-312-20427-2*) Picador.
Oates, Joyce Carol. The Tattooed Girl. 2003. 9p. pap. 89.95 (*0-7927-2897-1*); 7p. pap. 59.95 (*0-7927-2896-3*) BBC Audiobooks America.
—The Tattooed Girl. 320p. 2004. pap. 13.95 (*0-06-053107-X*); 2003. 25.95 (*0-06-053106-1*) Harper-Trade. (Ecco).
Olidort, Baila. Just Like Mommy. 1992. (Illus.). 8.00 (*0-8266-0359-9*, Merkos L'Inyonei Chinuch) Kehot Pubn. Society.
Oppenheim, Shulamith L. The Lily Cupboard. 1992. (Charlotte Zolotow Bk.). (Illus.). 32p. (J). (gr. 1-3). 15.00 o.p. (*0-06-024669-3*); lib. bdg. 14.89 o.p. (*0-06-024670-7*) HarperCollins Children's Bk. Group.
Organick, Avrum B. Blessings. 1999. iii, 250p. pap. 13.50 (*0-9671068-0-X*); 2nd ed. 2000. 270p. 22.95 (*0-9671068-2-6*); 2nd rev. ed. 2000. 270p. pap. 14.50 (*0-9671068-1-8*) Red Lake Pr.
Orgel, Doris. The Devil in Vienna. 1988. 256p. (J). (gr. 4-7). pap. 5.99 (*0-14-032500-X*, Puffin Bks.) Penguin Putnam Bks. for Young Readers.
Orner, Peter. Esther Stories. 2001. 224p. pap. 12.00 (*0-618-12873-5*, Mariner Bks.) Houghton Mifflin Co. Trade & Reference Div.
Ornitz, Samuel. Alrightniks Row: The Making of a Professional Jew, Haunch, Paunch & Jowl. 1986. (Masterworks of Modern Jewish Writing Ser.). 323p. reprint ed. pap. 9.95 (*0-910129-46-0*) Wiener, Markus Pubs., Inc.
Ossowski, Leonie. Star Without a Sky. 1985. Orig. Title: Stern Ohne Himmel. 216p. (J). (gr. 3-6). lib. bdg. 19.95 o.p. (*0-8225-0771-4*, Lerner Pubns.) Lerner Publishing Group.
Oz, Amos. The Hill of Evil Counsel. 1978. 216p. 7.95 o.p. (*0-15-140234-5*) Harcourt Trade Pubs.
—Where the Jackals Howl & Other Stories. De Lange, Nicholas R. M. & Simpson, Philip, trs. 1981. (Helen & Kurt Wolff Bk.). 228p. 12.95 o.p. (*0-15-196038-0*) Harcourt Trade Pubs.
Ozick, Cynthia. The Shawl. 1990. (Vintage International Ser.). 96p. pap. 9.00 (*0-679-72926-7*, Vintage) Knopf Publishing Group.
Packer, Miriam. Take Me to Coney Island, No. 25. 1993. (Prose Ser.: No. 25). 180p. pap. 15.00 (*0-920717-92-6*) Guernica Editions, Inc.
Page, Carole G. Bouquet of Good-Byes. 1992. (Kasey Carlone Ser.). (YA). pap. 4.99 o.p. (*0-8024-8180-9*) Moody Pr.
Paley, Grace. The Collected Stories. 1994. 386p. 27.50 o.s.i (*0-374-12636-4*) Farrar, Straus & Giroux.
—The Little Disturbances of Man. 1973. pap. 2.95 o.p. (*0-452-25073-0*); pap. 3.95 o.p. (*0-452-25304-7*) Dutton/Plume. (Plume).
—The Little Disturbances of Man. (American Fiction Ser.). 1985. 192p. 13.00 (*0-14-007557-7*); 1968. 4.50 o.p. (*0-670-43179-6*) Viking Penguin.
Pamensky, Robin. Avi's Adventures in the Mitzvah Car. 1995. (J). text 12.95 (*965-229-138-2*) Gefen Publishing Hse., Ltd ISR. *Dist:* Gefen Bks.
Pashman, Susan. The Speed of Light. 1997. 207p. 24.00 (*1-877946-86-9*) Permanent Pr., The.
Pastor, Irene. Silent Legacy. 2000. 208p. pap. 14.95 (*0-88739-290-3*) Creative Arts Bk. Co.
Paul, Terri. Glass Hearts. 1999. 326p. 24.95 (*0-89733-470-1*) Academy Chicago Pubs., Ltd.
Pears, Iain. The Dream of Scipio. 2003. 400p. pap. (*0-676-97292-6*, Vintage) Knopf Publishing Group.
—The Dream of Scipio. 2002. (Illus.). 608p. 27.99 o.s.i (*1-57322-202-X*, Riverhead Bks. (Hardcovers)) Putnam Publishing Group, The.
Penn, Malka. The Hanukkah Ghosts. 1997. 80p. (J). (gr. 3-7). pap. 3.99 o.p. (*0-380-72838-9*, Avon Bks.) Morrow/Avon.
Perutz, Leo. By Night under the Stone Bridge. Mosbacher, Eric, tr. from GER. 1990. 208p. lib. bdg. 18.95 o.s.i (*1-55970-055-6*) Arcade Publishing, Inc.
Pessin, Deborah. Aleph-Bet Story. 1989. (J). pap. 10.95 o.p. incl. audio (*0-8276-0304-5*) Jewish Pubn. Society.
Pfeffer, Susan Beth. Turning Thirteen. 1988. 144p. (J). (gr. 6-8). pap. 12.95 o.p. (*0-590-40764-3*) Scholastic, Inc.
Phillips, Caryl. The Nature of Blood. 1997. 224p. 23.00 o.s.i (*0-679-45470-5*) Knopf, Alfred A. Inc.
—The Nature of Blood. 1998. pap. o.s.i (*0-676-97104-0*, Vintage) Random Hse. of Canada, Ltd. CAN. *Dist:* Random Hse., Inc.
—The Nature of Blood. 1998. 224p. pap. 13.00 (*0-679-77675-3*) Random Hse., Inc.
Piercy, Marge & Wood, Ira. Storm Tide. 1998. 304p. 25.00 o.s.i (*0-449-00166-0*, Fawcett) Ballantine Bks.
Plain, Belva. Evergreen. 1991. 598p. reprint ed. lib. bdg. 38.95 (*0-89966-813-5*) Buccaneer Bks., Inc.
—Evergreen. 1980. 704p. mass mkt. 7.99 (*0-440-13278-9*); 1979. 19.95 o.s.i (*0-385-28299-0*, Delacorte Pr.) Dell Publishing.
—Evergreen. 1910. mass mkt. o.s.i (*0-385-31997-5*) Doubleday Publishing.
—Evergreen. 1980. (General Ser.). lib. bdg. 23.95 o.p. (*0-8161-3114-7*, Macmillan Reference USA) Gale Group.
Polacco, Patricia. The Keeping Quilt. 10th anniv. ed. 1988. (Illus.). 32p. (J). (ps-3). 16.00 (*0-671-64963-9*, Simon & Schuster Children's Publishing) Simon & Schuster Children's Publishing.
Pollack, Eileen. Paradise, New York: A Novel. 2000. 288p. 49.50 (*1-56639-657-3*); pap. 17.95 (*1-56639-789-8*) Temple Univ. Pr.
Potok, Chaim. The Book of Lights. 1997. pap. 12.00 o.s.i (*0-449-00114-8*); 1982. 400p. mass mkt. 7.99 (*0-449-24569-1*) Ballantine Bks. (Fawcett).
—The Book of Lights. l.t. ed. 1982. 660p. reprint ed. 13.95 o.p. (*0-89621-358-7*) Thorndike Pr.
—The Chosen. (Ballantine Reader's Circle Ser.). 1996. 304p. pap. 13.95 (*0-449-91154-3*); 1987. 304p. mass mkt. 6.99 (*0-449-21344-7*); 1985. mass mkt. 3.50 o.p. (*0-449-20962-8*); 1982. mass mkt. 2.95 o.p. (*0-449-20334-4*) Ballantine Bks. (Fawcett).
—The Chosen. 1994. reprint ed. lib. bdg. 35.95 (*1-56849-319-3*) Buccaneer Bks., Inc.
—The Chosen. 25th anniv. ed. 1992. 30.00 o.s.i (*0-679-40222-5*) Knopf, Alfred A. Inc.
—The Chosen. 1967. 9.95 o.p. (*0-671-13674-7*, Simon & Schuster) Simon & Schuster.
—The Chosen. l.t. ed. 1998. (Perennial Bestsellers Ser.). 413p. 27.95 (*0-7838-8450-8*) Thorndike Pr.
—The Chosen. 1976. 13.04 (*0-606-00469-6*) Turtleback Bks.
—Old Men at Midnight. 2002. 304p. pap. 14.95 (*0-345-43998-8*) Random Hse., Inc.
—The Promise. 1997. 384p. pap. 12.95 (*0-449-00116-4*); 1985. 384p. mass mkt. 7.99 (*0-449-20910-5*); 1982. mass mkt. 3.25 o.p. (*0-449-20076-0*) Ballantine Bks. (Fawcett).
—The Promise. l.t. ed. 1998. (Perennial Bestsellers Ser.). 512p. 26.95 (*0-7838-0256-0*) Thorndike Pr.
Powers, Richard. The Time of Our Singing. 2003. E-Book 15.00 o.p. (*0-374-70465-1*); 2003. 640p. 27.00 (*0-374-27782-6*); 2003. E-Book 15.00 (*0-374-70463-5*); 2002. E-Book (*0-374-70467-8*) Farrar, Straus & Giroux.
Pressburger, Giorgio & Pressburger, Nicola. Homage to the Eighth District: Tales from Budapest. Moore, Gerald, tr. from ITA. 1990. 200p. (Orig.). pap. 17.95 (*0-930523-75-X*); pap. 9.95 (*0-930523-76-8*) Readers International.
Prose, Francine. Stories from Our Living Past. Harlow, Jules, ed. 1974. (Illus.). 128p. pap., tchr. ed. 14.95 o.p. (*0-87441-082-7*); (J). (gr. 3-4). pap. 8.95 o.p. (*0-87441-081-9*);No. 1. (J). (gr. 3-4). pap., wbk. ed. 3.50 o.p. (*0-87441-083-5*);No. 2. (J). (gr. 3-4). pap., wbk. ed. 3.50 o.p. (*0-87441-084-3*) Behrman Hse., Inc.
Provost, Gary. Good If It Goes. 1990. 160p. (J). (gr. 4-7). pap. 3.95 o.s.i (*0-689-71381-9*, Aladdin) Simon & Schuster Children's Publishing.
Pushker, Gloria T. A Belfer Bar Mitzvah. 1995. (Illus.). 32p. (J). (gr. 4-7). 14.95 (*1-56554-095-6*) Pelican Publishing Co., Inc.
Rabinovich, Dalia. Flora's Suitcase. 1998. 256p. o.s.i (*0-06-019137-6*, HarperFlamingo) HarperCollins Pubs. Canada, Ltd.
—Flora's Suitcase: A Novel. 1999. 256p. pap. 13.00 (*0-06-093249-X*) HarperCollins Pubs.
Rabinyan, Dorit. Persian Brides. 2000. 236p. pap. 15.95 (*0-8076-1461-0*) Braziller, George Inc.
—Persian Brides. Lotan, Yael, tr. from HEB. 1998. 240p. 22.50 (*0-8076-1430-0*) Braziller, George Inc.
Raczymow, Henri. Writing the Book of Esther. Katz, Dori, tr. from FRE. 1995. (French Expressions Ser.). 220p. 24.00 (*0-8419-1335-8*) Holmes & Meier Pubs., Inc.
Ragen, Naomi. Chains Around the Grass. 2003. pap. 12.95 (*1-902881-82-6*); 2002. (Illus.). 256p. 26.95 (*1-902881-53-2*); 2003. 394p. 24.95 (*1-902881-72-9*) Toby Pr.
—The Ghost of Hannah Mendes. 5th ed. 2001. (Illus.). 384p. reprint ed. pap. 14.95 (*0-312-28125-0*, CPB1198, Saint Martin's Griffin) St. Martin's Pr.
—Jephte's Daughter. l.t. ed. 1990. (General Ser.). 538p. 21.95 o.p. (*0-8161-4826-0*, Macmillan Reference USA) Gale Group.
—Jephte's Daughter. 1990. 416p. 18.45 o.s.i (*0-446-51486-1*) Warner Bks., Inc.
—The Sacrifice of Tamar. l.t. ed. 2003. 674p. 24.95 (*1-902881-74-5*) Toby Pr.
—Sotah. 2002. 492p. pap. 14.95 (*1-902881-51-6*); 2003. 754p. 24.95 (*1-902881-73-7*) Toby Pr.
Ramati, Alexander. Barbed Wire on the Isle of Man. 1980. 252p. 10.95 o.p. (*0-15-110671-1*) Harcourt Trade Pubs.

Rand, Robert. My Suburban Shtetl: A Novel about Life in a Twentieth-Century Jewish American Village. 2001. (Library of Modern Jewish Literature). 232p. 22.95 (*0-8156-0721-0*) Syracuse Univ. Pr.

Raphael, David. The Alhambra Decree: A Historical Novel about the Expulsion of the Jews from Spain. 1988. 358p. (C). 25.00 (*0-9620772-0-8*) Carmi Hse. Pr.

—Cavalier of Malaga. 1989. 190p. 15.00 (*0-9620772-1-6*) Carmi Hse. Pr.

—El Decreto de la Alhambra: Novela Historica Sobre la Expulsion de los Judios de Espana en 1492. Santacruz, Daniel M., tr. from ENG. 1992. (SPA.). 357p. 25.00 (*0-9620772-4-0*); pap. 15.00 (*0-9620772-5-9*) Carmi Hse. Pr.

Raphael, Lev. Dancing on Tisha B'av. (Stonewall Inn Editions Ser.). 1991. 240p. pap. 8.95 (*0-312-06326-1*, Saint Martin's Griffin); 1990. 16.95 o.p. (*0-312-04862-9*) St. Martin's Pr.

—The German Money: A Novel. 2003. 212p. pap. 14.95 (*0-9679520-0-X*) Leapfrog Pr.

Reich, Tova. Mara: A Novel. 2001. (Library of Modern Jewish Literature). 256p. pap. 18.95 (*0-8156-0659-1*) Syracuse Univ. Pr.

—Master of the Return. 1988. 300p. 19.95 o.s.i (*0-15-157880-X*) Harcourt Trade Pubs.

—Master of the Return. 1999. (Library of Modern Jewish Literature). 256p. pap. text 17.95 (*0-8156-0620-6*) Syracuse Univ. Pr.

Reznikoff, Charles. By the Waters of Manhattan. 1986. (Masterworks of Modern Jewish Writings). (Illus.). 264p. (C). reprint ed. pap. 9.95 (*0-910129-55-X*) Wiener, Markus Pubs., Inc.

—Family Chronicle. 1988. (Masterworks of Modern Jewish Writings). 320p. reprint ed. 9.95 o.p. (*0-910129-73-8*); pap. 9.95 (*0-910129-74-6*) Wiener, Markus Pubs., Inc.

Richler, Mordecai. The Apprenticeship of Duddy Kravitz. 2000. 320p. 24.95 (*0-8488-2769-4*) Amereon, Ltd.

—The Apprenticeship of Duddy Kravitz. Young, George, ed. 1974. (Illus.). 288p. mass mkt. 1.50 o.p. (*0-345-24154-1*) Ballantine Bks.

—The Apprenticeship of Duddy Kravitz. 1981. 304p. pap. 2.95 o.p. (*0-553-14584-3*) Bantam Bks.

—The Apprenticeship of Duddy Kravitz. 1989. (New Canadian Library). 328p. mass mkt. 6.95 (*0-7710-9972-X*) McClelland & Stewart/Tundra Bks.

—The Apprenticeship of Duddy Kravitz. 1991. 384p. pap. 9.95 o.p. (*0-14-015296-2*, Penguin Bks.) Penguin Group (USA) Inc.

—The Apprenticeship of Duddy Kravitz. 1999. 384p. pap. 14.00 (*0-671-02847-2*, Pocket) Simon & Schuster.

—Barney's Version. 1999. 368p. pap. 14.00 (*0-671-02846-4*, Washington Square Pr.) Simon & Schuster.

Richler, Nancy. Your Mouth Is Lovely: A Novel. 368p. 2003. pap. 13.95 (*0-06-009678-0*); 2002. 25.95 (*0-06-009677-2*, Ecco) HarperTrade.

Rischin, Moses, ed. Yiddish Tales. Frank, Helena, tr. from YID. 1975. (Modern Jewish Experience Ser.). reprint ed. 52.95 (*0-405-06755-0*) Ayer Co. Pubs., Inc.

Rodburg, Maxine. Law of Return. 1999. (Carnegie Mellon Series in Short Fiction Ser.). pap. text 15.95 (*0-88748-313-5*) Carnegie-Mellon Univ. Pr.

Romm, J. Leonard. The Swastika on the Synagogue Door. 2nd ed. 1994. (Lazarus Family Mystery Ser.). (Illus.). 168p. (Orig.). (J). (gr. 7 up). reprint ed. pap. 6.95 (*1-881283-05-4*) Alef Design Group.

—The Swastika on the Synagogue Door. 1984. (Lazarus Family Mystery Ser.). 180p. (Orig.). (J). (gr. 3-10). pap. 6.95 o.p. (*0-940646-53-6*) Rossel Bks.

Ron-Feder, Galila. To Myself: The Story of a Foster Child. Arad, Miriam, tr. from HEB. 1987. (Illus.). 140p. (J). (gr. 4 up). 12.95 o.p. (*1-55774-003-8*) Lambda Pubs., Inc.

Rose, Deborah Lee. The Rose Horse. 1995. (Illus.). 80p. (J). (gr. 4-7). 16.00 (*0-15-200068-2*) Harcourt Children's Bks.

Rose, Howard. The Marrano. 1992. 256p. 20.00 (*1-878352-08-3*); pap. 10.00 (*1-878352-09-1*) Saroff, Raymond Pub.

Roseman, Kenneth D. The Tenth of Av. 1988. (Do-It-Yourself Jewish Adventure Ser.). (Illus.). 96p. (J). (gr. 4-7). pap. text 8.95 (*0-8074-0359-8*, 123928) UAHC Pr.

Rosen, Charley. The House of Moses All-Stars. 1998. (Harvest Book Ser.). 456p. pap. 13.00 (*0-15-600570-0*, Harvest Bks.) Harcourt Trade Pubs.

—The House of Moses All-Stars. 1996. 496p. 24.95 (*1-888363-33-9*) Seven Stories Pr.

Rosenbaum, Thane. Elijah Visible. 1996. 224p. 21.95 (*0-312-14325-7*) St. Martin's Pr.

—The Golems of Gotham. 2002. 384p. 25.95 (*0-06-018490-6*) HarperCollins Pubs.

—The Golems of Gotham. 2003. 384p. pap. 13.95 (*0-06-095945-2*, Perennial) HarperTrade.

—Second Hand Smoke. 320p. 2000. pap. 13.95 (*0-312-25418-0*, Saint Martin's Griffin); 1999. 24.95 (*0-312-19954-6*) St. Martin's Pr.

Rosenfeld, Dina. Peanut Butter & Jelly for Shabbos. 1995. (Illus.). 32p. (J). (ps-1). 9.95 (*0-922613-69-9*) Hachai Publishing.

Rosenfeld, Isaac. Passage from Home. 1988. (Masterworks of Modern Jewish Writings). 300p. reprint ed. pap. 9.95 (*0-910129-75-4*) Wiener, Markus Pubs., Inc.

Rosofsky, Iris. Miriam. 1988. (Charlotte Zolotow Bk.). 192p. (YA). (gr. 7 up). 11.95 (*0-06-024853-X*) HarperCollins Children's Bk. Group.

Ross, Fran. Oreo. 1974. 10.95 o.p. (*0-914870-00-9*) Greyfalcon Hse.

—Oreo. 2000. (Library of Black Literature). 212p. pap. 16.95 (*1-55553-464-3*) Northeastern Univ. Pr.

Ross, Lillian. The Little Old Man & His Dreams. 1990. (Charlotte Zolotow Bk.). (Illus.). 32p. (J). (gr. k-3). 14.95 (*0-06-025094-1*) HarperCollins Children's Bk. Group.

Roth-Hano, Renee. Safe Harbors. 1993. 224p. (YA). (gr. 12 up). 16.95 o.p. (*0-02-777795-2*, Simon & Schuster Children's Publishing) Simon & Schuster Children's Publishing.

Roth, Henry. Call It Sleep. ltd. ed. 1995. (Illus.). 482p. 700.00 (*0-910457-30-1*) Arion Pr.

—Call It Sleep. 1995. reprint ed. lib. bdg. 29.95 (*1-56849-634-6*) Buccaneer Bks., Inc.

—Call It Sleep. reprint ed. 20.00 o.p. (*0-8154-0198-1*) Cooper Square Pubs., Inc.

—Call It Sleep. 1992. 30.00 o.s.i (*0-374-11819-1*); 448p. pap. 16.00 (*0-374-52292-8*) Farrar, Straus & Giroux.

—Call It Sleep. 1976. mass mkt. 4.95 o.p. (*0-380-01002-X*, Avon Bks.) Morrow/Avon.

—Call It Sleep. l.t. ed. 1995. 655p. 24.95 (*0-7838-1564-6*) Thorndike Pr.

—A Diving Rock on the Hudson. 1996. (Mercy of a Rude Stream Ser.: Vol. 2). 432p. pap. 14.00 o.s.i (*0-312-14085-1*) Picador.

—A Diving Rock on the Hudson: Mercy of a Rude Stream, Vol. II. 1995. (Mercy of a Rude Stream Ser.). 1p. 23.95 o.p. (*0-312-11777-9*) St. Martin's Pr.

—From Bondage. 1997. (Mercy of a Rude Stream Ser.: Vol. 3). 416p. pap. 15.00 (*0-312-15532-8*) Picador.

—From Bondage. 1996. (Mercy of a Rude Stream Ser.: Vol. 3). 432p. 25.95 o.p. (*0-312-14341-9*) St. Martin's Pr.

—Requiem for Harlem. 1998. (Mercy of a Rude Stream Ser.: Vol. 4). 304p. pap. 14.00 (*0-312-20205-9*); 24.95 o.s.i (*0-312-16980-9*) Picador.

Roth, Philip. The Anatomy Lesson. 1984. 240p. mass mkt. 4.95 o.s.i (*0-449-20614-9*, Fawcett) Ballantine Bks.

—The Anatomy Lesson. 1983. 291p. 14.95 o.p. (*0-374-10491-3*); 60.00 o.s.i (*0-374-10492-1*) Farrar, Straus & Giroux.

—The Anatomy Lesson. 1996. 304p. pap. 13.00 (*0-679-74902-0*) Random Hse., Inc.

—The Ghost Writer. 1982. 224p. mass mkt. 4.95 o.s.i (*0-449-20009-4*); 1980. mass mkt. 2.95 o.p. (*0-449-24322-2*) Ballantine Bks. (Fawcett).

—The Ghost Writer. 1979. 180p. 8.95 o.p. (*0-374-16189-5*) Farrar, Straus & Giroux.

—The Ghost Writer. 1980. lib. bdg. 10.95 o.p. (*0-8161-3069-8*, Macmillan Reference USA) Gale Group.

—The Ghost Writer. 1995. 192p. pap. 12.00 (*0-679-74898-9*, Vintage) Knopf Publishing Group.

—Goodbye, Columbus. 1994. reprint ed. lib. bdg. 32.95 o.p. (*1-56849-325-8*) Buccaneer Bks., Inc.

—Goodbye, Columbus, 001. 1959. 9.95 o.p. (*0-395-08138-6*); 1989. 304p. reprint ed. pap. 8.95 o.p. (*0-395-51850-4*) Houghton Mifflin Co.

—Goodbye, Columbus. annuals (Modern Library Ser.). 1995. (Illus.). 320p. 17.95 o.s.i (*0-679-60159-7*); 1966. 3.95 o.s.i (*0-394-60374-5*) Random Hse., Inc.

—Goodbye, Columbus & Five Short Stories. 1994. 320p. pap. 13.00 (*0-679-74826-1*) Random Hse., Inc.

—The Human Stain. tchr. ed. 234.00 o.p. (*0-618-06598-9*); 2000. 368p. tchr. ed. 26.00 (*0-618-05945-8*) Houghton Mifflin Co.

—The Human Stain. 2001. (International Ser.). 384p. pap. 14.95 (*0-375-72634-9*, Vintage) Knopf Publishing Group.

—The Human Stain. l.t. ed. 2000. (Basic Ser.). 614p. 27.95 (*0-7862-2964-0*) Thorndike Pr.

—Letting Go. 1982. 657p. pap. 9.95 o.s.i (*0-374-51701-0*) Farrar, Straus & Giroux.

—Letting Go. 1997. 640p. pap. 15.00 (*0-679-76417-8*, Vintage) Knopf Publishing Group.

—Letting Go. 1962. 12.50 o.s.i (*0-394-43305-X*) Random Hse., Inc.

—Letting Go. 1991. 640p. pap. 10.95 o.s.i (*0-671-73616-7*, Touchstone) Simon & Schuster.

—Portnoy's Complaint. 1984. 320p. mass mkt. 5.99 o.s.i (*0-449-20291-7*, Fawcett) Ballantine Bks.

—Portnoy's Complaint. 1972. 320p. pap. 2.95 o.p. (*0-553-14350-6*) Bantam Bks.

—Portnoy's Complaint. 1994. reprint ed. lib. bdg. 32.95 o.p. (*1-56849-324-X*) Buccaneer Bks., Inc.

—Portnoy's Complaint. 1994. 304p. pap. 13.00 (*0-679-75645-0*, Vintage) Knopf Publishing Group.

—Portnoy's Complaint. 2002. 288p. 20.00 o.s.i (*0-375-50793-0*); 1983. 288p. 6.95 o.s.i (*0-394-60810-0*); 1969. 15.00 o.s.i (*0-394-44198-2*) Random Hse., Inc.

—Portnoy's Complaint. 1991. pap. 9.95 o.p. (*0-671-73615-9*, Touchstone) Simon & Schuster.

—The Prague Orgy. 1952. o.p. (*0-374-23679-8*) Farrar, Straus & Giroux.

—The Prague Orgy. 1996. 96p. pap. 10.00 (*0-679-74903-9*) Knopf, Alfred A. Inc.

—Zuckerman Bound: A Trilogy & Epilogue. 1986. 480p. mass mkt. 5.95 o.s.i (*0-449-21090-1*, Fawcett) Ballantine Bks.

—Zuckerman Bound: A Trilogy & Epilogue. 1985. 800p. 22.50 o.s.i (*0-374-29943-9*); 784p. pap. 9.95 o.p. (*0-374-51899-8*) Farrar, Straus & Giroux.

—Zuckerman Bound: A Trilogy & Epilogue. abr. ed. 1988. audio 14.00 o.s.i (*0-694-50958-2*, SWC 1768, HarperAudio) HarperTrade.

—Zuckerman Unbound. 1982. mass mkt. 3.50 o.s.i (*0-449-24521-7*, Fawcett) Ballantine Bks.

—Zuckerman Unbound. 1981. 225p. 10.95 o.p. (*0-374-29945-5*); 50.00 o.p. (*0-374-29946-3*) Farrar, Straus & Giroux.

—Zuckerman Unbound. l.t. ed. 1981. lib. bdg. 13.95 o.p. (*0-8161-3291-7*, Macmillan Reference USA) Gale Group.

—Zuckerman Unbound. 1995. 240p. pap. 13.00 (*0-679-74899-7*, Vintage) Knopf Publishing Group.

Rothchild, Sylvia. Family Stories for Every Generation. 229p. reprint ed. pap. 71.00 (*0-608-10553-8*, 207117300009) Bks. on Demand.

—Family Stories for Every Generation. 1989. 230p. (C). 24.95 o.p. (*0-8143-2240-9*) Wayne State Univ. Pr.

Rothstein, Chaya L. But Then I Remembered. 1991. 11.95 (*0-87306-558-1*) Feldheim, Philipp Inc.

—Mentchkins Make Friends. 1988. (J). (gr. 4-8). pap. 7.95 (*0-87306-453-4*) Feldheim, Philipp Inc.

Rothsteis, Shmuel. Heir to the Throne. 1990. (Illus.). 224p. (J). (gr. 5-8). 16.95 (*1-56062-043-9*, CFR106H); pap. 13.95 (*1-56062-044-7*, CFR106S) CIS Communications, Inc.

Rubens, Bernice. Brothers. 1984. 480p. 16.95 o.s.i (*0-385-29328-3*, Delacorte Pr.) Dell Publishing.

Ruby, Lois. Two Truths in My Pocket. 1983. 128p. mass mkt. 1.95 o.s.i (*0-449-70070-4*, Fawcett) Ballantine Bks.

—Two Truths in My Pocket. 1982. 156p. (J). (gr. 7 up). 9.95 o.p. (*0-670-73724-0*) Viking Penguin.

Ruffner, Sara S. A Liberal Education. 1991. 256p. (Orig.). pap. 10.95 o.p. (*0-931832-74-8*) Fithian Pr.

Rybakov, Anatoly. Heavy Sand. 1982. 384p. pap. 7.95 o.p. (*0-14-005535-5*, Penguin Bks.) Viking Penguin.

—Heavy Sand. Shukman, Harold, tr. from RUS. 1981. 384p. 13.95 o.p. (*0-670-36499-1*) Viking Penguin.

Sabato, Haim. Aleppo Tales. Simpson, Philip, tr. 2003. (HEB.). 250p. 19.95 (*1-59264-051-6*) Toby Pr.

Sachs, Marilyn. Peter & Veronica. 1995. 160p. (J). (gr. 4-7). pap. 5.99 (*0-14-037082-X*, Puffin Bks.) Penguin Putnam Bks. for Young Readers.

—Peter & Veronica. 1987. (Illus.). 176p. (J). (gr. 4-6). reprint ed. mass mkt. 2.50 o.p. (*0-590-40404-0*, Scholastic Paperbacks) Scholastic, Inc.

Sandgren, Leo Dupree. The Shadow of God: Stories from Early Judaism. 2003. 336p. 24.95 (*1-56563-605-8*) Hendrickson Pubs., Inc.

Schachter, Esty. Anya's Echoes: A Novel. 2003. 96p. pap. 10.00 (*1-56474-427-2*) Fithian Pr.

Schiffman, Ruth. Turning the Corner. 1981. 192p. (J). (gr. 6 up). 9.95 o.p. (*0-8037-9153-4*, Dial Bks. for Young Readers) Penguin Putnam Bks. for Young Readers.

Schleimer, Sarah M. One Good Turn. 1990. 10.95 o.p. (*0-87306-527-1*) Feldheim, Philipp Inc.

Schnitzler, Arthur. The Road into the Open. Byers, Roger, tr. 1992. 314p. (C). pap. 18.95 (*0-520-07774-1*); text 55.00 (*0-520-07575-7*) Univ. of California Pr.

Schnur, Steven. The Narrowest Bar Mitzvah. 1986. (Illus.). 48p. (Orig.). (J). (gr. 4-6). pap. text 6.95 o.p. (*0-8074-0316-4*, 123923) UAHC Pr.

—The Return of Morris Schumsky. 1987. (Illus.). 48p. (J). (gr. 4-7). pap. 6.95 (*0-8074-0358-X*, 123927) UAHC Pr.

—The Tie Man's Miracle: A Chanukah Tale. 1995. (Illus.). 32p. (J). (gr. k up). lib. bdg. 15.89 o.p. (*0-688-13464-5*, Morrow, William & Co.) Morrow/Avon.

Schonberg, Leonard. Legacy: A Novel of Three Generations. 2002. 336p. pap. 22.95 (*0-86534-357-8*) Sunstone Pr.

Schram, Peninnah. The Big Sukkah. 1986. (Illus.). 32p. (J). (ps-3). 10.95 o.p. (*0-930494-56-3*) Kar-Ben Publishing.

Schram, Peninnah, ed. Chosen Tales: Stories Told by Jewish Storytellers. 1995. 480p. 35.00 (*1-56821-352-2*) Aronson, Jason Pubs.

Schulz, Bruno. The Complete Fiction of Bruno Schulz: The Street of Crocodiles & Sanatorium Under the Sign of the Hourglass. 1989. 320p. 22.95 (*0-8027-1091-3*) Walker & Co.

Schur, Maxine R. The Peddler's Gift. Arico, Diane, ed. 1999. (Illus.). 32p. (J). (gr. k-4). 15.99 o.p. (*0-8037-1978-7*, Dial Bks. for Young Readers) Penguin Putnam Bks. for Young Readers.

Schurfranz, Vivian. Rachel, No. 21. 1986. 224p. (Orig.). (J). (gr. 7 up). pap. 2.50 o.p. (*0-590-40394-X*) Scholastic, Inc.

Schwartz, Amy. Mrs. Moskowitz & the Sabbath Candlesticks. 1983. (Illus.). 32p. (J). (gr. 4-7). pap. 7.95 (*0-8276-0372-X*) Jewish Pubn. Society.

Schwartz, Howard. The Four Who Entered Paradise. (Illus.). 256p. 2000. pap. 20.00 (*0-7657-6155-6*); 1995. 30.00 (*0-87668-579-3*) Aronson, Jason Pubs.

Schwartz, Steven. A Good Doctor's Son. 1998. 256p. 24.00 (*0-688-15401-8*, Morrow, William & Co.) Morrow/Avon.

Schwarz-Bart, Andre. The Last of the Just. 1973. 432p. pap. 2.95 o.p. (*0-553-10469-1*, 12510-9) Bantam Bks.

—The Last of the Just. Becker, Stephen, tr. from FRE. 1981. reprint ed. lib. bdg. 22.00 (*0-8376-0456-7*) Bentley Pubs.

—The Last of the Just. 1996. (Library of the Holocaust). 374p. reprint ed. 9.98 o.s.i (*1-56731-140-7*, MJF Bks.) Fine Communications.

—The Last of the Just. Becker, Stephen, tr. from FRE. 2000. 374p. 15.95 (*1-58567-016-2*) Overlook Pr., The.

—The Last of the Just. Becker, Stephen, tr. from FRE. 1973. 374p. (C). reprint ed. pap. 15.95 (*0-689-70365-1*, 202, Scribner) Simon & Schuster.

Schweiger-Dmi'el, Itzhak. Hannah's Sabbath Dress. 1996. (Illus.). 32p. (J). (ps-3). 15.00 (*0-689-80517-9*, Simon & Schuster Children's Publishing) Simon & Schuster Children's Publishing.

Scott, Walter, Sr. Ivanhoe. 2000. 536p. mass mkt. 3.99 (*0-8125-6565-7*, Tor Classics) Doherty, Tom Assocs., LLC.

—Ivanhoe. 2001. (Wishbone Classics Ser.: No. 12). 512p. (J). (gr. 3-7). mass mkt. 5.95 (*0-451-52799-2*) NAL.

Sebald, W. G. The Emigrants. Hulse, Michael, tr. from GER. Tr. of Ausgewanderten. (Illus.). 256p. 1997. pap. 14.95 (*0-8112-1366-8*, NDP853); 1996. 22.95 (*0-8112-1338-2*) New Directions Publishing Corp.

Segal, Brenda L. If I Forget Thee. 1985. 480p. mass mkt. 3.95 o.p. (*0-425-08384-5*) Berkley Publishing Group.

—If I Forget Thee. 1983. 480p. 16.95 o.p. (*0-312-40489-1*) St. Martin's Pr.

Segal, Jerry. The Place Where Nobody Stopped. 1991. (Illus.). 160p. (J). (gr. 6-8). 15.95 o.p. (*0-531-05897-2*); mass mkt. 16.99 o.p. (*0-531-08497-3*) Scholastic, Inc. (Orchard Bks.).

—The Place Where Nobody Stopped. Cohn, Amy, ed. 1994. (Illus.). 160p. (J). (gr. 5 up). reprint ed. pap. 4.95 o.p. (*0-688-12567-0*, Morrow, William & Co.) Morrow/Avon.

Seide, Michael. The Common Thread: A Book of Stories. 1975. (Modern Jewish Experience Ser.). reprint ed. 20.95 (*0-405-06748-8*) Ayer Co. Pubs., Inc.

Seletz, Jules. Abraham, Isaac & Jacob. 2000. E-Book 6.95 (*0-87714-473-7*) Denlingers Pubs., Ltd.

Seletz, Jules M. Abraham, Isaac & Jacob. 2001. 240p. pap. 14.95 (*0-87714-244-0*) Denlingers Pubs., Ltd.

Semel, Nava. Flying Lessons. Halkin, Hillel, tr. 1995. Orig. Title: Moris Havivel Melamid La-uf. (Illus.). 112p. (YA). (gr. 5 up). 14.00 o.p. (*0-689-80161-0*, Simon & Schuster Children's Publishing) Simon & Schuster Children's Publishing.

Sendak, Philip. In Grandpa's House. Barofsky, Semour, tr. from YID. 1985. (Illus.). 48p. (J). (ps up). 13.00 o.s.i (*0-06-025462-9*); lib. bdg. 9.89 o.s.i (*0-06-025463-7*) HarperCollins Children's Bk. Group.

Shalant, Phyllis. Shalom, Geneva Peace. 1992. 160p. (J). (gr. 7 up). 15.00 o.p. (*0-525-44868-3*, Dutton Children's Bks.) Penguin Putnam Bks. for Young Readers.

Shapiro, David. The Promise of God: A Novel. 2000. 335p. pap. 12.95 (*1-55874-744-3*, Simcha Pr.) Health Communications, Inc.

Sherman, Eileen B. The Odd Potato. 1984. (Illus.). 32p. (J). (gr. k-5). pap. 4.95 o.p. (*0-930494-37-7*) Kar-Ben Publishing.

Sherwood, Frances. The Book of Splendor. 2002. (Illus.). 352p. 25.95 (*0-393-02138-6*) Norton, W. W. & Co., Inc.

—The Book of Splendor: A Novel. 2003. (Illus.). 352p. pap. 14.95 (*0-393-32458-3*) Norton, W. W. & Co., Inc.

Sidi, Smadar S. The Dreidle Champ & Other Holiday Stories. 1987. (Illus.). 120p. (J). (gr. 3-9). 13.95 (*0-915361-89-2*) Lambda Pubs., Inc.

Siegel, Bruce H. Champion & Jewboy. 1995. (Illus.). 144p. (J). (gr. 8 up). 6.95 (*1-881283-11-9*) Alef Design Group.

Silbert, Layle. The Free Thinkers. 2001. 320p. pap. 14.95 (*1-58322-075-5*) Seven Stories Pr.

Silgal, Aranka. Grace in the Wilderness. 1986. 208p. mass mkt. 2.50 o.p. (*0-451-14624-7*, Signet Vista) NAL.
Silver, Norman. An Eye for Color. 1993. 192p. (YA). (gr. 8 up). 14.99 o.p. (*0-525-44859-4*, Dutton Children's Bks.) Penguin Putnam Bks. for Young Readers.
Sim, Dorrith M. In My Pocket. 1997. (Illus.). 32p. (J). (gr. k-3). 16.00 o.s.i (*0-15-201357-1*) Harcourt Trade Pubs.
Simon, Solomon. More Wise Men of Helm: And Their Merry Tales. 1979. (Illus.). (Orig.). reprint ed. pap. 9.50 o.p. (*0-87441-126-2*) Behrman Hse., Inc.
—Wise Men of Helm. 1942. (Illus.). (J). (gr. 3-7). pap. 10.95 (*0-87441-469-5*) Behrman Hse., Inc.
Singer, Isaac Bashevis. Gimpel the Fool & Other Stories. 1988. 208p. pap. 12.00 (*0-374-50052-5*); 1978. 205p. 9.95 o.p. (*0-374-16244-1*) Farrar, Straus & Giroux.
—The Golem. RS. (Illus.). (J). 1996. 96p. (ps-3). pap. 8.95 o.s.i (*0-374-42746-1*, Sunburst); 1982. 86p. (gr. 3 up). 40.00 o.p. (*0-374-32742-4*, Farrar, Straus & Giroux (BYR)); 1982. 86p. (gr. 3 up). 16.00 (*0-374-32741-6*, Farrar, Straus & Giroux (BYR)) Farrar, Straus & Giroux.
—Isaac Bashevis Singer: Three Complete Novels. Singer, Isaac Bashevis & Hemley, Cecil, trs. from YID. 1995. 464p. 11.99 o.s.i (*0-517-12273-1*) Random Hse. Value Publishing.
—Naftali the Storyteller & His Horse, Sus: And Other Stories. RS. (Sunburst Ser.). (Illus.). 144p. (J). (gr. 4-7). 1987. pap. 3.50 o.s.i (*0-374-45487-6*, Sunburst); 1976. 16.00 o.p. (*0-374-35490-1*, Farrar, Straus & Giroux (BYR)) Farrar, Straus & Giroux.
—Scum. Schwartz, Rosaline Dukalsky, tr. 1992. 224p. reprint ed. pap. 9.95 o.p. (*0-452-26786-2*, Plume) Dutton/Plume.
—Scum. 2003. pap. 19.00 (*0-374-52907-8*) Farrar, Straus & Giroux.
—Scum. Schwartz, Rosaline Dukalsky, tr. 1991. 224p. 19.95 o.p. (*0-374-25511-3*) Farrar, Straus & Giroux.
—Scum. 1993. 5.99 o.p. (*0-517-10827-5*) Random Hse. Value Publishing.
—Scum. Schwartz, Rosaline Dukalsky, tr. 1996. (Penguin Twentieth-Century Classics Ser.). 224p. pap. 11.95 o.s.i (*0-14-018842-8*, Viking) Viking Penguin.
—Shadows on the Hudson. Sherman, Joseph, tr. from YID. 1999. 560p. pap. 16.00 (*0-452-28003-6*, Plume) Dutton/Plume.
—Shadows on the Hudson. Sherman, Joseph, tr. from YID. 1998. 548p. 28.00 (*0-374-26186-5*) Farrar, Straus & Giroux.
—The Slave. Singer, Isaac Bashevis & Hemley, Cecil, trs. from YID. 1962. 311p. 10.95 o.p. (*0-374-26580-1*) Farrar, Straus & Giroux.
—A Tale of Three Wishes. RS. 1976. (Illus.). 32p. (J). (ps-3). 14.00 o.s.i (*0-374-37370-1*, Farrar, Straus & Giroux (BYR)) Farrar, Straus & Giroux.
—Zlateh the Goat & Other Stories. Shub, Elizabeth, tr. 1984. (Trophy Bk.). (Illus.). 104p. (J). (gr. 4-7). pap. 7.99 (*0-06-440147-2*, Harper Trophy) HarperCollins Children's Bk. Group.
Singer, Kalle. The Wholeness of a Broken Heart. 2000. 448p. pap. 14.00 (*1-57322-831-1*, Riverhead Trade (Paperbacks)) Berkley Publishing Group.
Singer, Katie. The Wholeness of a Broken Heart. 1999. 336p. 24.95 o.p. (*1-57322-147-3*, Riverhead Bks. (Hardcovers)) Putnam Publishing Group, The.
Skibell, Joseph. A Blessing on the Moon. 1997. 276p. tchr. ed. 21.95 (*1-56512-179-1*) Algonquin Bks. of Chapel Hill.
—A Blessing on the Moon. 1999. 288p. reprint ed. pap. 12.00 o.s.i (*0-425-16713-5*) Berkley Publishing Group.
Skvorecky, Josef. When Eve Was Naked: Stories of a Life's Journey. 2003. 368p. pap. 15.00 (*0-312-42173-7*) Picador.
Snyder, Carol. Ike & Mama & the Block Wedding. 1979. (Illus.). (J). (gr. 2-6). 7.95 o.s.i (*0-698-20461-1*, Coward-McCann) Putnam Publishing Group, The.
—Ike & Mama & the Once-a-Year Suit. 1992. (Illus.). 48p. (J). (gr. 2-5). reprint ed. pap. 5.95 (*0-8276-0418-1*) Jewish Pubn. Society.
—Ike & Mama & the Once-in-a-Lifetime Movie. 1981. (Illus.). 96p. (J). 7.95 o.p. (*0-698-20501-4*, Coward-McCann) Putnam Publishing Group, The.
—Ike & Mama & the Seven Surprises. 1985. (Illus.). 160p. (J). (gr. 3-6). 12.95 o.p. (*0-688-03732-1*) HarperCollins Children's Bk. Group.
—Ike & Mama & Trouble at School. 1983. (Illus.). (J). (gr. 4-7). 9.95 o.s.i (*0-698-20570-7*, Coward-McCann) Putnam Publishing Group, The.
Sofer, Barbara. Holiday Adventures of Achbar. 1983. (Illus.). 64p. (J). (gr. k-5). pap. 3.95 o.p. (*0-930494-22-9*) Kar-Ben Publishing.
Sohn, Amy. Run Catch Kiss: A Gratifying Novel. 256p. 2000. pap. 12.00 (*0-684-86753-2*); 1999. 23.00 (*0-684-85302-7*) Simon & Schuster. (Simon & Schuster).
Solotaroff, Ted. The Schocken Book of Contemporary Jewish Fiction. Rapoport, Nessa, ed. 1996. 416p. reprint ed. pap. 14.00 (*0-8052-1065-2*, Schocken) Knopf Publishing Group.
Speregen, Devra Newberger. Arielle & the Hanukkah Surprise. 1992. 32p. (J). (gr. k-3). mass mkt. 3.25 (*0-590-46125-7*, Cartwheel Bks.) Scholastic, Inc.
Spiegel, Isaiah. Ghetto Kingdom: Tales of the Lodz Ghetto. Hirsch, David H. & Hirsch, Roslyn, trs. from YID. 1998. (Jewish Lives Ser.). 184p. 44.00 o.p. (*0-8101-1624-3*); pap. 19.00 (*0-8101-1625-1*) Northwestern Univ. Pr.
Stark, Marisa K. Bring Us the Old People: A Novel. 1998. 208p. 22.95 (*1-56689-074-8*) Coffee Hse. Pr.
Stavans, Ilan, ed. The Oxford Book of Jewish Stories. 1998. 512p. 35.00 (*0-19-511019-6*) Oxford Univ. Pr., Inc.
Steiker, Valerie. The Leopard Hat: A Daughter's Story. 2003. 336p. pap. 13.00 (*0-375-72620-9*, Vintage) Knopf Publishing Group.
Steinberg, Milton. As a Driven Leaf. 1996. 480p. reprint ed. 40.00 o.s.i (*0-87668-994-2*) Aronson, Jason Pubs.
—As a Driven Leaf. 1996. pap. text 15.95 (*0-87441-103-3*) Behrman Hse., Inc.
Steinberg, Susan. The End of Free Love. 2003. 200p. pap. 13.95 (*1-57366-106-6*) Fiction Collective Two, Inc.
Steiner, Connie C. On Eagles Wings & Other Things. 1987. 32p. (J). (gr. k-4). 16.95 o.p. (*0-8276-0274-X*) Jewish Pubn. Society.
Steinfeld, J. J. Dancing at the Club Holocaust: Stories New & Selected. 1993. 224p. pap. 14.95 o.p. (*0-921556-30-6*) Ragweed Pr. CAN. *Dist:* LPC/InBook.
Stern, Daniel. Who Shall Live, Who Shall Die. 1994. 328p. pap. 11.95 (*0-89263-330-1*) Rice Univ. Pr.
—Who Shall Live, Who Shall Die. 1994. (First Rediscovered Modern Masterpieces Edition Ser.). 319p. 22.50 (*0-89263-329-8*) Texas A&M Univ. Pr.
Stern, Steve. Isaac & the Undertaker's Daughter. 1983. (Lost Roads Ser.: No. 22). 120p. (Orig.). (C). pap. 6.95 (*0-918786-27-4*) Lost Roads Pubs.
—Lazar Malkin Enters Heaven. 1987. 256p. 16.95 o.p. (*0-670-81379-6*) Viking Penguin.
—Plague of Dreamers: 3 Novellas. 1997. (Library of Modern Jewish Literature). 267p. pap. 17.95 (*0-8156-0453-X*) Syracuse Univ. Pr.
Stern, Steve & Grossman, B. A Plague of Dreamers: 3 Novellas. 1994. 256p. 20.00 o.p. (*0-684-19532-1*, Scribner) Simon & Schuster.
Stirling. Drums of Time. 1979. 12.95 o.p. (*0-312-22019-7*) St. Martin's Pr.
Stollman, Aryeh L. Far Euphrates: A Novel. 1998. 224p. 14.00 (*1-57322-697-1*, Riverhead Trade (Paperbacks)) Berkley Publishing Group.
Stollman, Aryeh Lev. The Dialogues of Time & Entropy. 2004. 240p. pap. 14.00 (*1-57322-375-1*, Riverhead Trade (Paperbacks)) Berkley Publishing Group.
—The Dialogues of Time & Entropy. 2003. (Illus.). 240p. 24.95 (*1-57322-235-6*, Riverhead Bks. (Hardcovers)) Putnam Publishing Group, The.
—Far Euphrates: A Novel. 1997. 224p. 21.95 o.s.i (*1-57322-075-2*, Riverhead Bks. (Hardcovers)) Putnam Publishing Group, The.
—The Illuminated Soul. 2003. 288p. pap. 14.00 (*1-57322-975-X*, Riverhead Trade (Paperbacks)) Berkley Publishing Group.
—The Illuminated Soul. 2002. (*1-57322-198-8*); 240p. 24.95 o.s.i (*1-57322-201-1*) Putnam Publishing Group, The. (Riverhead Bks. (Hardcovers)).
Sukenick, Ronald. Mosaic Man. 1999. 260p. pap. 23.00 (*1-57366-079-5*, Black Ice Bks.) Fiction Collective Two, Inc.
Sussman, Susan. There's No Such Thing as a Chanukah Bush, Sandy Goldstein. 1993. (J). (gr. 3-7). pap. 3.50 (*0-8075-7863-0*) Whitman, Albert & Co.
—There's No Such Thing as a Chanukah Bush, Sandy Goldstein. Tucker, Kathleen, ed. 1983. (Illus.). 48p. (J). (gr. 4-7). lib. bdg. 8.95 (*0-8075-7862-2*) Whitman, Albert & Co.
Swados, Elizabeth. Fabulous. 1998. 244p. 22.00 o.p. (*0-312-19547-8*) Picador.
Swartz, Leslie. First Passover. 1994. (Illus.). 32p. (J). (ps-3). pap. 5.95 (*0-671-88025-X*, Aladdin) Simon & Schuster Children's Publishing.
Syme, Deborah Shayne. Partners. 1990. (Illus.). 32p. (J). (ps-3). 8.95 (*0-8074-0435-7*, 103104) UAHC Pr.
Szeman, Sherri. The Kommandant's Mistress. 2000. 273p. pap. 13.95 (*1-55970-542-6*) Arcade Publishing, Inc.
—The Kommandant's Mistress. 1993. 224p. 17.50 o.p. (*0-06-017011-5*); 1994. 288p. reprint ed. pap. 12.50 o.p. (*0-06-092497-7*, Perennial) HarperTrade.
Tabak, Marsi. And Rachel Was His Wife. 1990. 16.95 (*0-87306-488-7*) Feldheim, Philipp Inc.
Tamar, Erika. Good-Bye, Glamour Girl. 1984. 224p. (J). (gr. 5 up). lib. bdg. 12.89 (*0-397-32088-4*) HarperCollins Children's Bk. Group.
—Good-Bye Glamour Girl. 1985. mass mkt. 2.50 o.p. (*0-451-14019-2*, Signet Vista) NAL.
Taube, Herman. My Baltimore Landsmen: A Documentary Novel. 1995. (Orig.). pap. 12.95 o.p. (*0-931848-90-3*) Dryad Pr.
Taylor, Kathrine Kressmann. Address Unknown. 2001. (Illus.). 64p. reprint ed. pap. 8.95 (*0-7434-1271-0*, Washington Square Pr.) Simon & Schuster.
Taylor, Kressmann. Address Unknown. 1995. 64p. 12.99 o.p. (*1-884910-17-3*, Story Pr.) F&W Pubns., Inc.
Taylor, Sydney. Danny Loves a Holiday. 1980. (Illus.). 80p. (J). (gr. 1-3). 8.95 o.p. (*0-525-28510-5*, Dutton) Dutton/Plume.
—A Papa Like Everyone Else. 1988. 160p. (J). (gr. k-6). pap. 2.95 o.s.i (*0-440-40129-1*, Yearling) Random Hse. Children's Bks.
Teitelbaum, Michael, adapted by. An American Tail: Escape from the Catsacks. 1986. (Illus.). 24p. (J). (ps-3). 2.25 o.s.i (*0-448-48614-8*, Grosset & Dunlap) Penguin Putnam Bks. for Young Readers.
Thoene, Bodie. Jerusalem Interlude. (Zion Covenant Ser.: No. 4). 2000. 448p. pap. 7.99 (*0-7642-2430-1*); 1990. 400p. pap. 12.99 (*1-55661-080-7*) Bethany Hse. Pubs.
—Munich Signature. (Zion Covenant Ser.: No. 3). 2000. 448p. pap. 7.99 (*0-7642-2429-8*); 1990. 400p. pap. 12.99 (*1-55661-079-3*) Bethany Hse. Pubs.
—Vienna Prelude. (Zion Covenant Ser.: No. 1). 2000. 464p. pap. 7.99 (*0-7642-2427-1*); 1989. 416p. pap. 12.99 (*1-55661-066-1*) Bethany Hse. Pubs.
—Warsaw Requiem. 2000. (Zion Covenant Ser.: No. 6). 544p. pap. 7.99 (*0-7642-2432-8*) Bethany Hse. Pubs.
Thoene, Bodie & Thoene, Brock. First Light. 2003. (Illus.). xix, 395p. pap. (*0-8423-7507-4*) Tyndale Hse. Pubs.
—The Jerusalem Scrolls. 2001. (Zion Legacy Ser.: No. 4). (Illus.). 304p. 24.95 o.s.i (*0-670-03012-0*, Viking) Viking Penguin.
—Jerusalem Vigil. 2001. (Zion Legacy Ser.: No. 1). 336p. pap. 13.00 (*0-14-029856-8*) Penguin Group (USA) Inc.
—Jerusalem Vigil. 2000. (Zion Legacy Ser.: No. 1). (Illus.). 352p. 19.95 o.p. (*0-670-88911-3*) Viking Penguin.
—Jerusalem's Hope, Vol. 6. 2002. (Illus.). 272p. 24.95 (*0-670-03084-8*, Viking) Viking Penguin.
—Stones of Jerusalem. 2002. (Zion Legacy Ser.: No. 5). (Illus.). 304p. 24.95 (*0-670-03051-1*, Viking) Viking Penguin.
—Thunder from Jerusalem. 2000. (Zion Legacy Ser.: No. 2). (Illus.). 352p. 19.95 o.s.i (*0-670-89206-8*, Viking); 4p. 25.95 o.s.i (*0-14-180237-5*, Penguin AudioBooks) Viking Penguin.
Thoene, Brock. The Jerusalem Scrolls: A Novel of Struggle for Jerusalem. 2002. 288p. pap. 13.00 (*0-14-200151-1*) Penguin Group (USA) Inc.
—Stones of Jerusalem: A Novel. 2003. 272p. pap. 13.00 (*0-14-200188-0*) Penguin Group (USA) Inc.
Thoene, Brock & Thoene, Bodie. Jerusalem's Heart. l.t. ed. 2002. lib. bdg. 27.95 (*1-58547-134-8*, Premier) Ctr. Point Large Print.
—Jerusalem's Hope. 2003. 272p. pap. 14.00 (*0-14-200357-3*) Penguin Group (USA) Inc.
Throssell, Ric, contrib. by. Tomorrow - 1997. 289p. (*0-646-28766-4*) Welles, Dorian Proprietary, Ltd.
Tisma, Aleksandar. The Book of Blam. 2000. 240p. pap. 13.00 o.s.i (*0-15-600841-6*) Harcourt Trade Pubs.
—The Book of Blam. Heim, Michael H., tr. from CRO. 1998. 240p. (C). 23.00 (*0-15-100235-5*) Harcourt Trade Pubs.
—Kapo. 1993. 24.95 o.s.i (*0-15-146693-9*) Harcourt Trade Pubs.
Tobias, Tobi. Pot Luck. 1993. (Illus.). (J). 32p. 15.00 o.p. (*0-688-09824-X*); lib. bdg. 14.93 o.p. (*0-688-09825-8*) HarperCollins Children's Bk. Group.
Topol, Edward. The Jewish Lover. E-Book 25.95 (*0-312-24613-7*); 1998. 496p. 25.95 (*0-312-19291-6*); 1998. 25.95 o.p. (*0-312-15557-3*) St. Martin's Pr.
Travis, Lucille. Tirzah. Garber, S. David, ed. 1991. 160p. (Orig.). (J). (gr. 4-7). pap. 5.99 (*0-8361-3546-6*) Herald Pr.
Tremain, Rose. Music & Silence. 2000. 485p. 25.00 o.s.i (*0-374-19989-2*) Farrar, Straus & Giroux.
Tulchinsky, Karen X. Love & Other Ruins. 2003. 317p. pap. 15.95 (*1-55192-554-0*, Polestar Book Pubs.) Raincoast Bk. Distribution CAN. *Dist:* Publishers Group West.
Tyberg, Sarah. El Al Hold That Flight. 1992. 10.95 o.p. (*0-87306-591-3*) Feldheim, Philipp Inc.
Uhlman, Fred. Reunion. 112p. 1997. pap. 10.00 (*0-374-52515-3*); 1977. 6.95 o.p. (*0-374-24951-2*) Farrar, Straus & Giroux.
Unger, David. Life in the Damn Tropics: A Novel. 2002. (Library of Modern Jewish Literature). 308p. 34.95 (*0-8156-0737-7*) Syracuse Univ. Pr.
Updike, John. Bech: A Book. 1999. pap. 12.00 (*0-449-45933-0*); 1998. 224p. pap. 12.95 (*0-449-00452-X*) Ballantine Bks. (Fawcett).
—Bech: A Book. 1970. 13.95 o.s.i (*0-394-41638-4*) Knopf, Alfred A. Inc.
—Bech at Bay: A Quasi-Novel. mass mkt. 7.50 (*0-449-00565-8*); 1999. 256p. pap. 12.00 (*0-449-00404-X*) Ballantine Bks. (Fawcett).
—Bech at Bay: A Quasi-Novel. 1998. 240p. 23.00 (*0-375-40368-X*) Knopf, Alfred A. Inc.
—Bech Is Back. 1999. pap. 12.00 (*0-449-45934-9*); 1998. 208p. pap. 12.00 (*0-449-00453-8*); 1983. 192p. mass mkt. 5.99 o.s.i (*0-449-20277-1*) Ballantine Bks. (Fawcett).
—Bech Is Back. 1982. (Illus.). 195p. 25.00 o.s.i (*0-394-52806-9*) Knopf, Alfred A. Inc.
—The Complete Henry Bech. 2001. (Everyman's Library). 544p. 23.00 (*0-375-41176-3*) Knopf, Alfred A. Inc.
Upton, Rosemary. The Court & the Kingdom. 1993. 304p. (Orig.). pap. 8.99 o.p. (*0-87788-159-6*, Shaw) WaterBrook Pr.
Uris, Leon. Exodus. 1983. (Illus.). 608p. mass mkt. 7.99 (*0-553-25847-8*) Bantam Bks.
—Exodus. 1994. reprint ed. lib. bdg. 35.95 (*1-56849-353-3*) Buccaneer Bks., Inc.
—Exodus. 1958. 648p. 21.95 o.s.i (*0-385-05082-8*) Doubleday Publishing.
—Exodus. 2000. (Modern Classics Ser.). (Illus.). 640p. 10.99 (*0-517-20798-2*) Random Hse., Inc.
—Exodus. 1959. 14.04 (*0-606-00621-4*) Turtleback Bks.
—A God in Ruins. 1999. 483p. 26.00 (*0-06-018377-2*); 656p. pap. 27.50 (*0-06-093304-6*) HarperCollins Pubs.
—A God in Ruins, Set. abr. ed. 1999. audio 25.00 (*0-694-52040-3*, HarperAudio) HarperTrade.
—A God in Ruins. 2000. 528p. mass mkt. 7.99 (*0-06-109793-4*, Avon Bks.) Morrow/Avon.
Van Gieson, Judith. Land of Burning Heat: A Claire Reynier Mystery. 2003. 272p. mass mkt. 5.99 (*0-451-20800-5*, Signet Bks.) NAL.
—Land of Burning Heat: A Claire Reynier Mystery. l.t. ed. 2003. (Senior Lifestyles Ser.). 28.95 (*0-7862-5470-X*) Thorndike Pr.
—Land of Burning Heat: A Claire Reynier Mystery. 2003. 264p. 24.95 (*0-8263-3172-6*) Univ. of New Mexico Pr.
Van Kampen, Robert. The Fourth Reich. 1997. 448p. (gr. 13 up). 24.99 o.p. (*0-8007-1745-7*); pap. 14.99 o.p. (*0-8007-5650-9*) Revell, Fleming H. Co.
Vapnyar, Lara. There Are Jews in My House: Stories. 2003. 160p. 17.95 (*0-375-42250-1*, Pantheon) Knopf Publishing Group.
Viereck, George S. & Eldridge, Paul. My First Two Thousand Years. 1932. 501p. reprint ed. 25.00 o.p. (*0-403-01254-6*) Scholarly Pr., Inc.
—My First Two Thousand Years: The Autobiography of the Wandering Jew. 1984. 501p. reprint ed. 25.00 o.s.i (*0-911378-16-2*) Sheridan Hse., Inc.
Viereck, George Sylvester & Eldridge, Paul. My First Two Thousand Years: The Autobiography of the Wandering Jew. 2001. xiii, 501p. reprint ed. pap. 20.00 (*1-57409-128-X*) Sheridan Hse., Inc.
Vogiel, Eva. A Weed among the Roses. 1993. 14.95 (*0-87306-635-9*); pap. 11.95 (*0-87306-637-5*) Feldheim, Philipp Inc.
Von Sacher-Masoch, Leopold. Jewish Life: Tales from Nineteenth-Century Euroope. Lewis, Virginia, tr. from GER. & afterword by by. 2002. (Studies in Austrian Literature, Culture, & Thought). (Illus.). 216p. 24.50 (*1-57241-114-7*) Ariadne Pr.
—A Light for Others & Other Jewish Tales from Galicia. 1994. (Studies in Austrian Literature, Culture & Thought). 350p. pap. 25.95 (*0-929497-93-7*) Ariadne Pr.
Wartofsky, Victor. Meeting the Pieman. 2001. 320p. reprint ed. pap. 12.95 (*0-88739-282-2*) Creative Arts Bk. Co.
Webster, Brenda S. Paradise Farm. 250p. (C). 2000. pap. text 19.95 (*0-7914-4100-8*); 1999. text 20.50 (*0-7914-4099-0*) State Univ. of New York Pr.
Weil, Jiri. Colors: Barvy. Harrell, Rachel, tr. from CZE. 2001. (Czech Translations Ser.: Vol. 2). 90p. (*0-930042-87-5*) Michigan Slavic Pubns.
Weilerstein, Sadie R. Best of K'tonton. 1980. (Illus.). 96p. (J). (gr. 1 up). 9.95 o.p. (*0-8276-0184-0*) Jewish Pubn. Society.
—K'tonton in the Circus: A Hanukkah Adventure. (Illus.). 96p. (J). (gr. 2 up). pap. 9.95 o.p. (*0-8276-0303-7*) Jewish Pubn. Society.
Weilerstein, Sadie Rose. Best of K'tonton. (Illus.). 94p. (J). (gr. 1 up). pap. 9.95 (*0-8276-0187-5*) Jewish Pubn. Society.
—K'tonton's Yom Kippur Kitten. 1995. (Illus.). 36p. (J). (ps-3). 9.95 (*0-8276-0541-2*) Jewish Pubn. Society.
Weinfeld, Chaya B. New Beginnings. 1999. 288p. 13.95 (*1-880582-46-5*) Judaica Pr., Inc., The.
Weinfeld, Chaya Baila. An Unexpected Detour: And Other Stories. 2003. (YA). 19.95 (*1-880582-20-1*, AUDH) Judaica Pr., Inc., The.
Weiss, David. The Mensch. 1998. (First Ser.). 192p. pap. 14.00 o.p. (*0-922811-32-6*) Mid-List Pr.
Weiss, Nicki. Stone Men. 1993. (Illus.). 32p. (J). (ps up). 14.00 o.p. (*0-688-11015-0*); lib. bdg. 13.93 o.p. (*0-688-11016-9*) HarperCollins Children's Bk. Group. (Greenwillow Bks.).

Welt, Elly. Berlin Wild. 1988. 400p. mass mkt. 4.50 o.p. (0-451-40028-3, Onyx) NAL.
—Berlin Wild. 1986. 384p. 17.95 o.p. (0-670-80925-X) Viking Penguin.
Wengrov, Charles. Zalman's Menorah: Based on Old Jewish Folktale. 1987. 10.95 (0-87306-450-X) Feldheim, Philipp Inc.
Wenner, Kate. Setting Fires. 2001. 352p. reprint ed. pap. 13.00 (0-425-18210-X) Berkley Publishing Group.
—Setting Fires. 2000. 304p. 24.00 o.s.i (0-684-83748-X, Scribner) Simon & Schuster.
Werthan, Libby Rosenbaum. The Fourth Corner. 2001. (Illus.). 144p. 16.95 (965-229-275-3) Gefen Publishing Hse., Ltd ISR. *Dist:* Gefen Bks.
Whiteman, Amram. Bar Kochba. 1985. 150p. 10.95 (0-8197-0499-7) Bloch Publishing Co.
Wiesel, Elie. Legends of Our Time. 1987. 198p. reprint ed. pap. 14.00 o.s.i (0-8052-0714-7, Schocken) Knopf Publishing Group.
—Night Trilogy. 2004. 318p. reprint ed. 25.00 (0-8090-7369-2, Hill & Wang) Farrar, Straus & Giroux.
—The Testament. 1982. 272p. mass mkt. 3.95 o.s.i (0-553-20810-1) Bantam Bks.
—The Testament. Wiesel, Marion, tr. from FRE. 1999. 352p. pap. 13.00 (0-8052-1115-2, Schocken) Knopf Publishing Group.
—The Testament. Wiesel, Marion, tr. 1990. pap. 9.95 o.s.i (0-671-65746-1, Touchstone) Simon & Schuster.
—The Testament. Wiesel, Marion, tr. 1981. 13.95 o.s.i (0-671-44833-1) Summit Bks.
—Le Testament d'un Poete Juif Assassine. 1981. (FRE.). pap. 16.95 (0-7859-2684-4) French & European Pubns., Inc.
—Twilight. Wiesel, Marion, tr. from FRE. 1995. 224p. pap. 12.00 (0-8052-1058-X, Schocken) Knopf Publishing Group.
—Twilight. 1988. 75.00 o.s.i (0-671-66435-2); 17.95 o.p. (0-671-64407-6) Summit Bks.
—Twilight. Wiesel, Marion, tr. 1989. 224p. pap. 9.95 (0-446-39066-6) Warner Bks., Inc.
Wiesel, Elie, ed. The Golem: The Story of a Legend. Borchardt, Anne, tr. 1983. (Illus.). 105p. 12.50 o.p. (0-671-45483-8); 50.00 o.p. (0-671-49624-7) Summit Bks.
Wills, Lawrence M., ed. & tr. from GEC. Ancient Jewish Novels: An Anthology. 2002. 320p. pap. 24.95 (0-19-515142-9); text 55.00 (0-19-515141-0) Oxford Univ. Pr., Inc.
Willson, Sarah. Let My Babies Go! A Passover Story. 1998. (Rugrats Ser.). (Illus.). 32p. (J). (ps-2). pap. 5.99 (0-689-81979-X, Simon Spotlight/ Nickelodeon) Simon & Schuster Children's Publishing.
Wilson, Jonathan. The Hiding Room. 1995. 272p. 23.95 o.p. (0-670-85603-7, Viking) Viking Penguin.
Winkler, Gershon. The Hostage Torah. 1981. (Judaica Youth Ser.). (Illus.). (J). (gr. 7 up). pap. 7.95 (0-910818-34-7) Judaica Pr., Inc., The.
Wisse, Ruth R. A Shtetl & Other Yiddish Novellas. 1973. (Library of Jewish Studies). 368p. 6.95 o.p. (0-87441-201-3) Behrman Hse., Inc.
Wisse, Ruth R., ed. A Shtetl & Other Yiddish Novellas. 1986. 344p. reprint ed. 34.95 o.p. (0-8143-1848-7); pap. 18.95 (0-8143-1849-5) Wayne State Univ. Pr.
Witham, Larry. The Negev Project. 1994. 301p. 17.95 (0-9640428-0-0) Meridian Bks. of Maryland.
Wojdowski, Bogdan. Bread for the Departed. Levine, Madeline G., tr. from ENG. 1997. (Jewish Lives Ser.). 304p. 59.95 (0-8101-1455-0); pap. 24.00 (0-8101-1456-9) Northwestern Univ. Pr.
Wolf, Janet. Her Book. 1982. (Illus.). 40p. (J). (ps-2). lib. bdg. 9.89 o.p. (0-06-026582-5) HarperCollins Children's Bk. Group.
Wolf, Leonard. False Messiah, 001. 1982. 13.95 o.p. (0-395-32528-5) Houghton Mifflin Co.
Wolff, Ferida. Pink Slippers, Bat Mitzvah Blues. (J). 1994. 138p. (gr. 4-7). pap. 9.95 (0-8276-0531-5); 1989. (gr. 3-7). 14.95 o.p. (0-8276-0332-0) Jewish Pubn. Society.
Wouk, Herman. The Hope. 1995. mass mkt. (0-316-99978-4); 1993. 693p. 24.95 o.s.i (0-316-95519-1); 1993. 693p. 125.00 o.p. (0-316-95521-3); 2002. 704p. reprint ed. pap. 15.95 (0-316-95441-1, Back Bay) Little Brown & Co.
Yaffe, Rachel. Lost & Found: And Other Stories. 2002. (Illus.). 106p. (J). 14.00 (0-8266-0330-0, Merkos L'Inyonei Chinuch) Kehot Pubn. Society.
Yedidya & the Esrog Tree. 1982. pap. 2.95 (0-87306-235-3) Feldheim, Philipp Inc.
Yehoshua, A. B. The Continuing Silence of a Poet: The Collected Stories of A. B. Yehoshua. 1991. 336p. pap. 9.95 o.p. (0-14-014844-2, Penguin Bks.) Penguin Group (USA) Inc.
Yezierska, Anzia. How I Found America: Collected Stories of Anzia Yezierska. 1995. 272p. (C). pap. 11.95 (0-89255-211-5); 1980. 352p. 24.95 o.p. (0-89255-160-7) Persea Bks., Inc.
—Hungry Hearts. lib. bdg. 21.95 (0-8488-2086-X) Amereon, Ltd.
—Hungry Hearts. 1975. (Modern Jewish Experience Ser.). reprint ed. 26.95 (0-405-06754-2) Ayer Co. Pubs., Inc.
—Hungry Hearts. 1997. (Twentieth Century Classics Ser.). 288p. pap. 12.00 (0-14-118005-6, Penguin Classics) Viking Penguin.
—Hungry Hearts & Other Stories. 1985. 364p. (Orig.). (C). pap. 9.95 o.p. (0-89255-093-7) Persea Bks., Inc.
—The Open Cage: An Anzia Yezierska Collection. 1993. 280p. (C). pap. 9.95 (0-89255-036-8) Persea Bks., Inc.
—The Open Cage: Collection. Harris, Alice K., ed. 1979. 12.95 o.p. (0-89255-035-X) Persea Bks., Inc.
—Salome of the Tenements. l.t. ed. 1998. 235p. text 27.95 (1-56000-478-9) Transaction Pubs.
—Salome of the Tenements. 1995. (Radical Novel Reconsidered Ser.). 160p. pap. text 15.95 (0-252-06435-6) Univ. of Illinois Pr.
Yolen, Jane. And Twelve Chinese Acrobats. 1995. (Illus.). 50p. (J). 15.95 o.p. (0-399-22691-5, Philomel) Penguin Putnam Bks. for Young Readers.
Zakon, Miriam S. The Cohens of Tzefat. 1985. (ArtScroll Youth Ser.). (Illus.). 128p. (YA). (gr. 6-12). 14.99 (0-89906-783-2) Mesorah Pubns., Ltd.
—The Egyptian Star. 1983. (Judaica Youth Ser.). (Illus.). 128p. (J). (gr. 3-9). pap. 6.95 (0-910818-48-7) Judaica Pr., Inc., The.
—Floating Minyan of Pirate's Cove. 1986. (Judaica Youth Ser.). (Illus.). 152p. (J). (gr. 3-9). 8.95 (0-910818-62-2) Judaica Pr., Inc., The.
Zalben, Jane Breskin. Beni's Family Treasury, ERS. 1998. (Illus.). 128p. (Orig.). (J). (ps-4). 18.95 (0-8050-5889-3, Holt, Henry & Co. Bks. For Young Readers) Holt, Henry & Co.
—Goldie's Purim, ERS. 1991. (Illus.). 32p. (J). (ps-2). 13.95 o.p. (0-8050-1227-3, Holt, Henry & Co. Bks. For Young Readers) Holt, Henry & Co.
—Papa's Latkes, ERS. 1996. (Illus.). 32p. (J). (ps-3). 13.95 o.s.i (0-8050-4634-8, Holt, Henry & Co. Bks. For Young Readers) Holt, Henry & Co.
—Papa's Latkes: Mini Book, ERS. 1994. 32p. (J). (ps-3). 5.95 o.s.i (0-8050-3099-9, Holt, Henry & Co. Bks. For Young Readers) Holt, Henry & Co.
—Unfinished Dreams: A Poignant Coming-of-Age Novel about Dreams Cut Short by AIDS. 1996. 176p. (J). (gr. 4-7). 16.00 o.s.i (0-689-80033-9, Simon & Schuster Children's Publishing) Simon & Schuster Children's Publishing.
Zamvil, Stella. In the Time of the Russias. 1985. 112p. (Orig.). pap. 10.00 o.p. (0-936784-02-4) Daniel, John & Co., Pubs.
Zangwill, Israel. Children of the Ghetto. 1977. (Victorian Library Ser.). (Illus.). 448p. reprint ed. text 15.75 o.p. (0-7185-5028-5) Brill Academic Pubs., Inc.
—Children of the Ghetto. 2001. (Works of Israel Zangwill). pap. text 56.00 (0-7426-8780-5) Classic Bks.
—Children of the Ghetto. 1998. 512p. reprint ed. pap. 27.95 (0-8143-2593-9) Wayne State Univ. Pr.
—The King of Schnorrers. E-Book 3.95 (0-594-01478-6) 1873 Pr.
—The King of Schnorrers. 2003. (Judaica Ser.). 128p. pap. 6.95 (0-486-42872-9) Dover Pubns., Inc.
—The King of Schnorrers. 1987. (Illus.). 156p. 14.95 (0-915361-98-1) Lambda Pubs., Inc.
—King of Schnorrers. 1983. pap. 1.50 o.p. (0-486-21354-4) Dover Pubns., Inc.
—King of Schnorrers. 1981. 5.00 o.p. (0-8446-3228-7) Smith, Peter Pub., Inc.
—Selected Works: Three Volumes in One. 1977. (Short Story Index Reprint Ser.). reprint ed. 63.95 (0-8369-4141-1) Ayer Co. Pubs., Inc.
Zimler, Richard. The Last Kabbalist of Lisbon. 2000. 318p. 15.95 (1-58567-022-7); 1998. 272p. 24.95 (0-87951-834-0) Overlook Pr., The.
Zipper, Jacob. The Far Side of the River: Selected Short Stories. Butovsky, M., tr. 1995. 96p. lib. bdg. 27.00 o.p. (0-8095-4873-9) Millefleurs.
—The Far Side of the River: Selected Short Stories. Butovsky, M., tr. from YID. 1994. 96p. pap. 8.95 (0-88962-287-6) Mosaic Pr.
Zucker, Benjamin. Blue. 2001. 248p. pap. 29.95 (1-58567-181-9); 2000. (Illus.). 224p. 40.00 (1-58567-000-6) Overlook Pr., The.
—Green. 2001. (Illus.). 288p. 40.00 (1-58567-174-6) Overlook Pr., The.
Zweig, Stefan. Jewish Legends. Paul, Eden & Paul, Cedar, trs. from GER. 1987. (Masterworks of Modern Jewish Writing Ser.). 300p. (Orig.). pap. 9.95 o.p. (0-910129-59-2) Wiener, Markus Pubs., Inc.

# M

## MENNONITES—FICTION

Birdsell, Sandra. The Russlander. 2002. 408p. pap. (0-7710-1451-1) McClelland & Stewart.
Block, Kevin James. Without Shedding of Blood. 1994. 185p. pap. (1-895308-17-8) Hyperion Pr., Ltd.
Dick, Janice L. Calm Before the Storm. 2002. (Crossings of Promise Ser.: Bk. 1). (Illus.). 368p. pap. 14.99 (0-8361-9201-X) Herald Pr.
—Eye of the Storm, 3 vols. 2003. (Crossings of Promise Ser.). 360p. pap. 14.99 (0-8361-9253-2) Herald Pr.
Epp, Margaret. Chariots in the Smoke. 1990. 350p. (Orig.). pap. 5.95 (0-921788-04-5) Kindred Productions.
—The Earth Is Round. 1974. 228p. (Orig.). pap. 4.50 o.p. (0-919797-00-8) Kindred Productions.
Epp, Margaret A. The Earth Is Round. 1998. 228 p. (Orig.). mass mkt. 4.95 (0-87813-575-8) Christian Light Pubns., Inc.
Martens, Wilfred. River of Glass. 1980. 232p. pap. 6.95 o.p. (0-8361-1913-4) Herald Pr.
Martin, Rebecca. Horse Called Willing. 1998. 165p. pap. 6.95 (0-87813-576-6) Christian Light Pubns., Inc.
Mueller, Amelia. A Quiet Strength: The Susanna Ruth Krehbiel Story. 1992. 146p. pap. 2.50 (0-87303-201-2) Faith & Life Pr.
Myers, Tamar. Between a Wok & a Hard Place. 1998. (Magdalena Yoda Ser.: Vol. 5). 272p. mass mkt. 5.99 (0-451-19230-3, Signet Bks.) NAL.
—Between a Wok & a Hard Place. l.t. ed. 2002. (Mystery Ser.). 373p. 29.45 (0-7862-4640-5) Thorndike Pr.
—The Crepes of Wrath: A Pennsylvania Dutch Mystery with Recipes. 2001. (Pennsylvania Dutch Mystery with Recipes Ser.). 240p. 19.99 o.s.i (0-451-20225-2) NAL.
—Custard's Last Stand: A Pennsylvania Dutch Mystery with Recipes. 2003. 240p. 19.95 (0-451-20782-3) NAL.
—Eat, Drink & Be Wary: A Pennsylvania Dutch Mystery with Recipes. 1998. (PennDutch Mysteries Ser.). 272p. mass mkt. 5.99 (0-451-19231-1, Signet Bks.) NAL.
—Eat, Drink & Be Wary: A Pennsylvania Dutch Mystery with Recipes. l.t. ed. 2001. 384p. 28.95 o.p. (0-7862-3455-5) Thorndike Pr.
—Hand That Rocks the Ladle. 2000. (Pennsylvania Dutch Mystery with Recipes Ser.). 272p. mass mkt. 5.99 (0-451-19755-0, Signet Bks.) NAL.
—Just Plain Pickled. 1997. 272p. mass mkt. 5.99 (0-451-19293-1, Signet Bks.) NAL.
—No Use Dying over Spilled Milk: A Pennsylvania-Dutch Mystery with Recipes. 1996. 272p. 20.95 o.p. (0-525-94099-5, Dutton) Dutton/Plume.
—No Use Dying over Spilled Milk: A Pennsylvania-Dutch Mystery with Recipes. 1997. 272p. mass mkt. 5.99 (0-451-18854-3, Signet Bks.) NAL.
—Parsley, Sage, Rosemary & Crime. 1996. (PennDutch Inn Mystery Ser.). 272p. mass mkt. 5.99 (0-451-18297-9, Signet Bks.) NAL.
—Play It Again Spam. 1999. (Pennsylvania Dutch Mystery with Recipes Ser.). 272p. mass mkt. 5.99 (0-451-19754-2, Signet Bks.) NAL.
—Too Many Crooks Spoil the Broth. 1995. (PennDutch Inn Mystery Ser.). 256p. mass mkt. 5.99 (0-451-18296-0, Signet Bks.) NAL.
—Too Many Crooks Spoil the Broth: A Pennsylvania-Dutch Mystery with Recipes. 1993. 256p. 17.00 o.s.i (0-385-47139-4) Doubleday Publishing.
Myers, Tamar & Myers, Les. Parsley, Sage, Rosemary & Crime. 1995. 256p. 21.95 o.s.i (0-385-47140-8) Doubleday Publishing.
Oke, Janette. The Calling of Emily Evans. 2003. (Classics for Girls Ser.). (Illus.). 176p. (J). 9.99 (0-7642-2713-0); 1998. (Women of the West Ser.: Bk. 1). 288p. mass mkt. 5.99 o.p. (0-7642-2098-5, 202098); 1990. (Women of the West Ser.). 224p. pap. 11.99 (1-55661-118-8); 1990. (Women of the West Ser.). 224p. pap. 12.99 o.p. (1-55661-121-8) Bethany Hse. Pubs.
—The Calling of Emily Evans. l.t. ed. 2000. (Christian Fiction Ser.). 345p. 26.95 (0-7862-2701-X) Thorndike Pr.
—Women of the West I: Calling of Emily Evans, Julia's Last Hope, Roses for Mama, Woman Named Damaris. 1991. (Women of the West Ser.). pap. 43.99 o.p. (1-55661-761-5) Bethany Hse. Pubs.
—Women of the West II, Vols. 5-8. 1993. (Women of the West Ser.). pap. 43.99 (1-55661-773-9, 252773) Bethany Hse. Pubs.
—Women of the West II: Drums of Change; Julia's Last Hope; Too Long a Stranger, 3 bks. 2000. (Women of the West Ser.). pap. 17.99 o.p. (0-7642-8648-X) Bethany Hse. Pubs.
—Women of the West III: Too Long Long a Stranger, The Bluebird & the Sparrow, 4 vols. 1996. (Women of the West Ser.). pap. 43.99 (0-7642-8025-2) Bethany Hse. Pubs.
Plett, Delbert F. Sarah's Prairie: A Novel. 1995. (1-895308-20-8) Windflower Communications.
Schwartz, Warren E. In the Far Country: A Portrait of Three Generations. 1984. (Illus.). 228p. (Orig.). pap. 12.00 (0-914222-14-7) American Historical Society of Germans from Russia.
Wiebe, Rudy. Sweeter Than All the World. 2002. 448p. pap. 14.00 (0-676-97341-8) Random Hse., Inc.
Yoder, James D. Black Spider over Tiegenhof. 1995. 232p. pap. 11.99 o.p. (0-8361-9012-2) Herald Pr.
—Black Spider over Tiegenhof. l.t. ed. 2000. (Christian Mystery Ser.). 335p. 23.95 (0-7862-2709-5) Thorndike Pr.
—Black Spider over Tiegenhof. 1995. E-Book 11.99 (0-585-22785-3) netLibrary, Inc.
Yoder, Paton. Tradition & Transition: Amish Mennonites & Old Order Amish, 1800-1900. 2000. 360p. pap. 31.00 (1-57910-468-1) Wipf & Stock Pubs.

## MEXICAN AMERICANS—FICTION

Anaya, Rudolfo A. Albuquerque. 1992. 13.04 (0-606-06168-1) Turtleback Bks.
—Albuquerque. 1992. 288p. 22.50 o.p. (0-8263-1359-0) Univ. of New Mexico Pr.
—Albuquerque. 1994. 304p. mass mkt. 7.50 (0-446-36544-0); 2000. 336p. reprint ed. pap. 13.95 (0-446-67615-2) Warner Bks., Inc.
—Rio Grande Fall. 1997. 352p. mass mkt. 6.99 (0-446-60486-0); 1996. 368p. 23.00 o.p. (0-446-51844-1) Warner Bks., Inc.
—Shaman Winter. 2000. 432p. mass mkt. 7.50 (0-446-60801-7); 1999. (Illus.). 374p. 30.00 o.p. (0-446-52374-7) Warner Bks., Inc.
—Zia Summer. 1996. 13.04 (0-606-17163-0) Turtleback Bks.
—Zia Summer. 1996. 368p. mass mkt. 7.50 (0-446-60316-3); 1995. 400p. (YA). 21.95 o.p. (0-446-51843-3) Warner Bks., Inc.
Bjorkquist, Elena D. Suffer Smoke. 1996. 202p. pap. 11.95 o.p. (1-55885-168-2) Arte Publico Pr.
Blake, James C. Borderlands. 1999. 256p. pap. 12.50 o.p. (0-380-79485-3); 241p. 24.00 o.p. (0-380-97807-5) Morrow/Avon. (Avon Bks.).
Candelaria, Nash. Memories of the Alhambra. 192p. 1977. 25.00 (0-9601086-1-0); 1982. reprint ed. pap. 15.00 (0-916950-32-8) Bilingual Pr./Editorial Bilingue.
Chavez Ballejos, Gilberto & Witt, Shirley H. El Indio Jesus: A Novel. 2000. (Politics & International Relations of Southeast Asia Ser.: Vol. 35). x, 257p. 29.95 (0-8061-3230-2) Univ. of Oklahoma Pr.
Chavez Ballejos, Gilberto & Witt, Shirley Hill. El Indio Jesus: A Novel. 2002. pap. 17.95 (0-8061-3376-7) Univ. of Oklahoma Pr.
Chavez, Denise. Face of an Angel. 1994. 356p. 23.00 o.p. (0-374-15204-7) Farrar, Straus & Giroux.
—The Face of an Angel. 1995. 480p. reprint ed. pap. 14.95 (0-446-67185-1) Warner Bks., Inc.
Cisneros, Sandra. Caramelo. 2003. 464p. pap. 13.95 (0-679-74258-1, Vintage); (SPA.). 496p. pap. 13.95 (1-4000-3099-4, Vintage); 464p. 24.00 (1-4000-4150-3) Knopf Publishing Group.
—Caramelo. 2002. 464p. 24.00 (0-679-43554-9) Knopf, Alfred A. Inc.
—Caramelo. 2002. (SPA.). 496p. 24.00 (0-375-41509-2) Random Hse., Inc.
—Caramelo. 2003. (Spanish Language Ser.). (SPA.). 28.95 (0-7862-5124-7); 30.95 (0-7862-5138-7) Thorndike Pr.
—La Casa en Mango Street. 2002. (SPA.). 150p. 27.95 (0-7862-4298-1) Thorndike Pr.
—La Casa en Mango Street. 1994. 16.00 (0-606-19185-2) Turtleback Bks.
—The House on Mango Street. 1989. 80p. 7.50 o.p. (0-934770-20-4) Arte Publico Pr.
—The House on Mango Street. 1991. (Contemporaries Ser.). 128p. pap. 9.95 (0-679-73477-5, RH4775, Vintage) Knopf Publishing Group.
—The House on Mango Street. 1996. (ESOL Companion Guide Ser.). 128p. pap. 13.13 (0-07-009429-2) McGraw-Hill Higher Education.
—The House on Mango Street. 1999. 11.95 (1-58130-559-1) Novel Units, Inc.
—The House on Mango Street. 1994. 160p. 24.00 (0-679-43335-X) Random Hse., Inc.
—The House on Mango Street. 1991. (Vintage Contemporaries Ser.). 16.00 (0-606-05352-2) Turtleback Bks.
Colman, Hila. That's the Way It Is, Amigo. 1975. (Illus.). 96p. (J). (gr. 6 up). 11.95 (0-690-00750-7) HarperCollins Children's Bk. Group.
Enright, Michael. Daisies in the Junkyard. 2002. 240p. 23.95 (0-7653-0144-X, Forge Bks.) Doherty, Tom Assocs., LLC.
Fernandez, Roberta. Fronterizas: Una Novela en Seis Cuentos. 2001. Orig. Title: Intaglio: A Novel in Six Stories. (SPA.). 192p. pap. 12.95 (1-55885-339-1) Arte Publico Pr.
Gilb, Dagoberto. Woodcuts of Women: Stories. 2001. (Illus.). 167p. 23.00 o.p. (0-8021-1679-5) Grove/ Atlantic, Inc.
Gomez-Pena, Guillermo. Friendly Cannibals. 1996. (Illus.). 64p. 15.00 (0-9631095-7-X) Artspace Bks.
Gonzalez, Genaro. The Quixote Cult. 1998. 224p. pap. 12.95 (1-55885-254-9) Arte Publico Pr.
Gonzalez, Rigoberto. Crossing Vines: A Novel. 2003. (Chicana & Chicano Visions of the Americas Ser.: Vol. 2). 216p. 24.95 (0-8061-3528-X) Univ. of Oklahoma Pr.

Guerrero, Lucrecia. Chasing Shadows. 2000. (Illus.). 175p. pap. 12.95 (*0-8118-2794-1*) Chronicle Bks. LLC.

Hinojosa, Rolando. Los Amigos de Becky. 1991. (Klail City Death Trip Ser.). (SPA.). 128p. pap. 9.50 o.p. (*1-55885-021-X*) Arte Publico Pr.

—Ask a Policeman: A Rafe Buenrostro Mystery. 1998. (Rafe Buenrostro Mysteries Ser.). 256p. pap. text 12.95 (*1-55885-226-3*) Arte Publico Pr.

—Becky & Her Friends. 1990. (Klail City Death Trip Ser.). 160p. pap. 9.50 (*1-55885-006-6*) Arte Publico Pr.

—Claros Varones de Belken: Fair Gentlemen of Belken County, Bilingual Edition. Cruz, Julia, tr. 1986. (United States Hispanic Creative Literature Ser.).Tr. of Fair Gentlemen of Belken County. (ENG & SPA.). 224p. pap. text 16.00 (*0-916950-65-4*); 223p. lib. bdg. 26.00 (*0-916950-64-6*) Bilingual Pr./Editorial Bilingue.

—El Condado de Belken-Klail City. 1994. (Clasicos Chicanos - Chicano Classics Ser.: No. 8). 168p. 25.00 (*0-927534-33-9*); pap. 15.00 (*0-927534-34-7*) Bilingual Pr./Editorial Bilingue.

—Dear Rafe. 1985. 136p. pap. 8.50 (*0-934770-38-7*) Arte Publico Pr.

—Estampas del Valle. 1994. (Clasicos Chicanos - Chicano Classics Ser.: No. 7). (SPA.). 144p. 24.00 (*0-927534-24-X*); pap. 13.00 (*0-927534-25-8*) Bilingual Pr./Editorial Bilingue.

—Klail City. 1987. (Klail City Death Trip Ser.). 144p. pap. 9.00 (*0-934770-54-9*) Arte Publico Pr.

—Mi Querido Rafa. 1981. (Klail City Death Trip Ser.). (SPA.). 112p. (C). pap. 8.50 o.p. (*0-934770-10-7*) Arte Publico Pr.

—Partners in Crime. 1985. 248p. (C). pap. 10.00 (*0-934770-37-9*) Arte Publico Pr.

—Rites & Witnesses. 1982. (Klail City Death Trip Ser.). 112p. pap. 8.50 o.p. (*0-934770-19-0*) Arte Publico Pr.

—The Useless Servants. 1993. 192p. (C). 8.95 (*1-55885-068-6*) Arte Publico Pr.

—The Valley. 1983. (Klail City Death Trip Ser.). 112p. 18.00 (*0-916950-37-9*); pap. 10.00 (*0-916950-38-7*) Bilingual Pr./Editorial Bilingue.

Houston-Davila, Daniel. Malinche's Children. 2003. 362p. 27.00 (*1-57806-521-6*) Univ. Pr. of Mississippi.

Lansdale, Joe R. Captains Outrageous. 2001. 336p. 24.45 o.p. (*0-89296-728-5*) Mysterious Pr.

—Captains Outrageous. 2003. 336p. pap. 12.95 (*0-446-67963-1*, Mysterious Pr. Paperback Bks.) Warner Bks., Inc.

Limon, Graciela. The Day of the Moon. 1999. 228p. pap. 12.95 (*1-55885-274-3*) Arte Publico Pr.

—The Memories of Ana Calderon. 200p. 2001. pap. 12.95 (*1-55885-355-3*); 1994. 9.95 (*1-55885-116-X*) Arte Publico Pr.

Lopez, Lorraine. Soy la Avon Lady & Other Stories. 2002. 233p. pap. 15.95 (*1-880684-86-1*) Curbstone Pr.

Martin, Patricia P. El Milagro & Other Stories. 1996. (Camino del Sol). 92p. 22.95 o.p. (*0-8165-1547-6*); pap. 9.95 (*0-8165-1548-4*) Univ. of Arizona Pr.

Martin, Patricia Preciado. Amor Eterno: Eleven Lessons in Love. 2000. (Camino del Sol). 121p. pap. 12.95 (*0-8165-1995-1*) Univ. of Arizona Pr.

—Amor Eterno: Eleven Lessons in Love. 2000. (Camino del Sol). 121p. 24.95 (*0-8165-1994-3*) Univ. of Arizona, Ctr. for Mineral Resources & U.S. Geological Survey.

Matiella, Ana Consuelo. The Truth about Alicia & Other Stories. 2002. (Camino del Sol). 150p. 24.95 (*0-8165-2161-1*); pap. 14.95 (*0-8165-2163-8*) Univ. of Arizona Pr.

Matinez, Manuel Luis. Drift. 2003. 256p. pap. 14.00 o.s.i (*0-312-30995-3*) Picador.

Mayo, Wendell. Centaur of the North. 1996. 140p. pap. 11.95 (*1-55885-165-8*) Arte Publico Pr.

Millar, Margaret. Ask for Me Tomorrow. l.t. ed. 1989. (Atlantic Mystery Ser.). 265p. pap. 14.95 o.p. (*1-55504-738-6*, 833) BBC Audiobooks America.

—Ask for Me Tomorrow. (Library of Crime Classics). 1991. 184p. pap. 8.95 o.p. (*1-55882-115-5*); 1985. 179p. reprint ed. pap. 4.95 o.p. (*0-930330-15-3*) International Polygonics, Ltd.

—Ask for Me Tomorrow. 1978. pap. 1.50 o.p. (*0-380-01805-5*, 35618, Avon Bks.) Morrow/Avon.

—Mermaid. 1982. 317p. (*0-89340-543-4*) BBC Audiobooks America.

—Mermaid. 1991. (Library of Crime Classics). 216p. pap. 8.95 (*1-55882-114-7*) International Polygonics, Ltd.

—The Murder of Miranda. 22.95 (*0-89190-156-6*) Amereon, Ltd.

—The Murder of Miranda. l.t. ed. 1980. 459p. lib. bdg. 5.95 o.p. (*0-89340-283-4*, 56) BBC Audiobooks America.

—The Murder of Miranda. 1988. 240p. reprint ed. pap. 4.95 o.p. (*0-930330-95-1*, Library of Crime Classics) International Polygonics, Ltd.

—The Murder of Miranda. 1979. 240p. 8.95 o.p. (*0-394-50509-3*) Random Hse., Inc.

Munoz, Manuel. Zigzagger. 2003. (Latino Voices Ser.). 184p. 49.95 (*0-8101-2098-4*); pap. 15.95 (*0-8101-2099-2*) Northwestern Univ. Pr.

Nava, Michael. The Burning Plain. 1999. 432p. mass mkt. 5.99 o.s.i (*0-553-58085-X*) Bantam Bks.

—The Burning Plain. 1998. 240p. 23.95 o.p. (*0-399-14310-6*, G. P. Putnam's Sons) Penguin Group (USA) Inc.

—Death of Friends. 1996. 288p. 22.95 o.p. (*0-399-13977-X*, G. P. Putnam's Sons) Penguin Group (USA) Inc.

—The Death of Friends. 1998. 256p. reprint ed. mass mkt. 5.99 o.s.i (*0-553-57763-8*) Bantam Bks.

—Goldenboy. 1988. 216p. 5.95 o.p. (*1-55583-141-9*); 1996. 224p. reprint ed. pap. 10.00 o.p. (*1-55583-366-7*); 1991. 215p. reprint ed. pap. 8.95 o.p. (*1-55583-130-3*) Alyson Pubns.

—The Hidden Law. 1994. (Los Angeles Mysteries Ser.). 192p. mass mkt. 4.99 o.s.i (*0-345-38406-7*) Ballantine Bks.

—The Hidden Law. 1992. 288p. 19.00 o.p. (*0-06-016783-1*) HarperTrade.

—How Town. 1991. (Los Angeles Mysteries Ser.). 240p. mass mkt. 4.99 o.s.i (*0-345-36987-4*) Ballantine Bks.

—How Town. 1990. 224p. 16.95 o.p. (*0-06-016207-4*) HarperTrade.

—The Little Death. 165p. 1986. pap. 7.95 o.p. (*0-932870-96-1*); 1997. reprint ed. pap. 9.95 o.p. (*1-55583-388-8*) Alyson Pubns.

—Rag & Bone: A Henry Rios Novel. 2001. 304p. 24.95 o.s.i (*0-399-14708-X*) Penguin Group (USA) Inc.

Nichols, John. The Magic Journey. 1996. 516p. pap. 12.95 o.s.i (*0-345-41033-5*); 1983. 546p. mass mkt. 5.99 o.s.i (*0-345-31049-7*, Ballantine Bks.) Ballantine Bks.

—The Magic Journey. 2000. (Illus.). 540p. pap. 15.00 (*0-8050-6339-0*, Owl Bks.); 1978. o.p. (*0-03-015356-5*); 1978. pap. o.p. (*0-03-042866-1*, Owl Bks.) Holt, Henry & Co.

—The Magic Journey. 1979. pap. 2.75 o.p. (*0-671-82311-6*, Pocket) Simon & Schuster.

—The Milagro Beanfield War. 1996. pap. 12.95 o.s.i (*0-345-41016-5*); 1987. 640p. mass mkt. 5.95 o.s.i (*0-345-34446-4*); 1986. mass mkt. 3.95 o.s.i (*0-345-33215-6*); 1978. mass mkt. 2.95 o.s.i (*0-345-28245-0*) Ballantine Bks.

—The Milagro Beanfield War. 2000. (Illus.). 464p. pap. 16.00 (*0-8050-6374-9*, Owl Bks.) Holt, Henry & Co.

—The Milagro Beanfield War. Facsimile Anniversary Edition. 1993. (Illus.). 484p. 27.50 o.p. (*0-8050-2805-6*) Holt, Henry & Co.

—The Nirvana Blues. 1996. pap. 12.95 o.s.i (*0-345-41037-8*); 1988. pap. o.p. (*0-345-00631-3*); 1983. 608p. mass mkt. 5.95 o.s.i (*0-345-30465-9*) Ballantine Bks.

—The Nirvana Blues. 2000. 528p. pap. 15.00 (*0-8050-6340-4*, Owl Bks.); 1981. 540p. o.p. (*0-03-059256-9*) Holt, Henry & Co.

Olivas, Daniel A. Assumption & Other Stories. 2003. 136p. pap. text 11.00 (*1-931010-19-6*) Bilingual Pr./Editorial Bilingue.

Palmer, Karen. Border Dogs: A Novel. 2002. 305p. 24.00 (*1-56947-315-3*) Soho Pr., Inc.

Ramos, Manuel. The Ballad of Gato Guerrero. 2004. (Latino Voices Ser.). 192p. pap. 14.00 (*0-8101-2091-7*) Northwestern Univ. Pr.

—The Ballad of Rocky Ruiz. 2004. (Latino Voices Ser.). 212p. pap. 14.00 (*0-8101-2090-9*) Northwestern Univ. Pr.

—Brown-on-Brown. 2003. ix, 178p. 21.95 (*0-8263-3169-6*) Univ. of New Mexico Pr.

—Moony's Road to Hell. 2002. 208p. 19.95 (*0-8263-2949-7*) Univ. of New Mexico Pr.

Rechy, John. Bodies & Souls: A Novel. 2001. 448p. pap. 14.00 (*0-8021-3846-2*, Grove Pr.) Grove/Atlantic, Inc.

—The Miraculous Day of Amalia Gomez: A Novel. 2001. 224p. pap. 13.00 (*0-8021-3847-0*, Grove Pr.) Grove/Atlantic, Inc.

Rivera, Rick P. Stars Always Shine. 2001. 192p. pap. 15.00 (*1-931010-03-X*) Bilingual Pr./Editorial Bilingue.

Saenz, Benjamin Alire. Carry Me Like Water. 1995. 512p. (J). 22.95 (*0-7868-6135-5*) Hyperion Pr.

Sanchez, Rosaura. He Walked in & Sat down & Other Stories. Pita, Beatrice, tr. 2000. 208p. 29.95 (*0-8263-2213-1*); 160p. pap. 16.95 (*0-8263-2214-X*) Univ. of New Mexico Pr.

Santora, The Good Daughter. 2002. 320p. per. 14.95 (*0-9712357-0-8*) Xipactli Publishing.

Serros, Michele M. How to Be a Chicana Role Model: A Novel. 2000. 240p. pap. 12.95 (*1-57322-824-9*, Riverhead Trade (Paperbacks)) Berkley Publishing Group.

Soto, Gary. Chato y los Amigos Pachangueros. 2004. Tr. of Chato & the Party Animals. (Illus.). 32p. 7.99 (*0-14-240033-5*, Puffin Bks.) Penguin Putnam Bks. for Young Readers.

—Nickel & Dime. 2000. 189p. 29.95 (*0-8263-2185-2*); pap. 16.95 (*0-8263-2186-0*) Univ. of New Mexico Pr.

—Poetry Lover. 2001. 206p. 24.95 (*0-8263-2319-7*) Univ. of New Mexico Pr.

Troncoso, Sergio. The Nature of Truth: Novel. 2003. (Latino Voices Ser.). 296p. 22.95 (*0-8101-1991-9*) Northwestern Univ. Pr.

Trujillo, Carla Mari. What Night Brings. 2003. 242p. pap. 15.95 (*1-880684-94-2*) Curbstone Pr.

Vea, Alfredo, Jr. La Maravilla. 320p. 1994. pap. 13.95 (*0-452-27160-6*, Plume); 1993. 21.00 o.p. (*0-525-93588-6*) Dutton/Plume.

Villarreal, Rosa Martha. Chronicles of Air & Dreams. 1999. (Illus.). 235p. 22.00 (*0-9662299-2-4*) Archer Bks.

Villatoro, Marcos McPeek. The Holy Spirit of My Uncle's Cojones. 1999. 298p. pap. 12.95 (*1-55885-283-2*) Arte Publico Pr.

Yanez, Richard. El Paso Del Norte: Stories on the Border. 2003. (Western Literature Ser.). 152p. pap. 16.00 (*0-87417-533-X*) Univ. of Nevada Pr.

**MORMONS—FICTION**

Anderson, Glenn L. The Doomsday Factor. 1987. 160p. 11.98 (*0-88290-319-5*) Horizon Pubs. & Distributors, Inc.

Barber, Phyllis. And the Desert Shall Blossom: A Novel. 285p. reprint ed. pap. 88.40 (*0-7837-3965-6*, 204379400011) Bks. on Demand.

—And the Desert Shall Blossom: A Novel. 1993. 288p. reprint ed. pap. 14.95 o.p. (*1-56085-036-1*) Signature Bks., Inc.

—And the Desert Shall Blossom: A Novel. 1991. 340p. 23.95 o.p. (*0-87480-363-2*) Univ. of Utah Pr.

Bell, Michele Ashman. Candle in the Window. 2001. 3.95 (*1-57734-904-0*) Covenant Communications.

—Pathway Home: A Novel. 2003. 14.95 (*1-59156-187-6*); 296p. 14.95 (*1-59156-186-8*) Covenant Communications.

—Written in the Stars. 2001. 249p. 14.95 (*1-57734-853-2*) Covenant Communications.

Blair, Kerry. Closing In: A Novel. 2002. (Illus.). 280p. 14.95 (*1-59156-012-8*) Covenant Communications.

Blair, Kerry Lynn. The Heart Only Knows. 2001. 266p. 14.95 (*1-57734-861-3*) Covenant Communications.

Brown, Marilyn. The Wine-Dark Sea of Grass: A People Struggling to Survive Suffer the Horror of the Mountain Meadows Massacre. 2000. 385p. 24.95 (*1-55517-529-5*, Salt Pr.) Cedar Fort, Inc./CFI Distribution.

Call, Jeff. Mormonville: A Big-City Reporter Spends a Year in Utah to Uncover the Truth about the LDS Church, but Uncovers Truths about Himself. 2002. 310p. pap. 16.95 (*1-55517-618-6*, 76186) Cedar Fort, Inc./CFI Distribution.

Crane, Cheri J. The Girls Next Door: A Novel. 2002. (Illus.). 325p. (*1-59156-072-1*) Covenant Communications.

Darrington, LaResa. Crossroads: A Novel. 2003. 215p. 14.95 (*1-59156-184-1*) Covenant Communications.

Edwards, Paul M. The Angel Acronym: A Mystery Introducing Toom Taggart. 2003. (Illus.). 250p. pap. 21.95 (*1-56085-166-X*) Signature Bks., Inc.

Eno, Thomas D. Deep Waters: A Novel. 2002. (Illus.). 170p. 14.95 (*1-57734-996-2*) Covenant Communications.

Gardner, Lynn. Diamonds & Danger, Set. 1997. audio 11.98 (*1-57734-109-0*, 07001509) Covenant Communications, Inc.

—Diamonds & Danger: A Novel. 1997. 300p. pap. 11.95 (*1-57734-108-2*, 01112805) Covenant Communications, Inc.

Gardner, Willard Boyd. Pursuit of Justice: A Novel. 2003. 231p. 14.95 (*1-59156-154-X*) Covenant Communications.

—Race Against Time: A Novel. 2001. (Illus.). 198p. 14.95 (*1-57734-805-2*) Covenant Communications.

Glenn, Sharlee. Circle Dance. 1998. (YA). pap. o.p. (*1-57008-570-6*, Bookcraft, Inc.) Deseret Bk. Co.

Green, Betsy Brannon. Never Look Back. 2002. 287p. 14.95 (*1-57734-982-2*) Covenant Communications.

—Until Proven Guilty: A Novel. 2002. 348p. 14.95 (*1-59156-061-6*) Covenant Communications.

Grey, Zane. The Desert Crucible: A Western Story. 2003. 344p. 25.95 (*0-7862-3784-8*, Five Star) Gale Group.

—The Desert Crucible: A Western Story. l.t. ed. 2004. 465p. 26.95 (*0-7862-3767-8*) Thorndike Pr.

Grossman, Jeni. Beneath the Surface. 2001. (Illus.). 271p. 14.95 (*1-57734-828-1*) Covenant Communications.

Hansen, Jennie L. Abandoned: A Novel. 2002. (Illus.). 262p. 14.95 (*1-59156-070-5*) Covenant Communications.

Hendershot, Eric. Jimmy Stillman, I Will Always Love You. 1994. o.p. (*0-88494-949-4*, Bookcraft, Inc.) Deseret Bk. Co.

Heuston, Kimberley B. The Shakeress. 2001. 176p. (J). (gr. 7 up). 16.95 (*1-886910-56-1*) Front Street, Inc.

Hoffman Kimball, Linda. Home to Roost. 1995. 193p. pap. 8.95 (*0-9624049-7-7*) Hatrack River Pubns.

Hughes, Dean. As Wide As the River. 1980. pap. o.p. (*0-87747-820-1*) Deseret Bk. Co.

—Brothers. 1986. 111p. (J). (gr. 7-12). 7.95 o.s.i (*0-87579-007-0*) Deseret Bk. Co.

—Jenny Haller. 1983. 134p. 6.95 o.p. (*0-87747-969-0*) Deseret Bk. Co.

Hulme, Joy N. Climbing the Rainbow. 2004. 224p. (J). 15.99 (*0-380-81572-9*); lib. bdg. 16.89 (*0-06-054304-3*) HarperCollins Pubs.

Jarvis, Sharon D. The Healing Place. 1994. 361p. pap. o.p. (*0-87579-817-9*) Deseret Bk. Co.

Jenson, Marcie Anne. Homeward: A Novel. 2002. (Illus.). 250p. (*1-57734-986-5*) Covenant Communications.

Johnson. Belief. Date not set. pap. (*0-312-29112-4*, Saint Martin's Griffin) St. Martin's Pr.

Johnson, Annabel & Johnson, Edgar. Wilderness Bride. 2003. 232p. (YA). 12.95 (*0-9714612-7-9*) Green Mansion Pr. LLC.

Johnson, Stephanie. Belief. 2000. (Illus.). 485p. (*1-86941-436-5*, Vintage) Knopf Publishing Group.

—Belief. 2002. 496p. 26.95 (*0-312-29110-8*) St. Martin's Pr.

Jolley, JoAnn. Keepers of the Heart: A Novel. 2001. 314p. 14.95 (*1-57734-960-1*) Covenant Communications.

Jones, Cleo. Prophet Motive. 1984. 192p. 12.95 o.p. (*0-312-65178-3*) St. Martin's Pr.

Kidd, Kathryn H. Paradise Vue. 1989. 205p. (Orig.). pap. 8.95 (*0-9624049-0-X*) Hatrack River Pubns.

Kijewski, Karen. Alley Kat Blues. 1995. 22.95 o.s.i (*0-385-46852-0*) Doubleday Publishing.

Lyon, Annette. Lost Without You: A Novel. 2002. 201p. 14.95 (*1-59156-019-5*) Covenant Communications.

Marshall, Richard J. The Burning Bush Patrol. 1991. pap. 7.95 o.p. (*0-88494-804-8*, Bookcraft, Inc.) Deseret Bk. Co.

McCloud, Susan Evans. Anna. 1992. pap. 4.95 o.p. (*0-88494-855-2*, Bookcraft, Inc.) Deseret Bk. Co.

—Beloved Stranger. 10.95 o.p. (*0-88494-761-0*, Bookcraft, Inc.) Deseret Bk. Co.

—By All We Hold Dear. 1994. pap. 6.95 o.p. (*0-88494-929-X*, Bookcraft, Inc.) Deseret Bk. Co.

—A Face in the Shadows. 1993. 10.95 o.p. (*0-88494-898-6*, Bookcraft, Inc.) Deseret Bk. Co.

—First Love, Last Love. 10.95 o.p. (*0-88494-596-0*, Bookcraft, Inc.) Deseret Bk. Co.

—The Heart That Truly Loves. 1994. 12.95 o.p. (*0-88494-952-4*, Bookcraft, Inc.) Deseret Bk. Co.

—Jennie. pap. 5.95 o.p. (*0-88494-736-X*, Bookcraft, Inc.) Deseret Bk. Co.

—Lady of Mystery. 9.95 o.p. (*0-88494-641-X*, Bookcraft, Inc.) Deseret Bk. Co.

—My Enemy, My Love. pap. 4.95 o.p. (*0-88494-749-1*, Bookcraft, Inc.) Deseret Bk. Co.

—Out of the Shadows. 1998. 16.95 (*1-57008-571-4*, Bookcraft, Inc.) Deseret Bk. Co.

—Voices from the Dust. 1996. pap. 10.95 (*1-57008-226-X*, Bookcraft, Inc.) Deseret Bk. Co.

—A Vow to Keep. 1989. 245p. 10.95 o.p. (*0-87579-180-8*) Deseret Bk. Co.

—Where the Heart Leads. pap. 4.95 o.p. (*0-88494-743-2*, Bookcraft, Inc.) Deseret Bk. Co.

—Who Goes There? 1995. pap. 8.95 o.p. (*0-88494-973-7*, Bookcraft, Inc.) Deseret Bk. Co.

McKendrick, Lisa. On a Whim. 2001. 156p. (J). (*1-57734-896-6*) Covenant Communications.

Montague, Terry. Fireweed. 1992. pap. 10.95 (*1-55503-407-1*, 01111078) Covenant Communications, Inc.

Mouritsen, Laurel. The Turning Point: A Novel. 2002. 241p. 14.95 (*1-59156-015-2*) Covenant Communications.

Neilson, DeAnne. Perfect Neighbors. 1994. 207p. pap. 7.95 (*0-9624049-6-9*) Hatrack River Pubns.

Nunes, Rachel A. Ariana: A Gift Most Precious. 1997. pap. 11.95 (*1-57734-129-5*, 01112929) Covenant Communications, Inc.

—Ariana: The Making of a Queen. 1996. pap. 10.95 (*1-57734-025-6*, 01112481) Covenant Communications, Inc.

Nunes, Rachel Ann. Ariana: A Novel: a Gift Most Precious. 2003. 221p. pap. 14.95 (*1-55517-646-1*, 76461) Cedar Fort, Inc./CFI Distribution.

—Ariana, the Making of a Queen: A Novel. 2003. (*1-55517-705-0*, Bonneville Bks.) Cedar Fort, Inc./CFI Distribution.

—Ties That Bind. 2002. 325p. 14.95 (*1-57734-939-3*) Covenant Communications.

Paine, Lauran. The Outcast. 1999. 158p. (*0-7540-8064-1*) BBC Audiobooks America.

—The Outcast. l.t. ed. 2003. 20.95 (*1-58724-435-7*, Wheeler Publishing, Inc.) Gale Group.

Peters, Dory J. The Warriors' Code. 2002. 138p. pap. 12.95 (*1-55517-613-5*) Cedar Fort, Inc./CFI Distribution.

Poulson, Clair. Relentless. 2002. 282p. 14.95 (*1-57734-977-6*) Covenant Communications.

—Samuel: Thunder in Paradise. 1996. audio 11.98 (*1-55503-922-7*, 07001363); pap. 10.95 (*1-55503-921-9*, 01112414) Covenant Communications, Inc.

Reid, Pamela. Something Familiar: A Novel. 2003. (Illus.). 214p. 14.95 (1-59156-161-2) Covenant Communications.

Rohrer, Alyce. The True Believers. 1987. 22.95 (0-87949-253-8) Ashley Bks., Inc.

Rowley, Brent. Light Traveler: The Adventure Begins: A Novel. 1998. 185 P. ;p. o.p. (1-57734-310-7) Covenant Communications, Inc.

Ryan, Gordon. Dangerous Legacy. 1994. iv, 379p. 14.95 (0-87579-905-1, Shadow Mountain) Deseret Bk. Co.

—Spirit of Union: Destiny. 1996. 354p. o.p. (1-57345-215-7) Deseret Bk. Co.

Savage, Jeffrey S. Cutting Edge. 2001. 241p. 14.95 (1-57734-844-3) Covenant Communications.

—Into the Fire. 2002. 214p. 14.95 (1-59156-042-X) Covenant Communications.

Siddoway, Richard M. Degrees of Glory. 2003. 82p. pap. 7.95 (1-55517-686-0, 76860, Bonneville Bks.) Cedar Fort, Inc./CFI Distribution.

Smith, Marion. Riptide: A Novel. 2000. 204p. pap. 14.95 (1-56085-131-7) Signature Bks., Inc.

Smurthwaite, Donald. Letters by a Half-Moon. 2003. 142p. (1-59038-175-0) Deseret Bk. Co.

Stansfield, Anita. Gables of Legacy: A Novel. 2002. (Illus.). 324p. 14.95 (1-59156-059-4); 149p. 12.95 (1-59156-111-6) Covenant Communications.

—Silver Linings: A Novel. 2003. (Illus.). 233p. 14.95 (1-59156-168-X) Covenant Communications.

—When Hearts Meet. 2001. (Illus.). 130p. 12.95 (1-57734-855-9) Covenant Communications.

—Where the Heart Leads. 2001. 246p. 14.95 (1-57734-848-6) Covenant Communications.

Taylor, Lorraine. Last Words: A Novel. 2003. 247p. 14.95 (1-59156-207-4) Covenant Communications.

Thayne, Carole. A Question of Trust: A Novel. 2003. 293p. 14.95 (1-59156-210-4) Covenant Communications.

Tunnell, Michael O. Brothers in Valor: Story of Resistance. 2001. 260p. (J). (gr. 6-10). tchr. ed. 16.95 (0-8234-1541-4) Holiday Hse., Inc.

Van Wagoner, Robert H. Dancing Naked: A Novel. 1999. 369p. 20.95 (1-56085-130-9) Signature Bks., Inc.

Weyland, Jack. Ashley & Jen. 2000. (Illus.). 287p. (YA). 16.95 (1-57345-803-1) Deseret Bk. Co.

Yates, Dan. Lack of Evidence: A Novel. 2003. 195p. (1-59156-206-6) Covenant Communications.

Yorgason, Blaine M. To Soar with the Eagle. 1993. 280p. o.p. (0-87579-745-8) Deseret Bk. Co.

Young, Margaret Blair & Gray, Darius. The Last Mile of the Way, 3. 2003. (Standing on the Promises Ser.: 3). xvi, 448p. 21.95 (1-57008-904-3, 5730) Deseret Bk. Co.

Young, Margaret Blair & Gray, Darius Aidan. One More River to Cross. 2000. (Standing on the Promises Ser.: Vol. 1). xxiii, 337p. 19.95 (1-57345-629-2, Bookcraft, Inc.) Deseret Bk. Co.

## P

### POLISH AMERICANS—FICTION

Algren, Nelson. Never Come Morning. 1987. 336p. reprint ed. pap. 10.95 (1-888363-22-3) Seven Stories Pr.

Bartoletti, Susan Campbell. Dancing with Dziadziu. 1997. (Illus.). 40p. (J). (ps-3). 15.00 (0-15-200675-3) Harcourt Children's Bks.

Blos, Joan W. Brooklyn Doesn't Rhyme. (Illus.). 96p. (gr. 3-7). 2000. pap. 4.50 (0-689-83557-4, Aladdin); 1994. (J). 16.00 o.s.i (0-684-19694-8, Atheneum) Simon & Schuster Children's Publishing.

Bukoski, Anthony. Children of Strangers: Stories. 1993. 200p. (Orig.). 22.50 (0-87074-350-3); pap. 10.95 (0-87074-364-3) Southern Methodist Univ. Pr.

—Polonaise: Stories. 1998. 192p. 19.95 (0-87074-434-8) Southern Methodist Univ. Pr.

—Time Between Trains. 2003. 200p. 22.50 (0-87074-479-8) Southern Methodist Univ. Pr.

Chernoff, Maxine. American Heaven. 1996. 256p. (C). 21.95 (1-56689-041-1) Coffee Hse. Pr.

Cohen, Arthur A. In the Days of Simon Stern. 1987. (Phoenix Fiction Ser.). vi, 466p. reprint ed. pap. 36.00 (0-226-11254-3) Univ. of Chicago Pr.

Estes, Eleanor. Los Cien Vestidos. Mlawer, Teresa, tr. 1994. (SPA., Illus.). (J). (gr. k-2). pap. 6.95 (1-880507-15-3, LC1571) Lectorum Pubns., Inc.

Glodek, Geraldine. Nine Bells at the Breaker: An Immigrant's Story. 1998. viii, 248p. 24.00 (0-9665943-0-4); pap. 15.00 (0-9665943-1-2) Barn Peg Pr., The.

Gray, Suzanne. Circe, Goodnight: A Novel. 2001. 188p. 24.95 (1-56474-357-8) Fithian Pr.

Kavanagh, Katie. Home Is Where Your Family Is. 1994. (Publish-a-Book Contest Ser.). (Illus.). (J). (gr. 1-6). lib. bdg. 22.83 o.p. (0-8114-4462-7) Raintree Pubs.

Klauprecht, Emil. Cincinnati, or The Mysteries of the West: Emil Klauprecht's German-American Novel. Rowan, Steven & Tolzmann, Don H., trs. from GER. 1996. (New German-American Studies: Vol. 10). XXV, 657p. (C). text 79.95 (0-8204-2681-4) Lang, Peter Publishing, Inc.

Leighton, Maxinne R. An Ellis Island Christmas. (Picture Puffins Ser.). (Illus.). 32p. (J). 1994. (ps-3). pap. 6.99 (0-14-055344-4, Puffin Bks.); 1992. (gr. 1-4). 15.00 o.s.i (0-670-83182-4, Viking Children's Bks.) Penguin Putnam Bks. for Young Readers.

Pellowski, Anne. First Farm in the Valley: Anna's Story. 1982. (Illus.). 192p. (J). (gr. 3-6). 9.95 o.s.i (0-399-20887-9, Philomel) Penguin Putnam Bks. for Young Readers.

—First Farm in the Valley Vol. 1: Anna's Story. rev. ed. 1997. (Polish American Girls Ser.). (Illus.). 192p. (J). (gr. 3-5). pap. 9.95 (0-88489-537-8) St. Mary's Pr.

—Willow Wind Farm Vol. 4: Betsy's Story. Nagel, Steve, ed. rev. ed. 1997. (Polish American Girls Ser.). (Illus.). 176p. (J). (gr. 3-5). pap. 9.95 (0-88489-525-4) St. Mary's Pr.

Petesch, Natalie L. The Immigrant Train & Other Stories. 1996. 208p. text 24.95 (0-8040-0991-0); pap. 14.95 (0-8040-0992-9) Swallow Pr.

Pietrzyk, Leslie. Pears on a Willow Tree. 1999. 288p. pap. 13.00 (0-380-79910-3, Perennial) HarperTrade.

—Pears on a Willow Tree. 1998. 272p. 23.00 o.p. (0-380-97667-6, Avon Bks.) Morrow/Avon.

Potok, Chaim. In the Beginning. 1975. 13.95 o.s.i (0-394-49960-3) Knopf, Alfred A. Inc.

Raphael, Lev. Winter Eyes. 1992. 256p. 18.95 o.p. (0-312-08338-6) St. Martin's Pr.

Shea, Suzanne Strempek. Hoopi Shoopi Donna. 1996. 368p. 22.00 o.p. (0-671-53544-7, Atria) Simon & Schuster.

—Selling the Lite of Heaven. 1995. 288p. pap. 12.95 (0-671-79865-0, Washington Square Pr.) Simon & Schuster.

—Selling the Lite of Heaven. Rosenman, Jane, ed. 1994. 288p. 20.00 o.s.i (0-671-79864-2, Atria) Simon & Schuster.

Slezak, Ellen. Last Year's Jesus: A Novella & Nine Stories. 2002. pap. 13.95 (0-7868-8638-2); 224p. 22.95 (0-7868-6741-8) Hyperion Pr.

Sontag, Susan. In America. 2001. E-Book 9.00 o.p. (0-374-97519-1); 2001. E-Book 9.00 o.p. (0-374-97517-5); 2000. E-Book 9.00 (0-374-97515-9); 2000. E-Book 9.00 (0-374-70020-6); 2000. (Illus.). 387p. 26.00 o.p. (0-374-17540-3); 1998. (0-374-94114-9) Farrar, Straus & Giroux.

—In America. l.t. ed. 2000. 540p. 28.95 (1-56895-898-6, Wheeler Publishing, Inc.) Gale Group.

—In America. 2001. 400p. pap. 14.00 (0-312-27320-7) Picador.

Strigenz, Geri K., illus. For Bread. 1992. (History's Children Ser.). 48p. (J). (gr. 4-5). pap. o.p. (0-8114-6426-1); lib. bdg. 21.36 o.p. (0-8114-3501-6) Raintree Pubs.

Thorman, Carolyn. Fifty Years of Eternal Vigilance & Other Stories. 1988. 192p. 14.95 o.p. (0-934601-62-3) Peachtree Pubs., Ltd.

# HISTORICAL EVENTS

## C

### CHINA—HISTORY—TAIPING REBELLION, 1850-1864—FICTION

Chin, Shunshin. The Taiping Rebellion. Fogel, Joshua, tr. from JPN. 2000. 672p. pap. 35.00 (0-7656-0100-1, East Gate Bk.) Sharpe, M.E. Inc.

Fraser, George MacDonald. Flashman & the Dragon. unabr. ed. 1995. (Flashman Ser.). audio 72.00 (0-7366-3053-8, 3735) Books on Tape, Inc.

—Flashman & the Dragon. 1987. (Flashman Ser.). 336p. 13.95 (0-452-26191-0); pap. 7.95 o.p. (0-452-25930-4) Dutton/Plume. (Plume).

Lee, C. Y. The Second Son of Heaven: A Novel. Drew, Lisa, ed. 1990. 384p. 19.95 o.p. (0-688-05140-5, Morrow, William & Co.) Morrow/Avon.

Patterson, Richard O. The Mandarin from Salem. 1979. 404p. 16.95 (0-8022-2244-7) Philosophical Library, Inc.

Sledge, Linda C. Empire of Heaven. 1991. 640p. mass mkt. 5.95 o.s.i (0-553-28693-5) Bantam Bks.

### CRIMEAN WAR, 1853-1856—FICTION

Bainbridge, Beryl. Master Georgie. 190p. 1999. pap. 11.95 (0-7867-0697-X); 1998. 21.00 o.p. (0-7867-0563-9) Avalon Publishing Group. (Carroll & Graf Pubs.).

—Master Georgie. l.t. ed. 1999. (General Ser.). 224p. pap. 23.95 (0-7862-1681-6) Thorndike Pr.

Darrell, Elizabeth. Forget the Glory. 2003. (Illus.). 432p. 26.99 (0-7278-5657-X) Severn Hse. Pubs., Ltd.

Drummond, Emma. Forget the Glory. 1987. pap. 3.95 o.p. (0-312-90678-1, St. Martin's Paperbacks); 1985. 480p. 15.95 o.p. (0-312-29892-7) St. Martin's Pr.

—Forget the Glory. l.t. ed. 1986. (Charnwood Large Print Ser.). 640p. 29.99 o.p. (0-7089-8336-7, Charnwood) Thorpe, F. A. Pubs. GBR. Dist: Ulverscroft Large Print Bks., Ltd., Ulverscroft Large Print Canada, Ltd.

Fraser, George MacDonald. Flashman at the Charge. unabr. ed. 1994. audio 69.95 o.p. (0-7451-4300-8, CAB 983) BBC Audiobooks America.

—Flashman at the Charge. unabr. ed. 1994. (Flashman Ser.). audio 64.00 (0-7366-2775-8, 3494) Books on Tape, Inc.

—Flashman at the Charge. 1986. (Flashman Ser.). pap. 7.95 o.p. (0-452-25957-6); 288p. pap. 14.00 (0-452-26413-8); pap. 6.95 o.p. (0-452-25765-4) Dutton/Plume. (Plume).

—Flashman at the Charge. (Flashman Ser.). 1975. mass mkt. 1.50 o.p. (0-451-06931-5); 1974. mass mkt. 1.25 o.p. (0-451-06094-6) NAL. (Signet Bks.).

Harrod-Eagles, Cynthia. Fleur. 1992. 22.95 o.p. (0-312-08782-9) St. Martin's Pr.

Kilworth, Garry Douglas. Attack on the Redan. 2003. 288p. 25.00 (0-7867-1260-0) Avalon Publishing Group.

Reeman, Douglas. Badge of Glory. unabr. ed. 2000. 10p. audio 84.95 (0-7540-0514-3, CAB1937) Chivers Audio Bks. GBR. Dist: BBC Audiobooks America.

—Badge of Glory. 1924. o.p. (0-688-05395-5, Morrow, William & Co.) Morrow/Avon.

—Badge of Glory. l.t. ed. 1986. 544p. 13.95 o.p. (0-7089-8352-9, Charnwood) Thorpe, F. A. Pubs. GBR. Dist: Ulverscroft Large Print Bks., Ltd.

—Badge of Glory: Royal Marines Saga, 4 vols. 2002. (Royal Marines Saga: Vol. 1). 384p. pap. 16.95 (1-59013-013-8) McBooks Pr., Inc.

Stuart, V. A. The Brave Captains. 2003. (Philip Hazard Novels Ser.: No. 2). 272p. pap. 14.95 (1-59013-040-5) McBooks Pr., Inc.

—The Brave Captains: Hazard 2. l.t. ed. 1991. (Ulverscroft Large Print Ser.). 29.99 o.p. (0-7089-2560-X, Ulverscroft) Thorpe, F. A. Pubs. GBR. Dist: Ulverscroft Large Print Bks., Ltd., Ulverscroft Large Print Canada, Ltd.

—The Valiant Sailors. 1979. (Hazard: No. 1). pap. 1.75 o.p. (0-523-40481-6, Pinnacle Bks.) Kensington Publishing Corp.

—The Valiant Sailors. 2003. (Philip Hazard Novels Ser.: No. 1). 272p. pap. 14.95 (1-59013-039-1) McBooks Pr., Inc.

—The Valiant Sailors: Hazard 1. l.t. ed. 1991. (Ulverscroft Large Print Ser.). 29.99 o.p. (0-7089-2470-0, Ulverscroft) Thorpe, F. A. Pubs. GBR. Dist: Ulverscroft Large Print Bks., Ltd., Ulverscroft Large Print Canada, Ltd.

—Victors & Lords Book #1: Alexander Sheridan Novels. 2001. (Alexander Sheridan Novels: No. 1). 272p. pap. 13.95 (0-935526-98-6) McBooks Pr., Inc.

Thompson. Paths of Destiny. 2003. 28.00 (0-316-85721-1) Time Warner Bks. UK GBR. Dist: Trafalgar Square.

### CRUSADES—FICTION

Ball, David. Ironfire. 2003. (Illus.). 688p. 24.95 (0-385-33601-2) Dell Publishing.

Beaufort, Simon. Murder in the Holy City. annuals 1998. (Sir Geoffrey Mappestone Mysteries Ser.). 240p. 22.95 (0-312-19566-4, Saint Martin's Minotaur) St. Martin's Pr.

Chaikin, Linda L. Behind the Veil. 1998. (Royal Pavilions Ser.). 256p. pap. 9.99 o.p. (1-55661-513-2) Bethany Hse. Pubs.

—Golden Palaces. 1996. (Royal Pavilions Ser.: No. 2). 352p. pap. 9.99 o.p. (1-55661-865-4) Bethany Hse. Pubs.

—Golden Palaces. l.t. ed. 1998. (Royal Pavilions Ser.: Vol. 2). 581p. 25.95 (0-7862-1467-8) Thorndike Pr.

—Swords & Scimitars. 1996. (Royal Pavilions Ser.: No. 1). 288p. pap. 9.99 o.p. (1-55661-881-6) Bethany Hse. Pubs.

—Swords & Scimitars. 1993. pap. 10.99 o.p. (0-8407-6728-5) Nelson, Thomas Inc.

—Swords & Scimitars. l.t. ed. 1997. (Christian Fiction Ser.: Vol. 1). 430p. 24.95 (0-7862-1236-5) Thorndike Pr.

Connell, Evan S. Deus lo Volt! A Chronicle of the Crusades. 2000. text o.p. (1-58243-092-6); (Illus.). 480p. text 28.00 o.p. (1-58243-065-9) Basic Bks. (Counterpoint Pr.).

—Deus lo Volt! A Chronicle of the Crusades. abr. ed. 2002. audio 24.95 (1-56511-596-1) HighBridge Co.

Crawford, F. Marion. El Via Crucis. rev. ed. 2000. 348p. E-Book 3.95 (0-594-02061-1) 1873 Pr.

—El Via Crucis. 1990. (Works of Francis Marion Crawford). reprint ed. lib. bdg. 79.00 (0-7812-2550-7) Reprint Services Corp.

Davis, William S. God Wills It. 1901. 25.00 o.p. (0-8196-1204-9) Biblo & Tannen Booksellers & Pubs., Inc.

Duggan, Alfred. Count Bohemond: A Novel. 2003. (Cassell Military Paperbacks Ser.). 288p. pap. 9.95 (0-304-36273-5) Cassell P L C GBR. Dist: Sterling Publishing Co., Inc.

Eisner, Michael Alexander. The Crusader: A Novel. (Illus.). 336p. 2003. pap. 13.00 (0-385-72141-2); 2001. 24.95 (0-385-50281-8, Currency) Doubleday Publishing.

—The Crusader: A Novel. l.t. ed. 2002. 567p. 29.95 (0-7862-3991-3) Gale Group.

Gordon, Alan. Jester Leaps In: A Medieval Mystery. 2002. 288p. mass mkt. 6.50 (0-312-97900-2, St. Martin's Paperbacks); 2000. 276p. 23.95 (0-312-24117-8, Saint Martin's Minotaur) St. Martin's Pr.

—Widow of Jerusalem: A Medieval Mystery. 2003. 288p. 23.95 (0-312-30089-1, Saint Martin's Minotaur) St. Martin's Pr.

Hoban, Russell. Pilgermann. 1986. mass mkt. 2.95 o.s.i (0-671-61893-8, Pocket) Simon & Schuster.

—Pilgermann. 1983. 13.50 o.p. (0-671-45968-6) Summit Bks.

Holland, Cecelia. Jerusalem. 1997. 405p. pap. text 6.99 (0-8125-5397-7); 1995. 320p. 23.95 o.p. (0-312-85956-2) Doherty, Tom Assocs., LLC. (Forge Bks.).

Hurley, Frank X. The Crusader. 1975. 112p. 4.95 o.p. (0-8059-2087-0) Dorrance Publishing Co., Inc.

Kay, Guy Gavriel. A Song for Arbonne. 1994. 512p. mass mkt. 6.99 o.s.i (0-451-45332-8, ROC) NAL.

—The Song for Arbonne. Chizmar, Richard & Morrish, Robert, eds. 2002. 512p. reprint ed. pap. 15.00 (0-451-45897-4) NAL.

Kurtz, Katherine, ed. On Crusade: More Tales of the Knights Templar. 2003. 304p. mass mkt. 6.50 (0-446-61317-7); 1998. 256p. reprint ed. pap. 15.99 (0-446-67339-0) Warner Bks., Inc. (Aspect).

Lamb, Harold. Durandal. 1981. (Illus.). 35.00 (0-937986-64-X); 15.00 o.p. (0-937986-45-3) Grant, Donald M. Pub., Inc.

Lawhead, Stephen R. The Black Rood. 2000. (Celtic Crusades Ser.: Bk. II). (Illus.). 448p. 25.00 (0-06-105034-2) HarperCollins Pubs.

—The Black Rood. 2001. (Celtic Crusades Ser.: Vol. 2). 624p. mass mkt. 7.50 (0-06-105110-1, Eos) Morrow/Avon.

—The Black Rood. 2001. (Illus.). 448p. pap. 16.99 (0-310-21783-0) Zondervan.

—The Iron Lance. (Celtic Crusades Ser.: Bk. 1). 2000. 656p. mass mkt. 7.99 (0-06-105109-8); 1998. 512p. 24.00 (0-06-105032-6) Morrow/Avon. (Eos).

—The Iron Lance, 1999. (Celtic Crusades Ser.: Bk. 1). 512p. pap. 16.99 (0-310-21782-2) Zondervan.

—The Mystic Rose. 2002. (Celtic Crusades Ser.: Bk. III). 624p. mass mkt. 7.99 (0-380-82018-8) HarperCollins Pubs.

—The Mystic Rose. 2001. (Celtic Crusades Ser.: Bk. III). (Illus.). 432p. 25.00 (0-06-105031-8, Eos) Morrow/Avon.

—The Mystic Rose. 2002. (Celtic Crusades Ser.: Bk. III). (Illus.). 432p. pap. 16.99 (0-310-21784-9) Zondervan.

Patterson, James & Gross, Andrew. The Jester. 2003. 464p. 27.95 (0-316-60205-1); 656p. 27.95 (0-316-14787-7) Little Brown & Co.

—The Jester. 2003. E-Book 15.95 (0-7595-8751-5); E-Book 15.95 (0-7595-4744-0) Time Warner Bk. Group.

—The Jester. 2003. 464p. pap. 16.00 (0-446-69051-1) Warner Bks., Inc.

Read, Piers Paul. Knights of the Cross. unabr. ed. 1998. audio 84.95 (0-7540-0129-6, CAB1552, Chivers Children's Audio Bks.) BBC Audiobooks America.

—Knights of the Cross. l.t. ed. 1998. (Ulverscroft Large Print Ser.). 512p. 29.99 (0-7089-3970-8, Ulverscroft) Thorpe, F. A. Pubs. GBR. Dist: Ulverscroft Large Print Bks., Ltd., Ulverscroft Large Print Canada, Ltd.

Rivele, Stephen J. A Booke of Days: A Journal of the Crusades. 1997. 448p. 24.00 o.p. (0-7867-0348-2, Carroll & Graf Pubs.) Avalon Publishing Group.

—A Booke of Days: A Novel of the Crusades. 1998. 448p. pap. 13.95 (0-7867-0462-4, Carroll & Graf Pubs.) Avalon Publishing Group.

Schoonover, Lawrence. The Golden Exile. 1981. 416p. mass mkt. 2.75 o.p. (0-345-29581-1) Ballantine Bks.

Scott, Walter, Sr. The Betrothed. (Works of Sir Walter Scott: Vol. 37). 550p. reprint ed. 2001. (Illus.). pap. text 28.00 (0-7426-5269-6); 1999. lib. bdg. 90.00 (1-58201-269-5) Classic Bks.

—The Talisman. unabr. collector's ed. 1988. (Jimcin Recording Ser.). (J). audio 88.00 (0-7366-3929-2, 9167) Books on Tape, Inc.

—The Talisman. 1999. (Works of Sir Walter Scott: Vol. 38). 538p. reprint ed. lib. bdg. 90.00 (1-58201-270-9) Classic Bks.

—The Talisman. 1972. 7.95 o.p. (0-460-01144-8, Dutton) Dutton/Plume.
—The Talisman. l.t. ed. 1549p. pap. 105.27 (0-7583-2494-4); 1024p. pap. 72.50 (0-7583-2492-8); 456p. pap. 34.80 (0-7583-2489-8); 800p. pap. 60.75 (0-7583-2491-X); 1259p. pap. 84.84 (0-7583-2493-6); 1796p. pap. 117.17 (0-7583-2495-2); 625p. pap. 42.96 (0-7583-2490-1); 365p. pap. 29.64 (0-7583-2488-X); 365p. lib. bdg. 35.64 (0-7583-2480-4); 1259p. lib. bdg. 96.84 (0-7583-2485-5); 1796p. lib. bdg. 135.17 (0-7583-2487-1); 625p. lib. bdg. 48.96 (0-7583-2482-0); 456p. lib. bdg. 40.80 (0-7583-2481-2); 1549p. lib. bdg. 123.27 (0-7583-2486-3); 800p. lib. bdg. 72.75 (0-7583-2483-9) Huge Print Pr.
—The Talisman. 1989. audio 69.00 Jimcin Recordings.
—The Talisman. E-Book 1.95 (1-58515-260-9) MesaView, Inc.
—The Talisman. Parker, W. M., ed. 1991. 336p. pap. 7.95 o.p. (0-460-87088-2, Everyman's Classic Library in Paperback) Tuttle Publishing.
—The Talisman. 1981. pap. 3.50 o.p. (0-14-005826-5, Penguin Bks.) Viking Penguin.
Shwartz, Susan. Cross & Crescent. 1998. mass mkt. 5.99 (0-8125-4816-7); 1997. 384p. 23.95 o.p. (0-312-85714-4) Doherty, Tom Assocs., LLC. (Tor Bks.).
Simpson, Rosemary. The Seven Hills of Paradise. 1980. 13.95 o.p. (0-385-15775-4) Doubleday Publishing.
Tarr, Judith. The Dagger & the Cross. 1991. 464p. mass mkt. 4.99 o.s.i (0-553-29416-4) Bantam Bks.
—The Dagger & the Cross. 1991. 480p. 21.95 o.s.i (0-385-41181-2) Doubleday Publishing.
—Pride of Kings. 2001. 464p. pap. 14.95 (0-451-45847-8, ROC) NAL.

**CUBAN MISSILE CRISIS, 1962—FICTION**

DuBois, Brendan. Resurrection Day. unabr. ed. 2000. audio 96.95 (0-7927-2328-7, CSL 217, Chivers Sound Library) BBC Audiobooks America.
—Resurrection Day. 2000. 480p. mass mkt. 7.50 o.s.i (0-515-12949-6, Jove) Berkley Publishing Group.
—Resurrection Day. 1999. 400p. (YA). 23.95 o.p. (0-399-14498-6) Penguin Group (USA) Inc.
Huidekoper, Peter. Shelter: A Cold War Memory. 1998. 150p. pap. 7.95 (0-9660861-0-4) Shippen Pr.
Kelley, Robert E. The First Book of Timothy: A Novel. 1995. 260p. text 24.95 o.p. (0-87451-725-7) Univ. Pr. of New England.

# F

**FRANCE—HISTORY—REVOLUTION, 1789-1799—FICTION**

Alleyn, Susanne. A Far Better Rest. 2000. 353p. 25.00 (1-56947-197-5) Soho Pr., Inc.
Center for Learning Network Staff & Orczy, Baroness Emmuska. The Scarlet Pimpernel: Curriculum Unit. 1999. (Novel Ser.). 77p. tchr. ed., spiral bd. 18.95 (1-56077-583-1) Ctr. for Learning, The.
Connery, Tom. Honour Redeemed. 2003. 336p. pap. 13.00 (0-425-18972-4) Berkley Publishing Group.
—Honour Redeemed. 2000. (Markham of the Marines Ser.: Vol. 2). 328p. 21.95 (0-89526-255-X) Regnery Publishing, Inc., An Eagle Publishing Co.
—Shred of Honour: A Markham of the Marines Novel. 1999. (Markham of the Marines Ser.). (Illus.). 328p. 21.95 (0-89526-269-X) Regnery Publishing, Inc., An Eagle Publishing Co.
—A Shred of Honour: A Markham of the Marines Novel. 2002. (Illus.). 320p. pap. 13.00 (0-425-18498-6) Berkley Publishing Group.
Dickens, Charles. A Tale of Two Cities. E-Book 2.49 (1-58744-083-0) Electric Umbrella Publishing.
Ducornet, Rikki. The Fan-Maker's Inquisition: A Novel of the Marquis de Sade. 2000. 240p. pap. 14.00 (0-345-44104-4, Ballantine Bks.) Ballantine Bks.
—The Fan-Maker's Inquisition: A Novel of the Marquis de Sade. 1999. 224p. 22.00 o.s.i (0-8050-5926-1) Holt, Henry & Co.
Grange, Amanda. Anything but a Gentleman. l.t. ed. 2002. (General Ser.). 289p. pap. 23.95 (0-7862-4225-6) Thorndike Pr.
Hugo, Victor. Ninety-Three. 1976. 27.95 (0-8488-0820-7) Amereon, Ltd.
—Ninety-Three. 1998. 400p. pap. 11.95 (0-7867-0590-6); 1988. 8.95 o.p. (0-88184-405-5) Avalon Publishing Group. (Carroll & Graf Pubs.).
—Ninety-Three. unabr. ed. 2000. audio 69.95 (0-7861-1768-0, 2571) Blackstone Audio Bks., Inc.
—Ninety-Three. 2001. (Illus.). 392p. per. 27.95 (1-58963-198-6) International Law & Taxation Pubs.
—Ninety-Three. Bair, Lowell, tr. 2002. 352p. 39.95 (1-889439-31-2) Paper Tiger, The.
—Ninety-Three. Bair, Lowell, tr. 1998. reprint ed. pap. (1-56114-264-6) Second Renaissance Bks.
Jolis, Alan & Atlantic Monthly Staff. Love & Terror. 1998. 352p. 24.00 o.p. (0-87113-715-1, Atlantic Monthly Pr.) Grove/Atlantic, Inc.
Lee, Tanith. The Gods Are Thirsty. 1996. 528p. 26.95 (0-87951-672-0) Overlook Pr., The.
Mantel, Hilary. A Place of Greater Safety. 1998. 768p. pap. 15.00 o.s.i (0-8050-5204-6, Owl Bks.) Holt, Henry & Co.
—A Place of Greater Safety. 1993. 864p. 25.00 o.p. (0-689-12168-7, Scribner) Simon & Schuster.
Orczy, Baroness Emmuska. Adventures of the Scarlet Pimpernel. 1983. 321p. reprint ed. lib. bdg. 35.95 (0-89966-459-8) Buccaneer Bks., Inc.
—Eldorado. lib. bdg. 22.95 (0-8488-2010-X) Amereon, Ltd.
—Eldorado. 1980. 435p. reprint ed. lib. bdg. 35.95 (0-89968-195-6, Lightyear Pr.) Buccaneer Bks., Inc.
—The Elusive Pimpernel. 288p. 23.95 (0-8488-2521-7) Amereon, Ltd.
—The Elusive Pimpernel. unabr. ed. 1998. audio 49.95 (0-7861-1279-4, 2169) Blackstone Audio Bks., Inc.
—The Elusive Pimpernel. 1984. 419p. lib. bdg. 35.95 (0-89966-488-1); 1976. lib. bdg. 31.95 o.p. (0-89968-073-9, Lightyear Pr.) Buccaneer Bks., Inc.
—I Will Repay. unabr. ed. 1994. audio 44.95 (0-7861-0778-2, 1506) Blackstone Audio Bks., Inc.
—I Will Repay. 2000. 192p. reprint ed. 29.95 (1-56849-732-6) Buccaneer Bks., Inc.
—The League of the Scarlet Pimpernel. Date not set. 282p. 23.95 (0-8488-2377-X) Amereon, Ltd.
—The League of the Scarlet Pimpernel. 1981. 238p. reprint ed. lib. bdg. 35.95 (0-89966-286-2) Buccaneer Bks., Inc.
—Lord Tony's Wife. 1986. (gr. 4-7). reprint ed. lib. bdg. 37.95 (0-89966-553-5) Buccaneer Bks., Inc.
—Pimpernel & Rosemary. 312p. 24.95 (0-8488-2543-8) Amereon, Ltd.
—Pimpernel & Rosemary. 1996. 37.95 (0-89966-462-8) Buccaneer Bks., Inc.
—The Scarlet Pimpernel. 1964. (Airmont Classics Ser.). (J). (gr. 7 up). mass mkt. 2.95 o.p. (0-8049-0028-0, CL-28) Airmont Publishing Co., Inc.
—The Scarlet Pimpernel. 20.95 (0-8488-0601-8) Amereon, Ltd.
—The Scarlet Pimpernel. 1994. (Illustrated Classics Collection). 64p. pap. 3.60 o.p. (1-56103-606-4); pap. 4.95 (0-7854-0755-3, 40518) American Guidance Service, Inc.
—The Scarlet Pimpernel. 1987. audio 41.95 (1-55685-110-3) Audio Bk. Contractors, Inc.
—The Scarlet Pimpernel. 1992. (Bantam Classics Ser.). 272p. mass mkt. 4.95 (0-553-21402-0, Bantam Classics) Bantam Bks.
—The Scarlet Pimpernel. unabr. ed. 1983. (J). audio 56.00 (0-7366-3882-2, 9106) Books on Tape, Inc.
—The Scarlet Pimpernel. unabr. ed. 1999. (Bookcassette Classic Collection). audio 57.25 (1-56740-678-5, 1807, Unabridged Library Editions) Brilliance Audio.
—The Scarlet Pimpernel. 1976. lib. bdg. 21.95 o.p. (0-89968-072-0, Lightyear Pr.); 1984. 256p. reprint ed. lib. bdg. 21.95 (0-89966-508-X) Buccaneer Bks., Inc.
—The Scarlet Pimpernel. 2002. (Dover Thrift Editions Ser.). 176p. pap. 2.50 (0-486-42122-8) Dover Pubns., Inc.
—The Scarlet Pimpernel. E-Book 2.49 (1-58627-775-8) Electric Umbrella Publishing.
—The Scarlet Pimpernel. (Reader's Request Ser.). 1984. lib. bdg. 12.95 o.p. (0-8161-3077-9, Macmillan Reference USA); 2002. 437p. 28.95 (0-7862-4012-1) Gale Group.
—The Scarlet Pimpernel. 1999. 320p. (gr. 8-12). 14.95 (0-375-40658-1) Knopf, Alfred A. Inc.
—The Scarlet Pimpernel. l.t. ed. 2002. (LRS Large Print Heritage Ser.). lib. bdg. 34.95 (1-58118-093-4) LRS.
—The Scarlet Pimpernel. E-Book 1.95 (1-58515-047-9) MesaView, Inc.
—The Scarlet Pimpernel. 2000. (Signet Classics). 288p. mass mkt. 4.95 (0-451-52762-3, Signet Bks.) NAL.
—The Scarlet Pimpernel. abr. ed. 1995. (Classic, Ultimate, Dove Ser.). (gr. 4-7). audio 19.95 o.p. (1-55800-924-8, 692917, Dove Audio) NewStar Media, Inc.
—The Scarlet Pimpernel. 2000. (Twelve-Point Ser.). 245p. reprint ed. lib. bdg. 24.00 o.p. (1-58287-122-1) North Bks.
—The Scarlet Pimpernel. 1985. 11.95 (0-396-08690-X, G. P. Putnam's Sons) Penguin Putnam Bks. for Young Readers.
—The Scarlet Pimpernel. 2000. (YA). pap., stu. ed. 73.20 incl. audio (0-7887-3191-2, 40926X4) Recorded Bks., LLC.
—The Scarlet Pimpernel. 1998. 304p. pap. 12.95 (0-89526-365-3, Gateway Editions) Regnery Publishing, Inc., An Eagle Publishing Co.
—The Scarlet Pimpernel. abr. ed. 1998. mass mkt. 16.95 incl. audio (1-85998-958-6) Trafalgar Square.
—The Scarlet Pimpernel. 1974. 11.00 (0-606-00955-8) Turtleback Bks.
—The Scarlet Pimpernel & Other Tales. Wellborn, Sandra, ed. 2000. cd-rom 9.95 (1-930430-02-7) Waltsan Publishing, LLC.
—Sir Percy Hits Back. 2000. 320p. reprint ed. 37.95 (1-56849-733-4) Buccaneer Bks., Inc.
—Sir Percy Leads the Band. 2002. reprint ed. lib. bdg. 35.95 (1-56849-737-7) Buccaneer Bks., Inc.
—The Triumph of the Scarlet Pimpernel. 320p. 24.95 (0-8488-2557-8) Amereon, Ltd.
—The Triumph of the Scarlet Pimpernel. 1983. 321p. reprint ed. lib. bdg. 35.95 (0-89966-460-1) Buccaneer Bks., Inc.
—The Triumph of the Scarlet Pimpernel. abr. ed. pap. incl. audio (1-85998-959-4) Hodder Children's Audio.
—The Triumph of the Scarlet Pimpernel. abr. ed. 1999. audio 16.85 (1-84032-118-0) Hodder Headline Audiobooks GBR. *Dist:* Ulverscroft Large Print Bks., Ltd.
—The Way of the Scarlet Pimpernel. 24.95 (0-8488-1442-8) Amereon, Ltd.
—The Way of the Scarlet Pimpernel. 1983. 318p. reprint ed. lib. bdg. 37.95 (0-89966-461-X) Buccaneer Bks., Inc.
Piercy, Marge. City of Darkness, City of Light. 1997. 496p. pap. 14.95 (0-449-91275-2, Fawcett) Ballantine Bks.
Sabatini, Rafael. Scaramouche. 1976. reprint ed. lib. bdg. 25.95 (0-89190-744-0, Rivercity Pr.) Amereon, Ltd.
—Scaramouche. 1976. mass mkt. 1.75 o.s.i (0-345-25162-8) Ballantine Bks.
—Scaramouche. unabr. collector's ed. 1983. (J). audio 80.00 (0-7366-0365-4, 1349) Books on Tape, Inc.
—Scaramouche. 1990. reprint ed. lib. bdg. 31.95 (0-89968-547-1) Buccaneer Bks., Inc.
—Scaramouche. E-Book 2.49 (1-58627-421-X) Electric Umbrella Publishing.
—Scaramouche, 001. 9999. 10.95 o.p. (0-395-08142-4) Houghton Mifflin Co.
—Scaramouche. 2001. 384p. mass mkt. 5.95 (0-451-52797-6) NAL.
—Scaramouche. 2002. (Twelve-Point Ser.). 400p. lib. bdg. 25.00 (1-58287-189-2); 500p. lib. bdg. 26.00 (1-58287-672-X) North Bks.
—Scaramouche. 2002. 406p. pap. 13.95 (0-393-32330-7) Norton, W. W. & Co., Inc.
—Scaramouche. 1999. (Gateway Movie Classics Ser.). 384p. pap. 14.95 o.s.i (0-89526-310-6, Gateway Editions) Regnery Publishing, Inc., An Eagle Publishing Co.
—Scaramouche. (Ebook Classic Ser.). E-Book 5.00 (0-7410-1054-2) SoftBook Pr.
—Scaramouche: A Historical Romance of the French Revolution. 1992. 320p. reprint ed. pap. 10.95 o.p. (0-8118-0190-X) Chronicle Bks. LLC.
Small, Bertrice. The Duchess. 2003. 448p. mass mkt. 6.99 (0-345-43695-4, Ivy Bks.); 2001. 384p. pap. 14.95 (0-345-43435-8, Ballantine Bks.) Ballantine Bks.
Stockwin, Julian. Artemis. 2003. 352p. pap. 13.00 (0-7432-1461-7); 2002. 336p. 24.00 (0-7432-1460-9) Simon & Schuster. (Scribner).
—Artemis. l.t. ed. 2002. 28.95 (0-7862-4588-3) Thorndike Pr.
—Kydd. 2002. 272p. pap. 13.00 (0-7432-1459-5, Touchstone); 2001. 256p. 24.00 o.s.i (0-7432-1458-7, Scribner) Simon & Schuster.
—Kydd. l.t. ed. 2001. 485p. 28.95 (0-7862-3564-0); 447p. (0-7540-1682-X); 447p. (0-7540-9080-9) Thorndike Pr.
Tuten, Frederic. Tallien: A Brief Romance. 1994. 152p. pap. 13.95 o.p. (0-7145-2990-7) Boyars, Marion Pubs., Inc.
—Tallien: A Brief Romance. 1988. 230p. 17.95 o.p. (0-374-27249-2) Farrar, Straus & Giroux.
Van Horne, Hollie. The Diary of Jean-Jacques Coupier. 2002. (Time Travelers Ser.: No. 5). 336p. mass mkt. 16.50 (0-9674552-1-9) Time Travelers.
Woodman, Richard. A King's Cutter. 1984. 224p. pap. 2.50 o.p. (0-523-41977-5, Pinnacle Bks.) Kensington Publishing Corp.
—A King's Cutter. 1995. (Illus.). 273p. mass mkt. o.s.i (0-7515-0895-0) Little Brown & Co.
—A King's Cutter. 1997. (Nathan DrinkWater Ser.: Bk. 2). 224p. mass mkt. 5.99 o.p. (0-446-60462-3) Warner Bks., Inc.
—A King's Cutter: A Nathaniel Drinkwater Novel. 2001. (Captain Drinkwater Ser.: Bk. 2). (Illus.). 176p. reprint ed. pap. 14.95 (1-57409-124-7) Sheridan Hse., Inc.

**FRONTIER AND PIONEER LIFE—FICTION**

Boggs, Johnny D. The Despoilers: A Frontier Story. 2002. (Five Star Western Ser.). 269p. 24.95 (0-7862-3535-7, Five Star) Gale Group.
Cooper, James Fenimore. The Pioneers. Date not set. 346p. 25.95 (0-8488-2544-6) Amereon, Ltd.
—The Pioneers. 1993. 608p. mass mkt. 4.50 o.s.i (0-553-21417-9, Bantam Classics) Bantam Bks.
—The Pioneers. 1976. lib. bdg. 26.95 (0-89968-157-3, Lightyear Pr.); 1984. 493p. reprint ed. lib. bdg. 26.95 o.p. (0-89966-492-X) Buccaneer Bks., Inc.
—The Pioneers. 1969. mass mkt. 0.75 o.p. (0-451-50480-1, Signet Classics); 1969. mass mkt. 0.60 o.p. (0-451-50214-0, Signet Classics); 1964. mass mkt. 1.95 o.p. (0-451-51156-5, Signet Classics); 1964. mass mkt. 1.50 o.p. (0-451-50921-8, Signet Classics); 1964. mass mkt. 1.25 o.p. (0-451-50746-0, Signet Classics); 1964. mass mkt. 2.50 o.p. (0-451-51416-5, Signet Classics); 1964. mass mkt. 3.50 o.p. (0-451-51621-4, Signet Classics); 1964. mass mkt. 3.95 o.p. (0-451-52145-5) NAL.
—The Pioneers. Wallace, James D., ed. & intro. by. 2000. (Oxford World's Classics Ser.). (Illus.). 496p. pap. 10.95 (0-19-283667-6) Oxford Univ. Pr., Inc.
—The Pioneers. Wallace, James D., ed. 1992. (Oxford World's Classics Ser.). (Illus.). 484p. pap. 7.95 o.p. (0-19-282802-9, 4581) Oxford Univ. Pr., Inc.
—The Pioneers. 1990. (Works of James Fenimore Cooper). reprint ed. lib. bdg. 79.00 (0-7812-2371-7) Reprint Services Corp.
—The Pioneers. Clark, Robert, ed. 1993. (Illus.). 444p. pap. 6.95 o.p. (0-460-87187-0, Everyman's Classic Library in Paperback) Tuttle Publishing.
—The Pioneers. Ringe, Donald A., ed. & intro. by. 1988. (Classics Ser.). 480p. pap. 11.00 (0-14-039007-3, Penguin Classics) Viking Penguin.
Cooper, Virgil R. Virg-2 A Helping Hand. per. 4.99 (0-9668804-3-9) A-bar-V Publishing.
—Virg-4 Pettiquah Crossing. per. 4.99 (0-9668804-5-5) A-bar-V Publishing.
Copeland, Lori. Ruth. l.t. ed. 2004. (Brides of the West 1872 Ser.: No. 6). 351p. 26.95 (0-7862-6058-0) Thorndike Pr.
—Ruth. 2002. (HeartQuest Ser.). (Illus.). 312p. pap. 9.99 (0-8423-1937-9) Tyndale Hse. Pubs.
Crawford, Dianna. Lady of the River. 2003. (HeartQuest Ser.). 352p. pap. 9.99 (0-8423-6011-5) Tyndale Hse. Pubs.
Crummey, Michael. River Thieves: A Novel. 2002. 432p. pap. (0-385-65817-6, Anchor Canada) Doubleday Canada, Ltd. CAN. *Dist:* Random Hse., Inc.
—River Thieves: A Novel. 2002. (Illus.). 352p. 24.00 (0-618-14531-1) Houghton Mifflin Co.
—River Thieves: A Novel. 2003. 352p. pap. 13.00 (0-618-34071-8, Mariner Bks.) Houghton Mifflin Co. Trade & Reference Div.
Dailey, Janet. Shifting Calder Wind. 2004. 384p. mass mkt. 7.99 (0-8217-7223-6); 2003. 304p. 24.00 (0-7582-0067-6) Kensington Publishing Corp.
—Shifting Calder Wind. l.t. ed. 2004. 495p. pap. 13.95 (1-59413-019-1, Large Print Pr.); 2003. 447p. 32.95 (0-7862-5652-4) Thorndike Pr.
Dumont, Julia L. Tecumseh & Other Stories of the Ohio River Valley. Parker, Sandra, ed. 2001. 195p. pap. 16.95 (0-87972-824-8, Popular Pr.) Univ. of Wisconsin Pr.
—Tecumseh & Other Stories of the Ohio River Valley. Parker, Sandra, ed. & intro. by. 2001. 195p. 49.95 (0-87972-823-X, Popular Pr.) Univ. of Wisconsin Pr.
Elliott, Diane. Strength of Stone: The Journal of Electa Bryan Plumer, 1862-1864. 2002. (Illus.). 288p. 19.95 (0-7627-2464-1, Falcon Guides) Globe Pequot Pr., The.
Glover, Ruth. Bittersweet Bliss: A Novel. 2003. (Saskatchewan Saga Ser.). 272p. pap. 11.99 (0-8007-5828-5) Revell, Fleming H. Co.
—The Shining Light. 2003. 206p. 25.95 (0-7862-5491-2, Five Star) Gale Group.
—A Time to Dream. 2003. (Wildrose Ser.). 189p. 25.95 (0-7862-5512-9, Five Star) Gale Group.
—Turn Northward, Love. 2003. 217p. 25.95 (0-7862-5509-9, Five Star) Gale Group.
Haruf, Kent. The Tie That Binds: A Vivid Saga of Pioneer Life. 1986. (Contemporary American Fiction Ser.). 256p. pap. 6.95 o.p. (0-14-008466-5, Penguin Bks.) Viking Penguin.
Kohler, George. The Texan. 2003. 638p. 27.95 (0-9729518-0-6, (734) 945-2189) El Paso City Bks., LLC.
Lawrence, D. H. The Boy in the Bush. 1972. pap. 2.95 o.p. (0-670-00331-X) Penguin Group (USA) Inc.
—The Boy in the Bush. 400p. 1992. pap. 9.95 o.p. (0-14-018446-5, Penguin Classics); 1981. pap. 6.95 o.p. (0-14-001935-9, Penguin Bks.) Viking Penguin.
Lawrence, D. H. & Skinner, M. L. The Boy in the Bush. Eggert, Paul, ed. 1990. (Cambridge Edition of the Works of D. H. Lawrence). (Illus.). 561p. 130.00 (0-521-30704-X) Cambridge Univ. Pr.
—The Boy in the Bush. Eggert, Paul, ed. 1996. (Penguin Twentieth-Century Classics Ser.). 432p. pap. 12.95 o.s.i (0-14-018817-7) Viking Penguin.
Lawton, Wendy. Ransom's Mark. 2003. (Daughters of the Faith Ser.: Bk. 4). 168p. (J). (gr. k-3). pap. 6.99 (0-8024-3638-2) Moody Pr.
McMahon, Thomas A. McKay's Bees: A Novel. 2003. (Phoenix Fiction Ser.). 288p. pap. 14.00 (0-226-56111-9) Univ. of Chicago Pr.

Morris, Gilbert & McCarver, Aaron. Around the River's Bend. 2002. (Spirit of Appalachia Ser.: No. 5). (Illus.). 288p. pap. 11.99 (*1-55661-889-1*) Bethany Hse. Pubs.

Oke, Janette. Julia's Last Hope. (Women of the West Ser.). 2000. 188p. mass mkt. 6.99 o.p. (*0-7642-2384-4*); 1990. 208p. pap. 11.99 (*1-55661-153-6*); 1990. 208p. pap. 10.99 o.p. (*1-55661-157-9*) Bethany Hse. Pubs.

—Julia's Last Hope. l.t. ed. 2002. lib. bdg. 28.95 (*1-58547-212-3*, Premier) Ctr. Point Large Print.

Reece, Colleen L. Storm Clouds over Chantel. l.t. ed. 2002. 282p. pap. 14.95 (*1-4104-0031-X*, Walker Large Print) Gale Group.

—Storm Clouds over Chantel. l.t. ed. 2002. (Christian Fiction Ser.). 282p. 25.95 (*0-7862-4527-1*) Thorndike Pr.

Robinson, Derek. Kentucky Blues. 2003. 544p. pap. 8.95 (*0-304-36566-1*); 2002. 520p. 27.50 (*0-304-36182-8*) Cassell P L C GBR. *Dist:* Trafalgar Square.

Shaw, Patricia. The Feather & the Stone. 1993. 320p. 21.95 o.p. (*0-312-10462-6*) St. Martin's Pr.

Stahl, Naomi. Gold Rush Dreams. 2004. (*1-59414-026-X*, Five Star) Gale Group.

Tanner, Janet. Shadows of the Past. 2003. 288p. 26.99 (*0-7278-5926-9*) Severn Hse. Pubs., Ltd.

Taylor, Phyllis. Joshua, the Word & the Light. Taylor, Phyllis & Minner, Rose, eds. 2004. 280p. pap. 13.95 (*0-9742233-1-X*) Daybreak Publishing.

Trollope, Anthony. Harry Heathcote of Gangoil: A Tale of Australian Bush Life. Hall, N. John, ed. 1981. (Selected Works of Anthony Trollope). reprint ed. lib. bdg. 38.95 (*0-405-14163-7*) Ayer Co. Pubs., Inc.

—Harry Heathcote of Gangoil: A Tale of Australian Bush Life. reprint ed. lib. bdg. 98.00 (*0-7426-2472-2*); 2001. 313p. pap. text 28.00 (*0-7426-7472-X*) Classic Bks.

—Harry Heathcote of Gangoil: A Tale of Australian Bush Life. 1987. 159p. reprint ed. pap. 4.95 o.p. (*0-486-25317-1*) Dover Pubns., Inc.

—Harry Heathcote of Gangoil: A Tale of Australian Bush Life. 1992. (Oxford World's Classics Ser.). 158p. pap. 6.95 o.p. (*0-19-282846-0*) Oxford Univ. Pr., Inc.

—Harry Heathcote of Gangoil: A Tale of Australian Bush Life. 1994. (Penguin Trollope Ser.: Vol. 35). 320p. pap. 6.95 o.p. (*0-14-043835-1*, Penguin Classics) Viking Penguin.

Williamson, Larry. Tallapoosa. 2001. 256p. pap. 17.95 (*1-58838-039-4*) NewSouth, Inc.

Yoder Miller, Evie. Eyes at the Window. 2003. 22.95 (*1-56148-405-9*) Good Bks.

## G

### GREAT BRITAIN—HISTORY—WARS OF THE ROSES, 1455-1485—FICTION

Abbey, Margaret. The Warwick Heiress. l.t. ed. 1995. (Nightingale Ser.). 269p. pap. 16.95 (*0-8161-7497-0*, Macmillan Reference USA) Gale Group.

Brandewyne, Rebecca. Rose of Rapture. 1991. (Orig.). reprint ed. pap. 22.95 o.p. (*0-7278-4244-7*) Severn Hse. Pubs., Ltd.

—Rose of Rapture. 1988. 480p. (Orig.). mass mkt. 5.95 o.s.i (*0-446-35652-2*) Warner Bks., Inc.

Falconieri, David. The Beggar's Throne. 2004. pap. 13.50 (*1-931561-57-5*); 2000. 391p. 24.00 (*0-9673701-0-8*) MacAdam/Cage Publishing, Inc.

Gower, Iris. Destiny's Child. l.t. ed. 1999. (Romance Ser.). 287p. 26.95 (*0-7838-8768-X*, Macmillan Reference USA) Gale Group.

—Destiny's Child. 1999. 224p. 25.00 (*0-7278-5403-8*) Severn Hse. Pubs., Ltd.

Martyn, Isolde. Moonlight & Shadow. 480p. 2003. mass mkt. 5.99 (*0-425-19328-4*); 2002. (Illus.). pap. 14.00 (*0-425-18608-3*) Berkley Publishing Group.

Penman, Sharon Kay. The Sunne in Splendour. 1990. 944p. pap. 15.95 (*0-345-36313-2*) Ballantine Bks.

—The Sunne in Splendour. 1982. o.p. (*0-03-061368-X*) Holt, Henry & Co.

—The Sunne in Splendour. 1984. 896p. pap. 8.95 o.p. (*0-14-006764-7*, Penguin Bks.) Viking Penguin.

Rebecca. Rose of Rapture. 1984. mass mkt. 6.95 (*0-446-37613-2*) Warner Bks., Inc.

Robertson, R. Garcia Y. Knight Errant. 2001. 480p. 27.95 (*0-312-86996-7*, Forge Bks.) Doherty, Tom Assocs., LLC.

Sedley, Kate. Brothers of Glastonbury. 279p. text 29.95 (*0-7472-2087-5*); 1998. pap. 11.95 (*0-7472-5877-5*) Headline Bk. Publishing, Ltd. GBR. *Dist:* Trafalgar Square.

—Death & the Chapman. l.t. ed. 1992. (Mystery Ser.). 315p. 29.99 o.p. (*0-7505-0420-X*) Magna Large Print Bks. GBR. *Dist:* Ulverscroft Large Print Bks., Ltd., Ulverscroft Large Print Canada, Ltd.

—Death & the Chapman. 1994. 272p. mass mkt. 4.50 o.p. (*0-06-104319-2*, HarperTorch) Morrow/Avon.

—Death & the Chapman. 1991. 224p. 17.95 o.p. (*0-312-06945-6*, Saint Martin's Minotaur) St. Martin's Pr.

—Eve of Saint Hyacinth. 1996. 288p. 21.95 o.p. (*0-312-14331-1*, Saint Martin's Minotaur) St. Martin's Pr.

—The Hanged Man. unabr. ed. 2000. (Chapman Mystery Ser.). audio 54.95 (*0-7540-0241-1*, CAB 1664) Chivers Audio Bks. GBR. *Dist:* BBC Audiobooks America.

—The Holy Innocents, Set. unabr. ed. 1999. audio 69.95 (*0-7540-0330-2*, CAB1753) Chivers Audio Bks. GBR. *Dist:* BBC Audiobooks America.

—The Holy Innocents. 1996. 304p. mass mkt. 4.99 o.s.i (*0-06-104379-6*, HarperTorch) Morrow/Avon.

—The Holy Innocents. 1995. 21.00 o.p. (*0-312-11823-6*, Saint Martin's Minotaur) St. Martin's Pr.

—The Plymouth Cloak. unabr. ed. 1998. audio 54.95 (*0-7540-0188-1*, CAB 1611) BBC Audiobooks America.

—The Plymouth Cloak. l.t. ed. 1994. (Magna Large Print Ser.). 317p. 29.99 o.p. (*0-7505-0614-8*) Magna Large Print Bks. GBR. *Dist:* Ulverscroft Large Print Bks., Ltd., Ulverscroft Large Print Canada, Ltd.

—The Plymouth Cloak. 1994. 224p. mass mkt. 4.50 o.p. (*0-06-104320-6*, HarperTorch) Morrow/Avon.

—The Plymouth Cloak. 1993. 192p. 16.95 o.p. (*0-312-08875-2*, Saint Martin's Minotaur) St. Martin's Pr.

—The Weaver's Tale. 1995. 224p. mass mkt. 4.50 o.p. (*0-06-104336-2*, HarperTorch) Morrow/Avon.

—The Weaver's Tale. 1994. 256p. 20.95 o.p. (*0-312-10474-X*, Saint Martin's Minotaur) St. Martin's Pr.

—The Wicked Winter. 1997. 282p. pap. 11.95 (*0-7472-5631-4*) Headline Bk. Publishing, Ltd. GBR. *Dist:* Trafalgar Square.

—The Wicked Winter. 2nd ed. 1999. 288p. 22.95 (*0-312-20625-9*, Saint Martin's Minotaur) St. Martin's Pr.

Stevenson, Robert Louis. The Black Arrow. 21.95 (*0-8488-1182-8*) Amereon, Ltd.

—The Black Arrow. 2001. per. 14.00 (*1-891355-81-3*) Blue Unicorn Editions.

—The Black Arrow. E-Book 2.49 (*1-58627-549-6*) Electric Umbrella Publishing.

—The Black Arrow. 2002. 252p. 24.99 (*1-58827-850-6*); per. 20.99 (*1-58827-851-4*) IndyPublish.com.

—The Black Arrow. 1981. (English As a Second Language Bk.). pap. text 5.95 o.p. (*0-582-53503-4*, 74102) Longman Publishing Group.

—The Black Arrow. 2003. 272p. mass mkt. 6.95 (*0-451-52916-2*, Signet Classics) NAL.

—The Black Arrow. 2002. (Twelve-Point Ser.). 235p. lib. bdg. 25.00 (*1-58287-194-9*); 377p. lib. bdg. 26.00 (*1-58287-677-0*) North Bks.

—The Black Arrow: A Tale of the Two Roses. 2001. 224p. pap. 9.95 (*1-873631-12-X*) B & W Publishing GBR. *Dist:* Interlink Publishing Group, Inc.

—The Black Arrow: A Tale of the Two Roses. deluxe ed. 1987. (Scribners Illustrated Classics Ser.). (Illus.). xii, 328p. 75.00 o.s.i (*0-684-18897-X*, Atheneum) Simon & Schuster Children's Publishing.

—The Black Arrow, the Misadventures of John Nicholson. (Works of Robert Louis Stevenson Valima Edition Ser.: Vol. 13). 484p. reprint ed. 2001. (Illus.). pap. text 28.00 (*0-7426-5171-1*); 1999. lib. bdg. 88.00 (*1-58201-171-0*) Classic Bks.

Zabka, Paula Simonds. Desire the Kingdom: A Story of the Last Plantagenets. Zabka, George G. & Zabka, Alisa E., eds. 2002. (Illus.). 307p. pap. 16.95 (*0-9717693-0-3*) Bosworth Publishing Co.

### GREAT BRITAIN—HISTORY—PURITAN REVOLUTION, 1642-1660—FICTION

Belle, Pamela. Herald of Joy. 1990. 22.95 o.p. (*0-312-04327-9*) St. Martin's Pr.

Morris, Gilbert. Fields of Glory. 1996. (Wakefield Dynasty Ser.: Vol. 4). 376p. pap. 11.99 o.p. (*0-8423-6229-0*) Tyndale Hse. Pubs.

### GREAT BRITAIN—HISTORY—CIVIL WAR, 1642-1649—FICTION

Belle, Pamela. The Chains of Fate. 1986. 432p. mass mkt. 3.95 o.p. (*0-425-09218-6*); 1984. pap. 6.95 o.p. (*0-425-07367-X*) Berkley Publishing Group.

—The Chains of Fate. 1991. o.p. (*1-55836-000-X*) Chain Sales Marketing, Inc.

—Wintercombe. 1988. 528p. 24.95 o.p. (*0-312-02320-0*) St. Martin's Pr.

Chadwick, Elizabeth. The Leopard Unleashed. 1993. 336p. 19.95 o.p. (*0-312-09323-3*) St. Martin's Pr.

Defoe, Daniel. Memoirs of a Cavalier. (Illus.). reprint ed. (*0-404-07915-6*) AMS Pr., Inc.

—Memoirs of a Cavalier. (Shakespeare Head Edition of the Writings of Daniel Defoe Ser.: Vol. 7). 318p. reprint ed. 2001. pap. text 28.00 (*0-7426-5059-6*); 1999. lib. bdg. 88.00 (*1-58201-059-5*) Classic Bks.

—Memoirs of a Cavalier. 1972. (Novel in England, 1700-1775 Ser.). lib. bdg. 61.00 o.p. (*0-8240-0546-5*) Garland Publishing, Inc.

—Memoirs of a Cavalier. Boulton, James T., ed. 1991. (Oxford World's Classics Ser.). 350p. pap. 7.95 o.p. (*0-19-282710-3*) Oxford Univ. Pr., Inc.

—Memoirs of a Cavalier. 2002. 276p. per. 27.50 (*0-89875-958-7*) Univ. Pr. of the Pacific.

Henty, G. A. Friends Though Divided: A Tale of the Civil War. 2000. 252p. E-Book 3.95 (*0-594-03458-2*) 1873 Pr.

Macaulay, Rose. They Were Defeated. 1986. (Twentieth Century Classics Ser.). 445p. pap. 6.95 o.p. (*0-19-281316-1*) Oxford Univ. Pr., Inc.

Motley, Annette. The Quickenberry Tree. 1984. 704p. 17.95 o.p. (*0-312-66069-3*) St. Martin's Pr.

Rossiter, Clare. Anne of Summer Ho. l.t. ed. 1997. (Nightingale Ser.). pap. 17.95 o.p. (*0-7838-2045-3*, Macmillan Reference USA) Gale Group.

—Anne of Summer Ho. 1977. 7.95 o.p. (*0-312-03850-X*) St. Martin's Pr.

Scott, Walter, Sr. Woodstock, Pt. 2. 2001. (Works of Sir Walter Scott: Vol. 40). (Illus.). 406p. reprint ed. pap. text 28.00 (*0-7426-5272-6*) Classic Bks.

—Woodstock. Inglis, Tony, ed. 2001. (Waverley Novels Ser.). 592p. text 52.50 (*0-7486-0583-5*) Edinburgh Univ. Pr. GBR. *Dist:* Columbia Univ. Pr.

Settle, Mary Lee. Prisons. 1981. 244p. mass mkt. 3.50 o.s.i (*0-345-29312-6*) Ballantine Bks.

—Prisons. 1987. 256p. pap. 8.95 o.s.i (*0-684-18845-7*, Scribner Paper Fiction) Simon & Schuster.

—Prisons. 1996. (Beulah Quintet Ser.: Bk. 1). pap. 12.95 (*1-57003-114-2*) Univ. of South Carolina Pr.

Whyte-Mellville, George John. Holmby House. 2000. 252p. pap. 9.95 (*0-594-00963-4*); E-Book 3.95 (*0-594-02631-8*) 1873 Pr.

## H

### HOLOCAUST, JEWISH (1939-1945)—FICTION

Akavia, Miriam. An End to Childhood. McLeary, Michael P. & Goldman, Jeanette, trs. 1994. 112p. pap. 14.45 (*0-85303-294-7*) Vallentine Mitchell Pubs. GBR. *Dist:* International Specialized Bk. Services.

Amis, Martin. Time's Arrow: Or the Nature of the Offense. 1992. 176p. pap. 11.00 (*0-679-73572-0*); pap. 7.00 o.p. (*0-679-74170-4*) Knopf Publishing Group. (Vintage).

Appelfeld, Aharon. The Iron Tracks. 1999. 208p. pap. 12.00 (*0-8052-1099-7*, Schocken) Knopf Publishing Group.

—Tzili: The Story of a Life. Bilu, Dalya, tr. 1983. 192p. 12.95 o.p. (*0-525-24187-6*, 1258-370, Dutton) Dutton/Plume.

—Tzili: The Story of a Life. Bilu, Dalya, tr. 1984. 192p. pap. 5.95 o.p. (*0-14-007058-3*, Penguin Bks.) Viking Penguin.

Becker, Jurek. Jacob the Liar. 1997. pap. 12.95 o.p. (*1-55970-374-1*) Arcade Publishing, Inc.

—Jacob the Liar. Vennewitz, Leila, tr. from GER. 1996. (Illus.). 256p. 21.95 (*1-55970-315-6*) Arcade Publishing, Inc.

—Jacob the Liar. Vennewitz, Leila, tr. from GER. 1997. 256p. pap. 11.95 o.s.i (*0-452-27903-8*, Plume) Dutton/Plume.

—Jacob the Liar. Kornfeld, Melvin, tr. 1975. (Helen & Kurt Wolff Bk.). 256p. 7.95 o.p. (*0-15-145975-4*) Harcourt Trade Pubs.

—Jacob the Liar. 1990. 19.95 o.p. (*0-8052-4097-7*, Schocken) Knopf Publishing Group.

Belliveau, G. K. Go down to Silence: A Novel. 2003. 352p. pap. 11.99 (*1-57673-736-5*) Multnomah Pubs., Inc.

Brand, Sandra. Roma: During Two Invasions. 1992. 237p. 18.95 o.p. (*0-88400-158-X*, Shengold Bks.) Schreiber Publishing, Inc.

—Roma: During Two Invasions. 2001. 237p. pap. 21.99 (*0-7388-5485-9*); text 31.99 (*0-7388-5484-0*); E-Book 8.00 (*1-4010-0359-1*) Xlibris Corp.

Bruce, David. Klaus & Max. 2000. 200p. pap. 13.95 (*0-88739-283-0*) Creative Arts Bk. Co.

Bukiet, Melvin Jules. Stories of an Imaginary Childhood. 2002. (Library of American Fiction). 201p. pap. 17.95 (*0-299-18074-3*) Univ. of Wisconsin Pr.

Canetti, Veza. The Tortoises. Mitchell, Ian, tr. from GER. 2001. 224p. 24.95 (*0-8112-1468-0*) New Directions Publishing Corp.

Deal, Paul H. Night Lessons. 2001. pap. 21.95 (*0-595-18464-2*) iUniverse, Inc.

Diamond, Sander A. The German Table. rev. ed. 1999. 261p. pap. 15.95 (*1-58444-100-3*) Disc-Us Bks., Inc.

—The German Table: Education of a Nation. 2000. E-Book 12.95 incl. cd-rom (*1-58444-029-5*) Disc-Us Bks., Inc.

Dunn, J. R. Days of Cain. 1997. 336p. 23.00 o.p. (*0-380-97433-9*, Avon Bks.) Morrow/Avon.

—Days of Cain. 1998. 9.09 o.p. (*0-606-13319-4*) Turtleback Bks.

—The Days of Cain. 1998. mass mkt. 6.50 (*0-380-79049-1*, Eos); 1997. pap. 13.00 o.p. (*0-380-79280-X*, Avon Bks.) Morrow/Avon.

Edelman, Gwen. War Story: A Novel. 2002. 176p. pap. 13.00 (*1-57322-939-3*, Riverhead Trade (Paperbacks)) Berkley Publishing Group.

—War Story: A Novel. l.t. ed. 2001. (Large Print Book Ser.). 150p. 26.95 (*1-58724-146-3*, Wheeler Publishing, Inc.) Gale Group.

—War Story: A Novel. 2001. 224p. 21.95 o.p. (*1-57322-189-9*, Riverhead Bks. (Hardcovers)) Putnam Publishing Group, The.

Elberg, Yehuda, tr. from YID. Ship of the Hunted. 1997. (Library of Modern Jewish Literature). 400p. reprint ed. 28.95 (*0-8156-0449-1*) Syracuse Univ. Pr.

Federman, Raymond. The Voice in the Closet. 2001. (ENG & FRE.). pap. 9.00 (*0-9703165-8-5*) Starcherone Bks.

—The Voice in the Closet. 1986. 80p. pap. 30.00 o.p. (*0-930956-05-2*) Station Hill Pr.

Fink, Ida. A Scrap of Time: And Other Stories. Prose, Francine & Levine, Madeline, trs. from POL. 1995. (Jewish Lives Ser.). 174p. pap. 16.00 (*0-8101-1259-0*) Northwestern Univ. Pr.

Fishtein, Oscar. I'll Sell You a Million Jews. 1995. 272p. 19.95 (*0-8158-0517-9*) Christopher Publishing Hse.

Fralon, Jose Alain. A Good Man in Evil Times: The Heroic Story of Aristides de Sousa Mendes - The Man Who Saved the Lives of Countless Refugees in World War II. Graham, Peter, tr. from FRE. 2001. (Illus.). 192p. 22.00 (*0-7867-0848-4*, Carroll & Graf Pubs.) Avalon Publishing Group.

Frister, Roman. The Cap: The Price of a Life. Halkin, Hillel, tr. from HEB. 2001. 384p. pap. 14.00 (*0-8021-3762-8*) Grove/Atlantic, Inc.

Gille, Elisabeth. Shadows of a Childhood: A Novel of War & Friendship. Coverdale, Linda, tr. 1999. (Illus.). 144p. pap. text 12.95 (*1-56584-528-5*) New Pr., The.

Gille, Elizabeth. Shadows of a Childhood: A Novel of War & Friendship. Coverdale, Linda, tr. from FRE. 1998. 144p. text 23.00 (*1-56584-388-6*) New Pr., The.

Goldman, Alex J. I Am a Holocaust Torah. 2000. (Illus.). 40p. (J). (gr. 4-7). 12.95 (*965-229-236-2*) Gefen Publishing Hse., Ltd ISR. *Dist:* Gefen Bks.

Goldsmith, Andrea. The Prosperous Thief. 2002. 291p. (*1-86508-756-4*) Allen & Unwin Pty., Ltd.

Govrin, Michal. The Name. Harshav, Barbara, tr. 1999. 464p. reprint ed. 13.00 (*1-57322-755-2*, Riverhead Trade (Paperbacks)) Berkley Publishing Group.

Grynberg, Henryk. Drohobycz, Drohobycz & Other Stories: True Tales from the Holocaust & Life After. Robertson, Theodosia S., ed. Nitecki, Alicia, tr. from POL. 2002. 272p. pap. 14.00 (*0-14-200165-1*) Penguin Group (USA) Inc.

—The Jewish War & the Victory. Lourie, Richard & Wieniewska, Celina, trs. from POL. 2001. (Jewish Lives Ser.). 152p. text 49.95 (*0-8101-1901-3*) Northwestern Univ. Pr.

—The Jewish War & the Victory. Wieniewska, Celina & Lourie, Richard, trs. from POL. 2001. (Jewish Lives Ser.). 152p. reprint ed. pap. 15.95 (*0-8101-1785-1*) Northwestern Univ. Pr.

Guttmann, B. J. Magdalene. 1996. 231 p. (*1-85863-742-2*) Minerva Pr. GBR. *Dist:* Unity Distribution.

Helmreich, Helaine. The Chimney Tree. 2003. 506p. 19.95 (*1-59264-031-1*) Toby Pr.

—The Chimney Tree. 2000. 296p. 24.95 (*0-87081-562-8*) Univ. Pr. of Colorado.

Kalman, Judith. The County of Birches. 192p. 2000. pap. 11.95 (*0-312-26724-X*, Saint Martin's Griffin); 1999. 21.95 (*0-312-20886-3*) St. Martin's Pr.

Kelby, N. M. In the Company of Angels: A Novel. 2002. (Illus.). 192p. pap. 12.00 (*0-7868-8583-1*) Hyperion Pr.

Keneally, Thomas. Schindler's List. l.t. ed. (Large Print Bks.). 1994. ix, 549p. 25.95 o.p. (*1-56895-105-1*, Wheeler Publishing, Inc.); 1985. xiii, 548p. 18.95 o.p. (*0-8161-3854-0*, Macmillan Reference USA) Gale Group.

—Schindler's List. 1994. (Illus.). 400p. 25.00 (*0-671-51688-4*, Simon & Schuster); 1994. 528p. pap. 6.50 o.s.i (*0-671-51171-8*, Touchstone); 1993. 400p. pap. 14.00 (*0-671-88031-4*, Touchstone); 1992. 400p. pap. 12.00 o.s.i (*0-671-77972-9*, Touchstone); 1982. (Illus.). 400p. 17.50 o.p. (*0-671-44977-X*, Simon & Schuster) Simon & Schuster.

—Schindler's List. 1993. 20.05 (*0-606-14311-4*) Turtleback Bks.

—Schindler's List. 1983. (Illus.). 400p. pap. 9.95 o.p. (*0-14-006784-1*, Penguin Bks.) Viking Penguin.

Kis, Danilo. Hourglass. Manheim, Ralph, tr. from SBC. 1990. 274p. 39.95 o.s.i (*0-374-17287-0*) Farrar, Straus & Giroux.

—Hourglass. Manheim, Ralph, tr. from SER. 1998. (European Classics Ser.). 274p. pap. 22.00 (*0-8101-1513-1*) Northwestern Univ. Pr.

Kohler, Sheila. Children of Pithiviers. 2001. 224p. 22.00 (*1-58195-032-2*, Zoland Bks., Inc.) Steerforth Pr.

Lenard-Cook, Lisa. Dissonance: A Novel. 2003. 186p. 21.95 (*0-8263-3090-8*) Univ. of New Mexico Pr.

Lentin, Ronit. Songs on the Death of Children. 1997. 220p. pap. 13.95 (*1-85371-625-1*) Poolbeg Pr. IRL. *Dist:* Dufour Editions, Inc.
MacMillan, Ian. Village of a Million Spirits: A Novel of the Treblinka Uprising. 1999. 257p. 24.00 o.p. (*1-883642-84-1*) Steerforth Pr.
—Village of a Million Spirits: A Novel of the Treblinka Uprising. 2000. 272p. 12.95 o.s.i (*0-14-029033-8*) Viking Penguin.
Martinusen, Cindy McCormick. North of Tomorrow. 2002. 416p. pap. 10.99 (*0-8423-5237-6*) Tyndale Hse. Pubs.
Menkes, John H. After the Tempest: A Novel. 2003. 304p. 24.95 (*1-56474-420-5*) Fithian Pr.
Monteleone, Thomas F. Night of Broken Souls. 1997. 400p. 21.00 o.p. (*0-446-52048-9*, Aspect) Warner Bks., Inc.
—The Night of Broken Souls. 1998. 448p. mass mkt. 6.50 (*0-446-60577-8*) Warner Bks., Inc.
Norman, Howard. The Museum Guard. 1998. 310p. 24.00 o.p. (*0-374-21649-5*); 1994. E-Book 13.00 (*0-374-70237-3*); 1994. E-Book 13.00 (*0-374-70236-5*); 1994. E-Book 13.00 o.p. (*0-374-70235-7*); 1994. E-Book 13.00 (*0-374-70234-9*) Farrar, Straus & Giroux.
—The Museum Guard. 1999. pap. (*0-312-24716-8*); 320p. pap. 14.00 (*0-312-20427-2*) Picador.
Pap, Karoly. Azarel: A Novel. Olchvary, Paul, tr. from HUN. 2001. 224p. pap. 14.00 (*1-58642-019-4*) Steerforth Pr.
Pilcer, Sonia. The Holocaust Kid. 2001. 176p. 23.95 (*0-89255-261-1*) Persea Bks., Inc.
Prager, Emily. Eve's Tattoo. 1992. pap. 10.00 o.s.i (*0-679-74053-8*, Vintage) Knopf Publishing Group.
Raphael, Linda S. & Raphael, Marc Lee, eds. When Night Fell: An Anthology of Holocaust Short Stories. 1999. (Illus.). 300p. (YA). (gr. 10-12). pap. 20.00 (*0-8135-2663-9*) Rutgers Univ. Pr.
—When Night Fell: Short Stories of the Holocaust. 1999. (Illus.). 336p. (YA). (gr. 10-12). text 50.00 (*0-8135-2662-0*) Rutgers Univ. Pr.
Rawicz, Piotr. Blood from the Sky. Wiles, Peter, tr. 2003. 320p. pap. 15.95 (*0-300-07829-3*) Yale Univ. Pr.
Rosner, Elizabeth. The Speed of Light. 2003. 272p. pap. 12.95 (*0-345-44225-3*); 2001. 256p. 23.95 (*0-345-44224-5*) Ballantine Bks. (Ballantine Bks.).
—The Speed of Light. l.t. ed. 2002. 398p. 28.95 (*0-7862-4041-5*) Gale Group.
Sasson, Jean. Ester's Child. 448p. 2003. pap. 12.95 (*0-9676737-7-1*); 2nd ed. 2001. (Illus.). 24.95 o.p. (*0-9676737-3-9*) Windsor-Brooke Bks.
Schachter, Esty. Anya's Echoes: A Novel. 2003. 96p. pap. 10.00 (*1-56474-427-2*) Fithian Pr.
Schulman, Helen. The Revisionist: A Novel. 2001. (Illus.). 246p. pap. 14.95 (*1-58234-172-9*) Bloomsbury Publishing.
—The Revisionist: A Novel. 1998. 256p. 3.99 o.s.i (*0-609-60208-X*) Crown Publishing Group.
Schunk, Laurel. A Clear North Light: Book One of the Lithuanian Trilogy. 2001. (Lithuanian Trilogy Ser.). 332p. 24.95 (*0-9661879-6-2*) St Kitts Pr.
Sebald, W. G. Austerlitz. 2001. E-Book (*1-59061-448-8*) Adobe Systems, Inc.
—Austerlitz. 2002. 304p. pap. 13.95 (*0-375-75656-6*, Modern Library) Random House Adult Trade Publishing Group.
—Austerlitz. 2001. E-Book 19.95 (*1-58836-061-X*) Random Hse., Inc.
—Austerlitz. Bell, Anthea, tr. from GER. 2001. (Illus.). 304p. 25.95 (*0-375-50483-4*) Random Hse., Inc.
—The Emigrants. Hulse, Michael, tr. from GER. Tr. of Ausgewanderten. (Illus.). 256p. 1997. pap. 14.95 (*0-8112-1366-8*, NDP853); 1996. 22.95 (*0-8112-1338-2*) New Directions Publishing Corp.
Tisma, Aleksandar. The Book of Blam. 2000. 240p. pap. 13.00 o.s.i (*0-15-600841-6*) Harcourt Trade Pubs.
—The Book of Blam. Heim, Michael H., tr. from CRO. 1998. 240p. (C). 23.00 (*0-15-100235-5*) Harcourt Trade Pubs.
Troncoso, Sergio. The Nature of Truth: Novel. 2003. (Latino Voices Ser.). 296p. 22.95 (*0-8101-1991-9*) Northwestern Univ. Pr.
Van Kampen, Robert. The Fourth Reich. 1997. 448p. (gr. 13 up). 24.99 o.p. (*0-8007-1745-7*); pap. 14.99 o.p. (*0-8007-5650-9*) Revell, Fleming H. Co.
Vogler, Peter Z. The Broken Cross. 1997. 220p. 24.95 (*0-9656650-3-8*) Danville Creek Publishing.
Weil, Grete. Last Trolley from Beethovenstraat. Barrett, John, tr. from GER. 1997. (Verba Mundi Ser.). 176p. 22.95 (*1-56792-031-4*) Godine, David R. Pub.
Weil, Jiri. Life with a Star. Schloss, Roslyn, tr. 1989. 280p. 22.95 o.s.i (*0-374-18737-1*) Farrar, Straus & Giroux.
—Life with a Star. 1991. 224p. pap. 8.95 o.p. (*0-14-013171-X*, Penguin Bks.) Penguin Group (USA) Inc.
—Life with a Star. Klimova, Rita & Schloss, Roslyn, trs. 1993. 224p. pap. 10.95 o.p. (*0-14-018766-9*, Penguin Classics) Viking Penguin.
—Life with a Star: A Novel. Klimova, Rita & Schloss, Roslyn, trs. 1998. (Jewish Lives Ser.). 224p. pap. 19.00 (*0-8101-1685-5*) Northwestern Univ. Pr.
—Mendelssohn Is on the Roof. Winn, Marie, tr. 1991. 228p. 23.95 (*0-374-20810-7*) Farrar, Straus & Giroux.
—Mendelssohn Is on the Roof. Winn, Marie, tr. 1998. (Jewish Lives Ser.). 240p. pap. 19.00 (*0-8101-1686-3*) Northwestern Univ. Pr.
—Mendelssohn Is on the Roof: A Novel. 1992. 240p. pap. 10.00 o.p. (*0-14-016776-5*, Penguin Bks.) Penguin Group (USA) Inc.
Wiesel, Elie. The Accident. 1982. 96p. pap. 2.50 o.p. (*0-553-22688-6*); 128p. mass mkt. 5.99 (*0-553-58170-8*) Bantam Bks.
—The Accident. Borchardt, Anne, tr. from FRE. 1991. 120p. pap. 9.00 o.p. (*0-374-52311-8*, Hill & Wang) Farrar, Straus & Giroux.
—The Accident, No. 9. Borchardt, Ann, tr. 1985. 128p. pap. 5.70 o.p. (*0-8090-1525-0*, Hill & Wang) Farrar, Straus & Giroux.
—The Accident. 1981. pap. 1.75 o.p. (*0-380-01004-6*, 22236, Avon Bks.) Morrow/Avon.
—Night Trilogy. 2004. 318p. reprint ed. 25.00 (*0-8090-7369-2*, Hill & Wang) Farrar, Straus & Giroux.
Wojdowski, Bogdan. Bread for the Departed. Levine, Madeline G., tr. from ENG. 1997. (Jewish Lives Ser.). 304p. 59.95 (*0-8101-1455-0*); pap. 24.00 (*0-8101-1456-9*) Northwestern Univ. Pr.
Wolff, Renate. The Abyssal Zone. 354p. 25.00 (*0-615-11830-5*) Wolff, Renate.
Yoder, James D. Black Spider over Tiegenhof. 1995. 232p. pap. 11.99 o.p. (*0-8361-9012-2*) Herald Pr.
—Black Spider over Tiegenhof. l.t. ed. 2000. (Christian Mystery Ser.). 335p. 23.95 (*0-7862-2709-5*) Thorndike Pr.
—Black Spider over Tiegenhof. 1995. E-Book 11.99 (*0-585-22785-3*) netLibrary, Inc.
Zelitch, Simone. Louisa. 2001. 400p. reprint ed. pap. 14.00 (*0-425-18195-2*) Berkley Publishing Group.
—Louisa. 2000. 384p. 24.95 o.s.i (*0-399-14659-8*) Penguin Group (USA) Inc.
Zelman, Aaron S. & Smith, L. Neil. The Mitzvah. 1999. 245p. (YA). (gr. 7 up). mass mkt. 7.95 (*0-9642304-3-7*) Jews For The Preservation of Firearms Ownership, Inc.


**HUNDRED YEARS' WAR, 1339-1453—FICTION**


Cornwell, Bernard. Vagabond. 2002. (Illus.). 416p. 25.95 (*0-06-621080-1*, HarperCollins); 688p. pap. 25.95 (*0-06-051743-3*, HarperLargePrint) HarperTrade.
—Vagabond. 2003. 480p. mass mkt. 7.99 (*0-06-053268-8*, HarperTorch) Morrow/Avon.
Doyle, Arthur Conan. The White Company. 2000. 252p. pap. 9.95 (*0-594-00357-1*); E-Book 9.95 (*0-594-02127-8*) 1873 Pr.
—The White Company. Date not set. 374p. 26.95 (*0-8488-2560-8*) Amereon, Ltd.
—The White Company. 1986. (ps-k). reprint ed. lib. bdg. 31.95 (*0-89966-517-9*) Buccaneer Bks., Inc.
—The White Company, 3. reprint ed. lib. bdg. 294.00 (*0-7426-2685-7*); 2001. pap. text 84.00 (*0-7426-7685-4*) Classic Bks.
—The White Company. E-Book 2.49 (*0-7574-0466-9*) Electric Umbrella Publishing.
—The White Company. E-Book 1.95 (*1-57799-811-1*) Logos Research Systems, Inc.
—The White Company. collector's ed. 2002. (Illus.). im. lthr. 38.85 (*1-4115-1247-2*); pap. 19.95 (*1-4115-0519-0*); 25.95 (*1-4115-0892-0*); pap. 17.95 (*1-4115-0321-X*) Polyglot Pr., Inc.
—The White Company. 2000. 276p. pap. 14.99 (*1-57646-296-X*); 276p. lib. bdg. 35.99 (*1-57646-297-8*); 709p. E-Book 3.99 o.p. incl. cd-rom (*1-57646-295-1*); 598p. pap. 34.99 (*1-57646-298-6*); 598p. lib. bdg. 46.99 (*1-57646-299-4*) Quiet Vision Publishing.
—The White Company. E-Book 5.00 (*0-7410-0513-1*) SoftBook Pr.
—The White Company. 1986. 16.95 o.p. (*0-7195-3225-6*) Transatlantic Arts, Inc.
—The White Company. 1998. (Classics Library). pap. 3.95 (*1-85326-289-7*, 2897WW) Wordsworth Editions, Ltd. GBR. *Dist:* Combined Publishing.
Hall, Daniel. Kemp: The Road to Crecy. l.t. ed. 1998. (Magna Large Print Ser.). (Illus.). 547p. (*0-7505-1301-2*) Magna Large Print Bks. GBR. *Dist:* Ulverscroft Large Print Canada, Ltd.
Lawrence, George A. Brakespeare. E-Book 3.95 (*0-594-02561-3*) 1873 Pr.


# I

**INDIA—HISTORY—BRITISH OCCUPATION, 1765-1947—FICTION**


Bhattacharya, Keron. The Pearls of Coromandel. 1996. 256p. 21.95 o.p. (*0-312-14389-3*) St. Martin's Pr.
—The Pearls of Coromandel. l.t. ed. 1997. (Ulverscroft Large Print Ser.). 576p. 29.99 o.p. (*0-7089-3679-2*, Ulverscroft) Thorpe, F. A. Pubs. GBR. *Dist:* Ulverscroft Large Print Bks., Ltd., Ulverscroft Large Print Canada, Ltd.
Chaikin, Linda L. Under the Eastern Stars. 1993. (Heart of India Ser.: Bk. 2). 384p. pap. 10.99 o.p. (*1-55661-366-0*) Bethany Hse. Pubs.
Chatterji, Bankim C. Anandamath: A Novel. 1991. (C). 14.00 (*81-7094-091-5*) Vision IND. *Dist:* South Asia Bks.
Diver, Maud. Lilamani: A Study of Possibilities. Crane, Ralph, ed. 2004. 368p. text 29.95 (*0-19-566622-4*) Oxford Univ. Pr., Inc.
Drummond, Emma. That Sweet & Savage Land. 1991. 288p. 17.95 o.p. (*0-312-05973-6*) St. Martin's Pr.
Henty, G. A. With Clive in India: The Beginnings of an Empire. 2000. 252p. E-Book 9.95 (*0-594-02909-0*) 1873 Pr.
—With Clive in India: The Beginnings of an Empire. 2002. 392p. 29.95 (*1-59087-175-8*, GAH175); per. 19.95 (*1-59087-174-X*, GAH174) Althouse Pr.
—With Clive in India: The Beginnings of an Empire. collector's ed. 2002. (Illus.). im. lthr. 38.85 (*1-4115-1366-5*); pap. 19.95 (*1-4115-0608-1*); 25.95 (*1-4115-0996-X*); pap. 17.95 (*1-4115-0127-6*) Polyglot Pr., Inc.
Jhabvala, Ruth Prawer. Heat & Dust. 1995. (Longman Literature Ser.). pap. text 50.95 (*0-582-25398-5*) Addison-Wesley Longman, Ltd. GBR. *Dist:* Trans-Atlantic Pubns., Inc.
—Heat & Dust. 1999. 190p. pap. text 14.50 (*1-58243-015-2*, Counterpoint Pr.) Basic Bks.
—Heat & Dust. unabr. ed. 2000. audio 49.95 (*0-7451-2715-0*, SAB 081) Chivers Audio Bks. GBR. *Dist:* BBC Audiobooks America.
—Heat & Dust. 1975. 181 p. (*0-7195-3401-1*) Murray, John Pubs., Ltd.
—Heat & Dust. 1987. 192p. pap. 13.00 (*0-671-64657-5*, Touchstone) Simon & Schuster.
—Heat & Dust. 1988. 26.50 (*0-8446-6335-2*) Smith, Peter Pub., Inc.
—Heat & Dust: Movie Tie in Edition. 1983. 181p. reprint ed. pap. o.p. (*0-06-080641-9*, P641) HarperCollins Pubs.
MacNeil, Duncan. By Command of the Viceroy. 1975. 224p. 8.95 o.p. (*0-312-11060-X*) St. Martin's Pr.
—By Command of the Viceroy. l.t. ed. 1979. (Ulverscroft Large Print Ser.). 29.99 o.p. (*0-7089-0341-X*, Ulverscroft) Thorpe, F. A. Pubs. GBR. *Dist:* Ulverscroft Large Print Bks., Ltd., Ulverscroft Large Print Canada, Ltd.
—Charge of Cowardice. 1978. 8.95 o.p. (*0-312-13006-6*) St. Martin's Pr.
—Cunningham's Revenge. l.t. ed. 1986. lib. bdg. 17.95 o.p. (*0-89340-949-9*, 113) BBC Audiobooks America.
—Cunningham's Revenge. 1985. 192p. 13.95 o.s.i (*0-8027-0847-1*) Walker & Co.
—The Restless Frontier. 1980. 8.95 o.p. (*0-312-67782-0*) St. Martin's Pr.
—Wolf in the Fold. 1977. 8.95 o.p. (*0-312-88637-3*) St. Martin's Pr.
Mason, Philip. Skinner's Horse. 1980. o.p. (*0-06-013036-9*) HarperCollins Pubs.
McCutchan, Philip. Captain at Arms, 1. 1999. 286p. 25.00 o.p. (*0-7278-2231-4*) Severn Hse. Pubs., Ltd.
—Captain at Arms. l.t. ed. 1999. (General Ser.). 426p. pap. 23.95 (*0-7862-2094-5*); (*0-7540-3921-8*); (*0-7540-3922-6*) Thorndike Pr.
—The First Command. 1999. 315p. (*0-7540-3471-2*); pap. (*0-7540-3472-0*) BBC Audiobooks America.
—The First Command. l.t. ed. 1999. (General Ser.). 315p. pap. 23.95 (*0-7862-1589-5*) Thorndike Pr.
—Honour & Empire. 1999. 224p. 25.00 (*0-7278-2293-4*) Severn Hse. Pubs., Ltd.
—Honour & Empire. l.t. ed. 2000. (General Ser.). 324p. pap. 23.95 (*0-7862-2303-0*); (*0-7540-3987-0*); (*0-7540-3988-9*) Thorndike Pr.
—Soldier of the Queen. l.t. ed. 1999. (General Ser.). 336p. pap. 23.95 o.p. (*0-7862-1667-0*) Thorndike Pr.
Mehta, Ved. Three Stories of the Raj. 1986. (Illus.). 64p. 85.00 o.p. (*0-85967-722-2*) Ashgate Publishing, Ltd. GBR. *Dist:* Ashgate Publishing Co.
Murari, T. N. The Imperial Agent. 1989. 19.95 o.p. (*0-312-02933-0*) St. Martin's Pr.
Ward, Andrew. The Blood Seed: A Novel of India. 1985. 592p. 17.95 o.p. (*0-670-58934-9*) Viking Penguin.


**INDIANS OF NORTH AMERICA—WARS—1866-1895—FICTION**


Chiaventone, Frederick J. A Road We Do Not Know: A Novel of Custer at the Little Bighorn. 1996. (Illus.). 336p. 24.00 (*0-684-83056-6*, Simon & Schuster) Simon & Schuster.
—A Road We Do Not Know: A Novel of Custer at the Little Bighorn. 1998. (Illus.). 333p. pap. 15.95 o.p. (*0-8263-1885-1*) Univ. of New Mexico, Schl. of Medicine, Biomedical Communications.
Crockett, Richard F. Trooper Smith. 1994. 18.95 o.p. (*0-533-11059-9*) Vantage Pr., Inc.
Cummings, Jack. The Indian Fighter's Return. l.t. ed. 1994. 268p. lib. bdg. 16.95 (*0-8161-5991-2*, Macmillan Reference USA) Gale Group.
—The Indian Fighter's Return. 1993. 182p. 19.95 (*0-8027-1268-1*) Walker & Co.
Haines, William W. The Winter War. l.t. ed. 1998. (Western Ser.). 384p. 20.95 (*0-7862-1377-9*) Thorndike Pr.
Izzard, Kathryn, ed. Adobe Walls Wars. 4th ed. 1993. (Illus.). 116p. mass mkt. 10.00 (*1-891584-00-6*) Tangleaire Pr.
—Heroes Here Have Been. 2nd ed. 1993. (Illus.). ix, 112p. pap. 10.00 (*1-891584-01-4*) Tangleaire Pr.
Jones, Douglas C. Roman. 1989. mass mkt. 4.95 o.p. (*0-8125-8455-4*, Tor Bks.) Doherty, Tom Assocs., LLC.
—Roman. 1986. 320p. o.p. (*0-03-060044-8*) Holt, Henry & Co.
Paine, Lauran. Apache Trail. l.t. ed. 2000. (G. K. Hall Paperback Ser.). 228p. pap. 23.95 (*0-7838-8928-3*, Macmillan Reference USA) Gale Group.
Ross, Dana Fuller, pseud. Dakota! 1983. 320p. mass mkt. 4.50 o.s.i (*0-553-26184-3*) Bantam Bks.
—Dakota! l.t. ed. 1984. (General Ser.). lib. bdg. 13.95 o.p. (*0-8161-3628-9*, Macmillan Reference USA) Gale Group.
Sanford, John A. Song of the Meadowlark. 1986. 352p. 16.95 o.p. (*0-06-015546-9*) HarperTrade.
Skimin, Robert & Moody, William E. Custer's Luck. 2000. 608p. 25.00 (*1-928746-14-4*) Herodias.
Sutcliff, Ann. Westering: An Epic Story of Hope, Bravery & Shameful Treachery. 1997. 486p. pap. 18.95 o.p. (*1-85756-286-0*) Janus Publishing Co. GBR. *Dist:* Paul & Co. Pubs. Consortium, Inc.
Weddle, Virginia B. The Moon of the Falling Leaves. 1994. 125p. per. (*0-9640352-0-0*) Weddle, Virginia B.


**IRELAND—HISTORY—EASTER RISING, 1916—FICTION**


De Rosa, Peter. Rebels: The Irish Rising of 1916. 1992. 560p. pap. 15.95 (*0-449-90682-5*, Fawcett) Ballantine Bks.
—Rebels: The Irish Rising of 1916. 1991. 560p. 25.00 o.s.i (*0-385-26752-5*) Doubleday Publishing.
—Rebels: The Irish Uprising of 1916. 1996. pap. 14.00 o.s.i (*0-449-45660-9*) Ballantine Bks.
Dillon, Anna. Seasons. 1989. 22.95 o.p. (*0-312-02978-0*) St. Martin's Pr.
Doyle, Roddy. A Star Called Henry. l.t. ed. 2000. (Illus.). 487p. 26.95 (*1-56895-818-8*, Wheeler Publishing, Inc.) Gale Group.
—A Star Called Henry. 2000. (Last Roundup Ser.: Vol. 1). (Illus.). 384p. pap. 14.00 (*0-14-029613-1*) Penguin Group (USA) Inc.
—A Star Called Henry. 2000. 20.05 (*0-606-19864-4*) Turtleback Bks.
—A Star Called Henry. 1999. (Last Roundup Ser.). 343p. 24.95 o.s.i (*0-670-88757-9*) Viking Penguin.
Hayden, Thomas. The Killing Frost. 1992. 544p. 22.95 o.p. (*0-312-07010-1*) St. Martin's Pr.
Llywelyn, Morgan. 1916: A Novel of the Irish Rebellion. unabr. ed. 1998. audio 28.95 (*1-56740-050-7*, 196, Bookcassette); audio 89.25 (*1-56740-579-7*, 784, Unabridged Library Editions) Brilliance Audio.
—1916: A Novel of the Irish Rebellion. (Illus.). 1999. 544p. pap. text 6.99 (*0-8125-7492-3*, Tor Bks.); 1998. 447p. 24.95 o.p. (*0-312-86101-X*, Forge Bks.) Doherty, Tom Assocs., LLC.
—1916: A Novel of the Irish Rebellion. 1999. 6.99 (*0-312-87140-6*) St. Martin's Pr.
Murdoch, Iris. The Red & the Green. l.t. ed. 2000. (Perennial Bestsellers Ser.). (Illus.). 432p. pap. 28.95 (*0-7838-9085-0*) Thorndike Pr.
—The Red & the Green. 1988. 288p. pap. 10.95 o.s.i (*0-14-002756-4*, Penguin Bks.); 1965. 5.00 o.p. (*0-670-59100-9*) Viking Penguin.
O'Neill, Jamie. At Swim, Two Boys. 2002. E-Book 28.00 (*1-4014-9977-5*) Barnes & Noble Digital.
—At Swim, Two Boys. 2003. 576p. pap. 15.00 (*0-7432-2295-4*); 2002. E-Book 28.00 (*0-7432-4187-8*); 2002. 576p. 28.00 (*0-7432-2294-6*); 2001. 643p. (*0-7432-0712-2*); 2001. 643p. pap. (*0-7432-0713-0*) Simon & Schuster. (Scribner).
Spellman, Cathy Cash. An Excess of Love. 1986. 640p. mass mkt. 3.95 o.s.i (*0-440-12394-1*); 1985. 526p. 16.95 o.p. (*0-385-29398-4*, Delacorte Pr.) Dell Publishing.
—An Excess of Love. 2000. 532p. pap. 29.95 o.p. (*0-595-16145-6*, Backinprint.com) iUniverse, Inc.
Uris, Leon. Trinity. 1983. 832p. mass mkt. 7.99 (*0-553-25846-X*) Bantam Bks.
—Trinity. 1976. 751p. 21.95 o.s.i (*0-385-03458-X*) Doubleday Publishing.


**ISRAEL-ARAB WAR, 1948-1949—FICTION**


Aved, Joe. Ami. 1981. 192p. 16.95 o.p. (*0-88400-077-X*, Shengold Bks.) Schreiber Publishing, Inc.
Thoene, Bodie. Jerusalem's Heart, Vol. 3. abr. ed. 2001. (Zion Legacy Ser.: No. 3). 4p. 25.95 o.p. incl. audio (*0-14-180275-8*) Viking Penguin.

Thoene, Bodie & Thoene, Brock. Jerusalem Vigil. 2001. (Zion Legacy Ser.: No. 1). 336p. pap. 13.00 (*0-14-029856-8*) Penguin Group (USA) Inc.
—Jerusalem Vigil. 2000. (Zion Legacy Ser.: No. 1). (Illus.). 352p. 19.95 o.p. (*0-670-88911-3*) Viking Penguin.
—Jerusalem's Heart. 2002. (Zion Legacy Ser.: No. 3). 336p. pap. 13.00 (*0-14-200038-8*) Penguin Group (USA) Inc.
—Thunder from Jerusalem. 2000. (Zion Legacy Ser.: No. 2). (Illus.). 352p. 19.95 o.s.i (*0-670-89206-8*, Viking); 4p. 25.95 o.s.i (*0-14-180237-5*, Penguin AudioBooks) Viking Penguin.
Thoene, Brock. The Jerusalem Scrolls: A Novel of Struggle for Jerusalem. 2002. 288p. pap. 13.00 (*0-14-200151-1*) Penguin Group (USA) Inc.
—Stones of Jerusalem: A Novel. 2003. 272p. pap. 13.00 (*0-14-200188-0*) Penguin Group (USA) Inc.
Thoene, Brock & Thoene, Bodie. Jerusalem Vigil. l.t. ed. 2001. (Illus.). 413p. lib. bdg. 27.95 (*1-58547-132-1*) Ctr. Point Large Print.
—Thunder in Jerusalem. 16th l.t. ed. 2002. 408p. lib. bdg. 27.95 (*1-58547-133-X*) Ctr. Point Large Print.

### ISRAEL-ARAB WAR, 1967—FICTION

Cleeve, Roger. Daughters of Jerusalem. 1986. 304p. 15.95 o.p. (*0-917561-02-3*) Adler & Adler Pubs., Inc.
Jones, Scott. Heaven's War. 1998. 400p. pap. 11.95 (*1-57856-021-7*) WaterBrook Pr.
Navon, Yitzhak. The Six Days & the Seven Gates. 1980. 6.00 (*0-930832-57-4*) Herzl Pr.
Thoene, Bodie & Thoene, Brock. The Jerusalem Scrolls. 2001. (Zion Legacy Ser.: No. 4). (Illus.). 304p. 24.95 o.s.i (*0-670-03012-0*, Viking) Viking Penguin.
—Jerusalem's Hope, Vol. 6. 2002. (Illus.). 272p. 24.95 (*0-670-03084-8*, Viking) Viking Penguin.
—Stones of Jerusalem. 2002. (Zion Legacy Ser.: No. 5). (Illus.). 304p. 24.95 (*0-670-03051-1*, Viking) Viking Penguin.
Thoene, Brock & Thoene, Bodie. Jerusalem's Heart. 2001. (Zion Legacy Ser.: No. 3). 304p. 23.95 o.s.i (*0-670-89487-7*, Viking) Viking Penguin.
West, Morris. The Tower of Babel. l.t. ed. 1986. (Charnwood Large Print Ser.). 512p. 29.99 o.p. (*0-7089-8311-1*, Charnwood) Thorpe, F. A. Pubs. GBR. *Dist:* Ulverscroft Large Print Bks., Ltd., Ulverscroft Large Print Canada, Ltd.

### ISRAEL-ARAB WAR, 1973—FICTION

Dayan, Yael. Three Weeks in October. 1979. 8.95 o.s.i (*0-440-07992-6*, Delacorte Pr.) Dell Publishing.
Magun, Carol. Circling Eden: A Novel of Israel in Stories. 1995. 200p. 19.95 (*0-89733-412-4*) Academy Chicago Pubs., Ltd.
Michael, Sami. Refuge. Grossman, Edward, tr. from HEB. 1988. 376p. 22.50 o.p. (*0-8276-0308-8*) Jewish Pubn. Society.

## J

### JACOBITE REBELLION, 1745-1746—FICTION

Cooper, James Fenimore. The Two Admirals. 1842. 504p. (YA). reprint ed. pap. text 34.00 (*1-4047-2388-9*) Classic Textbooks.
—The Two Admirals. 1990. (Works of James Fenimore Cooper). reprint ed. lib. bdg. 79.00 (*0-7812-2388-1*) Reprint Services Corp.
—The Two Admirals: A Tale. 1990. 511p. (C). (gr. 9-12). text 59.50 (*0-88706-905-3*); pap. text 20.95 (*0-88706-907-X*) State Univ. of New York Pr.
Fletcher, Inglis. The Scotswoman. (Carolina Ser.). 414p. reprint ed. lib. bdg. 32.95 (*0-89244-008-2*, Queens Hse., Inc.) Amereon, Ltd.
Gabaldon, Diana. Outlander. 1998. 640p. pap. 14.95 (*0-385-31995-9*, Delacorte Pr.); 1996. 864p. mass mkt. 3.99 o.s.i (*0-440-22291-5*); 1992. 864p. mass mkt. 7.99 (*0-440-21256-1*); 1991. 640p. 27.95 (*0-385-30230-4*, Delacorte Pr.) Dell Publishing.
—Outlander. 2001. 640p. pap. (*0-385-65868-0*) Doubleday Canada, Ltd. CAN. *Dist:* Random Hse., Inc.
Hardwick, Mollie. Charlie Is My Darling. 1977. 8.95 o.p. (*0-698-10867-1*) Putnam Publishing Group, The.
Jacob, Violet. Flemington & Tales from Angus. 1999. (ENG.). 544p. pap. 14.95 (*0-86241-784-8*) Canongate Bks. GBR. *Dist:* Interlink Publishing Group, Inc.
Scott, Walter, Sr. Waverley. 1999. (Works of Sir Walter Scott: Vol. 1). reprint ed. Pt. 1. 410p. lib. bdg. 90.00 (*1-58201-233-4*); Pt. 2. 434p. lib. bdg. 90.00 (*1-58201-234-2*) Classic Bks.
—Waverley. Lamont, Claire, ed. & intro. by. (Oxford World's Classics Ser.). 1998. 456p. pap. 10.95 (*0-19-283601-3*); 1986. 496p. pap. 6.95 o.p. (*0-19-281722-1*) Oxford Univ. Pr., Inc.
—Waverley. 1981. 89.00 o.p. (*0-19-812643-3*) Oxford Univ. Pr., Inc.
—Waverley. Hook, Andrew, ed. & intro. by. 1981. (English Library). 608p. 10.95 (*0-14-043071-7*, Penguin Classics) Viking Penguin.
—Waverley. 1976. 8.95 o.p. (*0-460-01075-1*) Viking Penguin.
Stephen, David. Alba, the Last Wolf. 1985. 256p. o.p. (*0-7126-0454-5*) Random Hse. of Canada, Ltd. CAN. *Dist:* Random Hse., Inc.
Thomson, George M. The Ball at Glenkerran. 1983. 229p. o.p. (*0-436-52044-3*) David & Charles Pubs.

## K

### KING PHILIP'S WAR, 1675-1676—FICTION

Cooper, James Fenimore. The Wept of Wish-Ton-Wish, 2 vols. in 1. (BCL Ser. I). reprint ed. 42.50 (*0-404-01715-0*) AMS Pr., Inc.
—The Wept of Wish-Ton-Wish. 1990. (Works of James Fenimore Cooper). reprint ed. lib. bdg. 79.00 (*0-7812-2378-4*) Reprint Services Corp.
—The Wept of Wish-Ton-Wish, 2 vols. in 1. 1971. reprint ed. 39.00 (*0-403-00432-2*) Scholarly Pr., Inc.
Hunt, Angela Elwell. Rehoboth. 1997. (Keepers of the Ring Ser.: No. 4). 356p. pap. 11.99 o.p. (*0-8423-2015-6*) Tyndale Hse. Pubs.
Kotker, Zane. White Rising. 1981. 288p. 11.95 o.p. (*0-394-40776-8*, Knopf Bks. for Young Readers) Random Hse. Children's Bks.

### KOREAN WAR, 1950-1953—FICTION

Ahn, Junghyo. Silver Stallion: A Novel of Korea. 1993. 269p. pap. 13.00 (*1-56947-003-0*); 1990. 320p. 19.95 o.s.i (*0-939149-30-3*) Soho Pr., Inc.
Baldwin, Gene. A Matter of Destiny. 2002. 328p. pap. 22.99 (*0-7388-0272-7*); text 32.99 (*0-7388-0271-9*) Xlibris Corp.
Brady, James. The Marines of Autumn: A Novel of the Korean War. E-Book 24.95 (*0-312-27444-0*); 2000. (Illus.). viii, 274p. 24.95 o.p. (*0-312-26200-0*); 2001. 304p. reprint ed. pap. 13.95 (*0-312-28081-5*, Saint Martin's Griffin) St. Martin's Pr.
Busch, Frederick. War Babies. 1989. 128p. 15.95 (*0-8112-1103-7*); 2001. 122p. reprint ed. pap. 12.95 (*0-8112-1476-1*) New Directions Publishing Corp.
Carson, Jerry. The Guilty of the Korean War. 2002. 173p. per. 16.95 (*0-9713832-9-4*) WordWright.biz, Inc.
Cheek, John. Stay Safe Buddy: A Story of Humor & Horror During the Korean War. 2003. 298p. pap. 24.95 (*1-59286-631-X*) PublishAmerica, Inc.
Crews, Harry. Celebration: A Novel. 1999. 272p. pap. 13.00 (*0-684-84810-4*, Touchstone); 1998. 256p. 22.50 (*0-684-83758-7*, Simon & Schuster) Simon & Schuster.
Douglas, Mark. USS Hoquiam PF-5: Resurrected. 2001. 320p. pap. (*1-55212-688-9*) Trafford Publishing.
—USS Hoquiam (pf-5) Road to Hungnam. 2002. (Illus.). 347p. pap. (*1-55369-076-1*) Trafford Publishing.
Flynn, Robert. Living with the Hyenas. 1995. 232p. 22.50 (*0-87565-144-5*) Texas Christian Univ. Pr.
Griffin, W. E. B. Retreat, Hell! 2004. 512p. 26.95 (*0-399-15081-1*, G. P. Putnam's Sons) Penguin Putnam Bks. for Young Readers.
Harding, John H., Jr. Shortchanged. 1998. 144p. pap. 13.95 (*1-883911-22-2*) Brandylane Pubs., Inc.
Hooker, Richard. M*A*S*H: A Novel about Three Army Doctors. 188p. reprint ed. lib. bdg. 20.95 (*0-88411-198-9*) Amereon, Ltd.
—M*A*S*H: A Novel about Three Army Doctors. 1997. (Illus.). 224p. (ps-3). reprint ed. pap. 13.00 (*0-688-14955-3*, Quill) HarperTrade.
Justice, Glenn M. Fightin' "George" Light Infantry. DeMeester, Karen, ed. 2001st ed. 2001. (Illus.). 488p. text 29.95 (*0-9702145-0-2*) Justpub.
Loring, Emilie Baker. A Candle in Her Heart. 1976. reprint ed. lib. bdg. 22.95 (*0-88411-353-1*) Amereon, Ltd.
—A Candle in Her Heart. 1980. 224p. pap. 1.75 o.p. (*0-553-13484-1*) Bantam Bks.
Maddron, Ernest. Love, Shame, & Honor. 1993. 204p. (Orig.). pap. text 9.95 (*1-882185-15-3*) Cornerstone Publishing.
Marshall, S. L. A. Pork Chop Hill. 2000. (Illus.). 256p. mass mkt. 6.99 (*0-425-17505-7*) Berkley Publishing Group.
Michener, James A. The Bridges at Toko-Ri. 1984. 128p. mass mkt. 6.99 (*0-449-20651-3*, Fawcett) Ballantine Bks.
—The Bridges at Toko-Ri. l.t. ed. 1981. 13.95 o.p. (*0-8161-3262-3*, Macmillan Reference USA) Gale Group.
—The Bridges at Toko-Ri. 1953. 16.95 o.s.i (*0-394-41780-1*) Random Hse., Inc.
—The Bridges at Toko-Ri. l.t. ed. 2000. (Perennial Bestsellers Ser.). 131p. 27.95 (*0-7838-9182-2*) Thorndike Pr.
—The Bridges at Toko-Ri. 1982. 13.04 (*0-606-00430-0*) Turtleback Bks.
Morris, Willie. Taps: A Novel. 2002. 352p. pap. 13.00 (*0-618-21902-1*) Houghton Mifflin Co.
Porcelli, Joe. The Photograph. Wyrick, Charles L., Jr., ed. 1995. 346p. 22.95 (*0-941711-30-7*) Wyrick & Co.
Potok, Chaim. I Am the Clay. Date not set. mass mkt. 5.99 (*0-449-22288-8*); 1997. 211p. pap. 11.00 o.s.i (*0-449-00112-1*); 1993. 256p. mass mkt. 6.99 (*0-449-22138-5*) Ballantine Bks. (Fawcett).
—I Am the Clay. 1993. 4.99 o.p. (*0-517-11257-4*) Random Hse. Value Publishing.
Potter, Jacob. Reluctant Hero. 2000. 224p. pap. 13.95 (*1-58597-013-1*) Leathers Publishing.
Rosenbaum, Ray. Eagles: Book Four of the Wings of War. 1997. 368p. 22.95 o.p. (*0-89141-557-2*, Presidio Pr.) Ballantine Bks.
Ruggero, Ed. Thirty-Eight North Yankee. 1990. 18.95 o.p. (*0-671-70021-9*, Atria) Simon & Schuster.
—Thirty-Eight North Yankee. McCarthy, Paul, ed. 1991. 480p. reprint ed. mass mkt. 5.99 (*0-671-70022-7*, Pocket) Simon & Schuster.
Salter, James. The Hunters: A Novel. 1999. (Vintage International Ser.). 256p. pap. 13.00 (*0-375-70392-6*, Vintage) Knopf Publishing Group.
Simmons, Edwin Howard. Dog Company Six. 2000. (Illus.). 303p. 24.95 (*1-55750-898-4*) Naval Institute Pr.
Smith, Sid. Something Like a House. 2004. 224p. 25.00 (*1-56649-271-8*) Welcome Rain Pubs.
Sprinkle, Patricia H. Carley's Song. 2001. 448p. pap. 12.99 (*0-310-22993-6*) Zondervan.
Styron, William. The Long March. 1981. 96p. pap. 2.95 o.p. (*0-553-24194-X*) Bantam Bks.
—The Long March. 1968. 10.95 o.s.i (*0-394-43387-4*, V-141, Vintage) Knopf Publishing Group.
—The Long March & In the Clap Shack. 1993. 240p. reprint ed. pap. 14.00 (*0-679-73675-1*, Vintage) Knopf Publishing Group.
Talbert, Dale. Duke: Stories. 2001. 100p. pap. 10.95 (*1-56474-369-1*) Fithian Pr.

## L

### LEBANON—HISTORY—CIVIL WAR, 1975-1990—FICTION

Adnan, Etel. Sitt Marie-Rose. Kleege, Georgina, tr. from FRE. (Orig.). 1982. 116p. reprint ed. pap. 7.50 o.p. (*0-942996-02-X*); 2nd ed. 1989. 105p. pap. 7.95 o.p. (*0-942996-13-5*); 3rd ed. 1990. 105p. pap. 9.95 o.p. (*0-942996-18-6*); 4th ed. 1997. 105p. pap. 11.00 o.p. (*0-942996-27-5*) Post-Apollo Pr., The.
—Sitt Marie Rose: A Novel. Kleege, Georgina, tr. from FRE. 1998. 106p. reprint ed. pap. 11.95 (*0-942996-33-X*) Post-Apollo Pr., The.
Alameddine, Rabih. Koolaids: The Art of War. 256p. 1999. pap. 13.00 (*0-312-20658-5*); 1998. 23.00 (*0-312-18693-2*) Picador.
—Koolaids: The Art of War, a Novel. 2000. 245p. reprint ed. 23.00 (*0-7881-9338-4*) DIANE Publishing Co.
Bache, Ellyn. Safe Passage. 1993. 234p. reprint ed. pap. 10.95 (*0-9635967-7-2*) Banks Channel Bks.
—Safe Passage. 1994. 256p. mass mkt. 4.99 o.s.i (*0-553-56964-3*) Bantam Bks.
—Safe Passage. 1995. E-Book 7.50 (*1-886420-09-2*, Boson Bks.) C&M Online Media, Inc.
Barakat, Hoda. The Stone of Laughter: A Novel. Bennett, Sophie, tr. 1995. (Emerging Voices Ser.).Tr. of Hajar al-Dahk. 240p. 29.95 (*1-56656-197-3*); pap. 12.95 (*1-56656-190-6*) Interlink Publishing Group, Inc.
Dye, Dale. Outrage: A Novel of Beirut. 1990. mass mkt. 3.95 o.s.i (*0-515-10206-7*, Jove) Berkley Publishing Group.
—Outrage: A Novel of Beirut. 1988. 17.95 (*0-316-20010-7*) Little Brown & Co.
Hazo, Samuel J. Stills. 1989. 17.95 o.s.i (*0-689-12058-3*, Scribner) Simon & Schuster.
—Stills: A Novel. 1998. 192p. pap. 16.95 (*0-8156-0537-4*) Syracuse Univ. Pr.
Khoury, Elias. The Journey of Little Gandhi. Haydar, Paula, tr. 1994. xx, 194p. 19.95 (*0-8166-1995-6*) Univ. of Minnesota Pr.
—The Kingdom of Strangers. Haydar, Paula, tr. from ARA. 2003. viii, 103p. (C). 24.00 (*1-55728-433-4*); pap. 17.95 (*1-55728-434-2*) Univ. of Arkansas Pr.
Labaky, Mansour. The Roads of Nowhere: A Child of Lebanon. Annelyse, Allen, tr. 1988. Orig. Title: Enfant du Liban: les Chemins de Nulle Part. 96p. pap. 8.95 (*0-932506-61-5*) St. Bede's Pubns.
Moreau, C. X. Distant Valor. 1999. 351p. reprint ed. text 24.00 (*0-7881-6623-9*) DIANE Publishing Co.
—Distant Valor. 1998. (Illus.). 416p. mass mkt. 6.99 (*0-8125-5389-6*); 1996. 352p. 23.95 o.p. (*0-312-85941-4*) Doherty, Tom Assocs., LLC. (Forge Bks.).
Samman, Ghada. Beirut Nightmares. Roberts, Nancy N., tr. from ARA. 1998. 268p. pap. 13.95 (*0-7043-8065-X*) Quartet Bks., Ltd. GBR. *Dist:* Interlink Publishing Group, Inc.

### LITTLE BIGHORN, BATTLE OF THE, MONT., 1876—FICTION

Black, Michelle. An Uncommon Enemy. (Illus.). 400p. pap. 6.99 (*0-7653-4065-8*); 2001. 416p. 26.95 (*0-7653-0103-2*) Doherty, Tom Assocs., LLC. (Forge Bks.).
Blake, Michael. Marching to Valhalla: A Novel of Custer's Last Days. l.t. ed. 1997. 304p. pap. 19.00 (*0-449-00044-3*, Fawcett) Ballantine Bks.
—Marching to Valhalla: A Novel of Custer's Last Days. 2002. 261p. 24.95 (*0-9724753-3-8*) Hrymfaxe.
—Marching to Valhalla: A Novel of Custer's Last Days. l.t. ed. 1997. (G. K. Hall Western Ser.). 403p. 25.95 (*0-7838-8091-X*) Thorndike Pr.
Chiaventone, Frederick J. A Road We Do Not Know: A Novel of Custer at the Little Bighorn. 1996. (Illus.). 336p. 24.00 (*0-684-83056-6*, Simon & Schuster) Simon & Schuster.
—A Road We Do Not Know: A Novel of Custer at the Little Bighorn. 1998. (Illus.). 333p. pap. 15.95 o.p. (*0-8263-1885-1*) Univ. of New Mexico, Schl. of Medicine, Biomedical Communications.
Garcia y Robertson, Rodrigo. American Woman. 2001. 352p. pap. 15.95 (*0-312-87629-7*, Forge Bks.) Doherty, Tom Assocs., LLC.
Garcia y Robertson, Rodrigo, et al. American Woman. 1998. 352p. 24.95 (*0-312-86146-X*, Forge Bks.) Doherty, Tom Assocs., LLC.
Henry, Will. No Survivors. 1991. 352p. mass mkt. 3.99 o.s.i (*0-553-23698-9*) Bantam Bks.
—No Survivors. l.t. ed. 2002. lib. bdg. 28.95 (*1-58547-250-6*, Western) Ctr. Point Large Print.
—No Survivors. 1996. (Illus.). 345p. pap. 12.00 (*0-8032-7282-0*, Bison Bks.) Univ. of Nebraska Pr.
Hoyt, Edwin P. The Last Stand: A Novel about George Armstrong Custer & the Indians of the Plains. 320p. 1998. pap. 14.95 (*0-312-86501-5*); 1995. 22.95 o.p. (*0-312-85533-8*) Doherty, Tom Assocs., LLC. (Forge Bks.).
Huebner, Andrew. American by Blood. E-Book 23.00 (*1-58945-121-X*) Adobe Systems, Inc.
—American by Blood. 256p. 2001. pap. 13.00 (*0-684-85771-5*); 2000. (Illus.). 23.00 (*0-684-85770-7*) Simon & Schuster. (Simon & Schuster).
Huebner, Kenneth H. & Andrew. American by Blood. 2000. 256p. 23.00 (*0-684-87358-3*, Simon & Schuster) Simon & Schuster.
Morris, Alan. Between Earth & Sky. 1998. (Guardians of the North Ser.: Vol. 4). 288p. pap. 9.99 o.p. (*1-55661-695-3*) Bethany Hse. Pubs.
—Between Earth & Sky. l.t. ed. 1999. (Christian Fiction Ser.). 448p. 25.95 (*0-7862-1692-1*) Thorndike Pr.
Patten, Lewis B. The Red Sabbath. 1987. 192p. 2.50 o.s.i (*0-441-71173-1*, Diamond Bks.) Berkley Publishing Group.
—The Red Sabbath. l.t. ed. 2001. 255p. lib. bdg. 24.95 (*1-58547-081-3*) Ctr. Point Large Print.
Wilhelmsen, Romain. The Curse of Destiny: The Betrayal of General George Armstrong Custer - a Novel. 2000. 223p. pap. 18.95 (*0-86534-314-4*) Sunstone Pr.

## M

### MEXICAN WAR, 1846-1848—FICTION

Martin, Larry J. Rush to Destiny. 1992. 400p. mass mkt. 3.99 o.s.i (*0-553-29410-5*) Bantam Bks.
Martin, Larry Jay. Rush to Destiny. 1998. 312p. reprint ed. lib. bdg. 29.95 (*0-7351-0028-4*) Replica Bks.
—Rush to Destiny. 2002. 431p. pap. 17.95 (*1-885339-03-8*) Wolfpack Publishing.
Parker, F. M. The Far Battleground. 1988. mass mkt. 3.50 o.p. (*0-451-15675-7*, Signet Bks.); 15.95 o.p. (*0-453-00585-3*) NAL.
Shaara, Jeff. Gone for Soldiers: A Novel of the Mexican War. 2000. (Illus.). 448p. 26.95 (*0-345-42750-5*, Ballantine Bks.) Ballantine Bks.
—Gone for Soldiers: A Novel of the Mexican War. l.t. ed. 2000. 688p. 26.95 (*0-375-43057-1*) Random Hse. Large Print.

### MEXICO—HISTORY—REVOLUTION, 1910-1920—FICTION

Azuela, Mariano. Three Novels by Mariano Azuela: The Trials of a Respectable Family; The Underdogs; The Firefly. Hendricks, Frances K. & Berler, Bernice, trs. from SPA. 2nd ed. 373p. 25.00 (*0-911536-78-7*) Trinity Univ. Pr.
—The Underdogs: A Novel of the Mexican Revolution. Date not set. Tr. of De abajo. 149p. 18.95 (*0-8488-2559-4*) Amereon, Ltd.
—The Underdogs: A Novel of the Mexican Revolution. 1986. Tr. of De abajo. 160p. reprint ed. lib. bdg. 21.95 (*0-89966-515-2*) Buccaneer Bks., Inc.

Historical Events

—The Underdogs: A Novel of the Mexican Revolution. 1996. Tr. of De abajo. 176p. mass mkt. 6.95 (*0-451-52625-2*, MS6252, Signet Classics) NAL.
—The Underdogs: A Novel of the Mexican Revolution. Munguia, E., Jr., tr. 1963. Tr. of De abajo. mass mkt. 3.50 o.p. (*0-451-52102-1*, CE1741, Signet Classics) NAL.
—The Underdogs: A Novel of the Mexican Revolution. 2002. Tr. of De abajo. 192p. pap. 9.95 (*0-375-75942-5*) Random House Adult Trade Publishing Group.
—The Underdogs: A Novel of the Mexican Revolution. Fornoff, Frederick H., tr. 1992. (Latin American Ser.).Tr. of De abajo. (ENG & SPA.). 184p. (C). 49.95 o.p. (*0-8229-3728-X*); (Illus.). pap. 14.95 o.p. (*0-8229-5484-2*) Univ. of Pittsburgh Pr.
Bonds, Parris Afton. Blue Moon. 1988. mass mkt. 4.50 o.s.i (*0-449-14568-9*, Fawcett); 1985. pap. o.s.i (*0-449-90154-8*) Ballantine Bks.
Burroway, Janet. Cutting Stone. 1992. 400p. 21.95 o.p. (*0-395-59300-X*) Houghton Mifflin Co.
—Cutting Stone. 1993. 480p. mass mkt. 4.50 o.s.i (*1-55817-757-4*) Kensington Publishing Corp.
—Cutting Stone. 404p. 4.98 o.p. (*0-8317-9071-7*) Smithmark Pubs., Inc.
Campobello, Nellie. Cartucho & My Mother's Hands. Meyer, Doris & Matthews, Irene, trs. 1988. (Texas Pan American Ser.). 143p. pap. 10.95 o.p. (*0-292-71111-5*); 19.95 o.p. (*0-292-71110-7*) Univ. of Texas Pr.
Cano, Daniel. Pepe Rios. 1991. (SPA.). 250p. pap. 9.50 o.p. (*1-55885-023-6*) Arte Publico Pr.
Cunningham, John. The Rainbow Runner. 288p. 1993. mass mkt. 4.99 (*0-8125-1359-2*); 1992. 19.95 o.p. (*0-312-85163-4*) Doherty, Tom Assocs., LLC. (Tor Bks.).
Day, Douglas. The Prison Notebooks of Ricardo Flores Magon. 1991. 21.95 (*0-15-174598-6*) Harcourt Trade Pubs.
Fleming, David L. Border Crossings. 1993. 304p. (C). 24.50 (*0-87565-116-X*); pap. 14.95 (*0-87565-117-8*) Texas Christian Univ. Pr.
—Border Crossings. 1993. E-Book 24.50 (*0-585-35547-9*) netLibrary, Inc.
Maginnis, Nick. Antonia's Island. 2001. 262p. 18.95 (*1-56164-221-5*) Pineapple Pr., Inc.
Poniatowska, Elena. Here's to You, Jesusa! Heikkinen, Deanna, tr. from SPA. 2001. Tr. of Hasta No Verte Jesus Mio. xxx, 303p. 24.00 (*0-374-16819-9*) Farrar, Straus & Giroux.
—Here's to You, Jesusa! 2002. Tr. of Hasta No Verte Jesus Mio. 336p. pap. 14.00 (*0-14-200122-8*) Penguin Group (USA) Inc.
Robe, Stanley L. Azuela & the Mexican Underdogs. 1979. 45.00 o.p. (*0-520-03293-4*) Univ. of California Pr.
Shorris, Earl. Under the Fifth Sun. 1980. 14.95 o.s.i (*0-440-09388-0*, Delacorte Pr.) Dell Publishing.
—Under the Fifth Sun. 1993. 624p. pap. 11.95 (*0-393-31083-3*) Norton, W. W. & Co., Inc.
Wright, Rosalind. Veracruz. 1986. 480p. 18.95 o.p. (*0-06-015541-8*) HarperTrade.
—Veracruz. 1987. (McGraw-Hill Paperbacks). 624p. pap. text 5.95 o.p. (*0-07-072077-0*) McGraw-Hill Cos., The.
Zollinger, Norman. Not of War Only: A Novel of the Mexican Revolution. 1995. 597p. mass mkt. 5.99 (*0-8125-3013-6*); 1994. 416p. 22.95 o.p. (*0-312-85529-X*) Doherty, Tom Assocs., LLC. (Forge Bks.).

# N

## NAPOLEONIC WARS, 1800-1815—FICTION

Anthony, Evelyn. Valentina. l.t. ed. 1993. pap. 18.95 o.p. (*0-7927-1586-1*); 20.95 o.p. (*0-7927-1587-X*) BBC Audiobooks America.
—Valentina. 1979. mass mkt. 2.25 o.p. (*0-451-08598-1*, E8598, Signet Bks.) NAL.
Balogh, Mary. One Night for Love. 1999. 384p. mass mkt. 6.50 (*0-440-22600-7*) Dell Publishing.
—One Night for Love. l.t. ed. 1999. (Wheeler Large Print Book Ser.). 454p. pap. 23.95 (*1-56895-795-5*, Wheeler Publishing, Inc.) Gale Group.
Brandewyne, Rebecca. The Love Knot. l.t. ed. 2003. 418p. 29.95 (*1-58724-493-4*, Wheeler Publishing, Inc.) Gale Group.
—The Love Knot. 2003. 400p. mass mkt. (*1-55166-685-5*, Mira Bks.) Harlequin Enterprises, Ltd.
Bronte, Charlotte. Shirley. 1975. reprint ed. 11.95 o.p. (*0-460-00288-0*) Biblio Distribution.
—Shirley. Smith, Margaret & Rosengarten, Herbert, eds. (Oxford World's Classics Ser.). 1998. 720p. pap. 7.95 (*0-19-283378-2*); 1983. 718p. pap. 6.95 o.p. (*0-19-281562-8*) Oxford Univ. Pr., Inc.
—Shirley. Rosengarten, Herbert & Smith, Margaret, eds. 1979. (Clarendon Edition of the Novels of the Brontes). (Illus.). text 125.00 o.p. (*0-19-812565-8*) Oxford Univ. Pr., Inc.
—Shirley. annuals 1997. (Modern Library Ser.). 688p. 19.50 o.s.i (*0-679-60275-5*, Modern Library) Random House Adult Trade Publishing Group.
—Shirley. 1999. 656p. pap. (*0-14-043469-0*, Penguin Classics) Viking Penguin.
—Shirley. Hook, Andrew & Hook, Judith, eds. 1974. (Classics Ser.). 624p. 7.95 (*0-14-043095-4*, Penguin Classics) Viking Penguin.
—Shirley. 1998. (Wordsworth Collection). 496p. pap. 3.95 (*1-85326-064-9*, 0649WW) Wordsworth Editions, Ltd. GBR. *Dist:* Casemate Pubs. & Bk. Distributors, LLC.
Buchan, John. The Free Fishers. 2001. 294p. pap. 12.95 (*1-873631-32-4*) B & W Publishing GBR. *Dist:* Interlink Publishing Group, Inc.
Cartland, Barbara. A Duke in Danger. l.t. ed. 2002. 204p. pap. 23.95 (*0-7862-3962-X*, Hall, G. K. & Co.) Gale Group.
Conrad, Joseph. The Rover. 1999. (Heart of Oak Sea Classics Ser.). 288p. pap. 14.00 o.s.i (*0-8050-6263-7*, Owl Bks.) Holt, Henry & Co.
Cooper, James Fenimore. The Wing & Wing. 1998. (Heart of Oak Sea Classics Ser.). 448p. 30.00 o.s.i (*0-8050-5987-3*);No. 4. 412p. pap. 15.00 o.s.i (*0-8050-5567-3*, Owl Bks.);No. 5. 470p. pap. 15.00 (*0-8050-5568-1*, Owl Bks.) Holt, Henry & Co.
Cornwell, Bernard. Sharpe's Eagle: Richard Sharpe & the Talavera Campaign, July 1809. 1982. (Richard Sharpe Adventure Ser.: No. 5). (Illus.). 352p. 3.25 o.s.i (*0-441-76091-0*) Ace Bks.
—Sharpe's Eagle: Richard Sharpe & the Talavera Campaign, July 1809, unabr. ed. 1993. (Richard Sharpe Adventure Ser.: No. 5). 69.95 incl. audio (*0-7451-5879-X*, CAB 429) BBC Audiobooks America.
—Sharpe's Eagle: Richard Sharpe & the Talavera Campaign, July 1809, unabr. ed. 1995. (Richard Sharpe Adventure Ser.: No. 5). 5p. audio 49.95 (*0-7861-0662-X*, 1564) Blackstone Audio Bks., Inc.
—Sharpe's Eagle: Richard Sharpe & the Talavera Campaign, July 1809. unabr. ed. 2000. (Richard Sharpe Adventure Ser.: No. 5). audio 42.00 Books on Tape, Inc.
—Sharpe's Eagle: Richard Sharpe & the Talavera Campaign, July 1809. 1991. (Richard Sharpe Adventure Ser.: No. 5). reprint ed. lib. bdg. 29.95 (*1-56849-076-3*) Buccaneer Bks., Inc.
—Sharpe's Eagle: Richard Sharpe & the Talavera Campaign, July 1809. 1989. (Richard Sharpe Adventure Ser.: No. 5). audio 64.95 o.p. (*0-8161-9664-8*) Thorndike Pr.
—Sharpe's Eagle: Richard Sharpe & the Talavera Campaign, July 1809. l.t. ed. 1983. (Richard Sharpe Adventure Ser.: No. 5). 480p. 29.99 o.p. (*0-7089-0945-0*, Ulverscroft) Thorpe, F. A. Pubs. GBR. *Dist:* Ulverscroft Large Print Bks., Ltd., Ulverscroft Large Print Canada, Ltd.
—Sharpe's Eagle: Richard Sharpe & the Talavera Campaign, July 1809. (Richard Sharpe Adventure Ser.: No. 5). 1987. 288p. pap. 10.95 o.s.i (*0-14-009921-2*, Penguin Bks.); 1981. 264p. 12.95 o.p. (*0-670-63944-3*) Viking Penguin.
—Sharpe's Enemy: Richard Sharpe & the Defense of Portugal, Christmas 1812. 1987. (Richard Sharpe Adventure Ser.: No. 10). 352p. pap. 11.95 o.s.i (*0-14-010430-5*, Penguin Bks.) Viking Penguin.
—Sharpe's Havoc: Richard Sharpe & the Campaign in Northern Portugal, Spring 1809. 2003. (Richard Sharpe Adventure Ser.). 320p. 25.95 (*0-06-053046-4*) HarperCollins Pubs.
—Sharpe's Havoc: Richard Sharpe & the Campaign in Northern Portugal, Spring 1809. 2004. 336p. pap. 12.95 (*0-06-056670-1*, Perennial) HarperTrade.
—Sharpe's Havoc: Richard Sharpe & the Campaign in Northern Portugal, Spring 1809. l.t. ed. 2003. (Sharpe Novels Ser.). 498p. 29.95 (*0-7862-5601-X*) Thorndike Pr.
—Sharpe's Regiment: Richard Sharpe & the Invasion of France, June to November 1913. 2001. (Sharpe's Adventures Ser.: Vol. 8). 304p. pap. 12.00 (*0-14-029436-8*) Penguin Group (USA) Inc.
—Sharpe's Rifles: Richard Sharpe & the French Invasion of Galicia, January 1809. l.t. ed. 1990. (Richard Sharpe Adventure Ser.: No. 4). 479p. 29.99 o.p. (*1-85057-547-9*) Magna Large Print Bks. GBR. *Dist:* Ulverscroft Large Print Bks., Ltd., Ulverscroft Large Print Canada, Ltd.
—Sharpe's Rifles: Richard Sharpe & the French Invasion of Galicia, January 1809. (Richard Sharpe Adventure Ser.: No. 4). 304p. 1989. pap. 11.95 o.s.i (*0-14-011014-3*, Penguin Bks.); 1988. 17.95 o.p. (*0-670-82222-1*) Viking Penguin.
—Sharpe's Trafalgar: Richard Sharpe & the Battle of Trafalgar, 21 October 1805. 2001. 19.95 (*0-06-621326-6*) HarperCollins Pubs.
—Sharpe's Trafalgar: Richard Sharpe & the Battle of Trafalgar, 21 October 1805. l.t. ed. 2001. (Thorndike Press Large Print Adventure Ser.). (Illus.). 571p. 29.95 (*0-7862-3699-X*) Thorndike Pr.
Doyle, Arthur Conan. The Exploits of Brigadier Gerard. 2001. (New York Review Books Classics Ser.). 464p. pap. 13.95 (*0-940322-73-0*) New York Review of Bks., Inc., The.
Forester, C. S. Beat to Quarters. 1974. (Hornblower Ser.: No. 5). pap. 1.25 o.p. (*0-523-22385-4*, Pinnacle Bks.) Kensington Publishing Corp.
—Beat to Quarters. 1985. (Hornblower Ser.: No. 6). 288p. pap. 13.00 (*0-316-28932-9*, Back Bay) Little Brown & Co.
—Flying Colours. 1975. (Hornblower Ser.: No. 7). 192p. pap. 1.25 o.p. (*0-523-22387-0*, Pinnacle Bks.) Kensington Publishing Corp.
—Flying Colours. 1989. (Hornblower Ser.: No. 8). 256p. pap. 13.00 (*0-316-28939-6*, Back Bay) Little Brown & Co.
—The Gun. 1940. 22.95 (*0-88411-634-4*) Amereon, Ltd.
—The Gun. 2001. 290p. reprint ed. pap. 29.95 (*1-931313-25-3*) Simon Pubns., Inc.
—The Gun. l.t. ed. 1973. (Ulverscroft Large Print Ser.). 29.99 o.p. (*0-85456-206-0*, Ulverscroft) Thorpe, F. A. Pubs. GBR. *Dist:* Ulverscroft Large Print Bks., Ltd., Ulverscroft Large Print Canada, Ltd.
—Lord Hornblower. 1981. (Hornblower Ser.: No. 9). 256p. pap. 2.50 o.p. (*0-523-41394-7*, Pinnacle Bks.) Kensington Publishing Corp.
—Rifleman Dodd. 1976. 18.95 (*0-8488-1008-2*) Amereon, Ltd.
—Rifleman Dodd. 1989. (Great War Stories Ser.). 160p. reprint ed. 19.95 (*0-933852-76-2*) Nautical & Aviation Publishing Co. of America, Inc., The.
—Ship of the Line. abr. ed. 1998. (Hornblower Ser.: No. 6). mass mkt. incl. audio (*1-85998-997-7*) Hodder Headline Audiobooks.
—Ship of the Line. 1980. (Hornblower Ser.: No. 6). 256p. pap. 2.50 o.p. (*0-523-41391-2*, Pinnacle Bks.) Kensington Publishing Corp.
—Ship of the Line. 1985. (Hornblower Ser.: No. 7). 304p. (gr. 8). pap. 13.00 (*0-316-28936-1*, Back Bay) Little Brown & Co.
—Ship of the Line. l.t. ed. 1999. (Hornblower Ser.: No. 6). 336p. 31.99 o.p. (*0-7089-4157-5*, Ulverscroft) Thorpe, F. A. Pubs. GBR. *Dist:* Ulverscroft Large Print Bks., Ltd., Ulverscroft Large Print Canada, Ltd.
Gillenwater, Sharon. Highland Call. 2003. (Alabaster Bks.). 352p. pap. 11.99 (*1-57673-275-4*) Multnomah Pubs., Inc.
Graham, Winston. The Twisted Sword: Cornwall - January 1815. 1991. (Poldark Novel Ser.). 512p. 21.95 o.p. (*0-88184-693-7*, Carroll & Graf Pubs.) Avalon Publishing Group.
—The Twisted Sword: Cornwall - January 1815, Bk. 11. 2002. (Poldark Saga Ser.: Vol. 11). (Illus.). 544p. pap. 8.95 (*0-330-31749-0*) Pan Bks. Ltd. GBR. *Dist:* Trafalgar Square.
—The Twisted Sword Pt. 1: Cornwall - January 1815. l.t. ed. 1995. (Charnwood Large Print Ser.). 496p. 29.99 o.p. (*0-7089-8822-9*, Charnwood) Thorpe, F. A. Pubs. GBR. *Dist:* Ulverscroft Large Print Bks., Ltd., Ulverscroft Large Print Canada, Ltd.
—The Twisted Sword Pt. 2: Cornwall - January 1815. l.t. ed. 1995. (Charnwood Large Print Ser.). 288p. 29.99 o.p. (*0-7089-8828-8*, Charnwood) Thorpe, F. A. Pubs. GBR. *Dist:* Ulverscroft Large Print Bks., Ltd., Ulverscroft Large Print Canada, Ltd.
Hall, James Norman. Doctor Dogbody's Leg. 1998. (Heart of Oak Sea Classics Ser.). 272p. 25.00 o.s.i (*0-8050-5564-9*); 258p. pap. 13.00 o.s.i (*0-8050-5831-1*, Owl Bks.) Holt, Henry & Co.
Holmes, Clare F. The Academy of Love. l.t. ed. 1993. 236p. lib. bdg. 15.95 (*0-8161-5841-X*, Macmillan Reference USA) Gale Group.
Kent, Alexander. Colors Aloft! 1987. mass mkt. 3.50 o.s.i (*0-425-10264-5*) Berkley Publishing Group.
—Colors Aloft! 1999. 288p. reprint ed. 31.95 (*1-56849-728-8*) Buccaneer Bks., Inc.
—Colors Aloft! 1986. 16.95 o.p. (*0-399-12988-X*) Putnam Publishing Group, The.
—Second to None. 2001. (Richard Bolitho Novels Ser.: Vol. 24). 350p. pap. 16.95 (*0-935526-94-3*) McBooks Pr., Inc.
Lambdin, Dewey. Jester's Fortune: An Alan Lewrie Naval Adventure. 1999. (Alan Lewrie Navel Adventures Ser.). (Illus.). 384p. 26.95 o.p. (*0-525-94482-6*) Dutton/Plume.
—Jester's Fortune: An Alan Lewrie Naval Adventure. l.t. ed. 1999. (Core Ser.). (Illus.). 618p. pap. 27.95 (*0-7838-8681-0*, Macmillan Reference USA) Gale Group.
Lapouge, Gilles. The Battle of Wagram. Brownjohn, J. Maxwell, tr. from FRE. 1988. 295p. (C). pap. 19.95 (*0-941533-32-8*); 1990. 240p. reprint ed. pap. 12.95 (*1-56131-013-1*) Dee, Ivan R. Pub. (New Amsterdam Bks).
Luke, Peter. The Other Side of the Hill. 1986. 256p. 18.95 o.p. (*0-575-03490-4*) Gollancz, Victor GBR. *Dist:* Trafalgar Square.
Mack, William P. Captain Kilburnie: A Novel. 1999. 367p. 25.95 (*1-55750-586-1*) Naval Institute Pr.
—Commodore Kilburnie: A Novel. 2002. 256p. 24.95 (*1-55750-480-6*) Naval Institute Pr.
Mallinson, Allan. A Close Run Thing: A Novel of Wellington's Army of 1815. 2000. 320p. pap. 19.00 (*0-553-38043-5*, Spectra) Bantam Bks.
Marryat, Frederick. Mr. Midshipman Easy. 2000. 252p. pap. 9.95 (*0-594-01690-8*); E-Book 3.95 (*0-594-02609-1*) 1873 Pr.
—Mr. Midshipman Easy. Date not set. lib. bdg. 24.95 (*0-8488-1678-1*) Amereon, Ltd.
—Mr. Midshipman Easy. unabr. collector's ed. 1996. audio 88.00 (*0-7366-3499-1*, 4139) Books on Tape, Inc.
—Mr. Midshipman Easy. 1972. 2.95 o.p. (*0-460-01082-4*, Dutton) Dutton/Plume.
—Mr. Midshipman Easy. 1998. (Heart of Oak Sea Classics Ser.). 368p. 30.00 o.s.i (*0-8050-5988-1*) Holt, Henry & Co.
—Mr. Midshipman Easy. 1997. (Classics of Nautical Fiction Ser.). 352p. reprint ed. pap. 14.95 (*0-935526-40-4*) McBooks Pr., Inc.
—Mr. Midshipman Easy. 2001. (Signet Classics). 384p. mass mkt. 5.95 (*0-451-52796-8*) NAL.
—Mr. Midshipman Easy. 1990. (Classics of Naval Literature Ser.). 448p. reprint ed. 34.95 (*0-87021-590-6*) Naval Institute Pr.
—Mr. Midshipman Easy. 1983. pap. 4.95 o.p. (*0-14-005295-X*, Penguin Bks.) Viking Penguin.
—Percival Keene. 1999. (Heart of Oak Sea Classics Ser.). 416p. pap. 15.00 o.s.i (*0-8050-6139-8*, Owl Bks.) Holt, Henry & Co.
—Peter Simple. unabr. ed. 2000. audio 85.95 (*0-7861-1753-2*, 2557) Blackstone Audio Bks., Inc.
—Peter Simple. 1970. 5.00 o.p. (*0-460-00232-5*, Dutton) Dutton/Plume.
—Peter Simple. 1998. (Heart of Oak Sea Classics Ser.). 483p. 30.00 o.s.i (*0-8050-5830-3*) Holt, Henry & Co.
—Peter Simple: Heart of Oak Sea Classics. 1998. (Heart of Oak Sea Classics Ser.). 480p. pap. 15.00 o.s.i (*0-8050-5565-7*, Owl Bks.) Holt, Henry & Co.
McDonough, James. The Limits of Glory: A Novel of Waterloo. 1991. (Illus.). 312p. 19.95 o.p. (*0-89141-384-7*, Presidio Pr.) Ballantine Bks.
O'Brian, Patrick. The Hundred Days. (Aubrey-Maturin Ser.). 288p. 1999. pap. 13.95 (*0-393-31979-2*); 1998. 24.00 (*0-393-04674-5*) Norton, W. W. & Co., Inc.
—The Hundred Days. l.t. ed. (Aubrey-Maturin Ser.). 461p. 2000. 26.95 (*0-7862-1749-9*); 1999. 29.95 (*0-7862-1748-0*) Thorndike Pr.
—Treason's Harbour. l.t. ed. 2002. 524p. 29.95 (*0-7862-1929-7*) Thorndike Pr.
Parkinson, C. Northcote. Dead Reckoning, 001. 1978. 10.95 o.p. (*0-395-27115-0*) Houghton Mifflin Co.
—Dead Reckoning. 1978. 276p. (J). (*0-7195-3484-4*) Murray, John Pubs., Ltd. GBR. *Dist:* Trafalgar Square.
—Devil to Pay. 1973. 278p. text (*0-7195-2838-0*) Murray, John Pubs., Ltd. GBR. *Dist:* Trafalgar Square.
—The Fireship. 1980. (Parkinson Hist Sea Adventure Ser.: No. 2). 208p. 2.25 (*0-87216-685-6*, Jove) Berkley Publishing Group.
—The Fireship, 001. 1975. 192p. 6.95 o.p. (*0-395-20428-3*) Houghton Mifflin Co.
—The Fireship. 1975. 187p. (J). (*0-7195-3175-6*) Murray, John Pubs., Ltd. GBR. *Dist:* Trafalgar Square.
—The Life & Times of Horatio Hornblower. 1994. reprint ed. lib. bdg. 32.95 (*1-56849-318-5*) Buccaneer Bks., Inc.
—The Life & Times of Horatio Hornblower. l.t. ed. 2000. (Charnwood Large Print Ser.). 432p. 31.99 (*0-7089-9193-9*, Ulverscroft) Thorpe, F. A. Pubs. GBR. *Dist:* Ulverscroft Large Print Bks., Ltd., Ulverscroft Large Print Canada, Ltd.
—The Life & Times of Horatio Hornblower. 1970. 304p. (*0-7181-0787-X*, Joseph, Michael) Viking Penguin.
—The Life & Times of Horatio Hornblower: A Fictional Biography. 1998. 320p. pap. 10.95 (*0-7509-2109-9*) Sutton Publishing.
—So Near So Far. 2003. (Richard Delancey Novels: No. 5). 272p. pap. 13.95 (*1-59013-037-5*) McBooks Pr., Inc.
—Touch & Go. 1980. 272p. 2.25 (*0-87216-713-5*, Jove) Berkley Publishing Group.
—Touch & Go. 1978. (General Ser.). lib. bdg. 13.50 o.p. (*0-8161-6592-0*, Macmillan Reference USA) Gale Group.
—Touch & Go, 001. 1977. (Illus.). 230p. 8.95 o.p. (*0-395-25592-9*) Houghton Mifflin Co.
—Touch & Go. 2003. (Richard Delancey Novels: No. 4). 224p. pap. 13.95 (*1-59013-025-1*) McBooks Pr., Inc.
—Touch & Go. 1977. 230p. (J). (*0-7195-3371-6*) Murray, John Pubs., Ltd. GBR. *Dist:* Trafalgar Square.
Pope, Dudley. Galleon. 2001. (Illus.). 330p. pap. 9.95 (*0-7551-0439-0*) House of Stratus, Inc. GBR. *Dist:* Midpoint Trade Bks., Inc.

—Galleon. 1988. 17.95 o.s.i (*0-8027-0989-3*) Walker & Co.
—Ramage. 1991. 350p. reprint ed. lib. bdg. 26.95 (*0-89966-840-2*) Buccaneer Bks., Inc.
—Ramage. l.t. ed. 1992. (Windsor Ser.). 376p. 23.95 o.p. (*0-7451-7410-8*, Macmillan Reference USA) Gale Group.
—Ramage. 2000. (Lord Ramage Novels Ser.: No. 1). 319p. reprint ed. pap. 14.95 (*0-935526-76-5*) McBooks Pr., Inc.
—Ramage & the Drumbeat. unabr. ed. 1994. audio 69.95 (*0-7451-4277-X*, CAB 960) BBC Audiobooks America.
—Ramage & the Drumbeat. 2000. (Lord Ramage Novels Ser.: No. 2). 287p. reprint ed. pap. 14.95 (*0-935526-77-3*) McBooks Pr., Inc.
—Ramage & the Freebooters. 2000. (Lord Ramage Novels Ser.: Vol. 3). 382p. reprint ed. pap. 15.95 (*0-935526-78-1*) McBooks Pr., Inc.
—Ramage & the Freebooters. 1969. 384p. (YA). (*0-297-17710-9*) Weidenfeld & Nicolson, Ltd. GBR. *Dist:* Trafalgar Square.
—Ramage & the Guillotine. 2000. (Lord Ramage Novels Ser.: Vol. 6). 288p. pap. 14.95 (*0-935526-81-1*) McBooks Pr., Inc.
—Ramage & the Guillotine. 1981. 256p. pap. 2.50 o.p. (*0-380-55491-7*, 55491-7, Avon Bks.) Morrow/Avon.
—Ramage & the Rebels. 1985. 286p. 13.95 o.p. (*0-8027-0842-0*) Walker & Co.
—Ramage & the Renegades Book #12. 1982. 288p. pap. 2.75 o.p. (*0-380-60137-0*, 60137-0, Avon Bks.) Morrow/Avon.
—Ramage & the Saracens. 2002. (Lord Ramage Novels: No. 17). (Illus.). 304p. pap. 15.95 (*1-59013-023-5*) McBooks Pr., Inc.
—Ramage at Trafalgar. 2002. (Lord Ramage Novels: 16). (Illus.). 256p. pap. 14.95 (*1-59013-022-7*) McBooks Pr., Inc.
—The Ramage Touch. 1984. 226p. 12.95 o.p. (*0-8027-0785-8*) Walker & Co.
—Ramage's Challenge. 2002. (Lord Ramage Novels Ser.: Vol. 14). (Illus.). 320p. pap. 15.95 (*1-59013-012-X*) McBooks Pr., Inc.
—Ramage's Devil. 2002. (Lord Ramage Novels Ser.: Vol. 13). (Illus.). 320p. pap. 15.95 (*1-59013-010-3*) McBooks Pr., Inc.
—Ramage's Diamond. 1982. 288p. pap. 2.50 o.p. (*0-380-57828-X*, 57828-X, Avon Bks.) Morrow/Avon.
—Ramage's Mutiny. 2001. (Lord Ramage Novels Ser.: Vol. 8). (Illus.). 286p. pap. 14.95 (*0-935526-90-0*) McBooks Pr., Inc.
—Ramage's Prize. 2000. (Lord Ramage Novels Ser.: Vol. 5). (Illus.). 350p. pap. 15.95 (*0-935526-80-3*) McBooks Pr., Inc.
—Ramage's Prize. 1975. 344p. (J). 8.95 (*0-671-21860-3*, Simon & Schuster) Simon & Schuster.
—Ramage's Signal. 1984. 256p. 12.95 o.s.i (*0-8027-0811-0*) Walker & Co.

Rambaud. Retreat. 2003. 24.00 (*0-8021-1740-6*) Grove/Atlantic, Inc.

Saxton, Judith. Waterloo Sunset. 1998. 192p. 24.00 (*0-7278-5373-2*) Severn Hse. Pubs., Ltd.
—Waterloo Sunset. l.t. ed. 1998. (Romance Ser.). 224p. 26.95 (*0-7862-1595-X*) Thorndike Pr.

Unsworth, Barry. Losing Nelson. 1999. 352p. 23.95 o.s.i (*0-385-48652-9*, Talese, Nan A.) Doubleday Publishing.
—Losing Nelson. 2000. 352p. pap. 14.00 (*0-393-32117-7*, Norton Paperbacks) Norton, W. W. & Co., Inc.

Wilson, T. R. The Straw Tower. 1991. 18.95 o.p. (*0-312-05969-8*) St. Martin's Pr.

Winterson, Jeanette. The Passion. 1997. 176p. pap. 12.00 (*0-8021-3522-6*, Grove Pr.); 1988. 180p. 16.95 o.p. (*0-87113-183-8*) Grove/Atlantic, Inc.
—The Passion. 1990. (Vintage International Ser.). pap. 10.00 o.s.i (*0-679-72437-0*, Vintage) Knopf Publishing Group.

Woodiwiss, Kathleen E. The Reluctant Suitor. 2003. 496p. 24.95 (*0-06-018570-8*, Morrow, William & Co.) Morrow/Avon.

Woodman, Richard. Baltic Mission. 1996. 320p. mass mkt. o.s.i (*0-7515-1495-0*) Little Brown & Co.
—Baltic Mission. l.t. ed. 2001. (Magna Large Print Ser.). 384p. (*0-7505-1735-2*) Magna Large Print Bks. GBR. *Dist:* Ulverscroft Large Print Canada, Ltd.
—Baltic Mission. 2000. (Mariner's Library Fiction Classics). 211p. pap. 14.95 (*1-57409-097-6*) Sheridan Hse., Inc.
—Beneath the Aurora. 1996. 312p. mass mkt. o.s.i (*0-7515-1142-0*) Little Brown & Co.
—Beneath the Aurora: A Nathaniel Drinkwater Novel. 2001. (Mariner's Library Fiction Classics: Vol. 12). 256p. pap. 14.95 (*1-57409-102-6*) Sheridan Hse., Inc.
—The Bomb Vessel. 1995. mass mkt. o.s.i (*0-7515-1018-1*) Little Brown & Co.
—The Bomb Vessel, Set. unabr. ed. 1994. (Nathaniel Drinkwater Ser.: No. 4). audio 42.00 (*0-7887-0002-2*, 94141) Recorded Bks., LLC.
—The Bomb Vessel. 1986. 215p. 15.95 o.p. (*0-8027-0886-2*) Walker & Co.
—A Brig of War. 1984. 224p. pap. 2.95 o.p. (*0-523-41978-3*, Pinnacle Bks.) Kensington Publishing Corp.
—A Brig of War. 1995. mass mkt. o.s.i (*0-7515-1304-0*) Little Brown & Co.
—A Brig of War. 1998. 320p. mass mkt. 5.99 o.p. (*0-446-60463-1*) Warner Bks., Inc.
—The Shadow of the Eagle Bk. 13: A Nathaniel Drinkwater Novel. 2002. (Mariner's Library Fiction Classics: Vol. 13). (Illus.). 272p. pap. 14.95 (*1-57409-103-4*) Sheridan Hse., Inc.
—The Shadow of the Eagle Bk. 13: A Nathaniel Drinkwater Novel. 1997. (Illus.). 372p. pap. o.s.i (*0-7515-2051-9*) Warner Futura GBR. *Dist:* Little Brown & Co.
—Under False Colours: A Nathaniel Drinkwater Novel. 1999. (Illus.). 256p. pap. 14.95 (*1-57409-079-8*) Sheridan Hse., Inc.
—1805. 1996. (Illus.). 306p. mass mkt. o.s.i (*0-7515-1479-9*) Little Brown & Co.
—1805. unabr. ed. 1993. (Nathaniel Drinkwater Ser.: No. 6). audio 49.00 (*1-55690-946-2*, 93428) Recorded Bks., LLC.
—1805: A Nathaniel Drinkwater Novel. 2001. (Mariner's Library Fiction Classics). (Illus.). 224p. pap. 14.95 (*1-57409-101-8*) Sheridan Hse., Inc.

### NAZIS—FICTION

Barwick, James. The Hangman's Crusade. 1982. mass mkt. 2.95 o.s.i (*0-345-30025-4*) Ballantine Bks.
—The Hangman's Crusade. 1981. 320p. 12.95 o.p. (*0-698-11037-4*) Putnam Publishing Group, The.

Berkewicz, Ulla. Angels Are Black & White. Willson, A. Leslie, tr. from GER. 1997. 300p. 39.95 (*1-57113-112-4*) Camden Hse.

Chacko, David. White Gamma. 1989. mass mkt. 3.95 (*0-312-91577-2*, St. Martin's Paperbacks); 1988. 208p. 15.95 o.p. (*0-312-02317-0*) St. Martin's Pr.

Davis, J. Madison. The Murder of Frau Schutz. 1988. 18.95 (*0-8027-1055-7*) Walker & Co.

Farren, Mick. Underland. 2002. (Renquist Quartet Ser.). 496p. 27.95 (*0-7653-0321-3*, Tor Bks.) Doherty, Tom Assocs., LLC.

Hakun, George J. Carpathian Story. 2003. 122p. pap. 17.95 (*1-59129-976-4*) PublishAmerica, Inc.

Higgins, Jack. Thunder Point. 1994. 368p. reprint ed. mass mkt. 7.99 (*0-425-14357-0*) Berkley Publishing Group.
—Thunder Point. 1995. reprint ed. lib. bdg. 26.95 (*1-56849-594-3*) Buccaneer Bks., Inc.
—Thunder Point. l.t. ed. 1993. 26.95 o.p. (*1-56895-037-3*, Wheeler Publishing, Inc.) Gale Group.
—Thunder Point. 1993. 320p. 22.95 o.p. (*0-399-13835-8*, G. P. Putnam's Sons) Penguin Group (USA) Inc.
—Thunder Point. 5.98 o.s.i (*0-8317-6524-0*) Smithmark Pubs., Inc.
—The Valhalla Exchange. 1981. mass mkt. 2.95 o.s.i (*0-449-23449-5*, Fawcett) Ballantine Bks.
—The Valhalla Exchange. 1977. lib. bdg. 12.50 o.p. (*0-8161-6496-7*, Macmillan Reference USA) Gale Group.
—The Valhalla Exchange. 1977. 8.95 o.s.i (*0-8128-1932-2*, Scarborough Hse.) Madison Bks., Inc.

Kurtz, Katherine & Harris, Deborah T. Dagger Magic. (Adept Ser.: No. 4). 1996. 384p. mass mkt. 6.99 (*0-441-00304-4*); 1995. 375p. 19.95 o.p. (*0-441-00149-1*) Ace Bks.

Monteleone, Thomas F. Night of Broken Souls. 1997. 400p. 21.00 o.p. (*0-446-52048-9*, Aspect) Warner Bks., Inc.
—The Night of Broken Souls. 1998. 448p. mass mkt. 6.50 (*0-446-60577-8*) Warner Bks., Inc.

Morris, M. E. The Icemen: A Novel of Antarctica. 1988. 336p. 17.95 o.p. (*0-89141-281-6*, Presidio Pr.) Ballantine Bks.
—The Icemen: A Novel of Antarctica. 1989. mass mkt. 4.95 o.p. (*0-671-67869-8*, Pocket) Simon & Schuster.

Pottinger, Stan. The Last Nazi. 2003. 352p. 24.95 (*0-312-27676-1*) St. Martin's Pr.
—The Last Nazi. l.t. ed. 2003. 598p. 29.95 (*0-7862-5956-6*) Thorndike Pr.

Stroyar, J. N. The Children's War. 2002. (Illus.). 1168p. pap. 16.00 (*0-7434-0740-7*, Washington Square Pr.); 2001. (Illus.). 1168p. 29.95 (*0-7434-0739-3*, Atria); 2001. reprint ed. E-Book 29.95 (*0-7434-1928-6*, Atria) Simon & Schuster.

## P

### PENINSULAR WAR, 1807-1814—FICTION

Cleeve, Brian. Sara. 1976. 384p. 8.95 o.p. (*0-698-10700-4*) Putnam Publishing Group, The.

Cornwell, Bernard. Sharpe's Battle: Richard Sharpe & the Battle of Fuentes de Onoro, May 1811. 1995. (Richard Sharpe Adventure Ser.: No. 7). 320p. 20.00 o.p. (*0-06-017677-6*) HarperTrade.
—Sharpe's Battle: Richard Sharpe & the Battle of Fuentes de Onoro, May 1811. 1996. (Richard Sharpe Adventure Ser.: No. 7). 432p. mass mkt. 6.50 o.s.i (*0-06-109537-0*, HarperTorch) Morrow/Avon.
—Sharpe's Battle: Richard Sharpe & the Battle of Fuentes de Onoro, May 1811. 1999. 18.05 (*0-606-21712-6*) Turtleback Bks.
—Sharpe's Battle: Spain 1811. 1999. (Richard Sharpe Adventure Ser.: No. 7). (Illus.). 368p. pap. 12.95 (*0-06-093228-7*, Perennial) HarperTrade.
—Sharpe's Eagle: Richard Sharpe & the Talavera Campaign, July 1809. 2001. (Richard Sharpe Adventure Ser.: No. 5). 288p. pap. 12.00 (*0-14-029430-9*) Penguin Group (USA) Inc.
—Sharpe's Enemy: Richard Sharpe & the Defense of Portugal, Christmas 1812. (Richard Sharpe Adventure Ser.: No. 10). 1987. 352p. pap. 11.95 o.s.i (*0-14-010430-5*, Penguin Bks.); 1984. 336p. 16.95 o.p. (*0-670-63940-0*) Viking Penguin.
—Sharpe's Havoc: Richard Sharpe & the Campaign in Northern Portugal, Spring 1809. 2003. (Richard Sharpe Adventure Ser.). 320p. 25.95 (*0-06-053046-4*) HarperCollins Pubs.
—Sharpe's Havoc: Richard Sharpe & the Campaign in Northern Portugal, Spring 1809. 2004. 336p. pap. 12.95 (*0-06-056670-1*, Perennial) HarperTrade.
—Sharpe's Havoc: Richard Sharpe & the Campaign in Northern Portugal, Spring 1809. l.t. ed. 2003. (Sharpe Novels Ser.). 498p. 29.95 (*0-7862-5601-X*) Thorndike Pr.
—Sharpe's Rifles: Richard Sharpe & the French Invasion of Galicia, January 1809. (Richard Sharpe Adventure Ser.: No. 4). 304p. 1989. pap. 11.95 o.s.i (*0-14-011014-3*, Penguin Bks.); 1988. 17.95 o.p. (*0-670-82222-1*) Viking Penguin.

Forester, C. S. Admiral Hornblower in the West Indies. unabr. ed. 1980. (Hornblower Ser.: No. 10). audio 48.00 Books on Tape, Inc.
—Admiral Hornblower in the West Indies. 1989. 17.95 o.p. (*0-316-28901-9*); 1963. 29.95 o.s.i (*0-316-28904-3*); 1989. (Hornblower Ser.: No. 11). 336p. reprint ed. pap. 13.00 (*0-316-28941-8*, Back Bay) Little Brown & Co.
—Commodore Hornblower. 1976. (Hornblower Ser.: No. 8). 24.95 (*0-88411-928-9*) Amereon, Ltd.
—Commodore Hornblower. 2002. audio 56.00 (*0-7366-9118-9*); 2002. audio compact disk 64.00 (*0-7366-9119-7*); 1980. (Hornblower Ser.: No. 8). audio 56.00 (*0-7366-3095-3*, 1347-A) Books on Tape, Inc.
—Commodore Hornblower. 1975. (Hornblower Ser.: No. 8). 320p. pap. 1.50 o.p. (*0-523-23388-4*, Pinnacle Bks.) Kensington Publishing Corp.
—Commodore Hornblower. 1945. (YA). (gr. 7 up). 17.95 o.p. (*0-316-28894-2*); 1989. (Hornblower Ser.: No. 9). 320p. reprint ed. pap. 13.00 (*0-316-28938-8*, Back Bay) Little Brown & Co.
—Commodore Hornblower. abr. ed. 1999. (Hornblower Ser.: No. 8). mass mkt. 16.85 incl. audio (*1-85998-999-3*) Ulverscroft Audio (U.S.A.).
—The Gun. 1940. 22.95 (*0-88411-634-4*) Amereon, Ltd.
—The Gun. 2001. 290p. reprint ed. pap. 29.95 (*1-931313-25-3*) Simon Pubns., Inc.
—The Gun. l.t. ed. 1973. (Ulverscroft Large Print Ser.). 29.99 o.p. (*0-85456-206-0*, Ulverscroft) Thorpe, F. A. Pubs. GBR. *Dist:* Ulverscroft Large Print Bks., Ltd., Ulverscroft Large Print Canada, Ltd.
—Hornblower & the Atropos. 1976. (Hornblower Ser.: No. 4). 25.95 (*0-8488-0487-2*, Queens Hse., Inc.) Amereon, Ltd.
—Hornblower & the Atropos. unabr. collector's ed. 1984. (Hornblower Ser.: No. 4). audio 56.00 (*0-7366-0653-X*, 1614) Books on Tape, Inc.
—Hornblower & the Atropos. 1953. 17.95 o.p. (*0-316-28911-6*); 1985. (Hornblower Ser.: No. 5). 352p. reprint ed. pap. 13.00 (*0-316-28929-9*, Back Bay) Little Brown & Co.
—Hornblower & the Atropos. abr. ed. 1999. (Hornblower Ser.: No. 4). audio 25.00 (*0-7871-1960-1*, Dove Audio) NewStar Media, Inc.
—Hornblower & the Atropos. abr. ed. 2000. mass mkt. 16.95 incl. audio (*1-85998-977-2*) Trafalgar Square.
—Hornblower & the Hotspur. 1976. (Hornblower Ser.: No. 3). 25.95 (*0-8488-0488-0*, Queens Hse., Inc.) Amereon, Ltd.
—Hornblower & the Hotspur. unabr. collector's ed. 1984. (Hornblower Ser.: No. 3). audio 64.00 (*0-7366-0652-1*, 1613) Books on Tape, Inc.
—Hornblower & the Hotspur. 1981. (Hornblower Ser.: No. 3). 352p. pap. 2.75 o.p. (*0-523-41790-X*, Pinnacle Bks.) Kensington Publishing Corp.
—Hornblower & the Hotspur. 1998. (Hornblower Ser.: No. 3). 400p. pap. 13.00 (*0-316-29046-7*, Back Bay); 1985. 344p. pap. 14.95 o.p. (*0-316-28928-0*, Back Bay); 1962. 17.95 o.p. (*0-316-28899-3*) Little Brown & Co.
—Hornblower & the Hotspur. abr. ed. 1999. (Hornblower Ser.: No. 3). audio 25.00 (*0-7871-1959-8*, Dove Audio) NewStar Media, Inc.
—Hornblower During the Crisis. unabr. collector's ed. 1988. (Hornblower Ser.: No. 11). audio 30.00 (*0-7366-1354-4*, 2255) Books on Tape, Inc.
—Hornblower During the Crisis. 1967. (Illus.). 162p. 17.95 o.p. (*0-316-28915-9*); 1990. (Hornblower Ser.: No. 4). 176p. reprint ed. pap. 13.00 (*0-316-28944-2*, Back Bay) Little Brown & Co.
—Lieutenant Hornblower. 1976. (Hornblower Ser.: No. 2). 24.95 (*0-8488-0489-9*, Queens Hse., Inc.) Amereon, Ltd.
—Lieutenant Hornblower. unabr. collector's ed. 1984. (Hornblower Ser.: No. 2). audio 48.00 (*0-7366-0651-3*, 1612) Books on Tape, Inc.
—Lieutenant Hornblower. (Hornblower Ser.: No. 2). 1980. 320p. pap. 2.50 o.p. (*0-523-41387-4*); 1974. pap. 1.50 o.p. (*0-523-00382-X*) Kensington Publishing Corp. (Pinnacle Bks.).
—Lieutenant Hornblower. 1998. (Hornblower Ser.: No. 2). 320p. pap. 13.00 (*0-316-29063-7*); 1984. 306p. pap. 14.95 o.p. (*0-316-28921-3*) Little Brown & Co. (Back Bay).
—Lieutenant Hornblower. abr. ed. 1999. (Hornblower Ser.: No. 2). audio 25.00 (*0-7871-1961-X*, Dove Audio) NewStar Media, Inc.
—Lieutenant Hornblower. abr. ed. 1998. (Hornblower Ser.: No. 2). audio 16.95 (*1-85998-976-4*) Trafalgar Square.
—Lord Hornblower. Date not set. (Hornblower Ser.: No. 9). 320p. (*0-8488-1324-3*) Amereon, Ltd.
—Lord Hornblower. 1991. (Hornblower Ser.: No. 9). lib. bdg. 21.95 (*1-56849-052-6*) Buccaneer Bks., Inc.
—Lord Hornblower. 1981. (Hornblower Ser.: No. 9). 256p. pap. 2.50 o.p. (*0-523-41394-7*, Pinnacle Bks.) Kensington Publishing Corp.
—Lord Hornblower. 1946. (J). (gr. 7 up). 17.95 o.p. (*0-316-28908-6*); 1989. (Hornblower Ser.: No. 10). 336p. reprint ed. pap. 13.00 (*0-316-28943-4*, Back Bay) Little Brown & Co.
—Mr. Midshipman Hornblower. 1991. (Hornblower Ser.: No. 1). lib. bdg. 21.95 (*1-56849-053-4*) Buccaneer Bks., Inc.
—Mr. Midshipman Hornblower. (Hornblower Ser.: No. 1). 1981. 172p. pap. 2.50 o.p. (*0-523-41672-5*); 1974. pap. 1.50 o.p. (*0-523-23381-7*) Kensington Publishing Corp. (Pinnacle Bks.).
—Mr. Midshipman Hornblower. 1998. 320p. 18.95 o.p. (*0-316-29060-2*); 1950. (YA). 17.95 o.p. (*0-316-28909-4*); 1984. (Hornblower Ser.: No. 1). 320p. reprint ed. pap. 13.00 (*0-316-28912-4*, Back Bay) Little Brown & Co.
—Mr. Midshipman Hornblower. Hedge, Tricia, ed. 2000. (Hornblower Ser.: No. 1). (Illus.). 96p. (J). pap. text 5.95 (*0-19-423041-4*) Oxford Univ. Pr., Inc.
—Rifleman Dodd. 1976. 18.95 (*0-8488-1008-2*) Amereon, Ltd.
—Rifleman Dodd. 1989. (Great War Stories Ser.). 160p. reprint ed. 19.95 (*0-933852-76-2*) Nautical & Aviation Publishing Co. of America, Inc., The.

Forester, C. S. & Gruffudd, Ioan. Hornblower & the Hotspur. abr. ed. 1998. (Hornblower Ser.: No. 3). audio 16.85 (*1-85998-995-0*) Ulverscroft Audio (U.S.A.).

Heyer, Georgette. The Spanish Bride. Date not set. 28.95 (*0-8488-2313-3*) Amereon, Ltd.
—The Spanish Bride. 1984. mass mkt. 2.95 o.p. (*0-451-13276-9*, Signet Bks.) NAL.

Joseph. 2001. (Illus.). 592p. pap. 15.00 (*0-349-11227-4*) Little Brown U.K. GBR. *Dist:* Trafalgar Square.

Luke, Peter. The Other Side of the Hill. 1986. 256p. 18.95 o.p. (*0-575-03490-4*) Gollancz, Victor GBR. *Dist:* Trafalgar Square.

### PERSIAN GULF WAR, 1991 —FICTION

Blinn, James W. The Aardvark Is Ready for War. 1997. 288p. (gr. 8). 22.95 o.p. (*0-316-09987-2*) Little Brown & Co.

Bosek, Jeff S. Desert Scopes. 1995. 122p. (Orig.). pap. 5.95 (*0-9648145-0-1*, PA703-745) Northstar Bks.

Duncan, Patrick S. Courage under Fire. 1996. 288p. 23.95 o.p. (*0-399-14151-0*, G. P. Putnam's Sons) Penguin Group (USA) Inc.

Duncan, Patrick S. Courage under Fire. 1996. mass mkt. 5.99 o.s.i (*1-57297-183-5*) Boulevard Bks.

Fell, Doris Elaine. Betrayal in Paris. 2003. 350p. pap. 12.99 (*1-58229-314-7*) Howard Publishing Co.

Forsyth, Frederick. The Fist of God. 1995. 592p. mass mkt. 7.99 (*0-553-57242-3*); 1995. 592p. mass mkt. 9.99 o.s.i (*0-552-13990-4*); 1995. 592p. mass mkt. 6.99 o.s.i (*0-553-84000-2*); 1994. 29.95 o.s.i (*0-593-02798-1*); 1994. 992p. 28.95 o.s.i (*0-553-09662-1*) Bantam Bks.

Gregory, Michael T. Desert Skies: A Story of Champions in the Gulf War. 2001. 466p. E-Book 8.00 (*0-7388-8803-6*) Xlibris Corp.

Hailstone, David. Six Faces. 1998. 196p. pap. 7.95 (*0-9663490-0-8*) Mother Lode Bks.

Holt, G. Richard. The Rising Storm: A Military Novel about the Persian Gulf War. 1993. 352p. (Orig.). pap. 14.95 (*0-89896-272-2*) Larksdale.

Hudson, Gabe. Dear Mr. President: Stories & a Novella. 2003. 176p. pap. 11.00 (*0-375-71340-9*, Vintage) Knopf Publishing Group.
—Dear Mr. President: Stories & a Novella. 2002. 176p. 19.00 (*0-375-41395-2*) Knopf, Alfred A. Inc.
Jaco, Charles. Dead Air. 1999. mass mkt. 6.99 o.s.i (*0-345-42184-1*) Ballantine Bks.
—Dead Air. abr. ed. 1998. audio (*1-56876-074-4*) Soundlines Entertainment, Inc.
Joy, Camden. Boy Island: A Novel. 2000. 24p. (J). pap. 12.00 (*0-688-17033-1*, Quill) HarperTrade.
Livingston, Harold. To Die in Babylon. 1995. pap. 5.99 (*0-312-95315-1*, St. Martin's Paperbacks); 1993. 400p. 21.95 o.p. (*0-312-09923-1*) St. Martin's Pr.
Melheim, Richard A. Unfinished Business: Saddam Hussein, George Bush, & an American Arab in Military Intelligence Who Knew Too Much. 1992. 240p. 20.00 (*0-9635106-0-6*) Creative Outlet.
Nance, John J. Scorpion Strike. 1993. 352p. mass mkt. 6.99 (*0-449-22221-7*, Fawcett) Ballantine Bks.
Rizzi, Timothy. The Phalanx Dragon. 2000. 480p. reprint ed. pap. 6.99 (*0-8439-3885-4*, Leisure Bks.) Dorchester Publishing Co., Inc.
—The Phalanx Dragon. 1994. (Illus.). 432p. 21.95 o.p. (*1-55611-391-9*) Fine, Donald I. Bks.
—The Phalanx Dragon. 1995. E-Book 9.95 (*0-585-29807-6*) netLibrary, Inc.
Sutherland, Grant. The Consignment. 2004. 416p. mass mkt. 7.50 (*0-553-58331-X*); 2003. 368p. 23.95 (*0-553-80187-2*) Bantam Bks.
Whiting, Charles. The Balkan Chase. l.t. ed. 2000. (Dales Large Print Ser.). 288p. pap. 20.99 (*1-84262-039-8*) Dales Large Print Bks. GBR. *Dist:* Ulverscroft Large Print Bks., Ltd., Ulverscroft Large Print Canada, Ltd.
—The Balkan Chase. l.t. ed. 2000. pap. 20.99 (*1-84137-068-1*) Magna Large Print Bks. GBR. *Dist:* Ulverscroft Large Print Bks., Ltd.
—The Balkan Chase. 1999. 185p. 26.00 (*0-7278-5447-X*) Severn Hse. Pubs., Ltd.
Willard, Tom. Sword of Valor. 2003. (Black Sabre Chronicles Ser.). (Illus.). 384p. 24.95 (*0-312-87385-9*, Tor Bks.) Doherty, Tom Assocs., LLC.
Yorgason, Brenton G. & Myers, Richard. The Garrity Test. 1992. 12.95 (*0-88494-840-4*, Bookcraft, Inc.) Deseret Bk. Co.

## S

### SOUTH AFRICAN WAR, 1899-1902—FICTION

Bowen, Peter. Imperial Kelly. 1993. 3.99 o.p. (*0-517-11272-8*) Random Hse. Value Publishing.
Cloete, Stuart. Rags of Glory. 1973. pap. 1.50 o.p. (*0-380-01516-1*, 15792, Avon Bks.) Morrow/Avon.
Crane, John Kenny. The Legacy of Ladysmith. unabr. ed. 1989. audio 91.00 (*1-55690-307-3*, 89190E7) Recorded Bks., LLC.
—The Legacy of Ladysmith. 1986. 17.45 o.p. (*0-671-60586-0*, Simon & Schuster) Simon & Schuster.
—The Legacy of Ladysmith. 1987. 400p. pap. 4.50 o.p. (*0-14-010064-4*, Penguin Bks.) Viking Penguin.
Denton, Kit. The Breaker. 1982. reprint ed. mass mkt. 3.50 o.s.i (*0-671-44762-9*, Pocket) Simon & Schuster.
—The Breaker. 1981. 288p. 11.95 o.p. (*0-312-09517-1*) St. Martin's Pr.
Drummond, Emma. The Burning Land. l.t. ed. 1987. 688p. 17.95 o.p. (*0-7089-8379-0*, Charnwood) Thorpe, F. A. Pubs. GBR. *Dist:* Ulverscroft Large Print Bks., Ltd.
—A Distant Hero. 1997. 432p. 24.95 o.p. (*0-312-17177-3*) St. Martin's Pr.
Hansen, Brooks. The Chess Garden: Or, the Twilight Letters of Gustav Uyterhoeven. 1996. (Illus.). 480p. reprint ed. 16.00 (*1-57322-563-0*, Riverhead Trade (Paperbacks)) Berkley Publishing Group.
—The Chess Garden: Or, the Twilight Letters of Gustav Uyterhoeven. 1995. (Illus.). 496p. 23.00 o.p. (*0-374-16015-5*) Farrar, Straus & Giroux.
—Chess Garden Readers. 1995. pap. (*0-374-99817-5*) Farrar, Straus & Giroux.
Henty, G. A. With Buller in Natal: A Born Leader. 2000. 252p. (J). E-Book 9.95 (*0-594-02415-3*) 1873 Pr.
—With Buller in Natal: A Born Leader. 2002. 402p. 29.95 (*1-59087-173-1*, GAH173); per. 19.95 (*1-59087-172-3*, GAH172) Althouse Pr.
—With Buller in Natal: A Born Leader. collector's ed. 2002. (Illus.). im. lthr. 38.85 (*1-4115-1285-5*); pap. 19.95 (*1-4115-0573-5*); 25.95 (*1-4115-0995-1*); pap. 17.95 (*1-4115-0160-8*) Polyglot Pr., Inc.
McCutchan, Philip. Halfhyde Goes to War. l.t. ed. 1998. (Dales Large Print Ser.). 304p. pap. 19.99 o.p. (*1-85389-834-1*) Dales Large Print Bks. GBR. *Dist:* Ulverscroft Large Print Bks., Ltd., Ulverscroft Large Print Canada, Ltd.
—Halfhyde Goes to War. 1987. 176p. 12.95 o.p. (*0-312-00603-9*) St. Martin's Pr.
Mda, Zakes. The Madonna of Excelsior. 2004. 272p. 23.00 (*0-374-20008-4*) Farrar, Straus & Giroux.
Smith, Wilbur. The Roar of Thunder. 1977. mass mkt. 2.95 o.s.i (*0-440-18146-1*) Dell Publishing.
—The Sound of Thunder. 1991. 416p. mass mkt. 6.99 (*0-449-14819-X*, Fawcett) Ballantine Bks.
Trollope, Joanna. The Steps of the Sun. 1984. 266p. 13.95 o.p. (*0-312-76165-1*) St. Martin's Pr.
—The Steps of the Sun. abr. ed. 1995. pap. 16.95 incl. audio (*1-85998-166-6*) Trafalgar Square.

### SOVIET UNION—HISTORY—REVOLUTION, 1917-1921—FICTION

Ageyev, M. Novel with Cocaine. unabr. ed. 1999. (World Classic Literature Ser.). (RUS.). pap. 8.95 (*2-87714-279-5*) Bookking International FRA. *Dist:* Distribooks, Inc.
Ageyev, M. Novel with Cocaine. Heim, Michael H., tr. 1984. 240p. 15.95 o.p. (*0-525-24294-5*, 01549-460, Dutton) Dutton/Plume.
—Novel with Cocaine. Heim, Michael H., tr. from RUS. 1985. 224p. reprint ed. mass mkt. 6.95 o.p. (*0-06-097000-6*, PL 7000, Perennial) HarperTrade.
—Novel with Cocaine. Heim, Michael, tr. from RUS. 1983. 212p. reprint ed. pap. 14.00 o.p. (*0-8101-0998-0*) Northwestern Univ. Pr.
Crane, Teresa. Strange Are the Ways. 570p. 4.98 o.p. (*0-8317-4637-8*) Smithmark Pubs., Inc.
—Strange Are the Ways. 1993. 576p. 25.95 o.p. (*0-312-09919-3*) St. Martin's Pr.
Hart-Davis, Duff. Horses of War. 1992. 288p. 18.95 o.p. (*0-312-07787-4*) St. Martin's Pr.
Herlin, Hans. Siberian Transfer. 1992. 304p. 19.95 o.p. (*0-312-07803-X*) St. Martin's Pr.
Kapralov, Yuri. Devil's Midnight. 2003. (Illus.). 294p. 22.95 (*1-888451-11-4*) Akashic Bks.
Lambton, Anthony. Elizabeth & Alexandra. 1986. 18.95 o.p. (*0-525-24395-X*, Dutton) Dutton/Plume.
Leon, Bonnie. Harvest of Truth. 2000. (Sowers Trilogy Ser.: Vol. 3). 320p. pap. 12.99 (*0-8054-1274-3*) Broadman & Holman Pubs.
Pasternak, Boris. Doctor Zhivago. 1997. pap. text o.p. (*0-17-556762-X*) Addison-Wesley Longman, Inc.
—Doctor Zhivago. 1991. 550p. reprint ed. lib. bdg. 36.95 (*0-89966-839-9*) Buccaneer Bks., Inc.
—Doctor Zhivago. l.t. ed. 2000. 25.95 (*1-56895-930-3*, Wheeler Publishing, Inc.) Gale Group.
—Doctor Zhivago. 1997. 592p. pap. 15.00 (*0-679-77438-6*); 1991. 592p. pap. 15.00 o.p. (*0-679-73123-7*); 1958. 19.95 o.s.i (*0-394-42223-6*) Knopf Publishing Group. (Pantheon).
—Doctor Zhivago. 1991. (Everyman's Library). 544p. 20.00 (*0-679-40759-6*) Knopf, Alfred A. Inc.
—Doctor Zhivago. 1969. mass mkt. 0.95 o.p. (*0-451-01802-8*); 1969. mass mkt. 0.95 o.p. (*0-451-02014-6*); 1969. mass mkt. 1.25 o.p. (*0-451-04058-9*); 1960. mass mkt. 1.75 o.p. (*0-451-06531-X*); 1960. mass mkt. 1.95 o.p. (*0-451-07197-2*); 1960. mass mkt. 1.50 o.p. (*0-451-05595-0*) NAL. (Signet Bks.).
—Doctor Zhivago. unabr. ed. 1997. 320p. reprint ed. pap. 14.95 o.p. (*1-57002-039-6*) University Publishing Hse., Inc.
—Dr. Zhivago. 1986. 576p. mass mkt. 5.95 o.s.i (*0-345-34100-7*); 1983. mass mkt. 3.95 o.p. (*0-345-30759-3*); 1981. mass mkt. 3.50 o.p. (*0-345-29310-X*) Ballantine Bks.
—Dr. Zhivago. 1999. (RUS.). pap. 16.95 (*5-8370-0375-4*) Limbus Pr. RUS. *Dist:* Distribooks, Inc.
—Dr. Zhivago. 1960. mass mkt. 2.50 o.p. (*0-451-08430-6*, E8430, Signet Bks.) NAL.
Rand, Ayn. We Are the Living. 60th anniv. ed. 1995. 464p. 29.95 (*0-525-94054-5*, Dutton) Dutton/Plume.
—We the Living: 60th Anniversary Edition. anniv. ed. 1996. 466p. mass mkt. 7.99 (*0-451-18784-9*, Signet Bks.) NAL.
Von Doderer, Heimito. The Secret of the Empire. Barrett, John S., tr. from GER. & afterword by by. 1998. (Studies in Austrian Literature, Culture & Thought). pap. 14.95 (*1-57241-061-2*) Ariadne Pr.
Walpole, Hugh. Secret City. 1998. (Pocket Classics Ser.). 464p. pap. 12.95 (*0-7509-1559-5*) Sutton Publishing, Ltd. GBR. *Dist:* International Publishers Marketing.

### SPAIN—HISTORY—CIVIL WAR, 1936-1939—FICTION

Aub, Max. Field of Honour. Martin, Gerald, tr. 1988. 240p. (gr. 13). 18.95 o.p. (*0-86091-218-3*) Verso.
Betanzos-Palacios, Odon. Diosdado de lo Alto: Con la Senal en la Frente. 1990. (SPA., Illus.). pap. 15.00 (*0-86515-000-1*) Editorial Mensaje.
Cela, Camilo José. Mazurka for Two Dead Men. Haugaard, Patricia, tr. from SPA. Tr. of Mazurca para Dos Muertos. 272p. 1992. 21.95 (*0-8112-1222-X*); 1994. reprint ed. pap. 10.95 (*0-8112-1277-7*, NDP789) New Directions Publishing Corp.
—San Camilo, 1936: The Eve, Feast, & Octave of St. Camillus of the Year 1936 in Madrid. Polt, John H., tr. 1991. 327p. pap. 21.95 (*0-8223-1196-8*); lib. bdg. 69.95 (*0-8223-1179-8*) Duke Univ. Pr.
Cercas, Javier. Soldiers of Salamis: A Novel. McLean, Anne, tr. from SPA. 2004. 224p. 23.95 (*1-58234-384-5*) Bloomsbury Publishing.
Clark, Rosemary, ed. Jose Luis Olaizola's la Guerra del General Escobar. 1993. (Hispanic Texts). 224p. text 17.95 o.s.i (*0-7190-3706-9*) Manchester Univ. Pr. GBR. *Dist:* Holtzbrinck Pubs.
De Luca, Teresa. A Distant Thunder. 1991. 624p. mass mkt. 5.95 (*0-380-71086-2*, Avon Bks.); 1990. 512p. reprint ed. 24.95 o.p. (*0-688-08920-8*, Morrow, William & Co.) Morrow/Avon.
Hemingway, Ernest. Ernest Hemingway's For Whom the Bell Tolls. 1985. (Barron's Book Notes Ser.). (YA). (gr. 10-12). pap. 2.95 (*0-8120-3515-1*) Barron's Educational Series, Inc.
—The Fifth Column & Four Stories of the Spanish Civil War. 160p. 1978. 40.00 (*0-684-15815-9*); 1972. pap. 9.95 (*0-684-12723-7*) Gale Group. (Macmillan Reference USA).
—The Fifth Column & Four Stories of the Spanish Civil War. 2003. E-Book 9.99 (*0-7432-3716-1*); 1998. 160p. pap. 11.00 (*0-684-83926-1*) Simon & Schuster. (Scribner).
—For Whom the Bell Tolls. 1982. 480p. pap. 5.95 o.s.i (*0-684-17660-2*); 1977. 472p. 40.00 o.p. (*0-684-15316-5*); 1940. 482p. 25.00 (*0-684-10239-0*); 1940. 472p. pap. 15.00 o.s.i (*0-684-71798-0*) Gale Group. (Macmillan Reference USA).
—For Whom the Bell Tolls. 2003. E-Book 9.99 (*0-7432-3717-X*); 2003. 480p. pap. 14.00 (*0-684-80335-6*); 1996. 496p. 27.50 (*0-684-83048-5*) Simon & Schuster. (Scribner).
—For Whom the Bell Tolls. (SparkNotes Literature Study Guides). 64-96p. pap., stu. ed. 4.95 (*1-58663-830-0*) Spark Publishing Group.
—For Whom the Bell Tolls. l.t. ed. 1994. 692p. lib. bdg. 24.95 (*0-8161-5968-8*) Thorndike Pr.
—For Whom the Bell Tolls. 1995. 19.05 (*0-606-00680-X*) Turtleback Bks.
Kenwood, Alun, ed. The Spanish Civil War: A Cultural & Historical Reader. 1993. (European Studies). 288p. (*0-85496-318-9*); pap. (*0-85496-338-3*) Berg Pubs.
Leavitt, David. While England Sleeps. rev. ed. 1995. 324p. 24.95 o.p. (*0-395-75937-4*); 304p. pap. 11.95 o.s.i (*0-395-75286-8*) Houghton Mifflin Co.
—While England Sleeps. 320p. 9999. pap. 10.95 o.s.i (*0-14-013361-5*, Penguin Bks.); 1993. (Illus.). 22.00 o.p. (*0-670-83349-5*, Viking) Viking Penguin.
Malraux, André. Man's Hope. Gilbert, Stuart & MacDonald, Alastair, trs. from FRE. 1979. reprint ed. pap. 12.50 o.s.i (*0-394-17093-8*, E740) Grove/Atlantic, Inc.
—Man's Hope. Gilbert, Stuart & Macdonald, Alastair, trs. 1984. 511p. 10.95 o.s.i (*0-394-60478-4*) Random Hse., Inc.
Matute, Ana M. Soldiers Cry by Night/Los Soldados Lloran de Noche: Bilingual Edition. Miller, Yvette E., ed. Nugent, Robert & De la Camara, Maria, trs. 1995. (Discoveries Ser.). (ENG & SPA.). 160p. pap. 15.95 (*0-935480-67-6*, BT0676) Latin American Literary Review Pr.
—The Trap. Jose De La Camara, Maria & Nugent, Robert, trs. from SPA. 1996. (Discoveries Ser.).Tr. of Trampa. 220p. (C). pap. 15.95 (*0-935480-81-1*, BT0811) Latin American Literary Review Pr.
Pawel, Rebecca. Death of a Nationalist. 280p. 2004. pap. 12.00 (*1-56947-344-7*, Soho Crime); 2003. 24.00 (*1-56947-304-8*) Soho Pr., Inc.
Rivas, Manuel. The Carpenter's Pencil. Dunne, Jonathan, tr. 2001. (Illus.). 160p. 24.95 (*1-58567-145-2*) Overlook Pr., The.
Rodoreda, Mercé. The Time of the Doves. Rosenthal, David H., tr. from CAT. 1986. 208p. reprint ed. pap. 14.00 (*0-915308-75-4*) Graywolf Pr.
—The Time of the Doves. Rosenthall, David, tr. 1980. 8.95 o.s.i (*0-8008-7731-4*) Taplinger Publishing Co., Inc.
Scurr, John. A Deep Song of Desire: A Story of Love in the Spanish Civil War. 2001. 198p. 26.50 (*1-85776-573-7*) Book Guild, Ltd. GBR. *Dist:* Trans-Atlantic Pubns., Inc.
Wolff, Milton. Another Hill: An Autobiographical Novel. 424p. 2002. (Illus.). pap. text 18.95 (*0-252-06983-8*); 1994. text 29.95 (*0-252-02091-X*) Univ. of Illinois Pr.

### SPANISH-AMERICAN WAR, 1898—FICTION

Bowen, Peter. Imperial Kelly. 1993. 3.99 o.p. (*0-517-11272-8*) Random Hse. Value Publishing.
Casemore, Robert F. Splendid Morning. l.t. ed. 1999. (Romance Ser.). 439p. 26.95 (*0-7838-8474-5*) Thorndike Pr.
Henry, Will. San Juan Hill. 1996. 368p. reprint ed. mass mkt. 4.99 (*0-8439-4045-X*, Leisure Bks.) Dorchester Publishing Co., Inc.
—San Juan Hill. 1996. E-Book 9.95 (*0-585-25332-3*) netLibrary, Inc.
Leonard, Elmore. Cuba Libre. 1999. 416p. mass mkt. 7.50 o.s.i (*0-440-22559-0*); 2000. 352p. reprint ed. pap. 9.95 o.s.i (*0-385-32384-0*, Delta) Dell Publishing.
—Cuba Libre. l.t. ed. 1998. (Wheeler Large Print Book Ser.). 28.95 (*1-56895-600-2*, Wheeler Publishing, Inc.) Gale Group.
—Cuba Libre. abr. ed. 1998. audio 23.95 (*0-553-47847-8*, RH Audio) Random Hse. Audio Publishing Group.
—Cuba Libre. E-Book 7.50 o.p. (*0-440-33426-8*) Random Hse., Inc.
—Cuba Libre, unabr. ed. 1998. audio 60.00 (*0-7887-1866-5*, 95288E7) Recorded Bks., LLC.
Lynch, Daniel. Yellow: A Novel. 1992. 211p. 19.95 o.s.i (*0-8027-1226-6*) Walker & Co.
Morris, Gilbert. The Rough Rider, Vol. 18. 1995. (House of Winslow Ser.: Vol. 18). 304p. pap. 11.99 (*1-55661-394-6*) Bethany Hse. Pubs.
—The Rough Rider. l.t. ed. 1996. 458p. lib. bdg. 22.95 (*0-7838-1853-X*, Macmillan Reference USA) Gale Group.
Shiel, M. P. Contraband of War. (Americans in Fiction Ser.). (Illus.). 258p. reprint ed. pap. text 6.95 (*0-89197-713-9*); lib. bdg. 22.00 (*0-8398-1857-2*) Irvington Pubs.
Thane, Elswyth. Ever After. 1976. reprint ed. lib. bdg. 26.95 (*0-88411-958-0*) Amereon, Ltd.
—Ever After. 1983. mass mkt. 3.50 o.s.i (*0-553-22933-8*) Bantam Bks.
—Ever After. 1993. reprint ed. lib. bdg. 31.95 (*1-56849-230-8*) Buccaneer Bks., Inc.
—Ever After. 1981. (Reader's Request Ser.). lib. bdg. 17.95 o.p. (*0-8161-3165-1*, Macmillan Reference USA) Gale Group.

## T

### TRANSVAAL (SOUTH AFRICA)—HISTORY—WAR OF 1880-1881—FICTION

McCutchan, Philip. Ogilvie at War. 1999. 221p. 25.00 (*0-7278-5471-2*) Severn Hse. Pubs., Ltd.
—Ogilvie at War. l.t. ed. 2000. (General Ser.). 343p. pap. 23.95 (*0-7862-2567-X*); (*0-7540-4156-5*); (*0-7540-4157-3*) Thorndike Pr.

## U

### UNITED STATES—HISTORY—FRENCH AND INDIAN WAR, 1755-1763—FICTION

Altsheler, Joseph A. The Lords of the Wild. 2000. 252p. E-Book 3.95 (*0-594-01820-X*) 1873 Pr.
—The Lords of the Wild. 24.95 (*0-8488-0905-X*) Amereon, Ltd.
—The Lords of the Wild. 1993. reprint ed. lib. bdg. 21.95 (*0-89968-563-3*) Buccaneer Bks., Inc.
—The Masters of the Peaks. 2000. 252p. E-Book 3.95 (*0-594-01822-6*) 1873 Pr.
—The Masters of the Peaks. 311p. reprint ed. lib. bdg. 24.95 (*0-88411-938-6*) Amereon, Ltd.
—The Masters of the Peaks. 1990. reprint ed. lib. bdg. 20.95 (*0-89968-464-5*) Buccaneer Bks., Inc.
—The Rulers of the Lakes. 2000. 252p. E-Book 3.95 (*0-594-01819-6*) 1873 Pr.
—The Rulers of the Lakes. 25.95 (*0-8488-0906-8*) Amereon, Ltd.
—The Rulers of the Lakes. 1993. reprint ed. lib. bdg. 21.95 (*0-89968-565-X*) Buccaneer Bks., Inc.
—The Shadow of the North. 2000. 252p. pap. 9.95 (*0-594-00666-X*); E-Book 3.95 (*0-594-01821-8*) 1873 Pr.
—The Shadow of the North. 1976. 357p. reprint ed. lib. bdg. 23.95 (*0-88411-944-0*) Amereon, Ltd.
—The Shadow of the North. 1990. reprint ed. lib. bdg. 19.95 (*0-89968-468-8*) Buccaneer Bks., Inc.
—A Soldier of Manhattan. 2000. 252p. E-Book 3.95 (*0-594-01835-8*) 1873 Pr.
—The Sun of Quebec. 2000. (Illus.). 252p. E-Book 3.95 (*0-594-01823-4*) 1873 Pr.
—The Sun of Quebec. 25.95 (*0-8488-0907-6*) Amereon, Ltd.
—The Sun of Quebec. 1993. reprint ed. lib. bdg. 21.95 (*0-89968-564-1*) Buccaneer Bks., Inc.
Ashton, Richard C. Du Quesne: Washington's First Campaign. 1994. 232p. pap. 10.00 (*1-56002-355-4*, University Editions) Aegina Pr., Inc.
Cooper, James Fenimore. The Deerslayer. 1964. (YA). (gr. 6 up). pap. 2.95 o.p. (*0-8049-0031-0*, CL31) Airmont Publishing Co., Inc.
—The Deerslayer. Date not set. 410p. 27.95 (*0-8488-2517-9*) Amereon, Ltd.
—The Deerslayer. 1991. (States & Their Symbols Ser.). 528p. (gr. 9-12). mass mkt. 5.95 (*0-553-21085-8*, Bantam Classics) Bantam Bks.
—The Deerslayer. unabr. collector's ed. 1983. Pt. A. (J). audio 64.00 (*0-7366-3981-0*, 9529A); Pt. B. audio 64.00 (*0-7366-3982-9*, 9529-B) Books on Tape, Inc.

Historical Events

—The Deerslayer. 1984. 517p. lib. bdg. 27.95 o.p. (*0-89966-490-3*); 1976. lib. bdg. 21.95 (*0-89968-162-X*, Lightyear Pr.) Buccaneer Bks., Inc.

—The Deerslayer. 1841. 572p. (YA). reprint ed. pap. text 34.00 (*1-4047-2387-0*) Classic Textbooks.

—The Deerslayer. 1963. 544p. (J). (gr. 7). mass mkt. 2.95 o.p. (*0-451-51645-1*); mass mkt. 5.95 (*0-451-52484-5*, CE1645) NAL. (Signet Classics).

—The Deerslayer. Peck, Daniel H., ed. 2000. (Oxford World's Classics Ser.). (Illus.). 592p. pap. 10.95 (*0-19-283725-7*) Oxford Univ. Pr., Inc.

—The Deerslayer. 1993. (Oxford World's Classics Ser.). (Illus.). 588p. pap. 7.95 o.p. (*0-19-282811-8*) Oxford Univ. Pr., Inc.

—The Deerslayer. 1990. (Works of James Fenimore Cooper). reprint ed. lib. bdg. 79.00 (*0-7812-2387-3*) Reprint Services Corp.

—The Deerslayer. Pease, Donald, ed. & intro. by. 1996. (Classics Ser.). 576p. pap. 10.95 (*0-14-039061-8*, Penguin Classics) Viking Penguin.

—The Deerslayer. 1998. (Classics Library). pap. 3.95 (*1-85326-552-7*, 5527WW) Wordsworth Editions, Ltd. GBR. *Dist:* Combined Publishing.

—The Deerslayer, or the First Warpath. 1990. (Scribner Illustrated Classics Ser.). (Illus.). 480p. (YA). (gr. 7 up). 27.00 (*0-684-19224-1*, Atheneum) Simon & Schuster Children's Publishing.

—The Deerslayer, or the First Warpath. 1987. 12.00 (*0-606-00553-6*) Turtleback Bks.

—The Deerslayer or the First Warpath. Schachterle, Lance, ed. & intro. by. 1987. (Writings of James Fenimore Cooper Ser.). 682p. (C). pap. text 19.95 (*0-87395-790-3*); text 59.50 (*0-87395-361-4*) State Univ. of New York Pr.

—The Deerslayer, or the First Warpath. deluxe ed. 1990. (Illustrated Classics Ser.). (Illus.). 480p. (YA). 75.00 o.s.i (*0-684-19234-9*, Atheneum) Simon & Schuster Children's Publishing.

—The Last of the Mohicans. 1997. (Classics Illustrated Study Guides). (Illus.). mass mkt. 4.99 (*1-57840-053-8*) Acclaim Bks.

—The Last of the Mohicans. 27.95 (*0-89190-895-1*) Amereon, Ltd.

—The Last of the Mohicans. 1994. (Illustrated Classics Collection). 64p. pap. 4.95 (*0-7854-0699-9*, 40459); pap. 3.60 o.p. (*1-56103-537-8*) American Guidance Service, Inc.

—The Last of the Mohicans. 1982. (Bantam Classics Ser.). (Illus.). 400p. mass mkt. 4.95 (*0-553-21329-6*, Bantam Classics) Bantam Bks.

—The Last of the Mohicans. unabr. collector's ed. 1994. (YA). audio 88.00 (*0-7366-2687-5*, 3422) Books on Tape, Inc.

—The Last of the Mohicans. 1983. 450p. reprint ed. lib. bdg. 26.95 o.p. (*0-89966-312-5*) Buccaneer Bks., Inc.

—The Last of the Mohicans. 2001. (Early Best Sellers Ser.). (Illus.). reprint ed. pap. text 28.00 (*0-7426-6013-3*) Classic Bks.

—The Last of the Mohicans. 1992. (Illus.). 434p. pap. text 3.99 (*0-8125-2297-4*, Tor Classics) Doherty, Tom Assocs., LLC.

—The Last of the Mohicans. 2003. (Dover Thrift Editions Ser.). 288p. 3.00 (*0-486-42678-5*) Dover Pubns., Inc.

—The Last of the Mohicans. 2003. (Barnes & Noble Classics Ser.). 480p. mass mkt. 4.95 (*1-59308-065-4*) Fine Communications.

—The Last of the Mohicans. 2002. 372p. 26.99 (*1-4043-1560-8*); per. 22.99 (*1-4043-1561-6*) IndyPublish.com.

—The Last of the Mohicans. E-Book 1.95 (*1-57799-933-9*) Logos Research Systems, Inc.

—The Last of the Mohicans. E-Book 1.95 (*1-58515-169-6*) MesaView, Inc.

—The Last of the Mohicans. (Signet Classics). 2000. (Illus.). 432p. mass mkt. 4.95 (*0-451-52765-8*, Signet Bks.); 1970. mass mkt. 0.75 o.p. (*0-451-50521-2*, Signet Classics); 1970. mass mkt. 0.60 o.p. (*0-451-50320-1*, Signet Classics); 1970. mass mkt. 0.50 o.p. (*0-451-50148-9*, Signet Classics); 1962. mass mkt. 2.50 o.p. (*0-451-51495-5*); 1962. mass mkt. 1.25 o.p. (*0-451-50866-1*, Signet Classics); 1962. mass mkt. 0.95 o.p. (*0-451-50707-X*, Signet Classics); 1962. mass mkt. 1.95 o.p. (*0-451-51282-0*, Signet Classics); 1962. mass mkt. 1.50 o.p. (*0-451-51054-2*, Signet Classics) NAL.

—The Last of the Mohicans. l.t. ed. 2003. 476p. E-Book 2.99 (*1-932681-32-9*) NuVision Pubns.

—The Last of the Mohicans. McWilliams, John, ed. & intro. by. 1998. (Oxford World's Classics Ser.). (Illus.). 464p. pap. 9.95 (*0-19-283505-X*) Oxford Univ. Pr., Inc.

—The Last of the Mohicans. McWilliams, John P., Jr., ed. 1990. (Oxford World's Classics Ser.). (Illus.). 408p. pap. 7.95 o.p. (*0-19-282638-7*) Oxford Univ. Pr., Inc.

—The Last of the Mohicans. 1984. 12.95 o.p. (*0-396-08260-2*) Putnam Publishing Group, The.

—The Last of the Mohicans. 1999. (Illus.). E-Book 3.99 incl. cd-rom (*1-57646-016-9*) Quiet Vision Publishing.

—The Last of the Mohicans. 2001. (Modern Library Classics). 400p. pap. 9.95 (*0-375-75764-3*, Modern Library) Random House Adult Trade Publishing Group.

—The Last of the Mohicans. 1986. 3.99 o.s.i (*0-517-62630-6*) Random Hse. Value Publishing.

—The Last of the Mohicans. 1984. (Illus.). 432p. 12.95 o.p. (*0-89577-199-3*) Reader's Digest Assn., Inc., The.

—The Last of the Mohicans. 1990. (Works of James Fenimore Cooper). reprint ed. lib. bdg. 79.00 (*0-7812-2374-1*) Reprint Services Corp.

—The Last of the Mohicans. Peters, Sally, ed. 1992. 432p. mass mkt. 5.99 (*0-671-75931-0*, Pocket) Simon & Schuster.

—The Last of the Mohicans. Shefter, Harry, ed. 1985. pap. 0.95 o.s.i (*0-671-47962-8*, Washington Square Pr.) Simon & Schuster.

—The Last of the Mohicans. Beard, James F., ed. & intro. by. 1983. (Writings of James Fenimore Cooper Ser.). 418p. (C). pap. text 19.95 (*0-87395-470-X*) State Univ. of New York Pr.

—The Last of the Mohicans. 1983. (Writings of James Fenimore Cooper Ser.). (Illus.). 418p. (C). text 20.50 (*0-87395-362-2*) State Univ. of New York Pr.

—The Last of the Mohicans. l.t. ed. 2003. 630p. 29.95 (*0-7862-5790-3*) Thorndike Pr.

—The Last of the Mohicans. 2000. (Signature Classics Ser.). 376p. 24.95 (*1-58279-089-2*); lib. bdg. 29.95 (*1-58279-085-X*) Trident Pr. International.

—The Last of the Mohicans. 1980. 11.00 (*0-606-02760-2*) Turtleback Bks.

—The Last of the Mohicans. 1970. 410p. pap. 3.95 o.p. (*0-460-87137-4*); 1994. 432p. pap. 5.95 (*0-460-87545-0*) Tuttle Publishing. (Everyman's Classic Library in Paperback).

—The Last of the Mohicans. 1992. (Illus.). 391p. reprint ed. 29.95 o.p. (*1-877767-70-0*) University Publishing Hse., Inc.

—The Last of the Mohicans. Slotkin, Richard, ed. & intro. by. 1986. (Penguin Classics Ser.). (Illus.). 384p. pap. 9.95 (*0-14-039024-3*, Penguin Classics) Viking Penguin.

—The Last of the Mohicans. 1997. (Classics Ser.). (Illus.). 336p. pap. 3.95 (*1-85326-049-5*, 0495WW) Wordsworth Editions, Ltd. GBR. *Dist:* Casemate Pubs. & Bk. Distributors, LLC.

—The Last of the Mohicans Read-Along. 1994. (Illustrated Classics Collection). 64p. pap. 14.95 incl. audio (*0-7854-0740-5*, 40461); pap. 13.50 o.p. incl. audio (*1-56103-539-4*) American Guidance Service, Inc.

—The Pathfinder. 1998. pap. 4.99 o.p. (*1-57840-198-4*) Acclaim Bks.

—The Pathfinder. 1964. (Airmont Classics Ser.). (YA). (gr. 6 up). mass mkt. 2.95 (*0-8049-0035-3*, CL-35) Airmont Publishing Co., Inc.

—The Pathfinder. 1976. lib. bdg. 26.95 (*0-89968-159-X*, Lightyear Pr.); 1984. 419p. reprint ed. lib. bdg. 26.95 o.p. (*0-89966-491-1*) Buccaneer Bks., Inc.

—The Pathfinder. 1840. 502p. (YA). reprint ed. pap. text 34.00 (*1-4047-2386-2*) Classic Textbooks.

—The Pathfinder. 1961. (Leatherstocking Tale Ser.). (Illus.). 448p. (J). (gr. k-10). mass mkt. 5.95 (*0-451-52257-5*, Signet Classics) NAL.

—The Pathfinder. 1990. (Works of James Fenimore Cooper). reprint ed. lib. bdg. 79.00 (*0-7812-2386-5*) Reprint Services Corp.

—The Pathfinder. 1961. 12.00 (*0-606-02759-9*) Turtleback Bks.

—The Pathfinder. House, Kay S., ed. & intro. by. 1989. (Classics Ser.). 512p. pap. 12.00 (*0-14-039071-5*, Penguin Classics) Viking Penguin.

—The Pathfinder: Or, the Inland Sea. Date not set. 351p. 25.95 (*0-8488-2541-1*) Amereon, Ltd.

—The Pathfinder: Or, the Inland Sea. Kelly, William P., ed. (Oxford World's Classics Ser.). 2000. 528p. pap. 11.95 (*0-19-283989-6*); 1993. 522p. pap. 7.95 o.p. (*0-19-282956-4*) Oxford Univ. Pr., Inc.

—The Pathfinder: Or, the Inland Sea. 1980. (Writings of James Fenimore Cooper Ser.). 569p. (C). text 59.50 o.p. (*0-87395-360-6*); pap. text 19.95 (*0-87395-477-7*) State Univ. of New York Pr.

—The Pathfinder: Or, the Inland Sea. 1992. (Illus.). 417p. reprint ed. lib. bdg. 31.95 o.p. (*1-877767-65-4*) University Publishing Hse., Inc.

Coyle, Harold. Savage Wilderness. unabr. ed. 1998. audio 76.95 (*0-7861-1304-9*, 2215) Blackstone Audio Bks., Inc.

—Savage Wilderness. 1998. pap. 6.99 o.s.i (*0-671-00387-9*, Pocket); 1997. 519p. 25.50 (*0-684-83433-2*, Simon & Schuster); 1984. (Illus.). 519p. pap. 2.25 o.p. (*0-671-00522-7*) Simon & Schuster.

Gregor, Elmer Russel. Jim Mason, Scout. 2000. 252p. pap. 9.95 (*0-594-00759-3*); E-Book 3.95 (*0-594-02297-5*) 1873 Pr.

Herr, Marilyn. Where the Heart Leads. 2003. 318p. (*0-8327-7557-6*) Kensington Publishing.

—Where the Heart Leads. 2003. 352p. mass mkt. 5.99 o.s.i (*0-8217-7447-6*) Kensington Publishing Corp.

Kilian, Michael. Major Washington. 1998. 349p. 25.95 (*0-312-18131-0*) St. Martin's Pr.

Moss, Robert. Fire Along the Sky. 1992. 352p. 19.95 o.p. (*0-312-07011-X*) St. Martin's Pr.

—Fire Keeper: A Narrative of the Eastern Frontier. 1995. 512p. 24.95 o.p. (*0-312-85738-1*, Forge Bks.) Doherty, Tom Assocs., LLC.

Parker, Gilbert. The Seats of the Mighty. 2000. 252p. E-Book 9.95 (*0-594-02709-8*) 1873 Pr.

—The Seats of the Mighty, 23 vols. 2001. (Works of Gilbert Parker ). reprint ed. pap. text 28.00 (*0-7426-8822-4*) Classic Bks.

Quiller-Couch, Arthur Thomas. Fort Amity. 2000. 252p. E-Book 9.95 (*0-594-02733-0*) 1873 Pr.

Roarke, Mike. Thunder in the East: Frontier I, Vol. 1. 1993. 346p. pap. text 4.50 o.p. (*0-312-95192-2*, St. Martin's Paperbacks) St. Martin's Pr.

Seno, William J. Enemies: A Saga of the Great Lakes Wilderness. 1993. 240p. pap. 12.95 (*1-879483-10-6*) Prairie Oak Pr., Inc.

Tottle, Edward L. War in the Woods: The Day the United States Began July 9, 1755. (American Freedom Ser.). (Illus.). 1992. (YA). (gr. 10 up). text 29.00 o.p. (*0-937117-05-6*); 1991. 544p. pap. 20.00 (*0-937117-06-4*) Educational Materials Co.

## UNITED STATES—HISTORY—REVOLUTION, 1775-1783—FICTION

Altsheler, Joseph A. The Texan Triumph. E-Book 3.95 (*0-594-01827-7*) 1873 Pr.

—The Texan Triumph. 24.95 (*0-8488-0731-6*); 1985. 21.95 (*0-8488-0203-9*) Amereon, Ltd.

—The Texan Triumph. 1993. reprint ed. lib. bdg. 21.95 (*0-89968-571-4*) Buccaneer Bks., Inc.

Boggs, Johnny D. The Despoilers: A Frontier Story. 2002. (Five Star Western Ser.). 269p. 24.95 (*0-7862-3535-7*, Five Star) Gale Group.

Bowen, Marjorie. The Soldier of Virginia: A Novel on George Washington. 1997. pap. 12.90 (*0-921100-99-X*) Inheritance Pubns.

Burke, James Lee. Two for Texas. l.t. ed. 2002. 293p. 29.95 (*0-7862-3402-4*) Gale Group.

Carmichael, G. Wade. Jack's Resolve: A True Patriot's Tale. 2000. 249p. (*1-883103-12-6*) United, Inc.

Carter, Jimmy. The Hornet's Nest: A Novel of the Revolutionary War. 2003. (Illus.). 480p. 27.00 (*0-7432-5542-9*, Simon & Schuster) Simon & Schuster.

—The Hornet's Nest: A Novel of the Revolutionary War. l.t. ed. 2004. 832p. 31.95 (*0-7862-6154-4*) Thorndike Pr.

Carter, Ron. The Hand of Providence. 2000. (Prelude to Glory Ser.: Vol. 4). (Illus.). xvii, 681p. 22.95 (*1-57345-783-3*, Bookcraft, Inc.) Deseret Bk. Co.

—Prelude to Glory Vol. 7: The Impending Storm. 2003. 560p. 25.95 (*1-57008-993-0*, 995-102, Shadow Mountain) Deseret Bk. Co.

Cooper, James Fenimore. The Spy. 1976. lib. bdg. 28.95 (*0-89968-161-1*, Lightyear Pr.) Buccaneer Bks., Inc.

—The Spy. (Early Best Sellers Ser.). reprint ed. lib. bdg. 48.00 (*0-7426-1012-8*); 2001. (Illus.). pap. text 28.00 (*0-7426-6012-5*) Classic Bks.

—The Spy. 1990. (Works of James Fenimore Cooper). reprint ed. lib. bdg. 79.00 (*0-7812-2370-9*) Reprint Services Corp.

—The Spy. Pickering, James H., ed. 1971. (Masterworks of Literature Ser.). 368p. pap. 23.95 (*0-8084-0027-4*) Rowman & Littlefield Pubs., Inc.

—The Spy. 2001. 389p. mass mkt. 8.95 (*0-9709840-0-6*) Sovereign Pubs.

—The Spy. l.t. ed. 2000. (G. K. Hall Perennial Bestsellers Ser. ). 287p. 26.95 (*0-7838-8490-7*) Thorndike Pr.

—The Spy. unabr. ed. 1997. 250p. reprint ed. pap. 14.95 o.p. (*1-57002-045-0*) University Publishing Hse., Inc.

Devereux, Mary. From Kingdom to Colony. E-Book 3.95 (*0-594-02097-2*) 1873 Pr.

Farmer, James Eugene. Brinton Eliot: From Yale to Yorktown. 2000. 252p. E-Book 3.95 (*0-594-02195-2*) 1873 Pr.

Fast, Howard. Bunker Hill: The Prequel to the Crossing. 2001. (Illus.). 208p. pap. 14.00 (*0-7434-2384-4*) ibooks, Inc.

—The Crossing. E-Book 11.95 (*1-58824-009-6*) ibooks, Inc.

—The Unvanquished. 1997. (American History Through Literature Ser.). 350p. (C). (gr. 13). 35.95 (*1-56324-594-9*); pap. 21.95 (*1-56324-595-7*) Sharpe, M.E. Inc.

Fender, J. E. The Private Revolution of Geoffrey Frost: Being an Account of the Life & Times of Geoffrey Frost, Mariner, of Portsmouth, in New Hampshire, As Faithfully Translated from the Ming Tsun Chronicles, & Diligently Compared with Other Contemporary Histories. 2002. (Hardscrabble Books). 364p. 25.95 (*1-58465-212-8*) Univ. Pr. of New England.

Fleming, Thomas J. The Dreams of Glory. 2000. 336p. 24.95 (*0-312-87743-9*, Forge Bks.) Doherty, Tom Assocs., LLC.

Ford, Paul Leicester. Janice Meredith. reprint ed. lib. bdg. 48.00 (*0-7426-1099-3*); 2001. pap. text 28.00 (*0-7426-6099-0*) Classic Bks.

Fowler, Robert H. Jeremiah Martin: A Revolutionary War Novel. 1989. (Illus.). 348p. 18.95 o.p. (*0-312-03370-2*) St. Martin's Pr.

French, Allen. The Colonials. E-Book 3.95 (*0-594-02223-1*) 1873 Pr.

Gabaldon, Diana. The Fiery Cross. 2002. 992p. pap. 14.95 (*0-385-33676-4*); 2002. E-Book 13.95 (*0-440-33388-1*, Delta); 2001. 992p. 27.95 (*0-385-31527-9*, Delacorte Pr.) Dell Publishing.

—The Fiery Cross. 2002. 992p. pap. (*0-385-65943-1*, Anchor Canada) Doubleday Canada, Ltd. CAN. *Dist:* Random Hse., Inc.

Gilbert Morris. The Spider Catcher. 2003. 352p. pap. 12.99 (*0-310-24698-9*) Zondervan.

Glover, Douglas. The Life & Times of Captain N. 2nd ed. 2001. (GLE Library). (Illus.). 185p. pap. (*0-86492-297-3*) Goose Lane Editions.

—The Life & Times of Captain N. A Novel. 1993. 20.00 o.p. (*0-679-41573-4*) Knopf, Alfred A. Inc.

—The Life & Times of Captain N. A Novel. 1993. pap. 16.99 o.s.i (*0-7710-3353-2*) McClelland & Stewart/Tundra Bks.

Guhrke, Laura Lee. The Charade. 2000. (Sonnet Bks.). 448p. pap. 6.50 (*0-671-02367-5*, Pocket) Simon & Schuster.

Harr, John Ensor. Dark Eagle: A Novel of Benedict Arnold & the American Revolution. 2001. 544p. 14.00 (*0-14-100178-X*) Viking Penguin.

Hodges, Lee. Freedom 'N' Me. 2000. 284p. pap. 21.99 (*0-7388-2848-3*); text 31.99 (*0-7388-2847-5*) Xlibris Corp.

Jakes, John. The Americans. abr. ed. 2000. (Kent Family Chronicles: No. 8). audio 12.99 (*1-57815-167-8*, 4416, Media Bks. Audio Publishing) Media Bks., L. L. C.

—The Warriors. unabr. collector's ed. 1993. (Kent Family Chronicles: No. 6). audio 96.00 (*0-7366-2479-1*, 3241) Books on Tape, Inc.

—The Warriors. abr. ed. 2000. (Kent Family Chronicles: No. 6). audio 12.99 (*1-57815-165-1*, 4414, Media Bks. Audio Publishing) Media Bks., L. L. C.

Johnston, Coleen L. Guardians. 1994. (Gairden Legacy Ser.: No. 2). mass mkt. 4.99 o.p. (*0-312-95125-6*, St. Martin's Paperbacks) St. Martin's Pr.

Jones, Douglas C. Shadow of the Moon. 1996. ix, 470p. 25.00 o.p. (*0-8050-3654-7*) Holt, Henry & Co.

—Shadow of the Moon. 1997. 480p. mass mkt. 5.99 o.p. (*0-06-101033-2*, HarperTorch) Morrow/Avon.

—Shadow of the Moon. l.t. ed. 1996. (Americana Ser.). 668p. 24.95 (*0-7862-0691-8*) Thorndike Pr.

Kennedy, John P. Horse-Shoe Robinson. E-Book 3.95 (*0-594-02535-4*) 1873 Pr.

—Horse-Shoe Robinson. Leisy, Ernest E., ed. 1962. (Library of Classics: No. 23). (Illus.). reprint ed. pap. 3.95 o.s.i (*0-02-847840-1*) Hafner Pr.

—Horse-Shoe Robinson. 1999. (Notable American Authors Ser.). reprint ed. lib. bdg. 125.00 (*0-7812-3666-5*) Reprint Services Corp.

Lambdin, Dewey. For King & Country: The Naval Adventures of Alan Lewrie. 1994. 1088p. pap. 19.95 o.s.i (*1-55611-413-3*, Fine, Donald I.) Fine, Donald I. Bks.

—The French Admiral. 1999. mass mkt. (*0-449-00359-0*, Fawcett) Ballantine Bks.

—The French Admiral. 1990. (Midshipman Alan Lewrie Adventure Ser.). 19.95 o.p. (*1-55611-208-4*) Fine, Donald I. Bks.

—The French Admiral. l.t. ed. 1999. (G. K. Hall Core Ser.). 637p. 27.95 (*0-7838-8788-4*, Macmillan Reference USA) Gale Group.

—The French Admiral. 1991. mass mkt. 4.95 o.s.i (*1-55817-491-5*, Pinnacle Bks.) Kensington Publishing Corp.

Lewis, William. Set a Course for Freedom: A Novel of the Revolutionary War. 2000. 231p. E-Book 8.00 (*0-7388-8479-0*) Xlibris Corp.

Ligotti, Gene. The Youngest Patriot: The Story of the British Occupation of Long Island. 2000. 167p. pap. 20.99 (*0-7388-1271-4*); text 30.99 (*0-7388-1270-6*) Xlibris Corp.

Lussier, Paul. Last Refuge of Scoundrels: A Revolutionary Novel. 320p. 2002. pap. 14.95 (*0-446-67813-9*); 2001. 26.95 o.p. (*0-446-52342-9*) Warner Bks., Inc.

Marlowe, Sara. Rebel Bride. 2000. 352p. mass mkt. 5.99 o.s.i (*0-8217-6680-5*, Zebra Bks.) Kensington Publishing Corp.

Massie, Elizabeth. The Son of Liberty, 1776. 2000. (Young Founders Ser.: No. 3). 215p. mass mkt. 4.99 (*0-8125-9094-5*, Tor Bks.) Doherty, Tom Assocs., LLC.

Mitchell, Silas Weir. Hugh Wynne, Free Quaker, 2 vols. 1897. (YA). reprint ed. pap. text 28.00 (*1-4047-5491-1*) Classic Textbooks.

—Hugh Wynne, Free Quaker, 2 vols in 1. (Americans in Fiction Ser.). 573p. reprint ed. lib. bdg. 17.00 (*0-8398-1265-5*) Irvington Pubs.

—Hugh Wynne, Free Quaker, 2 vols., Set. reprint ed. 1993. lib. bdg. 150.00 (*0-7812-5491-4*); 1992. lib. bdg. 150.00 (*0-7812-6800-1*) Reprint Services Corp.

Morris, Gilbert. Command the Sun. 2000. (Liberty Bell Ser.: 7). 288p. pap. 10.99 o.p. (*1-55661-571-X*) Bethany Hse. Pubs.

—The Gentle Rebel. 1988. (House of Winslow Ser.: Vol. 4). 288p. pap. 11.99 (*1-55661-006-8*) Bethany Hse. Pubs.

—The Saintly Buccaneer. 1989. (House of Winslow Ser.: Vol. 5). 304p. pap. 11.99 (*1-55661-048-3*) Bethany Hse. Pubs.

Nelson, James L. All the Brave Fellows. 416p. 2000. (Revolution at Sea Saga Ser.: Vol. 5). (Illus.). 25.95 o.s.i (*0-671-03846-X*); 2001. reprint ed. pap. 13.95 (*0-671-03847-8*) Simon & Schuster. (Atria).

—By Force of Arms. Wolverton, Peter, ed. 1996. (Revolution at Sea Trilogy Ser.: Vol. 1). 336p. pap. 14.00 (*0-671-51924-7*, Pocket) Simon & Schuster.

—The Continental Risque. 1998. (Revolution at Sea Saga Ser.: Vol. 3). 384p. pap. 14.00 (*0-671-01381-5*, Atria) Simon & Schuster.

—Lords of the Ocean. 368p. 1999. (Revolution at Sea Saga Ser.: Vol. 4). (Illus.). 23.00 o.s.i (*0-671-03490-1*); 2000. reprint ed. pap. 13.95 (*0-671-01383-1*) Simon & Schuster. (Atria).

—The Maddest Idea. 1997. (Revolution at Sea Trilogy Ser.: Vol. 2). 432p. pap. 14.00 (*0-671-51925-5*, Atria) Simon & Schuster.

Nevin, David. Treason. 2001. 467p. 27.95 (*0-312-85512-5*, Forge Bks.) Doherty, Tom Assocs., LLC.

Newton, David, ed. The Forayers or the Raid of the Dog Days. 2003. (Simms Ser.). (Illus.). 560p. pap. 34.95 (*1-55728-741-4*) Univ. of Arkansas Pr.

Nicastro, Nicholas. Between Two Fires. 2002. (John Paul Jones Trilogy Ser.: Vol. 2). 384p. pap. 16.95 (*1-59013-033-2*) McBooks Pr., Inc.

Norman, Diana. A Catch of Consequence. 2003. 400p. pap. 14.00 (*0-425-19015-3*) Berkley Publishing Group.

Oke, Janette & Bunn, T. Davis. The Beloved Land. 2002. (Song of Arcadia Ser.: No. 5). 288p. 16.99 (*0-7642-2723-8*); pap. 15.99 (*0-7642-2725-4*); 288p. pap. 11.99 (*0-7642-2722-X*); 432p. pap. 16.99 (*0-7642-2724-6*) Bethany Hse. Pubs.

—The Beloved Land. l.t. ed. 2003. (Song of Acadia Ser.). 494p. 28.95 (*0-7862-5087-9*) Thorndike Pr.

—The Distant Beacon. 2002. (Song of Acadia Ser.). 272p. 16.99 (*0-7642-2601-0*); 272p. pap. 11.99 (*0-7642-2600-2*); pap. 15.99 (*0-7642-2602-9*) Bethany Hse. Pubs.

Rae, Catherine M. Marike's World. E-Book 21.95 (*0-312-27585-4*); 2000. 186p. 21.95 (*0-312-26199-3*) St. Martin's Pr.

Robbins, Jerry. For Love & Liberty. 1998. 224p. (*1-892358-00-X*) Medea Publishing, Inc.

Roberts, Carey & Seely, Rebecca. Tidewater Dynasty: A Biographical Novel of the Lees of Stratford Hall. (Harvest Book Ser.). 1983. 456p. pap. 23.00 (*0-15-690336-9*, Harvest Bks.); 1981. 19.95 o.s.i (*0-15-190294-1*) Harcourt Trade Pubs.

Roberts, Kenneth. Rabble in Arms. 1981. 608p. mass mkt. 2.95 o.s.i (*0-449-24426-1*); 1975. mass mkt. 1.95 o.s.i (*0-449-30748-4*) Ballantine Bks. (Fawcett).

—Rabble in Arms. 1947. 8.95 o.p. (*0-385-04377-5*) Doubleday Publishing.

—Rabble in Arms. 1996. (Illus.). 592p. reprint ed. pap. 17.95 (*0-89272-386-6*) Down East Bks.

—Rabble in Arms. 1991. 586p. reprint ed. pap. 10.95 o.p. (*0-89909-341-8*) Rodale Pr., Inc.

Rowe, Robert H. Quest for Liberty. 2001. (Illus.). 256p. 23.95 (*0-914339-92-3*) Randall, Peter E. Pub.

Sedgwick, Catharine Maria. The Linwoods of "Sixty Years Since" in America. 2002. (Hardscrabble Books). 448p. reprint ed. pap. 18.95 (*1-58465-153-9*, Hardscrabble Bks.) Univ. Pr. of New England.

Shaara, Jeff. The Glorious Cause: A Novel of the American Revolution. 2003. 656p. pap. 15.95 (*0-345-42757-2*, Ballantine Bks.); 2003. 704p. mass mkt. 7.99 (*0-345-42758-0*, Fawcett); 2002. E-Book 19.50 (*0-345-45868-0*); 2002. (Illus.). 656p. 29.95 (*0-345-42756-4*) Ballantine Bks.

—The Glorious Cause: A Novel of the American Revolution. l.t. ed. 2003. 1,050p. 29.95 (*0-375-43245-0*) Random Hse. Large Print.

—Rise to Rebellion: A Novel of the American Revolution. 2004. 576p. pap. 15.95 (*0-345-42754-8*); 2001. (Illus.). 512p. 27.95 (*0-345-42753-X*, Ballantine Bks.) Ballantine Bks.

—Rise to Rebellion: A Novel of the American Revolution. l.t. ed. 2001. 864p. 26.95 (*0-375-43108-X*) Random Hse. Large Print.

Simms, William Gilmore. Woodcraft. E-Book 3.95 (*0-594-01550-2*) 1873 Pr.

—Woodcraft. Watson, Charles S., ed. 1986. 288p. pap. 29.95 (*0-8084-0423-7*) Rowman & Littlefield Pubs., Inc.

—Woodcraft: or, Hawks about the Dovecote: A Story of the South at the Close of the Revolution. rev. ed. (Americans in Fiction Ser.). 518p. reprint ed. lib. bdg. 20.00 (*0-8398-1862-9*); 1986. pap. text 9.95 (*0-8290-2000-4*) Irvington Pubs.

Sorrells, Russell B. The Yelling Boys: A Story of the American Revolution in the South. 1998. 317p. 18.95 (*0-9640019-1-8*) Sorrells, Russell B. Happy Valley Publishing.

Thane, Elswyth. Dawn's Early Light. reprint ed. lib. bdg. 26.95 (*0-88411-974-2*) Amereon, Ltd.

—Dawn's Early Light. 1982. 352p. pap. 2.95 o.p. (*0-553-22581-2*) Bantam Bks.

—Dawn's Early Light. 1996. lib. bdg. 28.95 (*1-56849-475-0*) Buccaneer Bks., Inc.

—Dawn's Early Light. 1943. 10.00 o.p. (*0-8015-1957-8*, Dutton) Dutton/Plume.

—Dawn's Early Light. 1981. (Reader's Request Ser.). lib. bdg. 16.95 o.p. (*0-8161-3167-8*, Macmillan Reference USA) Gale Group.

Thompson, Daniel P. The Green Mountain Boys. E-Book 3.95 (*0-594-01065-9*) 1873 Pr.

—The Green Mountain Boys. 1987. 496p. reprint ed. pap. 14.95 o.s.i (*0-87797-145-5*) Cherokee Publishing Co.

—The Green Mountain Boys. Washington, Carol E. & Washington, Ida H., eds. 2000. (Illus.). 242p. pap. 15.00 (*0-9666832-4-2*) Cherry Tree Bks.

Walther, Anne Newton. A Time for Treason: A Novel of the American Revolution. 2001. 451p. reprint ed. mass mkt. 7.99 (*0-9676703-3-0*) Tapestries.

Williams, Philip Lee. The True & Authentic History of Jenny Dorset: Consisting of a Narrative by a Retainer, Mr. Henry Hawthorne, along with the History of Two Households, That of Dorset & Smythe...: A Novel. 2001. 512p. reprint ed. pap. 17.95 (*0-8203-2334-9*) Univ. of Georgia Pr.

**UNITED STATES—HISTORY—WAR OF 1812—FICTION**

Altsheler, Joseph A. A Herald of the West. 2000. 252p. E-Book 3.95 (*0-594-03543-0*) 1873 Pr.

—A Herald of the West. Date not set. lib. bdg. 25.95 (*0-8488-2119-X*) Amereon, Ltd.

Block, Kevin James. Without Shedding of Blood. 1994. 185p. pap. (*1-895308-17-8*) Hyperion Pr., Ltd.

Eggleston, George Cary. Captain Sam. 2000. 252p. pap. 9.95 (*0-594-03293-8*); E-Book 3.95 (*0-594-03296-2*) 1873 Pr.

Forester, C. S. The Captain from Connecticut. 1941. (J). (gr. 7 up). 14.45 o.p. (*0-316-28892-6*) Little Brown & Co.

—The Captain from Connecticut. 1997. 256p. reprint ed. 24.95 (*1-877853-30-5*) Nautical & Aviation Publishing Co. of America, Inc., The.

Fowler, Robert H. Voyage to Honor. 1996. 576p. 29.95 (*0-8117-0913-2*) Stackpole Bks.

Nevin, David. 1812. unabr. ed. 2003. audio compact disk 34.95 (*0-7861-8973-8*) Blackstone Audio Bks., Inc.

—1812. 1997. 579p. mass mkt. 6.99 (*0-8125-2471-3*); 567p. mass mkt. 8.99 (*0-8125-7150-9*) Doherty, Tom Assocs., LLC. (Forge Bks.).

—1812. 1998. 4.98 o.p. (*0-7651-1075-X*) Smithmark Pubs., Inc.

—1812. 1997. 13.04 (*0-606-19643-9*) Turtleback Bks.

—1812: A Novel. 2000. 442p. reprint ed. text 25.00 (*0-7881-9050-4*) DIANE Publishing Co.

O'Brian, Patrick. The Far Side of the World. l.t. ed. 2002. (Aubrey-Maturin Ser.). 538p. 29.95 (*0-7862-1930-0*, Macmillan Reference USA) Gale Group.

—The Far Side of the World. 2003. 366p. pap. 13.95 (*0-393-32476-1*); 1994. 24.00 (*0-393-03710-X*) Norton, W. W. & Co., Inc.

—The Fortune of War. (Aubrey-Maturin Ser.). 1994. 24.00 (*0-393-03706-1*); 1991. 329p. pap. 13.95 (*0-393-30813-8*) Norton, W. W. & Co., Inc.

—The Fortune of War. l.t. ed. 2001. (Illus.). 311p. (*0-7540-1588-2*); (*0-7540-2449-0*) Thorndike Pr.

O'Neal, Reagan, pseud. The Fallon Pride. 1997. (Illus.). 531p. mass mkt. 6.99 (*0-8125-6760-9*, Forge Bks.); 1996. 384p. 24.95 o.p. (*0-312-86231-8*, Forge Bks.); 1981. (Fallon Chronicles Ser.: Vol. 2). mass mkt. 2.95 (*0-523-48002-4*, Tor Bks.) Doherty, Tom Assocs., LLC.

Rae Rao, Linda. Of Eagles & Ravens. 1996. (Eagle Wings Ser.: No. 3). 256p. (gr. 10). pap. 9.99 o.p. (*0-8007-5580-4*) Revell, Fleming H. Co.

Roberts, Kenneth. Captain Caution. 1975. mass mkt. 1.50 o.s.i (*0-449-30739-5*, Ballantine Bks.) Ballantine Bks.

—Captain Caution. 1988. 14.95 o.p. (*0-385-04794-0*) Doubleday Publishing.

—Captain Caution. 1999. (Chronicles of Arundel Ser.: Vol. 4). 224p. reprint ed. pap. 15.95 (*0-89272-467-6*) Down East Bks.

Roberts, Kenneth Lewis. The Lively Lady: A Chronicle of Arundel, of Privateering, & of the Circular Prison on Dartmoor. Date not set. 282p. 23.95 (*0-8488-2591-8*) Amereon, Ltd.

—The Lively Lady: A Chronicle of Arundel, of Privateering, & of the Circular Prison on Dartmoor. 1988. 15.95 o.p. (*0-385-04261-2*) Doubleday Publishing.

—The Lively Lady: A Chronicle of Arundel, of Privateering & of the Circular Prison on Dartmoor. 1982. mass mkt. 2.95 o.s.i (*0-449-24482-2*, Fawcett) Ballantine Bks.

—The Lively Lady: A Chronicle of Arundel, of Privateering, & of the Circular Prison on Dartmoor. 1997. 288p. reprint ed. pap. 15.95 (*0-89272-425-0*) Down East Bks.

—The Lively Lady: A Chronicle of Arundel, of Privateering, & of the Circular Prison on Dartmoor. l.t. ed. 1994. 405p. lib. bdg. 22.95 (*0-8161-5996-3*) Thorndike Pr.

Wiles, Gary H. & Brown, Delores M. Ponder the Path. 2nd rev. ed. 1996. (History As It Happens Ser.: Vol. 1 Second Edition). 279p. pap. 12.95 (*1-889252-02-6*) Photosensitive.

Woodman, Richard. The Flying Squadron. l.t. ed. 1994. (Magna Large Print Ser.). 424p. (*0-7505-0691-1*) Magna Large Print Bks. GBR. *Dist:* Ulverscroft Large Print Canada, Ltd.

—The Flying Squadron: A Nathaniel Drinkwater Novel. 1999. (Illus.). 256p. pap. 14.95 (*1-57409-077-1*) Sheridan Hse., Inc.

**UNITED STATES—HISTORY—CIVIL WAR, 1861-1865—FICTION**

Adams, Richard. Traveller. 1989. 368p. reprint ed. mass mkt. 4.95 o.s.i (*0-440-20493-3*) Dell Publishing.

—Traveller. 1990. 4.99 o.p. (*0-517-05728-X*) Random Hse. Value Publishing.

Adrian, Christine. Gob's Grief. 2001. E-Book 19.95 (*0-7679-0936-4*) Broadway Bks.

—Gob's Grief: A Novel. 2002. (Vintage Contemporaries Ser.). 400p. reprint ed. pap. 13.95 (*0-375-72624-1*, Vintage) Knopf Publishing Group.

Alcott, Louisa May. Louisa May Alcott's Civil War. 2001. 256p. pap. 16.95 (*1-889020-10-9*) Edinborough Pr.

Alger, Horatio. Frank's Campaign, or the Farm & the Camp. E-Book 2.49 (*1-58744-228-0*) Electric Umbrella Publishing.

—Frank's Campaign, or the Farm & the Camp. 2002. 212p. 18.99 (*1-4043-0406-1*); per. 13.99 (*1-4043-0407-X*) IndyPublish.com.

Allard, Meredith. My Brother's Battle: A Novel. 2000. 364p. pap. 22.99 (*0-7388-2121-7*); text 32.99 (*0-7388-2120-9*) Xlibris Corp.

Allen, Nancy Campbell. Faith of Our Fathers. 2001. (Illus.). 458p. 22.95 (*1-57734-897-4*) Covenant Communications.

—Love Beyond Time: A Novel. 1999. (Illus.). 196p. pap. 12.95 (*1-57734-540-1*, 01114344) Covenant Communications, Inc.

Alley, Howard Eugene. Presumed Dead: A Civil War Mystery. 2002. (Illus.). 256p. pap. 16.00 (*0-914875-36-1*, Historical Images) Bright Mountain Bks., Inc.

Altsheler, Joseph A. Before the Dawn. 2000. 252p. pap. 9.95 (*0-594-00336-9*); E-Book 3.95 (*0-594-01832-3*) 1873 Pr.

—Before the Dawn. 22.95 (*0-8488-1234-4*) Amereon, Ltd.

—Before the Dawn. 1976. lib. bdg. 21.95 o.s.i (*0-89968-000-3*, Lightyear Pr.); 1990. reprint ed. lib. bdg. 18.95 o.p. (*0-89968-456-4*) Buccaneer Bks., Inc.

—In Circling Camps. E-Book 3.95 (*0-594-02804-3*) 1873 Pr.

—In Circling Camps. 28.95 (*0-8488-0715-4*) Amereon, Ltd.

—The Rock of Chickamauga. 2000. 252p. E-Book 3.95 (*0-594-01829-3*) 1873 Pr.

—The Rock of Chickamauga. 25.95 (*0-8488-0071-0*) Amereon, Ltd.

—The Rock of Chickamauga. 1993. reprint ed. lib. bdg. 21.95 (*0-89968-567-6*) Buccaneer Bks., Inc.

—The Scouts of Stonewall. 2000. 252p. pap. 9.95 (*0-594-06069-9*); E-Book 3.95 (*0-594-06072-9*) 1873 Pr.

—The Scouts of Stonewall. 1985. (Joseph A. Altsheler Civil War Ser.). 25.95 (*0-8488-0070-2*) Amereon, Ltd.

—The Scouts of Stonewall. 1976. lib. bdg. 19.95 (*0-89968-004-6*, Lightyear Pr.); 1990. reprint ed. lib. bdg. 21.95 (*0-89968-466-1*) Buccaneer Bks., Inc.

—The Shades of the Wilderness. 2000. 252p. E-Book 3.95 (*0-594-01830-7*) 1873 Pr.

—The Shades of the Wilderness. 312p. reprint ed. lib. bdg. 25.95 (*0-88411-940-8*) Amereon, Ltd.

—The Shades of the Wilderness. 1990. reprint ed. lib. bdg. 21.95 (*0-89968-467-X*) Buccaneer Bks., Inc.

—The Star of Gettysburg. 2000. 252p. E-Book 3.95 (*0-594-05598-9*) 1873 Pr.

—The Star of Gettysburg. 1976. reprint ed. lib. bdg. 26.95 (*0-88411-945-9*) Amereon, Ltd.

—The Star of Gettysburg. 1990. reprint ed. lib. bdg. 22.95 (*0-89968-469-6*) Buccaneer Bks., Inc.

—The Tree of Appomattox. E-Book 3.95 (*0-594-01831-5*) 1873 Pr.

—The Tree of Appomattox. 1985. (Joseph A. Altsheler Civil War Ser.). 23.95 (*0-8488-0073-7*) Amereon, Ltd.

—The Tree of Appomattox. 1993. reprint ed. lib. bdg. 21.95 (*0-89968-568-4*) Buccaneer Bks., Inc.

Austin, Lynn. Fire by Night. 2003. (Refiners Fire Ser.). 432p. pap. 12.99 (*1-55661-443-8*) Bethany Hse. Pubs.

Bahr, Howard. The Black Flower: A Novel of the Civil War. unabr. ed. 1999. audio 56.95 Blackstone Audio Bks., Inc.

—The Black Flower: A Novel of the Civil War. 1998. 272p. pap. 13.00 o.s.i (*0-8050-5445-6*, Owl Bks.) Holt, Henry & Co.

—The Black Flower: A Novel of the Civil War. 3rd ed. 1997. (Illus.). 230p. (YA). (gr. 10-12). 24.95 (*1-877853-50-X*) Nautical & Aviation Publishing Co. of America, Inc., The.

—The Black Flower: A Novel of the Civil War. 2000. 272p. pap. 13.00 (*0-312-26507-7*) Picador.

—The Black Flower: A Novel of the Civil War. l.t. ed. 1997. (Niagara Large Print Ser.). 464p. 29.50 o.p. (*0-7089-5882-6*, Ulverscroft) Thorpe, F. A. Pubs. GBR. *Dist:* Ulverscroft Large Print Bks., Ltd.

—The Black Flower: A Novel of the Civil War. 2000. 19.05 (*0-606-21819-X*) Turtleback Bks.

—The Year of Jubilo: A Novel of the Civil War. 2000. 384p. 25.00 o.s.i (*0-8050-5972-5*) Holt, Henry & Co.

—The Year of Jubilo: A Novel of the Civil War. 2001. 384p. pap. 14.00 (*0-312-28069-6*) Picador.

Baker, Kevin. Paradise Alley: A Novel. 2002. 688p. 26.95 (*0-06-019582-7*) HarperCollins Pubs.

—Paradise Alley: A Novel. 2003. 688p. pap. 14.95 (*0-06-095521-X*, Perennial) HarperTrade.

Ballard, Allen B. Where I'm Bound. 2000. (Illus.). 320p. 24.00 o.s.i (*0-684-87031-2*, Simon & Schuster) Simon & Schuster.

—Where I'm Bound: A Novel. 2001. 320p. reprint ed. pap. 14.00 (*0-684-87032-0*, Simon & Schuster) Simon & Schuster.

Barry, Louise M. A Price Beyond Rubies: A Novel of the Civil War. 1996. (Illus.). 492p. pap. 25.95 (*0-89745-201-1*) Sunflower Univ. Pr.

Bartron, Harry. Drummer Boy: A Novel of the American Civil War. 1997. 24.95 (*0-533-12275-9*) Vantage Pr., Inc.

Benson, B. K. Who Goes There? 2000. 252p. E-Book 3.95 (*0-594-01873-0*) 1873 Pr.

Best, Steven M. When Philosophers Were Kings. 2002. (Illus.). 384p. 28.95 (*0-86534-362-4*) Sunstone Pr.

Bierce, Ambrose. Ambrose Bierce's An Occurrence at Owl Creek Bridge: A Critical Edition. Evans, Robert C. & Atkins, Eric W., eds. annot. ed. 2003. (Annotated Classic Texts Ser.: No. 1). xxi, 166p. (C). lib. bdg. 25.00 (*0-9722289-6-9*) Locust Hill Pr.

—Tales of Soldiers & Civilians. 1980. (Short Story Index Reprint Ser.). 30.95 (*0-8369-3478-4*) Ayer Co. Pubs., Inc.

—Tales of Soldiers & Civilians. Blume, Donald T., ed. 2003. 30.00 (*0-87338-789-9*); pap. 20.00 (*0-87338-777-5*) Kent State Univ. Pr.

—Tales of Soldiers & Civilians. 1989. (Principle Works of Ambrose Gwinett Bierce). reprint ed. lib. bdg. 79.00 (*0-7812-1959-0*) Reprint Services Corp.

—Tales of Soldiers & Civilians. 2000. (Classics Ser.). 304p. pap. 12.95 (*0-14-043756-8*, Penguin Classics) Viking Penguin.

Biondo, Steve. The True Story of Manse Jolly, Pt. 1. 2002. 242p. pap. 14.95 (*0-595-23800-9*, Writer's Showcase Pr.) iUniverse, Inc.

Blake, James Carlos. Wildwood Boys: A Novel. 2001. 384p. pap. 13.00 (*0-380-80593-6*, Perennial) HarperTrade.

Braver, Adam. Mr. Lincoln's Wars: A Novel in Thirteen Stories. 2004. 320p. pap. 12.95 (*0-06-008119-8*, Perennial) HarperTrade.

—Mr. Lincoln's Wars: A Novel in Thirteen Stories. 2003. 320p. 23.95 (*0-06-008118-X*, Morrow, William & Co.) Morrow/Avon.

Brown, Steve. Black Fire. 2000. 273p. pap. 13.95 (*0-9670273-2-2*) Chick Springs Publishing.

Bryan, Vernanne. Fields of Gold Pt. 1: A Romantic-Historical Novel of the Civil War Era in Two Parts. 2001. 254p. pap. 21.99 (*0-7388-4862-X*) Xlibris Corp.

—Fields of Gold Pt. II: A Romantic-Historical Novel of the Civil War Era in Two Parts. 2001. 371p. pap. 22.99 (*0-7388-4863-8*) Xlibris Corp.

Burke, James Lee. White Doves at Morning. 2004. 502p. pap. 12.95 (*1-4104-0173-1*, Wheeler Publishing, Inc.) Gale Group.

—White Doves at Morning. 2004. 448p. mass mkt. 7.99 (*0-7434-6662-4*, Pocket Star); 2002. 320p. 25.00 (*0-7432-4471-0*, Simon & Schuster) Simon & Schuster.

—White Doves at Morning. l.t. ed. 2003. (Core Ser.). 537p. 32.95 (*0-7862-4924-2*) Thorndike Pr.

Burton, Mary. Rafferty's Bride. 2002. (Harlequin Historicals Ser.: No. 632). 304p. mass mkt. (*0-373-29232-5*, Harlequin Bks.) Harlequin Enterprises, Ltd.

Butler, Luther. Amite County & Mississippi Woman. 1999. (Plata County Ser.: 2). 372p. pap. 15.95 (*1-58348-458-2*) iUniverse, Inc.

Cable, George W. Kincaid's Battery. E-Book 3.95 (*0-594-04697-1*) 1873 Pr.

—Kincaid's Battery. (Illus.). 424p. pap. 18.95 (*1-56554-978-3*, Firebird Pr.) Pelican Publishing Co., Inc.

—Kincaid's Battery. 1990. (Works of George Washington Cable). reprint ed. lib. bdg. 79.00 (*0-7812-1145-X*) Reprint Services Corp.

Campbell, Meredith. Righteous Warriors: The Civil War in Jefferson City, Missouri 1861. 2000. 348p. pap. 13.95 (*1-929311-05-2*) Two Trails Publishing.

Carter, Alden R. Bright Starry Banner: A Novel of the Civil War. 2004. 488p. 27.00 (*1-56947-355-2*) Soho Pr., Inc.

Cavanaugh, Jack. The Adversaries. (American Family Portrait Ser.). 500p. pap. 13.99 (*1-56476-535-0*, 6-3535) Cook Communications Ministries.

Chambers, Robert S. The God of War: When I Rode with N. B. Forrest, The Letters of Henry Wylie. 2000. (Journal of Confederate History Book Ser.: Vol. 22). 288p. pap. 16.95 (*1-889332-30-5*) Southern Heritage Pr.

Champlin, Tim. Raiders of the Western & Atlantic. 2004. mass mkt. 4.99 (*0-8439-5304-7*) Dorchester Publishing Co., Inc.

—Raiders of the Western & Atlantic. 2002. (Five Star Western Ser.). (Illus.). 244p. 24.95 (*0-7862-3538-1*, Five Star) Gale Group.

Charles, Christine. Heart's Bounty. 1996. 184p. E-Book 6.00 (*1-58200-001-8*); E-Book 6.00 (*1-58200-173-1*) Hard Shell Word Factory.

Chesnut, Mary Boykin Miller. Two Novels by Mary Chesnut. Muhlenfeld, Elisabeth, ed. & intro. by. 2002. (Publications of the Southern Texts Society). xx, 216p. 29.95 (*0-8139-2058-2*) Univ. Pr. of Virginia.

Cole, Les. Baker's Dozenth. 2000. (Pure Vanilla - Historic Sage Ser.). 500p. E-Book 10.95 incl. cd-rom (*1-58519-202-3*) Book-On-Disc.Com.

Collingwood, Herbert. Andersonville Violets: A Story of Northern & Southern Life. 2000. (Classics of Civil War Fiction Ser.). xxviii, 270p. pap. text 19.95 (*0-8173-1061-4*) Univ. of Alabama Pr.

Conquest, Ned. Virginia, the Gray & the Green. 1990. 160p. 19.95 (*0-9627485-1-X*) Apollonian Pr.

Cooke, John Esten. Surry of Eagle's Nest. 2000. 252p. pap. 9.95 (*0-594-00129-3*); E-Book 9.95 (*0-594-02033-6*) 1873 Pr.

—Surry of Eagle's Nest: Or, the Memoirs of a Staff Officer Serving in Virginia. (Americans in Fiction Ser.). 484p. reprint ed. lib. bdg. 37.00 (*0-8398-0273-0*); 1986. (C). pap. text 8.95 (*0-8290-2037-3*) Irvington Pubs.

Cord, Barry. Two Graves for a Gunman. l.t. ed. 2002. (Nightingale Ser.). 22.95 (*0-7862-4192-6*) Thorndike Pr.

Cornwell, Bernard. Battle Flag. 1995. 384p. 20.00 o.p. (*0-06-017634-2*) HarperCollins Pubs.

—Battle Flag. 2001. 432p. pap. 13.95 (*0-06-093718-1*, Perennial) HarperTrade.

—Battle Flag. 1996. (Starbuck Chronicles Ser.: Vol. 3). 448p. mass mkt. 6.99 (*0-06-109197-9*, HarperTorch) Morrow/Avon.

—The Bloody Ground. l.t. ed. 1996. 24.95 o.p. (*1-56895-371-2*, Wheeler Publishing, Inc.) Gale Group.

—The Bloody Ground. (Starbuck Chronicles Ser.: Vol. 4). 1997. 400p. mass mkt. 6.50 (*0-06-109198-7*); 1995. 79p. 24.00 o.p. (*0-06-017500-1*) HarperCollins Pubs.

—The Bloody Ground. 2001. (Nathaniel Starbuck Chronicles ). 368p. pap. 13.95 (*0-06-093719-X*, Perennial) HarperTrade.

—Copperhead. 2001. 432p. pap. 13.95 (*0-06-093462-X*, Perennial); 1994. (Starbuck Chronicles Ser.: Vol. 2). (Illus.). 352p. 15.95 o.p. (*0-06-017766-7*) HarperTrade.

—Copperhead. 1995. 448p. mass mkt. 6.99 o.s.i (*0-06-109196-0*, HarperTorch) Morrow/Avon.

—Rebel. (Nathaniel Starbuck Chronicles ). 2001. 416p. pap. 13.95 (*0-06-093461-1*, Perennial); 1993. 320p. 20.00 o.p. (*0-06-017713-6*) HarperTrade.

—Rebel. 1994. (Starbuck Chronicles Ser.: Vol. 1). 512p. mass mkt. 6.99 (*0-06-109187-1*, HarperTorch) Morrow/Avon.

Cotton, Ralph W. While Angels Dance: The Life & Times of Jeston Nash. 1995. 344p. pap. text 5.50 o.p. (*0-312-95461-1*, St. Martin's Paperbacks); 1994. 352p. 21.95 o.p. (*0-312-11098-7*) St. Martin's Pr.

Coyle, Harold. Look Away. 592p. 1997. (Illus.). mass mkt. 3.99 (*0-671-00991-5*); 1996. mass mkt. 6.99 (*0-671-52819-X*) Simon & Schuster. (Pocket).

—Until the End. 1997. 544p. pap. 6.99 (*0-671-89017-4*, Pocket); 1996. 464p. 24.50 o.p. (*0-684-81140-5*, Simon & Schuster) Simon & Schuster.

Crane, Stephen. The Red Badge of Courage. E-Book 3.95 (*0-594-03693-3*) 1873 Pr.

—The Red Badge of Courage. 1997. (Classics Illustrated Study Guides). (Illus.). mass mkt. 4.99 (*1-57840-040-6*) Acclaim Bks.

—The Red Badge of Courage. 17.95 (*0-89190-118-3*) Amereon, Ltd.

—The Red Badge of Courage. 1994. (Illustrated Classics Collection). 64p. pap. 4.95 (*0-7854-0669-7*, 40352) American Guidance Service, Inc.

—The Red Badge of Courage. 1997. 216p. pap. 14.95 incl. disk, cd-rom (*1-55701-230-X*) BNI Pubns., Inc.

—The Red Badge of Courage. 1986. (Bantam Classics Ser.). 208p. pap. 11.95 o.p. (*0-553-06415-0*) Bantam Bks.

—The Red Badge of Courage. Green, Frank & Seely, John, eds. 1999. (Classic Novels ). 200p. pap. 8.95 (*0-7641-1145-0*) Barron's Educational Series, Inc.

—The Red Badge of Courage. 2002. pap. 3.93 (*1-59109-097-0*) Booksurge, LLC.

—The Red Badge of Courage. reprint ed. lib. bdg. 48.00 (*0-7426-1071-3*); 2001. pap. text 28.00 (*0-7426-6071-0*) Classic Bks.

—The Red Badge of Courage. 1988. mass mkt. 4.95 (*0-938819-99-2*, Aerie) Doherty, Tom Assocs., LLC.

—The Red Badge of Courage. E-Book 2.49 (*1-58744-104-7*) Electric Umbrella Publishing.

—The Red Badge of Courage. (Reader's Request Ser.). 1980. lib. bdg. 8.95 o.p. (*0-8161-3078-7*); 2001. 155p. 27.95 (*0-7838-9527-5*) Gale Group. (Macmillan Reference USA).

—The Red Badge of Courage. 1999. 150p. pap. 9.95 o.p. (*1-930128-09-6*, JNMedia Bks.) JNMedia, Inc.

—The Red Badge of Courage. 1990. (Vintage-Library of America ). 168p. pap. 10.00 (*0-679-73223-3*, Vintage) Knopf Publishing Group.

—The Red Badge of Courage. 1998. (Cloth Bound Pocket Ser.). 7.95 (*3-89508-686-X*, 520038) Konemann.

—The Red Badge of Courage. l.t. ed. 1997. (Large Print Heritage Ser.). 233p. lib. bdg. 28.95 (*1-58118-019-5*, 21491) LRS.

—The Red Badge of Courage. E-Book 1.95 (*1-57799-934-7*) Logos Research Systems, Inc.

—The Red Badge of Courage, Level 3. 2000. pap. 11.67 (*0-582-34265-1*) Longman Publishing Group.

—The Red Badge of Courage. 1951. 187p. (C). pap. 7.50 (*0-07-555608-1*, McGraw-Hill Humanities, Social Sciences & World Languages) McGraw-Hill Higher Education.

—The Red Badge of Courage. 1999. E-Book 1.95 (*1-58515-248-X*) MesaView, Inc.

—The Red Badge of Courage. Binder, Henry, ed. 1987. pap. 3.50 (*0-380-70432-3*); 1983. 192p. mass mkt. 6.95 o.p. (*0-380-64113-5*, 64113) Morrow/Avon. (Avon Bks.).

—The Red Badge of Courage. Willard, Throp, ed. & intro. by. 1969. pap. NAL.

—The Red Badge of Courage. 1960. mass mkt. 0.50 o.p. (*0-451-50016-4*); mass mkt. 0.60 o.p. (*0-451-50671-5*); mass mkt. 1.50 o.p. (*0-451-51304-5*); mass mkt. 0.95 o.p. (*0-451-50971-4*); mass mkt. 0.75 o.p. (*0-451-50812-2*); mass mkt. 1.75 o.p. (*0-451-51433-5*); mass mkt. 1.25 o.p. (*0-451-51127-1*) NAL. (Signet Classics).

—The Red Badge of Courage. l.t. ed. reprint ed. 10.00 (*0-89064-053-X*) National Assn. for Visually Handicapped.

—The Red Badge of Courage. Green, Frank, ed. 1996. (Thornes Classic Novels Ser.). (Illus.). 194p. pap. 16.75 (*0-7487-2423-0*) Nelson Thornes GBR. *Dist:* Trans-Atlantic Pubns., Inc.

—The Red Badge of Courage. 1993. (Super Sound Buy, Dove Ser.). 8.99 o.p. (*1-55800-685-0*) NewStar Media, Inc.

—The Red Badge of Courage. l.t. ed. 2000. reprint ed. 250p. lib. bdg. 25.00 (*0-939495-99-6*); 155p. lib. bdg. 24.00 (*1-58287-123-X*) North Bks.

—The Red Badge of Courage. 1999. 192p. pap. 10.95 (*0-393-31954-7*) Norton, W. W. & Co., Inc.

—The Red Badge of Courage. Binder, Henry, ed. 1982. (Critical Editions Ser.). 14.95 o.p. (*0-393-01345-6*) Norton, W. W. & Co., Inc.

—The Red Badge of Courage. Pizer, Donald, ed. 3rd ed. 1993. (Critical Editions Ser.). (C). pap. text 9.00 (*0-393-96430-2*) Norton, W. W. & Co., Inc.

—The Red Badge of Courage. l.t. ed. 2003. 177p. E-Book 3.99 (*1-932681-36-1*) NuVision Pubns.

—The Red Badge of Courage. 1999. pap. 2.99 o.p. (*0-14-130548-7*); 1987. 186p. pap. 2.99 o.p. (*0-14-035055-1*) Penguin Putnam Bks. for Young Readers. (Puffin Bks.).

—The Red Badge of Courage. 1982. (Classics Ser.). 3.95 o.p. (*0-442-82531-5*) Peter Pauper Pr. Inc.

—The Red Badge of Courage. text (*0-13-981606-2*) Prentice Hall (Schl. Div.).

—The Red Badge of Courage. 1999. E-Book 3.99 incl. cd-rom (*1-57646-018-5*) Quiet Vision Publishing.

—The Red Badge of Courage. 1998. E-Book 4.95 (*0-679-64129-7*, Modern Library) Random House Adult Trade Publishing Group.

—The Red Badge of Courage. 1993. 252p. 13.50 o.s.i (*0-679-60044-2*); 1980. 251p. 10.95 o.s.i (*0-394-60493-8*) Random Hse., Inc.

—The Red Badge of Courage. 1982. (Illus.). 176p. 12.95 o.p. (*0-89577-155-1*) Reader's Digest Assn., Inc., The.

—The Red Badge of Courage. 1990. (Works of Stephen Crane). reprint ed. lib. bdg. 79.00 (*0-7812-2426-8*) Reprint Services Corp.

—The Red Badge of Courage. (Literary Classics Ser.). 1992. 128p. text 5.98 o.p. (*1-56138-115-2*, Courage Bks.); 1986. 160p. pap. 4.95 o.p. (*0-89471-482-1*); 1986. 160p. lib. bdg. 12.90 o.p. (*0-89471-483-X*) Running Pr. Bk. Pubs.

—The Red Badge of Courage. 1967. reprint ed. 40.00 (*0-8201-1010-8*) Scholars' Facsimiles & Reprints.

—The Red Badge of Courage. Shefter, Harry, ed. 1990. (Enriched Classics Ser.). 224p. mass mkt. (*0-671-74081-4*, 44003, Washington Square Pr.) Simon & Schuster.

—The Red Badge of Courage. 1996. (Enriched Classics Ser.). 224p. reprint ed. mass mkt. 5.99 (*0-671-00275-9*, Pocket) Simon & Schuster.

—The Red Badge of Courage. (Ebook Classic Ser.). E-Book 5.00 (*0-7410-0452-6*) SoftBook Pr.

—The Red Badge of Courage. l.t. ed. 1997. 190p. text 24.95 (*1-56000-528-9*) Transaction Pubs.

—The Red Badge of Courage. 1987. 8.60 o.p. (*0-606-03448-X*) Turtleback Bks.

—The Red Badge of Courage. Bradbury, Malcolm & Bigsby, Christopher, eds. 1993. 152p. pap. 7.95 (*0-460-87381-4*, Everyman's Classic Library in Paperback) Tuttle Publishing.

—The Red Badge of Courage. 1983. 133p. pap. 1.95 o.p. (*0-460-87138-2*, Everyman's Classic Library in Paperback) Tuttle Publishing.

—The Red Badge of Courage. unabr. ed. 1997. 135p. reprint ed. pap. 9.95 (*1-57002-051-5*) University Publishing Hse., Inc.

—The Red Badge of Courage. 1983. (American Library). 224p. pap. 2.95 o.p. (*0-14-039021-9*, Penguin Classics) Viking Penguin.

—The Red Badge of Courage. 2002. 184p. 29.95 (*1-59224-793-8*) Wildside Pr.

—The Red Badge of Courage. (Classics Ser.). 1999. pap. 3.95 (*1-85326-084-3*); 1997. 128p. pap. 3.95 o.s.i (*1-85326-567-5*, 5675WW) Wordsworth Editions, Ltd. GBR. *Dist:* Combined Publishing.

—The Red Badge of Courage: An Annotated Text with Critical Essays. Bradley, Sculley et al, eds. rev. ed. (Critical Editions Ser.). 1977. 12.50 o.p. (*0-393-04435-1*); 1976. (C). pap. o.p. (*0-393-09182-1*) Norton, W. W. & Co., Inc.

—The Red Badge of Courage: An Episode of the American Civil War. 1998. (Modern Library Ser.). 304p. 16.95 (*0-679-60296-8*) Random Hse., Inc.

—The Red Badge of Courage: An Historically Annotated Edition. LaRocca, Charles J., ed. 1995. (Illus.). 212p. pap. 18.00 o.p. (*0-935796-68-1*) Purple Mountain Pr., Ltd.

—The Red Badge of Courage: And Four Stories. Stallman, R. W., ed. & notes by. rev. ed. 1997. (Signet Classics). 240p. mass mkt. 3.95 (*0-451-52647-3*, Signet Classics) NAL.

—The Red Badge of Courage: And Selected Prose & Poetry. Gibson, William M., ed. 3rd ed. 1968. 652p. (C). pap. text 26.50 (*0-03-073360-X*) Harcourt College Pubs.

—The Red Badge of Courage: And Selected Stories. 1960. (Signet Classics Ser.). 10.00 (*0-606-00225-1*) Turtleback Bks.

—The Red Badge of Courage: The Comprehensive Edition: The December 1894 Newspaper Serial & the Novel. 1999. (Ironweed American Classics Ser.). 189p. (Orig.). pap. 10.95 (*0-9655309-2-2*) Ironweed Pr., Inc.

—The Red Badge of Courage & Maggie, a Girl of the Streets. l.t. ed. 2001. per. 15.50 (*1-58396-129-1*); 2000. 250p. per. 9.90 (*1-58396-033-3*) Blue Unicorn Editions.

—The Red Badge of Courage & Other Stories. 1960. 224p. mass mkt. 3.95 o.p. (*0-451-52368-7*, CW1592, Signet Classics) NAL.

—The Red Badge of Courage & Other Stories. Robertson, Fiona & Mellors, Anthony, eds. 1998. (Oxford World's Classics Ser.). 320p. pap. 8.95 (*0-19-283315-4*) Oxford Univ. Pr., Inc.

—The Red Badge of Courage & Other Stories, Set. unabr. ed. 1999. audio 44.98 BBC Audiobooks America.

—The Red Badge of Courage & Selected Stories. 1987. 224p. reprint ed. lib. bdg. 21.95 (*0-89966-620-5*) Buccaneer Bks., Inc.

—The Red Badge of Courage & Selected Stories. 1960. mass mkt. 1.50 o.p. (*0-451-51592-7*) NAL.

—The Red Badge of Courage Readalong. 1994. (Illustrated Classics Collection). 64p. pap. 14.95 incl. audio (*0-7854-0710-3*, 40354) American Guidance Service, Inc.

Crane, Stephen & Covici, Pascal, Jr. The Red Badge of Courage & Other Stories. Covici, Pascal, Jr., ed. 1991. (Classics Ser.). 336p. pap. 8.95 (*0-14-039081-2*, Penguin Classics) Viking Penguin.

Crane, Stephen, et al. The Red Badge of Courage & Other Stories. 1998. E-Book 8.35 (*0-585-36127-4*) netLibrary, Inc.

—Three Great Novels of the Civil War. Jaffe, Marc, ed. 1994. 944p. 14.99 o.s.i (*0-517-12196-4*) Random Hse. Value Publishing.

Croker, Richard. To Make Men Free: A Novel of the Battle of Antietam. 2004. 400p. 25.95 (*0-06-055908-X*, Morrow, William & Co.) Morrow/Avon.

Dallas, Sandra. Alice's Tulips. 2001. 256p. pap. 12.95 (*0-312-28378-4*, Saint Martin's Griffin); 2000. 246p. 22.95 (*0-312-20359-4*) St. Martin's Pr.

—Alice's Tulips. l.t. ed. 2001. (Thorndike Press Large Print Americana Ser.). 413p. 28.95 (*0-7862-3224-2*) Thorndike Pr.

Dann, Jack. The Silent. 1999. 304p. reprint ed. pap. 19.00 (*0-553-38038-9*) Bantam Bks.

De Forest, John W. Miss Ravenel's Conversion from Secession to Loyalty. 1988. (Collected Works of John W. De Forest). reprint ed. lib. bdg. 59.00 (*0-7812-1153-0*) Reprint Services Corp.

—Miss Ravenel's Conversion from Secession to Loyalty. reprint ed. 69.00 (*0-403-03090-0*) Somerset Pubs., Inc.

—Miss Ravenel's Conversion from Secession to Loyalty. 2000. (Classics Ser.). 544p. pap. 14.95 (*0-14-043757-6*, Penguin Classics) Viking Penguin.

Diffley, Kathleen Elizabeth, ed. To Live & Die: Collected Stories of the Civil War, 1861-1876. 2002. (Illus.). 448p. 34.95 (*0-8223-2887-9*) Duke Univ. Pr.

Dixon, Thomas, Jr. The Leopard's Spots. 2000. 252p. pap. 9.95 (*0-594-00453-5*); E-Book 3.95 (*0-594-02103-0*) 1873 Pr.

Dixon, Thomas, Jr. The Leopard's Spots: A Romance of the White Man's Burden. 1979. (Americans in Fiction Ser.). (Illus.). 481p. reprint ed. lib. bdg. 49.50 (*0-8398-0366-4*) Irvington Pubs.

Dopp, Peggy H. & Vroman, Barbara F. Tomorrow Is a River. 1977. 390p. 15.95 (*0-931762-00-6*) Phunn Pubs.

Dowdey, Clifford. Bugles Blow No More. 1990. 512p. reprint ed. 42.00 (*0-87797-176-5*) Cherokee Publishing Co.

Drake, Albert. Fast & Loose in Dixie: A Civil War Adventure. 1998. 220p. E-Book 8.00 (*0-7388-8027-2*) Xlibris Corp.

Drannan, Walt. The Land Aflame. 2002. 196p. pap. 11.95 (*0-87714-252-1*) Denlingers Pubs., Ltd.

—The Land Aflame. Ballard, Lynn, ed. 2000. E-Book 6.95 (*0-87714-517-2*) Denlingers Pubs., Ltd.

Dwyer, John J. Stonewall. 1998. pap. 14.99 (*0-8054-1663-3*) Broadman & Holman Pubs.

Easton, Robert Olney. Blood & Money. l.t. ed. 1999. (Western Ser.). 477p. 24.95 o.p. (*0-7862-1166-0*) Thorndike Pr.

Eberhart, Mignon G. Family Fortune. reprint ed. lib. bdg. 22.95 (*0-88411-769-3*) Amereon, Ltd.

—Family Fortune. l.t. ed. 2000. (G. K. Hall Romance Ser.). 384p. 27.95 (*0-7838-9044-3*, Macmillan Reference USA) Gale Group.

—Family Fortune. 1976. 7.95 o.p. (*0-394-40723-7*) Random Hse., Inc.

Edwards, Cassie. Forbidden Embrace. 2000. 448p. mass mkt. 5.99 o.s.i (*0-8217-6727-5*, Zebra Bks.); 1982. mass mkt. 3.50 o.p. (*0-8217-1105-9*) Kensington Publishing Corp.

Eggleston, George Cary. The Bale Marked Circle X. 2000. 252p. E-Book 3.95 (*0-594-02175-8*) 1873 Pr.

—The Master of Warlock. E-Book 3.95 (*0-594-02179-0*) 1873 Pr.

Ehrlich, Ev. Grant Speaks. 416p. 2000. (Illus.). 25.95 (*0-446-52387-9*); 2001. reprint ed. pap. 13.95 o.s.i (*0-446-67655-1*) Warner Bks., Inc.

Elwood, Roger. Across Fields of Dixie. 2001. pap. 12.99 (*0-8054-1698-6*) Broadman & Holman Pubs.

Faulkner, William. The Unvanquished. (Vintage International Ser.). 1991. 272p. pap. 12.95 (*0-679-73652-2*); Vol. 351. 1966. (Illus.). pap. 8.00 o.p. (*0-394-70351-0*, V351) Knopf Publishing Group. (Vintage).

Forstchen, William R. We Look Like Men of War. 192p. 2001. 21.95 (*0-7653-0114-8*); 2003. reprint ed. pap. 12.95 (*0-7653-0115-6*) Doherty, Tom Assocs., LLC. (Forge Bks.).

Fowler, Robert H. The Battle of Milroy Station: A Novel of the Nature of True Courage. 2003. (Illus.). 320p. 25.95 (*0-7653-0659-X*, Forge Bks.) Doherty, Tom Assocs., LLC.

Fox, John, Jr. The Little Shepherd of Kingdom Come. 2000. 252p. pap. 9.95 (*0-594-00462-4*); E-Book 3.95 (*0-594-02219-3*) 1873 Pr.

—The Little Shepherd of Kingdom Come. 1976. 23.95 (*0-8488-1327-8*) Amereon, Ltd.

—The Little Shepherd of Kingdom Come. 1976. lib. bdg. 29.95 (*0-89968-039-9*, Lightyear Pr.) Buccaneer Bks., Inc.

—The Little Shepherd of Kingdom Come. (Best Sellers of 1903 Ser.). reprint ed. lib. bdg. 48.00 (0-7426-1186-8); 2001. pap. text 28.00 (0-7426-6186-5) Classic Bks.

—The Little Shepherd of Kingdom Come. E-Book 2.49 (0-7574-0277-1) Electric Umbrella Publishing.

—The Little Shepherd of Kingdom Come. 2002. 252p. 24.99 (1-4043-1506-3); per. 20.99 (1-4043-1507-1) IndyPublish.com.

—The Little Shepherd of Kingdom Come. 1987. 336p. reprint ed. 30.00 o.p. (0-8131-1631-7); pap. 18.00 (0-8131-0172-7) Univ. Pr. of Kentucky.

Fox, Lyal LeClair. Reflections from the Riverbank. 2001. 151p. pap. (1-55212-559-9) Trafford Publishing.

Frazier, Charles. Cold Mountain. l.t. ed. 1997. (Large Print Ser.). lib. bdg. 27.95 o.s.i (1-57490-101-X) Beeler, Thomas T. Publisher.

—Cold Mountain. 1997. 368p. 19.95 (0-87113-679-1, Atlantic Monthly Pr.) Grove/Atlantic, Inc.

—Cold Mountain. 464p. 2003. pap. 14.95 (1-4000-7782-6); 1998. pap. 14.95 (0-375-70075-7) Knopf Publishing Group. (Vintage).

—Cold Mountain. aut. ed. 1998. pap. 13.00 o.p. (0-676-58288-5) Random Hse., Inc.

—Cold Mountain. 1998. 19.05 (0-606-16198-8) Turtleback Bks.

Fuller, Richard. Escape from Savannah. 2001. 397p. 27.95 (1-931055-40-8) SuperiorBooks.com, Inc.

Gaffney, Virginia. Magnolia Dreams. 1998. (Richmond Chronicles Ser.: No. 4). 403p. pap. 9.99 o.p. (1-56507-670-2) Harvest Hse. Pubs.

Gerson, Noel B. Clear for Action: A Biographical Novel about David Farragut. 22.95 (0-88411-641-7) Amereon, Ltd.

Gibbons, Kaye. On the Occasion of My Last Afternoon. l.t. ed. 1998. (Large Print Book Ser.). 26.95 (1-56895-624-X, Wheeler Publishing, Inc.) Gale Group.

—On the Occasion of My Last Afternoon. 1999. 288p. reprint ed. pap. 13.00 (0-380-73214-9, Perennial) HarperTrade.

—On the Occasion of My Last Afternoon. 1998. 208p. 22.95 (0-399-19408-8); 288p. (YA). 22.95 o.s.i (0-399-14299-1) Penguin Group (USA) Inc. (G. P. Putnam's Sons).

Gilliam, Richard, et al, eds. Confederacy of the Dead. 1995. 480p. mass mkt. 5.99 o.s.i (0-451-45477-4, ROC) NAL.

Gindlesperger, James. Escape from Libby Prison. 1996. 245p. 24.95 (0-942597-91-5, Burd Street Pr.) White Mane Publishing Co., Inc.

Gingrich, Newt. Gettysburg: A Novel of the Civil War. Date not set. pap. (0-312-30936-8, Saint Martin's Griffin); mass mkt. (0-312-98725-0, St. Martin's Paperbacks) St. Martin's Pr.

Gingrich, Newt & Forstchen, William R. Gettysburg: A Novel of the Civil War. 2003. (Illus.). 384p. 24.95 (0-312-30935-X) St. Martin's Pr.

Gingrich, Newt & William R. Forstchen. Gettysburg: A Novel of the Civil War. l.t. ed. 2003. 731p. 30.95 (0-7862-5957-4) Thorndike Pr.

Glass, Caleb D. Horse Soldiers: A Novel of the Civil War. 2000. 448p. 25.95 (0-9702918-0-9) Eynon Pubns.

Graham, Heather. Glory. l.t. ed. 1999. 27.95 (1-56895-645-2, Wheeler Publishing, Inc.) Gale Group.

—Glory, 1 vol. 1999. (Topaz Historical Romance Ser.). 352p. mass mkt. 6.99 o.s.i (0-451-40848-9) NAL.

—Surrender. 1998. (Star-Romance Ser.). 450p. 26.95 (0-7862-1602-6, Five Star); 26.95 (1-56895-579-0, Wheeler Publishing, Inc.) Gale Group.

—Surrender. 1998. 386p. mass mkt. 6.99 o.s.i (0-451-40690-7, Onyx) NAL.

—Triumph. l.t. ed. 2000. (Wheeler Romance Ser.). 664p. 25.95 (1-56895-131-0, Wheeler Publishing, Inc.) Gale Group.

—Triumph. 2000. 496p. mass mkt. 6.99 o.s.i (0-451-40849-7, Signet Bks.) NAL.

Greenberg, Martin H. Civil War Women II: Stories by & about Women. 1997. pap. text 9.95 (0-87483-487-2) August Hse. Pubs., Inc.

—Murder Most Confederate. 2003. 288p. 9.99 (0-517-22157-8) Gramercy Bks.

Greenberg, Martin H., ed. Civil War Fantastic. 2000. (Daw Book Collectors Ser.: Vol. 1159). 320p. mass mkt. 6.99 o.s.i (0-88677-903-0, D A W Fantasy) DAW Bks., Inc.

Greenwood, Randall. Burn, Missouri, Burn. 1995. 320p. (Orig.). mass mkt. 4.99 o.p. (0-8125-3455-7, Forge Bks.) Doherty, Tom Assocs., LLC.

Grove, Fred. The Spring of Valor: An Historical Story. 2003. 292p. 25.95 (0-7862-3776-7, Five Star) Gale Group.

Guest, James W. Love, Honour, & Civil War. 1993. 275p. 14.95 o.p. (0-9623065-5-X) Palmetto Bookworks.

Gurganus, Allan. Oldest Living Confederate Widow Tells All. 1996. 736p. pap. 15.00 o.s.i (0-449-91169-1, Fawcett); 1994. pap. 6.99 o.p. (0-8041-9826-8, Ivy Bks.); 1990. 912p. mass mkt. 6.99 o.s.i (0-8041-0643-6, Ivy Bks.) Ballantine Bks.

—Oldest Living Confederate Widow Tells All. 2001. 736p. reprint ed. pap. 16.00 (0-375-72663-2, Vintage) Knopf Publishing Group.

—Oldest Living Confederate Widow Tells All. 1992. 5.99 o.p. (0-517-08827-4); 1991. 5.99 o.p. (0-517-06769-2) Random Hse. Value Publishing.

Haeger, Diane. My Dearest Cecelia: A Novel of the Southern Belle Who Stole General Sherman's Heart. 2004. 320p. pap. 14.95 (0-312-32594-0, Saint Martin's Griffin); 2003. 288p. 24.95 (0-312-28200-1) St. Martin's Pr.

Hanna, James Milton. A Man Called Shiloh. 2000. 228p. pap. 12.95 (0-9640458-7-7) Cherokee Bks.

Harper, M. A. For the Love of Robert E. Lee. 1994. 325p. pap. 13.00 (1-56947-002-2); 1992. 330p. 20.00 o.s.i (0-939149-63-X) Soho Pr., Inc.

Harrison. The Carlyles. 2000. 252p. E-Book 9.95 (0-594-02327-0) 1873 Pr.

Harrison, Charles. No Longer Warriors. 2003. 196p. pap. 19.95 (1-59129-981-0) PublishAmerica, Inc.

Harrison, Delores. Purple Wisteria of Heart Haven. Hammond, Ray, ed. 2000. 160p. pap. 12.50 (0-9700486-5-3) Penman Publishing, Inc.

Harrison, Harry. Stars & Stripes Forever. 1998. 352p. 24.95 o.p. (0-345-40933-7, Del Rey) Ballantine Bks.

—Stars & Stripes Triumphant. 2003. 304p. mass mkt. 6.99 (0-345-40938-8); (Illus.). 256p. 24.95 (0-345-40937-X) Ballantine Bks. (Del Rey).

Hatcher, Robin Lee. Stormy Surrender. 432p. 1994. pap. 4.99 (0-8439-3573-1); 1988. pap. 3.95 (0-8439-2585-X); 1984. (Spring Haven Saga Ser.: Vol. I). pap. 3.75 o.p. (0-8439-2073-4) Dorchester Publishing Co., Inc.

—Stormy Surrender. 1999. (Romances Ser.). pap. 25.95 (0-7862-2087-2, Five Star) Gale Group.

Herrin, Lamar. The Unwritten Chronicles of Robert E. Lee. 1991. pap. 9.95 o.p. (0-312-05983-3, Saint Martin's Griffin); 1989. 256p. 17.95 o.p. (0-312-03448-2) St. Martin's Pr.

Hill, Morgan. Lost Patrol. 2003. (Lost Patrol Ser.). 272p. pap. 5.99 (1-59052-050-5) Multnomah Pubs., Inc.

Hord, Benjamin M. Nick Hardeman: A Civil War Novel with an Appendix of Selected Short Stories. Sikes, Lewright B., ed. 1993. 384p. pap. 75.50 (0-8191-9244-9); 336p. 48.00 (0-8191-9245-7) Univ. Pr. of America.

Hower, Edward. Shadows & Elephants. 2002. 317p. pap. 14.95 (0-9679520-3-4) Leapfrog Pr.

Huff Fisk, Sarah. Found among the Fragments: A Story of Love & Courage. 1997. (Illus.). 320p. (Orig.). pap. 15.95 (0-9655917-2-7) Pinhook Publishing Co.

Hummel, Maria. Wilderness Run: A Novel. 352p. 2003. pap. 13.95 (0-312-32047-7, Saint Martin's Griffin); 2002. 24.95 (0-312-28757-7) St. Martin's Pr.

Humphreys, Josephine. Nowhere Else on Earth. l.t. ed. 2000. (Large Print Bks.). 460p. 28.95 (1-56895-957-5, Wheeler Publishing, Inc.) Gale Group.

—Nowhere Else on Earth. 2000. (0-670-78270-X); (Illus.). 288p. 24.95 o.p. (0-670-89176-2, Viking) Viking Penguin.

Jacobs, William H. Dear Lizzie: A Civil War Novel. 2001. (Illus.). 248p. pap. (0-9706546-0-X) Converg Pubs.

—Dear Lizzie: Alone in Glory. 2002. (Illus.). xiv, 327p. (0-9706546-1-8) Converg Pubs.

Jakes, John. Love & War. 1985. (North & South Trilogy Ser.: Vol. 2). 1088p. mass mkt. 7.50 o.s.i (0-440-15016-7) Dell Publishing.

—Love & War. 1984. (North & South Trilogy Ser.: Vol. 2). 800p. 19.95 o.p. (0-15-154496-4) Harcourt Trade Pubs.

—Love & War. 2000. (North & South Trilogy Ser.: Vol. 2). 1088p. mass mkt. 7.99 (0-451-20082-9, Signet Bks.) NAL.

—North & South. 1985. (North & South Trilogy Ser.: Vol. 1). 816p. mass mkt. 7.50 o.s.i (0-440-16205-X) Dell Publishing.

—North & South. l.t. ed. 1985. (North & South Trilogy Ser.: Vol. 1). 1333p. 29.95 o.p. (0-8161-3952-0); 14.95 o.p. (0-8161-3953-9) Gale Group. (Macmillan Reference USA).

—North & South. 1982. (North & South Trilogy Ser.: Vol. 1). 752p. 24.95 o.s.i (0-15-166998-8) Harcourt Trade Pubs.

—North & South. 2000. (North & South Trilogy Ser.: Vol. 1). 816p. mass mkt. 7.99 (0-451-20081-0, Signet Bks.) NAL.

—On Secret Service. 2000. 416p. 25.95 o.s.i (0-525-94544-X, Dutton) Dutton/Plume.

—On Secret Service. l.t. ed. (Wheeler Press Paperback Ser.). 2001. pap. 12.95 o.p. (1-56895-177-9); 2000. 681p. 30.95 (1-56895-905-2) Gale Group. (Wheeler Publishing, Inc.).

—On Secret Service. 2001. 480p. reprint ed. mass mkt. 7.99 (0-451-20405-0, Signet Bks.) NAL.

Jakober, Marie. Only Call Us Faithful: A Novel of the Union Underground. 2002. (Illus.). 384p. 25.95 (0-7653-0316-7, Forge Bks.) Doherty, Tom Assocs., LLC.

Jiles, Paulette. Enemy Women. 2003. 336p. pap. 13.95 (0-06-093809-9, Perennial) HarperTrade.

—Enemy Women. l.t. ed. 2002. (Women's Fiction Ser.). 561p. 29.95 (0-7862-4396-1) Thorndike Pr.

—Enemy Women: A Novel. 2002. 336p. 24.95 (0-06-621444-0, Morrow, William & Co.) Morrow/Avon.

Johnston, Mary. Cease Firing. E-Book 3.95 (0-594-02503-6) 1873 Pr.

—The Long Roll. 2000. 252p. pap. 9.95 (0-594-01116-7); E-Book 3.95 (0-594-02509-5) 1873 Pr.

—The Long Roll. Date not set. 702p. 37.95 (0-8488-2343-5) Amereon, Ltd.

—The Long Roll. reprint ed. lib. bdg. 48.00 (0-7426-1210-4) Classic Bks.

—The Long Roll. 1996. 668p. reprint ed. pap. text 19.95 (0-8018-5524-1) Johns Hopkins Univ. Pr.

Jones, Alice. The Night Hawk. Davies, Gwendolyn, ed. 2001. (Fiction Treasures Ser.). (Illus.). 408p. pap. (0-88780-538-8) Formac Publishing Co., Ltd.

Jones, Ben. The Rope Eater: A Novel. 2003. 304p. 24.00 (0-385-50977-4) Doubleday Publishing.

Jones, Douglas C. Elkhorn Tavern. 1989. mass mkt. 4.95 o.p. (0-8125-8457-0, Tor Bks.) Doherty, Tom Assocs., LLC.

—Elkhorn Tavern. 1996. 368p. mass mkt. 4.99 o.p. (0-06-100923-7) HarperCollins Pubs.

—Elkhorn Tavern. 1985. 320p. pap. 5.95 o.p. (0-03-000097-1, Owl Bks.); 1980. 304p. o.p. (0-03-050926-2) Holt, Henry & Co.

—Elkhorn Tavern. l.t. ed. 1981. reprint ed. 12.95 o.p. (0-89621-273-4) Thorndike Pr.

Joshi, S. T. Civil War Memories: Nineteen Stories of Glory & Tragedy. 2003. 304p. 9.99 (0-517-22261-2) Gramercy Bks.

Joshi, S. T., ed. Civil War Memories. 2000. x, 292p. pap. 14.95 (1-55853-809-7) Rutledge Hill Pr.

Justus, James H., intro. Wilderness: A Tale of the Civil War. 2001. (Tennesseana Editions Ser.). (Illus.). xxii, 310p. reprint ed. pap. 19.50 (1-57233-134-8) Univ. of Tennessee Pr.

Kantor, MacKinlay. If the South Had Won the Civil War. 1994. reprint ed. lib. bdg. 25.95 (1-56849-528-5) Buccaneer Bks., Inc.

—If the South Had Won the Civil War. 128p. 2002. (Illus.). pap. 9.95 (0-312-86949-5); 2001. 19.95 (0-312-86553-8) Doherty, Tom Assocs., LLC. (Forge Bks.).

—Long Remember. 1934. (YA). reprint ed. pap. text 28.00 (1-4047-5475-X) Classic Textbooks.

—Long Remember. 2000. 416p. pap. 14.95 (0-312-87520-7); (Illus.). 24.95 (0-312-86552-X) Doherty, Tom Assocs., LLC. (Forge Bks.).

—Long Remember. 1993. reprint ed. lib. bdg. 89.00 (0-7812-5475-2) Reprint Services Corp.

Kellum, Rose. A Storm of Passion. 1999. 230p. pap. 10.95 (1-929416-11-3) Magner Publishing & American Binding & Publishing.

Kelton, Elmer. The Buckskin Line. l.t. ed. 2001. lib. bdg. 26.95 (1-58547-112-7) Ctr. Point Large Print.

—The Buckskin Line. 2000. 393p. mass mkt. 5.99 (0-8125-4020-4); 2nd ed. 1999. 287p. 22.95 (0-312-86522-8) Doherty, Tom Assocs., LLC. (Forge Bks.).

—The Buckskin Line. abr. ed. 1999. 25.00 incl. audio (0-7871-2005-7, Dove Audio) NewStar Media, Inc.

—The Buckskin Line. 2000. 12.04 (0-606-19646-3) Turtleback Bks.

Keneally, Thomas. Confederates. 1983. mass mkt. 3.95 o.s.i (0-425-06542-1); 1981. mass mkt. 3.50 o.s.i (0-425-05057-2) Berkley Publishing Group.

—Confederates. 1980. 427p. 13.50 o.p. (0-06-012299-4); 1987. 448p. reprint ed. pap. 13.00 o.p. (0-06-091446-7, PL/1446, Perennial) HarperTrade.

—Confederates. 2000. (Illus.). 427p. pap. 18.95 (0-8203-2263-6) Univ. of Georgia Pr.

Kilian, Michael. A Grave at Glorieta. 2004. 304p. mass mkt. 6.99 (0-425-19531-7) Berkley Publishing Group.

—The Ironclad Alibi: A Harrison Raines Civil War Mystery. 2002. 320p. 22.95 o.s.i (0-425-18325-4, Prime Crime) Berkley Publishing Group.

—A Killing at Ball's Bluff. 2002. 384p. reprint ed. mass mkt. 6.50 o.s.i (0-425-18314-9, Prime Crime) Berkley Publishing Group.

—A Killing at Ball's Bluff: A Harrison Raines Civil War Mystery. 2001. (Harrison Raines Civil War Mysteries Ser.). 384p. 21.95 o.s.i (0-425-17804-8, Prime Crime) Berkley Publishing Group.

—Murder at Manassas: A Harrison Raines Civil War Mystery. 2000. (Harrison Raines Civil War Mysteries Ser.). 320p. mass mkt. 5.99 (0-425-17743-2); 306p. 21.95 o.s.i (0-425-17233-3) Berkley Publishing Group. (Prime Crime).

King, Barrington. The Way Upcountry. 2002. (Five Star First Edition Romance Ser.). 260p. 26.95 (0-7862-4407-0, Five Star) Gale Group.

Knox, Dahk. The Danville Diaries Vol. 1: A Time of Turmoil. 2003. pap. 15.95 (1-58275-125-0) Black Forest Pr.

Kolbaker, Genieva. Kisatchie: The Big Thicket. Eyster, Warren, ed. (Illus.). 238p. pap. 12.95 (0-9725072-1-3); 1992. 25.00 (0-9725072-0-5) Kildara Pr.

Kope, Spencer. When the Drummer Falls. 1995. 191p. pap. 17.95 (0-9647183-0-8) Lion's Gate Publishing.

Lacy, Al. A Heart Divided: Mobile Bay, 8 vols. 2003. (Battles of Destiny Ser.: Vol. 2). 353p. pap. 9.99 (0-88070-591-4, Multnomah Bks.) Multnomah Pubs., Inc.

—Joy from Ashes: Fredericksburg, 8 vols. 2003. (Battles of Destiny Ser.: Vol. 5). 308p. pap. 9.99 (0-88070-720-8) Multnomah Pubs., Inc.

Lacy, Al & Lacy, Lew A. Wings of the Wind, 8 vols. 2003. (Battles of Destiny Ser.: Vol. 7). 366p. pap. 9.99 (1-57673-032-8, Multnomah Bks.) Multnomah Pubs., Inc.

Ladnier, Gene S. Fame's Eternal Camping Ground: The Civil War Battle of Brice's Crossroads. 1999. 363p. E-Book 8.00 (0-7388-8246-1) Xlibris Corp.

Larrigan, Tex. The Dam Breakers. l.t. ed. 2001. (Dales Large Print Ser.). 208p. pap. 21.99 (1-84262-121-1) Dales Large Print Bks. GBR. *Dist:* Ulverscroft Large Print Bks., Ltd., Ulverscroft Large Print Canada, Ltd.

Lent, Jeffrey. In the Fall. 2000. 560p. 25.00 o.p. (0-87113-765-8, Atlantic Monthly Pr.) Grove/Atlantic, Inc.

—In the Fall. 2000. pap. (0-375-72589-X, Vintage) Knopf Publishing Group.

—In the Fall. l.t. ed. 2000. (Americana Ser.). 967p. 28.95 (0-7862-2783-4) Thorndike Pr.

—In the Fall: A Novel. 2001. 528p. reprint ed. pap. 14.95 (0-375-70745-X, Vintage) Knopf Publishing Group.

Leonard, Ann Georgi. Hoops of Steel: A Civil War Novel. 2001. (Illus.). 352p. 22.00 (0-9708053-0-6) Authors & Artists Publishers of New York.

Lewis, Preston. The Redemption of Jesse James. Lewis, Preston, ed. 1995. 368p. mass mkt. 5.50 o.s.i (0-553-56542-7) Bantam Bks.

—The Redemption of Jesse James. l.t. ed. 1995. 496p. 20.95 o.p. (0-7838-1500-X, Macmillan Reference USA) Gale Group.

Ligotti, Eugene. The Youngest Patriot: The Story of the British Occupation of Long Island. 2000. 167p. E-Book 8.00 (0-7388-8382-4) Xlibris Corp.

Locust Alley: A Novel of the Civil War. 2000. 268p. pap. 15.00 (0-9677103-0-8) Wordsmith & Penn.

Lowe, Frances Noland. Anna, a Civil War Story. 1999. 204p. pap. 12.95 (1-929264-00-3) Blue & Grey Bk. Shoppe.

Macomber, Robert N. At the Edge of Honor: A Novel of the Naval Civil War. 2002. (Illus.). 278p. 19.95 (1-56164-252-5) Pineapple Pr., Inc.

—Point of Honor. 2003. (Illus.). vi, 327p. 19.95 (1-56164-270-3) Pineapple Pr., Inc.

Manton, Richard. Fancy Girl. 2003. 186p. mass mkt. 7.95 o.p. (1-56201-354-8); 1999. 192p. mass mkt. 7.95 (1-56201-120-0); 1990. pap. 4.95 o.p. (0-929654-33-1) Avalon Publishing Group. (Blue Moon Bks.).

Marlow, Herb. The Guns Are Silent. 2002. (Guns of the Civil War Ser.: No. 4). (Illus.). 150p. lib. bdg. 21.95 (1-893595-30-7) Four Seasons Bks., Inc.

—The Guns of Chickamauga. 2001. 150p. (Guns of the Civil War Ser.: No. 3). lib. bdg. 21.95 net. (1-893595-17-X); (Goerge Svage: The Guns of the Civil War: Vol. 3). per. 10.95 net. (1-893595-18-8) Four Seasons Bks., Inc.

—The Guns of Devil's Den. 2000. (Guns of the Civil War Ser.: No. 2). (Illus.). 150p. 21.95 (1-893595-12-9, Guns-2) Four Seasons Bks., Inc.

—The Guns of Prairie Grove. 1999. (Illus.). vi, 153p. pap. 10.95 (1-893595-03-X); (Guns of the Civil War Ser.: No. 1). lib. bdg. 21.95 (1-893595-02-1) Four Seasons Bks., Inc.

Massie, Elizabeth. 1863: The Battle of Gettysburg. 2000. (Young Founders Ser.: No. 4). 178p. (YA). (gr. 7-12). mass mkt. 4.99 (0-8125-9095-3, Tor Bks.) Doherty, Tom Assocs., LLC.

McColley, Kevin. The Other Side. 2002. 384p. pap. 21.95 (0-7432-4262-9, Simon & Schuster) Simon & Schuster.

—The Other Side: A Novel of the Civil War. 2000. 384p. 24.00 o.s.i (0-684-85762-6, Simon & Schuster) Simon & Schuster.

McCrumb, Sharyn. Ghost Riders. 2004. 416p. mass mkt. 7.99 (0-451-21184-7, Signet Bks.) NAL.

—Ghost Riders. l.t. ed. 2003. 630p. 32.95 (0-7862-5570-6) Thorndike Pr.

—Ghost Riders: A Novel. 2003. 336p. 24.95 (0-525-94718-3, Dutton) Dutton/Plume.

McDonald, Jerry W. The Reluctant Rebels. 2000. 148p. pap. 20.99 (0-7388-2525-5) Xlibris Corp.

McIntire, Dennis P. Lee at Chattanooga: A Novel of What Might Have Been. 2002. (Illus.). 320p. pap. 16.95 (1-58182-257-X) Cumberland Hse. Publishing.

McMillan, Ann. Civil Blood: A Civil War Mystery. l.t. ed. 2001. (Thorndike Press Large Print Americana Ser.). (Illus.). 447p. 28.95 o.p. (0-7862-3614-0) Gale Group.

—Civil Blood: A Civil War Mystery. 2003. 320p. mass mkt. 6.99 (0-14-200124-4) Penguin Group (USA) Inc.

Historical Events

—Civil Blood: A Civil War Mystery. 2001. (Illus.). 224p. 22.95 o.p. (*0-670-89997-6*, Viking) Viking Penguin.
—Dead March: A Civil War Mystery, Vol. 1. 1999. 288p. pap. 5.99 (*0-14-028020-0*) Penguin Group (USA) Inc.
Merriam, John Duke. Meade's Reprise: A Novel of Gettysburg, War, & Intrigue. 2002. 316p. 25.00 (*1-889274-18-6*) Posterity Pr., Inc.
Mitchell, Kirk. Fredericksburg: A Novel of the Irish at Marye's Heights. 1996. 384p. 23.95 o.p. (*0-312-13974-8*) St. Martin's Pr.
—Fredericksburg: A Novel of the Irish at Marye's Heights. 2003. 384p. mass mkt. 7.99 (*0-7434-5827-3*) ibooks, Inc.
Mitchell, Margaret. Gone with the Wind. l.t. unabr. ed. 1992. lib. bdg. (*0-8161-5531-3*);Set. 37.95 o.p. (*0-8161-5529-1*);Set. pap. 25.95 (*0-8161-5530-5*);Vol. 2. 19.95 (*0-8161-5532-1*) Gale Group. (Macmillan Reference USA).
—Gone with the Wind. 1976. 1024p. reprint ed. mass mkt. 6.50 (*0-380-00109-8*, Avon Bks.) Morrow/Avon.
—Gone with the Wind, 28 cass., Set. 2002. audio 79.99 (*0-7887-8957-0*, 00414) Recorded Bks., LLC.
—Gone with the Wind. 1936. 1048p. reprint ed. 26.00 (*0-684-83068-X*, Scribner) Simon & Schuster.
—Gone with the Wind. 1993. 1024p. mass mkt. 7.99 (*0-446-36538-6*); 1999. 1056p. reprint ed. pap. 15.95 (*0-446-67553-9*) Warner Bks., Inc.
Molstad, Stephen. The Patriot. 2000. (Illus.). 304p. mass mkt. 6.99 (*0-06-102076-1*, HarperEntertainment) Morrow/Avon.
Monfredo, Miriam G. Children of Cain. 2002. (Illus.). 352p. 22.95 (*0-425-18641-5*, Prime Crime) Berkley Publishing Group.
Monfredo, Miriam G. Brothers of Cain. 2001. (Illus.). 336p. 22.95 o.s.i (*0-425-18189-8*, Prime Crime) Berkley Publishing Group.
—Children of Cain. 2003. 352p. mass mkt. 6.99 (*0-425-19130-3*, Prime Crime) Berkley Publishing Group.
—Must the Maiden Die? 1999. (Seneca Falls Historical Mysteries Ser.: No. 6). 384p. 21.95 o.s.i (*0-425-16699-6*, Prime Crime) Berkley Publishing Group.
—The North Star Conspiracy. 1995. 368p. mass mkt. 6.99 (*0-425-14720-7*, Prime Crime) Berkley Publishing Group.
—Seneca Falls Inheritance. 1994. 304p. mass mkt. 6.99 (*0-425-14465-8*, Prime Crime) Berkley Publishing Group.
—Sisters of Cain: A Seneca Falls Civil War Mystery. 2000. (Illus.). 384p. 21.95 o.s.i (*0-425-17672-X*, Prime Crime) Berkley Publishing Group.
—The Stalking Horse. 1999. (Historical Mystery Ser.: Vol. 5). 352p. reprint ed. mass mkt. 6.99 o.s.i (*0-425-16695-3*, Prime Crime) Berkley Publishing Group.
—The Stalking Horse: A Seneca Falls Historical Mystery. 1998. (Glynis Tryon Historical Mysteries Ser.). 352p. 21.95 o.s.i (*0-425-15783-0*, Prime Crime) Berkley Publishing Group.
Moore, Ward. Bring the Jubilee. 1997. 240p. pap. 11.00 o.p. (*0-345-40502-1*) Ballantine Bks.
—Bring the Jubilee. 1976. (Science Fiction Rediscovery Ser.: Vol. 23). pap. 2.25 o.p. (*0-380-00756-8*, 30361, Avon Bks.) Morrow/Avon.
Moreau, C. X. A Promise of Glory. 2000. (Illus.). 302p. 24.95 (*0-312-87272-0*, Forge Bks.) Doherty, Tom Assocs., LLC.
Morris, Dorothy K. Secret Sins of the Mothers: A Novel. Finton, Kenneth H. & Thompson, Chaya, eds. 1999. 248p. 24.95 (*1-892977-03-6*) HT Communications.
Morris, Gilbert. The Dixie Widow. 1991. (House of Winslow Ser.: Bk. 9). 320p. pap. 11.99 (*1-55661-115-3*) Bethany Hse. Pubs.
—The Last Confederate. 1990. (House of Winslow Ser.: Vol. 8). 336p. pap. 11.99 (*1-55661-109-9*) Bethany Hse. Pubs.
Morton, Virginia B. Marching Through Culpeper: A Novel of Culpeper, Virginia - Crossroads of the Civil War. 2nd ed. 2000. (Illus.). 542p. (C). 27.99 (*0-615-11642-6*) Edgehill Bks.
Mrazek, Robert. Stonewall's Gold. 2001. pap., tchr.'s training gde. ed. (*0-312-28189-7*, Saint Martin's Griffin) St. Martin's Pr.
Mrazek, Robert J. Hookers Tale. Date not set. pap. (*0-312-30674-1*, Saint Martin's Griffin) St. Martin's Pr.
—Stonewall's Gold. l.t. ed. 2000. (G. K. Hall Paperback Ser.). (Illus.). 302p. pap. 23.95 (*0-7838-9288-8*, Macmillan Reference USA) Gale Group.
—Stonewall's Gold. unabr. ed. 2000. audio 53.00 (*0-7887-3119-X*, 95685E7) Recorded Bks., LLC.
—Stonewall's Gold. 2000. (Illus.). 240p. pap. 12.95 (*0-312-25422-9*, Saint Martin's Griffin); 1999. mass mkt. 4.99 (*0-312-97429-9*, St. Martin's Paperbacks); 1998. (Illus.). 240p. 22.95 (*0-312-20024-2*) St. Martin's Pr.
—Unholy Fire: A Novel of the Civil War. 2003. 336p. 24.95 (*0-312-30673-3*) St. Martin's Pr.
—Unholy Fire: A Novel of the Civil War. l.t. ed. 2003. 543p. 28.95 (*0-7862-5674-5*) Thorndike Pr.
Nagle, P. G. Galveston. E-Book 24.95 (*0-312-70631-6*, Tor Bks.); 2003. (Illus.). 384p. mass mkt. 6.99 o.s.i (*0-8125-6573-8*, Forge Bks.); 2002. (Illus.). 384p. 24.95 (*0-312-87614-9*, Forge Bks.) Doherty, Tom Assocs., LLC.
O'Brien, Patricia. The Glory Cloak: A Novel. 2004. 368p. pap. 14.00 (*0-7432-5750-2*, Touchstone) Simon & Schuster.
Okon, Phyllis. Winds of Destiny. 1999. 176p. pap. 13.00 (*0-8059-4559-8*) Dorrance Publishing Co., Inc.
O'Nan, Stewart. A Prayer for the Dying: A Novel. l.t. ed. 2000. (Wheeler Large Print Book Ser.). 196p. 26.95 (*1-56895-841-2*, Wheeler Publishing, Inc.) Gale Group.
—A Prayer for the Dying: A Novel. 1999. 195p. 22.00 o.s.i (*0-8050-6147-9*) Holt, Henry & Co.
—A Prayer for the Dying: A Novel. 2000. 208p. pap. 13.00 (*0-312-25501-2*) Picador.
Parry, Owen. Bold Sons of Erin: A Novel of Suspense. 2003. 352p. 24.95 (*0-06-051390-X*, Morrow, William & Co.) Morrow/Avon.
—Call Each River Jordan. l.t. ed. 2002. (Adventure Ser.). 514p. 29.95 (*0-7862-4015-6*) Gale Group.
—Call Each River Jordan. 2002. (Illus.). 384p. mass mkt. 7.50 (*0-06-000922-5*) HarperCollins Pubs.
—Call Each River Jordan. 2001. 336p. 25.00 (*0-06-018638-0*, Morrow, William & Co.) Morrow/Avon.
—Faded Coat of Blue. 2002. 352p. pap. 13.95 (*0-06-093766-1*, Perennial) HarperTrade.
—Faded Coat of Blue. 2000. 368p. mass mkt. 6.99 (*0-380-79739-9*); 1999. 352p. 23.00 (*0-380-97642-0*, Avon Bks.) Morrow/Avon.
—Honor's Kingdom. 2003. 448p. mass mkt. 7.99 (*0-06-051079-X*, HarperTorch); 2002. 336p. 25.95 (*0-06-018634-8*, Morrow, William & Co.) Morrow/Avon.
—Honor's Kingdom. 2002. (Adventure Ser.). 28.95 (*0-7862-4852-1*) Thorndike Pr.
—Our Simple Gifts: Civil War Christmas Tales. 2002. 160p. 14.95 (*0-06-001378-8*, Morrow, William & Co.) Morrow/Avon.
—Shadows of Glory. 2001. 384p. mass mkt. 6.99 (*0-380-82087-0*); 2000. 311p. 24.00 (*0-380-97643-9*, Morrow, William & Co.) Morrow/Avon.
Passarella, Lee. Swallowed up in Victory: A Civil War Narrative, Petersburg, 1864-1865. 2002. (Illus.). 273p. pap. 19.95 (*1-57249-301-1*, Burd Street Pr.) White Mane Publishing Co., Inc.
Peart, Jane. The Pledge. l.t. ed. 1998. (American Quilt Ser.: Vol. 2). 349p. 24.95 o.p. (*0-7862-1469-4*) Thorndike Pr.
—The Pledge. 1996. (American Quilt Ser.). 256p. pap. 16.99 (*0-310-20167-5*) Zondervan.
Philips, Ingram. Beyond Sundown. 2000. 280p. pap. 16.00 o.p. (*0-7388-1159-9*); text 25.00 o.p. (*0-7388-1158-0*) Xlibris Corp.
Phillips, Michael. Angels Watching over Me. 2002. (Shenandoah Sisters Ser.: Bk. 1). 320p. 16.99 (*0-7642-2705-X*); pap. 12.99 (*0-7642-2700-9*) Bethany Hse. Pubs.
Poyer, David. Fire on the Waters: A Novel of the Civil War at Sea. 448p. 2001. 25.00 (*0-684-87133-5*); 2003. reprint ed. pap. 13.00 (*0-671-04681-0*) Simon & Schuster. (Simon & Schuster).
—Fire on the Waters: A Novel of the Civil War at Sea. l.t. ed. 2001. (Large Print Adventure Ser.). 714p. 28.95 (*0-7862-3664-7*) Thorndike Pr.
Price, Charles. Hiwassee: A Novel of the Civil War. 2003. reprint ed. pap. 16.95 (*0-89733-517-1*) Academy Chicago Pubs., Ltd.
Quinn, Peter. Banished Children of Eve. 1995. 624p. pap. 14.00 (*0-14-023003-3*, Penguin Bks.) Penguin Group (USA) Inc.
—Banished Children of Eve. 1994. 624p. 22.95 o.p. (*0-670-85076-4*, Viking) Viking Penguin.
Randall, Alice. The Wind Done Gone. 2001. (Illus.). 224p. 22.00 (*0-618-10450-X*); 210p. 23.00 (*0-618-13309-7*) Houghton Mifflin Co.
—The Wind Done Gone: A Novel. 2002. (Illus.). 224p. pap. 12.00 (*0-618-21906-4*, Mariner Bks.) Houghton Mifflin Co. Trade & Reference Div.
Reasoner, James. Antietam: A Novel. 2002. (Civil War Battle Ser.: Vol. 3). 368p. reprint ed. pap. 16.95 (*1-58182-275-8*) Cumberland Hse. Publishing.
—Chickamauga: A Novel. 2002. (Civil War Battle Ser.: Vol. 7). 432p. 22.95 (*1-58182-253-7*) Cumberland Hse. Publishing.
—Shiloh. 1999. (Civil War Battle Ser.: Vol. 2). 352p. 22.95 (*1-58182-048-8*, Cumberland Hearthside) Cumberland Hse. Publishing.
—Shiloh: A Novel. 2002. (Civil War Battle Ser.: Vol. 2). 352p. reprint ed. pap. 16.95 (*1-58182-248-0*) Cumberland Hse. Publishing.
—Vicksburg. (Civil War Battle Ser.: Vol. 5). 2004. 400p. pap. 16.95 (*1-58182-372-X*); 2001. (Illus.). 368p. 22.95 (*1-58182-163-8*) Cumberland Hse. Publishing.
The Red Badge of Courage & Other Stories. unabr. collector's ed. Incl. Blue Hotel. audio Bride Comes to Yellow Sky. audio Open Boat. audio 1984. 1978. Set audio 48.00 (*0-7366-0100-7*, 1108) Books on Tape, Inc.
Reece, Colleen L. Legacy of Silver. l.t. ed. 2002. (Christian Romance Ser.). 254p. 24.95 (*0-7862-3823-2*) Gale Group.
Reed, Ishmael. Flight to Canada. 1989. 180p. pap. 11.00 (*0-689-70733-9*) Central Bureau voor Schimmelcultures NLD. *Dist:* Lubrecht & Cramer, Ltd.
—Flight to Canada. 1977. pap. 2.75 o.p. (*0-380-01798-9*, 52019, Avon Bks.) Morrow/Avon.
—Flight to Canada. 1998. 192p. pap. 11.00 (*0-684-84750-7*, Scribner) Simon & Schuster.
Renich, T. Elizabeth. Word of Honor. 1994. (Shadowcreek Chronicles Ser.: Bk. 1). 300p. pap. 9.99 (*1-883002-10-9*) Emerald Bks.
Roberts, Ralph. How the South Won the War & Perserved the Union. 1997. 9.95 (*1-57090-052-3*, Farthest Star) aBOOKS Distributing.
Robinson, Derek. Kentucky Blues. 2003. 544p. pap. 8.95 (*0-304-36566-1*); 2002. 520p. 27.50 (*0-304-36182-8*) Cassell P L C GBR. *Dist:* Trafalgar Square.
Roddy, Lee. Road to Freedom. 1999. (Between Two Flags Ser.: Vol. 4). 160p. (J). (gr. 6-9). pap. 5.99 o.p. (*0-7642-2028-4*) Bethany Hse. Pubs.
Roles, Joe B. Mary Jane's War. (*0-615-12327-9*) Roles, Joe B.
Santangelo, Elena. By Blood Possessed. 2001. (Transforming Government Ser.). 304p. mass mkt. 6.50 (*0-312-97723-9*, St. Martin's Paperbacks) St. Martin's Pr.
Savage, Douglas. The Court-Martial of Robert E. Lee: A Historical Novel. 1995. 480p. pap. 21.99 (*0-446-67056-1*) Warner Bks., Inc.
—Court-Martial of Robert E. Lee: A Historical Novel. 1993. 448p. text o.p. (*0-938289-26-8*, 289268, Combined Publishing) Da Capo Pr., Inc.
Schnurr, John W. Soldier Boy. 1998. 192p. 21.95 o.p. (*1-56167-428-1*) American Literary Pr., Inc.
Shaara, Jeff. The Last Full Measure. 1998. 576p. 27.95 (*0-345-40491-2*) Ballantine Bks.
—The Last Full Measure: A Novel. l.t. ed. 1998. pap. 25.00 o.s.i (*0-375-70291-1*) Random Hse. Large Print.
Shaara, Jeff, ed. The Last Full Measure. (Ballantine Reader's Circle Ser.). 1999. (Illus.). 576p. pap. 14.95 (*0-345-42548-0*); 1998. 25.95 o.s.i (*0-345-43003-4*) Ballantine Bks.
—The Last Full Measure. l.t. ed. 1998. pap. 25.00 o.p. (*0-7838-0155-6*, Macmillan Reference USA) Gale Group.
—The Last Full Measure. 2000. E-Book 12.50 (*0-345-43850-7*) Random Hse., Inc.
Shaara, Michael. The Killer Angels. 2001. 368p. 25.95 (*0-345-44412-4*, Ballantine Bks.); 1996. 400p. pap. 13.95 (*0-345-40727-X*); 1993. mass mkt. 5.99 o.p. (*0-345-01999-7*); 1987. (Illus.). 384p. mass mkt. 7.99 (*0-345-34810-9*); 1983. mass mkt. 2.95 o.p. (*0-345-31640-1*); 1980. mass mkt. 2.75 o.p. (*0-345-29535-8*); 1980. mass mkt. 2.50 o.p. (*0-345-28605-7*); 1978. mass mkt. 1.95 o.p. (*0-345-27652-3*); 1976. mass mkt. 1.95 o.p. (*0-345-25487-2*); 1975. mass mkt. 1.95 o.p. (*0-345-24528-8*) Ballantine Bks.
—The Killer Angels. 1974. 19.95 o.s.i (*0-679-50466-4*) McKay, David Co., Inc.
—The Killer Angels. l.t. ed. 2004. 592p. 27.95 (*0-375-43310-4*) Random Hse. Large Print.
—The Killer Angels. 1993. (Illus.). 400p. 25.00 o.s.i (*0-679-42541-1*) Random Hse., Inc.
—The Killer Angels. 1975. 14.04 (*0-606-01203-6*) Turtleback Bks.
Shenley, Paul. A Bit of Irish Earth. 1996. 158p. pap. 9.99 (*0-88092-179-X*, 179X) Royal Fireworks Publishing Co.
Sigafoos, Robert A. Wave the Bloody Shirt; A Civil War Novel: The Life & Times of General Nathan Bedford Forrest, C.S.A. 1999. (Illus.). 415p. pap. 19.95 (*0-938041-48-7*) Arc Pr.
Sinclair, Upton. Manassas: A Novel of the Civil War. (Collected Works of Upton Sinclair). 412p. 2001. pap. text 28.00 (*0-7426-5825-2*); 1999. reprint ed. lib. bdg. 118.00 (*1-58201-825-1*) Classic Bks.
—Manassas: A Novel of the Civil War. 1969. reprint ed. 39.00 (*0-403-00060-2*) Scholarly Pr., Inc.
—Manassas: A Novel of the Civil War. 2000. (Classics of Civil War Fiction Ser.). 438p. pap. text 21.95 (*0-8173-1044-4*) Univ. of Alabama Pr.
Sinclair, Upton & Gramm, Kent. Manassas: A Novel of the War. 2000. E-Book 21.95 (*0-585-34983-5*) netLibrary, Inc.
Slouka, Mark. God's Fool: A Novel. 2002. 288p. 24.00 (*0-375-40216-0*) Knopf, Alfred A. Inc.
Smith, Derek. The Sentinels. 2001. 234p. 24.95 (*1-929490-13-5*) Beil, Frederic C. Pub., Inc.
Snelling, Lauraine. Daughter of Twin Oaks. 2000. (Secret Refuge Ser.: Vol. 1). 288p. pap. 11.99 (*1-55661-839-5*) Bethany Hse. Pubs.
—Daughter of Twin Oaks. 2001. 350p. 24.95 o.p. (*0-7862-3684-1*, Five Star) Gale Group.
—Sisters of the Confederacy. 2000. (Secret Refuge Ser.: Vol. 2). (Illus.). 304p. pap. 11.99 (*1-55661-840-9*) Bethany Hse. Pubs.
—Sisters of the Confederacy. l.t. ed. 2002. 349p. 24.95 (*0-7862-3685-X*, Five Star) Gale Group.
Stewart, Fred M. Pomp & Circumstance. 1991. 320p. 19.95 o.p. (*0-525-93309-3*) Dutton/Plume.
—Pomp & Circumstance. l.t. ed. 1992. (General Ser.). 614p. 22.95 o.p. (*0-8161-5373-6*); 16.95 o.p. (*0-8161-5374-4*) Gale Group. (Macmillan Reference USA).
—Pomp & Circumstance. 1992. 496p. mass mkt. 5.99 o.s.i (*0-451-17227-2*, Signet Bks.) NAL.
Stone, Irving. Love Is Eternal: Biographical Novel of Mary Todd & Abraham Lincoln. 1961. 480p. 24.95 o.s.i (*0-385-02040-6*) Doubleday Publishing.
Sullivan, Paul. The Unforgiving Land. Kemnitz, Myrna, ed. 1996. 220p. (YA). pap. 9.99 (*0-88092-256-7*) Royal Fireworks Publishing Co.
Tennant, Emma. Gone with the Wind Sequel. Date not set. (*0-312-26251-5*) St. Martin's Pr.
Thane, Elswyth. Yankee Stranger. 1976. reprint ed. lib. bdg. 25.95 (*0-88411-963-7*) Amereon, Ltd.
—Yankee Stranger. 1993. reprint ed. lib. bdg. 31.95 (*1-56849-229-4*) Buccaneer Bks., Inc.
—Yankee Stranger. 1981. (Williamsburg Ser.: No. 2). lib. bdg. 16.95 o.p. (*0-8161-3166-X*, Macmillan Reference USA) Gale Group.
—Yankee Stranger. unabr. ed. 2001. audio 84.95 (*1-85089-622-4*, 91014) ISIS Audio Bks. GBR. *Dist:* Ulverscroft Large Print Bks., Ltd.
Thoene, Brock & Thoene, Bodie. Cannons of the Comstock. l.t. ed. 2002. lib. bdg. 27.95 (*1-58547-182-8*, Western) Ctr. Point Large Print.
Thomasson, Clarissa. Reconstructing Hillsborough. 1999. 304p. pap. 12.95 (*1-929202-01-6*) Salt Marsh Pubns.
Thompson, Lee B. Addie. 2001. (Five Star First Edition Romance Ser.). 305p. 25.95 (*0-7862-3364-8*, Five Star) Gale Group.
Trotter, William R. The Sands of Pride: A Novel of the Civil War. 2002. 768p. 28.00 (*0-7867-1013-6*, Carroll & Graf Pubs.) Avalon Publishing Group.
Truax, Carlton W. Banjo on My Knee. 1995. 325p. (Orig.). pap. 12.95 (*0-9636845-5-8*) Senior Pr.
Turtledove, Harry. The Great War: American Front. 1999. 576p. mass mkt. 7.99 (*0-345-40560-9*, Del Rey) Ballantine Bks.
—The Great War Vol. 1: American Front. 1998. (Great War Ser.: Vol. 1). 504p. (gr. 7). 25.00 o.s.i (*0-345-40615-X*) Ballantine Bks.
—Sentry Peak. 2001. 512p. pap. 7.99 (*0-671-31846-2*); 2000. 416p. 24.00 (*0-671-57887-1*) Baen Bks.
Van Wyck Mason, F. Armored Giants: A Novel of the Civil War. 1980. 352p. 13.95 o.p. (*0-316-54922-3*) Little Brown & Co.
Thomsen, Brian & Greenberg, Martin H., eds. 2002. 352p. mass mkt. 6.99 o.s.i (*0-425-18377-7*) Berkley Publishing Group.
Vidal, Gore. Lincoln: A Novel. 1988. mass mkt. 4.95 o.p. (*0-345-00885-5*); 1988. mass mkt. 4.95 o.p. (*0-345-00790-5*); 1985. 672p. mass mkt. 6.99 o.s.i (*0-345-31221-X*) Ballantine Bks.
—Lincoln: A Novel. 1995. reprint ed. lib. bdg. 37.95 (*1-56849-626-5*) Buccaneer Bks., Inc.
—Lincoln: A Novel. 2000. (Ace's Exambusters Ser.). 672p. pap. 16.00 (*0-375-70876-6*, Vintage) Knopf Publishing Group.
—Lincoln: A Novel. 1998. 21.00 o.s.i (*0-679-60284-4*); 1993. 768p. 25.00 o.s.i (*0-679-60048-5*); 1984. 657p. 75.00 o.p. (*0-394-53889-7*) Random Hse., Inc.
Vogt, Esther Loewen. The Flame & the Fury. 1998. 173p. pap. 9.99 (*0-88965-143-4*, Horizon Bks.) Christian Pubns., Inc.
—The Flame & the Fury. l.t. ed. 2000. (Candlelight Romance Ser.). 192p. 20.95 (*0-7862-2796-6*) Thorndike Pr.
—The Splendid Vista. 1989. 184p. pap. 5.95 o.p. (*0-8361-3485-0*) Herald Pr.
—The Splendid Vista. l.t. ed. 2000. (Christian Fiction Ser.). 262p. 24.95 o.p. (*0-7862-2799-0*) Thorndike Pr.
Walker, Margaret. Jubilee. 1983. 432p. mass mkt. 6.99 o.s.i (*0-553-27383-3*, Bantam Classics) Bantam Bks.
—Jubilee. 1999. 512p. pap. 8.95 (*0-395-92495-2*); 1966. 15.95 o.p. (*0-395-08288-9*) Houghton Mifflin Co.
—Jubilee. 1967. 11.60 o.p. (*0-606-01623-6*) Turtleback Bks.
West, Mark. Union Gold. 1998. (Illus.). 288p. pap. 19.95 (*1-889901-02-4*) Glencannon Pr.
Williams, Elmer. The Making of a Soldier. 2001. 141p. pap. 11.95 (*0-9714319-0-6*) Adventures In Creative Living.
Williams, Elmer A. The Making of a Soldier. 2002. 140p. E-Book 8.00 o.p. (*1-4010-3843-3*); (Illus.). pap. 20.99 o.p. (*1-4010-3841-7*); (Illus.). text 30.99 o.p. (*1-4010-3842-5*) Xlibris Corp.
Williams, William G. Days of Darkness: The Gettysburg Civilians. 1990. mass mkt. 6.99 o.s.i (*0-425-12353-7*) Berkley Publishing Group.

—Days of Darkness: The Gettysburg Civilians. (Illus.). 1994. 254p. 19.95 o.p. (*0-932751-05-9*); rev. ed. 2001. 268p. lib. bdg. 24.95 (*1-57249-262-7*); 2nd ed. 1994. 254p. 19.95 (*0-942597-59-1*) White Mane Publishing Co., Inc.
Youmans, Marly. The Wolf Pit. 2001. 352p. 24.00 o.p. (*0-374-29195-0*) Farrar, Straus & Giroux.
—The Wolf Pit. 2003. 352p. pap. 14.00 (*0-15-602714-3*, Harvest Bks.) Harcourt Trade Pubs.
Young, Stark. So Red the Rose. 1992. (Southern Classics Ser.). 453p. reprint ed. pap. 15.95 (*1-879941-12-0*, Sanders, J. S. & Co., Inc.) Dee, Ivan R. Pub.
—So Red the Rose. 1978. reprint ed. 18.00 o.p. (*0-89783-006-7*) Larlin Corp.

# V

## VIETNAMESE CONFLICT, 1961-1975—FICTION

Anderson, Kent. Sympathy for the Devil. 2000. 416p. mass mkt. 6.50 (*0-553-58087-6*) Bantam Bks.
—Sympathy for the Devil. 2000. 12.55 (*0-606-19291-3*) Turtleback Bks.
Anthony, Tony. Beneath Buddha's Eyes. 2002. 256p. 25.00 (*1-56649-252-1*) Welcome Rain Pubs.
Babcock, Richard. Bow's Boy: A Novel. 2003. 336p. pap. 14.00 (*0-7432-2728-X*, Scribner) Simon & Schuster.
Baldwin, Eugene. Silent Echoes: Story of a Man Torn Between Duty & Conscience. 2002. 297p. E-Book 8.00 (*1-4010-0698-1*) Xlibris Corp.
Baldwin, Gene. Silent Echoes: Story of a Man Torn Between Duty & Conscience. 2002. 297p. pap. 21.99 (*0-7388-4749-6*); text 31.99 (*0-7388-4750-X*) Xlibris Corp.
Barnes, H. Lee. Gunning for Ho: Vietnam Stories. 2000. (Western Literature Ser.). 170p. pap. 15.00 (*0-87417-346-9*) Univ. of Nevada Pr.
Beaver, Victor R. Sky Soldiers. 2001. pap. 33.95 (*0-7596-1299-4*) 1stBooks Library.
Berent, Mark. Eagle Station. 1993. mass mkt. 5.99 o.s.i (*0-515-11208-9*, Jove) Berkley Publishing Group.
—Eagle Station. 1992. 416p. 22.95 o.p. (*0-399-13722-X*, G. P. Putnam's Sons) Penguin Group (USA) Inc.
—Phantom Leader. 1992. 448p. mass mkt. 5.99 o.s.i (*0-515-10785-9*, Jove) Berkley Publishing Group.
—Rolling Thunder. 1989. mass mkt. 6.50 o.s.i (*0-515-10190-7*, Jove) Berkley Publishing Group.
—Rolling Thunder. 1989. 384p. 19.95 o.p. (*0-399-13439-5*, G. P. Putnam's Sons) Penguin Putnam Bks. for Young Readers.
—Steel Tiger. 1990. mass mkt. 5.99 o.s.i (*0-515-10467-1*, Jove) Berkley Publishing Group.
—Steel Tiger. 1990. 384p. 19.95 o.p. (*0-399-13538-3*, G. P. Putnam's Sons) Penguin Putnam Bks. for Young Readers.
—Storm Flight. 1994. 512p. reprint ed. mass mkt. 5.99 o.s.i (*0-515-11432-4*, Jove) Berkley Publishing Group.
—Storm Flight. 1993. 416p. 22.95 o.p. (*0-399-13814-5*, G. P. Putnam's Sons) Penguin Group (USA) Inc.
Borroel, Roger. The Teenager & the War: Vietnam War Stories of a Screaming Eagle. 1997. (Illus.). 78p. (Orig.). pap. 4.99 (*0-9624727-8-6*) La Villita Pubns.
Buckley, William F., Jr. Tucker's Last Stand: A Blackford Oakes Novel. 1998. (Blackford Oakes Novel Ser.). 320p. reprint ed. pap. 10.95 (*1-888952-73-3*) Cumberland Hse. Publishing.
—Tucker's Last Stand: A Blackford Oakes Novel. 1992. 352p. mass mkt. 5.99 o.p. (*0-06-104165-3*, HarperTorch) Morrow/Avon.
—Tucker's Last Stand: A Blackford Oakes Novel. 1992. 3.99 o.p. (*0-517-09025-2*) Random Hse. Value Publishing.
Buckman, Daniel. Morning Dark. 2003. 224p. 22.95 (*0-312-31462-0*) St. Martin's Pr.
Butler, Robert Olen. A Good Scent from a Strange Mountain: Stories. 2001. 269p. reprint ed. pap. 13.00 (*0-8021-3798-9*, Grove Pr.) Grove/Atlantic, Inc.
Caputo, Philip. Delcorso's Gallery. 1983. 374p. o.p. (*0-03-058277-6*) Holt, Henry & Co.
—DelCorso's Gallery. 2001. 368p. pap. 14.00 (*0-375-72509-1*, Vintage) Knopf Publishing Group.
—Delcorso's Gallery. 1991. 368p. reprint ed. pap. 11.00 (*0-06-098606-9*, Perennial) HarperTrade.
Carmichael, Don. A Trumpet for Freedom: The Legacy: Lost Heritage & War. 2002. (Illus.). 330p. pap. (*1-55369-150-4*) Trafford Publishing.
Carroll, Gerry. North SAR: A Novel of Navy Combat Pilots in Vietnam. McCarthy, Paul, ed. 1992. 416p. mass mkt. 5.99 (*0-671-73183-1*, Pocket) Simon & Schuster.
—North SAR: A Novel of Navy Combat Pilots in Vietnam. 1991. 320p. 21.00 (*0-671-73182-3*, Atria) Simon & Schuster.
Clark, Robert. Love among the Ruins. 2001. 352p. text 24.95 (*0-393-02015-0*) Norton, W. W. & Co., Inc.
—Love among the Ruins: A Novel. 2002. 336p. pap. 13.00 (*1-4000-3030-7*) Random Hse., Inc.
Cohen, Joe. The Minefield. 2002. 152p. pap. 12.00 (*1-58790-029-7*) Regent Pr.
Coonts, Stephen. Flight of the Intruder. abr. ed. 1990. audio 9.95 (*0-88690-314-9*, A20203, Audio Editions Bks. on Cassette) Audio Partners Publishing Corp.
—Flight of the Intruder. unabr. collector's ed. 1987. audio 72.00 (*0-7366-1175-4*, 2097) Books on Tape, Inc.
—Flight of the Intruder. unabr. ed. 1987. audio 19.95 o.p. (*0-930435-32-X*, 110, Bookcassette);Set. audio 73.25 o.p. (*1-56100-027-2*, 840) Brilliance Audio.
—Flight of the Intruder. l.t. ed. 1987. 523p. 19.95 o.p. (*0-8161-4295-5*); 11.95 o.p. (*0-8161-4296-3*) Gale Group. (Macmillan Reference USA).
—Flight of the Intruder. 1986. 329p. 26.95 (*0-87021-200-1*) Naval Institute Pr.
—Flight of the Intruder, unabr. ed. 1986. audio 70.00 (*1-55690-180-1*, 86980E7) Recorded Bks., LLC.
—Flight of the Intruder. 1991. mass mkt. 5.95 (*0-671-72470-3*, Pocket) Simon & Schuster.
—Flight of the Intruder. McCarthy, Paul, ed. 1990. 448p. mass mkt. 6.99 o.s.i (*0-671-70960-7*, Pocket) Simon & Schuster.
—Flight of the Intruder. 1987. mass mkt. 4.95 (*0-671-64012-7*, Pocket) Simon & Schuster.
Crumley, James. One to Count Cadence. unabr. ed. 1997. audio 64.00 (*0-7366-3816-4*, 4484) Books on Tape, Inc.
—One to Count Cadence. 1987. (Vintage Contemporaries Ser.). 352p. pap. 14.00 (*0-394-73559-5*, Vintage) Knopf Publishing Group.
—One to Count Cadence. 1996. 338p. reprint ed. pap. 16.95 o.p. (*0-330-32450-0*) Picador GBR. *Dist:* Trans-Atlantic Pubns., Inc.
Currey, Cecil B. Innocence Dies. 2001. pap. 23.35 (*0-7596-0688-9*) 1stBooks Library.
Currey, Richard. Fatal Light. 1988. 176p. 16.95 o.p. (*0-525-24622-3*, Dutton) Dutton/Plume.
—Fatal Light. 1997. 208p. pap. 12.00 o.p. (*0-395-85995-6*, Mariner Bks.) Houghton Mifflin Co. Trade & Reference Div.
—Fatal Light. 1989. 208p. pap. 10.00 o.p. (*0-14-011945-0*, Penguin Bks.) Viking Penguin.
Davis, Patrick A. The General. 1999. 416p. reprint ed. mass mkt. 6.99 (*0-425-16804-2*) Berkley Publishing Group.
—The General. abr. ed. 1999. audio 7.99 (*1-56740-284-4*, 1749, Paperback Nova Audio Bks.); 1998. audio 26.95 (*1-56740-063-9*, 1213, Bookcassette); 1998. 10p. audio 73.25 (*1-56740-592-4*, 1214, Unabridged Library Editions); Set. 1998. audio 17.95 o.p. (*1-56740-788-9*, 524, Nova Audio Bks.) Brilliance Audio.
—The General. 1998. 352p. 23.95 o.p. (*0-399-14411-0*, G. P. Putnam's Sons) Penguin Group (USA) Inc.
DeCourt, Ann. Never Forget: Greatest Love Story Ever Told. 1998. x, 208p. (Orig.). pap. 14.95 (*0-9664753-1-3*, 1-126) Wabokat Publishing.
Del Vecchio, John M. The 13th Valley. 1984. 688p. mass mkt. 5.95 o.s.i (*0-553-26020-0*) Bantam Bks.
—The 13th Valley. 1999. (Illus.). 640p. pap. 16.95 (*0-312-20081-1*, Saint Martin's Griffin) St. Martin's Pr.
DeMille, Nelson. Up Country. 2002. (Illus.). 720p. 26.95 o.p. (*0-446-51657-0*); 1184p. 26.95 o.p. (*0-446-52993-1*) Warner Bks., Inc.
DeMott, Wes. Walking K. 1998. 295p. 23.95 (*0-9659602-6-9*) Admiral Hse. Publishing.
Dickinson, Richard H. The Silent Men: A Novel. 2002. (Illus.). 304p. 19.95 (*1-59071-004-5*) Rugged Land.
Dinallo, Greg. Final Answers. 1993. 336p. mass mkt. 5.50 (*0-671-73312-5*, Pocket) Simon & Schuster.
—Final Answers. Grose, Ed & Grad, Doug, eds. 1992. 320p. 20.00 (*0-671-73311-7*, Atria) Simon & Schuster.
Duarte, Stella Pope. Let Their Spirits Dance. 2003. 336p. pap. 12.95 (*0-06-008948-2*, Rayo) HarperTrade.
—Let Their Spirits Dance: A Novel. 2002. 336p. 24.95 (*0-06-018637-2*, Rayo) HarperTrade.
—Que Bailen Sus Espiritus. 2003. 352p. pap. 12.95 (*0-06-054824-X*, Rayo) HarperTrade.
DuBois, Brendan. Betrayed. pap. (*0-312-31019-6*, St. Martin's Paperbacks); mass mkt. (*0-312-98757-9*, St. Martin's Paperbacks); 2003. 304p. 24.95 (*0-312-31018-8*, Saint Martin's Minotaur) St. Martin's Pr.
Eickhoff, Randy Lee. Return to Ithaca. 2001. 512p. 25.95 (*0-312-87446-4*); 2002. 496p. reprint ed. pap. 16.95 (*0-312-87538-X*) Doherty, Tom Assocs., LLC. (Forge Bks.).
Ellis, Mary. The Turtle Warrior. 2004. 384p. 24.95 (*0-670-03265-4*) Viking Penguin.
Evans, Elizabeth. Carter Clay: A Novel. 1999. 416p. o.s.i (*0-06-019265-8*, HarperFlamingo) HarperCollins Pubs. Canada, Ltd.
—Carter Clay: A Novel. 2000. 416p. pap. 14.00 (*0-06-092982-0*, Perennial) HarperTrade.
Fleming, Stephen. The Exile of Sergeant Nen. 1986. 186p. 14.95 o.p. (*0-912697-46-6*) Algonquin Bks. of Chapel Hill.
Freadhoff, Chuck. Blue Rain. 2000. 368p. mass mkt. 6.99 (*0-06-109727-6*); 1999. 336p. 24.00 o.p. (*0-06-019217-8*) HarperCollins Pubs.
—Blue Rain. l.t. ed. 1999. (Americana Ser.). 493p. 26.95 (*0-7862-2068-6*) Thorndike Pr.
Funderburk, Robert. Rainbow's End. 1997. (Innocent Years Ser.: Vol. 6). 256p. pap. 8.99 o.p. (*1-55661-465-9*) Bethany Hse. Pubs.
—The Rainbow's End. l.t. ed. 1998. (Innocent Years Ser.: Vol. 6). 339p. 25.95 (*0-7862-1405-8*) Thorndike Pr.
Gilroy, Jack. The Wisdom Box. 2002. 277p. pap. 14.00 (*1-58684-234-X*) Global Academic Publishing.
Gold, Jerome. Sergeant Dickinson. 1999. 180p. 20.00 (*1-56947-162-2*); 2002. 256p. reprint ed. pap. 11.00 (*1-56947-269-6*) Soho Pr., Inc.
Green, Norman. The Angel of Montague Street. 2003. 304p. 24.95 (*0-06-018819-7*) HarperCollins Pubs.
—The Angel of Montague Street: A Novel. 2004. 304p. pap. 13.95 (*0-06-093411-5*, Dark Alley) HarperTrade.
Griffin, W. E. B. The Aviators. 1989. (Brotherhood of War Ser.: No. 8). 464p. mass mkt. 7.99 (*0-515-10053-6*, Jove) Berkley Publishing Group.
—The Aviators. unabr. collector's ed. 1995. (Brotherhood of War Ser.: No. 8). audio 88.00 (*0-7366-3086-4*, 133384) Books on Tape, Inc.
—The Aviators. 2001. (Brotherhood of War Ser.: No. 8). 18.95 (*0-399-13683-5*) Penguin Group (USA) Inc.
—The Aviators. 1988. (Brotherhood of War Ser.: No. 8). 416p. 18.95 o.p. (*0-399-13380-1*, G. P. Putnam's Sons) Penguin Putnam Bks. for Young Readers.
—The Aviators. abr. ed. 1989. (Brotherhood of War Ser.: No. 8). audio 14.95 (*0-671-67501-X*, Simon & Schuster Audioworks) Simon & Schuster Audio.
—The Berets. 1986. (Brotherhood of War Ser.: No. 5). 416p. mass mkt. 7.99 (*0-515-09020-4*, Jove) Berkley Publishing Group.
—The Berets. unabr. ed. 1995. (Brotherhood of War Ser.: No. 5). audio 88.00 Books on Tape, Inc.
—The Berets. 1992. (Brotherhood of War Ser.: No. 5). o.p. (*0-7126-2515-1*) Random Hse. UK, Ltd. GBR. *Dist:* Random Hse. of Canada, Ltd.
—The New Breed. 1988. (Brotherhood of War Ser.: No. 7). 384p. mass mkt. 7.99 (*0-515-09226-6*, Jove) Berkley Publishing Group.
—The New Breed. unabr. ed. 1996. (Brotherhood of War Ser.: No. 7). audio 88.00. audio Books on Tape, Inc.
—The New Breed. 1987. (Brotherhood of War Ser.: No. 7). 416p. 16.95 o.p. (*0-399-13305-4*, G. P. Putnam's Sons) Penguin Putnam Bks. for Young Readers.
Grooms, Anthony. Bombingham. 2002. 320p. pap. 13.95 (*0-345-45293-3*) Random Hse., Inc.
—Bombingham. 2001. 320p. 24.00 (*0-7432-0558-8*, Free Pr.) Simon & Schuster.
Gunn, Gay G. Everlastin' Love. 1994. 220p. pap. 10.95 (*1-885478-02-X*) Genesis Pr., Inc.
Gustafson, Sid. Prisoners of Flight. 2003. 256p. pap. 16.00 (*1-57962-088-4*) Permanent Pr., The.
Hammarberg, Roger. The Pit Fighter. 2000. pap. 8.50 (*0-9671005-0-X*) Hammarberg, Roger .
Hart, William. Never Fade Away: A Novel. 2002. 202p. pap. 12.95 (*1-56474-386-1*) Fithian Pr.
Hasford, Gustav. The Phantom Blooper. 1990. 256p. 17.95 o.s.i (*0-553-05718-9*) Bantam Bks.
Hathaway, Stephen. A Kind of Redemption. 1991. 120p. 17.95 o.p. (*0-8071-1611-4*) Louisiana State Univ. Pr.
Henley, Patricia. In the River Sweet: A Novel. 2002. 304p. 24.00 (*0-375-42127-0*, Pantheon) Knopf Publishing Group.
Henschel, Lee, Jr. Deja 'Nam. 2000. 268p. pap. 21.99 (*0-7388-2979-X*) Xlibris Corp.
Higgins, Jack. Toll for the Brave. 1979. pap. 1.75 o.s.i (*0-449-14105-5*, Fawcett); 1976. mass mkt. 1.50 o.s.i (*0-449-13496-2*) Ballantine Bks.
—Toll for the Brave. 1984. 224p. mass mkt. 4.99 o.p. (*0-451-13271-8*, Signet Bks.) NAL.
—Toll for the Brave. abr. ed. 1995. 16.95 o.p. (*0-7871-0033-1*, 391793) NewStar Media, Inc.
—Toll for the Brave. 1994. mass mkt. o.p. (*0-09-914000-4*) Random Hse. of Canada, Ltd. CAN. *Dist:* Random Hse., Inc.
Hillerman, Tony. Finding Moon. 1995. ix, 319p. 24.00 o.p. (*0-06-017772-1*); 288p. 432.00 o.p. (*0-06-017669-5*); 336p. 150.00 o.p. (*0-06-017287-8*) HarperCollins Pubs.
—Finding Moon. 1996. 368p. mass mkt. 6.99 (*0-06-109261-4*, HarperTorch) Morrow/Avon.
—Finding Moon. l.t. ed. 1996. (Basic Ser.). 448p. 28.95 (*0-7862-0574-1*) Thorndike Pr.
—Finding Moon. 1996. lib. bdg. 13.04 (*0-606-16176-7*) Turtleback Bks.
Hoar, Jere. The Hit. 2003. 302p. 24.95 (*1-893956-34-2*) Context Bks.
—The Hit. 2004. 304p. pap. 14.00 (*0-451-21196-0*) NAL.
Ihimaera, Witi. The Uncle's Story. 2000. 373p. (*0-14-029892-4*) Penguin Group (USA) Inc.
—The Uncle's Story. 2002. (Talanoa: Contemporary Pacific Literature Ser.). 384p. (C). pap. 15.95 (*0-8248-2576-4*) Univ. of Hawaii Pr.
Irving, John. A Prayer for Owen Meany. 1999. 7.99 (*0-345-91555-0*); 1990. 640p. mass mkt. 7.99 (*0-345-36179-2*, Ballantine Bks.); 1989. mass mkt. 4.95 o.s.i (*0-345-36352-3*); 1997. 560p. reprint ed. pap. 14.95 (*0-345-41797-6*, Ballantine Bks.) Ballantine Bks.
—A Prayer for Owen Meany. 1990. (GER.). 864p. (*3-257-01850-9*) Diogenes Verlag AG CHE. *Dist:* International Bk. Import Service, Inc.
—A Prayer for Owen Meany. 2002. (Illus.). 672p. 22.95 (*0-679-64259-5*, Modern Library) Random House Adult Trade Publishing Group.
—A Prayer for Owen Meany. 1990. 14.04 (*0-606-16249-6*) Turtleback Bks.
Jaynes, Thomas E. Challenge the Death Angel. 1999. 280p. pap. 12.95 (*1-893652-08-4*, Writers Club Pr.) iUniverse, Inc.
Just, Ward. A Dangerous Friend. 2000. 256p. pap. 13.00 (*0-618-05670-X*) Houghton Mifflin Co.
Kilmer, Nicholas. Harmony in Flesh & Black, Vol. 23. 2000. (Missing Mysteries Ser.: Vol. 23). 222p. pap. 14.95 (*1-890208-47-7*) Poisoned Pen Pr.
King, Laurie R. Keeping Watch. 2004. 400p. pap. 12.00 (*0-553-38252-7*); 2003. 400p. 23.95 (*0-553-80191-0*); 2003. E-Book 19.50 (*0-553-89726-8*) Bantam Bks.
—Keeping Watch. audio 34.99 (*1-4025-3627-5*) Recorded Bks., LLC.
—Keeping Watch. l.t. ed. 2003. (Basic Ser.). 29.95 (*0-7862-5498-X*) Thorndike Pr.
King, Stephen. Hearts in Atlantis. 2001. E-Book 9.99 (*1-59061-258-2*) Adobe Systems, Inc.
—Hearts in Atlantis. l.t. ed. (Thorndike/G. K. Hall Paperback Bestsellers Ser.). 2000. 760p. pap. 28.95 (*0-7838-8738-8*); 1999. 732p. 31.95 (*0-7838-8737-X*) Gale Group. (Macmillan Reference USA).
—Hearts in Atlantis. 1999. 528p. 28.00 (*0-684-85351-5*, Scribner); 1999. E-Book 28.00 (*0-684-84490-7*, Scribner); 2000. 688p. reprint ed. pap. 7.99 (*0-671-02424-8*, Pocket); 2000. 528p. reprint ed. 7.99 (*0-671-04214-9*, Pocket); 2001. 688p. reprint ed. mass mkt. 7.99 o.s.i (*0-7434-3621-0*, Pocket) Simon & Schuster.
—Hearts in Atlantis. 2001. pap. 49.95 incl. audio compact disk (*0-7435-0987-0*); pap. 49.95 incl. audio compact disk (*0-7435-0987-0*) Simon & Schuster Audio. (Simon & Schuster Audioworks).
—Hearts in Atlantis. 2000. 14.04 (*0-606-19496-7*) Turtleback Bks.
Kingston, Maxine Hong. The Fifth Book of Peace. 2003. 416p. 26.00 (*0-679-44075-5*) Knopf, Alfred A. Inc.
Kraus, Lani S. Dura Mater. 2000. 300p. E-Book 24.95 incl. audio compact disk (*0-9701368-2-X*, Written Word, The) Hornkohl Communications.
La Fountaine, George. The Long Walk. 1986. 256p. 17.95 o.p. (*0-399-13130-2*) Putnam Publishing Group, The.
Laughton, K. C. Not Quite Men, No Longer Boys. 1999. (Illus.). 352p. pap. 17.95 (*1-86465-006-0*) IAD Pr./Jukurrpa Bks. AUS. *Dist:* International Specialized Bk. Services.
Lax, Scott. The Year That Trembled: A Novel. 1998. 192p. 21.95 (*0-8397-8660-3*) Eriksson, Paul S. Pub.
Leib, Franklin Allen. The Fire Dream. 2003. 592p. mass mkt. 7.99 (*0-7434-4556-2*) ibooks, Inc.
Levinson, Barry. Sixty-Six. 2003. 288p. 24.00 (*0-7679-1533-X*) Broadway Bks.
Maillard, Keith. The Clarinet Polka. Date not set. pap. (*0-312-30890-6*, Saint Martin's Griffin); mass mkt. (*0-312-98689-0*, St. Martin's Paperbacks) St. Martin's Pr.
McAuliffe, Lawrence. Purple Sun. 2003. 240p. per. 12.95 (*0-942679-27-X*) Upper Access, Inc.
McQ, Dan. Fly the Friendly Skies of Laos? 2001. 269p. pap. 21.99 (*1-4010-1935-8*); E-Book 8.00 (*1-4010-1883-1*) Xlibris Corp.
Mooney, Robert. Father of the Man: A Novel. 2002. 240p. 23.00 (*0-375-42204-8*, Pantheon) Knopf Publishing Group.
Moreau, Donna. Waiting Wives. 320p. 2005. pap. 13.00 (*0-7434-7078-8*); 2004. (*0-7434-7077-X*) Simon & Schuster. (Atria).
Morris, Mary McGarry. Fiona Range. l.t. ed. 2000. 28.95 (*1-56895-882-X*, Wheeler Publishing, Inc.) Gale Group.
—Fiona Range. 2000. 400p. 24.95 o.s.i (*0-670-89156-8*, Viking); 2001. 432p. reprint ed. 14.00 (*0-14-100184-4*) Viking Penguin.
Mulligan, John. Shopping Cart Soldiers. 1997. 239p. 22.95 (*1-880684-48-9*) Curbstone Pr.
—Shopping Cart Soldiers. 1999. 256p. pap. 12.00 (*0-684-85605-0*, Touchstone) Simon & Schuster.

Mullins, John F. Napalm Dreams. 2004. 352p. mass mkt. 6.99 (*0-7434-7767-7*, Pocket Star) Simon & Schuster.

Newman, Paul A., et al. Nine from the Ninth. 2002. 148p. pap. 11.95 (*0-595-25305-9*, Writers Club Pr.) iUniverse, Inc.

Norton, Bruce H. Stingray. 2000. (Illus.). 368p. mass mkt. 6.99 (*0-8041-1026-3*, Ballantine Bks.) Ballantine Bks.

Nunez, Sigrid. For Rouenna. 2001. 208p. 22.00 o.p. (*0-374-25430-3*) Farrar, Straus & Giroux.

—For Rouenna. l.t. ed. 2001. 273p. 27.95 (*1-58724-217-6*, Wheeler Publishing, Inc.) Gale Group.

—For Rouenna: A Novel. 2002. 240p. pap. 13.00 (*0-312-42063-3*) Picador.

O'Brien, Tim. The Things They Carried. 1998. 272p. pap. 14.95 (*0-7679-0289-0*) Broadway Bks.

—The Things They Carried. 1990. 273p. 19.95 o.p. (*0-395-51598-X*) Houghton Mifflin Co. Trade & Reference Div.

—The Things They Carried. 1997. (C). pap. text (*0-8013-3149-8*) Longman Publishing Group.

—The Things They Carried. 1991. (Contemporary American Fiction Ser.). 288p. (C). pap. 12.95 o.p. (*0-14-014773-X*) Penguin Group (USA) Inc.

Palmer, Catherine & Stoks, Peggy. The Loved One. 2003. (Moving Fiction Ser.). 175p. 12.99 (*0-8423-7214-8*) Tyndale Hse. Pubs.

Pearce, Jonathan. Thing with Feathers: A Different Romance. 2003. 179p. per. 14.95 (*1-59411-012-3*) Writers' Collective, The.

Pelecanos, George P. Hard Revolution. 2004. 384p. 24.95 (*0-316-60897-1*) Little Brown & Co.

—Hard Revolution. abr. ed. 2004. audio 25.98 (*1-58621-600-7*); audio compact disk 31.98 (*1-58621-601-5*) Time Warner AudioBooks.

Peterson, Robert. Rites of Passage: Odyssey of a Grunt. 2001. (Illus.). 576p. mass mkt. 6.99 (*0-345-44694-1*, Ballantine Bks.) Ballantine Bks.

Phillips, Jayne Anne. Machine Dreams. l.t. ed. 1985. (General Ser.). 456p. 18.95 o.p. (*0-8161-3819-2*, Macmillan Reference USA) Gale Group.

—Machine Dreams. 1999. 352p. pap. 14.00 (*0-375-70525-2*) Knopf, Alfred A. Inc.

—Machine Dreams. 1984. 352p. 16.95 o.p. (*0-525-24252-X*, 01646-490, Seymour Lawrence) NAL.

—Machine Dreams. 1985. mass mkt. 3.95 (*0-671-53290-1*, Pocket) Simon & Schuster.

—Machine Dreams. Rosenman, Jane, ed. 1992. 400p. reprint ed. pap. (*0-671-74235-3*, Pocket) Simon & Schuster.

Porcelli, Joe. The Photograph. Wyrick, Charles L., Jr., ed. 1995. 346p. 22.95 (*0-941711-30-7*) Wyrick & Co.

Potter, G. W. Lessons from a Secret War. 1997. 224p. pap. 12.95 (*0-533-12355-0*) Vantage Pr., Inc.

Pratt, George. Enemy Ace: War Idyll. Helfer, Andrew, ed. 1998. (Illus.). 128p. pap. 14.95 (*0-930289-78-1*); 1991. 144p. 75.00 o.s.i (*1-56389-010-0*); 1990. 128p. 24.95 o.s.i (*0-930289-65-X*) DC Comics.

—Enemy Ace: War Idyll. Helfer, Andrew, ed. 1992. (Illus.). 128p. reprint ed. mass mkt. 14.99 (*0-446-39365-7*) Warner Bks., Inc.

Price, Reynolds. Noble Norfleet. 2003. 320p. pap. 13.00 (*0-7432-0418-2*); 2002. E-Book (*0-7432-3393-X*); 2002. (Illus.). 320p. 26.00 (*0-7432-0417-4*) Simon & Schuster. (Scribner).

Quintana, Leroy V. La Promesa & Other Stories. 2002. (Chicana & Chicano Visions of the Americas Ser.: Vol. 1). 192p. 24.95 (*0-8061-3449-6*) Univ. of Oklahoma Pr.

Reife, Barbara. A Family Affair. 1999. (First Edition Romance Ser.). 179p. 25.95 (*0-7862-2138-0*, Five Star) Gale Group.

Riedel, Gary. Seasons of the Pearl. 2000. 212p. pap. 21.99 (*0-7388-2781-9*); text 31.99 (*0-7388-2780-0*) Xlibris Corp.

Salinger, Steven D. Behold the Fire. 1998. 432p. mass mkt. 6.99 (*0-446-60620-0*); 1997. 384p. 23.00 o.p. (*0-446-52079-9*) Warner Bks., Inc.

Schow, Vione I. Phay Vanneth: Dead or Alive? 2002. 180p. pap. 12.95 (*1-55517-605-4*, Bonneville Bks.) Cedar Fort, Inc./CFI Distribution.

Silver, Jim. Kill Zone: A Novel. 1999. 320p. 23.00 (*0-684-84289-0*, Simon & Schuster) Simon & Schuster.

Smeds, Dave. Piper in the Night. 2002. 244p. 37.95 (*1-58715-575-3*) Wildside Pr.

Spencer, Elizabeth. The Night Travellers. 2002. (Voices of the South Ser.). 384p. pap. 17.95 (*0-8071-2792-2*) Louisiana State Univ. Pr.

—The Night Travellers. 1992. (Contemporay American Fiction Ser.). 384p. reprint ed. pap. 10.00 o.p. (*0-14-015281-4*, Penguin Bks.) Penguin Group (USA) Inc.

—The Night Travellers. 1991. 352p. 21.95 o.p. (*0-670-83915-9*) Viking Penguin.

Standley, Gerald B. The Red Caduceus. 2003. 225p. 24.95 (*1-932162-16-X*) Benoy Publishing.

Stone, Robert. Dog Soldiers. 1978. 352p. mass mkt. 2.25 o.s.i (*0-345-27574-8*); 1975. mass mkt. 1.95 o.s.i (*0-345-24558-X*) Ballantine Bks.

—Dog Soldiers. 1974. 352p. reprint ed. 11.95 o.p. (*0-395-18481-9*) Houghton Mifflin Co.

—Dog Soldiers. rev. ed. 1997. 352p. pap. 13.00 (*0-395-86025-3*, Mariner Bks.) Houghton Mifflin Co. Trade & Reference Div.

—Dog Soldiers. 1987. 352p. pap. 12.95 o.p. (*0-14-009835-6*, Penguin Bks.) Viking Penguin.

Taylor, Robert. The Innocent: A Novel. 1997. 256p. (Orig.). pap. 14.95 (*1-56474-230-X*) Fithian Pr.

Tetrick, Byron R., ed. In the Shadow of the Wall: Vietnam Stories That Might Have Been. 2002. 320p. pap. 14.95 (*1-58182-252-9*) Cumberland Hse. Publishing.

Tomes, Jonathan P. Lawful Orders. 1998. 280p. 24.95 (*1-880483-00-9*) Veterans Pr.

Tuck, Lily. Siam: or The Woman Who Shot a Man. 2000. 192p. reprint ed. 12.00 (*0-452-28206-3*, Plume) Dutton/Plume.

Turnbull, Rick. Gum's Story. 2002. 304p. 24.95 (*1-891799-22-3*) Harbor Hse.

Van, Hong. Doi Vao Thu. 2002. Tr. of Autumn. (VIE.). 310p. pap. 10.00 (*1-889880-08-6*) Nguoi Dan.

Vega Yunqué, Edgardo. No Matter How Much You Promise to Cook or Pay the Rent You Blew It Cauze Bill Bailey Ain't Never Coming Home Again. 2003. 656p. 25.00 (*0-374-22311-4*); pap. (*0-374-96112-3*) Farrar, Straus & Giroux.

Watson, James, Jr. & Roberts, Mark. Operation Artful Dodger. 1998. (SEALs Top Secret Ser.: No. 1). pap. 5.99 (*0-380-78712-1*, Avon Bks.) Morrow/Avon.

Webb, James. Fields of Fire. 1982. 432p. mass mkt. 4.95 o.s.i (*0-553-25679-3*) Bantam Bks.

—The Fields of Fire. 2001. (Illus.). 496p. mass mkt. 7.50 (*0-553-58385-9*, Spectra) Bantam Bks.

—Fields of Fire. 2000. (Bluejacket Bks.). (Illus.). 344p. reprint ed. pap. 17.95 (*1-55750-963-8*) Naval Institute Pr.

—Fields of Fire. Rubenstein, Julie, ed. 1991. 432p. reprint ed. mass mkt. 6.99 (*0-671-73138-6*, Pocket) Simon & Schuster.

Wetterling, J. D. Son of Thunder. 1998. 280p. 22.95 (*0-9630731-8-4*, 9630731) Rivilo Bks.

White, Jack M. The Keeper of the Ferris Wheel. 1993. 260p. 10.00 (*0-9636031-9-1*) Ashleigh-Reid Pubs.

—The Keeper of the Ferris Wheel: A Novel. 1995. 272p. 21.50 o.p. (*1-55611-453-2*) Fine, Donald I. Bks.

Willard, Tom. The Stone Ponies. 320p. 2001. (Black Sabre Chronicles Ser.). mass mkt. 6.99 (*0-8125-6478-2*); 2000. (Black Sabre Chronicles Ser.: No. 4). 24.95 o.p. (*0-312-85763-2*) Doherty, Tom Assocs., LLC. (Forge Bks.).

Williamson, Richard. In Black & White. 2003. 184p. pap. 19.95 (*1-59286-594-1*) PublishAmerica, Inc.

Wilson, Edward. A River in May. 2002. 256p. pap. 13.95 (*1-900850-72-9*) Arcadia Bks. GBR. *Dist:* Consortium Bk. Sales & Distribution.

Wilson, Tom. Termite Hill. 2002. (Illus.). 624p. mass mkt. 7.99 (*0-7434-3481-1*) ibooks, Inc.

Wood, Robert W. Goodbye Vietnam. 2nd ed. 2003. (Illus.). 120p. 16.00 (*1-59096-000-9*) Varangon Corp.

Wortham, Rick. Altered Spring. 1998. 304p. pap. 12.95 o.p. (*1-56167-418-4*) American Literary Pr., Inc.

Wright, Stephen. Meditations in Green. 1984. 336p. pap. 3.95 o.p. (*0-553-24645-3*) Bantam Bks.

—Meditations in Green. 2nd ed. 1988. 352p. pap. 8.95 o.p. (*0-684-18973-9*, Macmillan Reference USA) Gale Group.

—Meditations in Green. 2003. 352p. pap. 14.00 (*0-375-71293-3*, Vintage) Knopf Publishing Group.

# W

## WORLD WAR, 1914-1918—FICTION

Anderson, David Martin. The Truth about Snipe. Abreau, Kevin, ed. 2000. 128p. pap. 9.99 (*1-892617-12-9*) Conroca Publishing.

Barker, Pat. The Eye in the Door. 288p. 1995. pap. 14.00 (*0-452-27272-6*, Abrahams, William Bks.); 1994. 20.95 o.p. (*0-525-93808-7*, Dutton) Dutton/Plume.

—The Eye in the Door. l.t. ed. 1996. 25.95 o.p. (*1-56895-350-X*, Wheeler Publishing, Inc.) Gale Group.

—The Eye in the Door. unabr. ed. 1997. audio 51.00 (*0-7887-0819-8*, 94969E7) Recorded Bks., LLC.

—The Ghost Road. 1995. 256p. 21.95 o.p. (*0-525-94191-6*, Abrahams, William Bks.) Dutton/Plume.

—The Ghost Road. 1996. o.p. (*0-452-15520-7*) NAL.

—Ghost Road. 1996. 288p. pap. 14.00 (*0-452-27672-1*, Plume) Dutton/Plume.

—The Ghost Road, Vol. 3. l.t. ed. 1996. 26.95 (*1-56895-380-1*, Wheeler Publishing, Inc.) Gale Group.

—Regeneration. (William Abrahams Book Ser.). 256p. 1993. pap. 14.00 (*0-452-27007-3*); 1992. 20.00 o.p. (*0-525-93427-8*) Dutton/Plume. (Abrahams, William Bks.).

—Regeneration. l.t. ed. 1996. 26.95 (*1-56895-320-8*, Wheeler Publishing, Inc.) Gale Group.

—Regeneration. unabr. ed. 1996. audio 60.00 (*0-7887-0658-6*, 94835E7) Recorded Bks., LLC.

Beach, Edward L., Jr. Run Silent, Run Deep. l.t. ed. 1992. 22.95 o.p. (*0-7927-1314-1*); pap. 20.95 o.p. (*0-7927-1313-3*) BBC Audiobooks America.

—Run Silent, Run Deep. 1988. 432p. mass mkt. 3.95 o.s.i (*0-8217-2408-8*, Zebra Bks.) Kensington Publishing Corp.

Besson, Philippe. In the Absence of Men. Wynne, Frank, tr. 2003. 176p. 21.00 (*0-7867-1161-2*, Carroll & Graf Pubs.) Avalon Publishing Group.

Boyd, Thomas. Through the Wheat: A Novel of the World War I Marines. 1978. (Lost American Fiction Ser.). 286p. reprint ed. 8.95 o.p. (*0-8093-0855-X*) Southern Illinois Univ. Pr.

—Through the Wheat: A Novel of the World War I Marines. 2000. 266p. pap. 13.95 (*0-8032-6168-3*, Bison Bks.) Univ. of Nebraska Pr.

Bromfield, Louis. The Green Bay Tree. 2002. 390p. pap. 14.00 (*1-888683-64-3*) Wooster Bk. Co., The.

Buchan, John. Greenmantle. 1999. E-Book 2.49 (*1-58627-246-2*) Electric Umbrella Publishing.

—Greenmantle. 1986. pap. 9.95 o.p. (*0-87923-598-5*); 1988. 345p. reprint ed. 19.95 o.p. (*0-933852-84-3*) Godine, David R. Pub.

—The Runagates Club. 1997. (Pocket Classics Ser.). 192p. pap. 10.95 (*0-7509-1159-X*) Sutton Publishing.

Burroughs, Edgar Rice. Beyond Thirty: The Lost Continent. 2001. (Bison Frontiers of Imagination Ser.). 124p. reprint ed. pap. 9.95 (*0-8032-6184-5*, Bison Bks.) Univ. of Nebraska Pr.

Carpenter, Clarence A. Take the Wings of the Morning. 2002. 272p. pap. (*1-55369-242-X*) Trafford Publishing.

Cavanaugh, Jack. The Allies. 2010. (American Family Portrait Ser.). 475p. pap. 13.99 (*1-56476-588-1*) Cook Communications Ministries.

Celine, Louis-Ferdinand. London Bridge. Di Bernardi, Dominic, tr. from FRE. 1995. 449p. 23.95 (*1-56478-071-6*); 1999. 390p. reprint ed. pap. 14.50 (*1-56478-175-5*) Dalkey Archive Pr.

Collins, Max Allan. The Lusitania Murders. 2002. 272p. mass mkt. 6.99 (*0-425-18688-1*, Prime Crime) Berkley Publishing Group.

Cook, Gloria. Touch the Silence. 2003. 288p. 26.99 (*0-7278-5894-7*) Severn Hse. Pubs., Ltd.

Cooper, Natasha. A Place of Safety: A Trish Maguire Mystery. 2003. 320p. 24.95 (*0-312-31936-3*, Saint Martin's Minotaur) St. Martin's Pr.

cummings, e e. The Enormous Room. 2002. (Dover Thrift Editions Ser.). (Illus.). 224p. pap. 3.00 (*0-486-42120-1*) Dover Pubns., Inc.

Daly, Lorraine. Sherlock Holmes & the Lusitania. Wilks, Ian, ed. 1998. 192p. 30.00 (*0-86025-291-4*) Henry, Ian Pubns. GBR. *Dist:* Empire Publishing Service.

Davey, Chris. The Aviator's Apprentice. 2000. (Will Turner Flight Logs Ser.: Pt. 1). (Illus.). 484p. pap. 18.95 (*0-9676050-3-2*) Lucky Pr., LLC.

Davis, Margaret Thomson. The Clydesiders. 2001. 278p. pap. 11.95 (*1-903265-06-1*) B & W Publishing GBR. *Dist:* Interlink Publishing Group, Inc.

Dos Passos, John. Three Soldiers. E-Book 3.95 (*0-594-04743-9*) 1873 Pr.

—Three Soldiers. 1988. 433p. pap. 9.95 o.p. (*0-88184-413-6*, Carroll & Graf Pubs.) Avalon Publishing Group.

—Three Soldiers. 1997. 464p. mass mkt. 5.95 o.s.i (*0-553-21456-X*, Bantam Classics) Bantam Bks.

—Three Soldiers, 001. 1964. pap. 12.95 o.p. (*0-395-08389-3*, 40) Houghton Mifflin Co. Trade & Reference Div.

—Three Soldiers. 1997. 432p. mass mkt. 6.95 o.s.i (*0-451-52645-7*, Signet Classics) NAL.

—Three Soldiers. 2002. (Modern Library Classics). 416p. pap. 9.95 (*0-375-76086-5*, Modern Library) Random House Adult Trade Publishing Group.

—Three Soldiers. 1997. (Twentieth Century Classics Ser.). 400p. pap. 11.00 (*0-14-118027-7*, Penguin Classics) Viking Penguin.

Drummond, Emma. Act of Valour. 1998. 25.95 o.p. (*0-312-18521-9*) St. Martin's Pr.

Dugain, Marc. The Officers' Ward. 2002. 136p. pap. 11.00 (*1-56947-307-2*) Soho Pr., Inc.

—The Officer's Ward. Curtis, Howard, tr. from FRE. 2001. 143p. 21.00 (*1-56947-265-3*) Soho Pr., Inc.

—The Officers' Ward. Curtis, Howard, tr. l.t. ed. 2002. (General Ser.). 24.95 (*0-7862-4482-8*) Thorndike Pr.

Farrell, J. G. Troubles. 1986. 448p. mass mkt. 4.95 o.p. (*0-88184-269-9*, Carroll & Graf Pubs.) Avalon Publishing Group.

—Troubles. 2002. (New York Review Books Classics Ser.). 512p. pap. 16.95 (*1-59017-018-0*) New York Review of Bks., Inc., The.

Findley, Timothy. The Wars. 1983. mass mkt. 3.95 o.s.i (*0-440-39239-X*); 1977. 8.95 o.s.i (*0-440-09397-X*, Delacorte Pr.) Dell Publishing.

Fisher, Alan. The Rage of Angels. 1997. 224p. 21.00 o.p. (*0-7867-0409-8*, Carroll & Graf Pubs.) Avalon Publishing Group.

Fitzgerald, F. Scott. This Side of Paradise. 2001. (Modern Library Classics). 352p. pap. 9.95 (*0-375-75886-0*, Modern Library) Random House Adult Trade Publishing Group.

Ford, Ford Madox. No Enemy: A Tale of Reconstruction. 2002. 220p. pap. 16.95 (*1-85754-565-6*) Carcanet Pr., Ltd. GBR. *Dist:* Independent Pubs. Group.

—No Enemy: A Tale of Reconstruction. 1984. 302p. reprint ed. pap. o.p. (*0-88001-062-2*, Ecco) HarperTrade.

—No More Parades: A Novel. 1999. 305p. text 29.95 (*1-56000-468-1*) Transaction Pubs.

—Parade's End. 1997. 600p. pap. 27.95 (*1-85754-342-4*) Carcanet Pr., Ltd. GBR. *Dist:* Paul & Co. Pubs. Consortium, Inc.

—Parade's End. 2001. 864p. pap. 19.00 (*0-14-118661-5*, Penguin Classics) Viking Penguin.

Fullerton, Alexander. The Blooding of the Guns. 1998. 286p. pap. text o.s.i (*0-7515-1620-1*) Little Brown & Co.

—The Blooding of the Guns. (Everard Naval Ser.: Vol. 1). 286p. 2002. pap. 13.00 (*1-56947-313-7*); 2001. 24.00 (*1-56947-259-9*) Soho Pr., Inc.

—The Blooding of the Guns. l.t. ed. 1987. (Ulverscroft Large Print Ser.). 512p. 29.99 o.p. (*0-7089-1726-7*, Ulverscroft) Thorpe, F. A. Pubs. GBR. *Dist:* Ulverscroft Large Print Bks., Ltd., Ulverscroft Large Print Canada, Ltd.

—The Blooding of the Guns. 1984. 192p. 12.95 o.s.i (*0-8027-0780-7*) Walker & Co.

—Sixty Minutes for St. George. 2003. 320p. pap. 13.00 (*1-56947-321-8*); 2002. 308p. 24.00 (*1-56947-293-9*) Soho Pr., Inc.

—Sixty Minutes for St. George. l.t. ed. 1988. (Ulverscroft Large Print Ser.). 480p. 29.99 o.p. (*0-7089-1761-5*, Ulverscroft) Thorpe, F. A. Pubs. GBR. *Dist:* Ulverscroft Large Print Bks., Ltd., Ulverscroft Large Print Canada, Ltd.

Gerard, Philip. Hatteras Light. 1997. (Salem Selections Ser.). 256p. (Orig.). pap. 12.95 (*0-89587-166-1*) Blair, John F. Pub.

Gibbon, Lewis Grassic. The Thirteenth Disciple. 2001. 274p. pap. 12.95 (*1-873631-55-3*) B & W Publishing GBR. *Dist:* Interlink Publishing Group, Inc.

Gilbert, Michael Francis. Over & Out. l.t. ed. 1999. (Paperback Ser.). 287p. pap. 22.95 (*0-7838-8736-1*, Macmillan Reference USA) Gale Group.

Glasgow, Ellen. The Sheltered Life. 24.95 (*0-88411-646-8*) Amereon, Ltd.

—The Sheltered Life. 1985. 408p. reprint ed. pap. 23.00 (*0-15-681690-3*, Harvest Bks.) Harcourt Trade Pubs.

—The Sheltered Life. 1994. 352p. (C). pap. 14.95 (*0-8139-1514-7*) Univ. Pr. of Virginia.

Goodrich, Marcus. Delilah: A Novel about a U.S. Navy Destroyer & the Epic Struggles of Her Crew. 2000. (Illus.). 526p. pap. 19.95 (*1-58574-129-9*, Lyons Pr.) Globe Pequot Pr., The.

Greene, Sheldon. Burnt Umber. 2001. 300p. pap. 14.95 o.p. (*0-9679520-1-8*) Leapfrog Pr.

Hemingway, Ernest. A Farewell to Arms. Bloom, Harold, ed. 1999. (Bloom's Reviews Comprehensive Research & Study Guides). 79p. (J). (gr. 4-7). pap. 4.95 (*0-7910-4120-4*) Chelsea Hse. Pubs.

—A Farewell to Arms. 1982. 336p. pap. 4.95 o.s.i (*0-684-17469-3*); 1978. 334p. 35.00 (*0-684-15562-1*); 1929. 332p. pap. 11.95 o.s.i (*0-684-71797-2*); 1920. 336p. 14.95 o.s.i (*0-684-10236-6*) Gale Group. (Macmillan Reference USA).

—A Farewell to Arms. 1929. (Illus.). 358p. (C). pap. text 24.20 o.p. (*0-02-352980-6*, Macmillan College) Prentice Hall PTR.

Hill, Grace Livingston. The Red Signal. reprint ed. lib. bdg. 23.95 (*0-89190-047-0*, Rivercity Pr.) Amereon, Ltd.

—The Red Signal, No. 51. 1978. pap. 1.75 o.p. (*0-553-13939-8*, X13939-8) Bantam Bks.

—The Red Signal. 1999. 295 p. (*0-7540-3616-2*, Macmillan Reference USA) Gale Group.

—The Red Signal. l.t. ed. 1999. 296p. pap. 23.95 (*0-7838-0420-2*) Thorndike Pr.

—The Red Signal. 1993. (Grace Livingston Hill Ser.: Vol. 51). pap. 4.99 o.p. (*0-8423-5402-6*) Tyndale Hse. Pubs.

Hill, Grace Livingston, contrib. by. The Red Signal. (*0-7540-3615-4*) BBC Audiobooks America.

Hull, Jonathan. Losing Julia. 2001. 400p. mass mkt. 6.99 (*0-440-23485-9*, Delta) Dell Publishing.

—Losing Julia. l.t. ed. 2000. 26.95 o.p. (*1-56895-827-7*, Wheeler Publishing, Inc.) Gale Group.

Itani, Frances. Deafening: A Novel. l.t. ed. 2003. 639p. 29.95 (*0-7862-6010-6*) Gale Group.

—Deafening: A Novel. 2003. 368p. 24.00 (*0-87113-902-2*, Atlantic Monthly Pr.) Grove/Atlantic, Inc.

Jack, Donald. Three Cheers for Me. 2001. 336p. pap. 0.00 (*0-7710-4380-5*) McClelland & Stewart/Tundra Bks.

Historical Events

Japrisot, Sebastien. A Very Long Engagement. Coverdale, Linda, tr. from FRE. 1994. Tr. of Long Dimanche de Finacailles. 336p. pap. 14.00 (*0-452-27297-1*, Plume) Dutton/Plume.
—A Very Long Engagement. 1993. Tr. of Long Dimanche de Finacailles. 327p. 23.00 o.p. (*0-374-28335-4*) Farrar, Straus & Giroux.
Jones, David. In Parenthesis. 2003. (New York Review Books Classics Ser.). (Illus.). 224p. 14.00 (*1-59017-036-9*) New York Review of Bks., Inc., The.
Jones, David & Jones, Pauline. In Parenthesis. 1963. pap. 2.45 o.p. (*0-670-00139-2*) Penguin Group (USA) Inc.
Kerschbaumer, Marie-Therese & Bangerter, Lowell A. Woman's Face of Resistance. Bangerter, Lowell A., tr. from GER. 1996. (Studies in Austrian Literature, Culture & Thought). Orig. Title: Der Weibliche Name des Widerstands. 260p. pap. 19.95 (*1-57241-027-2*) Ariadne Pr.
Kirk, Susan Van. CliffsNotes TM All Quiet on the Western Front. 1999. E-Book 5.99 (*0-8220-7005-7*, Cliff Notes) Wiley, John & Sons, Inc.
Kolesnikoff, Lee A. The Tempest: Calista's Song. 2002. (Illus.). 398p. pap. (*1-55369-385-X*) Trafford Publishing.
Linscott, Gillian. Hanging on the Wire. 1992. 215p. 17.95 o.p. (*0-312-08806-X*, Saint Martin's Minotaur) St. Martin's Pr.
Lussu, Emilio. Sardinian Brigade. 2000. (Lost Treasures Ser.). 286p. pap. 14.95 (*1-85375-360-2*) Prion GBR. *Dist:* Trafalgar Square.
MacLennan, Hugh. Barometer Rising. 1996. (New Canadian Library: Vol. 8). 240p. mass mkt. 6.95 (*0-7710-9991-6*) McClelland & Stewart/Tundra Bks.
MacNeil, Robert. Burden of Desire. 1993. 576p. mass mkt. 5.99 o.s.i (*0-440-21509-9*) Dell Publishing.
—Burden of Desire. l.t. ed. 1996. pap. 23.95 o.p. (*1-56895-303-8*, Wheeler Publishing, Inc.) Gale Group.
Major, Kevin. No Man's Land. 264p. 2001. (Illus.). pap. (*0-385-65886-9*, Anchor Canada); 1997. pap. o.s.i (*0-385-25579-9*) Doubleday Canada, Ltd. CAN. *Dist:* Random Hse., Inc.
Malouf, David. Fly Away Peter. l.t. ed. 1991. pap. 9.95 o.p. (*1-86340-109-1*, AUS019) BBC Audiobooks America.
—Fly Away Peter. 1998. 144p. pap. 15.00 (*0-679-77670-2*, Vintage) Knopf Publishing Group.
Malraux, André. The Walnut Trees of Altenburg. Fielding, A. W., tr. from FRE. 1989. 224p. lib. bdg. 35.00 (*0-86527-392-8*) Fertig, Howard Inc.
—The Walnut Trees of Altenburg. Fielding, A. W., tr. 1992. (Phoenix Fiction Ser.). 226p. pap. 14.00 (*0-226-50289-9*) Univ. of Chicago Pr.
Manning, Frederic. The Middle Parts of Fortune. 1979. pap. 4.95 o.p. (*0-452-25202-4*, Z5202, Plume) Dutton/Plume.
—The Middle Parts of Fortune. 1978. 8.95 o.p. (*0-312-53185-0*) St. Martin's Pr.
—The Middle Parts of Fortune. 1990. 272p. pap. 8.95 o.p. (*0-14-018461-9*, Penguin Classics) Viking Penguin.
Maugham, W. Somerset. Ashenden, or, The British Agent. 24.95 (*0-89190-213-9*) Amereon, Ltd.
—Ashenden, or, The British Agent. (Short Story Index Reprint Ser.). reprint ed. 14.50 (*0-8369-4052-0*); 1977. 27.95 (*0-405-07805-6*) Ayer Co. Pubs., Inc.
—Ashenden, or, The British Agent. l.t. ed. 1992. 512p. 22.95 (*1-85290-034-2*) ISIS Large Print Bks. GBR. *Dist:* Transaction Pubs.
—Ashenden, or, The British Agent. l.t. ed. 2000. 350p. 34.95 (*0-7658-0779-3*) Transaction Pubs.
—Ashenden, or, The British Agent. 1977. pap. 2.95 o.p. (*0-14-004493-0*, Penguin Bks.); 1976. 256p. pap. 8.00 o.p. (*0-14-017431-1*, Penguin Classics) Viking Penguin.
McKay, Sharon E. Charlie Wilcox. braille ed. 2000. (YA). (gr. 2). spiral bd. (*0-616-08847-7*) Canadian National Institute for the Blind/Institut National Canadien pour les Aveugles.
—Charlie Wilcox. 2000. 221p. (J). (gr. 7 up). pap. 7.95 (*0-7737-6093-8*) Stoddart Kids CAN. *Dist:* General Distribution Services, Inc.
McLeay, Alison. The Summer House. l.t. ed. 1998. (Romance Ser.). 432p. 28.95 (*0-7838-0164-5*) Thorndike Pr.
McLeay, Alison. The Summer House. 1997. 320p. 23.95 (*0-312-15666-9*) St. Martin's Pr.
McNiven, Daniel A. The Kilted Ladies from Hell. l.t. ed. 1996. 176p. (Orig.). pap. 12.95 (*0-9654680-2-X*) Pilgrimage Pr.
Mills, Scott. Trenches. 2002. 176p. pap. 14.95 (*1-891830-28-7*) Top Shelf Productions.
Mitchell, Judith Claire. The Last Day of the War. 2004. 400p. 24.95 (*0-375-42166-1*, Pantheon) Knopf Publishing Group.
Morris, Gilbert. The Amazon Quest. 2001. (House of Winslow Ser.: Vol. 28). 320p. pap. 11.99 (*0-7642-2117-5*) Bethany Hse. Pubs.
Murray, Les. Fredy Neptune. 2000. 272p. pap. 14.00 (*0-374-52676-1*) Farrar, Straus & Giroux.
Parkinson, Heather. Across Open Ground: A Novel. 2003. (Illus.). 256p. pap. 14.95 (*1-58234-289-X*); 2002. 288p. 23.95 (*1-58234-243-1*) Bloomsbury Publishing.
Perry, Anne. No Graves As Yet: A Novel of World War I. 2003. 352p. 25.95 (*0-345-45652-1*, Ballantine Bks.) Ballantine Bks.
Piepenburg, Matthew. Time & the Maiden. 1997. 256p. pap. 15.95 (*1-882897-15-3*) Lost Coast Pr.
Poland, Marguerite. Iron Love. 1999. (*0-670-88986-5*) Viking Penguin.
Pratt, George. Enemy Ace: War Idyll. Helfer, Andrew, ed. 1998. (Illus.). 128p. pap. 14.95 (*0-930289-78-1*); 1991. 144p. 75.00 o.s.i (*1-56389-010-0*); 1990. 128p. 24.95 o.s.i (*0-930289-65-X*) DC Comics.
—Enemy Ace: War Idyll. Helfer, Andrew, ed. 1992. (Illus.). 128p. reprint ed. mass mkt. 14.99 (*0-446-39365-7*) Warner Bks., Inc.
Prichard, Caradog. One Moonlit Night. 1995. xv, 76 p. (*0-86241-530-6*) Canongate Bks.
—One Moonlit Night. Mitchell, Philip, tr. from WEL. 1997. (Classics Ser.). 304p. pap. 12.95 (*0-8112-1342-0*, NDP835) New Directions Publishing Corp.
Rae, Catherine M. Julia's Story. 1990. 2.99 o.p. (*0-517-05817-0*) Random Hse. Value Publishing.
—Julia's Story. 1989. 15.95 o.p. (*0-312-02935-7*) St. Martin's Pr.
Remarque, Erich-Maria. All Quiet on the Western Front. 1998. (Classics Illustrated Study Guides). (Illus.). mass mkt. 4.99 (*1-57840-056-2*) Acclaim Bks.
—All Quiet on the Western Front. 20.95 (*0-8488-1459-2*) Amereon, Ltd.
—All Quiet on the Western Front. 1999. mass mkt. 2.22 o.s.i (*0-449-45942-X*); 1996. 304p. pap. 13.95 (*0-449-91149-7*, Fawcett); 1987. 304p. mass mkt. 6.99 (*0-449-21394-3*, Ballantine Bks.) Ballantine Bks.
—All Quiet on the Western Front. 1981. 391p. reprint ed. lib. bdg. 21.95 (*0-89966-292-7*) Buccaneer Bks., Inc.
—All Quiet on the Western Front. 1929. 248p. (gr. 8). 24.95 (*0-316-73992-8*) Little Brown & Co.
—All Quiet on the Western Front. 9999. pap. 2.50 o.s.i (*0-590-02981-9*) Scholastic, Inc.
—All Quiet on the Western Front. 1975. 13.04 (*0-606-00101-8*) Turtleback Bks.
—All Quiet on the Western Front: The Illustrated Edition. Wheen, A. W., tr. from GER. 1996. (Illus.). 208p. 29.95 o.p. (*0-8212-2312-7*) Little Brown & Co.
Remarque, Erich Maria. The Road Back. 1998. 352p. pap. 19.00 (*0-449-91246-9*) Ballantine Bks.
—The Road Back. 2002. 343p. (C). reprint ed. pap. 35.95 (*1-931541-74-4*) Simon Pubns., Inc.
Robins, Denise. Illusion of Love. 192p. 25.00 (*0-7278-5577-8*) Severn Hse. Pubs., Ltd.
—Illusion of Love. l.t. ed. 2001. (Thorndike General Ser.). 250p. pap. 22.95 (*0-7862-3188-2*) Thorndike Pr.
Romains, Jules. Verdun. 1964. (FRE.). 376p. pap. 17.95 (*0-7859-1598-2*, 2080602 11X) French & European Pubns., Inc.
—Verdun. 2000. (Lost Treasures Ser.). 500p. pap. 17.95 (*1-85375-358-0*) Prion GBR. *Dist:* Trafalgar Square.
Sapper. John Walters. 2001. 180p. pap. 9.95 (*1-84232-553-1*) House of Stratus, Inc. GBR. *Dist:* Midpoint Trade Bks., Inc.
Saxton, Judith. Still Waters. 1998. 504p. 26.95 o.p. (*0-312-18185-X*) St. Martin's Pr.
Sholokhov, Mikhail. Quiet Flows the Don. Murphy, Brian, ed. Daglish, Robert, tr. rev. ed. 1996. 1376p. 35.00 o.p. (*0-7867-0360-1*, Carroll & Graf Pubs.) Avalon Publishing Group.
—Quiet Flows the Don, 2 vols., Set, Vols. 1 & 2. Daglish, Robert, tr. 1988. 1612p. (C). 130.00 (*0-569-09106-3*) State Mutual Bk. & Periodical Service, Ltd.
Simon, Frank. The Third Dragon: A Novel. 2002. 352p. pap. 12.99 (*0-8054-2444-X*) Broadman & Holman Pubs.
Skinner, Richard. The Red Dancer: The Life & Times of Mata Hari. 2002. 272p. 24.95 (*0-06-621366-5*, Ecco) HarperTrade.
Solzhenitsyn, Aleksandr. August 1914. 1974. 736p. pap. 1.50 o.s.i (*0-553-04931-3*) Bantam Bks.
—August 1914. Willetts, H. T., tr. from RUS. (Red Wheel Ser.: Vol. 1). 2000. (Illus.). 896p. pap. 25.00 (*0-374-51999-4*); 1989. 1120p. 50.00 o.p. (*0-374-10683-5*) Farrar, Straus & Giroux.
—August 1914. Glenny, Michael, tr. from RUS. 1972. 512p. 10.00 o.p. (*0-374-10684-3*) Farrar, Straus & Giroux.
—August 1914. Willetts, H. T., tr. 1992. (Red Wheel Ser.: Vol. 1). 832p. reprint ed. pap. 18.95 o.s.i (*0-14-007122-9*) Penguin Group (USA) Inc.
—November 1916. Willetts, H. T., tr. from RUS. (Red Wheel Ser.: Vol. 2). 1040p. 2000. pap. 17.00 (*0-374-52703-2*); 1999. 35.00 o.p. (*0-374-22314-9*) Farrar, Straus & Giroux.
Stirling, Jessica. Shamrock Green. 2003. 480p. 26.95 (*0-312-31770-0*) St. Martin's Pr.
Swan, Mary. The Deep & Other Stories. 2004. 240p. pap. 12.95 (*0-8129-6650-3*, Random Hse. Trade Paperbacks) Random House Adult Trade Publishing Group.
—The Deep & Other Stories. 2003. 240p. 23.95 (*0-375-50851-1*) Random Hse., Inc.
Thane, Elswyth. The Light Heart. 1974. reprint ed. lib. bdg. 26.95 (*0-88411-951-3*) Amereon, Ltd.
—The Light Heart. 1996. lib. bdg. 29.95 (*1-56849-476-9*) Buccaneer Bks., Inc.
—The Light Heart. 1977. 10.00 o.p. (*0-8015-4543-9*, Dutton) Dutton/Plume.
—The Light Heart. 1981. (Williamsburg Ser.: No. 4). lib. bdg. 17.95 o.p. (*0-8161-3163-5*, Macmillan Reference USA) Gale Group.
Turtledove, Harry. The Great War: American Front. 1999. 576p. mass mkt. 7.99 (*0-345-40560-9*, Del Rey) Ballantine Bks.
—The Great War Vol. 1: American Front. 1998. (Great War Ser.: Vol. 1). 504p. (gr. 7). 25.00 o.s.i (*0-345-40615-X*) Ballantine Bks.
Urquhart, Jane. The Stone Carvers. 2003. 400p. pap. 14.00 (*0-14-200358-1*) Penguin Group (USA) Inc.
—The Stone Carvers. 2002. 400p. 25.95 (*0-670-03044-9*, Viking) Viking Penguin.
Weiner, Steve. The Yellow Sailor. 2002. 220p. pap. 13.95 (*1-58567-324-2*); 2001. 256p. 26.95 (*1-58567-169-X*) Overlook Pr., The.
West, Rebecca. The Return of the Soldier. 2002. (Thrift Editions Ser.). 128p. pap. 5.95 (*0-486-42207-0*) Dover Pubns., Inc.
Wharton, Edith. The Marne. 1998. (Collected Works of Edith Wharton). 138p. reprint ed. lib. bdg. 88.00 (*1-58201-987-8*) Classic Bks.
Williamson, Anne, intro. A Test to Destruction, Vol. 7. 1997. (Pocket Classics Ser.). 464p. pap. 12.95 (*0-7509-1470-X*) Sutton Publishing, Ltd. GBR. *Dist:* International Publishers Marketing.
Williamson, Henry. A Fox under My Cloak, Vol. 5. 1996. (Pocket Classics Ser.). 416p. pap. 12.95 o.p. (*0-7509-1214-6*) Sutton Publishing, Ltd. GBR. *Dist:* International Publishers Marketing.
—The Golden Virgin. Date not set. 448p. 29.95 (*0-8488-2417-2*) Amereon, Ltd.
—The Golden Virgin, Vol. 6. 1996. (Pocket Classics Ser.). 448p. pap. text 12.95 (*0-7509-1215-4*) Sutton Publishing, Ltd. GBR. *Dist:* International Publishers Marketing.
—Love & the Loveless, Vol. 6. 1997. (Chronicle of Ancient Sunlight Ser.: Vol. 7). 384p. pap. 12.95 o.p. (*0-7509-1471-8*) Sutton Publishing.
Windle, Janice Woods. Will's War: A Novel. 2002. 384p. 25.00 (*1-56352-639-5*) Longstreet Pr., Inc.
Winspear, Jacqueline. Maisie Dobbs. l.t. ed. 2004. lib. bdg. 28.95 (*1-58547-406-1*, Platinum) Ctr. Point Large Print.
—Maisie Dobbs. 2003. 336p. 24.00 (*1-56947-330-7*) Soho Pr., Inc.


## WORLD WAR, 1939-1945—FICTION


Aaron, David. Crossing by Night. 1994. 416p. mass mkt. 5.99 (*0-380-72191-0*, Avon Bks.); 1993. 22.00 o.p. (*0-688-09296-9*, Morrow, William & Co.) Morrow/Avon.
Abbott, Patricia. Goodbye Dear, I'll Be Back in a Year. 2003. 295p. pap. 13.95 (*1-4104-0108-1*, Five Star Trade); 2002. 320p. 26.95 (*0-7862-4077-6*, Five Star) Gale Group.
Adams, Alice. After the War. l.t. ed. 2001. (G. K. Hall Core Ser.). 367p. 31.95 (*0-7838-9392-2*, Macmillan Reference USA) Gale Group.
—After the War. 2001. 320p. reprint ed. pap. 14.00 (*0-7434-2222-8*, Washington Square Pr.) Simon & Schuster.
Allbeury, Ted. The Networks. 2002. 176p. 25.99 (*0-7278-5898-X*) Severn Hse. Pubs., Ltd.
Altman, John. A Game of Spies. 2003. 304p. reprint ed. mass mkt. 6.99 (*0-515-13463-5*, Jove) Berkley Publishing Group.
—A Game of Spies. l.t. ed. 2002. 373p. 28.95 (*0-7862-4104-7*) Gale Group.
—A Game of Spies. 2002. 320p. 25.95 o.s.i (*0-399-14837-X*) Putnam Publishing Group, The.
—A Gathering of Spies. abr. ed. 2000. audio 17.95 o.p. (*1-56740-919-9*, 2165, Nova Audio Bks.); audio 57.25 (*1-56740-744-7*, 2164, Unabridged Library Editions); audio 27.95 (*1-56740-377-8*, 2163, Brilliance Audio Unabridged) Brilliance Audio.
—A Gathering of Spies. 2000. (Illus.). 320p. 24.95 o.s.i (*0-399-14641-5*) Penguin Group (USA) Inc.
Amory, A. Lustwaffe Letters. 224p. pap. 6.95 (*0-7472-6239-X*) Headline Bk. Publishing, Ltd. GBR. *Dist:* Trafalgar Square.
Andersch, Alfred. Winterspelt: A Novel about the Last Days of World War II. 1980. 480p. 30.00 (*0-7206-0550-4*) Dufour Editions, Inc.
Anthony, Evelyn. Sleeping with the Enemy. 2003. 288p. 25.99 (*0-7278-5947-1*) Severn Hse. Pubs., Ltd.
Appel, Allen. Till the End of Time. 1990. 336p. 19.95 o.s.i (*0-385-24944-6*) Doubleday Publishing.
Azzopardi, Trezza. Remember Me. 2004. 192p. 23.00 (*0-8021-1767-8*, Grove Pr.) Grove/Atlantic, Inc.
Baddock, James. Emerald. 1991. 208p. 17.95 o.s.i (*0-8027-1144-8*) Walker & Co.
—The Faust Conspiracy. 1989. 192p. 18.95 o.p. (*0-8027-1081-6*) Walker & Co.
Baldwin, Faith. You Can't Escape. 1976. reprint ed. lib. bdg. 22.95 (*0-88411-625-5*) Amereon, Ltd.
—You Can't Escape. l.t. ed. 1998. (Romance Ser.). 275p. 25.95 o.p. (*0-7838-8408-7*, Macmillan Reference USA) Gale Group.
Ballard, J. G. Empire of the Sun, unabr. ed. 1996. audio 64.00 (*0-7366-3319-7*, 3971) Books on Tape, Inc.
—Empire of the Sun. 1997. reprint ed. lib. bdg. 39.95 (*1-56849-663-X*) Buccaneer Bks., Inc.
—Empire of the Sun. unabr. ed. 2001. audio 59.95 (*0-7451-5767-X*, CAB 152) Chivers Audio Bks. GBR. *Dist:* BBC Audiobooks America.
—Empire of the Sun. 1987. 384p. mass mkt. 5.99 (*0-671-64877-2*, Pocket); 1984. 320p. 16.45 o.p. (*0-671-53051-8*, Simon & Schuster); 1985. reprint ed. mass mkt. 4.50 (*0-671-53053-4*, Washington Square Pr.) Simon & Schuster.
—Empire of the Sun. l.t. ed. 1985. 480p. 13.95 o.p. (*0-7089-8270-0*, Charnwood) Thorpe, F. A. Pubs. GBR. *Dist:* Ulverscroft Large Print Bks., Ltd.
Ballard, Mignon F. The War in Sallie's Station. 275p. 2003. pap. 13.95 (*1-4104-0117-0*, Five Star Trade); 2001. 25.95 (*0-7862-3377-X*, Five Star) Gale Group.
Baly, Lindsay. Ironbottom Sound. l.t. ed. 1991. (Magna Large Print Ser.). 361p. o.p. (*1-85057-994-6*) Magna Large Print Bks. GBR. *Dist:* Ulverscroft Large Print Canada, Ltd.
—Ironbottom Sound. 1989. 240p. 18.95 o.p. (*0-8027-1063-8*) Walker & Co.
Barnett, Jill. Sentimental Journey. 2002. 528p. pap. 6.99 (*0-671-03534-7*, Pocket Star); 2001. 448p. 24.95 (*0-671-03533-9*, Atria) Simon & Schuster.
—Sentimental Journey. l.t. ed. 2002. (Basic Ser.). 741p. 29.95 (*0-7862-3638-8*) Thorndike Pr.
Barthelme, Donald. The King. 1990. (Illus.). 176p. 16.95 o.p. (*0-06-016195-7*) HarperTrade.
—The King. 1992. (Illus.). 160p. pap. 10.00 o.p. (*0-14-014992-9*, Penguin Bks.) Penguin Group (USA) Inc.
Barwick, James. The Hangman's Crusade. 1982. mass mkt. 2.95 o.s.i (*0-345-30025-4*) Ballantine Bks.
—The Hangman's Crusade. 1981. 320p. 12.95 o.p. (*0-698-11037-4*) Putnam Publishing Group, The.
Basu, Jay. The Stars Can Wait: A Novel. 2002. 192p. 21.00 o.s.i (*0-8050-6887-2*) Holt, Henry & Co.
—The Stars Can Wait: A Novel. 2003. 192p. pap. 12.00 (*0-312-42115-X*) Picador.
Beach, Edward L., Jr. Cold Is the Sea. 1978. o.p. (*0-03-013916-3*) Holt, Henry & Co.
—Cold Is the Sea. 1988. 416p. mass mkt. 3.95 o.p. (*0-8217-2507-6*, Zebra Bks.) Kensington Publishing Corp.
—Dust on the Sea. 1989. 448p. mass mkt. 3.95 o.s.i (*0-8217-2580-7*, Zebra Bks.) Kensington Publishing Corp.
—Run Silent, Run Deep. Date not set. 378p. 26.95 (*0-8488-2627-2*) Amereon, Ltd.
—Run Silent, Run Deep. 1996. (gr. 9 up). o.p. (*0-03-026645-9*) Holt, Henry & Co.
—Run Silent, Run Deep. 1977. pap. 1.95 o.p. (*0-671-81119-3*, Pocket) Simon & Schuster.
Beach, Edward L. Run Silent, Run Deep. 2003. (Cassell Military Paperbacks Ser.). 352p. pap. 9.95 (*0-304-36465-7*) Cassell P L C GBR. *Dist:* Sterling Publishing Co., Inc.
Beach, Edward L., Jr. Run Silent, Run Deep. 1986. (Classics of Naval Literature Ser.). 343p. reprint ed. 34.95 (*0-87021-557-4*) Naval Institute Pr.
Benford, Gregory & Greenberg, Martin H., eds. Hitler Victorious: Eleven Stories of the German Victory in World War II. 1987. 336p. mass mkt. 3.95 o.p. (*0-425-10137-1*) Berkley Publishing Group.
—Hitler Victorious: Eleven Stories of the German Victory in World War II. 1986. (Reference Library of the Humanities). 256p. lib. bdg. 30.00 o.p. (*0-8240-8658-9*) Garland Publishing, Inc.
Bhabra, H. S. Gestures: A Novel. 2003. 318p. 17.95 (*1-56792-235-X*) Godine, David R. Pub.
Binding, Tim. Lying with the Enemy. 1999. 360p. 24.00 (*0-7867-0657-0*); 2000. 368p. reprint ed. pap. 12.95 (*0-7867-0809-3*) Avalon Publishing Group. (Carroll & Graf Pubs.).
Bingham, Charlotte. The Blue Note. 2000. 566p. (*0-385-60063-1*) Doubleday Publishing.
—The Chestnut Tree. Date not set. pap. (*0-312-30760-8*, Saint Martin's Griffin); mass mkt. (*0-312-98593-2*, St. Martin's Paperbacks); E-Book (*0-312-70580-8*) St. Martin's Pr.
—The Chestnut Tree. l.t. ed. 2003. 555p. 28.95 (*0-7862-5951-5*) Thorndike Pr.
—The Chestnut Tree: A Novel of the Women of World War II. 2003. 336p. 24.95 (*0-312-30759-4*) St. Martin's Pr.

Birchard, Harry. Brandywine County: A Novel of World War II. 2002. 310p. pap. 22.99 (0-7388-2026-1); text 32.99 (0-7388-2025-3); E-Book 8.00 (0-7388-8680-7) Xlibris Corp.

Blum, Jenna. Those Who Save Us. 2004. 496p. (0-15-101019-6) Harcourt Trade Pubs.

Bock, Dennis. The Ash Garden. 2001. E-Book 18.50 (1-59061-597-2) Adobe Systems, Inc.

—The Ash Garden. 2003. 304p. pap. 13.00 (0-375-72749-3, Vintage) Knopf Publishing Group.

Bonner, Cindy. Right from Wrong: A Novel. 1999. 336p. tchr. ed. 19.95 (1-56512-104-X, 72104) Algonquin Bks. of Chapel Hill.

—Right from Wrong: A Novel. l.t. ed. 1999. (Basic Ser.). 472p. 28.95 (0-7862-1990-4) Thorndike Pr.

Boulle, Pierre. The Bridge on the River Kwai. 21.95 (0-89190-571-5) Amereon, Ltd.

Bove, Emmanuel. Quicksand. Di Bernardi, Dominic, tr. from FRE. 1993. 192p. pap. 11.95 (0-910395-70-5) Marlboro Pr., Inc., The.

—Quicksand. Di Bernado, Dominic, tr. from FRE. 1991. 192p. 29.95 (0-910395-69-1) Marlboro Pr., Inc., The.

Boyar, Jane & Boyar, Burt. Hitler Stopped by Franco. 2001. (Illus.). viii, 323p. (Orig.). pap. 19.95 (0-9710392-0-8) Marbella Hse.

Boyd, Bill. For Love & Glory: A Novel. 2000. 308p. 21.95 (1-892123-17-7) Capital Bks., Inc.

Boyd, W. Y. A Fight for Love & Glory. 2nd ed. 2003. 256p. per. 12.99 (1-58619-047-4) Elton-Wolf Publishing.

—The Gentle Infantryman. 3rd ed. 2003. 360p. per. 12.99 (1-58619-048-2) Elton-Wolf Publishing.

—A Rendezvous with Death. 2003. 204p. 21.95 (1-58619-046-6) Elton-Wolf Publishing.

Brady, James. Warning of War: A Novel of the North China Marines. (Illus.). 352p. 2002. 24.95 (0-312-28018-1); 2003. reprint ed. pap. 13.95 (0-312-30332-7, Saint Martin's Griffin) St. Martin's Pr.

—Warning of War: A Novel of the North China Marines. l.t. ed. 2002. (Americana Ser.). 31.95 (0-7862-4440-2) Thorndike Pr.

Bragg, Melvyn. The Soldier's Return. 2002. 384p. 25.95 (1-55970-639-2) Arcade Publishing, Inc.

—The Son of War: A Novel. 2003. 432p. 25.95 (1-55970-686-4) Arcade Publishing, Inc.

Brennan, Dan. Suicide Squadron. l.t. ed. 1998. (Magna Large Print Ser.). 419p. 29.99 (0-7505-1216-4) Magna Large Print Bks. GBR. Dist: Ulverscroft Large Print Bks., Ltd., Ulverscroft Large Print Canada, Ltd.

Brodrick, William. The 6th Lamentation: A Novel. 2003. 400p. 24.95 (0-670-03191-7, Viking) Viking Penguin.

Brown, Harry. A Walk in the Sun. 192p. reprint ed. lib. bdg. 20.95 (0-88411-075-3) Amereon, Ltd.

—A Walk in the Sun. 1985. 187p. mass mkt. 3.95 (0-88184-117-X, Carroll & Graf Pubs.) Avalon Publishing Group.

—A Walk in the Sun. 1993. reprint ed. lib. bdg. 25.95 (1-56849-191-3) Buccaneer Bks., Inc.

—A Walk in the Sun. 1998. 187p. pap. 12.00 (0-8032-6148-9, Bison Bks.) Univ. of Nebraska Pr.

Brown, Marilyn McMeen Miller. House on the Sound: A Novel. 2002. 235p. 22.50 (1-55517-584-8, Salt Pr.) Cedar Fort, Inc./CFI Distribution.

Buchan, John. Greenmantle. lib. bdg. 20.95 (0-8488-0925-4) Amereon, Ltd.

—Greenmantle. unabr. ed. 1997. audio 69.95 (0-7451-5813-7, CAB 229) BBC Audiobooks America.

—Greenmantle. unabr. ed. 1996. audio 49.95 (0-7861-1015-5, 1793) Blackstone Audio Bks., Inc.

—Greenmantle. 2002. 244p. 24.99 (1-4043-0500-9); per. 20.99 (1-4043-0501-7) IndyPublish.com.

—Greenmantle. Macdonald, Kate, ed. (Oxford World's Classics Ser.). 320p. 1999. pap. 9.95 (0-19-283684-6); 1994. pap. 8.95 o.p. (0-19-282953-X) Oxford Univ. Pr., Inc.

—Greenmantle. 1992. (Classic Crime Ser.). (Illus.). 272p. pap. 5.95 o.p. (0-14-001132-3, Penguin Bks.) Penguin Group (USA) Inc.

—Greenmantle. (Ebook Classic Ser.). E-Book 5.00 (0-7410-0825-4) SoftBook Pr.

—Greenmantle. 1998. (Classics Library). 225p. pap. 3.95 (1-85326-204-8, 2048WW) Wordsworth Editions, Ltd. GBR. Dist: Casemate Pubs. & Bk. Distributors, LLC.

Buckley, William F., Jr. Brothers No More. l.t. ed. 1996. pap. 22.95 o.p. (1-56895-283-X, Wheeler Publishing, Inc.) Gale Group.

Buckley, William F., Jr. & Hodges, Candace. Brothers No More. 1996. (Harvest Book Ser.). 304p. pap. 12.00 (0-15-600476-3) Harcourt Trade Pubs.

Buckman, Daniel. Morning Dark. 2003. 224p. 22.95 (0-312-31462-0) St. Martin's Pr.

Bull, Bartle. The Devil's Oasis. 2001. (Illus.). 356p. 25.00 (0-7867-0844-1); 2002. 336p. reprint ed. pap. 14.00 (0-7867-0990-1) Avalon Publishing Group. (Carroll & Graf Pubs.).

Bunn, T. Davis. The Amber Room. l.t. ed. 2001. (Christian Mystery Ser.). 519p. 24.95 o.p. (0-7862-3070-3) Thorndike Pr.

Burke, Warren. A Time of Innocence. 1986. 192p. 15.95 o.p. (0-8027-0888-9) Walker & Co.

Burnard, Bonnie. A Good House: A Novel. 2000. 309p. 25.00 o.s.i (0-8050-6495-8) Holt, Henry & Co.

—A Good House: A Novel. 2001. 320p. pap. 14.00 (0-312-42032-3) Picador.

Burns, John Horne. The Gallery. 1985. pap. 6.95 o.p. (0-87795-709-6, Morrow, William & Co.); 1984. pap. 2.25 o.p. (0-380-01667-2, 33357-0, Avon Bks.) Morrow/Avon.

—The Gallery. 2004. (New York Review Books Classics Ser.). 392p. pap. 14.95 (1-59017-080-6) New York Review of Bks., Inc., The.

Calaferte, Louis. C'est la Guerre: A Novel. Wainhouse, Austryn, tr. from FRE. 1999. 130p. 66.00 (0-8101-6032-3); pap. 14.95 (0-8101-6068-4) Northwestern Univ. Pr. (Marlboro Pr., The).

Callanan, Liam. The Cloud Atlas: A Novel. 2004. 368p. 22.95 (0-385-33694-2, Delacorte Pr.) Dell Publishing.

Callison, Brian R. The Stollenberg Legacy. 268p. 28.00 (0-00-225972-9) HarperCollins Pubs. Ltd. GBR. Dist: Trafalgar Square.

—The Stollenberg Legacy. l.t. ed. 2001. (Thorndike General Ser.). 380p. pap. 22.95 (0-7862-3200-5) Thorndike Pr.

Calvino, Italo. The Path to the Spiders' Nests. rev. ed. 2000. Orig. Title: The Path to the Nest of Spiders. 192p. pap. 12.00 (0-06-095658-5, Ecco) HarperTrade.

—The Path to the Spiders' Nests. McLaughlin, Martin, ed. Colquhoun, Archibald, tr. from ITA. rev. ed. 1998. Orig. Title: The Path to the Nest of Spiders. 192p. o.p. (0-88001-621-3, Ecco) HarperTrade.

Canin, Ethan. Carry Me Across the Water: A Novel. 2001. E-Book 19.00 (1-58945-887-7) Adobe Systems, Inc.

—Carry Me Across the Water: A Novel. 2002. 240p. pap. 12.95 (0-375-75993-X); 2001. E-Book 19.00 (1-58836-007-5) Random Hse., Inc.

Carcaterra, Lorenzo. Street Boys. 2003. 352p. mass mkt. 7.99 (0-345-41099-8); 2002. 336p. 25.95 (0-345-41096-3, Ballantine Bks.); 2002. E-Book 20.95 (0-345-46180-0, Ballantine Bks.) Ballantine Bks.

—Street Boys. 2002. (Basic Ser.). 30.95 (0-7862-4863-7) Thorndike Pr.

Carter, Vincent O. Such Sweet Thunder: A Novel. 2003. (Illus.). 560p. 25.95 (1-58642-058-5) Steerforth Pr.

Castellani, Christopher. A Kiss from Maddalena. 2003. 352p. tchr. ed. 23.95 (1-56512-389-1, 72389) Algonquin Bks. of Chapel Hill.

—A Kiss from Maddalena. 2004. 352p. pap. 13.00 (0-425-19642-9) Berkley Publishing Group.

Cavanaugh, Jack. His Watchful Eye. 2002. (Songs in the Night Ser.: Vol. 2). 384p. pap. 12.99 (0-7642-2308-9) Bethany Hse. Pubs.

Celine, Louis-Ferdinand. Rigadoon. Manheim, Ralph, tr. from FRE. 1997. 296p. reprint ed. pap. 13.50 (1-56478-162-3) Dalkey Archive Pr.

—Rigadoon. 1974. 273p. 8.95 o.p. (0-440-07364-2, Delacorte Pr.) Dell Publishing.

—Rigadoon. Manheim, Ralph, tr. from FRE. 1975. 304p. pap. 4.95 o.p. (0-14-004083-8, Penguin Bks.) Viking Penguin.

Chaikin, Linda L. Friday's Child. 2001. (Day to Remember Ser.: Bk. 5). (Illus.). 350p. pap. 10.99 (0-7369-0657-6) Harvest Hse. Pubs.

—Thursday's Child. 2001. (Day to Remember Ser.: Vol. 4). 358p. 10.99 (0-7369-0070-5) Harvest Hse. Pubs.

—Tuesday's Child. 2000. (Day to Remember Ser.: Bk. 2). (Illus.). 335p. pap. 10.99 o.p. (0-7369-0068-3) Harvest Hse. Pubs.

Christie, Agatha. N or M? (Agatha Christie Ser.). 1998. mass mkt. 3.99 o.s.i (0-425-16929-4); 1986. 240p. mass mkt. 5.99 o.s.i (0-425-09845-1); 1986. mass mkt. 2.95 o.s.i (0-425-09329-8); 1984. mass mkt. 2.95 o.s.i (0-425-06796-3) Berkley Publishing Group.

—N or M? 1974. 192p. pap. 2.50 o.s.i (0-440-16254-8) Dell Publishing.

—N or M? 2000. (Tommy & Tuppence Mysteries Ser.). 224p. mass mkt. 5.99 (0-451-20113-2, Signet Bks.) NAL.

—N or M? 1987. (Agatha Christie Ser.). 14.95 o.s.i (0-396-09163-6, G. P. Putnam's Sons) Penguin Putnam Bks. for Young Readers.

—N or M? l.t. ed. 1984. (Ulverscroft Large Print Ser.). 336p. 32.50 (0-7089-1156-0, Ulverscroft) Thorpe, F. A. Pubs. GBR. Dist: Ulverscroft Large Print Bks., Ltd., Ulverscroft Large Print Canada, Ltd.

Clarke, Arthur C. Glide Path: To the Heart of Experimental Technology. . in WW II! 2003. 288p. pap. 11.95 (0-7434-7531-3) ibooks, Inc.

Clarke, Caro. The Wolf Ticket: A Novel. 1998. 216p. pap. 12.95 (1-56341-098-2); lib. bdg. 24.95 (1-56341-099-0) Firebrand Bks.

Claus, Hugo. The Sorrow of Belgium. 1990. 24.95 o.s.i (0-394-56263-1, Pantheon) Knopf Publishing Group.

—The Sorrow of Belgium. 2003. (Tusk Ivories Ser.). 608p. pap. 17.95 (1-58567-238-6) Overlook Pr., The.

—The Sorrow of Belgium. Pomerans, Arnold J., tr. 1994. (Penguin Twentieth-Century Classics Ser.). 624p. pap. 11.95 o.p. (0-14-018801-0, Penguin Classics) Viking Penguin.

Coffman, Virginia. The Lombard Cavalcade. l.t. ed. 2001. 597p. 28.95 (0-7838-9400-7, Macmillan Reference USA) Gale Group.

—The Lombard Cavalcade. 1982. 464p. 15.50 o.p. (0-87795-355-4, Morrow, William & Co.) Morrow/Avon.

Colbert, Curt. Sayonaraville. 2003. 14.95 (0-9724412-1-2) UglyTown.

Colbert, Larry L. Songs of Zion. 2001. 448p. 23.99 (1-887399-03-8) Colbert Hse., The.

Collins, Ellwyn K. Deep Six. 2002. 385p. (1-55369-007-9) Trafford Publishing.

Collins, Max Allan. Saving Private Ryan. l.t. ed. 2001. 248p. lib. bdg. 27.95 (1-58547-126-7) Ctr. Point Large Print.

—Saving Private Ryan, Level 6. 2000. (Penguin Ser.). (C). pap. 7.66 (0-582-41983-2) Longman Publishing Group.

—Saving Private Ryan. 1998. 319p. mass mkt. 6.50 o.s.i (0-451-19727-5, Signet Bks.) NAL.

Coonts, Stephen, ed. Victory. 2003. 768p. 27.95 (0-312-87462-6, Forge Bks.) Doherty, Tom Assocs., LLC.

Corrick, Martin. The Navigation Log: A Novel. 2004. 304p. pap. 13.95 (0-375-76053-9, Random Hse. Trade Paperbacks) Random House Adult Trade Publishing Group.

—The Navigation Log: A Novel. 2003. 304p. 24.95 (0-375-50812-0) Random Hse., Inc.

Cottam, Francis. The Fire Fighter. 2001. 320p. o.p. (0-7011-6981-8) Random Hse. of Canada, Ltd. CAN. Dist: Random Hse., Inc.

—The Fire Fighter. 2002. 256p. 23.95 (0-312-28679-1) St. Martin's Pr.

Courtenay, Bryce. The Power of One. 1996. 528p. pap. 14.95 (0-345-41005-X); 1990. 544p. mass mkt. 6.99 o.s.i (0-345-35992-5); 1989. mass mkt. 5.95 o.p. (0-345-01848-6) Ballantine Bks.

Cozzens, James Gould. Guard of Honor. 1964. 648p. pap. 8.95 o.s.i (0-15-637609-1, Harvest Bks.) Harcourt Trade Pubs.

—Guard of Honor. annuals 1998. (Modern Library Ser.). 800p. 24.95 o.s.i (0-679-60305-0) Random Hse., Inc.

Creel, Ann Howard. The Magic of Ordinary Days. l.t. ed. 2001. 27.95 o.p. (0-7862-3741-4) Thorndike Pr.

—The Magic of Ordinary Days. 288p. 2002. 13.00 (0-14-200090-6); 2001. 24.95 o.p. (0-670-91027-9, Viking) Viking Penguin.

Dailey, Janet. Silver Wings Santiago Blue. l.t. ed. 1984. 15.95 o.p. (0-8161-3725-0); 10.95 o.p. (0-8161-3762-5) Gale Group. (Macmillan Reference USA).

—Silver Wings Santiago Blue. 1994. 400p. mass mkt. 6.99 (0-671-87515-9, Pocket); 1989. mass mkt. 5.95 (0-671-70280-7, Pocket); 1988. mass mkt. 4.95 (0-671-68141-9, Pocket); 1985. mass mkt. 4.50 (0-671-60072-9, Pocket); 1984. 480p. 40.00 o.s.i (0-671-50906-3, Simon & Schuster); 1984. 480p. 15.45 (0-671-50405-3, Simon & Schuster) Simon & Schuster.

Daley, Robert. The Innocents Within. 2001. 480p. mass mkt. 7.50 (0-449-00415-5, Ballantine Bks.) Ballantine Bks.

—The Innocents Within. 2001. 13.55 (0-606-20497-0) Turtleback Bks.

—The Innocents Within: A Novel. 1999. 448p. 25.95 o.s.i (0-375-50178-9, Villard Bks.) Random House Adult Trade Publishing Group.

Davis, Don. Appointment with the Squire: A Novel. 1995. 333p. 24.95 (1-55750-157-2) Naval Institute Pr.

Davis, Richard. Yours D3. 2000. 324p. pap. 12.95 (0-9665234-1-5) Alliance Hse., Inc.

Davison, Geoffrey W. The Last Waltz: Vienna May 1945. 2001. 288p. pap. 21.99 (0-7388-3143-3) Xlibris Corp.

De Graaf, Anne. Bread upon the Waters. 1995. (Hidden Harvest Ser.: Bk. 1). 352p. pap. 10.99 o.p. (1-55661-618-X) Bethany Hse. Pubs.

—Bread upon the Waters. 1999. 17.04 (0-606-18971-8) Turtleback Bks.

De Vries, Anne. Journey Through the Night. der Nederlanden, Harry, tr. from DUT. 2001. (Illus.). 373p. pap. 14.90 (0-921100-25-6) Inheritance Pubns.

Deal, Paul H. Night Lessons. 2001. pap. 21.95 (0-595-18464-2) iUniverse, Inc.

Dekker, Ted. When Heaven Weeps. 2001. (Martyr's Song Ser.: Vol. 2). v, 375p. pap. 14.99 (0-8499-4291-8) W Publishing Group.

DeSimone, Fred. Cold Sweat. 1999. 256p. pap. 17.00 (0-8059-4644-6) Dorrance Publishing Co., Inc.

Dickey, James. To the White Sea. 1994. 288p. pap. 11.95 (0-385-31309-8, Delta) Dell Publishing.

—To the White Sea. l.t. ed. 1994. 25.95 (1-56895-046-2, Wheeler Publishing, Inc.) Gale Group.

—To the White Sea. 1993. 275p. 22.95 o.s.i (0-395-47565-1) Houghton Mifflin Co.

Dietrich, Bill. Ice Reich. 1998. 375p. 25.00 o.p. (0-446-52339-9) Warner Bks., Inc.

Dobbs, Michael. At the Right Hand. 2002. 320p. (0-00-225414-X); pap. (0-00-713018-X) HarperCollins Pubs.

Doran, Elizabeth L. Wings - His Way. (0-9639986-0-9) Fielder Group.

Dorfman, Allan. A House at War: A Ship & a Family Do Battle Against the Sea & the Nazis. 2000. 492p. pap. 24.99 (0-7388-2201-9); E-Book 8.00 (0-7388-8787-0) Xlibris Corp.

Douglas, Garry. The Valley of Death. l.t. ed. 1999. (Ulverscroft Large Print Ser.). 392p. 31.99 o.p. (0-7089-4132-X, Ulverscroft) Thorpe, F. A. Pubs. GBR. Dist: Ulverscroft Large Print Bks., Ltd., Ulverscroft Large Print Canada, Ltd.

Dunmore, Siege. 2003. pap. 13.00 (0-8021-3958-2) Grove/Atlantic, Inc.

Dunmore, Helen. The Siege: A Novel. 2002. 304p. 24.00 o.p. (0-8021-1700-7, Grove Pr.) Grove/Atlantic, Inc.

Dunning, John. Two O'Clock, Eastern Wartime: A Novel. 2001. 480p. 26.00 o.s.i (0-7432-0195-7, Scribner) Simon & Schuster.

Eastlake, William. Castle Keep. 1999. 382p. reprint ed. pap. 13.95 (1-56478-208-5) Dalkey Archive Pr.

Eisenberg, Nora. The War at Home. 2002. 217p. pap. 14.95 (0-9679520-4-2) Leapfrog Pr.

Elkins, Aaron. Turncoat: A Novel of Suspense. 2002. 304p. 24.95 (0-06-019770-6, Morrow, William & Co.) Morrow/Avon.

Elliott, Ray. Wild Hands Toward the Sky: A Novel. 2002. (Illus.). 431p. 28.00 (0-9641423-7-6) Tales Pr.

Elwood, Roger. Code Name Bloody Winter. 1996. mass mkt. 5.99 o.p. (0-8499-3883-X); 1993. pap. 8.99 o.p. (0-8499-3388-9) W Publishing Group.

—Deadly Sanction. 1995. mass mkt. 5.99 o.p. (0-8499-3885-6); 1993. pap. 8.99 o.p. (0-8499-3387-0) W Publishing Group.

—Wolf's Lair. 1995. mass mkt. 5.99 o.p. (0-8499-3884-8); 1993. 224p. pap. 8.99 o.p. (0-8499-3386-2) W Publishing Group.

Evans, George Brinley. Boys of Gold. 2001. 78p. pap. 12.95 (1-902638-12-3) Parthian Bks. GBR. Dist: Dufour Editions, Inc.

Fast, Howard. The Bridge Builder's Story. 1995. 224p. (C). (gr. 13). 29.95 (1-56324-691-0) Sharpe, M.E. Inc.

—Second Generation. 1979. lib. bdg. 21.95 o.p. (0-8161-6715-X, Macmillan Reference USA) Gale Group.

—Second Generation. 2001. (Immigrants Ser.: Vol. 2). 448p. pap. 14.95 (0-7434-2372-0) ibooks, Inc.

Faulkner, William. The Unvanquished, Vol. 351. 1966. (Illus.). pap. 8.00 o.p. (0-394-70351-0, V351, Vintage) Knopf Publishing Group.

Faulks, Sebastian. Charlotte Gray. unabr. ed. 1999. audio 110.95 (0-7540-0395-7, CAB1818) BBC Audiobooks America.

—Charlotte Gray. 2001. 14p. audio compact disk 115.95 (0-7540-5438-1, CCD 129) Chivers Audio Bks. GBR. Dist: BBC Audiobooks America.

—Charlotte Gray. abr. ed. 1999. audio 25.95 (0-375-40598-4, RH Audio) Random Hse. Audio Publishing Group.

—Charlotte Gray. l.t. ed. 1999. (Charnwood Large Print Ser.). 592p. 31.99 (0-7089-9078-9, Linford) Thorpe, F. A. Pubs. GBR. Dist: Ulverscroft Large Print Bks., Ltd., Ulverscroft Large Print Canada, Ltd.

Feldman, Ian. The Sky Club. 2004. (Illus.). 544p. pap. 7.99 (0-9743673-1-1, 0-9743673-1-1); cd-rom 19.95 (0-9743673-2-X, 1); cd-rom 19.95 (0-9743673-3-8, 0-9743673-3-8); 29.95 (0-9743673-0-3, 0-9743673-0-3) SSI, Inc. Publishing.

Findley, Timothy. Famous Last Words. 1983. mass mkt. 3.95 o.s.i (0-440-32543-9, Laurel); 1982. 13.95 o.s.i (0-385-28271-0, Delacorte Pr.) Dell Publishing.

—Famous Last Words. l.t. ed. 1988. (Mainstream Ser.). 576p. reprint ed. lib. bdg. 18.95 o.p. (1-85089-229-6) ISIS Large Print Bks. GBR. Dist: Transaction Pubs.

Fischer, Tibor. Under the Frog. 1997. 256p. pap. 13.00 o.s.i (0-8050-5245-3, Owl Bks.) Holt, Henry & Co.

—Under the Frog. 2001. 256p. pap. 13.00 (0-312-27871-3) Picador.

Fish, Robert L. Pursuit: A Novel. 1978. 10.00 o.p. (0-385-13398-7) Doubleday Publishing.

Fishtein, Oscar. I'll Sell You a Million Jews. 1995. 272p. 19.95 (0-8158-0517-9) Christopher Publishing Hse.

Fitzgerald, Penelope. Offshore, Human Voices: The Beginning of Spring. 2003. 480p. 23.00 (1-4000-4125-2, Everyman's Library) Knopf Publishing Group.

Florence, Ronald. The Last Season. 2000. 348p. 24.95 (*0-312-84873-0*, Forge Bks.) Doherty, Tom Assocs., LLC.
Foer, Jonathan Safran. Everything Is Illuminated: A Novel. 2003. 288p. pap. 13.95 (*0-06-052970-9*, Perennial) HarperTrade.
—Everything Is Illuminated: A Novel. 2002. (Illus.). 288p. tchr. ed. 24.00 (*0-618-17387-0*) Houghton Mifflin Co.
Follett, Ken. Hornet Flight. 2002. 416p. 26.95 (*0-525-94689-6*) Dutton/Plume.
—Hornet Flight. 2003. 558p. pap. 13.95 (*1-4104-0167-7*, Wheeler Publishing, Inc.) Gale Group.
—Hornet Flight. 2003. 528p. mass mkt. 7.99 (*0-451-21074-3*, Signet Bks.) NAL.
—Hornet Flight. 2003. (Core Ser.). 32.95 (*0-7862-4685-5*) Thorndike Pr.
—Jackdaws. 2001. 464p. 26.95 o.s.i (*0-525-94628-4*, Dutton) Dutton/Plume.
—Jackdaws. 2002. 496p. pap. 7.99 (*0-451-20559-6*); 512p. reprint ed. mass mkt. 7.99 (*0-451-20752-1*, Signet Bks.) NAL.
—Jackdaws. 2003. E-Book 7.99 (*0-7865-3809-0*) Penguin Putnam, Inc E-Books.
—Jackdaws. l.t. ed. 2001. 688p. 26.95 (*0-375-43159-4*) Random Hse. Large Print.
—Jackdaws. abr. ed. 2001. 4p. audio 24.95 o.s.i (*0-14-280001-5*); 5p. audio compact disk 29.95 (*0-14-280002-3*); 8p. audio 44.95 o.s.i (*0-14-280003-1*) Viking Penguin. (Penguin AudioBooks).
—The Key to Rebecca. l.t. ed. 1993. 21.95 o.p. (*0-7927-1538-1*); 1992. pap. 16.95 o.p. (*0-7927-1537-3*) BBC Audiobooks America.
—The Key to Rebecca. 1994. reprint ed. lib. bdg. 32.95 (*1-56849-278-2*) Buccaneer Bks., Inc.
—The Key to Rebecca. 1981. lib. bdg. 16.95 o.p. (*0-8161-3151-1*); 1993. pap. 9.95 o.p. (*0-8161-3275-5*) Gale Group. (Macmillan Reference USA).
—The Key to Rebecca. 1980. 12.95 o.p. (*0-688-03734-8*, Morrow, William & Co.) Morrow/Avon.
—The Key to Rebecca. 1981. 352p. mass mkt. 4.95 o.p. (*0-451-15510-6*, Signet Bks.); 1981. 400p. mass mkt. 7.99 (*0-451-16349-4*, AE2788, Signet Bks.); 1981. mass mkt. 3.95 o.p. (*0-451-12788-9*, Signet Bks.); 1981. mass mkt. 3.95 o.p. (*0-451-11012-9*, Signet Bks.); 1981. mass mkt. 4.50 o.p. (*0-451-13509-1*, ROC); 2003. 352p. reprint ed. pap. 13.95 (*0-451-20779-3*) NAL.
Fontane, Theodor. Delusions, Confusions & the Poggenpuhl Family. Demetz, Peter, ed. 1989. (German Library Ser.: Vol. 47). 292p. 39.50 (*0-8264-0325-5*) Continuum International Publishing Group, Inc.
Forbes, Gordon. Goodbye to Some. 1982. (War Library). 272p. mass mkt. 2.50 o.s.i (*0-345-30641-4*) Ballantine Bks.
—Goodbye to Some. 1997. (Classics of Naval Literature Ser.). 328p. 34.95 (*1-55750-277-3*) Naval Institute Pr.
Fox, John. The Thunderbird Covenant. Dageforde, Linda J., ed. 1999. 448p. pap. 19.95 (*1-886225-46-X*, 5000) Dageforde Publishing, Inc.
Fox, William Price. Wild Blue Yonder. 2002. 235p. 24.95 (*1-57587-197-1*) Crane Hill Pubs.
Francis, H. E. The Invisible Country. 2003. 533p. 29.95 (*1-929490-06-2*) Beil, Frederic C. Pub., Inc.
Frayn, Michael. Spies: A Novel. 2002. 288p. 23.00 o.s.i (*0-8050-7058-3*, Metropolitan Bks.) Holt, Henry & Co.
—Spies: A Novel. 2003. 272p. pap. 13.00 (*0-312-42117-6*) Picador.
—Spies: A Novel. l.t. ed. (General Ser.). 25.95 (*0-7862-4480-1*) Thorndike Pr.
Fullerton, Alexander. All the Drowning Seas. l.t. ed. 1984. (Ulverscroft Large Print Ser.). 560p. 29.99 o.p. (*0-7089-1159-5*, Ulverscroft) Thorpe, F. A. Pubs. GBR. *Dist:* Ulverscroft Large Print Bks., Ltd., Ulverscroft Large Print Canada, Ltd.
—Return to the Field. l.t. ed. 1998. 544 p. (*0-7540-2128-9*) BBC Audiobooks America.
—Return to the Field. 1997. (Illus.). 378p. o.s.i (*0-316-88293-3*) Little Brown & Co.
—Return to the Field. l.t. ed. 1998. (Paperback Ser.). 544p. (gr. 7). pap. 24.95 (*0-7838-0205-6*) Thorndike Pr.
Furst, Alan. Blood of Victory: A Novel. 2003. (Illus.). 272p. pap. 12.95 (*0-8129-6872-7*, Modern Library) Random House Adult Trade Publishing Group.
—Blood of Victory: A Novel. 2002. (Illus.). 256p. 24.95 (*0-375-50574-1*) Random Hse., Inc.
—Blood of Victory: A Novel. 2002. (Core Ser.). 29.95 (*0-7862-4915-3*) Thorndike Pr.
—Dark Star. (Illus.). 390p. pap. 13.00 (*0-00-651131-7*) HarperCollins Pubs. Ltd. GBR. *Dist:* Trafalgar Square.
—Dark Star. 1991. 288p. 22.95 o.p. (*0-395-51064-3*) Houghton Mifflin Co.
—Dark Star. 1992. mass mkt. 6.99 o.p. (*0-312-92845-9*, St. Martin's Paperbacks) St. Martin's Pr.
—Kingdom of Shadows: A Novel. E-Book 19.95 (*1-58945-591-6*) Adobe Systems, Inc.
—Kingdom of Shadows: A Novel. l.t. ed. 2001. (Illus.). 359p. 28.95 (*0-7838-9427-9*); (*0-7540-1587-4*); pap. (*0-7540-2448-2*) Gale Group. (Macmillan Reference USA).
—Kingdom of Shadows: A Novel. 2001. 272p. pap. 11.95 (*0-375-75826-7*) Random House Adult Trade Publishing Group.
—The Polish Officer: A Novel. 2000. 352p. pap. 13.00 (*0-00-651129-5*) HarperCollins Pubs. Ltd. GBR. *Dist:* Trafalgar Square.
—The Polish Officer: A Novel. 2001. 304p. pap. 12.95 (*0-375-75827-5*) Random House Adult Trade Publishing Group.
—Red Gold. 2000. 283p. reprint ed. pap. 13.00 (*0-00-649903-1*) HarperCollins Pubs. Ltd. GBR. *Dist:* Trafalgar Square.
—Red Gold. l.t. ed. 2000. (Ulverscroft Large Print Ser.). 432p. 31.99 (*0-7089-4253-9*, Ulverscroft) Thorpe, F. A. Pubs. GBR. *Dist:* Ulverscroft Large Print Bks., Ltd., Ulverscroft Large Print Canada, Ltd.
—Red Gold: A Novel. 2002. 288p. pap. 11.95 (*0-375-75859-3*) Random House Adult Trade Publishing Group.
—Red Gold: A Novel. 1999. (Illus.). 288p. 23.95 o.s.i (*0-679-45186-2*) Random Hse., Inc.
—The World at Night. 2000. 320p. pap. 13.00 (*0-00-651097-3*) HarperCollins Pubs. Ltd. GBR. *Dist:* Trafalgar Square.
—The World at Night, abr. ed. 2000. audio compact disk 79.95 (*0-7531-0704-X*, 10704X); 1998. audio 69.95 (*0-7531-0383-4*, 980508) ISIS Audio Bks. GBR. *Dist:* Ulverscroft Large Print Bks., Ltd.
—The World at Night. l.t. ed. 1999. (Ulverscroft Large Print Ser.). 448p. 31.99 o.p. (*0-7089-4024-2*, Ulverscroft) Thorpe, F. A. Pubs. GBR. *Dist:* Ulverscroft Large Print Bks., Ltd., Ulverscroft Large Print Canada, Ltd.
—The World at Night: A Novel. 2002. (Illus.). 288p. pap. 11.95 (*0-375-75858-5*) Random House Adult Trade Publishing Group.
Gaddo, Don & Parks, Demaris H. War's Lost Love Found: An Enduring Story of Love, Mystery, & Miracles. 2002. (Illus.). 288p. (*0-9707087-1-8*) Palmaya Publishing.
Gardner, John. Bottled Spider. 29.99 (*0-7278-7200-1*); 2002. 384p. 26.99 (*0-7278-5829-7*) Severn Hse. Pubs., Ltd.
Garnett, Cliff. Hellstorm. 2000. (T.A.L.O.N. Force Ser.: No. 7). 224p. mass mkt. 5.99 o.s.i (*0-451-19984-7*, Signet Bks.) NAL.
—Zulu Plus Ten. 2000. (T.A.L.O.N. Force Ser.: No. 5). 224p. mass mkt. 5.99 o.s.i (*0-451-19979-0*, Signet Bks.) NAL.
Gartner, Chloe. Lower Than the Angels. 2000. 26.95 (*0-7862-2351-0*, Five Star) Gale Group.
George, Michael. Of Rain Barrels & Bridges. 2002. pap. 6.00 (*0-9721980-0-8*) MARUGE PUBLISHING.
Gibbins, James. Searching for Johnny. 2002. (Illus.). 400p. 25.95 (*0-312-28184-6*) St. Martin's Pr.
Gilpatric, Guy. Action in the North Atlantic. Jaffee, Walter W., ed. l.t. ed. 2000. xii, 210p. reprint ed. 29.95 (*1-889901-15-6*) Glencannon Pr.
Gilroy, Jack. Absolute Flanigan. 2002. 320p. pap. 14.00 (*1-58684-233-1*) Global Academic Publishing.
Glazener, Mary. The Cup of Wrath: The Story of Dietrich Bonhoeffer's Resistance to Hitler. 1990. 576p. 29.95 (*0-913720-71-2*) Beil, Frederic C. Pub., Inc.
Gobbell, John J. A Code for Tomorrow. E-Book 24.95 (*0-312-26449-6*); 2002. 496p. mass mkt. 7.50 (*0-312-97142-7*, St. Martin's Paperbacks); 2000. pap. (*0-312-97385-3*, St. Martin's Paperbacks); 1999. (Illus.). 316p. 24.95 (*0-312-20511-2*) St. Martin's Pr.
—The Last Lieutenant. 1997. (Last Lieutenant Ser.: Vol. 1). 480p. mass mkt. 6.99 (*0-312-95838-2*, St. Martin's Paperbacks); 1995. 384p. 23.95 o.p. (*0-312-13108-9*) St. Martin's Pr.
Goldreich, Gloria. That Year of Our War. l.t. ed. 1994. pap. 21.95 (*1-56895-081-0*, Wheeler Publishing, Inc.) Gale Group.
—That Year of Our War. 1994. 356p. 22.95 o.p. (*0-316-31943-0*) Little Brown & Co.
Goyer, Tricia. From Dust & Ashes: A Story of Liberation. 2003. 448p. pap. 12.99 (*0-8024-1554-7*) Moody Pr.
Gracq, Julien. Un Balcon en Foret. 1990. (FRE.). 256p. reprint ed. 29.95 o.p. (*0-8288-9820-0*, F104670); pap. 38.95 (*0-7859-4599-7*) French & European Pubns., Inc.
—Balcony in the Forest. Howard, Richard, tr. from FRE. & pref. by. 1989. (Twentieth-Century Continental Fiction Ser.). 213p. pap. 12.50 (*0-231-06643-0*) Columbia Univ. Pr.
—Balcony in the Forest. Howard, Richard, tr. 1987. 213p. text 46.00 (*0-231-06672-4*); pap. text 18.00 (*0-231-06673-2*) Columbia Univ. Pr.
—King Cophetua. Kohn, Ingeborg M., tr. from FRE. 2004. (Illus.). 96p. (gr. 13 up). pap. 12.95 (*1-885586-86-8*) Turtle Point Pr.
Grant, Jan. Shed the Rain & Dance into the Wind. 2001. pap. 23.35 (*0-7596-2509-3*) 1stBooks Library.
Grass, Gunter. The Call of the Toad. Manheim, Ralph, tr. from GER. (Harvest Book Ser.).Tr. of Unkenrufe. 1993. 256p. pap. 14.00 (*0-15-615340-8*, Harvest Bks.); 1992. (Illus.). 248p. (C). 19.95 o.s.i (*0-15-125743-4*) Harcourt Trade Pubs.
—The Call of the Toad. 1997. Tr. of Unkenrufe. pap. o.s.i (*0-7493-9878-7*) Random Hse. of Canada, Ltd.
—Cat & Mouse.Tr. of Katz & Maus. 17.95 (*0-8488-0112-1*) Amereon, Ltd.
—Cat & Mouse. Manheim, Ralph, tr. from GER. Tr. of Katz & Maus. 1991. 192p. pap. 13.00 (*0-15-615551-6*, Harvest Bks.); 1963. 189p. 10.95 o.p. (*0-15-116100-3*) Harcourt Trade Pubs.
—Crabwalk. Winston, Krishna, tr. from GER. 2003. 240p. 25.00 (*0-15-100764-0*) Harcourt Trade Pubs.
—The Tin Drum. 1999. Tr. of Blechtrommel. 592p. 20.00 (*0-375-42057-6*, Pantheon) Knopf Publishing Group.
—The Tin Drum. Manheim, Ralph, tr. from GER. 1990. (Vintage International Ser.).Tr. of Blechtrommel. 592p. pap. 15.95 (*0-679-72575-X*, Vintage) Knopf Publishing Group.
—The Tin Drum. 1964. Tr. of Blechtrommel. pap. 5.95 o.p. (*0-394-70300-6*, Vintage) Knopf Publishing Group.
—The Tin Drum. Manheim, Ralph, tr. from GER. 1993. (Everyman's Library).Tr. of Blechtrommel. xxxvii, 551p. 20.00 (*0-679-42033-9*) Knopf, Alfred A. Inc.
—The Tin Drum. 1963. Tr. of Blechtrommel. 10.95 o.s.i (*0-394-44902-9*) Random Hse., Inc.
Gray, Edwyn. Crash Dive Five Hundred. 1985. 220p. 13.95 o.s.i (*0-8027-0840-4*) Walker & Co.
Gray, Stephen. War Child. 2001. 256p. pap. 14.95 (*1-897959-01-X*) Serif GBR. *Dist:* Interlink Publishing Group, Inc.
Grayson, Emily. Waterloo Station. 2004. 304p. mass mkt. 6.99 (***0-06-001398-2**, HarperTorch); 2003. 208p. 21.95 (*0-06-001397-4*, Morrow, William & Co.) Morrow/Avon.
—Waterloo Station. l.t. ed. 2003. 232p. 29.95 (*0-7862-5789-X*) Thorndike Pr.
Green, Gerald. East & West. 1987. 512p. mass mkt. 4.95 o.s.i (*0-449-21366-8*, Fawcett) Ballantine Bks.
—East & West. 1986. 500p. 18.95 o.p. (*0-917657-56-X*) Fine, Donald I. Bks.
Greene, Sheldon. Burnt Umber. 2001. 300p. pap. 14.95 o.p. (*0-9679520-1-8*) Leapfrog Pr.
Greig, Andrew. The Clouds Above: A Novel of Love & War. 2001. 256p. 24.00 (*0-7432-0640-1*, Simon & Schuster) Simon & Schuster.
Griffin, Frank James. Till the Tide Comes In. 2003. (*0-945582-90-0*) Down The Shore Publishing.
Griffin, W. E. B. Battleground. 1991. (Corps Ser.: No. 4). 496p. mass mkt. 7.99 (*0-515-10640-2*, Jove) Berkley Publishing Group.
—Battleground. unabr. ed. 1993. (Corps Ser.: No. 4). audio 96.00 (*0-7366-2240-3*, 3030) Books on Tape, Inc.
—Battleground. 2001. 19.95 (*0-399-13794-7*); 1991. (Corps Ser.: No. 4). 416p. 19.95 o.s.i (*0-399-13550-2*, G. P. Putnam's Sons) Penguin Group (USA) Inc.
—Behind the Lines. 1996. (Corps Ser.: No. 7). 576p. mass mkt. 7.99 (*0-515-11938-5*, Jove) Berkley Publishing Group.
—Behind the Lines. unabr. ed. 1996. (Corps Ser.: No. 7). audio 104.00 (*0-7366-3307-3*, 3961) Books on Tape, Inc.
—Behind the Lines. l.t. ed. 1996. (Corps Ser.: No. 7). 800p. 26.95 (*0-7838-1722-3*, Macmillan Reference USA) Gale Group.
—Behind the Lines. 2001. 23.95 (*0-399-14336-X*); 1996. (Corps Ser.: No. 7). 384p. 23.95 o.p. (*0-399-14086-7*, G. P. Putnam's Sons) Penguin Group (USA) Inc.
—Blood & Honor. 1997. (Honor Bound Ser.: No. 2). 736p. mass mkt. 7.99 (*0-515-12194-0*, Jove) Berkley Publishing Group.
—Blood & Honor, Pt. 1. unabr. ed. 1996. (Honor Bound Ser.: No. 2). audio 80.00 (*0-7366-3594-7*, 4246A ) Books on Tape, Inc.
—Blood & Honor. l.t. ed. 1997. (Honor Bound Ser.: No. 2). 1105p. 28.95 (*0-7838-8125-8*, Macmillan Reference USA) Gale Group.
—Blood & Honor. 2001. 34.95 (*0-399-14481-1*); 1996. (Honor Bound Ser.: No. 2). 480p. 24.95 o.s.i (*0-399-14190-1*, G. P. Putnam's Sons); Set. 1996. (Honor Bound Ser.: No. 2). 4p. 24.95 o.p. (*0-399-14226-6*, 694560, Putnam Berkley Audio) Penguin Group (USA) Inc.
—Brotherhood of War. 2001. 816p. 14.98 (*0-399-14730-6*) Penguin Group (USA) Inc.
—Call to Arms. 1987. (Corps Ser.: No. 2). 384p. mass mkt. 7.99 (*0-515-09349-1*, Jove) Berkley Publishing Group.
—Call to Arms. unabr. collector's ed. 1992. (Corps Ser.: No. 2). audio 80.00 (*0-7366-2206-3*, 3001) Books on Tape, Inc.
—Close Combat. l.t. ed. 1994. (Corps Ser.: No. 6). 22.95 o.p. (*0-7927-1660-4*) BBC Audiobooks America.
—Close Combat. 1993. (Corps Ser.: No. 6). 416p. mass mkt. 7.99 (*0-515-11269-0*, Jove) Berkley Publishing Group.
—Close Combat. unabr. ed. 1993. (Corps Ser.: No. 6). audio 80.00 (*0-7366-2423-6*, 112719) Books on Tape, Inc.
—Close Combat. 1993. (Corps Ser.: No. 6). 416p. 22.95 o.p. (*0-399-13766-1*, G. P. Putnam's Sons) Penguin Group (USA) Inc.
—The Corps: Semper Fi. 1986. (Corps Ser.: No. 1). 352p. mass mkt. 7.99 (*0-515-08749-1*, Jove) Berkley Publishing Group.
—The Corps Boxed Set: Battleground, Line of Fire, Close Combat. 1995. (Corps Ser.: Nos. 4-6). 11.98 o.s.i (*0-399-14013-1*) Penguin Group (USA) Inc.
—The Corps Boxed Set: Semper Fi, Call to Arms, Counterattack, Battleground. 1991. (Corps Ser.: Nos. 1-4). 22.45 o.s.i (*0-515-10775-1*, Jove) Berkley Publishing Group.
—Counterattack. 1990. (Corps Ser.: No. 3). 512p. mass mkt. 7.99 (*0-515-10417-5*, Jove) Berkley Publishing Group.
—Counterattack. unabr. collector's ed. 1992. (Corps Ser.: No. 3). audio 104.00 (*0-7366-2211-X*, 3004) Books on Tape, Inc.
—Counterattack. 1990. (Corps Ser.: No. 3). 400p. 16.95 o.p. (*0-399-13493-X*, G. P. Putnam's Sons) Penguin Putnam Bks. for Young Readers.
—The Fighting Agents. 2001. (Men at War Ser.: Vol. 4). 448p. reprint ed. mass mkt. 7.99 (*0-515-13052-4*, Jove) Berkley Publishing Group.
—The Fighting Agents. 2000. (Men at War Ser.: Vol. 4). 311p. 25.95 o.s.i (*0-399-14612-1*) Penguin Group (USA) Inc.
—The Fighting Agents. 1990. (Men at War Ser.: Vol. 4). mass mkt. 4.95 (*0-671-73280-3*, Pocket) Simon & Schuster.
—The Fighting Agents. l.t. ed. 2001. pap. 29.95 (*0-7862-2830-X*); 2000. 674p. 31.95 (*0-7862-2829-6*) Thorndike Pr.
—Honor Bound. 1994. (Honor Bound Ser.: No. 1). 560p. mass mkt. 7.99 (*0-515-11486-3*, Jove) Berkley Publishing Group.
—Honor Bound, Pt. 1. unabr. ed. (Honor Bound Ser.: No. 1). audio 64.00 (*0-7366-2732-4*, 3460-A/B) Books on Tape, Inc.
—Honor Bound. unabr. ed. 1994. (Honor Bound Ser.: No. 1). audio 130.55 (*1-56100-184-8*, 901, Unabridged Library Editions); audio 29.95 (*1-56100-558-4*, 138, Bookcassette) Brilliance Audio.
—Honor Bound. l.t. ed. 1994. (Honor Bound Ser.: No. 1). 25.95 o.p. (*1-56895-100-0*, Wheeler Publishing, Inc.) Gale Group.
—Honor Bound. abr. ed. 2000. (Honor Bound Ser.: No. 1). audio 7.95 (*1-57815-012-4*, 1002, Media Bks. Audio Publishing) Media Bks., L. L. C.
—Honor Bound. 1994. (Honor Bound Ser.: No. 1). 384p. 22.95 o.p. (*0-399-13862-5*, G. P. Putnam's Sons) Penguin Group (USA) Inc.
—Honor Bound. 22.95 o.s.i (*0-399-14117-0*) Putnam Publishing Group, The.
—In Danger's Path, Vol. 8. 1999. (Corps Ser.: No. 8). 736p. reprint ed. mass mkt. 7.99 (*0-515-12698-5*, Jove) Berkley Publishing Group.
—In Danger's Path. l.t. ed. 1999. (Corps Ser.: No. 8). 883p. 31.95 (*1-56895-724-6*, Wheeler Publishing, Inc.) Gale Group.
—In Danger's Path, Set. abr. ed. 1999. (Corps Ser.: No. 8). audio 24.95 Highsmith Inc.
—In Danger's Path. 1999. (Corps Ser.: No. 8). 560p. 24.95 o.p. (*0-399-14421-8*);No. 8. 24.95 o.s.i (*0-399-14454-4*, 752354) Penguin Group (USA) Inc.
—The Last Heroes. 1998. (Men at War Ser.: No. 1). 400p. mass mkt. 7.99 (*0-515-12329-3*, Jove) Berkley Publishing Group.
—The Last Heroes, unabr. ed. 1998. (Men at War Ser.: No. 1). audio 64.00 (*0-7366-4097-5*, 4602) Books on Tape, Inc.
—The Last Heroes. l.t. ed. 1998. (Men at War Ser.: No. 1). pap. 24.95 o.p. (*1-56895-654-1*, Wheeler Publishing, Inc.) Gale Group.
—The Last Heroes. 1997. (Men at War Ser.: No. 1). 352p. 24.95 o.p. (*0-399-14289-4*, G. P. Putnam's Sons); 4p. 24.95 o.p. (*0-399-14296-7*, 695053) Penguin Group (USA) Inc.
—The Last Heroes. (Men at War Ser.: No. 1). 1988. mass mkt. 5.99 (*0-671-67822-1*); 1985. mass mkt. 3.50 (*0-671-49778-2*) Simon & Schuster. (Pocket).
—The Last Heroes. 1998. (Men at War Ser.). 13.55 (*0-606-15608-9*) Turtleback Bks.
—Line of Fire. 1993. (Corps Ser.: No. 5). 480p. mass mkt. 7.99 (*0-515-11013-2*, Jove) Berkley Publishing Group.
—Line of Fire. unabr. ed. 1992. (Corps Ser.: No. 5). audio 96.00 (*0-7366-2255-1*, 3044) Books on Tape, Inc.

—Line of Fire. 1992. (Corps Ser.: No. 5). 416p. 21.95 o.p. (*0-399-13671-1*, G. P. Putnam's Sons) Penguin Group (USA) Inc.
—Secret Honor. 2000. (Honor Bound Ser.: No. 3). 624p. mass mkt. 7.99 (*0-515-13009-5*, Jove) Berkley Publishing Group.
—Secret Honor. l.t. ed. 2000. (Honor Bound Ser.: No. 3). 28.95 (*1-56895-868-4*, Wheeler Publishing, Inc.) Gale Group.
—Secret Honor. 2000. (Honor Bound Ser.: No. 3). 544p. 25.95 o.s.i (*0-399-14568-0*) Penguin Group (USA) Inc.
—Secret Honor. (Honor Bound Ser.: No. 3). 512p. (*0-7278-5504-2*) Severn Hse. Pubs., Ltd.
—The Secret Warriors. 1999. (Men at War Ser.: No. 2). 416p. reprint ed. mass mkt. 7.99 (*0-515-12490-7*, Jove) Berkley Publishing Group.
—The Secret Warriors, unabr. ed. 1999. (Men at War Ser.: No. 2). audio 72.00 (*0-7366-4394-X*, 4856) Books on Tape, Inc.
—The Secret Warriors, abr. ed. 1999. (Men at War Ser.: No. 2). (J). audio 24.95 Highsmith Inc.
—The Secret Warriors. 1998. (Men at War Ser.: No. 2). 336p. 24.95 o.p. (*0-399-14381-5*, G. P. Putnam's Sons); 24.95 o.s.i (*0-399-14403-X*, 692928, Putnam Berkley Audio) Penguin Group (USA) Inc.
—The Secret Warriors. (Men at War Ser.: No. 2). 1989. mass mkt. 4.50 (*0-671-68443-4*); 1985. mass mkt. 3.50 (*0-671-49779-0*) Simon & Schuster. (Pocket).
—The Secret Warriors. l.t. ed. 1998. (Men at War Ser.: No. 2). 607p. 30.95 (*0-7862-1555-0*) Thorndike Pr.
—Semper Fi. unabr. collector's ed. 1992. (Corps Ser.: No. 1). audio 72.00 (*0-7366-2196-2*, 2991) Books on Tape, Inc.
—The Soldier Spies. 2000. (Men at War Ser.: No. 3). 432p. mass mkt. 7.99 (*0-515-12802-3*, Jove) Berkley Publishing Group.
—The Soldier Spies. l.t. ed. 2000. (Men at War Ser.: No. 3). 12.95 (*1-56895-978-8*); 562p. 27.95 (*1-56895-815-3*) Gale Group. (Wheeler Publishing, Inc.).
—The Soldier Spies. 1999. (Men at War Ser.: No. 3). 352p. 25.95 o.p. (*0-399-14494-3*, G. P. Putnam's Sons) Penguin Group (USA) Inc.
—The Soldier Spies. (Men at War Ser.: No. 3). 1989. mass mkt. 4.50 (*0-671-68444-2*); 1986. mass mkt. 3.95 (*0-671-60757-X*) Simon & Schuster. (Pocket).
Grimm, Jo. Putting on Her Face. 2001. 392p. pap. 25.50 (*0-7596-4366-0*) 1stBooks Library.
Grynberg, Henryk. The Jewish War & the Victory. Lourie, Richard & Wieniewska, Celina, trs. from POL. 2001. (Jewish Lives Ser.). 152p. text 49.95 (*0-8101-1901-3*) Northwestern Univ. Pr.
—The Jewish War & the Victory. Wieniewska, Celina & Lourie, Richard, trs. from POL. 2001. (Jewish Lives Ser.). 152p. reprint ed. pap. 15.95 (*0-8101-1785-1*) Northwestern Univ. Pr.
Guerard, Albert J. Maquisard: A Christmas Tale. 1995. 192p. 17.95 o.p. (*0-89141-585-8*, Presidio Pr.) Ballantine Bks.
Guilford, Irene. The Embrace, Vol. 1. 1999. (Prose Ser.: Vol. 55). 150p. pap. 13.00 (*1-55071-086-9*) Guernica Editions, Inc.
Haeffner, A. C. The Islander Bk. 2: White Woods Chronicles. 2001. 337p. pap. 22.99 (*1-4010-0374-5*) Xlibris Corp.
Haig, Kathryn. Apple Blossom Time. 2000. 458p. pap. 9.95 (*0-552-14537-8*) Transworld Publishers Ltd. GBR. *Dist:* Trafalgar Square.
Halpert, Sam. A Real Good War. 1999. 288p. pap. 12.95 (*0-385-49618-4*) Doubleday Publishing.
—A Real Good War. Kennedy, Byron, ed. 1997. (Illus.). 330p. (C). 19.95 (*0-941072-30-4*) Southern Heritage Pr., Inc.
Hamilton, Ruth. Billy London's Girls. 2000. (J). pap. 9.95 (*0-552-13897-5*) Transworld Publishers Ltd. GBR. *Dist:* Trafalgar Square.
Harding, Duncan. Slaughter in Singapore. 2003. 224p. 25.99 (*0-7278-5885-8*) Severn Hse. Pubs., Ltd.
Harington, Donald. When Angels Rest. 1998. 256p. 24.00 (*1-887178-07-4*, Counterpoint Pr.) Basic Bks.
Harris, Joanne. Five Quarters of the Orange. l.t. ed. 2001. 420p. lib. bdg. 28.95 (*1-58547-137-2*) Ctr. Point Large Print.
—Five Quarters of the Orange. 2002. 320p. pap. 13.95 (*0-06-095802-2*, Perennial) HarperTrade.
—Five Quarters of the Orange. 2001. 320p. 25.00 (*0-06-019813-3*, Morrow, William & Co.) Morrow/Avon.
Harris, Jonathan. Seizing Amber: A Novel. 2001. 272p. 22.00 o.p. (*1-57071-712-5*, Sourcebooks Landmark) Sourcebooks, Inc.
Harris, Robert. Enigma, Set. abr. ed. 1995. audio 3.99 o.s.i (*0-679-44549-8*, 693150, RH Audio) Random Hse. Audio Publishing Group.
—Enigma: A Novel. 1996. 384p. mass mkt. 6.99 (*0-8041-1548-6*, Ivy Bks.) Ballantine Bks.
—Enigma: A Novel. l.t. ed. 1996. (Large Print Bks.). 27.95 (*1-56895-275-9*, Wheeler Publishing, Inc.) Gale Group.
—Enigma: A Novel. 1995. pap. 22.00 o.p. (*0-679-76505-0*) Random Hse., Inc.
Harris, Thomas. Clearance & Fair & Just Reward. 2000. 316p. pap. 22.99 (*0-7388-3051-8*) Xlibris Corp.
Harrison. Flower That's Free. 767p. mass mkt. 11.95 (*0-7515-0233-2*) Warner Bks. GBR. *Dist:* Trafalgar Square.
Harrison, Sarah. A Flower That's Free. 1986. mass mkt. 4.50 o.s.i (*0-671-55206-6*, Pocket) Simon & Schuster.
—A Flower That's Free: A Novel. 1985. 17.45 o.p. (*0-671-55205-8*, Simon & Schuster) Simon & Schuster.
Harry, Lilian. A Girl Called Thursday. l.t. ed. 2003. (Magna Large Print Ser.). 576p. (*0-7505-2136-8*) Magna Large Print Bks. GBR. *Dist:* Ulverscroft Large Print Canada, Ltd.
—A Girl Called Thursday. 2003. 480p. mass mkt. (*0-7528-4950-6*) Orion Publishing Group, Ltd. GBR. *Dist:* Trafalgar Square.
—Lilian Harry: Two Great Novels. 2003. 800p. pap. 13.00 (*0-7528-5785-1*) Orion Publishing Group, Ltd. GBR. *Dist:* Trafalgar Square.
Harvey, Caroline, pseud. The Brass Dolphin. (Illus.). 1998. 413p. mass mkt. 8.99 (*0-552-14553-X*); 1997. 352p. 32.95 o.s.i (*0-385-40890-0*) Bantam Bks.
—The Brass Dolphin. 2000. 352p. mass mkt. 6.99 o.s.i (*0-425-17633-9*) Berkley Publishing Group.
—The Brass Dolphin. l.t. ed. 1998. (Charnwood Large Print Ser.). 448p. 29.99 o.p. (*0-7089-8987-X*, Ulverscroft) Thorpe, F. A. Pubs. GBR. *Dist:* Ulverscroft Large Print Bks., Ltd., Ulverscroft Large Print Canada, Ltd.
—The Brass Dolphin. 1999. 336p. 24.95 o.s.i (*0-670-88518-5*, Viking) Viking Penguin.
Hassel, Sven. Legion of the Damned. 2003. (Cassell Military Paperbacks Ser.). 312p. pap. 7.95 (*0-304-36631-5*) Cassell P L C GBR. *Dist:* Sterling Publishing Co., Inc.
—Monte Cassino. 2003. (Cassell Military Paperbacks Ser.). 256p. pap. 7.95 (*0-304-36632-3*) Cassell P L C GBR. *Dist:* Sterling Publishing Co., Inc.
—SS General. 2003. (Cassell Military Paperbacks Ser.). (DAN & ENG.). 288p. pap. 7.95 (*0-304-36634-X*) Cassell P L C GBR. *Dist:* Sterling Publishing Co., Inc.
Hazelgrove, William E. Tobacco Sticks. 1997. 352p. reprint ed. mass mkt. 5.99 o.s.i (*0-553-57559-7*) Bantam Bks.
—Tobacco Sticks. 1995. 308p. 18.95 (*0-9630052-8-6*) Pantonne Pr., Inc.
Heller, Joseph. Catch-22. 1973. 6.95 o.p. (*0-440-01098-5*); 1964. pap. 4.95 o.s.i (*0-385-28120-X*) Dell Publishing. (Delacorte Pr.).
—Catch-22. 1999. 19.15 (*0-8085-1402-4*) Econo-Clad Bks.
—Catch-22. o.p. (*0-394-60375-3*); 1995. 624p. 20.00 (*0-679-43722-3*) Knopf, Alfred A. Inc.
—Catch-22. 1971. (C). 3.95 (*0-671-00905-2*, Arco) Peterson's.
—Catch-22. 1987. 4.99 o.p. (*0-517-13313-X*) Random Hse. Value Publishing.
—Catch-22. (Simon & Schuster Classic Editions). 1999. (Illus.). 416p. 26.00 (*0-684-86513-0*); 1996. 464p. pap. 13.00 (*0-684-83339-5*); 1994. 415p. 26.00 (*0-671-50233-6*); 1961. 19.95 o.p. (*0-671-12805-1*); 1994. 432p. 75.00 o.p. (*0-671-89854-X*) Simon & Schuster. (Simon & Schuster).
—Catch-22. l.t. ed. 1984. 768p. 13.95 o.p. (*0-7089-8164-X*, Ulverscroft) Thorpe, F. A. Pubs. GBR. *Dist:* Ulverscroft Large Print Bks., Ltd.
—Catch-22. 1992. 455p. 13.50 o.p. (*0-606-00453-X*) Turtleback Bks.
—Closing Time: The Sequel to Catch-22. 1994. 464p. 24.00 (*0-671-74604-9*, Simon & Schuster) Simon & Schuster.
—Closing Time: The Sequel to Catch-22. 1999. pap. 12.90 (*0-671-04431-1*, Simon & Schuster Audioworks) Simon & Schuster Audio.
Hickam, Homer. The Keeper's Son. 2003. (Illus.). 352p. 24.95 (*0-312-30189-8*) St. Martin's Pr.
Higgins, Jack. Cold Harbour. 2003. 304p. mass mkt. 7.99 (*0-425-19320-9*) Berkley Publishing Group.
—Cold Harbour. 1990. 239.40 (*0-671-94343-X*); 19.95 o.p. (*0-671-68425-6*) Simon & Schuster. (Simon & Schuster).
—Cold Harbour. Grose, Bill, ed. 1990. reprint ed. mass mkt. 6.50 (*0-671-68426-4*, Pocket) Simon & Schuster.
—Cold Harbour. abr. ed. 1990. 15.95 incl. audio (*0-671-70194-0*, Simon & Schuster Audioworks) Simon & Schuster Audio.
—The Eagle Has Landed. 1946. pap. text o.p. (*0-17-556767-0*) Addison-Wesley Longman, Inc.
—The Eagle Has Landed. 1982. mass mkt. 4.50 o.s.i (*0-553-27042-7*); 368p. mass mkt. 3.95 o.s.i (*0-553-23345-9*) Bantam Bks.
—The Eagle Has Landed. 2000. 368p. mass mkt. 7.99 (*0-425-17718-1*) Berkley Publishing Group.
—The Eagle Has Landed. 1995. reprint ed. lib. bdg. 26.95 (*1-56849-593-5*) Buccaneer Bks., Inc.
—The Eagle Has Landed. l.t. ed. 1992. 17.95 o.p. (*0-8161-5474-0*); 1975. reprint ed. lib. bdg. 14.95 o.p. (*0-8161-6330-8*) Gale Group. (Macmillan Reference USA).
—The Eagle Has Landed. 1975. o.p. (*0-03-013746-2*) Holt, Henry & Co.
—The Eagle Has Landed. abr. ed. 1996. 24.95 o.p. (*0-7871-0960-6*); 39.95 o.p. (*0-7871-0959-2*, 103449) NewStar Media, Inc.
—The Eagle Has Landed. 1993. audio 15.99 o.s.i (*0-553-47143-0*, RH Audio) Random Hse. Audio Publishing Group.
—The Eagle Has Landed. 1997. 400p. pap. 19.95 o.p. (*0-671-01934-1*); 1989. bds. 4.95 (*0-671-66529-4*) Simon & Schuster. (Pocket).
—The Eagle Has Landed. Rubenstein, Julie, ed. 1990. 336p. reprint ed. mass mkt. 7.99 (*0-671-72773-7*, Pocket) Simon & Schuster.
—The Eagle Has Landed. rev. ed. 1991. 368p. 21.95 o.p. (*0-671-73310-9*, Simon & Schuster) Simon & Schuster.
—The Eagle Has Landed. l.t. ed. 1983. 528p. 12.50 o.p. (*0-7089-0973-6*, Ulverscroft) Thorpe, F. A. Pubs. GBR. *Dist:* Ulverscroft Large Print Bks., Ltd.
—Flight of Eagles. 1999. 336p. reprint ed. mass mkt. 7.99 (*0-425-16968-5*) Berkley Publishing Group.
—Flight of Eagles. l.t. ed. 1998. 28.95 o.p. (*1-56895-655-X*, Wheeler Publishing, Inc.) Gale Group.
—Flight of Eagles. 1998. 328p. 24.95 o.p. (*0-399-14376-9*, G. P. Putnam's Sons) Penguin Group (USA) Inc.
—A Game for Heroes. 2002. 320p. mass mkt. 7.99 (*0-425-18304-1*); 1986. 224p. mass mkt. 3.50 o.p. (*0-425-10088-X*); 1984. mass mkt. 2.95 o.s.i (*0-425-07195-2*) Berkley Publishing Group.
—A Game for Heroes. 1978. pap. 1.95 o.p. (*0-440-13262-2*) Dell Publishing.
—A Game for Heroes. abr. ed. 1995. 16.95 o.p. (*0-7871-0167-2*) NewStar Media, Inc.
—A Game for Heroes. Rubenstein, Julie, ed. 1990. 256p. reprint ed. mass mkt. 6.50 (*0-671-72455-X*, Pocket) Simon & Schuster.
—A Jack Higgins Trilogy. 1986. 736p. 17.95 o.s.i (*0-8128-3100-4*, Scarborough Hse.) Madison Bks., Inc.
—Night of the Fox. 1995. (Select Sound, Dove Ser.). 4.99 o.p. (*0-7871-0312-8*) Penguin Group (USA) Inc.
—Night of the Fox. 1991. 352p. mass mkt. 5.95 (*0-671-72820-2*, Pocket); 1987. mass mkt. 5.95 (*0-671-64058-5*, Pocket); 1987. (Illus.). 320p. bds. 17.45 o.p. (*0-671-63727-4*, Simon & Schuster) Simon & Schuster.
—Storm Warning. 2000. 320p. mass mkt. 7.99 (*0-425-17607-X*) Berkley Publishing Group.
—Storm Warning. 1977. lib. bdg. 12.50 o.p. (*0-8161-6439-8*, Macmillan Reference USA) Gale Group.
—Storm Warning. 1976. o.p. (*0-03-017761-8*) Holt, Henry & Co.
—Storm Warning. abr. ed. 1995. 16.95 o.p. (*0-7871-0166-4*) NewStar Media, Inc.
—Thunder Point. 1994. 368p. reprint ed. mass mkt. 7.99 (*0-425-14357-0*) Berkley Publishing Group.
—Thunder Point. 1995. reprint ed. lib. bdg. 26.95 (*1-56849-594-3*) Buccaneer Bks., Inc.
—Thunder Point. l.t. ed. 1993. 26.95 o.p. (*1-56895-037-3*, Wheeler Publishing, Inc.) Gale Group.
—Thunder Point. 1993. 320p. 22.95 o.p. (*0-399-13835-8*, G. P. Putnam's Sons) Penguin Group (USA) Inc.
—Thunder Point. 5.98 o.s.i (*0-8317-6524-0*) Smithmark Pubs., Inc.
—The Valhalla Exchange. 1981. mass mkt. 2.95 o.s.i (*0-449-23449-5*, Fawcett) Ballantine Bks.
—The Valhalla Exchange. 1977. lib. bdg. 12.50 o.p. (*0-8161-6496-7*, Macmillan Reference USA) Gale Group.
—The Valhalla Exchange. 1977. 8.95 o.s.i (*0-8128-1932-2*, Scarborough Hse.) Madison Bks., Inc.
Hijuelos, Oscar. A Simple Habana Melody: From When the World Was Good. l.t. ed. 2003. lib. bdg. 29.95 (*1-58547-298-0*, Platinum) Ctr. Point Large Print.
Hijuelos, Oscar. A Simple Habana Melody: From When the World Was Good. 2002. 352p. 24.95 (*0-06-017569-9*) HarperCollins Pubs.
—A Simple Habana Melody: From When the World Was Good. 2003. 368p. pap. 13.95 (*0-06-092869-7*, Perennial) HarperTrade.
Hill, Grace Livingston. All Through the Night. 1976. reprint ed. lib. bdg. 22.95 (*0-89190-001-2*, Rivercity Pr.) Amereon, Ltd.
—All Through the Night. l.t. ed. 2000. (Candlelight Romance Ser.). 387p. 22.95 o.p. (*0-7862-2786-9*) Thorndike Pr.
—All Through the Night, No. 6. 1996. (Grace Livingston Hill Ser.: Vol. 6). 224p. mass mkt. 4.99 o.p. (*0-8423-0018-X*) Tyndale Hse. Pubs.
—More Than Conqueror. 256p. reprint ed. lib. bdg. 22.95 (*0-89190-053-5*, Rivercity Pr.) Amereon, Ltd.
—More Than Conqueror. l.t. ed. 2001. (Thorndike Candlelight Romance Ser.). 392p. 24.95 (*0-7862-3278-1*) Thorndike Pr.
—More Than Conqueror. 1990. (Grace Livingston Hill Ser.: Vol. 11). pap. 4.95 o.p. (*0-8423-4559-0*, 074559-0) Tyndale Hse. Pubs.
Hirsch, Harvey. Grandma's Lost Gift: A Christmas Story. 1994. Orig. Title: The Creche of Krakow. (Illus.). 56p. pap. 7.95 (*0-929613-00-7*, 100GLG) Cobblestone Pr.
Hodgson, Ken. Surviving Wisdom. 2003. 218p. 25.95 (*0-7862-5437-8*, Five Star) Gale Group.
Hoel, Sigurd. Meeting at the Milestone. Lyngstad, Sverre, tr. from NOR. 2002. 284p. pap. 15.95 (*1-892295-31-8*) Green Integer.
Holt, Tate. Yamashita's Gold: A Novel. 1998. (Illus.). 428p. 23.95 (*0-9653774-6-6*) Berkeley Hills Bks.
Holthe, Tess Uriza. When the Elephants Dance: A Novel. 2002. (Illus.). 384p. 24.95 (*0-609-60952-1*, Crown) Crown Publishing Group.
—When the Elephants Dance: A Novel. 2003. 384p. pap. 14.00 (*0-14-200288-7*) Penguin Group (USA) Inc.
Hough, Richard. Fight of the Few. 1981. pap. 2.50 o.p. (*0-440-12771-8*) Dell Publishing.
Hoyt, Richard. Old Soldiers Sometimes Lie. E-Book 19.95 (*0-312-70863-7*, Tor Bks.); 2002. 432p. 25.95 (*0-7653-0331-0*, Forge Bks.) Doherty, Tom Assocs., LLC.
Hughes, Dean. As Long As I Have You. 2000. (Children of the Promise Ser.: Vol. 5). 471p. 22.95 (*1-57345-800-7*, Bookcraft, Inc.) Deseret Bk. Co.
—Far from Home. 1998. (Children of the Promise Ser.: Vol. 3). 492 p. 21.95 (*1-57345-406-0*) Deseret Bk. Co.
—Since You Went Away. (Children of the Promise Ser.: Vol. 2). 2003. audio 19.95 (*1-57345-293-9*); 1997. 507p. 17.95 (*1-57345-285-8*) Deseret Bk. Co.
Hughes, Richard Arthur Warren. The Fox in the Attic. 1962. o.p. (*0-06-011985-3*) HarperCollins Pubs.
—The Fox in the Attic. 2000. (New York Review Books Classics Ser.). 326p. reprint ed. pap. 12.95 (*0-940322-29-3*) New York Review of Bks., Inc., The.
Hunter, Alan. Over Here. l.t. ed. 2003. 245p. pap. 24.45 (*0-7862-5411-4*) Thorndike Pr.
Hyde, Catherine Ryan. Walter's Purple Heart: A Novel. 2002. (Illus.). 320p. 24.00 (*0-684-86723-0*, Simon & Schuster) Simon & Schuster.
Hyde, Christopher. A Gathering of Saints. 1997. 438p. per. 6.99 (*0-671-87581-7*, Pocket); 1996. 432p. 24.00 (*0-671-87580-9*, Atria) Simon & Schuster.
—The Second Assassin. 2002. 400p. (Orig.). mass mkt. 6.99 (*0-451-41030-0*, Onyx) NAL.
Ibuse, Masuji. Black Rain. 1985. 304p. mass mkt. 3.95 o.s.i (*0-553-24988-6*) Bantam Bks.
—Black Rain. Shaw, ed. Bester, John, tr. from JPN. 1988. 304p. pap. 12.00 (*0-87011-364-X*) Kodansha America, Inc.
—Black Rain. 1988. 18.05 (*0-606-20070-3*) Turtleback Bks.
Iles, Greg. Black Cross. l.t. ed. 1995. 528p. 19.95 o.p. (*0-525-93829-X*, Dutton) Dutton/Plume.
—Black Cross. l.t. ed. 1995. pap. 23.95 (*1-56895-225-2*, Wheeler Publishing, Inc.) Gale Group.
—Black Cross. 1995. 576p. mass mkt. 7.99 (*0-451-18519-6*); pap. 5.99 (*0-451-18746-6*) NAL. (Signet Bks.).
—Black Cross. abr. ed. 1995. pap. 23.95 o.p. incl. audio (*0-453-00935-2*, 692155) Penguin/HighBridge.
Ishiguro, Kazuo. An Artist of the Floating World. 1989. (Vintage International Ser.). 208p. pap. 12.00 (*0-679-72266-1*, Vintage) Knopf Publishing Group.
—An Artist of the Floating World. 1986. 208p. 15.95 o.p. (*0-399-13119-1*) Putnam Publishing Group, The.
—An Artist of the Floating World. 2000. 26.50 (*0-8446-7123-1*) Smith, Peter Pub., Inc.
—An Artist of the Floating World. l.t. ed. 2001. 262p. pap. 25.95 (*0-7862-3565-9*); 280p. (*0-7540-4619-2*); 280p. (*0-7540-4620-6*) Thorndike Pr.
—A Pale View of Hills. l.t. ed. 1999. (*0-7540-3914-5*); (*0-7540-3913-7*) Thorndike Pr.
Jack, Donald. That's Me in the Middle: The Bandy Papers, Vol. 2. 2001. 364p. pap. (*0-7710-4379-1*) McClelland & Stewart/Tundra Bks.
Jackson, Jeffrey. Island of Paradise & Hell. 2000. 14.95 (*0-533-13042-5*) Vantage Pr., Inc.
Jackson, Mick. Five Boys: A Novel. 2001. 239p. (*0-571-21401-0*); 248p. pap. (*0-571-20613-1*) Faber & Faber, Inc.
—Five Boys: A Novel. 2002. 288p. 24.95 (*0-06-001394-X*, Morrow, William & Co.) Morrow/Avon.
Jagendorf, Zvi. Wolfy & the Strudelbakers. 2002. 192p. pap. 13.95 (*1-899235-38-8*) Lewis, Dewi Publishing GBR. *Dist:* Consortium Bk. Sales & Distribution.
Janes, J. Robert. Dollmaker. 2003. pap. 12.00 (*1-56947-346-3*); 2002. 258p. 23.00 (*1-56947-285-8*) Soho Pr., Inc.

—Mayhem. 1999. 272p. pap. 12.00 (*1-56947-158-4*) Soho Pr., Inc.

Jefferson, M. T. The Victory Dance Murder. 2000. (Homefront Mysteries Ser.). 208p. mass mkt. 5.99 o.s.i (*0-425-17310-0*, Prime Crime) Berkley Publishing Group.

Jenkins, Robin. Guests of War. 1988. (Scottish Classic Ser.: No. 10). 286p. pap. text 19.95 o.p. (*0-7073-0544-6*) Ashgate Publishing Co.

—Guests of War. 2001. 298p. pap. 12.95 (*1-873631-70-7*) B & W Publishing GBR. *Dist:* Interlink Publishing Group, Inc.

Jensen, Liz. War Crimes for the Home. 2002. 288p. (*0-7475-5969-4*) Bloomsbury Pr.

Jones, James. The Pistol. 2003. 158p. pap. 12.00 (*0-226-39186-8*) Univ. of Chicago Pr.

—The Thin Red Line. 1999. E-Book 11.95 (*0-440-33411-X*) Random Hse., Inc.

Jones, Todd E. A Bend in the River. 2002. 39.50 (*0-7596-1452-0*); 2001. 608p. pap. 29.60 (*0-7596-1451-2*) 1stBooks Library.

Joyce, Brenda. The Chase. 2003. 29.95 (*1-57490-482-5*, Beeler Large Print Bks.) Beeler, Thomas T. Publisher.

—The Chase. E-Book 24.95 (*0-312-70731-2*); 2002. 384p. 24.95 (*0-312-28449-7*); 2003. 480p. reprint ed. mass mkt. 6.99 (*0-312-98376-X*, St. Martin's Paperbacks) St. Martin's Pr.

Katzenbach, John. Hart's War. 2002. E-Book 7.99 (*1-59061-829-7*) Adobe Systems, Inc.

—Hart's War. movie tie-in ed. 2000. 576p. mass mkt. 7.99 (*0-345-42625-8*, Ballantine Bks.) Ballantine Bks.

Kawano, Doris. Harue, Child of Hawaii. 1984. pap. 11.95 o.p. (*0-914916-64-5*) Ku Pa'a Publishing.

Keeley, Edmund. Some Wine for Remembrance. 2002. pap. 15.00 (*1-893996-15-8*) White Pine Pr.

Kelby, N. M. In the Company of Angels: A Novel. 2002. (Illus.). 192p. pap. 12.00 (*0-7868-8583-1*) Hyperion Pr.

Kelleher, Brian. Iron Star. 2001. 304p. mass mkt. 6.99 o.s.i (*0-515-13040-0*, Jove) Berkley Publishing Group.

Kendall, Jay. The Secret Keepers. 1998. 250p. pap. 14.95 (*1-884540-39-2*) Haley's.

Keneally, Thomas. An Angel in Australia. 2002. 336p. o.s.i (*1-86471-001-2*) Doubleday Publishing.

—The Office of Innocence. 2003. 336p. 25.00 (*0-385-50763-1*, Talese, Nan A.) Doubleday Publishing.

—Schindler's List. l.t. ed. (Large Print Bks.). 1994. ix, 549p. 25.95 o.p. (*1-56895-105-1*, Wheeler Publishing, Inc.); 1985. xiii, 548p. 18.95 o.p. (*0-8161-3854-0*, Macmillan Reference USA) Gale Group.

—Schindler's List. 400p. 1994. (Illus.). 25.00 (*0-671-51688-4*, Simon & Schuster); 1993. pap. 14.00 (*0-671-88031-4*, Touchstone); 1992. pap. 12.00 o.s.i (*0-671-77972-9*, Touchstone); 1982. (Illus.). 17.50 o.p. (*0-671-44977-X*, Simon & Schuster) Simon & Schuster.

—Schindler's List. 1993. 20.05 (*0-606-14311-4*) Turtleback Bks.

—Schindler's List. 1983. (Illus.). 400p. pap. 9.95 o.p. (*0-14-006784-1*, Penguin Bks.) Viking Penguin.

Kennedy, William P. The Himmler Equation. 1989. 304p. 18.95 o.p. (*0-312-03358-3*) St. Martin's Pr.

Kessler, Leo. Sirens of Dunkirk. 2003. 224p. 25.99 (*0-7278-5884-X*) Severn Hse. Pubs., Ltd.

Kesson, Jessie. Another Time, Another Place. 2001. 160p. pap. 9.95 (*1-873631-71-5*) B & W Publishing GBR. *Dist:* Interlink Publishing Group, Inc.

—Another Time, Another Place. l.t. ed. 1987. 16.95 o.p. (*0-86009-810-9*, Macmillan Reference USA) Gale Group.

—Another Time, Another Place. 1989. pap. o.p. (*0-7012-0835-X*) Random Hse. of Canada, Ltd. CAN. *Dist:* Random Hse., Inc.

Kingsbury, Kate. For Whom Death Tolls. 2002. (Manor House Mystery Ser.: No. 3). 208p. mass mkt. 5.99 (*0-425-18386-6*, Prime Crime) Berkley Publishing Group.

—Paint by Murder. 2003. 224p. mass mkt. 5.99 (*0-425-19215-6*, Prime Crime) Berkley Publishing Group.

Knauss, Sibylle. Eva's Cousin: A Novel. Bell, Anthea, tr. from GER. 2002. 336p. 24.95 (*0-345-44905-3*, Ballantine Bks.) Ballantine Bks.

—Eva's Cousin: A Novel. Bell, Anthea, tr. 2002. (Women's Fiction Ser.). 28.95 (*0-7862-4902-1*) Thorndike Pr.

Kogawa, Joy. Itsuka. 1993. 352p. pap. 19.00 (*0-385-46885-7*) Knopf, Alfred A. Inc.

Kohout, Pavel. The Widow Killer. 2000. 400p. pap. 14.00 (*0-312-25289-7*) Picador.

—The Widow Killer: A Novel. Bermel, Neil, tr. 1998. (Illus.). 391p. 24.95 o.p. (*0-312-19363-7*) Picador.

—The Widow Killer: A Novel. 1999. mass mkt. (*0-312-96920-1*, St. Martin's Paperbacks) St. Martin's Pr.

—The Widow Killer: A Novel. Bermel, Neil, tr. 1999. E-Book 24.95 (*0-312-24620-X*) St. Martin's Pr.

Koning, Hans. The Affair. 2002. 227p. pap. 14.00 (*1-58838-051-3*) NewSouth, Inc.

—Zeeland: or Elective Concurrences: A Novel of War, Death, Love & Loss. 2001. 256p. (*1-58838-050-5*) NewSouth, Inc.

Labro, Philippe. Le Petit Garcon. Coverdale, Linda, tr. 1992. 320p. 23.00 o.p. (*0-374-18448-8*) Farrar, Straus & Giroux.

—Le Petit Garcon. (Folio Ser.: No. 2389). (FRE.). pap. 13.95 (*2-07-038526-4*) Schoenhof's Foreign Bks., Inc.

Lambert, Derek. Vendetta. 1990. 176p. 16.95 (*0-8027-1120-0*) Walker & Co.

Landon, Christopher. Ice-Cold in Alex. 2003. (Cassell Military Paperbacks Ser.). (Illus.). 248p. pap. 9.95 (*0-304-36625-0*) Cassell P L C GBR. *Dist:* Sterling Publishing Co., Inc.

Larson, Elyse. The Hope Before Us. 2002. (Women of Valor Ser.: Vol. 3). 352p. pap. 12.99 (*0-7642-2376-3*) Bethany Hse. Pubs.

—So Shall We Stand. 2001. (Women of Valor Ser.: Vol. 2). 352p. pap. 12.99 (*0-7642-2375-5*) Bethany Hse. Pubs.

Lawton, John. Bluffing Mr. Churchill. 2005. 336p. 24.00 (*0-87113-907-3*, Atlantic Monthly Pr.) Grove/Atlantic, Inc.

Leavitt, David. While England Sleeps. rev. ed. 1995. 324p. 24.95 o.p. (*0-395-75937-4*); 304p. pap. 11.95 o.s.i (*0-395-75286-8*) Houghton Mifflin Co.

—While England Sleeps. 320p. 9999. pap. 10.95 o.s.i (*0-14-013361-5*, Penguin Bks.); 1993. (Illus.). 22.00 o.p. (*0-670-83349-5*, Viking) Viking Penguin.

Lee, Chang-Rae. A Gesture Life. 2000. 368p. pap. 14.00 (*1-57322-828-1*, Riverhead Trade (Paperbacks)) Berkley Publishing Group.

—A Gesture Life. 1999. 356p. 23.95 o.s.i (*1-57322-146-5*, Riverhead Bks. (Hardcovers)) Putnam Publishing Group, The.

Lee, George. Goat for Azazel: A World War II Story. 1999. 640p. E-Book 8.00 (*0-7388-8181-3*) Xlibris Corp.

Lee, George Oscar. Goat for Azazel: A World War II Story. 1999. 640p. pap. 28.99 (*0-7388-0545-9*); text 38.99 (*0-7388-0544-0*) Xlibris Corp.

Lee, Maureen. House by Princes Park. 2002. 512p. pap. (*0-7528-4835-6*); 406p. (*0-7528-3803-2*) Orion Publishing Group, Ltd. GBR. *Dist:* Trafalgar Square.

Lehrer, Jim. Special Prisoner. E-Book 19.50 (*1-58945-601-7*) Adobe Systems, Inc.

—Special Prisoner. 2002. 240p. pap. text 6.99 (*1-903985-30-7*) Perseus Bks. Group.

—Special Prisoner. 2001. 240p. pap. text 14.00 (*1-58648-042-1*) PublicAffairs.

—Special Prisoner. 2000. E-Book 19.50 (*0-375-50577-6*) Random Hse., Inc.

—Special Prisoner. l.t. ed. 2000. (Americana Ser.). 320p. 30.95 (*0-7862-3019-3*) Thorndike Pr.

Leon, Donna. A Noble Radiance. 2003. 304p. mass mkt. 6.99 (*0-14-200319-0*) Penguin Group (USA) Inc.

Litwak, Leo. The Medic: Life & Death in the Last Days of World War II. 2002. 240p. pap. 14.00 (*0-14-200219-4*) Penguin Group (USA) Inc.

Loh, Vyvyane. Breaking the Tongue. 2004. 448p. text 24.95 (*0-393-05792-5*) Norton, W. W. & Co., Inc.

London, Joan. Gilgamesh. 272p. 2004. pap. 13.00 (*0-8021-4121-8*); 2003. 23.00 (*0-8021-1741-4*) Grove/Atlantic, Inc. (Grove Pr.).

Lovell, Ron. Murder at Yaquina Head: A Thomas Martindale Mystery. 2002. 184p. pap. 18.95 (*0-86534-369-1*); 256p. 22.95 (*0-86534-345-4*) Sunstone Pr.

Loy, Rosetta. Hot Chocolate at Hanselmann's. Conti, Gregory, tr. from ITA. & intro. by. 2003. (European Women Writers Ser.). 176p. pap. 16.95 (*0-8032-8006-8*); text 50.00 (*0-8032-2945-3*) Univ. of Nebraska Pr.

Ludlum, Robert. The Tristan Betrayal: A Novel. Date not set. mass mkt. (*0-312-99774-4*, St. Martin's Paperbacks); 2003. 528p. 27.95 (*0-312-31669-0*); 2003. E-Book 27.95 (*0-312-71133-6*) St. Martin's Pr.

MacInnes, Helen. Horizon. 1985. 225p. mass mkt. 4.95 o.s.i (*0-449-20861-3*, Fawcett) Ballantine Bks.

—Horizon. 1971. 213p. 24.95 o.s.i (*0-15-142171-4*) Harcourt Trade Pubs.

—Horizon. l.t. ed. 1975. (Ulverscroft Large Print Ser.). 29.99 o.p. (*0-85456-316-4*, Ulverscroft) Thorpe, F. A. Pubs. GBR. *Dist:* Ulverscroft Large Print Bks., Ltd., Ulverscroft Large Print Canada, Ltd.

MacLean, Alistair. The Guns of Navarone. 1997. pap. text o.p. (*0-17-556608-9*) Addison-Wesley Longman, Inc.

—The Guns of Navarone. 1987. mass mkt. 5.99 o.s.i (*0-449-21472-9*, Fawcett); 1976. mass mkt. 1.75 o.s.i (*0-449-13537-3*) Ballantine Bks.

—The Guns of Navarone. 1994. reprint ed. lib. bdg. 27.95 (*1-56849-306-1*) Buccaneer Bks., Inc.

—The Guns of Navarone. 1984. 11.09 o.p. (*0-606-00780-6*) Turtleback Bks.

—Where Eagles Dare. 2002. (Adrenaline Classics Ser.). 320p. 13.95 (*1-56025-455-6*, Thunder's Mouth Pr.) Avalon Publishing Group.

MacMillan, Ian. Village of a Million Spirits: A Novel of the Treblinka Uprising. 1999. 257p. 24.00 o.p. (*1-883642-84-1*) Steerforth Pr.

—Village of a Million Spirits: A Novel of the Treblinka Uprising. 2000. 272p. 12.95 o.s.i (*0-14-029033-8*) Viking Penguin.

Mailer, Norman. The Naked & the Dead. 1994. lib. bdg. 65.00 (*1-56849-421-1*) Buccaneer Bks., Inc.

—The Naked & the Dead. 1988. 18.95 o.s.i (*0-8050-0522-6*); 1981. pap. o.p. (*0-03-059043-4*, Owl Bks.); 1980. 740p. pap. 16.00 o.s.i (*0-8050-0521-8*, Owl Bks.); 1990. 736p. 30.00 o.p. (*0-8050-1273-7*) Holt, Henry & Co.

—The Naked & the Dead. 1971. mass mkt. 1.50 o.p. (*0-451-04734-6*); 1969. mass mkt. 1.25 o.p. (*0-451-04087-2*); 1951. mass mkt. 1.75 o.p. (*0-451-06052-0*); 1951. mass mkt. 2.95 o.p. (*0-451-09051-9*); 1951. mass mkt. 0.75 o.p. (*0-451-01549-5*); 1951. mass mkt. 0.95 o.p. (*0-451-02460-5*); 1951. mass mkt. 2.25 o.p. (*0-451-07604-4*); 1951. mass mkt. 0.50 o.p. (*0-451-00837-5*); 1951. mass mkt. 3.50 o.p. (*0-451-09702-5*, E9702) NAL. (Signet Bks.).

—The Naked & the Dead. 2000. 752p. pap. 16.00 (*0-312-26505-0*) Picador.

—The Naked & the Dead. 2000. 22.05 (*0-606-19213-1*) Turtleback Bks.

—The Naked & the Dead: The 50th Anniversary Edition. 1998. 736p. pap. 17.00 o.s.i (*0-8050-6017-0*, Owl Bks.); 50th ed. 37.50 (*0-8050-6018-9*) Holt, Henry & Co.

Mairesse, Michelle & Mairesse, Jean. The Season Is Over. 1999. (Illus.). 300p. (C). E-Book (*1-929485-04-2*) Hermes Pr.

Malaparte, Curzio. The Skin. 1988. pap. 12.95 o.p. (*0-910395-37-3*) Marlboro Pr., Inc., The.

—The Skin. Moore, David, tr. 1997. (European Classics Ser.). 274p. pap. 21.00 (*0-8101-1572-7*) Northwestern Univ. Pr.

Mantle, John. The Bloody War, Mate. 2003. 320p. pap. 16.95 (*0-9713318-7-1*) Lucky Pr., LLC.

Marahimin, Ismail. And the War Is Over. McGlynn, John H., tr. from IND. 2002. (Pegasus Prize for Literature Ser.). 192p. pap. 13.00 (*0-8021-3922-1*, Grove Pr.) Grove/Atlantic, Inc.

Marks, Annie. An Enchanted Place. 2003. 242p. 29.95 (*0-7090-7148-5*) Hale, Robert Ltd. GBR. *Dist:* Trafalgar Square.

Marshall, James Vance. White-Out. (Illus.). 256p. 2002. pap. 13.00 (*1-56947-277-7*); 2000. 23.00 (*1-56947-224-6*) Soho Pr., Inc.

—White-Out. l.t. ed. 2001. (Adventure Ser.). 384p. 28.95 (*0-7862-3320-6*) Thorndike Pr.

Martinusen, Cindy McCormick. Blue Night: A Novel. 2001. 416p. pap. 10.99 (*0-8423-5236-8*) Tyndale Hse. Pubs.

Maruya, Saiichi. Grass for My Pillow. Keene, Dennis, tr. from JPN. 2002. (Modern Asian Literature Ser.). 320p. 24.50 (*0-231-12658-1*) Columbia Univ. Pr.

Maruya, Saiichi & Keene, Dennis. Grass for My Pillow. E-Book 24.50 (*0-231-50157-9*) Columbia Univ. Pr.

Matheson, Richard. The Beardless Warriors: A Novel of World War II. 2001. 320p. pap. 13.95 (*0-312-87831-1*, Forge Bks.) Doherty, Tom Assocs., LLC.

McBride, James. Miracle at St. Anna. l.t. ed. 2003. 345p. 29.95 (*1-58724-473-X*, Wheeler Publishing, Inc.) Gale Group.

—Miracle at St. Anna: A Novel. 2002. 64p. audio 25.95 (*0-06-009318-8*); 64p. audio compact disk 29.95 (*0-06-009319-6*); 128p. audio 34.95 (*0-06-009320-X*) HarperTrade. (Caedmon).

—Miracle at St. Anna: A Novel. 2002. 228p. 24.95 o.s.i (*1-57322-212-7*, Riverhead Bks. (Hardcovers)) Putnam Publishing Group, The.

McCledon, Lise. One O'Clock Jump: A Dorie Lennox Mystery. 2001. 276p. 23.95 (*0-312-25195-5*, Saint Martin's Minotaur) St. Martin's Pr.

McCown, Clint. War Memorials. 2000. 220p. 23.95 (*1-55597-312-4*) Graywolf Pr.

—War Memorials. 2001. 240p. reprint ed. pap. 13.00 (*0-618-12847-6*, Mariner Bks.) Houghton Mifflin Co. Trade & Reference Div.

McCunn, Ruthanne Lum. Sole Survivor: The True Account of 133 Days Adrift. 1999. (Illus.). 240p. (gr. 8-12). pap. 12.00 (*0-8070-7139-0*) Beacon Pr.

McCutchan, Philip. Cameron & the Kaiserhof. 1984. 192p. 10.95 o.p. (*0-312-11443-5*) St. Martin's Pr.

—Cameron Comes Through. 1986. 160p. 12.95 o.p. (*0-312-11444-3*) St. Martin's Pr.

—Cameron in Command. 1986. pap. 3.50 o.p. (*0-312-90468-1*, St. Martin's Paperbacks); 1984. 176p. 10.95 o.p. (*0-312-11446-X*) St. Martin's Pr.

—Cameron in the Gap. 1999. audio 44.95 Soundings, Ltd. GBR. *Dist:* Ulverscroft Large Print Bks., Ltd.

—Cameron in the Gap. 1983. 160p. 9.95 o.p. (*0-312-11448-6*) St. Martin's Pr.

—Cameron in the Gap. l.t. ed. 1999. (General Ser.). 232p. pap. 23.95 (*0-7862-1964-5*); (*0-7540-3810-6*); (*0-7540-3809-2*) Thorndike Pr.

—Cameron of the Castle Bay. unabr. ed. 2001. audio 44.95 (*1-85496-708-8*, 67088) Soundings, Ltd. GBR. *Dist:* Ulverscroft Large Print Bks., Ltd.

—Cameron's Chase. unabr. ed. 1997. audio 49.95 (*1-85496-934-X*, 6934X) Soundings, Ltd. GBR. *Dist:* Ulverscroft Large Print Bks., Ltd.

—Cameron's Chase. 1987. pap. 3.50 o.p. (*0-312-90703-6*, St. Martin's Paperbacks); 1986. 182p. 12.95 o.p. (*0-312-11450-8*) St. Martin's Pr.

—Cameron's Commitment. 1989. 192p. 14.95 o.p. (*0-312-02532-7*) St. Martin's Pr.

—Cameron's Convoy. 156p. 14.99 o.p. (*0-7278-4771-6*) Severn Hse. Pubs., Ltd.

—Cameron's Convoy. 2001. audio 44.95 (*1-85496-138-1*, 61381) Soundings, Ltd. GBR. *Dist:* Ulverscroft Large Print Bks., Ltd.

—Cameron's Convoy. l.t. ed. 1999. (General Ser.). 240p. pap. 23.95 (*0-7862-1821-5*) Thorndike Pr.

—Cameron's Crossing. 1993. 176p. 17.95 o.p. (*0-312-09762-X*) St. Martin's Pr.

—Cameron's Raid. unabr. ed. 1999. audio 54.95 (*1-86042-388-4*, 23884) Soundings, Ltd. GBR. *Dist:* Ulverscroft Large Print Bks., Ltd.

—Cameron's Raid. 1986. pap. 3.50 o.p. (*0-312-90081-3*, St. Martin's Paperbacks); 1985. 11.95 o.p. (*0-312-11452-4*) St. Martin's Pr.

—Cameron's Troop Lift. 1987. 208p. 13.95 o.p. (*0-312-01008-7*) St. Martin's Pr.

—Convoy South. 192p. 1996. pap. 8.95 o.p. (*0-312-14299-4*, Saint Martin's Griffin); 1988. 14.95 o.p. (*0-312-02178-X*) St. Martin's Pr.

—Lieutenant Cameron RNVR. unabr. ed. 1998. audio 63.95 (*1-85903-068-8*) Magna Story Sound GBR. *Dist:* Ulverscroft Large Print Bks., Ltd.

—Lieutenant Cameron RNVR. 1987. pap. 3.50 o.p. (*0-312-90691-9*, St. Martin's Paperbacks); 1985. 160p. 11.95 o.p. (*0-312-48373-2*) St. Martin's Pr.

—Orders for Cameron. l.t. ed. 1985. lib. bdg. 14.50 o.p. (*0-7451-0246-8*); 13.50 o.p. (*0-8166-0246-8*) Gale Group. (Macmillan Reference USA).

—Orders for Cameron. unabr. ed. 1996. audio 49.95 (*1-86042-123-7*, 21237) Soundings, Ltd. GBR. *Dist:* Ulverscroft Large Print Bks., Ltd.

—Orders for Cameron. 1983. 160p. 10.95 o.p. (*0-312-58722-8*) St. Martin's Pr.

McLaughlin, Ann L. The House on Q Street: A Novel. 2002. 292p. pap. 14.95 (*1-880284-59-6*) Daniel, John & Co., Pubs.

McMullan, Margaret. In My Mother's House. Date not set. mass mkt. (*0-312-99153-3*, St. Martin's Paperbacks); 2003. 272p. 23.95 (*0-312-31824-3*) St. Martin's Pr.

McSherry, Frank D., Jr. The Fantastic World War II. Greenberg, Martin H., ed. 1990. (Orig.). pap. 3.50 o.s.i (*0-671-69881-8*) Baen Bks.

Mesce, Bill, Jr. & Szilagyi, Steven G. The Advocate: A Novel of World War II. 2001. (Illus.). 416p. reprint ed. mass mkt. 6.50 (*0-553-58197-X*) Bantam Bks.

Michaels, Anne. Fugitive Pieces. 1997. 294p. 25.00 o.s.i (*0-679-45439-X*) Knopf, Alfred A. Inc.

—Fugitive Pieces. l.t. ed. 1997. (Basic Ser.). 384p. 26.95 (*0-7862-1200-4*) Thorndike Pr.

—Fugitive Pieces: A Novel. 1998. (Illus.). 304p. pap. 13.00 (*0-679-77659-1*, Vintage) Knopf Publishing Group.

Monsarrat, Nicholas. The Cruel Sea. 2000. (Classics of War Ser.). 509p. reprint ed. pap. 18.95 (*1-58080-046-7*) Burford Bks.

—The Cruel Sea. Sweetman, Jack, ed. 1988. (Classics of Naval Literature Ser.). (Illus.). 400p. 32.95 o.s.i (*0-87021-055-6*) Naval Institute Pr.

—The Cruel Sea. l.t. ed. 1984. 752p. 29.99 o.p. (*0-7089-8171-2*, Ulverscroft) Thorpe, F. A. Pubs. GBR. *Dist:* Ulverscroft Large Print Bks., Ltd.

Montagu, Ewen & Cooper, Duff, intros. The Man Who Never Was: Operation Heartbreak. 2003. (Illus.). 288p. 29.95 (*1-86227-187-9*) Spellmount Pubs. GBR. *Dist:* Casemate Pubs. & Bk. Distributors, LLC.

Montague, Terry. Fireweed. 1992. pap. 10.95 (*1-55503-407-1*, 01111078) Covenant Communications, Inc.

Mooney, Robert. Father of the Man: A Novel. 2002. 240p. 23.00 (*0-375-42204-8*, Pantheon) Knopf Publishing Group.

Moore, Philip N. What If Hitler Won the War: Where Would We Be Today. 1998. (Illus.). 190p. pap. 19.95 (*1-57915-996-6*) Rams Head Pr., International, The.

Morante, Elsa. History. 1983. pap. 2.95 o.p. (*0-380-41889-4*, Avon Bks.) Morrow/Avon.

—History: A Novel. Weaver, William, tr. from ITA. 2nd ed. 2000. (Steerforth Italia Ser.). 740p. pap. 19.50 (*1-58642-004-6*, Steerforth Italia) Steerforth Pr.

Morris, Gilbert. Flying Cavalier. 1999. (House of Winslow Ser.: Vol. 23). 320p. pap. 11.99 (*0-7642-2115-9*) Bethany Hse. Pubs.

—A Time of War. 1997. (American Odyssey Ser.: Bk. 5). 352p. (gr. 10). pap. 10.99 o.p. (*0-8007-5610-X*) Revell, Fleming H. Co.

Morris, Marion E. The Sand Crabs. 1999. 192p. 16.00 (*1-891954-30-X*) Russell Dean & Co.

Morrissey, Donna. Downhill Chance. 2003. (Illus.). 448p. pap. 14.00 (*0-618-18927-0*) Houghton Mifflin Co.

Mosley, Walter. Fearless Jones. l.t. ed. 2001. (Hardcover Ser.). 322p. 31.95 (*1-58724-050-5*, Wheeler Publishing, Inc.) Gale Group.
—Fearless Jones. Pietsch, Michael, ed. 2001. 320p. 24.95 o.p. (*0-316-59238-2*) Little Brown & Co.
Murray, Sabina. The Caprices: Stories of the Pacific Campaign. 2002. 208p. pap. 13.00 (*0-618-09525-X*) Houghton Mifflin Co.
Myrer, Anton. The Last Convertible. 1985. mass mkt. 4.50 o.p. (*0-425-08223-7*) Berkley Publishing Group.
—The Last Convertible. 1993. reprint ed. lib. bdg. 37.95 (*1-56849-240-5*) Buccaneer Bks., Inc.
—The Last Convertible. 2002. 624p. pap. 15.95 (*0-06-093405-0*, Perennial) HarperTrade.
—The Last Convertible. 2001. 624p. mass mkt. 7.50 (*0-380-81959-7*) Morrow/Avon.
—The Last Convertible. 1978. 10.95 o.p. (*0-399-12124-2*) Putnam Publishing Group, The.
Nathanson, E. M. The Dirty Dozen. 2002. (Illus.). 607p. 28.00 (*0-9704662-0-X*) Regenesis Pr.
Nathanson, E. M. & Bank, Aaron. Knight's Cross. unabr. collector's ed. 1995. audio 60.00 (*0-7366-2943-2*, 3638) Books on Tape, Inc.
—Knight's Cross: A Novel. 1995. 448p. mass mkt. 5.99 (*0-8439-3724-6*) Dorchester Publishing Co., Inc.
Niles, Douglas & Dobson, Michael. Fox at the Front. 2003. (Fox on the Rhine Ser.). 624p. 27.95 (*0-7653-0479-1*, Forge Bks.) Doherty, Tom Assocs., LLC.
—The Fox on the Rhine. 2000. (Illus.). 416p. reprint ed. 27.95 (*0-312-86894-4*, NHC 0121, Forge Bks.) Doherty, Tom Assocs., LLC.
Norfolk, Lawrence. In the Shape of a Boar. 2001. 336p. 25.00 o.p. (*0-8021-1701-5*) Grove/Atlantic, Inc.
Novak, Steve. Desert Duel with Satan. 2001. (Illus.). 195p. pap. (*1-55212-738-9*) Trafford Publishing.
O'Callahan, Jay. The Herring Shed. 1983. (YA). (gr. 9 up). 10.00 incl. audio (*1-877954-01-2*); 10.00 incl. audio (*1-877954-01-2*) Artana Productions.
—The Herring Shed. 1990. audio 9.98 o.p. National Storytelling Network.
—The Herring Shed. 1983. (J). (gr. 6 up). audio 9.95 Yellow Moon Pr.
Oda, Makoto. The Breaking Jewel. Keene, Donald, tr. from JPN. 2003. (Weatherhead Books on Asia). 136p. 49.50 (*0-231-12612-3*); pap. 14.50 (*0-231-12613-1*) Columbia Univ. Pr.
O'Grady, Myles. Colonfay. 2000. 263p. 25.00 (*1-57962-068-X*) Permanent Pr., The.
Oke, Janette & Bunn, T. Davis. Another Homecoming. 1997. 256p. pap. 11.99 (*1-55661-934-0*); 256p. text 15.99 o.p. (*1-55661-978-2*); 1p. audio 15.99 o.p. (*1-55661-980-4*); 384p. pap. 14.99 o.p. (*1-55661-979-0*) Bethany Hse. Pubs.
—Another Homecoming. l.t. ed. 1997. 25.95 (*0-7838-8332-3*, Macmillan Reference USA) Gale Group.
Oldfield, Jenny. All Fall Down. 1998. 551 p. (*0-7540-2120-3*, Macmillan Reference USA) Gale Group.
—All Fall Down. 2003. 392p. pap. (*0-330-34843-4*) Pan Macmillan.
—All Fall Down. l.t. ed. 1998. (Romance Ser.). 552p. 26.95 (*0-7862-1393-0*) Thorndike Pr.
—Paradise Court. l.t. ed. 1997. 603 p. (*0-7540-2011-8*, Galaxy Children's Large Print) BBC Audiobooks America.
—Paradise Court. 2003. 421p. pap. (*0-330-33886-2*) Macmillan Children's Bks.
Ollier, Claude. Disconnection. Di Bernardi, Dominic, tr. from FRE. 1989. 130p. 19.95 (*0-916583-47-3*) Dalkey Archive Pr.
O'Nan, Stewart. A World Away: A Novel. 352p. 1999. pap. 13.00 o.s.i (*0-8050-5775-7*, Owl Bks.); 1998. 23.00 o.s.i (*0-8050-5774-9*) Holt, Henry & Co.
—A World Away: A Novel. 2003. 352p. pap. 14.00 (*0-312-42277-6*) Picador.
Ondaatje, Michael. The English Patient. 1993. 320p. pap. 13.00 (*0-679-74520-3*); 1996. reprint ed. pap. 12.00 (*0-676-51420-0*) Knopf Publishing Group. (Vintage).
—The English Patient. 1993. 320p. pap. 10.50 (*0-394-28013-X*); 1993. pap. 7.00 o.p. (*0-679-74706-0*); 1992. 320p. 27.50 (*0-679-41678-1*) Knopf, Alfred A. Inc.
—The English Patient. abr. ed. 1993. audio 18.00 o.s.i (*0-679-42924-7*, 390725, RH Audio) Random Hse. Audio Publishing Group.
Ondaatje, Michael & Minghella, Anthony. The English Patient: A Screenplay. 1996. (Illus.). 208p. (J). pap. 10.95 (*0-7868-8245-X*) Hyperion Pr.
O'Regan, Judi. Urchin Along. 2000. 184p. pap. 20.99 (*0-7388-2929-3*) Xlibris Corp.
Oren, Michael B. Reunion: A Novel. 2003. 353p. 25.00 (*1-931561-26-5*) MacAdam/Cage Publishing, Inc.
Otsuka, Julie. When the Emperor Was Divine: A Novel. 2003. 160p. pap. 9.95 (*0-385-72181-1*) Doubleday Publishing.
—When the Emperor Was Divine: A Novel. 2002. 160p. 18.00 (*0-375-41429-0*) Knopf, Alfred A. Inc.
—When the Emperor Was Divine: A Novel. l.t. ed. 2003. 256p. 20.00 (*0-375-43278-7*) Random Hse. Large Print.
Ott, Wolfgang. Sharks & Little Fish: A Novel. Manheim, Ralph, tr. 2003. 432p. pap. 14.95 (*1-58574-809-9*, Lyons Pr.) Globe Pequot Pr., The.
Pagano, Emma Maria. Heart of a Girl. 2003. Orig. Title: Si Accade Il 2 Gennaio. (ITA.). 21.95 (*0-9729518-1-4*, Olive Tree Bks.) El Paso City Bks., LLC.
Paladin, J. Anthony. The One Who Leaves Never Returns: A Novel. 2001. (Illus.). 336p. pap. 14.95 (*1-56474-368-3*) Fithian Pr.
Parker, Alice Anne. The Last of the Dream People. 1998. 228p. pap. 12.95 (*0-915811-79-0*) Kramer, H.J. Inc.
Pastor, Ben. Liar Moon. 2001. 207p. pap. 18.00 (*1-929871-01-5*) Van Neste Bks.
Paton Walsh, Jill. A Presumption of Death. E-Book 24.95 (*0-312-70987-0*) St. Martin's Pr.
Paton Walsh, Jill & Sayers, Dorothy L. A Presumption of Death. l.t. ed. 2003. (New Lord Peter Wimsey/Harriet Vane Mystery Ser.). 449p. 28.95 (*0-7862-5561-7*) Thorndike Pr.
Paulsen, Gary. The Cookcamp. 1991. 10.55 (*0-606-00894-2*) Turtleback Bks.
Pavese, Cesare. The Moon & the Bonfire. Sinclair, Louis, tr. 1974. 15.95 o.p. (*0-7206-0383-8*) Dufour Editions, Inc.
—The Moon & the Bonfires. Flint, R. W., tr. from ITA. 2002. (New York Review Books Classics Ser.). 176p. pap. 12.95 (*1-59017-021-0*) New York Review of Bks., Inc., The.
—The Moon & the Bonfires. Sinclair, Louise, tr. from ITA. 2002. (Peter Owen Modern Classics Ser.). 189p. reprint ed. pap. 18.95 (*0-7206-1119-9*) Owen, Peter Ltd. GBR. *Dist:* Dufour Editions, Inc.
Pelham, Jackie. Under the Rose. 2002. 269p. pap. 21.95 (*1-57168-652-5*, Eakin Pr.) Eakin Pr.
Pella, Judith. Somewhere a Song. 2002. (Daughters of Fortune Ser.). 432p. 18.99 (*0-7642-2720-3*); 432p. pap. 13.99 (*0-7642-2422-0*); 720p. pap. 18.99 (*0-7642-2721-1*) Bethany Hse. Pubs.
—Toward the Sunrise. 2003. (Daughters of Fortune Ser.). 720p. pap. 16.99 (*0-7642-2845-5*); 464p. 16.99 (*0-7642-2846-3*); 464p. pap. 12.99 (*0-7642-2423-9*) Bethany Hse. Pubs.
—Written on the Wind. 2001. (Daughters of Fortune Ser.). 464p. pap. 13.99 (*0-7642-2421-2*); 464p. text 18.99 o.s.i (*0-7642-2608-8*); 720p. pap. 18.99 (*0-7642-2609-6*) Bethany Hse. Pubs.
Perec, Georges. W, or the Memory of Childhood. Bellos, David, tr. from FRE. 1988. 192p. 16.95 o.s.i (*0-87923-756-2*); 2002. 176p. reprint ed. 16.95 (*1-56792-158-2*) Godine, David R. Pub.
Peters, Dory J. The Warriors' Code. 2002. 138p. pap. 12.95 (*1-55517-613-5*) Cedar Fort, Inc./CFI Distribution.
Peterson, Tracie. Silent Star. 2003. 208p. pap. 10.99 (*0-7642-2824-2*) Bethany Hse. Pubs.
—Tidings of Peace. 2000. 304p. pap. 10.99 (*0-7642-2291-0*) Bethany Hse. Pubs.
Phillips, Michael R. & Pella, Judith. Shadows over Stonewycke. (Stonewycke Legacy Ser.: Bk. 2). (Orig.). 1995. 464p. mass mkt. 6.99 o.p. (*1-55661-632-5*); 1988. 400p. pap. 9.99 o.p. (*0-87123-901-9*) Bethany Hse. Pubs.
Pike, Arthur L. A River to Cross. 2001. 192p. pap. 17.50 o.s.i (*0-9578735-1-4*) International Specialized Bk. Services.
Pilcher, Rosamunde. Coming Home. 1995. 752p. 35.00 (*0-7710-7011-X*) McClelland & Stewart/Tundra Bks.
—Coming Home. 1996. 977p. mass mkt. 7.99 (*0-312-95812-9*, St. Martin's Paperbacks); 1995. 736p. 25.95 o.p. (*0-312-13451-7*) St. Martin's Pr.
—Coming Home. l.t. ed. 1995. (Basic Ser.). 1217p. 31.95 (*0-7862-0531-8*) Thorndike Pr.
Pimentel, Ricardo. Voices from the River. 2001. 144p. pap. 12.00 (*1-931010-00-5*) Bilingual Pr./Editorial Bilingue.
Platt, Randall Beth. The Cornerstone. 1998. 244p. 21.95 (*0-945774-40-0*) Catbird Pr.
Powell, Mark. Prodigals: A Novel. 2002. 193p. 26.95 (*1-57233-189-5*) Univ. of Tennessee Pr.
Poyer, David. The Only Thing to Fear. 1996. 596p. mass mkt. 6.99 o.p. (*0-8125-4815-9*); 1995. 432p. 22.95 (*0-312-85709-8*) Doherty, Tom Assocs., LLC. (Forge Bks.).
Pratt, James Michael. The Last Valentine. E-Book 6.99 (*1-58945-604-1*) Adobe Systems, Inc.
—The Last Valentine. l.t. ed. 1998. 24.95 (*1-57490-133-8*, Beeler Large Print Bks.) Beeler, Thomas T. Publisher.
—The Last Valentine. 1996. 268p. pap. 13.95 (*0-9651163-1-X*) Harkness Publishing Consultants, LLC.
—The Last Valentine. abr. ed. 1997. 18.00 o.p. (*0-7871-1674-2*) NewStar Media, Inc.
—The Last Valentine. E-Book 6.99 (*0-312-27983-3*); 1999. E-Book 6.99 (*0-312-20727-1*); 1999. 302p. mass mkt. 6.99 (*0-312-96822-1*, St. Martin's Paperbacks); 1997. 272p. 21.95 (*0-312-18121-3*) St. Martin's Pr.
—The Lighthouse Keeper. l.t. ed. 2000. (Wheeler Large Print Book Ser.). 277p. 28.95 (*1-56895-896-X*, Wheeler Publishing, Inc.) Gale Group.
—The Lighthouse Keeper. 2000. ix, 257p. 23.95 o.s.i (*0-312-24113-5*); 2001. 336p. reprint ed. mass mkt. 6.99 o.s.i (*0-312-97469-8*, 20-3283, St. Martin's Paperbacks) St. Martin's Pr.
Pye, Michael. The Pieces from Berlin. 2004. 352p. pap. 14.00 (*0-375-71416-2*, Vintage) Knopf Publishing Group.
—The Pieces from Berlin. 2003. 352p. 24.00 (*0-375-41436-3*) Knopf, Alfred A. Inc.
Quintana, Leroy V. La Promesa & Other Stories. 2002. (Chicana & Chicano Visions of the Americas Ser.: Vol. 1). 192p. 24.95 (*0-8061-3449-6*) Univ. of Oklahoma Pr.
Radcliffe, Robert. Under an English Heaven. 2001. (Illus.). 448p. (*0-316-85990-7*) Little Brown & Co.
Radiguet, Raymond. Count d'Orgel. 1970. pap. 1.25 o.p. (*0-394-17448-8*, B214, Grove Pr.) Grove/Atlantic, Inc.
—Count D'Orgel's Ball. Cancogni, Annapaola, tr. from FRE. 1989. 174p. reprint ed. 20.00 o.p. (*0-941419-31-2*); pap. 11.00 (*0-941419-30-4*) Marsilio Pubs. (Eridanos Library).
—Count D'Orgel's Ball. Schiff, Violet, tr. from FRE. 2001. 160p. pap. 14.00 (*1-901285-03-0*) Pushkin Pr., Ltd. GBR. *Dist:* Consortium Bk. Sales & Distribution.
Radiguet, Raymond. Count d'Orgel. Schiff, Violet, tr. from FRE. 2000. 160p. pap. 12.95 (*1-885586-02-7*) Turtle Point Pr.
Raspail, Jean. Blue Island. Leggatt, Jeremy, tr. from FRE. 1991. 208p. 17.95 (*0-916515-99-0*) Mercury Hse.
Rathbone, Julian. Blame Hitler. 288p. (*0-575-06284-3*) Gollancz, Victor.
—Blame Hitler. 288p. mass mkt. 10.95 (*0-575-40094-3*) Gollancz, Victor GBR. *Dist:* Trafalgar Square.
—Blame Hitler. l.t. ed. 1998. 24.95 (*0-7531-5582-6*) ISIS Large Print Bks. GBR. *Dist:* Transaction Pubs.
Ready, Roger A. Operation Killer Mouse: A Novel of World War II. 1985. 440p. 16.95 o.p. (*0-89015-517-8*) Eakin Pr.
Reasoner, James. Battle Lines: The Last Good War. 2001. 384p. 24.95 (*0-312-87345-X*, Forge Bks.) Doherty, Tom Assocs., LLC.
—Trial by Fire Bk. 2: The Last Good War. 2002. (Illus.). 448p. 25.95 (*0-312-87346-8*, Forge Bks.) Doherty, Tom Assocs., LLC.
Reece, Colleen L. The Hills of Hope. l.t. ed. 2001. (Christian Fiction Ser.). 259p. 25.95 (*0-7862-3071-1*) Thorndike Pr.
Reeman, Douglas. Battlecruiser. 2003. (Douglas Reeman Modern Naval Library). 320p. pap. 15.95 (*1-59013-043-X*) McBooks Pr., Inc.
—The Destroyers. 1974. 288p. 7.95 o.p. (*0-399-11399-1*) Putnam Publishing Group, The.
—Strike from the Sea. 1984. mass mkt. 3.50 o.s.i (*0-515-08087-X*, Jove); 1983. mass mkt. 2.95 o.s.i (*0-515-07065-3*, Jove); 1979. mass mkt. 2.25 o.s.i (*0-425-04189-1*) Berkley Publishing Group.
—Strike from the Sea. 1994. 255p. mass mkt. (*0-09-918780-9*) Random Hse. of Canada, Ltd. CAN. *Dist:* Random Hse., Inc.
—Surface with Daring. 272p. mass mkt. (*0-09-914540-5*) Arrow Bks., Ltd.
—Surface with Daring. 1984. mass mkt. 3.50 o.s.i (*0-515-07620-1*); 1982. mass mkt. 2.95 o.s.i (*0-515-06719-9*) Berkley Publishing Group. (Jove).
—Surface with Daring. 1977. 8.95 o.p. (*0-399-11891-8*) Putnam Publishing Group, The.
—Surface with Daring. l.t. ed. 1981. (Ulverscroft Large Print Ser.). 505p. 29.99 o.p. (*0-7089-0795-4*, Ulverscroft) Thorpe, F. A. Pubs. GBR. *Dist:* Ulverscroft Large Print Bks., Ltd., Ulverscroft Large Print Canada, Ltd.
—Torpedo Run. 1994. 290p. mass mkt. (*0-09-928380-8*) Random Hse. of Canada, Ltd. CAN. *Dist:* Random Hse., Inc.
—Torpedo Run. l.t. ed. 1983. (Ulverscroft Large Print Ser.). 512p. 29.99 o.p. (*0-7089-1061-0*, Ulverscroft) Thorpe, F. A. Pubs. GBR. *Dist:* Ulverscroft Large Print Bks., Ltd., Ulverscroft Large Print Canada, Ltd.
—Twelve Seconds to Live. 2003. 368p. pap. 15.95 (*1-59013-044-8*) McBooks Pr., Inc.
—The Volunteers. 1987. mass mkt. 3.95 o.p. (*0-425-10377-3*) Berkley Publishing Group.
—The Volunteers. 1986. 288p. 17.95 o.p. (*0-688-06356-X*, Morrow, William & Co.) Morrow/Avon.
Remarque, Erich Maria. Flotsam. 2002. 436p. (C). reprint ed. pap. 35.95 (*1-931541-73-6*) Simon Pubns., Inc.
Renault, Mary. The Charioteer. 2003. 352p. pap. 14.00 (*0-375-71418-9*, Vintage); 1983. pap. 6.95 o.s.i (*0-394-71480-6*, Pantheon) Knopf Publishing Group.
—Charioteer. 1994. (Harvest Book Ser.). 348p. pap. 10.95 o.s.i (*0-15-616768-9*, Harvest Bks.) Harcourt Trade Pubs.
—The Charioteer. unabr. ed. 1988. audio 85.00 (*1-55690-097-X*, 88760E7) Recorded Bks., LLC.
Rinaldi, Nicholas M. The Jukebox Queen of Malta. 368p. 2000. pap. 13.00 (*0-684-86742-7*); 1999. (Illus.). 25.00 (*0-684-85612-3*) Simon & Schuster. (Simon & Schuster).
Riols, Noreen. Where Hope Shines Through. 1994. (House of Annanbrae Ser.: Vol. 1). 320p. pap. 10.99 (*0-89107-790-1*) Crossway Bks.
—Where Hope Shines Through. l.t. ed. 1997. (G. K. Hall Inspirational Ser.). 492p. lib. bdg. 21.95 (*0-7838-8225-4*, Macmillan Reference USA) Gale Group.
Riviere, William. Kate Caterina. 2002. 384p. 25.00 (*0-87113-839-5*, Atlantic Monthly Pr.) Grove/Atlantic, Inc.
Robbins, David L. The End of War. 2001. 528p. reprint ed. mass mkt. 6.99 (*0-553-58138-4*) Bantam Bks.
—The Last Citadel: A Novel of the Battle of Kursk. 2003. (Illus.). 432p. 24.95 (*0-553-80177-5*) Bantam Bks.
—War of the Rats. 2000. (Illus.). 512p. mass mkt. 6.99 (*0-553-58135-X*) Bantam Bks.
—The War of the Rats. 1999. 416p. 23.95 o.s.i (*0-553-10817-4*) Bantam Bks.
—War of the Rats. unabr. ed. 2000. audio compact disk 119.00 (*0-7887-4203-5*, C1132E7); 1999. audio 96.00 (*0-7887-3743-0*, 95925E7) Recorded Bks., LLC.
Roberts, Michele. Daughters of the House. 1993. 223p. 18.00 o.p. (*0-688-04610-X*, Morrow, William & Co.); 1994. 224p. reprint ed. pap. 10.00 (*0-380-72139-2*, Avon Bks.) Morrow/Avon.
—Daughters of the House. 2001. (Illus.). 176p. pap. 12.00 (*0-312-42038-2*) Picador.
—Daughters of the House. 1993. 208p. o.s.i (*1-85381-600-0*) Random Hse., Inc.
—Daughters of the House. 1992. o.s.i (*1-85381-637-X*); o.s.i (*1-85381-550-0*) Virago Pr., Ltd. GBR. *Dist:* Random Hse. of Canada, Ltd.
Robinson, Derek. A Damned Good Show. 2002. 384p. 29.95 (*0-304-36310-3*) Cassell P L C GBR. *Dist:* Trafalgar Square.
—Damned Good Show. 2003. (Cassell Military Paperbacks Ser.). 400p. pap. 9.95 (*0-304-36311-1*) Cassell P L C GBR. *Dist:* Sterling Publishing Co., Inc.
Robinson, James. London's Dark. 2003. (Illus.). 48p. pap. 9.95 (*1-85286-157-6*) Titan Bks. Ltd. GBR. *Dist:* Client Distribution Services.
Rosenbaum, Ray. Condors: A Novel. 1995. 340p. 21.95 o.p. (*0-89141-478-9*, Presidio Pr.) Ballantine Bks.
—Falcons: A Novel. 1993. 362p. 21.95 o.p. (*0-89141-476-2*, Presidio Pr.) Ballantine Bks.
—Falcons Bk. 1: Wings of War. 1995. 416p. (Orig.). pap. 9.95 o.p. (*0-89141-559-9*, Presidio Pr.) Ballantine Bks.
—Hawks: A Novel. 1994. 314p. 21.95 o.p. (*0-89141-477-0*, Presidio Pr.) Ballantine Bks.
Rubin, Charles. 4-F Blues: A Novel of WWII Hollywood. 2002. 308p. pap. 14.00 (*0-9679790-0-5*) NewCentury Pubs.
Sachs, Herb. The Fifth Notebook. 2002. 342p. text 32.99 (*0-7388-6420-X*); E-Book 8.00 (*0-7388-6422-6*) Xlibris Corp.
Sakabe, Yoshio. Night Autopsy Room: Seven Tales of Life, Death & Hope. 1994. 350p. 39.95 (*0-940121-20-4*, H207, Cross Roads Books) Cross Cultural Pubns., Inc.
Sanchez, Thomas. Day of the Bees. 2001. 320p. pap. 13.00 (*0-375-70177-X*, Vintage) Knopf Publishing Group.
Sartre, Jean-Paul. The Age of Reason. Sutton, Eric, tr. 1992. (Roads To Freedom = les Chemins de la Liberte Ser.: Vol. 1). 416p. pap. 15.00 (*0-679-73895-9*, Vintage) Knopf Publishing Group.
—The Age of Reason. 1972. pap. 8.00 o.p. (*0-394-71838-0*) Random Hse., Inc.
—Troubled Sleep. 1972. pap. 9.95 o.p. (*0-394-71840-2*, Vintage) Knopf Publishing Group.
—Troubled Sleep: A Novel. Hopkins, Gerard Manley, tr. 1992. (Chemins de la Liberte = The Roads To Freedom Ser.: Vol. 3). 432p. pap. 16.00 (*0-679-74079-1*, Vintage) Knopf Publishing Group.
Savage, Alan. Battleground. 2002. 256p. 26.99 (*0-7278-5890-4*) Severn Hse. Pubs., Ltd.
Saxton, Judith. You Are My Sunshine. l.t. ed. 2001. (Magna Large Print Ser.). 496p. (*0-7505-1617-8*) Magna Large Print Bks. GBR. *Dist:* Ulverscroft Large Print Canada, Ltd.
—You Are My Sunshine. 2000. 448p. 26.95 o.p. (*0-312-26700-2*) St. Martin's Pr.
Sayers, Dorothy L. A Presumption of Death. Date not set. mass mkt. (*0-312-99138-X*, St. Martin's Paperbacks) St. Martin's Pr.

Sayers, Dorothy L. & Paton Walsh, Jill. A Presumption of Death. 2003. (Lord Peter Wimsey Mystery Ser.). 384p. 24.95 (*0-312-29100-0*, Saint Martin's Minotaur) St. Martin's Pr.

Schlink, Bernhard. The Reader. 2001. E-Book 11.95 (*1-58945-800-1*) Adobe Systems, Inc.

—The Reader. Janeway, Carol Brown, tr. from GER. (Oprah's Book Club Ser.). 224p. 1999. 22.00 o.s.i (*0-375-40826-6*, Pantheon); 1999. pap. 11.95 (*0-375-70797-2*, Vintage); 1998. pap. 11.00 o.s.i (*0-679-78130-7*, Vintage); 1997. 21.00 o.p. (*0-679-44279-0*, Pantheon) Knopf Publishing Group.

—The Reader. l.t. ed. 1999. 216p. pap. 24.95 (*0-7838-8646-2*) Thorndike Pr.

—The Reader. l.t. ed. 1999. (Ulverscroft Large Print Ser.). 240p. 31.99 (*0-7089-4064-1*, Linford) Thorpe, F. A. Pubs. GBR. *Dist:* Ulverscroft Large Print Bks., Ltd., Ulverscroft Large Print Canada, Ltd.

Schneider, Peter W. UX-6000: Battle of the Death Sub's Secret. Duffy, Michael, ed. 2001. (Illus.). 300p. 23.95 (*0-9703512-1-6*, 101); pap. 12.95 o.p. (*0-9703512-0-8*, 101) Andover Pr.

Schunk, Laurel. A Clear North Light: Book One of the Lithuanian Trilogy. 2001. (Lithuanian Trilogy Ser.). 332p. 24.95 (*0-9661879-6-2*) St Kitts Pr.

Scott, Peter. Something in the Water. 2000. 301p. pap. 16.95 (*0-89272-517-6*) Down East Bks.

Sebald, W. G. The Emigrants. Hulse, Michael, tr. from GER. Tr. of Ausgewanderten. (Illus.). 256p. 1997. pap. 14.95 (*0-8112-1366-8*, NDP853); 1996. 22.95 (*0-8112-1338-2*) New Directions Publishing Corp.

Seiffert, Rachel. The Dark Room: A Novel. 2002. 288p. pap. 13.00 (*0-375-72632-2*) Knopf, Alfred A. Inc.

Sellar, Maurice. The Allies. l.t. ed. 1999. (General Ser.). 384p. pap. 23.95 o.p. (*0-7862-1983-1*) Thorndike Pr.

Semprun, Jorge. The Long Voyage. 1999. pap. (*0-14-026262-8*) Viking Penguin.

—The Long Voyage. Seaver, Richard, tr. 1997. (Penguin Twentieth-Century Classics Ser.). 240p. pap. 11.95 o.s.i (*0-14-118029-3*) Viking Penguin.

Shute, Nevil. A Town Like Alice. 23.95 (*0-8488-0848-7*) Amereon, Ltd.

—A Town Like Alice. 1987. 288p. mass mkt. 6.99 (*0-345-35374-9*); 1985. mass mkt. 2.95 o.p. (*0-345-33029-3*); 1981. mass mkt. 2.75 o.p. (*0-345-30565-5*) Ballantine Bks.

—A Town Like Alice. l.t. ed. 2001. (Dales Large Print Ser.). pap. (*1-84262-100-9*) Dales Large Print Bks. GBR. *Dist:* Ulverscroft Large Print Canada, Ltd.

—A Town Like Alice. l.t. ed. 1976. (Ulverscroft Large Print Ser.). 12.00 o.p. (*0-85456-410-1*, Ulverscroft) Thorpe, F. A. Pubs. GBR. *Dist:* Ulverscroft Large Print Bks., Ltd., Ulverscroft Large Print Canada, Ltd.

Signorello, James W. Fifty Years of Silence: Forgotten & Betrayed: a World War II Story. 2002. (Illus.). 52p. pap. (*1-55369-774-X*) Trafford Publishing.

Silko, Leslie Marmon. Ceremony. 1978. mass mkt. 1.95 o.p. (*0-451-08017-3*); mass mkt. 2.25 o.p. (*0-451-09006-3*) NAL. (Signet Bks.).

—Ceremony. 1986. (Contemporay American Fiction Ser.). 272p. pap. 14.00 (*0-14-008683-8*) Penguin Group (USA) Inc.

—Ceremony. 1977. (Richard Seaver Bks.). 12.95 o.p. (*0-670-20986-4*) Viking Penguin.

Simenon, Georges. Across the Street. 1992. 18.95 (*0-15-103266-1*) Harcourt Trade Pubs.

Singleton, Elyse. This Side of the Sky. 2003. 336p. pap. 14.00 (*0-425-19312-8*); 2002. 304p. 24.95 o.s.i (*0-399-14920-1*) Putnam Publishing Group, The. (BlueHen Bks.).

Skvorecky, Josef. When Eve Was Naked: Stories of a Life's Journey. 2003. 368p. pap. 15.00 (*0-312-42173-7*) Picador.

Smith, Frederick E. 633 Squadron. 2003. (Cassell Military Paperbacks Ser.). 224p. pap. 9.95 (*0-304-36621-8*) Cassell P L C GBR. *Dist:* Sterling Publishing Co., Inc.

Smith, Henry T. The Last Campaign. 1985. 192p. 13.95 o.p. (*0-8027-0867-6*) Walker & Co.

Smith, Martin Cruz. December 6: A Novel. 2003. 558p. pap. 13.95 (*1-4104-0170-7*, Wheeler Publishing, Inc.) Gale Group.

—December 6: A Novel. 2003. 400p. mass mkt. 7.99 (*0-671-77592-8*, Pocket Star); 2003. E-Book 26.00 (*0-7432-5006-0*, Simon & Schuster); 2002. (Illus.). 352p. 26.00 (*0-684-87253-6*, Simon & Schuster); 2002. (Illus.). 352p. 26.00 (*0-7432-4352-8*, Simon & Schuster); 2002. 352p. 26.00 (*0-7432-4284-X*, Simon & Schuster) Simon & Schuster.

—December 6: A Novel. l.t. ed. 2003. (Basic Ser.). 632p. 32.95 (*0-7862-4683-9*) Thorndike Pr.

Solomon, James. Il Commandante. 2000. xiii, 243p. pap. 16.95 (*0-615-11244-7*) Solomon, James.

Spark, Muriel. The Girls of Slender Means. 1990. 128p. pap. 7.95 (*0-380-70937-6*, Avon Bks.) Morrow/Avon.

—The Girls of Slender Means. 1998. (Classics Ser.). 144p. pap. 10.95 (*0-8112-1379-X*, NDP859) New Directions Publishing Corp.

—The Girls of Slender Means. 1982. 192p. pap. 5.95 o.p. (*0-399-50659-4*) Putnam Publishing Group, The.

—The Girls of Slender Means. 1963. 4.95 o.p. (*0-394-42637-1*, Knopf Bks. for Young Readers) Random Hse. Children's Bks.

Spencer, James. Pilots. 2003. 288p. 23.95 (*0-399-14973-2*, Putnam & Grosset) Putnam Publishing Group, The.

—The Pilots. 2004. 288p. pap. 13.00 (*0-425-19416-7*) Berkley Publishing Group.

—The Pilots. 2003. 434p. 29.95 (*0-7862-5390-8*) Thorndike Pr.

Steinbeck, John. Steinbeck: Novels 1942-1952, Vol. 3. DeMott, Robert, ed. 2002. (Library of America: Vol. 132). (Illus.). 983p. 35.00 (*1-931082-07-3*) Library of America, The.

Stephens, Kay. Set in Stone. 2003. 192p. 26.99 (*0-7278-5871-8*) Severn Hse. Pubs., Ltd.

Stephenson, Neal. Cryptonomicon. E-Book 7.99 (*0-06-057547-6*); E-Book 7.99 (*0-06-057550-6*); E-Book 7.99 (*0-06-057549-2*); 2003. E-Book 12.95 (*0-06-057548-4*) HarperCollins Pubs.

—Cryptonomicon. 1999. 928p. 27.50 (*0-380-97346-4*, Eos) Morrow/Avon.

Stroyar, J. N. The Children's War. 2002. (Illus.). 1168p. pap. 16.00 (*0-7434-0740-7*, Washington Square Pr.); 2001. (Illus.). 1168p. 29.95 (*0-7434-0739-3*, Atria); 2001. reprint ed. E-Book 29.95 (*0-7434-1928-6*, Atria) Simon & Schuster.

Tanner, Janet. Women & War. 1989. mass mkt. 4.50 o.s.i (*1-55817-272-6*, Pinnacle Bks.) Kensington Publishing Corp.

—Women & War. 1988. 352p. 18.95 o.p. (*0-312-01538-0*) St. Martin's Pr.

Tapon, Philippe. The Mistress: A Novel. 192p. 2000. pap. 12.95 o.s.i (*0-452-28058-3*, Plume); 1999. 23.95 o.p. (*0-525-94461-3*, Abrahams, William Bks.) Dutton/Plume.

—The Mistress: A Novel. l.t. ed. 1999. (Wheeler Large Print Book Ser.). 213p. 26.95 (*1-56895-725-4*, Wheeler Publishing, Inc.) Gale Group.

Thackara, James. America's Children. 2001. 336p. 26.95 (*1-58567-111-8*) Overlook Pr., The.

Thane, Elswyth. Homing. 272p. reprint ed. lib. bdg. 23.95 (*0-88411-969-6*) Amereon, Ltd.

—Homing. 1994. lib. bdg. 29.95 (*1-56849-479-3*) Buccaneer Bks., Inc.

—Homing. l.t. ed. 1981. lib. bdg. 15.95 o.p. (*0-8161-3164-3*, Macmillan Reference USA) Gale Group.

—This Was Tomorrow. 1976. reprint ed. lib. bdg. 24.95 (*0-88411-962-9*) Amereon, Ltd.

—This Was Tomorrow. 1994. lib. bdg. 29.95 (*1-56849-478-5*) Buccaneer Bks., Inc.

—This Was Tomorrow. 1981. (Williamsburg Ser.: No. 6). lib. bdg. 14.95 o.p. (*0-8161-3161-9*, Macmillan Reference USA) Gale Group.

Thayer, James Stewart. Five Past Midnight. 1997. 320p. 23.00 (*0-684-80025-X*, Simon & Schuster) Simon & Schuster.

Thirkell, Angela. Cheerfulness Breaks In. 2002. 188p. pap. 12.95 (*1-55921-312-4*) Moyer Bell.

—The Headmistress. l.t. ed. 480p. 2003. pap. 21.99 (*0-7531-6732-8*); 2002. 32.50 (*0-7531-6731-X*) ISIS Large Print Bks. GBR. *Dist:* Ulverscroft Large Print Bks., Ltd., Ulverscroft Large Print Bks., Ltd., Ulverscroft Large Print Canada, Ltd.

Thirkell, Angela M. Cheerfulness Breaks In: A Barsetshire Novel. 1996. 320p. pap. 11.95 o.p. (*0-7867-0318-0*, Carroll & Graf Pubs.) Avalon Publishing Group.

—Cheerfulness Breaks In: A Barsetshire Novel. l.t. ed. 1999. (Magna Large Print Ser.). 448p. 31.99 o.p. (*0-7505-1339-X*) Magna Large Print Bks. GBR. *Dist:* Ulverscroft Large Print Bks., Ltd., Ulverscroft Large Print Canada, Ltd.

—Growing Up. 1995. 272p. pap. 12.95 (*1-55921-149-0*) Moyer Bell.

—The Headmistress. 1996. 296p. reprint ed. pap. 12.95 (*1-55921-150-4*) Moyer Bell.

—Northbridge Rectory. (Barsetshire Ser.). 320p. 1991. pap. 5.95 o.p. (*0-88184-718-6*); 2nd ed. 1997. pap. 12.95 o.p. (*0-7867-0380-6*) Avalon Publishing Group. (Carroll & Graf Pubs.).

—Northbridge Rectory. l.t. ed. 1999. (Magna Large Print Ser.). 480p. 31.99 (*0-7505-1340-3*) Magna Large Print Bks. GBR. *Dist:* Ulverscroft Large Print Bks., Ltd., Ulverscroft Large Print Canada, Ltd.

—Peace Breaks Out. 1997. (Angela Thirkell Barsetshire Ser.). 328p. pap. 12.95 (*1-55921-188-1*) Moyer Bell.

—Private Enterprise. 1997. 381p. pap. 13.95 (*1-55921-189-X*) Moyer Bell.

Thompson, Grace. Unwise Promises. 2002. 256p. 26.99 (*0-7278-5852-1*) Severn Hse. Pubs., Ltd.

Thoreson, Richard M., contrib. by. Someone to Remember. 1997. (*0-9653649-3-3*) Thirteenth Bomb Squadron Assn. (Korea).

Thornton, Margaret. Wish upon a Star. l.t. ed. 1999. (Magna Large Print Ser.). 448p. o.p. (*0-7505-1377-2*) Magna Large Print Bks. GBR. *Dist:* Ulverscroft Large Print Canada, Ltd.

Tilghman, Christopher. Mason's Retreat. Date not set. (*0-679-45240-0*) McKay, David Co., Inc.

—Mason's Retreat. 1997. 304p. pap. 13.00 o.p. (*0-312-15586-7*) Picador.

—Mason's Retreat. 1995. 290p. 22.00 o.s.i (*0-679-45143-9*) Random Hse., Inc.

Tillman, Barrett. The Dauntless Dive Bomber of World War II. 1976. (Illus.). 225p. 34.95 (*0-87021-569-8*) Naval Institute Pr.

—Hellcats: A Novel of War in the Pacific. 1996. (Illus.). 352p. 24.95 o.p. (*1-57488-093-4*) Brassey's, Inc.

Towler, Katherine. Snow Island: A Novel. 2003. 304p. pap. 13.00 (*0-452-28390-6*) Dutton/Plume.

—Snow Island: A Novel. 2002. 287p. 25.00 (*1-931561-01-X*) MacAdam/Cage Publishing, Inc.

Townsend, Lindsay. Voices in the Dark. l.t. ed. 1999. (Magna Large Print Ser.). 560p. 31.99 (*0-7505-1372-1*) Magna Large Print Bks. GBR. *Dist:* Ulverscroft Large Print Bks., Ltd., Ulverscroft Large Print Canada, Ltd.

Townsend, Tom. The Last Grey Wolf: A Novel of Treasure & Intrigue Surrounding the "Forgotten" Nazi U-Boat in the Gulf. 1982. 181p. 9.95 (*0-89896-009-6*); pap. 5.95 (*0-89896-010-X*) Larksdale.

Trapp, E. Philip. The Red-Ribboned Letters. 2003. (*0-9713470-3-4*) Phoenix International, Inc.

Trevor, William. Nights at the Alexandra. 1987. (Harper Short Novel Ser.). (Illus.). 80p. 10.95 o.p. (*0-06-015848-4*) HarperTrade.

—Nights at the Alexandra. 2001. 112p. 14.95 o.s.i (*0-375-50471-0*, Modern Library) Random House Adult Trade Publishing Group.

Trobaugh, Augusta. Sophie & the Rising Sun. 2002. 224p. pap. 13.00 (*0-452-28349-3*, Plume); 2001. 208p. 22.95 o.s.i (*0-525-94627-6*, Dutton) Dutton/Plume.

—Sophie & the Rising Sun. l.t. ed. 2002. (Women's Fiction Ser.). 291p. 28.95 (*0-7862-4052-0*) Gale Group.

Trotter, William R. Winter Fire. 2003. 464p. pap. 14.00 (*0-7867-1257-0*) Avalon Publishing Group.

—Winter Fire. 1993. 496p. 22.00 o.p. (*0-525-93581-9*) Dutton/Plume.

—Winter Fire. 1994. 464p. mass mkt. 4.99 o.p. (*0-451-17718-5*, Signet Bks.) NAL.

Tsukiyama, Gail. The Language of Threads. 2000. (Illus.). 288p. reprint ed. pap. 12.95 (*0-312-26756-8*, Saint Martin's Griffin) St. Martin's Pr.

Tugwell, Maurice. Herzl Street. 1997. 200p. pap. 21.99 (*0-7388-0036-8*); text 31.99 (*0-7388-0007-4*) Xlibris Corp.

Turtledove, Harry. Colonization: Aftershocks. 2001. (Colonization Ser.). 496p. 26.00 o.s.i (*0-345-43021-2*, Del Rey) Ballantine Bks.

—Colonization: Second Contact. 2002. E-Book 6.99 (*1-59061-765-7*) Adobe Systems, Inc.

—Colonization: Second Contact. 2000. 608p. mass mkt. 6.99 (*0-345-43022-0*); 1999. (Illus.). 496p. 25.95 o.s.i (*0-345-43019-0*) Ballantine Bks. (Del Rey).

—In the Presence of Mine Enemies. 2003. 464p. pap. 24.95 (*0-451-52902-2*) NAL.

—Jaws of the Darkness. 2003. 576p. 27.95 (*0-7653-0417-1*, Tor Bks.) Doherty, Tom Assocs., LLC.

—Through the Darkness. 2001. 512p. 27.95 (*0-312-87825-7*, Tor Bks.) Doherty, Tom Assocs., LLC.

Underhill, Robert. I'll See You Again: A Love Story Out of the Ashes of War. 2002. 210p. pap. 14.95 (*1-888223-31-6*) McMillen Publishing.

Van den Brink, H. M. On the Water. Vincent, Paul, tr. from DUT. 2001. 134p. 22.00 o.p. (*0-8021-1692-2*); 2002. 144p. reprint ed. pap. 11.00 (*0-8021-3895-0*) Grove/Atlantic, Inc. (Grove Pr.).

Van Kampen, Robert. The Fourth Reich. 1997. 448p. (gr. 13 up). 24.99 o.p. (*0-8007-1745-7*); pap. 14.99 o.p. (*0-8007-5650-9*) Revell, Fleming H. Co.

Van Steenwyk, Elizabeth. A Traitor among Us. 1999. 143p. (J). (gr. 4-7). pap. 6.00 (*0-8028-5157-6*, Eerdmans Bks For Young Readers) Eerdmans, William B. Publishing Co.

—A Traitor among Us. 1999. 12.05 (*0-606-17601-2*) Turtleback Bks.

Vaughan, Robert. His Truth Is Marching On: A World War II Novel. 2004. 320p. pap. 14.99 (*0-7852-6185-0*) Nelson, Thomas Inc.

—Touch the Face of God: A World War II Novel. 2002. 320p. pap. 14.99 (*0-7852-6627-5*) Nelson, Thomas Inc.

—Whose Voice the Waters Heard: A WWII Novel. 2003. 320p. pap. 14.99 (*0-7852-6315-2*) Nelson, Thomas Pubs.

Vidal, Gore. Williwaw. 2003. 222p. pap. 15.00 (*0-226-85585-6*) Univ. of Chicago Pr.

Vogler, Peter Z. The Broken Cross. 1997. 220p. 24.95 (*0-9656650-3-8*) Danville Creek Publishing.

Volpi, Jorge. In Search of Klingsor. 416p. 2003. pap. 14.00 (*0-7432-0119-1*); 2002. 26.00 (*0-7432-0118-3*) Simon & Schuster. (Scribner).

Von Drogas, Johann. As Once We Were: A Love Story. Wade, Virginia, ed. unabr. ed. 1999. 438p. 23.50 (*0-9620016-2-7*) Great Lakes Publishing Co.

Vreeland, Susan. Girl in Hyacinth Blue. 1999. 242p. 17.50 (*1-878448-90-0*); 150p. 17.50 o.p. MacMurray & Beck, Inc.

—Girl in Hyacinth Blue. 2000. (Illus.). 256p. pap. 13.00 (*0-14-029628-X*) Penguin Group (USA) Inc.

—Girl in Hyacinth Blue. l.t. ed. 2000. (Basic Ser.). 227p. 28.95 (*0-7862-2440-1*) Thorndike Pr.

—Girl in Hyacinth Blue. 2000. 17.05 (*0-606-20671-X*) Turtleback Bks.

Wagner, Ray C. Delayed Justice: A Mystery Novel. 1999. 340p. (*0-9670744-2-8*, 0325); 282p. pap. (*0-9670744-1-X*, 0324) MC Pr.

Wahl, Loren. The Invisible Glass. 2001. 232p. pap. 12.95 (*1-55583-575-9*) Alyson Pubns.

Walbert, Kate. The Gardens of Kyoto: A Novel. 288p. 2002. pap. 13.00 (*0-684-86949-7*); 2001. 24.00 (*0-684-86948-9*) Simon & Schuster. (Scribner).

—The Gardens of Kyoto: A Novel. l.t. ed. 2001. (Women's Fiction Ser.). 461p. 29.95 (*0-7862-3477-6*) Thorndike Pr.

Wales, Ken & Poling, David. Sea of Glory: A Novel Based on the True WWII Story of the Four Chaplains & the U. S. A. T. Dorchester. 2001. (Illus.). 353p. 21.99 (*0-8054-5000-9*) Broadman & Holman Pubs.

Walker, Jim. Murder at Pearl Harbor. 2000. (Mysteries in Time Ser.). 438p. pap. 14.99 (*0-8054-2160-2*) Broadman & Holman Pubs.

Wallace, Randel. Pearl Harbor. movie tie-in ed. 2001. (Illus.). 336p. mass mkt. 5.99 (*0-7868-9005-3*) Hyperion Pr.

Walsh, Michael. As Time Goes By. l.t. ed. 1999. (Charnwood Large Print Ser.). 384p. 31.99 o.p. (*0-7089-9092-4*, Ulverscroft) Thorpe, F. A. Pubs. GBR. *Dist:* Ulverscroft Large Print Bks., Ltd., Ulverscroft Large Print Canada, Ltd.

—As Time Goes By. 1998. 420p. 25.00 o.p. (*0-446-51900-6*) Warner Bks., Inc.

—As Time Goes By: A Novel of Casablanca. 1999. 416p. mass mkt. 7.50 (*0-446-60745-2*) Warner Bks., Inc.

Walton, C. S. The Voice of Leningrad: The Story of a Siege. 2003. 170p. per. 14.95 (*1-891053-82-5*) Garrett County Pr.

Watkins, Paul. The Forger. 2001. 336p. pap. 14.00 (*0-312-27696-6*); 2000. 352p. 25.00 (*0-312-26593-X*) Picador.

—Night over Day over Night. 1990. 304p. pap. 7.95 (*0-380-70737-3*, Avon Bks.) Morrow/Avon.

—Night over Day over Night. 1997. 304p. pap. 13.00 (*0-312-15608-1*) Picador.

Webb, James H. The Emperor's General. 2000. 480p. mass mkt. 6.99 (*0-553-57854-5*) Bantam Bks.

—The Emperor's General: A Novel. l.t. ed. 1999. (Basic Ser.). 712p. 29.95 (*0-7862-2037-6*) Thorndike Pr.

Webster, Donald A. Blood Son. 2001. 220p. 19.95 (*1-58345-619-8*); 213p. pap. 14.95 (*1-58345-620-1*) Domhan Bks.

Weil, Jiri. Colors: Barvy. Harrell, Rachel, tr. from CZE. 2001. (Czech Translations Ser.: Vol. 2). 90p. (*0-930042-87-5*) Michigan Slavic Pubns.

Weismiller, Edward. The Serpent Sleeping. 2nd ed. 1998. (Classics of Espionage Ser.: Vol. 4). 368p. 49.50 o.s.i (*0-7146-4729-2*); pap. 24.50 o.s.i (*0-7146-4279-7*) Cass, Frank Pubs. GBR. *Dist:* International Specialized Bk. Services.

Welcome, John. A Call to Arms. 1985. 316p. 15.95 o.p. (*0-312-11431-1*) St. Martin's Pr.

Wenzel, Lawrence A. Turnip Patch Infield & a Navajo. 1999. 256p. 22.95 (*0-918606-13-6*) Heidelberg Graphics.

Wesley, Mary. The Camomile Lawn. 1986. 336p. pap. 10.95 o.p. (*0-552-99126-0*) Bantam Bks.

—The Camomile Lawn. 1990. (King Penguin Ser.). 336p. pap. 14.00 (*0-14-012392-X*, Penguin Bks.) Penguin Group (USA) Inc.

—The Camomile Lawn. 1984. 297p. 15.50 o.p. (*0-671-50461-4*) Summit Bks.

—Part of the Furniture. 1997. 255p. o.p. (*0-593-04115-1*, Corgi) Bantam Bks.

—Part of the Furniture. 1998. 288p. pap. o.s.i (*0-552-99723-4*) Corgi Bks. Ltd. GBR. *Dist:* Doubleday Publishing.

—Part of the Furniture. l.t. ed. 1997. (G. K. Hall Core Ser.). 351p. lib. bdg. 25.95 (*0-7838-8223-8*, Macmillan Reference USA) Gale Group.

—Part of the Furniture. l.t. ed. 1998. 256p. pap. 12.95 o.s.i (*0-14-026628-3*) Penguin Group (USA) Inc.

—Part of the Furniture. abr. ed. 1997. mass mkt. 16.95 incl. audio (*1-85998-863-6*) Trafalgar Square.

—Part of the Furniture. l.t. ed. 1997. 256p. 22.95 o.s.i (*0-670-87363-2*) Viking Penguin.

Westin, Jeane. Love & Glory: A Novel. 1986. 528p. 17.45 o.p. (*0-671-55667-3*, Simon & Schuster) Simon & Schuster.

Wharton, William. A Midnight Clear. 1983. 256p. mass mkt. 4.99 o.s.i (*0-345-31291-0*) Ballantine Bks.

—A Midnight Clear. 2004. 288p. pap. 14.95 (*1-55704-257-8*) Newmarket Pr.

Widdecombe, Ann. The Act of Treachery. 2002. 257p. 24.95 (*0-297-64573-0*) Weidenfeld & Nicolson, Ltd. GBR. *Dist:* Trafalgar Square.

Wiggin, Helene. Dancing at the Victory Cafe. 1995. 256p. 21.95 o.p. (*0-312-13954-3*) St. Martin's Pr.
Wilson, Robert. The Company of Strangers. 2002. 496p. pap. 14.00 (*0-15-602710-0*, Harvest Bks.); 2001. 480p. 25.00 (*0-15-100745-4*); 2001. 480p. 25.00 o.s.i (*0-15-100846-9*) Harcourt Trade Pubs.
Wilson, Sloan. The Man in the Gray Flannel Suit. 20.95 (*0-8488-1512-2*) Amereon, Ltd.
—The Man in the Gray Flannel Suit. 1980. reprint ed. lib. bdg. 16.00 (*0-8376-0448-6*) Bentley Pubs.
—The Man in the Gray Flannel Suit. 1991. 250p. reprint ed. lib. bdg. 35.95 (*0-89966-862-3*) Buccaneer Bks., Inc.
—The Man in the Gray Flannel Suit. 2002. 288p. reprint ed. pap. 13.95 (*1-56858-246-3*) Four Walls Eight Windows.
—The Man in the Gray Flannel Suit. 356p. 1983. 8.50 o.p. (*0-87795-553-0*); 2nd ed. 1984. 16.95 o.p. (*0-87795-474-7*) Morrow/Avon. (Morrow, William & Co.).
—The Man in the Gray Flannel Suit. 2003. (Perennial Bestseller Ser.). lib. bdg. 29.95 (*0-7862-5104-2*) Thorndike Pr.
Wilson, Susan. Hawke's Cove. 2000. 282p. 23.95 (*0-671-03573-8*, Atria); 2003. (Illus.). 320p. reprint ed. pap. 6.99 (*0-671-03574-6*, Pocket); 2001. reprint ed. E-Book 23.95 (*0-7434-1737-2*, Atria) Simon & Schuster.
Wingate, John. Go Deep. 1985. 192p. 12.95 o.p. (*0-312-33062-6*) St. Martin's Pr.
Wise, Robert L. Be Not Afraid: A Novel. 2001. xii, 363p. pap. 12.99 (*0-7852-6977-0*) Nelson, Thomas Pubs.
Wojdowski, Bogdan. Bread for the Departed. Levine, Madeline G., tr. from ENG. 1997. (Jewish Lives Ser.). 304p. 59.95 (*0-8101-1455-0*); pap. 24.00 (*0-8101-1456-9*) Northwestern Univ. Pr.
Wood, Jane Roberts. Grace. 2001. 240p. 22.95 o.s.i (*0-525-94602-0*) Dutton/Plume.
—Grace. l.t. ed. 2001. (Americana Ser.). 397p. 28.95 (*0-7862-3457-1*) Thorndike Pr.
Woodman, Richard. The Corvette. 2000. (Nathaniel Drinkwater Ser.). (Illus.). 232p. reprint ed. pap. 14.95 (*1-57409-100-X*) Sheridan Hse., Inc.
Woodthorpe, Michael. The Riviera of Hades: Black Sea Assignment. 2003. 208p. 25.00 (*0-8028-2118-9*) Eerdmans, William B. Publishing Co.
Wouk, Herman. War & Remembrance. unabr. ed. 1982. Pt. 1. audio 88.00 (*0-7366-0611-4*, 1575-A); Pt. 2. audio 96.00; Pt. 3. audio 88.00 Books on Tape, Inc.
—War & Remembrance. 1995. mass mkt. (*0-316-95591-4*); 1992. 1392p. mass mkt. 8.99 (*0-316-95515-9*); 1978. 1042p. (YA). (gr. 8 up). 29.95 o.p. (*0-316-95501-9*); 2002. 1056p. reprint ed. pap. 15.95 (*0-316-95499-3*, Back Bay) Little Brown & Co.
—War & Remembrance. 1989. mass mkt. 5.95 o.p. (*0-671-67288-6*); 1983. mass mkt. 5.95 o.s.i (*0-671-46314-4*) Simon & Schuster. (Pocket).
—War & Remembrance. 1992. 15.04 (*0-606-12567-1*) Turtleback Bks.
—The Winds of War. unabr. ed. 1981. Pt. 1. audio 80.00 (*0-7366-0608-4*, 1574-A); Pt. II. audio 72.00; Pt. III. audio 72.00 Books on Tape, Inc.
—The Winds of War. 1995. mass mkt. (*0-316-95590-6*); 1992. (Illus.). 1056p. mass mkt. 8.99 (*0-316-95516-7*); 1971. 885p. (gr. 8). 35.00 o.p. (*0-316-95500-0*); 2002. 896p. reprint ed. pap. 15.95 (*0-316-95266-4*, Back Bay) Little Brown & Co.
—The Winds of War. 1989. mass mkt. 5.95 o.p. (*0-671-67287-8*); 1986. mass mkt. 5.95 o.s.i (*0-671-63472-0*) Simon & Schuster. (Pocket).
—The Winds of War. 1992. 14.04 (*0-606-12577-9*) Turtleback Bks.
—The Winds of War: T. V. Tie-In Edition. 1983. mass mkt. 4.95 o.s.i (*0-671-46319-5*, Pocket) Simon & Schuster.
—The Winds of War & War & Remembrance. 1978. 45.00 o.s.i (*0-316-95502-7*) Little Brown & Co.
Yarbrough, Steve. Prisoners of War. A Novel. 2004. 304p. 23.00 (*0-375-41478-9*) Knopf, Alfred A. Inc.
Yoder, James D. Black Spider over Tiegenhof. 1995. 232p. pap. 11.99 o.p. (*0-8361-9012-2*) Herald Pr.
—Black Spider over Tiegenhof. l.t. ed. 2000. (Christian Mystery Ser.). 335p. 23.95 (*0-7862-2709-5*) Thorndike Pr.
—Black Spider over Tiegenhof. 1995. E-Book 11.99 (*0-585-22785-3*) netLibrary, Inc.
Zimmermann, Frank W. Not by Arms Alone: A Novel of a U. S. Navy Destroyer in the Pacific Theater, 1941-1945. 1994. (Illus.). 626p. pap. 22.50 (*0-9644793-0-3*) Zimmermann Publishing.
Zollo, Burt. Prisoners. 2003. 22.50 (*0-89733-515-5*) Academy Chicago Pubs., Ltd.

### WORLD WAR III—FICTION

Anthony, Patricia. Cold Allies. 1994. 304p. mass mkt. 5.99 o.s.i (*0-441-00018-5*) Ace Bks.
—Cold Allies. 1993. 288p. 21.95 o.s.i (*0-15-118503-4*) Harcourt Trade Pubs.
Arthur, Robert P. Crazy Horse in Heaven. 2000. 320p. 22.95 (*0-9669930-1-2*) Stonehall Publishing.
Clancy, Tom. Red Storm Rising. 1986. Tr. of Tormenta Roja. 656p. 27.95 (*0-399-13149-3*, G. P. Putnam's Sons) Penguin Putnam Bks. for Young Readers.
—Red Storm Rising. l.t. ed. 1991. (Basic Ser.).Tr. of Tormenta Roja. 1289p. lib. bdg. 25.95 (*0-89621-885-6*) Thorndike Pr.
—Red Storm Rising. 1987. Tr. of Tormenta Roja. 13.09 o.p. (*0-606-00983-3*) Turtleback Bks.
—Tormenta Roja. 1998. (SPA.). 944p. 10.95 (*84-01-49521-0*, PJ9035) Plaza & Janés Editories, S.A. ESP. *Dist:* Lectorum Pubns., Inc.
Coyle, Harold. Team Yankee: A Novel of World War III. l.t. ed. 1988. (General Ser.). 480p. 19.95 o.p. (*0-8161-4641-1*, Macmillan Reference USA) Gale Group.
Coyle, Harold W. Team Yankee: A Novel of World War III. 1987. (Illus.). 320p. 17.95 o.p. (*0-89141-290-5*, Presidio Pr.) Ballantine Bks.
LaHaye, Tim. Nicolae: The Rise of Antichrist. 2002. (Left Behind Ser.: No. 3). E-Book 14.99 (*0-8423-7137-0*) Tyndale Hse. Pubs.
LaHaye, Tim & Jenkins, Jerry B. Nicolae: The Rise of Antichrist. 2000. (Left Behind Ser.: Bk. 3). (SPA.). pap. 9.99 (*0-7899-0457-8*) Editorial Unilit.
—Nicolae: The Rise of Antichrist. (Left Behind Ser.: Bk. 3). 1998. 432p. pap. 14.99 (*0-8423-2924-2*, 910666Q); 1997. 432p. 22.99 (*0-8423-2914-5*); 2002. 512p. pap. 19.99 (*0-8423-6552-4*) Tyndale Hse. Pubs.
Muehlberg, R. L. Jet Stream. 1996. (Breakup of America Ser.). vi, 130p. (Orig.). pap. 12.95 (*0-9653342-0-1*) Muehlberg Pr., The.

## Y

### YUGOSLAV WAR, 1991-1995—FICTION

Bradford, Barbara Taylor. Where You Belong. 2000. 464p. mass mkt. 7.99 (*0-440-23515-4*) Dell Publishing.
—Where You Belong. l.t. ed. 2000. 528p. pap. 13.95 (*0-375-72797-3*); 24.95 (*0-375-40974-2*) Random Hse. Large Print.
Goytisolo, Juan. State of Siege. Lane, Helen, tr. from SPA. 2002. 144p. (Orig.). pap. 13.95 (*0-87286-406-5*) City Lights Bks.
Jergovic, Miljenko. Sarajevo Marlboro. Tomasevic, Stela, tr. from MIS. 2004. Orig. Title: Sarajevski Marlboro. 180p. pap. 14.00 (*0-9728692-2-0*) Archipelago Bks.
—Sarajevo Marlboro. 1997. Orig. Title: Sarajevski Marlboro. 192p. pap. 13.95 (*0-14-026071-4*) Penguin Bks., Ltd. GBR. *Dist:* Trafalgar Square.
MacLean, Alistair. Force 10 from Navarone. 16th l.t. ed. 2001. 304p. 32.50 (*0-7531-6463-9*) Thorpe, F. A. Pubs. GBR. *Dist:* Ulverscroft Large Print Bks., Ltd., Ulverscroft Large Print Canada, Ltd.
Morrell, David. Double Image. l.t. ed. 1998. (Core Ser.). 599p. 28.95 (*0-7838-0144-0*) Thorndike Pr.
—Double Image. 1998. 448p. 25.00 o.p. (*0-446-51963-4*) Warner Bks., Inc.
—Double Image. Warner, ed. 1999. 528p. reprint ed. mass mkt. 7.50 (*0-446-60696-0*) Warner Bks., Inc.
Radojecic-Kane, Natasha. Homecoming: A Novel. 2002. 192p. 19.95 (*1-56858-239-0*) Four Walls Eight Windows.
Seymour, Gerald. The Heart of Danger. 1995. 368p. pap. 23.00 o.p. (*0-06-100968-7*) HarperTrade.

# MISCELLANEOUS

## A

### AIDS (DISEASE)—FICTION

Aiello, Barbara & Shulman, Jeffrey. Friends for Life: Featuring Amy Wilson. 1995. (Kids on the Block Bks.). (Illus.). 88p. (J). (gr. 5-8). lib. bdg. 14.98 o.p. (*0-8050-4137-0*, 21st Century Bks., Inc.) Millbrook Pr., Inc.
Alameddine, Rabih. Koolaids: The Art of War. 256p. 1999. pap. 13.00 (*0-312-20658-5*); 1998. 23.00 (*0-312-18693-2*) Picador.
—Koolaids: The Art of War, a Novel. 2000. 245p. reprint ed. 23.00 (*0-7881-9338-4*) DIANE Publishing Co.
Alexander, Earl, et al. My Dad Has HIV. 1996. (Illus.). 32p. (J). (gr. 1-4). 14.95 o.p. (*0-925190-99-3*) Fairview Pr.
Baer, Judy. The Discovery. 1993. (Cedar River Daydreams Ser.: No. 20). 128p. (YA). (gr. 7-10). mass mkt. 4.99 o.p. (*1-55661-330-X*) Bethany Hse. Pubs.
Balizet, Carol. Plague. 1994. 352p. (Orig.). (gr. 10). pap. 10.99 o.p. (*0-8007-9213-0*) Chosen Bks.
Bantle, Lee F. Diving for the Moon. 1995. 176p. (J). (gr. 4-7). per. 14.00 (*0-689-80004-5*, Atheneum) Simon & Schuster Children's Publishing.
Bellamy, Dodie & D'Allesandro, Sam. Real: The Letters of Mina Harker & Sam D'Allesandro. 1994. 218p. pap. 10.95 (*1-883689-16-3*); lib. bdg. 30.95 (*1-883689-17-1*) Talisman Hse., Pubs.
Bennett, Cherie. Sunset Heart. 1994. 224p. (Orig.). (J). (ps-3). mass mkt. 3.99 o.s.i (*0-425-14183-7*, Splash) Berkley Publishing Group.
Benning, Elizabeth. Losing David. 1994. 160p. (YA). mass mkt. 3.50 o.p. (*0-06-106147-6*, HarperTorch) Morrow/Avon.
Berger, John. To the Wedding: A Novel. 1995. 192p. 22.00 o.s.i (*0-679-43981-1*, Pantheon) Knopf Publishing Group.
Bess, Clayton. The Mayday Rampage. 1993. (Illus.). 208p. (YA). (gr. 9-12). 14.95 o.p. (*1-882405-00-5*); pap. 12.95 (*1-882405-01-3*) Lookout Pr.
Bourjaily, Vance N. Old Soldier. 1990. 18.95 o.s.i (*1-55611-198-3*) Fine, Donald I. Bks.
Brewer, Jeannie. A Crack in Forever. 1996. 304p. 21.50 (*0-684-80148-5*, Simon & Schuster) Simon & Schuster.
Brown, Rebecca. The Gifts of the Body. 1994. 176p. 17.50 o.p. (*0-06-017159-6*) HarperTrade.
Butler, Luther. Aids: No Place to Die. 2000. 208p. E-Book 8.00 (*0-7388-7780-8*) Xlibris Corp.
Ciresi, Rita. Pink Slip. 1999. 416p. pap. 12.95 (*0-385-32363-8*, Delta) Dell Publishing.
Cleage, Pearl. What Looks Like Crazy on an Ordinary Day. 256p. 1998. pap. 13.00 (*0-380-79487-X*, Avon Bks.); 1997. 20.00 (*0-380-97584-X*, Morrow, William & Co.) Morrow/Avon.
—What Looks Like Crazy on an Ordinary Day. l.t. ed. (Americana Ser.). 416p. 2000. pap. 26.95 (*0-7862-1760-X*); 1999. 29.95 (*0-7862-1759-6*) Thorndike Pr.
Coben, Harlan. Miracle Cure: A Novel. 1991. 440p. 20.00 o.s.i (*0-945167-39-3*) British American Publishing, Ltd.
—Miracle Cure: A Novel. 1992. pap. 5.50 (*1-56171-126-8*) SPI Bks.
Coe, Ian. Motions of the Blood. 1993. 317p. 22.95 o.s.i (*0-15-186426-8*) Harcourt Trade Pubs.
Cohen, Miriam. Laura Leonora's First Amendment. 1990. 128p. (J). (gr. 5-9). 14.95 o.p. (*0-525-67317-2*, Dutton Children's Bks.) Penguin Putnam Bks. for Young Readers.
Collard, Cyril. Savage Nights. 1995. 240p. pap. 11.95 (*0-87951-580-5*) Overlook Pr., The.
—Savage Nights. Rodarmor, William, tr. 1994. 240p. 18.95 (*0-87951-534-1*) Overlook Pr., The.
Cooper, Melrose. Life Magic, ERS. 1996. 128p. (J). (gr. 4-7). 14.95 o.p. (*0-8050-4114-1*, Holt, Henry & Co. Bks. For Young Readers) Holt, Henry & Co.
Corbin, Steven. A Hundred Days from Now. 1994. 223p. 18.95 o.p. (*1-55583-232-6*) Alyson Pubns.
Currier, Jameson. Dancing on the Moon. 1993. 208p. 20.00 o.p. (*0-670-84656-2*, Viking) Viking Penguin.
—Dancing on the Moon: Short Stories about AIDS. 1994. 208p. pap. 9.95 o.p. (*0-14-017272-6*, Penguin Bks.) Penguin Group (USA) Inc.
Dawson, David L. Double Blind. 1991. 240p. 17.95 o.p. (*0-312-07085-3*, Saint Martin's Minotaur) St. Martin's Pr.
Denker, Henry. A Place for Kathy. 1997. 320p. 24.00 (*0-688-14963-4*, Morrow, William & Co.) Morrow/Avon.
D'Haene, Elise. Licking Our Wounds. 1997. 208p. 24.00 (*1-877946-81-8*) Permanent Pr., The.
Donnelly, Nisa. The Love Songs of Phoenix Bay. (Stonewall Inn Editions Ser.). 1995. 320p. pap. 12.95 o.p. (*0-312-13561-0*, Saint Martin's Griffin); 1994. 304p. 13.99 o.p. (*0-312-11391-9*) St. Martin's Pr.
Edgerton, Dale. Goneaway Road. 2003. 320p. pap. 17.95 (*1-56023-434-2*); 39.95 (*1-56023-433-4*) Haworth Pr., Inc., The. (Southern Tier Editions).
Feinberg, David B. Eighty-Sixed. 1989. 336p. 18.95 o.p. (*0-670-82315-5*) Viking Penguin.
Grady, Rita M. Who's Gonna Notice Anyway: ER Nurse Manager Deals with AIDS. 2000. 168p. pap. 20.99 (*0-7388-1417-2*); text 30.99 (*0-7388-1416-4*); E-Book 8.00 (*0-7388-8440-5*) Xlibris Corp.
Guibert, Herve. The Compassion Protocol. Kirkup, James, tr. 1994. 200p. 20.00 (*0-8076-1352-5*) Braziller, George Inc.
—Protocole Compassionnel. 1991. (Folio Ser.: No. 2481). (FRE.). 226p. pap. 29.95 (*2-07-038731-3*) Schoenhof's Foreign Bks., Inc.
—To the Friend Who Did Not Save My Life. Coverdale, Linda, tr. from FRE. 1991. 272p. text 18.95 (*0-689-12120-2*) Central Bureau voor Schimmelcultures NLD. *Dist:* Lubrecht & Cramer, Ltd.
—To the Friend Who Did Not Save My Life. Coverdale, Linda, tr. from FRE. 1994. (High Risk Ser.). 240p. reprint ed. pap. (*1-85242-328-5*) Serpent's Tail Ltd.
Gurganus, Allan. Plays Well with Others. unabr. collector's ed. 1998. audio 96.00 (*0-7366-4206-4*, 4702) Books on Tape, Inc.
—Plays Well with Others. 1999. 368p. pap. 14.00 (*0-375-70203-2*, Vintage) Knopf Publishing Group.
—Plays Well with Others. 1997. 336p. 25.00 o.p. (*0-394-58914-9*) Knopf, Alfred A. Inc.
—Plays Well with Others. abr. ed. 1997. audio 18.00 o.s.i (*0-679-46055-1*, RH Audio) Random Hse. Audio Publishing Group.
Handis, Mikey. Watch Out, He's Got AIDS. 1998. (Illus.). 48p. (J). (gr. 4-7). 12.95 (*0-934953-58-9*) Water Row Pr.
Hunt, Angela Elwell. A Dream to Cherish. 1992. (Cassie Perkins Ser.: Vol. 4). 176p. (J). (gr. 4-8). pap. 4.99 o.p. (*0-8423-1064-9*) Tyndale Hse. Pubs.
—A Dream to Cherish. 2000. (Cassie Perkins Ser.: Vol. 4). 196p. (YA). (gr. 5-9). pap. 12.95 (*0-595-08995-X*) iUniverse, Inc.
Johnson, Fenton. Scissors, Paper, Rock. 1993. 240p. 20.00 (*0-671-79541-4*, Atria) Simon & Schuster.
Jordan, MaryKate. Losing Uncle Tim. Levine, Abby, ed. 1989. (Albert Whitman Concept Bks.). (Illus.). 32p. (J). (gr. 4-7). lib. bdg. 14.95 o.p. (*0-8075-4756-5*); (ps-3). pap. 5.95 o.p. (*0-8075-4758-1*) Whitman, Albert & Co.
Katz, Illana. Uncle Jimmy. 1994. (Illus.). 40p. (J). (gr. k-6). 16.95 (*1-882388-03-8*) Real Life Storybooks.
—Uncle Jimmy: AIDS. 1993. (J). (gr. k-6). pap. 9.95 (*1-882388-09-7*) Real Life Storybooks.
Kear, Cynthia. Searching for Grace. 1998. 24.95 (*0-947993-75-4*) Malvern Publishing Co., Ltd. GBR. *Dist:* British Bk. Co., Inc.
Kittle, Katrina. Traveling Light. l.t. ed. 2000. (G. K. Hall Core Ser.). 407p. 27.95 (*0-7838-9173-3*) Thorndike Pr.
—Traveling Light. 2000. 320p. 18.95 (*0-446-52480-8*); 2001. 336p. reprint ed. pap. 13.95 (*0-446-67694-2*) Warner Bks., Inc.
Kondoleon, Harry. Diary of a Lost Boy. 1995. 224p. 10.00 o.s.i (*1-57322-504-5*, Riverhead Trade (Paperbacks)) Berkley Publishing Group.
Labine, Claire & Pinsker, Judith. Robin's Diary. 1995. (Illus.). 192p. pap. 9.95 o.p. (*0-8019-8775-X*) Krause Pubns.
Levy, Marilyn. Rumors & Whispers. 1990. 160p. (YA). (gr. 8 up). mass mkt. 3.95 o.s.i (*0-449-70327-4*, Fawcett) Ballantine Bks.
Manfredi, Renee. Above the Thunder. 2004. 24.00 (*1-931561-59-1*) MacAdam/Cage Publishing, Inc.
Mars-Jones, Adam. Monopolies of Loss. 1994. pap. 11.00 o.s.i (*0-679-74415-0*, Vintage) Knopf Publishing Group.
McCollum, Thomas C., 3rd. Tainted Blood: A Frightening Possibility. 1996. 368p. 25.00 (*1-880404-11-7*) Bookwrights Pr.
McDaniel, Lurlene. Baby Alicia Is Dying. 1993. 192p. (YA). (gr. 7 up). mass mkt. 4.99 (*0-553-29605-1*) Bantam Bks.
McMurtry, Larry. The Late Child. l.t. ed. 1995. 26.95 o.p. (*1-56895-246-5*, Wheeler Publishing, Inc.) Gale Group.
—The Late Child. 1995. 461p. 25.00 (*0-684-80998-2*, Simon & Schuster) Simon & Schuster.
Merrifield, Margaret. Come Sit by Me. 1990. (Illus.). 32p. (J). reprint ed. pap. 6.95 (*0-88961-141-6*) Women's Pr. CAN. *Dist:* Univ. of Toronto Pr.
Miklowitz, Gloria D. Goodbye Tomorrow. 1987. 192p. (J). (gr. 7 up). 13.95 o.s.i (*0-385-29562-6*, Delacorte Pr.) Dell Publishing.
—Goodbye Tomorrow. 1988. 160p. (J). (gr. k-12). mass mkt. 3.25 o.s.i (*0-440-20081-4*, Laurel Leaf) Random Hse. Children's Bks.
Miller, K. D. A Litany in Time of Plague. 1994. 160p. pap. (*0-88984-145-4*) Porcupine's Quill, Inc.
Neale, Jonathan. Laughter of Heroes. 1993. 128p. pap. (*1-85242-279-3*) Serpent's Tail Ltd.
O'Brien, Thomas J. The TATA-Box Virus. 2000. 140p. pap. 20.99 (*0-7388-2371-6*) Xlibris Corp.
Olshan, Joseph. Vanitas. 2000. 272p. pap. 12.00 (*0-7475-4425-5*) Bloomsbury Publishing, Ltd. GBR. *Dist:* Trafalgar Square.
—Vanitas. 1998. 272p. 23.00 (*0-684-83396-4*, Simon & Schuster) Simon & Schuster.
Ortiz Taylor, Sheila. Coachella. 1998. x, 187p. pap. 14.95 (*0-8263-1843-6*) Univ. of New Mexico Pr.
Peck, Dale. Martin & John. 1994. 240p. reprint ed. pap. 13.00 (*0-06-097588-1*, Perennial) HarperTrade.
—Martin & John: A Novel. 1993. 227p. 21.00 o.p. (*0-374-20311-3*) Farrar, Straus & Giroux.
Peterson, Paula W. Women in the Grove. 2004. 144p. 22.00 (*0-8070-8352-6*) Beacon Pr.
Picano, Felice. Like People in History. 1995. 528p. 23.95 o.p. (*0-670-86047-6*) Viking Penguin.
Price, Reynolds. The Promise of Rest. 1996. 368p. pap. 13.00 (*0-684-82510-4*); 1995. 353p. 24.00 o.p. (*0-684-80149-3*) Simon & Schuster. (Scribner).
—The Promise of Rest. abr. ed. 1995. audio 23.00 (*0-671-52895-5*, Simon & Schuster Audioworks) Simon & Schuster Audio.

Reinken, Patrick. Judgment Day. 1996. 448p. 23.00 (*0-684-80762-9*, Simon & Schuster) Simon & Schuster.

Russell, Paul. War Against the Animals: A Novel. 2003. 320p. 24.95 (*0-312-20935-5*) St. Martin's Pr.

Ryman, Geoff. Was. 1993. 384p. pap. 13.95 (*0-14-017872-4*, Penguin Bks.) Penguin Group (USA) Inc.

—Was. 1994. 4.99 o.p. (*0-517-11656-1*) Random Hse. Value Publishing.

Saint, David A. The Winnowing. 1998. xiv, 331p. 24.95 (*0-9662818-0-2*) Topsail Pr., Inc.

Schamess, Lisa. Borrowed Light: A Novel. 2002. 208p. 22.50 (*0-87074-474-7*) Southern Methodist Univ. Pr.

Schulman, Sarah. Rat Bohemia. 240p. 1996. pap. 10.95 o.p. (*0-452-27182-7*, Plume); 1995. 19.95 o.p. (*0-525-93790-0*, Dutton) Dutton/Plume.

Self, Will. Dorian. 2004. 288p. pap. 13.00 (*0-8021-4047-5*, Grove Pr.) Grove/Atlantic, Inc.

Self, Will & Wilde, Oscar. Dorian: An Imitation. 2003. 288p. 23.00 (*0-8021-1729-5*, Grove Pr.) Grove/Atlantic, Inc.

Sherman, Charlotte W. Touch. 1995. 224p. 20.00 o.p. (*0-06-016925-7*) HarperTrade.

Spanbauer, Tom. In the City of Shy Hunters: A Novel. 2001. viii, 504p. 26.00 o.p. (*0-8021-1691-4*); 2002. 512p. reprint ed. pap. 14.00 (*0-8021-3898-5*) Grove/Atlantic, Inc. (Grove Pr.).

Starkman, Neal. I Used to Be Afraid. 1995. (Illus.). (J). 8.95 o.p. (*0-935529-96-9*) Comprehensive Health Education Foundation.

Svoboda, Terese. Cannibal. 1994. 138p. (C). 20.00 (*0-8147-8012-1*) New York Univ. Pr.

—Cannibal. 1994. E-Book 19.95 (*0-585-31629-5*) netLibrary, Inc.

Tapon, Philippe. Parisian from Kansas. (William Abrahams Book Ser.). 336p. 1998. pap. 13.95 o.s.i (*0-452-27735-3*, Plume); 1997. 23.95 o.s.i (*0-525-94239-4*) Dutton/Plume.

Thiele, Thom. Five Little Indians: A Novel. 1997. 215p. (Orig.). pap. 12.95 o.p. (*0-533-12350-X*) Vantage Pr., Inc.

Toibin, Colm. The Blackwater Lightship. 1999. 272p. 16.95 o.p. (*0-330-38985-8*) Picador GBR. *Dist:* Trans-Atlantic Pubns., Inc.

—The Blackwater Lightship. 288p. 2000. 24.00 o.s.i (*0-684-87389-3*); 2001. reprint ed. pap. 13.00 (*0-7432-0331-3*) Simon & Schuster. (Scribner).

Weir, John. The Irreversible Decline of Eddie Socket. 1989. 256p. 17.95 o.p. (*0-06-016162-0*) HarperTrade.

White, Edmund & Mars-Jones, Adam. The Darker Proof: Stories from a Crisis. 1988. 233p. pap. 8.95 o.p. (*0-452-26070-1*, Plume) Dutton/Plume.

Whitney, Ruth Linnea. Slim: A Novel. 2003. 320p. 24.95 (*0-87074-478-X*) Southern Methodist Univ. Pr.

Zimmerman, R. D. Hostage. 1998. 288p. pap. 10.95 o.s.i (*0-385-31892-8*, Delacorte Pr.) Dell Publishing.

# C

## CAT OWNERS—FICTION

Adamson, Lydia. A Cat by Any Other Name. unabr. collector's ed. 1997. (Alice Nestleton Ser.). audio 30.00 (*0-7366-3597-1*, 4248) Books on Tape, Inc.

—A Cat by Any Other Name: An Alice Nestleton Mystery. 1992. (Alice Nestleton Mystery Ser.). 208p. mass mkt. 5.50 o.s.i (*0-451-17231-0*, Signet Bks.) NAL.

—A Cat in a Chorus Line. unabr. ed. 1997. (Alice Nestleton Ser.: Vol. 12). audio 24.00 (*0-7366-4052-5*, 4561) Books on Tape, Inc.

—A Cat in a Chorus Line. 1996. (Alice Nestleton Mystery Ser.). 256p. mass mkt. 5.50 o.s.i (*0-451-18084-4*, Signet Bks.) NAL.

—A Cat in a Glass House. unabr. ed. 1997. (Alice Nestleton Ser.). audio 30.00 (*0-7366-3675-7*, 4354) Books on Tape, Inc.

—A Cat in a Glass House. 1993. (Alice Nestleton Mystery Ser.). 208p. mass mkt. 3.99 o.s.i (*0-451-17706-1*, Signet Bks.) NAL.

—A Cat in Fine Style. unabr. ed. 1997. (Alice Nestleton Ser.: Vol. 10). audio 30.00 (*0-7366-3831-8*, 4551) Books on Tape, Inc.

—A Cat in Fine Style: An Alice Nestleton Mystery. 1995. (Alice Nestleton Mystery Ser.). 224p. mass mkt. 5.99 o.s.i (*0-451-18083-6*, Signet Bks.) NAL.

—A Cat in the Manger. l.t. ed. 1991. 17.95 o.p. (*0-7451-8142-2*, AH0179); pap. 15.95 o.p. (*0-7927-0663-3*, AS0215) BBC Audiobooks America.

—A Cat in the Manger. unabr. collector's ed. 1997. (Alice Nestleton Ser.: Vol. 1). audio 30.00 (*0-7366-3556-4*, 4201) Books on Tape, Inc.

—A Cat in the Manger. 1990. (Alice Nestleton Mystery Ser.). 208p. mass mkt. 5.50 o.s.i (*0-451-16787-2*, Signet Bks.) NAL.

—A Cat in the Wings. unabr. collector's ed. 1997. (Alice Nestleton Ser.). audio 36.00 (*0-7366-3598-X*, 4249) Books on Tape, Inc.

—A Cat in the Wings. 1992. (Alice Nestleton Mystery Ser.: No. 5). 208p. mass mkt. 5.99 o.s.i (*0-451-17336-8*, Signet Bks.) NAL.

—A Cat in the Wings: An Alice Nestleton Mystery. l.t. ed. 2001. 301p. 28.95 o.p. (*0-7862-3676-0*) Thorndike Pr.

—A Cat in Wolf's Clothing. unabr. collector's ed. 1997. (Alice Nestleton Ser.: Vol. 3). audio 30.00 (*0-7366-3558-0*, 4203) Books on Tape, Inc.

—A Cat in Wolf's Clothing. 1991. (Alice Nestleton Mystery Ser.). 208p. mass mkt. 4.99 o.s.i (*0-451-17085-7*, Signet Bks.) NAL.

—A Cat in Wolf's Clothing: An Alice Nestleton Mystery. l.t. ed. 1993. (General Ser.). 223p. pap. 16.95 (*0-8161-5401-5*); lib. bdg. 18.95 o.p. (*0-8161-5400-7*) Gale Group. (Macmillan Reference USA).

—A Cat of a Different Color. unabr. collector's ed. 1997. (Alice Nestleton Ser.: Vol. 2). audio 30.00 (*0-7366-3557-2*, 4202) Books on Tape, Inc.

—A Cat of a Different Color. l.t. ed. 1992. (General Ser.). 200p. pap. 14.95 o.p. (*0-8161-5399-X*); lib. bdg. 18.95 o.p. (*0-8161-5398-1*) Gale Group. (Macmillan Reference USA).

—A Cat of a Different Color. 1991. (Alice Nestleton Mystery Ser.). 208p. mass mkt. 5.50 o.s.i (*0-451-16955-7*, Signet Bks.) NAL.

—A Cat of One's Own. 1999. (Alice Nestleton Mysteries Ser.: Bk. 17). 208p. 19.95 (*0-525-94428-1*) Dutton/Plume.

—A Cat of One's Own, 1. 2000. (Alice Nestleton Mysteries Ser.). 208p. mass mkt. 5.99 o.s.i (*0-451-19769-0*) NAL.

—A Cat of One's Own. l.t. ed. 1999. (Mystery Ser.). 216p. 28.95 (*0-7862-1884-3*) Thorndike Pr.

—A Cat on a Beach Blanket. unabr. ed. 1998. (Alice Nestleton Ser.). audio 30.00 (*0-7366-4260-9*, 4759) Books on Tape, Inc.

—A Cat on a Beach Blanket. 1997. (Alice Nestleton Mystery Ser.). (Illus.). 192p. 18.95 o.p. (*0-525-94304-8*) Dutton/Plume.

—A Cat on a Beach Blanket. 1998. (Alice Nestleton Mysteries Ser.). 256p. mass mkt. 5.99 o.s.i (*0-451-19259-1*, Signet Bks.) NAL.

—A Cat on a Beach Blanket: An Alice Nestleton Mystery. l.t. ed. 2001. 231p. 29.95 (*0-7862-2649-8*) Thorndike Pr.

—A Cat on a Winning Streak. unabr. ed. 1997. (Alice Nestleton Ser.). audio 24.00 (*0-7366-3746-X*, 4421) Books on Tape, Inc.

—A Cat on a Winning Streak. 1995. (Alice Nestleton Mystery Ser.). 240p. mass mkt. 4.50 o.s.i (*0-451-18082-8*, Signet Bks.) NAL.

—A Cat on Jingle Bell Rock. 1997. (Alice Nestleton Mystery Ser.). 192p. 19.95 o.p. (*0-525-94375-7*) Dutton/Plume.

—A Cat on Jingle Bell Rock. 1998. (Alice Nestleton Mystery Ser.). 340p. mass mkt. 5.99 o.s.i (*0-451-19458-6*, Signet Bks.) NAL.

—A Cat on Jingle Bell Rock: An Alice Nestleton Mystery. l.t. ed. 2000. (Mystery Ser.). 216p. 28.95 (*0-7862-2650-1*) Thorndike Pr.

—A Cat on Stage Left. 1998. (Alice Nestleton Mysteries Ser.: Vol. 16). (Illus.). 176p. 19.95 o.p. (*0-525-94419-2*) Dutton/Plume.

—A Cat on Stage Left: An Alice Nestleton Mystery, 1 vol., Vol. 16. 1999. (Alice Nestleton Mysteries Ser.: Vol. 16). 256p. mass mkt. 5.99 o.s.i (*0-451-19734-8*) NAL.

—A Cat on Stage Left: An Alice Nestleton Mystery. l.t. ed. 1998. (Mystery Ser.). 232p. 27.95 (*0-7862-1559-3*) Thorndike Pr.

—A Cat on the Cutting Edge. unabr. ed. 1997. (Alice Nestleton Ser.: Vol. 9). audio 24.00 (*0-7366-3745-1*, 4420) Books on Tape, Inc.

—A Cat on the Cutting Edge. l.t. ed. 1995. (Alice Nestleton Mystery Ser.). 178p. lib. bdg. 21.95 o.p. (*0-7838-1243-4*, Macmillan Reference USA) Gale Group.

—A Cat on the Cutting Edge. 1994. (Alice Nestleton Mystery Ser.). 224p. mass mkt. 4.50 o.s.i (*0-451-18080-1*, Signet Bks.) NAL.

—A Cat under the Mistletoe. 1997. (Alice Nestleton Mysteries Ser.). 256p. mass mkt. 5.99 o.s.i (*0-451-19105-6*, Signet Bks.) NAL.

—A Cat under the Mistletoe: A Christmas Cat Mystery. 1996. (Alice Nestleton Mystery Ser.). 224p. 18.95 o.p. (*0-525-94226-2*, Dutton) Dutton/Plume.

—A Cat under the Mistletoe: An Alice Nestleton Mystery. l.t. ed. 2000. (Mystery Ser.). 248p. 28.95 (*0-7862-2651-X*) Thorndike Pr.

—A Cat with No Regrets. unabr. ed. 1997. (Alice Nestleton Ser.). audio 30.00 (*0-7366-3744-3*, 4419) Books on Tape, Inc.

—A Cat with No Regrets. 1994. (Alice Nestleton Mystery Ser.: No. 8). 208p. mass mkt. 3.99 o.s.i (*0-451-18055-0*, Signet Bks.) NAL.

—A Cat with No Regrets. 1999. pap. (*0-525-93811-7*) Viking Penguin.

Allen, Garrison. Baseball Cat. (Big Mike Mystery Ser.: Vol. 4). 1998. 336p. mass mkt. 5.99 (*1-57566-309-0*); 1997. 304p. 18.95 o.s.i (*1-57566-183-7*) Kensington Publishing Corp.

—Dinosaur Cat. (Big Mike Mystery Ser.). 336p. 1999. mass mkt. 5.99 o.s.i (*1-57566-426-7*); 1998. (J). 20.00 o.s.i (*1-57566-304-X*, Kensington Bks.) Kensington Publishing Corp.

—Movie Cat. 1999. (Big Mike Mystery Ser.). 304p. 20.00 o.s.i (*1-57566-413-5*) Kensington Publishing Corp.

—Royal Cat: A Big Mike Mystery. 1996. (Big Mike Mystery Ser.: Vol. 2). 304p. mass mkt. 4.99 o.s.i (*1-57566-045-8*); 1995. mass mkt. 16.95 o.s.i (*0-8217-4957-9*, Zebra Bks.) Kensington Publishing Corp.

—Stable Cat. 304p. 1997. mass mkt. 5.50 o.s.i (*1-57566-188-8*); 1996. pap. 18.95 o.p. (*1-57566-042-3*) Kensington Publishing Corp.

Babson, Marian. Canapes for the Kitties. unabr. ed. 1999. audio 44.95 (*0-7861-1565-3*, 2396) Blackstone Audio Bks., Inc.

—Canapes for the Kitties. l.t. ed. 1998. (Large Print Book Ser.). pap. 23.95 (*1-56895-522-7*, Wheeler Publishing, Inc.) Gale Group.

—Canapes for the Kitties. 1997. 272p. 21.95 o.p. (*0-312-16929-9*, Saint Martin's Minotaur); 1999. 256p. reprint ed. mass mkt. 5.99 (*0-312-96897-3*, St. Martin's Paperbacks) St. Martin's Pr.

—The Company of Cats. l.t. ed. 1999. (Beeler Large Print Mystery Ser.). 216p. 24.95 (*1-57490-209-1*, Beeler Large Print Bks.) Beeler, Thomas T. Publisher.

—The Company of Cats. 2000. 192p. mass mkt. 5.99 (*0-312-97501-5*, St. Martin's Paperbacks); 1999. 183p. 20.95 o.p. (*0-312-19924-4*, Saint Martin's Minotaur) St. Martin's Pr.

—The Diamond Cat. l.t. ed. 1995. 256p. pap. 17.95 o.p. (*0-7838-1456-9*, Macmillan Reference USA) Gale Group.

—The Diamond Cat. unabr. ed. 2000. audio 46.00 (*1-84197-067-0*, H1064E7, Clipper Audio) Recorded Bks., LLC.

—The Diamond Cat. 1996. mass mkt. 5.99 (*0-312-95660-6*, St. Martin's Paperbacks); 1995. 224p. 20.95 o.p. (*0-312-13049-X*, Saint Martin's Minotaur) St. Martin's Pr.

—Nine Lives to Murder. 1995. mass mkt. 4.99 (*0-312-95580-4*, St. Martin's Paperbacks); 1994. 192p. 18.95 o.p. (*0-312-10511-8*, Saint Martin's Minotaur) St. Martin's Pr.

—Paws for Alarm. 1998. (Dead Letter Mysteries Ser.). 272p. reprint ed. pap. 6.50 (*0-312-96513-3*, St. Martin's Paperbacks) St. Martin's Pr.

—Whiskers & Smoke. 1997. (Dead Letter Mysteries Ser.). 214p. mass mkt. 5.99 (*0-312-96181-2*, St. Martin's Paperbacks) St. Martin's Pr.

—Whiskers & Smoke. abr. ed. 1997. audio 16.96 o.p. (*1-56431-214-3*) Sunset Products.

Barlow, Eleanor Poe. The Master's Cat: The Story of Charles Dickens as Told by His Cat. 1998. (Illus.). 132p. (YA). (gr. 7 up). 24.00 (*0-9518525-3-1*) Dickens Publishing GBR. *Dist:* Hood, Alan C. & Co., Inc.

—The Master's Cat: The Story of Charles Dickens as Told by His Cat. 1999. 132p. (YA). pap. 16.50 (*1-880158-22-1*) Townsend, J.N. Publishing.

Braun, Lilian Jackson. The Cat Who Ate Danish Modern. 1986. (Cat Who Ser.). 192p. mass mkt. 6.99 (*0-515-08712-2*, Jove) Berkley Publishing Group.

—The Cat Who Ate Danish Modern. l.t. ed. 1990. (Nightingale Ser.). 274p. 14.95 o.p. (*0-8161-4914-3*, Macmillan Reference USA) Gale Group.

—The Cat Who Ate Danish Modern. unabr. ed. 1990. (Cat Who Ser.). audio 35.00 (*1-55690-090-2*, 90081E7) Recorded Bks., LLC.

—The Cat Who Brought down the House. 2003. 256p. mass mkt. 6.99 (*0-515-13655-7*, Jove) Berkley Publishing Group.

—The Cat Who Brought down the House. 2003. 240p. 23.95 (*0-399-14942-2*); audio 24.95 (*0-399-14993-7*, Putnam Berkley Audio) Putnam Publishing Group, The.

—The Cat Who Brought down the House. 2003. 299p. 32.95 (*0-7862-5036-4*); 2004. 304p. pap. 13.95 (*1-59413-011-6*, Large Print Pr.) Thorndike Pr.

—The Cat Who Came to Breakfast. l.t. ed. 296p. 1995. 17.95 o.p. (*0-8161-5935-1*); 1994. lib. bdg. 23.95 o.p. (*0-8161-5934-3*) Gale Group. (Macmillan Reference USA).

—The Cat Who Came to Breakfast. abr. ed. 1993. audio 16.95 o.p. (*1-55800-937-X*, 393255, Dove Audio) NewStar Media, Inc.

—The Cat Who Came to Breakfast. 1994. 240p. 19.95 o.p. (*0-399-13868-4*, G. P. Putnam's Sons) Penguin Group (USA) Inc.

—The Cat Who Could Read Backwards. l.t. ed. 1991. 12.95 o.p. (*0-7927-0098-8*, C0139) BBC Audiobooks America.

—The Cat Who Could Read Backwards. 256p. 2003. pap. 10.00 (*0-425-19520-1*); 1986. mass mkt. 6.99 (*0-515-09017-4*, Jove) Berkley Publishing Group.

—The Cat Who Could Read Backwards. l.t. ed. 1997. (Large Print Book Ser.). 25.95 o.p. (*1-56895-470-0*, Wheeler Publishing, Inc.) Gale Group.

—The Cat Who Could Read Backwards. 1997. (Cat Who. . . Ser.). 240p. 19.95 o.p. (*0-399-14286-X*, G. P. Putnam's Sons) Penguin Group (USA) Inc.

—The Cat Who Could Read Backwards. unabr. ed. 1990. (Cat Who Ser.). audio 19.95 (*1-55690-091-0*, 90082) Recorded Bks., LLC.

—The Cat Who Had 14 Tales. 1988. (Cat Who Ser.). 256p. mass mkt. 6.99 (*0-515-09497-8*, Jove) Berkley Publishing Group.

—The Cat Who Had 14 Tales. l.t. ed. 1991. (Nightingale Ser.). 241p. 14.95 o.p. (*0-8161-4915-1*, Macmillan Reference USA) Gale Group.

—The Cat Who Knew a Cardinal. 1992. (Cat Who Ser.). 288p. mass mkt. 6.99 (*0-515-10786-7*, Jove) Berkley Publishing Group.

—The Cat Who Knew a Cardinal. l.t. ed. 1992. (General Ser.). 316p. 18.95 (*0-8161-5279-9*); lib. bdg. 19.95 o.p. (*0-8161-5278-0*) Gale Group. (Macmillan Reference USA).

—The Cat Who Knew Shakespeare. 1988. (Cat Who Ser.). 256p. mass mkt. 6.99 (*0-515-09582-6*, Jove) Berkley Publishing Group.

—The Cat Who Knew Shakespeare. unabr. ed. 1991. (Cat Who Ser.). (YA). (gr. 10 up). audio 24.95 (*1-55690-092-9*, 91115E7) Recorded Bks., LLC.

—The Cat Who Lived High. 1991. (Cat Who Ser.). 304p. mass mkt. 6.99 (*0-515-10566-X*, Jove) Berkley Publishing Group.

—The Cat Who Moved a Mountain. 1992. (Cat Who Ser.). 272p. mass mkt. 6.99 (*0-515-10950-9*, Jove) Berkley Publishing Group.

—The Cat Who Moved a Mountain. 1992. (Cat Who Ser.). 240p. 18.95 o.p. (*0-399-13646-0*, G. P. Putnam's Sons) Penguin Group (USA) Inc.

—The Cat Who Played Brahms. 1987. (Cat Who Ser.). 256p. mass mkt. 6.99 (*0-515-09050-6*, Jove) Berkley Publishing Group.

—The Cat Who Played Brahms. unabr. ed. 1992. (Cat Who Ser.). audio 24.95 (*1-55690-651-X*, 92133) Recorded Bks., LLC.

—The Cat Who Robbed a Bank. 2001. (Cat Who Ser.). 304p. mass mkt. 6.99 (*0-515-12994-1*, Jove) Berkley Publishing Group.

—The Cat Who Robbed a Bank. l.t. ed. 2000. pap. 22.95 o.p. (*0-7838-8710-8*, Macmillan Reference USA) Gale Group.

—The Cat Who Robbed a Bank. 2000. (Cat Who Ser.). 256p. 23.95 o.p. (*0-399-14570-2*) Penguin Group (USA) Inc.

—The Cat Who Robbed a Bank. l.t. ed. 2000. 400p. 23.95 (*0-375-40878-9*) Random Hse. Large Print.

—The Cat Who Saw Red. 1986. (Cat Who Ser.). 256p. mass mkt. 6.99 (*0-515-09016-6*, Jove) Berkley Publishing Group.

—The Cat Who Saw Red. unabr. ed. 1990. (Cat Who Ser.). (YA). (gr. 10 up). audio 35.00 (*1-55690-093-7*, 90083E7) Recorded Bks., LLC.

—The Cat Who Talked to Ghosts. 1990. (Cat Who Ser.). 288p. pap. 6.99 (*0-515-10265-2*, Jove) Berkley Publishing Group.

—The Cat Who Talked to Ghosts. unabr. ed. 1994. (Cat Who Ser.). audio 42.00 Recorded Bks., LLC.

—The Cat Who Talked Turkey. 2003. 288p. 23.95 (*0-399-15107-9*) Putnam Publishing Group, The.

—The Cat Who Turned on & Off. 1986. (Cat Who Ser.). 272p. mass mkt. 6.99 (*0-515-08794-7*, Jove) Berkley Publishing Group.

—The Cat Who Turned on & Off. l.t. ed. 1992. (Nightingale Ser.). 285p. 14.95 o.p. (*0-8161-4815-5*, Macmillan Reference USA) Gale Group.

—The Cat Who Turned on & Off. unabr. ed. 1991. (Cat Who Ser.). audio 44.00 (*1-55690-094-5*, 91402E7) Recorded Bks., LLC.

—The Cat Who Turned on & Off. 1986. 11.60 o.p. (*0-606-13255-4*) Turtleback Bks.

—The Cat Who Wasn't There. 1993. (Cat Who Ser.). 288p. mass mkt. 6.99 (*0-515-11127-9*, Jove) Berkley Publishing Group.

—The Cat Who Wasn't There. 1992. 240p. 18.95 o.p. (*0-399-13780-7*, G. P. Putnam's Sons) Penguin Group (USA) Inc.

—The Cat Who Went Underground. 1989. (Cat Who Ser.). 288p. mass mkt. 6.99 (*0-515-10123-0*, Jove) Berkley Publishing Group.

—El Gato Que Leia del Reves. 1997. Tr. of Cat Who Could Read Backwards. (SPA.). 248p. 14.58 (*84-01-47431-0*) Plaza & Janés Editories, S.A. ESP. *Dist:* Distribooks, Inc., Lectorum Pubns., Inc.

—Lilian Jackson Braun: Three Complete Novels. 1998. 640p. 12.98 o.p. (*0-399-14364-5*); 1996. 12.98 o.p. (*0-399-14127-8*); 1994. 608p. 11.98 o.s.i (*0-399-13984-2*) Penguin Group (USA) Inc. (G. P. Putnam's Sons).

—Three Complete Novels. 2002. 803p. 14.98 (*0-399-14813-2*) Penguin Group (USA) Inc.

—Three Complete Novels: The Cat Who Saw Red; The Cat Who Played Brahms; The Cat Who Played Post Office - Omnibus Edition. 1993. 608p. 12.98 o.s.i (*0-399-13885-4*, G. P. Putnam's Sons) Penguin Group (USA) Inc.

—Three Complete Novels: The Cat Who Talked to Ghosts; The Cat Who Knew a Cardinal; The Cat Who Lived High, 3 bks. in 1. 1997. 512p. 12.98 o.p. (*0-399-14258-4*, G. P. Putnam's Sons) Penguin Group (USA) Inc.

Brown, Rita Mae. Cat on the Scent. 336p. 1999. (Illus.). 23.95 o.s.i (*0-553-09971-X*); 2000. reprint ed. mass mkt. 7.50 (*0-553-57541-4*) Bantam Bks.

—Cat on the Scent. l.t. ed. 1999. 26.95 o.p. (*1-56895-749-1*, Wheeler Publishing, Inc.) Gale Group.

—Catch as Cat Can. l.t. ed. 2002. 504p. 31.95 (*0-7862-4045-8*) Gale Group.

—Catch as Cat Can. l.t. ed. 2003. (Paperback Bestsellers Ser.). pap. 13.95 (*0-7862-4044-X*) Thorndike Pr.

—Claws & Effect. 2002. (Mrs. Murphy Mystery Ser.). (Illus.). 320p. reprint ed. mass mkt. 7.50 (*0-553-58090-6*) Bantam Bks.

—Claws & Effect. l.t. ed. 2001. (Illus.). 433p. 30.95 (*0-7862-3484-9*) Thorndike Pr.

—Murder at Monticello, or, Old Sins. 1995. (Mrs. Murphy Mystery Ser.). 320p. mass mkt. 7.50 (*0-553-57235-0*, Crimeline) Bantam Bks.

—Murder on the Prowl. 1999. 400p. reprint ed. mass mkt. 7.50 (*0-553-57540-6*) Bantam Bks.

—Murder on the Prowl. l.t. ed. 1998. (Basic Ser.). 467p. 30.95 (*0-7862-1458-9*) Thorndike Pr.

—Murder, She Meowed. 1997. (Mrs. Murphy Mystery Ser.). (Illus.). 336p. mass mkt. 7.50 (*0-553-57237-7*) Bantam Bks.

—Pawing Through the Past. 2001. (Mrs. Murphy Mystery Ser.). 352p. mass mkt. 7.50 (*0-553-58025-6*) Bantam Bks.

—Pawing Through the Past. l.t. ed. 2000. (Wheeler Large Print Book Ser.). (Illus.). 360p. 28.95 o.p. (*1-56895-134-5*, Wheeler Publishing, Inc.) Gale Group.

—Pay Dirt. 1996. (Mrs. Murphy Mystery Ser.). 288p. mass mkt. 7.50 (*0-553-57236-9*, Crimeline) Bantam Bks.

—Rest in Pieces. 1993. (Mrs. Murphy Mystery Ser.). 368p. mass mkt. 7.50 (*0-553-56239-8*) Bantam Bks.

—The Tail of the Tip-Off. 2004. (Illus.). 400p. mass mkt. 7.50 (*0-553-58285-2*) Bantam Bks.

—Wish You Were Here. l.t. ed. 1992. pap. 20.95 o.p. (*0-7927-1189-0*); 22.95 o.p. (*0-7927-1188-2*, CH0250) BBC Audiobooks America.

—Wish You Were Here. 1991. (Mrs. Murphy Mystery Ser.). 304p. mass mkt. 7.50 (*0-553-28753-2*) Bantam Bks.

Brown, Rita Mae & Brown, Sneaky Pie. Catch As Cat Can. 2003. (Illus.). 368p. mass mkt. 7.50 (*0-553-58028-0*, Bantam) Bantam Bks.

—Catch As Cat Can. 2002. (Illus.). 304p. 24.95 (*0-553-10744-5*) Bantam Dell Publishing Group.

—Catch as Cat Can. l.t. ed. 13.95 (*1-4104-0084-0*, Large Print Pr.) Thorndike Pr.

—The Tail of the Tip-Off. 2003. (Mrs. Murphy Mystery Ser.). E-Book 19.95 (*0-553-89725-X*); (Illus.). 320p. 24.95 (*0-553-80158-9*) Bantam Bks.

—The Tail of the Tip-Off. audio 29.99 (*1-4025-3628-3*) Recorded Bks., LLC.

—The Tail of the Tip-Off. l.t. ed. 2003. 32.95 (*0-7862-4991-9*) Thorndike Pr.

Browne, L. Virginia, et al. Letters from Cleo & Tyrone: A Feline Perspective on Love, Life & Litter. 2000. (Illus.). 160p. 15.95 (*0-312-26706-1*, Saint Martin's Griffin) St. Martin's Pr.

Carroll, Noriko & Carroll, Don, photos by. Happy Birthday, the Cat: True Meow Stories. 2003. (Illus.). 176p. 16.95 (*0-7407-3317-6*) Andrews McMeel Publishing.

Douglas, Carole Nelson. The Cat & the King of Clubs. 1999. (Mystery Ser.). 227p. 20.95 (*0-7862-1920-3*, Five Star) Gale Group.

—The Cat & the Queen of Hearts. 1999. (Mystery Ser.). 223p. 21.95 (*0-7862-2173-9*, Five Star) Gale Group.

—Cat in a Crimson Haze: A Midnight Louie Mystery. 1996. mass mkt. 219.68 (*0-8125-6330-1*); 1996. 408p. mass mkt. 6.99 (*0-8125-4414-5*, Forge Bks.); 1995. 352p. 22.95 o.p. (*0-312-85901-5*, Forge Bks.) Doherty, Tom Assocs., LLC.

—Cat in a Crimson Haze: A Midnight Louie Mystery. l.t. ed. 1995. (Midnight Louie Mystery Ser.). 604p. 24.95 o.p. (*0-7838-1390-2*, Macmillan Reference USA) Gale Group.

—Cat in a Crimson Haze: A Midnight Louie Mystery. 1996. mass mkt. 223.68 (*0-8125-6329-8*) Holtzbrinck Pubs.

—Cat in a Diamond Dazzle: A Midnight Louie Mystery. (Midnight Louie Mystery Ser.). 1997. 411p. mass mkt. 6.99 (*0-8125-5506-6*); 1996. 416p. 24.95 o.p. (*0-312-86085-4*) Doherty, Tom Assocs., LLC. (Forge Bks.).

—Cat in a Flamingo Fedora: A Midnight Louie Mystery. (Midnight Louie Mystery Ser.). 1998. 373p. mass mkt. 6.99 (*0-8125-6535-5*); 1997. 384p. 24.95 o.p. (*0-312-86329-2*) Doherty, Tom Assocs., LLC. (Forge Bks.).

—Cat in a Golden Garland: A Midnight Louie Mystery. (Midnight Louie Mystery Ser.). 1998. 406p. mass mkt. 6.99 (*0-8125-3036-5*); 1997. 352p. 23.95 (*0-312-86386-1*) Doherty, Tom Assocs., LLC. (Forge Bks.).

—Cat in a Golden Garland: A Midnight Louie Mystery. l.t. ed. 1998. (G. K. Hall Core Ser.). 576p. 25.95 o.p. (*0-7838-8419-2*, Macmillan Reference USA) Gale Group.

—Cat in a Jeweled Jumpsuit: A Midnight Louie Mystery. 2000. 432p. mass mkt. 6.99 (*0-8125-6674-2*); 1999. 384p. 24.95 (*0-312-86817-0*) Doherty, Tom Assocs., LLC. (Forge Bks.).

—Cat in a Jeweled Jumpsuit: A Midnight Louie Mystery. l.t. ed. 2000. (Americana Ser.). 599p. 29.95 (*0-7862-2455-X*) Thorndike Pr.

—Cat in a Kiwi Con: A Midnight Louie Mystery. (Midnight Louie Mystery Ser.). 2001. 432p. mass mkt. 6.99 (*0-8125-8425-2*); 2000. 384p. 24.95 o.p. (*0-312-86955-X*) Doherty, Tom Assocs., LLC. (Forge Bks.).

—Cat in a Leopard Spot: A Midnight Louie Mystery. E-Book 24.95 (*0-312-70128-4*, Tor Bks.); 2002. 416p. pap. 6.99 (*0-8125-7022-7*, Forge Bks.); 2001. 384p. 24.95 (*0-312-85370-X*, Forge Bks.) Doherty, Tom Assocs., LLC.

—Cat in a Midnight Choir: A Midnight Louie Mystery. E-Book 24.95 (*0-312-70619-7*, Tor Bks.); 2003. 416p. mass mkt. 24.95 (*0-8125-7021-9*, Forge Bks.); 2002. 336p. 24.95 (*0-312-85797-7*, Forge Bks.) Doherty, Tom Assocs., LLC.

—Cat in an Indigo Mood: A Midnight Louie Mystery. l.t. ed. 2003. (Large Print Ser.). 29.95 (*1-57490-473-6*, Beeler Large Print Bks.) Beeler, Thomas T. Publisher.

—Cat in an Indigo Mood: A Midnight Louie Mystery. 1999. 384p. mass mkt. 6.99 (*0-8125-6187-2*); (Illus.). 381p. 24.95 (*0-312-86635-6*) Doherty, Tom Assocs., LLC. (Forge Bks.).

—Cat on a Blue Monday: A Midnight Louie Mystery. l.t. ed. 1994. o.p. (*0-7927-2111-X*); pap. o.p. (*0-7927-2110-1*) BBC Audiobooks America.

—Cat on a Blue Monday: A Midnight Louie Mystery. 1994. (Midnight Louie Mystery Ser.). 374p. mass mkt. 6.99 (*0-8125-3441-7*); 384p. 21.95 o.p. (*0-312-85607-5*) Doherty, Tom Assocs., LLC. (Forge Bks.).

—Cat on a Blue Monday: A Midnight Louie Mystery. l.t. ed. 1994. 540p. pap. 17.95 o.p. (*0-8161-7456-3*, Macmillan Reference USA) Gale Group.

—Cat on a Hyacinth Hunt: A Midnight Louie Mystery. (Midnight Louie Mystery Ser.). 384p. 1999. mass mkt. 6.99 (*0-8125-6186-4*); 1998. 23.95 (*0-312-86634-8*) Doherty, Tom Assocs., LLC. (Forge Bks.).

—Cat on a Hyacinth Hunt: A Midnight Louie Mystery. l.t. ed. 2000. pap. 23.95 (*1-56895-872-2*, Wheeler Publishing, Inc.) Gale Group.

—Cat with an Emerald Eye: A Midnight Louie Mystery. (Midnight Louie Mystery Ser.). 384p. 1997. mass mkt. 6.99 (*0-8125-4012-3*); 1996. 24.95 o.p. (*0-312-86228-8*) Doherty, Tom Assocs., LLC. (Forge Bks.).

—Catnap: A Midnight Louie Mystery. l.t. ed. 1993. (Midnight Louie Mystery Ser.). 23.95 o.p. (*0-7927-1644-2*) BBC Audiobooks America.

—Catnap: A Midnight Louie Mystery. (Midnight Louie Mystery Ser.). 1993. 241p. mass mkt. 6.99 (*0-8125-1682-6*, Forge Bks.); 1992. 256p. 17.95 o.p. (*0-312-85217-7*, Tor Bks.) Doherty, Tom Assocs., LLC.

—Pussyfoot: A Midnight Louie Mystery. l.t. ed. 1994. (Midnight Louie Mystery Ser.). 24.95 o.p. (*0-7927-1846-1*); pap. 22.95 o.p. (*0-7927-1845-3*) BBC Audiobooks America.

—Pussyfoot: A Midnight Louie Mystery. (Midnight Louie Mystery Ser.). 1994. 304p. mass mkt. 5.99 (*0-8125-1683-4*); 1993. 256p. 19.95 o.p. (*0-312-85218-5*) Doherty, Tom Assocs., LLC. (Tor Bks.).

Engleman, Paul. The Man with My Cat. 2000. 228p. 23.95 o.p. (*0-312-24651-X*, Saint Martin's Minotaur) St. Martin's Pr.

Feaster, Sharon A. The Cat Who . . . Companion: The Complete Guide to Lilian Jackson Braun's Beloved Cat Who . . . Mysteries. 1998. 336p. pap. 13.00 o.s.i (*0-425-16540-X*) Berkley Publishing Group.

Feldman, Steve, illus. Letters from Cleo & Tyrone: A Feline Perspective on Love, Life & Litter. l.t. ed. 2001. 176p. pap. 24.95 (*0-7838-9481-3*, Macmillan Reference USA) Gale Group.

Gorman, Ed, et al, eds. Murder Most Feline: Cunning Tales of Cats & Crime. 2001. (Murder Most Ser.). 256p. pap. 14.95 (*1-58182-215-4*) Cumberland Hse. Publishing.

Marshall, Evan. Icing Ivy: A Jan Stuart & Winky Mystery. 2002. (Jane Stuart & Winky Mystery Ser.). (Illus.). 304p. 22.00 (*0-7582-0224-5*) Kensington Publishing Corp.

—Stabbing Stephanie. (Jane Stuart & Winky Mystery Ser.). 2002. 352p. mass mkt. 5.99 (*1-57566-729-0*); 2001. 34p. 22.00 o.s.i (*1-57566-657-X*) Kensington Publishing Corp.

—Toasting Tina. 2003. 304p. 22.00 (*0-7582-0226-1*, Kensington Bks.) Kensington Publishing Corp.

Walters, Minette. The Shape of Snakes. 2002. 384p. reprint ed. mass mkt. 7.99 (*0-515-13306-X*, Jove) Berkley Publishing Group.

—The Shape of Snakes. l.t. ed. 2002. 27.95 (*1-58724-156-0*, Wheeler Publishing, Inc.) Gale Group.

—The Shape of Snakes. 2001. (Illus.). 352p. 24.95 o.s.i (*0-399-14733-0*) Penguin Group (USA) Inc.

## CHRISTIAN LIFE—FICTION

Allen, Nancy Campbell. Faith of Our Fathers. 2001. (Illus.). 458p. 22.95 (*1-57734-897-4*) Covenant Communications.

Atteberry, Mark. The Caleb Quest. 2004. 128p. 14.99 (*0-7852-6187-7*) Nelson, Thomas Pubs.

Austin, Lynn. Fire by Night. 2003. (Refiners Fire Ser.). 432p. pap. 12.99 (*1-55661-443-8*) Bethany Hse. Pubs.

Baumbich, Charlene. Dearest Dorothy, Slow down, You're Wearing Us Out! 2004. 256p. pap. 10.95 (*0-14-200418-9*) Penguin Group (USA) Inc.

Baumbich, Charlene Ann. Dearest Dorothy, Are We There Yet? 2004. 224p. pap. 10.95 (*0-14-200379-4*) Penguin Group (USA) Inc.

Bayly, Joseph. How Silently, How Silently. rev. ed. 1973. 128p. pap. 1.25 o.p. (*0-912692-24-3*) Cook, David C. Publishing Co.

Bedford, Deborah. When You Believe. 2003. 304p. pap. 13.95 (*0-446-69041-4*, Warner Faith) Warner Bks., Inc.

Bell, Derrick A. Gospel Choirs: Psalms of Survival in an Alien Land Called Home. 1997. 240p. pap. 13.00 (*0-465-02413-0*) Basic Bks.

Bradbury, Stefin. The Immortality King: A Novel. 2003. 183p. pap. 19.95 (*1-59286-431-7*) PublishAmerica, Inc.

Brouwer, Sigmund. Degrees of Guilt. 2003. (Degrees of Guilt Ser.). 225p. (YA). pap. 12.99 (*0-8423-8285-2*) Tyndale Hse. Pubs.

Bunyan, John. The Pilgrim's Progress. 1969. (Classics Ser.). mass mkt. 1.95 o.p. (*0-8049-0183-X*, CL-183) Airmont Publishing Co., Inc.

—The Pilgrim's Progress. 23.95 (*0-8488-0141-5*) Amereon, Ltd.

—The Pilgrim's Progress. l.t. ed. 1978. (Giant Summit Book Ser.). 396p. (gr. 10). pap. 14.99 o.p. (*0-8010-0732-1*) Baker Bks.

—The Pilgrim's Progress. 1981. 379p. reprint ed. 35.99 (*0-85151-259-3*) Banner of Truth, The.

—The Pilgrim's Progress. 9.95 o.p. (*1-55748-169-5*); 2000. 304p. 9.97 (*1-57748-916-0*); 1998. 432p. 9.97 (*1-57748-262-X*); 1993. 384p. mass mkt. 2.49 o.p. (*1-55748-345-0*); 1989. 384p. 8.97 o.p. (*0-916441-00-8*); 1998. 96p. pap. 0.99 o.p. (*1-55748-812-6*); 14.95 o.p. (*1-55748-074-5*); 1995. 384p. 8.97 o.p. (*1-55748-621-2*); 1998. 384p. pap. 3.97 (*0-916441-24-5*) Barbour Publishing, Inc.

—The Pilgrim's Progress. 2000. per. 12.50 (*1-58396-528-9*) Blue Unicorn Editions.

—The Pilgrim's Progress. 1985. 396p. pap. 4.95 o.p. (*1-85030-017-8*) Bridge-Logos Pubs.

—The Pilgrim's Progress. 1976. lib. bdg. 26.95 (*0-89968-156-5*, Lightyear Pr.) Buccaneer Bks., Inc.

—The Pilgrim's Progress. Cantelon House Publishers Staff, ed. & intro. by. 1994. 174p. pap. 19.95 (*0-9642116-0-2*) Cantelon Hse. Pubs.

—The Pilgrim's Progress. 1984. pap. 0.50 o.p. (*0-87508-048-0*) Christian Literature Crusade, Inc.

—The Pilgrim's Progress. (Early Best Sellers Ser.). reprint ed. lib. bdg. 48.00 (*0-7426-1008-X*); 2001. (Illus.). pap. text 28.00 (*0-7426-6008-7*) Classic Bks.

—The Pilgrim's Progress. 1928. 352p. (YA). reprint ed. pap. text 28.00 (*1-4047-7326-6*) Classic Textbooks.

—The Pilgrim's Progress. 2001. 19.99 (*0-7684-2051-2*) Destiny Image Pubs.

—The Pilgrim's Progress. 2003. (Dover Thrift Editions Ser.). 336p. pap. 3.00 (*0-486-42675-0*) Dover Pubns., Inc.

—The Pilgrim's Progress. 1972. 2.95 o.p. (*0-460-01204-5*); 1957. 10.50 o.p. (*0-460-00204-X*) Dutton/Plume. (Dutton).

—The Pilgrim's Progress. 1999. E-Book 2.49 (*1-58627-299-3*) Electric Umbrella Publishing.

—The Pilgrim's Progress. 2003. 440p. pap. 24.99 incl. cd-rom (*1-889893-93-5*, Ambassador-Emerald, International); 1997. (Illus.). 379p. pap. 9.99 (*0-907927-74-2*) Emerald Hse. Group, Inc.

—The Pilgrim's Progress. 1975. 18.99 o.p. (*0-87377-030-7*) GAM Pubns.

—The Pilgrim's Progress. 1984. 288p. 30.00 o.p. (*0-905418-29-8*) Gresham Bks. GBR. *Dist:* State Mutual Bk. & Periodical Service, Ltd.

—The Pilgrim's Progress. l.t. ed. 2003. pap. 16.95 (*0-340-86167-3*) Hodder & Stoughton, Ltd. GBR. *Dist:* Trafalgar Square.

—The Pilgrim's Progress. l.t. ed. 390p. pap. 31.08 (*0-7583-1833-2*); 684p. pap. 47.40 (*0-7583-1835-9*); 1077p. pap. 77.29 (*0-7583-1837-5*); 875p. pap. 66.07 (*0-7583-1836-7*); 1536p. pap. 107.40 (*0-7583-1839-1*); 1324p. pap. 88.58 (*0-7583-1838-3*); 534p. pap. 38.50 (*0-7583-1834-0*); 300p. pap. 25.98 (*0-7583-1832-4*); 300p. lib. bdg. 31.98 (*0-7583-1824-3*); 684p. lib. bdg. 53.40 (*0-7583-1827-8*); 1077p. lib. bdg. 89.29 (*0-7583-1829-4*); 534p. lib. bdg. 44.50 (*0-7583-1826-X*); 1536p. lib. bdg. 125.40 (*0-7583-1831-6*); 390p. lib. bdg. 37.08 (*0-7583-1825-1*); 875p. lib. bdg. 78.07 (*0-7583-1828-6*); 1324p. lib. bdg. 100.58 (*0-7583-1830-8*) Huge Print Pr.

—The Pilgrim's Progress. 1998. 466p. reprint ed. pap. 29.95 (*0-7661-0600-4*) Kessinger Publishing Co.

—The Pilgrim's Progress. 1995. 534p. 9.99 o.p. (*0-8254-5305-4*) Kregel Pubns.

—The Pilgrim's Progress. E-Book 2.95 (*1-57799-957-6*) Logos Research Systems, Inc.

—The Pilgrim's Progress. l.t. ed. 1983. 16.95 o.p. (*0-87983-335-1*); 1972. 352p. reprint ed. pap. 10.00 o.p. (*0-87983-011-5*) McGraw-Hill Trade. (Keats Publishing).

—The Pilgrim's Progress. 1984. (Moody Classics Ser.). mass mkt. 4.99 (*0-8024-0012-4*, 392) Moody Pr.

—The Pilgrim's Progress. 2002. 320p. mass mkt. 6.95 (*0-451-52833-6*); 1968. mass mkt. 0.60 o.p. (*0-451-50432-1*, Signet Classics); 1968. mass mkt. 0.50 o.p. (*0-451-50221-3*, Signet Classics); 1964. mass mkt. 2.50 o.p. (*0-451-51813-6*, Signet Classics); 1964. mass mkt. 2.75 o.p. (*0-451-51930-2*, Signet Classics); 1964. 304p. mass mkt. 6.95 o.s.i (*0-451-52399-7*, CE1813, Signet Classics); 1964. mass mkt. 0.75 o.p. (*0-451-50546-8*, Signet Classics); 1964. mass mkt. 0.95 o.p. (*0-451-50708-8*, Signet Classics); 1964. mass mkt. 1.25 o.p. (*0-451-50895-5*, Signet Classics); 1964. mass mkt. 1.50 o.p. (*0-451-51115-8*, Signet Classics); 1964. mass mkt. 1.95 o.p. (*0-451-51346-0*, Signet Classics); 1964. mass mkt. 2.25 o.p. (*0-451-51643-5*, Signet Classics); 1964. mass mkt. 2.95 o.p. (*0-451-52218-4*) NAL.

—The Pilgrim's Progress. 1999. (Royal Classics Ser.: Vol. 1). xvi, 267p. 18.99 (*0-7852-4222-8*); 9.97 o.p. (*0-7852-4245-7*) Nelson, Thomas Inc.

—The Pilgrim's Progress, Pt. 3. 2000. 86p. pap. 13.95 (*1-889058-11-4*) Old Paths Pubns., Inc.

—The Pilgrim's Progress. Keeble, N. H., ed. & intro. by. 1998. (Oxford World's Classics Ser.). 336p. pap. 7.95 (*0-19-283400-2*) Oxford Univ. Pr., Inc.

—The Pilgrim's Progress. 1984. (Oxford World's Classics Ser.). 334p. pap. 5.95 o.p. (*0-19-281607-1*) Oxford Univ. Pr., Inc.

—The Pilgrim's Progress. Owens, W. R., ed. 2nd ed. 2003. (Oxford World's Classics Ser.). (Illus.). 368p. pap. 7.95 (*0-19-280361-1*) Oxford Univ. Pr., Inc.

—The Pilgrim's Progress. Wharey, James B. & Sharrock, Roger, eds. 2nd ed. 1960. (Oxford English Texts). 55.00 o.p. (*0-19-811802-3*) Oxford Univ. Pr., Inc.

—The Pilgrim's Progress. 1982. (Living Library). (Illus.). 268p. pap. 12.95 (*0-941478-02-5*, 930-033) Paraclete Pr., Inc.

—The Pilgrim's Progress. 2001. E-Book 2.25 (*1-4011-0109-7*) PublishingOnline.

—The Pilgrim's Progress. 1992. (BCL1-PR English Literature Ser.). 352p. reprint ed. lib. bdg. 89.00 (*0-7812-7326-9*) Reprint Services Corp.

—The Pilgrim's Progress. 1989. 320p. (gr. 10). pap. 5.99 (*0-8007-8609-2*, Spire) Revell, Fleming H. Co.

—The Pilgrim's Progress. 1980. 320p. mass mkt. 2.50 o.s.i (*0-671-42460-2*, Pocket) Simon & Schuster.

—The Pilgrim's Progress. 1998. per. 8.95 (*1-929579-89-6*) Smarr Pubs.

—The Pilgrim's Progress. l.t. ed. 1982. (Charnwood Large Print Ser.). 416p. 29.99 o.p. (*0-7089-8072-4*, Charnwood) Thorpe, F. A. Pubs. GBR. *Dist:* Ulverscroft Large Print Bks., Ltd., Ulverscroft Large Print Canada, Ltd.

—The Pilgrim's Progress. 1998. 14.00 (*0-606-14293-2*) Turtleback Bks.

—The Pilgrim's Progress. 1999. 480p. pap. 13.99 (*0-8423-5145-0*); 1991. 446p. 16.99 o.p. (*0-8423-4787-9*) Tyndale Hse. Pubs.

—The Pilgrim's Progress. Helms, Hal M., ed. 1984. (Illus.). 268p. reprint ed. pap. 6.95 o.p. (*0-8358-0516-6*) Upper Room Bks.

—The Pilgrim's Progress. 2003. 112p. pap. (*1-84333-593-X*) Vega Bks.

—The Pilgrim's Progress. Sharrock, Roger, ed. 1965. (Classics Ser.). 336p. pap. 8.95 (*0-14-043004-0*, Penguin Classics) Viking Penguin.

—The Pilgrim's Progress. 1981. 400p. mass mkt. 7.99 (*0-88368-096-3*, 770963) Whitaker Hse.

—The Pilgrim's Progress. 1999. E-Book 5.99 (*0-8220-7164-9*, Cliff Notes) Wiley, John & Sons, Inc.

—The Pilgrim's Progress. 1999. (Classics of World Literature). 272p. pap. 5.95 (*1-85326-468-7*, 4687WW) Wordsworth Editions, Ltd. GBR. *Dist:* Combined Publishing.

—The Pilgrim's Progress. 1973. 256p. reprint ed. pap. 3.95 o.p. (*0-310-22142-0*, 6610S) Zondervan.

—The Pilgrim's Progress: A Modern-Day Abridgement for Today's Reader. 1995. (Little Library Ser.). 48p. pap. 0.99 (*1-55748-648-4*) Barbour Publishing, Inc.

—The Pilgrim's Progress: In Modern English. Hazelbaker, L. Edward, ed. 882nd rev. ed. 1998. (Illus.). 450p. pap. 12.99 (*0-88270-757-4*, Bridge) Bridge-Logos Pubs.

—The Pilgrim's Progress: In Modern English. 2000. 144p. 20.99 (*1-58960-013-4*) Sovereign Grace Pubs., Inc.

—The Pilgrim's Progress: In Today's English. 1964. pap. 8.99 (*0-8024-6520-X*) Moody Pr.

—The Pilgrim's Progress & Grace Abounding. 1991. 432p. (Orig.). pap. 6.95 o.p. (*0-460-87142-0*, Everyman's Classic Library in Paperback) Tuttle Publishing.

Bunyan, John & Thomas, James H. The Pilgrim's Progress: In Today's English. (Illus.). 144p. 15.99 o.p. (*0-8024-4964-6*, 249) Moody Pr.

—The Pilgrim's Progress: In Today's English. 1999. lib. bdg. 23.95 (*1-56723-201-9*) Yestermorrow, Inc.

Bunyan, John & Watson, Jean. The Pilgrim's Progress. 1982. 144p. pap. 6.95 o.p. (*0-310-22147-1*, 12578L) Zondervan.

Carlson, Melody. Degrees of Guilt. 2003. (Degrees of Guilt Ser.). 225p. (YA). pap. 9.99 (*0-8423-8283-6*) Tyndale Hse. Pubs.

Chick, Jack T. This Was Your Life. 24p. 2002. (MON., Illus.). pap. 0.14 (*0-7589-0477-0*, 1623); 2001. (DAN.). pap. 0.14 (*0-7589-0416-9*); 1999. (FAR., Illus.). pap. 0.14 (*0-7589-0323-5*); 1999. (MAL., Illus.). pap. 0.14 (*0-7589-0319-7*); 1999. (Illus.). pap. 0.14 (*0-7589-0324-3*); 1999. (TAM., Illus.). pap. 0.14 (*0-7589-0329-4*); 1999. (KAN., Illus.). pap. 0.14 (*0-7589-0337-5*); 1999. (TEL., Illus.). pap. 0.14 (*0-7589-0338-3*); 1998. (CRE., Illus.). pap. 0.14 (*0-7589-0322-7*); 1998. (SPA., Illus.). pap. 0.14 (*0-7589-0151-8*); 1997. (Illus.). pap. 0.14 (*0-7589-0311-1*); 1996. (THA., Illus.). pap. 0.14 (*0-7589-0307-3*); 1995. (SWA., Illus.). pap. 0.14 (*0-7589-0282-4*); 1995. (ARA., Illus.). pap. 0.14 (*0-7589-0291-3*); 1995. (CRO., Illus.). pap. 0.14 (*0-7589-0281-6*); 1995. (POR., Illus.). pap. 0.14 (*0-7589-0111-9*); 1995. (ARM., Illus.). pap. 0.14 (*0-7589-0087-2*); 1995. (SER., Illus.). pap. 0.14 (*0-7589-0100-3*); 1995. (HIN., Illus.). pap. 0.14 (*0-7589-0219-0*); 1994. (CAM., Illus.). pap. 0.14 (*0-7589-0098-8*); 1993. (SLO., Illus.). pap. 0.14 (*0-7589-0238-7*); 1993. (EST., Illus.). pap. 0.14 (*0-7589-0233-6*); 1993. (LIT., Illus.). pap. 0.14 (*0-7589-0220-4*); 1992. (RUM., Illus.). pap. 0.14 (*0-7589-0250-6*); 1991. (ALB., Illus.). pap. 0.14 (*0-7589-0293-X*); 1990. (DUT., Illus.). pap. 0.14 (*0-7589-0286-7*); 1990. (HUN., Illus.). pap. 0.14 (*0-7589-0284-0*); 1990. (SWE., Illus.). pap. 0.14 (*0-7589-0275-1*); 1990. (TUR., Illus.). pap. 0.14 (*0-7589-0285-9*); 1989. (RUS., Illus.). pap. 0.14 (*0-7589-0260-3*); 1989. (UKR., Illus.). pap. 0.14 (*0-7589-0266-2*); 1989. (NOR., Illus.). pap. 0.14 (*0-7589-0274-3*); 1989. (FIN., Illus.). pap. 0.14 (*0-7589-0522-X*, 768); 1989. (Illus.). pap. 0.14 (*0-7589-0244-1*); 1988. (VIE., Illus.). pap. 0.14 (*0-7589-0114-3*); 1988. (TAG., Illus.). pap. 0.14 (*0-7589-0123-2*); 1988. (KOR., Illus.). pap. 0.14 (*0-7589-0107-0*); 1988. (JPN., Illus.). pap. 0.14 (*0-7589-0240-9*); 1988. (Illus.). pap. 0.14 (*0-7589-0126-7*); 1988. (POL., Illus.). pap. 0.14 (*0-7589-0131-3*); 1988. (CHI., Illus.). pap. 0.14 (*0-7589-0232-8*); 1985. (CZE., Illus.). pap. 0.14 (*0-7589-0257-3*); 1977. (ITA., Illus.). pap. 0.14 (*0-7589-0242-5*); 1973. (ZUL., Illus.). pap. 0.14 (*0-7589-0239-5*); 1973. (CHI., Illus.). pap. 0.14 (*0-7589-0106-2*); 1972. pap. 0.14 (*0-7589-0000-7*); 1972. (GRE., Illus.). pap. 0.14 (*0-7589-0243-3*); 1972. (AFR., Illus.). pap. 0.14 (*0-7589-0258-1*); 1971. (FRE., Illus.). pap. 0.14 (*0-7589-0241-7*); 1971. (GER., Illus.). pap. 0.14 (*0-7589-0112-7*) Chick Pubns., Inc.

Clagon, Angelena E., as told by. Mother's Dreams, 200, 200. 2002. (Illus.). 54p. 19.95 (*0-9724301-0-5*) Clagon, Angelena E.

Coble, Colleen. Without a Trace. 2003. pap. 12.99 (*0-8499-4429-5*) W Publishing Group.

Doherty, Catherine. Not Without Parables: Stories of Yesterday, Today & Eternity. 2nd alt. ed. 1989. (Illus.). 187p. pap. (*0-921440-16-2*) Madonna Hse. Pubns.

Doherty, Catherine D. Not Without Parables: Stories of Yesterday, Today & Eternity. 1977. (Illus.). 192p. pap. 3.50 o.p. (*0-87793-127-5*) Ave Maria Pr.

Dooly, Paige Winship, et al. Church in the Wildwood: A Missouri Church Stands As a Landmark of Love for Four Generations. 2003. (Historical Collections). 352p. pap. 6.97 (*1-58660-966-1*) Barbour Publishing, Inc.

Draper, Jessica & Draper, Richard D. Seventh Seal: A Novel of the Last Days: A Novel. 2003. 499p. 16.95 (*1-59156-190-6*) Covenant Communications.

Dunn, Philip. The Promise of Dawn. 2003. 180p. 22.95 (*0-8245-2122-6*, Crossroad Carlisle) Crossroad Publishing Co.

Ellis, Jamellah. That Faith, That Trust, That Love: A Novel. 2003. (Strivers Row Ser.). 352p. pap. 12.95 (*0-8129-6656-2*, Villard Bks.) Random House Adult Trade Publishing Group.

Emerald House Group Inc., Staff. Pilgrim's Progress. deluxe ed. 1999. (Illus.). 440p. 29.99 (*1-889893-41-2*) Emerald Hse. Group, Inc.

Feehan, Christine. Untitled Christmas Novella. 2004. mass mkt. 6.99 (*0-7434-8296-4*, Pocket) Simon & Schuster.

Final Exam: Christian Novel of Heaven & Hell Battle for the Soul of Earth. 2001. 38.00 (*1-883707-76-5*) Protea Publishing Co.

Gates, Jay. The League: Reunion. 2003. 119p. pap. 16.95 (*1-59286-100-8*) PublishAmerica, Inc.

George, Margaret. Mary Called Magdalene: A Novel. 2003. 656p. pap. 16.00 (*0-14-200279-8*); 2002. 528p. 27.95 o.s.i (*0-670-03096-1*, Viking) Viking Penguin.

Grossman, Jeni. Beneath the Surface. 2001. (Illus.). 271p. 14.95 (*1-57734-828-1*) Covenant Communications.

Gulley, Philip. Home to Harmony. 240p. 2004. pap. 12.95 (*0-06-072766-7*); 2002. (Illus.). 17.95 (*0-06-000629-3*) HarperSanFrancisco.

—Home to Harmony. 2000. (Harmony Ser.). (Illus.). 219p. 14.99 o.p. (*1-57673-613-X*) Multnomah Pubs., Inc.

—Home to Harmony. l.t. ed. 2002. 28.95 (*0-7862-4517-4*) Thorndike Pr.

—Just Shy of Harmony. 256p. 2004. pap. 12.95 (*0-06-072708-X*); 2002. (Illus.). 17.95 (*0-06-000632-3*) HarperSanFrancisco.

—Just Shy of Harmony. 2001. (Harmony Ser.: Vol. 2). 200p. 12.99 (*1-57673-790-X*); audio 19.99 (*1-57673-789-6*) Multnomah Pubs., Inc.

—Just Shy of Harmony. 2002. (Americana Ser.). 28.95 (*0-7862-4514-X*) Thorndike Pr.

Guymon, Shannon. Never Letting Go of Hope. 2001. vi, 170p. pap. (*1-55517-534-1*, Bonneville Bks.) Cedar Fort, Inc./CFI Distribution.

Hamlin, Rick. Hidden Gifts. 2001. 320p. pap. 11.99 (*0-7642-2327-5*) Bethany Hse. Pubs.

Hansen, Jennie L. Beyond Summer Dreams. 2001. 282p. 14.95 (*1-57734-889-3*) Covenant Communications.

Hartley, Allan. Crossfire. 1975. (Illus.). pap. 0.49 o.p. (*0-8007-8525-8*) Revell, Fleming H. Co.

—In His Steps. 1977. pap. 0.79 o.p. (*0-8007-8530-4*) Revell, Fleming H. Co.

Hasta lo Ultimo de la Tierra. 2004. 15.99 (*0-8297-3826-6*) Zondervan.

Hatcher, Robin Lee. Dear Lady. 1997. 368p. mass mkt. 5.99 o.p. (*0-06-108687-8*) HarperCollins Pubs.

—Dear Lady. 2000. (Coming to America Bk.: No. 1). 304p. pap. 10.99 (*0-310-23083-7*) Zondervan.

—Patterns of Love. l.t. ed. 1998. 320p. 25.95 (*1-57490-143-5*, Beeler Large Print Bks.) Beeler, Thomas T. Publisher.

—Patterns of Love. 1998. 416p. mass mkt. 6.50 o.s.i (*0-06-108688-6*) HarperCollins Pubs.

—Patterns of Love. 2001. 320p. pap. 10.99 (*0-310-23105-1*) Zondervan.

—Ribbon of Years: A Novel. 2001. 312p. 12.99 (*0-8423-4009-2*) Tyndale Hse. Pubs.

Hawkins, Don. Flambeau 2.0. 2002. 144p. pap. 8.99 (*0-8254-2874-2*) Kregel Pubns.

Higgs, Liz Curtis, et al. Three Weddings & a Giggle. 2003. (Illus.). 416p. pap. 11.99 (*1-57673-656-3*) Multnomah Pubs., Inc.

Hijuelos, Oscar. Mr. Ives' Christmas. 1995. 272p. 19.00 o.p. (*0-06-017131-6*) HarperCollins Pubs.

—Mr. Ives' Christmas. 1996. 256p. pap. 13.95 (*0-06-092754-2*, Perennial) HarperTrade.

Hill, Morgan. Lost Patrol. 2003. (Lost Patrol Ser.). 272p. pap. 5.99 (*1-59052-050-5*) Multnomah Pubs., Inc.

Hollingsworth, Mary. Fireside Stories of Heaven, Hope & Hilarity. 2001. 200p. pap. 12.99 (*0-8499-4265-9*) W Publishing Group.

Hourihan, Paul. The Death of Thomas Merton, a Novel: A Confessional Portayal of the Last Day in the Life of the Famous Catholic Monk & Writer. 2003. 168p. per. 13.95 (*1-931816-01-8*) Vedantic Shores Pr.

Hutchens, Paul. Colorado Kidnapping. (Sugar Creek Gang Ser.: No. 27). (J). (gr. 3-7). mass mkt. 3.99 o.p. (*0-8024-4827-5*, 627) Moody Pr.

Johnson, Matthew. Rock of Ages. 2003. 87p. pap. 14.95 (*1-59286-105-9*) PublishAmerica, Inc.

King, Beverly. Unlikely Match: A Novel. 2003. 279p. 14.95 (*1-59156-193-0*) Covenant Communications.

Kingsbury, Karen & Smalley, Gary. Redemption Series POS kit. 2003. (*0-8423-8021-3*) Tyndale Hse. Pubs.

Kraus, Jim & Kraus, Terri. The Unfolding: God's Amazing Grace Unfolds in Story. 2003. (Stories from MacKenzie Street Ser.). 304p. pap. 11.99 (*1-58660-859-2*) Barbour Publishing, Inc.

Lacy, Al & Lacy, JoAnna. Let There Be Light. 2003. (Mail Order Bride Ser.). 320p. pap. 10.99 (*1-59052-042-4*) Multnomah Pubs., Inc.

LaHaye, Beverly & Blackstock, Terri. Times & Seasons. 2001. 371p. 16.99 (*0-310-23319-4*) Zondervan.

Langille, J. H. Snail-Shell Harbor. 2001. (Bigwater Classics Ser.: Vol. 3). (Illus.). 288p. reprint ed. pap. 14.95 (*0-923048-52-9*) Bigwater Publishing.

Larson, Elyse. The Hope Before Us. 2002. (Women of Valor Ser.: Vol. 3). 352p. pap. 12.99 (*0-7642-2376-3*) Bethany Hse. Pubs.

Lewis, Beverly. The Betrayal. 2003. (Abram's Daughters Ser.). 320p. 17.99 (*0-7642-2807-2*); 320p. pap. 12.99 (*0-7642-2331-3*); 432p. pap. 16.99 (*0-7642-2806-4*); audio 16.99 (*0-7642-2808-0*) Bethany Hse. Pubs.

Mandino, Og. The Christ Commission. 1983. 272p. mass mkt. 3.50 o.s.i (*0-553-24139-7*) Bantam Bks.

Martin, Charles. The Dead Don't Dance: A Novel. 2004. 320p. pap. 13.99 (*0-7852-6181-8*) Nelson, Thomas Pubs.

McBride, Gordon. Flying to Tombstone. 2003. 313p. pap. 24.95 (*1-59129-743-5*) PublishAmerica, Inc.

McGrath, Alister E. Knowing Christ. 2001. 17.95 (*0-340-75679-9*) Hodder & Stoughton, Ltd. GBR. *Dist:* Trafalgar Square.

Mings, Lonnie C. The Pure Land. 1979. pap. 4.95 o.p. (*0-8024-5989-7*) Moody Pr.

Moore, Stephanie Perry. Absolutely Worthy. 2003. (Laurel Shadrach Ser.: Vol. 4). 191p. (YA). pap. 6.99 (*0-8024-4038-X*) Moody Pr.

Nichols, Linda. If I Gained the World. 2003. 384p. 17.99 (*0-7642-2802-1*); 384p. pap. 12.99 (*0-7642-2728-9*); 464p. pap. 17.99 (*0-7642-2801-3*) Bethany Hse. Pubs.

Nunes, Rachel Ann. This Very Moment. 2001. 185p. 14.95 (*1-57734-934-2*) Covenant Communications.

Olson, John B. Adrenaline: Desperation Threatens to Carry Him Beyond the Limits of Medical Ethics. 2003. 304p. pap. 12.99 (*0-7642-2819-6*) Bethany Hse. Pubs.

Oulton, Carolyn. Literature & Religion in Mid-Victorian England: From Dickens to Eliot. 2003. 256p. 62.00 (*0-333-99337-3*) Palgrave Macmillan.

Peretti, Frank E. Peretti Three-pack. 2003. 500p. pap. 18.97 (*0-8423-8656-4*) Tyndale Hse. Pubs.

Peters, Dory J. Winds of Change: A Navajo Falls in Love with a White Woman. . . in His Struggle to Blend Cultures He Leans on His Grandfather's Wisdom. . . 2000. 143p. pap. 11.95 (*1-55517-523-6*) Cedar Fort, Inc./CFI Distribution.

Peterson, Eugene H. & Griffin, Emilie. Epiphanies: Stories for the Christian Year. 2nd ed. 2003. 208p. pap. 15.99 (*0-8010-6446-5*) Baker Bks.

Peterson, Tracie & Miller, Judith. These Tangled Threads. 2003. (Bells of Lowell Ser.). 384p. pap. 12.99 (*0-7642-2690-8*) Bethany Hse. Pubs.

Randalls, Vickie Mason. Red Moon Rising. 2001. 202p. pap. 12.95 (*1-55517-528-7*, Bonneville Bks.) Cedar Fort, Inc./CFI Distribution.

Reece, Colleen L. & Reece-DeMarco, Julie. The Heirloom: One Family's Courageous Sacrifice Sparks Hope in the Midst of Despair. 2002. (Illus.). 66p. 14.99 (*0-8254-3606-0*) Kregel Pubns.

Reid, Carol A. I Choose to Believe. Adams, Philip, ed. 2002. 297p. pap. 12.99 (*0-9718023-0-0*) Believer's Ink.

Roberts, Sally-Ann. Angelvision. 2002. 192p. 22.00 (*1-56554-907-4*) Pelican Publishing Co., Inc.

Rosas, Roberto. The Temptation of the Miracle Weaver. 2003. 284p. pap. 24.95 (*1-59129-598-X*) PublishAmerica, Inc.

Runk, Wesley T. Who Needs a Bigger Barn? 1977. pap. 2.95 o.p. (*0-89536-267-8*, 2328) CSS Publishing Co.

Sloan, David. The Heaven Factor. 2003. 245p. pap. 19.95 (*1-59286-116-4*) PublishAmerica, Inc.

Smith, Edward H. Knights in Athens: A Story of Conspiracy & Victory. 2002. 190p. pap. 13.95 (*0-615-11995-6*) Dime Pubs.

Smurthwaite, Donald S. A Wise, Blue Autumn: A Novel about Fathers, Daughters & Remembering. 2001. 151p. pap. 12.95 (*1-57345-922-4*, SKU 4132192, Bookcraft, Inc.) Deseret Bk. Co.

Snelling, Lauraine. A Dream to Follow: Return to Red River. 2001. (*0-7642-8856-3*); 416p. pap. 16.99 (*0-7642-2611-8*) Bethany Hse. Pubs.

—A Dream to Follow Bk #1. 2001. (Red River of the North Ser.). 320p. pap. 12.99 (*0-7642-2317-8*) Bethany Hse. Pubs.

—A Dream to Follow Bk. 1: Return to Red River. 2002. (Five Star Christian Fiction Ser.). 319p. 24.95 (*0-7862-4441-0*, Five Star) Gale Group.

Stoops, Alexander. The Good Reverend. 2003. 151p. pap. 19.95 (*1-59286-133-4*) PublishAmerica, Inc.

Strong, Joyce. A Dragon, a Dreamer & the Promise Giver. 2003. 208p. pap. 12.99 (*0-7684-2182-9*) Destiny Image Pubs.

Thoene, Bodie & Thoene, Brock. First Light Endcap Kit. 2003. (*0-8423-8520-7*) Tyndale Hse. Pubs.

Thomas, Mack. The Pilgrim's Progress. 1996. 64p. 14.99 o.p. (*0-88070-917-0*) Zonderkidz.

Thompson, Joel. Critter Sitters: And Other Stories That Teach Christian Values. 2002. (ClubZone Kids Ser.). (Illus.). 80p. (J). pap. 5.99 (*0-8010-4511-8*) Baker Bks.

—Shortcuts: And Other Stories That Teach Christian Values. 2002. (Clubzone Kids Ser.). (Illus.). 80p. (J). pap. 5.99 (*0-8010-4510-X*) Baker Bks.

—Tennis Shoes in a Tree: And Other Stories That Teach Christian Values. 2002. (ClubZone Kids Ser.). (Illus.). 80p. (J). pap. 5.99 (*0-8010-4509-6*) Baker Bks.

Tobin, Greg. The Council. 2002. 432p. 25.95 (*0-312-87353-0*, Forge Bks.) Doherty, Tom Assocs., LLC.

Vreeland, L. There's a Goat on My Roof. 2003. 134p. pap. 19.95 (*1-59286-179-2*) PublishAmerica, Inc.

Walker, Celeste Perrino. Prayer Warriors, the Final Chapter: A Story of Prevailing Prayer by the Author of Prayer Warriors & Guardians. 2004. pap. (*0-8163-2001-2*) Pacific Pr. Publishing Assn.

Wheeler, Joe L. Christmas in My Soul. 2000. (Illus.). 128p. 15.95 o.s.i (*0-385-49859-4*) Doubleday Publishing.

—Christmas in My Soul: A Second Collection. 2001. E-Book 13.50 (*1-59061-591-3*) Adobe Systems, Inc.

Wheeler, Joe L., ed. Christmas in My Soul: A Second Collection. 2001. 128p. 14.95 (*0-385-49860-8*, Currency) Doubleday Publishing.

Whitson, Stephanie Grace. Secrets on the Wind. 2003. (Pine Ridge Portraits Ser.). (Illus.). 320p. pap. 12.99 (*0-7642-2785-8*) Bethany Hse. Pubs.

Whittington, Brad. Welcome to Fred: A Novel. 2003. 256p. pap. 12.99 (*0-8054-2555-1*) Broadman & Holman Pubs.

Wick, Lori. Beyond the Picket Fence. 1998. 256p. pap. 10.99 (*0-7369-0055-1*) Harvest Hse. Pubs.

—Beyond the Picket Fence & Other Short Stories. l.t. ed. 2000. (Christian Fiction Ser.). 331p. 26.95 (*0-7862-2311-1*) Thorndike Pr.

# D

## DOG OWNERS—FICTION

Ackerley, Joe R. We Think the World of You. 1981. 190p. pap. 5.95 o.p. (*0-916870-36-7*) Creative Arts Bk. Co.

—We Think the World of You. 2000. (New York Review Books Classics Ser.). 211p. pap. 12.95 (*0-940322-26-9*) New York Review of Bks., Inc., The.

—We Think the World of You. 1988. pap. 12.95 o.p. (*0-14-011554-4*) Penguin Group (USA) Inc.

—We Think the World of You. 1989. pap. 7.95 o.s.i (*0-671-67811-6*, Simon & Schuster) Simon & Schuster.

Alwyn, Cynthia G. Scent of Murder. 2001. E-Book 23.95 (*1-59061-037-7*) Adobe Systems, Inc.

—Scent of Murder. 2001. 294p. 23.95 (*0-312-26559-X*, Saint Martin's Minotaur) St. Martin's Pr.

Auster, Paul. Timbuktu. 1999. 192p. 22.00 o.s.i (*0-8050-5407-3*) Holt, Henry & Co.

—Timbuktu. 2000. 192p. pap. 11.00 (*0-312-26399-6*); mass mkt. 7.99 o.s.i (*0-312-97528-7*) Picador.

Benjamin, Carol Lea. The Dog Who Knew Too Much: A Rachel Alexander & Dash Mystery. 1998. (Rachel Alexander & Dash Mystery Ser.: Vol. 2). 272p. reprint ed. mass mkt. 5.99 o.s.i (*0-440-22637-6*) Dell Publishing.

—The Dog Who Knew Too Much: A Rachel Alexander & Dash Mystery. 1997. (Rachel Alexander & Dash Mystery Ser.). 256p. 21.95 (*0-8027-3312-3*) Walker & Co.

—A Hell of a Dog. 1998. (Rachel Alexander & Dash Mystery Ser.). (Illus.). 276p. 22.95 (*0-8027-3325-5*) Walker & Co.

—A Hell of a Dog: A Rachel Alexander & Dash Mystery. 1999. (Rachel Alexander & Dash Mystery Ser.). 320p. mass mkt. 5.99 (*0-440-22548-5*) Dell Publishing.

—Lady Vanishes. 1999. (Rachel Alexander & Dash Mystery Ser.). 264p. 23.95 (*0-8027-3335-2*) Walker & Co.

—The Long Good Boy: A Rachel Alexander & Dash Mystery. 2001. 240p. 23.95 (*0-8027-3364-6*) Walker & Co.

—This Dog for Hire: A Rachel Alexander & Dash Mystery. 1997. (Rachel Alexander & Dash Mystery Ser.: Vol. 1). 304p. mass mkt. 6.50 (*0-440-22520-5*) Dell Publishing.

—This Dog for Hire: A Rachel Alexander & Dash Mystery. l.t. ed. 2002. 346p. 28.95 o.p. (*0-7862-4191-8*) Thorndike Pr.

—This Dog for Hire: A Rachel Alexander & Dash Mystery. 1996. (Rachel Alexander & Dash Mystery Ser.). 224p. 20.95 (*0-8027-3292-5*) Walker & Co.

Berenson, Laurien. Dog Eat Dog: A Melanie Travis Mystery. (Melanie Travis Mystery Ser.). 1997. 336p. mass mkt. 5.99 (*1-57566-227-2*); 1996. 352p. 18.95 o.s.i (*1-57566-103-9*) Kensington Publishing Corp.
—Hair of the Dog: A Melanie Travis Mystery. (Melanie Travis Mystery Ser.). 1998. 336p. mass mkt. 5.99 (*1-57566-356-2*); 1997. 320p. 18.95 o.s.i (*1-57566-222-1*) Kensington Publishing Corp.
—Hush Puppy. (Melanie Travis Mystery Ser.). 2000. 32p. mass mkt. 5.99 (*1-57566-600-6*); 1999. 304p. 20.00 o.s.i (*1-57566-469-0*, Kensington Bks.) Kensington Publishing Corp.
—A Pedigree to Die For: A Melanie Travis Mystery. l.t. ed. 1995. 347p. pap. 20.95 o.p. (*0-7838-1446-1*, Macmillan Reference USA) Gale Group.
—A Pedigree to Die For: A Melanie Travis Mystery, 1. 1998. mass mkt. 5.99 (*1-57566-374-0*); 1997. 288p. pap. 9.95 o.s.i (*1-57566-125-X*); 1996. 288p. mass mkt. 4.99 o.s.i (*1-57566-003-2*); 1996. mass mkt. 4.99 o.p. (*0-8217-5227-8*); 1995. 304p. mass mkt. 16.95 o.p. (*0-8217-4827-0*, Zebra Bks.) Kensington Publishing Corp.
—Underdog: A Melanie Travis Mystery. 1996. 336p. mass mkt. 4.99 o.s.i (*1-57566-108-X*); 320p. 18.95 o.s.i (*1-57566-011-3*); mass mkt. 16.95 o.s.i (*0-8217-5224-3*) Kensington Publishing Corp.
—Watchdog. (Melanie Travis Mystery Ser.). 1999. 320p. mass mkt. 5.99 (*1-57566-472-0*, Kensington Bks.); 1998. 314p. (J). (gr. 10 up). 20.00 o.s.i (*1-57566-350-3*) Kensington Publishing Corp.
Cassara, Ernest. Murder on Beacon Hill. 1995. 201p. (Orig.). pap. 10.00 (*0-9625794-6-7*) Miniver, Anne Pr.
—Murder on Boston Common: A Father Ballou & His Dog Spot Mystery. 1998. 174p. pap. 9.95 (*0-9662870-0-2*) Cambridge Cornerstone Pr.
Cleary, Melissa. And Your Little Dog, Too. 1998. (Dog Lover's Mysteries Ser.). 208p. mass mkt. 5.99 o.s.i (*0-425-16242-7*, Prime Crime) Berkley Publishing Group.
—Dead & Buried. 1994. 208p. (Orig.). mass mkt. 4.99 o.s.i (*0-425-14547-6*, Prime Crime) Berkley Publishing Group.
—Dog Collar Crime. 1993. 192p. (Orig.). 3.99 o.s.i (*1-55773-896-3*, Diamond Bks.) Ace Bks.
—A Dog Collar Crime. 1994. (Orig.). mass mkt. 4.99 o.s.i (*0-425-14857-2*, Prime Crime) Berkley Publishing Group.
—First Pedigree Murder: A Dog Lover's Mystery. 1994. 208p. (Orig.). mass mkt. 4.99 o.s.i (*0-425-14299-X*, Prime Crime) Berkley Publishing Group.
—Hounded to Death. 1993. 192p. mass mkt. 4.99 o.s.i (*0-425-14324-4*) Berkley Publishing Group.
—The Maltese Puppy. 1995. 256p. (Orig.). mass mkt. 4.99 o.s.i (*0-425-14721-5*, Prime Crime) Berkley Publishing Group.
—A Murder Most Beastly. 1996. 208p. (Orig.). mass mkt. 4.99 o.s.i (*0-425-15139-5*) Berkley Publishing Group.
—Old Dogs. 1997. (Dog Lover's Mysteries Ser.). 224p. mass mkt. 5.99 o.s.i (*0-425-15858-6*, Prime Crime) Berkley Publishing Group.
—Skull & Dog Bones. 1994. (Orig.). mass mkt. 4.99 o.s.i (*0-425-14541-7*); 208p. mass mkt. 4.50 o.s.i (*0-515-11279-8*, Jove) Berkley Publishing Group.
—Tail of Two Murders. 1993. 192p. (Orig.). mass mkt. 4.99 o.s.i (*0-425-15809-8*, Prime Crime) Berkley Publishing Group.
Cleary, Melissa & Jove Publications Staff. Hounded to Death. 1993. (Dog Lover's Mysteries Ser.). 184p. mass mkt. 3.99 o.s.i (*0-515-11190-2*, Jove) Berkley Publishing Group.
Conant, Susan. Animal Appetite: A Dog Lover's Mystery. 1998. (Dog Lover's Mysteries Ser.). 304p. reprint ed. mass mkt. 5.99 o.s.i (*0-553-57186-9*, Crimeline) Bantam Bks.
—The Barker Street Regulars: A Dog Lover's Mystery. 1999. (Dog Lover's Mysteries Ser.). 288p. mass mkt. 6.99 (*0-553-57655-0*) Bantam Bks.
—The Barker Street Regulars: A Dog Lover's Mystery. l.t. ed. 1998. (Large Print Book Ser.). pap. 23.95 (*1-56895-609-6*, Wheeler Publishing, Inc.) Gale Group.
—Bite of Death. 1991. 4.50 (*1-55773-490-9*) Ace Bks.
—Bite of Death. 1994. mass mkt. 5.99 o.s.i (*0-425-14542-5*) Berkley Publishing Group.
—Black Ribbon: A Dog Lover's Mystery. 1995. (Dog Lover's Mysteries Ser.). 288p. reprint ed. mass mkt. 5.99 o.s.i (*0-553-29875-5*, Crimeline) Bantam Bks.
—Bloodlines. 1993. (Dog Lover's Mysteries Ser.). 272p. mass mkt. 5.99 (*0-553-29886-0*) Bantam Bks.
—Bride & Groom. 2004. 272p. 22.95 (*0-425-19412-4*) Berkley Publishing Group.
—Creature Discomforts. 2001. (Dog Lover's Mysteries Ser.). 224p. mass mkt. 6.99 (*0-553-58059-0*, Spectra) Bantam Bks.
—Creature Discomforts: A Dog Lover's Mystery. l.t. ed. 2001. (Beeler Large Print Mystery Ser.). 228p. 25.95 (*1-57490-360-8*, Beeler Large Print Bks.) Beeler, Thomas T. Publisher.
—Creature Discomforts: A Dog Lover's Mystery. 2000. 256p. 22.95 o.s.i (*0-385-49446-7*) Doubleday Publishing.
—Dead & Doggone. 2003. (Mystery Ser.). 27.95 (*1-57490-466-3*) Beeler, Thomas T. Publisher.
—Dead & Doggone. 1990. mass mkt. 5.99 o.s.i (*0-425-14429-1*, Prime Crime) Berkley Publishing Group.
—Evil Breeding. 2000. (Dog Lover's Mysteries Ser.). 224p. reprint ed. mass mkt. 6.99 (*0-553-58052-3*) Bantam Bks.
—Gone to the Dogs: A Dog Lover's Mystery. 1992. (Dog Lover's Mysteries Ser.). 272p. mass mkt. 5.99 (*0-553-29734-1*) Bantam Bks.
—Gone to the Dogs: A Dog Lover's Mystery. l.t. ed. 2003. (Mystery Ser.). 27.95 (*1-57490-488-4*, Beeler Large Print Bks.) Beeler, Thomas T. Publisher.
—Gone to the Dogs: A Dog Lover's Mystery. 1992. 224p. 16.50 o.s.i (*0-385-42378-0*) Doubleday Publishing.
—New Leash on Death. 1990. 4.50 (*1-55773-385-6*) Berkley Publishing Group.
—A New Leash on Death. 1994. 192p. mass mkt. 5.99 (*0-425-14622-7*) Berkley Publishing Group.
—Paws Before Dying. 1991. 4.50 (*1-55773-550-6*) Ace Bks.
—Paws Before Dying. 1991. mass mkt. 5.99 o.s.i (*0-425-14430-5*) Berkley Publishing Group.
—Ruffly Speaking: A Dog Lover's Mystery. 1994. (Dog Lover's Mysteries Ser.). 304p. mass mkt. 6.99 (*0-553-29484-9*) Bantam Bks.
—Stud Rites: A Dog Lover's Mystery. 1997. (Dog Lover's Mysteries Ser.). 272p. mass mkt. 5.99 o.s.i (*0-553-57300-4*, Crimeline) Bantam Bks.
Constable, George. Where You Are. 1996. 336p. 21.95 o.s.i (*0-385-48438-0*) Doubleday Publishing.
Dianne, Jessup. The Dog Who Spoke to God. 2001. 400p. 23.95 (*0-312-26662-6*) St. Martin's Pr.
Fischer, Renaldo & St. George, Michele. The Shaman Bulldog: A Love Story. 1996. 104p. 11.50 o.p. (*0-446-52029-2*) Warner Bks., Inc.
Gaddis, Mike. Jenny Willow: A Novel. 288p. 2004. pap. 14.95 (*1-59228-492-2*, Lyons Pr.); 2002. 24.95 (*1-58574-451-4*) Globe Pequot Pr., The.
Gaskell, Whitney. Pushing 30. 2003. 352p. pap. 11.95 (*0-553-38224-1*); E-Book (*0-553-89805-1*) Bantam Bks.
Henry, Sue. Cold Company. l.t. ed. 2002. (Large Print Ser.). 27.95 (*1-57490-457-4*) Beeler, Thomas T. Publisher.
—Cold Company. 2002. (Alaska Mystery Ser.). (Illus.). 304p. 23.95 (*0-380-97882-2*, Morrow, William & Co.) Morrow/Avon.
Highsmith, Patricia. A Dog's Ransom. 2002. 271p. pap. 12.95 (*0-393-32336-6*) Norton, W. W. & Co., Inc.
—A Dog's Ransom. 1981. 256p. pap. 3.95 o.p. (*0-14-003944-9*, Penguin Bks.) Viking Penguin.
Lanier, Virginia. Blind Bloodhound Justice: A Jo Beth Sidden Mystery. unabr. ed. 2000. (Bloodhound Ser.). audio 59.95 (*0-7927-2261-2*, CSL 150) Chivers Audio Bks. GBR. *Dist:* BBC Audiobooks America.
—Blind Bloodhound Justice: A Jo Beth Sidden Mystery. 1998. 288p. 24.00 o.s.i (*0-06-017547-8*) HarperCollins Pubs.
—Blind Bloodhound Justice: A Jo Beth Sidden Mystery. 1999. (Bloodhound Ser.). 352p. mass mkt. 6.99 (*0-06-109971-6*, HarperTorch) Morrow/Avon.
—A Bloodhound to Die For. 2003. 240p. 23.95 (*0-06-019388-3*) HarperCollins Pubs.
—A Bloodhound to Die For. 2004. 320p. mass mkt. 6.99 (*0-06-109840-X*, Avon Bks.) Morrow/Avon.
—A Brace of Bloodhounds. (Bloodhound Ser.). 1998. 448p. mass mkt. 6.50 (*0-06-101087-1*); 1997. 336p. 23.00 o.p. (*0-06-101089-8*) HarperCollins Pubs.
—Death in Bloodhound Red. 1996. (Bloodhound Ser.). 544p. mass mkt. 6.50 (*0-06-101025-1*, HarperTorch) Morrow/Avon.
—Death in Bloodhound Red. 1995. (Bloodhound Ser.). 462p. 19.95 (*1-56164-076-X*) Pineapple Pr., Inc.
—House on Bloodhound Lane. 1996. 352p. mass mkt. 20.00 o.p. (*0-06-101088-X*, HarperTorch) Morrow/Avon.
—The House on Bloodhound Lane. 1997. (Bloodhound Ser.). 384p. mass mkt. 5.99 (*0-06-101086-3*, HarperTorch) Morrow/Avon.
—Ten Little Bloodhounds: A Jo Beth Sidden Mystery, Set. unabr. ed. 1999. audio 69.95 (*0-7927-2335-X*, CSL 224, Chivers Sound Library) BBC Audiobooks America.
—Ten Little Bloodhounds: A Jo Beth Sidden Mystery. 1999. (Bloodhound Ser.). 288p. 24.00 (*0-06-017548-6*) HarperCollins Pubs.
—Ten Little Bloodhounds: A Jo Beth Sidden Mystery. 2000. (Bloodhound Ser.). 352p. mass mkt. 6.50 (*0-06-109066-2*, Avon Bks.) Morrow/Avon.
Mayle, Peter. A Dog's Life. unabr. collector's ed. 1997. audio 24.00 (*0-913369-75-6*, 4330) Books on Tape, Inc.
—A Dog's Life. 1996. (Illus.). 208p. pap. 12.00 (*0-679-76267-1*, Vintage) Knopf Publishing Group.
—A Dog's Life. 1995. 192p. 20.00 o.s.i (*0-679-44122-0*) Knopf, Alfred A. Inc.
—A Dog's Life, Set. abr. ed. 1995. audio 16.00 o.s.i (*0-679-44328-2*, RH Audio) Random Hse. Audio Publishing Group.
Michaels, Fern. What You Wish For. l.t. ed. 2000. (Romance Ser.). 431p. 27.95 o.p. (*1-56895-998-2*, Wheeler Publishing, Inc.) Gale Group.
—What You Wish For. 2000. 32p. 24.00 o.s.i (*1-57566-573-5*); 2001. 352p. reprint ed. mass mkt. 7.99 (*0-8217-6828-X*) Kensington Publishing Corp.
Minear, Lola F. In the Dog House: A Collection of Short Stories. 1981. 47p. 6.95 o.p. (*0-533-04878-8*) Vantage Pr., Inc.
Murphy, Dallas. Don't Explain. 1997. 288p. mass mkt. 5.99 (*0-671-86688-5*, Pocket) Simon & Schuster.
—Don't Explain. Grose, Bill, ed. 1996. 304p. 22.00 o.p. (*0-671-86687-7*, Atria) Simon & Schuster.
—Lover Man. 1988. mass mkt. 5.50 (*0-671-66188-4*, Pocket) Simon & Schuster.
—Lover Man: A Mystery Introducing Artie Deemer. 1987. 14.95 o.p. (*0-684-18757-4*, Macmillan Reference USA) Gale Group.
—Lush Life. 1993. 288p. (Orig.). mass mkt. 4.99 (*0-671-68556-2*, Pocket) Simon & Schuster.
—Lush Life. Chelius, Jane, ed. 1992. 288p. (Orig.). pap. 20.00 (*0-671-68555-4*, Atria) Simon & Schuster.
North, Hailey. Tangled up in Love. 2002. 384p. mass mkt. 5.99 (*0-380-82069-2*) HarperCollins Pubs.
Shelton, Connie. Reunions Can Be Murder: The Seventh Charlie Parker Mystery. 2002. (The Charlie Parker Mystery Ser.: No. 7). 255p. 23.95 (*1-890768-46-4*, Intrigue Pr.) Corvus Publishing.
Van Meter, Homer. Day of the Little Guy. 1996. 196p. 18.50 (*1-880664-16-X*) E. M. Productions.
Watson, Brad. Last Days of the Dog-Men: Stories. 1997. 144p. pap. 9.95 o.s.i (*0-385-31827-8*) Doubleday Publishing.
—Last Days of the Dog-Men: Stories. 1996. 146p. 19.00 o.p. (*0-393-03926-9*) Norton, W. W. & Co., Inc.
Wood, Ted. Corkscrew. 1987. (Reid Bennett Mystery Ser.). 240p. 14.95 o.p. (*0-684-18853-8*, Macmillan Reference USA) Gale Group.
—Corkscrew. 1989. 224p. reprint ed. mass mkt. (*0-373-26024-5*, Harlequin Bks.) Harlequin Enterprises, Ltd.
—Corkscrew. 2001. E-Book 6.99 (*0-7592-1043-8*); 1999. 188p. per. 19.95 (*1-58586-863-9*) ereads.com.
—Dead in the Water. 1984. 160p. mass mkt. 2.95 o.s.i (*0-7704-2006-0*) Bantam Bks.
—Flashback. l.t. ed. 1994. 21.95 o.p. (*0-7927-1819-4*); pap. 19.95 o.p. (*0-7927-1818-6*) BBC Audiobooks America.
—Flashback. 1992. 256p. text 20.00 (*0-684-19414-7*, Macmillan Reference USA) Gale Group.
—Flashback. 1994. (WWL Mystery Ser.). per. (*0-373-26137-3*, 1-26137-9, Harlequin Bks.) Harlequin Enterprises, Ltd.
—Fool's Gold. 1986. 192p. 13.95 o.s.i (*0-684-18568-7*, Macmillan Reference USA) Gale Group.
—Fool's Gold. 1988. 224p. reprint ed. mass mkt. (*0-373-26019-9*, Harlequin Bks.) Harlequin Enterprises, Ltd.
—Live Bait. 1986. (Mystery Ser.). 208p. mass mkt. 2.95 o.s.i (*0-553-25558-4*) Bantam Bks.
—Live Bait. 1985. 192p. 12.95 o.s.i (*0-684-18330-7*, Macmillan Reference USA) Gale Group.
—Live Bait. 2002. 174p. pap. 6.99 (*1-58586-855-8*); E-Book 6.99 (*0-7592-0395-4*); E-Book 6.99 (*0-7592-1039-X*); E-Book 6.99 (*1-58586-852-3*) ereads.com.
—Murder on Ice. 1985. 176p. mass mkt. 2.95 o.s.i (*0-7704-2049-4*) Bantam Bks.
—Murder on Ice. 1984. 160p. 12.95 o.s.i (*0-684-18134-7*, Macmillan Reference USA) Gale Group.
—On the Inside: A Reid Bennett Mystery. 1990. 256p. 18.95 o.s.i (*0-684-19090-7*, Macmillan Reference USA) Gale Group.
—On the Inside: A Reid Bennett Mystery. 1991. 224p. reprint ed. pap. (*0-373-26076-8*, Harlequin Bks.) Harlequin Enterprises, Ltd.
—Snowjob. 1995. (Mystery Ser.). 251p. per. (*0-373-26182-9*, 1-26182-5, Worldwide Library) Harlequin Enterprises, Ltd.
—Snowjob. 1993. 256p. 20.00 o.p. (*0-684-19563-1*, Scribner) Simon & Schuster.
—When the Killing Starts. 1990. mass mkt. (*0-373-26043-1*, Harlequin Bks.) Harlequin Enterprises, Ltd.
—When the Killing Starts. 1989. 224p. 16.95 o.s.i (*0-684-18331-5*, Scribner) Simon & Schuster.
Woods, Stuart. Orchid Blues. 2002. 400p. reprint ed. mass mkt. 7.99 (*0-451-20671-1*, Signet Bks.) NAL.
—Orchid Blues. 2001. 350p. 24.95 o.s.i (*0-399-14777-2*) Penguin Group (USA) Inc.
—Orchid Blues. abr. ed. 2001. 4p. audio 24.95 o.s.i (*0-399-14820-5*, Putnam Berkley Audio) Putnam Publishing Group, The.
—Orchid Blues. l.t. ed. 2003. (Paperback Bestsellers Ser.). pap. 29.95 (*0-7838-9747-2*) Thorndike Pr.

# I

## INTERNET—FICTION

Allen, Phillip. Play Money: A Novel. 2003. 304p. 24.00 (*1-56947-338-2*) Soho Pr., Inc.
Anthony, Piers. Realty Check. 1999. 204p. pap. text 19.95 (*1-58445-000-2*) Pulpless.com, Inc.
—Realty Check. 2000. 181p. text 25.00 o.p. (*0-7388-1954-9*) Xlibris Corp.
Blum, Dan A. Lisa33: A Novel. 2004. 256p. 23.95 (*0-670-03165-8*, Viking) Viking Penguin.
Brownrigg, Sylvia. The Metaphysical Touch. 24.00 o.p. (*0-374-20873-5*); 1999. 390p. 24.00 o.s.i (*0-374-19965-5*) Farrar, Straus & Giroux.
—The Metaphysical Touch. 2000. 400p. pap. 15.00 (*0-312-26357-0*) Picador.
Couch-Jareb, Annette L. Cyber Bride. 1999. 184p. 18.95 (*0-8034-9364-9*, Avalon Bks.) Bouregy, Thomas & Co., Inc.
—Cyber Bride. l.t. ed. 2002. 311p. 24.95 (*0-7862-4090-3*) Gale Group.
Fitch, Stona. Senseless. 160p. 2002. pap. 12.00 (*1-56947-306-4*); 2001. 22.00 o.p. (*1-56947-268-8*) Soho Pr., Inc.
Forbes, Edith. Navigating the Darwin Straights: A Novel. 2001. 282p. pap. 13.95 (*1-58005-049-2*, Seal Pr.) Avalon Publishing Group.
Green, Jane. Jemima J. A Novel about Ugly Ducklings & Swans. 2001. (J). E-Book 15.95 (*0-7679-0738-8*); 384p. reprint ed. pap. 11.95 (*0-7679-0518-0*) Broadway Bks.
Grusky, Scott T. Silicon Sunset: Where the Information Highway Really Leads. 1998. pap. 15.95 (*0-9651190-0-9*) InfoNet Pubns.
Koretsky, J. Lea. Wall of Darkness. 2002. 119p. pap. 14.95 (*1-58790-020-3*) Regent Pr.
Mamet, David. Wilson: A Consideration of the Sources. 2000. xv, 336p. (*0-571-20187-3*) Faber & Faber, Inc.
—Wilson: A Consideration of the Sources. 2001. 336p. 26.95 (*1-58567-189-4*) Overlook Pr., The.
McCarty, Jerry. WWW.Wild, Wicked Web. 2000. 516p. E-Book 8.00 (*0-7388-8645-9*) Xlibris Corp.
Roberson, Matthew. 1998.6. 2002. (Illus.). 261p. pap. 13.95 (*1-57366-102-3*) Northwestern Univ. Pr.
Scott, Melissa. The Jazz. 320p. 2000. 23.95 (*0-312-86802-2*); 2001. reprint ed. pap. 14.95 (*0-312-87542-8*) Doherty, Tom Assocs., LLC. (Tor Bks.).
Sullivan, Caitlin & Bornstein, Kate. Nearly Roadkill: An Infobahn Erotic Adventure. 1996. (High Risk Ser.). 250p. (Orig.). pap. o.p. (*1-85242-418-4*) Serpent's Tail Ltd.
Taggart, Susan. Web of Intrigue. l.t. ed. 2001. (Christian Mystery Ser.). 419p. 23.95 (*0-7862-3072-X*) Thorndike Pr.
Taggart, Susan M. Web of Intrigue. 1998. (Portraits Ser.). 256p. pap. 8.99 o.p. (*0-7642-2069-1*, 212069) Bethany Hse. Pubs.
Ward, Gregory. The Internet Bride. 2000. 392p. pap. 21.95 (*1-55278-163-1*) McArthur & Co. CAN. *Dist:* HarperCollins Pubs. Canada, Ltd.
Watkins, Graham. Interception: An Internet Thriller. 1997. 416p. 24.00 o.p. (*0-7867-0354-7*, Carroll & Graf Pubs.) Avalon Publishing Group.
—Interception: An Internet Thriller. 1998. 416p. mass mkt. 5.99 o.s.i (*0-7860-0585-8*) Kensington Publishing Corp.
Weinberg, Robert & Gresh, Lois. The Termination Node. 1999. 320p. mass mkt. 6.99 o.s.i (*0-345-41246-X*, Del Rey) Ballantine Bks.
—The Termination Node. 1999. 13.04 (*0-606-18957-2*) Turtleback Bks.

# M

## MISSING PERSONS—FICTION

Adams, Jane. Mourning the Little Dead. 2002. 288p. 25.99 (*0-7278-5855-6*) Severn Hse. Pubs., Ltd.
Adler, Elizabeth A. All or Nothing. 2000. 368p. mass mkt. 6.99 (*0-440-23496-4*, Dell Bks.) Dell Publishing.
—All or Nothing. l.t. ed. 1999. 27.95 (*1-56895-825-0*, Wheeler Publishing, Inc.) Gale Group.
Alder, Elizabeth A. All or Nothing. E-Book 6.99 (*1-930161-75-1*) Adobe Systems, Inc.
Allyn, Douglas. Welcome to Wolf Country. 2001. (Five Star First Edition Mystery Ser.). 216p. 23.95 (*0-7862-3421-0*, Five Star) Gale Group.
Anastas, Benjamin. The Faithful Narrative of a Pastor's Disappearance. 2001. 24.00 o.p. (*0-374-15214-4*) Farrar, Straus & Giroux.

—The Faithful Narrative of a Pastor's Disappearance. 2002. 288p. pap. 13.00 (*0-312-42068-4*); pap. (*0-312-42108-7*) Picador.
Ansay, A. Manette. Sister. 1997. 240p. pap. 13.00 (*0-380-72976-8*, Perennial) HarperTrade.
—Sister. 1996. 224p. 24.00 o.p. (*0-688-14449-7*, Morrow, William & Co.) Morrow/Avon.
Anshaw, Carol. Seven Moves. 1996. 220p. tchr. ed. 21.95 o.p. (*0-395-69131-1*) Houghton Mifflin Co.
—Seven Moves. 1997. 240p. pap. 11.00 (*0-395-87756-3*, Mariner Bks.) Houghton Mifflin Co. Trade & Reference Div.
—Seven Moves. 1998. 242p. pap. o.s.i (*1-86049-436-6*) Virago Pr., Ltd. GBR. *Dist:* Little Brown & Co.
Atkins, Ace. Dark End of the Street. 2004. 416p. mass mkt. 7.50 (*0-06-000461-4*, HarperTorch); 2002. 336p. 23.95 (*0-06-000460-6*, Morrow, William & Co.) Morrow/Avon.
Atkins, P. W. Crossroad Blues. (Nick Travers Mysteries Ser.). 2000. 256p. mass mkt. 5.99 (*0-312-97192-3*, St. Martin's Paperbacks); 1998. 226p. 21.95 o.p. (*0-312-19254-1*, Saint Martin's Minotaur) St. Martin's Pr.
Atwood, Margaret. Surfacing. 1987. 240p. mass mkt. 5.99 o.s.i (*0-449-21375-7*, Fawcett) Ballantine Bks.
—Surfacing. 1995. 208p. pap. 10.95 o.s.i (*0-553-37780-9*) Bantam Bks.
—Surfacing. 1998. 208p. pap. 12.95 (*0-385-49105-0*) Doubleday Publishing.
—Surfacing. 1997. 200p. mass mkt. 6.95 (*0-7710-9899-5*) McClelland & Stewart/Tundra Bks.
—Surfacing. 1983. 224p. pap. 3.50 o.p. (*0-446-31107-3*) Warner Bks., Inc.
Auster, Paul. The Book of Illusions: A Novel. 2002. 336p. 24.00 (*0-8050-5408-1*) Holt, Henry & Co.
—The Book of Illusions: A Novel. l.t. ed. 2003. (Americana Ser.). 453p. 29.95 (*0-7862-4868-8*) Thorndike Pr.
—The Book of Illusions: A Novel: International Edition. 2003. mass mkt. 7.99 (*0-312-99096-0*) Picador.
Auster, Paul, ed. The Book of Illusions: A Novel. 2003. 336p. pap. 14.00 (*0-312-42181-8*) Picador.
Baker, James Robert. Testosterone: A Novel. viii, 200p. 2001. pap. 12.95 (*1-55583-714-X*); 2000. 22.95 o.p. (*1-55583-567-8*, Alyson Bks.) Alyson Pubns.
Baldacci, David. Total Control. l.t. ed. (Paperback Bestsellers Ser.). 784p. 1998. pap. 26.95 (*0-7862-0964-X*); 1997. 26.95 (*0-7862-0963-1*) Thorndike Pr.
—Total Control. 1997. 528p. 25.00 o.p. (*0-446-52095-0*); 1997. 720p. reprint ed. mass mkt. 7.99 (*0-446-60484-4*); 1996. 528p. reprint ed. pap. 14.95 (*0-446-67374-9*) Warner Bks., Inc.
Bannister, Jo. Echoes of Lies. 2001. 320p. 23.95 (*0-312-28432-2*, Saint Martin's Minotaur) St. Martin's Pr.
Barnard, Robert. No Place of Safety. 1998. 192p. 21.50 (*0-684-84503-2*, Scribner) Simon & Schuster.
—No Place of Safety. l.t. ed. 1998. (Basic Ser.). 312p. 28.95 (*0-7862-1452-X*); (*0-7540-3361-9*); (*0-7540-3362-7*) Thorndike Pr.
Barnes, Linda. The Big Dig. l.t. ed. 2003. lib. bdg. 29.95 (*1-58547-264-6*, Platinum) Ctr. Point Large Print.
—The Big Dig. 2003. 352p. mass mkt. 6.99 (*0-312-98969-5*, St. Martin's Paperbacks); 2002. 288p. 23.95 (*0-312-28270-2*, Saint Martin's Minotaur) St. Martin's Pr.
Barre, Richard. The Ghosts of Morning: A Will Hardesty Mystery. 1998. 336p. 21.95 o.s.i (*0-425-16300-8*); 1999. 320p. reprint ed. mass mkt. 6.50 o.s.i (*0-425-16931-6*, Prime Crime) Berkley Publishing Group.
Bausch, Richard. Mr. Field's Daughter. 1989. 18.95 o.p. (*0-671-64051-8*, Simon & Schuster) Simon & Schuster.
Bender, Karen E. Like Normal People. l.t. ed. 2000. (G. K. Hall Core Ser.). 384p. 27.95 (*0-7838-9301-9*, Macmillan Reference USA) Gale Group.
—Like Normal People. 2000. 288p. tchr. ed. 23.00 (*0-395-94515-1*) Houghton Mifflin Co.
—Like Normal People. 2001. 288p. pap. 13.00 (*0-618-12692-9*, Mariner Bks.) Houghton Mifflin Co. Trade & Reference Div.
Bergren, Lisa Tawn. Midnight Sun. 2000. (Northern Lights Ser.: Vol. 3). 384p. pap. 10.95 (*1-57856-113-2*) WaterBrook Pr.
Birch, Carol. Little Sister. 2001. 278p. pap. 13.00 (*1-86049-530-3*); 1998. o.s.i (*1-86049-434-X*); 1998. 278p. o.s.i (*1-86049-267-3*) Virago Pr., Ltd. GBR. *Dist:* Trafalgar Square, Little Brown & Co.
Blackstock, Terri. Line of Duty. 2003. (Newpointe 911 Ser.: Bk. 5). 384p. pap. 12.99 (*0-310-25064-1*) Zondervan.
Boggio, Sue. Sunlight & Shadows. 2004. 320p. pap. 12.95 (*0-451-21110-3*) NAL.
Borntrager, Mary Christner. Daniel. l.t. ed. 2000. (Christian Fiction Ser.). 191p. 23.95 (*0-7862-2859-8*) Thorndike Pr.
—Daniel. 1991. E-Book 7.99 (*0-585-16205-0*) netLibrary, Inc.
Boyle, Alistair. The Unholy Ghost: A Gil Yates Private Investigator Novel. 2003. (Gil Yates Private Investigator Ser.: 7). 271p. 23.00 (*1-888310-67-7*) Knoll, Allen A. Pubs.
Bradley, James. The Deep Field: A Novel. 2000. 358p. 26.00 o.s.i (*0-8050-6111-8*) Holt, Henry & Co.
Brand, Max. Seven Faces. l.t. ed. 1999. 271p. (*0-7540-3552-2*) BBC Audiobooks America.
—Seven Faces. l.t. ed. 1999. (Nightingale Ser.). 280p. pap. 21.95 (*0-7838-0360-5*) Thorndike Pr.
—Seven Faces. 1998. 180p. text 40.00 (*0-8032-1281-X*) Univ. of Nebraska Pr.
Brasfield, Lynette. Nature Lessons: A Novel. 2003. 288p. 23.95 (*0-312-31034-X*) St. Martin's Pr.
Brookner, Anita. Fraud. (Vintage Contemporaries Ser.). 1994. 272p. pap. 13.00 (*0-679-74308-1*); 1994. mass mkt. o.s.i (*0-394-22272-5*); 1993. 262p. 21.00 o.s.i (*0-679-41606-4*) Random Hse., Inc.
Buckley, Kristen. The Parker Grey Show. 2003. 240p. pap. 13.00 (*0-425-19109-5*) Berkley Publishing Group.
Buffett, Jimmy. Where Is Joe Merchant? l.t. ed. 1993. 22.95 o.p. (*1-56895-011-X*, Wheeler Publishing, Inc.) Gale Group.
—Where Is Joe Merchant? 1992. 19.95 o.p. (*0-15-196299-5*) Harcourt Trade Pubs.
—Where Is Joe Merchant? 2002. 416p. mass mkt. 7.99 (*0-380-72118-X*, Avon Bks.) Morrow/Avon.
—Where Is Joe Merchant? A Novel Tale. 1992. 416p. 25.00 (*0-15-196296-0*); 1992. 75.00 (*0-15-196297-9*); 2003. 496p. reprint ed. pap. 14.00 (*0-15-602699-6*, Harvest Bks.) Harcourt Trade Pubs.
Bunn, T. Davis. Winner Take All. 2003. 416p. mass mkt. 7.99 (*0-515-13652-2*, Jove) Berkley Publishing Group.
—Winner Take All. l.t. ed. 2003. lib. bdg. 28.95 (*1-58547-310-3*, Platinum) Ctr. Point Large Print.
—Winner Take All. 2003. 384p. 22.95 (*0-385-50370-9*) Doubleday Publishing.
Busch, Frederick. A Memory of War. 2004. 368p. pap. 14.95 (*0-345-46051-0*) Ballantine Bks.
—A Memory of War. l.t. ed. 2003. lib. bdg. 28.95 (*1-58547-350-2*, Platinum) Ctr. Point Large Print.
—A Memory of War. 2003. 352p. 25.95 (*0-393-04978-7*) Norton, W. W. & Co., Inc.
Chesney, Marion. The Constant Companion. 1987. mass mkt. 2.50 o.s.i (*0-449-21324-2*); 1980. 224p. mass mkt. 1.75 o.s.i (*0-449-50114-0*) Ballantine Bks. (Fawcett).
—The Constant Companion. l.t. ed. 2001. 248p. 27.95 (*0-7862-3634-5*); (*0-7540-4725-3*); (*0-7540-4724-5*) Thorndike Pr.
Childress, Mark. Gone for Good. 1999. (Ballantine Reader's Circle Ser.). 400p. pap. 12.95 (*0-345-41453-5*) Ballantine Bks.
Clark, Katharine. Steal Away. 368p. 1999. mass mkt. 6.50 o.s.i (*0-449-00319-1*); 1998. 24.00 o.s.i (*0-449-00276-4*) Ballantine Bks. (Fawcett).
Clarke, Brock. The Ordinary White Boy. 272p. text o.s.i (*0-15-100733-0*); 2002. pap. 13.00 (*0-15-602709-7*, Harvest Bks.); 2001. 24.00 o.s.i (*0-15-100810-8*, Harvest Bks.) Harcourt Trade Pubs.
Coben, Harlan. Gone for Good. 2003. 432p. mass mkt. 6.99 (*0-440-23673-8*); 2002. mass mkt. 6.99 (*0-440-29604-8*); 2002. 352p. 23.95 (*0-385-33558-X*, Delacorte Pr.) Dell Publishing.
—Gone for Good. l.t. ed. 2002. (Wheeler Hardcover Ser.). 29.95 (*1-58724-227-3*, Wheeler Publishing, Inc.) Gale Group.
—Gone for Good. abr. ed. 2002. audio compact disk 29.95 (*0-553-71298-5*, RH Audio) Random Hse. Audio Publishing Group.
—Gone for Good. l.t. ed. 2003. (Paperback Bestsellers Ser.). pap. 13.95 (*1-4104-0087-5*) Thorndike Pr.
Coe, Marian. Eve's Mountain: A Novel of Passion & Mystery in the Blue Ridge. (Illus.). 1998. 384p. pap. 14.98 o.p. (*0-9633341-5-8*); 4th ed. 2002. 363p. 18.95 (*0-9633341-7-4*) SouthLore Pr.
Coleman, Jane Candia. Lost River: A Western Story. 2003. 213p. 25.95 (*0-7862-3539-X*, Five Star) Gale Group.
Coleman, Reed Farrell. Walking the Perfect Square. 2001. 264p. 26.00 (*1-57962-039-6*) Permanent Pr., The.
Compton, Jodi. The 37th Hour. 2004. 326p. 21.95 (*0-385-33713-2*, Delacorte Pr.) Dell Publishing.
Conrad, Roxanne, tr. Exile, Texas. 2003. 302p. 25.95 (*1-59414-071-5*, Five Star) Gale Group.
Cookson, Catherine. The Silent Lady. 2002. 352p. 25.00 (*0-7432-2761-1*, Simon & Schuster) Simon & Schuster.
Cord, Barry. The Gun-Shy Kid. 1979. reprint ed. pap. 1.25 o.s.i (*0-505-51379-X*) Dorchester Publishing Co., Inc.
Craft, Mary Beth. Golden Grove. 1999. 183p. 16.95 (*1-885478-97-6*) Genesis Pr., Inc.
Crocker, H. W., III. The Old Limey. 2001. 250p. 19.95 (*0-89526-232-0*) Regnery Publishing, Inc., An Eagle Publishing Co.
Crumey, Andrew. Pfitz. 1998. 192p. pap. 12.00 (*0-312-19550-8*); 1997. 176p. 20.00 (*0-312-16964-7*) Picador.
Crumley, James. The Mexican Tree Duck. 1993. 256p. 19.95 (*0-89296-391-3*) Mysterious Pr.
—The Mexican Tree Duck. 1994. 272p. mass mkt. 5.99 (*0-446-40407-1*); 2001. 256p. reprint ed. pap. 11.95 (*0-446-67791-4*) Warner Bks., Inc.
—The Wrong Case. 1985. (Vintage Contemporaries Ser.). 288p. pap. 12.00 (*0-394-73558-7*) Random Hse., Inc.
Cussler, Clive. Blue Gold: A Novel from the NUMA Files. E-Book 16.00 (*1-58945-135-X*) Adobe Systems, Inc.
—Blue Gold: A Novel from the NUMA Files. 2002. E-Book 9.99 (*0-7434-2308-9*, Pocket) Simon & Schuster.
Cussler, Clive & Kemprecos, Paul. Blue Gold: A Novel from the NUMA Files. 2001. 416p. 7.99 (*0-7434-3790-X*); 2000. (NUMA Files Ser.: Vol. 2). (Illus.). 400p. pap. 16.00 (*0-671-78546-X*); 2001. (NUMA Files Ser.: Vol. 2). 416p. reprint ed. mass mkt. 7.99 (*0-7434-1822-0*) Simon & Schuster. (Pocket).
Czuchlewski, David. Empire of Light. 2003. 236p. 23.95 (*0-399-15103-6*) Putnam Publishing Group, The.
Dailey, Janet. Strange Bedfellows: Rhode Island. 1992. per. (*0-373-89889-4*, 1-89889-9); 1987. (Americana Ser.: No. 39). pap. (*0-373-89839-8*) Harlequin Enterprises, Ltd. (Harlequin Bks.).
—Strange Bedfellows: Rhode Island. l.t. ed. 2000. (Romance Ser.). 243p. 28.95 (*0-7862-2745-1*) Thorndike Pr.
—Strange Bedfellows: Rhode Island. 2002. 128p. pap. 6.99 (*0-7592-3829-4*); E-Book 6.99 (*0-7592-0167-6*); E-Book 6.99 (*0-7592-0911-1*); E-Book 6.99 (*1-58586-404-8*) ereads.com.
Darrieussecq, Marie. My Phantom Husband. Allen, Esther, tr. from FRE. 1999. 144p. text 19.95 (*1-56584-538-2*) New Pr., The.
Darty, Peggy. Spirits. 1998. (Palisades Pure Romance Ser.). 252p. pap. 9.99 o.s.i (*1-57673-460-9*) Multnomah Pubs., Inc.
Delinsky, Barbara. First Things First. 1992. mass mkt. (*0-373-83249-4*, 1-83249-2); 1985. mass mkt. (*0-373-25187-4*) Harlequin Enterprises, Ltd. (Harlequin Bks.).
—First Things First. l.t. ed. 2001. (Large Print Famous Authors Ser.). 334p. 29.95 (*0-7862-3101-7*) Thorndike Pr.
Deutermann, P. T. Hunting Season. 2001. 402p. 24.95 (*0-312-26979-X*) St. Martin's Pr.
Dickens, Charles. The Mystery of Edwin Drood. 2001. (Collected Works of Charles Dickens: Vol. 33). (Illus.). reprint ed. pap. text 28.00 (*0-7426-7339-1*) Classic Bks.
—The Mystery of Edwin Drood. 1961. mass mkt. 2.50 o.p. (*0-451-51425-4*, CE1425, Signet Classics) NAL.
—The Mystery of Edwin Drood. 1999. (Oxford World's Classics Ser.). (Illus.). 272p. pap. 7.95 (*0-19-283660-9*) Oxford Univ. Pr., Inc.
—The Mystery of Edwin Drood. Cardwell, Margaret, ed. 1982. (Oxford World's Classics Ser.). (Illus.). 266p. pap. 6.95 o.p. (*0-19-281593-8*) Oxford Univ. Pr., Inc.
—The Mystery of Edwin Drood. 1972. (Illus.). 42.00 o.p. (*0-19-812439-2*) Oxford Univ. Pr., Inc.
—The Mystery of Edwin Drood. E-Book 5.00 (*0-7410-0450-X*) SoftBook Pr.
—The Mystery of Edwin Drood. Maule, Jeremy, ed. 1999. pap. 7.95 (*0-14-043605-7*, Penguin Classics) Viking Penguin.
—The Mystery of Edwin Drood. Cox, Arthur J., ed. 1986. pap. 3.95 o.p. (*0-14-009258-7*, Penguin Bks.) Viking Penguin.
—The Mystery of Edwin Drood. Cox, A., ed. 1974. (Penguin English Library). 320p. pap. 7.95 o.s.i (*0-14-043092-X*, Penguin Classics) Viking Penguin.
—The Mystery of Edwin Drood. 1998. (Classics Library). 432p. pap. 3.95 (*1-85326-729-5*, 7295WW) Wordsworth Editions, Ltd. GBR. *Dist:* Combined Publishing.
Didion, Joan. A Book of Common Prayer. 1995. 272p. pap. 13.00 (*0-679-75486-5*, Vintage) Knopf Publishing Group.
—A Book of Common Prayer. 1986. mass mkt. 4.50 o.s.i (*0-671-63808-4*, Pocket); 1983. mass mkt. 3.50 o.s.i (*0-671-47098-1*, Pocket); 1983. 288p. mass mkt. 3.95 o.s.i (*0-671-49589-5*, Pocket); 1977. 8.95 o.p. (*0-671-22491-3*, Simon & Schuster) Simon & Schuster.
Dilke, Annabel. Present from the Past. 1994. 240p. 23.95 (*0-233-98800-9*) Andre Deutsch GBR. *Dist:* Trafalgar Square, Trans-Atlantic Pubns., Inc.
Dobyns, Stephen. The Church of Dead Girls. l.t. ed. 1997. (Large Print Book Ser.). 26.95 (*1-56895-478-6*, Wheeler Publishing, Inc.) Gale Group.
—The Church of Dead Girls. 400p. 1998. pap. 14.00 o.s.i (*0-8050-5104-X*, Owl Bks.); 1997. 23.00 o.s.i (*0-8050-5103-1*, Metropolitan Bks.) Holt, Henry & Co.
—The Church of Dead Girls. 2001. 432p. reprint ed. mass mkt. 6.99 (*0-312-97736-0*, St. Martin's Paperbacks) St. Martin's Pr.
Donaldson, Stephen R. The Man Who Killed His Brother. 2002. (Illus.). 256p. 24.95 (*0-7653-0203-9*, Forge Bks.) Doherty, Tom Assocs., LLC.
Dooling, Richard. White Man's Grave: A Novel. 1994. 356p. 22.00 o.p. (*0-374-28951-4*) Farrar, Straus & Giroux.
—White Man's Grave: A Novel. 1995. 400p. pap. 15.00 (*0-312-13214-X*) Picador.
Doss, James D. Dead Soul. Date not set. pap. (*0-312-31746-8*, St. Martin's Paperbacks); Date not set. mass mkt. (*0-312-99462-1*, St. Martin's Paperbacks); mass mkt. (*0-312-99109-6*, St. Martin's Paperbacks); 2003. 352p. 24.95 (*0-312-31744-1*, Saint Martin's Minotaur) St. Martin's Pr.
Driver, Lee. The Good Die Twice. (Chase Dagger Mystery Ser.). 2000. 304p. pap. 6.50 (*0-9666021-5-3*); 1999. 315p. 21.95 o.p. (*0-9666021-1-0*) Full Moon Publishing.
Edwards, Jane. What Happened to Amy? l.t. ed. 2000. (*0-7540-4107-7*) Thorndike Pr.
Edwards, Page, Jr. The Search for Kate Duval. 1996. 208p. pap. 14.95 o.p. (*0-7145-3000-X*) Boyars, Marion Pubs., Inc.
Egleton, Clive. A Double Deception. 1992. 288p. 18.95 o.p. (*0-312-07736-X*, Saint Martin's Minotaur) St. Martin's Pr.
—A Double Deception. l.t. ed. 1994. (Charnwood Large Print Ser.). 496p. 29.99 o.p. (*0-7089-8769-9*, Ulverscroft) Thorpe, F. A. Pubs. GBR. *Dist:* Ulverscroft Large Print Bks., Ltd., Ulverscroft Large Print Canada, Ltd.
Eidson, Bill. The Repo. 2003. 320p. 24.95 (*1-932112-11-1*, Kate's Mystery Bks.) Justin, Charles & Co. Pubs.
Ellis, Alice Thomas. Pillars of Gold. 2003. 186p. pap. 15.95 (*1-888173-54-8*) Akadine Pr., The.
—Pillars of Gold. 2000. 181p. 22.95 (*1-55921-284-5*) Moyer Bell.
—Pillars of Gold. l.t. ed. 2000. (General Ser.). 236p. 24.95 (*0-7862-2805-9*); (*0-7540-4247-2*); (*0-7540-4248-0*) Thorndike Pr.
Emerson, Scott, ed. The Case of the Cat with the Missing Ear: From the Notebooks of Dr. Edward R. Smithfield, D.V.M. 2003. (Adventures of Samuel Blackthorne Ser.). (Illus.). 240p. (J). 15.95 (*0-689-85861-2*, Simon & Schuster Children's Publishing) Simon & Schuster Children's Publishing.
Farris, John. Soon She Will Be Gone. 1998. 387p. mass mkt. 6.99 (*0-8125-0954-4*); 1997. 352p. 24.95 (*0-312-85375-0*) Doherty, Tom Assocs., LLC. (Forge Bks.).
Freeman, McGuinn C. The Place Last Seen. 2001. 304p. pap. 13.00 (*0-312-25407-5*) Picador.
Friedman, Kinky. Steppin' on a Rainbow. 2001. 208p. 23.00 (*0-684-86487-8*, Simon & Schuster) Simon & Schuster.
Fyfield, Frances. The Nature of the Beast. 2001. 280p. (*0-316-85746-7*); pap. (*0-316-85745-9*) Little Brown & Co.
Gallagher, Stephen. Nightmare, with Angel. 9999. pap. o.p. (*0-449-90866-6*, Fawcett); 1995. reprint ed. mass mkt. 5.99 o.s.i (*0-345-38966-2*, Ivy Bks.) Ballantine Bks.
Gilstrap, John. Even Steven. 2000. 368p. 24.95 o.s.i (*0-671-78666-0*, Atria); 2001. 464p. reprint ed. mass mkt. 7.99 (*0-671-78673-3*, Pocket) Simon & Schuster.
Glass, Leslie. Tracking Time. l.t. ed. 2001. (Wheeler Large Print Book Ser.). 437p. 28.95 (*1-58724-108-0*, Wheeler Publishing, Inc.) Gale Group.
—Tracking Time: An April Woo Suspense Novel. 2000. (April Woo Suspense Novels Ser.). 336p. 23.95 o.s.i (*0-525-94469-9*) Dutton/Plume.
Goddard, Robert. Caught in the Light: A Mystery. 1999. 444p. mass mkt. (*0-552-14597-1*); 1998. 352p. o.s.i (*0-593-04266-2*) Bantam Bks. (Corgi).
—Caught in the Light: A Mystery. 1999. 352p. 26.00 o.s.i (*0-8050-6155-X*) Holt, Henry & Co.
Goodman, Jo. With All My Heart. 2001. (Thorne Brothers Trilogy Ser.). (Illus.). 473p. (J). 26.95 (*0-7862-2959-4*, Five Star) Gale Group.
—With All My Heart, 1. 1999. 429p. mass mkt. 5.99 o.s.i (*0-8217-6145-5*) Kensington Publishing Corp.
Goodwin, Suzanne. The Rising Storm. 1993. 568p. 24.95 o.p. (*0-312-09372-1*) St. Martin's Pr.
Gower, Iris. When Night Closes In. l.t. ed. 2001. (Thorndike Romance Ser.). 448p. 27.95 (*0-7862-3203-X*) Thorndike Pr.
Graham, Heather. Tall, Dark & Deadly. l.t. ed. (Wheeler Press Paperback Ser.). 2000. pap. 11.95 (*1-56895-971-0*); 1999. 27.95 (*1-56895-799-8*) Gale Group. (Wheeler Publishing, Inc.).
Grayson, Emily. The Fountain: A Novel. l.t. ed. 2001. 261p. 29.95 (*0-7862-3493-8*) Thorndike Pr.
Greeley, Andrew M. The Bishop & the Beggar Girl of St. Germain: A Blackie Ryan Mystery. 2001. 304p. 24.95 (*0-312-86874-X*); 2002. 259p. reprint ed. mass mkt. 6.99 (*0-8125-7597-0*) Doherty, Tom Assocs., LLC. (Forge Bks.).

Green, Terence M. Shadow of Ashland. 2000. 223p. pap. 13.95 (*0-312-87301-8*, Forge Bks.); 1997. 223p. mass mkt. 5.99 (*0-8125-5526-0*, Tor Bks.); 1996. 224p. 17.95 o.p. (*0-312-85958-9*, Forge Bks.) Doherty, Tom Assocs., LLC.

Green, Tim. The First 48. 2004. 336p. 24.95 (*0-446-53144-8*) Warner Bks., Inc.

Gregg, Andy. Cannibal Lake: A Thriller. 2003. 214p. 25.95 (*1-59414-059-6*, Five Star) Gale Group.

Grimes, Martha. The Grave Maurice: A Richard Jury Mystery. l.t. ed. 2003. (Core Ser.). 574p. 31.95 (*0-7862-4929-3*) Thorndike Pr.

—The Grave Maurice: A Richard Jury Mystery. 2002. 432p. 25.95 o.s.i (*0-670-03045-7*) Viking Penguin.

Gross, Gwendolen. Field Guide. 2002. (Illus.). 288p. reprint ed. pap. 14.00 (*0-15-600766-5*, Harvest Bks.) Harcourt Trade Pubs.

—Field Guide: A Novel. 2001. (Harvest Book Ser.). (Illus.). 275p. 23.00 o.s.i (*0-8050-6492-3*) Holt, Henry & Co.

Guerard, Albert J. The Hotel in the Jungle. 1996. 392p. 23.00 (*1-880909-45-6*) Baskerville Pubs., Inc.

Haggard, H. Rider. King Solomon's Mines. Date not set. reprint ed. lib. bdg. 20.95 (*0-89190-703-3*, American Reprint Co.) Amereon, Ltd.

—King Solomon's Mines. Kay, Marilyn, ed. abr. ed. 1987. pap. 12.95 incl. audio (*1-882071-12-3*, 014) B&B Audio, Inc.

—King Solomon's Mines. 1976. reprint ed. lib. bdg. 19.95 (*0-89968-513-7*) Buccaneer Bks., Inc.

—King Solomon's Mines. l.t. ed. 1986. (Mainstream Ser.). (Illus.). xi, 317p. 15.95 o.p. (*1-85089-063-3*) ISIS Large Print Bks. GBR. *Dist:* Transaction Pubs.

—King Solomon's Mines. l.t. ed. 1998. (Large Print Heritage Ser.). 365p. lib. bdg. 33.95 (*1-58118-033-0*, 22014) LRS.

—King Solomon's Mines. 1981. (English As a Second Language Bk.). pap. text 5.95 o.p. (*0-582-53502-6*, 74101) Longman Publishing Group.

—King Solomon's Mines. l.t. ed. (Large Print Ser.). 1992. 382p. lib. bdg. 26.00 (*0-939495-49-X*); 1998. 240p. reprint ed. lib. bdg. 25.00 (*1-58287-044-6*) North Bks.

—King Solomon's Mines. Butts, Dennis, ed. & intro. by. 1998. (Oxford World's Classics Ser.). (Illus.). 368p. pap. 9.95 (*0-19-283485-1*) Oxford Univ. Pr., Inc.

—King Solomon's Mines. Butts, Dennis, ed. 1990. (Oxford World's Classics Ser.). (Illus.). 366p. pap. 5.95 o.p. (*0-19-282204-7*) Oxford Univ. Pr., Inc.

—King Solomon's Mines. 1999. (Gateway Movie Classics Ser.). 382p. pap. 14.95 (*0-89526-329-7*, Gateway Editions) Regnery Publishing, Inc., An Eagle Publishing Co.

—King Solomon's Mines. 1998. (Children's Classics). 224p. pap. 3.95 (*1-85326-105-X*, 105XWW) Wordsworth Editions, Ltd. GBR. *Dist:* Advanced Global Distribution Services.

Hall, Linda. Chat Room. 2003. (Teri Blake-Addision Mystery Series, Book 2 Ser.). 290p. pap. 11.99 (*1-59052-200-1*) Multnomah Pubs., Inc.

Hall, Oakley M. Ambrose Bierce & the One-Eyed Jacks. 2004. 224p. pap. 12.00 (*0-14-200014-0*) Penguin Group (USA) Inc.

—Ambrose Bierce & the One-Eyed Jacks: An Ambrose Bierce Mystery. 2003. 224p. 24.95 (*0-670-03180-1*, Viking) Viking Penguin.

Halligan, Marion. The Golden Dress. 1999. 380p. (*0-14-027302-6*) Penguin Group (USA) Inc.

Hamilton, Lyn. The Thai Amulet. 2004. 288p. mass mkt. 6.99 (*0-425-19487-6*); 2003. 256p. 22.95 (*0-425-19006-4*, Prime Crime) Berkley Publishing Group.

Hamilton, Steve. Blood Is the Sky: An Alex McKnight Mystery. 2003. 304p. 21.95 (*0-312-30115-4*, Saint Martin's Minotaur) St. Martin's Pr.

Harris, Mark. Speed. 1990. 285p. 19.95 o.p. (*1-55611-180-0*) Fine, Donald I. Bks.

—Speed. l.t. ed. 1991. (General Ser.). 431p. lib. bdg. 21.95 (*0-8161-5208-X*, Macmillan Reference USA) Gale Group.

—Speed. 1998. 285p. pap. 15.00 (*0-8032-7314-2*, HARSPX) Univ. of Nebraska Pr.

—Speed. 1991. mass mkt. 5.99 (*0-446-36211-5*) Warner Bks., Inc.

Harrison, William. The Blood Latitudes. 2000. 280p. 25.00 (*1-878448-97-8*) MacMurray & Beck, Inc.

Hart, Ellen. Merchant of Venus. mass mkt. (*0-312-97991-6*, St. Martin's Paperbacks); 2001. 389p. 24.95 (*0-312-26618-9*, Saint Martin's Minotaur) St. Martin's Pr.

Hart, Griffin. Wyakin. 2000. 314p. 24.95 (*1-929897-05-7*) Holdfast Bks.

Hartmann, William K. Mars Underground. 1999. (Illus.). 428p. pap. text 6.99 (*0-8125-8039-7*); 1997. 352p. 24.95 (*0-312-86342-X*) Doherty, Tom Assocs., LLC. (Tor Bks.).

—Mars Underground. 1999. 6.99 (*0-312-87123-6*) St. Martin's Pr.

Hiaasen, Carl. Stormy Weather. l.t. ed. 1996. 26.95 (*1-56895-276-7*, Wheeler Publishing, Inc.) Gale Group.

—Stormy Weather. 1995. 352p. 24.00 o.s.i (*0-679-41982-9*) Knopf, Alfred A. Inc.

—Stormy Weather. reprint ed. 2001. 416p. pap. 14.95 (*0-446-67716-7*); 1996. 400p. mass mkt. 7.99 (*0-446-60342-2*) Warner Bks., Inc.

Hoag, Tami. Dark Horse. 2004. 592p. mass mkt. 7.99 (*0-553-58357-3*); 2002. E-Book 21.95 (*0-553-89706-3*); 2002. 448p. 26.95 (*0-553-80192-9*) Bantam Bks.

—Dark Horse. l.t. ed. 2002. 768p. 28.95 (*0-375-43182-9*) Random Hse., Inc.

Hooper, Kay. Haunting Rachel. 1999. 368p. mass mkt. 7.50 (*0-553-57183-4*); 1998. 352p. 22.95 o.s.i (*0-553-09950-7*) Bantam Bks.

—Haunting Rachel. l.t. ed. 2000. (Wheeler Romance Ser.). 26.95 (*1-56895-987-7*, Wheeler Publishing, Inc.) Gale Group.

—Hiding in the Shadows. 2000. (Shadows Trilogy Ser.). 368p. mass mkt. 7.50 (*0-553-57692-5*) Bantam Bks.

—Hiding in the Shadows. l.t. ed. 2001. (Basic Ser.). 421p. 30.95 (*0-7862-3057-6*); 29.95 (*0-7862-3058-4*) Thorndike Pr.

Hubbard, S. W. Take the Bait. 2003. 336p. mass mkt. 6.50 (*0-7434-6653-5*, Pocket) Simon & Schuster.

Huggins, David. Me Me Me. 2001. 256p. pap. (*0-571-20936-X*) Faber & Faber, Inc.

Hughes, Kathleen. Dear Mrs. Lindbergh. 2003. 320p. text 24.95 (*0-393-05785-2*) Norton, W. W. & Co., Inc.

Hughes, Richard. Isla Grande. 1994. 215p. (Orig.). pap. 12.50 (*1-883721-10-5*) Silver Mountain Pr.

Hyde, Anthony. Double Helix. 1999. 320p. text (*0-670-87825-1*) Viking.

Iles, Greg. Dead Sleep. 2002. 480p. reprint ed. mass mkt. 7.99 (*0-451-20652-5*, Signet Bks.) NAL.

—Dead Sleep. 2001. 352p. 19.95 o.p. (*0-399-14735-7*) Penguin Group (USA) Inc.

—Dead Sleep. l.t. ed. 12.95 (*1-4104-0053-0*, Large Print Pr.); 2003. 703p. pap. 12.95 (*0-7862-3681-7*); 2001. 681p. 30.95 (*0-7862-3682-5*) Thorndike Pr.

Isaacs, Susan. Long Time No See. 2001. 368p. 26.00 (*0-06-019570-3*); 496p. pap. 26.00 (*0-06-621404-1*) HarperCollins Pubs.

Ishiguro, Kazuo. When We Were Orphans. E-Book 19.95 (*1-58945-537-1*) Adobe Systems, Inc.

—When We Were Orphans. 2001. 352p. reprint ed. pap. 14.00 (*0-375-72440-0*, Vintage) Knopf Publishing Group.

—When We Were Orphans. 2000. 352p. 25.00 (*0-375-41054-6*) Knopf, Alfred A. Inc.

—When We Were Orphans. 2001. E-Book 12.50 (*0-375-41265-4*) Random Hse., Inc.

Jackson, Loretta & Britton, Vickie. Arctic Legacy. 1997. 192p. lib. bdg. 18.95 (*0-8034-9359-2*, Avalon Bks.) Bouregy, Thomas & Co., Inc.

Jacobs, Mark. Stone Cowboy. 1997. 304p. 24.00 (*1-56947-098-7*) Soho Pr., Inc.

—Stone Cowboy: A Novel. 1999. 304p. pap. 13.00 (*1-56947-136-3*) Soho Pr., Inc.

Jacobson, Alan. The Hunted. 2001. 416p. 24.95 (*0-671-02680-1*); reprint ed. E-Book 24.95 (*0-7434-2202-3*) Simon & Schuster. (Atria).

John, Katherine. Without Trace. 1995. 426p. 24.95 o.p. (*0-312-13218-2*, Saint Martin's Minotaur) St. Martin's Pr.

Johnston, Velda. The Etruscan Smile. 1980. mass mkt. 2.25 o.p. (*0-451-09020-9*, E9020, Signet Bks.) NAL.

—The Etruscan Smile: A Novel of Suspense. l.t. ed. 2000. (Candlelight Romance Ser.). 271p. 22.95 (*0-7862-2449-5*) Thorndike Pr.

Jones, Pauline Baird. Missing You. 2002. (Five Star First Edition Romance Ser.). 335p. 26.95 (*0-7862-3748-1*, Five Star) Gale Group.

—Missing You. 2002. (Lonesome Lawman Ser.: Bk. 3). 240p. pap. 12.95 (*0-7599-0526-6*) Hard Shell Word Factory.

Joyce, Graham. Smoking Poppy. 288p. 2003. pap. 14.00 (*0-671-03940-7*, Washington Square Pr.); 2002. 23.00 (*0-671-03939-3*, Atria) Simon & Schuster.

Kagan, Elaine. Losing Mr. North: A Novel. 2002. 272p. 24.95 (*0-06-018474-4*, Morrow, William & Co.) Morrow/Avon.

Kelley, Norman. Black Heat. 228p. 1997. 22.00 o.p. (*1-887276-02-5*); 1996. (Illus.). pap. 12.95 (*1-887276-03-3*) Cool Grove Publishing, Inc. (Coolgrove Pr.).

—Black Heat: A Nina Halligan Mystery. 2001. 320p. 23.00 (*0-06-018542-2*) HarperTrade.

Kelly, Susan. Little Girl Lost: A Gregory Summers Mystery. 2002. (Gregory Summers Mystery Ser.). 282p. 24.95 (*0-7490-0533-5*) Allison & Busby, Ltd. GBR. *Dist:* International Publishers Marketing.

—Little Girl Lost: A Gregory Summers Mystery. l.t. ed. 2003. (Magna Large Print Ser.). 400p. 32.50 (*0-7505-2001-9*) Magna Large Print Bks. GBR. *Dist:* Ulverscroft Large Print Bks., Ltd., Ulverscroft Large Print Canada, Ltd.

King, Jonathon. Shadow Men. unabr. ed. 2004. (Max Freeman Ser.). audio 27.95 (*1-59355-306-4*, 4918, Brilliance Audio Unabridged); audio 69.25 (*1-59355-307-2*, 4919, Brilliance Audio Unabridged Lib Ed); audio compact disk 82.25 (*1-59355-309-9*, 4921, Brilliance Audio on CD Unabridged Lib Ed); audio compact disk 29.95 (*1-59355-308-0*, 4920, Brilliance Audio on CD Unabridged) Brilliance Audio.

—Shadow Men. 2004. 288p. 23.95 (*0-525-94807-4*, Dutton) Dutton/Plume.

King, Laurie R. The Game. 2004. 384p. 23.95 (*0-553-80194-5*) Bantam Bks.

Kosinski, Jerzy N. Pinball. 1989. 310p. reprint ed. pap. 8.95 o.p. (*1-55970-004-1*) Arcade Publishing, Inc.

—Pinball. 1982. pap. 3.95 o.p. (*0-553-23322-X*); o.p. (*0-553-01365-3*) Bantam Bks.

—Pinball. 1996. 320p. pap. 15.00 (*0-8021-3482-3*, Grove Pr.) Grove/Atlantic, Inc.

Krentz, Jayne Ann. The Waiting Game. 1998. mass mkt. (*0-373-83351-2*, 1-83351-6); 1995. per. (*0-373-45197-0*, 1-45197-0); 1985. mass mkt. (*0-373-22017-0*) Harlequin Enterprises, Ltd. (Harlequin Bks.).

—The Waiting Game. l.t. ed. 2002. 328p. 29.95 (*0-7862-3981-6*) Thorndike Pr.

Krist, Gary. Bad Chemistry. 2000. 368p. reprint ed. mass mkt. 7.50 o.s.i (*0-425-17300-3*) Berkley Publishing Group.

Krueger, William Kent. Boundary Waters. (Cork O'Connor Mysteries Ser.). 1999. 336p. 23.00 (*0-671-01698-9*, Atria); 2000. 416p. reprint ed. mass mkt. 6.99 (*0-671-01699-7*, Pocket Star) Simon & Schuster.

Kwitney, Alisa. The Dominant Blonde. 2002. 288p. pap. 13.95 (*0-06-008329-8*) Morrow/Avon.

Lapierre, Janet. Old Enemies. 1993. 256p. text 20.00 (*0-684-19614-X*, Macmillan Reference USA) Gale Group.

Lippman, Laura. Every Secret Thing. 2003. 400p. 24.95 (*0-06-050667-9*, Morrow, William & Co.) Morrow/Avon.

Liu, Aimee E. Flash House. 2004. 472p. pap. 13.95 (*0-446-69121-6*); 2003. (Illus.). 464p. 24.95 (*0-446-53097-2*) Warner Bks., Inc.

Lovell, Glenville. Too Beautiful to Die. 2004. 320p. mass mkt. 6.99 (*0-425-19702-6*) Berkley Publishing Group.

—Too Beautiful to Die. 2003. 304p. 23.95 (*0-399-15048-X*) Putnam Publishing Group, The.

Macomber, Debbie. Sooner or Later. l.t. ed. 2000. (Wheeler Softcover Ser.). 346p. pap. 25.95 (*1-56895-141-8*, Wheeler Publishing, Inc.) Gale Group.

—Sooner or Later. 1998. 368p. mass mkt. 3.99 o.p. (*0-06-104475-X*) HarperCollins Pubs.

—Sooner or Later. 1996. 368p. mass mkt. 6.99 (*0-06-108345-3*, HarperTorch) Morrow/Avon.

Marquis, Christopher. A Hole in the Heart: A Novel. 2003. 320p. 24.95 (*0-312-30630-X*) St. Martin's Pr.

Marshall, Evan. Missing Marlene. (Jane Stuart & Winky Mystery Ser.). 2000. 336p. mass mkt. 5.99 (*1-57566-555-7*, Kensington Bks.); 1999. 309p. 20.00 o.s.i (*1-57566-420-8*) Kensington Publishing Corp.

Martin, Emer. More Bread or I'll Appear. 2000. 288p. pap. 12.00 (*0-385-72009-2*) Doubleday Publishing.

—More Bread or I'll Appear. 1999. 268p. tchr. ed. 23.00 (*0-395-91871-5*) Houghton Mifflin Co.

Martinusen, Cindy McCormick. Blue Night: A Novel. 2001. 416p. pap. 10.99 (*0-8423-5236-8*) Tyndale Hse. Pubs.

Mathews, Francine. The Secret Agent. 2003. 528p. mass mkt. 6.99 (*0-553-58153-8*); 2002. (Illus.). 416p. 23.95 (*0-553-10913-8*) Bantam Bks.

May, Janis S. Where Shadows Linger. l.t. ed. 1993. 19.95 o.p. (*0-7927-1767-8*); pap. 18.95 o.p. (*0-7927-1766-X*) BBC Audiobooks America.

McCall, Wendell. Concerto in Dead Flat. l.t. ed. 2002. lib. bdg. 28.95 (*1-58547-157-7*, Premier) Ctr. Point Large Print.

—Concerto in Dead Flat. 2000. pap. 12.95 (*1-890208-52-3*); 1999. 277p. 23.95 (*1-890208-18-3*) Poisoned Pen Pr.

McCourtney, Lorena. Canyon. 1998. 240p. pap. 9.99 o.p. (*1-57673-287-8*, Palisades) Multnomah Pubs., Inc.

McGarrity, Michael. Tularosa. l.t. ed. 1996. pap. 23.95 (*1-56895-372-0*, Wheeler Publishing, Inc.) Gale Group.

—Tularosa. 1996. 304p. 25.00 (*0-393-03922-6*) Norton, W. W. & Co., Inc.

—Tularosa. 1998. 3.99 (*0-671-02373-X*, Pocket); 1997. (Illus.). 336p. mass mkt. 6.99 (*0-671-00252-X*, Pocket Star) Simon & Schuster.

McGregor, Elizabeth. The Ice Child. 2001. (Illus.). 400p. 24.95 o.p. (*0-525-94567-9*, Dutton) Dutton/Plume.

—The Ice Child. l.t. ed. 2001. (Wheeler Large Print Book Ser.). (Illus.). 540p. 29.95 o.p. (*1-58724-109-9*, Wheeler Publishing, Inc.) Gale Group.

—The Ice Child. 2002. pap. 6.99 (*0-451-20539-1*, Signet Bks.); 448p. reprint ed. mass mkt. 7.99 (*0-451-41061-0*, Onyx) NAL.

McInerny, Ralph. Still Life: A Novel. 2000. (First Edition Mystery Ser.). 255p. 21.95 (*0-7862-2895-4*, Five Star) Gale Group.

McKinney, Meagan. In the Dark. 1999. 304p. mass mkt. 6.99 o.s.i (*0-8217-6341-5*, Zebra Bks.); 1998. (Illus.). 288p. 23.00 o.s.i (*1-57566-371-6*) Kensington Publishing Corp.

—In the Dark. l.t. ed. 2000. (Basic Ser.). 448p. 27.95 (*0-7862-2452-5*) Thorndike Pr.

Meehan, Michael. The Salt of Broken Tears: A Novel. 2001. 304p. 24.95 (*1-55970-567-1*) Arcade Publishing, Inc.

Meek, M. R. D. The Vanishing Point. 2002. 256p. 26.99 (*0-7278-5840-8*) Severn Hse. Pubs., Ltd.

Memmi, Albert. The Scorpion, or the Imaginary Confession. Levieux, Eleanor, tr. 1986. (Folio Ser.: No. 1715). (FRE.). 270p. pap. 10.95 (*2-07-037715-6*) Schoenhof's Foreign Bks., Inc.

Michaels, Lisa. Grand Ambition: A Novel. l.t. ed. 2001. 275p. 26.95 (*1-57490-374-8*, Beeler Large Print Bks.) Beeler, Thomas T. Publisher.

—Grand Ambition: A Novel. 288p. 2002. pap. 13.95 (*0-393-32295-5*); 2001. (Illus.). 23.95 (*0-393-05047-5*) Norton, W. W. & Co., Inc.

Miller, Geoffrey. The Black Glove. 1984. 254p. pap. 3.50 o.p. (*0-88184-080-7*, Carroll & Graf Pubs.) Avalon Publishing Group.

—The Black Glove. 1981. 276p. 12.95 o.p. (*0-670-17166-2*) Viking Penguin.

Miscione, Lisa. Angel Fire. E-Book 17.95 (*0-312-70416-X*); 2003. 288p. mass mkt. 6.50 (*0-312-98918-0*, St. Martin's Paperbacks); 2002. 288p. 23.95 (*0-312-28304-0*, Saint Martin's Minotaur) St. Martin's Pr.

—The Darkness Gathers: A Novel. 2003. 304p. 23.95 (*0-312-28359-8*, Saint Martin's Minotaur) St. Martin's Pr.

Mitchell, Sharon. Sheer Necessity. 1999. 304p. 23.95 o.p. (*0-525-94523-7*) Dutton/Plume.

—Sheer Necessity. 2000. 352p. reprint ed. mass mkt. 6.99 o.s.i (*0-451-19947-2*, Signet Bks.) NAL.

—Sheer Necessity. 2000. 13.04 (*0-606-19634-X*) Turtleback Bks.

Morris, Gilbert. The Fiery Ring. 2002. (House of Winslow Ser.: Bk. 28). (Illus.). 320p. pap. 11.99 (*0-7642-2622-3*) Bethany Hse. Pubs.

Muller, Marcia. Cyanide Wells. 2003. (Illus.). 304p. 24.95 (*0-89296-781-1*) Mysterious Pr.

—Cyanide Wells. l.t. ed. 2003. 432p. 30.95 (*0-7862-5837-3*) Thorndike Pr.

—Cyanide Wells. 2004. mass mkt. (*0-446-61421-1*) Warner Bks., Inc.

Nagy, Gloria. Looking for Leo. 1993. 432p. mass mkt. 5.99 o.s.i (*0-440-21251-0*) Dell Publishing.

Nahal, Chaman. My True Faces: A Novel about India. 1978. 9.00 o.p. (*0-88253-254-5*) South Asia Bks.

Novak, Karen. Ordinary Monsters: A Novel. 2002. 288p. 24.95 (*1-58234-241-5*) Bloomsbury Publishing.

O'Brien, Maureen. Unauthorized Departure: A Mystery. 2003. 288p. 23.95 (*0-312-31600-3*, Saint Martin's Minotaur) St. Martin's Pr.

O'Brien, Tim. In the Lake of the Woods. 1994. 320p. tchr. ed. 21.95 o.p. (*0-395-48889-3*) Houghton Mifflin Co.

—In the Lake of the Woods. 1996. o.p. (*0-14-771179-7*); 1995. 320p. pap. 14.00 (*0-14-025094-8*, Penguin Bks.) Penguin Group (USA) Inc.

O'Grady, Timothy. Motherland. 1990. 240p. 19.95 o.p. (*0-8050-1230-3*) Holt, Henry & Co.

Peace, David. Nineteen Seventy-Four. 2000. 295p. pap. o.p. (*1-85242-634-9*) Serpent's Tail Ltd.

—Nineteen Seventy Four. 2000. (Red Riding Quartet Ser.: Bk. 1). 320p. pap. (*1-85242-741-8*) Serpent's Tail Ltd.

Prior, Lily. Ardor: A Novel of Enchantment. 2004. (*0-06-052786-2*, Ecco) HarperTrade.

Pritchett, V. S. Dead Man Leading. 1984. (Twentieth Century Classics Ser.). 224p. pap. 6.95 o.p. (*0-19-281469-9*) Oxford Univ. Pr., Inc.

Purdy, James. The Nephew. 1987. 176p. pap. 7.95 o.p. (*1-55584-085-X*) Grove/Atlantic, Inc.

—The Nephew. 1980. 152p. pap. 3.95 o.p. (*0-14-005670-X*, Penguin Bks.) Viking Penguin.

Reid, Van. Mrs. Roberto: Or the Widowy Worries of the Moosepath League. 2003. 352p. text 25.95 (*0-670-03225-5*, Viking) Viking Penguin.

Robb, Candace. A Trust Betrayed. 2002. 272p. pap. 12.95 (*0-446-67850-3*, Mysterious Pr. Paperback Bks.) Warner Bks., Inc.

—A Trust Betrayed: First Chapter of Margaret Kerr of Perth. 2001. 272p. E-Book 14.95 (*0-7595-8248-3*); E-Book 14.95 (*0-7595-6242-3*); E-Book 14.95 (*0-7595-9274-8*); E-Book 14.95 (*0-7595-4245-7*); E-Book 14.95 (*0-7595-0242-0*); (Illus.). 22.95 o.p. (*0-89296-708-0*) Mysterious Pr.

—A Trust Betrayed: First Chapter of Margaret Kerr of Perth. l.t. ed. 2001. (Illus.). 354p. 29.95 (*0-7862-3323-0*); 368p. (*0-7540-1663-3*); 368p. (*0-7540-9077-9*) Thorndike Pr.

Roberts, Les. The Chinese Fire Drill. 2003. 192p. pap. 13.95 (*1-4104-0114-6*, Five Star Trade); 2001. 188p. 23.95 (*0-7862-3760-0*, Five Star) Gale Group.

Rooke, Leon. The Fall of Gravity: A Novel. 2000. 271p. tchr. ed. (*0-919028-36-5*) Allen, Thomas & Son, Ltd.

Rose, M. J. Sheet Music. 336p. 2004. pap. 13.95 (*0-345-45107-4*); 2003. 22.95 (*0-345-45106-6*, Ballantine Bks.) Ballantine Bks.

Saylor, Steven. Have You Seen Dawn? 2003. 256p. 24.00 (*0-7432-1366-1*, Simon & Schuster) Simon & Schuster.

—Have You Seen Dawn? l.t. ed. 2003. 28.95 (*0-7862-5467-X*) Thorndike Pr.

Schow, Vione I. Phay Vanneth: Dead or Alive? 2002. 180p. pap. 12.95 (*1-55517-605-4*, Bonneville Bks.) Cedar Fort, Inc./CFI Distribution.

Sedley, Kate. Nine Men Dancing. 2003. 224p. 26.99 (*0-7278-5977-3*) Severn Hse. Pubs., Ltd.

Shelton, Connie. Reunions Can Be Murder: The Seventh Charlie Parker Mystery. 2002. (The Charlie Parker Mystery Ser.: No. 7). 255p. 23.95 (*1-890768-46-4*, Intrigue Pr.) Corvus Publishing.

Silvis, Randall. Disquiet Heart. E-Book 24.95 (*0-312-70623-5*); 2002. 336p. 24.95 (*0-312-26248-5*, Saint Martin's Minotaur) St. Martin's Pr.

Smith, Florence B. Labette County's Ultimate Deception. l.t. ed. 2001. (G. K. Hall Romance Ser.). 303p. 27.95 (*0-7838-9375-2*, Macmillan Reference USA) Gale Group.

Solomon, Nina. Single Wife: A Novel. 2003. 336p. tchr. ed. 23.95 (*1-56512-382-4*, 72382) Algonquin Bks. of Chapel Hill.

Spark, Muriel. Aiding & Abetting. 2001. E-Book 10.00 (*1-58945-957-1*) Adobe Systems, Inc.

—Aiding & Abetting. 2002. 176p. pap. 11.00 (*0-385-72090-4*, Knopf Bks. for Young Readers) Random Hse. Children's Bks.

—Aiding & Abetting. l.t. ed. 2001. (Thorndike Basic Ser.). 192p. 29.95 (*0-7862-3184-X*); (*0-7540-4515-3*); (*0-7540-4516-1*) Thorndike Pr.

Stevens, Marcus. The Curve of the World. 2002. 320p. tchr. ed. 24.95 (*1-56512-336-0*) Algonquin Bks. of Chapel Hill.

—The Curve of the World. 2003. 320p. pap. 14.00 (*0-7434-7082-6*, Washington Square Pr.) Simon & Schuster.

Straub, Peter. Lost Boy Lost Girl: A Novel. 2003. 304p. 24.95 (*1-4000-6092-3*) Random Hse., Inc.

Tapply, William G. A Fine Line: A Brady Coyne Novel. 2002. 320p. 24.95 (*0-312-30352-1*, Saint Martin's Minotaur) St. Martin's Pr.

—A Fine Line: A Brady Coyne Novel. l.t. ed. 2003. (Mystery Ser.). 30.95 (*0-7862-5208-1*) Thorndike Pr.

—Past Tense. 2004. mass mkt. 6.99 (*0-312-99551-2*, St. Martin's Paperbacks) St. Martin's Pr.

—Past Tense. l.t. ed. 2002. (Core Collection). 382p. 28.95 (*0-7862-4678-2*) Thorndike Pr.

Teran, Boston. Never Count Out the Dead. 2001. E-Book 23.95 (*1-58945-789-7*) Adobe Systems, Inc.

—Never Count Out the Dead. E-Book 23.95 (*0-312-70156-X*); 2002. 384p. mass mkt. 6.99 (*0-312-98020-5*, St. Martin's Paperbacks); 2001. 366p. 23.95 (*0-312-27115-8*, Saint Martin's Minotaur) St. Martin's Pr.

Thomas, Trisha R. Roadrunner: A Novel. 2003. 288p. pap. 12.00 (*1-4000-4791-9*) Crown Publishing Group.

—Roadrunner: A Novel. 2002. 288p. 22.95 (*0-609-60584-4*, Compass American Guides, Inc.) Fodor's Travel Pubns.

Tyler, Anne. Ladder of Years. 1997. 416p. mass mkt. 7.99 (*0-8041-1347-5*, Ivy Bks.); 1996. 352p. pap. 14.95 (*0-449-91057-1*); 1996. mass mkt. 6.99 o.s.i (*0-8041-1492-7*, Ivy Bks.); Bk. 5. Date not set. pap. (*0-449-91056-3*, Fawcett) Ballantine Bks.

—Ladder of Years. deluxe l.t. ed. 1995. 23.00 o.s.i (*0-676-50229-6*) Random Hse., Inc.

Ursu, Anne. The Disapparation of James. 2004. pap. 13.95 (*0-7868-8663-3*); 2003. 288p. 23.95 (*0-7868-6779-5*) Hyperion Pr.

Van Gieson, Judith. Vanishing Point: A Claire Reynier Mystery. 2001. 272p. mass mkt. 5.99 (*0-451-20240-6*) NAL.

—Vanishing Point: A Claire Reynier Mystery. l.t. ed. 2001. (Senior Lifestyles Ser.). 293p. 28.95 (*0-7862-3587-X*) Thorndike Pr.

—Vanishing Point: A Claire Reynier Mystery. 2001. (Claire Reynier Mysteries Ser.). 216p. 24.95 (*0-8263-2383-9*) Univ. of New Mexico Pr.

Vanderhaeghe, Guy. My Present Age. 1985. 239p. 15.95 o.p. (*0-89919-384-6*) Houghton Mifflin Co.

Victor, Barbara. Coriander. 1994. mass mkt. 5.99 o.s.i (*0-345-38454-7*) Ballantine Bks.

—Coriander. 1993. 22.00 o.p. (*1-55611-353-6*) Fine, Donald I. Bks.

—Coriander. l.t. ed. 1996. 24.95 o.p. (*1-56895-281-3*, Wheeler Publishing, Inc.) Gale Group.

Wall, Michael. The Cassino Legacy. 1999. 379p. (*0-14-028836-8*) Viking Penguin.

Wallace, David Foster. The Broom of the System. 1997. pap. 6.99 (*0-380-73030-8*); 1993. 480p. pap. 14.00 (*0-380-71991-6*) Morrow/Avon. (Avon Bks.).

—The Broom of the System. 1987. (Contemporary American Fiction Ser.). 467p. 18.95 o.p. (*0-670-81230-7*); 480p. pap. 7.95 o.p. (*0-14-009868-2*, Penguin Bks.) Viking Penguin.

Wallen, Jacqueline. Sudden Loss of Serenity. 2004. 220p. 12.95 (*1-892281-21-X*) New Victoria Pubs., Inc.

West, Morris. Vanishing Point. l.t. ed. 1997. (Wheeler Large Print Book Ser.). pap. 24.95 (*1-56895-474-3*, Wheeler Publishing, Inc.) Gale Group.

—Vanishing Point. 1997. 320p. mass mkt. 5.99 o.p. (*0-06-101222-X*, HarperTorch); 1996. 272p. mass mkt. 23.00 o.p. (*0-06-101069-3*, Eos) Morrow/Avon.

Westermann, John. Ladies of the Night. 1998. 288p. 23.00 (*0-671-87124-2*, Atria) Simon & Schuster.

Whitney, Phyllis A. Amethyst Dreams. 1998. 304p. mass mkt. 6.99 (*0-449-22618-2*, Fawcett) Ballantine Bks.

—Amethyst Dreams. l.t. ed. 1997. pap. 24.00 o.p. (*0-7838-8130-4*, Macmillan Reference USA) Gale Group.

—Amethyst Dreams. l.t. ed. 1997. (Large Print Ser.). pap. 25.00 o.s.i (*0-679-77436-X*) Random Hse., Inc.

—Amethyst Dreams. 1998. 13.04 (*0-606-14150-2*) Turtleback Bks.

Williams, Darren. Angel Rock: A Novel. 2003. 320p. pap. 13.00 (*0-375-71924-5*) Knopf, Alfred A. Inc.

Wilson, F. Paul. Conspiracies. 2000. (Repairman Jack Ser.). 405p. mass mkt. 6.99 (*0-8125-6699-8*, Tor Bks.); 317p. 24.95 (*0-312-86797-2*, Forge Bks.) Doherty, Tom Assocs., LLC.

—Conspiracies. aut. ltd. ed. 1999. (Repairman Jack Ser.). 324p. 50.00 (*1-887368-20-5*) Gauntlet, Inc.

Windle, Jeanette. The DMZ: A Novel. 2002. 512p. 15.99 (*0-8254-4118-8*) Kregel Pubns.

Winton, Tim. The Riders. l.t. ed. 1996. 392p. lib. bdg. 24.95 (*1-57490-036-6*) Beeler, Thomas T. Publisher.

—The Riders. 384p. 1996. pap. 12.00 (*0-684-82277-6*); 1995. 22.50 (*0-684-80296-1*) Simon & Schuster. (Scribner).

Woods, Stuart. Swimming to Catalina. l.t. ed. 1998. (Wheeler Large Print Book Ser.). 27.95 (*1-56895-620-7*, Wheeler Publishing, Inc.) Gale Group.

—Swimming to Catalina. 1998. 320p. 25.00 o.s.i (*0-06-018369-1*) HarperCollins Pubs.

—Swimming to Catalina. 1998. 416p. mass mkt. 7.99 (*0-06-109980-5*, HarperTorch) Morrow/Avon.

Wright, Eric. The Kidnapping of Rosie Dawn: A Joe Barley Mystery. 2000. 213p. pap. 12.95 (*1-880284-40-5*, Perseverance Pr.) Daniel, John & Co., Pubs.

—The Kidnapping of Rosie Dawn: A Joe Barley Mystery. l.t. ed. 2001. 306p. 27.95 (*0-7862-3478-4*); 296p. (*0-7540-4673-7*); 296p. (*0-7540-4674-5*) Thorndike Pr.

Wright, Laurali R. Prized Possessions, No. 5. 1997. 336p. mass mkt. 7.50 (*0-7704-2543-7*) Bantam Bks.

—Prized Possessions. 1994. (Crime Ser.). 272p. pap. 5.95 o.p. (*0-14-017146-0*, Penguin Bks.) Penguin Group (USA) Inc.

—Prized Possessions. 1993. 272p. 19.00 o.p. (*0-670-84565-5*, Viking) Viking Penguin.

Xiaolong, Qiu. A Loyal Character Dancer. 360p. 2003. pap. 13.00 (*1-56947-341-2*); 2002. 25.00 (*1-56947-301-3*) Soho Pr., Inc.

Yates, Dan. Lack of Evidence: A Novel. 2003. 195p. (*1-59156-206-6*) Covenant Communications.

Zoller, James S. Beyond the Bridge. 2001. 423p. pap. 20.95 (*0-595-17016-1*) iUniverse, Inc.

## P

### PEOPLE WITH DISABILITIES—FICTION

Anderson, Catherine. Phantom Waltz. l.t. ed. 2001. 447p. 27.95 (*1-57490-376-4*, Beeler Large Print Bks.) Beeler, Thomas T. Publisher.

Mapson, Jo-Ann. Bad Girl Creek. 2002. 384p. pap. 13.00 (*0-7432-1771-3*, Simon & Schuster) Simon & Schuster.

—Bad Girl Creek: A Novel. l.t. ed. 2001. 529p. 29.95 o.p. (*1-58724-126-9*, Wheeler Publishing, Inc.) Gale Group.

—Bad Girl Creek: A Novel. 2001. 384p. 24.00 (*0-7432-0256-2*, Simon & Schuster) Simon & Schuster.

Mavrikis, Anna. A Doll for Amy. 2003. 260p. pap. 15.95 (*0-88739-466-3*) Creative Arts Bk. Co.

Miller, Vassar, ed. Despite This Flesh: The Disabled in Stories & Poems. 1985. 166p. 15.95 o.p. (*0-292-72449-7*); pap. 8.95 o.p. (*0-292-71550-1*) Univ. of Texas Pr.

Wells, Leslie. The Curing Season. 2001. 256p. 22.95 o.p. (*0-446-52693-2*) Warner Bks., Inc.

Wick, Lori. The Long Road Home. 1991. (Fireside Ser.). 224p. pap. 6.99 o.s.i (*0-89081-885-1*); 1997. (Place Called Home Ser.: Vol. 3). 192p. reprint ed. pap. 8.99 (*1-56507-590-0*) Harvest Hse. Pubs.

—The Long Road Home. l.t. ed. 2001. (Christian Romance Ser.). (Illus.). 288p. 25.95 o.p. (*0-7862-2956-X*) Thorndike Pr.

## S

### SERIAL MURDERERS—FICTION

Ablow, Keith Russell. Psychopath: A Novel. abr. ed. 2003. (Illus.). audio 25.95 (*1-55927-878-1*) Audio Renaissance.

—Psychopath: A Novel. 2003. 320p. 19.95 (*0-312-26671-5*) St. Martin's Pr.

Alwyn, Cynthia G. Scent of Murder. 2001. E-Book 23.95 (*1-59061-037-7*) Adobe Systems, Inc.

—Scent of Murder. 2001. 294p. 23.95 (*0-312-26559-X*, Saint Martin's Minotaur) St. Martin's Pr.

Ashford, Jeffrey. Loyal Disloyalty. 1998. 192p. 20.95 (*0-312-19918-X*, Saint Martin's Minotaur) St. Martin's Pr.

—Loyal Disloyalty. l.t. ed. 1999. (Mystery Ser.). 295p. 26.95 (*0-7862-2048-1*); (*0-7540-3895-5*); (*0-7540-3896-3*) Thorndike Pr.

Barth, Richard. Jumper. l.t. ed. 2001. 240p. 25.95 (*1-57490-343-8*) Beeler, Thomas T. Publisher.

—Jumper. 2000. 218p. 22.95 (*0-312-26608-1*, Saint Martin's Minotaur); E-Book 22.95 (*0-312-27610-9*) St. Martin's Pr.

Billingham, Mark. Sleepyhead. 2002. 320p. 24.95 (*0-06-621299-5*, Morrow, William & Co.) Morrow/Avon.

Block, Lawrence. Small Town. 2003. mass mkt. 139.90 (*0-06-057957-9*, HarperTorch) Morrow/Avon.

Braithwaite, Kent. The Wonderland Murders. 2000. 324p. pap. 14.95 (*1-891929-33-X*) Four Seasons Pubs.

Burke, Jan. Nine. 2003. 544p. mass mkt. 7.50 (*0-7434-4454-X*, Pocket); 2002. 384p. 24.00 (*0-7432-2389-6*, Simon & Schuster); 2002. E-Book 14.99 (*0-7432-3334-4*, Simon & Schuster) Simon & Schuster.

Campbell, Ramsey. Silent Children. 2000. 352p. reprint ed. 24.95 (*0-312-87056-6*, MHC 0149, Tor Bks.) Doherty, Tom Assocs., LLC.

Conant, Susan. Bride & Groom. 2004. 272p. 22.95 (*0-425-19412-4*) Berkley Publishing Group.

Connelly, Michael. A Darkness More Than Night. 2001. 432p. 25.95 o.p. (*0-316-15407-5*); 400p. E-Book 14.95 (*0-7595-0067-3*); 400p. E-Book 14.95 (*0-7595-9076-1*); 400p. E-Book 14.95 (*0-7595-4069-1*) Little Brown & Co.

—A Darkness More Than Night. l.t. ed. 608p. 2002. 30.95 (*0-7862-2821-0*); 2001. 31.95 (*0-7862-2820-2*) Thorndike Pr.

—A Darkness More Than Night. deluxe ltd. ed. 2000. 150.00 (*1-890885-10-X*) Trice, B.E. Publishing.

—A Darkness More Than Night. 2002. 488p. reprint ed. mass mkt. 7.99 (*0-446-66790-0*) Warner Bks., Inc.

Connor, Bernadette Y. The Parcel Express Murders. 2002. 239p. 22.00 (*0-9715838-0-3*); pap. 13.00 (*0-9715838-1-1*) Bee Con Bks.

Cooke, John Peyton. Torsos. 1994. 368p. 19.95 o.s.i (*0-89296-522-3*) Mysterious Pr.

—Torsos. 1995. 352p. mass mkt. 5.99 o.s.i (*0-446-40454-3*) Warner Bks., Inc.

Cray, David. Partners: A Novel of Crime. 2004. 320p. 25.00 (*0-7867-1292-9*, Carroll & Graf Pubs.) Avalon Publishing Group.

Deaver, Jeffery. The Devil's Teardrop: A Novel of the Last Night of the Century. l.t. ed. 2000. pap. 11.95 (*1-56895-982-6*, Wheeler Publishing, Inc.) Gale Group.

—The Devil's Teardrop: A Novel of the Last Night of the Century. l.t. ed. 2002. (Charnwood Large Print Ser.). 520p. 32.50 o.p. (*0-7089-9298-6*, Charnwood) Thorpe, F. A. Pubs. GBR. *Dist:* Ulverscroft Large Print Bks., Ltd., Ulverscroft Large Print Canada, Ltd.

—Die Tranen des Teufels. 2003. (GER.). 448p. pap. 23.00 (*1-4000-5510-5*) Random Hse. Information Group.

Denton, Bradley. Blackburn: A Novel. 1995. 304p. pap. 12.00 (*0-312-13029-5*) Picador.

—Blackburn: A Novel. 1993. 19.95 o.p. (*0-312-08705-5*) St. Martin's Pr.

Dorsey, Tim. Cadillac Beach. 2004. 352p. 24.95 (*0-06-052046-9*, Morrow, William & Co.) Morrow/Avon.

—The Stingray Shuffle. 2004. 400p. mass mkt. 7.50 (*0-06-055693-5*, HarperTorch); 2003. 320p. 24.95 (*0-06-052045-0*, Morrow, William & Co.) Morrow/Avon.

Edwards, Grace F. No Time to Die. 2000. (Mali Anderson Mystery Ser.). 240p. mass mkt. 5.99 (*0-553-57956-8*) Bantam Bks.

—No Time to Die. 1999. 272p. 22.95 o.s.i (*0-385-49247-2*) Doubleday Publishing.

Ellroy, James. Killer on the Road. 1999. 272p. pap. 13.00 (*0-380-80896-X*, Perennial) HarperTrade.

—Killer on the Road. 1986. 288p. mass mkt. 5.99 (*0-380-89934-5*, Avon Bks.) Morrow/Avon.

Farrow, David A. The Root of All Evil. 2002. E-Book 20.00 o.p. (*0-941711-54-4*); 1997. 350p. 23.95 (*0-941711-36-6*) Wyrick & Co.

Ferrell, David. Screwball. 2004. 384p. mass mkt. 7.50 (*0-06-008742-0*, HarperTorch); 2003. 320p. 23.95 (*0-06-008741-2*, Morrow, William & Co.) Morrow/Avon.

—Screwball: A Novel. 2004. 320p. pap. 13.95 (*0-06-072600-8*, Dark Alley) HarperTrade.

Finch, Phillip. F2F. 1997. 320p. mass mkt. 6.50 o.s.i (*0-553-57216-4*) Bantam Bks.

—F2F: The Ultimate Thriller of High Tech Terror. abr. ed. 1996. audio 17.00 (*0-671-52282-5*, 393930, Simon & Schuster Audioworks) Simon & Schuster Audio.

Frasier, Anne. Hush. 2002. (Illus.). 384p. mass mkt. 6.99 (*0-451-41031-9*, Onyx) NAL.

Gardner, Lisa. The Killing Hour. 2004. 448p. mass mkt. 7.50 (*0-553-84046-0*); 2003. 336p. 23.95 (*0-553-80252-6*); 2003. 368p. E-Book 19.50 (*0-553-89766-7*) Bantam Bks.

—The Killing Hour. l.t. ed. 2004. 656p. pap. 12.95 (*1-59413-029-9*, Large Print Pr.); 2003. 696p. 31.95 (*0-7862-5867-5*) Thorndike Pr.

—The Other Daughter. 10p. 2003. pap. 94.95 incl. audio compact disk (*0-7927-2901-3*); 2000. audio 84.95 (*0-7927-2356-2*, CSL 245, Chivers Sound Library) BBC Audiobooks America.

—The Other Daughter. 1999. 416p. mass mkt. 7.50 (*0-553-57679-8*) Bantam Bks.

—The Other Daughter. l.t. ed. (Thorndike/G. K. Hall Paperback Bestsellers Ser.). 2000. 523p. 28.95 (*0-7862-2291-3*); 1999. 619p. 31.95 (*0-7862-2290-5*) Thorndike Pr.

Gear, Kathleen O'Neal & Gear, W. Michael. The Summoning God. (Illus.). 366p. pap. 15.95 (*0-312-87639-4*, Forge Bks.); 2000. (Anasazia Mysteries Ser.: Vol. 2). (Illus.). 352p. 25.95 (*0-312-86532-5*, Forge Bks.); 2001. (Anasazi Ser.). 576p. reprint ed. mass mkt. 7.99 (*0-8125-4034-4*, Tor Bks.) Doherty, Tom Assocs., LLC.

Gerritsen, Tess. The Apprentice. 2003. 384p. mass mkt. 7.99 (*0-345-44786-7*); 2002. 352p. 24.95 (*0-345-44785-9*) Ballantine Bks.

—The Apprentice. l.t. ed. 2002. 30.95 (*1-58724-322-9*, Wheeler Publishing, Inc.) Gale Group.

Grey, Dorien. The 9th Man: A Gay Mystery. 2001. (Dick Hardesty Series). 155p. pap. 14.95 (*1-879194-88-0*) GLB Pubs.

Gutman, Amy. The Anniversary. 2003. 352p. 21.95 (*0-316-38120-9*) Little Brown & Co.

—The Anniversary. 2004. 432p. mass mkt. 7.50 (*0-446-61417-3*) Warner Bks., Inc.

Hall, James W. Body Language. 1999. E-Book 24.95 o.s.i (*0-312-20761-1*); 1998. 352p. 24.95 (*0-312-19243-6*) St. Martin's Pr.

—Body Language. l.t. ed. 1998. (Americana Ser.). 527p. 28.95 (*0-7862-1686-7*) Thorndike Pr.

Hamilton, Steve. A Cold Day in Paradise. l.t. ed. 2001. 354p. lib. bdg. 28.95 (*1-58547-136-4*) Ctr. Point Large Print.

—A Cold Day in Paradise. (Alex McKnight Mysteries Ser.). 2000. 320p. mass mkt. 6.99 (*0-312-96919-8*, St. Martin's Paperbacks); 1998. 288p. 22.95 (*0-312-19248-7*, Saint Martin's Minotaur) St. Martin's Pr.

—A Cold Day in Paradise: A Mystery, Set. unabr. ed. 1999. (Chivers Sound Library American Collections). audio 54.95 (*0-7927-2326-0*, CSL 215, Chivers Sound Library) BBC Audiobooks America.

Harper, Andrew. Red Angel. 2004. 368p. mass mkt. 6.99 (*0-8439-5275-X*, Leisure Bks.) Dorchester Publishing Co., Inc.

Harper, Brian. Shudder. 1994. 416p. mass mkt. 4.99 o.s.i (*0-451-17693-6*, Signet Bks.) NAL.

Harris, Thomas. The Silence of the Lambs. l.t. ed. 2001. 367p. lib. bdg. 28.95 (*1-58547-110-0*) Ctr. Point Large Print.

—The Silence of the Lambs. 1989. 4.99 o.p. (*0-517-00503-4*) Random Hse. Value Publishing.

Hart, Ellen. Immaculate Midnight: A Jane Lawless Mystery. E-Book 24.95 (*0-312-70728-2*); 2003. 336p. pap. 13.95 (*0-312-31365-9*, Saint Martin's Griffin); 2002. 384p. 24.95 (*0-312-26676-6*, Saint Martin's Minotaur) St. Martin's Pr.

Henry, Sue. Cold Company. l.t. ed. 2002. (Large Print Ser.). 27.95 (*1-57490-457-4*) Beeler, Thomas T. Publisher.

—Cold Company. 2002. (Alaska Mystery Ser.). (Illus.). 304p. 23.95 (*0-380-97882-2*, Morrow, William & Co.) Morrow/Avon.

Hooper, Kay. Out of the Shadows. 2000. (Shadows Trilogy Ser.). 368p. mass mkt. 7.50 (*0-553-57695-X*) Bantam Bks.

—Out of the Shadows. l.t. ed. 504p. 2002. pap. 28.95 (*0-7862-3060-6*); 2001. 31.95 (*0-7862-3059-2*) Thorndike Pr.

Hunter, Jessie. One Two Buckle My Shoe. 1998. 464p. mass mkt. 6.50 o.s.i (0-06-101325-0) HarperCollins Pubs.

—One Two Buckle My Shoe. 1997. 304p. 22.50 (0-684-83170-8, Simon & Schuster) Simon & Schuster.

Jones, Tayari. Leaving Atlanta. 272p. 2003. pap. 13.95 (0-446-69089-9); 2002. 23.95 (0-446-52830-7) Warner Bks., Inc.

Jordan, Oakley. Death's Parallel. 2002. 406p. pap. 16.95 (1-56825-078-9) Rainbow Bks., Inc.

Joyce, Brenda. The Chase. 2003. 29.95 (1-57490-482-5, Beeler Large Print Bks.) Beeler, Thomas T. Publisher.

—The Chase. E-Book 24.95 (0-312-70731-2); 2002. 384p. 24.95 (0-312-28449-7); 2003. 480p. reprint ed. mass mkt. 6.99 (0-312-98376-X, St. Martin's Paperbacks) St. Martin's Pr.

Kadow, Jeannine. Dead Tide. 2003. 400p. mass mkt. 7.50 (0-451-21069-7, Signet Bks.); 2002. 352p. 23.95 (0-451-20632-0) NAL.

Kaminsky, Stuart M. A Few Minutes Past Midnight. l.t. ed. 2002. 347p. 29.95 (0-7862-4118-7) Gale Group.

Katzenbach, John. State of Mind. 1998. 544p. mass mkt. 6.99 (0-345-42253-8); 1997. 409p. 24.00 o.s.i (0-345-38631-0, Ballantine Bks.) Ballantine Bks.

—State of Mind. l.t. ed. 1998. (Large Print Book Ser.). 26.95 o.p. (1-56895-528-6, Wheeler Publishing, Inc.) Gale Group.

Keating, H. R. F. The Hard Detective. l.t. ed. 2000. (G. K. Hall Nightingale Ser.). 263p. pap. 20.95 (0-7838-9256-X); (0-7540-4298-7); (0-7540-4297-9) Gale Group. (Macmillan Reference USA).

—The Hard Detective. 2000. 236p. 21.95 o.p. (0-312-24648-X, Saint Martin's Minotaur) St. Martin's Pr.

King, Stephen. Black House. 2003. 688p. pap. 15.95 (0-345-47063-X) Ballantine Bks.

King, Stephen & Straub, Peter. Black House. 2001. E-Book 19.95 (1-59061-169-1) Adobe Systems, Inc.

—Black House. 2002. 672p. mass mkt. (0-345-45925-3); mass mkt. 7.99 (0-345-44103-6, Ballantine Bks.) Ballantine Bks.

—Black House, 2 vols. deluxe ed. 2001. 225.00 (1-880418-52-5) Grant, Donald M. Pub., Inc.

—Black House. unabr. ed. 2001. audio 54.95 (0-7393-0010-5, RH Audio) Random Hse. Audio Publishing Group.

—Black House. l.t. ed. 2001. 1056p. 28.95 (0-375-43151-9) Random Hse. Large Print.

—Black House. 2002. 672p. mass mkt. 7.99 (0-345-45121-X); 2001. E-Book 19.95 (1-58836-054-7) Random Hse., Inc.

Kohout, Pavel. The Widow Killer. 2000. 400p. pap. 14.00 (0-312-25289-7) Picador.

—The Widow Killer: A Novel. Bermel, Neil, tr. 1998. (Illus.). 391p. 24.95 o.p. (0-312-19363-7) Picador.

—The Widow Killer: A Novel. 1999. mass mkt. (0-312-96920-1, St. Martin's Paperbacks) St. Martin's Pr.

—The Widow Killer: A Novel. Bermel, Neil, tr. 1999. E-Book 24.95 (0-312-24620-X) St. Martin's Pr.

Laird, Thomas. Cutter. 2001. 256p. 24.00 (0-7867-0944-8, Carroll & Graf Pubs.) Avalon Publishing Group.

—Cutter. l.t. ed. 2002. (General Ser.). 320p. pap. 24.95 (0-7862-4228-0) Thorndike Pr.

Lansdale, Joe R. The Bottoms. l.t. ed. 2001. (Wheeler Large Print Book Ser.). 401p. 28.95 o.p. (1-58724-093-9, Wheeler Publishing, Inc.) Gale Group.

—The Bottoms. 2000. 336p. 24.95 (0-89296-704-8); 304p. E-Book 14.95 (0-446-91367-7); E-Book 14.95 (0-446-93137-3); 304p. E-Book 14.95 (0-446-92859-3); E-Book 14.95 (0-446-96088-8); 304p. E-Book 14.95 (0-446-92368-0) Mysterious Pr.

—The Bottoms. ltd. unabr. ed. 2000. (Illus.). 350p. 150.00 (1-892284-60-X) Subterranean Pr.

—The Bottoms. 2001. 336p. reprint ed. pap. 13.95 (0-446-67792-2) Warner Bks., Inc.

—The Bottoms: Lettered Edition. deluxe unabr. ed. 2000. (Illus.). 350p. 400.00 (1-892284-61-8) Subterranean Pr.

Lasdun, James. The Horned Man: A Novel. 2002. 208p. 24.95 (0-393-00336-1) Norton, W. W. & Co., Inc.

Leigh, Robert. The Turner Journals. 1996. 288p. 22.95 (0-8027-3260-7) Walker & Co.

Lescroart, John. The Second Chair. 2004. 400p. 25.95 (0-525-94775-2, Dutton) Dutton/Plume.

Lish, Gordon. Dear Mr. Capote. 3rd ed. 1996. 264p. reprint ed. pap. 12.95 (1-56858-079-7) Four Walls Eight Windows.

—Dear Mr. Capote. 1983. 264p. o.p. (0-03-061477-5) Holt, Henry & Co.

Lovesey, Peter. The Reaper. 2002. 304p. pap. 12.00 (1-56947-308-0); 2001. 295p. 23.00 (1-56947-227-0) Soho Pr., Inc.

—The Reaper. l.t. ed. 2001. 368p. 28.95 o.p. (0-7862-3438-5) Thorndike Pr.

Maness, Larry. Strangler: A Jake Eaton Mystery. 1998. 192p. 19.95 o.p. (0-89141-568-8, Presidio Pr.) Ballantine Bks.

Margolin, Phillip. Wild Justice. 2002. E-Book 7.99 (0-06-621026-7); 2002. E-Book 7.99 (0-06-621025-9); 2001. mass mkt. 186.37 o.s.i (0-06-008372-7); 2001. E-Book 7.99 (0-06-018919-3); 2000. 464p. pap. 26.00 (0-06-019913-X) HarperCollins Pubs.

—Wild Justice. 2000. 384p. 26.00 (0-06-019624-6, HarperCollins) HarperTrade.

Marshall, Michael. The Straw Men. 2002. 373p. pap. (0-00-715186-1) HarperCollins Pubs.

Masters, Priscilla. A Fatal Cut. l.t. ed. 2001. (Ulverscroft Large Print Ser.). 424p. 32.50 (0-7089-4448-5) Ulverscroft Large Print Bks., Ltd.

Matthews, Christine & Randisi, Robert J. Murder Is the Deal of the Day. 2003. (WWL Mystery Ser.: No. 472). 256p. mass mkt. (0-373-26472-0, Worldwide Library) Harlequin Enterprises, Ltd.

—Murder Is the Deal of the Day. 1998. 240p. 22.95 o.p. (0-312-19928-7, Saint Martin's Minotaur) St. Martin's Pr.

McDermid, Val. Killing the Shadows. l.t. ed. 2002. (Wheeler Large Print Book Ser.). 28.95 (1-58724-184-6, Wheeler Publishing, Inc.) Gale Group.

—Killing the Shadows. E-Book 24.95 (0-312-70297-3); 2002. 496p. mass mkt. 6.99 (0-312-98338-7, St. Martin's Paperbacks) St. Martin's Pr.

—The Last Temptation. 2002. (Illus.). 431p. (0-00-226109-X) HarperCollins Pubs.

—The Last Temptation. 2003. 496p. mass mkt. 6.99 (0-312-98631-9, St. Martin's Paperbacks) St. Martin's Pr.

McGarrity, Michael. Everyone Dies. l.t. ed. 2004. lib. bdg. 28.95 (1-58547-374-X, Platinum) Ctr. Point Large Print.

—Everyone Dies. 2003. (Kevin Kerney Novel Ser.). 336p. 23.95 (0-525-94761-2, Dutton) Dutton/Plume.

—Everyone Dies. 2004. 352p. mass mkt. 6.99 (0-451-41147-1, Onyx) NAL.

McGuire, Christine. Until Judgment Day. 2003. 368p. mass mkt. 6.99 (0-7434-2230-9, Pocket) Simon & Schuster.

McLaren, Philip. Scream Black Murder: A WorldKrime Mystery. 2002. 288p. 21.95 (1-890768-42-1, Intrigue Pr.) Corvus Publishing.

Miano, Mark. The Street Where She Lived: A Michael Carpo Mystery. 1998. (Michael Carpo Mystery Ser.). 320p. 20.00 o.s.i (1-57566-270-1, Kensington Bks.) Kensington Publishing Corp.

Miller, Rex. Butcher. Grad, Doug, ed. 1994. 320p. mass mkt. 5.50 (0-671-86882-9, Pocket) Simon & Schuster.

—Butcher. 2002. 273p. pap. 6.99 (1-58586-076-X); 2000. E-Book 6.99 (1-58586-235-5); 2000. 273p. E-Book 6.99 (1-58586-074-3); 2000. E-Book 6.99 (1-58586-075-1) ereads.com.

—Chaingang. Grad, Doug, ed. 1992. 320p. mass mkt. 4.99 (0-671-74847-5, Pocket) Simon & Schuster.

—Chaingang. 2002. 217p. pap. 6.99 (1-58586-079-4); 2000. 6.99 (1-58586-236-3); 2000. E-Book 6.99 (1-58586-078-6); 2000. 217p. E-Book 6.99 (1-58586-077-8) ereads.com.

—Savant. Grad, Doug, ed. 1994. 288p. mass mkt. 5.99 (0-671-74848-3, Pocket) Simon & Schuster.

—Savant. E-Book 6.99 (0-7592-0788-7); 2000. pap. 19.95 (1-58586-150-2); 2000. E-Book 6.99 (1-58586-271-1); 2000. E-Book 6.99 (1-58586-149-9); 2000. E-Book 6.99 (1-58586-148-0) ereads.com.

—Slob. 1988. mass mkt. 4.95 o.p. (0-451-40065-8, Onyx); 1987. 304p. mass mkt. 3.95 o.p. (0-451-15005-8, Signet Bks.) NAL.

—Slob. 2002. 168p. pap. 6.99 (1-58586-155-3); 2000. E-Book 6.99 (1-58586-154-5); 2000. E-Book 6.99 (1-58586-273-8); 1987. 168p. E-Book 6.99 (1-58586-153-7) ereads.com.

—Stone Shadow. 1989. mass mkt. 3.95 o.p. (0-451-40164-6, 036, Onyx) NAL.

—Stone Shadow. E-Book 6.99 (0-7592-0797-6); 2000. pap. 19.95 (1-58586-164-2); 2000. E-Book 6.99 (1-58586-163-4); 2000. E-Book 6.99 (1-58586-280-0); 2000. E-Book 6.99 (1-58586-162-6) ereads.com.

Mills, Kyle. Burn Factor. 2001. audio 64.00 (0-7366-6194-8) Books on Tape, Inc.

—Burn Factor. 2001. 368p. 25.00 (0-06-019334-4); 576p. pap. 25.00 (0-06-018558-9) HarperCollins Pubs.

—Burn Factor. 2002. 432p. mass mkt. 7.99 (0-06-109803-5, HarperTorch) Morrow/Avon.

Monsour, Theresa. Road Kill. 2004. 320p. 24.95 (0-399-15156-7) Putnam Publishing Group, The.

Montanari, Richard. Deviant Way. 1997. 336p. mass mkt. 6.50 (0-671-51109-2, Pocket); 1995. 288p. 22.00 o.p. (0-684-80357-7, Simon & Schuster) Simon & Schuster.

Niles, Chris. Hell's Kitchen. 2001. 280p. pap. 15.95 (1-888451-21-1) Akashic Bks.

O'Brien, Edna. In the Forest. 2002. 264p. tchr. ed. 24.00 (0-618-19730-3) Houghton Mifflin Co.

—In the Forest. 2003. 272p. pap. 13.00 (0-618-33965-5, Mariner Bks.) Houghton Mifflin Co. Trade & Reference Div.

—In the Forest. l.t. ed. 2003. 314p. 28.95 (0-7862-5728-8) Thorndike Pr.

O'Connor, Edward. The Yeare's Midnight. 2002. 256p. 23.00 (0-7867-1028-4, Carroll & Graf Pubs.) Avalon Publishing Group.

Parrish, P. J. Dead of Winter. 2001. 416p. (Orig.). mass mkt. 6.99 (0-7860-1189-0, Pinnacle Bks.) Kensington Publishing Corp.

Patterson, James. Cat & Mouse. 1997. 400p. 24.95 o.p. (0-316-69329-4) Little Brown & Co.

—Kiss the Girls. l.t. ed. 2001. 432p. 31.95 o.p. (0-7838-9437-6, Macmillan Reference USA) Gale Group.

—Kiss the Girls. 2002. E-Book 4.95 (0-7595-4718-1) Time Warner Bk. Group.

—Kiss the Girls. 2000. 496p. reprint ed. pap. 13.95 (0-446-67738-8) Warner Bks., Inc.

—1st to Die. 2001. 432p. 26.95 o.p. (0-316-66600-9) Little Brown & Co.

—1st to Die. l.t. ed. 2001. 464p. 32.95 (0-7862-3291-9); pap. 29.95 (0-7862-3292-7); (0-7540-2486-5); (0-7540-1631-5) Thorndike Pr.

—1st to Die. 2001. E-Book 4.95 (0-7595-8434-6) Time Warner Bk. Group.

—1st to Die. 2001. 432p. pap. 16.00 (0-446-67842-2); 2002. 488p. reprint ed. mass mkt. 7.99 (0-446-61003-8) Warner Bks., Inc.

—1st to Die. 2001. E-Book 4.95 (0-7595-6427-2) ereads.com.

—2nd Chance. 2002. 400p. pap. 16.00 (0-446-67876-7) Warner Bks., Inc.

Patterson, James & Gross, Andrew. 2nd Chance. 2002. 400p. 26.95 o.p. (0-316-69320-0); 512p. 26.95 o.p. (0-316-69597-1) Little Brown & Co.

—2nd Chance. 2003. 432p. reprint ed. mass mkt. 7.99 (0-446-61279-0) Warner Bks., Inc.

Peace, David. Nineteen Eighty. 2001. (Red Riding Quartet Ser.: Bk. 3). 382p. 24.00 (1-85242-683-7) Serpent's Tail Ltd. GBR. Dist: Consortium Bk. Sales & Distribution.

—Nineteen Eighty Three. 2003. (Red Riding Quartet Ser.: Vol. 4). 416p. pap. 16.00 (1-85242-684-5) Serpent's Tail Ltd. GBR. Dist: Consortium Bk. Sales & Distribution.

—Nineteen Seventy Seven. 2001. (Red Riding Quartet Ser.: Bk. 2). 344p. pap. 14.00 (1-85242-639-X) Serpent's Tail Ltd. GBR. Dist: Consortium Bk. Sales & Distribution.

Pearson, Ridley. Probable Cause. 1991. 401p. mass mkt. 6.99 (0-312-92385-6, St. Martin's Paperbacks); 1990. 320p. 18.95 o.p. (0-312-03914-X) St. Martin's Pr.

—Probable Cause. l.t. ed. 2000. (Basic Ser.). (Illus.). 501p. 29.95 (0-7862-2849-0) Thorndike Pr.

—Undercurrents. 2000. E-Book 4.99 (1-58910-004-2) PreviewPort.com.

—Undercurrents. 1992. mass mkt. 6.99 (0-312-92958-7, St. Martin's Paperbacks); 1989. mass mkt. 4.95 o.s.i (0-312-91485-7, St. Martin's Paperbacks); 1988. 416p. 18.95 o.p. (0-312-01841-X) St. Martin's Pr.

Pennac, Daniel. Monsieur Malaussene. l.t. ed. 1996. (French Ser.). (FRE.). Vol. 1. 450p. pap. 30.99 o.p. (2-84011-150-0); Vol. 2. 419p. pap. 30.99 o.p. (2-84011-151-9) Feryane, SA, Editions FRA. Dist: Ulverscroft Large Print Bks., Ltd., Ulverscroft Large Print Canada, Ltd.

—Monsieur Malaussene. 2003. 368p. pap. (1-84343-020-7) Harvill Pr., The GBR. Dist: Trafalgar Square.

Perry, Thomas. Pursuit. 2003. 416p. mass mkt. 7.50 (0-8041-1543-5, Ballantine Bks.) Ballantine Bks.

—Pursuit. l.t. ed. 2002. 715p. 28.95 (0-7862-4209-4) Gale Group.

Pozzessere, Heather G. If Looks Could Kill. 1997. 48p. mass mkt. (1-55166-285-X, 0-66285-8, Mira Bks.) Harlequin Enterprises, Ltd.

Preston, Douglas J. & Child, Lincoln. The Cabinet of Curiosities. 2003. 656p. mass mkt. 7.99 (0-446-61123-9); 2002. 480p. 25.95 (0-446-53022-0) Warner Bks., Inc.

Pye, Michael. Taking Lives. 2004. 304p. pap. 13.00 (1-4000-7573-4, Vintage) Knopf Publishing Group.

—Taking Lives. l.t. ed. 1999. (Basic Ser.). 535p. 27.95 (0-7862-2096-1) Thorndike Pr.

Queen, Ellery. A Study in Terror. l.t. ed. 2001. 192p. pap. 24.95 (0-7838-9485-6); (0-7540-4585-4); (0-7540-4586-2) Gale Group. (Macmillan Reference USA).

Rankin, Ian. Black & Blue. unabr. ed. 1998. audio 80.00 (0-7366-4176-9, 4675) Books on Tape, Inc.

—Black & Blue. Date not set. E-Book (0-312-70694-4); 1999. (Black & Blue Ser.: Vol. 1). 352p. mass mkt. 6.99 (0-312-96677-6, St. Martin's Paperbacks); 1997. (Inspector Rebus Novel Ser.). 394p. 24.95 (0-312-16783-0, Saint Martin's Minotaur) St. Martin's Pr.

—Black & Blue: An Inspector Rebus Novel. l.t. ed. 1998. (Mystery Ser.). 623p. 28.95 (0-7838-8443-5) Thorndike Pr.

Rendell, Ruth. Adam & Eve & Pinch Me. 2003. 368p. pap. 13.00 (1-4000-3118-4, Vintage) Knopf Publishing Group.

—Adam & Eve & Pinch Me. l.t. ed. 2002. 604p. 29.95 (0-7862-3815-1) Thorndike Pr.

Rice, Luanne. The Secret Hour. 2004. 432p. mass mkt. 7.50 (0-553-58401-4); 2003. 352p. 22.95 (0-553-80224-0) Bantam Bks.

—The Secret Hour. 2003. (Core Ser.). 482p. 31.95 (0-7862-5371-1) Thorndike Pr.

Ruth, Jenifer. The Protector. 2003. 258p. 26.95 (1-59414-027-8, Five Star) Gale Group.

Sacks, Jen. Nice. 1999. 256p. mass mkt. 5.99 (0-312-96925-2, St. Martin's Paperbacks); 1998. 208p. 21.95 (0-312-19306-8) St. Martin's Pr.

Sanderson, Mark. Audacious Perversion. 1999. 236p. pap. 14.95 (1-899344-32-2) DuFour, Howard.

Santlofer, Jonathan. The Death Artist: A Novel of Suspense. 2003. 448p. mass mkt. 7.50 (0-06-000442-8, HarperTorch); 2002. 352p. 24.95 (0-06-000441-X, Morrow, William & Co.) Morrow/Avon.

Stevens, Shane. By Reason of Insanity. 1990. 540p. mass mkt. 5.95 o.p. (0-88184-609-0); 2nd ed. 1997. 576p. pap. 13.95 (0-7867-0463-2) Avalon Publishing Group. (Carroll & Graf Pubs.).

—By Reason of Insanity. 1980. pap. 2.75 o.p. (0-440-11028-9) Dell Publishing.

—By Reason of Insanity. 1979. 11.95 o.s.i (0-671-24058-7, Simon & Schuster) Simon & Schuster.

Sturz, James. Sasso. 2002. 306p. 25.95 (0-8027-3372-7) Walker & Co.

Taylor, Andrew. The Four Last Things. 1997. (Roth Trilogy Ser.: Vol. 1). 304p. 22.95 (0-312-16845-4, Saint Martin's Minotaur) St. Martin's Pr.

—The Office of the Dead. 2000. (Roth Trilogy Ser.: Vol. 3). 352p. 24.95 (0-312-20348-9, Saint Martin's Minotaur) St. Martin's Pr.

Thayer, Steve. The Weatherman. 1996. 416p. mass mkt. 7.99 (0-451-18438-6, Signet Bks.) NAL.

—The Weatherman, Set. abr. ed. 1995. audio 16.95 (1-879371-88-X, 391877) Publishing Mills, Inc., The.

—The Weatherman, unabr. ed. 1995. audio 91.00 (0-7887-0267-X, 94476E7) Recorded Bks., LLC.

—The Weatherman. 1995. 22.95 (0-670-77309-3); 464p. 21.95 o.s.i (0-670-84958-8, Viking) Viking Penguin.

Thorne, Tamara. Eternity. 2001. 4p. mass mkt. 5.99 (0-7860-1310-9, Pinnacle Bks.) Kensington Publishing Corp.

Vasas-Brown, Cathy. Every Wickedness. 2002. 432p. mass mkt. (0-7704-2864-9) Seal Pr.

Walker, Robert W. Bitter Instinct. 400p. 2003. mass mkt. 6.99 (0-515-13569-0, Jove); 2001. 21.95 o.s.i (0-425-17963-X) Berkley Publishing Group.

Walter, Jess. Over Tumbled Graves. 2002. 416p. mass mkt. 7.50 (0-06-103200-X); 2000. pap. 13.00 (0-06-098867-3) HarperCollins Pubs.

—Over Tumbled Graves. 2001. (0-06-039417-X); 384p. 25.00 (0-06-039386-6) HarperTrade. (Regan-Books).

Waterhouse, Jane. Shadow Walk. 1999. (Prime Crime Mysteries Ser.). 320p. reprint ed. mass mkt. 5.99 o.s.i (0-425-16946-4, Prime Crime) Berkley Publishing Group.

—Shadow Walk. 1997. 320p. 23.95 o.p. (0-399-14305-X, G. P. Putnam's Sons) Penguin Group (USA) Inc.

Westlake, Donald E. The Ax. unabr. collector's ed. 1997. (Dortmunder Ser.). audio 56.00 (0-7366-3774-5, 4447) Books on Tape, Inc.

—The Ax. 1997. 288p. 22.50 o.p. (0-89296-587-8) Mysterious Pr.

—The Ax. 1998. mass mkt. (0-446-40434-9, Mysterious Pr. Paperback Bks.); mass mkt. 188.73 (0-446-16658-8); 352p. reprint ed. mass mkt. 6.99 (0-446-60608-1) Warner Bks., Inc.

White, Stephen. Blinded. 2004. 400p. 24.95 (0-385-33620-9, Delacorte Pr.) Dell Publishing.

Wilson, Robert. The Blind Man of Seville. 2003. 448p. 25.00 (0-15-100835-3) Harcourt Trade Pubs.

Woods, Stuart. Chiefs. 1982. pap. 3.95 o.p. (0-553-24080-3) Bantam Bks.

—Chiefs. 1999. 432p. mass mkt. 7.99 (0-380-70347-5, Avon Bks.) Morrow/Avon.

—Chiefs. 1981. 14.95 o.s.i (0-393-01461-4) Norton, W. W. & Co., Inc.

—Chiefs. l.t. ed. 2001. (Thorndike Basic Ser.). 701p. 30.95 (0-7862-3150-5) Thorndike Pr.

## SLAVES—FICTION

The Adventures of Tom Sawyer. 2001. 8.97 (0-673-58321-X) Addison-Wesley Longman, Inc.

The Adventures of Tom Sawyer. 2001. E-Book 2.95 (1-58853-036-1) Sensory Publishing, Inc.

Arthur, Kevyn A. The View from Belmont. 1997. 230p. pap. 14.95 (1-900715-02-3) Peepal Tree Pr., Ltd. GBR. Dist: Independent Pubs. Group, Paul & Co. Pubs. Consortium, Inc.

Balewa, Alhaji S. Shaihu Umar: A Historical Novel about Slavery in Africa. Hiskett, Mervin, tr. 1989. (Topics in World History Ser.). (Illus.). 144p. 18.95 (*1-55876-012-1*); 124p. pap. 9.95 (*1-55876-006-7*) Wiener, Markus Pubs., Inc.

Barnes, Steven. Lion's Blood: A Novel of Slavery & Freedom in an Alternate America. 2003. 624p. mass mkt. 6.99 (*0-446-61221-9*, Aspect) Warner Bks., Inc.

Behn, Aphra. Oroonoko. Todd, Janet M., ed. & tr. by. 2004. 144p. pap. 9.00 (*0-14-043988-9*, Penguin Classics) Viking Penguin.

—Oroonoko: The Royal Slave. 1997. (Critical Editions Ser.). (Illus.). v, 90p. pap. 8.95 (*0-393-31205-4*) Norton, W. W. & Co., Inc.

Bennerson, Denise. Daniel & the 150th Emancipation Celebration. 2001. (Illus.). 11p. (J). 4.00 (*0-9646279-5-7*) Bennerson, Denise.

Brink, André. A Chain of Voices. 1983. 528p. pap. 23.00 o.s.i (*0-14-006538-5*, Penguin Bks.) Penguin Group (USA) Inc.

Brown, William Wells. Clotel or the President's Daughter: A Narrative of Slave Life in the United States. 1969. (American Negro). reprint ed. 27.95 (*0-405-01853-3*) Ayer Co. Pubs., Inc.

—Clotel or the President's Daughter: A Narrative of Slave Life in the United States. 2000. (Bedford Cultural Editions Ser.). (Illus.). xv, 527p. pap. text 8.50 (*0-312-15265-5*) Bedford/Saint Martin's.

—Clotel or the President's Daughter: A Narrative of Slave Life in the United States. 1985. (Muckrakers Ser.). reprint ed. pap. text 6.50 o.p. (*0-89197-701-5*); lib. bdg. 19.95 o.p. (*0-8398-0176-9*) Irvington Pubs.

—Clotel or the President's Daughter: A Narrative of Slave Life in the United States. 2000. (Bedford Cultural Editions Ser.). (Illus.). xv, 527p. 45.00 o.p. (*0-312-22758-2*) Palgrave Macmillan.

—Clotel or the President's Daughter: A Narrative of Slave Life in the United States. 2001. (Modern Library Classics). 256p. pap. 10.95 (*0-679-78323-7*, Modern Library) Random House Adult Trade Publishing Group.

—Clotel or the President's Daughter: A Narrative of Slave Life in the United States. 1996. (American History Through Literature Ser.). 216p. (C). 76.95 (*1-56324-803-4*); (Illus.). pap. 22.95 (*1-56324-804-2*) Sharpe, M.E. Inc.

—Clotelle: Or, the Colored Heroine. 1977. (Black Heritage Library Collection). 11.95 (*0-8369-8517-6*) Ayer Co. Pubs., Inc.

—Clotelle: Or, the Colored Heroine. Wills, Susan, ed. rev. ed. 1998. (Illus.). 116p. (C). pap. 19.95 (*1-58112-899-1*) Dissertation.com.

—Clotelle: The Coloured Heroine. 1999. E-Book 2.49 (*1-58627-252-7*) Electric Umbrella Publishing.

Browne, Martha G. Autobiography of a Female Slave. 1970. 401p. reprint ed. 45.00 o.s.i (*0-8371-2194-9*, GRS&) Greenwood Publishing Group, Inc.

—Autobiography of a Female Slave. 1991. (American Biography Ser.). 401p. reprint ed. lib. bdg. 89.00 (*0-7812-8046-X*) Reprint Services Corp.

Courlander, Harold. The African. 1977. 7.95 o.s.i (*0-517-50680-7*, Crown) Crown Publishing Group.

—The African. 1993. 320p. pap. 12.95 o.p. (*0-8050-3000-X*, Owl Bks.) Holt, Henry & Co.

Crafts, Hannah. The Bondwoman's Narrative. l.t. ed. 2002. (African American Ser.). 29.95 (*0-7862-4471-2*) Thorndike Pr.

—The Bondwoman's Narrative. Gates, Henry Louis, Jr., ed. 2002. (Illus.). 416p. 24.95 (*0-446-53008-5*) Warner Bks., Inc.

—The Bondwoman's Narrative. Gates, Henry Louis, Jr., ed. & intro. by. fac. ed. 2003. (Illus.). 384p. 50.00 (*0-446-53173-1*) Warner Bks., Inc.

—The Bondwoman's Narrative. Gates, Henry Louis, Jr., ed. 2003. 464p. reprint ed. pap. 14.95 (*0-446-69029-5*) Warner Bks., Inc.

Crooks, Paul. Ancestors. 2002. (Illus.). 296p. pap. 12.95 (*1-901969-07-X*) BlackAmber Bks. GBR. *Dist:* SPD-Small Pr. Distribution.

—Ancestors. l.t. ed. 2003. (Ulverscroft Large Print Ser.). 456p. 32.50 (*0-7089-4791-3*) Thorpe, F. A. Pubs. GBR. *Dist:* Ulverscroft Large Print Bks., Ltd., Ulverscroft Large Print Canada, Ltd.

D'Aguiar, Fred. Feeding the Ghosts. 1999. 240p. o.p. (*0-88001-623-X*, Ecco) HarperTrade.

De Beaumont, Gustave. Marie, or Slavery in the United States. 1998. (Race in the Americas Ser.). 300p. pap. text 19.95 (*0-8018-6064-4*) Johns Hopkins Univ. Pr.

DeJarnett, Don Patrick. I Cry But I Shed No Tears. 2000. 136p. pap. 17.95 (*1-56167-587-3*) American Literary Pr., Inc.

Griffith, Mattie. Autobiography of a Female Slave. 1998. 408p. 48.00 (*1-57806-046-X*); pap. 18.00 (*1-57806-047-8*) Univ. Pr. of Mississippi. (A Banner Bk.).

Hauger, Torill Thorstad. Escape from the Vikings. Hamnes, Lisa, ed. Born, Anne, tr. from NOR. 2000. Orig. Title: Flukten Fra Vikingene. (Illus.). 175p. (J). (gr. 4-12). pap. (*1-57534-013-5*) Skandisk, Inc.

Hearn, Lafcadio. Youma: The Story of a West Indian Slave. E-Book 3.95 (*0-594-02347-5*) 1873 Pr.

—Youma: The Story of a West Indian Slave. reprint ed. 45.00 (*0-404-03208-7*) AMS Pr., Inc.

—Youma: The Story of a West Indian Slave. 1890. 193p. (YA). reprint ed. pap. text 28.00 (*1-4047-6737-1*) Classic Textbooks.

—Youma: The Story of a West Indian Slave. 1992. (BCL1-PS American Literature Ser.). 193p. reprint ed. lib. bdg. 69.00 (*0-7812-6737-4*) Reprint Services Corp.

Johnson, Charles. Oxherding Tale. 1995. 224p. pap. 12.95 o.s.i (*0-452-27503-2*, Plume) Dutton/Plume.

—Oxherding Tale. 1984. 192p. pap. 9.95 o.p. (*0-8021-5051-9*, Grove Pr.) Grove/Atlantic, Inc.

—Oxherding Tale. 1982. 192p. 15.00 o.p. (*0-253-16607-1*) Indiana Univ. Pr.

—Soulcatcher: Twelve Powerful Tales about Slavery. 2001. (Harvest Original Ser.). 132p. pap. 12.00 (*0-15-601112-3*, Harvest Bks.) Harcourt Trade Pubs.

Jones, Edward P. The Known World. unabr. ed. 2003. audio 39.95 (*0-06-056943-3*) HarperCollins Pubs.

—The Known World. 2003. 400p. 24.95 (*0-06-055754-0*, Amistad Pr.) HarperTrade.

Karlin, Wayne. The Wished-For Country. 2002. (Illus.). 340p. pap. 16.95 (*1-880684-89-6*) Curbstone Pr.

Lim, Catherine. The Bondmaid. 1997. 384p. 24.95 (*0-87951-790-5*) Overlook Pr., The.

—The Bondmaid. 1998. pap. (*0-446-67475-3*); 368p. mass mkt. 6.99 (*0-446-60734-7*) Warner Bks., Inc.

Mann, Mary Peabody. Juanita: A Romance of Real Life in Cuba Fifty Years Ago. Ard, Patricia M., ed. & intro. by. 2000. (New World Studies). (Illus.). xlvii, 222p. 55.00 (*0-8139-1955-X*); pap. 18.50 (*0-8139-1956-8*) Univ. Pr. of Virginia.

Mezlekia, Nega. The God Who Begat a Jackal. 2001. (Illus.). 288p. pap. (*0-14-100662-5*) Penguin Group (USA) Inc.

—The God Who Begat a Jackal. 2002. (Illus.). 256p. 23.00 (*0-312-28701-1*) Picador.

—The God Who Begat a Jackal: A Novel. 2003. 256p. pap. 13.00 (*0-312-30996-1*) Picador.

Myers, Mildred D. Miss Emily: Emily Howland, Teacher of Freed Slaves, Suffragist & Friend of Susan B. Anthony & Harriet Tubman. 1998. (Illus.). 240p. 14.95 (*1-881539-20-2*) Tabby Hse. Bks.

Philbrick, Rodman. Coffins. 320p. mass mkt. 6.99 (*0-8125-6651-3*, Tor Bks.); E-Book 23.95 (*0-312-70547-6*, Tor Bks.); 2002. 320p. 23.95 (*0-312-87273-9*, Forge Bks.) Doherty, Tom Assocs., LLC.

Rizzo, Kay D. Annie's Trust. 2001. (Serenity Inn Ser.: Vol. 6). 280p. pap. 7.99 (*0-8054-2132-7*) Broadman & Holman Pubs.

Robinson, Derek. Kentucky Blues. 2003. 544p. pap. 8.95 (*0-304-36566-1*); 2002. 520p. 27.50 (*0-304-36182-8*) Cassell P L C GBR. *Dist:* Trafalgar Square.

Ross, David W. Savage Plains. 1996. 480p. (Orig.). mass mkt. 5.99 (*0-380-78324-X*, Avon Bks.) Morrow/Avon.

Stockenberg, Antoinette. Beloved. 1993. 400p. mass mkt. 5.50 o.s.i (*0-440-21330-4*) Dell Publishing.

Stowe, Harriet Beecher. Uncle Tom's Cabin. 1997. (Classics Illustrated Notes). (Illus.). pap. text 4.99 (*1-57840-060-0*) Acclaim Bks.

—Uncle Tom's Cabin. 1997. (C). pap. text (*0-321-02606-3*) Addison-Wesley Educational Pubs., Inc.

—Uncle Tom's Cabin. 29.95 (*0-8488-0637-9*) Amereon, Ltd.

—Uncle Tom's Cabin. 1982. (Bantam Classics Ser.). 544p. reprint ed. mass mkt. 5.95 (*0-553-21218-4*) Bantam Dell Publishing Group.

—Uncle Tom's Cabin. E-Book 5.00 (*0-7607-1294-8*) Barnes & Noble, Inc.

—Uncle Tom's Cabin. 1982. reprint ed. lib. bdg. 27.95 (*0-89966-378-8*) Buccaneer Bks., Inc.

—Uncle Tom's Cabin. E-Book 2.49 (*1-58627-625-5*) Electric Umbrella Publishing.

—Uncle Tom's Cabin. Meserve, Walter J. & Meserve, Mollie A., eds. 1999. (Fateful Lightning Ser.). 75p. (C). 7.95 (*0-937657-49-2*) Feedback Theatrebooks & Prospero Pr.

—Uncle Tom's Cabin. 2003. (Barnes & Noble Classics Ser.). 560p. mass mkt. 5.95 (*1-59308-038-7*) Fine Communications.

—Uncle Tom's Cabin. l.t. ed. 1994. 688p. pap. 15.95 (*0-8161-5893-2*, Macmillan Reference USA) Gale Group.

—Uncle Tom's Cabin. 1970. 480p. mass mkt. 6.50 (*0-06-080618-4*, Perennial) HarperTrade.

—Uncle Tom's Cabin, 001. 1972. (Riverside Library). 512p. tchr. ed. 29.95 o.p. (*0-395-08129-7*) Houghton Mifflin Co.

—Uncle Tom's Cabin. 1995. (Everyman's Library). 538p. 20.00 (*0-679-44365-7*) Knopf, Alfred A. Inc.

—Uncle Tom's Cabin. 1991. E-Book 1.95 (*1-58515-015-0*) MesaView, Inc.

—Uncle Tom's Cabin. 1968. mass mkt. 0.75 o.p. (*0-451-50322-8*, Signet Classics); 1968. mass mkt. 0.75 o.p. (*0-451-50393-7*, Signet Classics); 1968. mass mkt. 0.85 o.p. (*0-451-50369-4*, Signet Classics); 1966. mass mkt. 0.95 o.p. (*0-451-50714-2*, Signet Classics); 1966. mass mkt. 2.25 o.p. (*0-451-51755-5*, Signet Classics); 1966. mass mkt. 2.75 o.p. (*0-451-51973-6*, Signet Classics); 1966. mass mkt. 2.75 o.p. (*0-451-51611-7*, Signet Classics); 1966. mass mkt. 1.50 o.p. (*0-451-51009-7*, Signet Classics); 1966. mass mkt. 1.95 o.p. (*0-451-51182-4*, Signet Classics); 1966. mass mkt. 2.25 o.p. (*0-451-51473-4*, Signet Classics); 1998. 512p. mass mkt. 5.95 (*0-451-52670-8*, Penguin Classics) NAL.

—Uncle Tom's Cabin. Yellin, Jean F., ed. 1998. (Oxford World's Classics Ser.). 576p. pap. 7.95 (*0-19-282787-1*) Oxford Univ. Pr., Inc.

—Uncle Tom's Cabin. (Modern Library Ser.). 1996. 656p. 19.95 (*0-679-60200-3*); 1985. 552p. 20.00 o.s.i (*0-394-60527-6*) Random Hse., Inc.

—Uncle Tom's Cabin. 1999. (Notable American Authors Ser.). reprint ed. lib. bdg. 125.00 (*0-7812-8957-2*) Reprint Services Corp.

—Uncle Tom's Cabin. 512p. 2004. mass mkt. 5.95 (*0-7434-8766-4*); 2005. (Illus.). reprint ed. pap. 5.99 (*0-7434-2190-6*) Simon & Schuster. (Pocket).

—Uncle Tom's Cabin. l.t. ed. 1993. 688p. lib. bdg. 22.95 (*0-8161-5714-6*) Thorndike Pr.

—Uncle Tom's Cabin. 1981. 12.00 (*0-606-02474-3*) Turtleback Bks.

—Uncle Tom's Cabin. Douglas, Ann, ed. & intro. by. 1981. (Penguin American Library). 640p. pap. 8.95 (*0-14-039003-0*, Penguin Classics) Viking Penguin.

—Uncle Tom's Cabin. 1997. (Classics Library). 432p. pap. 3.95 o.s.i (*1-85326-575-6*, 5756WW) Wordsworth Editions, Ltd. GBR. *Dist:* Combined Publishing.

Twain, Mark. Huckleberry Finn. Date not set. pap. text (*0-17-557047-7*) Addison-Wesley Longman, Inc.

—Huckleberry Finn. 1997. (Cyber Classics Ser.). 317p. pap. 14.95 incl. disk (*1-55701-199-0*); 435p. pap. 19.95 (*1-55701-228-8*) BNI Pubns., Inc.

—Huckleberry Finn. l.t. ed. 1997. 435p. pap. 19.95 (*1-58855-015-X*) Cyber Classics, Inc.

—Huckleberry Finn. 1942. 112p. pap. 5.60 (*0-87129-839-2*, H35) Dramatic Publishing Co.

—Huckleberry Finn. 1998. (SPA.). 384p. (*84-08-00303-8*) GeoPlaneta, Editorial, S. A.

—Huckleberry Finn. l.t. ed. 1995. 507p. lib. bdg. 26.00 (*0-939495-76-7*); 1998. 320p. reprint ed. lib. bdg. 25.00 (*1-58287-038-1*) North Bks.

—Huckleberry Finn. Teresa Agnes, ed. Heller, Rudolf, tr. 1979. (SPA., Illus.). 64p. pap. text 3.95 (*0-88301-450-5*) Pendulum Pr., Inc.

—Huckleberry Finn. 1985. 366p. 14.50 o.s.i (*0-394-60521-7*) Random Hse., Inc.

—Huckleberry Finn: Custom Edition. deluxe ed. 1983. 1000.00 o.p. (*0-8103-1636-6*, 00000512) Gale Group.

—Huckleberry Finn Readalong. 1994. (Illustrated Classics Collection: No. 1). 64p. pap. 14.95 incl. audio (*0-7854-0708-1*, 40348); pap. 13.50 o.p. incl. audio (*1-56103-431-2*) American Guidance Service, Inc.

Walker, Margaret. Jubilee. 1983. 432p. mass mkt. 6.99 o.s.i (*0-553-27383-3*, Bantam Classics) Bantam Bks.

—Jubilee. 1999. 512p. pap. 8.95 (*0-395-92495-2*); 1966. 15.95 o.p. (*0-395-08288-9*) Houghton Mifflin Co.

—Jubilee. 1967. 11.60 o.p. (*0-606-01623-6*) Turtleback Bks.

Wells Brown, William. Clotelle: Or, the Colored Heroine. 2000. per. 12.50 (*1-58396-520-3*) Blue Unicorn Editions.

Williams, Sherley A. Dessa Rose. 1987. mass mkt. 6.50 o.s.i (*0-425-10337-4*) Berkley Publishing Group.

—Dessa Rose. abr. ed. 2000. audio 7.95 (*1-57815-148-1*, 1107, Media Bks. Audio Publishing) Media Bks., L. L. C.

—Dessa Rose: A Novel. 1999. 240p. pap. 13.00 (*0-688-16643-1*, Quill) HarperTrade.

—Dessa Rose: A Riveting Story of the South During Slavery. 1986. 256p. 15.95 o.p. (*0-688-05113-8*, Morrow, William & Co.) Morrow/Avon.

Williams, Shirley A. Dessa Rose. abr. ed. 1993. audio 15.95 o.p. (*1-55800-001-1*, 40000, Dove Audio) NewStar Media, Inc.

Williamson, Denise. The Dark Sun Rises: A Novel. 1999. (Roots of Faith Ser.: Bk. 1). 448p. pap. 12.99 (*1-55661-882-4*) Bethany Hse. Pubs.

Wright, Susan. Slave Trade Tilogy. 2003. (Slave Trade Trilogy Ser.). 352p. mass mkt. 6.99 (*0-7434-5763-3*, Pocket Star) Simon & Schuster.

## T

### TERRORISM—FICTION

Blish, Nelson Adrian. Ishmael's Son. 2003. (Illus.). 288p. per. 19.95 (*1-889901-29-6*, Palo Alto Bks.) Glencannon Pr.

Boylan, Roger. The Great Pint-Pulling Olympiad: A Mostly Irish Farce. 2003. 445p. 14.00 (*0-8021-4032-7*, Grove Pr.) Grove/Atlantic, Inc.

Clancy, Tom. The Teeth of the Tiger. 2004. 496p. mass mkt. 7.99 (*0-425-19740-9*) Berkley Publishing Group.

—The Teeth of the Tiger. 2003. 448p. 27.95 (*0-399-15079-X*); 640p. 150.00 (*0-399-15136-2*) Putnam Publishing Group, The.

—The Teeth of the Tiger. l.t. ed. 2003. 32.95 (*0-7862-5691-5*) Thorndike Pr.

—The Teeth of the Tiger: Chapter Excerpt Booklets. 2003. (*0-399-19783-4*) Putnam Publishing Group, The.

Coonts, Stephen. Liberty. l.t. ed. 2003. 688p. 32.95 (*1-58724-442-X*, Wheeler Publishing, Inc.) Gale Group.

—Liberty. 2004. 544p. mass mkt. 7.99 (*0-312-98970-9*); 2003. mass mkt. 7.99 (*0-312-99062-6*) St. Martin's Pr. (St. Martin's Paperbacks).

Davidsen, Leif. Lime's Photograph. 2002. 352p. pap. 12.00 (*1-86046-988-4*) Random Hse. UK, Ltd. GBR. *Dist:* Trafalgar Square.

Foden, Giles. Zanzibar. 2002. 384p. (*0-571-20512-7*) Faber & Faber, Inc.

Hoyt, Richard. The Mongoose Man. 2000. 340p. mass mkt. 6.99 (*0-8125-4023-9*, Tor Bks.) Doherty, Tom Assocs., LLC.

Hoyt, Richard, et al. The Mongoose Man. 1998. 288p. 24.95 (*0-312-86476-0*, Forge Bks.) Doherty, Tom Assocs., LLC.

Kingsbury, Karen & Smalley, Gary. Return. 2003. (Redemption Ser.). 250p. pap. 12.99 (*0-8423-8289-5*) Tyndale Hse. Pubs.

Lawhead, Stephen R. & Lawhead, Ross. City of Dreams. 2003. 372p. 12.99 (*1-57683-499-9*) NavPress Publishing Group.

McNab, Andy. Liberation Day: A Nick Stone Mission. 400p. 2004. mass mkt. 7.99 (*0-7434-0631-1*); 2003. mass mkt. 7.99 (*0-7434-7437-6*) Simon & Schuster. (Pocket).

Nora, James. Panacea. 2002. 224p. pap. 16.00 (*0-9719155-3-9*) Skald Bks.

Patterson, James & Gross, Andrew. 3rd Degree. 2004. 352p. 26.95 (*0-316-60357-0*); 400p. 27.95 (*0-316-74386-0*) Little Brown & Co.

—3rd Degree. unabr. ed. 2004. audio 26.98 (*1-58621-598-1*); audio compact disk 31.98 (*1-58621-599-X*) Time Warner AudioBooks.

—3rd Degree. 2004. pap. 16.00 (*0-446-69258-1*) Warner Bks., Inc.

Pendleton, Don. Ramrod Intercept. 2004. (StonyMan Ser.: No. 70). 352p. mass mkt. (*0-373-61954-5*, Gold Eagle) Harlequin Enterprises, Ltd.

Pottinger, Stan. The Last Nazi. 2003. 352p. 24.95 (*0-312-27676-1*) St. Martin's Pr.

—The Last Nazi. l.t. ed. 2003. 598p. 29.95 (*0-7862-5956-6*) Thorndike Pr.

Reich, Christopher. The Devil's Banker. 2003. 400p. 25.95 (*0-385-33727-2*, Delacorte Pr.); E-Book 9.99 (*0-440-33454-3*) Dell Publishing.

—The Devil's Banker. l.t. ed. 2003. 716p. 27.95 (*0-375-43280-9*, Random House Large Print) Random Hse. Large Print.

Ritchie, Ruth & Elmore, Gene, des. The Return of D. B. Cooper. 2003. 229p. 9.95 (*1-889361-08-9*) Ruroanik Pubs.

Rodgers, Edwin. Red Sky in the Morning: An American Survival Story. 2003. 282p. pap. 24.95 (*1-59129-512-2*) PublishAmerica, Inc.

Roiphe, Anne. Secrets of the City. 2003. 320p. 24.00 (*1-4000-4945-8*, Shaye Areheart Bks.) Crown Publishing Group.

Schwartz, Bruce. The Twenty-First Century. 2003. 395p. 24.95 (*0-9729076-0-2*) Park Avenue Pr.

Storm, P. W. Force 5 Recon: Deployment: North Korea. 2004. 368p. mass mkt. 6.99 (*0-06-052350-6*, Avon Bks.) Morrow/Avon.

—Force 5 Recon: Deployment: Pakistan. 2003. 400p. mass mkt. 6.99 (*0-06-052349-2*, Avon Bks.) Morrow/Avon.

Trew, Antony. Ultimatum. 2003. 242p. 29.95 (*0-7090-7368-2*) Hale, Robert Ltd. GBR. *Dist:* Trafalgar Square.

—Ultimatum. 1976. 8.95 o.p. (*0-312-82845-4*) St. Martin's Pr.

—Ultimatum. l.t. ed. 2003. (General Ser.). lib. bdg. 24.95 (*0-7862-5669-9*) Thorndike Pr.

Wilson, Steven E. Winter in Kandahar. 2003. 464p. per. 14.95 (*0-9729480-0-7*) Hailey-Grey Bks.

Zietlow, E. R. Matada: Seeds of Terror. (*1-894694-11-2*) Granville Island Publishing.

Zubrin, Robert. The Holy Land. 2003. 308p. per. 14.95 (*0-9741443-0-4*) Polaris Bks.

### TERRORISTS—FICTION

Abdoh, Salar. The Poet Game. E-Book 12.00 (*0-312-27357-6*); 2001. 240p. pap. 12.00 (*0-312-20968-1*); 2000. 240p. 23.00 (*0-312-20954-1*) Picador.

Adler, Warren. We Are Holding the President Hostage. 1988. 304p. pap. (*0-373-97072-2*, Harlequin Bks.) Harlequin Enterprises, Ltd.

Aline, Countess of Romanones. The Well-Mannered Assassin. 1995. 368p. mass mkt. 5.99 o.s.i (*0-515-11533-9*, Jove) Berkley Publishing Group.
—The Well-Mannered Assassin. l.t. ed. 1994. 584p. lib. bdg. 24.95 (*0-8161-7447-4*, Macmillan Reference USA) Gale Group.
—The Well-Mannered Assassin. 1994. 320p. 22.95 o.p. (*0-399-13863-3*, G. P. Putnam's Sons) Penguin Group (USA) Inc.
Allbeury, Ted. The Stalking Angel. 208p. 1989. mass mkt. 3.95 o.s.i (*0-445-40834-0*); 1988. 17.95 (*0-89296-184-8*) Mysterious Pr.
Allen, Richard. Flashpoint. 1991. 19.95 o.p. (*1-55611-194-0*) Fine, Donald I. Bks.
Anderson, Kevin J. Ignition. abr. ed. 1997. audio 7.99 o.p. (*1-56740-232-1*, 661, Nova Audio Bks.) Brilliance Audio.
Anderson, Kevin J. & Beason, Doug. Ignition. abr. ed. 1997. audio 16.95 o.p. (*1-56100-910-5*, 1263, Nova Audio Bks.); audio 57.25 o.p. (*1-56100-328-X*, 906, Unabridged Library Editions); audio 23.95 o.p. (*1-56100-702-1*, 143, Bookcassette) Brilliance Audio.
—Ignition. 1998. 402p. mass mkt. 6.99 o.p. (*0-8125-4548-6*, Tor Bks.); 1997. 304p. 23.95 (*0-312-86270-9*, Forge Bks.) Doherty, Tom Assocs., LLC.
Antaki, Myriam. Verses of Forgiveness. de Jager, Marjolijn, tr. from FRE. 2002. 174p. 22.00 (*1-59051-038-0*) Other Pr., LLC.
Armstrong, Campbell. Jig. Congdon, Thomas, ed. 1987. 512p. 18.95 o.p. (*0-688-06879-0*, Morrow, William & Co.) Morrow/Avon.
—Jig. 1989. bds. 4.95 (*0-671-66524-3*, Pocket) Simon & Schuster.
Bayley, John. The Red Hat. 1998. 224p. 21.95 (*0-312-18658-4*) St. Martin's Pr.
—The Red Hat. 2001. 196p. pap. 14.00 (*1-56649-194-0*) Welcome Rain Pubs.
Bellacera, Carole. Border Crossing. 2000. 448p. mass mkt. 6.99 (*0-8125-7573-3*, Forge Bks.) Doherty, Tom Assocs., LLC.
—Border Crossings. 1999. 381p. 25.95 (*0-312-86858-8*, Forge Bks.) Doherty, Tom Assocs., LLC.
Bishop, Paul. Tequila Mockingbird. 1998. (Fey Croaker Novels Ser.). 400p. pap. 6.99 (*0-671-02531-7*, Pocket) Simon & Schuster.
—Tequila Mockingbird: A Fey Croaker Novel. 1997. (Fey Croaker Novels Ser.). 400p. 23.00 o.s.i (*0-684-83009-4*, Scribner) Simon & Schuster.
Blauner, Peter. Man of the Hour. 1999. 432p. 24.00 o.p. (*0-316-03817-2*) Little Brown & Co.
—The Man of the Hour. 2000. 496p. mass mkt. 7.99 o.s.i (*0-446-60541-7*) Warner Bks., Inc.
Bond, Larry. Day of Wrath. unabr. ed. 1998. audio 96.00 (*0-7366-4187-4*, 4685) Books on Tape, Inc.
—Day of Wrath. abr. ed. 1998. 5p. audio 25.00 (*0-671-58224-0*, 495728, Simon & Schuster Audioworks) Simon & Schuster Audio.
—Day of Wrath. l.t. ed. 1999. (Mystery Ser.). 725p. 30.95 o.p. (*0-7862-1616-6*) Thorndike Pr.
—Day of Wrath. 1999. 528p. mass mkt. 7.99 (*0-446-60705-3*); 1998. 496p. 25.00 (*0-446-51677-5*) Warner Bks., Inc.
—The Enemy Within. abr. ed. audio. 1999. audio 12.98 (*0-671-04632-2*, Simon & Schuster Audioworks-);Set. 1996. 192p. pap. 23.00 incl. audio (*0-671-57054-4*, 493929, Simon & Schuster Audioworks) Simon & Schuster Audio.
—The Enemy Within. 1997. 528p. mass mkt. 7.99 (*0-446-60385-6*); 1996. 496p. 32.00 (*0-446-51676-7*) Warner Bks., Inc.
Bond, Larry & Larkin, Patrick. The Enemy Within. unabr. ed. 1996. audio 104.00 (*0-7366-3388-X*, 4038) Books on Tape, Inc.
Brockmann, Suzanne. Into the Night. 2002. 480p. mass mkt. 6.99 (*0-8041-1972-4*, Ballantine Bks.) Ballantine Bks.
—Into the Night. 2002. 480p. 26.00 (*0-345-45885-0*) Random Hse., Inc.
—Into the Night. 2003. (Core Ser.). 28.95 (*0-7862-5149-2*) Thorndike Pr.
Brown, Alan. Princess. l.t. ed. 1991. 21.95 o.p. (*0-7927-0694-3*, CH010); pap. 19.95 o.p. (*0-7927-0695-1*, CS0112) BBC Audiobooks America.
Brown, Dale. Storming Heaven. 1995. 496p. mass mkt. 7.99 (*0-425-14723-1*) Berkley Publishing Group.
—Storming Heaven. abr. ed. 1994. 24.95 o.p. (*0-7871-0049-8*, 692317) NewStar Media, Inc.
—Storming Heaven. 1994. 480p. 22.95 o.p. (*0-399-13931-1*, G. P. Putnam's Sons) Penguin Group (USA) Inc.
—The Tin Man. 1999. 464p. reprint ed. mass mkt. 7.99 (*0-553-58000-0*, Bantam Classics) Bantam Bks.
—The Tin Man. l.t. ed. 1998. (Large Print Book Ser.). 26.95 (*1-56895-684-3*, Wheeler Publishing, Inc.) Gale Group.
Byrne, Robert. Mannequin. 1989. mass mkt. 3.95 o.s.i (*1-55817-300-5*, Pinnacle Bks.) Kensington Publishing Corp.
—Mannequin. 1988. 288p. 18.95 o.s.i (*0-689-11836-8*, Scribner) Simon & Schuster.
Clancy, Tom. Rainbow Six. 1999. 7.99 (*0-425-17005-5*); 912p. reprint ed. mass mkt. 8.50 (*0-425-17034-9*) Berkley Publishing Group.
—Rainbow Six. l.t. ed. 1999. pap. 27.95 o.p. (*0-7838-0160-2*, Macmillan Reference USA) Gale Group.
—Rainbow Six. 1998. 752p. 27.95 (*0-399-14390-4*); 800p. 150.00 (*0-399-14413-7*) Penguin Group (USA) Inc. (G. P. Putnam's Sons).
—Rainbow Six. l.t. ed. 1998. 800p. pap. 27.95 (*0-375-70324-1*) Random Hse. Large Print.
—Rainbow Six. 1998. 14.55 (*0-606-17207-6*) Turtleback Bks.
Clancy, Tom & Pieczenik, Steve, creators. Acts of War. 1997. (Op-Center Ser.: No. 4). 512p. mass mkt. 7.99 (*0-425-15601-X*) Berkley Publishing Group.
—Acts of War. l.t. ed. 1997. (Op-Center Ser.: No. 4). 678p. 29.95 (*0-7862-1218-7*) Thorndike Pr.
Coonts, Stephen. America: A Jake Grafton Novel. 2001. 390p. 25.95 (*0-312-25341-9*) St. Martin's Pr.
—America: A Jake Grafton Novel. l.t. ed. 2001. 657p. 31.95 (*0-7862-3641-8*); 28.95 (*0-7862-3645-0*) Thorndike Pr.
Coppel, Alfred. Show Me a Hero. 1988. 304p. mass mkt. 3.95 o.s.i (*0-8041-0232-5*, Ivy Bks.) Ballantine Bks.
—Show Me a Hero. 1987. 320p. 16.95 (*0-15-182080-5*) Harcourt Trade Pubs.
Daniel, Mark. The Bold Thing. 1994. 279p. 19.95 o.p. (*0-316-17266-9*) Little Brown & Co.
DeMille, Nelson. By the Rivers of Babylon. 1986. 432p. mass mkt. 3.95 o.s.i (*0-515-08761-0*, Jove) Berkley Publishing Group.
—By the Rivers of Babylon. 1978. 10.00 o.p. (*0-15-115278-0*) Harcourt Trade Pubs.
—By the Rivers of Babylon. l.t. ed. 1983. (Charnwood Large Print Ser.). 624p. 29.99 o.p. (*0-7089-8091-0*, Charnwood) Thorpe, F. A. Pubs. GBR. *Dist:* Ulverscroft Large Print Bks., Ltd., Ulverscroft Large Print Canada, Ltd.
—By the Rivers of Babylon. 432p. 2001. E-Book 6.95 (*0-7595-9287-X*); 2001. E-Book 6.95 (*0-7595-8260-2*); 2001. E-Book 6.95 (*0-7595-0254-4*); 2001. E-Book 6.95 (*0-7595-6254-7*); 2001. E-Book 6.95 (*0-7595-4257-0*); 1990. reprint ed. mass mkt. 7.99 (*0-446-35859-2*) Warner Bks., Inc.
—Cathedral. 1982. 576p. mass mkt. 5.95 o.s.i (*0-440-11620-1*); 1981. 13.95 o.s.i (*0-440-01140-X*, Delacorte Pr.) Dell Publishing.
—Cathedral, Set. abr. ed. 1998. audio 8.99 o.s.i (*0-375-40296-9*, RH Audio) Random Hse. Audio Publishing Group.
—Cathedral. l.t. ed. 1982. (Charnwood Large Print Ser.). 720p. 29.99 o.p. (*0-7089-8079-1*, Charnwood) Thorpe, F. A. Pubs. GBR. *Dist:* Ulverscroft Large Print Bks., Ltd., Ulverscroft Large Print Canada, Ltd.
—Cathedral. 2001. 575p. E-Book 6.95 (*0-7595-8261-0*); 2001. 575p. E-Book 6.95 (*0-7595-0255-2*); 2001. 575p. E-Book 6.95 (*0-7595-6255-5*); 2001. 575p. E-Book 6.95 (*0-7595-4258-9*); 2001. 575p. E-Book 6.95 (*0-7595-9288-8*); 1990. 576p. reprint ed. mass mkt. 7.99 (*0-446-35857-6*) Warner Bks., Inc.
—The Lion's Game. l.t. ed. (Thorndike General Ser.). 2001. 1049p. pap. 29.95 (*0-7862-2020-1*); 2000. 1037p. 31.95 (*0-7862-2019-8*) Thorndike Pr.
—The Lion's Game. 2000. E-Book 6.95 (*0-446-92370-2*) Time Warner Bk. Group.
—The Lion's Game. 2000. 944p. E-Book 6.95 (*0-446-91357-X*); 2000. 944p. E-Book 6.95 (*0-446-96090-X*); 2000. 944p. E-Book 6.95 (*0-446-92265-X*); 2000. E-Book 6.95 (*0-446-93138-1*); 2000. 944p. E-Book 6.95 (*0-446-92862-3*); 2000. 688p. 26.95 (*0-446-52065-9*); 2002. 720p. reprint ed. pap. 15.95 (*0-446-67909-7*); 2000. 944p. reprint ed. mass mkt. 7.99 (*0-446-60826-2*) Warner Bks., Inc.
—Plum Island. abr. ed. 1997. audio 24.00 o.s.i (*0-394-58389-2*, 495350, RH Audio) Random Hse. Audio Publishing Group.
—Plum Island. l.t. ed. 1998. (Paperback Bestsellers Ser.). 821p. pap. 28.95 (*0-7862-0980-1*) Thorndike Pr.
—Plum Island. 2001. 576p. E-Book 6.95 (*0-7595-9290-X*); 2001. 576p. E-Book 6.95 (*0-7595-6257-1*); 2001. 576p. E-Book 6.95 (*0-7595-8263-7*); 2001. 576p. E-Book 6.95 (*0-7595-0257-9*); 2001. 576p. E-Book 6.95 (*0-7595-4260-0*); 1998. mass mkt. 287.64 (*0-446-16544-1*); 1997. 528p. 24.50 o.p. (*0-446-51506-X*); 2002. 592p. reprint ed. pap. 15.95 (*0-446-67908-9*); 1998. 592p. reprint ed. mass mkt. 7.99 (*0-446-60540-9*) Warner Bks., Inc.
Deverell, Diana. 12 Drummers Drumming. 304p. 1999. mass mkt. 6.99 o.p. (*0-380-79594-9*); 1998. 23.00 (*0-380-97610-2*) Morrow/Avon. (Avon Bks.).
Dickey, Christopher. Innocent Blood. 1997. 336p. 23.00 (*0-684-84200-9*, Simon & Schuster) Simon & Schuster.
Dostoyevsky, Fyodor. Demons. Pevear, Richard, tr. from RUS. 2000. 784p. 23.00 (*0-375-41122-4*) Knopf, Alfred A. Inc.
Easterman, Daniel. Night of the Apocalypse. 1995. 430p. 24.00 o.p. (*0-06-017742-X*) HarperTrade.
—Night of the Apocalypse. 1996. 448p. mass mkt. 5.99 o.p. (*0-06-109205-3*, HarperTorch) Morrow/Avon.
Egleton, Clive. Warning Shot. 1997. 410p. 22.95 o.p. (*0-312-15685-5*) St. Martin's Pr.
—Warning Shot. l.t. ed. 1997. (Charnwood Large Print Ser.). 544p. 29.99 o.p. (*0-7089-8966-7*, Ulverscroft) Thorpe, F. A. Pubs. GBR. *Dist:* Ulverscroft Large Print Bks., Ltd., Ulverscroft Large Print Canada, Ltd.
Eversz, Robert M. Shooting Elvis. 224p. 1996. pap. 21.00 o.p. (*0-8021-1582-9*); 1997. reprint ed. pap. 12.00 (*0-8021-3501-3*) Grove/Atlantic, Inc. (Grove Pr.).
Flynn, Vince. Transfer of Power. 2001. 416p. E-Book 9.99 (*0-7434-4924-X*, Atria); 1999. (Illus.). 395p. pap. 24.00 (*0-671-02319-5*, Atria); 2000. (Illus.). 592p. reprint ed. mass mkt. 7.99 (*0-671-02320-9*, Pocket Star) Simon & Schuster.
—Transfer of Power. l.t. ed. 2004. 751p. 29.95 (*0-7862-5872-1*) Thorndike Pr.
Follett, Ken. The Hammer of Eden. 1999. 448p. mass mkt. 7.99 (*0-449-22754-5*, Fawcett) Ballantine Bks.
—The Hammer of Eden. l.t. ed. 1998. 672p. 25.95 o.p. (*0-7838-0265-X*, Macmillan Reference USA) Gale Group.
—The Hammer of Eden: A Novel. l.t. ed. 1998. 672p. pap. 25.95 o.s.i (*0-375-70419-1*) Random Hse., Inc.
Foote, Tom. The Undertow. 1998. 352p. pap. 14.95 (*0-8023-1320-5*) Dufour Editions, Inc.
—The Undertow. 1998. 352p. pap. 14.95 (*1-897648-93-6*) Salmon Publishing IRL. *Dist:* Dufour Editions, Inc.
Fouliard, Paul. Waltz with the Devil. 2003. 273p. (Orig.). pap. 12.95 (*1-878044-06-0*) Mayhaven Publishing.
Glanville, Brian. The Catacomb. 1988. 352p. 22.95 (*0-340-42327-7*) Hodder & Stoughton, Ltd. GBR. *Dist:* Lubrecht & Cramer, Ltd., Trafalgar Square.
Hagberg, David. Joshua's Hammer. (Kirk McGarvey Novels Ser.). 2000. (Illus.). 352p. 25.95 (*0-312-86128-1*, Forge Bks.); 2001. 544p. reprint ed. mass mkt. 7.99 (*0-8125-4439-0*, Tor Bks.) Doherty, Tom Assocs., LLC.
Hailey, Arthur. The Evening News. 592p. 1991. mass mkt. 6.99 o.s.i (*0-440-20851-3*); 1990. mass mkt. 5.50 o.s.i (*0-440-29514-9*) Dell Publishing.
—The Evening News. 1990. 576p. 27.95 o.s.i (*0-385-41405-6*) Doubleday Publishing.
Harcourt, Palma. Limited Options. 1987. 224p. 15.95 o.p. (*0-8253-0419-9*) Beaufort Bks., Inc.
—Limited Options. l.t. ed. 1988. (Ulverscroft Large Print Ser.). 400p. 29.99 o.p. (*0-7089-1847-6*, Ulverscroft) Thorpe, F. A. Pubs. GBR. *Dist:* Ulverscroft Large Print Bks., Ltd., Ulverscroft Large Print Canada, Ltd.
Harris, Thomas. Black Sunday. 1981. mass mkt. 4.50 o.s.i (*0-553-28116-X*); 1977. pap. 2.25 o.p. (*0-553-10940-5*) Bantam Bks.
—Black Sunday. 1991. 318p. reprint ed. lib. bdg. 24.95 o.p. (*0-89966-876-3*) Buccaneer Bks., Inc.
—Black Sunday. 1990. 384p. reprint ed. mass mkt. 7.50 o.s.i (*0-440-20614-6*) Dell Publishing.
—Black Sunday. 25th anniv. ed. 2000. 320p. 26.95 (*0-525-94555-5*, Abrahams, William Bks.) Dutton/Plume.
—Black Sunday. 2001. 320p. mass mkt. 7.99 (*0-451-20415-8*) NAL.
—Black Sunday. 1975. 320p. 7.95 o.p. (*0-399-11443-2*) Putnam Publishing Group, The.
Heide, C. L. Terrorist Cove. 2002. 178p. pap. (*1-55369-241-1*) Trafford Publishing.
Hellenga, Robert R. The Fall of a Sparrow, Set. abr. ed. 1999. audio 26.95 (*0-7871-1752-8*, 696024, Dove Audio) NewStar Media, Inc.
—The Fall of a Sparrow. 1998. 464p. 25.00 o.s.i (*0-684-85026-5*, Scribner) Simon & Schuster.
—The Fall of the Sparrow: A Novel. 1999. 464p. pap. 14.00 (*0-684-85027-3*, Scribner) Simon & Schuster.
Henderson, Dee. True Honor. 2002. (Uncommon Heroes Ser.). (Illus.). 352p. pap. 12.99 (*1-59052-043-2*) Multnomah Pubs., Inc.
Higgins, Jack. Angel of Death. 1996. 352p. mass mkt. 7.99 (*0-425-15223-5*) Berkley Publishing Group.
—Angel of Death. unabr. ed. 1995. 24.95 o.p. (*0-7871-0391-8*, 692879) NewStar Media, Inc.
—Angel of Death. 2001. 23.95 (*0-399-14274-6*); 1995. 311p. 23.95 (*0-399-14042-5*, G. P. Putnam's Sons) Penguin Group (USA) Inc.
—Angel of Death. l.t. ed. 1996. (Paperback Bestsellers Ser.). 402p. lib. bdg. 24.95 (*0-7862-0465-6*) Thorndike Pr.
—Midnight Runner. 2003. 304p. mass mkt. 7.99 (*0-425-18941-4*) Berkley Publishing Group.
—Midnight Runner. 2002. 288p. 25.95 o.s.i (*0-399-14833-7*, Riverhead Bks. (Hardcovers)) Penguin Group (USA) Inc.
—Midnight Runner. l.t. ed. 13.95 (*1-4104-0090-5*, Large Print Pr.); 2003. 449p. 13.95 (*0-7862-4107-1*); 2002. 449p. 32.95 (*0-7862-4106-3*) Thorndike Pr.
Hornig, Doug. Stinger. 1990. 400p. mass mkt. 4.95 o.p. (*0-451-16691-4*, Signet Bks.) NAL.
Hunter, Stephen. The Day Before Midnight. 1989. 432p. mass mkt. 7.99 (*0-553-28235-2*) Bantam Bks.
Huston, James W. Flash Point. 2001. E-Book 7.50 (*0-06-001124-6*) HarperCollins Pubs.
—Flash Point. 2001. 592p. mass mkt. 7.50 (*0-380-73282-3*, Avon Bks.); 2000. 462p. 26.00 (*0-688-17201-6*, Morrow, William & Co.) Morrow/Avon.
—The Price of Power. 1999. (Illus.). 431p. 25.00 (*0-688-15918-4*, Morrow, William & Co.) Morrow/Avon.
Kiefer, Warren. The Perpignon Exchange. 1990. 19.95 o.p. (*1-55611-227-0*) Fine, Donald I. Bks.
Kiely, David M. The Angel Tapes: A Blade Macken Mystery. 1997. (Blade Macken Mystery Ser.). 304p. text 23.95 o.p. (*0-312-16772-5*) St. Martin's Pr.
Land, Jon. Dead Simple. 1999. 404p. mass mkt. 6.99 (*0-8125-4001-8*); 1998. 320p. 23.95 (*0-312-86489-2*) Doherty, Tom Assocs., LLC. (Forge Bks.).
—Fires of Midnight. 1996. 361p. pap. text 6.99 (*0-8125-5252-0*); 1995. 320p. 22.95 o.p. (*0-312-85971-6*) Doherty, Tom Assocs., LLC. (Forge Bks.).
—Valhalla Testament. 1990. 352p. mass mkt. 5.95 o.s.i (*0-449-14634-0*, Fawcett) Ballantine Bks.
Liddy, G. Gordon. The Monkey Handlers. abr. ed. 1990. audio 15.95 o.p. (*1-55927-100-0*) Audio Renaissance.
—The Monkey Handlers. 1991. 352p. mass mkt. 5.99 (*0-312-92613-8*, St. Martin's Paperbacks); 1990. 19.95 o.p. (*0-312-05127-1*) St. Martin's Pr.
Ludlum, Robert. The Bourne Identity. 1984. 544p. mass mkt. 7.99 (*0-553-26011-1*); mass mkt. 3.99 o.s.i (*0-553-19941-2*) Bantam Bks.
—The Bourne Identity. 1980. 12.95 o.s.i (*0-399-90070-5*) Putnam Publishing Group, The.
—The Bourne Supremacy. 1989. 656p. mass mkt. 7.99 (*0-553-26322-6*); 1987. mass mkt. o.s.i (*0-553-26651-9*); 1987. 656p. mass mkt. 3.99 o.s.i (*0-553-19942-0*) Bantam Bks.
—The Bourne Supremacy. unabr. collector's ed. 1986. Pt. 1. audio 72.00 (*0-7366-0867-2*, 1818-A); Pt. 2. audio 64.00 (*0-7366-0868-0*, 1818-B) Books on Tape, Inc.
—The Bourne Supremacy. l.t. ed. 1987. 21.95 o.p. (*0-8161-4224-6*, Macmillan Reference USA) Gale Group.
—The Bourne Supremacy. abr. ed. 1989. audio 18.00 (*0-553-45159-6*, RH Audio) Random Hse. Audio Publishing Group.
—The Bourne Supremacy. 1986. 608p. 19.95 o.s.i (*0-394-54396-3*) Random Hse., Inc.
—The Bourne Ultimatum. 672p. 1991. mass mkt. 7.95 o.s.i (*0-553-29194-7*); 1991. mass mkt. 3.99 o.s.i (*0-553-19943-9*); 1991. mass mkt. 7.99 (*0-553-28773-7*); 1990. mass mkt. 5.50 o.s.i (*0-553-17342-1*) Bantam Bks.
—The Bourne Ultimatum. 1990. audio 14.39 o.s.i (*0-553-70028-6*, RH Audio) Random Hse. Audio Publishing Group.
—The Bourne Ultimatum. 1992. 6.99 o.p. (*0-517-08090-7*) Random Hse. Value Publishing.
Lyall, Gavin. Uncle Target. l.t. ed. 1989. (Ulverscroft Large Print Ser.). 487p. 29.99 o.p. (*0-7089-1945-6*, Ulverscroft) Thorpe, F. A. Pubs. GBR. *Dist:* Ulverscroft Large Print Bks., Ltd., Ulverscroft Large Print Canada, Ltd.
—Uncle Target. 1988. 256p. 16.95 o.p. (*0-670-82228-0*) Viking Penguin.
Mahoney, Dan. The Edge of the City. 1996. 514p. mass mkt. 6.99 (*0-312-95788-2*, St. Martin's Paperbacks); 1995. 464p. 14.99 o.p. (*0-312-13058-9*); 1995. 22.95 (*0-312-11812-0*) St. Martin's Pr.
Martini, Steve. Critical Mass. 1999. reprint ed. 384p. mass mkt. 7.99 (*0-515-12648-9*); 7.99 (*0-515-12583-0*) Berkley Publishing Group. (Jove).
—Critical Mass. l.t. ed. 1998. 28.95 (*1-56895-668-1*, Wheeler Publishing, Inc.) Gale Group.
—Critical Mass. 1998. 448p. 25.95 o.p. (*0-399-14362-9*) Penguin Group (USA) Inc.
Maxim, John R. Haven. abr. ed. 1998. audio 7.99 o.s.i (*1-56740-256-9*, 889, Paperback Nova Audio Bks.); 1997. audio 16.95 o.p. (*1-56740-750-1*, 519, Nova Audio Bks.); 1997. audio 89.25 (*1-56740-550-9*, 888, Unabridged Library Editions); 1997. audio 25.95 (*1-56100-771-4*, 329, Bookcassette) Brilliance Audio.
—Haven. 1998. 416p. mass mkt. 6.99 (*0-380-78669-9*); 1997. 384p. 24.00 (*0-380-97301-4*) Morrow/Avon. (Avon Bks.).
McBain, Ed, pseud. Money, Money, Money. 2001. E-Book 9.99 (*1-59061-377-5*) Adobe Systems, Inc.
—Money, Money, Money. 2002. 352p. mass mkt. 7.99 (*0-7434-4379-9*, Pocket); 2001. 272p. 25.00 (*0-7432-0269-4*, Simon & Schuster); 2001. 272p.

E-Book 25.00 (*0-7432-1767-5*, Simon & Schuster); 2003. 384p. pap. 25.00 (*0-7432-5445-7*, Simon & Schuster); 2001. 384p. 25.00 (*0-7432-2406-X*, Simon & Schuster); 2002. 352p. reprint ed. mass mkt. 7.99 (*0-7434-1032-7*, Pocket) Simon & Schuster.

Moran, Thomas. Water, Carry Me. 2000. 288p. 24.95 o.s.i (*1-57322-138-4*, Riverhead Bks. (Hardcovers)) Putnam Publishing Group, The.

—Water, Carry Me. l.t. ed. 2000. (Basic Ser.). 409p. 28.95 (*0-7862-2510-6*) Thorndike Pr.

Morris, M. E. Sword of the Shaheen. 1990. 320p. 18.95 o.p. (*0-89141-328-6*, Presidio Pr.) Ballantine Bks.

Nance, John J. Turbulence. 2003. 416p. mass mkt. 7.99 (*0-515-13486-4*, Jove) Berkley Publishing Group.

—Turbulence. 2002. 400p. 25.95 o.s.i (*0-399-14847-7*) Penguin Group (USA) Inc.

O'Brien, Edna. House of Splendid Isolation. unabr. ed. 2000. audio 59.95 (*0-7451-2733-9*, SAB 099) Chivers Audio Bks. GBR. *Dist:* BBC Audiobooks America.

—House of Splendid Isolation. 1995. 240p. pap. 14.00 (*0-452-27452-4*, Plume) Dutton/Plume.

—House of Splendid Isolation. 1994. 224p. 21.00 o.p. (*0-374-17309-5*) Farrar, Straus & Giroux.

O'Keefe, Bernard J., ed. Trapdoor. 1988. 192p. 17.95 o.p. (*0-395-48353-0*) Houghton Mifflin Co.

Pearson, Ryne Douglas. Capitol Punishment. 1996. 352p. mass mkt. 5.99 (*0-380-72228-3*, Avon Bks.); 1995. 320p. 22.00 o.p. (*0-688-12983-8*, Morrow, William & Co.) Morrow/Avon.

—Cloudburst. 1993. 23.00 o.p. (*0-688-12246-9*, Morrow, William & Co.) Morrow/Avon.

—Cloudburst, unabr. ed. 1993. audio 85.00 (*1-55690-901-2*, 93343E7) Recorded Bks., LLC.

—October's Ghost. 1994. 312p. 23.00 o.p. (*0-688-12984-6*, Morrow, William & Co.); 1995. 464p. reprint ed. mass mkt. 5.99 (*0-380-72227-5*, Avon Bks.) Morrow/Avon.

—October's Ghost, unabr. ed. 1995. audio 91.00 (*0-7887-0101-0*, 94342E7) Recorded Bks., LLC.

Pendleton, Don. Ring of Retaliation. 2002. (Executioner Ser.: No. 283). 224p. mass mkt. (*0-373-64283-0*, 1-64283-4, Worldwide Library) Harlequin Enterprises, Ltd.

Peters, Ralph. Traitor. 2000. 384p. mass mkt. 6.99 (*0-380-79738-0*); 1999. 320p. 23.00 (*0-380-97641-2*) Morrow/Avon. (Avon Bks.).

—Traitor. 2004. pap. (*0-8117-3107-3*) Stackpole Bks.

Petschull, Jurgen. The Martyr. Cappellari, Stephen G., tr. from GER. 1988. 296p. 18.95 o.p. (*0-916515-28-1*) Mercury Hse.

Pollock, Daniel. Lair of the Fox. 1990. 384p. mass mkt. 4.95 o.p. (*0-06-100087-6*, HarperTorch) Morrow/Avon.

—Lair of the Fox. 1989. 240p. 19.95 o.p. (*0-8027-1088-3*) Walker & Co.

Poyer, David. The Med. (Illus.). 1991. 576p. mass mkt. 6.99 (*0-312-92722-3*, St. Martin's Paperbacks); 1988. 512p. 19.95 o.p. (*0-312-01788-X*) St. Martin's Pr.

Prantera, Amanda. Letter to Lorenzo. 2000. 224p. pap. 13.00 (*0-7475-4509-X*) Bloomsbury Publishing, Ltd. GBR. *Dist:* Trafalgar Square.

Raines, Jeff. Unbalanced Acts. 1990. 272p. mass mkt. 4.50 (*0-380-76008-8*, Avon Bks.) Morrow/Avon.

Ramthun, Bonnie. Ground Zero. 1999. 304p. 24.95 o.p. (*0-399-14509-5*, G. P. Putnam's Sons) Penguin Group (USA) Inc.

Randall, John D. The Jihad Ultimatum: A Novel. 1989. mass mkt. 4.50 o.s.i (*1-55817-260-2*, Pinnacle Bks.) Kensington Publishing Corp.

—The Jihad Ultimatum: A Novel. 1988. (*0-933071-23-X*) Saybrook Publishing Co., Inc.

Reeves-Stevens, Garfield & Reeves-Stevens, Judith. Icefire. 1999. (Illus.). 736p. reprint ed. mass mkt. 7.99 (*0-671-01403-X*, Pocket) Simon & Schuster.

Reeves-Stevens, Judith & Reeves-Stevens, Garfield. Icefire. 1998. (Illus.). 384p. 23.00 (*0-671-01402-1*, Atria) Simon & Schuster.

Robb, J. D., pseud. Loyalty in Death. l.t. ed. 2000. (Americana Ser.). 539p. 30.95 (*0-7862-2443-6*) Thorndike Pr.

Rolf, Gerald. The Event. 1997. 350p. pap. 12.95 (*0-9661836-0-6*) Rolf, Gerald.

Royce, Kenneth. Patriots. 1989. 272p. mass mkt. 4.95 o.s.i (*0-446-35579-8*) Warner Bks., Inc.

—The President Is Dead. l.t. ed. 1989. (Ulverscroft Large Print Ser.). 518p. 29.99 o.p. (*0-7089-1967-7*, Ulverscroft) Thorpe, F. A. Pubs. GBR. *Dist:* Ulverscroft Large Print Bks., Ltd., Ulverscroft Large Print Canada, Ltd.

Shriver, Lionel. Bleeding Heart. 1990. 22.95 o.p. (*0-374-11432-3*) Farrar, Straus & Giroux.

Silva, Daniel. The Kill Artist. E-Book 20.95 (*1-58945-641-6*) Adobe Systems, Inc.

—The Kill Artist. 2002. 448p. mass mkt. 6.99 o.s.i (*0-449-00212-8*, Fawcett) Ballantine Bks.

—The Kill Artist. 2004. 448p. mass mkt. 7.99 (*0-451-20933-8*, Signet Bks.) NAL.

—The Kill Artist. 2001. E-Book 20.95 (*0-375-50672-1*) Random Hse., Inc.

—The Marching Season. 2000. 384p. mass mkt. 7.50 o.s.i (*0-449-00211-X*) Ballantine Bks.

—The Marching Season. l.t. ed. 1999. pap. 25.95 o.p. (*0-7838-8510-5*, Macmillan Reference USA) Gale Group.

—The Marching Season. 2004. 384p. mass mkt. 7.99 (*0-451-20932-X*, Signet Bks.) NAL.

—The Marching Season. abr. ed. 1999. audio compact disk 29.95 o.s.i (*0-553-45638-5*, RH Audio) Random Hse. Audio Publishing Group.

—The Marching Season. unabr. ed. 2000. audio compact disk 90.00 (*0-7887-3972-7*, C1009E7); 1999. audio 75.00 (*0-7887-3097-5*, 95808E7) Recorded Bks., LLC.

—The Mark of the Assassin. 2000. mass mkt. 6.99 (*0-449-45939-X*, Fawcett); 1999. 432p. mass mkt. 6.99 o.s.i (*0-449-22531-3*, Fawcett); 1998. mass mkt. (*0-449-00332-9*, Ballantine Bks.) Ballantine Bks.

—The Mark of the Assassin. l.t. ed. 1998. 464p. 25.00 o.p. (*0-7838-8342-0*, Macmillan Reference USA) Gale Group.

—The Mark of the Assassin. 2003. 432p. mass mkt. 7.99 (*0-451-20931-1*, Signet Bks.) NAL.

Simmons, Larry. Broken Seals: No Safe Place. 2001. 352p. E-Book 14.95 (*1-883955-20-3*) Penmarin Bks.

Smith, Michael A. Jeremiah: Terrorist Prophet. 384p. 1999. mass mkt. 6.99 (*0-8125-6189-9*); 1997. 24.95 (*0-312-86636-4*) Doherty, Tom Assocs., LLC. (Forge Bks.).

Snow, C. P. The Malcontents. l.t. ed. 2003. (Dales Large Print Ser.). 336p. pap. 21.99 (*1-84262-220-X*) Dales Large Print Bks. GBR. *Dist:* Ulverscroft Large Print Bks., Ltd., Ulverscroft Large Print Canada, Ltd.

—The Malcontents. 2000. 220p. pap. 9.95 (*1-84232-433-0*) Midpoint Trade Bks., Inc.

Sofer, Barbara. The Thirteenth Hour. 1996. 352p. 24.95 o.s.i (*0-525-94181-9*) Dutton/Plume.

—The Thirteenth Hour. 1997. 416p. mass mkt. 5.99 o.s.i (*0-451-19106-4*, Signet Bks.) NAL.

—The Thirteenth Hour, unabr. ed. 1997. audio 91.00 (*0-7887-0921-6*, 95061E7) Recorded Bks., LLC.

Stevens, Gordon. Do Not Go Gentle. 1989. 400p. reprint ed. mass mkt. (*0-373-97101-X*, Harlequin Bks.) Harlequin Enterprises, Ltd.

—Do Not Go Gentle. 1988. 384p. 17.95 o.p. (*0-312-01488-0*) St. Martin's Pr.

Stone, Robert. Damascus Gate. 1998. 512p. tchr. ed. 26.00 (*0-395-66569-8*) Houghton Mifflin Co.

—Damascus Gate. 1999. (Illus.). 528p. pap. 14.00 (*0-684-85911-4*, Touchstone) Simon & Schuster.

Thayer, James Stewart. Terminal Event. l.t. ed. 2000. 25.95 (*1-57490-304-7*, Beeler Large Print Bks.) Beeler, Thomas T. Publisher.

—Terminal Event. 1999. (Illus.). 352p. 25.00 (*0-684-84210-6*, Simon & Schuster); 2003. 448p. reprint ed. mass mkt. 7.99 (*0-671-01371-8*, Pocket) Simon & Schuster.

Thomas, Craig. Rat Trap. 1996. 318p. mass mkt. o.s.i (*0-7515-1292-3*) Little Brown & Co.

—Rat Trap. 1996. 79p. mass mkt. 3.99 o.p. (*0-06-101055-3*); 1992. 288p. mass mkt. 5.99 o.p. (*0-06-100397-2*) Morrow/Avon. (HarperTorch).

Wager, Walter. Tunnel. 2000. 317p. 23.95 (*0-312-86488-4*, Forge Bks.) Doherty, Tom Assocs., LLC.

—The Tunnel. 2001. 304p. mass mkt. 6.99 (*0-8125-6467-7*, Forge Bks.) Doherty, Tom Assocs., LLC.

Waller, Leslie. Embassy. 1988. 432p. pap. text 5.95 o.p. (*0-07-067944-4*); 1987. 256p. 15.95 o.p. (*0-07-067941-X*) McGraw-Hill Cos., The.

Weber, Joe. Assured Response. 2003. 384p. 25.95 (*0-89141-842-3*, Presidio Pr.) Ballantine Bks.

Wickert, Gary L. Dark Redemption. 1999. 475p. pap. 19.95 (*0-936389-70-2*) Tudor Pubs., Inc.

Zimmerman, R. D. Hostage. 1998. 288p. pap. 10.95 o.s.i (*0-385-31892-8*, Delacorte Pr.) Dell Publishing.

# V

## VAMPIRES—FICTION

Achilli, Justin. Clanbook: Cappadocian. 1997. (Vampire Ser.). (Illus.). 72p. (Orig.). pap. 12.00 (*1-56504-280-8*, 2805) White Wolf Publishing, Inc.

Achilli, Justin, et al. Kindred of the East. 1998. (Vampire Ser.). 220p. 25.00 (*1-56504-232-8*) White Wolf Publishing, Inc.

Adams, Scott Charles. . . .Never Dream. West, Carolyn, ed. 1999. 240p. pap. 15.00 o.p. (*0-9673045-0-4*) Adams, Scott Charles.

Anscombe, Roderick. The Secret Life of Laszlo, Count Dracula. 1994. 416p. 22.95 (*0-7868-6040-5*) Hyperion Pr.

—The Secret Life of Laszlo, Count Dracula. 1995. 480p. mass mkt. 6.50 o.p. (*0-06-100943-1*, HarperTorch) Morrow/Avon.

Augustyn, Michael. Vlad Dracula Vol. 1: The Dragon Prince. unabr. ed. 1995. (Illus.). 310p. pap. 14.99 (*0-9660865-0-3*, MA0001) Vasso Studios.

Baker, Nancy. Kiss of the Vampire. 1995. mass mkt. 5.99 o.s.i (*0-449-14957-9*, Fawcett) Ballantine Bks.

Baker, Scott. Ancestral Hungers. 320p. 1996. pap. 14.95 (*0-312-86305-5*); 1996. mass mkt. 5.99 (*0-8125-0259-0*); 1995. 21.95 o.p. (*0-312-85868-X*) Doherty, Tom Assocs., LLC. (Tor Bks.).

Baker, Trisha. Crimson Shadows. 2003. 384p. mass mkt. 5.99 o.s.i (*0-7860-1556-X*) Kensington Publishing Corp.

Banks, L. A. The Awakening: A Vampire Huntress Legend. 2004. 304p. pap. 12.95 (*0-312-31683-6*) St. Martin's Pr.

—Minion: A Vampire Huntress Legend. 2003. (Vampire Huntress Legend Ser.: Bk. 1). 288p. pap. 12.95 (*0-312-31680-1*, Saint Martin's Griffin) St. Martin's Pr.

Bedwell-Grime, Stephanie. The Bleeding Sun. 2000. E-Book 3.99 (*1-58608-126-8*); 1998. 190p. 4.99 (*1-58608-055-5*) New Concepts Publishing.

Bennett, Janice, et al. Lords of the Night: Tales of Vampire Love. 2001. 32p. pap. 12.00 (*0-7582-0049-8*) Kensington Publishing Corp.

Bennett, Nigel, et al. His Father's Son. 2001. 352p. 24.00 (*0-671-31981-7*) Baen Bks.

Bergstrom, Elaine. Nocturne. 2003. 384p. mass mkt. 6.50 (*0-441-01109-8*) Ace Bks.

Blacksin, Andrea. Revelations of the Dark Mother. 1998. (Vampire Ser.). (Illus.). pap. 10.95 (*1-56504-237-9*, 2024) White Wolf Publishing, Inc.

Bone, Patrick. The Aliens of Transylvania County. 2002. 160p. pap. 13.95 (*1-57072-175-0*); 23.95 (*1-57072-174-2*) Overmountain Pr. (Silver Dagger Mysteries).

Boulle, Philippe. Constantinople by Night. 1996. (Vampire Ser.). pap. text 15.00 (*1-56504-278-6*) White Wolf Publishing, Inc.

Bowen, Carl. Predator & Prey: Vampire. 2000. (Predator & Prey Ser.: Vol. 1). 288p. pap. 6.50 (*1-56504-969-1*) White Wolf Publishing, Inc.

Bowen, Gary. Diary of a Vampire. 1995. (Orig.). mass mkt. 6.95 (*1-56333-331-7*, Rhinoceros) Masquerade Bks., Inc.

—Winter of the Soul: Gay Vampire Fiction. 1995. 32p. pap. 5.00 (*1-887666-06-0*) Obelesk Bks.

Bradbury, Ray. From the Dust Returned. l.t. ed. 2002. 203p. 29.95 (*0-7862-4043-1*) Gale Group.

—From the Dust Returned. 2002. 288p. mass mkt. 6.99 (*0-380-78961-2*); 2001. (Illus.). 224p. 23.00 (*0-380-97382-0*, Morrow, William & Co.) Morrow/Avon.

Bridges, Bill, et al. War of Ages: Elysium/Anarch Cookbook. 1998. (Vampire Ser.). (Illus.). reprint ed. pap. 16.00 (*1-56504-243-3*, 2022) White Wolf Publishing, Inc.

Briery, Traci. The Vampire Journals. 2001. 352p. mass mkt. 5.99 o.s.i (*0-7860-1429-6*, Pinnacle Bks.) Kensington Publishing Corp.

—Vampire Journals. 1998. 352p. mass mkt. 4.99 o.s.i (*0-8217-6024-6*) Kensington Publishing Corp.

Brite, Poppy Z. Love in Vein II: 18 More Original Tales of Vampire Erotica. 2000. 375p. 9.99 (*0-7858-1211-3*) Book Sales, Inc.

Brownworth, Victoria A. Night Bites: Vampire Stories by Women. 1996. 280p. (Orig.). pap. 12.95 (*1-878067-71-0*, Seal Pr.) Avalon Publishing Group.

Byers, Richard L. World of Darkness: Vampire Netherworld. 1995. 336p. mass mkt. 4.99 o.p. (*0-06-105473-9*, Eos) Morrow/Avon.

Cacek, P. D. Night Prayers: A Vampire Novel. 1998. 240p. pap. 15.95 (*1-891946-01-3*) Design Image Group, Inc., The.

Campbell, Brian. Transylvania Chronicles: Dark Tides Rising, Vol. I. 1998. (Vampire Ser.). 120p. pap. 15.00 (*1-56504-290-5*) White Wolf Publishing, Inc.

Campbell, Brian & Rea, Nicky. Transylvania Chronicles: Son of the Dragon. 1998. (Vampire Ser.). (Illus.). pap. 15.00 (*1-56504-291-3*, 2812) White Wolf Publishing, Inc.

Carew, Henry. The Vampires of the Andes. Reginald, R. & Menville, Douglas A., eds. 1978. (Lost Race & Adult Fantasy Ser.). reprint ed. lib. bdg. 29.95 (*0-405-10962-8*) Ayer Co. Pubs., Inc.

Cartier, Crystal. Immortal Obsession: Book One: The Prophecy. 1993. (Immortal Obsession Ser.). 500p. (C). pap. 24.95 (*1-883111-00-5*) Love Story Publishing.

Cassada, Jackie & Rea, Nicky. World of Darkness: Hong Kong. 1998. (World of Darkness Ser.). (Illus.). 160p. pap. 18.00 (*1-56504-222-0*, 2009) White Wolf Publishing, Inc.

Cavelos, Jeanne, ed. The Many Faces of Van Helsing. 2004. 384p. pap. 14.95 (*0-441-01170-5*) Ace Bks.

Cervello, Mike. The Refuge of Night Vol. 1: A Modern Vampire Myth with a Bonus Tale of Renaissance Terror. 1996. (Illus.). 70p. (Orig.). pap. 4.95 (*0-9654364-0-3*) CVK Publishing.

Ciencin, Scott. The Vampire Odyssey. 1992. 416p. mass mkt. 4.50 o.s.i (*0-8217-3853-4*, Zebra Bks.) Kensington Publishing Corp.

Clark, Simon. Vampyrrhic. 2002. mass mkt. 5.99 (*0-8439-5031-5*) Dorchester Publishing Co., Inc.

Clauss, Jedediah. Victorian Vampires. 22.95 (*0-8488-0965-3*) Amereon, Ltd.

Collins, Nancy A. Midnight Blue: The Sonja Blue Collection. 1995. (Illus.). pap. 14.99 (*1-56504-900-4*, 13000) White Wolf Publishing, Inc.

The Count Dracula Book of Classic Vampire Tales. 1981. pap. 6.95 (*0-9611944-7-2*) Dracula Pr.

Cox, Greg & Weisskopf, T. K. Tomorrow Sucks: SF Vampire Stories. 1994. 288p. (Orig.). pap. 4.99 (*0-671-87626-0*) Baen Bks.

Cummings, J. A. Nightchild: A Clans Novel. 1999. (Vampire Clans Ser.). 328p. pap. 15.95 (*0-9670668-0-8*) Kresnak Pr., Ltd.

Curatola, Heather, et al. Hengeyokai: Shapeshifters of the East. 1998. (Werewolf Ser.). (Illus.). pap. 20.00 (*1-56504-338-3*, 3063) White Wolf Publishing, Inc.

Curtin, Joseph. Daughters of the Moon. 2000. 384p. mass mkt. 5.99 o.s.i (*0-7860-1309-5*, Pinnacle Bks.) Kensington Publishing Corp.

Dadey, Debbie & Jones, Marcia Thornton. Vampires Don't Wear Polka Dots. 9999. (Adventures of the Bailey School Kids Ser.: No. 1). Tr. of Vampires Ne Portent Pas de Robe a Pois. (FRE.). (J). (gr. 2-4). pap. 5.99 o.p. (*0-590-73545-4*) Scholastic, Inc.

Dakan, Richard. Ventrue. 2000. (Clanbook Ser.). (Illus.). 104p. pap. 14.95 (*1-56504-255-7*) White Wolf Publishing, Inc.

Dalby, Richard, ed. Vampire Stories. 1993. 7.98 (*1-55521-900-4*) Book Sales, Inc.

Dansky, Richard & Ditchburn, Elizabeth. Clanbook: LaSombra. 1996. (Vampire Ser.). (Illus.). 72p. pap., suppl. ed. 12.00 (*1-56504-211-5*, 2062) White Wolf Publishing, Inc.

Dansky, Richard, et al. Giovanni Chronicles No. II: Blood & Fire. 1996. (Vampire Ser.). (Illus.). 96p. (Orig.). pap. 18.00 (*1-56504-251-4*, 2091) White Wolf Publishing, Inc.

Datlow, Ellen. Blood Is Not Enough. 1994. 230p. mass mkt. 4.99 o.s.i (*0-441-00109-2*) Ace Bks.

—Blood Is Not Enough. 1990. mass mkt. 3.95 o.s.i (*0-425-12178-X*) Berkley Publishing Group.

—Blood Is Not Enough. 1989. 19.95 o.p. (*0-688-08526-1*, Morrow, William & Co.) Morrow/Avon.

Datlow, Ellen, ed. A Whisper of Blood. 1992. 288p. mass mkt. 4.99 o.p. (*0-425-13505-5*) Berkley Publishing Group.

—A Whisper of Blood. 1991. 320p. 22.00 o.p. (*0-688-10361-8*, Morrow, William & Co.) Morrow/Avon.

Dietz, Ulysses G. Desmond: A Novel about Love & the Modern Vampire. 1998. 300p. pap. 13.95 o.p. (*1-55583-470-1*) Alyson Pubns.

Dozois, Gardner. Isaac Asimov's Vampires. 1996. mass mkt. 5.50 o.s.i (*0-441-00387-7*) Ace Bks.

Drake, Shannon. Beneath a Blood Red Moon. 2000. (Five Star Romance Ser.). 394p. 27.95 (*0-7862-2500-9*, Five Star) Gale Group.

—Realm of Shadows. l.t. ed. 2003. (Romance Ser.). 30.95 (*1-58724-406-3*, Wheeler Publishing, Inc.) Gale Group.

—Realm of Shadows. 2002. 416p. mass mkt. 3.99 (*0-8217-7743-2*, Zebra Bks.); mass mkt. 6.99 (*0-8217-7227-9*) Kensington Publishing Corp.

Dufaux, Jean. Raptors. Johnson, Joe, tr. from SPA. (Illus.). 56p. Vol. 3. 2002. pap. 10.95 (*1-56163-298-8*); Vol. 4. 2003. pap. 10.95 (*1-56163-371-2*) NBM Publishing Co.

Dulabone, Christopher. Vampires & Oz. 2000. 148p. E-Book 8.00 (*0-7388-9239-4*) Xlibris Corp.

Eccarius, J. G. The Last Days of Christ the Vampire. 3rd rev. ed. 1996. 192p. (Orig.). pap. 10.00 (*1-886625-00-X*) III Publishing.

Eggleton, Bob, illus. A Coven of Vampires. 1998. xii, 292p. (*0-340-71542-1*) Hodder & Stoughton, Ltd.

Ellis, Jack. Nightlife. 2000. 384p. mass mkt. 5.99 o.s.i (*0-7860-1259-5*, Pinnacle Bks.) Kensington Publishing Corp.

Elrod, P. N. A Chill in the Blood. (Vampire Files Ser.: Vol. 7). 336p. 1998. 20.95 o.s.i (*0-441-00501-2*); 1999. reprint ed. mass mkt. 6.50 o.s.i (*0-441-00627-2*) Ace Bks.

—Cold Streets. 2003. 384p. mass mkt. 6.99 (*0-441-01103-9*); (Vampire Files Ser.: Bk. 9). 22.95 (*0-441-01009-1*) Ace Bks.

—Dance of Death. 1996. (Vampire Files Ser.). 352p. (Orig.). mass mkt. 5.99 o.s.i (*0-441-00309-5*) Ace Bks.

—Dark Sleep. (Vampire Files Ser.: Vol. 8). 368p. 2000. mass mkt. 6.99 (*0-441-00723-6*); 1999. 21.95 o.s.i (*0-441-00591-8*) Ace Bks.

—Death & the Maiden. 1994. (Vampire Files Ser.). 256p. (Orig.). mass mkt. 4.99 o.s.i (*0-441-00071-1*) Ace Bks.

—Death Masque. 1995. 272p. (Orig.). mass mkt. 4.99 o.s.i (*0-441-00143-2*) Ace Bks.

—Lady Crymsyn. 2001. 416p. reprint ed. mass mkt. 6.99 (*0-441-00873-9*) Ace Bks.

—Lady Crymsyn: A Novel of the Vampire Files. 2000. (Vampire Files Ser.: Vol. 9). (Illus.). 416p. 22.95 o.s.i (*0-441-00724-4*) Ace Bks.

—Quincey Morris, Vampire. 2001. 352p. pap. 6.99 (0-671-31988-4) Baen Bks.
—A Red Death. 1993. (Vampire Files Ser.). mass mkt. 4.99 o.s.i (0-441-71094-8) Ace Bks.
—Vampire Files: Blood Art. 1991. (Vampire Files Ser.: Vol. 4). 208p. mass mkt. 5.99 o.s.i (0-441-85945-3) Ace Bks.
—Vampire Files: Blood on the Water. 1992. (Vampire Files Ser.: Vol. 6). 208p. mass mkt. 5.99 o.s.i (0-441-85947-X) Ace Bks.
—Vampire Files: Fire in the Blood. 1991. (Vampire Files Ser.: Vol. 5). mass mkt. 5.99 o.s.i (0-441-85946-1) Ace Bks.
—Vampire Files: The Bloodlist, No. 1. 2003. 464p. pap. 14.00 (0-441-01090-3) Ace Bks.
—Vampire Files No. 01: Bloodlist. 1990. (Vampire Files Ser.). 208p. mass mkt. 6.50 o.s.i (0-441-06795-6) Ace Bks.
—Vampire Files No. 2: Lifeblood. 1990. (Vampire Files Ser.: Vol. 2). 208p. mass mkt. 5.99 o.s.i (0-441-84776-5) Ace Bks.
—Vampire Files No. 3: Bloodcircle. 1990. (Vampire Files Ser.: Vol. 3). mass mkt. 5.99 o.s.i (0-441-06717-4) Ace Bks.
Elrod, P. N., ed. Dracula in London. 2001. 272p. pap. 14.95 (0-441-00858-5) Ace Bks.
—Time of Vampires. 1996. 320p. mass mkt. 5.50 o.s.i (0-88677-693-7) DAW Bks., Inc.
Evans, Gloria E. Meh 'Yam. 2000. (Illus.). 259p. 17.95 (0-9702882-1-2); pap. 12.95 (0-9702882-0-4) T. Bo Publishing.
Farren, Mick. Darklost. 2000. 412p. 24.95 (0-312-86979-7, Tor Bks.) Doherty, Tom Assocs., LLC.
—Time of Feasting. 384p. 1996. 23.95 (0-312-86213-X); Vol. 1. 1998. (Time of Feasting Ser.: Vol. 1). mass mkt. 6.99 (0-8125-3874-9) Doherty, Tom Assocs., LLC. (Tor Bks.).
—Underland. 2002. (Renquist Quartet Ser.). 496p. 27.95 (0-7653-0321-3, Tor Bks.) Doherty, Tom Assocs., LLC.
Feehan, Christine. Dark Guardian. 2002. 384p. mass mkt. 6.99 (0-8439-4994-5, Leisure Bks.) Dorchester Publishing Co., Inc.
—Dark Symphony. 2003. 352p. mass mkt. 6.99 (0-515-13521-6, Jove) Berkley Publishing Group.
—Dark Symphony. l.t. ed. 2003. (Romance Ser.). 28.95 (0-7862-5587-0) Thorndike Pr.
Feehan, Christine, et al. Hot Blooded. 2004. 400p. mass mkt. 7.99 (0-515-13696-4, Jove) Berkley Publishing Group.
Fenyvesi, Angela S. Pilare the Vampire: The Untold Existence. 2002. 361p. pap. 24.95 (1-59129-105-4) PublishAmerica, Inc.
Ferrenz, Barbara J. Worse Than Death. 2003. 250p. 25.95 (0-7862-5395-9, Five Star) Gale Group.
Fleming, Gherbod. Nosferatu. 2000. (Clan Novel Ser.). 288p. pap. 6.50 (1-56504-835-0) White Wolf Publishing, Inc.
Ford, Michael Thomas. Masters of Midnight: Erotic Tales of the Vampire. 2003. 352p. pap. 14.00 (0-7582-0421-3) Kensington Publishing Corp.
Golden, Christie. Ravenloft: Vampire of the Mists. 1999. 341p. (Orig.). pap. 5.99 o.p. (1-56076-155-5) Wizards of the Coast.
Golden, Christopher. Of Saints & Shadows. 1998. (Shadow Saga Ser.: No. 1). 400p. mass mkt. 6.99 (0-441-00570-5) Ace Bks.
—Of Saints & Shadows. 1994. 400p. mass mkt. 5.99 o.s.i (0-515-11388-3, Jove) Berkley Publishing Group.
Golden, Christopher & Holder, Nancy. Immortal, Vol. 1. 2001. (Buffy the Vampire Slayer Ser.: Vol. 1). 320p. E-Book 9.99 (0-7434-3277-0, Simon Pulse) Simon & Schuster Children's Publishing.
Gottlieb, Sherry. Worse Than Death. 2000. 251p. 22.95 (0-312-87392-1, Forge Bks.) Doherty, Tom Assocs., LLC.
Greenberg, Martin H. Vampire Slayers. 2003. 240p. 8.99 (0-517-22197-7) Gramercy Bks.
—Weird Vampire Tales: 30 Blood-Chilling Stories from the Weird Fiction Pulps. 1992. 9.99 o.s.i (0-517-06018-3) Random Hse. Value Publishing.
Greenberg, Martin H., ed. Vampire Detectives. 1995. 320p. (Orig.). mass mkt. 4.99 o.s.i (0-88677-626-0) DAW Bks., Inc.
—Vampires: The Greatest Stories. 1997. (Greatest Stories Ser.). 320p. 9.98 (1-56731-167-9, MJF Bks.) Fine Communications.
Greenberg, Martin H. & Scarborough, Elizabeth Ann, eds. Vampire Slayers: Stories of Those Who Dare to Take Back the Night. 1999. (Slayers Ser.). 239p. pap. 12.95 (1-58182-036-4, Cumberland Hearthside) Cumberland Hse. Publishing.
Gresham, Stephen. In the Blood. 2001. 384p. mass mkt. 5.99 o.s.i (0-7860-1378-8, Pinnacle Bks.) Kensington Publishing Corp.
Guiley, Rosemary Ellen. Vampires among Us. Zion, Claire, ed. 1991. 288p. (Orig.). mass mkt. 5.99 (0-671-72361-8, Pocket) Simon & Schuster.
Hagen, Mark R., et al. Chicago Chronicles Vol. 1: For Vampire: The Masquerade. 1996. (Vampire Ser.). (Illus.). 336p. pap. 22.00 (1-56504-219-0, 2234) White Wolf Publishing, Inc.
Haining, Peter, ed. The Vampire Omnibus. 1998. 496p. pap. text 14.00 (0-7881-5649-7) DIANE Publishing Co.
Hambly, Barbara. Those Who Hunt the Night. 1995. mass mkt. 5.99 o.p. (0-345-90627-6); 1990. 352p. mass mkt. 5.99 o.s.i (0-345-36132-6) Ballantine Bks. (Del Rey).
—Traveling with the Dead. 1996. mass mkt. 5.99 o.s.i (0-345-40740-7, Del Rey) Ballantine Bks.
Hambly, Barbara & Greenberg, Martin H., eds. Sisters of the Night. 1995. 288p. pap. 17.99 (0-446-67143-6) Warner Bks., Inc.
Hamilton, Laurell K. Bloody Bones. 2002. 384p. mass mkt. 6.99 (0-515-13446-5) Berkley Publishing Group.
—Blue Moon. 1998. (Anita Blake Vampire Hunter Ser.: Bk. 8). 432p. mass mkt. 6.99 o.s.i (0-441-00574-8) Ace Bks.
—Burnt Offerings. 1998. (Anita Blake Vampire Hunter Ser.). 400p. mass mkt. 6.99 o.s.i (0-441-00524-1) Ace Bks.
—Burnt Offerings. 2002. 400p. mass mkt. 7.50 (0-515-13447-3) Berkley Publishing Group.
—Cerulean Sins. 2003. (Anita Blake Vampire Hunter Ser.). 416p. 23.95 (0-425-18836-1) Berkley Publishing Group.
—Circus of the Damned. 1995. (Anita Blake Vampire Hunter Ser.). 336p. (Orig.). mass mkt. 6.99 o.s.i (0-441-00197-1) Ace Bks.
—Circus of the Damned. (Orig.). 2004. 320p. 22.95 (0-425-19427-2); 2002. 336p. mass mkt. 6.99 (0-515-13448-1) Berkley Publishing Group.
—Guilty Pleasures. 1993. (Anita Blake Vampire Hunter Ser.). 272p. mass mkt. 6.99 o.s.i (0-441-30483-4) Ace Bks.
—Guilty Pleasures. 2004. 368p. pap. 13.00 (0-425-19754-9); 2002. 272p. mass mkt. 6.99 (0-515-13449-X); 2002. 320p. reprint ed. 21.95 (0-425-18756-X) Berkley Publishing Group.
—Guilty Pleasures. 2002. (Anita Blake Vampire Hunter Ser.). E-Book 6.99 (0-7865-2898-2) Penguin Putnam, Inc E-Books.
—The Killing Dance. 1997. (Anita Blake Vampire Hunter Ser.). 400p. mass mkt. 6.99 o.s.i (0-441-00452-0) Ace Bks.
—The Killing Dance. 2002. 400p. mass mkt. 7.99 (0-515-13451-1) Berkley Publishing Group.
—The Laughing Corpse. 1994. (Anita Blake Vampire Hunter Ser.). 304p. mass mkt. 6.99 o.s.i (0-441-00091-6) Ace Bks.
—The Laughing Corpse. 2003. 320p. 22.95 (0-425-19200-8); 2002. 304p. mass mkt. 7.50 (0-515-13444-9) Berkley Publishing Group.
—The Lunatic Cafe. 1996. (Anita Blake Vampire Hunter Ser.). 384p. mass mkt. 6.99 o.s.i (0-441-00293-5) Ace Bks.
—The Lunatic Cafe. 2002. 384p. mass mkt. 6.99 (0-515-13452-X) Berkley Publishing Group.
—Narcissus in Chains. 2001. 432p. 22.95 (0-425-18168-5); 2002. 656p. reprint ed. mass mkt. 7.99 (0-515-13387-6, Jove) Berkley Publishing Group.
—Obsidian Butterfly: An Anita Blake Vampire Hunter Novel. 2000. (Anita Blake Ser.). 400p. 21.95 (0-441-00684-1); 608p. reprint ed. mass mkt. 7.50 o.s.i (0-441-00781-3) Ace Bks.
—Obsidian Butterfly: An Anita Blake Vampire Hunter Novel. 2002. 608p. mass mkt. 7.99 (0-515-13450-3) Berkley Publishing Group.
Harbaugh, Karen. The Vampire Viscount. 1995. (Regency Romance Ser.). 224p. mass mkt. 3.99 o.s.i (0-451-18319-3, Signet Bks.) NAL.
Hartshorn, Jennifer & Skemp, Ethan. Storyteller's Screen. 1996. (Vampire Ser.). (Illus.). pap. 25.95 (1-56504-276-X, 2801) White Wolf Publishing, Inc.
Hatch, Robert. Clanbook: Ravnos. 1997. (Vampire Ser.). (Illus.). 72p. (Orig.). pap. 12.00 (1-56504-217-4, 2064) White Wolf Publishing, Inc.
Hatch, Robert & Achille, Justin, eds. Dark Tyrants: A Vampire: The Dark Ages Anthology. 1997. 393p. pap. 12.99 (1-56504-868-7, WW 11868, World of Darkness) White Wolf Publishing, Inc.
Hendee, Barb. Thief of Lives. 2004. 416p. mass mkt. 6.99 (0-451-45953-9, ROC) NAL.
Herbert, Brian & Landis, Marie. Blood on the Sun. 1996. (World of Darkness Vampire Ser.). 240p. mass mkt. 5.50 o.p. (0-06-105670-7, Eos) Morrow/Avon.
Herter, Lori. Confession. 1992. 288p. (Orig.). mass mkt. 4.99 o.p. (0-425-13358-3) Berkley Publishing Group.
—Eternity. 1993. 288p. (Orig.). mass mkt. 4.99 o.s.i (0-425-13978-6) Berkley Publishing Group.
—Obsession. 1991. mass mkt. 4.50 o.p. (0-425-12817-2) Berkley Publishing Group.
—Possession. 1992. mass mkt. 4.99 o.p. (0-425-13133-5) Berkley Publishing Group.
Hetherington, Grant. Evolution of the Vampire. 1998. 180p. E-Book 8.00 (0-7388-7981-9) Xlibris Corp.
Higgins, Kristie Lynn. Unexplained Unexpected: Vampiress. 2000. (Illus.). 242p. pap. 21.99 (0-7388-3971-X) Xlibris Corp.
Hill, William. Dawn of the Vampire. 2001. 48p. mass mkt. 5.99 (0-7860-1391-5); 2001. 480p. mass mkt. 6.99 (0-7860-1619-1, Pinnacle Bks.); 1998. 480p. mass mkt. 5.99 o.s.i (0-7860-0537-8, Pinnacle Bks.) Kensington Publishing Corp.
—Vampire's Kiss. 1994. 480p. mass mkt. 4.50 o.s.i (1-55817-886-4) Kensington Publishing Corp.
Hillyer, Vincent. Vampires. 1988. 128p. (Orig.). pap. 15.95 (0-944707-03-3) Loose Change.
Holder, Nancy. The Journals of Rupert Giles. 2002. (Buffy the Vampire Slayer Ser.: Vol. 23). (Illus.). 208p. (YA). pap. 5.99 (0-7434-2712-2, Simon Pulse) Simon & Schuster Children's Publishing.
Holder, Nancy & Mariotte, Jeff. The Unseen Book 1: The Burning. 2001. (Buffy the Vampire Slayer & Angel Crossover Ser.: No. 1). 288p. pap. 6.99 (0-7434-1893-X, Simon Pulse) Simon & Schuster Children's Publishing.
Howell, Richard. Deadbeats Vol. 1: New in Town! 1996. (Illus.). 160p. (Orig.). pap. 12.95 (0-9653109-2-2, Claypool Comics) Boffin Bks.
Huff, Tanya. Blood Debt. 1997. (Victory Nelson Ser.). 336p. mass mkt. 6.99 (0-88677-739-9) DAW Bks., Inc.
—Blood Lines, Bk. 3. 1993. (Daw Book Collectors Ser.: Vol. 901). 272p. (Orig.). mass mkt. 5.99 o.s.i (0-88677-530-2) DAW Bks., Inc.
—Blood Pact. 1993. (Daw Book Collectors Ser.: Vol. 931). 336p. mass mkt. 5.99 o.s.i (0-88677-582-5) DAW Bks., Inc.
—Blood Price. 1991. (Daw Book Collectors Ser.: Vol. 850). 272p. (Orig.). mass mkt. 6.99 (0-88677-471-3) DAW Bks., Inc.
—Blood Trail. 1992. (Victor Nelson Investigator Ser.: Vol. 3). 304p. (Orig.). mass mkt. 6.99 (0-88677-502-7) DAW Bks., Inc.
Jefferson, Jemiah. Wounds. 2002. 384p. mass mkt. 5.99 (0-8439-4998-8, Leisure Bks.) Dorchester Publishing Co., Inc.
Jones, Stephen, ed. The Mammoth Book of Dracula. 1997. (Mammoth Bks.). 512p. pap. 10.95 (0-7867-0428-4, Carroll & Graf Pubs.) Avalon Publishing Group.
—The Mammoth Book of Vampire Stories by Women. 2001. 512p. pap. 11.95 (0-7867-0918-9, Carroll & Graf Pubs.) Avalon Publishing Group.
—The Mammoth Book of Vampires. 1992. (Mammoth Bks.). 512p. pap. 9.95 (0-88184-796-8, Carroll & Graf Pubs.) Avalon Publishing Group.
—The Vampire Stories of R. Chetwynd-Hayes. 1997. (Illus.). 246p. 27.00 (1-878252-33-X) Fedogan & Bremer.
Kalogridis, Jeanne. Children of the Vampire. abr. ed. 1996. audio 7.99 o.p. (1-56740-135-X, 633, Paperback Nova Audio Bks.); 1995. audio 17.95 o.p. (1-56100-444-8, 1637, Nova Audio Bks.); 1995. audio 57.25 o.p. (1-56100-276-3, 1150, Unabridged Library Editions); 1995. audio 23.95 o.p. (1-56100-651-3, 62, Bookcassette) Brilliance Audio.
—Children of the Vampire. 1996. (Diaries of the Family Dracula: Vol. 2). 368p. mass mkt. 6.99 (0-440-22269-9) Dell Publishing.
—Covenant with the Vampire: The Diaries of the Family Dracula. abr. ed. 1994. audio 16.95 o.p. (1-56100-393-X, 1552, Nova Audio Bks.); audio 73.25 o.p. (1-56100-227-5, 849, Unabridged Library Editions); audio 23.95 o.p. (1-56100-602-5, 71, Bookcassette) Brilliance Audio.
—Covenant with the Vampire: The Diaries of the Family Dracula. 1995. (Diaries of the Family Dracula: Vol. 1). 384p. mass mkt. 6.99 (0-440-21543-9) Dell Publishing.
—Covenant with the Vampire: The Diaries of the Family Dracula. l.t. ed. 1995. (Charnwood Large Print Ser.). 448p. 29.99 o.p. (0-7089-8872-5, Charnwood) Thorpe, F. A. Pubs. GBR. *Dist:* Ulverscroft Large Print Bks., Ltd., Ulverscroft Large Print Canada, Ltd.
—Lord of the Vampires: The Diaries of the Family Dracul. 1997. (Diaries of the Family Dracula: Vol. 3). 384p. mass mkt. 6.50 (0-440-22442-X); 1996. 336p. 22.95 o.s.i (0-385-31414-0, Delacorte Pr.) Dell Publishing.
Keesey, Pam, ed. Dark Angels: Lesbian Vampire Stories. 1995. 200p. pap. 10.95 (1-57344-014-0); lib. bdg. 24.95 o.p. (1-57344-015-9) Cleis Pr.
—Daughters of Darkness: Lesbian Vampire Stories. 250p. 1993. 24.95 o.p. (0-939416-77-8); 1993. pap. 9.95 o.p. (0-939416-78-6); 2nd ed. 1998. pap. 14.95 (1-57344-076-0) Cleis Pr.
Kelly, Ronald. Blood Kin. 2001. 384p. mass mkt. 5.99 o.s.i (0-7860-1413-X) Kensington Publishing Corp.
Kiernan, Caitlin R. The Five of Cups. 2003. 370p. 40.00 (1-931081-80-8) Subterranean Pr.
Kilpatrick, Nancy. Bloodlover. 2000. (Power of the Blood Ser.: Vol. 4V). 273p. pap. (0-9686776-0-6) Baskerville Bks.
—The Vampire Stories of Nancy Kilpatrick: 16 Magical Stories of Short Fiction. 2000. 200p. pap. 15.00 (0-88962-726-6) Mosaic Pr.
King, Stephen. El Misterio de Salem's Lot. 2nd ed. 1999. (SPA., Illus.). 512p. (84-01-47456-6) Plaza & Janés Editories, S.A.
—El Misterio de Salem's Lot. 2001. (SPA.). 512p. pap. 9.50 (0-609-81086-3, RH13085, Living Language) Random Hse. Information Group.
—Salem's Lot. 1990. 464p. 35.00 (0-385-00751-5) Doubleday Publishing.
—Salem's Lot. 1991. (Stephen King Collectors Editions Ser.). (Illus.). 400p. pap. 14.95 o.p. (0-452-26721-8, Plume) Dutton/Plume.
—Salem's Lot. l.t. ed. 1994. 694p. lib. bdg. 23.95 (0-8161-5686-7, Macmillan Reference USA) Gale Group.
—Salem's Lot. 1979. mass mkt. 2.75 o.p. (0-451-09231-7); 1976. mass mkt. 1.95 o.p. (0-451-07112-3); 1976. mass mkt. 2.25 o.p. (0-451-08000-9); 1976. mass mkt. 3.50 o.p. (0-451-09827-7); 1976. mass mkt. 3.95 o.p. (0-451-12545-2); 1976. mass mkt. 4.50 o.p. (0-451-13969-0); 1976. mass mkt. 3.95 o.p. (0-451-12158-9); 1976. mass mkt. 2.95 o.p. (0-451-09545-6); 1976. mass mkt. 2.50 o.p. (0-451-09000-4); 1976. mass mkt. 4.95 o.p. (0-451-16588-8); 1976. mass mkt. 4.50 o.p. (0-451-15065-1); 1976. (Illus.). 448p. (YA). (gr. 10). reprint ed. mass mkt. 7.99 o.s.i (0-451-16808-9) NAL. (Signet Bks.).
—Salem's Lot. 1999. 656p. mass mkt. 7.99 (0-671-03974-1); 2000. 480p. pap. 13.95 (0-671-03975-X) Simon & Schuster. (Pocket).
—Salem's Lot. 1990. 14.04 (0-606-02434-4) Turtleback Bks.
King, William. Vampireslayer. Gascoigne, Marc, ed. 2003. (Gotrek & Felix Ser.). 320p. mass mkt. 6.99 (1-84416-053-X, Black Library, The) BL Publishing GBR. *Dist:* Simon & Schuster Canada.
—Vampireslayer. 2001. 288p. mass mkt. 6.95 o.p. (0-7434-1168-4, Games Workshop) Simon & Schuster.
Knight, Amarantha, ed. Love Bites. 1995. (Orig.). pap. 12.95 (1-56333-234-5, Kasak, Richard Bks.) Masquerade Bks., Inc.
Knight, Eric. Way of the Wolf: Book One of the Vampire Earth. 2003. 400p. mass mkt. 6.50 (0-451-45939-3, ROC) NAL.
Lackey, Mercedes. Burning Water. 1992. 314p. pap. text 6.99 (0-8125-2485-3, Tor Bks.) Doherty, Tom Assocs., LLC.
—Children of the Night. 1992. 313p. pap. text 6.99 (0-8125-2272-9); 1990. mass mkt. 3.95 o.s.i (0-8125-2112-9) Doherty, Tom Assocs., LLC. (Tor Bks.).
—Jinx High. 1991. 314p. (Orig.). pap. text 4.99 o.s.i (0-8125-2114-5, Tor Bks.) Doherty, Tom Assocs., LLC.
Lamb, Charlotte. Vampire Lover: (Presents Plus) 1995. (Harlequin Presents Ser.). 189p. pap. (0-373-11720-5, 1-11720-9, Harlequin Bks.) Harlequin Enterprises, Ltd.
Lauria, Frank. Raga Six. 2001. 275p. pap. 12.95 (1-58394-043-X) Frog, Ltd.
Laymon, Richard. Bite. 1999. (Love Spell Ser.). 384p. mass mkt. 5.50 (0-8439-4550-8, Leisure Bks.) Dorchester Publishing Co., Inc.
—Bite. 1997. 378p. pap. 11.95 (0-7472-5101-0) Headline Bk. Publishing, Ltd. GBR. *Dist:* Trafalgar Square.
—Bite. 1999. E-Book 9.95 (0-585-29846-7) netLibrary, Inc.
Lee, Diana. A Taste for Blood. 2003. 370p. pap. 19.95 (1-56023-461-X, Alice Street Editions) Haworth Pr., Inc., The.
Lee, Earl. Drakulya: The Lost Journal of Mircea Drakulya, Lord of the Undead. 1994. 224p. pap. 10.95 o.p. (1-884365-02-7) See Sharp Pr.
Lichtenberg, Jacqueline. Those of My Blood. 2003. 400p. pap. 14.95 (1-932100-09-1) BenBella Bks.
—Those of My Blood. 1988. 416p. 19.95 o.p. (0-312-02298-0) St. Martin's Pr.
Lord, David Thomas. Bound in Blood: The Erotic Journey of a Vampire. 2001. 352p. pap. 14.00 (1-57566-764-9) Kensington Publishing Corp.
—Bound in Flesh. 2002. pap. 14.00 (1-57566-765-7) Kensington Publishing Corp.
Lorrah, Jean. Blood Will Tell. 2002. pap. 14.95 (1-58749-134-6); 2001. E-Book 4.75 (1-58749-094-3); Romance/suspense. 2001. E-Book 4.75 incl. disk (1-58749-093-5) Awe-Struck E-Bks.
—Blood Will Tell. 2003. 304p. per. 14.95 (1-932100-03-2) BenBella Bks.
Lumley, Brian. A Coven of Vampires. 1998. 261p. 27.00 (1-878252-37-2) Fedogan & Bremer.
—Harry Keogh: Necroscope & Other Heroes! 2003. 320p. 25.95 (0-7653-0847-9, Tor Bks.) Doherty, Tom Assocs., LLC.
—Invaders. 2nd ed. 1999. (Necroscope Ser.: 10). 384p. 25.95 (0-312-86814-6, Tor Bks.) Doherty, Tom Assocs., LLC.
—Necroscope: Avengers. 2001. (Necroscope Ser.: Vol. 13). E-Book 25.95 (1-58945-853-2) Adobe Systems, Inc.

—Necroscope: Avengers. (Necroscope Ser.: Vol. 13). 2002. 560p. mass mkt. 7.99 (*0-8125-7019-7*); 2001. 448p. 25.95 (*0-312-87923-7*) Doherty, Tom Assocs., LLC. (Tor Bks.).

Lungu, Radu. Dracula. 2000. (Temporis Ser.). (Illus.). 206p. 55.00 (*1-85995-780-3*) Parkstone Pr.

Marffin, Kyle. Carmilla - The Return: A Vampire Novel. 1998. 336p. pap. 15.95 (*1-891946-02-1*) Design Image Group, Inc., The.

—Gothique: A Vampire Novel. 2000. 448p. pap. 15.95 (*1-891946-06-4*) Design Image Group, Inc., The.

Mariotte, Jeff, et al. Angel: The Angel Casefiles. 2002. (Angel Ser.). (Illus.). 368p. (YA). pap. 16.95 (*0-7434-2414-X*, Simon Pulse) Simon & Schuster Children's Publishing.

Matheson, Richard. I Am Legend. 1997. 317p. reprint ed. pap. 13.95 (*0-312-86504-X*, NPB 0275, Orb Bks.) Doherty, Tom Assocs., LLC.

McKean, Thomas. Vampire Vacation. 1986. pap. 2.50 (*0-380-89808-X*, Avon Bks.) Morrow/Avon.

McKinley, Robin. Sunshine. 2003. 400p. 23.95 (*0-425-19178-8*) Berkley Publishing Group.

McMahan, Jeffrey N. Vampires Anonymous. 1991. 256p. pap. 8.95 o.p. (*1-55583-183-4*) Alyson Pubns.

Miller, Linda Lael. Into the Night. 2002. 496p. pap. 14.00 (*0-425-18615-6*) Berkley Publishing Group.

Mitchell, Mary Ann. Cathedral of Vampires. 2002. 368p. mass mkt. 5.99 (*0-8439-5023-4*, Leisure Bks.) Dorchester Publishing Co., Inc.

Moore, Elaine. Retribution: Madonna of the Dark, Book II. 2002. 248p. pap. 12.95 (*1-928704-19-0*, Authorlink Pr.) Authorlink.

Moriarty, Tim. Vampire Nights. 1989. mass mkt. 3.95 o.s.i (*1-55817-180-0*, Pinnacle Bks.) Kensington Publishing Corp.

Morris, J. R. Vampyre Mystry. 2002. 320p. pap. 19.95 (*0-87714-236-X*); 2000. E-Book 6.95 (*0-87714-502-4*) Denlingers Pubs., Ltd.

Mosiman, Billie Sue. Malachi's Moon. 2002. 352p. mass mkt. 6.99 (*0-7564-0048-1*) DAW Bks., Inc.

—Red Moon Rising. 2001. 320p. mass mkt. 6.99 (*0-88677-955-3*) DAW Bks., Inc.

Murray, Doug. Blood Relations. 1996. (World of Darkness Vampire Ser.). 304p. mass mkt. 5.50 o.p. (*0-06-105674-X*, Eos) Morrow/Avon.

Muss-Barnes, Eric. The Gothic Rainbow. 1997. (Vampire Noctuaries Ser.: Vol. 1). (Illus.). 496p. pap. 21.95 (*0-9656318-2-6*) Dubh Sith Ink.

Muth, Jon J. Dracula: A Symphony in Moonlight & Nightmares. 1986. (Illus.). 80p. 7.95 o.p. (*0-87135-171-4*) Marvel Enterprises.

—Dracula: A Symphony in Moonlight & Nightmares. 1993. 80p. 45.00 o.p. (*1-56163-060-8*); 2nd ed. pap. 7.99 o.p. (*1-56163-059-4*) NBM Publishing Co.

Nasaw, Jonathan. Shadows. 1997. 384p. 24.95 o.s.i (*0-525-94065-0*) Dutton/Plume.

—Shadows. 1998. 400p. mass mkt. 6.99 o.s.i (*0-451-18659-1*, Signet Bks.) NAL.

Newman, Kim. Anno Dracula. 1994. 416p. mass mkt. 5.99 (*0-380-72345-X*, Avon Bks.) Morrow/Avon.

—The Bloody Red Baron. 1995. 320p. 21.00 o.p. (*0-7867-0252-4*, Carroll & Graf Pubs.) Avalon Publishing Group.

—Bloody Red Baron. 1997. mass mkt. 5.99 (*0-380-72714-5*, Avon Bks.) Morrow/Avon.

—Judgement of Tears: Anno Dracula 1959. 1998. 240p. 22.95 o.p. (*0-7867-0558-2*, Carroll & Graf Pubs.) Avalon Publishing Group.

Nox, Abraham R. Bloodfellow Book One: Separation. 2000. 536p. pap. 26.99 (*0-7388-2931-5*) Xlibris Corp.

—Bloodfellow Book Two: Transformation. 2000. 512p. pap. 26.99 (*0-7388-2932-3*) Xlibris Corp.

O'Connor, William. Three Pillars. 1997. (Vampire Ser.). (Illus.). pap. 18.00 (*1-56504-288-3*, 2809) White Wolf Publishing, Inc.

Pantaleo, Jack. Mother Julian & the Gentle Vampire. 2000. (New Voices in American Fiction Ser.). 230p. pap. 14.95 (*1-883938-66-X*) Dry Bones Pr.

Patterson, James. Violets Are Blue. 2001. 400p. 27.95 o.p. (*0-316-69323-5*); 432p. 27.95 o.p. (*0-316-68656-5*) Little Brown & Co.

—Violets Are Blue. 2001. pap. 16.00 o.s.i (*0-446-67860-0*) Warner Bks., Inc.

Pike, Christopher, pseud. Black Blood. MacDonald, Patricia, ed. 1994. (Last Vampire Ser.: No. 2). 208p. (YA). (gr. 7 up). pap. 3.99 (*0-671-87266-4*, Simon Pulse) Simon & Schuster Children's Publishing.

—The Last Vampire. MacDonald, Patricia, ed. 1994. 208p. (YA). (gr. 9 up). 14.00 o.p. (*0-671-87256-7*, Simon & Schuster Children's Publishing); (Last Vampire Ser.: Vol. 1). (gr. 7-12). mass mkt. 5.99 (*0-671-87264-8*, Simon Pulse) Simon & Schuster Children's Publishing.

—The Last Vampire. 1994. (Last Vampire Ser.: Vol. 1). (Illus.). (J). mass mkt. 3.99 (*0-671-89276-2*, Simon Pulse) Simon & Schuster Children's Publishing.

—The Last Vampire. 1994. 11.04 (*0-606-06522-9*) Turtleback Bks.

Pitt, Ingrid. The Ingrid Pitt Bedside Companion for Vampire Lovers. 1998. (Illus.). 192p. pap. text 19.95 (*0-7134-8277-X*) Batsford, B.T. Ltd. GBR. *Dist:* Branford, Charles T. Co.

Pocket, G. Buffy Adult. 2002. (Buffy the Vampire Slayer Ser.: Vol. 20). 240p. mass mkt. 6.99 (*0-7434-2774-2*, Simon & Schuster Children's Publishing) Simon & Schuster Children's Publishing.

Polidori, John William. The Vampyre. 2003. (Revolution & Romanticism, 1789-1834 Ser.). 84p. (*1-85477-255-4*); pap. (*1-85477-256-2*) Woodstock Books.

Polidori, John William, et al. Three Vampire Tales. Williams, Anne, ed. 2003. (New Riverside Edtions Ser.). viii, 481p. pap. 9.96 (*0-618-08490-8*) Houghton Mifflin Co.

Prest, Thomas P. Varney, the Vampire: or The Feast of Blood, 3 vols., Set. Varma, Devendra P., ed. 1972. (Gothic Novels II Ser.). 933p. reprint ed. 64.95 (*0-405-00801-5*) Ayer Co. Pubs., Inc.

Queen, Stephanie. Libra, Angel or Vampire. 1997. 304p. 21.95 (*1-57087-336-4*) Professional Pr.

Rice, Anne. Anne Rice's the Vampire Lestat: The Graphic Novel. 1991. (Illus.). 384p. (Orig.). pap. 25.00 o.s.i (*0-345-37394-4*) Ballantine Bks.

—Blackwood Farm. 2003. 640p. mass mkt. 7.99 (*0-345-44368-3*) Ballantine Bks.

—Blackwood Farm. 2002. (Vampire Chronicles). 544p. 26.95 (*0-375-41199-2*); (*0-676-97542-9*) Knopf, Alfred A. Inc.

—Blackwood Farm: The Vampire Chronicles. 2002. E-Book 6.99 (*1-4000-4020-5*) Knopf Publishing Group.

—Blood & Gold. E-Book 21.50 (*1-59061-268-X*) Adobe Systems, Inc.

—Blood & Gold. 2002. (Vampire Chronicles). 576p. mass mkt. 7.99 (*0-345-40932-9*, Ballantine Bks.) Ballantine Bks.

—Blood & Gold. 2001. (Vampire Chronicles). 480p. 26.95 (*0-679-45449-7*) Knopf, Alfred A. Inc.

—Blood & Gold. l.t. ed. 2001. 784p. 26.95 (*0-375-43133-0*) Random Hse. Large Print.

—Blood Canticle. 2003. (Vampire Chronicles). E-Book 25.95 (*1-4000-4194-5*) Knopf Publishing Group.

—Blood Canticle. 2003. (Vampire Chronicles). 320p. 25.95 (*0-375-41200-X*) Knopf, Alfred A. Inc.

—Blood Canticle. abr. ed. 2003. audio 25.95 (*0-7393-0467-4*, Listening Library); audio 25.95 (*0-7393-0467-4*, Listening Library); audio compact disk 29.95 (*0-7393-0630-8*, Listening Library); audio compact disk 29.95 (*0-7393-0630-8*, Listening Library); audio 39.95 (*0-7393-0631-6*) Random Hse. Audio Publishing Group.

—Entrevista con el Vampiro. 2000. (SPA.). pap. 11.95 (*84-406-4149-4*) B Ediciones S.A. ESP. *Dist:* Distribooks, Inc.

—Entrevista con el Vampiro. 4th ed. 2000. (SPA., Illus.). 464p. 9.00 (*84-95501-25-2*, SN12818) Suma de Letras, S.L. ESP. *Dist:* Lectorum Pubns., Inc., Santillana USA Publishing Co., Inc.

—Interview with the Vampire. 1997. (Vampire Chronicles: Bk. 1). pap. 14.00 o.s.i (*0-345-91272-1*); 1994. (Vampire Chronicles: Bk. 1). pap. 6.99 o.p. (*0-345-90444-3*); 1994. (Vampire Chronicles: Bk. 1). mass mkt. 6.99 o.p. (*0-345-90333-1*); 1991. (Vampire Chronicles: Bk. 1). 352p. mass mkt. 7.99 (*0-345-33766-2*); 1985. mass mkt. 3.50 o.p. (*0-345-32899-X*); 1982. mass mkt. 2.95 o.p. (*0-345-31059-4*); 1981. mass mkt. 2.75 o.p. (*0-345-29882-9*); 1979. mass mkt. 2.25 o.p. (*0-345-28126-8*); 20th ed. 1997. (Vampire Chronicles: Bk. 1). 352p. pap. 14.95 (*0-345-40964-7*) Ballantine Bks.

—Interview with the Vampire. 1991. (Vampire Chronicles: Bk. 1). 320p. reprint ed. lib. bdg. 35.95 (*0-89966-781-3*) Buccaneer Bks., Inc.

—Interview with the Vampire. (Vampire Chronicles: Bk. 1). 1994. 23.00 o.s.i (*0-394-26725-7*); 1993. o.s.i (*0-394-25662-X*); 1976. 352p. 27.95 (*0-394-49821-6*); 1996. 384p. 35.00 o.s.i (*0-679-45084-X*) Knopf, Alfred A. Inc.

—Interview with the Vampire. 1987. audio 14.95 o.p. (*0-394-55747-6*); Set. 1995. audio compact disk 25.00 (*0-679-44764-4*); Set. 1986. audio 17.00 (*0-394-55617-8*, 390985) Random Hse. Audio Publishing Group. (RH Audio).

—Interview with the Vampire. unabr. ed. (Vampire Chronicles: Bk. 1). 1999. audio compact disk 114.00 (*0-7887-3442-3*, C1048E7); 1994. audio 85.00 (*0-7887-0065-0*, 94321E7) Recorded Bks., LLC.

—Memnoch, the Devil. (Vampire Chronicles: Bk. 5). 1997. pap. 14.00 o.s.i (*0-345-91273-X*); 1996. mass mkt. 7.50 o.s.i (*0-345-40499-8*); 1996. 464p. pap. 14.95 (*0-345-38940-9*) Ballantine Bks.

—Memnoch, the Devil. 1995. (Vampire Chronicles: Bk. 5). 368p. 29.95 (*0-679-44101-8*) Knopf, Alfred A. Inc.

—Memnoch, the Devil. abr. ed. 1995. (Vampire Chronicles). audio 23.50 (*0-679-43832-7*, 493006, RH Audio) Random Hse. Audio Publishing Group.

—Memnoch, the Devil. deluxe ltd. num. ed. 1995. (Vampire Chronicles: Vol. 5). 354p. 195.00 (*0-9631925-4-X*) Trice, B.E. Publishing.

—Merrick. 2000. 320p. o.s.i (*0-676-97331-0*) Knopf Canada CAN. *Dist:* Random Hse. of Canada, Ltd., Random Hse., Inc.

—Merrick. 2000. (Vampire Chronicles). 320p. 26.95 (*0-679-45448-9*) Knopf, Alfred A. Inc.

—Merrick. l.t. ed. 2000. 544p. 26.95 (*0-375-43077-6*) Random Hse. Large Print.

—Pandora. 1998. (New Tales of the Vampires Ser.: Bk. 1). 368p. mass mkt. 7.99 (*0-345-42238-4*) Ballantine Bks.

—Pandora. l.t. ed. 1998. (New Tales of the Vampires Ser.: Bk. 1). 384p. pap. 19.95 o.p. (*0-7838-8337-4*, Macmillan Reference USA) Gale Group.

—Pandora. aut. ed. 1998. (New Tales of the Vampires Ser.: Bk. 1). 19.95 o.p. (*0-676-54921-7*) Random Hse., Inc.

—Pandora. ltd. ed. 1998. (New Tales of the Vampires Ser.: Bk. 1). 356p. 150.00 (*1-890885-02-9*) Trice, B.E. Publishing.

—Pandora: New Tales of the Vampires. l.t. ed. 1998. (New Tales of the Vampires Ser.: Bk. 1). 288p. pap. 19.95 (*0-375-70218-0*) Random Hse. Large Print.

—Pandora: New Tales of the Vampires. 1998. (New Tales of the Vampires Ser.: Bk. 1). 368p. 19.95 (*0-375-40159-8*) Random Hse., Inc.

—The Queen of the Damned. 1997. (Vampire Chronicles: Bk. 3). 464p. pap. 15.00 (*0-345-41962-6*); 1994. (Vampire Chronicles: Bk. 3). mass mkt. 6.99 o.p. (*0-345-90335-8*); 1989. (Vampire Chronicles: Bk. 3). 512p. mass mkt. 7.99 (*0-345-35152-5*); 1989. mass mkt. 5.95 o.s.i (*0-345-36260-8*); 1988. (Vampire Chronicles: Bk. 3). 464p. 27.95 (*0-394-55823-5*) Ballantine Bks.

—The Queen of the Damned. 1993. (Vampire Chronicles: Bk. 3). o.s.i (*0-394-25660-3*) Knopf, Alfred A. Inc.

—The Queen of the Damned. abr. ed. 1988. (Critical Edition Ser.). audio 18.00 (*0-394-57318-8*, 391430, RH Audio) Random Hse. Audio Publishing Group.

—The Queen of the Damned. 1990. 5.99 o.p. (*0-517-05227-X*) Random Hse. Value Publishing.

—The Queen of the Damned. unabr. ed. 1995. (Vampire Chronicles: Bk. 3). audio 120.00 (*0-7887-0100-2*, 94341E7) Recorded Bks., LLC.

—The Tale of the Body Thief. 1997. 448p. pap. 15.00 (*0-345-41963-4*); 1994. (Vampire Chronicles: Bk. 4). mass mkt. 6.99 o.p. (*0-345-90336-6*); 1993. (Vampire Chronicles: Bk. 4). 448p. mass mkt. 7.99 (*0-345-38475-X*); 1993. mass mkt. 5.99 o.s.i (*0-345-38388-5*) Ballantine Bks.

—The Tale of the Body Thief. 1992. (Vampire Chronicles). 428p. 23.50 o.s.i (*0-394-22317-9*) Knopf, Alfred A. Inc.

—The Tale of the Body Thief, Set. abr. ed. 1992. (Vampire Chronicles: No. 4). pap. 18.00 incl. audio (*0-679-41162-3*, RH Audio) Random Hse. Audio Publishing Group.

—The Tale of the Body Thief. unabr. ed. 1995. (Vampire Chronicles: Bk. 4). audio 112.00 (*0-7887-0096-0*, 94337E7) Recorded Bks., LLC.

—The Tale of the Body Thief: The Vampire Chronicles. 1992. (Vampire Chronicles: Bk. 4). 448p. 30.00 (*0-679-40528-3*) Knopf, Alfred A. Inc.

—The Vampire Armand. (Vampire Chronicles). 2002. E-Book 7.99 (*0-345-46453-2*, Ballantine Bks.); 1999. 400p. pap. 14.95 (*0-345-40927-2*) Ballantine Bks.

—The Vampire Armand. l.t. ed. 1999. (New Tales of the Vampires Ser.: Bk. 2). pap. 26.95 o.p. (*0-7838-0263-3*, Macmillan Reference USA) Gale Group.

—The Vampire Chronicles, 4 vols. (Vampire Chronicles). 1993. 31.96 (*0-345-38540-3*); Set. 1989. 20.97 (*0-345-36422-8*) Ballantine Bks.

—The Vampire Chronicles, 3 vols. 1990. (Vampire Chronicles). 99.50 o.s.i (*0-394-58186-5*) Random Hse., Inc.

—The Vampire Lestat. (Vampire Chronicles: Bk. 2). 1997. 496p. pap. 15.95 (*0-345-41964-2*); 1994. mass mkt. 6.99 o.p. (*0-345-90334-X*); 1986. 560p. mass mkt. 7.99 (*0-345-31386-0*) Ballantine Bks.

—The Vampire Lestat. (Vampire Chronicles: Bk. 2). 1993. o.s.i (*0-394-25661-1*); 1985. 496p. 27.95 (*0-394-53443-3*) Knopf, Alfred A. Inc.

—The Vampire Lestat, Set. abr. ed. 1989. (Vampire Chronicles). audio 18.00 (*0-394-57705-1*, 391846, RH Audio) Random Hse. Audio Publishing Group.

—The Vampire Lestat. unabr. ed. 1994. (Vampire Chronicles: Bk. 2). audio 128.00 (*0-7887-0098-7*, 94339E7) Recorded Bks., LLC.

—Vittorio, the Vampire: New Tales of the Vampires. 2001. (New Tales of the Vampires Ser.: Bk. 3). 304p. mass mkt. 7.99 (*0-345-42239-2*, Ballantine Bks.) Ballantine Bks.

—Vittorio, the Vampire: New Tales of the Vampires. l.t. ed. 1999. (New Tales of the Vampires Ser.: Bk. 3). pap. 30.00 o.p. (*0-7838-8486-9*, Macmillan Reference USA) Gale Group.

—Vittorio, the Vampire: New Tales of the Vampires. 1999. (New Tales of the Vampires Ser.: Bk. 3). o.s.i (*0-676-58668-6*); (Illus.). 304p. 19.95 (*0-375-40160-1*) Knopf, Alfred A. Inc.

—Vittorio, the Vampire: New Tales of the Vampires. l.t. ed. 1999. (New Tales of the Vampires Ser.: Bk. 3). 352p. pap. 19.95 (*0-375-70572-4*) Random Hse. Large Print.

—Vittorio, the Vampire: New Tales of the Vampires. ltd. ed. 1999. (New Tales of the Vampires Ser.: Bk. 3). 292p. 150.00 (*1-890885-07-X*) Trice, B.E. Publishing.

Robbins, David. Vampire Strike - Pipeline Strike, 2 vols. in 1, Set. 1992. (Blade Double Edition Ser.). 384p. mass mkt. 4.50 (*0-8439-3310-0*, Leisure Bks.) Dorchester Publishing Co., Inc.

Roberts, Bette B. Anne Rice. 1995. pap. 14.95 (*0-8057-9231-7*); 1994. (Twayne's United States Authors Ser.: No. 644). 192p. 33.00 (*0-8057-3961-0*) Gale Group. (Macmillan Reference USA).

Romkey, Michael. The London Vampire Panic. 2001. 304p. mass mkt. 6.99 (*0-449-00573-9*) Ballantine Bks.

—Vampire Hunter. 1998. 320p. mass mkt. 6.50 (*0-449-00200-4*, Fawcett) Ballantine Bks.

—The Vampire Princess. 1995. 352p. mass mkt. 6.99 (*0-449-14937-4*, Fawcett) Ballantine Bks.

Ronald, Bruce. Dracula, Baby - Musical Comedy. 1970. 104p. pap. 5.95 (*0-87129-626-8*, D01) Dramatic Publishing Co.

Ross, Clarissa. Secret of the Pale Lover. 2000. 196p. pap. 25.95 (*0-7862-2636-6*, Five Star) Gale Group.

Rowe, Michael. Brothers of the Night: Tales of Men, Blood & Immortality. 1997. 180p. pap. 14.95 o.p. (*1-57344-025-6*) Cleis Pr.

Ryan, Alan, ed. The Penguin Book of Vampire Stories. 1989. 640p. 14.95 (*0-14-012445-4*) Viking Penguin.

Saberhagen, Fred. A Coldness in the Blood. E-Book 25.95 (*0-312-70835-1*, Tor Bks.); 2002. 384p. 25.95 (*0-7653-0045-1*, Forge Bks.) Doherty, Tom Assocs., LLC.

—Dominion. (Orig.). 1992. 320p. mass mkt. 5.99 (*0-8125-2386-5*); 1990. pap. 3.95 o.s.i (*0-8125-0855-6*) Doherty, Tom Assocs., LLC. (Tor Bks.).

—The Dominion. 1982. 320p. (Orig.). mass mkt. 2.95 o.s.i (*0-523-48536-0*, Tor Bks.) Doherty, Tom Assocs., LLC.

—The Dracula Tape. 1985. 288p. mass mkt. 2.95 o.s.i (*0-441-16601-6*) Ace Bks.

—The Dracula Tape. 1999. 288p. mass mkt. 5.99 (*0-671-57839-1*) Baen Bks.

—The Dracula Tape. 1992. 280p. mass mkt. 5.99 (*0-8125-2383-0*); 1989. pap. 3.95 o.s.i (*0-8125-2581-7*) Doherty, Tom Assocs., LLC. (Tor Bks.).

—Holmes-Dracula File. 1982. mass mkt. 2.50 o.s.i (*0-441-34247-7*); 1981. mass mkt. 2.25 o.s.i (*0-441-34246-9*) Ace Bks.

—Holmes-Dracula File. 1992. 249p. mass mkt. 4.99 (*0-8125-2384-9*); 1989. pap. 3.95 o.s.i (*0-8125-0255-8*) Doherty, Tom Assocs., LLC. (Tor Bks.).

—A Matter of Taste. 1992. 288p. mass mkt. 3.99 (*0-8125-2575-2*); 1990. 16.95 o.p. (*0-312-85046-8*) Doherty, Tom Assocs., LLC. (Tor Bks.).

—An Old Friend of the Family. 1981. 256p. mass mkt. 2.50 o.s.i (*0-441-62161-9*) Ace Bks.

—An Old Friend of the Family. 1992. 247p. mass mkt. 4.99 (*0-8125-2385-7*); 1987. 256p. reprint ed. pap. 3.50 o.s.i (*0-8125-2550-7*) Doherty, Tom Assocs., LLC. (Tor Bks.).

—A Question of Time. 1993. 278p. pap. text 5.99 (*0-8125-2577-9*); 1992. 272p. 19.95 o.p. (*0-312-85129-4*) Doherty, Tom Assocs., LLC. (Tor Bks.).

—Seance for a Vampire. 1994. 288p. 21.95 o.p. (*0-312-85562-1*); Vol. 1. 1997. 310p. pap. 5.99 o.s.i (*0-8125-3348-8*) Doherty, Tom Assocs., LLC. (Tor Bks.).

—Thorn. 1980. mass mkt. 2.75 o.s.i (*0-441-80744-5*) Ace Bks.

—Thorn. 1990. mass mkt. 4.95 (*0-8125-0316-3*, Tor Bks.) Doherty, Tom Assocs., LLC.

—The Vlad Tapes. 2000. 544p. pap. 6.99 (*0-671-57878-2*) Baen Bks.

Saberhagen, Fred & Hart, James V. Bram Stoker's Dracula. 1992. 304p. mass mkt. 4.99 o.p. (*0-451-17575-1*, Signet Bks.) NAL.

Schiefelbein, Michael. Vampire Thrall: A Novel. 2003. 224p. pap. 13.95 (*1-55583-728-X*) Alyson Pubns.

Schildt, Chris. Night of Dracula. 2001. 192p. pap. 6.99 (*0-7434-3452-8*, Pocket) Simon & Schuster.

Schimel, Lawrence & Greenberg, Martin H., eds. Blood Lines: Vampire Stories from New England. 1997. (American Vampire Ser.). (Illus.). 240p. (Orig.). pap. 12.95 (*1-888952-50-4*) Cumberland Hse. Publishing.

—Southern Blood: Vampire Stories from the American South. 1997. (American Vampire Ser.). (Illus.). 240p. (Orig.). pap. 12.95 (*1-888952-49-0*) Cumberland Hse. Publishing.

Schimel, Lawrence & Greenburg, Martin, eds. Fields of Blood: Vampire Stories of the Heartland. 1998. (American Vampire Ser.). 224p. pap. 12.95 (*1-888952-79-2*) Cumberland Hse. Publishing.

—Streets of Blood: Vampires Stories from New York City. 1998. (American Vampire Ser.). 240p. pap. 12.95 (1-888952-78-4) Cumberland Hse. Publishing.

Shayne, Maggie B. Born in Twilight, abr. ed. 2000. (Silhouette Romance Ser.). audio 7.99 o.p. (1-56740-533-9, 1842, Silhouette Romance Audio) Brilliance Audio.

—Born in Twilight. 1997. 384p. per. (0-373-48338-4, 1-483387, Harlequin Bks.) Harlequin Enterprises, Ltd.

Shepard, Leslie. Classic Vampire Stories. 1995. 272p. pap. 9.95 o.s.i (0-8065-1664-X, Citadel Pr.) Kensington Publishing Corp.

Shepard, Leslie, ed. The Book of Dracula. 1991. 560p. reprint ed. 12.99 o.s.i (0-517-03758-0) Random Hse. Value Publishing.

—The Dracula Book of Great Vampire Stories. 1978. 1.95 o.s.i (0-515-04506-3, Jove) Berkley Publishing Group.

—The Dracula Book of Great Vampire Stories. 1989. 6.99 o.p. (0-517-03016-0) Random Hse. Value Publishing.

The Siddhi Kur: Tales of the Bewitched Vampire, the Vetalapan-cavimsatika. (Mongolia Society Special Papers: Issue III). 7.50 (0-910980-23-3) Mongolia Society, Inc., The.

Simmons, Dan. Children of the Night. unabr. ed. 1992. audio 23.95 o.p. (1-56100-470-7, 61, Bookcassette-);Set. audio 73.25 o.p. (1-56100-104-X, 825, Unabridged Library Editions) Brilliance Audio.

—Children of the Night. deluxe ed. 1992. 450p. (J). 125.00 (0-935716-63-7) Lord John Pr.

—Children of the Night. 320p. (J). 2015. 100.00 (0-399-13757-2); 1992. 21.95 o.p. (0-399-13717-3) Penguin Group (USA) Inc. (G. P. Putnam's Sons).

—Children of the Night. 1993. 464p. reprint ed. mass mkt. 6.99 (0-446-36475-4) Warner Bks., Inc.

Simmons, William Mark. One Foot in the Grave. 1996. 352p. pap. 5.99 (0-671-87721-6) Baen Bks.

Simmons, Wm. Mark. Dead on My Feet. 2003. 416p. 24.00 (0-7434-3610-5) Baen Bks.

Sipos, Thomas M. Vampire Nation. 2001. 260p. E-Book 8.00 (0-7388-8287-9) Xlibris Corp.

Sizemore, Susan. Heroes. 2003. (Laws of the Blood Ser.: No. 5). 288p. mass mkt. 6.50 (0-441-01108-X) Ace Bks.

—The Hunt, Vol. 1. 1999. (Laws of the Blood Ser.: Vol. 1). 288p. mass mkt. 6.50 (0-441-00660-4) Ace Bks.

—Laws of the Blood Vol. 4: Deceptions. 2002. 272p. mass mkt. 5.99 (0-441-00984-0) Ace Bks.

—Partners. 2000. (Laws of the Blood Ser.: No. 2). 288p. mass mkt. 6.50 (0-441-00783-X) Ace Bks.

—Untitled Vampire Romance. 384p. No. 2. 2004. mass mkt. (0-7434-6743-4, Pocket Star); No. 3. 2005. mass mkt. (0-7434-6744-2, Pocket) Simon & Schuster.

Skal, David J., ed. & comment. Vampires: Encounters with the Undead. 2001. (Illus.). 608p. tchr. ed. 29.99 (1-57912-209-4, 81209) Black Dog & Leventhal Pubs., Inc.

Skoog, Sven & Soulban, Lucien. Clanbook: Baali. 1998. (Vampire Ser.). (Illus.). pap. 12.00 (1-56504-213-1, 2817) White Wolf Publishing, Inc.

Smith, Beecher. The Guardian: Is Here. 1999. 364p. pap. 14.95 (0-9671667-0-5) Hot Biscuit Productions, Inc.

Smith, Guy N. The Knighton Vampires. 1993. text (0-7499-0180-2) Piatkus Bks. GBR. Dist: London Bridge.

Somtow, S. P. Vampire Junction. 1985. mass mkt. 3.50 o.s.i (0-425-07746-2) Berkley Publishing Group.

—Vampire Junction. 1991. 372p. mass mkt. 5.99 (0-8125-2596-5, Tor Bks.) Doherty, Tom Assocs., LLC.

—Vampire Junction. Reynolds, Kay, ed. (Illus.). 280p. 35.00 o.p. (0-89865-368-1); 15.95 o.p. (0-89865-367-3) Donning Co. Pubs. (Starblaze).

—Vanitas. 1997. (Middle Ages Ser.). 368p. pap. text 6.99 (0-8125-2478-0, Tor Bks.) Doherty, Tom Assocs., LLC.

—Vanitas: Escape from Vampire Junction. 1995. 384p. 23.95 o.p. (0-312-85513-3, Tor Bks.) Doherty, Tom Assocs., LLC.

Spinrad, Norman. Vampire Junkies. 1994. 80p. pap. 9.95 (0-936071-37-0) Gryphon Bks.

Staab, Thomas. Vampire's Waltz. 2000. 495p. mass mkt. 6.99 (0-9674172-0-1) Crazy Wolf Publishing.

Steakley, John. Vampires. (Orig.). 1992. 368p. mass mkt. 6.99 (0-451-45153-8); 1990. 38p. mass mkt. 8.95 o.p. (0-451-45033-7) NAL. (ROC).

Stephens, John R., ed. Vampires, Wine & Roses. 1997. 400p. (Orig.). pap. 14.00 o.s.i (0-425-15741-5) Berkley Publishing Group.

Stoker, Bram. Dracula. 2000. 252p. E-Book 9.95 (0-594-05212-2) 1873 Pr.

—Dracula. Date not set. pap. text (0-17-557040-X) Addison-Wesley Longman, Inc.

—Dracula. Date not set. reprint ed. lib. bdg. 27.95 (0-88411-131-8, Aeonian Pr.) Amereon, Ltd.

—Dracula. 2000. (SPA.). 496p. 10.95 (84-406-5500-2) B Ediciones S.A. ESP. Dist: Distribooks, Inc.

—Dracula. 1983. mass mkt. 1.95 o.s.i (0-553-21148-X, Bantam Classics) Bantam Bks.

—Dracula. E-Book 5.00 (0-7607-1358-8) Barnes & Noble, Inc.

—Dracula. Bennett, S. A., ed. 1992. (Illus.). 64p. pap. (0-944099-20-3) Bill Barry's Compass Bks.

—Dracula. 2002. pap. 4.50 (1-59109-321-X) Booksurge, LLC.

—Dracula. 1992. 320p. reprint ed. pap. 9.95 (0-86322-143-2) Brandon Bk. Pubs., Ltd. IRL. Dist: Irish Bks. & Media, Inc.

—Dracula. Byron, Glennis, ed. 1997. (Literary Texts Ser.). 400p. (C). pap. (1-55111-136-5) Broadview Pr.

—Dracula. 1990. reprint ed. lib. bdg. 26.95 (0-89966-692-2) Buccaneer Bks., Inc.

—Dracula. ed. 1999. (J). (gr. 2). spiral bd. (0-616-01788-X) Canadian National Institute for the Blind/Institut National Canadien pour les Aveugles.

—Dracula. reprint ed. lib. bdg. 98.00 (0-7426-2890-6); 2001. pap. text 28.00 (0-7426-7890-3) Classic Bks.

—Dracula. 1997. 384p. 21.95 (0-312-86358-6, Tor Bks.); 1992. 384p. mass mkt. 4.99 (0-8125-2301-6, Tor Classics); 1988. mass mkt. 4.95 (1-55902-006-7, Aerie) Doherty, Tom Assocs., LLC.

—Dracula. 1959. 7.95 o.p. (0-385-00383-8) Doubleday Publishing.

—Dracula. 2000. 320p. pap. 2.00 (0-486-41109-5) Dover Pubns., Inc.

—Dracula. 1980. 82p. (YA). (gr. 7 up). pap. 5.60 (0-87129-308-0, D35) Dramatic Publishing Co.

—Dracula. l.t. ed. 406p. pap. 32.00 (0-7583-3184-3); 528p. pap. 37.00 (0-7583-3185-1); 926p. pap. 64.00 (0-7583-3187-8); 1792p. pap. 110.00 (0-7583-3190-8); 2079p. pap. 123.00 (0-7583-3191-6); 723p. pap. 45.00 (0-7583-3186-X); 1185p. pap. 76.00 (0-7583-3188-6); 1457p. lib. bdg. 102.00 (0-7583-3181-9); 926p. lib. bdg. 76.00 (0-7583-3179-7); 2079p. lib. bdg. 148.00 (0-7583-3183-5); 528p. lib. bdg. 43.00 (0-7583-3177-0); 723p. lib. bdg. 51.00 (0-7583-3178-9); 1185p. lib. bdg. 88.00 (0-7583-3180-0); 406p. lib. bdg. 38.00 (0-7583-3176-2); 1792p. lib. bdg. 133.00 (0-7583-3182-7) Huge Print Pr.

—Dracula. 1998. (Cloth Bound Pocket Ser.). 240p. 7.95 (3-89508-096-9, 520018) Konemann.

—Dracula. 2002. (Classics for Young Readers Ser.). (SPA.). (YA). 14.95 (84-392-0934-7, EV30652) Lectorum Pubns., Inc.

—Dracula. 2000. (English As a Second Language Bk.). pap. text 5.95 o.p. (0-582-53523-9) Longman Publishing Group.

—Dracula. 1992. 392p. mass mkt. 3.99 o.p. (0-451-17581-6, Signet Classics); 1986. mass mkt. 2.50 o.p. (0-451-52097-1); 1973. mass mkt. 0.95 o.p. (0-451-05438-5, Signet Bks.); 1973. mass mkt. 0.60 o.p. (0-451-02793-0, Signet Bks.); 1965. mass mkt. 1.25 o.p. (0-451-50717-7, Signet Classics); 1965. mass mkt. 1.50 o.p. (0-451-51030-5, Signet Classics); 1965. mass mkt. 1.95 o.p. (0-451-51889-6, Signet Classics); 1965. mass mkt. 2.50 o.p. (0-451-51670-2, Signet Classics); 1965. mass mkt. 1.75 o.p. (0-451-51129-8, Signet Classics) NAL.

—Dracula. l.t. ed. (Large Print Ser.). 1993. 558p. lib. bdg. 26.00 (0-939495-43-0); 1998. 435p. reprint ed. lib. bdg. 25.00 (1-58287-024-1) North Bks.

—Dracula. l.t. ed. 2003. 448p. E-Book 2.99 (1-932681-17-5) NuVision Pubns.

—Dracula. Ellmann, Maud, ed. & intro. by. 1998. (Oxford World's Classics Ser.). 432p. pap. 9.95 (0-19-283386-3) Oxford Univ. Pr., Inc.

—Dracula. 1984. (Oxford World's Classics Ser.). 408p. pap. 4.95 o.p. (0-19-281598-9) Oxford Univ. Pr., Inc.

—Dracula. Ellman, Maud, ed. & intro. by. 2nd ed. 1996. (Oxford World's Classics Ser.). 428p. pap. 6.95 o.p. (0-19-282462-7) Oxford Univ. Pr., Inc.

—Dracula. Teresa Agnes, ed. Heller, Rudolf, tr. 1979. (SPA., Illus.). 64p. stu. ed. 1.50 (0-88301-566-8); pap. text 3.95 (0-88301-446-7) Pendulum Pr., Inc.

—Dracula. abr. ed. 1992. (Classics on Cassette). 15.95 o.p. incl. audio (0-453-00786-4) Penguin/HighBridge.

—Dracula. 1993. (SPA.). 464p. (84-01-49200-9) Plaza & Janés Editories, S.A.

—Dracula. (Paperback Classics Ser.). 2001. 432p. pap. 10.95 (0-375-75670-1); 2000. E-Book 4.95 (0-679-64197-1) Random House Adult Trade Publishing Group. (Modern Library).

—Dracula. (Modern Library Ser.). 1996. 448p. 17.95 o.s.i (0-679-60229-1); 1978. 6.95 o.s.i (0-394-60447-4) Random Hse., Inc.

—Dracula. 2002. E-Book 4.95 (0-9712207-1-9) Riverdale Electronic Bks.

—Dracula. unabr. ed. 1995. 528p. text 8.98 o.p. (1-56138-515-8, Courage Bks.) Running Pr. Bk. Pubs.

—Dracula. 2003. 528p. mass mkt. 5.99 (0-7434-7736-7, Pocket) Simon & Schuster.

—Dracula. l.t. ed. 1993. 592p. lib. bdg. 22.95 (0-8161-5692-1) Thorndike Pr.

—Dracula. Johnson, Beth, ed. & afterword by by. 2003. 428p. mass mkt. 2.00 (1-59194-003-6) Townsend Pr.

—Dracula. 2001. (Classics of Mystery & Suspense Ser.). 334p. (1-58279-187-2) Trident Pr. International.

—Dracula. 1965. (Signet Classics Ser.). 11.00 (0-606-00578-1) Turtleback Bks.

—Dracula. 1993. 432p. pap. 5.95 o.p. (0-460-87189-7, Everyman's Classic Library in Paperback) Tuttle Publishing.

—Dracula. Howes, Marjorie, ed. rev. ed. 1995. 400p. pap. 5.95 (0-460-87598-1, Everyman's Classic Library in Paperback) Tuttle Publishing.

—Dracula. (Penguin Classics Ser.). 560p. 2003. pap. 11.00 (0-14-143984-X, Penguin Classics); 1999. pap. (0-14-043381-3) Viking Penguin.

—Dracula. annuals Hindle, Maurice, ed. & intro. by. 1993. (Classics Ser.). 560p. 10.95 (0-14-043406-2, Penguin Classics) Viking Penguin.

—Dracula. 1979. 448p. pap. 4.95 o.p. (0-14-005280-1, Penguin Bks.) Viking Penguin.

—Dracula. 2002. 324p. pap. 18.95 (1-58715-588-5); lib. bdg. 29.95 (1-58715-589-3) Wildside Pr.

—Dracula. 1997. (Classics Library). 336p. pap. 3.95 (1-85326-086-X, 086XWW) Wordsworth Editions, Ltd. GBR. Dist: Casemate Pubs. & Bk. Distributors, LLC.

—Dracula. l.t. ed. 1994. 592p. pap. 14.95 o.p. (0-8161-5817-7) World Pubns., Inc.

—Dracula: Authoritative Text, Contexts, Reviews & Reactions, Criticism, Dramatic & Film Variations. Auerbach, Nina & Skal, David J., eds. 1996. (Critical Editions Ser.). (C). pap. text 14.20 (0-393-97012-4) Norton, W. W. & Co., Inc.

—Dracula Unearthed. Leatherdale, Clive, ed. & anno. by. 1998. 512p. 29.95 (1-874287-12-0) Desert Island Bks. GBR. Dist: Griffin Skye Co.

—Dracula's Guest. 1990. 160p. reprint ed. pap. 9.95 o.p. (0-86322-120-3) Brandon Bk. Pubs., Ltd. IRL. Dist: Irish Bks. & Media, Inc.

Stoker, Bram & Byron, Glennis. Dracula. 1998. E-Book 9.95 (0-585-29380-5) netLibrary, Inc.

Stoker, Bram & Shelley, Mary Wollstonecraft. Frankenstein, Dracula, Dr. Jekyll & Mr. Hyde. 1978. mass mkt. 4.50 o.p. (0-451-52170-6, Signet Classics) NAL.

Strauch, Thomas J., ed. The Darkest Thirst: A Vampire Anthology. 1998. 272p. pap. 15.95 (1-891946-00-5) Design Image Group, Inc., The.

Strieber, Whitley. The Last Vampire. 2001. 320p. 24.95 (0-7434-1720-8, Atria); 2002. 416p. reprint ed. pap. 6.99 (0-7434-1721-6, Pocket); 2001. reprint ed. E-Book 24.95 (0-7434-1808-5, Pocket) Simon & Schuster.

—Lilith's Dream: A Tale of the Vampire Life. 2003. E-Book 19.99 (0-7434-5309-3); 2002. 336p. 25.00 (0-7434-5152-X) Simon & Schuster. (Atria).

Summers, Cynthia. Libellus Sanguinis: Keepers of the Word. 1998. (Vampire Ser.). (Illus.). pap. 15.00 (1-56504-294-8, 2815) White Wolf Publishing, Inc.

Sumner, Mark. News from the Edge. 1999. (News from the Edge Ser.). 208p. mass mkt. 6.50 o.s.i (0-441-00628-0) Ace Bks.

Tan, Cecilia, ed. Cherished Blood: Vampire Erotica. 1997. 192p. (Orig.). pap. 14.95 (1-885865-18-X) Circlet Pr., Inc.

—Erotica Vampirica: Erotic Vampire Stories. 1996. 192p. pap. 12.95 (1-885865-08-2) Circlet Pr., Inc.

—A Taste of Midnight: Vampire Erotica. 2000. (Erotic Vampire Ser.: Vol. 4). 224p. pap. 14.95 (1-885865-23-6) Circlet Pr., Inc.

Tan, Cecilia, ed. & intro. Blood Kiss: Vampire Erotica. 1994. 138p. (Orig.). pap. 9.95 (1-885865-00-7) Circlet Pr., Inc.

Taylor, Karen E. Bitter Blood. (Vampire Legacy). 352p. 1998. mass mkt. 4.99 o.s.i (0-8217-6021-1); 1994. mass mkt. 4.50 o.s.i (0-8217-4722-3, Zebra Bks.) Kensington Publishing Corp.

—Blood of My Blood. 2000. (Vampire Legacy Ser.). 32p. mass mkt. 5.99 o.s.i (0-7860-1153-X, Pinnacle Bks.) Kensington Publishing Corp.

—Blood Secrets. (Vampire Legacy). 304p. 1998. mass mkt. 4.99 o.s.i (0-8217-6022-X); 1994. mass mkt. 4.50 o.s.i (0-8217-4437-2, Zebra Bks.) Kensington Publishing Corp.

—Blood Ties. (Vampire Legacy). 1998. 352p. mass mkt. 4.99 o.s.i (0-8217-6023-8); 1996. 352p. mass mkt. 2.99 o.p. (0-8217-5496-3); 1995. mass mkt. 4.99 o.s.i (0-8217-5114-X) Kensington Publishing Corp.

—The Vampire Vivienne. 2001. 32p. mass mkt. 5.99 o.s.i (0-7860-1206-4, Pinnacle Bks.) Kensington Publishing Corp.

Taylor, Lucy. Eternal Hearts. 1999. (Vampire Ser.). (Illus.). 128p. pap. 19.95 (1-56504-205-0, 2400) White Wolf Publishing, Inc.

Thompson, James. Immortal Blood. 2003. 314p. mass mkt. 5.99 (0-7860-1434-2) Kensington Publishing Corp.

Thompson, James M. Night Blood. 2001. 4p. mass mkt. 5.99 o.s.i (0-7860-1382-6, Pinnacle Bks.) Kensington Publishing Corp.

Thorne, Tamara. Candle Bay. 2001. 4p. mass mkt. 5.99 (0-7860-1311-7, Pinnacle Bks.) Kensington Publishing Corp.

Thurlo, David & Thurlo, Aimee. Second Sunrise: A Lee Nez Novel. 2002. (Lee Nez Novel Ser.). 336p. 24.95 (0-7653-0441-4, Forge Bks.) Doherty, Tom Assocs., LLC.

Timpone, Anthony, ed. Fangoria's Vampires. 1996. 240p. (Orig.). mass mkt. 5.50 o.p. (0-06-105666-9, Eos) Morrow/Avon.

Tournier, Michel. Le Vol du Vampire. 1983. (FRE.). pap. 12.95 (0-7859-2853-7) French & European Pubns., Inc.

Tower, Allen, et al. The Prince's Primer. 1996. (Vampire Ser.). (Illus.). 112p. (Orig.). pap. 10.95 o.p. (1-56504-201-8, 2232) White Wolf Publishing, Inc.

Viereck, George S. The House of the Vampire. Reginald, R. & Menville, Douglas A., eds. 1976. (Supernatural & Occult Fiction Ser.). reprint ed. lib. bdg. 26.95 (0-405-08171-5) Ayer Co. Pubs., Inc.

Warrington, Freda. A Taste of Blood Wine. 2001. pap. 16.00 (1-892065-48-7) Meisha Merlin Publishing, Inc.

Weinberg, Robert. Blood War Bk. 1: Vampire: Masquerade of the Red Death. 1995. (Masquerade of the Red Death Ser.: Vol. 1). 292p. pap. 5.99 (1-56504-840-7, 12400) White Wolf Publishing, Inc.

Whedon, Joss, et al. Buffy the Vampire Slayer: Tales of the Slayer. 2002. (Illus.). 96p. (YA). pap. 14.95 (1-56971-605-6) Dark Horse Comics.

White Wolf Publishing Staff, Wolf. Cities of Darkness: Dark Colony/Alien Hunger, Vol. 1. 1997. (Vampire Ser.). (Illus.). reprint ed. pap. 20.00 (1-56504-233-6, 2622) White Wolf Publishing, Inc.

—Vampire: The Masquerade. 3rd rev. ed. 1998. (Vampire Ser.). (Illus.). 29.95 (1-56504-249-2, 2300) White Wolf Publishing, Inc.

Wolf, Leonard, ed. Blood Thirst: 100 Years of Vampire Fiction. 2000. 379p. reprint ed. 25.00 (0-7881-9472-0) DIANE Publishing Co.

Wolf, Leonard, ed. & intro. Blood Thirst: 100 Years of Vampire Fiction. 1999. (Illus.). 384p. pap. 19.95 (0-19-513250-5) Oxford Univ. Pr., Inc.

Wolf, Leonard & Stoker, Bram. The Essential Dracula. 1993. (Essentials Ser.). (Illus.). 512p. pap. 16.95 o.p. (0-452-26943-1, Plume) Dutton/Plume.

Wong, Victor James. Vampire Hunter. 2002. per. 6.95 (1-892937-15-8) Special Pubns., Inc.

Woodruff, Teewynn. World of Darkness: Gypsies. 1994. (World of Darkness Ser.). (Illus.). 128p. per. 15.00 (1-56504-136-4, 2223) White Wolf Publishing, Inc.

Wright, T. Lucien. Thirst of the Vampire. 1992. 352p. mass mkt. 4.50 o.s.i (1-55817-649-7, Pinnacle Bks.) Kensington Publishing Corp.

Wright, T. M. The Last Vampire. 2001. 368p. mass mkt. 5.99 (0-8439-4939-2, Leisure Bks.) Dorchester Publishing Co., Inc.

Yarbro, Chelsea Quinn. The Angry Angel. (Sisters of the Night Ser.). (Illus.). 368p. 1999. pap. 13.50 (0-380-78984-1); 1998. 23.00 (0-380-97400-2) Morrow/Avon. (Avon Bks.).

—Better in the Dark. 1995. 412p. pap. 14.95 (0-312-85978-3, Orb Bks.); 1993. (Illus.). 416p. 23.95 o.p. (0-312-85504-4, Tor Bks.) Doherty, Tom Assocs., LLC.

—Blood Games. 1989. 480p. mass mkt. 4.95 (0-8125-2801-8, Tor Bks.) Doherty, Tom Assocs., LLC.

—Blood Games. 1980. mass mkt. 2.75 o.p. (0-451-09405-0, E9405, Signet Bks.) NAL.

—Blood Games. 1979. 458p. 11.95 o.p. (0-312-08441-2) St. Martin's Pr.

—Blood Games. 2004. 640p. mass mkt. 6.99 (0-446-61379-7) Warner Bks., Inc.

—Blood Roses: A Novel of Saint-Germain. 1999. 382p. pap. 15.95 (0-312-87248-8); 1998. 384p. 24.95 (0-312-86529-5) Doherty, Tom Assocs., LLC. (Tor Bks.).

—Come Twilight: A Novel of Count Saint-Germain. (Illus.). 2000. 479p. 27.95 (0-312-87330-1); 2001. 480p. reprint ed. pap. 17.95 (0-312-87371-9) Doherty, Tom Assocs., LLC. (Tor Bks.).

—Communion Blood: A Saint-Germain Novel. 2000. 477p. pap. 16.95 (0-312-86794-8); 1999. 472p. 26.95 (0-312-86793-X) Doherty, Tom Assocs., LLC. (Tor Bks.).

—Darker Jewels. 398p. 1995. pap. 14.95 (0-312-89031-1, Orb Bks.); 1993. 19.95 (0-312-85296-7, Tor Bks.) Doherty, Tom Assocs., LLC.

—Hotel Transylvania. 1988. 320p. mass mkt. 3.95 (0-8125-5850-2, Tor Bks.) Doherty, Tom Assocs., LLC.

—Hotel Transylvania. 1979. mass mkt. 1.95 o.p. (0-451-08461-6, J8461, Signet Bks.) NAL.

—Hotel Transylvania. 1978. 279p. 8.95 o.p. (0-312-39248-6) St. Martin's Pr.

—Mansions of Darkness. 1997. 432p. pap. 15.95 (0-312-86382-9, Tor Bks.) Doherty, Tom Assocs., LLC.

—Night Blooming. (Illus.). 2003. 672p. mass mkt. 6.99 (0-446-61102-6); 2002. 448p. 24.95 (0-446-52981-8, Aspect) Warner Bks., Inc.
—Out of the House of Life. 1994. 446p. pap. 15.95 (0-312-89026-5, Orb Bks.); Vol. 1. 1990. xi,446p. 19.95 (0-312-93126-3, Tor Bks.) Doherty, Tom Assocs., LLC.
—The Palace. 1988. 480p. mass mkt. 3.95 (0-8125-2802-6, Tor Bks.) Doherty, Tom Assocs., LLC.
—The Palace. 1979. mass mkt. 2.25 o.p. (0-451-08949-9, E8949, Signet Bks.) NAL.
—The Palace. 1978. 408p. 9.95 o.p. (0-312-59474-7) St. Martin's Pr.
—The Palace. 2003. 528p. reprint ed. mass mkt. 6.99 (0-446-61099-2) Warner Bks., Inc.
—Path of the Eclipse. 1989. mass mkt. 4.95 (0-8125-2810-7, Tor Bks.) Doherty, Tom Assocs., LLC.
—Path of the Eclipse. 1982. mass mkt. 3.50 o.p. (0-451-11340-3, AE1340, Signet Bks.) NAL.
—Path of the Eclipse. 1981. xi, 518p. 13.95 o.p. (0-312-59802-5) St. Martin's Pr.
—The St. Germain Chronicles. 1983. 256p. (Orig.). mass mkt. 2.95 o.s.i (0-671-45903-1, Pocket) Simon & Schuster.
—Tempting Fate. 1982. mass mkt. 3.95 o.p. (0-451-11865-0, AE1865, Signet Bks.) NAL.
—Tempting Fate. 1981. 662p. 17.95 o.p. (0-312-79087-2) St. Martin's Pr.
—Writ in Blood: A Novel of Saint-Germain. 1997. 544p. 26.95 o.p. (0-312-86318-7, Tor Bks.) Doherty, Tom Assocs., LLC.

# Y

## YOUNG WOMEN—FICTION

Alhadeff, Gini. Diary of a Djinn: A Novel. 2004. 224p. pap. 13.00 (1-4000-3461-2, Anchor) Knopf Publishing Group.
Ali, Monica. Brick Lane: A Novel. l.t. ed. 2003. 676p. 30.95 (0-7862-6018-1) Gale Group.
—Brick Lane: A Novel. 2003. 384p. 25.00 (0-7432-4330-7); E-Book (0-7432-4971-2) Simon & Schuster. (Scribner).
—Seven Seas, Thirteen Rivers. 2004. 288p. pap. 13.00 (0-7432-4331-5, Scribner) Simon & Schuster.
Andrews, V. C. Cinnamon. l.t. ed. 2002. (Core Collection). 186p. 29.95 (0-7838-9750-2) Gale Group.
—Eye of the Storm. 2001. (Hudson Ser.: No. 3). E-Book 7.99 (1-59061-063-6) Adobe Systems, Inc.
—Eye of the Storm. l.t. ed. 2001. 435p. (0-7540-2442-3); (0-7540-1580-7) Gale Group. (Macmillan Reference USA).
—Eye of the Storm. 2000. (Hudson Family Ser.: Vol. 3). 400p. 24.95 (0-671-03982-2, Atria); pap. 7.99 (0-671-03983-0, Pocket) Simon & Schuster.
—Eye of the Storm. l.t. ed. 2001. (Hudson Ser.). 435p. 31.95 (0-7838-9328-0) Thorndike Pr.
—Eye of the Storm. 2000. (Hudson Family Ser.). 14.04 (0-606-20221-8) Turtleback Bks.
—Falling Stars. 2001. 400p. 25.00 (0-671-03986-5, Atria); E-Book 7.99 (0-7434-2168-X, Pocket); (Illus.). 416p. pap. 7.99 (0-671-03987-3, Pocket) Simon & Schuster.
—Falling Stars. l.t. ed. 2002. 403p. 30.95 (0-7838-9753-7) Thorndike Pr.
—Lightning Strikes. 2001. 424p. (0-7540-2432-6); (0-7540-1570-X) Gale Group. (Macmillan Reference USA).
—Lightning Strikes. 2000. (Hudson Family Ser.: Vol. 2). 368p. 24.95 o.s.i (0-671-00768-8, Atria); 384p. pap. 7.99 (0-671-00769-6, Pocket) Simon & Schuster.
—Lightning Strikes. l.t. ed. 2001. (G. K. Hall Core Ser.). (Illus.). 352p. 31.95 (0-7838-9316-7) Thorndike Pr.
—Lightning Strikes. 2000. (Illus.). (J). 14.04 (0-606-18830-4) Turtleback Bks.
—Rose. 2002. E-Book 4.99 (1-59061-644-8) Adobe Systems, Inc.
Aston, Elizabeth. Mr. Darcy's Daughters: A Novel. 2003. 368p. pap. 14.00 (0-7432-4397-8, Touchstone) Simon & Schuster.
Austen, Jane. Emma. 2002. (World Digital Library). E-Book 3.95 (0-594-08158-0) 1873 Pr.
—Emma. 1997. (Modern Library Ser.). E-Book 4.95 (1-931208-08-5) Adobe Systems, Inc.
—Emma. 1966. (Airmont Classics Ser.). mass mkt. 2.95 o.p. (0-8049-0102-3, CL-102) Airmont Publishing Co., Inc.
—Emma. Date not set. 232p. 21.95 (0-8488-2522-5) Amereon, Ltd.
—Emma. l.t. ed. 1999. 630p. pap. 24.95 (1-55701-279-2) BNI Pubns., Inc.
—Emma. 1984. mass mkt. 1.95 o.s.i (0-553-21159-5, Bantam Classics); 432p. mass mkt. 4.95 (0-553-21273-7) Bantam Bks.
—Emma. 2002. audio compact disk 120.00 (0-7366-8766-1) Books on Tape, Inc.
—Emma. 1986. lib. bdg. 19.95 (0-89966-242-0) Buccaneer Bks., Inc.
—Emma, 3 Vols. (Collected Works of Jane Austen). reprint ed. lib. bdg. 294.00 (0-7426-2073-5); 2001. pap. text 84.00 (0-7426-7073-2) Classic Bks.
—Emma. l.t. ed. 1999. 630p. pap. 24.95 (1-58855-018-4) Cyber Classics, Inc.
—Emma. unabr. ed. 1999. 384p. pap. text 2.50 (0-486-40648-2) Dover Pubns., Inc.
—Emma. 1956. 10.50 o.p. (0-460-00024-1, Dutton) Dutton/Plume.
—Emma. E-Book 2.49 (1-58744-220-5) Electric Umbrella Publishing.
—Emma. 1998. (SPA.). 416p. (84-320-3877-6) GeoPlaneta, Editorial, S. A.
—Emma. l.t. ed. 2000. 624p. pap. 22.00 (0-06-095693-3, HarperCollins) HarperTrade.
—Emma. 2003. audio 14.95 (1-84032-771-5) Hodder Headline Audiobooks GBR. *Dist:* Trafalgar Square.
—Emma. Trilling, Lionel, ed. 1972. (C). pap. 16.36 (0-395-05115-0) Houghton Mifflin Co.
—Emma. l.t. ed. 1233p. pap. 88.84 (0-7583-0815-9); 708p. pap. 51.13 (0-7583-0812-4); 319p. pap. 27.06 (0-7583-0809-4); 555p. pap. 41.61 (0-7583-0811-6); 436p. pap. 33.67 (0-7583-0810-8); 254p. pap. 23.38 (0-7583-0808-6); 865p. pap. 68.70 (0-7583-0813-2); 1063p. pap. 79.19 (0-7583-0814-0); 555p. lib. bdg. 47.61 (0-7583-0803-5); 865p. lib. bdg. 81.13 (0-7583-0805-1); 1233p. lib. bdg. 100.84 (0-7583-0807-8); 254p. lib. bdg. 29.38 (0-7583-0800-0); 319p. lib. bdg. 33.06 (0-7583-0801-9); 436p. lib. bdg. 39.67 (0-7583-0802-7); 708p. lib. bdg. 57.13 (0-7583-0804-3); 1063p. lib. bdg. 91.19 (0-7583-0806-X) Huge Print Pr.
—Emma. 1996. (Illus.). 464p. reprint ed. pap. 9.95 (0-7868-8183-6) Hyperion Pr.
—Emma. 1991. (Everyman's Library). 484p. (1-85715-036-8, Everyman's Library) Knopf Publishing Group.
—Emma. 1999. (Cloth Bound Pocket Ser.). 7.95 (3-8290-0827-9, 520519) Konemann.
—Emma. E-Book 2.95 (1-57799-846-4); E-Book 2.95 (1-57799-980-0) Logos Research Systems, Inc.
—Emma. Cheetham, Paul, ed. 1984. (Study Texts Ser.). pap. text 4.29 (0-582-33153-6, 72058) Longman Publishing Group.
—Emma. E-Book 1.95 (1-58515-171-8) MesaView, Inc.
—Emma. (Signet Classics). 1996. 416p. mass mkt. 4.95 (0-451-52627-9, Signet Classics); 1968. mass mkt. 0.75 o.p. (0-451-50388-0, Signet Classics); 1968. mass mkt. 0.50 o.p. (0-451-50216-7, Signet Classics); 1964. mass mkt. 1.95 o.p. (0-451-51524-2, Signet Classics); 1964. mass mkt. 1.75 o.p. (0-451-51357-6, Signet Classics); 1964. mass mkt. 1.25 o.p. (0-451-50798-3, Signet Classics); 1964. mass mkt. 0.95 o.p. (0-451-50705-3, Signet Classics); 1964. mass mkt. 2.25 o.p. (0-451-51941-8); 1964. 400p. mass mkt. 4.95 o.p. (0-451-52306-7, Signet Classics); 1943. mass mkt. 1.50 o.p. (0-451-51010-0, Signet Classics) NAL.
—Emma. l.t. ed. reprint ed. 1997. 610p. lib. bdg. 26.00 (0-939495-08-2); 1998. 478p. lib. bdg. 25.00 (1-58287-025-X) North Bks.
—Emma. Parrish, Stephen M., ed. (Critical Editions Ser.). 430p. (C). 1972. pap. o.p. (0-393-09667-X); 2nd ed. 1993. pap. text o.p. (0-393-96014-5) Norton, W. W. & Co., Inc.
—Emma. 1999. (Oxford World's Classics Ser.). 464p. 13.00 o.p. (0-19-210030-0) Oxford Univ. Pr., Inc.
—Emma. Kinsley, James, ed. (Oxford World's Classics Ser.). 1998. 488p. pap. 6.95 o.p. (0-19-283357-X); 1990. 482p. pap. 4.50 o.p. (0-19-282756-1) Oxford Univ. Pr., Inc.
—Emma. Kinsley, James & Lodge, David, eds. 1980. (Oxford World's Classics Ser.). pap. 2.50 o.p. (0-19-281504-0) Oxford Univ. Pr., Inc.
—Emma. Pinch, Adela, ed. 2nd ed. 2003. (Oxford World's Classics Ser.). 672p. pap. 6.95 (0-19-280237-2) Oxford Univ. Pr., Inc.
—Emma. Kinsley, James, ed. 2nd ed. 1995. (Oxford World's Classics Ser.). 484p. pap. 4.95 o.p. (0-19-282432-5) Oxford Univ. Pr., Inc.
—Emma, Vol. IV. Chapman, R. W., ed. 3rd ed. 1988. (Illus.). 536p. reprint ed. 20.00 (0-19-254704-6) Oxford Univ. Pr., Inc.
—Emma. collector's ed. 2002. (Illus.). im. lthr. 38.85 (1-931927-22-7); pap. 19.95 (1-931927-23-5); 25.95 (1-931927-21-9); pap. 17.95 (1-931927-14-6) Polyglot Pr., Inc.
—Emma. (Jane Austen Works). 2000. 364p. lib. bdg. 41.99 (1-57646-332-X); 2000. 364p. pap. 19.99 o.p. (1-57646-261-7); 1999. 200p. E-Book 3.99 incl. audio compact disk (1-57646-144-0); 2000. 646p. pap. 39.99 (1-57646-333-8); 2000. 646p. lib. bdg. 49.99 (1-57646-334-6) Quiet Vision Publishing.
—Emma. (Modern Library Classics). 2001. 384p. pap. 7.95 (0-375-75742-2); 2001. E-Book 4.95 (0-679-64108-4); 1995. 14.95 o.s.i (0-679-60193-7) Random House Adult Trade Publishing Group. (Modern Library).
—Emma. 1988. (Zodiac Press Ser.). 520p. o.p. (0-7011-1232-8) Random Hse. of Canada, Ltd. CAN. *Dist:* Random Hse., Inc.
—Emma. 2002. (SPA.). 600p. mass mkt. 9.95 (1-4000-0083-1); 1997. 13.00 o.s.i (0-679-60257-7); 1991. 560p. 18.00 (0-679-40581-X); 1989. o.s.i (1-85381-096-7) Random Hse., Inc.
—Emma. 1994. (World's Best Reading Ser.). 391p. (0-89577-582-4) Reader's Digest Assn., Inc., The.
—Emma. 2000. E-Book 2.95 incl. cd-rom (1-58853-011-6) Sensory Publishing, Inc.
—Emma. E-Book 5.00 (0-7410-0560-3) SoftBook Pr.
—Emma. unabr. ed. 2003. audio 19.99 (1-59335-041-4, 30126) Soulmate Audio Bks., Inc.
—Emma. l.t. ed. 1985. (Charnwood Large Print Ser.). 547p. 29.99 (0-7089-8258-1, Charnwood) Thorpe, F. A. Pubs. GBR. *Dist:* Ulverscroft Large Print Bks., Ltd., Ulverscroft Large Print Canada, Ltd.
—Emma. Daleski, H. M., ed. 2003. 9.95 (1-59264-004-4); 510p. pap. 9.95 (1-59264-003-6) Toby Pr.
—Emma. 2000. (Signature Classics Ser.). 459p. 24.95 (1-58279-090-6); lib. bdg. 29.95 (1-58279-081-7) Trident Pr. International.
—Emma. 1997. 19.00 (0-606-17578-4); 1980. 11.00 (0-606-03147-2) Turtleback Bks.
—Emma. 1994. 464p. pap. 3.95 o.p. (0-460-87467-5); 1964. 432p. pap. 5.95 o.p. (0-460-15024-3) Tuttle Publishing. (Everyman's Classic Library in Paperback).
—Emma. 2000. 9.00 (81-85944-76-8) UBS Pubs. Distributions, Ltd. IND. *Dist:* South Asia Bks.
—Emma. (Classics Ser.). 2003. 512p. pap. 8.00 (0-14-143958-0, Penguin Classics); 1997. 448p. 7.95 (0-14-043415-1); 1971. 4.50 o.p. (0-460-01024-7) Viking Penguin.
—Emma. Blythe, Ronald, ed. 1966. (English Library). 480p. pap. 6.95 o.s.i (0-14-043010-5, Penguin Classics) Viking Penguin.
—Emma. 1999. E-Book 5.99 (0-8220-7063-4, Cliff Notes) Wiley, John & Sons, Inc.
—Emma. 1997. (Classics Library). 384p. pap. 3.95 (1-85326-028-2, 0282WW) Wordsworth Editions, Ltd. GBR. *Dist:* Casemate Pubs. & Bk. Distributors, LLC.
—Emma: Critical Edition. Parrish, Stephen M., ed. 3rd ed. 2000. (Critical Editions Ser.). (Illus.). ix, 449p. pap. 11.00 (0-393-97284-4) Norton, W. W. & Co., Inc.
—Emma, Northanger Abbey & Persuasion, Vol. 2. 1976. pap. 8.95 o.p. (0-394-71892-5, V-892) Random Hse., Inc.
—Jane Austen's Pride & Prejudice. Johnson, Claudia L. & Wolfson, Susan J., eds. 2002. (Longman Cultural Edition Ser.). 464p. pap. 16.00 (0-321-10507-9) Longman Publishing Group.
—Northanger Abbey. (Modern Library Ser.). E-Book 4.95 (1-931208-13-1) Adobe Systems, Inc.
—Northanger Abbey. Date not set. lib. bdg. 20.95 (0-8488-1244-1) Amereon, Ltd.
—Northanger Abbey. unabr. ed. 54.95 o.p. incl. audio (1-85549-915-0, CTC 055) BBC Audiobooks America.
—Northanger Abbey. 1999. 320p. pap. 4.95 (0-553-21494-2, Bantam Classics); 240p. mass mkt. 4.95 (0-553-21197-8) Bantam Bks.
—Northanger Abbey. Grogan, Claire, ed. (Illus.). 1996. 276p. (C). pap. text (1-55111-078-4); 2nd ed. 2002. 280p. pap. (1-55111-479-8) Broadview Pr.
—Northanger Abbey. 1986. 220p. reprint ed. lib. bdg. 18.95 o.p. (0-89966-539-X); lib. bdg. 18.95 (0-89966-534-9) Buccaneer Bks., Inc.
—Northanger Abbey. unabr. ed. 2000. (Thrift Editions Ser.). 192p. pap. 2.00 (0-486-41412-4) Dover Pubns., Inc.
—Northanger Abbey. 1977. 3.95 o.p. (0-460-01893-0, Dutton) Dutton/Plume.
—Northanger Abbey. 1999. E-Book 2.49 (1-58627-076-1) Electric Umbrella Publishing.
—Northanger Abbey. l.t. ed. 2001. 315p. 28.95 (0-7838-9633-6, Hall, G. K. & Co.) Gale Group.
—Northanger Abbey. 2000. (Green Integer Bks.: Vol. 99). 290p. pap. 11.95 (1-892295-92-X) Green Integer.
—Northanger Abbey. l.t. ed. 277p. pap. 26.95 (0-7583-1633-X); 379p. pap. 33.50 (0-7583-1634-8); 213p. pap. 22.00 (0-7583-1632-1); 486p. pap. 41.45 (0-7583-1635-6); 1091p. pap. 88.55 (0-7583-1639-9); 622p. pap. 50.95 (0-7583-1636-4); 764p. pap. 61.50 (0-7583-1637-2); 940p. pap. 74.00 (0-7583-1638-0); 213p. lib. bdg. 28.06 (0-7583-1624-0); 1091p. lib. bdg. 100.55 (0-7583-1631-3); 379p. lib. bdg. 39.54 (0-7583-1626-7); 940p. lib. bdg. 90.94 (0-7583-1630-5); 277p. lib. bdg. 32.95 (0-7583-1625-9); 622p. lib. bdg. 56.94 (0-7583-1628-3); 486p. lib. bdg. 47.45 (0-7583-1627-5); 764p. lib. bdg. 80.90 (0-7583-1629-1) Huge Print Pr.
—Northanger Abbey. l.t. ed. 1991. (Isis Large Print Bks.). 234p. 24.95 (1-85089-434-5) ISIS Large Print Bks. GBR. *Dist:* Transaction Pubs.
—Northanger Abbey. 2002. 204p. 24.99 (1-4043-2098-9); per. 19.99 (1-4043-2099-7) IndyPublish.com.
—Northanger Abbey. 1992. (Everyman's Library). 288p. 15.00 (0-679-41715-X) Knopf, Alfred A. Inc.
—Northanger Abbey. 1999. (Cloth Bound Pocket Ser.). 7.95 (3-8290-3001-0, 521272) Konemann.
—Northanger Abbey. l.t. ed. 1998. (Large Print Heritage Ser.). 357p. lib. bdg. 33.95 (1-58118-030-6, 22022) LRS.
—Northanger Abbey. E-Book 1.95 (1-57799-956-8) Logos Research Systems, Inc.
—Northanger Abbey. 1996. 240p. mass mkt. 4.95 (0-451-52636-8); 1965. mass mkt. 0.95 o.p. (0-451-50868-8, Signet Classics); 1965. 224p. mass mkt. 2.50 o.p. (0-451-51834-9, Signet Classics); 1965. 224p. mass mkt. 3.95 o.p. (0-451-52372-5, Signet Classics); 1965. mass mkt. 0.50 o.p. (0-451-50580-8, Signet Classics); 1965. mass mkt. 0.60 o.p. (0-451-50720-7, Signet Classics); 1965. mass mkt. 2.50 o.p. (0-451-51748-2, Signet Classics); 1965. mass mkt. 1.50 o.p. (0-451-51113-1, Signet Classics); 1965. mass mkt. 2.25 o.p. (0-451-51539-0, Signet Classics); 1965. mass mkt. 0.50 o.p. (0-451-50312-0, Signet Classics) NAL.
—Northanger Abbey. l.t. ed. 2000. reprint ed. 370p. lib. bdg. 26.00 (0-939495-48-1); 230p. lib. bdg. 25.00 (1-58287-121-3) North Bks.
—Northanger Abbey, Vol. V. Chapman, R. W., ed. 3rd ed. 1988. (Illus.). 348p. reprint ed. 20.00 (0-19-254705-4) Oxford Univ. Pr., Inc.
—Northanger Abbey. collector's ed. 2002. (Illus.). im. lthr. 38.85 (1-931927-35-9); pap. 19.95 (1-931927-36-7); 25.95 (1-931927-34-0); pap. 17.95 (1-931927-18-9) Polyglot Pr., Inc.
—Northanger Abbey. (Jane Austen Works: Vol. 4). 2000. 180p. lib. bdg. 29.99 (1-57646-341-9); 2000. 180p. pap. 14.99 o.p. (1-57646-264-1); 1999. 200p. E-Book 3.99 incl. audio compact disk (1-57646-147-5); 2000. 318p. pap. 24.99 (1-57646-342-7); 2000. 318p. lib. bdg. 32.99 (1-57646-343-5) Quiet Vision Publishing.
—Northanger Abbey. 2002. 256p. pap. 6.95 (0-375-75917-4); 2000. E-Book 4.95 (0-679-64110-6); 1995. 192p. 13.95 (0-679-60192-9) Random House Adult Trade Publishing Group. (Modern Library).
—Northanger Abbey. 1988. (Zodiac Press Ser.). 240p. o.p. (0-7011-1234-4) Random Hse. of Canada, Ltd. CAN. *Dist:* Random Hse., Inc.
—Northanger Abbey. 1989. o.s.i (1-85381-094-0) Random Hse., Inc.
—Northanger Abbey. E-Book 5.00 (0-7410-0423-2) SoftBook Pr.
—Northanger Abbey. l.t. ed. 1995. (Charnwood Large Print Ser.). 359p. 29.99 (0-7089-8876-8, Charnwood) Thorpe, F. A. Pubs. GBR. *Dist:* Ulverscroft Large Print Bks., Ltd., Ulverscroft Large Print Canada, Ltd.
—Northanger Abbey. 1998. 12.00 (0-606-20826-7) Turtleback Bks.
—Northanger Abbey. 1994. 304p. 3.95 o.p. (0-460-87434-9, Everyman's Classic Library in Paperback) Tuttle Publishing.
—Northanger Abbey. Butler, Marilyn, ed. 1996. (Penguin Classics Ser.). (Illus.). 288p. 6.95 (0-14-043413-5) Viking Penguin.
—Northanger Abbey. Ehrenpreis, Anne H., ed. 1972. (English Library). 256p. pap. 5.95 o.p. (0-14-043074-1, Penguin Classics) Viking Penguin.
—Northanger Abbey. 1998. (Classics Library). 208p. pap. 3.95 (1-85326-043-6, 0436WW) Wordsworth Editions, Ltd. GBR. *Dist:* Casemate Pubs. & Bk. Distributors, LLC.
—Persuasion. 2001. (Modern Library Classics). 224p. pap. 5.95 (0-375-75729-5, Modern Library) Random House Adult Trade Publishing Group.
—Pride & Prejudice. 2000. 252p. E-Book 9.95 (0-594-05313-7) 1873 Pr.
—Pride & Prejudice. 1998. pap. 4.99 o.p. (1-57840-200-X) Acclaim Bks.
—Pride & Prejudice. unabr. ed. 1962. (Classics Ser.). mass mkt. 4.95 (0-8049-0001-9, CL-1) Airmont Publishing Co., Inc.
—Pride & Prejudice. Date not set. lib. bdg. 25.95 (0-8488-0420-1) Amereon, Ltd.
—Pride & Prejudice. 2001. 7.95 (0-8010-1211-2) Baker Bks.
—Pride & Prejudice. 1983. mass mkt. 1.95 o.s.i (0-553-21215-X); 352p. reprint ed. mass mkt. 4.95 (0-553-21310-5, Bantam Classics) Bantam Bks.
—Pride & Prejudice. Kendrick, Walter, ed. 1980. (Mcdonald Classics Ser.). 410p. 19.95 (0-8464-1071-0) Beekman Pubs., Inc.
—Pride & Prejudice. 1988. lib. bdg. 19.95 (0-89966-243-9) Buccaneer Bks., Inc.
—Pride & Prejudice, 3 Vols. reprint ed. lib. bdg. 294.00 (0-7426-2071-9) Classic Bks.
—Pride & Prejudice. 1994. 332p. mass mkt. 3.99 (0-8125-2336-9, Tor Classics) Doherty, Tom Assocs., LLC.
—Pride & Prejudice. unabr. ed. 1995. (Thrift Editions Ser.). 272p. pap. 2.50 (0-486-28473-5) Dover Pubns., Inc.
—Pride & Prejudice. 1985. (Illus.). 352p. 20.00 o.p. (0-525-18381-7, Dutton) Dutton/Plume.
—Pride & Prejudice. 1997. pap. 8.25 (0-03-051487-8) Holt, Rinehart & Winston.

Miscellaneous

—Pride & Prejudice. Schorer, Mark, ed. 1956. pap. 16.36 (*0-395-05101-0*, Riverside Editions) Houghton Mifflin Co.

—Pride & Prejudice. l.t. ed. 1444p. pap. 95.94 (*0-7583-1943-6*); 1224p. pap. 85.50 (*0-7583-1942-8*); 995p. pap. 74.61 (*0-7583-1941-X*); 484p. pap. 36.91 (*0-7583-1938-X*); 276p. pap. 24.62 (*0-7583-1936-3*); 806p. pap. 63.79 (*0-7583-1940-1*); 623p. pap. 45.49 (*0-7583-1939-8*); 349p. pap. 29.76 (*0-7583-1937-1*); 806p. lib. bdg. 75.79 (*0-7583-1932-0*); 484p. lib. bdg. 42.91 (*0-7583-1930-4*); 1224p. lib. bdg. 97.50 (*0-7583-1934-7*); 1444p. lib. bdg. 107.94 (*0-7583-1935-5*); 276p. lib. bdg. 30.62 (*0-7583-1928-2*); 995p. lib. bdg. 86.61 (*0-7583-1933-9*); 349p. lib. bdg. 35.76 (*0-7583-1929-0*); 623p. lib. bdg. 51.49 (*0-7583-1931-2*) Huge Print Pr.

—Pride & Prejudice. 1991. 416p. 17.00 (*0-679-40542-9*) Knopf, Alfred A. Inc.

—Pride & Prejudice. (Longman Fiction Ser.). 1997. pap. 9.07 (*0-582-27508-3*); 1993. pap. text 6.50 o.p. (*0-582-09674-X*, 79823) Longman Publishing Group.

—Pride & Prejudice. Adams, Richard, ed. 1983. (Study Texts Ser.). pap. text 5.95 (*0-582-33086-6*, 72039) Longman Publishing Group.

—Pride & Prejudice. 9999. o.p.; 1950. 336p. mass mkt. 3.95 o.p. (*0-451-52365-2*); 1950. mass mkt. 2.25 o.p. (*0-451-52226-5*, Signet Classics) NAL.

—Pride & Prejudice. abr. ed. 1996. 19.95 o.p. (*0-7871-0306-3*) NewStar Media, Inc.

—Pride & Prejudice. Gray, Donald J., ed. 1966. (Critical Editions Ser.). 450p. (C). pap. o.p. (*0-393-09668-8*) Norton, W. W. & Co., Inc.

—Pride & Prejudice. 3rd ed. 2000. (Critical Editions Ser.). viii, 413p. (C). pap. 7.25 (*0-393-97604-1*, Norton Paperbacks) Norton, W. W. & Co., Inc.

—Pride & Prejudice. Kinsley, James, ed. 1990. (Oxford World's Classics Ser.). 390p. pap. 5.95 o.p. (*0-19-282760-X*) Oxford Univ. Pr., Inc.

—Pride & Prejudice. Kinsley, James & Bradbrook, F. W., eds. 1980. (Oxford World's Classics Ser.). pap. 2.25 o.p. (*0-19-281503-2*) Oxford Univ. Pr., Inc.

—Pride & Prejudice, Vol. II. Chapman, R. W., ed. 3rd ed. 1988. (Illus.). 432p. reprint ed. 21.50 (*0-19-254702-X*) Oxford Univ. Pr., Inc.

—Pride & Prejudice. text (*0-13-981465-5*) Prentice Hall (Schl. Div.).

—Pride & Prejudice. (Jane Austen Works: Vol. 7). 2000. 280p. lib. bdg. 36.99 (*1-57646-350-8*); 2000. 280p. pap. 19.99 o.p. (*1-57646-267-6*); 1999. 200p. E-Book 3.99 incl. audio compact disk (*1-57646-150-5*); 2000. 518p. pap. 34.99 (*1-57646-351-6*) Quiet Vision Publishing.

—Pride & Prejudice. (Modern Library Ser.). 2000. E-Book 4.95 (*0-679-64112-2*); 2000. 320p. pap. 7.95 (*0-679-78326-1*); 1995. (Illus.). 304p. 14.95 (*0-679-60168-6*) Random House Adult Trade Publishing Group. (Modern Library).

—Pride & Prejudice. 1988. (Zodiac Press Ser.). 248p. o.p. (*0-7011-1236-0*) Random Hse. of Canada, Ltd. CAN. *Dist:* Random Hse., Inc.

—Pride & Prejudice. 1989. o.s.i (*1-85381-097-5*); 1986. pap. 16.00 o.s.i incl. audio (*0-394-55731-X*); 1986. pap. 16.00 o.s.i incl. audio (*0-394-55731-X*) Random Hse., Inc.

—Pride & Prejudice. 1984. (Illus.). 368p. 25.00 o.p. (*0-89577-198-5*) Reader's Digest Assn., Inc., The.

—Pride & Prejudice. 1992. (Literary Classics Ser.). 368p. text 5.98 o.p. (*1-56138-171-3*, Courage Bks.) Running Pr. Bk. Pubs.

—Pride & Prejudice. 2000. 416p. mass mkt. 4.99 (*0-439-10135-2*) Scholastic, Inc.

—Pride & Prejudice. 2000. E-Book 2.95 (*1-58853-022-1*) Sensory Publishing, Inc.

—Pride & Prejudice. 2004. 400p. mass mkt. 4.95 (*0-7434-8759-1*); 1982. 464p. mass mkt. 2.95 o.s.i (*0-671-44389-5*) Simon & Schuster. (Pocket).

—Pride & Prejudice. l.t. ed. 1984. (Charnwood Large Print Ser.). 532p. 29.99 (*0-7089-8228-X*, Charnwood) Thorpe, F. A. Pubs. GBR. *Dist:* Ulverscroft Large Print Bks., Ltd., Ulverscroft Large Print Canada, Ltd.

—Pride & Prejudice. 1986. (Illus.). 352p. 25.95 o.p. (*0-7126-1011-1*) Trafalgar Square.

—Pride & Prejudice. 1999. (Signature Classics Ser.). (Illus.). 352p. 24.95 (*1-58279-032-9*); 29.95 (*1-58279-044-2*) Trident Pr. International.

—Pride & Prejudice. Norris, Pamela, ed. 1993. 384p. pap. 3.95 (*0-460-87212-5*, Everyman's Classic Library in Paperback) Tuttle Publishing.

—Pride & Prejudice. 1906. 352p. pap. 4.95 o.p. (*0-460-11022-5*, Everyman's Classic Library in Paperback) Tuttle Publishing.

—Pride & Prejudice. Tanner, Tony, ed. 1972. (English Library). 400p. pap. 7.95 o.s.i (*0-14-043072-5*, Penguin Classics) Viking Penguin.

—Pride & Prejudice. 2000. text 6.00 (*0-8220-7172-X*); text 6.00 (*0-8220-7172-X*) Wiley, John & Sons, Inc. (Cliff Notes).

—Pride & Prejudice. 1992. E-Book 8.98 (*0-585-25816-3*) netLibrary, Inc.

Austen, Jane & Butler, Marilyn. Northanger Abbey. 2003. (Classics Ser.). (Illus.). 288p. pap. 7.00 (*0-14-143979-3*, Penguin Classics) Viking Penguin.

Austen, Jane & Crogan, Claire. Northanger Abbey. 1996. E-Book 7.95 (*0-585-23088-9*) netLibrary, Inc.

Austen, Jane & Hemmant, Lynette. Pride & Prejudice. 1980. 14.95 o.p. (*0-437-24575-6*) Trafalgar Square.

Austen, Jane & Kinsley, James. Pride & Prejudice. 1990. E-Book 13.13 (*0-585-37761-8*) netLibrary, Inc.

Austen, Jane, et al. Emma. 1998. E-Book 7.30 (*0-585-36169-X*) netLibrary, Inc.

Austin, Lynn. Fire by Night. 2003. (Refiners Fire Ser.). 432p. pap. 12.99 (*1-55661-443-8*) Bethany Hse. Pubs.

Ballard-Jones, Anita. Rehoboth Road. 2003. 248p. 28.95 (*0-9729455-1-2*); per. 19.95 (*0-9729455-0-4*) Black Deer Bks.

Barr, Emily. Backpack. 2001. 320p. pap. 13.00 (*0-452-28293-4*, Plume) Dutton/Plume.

—Cuba. 2004. 13.00 (*0-452-28503-8*, Plume) Dutton/Plume.

Barrett, Julia, pseud. Presumption. 238p. pap. 11.95 (*1-85479-993-2*) O'Mara, Michael Bks., Ltd. GBR. *Dist:* Andrews McMeel Publishing.

Barrett, Julia, pseud & Austen, Jane. Presumption: An Entertainment: A Sequel to Pride & Prejudice. 1993. 240p. 19.95 o.p. (*0-87131-736-2*) Evans, M. & Co., Inc.

—Presumption: An Entertainment: A Sequel to Pride & Prejudice. 1995. 238p. reprint ed. pap. 12.00 (*0-226-03813-0*) Univ. of Chicago Pr.

Bedford, Sybille. Jigsaw: An Unsentimental Education. 1991. 352p. pap. 10.00 o.p. (*0-14-011388-6*, Penguin Bks.) Penguin Group (USA) Inc.

—Jigsaw: An Unsentimental Education, a Biographical Novel. 2001. 368p. pap. text 15.00 (*1-58243-143-4*, Counterpoint Pr.) Basic Bks.

Bialosky, Jill. House under Snow. 2003. 264p. pap. 14.00 (*0-15-602746-1*, Harvest Bks.); 2002. 256p. 24.00 (*0-15-100685-7*) Harcourt Trade Pubs.

Blair, Jessica. Time & Tide. l.t. ed. 2003. (Magna Large Print Ser.). 512p. 32.50 (*0-7505-2027-2*) Magna Large Print Bks. GBR. *Dist:* Ulverscroft Large Print Bks., Ltd., Ulverscroft Large Print Canada, Ltd.

Blake, Cindy. Girl Talk. 2002. 224p. 25.99 (*0-7278-5905-6*) Severn Hse. Pubs., Ltd.

Blensdorf, Jan. My Name Is Sei Shonagon. 2003. 248p. 19.95 (*1-58567-443-5*) Overlook Pr., The.

Bloom, Rebecca. Tangled up in Daydreams. 2003. 288p. 24.95 (*0-06-621258-8*, Morrow, William & Co.) Morrow/Avon.

Bowen, Elizabeth. The Last September. 2000. 320p. pap. 13.00 (*0-385-72014-9*, Knopf Bks. for Young Readers) Random Hse. Children's Bks.

—The Last September. (Penguin Twentieth-Century Classics Ser.). 208p. 1990. pap. 11.95 o.p. (*0-14-018304-3*, 83, Penguin Classics); 1987. pap. 5.95 o.p. (*0-14-000372-X*, Penguin Bks.) Viking Penguin.

Boyle, Kay. Process: A Novel. Spanier, Sandra Whipple, ed. & intro. by. 2002. (Illus.). 168p. 24.95 (*0-252-02668-3*) Univ. of Illinois Pr.

Bradford, Barbara Taylor. The Triumph of Katie Byrne. l.t. ed. 2001. 496p. 24.95 (*0-375-43097-0*) Random Hse. Large Print.

Brennan, Maeve. The Visitor. 2001. 96p. pap. text 10.00 (*1-58243-161-2*, Counterpoint Pr.) Basic Bks.

—Visitor. 2000. 96p. text 16.95 o.p. (*1-58243-083-7*, Counterpoint Pr.) Basic Bks.

Brink, André. The Other Side of Silence. 320p. 2004. pap. (*0-15-602964-2*, Harvest Bks.); 2003. 25.00 (*0-15-100770-5*) Harcourt Trade Pubs.

Brookner, Anita. The Bay of Angels. E-Book 9.95 (*1-58945-826-5*) Adobe Systems, Inc.

—The Bay of Angels. 2002. 208p. pap. 12.00 (*0-375-72760-4*) Knopf, Alfred A. Inc.

—The Bay of Angels. E-Book 19.00 (*1-58836-006-7*) Random Hse., Inc.

—The Bay of Angels. 2001. (Thorndike Press Large Print Women's Fiction Ser.). 335p. 29.95 (*0-7862-3654-X*) Thorndike Pr.

Brown, Mary. Here There Be Dragonnes. 2003. 832p. pap. 15.00 (*0-7434-3596-6*) Baen Bks.

Brown, Sandra. Hello, Darkness. 2003. 416p. 25.95 (*0-7432-4552-0*, Simon & Schuster) Simon & Schuster.

Buckley, Kristen. The Parker Grey Show. 2003. 240p. pap. 13.00 (*0-425-19109-5*) Berkley Publishing Group.

Bushnell, Candace. Trading Up. l.t. ed. 2003. 808p. 32.95 (*1-58724-549-3*, Wheeler Publishing, Inc.) Gale Group.

—Trading Up. 2003. pap. 13.95 (*0-7868-8706-0*); 416p. 24.95 (*0-7868-6818-X*); pap. 13.95 (*0-7868-8871-7*) Hyperion Pr.

Butler, Tajuana. The Night Before Thirty: A Novel. 2003. 240p. 19.95 (*1-4000-6020-6*, Villard Bks.) Random House Adult Trade Publishing Group.

Cambeira, Alan. Azucar! The Story of Sugar. 2001. 290p. pap. 14.50 (*0-9720821-1-5*) Belecam & Assocs.

Campbell, Rebecca. Slave to Fashion: A Novel. 2002. Orig. Title: The Favours & Fortunes of Katie Castle. 240p. 22.95 (*0-375-50713-2*); 288p. pap. 11.95 (*0-375-76062-8*) Random House Adult Trade Publishing Group. (Villard Bks.).

Carter, Emily. Glory Goes & Gets Some. 2000. 239p. 20.95 (*1-56689-101-9*) Coffee Hse. Pr.

—Glory Goes & Gets Some. 2001. 240p. pap. 13.00 (*0-312-28251-6*) Picador.

Ceely, Jonatha. Mina. 2004. 336p. 21.95 (*0-385-33690-X*, Delacorte Pr.) Dell Publishing.

Choi, Susan. American Woman: A Novel. 2003. 384p. 24.95 (*0-06-054221-7*) HarperCollins Pubs.

Clair, Maxine. October Suite: A Novel. 2002. E-Book 19.00 (*1-59061-867-X*) Adobe Systems, Inc.

—October Suite: A Novel. 2002. 352p. pap. 12.95 (*0-375-76095-4*) Random House Adult Trade Publishing Group.

—October Suite: A Novel. 2001. E-Book 19.00 (*1-58836-059-8*) Random Hse., Inc.

—October Suite: A Novel. l.t. ed. 2002. (African American Ser.). 563p. 28.95 (*0-7862-4094-6*) Thorndike Pr.

Clement, Alison. Pretty Is As Pretty Does: A Novel. 2001. 268p. 25.00 (*0-9673701-9-1*) MacAdam/Cage Publishing, Inc.

Constantine, Storm. Burying the Shadow. 2004. 16.00 (*1-892065-45-2*) Meisha Merlin Publishing, Inc.

Cook, David. Sunrising. 1990. pap. 8.95 o.p. (*0-87951-338-1*); 1990. 240p. pap. 9.95 o.s.i (*0-87951-261-X*); 1986. 248p. 16.95 o.p. (*0-87951-253-9*) Overlook Pr., The.

Cooney, Ellen. The White Palazzo. 2002. 219p. pap. 14.00 (*1-56689-134-5*) Coffee Hse. Pr.

Coyle, Neva. A Door of Hope. 2000. (Summerwind Ser.). 244p. 23.95 (*0-7862-2868-7*, Five Star) Gale Group.

Creamer, Hannah Gardner. Delia's Doctors; or, a Glance Behind the Scenes. 2003. 296p. text 39.95 (*0-252-02807-4*); pap. text 14.95 (*0-252-07108-5*) Univ. of Illinois Pr.

Crosby, Harry W. Portrait of Paloma: A Novel. 2001. (Illus.). 320p. pap. 14.95 (*0-916251-56-X*) Sunbelt Pubns., Inc.

Crowell, Jenn. Letting the Body Lead. 2002. 288p. 23.95 o.s.i (*0-399-14859-0*, Putnam & Grosset) Penguin Group (USA) Inc.

Cunnah, Michelle. 32AA. 2003. 320p. pap. 13.95 (*0-06-056012-6*) HarperCollins Pubs.

D'Ancona, Matthew. Going East. 2004. 384p. 25.00 (*0-385-51049-7*, Talese, Nan A.) Doubleday Publishing.

D'Arcy, Paula. Red Fire: A Quest for Awakening. 2001. (Illus.). 118p. pap. 13.95 (*1-880913-51-8*) Innisfree Pr.

Dart-Thornton, Cecilia. The Battle of Evernight. (Bitterbynde Ser.: Bk. III). 2003. (Illus.). 480p. 24.95 (*0-446-52807-2*); 2004. 608p. mass mkt. 6.99 (*0-446-61135-2*) Warner Bks., Inc. (Aspect).

Daugherty, Tracy. Axeman's Jazz: A Novel. 2003. 240p. 22.50 (*0-87074-481-X*) Southern Methodist Univ. Pr.

Davies, Luke. Isabelle the Navigator. 2002. 272p. pap. 12.95 (*0-425-18604-0*) Berkley Publishing Group.

Davis, Amanda. Circling the Drain. 2000. 208p. pap. 13.00 (*0-688-17909-6*, Perennial) HarperTrade.

—Circling the Drain: Stories. 1999. 191p. 23.00 (*0-688-16780-2*, Morrow, William & Co.) Morrow/Avon.

Davis-Goff, Annabel. This Cold Country. 368p. 2003. pap. 14.00 (*0-15-602738-0*, Harvest Bks.); 2002. (Illus.). 25.00 (*0-15-100847-7*) Harcourt Trade Pubs.

—This Cold Country. Date not set. (*0-312-28448-9*) St. Martin's Pr.

Davis, Kathleen Legeia. Serpentina: A Novel. 2003. (Illus.). 323p. 18.50 (*0-9715402-1-7*, 410-707-6686) Barnhardt & Ashe Publishing, Inc.

Delbanco, Francesca. Ask Me Anything. 2004. 256p. 23.95 (*0-393-05170-6*) Norton, W. W. & Co., Inc.

Delinsky, Barbara. Flirting with Pete. 2004. 544p. mass mkt. 7.99 (*0-7434-6984-4*, Pocket); 2003. 368p. 26.00 (*0-7432-4642-X*, Scribner) Simon & Schuster.

—Flirting with Pete. l.t. ed. 2004. 654p. pap. 13.95 (*1-59413-018-3*, Large Print Pr.); 2003. 663p. 32.95 (*0-7862-5100-X*) Thorndike Pr.

Desai, Anita. Fasting, Feasting. 2000. 240p. pap. 13.00 (*0-618-06582-2*, Mariner Bks.) Houghton Mifflin Co. Trade & Reference Div.

—Fasting, Feasting. 1999. 227p. (*0-7011-6894-3*) Random Hse. of Canada, Ltd. CAN. *Dist:* Random Hse., Inc.

—Fasting, Feasting. l.t. ed. 2000. (Basic Ser.). 323p. 27.95 (*0-7862-2638-2*); (*0-7540-4239-1*); (*0-7540-4240-5*) Thorndike Pr.

Donner, Rebecca. Sunset Terrace. 2003. 312p. 22.00 (*1-931561-34-6*) MacAdam/Cage Publishing, Inc.

Doughty, Anne. Beyond the Green Hills. 384p. 25.99 (*0-7278-5751-7*); 29.99 (*0-7278-7166-8*) Severn Hse. Pubs., Ltd.

Dreiser, Theodore. Sister Carrie. (Modern Library Ser.). E-Book 4.95 (*1-931208-42-5*) Adobe Systems, Inc.

—Sister Carrie. 1967. (Airmont Classics Ser.). mass mkt. 2.95 o.p. (*0-8049-0147-3*, CL-147) Airmont Publishing Co., Inc.

—Sister Carrie. 1976. 27.95 (*0-8488-0993-9*) Amereon, Ltd.

—Sister Carrie. 1982. 432p. mass mkt. 2.95 o.s.i (*0-553-21264-8*); mass mkt. 5.99 (*0-553-21374-1*) Bantam Bks. (Bantam Classics).

—Sister Carrie. 1971. 472p. reprint ed. lib. bdg. 20.00 (*0-8376-0401-X*) Bentley Pubs.

—Sister Carrie. 1980. 557p. reprint ed. lib. bdg. 37.95 (*0-89968-207-3*, Lightyear Pr.) Buccaneer Bks., Inc.

—Sister Carrie. (Collected Works of Theodore Dreiser). 382p. reprint ed. 2001. (Illus.). pap. text 28.00 (*0-7426-5625-X*); 1998. lib. bdg. 98.00 (*1-58201-625-9*) Classic Bks.

—Sister Carrie. E-Book 2.49 (*0-7574-0316-6*); E-Book 2.49 (*0-7574-0213-5*) Electric Umbrella Publishing.

—Sister Carrie. 1957. 474p. (C). pap. text 24.00 (*0-03-009075-X*) Harcourt College Pubs.

—Sister Carrie. Simpson, Claude, ed. 1972. pap. 12.36 o.p. (*0-395-05134-7*, Riverside Editions) Houghton Mifflin Co.

—Sister Carrie. l.t. ed. 590p. pap. 42.40 (*0-7583-2329-8*); 808p. pap. 60.08 (*0-7583-2330-1*); 1035p. pap. 71.70 (*0-7583-2331-X*); 1324p. pap. 85.64 (*0-7583-2332-8*); 2004p. pap. 123.01 (*0-7583-2334-4*); 2324p. pap. 145.14 (*0-7583-2335-2*); 1629p. pap. 108.27 (*0-7583-2333-6*); 808p. lib. bdg. 72.08 (*0-7583-2322-0*); 2324p. lib. bdg. 174.31 (*0-7583-2327-1*); 1629p. lib. bdg. 126.27 (*0-7583-2325-5*); 590p. lib. bdg. 48.40 (*0-7583-2321-2*); 472p. lib. bdg. 41.72 (*0-7583-2320-4*); 1035p. lib. bdg. 83.70 (*0-7583-2323-9*); 1324p. lib. bdg. 97.64 (*0-7583-2324-7*); 2004p. lib. bdg. 144.15 (*0-7583-2326-3*) Huge Print Pr.

—Sister Carrie. 1962. mass mkt. 2.25 o.p. (*0-451-51319-3*); 1962. mass mkt. 1.50 o.p. (*0-451-50904-8*); 1962. mass mkt. 0.75 o.p. (*0-451-50086-5*); 1962. mass mkt. 2.25 o.p. (*0-451-51725-3*); 1962. mass mkt. 2.95 o.p. (*0-451-51969-8*); 1962. 480p. mass mkt. 5.95 o.s.i (*0-451-52273-7*); 1962. mass mkt. 1.75 o.p. (*0-451-51206-5*); 1962. mass mkt. 0.95 o.p. (*0-451-50758-4*); 1962. mass mkt. 2.50 o.p. (*0-451-51462-9*); 2000. 512p. mass mkt. 5.95 (*0-451-52760-7*) NAL. (Signet Classics).

—Sister Carrie. l.t. ed. (Large Print Ser.). reprint ed. 1997. 632p. lib. bdg. 28.00 (*0-939495-16-3*); 1998. 453p. lib. bdg. 25.00 (*1-58287-071-3*) North Bks.

—Sister Carrie. 1970. (C). pap. o.p. (*0-393-09949-0*) Norton, W. W. & Co., Inc.

—Sister Carrie. Pizer, Donald, ed. 2nd ed. 1991. (Critical Editions Ser.). 600p. (C). pap. text 12.00 (*0-393-96042-0*, 9949) Norton, W. W. & Co., Inc.

—Sister Carrie. Mitchell, Lee Clark, ed. 1999. (Oxford World's Classics Ser.). 512p. pap. 12.95 (*0-19-283574-2*) Oxford Univ. Pr., Inc.

—Sister Carrie. 1991. (Oxford World's Classics Ser.). 508p. pap. 9.95 o.p. (*0-19-282742-1*, 9673) Oxford Univ. Pr., Inc.

—Sister Carrie. 2000. E-Book 4.95 (*0-679-64138-6*); 1999. 752p. pap. 12.95 (*0-375-75321-4*) Random House Adult Trade Publishing Group. (Modern Library).

—Sister Carrie. 1997. (Modern Library Ser.). 658p. 19.50 o.s.i (*0-679-60250-X*) Random Hse., Inc.

—Sister Carrie. E-Book 5.00 (*0-7410-0562-X*) SoftBook Pr.

—Sister Carrie. 1994. (Penguin Twentieth-Century Classics Ser.). 19.00 (*0-606-04903-7*) Turtleback Bks.

—Sister Carrie. Berkey, John C. et al, eds. 1997. (University of Pennsylvania Dreiser Edition Ser.). 544p. pap. 22.50 (*0-8122-1638-5*) Univ. of Pennsylvania Pr.

—Sister Carrie. West, James L. W., III et al, eds. 1981. (Dreiser Edition Ser.). (Illus.). 704p. 49.95 o.p. (*0-8122-7784-8*); pap. 24.95 o.p. (*0-8122-1110-3*) Univ. of Pennsylvania Pr.

—Sister Carrie. unabr. ed. 1997. 297p. reprint ed. pap. 14.95 o.p. (*1-57002-041-8*) University Publishing Hse., Inc.

—Sister Carrie. 1994. (Twentieth Century Classics Ser.). 496p. 12.95 (*0-14-018828-2*, Penguin Classics) Viking Penguin.

—Sister Carrie. Berkey, John C. et al, eds. 1981. (American Library). 528p. pap. 8.95 o.p. (*0-14-039002-2*, Penguin Classics) Viking Penguin.

—Sister Carrie: An Authoritative Text, Backgrounds & Sources Criticism. 1970. (Critical Editions Ser.). (Illus.). x, 591p. (*0-393-04325-8*) Norton, W. W. & Co., Inc.

—Sister Carrie, Jennie Gerhardt, Twelve Men. Lehan, Richard, ed. 1987. (Library of America). 1168p. 40.00 (*0-940450-41-0*) Library of America, The.

Edgeworth, Maria. The Works of Maria Edgeworth, 12 vols. Incl. Belinda. 91.66 (*1-85196-176-3*); 91.66 (*1-85196-175-5*); 91.66 (*1-85196-178-X*); 91.66 (*1-85196-179-8*); 91.66 (*1-85196-180-1*); 91.66 (*1-85196-181-X*); 91.66 (*1-85196-182-8*); 91.66 (*1-85196-183-6*); 91.66 (*1-85196-184-4*); 91.70 (*1-85196-185-2*); 91.70 (*1-85196-187-9*); 91.66 (*1-85196-177-1*); 1997. 4400p. 2003. 1100.00 (*1-85196-186-0*) Pickering & Chatto Pubs., Ltd. GBR. *Dist:* Ashgate Publishing Co.

Eliot, George. Middlemarch: A Study of English Provincial Life, 2 vols. 2001. 14.95 (*0-8010-1218-X*) Baker Bks.

—Middlemarch: A Study of English Provincial Life. 2002. Vol. 1. 420p. 27.99 (*1-4043-1964-6*); Vol. 1. 420p. per. 22.99 (*1-4043-1965-4*); Vol. 2. 396p. 27.99 (*1-4043-1966-2*); Vol. 2. 396p. per. 22.99 (*1-4043-1967-0*) IndyPublish.com.

—Middlemarch: A Study of English Provincial Life. 2003. 880p. pap. 10.00 (*0-14-143954-8*, Penguin Classics) Viking Penguin.

—The Mill on the Floss. 2003. (Dover Thrift Editions Ser.). 416p. 3.50 (*0-486-42680-7*) Dover Pubns., Inc.

—The Mill on the Floss. 1972. 3.95 o.p. (*0-460-01325-4*); 1956. 10.50 o.p. (*0-460-00325-9*) Dutton/Plume. (Dutton).

—The Mill on the Floss. 1968. mass mkt. 0.95 o.p. (*0-451-50438-0*); 1968. mass mkt. 0.75 o.p. (*0-451-50278-7*); 1965. mass mkt. 1.25 o.p. (*0-451-50672-3*); 1965. mass mkt. 1.95 o.p. (*0-451-51055-0*); 1965. mass mkt. 2.95 o.p. (*0-451-51472-6*); 1965. mass mkt. 1.50 o.p. (*0-451-50892-0*) NAL. (Signet Classics).

—The Mill on the Floss. 2001. (Modern Library Classics). 656p. pap. 8.95 (*0-375-75783-X*, Modern Library) Random House Adult Trade Publishing Group.

—The Mill on the Floss. 2000. (Signature Classics Ser.). 486p. 24.95 (*1-58279-088-4*); lib. bdg. 29.95 (*1-58279-083-3*) Trident Pr. International.

Elliott, George P. Middlemarch. 2003. 912p. mass mkt. 6.95 (*0-451-52917-0*, Signet Classics) NAL.

Elphinstone, Margaret. Hy Brasil. 2002. (Illus.). 320p. pap. (*1-84195-247-8*) Canongate Bks.

Eversz, Robert M. Shooting Elvis. 224p. 1996. pap. 21.00 o.p. (*0-8021-1582-9*); 1997. reprint ed. pap. 12.00 (*0-8021-3501-3*) Grove/Atlantic, Inc. (Grove Pr.).

Faber, Michel. The Crimson Petal & the White. 2002. 848p. 26.00 (*0-15-100692-X*) Harcourt Trade Pubs.

Farber, Thomas. The Beholder: A Novel. 2002. 208p. 22.00 (*0-8050-6972-0*, Metropolitan Bks.) Holt, Henry & Co.

—The Beholder: A Novel. 2003. 208p. pap. 13.00 (*0-312-42182-6*) Picador.

Foster, Barbara Spencer. Pecos Queen: A Novel. 2003. 192p. pap. 18.95 (*0-86534-391-8*) Sunstone Pr.

Fox, Paula. The God of Nightmares. 1990. 240p. 18.95 o.p. (*0-86547-432-X*, North Point Pr.) Farrar, Straus & Giroux.

—The God of Nightmares. 2002. 240p. pap. 13.95 (*0-393-32287-4*) Norton, W. W. & Co., Inc.

—The God of Nightmares. 1991. mass mkt. 5.95 (*0-446-36114-3*) Warner Bks., Inc.

Franklin, Miles. My Brilliant Career. 2002. 288p. pap. 13.95 (*0-207-19724-5*) Angus & Robertson, Ltd. GBR. *Dist:* Consortium Bk. Sales & Distribution.

—My Brilliant Career. l.t. ed. 1987. (General Ser.). 17.95 o.p. (*0-8161-4158-4*, Macmillan Reference USA) Gale Group.

—My Brilliant Career. 1992. 81p. pap. 14.00 o.p. (*0-207-18695-2*) HarperTrade.

—My Brilliant Career. 1982. 272p. mass mkt. 3.95 o.s.i (*0-671-45915-5*, Pocket) Simon & Schuster.

—My Brilliant Career. 1980. 252p. 9.95 o.p. (*0-312-55599-7*) St. Martin's Pr.

Gaffney, Patricia. Flight Lessons. 2002. 400p. 24.95 (*0-06-018528-7*); 608p. pap. 24.95 (*0-06-009392-7*) HarperCollins Pubs.

—Flight Lessons. 2003. 464p. mass mkt. 7.99 (*0-06-103144-5*, HarperTorch) Morrow/Avon.

Gardam, Jane. The Flight of the Maidens. 2002. 288p. pap. 13.00 (*0-452-28334-5*) Dutton/Plume.

—The Flight of the Maidens. 2000. 352p. (*0-7011-6963-X*) Random Hse. of Canada, Ltd. CAN. *Dist:* Random Hse., Inc.

Gardner, Katy. Losing Gemma: A Novel. 2002. 368p. pap. 13.00 (*1-57322-933-4*, Riverhead Bks. (Hardcovers)) Putnam Publishing Group, The.

Giordano, Marie. I Love You Like a Tomato. Date not set. mass mkt. (*0-7653-4588-9*, Forge Bks.); pap. (*0-7653-0669-7*, Forge Bks.); 2003. 480p. 24.95 (*0-7653-0668-9*, Forge Bks.); 2003. 477p. 21.95 (*0-7653-0927-0*, Tor Bks.) Doherty, Tom Assocs., LLC.

Glover, Ruth. Backroads to Bliss: A Novel. 2003. 272p. pap. 11.99 (*0-8007-5829-3*) Revell, Fleming H. Co.

Goodman, Allegra. Paradise Park. 2002. 368p. pap. 12.95 (*0-385-33418-4*, Delta) Dell Publishing.

Gowdy, Barbara. The Romantic: A Novel. 2003. 320p. 24.00 (*0-8050-7190-3*, Metropolitan Bks.) Holt, Henry & Co.

Graham, Laurie. The Great Husband Hunt. 2003. 368p. pap. 14.00 (*0-446-69132-1*) Warner Bks., Inc.

—The Unfortunates. 2002. (Illus.). 368p. pap. (*1-84115-314-1*, Fourth Estate) HarperTrade.

Green, Jane. Mr. Maybe. 2001. E-Book 16.00 (*1-59061-361-9*); E-Book 16.00 (*1-59061-495-X*) Adobe Systems, Inc.

—Mr. Maybe. 2002. 368p. reprint ed. pap. 11.95 (*0-7679-0520-2*) Broadway Bks.

Greenwood, Tammy. Undressing the Moon. 2003. 256p. pap. 13.95 (*0-312-30327-0*, Saint Martin's Griffin) St. Martin's Pr.

Greenwood, Tammy, ed. Undressing the Moon. 2002. 256p. 23.95 (*0-312-28473-X*) St. Martin's Pr.

Gross, Gwendolen. Getting Out: A Novel. 2002. 304p. 24.00 (*0-8050-6834-1*) Holt, Henry & Co.

Gwinne, Jean Q. Mollie O'neill. 1997. (Illus.). 224p. 22.95 (*1-879384-31-0*) Cypress Hse.

Hansen, Jennie L. Beyond Summer Dreams. 2001. 282p. 14.95 (*1-57734-889-3*) Covenant Communications.

Haulsey, Kuwana. The Red Moon: A Novel. 2001. (Illus.). 288p. 22.95 o.s.i (*0-375-50557-1*, Villard Bks.) Random House Adult Trade Publishing Group.

Hill, Grace Livingston. All Through the Night. 1976. reprint ed. lib. bdg. 22.95 (*0-89190-001-2*, River-city Pr.) Amereon, Ltd.

—All Through the Night. l.t. ed. 2000. (Candlelight Romance Ser.). 387p. 22.95 o.p. (*0-7862-2786-9*) Thorndike Pr.

—All Through the Night, No. 6. 1996. (Grace Livingston Hill Ser.: Vol. 6). 224p. mass mkt. 4.99 o.p. (*0-8423-0018-X*) Tyndale Hse. Pubs.

Hill, Pamela. The Gods Return. l.t. ed. 2001. 224p. (*0-7540-4390-8*); (*0-7540-4389-4*) Gale Group. (Macmillan Reference USA).

—The Gods Return. l.t. ed. 2001. (Nightingale Ser.). 224p. pap. 22.95 (*0-7838-9339-6*) Thorndike Pr.

Hoffman, Eva. The Secret. 2004. 272p. pap. 12.95 (*0-345-46536-9*) Ballantine Bks.

—The Secret. 2002. 272p. text 25.00 (*1-58648-150-9*) PublicAffairs.

Holden, Wendy. Gossip Hound. 2003. 304p. pap. 13.00 (*0-452-28393-0*, Plume) Dutton/Plume.

Hyde, Robin. The Godwits Fly. Sandbrook, Patrick, ed. 2001. xxxiv, 259p. pap. 24.95 (*1-86940-245-6*) Auckland Univ. Pr. NZL. *Dist:* Paul & Co. Pubs. Consortium, Inc.

Jackson, Faith Reyher. Meadow Fugue & Descant: A Novel. 2002. (*0-931846-66-8*); pap. (*0-931846-64-1*) Washington Writers' Publishing Hse.

Jaffe, Rona. The Best of Everything. 1976. reprint ed. lib. bdg. 28.95 o.p. (*0-89966-130-0*) Buccaneer Bks., Inc.

—The Best of Everything. 1986. 448p. pap. 6.95 o.s.i (*0-385-29468-9*, Delta) Dell Publishing.

James, Henry. The Bostonians. 1980. mass mkt. 2.95 o.p. (*0-451-51285-5*, Signet Classics) NAL.

—The Bostonians. 2003. 496p. pap. 8.95 (*0-8129-6996-0*, Modern Library) Random House Adult Trade Publishing Group.

—Daisy Miller. l.t. ed. 2001. per. 15.50 (*1-58396-130-5*) Blue Unicorn Editions.

—Daisy Miller. 1988. mass mkt. 4.95 (*1-55902-007-5*, Aerie) Doherty, Tom Assocs., LLC.

—Daisy Miller. l.t. ed. 2002. 172p. 28.95 (*0-7862-4386-4*) Gale Group.

—Daisy Miller. mass mkt. 0.25 o.p. (*0-451-00625-9*, Signet Bks.) NAL.

—Daisy Miller. l.t. ed. 2002. (Large Print Ser.). 213p. lib. bdg. 25.00 (*1-58287-661-4*) North Bks.

—Daisy Miller. 2002. (Modern Library Classics). 112p. pap. 5.95 (*0-375-75966-2*, Modern Library) Random House Adult Trade Publishing Group.

—Daisy Miller. (Ebook Classic Ser.). E-Book 3.00 (*0-7410-0413-5*) SoftBook Pr.

—The Wings of the Dove. 2003. 768p. pap. 9.95 (*0-8129-6719-4*, Modern Library) Random House Adult Trade Publishing Group.

Jewell, Lisa. One-Hit Wonder. 2002. 352p. 23.95 o.s.i (*0-525-94653-5*, Dutton) Dutton/Plume.

Jiles, Paulette. Enemy Women. 2003. 336p. pap. 13.95 (*0-06-093809-9*, Perennial) HarperTrade.

—Enemy Women. l.t. ed. 2002. (Women's Fiction Ser.). 561p. 29.95 (*0-7862-4396-1*) Thorndike Pr.

—Enemy Women: A Novel. 2002. 336p. 24.95 (*0-06-621444-0*, Morrow, William & Co.) Morrow/Avon.

Jong, Erica. Fanny: Being the True History of the Adventures of Fanny Hackabout-Jones. 1984. mass mkt. 1.95 o.p. (*0-451-13370-6*, Signet Bks.) NAL.

—Fanny: Being the True History of the Adventures of Fanny Hackabout-Jones. 2003. (Illus.). 512p. pap. 14.95 (*0-393-32435-4*) Norton, W. W. & Co., Inc.

Kaufman, Pamela. Banners of Gold: A Novel. 2002. 416p. pap. 9.95 (*0-609-80947-4*) Crown Publishing Group.

Keady, Walter. The Altruist: A Novel. 2003. 283p. pap. 13.50 (*1-931561-39-7*) MacAdam/Cage Publishing, Inc.

Kelman, Nicholas. Girls. 2003. 224p. 22.95 (*0-316-71153-5*) Little Brown & Co.

Kennedy, Raymond A. The Romance of Eleanor Gray: A Novel. 2003. (Hardscrabble Books). (Illus.). 255p. text 24.95 (*1-58465-291-8*) Univ. Pr. of New England.

Keyes, Marian. Last Chance Saloon. 2001. 384p. 25.00 (*0-688-18072-8*, Morrow, William & Co.) Morrow/Avon.

—Last Chance Saloon. 1999. 505p. (*1-85371-965-X*) Poolbeg Pr. IRL. *Dist:* Dufour Editions, Inc.

—Lucy Sullivan Is Getting Married. 2002. 624p. pap. 13.95 (*0-06-009037-5*, Perennial) HarperTrade.

—Lucy Sullivan Is Getting Married. 2000. 624p. mass mkt. 6.99 (*0-380-79610-4*); 1999. 448p. 24.00 (*0-380-97618-8*) Morrow/Avon. (Avon Bks.).

—Lucy Sullivan Is Getting Married. 1996. 740p. pap. 12.95 (*1-85371-615-4*) Poolbeg Pr. IRL. *Dist:* Dufour Editions, Inc.

—Rachel's Holiday. 2001. 528p. mass mkt. 6.99 (*0-380-81768-3*, Avon Bks.); 2000. 576p. 25.00 (*0-688-18071-X*, Morrow, William & Co.) Morrow/Avon.

—Rachel's Holiday. 1998. (*1-85371-896-3*) Poolbeg Pr. IRL. *Dist:* Dufour Editions, Inc.

—Sushi for Beginners. unabr. ed. 2003. audio 39.95 (*0-06-055780-X*, HarperAudio) HarperTrade.

—Sushi for Beginners. 2004. 560p. mass mkt. 7.99 (*0-06-055725-7*, HarperTorch); 2003. 432p. 24.95 (*0-06-052050-7*, Morrow, William & Co.) Morrow/Avon.

Kingsbury, Karen & Smalley, Gary. Remember. 2003. (Redemption Ser.). 432p. pap. 12.99 (*0-8423-5629-0*) Tyndale Hse. Pubs.

Kinsella, Sophie. Can You Keep a Secret? 2004. 368p. 21.95 (*0-385-33681-0*, Dial Bks.) Dell Publishing.

—Confessions of a Shopaholic. 2003. 384p. mass mkt. 6.99 (*0-440-24141-3*, Dell Bks.); 2001. (Illus.). 320p. pap. 11.95 (*0-385-33548-2*, Delta) Dell Publishing.

—Confessions of a Shopaholic. audio 29.99 (*1-4025-3603-8*) Recorded Bks., LLC.

—Shopaholic Takes Manhattan. Orig. Title: Shopaholic Abroad. 2004. 416p. mass mkt. 6.99 (*0-440-24181-2*); 2002. 336p. pap. 11.95 (*0-385-33588-1*, Delta) Dell Publishing.

—Shopaholic Takes Manhattan. Orig. Title: Shopaholic Abroad. audio 29.99 (*1-4025-3624-0*) Recorded Bks., LLC.

—Shopaholic Ties the Knot. 2003. 352p. pap. 10.95 (*0-385-33617-9*, Delta) Dell Publishing.

—Shopaholic Ties the Knot. audio 29.99 (*1-4025-3625-9*) Recorded Bks., LLC.

Kizis, Deanna. How to Meet Cute Boys: A Novel. 2003. (Illus.). 272p. 21.95 (*0-446-53072-7*) Warner Bks., Inc.

Krentz, Jayne Ann. Light in Shadow. 2003. 384p. mass mkt. 7.99 (*0-515-13618-2*, Jove) Berkley Publishing Group.

—Light in Shadow. 2003. 543p. pap. 13.95 (*1-4104-0164-2*, Wheeler Publishing, Inc.) Gale Group.

—Light in Shadow. 2002. 384p. 24.95 (*0-399-14938-4*, Putnam & Grosset) Putnam Publishing Group, The.

—Light in Shadow: A Whispering Spring Novel. l.t. ed. 2003. (Basic Ser.). 32.95 (*0-7862-5033-X*) Thorndike Pr.

Kusel, Lisa. Other Fish in the Sea. 2003. pap. 15.95 (*0-7868-8802-4*) Hyperion Pr.

LeClaire, Anne D. Leaving Eden. 2003. 320p. pap. 13.95 (*0-345-44575-9*); 2002. 304p. 23.95 (*0-345-44574-0*) Ballantine Bks. (Ballantine Bks.).

—Leaving Eden. l.t. ed. 2003. (Women's Fiction Ser.). 341p. 29.95 (*0-7862-4871-8*) Gale Group.

Libaire, Jardine. Here Kitty Kitty. 2004. 192p. 22.95 (*0-316-73688-0*) Little Brown & Co.

Livesey, Margot. Eva Moves the Furniture: A Novel. 2001. 272p. 23.00 o.s.i (*0-8050-6801-5*) Holt, Henry & Co.

—Eva Moves the Furniture: A Novel. 2002. 240p. pap. 13.00 (*0-312-42103-6*) Picador.

Luke, Pearl. Burning Ground. 2001. 256p. pap. 13.00 (*0-452-28267-5*, Plume) Dutton/Plume.

—Burning Ground. 2000. 249p. (*0-00-225504-9*) HarperCollins Pubs.

MacEnulty, Pat. Sweet Fire. 2003. 256p. pap. 14.00 (*1-85242-455-9*) Serpent's Tail Ltd. GBR. *Dist:* Consortium Bk. Sales & Distribution.

Marillier, Juliet. Son of the Shadows. 2001. 462p. 25.95 (*0-312-84880-3*); 2002. 608p. reprint ed. mass mkt. 6.99 (*0-7653-4326-6*); 2002. reprint ed. pap. 14.95 (*0-312-87529-0*) Doherty, Tom Assocs., LLC. (Tor Bks.).

Marino, Anne N. The Collapsible World. 2000. 171p. 22.95 (*0-393-04909-4*) Norton, W. W. & Co., Inc.

Marquis, Traci. I Can't Cry: A Journey from Shame to Redemption. 2002. ii, 190p. 25.00 (*0-9720310-0-6*); pap. 14.95 (*0-9720310-1-4*) Sterling Pubs.

Marshall, Catherine. Christy. abr. ed. 1995. pap. 19.95 o.p. incl. audio (*1-55927-324-0*); pap. 19.95 o.p. incl. audio (*1-55927-324-0*) Audio Renaissance.

—Christy. 1994. reprint ed. lib. bdg. 35.95 (*1-56849-309-6*) Buccaneer Bks., Inc.

—Christy. 1967. text 14.95 o.p. (*0-07-040605-7*) McGraw-Hill Cos., The.

—Christy. 1976. 512p. mass mkt. 6.99 (*0-380-00141-1*, Avon Bks.) Morrow/Avon.

—Christy. 1968. 348p. mass mkt. 4.50 o.p. (*0-8007-8008-6*); 1995. (Illus.). 160p. (J). (gr. 6-9). 10.99 o.p. (*0-8007-1708-2*) Revell, Fleming H. Co.

—Christy. 1968. 13.04 (*0-606-00470-X*) Turtleback Bks.

—Christy. 2001. 512p. pap. 12.99 (*0-310-24163-4*) Zondervan.

—Christy: The Collectors Edition. 2001. (Illus.). 480p. (gr. 13 up). 24.99 (*0-8007-9290-4*) Chosen Bks.

—Christy: The Collectors Edition. l.t. ed. 1987. 721p. 20.95 o.p. (*0-8161-4186-X*, Macmillan Reference USA) Gale Group.

—Christy: The Young Readers Edition. 2001. (Illus.). 160p. (J). (gr. 6-9). 9.99 (*0-8007-9293-9*) Chosen Bks.

—Christy Books. 1995. pap. 19.99 (*0-8499-3947-X*) W Publishing Group.

—Christy's Choice. 1996. (Christy Fiction Ser.: No. 6). 128p. (Orig.). (J). (gr. 4-8). mass mkt. 4.99 (*0-8499-3919-4*) Nelson, Tommy.

—The Macmillan International Film Encyclopedia. 4th ed. 2001. 1520p. reprint ed. pap. 12.99 (*0-333-90690-X*, HarperResource) HarperInformation.

Martin, Sarah Beth. The One True Ocean. 2003. 320p. pap. 14.00 (*1-4022-0143-5*, Sourcebooks Landmark) Sourcebooks, Inc.

Martin, Steve. Shopgirl: A Novella. l.t. ed. 2001. (Wheeler Large Print Book Ser.). 151p. 28.95 (*1-58724-012-2*, Wheeler Publishing, Inc.) Gale Group.

—Shopgirl: A Novella. 2001. 112p. pap. 10.95 (*0-7868-8568-8*); 2001. 144p. E-Book 12.95 (*0-7868-7165-2*); 2001. 144p. E-Book 12.95 (*0-7868-7162-8*); 2001. 144p. E-Book 12.95 (*0-7868-7160-1*); 2001. 144p. E-Book 12.95 (*0-7868-7163-6*); 2001. 144p. E-Book 12.95 (*0-7868-7161-X*); 2000. (Illus.). 130p. 17.95 (*0-7868-6658-6*) Hyperion Pr.

Matthews, Carole. For Better, for Worse. 2002. 352p. pap. 14.95 (*0-380-82044-7*, Avon Bks.) Morrow/Avon.

Maxted, Anna. Running in Heels. 432p. 2002. pap. 13.95 (*0-06-098825-8*); 2001. (Illus.). 25.00 (*0-06-039321-1*) HarperTrade. (ReganBooks).

McCafferty, Kate. Testimony of an Irish Slave Girl. 2003. 240p. pap. 13.00 (*0-14-200183-X*) Penguin Group (USA) Inc.

—Testimony of an Irish Slave Girl: A Novel. 2002. 224p. 24.95 o.s.i (*0-670-03065-1*, Viking) Viking Penguin.

McCaffrey, Anne & Scarborough, Elizabeth Ann. Acorna's Rebels. 2003. 384p. mass mkt. 7.50 (*0-380-81847-7*); 320p. 24.95 (*0-380-97899-7*); 320p. 24.95 (*0-380-97899-7*) Morrow/Avon. (Eos).

McDermid, Val. The Distant Echo. Date not set. mass mkt. (*0-312-99483-4*, St. Martin's Paperbacks); 2003. 384p. 24.95 o.s.i (*0-312-30199-5*, Saint Martin's Minotaur) St. Martin's Pr.

McGiffen, Steve. Tennant's Rock. 2001. 224p. 23.95 (*0-312-26657-X*) St. Martin's Pr.

McKoy-Hibbert, Erica. Mi Neva Know Sey. 2000. 167p. 12.95 (*1-930331-00-2*) Machibb Creations.

McMurtry, Larry. By Sorrow's River: A Novel. l.t. ed. 2004. (Berrybender Narratives Ser.). 495p. 32.95 (*1-58724-598-1*, Wheeler Publishing, Inc.) Gale Group.

—By Sorrow's River: A Novel. 2003. (Illus.). 368p. 26.00 (*0-7432-3304-2*, Simon & Schuster) Simon & Schuster.

—The Wandering Hill. l.t. ed. 2003. (Berrybender Narratives Ser.: Bk. 2). 421p. 31.95 (*1-58724-437-3*, Wheeler Publishing, Inc.) Gale Group.

—The Wandering Hill. 2003. (Berrybender Narratives Ser.: Bk. 2). 432p. mass mkt. 7.99 (*0-7434-5142-2*, Pocket Star); (Illus.). 320p. 26.00 (*0-7432-3303-4*, Simon & Schuster) Simon & Schuster.

Messina, Lynn. Fashionistas. 2003. 288p. pap. (*0-373-25025-8*, Red Dress Ink) Harlequin Enterprises, Ltd.

Millar, Margaret. Best Mysteries of All Time: A Stranger in My Grave. 2002. (Best Mysteries of All Time Ser.). 289p. (*0-7621-8887-1*, Impress) Scriptorium Pr., The.

Min, Anchee. Katherine. 2001. 240p. pap. 13.00 o.s.i (*0-425-18023-9*); 1996. 304p. mass mkt. 6.99 o.s.i (*0-425-15291-X*) Berkley Publishing Group.

—Katherine, Set. abr. ed. 1995. 17.95 o.p. (*0-7871-0252-0*, 392915) NewStar Media, Inc.

—Katherine. 1995. 241p. 22.95 o.p. (*1-57322-005-1*, Riverhead Bks. (Hardcovers)) Putnam Publishing Group, The.

Mohanraj, Mary Anne. Kathryn in the City. 2003. (Create Your Own Erotic Fantasy Ser.). 196p. pap. 12.00 (*1-59240-030-2*) Gothman Bks.

Montague, Terry. Fireweed. 1992. pap. 10.95 (*1-55503-407-1*, 01111078) Covenant Communications, Inc.
Moore, Lorrie. Self-Help: Stories. 1986. 176p. pap. 9.00 o.p. (*0-452-25821-9*, Plume) Dutton/Plume.
Moore, Stephanie Perry. A Lova' Like No Otha' l.t. ed. 2003. 300p. 28.95 (*0-7862-5941-8*) Gale Group.
—A Lova' Like No Otha' 2003. 256p. pap. 13.95 (*0-446-67967-4*, Walk Worthy Pr.) Warner Bks., Inc.
Munro, Alice. Lives of Girls & Women. 1983. pap. 6.95 o.p. (*0-452-25433-7*, Plume) Dutton/Plume.
—Lives of Girls & Women. 2001. 288p. pap. 13.00 (*0-375-70749-2*, Vintage) Knopf Publishing Group.
—Lives of Girls & Women. 1974. mass mkt. 3.95 o.p. (*0-451-13643-8*); mass mkt. 3.50 o.p. (*0-451-12294-1*); mass mkt. 4.50 o.p. (*0-451-14733-2*); mass mkt. 1.25 o.p. (*0-451-05740-6*); mass mkt. 2.50 o.p. (*0-451-11298-9*); mass mkt. 1.75 o.p. (*0-451-07961-2*); mass mkt. 4.95 o.p. (*0-451-16754-6*) NAL. (Signet Bks.).
Mylnowski, Sarah. Fishbowl. 2002. 368p. pap. (*0-373-25020-7*, Red Dress Ink) Harlequin Enterprises, Ltd.
Naylor, Clare. Dog Handling. 2004. 336p. mass mkt. 6.99 (*0-345-46539-3*); 2002. 352p. pap. 12.95 (*0-345-45338-7*) Ballantine Bks.
Newman, Sandra. The Only Good Thing Anyone Has Ever Done. 2003. 400p. 24.95 (*0-06-051498-1*) HarperCollins Pubs.
Nichols, Linda. Not a Sparrow Falls. 2002. 352p. pap. 12.99 (*0-7642-2727-0*) Bethany Hse. Pubs.
Nunes, Rachel Ann. Where I Belong. 2003. 208p. pap. 14.95 (*1-55517-715-8*, 77158, Bonneville Bks.) Cedar Fort, Inc./CFI Distribution.
Oates, Joyce Carol. Marya: A Life. 1988. mass mkt. 3.95 o.s.i (*0-425-10688-8*) Berkley Publishing Group.
—Marya: A Life. 1998. 320p. pap. 14.00 (*0-452-28020-6*, Plume); 1986. 288p. 16.95 o.p. (*0-525-24374-7*, Abrahams, William Bks.) Dutton/Plume.
—Marya: A Life. l.t. ed. 1987. 448p. 18.95 o.p. (*0-8161-4178-9*, Macmillan Reference USA) Gale Group.
—Marya: A Life. 1992. 4.99 o.p. (*0-517-08002-8*) Random Hse. Value Publishing.
O'Carroll, Brendan. The Young Wan: An Agnes Browne Novel. 2003. 224p. 23.95 (*0-670-03114-3*, Viking) Viking Penguin.
Olson, Shannon. Children of God Go Bowling. 2004. 304p. 24.95 (*0-670-03281-6*, Viking) Viking Penguin.
Osborn, Karen. The River Road. 2002. 288p. 23.95 (*0-688-15899-4*, Morrow, William & Co.) Morrow/Avon.
Packer, Ann. The Dive from Clausen's Pier. 2002. 384p. 24.00 (*0-375-41282-4*) Knopf, Alfred A. Inc.
Packer, Z. Z. Drinking Coffee Elsewhere. 2004. 304p. pap. 14.00 (*1-57322-378-6*, Riverhead Trade (Paperbacks)) Berkley Publishing Group.
—Drinking Coffee Elsewhere: Stories. 2003. 224p. 24.95 (*1-57322-234-8*, Riverhead Bks. (Hardcovers)) Putnam Publishing Group, The.
Paver, Michelle. The Shadow Catcher. 2003. 416p. mass mkt. (*0-552-15041-X*, Corgi) Bantam Bks.
—The Shadow Catcher. l.t. ed. 2003. 544p. 32.50 (*0-7531-6815-4*) ISIS Large Print Bks. GBR. *Dist:* Ulverscroft Large Print Bks., Ltd., Ulverscroft Large Print Canada, Ltd.
—The Shadow Catcher. 2003. (Illus.). 579p. pap. 9.95 (*0-552-14872-5*) Transworld Publishers Ltd. GBR. *Dist:* Trafalgar Square.
Pearce, Jonathan. Buds: A Story about Friendship. 2003. 154p. per. 12.95 (*1-59411-006-9*) Writers' Collective, The.
Peart, Jane. The Heart's Lonely Secret. 1994. (Orphan Train West Ser.). 312p. (gr. 10 up). pap. 9.99 o.p. (*0-8007-5542-1*) Revell, Fleming H. Co.
—The Heart's Lonely Secret. l.t. ed. 2001. (Christian Fiction Ser.). 423p. 27.95 (*0-7862-3286-2*) Thorndike Pr.
Plath, Sylvia. The Bell Jar. 1983. 320p. mass mkt. 4.50 o.s.i (*0-553-26008-1*); 1978. (Illus.). 224p. mass mkt. 7.50 o.s.i (*0-553-27835-5*, Bantam Classics) Bantam Bks.
—The Bell Jar. 1991. 300p. reprint ed. lib. bdg. 17.95 (*0-89966-815-1*) Buccaneer Bks., Inc.
—The Bell Jar. 20th anniv. ed. 1996. 320p. 20.00 (*0-06-017490-0*) HarperCollins Pubs.
—The Bell Jar. (Perennial Classics Ser.). 2000. 288p. pap. 13.00 (*0-06-093018-7*, Perennial); 1971. (Illus.). 16.95 o.p. (*0-06-013356-2*); 2003. 416p. pap. 19.95 (*0-06-057309-0*, HarperLargePrint); 2003. audio 34.95 (*0-06-056945-X*, HarperAudio) HarperTrade.
—The Bell Jar. 1998. (Everyman's Library: Vol. 212). 256p. 17.00 (*0-375-40463-5*) Knopf, Alfred A. Inc.
—The Bell Jar. l.t. ed. 1996. (Perennial Bestsellers Ser.). 336p. 24.95 o.p. (*0-7838-1987-0*) Thorndike Pr.
—The Bell Jar. 2000. 19.05 (*0-606-19807-5*); 1972. 11.09 o.p. (*0-606-02294-5*) Turtleback Bks.
Prentice-Hall Staff. Pride & Prejudice. 2nd ed. text, stu. ed. (*0-13-716978-7*) Prentice Hall (Schl. Div.).
Prior, Lily. Ardor: A Novel of Enchantment. 2004. (*0-06-052786-2*, Ecco) HarperTrade.
Rainey, Yvonne. Dear Lover. Taylor, Chandra Sparks, ed. 2001. 306p. pap. 19.99 (*0-9706847-2-X*) Beginning II End Publishing, Inc.
Raney, Deborah. After the Rains. l.t. ed. 2003. 25.95 (*0-7862-4945-5*) Thorndike Pr.
—After the Rains. 2002. 352p. pap. 11.99 (*1-57856-576-6*) WaterBrook Pr.
Rice, Patty. Somethin' Extra. 2003. 400p. mass mkt. 6.50 (*0-515-13526-7*, Jove) Berkley Publishing Group.
—Somethin' Extra: A Novel. 2000. 368p. 23.00 (*0-684-85340-X*, Simon & Schuster) Simon & Schuster.
Richmond, Michelle. Dream of the Blue Room. 2003. 297p. 23.00 (*1-931561-24-9*) MacAdam/Cage Publishing, Inc.
Riley, Gwendolyn. Cold Water. 2003. 176p. 20.00 (*0-7867-1109-4*, Carroll & Graf Pubs.) Avalon Publishing Group.
Robinson, Eden. Monkey Beach: A Novel. 2002. (Illus.). 384p. pap. 13.00 (*0-618-21905-6*, Mariner Bks.) Houghton Mifflin Co. Trade & Reference Div.
Rosenfeld, Lucinda. Why She Went Home: A Novel. 2004. 320p. 23.95 (*1-4000-6185-7*, Random House) Random House Adult Trade Publishing Group.
Saylor, Steven. Have You Seen Dawn? 2003. 256p. 24.00 (*0-7432-1366-1*, Simon & Schuster) Simon & Schuster.
—Have You Seen Dawn? l.t. ed. 2003. 28.95 (*0-7862-5467-X*) Thorndike Pr.
Schmais, Libby. The Perfect Elizabeth: A Tale of Two Sisters. E-Book 22.95 (*0-312-27589-7*); 2001. 240p. pap. 12.95 (*0-312-27080-1*, CPB1125, Saint Martin's Griffin); 2000. 228p. 22.95 o.p. (*0-312-25225-0*) St. Martin's Pr.
Schutt, Christine. Florida. 2003. 152p. 22.95 (*0-8101-5150-2*, TriQuarterly Bks.) Northwestern Univ. Pr.
Shames, Germaine W. Between Two Deserts. 2002. 155p. 24.00 (*1-931561-13-3*) MacAdam/Cage Publishing, Inc.
Shaw, Patricia. The Feather & the Stone. 1993. 320p. 21.95 o.p. (*0-312-10462-6*) St. Martin's Pr.
Shields, Jean. Air Burial. 2004. 244p. pap. 13.00 (*0-7867-1274-0*); 2003. 256p. 25.00 (*0-7867-1100-0*) Avalon Publishing Group. (Carroll & Graf Pubs.).
Siler, Jenny. Flashback. 2004. 272p. 24.00 (*0-8050-7211-X*) Holt, Henry & Co.
Sinclair, April. Coffee Will Make You Black: A Novel. 1995. 256p. pap. 12.00 (*0-380-72459-6*, Perennial) HarperTrade.
—Coffee Will Make You Black: A Novel. 1994. 256p. 19.95 o.p. (*1-56282-796-0*) Hyperion Pr.
—Coffee Will Make You Black: A Novel. 1995. 18.05 (*0-606-12860-3*) Turtleback Bks.
Smith, Andrea. Friday Night at Honeybee's. 2004. 400p. pap. 12.00 (*0-385-33698-5*, Delta) Dell Publishing.
Stark, Elizabeth. Shy Girl. 2000. (Illus.). 224p. (J). pap. 12.95 (*1-58005-047-6*, Seal Pr.) Avalon Publishing Group.
Stern, Amanda. The Long Haul. 2003. 128p. pap. 12.00 (*1-932360-06-9*) Soft Skull Pr., Inc.
Stevenson, Talitha. An Empty Room. 2004. 181p. pap. 12.00 (*0-7867-1279-1*, Carroll & Graf Pubs.) Avalon Publishing Group.
Strom, Dao. Grass Roof, Tin Roof: A Novel. 2003. 240p. pap. 12.00 (*0-618-14559-1*) Houghton Mifflin Co.
Sykes, Plum. Bergdorf Blondes. 2004. 24.95 (*1-4013-5196-4*) Hyperion Pr.
Taylor, Valerie. The Girls in 3-B. 2003. (Femmes Fatales Ser.). 208p. pap. 13.95 (*1-55861-456-7*); lib. bdg. 14.95 (*1-55861-462-1*) Feminist Pr. at The City Univ. of New York.
Templeton, Edith. Gordon. 2003. 240p. 22.00 (*0-375-42194-7*, Pantheon) Knopf Publishing Group.
Thirkell, Angela. Summer Half. l.t. ed. 2001. 296p. pap. 21.99 o.p. (*0-7531-6413-2*) ISIS Large Print Bks. GBR. *Dist:* Ulverscroft Large Print Bks., Ltd., Ulverscroft Large Print Canada, Ltd.
—Summer Half. 2003. (Angela Thirkell Barsetshire Ser.). 288p. pap. 12.95 (*1-55921-311-6*) Moyer Bell.
—Summer Half. 16th l.t. ed. 2001. 296p. 32.50 (*0-7531-6412-4*) Thorpe, F. A. Pubs. GBR. *Dist:* Ulverscroft Large Print Bks., Ltd., Ulverscroft Large Print Canada, Ltd.
Thomas, Jacquelin. Singsation. 352p. 2003. pap. 13.95 (*0-446-67886-4*, Walk Worthy Pr.); 2001. 21.95 o.p. (*0-446-52798-X*); 2001. E-Book 14.95 (*0-7595-6241-5*); 2001. E-Book 14.95 (*0-7595-8247-5*); 2001. E-Book 14.95 (*0-7595-0241-2*); 2001. E-Book 14.95 (*0-7595-9273-X*); 2001. E-Book 14.95 (*0-7595-4244-9*) Warner Bks., Inc.
Thompson, Alice. Pharos: A Ghost Story. 2003. 160p. 21.95 (*0-312-31810-3*) St. Martin's Pr.
Thompson, Flora. Candleford Green. l.t. ed. 2000. 224p. 32.50 (*0-7531-5731-4*) ISIS Large Print Bks. GBR. *Dist:* Ulverscroft Large Print Bks., Ltd., Ulverscroft Large Print Canada, Ltd.
—Candleford Green. l.t. ed. 2001. 224p. pap. 21.99 (*0-7531-5782-9*) Thorpe, F. A. Pubs. GBR. *Dist:* Ulverscroft Large Print Bks., Ltd., Ulverscroft Large Print Canada, Ltd.
Thompson, Nancy Robards. Reinventing Olivia. 2003. 291p. 26.95 (*0-7862-5536-6*, Five Star) Gale Group.
Tower, S. D. The Assassins of Tamurin. 2003. 464p. 25.95 (*0-380-97803-2*) HarperCollins Pubs.
—The Assassins of Tamurin. 2004. 464p. mass mkt. 7.50 (*0-380-80621-5*, Eos) Morrow/Avon.
Trigiani, Adriana. Lucia, Lucia: A Novel. 2004. 288p. pap. 13.95 (*0-8129-6779-8*) Ballantine Bks.
—Lucia, Lucia: A Novel. 2003. 272p. 24.95 (*1-4000-6005-2*) Random Hse., Inc.
—Lucia, Lucia: A Novel. l.t. ed. 2003. 440p. 31.95 (*0-7862-5863-2*, Large Print Pr.) Thorndike Pr.
Trollope, Joanna. Girl from the South. 2003. 352p. pap. 14.00 (*0-425-19350-0*) Berkley Publishing Group.
—Girl from the South. 2002. 304p. 24.95 (*0-670-03097-X*, Viking) Viking Penguin.
Trujillo, Carla Mari. What Night Brings. 2003. 242p. pap. 15.95 (*1-880684-94-2*) Curbstone Pr.
Tuomey, Nesta. Like One of the Family. 1999. 456p. pap. (*1-902011-12-0*) Mount Eagle Pubns., Ltd.
Vega Yunqué, Edgardo. No Matter How Much You Promise to Cook or Pay the Rent You Blew It Cauze Bill Bailey Ain't Never Coming Home Again. 2003. 656p. 25.00 (*0-374-22311-4*); pap. (*0-374-96112-3*) Farrar, Straus & Giroux.
Vera, Yvonne. Butterfly Burning. 2000. 151p. pap. 12.00 (*0-374-29186-1*) Farrar, Straus & Giroux.
—Without a Name & under the Tongue. 2002. (Illus.). 224p. pap. 13.00 (*0-374-52816-0*) Farrar, Straus & Giroux.
Vernon, Claire. The Dutiful Doctor. l.t. ed. 2002. (Nightingale Ser.). 23.95 (*0-7862-4252-3*) Thorndike Pr.
Vida, Vendela. And Now You Can Go. 2003. 208p. 19.95 (*1-4000-4027-2*) Knopf, Alfred A. Inc.
Viteritti, Laurette. The Jewel of the Lotus Flower. 2001. pap. 16.95 (*0-595-18251-8*) iUniverse, Inc.
Walbert, Kate. The Gardens of Kyoto: A Novel. 288p. 2002. pap. 13.00 (*0-684-86949-7*); 2001. 24.00 (*0-684-86948-9*) Simon & Schuster. (Scribner).
—The Gardens of Kyoto: A Novel. l.t. ed. 2001. (Women's Fiction Ser.). 461p. 29.95 (*0-7862-3477-6*) Thorndike Pr.
Waller, Pamela. The Glass Rose. 2003. 200p. per. 12.95 (*1-892343-32-0*, Timeless Love) Oak Tree Publishing.
Wang, Annie R. Lili: A Novel. 2002. 320p. pap. 13.00 (*0-385-72050-5*, Knopf Bks. for Young Readers) Random Hse. Children's Bks.
—Lili: A Novel of Tiananmen. 2001. 320p. 24.00 (*0-375-42085-1*, Pantheon) Knopf Publishing Group.
Watt-Evans, Lawrence. Ithanalin's Restoration. 2002. (Ethshar Ser.). 272p. 24.95 (*0-7653-0012-5*, Tor Bks.) Doherty, Tom Assocs., LLC.
Weinstein, Debra. Apprentice to the Flower Poet Z: A Novel. 2004. (Illus.). 256p. 23.95 (*1-4000-6155-5*) Random Hse., Inc.
Weisberger, Lauren. The Devil Wears Prada: A Novel. 2004. 368p. pap. 13.95 (*0-7679-1476-7*) Broadway Bks.
—The Devil Wears Prada: A Novel. 2003. 368p. 21.95 (*0-385-50926-X*) Doubleday Publishing.
—The Devil Wears Prada: A Novel. l.t. ed. 2003. 712p. 29.95 (*0-7862-5575-7*) Thorndike Pr.
Wharton, Edith. Ethan Frome & Summer. (Twelve-Point Ser.). 1998. lib. bdg. 25.00 (*1-58287-027-6*); 1993. 449p. reprint ed. lib. bdg. 26.00 (*0-939495-27-9*) North Bks.
—Ethan Frome & Summer. 2001. (Modern Library Classics). 304p. pap. 7.95 (*0-375-75728-7*, Modern Library) Random House Adult Trade Publishing Group.
Whyte, Anthony J. Ghetto Girls. 2002. 251p. pap. 14.95 (*0-9722771-2-9*) Black Print Publishing.
Wilhelm, Kate. Skeletons. 2002. 304p. 24.95 (*0-312-30075-1*, Saint Martin's Minotaur) St. Martin's Pr.
Wimer, Genevieve R. Honour & Humility. 2002. (Illus.). 592p. 19.95 (*0-915010-46-1*) Hemlock Hill Bk. Distributors.
Wing, Chrystal. Ariadne's Egg. 2001. (Illus.). 100p. pap. 14.00 (*0-9657993-7-9*) mwynhad.
Winston, Lolly. Good Grief. 2004. 18.00 (*0-446-53304-1*) Warner Bks., Inc.
Witchel, Alex. Me Times Three: A Novel. 2003. 320p. reprint ed. pap. 13.00 (*0-7432-4085-5*, Touchstone) Simon & Schuster.
Woolf, Virginia. The Voyage Out. 2001. (Modern Library Classics). 448p. pap. 11.95 (*0-375-75727-9*, Modern Library) Random House Adult Trade Publishing Group.
Wright, Richard B. Clara Callan: A Novel. 2002. 432p. 25.95 (*0-06-050606-7*) HarperCollins Pubs.
Yurk, Amy. The Language of Sisters. 2002. (Illus.). 256p. (Orig.). pap. 12.95 (*0-451-20700-9*) NAL.
Zabytko, Irene. When Luba Leaves Home: A Profile in Stories. 2003. 240p. tchr. ed. 22.95 (*1-56512-332-8*, 72332) Algonquin Bks. of Chapel Hill.
Zappa, Moon Unit. America the Beautiful: A Novel. 2001. 304p. pap. 14.00 (*0-7432-1383-1*); E-Book 9.99 (*0-7432-1913-9*) Simon & Schuster. (Touchstone).

# OCCUPATIONS

## A

### ACTORS—FICTION

Andrews, V. C. Cinnamon. l.t. ed. 2002. (Core Collection). 186p. 29.95 (*0-7838-9750-2*) Gale Group.
Babson, Marian. Nine Lives to Murder. 1995. mass mkt. 4.99 (*0-312-95580-4*, St. Martin's Paperbacks); 1994. 192p. 18.95 o.p. (*0-312-10511-8*, Saint Martin's Minotaur) St. Martin's Pr.
Banville, John. Eclipse. l.t. ed. 2001. (Thorndike General Ser.). 298p. pap. 24.95 (*0-7862-2994-2*) Thorndike Pr.
—Eclipse: A Novel. 2002. 224p. pap. 12.00 (*0-375-72529-6*) Knopf, Alfred A. Inc.
Barnes, Linda. Bitter Finish. 1985. 208p. mass mkt. 4.95 o.s.i (*0-449-20690-4*, Fawcett) Ballantine Bks.
—Bitter Finish. l.t. ed. 2000. 263p. lib. bdg. 28.95 (*1-58547-031-7*) Ctr. Point Large Print.
—Bitter Finish. 1994. 272p. mass mkt. 5.99 o.s.i (*0-440-21606-0*) Dell Publishing.
—Bitter Finish. 1983. 192p. 11.95 o.p. (*0-312-08236-3*) St. Martin's Pr.
—Blood Will Have Blood. 1986. 192p. mass mkt. 5.99 o.s.i (*0-449-20901-6*, Fawcett) Ballantine Bks.
—Blood Will Have Blood. 1985. 192p. pap. 2.25 o.p. (*0-380-79368-7*, 79368, Avon Bks.) Morrow/Avon.
—Cities of the Dead. l.t. ed. 1991. 8.95 o.p. (*0-7451-9581-4*, 5059); pap. 10.95 o.p. (*0-7927-0009-0*, 4616) BBC Audiobooks America.
—Cities of the Dead. 1987. mass mkt. 4.99 o.s.i (*0-449-21188-6*, Fawcett) Ballantine Bks.
—Cities of the Dead. 1996. 272p. mass mkt. 5.99 o.s.i (*0-440-22095-5*) Dell Publishing.
—Cities of the Dead. 1985. 224p. 14.95 o.p. (*0-312-13940-3*) St. Martin's Pr.
—Dead Heat. 1985. 256p. mass mkt. 4.99 o.s.i (*0-449-20689-0*, Fawcett) Ballantine Bks.
—Dead Heat. 1995. 288p. mass mkt. 5.99 o.s.i (*0-440-21862-4*) Dell Publishing.
—Dead Heat. 1984. 224p. 11.95 o.p. (*0-312-18498-0*) St. Martin's Pr.
Berkoff, Steven. Graft: Tales of an Actor. (Oberon Book Ser.). 2000. 160p. pap. 12.95 (*1-84002-038-5*); 1999. 144p. 25.00 (*1-84002-040-7*) Theatre Communications Group, Inc.
Bloom, Matt. A Death in the Hamptons. 2003. 248p. pap. 14.95 (*1-57826-150-3*); 2002. 200p. 22.95 (*1-57826-115-5*) Hatherleigh Co., Ltd., The.
Bradbury, Ray. Let's All Kill Constance. 2003. pap. 13.95 (*0-06-051585-6*); 224p. 23.95 (*0-06-051584-8*) HarperCollins Pubs.
—Let's All Kill Constance. 2004. 256p. mass mkt. 7.50 (*0-06-056178-5*, Avon Bks.) Morrow/Avon.
—Let's All Kill Constance. l.t. ed. 2003. (Core Ser.). 28.95 (*0-7862-5523-4*) Thorndike Pr.
Brett, Simon. An Amateur Corpse. l.t. ed. 1990. pap. 5.00 (*0-7451-1285-4*) BBC Audiobooks America.
—An Amateur Corpse. 1980. mass mkt. 1.95 o.p. (*0-425-04489-0*) Berkley Publishing Group.
—An Amateur Corpse. unabr. ed. 1994. audio 39.95 (*0-7861-0483-X*, 1435) Blackstone Audio Bks., Inc.
—An Amateur Corpse. unabr. ed. 2000. (Charles Paris Mystery Ser.: Bk. 4). audio 49.95 (*0-7451-6617-2*, CAB 1233) Chivers Audio Bks. GBR. *Dist:* BBC Audiobooks America.
—An Amateur Corpse. 1986. mass mkt. 3.50 o.s.i (*0-440-10185-9*) Dell Publishing.
—An Amateur Corpse. l.t. ed. 1990. (Nightingale Ser.). 300p. pap. 13.95 (*0-8161-5040-0*, Macmillan Reference USA) Gale Group.
—An Amateur Corpse. unabr. ed. 2000. (Charles Paris Mystery Ser. : Vol. 4). audio 44.00 (*0-7887-1286-1*, 95146E7) Recorded Bks., LLC.
—An Amateur Corpse. 1991. mass mkt. 3.95 o.p. (*0-446-35960-2*) Warner Bks., Inc.
—An Amateur Corpse. 2000. 196p. pap. 12.95 (*0-595-00359-1*) iUniverse, Inc.
—Cast, in Order of Disappearance. unabr. ed. 1993. audio 39.95 (*0-7451-5803-X*, CSL 052) BBC Audiobooks America.

—Cast, in Order of Disappearance. 1981. mass mkt. 2.25 o.p. (*0-425-04934-5*) Berkley Publishing Group.
—Cast, in Order of Disappearance. l.t. ed. 1990. (Nightingale Ser.). 279p. pap. 13.95 o.p. (*0-8161-4917-8*, Macmillan Reference USA) Gale Group.
—Cast, in Order of Disappearance. unabr. ed. 1997. (Charles Paris Mystery Ser. : Vol. 1). audio 35.00 (*0-7887-0858-9*, 94984E7) Recorded Bks., LLC.
—A Comedian Dies. 1980. mass mkt. 2.25 o.p. (*0-425-04702-4*) Berkley Publishing Group.
—A Comedian Dies. unabr. ed. 1999. audio 39.95 Blackstone Audio Bks., Inc.
—A Comedian Dies. unabr. ed. 1998. (Charles Paris Mystery Ser. : Vol. 5). audio 44.00 (*0-7887-1886-X*, 95308E7) Recorded Bks., LLC.
—A Comedian Dies. 1990. mass mkt. 3.95 o.p. (*0-446-35958-0*) Warner Bks., Inc.
—A Comedian Dies. 2000. 164p. pap. 11.95 (*0-595-00358-3*) iUniverse, Inc.
—Corporate Bodies. l.t. ed. 1993. 22.95 o.p. (*0-7927-1418-0*); pap. 20.95 o.p. (*0-7927-1417-2*) BBC Audiobooks America.
—Corporate Bodies, unabr. ed. 1993. audio 39.95 (*0-7861-0394-9*, 752393) Blackstone Audio Bks., Inc.
—Corporate Bodies. abr. ed. 1992. 2p. audio 16.99 (*0-88646-323-8*, 7323); Set. 1996. audio 9.99 (*1-55204-012-7*, 393577) Durkin Hayes Publishing Ltd.
—Corporate Bodies. 1992. 256p. 19.00 (*0-684-19397-3*, Macmillan Reference USA) Gale Group.
—Corporate Bodies. 1993. (Mystery Ser.). mass mkt. (*0-373-26130-6*, 1-26130-4, Harlequin Bks.) Harlequin Enterprises, Ltd.
—Corporate Bodies. unabr. ed. 2000. (Charles Paris Mystery Ser. : Vol. 15). audio 44.00 (*1-55690-654-4*, 92406E7) Recorded Bks., LLC.
—Dead Giveaway. 1987. 256p. mass mkt. 3.50 o.s.i (*0-440-11914-6*) Dell Publishing.
—Dead Giveaway. (Charles Paris Mystery Ser.). 1986. 169p. 13.95 o.p. (*0-684-18517-2*); 1987. 237p. 10.95 o.p. (*0-8161-4218-1*) Gale Group. (Macmillan Reference USA).
—Dead Giveaway. 2000. 180p. pap. 12.95 (*0-595-00357-5*) iUniverse, Inc.
—Dead Room Farce. unabr. ed. 1998. audio 54.95 (*0-7540-0150-4*, CAB 1573) BBC Audiobooks America.
—Dead Room Farce. unabr. ed. 1999. audio 39.95 (*0-7861-1642-0*, 2470) Blackstone Audio Bks., Inc.
—Dead Room Farce. 1998. 208p. 20.95 (*0-312-19251-7*, Saint Martin's Minotaur) St. Martin's Pr.
—Dead Room Farce. l.t. ed. 1998. (Mystery Ser.). 344p. 27.95 (*0-7862-1564-X*) Thorndike Pr.
—The Dead Side of the Mike. unabr. ed. 1997. audio 54.95 (*0-7451-6738-1*, CAB 1354) BBC Audiobooks America.
—The Dead Side of the Mike. unabr. ed. 1992. audio 39.95 (*0-7861-0340-X*, 1297) Blackstone Audio Bks., Inc.
—The Dead Side of the Mike. 1986. pap. 3.50 o.p. (*0-440-11763-1*) Dell Publishing.
—The Dead Side of the Mike. unabr. ed. 1998. (Charles Paris Mystery Ser. : No. 6). audio 44.00 (*0-7887-2520-3*, 95593E7) Recorded Bks., LLC.
—The Dead Side of the Mike. 1991. mass mkt. 3.95 o.p. (*0-446-35957-2*) Warner Bks., Inc.
—The Dead Side of the Mike. 2000. 180p. per. 11.95 (*0-595-00354-0*) iUniverse, Inc.
—Murder in the Title. unabr. ed. 2000. (Charles Paris Mystery Ser.: Bk. 9). audio 49.95 (*0-7451-4072-6*, CAB 769) Chivers Audio Bks. GBR. *Dist:* BBC Audiobooks America.
—Murder in the Title. 1986. pap. 3.50 o.p. (*0-440-16016-2*) Dell Publishing.
—Murder in the Title. 1983. 192p. 11.95 o.s.i (*0-684-17898-2*, Macmillan Reference USA) Gale Group.
—Murder in the Title. 1990. mass mkt. 3.95 o.p. (*0-446-35954-8*) Warner Bks., Inc.
—Murder in the Title. 2000. (Charles Paris Mystery Ser.). 196p. pap. 12.95 (*0-595-00353-2*) iUniverse, Inc.
—Murder Unprompted. unabr. ed. 1992. (Audio Bks.). audio 39.95 (*0-7451-5804-8*, CAB 686) BBC Audiobooks America.
—Murder Unprompted. unabr. ed. 1997. audio 32.95 (*0-7861-1081-3*, 1851) Blackstone Audio Bks., Inc.
—Murder Unprompted. 1986. (Murder Ink Mystery Ser.: No. 69). pap. 3.50 o.p. (*0-440-16145-2*) Dell Publishing.
—Murder Unprompted. (Nightingale Ser.). 1983. 290p. pap. 9.95 o.p. (*0-8161-3540-1*); 1982. 160p. 10.95 o.s.i (*0-684-17659-9*) Gale Group. (Macmillan Reference USA).
—Murder Unprompted. unabr. ed. 2001. audio compact disk 49.00 (*0-7887-3982-4*, C1145E7, Clipper Audio) Recorded Bks., LLC.
—Murder Unprompted. 1990. mass mkt. 3.95 o.p. (*0-446-35955-6*) Warner Bks., Inc.
—Not Dead, Only Resting. l.t. ed. 1985. (Nightingale Ser.). 304p. 10.95 o.p. (*0-8161-3831-1*, Macmillan Reference USA) Gale Group.
—Not Dead, Only Resting. 1990. mass mkt. 3.95 o.p. (*0-446-35952-1*) Warner Bks., Inc.
—Not Dead, Only Resting. 2000. 180p. pap. 12.95 (*0-595-00356-7*) iUniverse, Inc.
—Not Dead, Only Resting: A Charles Paris Mystery. 1984. 176p. 11.95 o.s.i (*0-684-18193-2*, Macmillan Reference USA) Gale Group.
—A Reconstructed Corpse. l.t. ed. 1994. 234p. 24.95 (*1-56895-117-5*, Wheeler Publishing, Inc.) Gale Group.
—A Reconstructed Corpse. 1996. (WWL Mystery Ser.). per. (*0-373-26194-2*, 1-26194-0, Worldwide Library) Harlequin Enterprises, Ltd.
—A Reconstructed Corpse. l.t. ed. 1994. (Magna Large Print Ser.). 302p. o.p. (*0-7505-0717-9*) Magna Large Print Bks. GBR. *Dist:* Ulverscroft Large Print Canada, Ltd.
—A Reconstructed Corpse. 1994. 192p. 20.00 (*0-684-19700-6*, Scribner) Simon & Schuster.
—A Series of Murders, unabr. ed. 1993. audio 39.95 (*0-7451-5801-3*, CAB 427) BBC Audiobooks America.
—A Series of Murders. 1989. 224p. 16.95 o.s.i (*0-684-19096-6*, Scribner) Simon & Schuster.
—A Series of Murders. 1990. mass mkt. 3.95 o.s.i (*0-446-35949-1*) Warner Bks., Inc.
—Sicken & So Die. unabr. ed. 1996. (Charles Paris Mystery Ser.). audio 54.95 (*0-7451-6698-9*, CAB1314) BBC Audiobooks America.
—Sicken & So Die. unabr. ed. (Charles Paris Mystery Ser.). 2000. audio compact disk 40.00 (*0-7861-9896-6*, z1874); 1997. audio 32.95 (*0-7861-1108-9*, 1874) Blackstone Audio Bks., Inc.
—Sicken & So Die. 1997. per. (*0-373-26262-0*, 1-26262-5, Worldwide Library) Harlequin Enterprises, Ltd.
—Sicken & So Die. 1997. 208p. 20.50 (*0-684-82459-0*, Scribner) Simon & Schuster.
—Situation Tragedy. unabr. ed. 1996. audio 32.95 (*0-7861-0965-3*, 1742) Blackstone Audio Bks., Inc.
—Situation Tragedy. 1986. pap. 3.50 o.p. (*0-440-18792-3*) Dell Publishing.
—Situation Tragedy. unabr. ed. 1998. audio 69.95 o.p. (*1-872672-11-6*) Magna Story Sound GBR. *Dist:* Ulverscroft Large Print Bks., Ltd.
—Situation Tragedy. 1981. (Charles Paris Mystery Ser. : Vol. 7). audio 44.00 (*0-7887-3491-1*, 95898E7) Recorded Bks., LLC.
—Situation Tragedy. 1981. 192p. 9.95 o.s.i (*0-684-17268-2*, Scribner) Simon & Schuster.
—Situation Tragedy. 1990. mass mkt. 3.95 o.s.i (*0-446-35956-4*) Warner Bks., Inc.
—So Much Blood. 1981. mass mkt. 2.25 o.s.i (*0-425-04935-3*); 1979. mass mkt. 1.75 o.s.i (*0-425-04159-X*) Berkley Publishing Group.
—So Much Blood. 1986. mass mkt. 3.50 o.s.i (*0-440-18069-4*) Dell Publishing.
—So Much Blood. 2000. 196p. pap. 12.95 (*0-595-00360-5*) iUniverse, Inc.
—Star Trap. unabr. ed. 1995. audio 54.95 (*0-7451-6481-1*, CAB 1097) BBC Audiobooks America.
—Star Trap. unabr. ed. 2000. audio 32.95 (*0-7861-1750-8*, 2554); audio compact disk 40.00 (*0-7861-9901-6*, z2554) Blackstone Audio Bks., Inc.
—Star Trap. 1986. mass mkt. 3.50 o.s.i (*0-440-18300-6*) Dell Publishing.
—Star Trap. l.t. ed. 1989. 315p. 13.95 o.p. (*0-8161-4774-4*, Macmillan Reference USA) Gale Group.
—Star Trap. unabr. ed. 1997. (Charles Paris Mystery Ser. : Vol. 3). audio 44.00 (*0-7887-1146-6*, 95084E7) Recorded Bks., LLC.
—Star Trap. 1990. mass mkt. 3.95 o.p. (*0-446-35959-9*) Warner Bks., Inc.
—What Bloody Man Is That? 1989. mass mkt. 3.50 o.s.i (*0-440-20344-9*) Dell Publishing.
—What Bloody Man Is That? l.t. ed. 1988. (Nightingale Ser.). 297p. 12.95 o.p. (*0-8161-4398-6*, Macmillan Reference USA) Gale Group.
—What Bloody Man Is That? 1987. 196p. 14.95 o.p. (*0-684-18824-4*, Scribner) Simon & Schuster.
—What Bloody Man Is That? 2000. 188p. pap. 12.95 (*0-595-00349-4*) iUniverse, Inc.
Busch, Charles. Whores of Lost Atlantis: A Novel. 1993. 304p. 21.95 o.p. (*1-56282-780-4*) Hyperion Pr.
Chase, Elaine Raco. Video Vixen. l.t. ed. 2000. (Romance Ser.). 203p. 25.95 (*0-7862-2490-8*) Thorndike Pr.
Chavez, Denise. Loving Pedro Infante. 2001. 325p. 24.00 (*0-374-19411-4*) Farrar, Straus & Giroux.
—Loving Pedro Infante. 2002. 336p. pap. 13.00 (*0-7434-4573-2*, Washington Square Pr.) Simon & Schuster.
Colette, Sidonie-Gabrielle. The Vagabond. McLeod, Enid, tr. from FRE. 2nd ed. 2001. 224p. pap. 12.00 (*0-374-52804-7*) Farrar, Straus & Giroux.
Corbin, Steven. Fragments That Remain. 1995. 318p. pap. 9.95 o.p. (*1-55583-274-1*); 1993. 280p. 19.95 o.p. (*1-55583-218-0*) Alyson Pubns.
Crace, Jim. Genesis. 2003. E-Book (*0-374-70476-7*); E-Book 15.00 (*0-374-70475-9*); E-Book (*0-374-70473-2*); E-Book 15.00 (*0-374-70474-0*); 256p. 23.00 (*0-374-22730-6*); E-Book (*0-374-93031-7*) Farrar, Straus & Giroux.
Craft, Michael. Rehearsing. 1993. 120p. (Orig.). pap. 9.95 (*1-879603-09-8*) Los Hombres Pr.
Craig, Michael D. The Ice Sculptures: A Novel of Hollywood. 2004. pap. (*1-56023-481-4*, Southern Tier Editions) Haworth Pr., Inc., The.
Dandola, John. Dead at the Box Office. 2nd rev. ed. 1993. Orig. Title: West of Orange. (Illus.). 240p. reprint ed. pap. 10.95 o.p. (*1-878452-15-0*, Jersey Yarns) Quincannon Publishing Group.
—Dead at the Box Office: An Edie Koslow - Tony Del Plato Mystery. 2001. (Illus.). 182p. pap. 12.95 (*1-878452-25-8*, Compass Point Mysteries) Quincannon Publishing Group.
Delman, David. The Bluestocking. 1994. 320p. 22.95 o.p. (*0-312-10432-4*) St. Martin's Pr.
Ewing, Barbara. The Actresses. 1997. 376p. o.s.i (*0-316-64074-3*); 384p. pap. o.s.i (*0-316-64280-0*) Little Brown & Co.
—The Actresses. 1998. 566p. mass mkt. 9.95 o.s.i (*0-7515-2137-X*) Warner Futura GBR. *Dist:* Trafalgar Square.
Fawcett, Quinn. The Scottish Ploy. 2001. 352p. reprint ed. pap. 15.95 (*0-312-87628-9*, Forge Bks.) Doherty, Tom Assocs., LLC.
—The Scottish Ploy: The A. Mycroft Holmes Novel Authorized by Dame Jean Conan Doyle. 2000. (Mycroft Holmes Novels Ser.). 352p. 24.95 (*0-312-87282-8*, Forge Bks.) Doherty, Tom Assocs., LLC.
Fenn, Lionel. Kent Montana & the Once & Future Thing. 1991. mass mkt. 3.95 o.s.i (*0-441-43537-8*) Ace Bks.
—Kent Montana & the Really Ugly Thing from Mars. 1990. mass mkt. 3.95 o.s.i (*0-441-43535-1*) Ace Bks.
—Kent Montana & the Reasonably Invisible Man. 1991. mass mkt. 3.95 o.s.i (*0-441-43536-X*) Ace Bks.
Findley, Timothy. Spadework: A Novel. 416p. 2003. pap. 13.95 (*0-06-093262-7*); 2002. 24.95 (*0-06-019472-3*) HarperCollins Pubs.
Forbes, Deloris. The Perils of Marie Louise. 2003. 232p. 25.95 (*1-59414-083-9*, Five Star) Gale Group.
Francis, Dick. Smokescreen. l.t. ed. 1993. 19.95 o.p. (*0-7927-1664-7*); 1993. pap. 17.95 o.p. (*0-7927-1663-9*); 1995. audio 54.95 (*0-7451-6832-9*, CAB 486) BBC Audiobooks America.
—Smokescreen. 1993. 272p. mass mkt. 6.99 (*0-449-22111-3*, Fawcett) Ballantine Bks.
—Smokescreen. unabr. ed. 1999. audio 32.95 (*0-7861-1514-9*, 2364) Blackstone Audio Bks., Inc.
—Smokescreen. unabr. ed. 1994. audio 42.00 (*0-7366-2838-X*, 3546) Books on Tape, Inc.
—Smokescreen. unabr. ed. 2000. audio 49.95 Chivers Audio Bks. GBR. *Dist:* BBC Audiobooks America.
—Smokescreen. 1973. (Harper Novel of Suspense Ser.). 224p. 8.95 o.p. (*0-06-011334-0*) HarperCollins Pubs.
—Smokescreen. 1990. audio 15.95; audio 15.95 o.p. (*1-55994-130-8*, CPN 2130) HarperTrade. (Harper-Audio).
—Smokescreen, unabr. ed. 1999. audio 32.95 Highsmith Inc.
—Smokescreen. abr. ed. 2000. audio 7.95 (*1-57815-049-3*, 1046, Media Bks. Audio Publishing) Media Bks., L. L. C.
—Smokescreen. unabr. ed. 2000. audio 44.00 (*0-7887-0231-9*, 94456E7) Recorded Bks., LLC.
—Smokescreen. 1990. mass mkt. 4.95 (*0-671-70470-2*); 1984. 224p. mass mkt. 3.50 (*0-671-50737-0*); 1982. mass mkt. 2.95 o.s.i (*0-671-45911-2*) Simon & Schuster. (Pocket).
—Smokescreen. l.t. ed. 1978. 12.00 o.p. (*0-7089-0126-3*, Ulverscroft) Thorpe, F. A. Pubs. GBR. *Dist:* Ulverscroft Large Print Bks., Ltd.
Graham, Heather. Long, Lean & Lethal. l.t. ed. 2000. (Large Print Book Ser.). 410p. 28.95 (*1-56895-928-1*, Wheeler Publishing, Inc.) Gale Group.
—Long, Lean & Lethal. 2000. 400p. mass mkt. 6.99 o.s.i (*0-451-40915-9*, Onyx) NAL.
Hagedorn, Jessica. Dream Jungle. 2003. 320p. 23.95 (*0-670-88458-8*, Viking) Viking Penguin.
Hall, Parnell. Actor. 1993. 288p. 19.95 (*0-89296-520-7*) Mysterious Pr.
—Actor. 1994. 304p. mass mkt. 5.50 (*0-446-40364-4*, Mysterious Pr. Paperback Bks.) Warner Bks., Inc.
—Blackmail. 1994. 288p. 19.95 o.p. (*0-89296-521-5*) Mysterious Pr.
—Blackmail. 1995. 304p. mass mkt. 5.99 o.s.i (*0-446-40365-2*) Warner Bks., Inc.
—Client. 1990. 18.95 o.p. (*1-55611-169-X*) Fine, Donald I. Bks.
—Client. 1991. 272p. mass mkt. 4.50 o.p. (*0-451-40249-9*, Onyx) NAL.
—Detective. 1987. 300p. 17.95 o.p. (*1-55611-026-X*) Fine, Donald I. Bks.
—Detective. 1988. 256p. mass mkt. 3.95 o.p. (*0-451-40070-4*, Onyx) NAL.
—Favor. 1988. 17.95 o.p. (*1-55611-096-0*) Fine, Donald I. Bks.
—Favor. 1989. mass mkt. 3.95 o.p. (*0-451-40161-1*, 035, Onyx) NAL.
—Favor. 2002. 186p. pap. 6.99 (*0-7592-1854-4*); E-Book 6.99 (*0-7592-1850-1*); E-Book 6.99 (*0-7592-1851-X*); E-Book 6.99 (*0-7592-1849-8*) ereads.com.
—Juror. 1990. 18.95 o.p. (*1-55611-230-0*) Fine, Donald I. Bks.
—Juror. 1992. 304p. mass mkt. 4.99 o.p. (*0-451-40316-9*, Onyx) NAL.
—Movie. 1995. 82p. 19.95 o.p. (*0-89296-569-X*) Mysterious Pr.
—Movie. 1996. 288p. mass mkt. 5.99 (*0-446-40395-4*) Warner Bks., Inc.
—Murder. 1988. 256p. 17.95 o.s.i (*1-55611-058-8*) Fine, Donald I. Bks.
—Murder. 2002. 256p. reprint ed. pap. 13.95 (*1-58754-111-4*, Olmstead Pr.) Moyer Bell.
—Murder. 1989. mass mkt. 3.95 o.p. (*0-451-40110-7*, Onyx) NAL.
—Murder. E-Book 6.99 (*0-7592-1545-6*) ereads.com.
—Scam. 1998. 336p. pap. 6.50 (*0-446-40469-1*, Mysterious Pr. Paperback Bks.) Warner Bks., Inc.
—Scam: A Stanley Hastings Mystery. l.t. ed. 1997. (Americana Ser.). 463p. 26.95 (*0-7862-1210-1*) Thorndike Pr.
—Scam: A Stanley Hastings Mystery. 1997. 320p. 21.50 o.p. (*0-89296-623-8*) Warner Bks., Inc.
—Shot. 1993. 320p. mass mkt. 4.99 o.p. (*0-451-40354-1*, Onyx) NAL.
—Shot: A Stanley Hastings Novel of Suspense. 1991. 18.95 o.p. (*1-55611-239-4*) Fine, Donald I. Bks.
—Strangler. 1989. 304p. 16.95 o.p. (*1-55611-125-8*) Fine, Donald I. Bks.
—Strangler. 1990. mass mkt. 4.50 o.p. (*0-451-40217-0*, Onyx) NAL.
—Suspense: A Stanley Hastings Mystery Novel. 1998. 320p. 23.00 o.p. (*0-89296-624-6*) Mysterious Pr.
—Trial. 1996. 82p. 21.95 o.s.i (*0-89296-570-3*) Mysterious Pr.
—Trial. 1997. 288p. mass mkt. 5.99 (*0-446-40396-2*) Warner Bks., Inc.
Hawke, Simon. Much Ado about Murder. E-Book 23.95 (*0-312-70933-1*, Tor Bks.); 2004. 240p. pap. 13.95 (*0-7653-0836-3*, Forge Bks.); 2002. 304p. 23.95 (*0-7653-0241-1*, Forge Bks.) Doherty, Tom Assocs., LLC.
—The Slaying of the Shrew. 2001. 255p. 23.95 (*0-312-87894-X*, Forge Bks.) Doherty, Tom Assocs., LLC.
Howard, Maureen. Natural History. 1999. (Illus.). 393p. pap. 12.95 (*0-7867-0632-5*, Carroll & Graf Pubs.) Avalon Publishing Group.
—Natural History. 1993. (Illus.). 416p. reprint ed. 12.00 o.p. (*0-06-097569-5*, Perennial) HarperTrade.
—Natural History. 1992. (Illus.). 512p. 22.95 o.p. (*0-393-03405-4*) Norton, W. W. & Co., Inc.
Huggins, David. Me Me Me. 2001. 256p. pap. (*0-571-20936-X*) Faber & Faber, Inc.
Indiana, Gary. Gone Tomorrow. 1995. 175p. reprint ed. pap. (*1-85242-336-6*) Serpent's Tail Ltd.
Iyer, Pico. Abandon: A Romance. 2003. 368p. 24.00 (*0-375-41505-X*) Knopf, Alfred A. Inc.
Kaplow, Robert. Me & Orson Welles: A Novel. 2003. 278p. 18.50 (*1-931561-49-4*) MacAdam/Cage Publishing, Inc.
Kazan, Elia. The Understudy. unabr. collector's ed. 1986. audio 72.00 (*0-7366-0978-4*, 1919) Books on Tape, Inc.
—The Understudy. 1975. 8.95 o.p. (*0-8128-1731-1*); pap. 3.95 o.p. (*0-8128-8193-1*) Madison Bks., Inc. (Scarborough Hse.).
—The Understudy. 1976. pap. 2.50 o.s.i (*0-446-81646-9*) Warner Bks., Inc.
Korda, Michael. Curtain: A Novel. abr. ed. 1991. audio 15.95 (*0-671-73380-X*, Simon & Schuster Audioworks) Simon & Schuster Audio.
—Curtain: A Novel. 1991. 448p. 19.95 o.p. (*0-671-68684-4*) Summit Bks.
—Curtain: A Novel. 1992. mass mkt. 5.99 o.s.i (*0-446-36227-1*) Warner Bks., Inc.
Kranz, Rachel. Leaps of Faith. 2000. 565p. 25.00 o.p. (*0-374-18444-5*) Farrar, Straus & Giroux.
L'Engle, Madeleine. Certain Women. 1992. 351p. 21.00 o.p. (*0-374-12025-0*) Farrar, Straus & Giroux.
—Certain Women. 1993. 368p. pap. 15.00 (*0-06-065207-1*) HarperSanFrancisco.
Litt, Toby. Corpsing. 2002. 373p. pap. 14.95 (*0-7145-3068-9*) Boyars, Marion Pubs., Inc.
Lovell, Glenville. Too Beautiful to Die. 2004. 320p. mass mkt. 6.99 (*0-425-19702-6*) Berkley Publishing Group.
—Too Beautiful to Die. 2003. 304p. 23.95 (*0-399-15048-X*) Putnam Publishing Group, The.
Mahon, Brid. A Time to Love. 1992. 484p. pap. 13.95 (*1-85371-221-3*) Poolbeg Pr. IRL. *Dist:* Dufour Editions, Inc.

Occupations

Malone, Michael. The Delectable Mountains: Or, Entertaining Strangers. 1977. 8.95 o.p. (0-394-49729-5) Random Hse., Inc.

—The Delectable Mountains: Or, Entertaining Strangers. 2002. (Illus.). 352p. pap. 15.00 (1-4022-0006-4) Sourcebooks, Inc.

Marston, Edward. The Fair Maid of Bohemia: A Novel. 2002. 271p. pap. 14.95 o.s.i (1-59058-005-2) Poisoned Pen Pr.

—The Fair Maid of Bohemia: A Novel. 1997. 229p. 21.95 o.p. (0-312-15606-5, Saint Martin's Minotaur) St. Martin's Pr.

—The Laughing Hangman. 2002. (Missing Mystery Ser.: Vol. 50). 200p. pap. 14.95 o.s.i (1-59058-023-0) Poisoned Pen Pr.

—The Laughing Hangman. 1996. 320p. 21.95 o.p. (0-312-14305-2, Saint Martin's Minotaur) St. Martin's Pr.

—The Mad Courtesan. 1994. reprint ed. mass mkt. 4.99 o.s.i (0-449-22246-2, Fawcett) Ballantine Bks.

—The Mad Courtesan. 1992. 240p. 18.95 o.p. (0-312-08259-2, Saint Martin's Minotaur) St. Martin's Pr.

—The Merry Devils. 1991. (Elizabethan Mystery Ser.). 240p. mass mkt. 3.95 o.s.i (0-449-21880-5, Fawcett) Ballantine Bks.

—The Merry Devils. 1989. 240p. 16.95 o.p. (0-312-03863-1, Saint Martin's Minotaur) St. Martin's Pr.

—The Nine Giants. 1993. mass mkt. 4.50 o.s.i (0-449-22128-8, Fawcett) Ballantine Bks.

—The Nine Giants. 1991. 224p. 17.95 o.p. (0-312-06426-8, Saint Martin's Minotaur) St. Martin's Pr.

—The Queen's Head. 1990. 224p. mass mkt. 3.95 o.s.i (0-449-21791-4, Fawcett) Ballantine Bks.

—The Queen's Head. 1989. mass mkt. o.s.i (0-552-13292-6, Corgi) Bantam Bks.

—The Queen's Head. 2000. (Missing Mysteries Ser.: No. 19). 300p. pap. 14.95 (1-890208-45-0) Poisoned Pen Pr.

—The Queen's Head. 1989. 16.95 o.p. (0-312-02970-5, Saint Martin's Minotaur) St. Martin's Pr.

—The Roaring Boy. 1996. 296p. mass mkt. 5.99 o.s.i (0-449-22431-7, Fawcett) Ballantine Bks.

—The Roaring Boy. 2002. 250p. pap. 14.95 o.s.i (1-59058-001-X) Poisoned Pen Pr.

—The Roaring Boy. 1995. 272p. 14.99 o.p. (0-312-13155-0, Saint Martin's Minotaur) St. Martin's Pr.

—The Silent Woman. 1995. mass mkt. 5.99 o.s.i (0-449-22375-2, Fawcett) Ballantine Bks.

—The Silent Woman. 2002. 240p. pap. 14.95 o.s.i (1-59058-000-1) Poisoned Pen Pr.

—The Silent Woman. 1994. 320p. 21.95 o.p. (0-312-11115-0, Saint Martin's Minotaur) St. Martin's Pr.

—The Trip to Jerusalem: An Elizabethan Whodunit. 1991. 240p. mass mkt. 3.99 o.s.i (0-449-21987-9, Fawcett) Ballantine Bks.

—The Trip to Jerusalem: An Elizabethan Whodunit. 1990. 224p. 15.95 o.p. (0-312-05174-3, Saint Martin's Minotaur) St. Martin's Pr.

—The Vagabond Clown: An Elizabethan Theater Mystery Featuring Nicholas Bracewell. Date not set. pap. (0-312-30790-X, Saint Martin's Griffin); mass mkt. (0-312-98612-2, St. Martin's Paperbacks); E-Book (0-312-70591-3); 2003. 352p. 24.95 (0-312-30789-6, Saint Martin's Minotaur) St. Martin's Pr.

—The Wanton Angel. 2nd ed. 1999. 288p. 23.95 (0-312-20391-8, Saint Martin's Minotaur) St. Martin's Pr.

McAlpine, Gordon. The Persistence of Memory. 1998. 176p. 29.95 (0-7206-1047-8) Owen, Peter Ltd. GBR. Dist: Dufour Editions, Inc.

McCarver, Sam. To Die, or Not to Die- A John Darnell Mystery. l.t. ed. 2003. (Five Star First Edition Mystery Ser.). 215p. 25.95 (0-7862-5444-0, Five Star) Gale Group.

Miller, Andrew. Oxygen. 2003. 352p. pap. 14.00 (0-15-602740-2, Harvest Bks.); 2002. 336p. 24.00 (0-15-100721-7) Harcourt Trade Pubs.

Murdoch, Iris. The Sea, the Sea. 2001. pap. (0-14-771593-8); 2001. 528p. pap. 15.00 (0-14-118616-X, Penguin Classics); 1980. 512p. pap. 14.95 o.s.i (0-14-005199-6, Penguin Bks.); 1978. 12.95 o.p. (0-670-62651-1) Viking Penguin.

Nathan, Melissa. Pride, Prejudice & Jasmin Field. 2001. 280p. pap. 6.50 (0-06-107233-8) HarperCollins Pubs.

—Pride, Prejudice, & Jasmine Field: A Novel. 2001. 288p. pap. 14.00 (0-06-018495-7, Avon Bks.) Morrow/Avon.

O'Conner, Varley. A Company of Three. 2003. 320p. 24.95 (1-56512-373-5) Algonquin Bks. of Chapel Hill.

Phillips, Pat. Invitation to Danger. l.t. ed. 2000. (Candlelight Romance Ser.). 195p. 19.95 (0-7862-2592-0); (0-7540-4195-6); (0-7540-4196-4) Thorndike Pr.

Putney, Mary Jo. The Spiral Path. 2002. 368p. mass mkt. 7.50 o.s.i (0-425-18301-7) Berkley Publishing Group.

—The Spiral Path. l.t. ed. 2002. lib. bdg. 29.95 (1-58547-219-0, Platinum) Ctr. Point Large Print.

Rann, Sheila. Anything for Love. 1995. 288p. 21.95 o.p. (0-446-51830-1) Warner Bks., Inc.

Roberts, Les. A Carrot for the Donkey: A Saxon Mystery. 1989. 256p. 16.95 o.p. (0-312-02554-8, Saint Martin's Minotaur) St. Martin's Pr.

—An Infinite Number of Monkeys. 1988. mass mkt. 2.95 (0-312-91095-9, St. Martin's Paperbacks); 1987. 176p. 12.95 o.p. (0-312-00610-1) St. Martin's Pr.

—The Lemon Chicken Jones. 1993. 288p. 20.95 o.p. (0-312-10490-1, Saint Martin's Minotaur) St. Martin's Pr.

—Not Enough Horses. 1988. 224p. mass mkt. 3.50 o.p. (0-312-91225-0, St. Martin's Paperbacks); 256p. 15.95 o.p. (0-312-01485-6, Saint Martin's Minotaur) St. Martin's Pr.

—Seeing the Elephant. 1992. 352p. 18.95 o.p. (0-312-07081-0, Saint Martin's Minotaur) St. Martin's Pr.

—Snake Oil. 1990. 17.95 o.p. (0-312-04424-0, Saint Martin's Minotaur) St. Martin's Pr.

Robertson, James. The Fanatic. 2003. 310p. pap. 12.00 (1-84115-189-0) Fourth Estate, Ltd. GBR. Dist: Trafalgar Square.

Sahgal, Ajay. Pool: A Novel. 224p. 1995. pap. 10.00 (0-8021-3343-6, Grove Pr.); 1994. 20.00 o.p. (0-87113-559-0, Atlantic Monthly Pr.) Grove/Atlantic, Inc.

Shaw, Simon. The Company of Knaves. 1997. (Philip Fletcher Mystery Ser.). 224p. 22.95 (0-312-18069-1, Saint Martin's Minotaur) St. Martin's Pr.

—Dead for a Ducat. 1996. 224p. 20.95 o.p. (0-312-14309-5, Saint Martin's Minotaur) St. Martin's Pr.

—Murder Out of Tune. unabr. ed. 1993. audio 54.95 (0-7451-4094-7, CAB 782) BBC Audiobooks America.

—Murder Out of Tune. 1992. 256p. mass mkt. 4.50 o.s.i (0-553-29592-6) Bantam Bks.

—Murder Out of Tune. 1988. 192p. o.s.i (0-385-24602-1) Doubleday Publishing.

—The Villain of the Earth. 1995. 189p. 19.95 o.p. (0-312-13201-8, Saint Martin's Minotaur) St. Martin's Pr.

Sherrill, Martha. My Last Movie Star: A Novel of Hollywood. 2004. 384p. pap. 13.95 (0-375-75949-2, Random Hse. Trade Paperbacks) Random House Adult Trade Publishing Group.

—My Last Movie Star: A Novel of Hollywood. 2003. 368p. 23.95 (0-375-50769-8) Random Hse., Inc.

Smith, Charlie. Chimney Rock: A Novel. 1997. 352p. pap. 14.00 o.p. (0-8050-5592-4, Owl Bks.); 1993. 400p. 22.50 o.p. (0-8050-2244-9) Holt, Henry & Co.

Steel, Danielle. The Cottage. 2003. 400p. mass mkt. 7.99 (0-440-23681-9, Dell Bks.); 2002. 312p. 200.00 (0-385-33622-5, Delacorte Pr.); 2002. 312p. 26.95 (0-385-33552-0, Delacorte Pr.) Dell Publishing.

—The Cottage. abr. ed. 2002. audio 26.95 (0-553-52893-9); audio compact disk 31.95 (0-553-71465-1); audio 39.95 (0-553-52899-8) Random Hse. Audio Publishing Group. (RH Audio).

—The Cottage. l.t. ed. 496p. 2003. pap. 15.95 (0-375-43198-5); 2002. 26.95 (0-375-43150-0) Random Hse. Large Print.

Thorne, Matt. Child Star. 2003. 320p. pap. (0-297-82908-4) Weidenfeld & Nicolson, Ltd.

Varley, John & McKillip, Patricia. The Golden Globe. 1998. 432p. 22.95 o.s.i (0-441-00558-6); 1999. 528p. reprint ed. mass mkt. 7.99 (0-441-00643-4) Ace Bks.

Wilcox, Collin. Bernhardt's Edge. 1991. pap. 3.95 o.p. (0-8125-1148-4); 1988. 320p. 17.95 o.p. (0-312-93076-3) Doherty, Tom Assocs., LLC. (Tor Bks.).

—Except for the Bones. 1991. 288p. 18.95 o.p. (0-312-93162-X, Tor Bks.) Doherty, Tom Assocs., LLC.

—Find Her a Grave. 1993. 288p. 19.95 o.p. (0-312-85244-4, Forge Bks.) Doherty, Tom Assocs., LLC.

—Silent Witness. 1992. mass mkt. 3.99 (0-8125-1149-2); 1990. 17.95 o.p. (0-312-93161-1) Doherty, Tom Assocs., LLC. (Tor Bks.).

Willis, Sarah. The Rehearsal. 2003. 304p. reprint ed. pap. 14.00 (0-425-18830-2) Berkley Publishing Group.

—The Rehearsal. 2001. 272p. 24.00 o.p. (0-374-24861-3) Farrar, Straus & Giroux.

## ACTRESSES—FICTION

Adamson, Lydia. A Cat on a Beach Blanket: An Alice Nestleton Mystery. l.t. ed. 2001. 231p. (0-7540-4552-8) Thorndike Pr.

—A Cat under the Mistletoe. 1997. (Alice Nestleton Mysteries Ser.). 256p. mass mkt. 5.99 o.s.i (0-451-19105-6, Signet Bks.) NAL.

—A Cat under the Mistletoe: A Christmas Cat Mystery. 1996. (Alice Nestleton Mystery Ser.). 224p. 18.95 o.p. (0-525-94226-2, Dutton) Dutton/Plume.

—A Cat under the Mistletoe: An Alice Nestleton Mystery. l.t. ed. 2000. (Mystery Ser.). 248p. 28.95 (0-7862-2651-X) Thorndike Pr.

—A Cat with the Blues. 2000. (Alice Nestleton Mysteries Ser.: Vol. 10). 208p. mass mkt. 5.99 (0-451-20196-5) NAL.

—A Cat with the Blues: An Alice Nestleton Mystery. l.t. ed. 2001. (Thorndike Mystery Ser.). 200p. 29.95 (0-7862-3076-2); (0-7540-4465-3) Thorndike Pr.

Arnold, Emily. Life Drawing. 1986. 288p. 15.95 o.s.i (0-385-29437-9, Delacorte Pr.); 1988. reprint ed. mass mkt. 4.95 o.s.i (0-440-20025-3, Laurel) Dell Publishing.

Babson, Marian. Break a Leg, Darlings. l.t. ed. 1997. (G. K. Hall Nightingale Ser.). 300p. lib. bdg. 18.95 o.p. (0-7838-8036-7, Macmillan Reference USA) Gale Group.

—Break a Leg, Darlings. 1997. 183p. 20.95 o.p. (0-312-15285-X, Saint Martin's Minotaur) St. Martin's Pr.

—Encore Murder. l.t. ed. 1991. (Nightingale Ser.). 275p. pap. 14.95 o.p. (0-8161-5139-3, Macmillan Reference USA) Gale Group.

—Encore Murder. 1990. 15.95 o.p. (0-312-04964-1, Saint Martin's Minotaur) St. Martin's Pr.

—Reel Murder, unabr. ed. 1993. audio 39.95 (0-7451-5753-X, CAT 4025) BBC Audiobooks America.

—Reel Murder. 1988. mass mkt. 3.50 o.s.i (0-553-27361-2) Bantam Bks.

—Reel Murder. l.t. ed. 1988. (Nightingale Ser.). 307p. 12.95 o.p. (0-8161-4492-3, Macmillan Reference USA) Gale Group.

—Reel Murder. 1987. 192p. 12.95 o.p. (0-312-00227-0) St. Martin's Pr.

—Reel Murder. 1988. audio 35.95 o.p. (0-8161-7780-5) Thorndike Pr.

—Shadows in Their Blood. l.t. ed. 1994. 322p. lib. bdg. 16.95 (0-8161-5952-1, Macmillan Reference USA) Gale Group.

—Shadows in Their Blood. 1993. 192p. 16.95 o.p. (0-312-09383-7, Saint Martin's Minotaur) St. Martin's Pr.

Bainbridge, Beryl. An Awfully Big Adventure. 224p. 1995. pap. 8.95 (0-7867-0184-6); 1993. pap. 9.95 o.p. (0-88184-961-8) Avalon Publishing Group. (Carroll & Graf Pubs.).

—An Awfully Big Adventure. 1989. 193 p. (0-7156-2204-8) Duckworth, Gerald & Co., Ltd. GBR. Dist: International Publishers Marketing.

—An Awfully Big Adventure. 1991. 240p. 19.95 o.p. (0-06-016544-8) HarperTrade.

—An Awfully Big Adventure. l.t. unabr. ed. 1999. 196p. pap. 19.95 (0-7531-5120-0, 151200) ISIS Large Print Bks. GBR. Dist: ISIS Publishing.

—An Awfully Big Adventure. l.t. ed. 1997. 24.95 (1-85695-264-9) Isis-Oasis GBR. Dist: Eye in the Ear Inc.

Baldwin, Faith. The Moon's Our Home. 1976. reprint ed. lib. bdg. 24.95 (0-88411-602-6) Amereon, Ltd.

—The Moon's Our Home. l.t. ed. 2001. (Thorndike Candlelight Romance Ser.). 331p. 23.95 (0-7862-3280-3); (0-7540-4520-X); (0-7540-4519-6) Thorndike Pr.

Barton, Wayne. Lockhart's Nightmare. 2000. 350p. mass mkt. 6.99 (0-8125-7196-7, Forge Bks.) Doherty, Tom Assocs., LLC.

Barton, Wayne & Williams, Stan. Lockharts Nightmare. 1998. 384p. 24.95 o.p. (0-312-86142-7, Forge Bks.) Doherty, Tom Assocs., LLC.

Brand, Rebecca. The Ruby Tear. 1998. 247p. mass mkt. 5.99 (0-8125-7132-0, Tor Bks.); 1997. 253p. 22.95 o.p. (0-312-86165-6, Forge Bks.) Doherty, Tom Assocs., LLC.

Brennan, Carol. In the Dark. l.t. ed. 1995. 288p. lib. bdg. 23.95 (1-57490-029-3, Beeler Large Print Bks.) Beeler, Thomas T. Publisher.

—In the Dark. 1995. 256p. mass mkt. 4.99 o.p. (0-425-14579-4, Prime Crime) Berkley Publishing Group.

—In the Dark. 1994. 288p. 21.95 o.p. (0-399-13940-0, G. P. Putnam's Sons) Penguin Group (USA) Inc.

Cartland, Barbara. Lights, Laughter, & a Lady. l.t. ed. 2001. (Candlelight Ser.). 238p. 24.95 o.p. (0-7862-3624-8) Thorndike Pr.

Chaikin, Linda. Desert Star. 2004. pap. 10.99 (0-7369-1235-5) Harvest Hse. Pubs.

Colette, Sidonie-Gabrielle. The Vagabond. 1982. 224p. mass mkt. 4.99 o.s.i (0-345-30061-0) Ballantine Bks.

—The Vagabond. McLeod, Enid, tr. from FRE. 1974. 223p. 8.95 o.p. (0-374-28233-1); pap. 12.00 o.p. (0-374-51175-6) Farrar, Straus & Giroux.

—The Vagabond. 1995. 7.99 o.s.i (0-517-12259-6) Random Hse. Value Publishing.

—The Vagabond. McLeod, Enid, tr. 1995. (Penguin Twentieth-Century Classics Ser.). 192p. pap. 10.95 o.p. (0-14-018325-6, Penguin Classics) Viking Penguin.

—La Vagabonde. 1993. 256p. mass mkt. 3.50 o.s.i (0-553-21423-3, Bantam Classics) Bantam Bks.

—La Vagabonde. 1958. (FRE.). 256p. pap. (0-7859-4722-1); pap. 11.95 o.p. (0-8288-9164-8, F97341) French & European Pubns., Inc.

Collins, Joan. Star Quality. 2003. 368p. mass mkt. 6.99 (0-7868-9048-7) Hyperion Pr.

—Star Quality: A Novel. 2003. mass mkt. 7.99 (0-7868-9060-6); 2002. 368p. 23.95 (1-4013-0000-6); 2002. mass mkt. 7.99 (0-7868-9064-9) Hyperion Pr.

—Star Quality: A Novel. 2003. (Core Ser.). 32.95 (0-7862-4694-4) Thorndike Pr.

Cookson, Catherine. Riley. l.t. ed. 2001. 480p. lib. bdg. 29.95 (1-58547-071-6) Ctr. Point Large Print.

Crusie, Jennifer. Welcome to Temptation. l.t. ed. 2000. (Wheeler Large Print Book Ser.). 479p. 28.95 (1-56895-906-0, Wheeler Publishing, Inc.) Gale Group.

—Welcome to Temptation. 2004. mass mkt. 3.99 (0-312-93280-4); 2000. 352p. 24.95 (0-312-25294-3); 2001. 416p. reprint ed. mass mkt. 7.50 (0-312-97425-6, St. Martin's Paperbacks) St. Martin's Pr.

Dennis, Patrick. Little Me: The Intimate Memoirs of That Great Star of Stage, Screen & Television, Belle Poitrine. 2002. (Illus.). 304p. reprint ed. pap. 15.95 (0-7679-1347-7) Broadway Bks.

Dentinger, Jane. Murder on Cue. 1984. (Murder Ink Mystery Ser.: No. 71). pap. 2.95 o.p. (0-440-16105-3) Dell Publishing.

—Murder on Cue. 1983. 192p. 11.95 o.p. (0-385-18411-5) Doubleday Publishing.

—Murder on Cue. 1992. (Jocelyn O'Roarke Mystery Ser.). 192p. reprint ed. pap. 5.95 o.p. (0-14-015841-3, Penguin Bks.) Penguin Group (USA) Inc.

Devereaux, Grant. Nevada Bluff. 2001. 288p. pap. 12.95 (0-9701466-1-2); 19.95 (0-9701466-0-4) Athenean Pr., Inc.

Farrell, Gillian B. Alibi for an Actress. Chelius, Jane, ed. 256p. 1992. 19.00 (0-671-75707-5, Atria); 1993. reprint ed. mass mkt. 5.50 (0-671-75708-3, Pocket) Simon & Schuster.

—Murder & a Muse. 1995. 288p. mass mkt. 5.99 (0-671-75711-3, Pocket); 1994. 256p. 20.00 (0-671-75710-5, Atria) Simon & Schuster.

Filipacchi, Amanda. Vapor. 1999. 320p. 22.95 (0-7867-0617-1, Carroll & Graf Pubs.) Avalon Publishing Group.

—Vapor: A Novel. 2003. 320p. pap. 14.00 (0-7867-1129-9, Carroll & Graf Pubs.) Avalon Publishing Group.

Goldstein, Rebecca. Mazel. 1996. 368p. pap. 12.95 o.s.i (0-14-023905-7, Penguin Bks.) Penguin Group (USA) Inc.

—Mazel. 2002. (Library of American Fiction). 368p. pap. 19.95 (0-299-18124-3) Univ. of Wisconsin Pr.

—Mazel. 1995. 368p. 23.95 o.s.i (0-670-85648-7, Viking) Viking Penguin.

Graham, Heather. Long, Lean & Lethal. l.t. ed. 2000. (Large Print Book Ser.). 410p. 28.95 (1-56895-928-1, Wheeler Publishing, Inc.) Gale Group.

—Long, Lean & Lethal. 2000. 400p. mass mkt. 6.99 o.s.i (0-451-40915-9, Onyx) NAL.

Harley, Don. Stranger in the Wings. E-Book (1-84045-051-7) Online Originals.

Harris, E. Lynn. Not a Day Goes By. 2000. 288p. 19.95 (0-385-49824-1) Doubleday Publishing.

—Not a Day Goes By. pap. (0-385-72885-9) Knopf Publishing Group.

—Not a Day Goes By. 2001. 304p. reprint ed. mass mkt. 6.99 (0-385-49825-X, Knopf Bks. for Young Readers) Random Hse. Children's Bks.

—Not a Day Goes By. l.t. ed. 347p. 2002. 28.95 (0-7862-3042-8); 2001. 31.95 (0-7862-3041-X) Thorndike Pr.

Harris, Joanne. Holy Fools. 2004. 368p. 24.95 (0-06-055912-8, Morrow, William & Co.) Morrow/Avon.

Heller, Jane. Lucky Stars. E-Book 24.95 (0-312-70995-1); 2004. 352p. mass mkt. 6.99 (0-312-99006-5, St. Martin's Paperbacks); 2003. 352p. 24.95 (0-312-28848-4) St. Martin's Pr.

Hughes, Dorothy B. In a Lonely Place. 1984. 240p. pap. 3.50 o.p. (0-88184-079-3, Carroll & Graf Pubs.) Avalon Publishing Group.

—In a Lonely Place. 2003. (Femmes Fatales Ser.). 256p. pap. 14.95 (1-55861-455-9); lib. bdg. 39.00 (1-55861-461-3) Feminist Pr. at The City Univ. of New York.

Jewsbury, Geraldine E. The Half Sisters. Wilkes, Joanne, ed. & intro. by. 1999. (Oxford World's Classics Ser.). 448p. pap. 12.95 (0-19-283757-5) Oxford Univ. Pr., Inc.

—The Half Sisters. Wilkes, Joanne, ed. 1994. (Oxford World's Classics Ser.). 442p. pap. 11.95 o.p. (0-19-283114-3) Oxford Univ. Pr., Inc.

—The Half-Sisters: A Tale, 2 vols., 1 bk. reprint ed. 44.50 (0-404-61945-2) AMS Pr., Inc.

Jong, Erica. Serenissima. unabr. ed. 1987. audio 17.95 o.p. (0-930435-33-8, 389); audio 57.25 o.p. (1-56100-028-0, 571) Brilliance Audio.

—Serenissima. 1988. 384p. mass mkt. 4.95 o.s.i (0-440-20104-7) Dell Publishing.

—Serenissima. 1987. 225p. 16.95 o.p. (0-395-42922-6) Houghton Mifflin Co.

—Serenissima. 1989. 3.99 o.p. (0-517-68552-3) Random Hse. Value Publishing.

Jordan, Neil. The Past. 1980. 8.95 o.p. (0-8076-0982-X) Braziller, George Inc.

Krantz, Judith. The Jewels of Tessa Kent. 1999. 480p. mass mkt. 7.99 (0-553-56137-5) Bantam Bks.

—The Jewels of Tessa Kent. l.t. ed. 1998. 672p. 25.95 o.p. (0-7838-0267-6, Macmillan Reference USA) Gale Group.

—The Jewels of Tessa Kent. l.t. ed. 1998. 672p. 25.95 (0-375-70421-3) Random Hse. Large Print.
Leigh, Wendy. The Secret Letters of Marilyn Monroe & Jacqueline Kennedy. 2003. 288p. 24.95 (0-312-30368-8) St. Martin's Pr.
—The Secret Letters of Marilyn Monroe & Jacqueline Kennedy. l.t. ed. 2003. (Women's Fiction Ser.). 28.95 (0-7862-5546-3) Thorndike Pr.
Levinson, Robert S. The Elvis & Marilyn Affair. 1999. (Neil Gulliver & Steve Marriner Novels Ser.). 304p. 24.95 (0-312-86968-1, Forge Bks.) Doherty, Tom Assocs., LLC.
—The Elvis & Marilyn Affair: A Neil Gulliver & Stevie Marriner Novel. 2000. 340p. mass mkt. 6.99 (0-8125-8432-5, Forge Bks.) Doherty, Tom Assocs., LLC.
—The James Dean Affair. 2000. (Neil Gulliver & Steve Marriner Novels Ser.). 320p. 24.95 o.p. (0-312-87268-2, Forge Bks.) Doherty, Tom Assocs., LLC.
Lovell, Glenville. Too Beautiful to Die. 2004. 320p. mass mkt. 6.99 (0-425-19702-6) Berkley Publishing Group.
—Too Beautiful to Die. 2003. 304p. 23.95 (0-399-15048-X) Putnam Publishing Group, The.
Matteson, Stefanie. Murder among the Angels. 1996. 256p. mass mkt. 5.99 o.s.i (0-425-15548-X); 19.95 o.p. (0-425-15149-2) Berkley Publishing Group. (Prime Crime).
—Murder at Teatime. 1991. 3.95 (1-55773-477-1) Ace Bks.
—Murder at Teatime. 1994. mass mkt. 4.50 o.s.i (0-425-14789-4) Berkley Publishing Group.
—Murder at the Falls. 1993. 240p. (Orig.). mass mkt. 5.50 o.s.i (0-425-14008-3) Berkley Publishing Group.
—Murder at the Spa. 1990. mass mkt. 4.50 o.s.i (0-425-14609-X); 3.95 (1-55773-411-9) Berkley Publishing Group.
—Murder on High. l.t. ed. 2000. (Beeler Large Print Mystery Ser.). 25.95 (1-57490-261-X, Beeler Large Print Bks.) Beeler, Thomas T. Publisher.
—Murder on High. 1995. 272p. mass mkt. 5.99 o.s.i (0-425-15050-X); 1994. 18.95 o.p. (0-425-14355-4, Prime Crime) Berkley Publishing Group.
—Murder on the Cliff. 1991. 3.99 (1-55773-596-4) Ace Bks.
—Murder on the Cliff. 1991. mass mkt. 4.50 o.s.i (0-425-14821-1) Berkley Publishing Group.
—Murder on the Silk Road. 1992. 240p. 3.99 o.p. (1-55773-814-9, Diamond Bks.) Ace Bks.
—Murder on the Silk Road. 1992. mass mkt. 5.50 o.s.i (0-425-14820-3, Prime Crime) Berkley Publishing Group.
—Murder under the Palms. l.t. ed. 1998. (Beeler Large Print Mystery Ser.). 25.95 (1-57490-137-0, Beeler Large Print Bks.) Beeler, Thomas T. Publisher.
—Murder under the Palms. 1997. 256p. (Charlotte Graham Mystery Ser.: Vol. 3). 21.95 o.s.i (0-425-15628-1); reprint ed. mass mkt. 5.99 o.s.i (0-425-16035-1) Berkley Publishing Group. (Prime Crime).
—Murder under the Palms. unabr. ed. 1999. audio 44.95 (0-7861-1653-6, 2481) Blackstone Audio Bks., Inc.
Maugham, W. Somerset. Theatre. 2001. 304p. pap. 13.00 (0-375-72463-X, Vintage) Knopf Publishing Group.
McElroy, Joseph. Actress in the House: A Novel. 2003. 445p. 26.95 (1-58567-350-1) Overlook Pr., The.
McHugh, Frances Y. The Rocking Chair. l.t. ed. 2001. 191p. pap. 23.95 (0-7838-9463-5, Macmillan Reference USA) Gale Group.
Morice, Anne. Dead on Cue. l.t. ed. 1986. (Nightingale Ser.). 291p. 11.95 o.p. (0-8161-4118-5, Macmillan Reference USA) Gale Group.
—Dead on Cue. 1985. 208p. 12.95 o.p. (0-312-18519-7) St. Martin's Pr.
—Death & the Dutiful Daughter. l.t. ed. 1986. (Nightingale Ser.). 288p. 10.95 o.p. (0-8161-3866-4, Macmillan Reference USA) Gale Group.
—Death in the Round. 1980. 192p. 8.95 o.p. (0-312-18616-9) St. Martin's Pr.
—Death in the Round. 1981. (Crime Monthly Ser.). 192p. pap. 2.95 o.p. (0-14-005997-0, Penguin Bks.) Viking Penguin.
—Death of a Wedding Guest. 1976. 7.95 o.p. (0-312-18830-7) St. Martin's Pr.
—Design for Dying. unabr. ed. 1991. (Audio Ser.). audio 39.95 (0-7451-6174-X, CAT 4070) BBC Audiobooks America.
—Design for Dying. 1988. 192p. 14.95 o.p. (0-312-01759-6, Saint Martin's Minotaur) St. Martin's Pr.
—Fatal Charm. l.t. ed. 1990. (Nightingale Ser.). 276p. pap. 13.95 o.p. (0-8161-4925-9, Macmillan Reference USA) Gale Group.
—Fatal Charm. 1989. 192p. 14.95 o.p. (0-312-03338-9, Saint Martin's Minotaur) St. Martin's Pr.
—Getting Away with Murder? l.t. ed. 1985. (Nightingale Ser.). 304p. 10.95 o.p. (0-8161-3865-6, Macmillan Reference USA) Gale Group.
—Getting Away with Murder? 1984. 11.95 o.p. (0-312-32633-5) St. Martin's Pr.
—Hollow Vengeance. 1982. 196p. 10.95 o.p. (0-312-38834-9) St. Martin's Pr.
—The Men in Her Death. 1981. 224p. 9.95 o.p. (0-312-52939-2) St. Martin's Pr.
—Murder in Outline. 1986. 176p. mass mkt. 2.95 o.s.i (0-553-25647-5) Bantam Bks.
—Murder in Outline. 1979. 8.95 o.p. (0-312-55303-X) St. Martin's Pr.
—Murder Post-Dated. 1986. 208p. mass mkt. 2.95 o.s.i (0-553-25652-1) Bantam Bks.
—Murder Post-Dated. l.t. ed. 1985. (Nightingale Ser.). 396p. pap. 11.95 o.p. (0-8161-3769-2, Macmillan Reference USA) Gale Group.
—Murder Post-Dated. 1984. 192p. 10.95 o.p. (0-312-55321-8) St. Martin's Pr.
—Planning for Murder. l.t. ed. 1991. (Nightingale Ser.). 267p. pap. 14.95 o.p. (0-8161-5246-2, Macmillan Reference USA) Gale Group.
—Planning for Murder. 1991. 15.95 o.p. (0-312-04869-6, Saint Martin's Minotaur) St. Martin's Pr.
—Publish & Be Killed. l.t. ed. 1988. (Nightingale Ser.). 294p. 12.95 o.p. (0-8161-4394-3, Macmillan Reference USA) Gale Group.
—Scared to Death. 1986. mass mkt. 2.95 o.s.i (0-553-25628-9) Bantam Bks.
—Scared to Death. 1978. (General Ser.). lib. bdg. 10.95 o.p. (0-8161-6584-X, Macmillan Reference USA) Gale Group.
—Scared to Death. (Mystery Bookshelf Selection Ser.). 1978. pap. 2.95 o.p. (0-312-70044-X, Saint Martin's Griffin); 1977. 7.95 o.p. (0-312-70043-1) St. Martin's Pr.
—Sleep of Death. 1986. mass mkt. 2.95 o.s.i (0-553-25877-X) Bantam Bks.
—Treble Exposure. l.t. ed. 1988. (Nightingale Ser.). 312p. 12.95 o.p. (0-8161-4622-5, Macmillan Reference USA) Gale Group.
—Treble Exposure. 1988. 192p. 13.95 o.p. (0-312-01525-9, Saint Martin's Minotaur) St. Martin's Pr.
Morris, Gilbert. The Silver Star, Vol. 20. 1997. (House of Winslow Ser.: Vol. 20). 336p. pap. 11.99 (1-55661-688-0) Bethany Hse. Pubs.
Munson, Ronald. Night Vision. 1995. 336p. 21.95 o.p. (0-525-93781-1, Dutton) Dutton/Plume.
—Night Vision. 1996. pap. 5.99 o.s.i (0-451-40659-1, Onyx); 416p. mass mkt. 5.99 o.s.i (0-451-18013-5, Signet Bks.) NAL.
O'Conner, Varley. A Company of Three. 2003. 320p. 24.95 (1-56512-373-5) Algonquin Bks. of Chapel Hill.
Perrin, Kayla. Again, My Love. 1999. 286p. mass mkt. 5.99 (0-345-43255-X) Ballantine Bks.
—Again, My Love. 1998. (Indigo Love Stories Ser.). 212p. pap. 10.95 (1-885478-23-2) Genesis Pr., Inc.
Phillips, David G. Susan Lenox: Her Fall & Rise, 2 vols. in 1. (Illus.). reprint ed. 35.00 (0-404-05029-8) AMS Pr., Inc.
—Susan Lenox: Her Fall & Rise, 2 vols., Set. (Muckrakers Ser.). 1076p. reprint ed. lib. bdg. 19.00 (0-8398-1568-9); 1986. pap. text 12.50 (0-8290-2038-1) Irvington Pubs.
—Susan Lenox: Her Fall & Rise, 2 vols., Set. 1988. (Collected Works of David G. Phillips). reprint ed. lib. bdg. 99.00 (0-7812-1346-0) Reprint Services Corp.
—Susan Lenox: Her Fall & Rise, 2 vols. 1917. reprint ed. 79.00 Somerset Pubs., Inc.
—Susan Lenox: Her Fall & Rise. 1977. (Lost American Fiction Ser.). 986p. reprint ed. 12.95 o.p. (0-8093-0773-1) Southern Illinois Univ. Pr.
—Susan Lenox: Her Fall & Rise. l.t. ed. 1999. 650p. text 34.95 (1-56000-479-7); Vol. 2. 2000. 470p. text 34.95 (1-56000-448-7) Transaction Pubs.
Porter, Margaret E. Toast of the Town. l.t. ed. 2001. 395p. (Orig.). 27.95 (0-7862-3345-1) Thorndike Pr.
Randall, Bob. The Fan. 1977. 7.95 o.p. (0-394-41203-6) Random Hse., Inc.
—The Fan. 1999. mass mkt. 2.50 o.s.i (0-446-91887-3); 1978. 288p. pap. 2.75 o.s.i (0-446-95887-5) Warner Bks., Inc.
Roberts, Nora. Dual Image. 1993. (Language of Love Ser.: No. 29). per. (0-373-51029-2, 1-51029-6, Silhouette); 1985. pap. (0-373-07123-X, Harlequin Bks.) Harlequin Enterprises, Ltd.
—Private Scandals. 2003. 416p. reprint ed. pap. 13.95 (0-425-19038-2) Berkley Publishing Group.
—Private Scandals. 19.95 o.s.i (0-399-14070-0) Putnam Publishing Group, The.
Sheldon, Sidney. A Stranger in the Mirror. 1976. 21.50 o.p. (0-688-03002-5, Morrow, William & Co.) Morrow/Avon.
—A Stranger in the Mirror. l.t. ed. 1983. (Charnwood Large Print Ser.). 400p. o.p. (0-7089-8111-9, Charnwood) Thorpe, F. A. Pubs. GBR. *Dist:* Ulverscroft Large Print Canada, Ltd.
—A Stranger in the Mirror. 1988. 320p. reprint ed. mass mkt. 7.99 (0-446-35657-3) Warner Bks., Inc.
Sobin, Gustaf. In Pursuit of Vanishing a Star: A Novel. 2002. 192p. 23.95 (0-393-04204-9) Norton, W. W. & Co., Inc.
Stanfill, Francesca. Wakefield Hall. 1994. 464p. mass mkt. 5.99 o.s.i (0-440-21788-1) Dell Publishing.
—Wakefield Hall. 1924. o.s.i (0-688-07597-5, Morrow, William & Co.) Morrow/Avon.
Sussman, Susan. Cruising for Murder. E-Book 23.95 (0-312-27575-7) St. Martin's Pr.
Sussman, Susan & Avidon, Sara Jane. Cruising for Murder. 2002. (WWL Mystery Ser.: No. 424). 256p. mass mkt. (0-373-26424-0, 1-26424-1, Worldwide Library) Harlequin Enterprises, Ltd.
Sussman, Susan & Avidon, Sarajane. Cruising for Murder: A Mystery. 2000. 288p. 23.95 (0-312-25220-X, Saint Martin's Minotaur) St. Martin's Pr.
Tsukiyama, Gail. Night of Many Dreams. unabr. ed. 1999. audio 29.95 (0-7861-1546-7); pap. 44.95 incl. audio (0-7861-1335-9, 2229) Blackstone Audio Bks., Inc.
—Night of Many Dreams. 1999. E-Book 12.95 o.s.i (0-312-20733-6); 1998. 288p. 22.95 o.p. (0-312-17194-3); 1998. 288p. reprint ed. pap. 12.95 (0-312-19940-6, NPB 0230, Saint Martin's Griffin) St. Martin's Pr.
Weber, Janice. Devil's Food. 1996. 480p. 22.95 o.p. (0-446-51772-0) Warner Bks., Inc.
Wright, Richard B. Clara Callan: A Novel. 2003. 432p. pap. 13.95 (0-06-050607-5, Perennial) HarperTrade.
Yeager, Dorian. Cancellation by Death. 1994. (WWL Mystery Ser.). per. (0-373-26159-4, 1-26159-3, Harlequin Bks.) Harlequin Enterprises, Ltd.
—Cancellation by Death. 1992. 240p. 17.95 o.p. (0-312-08152-9, Saint Martin's Minotaur) St. Martin's Pr.
—Eviction by Death. 1995. per. (0-373-26176-4, Harlequin Bks.) Harlequin Enterprises, Ltd.
—Eviction by Death: A Victoria Bowering Mystery. 1993. 192p. 17.95 o.p. (0-312-09803-0, Saint Martin's Minotaur) St. Martin's Pr.
—Libation by Death. 1998. (Vic Bowering Mystery Ser.). 240p. 21.95 (0-312-18128-0, 874692, Saint Martin's Minotaur) St. Martin's Pr.
—Ovation by Death. 1996. 208p. 20.95 o.p. (0-312-14022-3, Saint Martin's Minotaur) St. Martin's Pr.

### AIR PILOTS—FICTION

Brown, Dale. Air Battle Force. 2003. 448p. 25.95 (0-06-009409-5); E-Book 19.95 (0-06-058430-0) HarperCollins Pubs.
Hughes, Kathleen. Dear Mrs. Lindbergh. 2003. 320p. text 24.95 (0-393-05785-2) Norton, W. W. & Co., Inc.
Spencer, James. Pilots. 2003. 288p. 23.95 (0-399-14973-2, Putnam & Grosset) Putnam Publishing Group, The.
—The Pilots. 2004. 288p. pap. 13.00 (0-425-19416-7) Berkley Publishing Group.
Towell, David G. From Jennys to Jets. 2002. (Illus.). 274p. pap. (0-595-21189-5, Writers Club Pr.) iUniverse, Inc.
Walker, Nick. Blackbox. 2003. 320p. pap. 12.95 (0-06-053224-6, Perennial) HarperTrade.

### ANTHROPOLOGISTS—FICTION

Barker, Pat. Regeneration. (William Abrahams Book Ser.). 256p. 1993. pap. 14.00 (0-452-27007-3); 1992. 20.00 o.p. (0-525-93427-8) Dutton/Plume. (Abrahams, William Bks.).
—Regeneration. l.t. ed. 1996. 26.95 (1-56895-320-8, Wheeler Publishing, Inc.) Gale Group.
—Regeneration. unabr. ed. 1996. audio 60.00 (0-7887-0658-6, 94835E7) Recorded Bks., LLC.
Elkins, Aaron. Skeleton Dance. (Gideon Oliver Mystery Ser.). 2001. 352p. mass mkt. 6.99 (0-380-73163-0, Avon Bks.); 2000. 256p. 23.00 (0-688-15928-1, Morrow, William & Co.) Morrow/Avon.
—Skeleton Dance: A Novel. l.t. ed. 2000. (G. K. Hall Core Ser.). 343p. 30.95 (0-7838-9190-3, Macmillan Reference USA) Gale Group.
Gillison, Samantha. The King of America: A Novel. 2004. (Illus.). 240p. 21.95 (0-375-50819-8) Random Hse., Inc.
Gruber, Michael. Tropic of Night. 2003. 432p. 24.95 (0-06-050954-6) HarperCollins Pubs.
—Tropic of Night. 2004. 480p. mass mkt. 7.50 (0-06-050955-4, HarperTorch) Morrow/Avon.
Long, Jeff. Year Zero. 2002. 416p. 25.00 (0-7434-0611-7); E-Book 6.99 (0-7434-8231-X) Simon & Schuster. (Atria).
McKnight, Reginald. He Sleeps. 2001. 224p. 23.00 o.s.i (0-8050-4828-6) Holt, Henry & Co.
Nimmo, H. Arlo. The Songs of Salanda: And Other Stories of Sulu. E-Book 19.95 (0-295-98005-2); 1994. 248p. 22.50 o.p. (0-295-97334-X); 1994. x, 237p. pap. (0-295-97335-8) Univ. of Washington Pr.
Price, Richard & Price, Sally. Enigma Variations. (Illus.). 176p. 1995. (C). 18.95 (0-674-25726-X); 1997. reprint ed. 12.95 (0-674-25728-6) Harvard Univ. Pr.
Reichs, Kathy. Fatal Voyage. 2001. 368p. 25.00 (0-684-85972-6); E-Book (0-7432-1822-1); 368p. 25.00 o.s.i (0-7432-2281-4); 528p. 25.00 (0-7432-1662-8) Simon & Schuster. (Scribner).
—Fatal Voyage. abr. ed. 2001. audio 26.00 (0-7435-0462-3); audio compact disk 30.00 (0-7435-0463-1) Simon & Schuster Audio. (Simon & Schuster Audioworks).
—Grave Secrets. 2003. 400p. mass mkt. 7.99 (0-671-02838-3, Pocket Star) Simon & Schuster.

### ANTIQUE DEALERS—FICTION

Armstrong, Vivien. Smile Now, Die Later. 2002. 224p. 25.99 (0-7278-5896-3) Severn Hse. Pubs., Ltd.
Bunn, T. Davis. The Amber Room. 1992. (Priceless Collection). 336p. pap. 9.99 o.p. (1-55661-285-0) Bethany Hse. Pubs.
—The Amber Room. l.t. ed. 2001. (Christian Mystery Ser.). 519p. 24.95 o.p. (0-7862-3070-3) Thorndike Pr.
—Florian's Gate. 1992. (Priceless Collection). 352p. (ps up). pap. 9.99 o.p. (1-55661-244-3) Bethany Hse. Pubs.
—Florian's Gate. l.t. ed. 2000. (Christian Mystery Ser.). 563p. 24.95 (0-7862-2877-6) Thorndike Pr.
—Winter Palace. 1993. (Priceless Collection: No. 3). 352p. pap. 9.99 o.p. (1-55661-324-5) Bethany Hse. Pubs.
—Winter Palace. l.t. ed. 2001. (Thorndike Christian Mystery Ser.). (Illus.). 512p. 24.95 (0-7862-3179-3) Thorndike Pr.
Coe, Simon. The Gold Bokhara. 2002. 352p. pap. 21.95 (0-87714-826-0) Denlingers Pubs., Ltd.
—The Gold Bokhara. 2000. 387p. pap. 18.00 (0-7388-1835-6) Xlibris Corp.
Coomer, Joe. Apologizing to Dogs. 1999. (Illus.). 288p. 22.00 o.s.i (0-684-85946-7, Scribner) Simon & Schuster.
—Apologizing to Dogs. l.t. ed. 2000. (Americana Ser.). 416p. 26.95 (0-7862-2367-7) Thorndike Pr.
—Apologizing to Dogs: A Novel. 2000. E-Book 22.00 (0-684-87123-8, Scribner) Simon & Schuster.
Dickens, Charles. The Old Curiosity Shop. 2001. (Classics Ser.). (Illus.). 352p. 11.00 (0-14-043742-8, Penguin Classics) Viking Penguin.
Fennelly, Tony. The Closet Hanging. 1987. (Matt Sinclair Ser.). 224p. 14.95 o.p. (0-88184-306-7); pap. 3.50 o.p. (0-88184-393-8) Avalon Publishing Group. (Carroll & Graf Pubs.).
—Murder with a Twist: The Glory Hole Murders & the Closet Hanging. 1991. 432p. pap. 4.95 o.p. (0-88184-783-6, Carroll & Graf Pubs.) Avalon Publishing Group.
Fiffer, Sharon. The Wrong Stuff. Date not set. pap. (0-312-31415-9, St. Martin's Paperbacks); 2003. 320p. 24.95 (0-312-31414-0, Saint Martin's Minotaur) St. Martin's Pr.
Flynn, Lucine H. Antique & Deadly. 1988. 16.95 (0-8027-5702-2) Walker & Co.
Gash, Jonathan. Firefly Gadroon. 1985. (Lovejoy Mystery Ser.). 12.95 o.p. (0-525-24135-3, Dutton) Dutton/Plume.
—Firefly Gadroon. 1984. 208p. 11.95 o.p. (0-312-29205-8) St. Martin's Pr.
—Firefly Gadroon. l.t. ed. 1983. 352p. 15.95 o.p. (0-7089-1012-2, Ulverscroft) Thorpe, F. A. Pubs. GBR. *Dist:* Ulverscroft Large Print Bks., Ltd.
—Firefly Gadroon. 1985. (Lovejoy Mystery Ser.). 208p. pap. 5.95 o.s.i (0-14-008007-4, Penguin Bks.) Viking Penguin.
—Gold by Gemini. 1982. (Scene of the Crime Mystery Ser.: No. 36). pap. 2.25 o.p. (0-440-12749-1) Dell Publishing.
—Gold by Gemini. 1978. 186p. 8.95 (0-06-011463-0) HarperCollins Pubs.
—Gold by Gemini. 1988. (Lovejoy Mystery Ser.). 192p. mass mkt. 3.95 o.p. (0-451-82185-8) NAL.
—Gold by Gemini. unabr. ed. 1999. (Lovejoy Mystery Ser.). audio 53.00 (1-84197-020-4, H1020E7, Clipper Audio); audio compact disk 59.00 (1-84197-090-5, C1126E7);Set. audio 53.00 Recorded Bks., LLC.
—Gold by Gemini. l.t. ed. 1981. (Ulverscroft Large Print Ser.). 29.99 o.p. (0-7089-0575-7, Ulverscroft) Thorpe, F. A. Pubs. GBR. *Dist:* Ulverscroft Large Print Bks., Ltd., Ulverscroft Large Print Canada, Ltd.
—Gold by Gemini. 1988. 224p. pap. 3.95 o.p. (0-14-010529-8, Penguin Bks.); 224p. pap. 5.95 o.p. (0-14-023014-9, Penguin Bks.); pap. 39.50 o.p. (0-14-778299-6) Viking Penguin.
—The Gondola Scam. 1984. 256p. 12.95 o.p. (0-312-33828-7) St. Martin's Pr.
—The Gondola Scam. 1985. (Lovejoy Mystery Ser.). 256p. pap. 5.99 o.p. (0-14-007656-5, Penguin Bks.) Viking Penguin.
—The Grace in Older Women: A Lovejoy Novel. 1996. (Lovejoy Mystery Ser.). 288p. pap. 5.95 o.p. (0-14-024662-2, Penguin Bks.) Penguin Group (USA) Inc.
—The Grace in Older Women: A Lovejoy Novel. 1995. (Lovejoy Mystery Ser.). 288p. 19.95 o.p. (0-670-86128-6, Viking) Viking Penguin.
—The Grail Tree. 21.95 (0-88411-559-3) Amereon, Ltd.

—The Grail Tree. 1982. (Scene of the Crime Ser.: No. 48). 288p. pap. 2.50 o.p. (*0-440-13022-0*) Dell Publishing.

—The Grail Tree. 1980. o.p. (*0-06-011462-2*) HarperCollins Pubs.

—The Grail Tree. 1988. (Lovejoy Mystery Ser.). 224p. mass mkt. 3.95 o.p. (*0-451-82186-6*) NAL.

—The Grail Tree. l.t. ed. 1983. (Ulverscroft Large Print Ser.). 368p. 29.99 o.p. (*0-7089-0958-2*, Ulverscroft) Thorpe, F. A. Pubs. GBR. *Dist:* Ulverscroft Large Print Bks., Ltd., Ulverscroft Large Print Canada, Ltd.

—The Grail Tree. 1988. (Lovejoy Mystery Ser.). 224p. pap. 5.95 o.s.i (*0-14-023015-7*, Penguin Bks.); pap. 39.50 o.p. (*0-14-778300-3*); 224p. pap. 3.95 o.p. (*0-14-010530-1*, Penguin Bks.) Viking Penguin.

—The Great California Game. 1992. (Lovejoy Mystery Ser.). 256p. reprint ed. pap. 5.95 o.p. (*0-14-017224-6*, Penguin Bks.) Penguin Group (USA) Inc.

—The Great California Game. 1991. 288p. 19.95 o.p. (*0-312-06363-6*, Saint Martin's Minotaur) St. Martin's Pr.

—The Great California Game. l.t. ed. 1993. (Mystery Ser.). 512p. 29.99 o.p. (*0-7089-2930-3*, Ulverscroft) Thorpe, F. A. Pubs. GBR. *Dist:* Ulverscroft Large Print Bks., Ltd., Ulverscroft Large Print Canada, Ltd.

—Jade Woman. 1988. 288p. 17.95 o.p. (*0-312-02224-7*, Saint Martin's Minotaur) St. Martin's Pr.

—Jade Woman. l.t. ed. 1990. 18.95 o.p. (*0-7089-2189-2*, Ulverscroft) Thorpe, F. A. Pubs. GBR. *Dist:* Ulverscroft Large Print Bks., Ltd.

—Jade Woman. 1990. (Lovejoy Mystery Ser.). 288p. pap. 5.95 o.p. (*0-14-012280-X*, Penguin Bks.) Viking Penguin.

—The Judas Pair. 1981. (Scene of the Crime Mystery Ser.: No. 30). pap. 2.25 o.p. (*0-440-14354-3*) Dell Publishing.

—The Judas Pair. 1988. 39.50 o.p. (*0-14-778245-7*) Penguin Group (USA) Inc.

—The Judas Pair. 1999. (Lovejoy Mystery Ser.). audio 53.00 (*1-84197-004-2*, H1004E7); audio compact disk 61.00Set. audio 53.00 Recorded Bks., LLC.

—The Judas Pair. l.t. ed. 1982. (Ulverscroft Large Print Ser.). 368p. 29.99 o.p. (*0-7089-0856-X*, Ulverscroft) Thorpe, F. A. Pubs. GBR. *Dist:* Ulverscroft Large Print Bks., Ltd., Ulverscroft Large Print Canada, Ltd.

—The Judas Pair. (Lovejoy Mystery Ser.). 1989. 22p. pap. 6.95 o.p. (*0-14-012688-0*); 1988. 224p. pap. 3.95 o.p. (*0-14-010528-X*) Viking Penguin. (Penguin Bks.).

—The Lies of Fair Ladies. 1993. (Lovejoy Mystery Ser.). 272p. pap. 5.95 o.p. (*0-14-017630-6*, Penguin Bks.) Penguin Group (USA) Inc.

—The Lies of Fair Ladies. 1992. 288p. 19.95 o.p. (*0-312-07620-7*, Saint Martin's Minotaur) St. Martin's Pr.

—The Lies of Fair Ladies. l.t. ed. 1994. (Large Print Ser.). 592p. 29.99 o.p. (*0-7089-3006-9*, Ulverscroft) Thorpe, F. A. Pubs. GBR. *Dist:* Ulverscroft Large Print Bks., Ltd., Ulverscroft Large Print Canada, Ltd.

—Moonspender. 1987. 240p. 14.95 o.p. (*0-312-00156-8*) St. Martin's Pr.

—Moonspender. (Lovejoy Mystery Ser.). 1990. 224p. pap. 5.99 o.p. (*0-14-014339-4*); 1988. 272p. pap. 4.50 o.p. (*0-14-010646-4*) Viking Penguin. (Penguin Bks.).

—Paid & Loving Eyes. 1994. (Lovejoy Mystery Ser.). 272p. pap. 5.99 o.s.i (*0-14-023557-4*, Penguin Bks.) Penguin Group (USA) Inc.

—Paid & Loving Eyes. 1993. (Lovejoy Novel of Suspense Ser.). 288p. 19.95 o.p. (*0-312-09361-6*, Saint Martin's Minotaur) St. Martin's Pr.

—Paid & Loving Eyes. l.t. ed. 1994. (Ulverscroft Large Print Ser.). 608p. 29.99 o.p. (*0-7089-3164-2*, Ulverscroft) Thorpe, F. A. Pubs. GBR. *Dist:* Ulverscroft Large Print Bks., Ltd., Ulverscroft Large Print Canada, Ltd.

—Pearlhanger. 1985. 256p. 14.95 o.p. (*0-312-59970-6*) St. Martin's Pr.

—Pearlhanger. l.t. ed. 2000. (Mystery Ser.). 319p. 26.95 (*0-7862-2456-8*); (*0-7540-4138-7*); (*0-7540-4139-5*) Thorndike Pr.

—Pearlhanger. 1986. (Lovejoy Mystery Ser.). 24p. pap. 5.95 o.p. (*0-14-008468-1*, Penguin Bks.) Viking Penguin.

—The Possessions of a Lady. 1997. (Lovejoy Mystery Ser.). 336p. pap. 5.95 o.s.i (*0-14-025792-6*) Penguin Group (USA) Inc.

—The Possessions of a Lady. 1996. (Lovejoy Mystery Ser.). 332p. 21.95 o.s.i (*0-670-86933-3*, Viking) Viking Penguin.

—A Rag, a Bone & a Hank of Hair. 2001. (Lovejoy Mystery Ser.). 352p. pap. 5.99 o.s.i (*0-14-029857-6*) Penguin Group (USA) Inc.

—A Rag, a Bone & a Hank of Hair. 2000. (Lovejoy Mystery Ser.). 256p. 23.95 o.s.i (*0-670-88598-3*, Viking) Viking Penguin.

—The Rich & the Profane. l.t. ed. 1999. pap. 23.95 (*1-56895-794-7*, Wheeler Publishing, Inc.) Gale Group.

—The Rich & the Profane. 2000. (Lovejoy Mystery Ser.). 352p. pap. 5.99 (*0-14-028622-5*, Penguin Bks.) Penguin Group (USA) Inc.

—The Rich & the Profane. 1999. (Lovejoy Mystery Ser.). 288p. 22.95 o.s.i (*0-670-88346-8*) Viking Penguin.

—The Sin Within Her Smile. l.t. ed. 1994. 385p. 20.95 (*0-8161-1115-4*); lib. bdg. 21.95 (*0-7838-1115-2*) Gale Group. (Macmillan Reference USA).

—The Sin Within Her Smile. 1995. (Lovejoy Mystery Ser.). 240p. pap. 5.99 o.s.i (*0-14-023839-5*, Penguin Bks.) Penguin Group (USA) Inc.

—The Sin Within Her Smile. 1994. (Lovejoy Mystery Ser.). 240p. 18.95 o.p. (*0-670-85608-8*, Viking) Viking Penguin.

—The Sleepers of Erin. 1983. (Lovejoy Mystery Ser.). 228p. 13.95 o.p. (*0-525-24163-9*, 01354-410, Dutton) Dutton/Plume.

—The Sleepers of Erin. l.t. ed. 1985. 384p. 15.95 o.p. (*0-7089-1363-6*, Ulverscroft) Thorpe, F. A. Pubs. GBR. *Dist:* Ulverscroft Large Print Bks., Ltd.

—The Sleepers of Erin. 1984. (Crime Monthly Ser.). 224p. pap. 5.99 o.p. (*0-14-006970-4*, Penguin Bks.) Viking Penguin.

—Spend Game. 1981. (Joan Kahn Bk.). 204p. 9.95 o.p. (*0-89919-030-8*) Houghton Mifflin Co.

—Spend Game. unabr. ed. 2000. (Lovejoy Mystery Ser.). audio 53.00 (*1-84197-045-X*, H1050E7, Clipper Audio) Recorded Bks., LLC.

—Spend Game. l.t. ed. 1981. 360p. 12.00 o.p. (*0-7089-0673-7*, Ulverscroft) Thorpe, F. A. Pubs. GBR. *Dist:* Ulverscroft Large Print Bks., Ltd.

—Spend Game. 1982. (Crime Monthly Ser.). 208p. pap. 5.95 o.p. (*0-14-006190-8*, Penguin Bks.) Viking Penguin.

—The Tartan Sell. 1990. (Lovejoy Mystery Ser.). 24p. pap. 5.99 (*0-14-014596-6*, Penguin Bks.) Penguin Group (USA) Inc.

—The Tartan Sell. 1986. 240p. 14.95 o.p. (*0-312-78614-X*) St. Martin's Pr.

—The Tartan Sell. 1987. (Lovejoy Mystery Ser.). 240p. pap. 3.95 o.p. (*0-14-009745-7*, Penguin Bks.) Viking Penguin.

—The Vatican Rip. 1982. (Joan Kahn Bk.). 228p. 10.95 o.p. (*0-89919-080-4*) Houghton Mifflin Co.

—The Vatican Rip. l.t. ed. 1984. 368p. 15.95 o.p. (*0-7089-1101-3*, Ulverscroft) Thorpe, F. A. Pubs. GBR. *Dist:* Ulverscroft Large Print Bks., Ltd.

—The Vatican Rip. 1983. (Lovejoy Mystery Ser.). 224p. pap. 5.99 o.s.i (*0-14-006431-1*, Penguin Bks.) Viking Penguin.

—The Very Last Gambado. 1991. (Crime Monthly Ser.). 288p. reprint ed. pap. 5.95 o.p. (*0-14-014738-1*, Penguin Bks.) Penguin Group (USA) Inc.

—The Very Last Gambado. 1990. 18.95 o.p. (*0-312-05175-1*) St. Martin's Pr.

—The Very Last Gambado. l.t. ed. 1991. (Ulverscroft Large Print Ser.). 29.99 o.p. (*0-7089-2532-4*, Ulverscroft) Thorpe, F. A. Pubs. GBR. *Dist:* Ulverscroft Large Print Bks., Ltd., Ulverscroft Large Print Canada, Ltd.

Hamilton, Lyn. The African Quest: An Archaeological Mystery. 2001. (Archaeological Mystery Ser.). (Illus.). 304p. 21.95 o.s.i (*0-425-17806-4*) Berkley Publishing Group.

—The Celtic Riddle. 2000. 304p. mass mkt. 6.50 (*0-425-17775-0*, Prime Crime) Berkley Publishing Group.

—The Celtic Riddle: An Archaeological Mystery. 2000. 296p. 21.95 o.s.i (*0-425-17235-X*, Prime Crime) Berkley Publishing Group.

—The Maltese Goddess: An Archaeological Mystery. 1998. (Archaeological Mystery Ser.). 256p. mass mkt. 6.50 (*0-425-16240-0*, Prime Crime) Berkley Publishing Group.

—The Moche Warrior: An Archaeological Mystery. (Archaeological Mystery Ser.). 336p. 1999. 21.95 o.s.i (*0-425-16809-3*); 2000. reprint ed. mass mkt. 6.50 (*0-425-17308-9*) Berkley Publishing Group. (Prime Crime).

—The Thai Amulet. 2004. 288p. mass mkt. 6.99 (*0-425-19487-6*); 2003. 256p. 22.95 (*0-425-19006-4*, Prime Crime) Berkley Publishing Group.

—The Xibalba Murders: An Archeological Mystery. 1997. (Archaeological Mystery Ser.). 304p. mass mkt. 6.50 (*0-425-15722-9*, Prime Crime) Berkley Publishing Group.

Hardwick, Mollie. The Bandersnatch. 1994. mass mkt. 4.50 o.s.i (*0-449-22029-X*, Fawcett) Ballantine Bks.

—The Bandersnatch. 1989. 15.95 o.p. (*0-312-02865-2*, Saint Martin's Minotaur) St. Martin's Pr.

—The Bandersnatch. l.t. ed. 1991. (Ulverscroft Large Print Ser.). 29.99 o.p. (*0-7089-2534-0*, Ulverscroft) Thorpe, F. A. Pubs. GBR. *Dist:* Ulverscroft Large Print Bks., Ltd., Ulverscroft Large Print Canada, Ltd.

—Come Away, Death. 1997. 214p. mass mkt. 5.50 (*0-449-22421-X*, Fawcett) Ballantine Bks.

—The Dreaming Damozel. 1995. mass mkt. 4.99 o.s.i (*0-449-22073-7*, Fawcett) Ballantine Bks.

—The Dreaming Damozel. l.t. ed. 1992. (Nightingale Series Large Print Bks.). 337p. pap. 14.95 o.p. (*0-8161-5323-X*, Macmillan Reference USA) Gale Group.

—The Dreaming Damozel. 1991. 15.95 o.p. (*0-312-05421-1*, Saint Martin's Minotaur) St. Martin's Pr.

—Malice Domestic. 1992. mass mkt. 4.50 o.s.i (*0-449-22032-X*, Fawcett) Ballantine Bks.

—Malice Domestic. 1989. mass mkt. o.s.i (*0-552-13235-7*, Corgi) Bantam Bks.

—Malice Domestic. 1986. 208p. 13.95 o.p. (*0-312-50940-5*) St. Martin's Pr.

—Malice Domestic. l.t. ed. 1988. 400p. o.p. (*0-7089-1835-2*, Ulverscroft) Thorpe, F. A. Pubs.

—Parson's Pleasure. 1992. mass mkt. 4.50 o.s.i (*0-449-22031-1*, Fawcett) Ballantine Bks.

—Parson's Pleasure. 1989. mass mkt. o.s.i (*0-552-13236-5*, Corgi) Bantam Bks.

—Parson's Pleasure. 1987. 208p. 14.95 o.p. (*0-312-00642-X*) St. Martin's Pr.

—Parson's Pleasure. l.t. ed. 1989. 332p. 17.95 o.p. (*0-7089-1932-4*, Ulverscroft) Thorpe, F. A. Pubs. GBR. *Dist:* Ulverscroft Large Print Bks., Ltd.

—Perish in July. 1994. mass mkt. 4.99 o.s.i (*0-449-22028-1*, Fawcett) Ballantine Bks.

—Perish in July. 1991. mass mkt. o.s.i (*0-552-13664-6*, Corgi) Bantam Bks.

—Perish in July. 1990. 15.95 o.p. (*0-312-04402-X*, Saint Martin's Minotaur) St. Martin's Pr.

—Uneaseful Death. 1993. mass mkt. 5.99 o.s.i (*0-449-22030-3*, Fawcett) Ballantine Bks.

—Uneaseful Death. 1989. mass mkt. o.s.i (*0-552-13411-2*, Corgi) Bantam Bks.

—Uneaseful Death. 1988. 192p. 14.95 o.p. (*0-312-01842-8*, Saint Martin's Minotaur) St. Martin's Pr.

—Uneaseful Death. l.t. ed. 1990. (Ulverscroft Large Print Ser.). 29.99 o.p. (*0-7089-2252-X*, Ulverscroft) Thorpe, F. A. Pubs. GBR. *Dist:* Ulverscroft Large Print Bks., Ltd., Ulverscroft Large Print Canada, Ltd.

Heath, Roy A. The Ministry of Hope. 1996. 320p. 24.95 (*0-7145-3015-8*) Boyars, Marion Pubs., Inc.

Holtzer, Susan. Something to Kill For. 1995. 242p. mass mkt. 5.99 (*0-312-95589-8*, St. Martin's Paperbacks); 1994. 240p. 19.95 o.p. (*0-312-11117-7*, Saint Martin's Minotaur) St. Martin's Pr.

Hughes, Sean. The Detainees. 1997. 322p. o.p. (*0-684-82081-1*) Simon & Schuster.

Kaye, Gillian. The Kingowan Affair. l.t. ed. 2000. (Nightingale Ser.). 140p. pap. 20.95 (*0-7838-9094-X*) Thorndike Pr.

Massey, Sujata. The Bride's Kimono. 2001. 320p. 25.00 (*0-06-019933-4*) HarperCollins Pubs.

—The Bride's Kimono. 2002. 400p. mass mkt. 6.99 (*0-06-103115-1*, Avon Bks.) Morrow/Avon.

—The Floating Girl. 2000. 304p. 24.00 (*0-06-019229-1*) HarperCollins Pubs.

—The Floating Girl. 2001. 384p. mass mkt. 6.99 (*0-06-109735-7*, Avon Bks.) Morrow/Avon.

—The Flower Master. 1999. 304p. 24.00 (*0-06-019228-3*) HarperCollins Pubs.

—The Flower Master. 2000. 400p. mass mkt. 6.99 (*0-06-109734-9*, HarperTorch) Morrow/Avon.

—The Flower Master. 2000. 13.04 (*0-606-21840-8*) Turtleback Bks.

—The Salaryman's Wife. 1997. 432p. mass mkt. 7.50 (*0-06-104443-1*, HarperTorch) Morrow/Avon.

—Salarymans Wife Arc. 2000. 368p. pap. 5.99 (*0-06-104384-2*) HarperCollins Pubs.

—Zen Attitude. 1998. 320p. mass mkt. 6.99 (*0-06-104444-X*, HarperTorch) Morrow/Avon.

Morgan, Deborah. Death Is a Cabaret: An Antique Lover's Mystery. 2001. 240p. mass mkt. 5.99 (*0-425-18202-9*) Berkley Publishing Group.

Mortman, Doris. Rightfully Mine. 1990. 736p. mass mkt. 6.99 o.s.i (*0-553-28416-9*); 700p. mass mkt. 5.50 o.s.i (*0-553-17341-3*) Bantam Bks.

Myers, Tamar. Baroque & Desperate. 1999. (Den of Antiquity Ser.). 256p. mass mkt. 6.99 (*0-380-80225-2*, Avon Bks.) Morrow/Avon.

—Estate of Mind. 1999. 320p. mass mkt. 6.50 (*0-380-80227-9*, Avon Bks.) Morrow/Avon.

—Guilt by Association. 1996. (Den of Antiquity Ser.). 256p. mass mkt. 6.50 (*0-380-78237-5*, Avon Bks.) Morrow/Avon.

—Larceny & Old Lace. 1996. (Den of Antiquity Ser.). 224p. (Orig.). mass mkt. 6.99 (*0-380-78239-1*, Avon Bks.) Morrow/Avon.

—Ming & I. 1997. (Den of Antiquity Ser.). 256p. mass mkt. 6.99 (*0-380-79255-9*, Avon Bks.) Morrow/Avon.

—So Faux, So Good. 1998. (Den of Antiquity Ser.). 256p. mass mkt. 6.50 (*0-380-79254-0*, Avon Bks.) Morrow/Avon.

—Tiles & Tribulations. l.t. ed. 2003. (Mystery Ser.). 28.95 (*1-57490-509-0*) Beeler, Thomas T. Publisher.

—Tiles & Tribulations. 2003. 352p. mass mkt. 6.99 (*0-380-81965-1*, Avon Bks.) Morrow/Avon.

Orde, A. J., pseud. Death & the Dogwalker. 1993. mass mkt. 4.50 o.s.i (*0-449-22027-3*, Fawcett) Ballantine Bks.

—Death for Old Times' Sake. 1993. mass mkt. 4.50 o.s.i (*0-449-22193-8*, Fawcett) Ballantine Bks.

—Death for Old Times' Sake. 1992. 240p. 16.50 o.s.i (*0-385-41941-4*) Doubleday Publishing.

—A Little Neighborhood Murder. 1992. mass mkt. 4.50 o.s.i (*0-449-22026-5*, Fawcett) Ballantine Bks.

—A Little Neighborhood Murder. l.t. ed. 1992. (Linford Mystery Library). 448p. pap. 17.99 o.p. (*0-7089-7163-6*, Linford) Thorpe, F. A. Pubs. GBR. *Dist:* Ulverscroft Large Print Bks., Ltd., Ulverscroft Large Print Canada, Ltd.

—A Long Time Dead. 1995. mass mkt. 5.50 o.s.i (*0-449-22359-0*, Fawcett) Ballantine Bks.

Orde, A. J., pseud & Tepper, Sheri S. Death of Innocents. 1997. (Jason Lynx Mystery Ser.). mass mkt. 5.99 o.s.i (*0-449-22519-4*, Fawcett) Ballantine Bks.

Pye, Michael. The Pieces from Berlin. 2004. 352p. pap. 14.00 (*0-375-71416-2*, Vintage) Knopf Publishing Group.

—The Pieces from Berlin. 2003. 352p. 24.00 (*0-375-41436-3*) Knopf, Alfred A. Inc.

Roberts, Nora. Three Complete Novels. (Dream Ser.). 1999. 757p. 14.98 (*0-399-14480-3*); 1998. 768p. 14.98 (*0-399-14388-2*, G. P. Putnam's Sons) Penguin Group (USA) Inc.

—Three Complete Novels: Honest Illusions, Private Scandals & Hidden Riches. 2000. 864p. 14.98 (*0-399-14627-X*, G. P. Putnam's Sons) Penguin Group (USA) Inc.

Schaffert, Timothy. The Phantom Limbs of the Rollow Sisters. 2002. 240p. 23.95 o.s.i (*0-399-14900-7*, BlueHen Bks.) Putnam Publishing Group, The.

Wait, Lea. Shadows at the Fair: An Antique Print Mystery. (Illus.). 272p. 2003. mass mkt. 6.99 (*0-7434-5620-3*, Pocket); 2002. 24.00 (*0-7432-2553-8*, Scribner) Simon & Schuster.

—Shadows at the Fair: An Antique Print Mystery. 2003. (Americana Ser.). 28.95 (*0-7862-5003-8*) Thorndike Pr.

—Shadows on the Coast of Maine: An Antique Print Mystery. unabr. ed. 2003. audio 49.95 (*0-7861-2513-6*); audio compact disk 24.95 (*0-7861-8909-6*); audio compact disk 14.95 (*0-7861-9144-9*) Blackstone Audio Bks., Inc.

—Shadows on the Coast of Maine: An Antique Print Mystery. 2004. 272p. mass mkt. 6.99 (*0-7434-5621-1*, Pocket); 2003. 288p. 24.00 (*0-7432-2554-6*, Scribner) Simon & Schuster.

—Shadows on the Ivy: An Antique Print Mystery. 256p. Date not set. mass mkt. (*0-7434-7559-3*, Pocket); 2005. (*0-7432-4951-8*, Scribner); 2005. mass mkt. 5.99 (*0-7434-7558-5*, Pocket); 2004. 24.00 (*0-7432-4950-X*, Scribner) Simon & Schuster.

Warner, Sylvia Townsend. Music at the Long Verney: Twenty Stories. Steinman, Michael, ed. 2000. 224p. text 24.00 (*1-58243-112-4*, Counterpoint Pr.) Basic Bks.

## ARCHAEOLOGISTS—FICTION

Ackroyd, Peter. First Light. 1991. 336p. pap. 8.95 o.p. (*0-345-36887-8*) Ballantine Bks.

—First Light. 336p. 1989. 19.95 o.p. (*0-8021-1161-0*); 1996. reprint ed. pap. 12.00 (*0-8021-3481-5*, Grove Pr.) Grove/Atlantic, Inc.

Alten, Steve. Domain. E-Book 25.95 (*1-58945-659-9*) Adobe Systems, Inc.

—Domain. E-Book 25.95 (*0-312-70081-4*, Tor Bks.); 2001. (Illus.). 384p. 25.95 (*0-312-87476-6*, Forge Bks.); 2002. reprint ed. mass mkt. 7.99 (*0-8125-7956-9*, Tor Bks.) Doherty, Tom Assocs., LLC.

Anderson, Kevin J. Ruins. 1996. (X-Files Ser.). 304p. mass mkt. 22.00 o.p. (*0-06-105247-7*) HarperCollins Pubs.

—Ruins. (X-Files Ser.: Vol. 4). 1997. 272p. mass mkt. 6.50 o.s.i (*0-06-105736-3*, HarperEntertainment); 1996. 304p. 50.00 o.s.i (*0-06-105273-6*, Eos) Morrow/Avon.

Arnold, Margot, pseud. The Cape Cod Caper. 1982. (Murder Mystery Ser.). 192p. 2.50 (*0-86721-206-3*, Jove) Berkley Publishing Group.

—The Cape Cod Caper. 1988. (Penny Spring & Sir Toby Glendower Mystery Ser.). 192p. pap. 7.95 (*0-88150-116-6*, Foul Play) Norton, W. W. & Co., Inc.

—The Cape Cod Conundrum. (Penny Spring & Sir Toby Glendower Mystery Ser.). 224p. 1992. text 20.00 o.p. (*0-88150-244-8*); 1994. reprint ed. pap. 7.95 (*0-88150-293-6*) Norton, W. W. & Co., Inc. (Foul Play).

—The Catacomb Conspiracy. 1992. (Penny Spring & Sir Toby Glendower Mystery Ser.). 260p. 18.95 o.p. (*0-88150-208-1*) Countryman Pr.

—The Catacomb Conspiracy. 1993. (Penny Spring & Sir Toby Glendower Mystery Ser.). 240p. pap. 7.95 (*0-88150-255-3*, Foul Play) Norton, W. W. & Co., Inc.

—Death of a Voodoo Doll. 1989. 220p. reprint ed. pap. 7.95 (*0-88150-132-8*, Foul Play) Norton, W. W. & Co., Inc.

—Death on the Dragon's Tongue. 1982. 224p. 2.50 (*0-86721-150-4*, Jove) Berkley Publishing Group.
—Death on the Dragon's Tongue. 1990. (Penny Spring & Sir Toby Glendower Mystery Ser.). 224p. reprint ed. pap. 7.95 (*0-88150-158-1*, Foul Play) Norton, W. W. & Co., Inc.
—Dirge for a Dorset Druid. (Penny Spring & Sir Toby Glendower Mystery Ser.). 240p. 1995. pap. 7.95 (*0-88150-334-7*); 1993. 20.00 (*0-88150-266-9*) Norton, W. W. & Co., Inc. (Foul Play).
—Exit Actors, Dying. 1982. 176p. 2.50 (*0-86721-181-4*, Jove) Berkley Publishing Group.
—Exit Actors, Dying. 1988. (Penny Spring & Sir Toby Glendower Mystery Ser.). 176p. reprint ed. pap. 7.95 (*0-88150-115-8*, Foul Play) Norton, W. W. & Co., Inc.
—Lament for a Lady Laird. 1982. 224p. 2.50 (*0-86721-132-6*, Jove) Berkley Publishing Group.
—Lament for a Lady Laird. 1990. (Penny Spring & Sir Toby Glendower Mystery Ser.). 224p. reprint ed. pap. 7.95 (*0-88150-159-X*, Foul Play) Norton, W. W. & Co., Inc.
—The Menehune Murders. 1989. (Penny Spring & Sir Toby Glendower Mystery Ser.). 240p. 17.95 o.p. (*0-88150-149-2*) Countryman Pr.
—The Menehune Murders. 1991. (Penny Spring & Sir Toby Glendower Mystery Ser.). 260p. pap. 7.95 (*0-88150-196-4*, Foul Play) Norton, W. W. & Co., Inc.
—The Midas Murders. 1995. (Penny Spring & Sir Toby Glendower Mystery Ser.). 224p. 20.00 (*0-88150-340-1*, Foul Play) Norton, W. W. & Co., Inc.
—The Midas Murders: A Penny Spring & Sir Toby Glendower Mystery. 1997. (Penny Spring & Sir Toby Glendower Mystery Ser.). 224p. pap. 7.95 (*0-88150-394-0*) Norton, W. W. & Co., Inc.
—Toby's Folly. 1990. 256p. 18.95 o.p. (*0-88150-177-8*) Countryman Pr.
—Toby's Folly. 1992. (Penny Spring & Sir Toby Glendower Mystery Ser.). 256p. pap. 7.95 (*0-88150-228-6*, Foul Play) Norton, W. W. & Co., Inc.
—Zadok's Treasure. 1982. 192p. 2.50 (*0-86721-228-4*, Jove) Berkley Publishing Group.
—Zadok's Treasure. 1989. (Penny Spring & Sir Toby Glendower Mystery Ser.). 192p. reprint ed. pap. 7.95 (*0-88150-133-6*, Foul Play) Norton, W. W. & Co., Inc.
Bantock, Nick. Alexandria: In Which the Extraordinary Correspondence of Griffin & Sabine Unfolds. 19.95 o.s.i (*0-8118-3699-1*) Chronicle Bks. LLC.
—The Gryphon: In Which the Extraordinary Correspondence of Griffin & Sabine Is Rediscovered. 2001. 19.95 o.s.i (*0-8118-3384-4*); (Illus.). 56p. 19.95 (*0-8118-3162-0*) Chronicle Bks. LLC.
Bantock, Nick, illus. Alexandria: In Which the Extraordinary Correspondence of Griffin & Sabine Unfolds. 2002. 56p. 19.95 (*0-8118-3140-X*) Chronicle Bks. LLC.
Beaton, Roderick. Ariadne's Children. pap. 15.95 (*0-312-30457-9*, Saint Martin's Griffin); 1996. 384p. 24.95 o.p. (*0-312-13923-3*) St. Martin's Pr.
Blair, Clifford. Showdown at Viking Cave. l.t. ed. 1994. 255p. pap. 18.95 (*0-8161-7473-3*, Macmillan Reference USA) Gale Group.
—Showdown at Viking Cave. 1994. 198p. 19.95 (*0-8027-4136-3*) Walker & Co.
Bradley, James. Wrack. 340p. 2000. pap. 13.00 (*0-8050-6447-8*, Owl Bks.); 1999. 25.00 o.s.i (*0-8050-6108-8*) Holt, Henry & Co.
—Wrack. 1997. (Illus.). (*0-09-183494-5*) Trafalgar Square.
—Wrack: Roman. (GER.). 318p. (*3-612-65019-X*) Econ-Verlag GmbH DEU. *Dist:* International Bk. Import Service, Inc.
Burnham, Carol. Attic Light. 1997. 192p. 24.00 (*1-877946-88-5*) Permanent Pr., The.
Butler, Robert Olen. Countrymen of Bones. 1985. 256p. mass mkt. 2.95 o.s.i (*0-345-32118-9*) Ballantine Bks.
—Countrymen of Bones. 1994. 25.00 o.p. (*0-8050-3202-9*); 224p. pap. 11.00 o.s.i (*0-8050-3142-1*, Owl Bks.) Holt, Henry & Co.
Carter, Elizabeth E. Valley of the Kings: A Novel of Tutankhamun. 1977. 7.95 o.p. (*0-525-22777-6*, Dutton) Dutton/Plume.
Christie, Agatha. Murder in Mesopotamia. (Hercule Poirot Mystery Ser.). 1987. 272p. mass mkt. 5.99 (*0-425-10363-3*); 1986. mass mkt. 2.95 o.s.i (*0-425-09324-7*); 1984. mass mkt. 2.95 o.s.i (*0-425-06791-2*) Berkley Publishing Group.
—Murder in Mesopotamia. 1976. 192p. pap. 2.50 o.s.i (*0-440-15982-2*) Dell Publishing.
—Murder in Mesopotamia. l.t. ed. (G. K. Hall Large Print Book Ser.). 1992. 348p. 14.95 o.p. (*0-8161-4568-7*); 1991. 384p. 19.95 o.p. (*0-8161-4567-9*) Gale Group. (Macmillan Reference USA).
—Murder in Mesopotamia. l.t. ed. 1969. (Ulverscroft Large Print Ser.). 367p. 12.50 o.p. (*0-85456-667-8*, Ulverscroft) Thorpe, F. A. Pubs. GBR. *Dist:* Ulverscroft Large Print Bks., Ltd., Ulverscroft Large Print Canada, Ltd.
—Murder in Mesopotamia. 1984. 12.04 (*0-606-00965-5*) Turtleback Bks.
Connor, Beverly. Skeleton Crew: A Lindsay Chamberlain Novel. 2002. (Illus.). 432p. reprint ed. mass mkt. 7.99 (*1-58182-287-1*) Cumberland Hse. Publishing.
Easterman, Daniel. The Seventh Sanctuary. 1987. 456p. 17.95 o.s.i (*0-385-19814-0*) Doubleday Publishing.
—The Seventh Sanctuary. 1988. 608p. mass mkt. 4.50 o.p. (*0-8217-2451-7*, Zebra Bks.) Kensington Publishing Corp.
Ellis, Kate. The Bone Garden. 2003. 240p. 23.95 (*0-312-30037-9*, Saint Martin's Minotaur) St. Martin's Pr.
—The Merchant's House. l.t. ed. 1999. (Magna Large Print Ser.). 400p. o.p. (*0-7505-1438-8*) Magna Large Print Bks. GBR. *Dist:* Ulverscroft Large Print Canada, Ltd.
—The Merchant's House. 1999. 246p. 22.95 (*0-312-20562-7*, Saint Martin's Minotaur) St. Martin's Pr.
—An Unhallowed Grave. l.t. ed. 2001. (Magna Large Print Ser.). 400p. 31.99 (*0-7505-1627-5*) Magna Large Print Bks. GBR. *Dist:* Ulverscroft Large Print Bks., Ltd., Ulverscroft Large Print Canada, Ltd.
—An Unhallowed Grave. Date not set. E-Book 22.95 (*0-312-70164-0*) St. Martin's Pr.
—An Unhallowed Grave: Wesley Peterson Crime Novel. 2001. (Wesley Peterson Crime Novels Ser.). 240p. 22.95 (*0-312-27460-2*, Saint Martin's Minotaur) St. Martin's Pr.
Faust, Ron. Lord of the Dark Lake. 2000. 320p. pap. 13.95 (*0-312-87510-X*, Forge Bks.); 1998. mass mkt. 6.99 (*0-8125-3023-3*, Tor Bks.); 1996. 320p. 22.95 o.p. (*0-312-85535-4*, Forge Bks.) Doherty, Tom Assocs., LLC.
Freedman, J. F. Fallen Idols. 2003. 432p. 19.95 (*0-446-53189-8*) Warner Bks., Inc.
Gear, Kathleen O'Neal & Gear, W. Michael. Bone Walker. 2002. (Illus.). 352p. 26.95 (*0-312-87742-0*, Forge Bks.) Doherty, Tom Assocs., LLC.
Graham, Mark. The Fire Theft. l.t. ed. 1994. 607p. lib. bdg. 23.95 o.p. (*0-8161-5950-5*, Macmillan Reference USA) Gale Group.
—The Fire Theft. 406p. 4.98 o.p. (*0-8317-9315-5*) Smithmark Pubs., Inc.
—The Fire Theft. 1993. 400p. 21.00 o.p. (*0-670-84870-0*, Viking) Viking Penguin.
Gramling, Lee. Ninety-Mile Praire. 2002. (Cracker Western Ser.). (Illus.). 280p. pap. 8.95 (*1-56164-257-6*); 279p. 14.95 (*1-56164-255-X*) Pineapple Pr., Inc.
Hamilton, Lyn. The Magyar Venus. 2004. 256p. 22.95 (*0-425-19429-9*) Berkley Publishing Group.
Hart, Erin. Haunted Ground: A Crime Novel. 2003. (Illus.). 352p. 24.00 (*0-7432-3505-3*, Scribner) Simon & Schuster.
Hirschfield, Corson. Too High. 2001. 464p. 25.95 (*0-7653-0011-7*, Forge Bks.) Doherty, Tom Assocs., LLC.
Holland, Cecelia. Valley of the Kings. 1999. 231p. pap. 12.95 (*0-312-86862-6*, Forge Bks.) Doherty, Tom Assocs., LLC.
Hollyday, Thomas. Slave Graves. 2003. 284p. pap. 12.95 (*0-9741287-0-8*); E-Book 12.95 (*0-9741287-1-6*) Happy Bird Corp.
Howard, Linda. Heart of Fire. 1997. 320p. mass mkt. 7.99 (*0-671-01974-0*, Pocket) Simon & Schuster.
—Heart of Fire. Zion, Claire, ed. 1993. 320p. mass mkt. 6.99 (*0-671-72859-8*, Pocket) Simon & Schuster.
—Heart of Fire. l.t. ed. 2001. (Famous Authors Ser.). 531p. 28.95 o.p. (*0-7862-2850-4*) Thorndike Pr.
Johnson, Adam. Parasites Like Us. 2003. 368p. 24.95 (*0-670-03235-2*) Viking Penguin.
Johnston, Velda. The Etruscan Smile. 1980. mass mkt. 2.25 o.p. (*0-451-09020-9*, E9020, Signet Bks.) NAL.
—The Etruscan Smile: A Novel of Suspense. l.t. ed. 2000. (Candlelight Romance Ser.). 271p. 22.95 (*0-7862-2449-5*) Thorndike Pr.
Knight, Kathryn L. Mumbo Jumbo. 1991. 17.95 o.p. (*0-671-68448-5*, Simon & Schuster) Simon & Schuster.
—Mumbo Jumbo. Chelius, Jane, ed. 1992. 224p. reprint ed. mass mkt. 4.99 (*0-671-68447-7*, Pocket) Simon & Schuster.
LaHaye, Tim & Dinallo, Greg. Babylon Rising. 2003. 400p. 24.95 (*0-553-80322-0*) Bantam Bks.
—Babylon Rising. l.t. ed. 2003. 576p. 26.95 (*0-375-43237-X*) Random Hse. Large Print.
Lane, Christopher. Eden's Gate. 1994. 432p. pap. 12.99 (*0-310-41161-0*) Zondervan.
Lehrer, Jim. No Certain Rest. 2002. (Illus.). 240p. 23.95 (*0-375-50372-2*) Random Hse., Inc.
—No Certain Rest: A Novel. 2003. 240p. pap. 12.95 (*0-8129-6822-0*) Random House Adult Trade Publishing Group.
—No Certain Rest: A Novel. 2003. (Americana Ser.). 30.95 (*0-7862-5001-1*) Thorndike Pr.
Lewis, Roy. Angel of Death. l.t. ed. 1997. (Magna Large Print Ser.). 335p. o.p. (*0-7505-1204-0*) Magna Large Print Bks. GBR. *Dist:* Ulverscroft Large Print Canada, Ltd.
—Angel of Death. unabr. ed. 1999. audio 69.95 (*1-85903-264-8*) Ulverscroft Audio (U.S.A.).
—Bloodeagle. l.t. ed. 1994. 22.95 o.p. (*0-7927-1928-X*); pap. 20.95 o.p. (*0-7927-1927-1*) BBC Audiobooks America.
—The Cross Bearer. l.t. ed. 1995. (Magna Large Print Ser.). 378p. o.p. (*0-7505-0846-9*) Magna Large Print Bks. GBR. *Dist:* Ulverscroft Large Print Canada, Ltd.
—Cross Bearer: An Arnold Landon Mystery. 1994. 205p. 18.95 o.p. (*0-312-11765-5*, Saint Martin's Minotaur) St. Martin's Pr.
—The Devil Is Dead. l.t. ed. 1990. 17.95 o.p. (*0-7451-9920-8*, C0638); pap. 15.95 o.p. (*0-7927-0370-7*, C0832) BBC Audiobooks America.
—The Devil Is Dead. 1990. 208p. 15.95 o.p. (*0-312-04851-3*, Saint Martin's Minotaur) St. Martin's Pr.
—A Gathering of Ghosts. 1983. 192p. 10.95 o.p. (*0-312-31788-3*) St. Martin's Pr.
—Men of Subtle Craft. 1988. 192p. 13.95 (*0-312-81789-4*) St. Martin's Pr.
—Most Cunning Workmen. 1986. (Atlantic Ser.). 274 p. (*0-89340-966-9*) BBC Audiobooks America.
—Most Cunning Workmen. 1985. 182 p. 10.95 o.p. (*0-312-54907-5*) St. Martin's Pr.
—A Secret Dying: An Arthur Landon Mystery. l.t. ed. 1993. 21.95 o.p. (*0-7927-1546-2*); pap. 19.95 o.p. (*0-7927-1545-4*) BBC Audiobooks America.
—A Secret Dying: An Arthur Landon Mystery. 1993. 17.95 o.p. (*0-312-08887-6*, Saint Martin's Minotaur) St. Martin's Pr.
—A Wisp of Smoke. 1991. 208p. 17.95 o.p. (*0-312-07123-X*, Saint Martin's Minotaur) St. Martin's Pr.
Lewis, Roy H. Bloodeagle: An Arnold Landon Mystery. 1993. 224p. 19.95 o.p. (*0-312-10431-6*, Saint Martin's Minotaur) St. Martin's Pr.
—Men of Subtle Craft. l.t. ed. 1988. pap. 14.95 o.p. (*1-55504-661-4*, 462) BBC Audiobooks America.
—A Trout in the Milk: An Arnold Landon Novel. l.t. ed. 1988. (Atlantic Large Print Ser.). 285 p. (*1-55504-562-6*) BBC Audiobooks America.
—A Trout in the Milk: An Arnold Landon Novel. 1986. 208p. 13.95 o.p. (*0-312-82009-7*) St. Martin's Pr.
—A Wisp of Smoke. l.t. ed. 1992. (Magna Large Print Ser.). 326p. 29.99 (*0-7505-0355-6*) Magna Large Print Bks. GBR. *Dist:* Ulverscroft Large Print Bks., Ltd.
Long, Jeff. Year Zero. 2002. E-Book 6.99 (*0-7434-8231-X*, Atria) Simon & Schuster.
Lundin, Steve. A Ruin of Feathers. 1992. pap. text (*0-920661-23-8*) TSAR Pubns.
Mones, Nicole. Lost in Translation. 1999. 384p. pap. 13.95 (*0-385-31944-4*, Delta) Dell Publishing.
Morris, Gilbert. The Beloved Enemy. 2003. (House of Winslow Ser.). 320p. pap. 11.99 (*0-7642-2704-1*) Bethany Hse. Pubs.
Nolta, David D. Grave Circle: An Ivory Tower Mystery. 2003. 304p. 21.95 (*0-9713160-2-3*) Quality Words In Print.
Peters, Elizabeth, pseud. Children of the Storm. 2003. (Amelia Peabody Mystery Ser.). 416p. 25.95 (*0-06-621476-9*) HarperCollins Pubs.
—Children of the Storm. l.t. ed. 2003. 640p. pap. 25.95 (*0-06-053333-1*, HarperLargePrint) HarperTrade.
—Children of the Storm. 2004. 480p. mass mkt. 7.50 (*0-06-103248-4*, Avon Bks.) Morrow/Avon.
—The Jackal's Head. l.t. ed. 2000. 264p. lib. bdg. 26.95 (*1-58547-040-6*) Ctr. Point Large Print.
—The Jackal's Head. 1988. 245p. pap. 4.99 (*0-8125-0002-4*); pap. 3.50 o.s.i (*0-8125-0768-1*) Doherty, Tom Assocs., LLC. (Tor Bks.).
—The Jackal's Head. 1991. reprint ed. 18.95 o.p. (*0-7278-4257-9*) Severn Hse. Pubs., Ltd.
Pfaff, Eugene E., Jr. & Causey, Michael. Uwharrie. 1993. 256p. 19.95 (*0-936389-30-3*) Tudor Pubs., Inc.
Phillips, Michael. A Rift in Time. (Rift in Time Ser.). 2000. 512p. pap. 12.99 (*0-8423-5500-6*); 1997. 604p. 12.99 o.p. (*0-8423-5525-1*) Tyndale Hse. Pubs.
Rice, Luanne. Stone Heart. l.t. ed. 2001. 491p. 31.95 (*0-7838-9440-6*, Macmillan Reference USA) Gale Group.
—Stone Heart. 1990. 320p. 19.95 o.p. (*0-670-83267-7*, Viking) Viking Penguin.
Samuelson, Charmayne Pelt. Kachina Rain. 2000. 364p. pap. 22.99 o.p. (*0-7388-2752-5*); text 32.99 o.p. (*0-7388-2751-7*) Xlibris Corp.
Sawyer, Robert J. End of an Era. 1994. 240p. mass mkt. 4.99 o.s.i (*0-441-00114-9*) Ace Bks.
—End of an Era. E-Book 14.95 (*0-312-70256-6*); 2001. 256p. reprint ed. pap. 14.95 (*0-312-87693-9*) Doherty, Tom Assocs., LLC. (Tor Bks.).
Shuman, Malcolm. Assassin's Blood. 1999. 224p. mass mkt. 5.99 (*0-380-80485-9*) Morrow/Avon.
—Burial Ground. 1998. 224p. mass mkt. 5.50 (*0-380-79423-3*, Avon Bks.) Morrow/Avon.
—Meriweather Murder. 1998. (Alan Graham Mysteries Ser.: No. 2). 272p. mass mkt. 5.99 (*0-380-79424-1*, Avon Bks.) Morrow/Avon.
—Past Dying. 2000. (Alan Graham Mysteries Ser.). 224p. mass mkt. 5.99 (*0-380-80486-7*, Avon Bks.) Morrow/Avon.
Simon, Frank. Veiled Threats. 1996. 356p. pap. 12.99 o.p. (*0-89107-880-0*) Crossway Bks.
—Walls of Terror. 1997. 368p. pap. 12.99 o.p. (*0-89107-952-1*) Crossway Bks.
Stoker, Bram. The Jewel of Seven Stars. 25.95 (*0-89190-362-3*) Amereon, Ltd.
—The Jewel of Seven Stars. 1989. 256p. mass mkt. 3.95 o.p. (*0-88184-501-9*, Carroll & Graf Pubs.) Avalon Publishing Group.
—The Jewel of Seven Stars. reprint ed. lib. bdg. 98.00 (*0-7426-2894-9*); 2001. pap. text 28.00 (*0-7426-7894-6*) Classic Bks.
—The Jewel of Seven Stars. Leatherdale, Clive, ed. & anno. by. annot. unabr. ed. 1996. 256p. 29.95 (*1-874287-08-2*) Desert Island Bks. GBR. *Dist:* Griffin Skye Co.
—The Jewel of Seven Stars. 1999. 280p. mass mkt. 5.99 (*0-8125-6895-8*, Tor Bks.) Doherty, Tom Assocs., LLC.
—The Jewel of Seven Stars. 2002. 220p. 94.99 (*1-4043-1118-1*); per. 89.99 (*1-4043-1119-X*) IndyPublish.com.
—The Jewel of Seven Stars. 1981. mass mkt. 1.95 o.p. (*0-89083-416-4*, Zebra Bks.) Kensington Publishing Corp.
—The Jewel of Seven Stars. 1979. pap. 4.95 (*0-918172-05-5*) Leete's Island Bks.
—The Jewel of Seven Stars. 1996. (Oxford Popular Fiction Ser.). 238p. pap. 8.95 o.p. (*0-19-283219-0*) Oxford Univ. Pr., Inc.
—The Jewel of Seven Stars. 1996. (Pocket Classics Ser.). (Illus.). 192p. pap. 10.95 (*0-7509-0947-1*) Sutton Publishing.
—The Jewel of Seven Stars. 1999. 12.04 (*0-606-16659-9*) Turtleback Bks.
—The Jewel of Seven Stars. 2001. 304p. pap. 19.95 (*1-58715-576-1*); lib. bdg. 29.95 (*1-58715-577-X*) Wildside Pr.
Strauss, Victoria. Guardian of the Hills. 1995. (Illus.). 240p. (J). (gr. 7 up). 15.00 o.s.i (*0-688-06998-3*, Morrow, William & Co.) Morrow/Avon.
Stuart, Francis. King David Dances. 1997. 62p. pap. 12.95 (*1-874597-44-8*) Dufour Editions, Inc.
Sussman, Paul. The Lost Army of Cambyses. 2003. (Illus.). 384p. 24.95 (*0-312-30153-7*) St. Martin's Pr.
Talbot, Michael. The Bog. 1987. mass mkt. 3.95 o.s.i (*0-515-09049-2*, Jove) Berkley Publishing Group.
—The Bog. 1986. 320p. 17.95 o.p. (*0-688-05952-X*, Morrow, William & Co.) Morrow/Avon.
Tallent, Elizabeth. Museum Pieces. 1986. 240p. pap. 7.95 o.p. (*0-03-008003-7*, Owl Bks.) Holt, Henry & Co.
—Museum Pieces. Goerner, Lee, ed. 1985. 206p. 14.95 o.s.i (*0-394-53928-1*) Knopf, Alfred A. Inc.
Traylor, Ellen G. The Priest. 1998. 370 p. pap. 12.99 o.s.i (*0-8499-4099-0*) W Publishing Group.
Trow, M. J. Lestrade & the Kiss of Horus. 2001. (Lestrade Mystery Ser.: Vol. 15). (Illus.). 235p. (J). 19.95 (*0-89526-214-2*) Regnery Publishing, Inc., An Eagle Publishing Co.
Willey, Gordon R. Selena. 1995. (Mystery Ser.). 250p. per. (*0-373-26190-X*, 1-26190-8, Harlequin Bks.) Harlequin Enterprises, Ltd.
—Selena. 1993. 208p. 19.95 (*0-8027-3227-5*) Walker & Co.
Wolfe, Swain. The Parrot Trainer. (Illus.). mass mkt. (*0-312-98793-5*, St. Martin's Paperbacks); 2003. 288p. 24.95 (*0-312-31091-9*) St. Martin's Pr.

**ARTISTS—FICTION**

Agee, Jon. The Incredible Painting of Felix Clousseau, RS. 1988. (Illus.). 32p. (J). (ps-3). 15.00 o.p. (*0-374-33633-4*, Farrar, Straus & Giroux (BYR)) Farrar, Straus & Giroux.
—Incredible Painting of Felix Clousseau, RS. 1990. (Illus.). 32p. (J). (ps-3). pap. 4.95 (*0-374-43582-0*, Sunburst) Farrar, Straus & Giroux.
Alcock, Vivien. The Sylvia Game. 1997. 224p. (YA). (gr. 7-7). pap. 4.95 o.s.i (*0-395-81650-5*) Houghton Mifflin Co.
Alegria, Fernando. The Maypole Warriors. Miller, Yvette E., ed. Lozano, Carlos, tr. from SPA. 1992. (Discoveries Ser.). 192p. pap. 16.95 (*0-935480-58-7*) Latin American Literary Review Pr.
Alexander, Sidney. The Hand of Michelangelo. 1966. 693p. reprint ed. pap. 15.95 o.p. (*0-8214-0235-8*) Ohio Univ. Pr.
—Michelangelo the Florentine. 1985. 464p. pap. 17.95 o.p. (*0-8214-0236-6*) Ohio Univ. Pr.
—Nicodemus: The Roman Years of Michelangelo Buonarroti, 1534-1564. 1984. viii, 293p. 26.95 o.p. (*0-8214-0778-3*) Ohio Univ. Pr.

Anderson, Barbara. Portrait of the Artist's Wife. 1993. 320p. 21.95 o.p. (*0-393-03489-5*) Norton, W. W. & Co., Inc.

Anderson, M. The Unsinkable Molly Malone. 1991. 208p. (YA). (gr. 7 up). 16.95 (*0-15-213801-3*) Harcourt Children's Bks.

Andrews, Donna. Murder with Peacocks. l.t. ed. 2002. (Mystery Ser.). 26.95 (*1-57490-388-8*, Beeler Large Print Bks.) Beeler, Thomas T. Publisher.

—Murder with Peacocks. (Meg Langslow Mysteries Ser.). 2000. 320p. mass mkt. 6.50 (*0-312-97063-3*, St. Martin's Paperbacks); 1998. 332p. 23.95 (*0-312-19929-5*, Saint Martin's Minotaur) St. Martin's Pr.

—Murder with Puffins. l.t. ed. 2002. 26.95 (*1-57490-415-9*) Beeler, Thomas T. Publisher.

—Murder with Puffins. 2001. 320p. mass mkt. 6.50 o.s.i (*0-312-97886-3*, St. Martin's Paperbacks); 2000. 281p. 24.95 (*0-312-26221-3*, Saint Martin's Minotaur) St. Martin's Pr.

Anholt, Laurence. Camille & the Sunflowers. 1994. (Illus.). 32p. (J). (ps-2). 14.95 (*0-8120-6409-7*) Barron's Educational Series, Inc.

—Picasso & the Girl with a Ponytail. 1998. (Illus.). 32p. (J). (ps-2). 14.95 (*0-7641-5031-6*) Barron's Educational Series, Inc.

Arnold, Emily. Life Drawing. 1986. 288p. 15.95 o.s.i (*0-385-29437-9*, Delacorte Pr.); 1988. reprint ed. mass mkt. 4.95 o.s.i (*0-440-20025-3*, Laurel) Dell Publishing.

Atkinson, Charles. The Portrait. 1998. 272p. 23.95 o.p. (*0-312-18652-5*) St. Martin's Pr.

Auch, Mary Jane. Glass Slippers Give You Blisters. 1989. 176p. (J). (gr. 3-7). 14.95 o.p. (*0-8234-0752-7*) Holiday Hse., Inc.

—Glass Slippers Give You Blisters. 1990. (J). mass mkt. 2.75 o.p. (*0-590-43501-9*) Scholastic, Inc.

Bailey, Eleanor. Marlene Dietrich Lived Here. 439p. pap. 11.95 (*0-552-99863-X*) Corgi Bks. Ltd. GBR. *Dist:* Trafalgar Square.

—Marlene Dietrich Lived Here. 2002. 359p. (*0-385-60120-4*) Doubleday Publishing.

Bantock, Nick. Alexandria: In Which the Extraordinary Correspondence of Griffin & Sabine Unfolds. 19.95 o.s.i (*0-8118-3699-1*) Chronicle Bks. LLC.

—Griffin & Sabine: An Extraordinary Correspondence. 1991. (Illus.). 48p. 19.95 (*0-87701-788-3*) Chronicle Bks. LLC.

Bantock, Nick, illus. Alexandria: In Which the Extraordinary Correspondence of Griffin & Sabine Unfolds. 2002. 56p. 19.95 (*0-8118-3140-X*) Chronicle Bks. LLC.

Barrett, Neal, Jr. Bad Eye Blues, Vol. 1. (Wiley Moss Mystery Ser.). 1999. 352p. mass mkt. 5.99 o.s.i (*1-57566-484-4*); 1997. 288p. 21.95 o.p. (*1-57566-173-X*) Kensington Publishing Corp.

—Skinny Annie Blues. (Wiley Moss Mystery Ser.). 1997. 304p. mass mkt. 5.50 (*1-57566-134-9*); 1996. 256p. 21.95 o.p. (*1-57566-058-X*) Kensington Publishing Corp. (Kensington Bks.).

Barrows, Allison. The Artist's Friends. 1997. (Picture Bks.). (Illus.). 32p. (J). (gr. k-3). lib. bdg. 15.95 o.s.i (*1-57505-054-4*, Carolrhoda Bks.) Lerner Publishing Group.

—The Artist's Model. 1996. (Illus.). 32p. (J). (ps-3). lib. bdg. 15.95 o.s.i (*0-87614-948-4*, Carolrhoda Bks.) Lerner Publishing Group.

Bass, Rick. Fiber. aut. ltd. num. ed. 1998. (Illus.). 57p. text 100.00 (*0-8203-2086-2*) Univ. of Georgia Pr.

Begiebing, Robert J. The Adventures of Allegra Fullerton: Or a Memoir of Startling & Amusing Episodes from Itinerant Life - A Novel. 1999. (Illus.). 326p. text 30.00 (*0-87451-947-0*, Hardscrabble Bks.) Univ. Pr. of New England.

Bernardi, Adria. The Day Laid on the Altar. 2000. (Middlebury/Bread Loaf Book Ser.). (Illus.). 220p. 29.95 (*1-58465-044-3*) Univ. Pr. of New England.

Berry, Liz. Easy Connections. 1984. 180p. (J). (gr. 7-9). 12.95 o.p. (*0-670-28694-X*, Viking Children's Bks.) Penguin Putnam Bks. for Young Readers.

Bianchi, John. El Artista. Mendez, Nora, tr. 1992. Tr. of Artist. (SPA., Illus.). 32p. (J). (gr. k-3). pap. 5.95 o.p. (*0-921285-22-1*) Bungalo Bks. CAN. *Dist:* Firefly Bks., Ltd.

Biro, Val. Drango Dragon. 1989. (Picture Story Bks.: No. S8910-3). (J). pap. 3.95 o.s.i (*0-7214-9596-6*, Ladybird Bks.) Penguin Group (USA) Inc.

Bond, Michael. Paddington's Art Exhibition. 1986. (Paddington Ser.). Orig. Title: Paddington's Painting Exhibition. (Illus.). 32p. (J). (ps-3). 5.95 o.s.i (*0-399-21270-1*, G. P. Putnam's Sons) Penguin Putnam Bks. for Young Readers.

Bornstein, Ruth L. That's How It Is When We Draw. 1997. (Illus.). 32p. (J). (ps-2). 14.00 o.p. (*0-395-82509-1*) Houghton Mifflin Co.

Borovsky, Paul. The Strange Blue Creature. 1993. (Illus.). 32p. (J). (ps-2). 13.95 o.s.i (*1-56282-434-1*); lib. bdg. 13.89 o.s.i (*1-56282-435-X*) Hyperion Bks. for Children.

Boyd, William. Nat Tate. 1998. 69p. 15.95 o.p. (*1-901785-01-7*) 21 UK GBR. *Dist:* Distributed Art Pubs./D.A.P.

—Stars & Bars. 1985. 288p. 16.95 o.p. (*0-688-02599-4*, Morrow, William & Co.) Morrow/Avon.

—Stars & Bars. 1986. 336p. pap. 6.95 o.p. (*0-14-008889-X*, Penguin Bks.) Viking Penguin.

Boyle, Kay. My Next Bride. 1986. 336p. pap. 6.95 o.p. (*0-14-016147-3*, Penguin Bks.) Viking Penguin.

Bradberry, James. Eakins' Mistress: A Jamie Ramsgill Mystery. 1997. 169p. text 19.95 o.p. (*0-312-15518-2*, Saint Martin's Minotaur) St. Martin's Pr.

Braverman, Kate. The Incantation of Frida K. 240p. 2002. 23.95 (*1-58322-469-6*); 2003. reprint ed. pap. 11.95 (*1-58322-571-4*) Seven Stories Pr.

Brenner, Leah. An Artist Grows up in Mexico: Scenes from the Boyhood of Diego Rivera. 1987. (Illus.). 152p. pap. 9.95 o.p. (*0-8263-0924-0*) Univ. of New Mexico Pr.

Brooke, William J. A Brush with Magic. (Illus.). (J). (gr. 3 up). 1995. 80p. pap. 3.95 o.p. (*0-06-440490-0*, Harper Trophy); 1993. 160p. 15.00 o.p. (*0-06-022973-X*); 1993. 160p. lib. bdg. 14.89 o.p. (*0-06-022974-8*) HarperCollins Children's Bk. Group.

Brown, John Gregory. Audubon's Watch: A Novel. 2001. 224p. tchr. ed. 24.00 (*0-395-78607-X*) Houghton Mifflin Co.

—Audubon's Watch: A Novel. 2002. 224p. pap. 13.00 (*0-618-25731-4*, Mariner Bks.) Houghton Mifflin Co. Trade & Reference Div.

Brust, Steven. The Sun, the Moon, & the Stars. 1996. 210p. pap. 12.95 (*0-312-86039-0*, Orb Bks.) Doherty, Tom Assocs., LLC.

Buford, G. Dan. Separate but Equal, , Jasma, Ricardy & Morton, Randolph B., eds. 2003. (Politics of Black Love Novel Ser.: Vol. 2). 288p. pap. 15.00 (*0-9718191-4-9*) La Caille Nous Publishing Co.

Bulla, Clyde Robert. The Chalk Box Kid. 1987. (Stepping Stone Bks.). (Illus.). 64p. (gr. 1-4). lib. bdg. 11.99 (*0-394-99102-8*); 10th annot. ed. 80p. (gr. 2-4). pap. 3.99 (*0-394-89102-3*) Random Hse. Children's Bks. (Random Hse. Bks. for Young Readers).

—The Paint Brush Kid. 1999. (Stepping Stone Bks.). (Illus.). 80p. (J). (gr. 2-4). lib. bdg. 11.99 (*0-679-99282-0*, Random Hse. Bks. for Young Readers) Random Hse. Children's Bks.

Butenhoff, Lisa K. Nina's Magic. Thatch, Nancy R., ed. 1992. (Books for Students by Students). (Illus.). 26p. (J). (ps-3). lib. bdg. 15.95 (*0-933849-40-0*) Landmark Editions, Inc.

Carle, Eric. Draw Me a Star. (Illus.). (J). (ps-3). 1998. 40p. pap. 6.99 (*0-698-11632-1*, PaperStar); 1992. 32p. 16.99 (*0-399-21877-7*, Philomel) Penguin Putnam Bks. for Young Readers.

Carrick, Donald. Morgan & the Artist. (Illus.). 32p. (J). (ps-4). 1985. 14.95 o.p. (*0-89919-300-5*); 1991. reprint ed. pap. 4.95 o.p. (*0-395-58176-1*) Houghton Mifflin Co. Trade & Reference Div. (Clarion Bks.).

Carris, Joan D. The Greatest Idea Ever. 1990. (Illus.). 176p. (J). (gr. 3-7). lib. bdg. 13.89 o.p. (*0-397-32379-4*) HarperCollins Children's Bk. Group.

Catalanotto, Peter. The Painter. 1996. (Illus.). 32p. (J). (ps-3). pap. 15.95 (*0-531-09465-0*); lib. bdg. 16.99 (*0-531-08765-4*) Scholastic, Inc. (Orchard Bks.).

Chabon, Michael. The Amazing Adventures of Kavalier & Clay: A Novel. 2000. 656p. 26.95 (*0-679-45004-1*) Random Hse., Inc.

Chevalier, Tracy. Girl with a Pearl Earring. 240p. 2000. 21.95 (*0-525-94527-X*, Dutton); 2003. pap. 14.00 (*0-452-28493-7*, Plume) Dutton/Plume.

—Girl with a Pearl Earring. l.t. ed. 2001. 12.95 (*1-56895-186-8*); 2000. 283p. 26.95 o.p. (*1-56895-850-1*) Gale Group. (Wheeler Publishing, Inc.).

—Girl with a Pearl Earring. 1999. 248p. (*0-00-225890-0*) HarperCollins Pubs.

—Girl with a Pearl Earring. abr. ed. 2001. audio compact disk 26.95 (*1-56511-497-3*) HighBridge Co.

—Girl with a Pearl Earring. unabr. ed. 2000. audio 57.00 (*0-7887-4355-4*) Recorded Bks., LLC.

—Girl with a Pearl Earring. 2001. 18.05 (*0-606-20673-6*) Turtleback Bks.

Clarke, J. Riffraff, ERS. 1992. 112p. (YA). (gr. 9-12). 14.95 o.p. (*0-8050-1774-7*, Holt, Henry & Co. Bks. For Young Readers) Holt, Henry & Co.

Clement, Claude. The Painter & the Wild Swans. 32p. (J). (gr. k up). 1990. pap. 4.99 o.p. (*0-8037-0840-8*); 1986. (Illus.). 14.95 o.p. (*0-8037-0268-X*) Penguin Putnam Bks. for Young Readers. (Dial Bks. for Young Readers).

Coats, Laura J. Marcella & the Moon. 1986. (Illus.). 32p. (J). (gr. k-3). 12.95 o.s.i (*0-02-719050-1*, Simon & Schuster Children's Publishing) Simon & Schuster Children's Publishing.

Cohen, Arthur A. Artists & Enemies. 1987. 256p. 16.95 (*0-87923-650-7*) Godine, David R. Pub.

Cormier, Robert. Tunes for Bears to Dance To. 112p. 1994. (YA). (gr. 7-12). mass mkt. 5.50 (*0-440-21903-5*); 1992. (J). (gr. 5 up). 15.00 o.s.i (*0-385-30818-3*, Delacorte Pr.) Dell Publishing.

Crowell, Jenn. Necessary Madness. 1997. 212p. 21.95 o.p. (*0-399-14252-5*, G. P. Putnam's Sons) Penguin Group (USA) Inc.

—Necessary Madness. l.t. ed. 1998. (Niagara Large Print Ser.). 240p. 29.50 o.p. (*0-7089-5889-3*, Ulverscroft) Thorpe, F. A. Pubs. GBR. *Dist:* Ulverscroft Large Print Bks., Ltd., Ulverscroft Large Print Canada, Ltd.

—Necessary Madness. 1998. 256p. mass mkt. 6.99 (*0-446-60606-5*) Warner Bks., Inc.

Dann, Jack. The Memory Cathedral: A Secret History of Leonardo da Vinci. 1995. 512p. 22.95 o.s.i (*0-553-09637-0*); 1996. 508p. reprint ed. pap. 27.00 (*0-553-37857-0*) Bantam Bks.

Danner, Nikki. Face up to Love. 1994. (Sweet Dreams Ser.: No. 218). 160p. (YA). pap. 3.50 o.p. (*0-553-56483-8*) Bantam Bks.

Dartez, Cecilia Casrill. Jenny Giraffe Discovers the French Quarter. 1991. (Illus.). 32p. (J). (gr. 4-7). 14.95 (*0-88289-819-1*) Pelican Publishing Co., Inc.

de Paola, Tomie & Lear, Edward. Bonjour Mr. Satie. 1991. (Illus.). 32p. (J). (ps-3). 16.99 (*0-399-21782-7*, G. P. Putnam's Sons) Penguin Group (USA) Inc.

De Prada, Juan Manuel. Tempest. 2003. 341p. 24.95 (*1-58567-387-0*) Overlook Pr., The.

Deaver, Julie Reece. Chicago Blues. 1995. 192p. (J). (gr. 6-9). 15.95 (*0-06-024675-8*) HarperCollins Children's Bk. Group.

—Chicago Blues. 1995. 192p. (J). (gr. 6-9). lib. bdg. 14.89 o.p. (*0-06-024676-6*) HarperCollins Pubs.

Dee, Jonathan. Palladio. 2002. 400p. 24.95 (*0-385-50179-X*) Doubleday Publishing.

—Palladio. 2003. 400p. pap. 14.00 (*0-375-72641-1*) Knopf, Alfred A. Inc.

Defirenze, Rina. Mystery of the Mona Lisa: Leonardo Da Vinci's Greatest Painting. 1996. 354p. 22.95 o.p. (*0-8038-9381-7*) Hastings Hse. Daytrips Pubs.

Delahunt, Meaghan. In the Casa Azul: A Novel of Revolution & Betrayal. 2003. 320p. pap. 14.00 (*0-312-29107-8*) Picador.

—In the Casa Azul: A Novel of Revolution & Betrayal. 2002. 320p. 23.95 (*0-312-29106-X*) St. Martin's Pr.

Demi, Hitz. The Artist & the Architect, ERS. 1991. (Illus.). 32p. (J). (ps-2). 15.95 o.p. (*0-8050-1580-9*, Holt, Henry & Co. Bks. For Young Readers) Holt, Henry & Co.

Denoon, Anne. Back Flip: A Novel. 2002. (Illus.). 336p. pap. 24.95 (*0-88984-238-8*) Porcupine's Quill, Inc. CAN. *Dist:* Univ. of Toronto Pr.

Derwent, Lavinia. The Boy from Sula. 2002. (Kelpies Ser.). (Illus.). 160p. (J). pap. (*0-86315-400-X*) Floris Bks. GBR. *Dist:* SteinerBooks, Inc.

—Return to Sula. 1989. (Kelpie Ser.). 128p. (J). (gr. 5-8). pap. 6.95 o.p. (*0-86241-073-8*) Trafalgar Square.

—Song of Sula. 1989. (Kelpie Ser.). 128p. (J). (gr. 5-7). pap. 6.95 o.p. (*0-86241-135-1*) Trafalgar Square.

Diliberto, Gioia. I Am Madame X. 2003. (Illus.). 272p. 24.00 (*0-7432-1155-3*, Scribner) Simon & Schuster.

Dionetti, Michelle V. Painting the Wind: A Story of Vincent van Gogh. 1996. (Illus.). 32p. (J). (gr. 1-5). 15.95 (*0-316-18602-3*) Little Brown & Co.

Dunrea, Oliver. The Painter Who Loved Chickens, RS. 1995. (Illus.). 32p. (J). (ps-3). 15.00 o.p. (*0-374-35729-3*, Farrar, Straus & Giroux (BYR)) Farrar, Straus & Giroux.

Dunrea, Olivier. The Painter Who Loved Chickens, RS. 1998. (Illus.). 32p. (J). (gr. k-3). pap. 5.95 o.p. (*0-374-45708-5*, Sunburst) Farrar, Straus & Giroux.

Dye, Kitty. Meet George Winter: Pioneer Artist, Journalist, Entrepreneur. 2001. (Illus.). 232p. pap. 17.95 (*0-9702501-1-8*) LeClere Publishing Co.

Ebershoff, David. The Danish Girl: A Novel. 288p. 2001. 13.00 (*0-14-029848-7*); 2000. 24.95 o.s.i (*0-670-88808-7*, Viking) Viking Penguin.

Edwards, Michelle. A Baker's Portrait. 1991. (Illus.). 32p. (J). (gr. k up). lib. bdg. 13.88 o.p. (*0-688-09713-8*) HarperCollins Children's Bk. Group.

—Bakers Portrait. 1991. 13.95 o.p. (*0-688-09712-X*, Morrow, William & Co.) Morrow/Avon.

—Eve & Smithy. 1994. (J). (gr. 4 up). 15.00 o.p. (*0-688-11825-9*); (Illus.). 24p. lib. bdg. 14.93 o.p. (*0-688-11826-7*) HarperCollins Children's Bk. Group.

Ellison, Emily. The Picture Makers. l.t. ed. 1991. (General Ser.). 362p. lib. bdg. 20.95 (*0-8161-5166-0*, Macmillan Reference USA) Gale Group.

—The Picture Makers. 1990. 288p. 18.95 o.p. (*0-688-09581-X*, Morrow, William & Co.) Morrow/Avon.

Engel, Diana. Holding On. 1997. (Accelerated Reader Bks. ). (Illus.). 96p. (J). (gr. 3-7). 14.95 (*0-7614-5016-5*, Cavendish Children's Bks.) Cavendish, Marshall Corp.

Enquist, Anna. The Masterpiece. 2000. 278p. pap. 15.95 (*1-902881-21-4*) Toby Pr.

—The Masterpiece. Ringold, Jeannette K., tr. from DUT. 1999. 240p. 29.95 (*1-902881-05-2*) Toby Pr.

Eringer, Robert. Lo Mein. 2000. 224p. 19.95 (*1-929175-14-0*); pap. 14.95 (*1-929175-22-1*) Cote Literary Group, The. (Corinthian Bks.).

Ernst, Lisa Campbell. Hamilton's Art Show. 1986. (Illus.). 32p. (J). (ps-3). 12.95 o.p. (*0-688-04120-5*) HarperCollins Children's Bk. Group.

Farris, John. Soon She Will Be Gone. 1998. 387p. mass mkt. 6.99 (*0-8125-0954-4*); 1997. 352p. 24.95 (*0-312-85375-0*) Doherty, Tom Assocs., LLC. (Forge Bks.).

Feng Ji-cai. Let One Hundred Flowers Bloom. Smith, Christopher, tr. from CHI. 1996. 128p. (YA). (gr. 6 up). 13.99 o.s.i (*0-670-85805-6*, Viking Children's Bks.) Penguin Putnam Bks. for Young Readers.

Fielding, Brian. Rooster: An American Tragedy. 2000. x, 356p. 25.95 (*0-9676590-0-0*) Bodhisattva Pr., The.

Finney, Jack. From Time to Time: The Sequel to Time & Again. l.t. ed. 1995. (G. K. Hall Core Ser.). 610p. 25.95 o.p. (*0-7838-1387-2*, Macmillan Reference USA) Gale Group.

—From Time to Time: The Sequel to Time & Again. unabr. ed. 1995. audio 70.00 (*0-7887-0338-2*, 94530E7) Recorded Bks., LLC.

—From Time to Time: The Sequel to Time & Again. 1996. (Illus.). 304p. pap. 12.00 (*0-684-81844-2*, Touchstone); 1995. 288p. 22.50 o.p. (*0-671-89884-1*, Simon & Schuster) Simon & Schuster.

—From Time to Time: The Sequel to Time & Again. abr. ed. 1995. audio 23.00 (*0-671-52118-7*, 492039, Simon & Schuster Audioworks) Simon & Schuster Audio.

—Time & Again. 1995. reprint ed. lib. bdg. 25.95 (*0-89968-403-3*, Lightyear Pr.) Buccaneer Bks., Inc.

—Time & Again. l.t. ed. 1995. 512p. 25.95 o.p. (*0-7838-1386-4*, Macmillan Reference USA) Gale Group.

—Time & Again. unabr. ed. 1996. audio 97.00 (*0-7887-0344-7*, 94536E7) Recorded Bks., LLC.

—Time & Again. 1995. 25.00 (*0-684-80117-5*, Simon & Schuster); 1995. (Illus.). 400p. pap. 13.00 (*0-684-80105-1*, Touchstone); 1986. 400p. pap. 10.95 o.s.i (*0-671-24295-4*, Fireside) Simon & Schuster.

—Time & Again. abr. ed. 1995. audio 23.00 o.s.i (*0-671-52139-X*, 492983, Simon & Schuster Audioworks) Simon & Schuster Audio.

—Time & Again: Broadway Edition. 1997. pap. 11.00 (*0-684-83594-0*, Scribner Paper Fiction) Simon & Schuster.

Flanagan, Richard. Gould's Book of Fish: A Novel in Twelve Fish. 2003. 404p. pap. 14.00 (*0-8021-3959-0*); 2002. 416p. 27.50 (*0-8021-1711-2*) Grove/Atlantic, Inc. (Grove Pr.).

Fletcher, Jessica. A Palette for Murder: A Murder, She Wrote Mystery. 1996. (Murder She Wrote Ser.: Vol. 6). 304p. mass mkt. 6.50 (*0-451-18820-9*, Signet Bks.) NAL.

Florde, Katie. Dot to Dot. 2002. 320p. 24.95 (*0-312-27571-4*) St. Martin's Pr.

Foos, Laurie. Portrait of the Walrus by a Young Artist. 1997. 192p. 19.95 (*1-56689-057-8*) Coffee Hse. Pr.

—Portrait of the Walrus by a Young Artist. 1998. (Harvest Book Ser.). 176p. pap. 11.00 (*0-15-600543-3*, Harvest Bks.) Harcourt Trade Pubs.

Ford, Jeffrey. The Portrait of Mrs. Charbuque. 2003. 320p. pap. 12.95 (*0-06-093617-7*, Perennial) HarperTrade.

—The Portrait of Mrs. Charbuque. 2002. 320p. 24.95 (*0-06-621126-3*, Morrow, William & Co.) Morrow/Avon.

Francis, Dick. In the Frame. 1993. 272p. mass mkt. 6.99 (*0-449-22116-4*, Fawcett) Ballantine Bks.

—In the Frame. unabr. ed. 1996. audio 39.95 (*0-7861-1021-X*, 1799) Blackstone Audio Bks., Inc.

—In the Frame. unabr. ed. 2000. audio 49.95 (*0-7451-5952-4*, CAB 137) Chivers Audio Bks. GBR. *Dist:* BBC Audiobooks America.

—In the Frame. l.t. ed. 1994. 327p. lib. bdg. 22.95 o.p. (*0-8161-5783-9*, Macmillan Reference USA) Gale Group.

—In the Frame. unabr. ed. 1990. audio 44.00 (*1-55690-253-0*, 90026E7) Recorded Bks., LLC.

—In the Frame. 1989. 208p. mass mkt. 4.50 (*0-671-69648-3*); 1988. mass mkt. 3.95 (*0-671-67429-3*); 1987. mass mkt. 3.50 (*0-671-55658-4*); 1984. mass mkt. 3.50 (*0-671-50754-0*); 1982. mass mkt. 2.95 o.s.i (*0-671-45461-7*) Simon & Schuster. (Pocket).

—In the Frame. l.t. ed. 1977. (Ulverscroft Large Print Ser.). 12.00 o.p. (*0-7089-0060-7*, Ulverscroft) Thorpe, F. A. Pubs. GBR. *Dist:* Ulverscroft Large Print Bks., Ltd., Ulverscroft Large Print Canada, Ltd.

—To the Hilt. 1997. 352p. mass mkt. 6.99 (*0-515-12148-7*, Jove) Berkley Publishing Group.

—To the Hilt. unabr. ed. 1997. audio 56.00 (*0-913369-59-4*, 4287) Books on Tape, Inc.

—To the Hilt. 2015. 24.95 o.s.i (*0-399-14486-2*); 1996. 320p. 24.95 o.p. (*0-399-14185-5*, G. P. Putnam's Sons) Penguin Group (USA) Inc.

—To the Hilt. unabr. ed. 1997. audio 60.00 (*0-7887-0805-8*, 94954E7) Recorded Bks., LLC.

—To the Hilt. abr. ed. 1998. audio 14.40 (*0-671-57734-4*, 908766); 1996. audio 18.00 (*0-671-53630-3*, 394243) Simon & Schuster Audio. (Simon & Schuster Audioworks).

—To the Hilt. l.t. ed. 1996. (Basic Ser.). 492p. 28.95 (*0-7862-0892-9*) Thorndike Pr.

Furgerson, Celesta. Sculptured in Twilight. 1999. 202p. pap. 12.00 (*0-9679875-0-4*) River Bend Pr., Inc.

Futcher, Jane. Dream Lover. 1997. 260p. (Orig.). pap. 9.95 o.p. (*1-55583-375-6*) Alyson Pubns.

Geisert, Arthur. The Etcher's Studio. 1997. (Illus.). 32p. (J). (ps-3). lib. bdg., tchr. ed. 15.95 (*0-395-79754-3*) Houghton Mifflin Co.

Ghosh, Amitav. Circle of Reason. 2000. 423p. 19.95 (*81-7530-039-6*) Dayal, Ravi Pub. IND. *Dist:* South Asia Bks.

—Circle of Reason. 1986. 432p. 17.95 o.p. (*0-670-80984-5*) Viking Penguin.

—The Circle of Reason. 1990. 432p. pap. 8.95 o.p. (*0-14-013368-2*, Penguin Bks.) Viking Penguin.

Glass, Andrew. Jackson Makes His Move. 1982. (Illus.). 48p. (J). (gr. 1-4). 9.95 o.p. (*0-7232-6207-1*, Warne, Frederick) Penguin Putnam Bks. for Young Readers.

Gormley, Beatrice. Richard & the Vratch. 1987. (Illus.). 144p. pap. 2.95 o.p. (*0-380-75207-7*, Avon Bks.) Morrow/Avon.

Gray, Alasdair. Lanark: A Life in Four Books. 560p. 1986. pap. 9.95 (*0-8076-1162-X*); 1985. reprint ed. 20.00 (*0-8076-1108-5*) Braziller, George Inc.

—Lanark: A Life in Four Books, 4 bks., Set. 1996. (Harvest Book Ser.). 576p. pap. 16.00 o.s.i (*0-15-600361-9*, Harvest Bks.) Harcourt Trade Pubs.

—Lanark: A Life in Four Books. 1981. 488p. pap. o.p. (*0-06-090862-9*, CN 862) HarperCollins Pubs.

Greenan, Russell. It Happened in Boston? 2003. 304p. pap. 12.95 (*0-8129-7066-7*, Modern Library) Random House Adult Trade Publishing Group.

Greenan, Russell H. It Happened in Boston? 1987. 240p. (Orig.). mass mkt. 3.50 o.s.i (*0-553-25718-8*) Bantam Bks.

Greenleaf, Ann. Emily's New Ghost. 1993. (J). 2.99 o.s.i (*0-517-09159-3*) Random Hse. Value Publishing.

Grice, Julia. The Cutting Hours. 1995. 300p. mass mkt. 4.99 (*0-8125-1092-5*, Tor Bks.); 1993. 288p. 20.95 o.p. (*0-312-85677-6*, Forge Bks.) Doherty, Tom Assocs., LLC.

Gurganus, Allan. Plays Well with Others. unabr. collector's ed. 1998. audio 96.00 (*0-7366-4206-4*, 4702) Books on Tape, Inc.

—Plays Well with Others. 1999. 368p. pap. 14.00 (*0-375-70203-2*, Vintage) Knopf Publishing Group.

—Plays Well with Others. 1997. 336p. 25.00 o.p. (*0-394-58914-9*) Knopf, Alfred A. Inc.

—Plays Well with Others. abr. ed. 1997. audio 18.00 o.s.i (*0-679-46055-1*, RH Audio) Random Hse. Audio Publishing Group.

Gutcheon, Beth Richardson. Domestic Pleasures. 2001. 368p. pap. 13.00 (*0-06-093476-X*, Perennial) HarperTrade.

Halligan, Marion. The Golden Dress. 1999. 380p. (*0-14-027302-6*) Penguin Group (USA) Inc.

Hansen-Young, Diana. Mango Hill. 1988. pap. 6.95 o.p. (*0-89610-150-9*) Island Heritage Publishing.

Hanson, Rick. Extreme Odds. 1998. 240p. 22.00 o.s.i (*1-57566-333-3*) Kensington Publishing Corp.

—Mortal Remains. 1996. mass mkt. 4.99 o.s.i (*0-7860-0284-0*, Pinnacle Bks.); 1995. 256p. mass mkt. 18.95 o.p. (*0-8217-4955-2*, Zebra Bks.) Kensington Publishing Corp.

—Spare Parts. 1995. 256p. mass mkt. 4.99 o.s.i (*0-7860-0156-9*, Pinnacle Bks.); 1995. 256p. mass mkt. 4.99 (*0-8217-0156-8*, Zebra Bks.); 1994. 288p. mass mkt. 20.00 o.s.i (*0-8217-4738-X*, Zebra Bks.) Kensington Publishing Corp.

—Splitting Heirs. (Adam McCleet Mysteries Ser. ). 1998. 256p. mass mkt. 5.99 o.s.i (*1-57566-365-1*); 1997. 240p. 21.95 o.p. (*1-57566-194-2*, Kensington Bks.) Kensington Publishing Corp.

—Still Life. (Adam McCleet Mysteries Ser. ). 1997. 256p. mass mkt. 5.50 o.s.i (*1-57566-200-0*); 1996. 204p. 19.95 o.s.i (*1-57566-041-5*) Kensington Publishing Corp.

Harding, William H. Alvin's Famous No-Horse, ERS. 1992. (Redfeather Bks.). (Illus.). 80p. (J). (gr. 2-4). 14.95 o.p. (*0-8050-2227-9*, Holt, Henry & Co. Bks. For Young Readers) Holt, Henry & Co.

Harding, William Harry. Alvin's No-Horse, ERS. 1994. 80p. (J). pap. 4.95 o.s.i (*0-8050-3274-6*, Holt, Henry & Co. Bks. For Young Readers) Holt, Henry & Co.

Haskell, John. I Am Not Jackson Pollock: Stories. 2003. (Illus.). 192p. 20.00 (*0-374-17399-0*) Farrar, Straus & Giroux.

—I Am Not Jackson Pollock: Stories. 2004. 192p. pap. 12.00 (*0-312-42186-9*) Picador.

Hauser, Marianne. Shootout with Father. 2002. 100p. pap. 11.95 (*1-57366-100-7*) Fiction Collective Two, Inc.

Havill, Juanita. Sato & the Elephants. 1993. (Illus.). (J). (ps-3). 15.00 o.p. (*0-688-11155-6*); 32p. lib. bdg. 14.93 (*0-688-11156-4*) HarperCollins Children's Bk. Group.

Hawthorne, Nathaniel. The Marble Faun. 1966. (Airmont Classics Ser.). mass mkt. 1.95 o.p. (*0-8049-0104-X*, CL-104) Airmont Publishing Co., Inc.

—The Marble Faun. 2004. 288p. pap. 3.50 (*0-486-43411-7*) Dover Pubns., Inc.

—The Marble Faun. 2002. Vol. 1. 168p. 93.99 (*1-4043-1676-0*); Vol. 1. 168p. per. 88.99 (*1-4043-1677-9*); Vol. 2. 204p. 94.99 (*1-4043-1678-7*); Vol. 2. 204p. per. 89.99 (*1-4043-1679-5*) IndyPublish.com.

—The Marble Faun. 1968. mass mkt. 0.50 o.p. (*0-451-50112-8*, Signet Classics); 1968. mass mkt. 0.75 o.p. (*0-451-50423-2*, Signet Classics); 1968. mass mkt. 0.60 o.p. (*0-451-50321-X*, Signet Classics); 1961. pap. 3.95 o.p. (*0-452-00903-0*, Meridian Bks.); 1961. 352p. pap. 4.95 o.p. (*0-452-01012-8*); 1961. mass mkt. 1.95 o.p. (*0-451-51316-9*, Signet Classics); 1961. mass mkt. 3.50 o.p. (*0-451-51991-4*, CE1771, Signet Classics); 1961. mass mkt. 1.25 o.p. (*0-451-50851-3*, Signet Classics); 1961. mass mkt. 1.50 o.p. (*0-451-51084-4*, Signet Classics); 1961. mass mkt. 2.95 o.p. (*0-451-51771-7*, Signet Classics) NAL.

—The Marble Faun. 2001. (Twelve-Point Ser.). 450p. lib. bdg. 25.00 (*1-58287-159-0*); 570p. lib. bdg. 26.00 (*1-58287-642-8*) North Bks.

—The Marble Faun. Charvat, William et al, eds. 1969. (Centenary Edition of the Works of Nathaniel Hawthorne: Vol. 4). (Illus.). 610p. text 83.95 (*0-8142-0062-1*) Ohio State Univ. Pr.

—The Marble Faun. Manning, Susan, ed. 2002. (Oxford World's Classics Ser.). (Illus.). 432p. pap. 9.95 (*0-19-283976-4*) Oxford Univ. Pr., Inc.

—The Marble Faun. 1992. (Notable American Authors Ser.). reprint ed. lib. bdg. 75.00 (*0-7812-3041-1*) Reprint Services Corp.

—The Marble Faun. E-Book 5.00 (*0-7410-1449-1*); E-Book 5.00 (*0-7410-1275-8*) SoftBook Pr.

—The Marble Faun. l.t. ed. 2003. 652p. 28.95 (*0-7862-6106-4*, Large Print Pr.) Thorndike Pr.

—The Marble Faun. 1990. 16.00 (*0-606-20784-8*) Turtleback Bks.

—The Marble Faun. Bradbury, Malcolm, ed. 1995. 424p. pap. 6.95 (*0-460-87532-9*, Everyman's Classic Library in Paperback) Tuttle Publishing.

—The Marble Faun. 1990. (Classics Ser.). 480p. 9.95 (*0-14-039077-4*, Penguin Classics) Viking Penguin.

—The Marble Faun: Or the Romance of Monte Beni. 2001. E-Book 2.95 (*1-58882-564-7*) PublishingOnline.

—The Marble Faun: or The Romance of Monte Beni. 2002. (Modern Library Classics). 496p. pap. 9.95 (*0-375-75928-X*, Modern Library) Random House Adult Trade Publishing Group.

Haynes, Mary. Catch the Sea. 1990. 176p. pap. 3.95 o.p. (*0-14-034369-5*, Puffin Bks.) Penguin Putnam Bks. for Young Readers.

—Catch the Sea. 1989. 176p. (J). (gr. 4 up). lib. bdg. 13.95 o.p. (*0-02-743451-6*, Simon & Schuster Children's Publishing) Simon & Schuster Children's Publishing.

Heller, Murray. Placid's View: A Mike Diamond Mystery. 1997. 196p. 22.50 (*0-935796-81-9*) Purple Mountain Pr., Ltd.

Heller, Nicholas. The Giant. 1997. (Illus.). 24p. (J). (gr. k-3). 15.00 o.s.i (*0-688-15224-4*); lib. bdg. 14.93 o.p. (*0-688-15225-2*) HarperCollins Children's Bk. Group. (Greenwillow Bks.).

Hendry, Diana. The Rainbow Watchers. 1991. (Illus.). 48p. (J). (gr. 1 up). 10.95 o.p. (*0-688-10305-7*) HarperCollins Children's Bk. Group.

Henry, Marguerite. Benjamin West & His Cat Grimalkin. 2000. 160p. (J). per. 14.95 (*0-9705618-0-6*) Bradford Pr.

—Benjamin West & His Cat Grimalkin. rev. ed. 1985. (Illus.). 160p. (J). (gr. 3-7). 13.95 o.p. (*0-02-743660-8*, Simon & Schuster Children's Publishing) Simon & Schuster Children's Publishing.

Henry, O. The Last Leaf. 1980. (Creative's Classic Short Stories Ser.). (Illus.). 32p. (YA). (gr. 5-12). lib. bdg. 19.93 o.p. (*0-87191-774-2*, Creative Education) Creative Co., The.

Herman, George. A Comedy of Murders. 1994. 448p. 23.95 o.p. (*0-7867-0064-5*, Carroll & Graf Pubs.) Avalon Publishing Group.

—The Tears of the Madonna. 1996. 288p. 22.95 o.p. (*0-7867-0243-5*, Carroll & Graf Pubs.) Avalon Publishing Group.

Hest, Amy. Nana's Birthday Party. 1993. (Illus.). 32p. (J). (ps-3). 15.95 (*0-688-07497-9*) HarperCollins Children's Bk. Group.

—Nana's Birthday Party. 1993. (Illus.). 32p. (J). (gr. k up). lib. bdg. 14.93 o.p. (*0-688-07498-7*, Morrow, William & Co.) Morrow/Avon.

Highwater, Jamake. I Wear the Morning Star. 1986. (Charlotte Zolotow Bk.). 160p. (YA). (gr. 7 up). lib. bdg. 12.89 o.p. (*0-06-022356-1*) HarperCollins Children's Bk. Group.

Hoffman, Jill. Jilted. 1993. 320p. 20.00 o.p. (*0-671-79518-X*, Simon & Schuster) Simon & Schuster.

Houghton, John. A Distant Shore: A Novel. 1994. pap. 10.99 o.p. (*0-7852-8228-9*) Nelson, Thomas Inc.

Howard, Maureen. A Lover's Almanac. 1999. 288p. pap. 12.95 (*0-14-027512-6*, Penguin Classics) Penguin Group (USA) Inc.

—A Lover's Almanac. 1998. (Illus.). 288p. 24.95 (*0-670-87597-X*) Viking Penguin.

Howell, Brian. The Dance of Geometry. 2002. 214p. 24.95 (*1-902881-47-8*) Toby Pr.

Howker, Janni. The Topiary Garden. 1995. (Illus.). 64p. (YA). (gr. 2 up). mass mkt. 14.95 o.p. (*0-531-06891-9*, Orchard Bks.) Scholastic, Inc.

Hunter, Fred. Capital Queers. (Alex Reynolds Mysteries Ser.). 2000. 232p. pap. 12.95 (*0-312-26301-5*, Saint Martin's Griffin); 1999. 224p. 23.95 o.p. (*0-312-20463-9*, Saint Martin's Minotaur) St. Martin's Pr.

—Federal Fag. (Alex Reynolds Mysteries Ser.). 272p. 1999. pap. 11.95 (*0-312-20649-6*, Saint Martin's Griffin); 1998. 22.95 o.p. (*0-312-18580-4*, Saint Martin's Minotaur) St. Martin's Pr.

—Government Gay. (Alex Reynolds Mysteries Ser.). 1998. 224p. pap. 11.95 (*0-312-18721-1*, Saint Martin's Griffin); 1997. 215p. text 21.95 o.p. (*0-312-15536-0*, Saint Martin's Minotaur) St. Martin's Pr.

—National Nancys. 2000. (Alex Reynolds Mysteries Ser.). 240p. 22.95 (*0-312-25233-1*, Saint Martin's Minotaur) St. Martin's Pr.

Hurd, Thacher. Art Dog. (Trophy Picture Book Ser.). (Illus.). 32p. (J). (ps-3). 1998. pap. 6.99 (*0-06-443489-3*, Harper Trophy); 1996. 14.95 (*0-06-024424-0*); 1996. lib. bdg. 15.89 (*0-06-024425-9*) HarperCollins Children's Bk. Group.

Hustvedt, Siri. What I Loved: A Novel. 2003. 384p. 25.00 (*0-8050-7170-9*) Holt, Henry & Co.

—What I Loved: A Novel. 2004. 384p. pap. 14.00 (*0-312-42119-2*); 2003. mass mkt. 7.99 (*0-312-99387-0*) Picador.

Iles, Greg. Dead Sleep. 2002. 480p. reprint ed. mass mkt. 7.99 (*0-451-20652-5*, Signet Bks.) NAL.

—Dead Sleep. 2001. 352p. 19.95 o.p. (*0-399-14735-7*) Penguin Group (USA) Inc.

—Dead Sleep. l.t. ed. 12.95 (*1-4104-0053-0*, Large Print Pr.); 2003. 703p. pap. 12.95 (*0-7862-3681-7*); 2001. 681p. 30.95 (*0-7862-3682-5*) Thorndike Pr.

Innis, W. Joe. Also Rising. 1998. 22.95 o.p. (*1-57168-196-5*) Eakin Pr.

—Also Rising. 2000. 268p. pap. 16.95 (*0-595-15200-7*, Backinprint.com) iUniverse, Inc.

Ishiguro, Kazuo. An Artist of the Floating World. 1989. (Vintage International Ser.). 208p. pap. 12.00 (*0-679-72266-1*, Vintage) Knopf Publishing Group.

—An Artist of the Floating World. 1986. 208p. 15.95 o.p. (*0-399-13119-1*) Putnam Publishing Group, The.

—An Artist of the Floating World. 2000. 26.50 (*0-8446-7123-1*) Smith, Peter Pub., Inc.

—An Artist of the Floating World. l.t. ed. 2001. 262p. pap. 25.95 (*0-7862-3565-9*); 280p. (*0-7540-4620-6*); 280p. (*0-7540-4619-2*) Thorndike Pr.

Isom, Joan Shaddox. The First Starry Night. (Illus.). 32p. (J). (gr. k-7). 2001. pap. 6.95 (*1-58089-027-X*); 1998. 16.95 (*1-879085-96-8*) Charlesbridge Publishing, Inc. (Whispering Coyote).

Jenkins, Robin. Poor Angus. 2000. 320p. pap. 15.00 (*1-84195-002-5*) Canongate Bks. GBR. *Dist:* Grove/Atlantic, Inc.

Joyce, James. A Portrait of an Artist As a Young Man. 1992. 256p. mass mkt. 4.95 (*0-553-21404-7*, Bantam Classics) Bantam Bks.

—A Portrait of the Artist As a Young Man. 2001. (Illus.). E-Book 4.95 (*1-931208-62-X*) Adobe Systems, Inc.

—A Portrait of the Artist As a Young Man. 22.95 (*0-89190-725-4*) Amereon, Ltd.

—A Portrait of the Artist As a Young Man. abr. ed. 1993. audio 16.99 (*0-88646-343-2*) Durkin Hayes Publishing Ltd.

—A Portrait of the Artist As a Young Man. Gabler, Hans W. & Hettche, Walter, eds. 1993. 366p. text 61.00 (*0-8153-1278-4*) Garland Publishing, Inc.

—A Portrait of the Artist As a Young Man. abr. ed. audio 12.95 o.p. (*0-694-50084-4*, SWC 1110, Caedmon) HarperTrade.

—A Portrait of the Artist As a Young Man. 1993. 288p. pap. 10.00 (*0-679-73989-0*, Vintage) Knopf Publishing Group.

—A Portrait of the Artist As a Young Man. 1991. (Everyman's Library: Vol. 9). 368p. 17.00 (*0-679-40575-5*) Knopf, Alfred A. Inc.

—A Portrait of the Artist As a Young Man. 1991. 256p. mass mkt. 4.95 (*0-451-52544-2*, Signet Classics) NAL.

—A Portrait of the Artist As a Young Man. abr. ed. 1996. (Works of James Joyce). audio 17.98 (*962-634-570-5*, NA307014, Naxos AudioBooks) Naxos of America, Inc.

—A Portrait of the Artist As a Young Man. Johnson, Jeri, ed. & intro. by. 2001. 352p. pap. 7.95 (*0-19-283998-5*) Oxford Univ. Pr., Inc.

—A Portrait of the Artist As a Young Man. Kershner, R. B., ed. 1993. (Case Studies in Contemporary Criticism). 416p. (C). text 35.00 o.p. (*0-312-08987-2*) Palgrave Macmillan.

—A Portrait of the Artist As a Young Man. 2003. 384p. pap. 9.00 (*0-14-243734-4*); 1999. 240p. pap. 10.95 (*0-14-028328-5*); 1977. pap. 1.95 o.p. (*0-14-004579-1*); 1964. pap. 1.65 o.p. (*0-670-00009-4*) Penguin Group (USA) Inc.

—A Portrait of the Artist As a Young Man. 1996. (Modern Library Ser.). 368p. 17.95 (*0-679-60232-1*) Random Hse., Inc.

—A Portrait of the Artist As a Young Man. 1995. pap. 13.95 o.p. (*0-312-13845-8*) St. Martin's Pr.

—A Portrait of the Artist As a Young Man. 1916. 15.00 (*0-606-02826-9*) Turtleback Bks.

—A Portrait of the Artist As a Young Man. 1993. (Penguin Twentieth-Century Classics Ser.). 384p. pap. 8.95 o.s.i (*0-14-018683-2*, Penguin Classics) Viking Penguin.

—A Portrait of the Artist As a Young Man. Ellmann, Richard, ed. 1982. 17.50 o.p. (*0-670-56683-7*) Viking Penguin.

—A Portrait of the Artist As a Young Man. 1964. 256p. pap. 7.00 o.p. (*0-14-004221-0*, Penguin Bks.); 1964. 10.00 o.p. (*0-670-56682-9*); 1916. 3.50 o.p. (*0-670-56681-0*) Viking Penguin.

—A Portrait of the Artist As a Young Man. 1997. (Classics Ser.). 208p. pap. 3.95 (*1-85326-006-1*, 0061WW) Wordsworth Editions, Ltd. GBR. *Dist:* Casemate Pubs. & Bk. Distributors, LLC.

—A Portrait of the Artist As a Young Man. abr. ed. 1995. (Works of James Joyce). audio compact disk 19.98 (*962-634-070-3*, NA307012, Naxos AudioBooks) Naxos of America, Inc.

—A Portrait of the Artist As a Young Man, Set. unabr. ed. 1994. audio 41.95 (*1-55685-317-3*) Audio Bk. Contractors, Inc.

—A Portrait of the Artist As a Young Man. unabr. ed. 1995. audio 49.95 (*0-7861-0655-7*, 1559) Blackstone Audio Bks., Inc.

—A Portrait of the Artist As a Young Man. unabr. collector's ed. 1992. (J). audio 56.00 (*0-7366-2301-9*, 3085) Books on Tape, Inc.

—A Portrait of the Artist As a Young Man. 1992. 350p. reprint ed. lib. bdg. 26.95 (*0-89966-899-2*) Buccaneer Bks., Inc.

—A Portrait of the Artist As a Young Man. reprint ed. lib. bdg. 98.00 (*0-7426-3127-3*); 2001. pap. text 28.00 (*0-7426-8127-0*) Classic Bks.

—A Portrait of the Artist As a Young Man. 1994. (Thrift Editions Ser.). 192p. reprint ed. pap. 2.00 (*0-486-28050-0*) Dover Pubns., Inc.

—A Portrait of the Artist As a Young Man. unabr. ed. 1993. (YA). (gr. 11-12). audio 28.00 Jimcin Recordings.

—A Portrait of the Artist As a Young Man. l.t. ed. 1995. 410p. lib. bdg. 26.00 (*0-939495-86-4*); 1998. 255p. reprint ed. lib. bdg. 25.00 (*1-58287-057-8*) North Bks.

—A Portrait of the Artist As a Young Man, unabr. ed. 1999. audio 70.00 (*1-55690-421-5*, 91106E7) Recorded Bks., LLC.

—A Portrait of the Artist As a Young Man. 1998. (Enriched Classics Ser.). (Illus.). 288p. reprint ed. mass mkt. 5.99 (*0-671-01538-9*, Pocket) Simon & Schuster.

—A Portrait of the Artist As a Young Man: Text & Criticism. Anderson, Chester G., ed. (Critical Studies). 1977. 576p. 15.95 (*0-14-015503-1*); 1964. (J). (gr. 9 up). pap. 8.95 o.p. (*0-670-56648-9*) Viking Penguin.

—Stephen Hero. rev. ed. 1963. (Illus.). pap. 11.95 (*0-8112-0074-4*, NDP133) New Directions Publishing Corp.

—Ulysses. 2001. (Modern Library Ser.). E-Book 9.95 (*1-931208-63-8*) Adobe Systems, Inc.

—Ulysses. 2002. 800p. 26.00 (*0-375-50794-9*) Random Hse., Inc.

—Ulysses: A Reproduction of the 1922 First Edition. 2002. (Illus.). 736p. pap. 29.95 (*0-486-42444-8*) Dover Pubns., Inc.

Joyce, James, et al. A Portrait of the Artist As a Young Man. 1999. (Literature Made Easy Ser.). 85p. pap. 4.95 (*0-7641-0825-5*) Barron's Educational Series, Inc.

Kernan, Michael. The Lost Diaries of Frans Hals. 1995. pap. 13.95 (*0-312-13117-8*, Saint Martin's Griffin); 1994. 336p. 23.95 o.p. (*0-312-10946-6*) St. Martin's Pr.

Kidd, Richard. Almost Famous Daisy: Around the World in Famous Paintings. 2000. (Illus.). 32p. (J). (gr. k-4). pap. 9.99 (*0-7112-1070-5*) Lincoln, Frances Ltd. GBR. *Dist:* Antique Collectors' Club.

—Almost Famous Daisy: Around the World in Famous Paintings. 1996. (Illus.). 32p. (J). (ps-3). mass mkt. 16.00 o.s.i (*0-689-80390-7*, Simon & Schuster Children's Publishing) Simon & Schuster Children's Publishing.

Killien, Christi. Rusty Fertlanger, Lady's Man. 1989. 144p. (J). reprint ed. mass mkt. 2.95 o.s.i (*0-440-20414-3*) Dell Publishing.

—Rusty Fertlanger, Lady's Man. 1988. 144p. (J). (gr. 5-9). 13.95 o.p. (*0-395-46762-4*) Houghton Mifflin Co.

King, Ross. Domino. 2003. 448p. pap. 14.00 (*0-14-200336-0*) Penguin Group (USA) Inc.

Occupations

—Domino. 2002. 448p. 26.00 (*0-8027-3378-6*) Walker & Co.

Kingman, Lee. The Refiner's Fire, 001. 1981. (J). (gr. 7 up). 8.95 o.p. (*0-395-31606-5*) Houghton Mifflin Co.

Kinsey-Warnock, Natalie. The Canada Geese Quilt. 1989. (Illus.). 6p. (J). (gr. 4-7). 15.99 (*0-525-65004-0*, Dutton Children's Bks.) Penguin Putnam Bks. for Young Readers.

—The Canada Geese Quilt. 1992. (Illus.). 64p. (gr. 4-7). pap. text 3.99 o.s.i (*0-440-40719-2*, Yearling) Random Hse. Children's Bks.

Koch, Stephen. The Bachelor's Bride. 1986. 224p. 18.95 o.p. (*0-7145-2856-0*) Boyars, Marion Pubs., Inc.

Koho, Sharon Lewis. The Painting on the Pond. 2003. 198p. pap. 13.95 (*1-55517-703-4*, 77034, Bonneville Bks.) Cedar Fort, Inc./CFI Distribution.

Koren, Elaine Todd. Suzanne: Of Love & Art. Date not set. 21.95 (*0-9672355-3-7*); 2001. 377p. pap. 14.95 (*0-9672355-2-9*) Maverick Bks.

Koss, Amy Goldman. What Luck! A Duck! 1991. (Illus.). 32p. (J). (ps-2). 7.95 o.p. (*0-8431-1942-X*, Price Stern Sloan) Penguin Putnam Bks. for Young Readers.

Kozak, Harley Jane. Dating Dead Men. 2004. 336p. 22.95 (*0-385-51018-7*); pap. (*0-345-46521-0*) Doubleday Publishing.

Kruger, Michael. The Man in the Tower. 1993. 176p. 19.95 (*0-8076-1297-9*) Braziller, George Inc.

Laden, Nina. When Pigasso Met Mootisse. 1998. (Illus.). 40p. (J). (ps-5). 16.95 (*0-8118-1121-2*) Chronicle Bks. LLC.

Lager, Claude. A Tale of Two Rats. 1991. (Illus.). 32p. (J). (gr. k-3). 13.95 o.p. (*1-55670-228-0*) Stewart, Tabori & Chang.

Laurence, Janet. Canaletto & the Case of the Westminster Bridge, Vol. 1. 1998. (Canaletto & the Case of the Westminster Bridge Ser.: Vol. 1). 400p. 24.95 o.p. (*0-312-18551-0*, Saint Martin's Minotaur) St. Martin's Pr.

—Canaletto & the Case of Westminster Bridge. l.t. ed. 1999. (Magna Large Print Ser.). 416p. (*0-7505-1370-5*) Magna Large Print Bks. GBR. *Dist:* Ulverscroft Large Print Canada, Ltd.

Le Guin, Ursula K. & Sanders, Scott R. The Visionary, The Life Story of Flicker of the Serpentine & Wonders Hidden: Audubon's Early Years. 1988. (Capra Back-to-Back Ser.: No. 1). 133p. (C). reprint ed. lib. bdg. 27.00 o.p. (*0-8095-4100-9*) Millefleurs.

Leaf, Margaret. Eyes of the Dragon. 1987. (Illus.). 32p. (J). (ps-2). 18.00 o.p. (*0-688-06155-9*); lib. bdg. 16.93 o.p. (*0-688-06156-7*) HarperCollins Children's Bk. Group.

Leggat, Gillian. The Artist & the Bully. 1992. (Junior African Writers Ser.). (Illus.). (J). (gr. 5-6). pap. o.p. (*0-7910-2913-1*) Chelsea Hse. Pubs.

Lehan, Daniel. This Is Not a Book about Dodos. 1992. (Illus.). 320p. (J). (gr. k-3). 14.00 o.p. (*0-525-44878-0*, Dutton Children's Bks.) Penguin Putnam Bks. for Young Readers.

Levoy, Myron. A Shadow Like a Leopard. (Trophy Bk.). 192p. 1994. (J). (gr. 4-7). pap. 3.95 o.p. (*0-06-440458-7*, Harper Trophy); 1981. (YA). (gr. 7 up). lib. bdg. 12.89 o.p. (*0-06-023817-8*) HarperCollins Children's Bk. Group.

—A Shadow Like a Leopard. 1982. 144p. mass mkt. 2.50 o.p. (*0-451-13698-5*, Signet Vista) NAL.

—A Shadow Like a Leopard. 1995. 18.00 o.p. (*0-8446-6814-1*) Smith, Peter Pub., Inc.

Lewis, Beverly. Pickle Pizza. 1996. (Cul-de-Sac Kids Ser.: Vol. 8). 80p. (J). (gr. 2-5). pap. 3.99 (*1-55661-728-3*) Bethany Hse. Pubs.

Lewis, Wyndham. The Apes of God. 1992. (Illus.). 642p. reprint ed. 25.00 o.p. (*0-87685-513-3*, Black Sparrow Pr.) Godine, David R. Pub.

—The Apes of God. 1992. (Illus.). 642p. reprint ed. pap. 17.50 (*0-87685-512-5*) HarperCollins Pubs.

Lewitt, Shariann. Memento Mori. 1995. 288p. (YA). 21.95 o.p. (*0-312-85625-3*, Tor Bks.) Doherty, Tom Assocs., LLC.

Libera, Antoni. Madame. Kolakowska, Agniewska, tr. from POL. 2000. vi, 439p. 26.00 o.p. (*0-374-20006-8*) Farrar, Straus & Giroux.

Libonati, Gerald. The Artist's Life. 2002. (Illus.). 40p. pap. 11.95 (*1-886383-40-5*); 2000. 150p. pap. 12.95 (*1-883573-65-3*) Windstorm Creative Ltd.

Lionni, Leo. Matthew's Dream. 1991. (Illus.). 32p. (J). (ps-3). 15.00 o.s.i (*0-679-81075-7*, Knopf Bks. for Young Readers) Random Hse. Children's Bks.

—Matthew's Dream. 1995. (Illus.). 32p. (ps-3). pap. 5.99 (*0-679-87318-X*) Random Hse., Inc.

—Matthew's Dream. 1995. (J). 12.14 (*0-606-07847-9*) Turtleback Bks.

Littlesugar, Amy & Garrison, Barbara. Josiah True & the Art Maker. 1995. (J). 15.00 o.s.i (*0-671-88354-2*, Simon & Schuster Children's Publishing) Simon & Schuster Children's Publishing.

Littleton, Mark. Secrets of Moonlight Mountain. 1993. (J). mass mkt. 3.99 o.p. (*0-89081-960-2*) Harvest Hse. Pubs.

Llorente, Pilar Molina. The Apprentice. 1994. 11.00 (*0-606-16136-8*) Turtleback Bks.

—Apprentice, RS. 1993. 112p. (J). (gr. 4-7). 13.00 o.p. (*0-374-30389-4*, Farrar, Straus & Giroux (BYR)) Farrar, Straus & Giroux.

—The Apprentice, RS. 1994. (Illus.). 112p. (YA). (gr. 4-7). pap. 4.95 (*0-374-40432-1*, Sunburst) Farrar, Straus & Giroux.

Locker, Thomas. Miranda's Smile. (J). 2000. (Illus.). pap. 4.99 (*0-14-055669-9*, Puffin Bks.); 1994. 32p. 15.99 o.s.i (*0-8037-1688-5*, Dial Bks. for Young Readers); 1994. 32p. 15.89 o.s.i (*0-8037-1689-3*, Dial Bks. for Young Readers) Penguin Putnam Bks. for Young Readers.

—The Young Artist. (Illus.). 32p. (J). 1993. pap. 4.99 o.s.i (*0-14-054923-4*, Puffin Bks.); 1989. 15.89 o.s.i (*0-8037-0627-8*, Dial Bks. for Young Readers) Penguin Putnam Bks. for Young Readers.

Long, Joanna. An Artist Now Unknown. 2000. (Illus.). xiv, 210p. pap. 19.95 (*1-57736-201-2*, Hillsboro Pr.) Providence Hse. Pubs.

Lurie, Alison. Real People. 1998. 188p. pap. 12.00 o.s.i (*0-8050-5181-3*, Owl Bks.) Holt, Henry & Co.

Madden, Deirdre. Authenticity. 2002. 300p. pap. (*0-571-21446-0*) Faber & Faber, Inc.

Malcolm, Jahnna N. Libra: Into the Light. 1995. (Zodiac Ser.: No. 3). 176p. mass mkt. 3.99 o.p. (*0-06-106269-3*, HarperTorch) Morrow/Avon.

Mann, Helen R. Crawford's Horn Winding: A Biographical Novel about Ethan Allen Crawford & His Wife, Lucy, of Crawford Notch. 1997. 390p. 25.00 (*0-914339-63-X*) Randall, Peter E. Pub.

Mariconda, Barbara. Turn the Cup Around. 1998. 160p. (gr. 3-7). reprint ed. pap. text 3.99 o.s.i (*0-440-41311-7*, Yearling) Random Hse. Children's Bks.

Markun, Patricia Maloney. The Little Painter of Sabana Grande. 1993. (Illus.). 32p. (J). (ps-2). text 14.95 (*0-02-762205-3*, Simon & Schuster Children's Publishing) Simon & Schuster Children's Publishing.

Martin, Ann M. Claudia & the Genius of Elm Street. 1996. (Baby-Sitters Club Ser.: No. 49). (J). (gr. 3-7). lib. bdg. 21.27 o.p. (*0-8368-1573-4*) Stevens, Gareth Inc.

—Claudia & the Genius of Elm Street. 1991. (Baby-Sitters Club Ser.: No. 49). (J). (gr. 3-7). 9.30 (*0-606-00357-6*) Turtleback Bks.

—Claudia & the Mystery in the Painting. 1997. (Baby-Sitters Club Mystery Ser.: No. 32). 144p. (J). (gr. 3-7). mass mkt. 3.99 (*0-590-05972-6*) Scholastic, Inc.

—Claudia & the Mystery in the Painting. 1997. (Baby-Sitters Club Mystery Ser.: No. 32). (J). (gr. 3-7). 10.04 (*0-606-11076-3*) Turtleback Bks.

Maugham, W. Somerset. The Moon & Sixpence. 22.95 (*0-8488-2653-1*) Amereon, Ltd.

—The Moon & Sixpence. 1977. (Works of W. Somerset Maugham). reprint ed. 23.95 (*0-405-07816-1*) Ayer Co. Pubs., Inc.

—The Moon & Sixpence. 1995. 256p. mass mkt. 4.95 o.s.i (*0-553-21441-1*, Bantam Classics) Bantam Bks.

—The Moon & Sixpence. unabr. ed. 1995. (Thrift Editions Ser.). 176p. reprint ed. pap. text 2.00 (*0-486-28731-9*) Dover Pubns., Inc.

—The Moon & Sixpence. 2002. 244p. 18.99 (*1-4043-1902-6*); per. 13.99 (*1-4043-1903-4*) IndyPublish.com.

—The Moon & Sixpence. 2000. (Dover Thrift Editions Ser.). 288p. pap. 12.00 (*0-375-72456-7*, Vintage) Knopf Publishing Group.

—The Moon & Sixpence. 1993. 288p. mass mkt. 4.95 o.s.i (*0-451-52567-1*, Signet Classics) NAL.

—The Moon & Sixpence. 1998. 242p. reprint ed. lib. bdg. 25.00 (*1-58287-050-0*) North Bks.

—The Moon & Sixpence. 1997. (Ghosts of Fear Street Ser.: Vol. 22). 128p. (J). (gr. 3-6). pap. 3.99 (*0-671-00851-X*, Aladdin) Simon & Schuster Children's Publishing.

—The Moon & Sixpence. unabr. ed. 1997. 156p. reprint ed. pap. 14.95 o.p. (*1-57002-016-7*) University Publishing Hse., Inc.

—The Moon & Sixpence. (Twentieth Century Classics Ser.). 224p. 1993. 9.95 (*0-14-018597-6*, Penguin Classics); 1977. pap. 5.95 o.p. (*0-14-000468-8*, Penguin Bks.) Viking Penguin.

—Of Human Bondage. l.t. ed. 1998. 375p. text 39.95 (*1-56000-500-9*) Transaction Pubs.

—Of Human Bondage. 1992. (Twentieth Century Classics Ser.). 640p. pap. 11.95 (*0-14-018522-4*, Penguin Classics) Viking Penguin.

Maynard, Bill. Incredible Ned. 1997. (Illus.). 40p. (J). (ps-3). 15.95 o.s.i (*0-399-23023-8*, G. P. Putnam's Sons) Penguin Group (USA) Inc.

Mazzio, Joann. Leaving Eldorado. 1993. 176p. (YA). (gr. 7-9). tchr. ed. 16.00 (*0-395-64381-3*) Houghton Mifflin Co.

McClintock, Barbara. The Fantastic Drawings of Danielle. (Illus.). 32p. (J). (ps-3). 2004. pap. 5.95 (*0-618-43230-2*); 1996. tchr. ed. 17.00 o.p. (*0-395-73980-2*) Houghton Mifflin Co.

McGahan, Andrew. 1988. 1998. 320p. pap. 12.95 (*0-312-18032-2*, 837237, Saint Martin's Griffin); 1996. 314p. 22.95 o.p. (*0-312-15043-1*) St. Martin's Pr.

McKay, Hilary. Saffy's Angel. unabr. ed. 2002. (J). (gr. 13 up). audio 25.00 (*0-8072-0823-X*, Listening Library) Random Hse. Audio Publishing Group.

—Saffy's Angel. 2003. (Illus.). 160p. (J). pap. 4.99 (*0-689-84934-6*, Aladdin) Simon & Schuster Children's Publishing.

—Saffy's Angel. 2003. (Juvenile Ser.). 227p. (J). 21.95 (*0-7862-5500-5*) Thorndike Pr.

McPhail, David M. Lorenzo. 1984. (Illus.). 64p. (J). (gr. 1-3). 9.95 o.p. (*0-385-15590-5*); lib. bdg. 9.95 o.p. (*0-385-15591-3*) Doubleday Publishing.

—Something Special. (J). (ps-3). 1992. pap. 4.95 o.p. (*0-316-56333-1*, Joy Street Bks.); 1988. (Illus.). 32p. 12.95 o.p. (*0-316-56324-2*) Little Brown & Co.

Mendoza, George. Henri Mouse. 1986. (Picture Puffin Ser.). (Illus.). 32p. (J). (ps-3). pap. 3.95 o.p. (*0-14-050636-5*, Puffin Bks.) Penguin Putnam Bks. for Young Readers.

Mendoza, George & Boucher, Joelle. Henri Mouse. 1985. (J). (ps-3). 10.95 o.p. (*0-670-36689-7*, Viking Children's Bks.) Penguin Putnam Bks. for Young Readers.

Merrick, Gordon. The Quirk. 1998. 400p. reprint ed. pap. 12.95 o.p. (*1-55583-294-6*, Alyson Bks.) Alyson Pubns.

—The Quirk. 1978. pap. 3.95 o.p. (*0-380-38992-4*, 84970-4, Avon Bks.) Morrow/Avon.

Meyer, Carolyn. Brown Eyes Blue: A Novel. 2003. 352p. 23.95 (*1-882593-68-5*); 2004. 240p. reprint ed. pap. 15.95 (*1-882593-83-9*) Bridge Works Publishing Co., Inc.

Miller, Mary J. Going the Distance. 1994. 160p. (J). 14.99 o.p. (*0-670-84815-8*) Penguin Putnam Bks. for Young Readers.

Moggach, Deborah. Tulip Fever. l.t. ed. 2000. (General Ser.). 263p. pap. 22.95 (*0-7862-2300-6*) Thorndike Pr.

Molarsky, Osmond. A Sky Full of Kites. 1996. (Illus.). 32p. (J). (gr. k-2). 12.95 (*1-883672-26-0*) Tricycle Pr.

Morris, Gilbert. The Shadow Portrait. 1998. (House of Winslow Ser.: Vol. 21). 320p. pap. 11.99 (*1-55661-689-9*) Bethany Hse. Pubs.

Moss, Marissa. Regina's Big Mistake. 1990. (Illus.). 32p. (J). (ps-3). lib. bdg., tchr. ed. 16.00 (*0-395-55330-X*) Houghton Mifflin Co.

—Regina's Big Mistake. 1995. (Illus.). 32p. (J). (ps-3). pap. 6.95 (*0-395-70093-0*) Houghton Mifflin Co. Trade & Reference Div.

Moynihan, Danny. Boogie-Woogie. 2001. 256p. 22.95 (*0-312-27281-2*) St. Martin's Pr.

Naess, Atle. Doubting Thomas: A Novel about Caravaggio. 160p. 19.95 (*0-7206-1151-2*) Dufour Editions, Inc.

—Doubting Thomas: A Novel about Caravaggio. Born, Anne, tr. from NOR. 2000. 159p. 29.95 (*0-7206-1082-6*) Owen, Peter Ltd. GBR. *Dist:* Dufour Editions, Inc.

Natsume, Saoseki. The Three-Cornered World. 2003. (Peter Owen Modern Classics Ser.). 184p. pap. 19.95 (*0-7206-1156-3*) Owen, Peter Ltd. GBR. *Dist:* Dufour Editions, Inc.

Nolan, Han. Send Me down a Miracle. 1996. 256p. (YA). (gr. 7 up). 13.00 o.s.i (*0-15-200979-5*) Harcourt Trade Pubs.

Norman, Howard. The Bird Artist: A Novel. 1994. 320p. 20.00 o.s.i (*0-374-11330-0*) Farrar, Straus & Giroux.

—The Bird Artist: A Novel. l.t. ed. 1995. (Large Print Bks.). pap. 20.95 (*1-56895-094-2*, Wheeler Publishing, Inc.) Gale Group.

—The Bird Artist: A Novel. 7th ed. 1995. 289p. pap. 14.00 (*0-312-13027-9*) Picador.

Nunes, Lygia Bojunga. My Friend the Painter. Pontiero, Giovanni, tr. 1995. (Illus.). 96p. (J). (gr. 4-7). pap. 5.00 (*0-15-200872-1*, Harcourt Paperbacks) Harcourt Children's Bks.

—My Friend the Painter. Pontiero, Giovanni, tr. from POR. 1991. 96p. (J). (gr. 3-7). 13.95 (*0-15-256340-7*) Harcourt Trade Pubs.

Nye, Julie. Every Perfect Gift. Vogt, Carla, ed. 1990. (Illus.). 201p. (J). (gr. 9 up). pap. 6.49 o.p. (*0-89084-499-2*, 046896) Jones, Bob Univ. Pr.

Oneal, Zibby. In Summer Light. 1986. 160p. (YA). (gr. 6 up). mass mkt. 3.50 o.s.i (*0-553-25940-7*) Bantam Bks.

—In Summer Light. 1985. 16p. (J). (gr. 7 up). 12.95 o.p. (*0-670-80784-2*, Viking Children's Bks.) Penguin Putnam Bks. for Young Readers.

Otto, Whitney. The Passion Dream Book. 1998. 288p. pap. 13.00 (*0-06-109623-7*, Perennial); 1997. audio 18.00 o.p. (*0-694-51779-8*, CPN 2621, HarperAudio) HarperTrade.

—Passion Dream Book: A Novel. 1997. 288p. 22.00 o.s.i (*0-06-017824-8*) HarperCollins Pubs.

—The Passion Dream Book: A Novel. l.t. ed. 1997. (Americana Ser.). 432p. lib. bdg. 25.95 (*0-7862-1247-0*) Thorndike Pr.

Pagano, Michelina & Eubank, Mary G. Magic Paintbox. 1990. 24p. (J). (ps). pap. 1.79 o.s.i (*0-307-11680-8*, Golden Bks.) Random Hse. Children's Bks.

Page, Jake. A Certain Malice. 1997. mass mkt. 6.99 (*0-345-40539-0*) Ballantine Bks.

—The Deadly Canyon. 1994. 240p. 20.00 o.s.i (*0-345-37930-6*) Ballantine Bks.

—The Deadly Canyon. unabr. ed. 1994. audio 57.25 o.p. (*1-56100-168-6*, 859, Unabridged Library Editions); audio 21.95 o.p. (*1-56100-540-1*, 86, Bookcassette) Brilliance Audio.

—The Deadly Canyon. 1995. 272p. mass mkt. 4.99 o.s.i (*0-345-37931-4*, House of Collectibles) Random Hse. Information Group.

—The Deadly Canyon. 2002. (Illus.). 228p. pap. 13.95 (*0-8263-2861-X*) Univ. of New Mexico Pr.

—The Knotted Strings. 1995. mass mkt. 5.99 o.s.i (*0-345-38783-X*); 256p. 20.00 o.s.i (*0-345-38782-1*) Ballantine Bks.

—The Knotted Strings. abr. ed. 1995. audio 16.95 o.p. (*1-56100-406-5*, 1318, Nova Audio Bks.); audio 57.25 o.p. (*1-56100-238-0*, 921, Unabridged Library Editions); audio 23.95 o.p. (*1-56100-613-0*, 156, Bookcassette) Brilliance Audio.

—The Knotted Strings. abr. ed. 2000. audio 7.95 (*1-57815-016-7*, 1040, Media Bks. Audio Publishing) Media Bks., L. L. C.

—The Knotted Strings. 2003. 256p. pap. 13.95 (*0-8263-2862-8*) Univ. of New Mexico Pr.

—The Lethal Partner. 1996. 293p. mass mkt. 5.99 o.s.i (*0-345-38785-6*); 240p. 21.00 o.s.i (*0-345-38784-8*) Ballantine Bks.

—The Lethal Partner. unabr. ed. 1997. audio 48.00 (*0-913369-64-0*, 4305) Books on Tape, Inc.

—The Lethal Partner. 2003. 246p. pap. 13.95 (*0-8263-2863-6*) Univ. of New Mexico Pr.

—The Stolen Gods. (Southwest Mysteries Ser.). 1994. 272p. mass mkt. 4.99 o.s.i (*0-345-37929-2*); 1993. 256p. 19.00 o.s.i (*0-345-37928-4*) Ballantine Bks.

—The Stolen Gods. 2002. 260p. pap. 13.95 (*0-8263-2860-1*) Univ. of New Mexico Pr.

Palahniuk, Chuck. Diary: A Novel. 2003. 272p. 24.95 (*0-385-50947-2*) Doubleday Publishing.

Palmer, Elizabeth, contrib. by. Plucking the Apple. 1999. (*0-7540-1300-6*) BBC Audiobooks America.

Parks, Gordon. The Sun Stalker. 2003. 352p. 29.95 (*0-9640952-8-9*) Ruder Finn Pr.

Pascal, Francine, creator. Olivia's Story. 1991. (Sweet Valley High Super Star Ser.: No. 4). 224p. (YA). (gr. 7 up). mass mkt. 3.50 o.s.i (*0-553-29359-1*) Bantam Bks.

Paul. Monkey Fraggles' New Color. 1988. (J). 13.27 o.p. (*0-516-09076-3*, Children's Pr.) Scholastic Library Publishing.

Pauli, Emily. Mokey Fraggles New Colors. 1988. (J). o.p. (*0-02-689114-X*) Checkerboard Pr., Inc.

Paulsen, Gary. Monument. 1991. 160p. (J). 15.00 (*0-385-30518-4*, Delacorte Pr.) Dell Publishing.

—The Monument. 1993. 160p. (YA). (gr. 7 up). pap. text 5.50 (*0-440-40782-6*) Dell Publishing.

Peachment, Christopher. Caravaggio. Date not set. pap. (*0-312-31449-3*, St. Martin's Paperbacks) St. Martin's Pr.

—Caravaggio: A Novel. 2003. 240p. pap. (*0-330-48732-9*) Picador.

—Caravaggio: A Novel. 2003. 304p. 23.95 (*0-312-31448-5*) St. Martin's Pr.

Peet, Bill. Encore for Eleanor. 48p. (J). (ps-3). 1985. pap. 8.95 (*0-395-38367-6*); 1981. (Illus.). tchr. ed. 14.95 o.p. (*0-395-29860-1*) Houghton Mifflin Co.

Perutz, Leo. Leonardo's Judas. Mosbacher, Eric, tr. from GER. 1989. 160p. lib. bdg. 16.95 o.s.i (*1-55970-002-5*) Arcade Publishing, Inc.

Peusner, Stella. The Night the Whole Class Slept Over. McDonald, Patricia, ed. 1992. 176p. (J). (gr. 3-6). reprint ed. pap. 3.50 (*0-671-78157-X*, Aladdin) Simon & Schuster Children's Publishing.

Pevsner, Stella. The Night the Whole Class Slept Over. 1991. 176p. (J). (gr. 4-9). 14.95 o.p. (*0-89919-983-6*, Clarion Bks.) Houghton Mifflin Co. Trade & Reference Div.

Pfeffer, Susan Beth & Alcott, Louisa May. Amy Makes a Friend. 1998. (Portraits of Little Women Ser.). (Illus.). 112p. (gr. 3-7). text 9.95 o.s.i (*0-385-32584-3*, Dell Books for Young Readers) Random Hse. Children's Bks.

Pittman, Helena Clare. Gerald-Not-Practical. 1990. (Gerald Bks.). (Illus.). 32p. (J). (ps-3). lib. bdg. 18.95 o.s.i (*0-87614-430-X*, Carolrhoda Bks.) Lerner Publishing Group.

Plummer, Louise. My Name Is Sus5an Smith: The Five Is Silent. 1993. 224p. (YA). mass mkt. 3.50 o.s.i (*0-440-21451-3*) Dell Publishing.

Porte, Barbara Ann. Chickens! Chickens! 1995. (Illus.). 32p. (J). (ps-3). pap. 14.95 (*0-531-06877-3*); lib. bdg. 15.99 (*0-531-08727-1*) Scholastic, Inc. (Orchard Bks.).

Price, Reynolds. The Tongues of Angels. 1991. 244p. mass mkt. 5.99 o.s.i (*0-345-37102-X*, Ballantine Bks.) Ballantine Bks.

—The Tongues of Angels. 208p. 2000. pap. 11.00 (*0-7432-0221-X*); 1990. (J). 17.95 (*0-689-12093-1*) Simon & Schuster. (Scribner).
Provinzano, A. M. The Secret Spring of Edith Cooley. 2000. 138p. pap. 11.95 (*1-930185-00-6*, 101) Joan of Arc Publishing.
Purdy, James. Gertrude of Stony Island Avenue. 1999. 192p. pap. 13.00 o.s.i (*0-688-17226-1*, Quill) HarperTrade.
—Gertrude of Stony Island Avenue. 1998. 144p. 19.95 (*0-688-15901-X*, Morrow, William & Co.) Morrow/Avon.
—Gertrude of Stony Island Avenue. 1996. 256p. 27.95 (*0-7206-1011-7*) Owen, Peter Ltd. GBR. *Dist:* Dufour Editions, Inc.
Rawlins. Water Splashing on a Rock. 2005. pap. 12.95 (*0-8050-5239-9*, Owl Bks.); 2004. 27.00 (*0-8050-5240-2*) Holt, Henry & Co.
Redhill, Michael. Martin Sloane. 2001. 288p. pap. (*0-385-25987-5*, Anchor Canada) Doubleday Canada, Ltd. CAN. *Dist:* Random Hse., Inc.
—Martin Sloane. 2002. 288p. pap. 13.95 (*0-316-73936-7*, Back Bay) Little Brown & Co.
Reeves, James. Mr. Horrox & the Gratch. 1991. (Illus.). 32p. (J). (gr. 1-6). 13.95 (*0-922984-08-5*) Wellington Publishing, Inc.
Richardson, Nigel. Dog Days in Soho: One Man's Adventures in Fifties Bohemia. 2002. (Illus.). 256p. 29.95 (*0-575-06850-7*) Orion Publishing Group, Ltd. GBR. *Dist:* Trafalgar Square.
Robbins, Adreana. Paris Never Leaves You. unabr. ed. 1999. audio 83.95 (*0-7861-1630-7*, 2458) Blackstone Audio Bks., Inc.
—Paris Never Leaves You. 2000. 468p. mass mkt. 6.99 (*0-8125-7078-2*); 2nd ed. 1999. 384p. 25.95 (*0-312-86755-7*) Doherty, Tom Assocs., LLC. (Forge Bks.).
Roberts, Nora. The Art of Deception. l.t. ed. 2000. (G. K. Hall Romance Ser.). 274p. 29.95 (*0-7838-9055-9*); (*0-7540-4362-2*); (*0-7540-4363-0*) Gale Group. (Macmillan Reference USA).
—The Art of Deception. 1993. (NR Flowers Ser.: No. 27). mass mkt. (*0-373-51027-6*, 1-51027-0, Silhouette); 1986. per. (*0-373-07131-0*, Harlequin Bks.) Harlequin Enterprises, Ltd.
Robinson, Glen & Thomas, Jerry D. The Broken Dozen Mystery. 1996. (Shoebox Kids Ser.: Vol. 5). (J). 6.99 (*0-8163-1332-6*) Pacific Pr. Publishing Assn.
Rockwell, Anne F. Mr. Panda's Painting. 1993. (Illus.). 32p. (J). (ps-1). lib. bdg. 14.95 (*0-02-777451-1*, Simon & Schuster Children's Publishing) Simon & Schuster Children's Publishing.
Rogan, Barbara. Cafe Nevo. 1988. 324p. pap. 7.95 o.p. (*0-452-26141-4*, Plume) Dutton/Plume.
—Cafe Nevo. 1987. 320p. 19.95 o.s.i (*0-689-11840-6*, Scribner) Simon & Schuster.
Ross, Tom. Eggbert, the Slightly Cracked Egg. 1997. (Illus.). 32p. (J). (ps-3). pap. 5.99 (*0-698-11444-2*, PaperStar) Penguin Putnam Bks. for Young Readers.
Rucker, Rudolf V. B. As above, So Below: A Novel of Peter Bruegel. 2002. (Illus.). 320p. 23.95 (*0-7653-0403-1*, Forge Bks.) Doherty, Tom Assocs., LLC.
Rylant, Cynthia. All I See. (Illus.). 32p. (J). (gr. k-2). 1997. mass mkt. 11.40 (*0-531-07048-4*); 1988. mass mkt. 18.99 o.p. (*0-531-08377-2*); 1988. pap. 17.95 (*0-531-05777-1*) Scholastic, Inc. (Orchard Bks.).
—All I See. 1988. 13.10 (*0-606-08686-2*) Turtleback Bks.
Santlofer, Jonathan. The Death Artist: A Novel of Suspense. 2003. 448p. mass mkt. 7.50 (*0-06-000442-8*, HarperTorch); 2002. 352p. 24.95 (*0-06-000441-X*, Morrow, William & Co.) Morrow/Avon.
Saramago, José. La Caverna. (SPA., Illus.). 456p. 24.95 (*84-204-4228-3*) Alfaguara, Ediciones, S.A.- Grupo Santillana ESP. *Dist:* Santillana USA Publishing Co., Inc.
Saunders, Susan. Lauren's Double Disaster. 1991. (Sleepover Friends Ser.: No. 33). (J). (gr. 4-7). mass mkt. 2.75 o.p. (*0-590-43926-X*) Scholastic, Inc.
Say, Allen. The Ink-Keeper's Apprentice. 1994. (Illus.). 160p. (YA). (gr. 7-7). tchr. ed. 13.95 (*0-395-70562-2*) Houghton Mifflin Co.
—The Ink-Keeper's Apprentice. 1996. 160p. (YA). (gr. 7 up). pap. 4.99 o.s.i (*0-14-037826-X*, Puffin Bks.) Penguin Putnam Bks. for Young Readers.
Schmidt, Bernd. Our Friend the Painter. Young, Richard G., ed. 1989. (Illus.). 24p. (J). (gr. 1-3). lib. bdg. 14.60 o.p. (*0-944483-52-6*) Garrett Educational Corp.
Schreier, Joshua. Hank's Work. 1993. 320p. (J). (ps-2). 13.50 o.p. (*0-525-44970-1*, Dutton Children's Bks.) Penguin Putnam Bks. for Young Readers.
Schwartz, Alvin. The Blowtop. 2nd ed. 2001. xiii, 211p. (gr. 4-7). reprint ed. pap. (*1-58754-007-X*, Olmstead Pr.) Moyer Bell.
Scott, Joanna. Arrogance. 1991. 288p. pap. 13.00 (*0-393-30792-1*) Norton, W. W. & Co., Inc.
—Arrogance. 1990. 288p. bds. 18.95 o.p. (*0-671-69547-9*, Simon & Schuster) Simon & Schuster.
See, Carolyn. The Handyman. 2000. 272p. pap. 13.95 (*0-345-42660-6*, Ballantine Bks.) Ballantine Bks.
—The Handyman. unabr. ed. 1999. audio 24.95 (*1-57511-059-8*) Publishing Mills, Inc., The.
—The Handyman. l.t. ed. 1999. (Basic Ser.). 345p. 27.95 (*0-7862-2078-3*) Thorndike Pr.
—The Handyman: A Novel. 1999. 240p. 22.95 o.s.i (*0-375-50155-X*) Random Hse., Inc.
Seidler, Tor. A Rat's Tale, RS. 1986. (Illus.). 187p. (J). (gr. 1-8). 16.00 o.p. (*0-374-36185-1*, Farrar, Straus & Giroux (BYR)) Farrar, Straus & Giroux.
Shannon, Monica. Dobry. 1993. (Newbery Library). (Illus.). 192p. (J). (gr. 5 up). pap. 4.99 o.s.i (*0-14-036334-3*, Puffin Bks.) Penguin Putnam Bks. for Young Readers.
Sheehan, Patty. Gwendolyn's Gifts. 1991. (Illus.). 32p. (J). (ps-3). 14.95 (*0-88289-845-0*) Pelican Publishing Co., Inc.
Shimoda, Todd A. The Fourth Treasure. 2002. (Illus.). 368p. 24.95 (*0-385-50352-0*, Talese, Nan A.) Doubleday Publishing.
Shimoda, Todd A. & Shimoda, L. J. C. The Fourth Treasure. 2002. (Illus.). 349p. E-Book 22.50 (*0-385-50561-2*, Talese, Nan A.) Doubleday Publishing.
Sipherd, Ray. The Audubon Quartet. 1999. (WWL Mystery Ser.: No. 311). per. (*0-373-26311-2*, 1-26311-0, Worldwide Library) Harlequin Enterprises, Ltd.
—Audubon Quartet, Vol. 1. 1998. (Jonathan Wilder Mysteries Ser.). 272p. 22.95 o.p. (*0-312-18536-7*, Saint Martin's Minotaur) St. Martin's Pr.
—Dance of the Scarecrows. 1998. (WWL Mystery Ser.: Vol. 287). per. (*0-373-26287-6*, 1-26287-2, Worldwide Library) Harlequin Enterprises, Ltd.
—Dance of the Scarecrows. 1996. 256p. 21.95 o.p. (*0-312-14306-0*, Saint Martin's Minotaur) St. Martin's Pr.
Smith, Deborah. On Bear Mountain: A Novel. 2001. 352p. 23.95 o.p. (*0-316-80077-5*) Little Brown & Co.
Smith, Evelyn E. Miss Melville Regrets. 1987. mass mkt. 5.99 o.s.i (*0-449-21259-9*, Fawcett) Ballantine Bks.
—Miss Melville Regrets. 1986. 288p. 17.95 o.p. (*0-917657-45-4*) Fine, Donald I. Bks.
—Miss Melville Regrets. l.t. ed. 1989. (Ulverscroft Large Print Ser.). 29.99 o.p. (*0-7089-2110-8*, Ulverscroft) Thorpe, F. A. Pubs. GBR. *Dist:* Ulverscroft Large Print Bks., Ltd., Ulverscroft Large Print Canada, Ltd.
—Miss Melville Returns. 1988. mass mkt. 4.99 o.s.i (*0-449-21499-0*, Fawcett) Ballantine Bks.
—Miss Melville Returns. 1987. 272p. 17.95 o.s.i (*1-55611-015-4*) Fine, Donald I. Bks.
—Miss Melville Rides a Tiger. 1992. mass mkt. 4.99 o.s.i (*0-449-22105-9*, Fawcett) Ballantine Bks.
—Miss Melville Rides a Tiger. 1991. 18.95 o.p. (*1-55611-219-X*) Fine, Donald I. Bks.
—Miss Melville Rides a Tiger. l.t. ed. 1993. (General Ser.). 334p. 20.95 o.p. (*0-8161-5559-3*); pap. o.p. (*0-8161-5560-7*) Gale Group. (Macmillan Reference USA).
—Miss Melville's Revenge. 1990. 224p. mass mkt. 5.99 o.s.i (*0-449-21794-9*, Fawcett) Ballantine Bks.
—Miss Melville's Revenge. 1989. 288p. 17.95 o.p. (*1-55611-076-6*) Fine, Donald I. Bks.
Sorrentino, Gilbert. Imaginative Qualities of Actual Things. 1991. 243p. reprint ed. pap. 12.95 (*0-916583-86-4*) Dalkey Archive Pr.
—Imaginative Qualities of Actual Things. 1972. 30.00 (*0-394-47108-3*) SPD-Small Pr. Distribution.
St. Edmunds, Anne. Red Right Returning. 1997. (New England Mystery Ser.). per. (*0-373-26258-2*, 1-26258-3, Worldwide Library) Harlequin Enterprises, Ltd.
—Red Right Returning. 1996. 224p. 20.95 o.p. (*0-312-14033-9*, Saint Martin's Minotaur) St. Martin's Pr.
Stahl, Hilda. Hannah & the Daring Escape. 1993. (Best Friends Ser.: Vol. 12). 160p. (J). (gr. 4-7). pap. 4.99 o.p. (*0-89107-714-6*) Crossway Bks.
—Roxie & the Red Rose Mystery. 1992. (Best Friends Ser.: Vol. 5). 160p. (J). (gr. 4-7). pap. 4.99 o.p. (*0-89107-681-6*) Crossway Bks.
Steiner, Robert. The Catastrophe. 1995. (Sun & Moon Classics Ser.: No. 146). 450p. pap. 13.95 o.p. (*1-55713-233-X*) Sun & Moon Pr.
Steinke, Rene. Holy Skirts. 2003. 23.95 (*0-688-17694-1*, Morrow, William & Co.) Morrow/Avon.
Stevermer, Caroline. When the King Comes Home. 2000. 236p. 22.95 (*0-312-87214-3*); 2001. reprint ed. mass mkt. 6.99 (*0-8125-8981-5*) Doherty, Tom Assocs., LLC. (Tor Bks.).
Stolz, Mary. Pangur Ban. 1988. (Ursula Nordstrom Bk.). (Illus.). 196p. (YA). (gr. 7 up). lib. bdg. 13.89 o.p. (*0-06-025862-4*) HarperCollins Children's Bk. Group.
Stone, Irving. Agony & the Ecstasy. 1987. 776p. mass mkt. 5.95 o.p. (*0-451-15947-0*, AE2643); mass mkt. 4.95 o.p. (*0-451-14692-1*) NAL. (Signet Bks.).
—Agony & the Ecstasy. 1995. 15.04 (*0-606-04125-7*) Turtleback Bks.
—The Agony & the Ecstasy. Date not set. 774p. 38.95 (*0-8488-2402-4*) Amereon, Ltd.
—The Agony & the Ecstasy. unabr. ed. 1977. Pt. 1. audio 80.00; Pt. 2. audio 88.00 Books on Tape, Inc.
—The Agony & the Ecstasy. 1994. reprint ed. lib. bdg. 39.95 (*1-56849-340-1*) Buccaneer Bks., Inc.
—The Agony & the Ecstasy. 1976. mass mkt. 2.25 o.p. (*0-451-07444-0*); 1971. mass mkt. 1.75 o.p. (*0-451-05189-0*); 1969. mass mkt. 1.50 o.p. (*0-451-04050-3*); 1963. mass mkt. 4.50 o.p. (*0-451-14083-4*); 1963. mass mkt. 3.95 o.p. (*0-451-12643-2*); 1963. mass mkt. 1.25 o.p. (*0-451-02800-7*); 1963. mass mkt. 0.95 o.p. (*0-451-02246-7*); 1963. mass mkt. 1.75 o.p. (*0-451-04648-X*); 1963. mass mkt. 2.75 o.p. (*0-451-08276-1*); 1963. mass mkt. 3.95 o.p. (*0-451-11010-2*); 1963. mass mkt. 3.50 o.p. (*0-451-09284-8*); 1963. mass mkt. 1.95 o.p. (*0-451-06378-3*) NAL. (Signet Bks.).
—The Agony & the Ecstasy. abr. l.t. ed. 1976. (Ulverscroft Large Print Ser.). 12.00 o.p. (*0-85456-561-2*, Ulverscroft) Thorpe, F. A. Pubs. GBR. *Dist:* Ulverscroft Large Print Bks., Ltd., Ulverscroft Large Print Canada, Ltd.
—The Agony & the Ecstasy, Pts. 1 & 2. unabr. ed. Incl. Pt. 1. audio 80.00 Pt. 2. audio 88.00 1977. Set audio 168.00 (*0-7366-0048-5*, 1061-A/B) Books on Tape, Inc.
—The Agony & the Ecstasy: A Biographical Novel of Michelangelo. 1987. 776p. mass mkt. 8.99 (*0-451-17135-7*, Signet Classics) NAL.
—The Agony & the Ecstasy: A Novel of Michelangelo. 1961. 19.95 o.s.i (*0-385-01092-3*) Doubleday Publishing.
—Depths of Glory: A Biographical Novel of Camille Pissarro, Pt. 1. unabr. ed. 1988. audio 80.00 (*0-7366-1262-9*, 2175-A) Books on Tape, Inc.
—Depths of Glory: A Biographical Novel of Camille Pissarro. 1995. 624p. pap. 14.95 o.p. (*0-452-27501-6*, Plume) Dutton/Plume.
—Depths of Glory: A Biographical Novel of Camille Pissarro. 1987. mass mkt. 4.95 o.p. (*0-451-14602-6*); 624p. mass mkt. 5.95 o.p. (*0-451-16497-0*); mass mkt. 2.95 o.p. (*0-451-15790-7*) NAL. (Signet Bks.).
—Lust for Life. 29.95 (*0-89190-127-2*) Amereon, Ltd.
—Lust for Life. 1994. lib. bdg. 29.95 (*1-56849-480-7*) Buccaneer Bks., Inc.
—Lust for Life. 1959. 17.95 o.s.i (*0-385-04270-1*) Doubleday Publishing.
—Lust for Life. 1984. 512p. pap. 15.95 (*0-452-26249-6*, Plume) Dutton/Plume.
—Lust for Life. 1984. pap. 8.95 o.p. (*0-452-25517-1*); 1981. mass mkt. 3.95 o.p. (*0-451-09898-6*, E9898, Signet Bks.) NAL.
Strachan, Ian. The Soutar Retrospective. 1987. 176p. (J). 13.95 o.p. (*0-19-271464-3*) Oxford Univ. Pr., Inc.
Strigenz, Geri K., illus. For Bread. 1992. (History's Children Ser.). 48p. (J). (gr. 4-5). pap. o.p. (*0-8114-6426-1*); lib. bdg. 21.36 o.p. (*0-8114-3501-6*) Raintree Pubs.
Styron, William. Set This House on Fire. 1981. 528p. pap. 3.95 o.p. (*0-553-14666-1*) Bantam Bks.
—Set This House on Fire. unabr. collector's ed. 1986. Pt. 1. audio 72.00 (*0-7366-0557-6*, 1530-A); Pt. 2. audio 72.00 (*0-7366-0558-4*, 1530-B) Books on Tape, Inc.
—Set This House on Fire. 1977. mass mkt. 0.95 o.p. (*0-451-01944-X*, Signet Bks.) NAL.
—Set This House on Fire. 1993. 528p. pap. 15.00 (*0-679-73674-3*); 1960. 15.00 o.s.i (*0-394-44482-5*) Random Hse., Inc.
Tada, Joni Eareckson. I'll Be with You Always. 1998. (Illus.). 32p. (J). (gr. 8-12). 14.99 (*1-58134-000-1*) Crossway Bks.
Thomas, Abigail. Pearl Paints, ERS. 1996. (Illus.). 32p. (J). pap. 5.95 o.p. (*0-8050-4071-4*, Holt, Henry & Co. Bks. For Young Readers) Holt, Henry & Co.
—Pearl's Paints, ERS. 1994. (J). 15.95 o.p. (*0-8050-2976-1*, Holt, Henry & Co. Bks. For Young Readers) Holt, Henry & Co.
Toles, Tom. My School Is Worse Than Yours. 1997. (Illus.). 80p. (J). 13.99 o.s.i (*0-670-87336-5*) Penguin Putnam Bks. for Young Readers.
Turner, Ann Warren. Time of the Bison. 1987. (Illus.). 64p. (J). (gr. 2-6). 13.95 o.p. (*0-02-789300-6*, Simon & Schuster Children's Publishing) Simon & Schuster Children's Publishing.
Tyler, Anne. Celestial Navigation. l.t. ed. 1994. 366p. 24.95 o.p. (*0-7927-1977-8*); pap. 22.95 o.p. (*0-7927-1976-X*) BBC Audiobooks America.
—Celestial Navigation. 1996. 288p. pap. 13.95 (*0-449-91180-2*, Fawcett); 1992. 256p. mass mkt. 5.99 o.s.i (*0-8041-0888-9*, Ivy Bks.) Ballantine Bks.
—Celestial Navigation. mass mkt. 3.95 o.s.i (*0-425-08638-0*); 1986. 256p. mass mkt. 5.95 o.p. (*0-425-09840-0*); 1985. mass mkt. 3.95 o.s.i (*0-425-09142-2*); 1984. mass mkt. 3.50 o.s.i (*0-425-07013-1*) Berkley Publishing Group.
—Celestial Navigation. 1974. 7.95 o.p. (*0-394-49038-X*, Knopf Bks. for Young Readers) Random Hse. Children's Bks.
—Celestial Navigation. 1983. 256p. pap. 3.50 o.p. (*0-446-31169-3*) Warner Bks., Inc.
Updike, John. Seek My Face. 2003. 288p. pap. 13.95 (*0-345-46086-3*, Ballantine Bks.) Ballantine Bks.
—Seek My Face. l.t. ed. 2003. lib. bdg. 29.95 (*1-58547-318-9*, Platinum) Ctr. Point Large Print.
—Seek My Face. 2002. 288p. 23.00 (*0-375-41490-8*) Knopf, Alfred A. Inc.
Urquhart, Jane. The Underpainter. 256p. 1998. 14.00 (*0-14-026973-8*); 1997. 22.95 o.s.i (*0-670-87726-3*) Viking Penguin.
Van Dine, Lynn. The Search for Peter Hunt. 2003. (ENG., Illus.). xiv, 248p. 34.95 (*0-9711835-4-6*) Local History Co., The.
Vandermeer, Jeff. Veniss Underground. 2003. 188p. pap. 15.00 (*1-894815-64-5*) Prime.
Vargas Llosa, Mario. The Way to Paradise. 2003. 384p. 25.00 (*0-374-22803-5*); pap. (*0-374-98281-3*) Farrar, Straus & Giroux.
Varvasovsky, Lazlo. Henry in Shadowland. 1989. (Illus.). 32p. (J). (gr. 2-7). 17.95 (*0-87923-785-6*) Godine, David R. Pub.
Ventura, Piero & Ventura, Marisa M. The Painter's Trick. 1977. (Illus.). (J). (gr. k-2). 5.95 o.p. (*0-394-83320-1*, Random Hse. Bks. for Young Readers) Random Hse. Children's Bks.
Von Rosenburg, Marjorie. Artists Who Painted Texas. Date not set. (Illus.). 96p. (J). (gr. 5). 16.95 (*1-57168-203-1*) Eakin Pr.
Vonnegut, Kurt, Jr. Bluebeard. l.t. ed. 1988. 21.95 o.p. (*1-55504-592-8*); 343p. pap. 19.95 o.p. (*1-55504-600-2*) BBC Audiobooks America.
—Bluebeard. 1987. 300p. 17.95 o.s.i (*0-385-29590-1*, Delacorte Pr.) Dell Publishing.
Vreeland, Susan. The Forest Lover. 2004. 352p. 24.95 (*0-670-03267-0*) Viking Penguin.
—Girl in Hyacinth Blue. 1999. 242p. 17.50 (*1-878448-90-0*); 150p. 17.50 o.p. MacMurray & Beck, Inc.
—Girl in Hyacinth Blue. 2000. (Illus.). 256p. pap. 13.00 (*0-14-029628-X*) Penguin Group (USA) Inc.
—Girl in Hyacinth Blue. l.t. ed. 2000. (Basic Ser.). 227p. 28.95 (*0-7862-2440-1*) Thorndike Pr.
—Girl in Hyacinth Blue. 2000. 17.05 (*0-606-20671-X*) Turtleback Bks.
—The Passion of Artemesia. l.t. ed. 2002. 497p. 29.95 (*0-7862-3856-9*) Gale Group.
—The Passion of Artemesia. abr. unabr. ed. 2002. audio 34.95 (*1-56511-525-2*) HighBridge Co.
—The Passion of Artemesia. 2002. 352p. pap. 13.00 (*0-14-200182-1*) Penguin Group (USA) Inc.
—The Passion of Artemesia. 2002. 320p. 24.95 o.s.i (*0-670-89449-4*, Viking) Viking Penguin.
Waddell, Martin. Alice the Artist. 1988. (Illus.). 32p. (J). (ps-1). 10.95 o.p. (*0-525-44385-1*, 01063-320, Dutton Children's Bks.) Penguin Putnam Bks. for Young Readers.
Warhol, Andy. A: A Novel. 1998. o.p. (*0-8021-3538-2*, Grove Pr.) Grove/Atlantic, Inc.
Watson, Larry. Orchard: A Novel. 2004. 256p. pap. 13.95 (*0-375-75854-2*, Random Hse. Trade Paperbacks) Random House Adult Trade Publishing Group.
—Orchard: A Novel. 2003. 256p. 24.95 (*0-375-50723-X*) Random Hse., Inc.
Webb, Charles. New Cardiff. 2002. (Illus.). 368p. pap. 14.00 (*0-7434-4416-7*, Washington Square Pr.) Simon & Schuster.
Williams, Carol Lynch. Anna's Gift. 1995. (Latter-Day Daughters Ser.: Vol. 1). 80p. (J). (gr. 2 up). pap. 4.95 (*1-56236-501-0*) Aspen Bks.
Wilson, James. Dark Clue. 2003. 320p. pap. (*0-385-65806-0*, Anchor Canada) Doubleday Canada, Ltd. CAN. *Dist:* Random Hse., Inc.
—The Dark Clue: A Novel of Suspense. 2001. 400p. 25.00 o.p. (*0-87113-831-X*, Atlantic Monthly Pr.) Grove/Atlantic, Inc.
Wilson, Jonathan. A Palestine Affair. 272p. 2004. pap. 13.00 (*1-4000-3122-2*, Anchor); 2003. 23.00 (*0-375-42209-9*, Pantheon) Knopf Publishing Group.
Winter, Jeanette. Josefina. 1996. (Illus.). 36p. (J). (ps-3). 16.00 (*0-15-201091-2*) Harcourt Children's Bks.
Wooding, Sharon. The Painter's Cat. 1994. (Illus.). 32p. (J). (ps-3). 14.95 o.p. (*0-399-22414-9*) Penguin Group (USA) Inc.
Wubbels, Lance. In the Shadow of a Secret. 2001. (Christian Fiction Ser.). 347p. 24.95 (*0-7862-3300-1*, Five Star) Gale Group.
Zappa, Moon Unit. America the Beautiful: A Novel. 2001. 304p. pap. 14.00 (*0-7432-1383-1*); E-Book 9.99 (*0-7432-1913-9*) Simon & Schuster. (Touchstone).
Zelinsky, Paul O. The Lion & the Stoat. 1984. (Illus.). 40p. (J). (gr. 1-3). 11.95 o.p. (*0-688-02562-5*); lib. bdg. 11.93 o.p. (*0-688-02563-3*) HarperCollins Children's Bk. Group. (Greenwillow Bks.).

**AUTHORS—FICTION**

Adair, Gilbert. Closed Book. 1999. 258p. pap. (0-571-20081-8) Faber & Faber, Inc.

Agualusa, Jose Eduardo. Creole Nation. 2002. 288p. pap. 16.00 (1-900850-61-3) Arcadia Bks. GBR. Dist: Consortium Bk. Sales & Distribution.

Andahazi, Federico. The Merciful Women. Manguel, Alberto, tr. from SPA. 2000. (Illus.). 188p. 22.00 o.p. (0-8021-1674-4); 2002. 192p. reprint ed. pap. 13.00 (0-8021-3826-8) Grove/Atlantic, Inc. (Grove Pr.).

Atwood, Margaret. The Blind Assassin. 2000. 544p. 26.00 (0-385-47572-1, Talese, Nan A.) Doubleday Publishing.

—The Blind Assassin. pap. (0-385-72856-5) Knopf Publishing Group.

—The Blind Assassin. 2001. 544p. pap. 14.95 (0-385-72095-5, Knopf Bks. for Young Readers) Random Hse. Children's Bks.

—The Blind Assassin. l.t. ed. 2000. 832p. 26.00 (0-375-43085-7) Random Hse. Large Print.

—Lady Oracle. 1987. 384p. mass mkt. 5.95 o.s.i (0-449-21376-5, Fawcett) Ballantine Bks.

—Lady Oracle. 1995. 352p. pap. 10.95 o.s.i (0-553-37781-7); 1984. 352p. mass mkt. 8.99 o.s.i (0-7704-2299-3); 1984. mass mkt. 4.50 o.s.i (0-7704-2179-2) Bantam Bks.

—Lady Oracle. 1998. 352p. pap. 12.95 (0-385-49108-5) Doubleday Publishing.

—Lady Oracle. 1978. pap. 3.95 o.p. (0-380-01799-7, Avon Bks.) Morrow/Avon.

Bach, Richard. Writer Ferrets Chasing the Muse. 2003. (Ferret Chronicles: No. 3). (Illus.). 208p. 15.00 (0-7432-2754-9, Scribner) Simon & Schuster.

Bain, Donald. Murder She Wrote: A Palette for Murder. l.t. ed. 2001. (G. K. Hall Nightingale Ser.). 274p. 23.95 (0-7838-9319-1) Thorndike Pr.

—Trick or Treachery: A Murder, She Wrote Mystery. l.t. ed. 2001. (Large Print Mystery Ser.). 252p. pap. 23.95 (0-7838-9496-1, Macmillan Reference USA) Gale Group.

Bainbridge, Beryl. According to Queeney. 224p. 2001. 22.00 (0-7867-0773-9); 2002. reprint ed. pap. 12.00 (0-7867-0982-0) Avalon Publishing Group. (Carroll & Graf Pubs.).

—According to Queeney. l.t. ed. 2002. 242p. pap. 23.95 (0-7862-3958-1) Gale Group.

Barlow, Eleanor Poe. The Master's Cat: The Story of Charles Dickens as Told by His Cat. 1998. (Illus.). 132p. (YA). (gr. 7 up). 24.00 (0-9518525-3-1) Dickens Publishing GBR. Dist: Hood, Alan C. & Co., Inc.

—The Master's Cat: The Story of Charles Dickens as Told by His Cat. 1999. 132p. (YA). pap. 16.50 (1-880158-22-1) Townsend, J.N. Publishing.

Barron, Stephanie. Jane & the Ghosts of Netley. 2004. 336p. mass mkt. 6.99 (0-553-58406-5); 7th ed. 2003. 304p. 23.95 (0-553-80222-4) Bantam Bks.

—Jane & the Prisoner of Wool House. 2002. (Jane Austen Mystery Ser.: Bk. 6). 384p. mass mkt. 6.50 (0-553-57840-5, Crimeline) Bantam Bks.

—Jane & the Prisoner of Wool House. unabr. ed. 2001. (Jane Austen Ser.: Bk. 6). audio 56.00 (0-7366-8483-2) Books on Tape, Inc.

—Jane & the Stillroom Maid. 2001. (Jane Austen Mystery Ser.: Vol. 5). 336p. reprint ed. mass mkt. 6.50 (0-553-57837-5) Bantam Bks.

Barth, John. The Tidewater Tales: A Novel. 1988. 656p. pap. 15.00 o.s.i (0-449-90293-5, Fawcett) Ballantine Bks.

—The Tidewater Tales: A Novel. 1987. 624p. 21.95 o.p. (0-399-13247-3, G. P. Putnam's Sons) Penguin Putnam Bks. for Young Readers.

Barth, John & Johnston, Mary. The Tidewater Tales: A Novel. 1997. (Maryland Paperback Bookshelf Ser.). (Illus.). 655p. reprint ed. pap. 19.95 (0-8018-5556-X) Johns Hopkins Univ. Pr.

Battrick, Elizabeth. Beatrix Potter's Tale. l.t. ed. 1998. (Ulverscroft Large Print Ser.). 432p. 29.99 (0-7089-3891-4, Ulverscroft) Thorpe, F. A. Pubs. GBR. Dist: Ulverscroft Large Print Bks., Ltd., Ulverscroft Large Print Canada, Ltd.

Bedford, Sybille. Quicksands. 2004. text 24.00 (1-58243-169-8, Counterpoint Pr.) Basic Bks.

Begley, Louis. Shipwreck. 2003. 256p. 23.00 (1-4000-4098-1) Knopf, Alfred A. Inc.

Bell, Albert A., Jr. All Roads Lead to Murder: A Case from the Notebooks of Pliny the Younger. 2002. (Illus.). 246p. 21.95 (0-9713045-3-X) High Country Pubs., Ltd.

Binchy, Maeve, et al. Ladies' Night at Finbar's Hotel. Bolger, Dermot, ed. 2000. (Harvest Original Ser.). 276p. pap. 14.00 (0-15-600866-1, Harvest Bks.) Harcourt Trade Pubs.

Blacker, Terence. Kill Your Darlings. 2001. 320p. 24.95 (0-312-28329-6) St. Martin's Pr.

—Kill Your Darlings: A Novel. 2003. 304p. pap. 14.95 (0-312-30283-5, Saint Martin's Griffin) St. Martin's Pr.

Bochco, Steven. Death by Hollywood. 2004. 256p. mass mkt. 7.99 (0-345-46687-X, Fawcett) Ballantine Bks.

—Death by Hollywood. l.t. ed. 2003. 352p. 26.95 (0-375-43298-1) Random Hse. Large Print.

—Death by Hollywood: A Novel. 2003. 288p. 24.95 (1-4000-6156-3) Random Hse., Inc.

Bolger, Dermot, ed. Ladies' Night at Finbars Hotel. 2000. (0-15-100608-3) Harcourt Trade Pubs.

Boyd, William. Any Human Heart: A Novel. 2003. 512p. 24.95 (0-375-41493-2) Knopf Publishing Group.

Bradbury, Malcolm. To the Hermitage. 2002. 510p. 16.95 (1-58567-256-4) Overlook Pr., The.

Brothers, William P. The Sabbatical. 2000. pap. 18.95 o.p. (0-533-13215-0) Vantage Pr., Inc.

Brown, Sandra. Envy. 2001. 496p. 25.95 o.p. (0-446-52713-0) Warner Bks., Inc.

Bryan, Mike. The Afterword: A Novel. 2003. 208p. 16.00 (0-375-42212-9) Knopf, Alfred A. Inc.

Bugge, Carole. Who Killed Blanche Dubois? 1999. (Whodunnit Ser.). 256p. mass mkt. 5.99 o.s.i (0-425-17195-7, Prime Crime) Berkley Publishing Group.

—Who Killed Dorian Gray? 2000. (Claire Rawlings Mysteries Ser.). 48p. mass mkt. 5.99 o.s.i (0-425-17553-7) Berkley Publishing Group.

Bukowski, Charles. Ham on Rye. 2001. 336p. pap. 9.83 (1-84195-163-3) Canongate Bks. GBR. Dist: Grove/Atlantic, Inc.

—Ham on Rye. 1998. 288p. reprint ed. 25.00 (0-87685-558-3); pap. 16.00 (0-87685-557-5) HarperCollins Pubs.

Busch, Frederick. The Mutual Friend. 1983. (Nonpareil Bk.). 224p. reprint ed. pap. 8.95 o.p. (0-87923-482-2) Godine, David R. Pub.

—The Mutual Friend. 1978. 8.95 o.p. (0-06-010527-5) HarperCollins Pubs.

—The Mutual Friend. 1994. (Paperbook Ser.: Vol. 774). 240p. reprint ed. pap. 9.95 (0-8112-1258-0, NDP774) New Directions Publishing Corp.

Byatt, A. S. The Biographer's Tale. 2001. E-Book 12.50 (1-58945-774-9) Adobe Systems, Inc.

—The Biographer's Tale. 2001. 320p. reprint ed. pap. 14.00 (0-375-72508-3, Vintage) Knopf Publishing Group.

—The Biographer's Tale. 2000. (Illus.). 224p. (0-7011-6945-1) Random Hse. of Canada, Ltd. CAN. Dist: Random Hse., Inc.

—The Biographer's Tale. 2001. E-Book 12.50 (0-375-41342-1) Random Hse., Inc.

—The Biographer's Tale. l.t. ed. 2001. 240p. pap. 24.95 (0-7862-3523-3) Thorndike Pr.

Byrnes, Robert. The Night We Met. 2002. 320p. 23.00 (0-7582-0193-1) Kensington Publishing Corp.

Cameron, Peter. The City of Your Final Destination. 2003. 320p. reprint ed. pap. 14.00 (0-452-28430-9, Plume) Dutton/Plume.

—The City of Your Final Destination. 2002. 320p. 24.00 (0-374-28197-1) Farrar, Straus & Giroux.

Capote, Truman. Answered Prayers: The Unfinished Novel. 1988. pap. 8.95 o.p. (0-452-26137-6); 210p. pap. 11.95 o.s.i (0-452-26483-9) Dutton/Plume. (Plume).

—Answered Prayers: The Unfinished Novel. 1994. 208p. pap. 12.00 (0-679-75182-3, Vintage) Knopf Publishing Group.

Carroll, Jonathan. The Land of Laughs. 1983. 256p. mass mkt. 2.50 o.s.i (0-441-46987-6) Ace Bks.

—The Land of Laughs. E-Book 13.95 (1-58945-668-8) Adobe Systems, Inc.

—The Land of Laughs. 2001. 256p. pap. 13.95 (0-312-87311-5, Orb Bks.) Doherty, Tom Assocs., LLC.

—The Land of Laughs. 1980. 252p. 10.95 o.p. (0-670-41755-6) Viking Penguin.

Carter, Steven. I Was Howard Hughes: A Novel. 2003. 240p. pap. 14.95 (1-58234-375-6) Bloomsbury Publishing.

Chabon, Michael. The Amazing Adventures of Kavalier & Clay: A Novel. 2001. (Illus.). pap. 180.00 (0-312-28882-4); 656p. pap. 15.00 (0-312-28299-0) Picador.

Coetzee, J. M. Elizabeth Costello. 2003. 240p. 21.95 (0-670-03130-5) Viking Penguin.

—Youth: Scenes from Provincial Life II. 2002. 176p. 22.95 (0-670-03102-X, Viking) Viking Penguin.

Coffman, Virginia. The Wine-Dark Opal. l.t. ed. 1997. (Romance-Hall Ser.). 407p. 24.95 o.p. (0-7838-8105-3, Macmillan Reference USA) Gale Group.

—The Wine-Dark Opal, Vol. 2. 1996. (Jewels Ser.). 320p. 24.00 (0-7278-5139-X) Severn Hse. Pubs., Ltd.

Colapinto, John. About the Author. 2001. 272p. 25.00 (0-06-019417-0) HarperCollins Pubs.

—About the Author. 2002. 272p. pap. 12.95 (0-06-093217-1, Perennial) HarperTrade.

Collins, Max Allan. The Baby Blue Rip-Off. 1987. 224p. pap. 2.95 o.p. (0-8125-0154-3, Tor Bks.) Doherty, Tom Assocs., LLC.

—The Baby Blue Rip-Off. 1983. 11.95 o.s.i (0-8027-5475-9) Walker & Co.

—Kill Your Darlings. 1988. 224p. pap. 3.95 o.p. (0-8125-0161-6, Tor Bks.) Doherty, Tom Assocs., LLC.

—Kill Your Darlings. 1984. 192p. 13.95 o.s.i (0-8027-5594-1) Walker & Co.

—Nice Weekend for a Murder. 1986. 192p. 15.95 o.s.i (0-8027-5656-5) Walker & Co.

—A Nice Weekend for a Murder. 1994. 208p. mass mkt. 3.99 (0-8125-0138-1, Tor Bks.) Doherty, Tom Assocs., LLC.

—No Cure for Death. 1987. 288p. reprint ed. pap. 3.50 o.p. (0-8125-0157-8, Tor Bks.) Doherty, Tom Assocs., LLC.

—No Cure for Death. 1983. 192p. 12.95 o.p. (0-8027-5488-0) Walker & Co.

—A Shroud for Aquarius. 1988. 256p. pap. 3.95 o.p. (0-8125-0163-2, Tor Bks.) Doherty, Tom Assocs., LLC.

—A Shroud for Aquarius. 1985. (Mallory Mystery Ser.). 175p. 14.95 o.p. (0-8027-5629-8) Walker & Co.

Conley, Robert J. Wilder & Wilder. l.t. ed. 2002. (Paperback Ser.). 247p. pap. 24.95 (0-7862-4424-0) Thorndike Pr.

Conran, Shirley. Crimson. l.t. ed. 1993. 23.95 o.p. (0-7927-1402-4); pap. o.p. (0-7927-1401-6) BBC Audiobooks America.

—Crimson. 1992. 544p. 23.00 o.p. (0-671-50149-6, Simon & Schuster) Simon & Schuster.

—Crimson. Rubenstein, Julie, ed. 1992. 544p. reprint ed. mass mkt. 5.99 (0-671-79161-3, Pocket) Simon & Schuster.

—Crimson. Set. abr. ed. 1992. audio 17.00 (0-671-75959-0, Simon & Schuster Audioworks) Simon & Schuster Audio.

Cooper, Susan Rogers. A Crooked Little House. 1999. (E. J. Pugh Mysteries Ser.: No. 6). 352p. mass mkt. 5.99 o.s.i (0-380-79469-1, Avon Bks.) Morrow/Avon.

—Don't Drink the Water. 2000. (E. J. Pugh Mysteries Ser.). 192p. mass mkt. 5.99 o.s.i (0-380-80533-2, Avon Bks.) Morrow/Avon.

—Don't Drink the Water: An E. J. Pugh Mystery. l.t. ed. 2001. 192p. pap. 24.95 (0-7838-9521-6); 239p. (0-7540-4631-1); 239p. pap. (0-7540-4632-X) Gale Group. (Macmillan Reference USA).

—Hickory Dickory Stalk. 1996. (E. J. Pugh Mysteries Ser.). (Orig.). mass mkt. 5.50 o.s.i (0-380-78155-7, Avon Bks.) Morrow/Avon.

—Home Again, Home Again. 1997. (E. J. Pugh Mysteries Ser.). mass mkt. 5.99 o.s.i (0-380-78156-5, Avon Bks.) Morrow/Avon.

—Not in My Backyard. 1999. (E. J. Pugh Mysteries Ser.). 256p. mass mkt. 5.99 o.s.i (0-380-80532-4, Avon Bks.) Morrow/Avon.

—One, Two, What Did Daddy Do? 1996. (E. J. Pugh Mysteries Ser.). mass mkt. 5.50 o.s.i (0-380-78417-3, Avon Bks.) Morrow/Avon.

—One, Two, What Did Daddy Do? 1992. 224p. 17.95 o.p. (0-312-08209-6, Saint Martin's Minotaur) St. Martin's Pr.

—There Was a Little Girl. 1998. (E. J. Pugh Mysteries Ser.). 224p. mass mkt. 5.50 o.s.i (0-380-79468-3, Avon Bks.) Morrow/Avon.

Cunningham, Michael. The Hours. E-Book 13.00 (0-374-91952-6); 2003. E-Book 9.00 (0-374-70468-6); 1998. 230p. 23.00 (0-374-17289-7); 1998. E-Book 23.00 o.p. (0-374-70011-7); 1998. E-Book 9.00 o.p. (0-374-70006-0); 1998. E-Book 9.00 (0-374-70016-8); 1998. E-Book 9.00 (0-374-70009-5); 1998. pap. o.s.i (0-374-93947-0) Farrar, Straus & Giroux.

—The Hours. 240p. 2000. pap. 13.00 (0-312-24302-2); 2002. pap. 13.00 (0-312-30506-0) Picador.

—The Hours. l.t. ed. (Paperback Bestsellers Ser.). 2000. 253p. pap. 30.00 (0-7838-8714-0); 1999. 250p. pap. 30.95 (0-7838-8715-9) Thorndike Pr.

—The Hours. 2000. 19.05 (0-606-19100-3) Turtleback Bks.

Daly, Elizabeth. And Dangerous to Know. 1984. 176p. pap. 2.95 o.p. (0-553-24616-X) Bantam Bks.

—And Dangerous to Know. 1991. 9.95 o.p. (0-8050-0805-5) Holt, Henry & Co.

—Any Shape or Form. 1981. (Murder Ink Mystery Ser.: No. 27). pap. 2.25 o.p. (0-440-10108-5) Dell Publishing.

—Arrow Pointing Nowhere. 1983. pap. 3.25 o.p. (0-440-10021-6) Dell Publishing.

—The Book of the Lion. 1985. 160p. pap. 2.95 o.p. (0-553-24883-9) Bantam Bks.

—The Book of the Lion. 1950. 9.95 o.p. (0-8050-0806-3) Holt, Henry & Co.

—Deadly Nightshade. 1993. audio 44.20 (1-56544-034-X, 250013); audio Literate Ear, Inc.

—Death & Letters. 1981. pap. 2.25 o.p. (0-440-11791-7) Dell Publishing.

—Death & Letters. Barzun, Jacques & Taylor, W. H., eds. 1982. (Crime Fiction 1950-1975 Ser.). 131p. lib. bdg. 18.00 o.p. (0-8240-4979-9) Garland Publishing, Inc.

—The House Without the Door. 1984. 192p. pap. 2.95 o.p. (0-553-24610-0) Bantam Bks.

—Murders in Volume Two: A Henry Gamadge Mystery. 1993. audio 41.00 (1-56544-054-4, 250016); audio Literate Ear, Inc.

—Murders in Volume Two: A Henry Gamadge Mystery. 1994. 320p. reprint ed. pap. 6.95 (1-883402-52-2, Scribner) Simon & Schuster.

—Night Walk. 1982. (Murder Ink Mystery Ser.: No. 55). pap. 2.50 o.p. (0-440-16609-8) Dell Publishing.

—Nothing Can Rescue Me. 1984. 192p. pap. 2.95 o.p. (0-553-24605-4) Bantam Bks.

—Somewhere in the House. 1984. 192p. pap. 2.95 o.p. (0-553-24267-9) Bantam Bks.

—Unexpected Night: A Henry Gamadge Mystery. 1986. (Mystery Ser.). 224p. pap. 2.95 o.p. (0-553-25129-5) Bantam Bks.

—Unexpected Night: A Henry Gamadge Mystery. 1991. 9.95 o.p. (0-8050-0807-1) Holt, Henry & Co.

—Unexpected Night: A Henry Gamadge Mystery. 1993. audio. audio 39.20 (1-56544-033-1, 250003) Literate Ear, Inc.

—Unexpected Night: A Henry Gamadge Mystery. 1995. pap. 6.95 (1-883402-14-X); 1994. 240p. reprint ed. per. 7.00 (1-883402-51-4) Simon & Schuster. (Scribner).

—The Wrong Way Down. 1986. mass mkt. 9.95 o.p. (0-553-06515-7) Bantam Bks.

Davis, Patricia K. A Midnight Carol: A Novel of How Charles Dickens Saved Christmas. 1999. 192p. 16.95 o.p. (0-312-24523-8); 2000. 208p. reprint ed. mass mkt. 4.99 (0-312-97698-4, St. Martin's Paperbacks) St. Martin's Pr.

DeAndrea, William L. The Fatal Elixir: A Lobo Blacke-Quinn Booker Mystery. 1997. (Lobo Black/Quinn Booker Mystery Ser.). 208p. 22.95 (0-8027-3289-5) Walker & Co.

—Written in Fire: A Lobo Blacke-Quinn Booker Mystery. 1995. 168p. 19.95 (0-8027-3270-4) Walker & Co.

Delinsky, Barbara. Bronze Mystique. (Mira Bks.). 1997. mass mkt. (1-55166-423-2, 1-66423-4, Mira Bks.); 1992. mass mkt. (0-373-83252-4, 1-83252-6, Harlequin Bks.); 1984. pap. o.s.i (0-373-25117-3, Harlequin Bks.) Harlequin Enterprises, Ltd.

—Bronze Mystique. l.t. ed. 2000. (Romance Ser.). 277p. pap. 28.95 (0-7838-9047-8) Thorndike Pr.

Duffy, Margaret. Brass Eagle. 1990. 256p. mass mkt. 3.95 o.s.i (0-449-21887-2, Fawcett) Ballantine Bks.

—Brass Eagle. unabr. ed. 1998. audio 83.95 (1-85903-017-3) Magna Story Sound GBR. Dist: Ulverscroft Large Print Bks., Ltd.

—Brass Eagle. 1989. 15.95 o.p. (0-312-02880-6, Saint Martin's Minotaur) St. Martin's Pr.

—Brass Eagle. l.t. ed. 1991. (Ulverscroft Large Print Ser.). 29.99 o.p. (0-7089-2347-X, Ulverscroft) Thorpe, F. A. Pubs. GBR. Dist: Ulverscroft Large Print Bks., Ltd., Ulverscroft Large Print Canada, Ltd.

—Death of a Raven. 1989. 240p. mass mkt. 3.50 o.s.i (0-449-21741-8, Fawcett) Ballantine Bks.

—Death of a Raven. 1988. 224p. 15.95 o.p. (0-312-02567-X, Saint Martin's Minotaur) St. Martin's Pr.

—Death of a Raven. l.t. ed. 1990. (Ulverscroft Large Print Ser.). 29.99 o.p. (0-7089-2202-3, Ulverscroft) Thorpe, F. A. Pubs. GBR. Dist: Ulverscroft Large Print Bks., Ltd., Ulverscroft Large Print Canada, Ltd.

—A Murder of Crows. 1988. mass mkt. 3.50 o.s.i (0-449-21563-6, Fawcett) Ballantine Bks.

—A Murder of Crows. 1988. 240p. 15.95 o.p. (0-312-01483-X, Saint Martin's Minotaur) St. Martin's Pr.

—A Murder of Crows. l.t. ed. 1989. (Ulverscroft Large Print Ser.). 531p. 29.99 o.p. (0-7089-1929-4, Ulverscroft) Thorpe, F. A. Pubs. GBR. Dist: Ulverscroft Large Print Bks., Ltd., Ulverscroft Large Print Canada, Ltd.

—Rook-Shoot. l.t. ed. 1993. (Dales Mystery Ser.). 392p. pap. 19.99 (1-85389-399-4) Dales Large Print Bks. GBR. Dist: Ulverscroft Large Print Bks., Ltd.

—Rook-Shoot. 1991. 240p. 17.95 o.p. (0-312-06456-X, Saint Martin's Minotaur) St. Martin's Pr.

—Who Killed Cock Robin? 1990. 224p. 16.95 o.p. (0-312-04988-9, Saint Martin's Minotaur) St. Martin's Pr.

Dufresne, John. Love Warps the Mind a Little. l.t. ed. 1997. 352p. 23.00 (0-393-04013-5) Norton, W. W. & Co., Inc.

Duve, Karen. Rain: A Novel. Bell, Anthea, tr. from GER. 2003. 221p. pap. 14.95 (1-58234-179-6) Bloomsbury Publishing.

Edelman, Maurice. Disraeli Rising. 1978. 282p. 1.95 o.p. (0-8128-7007-7); 1975. 3.95 o.p. (0-8128-1675-7) Madison Bks., Inc. (Scarborough Hse.).

Edwards, Louis. Oscar Wilde Discovers America. 2003. 304p. 24.00 (0-7432-3689-0, Scribner) Simon & Schuster.

Eisner, William. The Sevigne Letters. Putnam, Jeff, ed. 1994. 201p. 18.00 (1-880909-27-8) Baskerville Pubs., Inc.

Evans, Richard Paul. A Perfect Day. 2003. 288p. 22.95 (0-525-94765-5) Dutton/Plume.

—A Perfect Day. l.t. ed. 2004. 374p. 32.95 (1-58724-563-9, Wheeler Publishing, Inc.) Gale Group.

Fawcett, Quinn. Siren Song: Ian Fleming #2. 2003. (Ian Fleming Ser.). 368p. 25.95 (*0-312-86928-2*, Tor Bks.) Doherty, Tom Assocs., LLC.
Feinstein, Elaine. Dark Inheritance. l.t. ed. 2001. 258p. pap. 22.95 (*0-7862-3566-7*); 274p. (*0-7540-4623-0*); 274p. (*0-7540-4624-9*) Thorndike Pr.
—Dark Inheritance. 2001. 154p. pap. 13.95 (*0-7043-4725-3*); 234p. pap. 16.95 (*0-7043-4671-0*) Women's Pr., Ltd., The GBR. *Dist:* Trafalgar Square.
Fenady, Andrew J. The Summer of Jack London. 1997. 240p. mass mkt. 5.99 o.s.i (*0-425-16096-3*) Berkley Publishing Group.
—The Summer of Jack London. l.t. ed. 2002. pap. 24.95 (*0-7862-4079-2*) Gale Group.
Fenady, Andrew Y. The Summer of Jack London. 1985. 192p. 13.95 o.s.i (*0-8027-4040-5*) Walker & Co.
Fforde, Jasper. The Well of Lost Plots: A Thursday Next Novel. 2004. 400p. 24.95 (*0-670-03289-1*) Viking Penguin.
Fitzwater, Judy. Dying for a Clue. 1999. (Jennifer Marsh Mysteries Ser.). 240p. mass mkt. 7.99 (*0-449-00426-0*, Fawcett) Ballantine Bks.
—Dying for a Clue. l.t. ed. 2000. (G. K. Hall Paperback Ser.). 271p. pap. 23.95 (*0-7838-9113-X*, Macmillan Reference USA) Gale Group.
—Dying to Get Published. (Jennifer Marsh Mysteries Ser.). 240p. 1998. mass mkt. 5.99 (*0-449-00294-2*, Fawcett); 1995. pap. 15.00 (*0-345-46381-1*, Ballantine Bks.) Ballantine Bks.
—Dying to Get Published. l.t. ed. 2000. (G. K. Hall Paperback Ser.). 264p. pap. 23.95 (*0-7838-8855-4*, Macmillan Reference USA) Gale Group.
—Dying to Remember. 2000. (Jennifer Marsh Mysteries Ser.). 240p. mass mkt. 6.50 (*0-449-00639-5*, Fawcett) Ballantine Bks.
—Dying to Remember. l.t. ed. 2001. 272p. (*0-7540-4425-4*); (*0-7540-4426-2*) Gale Group. (Macmillan Reference USA).
—Dying to Remember. l.t. ed. 2001. (Paperback Ser.). 272p. pap. 24.95 (*0-7838-9333-7*) Thorndike Pr.
Foer, Jonathan Safran. Everything Is Illuminated: A Novel. 2003. 288p. pap. 13.95 (*0-06-052970-9*, Perennial) HarperTrade.
—Everything Is Illuminated: A Novel. 2002. (Illus.). 288p. tchr. ed. 24.00 (*0-618-17387-0*) Houghton Mifflin Co.
Foley, Michael. The Road to Notown. 1997. 342p. pap. 16.95 (*0-85640-576-0*) Blackstaff Pr., The IRL. *Dist:* Dufour Editions, Inc.
Foreman, Walter C., Jr. Fairy Tale. 2003. 350p. 22.95 (*1-880909-63-4*) Baskerville Pubs., Inc.
Forrest, Richard. A Child's Garden of Death. 1982. (Scene of the Crime Ser.: No. 44). pap. 2.25 o.p. (*0-440-11325-3*) Dell Publishing.
—A Child's Garden of Death. 1977. pap. 1.50 o.p. (*0-671-80924-5*, Pocket) Simon & Schuster.
—The Death at Yew Corner. 1984. 176p. pap. 2.95 o.p. (*0-440-11782-8*) Dell Publishing.
—The Death at Yew Corner. 1981. (Rinehart Suspense Novel Ser.). 228p. o.p. (*0-03-053386-4*) Holt, Henry & Co.
—The Death in the Willows. 1979. (Rinehart Suspense Novel Ser.). 228p. o.p. (*0-03-049296-3*) Holt, Henry & Co.
—Death on the Mississippi. 1989. 224p. 15.95 o.p. (*0-312-03323-0*, Saint Martin's Minotaur) St. Martin's Pr.
—Death Through the Looking Glass. 1979. pap. 1.75 o.s.i (*0-671-82157-1*, Pocket) Simon & Schuster.
—Death under the Lilacs. 1985. 208p. 13.95 o.p. (*0-312-18878-1*) St. Martin's Pr.
—Pied Piper of Death: A Lyon & Bea Wentworth Mystery. 1997. 240p. 21.95 o.p. (*0-312-15292-2*, Saint Martin's Minotaur) St. Martin's Pr.
Fraser, Anthea. Motive for Murder. l.t. ed. 2002. (General Ser.). 272p. pap. 22.95 (*0-7862-3689-2*) Gale Group.
—Motive for Murder. 1996. 224p. 24.00 o.p. (*0-7278-5140-3*) Severn Hse. Pubs., Ltd.
Gould, Judith. The Greek Villa. 2003. 352p. 23.95 (*0-451-21047-6*) NAL.
Gutteridge, Rene. Boo. 2003. 256p. pap. 11.99 (*1-57856-573-1*) WaterBrook Pr.
Haddam, Jane. Act of Darkness. 1991. 288p. mass mkt. 4.50 o.s.i (*0-553-29086-X*) Bantam Bks.
—And One to Die On: A Birthday Mystery. 1997. 304p. mass mkt. 5.99 o.s.i (*0-553-56448-X*) Bantam Bks.
—Baptism in Blood. 1996. 352p. mass mkt. 5.99 o.s.i (*0-553-57464-7*, Crimeline) Bantam Bks.
—Bleeding Hearts. 1995. 368p. mass mkt. 5.50 o.s.i (*0-553-56936-8*) Bantam Bks.
—Deadly Beloved. 1998. 336p. mass mkt. 5.99 o.s.i (*0-553-57200-8*) Bantam Bks.
—Dear Old Dead. 1994. 352p. mass mkt. 5.50 o.s.i (*0-553-56447-1*) Bantam Bks.
—Feast of Murder. 1992. 336p. mass mkt. 5.50 o.s.i (*0-553-29389-3*) Bantam Bks.
—A Festival of Deaths. 1994. 384p. mass mkt. 5.99 o.s.i (*0-553-56085-9*) Bantam Bks.
—The Fountain of Death. 1995. 352p. (Orig.). mass mkt. 5.50 o.s.i (*0-553-56449-8*, Crimeline) Bantam Bks.
—A Great Day for the Deadly. 1992. 288p. mass mkt. 5.50 o.s.i (*0-553-29388-5*) Bantam Bks.
—Murder Superior. 1993. 304p. mass mkt. 5.99 o.s.i (*0-553-56084-0*) Bantam Bks.
—Not a Creature Was Stirring: A Gregor Demarkian Holiday Mystery. 1990. 320p. mass mkt. 5.99 o.s.i (*0-553-28792-3*) Bantam Bks.
—Precious Blood. 1991. 336p. mass mkt. 5.99 o.s.i (*0-553-28913-6*) Bantam Bks.
—Quoth the Raven. 1991. 288p. mass mkt. 5.99 o.s.i (*0-553-29255-2*) Bantam Bks.
—Skeleton Key. 2000. 276p. 23.95 o.p. (*0-312-20909-6*, Saint Martin's Minotaur) St. Martin's Pr.
—A Stillness in Bethlehem. 1993. (Gregor Demarkian Holiday Mystery Ser.). 368p. mass mkt. 5.50 o.s.i (*0-553-29390-7*) Bantam Bks.
Hall, James W. Rough Draft. l.t. ed. 2000. (Wheeler Softcover Ser.). 452p. pap. 24.95 (*1-56895-130-2*, Wheeler Publishing, Inc.) Gale Group.
—Rough Draft. E-Book 6.99 (*0-312-27347-9*); 2000. 352p. 24.95 o.p. (*0-312-20383-7*); 2001. 368p. reprint ed. mass mkt. 6.99 (*0-312-97492-2*, St. Martin's Paperbacks) St. Martin's Pr.
Hamsun, Knut. Hunger. 2001. 224p. pap. 9.83 (*1-84195-206-0*) Canongate Bks. GBR. *Dist:* Grove/Atlantic, Inc.
—Hunger. reprint ed. 2001. pap. text 28.00 (*0-7426-9475-5*); 1923. 118.00 (*0-7426-4475-8*) Classic Bks.
—Hunger. Egerton, George, tr. from NOR. 2003. 144p. pap. 5.95 (*0-486-43168-1*) Dover Pubns., Inc.
—Hunger. Bly, Robert, tr. & afterword by by. 1998. 240p. pap. 14.00 (*0-374-52528-5*) Farrar, Straus & Giroux.
—Hunger. Bly, Robert, tr. from NOR. 1967. 256p. pap. 10.00 o.s.i (*0-374-50520-9*) Farrar, Straus & Giroux.
—Hunger. Bly, Robert, tr. 1980. pap. 1.75 o.p. (*0-380-00556-5*, 42028, Avon Bks.) Morrow/Avon.
—Hunger. 2002. (YID.). (C). reprint ed. pap. 29.00 (*0-657-03477-0*); pap. 29.00 (*0-657-07069-6*); pap. 29.00 (*0-657-07065-3*) National Yiddish Bk. Ctr.
—Hunger. Lyngstad, Sverre, tr. from NOR. 1996. 194p. reprint ed. pap. 14.95 (*0-86241-625-6*) Rebel, Inc. GBR. *Dist:* AK Pr. Distribution.
—Hunger. Lyngstad, Sverre, ed. & tr. by. 1998. (Twentieth Century Classics Ser.). 224p. 13.00 (*0-14-118064-1*, Penguin Classics) Viking Penguin.
Harris, Joanne. Blackberry Wine. 336p. 2002. pap. (*0-385-65945-8*); 2001. (Illus.). pap. (*0-385-25776-7*) Doubleday Canada, Ltd. CAN. *Dist:* Random Hse., Inc.
—Blackberry Wine. l.t. ed. 2001. (G. K. Hall Core Ser.). 416p. 28.95 (*0-7838-9453-8*, Macmillan Reference USA) Gale Group.
—Blackberry Wine. 2001. 368p. pap. 13.00 (*0-380-81592-3*, Perennial) HarperTrade.
—Blackberry Wine. 2000. 368p. 24.00 (*0-380-97872-5*, Morrow, William & Co.) Morrow/Avon.
Hart, Josephine. The Stillest Day. l.t. ed. 1999. 192p. 32.50 (*0-7531-5974-0*); pap. (*0-7531-5987-2*, 159872) ISIS Large Print Bks. GBR. *Dist:* Ulverscroft Large Print Bks., Ltd., Ulverscroft Large Print Canada, Ltd., Ulverscroft Large Print Canada, Ltd.
—The Stillest Day. 224p. 1999. 13.95 (*0-87951-727-1*); 1998. 23.95 (*0-87951-894-4*) Overlook Pr., The.
Heller, Zoe. Everything You Know. 2000. 224p. 22.00 o.s.i (*0-375-40724-3*) Knopf, Alfred A. Inc.
—Everything You Know. 2001. (Illus.). 224p. reprint ed. pap. 12.95 (*0-7434-1195-1*, Washington Square Pr.) Simon & Schuster.
Hill, Grace Livingston. Kerry. 24.95 (*0-89190-357-7*) Amereon, Ltd.
—Kerry. l.t. ed. 2001. (Thorndike Candlelight Romance Ser.). 424p. 24.95 (*0-7862-3135-1*, Macmillan Reference USA) Gale Group.
—Kerry. 1995. (Grace Livingston Hill Ser.: Vol. 5). 288p. mass mkt. 4.99 o.p. (*0-8423-2044-X*) Tyndale Hse. Pubs.
Ireland, Ann. Exile: A Novel. 2002. 300p. 34.99 (*1-55002-400-0*) Dundurn Pr. CAN. *Dist:* Univ. of Toronto Pr.
James, Dean. Faked to Death: A Simon Kirby-Jones Mystery. 2003. 288p. 22.00 (*1-57566-887-4*) Kensington Publishing Corp.
Kaminsky, Stuart M. Retribution. mass mkt. 6.99 (*0-8125-4036-0*); 2001. 272p. 24.95 (*0-312-87452-9*) Doherty, Tom Assocs., LLC. (Forge Bks.).
Karasu, Bilge. Night: A Novel. Gun, Guneli, tr. 1994. 152p. (C). 19.95 (*0-8071-1849-4*) Louisiana State Univ. Pr.
Kauffman, Donna. The Big Bad Wolf Tells All. 2003. 368p. pap. 10.95 (*0-553-38222-5*) Bantam Bks.
Kelly, Susan. The Gemini Man. 1986. 304p. mass mkt. 2.95 o.s.i (*0-345-33113-3*) Ballantine Bks.
—The Gemini Man. 1985. 221p. 14.95 o.s.i (*0-8027-5613-1*) Walker & Co.
—Out of the Darkness. unabr. ed. 1992. audio 21.95 o.p. (*1-56100-478-2*, 204, Bookcassette); audio 57.25 o.p. (*1-56100-112-0*, 974, Unabridged Library Editions) Brilliance Audio.
—Out of the Darkness. 1994. 352p. mass mkt. 4.50 o.s.i (*0-8217-4620-0*) Kensington Publishing Corp.
—Out of the Darkness. 1992. 278p. 18.00 o.s.i (*0-679-41131-3*, Villard Bks.) Random House Adult Trade Publishing Group.
—The Summertime Soldiers. 1986. 192p. 14.95 o.p. (*0-8027-5646-8*) Walker & Co.
—Trail of the Dragon. 1990. 256p. mass mkt. 3.95 o.s.i (*0-345-35749-3*) Ballantine Bks.
—Trail of the Dragon. 1988. 282p. 17.95 (*0-8027-5696-4*) Walker & Co.
—Until Proven Innocent. unabr. ed. 1991. audio 57.25 o.p. (*1-56100-067-1*, 593); audio 21.95 o.p. (*0-930435-73-7*, 411) Brilliance Audio.
—Until Proven Innocent. 1990. 288p. 16.95 o.s.i (*0-394-58414-7*, Villard Bks.) Random House Adult Trade Publishing Group.
Kelman, Judith. Every Step You Take. 2004. 384p. mass mkt. 7.99 (*0-515-13792-8*, Jove) Berkley Publishing Group.
—Every Step You Take. 2003. 336p. 24.95 (*0-399-15109-5*) Putnam Publishing Group, The.
Kinder, Chuck. The Honeymooners: A Cautionary Tale. 2001. 384p. 24.00 o.p. (*0-374-17258-7*) Farrar, Straus & Giroux.
King, Beverly. Unlikely Match: A Novel. 2003. 279p. 14.95 (*1-59156-193-0*) Covenant Communications.
King, Stephen. Bag of Bones. 2000. (RUS.). Vol. 1. pap. 14.95 (*5-237-01450-X*); Vol. 2. pap. 14.95 (*5-237-01451-8*) AST, Izdatel'stvo, OOO, firma RUS. *Dist:* Distribooks, Inc.
—Bag of Bones. 2002. E-Book 9.99 (*1-59061-785-1*) Adobe Systems, Inc.
—Bag of Bones. unabr. ed. 1999. audio 59.95 Highsmith Inc.
—Bag of Bones. unabr. ed. 1999. audio 56.00 (*1-84032-192-X*) Hodder Headline Audiobooks GBR. *Dist:* Ulverscroft Large Print Bks., Ltd.
—Bag of Bones. 1999. E-Book 28.00 (*0-684-83541-X*, Scribner); 1998. 544p. 28.00 (*0-684-85350-7*, Scribner); 1988. pap. 7.99 (*0-671-02607-0*, Pocket); 1999. 752p. reprint ed. mass mkt. 7.99 (*0-671-02423-X*, Pocket) Simon & Schuster.
—Bag of Bones. unabr. ed. 1998. audio 59.95 (*0-671-58234-8*, 136013); audio compact disk 79.95 (*0-671-04306-4*) Simon & Schuster Audio. (Simon & Schuster Audioworks).
—Bag of Bones. l.t. ed. 1999. (Thorndike/G. K. Hall Paperback Bestsellers Ser.). 901p. pap. 28.95 (*0-7862-1721-9*); 30.95 o.p. (*0-7862-1720-0*) Thorndike Pr.
—Bag of Bones. 1999. 14.04 (*0-606-17066-9*) Turtleback Bks.
—The Dark Half. l.t. ed. 1991. (General Ser.). 623p. 14.95 o.p. (*0-8161-5123-7*); xxiii, 608p. lib. bdg. 22.95 o.p. (*0-8161-5109-1*) Gale Group. (Macmillan Reference USA).
—The Dark Half. 496p. 1993. mass mkt. 5.99 o.p. (*0-451-17181-0*); 1990. reprint ed. mass mkt. 7.99 (*0-451-16731-7*) NAL. (Signet Bks.).
—The Dark Half. 1990. 14.04 (*0-606-04648-8*) Turtleback Bks.
—The Dark Half. 1989. 448p. text 27.95 (*0-670-82982-X*) Viking Penguin.
Lane, Simon. Fear: A Novel. 1998. 211p. 21.95 (*1-882593-22-7*) Bridge Works Publishing Co., Inc.
Lelchuk, Alan. Ziff - A Life? A Novel. 2003. 432p. 25.00 (*0-7867-1115-9*, Carroll & Graf Pubs.) Avalon Publishing Group.
L'Heureux, John. A Woman Run Mad. 2000. 258p. reprint ed. pap. 13.00 (*0-8021-3731-8*, Grove Pr.) Grove/Atlantic, Inc.
—A Woman Run Mad. 1989. 240p. reprint ed. mass mkt. 4.99 (*0-380-70686-5*, Avon Bks.) Morrow/Avon.
—A Woman Run Mad. 1999. pap. (*0-14-010194-2*, Viking); 1988. 17.95 o.p. (*0-670-81752-X*) Viking Penguin.
Lodge, David. Home Truths: A Novella. 2000. 128p. 11.95 (*0-14-029180-6*) Viking Penguin.
Luzkow, Jack Lawerence. The Birthday Present. 2001. 260p. pap. 14.00 (*0-9701723-1-1*) Parma Hse., Ltd.
Maddison, Lauren. Epitaph for an Angel: A Connor Hawthorne Mystery. 2003. (Connor Hawthorne Mystery Ser.). 400p. pap. 14.95 (*1-55583-812-X*, Alyson Bks.) Alyson Pubns.
Marshall, Evan. Toasting Tina. 2003. 304p. 22.00 (*0-7582-0226-1*, Kensington Bks.) Kensington Publishing Corp.
Maso, Carole. The American Woman in the Chinese Hat. 1994. 200p. 19.95 (*1-56478-045-7*) Dalkey Archive Pr.
Maugham, W. Somerset. Cakes & Ale. 2000. 320p. pap. 13.00 (*0-375-72502-4*, Vintage) Knopf Publishing Group.
McConkey, James. To a Distant Island. 2000. (Illus.). 203p. reprint ed. pap. 14.95 (*0-9664913-5-1*) Dry, Paul Bks., Inc.
McConnell, David. The Firebrat. 2003. 246p. 22.00 (*0-929435-71-0*) AttaGirl Pr.
McCrae, Jackson Tippett. The Bark of the Dogwood: A Tour of Southern Homes & Gardens. 2002. 563p. 28.00 (*0-9715536-0-2*) Enolam Group, Inc., The.
McCrumb, Sharyn. Bimbos of the Death Sun. 1996. 224p. mass mkt. 6.50 (*0-345-41215-X*) Ballantine Bks.
—Bimbos of the Death Sun. unabr. ed. 1988. audio 35.00 (*0-7887-3758-9*, 95942E7) Recorded Bks., LLC.
—Bimbos of the Death Sun. 1988. pap. 3.95 o.p. (*0-88038-455-7*) Wizards of the Coast.
—Zombies of the Gene Pool. 1993. 288p. mass mkt. 6.99 (*0-345-37914-4*) Ballantine Bks.
McDermid, Val. Killing the Shadows. 2000. 422p. (*0-00-226108-1*) HarperCollins Pubs.
—Killing the Shadows. E-Book 24.95 (*0-312-70297-3*); 2001. 432p. 24.95 (*0-312-26615-4*, Saint Martin's Minotaur) St. Martin's Pr.
McElroy, Joseph. A Smuggler's Bible. 2003. 435p. pap. 15.95 (*1-58567-351-X*) Overlook Pr., The.
McGahan, Andrew. 1988. 1998. 320p. pap. 12.95 (*0-312-18032-2*, 837237, Saint Martin's Griffin); 1996. 314p. 22.95 o.p. (*0-312-15043-1*) St. Martin's Pr.
McGahern, John. The Pornographer. 1979. 11.45 o.p. (*0-06-013021-0*) HarperCollins Pubs.
—The Pornographer. 1983. 256p. pap. 6.95 o.p. (*0-14-006489-3*, Penguin Bks.) Viking Penguin.
McHugh, Stuart D. Knock on the Nursery Door: Tales of the Dickens Children. 1973. 9.95 o.p. (*0-7181-1031-5*) Transatlantic Arts, Inc.
McInerny, Ralph. Sub Rosa: An Egidio Manfredi Mystery. 2001. (Five Star First Edition Mystery Ser.). 200p. 24.95 (*0-7862-3559-4*, Five Star) Gale Group.
Michaels, Fern. The Guest List. 2000. (Five Star Romance Ser.). 398p. 27.95 (*0-7862-2985-3*, Five Star); 468p. 27.95 (*1-56895-943-5*, Wheeler Publishing, Inc.) Gale Group.
—The Guest List. 2002. mass mkt. 7.99 (*0-8217-7602-9*); 2000. 4p. mass mkt. 7.50 o.s.i (*0-8217-6657-0*, Zebra Bks.) Kensington Publishing Corp.
Michaels, Kasey. Maggie Needs an Alibi. 2003. 333p. mass mkt. 6.99 (*1-57566-880-7*) Kensington Publishing Corp.
—Maggie Needs an Alibi. l.t. ed. 2002. (Americana 5 Ser.). 560p. 28.95 (*0-7862-4765-7*) Thorndike Pr.
Miscione, Lisa. The Gathering Darkness. 2004. mass mkt. 6.99 (*0-312-99002-2*, St. Martin's Paperbacks) St. Martin's Pr.
Montgomery, Ian A. Dead Duck: A Jud Carson Mystery. Spafford, Jacalyn A., ed. 1993. 120p. (Orig.). pap. 9.95 (*1-890538-15-9*) Rhiannon Pubns.
Morton, Brian. A Window Across the River. 2003. 304p. 25.00 (*0-15-100757-8*) Harcourt Trade Pubs.
Mossman, Dow. The Stones of Summer. 2003. 576p. 19.95 (*0-7607-4884-5*) Barnes & Noble, Inc.
Murphy, Pat. Adventures in Time & Space with Max Merriwell. 2002. E-Book 24.95 (*1-59061-722-3*) Adobe Systems, Inc.
—Adventures in Time & Space with Max Merriwell. 2001. 288p. text 24.95 (*0-312-86643-7*, Tor Bks.) Doherty, Tom Assocs., LLC.
Naipaul, V. S. Half a Life. 2001. 224p. 24.00 (*0-375-40737-5*) Knopf, Alfred A. Inc.
—Half a Life: A Novel. 2002. 224p. pap. 13.00 (*0-375-70728-X*) Knopf, Alfred A. Inc.
—Vintage Naipaul. 2004. 208p. pap. 9.95 (*1-4000-3400-0*, Vintage) Knopf Publishing Group.
Nicholson, Geoff. Bedlam Burning. 298p. 2003. pap. 15.95 (*1-58567-453-2*); 2002. 26.95 (*1-58567-239-4*) Overlook Pr., The.
Nighbert, David F. Shutout. 1995. 307p. 21.95 o.p. (*0-312-11890-2*, Saint Martin's Minotaur) St. Martin's Pr.
—Squeezeplay: A Mystery. 1992. 272p. 18.95 o.p. (*0-312-07847-1*, Saint Martin's Minotaur) St. Martin's Pr.
—Strikezone. 1989. 14.95 o.p. (*0-312-02987-X*, Saint Martin's Minotaur) St. Martin's Pr.
Norfolk, Lawrence. In the Shape of a Boar. 2001. 336p. 25.00 o.p. (*0-8021-1701-5*) Grove/Atlantic, Inc.
Nunez, Sigrid. For Rouenna. 2001. 208p. 22.00 o.p. (*0-374-25430-3*) Farrar, Straus & Giroux.
—For Rouenna. l.t. ed. 2001. 273p. 27.95 (*1-58724-217-6*, Wheeler Publishing, Inc.) Gale Group.
—For Rouenna: A Novel. 2002. 240p. pap. 13.00 (*0-312-42063-3*) Picador.
Oates, Joyce Carol. The Tattooed Girl. 2003. 7p. pap. 59.95 (*0-7927-2896-3*); 9p. pap. 89.95 (*0-7927-2897-1*) BBC Audiobooks America.
—The Tattooed Girl. 320p. 2004. pap. 13.95 (*0-06-053107-X*); 2003. 25.95 (*0-06-053106-1*) HarperTrade. (Ecco).
O'Brien, Meg. Crashing Down. abr. ed. 1999. audio 7.99 (*1-55204-178-6*, MIR-1178) Durkin Hayes Publishing Ltd.

—Crashing Down. 1999. (Mira Bks.). 408p. mass mkt. (*1-55166-516-6*, 1-66516-5, Mira Bks.) Harlequin Enterprises, Ltd.

O'Kane, Leslie. The Fax of Life, 1. 1999. 256p. mass mkt. 5.99 o.s.i (*0-449-00160-1*, Fawcett) Ballantine Bks.

—The Fax of Life. l.t. ed. 2000. (Mystery Ser.). 381p. 26.95 (*0-7862-2328-6*) Thorndike Pr.

Olson, Toby. The Blond Box. 2003. 220p. pap. 14.95 (*1-57366-110-4*) Fiction Collective Two, Inc.

Ong, Han. Fixer Chao. 2001. 377p. 25.00 (*0-374-15575-5*) Farrar, Straus & Giroux.

—Fixer Chao. 2002. 384p. pap. 14.00 (*0-312-42053-6*) Picador.

Pall, Ellen. Slightly Abridged: A Nine Muses Mystery: Erato. 2003. 288p. 23.95 (*0-312-28185-4*, Saint Martin's Minotaur) St. Martin's Pr.

—Slightly Abridged: A Nine Muses Mystery: Erato. l.t. ed. 2003. (Nine Muses Mystery: Erato Ser.). 420p. 28.95 (*0-7862-5817-9*) Thorndike Pr.

Palmer, Diana. Heart of Ice. 1995. (Western Lovers Ser.). mass mkt. (*0-373-88524-5*, 1-88524-3, Harlequin Bks.) Harlequin Enterprises, Ltd.

Palmer, William J. The Detective & Mr. Dickens: A Secret Victorian Journal. 1992. reprint ed. mass mkt. 3.99 o.s.i (*0-345-37471-1*) Ballantine Bks.

—The Highwayman & Mr. Dickens: A Secret Victorian Journal, Attributed to Wilkie Collins. 1993. reprint ed. mass mkt. 4.99 o.s.i (*0-345-38252-8*) Ballantine Bks.

—The Hoydens & Mr. Dickens. 1996. 256p. 21.95 o.p. (*0-312-15145-4*) St. Martin's Pr.

Palmer, William J., ed. The Detective & Mr. Dickens: A Secret Victorian Journal. 1990. 320p. 17.95 o.p. (*0-312-05073-9*) St. Martin's Pr.

—The Highwayman & Mr. Dickens: A Secret Victorian Journal, Attributed to Wilkie Collins. 1992. 288p. text 18.95 o.p. (*0-312-08207-X*, Saint Martin's Minotaur) St. Martin's Pr.

Peachment, Christopher. The Green & the Gold. 2003. 200p. (*0-330-48733-7*) Picador.

Pearl, Matthew. The Dante Club. l.t. ed. 2003. 615p. 32.95 (*1-58724-465-9*, Wheeler Publishing, Inc.) Gale Group.

—The Dante Club: A Novel. 2004. 400p. pap. 13.95 (*0-8129-7104-3*, Random Hse. Trade Paperbacks) Random House Adult Trade Publishing Group.

—The Dante Club: A Novel. 2003. (Illus.). 384p. 24.95 (*0-375-50529-6*); E-Book 17.50 (*1-58836-310-4*) Random Hse., Inc.

—The Dante Club: A Novel. 2003. audio compact disk 30.00 (*0-7435-1792-X*); audio compact disk 30.00 (*0-7435-1792-X*) Simon & Schuster Audio. (Simon & Schuster Audioworks).

Phillips, Michael. The Garden at the Edge of Beyond. 1998. 160p. text 12.99 o.p. (*0-7642-2042-X*) Bethany Hse. Pubs.

—The Garden at the Edge of Beyond. l.t. ed. 1999. (Inspirational Ser.). 181p. 25.95 (*0-7838-8515-6*) Thorndike Pr.

Quosaybai, Ghaazai Abd al-Raohmaan. A Love Story. 2002. 140p. pap. 12.50 (*0-86356-320-1*) I.B.Tauris & Co., Ltd. GBR. *Dist:* Holtzbrinck Pubs., Palgrave Macmillan.

Raban, Jonathan. Waxwings: A Novel. 2003. 288p. 24.00 (*0-375-41008-2*, Pantheon) Knopf Publishing Group.

Redonnet, Marie. Candy Story. Quinn, Alexandra, tr. from FRE. 1995. (European Women Writers Ser.). 99p. text 20.00 o.p. (*0-8032-3915-7*); pap. 10.00 (*0-8032-8958-8*) Univ. of Nebraska Pr.

Rhode, Will. Paperback Original. 2004. 464p. pap. 14.00 (*1-59448-014-1*) Putnam Publishing Group, The.

Roberts, Les. The Chinese Fire Drill. 2003. 192p. pap. 13.95 (*1-4104-0114-6*, Five Star Trade); 2001. 188p. 23.95 (*0-7862-3760-0*, Five Star) Gale Group.

Roberts, Michele. The Mistressclass. 2003. 304p. 23.00 (*0-8050-7440-6*) Holt, Henry & Co.

Roberts, Nora. Brazen Virtue. 2002. 304p. mass mkt. 7.99 (*0-553-27283-7*, Spectra) Bantam Bks.

—Brazen Virtue. l.t. ed. 2001. 464p. 18.95 (*0-375-43112-8*) Random Hse. Large Print.

Rogan, Barbara. Suspicion. l.t. ed. 2000. pap. 23.95 (*1-56895-874-9*, Wheeler Publishing, Inc.) Gale Group.

—Suspicion. 1999. 352p. 24.00 (*0-684-81415-3*, Simon & Schuster); 2000. 432p. reprint ed. pap. 6.99 (*0-7434-0057-7*, Pocket) Simon & Schuster.

Rogow, Roberta. The Problem of the Evil Editor: A Charles Dodgson/Arthur Conan Doyle Mystery. 2000. (Charles Dodgson/Arthur Conan Doyle Mysteries Ser.). 298p. 23.95 (*0-312-20903-7*, Saint Martin's Minotaur) St. Martin's Pr.

Roiphe, Katie. Still She Haunts Me. 2002. 240p. pap. 12.95 (*0-385-33530-X*, Delta) Dell Publishing.

—Still She Haunts Me: A Novel of Lewis Carroll & Alice Liddell. 2002. E-Book 11.50 (*0-440-33385-7*, Delta) Dell Publishing.

Rolens, Sharon. Worthy's Town: A Novel. 2000. 230p. 22.95 (*1-882593-35-9*); 2002. 288p. reprint ed. pap. 13.95 (*1-882593-57-X*) Bridge Works Publishing Co., Inc.

—Worthy's Town: A Novel. l.t. ed. 2001. 343p. 28.95 (*0-7862-3376-1*) Thorndike Pr.

Rosenbaum, Thane. The Golems of Gotham. 2002. 384p. 25.95 (*0-06-018490-6*) HarperCollins Pubs.

—The Golems of Gotham. 2003. 384p. pap. 13.95 (*0-06-095945-2*, Perennial) HarperTrade.

Rosenstone, Richard A. The King of Odessa: A Novel of Isaac Babel. 2003. 256p. 24.95 (*0-8101-1992-7*) Northwestern Univ. Pr.

Ross, Veronica. The Anastasia Connection. 204p. pap. 15.95 (*1-55128-038-8*) Mercury Bks. CAN. *Dist:* LPC/InBook.

—Millicent: A Mystery. 2001. 256p. pap. 7.99 (*1-55128-042-6*) Mercury Bks. CAN. *Dist:* LPC/InBook.

Roszak, Theodore. The Devil & Daniel Silverman. 2003. 348p. pap. 15.95 (*0-9679520-7-7*) Leapfrog Pr.

Rowlands, Betty. Exhaustive Enquiries: A Melissa Craig Mystery. 1995. 240p. mass mkt. 4.99 o.p. (*0-425-14689-8*, Prime Crime) Berkley Publishing Group.

—Exhaustive Enquiries: A Melissa Craig Mystery. 1994. 252p. 19.95 o.p. (*0-8027-3180-5*) Walker & Co.

—Finishing Touch: A Melissa Craig Mystery. 1993. 256p. mass mkt. 4.50 o.s.i (*0-515-11059-0*, Jove) Berkley Publishing Group.

—Finishing Touch: A Melissa Craig Mystery. 1992. 253p. 19.95 (*0-8027-3209-7*) Walker & Co.

—A Little Gentle Sleuthing. 1992. 240p. mass mkt. 3.99 o.s.i (*0-515-10878-2*, Jove) Berkley Publishing Group.

—A Little Gentle Sleuthing. l.t. ed. 1992. (Mystery Ser.). 512p. 29.99 o.p. (*0-7089-2736-X*, Ulverscroft) Thorpe, F. A. Pubs. GBR. *Dist:* Ulverscroft Large Print Bks., Ltd., Ulverscroft Large Print Canada, Ltd.

—A Little Gentle Sleuthing. 1991. 272p. 18.95 o.s.i (*0-8027-5781-2*) Walker & Co.

—Over the Edge: A Melissa Craig Mystery. 1994. 240p. reprint ed. mass mkt. 4.50 o.p. (*0-425-14329-5*, Prime Crime) Berkley Publishing Group.

—Over the Edge: A Melissa Craig Mystery. 1993. 252p. 19.95 (*0-8027-3228-3*) Walker & Co.

Saum, Karen. Murder Is Germane. 1991. (Brigid Donovan Mystery Ser.). 288p. (Orig.). pap. 8.95 o.p. (*0-941483-98-3*) Naiad Pr., Inc.

—Murder Is Germane. 1991. (Brigid Donovan Mystery Ser.). 224p. (Orig.). pap. 8.95 (*0-934678-56-1*) New Victoria Pubs., Inc.

—Murder Is Material. 1994. (Brigid Donovan Mystery Ser.). 192p. (Orig.). pap. 9.95 (*0-934678-57-X*) New Victoria Pubs., Inc.

—Murder Is Relative. 1990. 256p. pap. 8.95 o.p. (*0-941483-70-3*) Naiad Pr., Inc.

—Murder Is Relative. 1990. (Brigid Donovan Mystery Ser.). 256p. pap. 8.95 (*0-934678-55-3*) New Victoria Pubs., Inc.

Saylor, Steven. A Twist at the End: A Novel of O. Henry. 2000. 464p. 25.00 o.s.i (*0-684-85681-6*, Simon & Schuster) Simon & Schuster.

Schechter, Harold. The Hum Bug. 2001. 400p. 25.00 (*0-671-04115-0*, Atria); 2002. 512p. reprint ed. mass mkt. 6.99 o.s.i (*0-671-04116-9*, Pocket) Simon & Schuster.

—Nevermore. 2000. 480p. reprint ed. pap. 6.99 (*0-671-79856-1*, Pocket) Simon & Schuster.

—Nevermore. l.t. ed. 1999. (Basic Ser.). 599p. 28.95 (*0-7862-1939-4*) Thorndike Pr.

—Nevermore: A Novel. 1999. 352p. 23.00 (*0-671-79855-3*, Atria) Simon & Schuster.

Schorb, E. M. Paradise Square. 2001. 264p. pap. 16.95 (*0-87714-711-6*); 2000. E-Book 6.95 (*0-87714-595-4*); 2000. E-Book 6.95 (*0-87714-570-9*) Denlingers Pubs., Ltd.

Sherman, Jory. The Ballad of Pinewood Lake. 2002. 192p. mass mkt. 5.99 (*0-8125-8879-7*); 2001. 224p. 21.95 (*0-312-85774-8*); 2002. reprint ed. pap. (*0-7653-0248-9*) Doherty, Tom Assocs., LLC. (Forge Bks.).

Shreve, Porter. The Obituary Writer. 2000. 224p. pap. 12.00 (*0-395-98132-8*) Houghton Mifflin Co.

Simmons, Charles. Wrinkles. 1978. 182p. 8.95 o.p. (*0-374-29333-3*) Farrar, Straus & Giroux.

—Wrinkles. 1988. 192p. pap. 6.95 o.p. (*0-14-011419-X*, Penguin Bks.) Viking Penguin.

Simmons, Dan. A Winter Haunting. 2002. 320p. 25.95 (*0-380-97886-5*, Morrow, William & Co.) Morrow/Avon.

Sklepowich, Edward. Black Bridge: A Mystery of Venice. 1995. 224p. 20.50 (*0-684-81520-6*); o.s.i (*1-883402-84-0*) Simon & Schuster. (Scribner).

—Death in a Serene City. 1992. 304p. pap. 4.50 (*0-380-71636-4*, Avon Bks.); 1990. 18.95 o.p. (*0-688-09180-6*, Morrow, William & Co.) Morrow/Avon.

—Death in the Palazzo: A Venetian Mystery. 1997. 250p. 21.50 o.p. (*0-684-83031-0*, Scribner) Simon & Schuster.

—Farewell to the Flesh: An Urbino Macintyre Mystery. 1993. 288p. pap. 4.99 (*0-380-71814-6*, Avon Bks.); 1991. 352p. 19.00 o.p. (*0-688-11006-1*, Morrow, William & Co.) Morrow/Avon.

—Liquid Desires: An Urbino Macintyre Mystery. 1993. 315p. 22.00 o.p. (*0-688-11165-3*, Morrow, William & Co.); 1994. 320p. reprint ed. mass mkt. 4.99 (*0-380-72150-3*, Avon Bks.) Morrow/Avon.

—Liquid Desires: An Urbino Macintyre Mystery. 316p. 4.98 o.p. (*0-7651-0268-4*) Smithmark Pubs., Inc.

Smith, Julie. Huckleberry Fiend. 1987. (Paul McDonald Mystery Ser.). 224p. 15.95 (*0-89296-237-2*) Mysterious Pr.

—Huckleberry Fiend. 1988. 224p. mass mkt. 5.50 (*0-445-40696-8*, Mysterious Pr. Paperback Bks.) Warner Bks., Inc.

—Louisiana Bigshot. 2002. 304p. 24.95 (*0-7653-0059-1*, Forge Bks.) Doherty, Tom Assocs., LLC.

—True-Life Adventure. 1986. 15.45 o.p. (*0-89296-120-1*) Mysterious Pr.

—True-Life Adventure. 1986. 256p. reprint ed. mass mkt. 4.99 o.s.i (*0-445-40505-8*, Mysterious Pr. Paperback Bks.) Warner Bks., Inc.

Smith, Mary-Ann Tirone. An American Killing. 1999. 352p. mass mkt. 6.99 (*0-449-00579-8*, Fawcett) Ballantine Bks.

—An American Killing. abr. ed. 1998. audio 17.95 o.p. (*1-56740-801-X*, 1447, Nova Audio Bks.); audio 26.95 o.s.i (*1-56740-077-9*, 1446, Bookcassette); audio 73.25 (*1-56740-606-8*, 1448, Unabridged Library Editions) Brilliance Audio.

—An American Killing. 1999. E-Book 6.99 (*0-8050-6250-5*); 1998. 368p. 23.00 o.s.i (*0-8050-5702-1*) Holt, Henry & Co.

Stuart, Sebastian. The Mentor. 2000. 288p. mass mkt. 5.99 o.s.i (*0-553-58031-0*) Bantam Bks.

Tennant, Emma. The Story of Sylvia & Ted: A Novel. 2001. (John MacRae Bks.). 192p. 22.00 (*0-8050-6675-6*) Holt, Henry & Co.

Tosches, Nick. In the Hand of Dante. 384p. 2002. 24.95 (*0-316-89524-5*); 2003. reprint ed. pap. 13.95 (*0-316-73564-7*, Back Bay) Little Brown & Co.

Trevor, William. My House in Umbria: Movie Tie Edition. 2003. 160p. pap. 10.00 (*0-14-200365-4*) Penguin Group (USA) Inc.

Tsypkin, Leonid. Summer in Baden-Baden: A Novel. 2003. 176p. pap. 13.95 (*0-8112-1548-2*) New Directions Publishing Corp.

—Summer in Baden-Baden: A Novel. Keys, Roger & Keys, Angela, trs. from RUS. 2001. 160p. 23.95 (*0-8112-1484-2*) New Directions Publishing Corp.

Updike, John. The Complete Henry Bech. 2001. (Everyman's Library). 544p. 23.00 (*0-375-41176-3*) Knopf, Alfred A. Inc.

Van Gieson, Judith. Vanishing Point: A Claire Reynier Mystery. 2001. 272p. mass mkt. 5.99 (*0-451-20240-6*) NAL.

—Vanishing Point: A Claire Reynier Mystery. l.t. ed. 2001. (Senior Lifestyles Ser.). 293p. 28.95 (*0-7862-3587-X*) Thorndike Pr.

—Vanishing Point: A Claire Reynier Mystery. 2001. (Claire Reynier Mysteries Ser.). 216p. 24.95 (*0-8263-2383-9*) Univ. of New Mexico Pr.

Vassilikos, Vassilis. The Few Things I Know about Glafkos Thrassakis. Emmerich, Karen, tr. from GRE. 2002. 368p. 24.95 (*1-58322-527-7*) Seven Stories Pr.

Veronesi, Sandro. The Force of the Past. 2004. pap. (*0-06-093661-4*, Ecco) HarperTrade.

—The Force of the Past: A Novel. McEwen, Alastair, tr. from ITA. 2003. 240p. 23.95 (*0-06-621245-6*, Ecco) HarperTrade.

Vickers, Salley. Mr. Golightly's Holiday. 2004. 368p. 24.00 (*0-374-21489-1*) Farrar, Straus & Giroux.

Walker, Alice. The Way Forward Is with a Broken Heart. l.t. ed. 2001. (Women's Fiction Ser.). 224p. 29.95 (*0-7862-3355-9*) Thorndike Pr.

Watts, Alan S. The Confessions of Charles Dickens: A Very Factual Fiction. 1992. (Dickens' Universe Ser.: Vol. 1). 179p. (C). text 24.00 o.p. (*0-8204-1533-2*) Lang, Peter Publishing, Inc.

Wehrenberg, Charles C. The Ploy of Cooking. 1995. 224p. pap. 11.00 (*1-886163-03-0*) Solo Zone Publishing.

Wenzel, Kurt. Gotham Tragic. 2004. 320p. 23.95 (*0-316-09400-5*) Little Brown & Co.

Williams, Elmer A. Au Revoir Parisienne. 1999. 112p. pap. 11.00 o.p. (*0-8059-4542-3*) Dorrance Publishing Co., Inc.

Wilson, Edmund. I Thought of Daisy. 2001. vii, 278p. 12.95 (*0-87745-769-7*) Univ. of Iowa Pr.

Wilson, Wayne. Eddie & Bella: A Novel. 2001. 304p. tchr. ed. 21.95 (*1-56512-297-6*) Algonquin Bks. of Chapel Hill.

Witting, Amy. Isobel on the Way to the Corner Shop. 1999. 352p. (*0-14-028634-9*) Penguin Group (USA) Inc.

Wolff, Tobias. Old School: A Novel. 2003. 208p. 22.00 (*0-375-40146-6*) Knopf, Alfred A. Inc.

Ying, Hong. Summer of Betrayal: A Novel. Avery, Martha, tr. from CHI. 1997. 208p. 22.00 o.p. (*0-374-27175-5*) Farrar, Straus & Giroux.

—Summer of Betrayal: A Novel. Avery, Martha, tr. from CHI. 1999. 192p. pap. 12.00 (*0-8021-3594-3*) Grove/Atlantic, Inc.

Youngblood, Shay. Black Girl in Paris. 2001. (Illus.). 256p. pap. 12.00 (*1-57322-851-6*, Riverhead Trade (Paperbacks)) Berkley Publishing Group.

—Black Girl in Paris. 2000. (Illus.). 300p. 23.95 o.p. (*1-57322-151-1*, Riverhead Bks. (Hardcovers)) Putnam Publishing Group, The.

Zackheim, Michele. Violette's Embrace. 1997. 224p. reprint ed. 12.00 o.s.i (*1-57322-608-4*, Riverhead Trade (Paperbacks)) Berkley Publishing Group.

—Violette's Embrace. 1996. 256p. 23.95 o.s.i (*1-57322-036-1*, Riverhead Bks. (Hardcovers)) Putnam Publishing Group, The.

Zimmerman, R. D. Blood Trance. 1994. 304p. mass mkt. 4.99 o.s.i (*0-440-21518-8*) Dell Publishing.

—Blood Trance. 1993. 236p. 20.00 o.p. (*0-688-12139-X*, Morrow, William & Co.) Morrow/Avon.

—Death Trance. 1993. 304p. mass mkt. 4.99 o.s.i (*0-440-21326-6*) Dell Publishing.

—Death Trance: A Novel of Hypnotic Detection. 1992. 256p. 20.00 o.p. (*0-688-11451-2*, Morrow, William & Co.) Morrow/Avon.

—Red Trance. 1995. 320p. mass mkt. 4.99 o.s.i (*0-440-21763-6*) Dell Publishing.

—Red Trance. 1994. 237p. 20.00 o.p. (*0-688-13030-5*, Morrow, William & Co.) Morrow/Avon.

## B

### BASEBALL PLAYERS—FICTION

Bennett, James W. & Raycraft, Donald R. Old Hoss: A Fictional Baseball Biography of Charles Radbourn. 2002. (Illus.). 201p. per. 24.95 (*0-7864-1321-2*) McFarland & Co., Inc. Pubs.

Blair, Kerry Lynn. The Heart Only Knows. 2001. 266p. 14.95 (*1-57734-861-3*) Covenant Communications.

Bookbinder, Bernie. Out at the Old Ball Game: A Novel. 1995. 347p. 21.95 o.s.i (*1-882593-09-X*); 2002. 262p. reprint ed. pap. 13.95 (*1-882593-56-1*) Bridge Works Publishing Co., Inc.

Cochrane, Mick. Sport. E-Book 22.95 (*1-58945-580-0*) Adobe Systems, Inc.

—Sport. E-Book 22.95 (*0-312-70059-8*); 2001. 246p. 22.95 (*0-312-26994-3*) St. Martin's Pr.

—Sport: A Novel. 2003. 256p. pap. 14.95 (*0-8166-4085-8*) Univ. of Minnesota Pr.

Dinger, Ed. A Prince at First: The Fictional Autobiography of Baseball's Hal Chase. 2002. 224p. per. 24.95 (*0-7864-1330-1*) McFarland & Co., Inc. Pubs.

Ferrell, David. Screwball. 2004. 384p. mass mkt. 7.50 (*0-06-008742-0*, HarperTorch); 2003. 320p. 23.95 (*0-06-008741-2*, Morrow, William & Co.) Morrow/Avon.

—Screwball: A Novel. 2004. 320p. pap. 13.95 (*0-06-072600-8*, Dark Alley) HarperTrade.

Forbes, Deloris. One Man Died on Base. l.t. ed. 2001. (Mystery Ser.). 168p. 23.95 (*0-7862-3005-3*, Five Star) Gale Group.

Fromm, Pete. How All This Started. 2001. 320p. pap. 14.00 (*0-312-27697-4*); 2000. 305p. 23.00 o.s.i (*0-312-20933-9*) Picador.

Hemphill, Paul. Long Gone: A Novel. 2002. 288p. reprint ed. pap. 14.95 (*1-56663-417-2*) Dee, Ivan R. Pub.

Lehmann, Donald. Courtland's Spirits. 2001. 324p. pap. 17.95 (*0-595-19859-7*, Writers Club Pr.) iUniverse, Inc.

Lupica, Mike. Wild Pitch. 2003. 352p. mass mkt. 7.99 (*0-425-19204-0*) Berkley Publishing Group.

—Wild Pitch. 2002. 352p. 24.95 (*0-399-14927-9*, Putnam & Grosset) Putnam Publishing Group, The.

Mathewson, Christy. First Base Faulkner. Date not set. 336p. 25.95 (*0-8488-2789-9*); 1976. 30.95 (*0-8488-1547-5*) Amereon, Ltd.

O'Rourke, Frank. The Heavenly World Series: Timeless Baseball Fiction. 2002. 320p. 25.00 (*0-7867-0950-2*, Carroll & Graf Pubs.) Avalon Publishing Group.

Shawver, Brian. Cuban Prospect: A Novel. 2003. 286p. 24.95 (*1-58567-344-7*) Overlook Pr., The.

Tooke, C. W. Ballpark Blues: A Novel. 2003. 304p. 22.95 (*0-385-50640-6*) Doubleday Publishing.

### BOOKSELLERS AND BOOKSELLING—FICTION

Allen, Garrison. Baseball Cat. (Big Mike Mystery Ser.: Vol. 4). 1998. 336p. mass mkt. 5.99 (*1-57566-309-0*); 1997. 304p. 18.95 o.s.i (*1-57566-183-7*) Kensington Publishing Corp.

—Dinosaur Cat. (Big Mike Mystery Ser.). 336p. 1999. mass mkt. 5.99 o.s.i (*1-57566-426-7*); 1998. (J). 20.00 o.s.i (*1-57566-304-X*, Kensington Bks.) Kensington Publishing Corp.

—Royal Cat: A Big Mike Mystery. 1996. (Big Mike Mystery Ser.: Vol. 2). 304p. mass mkt. 4.99 o.s.i (1-57566-045-8); 1995. mass mkt. 16.95 o.s.i (0-8217-4957-9, Zebra Bks.) Kensington Publishing Corp.
—Stable Cat. 304p. 1997. mass mkt. 5.50 o.s.i (1-57566-188-8); 1996. pap. 18.95 o.p. (1-57566-042-3) Kensington Publishing Corp.
Block, Lawrence. The Burglar in the Closet. 1997. (Bernie Rhodenbarr Mystery Ser.: No. 2). 320p. mass mkt. 6.99 (0-451-18074-7, Signet Bks.) NAL.
—The Burglar in the Closet. 1978. (Bernie Rhodenbarr Mystery Ser.: No. 2). 6.95 o.p. (0-394-42374-7) Random Hse., Inc.
—The Burglar in the Closet. 1986. (Bernie Rhodenbarr Mystery Ser.: No. 2). mass mkt. 3.50 o.s.i (0-671-61704-4, Pocket) Simon & Schuster.
—The Burglar in the Closet. l.t. ed. 1996. (Bernie Rhodenbarr Mystery Ser.: No. 2). 277p. 25.95 o.p. (0-7862-0548-2) Thorndike Pr.
—The Burglar in the Library. 1997. (Bernie Rhodenbarr Mystery Ser.: No. 8). 320p. 23.95 o.p. (0-525-94301-3, Dutton) Dutton/Plume.
—The Burglar in the Library. 1998. (Bernie Rhodenbarr Mystery Ser.: No. 8). 368p. mass mkt. 6.99 (0-451-40783-0, Signet Bks.) NAL.
—The Burglar in the Library. l.t. ed. 1998. (Bernie Rhodenbarr Mystery Ser.: No. 8). 464p. 27.95 o.p. (0-7862-1280-2) Thorndike Pr.
—The Burglar in the Library. abr. ed. 1997. (Bernie Rhodenbarr Mystery Ser.: No. 8). 2p. audio 16.95 (0-14-086582-9, Penguin AudioBooks) Viking Penguin.
—The Burglar Who Dropped in on Elvis. unabr. ed. 1999. audio 5.99 (1-55204-601-X, PAC-8601) Durkin Hayes Publishing Ltd.
—The Burglar Who Liked to Quote Kipling. 1996. (Bernie Rhodenbarr Mystery Ser.: No. 3). 256p. 22.95 o.s.i (0-525-94159-2, Dutton) Dutton/Plume.
—The Burglar Who Liked to Quote Kipling. 1997. (Bernie Rhodenbarr Mystery Ser.: No. 3). 320p. mass mkt. 6.99 o.s.i (0-451-18075-5, Signet Bks.) NAL.
—The Burglar Who Liked to Quote Kipling. 1979. (Bernie Rhodenbarr Mystery Ser.: No. 3). 7.95 o.p. (0-394-50417-8) Random Hse., Inc.
—The Burglar Who Liked to Quote Kipling. 1998. (Bernie Rhodenbarr Mystery Ser.: No. 3). audio 44.00 (0-7887-0810-4, 94959E7 ) Recorded Bks., LLC.
—The Burglar Who Liked to Quote Kipling. 1986. (Bernie Rhodenbarr Mystery Ser.: No. 3). mass mkt. 3.50 o.s.i (0-671-61831-8, Pocket) Simon & Schuster.
—The Burglar Who Liked to Quote Kipling. abr. ed. 1996. (Bernie Rhodenbarr Mystery Ser.: No. 3). audio 16.95 o.s.i (0-14-086345-1, Penguin AudioBooks) Viking Penguin.
—The Burglar Who Painted Like Mondrian. 1998. (Bernie Rhodenbarr Mystery Ser.: No. 5). 224p. 23.95 o.p. (0-525-94382-X) Dutton/Plume.
—The Burglar Who Painted Like Mondrian. l.t. ed. 1999. (Bernie Rhodenbarr Mystery Ser.: No. 5). 27.95 (1-56895-726-2, Wheeler Publishing, Inc.) Gale Group.
—The Burglar Who Painted Like Mondrian. 1999. (Bernie Rhodenbarr Mystery Ser.: No. 5). 320p. reprint ed. mass mkt. 6.99 o.p. (0-451-18076-3, Signet Bks.) NAL.
—The Burglar Who Painted Like Mondrian. unabr. ed. 1993. (Bernie Rhodenbarr Mystery Ser.: No. 5). audio 46.00 (0-7887-3214-5, 95846E7) Recorded Bks., LLC.
—The Burglar Who Painted Like Mondrian. 1986. (Bernie Rhodenbarr Mystery Ser.: No. 5). mass mkt. 3.50 o.s.i (0-671-49581-X, Pocket) Simon & Schuster.
—The Burglar Who Painted Like Mondrian. abr. ed. 1998. (Bernie Rhodenbarr Mystery Ser.: No. 5). 2p. audio 17.95 o.p. (0-14-086817-8, Penguin AudioBooks) Viking Penguin.
—The Burglar Who Studied Spinoza. 1997. (Bernie Rhodenbarr Mystery Ser.: No. 4). 240p. 23.95 o.s.i (0-525-94180-0, Signet Bks.) Dutton/Plume.
—The Burglar Who Studied Spinoza. l.t. ed. 1998. (Bernie Rhodenbarr Mystery Ser.: No. 4). 26.95 (1-56895-602-9, Wheeler Publishing, Inc.) Gale Group.
—The Burglar Who Studied Spinoza. 1998. (Bernie Rhodenbarr Mystery Ser.: No. 4). 320p. mass mkt. 6.99 o.s.i (0-451-19488-8, Signet Bks.) NAL.
—The Burglar Who Studied Spinoza. 1981. (Bernie Rhodenbarr Mystery Ser.: No. 4). 8.95 o.p. (0-394-51065-8) Random Hse., Inc.
—The Burglar Who Studied Spinoza. 1986. (Bernie Rhodenbarr Mystery Ser.: No. 4). mass mkt. 3.50 o.s.i (0-671-62485-7, Pocket) Simon & Schuster.
—The Burglar Who Thought He Was Bogart. unabr. ed. 1997. (Bernie Rhodenbarr Mystery Ser.: No. 7). audio 44.95 (0-7861-1196-8, 1957) Blackstone Audio Bks., Inc.
—The Burglar Who Thought He Was Bogart. 1996. (Bernie Rhodenbarr Mystery Ser.: No. 7). 384p. mass mkt. 6.99 o.s.i (0-451-18634-6, Onyx) NAL.
—The Burglar Who Thought He Was Bogart. unabr. ed. 1997. (Bernie Rhodenbarr Mystery Ser.: No. 7). audio 51.00 (0-7887-0476-1, 94669E7) Recorded Bks., LLC.
—The Burglar Who Thought He Was Bogart. abr. ed. 1995. (Bernie Rhodenbarr Mystery Ser.: No. 7). audio 16.95 o.s.i (0-14-086190-4, Penguin AudioBooks) Viking Penguin.
—The Burglar Who Traded Ted Williams. unabr. ed. 1997. (Bernie Rhodenbarr Mystery Ser.: No. 6). audio 44.95 (0-7861-1166-6, 1937) Blackstone Audio Bks., Inc.
—The Burglar Who Traded Ted Williams. 1994. (Bernie Rhodenbarr Mystery Ser.: No. 6). 272p. 19.95 o.p. (0-525-93807-9, Dutton) Dutton/Plume.
—The Burglar Who Traded Ted Williams. 1995. (Bernie Rhodenbarr Mystery Ser.: No. 6). 384p. mass mkt. 6.99 o.s.i (0-451-18426-2, Onyx) NAL.
—The Burglar Who Traded Ted Williams. abr. ed. 1994. (Bernie Rhodenbarr Mystery Ser.: No. 6). pap. 16.00 o.p. incl. audio (0-453-00890-9, 25024-31224) Penguin/HighBridge.
—The Burglar Who Traded Ted Williams. unabr. ed. 1994. (Bernie Rhodenbarr Mystery Ser.: No. 6). audio 51.00 (0-7887-1302-7, 95138E7) Recorded Bks., LLC.
—Burglars Can't Be Choosers. 1978. (Bernie Rhodenbarr Mystery Ser.: No. 1). pap. 1.75 o.s.i (0-515-04584-5, Jove) Berkley Publishing Group.
—Burglars Can't Be Choosers. unabr. ed. 1997. (Bernie Rhodenbarr Mystery Ser.: No. 1). audio 39.95 (0-7861-1136-4, 755302) Blackstone Audio Bks., Inc.
—Burglars Can't Be Choosers. 1995. (Bernie Rhodenbarr Mystery Ser.: No. 1). 256p. 19.95 o.p. (0-525-93943-1, Dutton) Dutton/Plume.
—Burglars Can't Be Choosers. 2004. 320p. mass mkt. 6.99 (0-06-058255-3, HarperTorch) Morrow/Avon.
—Burglars Can't Be Choosers. 1995. (Bernie Rhodenbarr Mystery Ser.: No. 1). 304p. mass mkt. 5.99 o.s.i (0-451-18073-9, Signet Bks.) NAL.
—Burglars Can't Be Choosers. abr. ed. 1995. (Bernie Rhodenbarr Mystery Ser.: No. 1). pap. 16.95 o.p. incl. audio (0-453-00932-8, 25024-39151) Penguin/HighBridge.
—Burglars Can't Be Choosers. 1977. (Bernie Rhodenbarr Mystery Ser.: No. 1). (Illus.). 6.95 o.p. (0-394-41183-8) Random Hse., Inc.
—Burglars Can't Be Choosers. unabr. ed. 1998. (Bernie Rhodenbarr Mystery Ser.: No. 1). audio 44.00 (0-7887-1990-4, 95377E7) Recorded Bks., LLC.
Cheek, Mavis. Getting Back Brahms. l.t. ed. 2001. 293p. pap. 24.95 (0-7862-3508-X) Thorndike Pr.
Fitzgerald, Penelope. The Bookshop. 1978. 118p. (0-7156-1320-0) Duckworth, Gerald & Co., Ltd.
—The Bookshop. l.t. ed. 1999. (General Ser.). 168p. pap. 21.95 o.p. (0-7862-2167-4); (0-7540-3910-2); (0-7540-3909-9) Thorndike Pr.
—The Bookshop: A Novel. 1997. 128p. pap. 11.00 (0-395-86946-3, Mariner Bks.) Houghton Mifflin Co. Trade & Reference Div.
—The Bookshop; The Gate of Angels; The Blue Flower. 2003. 512p. 23.00 (1-4000-4126-0, Everyman's Library) Knopf Publishing Group.
Gottlieb, Samuel H. Overbooked in Arizona. (Illus.). 112p. 1995. 20.00 (0-9639966-1-4); 1994. pap. 9.95 (0-9639966-0-6) Camelback Gallery.
Hart, Carolyn G. April Fool Dead. 2002. 304p. 23.95 (0-380-97774-5) Morrow/Avon.
—The Christie Caper. 1992. (Annie Darling Ser.). 400p. mass mkt. 6.99 (0-553-29569-1) Bantam Bks.
—The Christie Caper. unabr. ed. 1996. (Annie Laurance Darling Ser.). audio 64.00 (0-7366-3457-6, 4101) Books on Tape, Inc.
—Crime on Her Mind: A Collection of Short Stories. 1999. (Mystery Ser.). 268p. 21.95 (0-7862-1735-9, Five Star) Gale Group.
—Deadly Valentine. 1991. (Death on Demand Ser.). 272p. mass mkt. 6.99 incl. audio (0-553-28847-4) Bantam Bks.
—Deadly Valentine. l.t. ed. 1998. (Beeler Large Print Mystery Ser.). 25.95 (1-57490-189-3, Beeler Large Print Bks.) Beeler, Thomas T. Publisher.
—Deadly Valentine. 1990. 192p. 14.95 o.s.i (0-385-26518-2) Doubleday Publishing.
—Death on Demand. 1989. 208p. mass mkt. 1.95 o.s.i (0-553-18502-0); 1987. 224p. mass mkt. 6.99 (0-553-26351-X) Bantam Bks.
—Death on Demand. l.t. ed. 2000. (Mystery Ser.). (Illus.). 227p. 26.95 (1-57490-276-8, Beeler Large Print Bks.) Beeler, Thomas T. Publisher.
—Death on Demand. l.t. ed. 2000. (Wheeler Softcover Ser.). 280p. pap. 24.95 (1-56895-914-1, Wheeler Publishing, Inc.) Gale Group.
—Design for Murder. 1988. 320p. mass mkt. 6.99 (0-553-26562-8) Bantam Bks.
—Design for Murder. l.t. ed. 2000. (Beeler Large Print Mystery Ser.). 208p. (1-57490-291-1, Beeler Large Print Bks.) Beeler, Thomas T. Publisher.
—Design for Murder. l.t. ed. 2001. (Large Print Bks.). (Illus.). 345p. pap. 23.95 o.p. (1-58724-112-9, Wheeler Publishing, Inc.) Gale Group.
—Engaged to Die. 2003. 320p. 23.95 (0-06-000469-X, Morrow, William & Co.) Morrow/Avon.
—Engaged to Die: A Death on Demand Mystery. l.t. ed. 2003. (Core Ser.). 31.95 (0-7862-5553-6) Thorndike Pr.
—Honeymoon for Murder. 1994. 20.00 o.p. (0-7278-4590-X) Severn Hse. Pubs., Ltd.
—Honeymoon with Murder. 1988. 256p. mass mkt. 6.99 (0-553-27608-5) Bantam Bks.
—A Little Class on Murder. l.t. ed. 1992. pap. 21.95 o.p. (0-7927-1140-8, CS0306); 1991. 23.95 o.p. (0-7927-1139-4, CH0234) BBC Audiobooks America.
—A Little Class on Murder. 1989. 272p. mass mkt. 6.99 (0-553-28208-5) Bantam Bks.
—A Little Class on Murder. unabr. collector's ed. 1996. (Annie Laurance Darling Ser.). audio 48.00 (0-7366-3419-3, 894409) Books on Tape, Inc.
—A Little Class on Murder. 1989. 12.95 o.s.i (0-385-26452-6) Doubleday Publishing.
—Mint Julep Murder. 1996. 256p. mass mkt. 6.99 (0-553-57202-4); 1995. 288p. 19.95 o.s.i (0-553-09463-7) Bantam Bks.
—Mint Julep Murder. unabr. ed. 1996. (Annie Laurance Darling Ser.). audio 48.00 (0-7366-3498-3, 4138) Books on Tape, Inc.
—Mint Julep Murder. l.t. ed. 1996. 362p. 23.95 o.p. (0-7838-1496-8, Macmillan Reference USA) Gale Group.
—Something Wicked. 1988. 256p. mass mkt. 6.99 (0-553-27222-5) Bantam Bks.
—Something Wicked. 1994. 20.00 (0-7278-4656-6) Severn Hse. Pubs., Ltd.
—Southern Ghost. 1993. (Annie Darling Ser.). 320p. mass mkt. 6.99 (0-553-56275-4) Bantam Bks.
—Southern Ghost. unabr. ed. 1996. (Annie Laurance Darling Ser.). audio 56.00 (0-7366-3501-7, 4141) Books on Tape, Inc.
—White Elephant Dead. (Death on Demand Mysteries Ser.). 2000. 304p. mass mkt. 6.99 (0-380-79325-3); 1999. 277p. 23.00 (0-380-97530-0) Morrow/Avon. (Avon Bks.).
—White Elephant Dead. l.t. ed. 2000. (Mystery Ser.). 431p. 29.95 o.p. (0-7862-2341-3) Thorndike Pr.
—Yankee Doodle Dead. l.t. ed. 1999. pap. 24.95 (1-56895-718-1, Wheeler Publishing, Inc.) Gale Group.
—Yankee Doodle Dead. 1999. 304p. mass mkt. 6.99 (0-380-79326-1); 1998. 288p. 21.00 (0-380-97529-7) Morrow/Avon. (Avon Bks.).
Hess, Joan. Busy Bodies. 1995. (Claire Malloy Mystery Ser.). 256p. 19.95 o.p. (0-525-93910-5) Dutton/Plume.
—Busy Bodies. 1996. (Claire Malloy Mystery Ser.). 272p. mass mkt. 5.50 o.s.i (0-451-40560-9, Onyx) NAL.
—Closely Akin to Murder. 1996. (Claire Malloy Mystery Ser.). 240p. 21.95 o.s.i (0-525-93911-3, Dutton) Dutton/Plume.
—Closely Akin to Murder. 1997. (Claire Malloy Mysteries Ser.). 272p. mass mkt. 5.99 o.s.i (0-451-40561-7, Onyx) NAL.
—A Conventional Corpse. l.t. ed. 2000. (Wheeler Softcover Ser.). 293p. pap. 24.95 (1-56895-995-8, Wheeler Publishing, Inc.) Gale Group.
—A Conventional Corpse. 2001. 304p. mass mkt. 6.50 o.s.i (0-312-97726-3, St. Martin's Paperbacks); 2000. 275p. 23.95 (0-312-24662-5, Saint Martin's Minotaur) St. Martin's Pr.
—Dear Miss Demeanor. 1990. (Claire Malloy Ser.: No. 3). 195p. mass mkt. 4.99 o.s.i (0-345-34911-3) Ballantine Bks.
—Dear Miss Demeanor. (Claire Malloy Mysteries Ser.). 2000. 208p. mass mkt. 5.99 (0-312-97313-6, St. Martin's Paperbacks); 1987. 192p. 13.95 o.p. (0-312-00702-7, Saint Martin's Minotaur) St. Martin's Pr.
—Death by the Light of the Moon. 208p. 1995. pap. 15.00 (0-345-47171-7); 1994. mass mkt. 6.50 (0-345-37838-5) Ballantine Bks.
—Death by the Light of the Moon. (Claire Malloy Mystery Ser.). 240p. 2003. mass mkt. 6.99 (0-312-99101-0, St. Martin's Paperbacks); 1992. 18.95 o.p. (0-312-06949-9, Saint Martin's Minotaur) St. Martin's Pr.
—A Diet to Die For. 1992. (Claire Mallory Mystery Ser.). reprint ed. mass mkt. 5.50 o.s.i (0-345-36654-9) Ballantine Bks.
—A Diet to Die For. 1989. 192p. 14.95 o.p. (0-312-03326-5, Saint Martin's Minotaur) St. Martin's Pr.
—A Holly, Jolly Murder. l.t. ed. 2003. (Mystery Ser.). 27.95 (1-57490-531-7) Beeler, Thomas T. Publisher.
—A Holly, Jolly Murder. 1997. (Claire Malloy Mystery Ser.). 272p. 22.95 o.s.i (0-525-94240-8) Dutton/Plume.
—A Holly, Jolly Murder. 1998. (Claire Malloy Mystery Ser.). 288p. mass mkt. 5.99 o.s.i (0-451-40728-8, Onyx) NAL.
—The Murder at the Murder at the Mimosa Inn. 1987. mass mkt. 4.99 o.s.i (0-345-34324-7) Ballantine Bks.
—The Murder at the Murder at the Mimosa Inn. 1999. 192p. mass mkt. 5.99 (0-312-97178-8, St. Martin's Paperbacks); 1986. 208p. 13.95 o.p. (0-312-55293-9) St. Martin's Pr.
—Out on a Limb. E-Book 17.95 (0-312-70895-5); 2003. 336p. mass mkt. 6.99 (0-312-98632-7, St. Martin's Paperbacks); 2003. mass mkt. o.p. (0-312-98967-9, St. Martin's Paperbacks); 2002. 304p. 23.95 (0-312-26680-4, Saint Martin's Minotaur) St. Martin's Pr.
—Out on a Limb. 2003. (Americana Ser.). 28.95 (0-7862-5102-6) Thorndike Pr.
—Poisoned Pins. 1993. (Claire Malloy Mystery Ser.). 256p. 18.00 o.p. (0-525-93591-6) Dutton/Plume.
—Poisoned Pins. 1994. (Claire Malloy Mystery Ser.). 256p. mass mkt. 5.99 o.s.i (0-451-40390-8, Onyx) NAL.
—A Really Cute Corpse. 1988. 192p. 14.95 o.p. (0-312-02271-9, Saint Martin's Minotaur) St. Martin's Pr.
—Roll over & Play Dead. 1992. reprint ed. mass mkt. 5.50 o.s.i (0-345-37586-6) Ballantine Bks.
—Roll over & Play Dead. (Claire Mallory Mystery Ser.). 2003. 208p. mass mkt. 5.99 (0-312-98828-1, St. Martin's Paperbacks); 1991. 17.95 o.p. (0-312-05956-6, Saint Martin's Minotaur) St. Martin's Pr.
—Strangled Prose. 1987. mass mkt. 5.99 o.s.i (0-345-34059-0) Ballantine Bks.
—Strangled Prose. 192p. 1998. mass mkt. 5.99 (0-312-96864-7, St. Martin's Paperbacks); 1985. 12.95 o.p. (0-312-76428-6) St. Martin's Pr.
—Tickled to Death. 1994. (Claire Malloy Mystery Ser.). 224p. 18.95 o.p. (0-525-93810-9) Dutton/Plume.
—Tickled to Death. l.t. ed. 1994. pap. 19.95 o.p. (1-56895-079-9, Wheeler Publishing, Inc.) Gale Group.
—Tickled to Death. 1995. (Claire Malloy Mystery Ser.). 304p. mass mkt. 5.99 o.s.i (0-451-40550-1, Onyx) NAL.
King, Ross. Ex-Libris. 2002. 400p. reprint ed. 13.00 (0-14-200080-9) Viking Penguin.
MacDonald, Marianne. Death's Autograph. abr. ed. 1998. audio 54.95 (0-7540-0089-3, CAB1512) BBC Audiobooks America.
—Death's Autograph: A Mystery. 1999. (Antiquarian Book Mysteries Ser.). 352p. mass mkt. 5.99 (0-06-109742-X, HarperTorch) Morrow/Avon.
—Death's Autograph: A Mystery. 1997. (Dido Hoare Mysteries Ser.). 224p. 22.95 o.p. (0-312-16815-2, Saint Martin's Minotaur) St. Martin's Pr.
—Ghost Walk. 2000. (Antiquarian Book Mysteries Ser.). 304p. mass mkt. 5.99 (0-06-101426-5) HarperCollins Pubs.
—Ghost Walk. 1998. (Dido Hoare Mysteries Ser.). 256p. 21.95 o.p. (0-312-19417-X, Saint Martin's Minotaur) St. Martin's Pr.
—Smoke Screen. 1999. 255p. 23.95 o.p. (0-312-24243-3, Saint Martin's Minotaur) St. Martin's Pr.
Petsinis, Tom. The Twelfth Dialogue. 2000. 446p. (0-14-027936-9) Penguin Group (USA) Inc.
Simonson, Sheila. Larkspur. 1991. 224p. reprint ed. mass mkt. (0-373-26074-1, Harlequin Bks.) Harlequin Enterprises, Ltd.
—Larkspur: A Mystery. 1990. 16.95 o.p. (0-312-04338-4, Saint Martin's Minotaur) St. Martin's Pr.
—Malarkey. 1998. (WWL Mystery Ser.). per. (0-373-26275-2, 1-26275-7, Worldwide Library) Harlequin Enterprises, Ltd.
—Malarkey. 1996. 288p. 23.95 o.p. (0-312-15168-3, Saint Martin's Minotaur) St. Martin's Pr.
—Meadowlark. 1997. (WWL Mystery Ser.: No. 240). per. (0-373-26240-X, 1-26240-1, Worldwide Library) Harlequin Enterprises, Ltd.
—Meadowlark. 1996. 256p. 21.95 o.p. (0-312-14013-4, Saint Martin's Minotaur) St. Martin's Pr.
—Skylark. 1994. per. (0-373-26145-4, 1-26145-2, Harlequin Bks.) Harlequin Enterprises, Ltd.
—Skylark. 1992. 272p. 17.95 o.p. (0-312-08294-0, Saint Martin's Minotaur) St. Martin's Pr.
Wall, Alan. The Lightning Cage. 1999. 300p. (0-436-20491-6) Secker, Martin & Warburg, Ltd.
—The Lightning Cage: A Novel. 2003. 320p. 24.95 (0-312-28772-0) St. Martin's Pr.
Warga, Wayne. Fatal Impressions. 1989. 224p. 16.95 o.p. (0-87795-990-0, Morrow, William & Co.) Morrow/Avon.
—Fatal Impressions. 1990. 224p. pap. 3.95 o.p. (0-14-012431-4, Penguin Bks.) Viking Penguin.
—Hardcover. 1985. 256p. 15.95 o.p. (0-87795-749-5, Morrow, William & Co.) Morrow/Avon.
—Hardcover. 1987. (Illus.). 288p. pap. o.s.i (0-14-012875-1); pap. 3.95 o.p. (0-14-009703-1) Viking Penguin. (Penguin Bks.).

—Singapore Transfer: A Jeffrey Dean Mystery. 1992. (Jeffrey Dean Ser.). 160p. reprint ed. pap. 4.95 o.p. (0-14-014383-1, Penguin Bks.) Penguin Group (USA) Inc.
—Singapore Transfer: A Jeffrey Dean Mystery. 1991. (Jeffrey Dean Ser.). 224p. 17.95 o.p. (0-670-83569-2) Viking Penguin.
Warren, Susan. Happily Ever After. 2003. 384p. pap. 9.99 (0-8423-8117-1) Tyndale Hse. Pubs.
Wren, M. K. Curiosity Didn't Kill the Cat. 1988. 272p. mass mkt. 4.95 o.s.i (0-345-35002-2) Ballantine Bks.
—Dead Matter. 1993. (Northwest Mysteries Ser.). 283p. mass mkt. 4.99 o.s.i (0-345-37821-0) Ballantine Bks.
—King of the Mountain. 1994. mass mkt. 4.99 o.s.i (0-345-39019-9) Ballantine Bks.
—A Multitude of Sins. 1989. mass mkt. 3.50 o.s.i (0-345-35001-4) Ballantine Bks.
—Nothing's Certain but Death. 1989. 256p. mass mkt. 3.95 o.s.i (0-345-35000-6) Ballantine Bks.
—Nothing's Certain but Death. 1978. 6.95 o.p. (0-385-13283-2) Doubleday Publishing.
—Oh, Bury Me Not! 1989. 256p. mass mkt. 4.99 o.s.i (0-345-35004-9) Ballantine Bks.
—Seasons of Death. 1989. 192p. mass mkt. 4.99 o.s.i (0-345-35003-0) Ballantine Bks.
—Seasons of Death. 1981. (Crime Club Ser.). 192p. 9.95 o.p. (0-385-17413-6) Doubleday Publishing.
—Wake up, Darlin' Corey. 1990. 224p. mass mkt. 4.95 o.s.i (0-345-35071-5) Ballantine Bks.
—Wake up, Darlin' Corey. 1984. (Crime Club Ser.). 192p. 11.95 o.p. (0-385-19292-4) Doubleday Publishing.

## C

### CATERERS AND CATERING—FICTION

Binchy, Maeve. Scarlet Feather. 2001. 528p. 25.95 o.s.i (0-525-94593-8, Dutton) Dutton/Plume.
—Scarlet Feather. 2001. 560p. mass mkt. 7.99 (0-451-20446-8, Signet Bks.) NAL.
—Scarlet Feather. l.t. ed. 2001. 912p. 25.95 (0-375-43106-3) Random Hse. Large Print.
Davidson, Diane Mott. Catering to Nobody. 1998. pap. 5.99 (0-449-45882-2); 1998. pap. 5.99 (0-449-45833-4); 1992. 320p. reprint ed. mass mkt. 5.99 o.s.i (0-449-22046-X) Ballantine Bks. (Fawcett).
—Catering to Nobody. l.t. ed. 1999. (Beeler Large Print Mystery Ser.). 25.95 (1-57490-204-0, Beeler Large Print Bks.) Beeler, Thomas T. Publisher.
—Catering to Nobody. 1990. 17.95 (0-312-04277-9, Saint Martin's Minotaur) St. Martin's Pr.
—The Cereal Murders. 1994. 368p. mass mkt. 6.99 (0-553-56773-X) Bantam Bks.
—The Cereal Murders. l.t. ed. 1999. pap. 23.95 o.p. (1-56895-743-2, Wheeler Publishing, Inc.) Gale Group.
—Dying for Chocolate. 1993. (Culinary Mysteries Ser.). (Illus.). 352p. mass mkt. 6.99 (0-553-56024-7) Bantam Bks.
—Dying for Chocolate. l.t. ed. 2000. pap. 22.95 o.p. (1-56895-821-8, Wheeler Publishing, Inc.) Gale Group.
—The Grilling Season. 1998. 432p. reprint ed. mass mkt. 6.99 (0-553-57466-3) Bantam Bks.
—The Grilling Season. abr. ed. 1997. (Culinary Mysteries Ser.). audio 22.95 (0-553-47912-1, 695429, RH Audio) Random Hse. Audio Publishing Group.
—Killer Pancake. 1996. 368p. mass mkt. 6.99 (0-553-57204-0) Bantam Bks.
—Killer Pancake. unabr. ed. 2003. audio compact disk 59.95 (1-59007-439-4) New Millennium Entertainment.
—The Last Suppers. 1995. 304p. mass mkt. 6.99 (0-553-57258-X, Crimeline) Bantam Bks.
—The Last Suppers. l.t. ed. 1999. pap. 24.95 o.p. (1-56895-640-1, Wheeler Publishing, Inc.) Gale Group.
—The Main Corpse. 1997. (Culinary Mysteries Ser.). 384p. reprint ed. mass mkt. 6.99 (0-553-57463-9, Crimeline) Bantam Bks.
—The Main Corpse. l.t. ed. 1997. (Large Print Bks.). 25.95 o.p. (1-56895-409-3, Wheeler Publishing, Inc.) Gale Group.
—Prime Cut. 2000. (Illus.). 384p. reprint ed. mass mkt. 6.99 (0-553-57467-1) Bantam Bks.
—Prime Cut. l.t. ed. 1999. 27.95 o.p. (1-56895-588-X, Wheeler Publishing, Inc.) Gale Group.
—Prime Cut. abr. ed. 1998. (Culinary Mysteries Ser.). audio 25.00 (0-553-52535-2, 693716, RH Audio) Random Hse. Audio Publishing Group.
—Prime Cut. unabr. ed. 1999. (Catering Mystery Ser.). audio 72.00 (0-7887-2922-5, 95647E7); audio compact disk 83.00 (0-7887-3432-6, C1038E7) Recorded Bks., LLC.
—Sticks & Scones. l.t. ed. 2001. (Large Print Book Ser.). 410p. 29.95 (1-58724-027-0, Wheeler Publishing, Inc.) Gale Group.
—Tough Cookie. l.t. ed. 2000. (Wheeler Large Print Book Ser.). 31.95 (1-56895-892-7, Wheeler Publishing, Inc.) Gale Group.
Farmer, Jerrilyn. Immaculate Reception. l.t. ed. 2002. (Mystery Ser.). 396p. 28.95 (0-7862-4755-X) Gale Group.
—Immaculate Reception. 1999. (Madeline Bean Catering Mysteries Ser.). 256p. mass mkt. 6.50 (0-380-79597-3, Avon Bks.) Morrow/Avon.
—Killer Wedding. 2000. (Madeline Bean Catering Mysteries Ser.). 256p. mass mkt. 6.50 (0-380-79598-1, Avon Bks.) Morrow/Avon.
—Mumbo Gumbo: A Madeline Bean Novel. 2004. 368p. mass mkt. 6.99 (0-380-81719-5, Avon Bks.); 2003. 272p. 19.95 (0-380-97889-X, Morrow, William & Co.) Morrow/Avon.
—Perfect Sax: A Madeline Bean Novel. 2004. 304p. 22.95 (0-380-97890-3, Morrow, William & Co.) Morrow/Avon.
—Sympathy for the Devil. 1998. (Madeline Bean Mystery Ser.). 256p. mass mkt. 5.99 (0-380-79596-5, Avon Bks.) Morrow/Avon.
—Sympathy for the Devil. l.t. ed. 2002. (Mystery Ser.). 404p. 28.95 (0-7862-4743-6) Thorndike Pr.
John, Cathie, et al. Add One Dead Critic: Journals of Kate Cavanaugh. 1997. 249p. pap. 12.95 (0-9634183-4-3, Journey Bk. Pr.) C C Publishing.
—Beat a Rotten Egg to the Punch: Journals of Kate Cavanaugh. 1998. (Journals of Kate Cavanaugh Ser.). 287p. pap. 12.95 (0-9634183-5-1) C C Publishing.
—Carve a Witness to Shreds: A Kate Cavanaugh Mystery. 1999. (Journals of Kate Cavanaugh Ser.). 260p. (Orig.). pap. 12.95 (0-9634183-6-X, Journey Bk. Pr.) C C Publishing.
Laurence, Janet. Death & the Epicure. l.t. ed. 1994. (Magna Large Print Ser.). 384p. (0-7505-0702-0) Magna Large Print Bks. GBR. *Dist:* Ulverscroft Large Print Canada, Ltd.
—Death & the Epicure. 1993. 208p. 18.95 o.p. (0-312-10451-0, Saint Martin's Minotaur) St. Martin's Pr.
—Death at the Table. l.t. ed. 1997. (Paperback Ser.). 360p. lib. bdg. 21.95 (0-7838-8255-6, Macmillan Reference USA) Gale Group.
—Death at the Table. 1999. (Mystery Ser.: Bk. 316). per. (0-373-26316-3, 1-26316-9, Worldwide Library) Harlequin Enterprises, Ltd.
—Death at the Table. l.t. ed. 1997. 224p. 20.95 o.p. (0-312-15105-5, Saint Martin's Minotaur) St. Martin's Pr.
—A Deep Coffyn. 1989. 14.95 o.s.i (0-385-26626-X) Doubleday Publishing.
—Hotel Morgue. l.t. ed. 1992. (Mystery Ser.). 431p. 29.99 o.p. (0-7505-0298-3) Magna Large Print Bks. GBR. *Dist:* Ulverscroft Large Print Bks., Ltd., Ulverscroft Large Print Canada, Ltd.
Michaels, Fern. Listen to Your Heart. l.t. ed. 2000. 27.95 (1-56895-876-5, Wheeler Publishing, Inc.) Gale Group.
—Listen to Your Heart. 2004. 256p. mass mkt. 6.99 (0-8217-7463-8, Zebra Bks.); 2000. 214p. 20.00 o.s.i (1-57566-572-7) Kensington Publishing Corp.
—Listen to Your Heart. l.t. ed. 2004. 229p. pap. 13.95 (1-59413-027-2, Large Print Pr.) Thorndike Pr.
Neely, Barbara. Blanche Passes Go. 2001. 288p. 5.99 (0-14-100197-6); 2000. 272p. 22.95 o.s.i (0-670-89165-7, Viking) Viking Penguin.
Page, Katherine Hall. The Body in the Basement. l.t. ed. 1999. (Beeler Large Print Mystery Ser.). 25.95 (1-57490-206-7, Beeler Large Print Bks.) Beeler, Thomas T. Publisher.
—The Body in the Basement. 1995. (Faith Fairchild Mystery Ser.). 368p. reprint ed. mass mkt. 6.99 (0-380-72339-5, Avon Bks.) Morrow/Avon.
—The Body in the Basement. 1994. 272p. 20.95 o.p. (0-312-11470-2, Saint Martin's Minotaur) St. Martin's Pr.
—The Body in the Belfry. 1991. 320p. reprint ed. mass mkt. 6.99 (0-380-71328-4, Avon Bks.) Morrow/Avon.
—The Body in the Belfry. 1990. 272p. 16.95 (0-312-03798-8, Saint Martin's Minotaur) St. Martin's Pr.
—The Body in the Big Apple. l.t. ed. 2001. (Beeler Large Print Mystery Ser.). 272p. 26.95 (1-57490-367-5, Beeler Large Print Bks.) Beeler, Thomas T. Publisher.
—The Body in the Big Apple. 1999. 239p. 22.00 (0-688-15748-3, Morrow, William & Co.) Morrow/Avon.
—The Body in the Bog. l.t. ed. 1997. 299p. lib. bdg. 23.95 (1-57490-087-0, Beeler Large Print Bks.) Beeler, Thomas T. Publisher.
—The Body in the Bog. 1997. 384p. mass mkt. 6.99 (0-380-72712-9, Avon Bks.); 1996. 256p. 22.00 o.p. (0-688-14573-6, Morrow, William & Co.) Morrow/Avon.
—The Body in the Bonfire. 2002. 256p. 23.95 (0-380-97843-1, Morrow, William & Co.) Morrow/Avon.
—The Body in the Bookcase. l.t. ed. 2001. (Wheeler Large Print Book Ser.). 333p. pap. 22.95 (1-58724-018-1, Wheeler Publishing, Inc.) Gale Group.
—The Body in the Bookcase. (Faith Fairchild Mysteries Ser.). 1999. 384p. mass mkt. 6.99 (0-380-73237-8, Avon Bks.); 1998. 272p. 22.00 (0-688-15747-5, Morrow, William & Co.) Morrow/Avon.
—The Body in the Bouillon. 1992. 304p. mass mkt. 6.99 (0-380-71896-0, Avon Bks.) Morrow/Avon.
—The Body in the Bouillon. 1991. 224p. text 17.95 o.p. (0-312-06309-1, Saint Martin's Minotaur) St. Martin's Pr.
—The Body in the Cast. l.t. ed. 1999. (Beeler Large Print Mystery Ser.). 24.95 (1-57490-239-3, Beeler Large Print Bks.) Beeler, Thomas T. Publisher.
—The Body in the Cast. 1994. 368p. mass mkt. 6.99 (0-380-72338-7, Avon Bks.) Morrow/Avon.
—The Body in the Cast. 1993. 224p. 19.95 o.p. (0-312-09755-7, Saint Martin's Minotaur) St. Martin's Pr.
—The Body in the Fjord. l.t. ed. 1998. pap. 24.95 (1-56895-562-6, Wheeler Publishing, Inc.) Gale Group.
—The Body in the Fjord. 1998. 304p. mass mkt. 6.99 (0-380-73129-0, Avon Bks.); 1997. 272p. 22.00 (0-688-14574-4, Morrow, William & Co.) Morrow/Avon.
—The Body in the Kelp. l.t. ed. 1998. (Beeler Large Print Mystery Ser.). (Illus.). 246p. 25.95 (1-57490-188-5, Beeler Large Print Bks.) Beeler, Thomas T. Publisher.
—The Body in the Kelp. 1992. 304p. mass mkt. 6.99 (0-380-71329-2, Avon Bks.) Morrow/Avon.
—The Body in the Kelp. 1990. 16.95 o.p. (0-312-05392-4, Saint Martin's Minotaur) St. Martin's Pr.
—The Body in the Lighthouse. l.t. ed. 2003. (Mystery Ser.). 28.95 (1-57490-508-2) Beeler, Thomas T. Publisher.
—The Body in the Lighthouse. 2004. 352p. mass mkt. 6.99 (0-380-81386-6, Avon Bks.); 2003. 256p. 23.95 (0-380-97844-X, Morrow, William & Co.) Morrow/Avon.
—The Body in the Moonlight. 2001. (Faith Fairchild Mysteries Ser.). 256p. 23.00 (0-380-97842-3, Morrow, William & Co.) Morrow/Avon.
—The Body in the Vestibule. l.t. ed. 2000. (Beeler Large Print Mystery Ser.). 223p. 26.95 (1-57490-318-7, Beeler Large Print Bks.) Beeler, Thomas T. Publisher.
—The Body in the Vestibule. 1993. 352p. mass mkt. 6.99 (0-380-72079-5, Avon Bks.) Morrow/Avon.
—The Body in the Vestibule. 1992. 234p. 17.95 o.p. (0-312-08148-0, Saint Martin's Minotaur) St. Martin's Pr.

### CATHOLIC CHURCH—CLERGY—FICTION

Bernanos, Georges. The Impostor. Whitehouse, J. C., tr. from FRE. 1999. 250p. pap. 20.00 (0-8032-6153-5); text 50.00 (0-8032-1290-9) Univ. of Nebraska Pr.
Calia, Charles L. The Unspeakable. 1924. pap. (0-688-16642-3, Quill) HarperTrade.
—The Unspeakable. 1998. 224p. 23.00 (0-688-15119-1, Morrow, William & Co.) Morrow/Avon.
—The Unspeakable: A Novel. 1999. 224p. reprint ed. pap. 12.00 o.s.i (0-688-16710-1, Quill) HarperTrade.
Chesterton, G. K. The Annotated Innocence of Father Brown. 1998. (Illus.). 336p. pap. 12.95 (0-486-29859-0) Dover Pubns., Inc.
—The Annotated Innocence of Father Brown. Gardner, Martin, ed. 1988. 288p. pap. 7.95 o.p. (0-19-282164-4); 1987. (Illus.). 256p. 18.95 o.p. (0-19-217748-6) Oxford Univ. Pr., Inc.
—The Astonishing Father Brown. 1998. (Father Brown Mystery Ser.). audio 21.95 o.s.i (1-55656-301-9); audio 16.95 o.p. (1-55656-300-0) Dercum Audio.
—The Best of Father Brown. 1991. (Father Brown Mystery Ser.). 282p. pap. 7.95 o.p. (0-460-87073-4, Everyman's Classic Library in Paperback) Tuttle Publishing.
—The Best of Father Brown. Keating, H. R. F., ed. abr. ed. 1993. (Father Brown Mystery Ser.). 310p. pap. 9.95 (0-460-87395-4, Everyman's Classic Library in Paperback) Tuttle Publishing.
—The Blue Cross - A Father Brown Mystery. abr. ed. 1997. (Father Brown Mysteries Ser.). 3p. audio 16.99 (0-88646-447-1, 7447) Durkin Hayes Publishing Ltd.
—The Book of Father Brown. (Father Brown Mystery Ser.). reprint ed. lib. bdg. 19.95 (0-89190-576-6, Rivercity Pr.) Amereon, Ltd.
—The Book of Father Brown. 1990. (Father Brown Mystery Ser.). reprint ed. lib. bdg. 16.95 (0-89968-494-7) Buccaneer Bks., Inc.
—The Complete Father Brown. 1987. (Father Brown Mystery Ser.). 720p. pap. 16.95 (0-14-009766-X, Penguin Bks.) Penguin Group (USA) Inc.
—Father Brown: Selected Stories. 1995. (Father Brown Mystery Ser.). 582p. pap. (0-19-282309-4) Oxford Univ. Pr., Inc.
—Father Brown: Selected Stories. 1998. (Father Brown Mystery Ser.). pap. 3.95 (1-85326-003-7, 0037WW) Wordsworth Editions, Ltd. GBR. *Dist:* Casemate Pubs. & Bk. Distributors, LLC.
—Father Brown & the Church of Rome. 270p. 2002. pap. 13.95 (0-89870-953-9); 1996. 17.95 (0-89870-590-8) Ignatius Pr.
—Father Brown Crime Stories. 1990. (Father Brown Mystery Ser.). 12.99 o.s.i (0-517-00182-9) Random Hse. Value Publishing.
—The Father Brown Stories, Set. 1992. (Father Brown Mystery Ser.). audio 65.95 (1-55685-269-X) Audio Bk. Contractors, Inc.
—Favorite Father Brown Stories. 1993. (Father Brown Mystery Ser.). (Illus.). 96p. reprint ed. pap. 1.00 (0-486-27545-0) Dover Pubns., Inc.
—Following Father Brown. unabr. ed. (Father Brown Mystery Ser.). audio 21.95 o.p. (1-55656-013-3, DAB 038) BBC Audiobooks America.
—The Incredulity of Father Brown. (Father Brown Mystery Ser.). 20.95 (0-89190-339-9) Amereon, Ltd.
—The Incredulity of Father Brown. unabr. ed. 1992. (Father Brown Ser.). audio 44.95 (0-7861-0126-1, 1112) Blackstone Audio Bks., Inc.
—The Incredulity of Father Brown. unabr. collector's ed. 1986. (Father Brown Mystery Ser.). audio 48.00 (0-7366-0893-1, 1837) Books on Tape, Inc.
—The Incredulity of Father Brown. l.t. ed. 1984. (Father Brown Mystery Ser.). 9.95 o.p. (0-8161-3680-7); lib. bdg. 11.95 o.p. (0-8161-3732-3) Gale Group. (Macmillan Reference USA).
—The Incredulity of Father Brown. audio 38.95 NorthStar Audio Bks.
—The Incredulity of Father Brown. 1975. (Father Brown Mystery Ser.). pap. 3.95 o.p. (0-14-001069-6) Penguin Group (USA) Inc.
—The Incredulity of Father Brown. 1987. (Father Brown Mystery Ser.). 192p. pap. 4.95 o.p. (0-14-008258-1, Penguin Bks.) Viking Penguin.
—The Innocence of Father Brown. (Father Brown Mystery Ser.). 22.95 (0-89190-338-0) Amereon, Ltd.
—The Innocence of Father Brown. l.t. ed. 1991. (Father Brown Mystery Ser.). pap. 16.95 o.p. (0-7927-0373-1, CS042) BBC Audiobooks America.
—The Innocence of Father Brown. 1976. (Father Brown Mystery Ser.). reprint ed. lib. bdg. 21.00 o.p. (0-8240-2359-5) Garland Publishing, Inc.
—The Innocence of Father Brown. 1975. (Father Brown Mystery Ser.). pap. 3.95 o.p. (0-14-000765-2) Penguin Group (USA) Inc.
—The Innocence of Father Brown. 1987. (Father Brown Mystery Ser.). 256p. pap. 4.95 o.p. (0-14-008257-3, Penguin Bks.) Viking Penguin.
—The Invisible Man - A Father Brown Mystery. unabr. ed. 1998. (Father Brown Mysteries Ser.). audio 16.99 (0-88646-455-2, 7455) Durkin Hayes Publishing Ltd.
—The Scandal of Father Brown. unabr. ed. 1993. (Father Brown Mystery Ser.). audio 39.95 (0-7451-5828-5, CAT 4027) BBC Audiobooks America.
—The Scandal of Father Brown. unabr. ed. 1988. (Father Brown Ser.). audio 32.95 (0-7861-0058-3, 1055) Blackstone Audio Bks., Inc.
—The Scandal of Father Brown. unabr. collector's ed. 1994. (Father Brown Mystery Ser.). audio 36.00 (0-7366-2756-1, 3479) Books on Tape, Inc.
—The Scandal of Father Brown. l.t. ed. 1986. (Father Brown Mystery Ser.). 292p. 10.95 o.p. (0-8161-3930-X, Macmillan Reference USA) Gale Group.
—The Scandal of Father Brown. 2000. 182p. pap. 9.95 (0-7551-0026-3) House of Stratus, Inc. GBR. *Dist:* Midpoint Trade Bks., Inc.
—The Scandal of Father Brown. 1988. (Father Brown Mystery Ser.). audio 35.95 o.s.i (0-8161-7782-1) Thorndike Pr.
—The Scandal of Father Brown. (Father Brown Mystery Ser.). 1988. 176p. pap. 4.95 o.p. (0-14-008256-5); 1982. pap. 3.50 o.p. (0-14-004739-5) Viking Penguin. (Penguin Bks.).
—The Secret of Father Brown. (Father Brown Mystery Ser.). 20.95 (0-89190-337-2) Amereon, Ltd.
—The Secret of Father Brown. unabr. ed. 1999. (Father Brown Mystery Ser.). audio 39.95 (0-7861-0016-8, 1016) Blackstone Audio Bks., Inc.
—The Secret of Father Brown. unabr. collector's ed. 1994. (Father Brown Mystery Ser.). audio 42.00 (0-7366-2755-3, 3478) Books on Tape, Inc.
—The Secret of Father Brown. unabr. ed. 2000. (Father Brown Mystery Ser). audio 49.95 (0-7451-5829-3, CAB 428) Chivers Audio Bks. GBR. *Dist:* BBC Audiobooks America.
—The Secret of Father Brown. l.t. ed. 1985. (Father Brown Mystery Ser.). 312p. 9.95 o.p. (0-8161-3929-6, Macmillan Reference USA) Gale Group.
—The Secret of Father Brown. 2000. 204p. pap. 9.95 (0-7551-0027-1) House of Stratus, Inc. GBR. *Dist:* Midpoint Trade Bks., Inc.
—The Secret of Father Brown. unabr. ed. 2001. audio 38.95 NorthStar Audio Bks.

Occupations

—The Secret of Father Brown. 1975. (Father Brown Mystery Ser.). pap. 3.50 o.p. (*0-14-003807-8*) Penguin Group (USA) Inc.

—The Secret of Father Brown. 1989. (Father Brown Mystery Ser.). audio 53.95 o.s.i (*0-8161-7726-0*) Thorndike Pr.

—The Secret of Father Brown. 1987. (Father Brown Mystery Ser.). 176p. pap. 4.95 o.p. (*0-14-008255-7*, Penguin Bks.) Viking Penguin.

—The Wisdom of Father Brown. (Father Brown Mystery Ser.). 21.95 (*0-89190-336-4*) Amereon, Ltd.

—The Wisdom of Father Brown. unabr. ed. 1992. (Father Brown Mystery Ser.). audio 44.95 (*0-7861-0125-3*, 1111) Blackstone Audio Bks., Inc.

—The Wisdom of Father Brown. unabr. collector's ed. 1986. (Father Brown Mystery Ser.). audio 48.00 (*0-7366-0813-3*, 1763) Books on Tape, Inc.

—The Wisdom of Father Brown. 2001. audio 42.95 NorthStar Audio Bks.

—The Wisdom of Father Brown. 1975. (Father Brown Mystery Ser.). pap. 3.50 o.p. (*0-14-003118-9*) Penguin Group (USA) Inc.

—The Wisdom of Father Brown. l.t. ed. 2000. (Father Brown Mystery Ser.). 280p. pap. 18.95 (*1-888725-27-3*, MacroPrintBooks) Science & Humanities Pr.

—The Wisdom of Father Brown. 1987. (Father Brown Mystery Ser.). 208p. pap. 4.95 o.p. (*0-14-008159-3*, Penguin Bks.) Viking Penguin.

Coel, Margaret. The Dream Stalker. 1997. 256p. 21.95 o.s.i (*0-425-15967-1*); 1998. 272p. reprint ed. mass mkt. 6.50 (*0-425-16533-7*) Berkley Publishing Group. (Prime Crime).

—The Spirit Woman. 2000. 272p. 21.95 o.s.i (*0-425-17597-9*); 2001. 304p. reprint ed. mass mkt. 6.50 (*0-425-18090-5*, Prime Crime) Berkley Publishing Group.

—The Spirit Woman. l.t. ed. 2001. 294p. lib. bdg. 28.95 (*1-58547-063-5*) Ctr. Point Large Print.

Cooney, John. Acts of Contrition. 1994. 416p. mass mkt. 5.99 (*0-671-78316-5*, Pocket) Simon & Schuster.

Cosse, Laurence. A Corner of the Veil. Asher, Linda, tr. from FRE. 1999. 272p. 23.00 (*0-684-84667-5*, Scribner) Simon & Schuster.

De Rosa, Peter. Pope Patrick. 1997. 352p. 23.95 o.s.i (*0-385-48548-4*) Doubleday Publishing.

Disch, Thomas M. The Priest: A Gothic Romance. 1995. 24.00 (*0-679-42880-1*) Knopf, Alfred A. Inc.

Flynn, Raymond & Moore, Robin. The Accidental Pope. 2000. 394p. 24.95 (*0-312-26801-7*) St. Martin's Pr.

Following Father Brown. unabr. ed. Incl. Absence of Mr. Glass. audio o.p. Blast of the Book. audio o.p. Man in the Passage. audio o.p. Oracle of the Dog. audio o.p. 1986. (Father Brown Mystery Ser.). 1986. Set audio 16.95 o.p. (*1-55656-008-7*) Dercum Audio.

Folsom, Allan. Day of Confession. l.t. ed. 1999. 27.95 (*1-56895-648-7*, Wheeler Publishing, Inc.) Gale Group.

—Day of Confession. 1998. 576p. (gr. 8). 25.00 (*0-316-28755-5*) Little Brown & Co.

—Day of Confession. 1999. 688p. mass mkt. 7.99 (*0-446-60453-4*) Warner Bks., Inc.

Gifford, Thomas. The Assassini. 1991. 688p. mass mkt. 6.99 o.s.i (*0-553-28740-0*); 1990. (*0-593-02172-X*); 1990. 688p. pap. 29.00 (*0-553-76236-2*) Bantam Bks.

—The Assassini. 1924. o.s.i (*0-688-04723-8*, Morrow, William & Co.) Morrow/Avon.

—The Assassini. 1991. audio 12.79 o.s.i (*0-553-70023-5*); 1999. audio 9.99 o.s.i (*0-553-70203-3*) Random Hse. Audio Publishing Group. (RH Audio).

Greeley, Andrew M. The Bishop & the Beggar Girl of St. Germain: A Blackie Ryan Mystery. 2001. 304p. 24.95 (*0-312-86874-X*); 2002. 259p. reprint ed. mass mkt. 6.99 (*0-8125-7597-0*) Doherty, Tom Assocs., LLC. (Forge Bks.).

—The Bishop & the Missing L Train: A Blackie Ryan Mystery. 2002. lib. bdg. 27.95 (*1-58547-254-9*, Premier) Ctr. Point Large Print.

—The Bishop & the Missing L Train: A Blackie Ryan Mystery. E-Book 6.99 (*0-312-70218-3*, Tor Bks.); 2001. 304p. reprint ed. mass mkt. 6.99 (*0-8125-7596-2*, Forge Bks.); 2000. 288p. reprint ed. 24.95 o.p. (*0-312-86875-8*, NHC 0141, Forge Bks.) Doherty, Tom Assocs., LLC.

—The Bishop & the Three Kings: A Blackie Ryan Mystery. 1998. (Blackie Ryan Novels Ser.). (Illus.). 320p. mass mkt. 6.99 (*0-425-16617-1*) Berkley Publishing Group.

—The Bishop at Sea: A Blackie Ryan Mystery. 1997. (Blackie Ryan Novels Ser.). 304p. mass mkt. 6.99 (*0-425-16080-7*) Berkley Publishing Group.

—The Bishop at Sea: A Blackie Ryan Mystery. l.t. ed. 2000. (Americana Ser.). 407p. 27.95 (*0-7862-2322-7*) Thorndike Pr.

—The Bishop in the West Wing: A Blackie Ryan Story. l.t. ed. 2003. lib. bdg. 28.95 (*1-58547-280-8*, Platinum) Ctr. Point Large Print.

—The Bishop in the West Wing: A Blackie Ryan Story. E-Book 24.95 (*0-312-70724-X*, Tor Bks.); 2002. (Illus.). 288p. 24.95 (*0-312-86873-1*, Forge Bks.); 2003. (Illus.). 320p. reprint ed. mass mkt. 6.99 (*0-8125-7598-9*, Forge Bks.) Doherty, Tom Assocs., LLC.

—The Cardinal Virtues. 1990. 19.45 o.s.i (*0-446-51478-0*) Warner Bks., Inc.

—Cardinal Virtues. 1991. mass mkt. 5.95 o.s.i (*0-446-36094-5*) Warner Bks., Inc.

—The Cardinal Virtues. l.t. ed. 1992. 16.95 o.p. (*0-7927-0650-1*); 1991. 21.95 o.p. (*0-7927-0624-2*, E0009) BBC Audiobooks America.

—Fall from Grace. 1994. 384p. mass mkt. 6.99 o.s.i (*0-515-11404-9*, Jove) Berkley Publishing Group.

—Fall from Grace. 1993. 384p. 22.95 o.p. (*0-399-13723-8*, G. P. Putnam's Sons) Penguin Group (USA) Inc.

—Happy Are the Clean of Heart: A Blackie Ryan Novel. l.t. ed. 1987. 412p. 18.95 o.p. (*0-8161-4278-5*, Macmillan Reference USA) Gale Group.

—Happy Are the Clean of Heart: A Blackie Ryan Novel. 1988. mass mkt. 4.95 (*0-446-35722-7*) Warner Bks., Inc.

—Happy Are the Meek: A Blackie Ryan Novel. l.t. ed. 1986. (General Ser.). 373p. 16.95 o.p. (*0-8161-4029-4*, Macmillan Reference USA) Gale Group.

—Happy Are the Meek: A Blackie Ryan Novel. 1985. 288p. mass mkt. 3.95 (*0-446-32706-9*) Warner Bks., Inc.

—Happy Are the Merciful: A Blackie Ryan Novel. 1992. 336p. mass mkt. 6.99 o.s.i (*0-515-10726-3*, Jove) Berkley Publishing Group.

—Happy Are the Oppressed: A Blackie Ryan Novel. l.t. ed. 1997. lib. bdg. 24.95 (*1-57490-083-8*, Beeler Large Print Bks.) Beeler, Thomas T. Publisher.

—Happy Are the Oppressed: A Blackie Ryan Novel. 1996. (Illus.). 320p. mass mkt. 7.50 (*0-515-11921-0*, Jove) Berkley Publishing Group.

—Happy Are the Peace Makers: A Blackie Ryan Novel. l.t. ed. 1993. 24.95 o.p. (*0-7927-1680-9*); 22.95 o.p. (*0-7927-1679-5*) BBC Audiobooks America.

—Happy Are the Peace Makers: A Blackie Ryan Novel. 1993. 320p. mass mkt. 6.99 o.s.i (*0-515-11075-2*, Jove) Berkley Publishing Group.

—Happy Are the Poor in Spirit: A Blackie Ryan Novel. 1994. (Blackie Ryan Novels Ser.). (Illus.). 304p. mass mkt. 6.99 o.s.i (*0-515-11502-9*, Jove) Berkley Publishing Group.

—Happy Are the Poor in Spirit: A Blackie Ryan Novel. l.t. ed. 2000. (Americana Ser.). 392p. 28.95 (*0-7862-2323-5*) Thorndike Pr.

—Happy Are Those Who Mourn: A Blackie Ryan Novel. l.t. ed. 1996. (Large Print Ser.). 352p. lib. bdg. 23.95 (*1-57490-038-2*, Beeler Large Print Bks.) Beeler, Thomas T. Publisher.

—Happy Are Those Who Mourn: A Blackie Ryan Novel. 1995. (Illus.). 304p. mass mkt. 6.99 o.s.i (*0-515-11761-7*, Jove) Berkley Publishing Group.

—Happy Are Those Who Thirst for Justice: A Blackie Ryan Novel. l.t. ed. 1988. (General Ser.). 440p. 18.95 o.p. (*0-8161-4488-5*, Macmillan Reference USA) Gale Group.

—Happy Are Those Who Thirst for Justice: A Blackie Ryan Novel. 1987. 320p. 16.95 (*0-89296-180-5*) Mysterious Pr.

—Happy Are Those Who Thirst for Justice: A Blackie Ryan Novel. 1988. mass mkt. 4.50 (*0-446-34946-1*) Warner Bks., Inc.

—White Smoke: A Novel about the Next Papal Conclave. 1997. 466p. mass mkt. 6.99 (*0-8125-9055-4*); 1996. 384p. 24.95 (*0-312-85814-0*) Doherty, Tom Assocs., LLC. (Forge Bks.).

—White Smoke: A Novel about the Next Papal Conclave, Set. abr. ed. 1996. audio 24.99 (*0-88646-413-7*, 693997) Durkin Hayes Publishing Ltd.

—White Smoke: A Novel about the Next Papal Conclave. 1997. 6.99 (*0-312-87118-X*) St. Martin's Pr.

Hailey, Arthur. Detective. 1998. 608p. reprint ed. mass mkt. 7.99 (*0-425-16386-5*) Berkley Publishing Group.

—Detective. l.t. ed. 1997. pap. 24.00 o.p. (*0-7838-8132-0*, Macmillan Reference USA) Gale Group.

—Detective. 1999. (SPA.). (*84-08-02910-X*) GeoPlaneta, Editorial, S. A.

Hassler, Jon. North of Hope: A Novel. 1996. 518p. pap. 12.95 o.s.i (*0-345-41010-6*) Ballantine Bks.

Hogan, Judy. The Shade. McClelland, Lucille A., ed. 1997. (Illus.). 391p. pap. 16.95 (*0-9652673-0-X*) Black Oaks Publishing.

Johnston, Wayne. The Divine Ryans. 1999. 224p. pap. 12.95 o.s.i (*0-385-49544-7*) Doubleday Publishing.

—The Divine Ryans. 1996. mass mkt. 6.99 o.p. (*0-7710-4436-4*); 1990. 0.00 o.p. (*0-7710-4447-X*) McClelland & Stewart/Tundra Bks.

Kienzle, William X. Assault with Intent. 1987. (Father Koesler Mystery Ser.: No. 4). 273p. 9.95 o.p. (*0-8362-6117-8*) Andrews McMeel Publishing.

—Assault with Intent. 1985. (Father Koesler Mystery Ser.: No. 4). 320p. mass mkt. 5.99 o.s.i (*0-345-33283-0*); 1983. mass mkt. 2.95 o.p. (*0-345-30812-3*) Ballantine Bks.

—Assault with Intent. unabr. collector's ed. 1997. (Father Koesler Mystery Ser.). audio 56.00 (*0-7366-3994-2*, 4459) Books on Tape, Inc.

—Bishop As Pawn. 1994. (Father Koesler Mystery Ser.: No. 16). xiii, 266p. 18.95 o.p. (*0-8362-6130-5*) Andrews McMeel Publishing.

—Bishop As Pawn. 1995. (Father Koesler Mystery Ser.: No. 16). mass mkt. 5.99 o.s.i (*0-345-38800-3*) Ballantine Bks.

—Body Count. 1992. (Father Koesler Mystery Ser.: No. 14). viii, 266p. 18.95 o.p. (*0-8362-6128-3*) Andrews McMeel Publishing.

—Body Count. 1993. (Father Koesler Mystery Ser.: No. 14). reprint ed. mass mkt. 5.99 o.s.i (*0-345-37767-2*) Ballantine Bks.

—Call No Man Father. 1995. (Father Koesler Mystery Ser.: No. 17). 272p. 18.95 o.p. (*0-8362-6131-3*) Andrews McMeel Publishing.

—Call No Man Father. 1996. (Father Koesler Mystery Ser.: No. 17). mass mkt. 5.99 o.s.i (*0-345-38801-1*) Ballantine Bks.

—Chameleon. 1991. (Father Koesler Mystery Ser.: No. 13). 289p. pap. 16.95 o.p. (*0-8362-6127-5*) Andrews McMeel Publishing.

—Chameleon. 1992. (Father Koesler Mystery Ser.: No. 13). mass mkt. 5.99 o.s.i (*0-345-36621-2*) Ballantine Bks.

—Dead Wrong. 1993. (Father Koesler Mystery Ser.: No. 15). 269p. 18.95 o.p. (*0-8362-6129-1*) Andrews McMeel Publishing.

—Dead Wrong. 1994. (Father Koesler Mystery Ser.: No. 15). mass mkt. 5.99 o.s.i (*0-345-37766-4*) Ballantine Bks.

—Deadline for a Critic. 1987. (Father Koesler Mystery Ser.: No. 9). 263p. 14.95 o.p. (*0-8362-6123-2*) Andrews McMeel Publishing.

—Deadline for a Critic. 1988. (Father Koesler Mystery Ser.: No. 9). 352p. mass mkt. 5.99 o.s.i (*0-345-33190-7*) Ballantine Bks.

—Deadline for a Critic. 1990. (Father Koesler Mystery Ser.: No. 9). 2.99 o.p. (*0-517-05975-4*) Random Hse. Value Publishing.

—Death Bed. 1987. (Father Koesler Mystery Ser.: No. 8). mass mkt. 5.99 o.s.i (*0-345-33189-3*) Ballantine Bks.

—Death Wears a Red Hat. 1980. (Father Koesler Mystery Ser.: No. 2). 304p. 9.95 o.p. (*0-8362-6111-9*) Andrews McMeel Publishing.

—Death Wears a Red Hat. 1989. (Father Koesler Mystery Ser.: No. 2). mass mkt. 5.99 o.s.i (*0-345-35669-1*) Ballantine Bks.

—Death Wears a Red Hat. 1981. (Father Koesler Mystery Ser.: No. 2). 288p. pap. 3.50 o.p. (*0-553-26524-5*) Bantam Bks.

—Death Wears a Red Hat. unabr. collector's ed. 1997. (Father Koesler Mystery Ser.). audio 56.00 (*0-7366-4063-0*, 4574) Books on Tape, Inc.

—Death Wears a Red Hat. l.t. ed. 1981. (Father Koesler Mystery Ser.: No. 2). 553p. 29.99 o.p. (*0-7089-0647-8*, Ulverscroft) Thorpe, F. A. Pubs. GBR. *Dist:* Ulverscroft Large Print Bks., Ltd., Ulverscroft Large Print Canada, Ltd.

—Deathbed. 1985. (Father Koesler Mystery Ser.: No. 8). 258p. 14.95 o.p. (*0-8362-6122-4*) Andrews McMeel Publishing.

—Eminence. 1989. (Father Koesler Mystery Ser.: No. 11). 312p. 15.95 o.p. (*0-8362-6125-9*) Andrews McMeel Publishing.

—Eminence. 1990. (Father Koesler Mystery Ser.: No. 11). 368p. mass mkt. 5.99 o.s.i (*0-345-35395-1*) Ballantine Bks.

—Eminence. 1990. 3.99 o.p. (*0-517-05976-2*) Random Hse. Value Publishing.

—The Greatest Evil. 1998. (Father Koesler Mystery Ser.: No. 20). vii, 278p. 19.95 o.p. (*0-8362-5206-3*) Andrews McMeel Publishing.

—The Greatest Evil. 1999. (Father Koesler Mystery Ser.: No. 20). 294p. mass mkt. 6.99 (*0-345-42638-X*) Ballantine Bks.

—The Greatest Evil. unabr. collector's ed. 1998. (Father Koesler Mystery Ser.). audio 56.00 (*0-7366-4529-2*, 4720) Books on Tape, Inc.

—Kill & Tell. 1984. (Father Koesler Mystery Ser.: No. 6). 250p. 12.95 o.p. (*0-8362-6120-8*) Andrews McMeel Publishing.

—Kill & Tell. 1985. (Father Koesler Mystery Ser.: No. 6). mass mkt. 5.99 o.s.i (*0-345-31856-0*) Ballantine Bks.

—Kill & Tell. l.t. ed. 1984. (Father Koesler Mystery Ser.: No. 6). 378p. 15.95 o.p. (*0-8161-3779-X*, Macmillan Reference USA) Gale Group.

—The Man Who Loved God. 1997. (Father Koesler Mystery Ser.: No. 19). 274p. 19.95 (*0-8362-2754-9*) Andrews McMeel Publishing.

—The Man Who Loved God. 1998. (Father Koesler Mystery Ser.: No. 19). 304p. mass mkt. 6.99 o.s.i (*0-345-40290-1*) Ballantine Bks.

—Marked for Murder. 1988. (Father Koesler Mystery Ser.: No. 10). 281p. 14.95 o.p. (*0-8362-6124-0*) Andrews McMeel Publishing.

—Marked for Murder. 1989. (Father Koesler Mystery Ser.: No. 10). mass mkt. 5.99 o.s.i (*0-345-35397-8*) Ballantine Bks.

—Masquerade. 1990. (Father Koesler Mystery Ser.: No. 12). 267p. 15.95 o.p. (*0-8362-6126-7*) Andrews McMeel Publishing.

—Masquerade. 1991. (Father Koesler Mystery Ser.: No. 12). 384p. mass mkt. 5.99 o.s.i (*0-345-36620-4*) Ballantine Bks.

—Mind over Murder. 1981. (Father Koesler Mystery Ser.: No. 3). v, 296p. 9.95 o.p. (*0-8362-6114-3*) Andrews McMeel Publishing.

—Mind over Murder. 1989. (Father Koesler Mystery Ser.: No. 3). mass mkt. 5.99 o.s.i (*0-345-35667-5*) Ballantine Bks.

—Mind over Murder. 1982. (Father Koesler Mystery Ser.: No. 3). pap. 3.50 o.p. (*0-553-25008-6*) Bantam Bks.

—Mind over Murder. unabr. collector's ed. 1997. (Father Koesler Mystery Ser.). audio 64.00 (*0-7366-4064-9*, 4575) Books on Tape, Inc.

—No Greater Love. 2000. (Father Koesler Mystery Ser.). 304p. mass mkt. 6.99 (*0-345-42639-8*, Fawcett) Ballantine Bks.

—Requiem for Moses. 1996. (Father Koesler Mystery Ser.: No. 18). 272p. 19.95 o.p. (*0-8362-1042-5*) Andrews McMeel Publishing.

—Requiem for Moses. 1997. (Father Koesler Mystery Ser.: No. 19). 322p. mass mkt. 5.99 o.s.i (*0-345-40291-X*) Ballantine Bks.

—The Rosary Murders. 1979. (Father Koesler Mystery Ser.: No. 1). 257p. 9.95 o.p. (*0-8362-6101-1*) Andrews McMeel Publishing.

—The Rosary Murders. 1989. (Father Koesler Mystery Ser.: No. 1). 304p. mass mkt. 5.99 o.s.i (*0-345-35668-3*) Ballantine Bks.

—The Rosary Murders. 1984. mass mkt. 3.50 o.s.i (*0-553-25084-1*); 1980. (Father Koesler Mystery Ser.: No. 1). 304p. mass mkt. 3.50 o.s.i (*0-553-26406-0*) Bantam Bks.

—Shadow of Death. 1983. (Father Koesler Mystery Ser.: No. 5). 252p. 10.95 o.p. (*0-8362-6119-4*) Andrews McMeel Publishing.

—Shadow of Death. (Father Koesler Mystery Ser.: No. 5). 1985. mass mkt. 5.99 o.s.i (*0-345-33110-9*); 1984. mass mkt. 2.95 o.p. (*0-345-31251-1*) Ballantine Bks.

—Shadow of Death. unabr. collector's ed. 1999. (Father Koesler Mystery Ser.). audio 56.00 (*0-7366-4330-3*, 4824) Books on Tape, Inc.

—Shadow of Death. l.t. ed. 1983. (Father Koesler Mystery Ser.: No. 5). lib. bdg. 16.95 o.p. (*0-8161-3582-7*, Macmillan Reference USA) Gale Group.

—Sudden Death. 1985. (Father Koesler Mystery Ser.: No. 7). 257p. 12.95 o.p. (*0-8362-6121-6*) Andrews McMeel Publishing.

—Sudden Death. 1986. (Father Koesler Mystery Ser.: No. 7). mass mkt. 5.99 o.s.i (*0-345-32851-5*) Ballantine Bks.

—Sudden Death. l.t. ed. 1986. (Father Koesler Mystery Ser.: No. 7). 416p. 16.95 o.p. (*0-8161-3965-2*, Macmillan Reference USA) Gale Group.

—Till Death. 2000. 279p. 19.95 (*0-7407-0489-3*) Andrews McMeel Publishing.

L'Heureux, John. The Clang Birds. 1993. 224p. pap. 11.00 o.p. (*0-14-015227-X*, Penguin Bks.) Penguin Group (USA) Inc.

—Tight White Collar. 1993. 224p. pap. 11.00 o.p. (*0-14-015226-1*, Penguin Bks.) Penguin Group (USA) Inc.

—Tight White Collar. 1993. 224p. pap. 10.00 (*0-14-015526-0*, Penguin Bks.) Viking Penguin.

Liloia, C. Tony. Father Anthony's Sin: Beyond the Lure of Lust & Love. 2000. 271p. pap. 21.99 (*0-7388-1187-4*); text 31.99 (*0-7388-1186-6*) Xlibris Corp.

MacLaverty, Bernard. Lamb. l.t. ed. 1999. (*0-7540-3475-5*); 200p. pap. (*0-7540-3476-3*) BBC Audiobooks America.

—Lamb. 1997. 160p. pap. 11.00 (*0-393-31701-3*) Norton, W. W. & Co., Inc.

—Lamb. l.t. ed. 1998. (General Ser.). 208p. pap. 23.95 (*0-7862-1609-3*) Thorndike Pr.

—Lamb. 1981. 160p. pap. 5.95 o.p. (*0-14-005769-2*, Penguin Bks.) Viking Penguin.

Mantel, Hilary. Fludd. 2000. 181p. pap. 13.00 (*0-8050-6273-4*, Owl Bks.) Holt, Henry & Co.

—Fludd. l.t. ed. 2001. (Thorndike General Ser.). 256p. pap. 25.95 (*0-7862-2993-4*); (*0-7540-4337-1*); (*0-7540-4336-3*) Thorndike Pr.

Martin, Malachi. Vatican. 1988. mass mkt. 5.95 o.s.i (*0-515-09654-7*, Jove) Berkley Publishing Group.

—Vatican. 1986. 672p. 18.95 o.p. (*0-06-015478-0*) HarperTrade.

—Windswept House: A Vatican Novel. 656p. 1998. pap. 18.95 (*0-385-49231-6*); 1996. 24.95 o.s.i (*0-385-48408-9*) Doubleday Publishing.

McCullough, Colleen. The Thorn Birds. 1998. lib. bdg. 11.95 (*1-56849-697-4*) Buccaneer Bks., Inc.

—The Thorn Birds. 1977. 19.95 o.p. (*0-06-012956-5*) HarperTrade.
—The Thorn Birds. 1978. 704p. mass mkt. 7.99 (*0-380-01817-9*, Avon Bks.) Morrow/Avon.
—The Thorn Birds. 1998. (Modern Classics Ser.). 704p. 9.99 o.s.i (*0-517-20165-8*) Random Hse. Value Publishing.
—The Thorn Birds. 1978. 13.04 (*0-606-01301-6*) Turtleback Bks.
McGinley, Patrick. The Devil's Diary. 1988. 256p. 16.95 o.p. (*0-312-02193-3*) St. Martin's Pr.
McInerny, Ralph. Abracadaver. l.t. ed. 1990. (Nightingale Ser.). pap. 12.95 o.p. (*0-8161-4904-6*, Macmillan Reference USA) Gale Group.
—Abracadaver. 1994. (WWL Mystery Ser.). per. (*0-373-26152-7*, 1-26152-8, Harlequin Bks.) Harlequin Enterprises, Ltd.
—Abracadaver. 1989. 176p. 14.95 o.p. (*0-312-02533-5*, Saint Martin's Minotaur) St. Martin's Pr.
—The Basket Case. l.t. ed. 1992. (Nightingale Ser.). 280p. pap. 14.95 o.p. (*0-8161-5569-0*, Macmillan Reference USA) Gale Group.
—The Basket Case. 1988. mass mkt. 3.50 (*0-312-91157-2*, St. Martin's Paperbacks); 1987. 208p. 14.95 o.p. (*0-312-00997-6*, Saint Martin's Minotaur) St. Martin's Pr.
—A Cardinal Offense. 1994. 384p. 21.95 o.p. (*0-312-11283-1*, Saint Martin's Minotaur) St. Martin's Pr.
—Desert Sinner. 1994. (WWL Mystery Ser.). per. (*0-373-26158-6*, 1-26158-5, Harlequin Bks.) Harlequin Enterprises, Ltd.
—Desert Sinner. 1992. (Father Dowling Mysteries Ser.). 192p. 16.95 o.p. (*0-312-08177-4*, Saint Martin's Minotaur) St. Martin's Pr.
—Easeful Death. 1994. 3.99 o.p. (*0-517-11437-2*) Random Hse. Value Publishing.
—Easeful Death. 1991. 256p. 19.95 o.s.i (*0-689-12131-8*, Scribner) Simon & Schuster.
—Four on the Floor. 1994. pap. (*0-373-26154-3*, Harlequin Bks.) Harlequin Enterprises, Ltd.
—Four on the Floor. 1989. 192p. 15.95 o.p. (*0-312-03345-1*, Saint Martin's Minotaur) St. Martin's Pr.
—Getting a Way with Murder. l.t. ed. 1985. (Nightingale Ser.). 256p. 9.95 o.p. (*0-8161-3924-5*, Macmillan Reference USA) Gale Group.
—Grave Undertakings: A Father Dowling Mystery. 2000. (Father Dowling Mysteries Ser.). 374p. 24.95 (*0-312-20309-8*, Saint Martin's Minotaur) St. Martin's Pr.
—Grave Undertakings: A Father Dowling Mystery. l.t. ed. 2000. (Basic Ser.). 448p. 29.95 (*0-7862-2925-X*) Thorndike Pr.
—Her Death of Cold. 1979. (Father Dowling Mysteries Ser.). 224p. 1.95 o.s.i (*0-441-32780-X*) Ace Bks.
—Infra Dig. l.t. ed. 1993. 21.95 o.p. (*0-7927-1461-X*); pap. 19.95 o.p. (*0-7927-1460-1*) BBC Audiobooks America.
—Infra Dig. 1992. 218p. 19.00 o.s.i (*0-689-12132-6*) Central Bureau voor Schimmelcultures NLD. *Dist:* Lubrecht & Cramer, Ltd.
—Judas Priest: A Father Dowling Mystery. 1994. per. (*0-373-26156-X*, 1-26156-9, Harlequin Bks.) Harlequin Enterprises, Ltd.
—Judas Priest: A Father Dowling Mystery. 1991. 208p. 17.95 o.p. (*0-312-06375-X*, Saint Martin's Minotaur) St. Martin's Pr.
—Lying Three. 1980. 256p. 2.25 o.s.i (*0-441-50515-5*) Ace Bks.
—Lying Three. l.t. ed. 1981. 374p. reprint ed. 11.95 o.p. (*0-89621-304-8*) Thorndike Pr.
—Prodigal Father. l.t. ed. 2003. (Mystery Ser.). 28.95 (*1-57490-487-6*, Beeler Large Print Bks.) Beeler, Thomas T. Publisher.
—Prodigal Father. E-Book 24.95 (*0-312-70741-X*); 2002. 384p. 24.95 (*0-312-29129-9*, Saint Martin's Minotaur) St. Martin's Pr.
—The Red Hat: A Novel. 1998. 600p. 24.95 (*0-89870-681-5*) Ignatius Pr.
—Rest in Pieces. l.t. ed. 1991. (Nightingale Ser.). 280p. lib. bdg. 13.95 o.p. (*0-8161-5107-5*, Macmillan Reference USA) Gale Group.
—Second Vespers. 1981. (Father Dowling Mysteries Ser.). 2.50 o.s.i (*0-441-75724-3*) Ace Bks.
—Second Vespers. l.t. ed. 1981. reprint ed. 10.95 o.p. (*0-89621-272-6*) Thorndike Pr.
—Seed of Doubt. 1993. 352p. 19.95 o.p. (*0-312-09381-0*) St. Martin's Pr.
—The Seventh Station. 1979. (Father McDowling Ser.). 224p. 1.95 o.s.i (*0-441-75947-5*) Ace Bks.
—The Tears of Things. 1996. o.p. (*0-03-214746-5*); 368p. text 24.95 o.p. (*0-312-14746-5*, Saint Martin's Minotaur) St. Martin's Pr.
—Triple Pursuit: A Father Dowling Mystery. 2002. E-Book 24.95 (*1-59061-754-1*) Adobe Systems, Inc.
—Triple Pursuit: A Father Dowling Mystery. 2001. (Father Dowling Mysteries Ser.). 371p. 24.95 (*0-312-26948-X*, Saint Martin's Minotaur) St. Martin's Pr.
—Triple Pursuit: A Father Dowling Mystery. l.t. ed. 2001. 547p. (*0-7862-3295-1*) Thorndike Pr.
Miller, Hugh. Ballykissangel: The New Arrival. 1998. 222p. pap. 10.95 o.p. (*0-912333-62-6*) Bay Soma Publishing.
Moore, Brian. The Color of Blood. 1987. 208p. 16.95 o.p. (*0-525-24539-1*, Abrahams, William Bks.) Dutton/Plume.
—The Color of Blood. 1995. 80p. pap. 10.00 o.p. (*0-586-08737-0*) HarperCollins Pubs. Ltd. GBR. *Dist:* HarperCollins Pubs.
—The Color of Blood. 1988. mass mkt. 4.95 (*0-7710-6422-5*) McClelland & Stewart/Tundra Bks.
—The Color of Blood. 1988. 192p. pap. 7.95 o.p. (*0-525-48422-1*, Obelisk) NAL.
—No Other Life. 1997. (William Abrahams Book Ser.). 224p. pap. 11.95 o.s.i (*0-452-27878-3*, Plume) Dutton/Plume.
—No Other Life. l.t. ed. 1993. 277p. lib. bdg. 22.95 (*0-8161-5897-5*, Macmillan Reference USA) Gale Group.
Patterson, James. Cradle & All. l.t. ed. 2000. (Large Print Book Ser.). 305p. 31.95 (*1-56895-879-X*, Wheeler Publishing, Inc.) Gale Group.
—Cradle & All. 2000. 368p. 25.95 o.p. (*0-316-69061-9*) Little Brown & Co.
—Cradle & All. 2001. 384p. reprint ed. mass mkt. 7.99 (*0-446-60940-4*) Warner Bks., Inc.
Powers, J. F. Morte D'Urban. 2000. (New York Review Books Classics Ser.). xviii, 336p. pap. 12.95 (*0-940322-23-4*) New York Review of Bks., Inc., The.
—The Stories of J. F. Powers. 2000. (New York Review Books Classics Ser.). xii, 570p. pap. 14.95 (*0-940322-22-6*) New York Review of Bks., Inc., The.
Pérez-Reverte, Arturo. The Seville Communion. Soto, Sonia, tr. from SPA. (Illus.). 1999. 416p. (C). pap. 14.00 (*0-15-600639-1*, Harvest Bks.); 1998. 400p. 24.00 (*0-15-100283-5*) Harcourt Trade Pubs.
—The Seville Communion. abr. ed. 1999. audio 25.00 (*0-7871-1910-5*, Dove Audio) NewStar Media, Inc.
Rivabella, Omar. Requiem for a Woman's Soul. 1986. 128p. 14.95 o.s.i (*0-394-54917-1*) Random Hse., Inc.
Schwab, Brian. The Sacred Robe. 2001. 262p. pap. 11.95 (*0-9707311-0-8*) Barrier Reef Publishing.
Shapiro, David. The Promise of God: A Novel. 2000. 335p. pap. 12.95 (*1-55874-744-3*, Simcha Pr.) Health Communications, Inc.
Sheehan, Edward R. Cardinal Galsworthy: A Romance. 1997. 512p. 26.95 o.s.i (*0-670-85541-3*) Viking Penguin.
Silva, Daniel. The Confessor. 2004. 416p. mass mkt. 7.99 (*0-451-21148-0*, Signet Bks.) NAL.
Strieber, Whitley. Unholy Fire. 1992. 336p. 21.00 o.p. (*0-525-93415-4*, Dutton) Dutton/Plume.
Tobin, Greg. Conclave. 2002. 453p. mass mkt. 7.99 (*0-8125-7921-6*, Tor Bks.); 2001. 432p. 25.95 (*0-312-87352-2*, Forge Bks.) Doherty, Tom Assocs., LLC.
Vetere, Richard. The Third Miracle. 1997. 256p. 22.00 o.p. (*0-7867-0413-6*, Carroll & Graf Pubs.) Avalon Publishing Group.
—The Third Miracle. 240p. 2000. per. 11.00 (*0-7432-0034-9*, Touchstone); 1998. pap. 11.00 (*0-684-84742-6*, Scribner Paper Fiction) Simon & Schuster.
West, Morris. The Devil's Advocate. 1959. 17.95 o.p. (*0-688-01453-4*, Morrow, William & Co.) Morrow/Avon.
—Eminence. l.t. ed. 2000. 424p. lib. bdg. 27.95 (*1-58547-044-9*) Ctr. Point Large Print.
—Eminence. 1998. 336p. 25.00 o.s.i (*0-15-100439-0*) Harcourt Trade Pubs.
—Eminence. 1998. (*0-7322-6704-8*) HarperCollins Pubs.
—Eminence. 2003. 328p. pap. 14.95 (*1-902881-69-9*) Toby Pr.
—Morris West: Three Complete Novels: The Shoes of the Fisherman, The Clowns of the Gods, Lazarus. 1993. 13.99 o.s.i (*0-517-09390-1*) Random Hse. Value Publishing.
Zola, Emile. Lourdes. 7.95 French & European Pubns., Inc.
—Lourdes. 2000. (Literary Classics). 504p. pap. 11.00 (*1-57392-828-3*) Prometheus Bks., Pubs.
—Lourdes. Vizetelly, Ernest Alfred, tr. from FRE. 1993. (Pocket Classics Ser.). xii, 492p. pap. 10.95 (*0-7509-0452-6*) Sutton Publishing, Ltd. GBR. *Dist:* International Publishers Marketing.
Zubro, Mark Richard. The Only Good Priest. (Tom & Scott Mystery Ser.). 1992. 192p. pap. 10.95 (*0-312-07054-3*, Saint Martin's Griffin); 1991. 8.99 o.p. (*0-312-05486-6*, Saint Martin's Minotaur) St. Martin's Pr.

**CLERGY—FICTION**

Adams, Henry. Esther: A Novel. 1997. (Literary Classics). 310p. pap. 11.00 (*1-57392-132-7*) Prometheus Bks., Pubs.
—Esther: A Novel. 1989. (Works of Henry Adams). reprint ed. lib. bdg. 79.00 (*0-7812-1439-4*) Reprint Services Corp.
—Esther: A Novel. 1976. reprint ed. 36.00 o.p. (*0-403-05725-6*) Scholarly Pr., Inc.
—Esther: A Novel. Spiller, Robert E., ed. 1976. reprint ed. lib. bdg. 50.00 (*0-8201-1187-2*) Scholars' Facsimiles & Reprints.
—Esther: A Novel. MacFarlane, Lisa, ed. & intro. by. 1999. (Classics Ser.). 256p. pap. 9.95 (*0-14-044754-7*, Penguin Classics) Viking Penguin.
Alexander, Hannah. Urgent Care. 2003. (Healing Touch Ser.: Vol. 3). 352p. pap. 11.99 (*0-7642-2530-8*) Bethany Hse. Pubs.
Andrews, Robert. A Murder of Honor. 2001. 304p. 23.95 o.s.i (*0-399-14684-9*, Wood, Marian Bks.) Penguin Group (USA) Inc.
Anthony, Michael D. Becket Factor. 1991. 17.95 o.p. (*0-312-05821-7*, Saint Martin's Minotaur) St. Martin's Pr.
—Dark Provenance. 1995. 256p. 21.00 o.p. (*0-312-11767-1*, Saint Martin's Minotaur) St. Martin's Pr.
—Dark Provenance. l.t. ed. 1995. (Ulverscroft Large Print Ser.). 528p. 29.99 o.p. (*0-7089-3324-6*, Ulverscroft) Thorpe, F. A. Pubs. GBR. *Dist:* Ulverscroft Large Print Bks., Ltd., Ulverscroft Large Print Canada, Ltd.
—Midnight Come. 1999. 302p. 22.95 (*0-312-20058-7*, Saint Martin's Minotaur) St. Martin's Pr.
Arditti, Michael. The Celibate. 341p. 2000. pap. 13.00 (*1-56947-184-3*); 1997. 24.00 o.p. (*1-56947-089-8*) Soho Pr., Inc.
Arthur, Randall. Brotherhood of Betrayal. 2003. 350p. pap. 11.99 (*1-59052-258-3*) Multnomah Pubs., Inc.
Atherton, Charles. The First Stone: A Novel. 2001. 15.95 (*1-58838-037-8*, Court Street Pr.) NewSouth, Inc.
Aycliffe, Jonathan. A Shadow on the Wall. 224p. 26.00 (*0-7278-5505-0*) Severn Hse. Pubs., Ltd.
—A Shadow on the Wall. 2001. 263p. (*0-7540-4416-5*); pap. 24.95 (*0-7862-3183-1*); (*0-7540-4417-3*) Thorndike Pr.
Bach, Alice. He Will Not Walk with Me. 1985. (Illus.). 192p. (J). (gr. 7 up). 15.95 o.p. (*0-385-29410-7*, Delacorte Pr.) Dell Publishing.
Bagdon, Paul. The Stranger from Medina: A Novel. 2003. 192p. pap. 11.99 (*0-8007-5835-8*) Revell, Fleming H. Co.
Bage, Robert. Hermsprong; or, Man as He Is Not. Perkins, Pamela Ann, ed. 2002. (Broadview Literary Texts Ser.). 387p. (*1-55111-279-5*) Broadview Pr.
Ballard-Jones, Anita. Rehoboth Road. 2003. 248p. 28.95 (*0-9729455-1-2*); per. 19.95 (*0-9729455-0-4*) Black Deer Bks.
Balzac, Honoré de. Le Cure de Tours. (Folio Ser.: No. 747). (FRE.). pap. 9.95 (*2-07-036717-7*) Schoenhof's Foreign Bks., Inc.
Barnard, Robert. The Bad Samaritan. unabr. ed. 1997. audio 54.95 (*0-7531-0046-0*, 961104) ISIS Audio Bks. GBR. *Dist:* Ulverscroft Large Print Bks., Ltd.
—The Bad Samaritan. 1996. (Crime Ser.). 240p. pap. 5.95 o.p. (*0-14-025730-6*) Penguin Group (USA) Inc.
—The Bad Samaritan. 1995. 240p. 21.00 (*0-684-81334-3*, Scribner) Simon & Schuster.
—Unholy Dying. l.t. ed. 2002. (Magna Large Print Ser.). 368p. (*0-7505-1822-7*) Magna Large Print Bks. GBR. *Dist:* Ulverscroft Large Print Canada, Ltd.
—Unholy Dying. 2001. 288p. 23.00 o.s.i (*0-7432-0149-3*, Scribner) Simon & Schuster.
—Unholy Dying. l.t. ed. 2001. 399p. 28.95 (*0-7862-3333-8*) Thorndike Pr.
Barrie, J. M. The Little Minister. 1968. (Airmont Classics Ser.). (J). (gr. 10 up). mass mkt. 0.75 o.p. (*0-8049-0187-2*, CL-187) Airmont Publishing Co., Inc.
Basch, Rachel. The Passion of Reverend Nash: A Novel. 2003. 288p. 23.95 (*0-393-05768-2*) Norton, W. W. & Co., Inc.
Bazan, Emilia P. The House of Ulloa. O'Prey, Paul & Graves, Lucia, trs. from SPA. 1991. 288p. pap. 8.95 o.p. (*0-14-044502-1*, Penguin Classics) Viking Penguin.
Beatty, Patricia. Behave Yourself, Bethany Brant. 1986. 160p. (J). (gr. 5-9). 16.00 o.p. (*0-688-05923-6*, Morrow, William & Co.) Morrow/Avon.
Benson, Angela. Abiding Hope. 2003. 256p. mass mkt. 6.99 (*1-58314-323-8*, New Spirit) BET Bks.
—Abiding Hope. 2001. (HeartQuest Ser.). (Illus.). 256p. pap. 9.99 (*0-8423-1940-9*) Tyndale Hse. Pubs.
Bernanos, Georges. The Diary of a Country Priest. 304p. 2001. pap. 14.00 (*0-7867-0961-8*); 1984. pap. 10.95 (*0-88184-013-0*) Avalon Publishing Group. (Carroll & Graf Pubs.).
—The Diary of a Country Priest. Morris, Pamela, tr. 1983. (Thomas More Books to Live). (FRE.). 15.95 o.p. (*0-88347-155-8*, More, Thomas) Ave Maria Pr.
—The Diary of a Country Priest. 1974. 240p. pap. 2.95 o.p. (*0-385-09600-3*) Doubleday Publishing.
Blackstock, Terri. Cape Refuge. 2003. 615p. pap. 16.95 (*1-4104-0139-1*, Walker Large Print) Gale Group.
—Cape Refuge. l.t. ed. 2003. (Cape Refuge Ser.). 615p. 27.95 (*0-7862-5521-8*) Thorndike Pr.
—Trial by Fire. 2000. (Newpointe 911 Ser.: Bk. 4). (Illus.). 352p. pap. 12.99 (*0-310-21760-1*) Zondervan.
Blake, Michelle. The Book of Light: A Lilly Connor Mystery. 2003. 224p. 24.95 (*0-399-15046-3*) Putnam Publishing Group, The.
—The Tentmaker: A Lily Connor Mystery. 1999. (Lily Connor Mysteries Ser.). 273p. 23.95 o.p. (*0-399-14577-X*, G. P. Putnam's Sons) Penguin Group (USA) Inc.
Bowen, Michele Andrea. Second Sunday. 2003. 336p. 22.95 (*0-446-53033-6*, Walk Worthy Pr.) Warner Bks., Inc.
Bream, Freda. The Vicar Investigates. l.t. ed. 1990. (Linford Mystery Library). 277p. pap. 17.99 o.p. (*0-7089-6849-X*, Ulverscroft) Thorpe, F. A. Pubs. GBR. *Dist:* Ulverscroft Large Print Bks., Ltd., Ulverscroft Large Print Canada, Ltd.
Breslin, Jimmy. I Don't Want to Go to Jail: A Good Novel. Clain, Judy, ed. 2001. 320p. 24.95 o.p. (*0-316-11845-1*) Little Brown & Co.
Brown, Sandra. Tempest in Eden. 1983. 192p. 1.95 o.s.i (*0-515-07579-5*, Jove) Berkley Publishing Group.
—Tempest in Eden. l.t. ed. 2000. (Americana Ser.). 261p. 30.95 o.p. (*0-7862-2294-8*) Thorndike Pr.
—Tempest in Eden. 1996. 256p. reprint ed. mass mkt. 6.99 (*0-446-36431-2*) Warner Bks., Inc.
Buchan, John. Prester John. unabr. ed. 1994. audio 44.95 (*0-7861-0744-8*, 892516) Blackstone Audio Bks., Inc.
—Prester John. 1994. (Oxford World's Classics Ser.). (Illus.). 256p. pap. 8.95 o.p. (*0-19-282936-X*) Oxford Univ. Pr., Inc.
—Prester John. 1988. reprint ed. lib. bdg. 49.00 (*0-7812-0160-8*) Reprint Services Corp.
—Prester John. 1970. (Illus.). 65.00 (*0-403-00537-X*) Scholarly Pr., Inc.
Buechner, Frederick. The Final Beast. 1982. 14.95 o.p. (*0-06-061159-6*) HarperSanFrancisco.
—Love Feast. 1984. (Books of Bebb). 380p. mass mkt. 3.95 o.p. (*0-06-061167-7*, P-5009) HarperSanFrancisco.
—Love Feast. 1974. 7.95 o.p. (*0-689-10612-2*, Atheneum) Simon & Schuster Children's Publishing.
—Open Heart. 1984. (Books of Bebb). mass mkt. 3.95 o.p. (*0-06-061166-9*, P-5008) HarperSanFrancisco.
—Open Heart. 1972. 5.95 o.p. (*0-689-10498-7*, Atheneum) Simon & Schuster Children's Publishing.
—Treasure Hunt. 1984. (Books of Bebb). mass mkt. 3.95 o.p. (*0-06-061168-5*, P-5010) HarperSanFrancisco.
—Treasure Hunt. 1977. 7.95 o.p. (*0-689-10800-1*, Atheneum) Simon & Schuster Children's Publishing.
Cameron, Angie. The Education of Annie. 2002. 359p. 28.95 (*0-9717610-0-0*) AM & K Publishing.
Carey, Peter. Oscar & Lucinda. 448p. 1988. 18.95 o.p. (*0-06-015908-1*); 1992. reprint ed. pap. 13.00 o.p. (*0-06-091592-7*, PL 1592, Perennial) HarperTrade.
—Oscar & Lucinda. l.t. ed. 1989. 818p. reprint ed. 20.95 (*1-85089-318-7*) ISIS Large Print Bks. GBR. *Dist:* Transaction Pubs.
—Oscar & Lucinda. 1997. 448p. pap. 14.95 (*0-679-77750-4*) Knopf Publishing Group.
—Oscar & Lucinda. pap. 18.95 (*0-7022-2760-9*) Univ. of Queensland Pr. AUS. *Dist:* International Specialized Bk. Services.
Cassara, Ernest. Murder on Beacon Hill. 1995. 201p. (Orig.). pap. 10.00 (*0-9625794-6-7*) Miniver, Anne Pr.
—Murder on Boston Common: A Father Ballou & His Dog Spot Mystery. 1998. 174p. pap. 9.95 (*0-9662870-0-2*) Cambridge Cornerstone Pr.
Cassity, Martin M., Jr. Fifty-Nine Front Street. 1993. pap. 13.95 (*1-881399-09-5*) Beaver Pond Publishing & Printing, Inc.
Cecala, Kathy. Secret Vow. 1997. 192p. 19.95 o.p. (*0-525-94290-4*) Dutton/Plume.
—Secret Vow. 1998. 288p. mass mkt. 6.99 o.s.i (*0-451-19227-3*, Onyx) NAL.
Chamberlain, Diane. Reflection. 1996. 384p. 24.00 o.p. (*0-06-017652-0*) HarperCollins Pubs.
—Reflection. 1997. 416p. mass mkt. 5.99 o.s.i (*0-06-109396-3*, HarperTorch) Morrow/Avon.
Chappell, Fred. The Fred Chappell Reader. 1990. pap. 14.95 (*0-312-05092-5*, Saint Martin's Griffin); 1987. 512p. 22.95 o.p. (*0-312-00012-X*) St. Martin's Pr.
Charles, Kate. Appointed to Die. 1994. 368p. 19.95 o.s.i (*0-89296-548-7*) Mysterious Pr.
—Appointed to Die. 1995. 352p. mass mkt. 5.99 o.s.i (*0-446-40361-X*) Warner Bks., Inc.
—A Dead Man Out of Mind. l.t. ed. 1996. (G. K. Hall Mystery Ser.). 429p. 22.95 o.p. (*0-7838-1706-1*, Macmillan Reference USA) Gale Group.
—A Dead Man Out of Mind. 1995. 82p. 19.95 o.p. (*0-89296-585-1*) Mysterious Pr.

—A Dead Man Out of Mind. 1996. 288p. mass mkt. 5.99 o.p. (*0-446-40432-2*) Warner Bks., Inc.
—A Drink of Deadly Wine. 1992. 336p. 17.95 (*0-89296-501-0*) Mysterious Pr.
—A Drink of Deadly Wine. 1993. (Book of Psalms Mysteries Ser.). 304p. mass mkt. 5.99 o.s.i (*0-446-40194-3*) Warner Bks., Inc.
—Evil Angels among Them. l.t. ed. 1997. (G. K. Hall Mystery Ser.). 371p. lib. bdg. 25.95 o.p. (*0-7838-2024-0*, Macmillan Reference USA) Gale Group.
—Evil Angels among Them. 352p. 1997. mass mkt. 6.50 (*0-446-40521-3*, Mysterious Pr. Paperback Bks.); 1996. 21.50 o.p. (*0-89296-639-4*) Warner Bks., Inc.
—The Snares of Death. 1993. 368p. 18.95 (*0-89296-498-7*) Mysterious Pr.
—The Snares of Death. 1994. 352p. mass mkt. 5.50 (*0-446-40195-1*) Warner Bks., Inc.
—Unruly Passions. 2001. 440p. pap. 8.95 (*0-7515-2437-9*) Warner Bks. GBR. *Dist:* Trafalgar Square.
Coel, Margaret. The Dream Stalker. unabr. ed. 1999. (O'Malley Mystery Ser.). audio 39.95 (*1-55686-873-1*) Books in Motion.
—The Ghost Walker. 256p. 1996. 21.95 o.p. (*0-425-15468-8*); 1997. reprint ed. mass mkt. 6.50 (*0-425-15961-2*) Berkley Publishing Group. (Prime Crime).
—The Ghost Walker. unabr. ed. 1999. (O'Malley Mystery Ser.). audio 39.95 (*1-55686-865-0*) Books in Motion.
—The Lost Bird. 2000. 304p. mass mkt. 6.50 (*0-425-17030-6*) Berkley Publishing Group.
—The Lost Bird. l.t. ed. 2000. (G. K. Hall Core Ser.). 332p. 28.95 (*0-7838-8958-5*, Macmillan Reference USA) Gale Group.
—The Lost Bird: A Mystery. 1999. 304p. 21.95 o.s.i (*0-425-17059-4*, Prime Crime) Berkley Publishing Group.
—The Shadow Dancer. 2002. 304p. 22.95 (*0-425-18640-7*, Prime Crime) Berkley Publishing Group.
—The Shadow Dancer. l.t. ed. 2003. lib. bdg. 28.95 (*1-58547-284-0*, Platinum) Ctr. Point Large Print.
—The Story Teller. (Wind River Arapaho Ser.). 256p. 1998. 21.95 o.s.i (*0-425-16538-8*); 1999. reprint ed. mass mkt. 6.50 (*0-425-17025-X*) Berkley Publishing Group. (Prime Crime).
—The Story Teller. unabr. ed. 1999. (O'Malley Mystery Ser.). audio 49.95 (*1-55686-891-X*) Books in Motion.
Connor, Ralph. The Company of the Noble Seven. 1996. mass mkt. 5.99 o.p. (*0-7852-7578-9*) Nelson, Thomas Inc.
—Thomas Skyler: Foothills Preacher. Phillips, Michael R., ed. 1988. (Stories of Yesteryear Ser.: Vol. 2). Orig. Title: The Sky Pilot. 169p. pap. 6.95 (*0-940652-07-2*) Inheritance Pubns.
Corcoran, Barbara. Annie's Monster. 1990. 192p. (J). (gr. 3-7). lib. bdg. 14.95 o.s.i (*0-689-31632-1*, Atheneum) Simon & Schuster Children's Publishing.
Crow, Donna Fletcher. Treasures of the Heart. l.t. ed. 1994. (Cambridge Chronicles: Vol. 2). 224p. pap. 9.99 o.p. (*0-89107-807-X*) Crossway Bks.
Davis, Rod. Corina's Way: A Novel. 2003. 288p. 24.95 (*1-58838-129-3*, NewSouth Bks.) NewSouth, Inc.
Deford, Frank. Love & Infamy. 1995. 576p. mass mkt. 5.99 (*0-8217-0122-3*, Zebra Bks.); mass mkt. 5.99 o.s.i (*0-7860-0122-4*, Pinnacle Bks.) Kensington Publishing Corp.
—Love & Infamy. 1993. 576p. 24.00 o.p. (*0-670-82995-1*) Viking Penguin.
Delffs, Dudley J. The Judas Tree. 1999. (Father Grif Mystery Ser.: Vol. 2). 320p. pap. 10.99 o.p. (*0-7642-2087-X*) Bethany Hse. Pubs.
—The Judas Tree. l.t. ed. 2002. 557p. 25.95 (*0-7862-4245-0*) Gale Group.
Edwards, Amelia B. Hand & Glove: A Novel. 2000. 294p. pap. 15.95 (*0-948695-63-3*) Rubicon Pr., The GBR. *Dist:* Brown, David Bk. Co.
Edwards, Ruth Dudley. Murder in a Cathedral. 1997. 317 p. (*0-7540-3117-9*) BBC Audiobooks America.
—Murder in a Cathedral. l.t. ed. 1997. 192p. 20.95 (*0-312-15597-2*, Saint Martin's Minotaur) St. Martin's Pr.
—Murder in a Cathedral. l.t. ed. 1997. (Mystery Ser.). 326p. lib. bdg. 25.95 (*0-7838-8284-X*) Thorndike Pr.
Eliot, George. Adam Bede. 1976. (Airmont Classics Ser.). mass mkt. 1.95 o.p. (*0-8049-0103-1*, CL 103) Airmont Publishing Co., Inc.
—Adam Bede. 1976. 29.95 (*0-8488-0481-3*) Amereon, Ltd.
—Adam Bede. 2000. Vol. 2. per. (*1-891355-21-X*); Vol.1. per. 14.00 (*1-891355-20-1*) Blue Unicorn Editions.
—Adam Bede. reprint ed. 1992. lib. bdg. 27.95 (*0-89968-276-6*, Lightyear Pr.); 1977. 466p. lib. bdg. 27.95 o.s.i (*0-89966-265-X*) Buccaneer Bks., Inc.
—Adam Bede. reprint ed. Pt. 1. 2001. (Writings of George Eliot Ser.: Vol. 3). 420p. pap. text 28.00 (*0-7426-5070-7*); Pt. 1. 1999. (Writings of George Eliot Ser.: Vol. 3). 420p. lib. bdg. 88.00 (*1-58201-070-6*); Pt. 2. 2001. 364p. pap. text 28.00 (*0-7426-5071-5*); Pt. 2. 1999. (Writings of George Eliot Ser.: Vol. 4). 364p. lib. bdg. 88.00 (*1-58201-071-4*) Classic Bks.
—Adam Bede. E-Book 2.49 (*1-58744-086-5*) Electric Umbrella Publishing.
—Adam Bede. 1973. (Collins Classics Ser.). 478p. (*0-00-424521-0*) HarperSanFrancisco.
—Adam Bede. Paterson, John, ed. 1968. pap. 13.16 o.p. (*0-395-05204-1*, Riverside Editions) Houghton Mifflin Co.
—Adam Bede, 4 vols. l.t. ed. 2000. 2698p. 193.58 (*0-7583-0007-7*); 1891p. 138.36 (*0-7583-0005-0*); 685p. 53.78 (*0-7583-0001-8*); 2326p. 174.41 (*0-7583-0006-9*); 1538p. 120.93 (*0-7583-0004-2*); 548p. 46.02 (*0-7583-0000-X*); 1201p. 91.44 (*0-7583-0003-4*); 938p. 78.54 (*0-7583-0002-6*); 548p. pap. 40.02 (*0-7583-0008-5*); 1891p. pap. 119.19 (*0-7583-0013-1*); 2326p. pap. 143.57 (*0-7583-0014-X*); 2698p. pap. 159.27 (*0-7583-0015-8*); 1201p. pap. 79.44 (*0-7583-0011-5*); 685p. pap. 47.78 (*0-7583-0009-3*); 938p. pap. 66.54 (*0-7583-0010-7*); 1538p. pap. 102.93 (*0-7583-0012-3*) Huge Print Pr.
—Adam Bede. 2001. 516p. 29.99 (*1-58827-312-1*); per. 24.99 (*1-58827-313-X*) IndyPublish.com.
—Adam Bede. 1999. (Cloth Bound Pocket Ser.). 7.95 (*3-8290-3005-3*, 521122) Konemann.
—Adam Bede. E-Book 1.95 (*1-57799-953-3*) Logos Research Systems, Inc.
—Adam Bede. 1992. (Everyman's Library: Vol. 59 0). 20.00 (*0-679-40991-2*) McKay, David Co., Inc.
—Adam Bede. 1969. mass mkt. 0.95 o.p. (*0-451-50483-6*, Signet Classics); 1969. mass mkt. 0.75 o.p. (*0-451-50076-8*, Signet Classics); 1961. mass mkt. 2.95 o.p. (*0-451-51578-1*, Signet Classics); 1961. mass mkt. 4.50 o.p. (*0-451-52110-2*); 1961. mass mkt. 1.95 o.p. (*0-451-51342-8*, Signet Classics); 1961. mass mkt. 1.75 o.p. (*0-451-51015-1*, Signet Classics); 1961. mass mkt. 3.50 o.p. (*0-451-51848-9*); 1961. mass mkt. 1.50 o.p. (*0-451-50790-8*, Signet Classics); 1961. 512p. mass mkt. 6.95 (*0-451-52527-2*, Signet Classics); 1961. mass mkt. 4.95 o.p. (*0-451-52256-7*, Signet Classics) NAL.
—Adam Bede. 2001. (Twelve-Point Ser.). lib. bdg. 27.00 (*1-58287-138-8*) North Bks.
—Adam Bede. Martin, Carol A., ed. 2001. (Clarendon Edition of the Novels of George Eliot Ser.). (Illus.). 688p. text 165.00 (*0-19-812595-X*) Oxford Univ. Pr., Inc.
—Adam Bede. (Oxford World's Classics Ser.). 1998. 656p. pap. 8.95 (*0-19-283495-9*); 1996. 646p. (C). pap. 5.95 o.p. (*0-19-283166-6*) Oxford Univ. Pr., Inc.
—Adam Bede. 2002. (Modern Library Classics). 624p. pap. 8.95 (*0-375-75901-8*, Modern Library) Random House Adult Trade Publishing Group.
—Adam Bede. 2001. 549p. E-Book 4.00 (*1-929670-68-0*) Renaissance E Bks.
—Adam Bede. 1971. pap. 0.95 o.s.i (*0-671-47190-2*, Washington Square Pr.) Simon & Schuster.
—Adam Bede. (Ebook Classic Ser.). E-Book 5.00 (*0-7410-1117-4*) SoftBook Pr.
—Adam Bede. 1985. 15.00 (*0-606-17254-8*) Turtleback Bks.
—Adam Bede. 1994. 528p. pap. 5.50 o.p. (*0-460-87461-6*, Everyman's Classic Library in Paperback) Tuttle Publishing.
—Adam Bede. Gill, Stephen, ed. 1980. (Classics Ser.). 608p. 8.95 (*0-14-043121-7*, Penguin Classics) Viking Penguin.
—Adam Bede. 1972. 4.95 o.p. (*0-460-01027-1*) Viking Penguin.
—Adam Bede. 1999. E-Book 5.99 (*0-8220-7250-5*); E-Book 5.99 (*0-8220-7250-5*) Wiley, John & Sons, Inc. (Cliff Notes).
—Scenes of Clerical Life. (Writings of George Eliot Ser.: Vol. 1). reprint ed. Pt. 1. 2001. 302p. pap. text 28.00 (*0-7426-5068-5*); Pt. 1. 1999. 302p. lib. bdg. 88.00 (*1-58201-068-4*); Pt. 2. 2001. 314p. pap. text 28.00 (*0-7426-5069-3*); Pt. 2. 1999. 314p. lib. bdg. 88.00 (*1-58201-069-2*) Classic Bks.
—Scenes of Clerical Life. 1978. 8.00 o.p. (*0-460-00468-9*); 1977. 3.95 o.p. (*0-460-01468-4*) Dutton/Plume. (Dutton).
—Scenes of Clerical Life. Wolff, Robert L., ed. 1975. (Victorian Fiction Ser.). 366p. reprint ed. lib. bdg. 73.00 o.p. (*0-8240-1567-3*) Garland Publishing, Inc.
—Scenes of Clerical Life. Noble, Thomas A., ed. 2002. (Oxford World's Classics Ser.). 338p. pap. 8.95 (*0-19-283780-X*) Oxford Univ. Pr., Inc.
—Scenes of Clerical Life. 1989. (Oxford World's Classics Ser.). 328p. pap. 6.95 o.p. (*0-19-281786-8*) Oxford Univ. Pr., Inc.
—Scenes of Clerical Life. Noble, Thomas A., ed. 1985. (Clarendon Edition of the Novels of George Eliot Ser.). 374p. text 89.00 o.p. (*0-19-812559-3*) Oxford Univ. Pr., Inc.
—Scenes of Clerical Life. 1999. (Literary Classics). 340p. pap. 11.00 (*1-57392-780-5*) Prometheus Bks., Pubs.
—Scenes of Clerical Life. 1994. 304p. pap. 4.95 (*0-460-87463-2*, Everyman's Classic Library in Paperback) Tuttle Publishing.
—Scenes of Clerical Life. Gribble, Jennifer, ed. & intro. by. 1999. (Penguin Classics Ser.). (Illus.). 416p. 8.95 (*0-14-043638-3*, Penguin Classics) Viking Penguin.
—Scenes of Clerical Life. Lodge, David, ed. 1973. (Penguin Classics Ser.). 432p. pap. 8.95 o.s.i (*0-14-043087-3*, Penguin Classics) Viking Penguin.
Erdrich, Louise. The Last Report on the Miracles at Little No Horse: A Novel. 2001. 368p. 26.00 (*0-06-018727-1*); E-Book 19.95 (*0-06-000563-7*) HarperCollins Pubs.
—The Last Report on the Miracles at Little No Horse: A Novel. l.t. ed. 2001. 677p. 29.95 (*0-7862-3520-9*) Thorndike Pr.
Evans, Richard Paul. The Looking Glass. l.t. ed. 1999. 25.95 (*1-56895-803-X*, Wheeler Publishing, Inc.) Gale Group.
Feldmeyer, Dean. Pitchfork Hollow. Chelius, Jane, ed. 1995. 256p. (Orig.). mass mkt. 5.50 (*0-671-76983-9*, Pocket) Simon & Schuster.
—Viper Quarry. 1994. 256p. mass mkt. 4.99 (*0-671-76982-0*, Pocket) Simon & Schuster.
Ferguson, Bruce. Every Day Is Sunday. 1998. 196p. (Orig.). pap. 14.95 (*1-880090-43-0*) Galde Pr., Inc.
Fielding, Henry. Joseph Andrews & Shamela. 1978. 8.00 o.p. (*0-460-00467-0*); 1976. 4.50 o.p. (*0-460-01467-6*) Dutton/Plume. (Dutton).
—Joseph Andrews & Shamela. (Oxford World's Classics Ser.). 1988. 420p. pap. 6.95 o.p. (*0-19-281550-4*); 2nd ed. 1999. (Illus.). 464p. pap. 9.95 (*0-19-283343-X*) Oxford Univ. Pr., Inc.
—Joseph Andrews & Shamela. Humphreys, Arthur Raleigh, ed. 1993. 412p. pap. 7.95 (*0-460-87385-7*, Everyman's Classic Library in Paperback) Tuttle Publishing.
—Joseph Andrews & Shamela. 1992. 422p. pap. 7.95 o.p. (*0-460-87115-3*, Everyman's Classic Library in Paperback) Tuttle Publishing.
—Joseph Andrews & Shamela. 1999. (Classics Ser.). 432p. 9.95 (*0-14-043386-4*, Penguin Classics) Viking Penguin.
Frederic, Harold. The Damnation of Theron Ware. unabr. ed. 1993. audio 53.95 (*1-55685-272-X*) Audio Bk. Contractors, Inc.
—The Damnation of Theron Ware. Raleigh, John H., ed. 1960. (Rinehart Editions Ser.). 378p. (C). pap. text 26.50 o.s.i (*0-03-010200-6*) Harcourt College Pubs.
—The Damnation of Theron Ware. Carter, Everett, ed. 1996. (John Harvard Library). (Illus.). 384p. pap. 14.95 (*0-674-19001-7*, Belknap Pr.) Harvard Univ. Pr.
—The Damnation of Theron Ware. 1987. audio 39.00 Jimcin Recordings.
—The Damnation of Theron Ware. 1997. (Literary Classics). 315p. pap. 11.00 (*1-57392-169-6*) Prometheus Bks., Pubs.
—The Damnation of Theron Ware. 1988. (Collected Works of Harold Frederic). reprint ed. lib. bdg. 79.00 (*0-7812-1192-1*) Reprint Services Corp.
—The Damnation of Theron Ware. 1984. 6.50 o.p. (*0-8446-2090-4*) Smith, Peter Pub., Inc.
—The Damnation of Theron Ware. reprint ed. 69.00 Somerset Pubs., Inc.
—The Damnation of Theron Ware. l.t. ed. 1999. 530p. text 32.95 (*1-56000-488-6*) Transaction Pubs.
—The Damnation of Theron Ware. 1986. (Classics Ser.). 512p. 13.95 (*0-14-039025-1*, Penguin Classics) Viking Penguin.
—The Damnation of Theron Ware: or Illumination. 1985. (Harold Frederic Edition Ser.: Vol. 3). 515p. reprint ed. pap. 159.70 (*0-608-07071-8*, 206728500009) Bks. on Demand.
—The Damnation of Theron Ware: or Illumination. Dodge, Charlyne & Garner, Stanton, eds. 1985. (Harold Frederic Edition Ser.: Vol. 3). 506p. text 40.00 o.p. (*0-8032-1967-9*) Univ. of Nebraska Pr.
Friedman, Donald. The Hand Before the Eye. 1999. (First Series Award). 266p. 24.00 (*0-922811-42-3*) Mid-List Pr.
Gansky, Alton L. By My Hands: A Novel. l.t. ed. 2001. (Christian Mystery Ser.). 505 psp. 23.95 (*0-7862-3245-5*) Thorndike Pr.
Garwood, Julie. Heartbreaker. 2001. E-Book 9.99 (*1-58945-199-6*) Adobe Systems, Inc.
—Heartbreaker. l.t. ed. 2000. (Large Print Book Ser.). 556p. 30.95 (*1-56895-918-4*, Wheeler Publishing, Inc.) Gale Group.
—Heartbreaker. 2003. 544p. pap. 10.00 (*0-7434-7419-8*, Pocket); 2001. 544p. mass mkt. 7.99 (*0-671-03400-6*, Pocket); 2000. 432p. 24.95 o.s.i (*0-671-03299-2*, Atria) Simon & Schuster.
Gill, Bartholomew. The Death of an Irish Sinner. 2001. (Inspector Peter McGarr Mysteries Ser.). 288p. 24.00 (*0-380-97798-2*, Morrow, William & Co.) Morrow/Avon.
Godwin, Gail. Evensong. 2000. (Ballantine Reader's Circle Ser.). 432p. pap. 14.00 (*0-345-43477-3*) Ballantine Bks.
—Evensong. l.t. ed. 1999. (Basic Ser.). 29.95 o.p. (*0-7862-2008-2*, Macmillan Reference USA) Gale Group.
Gorman, Ed. Harlot's Moon. 1998. 256p. 21.95 o.p. (*0-312-18108-6*, Saint Martin's Minotaur) St. Martin's Pr.
Greene, Graham. The Power & the Glory. 24.95 (*0-88411-656-5*) Amereon, Ltd.
—The Power & the Glory. l.t. ed. 1992. pap. 21.95 o.p. (*0-7927-1142-4*, CSO307); 1991. 23.95 o.p. (*0-7927-1141-6*, CHO235) BBC Audiobooks America.
—The Power & the Glory. l.t. ed. 2002. 28.95 (*0-7862-4131-4*) Gale Group.
—The Power & the Glory. 1977. 19.00 (*0-606-12485-3*) Turtleback Bks.
—The Power & the Glory. 2003. (Twentieth Century Classics Ser.). 240p. pap. 14.00 (*0-14-243730-1*, Penguin Classics); 1991. (Penguin Twentieth-Century Classics Ser.). 240p. pap. 14.00 o.s.i (*0-14-018499-6*, Penguin Classics); 1977. (Critical Studies: No. 6). (Illus.). 224p. pap. 6.00 o.p. (*0-14-001791-7*, Penguin Bks.); 1946. 276p. 16.95 o.p. (*0-670-56979-8*); 1990. 320p. 25.00 o.p. (*0-670-83536-6*); 1968. 8.50 o.p. (*0-670-57012-5*, LT3) Viking Penguin.
Greenwood, D. M. Idol Bones. 1993. 224p. 18.95 o.p. (*0-312-09829-4*, Saint Martin's Minotaur) St. Martin's Pr.
—Unholy Ghosts. 1992. 224p. 17.95 o.p. (*0-312-08515-X*, Saint Martin's Minotaur) St. Martin's Pr.
—Unholy Ghosts. l.t. ed. 2001. 288p. pap. 23.95 (*0-7838-9596-8*) Thorndike Pr.
Gulley, Philip. Home to Harmony. 240p. 2004. pap. 12.95 (*0-06-072766-7*); 2002. (Illus.). 17.95 (*0-06-000629-3*) HarperSanFrancisco.
—Home to Harmony. 2000. (Harmony Ser.). (Illus.). 219p. 14.99 o.p. (*1-57673-613-X*) Multnomah Pubs., Inc.
—Home to Harmony. l.t. ed. 2002. 28.95 (*0-7862-4517-4*) Thorndike Pr.
—Signs & Wonders: A Harmony Novel. 2003. (Illus.). 224p. 17.95 (*0-06-000633-1*) HarperSanFrancisco.
—Signs & Wonders: A Harmony Novel. l.t. ed. 2003. 285p. 28.95 (*0-7862-5639-7*) Thorndike Pr.
Gunn, Neil M. The Key of the Chest. 1999. 304p. pap. 12.95 (*0-86241-770-8*) Canongate Bks. GBR. *Dist:* Interlink Publishing Group, Inc.
Gunn, Neil M. The Key of the Chest. 27.95 (*0-8027-1052-2*) Walker & Co.
Guterson, David. Our Lady of the Forest. 2003. 336p. 25.95 (*0-375-41211-5*) Knopf, Alfred A. Inc.
—Our Lady of the Forest. unabr. ed. 2003. audio 39.95 (*0-7393-0637-5*) Random Hse. Audio Publishing Group.
—Our Lady of the Forest. l.t. ed. 2003. 544p. 27.95 (*0-375-43293-0*) Random Hse. Large Print.
Hailey, Arthur. Detective. 1998. 608p. reprint ed. mass mkt. 7.99 (*0-425-16386-5*) Berkley Publishing Group.
—Detective. l.t. ed. 1997. pap. 24.00 o.p. (*0-7838-8132-0*, Macmillan Reference USA) Gale Group.
—Detective. 1999. (SPA.). (*84-08-02910-X*) GeoPlaneta, Editorial, S. A.
Harding, Paul T., pseud. The House of Crows: The Sorrowful Mysteries of Brother Athelstan. 1996. (Illus.). 280p. pap. 13.95 (*0-7472-4918-0*) Headline Bk. Publishing, Ltd. GBR. *Dist:* Trafalgar Square.
—The Nightingale Gallery: Being the First of the Sorrowful Mysteries of Brother Athelstan. 1993. 256p. mass mkt. 4.99 (*0-380-71751-4*, Avon Bks.); 1992. 20.00 o.p. (*0-688-11225-0*, Morrow, William & Co.) Morrow/Avon.
Henegar, R. Michael. Ten Days in Canaan. 1993. 313p. (Orig.). pap. 9.99 (*1-881379-05-1*) Samaritan Pr.
Herrick, Rick. A Week in October. 2002. xii, 195p. 14.95 (*1-887905-65-0*) Parkway Pubs., Inc.
Holland, David. The Devil's Acre. Date not set. mass mkt. (*0-312-99197-5*, St. Martin's Paperbacks); 2003. 256p. 23.95 (*0-312-31866-9*) St. Martin's Pr.
Holland, Isabelle. Darcourt. 1977. pap. 1.75 o.s.i (*0-449-23224-7*, Fawcett) Ballantine Bks.
—Darcourt. l.t. ed. 1982. 529p. reprint ed. 13.95 o.p. (*0-89621-397-8*) Thorndike Pr.
—Death at St. Anselm's. 1984. 240p. 13.95 o.p. (*0-385-18332-1*) Doubleday Publishing.
—A Fatal Advent: A St. Anselm's Mystery. 1990. (St. Anselm's Mystery Ser.). 256p. mass mkt. 3.95 o.s.i (*0-449-21879-1*, Fawcett) Ballantine Bks.
—Flight of the Archangel. 1986. mass mkt. 2.95 o.s.i (*0-449-20977-6*, Fawcett) Ballantine Bks.
—The Long Search. 1992. mass mkt. 3.99 o.s.i (*0-449-22009-5*, Fawcett) Ballantine Bks.
—The Long Search. 1990. 272p. 16.95 o.s.i (*0-385-26545-X*) Doubleday Publishing.
—The Long Search. l.t. ed. 1993. (Magna Large Print Ser.). 435p. (*0-7505-0444-7*) Magna Large Print Bks. GBR. *Dist:* Ulverscroft Large Print Canada, Ltd.
—A Lover Scorned. 1987. 256p. mass mkt. 2.95 o.s.i (*0-449-21369-2*, Fawcett) Ballantine Bks.
—A Lover Scorned. 1986. 240p. 15.95 o.p. (*0-385-23169-5*) Doubleday Publishing.

Occupations

 

Howatch, Susan. Absolute Truths. 1996. mass mkt. 6.50 o.s.i (*0-449-22392-2*); 1996. 640p. mass mkt. 7.50 (*0-449-22555-0*); 1996. mass mkt. o.p. (*0-449-22121-0*); 1995. mass mkt. 6.99 o.s.i (*0-449-22417-1*) Ballantine Bks. (Fawcett).

—Absolute Truths. l.t. ed. 1995. (G. K. Hall Core Ser.). 967p. lib. bdg. 26.95 (*0-7838-1219-1*, Macmillan Reference USA) Gale Group.

—Glamorous Powers. l.t. ed. 1990. (General Ser.). 674p. 20.95 o.p. (*0-8161-4863-5*, Macmillan Reference USA) Gale Group.

—Glamorous Powers. 1990. 4.99 o.p. (*0-517-05075-7*) Random Hse. Value Publishing.

—Glittering Images. l.t. ed. 1989. 680p. lib. bdg. 20.95 o.p. (*0-8161-4668-3*, Macmillan Reference USA) Gale Group.

—Mystical Paths. 1993. 512p. mass mkt. 6.99 (*0-449-22122-9*, Fawcett) Ballantine Bks.

—Mystical Paths. l.t. ed. 1993. (General Ser.). 800p. lib. bdg. 23.95 o.p. (*0-8161-5671-9*, Macmillan Reference USA) Gale Group.

—Mystical Paths. 1994. 5.99 o.p. (*0-517-11629-4*) Random Hse. Value Publishing.

—Ultimate Prizes. 1990. mass mkt. 5.95 o.s.i (*0-449-21913-5*) Ballantine Bks.

—Ultimate Prizes. l.t. ed. 1990. (General Ser.). 668p. 21.95 o.p. (*0-8161-4994-1*, Macmillan Reference USA) Gale Group.

—Ultimate Prizes. 1991. 4.99 o.p. (*0-517-06772-2*) Random Hse. Value Publishing.

—The Wonder Worker. 1998. 560p. pap. 14.00 (*0-449-00150-4*, Fawcett) Ballantine Bks.

—The Wonder Worker. 1997. 544p. 25.95 o.s.i (*0-375-40102-4*) Knopf, Alfred A. Inc.

Huntington, Lee P. Maybe a Miracle. 1984. (Illus.). 80p. (J). (gr. 3-7). 9.95 o.p. (*0-698-20602-9*, Coward-McCann) Putnam Publishing Group, The.

James, P. D. Death in Holy Orders. l.t. ed. 2001. 640p. 25.00 (*0-375-43117-9*) Random Hse. Large Print.

Jinks, Catherine. The Inquisitor. 1999. 393p. (*0-7329-0972-4*) Macmillan Education Australia.

—The Inquisitor. mass mkt. (*0-312-98644-0*, St. Martin's Paperbacks); E-Book 25.95 (*0-312-70852-1*) St. Martin's Pr.

—The Inquisitor: A Novel. 2002. 400p. 25.95 (*0-312-30815-9*, Saint Martin's Minotaur) St. Martin's Pr.

Jobe, Pat. 365 Ways to Criticize the Preacher: A Very Short Novel. 2002. 117p. pap. 12.00 (*1-57312-361-7*) Smyth & Helwys Publishing, Inc.

Jones, Annie. The Snowbirds. 2003. 336p. pap. 11.99 (*1-57673-623-7*) Multnomah Pubs., Inc.

—The Snowbirds. l.t. ed. 2003. 25.95 (*0-7862-5490-4*) Thorndike Pr.

Karon, Jan. At Home in Mitford. l.t. ed. (Mitford Ser.: No.1). 21.95 (*1-57490-254-7*); 1996. lib. bdg. 26.95 (*1-57490-071-4*, Beeler Large Print Bks.) Beeler, Thomas T. Publisher.

—At Home in Mitford. (Mitford Ser.: No. 1). 448p. pap. 12.99 (*0-7459-2629-0*) Lion Publishing.

—At Home in Mitford. (Mitford Ser.: No. 1). 1998. 432p. 24.95 (*0-670-88225-9*); 1996. 448p. 12.95 (*0-14-025448-X*); 1996. 2p. pap. 16.95 incl. audio (*0-14-086501-2*, Penguin AudioBooks) Viking Penguin.

—A Light in the Window. l.t. ed. (Mitford Ser.: No. 2). 21.95 (*1-57490-255-5*); 1996. (Illus.). 492p. lib. bdg. 26.95 (*1-57490-072-2*, Beeler Large Print Bks.) Beeler, Thomas T. Publisher.

—A Light in the Window. 2003. (Mitford Ser.: No. 2). (Illus.). 413p. pap. 12.99 (*0-7459-2803-X*) Lion Publishing.

—A Light in the Window. unabr. ed. (Mitford Ser.: No. 2). audio. 1999. audio 97.00 (*0-7887-0646-2*, 94823K8) Recorded Bks., LLC.

—A Light in the Window. (Mitford Ser.: No. 2). 1998. 400p. 24.95 (*0-670-88226-7*); 1996. 432p. 12.95 (*0-14-025454-4*); 1997. 2p. audio 16.95 (*0-14-086596-9*, 394980, Penguin AudioBooks) Viking Penguin.

—The Mitford Years: At Home in Mitford; A Light in the Window; These High, Green Hills; Out to Canaan, 4 vols. 1999. (Illus.). pap. 51.80 (*0-14-771256-4*) Penguin Group (USA) Inc.

—The Mitford Years: At Home in Mitford; A Light in the Window; These High, Green Hills; Out to Canaan; A New Song, 5 vols. 2001. pap. 64.75 o.p. (*0-14-771596-2*); 1997. pap. 38.85 (*0-14-771203-3*); Vols. 4-6. 2002. 38.90 (*0-14-771728-0*) Penguin Group (USA) Inc.

—A New Song. l.t. ed. 1999. (Mitford Ser.: No. 5 ). 28.95 (*1-57490-190-7*, Beeler Large Print Bks.) Beeler, Thomas T. Publisher.

—A New Song. abr. ed. 1999. (Mitford Ser.: No. 5). audio 24.95. audio 55.95 Highsmith Inc.

—A New Song. unabr. ed. 1999. (Mitford Ser.: No. 5). audio 102.00 (*0-7887-3098-3*, 95809E7) Recorded Bks., LLC.

—A New Song. (Mitford Ser.: No. 5). 2000. (Illus.). 416p. 12.95 (*0-14-027059-0*); 1999. (Illus.). 368p. 24.95 (*0-670-87810-3*); 1999. 2p. audio 24.95 (*0-14-086901-8*, Penguin AudioBooks); 1999. audio 55.95 (*0-14-180013-5*, Penguin AudioBooks) Viking Penguin.

—Out to Canaan. l.t. ed. (Mitford Ser.: o. 4). 21.95 (*1-57490-257-1*); 1997. (Illus.). 412p. lib. bdg. 26.95 (*1-57490-104-4*, Beeler Large Print Bks.) Beeler, Thomas T. Publisher.

—Out to Canaan. unabr. ed. 1997. (Mitford Ser.: o. 4). audio 83.00 (*0-7887-0973-9*, 95081E7) Recorded Bks., LLC.

—Out to Canaan. (Mitford Ser.: No. 4). 1998. (Illus.). 352p. 12.95 (*0-14-026568-6*); 1997. (Illus.). 368p. 23.95 (*0-670-87485-X*); 1997. 2p. audio 16.95 (*0-14-086597-7*, Penguin AudioBooks) Viking Penguin.

—These High, Green Hills. l.t. ed. (Mitford Ser.: No. 3). 21.95 (*1-57490-256-3*); 1997. (Illus.). 414p. lib. bdg. 26.95 (*1-57490-103-6*, Beeler Large Print Bks.) Beeler, Thomas T. Publisher.

—These High, Green Hills. (Mitford Ser.: o. 3). (Illus.). 333p. pap. 12.99 (*0-7459-3741-1*) Cook Communications Ministries.

—These High, Green Hills. unabr. ed. 1999. (Mitford Ser.: No. 3). audio 85.00 (*0-7887-0664-0*, 94841K8) Recorded Bks., LLC.

—These High, Green Hills. (Mitford Ser.: No. 3). 1997. (Illus.). 368p. 12.95 (*0-14-025793-4*); 1996. 352p. 22.95 (*0-670-86934-1*, Viking); 1996. pap. o.s.i (*0-670-87320-9*, Viking); 1997. 2p. pap. 16.95 incl. audio (*0-14-086598-5*, Penguin AudioBooks) Viking Penguin.

Keady, Walter. Celibates & Other Lovers. 1998. (Harvest Book Ser.). 240p. pap. 13.00 o.s.i (*0-15-600571-9*, Harvest Bks.) Harcourt Trade Pubs.

—Celibates & Other Lovers. 1997. 225p. 20.00 (*1-878448-77-3*) MacMurray & Beck, Inc.

Kendrick, Stephen. Night Watch: A Long-Lost Adventure in Which Sherlock Holmes Meets Father Brown. 2001. (Illus.). 272p. 23.00 (*0-375-40367-1*, Pantheon) Knopf Publishing Group.

Keneally, Thomas. The Office of Innocence. 2003. 336p. 25.00 (*0-385-50763-1*, Talese, Nan A.) Doubleday Publishing.

Kienzle, William X. The Gathering. 2002. 288p. 22.95 (*0-7407-2229-8*) Andrews McMeel Publishing.

—The Gathering. 2003. 304p. mass mkt. 6.99 (*0-345-45794-3*, Fawcett) Ballantine Bks.

—No Greater Love. 1999. (Father Koesler Mystery Ser.: No. 21). 292p. 19.95 o.p. (*0-8362-7865-8*) Andrews McMeel Publishing.

Kimmel, Haven. The Solace of Leaving Early. 2003. 288p. reprint ed. pap. 13.00 (*1-4000-3334-9*, Anchor) Knopf Publishing Group.

—The Solace of Leaving Early: A Novel. 2002. 272p. 23.95 (*0-385-49983-3*) Doubleday Publishing.

King, Cassandra. The Sunday Wife. 2004. mass mkt. 7.99 (*0-7868-9070-3*); 2002. 400p. 23.95 (*0-7868-6905-4*) Hyperion Pr.

—The Sunday Wife. 2003. (Core Ser.). 30.95 (*0-7862-5040-2*) Thorndike Pr.

Klauprecht, Emil. Cincinnati, or The Mysteries of the West: Emil Klauprecht's German-American Novel. Rowan, Steven & Tolzmann, Don H., trs. from GER. 1996. (New German-American Studies: Vol. 10). XXV, 657p. (C). text 79.95 (*0-8204-2681-4*) Lang, Peter Publishing, Inc.

Klima, Ivan. The Ultimate Intimacy. Brain, A. G., tr. from CZE. Tr. of Posledni Stupen Duvernosti. 400p. 1998. 25.00 o.p. (*0-8021-1625-6*); 1999. reprint ed. pap. 14.00 (*0-8021-3601-X*) Grove/Atlantic, Inc. (Grove Pr.).

Kraus, Jim & Kraus, Terri. The Price: A Novel. 2000. (Circle of Destiny Ser.). 368p. pap. 8.99 o.p. (*0-8423-1835-6*) Tyndale Hse. Pubs.

Kritlow, William. Blood Money: A Novel. 1997. (Lake Champlain Mysteries Ser.). 288p. 10.99 (*0-7852-8027-8*) Nelson, Thomas Inc.

—Crimson Snow: A Novel. 1995. 10.99 o.p. (*0-7852-8098-7*) Nelson, Thomas Inc.

—Fire on the Lake: A Novel. 1996. (Lake Champlain Mysteries Ser.: Bk. 2). 288p. pap. 11.99 (*0-7852-8099-5*) Nelson, Thomas Inc.

Lansdowne, Judith. Just in Time. 2003. (Zebra Historical Romance Ser.). 32p. mass mkt. 5.99 (*0-8217-7421-2*) Kensington Publishing Corp.

Leonard, Elmore. Pagan Babies. l.t. ed. 2000. 352p. 24.95 o.s.i (*0-375-43086-5*) Random Hse. Large Print.

Lewis, Sinclair. Elmer Gantry. 1979. reprint ed. lib. bdg. 16.95 o.p. (*0-8376-0441-9*) Bentley Pubs.

L'Heureux, John. The Miracle: A Novel. 2002. 240p. 24.00 (*0-87113-857-3*, Atlantic Monthly Pr.) Grove/Atlantic, Inc.

Lindvall, Michael L. Leaving North Haven: The Further Adventures of a Small Town Pastor: A Novel. 2002. 224p. pap. 16.95 (*0-8245-2013-0*) Crossroad Publishing Co.

Lovesey, Peter. The Reaper. 2002. 304p. pap. 12.00 (*1-56947-308-0*); 2001. 295p. 23.00 (*1-56947-227-0*) Soho Pr., Inc.

—The Reaper. l.t. ed. 2001. 368p. 28.95 o.p. (*0-7862-3438-5*) Thorndike Pr.

MacDonald, George. George MacDonald: The Parish Papers: Edited for Today's Readers. Hamilton, Dan, ed. 1997. 500p. 14.99 (*1-56476-618-7*) Cook Communications Ministries.

—The Vicar's Daughter. 1985. 216p. 5.95 o.p. (*0-89693-330-X*) Cook Communications Ministries.

MacDonald, George, et al. The Curate of Glaston. 2002. 624p. pap. 12.99 (*0-7642-2591-X*) Bethany Hse. Pubs.

Manning, Jo. Seducing Mr. Heywood. 2002. 248p. pap. 13.95 (*1-4104-0071-9*, Five Star Trade); 245p. 25.95 (*0-7862-3400-8*, Five Star) Gale Group.

—Seducing Mr. Heywood. 2003. (Core Ser.). 28.95 (*0-7862-5052-6*) Thorndike Pr.

Mano, D. Keith. Topless. 1992. mass mkt. 4.99 o.s.i (*0-449-22165-2*, Fawcett) Ballantine Bks.

Mawer, Simon. The Gospel of Judas. Clain, Judy, ed. 2001. (Illus.). 336p. 24.95 o.p. (*0-316-09750-0*) Little Brown & Co.

—The Gospel of Judas. 2002. 368p. reprint ed. pap. 13.95 (*0-316-97374-2*, Back Bay) Little Brown & Co.

Maxwell, Jan. Baptism by Murder. 1995. 224p. (Orig.). mass mkt. 4.99 (*0-380-77621-9*, Avon Bks.) Morrow/Avon.

McCafferty, Taylor. Funny Money. 2000. (Haskell Blevins Mysteries Ser.). 304p. pap. 6.99 (*0-671-00129-9*, Pocket) Simon & Schuster.

McCullough, Colleen. The Thorn Birds. 1978. 540p. mass mkt. 6.95 o.p. (*0-380-56390-8*, 56390-8, Avon Bks.) Morrow/Avon.

McInerny, Ralph. Last Things. Date not set. pap. (*0-312-30900-7*, Saint Martin's Griffin); mass mkt. (*0-312-98690-4*, St. Martin's Paperbacks); 2003. 352p. 24.95 (*0-312-30899-X*, Saint Martin's Minotaur) St. Martin's Pr.

—Last Things. l.t. ed. 2003. (Father Dowling Mystery Ser.). 460p. 29.95 (*0-7862-5735-0*) Thorndike Pr.

McInerny, Ralph, ed. Murder Most Divine: Ecclesiastical Tales of Unholy Crimes. 2000. ([Murder Most Series]). xi, 348p. 19.95 (*1-58182-121-2*) Cumberland Hse. Publishing.

—Murder Most Divine: Ecclesiastical Tales of Unholy Crimes. 2004. 368p. 9.99 (*0-517-22163-2*, Gramercy) Random Hse. Value Publishing.

Meyer, Charles. Beside the Still Waters. 1997. (Reverend Lucas Holt Mystery Ser.). 232p. pap. 6.50 (*0-9631149-4-8*) Stone Angel Bks.

—Blessed Are the Merciless. 1996. 272p. mass mkt. 5.50 o.s.i (*0-425-15140-9*) Berkley Publishing Group.

—Blessed Are the Merciless. 2nd ed. 1997. (Reverend Lucas Holt Mystery Ser.). 266p. reprint ed. pap. 6.50 (*0-9631149-5-6*) Stone Angel Bks.

—Deathangel. 1999. 288p. 24.95 (*0-9651879-7-7*) Boaz Publishing Co.

—The Saints of God Murders. 1995. 256p. (Orig.). mass mkt. 5.99 o.s.i (*0-425-14869-6*, Prime Crime) Berkley Publishing Group.

Miller, Calvin. The Sermon Maker. 2002. 160p. 15.99 (*0-310-24656-3*) Zondervan.

Miller, Walter M., Jr. Saint Leibowitz & the Wild Horse Woman. 2000. 448p. pap. 23.00 (*0-553-38079-6*) Bantam Bks.

Montalbano, William D. Basilica. 2000. 368p. reprint ed. mass mkt. 6.99 o.s.i (*0-515-12723-X*, Jove) Berkley Publishing Group.

—Basilica. 1998. 304p. 23.95 o.p. (*0-399-14418-8*) Penguin Group (USA) Inc.

Montecino, Marcel. Sacred Heart. 1998. mass mkt. 6.99 (*0-671-01540-0*, Pocket Star); 1997. 375p. 23.00 (*0-671-01539-7*, Atria) Simon & Schuster.

Morgan, Kathleen. Child of Promise. 2002. (Brides of Culdee Creek Ser.: Bk. 4). 304p. (gr. 13 up). pap. 11.99 (*0-8007-5761-0*) Revell, Fleming H. Co.

Morson, Ian. A Psalm for Falconer, Vol. 1. Date not set. mass mkt. (*0-312-96534-6*, St. Martin's Paperbacks) St. Martin's Pr.

—A Psalm for Falconer: A William Falconer Medieval Mystery. 1997. 220p. 21.95 o.p. (*0-312-16833-0*, Saint Martin's Minotaur) St. Martin's Pr.

Mosher, Howard Frank. The Fall of the Year: A Novel. 1999. 288p. tchr. ed. 24.00 (*0-395-98416-5*); E-Book 24.00 (*0-618-15331-4*) Houghton Mifflin Co.

—The Fall of the Year: A Novel. 2000. 288p. pap. 13.00 (*0-618-08236-0*, Mariner Bks.) Houghton Mifflin Co. Trade & Reference Div.

Munnings, Claire, et al. Overnight Float: A Mystery. 2000. 288p. text 23.95 (*0-393-03849-1*) Norton, W. W. & Co., Inc.

Murphy, Jim. Carneyville: A Young Man's Journey Through the Old Catholic Seminary: A Novel. 2003. 16.95 (*0-9728969-2-9*) Acorn Publishing.

Myers, Bill. The Face of God. E-Book 10.99 (*0-310-25702-6*); 2002. 368p. pap. 12.99 (*0-310-22755-0*) Zondervan.

Myers, Virginia. Vessels of Honor. 1995. 10.99 o.p. (*0-7852-8004-9*) Nelson, Thomas Inc.

—Vessels of Honor. 1999. 208p. per. 15.95 (*0-7592-2664-4*) ereads.com.

Newton, Suzanne. I Will Call It Georgie's Blues. 1990. 208p. (YA). (gr. 7 up). pap. 5.99 (*0-14-034536-1*, Puffin Bks.); 1983. 204p. (J). (gr. 6 up). 12.95 o.p. (*0-670-39131-X*, Viking Children's Bks.) Penguin Putnam Bks. for Young Readers.

O'Doherty, Brian. The Deposition of Father McGreevy. 2001. 313p. pap. 14.95 (*1-900850-48-6*) Arcadia Bks. GBR. *Dist:* Consortium Bk. Sales & Distribution.

—The Deposition of Father McGreevy. 1999. 417p. 25.00 (*1-885983-39-5*) Turtle Point Pr.

O'Hara, Mary. The Devil Enters by a North Window. 1999. Orig. Title: The Son of Adam Wyngate. 440p. reprint ed. pap. 9.95 o.p. (*0-89733-354-3*) Academy Chicago Pubs., Ltd.

Pallamary, Matthew J. Land Without Evil. unabr. ed. 2000. (Illus.). 358p. 23.95 (*0-912880-09-0*) Charles Publishing Co.

Pardo Bazán, Emilia. The House of Ulloa: A Novel by Emilia Pardo Bazan. 1992. 352p. 35.00 o.p. (*0-8203-1372-6*) Univ. of Georgia Pr.

Parker, Gary E. Beyond a Reasonable Doubt. 1994. 253p. pap. 10.99 (*0-8407-4148-0*) Nelson, Thomas Inc.

Parshall, Craig. The Resurrection File. 2002. (Chambers of Justice Ser.). 396p. pap. 11.99 (*0-7369-0847-1*) Harvest Hse. Pubs.

Patrick, John, ed. Tarnished Angels. 1992. 192p. (Orig.). pap. 1.95 o.p. (*1-877978-33-7*, STARbooks Pr.) Florida Literary Foundation.

Peretti, Frank E. This Present Darkness. 1990. 416p. 15.95 o.p. (*0-89107-589-5*); 1986. 375p. pap. 12.99 (*0-89107-390-6*); 1996. 384p. 25.00 o.p. (*0-89107-919-X*) Crossway Bks.

—This Present Darkness. l.t. ed. 1993. (General Ser.). 713p. lib. bdg. 23.95 (*0-8161-5698-0*, Macmillan Reference USA) Gale Group.

Peters, Ellis, pseud. The Benediction of Brother Cadfael. 1992. (Chronicles of Brother Cadfael Ser.). 364p. 35.00 o.p. (*0-89296-449-9*) Mysterious Pr.

—Brother Cadfael's Penance. l.t. ed. 1995. (Chronicles of Brother Cadfael Ser.: Vol. 20). 352p. 21.95 o.p. (*0-7838-1175-6*, Macmillan Reference USA) Gale Group.

—Brother Cadfael's Penance. 1994. (Chronicles of Brother Cadfael Ser.: Vol. 20). 292p. 18.95 (*0-89296-599-1*) Mysterious Pr.

—Brother Cadfael's Penance. 1996. (Chronicles of Brother Cadfael Ser.: Vol. 20). 272p. mass mkt. 6.99 (*0-446-40453-5*) Warner Bks., Inc.

—The Confession of Brother Haluin. l.t. ed. 1990. (Chronicles of Brother Cadfael Ser.: Vol. 15). 282p. lib. bdg. 20.95 (*0-8161-4859-7*, Macmillan Reference USA) Gale Group.

—The Confession of Brother Haluin. 1990. (Chronicles of Brother Cadfael Ser.: Vol. 15). 15.95 o.p. (*0-89296-349-2*) Mysterious Pr.

—The Confession of Brother Haluin. l.t. ed. 1989. (Ulverscroft Large Print Ser.). 336p. 17.95 o.p. (*0-7089-2032-2*, Ulverscroft) Thorpe, F. A. Pubs. GBR. *Dist:* Ulverscroft Large Print Bks., Ltd., Ulverscroft Large Print Canada, Ltd.

—The Confession of Brother Haluin. 1989. (Chronicles of Brother Cadfael Ser.: Vol. 15). 208p. mass mkt. 6.99 (*0-445-40855-3*) Warner Bks., Inc.

—Dead Man's Ransom. 1986. (Chronicles of Brother Cadfael Ser.: Vol. 9). mass mkt. 4.95 o.s.i (*0-449-20819-2*, Fawcett) Ballantine Bks.

—Dead Man's Ransom. 1995. (Chronicles of Brother Cadfael Ser.: Vol. 9). 271p. mass mkt. o.s.i (*0-7515-1109-9*) Little Brown & Co.

—Dead Man's Ransom. Williams, Jennifer, ed. 1985. (Chronicles of Brother Cadfael Ser.: Vol. p). 224p. reprint ed. 13.95 o.p. (*0-688-04194-9*, Morrow, William & Co.) Morrow/Avon.

—Dead Man's Ransom. l.t. ed. 1999. (Chronicles of Brother Cadfael Ser.: Vol. 9). 304p. pap. 24.95 (*0-7862-1829-0*) Thorndike Pr.

—Dead Man's Ransom. l.t. ed. 1986. (Chronicles of Brother Cadfael Ser.: Vol. 9). 384p. 12.50 o.p. (*0-7089-1407-1*, Ulverscroft) Thorpe, F. A. Pubs. GBR. *Dist:* Ulverscroft Large Print Bks., Ltd.

—Dead Man's Ransom. 1997. (Chronicles of Brother Cadfael Ser.: Vol. 9). 288p. mass mkt. 6.99 (*0-446-40516-7*) Warner Bks., Inc.

—The Devil's Novice. 1985. (Chronicles of Brother Cadfael Ser.: Vol. 8). 224p. mass mkt. 3.95 o.s.i (*0-449-20701-3*, Fawcett) Ballantine Bks.

—The Devil's Novice. 1995. (Chronicles of Brother Cadfael Ser.: Vol. 8). (Illus.). 286p. mass mkt. o.s.i (*0-7515-1399-7*) Little Brown & Co.

—The Devil's Novice. Williams, Jennifer, ed. 1984. (Chronicles of Brother Cadfael Ser.: Vol. 8). 192p. 13.95 o.p. (*0-688-03247-8*, Morrow, William & Co.) Morrow/Avon.

—The Devil's Novice. l.t. ed. 1999. (Chronicles of Brother Cadfael Ser.: Vol. 8). 304p. pap. 24.95 (*0-7862-1668-9*) Thorndike Pr.

—The Devil's Novice. l.t. ed. 1985. (Chronicles of Brother Cadfael Ser.: Vol. 8). 368p. 12.50 o.p. (*0-7089-1342-3*, Ulverscroft) Thorpe, F. A. Pubs. GBR. *Dist:* Ulverscroft Large Print Bks., Ltd.

—The Devil's Novice. 1997. (Chronicles of Brother Cadfael Ser.: Vol. 8). 288p. mass mkt. 6.99 (*0-446-40515-9*) Warner Bks., Inc.

—An Excellent Mystery. 1987. mass mkt. 4.95 o.s.i (*0-449-21224-6*, Fawcett) Ballantine Bks.

—An Excellent Mystery. 1995. (Chronicles of Brother Cadfael Ser.). 253p. pap. text o.s.i (*0-7515-1111-0*) Little Brown & Co.
—An Excellent Mystery. Williams, Jennifer, ed. 1986. (Chronicles of Brother Cadfael Ser.: Vol. 11). 224p. reprint ed. 15.95 o.p. (*0-688-06250-4*, Morrow, William & Co.) Morrow/Avon.
—An Excellent Mystery. l.t. ed. 2000. (General Ser.). 299p. pap. 24.95 (*0-7862-2269-7*) Thorndike Pr.
—An Excellent Mystery. l.t. ed. 1987. 384p. 14.50 o.p. (*0-7089-1660-0*, Ulverscroft) Thorpe, F. A. Pubs. GBR. *Dist:* Ulverscroft Large Print Bks., Ltd.
—An Excellent Mystery. 1997. (Chronicles of Brother Cadfael Ser.: Vol. 11). 224p. mass mkt. 6.99 (*0-446-40532-9*) Warner Bks., Inc.
—The Heretic's Apprentice. l.t. ed. 2001. (Chronicles of Brother Cadfael Ser.: Vol. 16). 342p. lib. bdg. 25.95 (*1-58547-138-0*) Ctr. Point Large Print.
—The Heretic's Apprentice. 1990. (Chronicles of Brother Cadfael Ser.: Vol. 16). 16.95 o.p. (*0-89296-381-6*) Mysterious Pr.
—The Heretic's Apprentice. 1991. (Chronicles of Brother Cadfael Ser.: Vol. 16). 256p. mass mkt. 6.99 (*0-446-40000-9*) Warner Bks., Inc.
—The Hermit of Eyton Forest. l.t. ed. 1989. (Chronicles of Brother Cadfael Ser.: Vol. 14). 329p. lib. bdg. 19.95 o.p. (*0-8161-4677-2*, Macmillan Reference USA) Gale Group.
—The Hermit of Eyton Forest. 1987. (Chronicles of Brother Cadfael Ser.: Vol. 14). 224p. (*0-7472-0037-8*) Headline Bk. Publishing, Ltd.
—The Hermit of Eyton Forest. 1988. (Chronicles of Brother Cadfael Ser.: Vol. 14). 15.45 o.p. (*0-89296-290-9*) Mysterious Pr.
—The Hermit of Eyton Forest. 1989. (Chronicles of Brother Cadfael Ser.: Vol. 14). 240p. mass mkt. 6.50 (*0-445-40347-0*) Warner Bks., Inc.
—The Holy Thief. l.t. ed. 1994. (Chronicles of Brother Cadfael Ser.: Vol. 19). 19.95 o.p. (*0-7927-1744-9*); pap. 18.95 o.p. (*0-7927-1743-0*) BBC Audiobooks America.
—The Holy Thief. 1993. (Chronicles of Brother Cadfael Ser.: Vol. 19). 256p. 17.95 (*0-89296-524-X*) Mysterious Pr.
—The Holy Thief. 1994. (Chronicles of Brother Cadfael Ser.: Vol. 19). 256p. mass mkt. 6.99 (*0-446-40363-6*) Warner Bks., Inc.
—Monk's Hood. 1986. (Chronicles of Brother Cadfael Ser.: Vol. 3). 224p. mass mkt. 4.95 o.s.i (*0-449-20699-8*, Fawcett) Ballantine Bks.
—Monk's Hood. 1995. (Chronicles of Brother Cadfael Ser.: Vol. 3). (Illus.). 268p. mass mkt. o.s.i (*0-7515-1103-X*) Little Brown & Co.
—Monk's Hood. l.t. ed. 1982. (Chronicles of Brother Cadfael Ser.: Vol. 3). 368p. 12.50 o.p. (*0-7089-0829-2*, Ulverscroft) Thorpe, F. A. Pubs. GBR. *Dist:* Ulverscroft Large Print Bks., Ltd.
—Monk's Hood. 1992. (Chronicles of Brother Cadfael Ser.: Vol. 3). 224p. mass mkt. 6.99 (*0-446-40300-8*) Warner Bks., Inc.
—A Morbid Taste for Bones. 1985. (Chronicles of Brother Cadfael Ser.: Vol. 1). 224p. mass mkt. 4.95 o.s.i (*0-449-20700-5*, Fawcett) Ballantine Bks.
—A Morbid Taste for Bones. 1995. (Chronicles of Brother Cadfael Ser.: Vol. 1). pap. o.s.i (*0-7515-1101-3*) Little Brown & Co.
—A Morbid Taste for Bones. l.t. ed. 1981. (Chronicles of Brother Cadfael Ser.: Vol. 1). 344p. 12.00 o.p. (*0-7089-0659-1*, Ulverscroft) Thorpe, F. A. Pubs. GBR. *Dist:* Ulverscroft Large Print Bks., Ltd.
—A Morbid Taste for Bones. 1994. (Chronicles of Brother Cadfael Ser.: Vol. 1). 208p. mass mkt. 6.99 (*0-446-40015-7*) Warner Bks., Inc.
—One Corpse Too Many. 1985. (Chronicles of Brother Cadfael Ser.: Vol. 2). 224p. mass mkt. 4.95 o.s.i (*0-449-20702-1*, Fawcett) Ballantine Bks.
—One Corpse Too Many. 1995. (Chronicles of Brother Cadfael Ser.: Vol. 2). (Illus.). 254p. mass mkt. o.s.i (*0-7515-1102-1*) Little Brown & Co.
—One Corpse Too Many. 1994. (Chronicles of Brother Cadfael Ser.: Vol. 2). 224p. mass mkt. 6.99 (*0-446-40051-3*) Warner Bks., Inc.
—The Pilgrim of Hate. 1986. (Chronicles of Brother Cadfael Ser.: Vol. 10). mass mkt. 4.95 o.s.i (*0-449-21223-8*, Fawcett) Ballantine Bks.
—The Pilgrim of Hate. (Chronicles of Brother Cadfael Ser.: Vol. 10). 1999. mass mkt. o.s.i (*0-7515-0220-0*); 1995. 271p. mass mkt. o.s.i (*0-7515-1110-2*) Little Brown & Co.
—The Pilgrim of Hate. Williams, Jennifer, ed. 1985. (Chronicles of Brother Cadfael Ser.: Vol. 10). 190p. reprint ed. 14.95 o.p. (*0-688-04964-8*, Morrow, William & Co.) Morrow/Avon.
—The Pilgrim of Hate. l.t. ed. 1999. (General Ser.). 288p. pap. 24.95 (*0-7862-1945-9*) Thorndike Pr.
—The Pilgrim of Hate. l.t. ed. 1986. (Chronicles of Brother Cadfael Ser.: Vol. 10). 368p. o.p. (*0-7089-1535-3*, Ulverscroft) Thorpe, F. A. Pubs.
—The Pilgrim of Hate. 1997. (Chronicles of Brother Cadfael Ser.: Vol. 10). 256p. mass mkt. 6.99 (*0-446-40531-0*) Warner Bks., Inc.
—The Potter's Field. l.t. ed. 1991. (Chronicles of Brother Cadfael Ser.: Vol. 17). 303p. lib. bdg. 19.95 o.p. (*0-8161-5194-6*, Macmillan Reference USA) Gale Group.
—The Potter's Field. 1990. (Chronicles of Brother Cadfael Ser.: Vol. 17). 240p. 16.95 o.p. (*0-89296-419-7*) Mysterious Pr.
—The Potter's Field. 1991. (Chronicles of Brother Cadfael Ser.: Vol. 17). 224p. mass mkt. 6.99 (*0-446-40058-0*) Warner Bks., Inc.
—The Raven in the Foregate. 1987. (Chronicles of Brother Cadfael Ser.: Vol. 12). 208p. mass mkt. 4.95 o.s.i (*0-449-21225-4*, Fawcett) Ballantine Bks.
—The Raven in the Foregate, Bk 12. 1995. (Chronicles of Brother Cadfael Ser.: Vol. 12). (Illus.). 252p. mass mkt. o.s.i (*0-7515-1740-2*) Little Brown & Co.
—The Raven in the Foregate. Williams, Jennifer, ed. 1986. (Chronicles of Brother Cadfael Ser.: Vol 12). 204p. reprint ed. 15.95 o.p. (*0-688-06558-9*, Morrow, William & Co.) Morrow/Avon.
—The Raven in the Foregate. l.t. ed. 1987. (Chronicles of Brother Cadfael Ser.: Vol. 12). 368p. 16.95 o.p. (*0-7089-1731-3*, Ulverscroft) Thorpe, F. A. Pubs. GBR. *Dist:* Ulverscroft Large Print Bks., Ltd.
—The Raven in the Foregate. 1997. (Chronicles of Brother Cadfael Ser.: Vol. 12). 240p. mass mkt. 6.99 (*0-446-40534-5*) Warner Bks., Inc.
Pruett, Lynn. Ruby River. 2004. 288p. pap. 13.00 (*0-8021-4039-4*, Grove Pr.); 2002. 336p. 24.00 (*0-87113-855-7*, Atlantic Monthly Pr.) Grove/ Atlantic, Inc.
—Ruby River. 2003. (Americana Ser.). 28.95 (*0-7862-5144-1*) Thorndike Pr.
Pym, Barbara. Crampton Hodnet. unabr. ed. 1997. audio 54.95 (*0-7451-6209-6*, CAB 150) BBC Audiobooks America.
—Crampton Hodnet. 1986. 224p. pap. 8.95 o.p. (*0-452-25816-2*, Plume); 1986. 22p. pap. 9.00 o.p. (*0-452-26492-8*, Plume); 1985. 224p. 14.95 o.p. (*0-525-24333-X*, Dutton) Dutton/Plume.
—Crampton Hodnet. l.t. ed. 1986. (General Ser.). 345p. 14.95 o.p. (*0-8161-3968-7*, Macmillan Reference USA) Gale Group.
—Crampton Hodnet. 2000. viii, 216p. pap. 12.95 (*1-55921-243-8*) Moyer Bell.
Reece, Colleen L. The Calling of Elizabeth Cortland. l.t. ed. 2002. 24.95 (*0-7862-4087-3*) Gale Group.
Reece, Colleen L. & Reece-DeMarco, Julie. The Heirloom: One Family's Courageous Sacrifice Sparks Hope in the Midst of Despair. 2002. (Illus.). 66p. 14.99 (*0-8254-3606-0*) Kregel Pubns.
Reynolds, Sheri. The Rapture of Canaan. 336p. 1997. pap. 12.00 (*0-425-16244-3*); 1996. reprint ed. mass mkt. 7.99 (*0-425-15543-9*) Berkley Publishing Group.
—The Rapture of Canaan. 1997. audio 48.00. audio 48.00 (*0-913369-87-X*) Books on Tape, Inc.
—The Rapture of Canaan. 1999. 320p. reprint ed. pap. text 12.00 (*0-7881-6169-5*) DIANE Publishing Co.
—The Rapture of Canaan. unabr. ed. 1999. audio NorthStar Audio Bks.
—The Rapture of Canaan. 1997. 22.95 o.s.i (*0-399-14352-1*); 1996. 336p. 22.95 o.p. (*0-399-14112-X*, G. P. Putnam's Sons) Penguin Group (USA) Inc.
—The Rapture of Canaan. 2001. audio compact disk 78.00 (*0-7887-5205-7*, C1362E7); 1997. audio 48.00 (*0-7887-1315-9*, 95173E7) Recorded Bks., LLC.
—The Rapture of Canaan. l.t. ed. 1997. (Core Ser.). 364p. lib. bdg. 30.95 (*0-7838-8270-X*) Thorndike Pr.
Richards, Jeffrey J. The Great Journey. 2002. (Illus.). ix, 130p. pap. (*1-930566-24-7*, Smithfield Pr.) Scott, D.&F. Publishing, Inc.
Rickman, Phil. A Crown of Lights. 2002. 566p. pap. 7.95 (*0-330-48450-8*) Pan Bks. Ltd. GBR. *Dist:* Trafalgar Square.
—The Lamp of the Wicked. 2003. 356p. 19.95 (*0-333-90805-8*) Macmillan U.K. GBR. *Dist:* Trafalgar Square.
—Midwinter of the Spirit. 2001. 539p. pap. 7.95 (*0-330-37401-X*) Pan Bks. Ltd. GBR. *Dist:* Trafalgar Square.
—The Wine of Angels. 2001. 631p. pap. 7.95 (*0-330-34268-1*) Pan Bks. Ltd. GBR. *Dist:* Trafalgar Square.
Rivers, Francine. And the Shofar Blew. 448p. 2004. pap. 13.99 (*0-8423-6583-4*); 2003. audio compact disk 26.99 (*0-8423-6585-0*) Tyndale Hse. Pubs.
—And the Shofar Blew: A Novel. 2003. 464p. 22.99 (*0-8423-6582-6*) Tyndale Hse. Pubs.
Roby, Kimberla Lawson. Casting the First Stone. 2000. x, 300p. 22.00 o.s.i (*1-57566-489-5*, Kensington Bks.); 2001. 32p. reprint ed. pap. 14.00 (*1-57566-633-2*) Kensington Publishing Corp.
Segerhammar, Robert E. Peter Pulpitpounder, B. D. 2nd ed. 1995. (Illus.). 56p. (Orig.). pap. 7.25 (*0-7880-0432-8*) CSS Publishing Co.
Shand, Rosa. The Gravity of Sunlight. 2001. 256p. 24.00 (*1-56947-192-4*); reprint ed. pap. 13.00 (*1-56947-240-8*) Soho Pr., Inc.
Shepard, Roy. The Latest Epistle of Jim. 1996. 192p. (Orig.). pap. 14.00 (*0-922811-26-1*) Mid-List Pr.
Shockley, Ann A. Say Jesus & Come to Me. 1985. 288p. pap. 2.95 o.p. (*0-380-79657-0*, 79657-0, Avon Bks.) Morrow/Avon.
—Say Jesus & Come to Me. 1987. 288p. reprint ed. pap. 8.95 o.p. (*0-930044-98-3*) Naiad Pr., Inc.
Smith, D. L. The Miracles of Santo Fico. 2003. 28.95 (*0-7862-5243-X*) Thorndike Pr.
—The Miracles of Santo Fico. 368p. 2004. pap. 16.00 (*0-446-69036-8*); 2003. 22.95 (*0-446-53103-0*) Warner Bks., Inc.
Smith, Lee. Saving Grace. 1996. 304p. pap. 13.95 (*0-345-40333-9*) Ballantine Bks.
—Saving Grace. 1995. 273p. (YA). 22.95 o.s.i (*0-399-14050-6*, G. P. Putnam's Sons) Penguin Group (USA) Inc.
Spencer-Fleming, Julia. A Fountain Filled with Blood. E-Book 23.95 (*0-312-71002-X*); 2004. mass mkt. 6.99 (*0-312-99543-1*, St. Martin's Paperbacks); 2003. 304p. 23.95 (*0-312-30410-2*, Saint Martin's Minotaur) St. Martin's Pr.
—In the Bleak Midwinter. E-Book 17.95 (*0-312-70446-1*); 2003. 384p. mass mkt. 6.99 (*0-312-98676-9*, St. Martin's Paperbacks); 2002. 272p. 23.95 (*0-312-28847-6*, Saint Martin's Minotaur) St. Martin's Pr.
Sprinkle, Patricia. The Remember Box. 2000. (Illus.). 416p. pap. 11.99 (*0-310-22992-8*) Zondervan.
Stirling, Jessica. The Workhouse Girl. unabr. ed. 1997. audio 110.95 (*0-7451-8786-2*, CAB 1421) BBC Audiobooks America.
—The Workhouse Girl. 1997. 472p. text 25.95 o.p. (*0-312-15698-7*) St. Martin's Pr.
—The Workhouse Girl. l.t. ed. 1998. (Romance Ser.). 616p. 28.95 (*0-7838-0124-6*) Thorndike Pr.
Summers, Cristina. Crooked Heart. 2003. 336p. mass mkt. 6.99 (*0-553-58430-8*); 2002. 304p. 23.95 (*0-553-80303-4*); 2002. E-Book 19.50 (*0-553-89710-1*) Bantam Bks.
Svee, Gary D. Sanctuary. 2003. 240p. mass mkt. 5.99 (*0-7434-6350-1*, Pocket Star); E-Book (*0-7434-8013-9*, Pocket) Simon & Schuster.
—Sanctuary. 1990. 192p. 18.95 (*0-8027-4113-4*) Walker & Co.
Tanneberg, Ward M. September Strike. 1994. (Ward Tanneberg Ser.: No. 1). pap. 11.99 (*1-56476-339-0*, 6-3339) Cook Communications Ministries.
Taylor, Andrew. Judgement of Strangers. pap. 14.95 (*0-312-28730-5*, Saint Martin's Griffin); 1998. (Roth Trilogy Ser.: Vol. 2). 304p. 22.95 o.p. (*0-312-19292-4*, Saint Martin's Minotaur) St. Martin's Pr.
Taylor, Phyllis. Joshua, the Word & the Light. Taylor, Phyllis & Minner, Rose, eds. 2004. 280p. pap. 13.95 (*0-9742233-1-X*) Daybreak Publishing.
Trollope, Anthony. Barchester Towers. 1992. (Everyman's Library). 20.00 (*0-679-40587-9*) McKay, David Co., Inc.
—Barchester Towers. Page, Frederick & Sadleir, Michael, eds. 1989. 308p. 21.00 (*0-19-520813-7*) Oxford Univ. Pr., Inc.
—Barchester Towers. Sadleir, Michael & Page, Frederick, eds. 2nd ed. 1997. (Oxford World's Classics Ser.). (Illus.). 656p. pap. 5.95 o.p. (*0-19-282393-0*) Oxford Univ. Pr., Inc.
—The Vicar of Bullhampton. 1979. (Illus.). pap. 7.50 o.p. (*0-486-23824-5*) Dover Pubns., Inc.
—The Vicar of Bullhampton. Skilton, David, ed. 1988. (Oxford World's Classics Ser.). 566p. pap. 9.95 o.p. (*0-19-282163-6*) Oxford Univ. Pr., Inc.
Trollope, Frances M. The Vicar of Wrexhill. (Bentley's Standard Novels Ser.: No. 78). reprint ed. 27.50 o.p. (*0-404-54478-9*) AMS Pr., Inc.
—The Vicar of Wrexhill. Wolff, Robert L., ed. 1975. (Victorian Fiction Ser.). reprint ed. lib. bdg. 66.00 o.p. (*0-8240-1563-0*) Garland Publishing, Inc.
Trollope, Joanna. The Choir. l.t. ed. 1994. 322p. 20.95 o.p. (*0-7927-2089-X*); pap. 19.95 o.p. (*0-7927-2088-1*) BBC Audiobooks America.
—The Choir. 2002. 320p. pap. 14.00 (*0-425-18457-9*); 1997. 336p. reprint ed. mass mkt. 7.50 (*0-425-15718-0*) Berkley Publishing Group.
—The Choir. 1995. 261p. 22.00 o.s.i (*0-679-44454-8*) Random Hse., Inc.
—The Rector's Wife. l.t. ed. 1992. 316p. 18.95 o.p. (*0-7927-1363-X*) BBC Audiobooks America.
—The Rector's Wife. 1993. 288p. pap. 10.95 (*0-552-99470-7*) Bantam Bks.
—The Rector's Wife. 1999. 368p. pap. 14.00 (*0-425-17055-1*); 1996. 336p. mass mkt. 6.99 (*0-425-15529-3*) Berkley Publishing Group.
Tuft, John T. Even the Darkness: A Novel. 1994. pap. 10.99 o.p. (*0-7852-8226-2*) Nelson, Thomas Inc.
Updike, John. In the Beauty of the Lilies. 9999. mass mkt. 12.95 o.p. (*0-449-22490-2*); 1997. 512p. pap. 14.95 (*0-449-91121-7*); 1996. mass mkt. 6.99 (*0-449-22551-8*) Ballantine Bks. (Fawcett).
—In the Beauty of the Lilies. 1996. 512p. 29.95 (*0-679-44640-0*) Knopf, Alfred A. Inc.
—In the Beauty of the Lilies. l.t. ed. 1996. (Core Ser.). 653p. 29.95 (*0-7838-1721-5*) Thorndike Pr.
—A Month of Sundays. 1996. 240p. pap. 13.95 (*0-449-91220-5*); 1985. 272p. mass mkt. 5.99 o.s.i (*0-449-20795-1*); 1982. mass mkt. 2.75 o.p. (*0-449-20109-0*) Ballantine Bks. (Fawcett).
—A Month of Sundays. 1975. 228p. 16.95 (*0-394-49551-9*) Knopf, Alfred A. Inc.
Upton, Peter. Green Hill Far Away. 1978. mass mkt. 2.25 o.s.i (*0-345-27208-0*) Ballantine Bks.
—Green Hill Far Away. 1977. 10.95 o.s.i (*0-671-22344-5*, Simon & Schuster) Simon & Schuster.
Urquhart, Jane. The Stone Carvers. 2003. 400p. pap. 14.00 (*0-14-200358-1*) Penguin Group (USA) Inc.
—The Stone Carvers. 2002. 400p. 25.95 (*0-670-03044-9*, Viking) Viking Penguin.
Valentine, Katherine. A Gathering of Angels: A Novel. 2003. (Dorsetville Ser.). 288p. text 23.95 (*0-670-03229-8*, Viking) Viking Penguin.
—A Miracle for St. Cecilia's: A Novel. 2002. (Americana Ser.). 28.95 (*0-7862-4739-8*) Thorndike Pr.
—A Miracle for St. Cecilia's: A Novel. 2002. 288p. 23.95 o.s.i (*0-670-03113-5*, Viking) Viking Penguin.
Van Adler, T. C. The Evil That Boys Do: A Novel. 2003. 304p. pap. 13.95 (*1-55583-660-7*) Alyson Pubns.
—St. Agatha's Breast. 2001. 292p. pap. 13.95 (*1-55583-708-5*, Alyson Bks.) Alyson Pubns.
—St. Agatha's Breast. 1998. 292p. 22.95 (*0-312-20019-6*) St. Martin's Pr.
Vernon, Louise A. A Heart Strangely Warmed. 1994. 130p. (J). (gr. 4-8). pap. 7.95 (*1-882514-14-9*) Greenleaf Pr.
Waldron, Robert G. Blue Hope: A Novella. 2002. 128p. pap. 13.95 (*1-55725-290-4*) Paraclete Pr., Inc.
Wales, Ken & Poling, David. Sea of Glory: A Novel Based on the True WWII Story of the Four Chaplains & the U. S. A. T. Dorchester. 2001. (Illus.). 353p. 21.99 (*0-8054-5000-9*) Broadman & Holman Pubs.
Wangerin, Walter, Jr. Orphean Passages: The Drama of Faith. 1996. 308p. pap. 12.99 (*0-310-20568-9*) Zondervan.
Warmus, John. The Institut: A Novel. 2001. 378p. pap. 15.95 (*1-931402-09-4*) Barclay Bks., LLC.
Watkins, T. Wyatt. Gospel, Grits & Grace: Encountering the Holy in the Ridiculous, Sublime & Unexpected. 1999. (Illus.). xiii, 193p. pap. 15.00 (*0-8170-1311-3*) Judson Pr.
Wentworth, Kimberly Miller. The Tare in the Wheat. 361p. 2002. 34.95 (*1-59286-270-5*); 2001. pap. 24.95 (*1-58851-945-7*) PublishAmerica, Inc.
Wheelas, Jamie. Wild Plum at Night: A Novel. 1996. 192p. pap. 18.95 (*0-86534-049-8*) Sunstone Pr.
White, Michael C. The Blind Side of the Heart: A Novel. 1999. 368p. 24.00 (*0-06-019431-6*) HarperCollins Pubs.
Williams, Carolyn D. Teach My Heart To Sing. 2000. vi, 304p. (C). pap. 14.95 (*0-9705620-0-4*, 540228TMH) Williams, Carolyn D.
Williamson, Penelope. Wages of Sin. 2004. 496p. mass mkt. 7.50 (*0-446-61383-5*); 2003. 416p. 19.95 (*0-446-52841-2*) Warner Bks., Inc.
Wilson, A. N. The Vicar of Sorrows. unabr. ed. 1996. audio 76.95 (*0-7861-0972-6*, 1749) Blackstone Audio Bks., Inc.
—The Vicar of Sorrows. 1995. 400p. pap. 12.00 (*0-393-31294-1*, Norton Paperbacks); 1994. 384p. 23.00 o.p. (*0-393-03610-3*) Norton, W. W. & Co., Inc.
Wolfe, Gene. Lake of the Long Sun. 1993. 352p. 22.95 o.p. (*0-312-85494-3*, Tor Bks.) Doherty, Tom Assocs., LLC.
Wratchford, Eugene P. The Snows of Pine Ridge. 2002. 180p. pap. (*0-87012-672-5*) McClain Printing Co.
Wright, Harold Bell. The Calling of Dan Matthews. Date not set. 370p. 26.95 (*0-8488-2509-8*) Amereon, Ltd.
—The Calling of Dan Matthews. 363p. reprint ed. lib. bdg. 98.00 (*0-7222-0745-X*) Best Bks.
—The Calling of Dan Matthews. (Collected Works of Harold Bell Wright). 363p. 2001. pap. text 28.00 (*0-7426-5888-0*); 1999. reprint ed. lib. bdg. 98.00 (*1-58201-888-X*) Classic Bks.
—The Calling of Dan Matthews. 1995. 368p. pap. 5.99 (*1-56554-048-4*) Pelican Publishing Co., Inc.
—A Higher Call. Phllips, Michael R., ed. 1990. 304p. reprint ed. pap. 8.99 o.p. (*1-55661-136-6*) Bethany Hse. Pubs.
—The Shepherd of the Hills. 347p. reprint ed. lib. bdg. 98.00 (*0-7222-0733-6*) Best Bks.
—The Shepherd of the Hills. Phillips, Michael R., ed. rev. ed. 1988. 256p. pap. 9.99 (*0-87123-916-7*) Bethany Hse. Pubs.
—The Shepherd of the Hills. 1975. lib. bdg. 27.95 (*0-89966-206-4*) Buccaneer Bks., Inc.
—The Shepherd of the Hills. (Collected Works of Harold Bell Wright). 347p. 2001. pap. text 28.00 (*0-7426-5893-7*); 1999. reprint ed. lib. bdg. 98.00 (*1-58201-893-6*) Classic Bks.
—The Shepherd of the Hills. 1987. 269p. reprint ed. (*0-911978-04-6*) McCormick-Armstrong Co., Inc.
—The Shepherd of the Hills. 7th ed. 1992. 304p. pap. 5.99 (*0-88289-884-1*) Pelican Publishing Co., Inc.

—The Shepherd of the Hills. 1958. 9.95 o.s.i (*0-448-01056-9*, Grosset & Dunlap) Penguin Putnam Bks. for Young Readers.

Wright, Harold Bell & Phillips, Michael R. The Shepherd of the Hills. l.t. ed. 2000. (G. K. Hall Inspirational Ser.). 326p. 27.95 (*0-7838-8941-0*, Macmillan Reference USA) Gale Group.

Young, Douglas H. Jack-O-Lantern. 2003. 474p. 24.95 (*0-9606510-4-7*) Writer's Publishing Hse.

Zola, Emile. Paris. Vizetelly, Ernest Alfred, tr. 1993. (Pocket Classics Ser.). pap. text 10.95 (*0-7509-0450-X*) Sutton Publishing.

## COLLEGE TEACHERS—FICTION

Abu-Jaber, Diana. Crescent. 2003. 352p. 24.95 (*0-393-05747-X*) Norton, W. W. & Co., Inc.

Adams, Hazard. Home: A Novel. (SUNY Series in Postmodern Culture). (Illus.). xi, 205p. (C). 2002. pap. text 17.95 (*0-7914-5094-5*); 2001. E-Book 29.50 (*0-7914-5093-7*) State Univ. of New York Pr.

Amis, Kingsley. Jake's Thing. 1980. 288p. pap. 7.95 o.p. (*0-14-005096-5*, Penguin Bks.); 1979. 11.95 o.p. (*0-670-40471-3*) Viking Penguin.

Argiri, Laura. The God in Flight. 1996. 496p. pap. 22.00 o.s.i (*0-14-025413-7*, Penguin Bks.) Penguin Group (USA) Inc.

Banks, Carolyn. Mr. Right. 1999. 352p. 25.00 (*0-933256-91-4*) Second Chance Pr.

—Mr. Right. 1979. 9.95 o.p. (*0-670-49318-X*) Viking Penguin.

—Mr. Right. 1980. pap. 2.50 o.s.i (*0-446-91191-7*) Warner Bks., Inc.

Barrow, Adam. Blind Spot. 1997. 304p. 22.95 o.p. (*0-525-94186-X*) Dutton/Plume.

—Blind Spot. 1998. 416p. mass mkt. 5.99 o.s.i (*0-451-19187-0*, Signet Bks.) NAL.

Bernays, Anne. Professor Romeo. 1989. 288p. 18.95 o.p. (*1-55584-218-6*) Grove/Atlantic, Inc.

—Professor Romeo. 1997. 287p. reprint ed. pap. 15.95 (*0-87451-809-1*, Hardscrabble Bks.) Univ. Pr. of New England.

—Professor Romeo. 1990. 288p. reprint ed. pap. 7.95 o.p. (*0-14-014416-1*, Penguin Bks.) Viking Penguin.

Bowen, Gail. A Colder Kind of Death. 2001. (Joanne Kilbourn Mystery Ser.). 224p. mass mkt. 7.95 (*0-7710-1495-3*) McClelland & Stewart/Tundra Bks.

—A Colder Kind of Death: A Joanne Kilbourn Mystery. 1999. 240p. 19.95 o.p. (*0-7710-1482-1*); 1995. 232p. mass mkt. 7.99 (*0-7710-1483-X*) McClelland & Stewart/Tundra Bks.

—Deadly Appearances. 2000. (Joanne Kilbourn Mystery Ser.). 280p. mass mkt. 7.99 (*0-7710-1491-0*) McClelland & Stewart/Tundra Bks.

—Deadly Appearances: A Joanne Kilbourn Mystery. 1992. mass mkt. 5.99 o.s.i (*0-7704-2433-3*) Bantam Bks.

—Deadly Appearances: A Joanne Kilbourn Mystery. (*0-88894-703-8*) Douglas & McIntyre, Ltd.

—Deadly Appearances: A Joanne Kilbourn Mystery. 1997. 280p. mass mkt. 7.99 (*0-7710-1485-6*) McClelland & Stewart/Tundra Bks.

—A Killing Spring. 1997. (Joanne Kilbourn Mystery Ser.). 272p. mass mkt. 5.95 (*0-7710-1486-4*) McClelland & Stewart/Tundra Bks.

—A Killing Spring: A Joanne Kilburn Mystery. 1997. 264p. 22.95 o.p. (*0-7710-1484-8*) McClelland & Stewart/Tundra Bks.

—Love & Murder. 1993. 224p. 17.95 o.p. (*0-312-09344-6*, Saint Martin's Minotaur) St. Martin's Pr.

—Murder at the Mendel. 2000. (Joanne Kilbourn Mystery Ser.). 216p. mass mkt. 7.99 (*0-7710-1492-9*) McClelland & Stewart/Tundra Bks.

—Murder at the Mendel: A Joanne Kilbourn Mystery. 1992. mass mkt. 7.99 o.s.i (*0-7710-1480-5*) McClelland & Stewart/Tundra Bks.

—Verdict in Blood. (Joanne Kilbourn Mystery Ser.). 264p. 1999. mass mkt. 7.95 (*0-7710-1489-9*); 1998. 20.95 o.s.i (*0-7710-1487-2*) McClelland & Stewart/Tundra Bks.

—The Wandering Soul Murders: A Joanne Kilbourn Mystery. 1993. 216p. mass mkt. 7.99 (*0-7710-1481-3*) McClelland & Stewart/Tundra Bks.

—The Wandering Soul Murders: A Joanne Kilbourn Mystery. 1994. 207p. 19.95 o.p. (*0-312-10574-6*, Saint Martin's Minotaur) St. Martin's Pr.

Bowers, Neal. Loose Ends. 2001. E-Book 18.50 (*1-58945-778-1*) Adobe Systems, Inc.

—Loose Ends: A Novel. 2001. E-Book 18.50 (*0-375-50691-8*) Random Hse., Inc.

Bradberry, James. Eakins' Mistress: A Jamie Ramsgill Mystery. 1997. 169p. text 19.95 o.p. (*0-312-15518-2*, Saint Martin's Minotaur) St. Martin's Pr.

—Ruins of Civility. 1996. 256p. 21.95 o.p. (*0-312-14041-X*, Saint Martin's Minotaur) St. Martin's Pr.

—The Seventh Sacrament. 1994. 208p. 19.95 o.p. (*0-312-11059-6*, Saint Martin's Minotaur); Vol. 1. 1995. (Seventh Sacrament Ser.: Vol. 1). 209p. mass mkt. 4.99 (*0-312-95636-3*, St. Martin's Paperbacks) St. Martin's Pr.

Bradbury, Malcolm. Eating People Is Wrong. 1991. 248p. reprint ed. pap. 12.00 (*0-89733-189-3*) Academy Chicago Pubs., Ltd.

Callaghan, Mary R. I Met a Man Who Was Not There. 1997. 280p. 24.95 o.p. (*0-7145-3019-0*) Boyars, Marion Pubs., Inc.

Carter, Stephen L. The Emperor of Ocean Park: A Novel. 2003. 672p. reprint ed. pap. 14.00 (*0-375-71292-5*, Vintage) Knopf Publishing Group.

—The Emperor of Ocean Park: A Novel. 2002. 672p. 26.95 (*0-375-41363-4*) Knopf, Alfred A. Inc.

—The Emperor of Ocean Park: A Novel. l.t. ed. 2002. 1152p. 26.95 (*0-375-43165-9*) Random Hse. Large Print.

Chappell, Fred. The Gaudy Place. 1994. (Voices of the South Ser.). 192p. reprint ed. pap. 14.95 (*0-8071-1934-2*) Louisiana State Univ. Pr.

Cheever, John. Falconer. 1992. (Vintage International Ser.). 224p. pap. 12.00 (*0-679-73786-3*, Vintage) Knopf Publishing Group.

Childers, Max. The Congregation of the Dead. 1996. 282p. 21.95 (*0-941711-32-3*) Wyrick & Co.

Clarke, Anna. Cabin Three Thousand Thirty-Three. 1989. 3.50 (*1-55773-251-5*, Diamond Bks.) Berkley Publishing Group.

—Cabin Three Thousand Thirty-Three. 1986. (Crime Club Ser.). 192p. 12.95 o.p. (*0-385-23264-0*) Doubleday Publishing.

—Cabin Three Thousand Thirty-Three. l.t. ed. 1988. (Nightingale Ser.). 285p. 12.95 o.p. (*0-8161-4387-0*, Macmillan Reference USA) Gale Group.

—The Case of the Anxious Aunt. 1996. 208p. mass mkt. 5.99 o.p. (*0-425-15311-8*) Berkley Publishing Group.

—The Case of the Ludicrous Letters. 1994. 208p. (Orig.). mass mkt. 4.50 o.p. (*0-425-14048-2*) Berkley Publishing Group.

—The Case of the Paranoid Patient. 1993. 192p. mass mkt. 3.99 o.p. (*0-425-13858-5*) Berkley Publishing Group.

—The Case of the Paranoid Patient. l.t. ed. 1993. (Nightingale Ser.). 300p. lib. bdg. 15.95 (*0-8161-5845-2*, Macmillan Reference USA) Gale Group.

—Last Judgment. 1985. (Crime Club Ser.). 192p. 11.95 o.p. (*0-385-19666-0*) Doubleday Publishing.

—Last Seen in London. 1987. (Crime Club Ser.). 192p. o.s.i (*0-385-23559-3*) Doubleday Publishing.

—Last Seen in London. l.t. ed. 1992. 340p. pap. 14.95 o.p. (*0-8161-5452-X*, Macmillan Reference USA) Gale Group.

—Murder in Writing. 1990. 3.50 (*1-55773-326-0*, Diamond Bks.) Berkley Publishing Group.

—Murder in Writing. 1988. (Crime Club Ser.). 192p. pap. 15.00 (*0-385-24325-1*) Doubleday Publishing.

—Mystery Lady. 1986. (Crime Club Ser.). 192p. 12.95 o.p. (*0-385-23546-1*) Doubleday Publishing.

—The Whitelands Affair. 1992. mass mkt. 3.99 o.p. (*0-425-13268-4*) Berkley Publishing Group.

Cleary, Melissa. And Your Little Dog, Too. 1998. (Dog Lover's Mysteries Ser.). 208p. mass mkt. 5.99 o.s.i (*0-425-16242-7*, Prime Crime) Berkley Publishing Group.

—Dead & Buried. 1994. 208p. (Orig.). mass mkt. 4.99 o.s.i (*0-425-14547-6*, Prime Crime) Berkley Publishing Group.

—Dog Collar Crime. 1993. 192p. (Orig.). 3.99 o.s.i (*1-55773-896-3*, Diamond Bks.) Ace Bks.

—A Dog Collar Crime. 1994. (Orig.). mass mkt. 4.99 o.s.i (*0-425-14857-2*, Prime Crime) Berkley Publishing Group.

—First Pedigree Murder: A Dog Lover's Mystery. 1994. 208p. (Orig.). mass mkt. 4.99 o.s.i (*0-425-14299-X*, Prime Crime) Berkley Publishing Group.

—Hounded to Death. 1993. 192p. mass mkt. 4.99 o.s.i (*0-425-14324-4*) Berkley Publishing Group.

—The Maltese Puppy. 1995. 256p. (Orig.). mass mkt. 4.99 o.s.i (*0-425-14721-5*, Prime Crime) Berkley Publishing Group.

—A Murder Most Beastly. 1996. 208p. (Orig.). mass mkt. 4.99 o.s.i (*0-425-15139-5*) Berkley Publishing Group.

—Old Dogs. 1997. (Dog Lover's Mysteries Ser.). 224p. mass mkt. 5.99 o.s.i (*0-425-15858-6*, Prime Crime) Berkley Publishing Group.

—Skull & Dog Bones. 1994. (Orig.). mass mkt. 4.99 o.s.i (*0-425-14541-7*); 208p. mass mkt. 4.50 o.s.i (*0-515-11279-8*, Jove) Berkley Publishing Group.

—Tail of Two Murders. 1993. 192p. (Orig.). mass mkt. 4.99 o.s.i (*0-425-15809-8*, Prime Crime) Berkley Publishing Group.

Cleary, Melissa & Jove Publications Staff. Hounded to Death. 1993. (Dog Lover's Mysteries Ser.). 184p. mass mkt. 3.99 o.s.i (*0-515-11190-2*, Jove) Berkley Publishing Group.

Cory, Desmond. The Catalyst. 1991. 15.95 o.p. (*0-312-05832-2*, Saint Martin's Minotaur) St. Martin's Pr.

—The Dobie Paradox. 1994. 240p. 19.95 o.p. (*0-312-10969-5*, Saint Martin's Minotaur) St. Martin's Pr.

—The Mask of Zeus. 1993. 256p. 19.95 o.p. (*0-312-09873-1*, Saint Martin's Minotaur) St. Martin's Pr.

Cowasjee, Saros. The Assistant Professor. 1996. 160p. pap. 13.95 (*0-920661-50-5*) TSAR Pubns. CAN. *Dist:* LPC/InBook.

Craft, Michael. Desert Winter: A Claire Gray Mystery. 2003. 288p. 23.95 (*0-312-30501-X*, Saint Martin's Minotaur) St. Martin's Pr.

Crider, Bill. A Dangerous Thing. 1996. per. (*0-373-26216-7*, 1-26216-1, Worldwide Library) Harlequin Enterprises, Ltd.

—A Dangerous Thing. 1994. 200p. 19.95 (*0-8027-3187-2*) Walker & Co.

—Dying Voices. 1989. 192p. 14.95 o.p. (*0-312-03328-1*, Saint Martin's Minotaur) St. Martin's Pr.

—Murder Is an Art. 1999. 256p. 21.95 o.p. (*0-312-19927-9*, Saint Martin's Minotaur) St. Martin's Pr.

—One Dead Dean. 1988. 208p. 17.95 (*0-8027-5711-1*) Walker & Co.

Crispin, Edmund. Buried for Pleasure. 191p. reprint ed. lib. bdg. 20.95 (*0-89190-691-6*, Rivercity Pr.) Amereon, Ltd.

—Buried for Pleasure. Barzum, Jacques & Taylor, Wendell H., eds. 1976. (Crime Fiction Ser.). reprint ed. lib. bdg. 21.00 o.p. (*0-8240-2362-5*) Garland Publishing, Inc.

—Buried for Pleasure. 1980. mass mkt. 3.50 o.p. (*0-06-080506-4*, P 506, Perennial) HarperTrade.

—The Case of the Gilded Fly. l.t. ed. 1980. (YA). (gr. 7-12). lib. bdg. 13.95 o.p. (*0-8161-3018-3*, Macmillan Reference USA) Gale Group.

—The Case of the Gilded Fly. 1992. 224p. pap. 8.95 o.p. (*1-55882-108-2*) International Polygonics, Ltd.

—The Case of the Gilded Fly. 1980. pap. 2.95 o.p. (*0-380-50187-2*, 63552-6, Avon Bks.) Morrow/Avon.

—The Case of the Gilded Fly. 1979. (Walker Mystery Ser.). 223p. reprint ed. 8.95 o.s.i (*0-8027-5410-4*) Walker & Co.

—Frequent Hearses. l.t. ed. 1994. (General Ser.). 311p. lib. bdg. 16.95 (*0-8161-5860-6*, Macmillan Reference USA) Gale Group.

—Frequent Hearses. 1982. pap. 2.95 o.p. (*0-14-006325-0*) Penguin Group (USA) Inc.

—Frequent Hearses. 1987. (Classic Crime Ser.). 224p. pap. 5.95 o.p. (*0-14-009355-9*, Penguin Bks.) Viking Penguin.

—The Glimpses of the Moon. 23.95 (*0-89190-695-9*) Amereon, Ltd.

—The Glimpses of the Moon. 1979. pap. 2.95 o.p. (*0-380-45062-3*, 69021-7, Avon Bks.) Morrow/Avon.

—The Glimpses of the Moon. 1978. 8.95 o.s.i (*0-8027-5391-4*) Walker & Co.

—Holy Disorders. 1976. 22.95 (*0-8488-0468-6*) Amereon, Ltd.

—Holy Disorders. 1980. (General Ser.). lib. bdg. 13.95 o.p. (*0-8161-3111-2*, Macmillan Reference USA) Gale Group.

—Holy Disorders. 1980. 240p. pap. 2.95 o.p. (*0-380-51508-3*, Avon Bks.) Morrow/Avon.

—Holy Disorders. 1979. (Walker Mystery Ser.). 254p. 9.95 o.s.i (*0-8027-5411-2*) Walker & Co.

—The Long Divorce. 1981. (Crime Monthly Ser.). 256p. pap. 3.95 o.p. (*0-14-001304-0*, Penguin Bks.) Viking Penguin.

—Love Lies Bleeding. 20.95 (*0-89190-693-2*) Amereon, Ltd.

—Love Lies Bleeding. 1982. (Crime Monthly Ser.). pap. 3.95 o.p. (*0-14-000974-4*, Penguin Bks.) Viking Penguin.

—Love Lies Bleeding. 1981. 9.95 o.s.i (*0-8027-5444-9*) Walker & Co.

—The Moving Toy Shop. 20.95 (*0-8488-0104-0*) Amereon, Ltd.

—The Moving Toy Shop. 1989. (Penguin Classic Crime Ser.). 208p. pap. 6.99 (*0-14-008817-2*, Penguin Bks.) Penguin Group (USA) Inc.

—Swan Song. 1980. 192p. 16.95 (*0-8027-5420-1*) Boulevard Bks.

—Swan Song. 1993. reprint ed. lib. bdg. 16.95 (*1-56849-195-6*) Buccaneer Bks., Inc.

—Swan Song. 1982. 192p. pap. 2.50 o.p. (*0-380-55145-4*, 70020, Avon Bks.) Morrow/Avon.

—Swan Song. l.t. ed. 1987. (Linford Mystery Library). 336p. pap. 17.99 o.p. (*0-7089-6361-7*, Linford) Thorpe, F. A. Pubs. GBR. *Dist:* Ulverscroft Large Print Bks., Ltd., Ulverscroft Large Print Canada, Ltd.

Cross, Amanda. Amanda Cross: The Collected Stories. l.t. ed. 1997. (Wheeler Large Print Book Ser.). pap. 24.95 (*1-56895-453-0*, Wheeler Publishing, Inc.) Gale Group.

—Collected Stories of Amanda Cross. 1998. 192p. pap. 12.00 (*0-345-42113-2*) Ballantine Bks.

—Death in a Tenured Position. (Kate Fansler Novels Ser.). 1986. 208p. mass mkt. 6.99 (*0-345-34041-8*); 1982. mass mkt. 2.50 o.p. (*0-345-30215-X*) Ballantine Bks.

—Death in a Tenured Position. 1981. 10.50 o.p. (*0-525-08935-7*, 01019-310, Dutton) Dutton/Plume.

—Death in a Tenured Position. l.t. ed. 1981. reprint ed. 11.95 o.p. (*0-89621-321-8*) Thorndike Pr.

—An Imperfect Spy. 1995. (Kate Fansler Novels Ser.). 224p. mass mkt. 6.99 (*0-345-39005-9*); 240p. 20.00 o.p. (*0-345-38917-4*); 224p. pap. 15.00 (*0-345-46493-1*) Ballantine Bks.

—An Imperfect Spy. l.t. ed. 1995. 232p. pap. 18.95 o.p. (*0-7838-1299-X*, Macmillan Reference USA) Gale Group.

—An Imperfect Spy. unabr. ed. 1996. audio 49.95 o.p. (*1-85903-093-9*, 30939) Magna Story Sound GBR. *Dist:* Ulverscroft Large Print Bks., Ltd.

—In the Last Analysis. 2001. (Kate Fansler Novels Ser.: Vol. 1). 224p. mass mkt. 6.50 (*0-449-00711-1*, Fawcett) Ballantine Bks.

—In the Last Analysis. Barzun, Jacques & Taylor, W. H., eds. 1983. (Crime Fiction 1950-1975 Ser.). 187p. lib. bdg. 18.00 o.p. (*0-8240-4960-8*) Garland Publishing, Inc.

—In the Last Analysis. 1981. 176p. mass mkt. 5.50 (*0-380-54510-1*, Avon Bks.) Morrow/Avon.

—In the Last Analysis. l.t. ed. 1982. 305p. reprint ed. 10.95 o.p. (*0-89621-335-8*) Thorndike Pr.

—James Joyce Murder. 1985. mass mkt. 2.95 o.p. (*0-345-33141-9*) Ballantine Bks.

—The James Joyce Murders. 1987. (Kate Fansler Novels Ser.). 208p. mass mkt. 6.50 (*0-345-34686-6*) Ballantine Bks.

—The James Joyce Murders. 1982. 176p. 9.95 o.p. (*0-525-24101-9*, 0995-300, Dutton) Dutton/Plume.

—The James Joyce Murders. l.t. ed. 1993. (Nightingale Ser.). 282p. pap. 16.95 o.p. (*0-8161-5779-0*, Macmillan Reference USA) Gale Group.

—The James Joyce Murders. l.t. ed. 1982. 275p. reprint ed. 9.95 o.p. (*0-89621-373-0*) Thorndike Pr.

—No Word from Winifred. 1988. pap. 3.95 o.p. (*0-345-00728-X*); 1987. 272p. mass mkt. 6.99 (*0-345-33381-0*) Ballantine Bks.

—No Word from Winifred. 1986. 14.95 o.p. (*0-525-24432-8*, Dutton) Dutton/Plume.

—The Players Come Again. 1991. (Kate Fansler Novels Ser.). 240p. mass mkt. 6.99 (*0-345-36998-X*, Ballantine Bks.) Ballantine Bks.

—The Players Come Again. l.t. ed. 1994. 300p. lib. bdg. 15.95 o.p. (*0-8161-5990-4*, Macmillan Reference USA) Gale Group.

—The Players Come Again. 1992. 3.99 o.p. (*0-517-09455-X*) Random Hse. Value Publishing.

—The Players Come Again. l.t. ed. 1991. (Charnwood Large Print Ser.). 29.99 o.p. (*0-7089-8615-3*, Charnwood) Thorpe, F. A. Pubs. GBR. *Dist:* Ulverscroft Large Print Bks., Ltd., Ulverscroft Large Print Canada, Ltd.

—Poetic Justice. 2001. (Kate Fansler Novels Ser.). 224p. mass mkt. 6.50 (*0-449-00703-0*, Fawcett) Ballantine Bks.

—Poetic Justice. 1979. 176p. mass mkt. 4.99 (*0-380-44222-1*, Avon Bks.) Morrow/Avon.

—Poetic Justice. l.t. ed. 1981. 286p. reprint ed. 9.95 o.p. (*0-89621-291-2*) Thorndike Pr.

—The Puzzled Heart. 1998. (Kate Fansler Novels Ser.). 256p. mass mkt. 6.99 (*0-345-41884-0*) Ballantine Bks.

—The Puzzled Heart. l.t. ed. 1998. (*0-7540-3401-1*); (*0-7540-3402-X*) Thorndike Pr.

—The Question of Max. 1987. (Kate Fansler Novels Ser.). 224p. mass mkt. 6.50 (*0-345-35489-3*) Ballantine Bks.

—The Question of Max. 1977. lib. bdg. 10.95 o.p. (*0-8161-6451-7*, Macmillan Reference USA) Gale Group.

—The Question of Max. 1984. 7.95 o.p. (*0-394-48223-9*); mass mkt. 2.50 o.p. (*0-345-31385-2*) Knopf, Alfred A. Inc.

—Sweet Death, Kind Death. 1995. 224p. pap. 15.00 (*0-345-46763-9*); 1987. 244p. mass mkt. 5.99 (*0-345-35254-8*); 1985. mass mkt. 2.95 o.s.i (*0-345-31177-9*) Ballantine Bks.

—Sweet Death, Kind Death. 1984. 192p. 13.95 o.p. (*0-525-24241-4*, 01354-410, Dutton) Dutton/Plume.

—Sweet Death, Kind Death. l.t. ed. 1987. (Nightingale Ser.). 279p. pap. 11.95 o.p. (*0-8161-4222-X*, Macmillan Reference USA) Gale Group.

—The Theban Mysteries. 2001. (Kate Fansler Novels Ser.). 224p. mass mkt. 6.50 (*0-449-00706-5*, Fawcett) Ballantine Bks.

—The Theban Mysteries. 1979. 192p. pap. 4.99 (*0-380-45021-6*, Avon Bks.) Morrow/Avon.

—The Theban Mysteries. l.t. ed. 1982. 275p. reprint ed. 11.95 o.p. (*0-89621-362-5*) Thorndike Pr.

—A Trap for Fools. l.t. ed. 1990. pap. 5.00 (*0-7451-1286-2*) BBC Audiobooks America.

—A Trap for Fools. 1990. (Kate Fansler Novels Ser.). 224p. mass mkt. 5.99 (*0-345-35947-X*) Ballantine Bks.

—A Trap for Fools. 1989. 160p. 16.95 o.p. (*0-525-24754-8*, Dutton) Dutton/Plume.

—A Trap for Fools. l.t. ed. 1990. (Nightingale Ser.). 263p. 14.95 o.p. (*0-8161-4935-6*, Macmillan Reference USA) Gale Group.

Cullin, Mitch. The Cosmology of Bing. 2001. (Illus.). 192p. 24.00 (*1-57962-030-2*) Permanent Pr., The.

Cumyn, Alan. Losing It. Date not set. pap. (*0-312-30692-X*, Saint Martin's Griffin); mass mkt. (*0-312-98569-X*, St. Martin's Paperbacks); E-Book (*0-312-70532-8*); 2003. 384p. 24.95 (*0-312-30691-1*) St. Martin's Pr.

DeAndrea, William L. The Hog Murders. 1999. (*0-7862-1942-4*, Five Star) Gale Group.

—The Hog Murders. 1999. 210p. pap. 8.95 o.p. (*1-55882-030-2*, Library of Crime Classics) International Polygonics, Ltd.

—The Hog Murders. 1985. pap. 1.95 o.p. (*0-380-47548-0*, 47548-0, Avon Bks.) Morrow/Avon.

—The Manx Murders: A Professor Niccolo Benedetti Mystery. 1994. 17.00 o.s.i (*0-385-42500-7*) Doubleday Publishing.

—The Manx Murders: A Professor Niccolo Benedetti Mystery. 1994. 256p. 20.00 (*1-883402-66-2*, Scribner) Simon & Schuster.

—The Werewolf Murders. 1992. 240p. 16.50 o.s.i (*0-385-42089-7*) Doubleday Publishing.

DeLillo, Don. White Noise. (Contemporary American Fiction Ser.). 1986. 336p. 14.00 (*0-14-007702-2*); 1985. 352p. 16.95 o.p. (*0-670-80373-1*) Viking Penguin.

Dobson, Joanne. The Raven & the Nightingale. 2000. 320p. mass mkt. 5.99 (*0-553-57999-1*) Bantam Bks.

—The Raven & the Nightingale: A Modern Mystery of Edgar Allen Poe. 1999. 288p. 21.95 o.s.i (*0-385-49339-8*) Doubleday Publishing.

Donohue, John. Sensei: A Thriller. 2003. 288p. 23.95 (*0-312-28812-3*, Saint Martin's Minotaur) St. Martin's Pr.

Downing, Michael. Perfect Agreement. 1997. 224p. 22.00 (*1-887178-45-7*, Counterpoint Pr.) Basic Bks.

—Perfect Agreement. 1998. 288p. reprint ed. pap. 12.95 o.s.i (*0-425-16628-7*) Berkley Publishing Group.

Dressler, Mylene. The Deadwood Beetle. 2002. 256p. pap. 13.00 (*0-425-18760-8*) Berkley Publishing Group.

—The Deadwood Beetle. 2001. 208p. 23.95 o.p. (*0-399-14805-1*, BlueHen Bks.) Putnam Publishing Group, The.

—The Deadwood Beetle. l.t. ed. 2001. 289p. 28.95 (*0-7838-9665-4*) Thorndike Pr.

Ellenberg, Jordan. The Grasshopper King: A Debut Novel. 2003. 200p. pap. 14.00 (*1-56689-139-6*) Coffee Hse. Pr.

Elward, James. Monday's Child Is Dead. 1995. 240p. 19.00 o.p. (*0-7867-0130-7*, Carroll & Graf Pubs.) Avalon Publishing Group.

Ferrars, E. X. Thy Brother Death. 1993. 17.00 o.s.i (*0-385-48092-X*) Doubleday Publishing.

—Thy Brother Death. l.t. ed. 1994. (Ulverscroft Large Print Ser.). 336p. 29.99 o.p. (*0-7089-3202-9*, Ulverscroft) Thorpe, F. A. Pubs. GBR. *Dist:* Ulverscroft Large Print Bks., Ltd., Ulverscroft Large Print Canada, Ltd.

Follett, Ken. The Third Twin. 1998. pap. 7.99 (*0-449-45862-8*); 1997. pap. text 7.99 (*0-449-45794-X*); 1997. 480p. mass mkt. 7.99 (*0-449-22742-1*); 1997. mass mkt. 6.99 o.s.i (*0-449-22761-8*) Ballantine Bks. (Fawcett).

—The Third Twin. Set. abr. ed. 1996. audio 24.00 o.s.i (*0-679-45272-9*, 494389, RH Audio) Random Hse. Audio Publishing Group.

—The Third Twin. l.t. ed. 1996. 672p. pap. 25.95 o.p. (*0-7838-1923-4*) Random Hse. Large Print.

—The Third Twin. l.t. ed. 1996. (Large Print Ser.). 25.95 o.s.i (*0-679-75897-6*) Random Hse., Inc.

Frayn, Michael. The Trick of It. 1991. 176p. pap. 8.95 o.p. (*0-14-012651-1*) Penguin Group (USA) Inc.

—The Trick of It. 1990. 176p. 17.95 o.p. (*0-670-82985-4*, Viking) Viking Penguin.

—The Trick of It: A Novel. 2002. 176p. pap. 12.00 (*0-312-42144-3*) Picador.

French, Linda. Coffee to Die For. 1998. (Professor Teodora Morelli Mystery Ser.: No. 2). 224p. mass mkt. 5.99 (*0-380-79575-2*, Avon Bks.) Morrow/Avon.

—Steeped in Murder. 1999. (Professor Teodora Morelli Mystery Ser.). 256p. mass mkt. 5.99 (*0-380-79576-0*, Avon Bks.) Morrow/Avon.

—Talking Rain: A Professor Teodora Morelli Mystery. 1998. (Professor Teodora Morelli Mystery Ser.). 224p. mass mkt. 5.99 (*0-380-79573-6*, Avon Bks.) Morrow/Avon.

Gabriel, Richard. Sebastian's Cross. 2001. pap. 18.95 (*0-595-19156-8*) iUniverse, Inc.

Gaddis, William. A Frolic of His Own: A Novel. 1994. 586p. 25.00 (*0-671-66984-2*, Simon & Schuster) Simon & Schuster.

Galbraith, John Kenneth. A Tenured Professor. 1991. 208p. pap. 12.95 o.p. (*0-395-57424-2*); 1990. 224p. 19.95 o.p. (*0-395-47100-1*) Houghton Mifflin Co.

Galef, David. Flesh. 1995. 256p. 28.00 (*1-877946-55-9*) Permanent Pr., The.

Gass, William H. The Tunnel. 1999. (Illus.). 672p. reprint ed. pap. 15.95 (*1-56478-213-1*) Dalkey Archive Pr.

—The Tunnel. 1996. 79p. pap. 17.50 o.p. (*0-06-097686-1*) HarperCollins Pubs.

Gaus, P. L. Blood of the Prodigal: An Ohio Amish Mystery. 1999. (Ohio Amish Mysteries Ser.). 230p. pap. 12.95 (*0-8214-1277-9*); 24.95 (*0-8214-1276-0*) Ohio Univ. Pr.

—Broken English: An Ohio Amish Mystery. 2000. (Ohio Amish Mysteries Ser.). 205p. 24.95 (*0-8214-1325-2*); pap. 12.95 (*0-8214-1326-0*) Ohio Univ. Pr. (Ohio Univ. Ctr. for International Studies).

—Cast a Blue Shadow: An Ohio Amish Mystery. 2003. (Ohio Amish Mysteries Ser.). 24.95 (*0-8214-1529-8*); pap. 12.95 (*0-8214-1530-1*) Ohio Univ. Pr.

Gilmour, David. Sparrow Nights. 2002. 224p. text 24.00 (*1-58243-203-1*, Counterpoint Pr.) Basic Bks.

Gischler, Victor. The Pistol Poets. 2004. 336p. 22.95 (*0-385-33724-8*, Delacorte Pr.) Dell Publishing.

Godwin, Gail. The Good Husband. 1995. 496p. pap. 13.95 (*0-345-39645-6*) Ballantine Bks.

—The Good Husband. l.t. ed. 1994. (Large Print Bks.). 620p. pap. 24.95 (*1-56895-086-1*, Wheeler Publishing, Inc.) Gale Group.

Gonzalez, Edward. Ernesto's Ghost. 2002. 360p. 29.95 (*0-7658-0135-3*) Transaction Pubs.

Gordon, Mary. Men & Angels. l.t. ed. 1986. (General Ser.). 425p. 18.95 o.p. (*0-8161-3988-1*, Macmillan Reference USA) Gale Group.

Grayson, Emily. Waterloo Station. 2004. 304p. mass mkt. 6.99 (***0-06-001398-2**, HarperTorch); 2003. 208p. 21.95 (*0-06-001397-4*, Morrow, William & Co.) Morrow/Avon.

—Waterloo Station. l.t. ed. 2003. 232p. 29.95 (*0-7862-5789-X*) Thorndike Pr.

Hariharan, Githa. In Times of Siege: A Novel. 2004. 224p. pap. 13.00 (*1-4000-3337-3*, Vintage) Knopf Publishing Group.

—In Times of Siege: A Novel. 2003. 224p. 22.00 (*0-375-42239-0*) Knopf, Alfred A. Inc.

Harris, Mark. The Tale Maker. 1994. 224p. 21.00 o.p. (*1-55611-397-8*) Fine, Donald I. Bks.

—The Tale Maker. 1995. 215p. pap. 12.00 (*0-8032-7280-4*, Bison Bks.) Univ. of Nebraska Pr.

Hassler, Jon. Rookery Blues. 1997. 512p. mass mkt. 6.99 o.s.i (*0-345-42308-9*); 1996. 496p. pap. 12.00 o.s.i (*0-345-40641-9*) Ballantine Bks.

—Rookery Blues. abr. ed. audio 24.95 (*0-9650850-0-7*, PCAB-3500) Pine Curtain Audiobooks.

Hawley, Noah. A Conspiracy of Tall Men. 1998. 304p. 23.00 o.s.i (*0-609-60280-2*, Harmony) Crown Publishing Group.

—A Conspiracy of Tall Men. 1999. E-Book 12.50 (*0-609-60561-5*) Random Hse., Inc.

—A Conspiracy of Tall Men. 1999. 384p. pap. 19.95 (*0-671-03824-9*, Pocket) Simon & Schuster.

Hellenga, Robert R. The Fall of a Sparrow. Set. abr. ed. 1999. audio 26.95 (*0-7871-1752-8*, 696024, Dove Audio) NewStar Media, Inc.

—The Fall of a Sparrow. 1998. 464p. 25.00 o.s.i (*0-684-85026-5*, Scribner) Simon & Schuster.

—The Fall of the Sparrow: A Novel. 1999. 464p. pap. 14.00 (*0-684-85027-3*, Scribner) Simon & Schuster.

Heymann, Jody. Greystone's Dilemma. 2000. 300p. 22.95 (*0-9651376-4-3*) Bullion Bks.

Hynes, James. The Lecturer's Tale. 2001. x, 388p. 25.00 o.s.i (*0-312-20332-2*) Picador.

—Publish & Perish: Three Tales of Tenure & Terror. 1998. 352p. pap. 14.00 (*0-312-18696-7*); 1997. 3834p. 24.00 o.p. (*0-312-15628-6*) Picador.

Ingalls, Rachel. Binstead's Safari. 1988. 15.45 o.p. (*0-671-63934-X*, Simon & Schuster); pap. 6.95 o.s.i (*0-671-65955-3*, Touchstone) Simon & Schuster.

Isenberg, Jane. Death in a Hot Flash: A Bel Barrett Mystery. 2000. (Bel Barrett Mysteries Ser.). 224p. mass mkt. 5.99 (*0-380-80281-3*, Avon Bks.) Morrow/Avon.

—Hot & Bothered. 2003. 288p. mass mkt. 6.99 (*0-380-81888-4*, Avon Bks.) Morrow/Avon.

—The "M" Word: A Bel Barrett Mystery. 1999. 224p. mass mkt. 5.99 (*0-380-80280-5*, Avon Bks.) Morrow/Avon.

Jacobson, Howard. Coming from Behind. 1985. 202p. reprint ed. pap. 12.00 (*0-89733-155-9*) Academy Chicago Pubs., Ltd.

—Coming from Behind. 1984. 208p. 12.95 o.p. (*0-312-15101-2*) St. Martin's Pr.

Jin, Ha. The Crazed. 2004. 336p. pap. 13.95 (*0-375-71411-1*, Vintage) Knopf Publishing Group.

—The Crazed: A Novel. 2002. 336p. 24.00 (*0-375-42181-5*, Pantheon) Knopf Publishing Group.

Johnson, Denis. The Name of the World. 2000. 144p. 22.00 (*0-06-019248-8*) HarperCollins Pubs.

—The Name of the World: A Novel. 2001. 144p. pap. 12.00 (*0-06-092965-0*, Perennial) HarperTrade.

Jolley, Elizabeth. The Sugar Mother. 1988. 192p. 16.95 o.p. (*0-06-015940-5*) HarperTrade.

Jones, D. J. Murder at the MLA. 1993. 224p. text 12.95 (*0-8203-1502-8*) Univ. of Georgia Pr.

Jones, D. J. H. Murder at the MLA: A Novel. 2000. 224p. pap. 13.95 (*0-8263-2150-X*) Univ. of New Mexico Pr.

—Murder in the New Age. 192p. 2000. pap. 13.95 (*0-8263-2236-0*); 1997. 19.95 (*0-8263-1813-4*) Univ. of New Mexico Pr.

Kenney, Susan. Garden of Malice. 1984. 288p. mass mkt. 2.95 o.s.i (*0-345-31712-2*, Ballantine Bks.) Ballantine Bks.

—Garden of Malice. 1992. (Crime Ser.). 288p. reprint ed. pap. 5.95 o.p. (*0-14-016966-0*, Penguin Bks.) Penguin Group (USA) Inc.

—Graves in Academe. 1990. 28p. pap. 5.95 o.p. (*0-14-013349-6*, Penguin Bks.); 1986. 224p. pap. 3.95 o.p. (*0-14-009386-9*, Penguin Bks.); 1985. 288p. 14.95 o.p. (*0-670-80734-6*) Viking Penguin.

—One Fell Sloop. 1991. (Crime Monthly Ser.). 304p. reprint ed. pap. 5.95 o.p. (*0-14-015406-X*, Penguin Bks.) Penguin Group (USA) Inc.

—One Fell Sloop. 1990. 288p. 16.95 o.p. (*0-670-83537-4*) Viking Penguin.

Kiecolt-Glaser, Janice K. Detecting Lies. 1997. 256p. (Orig.). mass mkt. 5.50 (*0-380-78991-4*, Avon Bks.) Morrow/Avon.

—Unconscious Truths. 1998. mass mkt. 5.99 (*0-380-78992-2*, Avon Bks.) Morrow/Avon.

King, Laurie R. A Darker Place. 1999. (Illus.). 512p. mass mkt. 6.99 (*0-553-57824-3*); mass mkt. (*0-553-84027-4*); (Illus.). 400p. 23.95 o.s.i (*0-553-10711-9*) Bantam Bks.

—A Darker Place. l.t. ed. 1999. (Large Print Book Ser.). (Illus.). 27.95 (*1-56895-738-6*, Wheeler Publishing, Inc.) Gale Group.

—A Darker Place. unabr. ed. 1999. audio 87.00 (*0-7887-3121-1*, 95648 E7) Recorded Bks., LLC.

King, Stephen, et al. The Student Body: Short Stories about College Students & Professors. McNally, John, ed. 2001. ix, 280p. pap. 16.95 (*0-299-17404-2*) Univ. of Wisconsin Pr.

Kirshenbaum, Binnie. Hester among the Ruins: A Novel. 2002. 288p. 24.95 (*0-393-04152-2*) Norton, W. W. & Co., Inc.

Kitt, Sandra. Close Encounters. l.t. ed. 2000. (G. K. Hall Core Ser.). 432p. 27.95 (*0-7838-9271-3*, Macmillan Reference USA) Gale Group.

—Close Encounters. 2000. 368p. mass mkt. 6.99 (*0-451-20048-9*, Signet Bks.) NAL.

Krauss, Nicole. Man Walks into a Room. 2003. 256p. pap. 13.00 (*0-385-72191-9*) Broadway Bks.

—Man Walks into a Room. 2002. 256p. 23.95 (*0-385-50399-7*) Doubleday Publishing.

Krupat, Arnold. Woodsmen: or Thoreau & the Indians: A Novel. 1994. (American Indian Literature & Critical Studies Ser.: Vol. 11). 140p. reprint ed. pap. 10.95 (*0-8061-2671-X*) Univ. of Oklahoma Pr.

Langton, Jane. The Dante Game: A Homer Kelly Mystery. 1992. (Homer Kelly Mystery Ser.). (Illus.). 336p. pap. 6.99 o.s.i (*0-14-013887-0*, Penguin Bks.) Penguin Group (USA) Inc.

—The Dante Game: A Homer Kelly Mystery. 1991. (Homer Kelly Mystery Ser.). (Illus.). 336p. 18.95 o.p. (*0-670-83439-4*) Viking Penguin.

—Dark Nantucket Noon. 1993. (Black Dagger Crime Ser.). (Illus.). 304p. 16.50 o.p. (*0-7451-8604-1*, Black Dagger) BBC Audiobooks America.

—Dark Nantucket Noon. unabr. ed. 1982. audio 48.00 (*0-7366-0630-0*, 1591) Books on Tape, Inc.

—Dark Nantucket Noon. 1981. (Fiction Ser.). 304p. pap. 5.99 (*0-14-005836-2*, Penguin Bks.) Penguin Group (USA) Inc.

—Dead as a Dodo: A Homer Kelly Mystery. 1997. (Homer Kelly Mystery Ser.). (Illus.). 256p. pap. 6.95 o.s.i (*0-14-024795-5*) Penguin Group (USA) Inc.

—Dead as a Dodo: A Homer Kelly Mystery. 1996. (Homer Kelly Mystery Ser.). 352p. 21.95 o.s.i (*0-670-86221-5*) Viking Penguin.

—Dead As a Dodo: A Homer Kelly Mystery. unabr. ed. 1997. audio 56.00 (*0-913369-62-4*, 4295) Books on Tape, Inc.

—The Deserter: Murder at Gettysburg. 2003. (Illus.). 256p. 23.95 (*0-312-30186-3*, Saint Martin's Minotaur) St. Martin's Pr.

—Divine Inspiration: A Homer Kelly Mystery. unabr. collector's ed. 1994. audio 56.00 (*0-7366-2722-7*, 3452) Books on Tape, Inc.

—Divine Inspiration: A Homer Kelly Mystery. abr. ed. 1994. (Homer Kelly Mystery Ser.). audio 16.00 o.p. (*0-453-00888-7*, Penguin AudioBooks) HighBridge Co.

—Divine Inspiration: A Homer Kelly Mystery. 1994. (Homer Kelly Mystery Ser.). (Illus.). 416p. reprint ed. pap. 5.99 o.s.i (*0-14-017376-5*, Penguin Bks.) Penguin Group (USA) Inc.

—Divine Inspiration: A Homer Kelly Mystery. 1993. (Homer Kelly Mystery Ser.). (Illus.). 416p. 20.00 o.p. (*0-670-84709-7*, Viking) Viking Penguin.

—Emily Dickinson Is Dead. unabr. collector's ed. 1987. audio 48.00 (*0-7366-1077-4*, 2004) Books on Tape, Inc.

—Emily Dickinson Is Dead. 1984. 256p. 13.95 o.p. (*0-312-24434-7*) St. Martin's Pr.

—Emily Dickinson Is Dead. l.t. ed. 1992. (Linford Mystery Large Print Ser.). 448p. pap. 17.99 o.p. (*0-7089-7162-8*, Ulverscroft) Thorpe, F. A. Pubs. GBR. *Dist:* Ulverscroft Large Print Bks., Ltd., Ulverscroft Large Print Canada, Ltd.

—Emily Dickinson Is Dead. 1985. (Crime Ser.). 256p. pap. 5.95 o.p. (*0-14-007771-5*, Penguin Bks.) Viking Penguin.

—The Escher Twist: A Homer Kelly Mystery. 2002. (Homer Kelly Mystery Ser.). (Illus.). 256p. 22.95 o.s.i (*0-670-03067-8*, Viking) Viking Penguin.

—The Face on the Wall: A Homer Kelly Mystery. l.t. ed. 1999. (Large Print Mystery Ser.). 25.95 (*1-57490-205-9*, Beeler Large Print Bks.) Beeler, Thomas T. Publisher.

—The Face on the Wall: A Homer Kelly Mystery, , unabr. ed. 1999. audio 48.00 (*0-7366-4369-9*, 4827) Books on Tape, Inc.

—The Face on the Wall: A Homer Kelly Mystery. 1999. (Homer Kelly Mystery Ser.). (Illus.). 304p. pap. 5.99 o.s.i (*0-14-028157-6*) Penguin Group (USA) Inc.

—The Face on the Wall: A Homer Kelly Mystery. 1998. (Homer Kelly Mystery Ser.). (Illus.). 288p. 21.95 o.p. (*0-670-87674-7*) Viking Penguin.

—God in Concord: A Homer Kelly Mystery. 1993. (Homer Kelly Mystery Ser.). (Illus.). 352p. pap. 6.99 (*0-14-016594-0*, Penguin Bks.) Penguin Group (USA) Inc.

—God in Concord: A Homer Kelly Mystery. 1992. (Homer Kelly Mystery Ser.). 384p. 19.00 o.p. (*0-670-84260-5*, Viking) Viking Penguin.

—Good & Dead. unabr. collector's ed. 1992. audio 48.00 (*0-7366-2223-3*, 3013) Books on Tape, Inc.

—Good & Dead. 1986. 320p. 15.95 o.p. (*0-312-33865-1*) St. Martin's Pr.

—Good & Dead. (Homer Kelly Mystery Ser.). 256p. 1989. pap. 5.95 o.s.i (*0-14-012687-2*); 1987. pap. 3.95 o.p. (*0-14-010088-1*) Viking Penguin. (Penguin Bks.).

—The Memorial Hall Murder. unabr. ed. 1982. audio 48.00 (*0-7366-0631-9*, 1592) Books on Tape, Inc.

—The Memorial Hall Murder. 1996. pap. (*0-14-771166-5*) Penguin Group (USA) Inc.

—The Memorial Hall Murder. 1981. (Fiction Ser.). 272p. pap. 5.95 o.p. (*0-14-005704-8*, Penguin Bks.) Viking Penguin.

—Murder at the Gardner. unabr. collector's ed. 1990. audio 56.00 (*0-7366-1741-8*, 2581) Books on Tape, Inc.

—Murder at the Gardner. 1989. (Penguin Crime Fiction Ser.). 368p. pap. 6.99 (*0-14-011382-7*, Penguin Bks.) Penguin Group (USA) Inc.

—Murder at the Gardner. 1988. (Illus.). 288p. 17.95 o.p. (*0-312-01479-1*, Saint Martin's Minotaur) St. Martin's Pr.

—Natural Enemy. unabr. collector's ed. 1992. audio 48.00 (*0-7366-2231-4*, 3021) Books on Tape, Inc.

—Natural Enemy. 1982. (Joan Kahn Bk.). (Illus.). 288p. 11.95 o.p. (*0-89919-081-2*) Houghton Mifflin Co.

—Natural Enemy. (Homer Kelly Mystery Ser.). 1990. 28p. pap. 5.95 o.p. (*0-14-013393-3*); 1987. (Illus.). 228p. pap. 3.95 o.p. (*0-14-009345-1*) Viking Penguin. (Penguin Bks.).

—The Shortest Day: Murder at the Revels. 1996. (Homer Kelly Mystery Ser.). (Illus.). 272p. pap. 5.95 o.s.i (*0-14-017377-3*, Viking) Penguin Group (USA) Inc.

—The Shortest Day: Murder at the Revels. 1995. (Homer Kelly Mystery Ser.). (Illus.). 272p. 19.95 o.p. (*0-670-84710-0*) Viking Penguin.

—The Thief of Venice: A Homer Kelly Mystery. 2000. (Homer Kelly Mystery Ser.). (Illus.). 256p. pap. 5.99 (*0-14-029189-X*) Penguin Group (USA) Inc.

—The Thief of Venice: A Homer Kelly Mystery. 1999. (Homer Kelly Mystery Ser.). 256p. 22.95 o.p. (*0-670-88210-0*, Viking) Viking Penguin.

—The Transcendental Murder. unabr. collector's ed. 1982. audio 48.00 (*0-7366-0499-5*, 1473) Books on Tape, Inc.

—The Transcendental Murder. (Homer Kelly Mystery Ser.). 1990. 36p. pap. 6.95 o.p. (*0-14-014852-3*); 1989. 288p. pap. 3.95 o.p. (*0-14-011384-3*) Viking Penguin. (Penguin Bks.).

Lasdun, James. The Horned Man: A Novel. 2003. 204p. pap. 13.95 (*0-393-32438-9*); 2002. 208p. 24.95 (*0-393-00336-1*) Norton, W. W. & Co., Inc.

Law, Janice. The Lost Diaires of Iris Weed. Date not set. pap. (*0-7653-0274-8*, Forge Bks.) Doherty, Tom Assocs., LLC.

—The Lost Diaries of Iris Weed. Date not set. mass mkt. (*0-7653-4615-X*); 2002. 320p. 24.95 (*0-7653-0273-X*) Doherty, Tom Assocs., LLC. (Forge Bks.).

Lentricchia, Frank. Lucchesi & the Whale. Fish, Stanley & Jameson, Fredric, eds. 2003. 128p. pap. 16.95 (*0-8223-3171-3*) Duke Univ. Pr.

—Lucchesi & the Whale. 2001. (Post-Contemporary Interventions Ser.). 104p. pap. 24.95 (*0-8223-2654-X*) Duke Univ. Pr.

Llewellyn, Caroline. False Light. l.t. ed. 1997. (Large Print Bks.). pap. 23.95 (*1-56895-403-4*, Wheeler Publishing, Inc.) Gale Group.

Occupations

—False Light. 1996. 315p. 21.50 o.p. (*0-684-82460-4*, Scribner) Simon & Schuster.
Lodge, David. Thinks... 2001. 320p. (*0-436-44502-6*) Secker, Martin & Warburg, Ltd. GBR. *Dist:* Random Hse. of Canada, Ltd.
—Thinks... 2002. 352p. 14.00 (*0-14-200086-8*) Viking Penguin.
—Thinks. . . A Novel. 2001. 288p. 24.95 o.p. (*0-670-89984-4*, Viking) Viking Penguin.
Lorens, M. K. Deception Island. 1990. 240p. mass mkt. 3.95 o.s.i (*0-553-28793-1*) Bantam Bks.
—Dreamland. 1993. 320p. mass mkt. 4.99 o.s.i (*0-553-29437-7*) Bantam Bks.
—Dreamland. 1992. 304p. 16.50 o.s.i (*0-385-42237-7*) Doubleday Publishing.
—Ropedancer's Fall. 1990. 288p. mass mkt. 3.95 o.s.i (*0-553-28312-X*) Bantam Bks.
—Sorrowheart. 1994. (Winston Marlowe Sherman Mystery Ser.). 416p. mass mkt. 4.99 o.s.i (*0-553-29441-5*) Bantam Bks.
—Sorrowheart: A Winston Marlowe Sherman Mystery. 1993. 384p. 17.00 o.s.i (*0-385-46781-8*) Doubleday Publishing.
—Sweet Narcissus. 1989. 288p. mass mkt. 3.95 o.s.i (*0-553-28005-8*) Bantam Bks.
MacLeod, Charlotte. The Corpse in Oozak's Pond. 1987. 224p. 15.45 o.p. (*0-89296-188-0*) Mysterious Pr.
—The Corpse in Oozak's Pond. 1989. 2.99 o.p. (*0-517-00184-5*) Random Hse. Value Publishing.
—The Corpse in Oozak's Pond. 1988. 203p. mass mkt. 5.99 o.p. (*0-445-40683-6*, Mysterious Pr. Paperback Bks.) Warner Bks., Inc.
—Curse of the Giant Hogweed. 1986. (Peter Shandy Ser.). 176p. pap. 3.50 (*0-380-70051-4*, Avon Bks.) Morrow/Avon.
—Exit the Milkman. l.t. ed. 1996. 22.95 o.p. (*1-56895-388-7*, Wheeler Publishing, Inc.) Gale Group.
—Exit the Milkman. 1996. 364p. 21.95 o.s.i (*0-89296-572-X*) Mysterious Pr.
—Exit the Milkman. 1997. 256p. mass mkt. 5.99 o.p. (*0-446-40398-9*) Warner Bks., Inc.
—Exit the Milkman. 2003. 320p. pap. 6.99 (*0-7434-4537-6*) ibooks, Inc.
—The Luck Runs Out. 1981. 192p. pap. 3.50 (*0-380-54171-8*, Avon Bks.) Morrow/Avon.
—An Owl Too Many. l.t. ed. 1991. (General Ser.). 355p. lib. bdg. 20.95 (*0-8161-5235-7*, Macmillan Reference USA) Gale Group.
—An Owl Too Many. 1991. 17.95 o.p. (*0-89296-431-6*) Mysterious Pr.
—An Owl Too Many. 1992. 240p. mass mkt. 4.99 o.p. (*0-446-40101-3*, Mysterious Pr. Paperback Bks.) Warner Bks., Inc.
—Rest You Merry. 1979. (General Ser.). lib. bdg. 13.50 o.p. (*0-8161-3000-0*, Macmillan Reference USA) Gale Group.
—Rest You Merry. 1980. 224p. reprint ed. mass mkt. 4.99 o.p. (*0-380-47530-8*, Avon Bks.) Morrow/Avon.
—Something in the Water. 1994. 272p. 18.95 o.s.i (*0-89296-430-8*) Mysterious Pr.
—Something in the Water. 1995. 240p. mass mkt. 5.50 o.p. (*0-446-40446-2*, Mysterious Pr. Paperback Bks.) Warner Bks., Inc.
—Something the Cat Dragged In. l.t. ed. 1984. (Nightingale Ser.). 10.95 o.p. (*0-8161-3710-2*, Macmillan Reference USA) Gale Group.
—Something the Cat Dragged In. 1984. 208p. mass mkt. 3.99 (*0-380-69096-9*, Avon Bks.) Morrow/Avon.
—Vane Pursuit: A Peter Shandy Mystery. l.t. ed. 1990. 368p. lib. bdg. 19.95 o.p. (*0-8161-4850-3*, Macmillan Reference USA) Gale Group.
—Vane Pursuit: A Peter Shandy Mystery. 1989. 15.95 o.p. (*0-89296-369-7*) Mysterious Pr.
—Vane Pursuit: A Peter Shandy Mystery. 1990. 224p. mass mkt. 5.50 o.p. (*0-445-40780-8*, Mysterious Pr. Paperback Bks.) Warner Bks., Inc.
—Wrack & Rune. 1983. 208p. mass mkt. 3.99 (*0-380-61911-3*, Avon Bks.) Morrow/Avon.
—Wrack & Rune. l.t. ed. 1982. 322p. reprint ed. 11.95 o.p. (*0-89621-372-2*) Thorndike Pr.
Malone, Michael. Foolscap: Or, the Stages of Love. 2002. 400p. pap. 14.95 (*1-57071-757-5*, Sourcebooks Landmark) Sourcebooks, Inc.
Manrique, Jaime. Twilight at the Equator: A Novel. 1997. 224p. 23.95 o.s.i (*0-571-19901-1*) Faber & Faber, Inc.
—Twilight at the Equator: A Novel. 1997. pap. 18.00 (*1-891305-18-2*) Painted Leaf Pr.
—Twilight at the Equator: A Novel. 2003. 198p. pap. 15.95 (*0-299-18774-8*) Univ. of Wisconsin Pr.
Marsigli, Annalita. The Written Script. 1998. 320p. 24.95 (*0-87951-820-0*) Overlook Pr., The.
McCarver, Sam. The Case of Cabin 13. 1999. (John Darnell Mysteries Ser.). 256p. mass mkt. 5.99 o.s.i (*0-451-19690-2*) NAL.
—The Case of Cabin 13: A John Darnell Mystery. l.t. ed. 2000. (Mystery Ser.). 344p. 26.95 (*0-7862-2487-8*) Thorndike Pr.
—Case of Compartment 7. 2000. (John Darnell Mysteries Ser.). 256p. mass mkt. 5.99 o.s.i (*0-451-19959-6*, Signet Bks.) NAL.
McCrumb, Sharyn. Bimbos of the Death Sun. 1996. 224p. mass mkt. 6.50 (*0-345-41215-X*) Ballantine Bks.
—Bimbos of the Death Sun. unabr. ed. 1988. audio 35.00 (*0-7887-3758-9*, 95942E7) Recorded Bks., LLC.
—Bimbos of the Death Sun. 1988. pap. 3.95 o.p. (*0-88038-455-7*) Wizards of the Coast.
—Zombies of the Gene Pool. 1993. 288p. mass mkt. 6.99 (*0-345-37914-4*) Ballantine Bks.
McDermid, Val. Killing the Shadows. l.t. ed. 2002. (Wheeler Large Print Book Ser.). 28.95 (*1-58724-184-6*, Wheeler Publishing, Inc.) Gale Group.
—Killing the Shadows. 2002. 496p. mass mkt. 6.99 (*0-312-98338-7*, St. Martin's Paperbacks) St. Martin's Pr.
McInerny, Ralph. The Book of Kills: A Mystery Set at the University of Notre Dame. E-Book 23.95 (*0-312-27604-4*); 2000. 275p. 23.95 o.p. (*0-312-20346-2*, Saint Martin's Minotaur); 2001. 288p. reprint ed. mass mkt. 6.50 o.s.i (*0-312-97922-3*, St. Martin's Paperbacks) St. Martin's Pr.
—The Book of Kills: A Mystery Set at the University of Notre Dame. 2001. (Basic Ser.). 375p. 28.95 o.p. (*0-7862-3642-6*) Thorndike Pr.
—Celt & Pepper: A Mystery Set at the University of Notre Dame. 2002. 240p. 22.95 (*0-312-29117-5*, Saint Martin's Minotaur) St. Martin's Pr.
—Celt & Pepper: A Mystery Set at the University of Notre Dame. 2003. 28.95 (*0-7862-5179-4*) Thorndike Pr.
—Emerald Aisle: A Mystery Set at the University of Notre Dame. 2002. E-Book 23.95 (*1-59061-743-6*) Adobe Systems, Inc.
—Emerald Aisle: A Mystery Set at the University of Notre Dame. l.t. ed. 2002. 344p. 28.95 (*0-7862-4345-7*) Gale Group.
—Emerald Aisle: A Mystery Set at the University of Notre Dame. mass mkt. (*0-312-98277-1*, St. Martin's Paperbacks); E-Book 23.95 (*0-312-70326-0*); 2001. 288p. 22.95 (*0-312-26938-2*, Saint Martin's Minotaur) St. Martin's Pr.
—Irish Coffee. Date not set. pap. (*0-312-30902-3*, Saint Martin's Griffin); mass mkt. (*0-312-98691-2*, St. Martin's Paperbacks); 2003. 288p. 23.95 (*0-312-30901-5*, Saint Martin's Minotaur) St. Martin's Pr.
—Irish Tenure: A Mystery Set at the University of Notre Dame. 2000. 263p. mass mkt. 5.99 (*0-312-97320-9*, St. Martin's Paperbacks); 1999. 246p. 22.95 o.p. (*0-312-20345-4*, Saint Martin's Minotaur) St. Martin's Pr.
—Irish Tenure: A Mystery Set at the University of Notre Dame. l.t. ed. 2000. (Basic Ser.). 336p. 28.95 (*0-7862-2667-6*) Thorndike Pr.
McKinney, Meagan. Still of the Night. l.t. ed. 2001. (Wheeler Large Print Book Ser.). 424p. 29.95 (*1-58724-132-3*, Wheeler Publishing, Inc.) Gale Group.
—Still of the Night. 2002. 352p. mass mkt. 6.50 o.s.i (*0-8217-6832-8*) Kensington Publishing Corp.
Mendez, Miguel. From Labor to Letters: A Novel Autobiography. Foster, David W., tr. from SPA. 1997. 128p. 20.00 (*0-927534-70-3*); pap. 11.00 (*0-927534-66-5*) Bilingual Pr./Editorial Bilingue.
Merlis, Mark. American Studies. 1994. 288p. 21.95 o.p. (*0-395-68992-9*) Houghton Mifflin Co.
—American Studies. 1996. 286p. reprint ed. pap. 13.00 o.s.i (*0-14-025090-5*) Penguin Group (USA) Inc.
Minear, Lola F. In the Dog House: A Collection of Short Stories. 1981. 47p. 6.95 o.p. (*0-533-04878-8*) Vantage Pr., Inc.
Moore, Jeffrey. Prisoner in a Red-Rose Chain. 2002. 385p. 24.95 o.s.i (*0-399-14864-7*, Putnam & Grosset) Penguin Group (USA) Inc.
Moore, Robin. The Sparrowhook Curse. 1996. 424p. (Orig.). pap. 12.95 (*0-924771-70-4*, Covered Bridge Pr.) Douglas Charles, Ltd.
Moore, Susanna. In the Cut: A Novel. 1999. 192p. pap. 12.95 (*0-452-28129-6*, Plume) Dutton/Plume.
—In the Cut: A Novel. 1995. 177p. 21.00 o.s.i (*0-679-42258-7*) Knopf, Alfred A. Inc.
Moravia, Alberto. The Voyeur. Parks, Tim, tr. from ITA. 1987. 280p. 18.95 o.s.i (*0-374-28544-6*) Farrar, Straus & Giroux.
Morson, Ian. Falconer & the Face of God. 1997. 208p. mass mkt. 5.99 (*0-312-96410-2*, St. Martin's Paperbacks) St. Martin's Pr.
—Falconer & the Face of God: A William Falconer Medieval Mystery. 1997. 192p. text 21.95 o.p. (*0-312-15124-1*, Saint Martin's Minotaur) St. Martin's Pr.
—Falconer & the Great Beast. l.t. unabr. ed. 1998. (Illus.). 272p. 32.50 (*0-7531-5938-4*, 159384) ISIS Large Print Bks. GBR. *Dist:* Ulverscroft Large Print Bks., Ltd., Ulverscroft Large Print Canada, Ltd.
—Falconer & the Great Beast: A Medieval Oxford Mystery. 1999. (Medieval Oxford Mysteries Ser.). (Illus.). 220p. (YA). 21.95 (*0-312-20543-0*, Saint Martin's Minotaur) St. Martin's Pr.
—Falconer's Crusade. 1996. mass mkt. 4.99 (*0-312-95697-5*, St. Martin's Paperbacks); 1995. 190p. 18.95 o.p. (*0-312-11784-1*, Saint Martin's Minotaur) St. Martin's Pr.
—Falconer's Judgement. (Dead Letter Mysteries Ser.). 1997. 224p. mass mkt. 5.99 (*0-312-96151-0*, St. Martin's Paperbacks); 1996. 192p. 20.95 o.p. (*0-312-13971-3*, Saint Martin's Minotaur) St. Martin's Pr.
—A Psalm for Falconer, Vol. 1. Date not set. mass mkt. (*0-312-96534-6*, St. Martin's Paperbacks) St. Martin's Pr.
—A Psalm for Falconer: A William Falconer Medieval Mystery. 1997. 220p. 21.95 o.p. (*0-312-16833-0*, Saint Martin's Minotaur) St. Martin's Pr.
Mouse Works Staff. Flubber. 1997. (J). 6.98 (*1-57082-607-2*) Mouse Works.
Murdoch, Iris. The Book & the Brotherhood. 1989. 624p. pap. 16.00 (*0-14-010470-4*, Penguin Bks.) Penguin Group (USA) Inc.
—The Book & the Brotherhood. 1989. 4.99 o.p. (*0-517-02631-7*) Random Hse. Value Publishing.
—The Book & the Brotherhood. 1988. 19.95 o.p. (*0-670-81912-3*) Viking Penguin.
Nemec, David. Stonesifer. 2001. 276p. pap. 25.00 (*1-885003-19-6*) Reed, Robert D. Pubs.
Nevins, Francis M. Corrupt & Ensnare. 1978. 8.95 o.p. (*0-399-12203-6*) Putnam Publishing Group, The.
—Corrupt & Ensnare. 2000. 232p. pap. 14.95 (*1-58348-998-3*) iUniverse, Inc.
—Into the Same River Twice. 1996. 224p. 21.00 o.p. (*0-7867-0314-8*, Carroll & Graf Pubs.) Avalon Publishing Group.
—Into the Same River Twice. 2000. 228p. pap. 14.95 (*0-595-00001-0*, Authors Choice Pr.) iUniverse, Inc.
—Publish & Perish. 2000. 192p. pap. 12.95 (*0-595-00059-2*) iUniverse, Inc.
Nichols, John. Sterile Cuckoo. 1996. (Norton Paperback Fiction Ser.). 224p. reprint ed. pap. 13.00 (*0-393-31535-5*) Norton, W. W. & Co., Inc.
Palliser, Charles. The Unburied. 1999. 400p. 24.00 (*0-374-28035-5*) Farrar, Straus & Giroux.
—The Unburied. 2000. 432p. reprint ed. pap. 13.95 (*0-7434-1051-3*, Washington Square Pr.) Simon & Schuster.
—The Unburied. l.t. ed. 2000. (Basic Ser.). 655p. 29.95 (*0-7862-2543-2*) Thorndike Pr.
Parkin, Frank. The Mind & Body Shop. 1987. 224p. 14.95 o.p. (*0-689-11895-3*, Scribner) Simon & Schuster.
Parks, Tim. Europa. 1999. 272p. pap. 12.95 (*1-55970-506-X*) Arcade Publishing, Inc.
—Europa. 1997. 261p. (*0-436-20213-1*) Secker, Martin & Warburg, Ltd.
—Europa: A Novel. 1998. 272p. 23.95 (*1-55970-444-6*) Arcade Publishing, Inc.
Peterson, Audrey. Dartmoor Burial. Isaacson, Dana, ed. 1992. 256p. (Orig.). mass mkt. 5.50 o.s.i (*0-671-72970-5*, Pocket) Simon & Schuster.
—Death Too Soon. Isaacson, Dana, ed. 1994. 288p. (Orig.). mass mkt. 4.99 o.s.i (*0-671-79509-0*, Pocket) Simon & Schuster.
—Shroud for a Scholar. 1995. 272p. mass mkt. 5.50 o.s.i (*0-671-79510-4*, Pocket) Simon & Schuster.
Raphael, Lev. Burning down the House: A Nick Hoffman Novel. 2001. 256p. 23.95 (*0-8027-3365-4*) Walker & Co.
—Death of a Constant Lover. 2000. (Nick Hoffman Mystery Ser.). 288p. pap. 12.95 (*0-312-26496-8*, Saint Martin's Griffin) St. Martin's Pr.
—Death of a Constant Lover. 1999. (Nick Hoffman Mystery Ser.). 288p. 22.95 (*0-8027-3326-3*) Walker & Co.
—The Edith Wharton Murders: A Nick Hoffman Mystery. (Stonewall Inn Editions Ser.). 1998. 240p. pap. 11.95 (*0-312-19863-9*, Saint Martin's Griffin); 1997. 208p. 21.95 o.p. (*0-312-15519-0*, Saint Martin's Minotaur) St. Martin's Pr.
—Let's Get Criminal. 1996. 240p. 20.95 o.p. (*0-312-13999-3*, Saint Martin's Minotaur); 2nd ed. 1997. 244p. pap. 11.95 (*0-312-15160-8*, Saint Martin's Griffin) St. Martin's Pr.
—Little Miss Evil: A Nick Hoffman Mystery. 2000. (Nick Hoffman Mystery Ser.). 184p. 23.95 (*0-8027-3342-5*) Walker & Co.
Roth, Philip. The Breast. rev. ed. 1982. pap. 5.95 o.p. (*0-374-51699-5*) Farrar, Straus & Giroux.
—The Breast. 1994. 96p. pap. 11.00 (*0-679-74901-2*, Vintage) Knopf Publishing Group.
—The Breast. 1985. (Fiction Ser.). 96p. pap. 5.95 o.p. (*0-14-007679-4*, Penguin Bks.) Viking Penguin.
—The Dying Animal. 2001. 176p. 22.00 (*0-618-15272-5*); 156p. tchr. ed. 23.00 (*0-618-13587-1*) Houghton Mifflin Co.
—The Dying Animal. 2002. 176p. pap. 12.00 (*0-375-71412-X*) Knopf, Alfred A. Inc.
—The Human Stain. tchr. ed. 234.00 o.p. (*0-618-06598-9*); 2000. 368p. tchr. ed. 26.00 (*0-618-05945-8*) Houghton Mifflin Co.
—The Human Stain. 2001. (International Ser.). 384p. pap. 14.95 (*0-375-72634-9*, Vintage) Knopf Publishing Group.
—The Human Stain. l.t. ed. 2000. (Basic Ser.). 614p. 27.95 (*0-7862-2964-0*) Thorndike Pr.
—Letting Go. 1982. 657p. pap. 9.95 o.s.i (*0-374-51701-0*) Farrar, Straus & Giroux.
—Letting Go. 1997. 640p. pap. 15.00 (*0-679-76417-8*, Vintage) Knopf Publishing Group.
—Letting Go. 1962. 12.50 o.s.i (*0-394-43305-X*) Random Hse., Inc.
—Letting Go. 1991. 640p. pap. 10.95 o.s.i (*0-671-73616-7*, Touchstone) Simon & Schuster.
Rubin, Louis D. The Heat of the Sun. 1995. 448p. 21.95 (*1-56352-233-0*) Longstreet Pr., Inc.
Russell, E. S. Death of a Cloudwalker. 1991. 192p. 18.95 (*0-8027-5784-7*) Walker & Co.
Russo, Richard. The Straight Man. 1998. 416p. pap. 14.00 (*0-375-70190-7*, Vintage) Knopf Publishing Group.
Shaber, Sarah R. Simon Said. (Simon Shaw Mysteries Ser.). 224p. 1998. pap. 5.99 (*0-312-96555-9*, St. Martin's Paperbacks); 1997. 20.95 o.p. (*0-312-15207-8*, Saint Martin's Minotaur) St. Martin's Pr.
—Snipe Hunt. 2000. (Professor Simon Shaw Mysteries Ser.). 288p. 23.95 (*0-312-25337-0*, Saint Martin's Minotaur) St. Martin's Pr.
—Snipe Hunt: A Professor Simon Shaw Mystery. E-Book 6.50 (*0-312-27376-2*); 2001. 304p. reprint ed. mass mkt. 6.50 (*0-312-97470-1*, 20-3260, St. Martin's Paperbacks) St. Martin's Pr.
Shapiro, Lisa. Endless Love. 1998. 256p. pap. 11.95 (*1-56280-213-5*) Naiad Pr., Inc.
Sharpe, Tom. Porterhouse Blue. 1989. 224p. pap. 12.00 (*0-87113-279-6*, Atlantic Monthly Pr.) Grove/Atlantic, Inc.
—Porterhouse Blue. l.t. unabr. ed. 1998. 344p. reprint ed. 19.95 (*1-85089-308-X*, 89308X) ISIS Large Print Bks. GBR. *Dist:* Transaction Pubs.
—Wilt. 1984. pap. 9.00 o.s.i (*0-394-72418-6*) Random Hse., Inc.
—The Wilt Alternative. 1984. 224p. pap. 3.95 o.s.i (*0-394-72621-9*, Vintage) Knopf Publishing Group.
—The Wilt Alternative. 1980. 9.95 o.p. (*0-312-88212-2*) St. Martin's Pr.
—Wilt on High. 1985. 13.95 o.p. (*0-394-54480-3*) Random Hse., Inc.
—Wilt on High: Being the Further Misadventures of One Henry Wilt. 1986. 224p. pap. 4.95 o.s.i (*0-394-74321-0*, Vintage) Knopf Publishing Group.
Shields, Carol. Small Ceremonies. l.t. ed. 1996. (G. K. Hall Core Ser.). 241p. lib. bdg. 24.95 (*0-7838-1830-0*, Macmillan Reference USA) Gale Group.
—Small Ceremonies. 1976. text 7.95 o.p. (*0-07-082340-5*) McGraw-Hill Cos., The.
—Small Ceremonies. 1996. 194p. pap. 12.00 (*0-14-025145-6*, Penguin Bks.) Penguin Group (USA) Inc.
Shreve, Anita. All He Ever Wanted. 2004. (Illus.). 336p. pap. 14.95 (*0-316-73573-6*, Back Bay); 2003. 320p. 25.95 (*0-316-78226-2*); 2003. 496p. 25.95 (*0-316-71112-8*) Little Brown & Co.
Skom, Edith. The Charles Dickens Murders: A Beth Austin Mystery. (Beth Austin Mysteries Ser.). 304p. 1999. mass mkt. 5.99 (*0-440-21776-8*); 1998. 21.95 o.s.i (*0-385-31230-X*) Dell Publishing.
—The George Eliot Murders: A Beth Austin Mystery. (Beth Austin Mysteries Ser.). 1996. 288p. mass mkt. 5.99 o.s.i (*0-440-21775-X*); 1995. 243p. 19.95 o.s.i (*0-385-31228-8*, Delacorte Pr.) Dell Publishing.
—The Mark Twain Murders: A Beth Austin Mystery. 1989. (Brown Bag Mystery Line Ser.). 277p. 12.95 o.p. (*0-933031-17-3*) Council Oak Bks.
—The Mark Twain Murders: A Beth Austin Mystery. 1990. (Beth Austin Mysteries Ser.). 304p. mass mkt. 5.99 o.s.i (*0-440-20608-1*) Dell Publishing.
Skvorecky, Josef. Two Murders in My Double Life. 2001. 175p. 22.00 o.p. (*0-374-28025-8*) Farrar, Straus & Giroux.
—Two Murders in My Double Life. 1999. 183p. pap. (*1-55263-021-8*) Key Porter Bks. CAN. *Dist:* BookWorld Services, Inc.
—Two Murders in My Double Life. 2002. 192p. pap. 12.00 (*0-312-42026-9*) Picador.
Smith, Gregory B. The Divine Comedy of John Venner. 1992. 272p. 20.00 (*0-671-78854-X*, Simon & Schuster) Simon & Schuster.
Soto, Gary. Amnesia in a Republican County: A Novel. 2003. 208p. 23.95 (*0-8263-2931-4*) Univ. of New Mexico Pr.
Tarrant, Desmond. Priceless Souls. 1996. 192p. 16.95 (*0-913720-85-2*) Beil, Frederic C. Pub., Inc.
Tartt, Donna. The Secret History: A Novel. 1996. 592p. pap. 14.95 (*0-449-91151-9*, Fawcett); 1993. 512p. mass mkt. 7.99 (*0-8041-1135-9*, Ivy Bks.) Ballantine Bks.
—The Secret History: A Novel. 1992. 544p. 27.95 (*0-679-41032-5*) Knopf, Alfred A. Inc.

—The Secret History: A Novel. 1994. 6.99 o.p. (*0-517-11658-8*) Random Hse. Value Publishing.

Theroux, Alexander. Darconville's Cat. 1996. 720p. pap. 16.00 o.s.i (*0-8050-4365-9*, Owl Bks.) Holt, Henry & Co.

Thomas-Graham, Pamela. Blue Blood. (Ivy League Mysteries Ser.). 1999. 288p. 23.00 (*0-684-84527-X*, Simon & Schuster); 2000. 320p. reprint ed. pap. 6.99 (*0-671-01671-7*, Pocket) Simon & Schuster.

—A Darker Shade of Crimson: An Ivy League Mystery. (Ivy League Mysteries Ser.). 1999. (Illus.). 416p. pap. 6.99 (*0-671-01670-9*, Pocket); 1998. 288p. 23.00 (*0-684-84526-1*, Simon & Schuster) Simon & Schuster.

Waller, Robert James. Slow Waltz in Cedar Bend. unabr. ed. 1994. audio 30.00 o.p. Books on Tape, Inc.

—Slow Waltz in Cedar Bend. unabr. ed. 1993. audio 22.95 o.p. (*1-55800-876-4*, 592099); audio compact disk 59.95 o.p. (*1-55800-880-2*) NewStar Media, Inc.

—Slow Waltz in Cedar Bend. 1994. 227p. mass mkt. 4.99 o.s.i (*0-446-60164-0*); 1993. 200p. 25.00 (*0-446-51653-8*) Warner Bks., Inc.

—Slow Waltz in Cedar Bend & the Bridges of Madison County. 1993. audio 19.88 o.p. (*1-55800-927-2*, Dove Audio) NewStar Media, Inc.

Wright, Eric. The Kidnapping of Rosie Dawn: A Joe Barley Mystery. 2000. 213p. pap. 12.95 (*1-880284-40-5*, Perseverance Pr.) Daniel, John & Co., Pubs.

—The Kidnapping of Rosie Dawn: A Joe Barley Mystery. l.t. ed. 2001. 306p. 27.95 (*0-7862-3478-4*); 296p. (*0-7540-4673-7*); 296p. (*0-7540-4674-5*) Thorndike Pr.

Yorke, Margaret. Cast for Death. 1996. 18.50 o.p. (*0-7451-8685-8*, Black Dagger) BBC Audiobooks America.

—Cast for Death. 1983. pap. 2.25 o.p. (*0-553-22828-5*) Bantam Bks.

—Cast for Death. l.t. unabr. ed. 1999. 214p. 25.95 (*0-7531-6029-3*, 160293) ISIS Large Print Bks. GBR. *Dist:* ISIS Publishing.

—Cast for Death. l.t. ed. 1980. 12.00 o.p. (*0-7089-0408-4*, Ulverscroft) Thorpe, F. A. Pubs. GBR. *Dist:* Ulverscroft Large Print Bks., Ltd.

—Cast for Death. 1976. 6.95 o.p. (*0-8027-5353-1*) Walker & Co.

—Dead in the Morning. 2000. 224p. 21.95 (*0-7540-8560-0*, Black Dagger) BBC Audiobooks America.

—Dead in the Morning. 1982. pap. 2.25 (*0-553-22858-7*) Bantam Bks.

—Dead in the Morning. unabr. ed. 2000. audio 34.95 (*0-7451-6378-5*, CSL 079) Chivers Audio Bks. GBR. *Dist:* BBC Audiobooks America.

—Dead in the Morning. l.t. ed. 2000. (G. K. Hall Nightingale Ser.). 253p. 30.00 (*0-7838-8760-4*, Macmillan Reference USA) Gale Group.

—Dead in the Morning. l.t. ed. 1975. (Ulverscroft Large Print Ser.). 29.99 o.p. (*0-85456-390-3*, Ulverscroft) Thorpe, F. A. Pubs. GBR. *Dist:* Ulverscroft Large Print Bks., Ltd., Ulverscroft Large Print Canada, Ltd.

—Grave Matters. 1983. pap. 2.50 (*0-553-22914-1*) Bantam Bks.

—Grave Matters. l.t. ed. 1975. (Ulverscroft Large Print Ser.). 29.99 o.p. (*0-85456-333-4*, Ulverscroft) Thorpe, F. A. Pubs. GBR. *Dist:* Ulverscroft Large Print Bks., Ltd., Ulverscroft Large Print Canada, Ltd.

—Mortal Remains. l.t. ed. 1990. 18.95 o.p. (*0-7089-2163-9*, Ulverscroft) Thorpe, F. A. Pubs. GBR. *Dist:* Ulverscroft Large Print Bks., Ltd.

—Silent Witness. l.t. unabr. ed. 1999. 208p. 32.50 o.p. (*0-7531-6028-5*, 160285) ISIS Large Print Bks. GBR. *Dist:* Ulverscroft Large Print Bks., Ltd., Ulverscroft Large Print Canada, Ltd.

—Silent Witness. l.t. ed. 1976. o.p. (*0-85456-455-1*, Ulverscroft) Thorpe, F. A. Pubs.

—Silent Witness. 1975. 5.95 (*0-8027-5318-3*) Walker & Co.

**COMPOSERS—FICTION**

Bassett, Jennifer. The Phantom of the Opera. 1993. (Illus.). 48p. pap. text 5.95 o.p. (*0-19-422707-3*) Oxford Univ. Pr., Inc.

Champion, David. Phantom Virus: A Bomber Hanson Mystery. 1999. 275p. 23.00 (*1-888310-93-6*) Knoll, Allen A. Pubs.

Cobb, Thomas. Crazy Heart. 256p. 1987. 15.95 o.p. (*0-06-015803-4*); 1988. reprint ed. 15.75 (*0-00-002379-5*, PL1519, Perennial); 1988. reprint ed. pap. 7.95 o.p. (*0-06-091519-6*, Perennial) HarperTrade.

—Crazy Heart. unabr. ed. 1989. audio 51.00 (*1-55690-124-0*, 89110E7) Recorded Bks., LLC.

Cowell, Stephanie. Marrying Mozart: A Novel. 2004. 368p. 24.95 (*0-670-03268-9*, Viking) Viking Penguin.

Deverell, William. Platinum Blues. 1990. 18.95 o.s.i (*0-945167-33-4*) British American Publishing, Ltd.

—Platinum Blues. 1996. 261p. mass mkt. 5.95 o.p. (*0-7710-2662-5*) McClelland & Stewart/Tundra Bks.

Forsyth, Frederick. The Phantom of Manhattan. 2000. 320p. mass mkt. 6.50 (*0-312-97585-6*, St. Martin's Paperbacks); 1999. 192p. 19.95 o.p. (*0-312-24656-0*) St. Martin's Pr.

—The Phantom of Manhattan. l.t. ed. (Paperback Bestsellers Ser.). 232p. 2001. 28.95 (*0-7862-2203-4*); 2000. (*0-7540-1395-2*); 2000. (*0-7540-2297-8*); 2000. (Illus.). 30.95 (*0-7862-2202-6*) Thorndike Pr.

Hamilton-Paterson, James. Gerontius. 264p. 1992. 10.95 (*0-939149-69-9*); 1991. 19.95 (*0-939149-48-6*) Soho Pr., Inc.

Hartling, Peter. Schubert. Smith, Rosemary, tr. from GER. 1995. 260p. 27.95 (*0-8419-1347-1*) Holmes & Meier Pubs., Inc.

Harwood, Ronald. Cesar & Augusta. 1980. 10.95 o.p. (*0-316-34991-7*) Little Brown & Co.

Hijuelos, Oscar. A Simple Habana Melody: From When the World Was Good. l.t. ed. 2003. lib. bdg. 29.95 (*1-58547-298-0*, Platinum) Ctr. Point Large Print.

Hijuelos, Oscar. A Simple Habana Melody: From When the World Was Good. 2002. 352p. 24.95 (*0-06-017569-9*) HarperCollins Pubs.

—A Simple Habana Melody: From When the World Was Good. 2003. 368p. pap. 13.95 (*0-06-092869-7*, Perennial) HarperTrade.

Kennedy, Margaret. The Constant Nymph. 1984. 336p. mass mkt. 8.95 o.p. (*0-385-27977-9*) Doubleday Publishing.

—The Constant Nymph. l.t. ed. 1987. (Mainstream Ser.). 250p. lib. bdg. 18.95 o.p. (*1-85089-153-2*) ISIS Large Print Bks. GBR. *Dist:* Transaction Pubs.

—The Constant Nymph. 2001. (Modern Classics). 326p. 13.95 (*0-86068-354-0*) Virago Pr., Ltd. GBR. *Dist:* Trafalgar Square.

Landis, J. D. Longing: A Novel. 2000. 464p. 26.00 o.s.i (*0-15-100453-6*) Harcourt Trade Pubs.

Lenard-Cook, Lisa. Dissonance: A Novel. 2003. 186p. 21.95 (*0-8263-3090-8*) Univ. of New Mexico Pr.

Leroux, Gaston. The Phantom of the Opera. 2002. (World Digital Library). E-Book 3.95 (*0-594-08398-2*) 1873 Pr.

—The Phantom of the Opera. Date not set. lib. bdg. 26.95 (*0-8488-1652-8*) Amereon, Ltd.

—The Phantom of the Opera. 1986. 269p. reprint ed. pap. 3.95 o.p. (*0-88184-249-4*, Carroll & Graf Pubs.) Avalon Publishing Group.

—The Phantom of the Opera. 1990. (Bantam Classics Ser.). 288p. mass mkt. 4.95 (*0-553-21376-8*) Bantam Bks.

—The Phantom of the Opera. E-Book 5.00 (*0-7607-1322-7*) Barnes & Noble, Inc.

—The Phantom of the Opera. 2002. pap. 3.95 (*1-59109-403-8*) Booksurge, LLC.

—The Phantom of the Opera. 1975. lib. bdg. 28.95 (*0-89966-136-X*) Buccaneer Bks., Inc.

—The Phantom of the Opera. E-Book 2.49 (*1-58627-839-8*) Electric Umbrella Publishing.

—The Phantom of the Opera. 1990. 300p. pap. 9.95 o.s.i (*0-87052-937-4*) Hippocrene Bks., Inc.

—The Phantom of the Opera. l.t. ed. 1988. (Mainstream Ser.). 432p. reprint ed. lib. bdg. 18.95 o.p. (*1-85089-234-2*) ISIS Large Print Bks. GBR. *Dist:* Transaction Pubs.

—The Phantom of the Opera, Level 5. 2002. pap. 7.67 (*0-582-50502-X*) Longman Publishing Group.

—The Phantom of the Opera. 1988. (Illus.). 25.00 o.p. (*0-89296-279-8*) Mysterious Pr.

—The Phantom of the Opera. 2001. 288p. mass mkt. 4.95 (*0-451-52815-8*, Signet Classics); 1989. 288p. mass mkt. 4.95 o.s.i (*0-451-52482-9*, Signet Classics); 1987. mass mkt. 4.50 o.p. (*0-451-52432-2*, Signet Classics); 1987. mass mkt. 3.95 o.p. (*0-451-52173-0*) NAL.

—The Phantom of the Opera. 1989. (Bullseye Chillers Ser.). (Illus.). 96p. (J). (gr. 3-7). 5.99 o.s.i (*0-394-93847-X*, Random Hse. Bks. for Young Readers) Random Hse. Children's Bks.

—The Phantom of the Opera. 2002. (Modern Library Classics). 320p. pap. 8.95 (*0-375-76113-6*) Random Hse., Inc.

—The Phantom of the Opera. 1938. 10.60 o.p. (*0-606-03258-4*) Turtleback Bks.

—The Phantom of the Opera. 1995. mass mkt. 5.95 (*0-352-31716-7*) Virgin Bks. GBR. *Dist:* London Bridge.

—The Phantom of the Opera. 1986. 272p. mass mkt. 5.99 (*0-446-30120-5*) Warner Bks., Inc.

—The Phantom of the Opera. 1998. (Classics Library). 224p. pap. 3.95 (*1-85326-273-0*, 2730WW) Wordsworth Editions, Ltd. GBR. *Dist:* Combined Publishing.

—The Phantom of the Opera: The Original Novel. 1988. 368p. reprint ed. mass mkt. 7.00 (*0-06-080924-8*, PL-7140, Perennial) HarperTrade.

—The Phantom of the Opera: The Play. 1979. pap. 5.60 (*0-87129-363-3*, P45) Dramatic Publishing Co.

MacLaverty, Bernard. Grace Notes: A Novel. 1998. 288p. pap. 13.00 (*0-393-31841-9*, Norton Paperbacks); 1997. 224p. 23.00 (*0-393-04542-0*) Norton, W. W. & Co., Inc.

—Grace Notes: A Novel. 1997. 277p. o.p. (*0-224-04429-X*) Random Hse. UK, Ltd.

Miller, Christopher. Simon Silber: Works for Solo Piano. 2002. 240p. tchr. ed. 23.00 (*0-618-14336-X*) Houghton Mifflin Co.

Paul, Barbara. A Cadenza for Caruso: An Operatic Mystery. l.t. ed. 1986. (Nightingale Ser.). 227p. 10.95 o.p. (*0-8161-3781-1*, Macmillan Reference USA) Gale Group.

—A Cadenza for Caruso: An Operatic Mystery. 1986. mass mkt. 2.95 o.p. (*0-451-14523-2*, Signet Bks.) NAL.

—A Cadenza for Caruso: An Operatic Mystery. 1984. 175p. 11.95 o.p. (*0-312-11328-5*) St. Martin's Pr.

The Phantom of the Opera. 1998. 16p. pap. 6.95 (*0-7935-9664-5*) Leonard, Hal Corp.

Purdy, James. Out with the Stars. 1993. 192p. pap. 9.95 o.p. (*0-87286-284-4*) City Lights Bks.

Ridley, Ruth Ann. Bach's Passion: The Life of Johann Sebastian Bach - a Novel. 1999. 400p. pap. 16.99 o.p. (*1-57921-170-4*) WinePress Publishing.

Riley, Philip J. The Phantom of the Opera: The Original Shooting Script. Conforti, John, ed. 1999. (Universal Filmscript Series: Classic Silents: 1). (Illus.). pap. text 24.95 (*1-882127-33-1*) Magicimage Filmbooks.

Roberts, Nora. Tears of the Moon. 2000. 384p. mass mkt. 7.99 (*0-515-12854-6*, Jove) Berkley Publishing Group.

—Tears of the Moon. abr. ed. 2000. (Irish Jewels Trilogy Ser.). audio 24.95 o.p. (*1-56740-870-2*, 1913, Nova Audio Bks.); 10p. audio 73.25 (*1-56740-692-0*, 1911, Unabridged Library Editions); audio 32.95 (*1-56740-469-3*, 1910, Brilliance Audio Unabridged) Brilliance Audio.

—Tears of the Moon. l.t. ed. 2000. (Core Ser.). 400p. 31.95 (*0-7838-8991-7*); (Illus.). pap. 29.95 (*0-7838-8992-5*) Thorndike Pr.

Robinette, Joseph & Chauls, Robert. The Phantom of the Opera: Musical. 1992. pap. 5.95 (*0-87129-173-8*, P08) Dramatic Publishing Co.

Ross-Russell, Noel, contrib. by. A Voice Within. 1998. (*1-871871-39-5*) Open Gate Pr. GBR. *Dist:* Paul & Co. Pubs. Consortium, Inc.

Rudel, Anthony J. Imagining Don Giovanni. 2001. 288p. 24.00 (*0-87113-827-1*, Atlantic Monthly Pr.) Grove/Atlantic, Inc.

Rushdie, Salman. The Ground Beneath Her Feet: A Novel. l.t. ed. 2000. (Thorndike/G. K. Hall Paperback Bestsellers Ser.). 816p. pap. 30.95 (*0-7838-8712-4*, Macmillan Reference USA) Gale Group.

—The Ground Beneath Her Feet: A Novel. 1999. 592p. 27.50 o.s.i (*0-8050-5308-5*) Holt, Henry & Co.

—The Ground Beneath Her Feet: A Novel. abr. ed. 1999. audio 25.00 (*0-7871-1917-2*, Dove Audio) NewStar Media, Inc.

—The Ground Beneath Her Feet: A Novel. 2000. 592p. pap. 16.00 (*0-312-25499-7*) Picador.

—The Ground Beneath Her Feet: A Novel. unabr. ed. 1999. audio 104.00 (*0-7887-3747-3*, 95939E5); audio 163.00 (*0-7887-4350-3*, 95939E7) Recorded Bks., LLC.

—The Ground Beneath Her Feet: A Novel. l.t. ed. 1999. (G. K. Hall Core Ser.). 816p. 31.95 (*0-7838-8713-2*) Thorndike Pr.

Segal, Susan. Aria: Novel. 2001. 23.95 (*1-882593-45-6*) Bridge Works Publishing Co., Inc.

Siciliano, Sam. The Angel of the Opera: Sherlock Holmes Meets the Phantom of the Opera. 1994. 272p. 21.95 (*1-883402-46-8*, Scribner) Simon & Schuster.

Slater, Harrison Gradwell. Night Music. 2003. 576p. pap. 14.95 (*0-451-20972-9*) NAL.

Snyder, Keith. Coffin's Got the Dead Guy on the Inside. l.t. ed. 1998. (Jason Keltner Mysteries Ser.). 300p. 22.95 (*0-8027-3320-4*) Walker & Co.

—Show Control. 1996. 267p. 20.95 o.p. (*1-885173-11-3*) Write Way Publishing.

—Trouble Comes Back. 1999. (Jason Keltner Mysteries Ser.). 318p. 22.95 (*0-8027-3338-7*) Walker & Co.

Stafford, Joyce T. Mozart & Me. 2003. 720p. 29.95 (*1-929490-05-4*) Beil, Frederic C. Pub., Inc.

Trotter, William R. Winter Fire. 2003. 464p. pap. 14.00 (*0-7867-1257-0*) Avalon Publishing Group.

—Winter Fire. 1993. 496p. 22.00 o.p. (*0-525-93581-9*) Dutton/Plume.

—Winter Fire. 1994. 464p. mass mkt. 4.99 o.p. (*0-451-17718-5*, Signet Bks.) NAL.

Westmacott, Mary, pseud. Absent in the Spring: And Other Novels. 2001. (Mary Westmacott Omnibus Ser.: No. 1). 576p. pap. 18.95 (*0-312-27322-3*, Saint Martin's Griffin) St. Martin's Pr.

Wilson, Edmund. The Higher Jazz. Reinitz, Neale, ed. 1998. 224p. pap. 17.95 (*0-87745-655-0*); text 34.95 (*0-87745-653-4*) Univ. of Iowa Pr.

**COMPUTER INDUSTRY—FICTION**

Scoville, Thomas. Silicon Follies: A Dot.Comedy. 2002. 336p. pap. 13.00 (*0-7434-1121-8*, Washington Square Pr.); 2001. 336p. 23.95 o.s.i (*0-7434-1120-X*, Atria); 2001. reprint ed. E-Book 22.95 (*0-7434-1945-6*, Atria) Simon & Schuster.

Shuster, Bud. Chances. 2002. 240p. 24.95 (*1-57249-314-3*, Burd Street Pr.) White Mane Publishing Co., Inc.

Ullman, Ellen. The Bug. 2003. 368p. 23.95 (*0-385-50860-3*, Talese, Nan A.) Doubleday Publishing.

—The Bug. 2004. 368p. pap. 13.95 (*1-4000-3235-0*, Anchor) Knopf Publishing Group.

**CRIME AND CRIMINALS—FICTION**

Alibrandi, Tom. Killshot. 1979. pap. 2.25 o.p. (*0-523-40375-5*, Pinnacle Bks.) Kensington Publishing Corp.

Allen, Tricia. A Well-Respected Dead Man. 2003. (Five Star First Edition Mystery Ser.). 319p. 25.95 (*0-7862-5441-6*, Five Star) Gale Group.

Arnott, Jake. He Kills Coppers: A Novel. 2002. 336p. pap. 13.00 (*0-15-602693-7*, Harvest Bks.) Harcourt Trade Pubs.

—He Kills Coppers: A Novel. 2002. 340p. 25.00 (*1-56947-271-8*) Soho Pr., Inc.

—The Long Firm. 2001. 343p. reprint ed. 25.00 (*1-56947-169-X*) Soho Pr., Inc.

Bendis, Brian Michael & Andreyko, Marc. Torso: The Definitive Collection. 2001. (Illus.). 280p. pap. 24.95 (*1-58240-174-8*) Image Comics.

Blauner, Peter. Casino Moon. 1996. 320p. mass mkt. 5.99 o.p. (*0-380-72589-4*, Avon Bks.) Morrow/Avon.

—Casino Moon. 1994. 288p. 21.00 o.p. (*0-671-88177-9*, Simon & Schuster) Simon & Schuster.

Block, Lawrence. The Burglar in the Closet. 1997. (Bernie Rhodenbarr Mystery Ser.: No. 2). 320p. mass mkt. 6.99 (*0-451-18074-7*, Signet Bks.) NAL.

—The Burglar in the Closet. 1978. (Bernie Rhodenbarr Mystery Ser.: No. 2). 6.95 o.p. (*0-394-42374-7*) Random Hse., Inc.

—The Burglar in the Closet. 1986. (Bernie Rhodenbarr Mystery Ser.: No. 2). mass mkt. 3.50 o.s.i (*0-671-61704-4*, Pocket) Simon & Schuster.

—The Burglar in the Closet. l.t. ed. 1996. (Bernie Rhodenbarr Mystery Ser.: No. 2). 277p. 25.95 o.p. (*0-7862-0548-2*) Thorndike Pr.

—The Burglar in the Library. 1997. (Bernie Rhodenbarr Mystery Ser.: No. 8). 320p. 23.95 o.p. (*0-525-94301-3*, Dutton) Dutton/Plume.

—The Burglar in the Library. 1998. (Bernie Rhodenbarr Mystery Ser.: No. 8). 368p. mass mkt. 6.99 (*0-451-40783-0*, Signet Bks.) NAL.

—The Burglar in the Library. l.t. ed. 1998. (Bernie Rhodenbarr Mystery Ser.: No. 8). 464p. 27.95 o.p. (*0-7862-1280-2*) Thorndike Pr.

—The Burglar in the Library. abr. ed. 1997. (Bernie Rhodenbarr Mystery Ser.: No. 8). 2p. audio 16.95 (*0-14-086582-9*, Penguin AudioBooks) Viking Penguin.

—The Burglar Who Dropped in on Elvis. unabr. ed. 1999. audio 5.99 (*1-55204-601-X*, PAC-8601) Durkin Hayes Publishing Ltd.

—The Burglar Who Liked to Quote Kipling. 1997. (Bernie Rhodenbarr Mystery Ser.: No. 3). 320p. mass mkt. 6.99 o.s.i (*0-451-18075-5*, Signet Bks.) NAL.

—The Burglar Who Liked to Quote Kipling. 1979. (Bernie Rhodenbarr Mystery Ser.: No. 3). 7.95 o.p. (*0-394-50417-8*) Random Hse., Inc.

—The Burglar Who Liked to Quote Kipling. 1998. (Bernie Rhodenbarr Mystery Ser.: No. 3). audio 44.00 (*0-7887-0810-4*, 94959E7 ) Recorded Bks., LLC.

—The Burglar Who Liked to Quote Kipling. 1986. (Bernie Rhodenbarr Mystery Ser.: No. 3). mass mkt. 3.50 o.s.i (*0-671-61831-8*, Pocket) Simon & Schuster.

—The Burglar Who Liked to Quote Kipling. abr. ed. 1996. (Bernie Rhodenbarr Mystery Ser.: No. 3). audio 16.95 o.s.i (*0-14-086345-1*, Penguin AudioBooks) Viking Penguin.

—The Burglar Who Painted Like Mondrian. 1998. (Bernie Rhodenbarr Mystery Ser.: No. 5). 224p. 23.95 o.p. (*0-525-94382-X*) Dutton/Plume.

—The Burglar Who Painted Like Mondrian. 1983. (Bernie Rhodenbarr Mystery Ser.: No. 5). 217p. 14.50 o.p. (*0-87795-517-4*, Morrow, William & Co.) Morrow/Avon.

—The Burglar Who Painted Like Mondrian. 1999. (Bernie Rhodenbarr Mystery Ser.: No. 5). 320p. reprint ed. mass mkt. 6.99 o.p. (*0-451-18076-3*, Signet Bks.) NAL.

—The Burglar Who Painted Like Mondrian. unabr. ed. 1993. (Bernie Rhodenbarr Mystery Ser.: No. 5). audio 46.00 (*0-7887-3214-5*, 95846E7) Recorded Bks., LLC.

—The Burglar Who Painted Like Mondrian. abr. ed. 1998. (Bernie Rhodenbarr Mystery Ser.: No. 5). 2p. audio 17.95 o.p. (*0-14-086817-8*, Penguin AudioBooks) Viking Penguin.

—The Burglar Who Studied Spinoza. 1997. (Bernie Rhodenbarr Mystery Ser.: No. 4). 240p. 23.95 o.s.i (*0-525-94180-0*, Signet Bks.) Dutton/Plume.

—The Burglar Who Studied Spinoza. l.t. ed. 1998. (Bernie Rhodenbarr Mystery Ser.: No. 4). 26.95 (*1-56895-602-9*, Wheeler Publishing, Inc.) Gale Group.

—The Burglar Who Studied Spinoza. 1998. (Bernie Rhodenbarr Mystery Ser.: No. 4). 320p. mass mkt. 6.99 o.s.i (*0-451-19488-8*, Signet Bks.) NAL.

—The Burglar Who Studied Spinoza. 1981. (Bernie Rhodenbarr Mystery Ser.: No. 4). 8.95 o.p. (*0-394-51065-8*) Random Hse., Inc.

—The Burglar Who Studied Spinoza. 1986. (Bernie Rhodenbarr Mystery Ser.: No. 4). mass mkt. 3.50 o.s.i (*0-671-62485-7*, Pocket) Simon & Schuster.

—The Burglar Who Thought He Was Bogart. unabr. ed. 1997. (Bernie Rhodenbarr Mystery Ser.: No. 7). audio 44.95 (*0-7861-1196-8*, 1957) Blackstone Audio Bks., Inc.

—The Burglar Who Thought He Was Bogart. 1996. (Bernie Rhodenbarr Mystery Ser.: No. 7). 384p. mass mkt. 6.99 o.s.i (*0-451-18634-6*, Onyx) NAL.

—The Burglar Who Thought He Was Bogart. unabr. ed. 1997. (Bernie Rhodenbarr Mystery Ser.: No. 7). audio 51.00 (*0-7887-0476-1*, 94669E7) Recorded Bks., LLC.

—The Burglar Who Thought He Was Bogart. abr. ed. 1995. (Bernie Rhodenbarr Mystery Ser.: No. 7). audio 16.95 o.s.i (*0-14-086190-4*, Penguin Audio-Books) Viking Penguin.

—The Burglar Who Traded Ted Williams. unabr. ed. 1997. (Bernie Rhodenbarr Mystery Ser.: No. 6). audio 44.95 (*0-7861-1166-6*, 1937) Blackstone Audio Bks., Inc.

—The Burglar Who Traded Ted Williams. 1994. (Bernie Rhodenbarr Mystery Ser.: No. 6). 272p. 19.95 o.p. (*0-525-93807-9*, Dutton) Dutton/Plume.

—The Burglar Who Traded Ted Williams. 1995. (Bernie Rhodenbarr Mystery Ser.: No. 6). 384p. mass mkt. 6.99 o.s.i (*0-451-18426-2*, Onyx) NAL.

—The Burglar Who Traded Ted Williams. abr. ed. 1994. (Bernie Rhodenbarr Mystery Ser.: No. 6). pap. 16.00 o.p. incl. audio (*0-453-00890-9*, 25024-31224) Penguin/HighBridge.

—The Burglar Who Traded Ted Williams. unabr. ed. 1994. (Bernie Rhodenbarr Mystery Ser.: No. 6). audio 51.00 (*0-7887-1302-7*, 95138E7) Recorded Bks., LLC.

—Burglars Can't Be Choosers. 1978. (Bernie Rhodenbarr Mystery Ser.: No. 1). pap. 1.75 o.s.i (*0-515-04584-5*, Jove) Berkley Publishing Group.

—Burglars Can't Be Choosers. unabr. ed. 1997. (Bernie Rhodenbarr Mystery Ser.: No. 1). audio 39.95 (*0-7861-1136-4*, 755302) Blackstone Audio Bks., Inc.

—Burglars Can't Be Choosers. 1995. (Bernie Rhodenbarr Mystery Ser.: No. 1). 256p. 19.95 o.p. (*0-525-93943-1*, Dutton) Dutton/Plume.

—Burglars Can't Be Choosers. 2004. 320p. mass mkt. 6.99 (*0-06-058255-3*, HarperTorch) Morrow/Avon.

—Burglars Can't Be Choosers. 1995. (Bernie Rhodenbarr Mystery Ser.: No. 1). 304p. mass mkt. 5.99 o.s.i (*0-451-18073-9*, Signet Bks.) NAL.

—Burglars Can't Be Choosers. abr. ed. 1995. (Bernie Rhodenbarr Mystery Ser.: No. 1). pap. 16.95 o.p. incl. audio (*0-453-00932-8*, 25024-39151) Penguin/HighBridge.

—Burglars Can't Be Choosers. 1977. (Bernie Rhodenbarr Mystery Ser.: No. 1). (Illus.). 6.95 o.p. (*0-394-41183-8*) Random Hse., Inc.

—Burglars Can't Be Choosers. unabr. ed. 1998. (Bernie Rhodenbarr Mystery Ser.: No. 1). audio 44.00 (*0-7887-1990-4*, 95377E7) Recorded Bks., LLC.

Bowker, David. The Death You Deserve: A Novel. 2003. 256p. pap. 12.95 (*0-312-31178-8*, Saint Martin's Griffin) St. Martin's Pr.

Breslin, Jimmy. The Gang That Couldn't Shoot Straight. 1997. 256p. pap. 12.95 (*0-316-11174-0*, Back Bay) Little Brown & Co.

—The Gang That Couldn't Shoot Straight. l.t. ed. 2001. (G. K. Hall Paperback Ser.). 328p. 24.95 (*0-7838-9391-4*) Thorndike Pr.

—The Gang That Couldn't Shoot Straight. 1987. 256p. mass mkt. 4.50 o.p. (*0-14-010308-2*, Penguin Bks.); 1969. 5.95 o.p. (*0-670-33396-4*) Viking Penguin.

Brooks, Bill. Pretty Boy. 2003. 352p. 24.95 (*0-7653-0473-2*, Forge Bks.) Doherty, Tom Assocs., LLC.

Broussard, John. The Death of the Tin Man's Wife. 2001. 218p. E-Book (*0-9707413-2-4*) Shyflower Pr., The.

Bruen, Ken. London Boulevard. 2002. 238p. 29.95 (*1-899344-76-4*); pap. 14.95 (*1-899344-77-2*) Do-Not Pr., The GBR. *Dist:* Dufour Editions, Inc.

Bunker, Edward. Dog Eat Dog. 240p. 1997. pap. 13.95 (*0-312-16818-7*, Saint Martin's Griffin); 1996. 22.95 o.p. (*0-312-14314-1*) St. Martin's Pr.

Carcaterra, Lorenzo. Gangster. l.t. ed. 2001. 583p. 30.95 (*0-7838-9499-6*, Macmillan Reference USA) Gale Group.

Carey, Peter. Jack Maggs. 1999. 368p. pap. 13.00 (*0-679-76037-7*, Vintage) Knopf Publishing Group.

—Jack Maggs. 1998. 309p. 24.00 (*0-679-44008-9*) Knopf, Alfred A. Inc.

—Jack Maggs. l.t. ed. 1998. (Core Ser.). 535p. 28.95 (*0-7838-0285-4*) Thorndike Pr.

—Jack Maggs. 1998. 417p. pap. 16.95 (*0-7022-3049-9*) Univ. of Queensland Pr. AUS. *Dist:* International Specialized Bk. Services.

—True History of the Kelly Gang. 2001. (Illus.). 368p. 25.00 (*0-375-41084-8*) Knopf, Alfred A. Inc.

—True History of the Kelly Gang. 2000. (Illus.). 400p. pap. 30.00 (*0-7022-3188-6*) Univ. of Queensland Pr. AUS. *Dist:* International Specialized Bk. Services.

—True History of the Kelly Gang: A Novel. 2001. (Illus.). 384p. reprint ed. pap. 14.00 (*0-375-72467-2*, Vintage) Knopf Publishing Group.

Cheatham, Tony M. Father's Footsteps. Morton, Randolph B. & Cadet, Guichard, eds. 2002. 300p. pap. 15.00 (*0-9718191-1-4*) La Caille Nous Publishing Co.

Child, Lincoln. Utopia: A Novel. 2002. (Illus.). 400p. 24.95 (*0-385-50668-6*) Doubleday Publishing.

Chute, Carolyn. Snow Man. 256p. 2001. (Illus.). pap. 14.00 (*0-15-601140-9*, Harvest Bks.); 1999. 23.00 o.s.i (*0-15-100390-4*) Harcourt Trade Pubs.

Clarke, George Elliott. Beatrice Chancy. 1999. (Illus.). 160p. pap. 14.95 (*1-896095-94-1*, Polestar Book Pubs.) Raincoast Bk. Distribution CAN. *Dist:* Orca Bk. Pubs.

Collins, Jackie. Lethal Seduction. 2003. E-Book 26.00 (*0-7432-1112-X*); 2000. 480p. 26.00 (*0-684-85031-1*) Simon & Schuster. (Simon & Schuster).

—Lethal Seduction. l.t. ed. 2001. 720p. 32.50 o.p. (*0-7432-0425-5*) Thorpe, F. A. Pubs. GBR. *Dist:* Ulverscroft Large Print Bks., Ltd.

Collins, Max Allan. Bait Money, No. 1. 1981. 192p. pap. 1.95 o.p. (*0-523-41159-6*, Pinnacle Bks.) Kensington Publishing Corp.

—Blood Money. rev. ed. 1981. 192p. pap. 1.95 o.p. (*0-523-41160-X*, Pinnacle Bks.) Kensington Publishing Corp.

—The Broker's Wife. 1976. (Quarry Ser.). 1.50 o.p. (*0-425-03187-X*) Berkley Publishing Group.

—Fly Paper. 1981. 192p. pap. 1.95 o.p. (*0-523-41161-8*, Pinnacle Bks.) Kensington Publishing Corp.

—Hush Money. 1981. (Nolan Ser.: No.4). 192p. pap. 1.95 o.p. (*0-523-41162-6*, Pinnacle Bks.) Kensington Publishing Corp.

—Primary Target. 1987. (Quarry Novel Ser.). 208p. 14.95 o.p. (*0-88150-098-4*) Countryman Pr.

—Quarry. 1985. (Quarry Ser.). 224p. pap. 4.95 o.p. (*0-88150-057-7*) Countryman Pr.

—Quarry's Cut. 1986. (Quarry Ser.). 224p. reprint ed. pap. 4.95 o.p. (*0-88150-069-0*) Countryman Pr.

—Quarry's Deal. 1986. (Quarry Ser.). 192p. reprint ed. pap. 4.95 o.p. (*0-88150-068-2*) Countryman Pr.

—Quarry's List. 1985. (Quarry Ser.). 192p. pap. 4.95 o.p. (*0-88150-058-5*) Countryman Pr.

—Scratch Fever. 1982. 192p. pap. 1.95 o.p. (*0-523-41164-2*, Pinnacle Bks.) Kensington Publishing Corp.

—Spree. 320p. 1988. pap. 3.95 o.p. (*0-8125-0165-9*); 1987. 15.95 o.p. (*0-312-93029-1*) Doherty, Tom Assocs., LLC. (Tor Bks.).

Collins, Max Allan & Gelb, Jeff, eds. Flesh & Blood: Erotic Tales of Crime & Passion. 2001. 368p. pap. 12.95 (*0-446-67777-9*) Warner Bks., Inc.

Condon, Richard. Prizzi's Family. 1987. 320p. mass mkt. 4.50 o.s.i (*0-515-09106-5*, Jove) Berkley Publishing Group.

—Prizzi's Family. unabr. collector's ed. 1991. audio 40.00 (*0-7366-2009-5*, 2825) Books on Tape, Inc.

—Prizzi's Family. 1986. 17.95 o.p. (*0-399-13210-4*) Putnam Publishing Group, The.

—Prizzi's Glory. unabr. collector's ed. 1991. audio 48.00 (*0-7366-2076-1*, 2882) Books on Tape, Inc.

—Prizzi's Glory. 1988. 17.95 o.p. (*0-525-24689-4*, Dutton) Dutton/Plume.

—Prizzi's Glory. 1990. 368p. mass mkt. 4.95 o.p. (*0-451-16468-7*, NAL Bks.) NAL.

—Prizzi's Honor. 1986. 320p. mass mkt. 4.95 o.p. (*0-425-09507-X*) Berkley Publishing Group.

—Prizzi's Honor. unabr. collector's ed. 1985. audio 56.00 (*0-7366-0837-0*, 1788) Books on Tape, Inc.

—Prizzi's Honor, Set. abr. ed. 1987. audio 16.99 (*0-88646-193-6*, 7194) Durkin Hayes Publishing Ltd.

—Prizzi's Honor. 1982. 320p. 13.95 o.p. (*0-698-11143-5*) Putnam Publishing Group, The.

—Prizzi's Honor. l.t. ed. 1982. 480p. reprint ed. 14.95 o.p. (*0-89621-403-6*) Thorndike Pr.

—Prizzi's Money. 1995. 384p. mass mkt. 5.99 o.s.i (*0-7860-0167-4*) Kensington Publishing Corp.

Connelly, Michael. Void Moon. l.t. ed. 2000. 592p. 25.00 (*0-375-40862-2*) Random Hse. Large Print.

Connelly, Michael, contrib. by. Angels Flight. 1999. (*0-7540-1281-6*) BBC Audiobooks America.

Copeland, Lori. Child of Grace. 2001. 256p. pap. 11.99 (*0-8423-4260-5*) Tyndale Hse. Pubs.

Curry, John A. Two & Out. 2001. 304p. pap. 22.95 (*0-7596-6965-1*) 1stBooks Library.

Dalby, Richard, ed. Crime for Christmas. 1993. mass mkt. 4.99 o.p. (*0-312-95148-5*, St. Martin's Paperbacks); 1992. 288p. 18.95 o.p. (*0-312-08170-7*, Saint Martin's Minotaur) St. Martin's Pr.

Dezenhall, Eric. Money Wanders. E-Book 13.95 (*0-312-70428-3*); 2002. 338p. 24.95 (*0-312-28275-3*) St. Martin's Pr.

Dickens, Charles. Oliver Twist. 2002. (World Digital Library). E-Book 3.95 (*0-594-08303-6*) 1873 Pr.

—Oliver Twist. unabr. ed. 1963. (Classics Ser.). mass mkt. 3.50 (*0-8049-0009-4*, CL-9) Airmont Publishing Co., Inc.

—Oliver Twist. Date not set. 478p. 30.95 (*0-8488-2536-5*) Amereon, Ltd.

—Oliver Twist. l.t. ed. 1999. 657p. pap. 24.95 (*1-55701-274-1*) BNI Pubns., Inc.

—Oliver Twist. 1982. (Bantam Classics Ser.). 448p. mass mkt. 4.95 (*0-553-21102-1*, Bantam Classics) Bantam Bks.

—Oliver Twist. (J). E-Book 5.00 (*0-7607-1286-7*) Barnes & Noble, Inc.

—Oliver Twist. rev. ed. 2000. 500p. per. 14.00 (*1-58396-003-1*) Blue Unicorn Editions.

—Oliver Twist. 1982. reprint ed. lib. bdg. 28.95 (*0-89966-372-9*) Buccaneer Bks., Inc.

—Oliver Twist. (Early Best Sellers Ser.). reprint ed. lib. bdg. 48.00 (*0-7426-1017-9*); lib. bdg. 98.00 (*0-7426-2308-4*); 2001. (Illus.). pap. text 28.00 (*0-7426-7308-1*); 2001. (Illus.). pap. text 28.00 (*0-7426-6017-6*) Classic Bks.

—Oliver Twist. l.t. ed. 1999. 657p. pap. 24.95 (*1-58855-016-8*) Cyber Classics, Inc.

—Oliver Twist. 1998. 496p. mass mkt. 4.99 (*0-8125-8003-6*, Tor Classics) Doherty, Tom Assocs., LLC.

—Oliver Twist. 2002. (Thrift Editions Ser.). 384p. pap. 3.00 (*0-486-42453-7*) Dover Pubns., Inc.

—Oliver Twist. 1972. 2.95 o.p. (*0-460-01233-9*); 1957. 12.95 o.p. (*0-460-00233-3*) Dutton/Plume. (Dutton).

—Oliver Twist. (SPA.). pap. (*968-416-762-8*, 884) Fernandez USA Publishing.

—Oliver Twist. 2003. (Barnes & Noble Classics Ser.). 560p. pap. 4.95 (*1-59308-030-1*) Fine Communications.

—Oliver Twist. l.t. ed. 2002. 637p. 28.95 (*0-7862-4325-2*) Gale Group.

—Oliver Twist. 1988. (SPA.). 448p. (*84-320-3993-4*) GeoPlaneta, Editorial, S. A.

—Oliver Twist. 1991. (Complete Novels of Charles Dickens Ser.). (Illus.). 472p. (C). pap. 3.95 o.p. (*0-7493-0755-2*, A0527) Heinemann.

—Oliver Twist. l.t. ed. 1021p. pap. 71.03 (*0-7583-1731-X*); 797p. pap. 59.53 (*0-7583-1730-1*); 582p. pap. 41.94 (*0-7583-1729-8*); 1306p. pap. 84.84 (*0-7583-1732-8*); 466p. pap. 35.36 (*0-7583-1728-X*); 2293p. pap. 143.93 (*0-7583-1735-2*); 1976p. pap. 121.94 (*0-7583-1734-4*); 1607p. pap. 107.34 (*0-7583-1733-6*); 797p. lib. bdg. 71.53 (*0-7583-1722-0*); 2293p. lib. bdg. 172.68 (*0-7583-1727-1*); 1976p. lib. bdg. 142.75 (*0-7583-1726-3*); 1607p. lib. bdg. 125.34 (*0-7583-1725-5*); 582p. lib. bdg. 47.94 (*0-7583-1721-2*); 1306p. lib. bdg. 96.84 (*0-7583-1724-7*); 1021p. lib. bdg. 83.03 (*0-7583-1723-9*); 466p. lib. bdg. 41.36 (*0-7583-1720-4*) Huge Print Pr.

—Oliver Twist. 2002. 448p. 98.99 (*1-4043-2242-6*); per. 93.99 (*1-4043-2243-4*) IndyPublish.com.

—Oliver Twist. Ba'Albaki, Munir, tr. 1982. (ARA.). 200p. pap. 14.95 (*0-86685-138-0*) International Bk. Ctr., Inc.

—Oliver Twist. 1992. (Everyman's Library). 528p. 20.00 (*0-679-41724-9*) Knopf, Alfred A. Inc.

—Oliver Twist. 1999. (Cloth Bound Pocket Ser.). (Illus.). 7.95 (*3-8290-3004-5*, 521121) Konemann.

—Oliver Twist. 1996. (Longman Fiction Ser.). pap. text 5.90 o.s.i (*0-582-27519-9*) Longman Publishing Group.

—Oliver Twist. Adams, Richard, ed. 1988. (Study Texts Ser.). pap. text 5.95 (*0-582-33150-1*, 72056) Longman Publishing Group.

—Oliver Twist. 1988. (English As a Second Language Bk.). pap. text 4.46 net. (*0-582-53496-8*, 74097) Longman Publishing Group.

—Oliver Twist. E-Book 1.95 (*1-58515-055-X*) MesaView, Inc.

—Oliver Twist. 1994. (Books of Wonder). (Illus.). 464p. 20.00 (*0-688-12911-0*, Morrow, William & Co.) Morrow/Avon.

—Oliver Twist. 1970. mass mkt. 0.60 o.p. (*0-451-50102-0*); 1970. mass mkt. 0.75 o.p. (*0-451-50512-3*); 1961. 496p. mass mkt. 4.95 (*0-451-52351-2*); 1961. mass mkt. 2.25 o.p. (*0-451-51334-7*); 1961. mass mkt. 1.95 o.p. (*0-451-51143-3*); 1961. mass mkt. 1.50 o.p. (*0-451-50947-1*); 1961. mass mkt. 0.95 o.p. (*0-451-50804-1*); 1961. mass mkt. 2.50 o.p. (*0-451-51516-1*); 1961. 496p. mass mkt. 2.50 o.p. (*0-451-51685-0*) NAL. (Signet Classics).

—Oliver Twist. l.t. ed. 1998. (Large Print Ser.). 560p. lib. bdg. 28.00 (*0-939495-52-X*); 482p. reprint ed. lib. bdg. 25.00 (*1-58287-054-3*) North Bks.

—Oliver Twist. Kaplan, Fred, ed. 1992. (Critical Editions Ser.). 611p. (C). pap. text 14.50 (*0-393-96292-X*) Norton, W. W. & Co., Inc.

—Oliver Twist. Tillotson, Kathleen, ed. & intro. by. 1998. (Oxford World's Classics Ser.). (Illus.). 392p. pap. 5.95 o.p. (*0-19-283439-8*) Oxford Univ. Pr., Inc.

—Oliver Twist. 1987. (Illus.). 446p. 17.95 (*0-19-254505-1*) Oxford Univ. Pr., Inc.

—Oliver Twist. Tillotson, Kathleen, ed. (Oxford World's Classics Ser.). 1982. (Illus.). 392p. pap. 5.95 o.p. (*0-19-281591-1*); 1967. 55.00 o.p. (*0-19-811454-0*); 2nd ed. 1999. (Illus.). 544p. pap. 5.95 (*0-19-283339-1*) Oxford Univ. Pr., Inc.

—Oliver Twist. 1999. E-Book 3.99 incl. cd-rom (*1-57646-089-4*) Quiet Vision Publishing.

—Oliver Twist. 2001. (Modern Library Classics). (Illus.). 480p. pap. 7.95 (*0-375-75784-8*, Modern Library) Random House Adult Trade Publishing Group.

—Oliver Twist. 1987. (Illus.). 416p. 12.95 o.p. (*0-89577-258-2*) Reader's Digest Assn., Inc., The.

—Oliver Twist. 1996. 480p. text 8.98 o.p. (*1-56138-715-0*, Courage Bks.) Running Pr. Bk. Pubs.

—Oliver Twist. Shefter, Harry, ed. 1981. (Enriched Classics Ser.). 512p. mass mkt. 3.50 o.s.i (*0-671-44242-2*, Pocket) Simon & Schuster.

—Oliver Twist. (SPA.). 104p. 5.95 (*84-305-1317-5*) Susaeta Ediciones, S.A. ESP. *Dist:* AIMS International Bks., Inc.

—Oliver Twist. l.t. ed. 1982. (Classics Ser.). 29.99 o.p. (*0-7089-8019-8*, Charnwood) Thorpe, F. A. Pubs. GBR. *Dist:* Ulverscroft Large Print Bks., Ltd., Ulverscroft Large Print Canada, Ltd.

—Oliver Twist. Daleski, H. M., ed. 2003. 560p. 9.95 (*1-59264-007-9*); pap. 7.95 (*1-59264-006-0*) Toby Pr.

—Oliver Twist. 1999. (Signature Classics Ser.). (Illus.). xiii, 438p. 24.95 (*1-58279-037-X*); 29.95 (*1-58279-049-3*) Trident Pr. International.

—Oliver Twist. (Saddleback Classics). 2001. (Illus.). 13.10 (*0-606-21564-6*); 1986. 11.00 (*0-606-16029-9*); 1961. 11.00 (*0-606-00928-0*) Turtleback Bks.

—Oliver Twist. 1994. (Everyman Paperback Classics Ser.). 432p. pap. 3.95 (*0-460-87490-X*, Everyman's Classic Library in Paperback) Tuttle Publishing.

—Oliver Twist. 1992. (Illus.). 373p. reprint ed. lib. bdg. 29.95 o.p. (*1-877767-69-7*) University Publishing Hse., Inc.

—Oliver Twist. 2003. (Classics Ser.). (Illus.). 608p. pap. 7.00 (*0-14-143974-2*, Penguin Classics) Viking Penguin.

—Oliver Twist. Horne, Philip, ed. & intro. by. 2002. (Classics Ser.). (Illus.). 464p. 7.00 (*0-14-043522-0*) Viking Penguin.

—Oliver Twist. Fairclough, Peter, ed. 1966. (Penguin Classics Ser.). 496p. pap. 6.95 (*0-14-043017-2*, Penguin Classics) Viking Penguin.

—Oliver Twist. 1997. (Wordsworth Collection). 400p. pap. 3.95 (*1-85326-012-6*, 0126WW) Wordsworth Editions, Ltd. GBR. *Dist:* Casemate Pubs. & Bk. Distributors, LLC.

—Oliver Twist: Digital Reprint of 1902 Harper & Brothers Edition. Exams Unlimited, Inc. Staff, ed. 2001. (Illus.). 589p. (C). reprint ed. cd-rom 8.25 (*1-59132-017-8*) Exams Unlimited, Inc.

Dickens, Charles, et al. Oliver Twist. 1999. E-Book 6.25 (*0-585-35371-9*) netLibrary, Inc.

Dickey, Eric Jerome. Thieves' Paradise: A Novel. 2002. 320p. 19.95 (*0-525-94663-2*, Dutton) Dutton/Plume.

Dorsey, Tim. Florida Roadkill. 2000. 384p. mass mkt. 6.99 (*0-380-73233-5*, HarperTorch); 1999. 273p. 24.00 o.p. (*0-688-16782-9*, Morrow, William & Co.) Morrow/Avon.

Doyle, Arthur Conan. Masterworks of Crime & Mystery. Tracy, Jack W., ed. 1982. 320p. 14.95 o.p. (*0-385-27688-5*, Dial Bks.) Dell Publishing.

Duve, Karen. Rain: A Novel. Bell, Anthea, tr. from GER. 2003. 221p. pap. 14.95 (*1-58234-179-6*) Bloomsbury Publishing.

Ellroy, James. American Tabloid: A Novel. 1997. 592p. pap. 12.00 o.s.i (*0-449-00090-7*, Fawcett); 1996. mass mkt. o.p. (*0-449-22454-6*, Fawcett); 1995. 544p. mass mkt. 6.99 o.s.i (*0-8041-1449-8*, Ivy Bks.) Ballantine Bks.

—American Tabloid: A Novel. unabr. collector's ed. 1996. audio 112.00 (*0-7366-3279-4*, 3935) Books on Tape, Inc.

Enger, Leif. Peace Like a River. l.t. ed. 2002. (Wheeler Large Print Book Ser.). 28.95 (*1-58724-212-5*, Wheeler Publishing, Inc.) Gale Group.

—Peace Like a River. 320p. 2002. pap. 13.00 (*0-8021-3925-6*, Grove Pr.); 2001. 24.00 (*0-87113-795-X*, Atlantic Monthly Pr.) Grove/Atlantic, Inc.

Estleman, Loren D. Red Highway. 1994. 212p. 3.95 o.p. (*0-7867-0178-1*, Carroll & Graf Pubs.) Avalon Publishing Group.

—Red Highway. l.t. ed. 1988. pap. 17.95 o.p. (*1-55504-648-7*); lib. bdg. 19.95 o.p. (*1-55504-647-9*) BBC Audiobooks America.

—Red Highway. 1999. (Mystery Ser.). 195p. 19.95 (*0-7862-2180-1*, Five Star) Gale Group.

Ferrars, E. X. Beware of the Dog. l.t. ed. 1993. (Mystery Ser.). 304p. 29.99 o.p. (*0-7505-0490-0*) Magna Large Print Bks. GBR. *Dist:* Ulverscroft Large Print Bks., Ltd., Ulverscroft Large Print Canada, Ltd.
—Death of a Minor Character. 1983. (Crime Club Ser.). 192p. 11.95 o.p. (*0-385-18839-0*) Doubleday Publishing.
—Death of a Minor Character. l.t. ed. 1984. (Ulverscroft Large Print Ser.). 320p. 12.50 o.p. (*0-7089-1225-7*, Ulverscroft) Thorpe, F. A. Pubs. GBR. *Dist:* Ulverscroft Large Print Bks., Ltd., Ulverscroft Large Print Canada, Ltd.
—Frog in the Throat. 1981. 112p. pap. 1.95 o.p. (*0-553-20040-2*) Bantam Bks.
—Frog in the Throat. 1980. (Crime Club Ser.). 192p. 8.95 o.p. (*0-385-17207-9*) Doubleday Publishing.
—Frog in the Throat. unabr. ed. 1998. audio 54.95 (*0-7531-0239-0*, 980209) ISIS Audio Bks. GBR. *Dist:* Ulverscroft Large Print Bks., Ltd.
—Frog in the Throat. l.t. ed. 1986. (Ulverscroft Large Print Ser.). 304p. 12.50 o.p. (*0-7089-1430-6*, Ulverscroft) Thorpe, F. A. Pubs. GBR. *Dist:* Ulverscroft Large Print Bks., Ltd., Ulverscroft Large Print Canada, Ltd.
—I Met Murder. 1986. (Crime Club Ser.). 192p. 12.95 o.p. (*0-385-23367-1*) Doubleday Publishing.
—I Met Murder. unabr. ed. 1998. audio 49.95 (*0-7531-0408-3*, 970704) ISIS Audio Bks. GBR. *Dist:* Ulverscroft Large Print Bks., Ltd.
—I Met Murder. l.t. ed. 1987. (Ulverscroft Large Print Ser.). 320p. 14.50 o.p. (*0-7089-1586-8*, Ulverscroft) Thorpe, F. A. Pubs. GBR. *Dist:* Ulverscroft Large Print Bks., Ltd., Ulverscroft Large Print Canada, Ltd.
—In at the Kill. 1979. 9.95 o.p. (*0-385-14913-1*) Doubleday Publishing.
—In at the Kill. 1980. 192p. pap. 3.95 o.p. (*0-14-005644-0*, Penguin Bks.) Viking Penguin.
—Last Will & Testament. 1981. 160p. pap. 1.95 o.p. (*0-553-14795-1*) Bantam Bks.
—Last Will & Testament. 1978. 7.95 o.p. (*0-385-14455-5*) Doubleday Publishing.
—Last Will & Testament. unabr. ed. 2001. audio 39.95 (*1-85496-692-8*, 980704) Soundings, Ltd. GBR. *Dist:* Ulverscroft Large Print Bks., Ltd.
—Last Will & Testament. l.t. ed. 1980. 284p. 12.00 o.p. (*0-7089-0505-6*, Ulverscroft) Thorpe, F. A. Pubs. GBR. *Dist:* Ulverscroft Large Print Bks., Ltd.
—Thinner Than Water. unabr. ed. 1993. 39.95 incl. audio (*0-7451-5925-7*, CAT 4063) BBC Audiobooks America.
—Thinner Than Water. 1982. (Crime Club Ser.). 192p. 10.95 o.p. (*0-385-17946-4*) Doubleday Publishing.
—Woman Slaughter. unabr. ed. 2001. audio 49.95 (*1-85089-823-5*, 20891) ISIS Audio Bks. GBR. *Dist:* Ulverscroft Large Print Bks., Ltd.
Ford, John M. The Last Hot Time. 2000. 224p. 22.95 (*0-312-85545-1*); 2001. reprint ed. pap. 12.95 (*0-312-87578-9*) Doherty, Tom Assocs., LLC. (Tor Bks.).
Gansky, Alton. Distant Memory. l.t. ed. 2000. (Christian Mystery Ser.). 448p. 23.95 (*0-7862-2915-2*) Thorndike Pr.
Gansky, Alton L. Distant Memory. 2000. 304p. pap. 10.95 o.s.i (*1-57856-121-3*) WaterBrook Pr.
Gantos, Jack. Zip Six: A Novel. 1996. 224p. 21.95 (*1-882593-15-4*); 2000. 312p. reprint ed. 13.95 (*1-882593-39-1*) Bridge Works Publishing Co., Inc.
Gores, Joe. Speak of the Devil: 14 Tales of Crimes & Their Punishments. 1999. (Mystery Ser.). 220p. 20.95 (*0-7862-2035-X*, Five Star) Gale Group.
Greenburg, Martin H. & Davis, Russell, eds. Mardi Gras Madness: Stories of Murder & Mayhem in New Orleans. 2000. 239p. pap. 16.95 (*1-58182-077-1*, Cumberland Hearthside) Cumberland Hse. Publishing.
Hale, Hilary, ed. Winter's Crimes, No. 18. 1987. 224p. 13.95 o.p. (*0-312-00101-0*) St. Martin's Pr.
Highsmith, Patricia. The Boy Who Followed Ripley. 1993. (Mr. Ripley Ser.). 304p. pap. 12.00 (*0-679-74567-X*, Vintage) Knopf Publishing Group.
—The Boy Who Followed Ripley. 1985. (Mr. Ripley Ser.). 336p. pap. 3.95 o.p. (*0-14-005739-0*, Penguin Bks.) Viking Penguin.
—The Mysterious Mr. Ripley. 1985. (Crime Ser.). 656p. pap. 10.95 o.p. (*0-14-007196-2*, Penguin Bks.) Viking Penguin.
—Ripley under Ground. unabr. ed. 1993. (Mr. Ripley Ser.). audio 69.95 (*1-85088-853-1*, 91094) Eye in the Ear Inc.
—Ripley under Ground. l.t. ed. 1990. (Mr. Ripley Ser.). 416p. 19.95 (*1-85089-304-7*) ISIS Large Print Bks. GBR. *Dist:* Transaction Pubs.
—Ripley under Ground. 1992. (Mr. Ripley Ser.). 320p. pap. 12.95 (*0-679-74230-1*, Vintage) Knopf Publishing Group.
—Ripley under Water. unabr. ed. 2001. (Mr. Ripley Series). audio 69.95 (*1-85089-888-X*, 92061) ISIS Audio Bks. GBR. *Dist:* Ulverscroft Large Print Bks., Ltd.
—Ripley under Water. 1993. (Mr. Ripley Ser.). 320p. pap. 12.00 (*0-679-74809-1*, Vintage) Knopf Publishing Group.
—Ripley under Water. 1994. (Mr. Ripley Ser.). 4.99 o.p. (*0-517-11787-8*) Random Hse. Value Publishing.
—Ripley's Game. l.t. ed. 1991. (Mr. Ripley Ser.). 376p. 32.50 o.p. (*1-85089-423-X*) ISIS Large Print Bks. GBR. *Dist:* Ulverscroft Large Print Bks., Ltd.
—Ripley's Game. 1993. (Mr. Ripley Ser.). 288p. pap. 12.95 (*0-679-74568-8*, Vintage) Knopf Publishing Group.
—The Talented Mr. Ripley. unabr. ed. 2001. (Mr. Ripley Series). audio 69.95 (*1-85089-775-1*, 89102) ISIS Audio Bks. GBR. *Dist:* Ulverscroft Large Print Bks., Ltd.
—The Talented Mr. Ripley. l.t. ed. 1988. (Mr. Ripley Ser.). 392p. reprint ed. lib. bdg. 18.95 o.p. (*1-85089-184-2*) ISIS Large Print Bks. GBR. *Dist:* Transaction Pubs.
—The Talented Mr. Ripley. (Mr. Ripley Ser.). 304p. 1999. pap. 13.00 (*0-676-58972-3*); 1992. pap. 13.00 (*0-679-74229-8*) Knopf Publishing Group. (Vintage).
—The Talented Mr. Ripley, Set. unabr. ed. 1999. (Mr. Ripley Ser.). audio 39.95 (*0-375-40511-9*, RH Audio) Random Hse. Audio Publishing Group.
—The Talented Mr. Ripley. 2000. (Mr. Ripley Ser.). 287p. (*0-7621-8856-1*) Reader's Digest Assn., Inc., The.
—The Talented Mr. Ripley. 1982. (Mr. Ripley Ser.). 256p. pap. 4.95 o.p. (*0-14-004020-X*, Penguin Bks.) Viking Penguin.
—The Talented Mr. Ripley, Ripley Under Ground, Ripley's Game. 1999. (Mr. Ripley Ser.). 880p. 26.00 (*0-375-40792-8*) Knopf, Alfred A. Inc.
Hogan, Chuck. The Standoff. 1996. 368p. mass mkt. 6.50 o.s.i (*0-553-57446-9*) Bantam Bks.
—The Standoff. l.t. ed. 1995. 25.95 o.p. (*1-56895-231-7*, Wheeler Publishing, Inc.) Gale Group.
Hogg, James. Private Memoirs & Confessions of a Justified Sinner. 2002. (New York Review Books Classics Ser.). 296p. pap. 12.95 (*1-59017-025-3*) New York Review of Bks., Inc., The.
—Private Memoirs & Confessions of a Justified Sinner. 2001. 192p. pap. 3.95 (*1-85326-188-2*) Wordsworth Editions, Ltd. GBR. *Dist:* Combined Publishing.
Holden, Craig. The Jazz Bird: A Novel. l.t. ed. 2002. 408p. lib. bdg. 29.95 (*1-58547-165-8*, Platinum) Ctr. Point Large Print.
—The Jazz Bird: A Novel. 2003. 400p. mass mkt. 6.99 (*0-7434-1881-6*, Pocket); 2002. 320p. 25.00 (*0-7432-1296-7*, Simon & Schuster); 2002. E-Book 5.99 (*0-7432-1757-8*, Simon & Schuster) Simon & Schuster.
Jakubowski, Maxim, ed. The Mammoth Book of Pulp Action. 2001. 512p. pap. 11.95 (*0-7867-0920-0*, Carroll & Graf Pubs.) Avalon Publishing Group.
Jefferson, Roland S. Damaged Goods. 2003. 250p. (YA). 22.95 (*1-881524-93-0*) Milligan Bks.
Johnnie D. 2001. mass mkt. 6.99 (*0-8125-7087-1*, Forge Bks.) Doherty, Tom Assocs., LLC.
Kaste, Harry, ed. CliffsNotes TM Oliver Twist. 1999. E-Book 5.99 (*0-8220-7152-5*, Cliff Notes) Wiley, John & Sons, Inc.
Kelly, Jack. Protection. 1989. 320p. 18.95 o.p. (*0-525-24778-5*, Dutton) Dutton/Plume.
—Protection. 1990. 320p. mass mkt. 4.50 o.p. (*0-451-40229-4*, Onyx) NAL.
—Protection. 1991. 2.99 o.p. (*0-517-06392-1*) Random Hse. Value Publishing.
Kelly, Nora. My Sister's Keeper. 2000. (Missing Mysteries Ser.: Vol. 15). 221p. pap. 14.95 (*1-890208-28-0*) Poisoned Pen Pr.
Kennedy, William. Legs. 1975. 322p. 8.95 o.p. (*0-698-10672-5*) Putnam Publishing Group, The.
—Legs. l.t. ed. 2000. (Perennial Bestsellers Ser.). 427p. 29.95 (*0-7838-8860-0*) Thorndike Pr.
—Legs. 1983. 320p. 14.00 (*0-14-006484-2*) Viking Penguin.
—Legs. 1976. pap. 1.75 o.s.i (*0-446-84140-4*) Warner Bks., Inc.
King, Danny. The Bank Robber Diaries. 2002. 256p. pap. 13.00 (*1-85242-665-9*) Serpent's Tail Ltd. GBR. *Dist:* Consortium Bk. Sales & Distribution.
Knight, Michael. Divining Rod: A Novel. 1998. 256p. 23.95 o.p. (*0-525-94379-X*) Dutton/Plume.
Korelitz, Jean Hanff. The Sabbathday River. 2001. 528p. mass mkt. 7.99 o.s.i (*0-515-13011-7*, Jove) Berkley Publishing Group.
Kublicki, Nicolas. The Diamond Conspiracy. 2003. 512p. pap. 15.00 (*1-4022-0154-0*, Sourcebooks MediaFusion); mass mkt. 6.99 (*1-4022-0226-1*, Sourcebooks Landmark) Sourcebooks, Inc.
Latour, Jose. Outcast. 1999. 217p. pap. 13.95 o.p. (*1-888451-07-6*, AKB04) Akashic Bks.
—Outcast. 2001. 304p. 24.00 (*0-06-018488-4*, Morrow, William & Co.) Morrow/Avon.
Leitch, Maurice. Eggman's Apprentice. 2001. 276p. pap. (*0-436-40403-6*) Random Hse. of Canada, Ltd. CAN. *Dist:* Random Hse., Inc.
Leonard, Elmore. Get Shorty. 2000. 368p. mass mkt. 4.99 o.s.i (*0-440-23614-2*); 1998. 304p. pap. 9.95 o.s.i (*0-385-32398-0*); 1995. 304p. pap. 8.95 o.s.i (*0-385-31567-8*, Delacorte Pr.); 1991. 384p. mass mkt. 6.99 o.s.i (*0-440-20980-3*) Dell Publishing.
—Get Shorty. l.t. ed. 1993. pap. 18.95 (*0-8161-5809-6*, Macmillan Reference USA) Gale Group.
—Killshot. l.t. ed. 1990. (General Ser.). 432p. reprint ed. lib. bdg. 20.95 o.p. (*0-8161-4865-1*, Macmillan Reference USA) Gale Group.
—Killshot. 1999. 288p. pap. 12.00 (*0-688-16638-5*, Quill) HarperTrade.
—Killshot. 2003. 416p. mass mkt. 7.50 (*0-06-051224-5*, HarperTorch); 1989. 288p. 18.95 o.p. (*1-55710-041-1*, Morrow, William & Co.) Morrow/Avon.
—Killshot. 1994. (Super Sound Buy, Dove Ser.). 8.99 o.p. (*0-7871-0112-5*) Penguin Group (USA) Inc.
—Killshot. 1991. 4.99 o.p. (*0-517-07549-0*) Random Hse. Value Publishing.
—Killshot. 1990. 352p. reprint ed. mass mkt. 5.95 (*0-446-35041-9*) Warner Bks., Inc.
—Swag. unabr. collector's ed. 1996. audio 42.00 (*0-7366-3234-4*, 3895) Books on Tape, Inc.
—Swag. l.t. ed. 2000. 279p. lib. bdg. 28.95 (*1-58547-041-4*) Ctr. Point Large Print.
—Swag. 240p. 1978. mass mkt. 6.99 o.s.i (*0-440-18424-X*); 1976. pap. 7.95 o.s.i (*0-440-08449-0*, Delacorte Pr.) Dell Publishing.
—Swag, Set. abr. ed. 1987. audio 16.99 (*0-88646-221-5*, 7221) Durkin Hayes Publishing Ltd.
—Swag. unabr. ed. 1997. audio 44.00 (*0-7887-0502-4*, 94698E7) Recorded Bks., LLC.
Lester, Mike. An Occasional Dream. 2002. 167p. 13.00 (*0-9663473-8-2*) UglyTown.
Levison, Iain. Since the Layoffs: A Novel. 2003. 176p. 20.00 (*1-56947-335-8*) Soho Pr., Inc.
Lewis, Jed. Deliberate Indifference. 2000. 296p. 18.95 (*0-9674922-0-3*) Laughing Fire Pr.
Lindsey, David L. The Rules of Silence. 2003. 12p. pap. 10.95 (*0-7927-2881-5*); 10p. pap. 84.95 (*0-7927-2880-7*) BBC Audiobooks America.
—The Rules of Silence. 2004. mass mkt. (*0-446-61292-8*); 2003. 416p. 24.95 (*0-446-53163-4*) Warner Bks., Inc.
MacDonald, John D. Cape Fear. 1986. mass mkt. 5.99 o.s.i (*0-449-13190-4*, Fawcett) Ballantine Bks.
—Cape Fear. 1994. reprint ed. lib. bdg. 27.95 o.p. (*1-56849-304-5*) Buccaneer Bks., Inc.
Mareth, Paul. Fidel & Leo. 2001. 408p. pap. 25.50 (*0-7596-4738-0*) 1stBooks Library.
McCoy, Horace. Kiss Tomorrow Goodbye. 1997. 250p. (Orig.). (C). reprint ed. pap. text (*1-85242-433-8*) Serpent's Tail Ltd.
Meno, Joe. How the Hula Girl Sings: A Novel. 2001. 304p. 25.00 o.s.i (*0-06-039433-1*, ReganBooks) HarperTrade.
Morris, Monique W. Too Beautiful for Words. 288p. 2002. pap. 11.95 (*0-06-093594-4*); 2001. 24.00 (*0-06-621105-0*) HarperTrade. (Amistad Pr.).
Morrison, Toni. Tar Baby. (Contemporary Fiction Ser.). 1987. 320p. pap. 12.95 (*0-452-26479-0*); 1987. pap. 8.95 o.p. (*0-452-25258-X*); 1982. pap. 6.95 o.p. (*0-452-25326-8*) Dutton/Plume. (Plume).
—Tar Baby. 2004. 320p. pap. 13.00 (*1-4000-3344-6*, Vintage) Knopf Publishing Group.
—Tar Baby. 1981. 320p. 26.95 (*0-394-42329-1*) Knopf, Alfred A. Inc.
—Tar Baby. 1993. pap. 5.99 o.s.i (*0-451-18238-3*); 1983. 320p. mass mkt. 4.50 o.p. (*0-451-15260-3*); 1983. 272p. mass mkt. 5.99 o.p. (*0-451-16639-6*); 1983. mass mkt. 3.95 o.p. (*0-451-12224-0*) NAL. (Signet Bks.).
—Tar Baby. 1983. 19.00 (*0-606-01962-6*) Turtleback Bks.
O'Connell, Jack. Word Made Flesh. 1999. 336p. 24.00 o.p. (*0-06-019209-7*) HarperCollins Pubs.
—Word Made Flesh. 2000. 336p. pap. 13.00 (*0-06-109722-5*, Perennial) HarperTrade.
O'Nan, Stewart. The Speed Queen. 2001. 224p. 13.00 (*0-8021-3853-5*, Grove Pr.) Grove/Atlantic, Inc.
Ore, Rebecca. Outlaw School. 2000. 310p. pap. 13.50 (*0-380-79250-8*, Eos) Morrow/Avon.
Owen, Howard. The Rail. 2002. 256p. 25.00 (*1-57962-043-4*) Permanent Pr., The.
Perry, Thomas. Blood Money. l.t. ed. 2000. (Large Print Book Ser.). 513p. pap. 26.95 (*1-56895-925-7*, Wheeler Publishing, Inc.) Gale Group.
—Blood Money. 2000. audio 30.00 (*0-7871-2284-X*) NewStar Media, Inc.
—Blood Money: A Novel. 1999. (Illus.). 368p. 24.95 o.s.i (*0-679-45304-0*) Random Hse., Inc.
Petit, Chris. The Hard Shoulder. 2002. 224p. pap. 10.95 (*1-86207-529-8*) Granta.
Pickard, Nancy. The Whole Truth. (Marie Lightfoot Mysteries Ser.). 2000. 272p. 22.95 o.s.i (*0-671-88795-5*, Atria); 2001. reprint ed. E-Book 22.95 (*0-7434-1804-2*, Atria); 2001. (Illus.). 368p. reprint ed. mass mkt. 6.99 o.s.i (*0-671-88794-7*, Pocket) Simon & Schuster.
—The Whole Truth. l.t. ed. 2000. (Marie Lightfoot Mysteries Ser.). 439p. 29.95 (*0-7862-2577-7*) Thorndike Pr.
Pineiro, R. J. Shutdown. 2000. 320p. 24.95 (*0-312-86909-6*); 2002. reprint ed. mass mkt. 7.99 (*0-8125-7504-0*) Doherty, Tom Assocs., LLC. (Forge Bks.).
Puzo, Mario. Omerta. 2001. E-Book 7.99 (*1-58945-647-5*) Adobe Systems, Inc.
—Omerta. 2000. (SPA.). pap. 22.95 (*84-406-9876-3*, EB12029) B Ediciones S.A. ESP. *Dist:* Lectorum Pubns., Inc.
—Omerta. l.t. ed. 448p. 2001. pap. 13.95 (*0-375-72808-2*); 2000. 25.95 (*0-375-43058-X*) Random Hse. Large Print.
—Omerta. 2001. E-Book 7.99 (*0-375-50568-7*) Random Hse., Inc.
—The Sicilian. 1985. 416p. mass mkt. 6.99 o.s.i (*0-553-25282-8*) Bantam Bks.
—The Sicilian. unabr. ed. 1985. audio 19.95 (*0-930435-13-3*, 357, Bookcassette); audio 73.25 o.p. (*1-56100-008-6*, 1042, Unabridged Library Editions) Brilliance Audio.
—The Sicilian. l.t. ed. 1985. (Special Editions Ser.). 560p. 19.95 o.p. (*0-8161-3837-0*, Macmillan Reference USA) Gale Group.
—The Sicilian. unabr. ed. 1992. audio 91.00 (*1-55690-730-3*, 92230E7) Recorded Bks., LLC.
—The Sicilian. 1984. 448p. 17.45 o.p. (*0-671-43564-7*, Simon & Schuster) Simon & Schuster.
—The Sicilian. l.t. ed. 1986. (Charnwood Large Print Ser.). 574p. 29.99 o.p. (*0-7089-8317-0*, Charnwood) Thorpe, F. A. Pubs. GBR. *Dist:* Ulverscroft Large Print Bks., Ltd., Ulverscroft Large Print Canada, Ltd.
Ridley, John. Love Is a Racket. 352p. 2003. pap. 13.95 (*0-345-42146-9*); 1999. mass mkt. 6.99 (*0-345-43409-9*) Ballantine Bks.
—Love Is a Racket. aut. ed. 1998. 24.00 o.s.i (*0-676-54304-9*) Random Hse., Inc.
Robin, Robert. Above the Law. Rosenman, Jane, ed. 1992. 320p. 20.00 (*0-671-74423-2*); 20.00 (*0-671-74425-9*) Simon & Schuster. (Atria).
Rosenfeld, Arthur. A Cure for Gravity. 2001. 384p. mass mkt. 6.99 (*0-8125-6566-5*); 2000. 269p. 23.95 (*0-312-87455-3*) Doherty, Tom Assocs., LLC. (Forge Bks.).
Ruggiero, L. A. Burning Sand: A Novel. 2001. pap. (*0-9704135-8-0*) Beaconridge Pr.
Russo, Richard Paul. Carlucci 3 in 1. 2003. 624p. pap. 16.00 (*0-441-01054-7*) Ace Bks.
Sandford, John, pseud. The Devil's Code. l.t. ed. 2001. 375p. (*0-7540-1583-1*, Macmillan Reference USA) Gale Group.
—The Devil's Code. 2000. (Kidd Ser.). 320p. 25.95 o.s.i (*0-399-14650-4*) Penguin Group (USA) Inc.
—The Devil's Code. l.t. ed. 375p. 2002. pap. 29.95 (*0-7838-9371-X*); 2001. 32.95 (*0-7838-9370-1*) Thorndike Pr.
Savage, Marc. Paradise. 1994. 320p. mass mkt. 4.99 o.s.i (*0-553-56018-2*) Bantam Bks.
—Paradise. 1993. 17.00 o.s.i (*0-385-46770-2*); 368p. 17.00 o.s.i (*0-385-46779-6*) Doubleday Publishing.
Sister Souljah. The Coldest Winter Ever: A Novel. (Ann Rule's Crime Files Ser.). 1999. 352p. 23.00 o.s.i (*0-671-02578-3*, Atria); 2000. 432p. reprint ed. mass mkt. 7.99 (*0-671-02536-8*, Pocket) Simon & Schuster.
Smolens, John. Cold. 2003. 320p. pap. 12.00 (*1-4000-5087-1*, Three Rivers Pr.) Crown Publishing Group.
Stark, Richard. Flashfire. 2000. 288p. 22.95 o.p. (*0-89296-710-2*); 304p. E-Book 14.95 (*0-7595-8032-4*); E-Book 14.95 (*0-7595-6031-5*); 304p. E-Book 14.95 (*0-7595-4031-4*); 304p. E-Book 14.95 (*0-7595-9036-2*) Mysterious Pr.
—Flashfire. l.t. ed. 2001. (Mystery Ser.). 328p. 29.95 (*0-7862-2940-3*) Thorndike Pr.
—Flashfire. 2001. 288p. reprint ed. pap. 12.95 (*0-446-67790-6*) Warner Bks., Inc.
Stella, Charles P. Eddie's World. 2001. 256p. 24.00 (*0-7867-0893-X*, Carroll & Graf Pubs.) Avalon Publishing Group.
Stella, Charlie. Jimmy Bench-Press. 2002. 224p. 24.00 (*0-7867-1057-8*, Carroll & Graf Pubs.) Avalon Publishing Group.
Thompson, Jim. The Nothing Man. 1997. 224p. pap. 11.00 (*0-375-70031-5*, Vintage) Knopf Publishing Group.
—The Nothing Man. 1988. 208p. mass mkt. 4.50 o.s.i (*0-445-40570-8*, Mysterious Pr. Paperback Bks.) Warner Bks., Inc.
Thompson, Thomas. Serpentine. 2000. 576p. pap. 16.00 (*0-7867-0749-6*, Carroll & Graf Pubs.) Avalon Publishing Group.
Thorne, Nicola. My Name Is Martha Brown. 2000. 312p. (*0-00-225949-4*) HarperCollins Pubs.
Turner, Nikki. A Hustler's Wife. 2003. 315p. pap. 15.00 (*0-9702472-5-7*) TripleCrown Pubns.
Vachss, Andrew. The Getaway Man. 2003. (Vintage Crime/Black Lizard Ser.). 208p. pap. 11.00 (*1-4000-3119-2*) Knopf Publishing Group.

—Only Child: A Burke Novel. 2003. 304p. pap. 13.00 (*1-4000-3098-6*, Vintage) Knopf Publishing Group.
—Only Child: A Burke Novel. 2002. 288p. 24.00 (*0-375-41487-8*) Knopf, Alfred A. Inc.
Van Alder, Piet. Dropback. 2000. 368p. 24.95 o.p. (*0-9643256-7-5*) Palancar.
Westlake, Donald E. Bank Shot. unabr. collector's ed. 1996. (Dortmunder Ser.). audio 36.00 (*0-7366-3455-X*, 4099) Books on Tape, Inc.
—Bank Shot. 1987. mass mkt. 3.95 o.s.i (*0-445-40610-0*); 1989. 192p. reprint ed. mass mkt. 5.50 o.s.i (*0-445-40883-9*) Warner Bks., Inc.
—Don't Ask. unabr. collector's ed. 1997. (Dortmunder Ser.). audio 64.00 (*0-7366-3491-6*, 4131) Books on Tape, Inc.
—Don't Ask. 1993. 336p. 18.95 (*0-89296-469-3*) Mysterious Pr.
—Don't Ask. 1994. (Dortmunder Novel Ser.). 352p. reprint ed. mass mkt. 7.50 (*0-446-40095-5*) Warner Bks., Inc.
—Drowned Hopes. unabr. collector's ed. 1997. (Dortmunder Ser.). audio 88.00 (*0-7366-3677-3*, 4357) Books on Tape, Inc.
—Drowned Hopes. 1990. 75.00 (*0-89296-421-9*); 18.95 o.p. (*0-89296-178-3*) Mysterious Pr.
—Drowned Hopes. abr. ed. 1993. 15.95 o.p. (*1-55800-316-9*) NewStar Media, Inc.
—Drowned Hopes. 1991. 464p. mass mkt. 5.99 o.s.i (*0-446-40006-8*) Warner Bks., Inc.
—Good Behavior. unabr. collector's ed. 1997. (Dortmunder Ser.). audio 48.00 (*0-7366-3673-0*, 4350) Books on Tape, Inc.
—Good Behavior. 1988. mass mkt. 3.95 (*0-8125-1060-7*, Tor Bks.) Doherty, Tom Assocs., LLC.
—Good Behavior. l.t. ed. 1987. (General Ser.). 383p. 17.95 o.p. (*0-8161-4275-0*, Macmillan Reference USA) Gale Group.
—Good Behavior. 1986. 256p. 15.45 o.p. (*0-89296-240-2*) Mysterious Pr.
—Good Behavior. 1990. 2.99 o.p. (*0-517-68035-1*) Random Hse. Value Publishing.
—The Hot Rock. unabr. collector's ed. 1996. (Dortmunder Ser.). audio 42.00 (*0-7366-3417-7*, 4063) Books on Tape, Inc.
—The Hot Rock. 1987. 256p. reprint ed. mass mkt. 5.50 o.s.i (*0-445-40608-9*) Warner Bks., Inc.
—Jimmy the Kid. 1975. mass mkt. 1.50 o.p. (*0-345-24650-0*) Ballantine Bks.
—Jimmy the Kid. unabr. collector's ed. 1996. audio 36.00 (*0-7366-3517-3*, 4154) Books on Tape, Inc.
—Jimmy the Kid. 1974. 192p. 6.95 o.p. (*0-87131-157-7*) Holt, Henry & Co.
—Jimmy the Kid. 192p. 1994. mass mkt. 5.50 (*0-446-40409-8*, Mysterious Pr. Paperback Bks.); 1989. mass mkt. 5.50 o.s.i (*0-445-40747-6*) Warner Bks., Inc.
—Nobody's Perfect. 1979. mass mkt. 1.95 o.s.i (*0-449-23909-8*, Fawcett) Ballantine Bks.
—Nobody's Perfect. unabr. collector's ed. 1996. (Dortmunder Ser.: Vol. 4). audio 42.00 (*0-7366-3542-4*, 4189) Books on Tape, Inc.
—Nobody's Perfect. 1977. 228p. 7.95 o.p. (*0-87131-249-2*) Holt, Henry & Co.
—Nobody's Perfect. 1994. pap. (*0-446-40715-1*, Mysterious Pr. Paperback Bks.); 1989. 240p. mass mkt. 5.50 o.s.i (*0-445-40715-8*) Warner Bks., Inc.
—What's the Worst That Could Happen? unabr. collector's ed. 1997. (Dortmunder Ser.). audio 56.00 (*0-7366-3773-7*, 4446) Books on Tape, Inc.
—What's the Worst That Could Happen? 1996. 384p. 22.00 o.p. (*0-89296-586-X*) Mysterious Pr.
—What's the Worst That Could Happen? movie tie-in ed. 1997. (Dortmunder Novel Ser.). 336p. reprint ed. mass mkt. 6.50 (*0-446-60471-2*) Warner Bks., Inc.
—Why Me? unabr. collector's ed. 1997. (Dortmunder Ser.). audio 42.00 (*0-7366-3653-6*, 4318) Books on Tape, Inc.
—Why Me? 1985. 288p. reprint ed. mass mkt. 3.50 (*0-8125-1052-6*, Tor Bks.) Doherty, Tom Assocs., LLC.
—Why Me? 1983. 204p. 13.50 o.p. (*0-670-76569-4*) Viking Penguin.
—Why Me? 1994. 240p. mass mkt. 5.50 (*0-446-40346-6*) Warner Bks., Inc.
Yorke, Margaret. The Smooth Face of Evil. 1984. 208p. 10.95 o.p. (*0-312-73020-9*) St. Martin's Pr.
—The Smooth Face of Evil. l.t. ed. 2000. (Mystery Ser.). 375p. 27.95 (*0-7862-2678-1*) Thorndike Pr.
—The Smooth Face of Evil. l.t. ed. 1986. (Ulverscroft Large Print Ser.). 432p. 29.99 o.p. (*0-7089-1453-5*, Ulverscroft) Thorpe, F. A. Pubs. GBR. *Dist:* Ulverscroft Large Print Bks., Ltd., Ulverscroft Large Print Canada, Ltd.
—The Smooth Face of Evil. 1985. 208p. mass mkt. 2.95 o.s.i (*0-445-20033-2*) Warner Bks., Inc.
Young, Jim. Armed Memory. 1996. 246p. pap. text 5.99 (*0-8125-5027-7*); 1995. 256p. 21.95 o.p. (*0-312-85766-7*) Doherty, Tom Assocs., LLC. (Tor Bks.).

# F

## FORENSIC PATHOLOGISTS—FICTION

Ablow, Keith Russell. Denial. 1998. (Denial Ser.: Vol. 1). 368p. mass mkt. 6.99 o.s.i (*0-312-96596-6*, St. Martin's Paperbacks) St. Martin's Pr.
Andrews, Sarah. Bone Hunter. 2nd ed. 1999. 320p. 24.95 (*0-312-20381-0*, Saint Martin's Minotaur) St. Martin's Pr.
—Bone Hunter: An Em Hansen Mystery. 2000. (Em Hansen Mysteries Ser.). 353p. mass mkt. 6.50 (*0-312-97317-9*, St. Martin's Paperbacks) St. Martin's Pr.
—An Eye for Gold. 2000. ix, 387p. 24.95 (*0-312-25349-4*, Saint Martin's Minotaur) St. Martin's Pr.
—A Fall in Denver: An Em Hansen Mystery. 1996. (Em Hansen Mystery Ser.). 272p. mass mkt. 5.50 o.s.i (*0-451-18793-8*) NAL.
—A Fall in Denver: An Em Hansen Mystery. 1995. 288p. 20.00 o.p. (*0-684-81523-0*); 20.00 (*1-883402-34-4*) Simon & Schuster. (Scribner).
—Fault Line. 2003. 336p. mass mkt. 6.50 (*0-312-98445-6*, St. Martin's Paperbacks); 2002. 304p. 23.95 (*0-312-25350-8*, Saint Martin's Minotaur) St. Martin's Pr.
—Mother Nature. 1997. 352p. 23.95 (*0-312-15591-3*, Saint Martin's Minotaur) St. Martin's Pr.
—Only Flesh & Bones. 1999. (Dead Letter Mysteries Ser.: Vol. 1). 368p. mass mkt. 6.50 (*0-312-96702-0*, St. Martin's Paperbacks); 1998. 336p. 23.95 (*0-312-18642-8*, Saint Martin's Minotaur) St. Martin's Pr.
—Tensleep: An Em Hansen Mystery. 1995. (Em Hansen Mystery Ser.). 304p. mass mkt. 4.99 o.s.i (*0-451-18606-0*, Signet Bks.) NAL.
—Tensleep: An Em Hansen Mystery. 1994. 288p. 20.00 (*1-883402-33-6*, Scribner) Simon & Schuster.
Ayres, Noreen. Carcass Trade. unabr. ed. 1995. audio 56.00 (*0-7366-2934-3*, 3630) Books on Tape, Inc.
—Carcass Trade. 1994. 285p. 20.00 o.p. (*0-688-10875-X*, Morrow, William & Co.); 1995. 352p. reprint ed. mass mkt. 4.99 o.p. (*0-380-71572-4*, Avon Bks.) Morrow/Avon.
—A World the Color of Salt. unabr. ed. 1992. audio 32.00 (*0-7366-2321-3*, 3101) Books on Tape, Inc.
—A World the Color of Salt. 1993. 304p. mass mkt. 4.99 (*0-380-71571-6*, Avon Bks.); 1992. 352p. 19.00 o.p. (*0-688-10824-5*, Morrow, William & Co.) Morrow/Avon.
Bahr, Arthur W. Certifiably Insane: A Novel. 1999. 272p. 23.00 (*0-684-80232-5*, Simon & Schuster) Simon & Schuster.
Connor, Beverly. Dressed to Die: A Lindsay Chamberlain Novel. 1998. (Lindsay Chamberlain Mysteries Ser.). 320p. 20.95 (*1-888952-89-X*) Cumberland Hse. Publishing.
—A Rumor of Bones. 1996. (Lindsay Chamberlain Mysteries Ser.: Vol. 1). (Illus.). 254p. 20.95 o.p. (*1-888952-08-3*) Cumberland Hse. Publishing.
—Skeleton Crew. 1999. (Lindsay Chamberlain Mysteries Ser.: Vol. 3). (Illus.). 352p. 20.95 (*1-58182-042-9*, Cumberland Hearthside) Cumberland Hse. Publishing.
Cook, Robin. Chromosome 6. 1997. 7.50 (*0-425-16282-6*); 1998. 480p. mass mkt. 7.99 (*0-425-16124-2*) Berkley Publishing Group.
—Chromosome 6. unabr. ed. 1997. audio 80.00 (*0-913369-74-8*, 4328) Books on Tape, Inc.
—Chromosome 6. 1997. 400p. 24.95 o.s.i (*0-399-14207-X*, G. P. Putnam's Sons); 24.95 (*0-399-14227-4*, 694561, Putnam Berkley Audio) Penguin Group (USA) Inc.
—Chromosome 6. l.t. ed. 1998. (Paperback Bestsellers Ser.). 734p. pap. 26.95 o.p. (*0-7862-1099-0*) Thorndike Pr.
—Chromosome 6. 1998. 14.04 (*0-606-16388-3*) Turtleback Bks.
Cornwell, Patricia. All That Remains. unabr. ed. 1996. 10p. audio 84.95 (*0-7451-6665-2*, CAB1281) BBC Audiobooks America.
—All That Remains. unabr. collector's ed. 1992. (Kay Scarpetta Mystery Ser.). audio 56.00 (*0-7366-2239-X*, 3029) Books on Tape, Inc.
—All That Remains. unabr. ed. 1992. audio 22.95 o.p. (*1-56100-468-5*, 421, Bookcassette); audio 57.25 o.p. (*1-56100-102-3*, 604, Unabridged Library Editions) Brilliance Audio.
—All That Remains. l.t. ed. 1992. (G. K. Hall Hardcover Ser.). 447p. 23.95 (*0-8161-5526-7*, Macmillan Reference USA) Gale Group.
—All That Remains. abr. ed. 1994. (Kay Scarpetta Mystery Ser.). audio 18.00 (*0-694-51471-3*, 390332, HarperAudio) HarperTrade.
—All That Remains. 1993. (Kay Scarpetta Mystery Ser.). 416p. mass mkt. 7.99 (*0-380-71833-2*, Avon Bks.) Morrow/Avon.
—All That Remains. unabr. ed. 1995. (Kay Scarpetta Mystery Ser. : Vol. 3). audio 78.00 (*0-7887-0168-1*, 94393E7) Recorded Bks., LLC.
—All That Remains. 1992. 416p. 26.00 (*0-684-19395-7*); 21.95 (*0-684-19515-1*) Simon & Schuster. (Scribner).
—Black Notice. 2000. 464p. mass mkt. 7.99 (*0-425-17540-5*) Berkley Publishing Group.
—Black Notice. l.t. ed. 1999. 25.95 o.p. (*0-7838-8688-8*, Macmillan Reference USA) Gale Group.
—Black Notice. abr. ed. 1999. 24.95 o.s.i (*0-399-14515-X*); 368p. 150.00 (*0-399-14522-2*, G. P. Putnam's Sons);Set. 5p. 39.95 o.s.i (*0-399-14516-8*, Putnam Berkley Audio) Penguin Group (USA) Inc.
—Black Notice. 2002. 25.95 o.s.i (*0-399-15031-5*); 1999. 415p. 25.95 o.p. (*0-399-14508-7*) Putnam Publishing Group, The.
—Black Notice. l.t. ed. 2000. 544p. pap. 13.95 (*0-375-70771-9*); 1999. 576p. 25.95 (*0-375-40845-2*) Random Hse. Large Print.
—Black Notice. 2000. 14.04 (*0-606-19510-6*) Turtleback Bks.
—The Body Farm. 1995. 368p. mass mkt. 7.99 (*0-425-14762-2*); 6.99 (*0-425-14863-7*, Prime Crime) Berkley Publishing Group.
—The Body Farm. 1994. 400p. 23.00 (*0-684-19597-6*); 403p. lib. bdg. 26.95 o.p. (*0-7838-1122-5*) Gale Group. (Macmillan Reference USA).
—The Body Farm. 1999. audio 9.98 (*0-671-04687-X*, Simon & Schuster Audioworks) Simon & Schuster Audio.
—The Body Farm. l.t. ed. 1996. (Paperback Bestsellers Ser.). pap. 20.95 (*0-7838-1123-3*) Thorndike Pr.
—Body of Evidence. unabr. ed. 1996. audio 69.95 (*0-7451-6580-X*, CAB1196) BBC Audiobooks America.
—Body of Evidence. unabr. collector's ed. 1991. (Kay Scarpetta Mystery Ser.). audio 56.00 (*0-7366-2001-X*, 2818) Books on Tape, Inc.
—Body of Evidence. unabr. ed. 1992. audio 22.95 o.p. (*1-56100-457-X*, 427); audio 57.25 o.p. (*1-56100-091-4*, 609) Brilliance Audio. (Bookcassette).
—Body of Evidence. 1991. 400p. 18.95 (*0-684-19240-3*); 1994. lib. bdg. 16.95 o.p. (*0-8161-5867-3*) Gale Group. (Macmillan Reference USA).
—Body of Evidence. abr. ed. 1995. audio 18.00 (*0-694-51592-2*, CPN 2267, HarperAudio) HarperTrade.
—Body of Evidence. 1992. (Kay Scarpetta Mystery Ser.). 416p. mass mkt. 6.99 (*0-380-71701-8*, Avon Bks.) Morrow/Avon.
—Body of Evidence. unabr. ed. 1994. audio 78.00 (*0-7887-0048-0*, 94247E7) Recorded Bks., LLC.
—Body of Evidence. Pocket Books Staff, ed. 1999. 416p. pap. 7.99 (*0-671-03856-7*, Pocket) Simon & Schuster.
—Body of Evidence. 1900. mass mkt. (*0-671-03880-X*, Pocket) Simon & Schuster.
—Body of Evidence. l.t. ed. 1994. (Mystery Ser.). lib. bdg. 26.95 (*0-8161-5866-5*) Thorndike Pr.
—Cause of Death. 1997. 368p. mass mkt. 7.99 (*0-425-15861-6*); 7.50 (*0-425-16198-6*) Berkley Publishing Group.
—Cause of Death. l.t. ed. 1998. (Thorndike/G. K. Hall Paperback Bestsellers Ser.). 430p. pap. 25.95 o.p. (*0-7838-1793-2*, Macmillan Reference USA) Gale Group.
—Cause of Death. 1996. 352p. 25.95 o.p. (*0-399-14146-4*); 340p. 150.00 (*0-399-14170-7*) Penguin Group (USA) Inc. (G. P. Putnam's Sons).
—Cause of Death. 25.95 o.s.i (*0-399-14482-X*) Putnam Publishing Group, The.
—Cause of Death. abr. ed. 1996. 23.50 o.s.i incl. audio (*0-679-44508-0*, RH Audio) Random Hse. Audio Publishing Group.
—Cause of Death. 1998. 7.98 o.p. (*0-7651-1040-7*) Smithmark Pubs., Inc.
—Cause of Death. l.t. ed. 1996. (Core Collection). 407p. lib. bdg. 29.95 (*0-7838-1792-4*) Thorndike Pr.
—Cruel & Unusual. unabr. ed. 1996. audio 84.95 (*0-7451-4358-X*, CAB1041) BBC Audiobooks America.
—Cruel & Unusual. unabr. collector's ed. 1993. (Kay Scarpetta Mystery Ser.). audio 64.00 (*0-7366-2518-6*, 3273) Books on Tape, Inc.
—Cruel & Unusual. unabr. ed. 1993. audio 23.95 o.p. (*1-56100-506-1*, 76, Bookcassette); audio 73.25 o.p. (*1-56100-135-X*, 1164, Unabridged Library Editions) Brilliance Audio.
—Cruel & Unusual. 1993. 21.00 (*0-684-19599-2*); 448p. 23.00 (*0-684-19612-3*); 439p. 25.00 o.p. (*0-8161-5727-8*) Gale Group. (Macmillan Reference USA).
—Cruel & Unusual. abr. ed. 1993. (Kate Scarpetta Mystery Ser.). 3p. audio 18.00 (*1-55994-712-8*, 390583, HarperAudio) HarperTrade.
—Cruel & Unusual. 1994. 416p. mass mkt. 7.99 (*0-380-71834-0*, Avon Bks.) Morrow/Avon.
—Cruel & Unusual. unabr. ed. 2000. (Kay Scarpetta Mystery Ser. : No. 4). audio 70.00 (*1-55690-849-0*, 93217E7) Recorded Bks., LLC.
—Cruel & Unusual. 1993. 384p. 25.00 (*0-684-19530-5*, Scribner) Simon & Schuster.
—From Potter's Field. l.t. ed. 1996. 384p. mass mkt. 7.99 (*0-425-15409-2*) Berkley Publishing Group.
—From Potter's Field. unabr. ed. 1996. (Kay Scarpetta Mystery Ser.). audio 56.00 (*0-7366-3241-7*, 3900) Books on Tape, Inc.
—From Potter's Field. 1995. 29.50 (*0-684-81318-1*); 416p. 24.00 (*0-684-19598-4*, Scribner) Simon & Schuster.
—From Potter's Field. abr. ed. 1995. (Kay Scarpetta Mystery Ser.). audio 24.00 (*0-671-86881-0*, 493119, Simon & Schuster Audioworks) Simon & Schuster Audio.
—From Potter's Field. 1997. 7.98 o.p. (*0-7651-0544-6*) Smithmark Pubs., Inc.
—From Potter's Field. l.t. ed. (Thorndike/G. K. Hall Paperback Bestsellers Ser.). 434p. 1997. pap. 25.95 (*0-7838-1292-2*); 1995. 28.95 (*0-7838-1291-4*) Thorndike Pr.
—Patricia Cornwell: 3 Complete Novels: Postmortem; Body of Evidence; All That Remains. 1997. 832p. 14.98 (*0-7651-9112-1*) Smithmark Pubs., Inc.
—Point of Origin. l.t. ed. 1998. 542p. (*0-7540-2149-1*) BBC Audiobooks America.
—Point of Origin. 1999. 416p. reprint ed. mass mkt. 7.99 (*0-425-16986-3*) Berkley Publishing Group.
—Point of Origin. 1998. 25.95 o.s.i (*0-399-14769-1*); 368p. 25.95 o.p. (*0-399-14394-7*, G. P. Putnam's Sons); 350p. 150.00 (*0-399-14412-9*, G. P. Putnam's Sons) Penguin Group (USA) Inc.
—Point of Origin. l.t. ed. (Paperback Bestsellers Ser.). 543p. 1999. pap. 28.95 (*0-7862-1478-3*); 1998. 31.95 (*0-7862-1477-5*) Thorndike Pr.
—Postmortem. unabr. ed. 1996. audio 69.95 (*0-7451-6482-X*, CAB 1098) BBC Audiobooks America.
—Postmortem. unabr. collector's ed. 1991. (Kay Scarpetta Mystery Ser.). audio 56.00 (*0-7366-2071-0*, 2879) Books on Tape, Inc.
—Postmortem. unabr. ed. 1993. 73.25 o.p. incl. audio (*1-56100-172-4*, 990, Unabridged Library Editions-);Set. audio 23.95 o.p. (*1-56100-545-2*, 217, Bookcassette) Brilliance Audio.
—Postmortem. 1999. (SPA.). pap. 14.95 (*970-05-0943-5*) Distribooks, Inc.
—Postmortem. l.t. ed. 1994. 441p. lib. bdg. 16.95 o.p. (*0-8161-5865-7*); lib. bdg. 23.95 o.p. (*0-8161-5864-9*) Gale Group. (Macmillan Reference USA).
—Postmortem. abr. ed. 1999. audio 18.00 (*0-694-52281-3*) HarperCollins Pubs.
—Postmortem, Set. abr. ed. 1992. audio 16.00 (*1-55994-528-1*, DCN 2268, HarperAudio) HarperTrade.
—Postmortem, Set. unabr. ed. 1999. audio 73.25 Highsmith Inc.
—Postmortem. 1991. 352p. pap. 6.49 (*0-380-71021-8*, Avon Bks.) Morrow/Avon.
—Postmortem. 2000. (Best Mysteries of All Time Ser.). 333p. (*0-7621-8859-6*) Reader's Digest Assn., Inc., The.
—Postmortem. unabr. ed. 1993. (Kay Scarpetta Mystery Ser. : Vol. 1). audio 70.00 (*1-55690-892-X*, 93334E7) Recorded Bks., LLC.
—Postmortem. 2004. 352p. mass mkt. 7.99 (*0-7434-7715-4*, Pocket); 1990. 293p. 21.00 o.s.i (*0-684-19141-5*, Scribner); 1998. 352p. mass mkt. 7.99 (*0-671-02361-6*, Pocket) Simon & Schuster.
—The Scarpetta Collection Vol. I: Postmortem & Body of Evidence. 2003. 640p. 26.95 (*0-7432-5580-1*, Scribner) Simon & Schuster.
—The Scarpetta Collection Vol. II: All That Remains & Cruel & Unusual. 2003. 672p. 26.95 (*0-7432-5581-X*, Scribner) Simon & Schuster.
—Scarpetta's Winter Table. 1998. (Illus.). 96p. 19.95 (*0-941711-42-0*) Penguin Group (USA) Inc.
—Unnatural Exposure. 1998. 384p. mass mkt. 7.99 (*0-425-16340-7*) Berkley Publishing Group.
—Unnatural Exposure. 25.95 (*0-399-14544-3*); 1997. 352p. 25.95 o.p. (*0-399-14285-1*, G. P. Putnam's Sons); 1997. 352p. 150.00 (*0-399-14295-9*, G. P. Putnam's Sons) Penguin Group (USA) Inc.
—Unnatural Exposure. l.t. ed. (Paperback Bestsellers Ser.). 415p. 1998. pap. 28.95 (*0-7838-8088-X*); 1997. lib. bdg. 30.95 (*0-7838-8087-1*) Thorndike Pr.
—Unnatural Exposure: A Novel, Set. abr. ed. 1997. (Kay Scarpetta Mystery Ser.). audio 24.00 o.s.i (*0-679-44509-9*, 495252, RH Audio) Random Hse. Audio Publishing Group.
Deaver, Jeffery. The Bone Collector: A Lincoln Rhyme Novel. l.t. ed. 1998. (Large Print Bks.). pap. 23.95 o.p. (*1-56895-524-3*, Wheeler Publishing, Inc.) Gale Group.
—The Bone Collector: A Lincoln Rhyme Novel. 1998. 432p. mass mkt. 7.99 (*0-451-18845-4*, Signet Bks.) NAL.
—The Bone Collector: A Lincoln Rhyme Novel. 1997. 432p. 22.95 o.s.i (*0-670-86871-X*) Viking Penguin.
—The Coffin Dancer: A Lincoln Rhyme Novel. l.t. ed. 1998. 27.95 (*1-56895-698-3*, Wheeler Publishing, Inc.) Gale Group.
—The Coffin Dancer: A Lincoln Rhyme Novel. 1999. E-Book 25.00 (*0-684-86805-9*, Simon & Schuster); 1999. pap. 6.99 (*0-671-02606-2*, Pocket); 1998.

368p. 25.00 o.s.i (*0-684-85285-3*, Simon & Schuster); 1999. (Illus.). 560p. reprint ed. mass mkt. 7.99 (*0-671-02409-4*, Pocket) Simon & Schuster.

—The Devil's Teardrop: A Novel of the Last Night of the Century. E-Book 25.00 (*1-930161-37-9*) Adobe Systems, Inc.

—The Devil's Teardrop: A Novel of the Last Night of the Century. l.t. ed. 2000. pap. 11.95 (*1-56895-982-6*); 1999. 527p. 26.95 o.p. (*1-56895-804-8*) Gale Group. (Wheeler Publishing, Inc.).

—The Devil's Teardrop: A Novel of the Last Night of the Century. 2000. E-Book 9.99 (*0-684-85659-X*, Simon & Schuster); 1999. 400p. mass mkt. 7.99 (*0-671-03712-9*, Pocket); 1999. 400p. 25.00 o.s.i (*0-684-85292-6*, Simon & Schuster); 2000. (Illus.). 480p. reprint ed. pap. 7.99 (*0-671-03844-3*, Pocket) Simon & Schuster.

—The Devil's Teardrop: A Novel of the Last Night of the Century. abr. ed. 1999. 352p. audio 24.00 (*0-671-04569-5*, Simon & Schuster Audioworks) Simon & Schuster Audio.

—The Devil's Teardrop: A Novel of the Last Night of the Century. l.t. ed. 2002. (Charnwood Large Print Ser.). 520p. 32.50 o.p. (*0-7089-9298-6*, Charnwood) Thorpe, F. A. Pubs. GBR. *Dist:* Ulverscroft Large Print Bks., Ltd., Ulverscroft Large Print Canada, Ltd.

—The Empty Chair: A Lincoln Rhyme Novel. 2000. E-Book 25.00 (*0-7432-1165-0*); (Illus.). 416p. 25.00 o.s.i (*0-684-85563-1*); 416p. 25.00 (*0-7432-0162-0*); 624p. 25.00 o.s.i (*0-7432-0424-7*) Simon & Schuster. (Simon & Schuster).

—The Empty Chair: A Lincoln Rhyme Novel. abr. ed. 2000. audio 25.00 (*0-7435-0052-0*, Simon & Schuster Audioworks) Simon & Schuster Audio.

—Speaking in Tongues: A Novel. 2000. 336p. 25.00 o.s.i (*0-684-87126-2*, Simon & Schuster) Simon & Schuster.

—Speaking in Tongues: A Novel. 1999. 21.95 (*0-670-86073-5*, Viking) Viking Penguin.

Donaldson, D. J. Blood on the Bayou. 1991. 16.95 o.p. (*0-312-05387-8*, Saint Martin's Minotaur) St. Martin's Pr.

—Cajun Nights. 1989. pap. 3.95 o.p. (*0-312-91610-8*, St. Martin's Paperbacks); 1988. 256p. 16.95 o.p. (*0-312-02175-5*, Saint Martin's Minotaur) St. Martin's Pr.

—Louisiana Fever. (Andy Broussard/Kit Franklyn Mysteries Ser.). 288p. 1997. mass mkt. 5.99 o.p. (*0-312-96257-6*, St. Martin's Paperbacks); 1996. 21.95 o.p. (*0-312-14362-1*, Saint Martin's Minotaur) St. Martin's Pr.

—New Orleans Requiem. 1995. (Mystery Ser.). 250p. per. (*0-373-26188-8*, 1-26188-2, Worldwide Library) Harlequin Enterprises, Ltd.

—New Orleans Requiem. 1994. 240p. 19.95 o.p. (*0-312-10495-2*, Saint Martin's Minotaur) St. Martin's Pr.

—No Mardi Gras for the Dead. 1995. (WWL Mystery Ser.). mass mkt. (*0-373-26163-2*, 1-26163-5, Harlequin Bks.) Harlequin Enterprises, Ltd.

—No Mardi Gras for the Dead. 1992. (Andy Broussard - Kit Franklyn Mystery Ser.). 216p. 17.95 o.p. (*0-312-08271-1*) St. Martin's Pr.

—Sleeping with the Crawfish: An Andy Broussard & Kit Franklyn Mystery. (Andy Broussard/Kit Franklyn Mysteries Ser.). 272p. 1998. mass mkt. 5.99 (*0-312-96681-4*, St. Martin's Paperbacks); 1997. 21.95 o.p. (*0-312-17025-4*, Saint Martin's Minotaur) St. Martin's Pr.

Goldberg, Leonard S. Deadly Care. 1996. 336p. 23.95 o.s.i (*0-525-94092-8*, Dutton) Dutton/Plume.

—Deadly Care. 1997. 416p. mass mkt. 6.99 o.s.i (*0-451-18742-3*, Signet Bks.) NAL.

—Deadly Exposure. 1998. 336p. 23.95 o.p. (*0-525-94427-3*) Dutton/Plume.

—Deadly Exposure. 2000. 416p. reprint ed. mass mkt. 6.99 (*0-451-40872-1*, Signet Bks.) NAL.

—Deadly Harvest. 1997. 320p. 23.95 o.s.i (*0-525-94093-6*) Dutton/Plume.

—Deadly Harvest. 1998. 416p. mass mkt. 6.99 o.s.i (*0-451-18743-1*, Signet Bks.) NAL.

—Deadly Medicine. 1992. 352p. (Orig.). mass mkt. 6.99 (*0-451-17439-9*, Signet Bks.) NAL.

—Deadly Practice. 1994. 320p. (Orig.). mass mkt. 6.99 (*0-451-17945-5*) NAL.

—Lethal Measures: A Novel of Medical Suspense. 2000. (Illus.). 304p. 24.95 o.s.i (*0-525-94528-8*, Dutton) Dutton/Plume.

—Lethal Measures: A Novel of Medical Suspense. 2000. 416p. mass mkt. 6.99 o.s.i (*0-451-20156-6*, Onyx) NAL.

McCrery, Nigel. Silent Witness. pap. (*0-312-30022-0*, Saint Martin's Griffin); 2001. 324p. per. 15.95 (*0-312-29197-3*, Dunne, Thomas Bks.); 1998. 320p. 23.95 (*0-312-18178-7*, Saint Martin's Minotaur) St. Martin's Pr.

—Silent Witness. l.t. ed. 1999. (Charnwood Large Print Ser.). 344p. 31.99 o.p. (*0-7089-9116-5*, Ulverscroft) Thorpe, F. A. Pubs. GBR. *Dist:* Ulverscroft Large Print Bks., Ltd., Ulverscroft Large Print Canada, Ltd.

—The Spider's Web. 1999. 320p. 22.95 o.p. (*0-312-20017-X*, Saint Martin's Minotaur) St. Martin's Pr.

—Strange Screams of Death. l.t. ed. 2001. (Charnwood Large Print Ser.). 408p. 32.50 (*0-7089-9191-2*) Ulverscroft Large Print Bks., Ltd.

McCrumb, Sharyn. Lovely in Her Bones. 1999. 5.99 (*0-345-91574-7*); 1998. mass mkt. o.s.i (*0-345-42947-8*); 1990. 224p. reprint ed. mass mkt. 5.99 (*0-345-36035-4*) Ballantine Bks.

—Lovely in Her Bones. l.t. ed. 2000. (Wheeler Large Print Book Ser.). 249p. pap. 23.95 (*1-56895-859-5*, Wheeler Publishing, Inc.) Gale Group.

—Lovely in Her Bones. 1985. 224p. pap. 2.95 o.p. (*0-380-89592-7*, Avon Bks.) Morrow/Avon.

—Lovely in Her Bones. 1993. 224p. lib. bdg. 20.00 o.p. (*0-7278-4495-4*) Severn Hse. Pubs., Ltd.

—MacPherson's Lament. (Elizabeth MacPherson Ser.). 304p. 1993. mass mkt. 6.99 (*0-345-38474-1*); 1992. 17.00 o.p. (*0-345-36576-3*) Ballantine Bks.

—MacPherson's Lament. l.t. ed. 2002. 30.95 (*1-58724-230-3*, Wheeler Publishing, Inc.) Gale Group.

—MacPherson's Lament. unabr. ed. 2000. audio 46.00 (*0-7887-3109-2*, 95820E7) Recorded Bks., LLC.

—Missing Susan. 2000. mass mkt. 6.99 (*0-345-91578-X*); 1992. 256p. reprint ed. mass mkt. 5.99 (*0-345-37945-4*) Ballantine Bks.

—Missing Susan. l.t. ed. 1993. (General Ser.). 408p. pap. 18.95 (*0-8161-5566-6*, Macmillan Reference USA) Gale Group.

—Missing Susan. unabr. ed. 1998. audio 51.00 (*0-7887-1993-9*, 95380E7) Recorded Bks., LLC.

—Paying the Piper. 1999. 5.99 (*0-345-91576-3*); 1988. 192p. mass mkt. 5.99 (*0-345-34518-5*) Ballantine Bks.

—Paying the Piper. unabr. ed. 1993. audio 35.00 (*1-55690-709-5*, 93109E7) Recorded Bks., LLC.

—Paying the Piper. 1991. reprint ed. 18.95 o.p. (*0-7278-4247-1*) Severn Hse. Pubs., Ltd.

—Sick of Shadows. 1999. 5.99 (*0-345-91573-9*); 1998. mass mkt. o.s.i (*0-345-42946-X*); 1989. 240p. mass mkt. 6.99 (*0-345-35653-5*) Ballantine Bks.

—Sick of Shadows. 240p. 1984. pap. 2.95 o.p. (*0-380-87189-0*, 87189); 1992. reprint ed. 19.00 o.p. (*0-7278-4334-6*) Severn Hse. Pubs., Ltd.

—Sick of Shadows. l.t. ed. 2000. (Basic Ser.). 352p. 29.95 (*0-7862-2370-7*) Thorndike Pr.

Pomidor, Bill. Anatomy of a Murder. 1996. (Cal & Plato Marley Mystery Ser.). 272p. mass mkt. 5.50 o.s.i (*0-451-18417-3*, Signet Bks.) NAL.

—Mind over Murder. 1998. (Cal & Plato Marley Mystery Ser.). 288p. mass mkt. 5.99 o.s.i (*0-451-19216-8*, Signet Bks.) NAL.

—Murder by Prescription. 1995. (Cal & Plato Marley Ser.). 288p. mass mkt. 4.99 o.s.i (*0-451-18416-5*, Signet Bks.) NAL.

—Skeletons in the Closet. 1997. (Cal & Plato Marley Mystery Ser.). 288p. mass mkt. 5.50 o.s.i (*0-451-18418-1*, Signet Bks.) NAL.

—Ten Little Medicine Men. 1998. (Cal & Plato Marley Mystery Ser.). 288p. mass mkt. 5.99 o.s.i (*0-451-19214-1*, Signet Bks.) NAL.

Rayner, Claire. First Blood. l.t. ed. 1995. (Charnwood Large Print Ser.). 480p. 29.99 o.p. (*0-7089-8825-3*, Charnwood) Thorpe, F. A. Pubs. GBR. *Dist:* Ulverscroft Large Print Bks., Ltd., Ulverscroft Large Print Canada, Ltd.

—Fourth Attempt. l.t. ed. 1997. (Charnwood Large Print Ser.). 496p. 29.99 o.p. (*0-7089-8975-6*, Ulverscroft) Thorpe, F. A. Pubs. GBR. *Dist:* Ulverscroft Large Print Bks., Ltd., Ulverscroft Large Print Canada, Ltd.

—Second Opinion. unabr. ed. 1995. audio 84.95 (*0-7451-6539-7*, CAB 1155) BBC Audiobooks America.

—Second Opinion. l.t. ed. 1996. (Charnwood Large Print Ser.). 528p. 29.99 o.p. (*0-7089-8897-0*, Ulverscroft) Thorpe, F. A. Pubs. GBR. *Dist:* Ulverscroft Large Print Bks., Ltd., Ulverscroft Large Print Canada, Ltd.

Reichs, Kathy. Deadly Decisions. 2000. 336p. 25.00 (*0-684-85971-8*); E-Book 25.00 (*0-7432-1077-8*); 464p. 25.00 o.s.i (*0-7432-0429-8*) Simon & Schuster. (Scribner).

—Deadly Decisions. abr. ed. 2000. audio 25.00 (*0-7435-0054-7*, Simon & Schuster Audioworks) Simon & Schuster Audio.

—Death du Jour. unabr. ed. 2002. audio compact disk 110.95; 2000. audio 96.95 (*0-7927-2346-5*, CSL235, Chivers Sound Library) BBC Audiobooks America.

—Death du Jour. unabr. ed. 2000. 12p. audio compact disk 110.95 (*0-7540-5330-X*, CCD 021) Chivers Audio Bks. GBR. *Dist:* BBC Audiobooks America.

—Death du Jour. 1999. 384p. mass mkt. 7.99 (*0-671-03472-3*, Pocket); 1999. E-Book 25.00 (*0-7432-0080-2*, Scribner); 1999. 384p. 25.00 (*0-684-84118-5*, Scribner); 1999. 384p. 25.00 (*0-684-86906-3*, Scribner); 2000. (Illus.). 480p. reprint ed. mass mkt. 7.99 (*0-671-01137-5*, Pocket) Simon & Schuster.

—Death du Jour, Set. abr. ed. 1999. audio 24.00 (*0-671-04370-6*, 599126, Simon & Schuster Audioworks) Simon & Schuster Audio.

—Death du Jour. l.t. ed. (Thorndike/G. K. Hall Paperback Bestsellers Ser.). 632p. 2000. (FRE.). pap. 27.95 (*0-7862-1997-1*); 1999. 30.95 (*0-7862-1996-3*) Thorndike Pr.

—Death du Jour. abr. ed. 1999. audio 24.35 (*1-85686-522-3*) Ulverscroft Audio (U.S.A.).

—Deja Dead. 2001. E-Book 9.99 (*1-58945-168-6*) Adobe Systems, Inc.

—Deja Dead. 1998. (Illus.). 411p. (J). o.p. (*0-434-00427-8*) Random Hse. of Canada, Ltd. CAN. *Dist:* Random Hse., Inc.

—Deja Dead, unabr. ed. 1998. audio 96.00 (*0-7887-1750-2*, 95228E7) Recorded Bks., LLC.

—Deja Dead. 2000. E-Book 9.99 (*0-684-83906-7*, Scribner); 1998. (Illus.). 560p. mass mkt. 7.99 (*0-671-01136-7*, Pocket); 1997. 282.00 (*0-684-00611-1*, Scribner); 1997. (Illus.). 416p. 24.00 (*0-684-84117-7*, Scribner) Simon & Schuster.

—Deja Dead. abr. ed. 1997. 5p. audio 24.00 (*0-671-57706-9*, 495419, Simon & Schuster Audioworks) Simon & Schuster Audio.

—Deja Dead. l.t. ed. 1998. (Basic Ser.). 664p. 30.95 (*0-7862-1265-9*) Thorndike Pr.

Slater, Susan. The Pumpkin Seed Massacre. Ellison, Lee, ed. 1999. (Ben Pecos Mysteries Ser.: Vol. 1). 240p. 22.95 o.p. (*1-890768-17-0*, Intrigue Pr.) Corvus Publishing.

—Yellow Lies: A Ben Pecos Mystery. 2000. (Ben Pecos Mysteries Ser.). 297p. 22.95 (*1-890768-26-X*, Intrigue Pr.) Corvus Publishing.

Stephens, Kay. Sign of the Moon. 1999. (*0-7540-1263-8*); 373p. (*0-7540-2192-0*) BBC Audiobooks America.

—Sign of the Moon. 1998. 256p. 24.00 o.p. (*0-7278-5268-X*) Severn Hse. Pubs., Ltd.

—Sign of the Moon. l.t. ed. 1999. (Romance Ser.). 375p. 25.95 (*0-7862-1783-9*) Thorndike Pr.

Walker, Robert W. Blind Instinct: A Jessica Coren Novel. 2000. 369p. 21.95 o.s.i (*0-425-17234-1*) Berkley Publishing Group.

—Darkest Instinct. 1996. 464p. mass mkt. 6.99 o.s.i (*0-515-11856-7*, Jove) Berkley Publishing Group.

—Extreme Instinct. 1998. 400p. mass mkt. 6.99 o.s.i (*0-515-12195-9*, Jove) Berkley Publishing Group.

—Fatal Instinct. 1993. 5.99 o.s.i (*1-55773-950-1*, Diamond Bks.) Ace Bks.

—Fatal Instinct. 1995. 320p. mass mkt. 6.99 o.s.i (*0-515-11913-X*, Jove) Berkley Publishing Group.

—Killer Instinct. 1992. 336p. 5.99 o.s.i (*1-55773-743-6*, Diamond Bks.) Ace Bks.

—Killer Instinct. 1995. 336p. mass mkt. 6.99 o.s.i (*0-515-11790-0*, Jove) Berkley Publishing Group.

—Primal Instinct. 1994. 368p. (Orig.). pap. 5.99 o.s.i (*0-7865-0055-7*, Diamond Bks.) Ace Bks.

—Primal Instinct. 1995. 368p. (Orig.). mass mkt. 6.99 o.s.i (*0-515-11949-0*, Jove) Berkley Publishing Group.

—Pure Instinct. 1995. 432p. (Orig.). mass mkt. 6.99 (*0-515-11755-2*, Jove) Berkley Publishing Group.

**FORENSIC PSYCHIATRISTS—FICTION**

Ablow, Keith Russell. Compulsion: A Novel. E-Book 24.95 (*0-312-70706-1*); 2002. 320p. 24.95 (*0-312-26641-3*); 2003. 384p. reprint ed. mass mkt. 6.99 (*0-312-98824-9*, St. Martin's Paperbacks) St. Martin's Pr.

Carr, Caleb. The Alienist. 1995. 608p. mass mkt. 7.99 (*0-553-57299-7*); mass mkt. 6.99 o.s.i (*0-553-84001-0*) Bantam Bks.

—The Alienist. unabr. ed. 1995. audio 104.00 (*0-7366-2898-3*, 3598) Books on Tape, Inc.

—The Alienist. l.t. ed. 1994. pap. 22.95 o.p. (*1-56895-078-0*, Wheeler Publishing, Inc.) Gale Group.

—The Alienist. 1994. 496p. 29.95 o.s.i (*0-679-41779-6*) Random Hse., Inc.

—The Alienist. abr. ed. 1994. audio 22.00 (*0-671-88757-2*, 492028, Simon & Schuster Audioworks) Simon & Schuster Audio.

—The Angel of Darkness. 1998. mass mkt. 7.99 o.s.i (*0-345-42514-6*); 768p. mass mkt. 7.99 (*0-345-42763-7*) Ballantine Bks.

—The Angel of Darkness. unabr. ed. 1998. audio 72.00 (*0-7366-4114-9*, 4619-A); audio 72.00 (*0-7366-4115-7*, 4619-B) Books on Tape, Inc.

—The Angel of Darkness. l.t. ed. 1999. pap. 25.95 o.p. (*0-7838-8242-4*, Macmillan Reference USA) Gale Group.

—The Angel of Darkness. abr. ed. 1997. audio 25.00 (*0-671-57748-4*, 595482, Simon & Schuster Audioworks) Simon & Schuster Audio.

Ephron, G. H. Addiction. 2001. 304p. 23.95 (*0-312-26677-4*, Saint Martin's Minotaur) St. Martin's Pr.

—Obsessed. Date not set. mass mkt. (*0-312-99470-2*, St. Martin's Paperbacks); 2003. 320p. 24.95 (*0-312-30531-1*, Saint Martin's Minotaur) St. Martin's Pr.

Glass, Joseph. Blood: A Susan Shader Novel. 2000. (Susan Shader Novels Ser.). 400p. 24.00 (*0-684-85963-7*, Simon & Schuster) Simon & Schuster.

—Eyes. 1999. mass mkt. 6.99 o.s.i (*0-449-00512-7*, Fawcett) Ballantine Bks.

Jones, Dylan. Outside the Rules. l.t. ed. 2003. (Magna Large Print Ser.). 448p. 32.50 (*0-7505-2053-1*) Magna Large Print Bks. GBR. *Dist:* Ulverscroft Large Print Bks., Ltd., Ulverscroft Large Print Canada, Ltd.

—Outside the Rules. 1995. 21.00 o.p. (*0-312-11873-2*, Saint Martin's Minotaur) St. Martin's Pr.

Lovett, Sarah. Acquired Motives: A Novel. 1997. mass mkt. 5.99 o.s.i (*0-8041-1298-3*, Ivy Bks.) Ballantine Bks.

—Acquired Motives: A Novel. aut. ed. 1996. 22.95 o.s.i (*0-676-51776-5*, Villard Bks.) Random House Adult Trade Publishing Group.

—Acquired Motives: A Novel. 2003. (Illus.). 368p. pap. 6.99 (*0-7434-6335-8*, Pocket) Simon & Schuster.

—Dangerous Attachments. 1996. 344p. mass mkt. 5.99 o.s.i (*0-8041-1297-5*, Ivy Bks.) Ballantine Bks.

—Dangerous Attachments: A Dr. Sylvia Strange Novel. 2003. 400p. pap. 6.99 (*0-7434-6334-X*, Pocket) Simon & Schuster.

—Dante's Inferno. 2001. (Dr. Sylvia Strange Novels Ser.: No. 4). 320p. 24.00 (*0-684-85598-4*, Simon & Schuster) Simon & Schuster.

—Dark Alchemy. 2003. 304p. 24.00 (*0-684-85599-2*, Simon & Schuster) Simon & Schuster.

—A Desperate Silence: A Novel. 1998. mass mkt. 5.99 o.s.i (*0-8041-1299-1*, Ivy Bks.) Ballantine Bks.

—A Desperate Silence: A Novel. l.t. ed. 1998. 24.95 (*1-57490-152-4*) Beeler, Thomas T. Publisher.

—A Desperate Silence: A Novel. 2003. (Illus.). 400p. pap. 7.50 (*0-7434-6336-6*, Pocket) Simon & Schuster.

McFadden, Joseph T. Hermes' Viper. E-Book 4.95 (*1-58820-675-0*); 2002. 338p. 28.04 (*1-58820-674-2*); 2001. 338p. pap. 20.23 (*1-58820-673-4*) 1stBooks Library.

—Hermes' Viper. 2000. 450p. pap. 21.95 (*0-9703526-0-3*) Angus Publishing.

—Hermes' Viper. 2000. (*1-892693-14-3*) Hughes Henshaw Pubns.

O'Connell, Carol. Judas Child. 1999. 432p. reprint ed. mass mkt. 7.99 (*0-515-12549-0*, Jove) Berkley Publishing Group.

—Judas Child. abr. ed. 1999. audio 7.99 o.s.i (*1-56740-294-1*, 1863, Paperback Nova Audio Bks.); 1998. audio 28.95 (*1-56100-797-8*, 16, Bookcassette); 1998. audio 89.25 (*1-56740-576-2*, 913, Unabridged Library Editions); Set. 1998. audio 17.95 o.p. (*1-56740-771-4*, 447, Nova Audio Bks.) Brilliance Audio.

—Judas Child. 1998. 340p. 24.95 o.p. (*0-399-14380-7*, G. P. Putnam's Sons) Penguin Group (USA) Inc.

Philpin, John. Dreams in the Key of Blue. 2000. 368p. mass mkt. 6.50 (*0-553-58006-X*) Bantam Bks.

—The Prettiest Feathers. 1997. 336p. pap. 23.00 (*0-553-76244-3*) Bantam Bks.

—Tunnel of Night. 1999. 384p. pap. 19.00 (*0-553-76201-X*) Bantam Bks.

Philpin, John & Sierra, Patricia. The Prettiest Feathers. 1997. 336p. mass mkt. 5.50 o.s.i (*0-553-57555-4*) Bantam Bks.

—Tunnel of Night. 1999. 384p. mass mkt. 6.50 o.s.i (*0-553-57954-1*) Bantam Bks.

Salter, Anna. Fault Lines. 1998. E-Book 22.00 (*0-671-03696-3*, Atria); 1998. 272p. 22.00 (*0-671-00312-7*, Atria); 1999. 368p. reprint ed. mass mkt. 6.99 o.s.i (*0-671-00313-5*, Pocket Star); Vol. 2. Date not set. (*0-671-02352-7*, Atria) Simon & Schuster.

—Shiny Water. 1998. 320p. per. 6.50 (*0-671-00311-9*, Pocket Star); 1997. 272p. 23.00 (*0-671-00310-0*, Atria) Simon & Schuster.

Wooley, Marilyn. Jackpot Justice. E-Book 24.95 (*0-312-27384-3*); 2000. 352p. 24.95 (*0-312-25455-5*, Saint Martin's Minotaur) St. Martin's Pr.

## G

**GOLFERS—FICTION**

Bernhardt, William. Final Round. 2003. 336p. mass mkt. 7.50 (*0-345-44963-0*); 2002. 256p. 23.95 (*0-345-44962-2*) Ballantine Bks. (Ballantine Bks.).

—Final Round. l.t. ed. 2003. 307p. 25.95 (*0-375-43276-0*, Random House Large Print) Random Hse. Large Print.

Breaznell, Gene. Deadly Divots: A Golf Murder Mystery. 2003. 264p. 23.95 (*1-882593-74-X*) Bridge Works Publishing Co., Inc.

Coyne, Tom. A Gentleman's Game. l.t. ed. 2001. 352p. 25.00 (*0-06-620996-X*, HarperLargePrint) HarperTrade.

—A Gentleman's Game: A Novel. 2001. 224p. 24.00 o.p. (*0-87113-791-7*, Atlantic Monthly Pr.); 2002. 272p. reprint ed. pap. 13.00 (*0-8021-3890-X*, Grove Pr.) Grove/Atlantic, Inc.

—A Gentleman's Game: A Novel. unabr. ed. 2001. audio 34.95 (*0-694-52522-7*, H227, HarperAudio) HarperTrade.

Cullen, Robert. A Mulligan for Bobby Jobe. 2001. 400p. 26.00 (*0-06-018554-6*) HarperCollins Pubs.
—A Mulligan for Bobby Jobe: A Novel. 2002. 400p. pap. 13.95 (*0-06-093352-6*, Perennial) HarperTrade.
Forse, Harry. A Storm at Pebble Beach. 2000. 214p. 22.00 (*1-886947-84-8*) Clock Tower Pr. LLC.
Griffith, Michael. Spikes. 2002. 288p. pap. 12.95 (*1-55970-633-3*); 2001. 258p. 24.95 (*1-55970-536-1*) Arcade Publishing, Inc.
Jenkins, Dan. Dead Solid Perfect. 2000. (Illus.). 256p. pap. 13.95 (*0-385-49885-3*, Main St. Bks.) Broadway Bks.
—The Money-Whipped Steer-Job Three-Jack Give-Up Artist. 2002. 272p. reprint ed. pap. 14.95 (*0-7679-0587-3*) Broadway Bks.
Labbance, Bob. Golf in the Year 2100: A Fanciful Glimpse at the Future of Golf. 2003. (Good Golf! Ser.). (Illus.). 144p. 12.95 (*1-931249-23-7*) Towle-House Publishing Co.
Lipman, Elinor. The Dearly Departed. 2001. E-Book 8.95 (*1-58945-947-4*) Adobe Systems, Inc.
—The Dearly Departed. 2002. 288p. pap. 13.00 (*0-375-72458-3*, Vintage) Knopf Publishing Group.
—The Dearly Departed: A Novel. 2001. E-Book 19.00 (*1-58836-013-X*) Random Hse., Inc.
Shrake, Bud. Billy Boy. 2001. (Illus.). 240p. 21.00 (*0-7432-2480-9*, Simon & Schuster) Simon & Schuster.
Snyder, Don J. Winter Dreams: A Novel. 2004. 256p. 23.95 (*0-385-50850-6*) Doubleday Publishing.
Veron, J. Michael. The Greatest Course That Never Was. 2001. 384p. 22.95 (*1-886947-92-9*) Clock Tower Pr. LLC.
—The Greatest Course That Never Was: A Novel. 2002. 384p. reprint ed. pap. 12.95 (*0-7679-0717-5*) Broadway Bks.
Viall, W. Shelley. Golf, a Dreadful Hazard. 2002. pap. 6.95 (*0-87714-277-7*) Denlingers Pubs., Ltd.

# J

## JOCKEYS—FICTION

Baker, Donna. Ride for a Fall. 1998. 192p. 24.00 (*0-7278-5305-8*) Severn Hse. Pubs., Ltd.
—Ride for a Fall. l.t. ed. 2000. (Romance Ser.). 266p. 25.95 (*0-7862-2648-X*); (*0-7540-4231-6*); (*0-7540-4232-4*) Thorndike Pr.
Daniel, Mark. The Devil to Pay. l.t. ed. 1995. 391p. pap. 20.95 o.p. (*0-7838-1351-1*, Macmillan Reference USA) Gale Group.
—The Devil to Pay. 1993. 260p. 19.95 o.p. (*0-316-17265-0*) Little Brown & Co.
—The Devil to Pay. l.t. ed. 1995. (Magna Large Print Ser.). 442p. o.p. (*0-7505-0773-X*) Magna Large Print Bks. GBR. *Dist:* Ulverscroft Large Print Canada, Ltd.
—The Devil to Pay. 1995. 256p. mass mkt. 4.99 (*0-380-72328-X*, Avon Bks.) Morrow/Avon.
—Pity the Sinner. l.t. ed. 1994. (Magna Large Print Ser.). 460p. 29.99 o.p. (*0-7505-0728-4*) Magna Large Print Bks. GBR. *Dist:* Ulverscroft Large Print Bks., Ltd., Ulverscroft Large Print Canada, Ltd.
—Pity the Sinner. 1996. 288p. 22.95 (*0-312-14027-4*, Saint Martin's Minotaur) St. Martin's Pr.
—Unbridled. 1990. 224p. 17.95 o.p. (*0-89919-922-4*) Houghton Mifflin Co.
—Unbridled. 1992. 256p. mass mkt. 4.99 (*0-380-71443-4*, Avon Bks.) Morrow/Avon.
Francis, Dick. Bolt. 1996. audio 29.95 (*0-7451-2842-4*) BBC Audiobooks America.
—Bolt. 1988. 336p. mass mkt. 5.95 o.s.i (*0-449-21239-4*, Fawcett) Ballantine Bks.
—Bolt. unabr. ed. 1993. (Kit Fielding Adventure Ser.: Bk. 2). audio 49.95 (*0-7451-4169-2*, CAB 852) Chivers Audio Bks. GBR. *Dist:* BBC Audiobooks America.
—Bolt. abr. ed. 1990. 2p. audio 16.99 (*0-88646-219-3*, 7219) Durkin Hayes Publishing Ltd.
—Bolt. l.t. ed. 1988. 388p. 19.95 o.p. (*0-8161-4329-3*); 12.95 o.p. (*0-8161-4330-7*) Gale Group. (Macmillan Reference USA).
—Bolt. 1987. 320p. 17.95 o.s.i (*0-399-13226-0*, G. P. Putnam's Sons) Penguin Putnam Bks. for Young Readers.
—Bolt. unabr. ed. 1999. audio 51.00 (*0-7887-2937-3*, 95719E7); audio compact disk 66.00 (*0-7887-3435-0*, C1041E7) Recorded Bks., LLC.
—Break In. 1987. 384p. mass mkt. 5.99 o.s.i (*0-449-20755-2*, Fawcett) Ballantine Bks.
—Break In. abr. ed. 1987. (gr. 8-10). pap. 29.99 incl. audio (*0-88646-824-8*, R7128) Durkin Hayes Publishing Ltd.
—Break In. l.t. ed. 1987. (General Ser.). 18.95 o.p. (*0-8161-4161-4*); pap. 11.95 o.p. (*0-8161-4162-2*) Gale Group. (Macmillan Reference USA).
—Break In. 2001. 17.95 (*0-399-13685-1*) Penguin Group (USA) Inc.
—Break In. 1986. 17.95 o.p. (*0-399-13121-3*, G. P. Putnam's Sons) Penguin Putnam Bks. for Young Readers.
—Dead Cert. 1987. mass mkt. 6.99 o.s.i (*0-449-21263-7*, Fawcett) Ballantine Bks.
—Dead Cert. 288p. 2004. mass mkt. 6.99 (*0-425-19497-3*); 2000. mass mkt. 6.99 (*0-515-12726-4*, Jove) Berkley Publishing Group.
—Dead Cert. unabr. ed. 1994. audio 48.00 (*0-7366-2721-9*, 3451) Books on Tape, Inc.
—Dead Cert. l.t. ed. 1994. 365p. 22.95 (*0-8161-5784-7*, Macmillan Reference USA) Gale Group.
—Dead Cert. Barzun, Jacques & Taylor, W. H., eds. 1983. (Crime Fiction 1950-1975 Ser.). 220p. lib. bdg. 18.00 o.p. (*0-8240-4991-8*) Garland Publishing, Inc.
—Dead Cert. 1990. audio 15.95; audio 16.00 o.s.i (*1-55994-142-1*, CPN 2139) HarperTrade. (HarperAudio).
—Dead Cert, unabr. ed. 1996. audio 51.00 Recorded Bks., LLC.
—Dead Cert; Nerve; For Kicks. 1996. mass mkt. 7.99 o.s.i (*0-449-28768-8*, Fawcett) Ballantine Bks.
—Enquiry. 1987. 280p. mass mkt. 6.99 o.s.i (*0-449-21268-8*, Fawcett) Ballantine Bks.
—Enquiry. 2000. 272p. mass mkt. 6.99 (*0-515-12867-8*, Jove) Berkley Publishing Group.
—Enquiry. unabr. ed. 2000. audio compact disk 49.99 (*0-7861-9933-4*, z1736); 1996. audio 32.95 (*0-7861-0959-9*, 1736) Blackstone Audio Bks., Inc.
—Enquiry. unabr. ed. 1993. audio 49.95 (*0-7451-5949-4*, CAB 051) Chivers Audio Bks. GBR. *Dist:* BBC Audiobooks America.
—Enquiry. l.t. ed. 1995. 305p. lib. bdg. 22.95 o.p. (*0-7838-1142-X*, Macmillan Reference USA) Gale Group.
—Enquiry. unabr. ed. 1990. audio 44.00 (*1-55690-169-0*, 90088E7) Recorded Bks., LLC.
—Enquiry. 1984. mass mkt. 3.50 (*0-671-54362-8*); 1981. pap. 2.95 o.s.i (*0-671-44926-5*) Simon & Schuster. (Pocket).
—Enquiry. unabr. ed. 1983. audio 53.95 o.p. (*0-8161-9771-7*) Thorndike Pr.
—Enquiry. l.t. ed. 1980. (Ulverscroft Large Print Ser.). 12.00 o.p. (*0-7089-0399-1*, Ulverscroft) Thorpe, F. A. Pubs. GBR. *Dist:* Ulverscroft Large Print Bks., Ltd., Ulverscroft Large Print Canada, Ltd.
—Flying Finish. 1997. mass mkt. 6.99 (*0-449-45726-5*); 1987. mass mkt. 6.99 o.s.i (*0-449-21265-3*) Ballantine Bks. (Fawcett).
—Flying Finish. 1999. 288p. mass mkt. 6.99 (*0-515-12560-1*, Jove) Berkley Publishing Group.
—Flying Finish. unabr. ed. 1994. audio 48.00 (*0-7366-2676-X*, 3413) Books on Tape, Inc.
—Flying Finish. unabr. ed. 2000. audio 49.95 (*0-7451-6829-9*, CAB 453) Chivers Audio Bks. GBR. *Dist:* BBC Audiobooks America.
—Flying Finish. l.t. ed. 1995. 349p. reprint ed. 23.95 o.p. (*0-7838-1141-1*, Macmillan Reference USA) Gale Group.
—Flying Finish. abr. ed. audio 15.95 o.p. (*1-55994-137-5*, CPN 2137, HarperAudio) HarperTrade.
—Flying Finish. unabr. ed. 1997. audio 51.00 (*0-7887-0252-1*, 94461E7) Recorded Bks., LLC.
—Flying Finish. 1984. mass mkt. 3.50 (*0-671-50926-8*); 1983. mass mkt. 2.95 (*0-671-47020-5*) Simon & Schuster. (Pocket).
—Flying Finish. l.t. ed. 1979. 12.00 o.p. (*0-7089-0298-7*, Ulverscroft) Thorpe, F. A. Pubs. GBR. *Dist:* Ulverscroft Large Print Bks., Ltd.
—For Kicks. l.t. ed. 1994. 19.95 o.p. (*0-7927-1740-6*); 1994. pap. 18.95 o.p. (*0-7927-1739-2*); 1993. audio 54.95 o.p. (*0-7451-5950-8*) BBC Audiobooks America.
—For Kicks. 1987. 336p. mass mkt. 5.95 o.s.i (*0-449-21264-5*, Fawcett) Ballantine Bks.
—For Kicks. 304p. 2004. mass mkt. 6.99 (*0-425-19498-1*); 1998. mass mkt. 6.99 (*0-515-12386-2*, Jove) Berkley Publishing Group.
—For Kicks. unabr. ed. 1991. audio 56.00 (*0-7366-1918-6*, 2742) Books on Tape, Inc.
—For Kicks. 1984. mass mkt. 3.50 o.s.i (*0-671-53265-0*); 1982. mass mkt. 2.95 o.s.i (*0-671-45460-9*) Simon & Schuster. (Pocket).
—For Kicks. l.t. ed. 1973. o.p. (*0-85456-164-1*, Ulverscroft) Thorpe, F. A. Pubs.
—For Kicks. abr. ed. 1996. 2p. audio 16.95 o.s.i (*0-14-086222-6*) Viking Penguin.
—Nerve. l.t. ed. 1994. 18.95 o.p. (*0-7927-1755-4*); pap. o.p. (*0-7927-1754-6*) BBC Audiobooks America.
—Nerve. 1987. mass mkt. 5.95 o.s.i (*0-449-21266-1*, Fawcett) Ballantine Bks.
—Nerve. 1998. 320p. reprint ed. mass mkt. 6.99 (*0-515-12346-3*, Jove) Berkley Publishing Group.
—Nerve. 1965. mass mkt. 0.60 o.p. (*0-451-02607-1*, Signet Bks.) NAL.
—Nerve. 1984. mass mkt. 3.50 (*0-671-52522-0*); 1982. mass mkt. 2.95 (*0-671-45072-7*) Simon & Schuster. (Pocket).
—Nerve. l.t. ed. 1978. o.p. (*0-7089-0171-9*, Ulverscroft) Thorpe, F. A. Pubs.
—Odds Against. unabr. ed. audio 54.95 o.p. (*1-85549-031-5*); 1998. audio 69.95 (*0-7540-0086-9*, CAB1509) BBC Audiobooks America.
—Odds Against. 1987. 320p. mass mkt. 5.99 o.s.i (*0-449-21269-6*, Fawcett) Ballantine Bks.
—Odds Against. 2000. 288p. mass mkt. 6.99 (*0-515-12551-2*, Jove) Berkley Publishing Group.
—Odds Against. unabr. ed. 1999. audio 39.95 Blackstone Audio Bks., Inc.
—Odds Against. unabr. ed. 2000. (Sid Halley Adventure Ser.: Bk. 1). audio 59.95 Chivers Audio Bks. GBR. *Dist:* BBC Audiobooks America.
—Odds Against. l.t. ed. 1991. (General Ser.). 272p. 15.95 o.s.i (*0-8161-5034-6*); lib. bdg. 21.95 o.p. (*0-8161-5033-8*) Gale Group. (Macmillan Reference USA).
—Odds Against. abr. ed. 1991. audio 15.95 o.s.i (*1-55994-138-3*, CPN 2138, HarperAudio) HarperTrade.
—Odds Against, unabr. ed. 1999. audio 39.95 Highsmith Inc.
—Odds Against. 1982. mass mkt. 2.95 o.s.i (*0-671-45076-X*, Pocket) Simon & Schuster.
—Reflex. unabr. ed. 2000. audio 34.95 (*1-57270-135-8*, N81135u, Audio Editions Mystery Masters) Audio Partners Publishing Corp.
—Reflex. 1997. mass mkt. (*0-449-45727-3*); 1986. 352p. mass mkt. 5.99 o.s.i (*0-449-21173-8*); 1986. mass mkt. 4.50 o.p. (*0-449-21036-7*); 1984. mass mkt. 3.95 o.p. (*0-449-20713-7*); 1982. mass mkt. 3.50 o.p. (*0-449-24500-4*) Ballantine Bks. (Fawcett).
—Reflex. 2003. 304p. mass mkt. 6.99 (*0-515-13509-7*, Jove) Berkley Publishing Group.
—Reflex. l.t. ed. 1981. (General Ser.). lib. bdg. 14.95 o.p. (*0-8161-3255-0*, Macmillan Reference USA) Gale Group.
—Straight. 1998. mass mkt. 5.99 (*0-449-45788-5*); 1991. 320p. mass mkt. 5.95 o.p. (*0-449-45310-3*); 1991. 320p. mass mkt. 5.99 o.s.i (*0-449-21720-5*) Ballantine Bks. (Fawcett).
—Straight. 2003. 320p. mass mkt. 6.99 (*0-515-13465-1*, Jove) Berkley Publishing Group.
—Straight. l.t. ed. 1990. (General Ser.). 437p. 15.95 o.p. (*0-8161-4995-X*); lib. bdg. 21.95 o.p. (*0-8161-4991-7*) Gale Group. (Macmillan Reference USA).
—Straight. abr. ed. 1989. audio 15.95 (*1-55994-118-9*, CPN 2128, Caedmon) HarperTrade.
—Straight. 1989. 324p. 18.95 o.p. (*0-399-13470-0*, G. P. Putnam's Sons) Penguin Putnam Bks. for Young Readers.
—Straight. unabr. ed. 1994. audio 70.00 (*1-55690-993-4*, 94132E7) Recorded Bks., LLC.
—Trial Run. 1983. mass mkt. 3.50 o.s.i (*0-671-50732-X*, Pocket) Simon & Schuster.
Mount, Ferdinand. The Man Who Rode Ampersand. 2002. 256p. 25.00 (*0-7867-1007-1*, Carroll & Graf Pubs.) Avalon Publishing Group.

## JOURNALISTS—FICTION

Adamson, Isaac. Dreaming Pachinko. 2003. 368p. pap. 12.95 (*0-06-051623-2*, Perennial) HarperTrade.
Akst, Daniel. St. Burl's Obituary. 1997. (Harvest American Writing Ser.). 384p. pap. 12.00 (*0-15-600514-X*, Harvest Bks.) Harcourt Trade Pubs.
—St. Burl's Obituary. 1996. 370p. 22.95 (*1-878448-68-4*) MacMurray & Beck, Inc.
—The Webster Chronicle. 2002. 320p. pap. 14.00 (*0-425-18761-6*) Penguin Group (USA) Inc.
—The Webster Chronicle. 2001. 320p. 24.95 o.s.i (*0-399-14812-4*, BlueHen Bks.) Putnam Publishing Group, The.
Alcorn, Randy. Dominion. 2003. 612p. pap. 14.99 (*1-57673-661-X*, Multnomah Bks.); 2003. audio 24.99 (*1-57673-682-2*); 1986. 612p. pap. 14.99 o.p. (*0-88070-939-1*, Multnomah Bks.) Multnomah Pubs., Inc.
Allbeury, Ted. The Reckoning. l.t. ed. 2000. (Mystery Ser.). 392p. 26.95 (*0-7862-2664-1*); (*0-7540-1471-1*); (*0-7540-2356-7*) Thorndike Pr.
Allman, Kevin. Hot Shot. 1998. 256p. 22.95 (*0-312-16866-7*, Saint Martin's Minotaur) St. Martin's Pr.
—Tight Shot. 1995. 262p. 21.00 o.p. (*0-312-11904-6*, Saint Martin's Minotaur) St. Martin's Pr.
Arsenault, Mark. Spiked. 2003. 240p. 24.95 o.s.i (*1-59058-059-1*); 420p. pap. 22.95 o.s.i (*1-59058-085-0*) Poisoned Pen Pr.
Baldacci, David. The Christmas Train. 2002. E-Book 14.95 (*0-7595-4736-X*) Time Warner Bk. Group.
—The Christmas Train. 74.75 (*0-446-17408-4*); 2003. 272p. 12.95 (*0-446-53327-0*); 2002. 272p. 19.95 (*0-446-52573-1*); 2002. 400p. 19.95 (*0-446-53147-2*) Warner Bks., Inc.
Barker, Pat. Double Vision. 2004. (*0-374-14330-7*) Farrar, Straus & Giroux.
—Mind to Kill. 2003. 272p. 23.00 (*0-374-20905-7*) Farrar, Straus & Giroux.
Barnard, Robert. Unholy Dying. l.t. ed. 2002. (Magna Large Print Ser.). 368p. (*0-7505-1822-7*) Magna Large Print Bks. GBR. *Dist:* Ulverscroft Large Print Canada, Ltd.
—Unholy Dying. 2001. 288p. 23.00 o.s.i (*0-7432-0149-3*, Scribner) Simon & Schuster.
—Unholy Dying. l.t. ed. 2001. 399p. 28.95 (*0-7862-3333-8*) Thorndike Pr.
Bateman, Colin. Cycle of Violence. 1997. pap. 12.95 (*1-55970-378-4*); 1996. 256p. 21.95 (*1-55970-349-0*) Arcade Publishing, Inc.
—Divorcing Jack. 1996. 288p. pap. 11.95 (*1-55970-359-8*); 1995. 272p. 19.95 (*1-55970-310-5*) Arcade Publishing, Inc.
—Of Wee Sweetie Mice & Men. 1997. 326p. 23.95 (*1-55970-376-8*) Arcade Publishing, Inc.
Beck, K. K. Death in a Deck Chair. 1987. 176p. mass mkt. 4.99 o.s.i (*0-8041-0118-3*, Ivy Bks.) Ballantine Bks.
—Death in a Deck Chair. 1984. 12.95 (*0-8027-5601-8*) Walker & Co.
—Murder in a Mummy Case. l.t. ed. 1989. pap. 8.95 o.p. (*1-55504-841-2*) BBC Audiobooks America.
—Murder in a Mummy Case. 1987. 176p. mass mkt. 3.95 o.s.i (*0-8041-0117-5*, Ivy Bks.) Ballantine Bks.
—Murder in a Mummy Case. 1986. 176p. 15.95 o.s.i (*0-8027-5655-7*) Walker & Co.
—Peril under the Palms. 1990. 176p. mass mkt. 4.99 o.s.i (*0-8041-0594-4*, Ivy Bks.) Ballantine Bks.
—Peril under the Palms. 1989. 208p. 18.95 (*0-8027-5715-4*) Walker & Co.
Belsky, R. G. Playing Dead. 1999. mass mkt. 6.50 (*0-380-79069-6*, Avon Bks.) Morrow/Avon.
Benson, Christopher. Special Interest. 2001. 300p. 24.95 (*0-88378-227-8*) Third World Press.
Berger, Leon. Tabloid Trash: A Murder Mystery. 2002. 200p. pap. 14.95 (*1-55022-420-4*) ECW Pr. CAN. *Dist:* Independent Pubs. Group.
Berry, Venise. All of Me: A Voluptuous Tale. 2001. 288p. reprint ed. pap. 13.95 (*0-451-20262-7*) NAL.
Bloch, Jon. Touchdown to Murder. Date not set. pap. (*0-312-31313-6*); mass mkt. (*0-312-98910-5*) St. Martin's Pr. (St. Martin's Paperbacks).
Boyle, Gerry. Bloodline. 1996. 336p. mass mkt. 5.99 o.s.i (*0-425-15182-4*) Berkley Publishing Group.
—Bloodline. 1995. 21.95 o.p. (*0-399-14030-1*, G. P. Putnam's Sons) Penguin Group (USA) Inc.
—Borderline. (Jack McMorrow Mystery Ser.). 368p. 1998. 22.95 o.s.i (*0-425-16147-1*); 2000. reprint ed. mass mkt. 6.99 o.s.i (*0-425-16964-2*, Prime Crime) Berkley Publishing Group.
—Cover Story. 2000. (Jack McMorrow Mystery Ser.: No. 7). 371p. 22.95 o.s.i (*0-425-16893-X*, Prime Crime) Berkley Publishing Group.
—The Cover Story. 2001. (Jack McMorrow Mystery Ser.: No. 7). 384p. 6.99 (*0-425-17852-8*, Prime Crime) Berkley Publishing Group.
—Deadline: A Jack McMorrow Mystery. 1995. 288p. mass mkt. 6.50 o.s.i (*0-425-14637-5*, Prime Crime) Berkley Publishing Group.
—Deadline: A Jack McMorrow Mystery. 1993. 17.95 (*0-945980-44-2*) North Country Pr.
—Lifeline. 1997. (Jack McMorrow Mystery Ser.). 368p. mass mkt. 5.99 o.s.i (*0-425-15688-5*) Berkley Publishing Group.
—Lifeline. 1996. 288p. 22.95 o.s.i (*0-399-14150-2*, G. P. Putnam's Sons) Penguin Group (USA) Inc.
—Potshot. 1998. (Jack McMorrow Mystery Ser.). 336p. mass mkt. 5.99 o.s.i (*0-425-16233-8*) Berkley Publishing Group.
—Potshot. 1997. 304p. 23.95 o.p. (*0-399-14259-2*, G. P. Putnam's Sons) Penguin Group (USA) Inc.
Brady, James. Further Lane. 1999. E-Book 6.50 o.s.i (*0-312-20716-6*); 1998. (Further Lane Ser.: Vol. 1). 304p. pap. 6.50 (*0-312-96598-2*, St. Martin's Paperbacks); 1997. 224p. 22.95 (*0-312-15533-6*) St. Martin's Pr.
—Gin Lane: A Novel of Southampton. 1999. (Gin Lane Ser.: Vol. 1). 314p. mass mkt. 6.99 (*0-312-96706-3*, St. Martin's Paperbacks); 1998. 256p. 22.95 (*0-312-18579-0*) St. Martin's Pr.
Brady, John. Kaddish in Dublin. 2002. (Matt Minogue Mystery Ser.). 253p. pap. 14.95 (*1-58642-042-9*) Steerforth Pr.
Brandt, Nat & Brandt, Yanna. A Death in the Bulloch Parish: A Mitch Stevens Mystery. 1993. (Mitch Stevens Ser.). 224p. 19.00 o.p. (*0-88150-265-0*) Countryman Pr.
Braun, Lilian Jackson. The Cat Who Ate Danish Modern. 1989. (Black Dagger Crime Ser.). 200p. reprint ed. text 12.95 o.p. (*0-86220-755-X*) Chivers Pr. GBR. *Dist:* BBC Audiobooks America.
—The Cat Who Ate Danish Modern. 1986. 13.04 (*0-606-13246-5*) Turtleback Bks.
—The Cat Who Blew the Whistle. 1996. (Cat Who Ser.). 320p. mass mkt. 6.99 (*0-515-11824-9*, Jove) Berkley Publishing Group.
—The Cat Who Blew the Whistle. abr. ed. 1995. (J). audio 17.95 o.p. (*0-7871-0229-6*, 393238) NewStar Media, Inc.
—The Cat Who Blew the Whistle. 1995. 240p. 21.95 o.p. (*0-399-13981-8*, G. P. Putnam's Sons) Penguin Group (USA) Inc.
—The Cat Who Blew the Whistle. l.t. ed. (Paperback Bestsellers Ser.). 270p. 1996. lib. bdg. 18.95 (*0-7838-1253-1*); 1995. lib. bdg. 24.95 (*0-7838-1252-3*) Thorndike Pr.

—The Cat Who Blew the Whistle. 1996. 13.04 (*0-606-12643-0*) Turtleback Bks.
—The Cat Who Came to Breakfast. 1995. (Cat Who Ser.). 272p. (J). pap. 6.99 (*0-515-11564-9*, Jove) Berkley Publishing Group.
—The Cat Who Came to Breakfast. 1995. 13.04 (*0-606-12644-9*) Turtleback Bks.
—The Cat Who Could Read Backwards. l.t. ed. 1991. 12.95 o.p. (*0-7927-0098-8*, C0139) BBC Audiobooks America.
—The Cat Who Could Read Backwards. 2003. 256p. pap. 10.00 (*0-425-19520-1*) Berkley Publishing Group.
—The Cat Who Could Read Backwards. l.t. ed. 1997. (Large Print Book Ser.). 25.95 o.p. (*1-56895-470-0*, Wheeler Publishing, Inc.) Gale Group.
—The Cat Who Could Read Backwards. 1997. (Cat Who. . . Ser.). 240p. 19.95 o.p. (*0-399-14286-X*, G. P. Putnam's Sons) Penguin Group (USA) Inc.
—The Cat Who Had 14 Tales. l.t. ed. 1991. (Nightingale Ser.). 241p. 14.95 o.p. (*0-8161-4915-1*, Macmillan Reference USA) Gale Group.
—The Cat Who Knew a Cardinal. abr. ed. 1993. 15.95 o.p. (*1-55800-444-0*, 390492) NewStar Media, Inc.
—The Cat Who Knew a Cardinal. 1992. 13.04 (*0-606-12645-7*) Turtleback Bks.
—The Cat Who Knew a Cardinal; The Cat Who Moved a Mountain; The Cat Who Wasn't There. unabr. ed. 1993. audio 19.95 o.p. (*1-55800-782-2*) NewStar Media, Inc.
—The Cat Who Knew Shakespeare. l.t. ed. 1989. 284p. 12.95 o.p. (*0-8161-4790-6*, Macmillan Reference USA) Gale Group.
—The Cat Who Knew Shakespeare. 1991. 13.04 (*0-606-13248-1*) Turtleback Bks.
—The Cat Who Lived High. l.t. ed. 1991. lib. bdg. 19.95 o.p. (*0-8161-5126-1*, Macmillan Reference USA) Gale Group.
—The Cat Who Lived High. 1990. 240p. 17.95 o.p. (*0-399-13554-5*, G. P. Putnam's Sons) Penguin Putnam Bks. for Young Readers.
—The Cat Who Lived High. unabr. ed. 1994. (Cat Who Ser.: No. 11). audio 32.95 (*1-55690-992-6*, 94131) Recorded Bks., LLC.
—The Cat Who Lived High. 1991. 13.04 (*0-606-12646-5*) Turtleback Bks.
—The Cat Who Moved a Mountain. l.t. ed. 1993. (General Ser.). 379p. 18.95 o.p. (*0-8161-5551-8*); 20.95 o.p. (*0-8161-5550-X*) Gale Group. (Macmillan Reference USA).
—The Cat Who Moved a Mountain. abr. ed. 1993. 15.95 o.p. (*1-55800-470-X*, 390493) NewStar Media, Inc.
—The Cat Who Moved a Mountain. 1992. 13.04 (*0-606-12647-3*) Turtleback Bks.
—The Cat Who Played Brahms. l.t. ed. 1990. 18.95 o.p. (*0-7927-0335-9*, C0029); pap. 16.95 o.p. (*0-7927-0345-6*) BBC Audiobooks America.
—The Cat Who Played Brahms. 1990. 13.04 (*0-606-13249-X*) Turtleback Bks.
—The Cat Who Played Post Office. l.t. ed. 2000. (Wheeler Large Print Book Ser.). (Illus.). 230p. 27.95 o.p. (*1-56895-840-4*, Wheeler Publishing, Inc.) Gale Group.
—The Cat Who Played Post Office. 1987. 13.04 (*0-606-13250-3*) Turtleback Bks.
—The Cat Who Robbed a Bank. 2001. (Cat Who Ser.). 304p. mass mkt. 6.99 (*0-515-12994-1*, Jove) Berkley Publishing Group.
—The Cat Who Robbed a Bank. l.t. ed. 2000. pap. 22.95 o.p. (*0-7838-8710-8*, Macmillan Reference USA) Gale Group.
—The Cat Who Robbed a Bank. 2000. (Cat Who Ser.). 256p. 23.95 o.p. (*0-399-14570-2*) Penguin Group (USA) Inc.
—The Cat Who Robbed a Bank, No. 2. abr. ed. 2000. (Cat Who Ser.: Vol. 22). 3p. 17.95 o.s.i (*0-399-14582-6*, Putnam Berkley Audio) Putnam Publishing Group, The.
—The Cat Who Robbed a Bank. l.t. ed. 2000. 400p. 23.95 (*0-375-40878-9*) Random Hse. Large Print.
—The Cat Who Robbed a Bank. unabr. ed. 1999. (Cat Who Ser.). audio 29.95 (*0-7887-4032-6*, 96010 ) Recorded Bks., LLC.
—The Cat Who Said Cheese. 1997. (Cat Who Ser.). 272p. reprint ed. pap. 6.99 (*0-515-12027-8*, Jove) Berkley Publishing Group.
—The Cat Who Said Cheese. l.t. ed. 1997. pap. 23.95 o.p. (*0-7838-1632-4*, Macmillan Reference USA) Gale Group.
—The Cat Who Said Cheese. abr. ed. 1996. 17.95 o.p. (*0-7871-0610-0*) NewStar Media, Inc.
—The Cat Who Said Cheese. 1996. (Cat Who Ser.). (*0-399-19300-6*); 256p. 22.95 o.p. (*0-399-14075-1*, G. P. Putnam's Sons) Penguin Group (USA) Inc.
—The Cat Who Said Cheese. l.t. ed. 1996. (Core Collection). 303p. 27.95 (*0-7838-1631-6*) Thorndike Pr.
—The Cat Who Said Cheese. 1997. 13.04 (*0-606-12648-1*) Turtleback Bks.
—The Cat Who Sang for the Birds. 1999. (Cat Who Ser.). (Illus.). 272p. reprint ed. mass mkt. 6.99 (*0-515-12463-X*, Jove) Berkley Publishing Group.
—The Cat Who Sang for the Birds. l.t. ed. 1998. 26.95 o.p. (*1-56895-555-3*, Wheeler Publishing, Inc.) Gale Group.
—The Cat Who Sang for the Birds. 1998. (Cat Who. . . Ser.). 256p. (YA). 22.95 o.p. (*0-399-14333-5*, G. P. Putnam's Sons) Penguin Group (USA) Inc.
—The Cat Who Saw Red. 1986. mass mkt. 2.95 o.s.i (*0-515-08491-3*, Jove) Berkley Publishing Group.
—The Cat Who Saw Red. l.t. ed. 1989. 13.95 o.p. (*0-8161-4388-9*, Macmillan Reference USA) Gale Group.
—The Cat Who Saw Red. 1986. 13.04 (*0-606-13251-1*) Turtleback Bks.
—The Cat Who Saw Stars. 2000. (Cat Who Ser.). 304p. reprint ed. mass mkt. 6.99 (*0-515-12739-6*, Jove) Berkley Publishing Group.
—The Cat Who Saw Stars. l.t. ed. 2000. 11.95 (*1-56895-980-X*); 1999. 27.95 (*1-56895-595-2*) Gale Group. (Wheeler Publishing, Inc.).
—The Cat Who Saw Stars. 1999. (Cat Who. . . Ser.). 240p. 22.95 o.p. (*0-399-14431-5*) Penguin Group (USA) Inc.
—The Cat Who Smelled a Rat. l.t. ed. 293p. 2002. pap. 29.95 (*0-7862-2823-7*); 2001. 32.95 (*0-7862-2822-9*) Thorndike Pr.
—The Cat Who Sniffed Glue. l.t. ed. 1990. (Nightingale Ser.). 312p. 13.95 o.p. (*0-8161-4864-3*, Macmillan Reference USA) Gale Group.
—The Cat Who Sniffed Glue. 1988. (Cat Who. . . Ser.). 192p. 14.95 o.p. (*0-399-13381-X*, G. P. Putnam's Sons) Penguin Putnam Bks. for Young Readers.
—The Cat Who Sniffed Glue. 1989. 13.04 (*0-606-13252-X*) Turtleback Bks.
—The Cat Who Tailed a Thief. 1998. (Cat Who. . . Ser.). 272p. mass mkt. 6.99 (*0-515-12240-8*, Jove) Berkley Publishing Group.
—The Cat Who Tailed a Thief. l.t. ed. 1997. 293p. 27.95 o.p. (*0-7838-8046-4*, Macmillan Reference USA) Gale Group.
—The Cat Who Tailed a Thief. abr. ed. 1997. 17.95 o.p. (*0-7871-1352-2*, 394616) NewStar Media, Inc.
—The Cat Who Tailed a Thief. 1997. (Cat Who. . . Ser.). 256p. 22.95 o.p. (*0-399-14210-X*, G. P. Putnam's Sons) Penguin Group (USA) Inc.
—The Cat Who Tailed a Thief. l.t. ed. 1998. (Paperback Bestsellers Ser.). 293p. pap. 27.95 (*0-7838-8047-2*) Thorndike Pr.
—The Cat Who Tailed a Thief. 1998. 13.04 (*0-606-13253-8*) Turtleback Bks.
—The Cat Who Talked to Ghosts. l.t. ed. 1991. (General Ser.). 300p. 21.95 (*0-8161-5081-8*, Macmillan Reference USA) Gale Group.
—The Cat Who Talked to Ghosts. 1990. 224p. 15.95 o.p. (*0-399-13477-8*, G. P. Putnam's Sons) Penguin Putnam Bks. for Young Readers.
—The Cat Who Talked to Ghosts. 1990. 13.04 (*0-606-13254-6*) Turtleback Bks.
—The Cat Who Talked Turkey. 2003. 288p. 23.95 (*0-399-15107-9*) Putnam Publishing Group, The.
—The Cat Who Turned on & Off. 1986. (Cat Who Ser.). 272p. mass mkt. 6.99 (*0-515-08794-7*, Jove) Berkley Publishing Group.
—The Cat Who Turned on & Off. l.t. ed. 1992. (Nightingale Ser.). 285p. 14.95 o.p. (*0-8161-4815-5*, Macmillan Reference USA) Gale Group.
—The Cat Who Turned on & Off. 1986. 11.60 o.p. (*0-606-13255-4*) Turtleback Bks.
—The Cat Who Wasn't There. abr. ed. 1993. 16.95 o.p. (*1-55800-667-2*) NewStar Media, Inc.
—The Cat Who Went into the Closet. 1994. (Cat Who Ser.). 288p. mass mkt. 6.99 (*0-515-11332-8*, Jove) Berkley Publishing Group.
—The Cat Who Went into the Closet. l.t. ed. 1993. 24.95 o.p. (*1-56895-050-0*, Wheeler Publishing, Inc.) Gale Group.
—The Cat Who Went into the Closet. abr. ed. 1993. (Jim Qwilleran Mystery Ser.). audio 16.95 o.p. (*1-55800-785-7*, 390495) NewStar Media, Inc.
—The Cat Who Went into the Closet. 1993. (Cat Who Ser.). 240p. 19.95 o.p. (*0-399-13830-7*, G. P. Putnam's Sons) Penguin Group (USA) Inc.
—The Cat Who Went into the Closet. 5.98 o.p. (*0-8317-5327-7*) Smithmark Pubs., Inc.
—The Cat Who Went into the Closet. 1994. 13.04 (*0-606-13256-2*) Turtleback Bks.
—The Cat Who Went Underground. l.t. ed. 1990. (General Ser.). 324p. 19.95 o.p. (*0-8161-4941-0*, Macmillan Reference USA) Gale Group.
—The Cat Who Went Underground. 1989. (Cat Who. . . Ser.). 224p. 14.95 o.p. (*0-399-13431-X*, G. P. Putnam's Sons) Penguin Putnam Bks. for Young Readers.
—El Gato Que Leia del Reves. 1997. Tr. of Cat Who Could Read Backwards. (SPA.). 248p. 14.58 (*84-01-47431-0*) Plaza & Janés Editories, S.A. ESP. *Dist:* Distribooks, Inc., Lectorum Pubns., Inc.
—Lilian Jackson Braun: Three Complete Novels. 1998. 640p. 12.98 o.p. (*0-399-14364-5*); 1996. 12.98 o.p. (*0-399-14127-8*); 1994. 608p. 11.98 o.s.i (*0-399-13984-2*) Penguin Group (USA) Inc. (G. P. Putnam's Sons).
—The Private Life of the Cat Who... Tales of Koko & Yum Yum from the Journals of James Mackintosh Qwilleran. 2003. 144p. 10.95 (*0-399-15132-X*, Putnam & Grosset) Putnam Publishing Group, The.
—Three Complete Novels. 2002. 803p. 14.98 (*0-399-14813-2*) Penguin Group (USA) Inc.
—Three Complete Novels: The Cat Who Saw Red; The Cat Who Played Brahms; The Cat Who Played Post Office - Omnibus Edition. 1993. 608p. 12.98 o.s.i (*0-399-13885-4*, G. P. Putnam's Sons) Penguin Group (USA) Inc.
—Three Complete Novels: The Cat Who Talked to Ghosts; The Cat Who Knew a Cardinal; The Cat Who Lived High, 3 bks. in 1. 1997. 512p. 12.98 o.p. (*0-399-14258-4*, G. P. Putnam's Sons) Penguin Group (USA) Inc.
Brink, André. The Devil's Valley. 1999. 416p. 24.00 o.s.i (*0-15-100440-4*); 2001. 420p. reprint ed. pap. 14.00 (*0-15-601208-1*, Harvest Bks.) Harcourt Trade Pubs.
Briody, Thomas G. Rogue's Isles. 1995. 273p. 21.95 o.p. (*0-312-13157-7*, Saint Martin's Minotaur) St. Martin's Pr.
—Rogue's Justice: A Michael Carolina Mystery. 1996. 288p. 22.95 o.p. (*0-312-14402-4*, Saint Martin's Minotaur) St. Martin's Pr.
—Rogues Regatta. 1999. 272p. 23.95 (*0-312-24235-2*, Saint Martin's Minotaur) St. Martin's Pr.
—Rogue's Wager: A Michael Carolina Mystery. 1997. (Michael Carolina Mystery Ser.). 160p. 21.95 (*0-312-16990-6*, Saint Martin's Minotaur) St. Martin's Pr.
Brookmyre, Christopher. Country of the Blind. 2002. 416p. pap. 12.00 (*0-8021-3919-1*, Grove Pr.) Grove/Atlantic, Inc.
—Quite Ugly One Morning. 2002. 224p. pap. 12.00 (*0-8021-3861-6*, Grove Pr.) Grove/Atlantic, Inc.
—Quite Ugly One Morning. 1996. 224p. o.s.i (*0-316-87883-9*) Little Brown & Co.
Brown, Sandra. Exclusive, Set. unabr. ed. 1999. audio 49.95 Highsmith Inc.
—Exclusive, Set. abr. ed. 1996. 17.95 o.p. (*0-7871-0880-4*, 394140); 49.95 o.p. (*0-7871-0881-2*, 104018) NewStar Media, Inc.
—Exclusive. l.t. ed. 1996. (Basic Ser.). 688p. 28.95 (*0-7862-0698-5*) Thorndike Pr.
—Exclusive. 1996. 464p. 22.95 o.s.i (*0-446-51978-2*); 1997. 496p. reprint ed. mass mkt. 7.99 (*0-446-60423-2*) Warner Bks., Inc.
Brownstein, Michael. Self-Reliance. 1994. 280p. (Orig.). pap. 12.95 (*1-56689-018-7*) Coffee Hse. Pr.
Bruns, Donn. Jamaica Blue. Date not set. pap. (*0-312-30491-9*, Saint Martin's Griffin); E-Book 18.95 (*0-312-70853-X*); E-Book 24.95 (*0-312-70486-0*); 2003. 336p. mass mkt. 6.99 (*0-312-98506-1*, St. Martin's Paperbacks); 2002. 320p. 24.95 (*0-312-30490-0*, Saint Martin's Minotaur) St. Martin's Pr.
Bruns, Jana. Jamaica Blue. 2003. mass mkt. (*0-312-99221-1*, St. Martin's Paperbacks) St. Martin's Pr.
Buchanan, Edna. Miami, It's Murder. 1994. 256p. 21.95 o.p. (*1-56282-802-9*) Hyperion Pr.
—Miami, It's Murder. 1995. (Britt Montero Mysteries Ser.). 320p. mass mkt. 6.99 (*0-380-72261-5*, Avon Bks.) Morrow/Avon.
Buckley, Christopher. Little Green Men. 2000. 320p. pap. 13.00 (*0-06-095557-0*, Perennial) HarperTrade.
Bunn, T. Davis. One False Move. 1997. 400p. (Orig.). pap. 12.99 o.p. (*0-7852-7368-9*) Nelson, Thomas Inc.
Cabrera, Vicente. La Sombra del Espia. 2002. (SPA.). 297p. pap. 8.00 (*9978-42-083-5*) Editorial Gutenberg.
Call, Jeff. Mormonville: A Big-City Reporter Spends a Year in Utah to Uncover the Truth about the LDS Church, but Uncovers Truths about Himself. 2002. 310p. pap. 16.95 (*1-55517-618-6*, 76186) Cedar Fort, Inc./CFI Distribution.
Campbell, Ramsey. The Last Voice They Hear. 1999. 384p. pap. 6.99 (*0-8125-4194-4*, Tor Bks.) Doherty, Tom Assocs., LLC.
—The Last Voice They Hear. 1998. 6.99 (*0-312-87078-7*) St. Martin's Pr.
Campbell, Ramsey & Robbins, Harold. The Last Voice They Hear. 1998. 384p. 24.95 o.p. (*0-312-86611-9*, Forge Bks.) Doherty, Tom Assocs., LLC.
Caputo, Philip. Horn of Africa: A Novel. 1983. 544p. mass mkt. 4.95 o.s.i (*0-440-33675-9*, Laurel) Dell Publishing.
—Horn of Africa: A Novel. 1991. 544p. pap. 11.00 o.p. (*0-06-098605-0*, Perennial) HarperTrade.
—Horn of Africa: A Novel. 1980. 528p. 12.95 o.p. (*0-03-042136-5*) Holt, Henry & Co.
—Horn of Africa: A Novel. 2002. (Vintage Contemporaries Ser.). 496p. pap. 15.00 (*0-375-72511-3*, Vintage) Knopf Publishing Group.
Case, John. The First Horseman. l.t. ed. 1998. (Basic Ser.). 584p. 29.95 (*0-7862-1619-0*) Thorndike Pr.
Case, John, et al. The First Horseman. 1999. 384p. mass mkt. 6.99 (*0-345-43579-6*) Ballantine Bks.
Cawood, Chris. 1998: The Year of the Beast. Seale, Gaynell, ed. 1996. 312p. (Orig.). pap. 12.95 (*0-9642231-9-8*) Magnolia Hill Pr.
Cheever, Benjamin. The Plagiarist. 1992. 352p. 20.00 o.s.i (*0-689-12153-9*, Scribner) Simon & Schuster.
Collins, Michael. The Keepers of Truth. 2001. 320p. pap. 13.00 (*0-7432-1803-5*, Scribner); E-Book 9.99 (*0-7432-2361-6*, Simon & Schuster) Simon & Schuster.
Collins, Stephen. Double Exposure. 1999. 310p. pap. 6.99 (*0-380-73232-7*, Avon Bks.) Morrow/Avon.
—Double Exposure: A Novel. 1998. 256p. 24.00 (*0-688-15893-5*, Morrow, William & Co.) Morrow/Avon.
Conant, Susan. Bride & Groom. 2004. 272p. 22.95 (*0-425-19412-4*) Berkley Publishing Group.
Connelly, Michael. The Poet. l.t. ed. 2000. pap. 25.95 o.p. (*1-56895-330-5*, Wheeler Publishing, Inc.) Gale Group.
Courtemanche, Gil. A Sunday at the Pool in Kigali. Claxton, Patricia, tr. from FRE. 2003. 272p. 23.00 (*1-4000-4107-4*, Everyman's Library) Knopf Publishing Group.
Craft, Michael. Body Language. 1999. (Mark Manning Mystery Ser.). 273p. 22.00 o.s.i (*1-57566-419-4*) Kensington Publishing Corp.
—Flight Dreams. 2000. (Mark Manning Mystery Ser.: Vol. 1). 24p. pap. 13.00 (*1-57566-854-8*); 1998. 256p. pap. 10.95 o.s.i (*1-57566-294-9*, Kensington Bks.); 1997. (Mark Manning Mystery Ser.: Vol. 1). 224p. 19.95 o.s.i (*1-57566-174-8*, Kensington Bks.) Kensington Publishing Corp.
Cullen, Robert. Heirs of the Fire. 1998. 357p. mass mkt. 6.99 o.s.i (*0-8041-1445-5*, Ivy Bks.); 1997. 368p. 23.00 o.p. (*0-449-00025-7*, Fawcett) Ballantine Bks.
—Soviet Sources. 1990. 19.95 o.p. (*0-87113-358-X*) Grove/Atlantic, Inc.
Daheim, Mary R. Alpine Journey. l.t. ed. 2003. 512p. 25.95 (*0-375-43268-X*, Random House Large Print) Random Hse. Large Print.
D'Amato, Barbara. Hard Evidence: A Cat Marsala Mystery. 1999. (Cat Marsala Mysteries Ser.). 256p. 22.00 (*0-684-83354-9*, Scribner) Simon & Schuster.
Daniels, B. J. Premeditated Marriage. 2002. (Harlequin Intrigue Ser.: No. 691). 256p. mass mkt. o.s.i (*0-373-22687-X*, Harlequin Bks.) Harlequin Enterprises, Ltd.
De Haven, Tom. Funny Papers. (American Fiction Ser.). 384p. 1986. pap. 6.95 o.p. (*0-14-008680-3*, Penguin Bks.); 1985. 15.95 o.p. (*0-670-33251-8*) Viking Penguin.
—Funny Papers: A Novel. 2002. 384p. pap. 14.00 (*0-312-42134-6*) Picador.
Debin, David. The Big O: An Albie Marx Caper. 1994. 256p. 19.95 o.p. (*0-7867-0005-X*, Carroll & Graf Pubs.) Avalon Publishing Group.
—Murder Live at Five. 1995. 304p. 21.00 o.p. (*0-7867-0190-0*, Carroll & Graf Pubs.) Avalon Publishing Group.
DeBrosse, Jim. Hidden City: A Rick Decker Mystery. 1991. 304p. 18.95 o.p. (*0-312-06368-7*, Saint Martin's Minotaur) St. Martin's Pr.
—The Serpentine Wall. 1988. 336p. 17.95 o.p. (*0-312-02278-6*, Saint Martin's Minotaur) St. Martin's Pr.
—Southern Cross. 1994. 240p. 19.95 o.p. (*0-312-11070-7*, Saint Martin's Minotaur) St. Martin's Pr.
Decker, Rod. An Environment for Murder. 1994. 236p. (Orig.). pap. 14.95 o.p. (*1-56085-063-9*) Signature Bks., Inc.
DeLillo, Don. Bluthunde: Roman. 2003. (GER.). 288p. pap. 19.00 (*1-4000-3985-1*) Random Hse. Information Group.
Delinsky, Barbara. Lake News. 2002. E-Book 9.99 (*1-59061-637-5*) Adobe Systems, Inc.
—Lake News. unabr. ed. 2000. audio 84.95 (*0-7927-2350-3*, CSL 239, Chivers Sound Library) BBC Audiobooks America.
—Lake News. 2000. E-Book 9.99 (*0-684-85379-5*, Simon & Schuster); 1999. 384p. mass mkt. 7.99 (*0-671-03711-0*, Pocket); 1999. 384p. 24.00 (*0-684-86432-0*, Simon & Schuster); 2000. 544p. reprint ed. pap. 7.99 (*0-671-03619-X*, Pocket) Simon & Schuster.
—Lake News. abr. ed. 1999. audio 18.00 (*0-671-58221-6*, Simon & Schuster Audioworks) Simon & Schuster Audio.
—Lake News. l.t. ed. (Paperback Bestsellers Ser.). 584p. 2000. 28.95 (*0-7838-8660-8*); 1999. 31.95 (*0-7838-8659-4*) Thorndike Pr.
Dibdin, Michael. Thanksgiving. 2002. 192p. pap. 12.00 (*0-375-72607-1*, Vintage) Knopf Publishing Group.
—Thanksgiving. l.t. ed. 2001. 213p. pap. 24.95 (*0-7862-3308-7*); 190p. (*0-7540-4502-1*); 190p. (*0-7540-4501-3*) Thorndike Pr.
Dickinson, Peter. Tefuga. l.t. ed. 1987. 464p. 20.95 o.p. (*1-55504-178-7*); pap. 18.95 o.p. (*1-55504-202-3*) BBC Audiobooks America.
Diehl, William. Chameleon. 1996. mass mkt. 5.99 (*0-345-90986-0*); 1982. 480p. mass mkt. 6.99 (*0-345-29445-9*) Ballantine Bks.

—Chameleon. 1981. 14.50 o.p. (*0-394-51961-2*) Random Hse., Inc.

Dinallo, Greg. Red Ink. Grad, Doug, ed. 1994. 352p. 22.00 o.p. (*0-671-73313-3*, Atria) Simon & Schuster.

Djerassi, Carl. Marx, Deceased: A Novel. 1996. 232p. (C). 21.95 o.p. (*0-8203-1835-3*) Univ. of Georgia Pr.

Dockendorf, Margo. The Mahdi: A Millennium Thriller. 1999. 440p. 24.95 (*1-879384-35-3*) Cypress Hse.

Doe, Jean. Party Favours. 1997. 256p. 21.50 (*0-00-224562-0*) HarperCollins Pubs.

Downey, Timothy. A Splendid Executioner. 1987. 17.95 o.p. (*0-525-24486-7*, Dutton) Dutton/Plume.

Dreyer, Eileen. Brain Dead. 1997. 416p. mass mkt. 22.00 o.p. (*0-06-101095-2*) HarperCollins Pubs.

—Brain Dead. 1998. 512p. mass mkt. 6.99 (*0-06-101096-0*, HarperTorch) Morrow/Avon.

DuBois, Brendan. Black Tide: A Lewis Cole Mystery. 1996. 400p. mass mkt. 5.99 (*0-671-89999-6*, Pocket); 1995. 398p. 21.50 (*1-883402-58-1*, Scribner) Simon & Schuster.

—Dead Sand: A Lewis Cole Mystery. 1996. 320p. mass mkt. 5.99 (*0-671-54521-3*, Pocket) Simon & Schuster.

—Dead Sand: A Lewis Cole Mystery. Grose, Bill, ed. 1995. 336p. mass mkt. 5.50 (*0-671-89998-8*, Pocket) Simon & Schuster.

—Dead Sand: A Lewis Cole Mystery. 1994. 304p. 21.00 (*1-883402-45-X*, Scribner) Simon & Schuster.

—The Killer Waves: A Lewis Cole Mystery. 2002. 352p. 24.95 (*0-312-28487-X*, Saint Martin's Minotaur) St. Martin's Pr.

—Resurrection Day. unabr. ed. 2000. audio 96.95 (*0-7927-2328-7*, CSL 217, Chivers Sound Library) BBC Audiobooks America.

—Resurrection Day. 2000. 480p. mass mkt. 7.50 o.s.i (*0-515-12949-6*, Jove) Berkley Publishing Group.

—Resurrection Day. 1999. 400p. (YA). 23.95 o.p. (*0-399-14498-6*) Penguin Group (USA) Inc.

—Shattered Shell. 2nd ed. 1999. 368p. 24.95 (*0-312-19332-7*, Saint Martin's Minotaur) St. Martin's Pr.

Dunne, Dominick. Another City, Not My Own: A Novel in the Form of a Memoir. 1999. mass mkt. 7.99 (*0-449-00419-8*, Fawcett); 1998. 406p. mass mkt. 7.99 (*0-345-43051-4*); 1998. mass mkt. o.p. (*0-345-42703-3*) Ballantine Bks.

—Another City, Not My Own: A Novel in the Form of a Memoir. 1998. mass mkt. o.s.i (*0-553-57986-X*) Bantam Bks.

—Another City, Not My Own: A Novel in the Form of a Memoir. l.t. ed. 1997. pap. 25.00 o.p. (*0-7838-8248-3*, Macmillan Reference USA) Gale Group.

—Another City, Not My Own: A Novel in the Form of a Memoir. abr. ed. 1997. 25.00 o.p. (*0-7871-1612-2*) NewStar Media, Inc.

Dunne, John Gregory. The Red, White, & Blue. 1987. 464p. 18.45 o.p. (*0-671-46380-2*, Simon & Schuster) Simon & Schuster.

—The Red, White, & Blue. 1988. mass mkt. 4.95 o.p. (*0-312-90965-9*, St. Martin's Paperbacks) St. Martin's Pr.

Dunning, John. Two O'Clock, Eastern Wartime: A Novel. 2001. 480p. 26.00 o.s.i (*0-7432-0195-7*, Scribner) Simon & Schuster.

Egan, Greg. Distress. 1998. 464p. mass mkt. 6.50 (*0-06-105727-4*); 1997. 304p. 21.00 o.p. (*0-06-105264-7*) Morrow/Avon. (Eos).

Eisenberg, Nora. Just the Way You Want Me: A Novel. 2003. 220p. pap. 14.95 (*0-9679520-8-5*) Leapfrog Pr.

Farley, Christopher John. My Favorite War: A Novel. 1996. 220p. 20.00 o.p. (*0-374-21696-7*) Farrar, Straus & Giroux.

—My Favorite War: A Novel. 1998. pap. 13.00 o.p. (*0-88001-590-X*) HarperCollins Pubs.

Ferrigno, Robert. The Cheshire Moon. 1993. 285p. 20.00 o.p. (*0-688-10314-6*, Morrow, William & Co.) Morrow/Avon.

—Scavenger Hunt. 336p. 2004. pap. 13.00 (*1-4000-3254-7*, Vintage); 2003. 24.95 (*0-375-42173-4*, Pantheon) Knopf Publishing Group.

Flynn, Robert. The Last Klick. 1994. 363p. 21.00 (*1-880909-21-9*) Baskerville Pubs., Inc.

Ford, G. M. A Blind Eye: A Novel. 2003. 304p. 23.95 (*0-380-97875-X*) HarperCollins Pubs.

—Fury: A Novel. 2001. 336p. 24.00 (*0-380-97724-9*, Morrow, William & Co.) Morrow/Avon.

Forster, Gwynne. When Twilight Comes. 2003. 34p. pap. 15.00 (*0-7582-0009-9*) Kensington Publishing Corp.

Francis, Dick. Forfeit. unabr. ed. 1993. audio 54.95 o.p. (*0-7451-5951-6*) BBC Audiobooks America.

—Forfeit. 1987. mass mkt. 5.95 o.s.i (*0-449-21272-6*, Fawcett) Ballantine Bks.

—Forfeit. 1999. 256p. pap. 6.99 (*0-515-12445-1*, Jove) Berkley Publishing Group.

—Forfeit. unabr. ed. 1991. audio 48.00 (*0-7366-1885-6*, 2714) Books on Tape, Inc.

—Forfeit. l.t. ed. 1994. 22.95 (*0-8161-5781-2*, Macmillan Reference USA) Gale Group.

—Forfeit. 1969. (Harper Novel of Suspense Ser.). 6.95 o.p. (*0-06-011328-6*) HarperCollins Pubs.

—Forfeit. 1985. mass mkt. 3.50 (*0-671-54692-9*, Pocket) Simon & Schuster.

—Forfeit. l.t. ed. 1979. (Ulverscroft Large Print Ser.). 12.00 o.p. (*0-7089-0373-8*, Ulverscroft) Thorpe, F. A. Pubs. GBR. *Dist:* Ulverscroft Large Print Bks., Ltd., Ulverscroft Large Print Canada, Ltd.

—Longshot. 1999. mass mkt. (*0-449-45825-3*); 1992. 336p. mass mkt. 6.99 o.s.i (*0-449-21955-0*); 1992. mass mkt. 5.99 o.p. (*0-449-45309-X*) Ballantine Bks. (Fawcett).

—Longshot. unabr. ed. 1994. audio 56.00 (*0-7366-2739-1*, 3465) Books on Tape, Inc.

—Longshot. l.t. ed. 1992. (General Ser.). 412p. pap. 16.95 o.p. (*0-8161-5417-1*); lib. bdg. 21.95 o.p. (*0-8161-5416-3*) Gale Group. (Macmillan Reference USA).

—Longshot. abr. ed. audio 15.95 o.p. (*1-55994-345-9*, CPN 2187, HarperAudio) HarperTrade.

—Longshot. abr. ed. 2000. audio 7.95 (*1-57815-047-7*, 1019, Media Bks. Audio Publishing) Media Bks., L. L. C.

—Longshot. 1990. 324p. 19.95 o.s.i (*0-399-13581-2*, G. P. Putnam's Sons) Penguin Putnam Bks. for Young Readers.

—Longshot. 1992. 4.99 o.p. (*0-517-09581-5*) Random Hse. Value Publishing.

—Longshot: Open Market. 1991. mass mkt. 5.99 o.s.i (*0-449-22084-2*, Fawcett) Ballantine Bks.

Frank, Jeffrey. The Columnist. 2002. (Harvest Book Ser.). 240p. reprint ed. pap. 13.00 (*0-15-601198-0*, Harvest Bks.) Harcourt Trade Pubs.

—The Columnist. 2001. (Illus.). 240p. 22.00 (*0-7432-1253-3*, Simon & Schuster) Simon & Schuster.

Freadhoff, Chuck. Blue Rain. 2000. 368p. mass mkt. 6.99 (*0-06-109727-6*); 1999. 336p. 24.00 o.p. (*0-06-019217-8*) HarperCollins Pubs.

—Blue Rain. l.t. ed. 1999. (Americana Ser.). 493p. 26.95 (*0-7862-2068-6*) Thorndike Pr.

—A Permanent Twilight. 2000. 352p. 25.00 (*0-06-019216-X*) HarperCollins Pubs.

Fremlin, Celia. Dangerous Thoughts. 1992. 192p. 16.50 o.s.i (*0-385-41976-7*) Doubleday Publishing.

—Dangerous Thoughts. l.t. ed. 1993. (Ulverscroft Large Print Ser.). 352p. 29.99 o.p. (*0-7089-2953-2*, Ulverscroft) Thorpe, F. A. Pubs. GBR. *Dist:* Ulverscroft Large Print Bks., Ltd., Ulverscroft Large Print Canada, Ltd.

Friedman, Melanie. Jennifer No. 2: No Way, Jennifer. 1991. (J). mass mkt. 2.75 o.p. (*0-425-12604-8*, Splash) Berkley Publishing Group.

Fullerton, John. The Monkey House. abr. ed. 1997. audio 7.99 o.p. (*1-56740-180-5*, 676, Paperback Nova Audio Bks.); 1996. audio 16.95 o.p. (*1-56100-922-9*, 1297); 1996. audio 23.95 o.p. (*1-56100-712-9*, 178, Bookcassette); 1996. audio 57.25 o.p. (*1-56100-337-9*, 944, Unabridged Library Editions) Brilliance Audio.

—The Monkey House. 1996. o.s.i (*0-517-70695-4*) Crown Publishing Group.

—The Monkey House. 1996. 384p. 23.00 o.s.i (*0-517-70660-1*) Random Hse. Value Publishing.

—The Monkey House. 2000. 286p. 27.50 (*0-593-04052-X*); 347p. pap. 10.95 (*0-553-50475-4*) Transworld Publishers Ltd. GBR. *Dist:* Trafalgar Square.

Fuqua, Jonathon Scott. Darby. 2002. 256p. (J). (gr. 5 up). 15.99 (*0-7636-1417-3*) Candlewick Pr.

Galt, George. Scribes & Scoundrels. 1997. 220p. pap. (*1-55022-333-X*) ECW Pr.

Gantschev, Ivan. The Christmas Train. 1991. 3.99 o.p. (*0-517-07210-6*) Random Hse. Value Publishing.

Garlock, Dorothy. With Heart. l.t. ed. 1999. (Basic Ser.). 551p. 30.95 (*0-7862-2265-4*) Thorndike Pr.

—With Heart. 1999. 464p. reprint ed. mass mkt. 6.99 (*0-446-60589-1*) Warner Bks., Inc.

Garrett, George P. The King of Babylon Shall Not Come Against You. 352p. 1998. pap. 13.00 (*0-15-600553-0*, Harvest Bks.); 1996. 24.00 o.s.i (*0-15-157554-1*) Harcourt Trade Pubs.

Gilligan, Shannon. The Terrorist Trap. 1991. (Choose Your Own Adventure Ser.: No. 119). 128p. (J). (gr. 4-8). pap. 3.25 o.s.i (*0-553-29289-7*) Bantam Bks.

Glass, Stephen. The Fabulist. 2003. 352p. 24.00 (*0-7432-2712-3*, Simon & Schuster) Simon & Schuster.

Gray, John MacLachlan. The Fiend in Human. 2003. 352p. 24.95 (*0-312-28284-2*) St. Martin's Pr.

Greene, Graham. The Quiet American. l.t. ed. 1993. 19.95 o.p. (*0-7927-1420-2*); pap. 17.95 o.p. (*0-7927-1419-9*) BBC Audiobooks America.

—The Quiet American. 19th ed. 1992. (Modern Library Ser.). 272p. 14.95 (*0-679-60014-0*) Random Hse., Inc.

Grippando, James M. The Informant. l.t. ed. 1997. lib. bdg. 24.95 (*1-57490-079-X*, Beeler Large Print Bks.) Beeler, Thomas T. Publisher.

Guterson, David. Snow Falling on Cedars. 1999. 352p. 20.00 o.s.i (*0-15-100443-9*, Harvest Bks.); 1994. 100.00 o.s.i (*0-15-100242-8*); 1994. 368p. 21.95 (*0-15-100100-6*) Harcourt Trade Pubs.

—Snow Falling on Cedars. 1998. 512p. pap. 14.00 (*0-676-57609-5*); 1995. 480p. pap. 14.00 (*0-679-76402-X*) Knopf Publishing Group. (Vintage).

—Snow Falling on Cedars, Level 6. 2000. pap. 7.93 (*0-582-41928-X*) Longman Publishing Group.

—Snow Falling on Cedars. 1995. (Vintage Contemporaries Ser.). 20.05 (*0-606-12140-4*) Turtleback Bks.

Guy, David. The Autobiography of My Body. 1999. 323p. reprint ed. text 20.00 (*0-7881-6654-9*) DIANE Publishing Co.

—The Autobiography of My Body. 1995. 336p. pap. 12.95 o.p. (*0-452-27453-2*, Plume); 1991. 320p. 19.95 o.p. (*0-525-24974-5*, Dutton) Dutton/Plume.

—The Autobiography of My Body. 1992. 400p. mass mkt. 5.99 o.p. (*0-451-17252-3*, Signet Bks.) NAL.

Habila, Helon. Waiting for an Angel: A Novel. 2004. 236p. pap. 13.95 (*0-393-32511-3*); 2003. 256p. 23.95 (*0-393-05193-5*) Norton, W. W. & Co., Inc.

Hagedorn, Jessica. Dream Jungle. 2003. 320p. 23.95 (*0-670-88458-8*, Viking) Viking Penguin.

Hailey, Arthur. The Evening News. 592p. 1991. mass mkt. 6.99 o.s.i (*0-440-20851-3*); 1990. mass mkt. 5.50 o.s.i (*0-440-29514-9*) Dell Publishing.

—The Evening News. 1990. 576p. 27.95 o.s.i (*0-385-41405-6*) Doubleday Publishing.

Hall, Oakley M. Ambrose Bierce & the Death of Kings. 2001. 288p. 22.95 o.s.i (*0-670-03007-4*, Viking) Viking Penguin.

—Ambrose Bierce & the One-Eyed Jacks. 2004. 224p. pap. 12.00 (*0-14-200014-0*) Penguin Group (USA) Inc.

—Ambrose Bierce & the One-Eyed Jacks: An Ambrose Bierce Mystery. 2003. 224p. 24.95 (*0-670-03180-1*, Viking) Viking Penguin.

—Ambrose Bierce & the Queen of Spades: A Novel. 2000. 288p. pap. 5.99 (*0-14-028860-0*, Penguin Bks.) Penguin Group (USA) Inc.

—Ambrose Bierce & the Queen of Spades: A Novel. 1998. 321p. text 22.95 (*0-520-21555-9*) Univ. of California Pr.

—Ambrose Bierce & the Trey of Pearls. 2004. 224p. 24.95 (*0-670-03270-0*, Viking) Viking Penguin.

Hamill, Denis. A Long Time Gone. 2002. 416p. 25.00 (*0-7434-0709-1*, Atria) Simon & Schuster.

—The Sins of Two Fathers. 2003. 384p. 25.00 (*0-7434-6298-X*, Atria) Simon & Schuster.

Handberg, Ron. Dead Silence. 1999. 464p. (Orig.). mass mkt. 6.99 (*0-06-101247-5*) HarperCollins Pubs.

Harrison, Colin. Manhattan Nocturne. 1997. o.s.i (*0-517-70696-2*); 1996. 384p. 5.99 o.s.i (*0-517-58492-1*) Crown Publishing Group.

—Manhattan Nocturne. 1997. 416p. mass mkt. 6.99 o.s.i (*0-440-22433-0*) Dell Publishing.

—Manhattan Nocturne. unabr. ed. 1996. 24.95 o.p. (*0-7871-1115-5*) NewStar Media, Inc.

—Manhattan Nocturne. 2004. 416p. mass mkt. 6.99 (*0-312-99303-X*, St. Martin's Paperbacks) St. Martin's Pr.

Harrison, William. The Blood Latitudes. 2000. 280p. 25.00 (*1-878448-97-8*) MacMurray & Beck, Inc.

Hasluck, Nicholas P. Our Man K. 1999. 359p. (*0-14-028249-1*) Penguin Group (USA) Inc.

Hays, Clark & McFall, Kathleen. The Cowboy & the Vampire: A Very Unusual Romance. Hill, Connie, ed. 336p. pap. 12.95 (*1-56718-451-0*, K451) Llewellyn Pubns.

Heald, Tim. Stop the Press. 1998. 352p. pap. 17.95 (*0-297-84226-9*) Weidenfeld & Nicolson, Ltd. GBR. *Dist:* Trafalgar Square.

Heffernan, William. Cityside: William Heffernan. 1999. 276p. 24.00 (*0-688-16406-4*, Morrow, William & Co.) Morrow/Avon.

Heller, Jean. Maximum Impact. 1995. 627p. pap. 5.99 (*0-8125-1619-2*); 1993. 432p. 22.95 o.p. (*0-312-85203-7*) Doherty, Tom Assocs., LLC. (Forge Bks.).

Henderson, M. R. Victim. 2002. (Five Star First Edition Mystery Ser.). 250p. 24.95 (*0-7862-3930-1*, Five Star) Gale Group.

Herr, Michael. Walter Winchell: A Novel. 1991. 176p. pap. 9.00 o.s.i (*0-679-73393-0*, Vintage) Knopf Publishing Group.

Hiaasen, Carl. Basket Case. 2002. E-Book 20.95 (*1-59061-759-2*) Adobe Systems, Inc.

—Basket Case. 2002. 336p. 25.95 (*0-375-41107-0*) Knopf, Alfred A. Inc.

—Basket Case. abr. ed. 2002. audio 25.00 (*0-553-71485-6*) Random Hse. Audio Publishing Group.

—Basket Case. l.t. ed. 2003. 13.95 (*1-4104-0083-2*, Large Print Pr.) Thorndike Pr.

—Basket Case. 2003. 432p. mass mkt. 7.99 (*0-446-61193-X*) Warner Bks., Inc.

—Native Tongue. 1992. (Florida Mysteries Ser.). 416p. mass mkt. 7.50 o.s.i (*0-449-22118-0*, Fawcett) Ballantine Bks.

—Native Tongue. l.t. ed. 1996. (Large Print Bks.). pap. 21.95 o.p. (*1-56895-344-5*, Wheeler Publishing, Inc.) Gale Group.

—Native Tongue, Set. abr. ed. 1991. audio 16.00 o.s.i (*0-394-58966-1*, 391249, RH Audio) Random Hse. Audio Publishing Group.

—Native Tongue. 1993. 4.99 o.p. (*0-517-10755-4*) Random Hse. Value Publishing.

—Native Tongue, unabr. ed. 1992. audio 91.00 (*1-55690-761-3*, 92421E7) Recorded Bks., LLC.

—Native Tongue. 2003. mass mkt. 7.99 (*0-446-61320-7*) Warner Bks., Inc.

Hilden, Julie. Three: A Novel. 2003. 224p. pap. 13.00 (*0-452-28443-0*, Plume) Dutton/Plume.

Hill, Grace Livingston. Partners. 21.95 (*0-89190-071-3*) Amereon, Ltd.

—Partners, No. 35. 1980. 224p. pap. 1.95 o.p. (*0-553-14173-2*) Bantam Bks.

—Partners. l.t. ed. 1999. (Candlelight Romance Ser.). 347p. 21.95 (*0-7862-1755-3*) Thorndike Pr.

—Partners. 1994. (Grace Livingston Hill Ser.: Vol. 35). 256p. pap. 4.99 o.p. (*0-8423-5022-5*); 1988. 218p. pap. 7.95 o.p. (*0-8423-4777-1*) Tyndale Hse. Pubs.

Hill, Reginald. Singleton's Law. l.t. ed. 1997. (Myst-Hall Ser.). 295p. lib. bdg. 24.95 o.p. (*0-7838-8106-1*, Macmillan Reference USA) Gale Group.

—Singleton's Law. 1997. 224p. 24.00 o.p. (*0-7278-4994-8*) Severn Hse. Pubs., Ltd.

Hillerman, Tony. The Fly on the Wall. unabr. ed. 1993. audio 42.00 (*0-7366-2571-2*, 3320) Books on Tape, Inc.

—The Fly on the Wall. l.t. ed. 1992. (General Ser.). 308p. 20.95 o.p. (*0-8161-5381-7*); 15.95 o.p. (*0-8161-5382-5*) Gale Group. (Macmillan Reference USA).

—The Fly on the Wall. Barzun, Jacques & Taylor, W. H., eds. 1983. (Crime Fiction 1950-1975 Ser.). 212p. lib. bdg. 18.00 o.p. (*0-8240-4993-4*) Garland Publishing, Inc.

—The Fly on the Wall. 1990. audio 15.95; 2000. audio 9.99 (*0-694-52326-7*); 1995. 3p. audio 15.95 o.s.i (*1-55994-196-0*, 390794) HarperTrade. (HarperAudio).

—The Fly on the Wall. 1990. 368p. mass mkt. 6.99 (*0-06-100028-0*, HarperTorch); 1979. 224p. pap. 3.95 (*0-380-44156-X*, Avon Bks.) Morrow/Avon.

—The Fly on the Wall. 1990. 13.04 (*0-606-16168-6*) Turtleback Bks.

Hirschfeld, Corson. Aloha Mr. Lucky. 2000. 381p. 24.95 (*0-312-87002-7*, Forge Bks.) Doherty, Tom Assocs., LLC.

Hoag, Tami. Heart of Dixie. 1991. (Loveswept Ser.: No. 492). 192p. mass mkt. 2.75 o.s.i (*0-553-44163-9*) Bantam Bks.

—Heart of Dixie. l.t. ed. 2002. 266p. 29.95 (*0-7862-3487-3*) Gale Group.

Hodges, Sam. B-Four. 2000. (Deep South Bks.). 278p. pap. 17.95 (*0-8173-1049-5*) Univ. of Alabama Pr.

—B-Four: A Novel. 1992. 288p. 18.95 o.p. (*0-312-07647-9*) St. Martin's Pr.

Hoff, B. J. Masquerade. 1996. (Portraits Ser.: No. 1). 224p. pap. 8.99 o.p. (*1-55661-860-3*) Bethany Hse. Pubs.

—Masquerade. l.t. ed. 2000. (Christian Mystery Ser.). 279p. 24.95 (*0-7862-2376-6*) Thorndike Pr.

Holden, Wendy. Azur Like It. 2004. 368p. pap. 13.00 (*0-452-28517-8*, Plume) Dutton/Plume.

Hollingshead, Greg. The Healer: A Novel. 1999. 336p. 24.00 o.s.i (*0-06-019227-5*) HarperCollins Pubs.

—The Healer: A Novel. 2000. 336p. pap. 14.00 (*0-06-092967-7*, Perennial) HarperTrade.

Hoopes, Roy. Our Man in Washington. 2000. 380p. 24.95 (*0-312-86849-9*, Forge Bks.) Doherty, Tom Assocs., LLC.

—A Watergate Tape. E-Book 24.95 (*0-312-70650-2*, Tor Bks.); 2002. 384p. 24.95 (*0-312-87899-0*, Forge Bks.) Doherty, Tom Assocs., LLC.

Houston, James D. Continental Drift. 1987. 336p. pap. text 4.95 o.p. (*0-07-030488-2*) McGraw-Hill Cos., The.

—Continental Drift. 1978. 8.95 o.p. (*0-394-50124-1*, Knopf Bks. for Young Readers) Random Hse. Children's Bks.

—Continental Drift. 1996. (California Fiction Ser.). 337p. (C). pap. 15.95 (*0-520-20713-0*) Univ. of California Pr.

Howells, William Dean. A Modern Instance, unabr. ed. 1997. (J). (gr. 10 up). audio 65.95 (*1-55685-461-7*, 461-7) Audio Bk. Contractors, Inc.

—A Modern Instance. 1882. 255p. (YA). reprint ed. pap. text 28.00 (*1-4047-3235-7*) Classic Textbooks.

—A Modern Instance, 001. Gibson, W., ed. 1957. (YA). (gr. 9 up). pap. 13.16 o.p. (*0-395-05119-3*, Riverside Editions) Houghton Mifflin Co.

—A Modern Instance. 1977. (Selected Edition of W. D. Howells Ser.: Vol. 10). 608p. 20.00 o.p. (*0-253-33864-6*) Indiana Univ. Pr.

—A Modern Instance. mass mkt. 0.75 o.p. (*0-451-50249-3*, Signet Classics) NAL.

—A Modern Instance. 2003. (Twelve-Point Ser.). lib. bdg. 25.00 (*1-58287-220-1*); lib. bdg. 26.00 (*1-58287-704-1*) North Bks.

—A Modern Instance. 1992. (Notable American Authors Ser.). reprint ed. lib. bdg. 75.00 (*0-7812-3235-X*) Reprint Services Corp.

—A Modern Instance. l.t. ed. 1999. 524p. text 27.95 (*1-56000-487-8*) Transaction Pubs.

—A Modern Instance. 1984. (Classics Ser.). 480p. (C). 14.00 (*0-14-039027-8*, Penguin Classics) Viking Penguin.
Hower, Edward. Shadows & Elephants. 2002. 317p. pap. 14.95 (*0-9679520-3-4*) Leapfrog Pr.
Hunter, Jack D. Slingshot. unabr. ed. 1995. 5p. audio 62.95 (*0-7861-0872-X*, 113377) Blackstone Audio Bks., Inc.
—Slingshot. 1996. 432p. pap. text 6.99 o.p. (*0-8125-2457-8*); 1994. 384p. 22.95 o.p. (*0-312-85500-1*) Doherty, Tom Assocs., LLC. (Forge Bks.).
—Slingshot. 2000. 29.95 (*0-7351-0450-6*) Replica Bks.
Hyman, Jackie. The Eyes of a Stranger. 1987. 304p. 17.95 o.p. (*0-312-01017-6*) St. Martin's Pr.
Ignatieff, Michael. Charlie Johnson in the Flames. 2003. 224p. 24.00 (*0-8021-1755-4*, Grove Pr.) Grove/Atlantic, Inc.
Ignatius, David. A Firing Offense. 1998. mass mkt. 6.99 o.s.i (*0-8041-1802-7*, Ivy Bks.) Ballantine Bks.
—A Firing Offense. unabr. ed. 1998. audio 85.00 (*0-7887-2167-4*, 95463E7) Recorded Bks., LLC.
—The Sun King. E-Book 17.50 (*1-58945-558-4*) Adobe Systems, Inc.
—The Sun King. 2000. E-Book 17.50 (*0-375-50455-9*) Random Hse., Inc.
Irving, John. The Fourth Hand. 2001. E-Book 21.95 (*1-58945-955-5*) Adobe Systems, Inc.
—The Fourth Hand. 2003. 368p. mass mkt. 7.99 (*0-345-46315-3*, Ballantine Bks.); 2002. 352p. pap. 14.95 (*0-345-44934-7*) Ballantine Bks.
—The Fourth Hand. l.t. ed. 2001. 448p. 26.95 (*0-375-43121-7*) Random Hse. Large Print.
—The Fourth Hand. 2001. 336p. 26.95 (*0-375-50627-6*); E-Book 21.95 (*1-58836-017-2*) Random Hse., Inc.
Isaacs, Susan. Red, White & Blue. unabr. ed. 1999. audio 83.95 (*0-7861-1519-X*, 2369) Blackstone Audio Bks., Inc.
—Red, White & Blue. 1998. 416p. 25.00 o.s.i (*0-06-017608-3*) HarperCollins Pubs.
—Red, White & Blue. abr. ed. 1998. audio 25.00 (*0-694-51982-0*, 696054, HarperAudio) HarperTrade.
—Red, White & Blue. abr. ed. 1999. audio 25.00 Highsmith Inc.
—Red, White & Blue. l.t. ed. (Thorndike/G. K. Hall Paperback Bestsellers Ser.). 749p. 2000. pap. 27.95 (*0-7862-1742-1*); 1999. 30.95 (*0-7862-1741-3*) Thorndike Pr.
—Red, White & Blue: A Novel. 1999. 592p. mass mkt. 6.99 (*0-06-109310-6*, HarperTorch) Morrow/Avon.
Jackson, Edwardo. Neva Hafta: A Novel. 368p. 2003. pap. 13.95 (*0-375-75774-0*); 2002. 22.95 (*0-375-50637-3*, Villard Bks.) Random House Adult Trade Publishing Group.
Jaco, Charles. Dead Air. 1999. mass mkt. 6.99 o.s.i (*0-345-42184-1*) Ballantine Bks.
—Dead Air. abr. ed. 1998. audio (*1-56876-074-4*) Soundlines Entertainment, Inc.
Jaffe, John. Thief of Words. 2005. mass mkt. (*0-446-61391-6*); 2003. 256p. 19.95 (*0-446-53080-8*) Warner Bks., Inc.
Jenkins, Dan. Fast Copy. 1988. 400p. 19.95 o.p. (*0-671-60206-3*, Simon & Schuster) Simon & Schuster.
Johnson, Diane. Le Mariage. 2001. 336p. pap. 13.00 (*0-452-28226-8*, Plume); 2000. 320p. 23.95 o.s.i (*0-525-94518-0*, Dutton) Dutton/Plume.
—Le Mariage. l.t. ed. 2000. 457p. 27.95 (*1-56895-936-2*, Wheeler Publishing, Inc.) Gale Group.
Johnson, Mat. Hunting in Harlem. 2003. 300p. 23.95 (*1-58234-272-5*) Bloomsbury Publishing.
Johnston, Wayne. The Colony of Unrequited Dreams. 1999. (Illus.). 576p. 24.95 o.s.i (*0-385-49542-0*) Doubleday Publishing.
Jones, Gwyneth. White Queen. 1994. 316p. pap. 12.95 o.s.i (*0-312-89013-3*, Orb Bks.); 1993. 320p. (YA). 19.95 o.p. (*0-312-85492-7*, Tor Bks.) Doherty, Tom Assocs., LLC.
Jordan, Elizabeth G. Tales of the City Room. 1977. (Short Story Index Reprint Ser.). 19.95 (*0-8369-3462-8*) Ayer Co. Pubs., Inc.
Kallen, Lucille. C. B. Greenfield: No Lady in the House. 1984. 208p. mass mkt. 3.95 o.s.i (*0-345-32396-3*) Ballantine Bks.
—C. B. Greenfield: No Lady in the House. 1982. 12.95 o.p. (*0-671-43240-0*, Simon & Schuster) Simon & Schuster.
—C. B. Greenfield: No Lady in the House. l.t. ed. 1982. 374p. reprint ed. 10.95 o.p. (*0-89621-365-X*) Thorndike Pr.
—C. B. Greenfield: The Piano Bird. 1985. 224p. mass mkt. 3.95 o.s.i (*0-345-31118-3*, Ballantine Bks.) Ballantine Bks.
—C. B. Greenfield: The Piano Bird. 1984. 175p. 13.95 o.p. (*0-394-53081-0*) Random Hse., Inc.
—C. B. Greenfield: The Tanglewood Murder. 1985. mass mkt. 3.95 o.s.i (*0-345-33143-5*) Ballantine Bks.
—Introducing C. B. Greenfield. 1985. 208p. mass mkt. 3.95 o.s.i (*0-345-33426-4*); 1984. mass mkt. 2.50 o.p. (*0-345-32159-6*) Ballantine Bks.
—Introducing C. B. Greenfield. l.t. ed. 1980. 363p. reprint ed. 11.95 o.p. (*0-89621-260-2*) Thorndike Pr.
Kanon, Joseph. The Good German: A Novel. l.t. ed. 2002. (Basic Ser.). 809p. 31.95 (*0-7862-3655-8*) Gale Group.
—The Good German: A Novel. 2001. (Illus.). 496p. 26.00 o.s.i (*0-8050-6422-2*) Holt, Henry & Co.
—The Good German: A Novel. 2002. mass mkt. 7.99 o.s.i (*0-312-98253-4*); 496p. pap. 14.00 (*0-312-42126-5*); pap. (*0-312-42139-7*) Picador.
—The Good German: A Novel. l.t. ed. 2002. 805p. 28.95 (*0-7862-3656-6*); (*0-7540-1734-6*) Thorndike Pr.
Karaim, Reed. If Men Were Angels. abr. ed. 2000. audio 7.99 o.s.i (*1-56740-983-0*, 2106, Paperback Nova Audio Bks.); 1999. audio 26.95 (*1-56740-433-2*, 1725, Bookcassette); 1999. audio 73.25 (*1-56740-658-0*, 1726, Unabridged Library Editions) Brilliance Audio.
—If Men Were Angels. 1999. 320p. 24.95 o.p. (*0-393-04780-6*) Norton, W. W. & Co., Inc.
Karnezis, Panos. The Maze. 2004. 224p. 24.00 (*0-374-20480-2*) Farrar, Straus & Giroux.
Katzenbach, John. In the Heat of the Summer. 1982. 13.95 o.p. (*0-689-11269-6*, Scribner) Simon & Schuster.
Kendrick, Jeana. St. Abient Run. 2002. 188p. pap. 14.95 (*0-9678343-8-4*) Panther Creek Pr.
Kenney, Charles. Code of Vengeance. 1997. mass mkt. 5.99 o.s.i (*0-449-28779-3*, Fawcett) Ballantine Bks.
—Code of Vengeance. 1995. 303p. 22.00 (*0-671-89697-0*, Simon & Schuster) Simon & Schuster.
Kizis, Deanna. How to Meet Cute Boys: A Novel. 2003. (Illus.). 272p. 21.95 (*0-446-53072-7*) Warner Bks., Inc.
Klavan, Andrew. True Crime. 1996. mass mkt. 6.99 (*0-449-22512-7*, Fawcett) Ballantine Bks.
—True Crime. 1997. 400p. mass mkt. 6.99 (*0-440-22403-9*) Dell Publishing.
—True Crime. l.t. ed. 1995. 522p. 24.95 o.p. (*0-7838-1438-0*, Macmillan Reference USA) Gale Group.
—True Crime. abr. ed. 1996. audio 8.99 o.s.i (*0-679-45596-5*, 391811); 1995. audio 17.00 o.s.i (*0-679-44455-6*) Random Hse. Audio Publishing Group. (RH Audio).
Klein, Robin. Penny Pollard in Print. 1988. (Illus.). 64p. (J). (gr. 4 up). bds. 10.95 o.p. (*0-19-554638-5*) Oxford Univ. Pr., Inc.
Kliewer, Dorothy. Murder in the Swamp. 2004. (WWL Mystery Ser.: No. 490). 256p. mass mkt. (*0-373-26490-9*, Worldwide Library) Harlequin Enterprises, Ltd.
Knipfel, Jim. The Buzzing: A Novel. 2003. 272p. pap. 12.00 (*1-4000-3183-4*, Vintage) Knopf Publishing Group.
Kohler, Vincent. Banjo Boy. 1994. 226p. 19.95 o.p. (*0-312-11475-3*, Saint Martin's Minotaur) St. Martin's Pr.
—Rainy North Woods. 1990. 256p. 16.95 o.p. (*0-312-03918-2*, Saint Martin's Minotaur) St. Martin's Pr.
—Raven's Widows. 1997. 256p. text 22.95 o.p. (*0-312-14714-7*, Saint Martin's Minotaur) St. Martin's Pr.
—Rising Dog. 1992. 288p. 18.95 o.p. (*0-312-07075-6*, Saint Martin's Minotaur) St. Martin's Pr.
Koontz, Dean. Cold Fire. 1991. 432p. mass mkt. 7.99 (*0-425-13071-1*) Berkley Publishing Group.
—Cold Fire. 1991. 14.04 (*0-606-00937-X*) Turtleback Bks.
Kranes, David. Keno Runner: A Dark Romance. 1995. (Western Literature Ser.). 288p. reprint ed. pap. 15.00 (*0-87417-276-4*) Univ. of Nevada Pr.
—Keno Runner: A Romance. 1989. (Fiction Ser.). 17.95 o.p. (*0-87480-320-9*) Univ. of Utah Pr.
Kristeva, Julia. Possessions. Bray, Barbara, tr. from FRE. 1998. 256p. 33.50 (*0-231-10998-9*) Columbia Univ. Pr.
Kurland, Michael. Girls in High Heeled Shoes. 1998. (Alexander Brass Mysteries Ser.). 256p. 22.95 (*0-312-18104-3*, 874694, Saint Martin's Minotaur) St. Martin's Pr.
—Too Soon Dead. 1997. 288p. 22.95 o.p. (*0-312-15228-0*, Saint Martin's Minotaur) St. Martin's Pr.
Lamb, Fay. Tatted Angels. 2000. 108p. pap. 14.95 o.p. (*1-929925-50-6*) FirstPublish.
Lamb, Joyce. Caught in the ACT. 2003. 333p. 26.95 (*0-7862-5335-5*, Five Star) Gale Group.
—Relative Strangers. 2003. 272p. pap. 13.95 (*1-4104-0110-3*, Five Star Trade); 2002. 250p. 26.95 (*0-7862-3730-9*, Five Star) Gale Group.
Landis, Catherine E. Some Days There's Pie Easel. 2003. pap. 0.01 (*0-312-31737-9*, Saint Martin's Griffin) St. Martin's Pr.
Lantz, Francess L. Dear Celeste, My Life Is a Mess. 1991. 160p. (J). (gr. 4-7). pap. 3.25 o.s.i (*0-553-15961-5*) Bantam Bks.
Larsen, Michael. Uncertainty. 1998. Tr. of Uden Sikker Viden. 272p. pap. 12.00 o.s.i (*0-449-91236-1*, Fawcett) Ballantine Bks.
—Uncertainty. Blecher, Lone T. & Blecher, George, trs. from DAN. 1996. Tr. of Uden Sikker Viden. 272p. 22.00 o.s.i (*0-15-100202-9*) Harcourt Trade Pubs.
Ledford, Jan R. The Cloning. 2001. 346p. pap. 12.95 (*0-9625220-6-6*) Millennium III Pubs., L.P.
Lehrer, Jim. Last Debate. 2000. 368p. pap. text 13.00 (*1-58648-004-9*) PublicAffairs.
—Last Debate. l.t. ed. 1996. (Niagara Large Print Ser.). 485p. 29.50 o.p. (*0-7089-5838-9*, Ulverscroft) Thorpe, F. A. Pubs. GBR. *Dist:* Ulverscroft Large Print Bks., Ltd.
Lemann, Nancy. Malaise. l.t. ed. 2002. 28.95 (*1-58724-338-5*, Wheeler Publishing, Inc.) Gale Group.
—Malaise. 256p. 2003. pap. 13.00 (*0-7432-1549-4*); 2002. 24.00 (*0-7432-1548-6*) Simon & Schuster. (Scribner).
Leroux, Gaston. The Mystery of the Yellow Room: Extraordinary Adventures of Joseph Rouletabille, Reporter. 1976. (Literature of Mystery & Detection Ser.). reprint ed. 33.95 (*0-405-07883-8*) Ayer Co. Pubs., Inc.
—The Mystery of the Yellow Room: Extraordinary Adventures of Joseph Rouletabille, Reporter. 1992. lib. bdg. 27.95 (*0-89966-141-6*) Buccaneer Bks., Inc.
—The Mystery of the Yellow Room: Extraordinary Adventures of Joseph Rouletabille, Reporter. Hale, Terry, ed. 2003. (European Classics Ser.). 236p. pap. 12.99 (*1-873982-38-0*) Dedalus, Ltd.
Leto, Julie Elizabeth. Double the Pleasure. 2002. (Harlequin Blaze Ser.). mass mkt. (*0-373-79053-8*, Harlequin Bks.) Harlequin Enterprises, Ltd.
Levinson, Robert S. Hot Paint: A Neil Gulliver & Stevie Marriner Novel. 2002. 352p. 26.95 (*0-7653-0231-4*, Forge Bks.) Doherty, Tom Assocs., LLC.
—The James Dean Affair. 2000. (Neil Gulliver & Steve Marriner Novels Ser.). 320p. 24.95 o.p. (*0-312-87268-2*, Forge Bks.) Doherty, Tom Assocs., LLC.
Lilliefors, Jim. Bananaville. 1996. 288p. text 22.95 o.p. (*0-312-14548-9*, Saint Martin's Minotaur) St. Martin's Pr.
Lindsey, David L. Black Gold, Red Death. 1986. 256p. mass mkt. 5.99 o.s.i (*0-449-13121-1*, Fawcett) Ballantine Bks.
Llewellyn, Sam. Blood Knot. Chelius, Jane, ed. 1992. 320p. 20.00 (*0-671-67046-8*, Atria) Simon & Schuster.
Llywelyn, Morgan. 1921. 2002. E-Book 25.95 (*1-59061-720-7*) Adobe Systems, Inc.
—1921. 2001. 432p. 25.95 (*0-312-86754-9*); 2002. 560p. reprint ed. mass mkt. 7.99 (*0-8125-7079-0*) Doherty, Tom Assocs., LLC. (Forge Bks.).
Lyons, Genevieve. Alice's Awakening. l.t. ed. 2000. 248p. (*0-7540-4205-7*, Macmillan Reference USA) Gale Group.
—Alice's Awakening. 224p. 26.00 (*0-7278-5506-9*) Severn Hse. Pubs., Ltd.
—Alice's Awakening. l.t. ed. 2000. (Nightingale Ser.). 248p. pap. 20.95 (*0-7838-9109-1*) Thorndike Pr.
Mackay, Colin. Fires in the Night. E-Book (*1-84045-041-X*) Online Originals.
Mackin, Jeanne. The Sweet By & By. 2001. 293p. 24.95 o.p. (*0-312-26997-8*) St. Martin's Pr.
Marks, John. War Torn. 2003. 320p. 25.95 (*1-57322-254-2*, Riverhead Bks. (Hardcovers)) Putnam Publishing Group, The.
Martinez, Al. The Last City Room. 2000. 259p. 22.95 (*0-312-20901-0*) St. Martin's Pr.
Mason, Diane Baker. Last Summer at Barebones. 2002. 416p. 17.95 (*1-55278-239-5*) McArthur & Co. CAN. *Dist:* National Bk. Network.
Maynard, Roy. The Old Man. 1994. (Emerson Dunn Mystery Ser.). 192p. pap. 7.99 o.p. (*0-89107-772-3*) Crossway Bks.
—A Quick Thirty Seconds. 1993. (Emerson Dunn Mystery Ser.). 192p. (YA). pap. 7.99 o.p. (*0-89107-745-6*) Crossway Bks.
—Thirty-Eight Caliber. 1992. (Emerson Dunn Mystery Ser.). 192p. (Orig.). pap. 7.99 o.p. (*0-89107-674-3*) Crossway Bks.
—Twenty-Two Automatic. 1993. (Emerson Dunn Mystery Ser.). 192p. pap. 7.99 o.p. (*0-89107-696-4*) Crossway Bks.
McCabe, Peter. City of Lies: A Novel. 1993. 271p. 20.00 o.p. (*0-688-12118-7*, Morrow, William & Co.) Morrow/Avon.
McCormack, Eric. The Mysterium: A Novel of Deconstructionism. 1994. 272p. 20.95 o.p. (*0-312-11320-X*, Saint Martin's Minotaur) St. Martin's Pr.
McGregor, Elizabeth. The Ice Child. 2001. (Illus.). 400p. 24.95 o.p. (*0-525-94567-9*, Dutton) Dutton/Plume.
—The Ice Child. l.t. ed. 2001. (Wheeler Large Print Book Ser.). (Illus.). 540p. 29.95 o.p. (*1-58724-109-9*, Wheeler Publishing, Inc.) Gale Group.
—The Ice Child. 2002. pap. 6.99 (*0-451-20539-1*, Signet Bks.); 448p. reprint ed. mass mkt. 7.99 (*0-451-41061-0*, Onyx) NAL.
Millar, Peter. Stealing Thunder. 1999. 23.95 (*1-58234-016-1*) Bloomsbury Publishing.
Milofsky, David. Color of Law. 2000. viii, 377p. 24.95 (*0-87081-581-4*) Univ. Pr. of Colorado.
Miscione, Lisa. Angel Fire. E-Book 17.95 (*0-312-70416-X*); 2003. 288p. mass mkt. 6.50 (*0-312-98918-0*, St. Martin's Paperbacks); 2002. 288p. 23.95 (*0-312-28304-0*, Saint Martin's Minotaur) St. Martin's Pr.
Morrell, David. Desperate Measures. 1994. 416p. 22.95 o.s.i (*0-446-51791-7*); 1999. reprint ed. mass mkt. 3.99 (*0-446-60750-9*); 1995. 512p. reprint ed. mass mkt. 7.50 (*0-446-60239-6*) Warner Bks., Inc.
Muller, Eddie. The Distance: A Crime Novel Introducing Billy Nichols. 2002. 304p. 25.00 (*0-7432-1762-4*); (Illus.). 25.00 (*0-7432-1443-9*) Simon & Schuster. (Scribner).
Muller, Marcia. Point Deception. 2001. (Illus.). 320p. 23.95 o.p. (*0-89296-690-4*) Mysterious Pr.
—Point Deception. l.t. ed. 2001. 484p. 30.95 (*0-7862-3367-2*) Thorndike Pr.
Myers, Bill. Eli. (SPA.). (*0-7899-0953-7*) Editorial Unilit.
—Eli. 2002. E-Book 9.99 (*0-310-24754-3*); 2000. 24.99 incl. audio (*0-310-23622-3*) Zondervan.
—Eli: A Novel. 2000. 352p. pap. 12.99 (*0-310-21803-9*) Zondervan.
Nadelson, Reggie. Hot Poppies. l.t. ed. 1999. (Ulverscroft Large Print Ser.). 384p. 31.99 (*0-7089-4077-3*, Ulverscroft) Thorpe, F. A. Pubs. GBR. *Dist:* Ulverscroft Large Print Bks., Ltd., Ulverscroft Large Print Canada, Ltd.
—Hot Poppies: An Artie Cohen Mystery. 1998. 256p. 22.95 o.p. (*0-312-19986-4*, Saint Martin's Minotaur) St. Martin's Pr.
—Red Hot Blues. 1998. Orig. Title: Red Mercury Blues. 272p. 22.95 (*0-312-18166-3*, Saint Martin's Minotaur) St. Martin's Pr.
Naipaul, V. S. A House for Mr. Biswas. 1984. pap. 10.95 o.s.i (*0-394-72050-4*, Vintage) Knopf Publishing Group.
—A House for Mr. Biswas. 1995. (Everyman's Library: Vol. 213). 508p. 20.00 (*0-679-44458-0*) Knopf, Alfred A. Inc.
—A House for Mr. Biswas. (Penguin Twentieth-Century Classics Ser.). 1993. 608p. pap. 13.95 o.s.i (*0-14-018604-2*, Penguin Classics); 1976. 592p. pap. 10.95 o.p. (*0-14-003025-5*, Penguin Bks.) Viking Penguin.
—A House for Mr. Biswas: A Novel. 2001. 576p. pap. 15.00 (*0-375-70716-6*, Vintage) Knopf Publishing Group.
O'Connell, Jennifer. Bachelorette #1. 2003. 256p. pap. 12.95 (*0-451-21098-0*) NAL.
Orcutt, Christopher. Nick Chase's Great Escape. 1999. 267p. pap. 21.99 (*0-7388-0603-X*); text 31.99 (*0-7388-0602-1*) Xlibris Corp.
O'Reilly, Bill. Those Who Trespass: A Novel of Murder & Television. 1998. 332p. pap. 24.00 (*0-9631246-8-4*) Bancroft Pr.
—Those Who Trespass: A Novel of Murder & Television. 1999. 384p. reprint ed. mass mkt. 6.99 o.s.i (*0-451-40882-9*, Onyx) NAL.
—Those Who Trespass: A Novel of Murder & Television. l.t. ed. 2004. 464p. 24.95 (*0-375-43306-6*) Random Hse. Large Print.
—Those Who Trespass: A Novel of Television & Murder. 2004. 320p. pap. 14.00 (*0-7679-1381-7*) Broadway Bks.
Orlando, Jordon. The Object Lesson: A Novel. 1993. 560p. 23.00 o.p. (*0-671-66978-8*, Simon & Schuster) Simon & Schuster.
Palahniuk, Chuck. Lullaby. 2003. 272p. pap. 13.95 (*0-385-72219-2*); 2002. 272p. 24.95 (*0-385-50447-0*); 2002. E-Book 9.95 (*0-385-50449-7*) Doubleday Publishing.
—Lullaby. 2003. (Basic Ser.). 28.95 (*0-7862-5098-4*) Thorndike Pr.
Palmer, Diana. Roomful of Roses. 2000. 248p. mass mkt. (*1-55166-641-3*, Harlequin Bks.); 1997. per. (*1-55166-418-6*, 1-66418-4, Mira Bks.) Harlequin Enterprises, Ltd.
—Roomful of Roses. l.t. ed. 2000. (Romance Ser.). 215p. 27.95 (*0-7862-2613-7*); (*0-7540-4358-4*); (*0-7540-4359-2*) Thorndike Pr.
Palmer, Jessica. Cradlesong. Todd, Rebecca, ed. 1993. 320p. (Orig.). mass mkt. 4.99 (*0-671-73421-0*, Pocket) Simon & Schuster.
Pascal, Francine, creator. Beware the Wolfman. 1994. (Sweet Valley High Ser.: No. 106). 240p. (YA). (gr. 7 up). mass mkt. 3.99 o.s.i (*0-553-56234-7*) Bantam Bks.
—Love & Death in London. 1994. (Sweet Valley High Ser.: No. 104). 224p. (YA). (gr. 7 up). mass mkt. 3.50 o.s.i (*0-553-56227-4*) Bantam Bks.
Patterson, Richard North. No Safe Place. 1999. mass mkt. 7.99 (*0-345-38612-4*);Vol. 2. 544p. mass mkt. 7.99 (*0-345-40477-7*) Ballantine Bks.
—No Safe Place. l.t. ed. 1998. pap. 25.95 o.p. (*0-7838-0161-0*, Macmillan Reference USA) Gale Group.
—No Safe Place. aut. ed. 1998. 25.95 o.s.i (*0-676-54935-7*) Random Hse., Inc.
—No Safe Place: A Novel. l.t. ed. 1998. 512p. pap. 25.95 o.s.i (*0-375-70296-2*) Random Hse., Inc.
Peace, David. Nineteen Seventy-Four. 2000. 295p. pap. o.p. (*1-85242-634-9*) Serpent's Tail Ltd.

Occupations

—Nineteen Seventy Four. 2000. (Red Riding Quartet Ser.: Bk. 1). 320p. pap. (*1-85242-741-8*) Serpent's Tail Ltd.

—Nineteen Seventy Seven. 2001. (Red Riding Quartet Ser.: Bk. 2). 344p. pap. 14.00 (*1-85242-639-X*) Serpent's Tail Ltd. GBR. *Dist:* Consortium Bk. Sales & Distribution.

Peretti, Frank E. This Present Darkness. 1986. 375p. pap. 12.99 (*0-89107-390-6*); 1996. 384p. 25.00 o.p. (*0-89107-919-X*) Crossway Bks.

—This Present Darkness. l.t. ed. 1993. (General Ser.). 713p. lib. bdg. 23.95 (*0-8161-5698-0*, Macmillan Reference USA) Gale Group.

Perona, Tony. Second Advent: A Novel. 2002. (Five Star First Edition Mystery Ser.). 285p. 24.95 (*0-7862-4327-9*, Five Star) Gale Group.

Phillips, Michael. Depths of Destiny. 1992. pap. 11.99 o.p. (*0-8024-6319-3*) Moody Pr.

Phillips, Mike. Blood Rights. 1990. 208p. reprint ed. mass mkt. 3.95 o.s.i (*0-440-20702-9*) Dell Publishing.

—Blood Rights. 1989. 15.95 o.p. (*0-312-02874-1*, Saint Martin's Minotaur) St. Martin's Pr.

—Image to Die For: A Sam Dean Mystery. 1997. 239p. 22.95 o.p. (*0-312-15147-0*, Saint Martin's Minotaur) St. Martin's Pr.

—The Late Candidate. 1991. 320p. mass mkt. 3.99 o.s.i (*0-440-20942-0*) Dell Publishing.

—The Late Candidate. 1990. 256p. 17.95 o.p. (*0-312-04866-1*, Saint Martin's Minotaur) St. Martin's Pr.

—Point of Darkness: A Sam Dean Mystery. 1995. 310p. 21.95 o.p. (*0-312-11875-9*, Saint Martin's Minotaur) St. Martin's Pr.

Piglia, Ricardo. The Absent City. Waisman, Sergio, tr. from SPA. 2000. 136p. lib. bdg. 54.95 (*0-8223-2557-8*) Duke Univ. Pr.

—The Absent City. Waisman, Sergio, tr. from SPA. & intro. by. 2000. 136p. pap. 17.95 (*0-8223-2586-1*) Duke Univ. Pr.

Pike, Christopher, pseud. The Cold One. 1995. 394p. pap. text 5.99 o.s.i (*0-8125-1245-6*); 1994. 352p. 21.00 o.p. (*0-312-85117-0*) Doherty, Tom Assocs., LLC. (Tor Bks.).

Poe, Robert. The Black Cat. 1998. 278p. mass mkt. 6.99 (*0-8125-4932-5*, Tor Bks.); 1997. 384p. 23.95 (*0-312-86013-7*, Forge Bks.) Doherty, Tom Assocs., LLC.

Pollack, Neal. Never Mind the Pollacks. 2003. 272p. 23.95 (*0-06-052790-0*) HarperCollins Pubs.

Pratchett, Terry. The Truth. 2001. 443p. mass mkt. (*0-552-14768-0*, Corgi) Bantam Bks.

—The Truth. 2002. (Methuen Drama Ser.). ix, 125p. pap. 12.95 (*0-413-77116-4*) Methuen Publishing Ltd. GBR. *Dist:* Consortium Bk. Sales & Distribution.

—The Truth. 2001. 368p. mass mkt. 6.99 (*0-380-81819-1*); 2000. (Illus.). 324p. 24.00 (*0-380-97895-4*) Morrow/Avon.

Preston, Douglas J. & Child, Lincoln. The Cabinet of Curiosities. 2003. 656p. mass mkt. 7.99 (*0-446-61123-9*); 2002. 480p. 25.95 (*0-446-53022-0*) Warner Bks., Inc.

Priest, Christopher. Prestige. 1997. 416p. reprint ed. pap. 14.95 (*0-312-85886-8*, NPB 0236, Tor Bks.) Doherty, Tom Assocs., LLC.

—Prestige. 1999. 404p. 36.00 (*0-671-71924-6*, Simon Pulse) Simon & Schuster Children's Publishing.

—Prestige. 1996. 416p. 24.95 o.p. (*0-312-14705-8*) St. Martin's Pr.

Quittner, Joshua & Slatalla, Michelle. Mother's Day. 1993. 245p. 18.95 o.p. (*0-312-08850-7*, Saint Martin's Minotaur) St. Martin's Pr.

—Shoo-Fly Pie to Die. 1992. 224p. 17.95 o.p. (*0-312-06943-X*, Saint Martin's Minotaur) St. Martin's Pr.

Radley, Gail. Dear Gabby, Things Are Getting Out of Hand . . 1998. pap. 3.99 o.p. (*0-380-78357-6*, Avon Bks.) Morrow/Avon.

Randisi, Robert J. The Ham Reporter. 1986. (Double D Western Ser.). 192p. 12.95 o.p. (*0-385-23006-0*) Doubleday Publishing.

Raskin, Barbara. Current Affairs. 1991. 336p. mass mkt. 5.95 o.s.i (*0-8041-0537-5*, Ivy Bks.) Ballantine Bks.

Rayner, Richard. The Elephant. 2002. 276p. reprint ed. 25.00 (*0-7881-9107-1*) DIANE Publishing Co.

—The Elephant. 1993. 3.99 o.p. (*0-517-10669-8*) Random Hse. Value Publishing.

Rhode, William. Paperback Orginal: When the Travelling Ends, & the Drugs Wear Off, the Writing Must Begin. 2003. 464p. pap. 14.00 o.p. (*1-57322-980-6*, Riverhead Trade (Paperbacks)) Berkley Publishing Group.

Richler, Mordecai. Joshua Then & Now. 1997. 384p. mass mkt. 7.95 (*0-7710-9864-2*) McClelland & Stewart/Tundra Bks.

—Joshua Then & Now. 1991. 448p. pap. 9.95 o.p. (*0-14-015280-6*, Penguin Bks.) Penguin Group (USA) Inc.

Rickman, Phil. Candlenight. 1995. 480p. mass mkt. 5.99 o.s.i (*0-515-11715-3*, Jove) Berkley Publishing Group.

Riggs, John R. Cold Hearts & Gentle People. 1994. 272p. 17.95 (*1-56980-021-9*) Barricade Bks., Inc.

—Dead Letter. 1992. 15.95 (*0-942637-40-2*) Barricade Bks., Inc.

—Dead Letter. 1994. 208p. mass mkt. 4.50 o.s.i (*0-515-11280-1*, Jove) Berkley Publishing Group.

—A Dragon Lives Forever. 1992. (Garth Ryland Mystery Ser.). 344p. 17.95 (*0-942637-78-X*) Barricade Bks., Inc.

—A Dragon Lives Forever. 1994. 224p. reprint ed. mass mkt. 4.50 o.p. (*0-425-14301-5*, Prime Crime) Berkley Publishing Group.

—Glory Hound. 1986. (Garth Ryland Mystery Ser.). 14.95 o.p. (*0-934878-78-1*, Dembner Bks.) Barricade Bks., Inc.

—Haunt of the Nightingale. (Garth Ryland Mystery Ser.). 224p. 15.95 o.p. (*0-934878-97-8*, Dembner Bks.) Barricade Bks., Inc.

—Haunt of the Nightingale. 1992. 192p. mass mkt. 3.99 o.s.i (*0-515-10953-3*, Jove) Berkley Publishing Group.

—He Who Waits: A Garth Ryland Mystery. 1997. (Garth Ryland Mystery Ser.). 288p. 17.95 (*1-56980-096-0*) Barricade Bks., Inc.

—Killing Frost: A Garth Ryland Mystery. 1995. 304p. 17.95 (*1-56980-053-7*) Barricade Bks., Inc.

—The Last Laugh. l.t. ed. 1992. 19.95 o.p. (*0-7927-1394-X*); pap. 17.95 o.p. (*0-7927-1393-1*) BBC Audiobooks America.

—The Last Laugh. 1984. (Garth Ryland Mystery Ser.). 191p. 13.95 o.p. (*0-934878-37-4*, Dembner Bks.) Barricade Bks., Inc.

—The Last Laugh. 1993. 192p. mass mkt. 3.99 o.s.i (*0-515-11134-1*, Jove) Berkley Publishing Group.

—The Last Laugh. 1988. mass mkt. 2.95 (*0-312-91131-9*, St. Martin's Paperbacks) St. Martin's Pr.

—Let Sleeping Dogs Lie. 1986. (Garth Ryland Mystery Ser.). 14.95 o.p. (*0-934878-67-6*, Dembner Bks.) Barricade Bks., Inc.

—Let Sleeping Dogs Lie. 1993. mass mkt. 4.50 o.s.i (*0-515-11211-9*, Jove) Berkley Publishing Group.

—Let Sleeping Dogs Lie. 1988. mass mkt. 3.50 (*0-312-91140-8*, St. Martin's Paperbacks) St. Martin's Pr.

—The Lost Scout: A Garth Ryland Mystery. 1998. 352p. 17.95 (*1-56980-121-5*) Barricade Bks., Inc.

—One Man's Poison. 1991. (Garth Ryland Mystery Ser.). 17.95 o.p. (*0-942637-31-3*, Dembner Bks.) Barricade Bks., Inc.

—One Man's Poison, No. 4. 1993. 208p. mass mkt. 3.99 o.s.i (*0-515-11078-7*, Jove) Berkley Publishing Group.

—Snow on the Roses: A Garth Ryland Mystery. 1996. 272p. 17.95 (*1-56980-072-3*) Barricade Bks., Inc.

—Wolf in Sheep's Clothing. 1993. 192p. (Orig.). mass mkt. 3.99 o.s.i (*0-515-11016-7*, Jove) Berkley Publishing Group.

—Wolf in Sheep's Clothing: A Garth Ryland Mystery. 1989. 16.95 o.p. (*0-942637-16-X*, Dembner Bks.) Barricade Bks., Inc.

Riley, Mildred. Bad to the Bone. 2003. 28p. mass mkt. 5.99 (*1-58314-390-4*) Kensington Publishing Corp.

Robinson, Kevin. Mall Rats: A Stick Foster Mystery. 1992. 202p. 19.95 o.p. (*0-8027-3215-1*) Walker & Co.

—A Matter of Perspective. 1993. (Stick Foster Mystery Ser.). 217p. 19.95 o.p. (*0-8027-3242-9*) Walker & Co.

—Split Seconds. 1991. 208p. 18.95 (*0-8027-5785-5*) Walker & Co.

Rolens, Sharon. What Else but Home: A Novel. 2003. 336p. 23.95 (*1-882593-75-8*) Bridge Works Publishing Co., Inc.

Ryan, Courtney. Absolute Beginners, No. 462. 1989. 2.50 o.p. (*0-425-11591-7*) Berkley Publishing Group.

—Absolute Beginners. l.t. ed. 2000. (Romance Ser.). 220p. 25.95 (*0-7862-2489-4*) Thorndike Pr.

Ryan, Paul R. Khmer Rouge End Game. 1998. x, 236p. pap. 16.95 (*0-9662707-4-6*); xvi, 192 p. (*0-9662707-3-8*) Munewata Pr.

Safire, William. Scandalmonger. E-Book 27.00 (*1-58945-508-8*) Adobe Systems, Inc.

—Scandalmonger. 2001. (Harvest Book Ser.). (Illus.). 496p. reprint ed. pap. 14.00 (*0-15-601323-1*, Harvest Bks.) Harcourt Trade Pubs.

—Scandalmonger. 2000. (Illus.). 496p. 27.00 o.s.i (*0-684-86719-2*, Simon & Schuster) Simon & Schuster.

—Sleeper Spy. 2nd ed. 1997. 416p. mass mkt. 6.99 (*0-312-96156-1*, St. Martin's Paperbacks) St. Martin's Pr.

Saul, John Ralston. The Paradise Eater. 1989. 272p. text 17.95 o.p. (*0-07-054865-X*) McGraw-Hill Cos., The.

Saulnier, Beth. Bad Seed. 2002. 384p. 23.95 (*0-89296-749-8*) Mysterious Pr.

—Bad Seed. 2003. (Alex Bernier Mysteries Ser.). 432p. mass mkt. 6.99 (*0-446-61206-5*) Warner Bks., Inc.

—Distemper. unabr. ed. 2000. audio 54.95 (*0-7927-2417-8*, CSL 306, Chivers Sound Library) BBC Audiobooks America.

—Distemper. 2000. (Alex Bernier Mysteries Ser.). 400p. reprint ed. mass mkt. 6.50 (*0-446-60861-0*) Warner Bks., Inc.

—Ecstasy. 2003. (Alex Bernier Mystery Ser.). 352p. 23.95 (*0-89296-750-1*) Mysterious Pr.

—Ecstasy. 2004. (Illus.). 752p. mass mkt. 7.99 (*0-446-61370-3*) Warner Bks., Inc.

—The Fourth Wall. 2001. 432p. reprint ed. mass mkt. 6.99 (*0-446-60998-6*) Warner Bks., Inc.

—Reliable Sources. 1999. 352p. reprint ed. mass mkt. 6.50 (*0-446-60781-9*) Warner Bks., Inc.

Schiller, Gerald A. Death Underground. unabr. ed. 1999. 220p. pap. 9.95 (*1-881164-84-5*) Intercontinental Publishing, Inc.

Sennett, Frank. Nash, Rambler. 2003. (Five Star First Edition Mystery Ser.). 339p. 25.95 (*0-7862-5034-8*, Five Star) Gale Group.

Serote, Mongane. To Every Birth Its Blood. 1984. (African Writers Ser.). 206p. (Orig.). (C). pap. 10.95 (*0-435-90263-6*, 90263) Heinemann.

—To Every Birth Its Blood: A Novel. 1997. (Ravan Writers Ser.). 368p. (Orig.). pap. text 14.95 (*0-86975-216-2*) Ravan Pr. ZMB. *Dist:* Ohio Univ. Pr.

—To Every Birth Its Blood: A Novel of South Africa. 1989. 208p. 19.95 o.p. (*0-938410-71-7*); pap. 10.95 (*0-938410-70-9*) Avalon Publishing Group. (Thunder's Mouth Pr.).

Shirley, John. Spider Moon. 2002. 180p. 35.00 (*1-58767-054-2*) Cemetery Dance Pubns.

Siddons, Anne Rivers. Homeplace. 1988. mass mkt. 5.99 (*0-345-35457-5*) Ballantine Bks.

—Homeplace. l.t. ed. 1988. (General Ser.). 512p. 19.95 o.p. (*0-8161-4473-7*, Macmillan Reference USA) Gale Group.

—Homeplace. 1987. 320p. 17.95 o.p. (*0-06-015758-5*) HarperTrade.

—Homeplace. 1996. 432p. mass mkt. 7.99 (*0-06-101141-X*, HarperTorch) Morrow/Avon.

Silvis, Randall. Disquiet Heart. E-Book 24.95 (*0-312-70623-5*); 2002. 336p. 24.95 (*0-312-26248-5*, Saint Martin's Minotaur) St. Martin's Pr.

—On Night's Shore. E-Book 24.95 (*1-58945-579-7*) Adobe Systems, Inc.

—On Night's Shore. 2001. 352p. 24.95 o.s.i (*0-312-26201-9*, Saint Martin's Minotaur); 2002. 384p. reprint ed. mass mkt. 6.99 (*0-312-98210-0*, St. Martin's Paperbacks) St. Martin's Pr.

Slovo, Gillian. Catnap. 1996. 288p. 23.95 o.p. (*0-312-14561-6*, Saint Martin's Minotaur) St. Martin's Pr.

—Catnap. 1995. 276p. pap. o.s.i (*1-85381-815-1*) Virago Pr., Ltd. GBR. *Dist:* Little Brown & Co.

—Close Call: A Kate Baeier Mystery. 1996. 314p. mass mkt. o.s.i (*1-85381-816-X*) Virago Pr., Ltd. GBR. *Dist:* Little Brown & Co.

Smith, Julie. Huckleberry Fiend. 1987. (Paul McDonald Mystery Ser.). 224p. 15.95 (*0-89296-237-2*) Mysterious Pr.

—Huckleberry Fiend. 1988. 224p. mass mkt. 5.50 (*0-445-40696-8*, Mysterious Pr. Paperback Bks.) Warner Bks., Inc.

—True-Life Adventure. 1986. 15.45 o.p. (*0-89296-120-1*) Mysterious Pr.

—True-Life Adventure. 1986. 256p. reprint ed. mass mkt. 4.99 o.s.i (*0-445-40505-8*, Mysterious Pr. Paperback Bks.) Warner Bks., Inc.

Snelling, Lauraine. Believing the Dream. 2002. (Return to the Red River Ser.: Vol. 2). 320p. pap. 12.99 (*0-7642-2318-6*); (Return to Red River Ser.). 512p. pap. 16.99 (*0-7642-2684-3*) Bethany Hse. Pubs.

Squires, Susan. No More Lies. 2004. mass mkt. 6.99 (*0-505-52566-6*, 53741965, Love Spell) Dorchester Publishing Co., Inc.

Stangerup, Henrik. Snake in the Heart. Born, Anne, tr. 1996. (DAN.). 256p. 24.95 o.p. (*0-7145-2996-6*) Boyars, Marion Pubs., Inc.

Stone, Robert. Damascus Gate. 1998. 512p. tchr. ed. 26.00 (*0-395-66569-8*) Houghton Mifflin Co.

—Damascus Gate. 1999. (Illus.). 528p. pap. 14.00 (*0-684-85911-4*, Touchstone) Simon & Schuster.

—Dog Soldiers. 1978. 352p. mass mkt. 2.25 o.s.i (*0-345-27574-8*); 1975. mass mkt. 1.95 o.s.i (*0-345-24558-X*) Ballantine Bks.

—Dog Soldiers. 1974. 352p. reprint ed. 11.95 o.p. (*0-395-18481-9*) Houghton Mifflin Co.

—Dog Soldiers. rev. ed. 1997. 352p. pap. 13.00 (*0-395-86025-3*, Mariner Bks.) Houghton Mifflin Co. Trade & Reference Div.

—Dog Soldiers. 1987. 352p. pap. 12.95 o.p. (*0-14-009835-6*, Penguin Bks.) Viking Penguin.

Stone, Scott C. Song of the Wolf. 1985. 16.95 o.p. (*0-87795-678-2*, Morrow, William & Co.) Morrow/Avon.

—Song of the Wolf. 1987. mass mkt. 3.95 o.p. (*0-451-14775-8*, Signet Bks.) NAL.

—Song of the Wolf. 1999. 388p. reprint ed. pap. 13.95 (*1-58348-001-3*) iUniverse, Inc.

Strupp, Joe. The City & County: A Novel of San Francisco's Newsmakers. 2001. 425p. per. 19.95 (*1-931333-01-7*) Dry Bones Pr.

Tabucchi, Antonio. The Missing Head of Damasceno Monteiro. 2003. 181p. pap. 16.95 (*1-86046-770-9*) Harvill Pr., The GBR. *Dist:* Trafalgar Square.

—The Missing Head of Damasceno Monteiro. Creagh, Patrick, tr. 2000. (ITA.). 192p. 23.95 (*0-8112-1393-5*) New Directions Publishing Corp.

Taibo, Paco Ignacio, II. Four Hands. Dail, Laura C., tr. from SPA. 1995. 384p. pap. 13.00 (*0-312-13079-1*) Picador.

—Four Hands. Dail, Laura C., tr. 1994. 480p. 22.95 o.p. (*0-312-10987-3*) St. Martin's Pr.

Tasker, Peter. Dragon Dance. 2003. 272p. 22.95 (*4-7700-2948-9*) Kodansha International JPN. *Dist:* Kodansha America, Inc.

Tatlock, Ann. All the Way Home: A Friendship That Once Bridged Two Cultural Will It Survive The Span of Time. 2002. 448p. pap. 12.99 (*0-7642-2663-0*) Bethany Hse. Pubs.

Thayer, Steve. Silent Snow. 2000. 416p. reprint ed. mass mkt. 6.99 (*0-451-18664-8*, Signet Bks.) NAL.

—Silent Snow. abr. ed. 2000. audio 18.00 (*0-7871-1980-6*); 1999. audio 30.00 (*0-7871-1979-2*) NewStar Media, Inc. (Dove Audio).

—Silent Snow. unabr. ed. 1999. audio 66.00 (*0-7887-3767-8*, 95984E7) Recorded Bks., LLC.

—Silent Snow. 1999. 416p. 24.95 o.s.i (*0-670-86572-9*, Viking) Viking Penguin.

—The Weatherman. 1996. 416p. mass mkt. 7.99 (*0-451-18438-6*, Signet Bks.) NAL.

—The Weatherman, Set. abr. ed. 1995. audio 16.95 (*1-879371-88-X*, 391877) Publishing Mills, Inc., The.

—The Weatherman. unabr. ed. 1995. audio 91.00 (*0-7887-0267-X*, 94476E7) Recorded Bks., LLC.

—The Weatherman. 1995. 464p. 21.95 o.s.i (*0-670-84958-8*, Viking); 22.95 (*0-670-77309-3*) Viking Penguin.

Thomas, Herbert. Superlative Man. 1997. 288p. 22.00 o.p. (*0-374-27209-3*) Farrar, Straus & Giroux.

Thomas, R. J. The Fate of Generations. 500th ed. 2001. 252p. per. 19.95 (*0-9709394-0-X*) Temple Publishing.

Thompson, Hunter S. The Rum Diary: A Novel. 1999. (Illus.). 224p. pap. 12.00 (*0-684-85647-6*); 1998. pap. 15.99 (*0-684-85224-1*) Simon & Schuster. (Simon & Schuster).

Tooke, C. W. Ballpark Blues: A Novel. 2003. 304p. 22.95 (*0-385-50640-6*) Doubleday Publishing.

Trigoboff, Joseph. The Shooting Gallery: A Detective Yablonsky Mystery. 320p. 2004. pap. 14.95 (*1-59228-143-5*); 2002. 19.95 (*1-58574-547-2*) Globe Pequot Pr., The. (Lyons Pr.).

Tucker, Ernest. Underworld Dwellers. 1994. 160p. 15.95 o.p. (*0-944957-22-6*) Rivercross Publishing, Inc.

Turner, Jamie L. The Suncatchers. 1995. 400p. pap. 12.99 o.p. (*0-7852-7911-3*) Nelson, Thomas Inc.

Turner, Jamie Langston. Suncatchers. rev. ed. 2000. 400p. pap. 12.99 (*0-7642-2415-8*) Bethany Hse. Pubs.

Van Wormer, Laura. The Kill Fee. 2003. 352p. (*1-55166-744-4*, Mira Bks.) Harlequin Enterprises, Ltd.

Victor, Daniel. The Seventh Bullet: A Holmes & Watson American Adventure. 1992. 208p. 17.95 o.p. (*0-312-08291-6*, Saint Martin's Minotaur) St. Martin's Pr.

Walker, Blair S. Hidden in Plain View: A Darryl Billups Mystery. 2000. (Darryl Billups Ser.). 240p. mass mkt. 5.99 o.s.i (*0-380-79026-2*, Avon Bks.) Morrow/Avon.

—Up Jumped the Devil. abr. ed. 2001. audio 12.99 (*1-57815-210-0*, Media Bks. Audio Publishing) Media Bks., L. L. C.

—Up Jumped the Devil. 1999. 272p. mass mkt. 5.99 o.s.i (*0-380-79025-4*, Avon Bks.) Morrow/Avon.

—Up Jumped the Devil, Set. abr. ed. 1997. audio 24.95 (*1-57511-027-X*) Publishing Mills, Inc., The.

Wall, Michael. Friendly Fire. 1998. 358p. (*0-14-027768-4*) Penguin Group (USA) Inc.

Walters, Minette. The Echo. 1998. 368p. mass mkt. 7.99 (*0-515-12256-4*, Jove) Berkley Publishing Group.

—The Echo. l.t. ed. 1997. (Large Print Book Ser.). (Illus.). 449p. 25.95 o.p. (*1-56895-471-9*, Wheeler Publishing, Inc.) Gale Group.

—The Echo. 1998. 424p. mass mkt. 8.99 o.s.i (*0-7710-8754-3*) McClelland & Stewart/Tundra Bks.

—The Echo. 1997. (Illus.). 338p. 23.95 o.s.i (*0-399-14251-7*, G. P. Putnam's Sons) Penguin Group (USA) Inc.

—The Echo. unabr. ed. 1997. audio 70.00 (*0-7887-4044-X*, 96153E7) Recorded Bks., LLC.

Warner, Penny. Silence Is Golden: A Connor Westphal Mystery. 2003. 216p. pap. 13.95 (*1-880284-66-9*) Daniel, John & Co., Pubs.

Weaver, Michael. Impulse. abr. ed. 2001. audio 7.95 (*1-57815-216-X*, Media Bks. Audio Publishing) Media Bks., L. L. C.

—Impulse. 450p. 4.98 o.p. (*0-8317-5393-5*) Smithmark Pubs., Inc.

—Impulse. abr. ed. 1993. audio 12.98 (*1-57042-001-7*, 4-520017) Time Warner AudioBooks.
—Impulse. 1993. 464p. 18.95 o.s.i (*0-446-51611-2*); 1994. 512p. reprint ed. mass mkt. 5.99 o.s.i (*0-446-60073-3*) Warner Bks., Inc.
Weisman, John. Blood Cries. 1987. 17.95 o.p. (*0-670-81381-8*) Viking Penguin.
Westlake, Donald E. Baby, Would I Lie? unabr. ed. 2000. audio 29.95 (*1-57270-139-0*, N61139u, Audio Editions Mystery Masters) Audio Partners Publishing Corp.
—Baby, Would I Lie? abr. ed. 1994. audio 17.00 o.p. (*1-56100-374-3*, 799, Nova Audio Bks.); audio 57.25 o.p. (*1-56100-197-X*, 1127, Unabridged Library Editions); audio 21.95 o.p. (*1-56100-571-1*, 35, Bookcassette) Brilliance Audio.
—Baby, Would I Lie? unabr. ed. 2000. audio 59.95 (*0-7927-2275-2*, CSL 164) Chivers Audio Bks. GBR. *Dist:* BBC Audiobooks America.
—Baby, Would I Lie? 1994. 304p. 19.95 o.s.i (*0-89296-532-0*) Mysterious Pr.
—Baby, Would I Lie? 1995. 320p. mass mkt. 5.99 (*0-446-40342-3*) Warner Bks., Inc.
—The Hook. 2000. 288p. 23.95 (*0-89296-588-6*) Mysterious Pr.
—The Hook. l.t. ed. 2000. (Americana Ser.). 392p. 29.95 (*0-7862-2466-5*) Thorndike Pr.
Wheeler, Richard S. Flint's Gift. unabr. ed. 1999. audio 56.95 (*0-7861-1355-3*, 106028) Blackstone Audio Bks., Inc.
—Flint's Gift. 1999. 351p. mass mkt. 5.99 (*0-8125-5019-6*); 1997. 384p. 23.95 o.p. (*0-312-86366-7*) Doherty, Tom Assocs., LLC. (Forge Bks.).
—Flint's Gift. unabr. ed. 1998. audio 70.00 (*0-7887-2280-8*, 95449E7 ) Recorded Bks., LLC.
—Flint's Gift. l.t. ed. 1998. (Western Ser.). 479p. 25.95 (*0-7838-0270-6*) Thorndike Pr.
—Flint's Honor. 2001. 384p. mass mkt. 6.99 (*0-8125-5022-6*); 2nd ed. 1999. 320p. 23.95 (*0-312-86368-3*) Doherty, Tom Assocs., LLC. (Forge Bks.).
—Flint's Honor. l.t. ed. 2001. (G. K. Hall Western Ser.). 462p. 25.95 (*0-7838-9503-8*, Macmillan Reference USA) Gale Group.
—Flint's Truth. unabr. ed. 1998. audio 56.95 (*0-7861-1373-1*, 2280) Blackstone Audio Bks., Inc.
—Flint's Truth. 1998. (Sam Flint Novels Ser.). 352p. 23.95 o.p. (*0-312-86367-5*, Forge Bks.) Doherty, Tom Assocs., LLC.
—Flint's Truth. l.t. ed. 1998. (Western Ser.). 432p. 25.95 (*0-7838-0333-8*) Thorndike Pr.
—Sun Mountain: A Comstock Memoir. 1999. 304p. 24.95 (*0-312-86725-5*, Forge Bks.) Doherty, Tom Assocs., LLC.
Whitehead, Colson. John Henry Days: A Novel. 2002. 400p. pap. 14.00 (*0-385-49820-9*, Knopf Bks. for Young Readers) Random Hse. Children's Bks.
Whitney, Ruth Linnea. Slim: A Novel. 2003. 320p. 24.95 (*0-87074-478-X*) Southern Methodist Univ. Pr.
Wiggins, Marianne. Eveless Eden. 1995. 337p. 23.00 o.p. (*0-06-016951-6*) HarperTrade.
Wilcox, Stephen F. All the Dead Heroes. 1992. 224p. 18.95 o.p. (*0-312-06896-4*, Saint Martin's Minotaur) St. Martin's Pr.
—The Dry White Tear. 1989. 15.95 o.p. (*0-312-02909-8*, Saint Martin's Minotaur) St. Martin's Pr.
—The Green Mosaic. 1994. 272p. 20.95 o.p. (*0-312-11428-1*, Saint Martin's Minotaur) St. Martin's Pr.
—The Nimby Factor. 1992. 256p. 18.95 o.p. (*0-312-08270-3*, Saint Martin's Minotaur) St. Martin's Pr.
—The Painted Lady. 1993. 272p. 21.95 o.p. (*0-312-10520-7*, Saint Martin's Minotaur) St. Martin's Pr.
—St. Lawrence Run. 1991. mass mkt. 3.95 o.p. (*0-312-92488-7*, St. Martin's Paperbacks); 1990. 16.95 o.p. (*0-312-04430-5*, Saint Martin's Minotaur) St. Martin's Pr.
—The Twenty-Acre Plot. 1991. 16.95 o.p. (*0-312-05846-2*, Saint Martin's Minotaur) St. Martin's Pr.
Wilson, John Morgan. Blind Eye: A Benjamin Justice Novel. 2003. 288p. 23.95 (*0-312-30919-8*, Saint Martin's Minotaur) St. Martin's Pr.
—Justice at Risk: A Benjamin Justice Mystery. 2000. (Benjamin Justice Mystery Ser.). 368p. mass mkt. 6.50 (*0-553-57860-X*) Bantam Bks.
—Justice at Risk: A Benjamin Justice Mystery. 1999. (Benjamin Justice Mystery Ser.). 304p. 22.95 o.s.i (*0-385-49116-6*) Doubleday Publishing.
—Revision of Justice: A Benjamin Justice Mystery. 1999. (Benjamin Justice Mystery Ser.). 416p. mass mkt. 5.99 (*0-553-57533-3*) Bantam Bks.
—Simple Justice: A Benjamin Justice Mystery. 1997. (Benjamin Justice Mystery Ser.). 304p. mass mkt. 6.50 o.s.i (*0-553-57532-5*) Bantam Bks.
—Simple Justice: A Benjamin Justice Mystery. 1996. 256p. 21.00 o.s.i (*0-385-48234-5*) Doubleday Publishing.
Witchel, Alex. Me Times Three: A Novel. 2003. 320p. reprint ed. pap. 13.00 (*0-7432-4085-5*, Touchstone) Simon & Schuster.
Woods, Stuart. Under the Lake. 1999. 368p. mass mkt. 7.99 (*0-06-101417-6*) HarperCollins Pubs.
—Under the Lake. 1988. 288p. pap. 6.50 (*0-380-70519-2*, Avon Bks.) Morrow/Avon.
—Under the Lake, unabr. ed. audio 60.00 (*0-7887-0496-6*, 94688E7) Recorded Bks., LLC.
—Under the Lake. 1987. 17.45 o.p. (*0-671-63332-5*, Simon & Schuster) Simon & Schuster.
—Under the Lake. l.t. ed. 1988. (Charnwood Large Print Ser.). 416p. 19.95 o.p. (*0-7089-8490-8*, Charnwood) Thorpe, F. A. Pubs. GBR. *Dist:* Ulverscroft Large Print Bks., Ltd., Ulverscroft Large Print Canada, Ltd.
Wright, Jim. The Last Man Standing. 1991. 224p. 18.95 o.p. (*0-88184-744-5*, Carroll & Graf Pubs.) Avalon Publishing Group.
Zimmerman, R. D. Hostage. 1998. 288p. pap. 10.95 o.s.i (*0-385-31892-8*, Delacorte Pr.) Dell Publishing.

## L

### LAWYERS—FICTION

Auchincloss, Louis. The Education of Oscar Fairfax. 1995. 256p. 22.95 o.p. (*0-395-73918-7*) Houghton Mifflin Co.
Axelrood, Larry. The Advocate: A Novel. 2002. 230p. mass mkt. 7.99 (*1-58182-292-8*) Cumberland Hse. Publishing.
Berman, Richard. Hostile Witness. 1996. 304p. (Orig.). mass mkt. 5.99 (*0-380-77813-0*, Avon Bks.) Morrow/Avon.
—Unjust Death. 1995. 352p. (Orig.). mass mkt. 5.50 (*0-380-77812-2*, Avon Bks.) Morrow/Avon.
Bernhardt, William. Blind Justice. 1997. mass mkt. 3.50 o.s.i (*0-345-41806-9*); 1992. 320p. mass mkt. 6.99 (*0-345-37483-5*) Ballantine Bks.
—Blind Justice. l.t. ed. 1993. 80.95 o.p. (*0-7862-9989-4*, Macmillan Reference USA) Gale Group.
—Cruel Justice. 1997. mass mkt. 3.50 o.s.i (*0-345-41807-7*); 1996. 480p. mass mkt. 7.50 (*0-345-40803-9*) Ballantine Bks.
—Cruel Justice, unabr. ed. 1998. (Justice Ser.). audio 72.00 (*0-7366-4180-7*, 4678) Books on Tape, Inc.
—Cruel Justice. l.t. ed. 1996. pap. 23.95 (*1-56895-323-2*, Wheeler Publishing, Inc.) Gale Group.
—Dark Justice. 1999. 448p. mass mkt. 6.99 (*0-345-43476-5*) Ballantine Bks.
—Deadly Justice. 1997. mass mkt. 3.50 o.s.i (*0-345-41808-5*); 1993. 320p. mass mkt. 7.50 (*0-345-38027-4*) Ballantine Bks.
—Deadly Justice. unabr. ed. 1998. (Justice Ser.: Vol. 3). audio 48.00 (*0-7366-4107-6*, 4612) Books on Tape, Inc.
—Deadly Justice. l.t. ed. 1994. 65.95 o.p. (*0-7862-9988-6*, Macmillan Reference USA) Gale Group.
—Double Jeopardy. 1996. 416p. mass mkt. 7.99 (*0-345-39784-3*) Ballantine Bks.
—Double Jeopardy. l.t. ed. 1996. (Niagara Large Print Ser.). 431p. 29.50 o.p. (*0-7089-5828-1*, Ulverscroft) Thorpe, F. A. Pubs. GBR. *Dist:* Ulverscroft Large Print Bks., Ltd.
—Extreme Justice. 1998. (Ben Kincaid Ser.). 384p. mass mkt. 6.99 (*0-345-42481-6*) Ballantine Bks.
—Naked Justice. 1997. 448p. mass mkt. 6.99 (*0-449-00087-7*, Fawcett) Ballantine Bks.
—Naked Justice. unabr. ed. 1997. (Justice Ser.). audio 88.00 (*0-7366-3789-3*, 4463) Books on Tape, Inc.
—Naked Justice. l.t. ed. 1997. (Niagara Large Print Ser.). 688p. 29.50 o.p. (*0-7089-5879-6*, Ulverscroft) Thorpe, F. A. Pubs. GBR. *Dist:* Ulverscroft Large Print Bks., Ltd.
—Perfect Justice. 1997. mass mkt. 3.50 o.s.i (*0-345-41809-3*) Ballantine Bks.
—Perfect Justice. unabr. ed. 1998. (Justice Ser.: Vol. 4). audio 56.00 (*0-7366-4108-4*, 4613) Books on Tape, Inc.
—Perfect Justice, Set. l.t. ed. 1994. (Studio Ser.). 64.95 o.p. incl. audio (*0-7862-9987-8*, Macmillan Reference USA) Gale Group.
—Perfect Justice. 1995. 416p. mass mkt. 6.99 (*0-345-39133-0*, House of Collectibles) Random Hse. Information Group.
—Primary Justice. 1997. mass mkt. 3.50 o.s.i (*0-345-41810-7*); 1991. 320p. mass mkt. 6.99 (*0-345-37479-7*) Ballantine Bks.
—Primary Justice. unabr. ed. 1998. (Justice Ser.: Vol. 1). audio 48.00 (*0-7366-4105-X*, 4610) Books on Tape, Inc.
—Primary Justice. (Mystery Ser.). 1998. 309p. 22.95 (*0-7862-1659-X*, Five Star); Set. 1993. 79.95 o.p. incl. audio (*0-7862-9991-6*, Macmillan Reference USA) Gale Group.
Berry, Sheila M. My Name Is Legion. 1999. 306p. 25.00 (*0-9662299-1-6*) Archer Bks.
Biehl, Michael. Lawyered to Death: A Karen Hayes Mystery. 2003. 320p. 23.95 (*1-882593-76-6*) Bridge Works Publishing Co., Inc.
Blackstock, Terri. Word of Honor. 2000. (Newpointe 911 Ser.: Bk. 3). (Illus.). 368p. 24.95 (*0-7862-2572-6*, Five Star) Gale Group.
Blauner, Peter. The Intruder. l.t. ed. 1996. 26.95 (*1-56895-348-8*, Wheeler Publishing, Inc.) Gale Group.
—The Intruder. unabr. ed. audio 1999. audio 70.00 (*0-7887-0627-6*, 94801E7) Recorded Bks., LLC.
—The Intruder. 1996. 384p. 22.50 o.p. (*0-684-81094-8*, Simon & Schuster) Simon & Schuster.
—The Intruder. abr. ed. 1999. audio; 1996. 192p. pap. 18.00 incl. audio (*0-671-57041-2*, 394045, Simon & Schuster Audioworks) Simon & Schuster Audio.
—The Intruder. 1997. 464p. reprint ed. mass mkt. 6.99 (*0-446-60505-0*) Warner Bks., Inc.
Blum, Bill. The Last Appeal. 1997. 416p. mass mkt. 6.99 o.s.i (*0-451-18311-8*, Signet Bks.) NAL.
Brandon, Jay. Fade the Heat. 1991. 368p. mass mkt. 6.99 (*0-671-70261-0*, Pocket) Simon & Schuster.
—Fade the Heat. Gross, Bill, ed. 1990. 352p. 18.95 o.p. (*0-671-70260-2*, Atria) Simon & Schuster.
—Fade the Heat. abr. ed. 1990. audio 14.95 (*0-671-70893-7*, Simon & Schuster Audioworks) Simon & Schuster Audio.
—Loose among the Lambs. Grose, Bill, ed. 1993. 384p. 22.00 (*0-671-76032-7*, Atria); 1994. 400p. reprint ed. mass mkt. 5.99 (*0-671-76033-5*, Pocket); 1994. reprint ed. pap. 6.50 (*0-671-88315-1*, Pocket) Simon & Schuster.
Brown, Herb. Shadows of Doubt. 1994. 288p. 21.50 o.p. (*1-55611-394-3*) Fine, Donald I. Bks.
Buchan, John. The Leithen Stories: The Power House; John Macnab; Dancing Floor; Sick Heart River. 2000. 190p. pap. 16.00 (*0-86241-995-6*) Canongate Bks. GBR. *Dist:* Grove/Atlantic, Inc.
Buckley, Christopher. No Way to Treat a First Lady. 2002. 304p. 24.95 (*0-375-50734-5*) Random House Adult Trade Publishing Group.
—No Way to Treat a First Lady. 2002. E-Book 19.95 (*1-58836-257-4*) Random Hse., Inc.
—No Way to Treat a First Lady: A Novel. 2003. 304p. pap. 13.95 (*0-375-75875-5*, Random Hse. Trade Paperbacks) Random House Adult Trade Publishing Group.
—No Way to Treat a First Lady: A Novel. 2003. (Americana Ser.). 29.95 (*0-7862-5044-5*) Thorndike Pr.
Buffa, D. W. The Defense. 1997. 320p. 20.00 o.s.i (*0-8050-5307-7*) Holt, Henry & Co.
Bunn, T. Davis. The Great Divide. 2000. (Illus.). 432p. 19.95 o.s.i (*1-57856-373-9*) WaterBrook Pr.
Byrd, Adrianne. My Destiny. 2003. 28p. mass mkt. 6.99 (*1-58314-292-4*) Kensington Publishing Corp.
Champion, David. Celebrity Trouble: A Bomber Hanson Mystery. 1997. 200p. 20.00 (*1-888310-97-9*) Knoll, Allen A. Pubs.
—The Mountain Massacres: A Bomber Hanson Mystery. 1995. 161p. 14.95 (*0-9627297-4-4*) Knoll, Allen A. Pubs.
—Phantom Virus: A Bomber Hanson Mystery. 1999. 275p. 23.00 (*1-888310-93-6*) Knoll, Allen A. Pubs.
Clark, Robert. In Deep Midwinter. 1996. 288p. 23.00 o.p. (*0-312-15149-7*) Picador.
Cooper, Natasha. A Place of Safety: A Trish Maguire Mystery. 2003. 320p. 24.95 (*0-312-31936-3*, Saint Martin's Minotaur) St. Martin's Pr.
Costopoulos, William C. Guilty of Innocence. 1999. 216p. 22.00 (*0-940159-57-0*) Camino Bks., Inc.
Coughlin, William Jeremiah. Death Penalty. l.t. ed. 1993. pap. 22.95 o.p. (*0-7927-1541-1*); 22.95 o.p. (*0-7927-1542-X*) BBC Audiobooks America.
—Death Penalty. 1992. 304p. 20.00 o.p. (*0-06-017701-2*) HarperTrade.
—Death Penalty. 1993. 432p. mass mkt. 5.99 o.s.i (*0-06-109053-0*, HarperTorch) Morrow/Avon.
—In the Presence of Enemies. l.t. ed. 1993. (General Ser.). 575p. lib. bdg. 22.95 o.p. (*0-8161-5695-6*, Macmillan Reference USA) Gale Group.
—In the Presence of Enemies. 1994. mass mkt. 6.99 (*0-312-95164-7*, St. Martin's Paperbacks); 1993. 309p. 21.95 o.p. (*0-312-08818-3*) St. Martin's Pr.
—The Judgement. abr. l.t. ed. 1995. 352p. lib. bdg. 27.00 incl. audio (*1-57490-025-0*, Beeler Large Print Bks.) Beeler, Thomas T. Publisher.
—The Judgement. 1999. mass mkt. 223.68 (*0-312-96877-9*); 1997. 352p. 24.95 o.p. (*0-312-15558-1*) St. Martin's Pr.
—Shadow of a Doubt. l.t. ed. 1992. (General Ser.). 562p. 18.95 (*0-8161-5346-9*); lib. bdg. 21.95 (*0-8161-5345-0*) Gale Group. (Macmillan Reference USA).
—Shadow of a Doubt. 1993. 407p. mass mkt. 6.99 (*0-312-92745-2*, St. Martin's Paperbacks); 1991. 19.95 o.p. (*0-312-05961-2*) St. Martin's Pr.
Cozzens, James Gould. By Love Possessed. 1998. 570p. pap. 13.95 (*0-7867-0503-5*, Carroll & Graf Pubs.) Avalon Publishing Group.
—By Love Possessed. 1977. mass mkt. 2.25 o.s.i (*0-449-22954-8*, Fawcett) Ballantine Bks.
—By Love Possessed. 1994. reprint ed. lib. bdg. 21.95 (*1-56849-549-8*) Buccaneer Bks., Inc.
—By Love Possessed. 1957. 8.50 o.s.i (*0-15-115113-X*); 1901. pap. 2.95 o.p. (*0-15-614870-6*, Harvest Bks.) Harcourt Trade Pubs.
Cronin, A. J. Beyond This Place. 1976. 25.95 (*0-88411-525-9*) Amereon, Ltd.
—Beyond This Place. 1984. 320p. reprint ed. mass mkt. 6.95 o.s.i (*0-316-16192-6*) Little Brown & Co.
Dana, Barbara. Necessary Parties. 1986. (Charlotte Zolotow Bk.). 352p. (YA). (gr. 7 up). lib. bdg. 14.89 o.p. (*0-06-021409-0*) HarperCollins Children's Bk. Group.
—Necessary Parties. (J). 1991. mass mkt. o.s.i (*0-553-54043-2*, Dell Books for Young Readers); 1987. 320p. mass mkt. 3.50 o.s.i (*0-553-26984-4*, Starfire) Random Hse. Children's Bks.
Darden, Christopher A. & Lochte, Dick. The Last Defense. 2002. 368p. 24.95 (*0-451-20732-7*) NAL.
—The Trials of Nikki Hill. 2001. 496p. mass mkt. 7.50 o.s.i (*0-446-60798-3*); 1999. 448p. 25.00 (*0-446-52326-7*) Warner Bks., Inc.
Decure, John. Reef Dance. 2001. 384p. 24.95 (*0-312-27297-9*, Saint Martin's Minotaur) St. Martin's Pr.
Denker, Henry. Labyrinth: A Novel. 1994. 299p. 23.00 o.p. (*0-688-13700-8*, Morrow, William & Co.) Morrow/Avon.
Deverell, William. Kill All the Lawyers. 1995. 356p. mass mkt. 7.99 (*0-345-39817-3*, Ballantine Bks.) Ballantine Bks.
—Kill All the Lawyers. 2001. 416p. mass mkt. 6.99 (*0-7704-2869-X*) Bantam Bks.
Dias, Dexter. False Witness. l.t. ed. 2002. (Magna Large Print Ser.). 480p. (*0-7505-1883-9*) Magna Large Print Bks. GBR. *Dist:* Ulverscroft Large Print Canada, Ltd.
—False Witness. 1995. 82p. 19.95 o.p. (*0-89296-612-2*) Mysterious Pr.
—False Witness. 1996. 352p. mass mkt. 5.99 o.s.i (*0-446-40492-6*) Warner Bks., Inc.
Diehl, William. Primal Fear. 1998. pap. 6.99 (*0-345-91452-X*); 1995. mass mkt. 6.99 o.p. (*0-345-90885-6*); 1995. mass mkt. 6.99 o.p. (*0-345-90644-6*); 1994. 432p. mass mkt. 7.99 (*0-345-38877-1*, Ballantine Bks.); 1993. mass mkt. 6.99 (*0-345-38391-5*) Ballantine Bks.
—Primal Fear. unabr. ed. 1993. audio 25.95 o.p. (*1-56100-490-1*, 220, Bookcassette);Set. audio 89.25 o.p. (*1-56100-124-4*, 993) Brilliance Audio.
—Primal Fear. 1994. audio 8.99 o.s.i (*0-679-43414-3*); 1993. audio 18.00 o.s.i (*0-679-42014-2*, 391398); Set. 1999. audio 8.99 o.s.i (*0-375-40574-7*) Random Hse. Audio Publishing Group. (RH Audio).
Dooling, Richard. Brain Storm, unabr. collector's ed. 1998. audio 104.00 (*0-7366-4335-4*, 4816) Books on Tape, Inc.
—Brain Storm. 1999. 416p. pap. 14.00 (*0-312-20399-3*) Picador.
—Brain Storm. unabr. ed. 1998. audio 97.00 (*0-7887-1988-2*, 95375E7) Recorded Bks., LLC.
Downing, Warwick. A Lingering Doubt. Isaacson, Dana, ed. 1993. 320p. (Orig.). mass mkt. 4.99 (*0-671-76034-3*, Pocket) Simon & Schuster.
Dunbar, Tony. City of Beads. 1996. 256p. mass mkt. 5.99 o.s.i (*0-425-15578-1*, Prime Crime) Berkley Publishing Group.
—City of Beads. 1996. 256p. 21.95 o.p. (*0-399-14081-6*, G. P. Putnam's Sons) Penguin Group (USA) Inc.
—The Crime Czar: A Tubby Dubonnet Mystery. 1998. (Tubby Dubonnet Mysteries Ser.). 240p. mass mkt. 5.99 o.s.i (*0-440-22658-9*) Dell Publishing.
—Crooked Man. 1996. 208p. mass mkt. 4.99 o.s.i (*0-425-15138-7*) Berkley Publishing Group.
—Crooked Man. 1994. 240p. 21.95 o.p. (*0-399-13973-7*, G. P. Putnam's Sons) Penguin Group (USA) Inc.
—Lucky Man. 1999. (Tubby Dubonnet Mysteries Ser.). 240p. mass mkt. 5.99 o.s.i (*0-440-22662-7*) Dell Publishing.
—Shelter from the Storm. 1998. 224p. mass mkt. 5.99 o.s.i (*0-425-16644-9*) Berkley Publishing Group.
—Shelter from the Storm. l.t. ed. 1998. (Large Print Book Ser.). pap. 23.95 (*1-56895-607-X*, Wheeler Publishing, Inc.) Gale Group.
—Shelter from the Storm. 1997. 256p. 24.95 o.p. (*0-399-14301-7*, G. P. Putnam's Sons) Penguin Group (USA) Inc.
—Trick Question. l.t. ed. 1997. (Tubby Dubonnet Mysteries Ser.). 224p. mass mkt. 5.99 o.s.i (*0-425-16092-0*, Prime Crime) Berkley Publishing Group.
—Trick Question. 1997. 256p. 22.95 o.p. (*0-399-14184-7*, G. P. Putnam's Sons) Penguin Group (USA) Inc.
Eberhardt, Michael C. Body of a Crime. 1994. 368p. 19.95 o.p. (*0-525-93623-8*, Dutton) Dutton/Plume.
—Body of a Crime. unabr. ed. 1998. audio 103.95 (*1-85903-136-6*) Magna Story Sound GBR. *Dist:* Ulverscroft Large Print Bks., Ltd.
—Body of a Crime. 1995. 448p. mass mkt. 5.99 o.s.i (*0-451-40569-2*, Onyx) NAL.
—Body of a Crime. l.t. ed. 1997. (Niagara Large Print Ser.). 546p. 29.50 o.p. (*0-7089-5803-6*, Ulverscroft) Thorpe, F. A. Pubs. GBR. *Dist:* Ulverscroft Large Print Bks., Ltd., Ulverscroft Large Print Canada, Ltd.

Edwards, Martin. All the Lonely People. 2003. (Five Star First Edition Titles Ser.). 278p. 25.95 (*1-59414-069-3*, Five Star) Gale Group.

—Eve of Destruction: A Harry Devlin Mystery. 1998. 208p. 22.95 (*0-393-04635-4*) Norton, W. W. & Co., Inc.

—Suspicious Minds. l.t. ed. 1995. (Magna Large Print Ser.). 365p. o.p. (*0-7505-0865-5*) Magna Large Print Bks. GBR. *Dist:* Ulverscroft Large Print Canada, Ltd.

—Yesterday's Papers. l.t. ed. 1996. (Magna Large Print Ser.). 380p. (*0-7505-0867-1*) Magna Large Print Bks. GBR. *Dist:* Ulverscroft Large Print Canada, Ltd.

Egan, Lesley. Chain of Violence. 1985. (Crime Club Ser.). 192p. 12.95 o.p. (*0-385-19807-8*) Doubleday Publishing.

—Little Boy Lost. 1983. (Crime Club Ser.). (Illus.). 192p. 11.95 o.p. (*0-385-18840-4*) Doubleday Publishing.

—Little Boy Lost. l.t. ed. 1986. (Ulverscroft Large Print Ser.). 384p. 29.99 o.p. (*0-7089-1417-9*, Ulverscroft) Thorpe, F. A. Pubs. GBR. *Dist:* Ulverscroft Large Print Bks., Ltd., Ulverscroft Large Print Canada, Ltd.

—Look Back on Death. l.t. ed. 1981. reprint ed. 9.95 o.p. (*0-89621-267-X*) Thorndike Pr.

—The Miser. 1981. (Crime Club Ser.). 192p. 9.95 o.p. (*0-385-17626-0*) Doubleday Publishing.

—The Miser. l.t. ed. 1984. 368p. o.p. (*0-7089-1069-6*, Ulverscroft) Thorpe, F. A. Pubs.

—Motive in Shadow. 1980. (Crime Club Ser.). 10.95 o.p. (*0-385-15605-7*) Doubleday Publishing.

—Motive in Shadow. l.t. ed. 1986. (Ulverscroft Large Print Ser.). 384p. 29.99 o.p. (*0-7089-1471-3*, Ulverscroft) Thorpe, F. A. Pubs. GBR. *Dist:* Ulverscroft Large Print Bks., Ltd., Ulverscroft Large Print Canada, Ltd.

Elliot, Harry. The Dances They Do. 2000. 261p. 23.50 (*1-890791-95-4*) Plymouth Rock Publishing.

Fallon, Ann C. Blood Is Thicker. 1990. 256p. (Orig.). mass mkt. 3.95 (*0-671-70623-3*, Pocket) Simon & Schuster.

—Dead Ends. Isaacson, Dana, ed. 1992. 256p. (Orig.). mass mkt. 4.99 (*0-671-75134-4*, Pocket) Simon & Schuster.

—Hour of Our Death. Chelius, Jane, ed. 1995. 256p. (Orig.). mass mkt. 5.50 (*0-671-88515-4*, Pocket) Simon & Schuster.

—Potter's Field. Isaacson, Dana, ed. 1993. 256p. (Orig.). mass mkt. 4.99 (*0-671-75136-0*, Pocket) Simon & Schuster.

—Where Death Lies. Isaacson, Dana, ed. 1991. 256p. mass mkt. 4.99 (*0-671-70624-1*, Pocket) Simon & Schuster.

Farris, Michael. Guilt by Association: A Novel. 1997. pap. text 12.99 o.p. (*0-8054-0151-2*); pap. text 12.99 (*0-8054-0155-5*) Broadman & Holman Pubs.

Fishkin, Shelley Fisher, ed. The Tragedy of Pudd'nhead Wilson & the Comedy Those Extraordinary Twins (1894) 1996. (Oxford Mark Twain Ser.). (Illus.). 512p. 19.95 (*0-19-510147-2*) Oxford Univ. Pr., Inc.

Fletcher, Jessica & Bain, Donald. Deadly Judgement. 1996. (Murder She Wrote Ser.). 304p. mass mkt. 6.50 (*0-451-18771-7*) NAL.

Folsom, Allan. Day of Confession. l.t. ed. 1999. 27.95 (*1-56895-648-7*, Wheeler Publishing, Inc.) Gale Group.

—Day of Confession. 1998. 576p. (gr. 8). 25.00 (*0-316-28755-5*) Little Brown & Co.

—Day of Confession. 1999. 688p. mass mkt. 7.99 (*0-446-60453-4*) Warner Bks., Inc.

Francis, Clare. A Dark Devotion: A Novel. 2003. 304p. 25.00 (*1-56947-325-0*) Soho Pr., Inc.

Fredrickson, Michael. A Cinderella Affidavit. 2000. 450p. mass mkt. 6.99 (*0-8125-8013-3*, Tor Bks.); 1999. 384p. 25.95 (*0-312-86723-9*, Forge Bks.) Doherty, Tom Assocs., LLC.

—A Cinderella Affidavit. unabr. ed. 2000. audio compact disk 119.00 (*0-7887-4210-8*, C1139E7); 1999. audio 96.00 (*0-7887-3764-3*, 95981E7) Recorded Bks., LLC.

Freeborn, Peter. The Stark Truth. 1989. 18.95 o.p. (*0-395-51389-8*) Houghton Mifflin Co.

—The Stark Truth. 1990. mass mkt. 4.95 (*0-380-71162-1*, Avon Bks.) Morrow/Avon.

Friedman, Donald. The Hand Before the Eye. 1999. (First Series Award). 266p. 24.00 (*0-922811-42-3*) Mid-List Pr.

Friedman, Philip. Inadmissible Evidence. 1993. 640p. mass mkt. 7.99 (*0-8041-0852-8*, Ivy Bks.) Ballantine Bks.

—Inadmissible Evidence. unabr. ed. 1993. Pt. 1. audio 64.00; Pt. 2. audio 64.00 Books on Tape, Inc.

—Inadmissible Evidence. 1992. 480p. 23.00 o.p. (*1-55611-330-7*) Fine, Donald I. Bks.

—Inadmissible Evidence. abr. ed. 1993. audio 25.00 (*0-671-86568-4*, Simon & Schuster Audioworks) Simon & Schuster Audio.

Garcia-Aguilera, Carolina. One Hot Summer. 2002. 288p. (gr. 5 up). 23.95 (*0-06-000980-2*, Rayo) HarperTrade.

Gardner, Erle Stanley. The Case of the Amorous Aunt. 1994. mass mkt. 4.50 o.s.i (*0-345-37878-4*) Ballantine Bks.

—The Case of the Amorous Aunt. l.t. ed. 1985. (Nightingale Ser.). 11.95 o.p. (*0-8161-3752-8*, Macmillan Reference USA) Gale Group.

—The Case of the Angry Mourner. 1989. (*1-55504-971-0*); 1991. 12.95 o.p. (*1-55504-970-2*, 215) BBC Audiobooks America.

—The Case of the Angry Mourner. 1993. mass mkt. 4.50 o.s.i (*0-345-37870-9*) Ballantine Bks.

—The Case of the Baited Hook. (Perry Mason Bks.). 288p. reprint ed. lib. bdg. 23.95 (*0-88411-416-3*) Amereon, Ltd.

—The Case of the Baited Hook. (Perry Mason Mysteries Ser.). 1999. mass mkt. 4.99 (*0-345-91478-3*); 1995. 224p. pap. 15.00 (*0-345-46896-1*); 1986. 224p. mass mkt. 5.99 (*0-345-32942-2*) Ballantine Bks.

—The Case of the Beautiful Beggar. 1976. 21.95 (*0-8488-0498-8*) Amereon, Ltd.

—The Case of the Beautiful Beggar. 1986. mass mkt. 3.50 o.s.i (*0-345-34318-2*) Ballantine Bks.

—The Case of the Beautiful Beggar. l.t. ed. 1998. (G. K. Hall Paperback Ser.). 272p. 22.95 o.p. (*0-7838-0269-2*, Macmillan Reference USA) Gale Group.

—The Case of the Beautiful Beggar. abr. ed. 1988. audio 14.95 (*1-55800-118-2*, 40450, Dove Audio) NewStar Media, Inc.

—The Case of the Bigamous Spouse. l.t. ed. 1988. pap. 18.95 o.p. (*1-55504-668-1*); lib. bdg. 20.95 o.p. (*1-55504-687-8*) BBC Audiobooks America.

—The Case of the Bigamous Spouse. 1987. mass mkt. 2.95 o.s.i (*0-345-34378-6*) Ballantine Bks.

—The Case of the Bigamous Spouse. 1972. pap. 0.95 o.p. (*0-671-77865-X*, Pocket) Simon & Schuster.

—The Case of the Black-Eyed Blonde. 1976. 21.95 (*0-8488-0271-3*) Amereon, Ltd.

—The Case of the Black-Eyed Blonde. 1985. 208p. mass mkt. 3.50 o.s.i (*0-345-32311-4*) Ballantine Bks.

—The Case of the Black-Eyed Blonde. 1975. pap. 1.50 o.p. (*0-671-78782-9*, Pocket) Simon & Schuster.

—The Case of the Blonde Bonanza. 1994. mass mkt. 4.50 o.s.i (*0-345-37877-6*) Ballantine Bks.

—The Case of the Blonde Bonanza. l.t. ed. 1987. (Nightingale Ser.). 291p. pap. 11.95 o.p. (*0-8161-4283-1*, Macmillan Reference USA) Gale Group.

—The Case of the Borrowed Brunette. 1987. 224p. mass mkt. 4.99 o.s.i (*0-345-34374-3*) Ballantine Bks.

—The Case of the Borrowed Brunette. 1976. pap. 1.95 o.p. (*0-671-80470-7*, Pocket) Simon & Schuster.

—The Case of the Buried Clock. 1976. 22.95 (*0-8488-0273-X*) Amereon, Ltd.

—The Case of the Buried Clock. 1997. mass mkt. 4.99 (*0-345-90799-X*); 1986. mass mkt. 3.95 o.s.i (*0-345-33691-7*); 1983. mass mkt. 4.99 o.s.i (*0-345-31013-6*, Ballantine Bks.) Ballantine Bks.

—The Case of the Buried Clock. l.t. ed. 1998. (Paperback Ser.). 312p. pap. 24.95 (*0-7838-0366-4*) Thorndike Pr.

—The Case of the Calendar Girl. 1976. 21.95 (*0-8488-0499-6*) Amereon, Ltd.

—The Case of the Calendar Girl. 1987. 224p. mass mkt. 4.99 o.s.i (*0-345-34375-1*) Ballantine Bks.

—The Case of the Careless Cupid. 1995. mass mkt. 4.99 o.s.i (*0-345-39226-4*) Ballantine Bks.

—The Case of the Careless Cupid. l.t. ed. 2003. (Dales Large Print Ser.). 304p. pap. 21.99 (*1-84262-216-1*) Dales Large Print Bks. GBR. *Dist:* Ulverscroft Large Print Bks., Ltd., Ulverscroft Large Print Canada, Ltd.

—The Case of the Careless Cupid. 1977. lib. bdg. 9.95 o.p. (*0-8161-6447-9*, Macmillan Reference USA) Gale Group.

—The Case of the Careless Kitten. 1976. 23.95 (*0-8488-0272-1*) Amereon, Ltd.

—The Case of the Careless Kitten. 1989. (Perry Mason Mysteries Ser.). 224p. mass mkt. 4.99 o.s.i (*0-345-36223-3*) Ballantine Bks.

—The Case of the Caretaker's Cat. 1976. (Perry Mason Bks.). reprint ed. lib. bdg. 24.95 (*0-88411-407-4*) Amereon, Ltd.

—The Case of the Caretaker's Cat. 1985. (Perry Mason Mysteries Ser.). reprint ed. mass mkt. 4.99 o.s.i (*0-345-32156-1*) Ballantine Bks.

—The Case of the Caretaker's Cat. l.t. ed. 1998. (Perry Mason Mysteries Ser.). 283p. 21.95 o.p. (*0-7838-8439-7*, Macmillan Reference USA) Gale Group.

—The Case of the Cautious Coquette. 1997. 18.95 (*0-88411-440-6*); 1976. 21.95 (*0-8488-0500-3*) Amereon, Ltd.

—The Case of the Cautious Coquette. l.t. ed. 1991. 19.95 o.p. (*0-7927-0847-4*, CS0189); pap. 17.95 o.p. (*0-7927-0848-2*) BBC Audiobooks America.

—The Case of the Cautious Coquette. 1988. 240p. reprint ed. mass mkt. 4.99 o.s.i (*0-345-35202-5*) Ballantine Bks.

—The Case of the Counterfeit Eye. 1976. (Perry Mason Books Ser.). reprint ed. lib. bdg. 24.95 (*0-88411-406-6*) Amereon, Ltd.

—The Case of the Counterfeit Eye. (*0-7540-3701-0*); 1999. 296 p. (*0-7540-3702-9*) BBC Audiobooks America.

—The Case of the Counterfeit Eye. (Perry Mason Mysteries Ser.). 1998. mass mkt. 4.99 (*0-345-91229-2*); 1986. 256p. mass mkt. 4.99 o.s.i (*0-345-33195-8*) Ballantine Bks.

—The Case of the Counterfeit Eye. 1974. pap. 0.95 o.p. (*0-671-77895-1*, Pocket) Simon & Schuster.

—The Case of the Counterfeit Eye. l.t. ed. 1999. (Paperback Ser.). 296p. pap. 23.95 o.p. (*0-7838-8522-9*) Thorndike Pr.

—The Case of the Crimson Kiss. 1972. pap. 0.95 o.p. (*0-671-77881-1*, Simon Pulse) Simon & Schuster Children's Publishing.

—The Case of the Crooked Candle. 1976. 21.95 (*0-8488-0275-6*) Amereon, Ltd.

—The Case of the Crooked Candle. l.t. ed. 1989. vi, 339 p. (*1-55504-787-4*) BBC Audiobooks America.

—The Case of the Crooked Candle. 1989. mass mkt. 3.99 o.p. (*0-345-01834-6*); 1987. mass mkt. 3.99 o.s.i (*0-345-34164-3*) Ballantine Bks.

—The Case of the Crooked Candle. 1976. (Crime Fiction Ser.). reprint ed. lib. bdg. 21.00 o.p. (*0-8240-2368-4*) Garland Publishing, Inc.

—The Case of the Crying Swallow: A Perry Mason Novelette & Other Stories. l.t. ed. 1987. (Nightingale Ser.). 295p. 11.95 o.p. (*0-8161-4284-X*, Macmillan Reference USA) Gale Group.

—The Case of the Curious Bride. 1976. (Perry Mason Bks.). reprint ed. lib. bdg. 23.95 (*0-88411-405-8*) Amereon, Ltd.

—The Case of the Curious Bride. (Perry Mason Mysteries Ser.). 2000. 192p. mass mkt. 5.99 o.s.i (*0-345-43783-7*, Fawcett); 1989. 224p. mass mkt. 4.99 o.s.i (*0-345-36222-5*) Ballantine Bks.

—The Case of the Curious Bride. l.t. ed. 2001. (G. K. Hall Paperback Ser.). 319p. pap. 24.95 (*0-7838-9432-5*); (*0-7540-4536-6*) Gale Group. (Macmillan Reference USA).

—The Case of the Curious Bride. 1992. pap. 46.00 o.p. (*0-671-82708-1*, Pocket) Simon & Schuster.

—The Case of the Dangerous Dowager. 1976. (Perry Mason Bks.). reprint ed. lib. bdg. 19.95 (*0-88411-410-4*) Amereon, Ltd.

—The Case of the Dangerous Dowager. (Perry Mason Mysteries Ser.). 1998. mass mkt. 4.99 (*0-345-91231-4*); 1986. 224p. mass mkt. 4.99 o.s.i (*0-345-33192-3*) Ballantine Bks.

—The Case of the Dangerous Dowager. l.t. ed. 2000. (G. K. Hall Paperback Ser.). 299p. pap. 23.95 (*0-7838-9225-X*, Macmillan Reference USA) Gale Group.

—The Case of the Daring Decoy. 1989. (Perry Mason Mysteries Ser.). 224p. mass mkt. 4.99 o.s.i (*0-345-36220-9*) Ballantine Bks.

—The Case of the Daring Divorcee. 1984. 192p. mass mkt. 3.95 o.s.i (*0-345-32003-4*) Ballantine Bks.

—The Case of the Deadly Toy. (Perry Mason Mysteries Ser.). 224p. 2000. mass mkt. 6.99 (*0-345-43784-5*, Fawcett); 1985. mass mkt. 3.50 o.s.i (*0-345-33494-9*) Ballantine Bks.

—The Case of the Deadly Toy. 1981. 288p. reprint ed. lib. bdg. 18.00 (*0-8376-0397-8*) Bentley Pubs.

—The Case of the Deadly Toy. l.t. ed. 1993. (Nightingale Ser.). 378p. lib. bdg. 15.95 o.p. (*0-8161-5632-8*, Macmillan Reference USA) Gale Group.

—The Case of the Demure Defendant. 1991. 192p. mass mkt. 3.95 o.s.i (*0-345-37148-8*, Ballantine Bks.) Ballantine Bks.

—The Case of the Demure Defendant. l.t. ed. 1988. 336p. 15.95 o.p. (*0-7089-1785-2*, Ulverscroft) Thorpe, F. A. Pubs. GBR. *Dist:* Ulverscroft Large Print Bks., Ltd.

—The Case of the Drowning Duck. (Perry Mason Bks.). 284p. reprint ed. lib. bdg. 23.95 (*0-88411-420-1*) Amereon, Ltd.

—The Case of the Drowning Duck. l.t. ed. 1990. (Perry Mason Mystery Ser.). 21.95 o.p. (*0-7927-0635-8*, C0595); pap. 19.95 o.p. (*0-7927-0636-6*) BBC Audiobooks America.

—The Case of the Drowning Duck. 1993. reprint ed. mass mkt. 4.50 o.s.i (*0-345-37868-7*) Ballantine Bks.

—The Case of the Drowning Duck. 1976. pap. 1.95 o.p. (*0-671-80281-X*, Pocket) Simon & Schuster.

—The Case of the Drowsy Mosquito. 1976. 22.95 (*0-8488-0274-8*) Amereon, Ltd.

—The Case of the Drowsy Mosquito. 1994. reprint ed. mass mkt. 4.99 o.s.i (*0-345-37869-5*) Ballantine Bks.

—The Case of the Drowsy Mosquito. 1976. (Two-in-One Ser.). pap. 1.95 o.p. (*0-671-80390-5*, Pocket) Simon & Schuster.

—The Case of the Drowsy Mosquito. l.t. ed. 1978. 12.00 o.p. (*0-7089-0235-9*, Ulverscroft) Thorpe, F. A. Pubs. GBR. *Dist:* Ulverscroft Large Print Bks., Ltd.

—The Case of the Dubious Bridegroom. l.t. ed. 1994. 22.95 o.p. (*0-7927-2103-9*); pap. 21.95 o.p. (*0-7927-2102-0*) BBC Audiobooks America.

—The Case of the Dubious Bridegroom. 1986. 224p. mass mkt. 3.50 o.s.i (*0-345-34186-4*); 1984. mass mkt. 2.50 o.p. (*0-345-31811-0*); 1983. mass mkt. 4.99 o.s.i (*0-345-30881-6*) Ballantine Bks.

—The Case of the Duplicate Daughter. 1988. mass mkt. 3.50 o.s.i (*0-345-35681-0*) Ballantine Bks.

—The Case of the Duplicate Daughter. 1975. pap. 1.50 o.p. (*0-671-78779-9*, Pocket) Simon & Schuster.

—The Case of the Empty Tin. (Perry Mason Bks.). 282p. reprint ed. lib. bdg. 23.95 (*0-88411-419-8*) Amereon, Ltd.

—The Case of the Empty Tin. 1985. 240p. mass mkt. 4.99 o.s.i (*0-345-33198-2*); 1996. reprint ed. mass mkt. 4.99 (*0-345-90798-1*) Ballantine Bks.

—The Case of the Empty Tin. l.t. ed. 1979. (Ulverscroft Large Print Ser.). 12.00 o.p. (*0-7089-0244-8*, Ulverscroft) Thorpe, F. A. Pubs. GBR. *Dist:* Ulverscroft Large Print Bks., Ltd., Ulverscroft Large Print Canada, Ltd.

—The Case of the Fabulous Fake. l.t. ed. 1990. (Perry Mason Mystery Ser.). pap. 10.95 o.p. (*0-89340-024-6*, C0148) BBC Audiobooks America.

—The Case of the Fabulous Fake. 1986. mass mkt. 3.95 o.s.i (*0-345-33548-1*) Ballantine Bks.

—The Case of the Fabulous Fake. 1969. 7.95 o.p. (*0-688-01276-0*, Morrow, William & Co.) Morrow/Avon.

—The Case of the Fan-Dancer's Horse. 1992. reprint ed. mass mkt. 4.99 o.s.i (*0-345-37144-5*) Ballantine Bks.

—The Case of the Fan-Dancer's Horse & the Case of the Hesitant Hostess. 1977. pap. 1.95 o.p. (*0-671-81386-2*, Pocket) Simon & Schuster.

—The Case of the Fenced-In Woman. 1994. (Perry Mason Mysteries Ser.). 224p. mass mkt. 5.99 o.s.i (*0-345-39223-X*) Ballantine Bks.

—The Case of the Fiery Fingers. 1987. mass mkt. 3.50 o.s.i (*0-345-35161-4*) Ballantine Bks.

—The Case of the Fiery Fingers. 1975. pap. 1.50 o.p. (*0-671-78783-7*, Pocket) Simon & Schuster.

—The Case of the Foot-Loose Doll. 1983. mass mkt. 2.50 o.p. (*0-345-31273-2*); Vol. 1. 1999. mass mkt. 4.99 (*0-345-91479-1*) Ballantine Bks.

—The Case of the Foot-Loose Doll. 1975. pap. 24.95 o.p. (*0-671-78787-X*, Atria) Simon & Schuster.

—The Case of the Fugitive Nurse. 1993. mass mkt. 4.99 o.s.i (*0-345-37873-3*) Ballantine Bks.

—The Case of the Gilded Lily. l.t. ed. 1991. 8.95 o.p. (*1-55504-899-4*, 16) BBC Audiobooks America.

—The Case of the Gilded Lily. 1999. mass mkt. 4.99 (*0-345-91480-5*); 1985. 199p. mass mkt. 5.99 o.s.i (*0-345-32318-1*) Ballantine Bks.

—The Case of the Gilded Lily. 1981. (Perry Mason Mysteries Ser.). 256p. reprint ed. lib. bdg. 18.00 (*0-8376-0396-X*) Bentley Pubs.

—The Case of the Glamorous Ghost. l.t. ed. 1992. pap. 20.95 o.p. (*0-7927-1044-4*, CS0279); 1991. 22.95 o.p. (*0-7927-1043-6*, CH0211) BBC Audiobooks America.

—The Case of the Glamorous Ghost. 240p. 2000. mass mkt. 5.99 (*0-345-43786-1*, Fawcett); 1986. mass mkt. 3.95 o.s.i (*0-345-34440-5*) Ballantine Bks.

—The Case of the Glamorous Ghost. 1977. pap. 1.95 o.p. (*0-671-81691-8*, Pocket) Simon & Schuster.

—The Case of the Golddigger's Purse. 1997. mass mkt. 4.99 (*0-345-90800-7*); 1984. 224p. mass mkt. 4.99 o.s.i (*0-345-31680-0*, Ballantine Bks.) Ballantine Bks.

—The Case of the Golddigger's Purse. l.t. ed. 2002. 370p. pap. 25.95 (*0-7862-4251-5*) Gale Group.

—The Case of the Green-Eyed Sister. 1978. xii, 426p. (*0-89340-140-4*) BBC Audiobooks America.

—The Case of the Green-Eyed Sister. 1993. mass mkt. 4.50 o.s.i (*0-345-37872-5*) Ballantine Bks.

—The Case of the Green-Eyed Sister. 1975. pap. 1.50 o.p. (*0-671-80074-4*, Pocket) Simon & Schuster.

—The Case of the Grinning Gorilla. 1986. mass mkt. 2.95 o.s.i (*0-345-34187-2*) Ballantine Bks.

—The Case of the Grinning Gorilla. 1973. pap. 0.95 o.p. (*0-671-77889-7*, Star Trek) Simon & Schuster.

—The Case of the Half-Wakened Wife. 1991. 256p. mass mkt. 4.99 o.s.i (*0-345-37147-X*, Ballantine Bks.) Ballantine Bks.

—The Case of the Haunted Husband. 281p. reprint ed. lib. bdg. 23.95 (*0-88411-418-X*) Amereon, Ltd.

—The Case of the Haunted Husband. 1986. vii, 374 p. (*1-55504-067-5*) BBC Audiobooks America.

—The Case of the Haunted Husband. 1985. 208p. mass mkt. 4.99 o.s.i (*0-345-33495-7*) Ballantine Bks.

—The Case of the Haunted Husband. abr. ed. 1991. 2p. audio 16.99 (*0-88646-299-1*) Durkin Hayes Publishing Ltd.

—The Case of the Hesitant Hostess. 1993. mass mkt. 4.50 o.s.i (*0-345-37871-7*) Ballantine Bks.

—The Case of the Hesitant Hostess. l.t. ed. 1991. 377p. pap. 15.95 o.p. (*0-8161-5064-8*, Macmillan Reference USA) Gale Group.

—The Case of the Horrified Heirs. 1995. 192p. mass mkt. 5.99 (*0-345-39227-2*); pap. 15.00 (*0-345-47043-5*) Ballantine Bks.

—The Case of the Howling Dog. 1976. (Perry Mason Bks.). reprint ed. lib. bdg. 24.95 (0-88411-404-X) Amereon, Ltd.
—The Case of the Howling Dog. 1987. mass mkt. 4.99 o.s.i (0-345-34783-8); 1984. mass mkt. 2.50 o.p. (0-345-31679-7) Ballantine Bks.
—The Case of the Howling Dog. l.t. ed. 1999. (Paperback Ser.). 279p. pap. 23.95 (0-7838-8775-2, Macmillan Reference USA) Gale Group.
—The Case of the Ice-Cold Hands. 1989. mass mkt. 3.95 o.s.i (0-345-35939-9) Ballantine Bks.
—The Case of the Ice-Cold Hands. 1980. (General Ser.). lib. bdg. 11.95 o.p. (0-8161-3174-0, Macmillan Reference USA) Gale Group.
—The Case of the Irate Witness. 1973. pap. 0.95 o.p. (0-671-77883-8, Pocket) Simon & Schuster.
—The Case of the Lame Canary. (Perry Mason Bks.). 281p. reprint ed. lib. bdg. 23.95 (0-88411-411-2) Amereon, Ltd.
—The Case of the Lame Canary. 1996. mass mkt. 4.99 (0-345-90796-5); 1987. 256p. mass mkt. 4.99 o.s.i (0-345-35162-2); 1984. mass mkt. 2.50 o.s.i (0-345-31547-2) Ballantine Bks.
—The Case of the Lazy Lover. l.t. ed. 1982. vii, 438 p. (0-89340-362-8) BBC Audiobooks America.
—The Case of the Lazy Lover. 1997. mass mkt. 4.99 (0-345-90801-5); 1987. mass mkt. 2.95 o.s.i (0-345-35007-3); 1981. mass mkt. 4.99 o.s.i (0-345-29496-3) Ballantine Bks.
—The Case of the Lazy Lover. l.t. ed. 1997. 21.95 (0-7838-8348-X, Macmillan Reference USA) Gale Group.
—The Case of the Lazy Lover. abr. ed. 1989. audio 14.95 (1-55800-119-0, 40460, Dove Audio) NewStar Media, Inc.
—The Case of the Lonely Heiress. (Perry Mason Mysteries Ser.). 1997. mass mkt. 4.99 (0-345-90802-3); 1986. 224p. mass mkt. 3.95 o.s.i (0-345-34012-4); 1984. mass mkt. 2.50 o.p. (0-345-31797-1); 1983. 224p. mass mkt. 5.99 o.s.i (0-345-31012-8, Ballantine Bks.) Ballantine Bks.
—The Case of the Lonely Heiress. l.t. ed. 2001. 216p. pap. 24.95 (0-7838-9506-2, Macmillan Reference USA) Gale Group.
—The Case of the Lonely Heiress. 1973. pap. 0.95 o.p. (0-671-77886-2, Atria) Simon & Schuster.
—The Case of the Long-Legged Models. 1994. mass mkt. 4.99 o.s.i (0-345-37876-8) Ballantine Bks.
—The Case of the Long-Legged Models. 1971. pap. 0.75 o.p. (0-671-75556-0, Pimsleur) Simon & Schuster Audio.
—The Case of the Lucky Legs. 1976. (Perry Mason Bks.). reprint ed. lib. bdg. 23.95 (0-88411-403-1) Amereon, Ltd.
—The Case of the Lucky Legs. 1999. (0-7540-3827-0); (0-7540-3826-2) BBC Audiobooks America.
—The Case of the Lucky Legs. 1973. pap. 0.95 o.p. (0-671-77891-9, Simon & Schuster Audioworks) Simon & Schuster Audio.
—The Case of the Lucky Legs. l.t. ed. 1999. (G. K. Hall Paperback Ser.). 320p. pap. 23.95 (0-7838-8612-8) Thorndike Pr.
—The Case of the Lucky Loser. l.t. ed. 1991. 12.95 o.p. (0-7927-0227-1, 4764); 1990. pap. 17.95 o.p. (0-7927-0228-X, C0247) BBC Audiobooks America.
—The Case of the Lucky Loser. 1990. 192p. mass mkt. 4.99 o.s.i (0-345-36497-X) Ballantine Bks.
—The Case of the Mischievous Doll. 1989. mass mkt. 4.99 o.s.i (0-345-35940-2) Ballantine Bks.
—The Case of the Mischievous Doll. 1981. (General Ser.). lib. bdg. 11.95 o.p. (0-8161-3215-1, Macmillan Reference USA) Gale Group.
—The Case of the Moth-Eaten Mink. 1990. (Perry Mason Mysteries Ser.: No. 57). 240p. mass mkt. 3.95 o.p. (0-345-36928-9) Ballantine Bks.
—The Case of the Moth-Eaten Mink. l.t. ed. 1992. (General Ser.). 365p. lib. bdg. 19.95 o.p. (0-8161-5063-X, Macmillan Reference USA) Gale Group.
—The Case of the Moth-Eaten Mink. 1971. pap. 0.75 o.p. (0-671-75539-0, Star Trek) Simon & Schuster.
—The Case of the Mythical Monkeys. 1984. mass mkt. 3.95 o.s.i (0-345-31404-2) Ballantine Bks.
—The Case of the Mythical Monkeys. 1981. 288p. reprint ed. lib. bdg. 18.00 (0-8376-0398-6) Bentley Pubs.
—The Case of the Mythical Monkeys. l.t. ed. 1993. 13.95 o.p. (0-8161-3384-0, Macmillan Reference USA) Gale Group.
—The Case of the Negligent Nymph. 1986. 176p. mass mkt. 3.95 o.s.i (0-345-34013-2) Ballantine Bks.
—The Case of the Negligent Nymph. 1973. pap. 0.95 o.p. (0-671-77892-7, Pocket) Simon & Schuster.
—The Case of the Nervous Accomplice. 1992. mass mkt. 3.99 o.s.i (0-345-37874-1) Ballantine Bks.
—The Case of the Nervous Accomplice. 1974. pap. 0.95 o.p. (0-671-77926-5, Pocket) Simon & Schuster.
—The Case of the One-Eyed Witness. 1995. 240p. mass mkt. 5.99 (0-345-39225-6) Ballantine Bks.
—The Case of the One-Eyed Witness. l.t. ed. 1990. pap. 15.95 o.p. (0-8161-5062-1, Macmillan Reference USA) Gale Group.
—The Case of the One-Eyed Witness. 1971. pap. 0.75 o.p. (0-671-75536-6, Star Trek) Simon & Schuster.
—The Case of the Perjured Parrot. (Perry Mason Bks.). 288p. reprint ed. lib. bdg. 23.95 (0-88411-414-7) Amereon, Ltd.
—The Case of the Perjured Parrot. (Perry Mason Mysteries Ser.). 1987. mass mkt. 4.99 o.s.i (0-345-34685-8); 1982. mass mkt. 2.25 o.p. (0-345-30396-2) Ballantine Bks.
—The Case of the Perjured Parrot. l.t. ed. 2001. 253p. (0-7540-4401-7); (0-7540-4402-5) Gale Group. (Macmillan Reference USA).
—The Case of the Perjured Parrot. 1975. pap. 1.50 o.p. (0-671-78944-9, Pocket) Simon & Schuster.
—The Case of the Perjured Parrot. l.t. ed. 2001. (G. K. Hall Nightingale Ser.). 253p. pap. 23.95 (0-7838-9322-1) Thorndike Pr.
—The Case of the Phantom Fortune. 1986. mass mkt. 3.50 o.s.i (0-345-33191-5) Ballantine Bks.
—The Case of the Phantom Fortune. l.t. ed. 1984. (Nightingale Ser.). 9.95 o.p. (0-8161-3754-4, Macmillan Reference USA) Gale Group.
—The Case of the Phantom Fortune. 1974. pap. 0.95 o.p. (0-671-77896-X, Pocket) Simon & Schuster.
—The Case of the Postponed Murder. 1995. mass mkt. 4.99 o.s.i (0-345-39229-9) Ballantine Bks.
—The Case of the Postponed Murder. 1973. (General Ser.). reprint ed. lib. bdg. 8.95 o.p. (0-8161-6090-2, Macmillan Reference USA) Gale Group.
—The Case of the Postponed Murder. 1973. 7.95 o.p. (0-688-00033-9, Morrow, William & Co.) Morrow/Avon.
—The Case of the Postponed Murder. 1974. pap. 0.95 o.p. (0-671-77894-3, Pocket) Simon & Schuster.
—The Case of the Queenly Contestant. l.t. ed. 1990. (Perry Mason Mystery Ser.). pap. 18.95 o.p. (0-89340-025-4, C0160) BBC Audiobooks America.
—The Case of the Queenly Contestant. 1993. reprint ed. mass mkt. 4.50 o.s.i (0-345-37879-2) Ballantine Bks.
—The Case of the Reluctant Model. 1990. 208p. mass mkt. 3.95 o.s.i (0-345-36689-1) Ballantine Bks.
—The Case of the Reluctant Model. abr. ed. audio 16.99 (0-88646-301-7, DHA7301) Durkin Hayes Publishing Ltd.
—The Case of the Restless Redhead. 1980. xiv, 435 p. (0-89340-261-3) BBC Audiobooks America.
—The Case of the Restless Redhead. 1985. mass mkt. 3.95 o.s.i (0-345-33199-0) Ballantine Bks.
—The Case of the Rolling Bones. (Perry Mason Bks.). 288p. reprint ed. lib. bdg. 23.95 (0-88411-415-5) Amereon, Ltd.
—The Case of the Rolling Bones. 1999. 4.99 (0-345-91481-3); 1985. 208p. reprint ed. mass mkt. 4.99 o.s.i (0-345-32979-1) Ballantine Bks.
—The Case of the Rolling Bones. l.t. ed. 1986. (Nightingale Ser.). 350p. 11.95 o.p. (0-8161-4080-4, Macmillan Reference USA) Gale Group.
—The Case of the Rolling Bones. 1976. (Two-in-One Ser.). pap. 1.95 o.p. (0-671-80583-5, Pocket) Simon & Schuster.
—The Case of the Runaway Corpse. 1990. 224p. mass mkt. 4.99 o.s.i (0-345-36498-8) Ballantine Bks.
—The Case of the Runaway Corpse. l.t. ed. 1988. lib. bdg. 14.95 o.p. (1-85057-453-7, Macmillan Reference USA) Gale Group.
—The Case of the Screaming Woman. l.t. ed. 1992. pap. 18.95 o.p. (0-7927-0969-1) BBC Audiobooks America.
—The Case of the Screaming Woman. 1994. mass mkt. 4.99 o.s.i (0-345-37875-X); 1992. 20.95 o.p. (0-7927-1228-5, CH0260) Ballantine Bks.
—The Case of the Shapely Shadow. 1986. mass mkt. 3.50 o.s.i (0-345-33496-5) Ballantine Bks.
—The Case of the Shoplifter's Shoe. (Perry Mason Bks.). 312p. reprint ed. lib. bdg. 24.95 (0-88411-413-9) Amereon, Ltd.
—The Case of the Shoplifter's Shoe. 1998. mass mkt. 4.99 (0-345-91233-0); 1986. 224p. mass mkt. 5.99 o.s.i (0-345-32943-0) Ballantine Bks.
—The Case of the Shoplifter's Shoe. 1973. pap. 0.95 o.p. (0-671-77888-9, Pocket) Simon & Schuster.
—The Case of the Silent Partner. (Perry Mason Bks.). reprint ed. lib. bdg. 23.95 (0-88411-417-1) Amereon, Ltd.
—The Case of the Silent Partner. 1999. 4.99 (0-345-91482-1); 1986. 224p. mass mkt. 4.99 o.s.i (0-345-33684-4) Ballantine Bks.
—The Case of the Silent Partner. 2003. (Paperback Ser.). pap. 25.95 (0-7862-5047-X) Thorndike Pr.
—The Case of the Singing Skirt. 1992. mass mkt. 3.99 o.s.i (0-345-37149-6) Ballantine Bks.
—The Case of the Singing Skirt. 1981. 256p. reprint ed. 18.00 (0-8376-0399-4) Bentley Pubs.
—The Case of the Singing Skirt. l.t. ed. 1988. (Nightingale Ser.). 183p. 12.95 o.p. (0-8161-4515-6, Macmillan Reference USA) Gale Group.
—The Case of the Sleepwalker's Niece. 1976. (Perry Mason Bks.). reprint ed. lib. bdg. 21.95 (0-88411-408-2) Amereon, Ltd.
—The Case of the Sleepwalker's Niece. 1991. (Perry Mason Mysteries Ser.). mass mkt. 3.99 o.s.i (0-345-37146-1, Ballantine Bks.) Ballantine Bks.
—The Case of the Sleepwalker's Niece. l.t. ed. 1993. (Nightingale Ser.). 344p. 14.95 o.p. (0-8161-5633-6, Macmillan Reference USA) Gale Group.
—The Case of the Sleepwalker's Niece. 1973. pap. 0.95 o.p. (0-671-77893-5, Pocket) Simon & Schuster.
—The Case of the Spurious Spinster. 1988. mass mkt. 3.50 o.s.i (0-345-35203-3) Ballantine Bks.
—The Case of the Stepdaughter's Secret. 1989. (Perry Mason Mysteries Ser.). 192p. mass mkt. 3.95 o.s.i (0-345-36221-7) Ballantine Bks.
—The Case of the Stepdaughter's Secret. l.t. ed. 1985. (Nightingale Ser.). 288p. 9.95 o.p. (0-8161-3753-6, Macmillan Reference USA) Gale Group.
—The Case of the Stepdaughter's Secret. 1977. pap. 1.95 o.p. (0-671-80968-7, Pocket) Simon & Schuster.
—The Case of the Stuttering Bishop. 1976. (Perry Mason Bks.). reprint ed. lib. bdg. 23.95 (0-88411-409-0) Amereon, Ltd.
—The Case of the Stuttering Bishop. l.t. ed. 1994. 21.95 o.p. (0-7927-1907-7); pap. 19.95 o.p. (0-7927-1906-9) BBC Audiobooks America.
—The Case of the Stuttering Bishop. 1998. mass mkt. 4.99 (0-345-91230-6); 1988. 192p. mass mkt. 6.99 (0-345-35680-2) Ballantine Bks.
—The Case of the Substitute Face. (Perry Mason Bks.). 310p. reprint ed. lib. bdg. 24.95 (0-88411-412-0) Amereon, Ltd.
—The Case of the Substitute Face. l.t. ed. 1993. 22.95 o.p. (0-7927-1562-4); pap. 20.95 o.p. (0-7927-1561-6) BBC Audiobooks America.
—The Case of the Substitute Face. (Perry Mason Mysteries Ser.). 1998. mass mkt. 4.99 (0-345-91232-2); 1987. pap. o.s.i (0-345-01849-4); 1987. 256p. mass mkt. 4.99 o.s.i (0-345-34377-8) Ballantine Bks.
—The Case of the Substitute Face. 1974. pap. 1.25 o.p. (0-671-78448-X, Pocket) Simon & Schuster.
—The Case of the Sulky Girl. 1976. (Perry Mason Books Ser.). reprint ed. lib. bdg. 24.95 (0-88411-402-3) Amereon, Ltd.
—The Case of the Sulky Girl. 1992. mass mkt. 4.99 o.s.i (0-345-37145-3) Ballantine Bks.
—The Case of the Sulky Girl, unabr. ed. 1991. (Listen for Pleasure Ser.). audio 16.99 (0-88646-298-3, LFP 7298) Durkin Hayes Publishing Ltd.
—The Case of the Sun Bather's Diary. 1995. 244p. pap. 15.00 (0-345-47042-7, Fawcett); 1985. 208p. mass mkt. 2.95 o.s.i (0-345-33503-1) Ballantine Bks.
—The Case of the Sun Bather's Diary. 1971. pap. 1.25 o.p. (0-671-82704-9, Pocket) Simon & Schuster.
—The Case of the Sun Bather's Diary. l.t. ed. 2001. (Paperback Ser.). 328p. 24.95 (0-7838-9338-8) Thorndike Pr.
—The Case of the Sun Bather's Diary: A Perry Mason Mystery. 2000. (Perry Mason Mysteries Ser.). 240p. mass mkt. 5.99 (0-345-43788-8, Fawcett) Ballantine Bks.
—The Case of the Terrified Typist. 1999. 4.99 (0-345-91483-X); 1987. 192p. mass mkt. 5.99 o.s.i (0-345-34165-1) Ballantine Bks.
—The Case of the Terrified Typist. l.t. ed. 1989. 296p. 14.95 o.p. (0-8161-4514-8, Macmillan Reference USA) Gale Group.
—The Case of the Terrified Typist. 1975. pap. 1.50 o.p. (0-671-78780-2, Simon Pulse) Simon & Schuster Children's Publishing.
—The Case of the Troubled Trustee. 1995. mass mkt. 4.99 o.s.i (0-345-39224-8) Ballantine Bks.
—The Case of the Vagabond Virgin. l.t. ed. 1990. pap. 17.95 o.p. (0-7927-0534-3, C0794); 19.95 o.p. (0-7927-0533-5, C0286) BBC Audiobooks America.
—The Case of the Vagabond Virgin. 1997. pap. 4.99 (0-345-90803-1); 1986. mass mkt. 3.50 o.s.i (0-345-34319-0); 1982. mass mkt. 4.99 o.s.i (0-345-30393-8) Ballantine Bks.
—The Case of the Vagabond Virgin. 1973. pap. 0.95 o.p. (0-671-77885-4, Simon Pulse) Simon & Schuster Children's Publishing.
—The Case of the Velvet Claws. 1976. (Perry Mason Books Ser.). reprint ed. lib. bdg. 24.95 (0-88411-401-5) Amereon, Ltd.
—The Case of the Velvet Claws. 1996. mass mkt. 4.99 (0-345-90793-0); 1985. 224p. mass mkt. 5.99 o.s.i (0-345-32317-3) Ballantine Bks.
—The Case of the Velvet Claws. 2002. (Best Mysteries of All Time Ser.). 261p. (0-7621-8878-2, IM Pr.) Reader's Digest Assn., Inc., The.
—The Case of the Waylaid Wolf. 1990. (Perry Mason Mysteries Ser.). 208p. mass mkt. 3.95 o.s.i (0-345-36690-5) Ballantine Bks.
—The Case of the Waylaid Wolf. 1976. pap. 1.95 o.p. (0-671-80860-5, Pocket) Simon & Schuster.
—The Case of the Worried Waitress. 1986. 160p. mass mkt. 2.95 o.s.i (0-345-33193-1) Ballantine Bks.
—Perry Mason: Seven Complete Novels. 19th ed. 1994. 832p. 13.99 o.s.i (0-517-29363-3) Random Hse. Value Publishing.
Garwood, Julie. Mercy. 2001. E-Book 9.99 (1-59061-151-9) Adobe Systems, Inc.
—Mercy. l.t. ed. 2002. (Wheeler Large Print Book Ser.). 29.95 (1-58724-167-6, Wheeler Publishing, Inc.) Gale Group.
—Mercy. 2002. (Illus.). 496p. mass mkt. 7.99 (0-671-03402-2, Pocket); 2001. 416p. 25.00 (0-671-03401-4, Atria); 2001. E-Book 25.00 (0-7434-1933-2, Atria) Simon & Schuster.
—Mercy. l.t. ed. 2002. 13.95 (1-4104-0046-8, Large Print Pr.) Thorndike Pr.
Geary, Nancy. Misfortune. 2002. 480p. reprint ed. mass mkt. 7.50 (0-446-61094-1) Warner Bks., Inc.
Gifford, Thomas. The Assassini. 1991. 688p. mass mkt. 6.99 o.s.i (0-553-28740-0); 1990. (0-593-02172-X); 1990. 688p. pap. 29.00 (0-553-76236-2) Bantam Bks.
—The Assassini. 1924. o.s.i (0-688-04723-8, Morrow, William & Co.) Morrow/Avon.
—The Assassini. 1991. audio 12.79 o.s.i (0-553-70023-5); 1999. audio 9.99 o.s.i (0-553-70203-3) Random Hse. Audio Publishing Group. (RH Audio).
—Saints Rest. 1997. 448p. mass mkt. 6.99 o.s.i (0-553-57226-1) Bantam Bks.
—Saint's Rest. 1997. 448p. pap. 23.00 (0-553-76269-9, Crimeline) Bantam Bks.
Giroux, E. X. A Death for a Dancer: A Robert Forsythe Mystery. 1986. mass mkt. 2.95 o.s.i (0-345-33408-6) Ballantine Bks.
—A Death for a Dancer: A Robert Forsythe Mystery. 1985. 192p. 12.95 o.p. (0-312-18868-4) St. Martin's Pr.
—A Death for a Dancing Doll. 1992. mass mkt. 3.99 o.s.i (0-345-37609-9) Ballantine Bks.
—A Death for a Dancing Doll. 1991. 17.95 o.p. (0-312-05848-9, Saint Martin's Minotaur) St. Martin's Pr.
—A Death for a Darling. 1986. 192p. mass mkt. 3.50 o.s.i (0-345-33024-2) Ballantine Bks.
—A Death for a Darling. 1985. 192p. 13.95 o.p. (0-312-18607-X) St. Martin's Pr.
—A Death for a Dietician. 1989. 192p. mass mkt. 3.95 o.s.i (0-345-35767-1) Ballantine Bks.
—A Death for a Dietitian. 1988. 176p. 13.95 o.p. (0-312-01417-1, Saint Martin's Minotaur) St. Martin's Pr.
—A Death for a Dilettante. 1987. 176p. mass mkt. 3.50 o.s.i (0-345-34758-7) Ballantine Bks.
—A Death for a Dilettante. 1987. (Robert Forsythe Mystery Ser.). 208p. 13.95 o.p. (0-312-00044-8) St. Martin's Pr.
—A Death for a Doctor: A Robert Forsythe Mystery. 1986. 208p. 13.95 o.p. (0-312-18603-7) St. Martin's Pr.
—A Death for a Dodo. 1993. 17.95 o.p. (0-312-08762-4, Saint Martin's Minotaur) St. Martin's Pr.
—A Death for a Double. 1991. 192p. mass mkt. 3.95 o.s.i (0-345-36833-9) Ballantine Bks.
—A Death for a Double. 1992. 2.99 o.p. (0-517-09039-2) Random Hse. Value Publishing.
—A Death for a Double. 1990. 208p. 15.95 o.p. (0-312-03809-7, Saint Martin's Minotaur) St. Martin's Pr.
—A Death for a Dreamer. 1990. (Death Ser.). 192p. mass mkt. 3.95 o.s.i (0-345-36528-3) Ballantine Bks.
—A Death for a Dreamer. 1989. 14.95 o.p. (0-312-02901-2, Saint Martin's Minotaur) St. Martin's Pr.
—A Death for Adonis. 1985. 160p. mass mkt. 4.95 o.s.i (0-345-32889-2) Ballantine Bks.
—A Death for Adonis. 1984. 160p. 11.95 o.p. (0-312-18610-X) St. Martin's Pr.
Giroux, E. X. & Giroux, Leo. A Death for a Doctor: A Robert Forsythe Mystery. 1987. 192p. mass mkt. 4.95 o.s.i (0-345-34231-3) Ballantine Bks.
Gool, Reshard. Cape Town Coolie. 1990. (African Writers Ser.). 185p. (Orig.). (C). pap. 7.95 (0-435-90568-6, 90568) Heinemann.
—Cape Town Coolie: A Novel. 1989. pap. text (0-920661-09-2) TSAR Pubns.
Gorman, Ed. The Day the Music Died. 1999. 212p. 22.95 (0-7867-0569-8, Carroll & Graf Pubs.) Avalon Publishing Group.
—The Day the Music Died. 2000. (Sam McCain Mystery Ser.). 258p. mass mkt. 5.99 o.s.i (0-425-17411-5) Berkley Publishing Group.
—The Day the Music Died. l.t. ed. 1999. (Mystery Ser.). 323p. 27.95 (0-7862-2032-5) Thorndike Pr.
—The Day the Music Died. 2000. (Illus.). 12.04 (0-606-18007-9) Turtleback Bks.
—Wake up Little Susie: A Sam McCain Mystery. 2000. 225p. 22.95 (0-7867-0665-1, Carroll & Graf Pubs.) Avalon Publishing Group.
—Will You Still Love Me Tomorrow? 2001. 256p. 22.95 (0-7867-0775-5, Carroll & Graf Pubs.) Avalon Publishing Group.
—Will You Still Love Me Tomorrow? l.t. ed. 2001. 301p. 29.95 (0-7862-3672-8); 280p. (0-7540-4739-3); 280p. (0-7540-4738-5) Thorndike Pr.

Gotti, Victoria. The Senator's Daughter. 1998. 320p. mass mkt. 6.99 o.p. (0-8125-7176-2); 1997. 304p. 23.95 o.p. (0-312-86323-3) Doherty, Tom Assocs., LLC. (Forge Bks.).
—The Senator's Daughter. l.t. ed. 1997. (Core Ser.). 464p. 26.95 (0-7838-8196-7, Macmillan Reference USA) Gale Group.
—The Senator's Daughter. abr. ed. 1997. audio 23.00 (1-56876-065-5) Soundlines Entertainment, Inc.
—The Senator's Daughter. 1999. 6.99 (0-312-87111-2) St. Martin's Pr.
Gray, A. W. Bino. 1988. 208p. 16.95 o.p. (0-525-24590-1, Dutton) Dutton/Plume.
—Bino. 1989. mass mkt. 3.95 o.p. (0-451-40129-8, Onyx) NAL.
—Bino's Blues. 1995. 256p. 20.00 (0-671-88186-8, Simon & Schuster) Simon & Schuster.
—In Defense of Judges. 1990. 18.95 o.p. (0-525-24875-7, Dutton) Dutton/Plume.
—In Defense of Judges. 1991. 368p. mass mkt. 5.99 o.s.i (0-451-40271-5, Onyx) NAL.
—Killings. 1993. 304p. 20.00 o.p. (0-525-93625-4, Dutton) Dutton/Plume.
—Killings. 1994. 384p. mass mkt. 4.99 o.p. (0-451-40525-0, Onyx) NAL.
Grayson, George. The Revolutionary's Confession. 2000. 331p. 24.95 (1-890768-21-9, Intrigue Pr.) Corvus Publishing.
Green, Tim. The Fifth Angel. 384p. 2004. mass mkt. 6.99 (0-446-61377-0, Warner Vision); 2003. 24.95 (0-446-53085-9) Warner Bks., Inc.
Grippando, James M. Under Cover of Darkness. 2000. 416p. 25.00 (0-06-019240-2, HarperCollins) HarperTrade.
Grisham, John. The Client. l.t. ed. 1993. 432p. 29.95 (0-385-42471-X); (YA). 26.00 o.s.i (0-385-46865-2); 432p. 200.00 o.s.i (0-385-47015-0) Bantam Doubleday Dell Large Print Group, Inc. (Doubleday Large Type).
—The Client. 1994. 576p. mass mkt. 7.99 (0-440-21352-5); mass mkt. (0-440-21807-1) Dell Publishing.
—The Client. 1994. (Illus.). 14.04 (0-606-18101-6) Turtleback Bks.
—The Client: International Edition. 1993. 512p. mass mkt. 6.99 o.s.i (0-440-29526-2) Dell Publishing.
—El Cliente. 2nd ed. 1998. (SPA.). 424p. (84-08-02141-9) GeoPlaneta, Editorial, S. A.
—El Cliente. 1994. (SPA.). 16.30 (0-606-18347-7) Turtleback Bks.
—The Partner. 1998. 480p. pap. 7.99 (0-440-22604-X); 1998. 480p. mass mkt. 7.99 (0-440-22476-4); 1997. mass mkt. 7.99 (0-440-29555-6) Dell Publishing.
—The Partner. 1997. 368p. 27.95 (0-385-47295-1); 528p. 31.95 o.s.i (0-385-48578-6); 368p. 250.00 o.s.i (0-385-48592-1) Doubleday Publishing.
—The Partner, Level 5. 2001. pap. 7.66 (0-582-43406-8) Longman Publishing Group.
—The Partner. abr. ed. 1997. audio 26.95 (0-553-47283-6, 694963); audio compact disk 29.95 (0-553-45553-2) Random Hse. Audio Publishing Group. (RH Audio).
—The Partner. 1998. 14.04 (0-606-15672-0) Turtleback Bks.
—The Rainmaker. abr. ed. audio 22.95 Books on Tape, Inc.
—The Rainmaker. 1996. 608p. mass mkt. 7.99 (0-440-22165-X); 1995. (YA). mass mkt. 9.99 o.s.i (0-440-91092-7) Dell Publishing.
—The Rainmaker. 1995. (YA). mass mkt. 7.50 (0-440-29542-4); 448p. 27.95 (0-385-42473-6); 784p. 29.95 o.s.i (0-385-47512-8); (YA). 250.00 o.s.i (0-385-47513-6) Doubleday Publishing.
—The Rainmaker. unabr. ed. 1999. audio 49.95 Highsmith Inc.
—The Rainmaker, Level 5. 2000. (Penguin Reader Ser.). pap. 7.93 (0-582-36412-4) Longman Publishing Group.
—The Rainmaker. abr. ed. 1995. audio 27.95 (0-553-47305-0, 692837, RH Audio) Random Hse. Audio Publishing Group.
—Tiempo de Matar. 1995. (SPA., Illus.). 472p. 9.95 (84-08-01475-7, PT9159) GeoPlaneta, Editorial, S. A. ESP. *Dist:* Lectorum Pubns., Inc., Planeta Publishing Corp.
—A Time to Kill. 1992. 528p. mass mkt. 7.99 (0-440-21172-7) Dell Publishing.
—A Time to Kill. 1993. 496p. 30.00 (0-385-47081-9); 800p. 27.00 o.s.i (0-385-47078-9); 496p. 200.00 o.s.i (0-385-47112-2) Doubleday Publishing.
—A Time to Kill. l.t. ed. 1993. (0-8161-5590-9, Macmillan Reference USA) Gale Group.
—A Time to Kill, Level 5. 2000. pap. 7.93 (0-582-36410-8) Longman Publishing Group.
—A Time to Kill. 1993. 415p. o.s.i (0-7126-5906-4) Random Hse. of Canada, Ltd. CAN. *Dist:* Random Hse., Inc.
—A Time to Kill. 1992. 14.04 (0-606-14351-3) Turtleback Bks.
—A Time to Kill. 1991. 416p. pap. 9.95 o.p. (0-922066-72-8); 1989. 384p. 18.95 o.p. (0-922066-03-5) Wynwood.
Guhrke, Laura L. Breathless. 1999. (Sonnet Bks.). (Illus.). 416p. pap. 6.50 (0-671-02368-3, Pocket) Simon & Schuster.
Haddock, Richard. Arkalalah. 2002. 293p. pap. 16.95 (0-595-21522-X, Writers Club Pr.) iUniverse, Inc.
Hamill, Denis. Three Quarters. 1999. 352p. pap. 6.99 (0-671-00250-3, Pocket Star); 1998. 320p. 23.00 o.s.i (0-671-00249-X, Atria) Simon & Schuster.
—Throwing 7's. 1999. 319p. 24.00 (0-671-02614-3, Atria); 2000. (Illus.). 592p. reprint ed. pap. 6.99 (0-671-02615-1, Pocket Star) Simon & Schuster.
Hare, Cyril. Death Walks the Woods: A Francis Pettigrew Mystery. 1991. 288p. reprint ed. pap. 8.00 o.p. (0-06-092136-6, Perennial) HarperTrade.
—Tragedy at Law: An Inspector Mallett & Francis Pettigrew Mystery. 1986. mass mkt. 9.95 o.p. (0-553-06518-1) Bantam Bks.
—Tragedy at Law: An Inspector Mallett & Francis Pettigrew Mystery. 1991. 400p. pap. 5.95 o.p. (0-06-080522-6, Perennial) HarperTrade.
—Untimely Death: An Inspector Mallett & Francis Pettigrew Mystery. 1992. 192p. reprint ed. pap. 8.00 o.p. (0-06-092252-4, Perennial) HarperTrade.
—When the Wind Blows. l.t. ed. 2001. (Dales Large Print Ser.). 304p. pap. 21.99 (1-84262-104-1) Dales Large Print Bks. GBR. *Dist:* Ulverscroft Large Print Bks., Ltd., Ulverscroft Large Print Canada, Ltd.
—When the Wind Blows. 1976. (Crime Fiction Ser.). reprint ed. lib. bdg. 21.00 o.p. (0-8240-2373-0) Garland Publishing, Inc.
—When the Wind Blows. 1978. reprint ed. pap. 1.95 o.p. (0-06-080454-8, P 454) HarperCollins Pubs.
—The Wind Blows Death: A Francis Pettigrew Mystery. 1991. 272p. reprint ed. pap. 8.00 o.p. (0-06-092138-2, Perennial) HarperTrade.
—With a Bare Bodkin: A Francis Pettigrew Mystery. 1991. 256p. reprint ed. pap. 8.00 o.p. (0-06-092139-0, Perennial) HarperTrade.
Harris, E. Lynn. Abide with Me. 1999. (Abide with Me Ser.: Vol. 3). 368p. 24.95 (0-385-48657-X) Doubleday Publishing.
—Abide with Me. 2000. 368p. pap. 13.00 (0-385-48658-8, Knopf Bks. for Young Readers) Random Hse. Children's Bks.
—Abide with Me. 2003. (African American Ser.). 535p. 29.95 (0-7862-5062-3) Thorndike Pr.
Henry, Diane & Horrock, Nicholas. Blood Red, Snow White. 1992. 19.95 o.p. (0-316-35752-9) Little Brown & Co.
—Blood Red, Snow White. Peters, Sally, ed. 1993. 352p. mass mkt. 5.50 (0-671-79551-1, Pocket) Simon & Schuster.
Hensley, Joe L. Robak's Witch: A Dan Robak Mystery. 1997. 256p. 21.95 o.p. (0-312-15642-1, Saint Martin's Minotaur) St. Martin's Pr.
Higgins, George V. Defending Billy Ryan. unabr. ed. 1997. audio 39.95 (0-7861-1234-4) Blackstone Audio Bks., Inc.
—Defending Billy Ryan. l.t. ed. 1993. 50.95 (0-7838-1112-8, Macmillan Reference USA) Gale Group.
—Defending Billy Ryan. 1992. 320p. 21.95 o.p. (0-8050-1677-5) Holt, Henry & Co.
—Defending Billy Ryan. 1994. 304p. mass mkt. 4.99 o.s.i (0-8217-4586-7) Kensington Publishing Corp.
—Kennedy for the Defense. 1985. 224p. mass mkt. 2.95 o.p. (0-345-32612-1) Ballantine Bks.
—Kennedy for the Defense. 1992. mass mkt. 4.50 o.s.i (0-8217-3724-4, Zebra Bks.) Kensington Publishing Corp.
—Kennedy for the Defense. 1980. 9.95 o.p. (0-394-42406-9, Knopf Bks. for Young Readers) Random Hse. Children's Bks.
—Kennedy for the Defense: A Novel. 1995. pap. 12.00 o.p. (0-8050-4182-6, Owl Bks.) Holt, Henry & Co.
—Penance for Jerry Kennedy. 1986. 320p. pap. 3.50 o.p. (0-88184-224-9, Carroll & Graf Pubs.) Avalon Publishing Group.
—Sandra Nichols Found Dead: A Jerry Kennedy Novel. 1997. 256p. pap. 12.00 o.s.i (0-8050-5222-4, Owl Bks.); 1996. 89p. 23.00 o.p. (0-8050-3747-0) Holt, Henry & Co.
Hogan, Michael. Man Out of Time. 2003. 320p. pap. 11.95 (0-385-33693-4, Delta) Dell Publishing.
Holms, Joyce. Hot Potato. 2003. 240p. 24.95 (0-7490-0605-6) Allison & Busby, Ltd. GBR. *Dist:* International Publishers Marketing.
Huffman, Bob. Legal Fiction. 1999. 200p. pap. 13.95 (0-88739-205-9) Creative Arts Bk. Co.
Iles, Greg. 24 Hours. l.t. ed. 2000. (Wheeler Large Print Book Ser.). 448p. 29.95 (1-56895-931-1, Wheeler Publishing, Inc.) Gale Group.
Johnston, Joan. The Price. 2004. (Illus.). 432p. mass mkt. 7.99 (0-7434-5437-5, Pocket Star); 2003. 336p. 23.00 (0-7434-5432-4, Atria) Simon & Schuster.
—The Price. l.t. ed. 2003. 494p. 31.95 (0-7862-5618-4) Thorndike Pr.
Kane, Stephanie. Extreme Indifference. 2004. mass mkt. 6.99 (0-7434-6681-0, Pocket); 2003. 304p. 24.00 (0-7432-4556-3, Scribner) Simon & Schuster.
Kerr, Baine. Harmful Intent. 2000. 384p. reprint ed. mass mkt. 6.99 (0-515-12924-0, Jove) Berkley Publishing Group.
—Harmful Intent. 1999. 368p. 25.00 (0-684-85413-9, Scribner) Simon & Schuster.
Landesman, Peter. Blood Acre. 2000. 272p. pap. 12.95 o.s.i (0-14-028236-X) Penguin Group (USA) Inc.
Lashner, William. Hostile Witness. l.t. ed. 1995. (Large Print Bks.). 25.95 o.p. (1-56895-248-1, Wheeler Publishing, Inc.) Gale Group.
—Hostile Witness. 1995. 501p. 23.00 o.p. (0-06-039146-4) HarperCollins Pubs.
—Hostile Witness. 1996. 608p. mass mkt. 7.50 (0-06-100988-1, ReganBooks); 1995. audio 17.00 o.p. (0-694-51559-0, HarperAudio) HarperTrade.
—Hostile Witness. unabr. ed. 1998. audio 112.00 (0-7887-1954-8, 95352E7) Recorded Bks., LLC.
—Veritas. 1997. 464p. 25.00 o.p. (0-06-039147-2, ReganBooks);Set. audio 18.00 (0-694-51789-5, 392878, HarperAudio) HarperTrade.
—Veritas. 1997. 592p. mass mkt. 6.50 o.s.i (0-06-101023-5, HarperTorch) Morrow/Avon.
—Veritas, unabr. ed. 1997. audio 112.00 (0-7887-1768-5, 95246E5) Recorded Bks., LLC.
Latreille, Stan. Perjury. 1999. 384p. reprint ed. mass mkt. 6.99 o.s.i (0-451-19687-2, Onyx) NAL.
Lee, Gus. No Physical Evidence. 1998. 400p. 24.95 o.s.i (0-449-91139-X, Fawcett) Ballantine Bks.
—No Physical Evidence: A Courtroom Novel. 2000. 384p. mass mkt. 6.99 o.s.i (0-8041-1779-9, Ivy Bks.) Ballantine Bks.
Lescroart, John. Dead Irish. 1996. 416p. mass mkt. 7.99 (0-440-20783-5) Dell Publishing.
—Dead Irish. 1990. 18.95 o.p. (1-55611-159-2) Fine, Donald I. Bks.
—Hard Evidence. 1994. (Northern California Mysteries Ser.). 512p. mass mkt. 6.99 o.s.i (0-8041-1275-4, Ivy Bks.) Ballantine Bks.
—Hard Evidence. 1993. 478p. 21.95 o.p. (1-55611-344-7) Fine, Donald I. Bks.
—The Mercy Rule. 1999. 640p. mass mkt. 7.99 (0-440-22282-6) Dell Publishing.
—The Mercy Rule. l.t. ed. (Paperback Bestsellers Ser.). 684p. 1999. pap. 27.95 (0-7838-0394-X); 1998. 30.95 (0-7838-0344-3) Thorndike Pr.
—The Vig. 1998. 384p. mass mkt. 7.99 (0-440-20986-2) Dell Publishing.
—The Vig. 1991. 18.95 o.p. (1-55611-221-1) Fine, Donald I. Bks.
—The Vig. abr. ed. 1998. audio 16.99 o.p. Random Hse. Audio Publishing Group.
—The 13th Juror. 1995. 560p. mass mkt. 7.99 (0-440-22079-3) Dell Publishing.
—The 13th Juror. 1994. 480p. 22.95 o.s.i (1-55611-402-8) Fine, Donald I. Bks.
—The 13th Juror. l.t. ed. 1994. 803p. lib. bdg. 24.95 o.p. (0-8161-7448-2, Macmillan Reference USA) Gale Group.
Levine, Paul. False Dawn. 1993. 320p. 21.95 o.s.i (0-553-08995-1) Bantam Bks.
—False Dawn. 1993. audio 15.99 o.s.i (0-553-47136-8, RH Audio) Random Hse. Audio Publishing Group.
—The False Dawn. 1994. 368p. mass mkt. 5.99 o.s.i (0-553-56504-4) Bantam Bks.
—Flesh & Bones. 1998. (Jake Lassiter Mystery Ser.). 352p. mass mkt. 5.99 (0-380-72591-6, Avon Bks.) Morrow/Avon.
—Flesh & Bones: A Jake Lassiter Novel. l.t. ed. 1997. (G. K. Hall Core Ser.). 468p. 26.95 (0-7838-8065-0, Macmillan Reference USA) Gale Group.
—Flesh & Bones: A Jake Lassiter Novel. l.t. ed. 1997. 336p. 23.00 (0-688-14305-9, Morrow, William & Co.) Morrow/Avon.
—Fool Me Twice. 1996. 352p. mass mkt. 5.99 (0-380-72590-8, Avon Bks.) Morrow/Avon.
—Fool Me Twice: A Jake Lassiter Novel. 1996. 356p. 22.00 o.p. (0-688-14304-0, Morrow, William & Co.) Morrow/Avon.
—Mortal Sin. 1995. 352p. mass mkt. 5.50 (0-380-72161-9, Avon Bks.); 1994. 20.00 o.p. (0-688-12717-7, Morrow, William & Co.) Morrow/Avon.
—Night Vision. 1992. 448p. mass mkt. 5.99 o.s.i (0-553-29762-7); 1991. 352p. 20.00 o.s.i (0-553-07796-1) Bantam Bks.
—Slashback. abr. ed. 1995. audio 16.95 o.p. (1-56100-415-4, 1375, Nova Audio Bks.); audio 57.25 o.p. (1-56100-246-1, 1049, Unabridged Library Editions) Brilliance Audio.
—Slashback. abr. ed. 2000. audio 7.95 (1-57815-144-9, 1103, Media Bks. Audio Publishing) Media Bks., L. L. C.
—Slashback. 1995. pap. 5.99 o.p. (0-380-72162-7, Avon Bks.) Morrow/Avon.
—Slashback: A Jake Lassiter Novel. 1995. 350p. 22.00 o.p. (0-688-12718-5, Morrow, William & Co.) Morrow/Avon.
—To Speak for the Dead. 1991. 400p. mass mkt. 5.99 o.s.i (0-553-29172-6) Bantam Bks.
Levine, Paul J. To Speak for the Dead. 1990. 304p. 17.95 o.s.i (0-553-05747-2) Bantam Bks.
Lewis, Roy H. A Blurred Reality. 1985. 192p. 12.95 o.p. (0-312-08725-X) St. Martin's Pr.
—Dwell in Danger. 1982. 192p. 10.95 o.p. (0-312-22286-6) St. Martin's Pr.
—Once Dying, Twice Dead. l.t. ed. 1985. 12.95 o.p. (0-8166-0110-0, Macmillan Reference USA) Gale Group.
—Once Dying, Twice Dead. 1984. 192p. 10.95 o.p. (0-312-58476-8) St. Martin's Pr.
—Premium on Death: An Eric Ward Novel. 1987. 208p. 13.95 o.p. (0-312-00019-7) St. Martin's Pr.
—The Salamander Chill. l.t. ed. 1991. 8.95 o.p. (0-7451-9504-0, 73); pap. 10.95 o.p. (1-55504-903-6, 359) BBC Audiobooks America.
—The Salamander Chill. 1988. 192p. 14.95 o.p. (0-312-02637-4, Saint Martin's Minotaur) St. Martin's Pr.
Lodge, Marc. Within the Bounds. 1994. 336p. mass mkt. 5.99 o.s.i (0-425-14457-7) Berkley Publishing Group.
—Within the Bounds. 1993. 352p. 22.95 o.p. (0-399-13881-1, G. P. Putnam's Sons) Penguin Group (USA) Inc.
Margolin, Phillip, ed. The Last Innocent Man. 1995. 352p. reprint ed. mass mkt. 7.99 (0-553-56979-1) Bantam Bks.
—The Last Innocent Man. unabr. ed. 1996. audio 48.00 Books on Tape, Inc.
—The Last Innocent Man. 2002. lib. bdg. 29.95 (1-58547-247-6, Premier) Ctr. Point Large Print.
—The Last Innocent Man. 1981. 252p. 11.95 o.p. (0-316-54617-8) Little Brown & Co.
—The Last Innocent Man. l.t. ed. 1999. (Charnwood Large Print Ser.). 352p. 31.99 o.p. (0-7089-9071-1, Ulverscroft) Thorpe, F. A. Pubs. GBR. *Dist:* Ulverscroft Large Print Bks., Ltd., Ulverscroft Large Print Canada, Ltd.
Marson, Bonnie. Sleeping with Schubert: A Novel. 2004. 400p. 21.95 (1-4000-6041-9) Random Hse., Inc.
Marston, Edward. The Dragons of Archenfield. 1996. mass mkt. 5.99 o.s.i (0-449-22545-3, Fawcett) Ballantine Bks.
—The Dragons of Archenfield. 1995. 256p. 14.30 o.p. (0-312-13472-X, Saint Martin's Minotaur) St. Martin's Pr.
—The Hawks of Delamere. 2000. (Domesday Bks.: Vol. 7). (Illus.). 246p. 22.95 (0-312-20948-7, Saint Martin's Minotaur) St. Martin's Pr.
—The Lions of the North. 1996. 227p. 21.95 (0-312-14671-X, Saint Martin's Minotaur) St. Martin's Pr.
—The Ravens of Blackwater. 1996. mass mkt. 5.99 o.s.i (0-449-22410-4, Fawcett) Ballantine Bks.
—The Ravens of Blackwater. 1994. 20.95 o.p. (0-312-11330-7, Saint Martin's Minotaur) St. Martin's Pr.
—The Serpents of Harbledown: A Novel. 1998. (Domesday Bks.: Vol. 5). 288p. 22.95 (0-312-18021-7, Saint Martin's Minotaur) St. Martin's Pr.
—The Stallions of Woodstock. 1998. (Domesday Bks.: Vol. 6). 288p. 22.95 (0-312-20021-8, Saint Martin's Minotaur) St. Martin's Pr.
—The Wolves of Savernake. 1995. mass mkt. 5.99 o.s.i (0-449-22310-8, Fawcett) Ballantine Bks.
—The Wolves of Savernake. 1993. 256p. 19.95 o.p. (0-312-09942-8, Saint Martin's Minotaur) St. Martin's Pr.
Martel, John. The Alternate. 1999. 480p. 24.95 o.p. (0-525-94487-7) Dutton/Plume.
—Billy Strobe. 2001. 400p. 25.95 o.p. (0-525-94618-7, Dutton) Dutton/Plume.
—Billy Strobe. 2002. 544p. reprint ed. mass mkt. 7.99 (0-451-20668-1, Signet Bks.) NAL.
Martini, Steve. The Attorney. 2001. 448p. mass mkt. 7.99 (0-515-13004-4, Jove) Berkley Publishing Group.
—The Attorney. 2000. 448p. 25.95 o.s.i (0-399-14536-2) Penguin Group (USA) Inc.
—The Attorney. l.t. ed. 2000. (Basic Ser.). 613p. 31.95 (0-7862-2433-9) Thorndike Pr.
—Compelling Evidence. 1993. 448p. mass mkt. 7.99 (0-515-11039-6, Jove) Berkley Publishing Group.
—Compelling Evidence. l.t. ed. 1992. (General Ser.). 608p. lib. bdg. 23.95 o.p. (0-8161-5548-8, Macmillan Reference USA) Gale Group.
—Compelling Evidence. abr. ed. 1993. 15.95 o.p. (1-55800-613-3) NewStar Media, Inc.
—Compelling Evidence. 1992. 384p. 21.95 o.p. (0-399-13712-2, G. P. Putnam's Sons) Penguin Group (USA) Inc.
—Compelling Evidence. l.t. ed. 1993. (G. K. Hall Large Print Book Ser.). 657p. pap. 19.95 (0-8161-5549-6) Thorndike Pr.
—Compelling Evidence & Prime Witness. abr. ed. 1998. (Steve Martini Collections). audio 25.00 (0-7871-1759-5, Dove Audio) NewStar Media, Inc.
—The Judge. 1996. 512p. mass mkt. 6.99 o.s.i (0-515-11915-6, Jove); reprint ed. pap. 7.99 (0-515-11964-4) Berkley Publishing Group.
—The Judge. 1996. 400p. 23.95 o.p. (0-399-14043-3, G. P. Putnam's Sons) Penguin Group (USA) Inc.

Occupations

—The Judge, unabr. ed. audio 85.00 (*0-7887-0466-4*, 94659E7) Recorded Bks., LLC.
—The Judge. abr. ed. 1996. audio 24.00 (*0-671-53453-X*); Set. 1998. audio 12.98 (*0-671-58209-7*, 493061) Simon & Schuster Audio. (Simon & Schuster Audioworks).
—The Judge. l.t. ed. 1996. (Thorndike/G. K. Hall Paperback Bestsellers Ser.). 567p. pap. 27.95 (*0-7838-1611-1*); lib. bdg. 28.95 (*0-7838-1610-3*) Thorndike Pr.
—Prime Witness. 1994. 416p. mass mkt. 7.99 (*0-515-11264-X*, Jove) Berkley Publishing Group.
—Prime Witness. l.t. ed. 590p. 1994. 19.95 o.p. (*0-8161-5870-3*); 1993. 23.95 o.p. (*0-8161-5869-X*) Gale Group. (Macmillan Reference USA).
—Prime Witness. abr. ed. 1993. audio 16.95 o.p. (*1-55800-813-6*, 391400) NewStar Media, Inc.
—Prime Witness. 1993. 384p. 21.95 o.p. (*0-399-13802-1*, G. P. Putnam's Sons) Penguin Group (USA) Inc.
—Undue Influence. 480p. 1995. mass mkt. 7.99 (*0-515-11605-X*); 1996. pap. 6.99 o.s.i (*0-515-12072-3*) Berkley Publishing Group. (Jove).
—Undue Influence. l.t. ed. 1996. 567p. 19.95 o.p. (*0-7838-1129-2*); 1994. 714p. lib. bdg. 25.95 o.p. (*0-7838-1128-4*) Gale Group. (Macmillan Reference USA).
—Undue Influence. 1994. 400p. 22.95 o.p. (*0-399-13932-X*) Penguin Group (USA) Inc.
—Undue Influence, unabr. ed. 1995. audio 85.00 (*0-7887-0190-8*, 94425E7) Recorded Bks., LLC.
—Undue Influence. abr. ed. 1994. audio 17.00 (*0-671-89520-6*); Set. 1998. audio 9.98 (*0-671-58129-5*, 391836) Simon & Schuster Audio. (Simon & Schuster Audioworks).
—Undue Influence, Compelling Evidence, Prime Witness. 1995. 20.97 o.s.i (*0-515-11795-1*, Jove) Berkley Publishing Group.
McBain, Ed, pseud. Beauty & the Beast. unabr. ed. 1985. (Matthew Hope Ser.). audio 42.00 (*0-7366-1034-0*, 1964) Books on Tape, Inc.
—Beauty & the Beast. 1983. 228p. o.p. (*0-03-062198-4*) Holt, Henry & Co.
—Beauty & the Beast. 1988. 256p. mass mkt. 3.99 o.s.i (*1-55817-662-4*); mass mkt. 3.95 o.p. (*1-55817-134-7*) Kensington Publishing Corp. (Pinnacle Bks.).
—Beauty & the Beast. 1994. 224p. mass mkt. 5.99 o.s.i (*0-446-60131-4*) Warner Bks., Inc.
—Cinderella. unabr. ed. 1992. (Matthew Hope Ser.). audio 48.00 (*0-7366-2245-4*, 3035) Books on Tape, Inc.
—Cinderella. 1986. (Matthew Hope Ser.). 256p. (J). o.p. (*0-03-004959-8*) Holt, Henry & Co.
—Cinderella. 1993. 15.95 o.p. (*1-55800-396-7*); audio 8.95 o.p. (*1-55800-494-7*, Dove Audio) NewStar Media, Inc.
—Cinderella. 272p. 1994. mass mkt. 5.99 o.s.i (*0-446-60134-9*); 1989. mass mkt. 4.99 (*0-445-40898-7*, Mysterious Pr. Paperback Bks.); 1987. mass mkt. 3.95 o.s.i (*0-445-40618-6*) Warner Bks., Inc.
—Gladly the Cross-Eyed Bear. unabr. ed. 1997. (Matthew Hope Ser.). audio 48.00 (*0-913369-38-1*, 4214) Books on Tape, Inc.
—Gladly the Cross-Eyed Bear, Set. abr. ed. 1996. (Matthew Hope Mystery Ser.). 3p. audio 16.99 (*0-88646-423-4*, 394439) Durkin Hayes Publishing Ltd.
—Gladly the Cross-Eyed Bear. l.t. ed. 1996. (G. K. Hall Core Ser.). 424p. 25.95 (*0-7838-1899-8*, Macmillan Reference USA) Gale Group.
—Gladly the Cross-Eyed Bear. l.t. ed. 1998. (Paperback Bestsellers Ser.). 424p. pap. 25.95 (*0-7838-1900-5*) Thorndike Pr.
—Gladly the Cross-Eyed Bear. (Matthew Hope Novels Ser.). 336p. 1998. mass mkt. 6.50 o.s.i (*0-446-60494-1*); 1996. 22.50 o.p. (*0-446-51989-8*) Warner Bks., Inc.
—Goldilocks. 1979. pap. 2.25 o.p. (*0-553-12158-8*, 13158-3) Bantam Bks.
—Goldilocks. unabr. ed. 1985. (Matthew Hope Ser.). audio 36.00 (*0-7366-1032-4*, 1962) Books on Tape, Inc.
—Goldilocks. 224p. 1988. mass mkt. 3.95 o.s.i (*1-55817-108-8*); 1985. pap. 3.50 o.p. (*0-523-42452-3*) Kensington Publishing Corp. (Pinnacle Bks.).
—Goldilocks. 1978. 8.95 o.p. (*0-87795-177-2*, Morrow, William & Co.) Morrow/Avon.
—Goldilocks. 1996. 224p. mass mkt. 5.99 o.s.i (*0-446-60305-8*) Warner Bks., Inc.
—The House That Jack Built. unabr. ed. 1992. (Matthew Hope Ser.). audio 48.00 (*0-7366-2177-6*, 2974) Books on Tape, Inc.
—The House That Jack Built. l.t. ed. 1989. (General Ser.). 320p. 13.95 o.p. (*0-8161-4934-8*); lib. bdg. 20.95 (*0-8161-4758-2*) Gale Group. (Macmillan Reference USA).
—The House That Jack Built. 1988. 16.95 o.p. (*0-8050-0787-3*) Holt, Henry & Co.
—The House That Jack Built. 256p. 1994. mass mkt. 5.99 o.s.i (*0-446-60136-5*); 1989. mass mkt. 4.99 (*0-445-40623-2*, Mysterious Pr. Paperback Bks.) Warner Bks., Inc.
—Jack & the Beanstalk. unabr. ed. 1985. (Matthew Hope Ser.). audio 48.00 Books on Tape, Inc.
—Jack & the Beanstalk. 1984. o.p. (*0-03-062197-6*) Holt, Henry & Co.
—Jack & the Beanstalk. 288p. 1992. mass mkt. 3.99 o.s.i (*1-55817-663-2*); 1985. pap. 3.50 o.p. (*0-523-42559-7*) Kensington Publishing Corp. (Pinnacle Bks.).
—Jack & the Beanstalk. 1994. 256p. mass mkt. 5.99 (*0-446-60132-2*) Warner Bks., Inc.
—The Last Best Hope, unabr. ed. 1998. (Matthew Hope Ser.). audio 40.00 (*0-7366-4215-3*, 4713) Books on Tape, Inc.
—The Last Best Hope. l.t. ed. 1998. (Basic Ser.). 397p. pap. 29.95 (*0-7862-1605-0*) Thorndike Pr.
—The Last Best Hope. (Matthew Hope Novels Ser.). 1999. 304p. mass mkt. 7.50 o.s.i (*0-446-60673-1*); 1998. 320p. 24.00 o.p. (*0-446-51990-1*) Warner Bks., Inc.
—Mary, Mary. l.t. ed. 1993. 24.95 o.p. (*0-7927-1662-0*); pap. 22.95 o.p. (*0-7927-1661-2*) BBC Audiobooks America.
—Mary, Mary. unabr. ed. 1993. (Matthew Hope Ser.). audio 72.00 (*0-7366-2480-5*, 3242) Books on Tape, Inc.
—Mary, Mary. unabr. ed. 1993. 73.25 o.p. incl. audio (*1-56100-137-6*, 1280, Unabridged Library Editions); audio 23.95 o.p. (*1-56100-508-8*, 173, Bookcassette) Brilliance Audio.
—Mary, Mary. 384p. 1994. mass mkt. 5.99 o.s.i (*0-446-60054-7*); 1993. 19.95 o.s.i (*0-446-51738-0*) Warner Bks., Inc.
—Puss in Boots. 1987. 15.95 o.p. (*0-8050-0371-1*) Holt, Henry & Co.
—Puss in Boots. 1994. 224p. mass mkt. 5.99 o.s.i (*0-446-60135-7*); 1988. mass mkt. 4.95 o.s.i (*0-445-40621-6*) Warner Bks., Inc.
—Rumpelstiltskin. 1985. 240p. mass mkt. 4.95 o.s.i (*0-345-33149-4*); 1982. mass mkt. 2.50 o.p. (*0-345-30436-5*) Ballantine Bks.
—Rumpelstiltskin. 1981. (Matthew Hope Mystery Ser.). 12.95 o.p. (*0-670-61059-3*) Viking Penguin.
—Rumpelstiltskin. 1994. 240p. mass mkt. 5.99 o.s.i (*0-446-60130-6*) Warner Bks., Inc.
—Snow White & Rose Red. unabr. ed. 1995. audio 54.95 (*0-7451-6155-3*, CAB 162) BBC Audiobooks America.
—Snow White & Rose Red. unabr. ed. 1986. (Matthew Hope Ser.). audio 48.00 (*0-7366-1036-7*, 1966) Books on Tape, Inc.
—Snow White & Rose Red. 1985. o.p. (*0-03-002603-2*) Holt, Henry & Co.
—Snow White & Rose Red. abr. ed. 1993. audio 15.95 o.p. (*1-55800-256-1*, Dove Audio) NewStar Media, Inc.
—Snow White & Rose Red. 256p. 1994. mass mkt. 5.99 o.p. (*0-446-60133-0*); 1986. reprint ed. mass mkt. 4.99 o.s.i (*0-445-40513-9*) Warner Bks., Inc.
—There Was a Little Girl. l.t. ed. 1995. 424p. pap. 19.95 o.p. (*0-7838-1181-0*); 480p. 24.95 o.p. (*0-7838-1180-2*) Gale Group. (Macmillan Reference USA).
—There Was a Little Girl. 1995. 352p. mass mkt. 6.50 (*0-446-60214-0*); 1994. 336p. 21.95 o.s.i (*0-446-51739-9*) Warner Bks., Inc.
—Three Blind Mice. unabr. ed. 1991. (Matthew Hope Ser.). audio 56.00 (*0-7366-1963-1*, 2784) Books on Tape, Inc.
—Three Blind Mice. l.t. ed. 1991. (General Ser.). 396p. lib. bdg. 21.95 (*0-8161-5169-5*, Macmillan Reference USA) Gale Group.
—Three Blind Mice. abr. ed. (Super Sound Buy, Dove Ser.). 1994. audio 8.99 o.p. (*0-7871-0233-4*); 1993. 15.95 o.p. (*1-55800-392-4*, 41460) NewStar Media, Inc.
—Three Blind Mice. 1994. 304p. mass mkt. 5.99 o.s.i (*0-446-60137-3*); 1991. mass mkt. 4.99 o.s.i (*0-446-40035-1*) Warner Bks., Inc.
McInerny, Ralph. Body & Soil: An Andrew Broom Mystery. 1990. mass mkt. (*0-373-26063-6*, Harlequin Bks.) Harlequin Enterprises, Ltd.
—Body & Soil: An Andrew Broom Mystery. 1989. 224p. 17.95 o.p. (*0-689-12036-2*, Scribner) Simon & Schuster.
—Cause & Effect: An Andrew Broom Mystery. 1990. mass mkt. (*0-373-26046-6*, Harlequin Bks.) Harlequin Enterprises, Ltd.
—Cause & Effect: An Andrew Broom Mystery. 1987. 224p. 15.95 o.p. (*0-689-11894-5*, Scribner) Simon & Schuster.
—Frigor Mortis. l.t. ed. 1991. 19.95 o.p. (*0-7927-0733-8*, CH017); pap. 17.95 o.p. (*0-7927-0734-6*, CS0121) BBC Audiobooks America.
—Frigor Mortis. 1991. reprint ed. mass mkt. (*0-373-26080-6*, Harlequin Bks.) Harlequin Enterprises, Ltd.
—Frigor Mortis. 1989. 288p. 18.95 o.s.i (*0-689-12081-8*, Scribner) Simon & Schuster.
—Heirs & Parents: An Andrew Broom Mystery. 2000. (Andrew Broom Mysteries Ser.). 240p. 23.95 (*0-312-20311-X*, Saint Martin's Minotaur) St. Martin's Pr.
—Law & Ardor: An Andrew Broom Mystery. 1995. 256p. 21.00 (*0-684-80462-X*, Scribner) Simon & Schuster.
—Mom & Dead: An Andrew Broom Mystery. 1994. 256p. 20.00 o.p. (*0-689-12181-4*, Scribner) Simon & Schuster.
—Savings & Loam: An Andrew Broom Mystery. 1992. (WWL Mystery Ser.: No. 91). mass mkt. (*0-373-26091-1*, 1-26091-8, Harlequin Bks.) Harlequin Enterprises, Ltd.
—Savings & Loam: An Andrew Broom Mystery. 1993. 2.99 o.p. (*0-517-09633-1*) Random Hse. Value Publishing.
—Savings & Loam: An Andrew Broom Mystery. 1990. 224p. 17.95 o.s.i (*0-689-12037-0*, Scribner) Simon & Schuster.
Meador, Daniel J. Unforgotten. 1999. 400p. 25.00 (*1-56554-349-1*) Pelican Publishing Co., Inc.
Meek, M. R. D. A House to Die For. l.t. ed. 2000. (Dales Large Print Ser.). 368p. pap. 20.99 o.p. (*1-84262-044-4*) Dales Large Print Bks. GBR. *Dist:* Ulverscroft Large Print Bks., Ltd., Ulverscroft Large Print Canada, Ltd.
—A House to Die For. l.t. ed. 2000. pap. 20.99 (*1-84137-069-X*) Magna Large Print Bks. GBR. *Dist:* Ulverscroft Large Print Bks., Ltd.
—A House to Die For. 1999. 219p. 25.00 (*0-7278-5442-9*) Severn Hse. Pubs., Ltd.
—The Vanishing Point. 2002. 256p. 26.99 (*0-7278-5840-8*) Severn Hse. Pubs., Ltd.
Meltzer, Brad. Dead Even. 2003. audio 14.95 (*0-06-053571-7*); 1998. 6p. pap. 25.00 o.s.i incl. audio (*0-694-51991-X*) HarperTrade. (HarperAudio).
—Dead Even. 1998. 368p. 25.00 o.p. (*0-688-15090-X*, Morrow, William & Co.) Morrow/Avon.
—Dead Even. 1999. 544p. reprint ed. mass mkt. 7.99 (*0-446-60733-9*) Warner Bks., Inc.
Meredith, Doris R. Murder by Deception. 1989. mass mkt. 4.99 o.s.i (*0-345-35243-2*) Ballantine Bks.
—Murder by Deception. 2004. 288p. mass mkt. 6.99 (*0-7434-7999-8*) ibooks, Inc.
—Murder by Impulse. 1987. 288p. mass mkt. 4.99 o.s.i (*0-345-34671-8*) Ballantine Bks.
—Murder by Impulse. Holland, Steve, ed. abr. ed. 1993. audio 24.95 (*1-883268-05-2*) Spellbinders, Inc.
—Murder by Impulse. 2003. 288p. mass mkt. 6.99 (*0-7434-7968-8*) ibooks, Inc.
—Murder by Masquerade. 1990. (John Lloyd Branson Ser.). 256p. mass mkt. 4.99 o.s.i (*0-345-35986-0*) Ballantine Bks.
—Murder by Masquerade. Holland, Stephen, ed. abr. ed. 1994. audio 24.95 (*1-883268-11-7*) Spellbinders, Inc.
—Murder by Reference. 1991. 272p. mass mkt. 4.99 o.s.i (*0-345-36861-4*) Ballantine Bks.
—Murder by Reference. abr. ed. 1997. audio 25.00 (*1-883268-28-1*) Spellbinders, Inc.
—Murder by Sacrilege. 1993. mass mkt. 4.99 o.s.i (*0-345-37693-5*) Ballantine Bks.
Mesce, Bill, Jr. & Szilagyi, Steven G. The Advocate: A Novel of World War II. 2001. (Illus.). 416p. reprint ed. mass mkt. 6.50 (*0-553-58197-X*) Bantam Bks.
Millar, Margaret. Ask for Me Tomorrow. l.t. ed. 1989. (Atlantic Mystery Ser.). 265p. pap. 14.95 o.p. (*1-55504-738-6*, 833) BBC Audiobooks America.
—Ask for Me Tomorrow. (Library of Crime Classics). 1991. 184p. pap. 8.95 o.p. (*1-55882-115-5*); 1985. 179p. reprint ed. pap. 4.95 o.p. (*0-930330-15-3*) International Polygonics, Ltd.
—Ask for Me Tomorrow. 1978. pap. 1.50 o.p. (*0-380-01805-5*, 35618, Avon Bks.) Morrow/Avon.
—Mermaid. 1982. 317p. (*0-89340-543-4*) BBC Audiobooks America.
—Mermaid. 1991. (Library of Crime Classics). 216p. pap. 8.95 (*1-55882-114-7*) International Polygonics, Ltd.
—The Murder of Miranda. 22.95 (*0-89190-156-6*) Amereon, Ltd.
—The Murder of Miranda. l.t. ed. 1980. 459p. lib. bdg. 5.95 o.p. (*0-89340-283-4*, 56) BBC Audiobooks America.
—The Murder of Miranda. 1988. 240p. reprint ed. pap. 4.95 o.p. (*0-930330-95-1*, Library of Crime Classics) International Polygonics, Ltd.
—The Murder of Miranda. 1979. 240p. 8.95 o.p. (*0-394-50509-3*) Random Hse., Inc.
Minds Eye Staff. Rumpole 2. 14.95 (*0-559-35014-7*) Penguin Group (USA) Inc.
Mishima, Yukio. The Temple of Dawn. Saunders, E. Dale & Seigle, Cecilia S., trs. 1990. (Sea of Fertility Ser.: Vol. 3). 352p. pap. 14.00 (*0-679-72242-4*, Vintage) Knopf Publishing Group.
Mortimer, John. The Best of Rumpole. 1994. (Rumpole Ser.). 288p. reprint ed. pap. 14.00 (*0-14-017684-5*, Penguin Bks.) Penguin Group (USA) Inc.
—The Best of Rumpole. 1993. (Rumpole Ser.). 288p. 21.00 o.p. (*0-670-84978-2*, Viking) Viking Penguin.
—A First Rumpole Omnibus. 1984. (Crime Monthly Ser.). 560p. pap. 18.00 (*0-14-006768-X*, Penguin Bks.) Penguin Group (USA) Inc.
—Like Men Betrayed. l.t. ed. 1994. 21.95 o.p. (*0-7927-1930-1*); pap. 19.95 o.p. (*0-7927-1929-8*) BBC Audiobooks America.
—Rumpole a la Carte. l.t. ed. 1992. pap. 14.95 o.p. (*0-7927-1002-9*); 18.95 o.p. (*0-7927-1001-0*, E0023) BBC Audiobooks America.
—Rumpole a la Carte. unabr. ed. 1992. audio 49.95 (*0-7861-0351-5*, 1308) Blackstone Audio Bks., Inc.
—Rumpole a la Carte. unabr. ed. 1992. audio 4.99 (*0-88646-608-3*); Set. 1991. audio 16.99 (*0-88646-276-2*, LFP 7276) Durkin Hayes Publishing Ltd.
—Rumpole a la Carte. (Rumpole Ser.). 256p. 1993. pap. 10.00 o.p. (*0-14-017981-X*); 1991. reprint ed. pap. 12.00 (*0-14-015609-7*) Penguin Group (USA) Inc. (Penguin Bks.).
—Rumpole a la Carte. 1990. (Rumpole Ser.). 256p. 18.95 o.p. (*0-670-83284-7*) Viking Penguin.
—Rumpole & the Age of Miracles. l.t. ed. 1995. pap. 19.95 o.p. (*0-7838-1188-8*, Macmillan Reference USA) Gale Group.
—Rumpole & the Age of Miracles. 1989. (Rumpole Ser.). 240p. pap. 10.95 o.s.i (*0-14-013116-7*, Penguin Bks.) Penguin Group (USA) Inc.
—Rumpole & the Age of Miracles. unabr. ed. 1988. audio 62.00 (*0-7887-3483-0*, 95892E7) Recorded Bks., LLC.
—Rumpole & the Age of Retirement. unabr. ed. 1994. audio 4.99 (*0-88646-700-4*) Durkin Hayes Publishing Ltd.
—Rumpole & the Angel of Death. unabr. ed. 1996. audio 49.95 (*0-7861-0974-2*, 1751) Blackstone Audio Bks., Inc.
—Rumpole & the Angel of Death. l.t. ed. 1996. 426p. lib. bdg. 22.95 o.p. (*0-7838-1794-0*, Macmillan Reference USA) Gale Group.
—Rumpole & the Angel of Death. 1997. 272p. reprint ed. pap. 9.95 o.s.i (*0-14-026314-4*) Penguin Group (USA) Inc.
—Rumpole & the Angel of Death. unabr. ed. 1996. (Rumpole of the Bailey Ser.: Vol. 7). audio 70.00 (*0-7887-0514-8*, 94708E7) Recorded Bks., LLC.
—Rumpole & the Angel of Death. 1996. 272p. 22.95 o.p. (*0-670-86451-X*); 2p. audio 16.95 (*0-14-086197-1*, Penguin AudioBooks) Viking Penguin.
—Rumpole & the Golden Thread. l.t. ed. 1993. pap. 16.95 o.p. (*0-7927-1370-2*); 1992. 18.95 o.p. (*0-7927-1371-0*) BBC Audiobooks America.
—Rumpole & the Golden Thread. unabr. ed. 1995. audio 49.95 (*0-7861-0855-X*, 1653) Blackstone Audio Bks., Inc.
—Rumpole & the Golden Thread. unabr. ed. 1991. (Rumpole of the Bailey Ser.: Vol. 5). audio 60.00 (*1-55690-451-7*, 91211E7) Recorded Bks., LLC.
—Rumpole & the Golden Thread. 1984. (Crime Ser.). 256p. pap. 5.95 o.p. (*0-14-006331-5*, Penguin Bks.); pap. 9.95 o.s.i (*0-14-025014-X*, Penguin Classics) Viking Penguin.
—Rumpole & the Judge's Elbow. unabr. ed. 1992. audio 5.99 (*0-88646-607-5*, PAC-7607) Durkin Hayes Publishing Ltd.
—Rumpole & the Man of God. abr. ed. 1996. (Paperback Audio Ser.). audio 9.99 (*0-88646-882-5*, 7882) Durkin Hayes Publishing Ltd.
—Rumpole & the Primrose Path. 2003. (Rumpole Ser.). 224p. 24.95 (*0-670-03146-1*, Viking) Viking Penguin.
—Rumpole & the Younger Generation. 1995. 64p. pap. 0.95 o.p. (*0-14-600006-4*) Penguin Group (USA) Inc.
—Rumpole at the Bar. abr. ed. 1989. audio 16.99 (*0-88646-238-X*, LFP 7238) Durkin Hayes Publishing Ltd.
—The Rumpole Collection, 2 bks., Set. deluxe ed. 1992. (Rumpole Ser.). pap. 22.00 o.p. (*0-14-095385-X*, Penguin Bks.) Penguin Group (USA) Inc.
—Rumpole for the Defence. l.t. ed. 1994. pap. 16.95 o.p. (*0-7927-1604-3*); 1993. 18.95 o.p. (*0-7927-1605-1*) BBC Audiobooks America.
—Rumpole for the Defence. unabr. ed. 1991. audio 39.95 (*0-7861-0236-5*, 1206) Blackstone Audio Bks., Inc.
—Rumpole for the Defence. 1984. 192p. pap. 9.95 o.s.i (*0-14-025013-1*) Penguin Group (USA) Inc.
—Rumpole for the Defence. unabr. ed. 1991. (Rumpole of the Bailey Ser.: Vol. 4). audio 51.00 (*1-55690-452-5*, 91108E7) Recorded Bks., LLC.
—Rumpole for the Defence. 1984. (Crime Monthly Ser.). 192p. pap. 5.95 o.p. (*0-14-006060-X*, Penguin Bks.) Viking Penguin.
—Rumpole for the Prosecution, Set. unabr. ed. 1992. audio 16.99 (*0-88646-283-5*, 7283) Durkin Hayes Publishing Ltd.
—Rumpole of the Bailey. 17.95 (*0-89190-275-9*) Amereon, Ltd.
—Rumpole of the Bailey. l.t. ed. 1993. (Eagle Large Print Ser.). 19.95 o.p. (*0-7927-1532-2*); pap. o.p. (*0-7927-1531-4*) BBC Audiobooks America.
—Rumpole of the Bailey, unabr. ed. 1991. audio 44.95 (*0-7861-0255-1*, 1223) Blackstone Audio Bks., Inc.

Occupations

—Rumpole of the Bailey. abr. ed. 1983. audio 16.99 (*0-88646-084-0*, TC-LFP 7110) Durkin Hayes Publishing Ltd.
—Rumpole of the Bailey. unabr. ed. 1993. (Rumpole of the Bailey Ser.: Vol. 1). audio 51.00 (*1-55690-920-9*, 93416E7) Recorded Bks., LLC.
—Rumpole of the Bailey. 1980. 208p. pap. 9.95 o.s.i (*0-14-025012-3*); pap. 5.95 o.p. (*0-14-004670-4*, Penguin Bks.) Viking Penguin.
—Rumpole on Trial. 1993. (Rumpole Ser.). 256p. reprint ed. pap. 10.00 o.s.i (*0-14-017510-5*, Penguin Bks.) Penguin Group (USA) Inc.
—Rumpole on Trial. 1992. (Rumpole Ser.). 256p. 21.00 o.p. (*0-670-84459-4*, Viking) Viking Penguin.
—Rumpole Rests His Case. 2002. 224p. 24.95 (*0-670-03139-9*, Viking) Viking Penguin.
—Rumpole Unabridged, Set. unabr. ed. lib. bdg. 29.99 incl. audio (*1-55204-723-7*, PAUB-024) Durkin Hayes Publishing Ltd.
—Rumpole's Last Case. unabr. ed. 1995. audio 44.95 (*0-7861-0801-0*, 1625) Blackstone Audio Bks., Inc.
—Rumpole's Last Case. abr. ed. 1988. audio 16.99 (*0-88646-233-9*, LFP 7233); 1993. audio 4.99 (*0-88646-652-0*) Durkin Hayes Publishing Ltd.
—Rumpole's Last Case. l.t. ed. 1988. (General Ser.). 393p. 18.95 o.p. (*0-8161-4660-8*, Macmillan Reference USA) Gale Group.
—Rumpole's Last Case. 140th ed. 1990. (Rumpole Ser.). 288p. pap. 10.95 o.s.i (*0-14-012695-3*, Penguin Bks.) Penguin Group (USA) Inc.
—Rumpole's Last Case. unabr. ed. 1994. (Rumpole of the Bailey Ser.: Vol. 6). audio 60.00 (*0-7887-0057-X*, 94256E7) Recorded Bks., LLC.
—Rumpole's Last Case. 1988. (Rumpole Ser.). 288p. pap. 3.95 o.p. (*0-14-010447-X*, Penguin Bks.) Viking Penguin.
—Rumpole's Return. 18.95 (*0-89190-277-5*) Amereon, Ltd.
—Rumpole's Return, Set. abr. ed. 1990. audio 16.99 (*0-88646-162-6*, 7163) Durkin Hayes Publishing Ltd.
—Rumpole's Return. unabr. ed. 1991. (Rumpole of the Bailey Ser.: Vol. 3). audio 35.00 (*1-55690-453-3*, 91102E7) Recorded Bks., LLC.
—Rumpole's Return. 1982. 160p. pap. 9.95 o.s.i (*0-14-024698-3*, Penguin Classics); pap. 6.00 o.p. (*0-14-005571-1*, Penguin Bks.) Viking Penguin.
—The Second Rumpole Omnibus: Rumpole & the Golden Thread, Rumpole for the Defence & Rumpole's Last Case. 1988. (Rumpole Ser.). 672p. pap. 16.95 (*0-14-008958-6*, Penguin Bks.) Penguin Group (USA) Inc.
—The Second Rumpole Omnibus: Rumpole & the Golden Thread, Rumpole for the Defence & Rumpole's Last Case. 1987. (Rumpole Ser.). 672p. 18.95 o.p. (*0-670-81125-4*) Viking Penguin.
—The Third Rumpole Omnibus: Rumpole a la Carte, Rumpole on Trial, Rumpole & the Angel of Death. 150th ed. 1998. (Rumpole Ser.). 752p. pap. 18.00 (*0-14-025741-1*, Penguin Bks.) Penguin Group (USA) Inc.
—The Trials of Rumpole. 20.95 (*0-89190-276-7*) Amereon, Ltd.
—The Trials of Rumpole. unabr. ed. 1993. audio 39.95 (*0-7861-0422-8*, 1374) Blackstone Audio Bks., Inc.
—The Trials of Rumpole. abr. ed. 1986. audio 16.99 (*0-88646-118-9*, TC-LFP 7118) Durkin Hayes Publishing Ltd.
—The Trials of Rumpole. unabr. ed. 1993. (Rumpole of the Bailey Ser.: Vol. 2). audio 51.00 (*1-55690-825-3*, 93126E7) Recorded Bks., LLC.
—The Trials of Rumpole. 1981. 208p. pap. 9.95 o.s.i (*0-14-024697-5*); pap. 6.00 o.p. (*0-14-005162-7*) Viking Penguin. (Penguin Bks.).
Nava, Michael. The Burning Plain. 1999. 432p. mass mkt. 5.99 o.s.i (*0-553-58085-X*) Bantam Bks.
—The Burning Plain. 1998. 240p. 23.95 o.p. (*0-399-14310-6*, G. P. Putnam's Sons) Penguin Group (USA) Inc.
—Death of Friends. 1996. 288p. 22.95 o.p. (*0-399-13977-X*, G. P. Putnam's Sons) Penguin Group (USA) Inc.
—The Death of Friends. 1998. 256p. reprint ed. mass mkt. 5.99 o.s.i (*0-553-57763-8*) Bantam Bks.
—Goldenboy. 1988. 216p. 5.95 o.p. (*1-55583-141-9*); 1996. 224p. reprint ed. pap. 10.00 o.p. (*1-55583-366-7*); 1991. 215p. reprint ed. pap. 8.95 o.p. (*1-55583-130-3*) Alyson Pubns.
—The Hidden Law. 1994. (Los Angeles Mysteries Ser.). 192p. mass mkt. 4.99 o.s.i (*0-345-38406-7*) Ballantine Bks.
—The Hidden Law. 1992. 288p. 19.00 o.p. (*0-06-016783-1*) HarperTrade.
—How Town. 1991. (Los Angeles Mysteries Ser.). 240p. mass mkt. 4.99 o.s.i (*0-345-36987-4*) Ballantine Bks.
—How Town. 1990. 224p. 16.95 o.p. (*0-06-016207-4*) HarperTrade.
—The Little Death. 165p. 1986. pap. 7.95 o.p. (*0-932870-96-1*); 1997. reprint ed. pap. 9.95 o.p. (*1-55583-388-8*) Alyson Pubns.
O'Brien, Kevin. The Next to Die. 2001. 416p. mass mkt. 6.99 (*0-7860-1237-4*, Pinnacle Bks.) Kensington Publishing Corp.
Parker, Barbara. Criminal Justice. 1997. 320p. 22.95 o.p. (*0-525-93977-6*) Dutton/Plume.
—Criminal Justice. l.t. ed. 1997. 26.95 (*1-56895-498-0*, Wheeler Publishing, Inc.) Gale Group.
—Criminal Justice. 1998. 448p. mass mkt. 6.99 (*0-451-18474-2*, Signet Bks.) NAL.
—Suspicion of Betrayal. 1999. 352p. 23.95 o.s.i (*0-525-94468-0*, Dutton Studio) Dutton/Plume.
—Suspicion of Betrayal. l.t. ed. 1999. (Mystery Ser.). 568p. 29.95 (*0-7862-2000-7*) Thorndike Pr.
—Suspicion of Deceit. 1998. 368p. 23.95 o.p. (*0-525-94401-X*) Dutton/Plume.
—Suspicion of Deceit. 1999. 432p. reprint ed. mass mkt. 6.99 (*0-451-19549-3*, Signet Bks.) NAL.
—Suspicion of Deceit. l.t. ed. 1998. (Cloak & Dagger Ser.). 615p. 26.95 o.p. (*0-7862-1460-0*) Thorndike Pr.
—Suspicion of Innocence. 344p. 4.98 o.p. (*0-8317-4569-X*) Smithmark Pubs., Inc.
Passaro, Vincent. Violence, Nudity, Adult Content: A Novel. 304p. 2002. 24.00 (*0-684-85726-X*); 2003. reprint ed. pap. 13.00 (*0-7432-3425-1*) Simon & Schuster. (Simon & Schuster).
Patterson, Richard North. Degree of Guilt. 1998. pap. 7.99 (*0-345-91454-6*); 1997. pap. 12.00 o.s.i (*0-345-41811-5*); 1992. mass mkt. o.s.i (*0-345-38408-3*); 1993. 544p. reprint ed. mass mkt. 7.99 (*0-345-38184-X*) Ballantine Bks.
—Degree of Guilt. unabr. collector's ed. 1994. audio 104.00 (*0-7366-2612-3*, 3354) Books on Tape, Inc.
—Degree of Guilt. unabr. ed. 1993. audio 16.00 o.s.i (*0-679-42131-9*); Set. 1994. audio 8.99 o.s.i (*0-679-43409-7*) Random Hse. Audio Publishing Group. (RH Audio).
—Degree of Guilt. l.t. ed. 1993. 25.00 o.s.i (*0-679-42211-0*) Random Hse., Inc.
—Eyes of a Child. 1998. pap. 7.99 (*0-345-91463-5*); 1995. 576p. mass mkt. 7.99 (*0-345-38613-2*); 1995. mass mkt. 6.99 o.s.i (*0-345-40007-0*); 1994. mass mkt. o.p. (*0-345-39526-3*) Ballantine Bks.
—Eyes of a Child. l.t. ed. 1995. pap. 23.00 o.s.i (*0-679-76031-8*) Random Hse., Inc.
—The Lasko Tangent. 1997. pap. 12.00 o.s.i (*0-345-41814-X*); 1994. mass mkt. 5.99 o.p. (*0-345-90128-2*); 1985. 368p. mass mkt. 7.99 (*0-345-32532-X*); 1980. mass mkt. 1.95 o.p. (*0-345-28705-3*) Ballantine Bks.
—The Lasko Tangent. l.t. ed. 2000. 11.95 (*1-56895-984-2*); 26.95 o.p. (*1-56895-830-7*) Gale Group. (Wheeler Publishing, Inc.).
—The Lasko Tangent. 1979. 9.95 o.p. (*0-393-01190-9*) Norton, W. W. & Co., Inc.
—The Lasko Tangent, Set. abr. ed. 1999. audio 8.99 o.s.i (*0-375-40571-2*, RH Audio) Random Hse. Audio Publishing Group.
Perison, Paul Eben. A Breach of Confidence. 2002. (Illus.). 304p. mass mkt. 6.99 o.s.i (*0-451-41028-9*, Onyx) NAL.
Phillips, Edward O. Buried on Sunday: A Geoffrey Chadwick Novel. 2000. 240p. pap. 11.99 (*1-896332-12-9*) Riverbank, Pr., The CAN. *Dist:* General Distribution Services, Inc.
—Buried on Sunday: A Geoffrey Chadwick Novel. 1988. 192p. 13.95 o.p. (*0-312-01742-1*, Saint Martin's Minotaur) St. Martin's Pr.
—Sunday's Child: A Geoffry Chadwick Novel. 2000. 280p. pap. 11.99 (*1-896332-07-2*) Riverbank, Pr., The CAN. *Dist:* General Distribution Services, Inc.
—Sunday's Child: A Geoffry Chadwick Novel. (Stonewall Inn Editions Ser.). 240p. 1988. pap. 7.95 o.p. (*0-312-02294-8*, Saint Martin's Griffin); 1987. 15.95 o.p. (*0-312-01097-4*) St. Martin's Pr.
Phillips, Scott. The Ice Harvest. 2000. 224p. 19.95 (*0-345-44018-8*, Ballantine Bks.) Ballantine Bks.
Pierce, Donna. A Secret of Color. l.t. ed. 1999. E-Book 14.99 incl. cd-rom (*1-929077-19-X*, Books OnScreen) PageFree Publishing, Inc.
Plain, Belva. Fortune's Hand. unabr. ed. 2000. audio 69.95 (*0-7540-0415-5*, CAB 1838);Set. 8p. audio compact disk 99.95 (*0-7540-5324-5*, CCD 015) Chivers Audio Bks. GBR. *Dist:* BBC Audiobooks America.
—Fortune's Hand. 2000. 432p. mass mkt. 7.99 (*0-440-22641-4*); 1999. mass mkt. 7.99 (*0-440-29575-0*) Dell Publishing.
—Fortune's Hand, Set. abr. ed. 1999. audio 25.00 Highsmith Inc.
—Fortune's Hand. abr. ed. 1999. audio Random Hse. Audio Publishing Group.
—Fortune's Hand. l.t. ed. 2000. (Thorndike/G. K. Hall Paperback Bestsellers Ser.). 519p. pap. 30.95 (*0-7862-2013-9*) Thorndike Pr.
—Fortune's Hand. 2000. (Illus.). 14.04 (*0-606-18103-2*) Turtleback Bks.
Pottinger, Stan. The Last Nazi. 2003. 352p. 24.95 (*0-312-27676-1*) St. Martin's Pr.
—The Last Nazi. l.t. ed. 2003. 598p. 29.95 (*0-7862-5956-6*) Thorndike Pr.
Reuland, Rob. Hollowpoint. 2001. E-Book 19.95 (*0-375-50698-5*) Random Hse., Inc.
Rice, Luanne. The Secret Hour. 2004. 432p. mass mkt. 7.50 (*0-553-58401-4*); 2003. 352p. 22.95 (*0-553-80224-0*) Bantam Bks.
—The Secret Hour. 2003. (Core Ser.). 482p. 31.95 (*0-7862-5371-1*) Thorndike Pr.
Roberts, Barrie. Crowner & Justice. 2002. 192p. 24.95 (*0-7490-0528-9*) Allison & Busby, Ltd. GBR. *Dist:* International Publishers Marketing.
Rodi, Robert. Drag Queen. 272p. 1996. pap. 12.95 o.s.i (*0-452-27344-7*, Plume); 1995. 21.95 o.p. (*0-525-93925-3*, Dutton) Dutton/Plume.
Sanders, Marcella. My Soul to Keep. 2003. 28p. mass mkt. 5.99 (*1-58314-281-9*) Kensington Publishing Corp.
Sawikin, Harvey. The Education of Rick Green, Esquire. 1995. 320p. 23.00 (*0-684-80363-1*, Simon & Schuster) Simon & Schuster.
Sawyer, Robert J. Illegal Alien. 1997. 304p. 21.95 o.s.i (*0-441-00476-8*); 1999. 320p. reprint ed. mass mkt. 5.99 o.s.i (*0-441-00592-6*) Ace Bks.
Simmons, Suzanne. Lip Service. 2001. 304p. mass mkt. 6.50 o.s.i (*0-312-97299-7*, 20-3464, St. Martin's Paperbacks) St. Martin's Pr.
Smith, Janet L. Practice to Deceive. 1993. (Northwest Mysteries Ser.). mass mkt. 4.99 o.s.i (*0-8041-0978-8*, Ivy Bks.) Ballantine Bks.
—Sea of Troubles. 1991. 224p. mass mkt. 4.99 o.s.i (*0-8041-0759-9*, Ivy Bks.) Ballantine Bks.
—Sea of Troubles. 1990. 197p. pap. 8.95 o.p. (*0-9602676-9-7*, Perseverance Pr.) Daniel, John & Co., Pubs.
—Sea of Troubles. 1990. 200p. (C). reprint ed. lib. bdg. 29.00 o.p. (*0-8095-4208-0*) Millefleurs.
—A Vintage Murder. 1995. mass mkt. 5.99 o.s.i (*0-8041-1385-8*, Ivy Bks.); 1994. 240p. 20.00 o.s.i (*0-449-90871-2*, Fawcett) Ballantine Bks.
Smith, Rosamond, pseud. Snake Eyes. 1992. 272p. 20.00 o.p. (*0-525-93404-9*, Abrahams, William Bks.) Dutton/Plume.
—Snake Eyes. 1993. 352p. reprint ed. mass mkt. 4.99 o.s.i (*0-451-40382-7*, Onyx) NAL.
Snow, C. P. The Malcontents. l.t. ed. 2003. (Dales Large Print Ser.). 336p. pap. 21.99 (*1-84262-220-X*) Dales Large Print Bks. GBR. *Dist:* Ulverscroft Large Print Bks., Ltd., Ulverscroft Large Print Canada, Ltd.
—The Malcontents. 2000. 220p. pap. 9.95 (*1-84232-433-0*) Midpoint Trade Bks., Inc.
Stewart, Mike. Sins of the Brother. 1999. 304p. 23.95 o.p. (*0-399-14537-0*, G. P. Putnam's Sons) Penguin Group (USA) Inc.
Stockley, Grif. Blind Judgment. 1999. (Gideon Page Mystery Ser.). 384p. mass mkt. 6.50 o.s.i (*0-06-101317-X*) HarperCollins Pubs.
—Blind Judgment. 1997. 21.50 (*0-684-81564-8*, Simon & Schuster) Simon & Schuster.
—Expert Testimony. 1994. pap. 5.99 o.p. (*0-8041-9832-2*); 1993. pap. 5.99 o.p. (*0-8041-9810-1*); 1992. mass mkt. 5.99 o.s.i (*0-8041-1094-8*) Ballantine Bks. (Ivy Bks.).
—Expert Testimony. 1991. 19.95 o.p. (*0-671-70920-8*) Summit Bks.
—Illegal Motion: A Gideon Page Mystery. 1997. 408p. mass mkt. 6.99 o.s.i (*0-449-18332-7*, Fawcett); 1996. mass mkt. 6.99 o.p. (*0-449-22557-7*, Fawcett); 1995. mass mkt. 5.99 o.s.i (*0-8041-1401-3*, Ivy Bks.) Ballantine Bks.
—Illegal Motion: A Gideon Page Mystery. 1995. 301p. 21.00 (*0-684-80355-0*, Simon & Schuster) Simon & Schuster.
—Probable Cause. 1993. (Southern Mysteries Ser.). mass mkt. 5.99 o.s.i (*0-8041-1133-2*, Ivy Bks.) Ballantine Bks.
—Probable Cause. 1992. 287p. 19.00 o.p. (*0-671-74601-4*, Simon & Schuster) Simon & Schuster.
—Religious Conviction. 1995. reprint ed. mass mkt. 5.99 o.s.i (*0-8041-1255-X*, Ivy Bks.) Ballantine Bks.
—Religious Conviction. 1994. 286p. 21.00 (*0-671-79869-3*, Simon & Schuster) Simon & Schuster.
Stream, Arnold C. Until Proven Guilty. 1992. 320p. mass mkt. 4.99 o.p. (*0-425-13373-7*) Berkley Publishing Group.
—Until Proven Guilty. 1991. 272p. 19.95 o.p. (*0-8128-4010-0*, Scarborough Hse.) Madison Bks., Inc.
Tanenbaum, Robert K. Act of Revenge. l.t. ed. 2001. (Large Print Book Ser.). 575p. 28.95 (*1-58724-025-4*, Wheeler Publishing, Inc.) Gale Group.
—Act of Revenge. 1999. 416p. o.p. (*0-06-019218-6*, HarperFlamingo) HarperCollins Pubs. Canada, Ltd.
—Act of Revenge. 2000. 544p. mass mkt. 7.50 (*0-06-109730-6*, HarperTorch) Morrow/Avon.
—Corruption of Blood. unabr. ed. 1998. (Butch Karp Mystery Ser.). audio 80.00 (*0-7366-4045-2*, 4544) Books on Tape, Inc.
—Corruption of Blood. 1995. 368p. 22.95 o.p. (*0-525-93870-2*, Dutton) Dutton/Plume.
—Corruption of Blood. 1996. 416p. mass mkt. 7.99 (*0-451-18196-4*, Signet Bks.) NAL.
—Depraved Indifference. 1989. 18.95 o.p. (*0-453-00679-5*); 1990. 400p. reprint ed. mass mkt. 7.99 (*0-451-16842-9*, Signet Bks.) NAL.
—Falsely Accused. unabr. ed. 1998. (Butch Karp Mystery Ser.). audio 56.00 (*0-7366-4026-6*, 452511.95) Books on Tape, Inc.
—Falsely Accused. 1997. 448p. mass mkt. 7.99 (*0-451-19000-9*, Signet Bks.) NAL.
—Immoral Certainty. unabr. ed. 1997. (Butch Karp Mystery Ser.). audio 64.00 (*0-7366-3689-7*, 4368) Books on Tape, Inc.
—Immoral Certainty. 1991. 304p. 18.95 o.p. (*0-525-24941-9*, Dutton) Dutton/Plume.
—Immoral Certainty. 1992. 400p. reprint ed. mass mkt. 7.99 (*0-451-17186-1*, Signet Bks.) NAL.
—Irresistible Impulse. unabr. ed. 1998. (Butch Karp Mystery Ser.). audio 64.00 (*0-7366-4134-3*, 4639) Books on Tape, Inc.
—Irresistible Impulse. 1997. 352p. 24.95 o.p. (*0-525-94310-2*) Dutton/Plume.
—Irresistible Impulse. 1998. 445p. mass mkt. 6.99 (*0-451-19261-3*, Signet Bks.) NAL.
—Justice Denied. unabr. ed. 1997. (Butch Karp Mystery Ser.). audio 64.00 (*0-7366-3688-9*, 4367) Books on Tape, Inc.
—Justice Denied. 1994. 320p. 18.95 o.p. (*0-525-93814-1*) Dutton/Plume.
—Justice Denied. abr. ed. 1994. pap. 16.00 o.p. incl. audio (*0-453-00903-4*, 25024-33894) Penguin/HighBridge.
—Material Witness. unabr. ed. 1997. (Butch Karp Mystery Ser.). audio 64.00 (*0-7366-3687-0*, 4366) Books on Tape, Inc.
—Material Witness. 1993. 320p. 20.00 o.p. (*0-525-93579-7*, Dutton) Dutton/Plume.
—Material Witness. 1994. 416p. mass mkt. 7.99 (*0-451-18020-8*, Signet Bks.) NAL.
—No Lesser Plea. 1988. 368p. reprint ed. mass mkt. 7.99 (*0-451-15496-7*, Signet Bks.) NAL.
—No Lesser Plea. 1987. 17.95 o.p. (*0-531-09783-8*, Watts, Franklin) Scholastic Library Publishing.
—Reckless Endangerment. unabr. ed. 1999. (Butch Karp Mystery Ser.). audio 88.00 (*0-7366-4351-6*, 4828) Books on Tape, Inc.
—Reckless Endangerment. abr. ed. 1998. audio 17.95 o.p. (*1-56740-784-6*, 443, Nova Audio Bks.); audio 26.95 (*1-56740-059-0*, 10, Bookcassette); audio 73.25 o.p. (*1-56740-588-6*, 1001) Brilliance Audio.
—Reckless Endangerment. 1998. 352p. 23.95 o.p. (*0-525-94347-1*) Dutton/Plume.
—Reckless Endangerment. 1999. 448p. reprint ed. mass mkt. 7.99 (*0-451-19328-8*, Signet Bks.) NAL.
—Reversible Error. unabr. ed. 1997. (Butch Karp Mystery Ser.). audio 56.00 (*0-7366-3686-2*, 4365) Books on Tape, Inc.
—Reversible Error. 1992. 288p. 20.00 o.p. (*0-525-93423-5*, Dutton) Dutton/Plume.
—Reversible Error. 1993. 448p. reprint ed. mass mkt. 7.99 (*0-451-17519-0*, Signet Bks.) NAL.
Tapply, William G. Client Privilege. l.t. ed. 1991. 23.95 o.p. (*0-7927-0888-1*, CH099); pap. 21.95 o.p. (*0-7927-0889-X*, CS0199) BBC Audiobooks America.
—Client Privilege. 1991. 288p. mass mkt. 4.50 o.s.i (*0-440-20866-1*) Dell Publishing.
—Close to the Bone: A Brady Coyne Mystery. unabr. ed. 2000. audio 49.95 (*0-7927-2212-4*, CSL 101) Chivers Audio Bks. GBR. *Dist:* BBC Audiobooks America.
—Cutter's Run. l.t. ed. 1999. pap. 24.95 (*1-56895-706-8*, Wheeler Publishing, Inc.) Gale Group.
—Cutter's Run. 1998. (Brady Coyne Mysteries Ser.). 274p. 23.95 (*0-312-18561-8*, Saint Martin's Minotaur) St. Martin's Pr.
—Dead Meat. l.t. ed. 1991. pap. 8.95 o.p. (*1-55504-857-9*, 162); 1989. 15.95 o.p. (*0-7451-9473-7*, 546) BBC Audiobooks America.
—Dead Meat. 1988. 240p. mass mkt. 3.50 o.s.i (*0-345-34730-7*) Ballantine Bks.
—Dead Meat: A Brady Coyne Mystery. 1987. 14.95 o.p. (*0-684-18682-9*, Macmillan Reference USA) Gale Group.
—Dead Winter. 1990. 240p. mass mkt. 3.95 o.s.i (*0-440-20566-2*); 1989. 16.95 o.s.i (*0-440-50171-7*, Delacorte Pr.) Dell Publishing.
—Dead Winter. l.t. ed. 1991. (General Ser.). 350p. lib. bdg. 18.95 o.p. (*0-8161-5003-6*, Macmillan Reference USA) Gale Group.
—Dead Winter. l.t. ed. 1991. (Magna Large Print Ser.). 318p. o.p. (*0-7505-0126-X*) Magna Large Print Bks. GBR. *Dist:* Ulverscroft Large Print Canada, Ltd.
—Death at Charity's Point. l.t. ed. 1991. pap. 10.95 o.p. (*0-7927-0109-7*, C0136) BBC Audiobooks America.
—Death at Charity's Point. 1985. 240p. mass mkt. 2.95 o.s.i (*0-345-32014-X*) Ballantine Bks.
—Death at Charity's Point. 1984. 224p. 12.95 o.p. (*0-684-18056-1*, Macmillan Reference USA) Gale Group.
—Death at Charity's Point. 1997. (Missing Mysteries Ser.: Vol. 2). 244p. reprint ed. pap. 7.95 (*1-890208-02-7*) Poisoned Pen Pr.

—The Dutch Blue Error. 1985. 224p. mass mkt. 2.95 o.s.i (*0-345-32341-6*) Ballantine Bks.
—The Dutch Blue Error. 1984. 240p. 12.95 o.s.i (*0-684-18213-0*, Macmillan Reference USA) Gale Group.
—Dutch Blue Error. l.t. ed. 1986. 321p. 16.95 o.p. (*0-89340-937-5*) BBC Audiobooks America.
—A Fine Line. 2004. mass mkt. (*0-312-98978-4*, St. Martin's Paperbacks) St. Martin's Pr.
—Follow the Sharks. 1985. (Brady Coyne Mystery Ser.). 224p. 13.95 o.p. (*0-684-18446-X*, Macmillan Reference USA) Gale Group.
—Follow the Sharks! 1986. mass mkt. 4.99 o.s.i (*0-345-32906-6*) Ballantine Bks.
—Follow the Sharks. l.t. ed. 1988. pap. 8.95 o.p. (*1-55504-346-1*) BBC Audiobooks America.
—The Marine Corpse. 1987. 240p. mass mkt. 3.95 o.s.i (*0-345-34057-4*) Ballantine Bks.
—The Marine Corpse: A Brady Coyne Mystery. 1986. 240p. 13.95 o.s.i (*0-684-18681-0*, Macmillan Reference USA) Gale Group.
—Seventh Enemy: A Brady Coyne Mystery. 1995. 234p. 21.00 (*1-883402-99-9*, Scribner) Simon & Schuster.
—The Snake Eater. 1993. 273p. 20.00 o.p. (*1-883402-04-2*, Scribner) Simon & Schuster.
—The Spotted Cats: A Brady Coyne Mystery. 1992. 256p. mass mkt. 4.50 o.s.i (*0-440-21191-3*) Dell Publishing.
—Tight Lines. l.t. ed. 1995. (Magna Large Print Ser.). 421p. (*0-7505-0796-9*) Magna Large Print Bks. GBR. *Dist:* Ulverscroft Large Print Canada, Ltd.
—Tight Lines: A Brady Coyne Mystery. 1993. 288p. mass mkt. 4.99 o.s.i (*0-440-21410-6*) Dell Publishing.
—A Void in Hearts. 1990. 192p. mass mkt. 3.95 o.s.i (*0-345-35868-6*) Ballantine Bks.
—A Void in Hearts. l.t. ed. 1990. (General Ser.). 427p. lib. bdg. 18.95 o.p. (*0-8161-4822-8*, Macmillan Reference USA) Gale Group.
—A Void in Hearts. 1988. (Brady Coyne Mystery Ser.: No. 7). 224p. 16.95 o.s.i (*0-684-18793-0*, Scribner) Simon & Schuster.
—The Vulgar Boatman. l.t. ed. 1991. 8.95 o.p. (*0-7451-9583-0*, 5054); pap. 10.95 o.p. (*0-7927-0011-2*, 618) BBC Audiobooks America.
—The Vulgar Boatman. 1989. 256p. mass mkt. 3.95 o.s.i (*0-345-35577-6*) Ballantine Bks.
—The Vulgar Boatman. l.t. ed. 1989. viii, 315 p. pap. (*0-7451-9595-4*) Chivers Pr.
—The Vulgar Boatman. 1988. (Brady Coyne Mystery Ser.). 240p. 14.95 o.s.i (*0-684-18792-2*, Scribner) Simon & Schuster.
Topor, Tom. The Codicil. abr. ed. 1996. audio 7.99 o.p. (*1-56740-106-6*, 826, Paperback Nova Audio Bks.); 1995. audio 16.95 o.p. (*1-56100-429-4*, 1146, Nova Audio Bks.); 1995. audio 89.25 o.p. (*1-56100-262-3*, 827, Unabridged Library Editions); 1995. audio 25.95 o.p. (*1-56100-637-8*, 66, Bookcassette) Brilliance Audio.
—The Codicil. 1995. 352p. 21.95 (*0-7868-6153-3*); 1996. 576p. reprint ed. mass mkt. 5.99 (*0-7868-8906-3*) Hyperion Pr.
—The Codicil. l.t. ed. 1995. 600p. 24.95 o.p. (*0-7838-1375-9*) Thorndike Pr.
Turow, Scott. The Burden of Proof. unabr. collector's ed. 1990. audio 96.00 (*0-7366-1786-8*, 2623) Books on Tape, Inc.
—The Burden of Proof. 1990. 367.20 o.p. (*0-374-11735-7*); 640p. 30.00 (*0-374-11734-9*); E-Book 22.95 (*0-374-70093-1*); 640p. E-Book 9.95 o.p. (*0-374-70091-5*); E-Book 22.92 (*0-374-70092-3*) Farrar, Straus & Giroux.
—The Burden of Proof. l.t. ed. 1991. (General Ser.). 690p. 14.95 o.p. (*0-8161-5125-3*); 14.95 o.p. (*0-8161-5132-6*) Gale Group. (Macmillan Reference USA).
—The Burden of Proof. abr. ed. 1990. audio 17.00 (*0-671-70743-4*, Simon & Schuster Audioworks) Simon & Schuster Audio.
—The Burden of Proof. reprint ed. 2000. 608p. pap. 14.95 (*0-446-67712-4*); 1991. 576p. mass mkt. 7.99 (*0-446-36058-9*) Warner Bks., Inc.
—Personal Injuries. stu. ed. (*0-374-96409-2*); 1999. 384p. 27.00 (*0-374-28194-7*); 1999. E-Book 27.00 (*0-374-70194-6*); 1999. E-Book 9.00 (*0-374-70018-4*); 1999. E-Book 9.00 o.p. incl. cd-rom (*0-374-70007-9*) Farrar, Straus & Giroux.
—Personal Injuries. l.t. ed. 1999. (Basic Ser.). 731p. 31.95 (*0-7862-2014-7*) Thorndike Pr.
—Personal Injuries. 2000. 528p. reprint ed. mass mkt. 7.99 (*0-446-60860-2*) Warner Bks., Inc.
—Personal Injuries: Special Edition. E-Book 6.00 (*1-58945-505-3*) Adobe Systems, Inc.
—Pleading Guilty. unabr. ed. 1993. audio 64.00 (*0-7366-2605-0*, 3348) Books on Tape, Inc.
—Pleading Guilty. E-Book 4.95 (*0-374-70105-9*); E-Book 4.95 (*0-374-70118-0*); 2001. E-Book 4.95 o.p. (*0-374-70104-0*); 1993. 400p. 24.00 (*0-374-23457-4*); 1993. E-Book 24.00 (*0-374-70106-7*) Farrar, Straus & Giroux.
—Pleading Guilty. l.t. ed. 1993. 495p. pap. 19.95 o.p. (*0-8161-5747-2*); lib. bdg. 25.95 (*0-8161-5746-4*) Gale Group. (Macmillan Reference USA).
—Pleading Guilty. abr. ed. 1993. audio 24.00 (*0-671-87043-2*, Simon & Schuster Audioworks) Simon & Schuster Audio.
—Pleading Guilty. 1994. 480p. reprint ed. mass mkt. 7.99 (*0-446-36550-5*) Warner Bks., Inc.
—Presumed Innocent. 1987. 480p. 30.00 (*0-374-23713-1*); E-Book 4.95 o.p. (*0-374-70108-3*); E-Book 4.95 (*0-374-70111-3*); E-Book 4.95 (*0-374-70117-2*); E-Book 4.95 (*0-374-70109-1*) Farrar, Straus & Giroux.
—Presumed Innocent. l.t. ed. 1988. (General Ser.). 606p. 13.95 o.p. (*0-8161-4470-2*, Macmillan Reference USA) Gale Group.
—Presumed Innocent. 1999. (*0-7621-0254-3*) Reader's Digest Assn., Inc., The.
—Presumed Innocent. abr. ed. 1988. 17.00 incl. audio (*0-671-65218-4*, Simon & Schuster Audioworks) Simon & Schuster Audio.
—Presumed Innocent. reprint ed. 2000. 512p. pap. 14.95 (*0-446-67644-6*); 1989. 432p. mass mkt. 7.99 (*0-446-35986-6*) Warner Bks., Inc.
—Reversible Errors: A Novel. 2002. E-Book 15.00 o.p. (*0-374-70395-7*); E-Book 15.00 (*0-374-70394-9*); (Illus.). 448p. 28.00 (*0-374-28160-2*); E-Book (*0-374-70397-3*); pap. (*0-374-96781-4*) Farrar, Straus & Giroux.
—Reversible Errors: A Novel. l.t. ed. 2003. 720p. pap. 13.95 (*1-4104-0161-8*, Wheeler Publishing, Inc.) Gale Group.
—Reversible Errors: A Novel. pap. o.p. (*0-7862-4269-8*) Thorndike Pr.
—Reversible Errors: A Novel. 2003. 576p. mass mkt. 7.99 (*0-446-61262-6*, Warner Vision) Warner Bks., Inc.
Twain, Mark. Pudd'nhead Wilson & Other Tales. Gooder, R. D., ed. 1992. (Oxford World's Classics Ser.). 312p. pap. 7.95 o.p. (*0-19-281806-6*) Oxford Univ. Pr., Inc.
—Pudd'nhead Wilson & Other Tales: Those Extraordinary Twins, The Man that Corrupted Hadleyburg. Gooder, R. D., ed. 1999. (Oxford World's Classics Ser.). 320p. pap. 8.95 (*0-19-283730-3*) Oxford Univ. Pr., Inc.
—Pudd'nhead Wilson & Those Extraordinary Twins. Berger, Sidney E., ed. 1981. (Critical Editions Ser.). (Illus.). 384p. 22.50 o.p. (*0-393-01337-5*); (C). pap. text 9.00 (*0-393-95027-1*) Norton, W. W. & Co., Inc.
—Pudd'nhead Wilson & Those Extraordinary Twins. 2002. (Modern Library Classics). (Illus.). 288p. pap. 9.95 (*0-8129-6622-8*) Random House Adult Trade Publishing Group.
Van Gieson, Judith. Ditch Rider: A Neil Hamel Mystery. (Neil Hamel Mystery Ser.). 240p. 1999. mass mkt. 5.99 (*0-06-109515-X*); 1998. 23.00 (*0-06-017513-3*) HarperCollins Pubs.
—The Lies That Bind: A Neil Hamel Mystery. 1994. 304p. mass mkt. 4.99 o.p. (*0-06-109051-4*) HarperCollins Pubs.
—The Lies That Bind: A Neil Hamel Mystery. 1993. 256p. 20.00 o.p. (*0-06-017705-5*) HarperTrade.
—North of the Border: A Neil Hamel Mystery. 1993. 176p. mass mkt. 4.99 (*0-671-76967-7*, Pocket) Simon & Schuster.
—North of the Border: A Neil Hamel Mystery. 1988. 16.95 o.p. (*0-8027-5706-5*) Walker & Co.
—The Other Side of Death. 1991. 224p. 18.95 o.p. (*0-06-016581-2*) HarperTrade.
—The Other Side of Death. 2003. 224p. pap. 13.95 (*0-8263-3207-2*) Univ. of New Mexico Pr.
—Parrot Blues. 1995. 256p. 20.00 o.p. (*0-06-017706-3*) HarperTrade.
—Parrot Blues. 1995. 272p. mass mkt. 4.99 o.p. (*0-06-109048-4*, HarperTorch) Morrow/Avon.
—Raptor. 1990. 17.95 o.p. (*0-06-016167-1*) HarperTrade.
—Raptor. Isaacson, Dana, ed. 1991. 256p. reprint ed. mass mkt. 4.99 (*0-671-73243-9*, Pocket) Simon & Schuster.
—Raptor. 2002. 252p. pap. 13.95 (*0-8263-2974-8*) Univ. of New Mexico Pr.
—The Wolf Path: A Neil Hamel Mystery. 1992. 224p. 19.00 o.p. (*0-06-016804-8*) HarperTrade.
—The Wolf Path: A Neil Hamel Mystery. 1993. 256p. mass mkt. 4.50 o.p. (*0-06-109139-1*, HarperTorch) Morrow/Avon.
Warfield, Gallatin. Raising Cain. 1998. 400p. mass mkt. 6.99 (*0-446-60513-1*); 1996. 352p. 23.45 o.p. (*0-446-51850-6*) Warner Bks., Inc.
—Silent Son. 1994. 336p. 21.95 o.s.i (*0-446-51725-9*) Warner Bks., Inc.
—The Silent Son. 1995. 384p. mass mkt. 5.99 o.s.i (*0-446-60199-3*) Warner Bks., Inc.
—State vs. Justice, Set. unabr. ed. 1998. audio 103.95 (*1-85903-130-7*) Magna Story Sound GBR. *Dist:* Ulverscroft Large Print Bks., Ltd.
—State vs. Justice. 1993. 384p. mass mkt. 5.99 o.s.i (*0-446-36477-0*); 1992. 336p. 18.95 o.p. (*0-446-51688-0*) Warner Bks., Inc.
Welch, James. The Indian Lawyer. 1990. 19.95 o.p. (*0-393-02896-8*) Norton, W. W. & Co., Inc.
Wideman, John Edgar. Reuben. 1987. 16.95 o.p. (*0-8050-0375-4*) Holt, Henry & Co.
—Reuben. 1988. 224p. pap. 7.95 o.p. (*0-14-010595-6*, Penguin Bks.) Viking Penguin.
Willett, Sabin. The Deal. 1997. 496p. mass mkt. 6.99 o.s.i (*0-515-12182-7*, Jove) Berkley Publishing Group.
Woods, Sara. Away with Them to Prison. 1989. 224p. pap. 3.50 (*0-380-70589-3*, Avon Bks.) Morrow/Avon.
—Away with Them to Prison. 1985. 12.95 o.p. (*0-312-06311-3*) St. Martin's Pr.
—Away with Them to Prison. l.t. ed. 1988. 464p. 17.95 o.p. (*0-7089-1811-5*, Ulverscroft) Thorpe, F. A. Pubs. GBR. *Dist:* Ulverscroft Large Print Bks., Ltd.
—Bloody Instructions. 1986. pap. 2.95 (*0-380-69858-7*, Avon Bks.) Morrow/Avon.
—Call Back Yesterday. 1983. 224p. 10.95 o.p. (*0-312-11424-9*) St. Martin's Pr.
—Call Back Yesterday. l.t. ed. 1985. (Ulverscroft Large Print Ser.). 368p. 12.50 o.p. (*0-7089-1358-X*, Ulverscroft) Thorpe, F. A. Pubs. GBR. *Dist:* Ulverscroft Large Print Bks., Ltd., Ulverscroft Large Print Canada, Ltd.
—Cry Guilty. 1981. 192p. 9.95 o.p. (*0-312-17802-6*) St. Martin's Pr.
—Dearest Enemy. 1981. 196p. 9.95 o.p. (*0-312-18546-4*) St. Martin's Pr.
—Dearest Enemy. l.t. ed. 1984. (Ulverscroft Large Print Ser.). 416p. 12.50 o.p. (*0-7089-1235-4*, Ulverscroft) Thorpe, F. A. Pubs. GBR. *Dist:* Ulverscroft Large Print Bks., Ltd., Ulverscroft Large Print Canada, Ltd.
—Defy the Devil. 1984. 304p. 11.95 o.p. (*0-312-19121-9*) St. Martin's Pr.
—Defy the Devil. l.t. ed. 1986. 328p. 15.95 o.p. (*0-7089-1481-0*, Ulverscroft) Thorpe, F. A. Pubs. GBR. *Dist:* Ulverscroft Large Print Bks., Ltd.
—Error of the Moon. 1986. 176p. pap. 2.95 (*0-380-69859-5*, Avon Bks.) Morrow/Avon.
—Exit Murderer. (Fingerprint Mysteries Ser.). 1983. 192p. pap. 5.95 o.p. (*0-312-27588-9*, Saint Martin's Griffin); 1978. 7.95 o.p. (*0-312-27587-0*) St. Martin's Pr.
—The Law's Delay. 1977. 7.95 o.p. (*0-312-47565-9*) St. Martin's Pr.
—Let's Choose Executors. 1986. (Anthony Maitland Detective Ser.). 224p. pap. 2.95 o.p. (*0-380-69860-9*, Avon Bks.) Morrow/Avon.
—The Lie Direct. 1989. 160p. pap. 3.95 (*0-380-70588-5*, Avon Bks.) Morrow/Avon.
—The Lie Direct. 1983. 192p. 10.95 o.p. (*0-312-48369-4*) St. Martin's Pr.
—The Lie Direct. l.t. ed. 1986. 336p. o.p. (*0-7089-1551-5*, Ulverscroft) Thorpe, F. A. Pubs.
—Most Deadly Hate. 1987. 240p. pap. 3.50 (*0-380-70477-3*, Avon Bks.) Morrow/Avon.
—Most Deadly Hate. 1986. 224p. 13.95 o.p. (*0-312-54914-8*) St. Martin's Pr.
—Most Deadly Hate. l.t. ed. 1987. 496p. 14.95 o.p. (*0-7089-1663-5*, Ulverscroft) Thorpe, F. A. Pubs. GBR. *Dist:* Ulverscroft Large Print Bks., Ltd.
—Most Grievous Murder. 1982. 192p. 10.95 o.p. (*0-312-54908-3*) St. Martin's Pr.
—Most Grievous Murder. l.t. ed. 1984. (Ulverscroft Large Print Ser.). 288p. o.p. (*0-7089-1179-X*, Ulverscroft) Thorpe, F. A. Pubs. GBR. *Dist:* Ulverscroft Large Print Canada, Ltd.
—Murder's Out of Tune. l.t. ed. 1986. (Nightingale Ser.). 314p. pap. 10.95 o.p. (*0-8161-4002-2*, Macmillan Reference USA) Gale Group.
—Murder's Out of Tune. 1988. 192p. pap. 3.50 (*0-380-70586-9*, Avon Bks.) Morrow/Avon.
—Murder's Out of Tune. 1984. 208p. 11.95 o.p. (*0-312-55345-5*) St. Martin's Pr.
—Naked Villainy. l.t. ed. 1988. (General Ser.). 379p. 17.95 o.p. (*0-8161-4395-1*, Macmillan Reference USA) Gale Group.
—Naked Villainy. 1988. 288p. pap. 3.50 (*0-380-70479-X*, Avon Bks.) Morrow/Avon.
—Naked Villainy. 1987. 256p. 14.95 o.p. (*0-312-00163-0*) St. Martin's Pr.
—Nor Live So Long. l.t. ed. 1987. (Nightingale Ser.). 331p. 10.95 o.p. (*0-8161-4225-4*, Macmillan Reference USA) Gale Group.
—Nor Live So Long. 1988. 224p. pap. 3.50 (*0-380-70478-1*, Avon Bks.) Morrow/Avon.
—Nor Live So Long. 1986. 208p. 13.95 o.p. (*0-312-57740-0*) St. Martin's Pr.
—An Obscure Grave. 1985. 11.95 o.p. (*0-312-58053-3*) St. Martin's Pr.
—An Obscure Grave. l.t. ed. 1987. 384p. 14.95 o.p. (*0-7089-1607-4*, Ulverscroft) Thorpe, F. A. Pubs. GBR. *Dist:* Ulverscroft Large Print Bks., Ltd.
—Proceed to Judgment. 1980. 8.95 o.p. (*0-312-64776-X*) St. Martin's Pr.
—A Show of Violence. l.t. ed. 1980. 238p. o.p. (*0-7089-0436-X*, Ulverscroft) Thorpe, F. A. Pubs.
—They Stay for Death. 1988. 192p. mass mkt. 3.50 (*0-380-70587-7*, Avon Bks.) Morrow/Avon.
—They Stay for Death. 1980. 8.95 o.p. (*0-312-79983-7*) St. Martin's Pr.
—Third Encounter. 1986. pap. 3.50 (*0-380-69863-3*, Avon Bks.) Morrow/Avon.
—This Fatal Writ. 1979. 7.95 o.p. (*0-312-80050-9*) St. Martin's Pr.
—This Fatal Writ. l.t. ed. 1983. (Ulverscroft Large Print Ser.). 336p. 29.99 o.p. (*0-7089-0967-1*, Ulverscroft) Thorpe, F. A. Pubs. GBR. *Dist:* Ulverscroft Large Print Bks., Ltd., Ulverscroft Large Print Canada, Ltd.
—This Little Measure. 1986. (Anthony Maitland Detective Ser.). 192p. mass mkt. 2.95 (*0-380-69862-5*, Avon Bks.) Morrow/Avon.
—Villains by Necessity. 1982. 224p. 10.95 o.p. (*0-312-84683-5*) St. Martin's Pr.
—Villains by Necessity. l.t. ed. 1988. (Ulverscroft Large Print Ser.). 384p. 29.99 o.p. (*0-7089-1781-X*, Ulverscroft) Thorpe, F. A. Pubs. GBR. *Dist:* Ulverscroft Large Print Bks., Ltd., Ulverscroft Large Print Canada, Ltd.
—Weep for Her. 1981. 224p. 9.95 o.p. (*0-312-86019-6*) St. Martin's Pr.
—Where Should He Die? 1983. 224p. 10.95 o.p. (*0-312-86702-6*) St. Martin's Pr.
Woods, Sara, ed. Malice Domestic. 1986. pap. 3.50 (*0-380-69861-7*, Avon Bks.) Morrow/Avon.
Zion, Sidney. Markers. 1990. 426p. 19.95 o.p. (*0-917657-08-X*) Fine, Donald I. Bks.

**LIBRARIANS—FICTION**

Abbey, Lynn. Out of Time. 2000. 320p. mass mkt. 6.50 (*0-441-00751-1*) Ace Bks.
Abbott, Jeff. Distant Blood. 1996. 352p. mass mkt. 6.99 (*0-345-39470-4*) Ballantine Bks.
—Do unto Others. 1994. (Southwest Mysteries Ser.). 256p. mass mkt. 6.99 (*0-345-38948-4*) Ballantine Bks.
—The Only Good Yankee. 1995. 256p. mass mkt. 6.50 (*0-345-39438-0*, Del Rey) Ballantine Bks.
—Promises of Home. 1996. 288p. mass mkt. 6.99 (*0-345-39469-0*) Ballantine Bks.
Beasley, David. The Grand Conspiracy: A New York Library Mystery. 1997. 176p. pap. 10.95 (*0-915317-06-0*) Davus Publishing.
—The Jenny: A New York Library Detective Novel. 1994. 120p. pap. 7.95 (*0-915317-03-6*) Davus Publishing.
Betts, Doris. Heading West. 1981. 320p. 13.50 o.p. (*0-394-51798-9*) Knopf, Alfred A. Inc.
—Heading West. 1982. mass mkt. 3.50 o.p. (*0-451-11913-4*, AE1913, Signet Bks.) NAL.
—Heading West. 1995. 368p. pap. 17.00 (*0-684-80115-9*, Touchstone) Simon & Schuster.
Brookner, Anita. Look at Me. l.t. ed. 1991. 259p. 22.95 o.p. (*1-85089-404-3*) ISIS Large Print Bks. GBR. *Dist:* Transaction Pubs.
—Look at Me. 1997. 208p. pap. 12.00 (*0-679-73813-4*, Vintage) Knopf Publishing Group.
—Look at Me. 1985. pap. 7.95 o.p. (*0-525-48156-7*, Obelisk) NAL.
Browne, Marshall. Inspector Anders & the Ship of Fools. 2002. 272p. 23.95 (*0-312-27821-7*, Saint Martin's Minotaur) St. Martin's Pr.
Bulock, Lynn. And Mommy Makes Three. 1996. (Harlequin Romance Ser.). per. (*0-373-19154-5*, 1-19154-3, Silhouette) Harlequin Enterprises, Ltd.
Carr, Josephine. The Dewey Decimal System of Love. 2003. 272p. pap. 12.95 (*0-451-20971-0*) NAL.
—The Dewey Decimal System of Love. l.t. ed. 2004. 330p. 28.95 (*0-7862-6226-5*) Thorndike Pr.
Cecil, Henry. Cross Purposes. 1997. (Henry Cecil Reprint Ser.). 186p. reprint ed. 55.00 (*1-56169-272-7*) Gaunt, Inc.
Cooley, Martha. The Archivist. 336p. 1999. pap. 13.00 (*0-316-15846-1*, Back Bay); 1998. (YA). (gr. 8 up). 22.95 o.p. (*0-316-15872-0*) Little Brown & Co.
Coomer, Joe. The Loop. 228p. 1993. pap. 10.95 o.p. (*0-571-19823-6*); 1992. 21.95 o.p. (*0-571-12949-8*) Faber & Faber, Inc.
Dale, Ruth Jean. The Red-Blooded Yankee! 1992. (Harlequin Temptation Ser.). mass mkt. (*0-373-25513-6*, 1-25513-2, Harlequin Bks.) Harlequin Enterprises, Ltd.
Denison, Lyn. Gold Fever. 1998. 224p. (Orig.). pap. 11.95 (*1-56280-201-1*) Naiad Pr., Inc.
Dereske, Jo. Final Notice, Bk. 3. 1998. (Miss Zukas Mystery Ser.). 240p. mass mkt. 5.99 (*0-380-78245-6*, Avon Bks.) Morrow/Avon.
—Miss Zukas & Stroke of Death. 1995. (Miss Zukas Mystery Ser.: No. 3). 224p. mass mkt. 6.50 (*0-380-77033-4*, Avon Bks.) Morrow/Avon.
—Miss Zukas & the Island Murders. 1995. (Miss Zukas Mystery Ser.). 224p. (Orig.). mass mkt. 5.99 (*0-380-77031-8*, Avon Bks.) Morrow/Avon.
—Miss Zukas & the Library Murders. l.t. ed. 2003. (Mystery Ser.). (Orig.). 27.95 (*1-57490-511-2*) Beeler, Thomas T. Publisher.

Occupations

—Miss Zukas & the Library Murders. 1994. (Miss Zukas Mystery Ser.). 224p. (Orig.). mass mkt. 5.99 (*0-380-77030-X*, Avon Bks.) Morrow/Avon.
—Miss Zukas & the Raven's Dance. 1996. (Miss Zukas Mystery Ser.). 256p. mass mkt. 5.99 (*0-380-78243-X*, Avon Bks.) Morrow/Avon.
—Miss Zukas in Death's Shadow. 1999. 224p. mass mkt. 5.99 (*0-380-80472-7*, Avon Bks.) Morrow/Avon.
—Miss Zukas Shelves the Evidence. l.t. ed. 2002. (Paperback Ser.). 310p. pap. 25.95 (*0-7838-9734-0*) Gale Group.
—Miss Zukas Shelves the Evidence. 2001. (Miss Zukas Mystery Ser.). 256p. mass mkt. 5.99 (*0-380-80474-3*, Avon Bks.) Morrow/Avon.
—Out of Circulation. 1997. (Miss Zukas Mystery Ser.). mass mkt. 5.99 (*0-380-78244-8*, Avon Bks.) Morrow/Avon.
Douglas, Kirk. Last Tango in Brooklyn. l.t. ed. 1994. 392p. lib. bdg. 24.95 (*0-8161-7465-2*, Macmillan Reference USA) Gale Group.
—Last Tango in Brooklyn. abr. ed. 1994. audio 21.00 o.s.i (*1-57042-085-8*, 4-520858) Time Warner AudioBooks.
—Last Tango in Brooklyn. 352p. 1995. mass mkt. 6.50 o.s.i (*0-446-60201-9*); 1994. 30.00 (*0-446-51695-3*) Warner Bks., Inc.
Goodrum, Charles. The Best Cellar: A Werner-Bok Library Mystery. 1988. 288p. reprint ed. mass mkt. 3.95 o.p. (*0-06-080931-0*, P 931, Perennial) HarperTrade.
—Carnage of the Realm: A Werner-Bok Library Mystery. 1988. 240p. reprint ed. mass mkt. 3.95 o.p. (*0-06-080932-9*, Perennial) HarperTrade.
—Dewey Decimated: A Werner-Bok Library Mystery. 1988. 304p. reprint ed. mass mkt. 3.95 o.p. (*0-06-080933-7*, P 933, Perennial) HarperTrade.
—A Slip of the Tong. 1992. 192p. 16.95 o.p. (*0-312-07806-4*); Vol. 1. 1958. 17.95 o.p. (*0-312-08296-7*) St. Martin's Pr. (Saint Martin's Minotaur).
Goodrum, Charles A. The Best Cellar: Murder & Mystery at the Werner-Bok Library. 1987. 160p. 13.95 o.p. (*0-312-00008-1*) St. Martin's Pr.
—Carnage of the Realm. 1988. 1.99 o.p. (*0-517-53504-1*) Random Hse. Value Publishing.
Griffith, Michael. Bibliophilia: A Novella & Stories. 2003. (Illus.). 256p. 24.95 (*1-55970-676-7*) Arcade Publishing, Inc.
Harris, Charlaine. A Bone to Pick. 1993. (WWL Mystery Ser.). per. (*0-373-26136-5*, 1-26136-1, Harlequin Bks.) Harlequin Enterprises, Ltd.
—A Bone to Pick. 1992. 168p. 18.95 o.s.i (*0-8027-1245-2*) Walker & Co.
—Dead over Heels. 1997. per. (*0-373-26260-4*, 1-26260-9, Worldwide Library) Harlequin Enterprises, Ltd.
—Dead over Heels. 1996. 208p. 20.50 o.p. (*0-684-80429-8*, Scribner) Simon & Schuster.
—A Fool & His Honey. 2001. (WWL Mystery Ser.: No. 384). 253p. mass mkt. (*0-373-26384-8*, 1-26384-7, Worldwide Library) Harlequin Enterprises, Ltd.
—A Fool & His Honey. 1999. 224p. 22.95 (*0-312-20306-3*, Saint Martin's Minotaur) St. Martin's Pr.
—A Fool & His Honey. l.t. ed. 2000. (Mystery Ser.). 304p. 28.95 (*0-7862-2467-3*) Thorndike Pr.
—The Julius House. 1996. per. (*0-373-26217-5*, 1-26217-9, Worldwide Library) Harlequin Enterprises, Ltd.
—The Julius House. 1995. 221p. 20.00 (*0-684-19640-9*, Scribner) Simon & Schuster.
—Real Murders. l.t. ed. 1991. 17.95 o.p. (*0-7451-8204-6*, AH0240) BBC Audiobooks America.
—Real Murders. 1992. mass mkt. (*0-373-26104-7*, 1-26104-9, Harlequin Bks.) Harlequin Enterprises, Ltd.
—Real Murders. 1990. 192p. 18.95 o.s.i (*0-8027-5769-3*) Walker & Co.
—Three Bedrooms, One Corpse. 1995. per. (*0-373-26177-2*, Harlequin Bks.) Harlequin Enterprises, Ltd.
—Three Bedrooms, One Corpse. 2001. 224p. pap. 14.95 o.p. (*0-7432-2891-X*); 1994. 256p. 20.00 (*0-684-19643-3*) Simon & Schuster. (Scribner).
Hegi, Ursula. Stones from the River. (Reading Group Guides Ser.). 1997. pap. (*0-684-00597-2*, Touchstone); 1997. 528p. pap. 14.00 (*0-684-84477-X*, Touchstone); 1995. 528p. pap. 12.00 (*0-684-80035-7*, Scribner); 1994. 507p. 25.50 o.s.i (*0-671-78075-1*, Simon & Schuster); 1997. 26.00 (*0-684-84472-9*, Simon & Schuster) Simon & Schuster.
—Stones from the River. 1994. 20.05 (*0-606-19627-7*) Turtleback Bks.
Heller, Murray. Placid's View: A Mike Diamond Mystery. 1997. 196p. 22.50 (*0-935796-81-9*) Purple Mountain Pr., Ltd.
Holt, Hazel. The Cruellest Month. l.t. ed. 1992. 240p. 14.95 o.p. (*0-7451-1491-1*, Macmillan Reference USA) Gale Group.
—The Cruellest Month. 1992. (Mrs. Malory Mystery Ser.). 224p. mass mkt. 4.50 o.s.i (*0-451-40313-4*, Onyx) NAL.
—The Cruellest Month. 1991. 15.95 o.p. (*0-312-05840-3*, Saint Martin's Minotaur) St. Martin's Pr.
Howard, Linda. Open Season. l.t. ed. 2002. (Basic Ser.). 458p. 31.95 (*0-7862-3744-9*) Gale Group.
—Open Season. 2001. 320p. 24.95 o.s.i (*0-671-03442-1*, Atria) Simon & Schuster.
—Open Season. l.t. ed. 2002. 28.95 (*0-7862-3750-3*) Thorndike Pr.
Jones, Linda. Desperado's Gold. 1996. 400p. (Orig.). pap. 5.50 (*0-505-52140-7*, Love Spell) Dorchester Publishing Co., Inc.
King, Stephen. The Library Policeman. abr. unabr. ed. 1991. (Four Past Midnight Ser.). audio 30.95 (*0-453-00748-1*, 892527) Penguin/HighBridge.
—Policia de la Biblioteca. 1999. Tr. of Library Policeman. (SPA.). mass mkt. 4.99 (*0-451-18660-5*, Signet Bks.) NAL.
Lattany, Kristin Hunter. Do unto Others. E-Book 19.95 (*1-58945-572-X*) Adobe Systems, Inc.
—Do unto Others. E-Book 19.50 (*0-345-44329-2*, Ballantine Bks.) Ballantine Bks.
LeClaire, Anne D. Sideshow. 1995. 400p. mass mkt. 5.99 o.s.i (*0-451-40610-9*, Onyx) NAL.
—Sideshow. 308p. 3.98 o.p. (*0-8317-4551-7*) Smithmark Pubs., Inc.
—Sideshow. 1994. 320p. 20.95 o.p. (*0-670-84328-8*, Viking) Viking Penguin.
Linz, Cathie. Too Smart for Marriage. 1998. (Love & Laughter Ser.: Vol. 51). per. (*0-373-44051-0*, 1-44051-0, Harlequin Bks.) Harlequin Enterprises, Ltd.
Macomber, Debbie. Morning Comes Softly. 1993. 352p. mass mkt. 5.50 o.s.i (*0-06-108063-2*, HarperTorch) Morrow/Avon.
McCracken, Elizabeth. The Giant's House: A Romance. 1997. 304p. pap. 13.00 (*0-380-73020-0*, Avon Bks.) Morrow/Avon.
Meier, Leslie. Back to School Murder: A Lucy Stone Mystery. (Lucy Stone Mysteries Ser.). 1998. 272p. mass mkt. 5.99 (*1-57566-330-9*); 1997. 256p. 18.95 o.s.i (*1-57566-216-7*) Kensington Publishing Corp.
—Christmas Cookie Murder, Vol. 1. 1999. (Lucy Stone Mysteries Ser.). 256p. (J). pap. 20.00 o.s.i (*1-57566-476-3*) Kensington Publishing Corp.
—Mail-Order Murder. 1999. pap. 5.95 (*0-14-015832-4*, Viking) Viking Penguin.
—Mail-Order Murder: A Christmas Mystery. 1991. 192p. 18.95 o.p. (*0-670-84111-0*, Viking) Viking Penguin.
—Mail-Order Murders. 1993. 256p. mass mkt. 4.99 o.s.i (*0-440-21452-1*) Dell Publishing.
—Mistletoe Murder. 1998. Orig. Title: Mail-Order Murder. 224p. mass mkt. 6.50 (*0-7582-0337-3*); mass mkt. 5.99 o.s.i (*1-57566-370-8*, Kensington Bks.) Kensington Publishing Corp.
—Tippy Toe Murder. (Lucy Stone Mysteries Ser.). 1999. 352p. mass mkt. 5.99 (*1-57566-392-9*); 1996. 256p. mass mkt. 4.99 o.s.i (*1-57566-099-7*) Kensington Publishing Corp.
—Tippy Toe Murder. 1994. 240p. 18.95 o.p. (*0-670-84791-7*, Viking) Viking Penguin.
—Trick or Treat Murder. (Lucy Stone Mysteries Ser.). 256p. 1997. mass mkt. 5.99 (*1-57566-219-1*); 1996. 18.95 o.s.i (*1-57566-093-8*, Kensington Bks.) Kensington Publishing Corp.
—Valentine Murder. (Lucy Stone Mysteries Ser.). 2000. 272p. mass mkt. 5.99 (*1-57566-499-2*); 1999. 248p. 20.00 o.s.i (*1-57566-390-2*) Kensington Publishing Corp.
Meredith, Doris R. By Hook or by Book. 2000. (Prime Crime Mysteries Ser.). 272p. mass mkt. 5.99 (*0-425-17465-4*, Prime Crime) Berkley Publishing Group.
—Murder in Volume. 2000. (Prime Crime Mysteries Ser.). 256p. mass mkt. 6.50 (*0-425-17309-7*, Prime Crime) Berkley Publishing Group.
—Murder Past Due. 2001. 240p. mass mkt. 5.99 (*0-425-17800-5*, Prime Crime) Berkley Publishing Group.
Monfredo, Miriam G. Blackwater Spirits. 1996. 368p. reprint ed. mass mkt. 6.99 o.s.i (*0-425-15266-9*) Berkley Publishing Group.
—Blackwater Spirits. 1995. vii, 328p. 21.95 o.p. (*0-312-11754-X*, Saint Martin's Minotaur) St. Martin's Pr.
—Must the Maiden Die? 1999. (Seneca Falls Historical Mysteries Ser.: No. 6). 384p. 21.95 o.s.i (*0-425-16699-6*, Prime Crime) Berkley Publishing Group.
—Must the Maiden Die: A Seneca Falls Historical Mystery. 2000. (Seneca Falls Historical Mysteries Ser.). 384p. mass mkt. 6.99 o.s.i (*0-425-17610-X*) Berkley Publishing Group.
—North Star Conspiracy. 1993. 256p. 21.95 o.p. (*0-312-09355-1*, Saint Martin's Minotaur) St. Martin's Pr.
—The North Star Conspiracy. 1995. 368p. mass mkt. 6.99 (*0-425-14720-7*, Prime Crime) Berkley Publishing Group.
—Seneca Falls Inheritance. 1994. 304p. mass mkt. 6.99 (*0-425-14465-8*, Prime Crime) Berkley Publishing Group.
—Seneca Falls Inheritance. 1992. 320p. 19.95 o.p. (*0-312-07082-9*, Saint Martin's Minotaur) St. Martin's Pr.
—Sisters of Cain: A Seneca Falls Civil War Mystery. 2000. (Illus.). 384p. 21.95 o.s.i (*0-425-17672-X*, Prime Crime) Berkley Publishing Group.
—The Stalking Horse. 1999. (Historical Mystery Ser.: Vol. 5). 352p. reprint ed. mass mkt. 6.99 o.s.i (*0-425-16695-3*, Prime Crime) Berkley Publishing Group.
—The Stalking Horse: A Seneca Falls Historical Mystery. 1998. (Glynis Tryon Historical Mysteries Ser.). 352p. 21.95 o.s.i (*0-425-15783-0*, Prime Crime) Berkley Publishing Group.
—Through a Gold Eagle: A Glynis Tryon Mystery. 1997. 384p. mass mkt. 6.50 o.s.i (*0-425-15898-5*); 1996. 400p. 21.95 o.p. (*0-425-15318-5*) Berkley Publishing Group. (Prime Crime).
Morgan, Kate. Days of Crime & Roses. 1992. 192p. (Orig.). mass mkt. 3.99 o.p. (*0-425-13471-7*) Berkley Publishing Group.
—Home Sweet Homicide. 1991. mass mkt. 3.95 o.p. (*0-425-12895-4*) Berkley Publishing Group.
—Murder Most Fowl. 1991. mass mkt. 3.50 o.p. (*0-425-12610-2*) Berkley Publishing Group.
—Mystery Loves Company. 1992. mass mkt. 3.99 o.p. (*0-425-13237-4*) Berkley Publishing Group.
—The Old School Dies. 1996. 240p. (Orig.). mass mkt. 5.99 o.s.i (*0-425-15552-8*, Prime Crime) Berkley Publishing Group.
—Slay at the Races. 1990. mass mkt. 3.50 o.p. (*0-425-12166-6*) Berkley Publishing Group.
—Wanted: Dude or Alive. 1994. 208p. (Orig.). mass mkt. 4.50 o.p. (*0-425-14330-9*, Prime Crime) Berkley Publishing Group.
Pappano, Marilyn. You Must Remember This. 1998. (Thirty-Six Hours Ser.). 251p. per. (*0-373-65017-5*, 1-65017-5, Harlequin Bks.) Harlequin Enterprises, Ltd.
Peters, Elizabeth, pseud. Die for Love. unabr. ed. 1999. audio 49.95 (*0-7861-1476-2*, 108962) Blackstone Audio Bks., Inc.
—Die for Love. 1992. 288p. mass mkt. 4.50 (*0-8125-2470-5*, Forge Bks.); 1988. pap. 3.95 o.s.i (*0-8125-0791-6*, Tor Bks.) Doherty, Tom Assocs., LLC.
—Die for Love, Set. unabr. ed. 1999. audio 49.95 Highsmith Inc.
—Die for Love. unabr. ed. 2001. audio 54.95 (*1-85695-829-9*, 941203); 2000. audio compact disk 89.95 (*0-7531-0694-9*, 106949) ISIS Audio Bks. GBR. *Dist:* Ulverscroft Large Print Bks., Ltd., ISIS Publishing.
—Die for Love. 1993. 288p. reprint ed. lib. bdg. 20.00 o.p. (*0-7278-4491-1*) Severn Hse. Pubs., Ltd.
—Die for Love. 1990. mass mkt. 3.95 o.s.i (*0-312-92137-3*, St. Martin's Paperbacks) St. Martin's Pr.
—Naked Once More. unabr. ed. 1995. audio 62.95 (*0-7861-0809-6*, 1632) Blackstone Audio Bks., Inc.
—Naked Once More. l.t. ed. 1990. (General Ser.). 550p. pap. 13.95 o.p. (*0-8161-4940-2*); lib. bdg. 20.95 o.p. (*0-8161-4939-9*) Gale Group. (Macmillan Reference USA).
—Naked Once More. 1991. 3.99 o.p. (*0-517-07443-5*) Random Hse. Value Publishing.
—Naked Once More. unabr. ed. 1997. audio 85.00 (*0-7887-0928-3*, 95068E7) Recorded Bks., LLC.
—Naked Once More. 1990. 368p. mass mkt. 6.99 (*0-446-36032-5*); 1989. 17.45 o.s.i (*0-446-51482-9*) Warner Bks., Inc.
Pym, Barbara. An Unsuitable Attachment. 1982. 224p. 13.95 o.p. (*0-525-24117-5*, Dutton) Dutton/Plume.
—An Unsuitable Attachment. 256p. 1983. mass mkt. o.p. (*0-06-080653-2*, P 653); 1986. reprint ed. pap. 7.95 o.p. (*0-06-097055-3*, PL/7055) HarperTrade. (Perennial).
Sanders, Glenda. Look into My Eyes. 1995. 217p. per. (*0-373-25666-3*, 1-25666-8, Harlequin Bks.) Harlequin Enterprises, Ltd.
Sessions, Ellen S. Jennifer's True Love. 1996. 192p. 18.95 o.s.i (*0-8034-9218-9*, Avalon Bks.) Bouregy, Thomas & Co., Inc.
Shelley, Deborah. Talk about Love. 1999. 171p. pap. 1.96 (*0-8217-6328-8*) Kensington Publishing Corp.
Stone, Katherine. The Island of Dreams. 2001. 336p. mass mkt. 6.99 (*0-446-60954-4*); 2000. 272p. 23.95 (*0-446-52182-5*) Warner Bks., Inc.
—Island of Dreams. l.t. ed. 2000. (Large Print Bks.). 263p. 28.95 (*1-56895-955-9*, Wheeler Publishing, Inc.) Gale Group.
Storey, Gail D. The Lord's Motel. 1993. reprint ed. pap. 12.95 (*0-89255-194-1*) Persea Bks., Inc.
—The Lord's Motel: A Novel. 1992. 224p. 19.95 o.p. (*0-89255-178-X*) Persea Bks., Inc.
Sumner, Penny. Crosswords: The 2nd Victoria Cross Mystery. 1994. 256p. pap. 9.95 (*1-56280-064-7*) Naiad Pr., Inc.
—The End of April. 1992. (Victoria Cross Mystery Ser.). 256p. pap. 8.95 o.p. (*1-56280-007-8*) Naiad Pr., Inc.
Wesley, Valerie Wilson. Ain't Nobody's Business If I Do. 2000. 384p. mass mkt. 6.99 (*0-380-80304-6*); 1999. 323p. 24.00 (*0-380-97703-6*) Morrow/Avon. (Avon Bks.).
Wright, Eric. Death of a Sunday Writer. 1996. 224p. text 21.00 (*0-88150-377-0*) Norton, W. W. & Co., Inc.
—Death on the Rocks: A Lucy Trimble Mystery. 1999. 240p. 15.95 (*0-312-20525-2*, Saint Martin's Minotaur) St. Martin's Pr.
—Death on the Rocks: A Lucy Trimble Mystery. l.t. ed. 1999. (Mystery Ser.). 343p. 27.95 (*0-7862-2205-0*) Thorndike Pr.
Wright, Laurali R. Acts of Murder. 1998. 288p. 22.00 (*0-684-81381-5*, Scribner) Simon & Schuster.
—Acts of Murder. l.t. ed. 1998. (Mystery Ser.). 381p. 27.95 (*0-7862-1678-6*) Thorndike Pr.

# M

## MIDWIVES—FICTION

Bohjalian, Chris. Midwives: A Novel. 1998. E-Book 11.50 (*0-609-60630-1*); 1997. 312p. 24.00 o.s.i (*0-517-70396-3*, Harmony) Crown Publishing Group.
—Midwives: A Novel. 1998. 384p. pap. 14.00 (*0-375-70677-1*); 400p. pap. 13.00 o.p. (*0-679-77146-8*) Knopf Publishing Group. (Vintage).
—Midwives: A Novel. l.t. ed. 1998. (Niagara Large Print Ser.). 496p. 29.50 o.p. (*0-7089-5880-X*, Ulverscroft) Thorpe, F. A. Pubs. GBR. *Dist:* Ulverscroft Large Print Bks., Ltd., Ulverscroft Large Print Canada, Ltd.
Henley, Patricia. The Hummingbird House. 2000. pap. 13.00 (*1-878448-98-6*); 1999. 399p. 22.00 (*1-878448-87-0*) MacMurray & Beck, Inc.
Jennings, Maureen. Under the Dragon's Tail. 1999. 304p. mass mkt. 5.99 (*0-06-109740-3*, HarperTorch) Morrow/Avon.
—Under the Dragon's Tail. 1998. 256p. 21.95 o.p. (*0-312-19348-3*, Saint Martin's Minotaur) St. Martin's Pr.
Lawrence, Margaret. Blood Red Roses: A Novel of Historical Suspense. 1998. 416p. mass mkt. 6.50 (*0-380-78880-2*); 1997. 368p. 23.00 (*0-380-97352-9*) Morrow/Avon. (Avon Bks.).
—The Burning Bride. 400p. 1999. mass mkt. 6.99 (*0-380-79612-0*); 1998. 23.00 (*0-380-97620-X*) Morrow/Avon. (Avon Bks.).
—Hearts & Bones. 1997. 352p. mass mkt. 6.50 (*0-380-78879-9*); 1996. 304p. 23.00 (*0-380-97351-0*) Morrow/Avon. (Avon Bks.).
Lewis, Stephen. The Blind in Darkness. 2000. (Mystery of Colonial Times Ser.). 272p. mass mkt. 5.99 o.s.i (*0-425-17466-2*, Prime Crime) Berkley Publishing Group.
—The Dumb Shall Sing: A Mystery of Colonial Times. 1999. 272p. mass mkt. 5.99 o.s.i (*0-425-16997-9*, Prime Crime) Berkley Publishing Group.
Parr, Delia. Home to Trinity: A Novel. 2003. 352p. 25.95 (*0-312-27098-4*) St. Martin's Pr.
—A Place Called Trinity. 2002. (Illus.). 304p. 24.95 (*0-312-28288-5*) St. Martin's Pr.
—A Place Called Trinity. l.t. ed. 2002. (Americana Ser.). 491p. 28.95 (*0-7862-4443-7*) Thorndike Pr.
—A Place Called Trinity: A Novel. 2003. 320p. reprint ed. pap. 12.95 (*0-312-31005-6*, Saint Martin's Griffin) St. Martin's Pr.
Thompson, Victoria. Murder on Astor Place. 1999. (Gaslight Mysteries Ser.). 288p. mass mkt. 6.99 (*0-425-16896-4*, Prime Crime) Berkley Publishing Group.
—Murder on St. Mark's Place. 2000. (Gaslight Mysteries Ser.). 288p. mass mkt. 6.99 (*0-425-17361-5*, Prime Crime) Berkley Publishing Group.

## MISSIONARIES—FICTION

Arthur, Randall. Brotherhood of Betrayal. 2003. 350p. pap. 11.99 (*1-59052-258-3*) Multnomah Pubs., Inc.
Blackburn, Julia. The Book of Color. 1996. 192p. pap. 15.00 (*0-679-75837-2*) Random Hse., Inc.
Caldwell, Bo. The Distant Land of My Father: A Novel of Shanghai. 2001. (Illus.). 384p. 23.95 (*0-8118-3240-6*) Chronicle Bks. LLC.
—The Distant Land of My Father: A Novel of Shanghai. l.t. ed. 2003. (Charnwood Large Print Ser.). 496p. 32.50 (*0-7089-9446-6*) Thorpe, F. A. Pubs. GBR. *Dist:* Ulverscroft Large Print Bks., Ltd., Ulverscroft Large Print Canada, Ltd.
Crouch, Howard E. Damien & Dutton, Two Josephs on Molokai. 1998. 336p. 18.00 (*0-9606330-4-9*) Damien-Dutton Society for Leprosy Aid, Inc.
Crouch, Howard E. & Augustine, Mary. After Damien - Dutton: Yankee Soldier at Molokai. 1981. (Illus.). 144p. pap. 5.95 (*0-9606330-0-6*) Damien-Dutton Society for Leprosy Aid, Inc.
Eaton, Robert I. Thrust in Your Sickle but Watch Your Fingers. 1998. 192p. pap. 15.98 (*0-88290-642-9*, 1975) Horizon Pubs. & Distributors, Inc.
Herman, Kathy. Vital Signs. 2002. (Baxter Ser.). 320p. pap. 11.99 (*1-59052-040-8*) Multnomah Pubs., Inc.
Hersey, John. The Call. 1986. 704p. pap. 8.95 o.p. (*0-14-008695-1*, Penguin Bks.) Viking Penguin.

Hill, Chip. The Invisible Wilderness. 1993. 140p. (Orig.). pap. 6.99 o.p. (*1-56043-657-3*) Destiny Image Pubs.

Jeal, Tim. For God & Glory. 1996. 448p. 25.00 o.p. (*0-688-11871-2*, Morrow, William & Co.) Morrow/Avon.

Keidel, Levi. Caught in the Crossfire. 1979. 256p. pap. 7.95 o.p. (*0-8361-1888-X*) Herald Pr.

Keidel, Levi O. Caught in the Crossfire: The Trials & Triumphs of African Believers Through an Era of Tribulation. l.t. ed. 2000. (G. K. Hall Inspirational Ser.). 294p. 26.95 o.p. (*0-7838-9008-7*, Macmillan Reference USA) Gale Group.

Kingsolver, Barbara. The Poisonwood Bible. unabr. ed. 1998. audio 44.95 (*1-56740-408-1*, 1498, Brilliance Audio Unabridged); 16p. audio 89.25 (*1-56740-610-6*, 1630, Unabridged Library Editions) Brilliance Audio.

—The Poisonwood Bible. l.t. ed. (Thorndike/G. K. Hall Paperback Bestsellers Ser.). 712p. 2000. pap. 27.95 (*0-7838-8468-0*); 1999. 29.95 o.p. (*0-7838-8467-2*) Gale Group. (Macmillan Reference USA).

—The Poisonwood Bible. 1998. (Oprah's Book Club Ser.). 560p. 26.00 (*0-06-017540-0*) HarperCollins Pubs.

—The Poisonwood Bible: A Novel. 1999. 560p. pap. 15.00 (*0-06-093053-5*, Perennial) HarperTrade.

Leanne, Shelly. Joshua's Bible. 2003. 384p. 23.95 (*0-446-53032-8*, Walk Worthy Pr.) Warner Bks., Inc.

Mantel, Hilary. A Change of Climate. 1997. 336p. pap. 14.00 o.s.i (*0-8050-5205-4*, Owl Bks.) Holt, Henry & Co.

—A Change of Climate. 1994. 354p. 22.00 (*0-689-12201-2*, Scribner) Simon & Schuster.

Martin, LaJoyce. Ordered Steps. 1996. (Path of Promise Ser.). 208p. pap. 9.99 (*1-56722-190-4*) Word Aflame Pr.

Matthiessen, Peter. At Play in the Fields of the Lord. 1991. 384p. pap. 14.00 (*0-679-73741-3*); 1987. pap. 10.95 o.p. (*0-394-75083-7*) Knopf Publishing Group. (Vintage).

—At Play in the Fields of the Lord. 1967. mass mkt. 1.25 o.p. (*0-451-03057-5*, Signet Bks.) NAL.

—At Play in the Fields of the Lord. unabr. ed. 1999. audio 91.00 (*1-55690-701-X*, 92414E7) Recorded Bks., LLC.

—At Play in the Fields of the Lord. 1992. 26.75 (*0-8446-6636-X*) Smith, Peter Pub., Inc.

Meyers, Margaret. Swimming in the Congo. 1995. 280p. pap. 13.95 (*1-57131-006-1*) Milkweed Editions.

Moore, Brian. Black Robe. 1991. mass mkt. 4.99 o.p. (*0-449-45066-X*, Fawcett); 1986. mass mkt. 5.99 o.s.i (*0-449-20947-4*) Ballantine Bks.

—Black Robe. 1997. 256p. pap. 14.00 (*0-452-27865-1*, Plume); 1985. 15.95 o.p. (*0-525-24311-9*, Dutton) Dutton/Plume.

—Black Robe. 1995. 80p. pap. 10.00 o.p. (*0-586-08615-3*) HarperCollins Pubs. Ltd. GBR. *Dist:* HarperCollins Pubs.

Moore, Marvin. Conquering High Mountains. 1979. (Destiny Ser). pap. 4.95 o.p. (*0-8163-0327-4*, 03514-7) Pacific Pr. Publishing Assn.

Morris, Alan. Bright Sword of Justice. 1997. (Guardians of the North Ser.: Vol. 3). 256p. pap. 9.99 o.p. (*1-55661-694-5*) Bethany Hse. Pubs.

—Bright Sword of Justice. l.t. ed. 1998. (Guardians of the North Ser.: Vol. 3). 376p. 24.95 (*0-7862-1470-8*) Thorndike Pr.

—Wings of Healing. 1999. (Guardians of the North Ser.: Vol. 5). 272p. pap. 9.99 (*1-55661-696-1*) Bethany Hse. Pubs.

—Wings of Healing. l.t. ed. 2000. (Christian Fiction Ser.). 408p. 24.95 (*0-7862-2378-2*) Thorndike Pr.

Ngugi wa Thiong'o. The River Between. 1965. (African Writers Ser.). pap. text 6.50 o.p. (*0-435-90017-X*); 152p. (C). pap. 10.95 (*0-435-90548-1*, 90548, African Writers Series) Heinemann.

Palmer, Catherine. The Treasure of Timbuktu. 1997. (HeartQuest Ser.: No. 1). pap. 10.99 o.p. (*0-8423-5775-0*) Tyndale Hse. Pubs.

Parkinson, Benson Y. The MTC: Set Apart. 1995. 302p. pap. 9.95 (*1-56236-310-7*) Aspen Bks.

Singer, Randy D. Directed Verdict. 2002. 496p. pap. 13.99 (*1-57856-633-9*) WaterBrook Pr.

Upton, Peter. Green Hill Far Away. 1978. mass mkt. 2.25 o.s.i (*0-345-27208-0*) Ballantine Bks.

—Green Hill Far Away. 1977. 10.95 o.s.i (*0-671-22344-5*, Simon & Schuster) Simon & Schuster.

Vitti, James A. A Little Piece of Paradise. 1996. 336p. pap. 12.99 o.p. (*0-7852-7780-3*) Nelson, Thomas Inc.

Weld, John. The Missionary. 1980. 180p. 15.00 (*0-89002-176-7*); pap. 7.95 (*0-89002-175-9*) American History Pr.

**MOTION PICTURE INDUSTRY—FICTION**

Bochco, Steven. Death by Hollywood. 2004. 256p. mass mkt. 7.99 (*0-345-46687-X*, Fawcett) Ballantine Bks.

—Death by Hollywood. l.t. ed. 2003. 352p. 26.95 (*0-375-43298-1*) Random Hse. Large Print.

—Death by Hollywood: A Novel. 2003. 288p. 24.95 (*1-4000-6156-3*) Random Hse., Inc.

Buschlen, Jack P. Heil Hollywood. Kupelnick, Bruce S., ed. 1978. (Classics of Film Literature Ser.). lib. bdg. 11.00 o.p. (*0-8240-2869-4*) Garland Publishing, Inc.

Cannell, Stephen J. Hollywood Tough: A Shane Scully Novel. l.t. ed. 2003. 30.95 (*1-58724-416-0*, Wheeler Publishing, Inc.) Gale Group.

—Hollywood Tough: A Shane Scully Novel. 2003. 352p. 24.95 (*0-312-29102-7*) St. Martin's Pr.

Cort, Robert. Action! A Novel. 2004. 400p. pap. 13.95 (*0-8129-7216-3*, Random Hse. Trade Paperbacks) Random House Adult Trade Publishing Group.

—Action! A Novel. 2003. 400p. 24.95 (*0-679-45232-X*); E-Book 17.50 (*1-58836-293-0*) Random Hse., Inc.

Deaver, Jeffery. Shallow Graves. 2001. E-Book 6.99 (*0-7434-2401-8*, Pocket) Simon & Schuster.

Grazer, Gigi Levangie. Maneater. 320p. 2004. pap. 13.00 (*0-7434-6400-1*, Downtown Pr.); 2003. 21.95 (*0-7432-2685-2*, Simon & Schuster) Simon & Schuster.

Heller, Jane. Lucky Stars. E-Book 24.95 (*0-312-70995-1*); 2004. 352p. mass mkt. 6.99 (*0-312-99006-5*, St. Martin's Paperbacks); 2003. 352p. 24.95 (*0-312-28848-4*) St. Martin's Pr.

Jeffries, William, pseud. Shallow Graves. E-Book 6.99 (*1-59061-257-4*) Adobe Systems, Inc.

—Shallow Graves: A Location Scout Mystery. l.t. ed. 2000. (G. K. Hall Core Ser.). 380p. 31.95 (*0-7838-9296-9*, Macmillan Reference USA) Gale Group.

—Shallow Graves: A Location Scout Mystery. 1992. (Location Scout Mystery Ser.). 272p. mass mkt. 4.50 (*0-380-76669-8*, Avon Bks.) Morrow/Avon.

—Shallow Graves: A Location Scout Mystery. 2000. (Illus.). 368p. pap. 6.99 (*0-671-04748-5*, Pocket) Simon & Schuster.

—Shallow Graves: A Location Scout Mystery. l.t. ed. 2001. pap. 29.95 o.p. (*0-7838-9297-7*) Thorndike Pr.

Knode, Helen. The Ticket Out. 352p. 2004. pap. 13.00 (*0-15-602905-7*, Harvest Bks.); 2003. 24.00 (*0-15-100184-7*) Harcourt Trade Pubs.

McElroy, Joseph. Lookout Cartridge. 2003. 531p. pap. 16.95 (*1-58567-352-8*) Overlook Pr., The.

Rechy, John. The Life & Adventures of Lyle Clemens. 2003. (Illus.). 352p. 24.00 (*0-8021-1746-5*, Grove Pr.) Grove/Atlantic, Inc.

Robinson, Elisabeth. The True & Outstanding Adventures of the Hunt Sisters. 2004. (Illus.). 336p. 23.95 (*0-316-73502-7*) Little Brown & Co.

Schine, Cathleen. She Is Me: A Novel. 2003. 272p. 23.95 (*0-316-78609-8*) Little Brown & Co.

**MUSICIANS—FICTION**

Andorka, Catherine. Once upon a Secret. 2002. (Five Star Romance Ser.). 252p. 25.95 (*0-7862-4601-4*, Five Star) Gale Group.

Atkins, Ace. Dirty South. 2004. 304p. 24.95 (*0-06-000462-2*, Morrow, William & Co.) Morrow/Avon.

Baldino, Georgiann. The Prodigy. 2000. 587p. E-Book 24.95 incl. audio compact disk (*0-9701368-4-6*) Hornkohl Communications.

Bastable, Bernard. Dead Mr. Mozart. 1996. 183p. mass mkt. o.s.i (*0-7515-1092-0*) Little Brown & Co.

—Dead Mr. Mozart. 1995. 19.95 o.p. (*0-312-11771-X*, Saint Martin's Minotaur) St. Martin's Pr.

—To Die Like a Gentleman. 1993. 192p. 16.95 o.p. (*0-312-09402-7*, Saint Martin's Minotaur) St. Martin's Pr.

—Too Many Notes, Mr. Mozart. 1996. 192p. 21.00 o.p. (*0-7867-0315-6*, Carroll & Graf Pubs.) Avalon Publishing Group.

—Too Many Notes, Mr. Mozart. 1998. 250p. mass mkt. o.s.i (*0-7515-1806-9*) Little Brown & Co.

Becker, Geoffrey. Bluestown. pap. 15.95 (*0-312-30456-0*, Saint Martin's Griffin); 1997. pap. 11.95 o.p. (*0-312-15481-X*, Saint Martin's Griffin); 1996. 280p. 21.95 o.p. (*0-312-14223-4*) St. Martin's Pr.

Bellacera, Carole. The Spotlight. 352p. 2000. 25.95 o.s.i (*0-312-87451-0*); 2001. reprint ed. mass mkt. 6.99 (*0-8125-6158-9*) Doherty, Tom Assocs., LLC. (Forge Bks.).

Bentz, Joseph. Song of Fire. 1995. 448p. (Orig.). pap. 12.99 (*0-7852-7882-6*) Nelson, Thomas Inc.

Blechta, Rick. Shooting Straight in the Dark. 2002. 328p. pap. 18.95 (*0-7710-1534-8*) McClelland & Stewart/Tundra Bks.

Block, Lawrence. The Burglar Who Dropped in on Elvis. unabr. ed. 1999. audio 5.99 (*1-55204-601-X*, PAC-8601) Durkin Hayes Publishing Ltd.

Bocelli, Andrea. The Music of Silence. l.t. ed. 2002. (Thorndike Press Large Print Biography Ser.). 400p. 29.45 (*0-7862-3900-X*) Gale Group.

—The Music of Silence. 2000. pap. 13.00 (*0-06-093749-1*) HarperCollins Pubs.

—The Music of Silence. 2001. (Illus.). 256p. 25.00 (*0-06-621286-3*, HarperEntertainment) Morrow/Avon.

Borders, Lisa. Cloud Cuckoo Land: A Novel. 2002. 453p. 27.95 (*1-57966-030-4*) River City Publishing.

Bowen, Peter. A Murder in Mayfair. 2002. (Missing Mystery Ser.: Vol. 40). 260p. pap. 13.95 (*1-890208-64-7*) Poisoned Pen Pr.

Bruns, Donn. Barbados Heat. Date not set. mass mkt. (*0-312-99459-1*, St. Martin's Paperbacks); 2003. 320p. 24.95 (*0-312-30492-7*) St. Martin's Pr.

Bull, Emma. War for the Oaks. Date not set. mass mkt. (*0-7653-4915-9*, Tor Bks.); 4th ed. 2001. 320p. pap. 13.95 (*0-7653-0034-6*, CPB1150, Orb Bks.) Doherty, Tom Assocs., LLC.

Burke, James Lee. Half of Paradise. Date not set. lib. bdg. 24.95 (*0-8488-1778-8*) Amereon, Ltd.

—Half of Paradise. 1998. 469p. mass mkt. 6.50 (*0-7868-8946-2*); 1995. 288p. pap. 10.95 (*0-7868-8117-8*) Hyperion Pr.

—Half of Paradise. l.t. ed. 2001. 482p. 29.95 (*0-7862-3398-2*); 487p. (*0-7540-1683-8*); 487p. (*0-7540-9079-5*) Thorndike Pr.

Burke, Martyn. Ivory Joe. 303p. 2002. 24.91 (*1-58721-540-3*); 2000. pap. 17.10 (*1-58721-515-2*) 1stBooks Library.

Burns, Donald. Piano People: Upright Grand - Downright Nuts. Nyhuis, Philip, ed. 2002. (Illus.). 300p. per. (*0-9716030-0-6*, SCP 3599) Sundown Canyon Productions, Inc.

Carter, Charlotte. Coq Au Vin. 1999. (Nanette Hayes Mystery Ser.). 200p. 22.00 o.s.i (*0-89296-678-5*) Mysterious Pr.

—Coq Au Vin. 2000. (Nanette Hayes Mysteries Ser.). 224p. mass mkt. 6.50 (*0-446-60787-8*) Warner Bks., Inc.

—Drumsticks. 2000. (Nanette Hayes Mystery Ser.). 208p. 22.95 (*0-89296-679-3*) Mysterious Pr.

—Rhode Island Red. (Mask Noir Ser.). 1998. 176p. pap. (*1-85242-591-1*); Vol. 1. 1997. 250p. (*1-85242-564-4*) Serpent's Tail Ltd.

—Rhode Island Red. 1999. (Nanette Hayes Mysteries Ser.). 224p. mass mkt. 5.99 (*0-446-60664-2*) Warner Bks., Inc.

Carter, Vincent O. Such Sweet Thunder: A Novel. 2003. (Illus.). 560p. 25.95 (*1-58642-058-5*) Steerforth Pr.

Charles, Paul. The Hissing of the Silent Lonely Room. 2002. (Inspector Christy Kennedy Mystery Ser.: No. 5). 286p. 29.95 (*1-899344-70-5*); pap. 15.95 (*1-899344-71-3*) Do-Not Pr., The GBR. *Dist:* Dufour Editions, Inc.

—I Love the Sound of Breaking Glass: An Inspector Christy Kennedy Mystery. 1997. (Bloodlines Ser.). 232p. pap. 14.95 (*1-899344-16-0*) Do-Not Pr., The GBR. *Dist:* Dufour Editions, Inc.

Charters, Samuel B. Elvis Presley Calls His Mother after the Ed Sullivan Show. 1992. 128p. pap. 10.95 (*0-918273-98-6*) Coffee Hse. Pr.

Cobb, Thomas. Crazy Heart. 256p. 1987. 15.95 o.p. (*0-06-015803-4*); 1988. reprint ed. 15.75 (*0-00-002379-5*, PL1519, Perennial); 1988. reprint ed. pap. 7.95 o.p. (*0-06-091519-6*, Perennial) HarperTrade.

—Crazy Heart. unabr. ed. 1989. audio 51.00 (*1-55690-124-0*, 89110E7) Recorded Bks., LLC.

Cohen, Paula. Gramercy Park: A Novel. 368p. 2002. 24.95 (*0-312-27552-8*); 2003. reprint ed. pap. 13.95 (*0-312-30997-X*, Saint Martin's Griffin) St. Martin's Pr.

Cook, Christopher. Robbers. 2000. 372p. 24.95 (*0-7867-0776-3*, Carroll & Graf Pubs.) Avalon Publishing Group.

—Robbers. 2002. 368p. pap. 14.00 (*0-425-18346-7*) Berkley Publishing Group.

Coulter, Catherine. False Pretenses. l.t. ed. 1998. (Large Print Book Ser.). 26.95 (*1-56895-594-4*, Wheeler Publishing, Inc.) Gale Group.

—False Pretenses. 1988. 19.95 o.p. (*0-453-00641-8*); 1989. 352p. reprint ed. mass mkt. 7.50 o.s.i (*0-451-40127-1*, Onyx) NAL.

Crouch, Stanley. Don't the Moon Look Lonesome? A Novel in Blues & Swing. 2000. 560p. 26.95 o.s.i (*0-375-40932-7*, Pantheon) Knopf Publishing Group.

Danziger, Robert. The Musical Ascent of Herman Being: A How-To Novel. (Illus.). 1985. 100p. pap. 7.95 o.p. (*0-9613427-4-9*); rev. ed. 1988. pap. 9.95 o.p. (*0-9613427-5-7*); 3rd rev. ed. 1995. 112p. (C). pap. 11.95 (*0-9613427-8-1*) Jordan Pr.

Davidson, Donald. The Big Ballad Jamboree. Ellison, Curtis W. & Pratt, William, eds. 295p. 1996. 27.00 (*0-87805-853-2*); 2nd ed. 1998. reprint ed. pap. 17.00 (*1-57806-098-2*) Univ. Pr. of Mississippi.

Dejohn, Jacqueline. Antonio's Wife. 2004. 368p. 24.95 (*0-06-055800-8*, ReganBooks) HarperTrade.

Delelis, Philippe. The Last Cantata. 2000. 352p. pap. 15.95 (*1-902881-31-1*); (*1-902881-30-3*) Toby Pr.

DeMarco, Gordon. Elvis in Aspic. 1994. 224p. pap. 9.00 o.p. (*1-883303-11-7*, West Coast Crime) Blue Heron Publishing.

Duchin, Peter. Blue Moon. 2003. 320p. mass mkt. 6.99 (*0-425-19306-3*) Berkley Publishing Group.

Duchin, Peter & Wilson, John Morgan. Blue Moon: A Philip Damon Mystery. 2002. 320p. 22.95 (*0-425-18645-8*, Prime Crime) Berkley Publishing Group.

—Good Morning, Heartache. 2003. 304p. 22.95 (*0-425-19180-X*, Prime Crime) Berkley Publishing Group.

Edwards, Arthur. Stuck Outside of Phoenix. 2003. 128p. pap. 11.95 (*0-595-28109-5*) iUniverse, Inc.

Egolf, Tristan. Skirt & the Fiddle: A Novel. 208p. 2004. pap. 12.00 (*0-8021-4042-4*); 2002. 24.00 (*0-8021-1722-8*) Grove/Atlantic, Inc. (Grove Pr.).

Ellison, Harlan. Spider Kiss. 1983. 240p. mass mkt. 2.95 o.s.i (*0-441-77795-3*); 1982. mass mkt. 2.25 o.s.i (*0-441-77793-7*) Ace Bks.

—Spider Kiss. 1975. pap. 1.50 o.s.i (*0-515-03883-0*, Jove) Berkley Publishing Group.

—Spider Kiss. E-Book 9.99 (*1-58586-379-3*); E-Book 9.99 (*0-7592-0909-X*) ereads.com.

Enquist, Anna. The Secret. Ringold, Jennette K., tr. from DUT. 2000. 274p. 29.95 (*1-902881-07-9*); pap. 15.95 (*1-902881-12-5*) Toby Pr.

Estleman, Loren D. Billy Gashade. l.t. ed. 2001. (Wheeler Large Print Book Ser.). 19.95 o.p. (*1-58724-088-2*, Wheeler Publishing, Inc.) Gale Group.

Falconer, Helen. Sky High. 2003. 224p. 24.95 (*0-89255-301-4*); pap. 12.95 (*0-89255-304-9*) Persea Bks., Inc.

Flagg, Fannie. Standing in the Rainbow: A Novel. 2003. 544p. mass mkt. 7.99 (*0-8041-1935-X*, Ballantine Bks.) Ballantine Bks.

—Standing in the Rainbow: A Novel. 2002. 512p. 25.95 (*0-679-42615-9*); 816p. 27.95 (*0-375-43172-1*) Random Hse., Inc.

Flanagan, Bill. A & R. E-Book 19.50 (*1-58945-563-0*) Adobe Systems, Inc.

— A & R. 2001. 352p. pap. 12.95 (*0-375-75830-5*) Random House Adult Trade Publishing Group.

— A & R. 2000. E-Book 19.50 (*0-375-50575-X*) Random Hse., Inc.

— A & R: A Novel. 2000. 352p. 23.95 o.s.i (*0-375-50266-1*) Random Hse., Inc.

Forman, Bruce. Trust Me: A Novel. 2003. 285p. pap. (*1-882897-75-7*) Lost Coast Pr.

Frommer, Sara H. Buried in Quilts. 1996. (WWL Mystery Ser.). per. (*0-373-26204-3*, 1-26204-7, Worldwide Library) Harlequin Enterprises, Ltd.

—Buried in Quilts. 1994. (Joan Spencer Mystery Ser.). 224p. 19.95 o.p. (*0-312-11472-9*, Saint Martin's Minotaur) St. Martin's Pr.

—Murder & Sullivan: A Joan Spencer Mystery. 1998. (WWL Mystery Ser.). per. (*0-373-26285-X*, 1-26285-6, Worldwide Library) Harlequin Enterprises, Ltd.

—Murder & Sullivan: A Joan Spencer Mystery. 1997. 256p. 21.95 o.p. (*0-312-15595-6*, Saint Martin's Minotaur) St. Martin's Pr.

—Murder in C Major. 1988. 224p. reprint ed. spiral bd. (*0-373-26017-2*, Harlequin Bks.) Harlequin Enterprises, Ltd.

—Murder in C Major. 2000. (Missing Mysteries Ser.: Vol. 17). 183p. pap. 14.95 (*1-890208-31-0*) Poisoned Pen Pr.

—Murder in C Major. 1986. 240p. 14.95 o.p. (*0-312-55299-8*) St. Martin's Pr.

—Murder in C Major. l.t. ed. 2003. 331p. 24.95 (*0-7862-5987-6*) Thorndike Pr.

—The Vanishing Violinist. 2000. (WWL Mystery Ser.: No. 359). 256p. mass mkt. (*0-373-26359-7*, 1-26359-9, Worldwide Library) Harlequin Enterprises, Ltd.

—The Vanishing Violinist: A Joan Spencer Mystery. 2nd ed. 1999. 272p. 23.95 (*0-312-24104-6*, Saint Martin's Minotaur) St. Martin's Pr.

Fuller, Jack. The Best of Jackson Payne. 2000. 336p. 25.00 (*0-375-40535-6*) Knopf, Alfred A. Inc.

—The Best of Jackson Payne: Novel. 2001. (Phoenix Fiction Ser.). 321p. pap. 15.00 (*0-226-26868-3*) Univ. of Chicago Pr.

Gailly, Christian. An Evening at the Club. Fairfield, Susan, tr. from FRE. 2003. 133p. 22.00 (*1-59051-049-6*); pap. (*1-59051-073-9*) Other Pr., LLC.

Gallison, Kate. Unholy Angels: A Mother Lavinia Grey Mystery. 1996. (Mother Lavinia Grey Mysteries Ser.). 272p. mass mkt. 5.99 o.s.i (*0-440-22220-6*) Dell Publishing.

Galloway, Janice. Clara. 2003. (Illus.). 432p. 25.00 (*0-684-84449-4*, Simon & Schuster) Simon & Schuster.

George, Elizabeth. A Traitor to Memory. 2002. mass mkt. 7.99 (*0-553-84037-1*) Bantam Bks.

—A Traitor to Memory. l.t. ed. 2001. 1184p. 26.95 (*0-375-43113-6*) Random Hse. Large Print.

Gibson, William. Idoru. 2003. 320p. pap. 13.95 (*0-425-19045-5*) Berkley Publishing Group.

Glatzer, Hal. A Fugue in Hell's Kitchen: A Katy Green Mystery. 2003. 240p. pap. 13.95 (*1-880284-70-7*) Daniel, John & Co., Pubs.

Goldmark, Kathi Kamen. And My Shoes Keep Walking Back: A Novel. pap. 13.95 (*0-8118-4315-7*); 2002. 288p. 22.95 (*0-8118-3495-6*) Chronicle Bks. LLC.

Gollin, James. Eliza's Galiardo. 1986. 180p. pap. 4.95 (*0-930330-54-4*) International Polygonics, Ltd.

—Eliza's Galiardo. 1983. 160p. 10.95 o.p. (*0-312-24244-1*) St. Martin's Pr.

Gould, Judith. Rhapsody: A Love Story. 1999. 352p. 23.95 o.s.i (*0-525-94516-4*, Dutton) Dutton/Plume.

—Rhapsody: A Love Story. l.t. ed. 2000. (Wheeler Large Print Book Ser.). 548p. 26.95 (*1-56895-849-8*, Wheeler Publishing, Inc.) Gale Group.

—Rhapsody: A Love Story. 2000. 432p. mass mkt. 6.99 (*0-451-40933-7*, Onyx) NAL.

Grabien, Deborah. The Weaver & the Factory Maid. Date not set. pap. (*0-312-31423-X*, St. Martin's Paperbacks); Date not set. mass mkt. (*0-312-98954-7*, St. Martin's Paperbacks); 2003. 192p. 22.95 (*0-312-31422-1*) St. Martin's Pr.

Graham, Robert & Baty, Keith. Elvis: The Novel. 1997. 222p. pap. 14.95 (*1-899344-19-5*) Do-Not Pr., The GBR. *Dist:* Dufour Editions, Inc.

Graham, Robert & Baty, Keith, contrib. by. Elvis: The Novel. 1984. pap. o.p. (*0-586-06162-2*) Flamingo GBR. *Dist:* Trafalgar Square.

Gray, Denis. Benny's Last Blast. 2002. 95p. pap. 8.00 (*0-8059-5314-0*) Dorrance Publishing Co., Inc.

Grenier, Roger. Piano Music for Four Hands. Kaplan, Alice, tr. from FRE. 2001. 153p. pap. 15.00 (*0-8032-7087-9*) Univ. of Nebraska Pr.

—Piano Music for Four Hands. Kaplan, Alice, tr. from FRE. & pref. by. 2001. 153p. text 45.00 (*0-8032-2181-9*) Univ. of Nebraska Pr.

Hamilton, Jane. Disobedience: A Novel. 2001. 288p. pap. 13.00 (*0-385-72046-7*, Knopf Bks. for Young Readers) Random Hse. Children's Bks.

—Disobedience: A Novel. l.t. ed. 2001. (Thorndike Basic Ser.). 463p. 31.95 (*0-7862-3159-9*); pap. 29.95 (*0-7862-3158-0*) Thorndike Pr.

Hansen, Erik F. Psalm at Journey's End. Tate, Joan, tr. 1996. 388p. 24.00 o.p. (*0-374-23868-5*) Farrar, Straus & Giroux.

—Psalm at Journey's End. Tate, Joana, tr. 1997. (Harvest Book Ser.). 384p. pap. 13.00 o.s.i (*0-15-600527-1*, Harvest Bks.) Harcourt Trade Pubs.

Hassler, Jon. Rookery Blues. 1997. 512p. mass mkt. 6.99 o.s.i (*0-345-42308-9*); 1996. 496p. pap. 12.00 o.s.i (*0-345-40641-9*) Ballantine Bks.

—Rookery Blues. abr. ed. audio 24.95 (*0-9650850-0-7*, PCAB-3500) Pine Curtain Audiobooks.

Hayes, Teddy. Dead by Popular Demand. 2003. 240p. pap. 10.95 (*1-902934-02-4*) X Pr., The GBR. *Dist:* National Bk. Network.

Henderson, William M. Stark Raving Elvis. 1997. 272p. mass mkt. 6.99 o.s.i (*0-425-15935-3*) Berkley Publishing Group.

—Stark Raving Elvis. 1984. 224p. 14.95 o.p. (*0-525-24264-3*, 01451-440, Dutton) Dutton/Plume.

—Stark Raving Elvis. 1987. 224p. pap. 5.95 o.p. (*0-671-64081-X*, Fireside) Simon & Schuster.

Hersey, John. Antonietta. 1993. 304p. pap. 19.00 (*0-679-74181-X*) Knopf, Alfred A. Inc.

—Antonietta. 1993. 4.99 o.p. (*0-517-10970-0*) Random Hse. Value Publishing.

Hijuelos, Oscar. The Mambo Kings Play Songs of Love. 1989. 384p. 18.95 o.s.i (*0-374-20125-0*) Farrar, Straus & Giroux.

—The Mambo Kings Play Songs of Love. (Perennial Classics Ser.). 2004. 464p. pap. 14.00 (*0-06-095545-7*); 1994. 416p. pap. 13.00 (*0-06-097327-7*); 1992. 416p. reprint ed. pap. 12.00 o.p. (*0-06-097451-6*) HarperTrade. (Perennial).

—Los Reyes del Mambo Tocan Canciones de Amor. 1996. (SPA.). 560p. pap. 14.00 (*0-06-095214-8*, HC12648, Perennial) HarperTrade.

—Una Sencilla Melodia Habanera. 2003. (SPA.). 368p. pap. 13.95 (*0-06-054353-1*, Rayo) HarperTrade.

Hill, Donna. Through the Fire. 2001. (Arabesque Ser.). 352p. mass mkt. 5.99 (*1-58314-130-8*) BET Bks.

Hower, Edward. Queen of the Silver Dollar. 1997. 220p. 24.00 (*1-877946-92-3*) Permanent Pr., The.

Hynd, Noel. The Prodigy. 1999. 352p. mass mkt. 5.99 o.s.i (*0-7860-0614-5*); 1998. 336p. 23.00 o.s.i (*1-57566-240-X*) Kensington Publishing Corp.

Ishiguro, Kazuo. The Unconsoled. unabr. collector's ed. 1997. audio 112.00 (*0-7366-4040-1*, 4539) Books on Tape, Inc.

—The Unconsoled. 1996. 544p. pap. 15.95 (*0-679-73587-9*) Knopf, Alfred A. Inc.

—The Unconsoled. 1999. pap. 2.99 (*0-517-48426-9*) Random Hse. Value Publishing.

Jackson, Faith Reyher. Meadow Fugue & Descant: A Novel. 2002. (*0-931846-66-8*); pap. (*0-931846-64-1*) Washington Writers' Publishing Hse.

Jeffers, H. Paul. Rubout at the Onyx. 1987. mass mkt. 2.95 o.s.i (*0-345-34676-9*) Ballantine Bks.

—Rubout at the Onyx. l.t. ed. 2001. 264p. (*0-7540-4427-0*); (*0-7540-4428-9*) Gale Group. (Macmillan Reference USA).

—Rubout at the Onyx. 1981. (Joan Kahn Bk.). 192p. 10.95 o.p. (*0-89919-046-4*) Houghton Mifflin Co.

—Rubout at the Onyx. l.t. ed. 2001. (Paperback Ser.). 264p. 24.95 (*0-7838-9330-2*) Thorndike Pr.

Jewell, Lisa. One-Hit Wonder. 2002. 352p. 23.95 o.s.i (*0-525-94653-5*, Dutton) Dutton/Plume.

—One-Hit Wonder. 464p. (*0-7278-5910-2*) Severn Hse. Pubs., Ltd.

Jones, Vanessa. Kindest Use of a Knife. 2003. 208p. pap. 12.00 (*0-00-655239-0*) HarperCollins Pubs. Ltd. GBR. *Dist:* Trafalgar Square.

Joy, Camden. Boy Island: A Novel. 2000. 24p. (J). pap. 12.00 (*0-688-17033-1*, Quill) HarperTrade.

Kallen, Lucille. C. B. Greenfield: No Lady in the House. 1984. 208p. mass mkt. 3.95 o.s.i (*0-345-32396-3*) Ballantine Bks.

—C. B. Greenfield: No Lady in the House. l.t. ed. 1982. 374p. reprint ed. 10.95 o.p. (*0-89621-365-X*) Thorndike Pr.

—C. B. Greenfield: The Piano Bird. 1985. 224p. mass mkt. 3.95 o.s.i (*0-345-31118-3*, Ballantine Bks.) Ballantine Bks.

—C. B. Greenfield: The Tanglewood Murder. 1985. mass mkt. 3.95 o.s.i (*0-345-33143-5*) Ballantine Bks.

—Introducing C. B. Greenfield. 1985. 208p. mass mkt. 3.95 o.s.i (*0-345-33426-4*); 1984. mass mkt. 2.50 o.p. (*0-345-32159-6*) Ballantine Bks.

—Introducing C. B. Greenfield. l.t. ed. 1980. 363p. reprint ed. 11.95 o.p. (*0-89621-260-2*) Thorndike Pr.

Kalpakian, Laura. Graced Land. 2nd ed. 1997. 304p. reprint ed. pap. 14.95 (*0-936085-39-8*) Blue Heron Publishing.

—Graced Land. 1992. 18.95 o.p. (*0-8021-1474-1*) Grove/Atlantic, Inc.

Kelley, Norman. A Phat Death: A Nina Halligan Mystery. 2003. 260p. pap. 14.95 (*1-888451-48-3*) Akashic Bks.

Kennedy, Pagan. The Exes. 1999. 208p. pap. 14.00 (*0-684-85442-2*, Scribner) Simon & Schuster.

Klein, Daniel. Kill Me Tender. 2000. 227p. 22.95 (*0-312-26187-X*, Saint Martin's Minotaur) St. Martin's Pr.

—Viva las Vengeance: A Murder Mystery Featuring Elvis Presley. 2003. 288p. 23.95 (*0-312-28806-9*, Saint Martin's Minotaur) St. Martin's Pr.

Klein, Daniel M. Kill Me Tender: A Murder Mystery Featuring Elvis Presley. E-Book 17.95 (*0-312-27583-8*) St. Martin's Pr.

Kosinski, Jerzy N. Pinball. 1989. 310p. reprint ed. pap. 8.95 o.p. (*1-55970-004-1*) Arcade Publishing, Inc.

—Pinball. 1982. pap. 3.95 o.p. (*0-553-23322-X*); o.p. (*0-553-01365-3*) Bantam Bks.

—Pinball. 1996. 320p. pap. 15.00 (*0-8021-3482-3*, Grove Pr.) Grove/Atlantic, Inc.

Lackey, Mercedes. Spirits White as Lightning. 2003. 512p. pap. 7.99 (*0-7434-3608-3*) Baen Bks.

Lackey, Mercedes & Edghill, Rosemary. Spirits White as Lightning. 2001. 448p. 24.00 (*0-671-31853-5*) Baen Bks.

Landis, J. D. Longing: A Novel. 2000. 464p. 26.00 o.s.i (*0-15-100453-6*) Harcourt Trade Pubs.

Leblance, Whitney J. Blues in the Wind. 2002. 330p. 23.95 (*0-913515-47-7*) River City Publishing.

Lebrecht, Norman. The Song of Names. 2004. 320p. pap. 14.00 (*1-4000-3489-2*) Knopf Publishing Group.

Levinson, Robert S. The Elvis & Marilyn Affair. 1999. (Neil Gulliver & Steve Marriner Novels Ser.). 304p. 24.95 (*0-312-86968-1*, Forge Bks.) Doherty, Tom Assocs., LLC.

—The Elvis & Marilyn Affair: A Neil Gulliver & Stevie Marriner Novel. 2000. 340p. mass mkt. 6.99 (*0-8125-8432-5*, Forge Bks.) Doherty, Tom Assocs., LLC.

Like Hell. 2001. 196p. per. 12.00 (*0-9707458-2-6*) Hope & Nonthings.

Livingston, Julian. The Anonymous North American Tour of Franz Liszt. 1999. 150p. E-Book 8.00 (*0-7388-8249-6*) Xlibris Corp.

Ludington, Max. Tiger in a Trance. 2003. 400p. 21.95 (*0-385-50704-6*, 53435432) Doubleday Publishing.

Machlis, Joseph. Allegro: A Novel. 1997. 224p. 23.00 o.p. (*0-393-04075-5*) Norton, W. W. & Co., Inc.

Magrs, Paul. All the Rage. 2003. 288p. reprint ed. pap. 9.95 (*0-7490-0568-8*) Allison & Busby, Ltd. GBR. *Dist:* International Publishers Marketing.

—All the Rage: Two Boys, Two Girls, & a Dream of Pop Stardom... 2002. pap. 14.95 (*0-7490-0536-X*) Allison & Busby, Ltd. GBR. *Dist:* International Publishers Marketing.

Makine, Andrei. The Music of a Life: Novel. Strachan, Geoffrey, tr. from FRE. 2002. 144p. pap. 21.95 (*1-55970-637-6*) Arcade Publishing, Inc.

Mansbach, Adam. Shackling Water. 2002. 240p. 22.95 (*0-385-50205-2*) Doubleday Publishing.

—Shackling Water. 2003. 240p. reprint ed. pap. 12.00 (*1-4000-3159-1*, Anchor) Knopf Publishing Group.

Margoshes, Dave. I'm Frankie Sterne. 2001. 287p. pap. 14.95 (*1-896300-23-5*) NeWest Pubs., Ltd. CAN. *Dist:* Strauss Consultants.

Marks, Walter. Dangerous Behavior. Penzler, Otto, ed. 2002. 288p. 24.00 (*0-7867-1043-8*, Carroll & Graf Pubs.) Avalon Publishing Group.

Marley, Louise. The Glass Harmonica: A Novel. 2000. 352p. pap. 13.95 o.s.i (*0-441-00729-5*) Ace Bks.

Marshall, Paule. The Fisher King: A Novel. l.t. ed. 2001. 256p. lib. bdg. 27.95 (*1-58547-074-0*) Ctr. Point Large Print.

—The Fisher King: A Novel. 224p. 2000. 23.00 o.s.i (*0-684-87283-8*); 2001. reprint ed. pap. 12.00 (*0-684-86970-5*) Simon & Schuster. (Scribner).

Martineau, Michael James. Let's Get Rowdy! 2000. 300p. pap. 12.98 (*1-930739-17-6*); E-Book (*1-930739-16-8*) Internet Book Co., Inc.

Maurensig, Paolo. Canone Inverso: A Novel. 1999. 208p. pap. 12.00 (*0-8050-6302-1*, Owl Bks.) Holt, Henry & Co.

Maxwell, Evan. Season of the Swan. l.t. ed. 1998. 23.95 (*1-57490-132-X*, Beeler Large Print Bks.) Beeler, Thomas T. Publisher.

—Season of the Swan. 256p. 1998. mass mkt. 6.50 o.s.i (*0-06-109975-9*); 1997. 19.00 o.p. (*0-06-017529-X*) HarperCollins Pubs.

—Season of the Swan, unabr. ed. 1998. audio 51.00 (*0-7887-2005-8*, 95392E7) Recorded Bks., LLC.

Maxwell, John. Point Fury. 2003. 384p. mass mkt. 6.99 (*0-7434-5340-9*, Pocket Star); 2002. 320p. 25.00 (*0-7432-2207-5*, Scribner) Simon & Schuster.

McComas, Paul. Unplugged: A Novel. 2002. 272p. pap. 14.95 (*1-880284-60-X*) Daniel, John & Co., Pubs.

McDonough, Yona Zeldis. The Four Temperaments. 2002. 320p. 23.95 (*0-385-50361-X*) Doubleday Publishing.

Mendelson, Cheryl. Morningside Heights: A Novel. 2003. 336p. 24.95 (*0-375-50836-8*) Random Hse., Inc.

Milofsky, David. Playing from Memory. 1982. 304p. pap. 2.95 o.p. (*0-380-57166-8*, 57166-8, Avon Bks.) Morrow/Avon.

—Playing from Memory. 1981. 12.95 o.p. (*0-671-25252-6*, Simon & Schuster) Simon & Schuster.

—Playing from Memory. 1999. 270p. reprint ed. pap. 14.95 (*0-87081-526-1*) Univ. Pr. of Colorado.

Monteros, Maria. Flamenco. 1999. 80p. pap. 8.00 o.p. (*0-8059-4740-X*) Dorrance Publishing Co., Inc.

Moody, Bill. Bird Lives! An Evan Horne Mystery. 2000. (Evan Horne Mysteries Ser.: Bk. 350). per. (*0-373-26350-3*, 1-26350-8, Worldwide Library) Harlequin Enterprises, Ltd.

—Bird Lives! An Evan Horne Mystery. 1999. (Evan Horne Mysteries Ser.). 256p. 22.95 (*0-8027-3327-1*) Walker & Co.

—Death of A Tenor Man: An Evan Horne Mystery. 1995. 240p. 21.95 (*0-8027-3269-0*) Walker & Co.

—Death of a Tenor Man: An Evan Horne Mystery. 1997. 288p. mass mkt. 5.50 o.s.i (*0-440-22324-5*) Dell Publishing.

—Looking for Chet Baker: An Evan Horne Mystery. 2003. (WWL Mystery Ser.: No. 450). 272p. mass mkt. (*0-373-26450-X*, Worldwide Library) Harlequin Enterprises, Ltd.

—Looking for Chet Baker: An Evan Horne Mystery. 2002. 253p. 23.95 (*0-8027-3368-9*) Walker & Co.

—Solo Hand. 1996. 304p. mass mkt. 5.50 o.s.i (*0-440-22322-9*) Dell Publishing.

—Solo Hand. 2003. 193p. pap. 13.95 (*0-9644138-3-3*, Dark City Bks.) OffByOne Pr.

—Solo Hand. 1994. 19.95 (*0-8027-3248-8*) Walker & Co.

—The Sound of the Trumpet: An Evan Horne Mystery. 1998. (Evan Horne Mysteries Ser.: Vol. 3). 304p. mass mkt. 5.99 o.s.i (*0-440-22194-3*) Dell Publishing.

—The Sound of the Trumpet: An Evan Horne Mystery. 1997. (Evan Horne Mysteries Ser.). 240p. 21.95 (*0-8027-3291-7*) Walker & Co.

Mortman, Doris. The Wild Rose. 1992. 848p. mass mkt. 6.99 o.s.i (*0-553-29761-9*) Bantam Bks.

Mosley, Walter. RL's Dream. abr. ed. 1995. audio 16.95 (*1-55927-345-3*, 392939) Audio Renaissance.

—RL's Dream. unabr. ed. 1996. audio 48.00 Books on Tape, Inc.

—RL's Dream. 1995. 288p. 22.00 (*0-393-03802-5*) Norton, W. W. & Co., Inc.

—RL's Dream. 1996. 272p. pap. 14.00 (*0-671-88428-X*, Washington Square Pr.) Simon & Schuster.

Neate, Patrick. Twelve Bar Blues. 416p. 2004. pap. 14.00 (*0-8021-4056-4*); 2002. 24.00 (*0-8021-1727-9*) Grove/Atlantic, Inc. (Grove Pr.).

Nehring, Radine Trees. Music to Die For. 2003. (Something to Die for Ser.: Vol. 2). 273p. pap. 14.00 (*0-9661879-8-9*) St Kitts Pr.

O'Keefe, Matt. You Think You Hear. E-Book 23.95 (*0-312-70147-0*); 2001. 295p. 23.95 (*0-312-26903-X*) St. Martin's Pr.

Outlet Book Company Staff. Murder in C Major. 1987. 1.99 o.p. (*0-517-65735-X*) Random Hse. Value Publishing.

Parker, Graham. Carp Fishing on Valium. 2000. 227p. 22.95 (*0-312-26485-2*) St. Martin's Pr.

—The Other Life of Brian. 2003. 272p. 13.95 (*1-56025-549-8*, Thunder's Mouth Pr.) Avalon Publishing Group.

Parker, Thomas T. Anna, Ann, Annie. 336p. 1994. pap. 10.95 o.p. (*0-452-27225-4*, Plume); 1993. 21.00 o.p. (*0-525-93607-6*, Dutton) Dutton/Plume.

Patchett, Ann. Taft. 1999. 272p. pap. 13.00 o.s.i (*0-345-43353-X*, Ballantine Bks.); 1995. mass mkt. 5.99 o.s.i (*0-8041-1388-2*, Ivy Bks.) Ballantine Bks.

—Taft. 2003. 256p. pap. 12.95 (*0-06-054076-1*, Perennial) HarperTrade.

Perry, Steve. Windowpane. 2003. 440p. pap. 13.95 (*1-4104-0154-5*, Five Star Trade); 413p. 25.95 (*0-7862-5050-X*, Five Star) Gale Group.

Pina, Gabrielle. Bliss: A Novel. 2002. 272p. pap. 12.95 (*0-375-76103-9*, Villard Bks.) Random House Adult Trade Publishing Group.

Pollack, Neal. Never Mind the Pollacks. 2003. 272p. 23.95 (*0-06-052790-0*) HarperCollins Pubs.

Proulx, E. Annie. Accordion Crimes. 1997. 432p. pap. 13.00 (*0-684-83154-6*); 1996. 381p. 25.00 (*0-684-19548-8*); 1996. 544p. pap. 7.50 (*0-684-83282-8*) Simon & Schuster. (Scribner).

—Accordion Crimes. 1998. 4.98 o.p. (*0-7651-0770-8*) Smithmark Pubs., Inc.

Rice, Anne. The Violin. 2002. (SPA.). pap. 17.95 (*950-08-2295-4*, AA11960) Atlantida ARG. *Dist:* Lectorum Pubns., Inc.

—The Violin. 1999. 384p. mass mkt. 7.99 (*0-345-42530-8*); 1998. 304p. pap. 14.00 (*0-345-38942-5*); 1998. 7.50 (*0-345-42446-8*, Del Rey) Ballantine Bks.

—The Violin. l.t. ed. 1997. pap. 25.95 o.p. (*0-7838-8247-5*, Macmillan Reference USA) Gale Group.

—The Violin. 1997. 289p. 25.95 (*0-679-43302-3*) Knopf, Alfred A. Inc.

—The Violin. unabr. ed. 1997. audio 39.95 (*0-679-46066-7*, 105975, RH Audio) Random Hse. Audio Publishing Group.

—The Violin. l.t. ed. 1997. (Large Print Ser.). 496p. pap. 25.95 (*0-679-77444-0*) Random Hse. Large Print.

—The Violin. deluxe ltd. ed. 1997. 304p. 150.00 (*1-890885-00-2*) Trice, B.E. Publishing.

Ripley, J. R. The Body from Ipanema: A Tony Kozol Mystery. 2002. (Tony Kozol Mystery Ser.: Vol. 4). 244p. (YA). kivar 22.95 (*1-892695-08-1*) Long Wind Publishing.

Rolland, Romain. Jean-Christophe. 1996. 1584p. 35.00 o.p. (*0-7867-0307-5*, Carroll & Graf Pubs.) Avalon Publishing Group.

—Jean-Christophe. 1978. (FRE.). 1656p. 115.00 (*0-7859-5283-7*) French & European Pubns., Inc.

Rose, M. L. The Road to Eden's Ridge. 2002. 256p. 21.99 (*1-55853-993-X*) Rutledge Hill Pr.

Rushdie, Salman. The Ground Beneath Her Feet: A Novel. l.t. ed. 2000. (Thorndike/G. K. Hall Paperback Bestsellers Ser.). 816p. pap. 30.95 (*0-7838-8712-4*, Macmillan Reference USA) Gale Group.

—The Ground Beneath Her Feet: A Novel. 1999. 592p. 27.50 o.s.i (*0-8050-5308-5*) Holt, Henry & Co.

—The Ground Beneath Her Feet: A Novel. abr. ed. 1999. audio 25.00 (*0-7871-1917-2*, Dove Audio) NewStar Media, Inc.

—The Ground Beneath Her Feet: A Novel. 2000. 592p. pap. 16.00 (*0-312-25499-7*) Picador.

—The Ground Beneath Her Feet: A Novel. unabr. ed. 1999. audio 104.00 (*0-7887-3747-3*, 95939E5); audio 163.00 (*0-7887-4350-3*, 95939E7) Recorded Bks., LLC.

—The Ground Beneath Her Feet: A Novel. l.t. ed. 1999. (G. K. Hall Core Ser.). 816p. 31.95 (*0-7838-8713-2*) Thorndike Pr.

Salzman, Mark. The Soloist. 1995. 304p. pap. 13.00 (*0-679-75926-3*, Vintage) Knopf Publishing Group.

—The Soloist. l.t. ed. 2000. 300p. 34.95 (*1-56000-446-0*) Transaction Pubs.

Schneider, Robert. Brother of Sleep. 224p. 1996. pap. 13.95 (*0-87951-659-3*); 1995. 21.95 (*0-87951-595-3*) Overlook Pr., The.

Schwartzman, J. I. Grace Note. 1999. 307p. pap. 15.95 (*1-928863-03-5*, Aventura Bks.) Great Marsh Pr.

Seth, Vikram. An Equal Music. abr. ed. 1999. audio 25.00 o.s.i (*0-553-52636-7*, RH Audio) Random Hse. Audio Publishing Group.

—An Equal Music. unabr. ed. 2000. audio 102.00 (*0-7887-4493-3*, H1080E7, Clipper Audio) Recorded Bks., LLC.

—An Equal Music: A Novel. 2000. (International Ser.). 400p. pap. 14.00 (*0-375-70924-X*, Vintage) Knopf Publishing Group.

Sheepshanks, Mary. Facing the Music. 1997. 320p. 22.95 o.p. (*0-312-16832-2*) St. Martin's Pr.

Skvorecky, Josef. The Bass Saxophone. Polackvoa-Henley, Kaca, tr. 1979. 8.95 o.s.i (*0-394-50267-1*, Knopf Bks. for Young Readers) Random Hse. Children's Bks.

—The Bass Saxophone. 1985. mass mkt. 5.95 (*0-671-55681-9*, Washington Square Pr.) Simon & Schuster.

—Bass Saxophone. 1999. 256p. pap. 12.00 (*0-88001-370-2*, Ecco) HarperTrade.

Sloan, Kay & Pierce, Constance, eds. Elvis Rising: Stories of the King. 1993. 176p. (Orig.). pap. 10.00 (*0-380-77216-7*, Avon Bks.) Morrow/Avon.

—Elvis Rising: Stories on the King. 1997. 262p. reprint ed. pap. text 7.00 o.p. (*0-7881-5120-7*) DIANE Publishing Co.

Smith, Andrea. Friday Night at Honeybee's. 2004. 400p. pap. 12.00 (*0-385-33698-5*, Delta) Dell Publishing.

Sorrentino, Christopher. Sound on Sound. 1995. 200p. 19.95 (*1-56478-073-2*) Dalkey Archive Pr.

St. Marc, Jehan. To Walk in Newness of Life. 2001. 408p. pap. 20.95 (*0-595-19989-5*) iUniverse, Inc.

Steen, Fred. Bluesman. 1998. 190p. pap. 16.95 (*1-85756-353-0*) Janus Publishing Co. GBR. *Dist:* Independent Pubs. Group, Paul & Co. Pubs. Consortium, Inc.

Stern, Amanda. The Long Haul. 2003. 128p. pap. 12.00 (*1-932360-06-9*) Soft Skull Pr., Inc.

Suarez, Virgil. Latin Jazz. 2002. (Voices of the South Ser.). 304p. pap. 16.95 (*0-8071-2790-6*) Louisiana State Univ. Pr.

—Latin Jazz. 1989. 290p. 18.95 o.p. (*0-688-08475-3*, Morrow, William & Co.) Morrow/Avon.

—Latin Jazz. 1990. pap. 9.95 o.p. (*0-671-70535-0*, Fireside) Simon & Schuster.

Sublett, Jesse. Boiled in Concrete. 1999. pap. 3.95 (*0-14-015230-X*); 1992. 320p. 20.00 o.p. (*0-670-83888-8*) Viking Penguin. (Viking).

—Rock Critic Murders. 1990. 240p. mass mkt. 3.50 o.s.i (*0-440-20703-7*) Dell Publishing.

—Rock Critic Murders. 1989. pap. 3.95 o.p. (*0-14-011208-1*) Penguin Group (USA) Inc.

—Rock Critic Murders. 1989. 240p. 16.95 o.p. (*0-670-82302-3*) Viking Penguin.

—Tough Baby. 1999. pap. 4.95 (*0-14-012397-0*); 1990. 256p. 16.95 o.p. (*0-670-83325-8*) Viking Penguin. (Viking).

Sutherland. Jelly Roll. 2000. 413p. pap. 11.95 (*1-86230-030-5*) Transworld Publishers Ltd. GBR. *Dist:* Trafalgar Square.

Thomas, D. M. The Flute-Player. 1979. 8.95 o.p. (*0-525-10727-4*, Dutton) Dutton/Plume.

—The Flute-Player. 1979. 192 p. (*0-575-02642-1*) Gollancz, Victor.

—The Flute-Player. 1984. mass mkt. 3.95 o.s.i (*0-671-50885-7*); 1982. 224p. reprint ed. mass mkt. 3.95 o.p. (*0-671-44211-2*) Simon & Schuster. (Pocket).

Townsend, Lindsay. Voices in the Dark. l.t. ed. 1999. (Magna Large Print Ser.). 560p. 31.99 (*0-7505-1372-1*) Magna Large Print Bks. GBR. *Dist:* Ulverscroft Large Print Bks., Ltd., Ulverscroft Large Print Canada, Ltd.

Turner, Frederick. 1929: A Novel of the Jazz Age. 2003. 400p. text 25.00 (*1-58243-265-1*, Basic Civitas Bks.) Basic Bks.

Vaughn, Michael. Gabriella's Voice. 2000. E-Book 7.99 (*1-929429-47-9*) Dead End Street, LLC.

Vaughn, Michael J. Gabriella's Voice. 2000. E-Book 9.97 (*1-929429-48-7*) Dead End Street, LLC.

—Gabriella's Voice. Mrazovich, Christine & Rutledge, John P., eds. rev. ed. 2001. 244p. pap. 14.99 (*1-929429-95-9*) Dead End Street, LLC.

Voss, Louise. To Be Someone: A Novel. 2001. 400p. 23.00 o.s.i (*0-609-60892-4*, Crown) Crown Publishing Group.

Warner, Alan. The Sopranos. 1999. 256p. 24.00 o.p. (*0-374-26670-0*) Farrar, Straus & Giroux.

—The Sopranos. 2000. (Harvest Book Ser.). 336p. pap. 14.00 (*0-15-601201-4*, Harvest Bks.) Harcourt Trade Pubs.

Weber, Janice. Hot Ticket. 2000. 384p. mass mkt. 6.50 (*0-446-60788-6*); 1998. 337p. 24.00 o.p. (*0-446-51773-9*) Warner Bks., Inc.

Wheatcroft, John. Trio with Four Players. 1996. 144p. 19.95 (*0-8453-4856-6*, Cornwall Bks.) Associated Univ. Presses.

Williams, John. Lake Moon: A Novel. 2002. (Illus.). 304p. 24.95 (*0-86554-802-1*) Mercer Univ. Pr.

Williams, Niall. As It Is in Heaven. abr. ed. 2001. audio (*0-333-78257-7*) Macmillan U.K. GBR. *Dist:* Macmillan Publishing Co., Inc.

—As It Is in Heaven. 2000. 310p. E-Book 9.95 (*0-446-92334-6*); 1999. E-Book 9.95 (*0-446-96005-5*) Time Warner Bk. Group.

Womack, Jack. Elvissey: A Novel of Elvis Past & Elvis Future. 1997. 319p. reprint ed. pap. text 13.00 o.p. (*0-7881-5117-7*) DIANE Publishing Co.

—Elvissey: A Novel of Elvis Past & Elvis Future. 1997. 320p. reprint ed. pap. 13.50 (*0-8021-3495-5*, Grove Pr.) Grove/Atlantic, Inc.

York, Lynn. The Piano Teacher: A Novel of Swan's Knob. 2004. 304p. pap. 13.00 (*0-452-28477-5*, Plume) Dutton/Plume.

## N

### NUNS—FICTION

Black, Veronica. A Vow of Adoration: A Sister Joan Mystery. 1997. (Sister Joan Mystery Ser.: Vol. 9). 190p. 20.95 (*0-312-18205-8*, Saint Martin's Minotaur) St. Martin's Pr.

—A Vow of Chastity: A Sister Joan Mystery. 1993. mass mkt. 4.50 o.s.i (*0-8041-1055-7*, Ivy Bks.) Ballantine Bks.

—A Vow of Chastity: A Sister Joan Mystery. 1992. 192p. 16.95 o.p. (*0-312-07112-4*, Saint Martin's Minotaur) St. Martin's Pr.

—A Vow of Chastity: A Sister Joan Mystery. l.t. ed. 1992. (Linford Mystery Library). 400p. pap. 17.99 o.p. (*0-7089-7262-4*, Linford) Thorpe, F. A. Pubs. GBR. *Dist:* Ulverscroft Large Print Bks., Ltd., Ulverscroft Large Print Canada, Ltd.

—A Vow of Compassion: A Sister Joan Mystery. 1998. (Sister Joan Mystery Ser.: Vol. 10). 208p. 20.95 (*0-312-19354-8*, Saint Martin's Minotaur) St. Martin's Pr.

—A Vow of Compassion: A Sister Joan Mystery. l.t. ed. 1998. (Ulverscroft Large Print Ser.). 336p. 29.99 (*0-7089-3972-4*, Ulverscroft) Thorpe, F. A. Pubs. GBR. *Dist:* Ulverscroft Large Print Bks., Ltd., Ulverscroft Large Print Canada, Ltd.

—A Vow of Devotion: A Sister Joan Mystery. (Sister Joan Mystery Ser.). 1997. mass mkt. 5.50 o.s.i (*0-312-96005-0*, St. Martin's Paperbacks); 1995. 186p. 20.95 o.p. (*0-312-13206-9*, Saint Martin's Minotaur) St. Martin's Pr.

—A Vow of Devotion: A Sister Joan Mystery. l.t. ed. 1998. (Nightingale Ser.). 276p. pap. 20.95 (*0-7838-8388-9*) Thorndike Pr.

—A Vow of Fidelity: A Sister Joan Mystery. 1996. 208p. text 19.95 o.p. (*0-312-14064-9*, Saint Martin's Minotaur); Vol. 1. 1997. (Vow of Fidelity Ser.: Vol. 1). 192p. mass mkt. 5.50 (*0-312-96259-2*, St. Martin's Paperbacks) St. Martin's Pr.

—A Vow of Fidelity: A Sister Joan Mystery. l.t. ed. 1997. (Ulverscroft Large Print Ser.). 352p. 29.99 (*0-7089-3697-0*, Ulverscroft) Thorpe, F. A. Pubs. GBR. *Dist:* Ulverscroft Large Print Bks., Ltd., Ulverscroft Large Print Canada, Ltd.

—A Vow of Obedience: A Sister Joan Mystery. 1995. (Sister Joan Mystery Ser.). mass mkt. 5.50 o.s.i (*0-8041-1245-2*, Ivy Bks.) Ballantine Bks.

—A Vow of Obedience: A Sister Joan Mystery. l.t. ed. 1994. 298p. pap. 19.95 (*0-8161-7472-5*, Macmillan Reference USA) Gale Group.

—A Vow of Obedience: A Sister Joan Mystery. 1996. mass mkt. 143.76 (*0-312-95718-1*); 1994. 192p. 18.95 o.p. (*0-312-10573-8*, Saint Martin's Minotaur) St. Martin's Pr.

—A Vow of Penance: A Sister Joan Mystery. 1996. mass mkt. 5.50 (*0-312-95850-1*, St. Martin's Paperbacks); 1994. 270p. 19.95 o.p. (*0-312-11092-8*, Saint Martin's Minotaur) St. Martin's Pr.

—A Vow of Penance: A Sister Joan Mystery. l.t. ed. 1995. (Ulverscroft Large Print Ser.). 352p. 29.99 (*0-7089-3326-2*, Ulverscroft) Thorpe, F. A. Pubs. GBR. *Dist:* Ulverscroft Large Print Bks., Ltd., Ulverscroft Large Print Canada, Ltd.

—A Vow of Poverty: A Sister Joan Mystery. 1996. 208p. 20.95 o.p. (*0-312-14756-2*, Saint Martin's Minotaur) St. Martin's Pr.

—A Vow of Poverty: A Sister Joan Mystery. l.t. ed. 1997. (Ulverscroft Large Print Ser.). 388p. 29.99 (*0-7089-3733-0*, Ulverscroft) Thorpe, F. A. Pubs. GBR. *Dist:* Ulverscroft Large Print Bks., Ltd., Ulverscroft Large Print Canada, Ltd.

—A Vow of Sanctity: A Sister Joan Mystery. 1994. mass mkt. 4.99 o.s.i (*0-8041-1244-4*, Ivy Bks.) Ballantine Bks.

—A Vow of Sanctity: A Sister Joan Mystery. 1993. 192p. 16.95 (*0-312-09408-6*, Saint Martin's Minotaur) St. Martin's Pr.

—A Vow of Sanctity: A Sister Joan Mystery. l.t. ed. 1994. (Ulverscroft Large Print Ser.). 400p. 29.99 o.p. (*0-7089-3197-9*, Ulverscroft) Thorpe, F. A. Pubs. GBR. *Dist:* Ulverscroft Large Print Bks., Ltd., Ulverscroft Large Print Canada, Ltd.

—A Vow of Silence: A Sister Joan Mystery. 1991. mass mkt. 4.99 o.s.i (*0-8041-0814-5*, Ivy Bks.) Ballantine Bks.

—A Vow of Silence: A Sister Joan Mystery. 1990. 15.95 o.p. (*0-312-04441-0*, Saint Martin's Minotaur) St. Martin's Pr.

—A Vow of Silence: A Sister Joan Mystery. l.t. ed. 1991. (Ulverscroft Large Print Ser.). 29.99 (*0-7089-2529-4*, Ulverscroft) Thorpe, F. A. Pubs. GBR. *Dist:* Ulverscroft Large Print Bks., Ltd., Ulverscroft Large Print Canada, Ltd.

Boucher, Anthony. Nine Times Nine. 1986. 254p. pap. 4.95 o.p. (*0-930330-37-4*) International Polygonics, Ltd.

—Rocket to the Morgue. 1988. 176p. pap. 4.95 (*0-930330-82-X*) International Polygonics, Ltd.

Frazer, Margaret. The Bastard's Tale: A Dame Frevisse Mystery. 2003. (Dame Frevisse Mystery Ser.). 320p. 22.95 (*0-425-18649-0*, Prime Crime) Berkley Publishing Group.

—The Bishop's Tale. 1994. 208p. mass mkt. 6.50 (*0-425-14492-5*, Prime Crime) Berkley Publishing Group.

—The Boy's Tale. 1995. (Dame Frevisse Mystery Ser.). 240p. (Orig.). mass mkt. 6.50 (*0-425-14899-8*) Berkley Publishing Group.

—The Clerk's Tale. 2002. (Dame Frevisse Mystery Ser.). 320p. 22.95 (*0-425-18324-6*, Prime Crime) Berkley Publishing Group.

—The Maiden's Tale. 1998. (Dame Frevisse Mystery Ser.). 256p. mass mkt. 6.99 (*0-425-16407-1*, Prime Crime) Berkley Publishing Group.

—The Murderer's Tale. 1996. 240p. mass mkt. 5.99 o.s.i (*0-425-15406-8*, Prime Crime) Berkley Publishing Group.

—The Novice's Tale. 1993. (Dame Frevisse Mystery Ser.). 240p. (Orig.). mass mkt. 6.99 (*0-425-14321-X*) Berkley Publishing Group.

—The Outlaw's Tale. 224p. 1995. mass mkt. 5.99 o.s.i (*0-425-15119-0*); 1994. mass mkt. 4.50 o.s.i (*0-515-11335-2*, Jove) Berkley Publishing Group.

—The Prioress' Tale. 1997. (Dame Frevisse Mystery Ser.). 256p. mass mkt. 6.99 (*0-425-15944-2*, Prime Crime) Berkley Publishing Group.

—The Reeve's Tale. (Dame Frevisse Mystery Ser.). 288p. 1999. 21.95 o.s.i (*0-425-17232-5*, Prime Crime); 2000. reprint ed. mass mkt. 6.99 (*0-425-17667-3*) Berkley Publishing Group.

—The Reeve's Tale. l.t. ed. 2000. (Basic Ser.). 424p. 27.95 (*0-7862-2548-3*) Thorndike Pr.

—The Servant's Tale. 1993. (Dame Frevisse Mystery Ser.). mass mkt. 6.99 (*0-425-14389-9*); 240p. mass mkt. 4.50 o.s.i (*0-515-11163-5*, Jove) Berkley Publishing Group.

—The Squire's Tale. 2000. (Dame Frevisse Mystery Ser.). 288p. 21.95 o.s.i (*0-425-17678-9*) Berkley Publishing Group.

Frazer, Margaret, et al. The Novice's Tale. 1992. (Orig.). mass mkt. 4.50 o.s.i (*0-515-10900-2*, Jove) Berkley Publishing Group.

Gallison, Kate. Grave Misgivings: A Mother Lavinia Grey Mystery. 1999. (Mother Lavinia Grey Mysteries Ser.). 256p. mass mkt. 5.99 o.s.i (*0-440-22413-6*) Dell Publishing.

—Hasty Retreat: A Mother Lavinia Grey Mystery. 1998. (Mother Lavinia Grey Mysteries Ser.). 256p. mass mkt. 5.99 o.s.i (*0-440-22410-1*, Dell Bks.) Dell Publishing.

Gilman, Dorothy. A Nun in the Closet. 1986. 224p. mass mkt. 6.50 (*0-449-21167-3*); 1984. mass mkt. 2.50 o.p. (*0-449-20662-9*) Ballantine Bks. (Fawcett).

—A Nun in the Closet. 1975. 192p. 5.95 o.p. (*0-385-05635-4*) Doubleday Publishing.

—A Nun in the Closet. 1975. lib. bdg. 10.95 o.p. (*0-8161-6296-4*); 1993. 296p. pap. 16.95 o.p. (*0-8161-5719-7*) Gale Group. (Macmillan Reference USA).

Harris, Joanne. Holy Fools. 2004. 368p. 24.95 (*0-06-055912-8*, Morrow, William & Co.) Morrow/Avon.

Hilger, Christine. A Force of Habit: A Sister Abigail Mystery. l.t. ed. 2001. 288p. 24.95 (*0-7838-9638-7*) Thorndike Pr.

—A Force of Habit: A Sister Abigail Mystery. 2000. (Sister Abigail Mysteries Ser.). 326p. pap. 7.99 o.s.i (*0-87788-261-4*, Shaw) WaterBrook Pr.

Hough, R. Sister Agnes. 1998. (Illus.). x, 196p. text 45.00 (*0-7195-5561-2*) Murray, John Pubs., Ltd. GBR. *Dist:* Trafalgar Square.

Joseph, Alison. The Hour of Our Death: A Sister Agnes Mystery. 1997. 288p. text 23.95 o.p. (*0-312-15142-X*, Saint Martin's Minotaur) St. Martin's Pr.

—Sacred Hearts: A Mystery Introducing Sister Agnes. 1996. 256p. 22.95 o.p. (*0-312-14405-9*, Saint Martin's Minotaur) St. Martin's Pr.

Kelby, N. M. In the Company of Angels: A Novel. 2002. (Illus.). 192p. pap. 12.00 (*0-7868-8583-1*) Hyperion Pr.

Leonardi, Susan J. And Then They Were Nuns. 2003. pap. 14.95 (*1-56341-126-1*) Firebrand Bks.

Lira, Gonzalo. Counterparts. 1999. 400p. reprint ed. mass mkt. 6.99 o.s.i (*0-515-12429-X*, Jove) Berkley Publishing Group.

—Counterparts. 1997. 343p. 24.95 o.p. (*0-399-14312-2*, G. P. Putnam's Sons) Penguin Group (USA) Inc.

—Counterparts. 1998. o.p. (*0-399-14361-0*) Putnam Publishing Group, The.

McConnell, Frank. Blood Lake: A Harry Garnish/Bridget O'Toole Mystery. l.t. ed. 1988. 19.95 o.p. (*1-55504-590-1*); pap. 17.95 o.p. (*1-55504-573-1*) BBC Audiobooks America.

—Blood Lake: A Harry Garnish/Bridget O'Toole Mystery. 1988. (Crime Ser.). 256p. pap. 3.95 o.p. (*0-14-010755-X*, Penguin Bks.); 39.50 o.p. (*0-14-778359-3*) Viking Penguin.

—Blood Lake: A Harry Garnish/Bridget O'Toole Mystery. 1987. 256p. 16.95 o.s.i (*0-8027-5673-5*) Walker & Co.

—The Frog King: A Harry Garnish/Bridget O'Toole Mystery. l.t. ed. 1992. pap. 19.95 o.p. (*0-7927-1175-0*); 21.95 o.p. (*0-7927-1149-1*, CH0241) BBC Audiobooks America.

—The Frog King: A Harry Garnish/Bridget O'Toole Mystery. 1990. 192p. 18.95 o.p. (*0-8027-5748-0*) Walker & Co.

—Liar's Poker: A Harry Garnish/Bridget O'Toole Mystery. 1993. 234p. 19.95 (*0-8027-3229-1*) Walker & Co.

—Murder among Friends: A Harry Garnish/Bridget O'Toole Mystery. l.t. ed. 1986. pap. 13.95 o.p. (*0-7451-9149-5*) BBC Audiobooks America.

—Murder among Friends: A Harry Garnish/Bridget O'Toole Mystery. 1988. pap. 39.50 o.p. (*0-14-778313-5*); 192p. mass mkt. 3.95 o.p. (*0-451-82189-0*, Penguin Bks.) Viking Penguin.

—Murder among Friends: A Harry Garnish/Bridget O'Toole Mystery. 1983. 192p. 12.95 o.s.i (*0-8027-5567-4*) Walker & Co.

Newman, Sharan. Death Comes As Epiphany. 1995. 322p. mass mkt. 5.99 (*0-8125-2293-1*, Forge Bks.); 1993. 320p. 19.95 (*0-312-85419-6*, Tor Bks.); 2002. reprint ed. pap. 14.95 (*0-7653-0374-4*, Forge Bks.) Doherty, Tom Assocs., LLC.

—The Devil's Door. 1995. 416p. mass mkt. 6.99 (*0-8125-2295-8*); 1994. 384p. 21.95 o.p. (*0-312-85420-X*) Doherty, Tom Assocs., LLC. (Forge Bks.).

—Strong As Death. unabr. collector's ed. 1999. (Catherine LeVendeur Ser.: 4). audio 72.00 (*0-7366-4862-3*, 5189) Books on Tape, Inc.

—Strong As Death. (Catherine Levendeur Mystery Ser.). 384p. 1997. mass mkt. 5.99 (*0-8125-3935-4*); 1996. 23.95 o.p. (*0-312-86179-6*) Doherty, Tom Assocs., LLC. (Forge Bks.).

—The Wandering Arm. 2001. pap. 14.95 (*0-312-87733-1*); 1996. 372p. mass mkt. 5.99 (*0-8125-5089-7*); 1995. 352p. 23.95 o.p. (*0-312-85829-9*) Doherty, Tom Assocs., LLC. (Forge Bks.).

O'Marie, Carol Anne. Advent of Dying: A Sister Mary Helen Mystery. 1987. 256p. mass mkt. 4.99 o.s.i (*0-440-10052-6*); 1986. 288p. 14.95 o.p. (*0-385-29506-5*, Delacorte Pr.) Dell Publishing.

—The Corporal Works of Murder. 2002. (Sister Mary Helen Mystery Ser.). 208p. 22.95 (*0-312-20917-7*, Saint Martin's Minotaur) St. Martin's Pr.

—Death Goes on Retreat: A Sister Mary Helen Mystery. 1996. 272p. mass mkt. 5.50 o.s.i (*0-440-21610-9*) Dell Publishing.

—Death of an Angel: A Sister Mary Helen Mystery. l.t. ed. 1997. pap. 23.95 (*1-56895-442-5*, Wheeler Publishing, Inc.) Gale Group.

—Death of an Angel: A Sister Mary Helen Mystery. 1996. 256p. 21.95 (*0-312-15107-1*, Saint Martin's Minotaur); 3rd ed. 1997. 304p. mass mkt. 6.50 (*0-312-96396-3*, St. Martin's Paperbacks) St. Martin's Pr.

—Death Takes up a Collection: A Sister Mary Helen Mystery. (Sister Mary Helen Mystery Ser.: Vol. 8). 1998. 224p. 21.95 o.p. (*0-312-19256-8*, Saint Martin's Minotaur); 1999. 256p. reprint ed. mass mkt. 6.50 (*0-312-97193-1*, St. Martin's Paperbacks) St. Martin's Pr.

—Death Takes up a Collection: A Sister Mary Helen Mystery. l.t. ed. 1999. (Mystery Ser.). 347p. 27.95 (*0-7862-1663-8*) Thorndike Pr.

—The Missing Madonna: A Sister Mary Helen Mystery. 1989. 272p. reprint ed. mass mkt. 4.99 o.s.i (*0-440-20473-9*) Dell Publishing.

—The Missing Madonna: A Sister Mary Helen Mystery. l.t. ed. 1990. (General Ser.). 371p. lib. bdg. 20.95 o.p. (*0-8161-4814-7*, Macmillan Reference USA) Gale Group.

—Murder in Ordinary Time: A Sister Mary Helen Mystery. 256p. 1992. mass mkt. 4.99 o.s.i (*0-440-21353-3*); 1991. 18.00 o.s.i (*0-385-30226-6*, Delacorte Pr.) Dell Publishing.

—Murder in Ordinary Time: A Sister Mary Helen Mystery. l.t. ed. 1992. (General Ser.). 352p. lib. bdg. 20.95 o.p. (*0-8161-5425-2*); lib. bdg. 16.95 o.p. (*0-8161-5426-0*) Gale Group. (Macmillan Reference USA).

—Murder Makes a Pilgrimage: A Sister Mary Helen Mystery. 1994. 320p. mass mkt. 5.50 o.s.i (*0-440-21613-3*) Dell Publishing.

—Murder Makes a Pilgrimage: A Sister Mary Helen Mystery. l.t. ed. 1994. 336p. lib. bdg. 21.95 o.p. (*0-8161-5951-3*, Macmillan Reference USA) Gale Group.

—A Novena for Murder: A Sister Mary Helen Mystery. 1986. 192p. mass mkt. 4.99 o.s.i (*0-440-16469-9*) Dell Publishing.

—A Novena for Murder: A Sister Mary Helen Mystery. 1984. 224p. 12.95 o.s.i (*0-684-18087-1*, Macmillan Reference USA) Gale Group.

—Requiem at the Refuge: A Sister Mary Helen Mystery. 2000. (Sister Mary Helen Mystery Ser.). 276p. 23.95 (*0-312-20906-1*, Saint Martin's Minotaur) St. Martin's Pr.

—Requiem at the Refuge: A Sister Mary Helen Mystery. l.t. ed. 2000. (Mystery Ser.). 421p. 29.95 (*0-7862-2844-X*) Thorndike Pr.

O'Riordan, Kate. Angel in the House. 2000. 336p. pap. (*0-00-225880-3*) HarperCollins Pubs.

Quill, Monica. Half Past Nun: A Sister Mary Teresa Mystery. 1997. 198p. 20.95 o.p. (*0-312-15541-7*, Saint Martin's Minotaur) St. Martin's Pr.

—Nun Plussed: A Sister Mary Teresa Mystery. 1995. 250p. per. (*0-373-26187-X*, Worldwide Library) Harlequin Enterprises, Ltd.

—Nun Plussed: A Sister Mary Teresa Mystery. 1993. 224p. 18.95 o.p. (*0-312-09890-1*, Saint Martin's Minotaur) St. Martin's Pr.

Occupations

—Sister Hood: A Sister Mary Teresa Mystery. 1991. 16.95 o.p. (*0-312-04602-2*, Saint Martin's Minotaur) St. Martin's Pr.
—The Veil of Ignorance: A Sister Mary Teresa Mystery. 1988. 208p. 15.95 o.p. (*0-312-02308-1*, Saint Martin's Minotaur) St. Martin's Pr.
Reece, Colleen L. Angel of the North. l.t. ed. 2001. (Thorndike Press Large Print Christian Romance Ser.). 236p. 24.95 (*0-7862-3663-9*) Thorndike Pr.
Salzman, Mark. Lying Awake. 2001. (Illus.). 192p. reprint ed. pap. 12.00 (*0-375-70606-2*, Vintage) Knopf Publishing Group.
—Lying Awake, 4 cass. 2002. audio 19.99 (*1-4025-0174-9*, 00604) Recorded Bks., LLC.
—Lying Awake: A Novel. 2000. (Illus.). 192p. 22.00 (*0-375-40632-8*) Knopf, Alfred A. Inc.
—Lying Awake: A Novel. l.t. ed. 2001. (G. K. Hall Inspirational Ser.). 183p. 27.95 (*0-7838-9395-7*) Thorndike Pr.
Schreiber, Mordecai. The Rabbi & the Nun: A Love Story. 1991. 253p. 18.95 (*0-88400-150-4*, Shengold Bks.) Schreiber Publishing, Inc.
Spencer, LaVyrle. Then Came Heaven. 368p. 2003. pap. 10.00 (*0-425-19576-7*); 1999. reprint ed. pap. 7.99 (*0-515-12462-1*, Jove) Berkley Publishing Group.
—Then Came Heaven. l.t. ed. 1998. (Large Print Book Ser.). 28.95 (*1-56895-535-9*, Wheeler Publishing, Inc.) Gale Group.
—Then Came Heaven. abr. ed. 1997. 18.00 o.p. (*0-7871-1676-9*, 395617) NewStar Media, Inc.
—Then Came Heaven. 1997. xiii, 332p. 24.95 o.p. (*0-399-14369-6*, G. P. Putnam's Sons); 24.95 o.s.i (*0-399-14699-7*) Penguin Group (USA) Inc.
—Then Came Heaven. l.t. ed. 2000. (Charnwood Large Print Ser.). 376p. (*0-7089-9139-4*, Ulverscroft) Thorpe, F. A. Pubs. GBR. *Dist:* Ulverscroft Large Print Bks., Ltd., Ulverscroft Large Print Canada, Ltd.
Sullivan, Winona. Dead South: A Sister Cecile Mystery. 1997. (Sister Cecile Mystery Ser.). 275p. mass mkt. 5.99 o.s.i (*0-8041-1513-3*, Ivy Bks.) Ballantine Bks.
—Dead South: A Sister Cecile Mystery. 1996. 288p. 21.95 o.p. (*0-312-13959-4*, Saint Martin's Minotaur) St. Martin's Pr.
—Death's a Beach: A Sister Cecile Mystery. 1997. (Sister Cecile Mystery Ser.). 276p. mass mkt. 5.99 o.s.i (*0-8041-1568-0*, Ivy Bks.) Ballantine Bks.
—Saving Death: A Sister Cecile Mystery. 2000. 256p. mass mkt. 6.50 (*0-8041-1899-X*, Ivy Bks.) Ballantine Bks.
—A Sudden Death at the Norfolk Cafe: A Sister Cecile Mystery. 1995. (Sister Cecile Mystery Ser.). mass mkt. 5.99 o.s.i (*0-8041-1213-4*, Ivy Bks.) Ballantine Bks.
—A Sudden Death at the Norfolk Cafe: A Sister Cecile Mystery. 1993. 214p. 17.95 o.p. (*0-312-08899-X*, Saint Martin's Minotaur) St. Martin's Pr.
Tremayne, Peter. Absolution by Murder: A Sister Fidelma Mystery. l.t. ed. 1996. (Magna Large Print Ser.). 351p. 29.99 o.p. (*0-7505-0929-5*) Magna Large Print Bks. GBR. *Dist:* Ulverscroft Large Print Bks., Ltd., Ulverscroft Large Print Canada, Ltd.
—Absolution by Murder: A Sister Fidelma Mystery. 1997. (Sister Fidelma Mysteries Ser.). 272p. mass mkt. 6.50 (*0-451-19299-0*, Signet Bks.) NAL.
—Absolution by Murder: A Sister Fidelma Mystery. 1995. 288p. 21.95 o.p. (*0-312-13918-7*, Saint Martin's Minotaur) St. Martin's Pr.
—Hemlock at Vespers: Fifteen Sister Fidelma Mysteries. 2000. xiii, 398p. pap. 15.95 (*0-312-25288-9*, Saint Martin's Griffin) St. Martin's Pr.
—Shroud for the Archbishop: A Sister Fidelma Mystery. l.t. ed. 1996. (Magna Large Print Ser.). (Illus.). 436p. 29.99 (*0-7505-0930-9*) Magna Large Print Bks. GBR. *Dist:* Ulverscroft Large Print Bks., Ltd.
—Shroud for the Archbishop: A Sister Fidelma Mystery. 1998. (Sister Fidelma Mysteries Ser.). 304p. mass mkt. 6.99 (*0-451-19300-8*, Signet Bks.) NAL.
—Shroud for the Archbishop: A Sister Fidelma Mystery. 1996. (Sister Fidelma Mysteries Ser.). 352p. 23.95 (*0-312-14734-1*, Saint Martin's Minotaur) St. Martin's Pr.
—The Spider's Web: A Celtic Mystery. l.t. ed. 1998. (Magna Large Print Ser.). 512p. (*0-7505-1245-8*) Magna Large Print Bks. GBR. *Dist:* Ulverscroft Large Print Canada, Ltd.
—The Spider's Web: A Celtic Mystery. 1999. (Celtic Mysteries Ser.). (Illus.). 352p. 23.95 (*0-312-20589-9*, Saint Martin's Minotaur) St. Martin's Pr.
—The Subtle Serpent. l.t. ed. 1998. (Magna Large Print Ser.). 488p. o.p. (*0-7505-1244-X*) Magna Large Print Bks. GBR. *Dist:* Ulverscroft Large Print Canada, Ltd.
—The Subtle Serpent: A Celtic Mystery. 1998. (Sister Fidelma Mysteries Ser.). 352p. 23.95 (*0-312-18670-3*, Saint Martin's Minotaur) St. Martin's Pr.
—The Subtle Serpent: A Mystery of Ancient Ireland, 1, 4. 1999. (Sister Fidelma Mysteries Ser.). 320p. mass mkt. 6.99 (*0-451-19558-2*, Signet Bks.) NAL.
—Suffer Little Children: A Sister Fidelma Mystery, 1 vol. 1999. (Sister Fidelma Mysteries Ser.). 320p. mass mkt. 6.50 (*0-451-19557-4*) NAL.
—Suffer Little Children: A Sister Fidelma Mystery. 1997. (Sister Fidelma Mysteries Ser.). 352p. 23.95 (*0-312-15665-0*, Saint Martin's Minotaur) St. Martin's Pr.
Uppal, Priscila. The Divine Economy of Salvation. 2002. 416p. 24.95 (*1-56512-365-4*, 72365) Algonquin Bks. of Chapel Hill.
—The Divine Economy of Salvation. 2003. 416p. pap. (*0-385-65805-2*, Anchor Canada) Doubleday Canada, Ltd. CAN. *Dist:* Random Hse., Inc.
Woodworth, Deborah. Deadly Shaker Spring. 1998. (Sister Rose Callahan Mystery Ser.). 304p. mass mkt. 5.99 (*0-380-79203-6*, Avon Bks.) Morrow/Avon.
—The Death of a Winter Shaker. 1997. (Sister Rose Callahan Mystery Ser.). 224p. mass mkt. 5.50 (*0-380-79201-X*, Avon Bks.) Morrow/Avon.
—A Simple Shaker Murder. 2000. (Sister Rose Callahan Mystery Ser.). 256p. mass mkt. 5.99 (*0-380-80425-5*, Avon Bks.) Morrow/Avon.
—The Sins of a Shaker Summer: A Sister Rose Callahan Mystery. 1999. 272p. mass mkt. 5.99 (*0-380-79204-4*, Avon Bks.) Morrow/Avon.

# P

## PARK RANGERS—FICTION

Adams, Kelly. Wildfire. 1985. (Second Chance at Love Ser.). 192p. 2.25 o.s.i (*0-425-08153-2*) Berkley Publishing Group.
—Wildfire. l.t. ed. 2001. (Thorndike Press Large Print Romance Ser.). 304p. 27.95 (*0-7862-3347-8*) Thorndike Pr.
Barr, Nevada. Blind Descent. l.t. ed. 1998. 25.95 o.p. (*1-56895-547-2*, Wheeler Publishing, Inc.) Gale Group.
—Blind Descent. 1999. (Anna Pigeon Mysteries Ser.). (Illus.). 384p. mass mkt. 7.99 (*0-380-72826-5*, Avon Bks.) Morrow/Avon.
—Blind Descent. 1998. 352p. (gr. 5 up). 22.95 o.p. (*0-399-14371-8*, G. P. Putnam's Sons) Penguin Group (USA) Inc.
—Blind Descent. 1999. audio compact disk 99.00; 1998. audio 83.00 (*0-7887-2038-4*, 95402E7) Recorded Bks., LLC.
—Blood Lure. l.t. ed. 2001. (Large Print Book Ser.). 417p. 29.95 (*1-58724-001-7*, Wheeler Publishing, Inc.) Gale Group.
—Blood Lure. 2001. 320p. 24.95 o.p. (*0-399-14702-0*) Penguin Group (USA) Inc.
—Deep South. 2001. (Anna Pigeon Mysteries Ser.). 384p. mass mkt. 6.99 (*0-425-17895-1*) Berkley Publishing Group.
—Deep South. l.t. ed. 2000. 25.95 o.p. (*1-56895-867-6*, Wheeler Publishing, Inc.) Gale Group.
—Deep South. 2000. (Anna Pigeon Mysteries Ser.). 340p. 23.95 o.s.i (*0-399-14586-9*) Penguin Group (USA) Inc.
—Endangered Species. l.t. ed. 1997. 25.95 (*1-57490-108-7*, Beeler Large Print Bks.) Beeler, Thomas T. Publisher.
—Endangered Species. 1998. (Anna Pigeon Mysteries Ser.). 400p. mass mkt. 7.99 (*0-380-72583-5*, Avon Bks.) Morrow/Avon.
—Endangered Species, Set. abr. ed. 1997. 18.00 o.p. (*0-7871-1373-5*, 395114) NewStar Media, Inc.
—Endangered Species. 1997. 320p. 22.95 o.p. (*0-399-14246-0*, G. P. Putnam's Sons) Penguin Group (USA) Inc.
—Firestorm. l.t. ed. 1997. (Large Print Bks.). 24.95 o.p. (*1-56895-399-2*, Wheeler Publishing, Inc.) Gale Group.
—Firestorm. 1997. (Anna Pigeon Mysteries Ser.). 336p. reprint ed. mass mkt. 7.99 (*0-380-72582-7*, Avon Bks.) Morrow/Avon.
—Firestorm. 1996. 320p. 22.95 o.p. (*0-399-14126-X*, G. P. Putnam's Sons) Penguin Group (USA) Inc.
—Flashback. 2004. 416p. mass mkt. 7.99 (*0-425-19449-3*) Berkley Publishing Group.
—Flashback. 2004. 543p. pap. 13.95 (*1-4104-0172-3*); 2003. 32.95 (*1-58724-380-6*) Gale Group. (Wheeler Publishing, Inc.).
—Flashback. 2003. (Illus.). 400p. 24.95 (*0-399-14975-9*, Putnam & Grosset) Putnam Publishing Group, The.
—Flashback. audio 34.99 (*1-4025-3633-X*) Recorded Bks., LLC.
—High Country. 2004. 336p. 24.95 (*0-399-15144-3*) Putnam Publishing Group, The.
—Hunting Season. 2002. (Illus.). 320p. 24.95 o.s.i (*0-399-14846-9*); 249.50 o.p. (*0-399-19628-5*) Putnam Publishing Group, The.
—Hunting Season, 7 cass. 2002. audio 29.99 (*1-4025-0861-1*, 00974) Recorded Bks., LLC.
—Hunting Season. l.t. ed. 2003. (Paperback Bestsellers Ser.). 12.95 (*1-4104-0088-3*, Large Print Pr.) Thorndike Pr.
—Ill Wind. 2004. 320p. mass mkt. 6.99 (*0-425-19725-5*) Berkley Publishing Group.
—Ill Wind. l.t. ed. 1995. (Large Print Bks.). pap. 21.95 o.p. (*1-56895-252-X*, Wheeler Publishing, Inc.) Gale Group.
—Ill Wind. abr. ed. 1995. 17.95 o.p. (*0-7871-0370-5*) NewStar Media, Inc.
—Ill Wind. 1995. 309p. 19.95 o.p. (*0-399-14015-8*, G. P. Putnam's Sons) Penguin Group (USA) Inc.
—Ill Wind. unabr. ed. 1999. (Anna Pigeon Mystery Ser. : No. 3). audio 62.00 (*0-7887-2932-2*, 95717E7) Recorded Bks., LLC.
—Liberty Falling. l.t. ed. 1999. (Wheeler Large Print Bks.). 26.95 (*1-56895-711-4*, Wheeler Publishing, Inc.) Gale Group.
—Liberty Falling. 2000. (Anna Pigeon Mysteries Ser.). (Illus.). 384p. mass mkt. 7.99 (*0-380-72827-3*, Avon Bks.) Morrow/Avon.
—Liberty Falling. 1999. (Anna Pigeon Mysteries Ser.). 321p. 23.95 o.s.i (*0-399-14459-5*) Penguin Group (USA) Inc.
—Liberty Falling. unabr. ed. 1999. (Anna Pigeon Mystery Ser. : No. 7). (Illus.). audio 83.00 (*0-7887-3465-2*, 95649E7) Recorded Bks., LLC.
—A Superior Death. 2003. 320p. mass mkt. 6.99 (*0-425-19471-X*) Berkley Publishing Group.
—A Superior Death. 2002. (Anna Pigeon Mysteries Ser.: No. 2). 384p. mass mkt. 7.50 o.s.i (*0-380-72362-X*, Avon Bks.) Morrow/Avon.
—A Superior Death. 1994. 303p. 19.95 o.s.i (*0-399-13916-8*, G. P. Putnam's Sons) Penguin Group (USA) Inc.
—A Superior Death. unabr. ed. 1998. (Anna Pigeon Mystery Ser. : No. 2). audio 72.00 (*0-7887-1896-7*, 95318E7) Recorded Bks., LLC.
—A Superior Death. l.t. ed. 1994. 431p. lib. bdg. 23.95 (*0-8161-7446-6*) Thorndike Pr.
—Track of the Cat. 2003. 272p. mass mkt. 6.99 (*0-425-19083-8*) Berkley Publishing Group.
—Track of the Cat. l.t. ed. 1998. pap. 23.95 o.p. (*1-56895-572-3*, Wheeler Publishing, Inc.) Gale Group.
—Track of the Cat. 2002. (Anna Pigeon Mysteries Ser.: No. 1). 320p. reprint ed. mass mkt. 6.99 o.s.i (*0-380-72164-3*, Avon Bks.) Morrow/Avon.
—Track of the Cat. 1993. 240p. 19.95 o.s.i (*0-399-13824-2*, G. P. Putnam's Sons) Penguin Group (USA) Inc.
Charbonneau, Eileen. Waltzing in Ragtime. 1996. 480p. 26.95 o.p. (*0-312-86180-X*, Forge Bks.) Doherty, Tom Assocs., LLC.
Plowman, Mary S. White Powder. Goodfellow, Pamela R., ed. 1996. pap. 9.99 (*0-9639882-6-3*) Goodfellow Pr., Inc.

## PHOTOGRAPHERS—FICTION

Adams, Kelly. The Silent Heart, No. 461. 1989. 2.50 o.s.i (*0-425-11544-5*) Berkley Publishing Group.
—The Silent Heart. l.t. ed. 2001. 240p. pap. 23.95 (*0-7838-9504-6*); (*0-7540-4584-6*); (*0-7540-4583-8*) Gale Group. (Macmillan Reference USA).
Allbeury, Ted. The Reckoning. l.t. ed. 2000. (Mystery Ser.). 392p. 26.95 (*0-7862-2664-1*); (*0-7540-1471-1*); (*0-7540-2356-7*) Thorndike Pr.
Anderson, Scott. Triage. 1999. 240p. pap. 12.00 (*0-684-85653-0*, Scribner Paper Fiction) Simon & Schuster.
—Triage: A Novel. 1998. 240p. 23.00 (*0-684-84695-0*, Scribner) Simon & Schuster.
—Triage: A Novel. l.t. ed. 1999. (Ulverscroft Large Print Ser.). 408p. 31.99 o.p. (*0-7089-4117-6*, Ulverscroft) Thorpe, F. A. Pubs. GBR. *Dist:* Ulverscroft Large Print Bks., Ltd., Ulverscroft Large Print Canada, Ltd.
Bellacera, Carole. The Spotlight. 352p. 2000. 25.95 o.s.i (*0-312-87451-0*); 2001. reprint ed. mass mkt. 6.99 (*0-8125-6158-9*) Doherty, Tom Assocs., LLC. (Forge Bks.).
Blackstock, Terri. Seaside: A Novella. l.t. ed. 2001. 137p. 26.95 (*0-7838-9511-9*, Macmillan Reference USA) Gale Group.
Bradley, James. The Deep Field: A Novel. 2000. 358p. 26.00 o.s.i (*0-8050-6111-8*) Holt, Henry & Co.
Brennan, Kevin. Parts Unknown: A Novel. 2004. 320p. pap. 13.95 (*0-06-001277-3*, Perennial) HarperTrade.
—Parts Unknown: A Novel. 2003. 320p. 24.95 (*0-06-001276-5*, Morrow, William & Co.) Morrow/Avon.
Brown, Sandra. The Devil's Own. l.t. ed. 2002. 394p. 31.95 (*0-7862-3952-2*) Gale Group.
—The Devil's Own. 2001. 232p. (*1-55166-793-2*); 1994. 256p. per. (*1-55166-001-6*, 1-66001-8) Harlequin Enterprises, Ltd. (Mira Bks.).
—The Devil's Own. l.t. ed. 2002. pap. 28.95 (*0-7862-3978-6*) Thorndike Pr.
Burnside, John. The Locust Room. 2001. 224p. pap. o.p. (*0-224-05292-6*) Random Hse. UK, Ltd.
Campisi, Mary. Butterfly Garden. 2003. 32p. mass mkt. 5.99 (*0-8217-7499-9*) Kensington Publishing Corp.
Champlin, Tim. Shadow Catcher. l.t. ed. 2001. 273p. 24.95 (*0-7838-9494-5*, Macmillan Reference USA) Gale Group.
Clayton, Meg Waite. The Language of Light. Date not set. pap. (*0-312-31803-0*, St. Martin's Paperbacks); Date not set. mass mkt. (*0-312-99126-6*, St. Martin's Paperbacks); 2003. 352p. 24.95 (*0-312-31801-4*) St. Martin's Pr.
Colegate, Isabel. Winter Journey. l.t. ed. 2001. (Senior Lifestyles Ser.). 323p. 28.95 (*0-7862-3374-5*) Thorndike Pr.
—A Winter Journey. 2002. 208p. reprint ed. pap. text 14.00 (*1-58243-250-3*, Counterpoint Pr.) Basic Bks.
Corcoran, Tom. Gumbo Limbo. 1999. 293p. 23.95 (*0-312-24194-1*, Saint Martin's Minotaur) St. Martin's Pr.
—Gumbo Limbo: An Alex Rutledge Mystery. 2000. 304p. mass mkt. 6.50 (*0-312-97570-8*, St. Martin's Paperbacks) St. Martin's Pr.
—The Mango Opera. 304p. 1999. mass mkt. 6.99 (*0-312-96988-0*, St. Martin's Paperbacks); Vol. 1. 1998. (Mango Opera Ser.: Vol. 1). 22.95 (*0-312-18628-2*, Saint Martin's Minotaur) St. Martin's Pr.
—Octopus Alibi: An Alex Rutledge Mystery. 2003. (Alex Rutledge Mystery Ser.). 304p. 24.95 (*0-312-29127-2*, Saint Martin's Minotaur) St. Martin's Pr.
Eversz, Robert M. Burning Garbo: A Nina Zero Novel. 2003. 288p. 23.00 (*0-7432-5013-3*); E-Book (*0-7432-5356-6*) Simon & Schuster. (Simon & Schuster).
Falconer, Delia. The Service of Clouds. 1998. 256p. 23.00 o.p. (*0-374-26105-9*) Farrar, Straus & Giroux.
—The Service of Clouds. 1999. 336p. pap. 13.00 o.p. (*0-312-20969-X*) Picador.
Forbes, Leslie. Fish, Blood & Bone. 2002. 448p. pap. 13.95 (*0-553-38163-6*) Bantam Bks.
—Fish, Blood & Bone. 2001. (Illus.). 436p. 25.00 o.p. (*0-374-15506-2*); 2000. (*0-374-92746-4*) Farrar, Straus & Giroux.
Garrison, Paul. Sea Hunter: A Novel of Suspense. 2003. 352p. 25.95 (*0-06-008167-8*) HarperCollins Pubs.
—Sea Hunter: A Novel of Suspense. 2003. 384p. mass mkt. 7.99 (*0-06-008168-6*, HarperTorch) Morrow/Avon.
Goddard, Robert. Caught in the Light: A Mystery. 1999. 444p. mass mkt. (*0-552-14597-1*); 1998. 352p. o.s.i (*0-593-04266-2*) Bantam Bks. (Corgi).
—Caught in the Light: A Mystery. 1999. 352p. 26.00 o.s.i (*0-8050-6155-X*) Holt, Henry & Co.
Goodweather, Hartley, pseud. Dreadful Water Work 1. 2004. 256p. mass mkt. 6.99 (*0-7434-6396-X*, Pocket) Simon & Schuster.
—DreadfulWater Shows Up: A Novel. 2003. 272p. 24.00 (*0-7432-4392-7*, Scribner) Simon & Schuster.
Gorman, Ed. Cold Blue Midnight. 1998. 352p. reprint ed. mass mkt. 4.99 (*0-8439-4417-X*, Leisure Bks.) Dorchester Publishing Co., Inc.
—Cold Blue Midnight. 1996. 352p. 23.95 o.p. (*0-312-14568-3*, Saint Martin's Minotaur) St. Martin's Pr.
—Cold Blue Midnight. 1998. E-Book 9.95 (*0-585-28972-7*) netLibrary, Inc.
Hall, James W. Body Language. 1999. E-Book 24.95 o.s.i (*0-312-20761-1*); 1998. 352p. 24.95 (*0-312-19243-6*) St. Martin's Pr.
—Body Language. l.t. ed. 1998. (Americana Ser.). 527p. 28.95 (*0-7862-1686-7*) Thorndike Pr.
Hart, Virginia. A Rocky Romance. 1998. 192p. 18.95 (*0-8034-9325-8*, Avalon Bks.) Bouregy, Thomas & Co., Inc.
Hassinger, Amy. Nina: Adolescence. 2003. 320p. 23.95 (*0-399-15062-5*, Putnam & Grosset) Putnam Publishing Group, The.
Hecht, Julie. The Unprofessionals. 2003. 23.95 (*0-06-053247-5*) HarperCollins Pubs.
Jones, Susanna. The Earthquake Bird. 2001. 224p. 22.45 o.p. (*0-89296-742-0*) Mysterious Pr.
—The Earthquake Bird. l.t. ed. 2002. 236p. 28.95 (*0-7862-4136-5*) Thorndike Pr.
—The Earthquake Bird. 2003. 224p. pap. 12.95 (*0-446-67975-5*, Mysterious Pr. Paperback Bks.) Warner Bks., Inc.
Kachtick, Keith. Hungry Ghost: A Novel. 2003. 336p. 24.95 (*0-06-052390-5*) HarperCollins Pubs.
Kennedy, Douglas. The Big Picture. unabr. collector's ed. 1998. audio 72.00 (*0-7366-4078-9*, 4587) Books on Tape, Inc.
—The Big Picture. l.t. ed. 1997. (Wheeler Large Print Book Ser.). 491p. 27.95 (*1-56895-459-X*, Wheeler Publishing, Inc.) Gale Group.
—The Big Picture. 1998. 496p. mass mkt. 6.99 o.p. (*0-7868-8937-3*); 1997. 374p. 23.95 o.p. (*0-7868-6298-X*) Hyperion Pr.
—The Big Picture. abr. ed. 1990. audio 24.00 (*0-671-57564-3*, 495078, Simon & Schuster Audioworks) Simon & Schuster Audio.

Kesavan, Mukul. Looking Through Glass. 1995. (C). 19.50 (*0-02-516006-0*) Dayal, Ravi Pub. IND. *Dist:* South Asia Bks.
—Looking Through Glass. 1995. 375p. 25.00 o.p. (*0-374-19085-2*) Farrar, Straus & Giroux.
Kok, Marilyn. On Assignment. 1998. (Palisades Pure Romance Ser.). 266p. pap. 9.99 o.s.i (*1-57673-279-7*, Palisades) Multnomah Pubs., Inc.
—On Assignment. l.t. ed. 1999. (Christian Fiction Ser.). 383p. 24.95 (*0-7862-1966-1*) Thorndike Pr.
Leviant, Curt. Diary of an Adulterous Woman: A Novel. 2000. (Library of Modern Jewish Literature). 389p. 29.95 (*0-8156-0670-2*) Syracuse Univ. Pr.
Moody, Susan. Penny Black. 1986. 272p. mass mkt. 2.95 o.s.i (*0-449-12864-4*, Fawcett) Ballantine Bks.
—Penny Black. 1997. (Missing Mysteries Ser.: Vol. 1). pap. 7.95 (*1-890208-01-9*) Poisoned Pen Pr.
—Penny Black. l.t. ed. 1985. (Ulverscroft Large Print Ser.). 464p. 29.99 o.p. (*0-7089-1391-1*, Ulverscroft) Thorpe, F. A. Pubs. GBR. *Dist:* Ulverscroft Large Print Bks., Ltd., Ulverscroft Large Print Canada, Ltd.
—Penny Dreadful. 1986. mass mkt. 2.95 o.s.i (*0-449-12865-2*, Fawcett) Ballantine Bks.
—Penny Dreadful. unabr. ed. 2000. (Penny Wanawake Mystery Ser.). audio 59.95 (*0-7451-4183-8*, CAB 866) Chivers Audio Bks. GBR. *Dist:* BBC Audiobooks America.
—Penny Dreadful. l.t. ed. 1987. (Ulverscroft Large Print Ser.). 432p. 29.99 o.p. (*0-7089-1603-1*, Ulverscroft) Thorpe, F. A. Pubs. GBR. *Dist:* Ulverscroft Large Print Bks., Ltd., Ulverscroft Large Print Canada, Ltd.
—Penny Pinching. 1989. 240p. mass mkt. 3.50 o.s.i (*0-449-13237-4*, Fawcett) Ballantine Bks.
—Penny Pinching. l.t. ed. 1991. (Ulverscroft Large Print Ser.). 29.99 o.p. (*0-7089-2374-7*, Ulverscroft) Thorpe, F. A. Pubs. GBR. *Dist:* Ulverscroft Large Print Bks., Ltd., Ulverscroft Large Print Canada, Ltd.
—Penny Post. 1986. mass mkt. 2.95 o.s.i (*0-449-12866-0*, Fawcett) Ballantine Bks.
—Penny Post. l.t. ed. 1987. (Ulverscroft Large Print Ser.). 416p. 29.99 o.p. (*0-7089-1703-8*, Ulverscroft) Thorpe, F. A. Pubs. GBR. *Dist:* Ulverscroft Large Print Bks., Ltd., Ulverscroft Large Print Canada, Ltd.
—Penny Royal. 1987. 304p. mass mkt. 2.95 o.s.i (*0-449-12867-9*, Fawcett) Ballantine Bks.
—Penny Royal. l.t. ed. 1988. (Ulverscroft Large Print Ser.). 464p. 29.99 o.p. (*0-7089-1763-1*, Ulverscroft) Thorpe, F. A. Pubs. GBR. *Dist:* Ulverscroft Large Print Bks., Ltd., Ulverscroft Large Print Canada, Ltd.
—Penny Saving. unabr. ed. 2000. (Penny Wanawake Mystery Ser.). audio 59.95 (*0-7451-4007-6*, CAB 704) Chivers Audio Bks. GBR. *Dist:* BBC Audiobooks America.
—Penny Saving. l.t. ed. 1993. (Mystery Ser.). 464p. 29.99 o.p. (*0-7089-2938-9*, Ulverscroft) Thorpe, F. A. Pubs. GBR. *Dist:* Ulverscroft Large Print Bks., Ltd., Ulverscroft Large Print Canada, Ltd.
—Penny Wise. unabr. ed. 1992. (Penny Wanawake Mysteries Ser.). 69.95 incl. audio (*0-7451-4066-1*, CAB 763) BBC Audiobooks America.
—Penny Wise, No. 5. 1989. mass mkt. 3.50 o.s.i (*0-449-13236-6*, Fawcett) Ballantine Bks.
Morrell, David. Double Image. l.t. ed. 1998. (Core Ser.). 599p. 28.95 (*0-7838-0144-0*) Thorndike Pr.
—Double Image. 1998. 448p. 25.00 o.p. (*0-446-51963-4*) Warner Bks., Inc.
—Double Image. Warner, ed. 1999. 528p. reprint ed. mass mkt. 7.50 (*0-446-60696-0*) Warner Bks., Inc.
Norman, Howard. The Haunting of L. 2002. E-Book 9.00 (*0-374-70353-1*); E-Book 9.00 (*0-374-70355-8*); E-Book (*0-374-70358-2*); E-Book 9.00 o.p. (*0-374-70356-6*); 336p. 24.00 (*0-374-16825-3*); E-Book 9.00 (*0-374-70357-4*) Farrar, Straus & Giroux.
—The Haunting of L. 2003. 336p. pap. (*0-676-97500-3*, Vintage) Random Hse. of Canada, Ltd. CAN. *Dist:* Random Hse., Inc.
Nunn, Kem. The Dogs of Winter. 1998. 368p. pap. 14.00 o.s.i (*0-671-79334-9*); 1997. 400p. 23.50 (*0-684-82647-X*) Simon & Schuster. (Scribner).
O'Connor, Rebecca K. Falcon's Return. 2002. 186p. text 19.95 (*0-8034-9532-3*, Avalon Bks.) Bouregy, Thomas & Co., Inc.
O'Cork, Shannon. End of the Line. 1983. (A.T.T. Baldwin Mystery Ser.). mass mkt. 2.95 o.s.i (*0-671-44488-3*, Pocket) Simon & Schuster.
—End of the Line. 1981. 224p. 10.95 o.p. (*0-312-25102-5*) St. Martin's Pr.
—Hell Bent for Heaven. 1983. 224p. 12.95 o.p. (*0-312-36698-1*) St. Martin's Pr.
—Sports Freak. 1980. 8.95 o.p. (*0-312-75331-4*) St. Martin's Pr.
O'Reilly, Victor. The Devil's Footprint. 1998. 448p. mass mkt. 7.50 o.s.i (*0-425-16186-2*) Berkley Publishing Group.
—The Devil's Footprint. 1997. 400p. 24.95 o.p. (*0-399-14137-5*, G. P. Putnam's Sons) Penguin Group (USA) Inc.
—Games of the Hangman. 1992. 512p. mass mkt. 7.50 o.s.i (*0-425-13456-3*) Berkley Publishing Group.
—Games of the Hangman. 1991. 512p. 19.95 o.p. (*0-8021-1431-8*) Grove/Atlantic, Inc.
—Rules of the Hunt. 1995. 512p. mass mkt. 6.99 o.s.i (*0-425-15097-6*) Berkley Publishing Group.
—Rules of the Hunt. abr. ed. 1996. audio 7.99 o.p. (*1-56740-104-X*, 694, Paperback Nova Audio Bks.); 1995. audio 16.95 o.p. (*1-56100-413-8*, 1358, Nova Audio Bks.); 1995. audio 89.25 o.p. (*1-56100-244-5*, 1020, Unabridged Library Editions); 1995. audio 25.95 o.p. (*1-56100-619-X*, 242, Bookcassette) Brilliance Audio.
—Rules of the Hunt. 1995. 416p. 23.95 o.p. (*0-399-13869-2*, G. P. Putnam's Sons) Penguin Group (USA) Inc.
—Rules of the Hunt. 402p. pap. 4.98 o.p. (*0-7651-0430-X*) Smithmark Pubs., Inc.
Pattinson, James. Life-Preserver. l.t. ed. 2001. 225p. pap. 23.95 (*0-7838-9597-6*) Thorndike Pr.
Peterson, Tracie. Framed. 1998. (Portraits Ser.). 240p. pap. 8.99 o.p. (*1-55661-992-8*) Bethany Hse. Pubs.
—Framed. l.t. ed. 2000. (Christian Mystery Ser.). 367p. 24.95 (*0-7862-2696-X*) Thorndike Pr.
Roiphe, Katie. Still She Haunts Me. 2002. 240p. pap. 12.95 (*0-385-33530-X*, Delta) Dell Publishing.
—Still She Haunts Me: A Novel of Lewis Carroll & Alice Liddell. 2002. E-Book 11.50 (*0-440-33385-7*, Delta) Dell Publishing.
Seiffert, Rachel. The Dark Room: A Novel. 2002. 288p. pap. 13.00 (*0-375-72632-2*) Knopf, Alfred A. Inc.
Thayne, Carole. A Question of Trust: A Novel. 2003. 293p. 14.95 (*1-59156-210-4*) Covenant Communications.
Theis, David. Rio Ganges. 2002. 272p. pap. 20.00 (*0-9701525-6-6*) Winedale Publishing.
Trollope, Joanna. Girl from the South. 2003. 352p. pap. 14.00 (*0-425-19350-0*) Berkley Publishing Group.
—Girl from the South. 2002. 304p. 24.95 (*0-670-03097-X*, Viking) Viking Penguin.
Whipple, Dan. Click: A Novel. 2001. 258p. 35.00 (*0-87081-632-2*) Univ. Pr. of Colorado.
Wiggs, Susan. Home Before Dark. 2004. 416p. mass mkt. (*0-7783-2019-7*, Mira Bks.); 2003. 384p. (*1-55166-673-1*) Harlequin Enterprises, Ltd.
Wynne, Marcus. Warrior in the Shadows. 2002. 352p. 24.95 (*0-7653-0443-0*, Forge Bks.) Doherty, Tom Assocs., LLC.


**PHYSICIANS—FICTION**


Abse, Dannie. The Strange Case of Dr. Simmonds & Dr. Glas. 2003. 208p. 23.00 (*0-7867-1201-5*, Carroll & Graf Pubs.) Avalon Publishing Group.
Adams, Alice. Medicine Men. l.t. ed. 2000. 302p. lib. bdg. 28.95 (*1-58547-022-8*) Ctr. Point Large Print.
—Medicine Men, 000. 1997. 23.00 o.p. (*0-676-52928-3*) Random Hse., Inc.
—Medicine Men. 1998. 256p. pap. 14.00 (*0-671-02067-6*, Washington Square Pr.) Simon & Schuster.
Aiken, Ginny. Camellia. 2001. (HeartQuest Ser.: Vol. 3). 352p. pap. 9.99 (*0-8423-3561-7*) Tyndale Hse. Pubs.
Alexander, Hannah. Necessary Measures. 2002. (Healing Touch Ser.: Bk. 2). 352p. pap. 11.99 (*0-7642-2529-4*) Bethany Hse. Pubs.
—Silent Pledge. 2000. 352p. pap. 11.99 (*0-7642-2444-1*) Bethany Hse. Pubs.
—Solemn Oath. 2000. 352p. pap. 11.99 (*0-7642-2348-8*) Bethany Hse. Pubs.
—Urgent Care. 2003. (Healing Touch Ser.: Vol. 3). 352p. pap. 11.99 (*0-7642-2530-8*) Bethany Hse. Pubs.
Andrews, Brian. Knife under Fire. 1993. (*1-881529-01-0*) Custom & Limited Editions.
Armour, John. Death of a Doctor. l.t. ed. 2000. (Linford Mystery Large Print Ser.). 296p. pap. 18.99 o.p. (*0-7089-5718-8*, Ulverscroft) Thorpe, F. A. Pubs. GBR. *Dist:* Ulverscroft Large Print Bks., Ltd., Ulverscroft Large Print Canada, Ltd.
Auerbach, Paul S. Bad Medicine. 1998. 355p. pap. 16.95 (*0-9639960-7-X*) Specialized Pubns. Co.
Avery, Chris. Cut Loose. 2000. 432p. mass mkt. 5.99 o.s.i (*0-7860-1115-7*, Pinnacle Bks.) Kensington Publishing Corp.
Baggette, Susan K. Jonathan Goes to the Doctor. 1998. (Jonathan Adventures Ser.). (Illus.). 16p. (J). (ps-k). bds. 5.95 (*0-9660172-1-8*) Brookfield Reader, Inc., The.
Ballard, J. G. The Day of Creation. 1988. 17.95 o.s.i (*0-374-13527-4*) Farrar, Straus & Giroux.
Barrett, Linda. The Apple Orchard. 2002. (Harlequin Superromance Ser.). 304p. mass mkt. (*0-373-71073-9*, Harlequin Bks.) Harlequin Enterprises, Ltd.
Becker, Stephen. Dog Tags: A Novel. 1987. (Shoreline Bks.). pap. 7.95 o.p. (*0-393-30504-X*) Norton, W. W. & Co., Inc.
Bell, Madison Smartt. Doctor Sleep. 1991. 320p. 19.95 (*0-15-126100-8*) Harcourt Trade Pubs.
Benjamin, Cynthia. I Am a Doctor. 1994. (I Am a . . . Ser.). (Illus.). 24p. (J). (ps-k). 7.95 (*0-8120-6380-5*) Barron's Educational Series, Inc.
—Yo Soy un Medico. 1994. (SPA., Illus.). 24p. (J). (ps). 6.95 (*0-8120-6414-3*) Barron's Educational Series, Inc.
Bergen, Lara Rice. The Wee Bear Who Didn't Want to Go to the Doctor. 1995. (All Aboard Bks.). (Illus.). 32p. (J). (ps-3). 2.50 o.p. (*0-448-40484-2*, Grosset & Dunlap) Penguin Putnam Bks. for Young Readers.
Bergren, Lisa Tawn. Pathways. 2001. (Full Circle Ser.). 288p. pap. 10.99 (*1-57856-462-X*) WaterBrook Pr.
Blackwood, Algernon. Complete John Silence Stories. Joshi, S. T., ed. & intro. by. 1998. (Illus.). 380p. reprint ed. pap. 9.95 (*0-486-29942-2*) Dover Pubns., Inc.
Borthwick, J. S. Bodies of Water. 1991. 287p. mass mkt. 5.99 (*0-312-92603-0*, St. Martin's Paperbacks) St. Martin's Pr.
—The Case of the Hook-Billed Kites. 1991. (Dead Letter Mysteries Ser.). (Illus.). 256p. mass mkt. 5.99 (*0-312-92604-9*, St. Martin's Paperbacks) St. Martin's Pr.
—The Down-East Murders. 1991. 296p. mass mkt. 6.50 (*0-312-92606-5*, St. Martin's Paperbacks) St. Martin's Pr.
—The Down-East Murders: A Mystery Set on the Coast of Maine. 1985. 288p. 14.95 o.p. (*0-312-21855-9*) St. Martin's Pr.
—My Body Lies over the Ocean. (Sarah Deane Mysteries Ser.). 304p. 2000. mass mkt. 6.50 (*0-312-97040-4*, St. Martin's Paperbacks); 1998. 22.95 o.p. (*0-312-19991-0*, Saint Martin's Minotaur) St. Martin's Pr.
—The Student Body. 1991. 293p. mass mkt. 6.50 (*0-312-92605-7*, St. Martin's Paperbacks); 1987. mass mkt. 3.50 o.s.i (*0-312-90738-9*, St. Martin's Paperbacks); 1986. 320p. 16.95 o.p. (*0-312-76934-2*) St. Martin's Pr.
Boullosa, Carmen. They're Cows, We're Pigs. Chambers, Leland H., tr. 192p. 2001. pap. 12.00 (*0-8021-3786-5*); 1997. 23.00 o.p. (*0-8021-1610-8*, Grove Pr.) Grove/Atlantic, Inc.
Boyer, Rick. Billingsgate Shoal. 1989. 320p. mass mkt. 5.99 o.s.i (*0-8041-0551-0*, Ivy Bks.) Ballantine Bks.
—Billingsgate Shoal. unabr. ed. 1997. audio 56.95 Blackstone Audio Bks., Inc.
—Billingsgate Shoal, 001. 1982. 288p. 11.95 o.p. (*0-395-32041-0*) Houghton Mifflin Co.
—Billingsgate Shoal. 1985. 258p. mass mkt. 3.50 o.s.i (*0-446-32739-5*) Warner Bks., Inc.
—The Daisy Ducks. 1988. 288p. reprint ed. mass mkt. 3.50 o.s.i (*0-8041-0293-7*, Ivy Bks.) Ballantine Bks.
—The Daisy Ducks, 001. 1986. 276p. 15.95 o.p. (*0-395-35289-4*) Houghton Mifflin Co.
—Gone to Earth. 1991. (Boston Mysteries Ser.). mass mkt. 4.99 o.s.i (*0-8041-0611-8*, Ivy Bks.) Ballantine Bks.
—The Man Who Whispered. 1998. (Doc Adams Mysteries Ser.). 272p. mass mkt. 6.50 o.s.i (*0-8041-1044-1*, Ivy Bks.) Ballantine Bks.
—Moscow Metal. l.t. ed. 1991. pap. 8.95 o.p. (*1-55504-884-6*, 182); 1989. 21.95 o.p. (*1-55504-883-8*, 699) BBC Audiobooks America.
—Moscow Metal. 1988. 288p. reprint ed. mass mkt. 3.95 o.s.i (*0-8041-0292-9*, Ivy Bks.) Ballantine Bks.
—Moscow Metal: A Doc Adams Suspense Novel. 1987. 15.95 o.p. (*0-395-42737-1*) Houghton Mifflin Co.
—The Penny Ferry. 1990. 304p. mass mkt. 4.99 o.s.i (*0-8041-0550-2*, Ivy Bks.) Ballantine Bks.
—The Penny Ferry, 001. 1984. 13.95 o.p. (*0-395-35288-6*) Houghton Mifflin Co.
—The Penny Ferry. 1986. 272p. mass mkt. 3.50 o.s.i (*0-446-32741-7*) Warner Bks., Inc.
—Pirate Trade. 1994. (Doc Adams Mysteries Ser.). mass mkt. 4.99 o.s.i (*0-8041-0612-6*, Ivy Bks.) Ballantine Bks.
—The Whale's Footprints. 1989. 288p. mass mkt. 4.99 o.s.i (*0-8041-0450-6*, Ivy Bks.) Ballantine Bks.
—The Whale's Footprints. l.t. ed. 1989. (General Ser.). 392p. lib. bdg. 18.95 o.p. (*0-8161-4764-7*, Macmillan Reference USA) Gale Group.
—The Whale's Footprints. 1988. 288p. 17.95 o.p. (*0-395-42738-X*) Houghton Mifflin Co.
—Yellow Bird. (Boston Mysteries Ser.). 1992. mass mkt. 4.99 o.s.i (*0-8041-1036-0*, Ivy Bks.); 1991. 352p. 17.00 o.p. (*0-449-90506-3*, Fawcett) Ballantine Bks.
Brand, Max. Calling Dr. Kildare. l.t. ed. 1993. (General Ser.). lib. bdg. 15.95 (*0-8161-5717-0*, Macmillan Reference USA) Gale Group.
—Dr. Kildare Takes Charge. 160p. reprint ed. lib. bdg. 18.95 (*0-88411-531-3*) Amereon, Ltd.
—Dr. Kildare Takes Charge. l.t. ed. 1997. (G. K. Hall Nightingale Ser.). pap. 17.95 o.p. (*0-7838-1847-5*, Macmillan Reference USA) Gale Group.
—Dr. Kildare's Crisis. l.t. ed. 1994. 210p. lib. bdg. 16.95 (*0-8161-5873-8*, Macmillan Reference USA) Gale Group.
—Dr. Kildare's Search & Dr. Kildare's Hardest Case. l.t. ed. 1994. 173p. lib. bdg. 16.95 (*0-8161-5896-7*, Macmillan Reference USA) Gale Group.
—The Secret of Dr. Kildare. 180p. reprint ed. lib. bdg. 19.95 (*0-88411-530-5*, Rivercity Pr.) Amereon, Ltd.
Brashear, Jean. The Healer. 2003. (Harlequin Superromance Ser.: No. 1105). 304p. mass mkt. o.s.i (*0-373-71105-0*, Harlequin Bks.) Harlequin Enterprises, Ltd.
Brown, Carrie. The Hatbox Baby. 2000. 333p. tchr. ed. 22.95 (*1-56512-299-2*) Algonquin Bks. of Chapel Hill.
—The Hatbox Baby. 2002. 352p. pap. 14.00 (*0-425-18465-X*) Berkley Publishing Group.
—The Hatbox Baby. l.t. ed. 2000. (Compass Press Large Print Book Ser.). 410p. 26.95 (*1-56895-962-1*, Wheeler Publishing, Inc.) Gale Group.
Brown, John Gregory. Audubon's Watch: A Novel. 2001. 224p. tchr. ed. 24.00 (*0-395-78607-X*) Houghton Mifflin Co.
—Audubon's Watch: A Novel. 2002. 224p. pap. 13.00 (*0-618-25731-4*, Mariner Bks.) Houghton Mifflin Co. Trade & Reference Div.
Canin, Ethan. Blue River. 1991. 224p. 19.95 o.s.i (*0-395-49854-6*) Houghton Mifflin Co.
—Blue River. 1992. 240p. reprint ed. pap. 12.99 o.p. (*0-446-39447-5*) Warner Bks., Inc.
Carr, M. J. The Cabbage Patch Kids Visit the Doctor. 1993. 32p. (J). (ps-3). pap. 2.50 (*0-590-46631-3*) Scholastic, Inc.
Celine, Louis-Ferdinand. Rigadoon. Manheim, Ralph, tr. from FRE. 1997. 296p. reprint ed. pap. 13.50 (*1-56478-162-3*) Dalkey Archive Pr.
Ch, Weir. Madame Bovary. 1948. (C). pap. text 4.50 o.p. (*0-03-009895-5*) Harcourt College Pubs.
Chase, Elaine Raco. No Easy Way Out. l.t. ed. 2003. 105p. 26.95 (*0-7862-5620-6*, Five Star) Gale Group.
Chekhov, Anton. Chekhov's Doctors: A Collection of Chekhov's Medical Tales. Coulehan, John L., ed. 2003. 18.00 (*0-87338-780-5*) Kent State Univ. Pr.
Chittum, Ida. The Ghost Boy of el Toro. 1978. (J). (gr. 4 up). 8.00 o.p. (*0-8309-0201-5*, Independence Pr.) Herald Publishing Hse.
Clarke, Hope C. Shadow Lover: He Heard Her Cries & Out of the Shadows He Came. 1999. pap. 15.00 (*1-929279-00-0*) A New Hope Publishing.
Clement, Peter. Death Rounds. 1999. 345p. mass mkt. 6.99 (*0-449-00450-3*, Fawcett) Ballantine Bks.
—Lethal Practice. 1998. mass mkt. 6.99 (*0-8041-1781-0*, Ivy Bks.); 1998. 352p. mass mkt. 7.99 (*0-449-00281-0*, Fawcett); 1997. mass mkt. 6.99 (*0-345-40776-8*) Ballantine Bks.
Clifford, Eth. The Wild One, 001. 1974. (Illus.). 208p. (J). (gr. 5-9). 5.95 o.p. (*0-395-19491-1*) Houghton Mifflin Co.
Coben, Harlan. Tell No One. 2001. 352p. 22.95 (*0-385-33555-5*, Delacorte Pr.); 2002. 400p. reprint ed. mass mkt. 6.99 (*0-440-23670-3*) Dell Publishing.
—Tell No One. l.t. ed. 2002. 12.95 (*1-56895-192-2*); 2001. 384p. 29.95 o.p. (*1-58724-063-7*) Gale Group. (Wheeler Publishing, Inc.).
Coleman, Clay. Mutiny. 1991. (Escape from Lost Island Ser.: No. 3). 144p. (J). (gr. 4-7). mass mkt. 2.95 o.p. (*0-06-106039-9*, Perennial) HarperTrade.
Coles, Allison. Mandy & the Hospital. 1985. (Michael & Mandy Ser.). (Illus.). 28p. (J). (ps up). 3.95 o.p. (*0-88110-269-5*) EDC Publishing.
Collins, Lynne. Duel for the Doctor. l.t. ed. 1994. 18.95 o.p. (*0-7927-1926-3*); pap. 16.95 o.p. (*0-7927-1925-5*) BBC Audiobooks America.
Connor, Alexandra. Midnight's Smiling. l.t. ed. 1999. (Ulverscroft Large Print Ser.). 400p. 31.99 o.p. (*0-7089-4096-X*, Linford) Thorpe, F. A. Pubs. GBR. *Dist:* Ulverscroft Large Print Bks., Ltd., Ulverscroft Large Print Canada, Ltd.
Cook, Robin. Harmful Intent. 1991. 368p. mass mkt. 7.99 (*0-425-12546-7*) Berkley Publishing Group.
—Harmful Intent. 1990. 368p. 18.95 o.p. (*0-399-13481-6*, G. P. Putnam's Sons) Penguin Putnam Bks. for Young Readers.
—Harmful Intent. 18.95 o.s.i (*0-399-13700-9*) Putnam Publishing Group, The.
—Harmful Intent. l.t. ed. 2000. (Famous Authors Ser.). 663p. 28.95 (*0-7862-2504-1*) Thorndike Pr.
—Harmful Intent. 1991. 14.04 (*0-606-00927-2*) Turtleback Bks.
—The Year of the Intern. 1972. 6.75 o.p. (*0-15-199740-3*) Harcourt Trade Pubs.
Copeland, Carolyn F. The Last Colonial. 1992. 17.95 o.p. (*0-533-09645-6*) Vantage Pr., Inc.
Cote, Lyn. Summer's End. 2003. (HeartQuest Ser.). 300p. pap. 9.99 (*0-8423-3558-7*) Tyndale Hse. Pubs.
Cowell, Stephanie. Nicholas Cooke: Actor, Soldier, Physician, Priest. 1994. 448p. reprint ed. pap. 12.00 o.s.i (*0-345-39016-4*) Ballantine Bks.

—Nicholas Cooke: Actor, Soldier, Physician, Priest. 1993. 442p. 24.00 o.p. (*0-393-03543-3*) Norton, W. W. & Co., Inc.

—The Physician of London: The 2nd Part of the Seventeenth-Century Trilogy of Nicholas Cooke. 1995. 416p. 23.00 o.p. (*0-393-03873-4*) Norton, W. W. & Co., Inc.

Creamer, Hannah Gardner. Delia's Doctors; or, a Glance Behind the Scenes. 2003. 296p. text 39.95 (*0-252-02807-4*) Univ. of Illinois Pr.

Cronin, A. J. The Citadel. 1983. (J). 16.95 (*0-316-16158-6*) Little Brown & Co.

Cutrer, William & Glahn, Sandra. Lethal Harvest. 2000. 416p. pap. 11.99 (*0-8254-2371-6*) Kregel Pubns.

Dalmatian Press Staff, adapted by. Dr. Jekyll & Mr. Hyde. 1994. (Review Ser.: No. 3). 136p. pap. 6.00 (*0-9641292-5-6*) Global City Pr.

Danish, Barbara. The Dragon & the Doctor. 2nd rev. ed. 2004. (Illus.). 40p. (J). (ps-3). pap. 5.95 (*1-55861-117-7*) Feminist Pr. at The City Univ. of New York.

Danner, Craig Joseph. Himalayan Dhaba: A Novel. 2001. 256p. 24.00 (*0-9706405-9-5*, HD134) Crispin/Hammer Pr.

—Himalayan Dhaba: A Novel. 2002. 23.95 o.s.i (*0-525-94690-X*); 2003. 320p. reprint ed. pap. 13.00 (*0-452-28387-6*, Plume) Dutton/Plume.

Davies, June W. Storm Before Sunrise. 1993. 574p. 24.95 o.p. (*0-312-10552-5*) St. Martin's Pr.

Davies, Robertson. The Cunning Man. unabr. ed. 1996. audio 76.95 (*0-7861-1060-0*, 1831) Blackstone Audio Bks., Inc.

—The Cunning Man. l.t. ed. 1995. pap. 23.95 o.p. (*1-56895-230-9*, Wheeler Publishing, Inc.) Gale Group.

—The Cunning Man. 1994. 472p. (*0-7710-2581-5*) McClelland & Stewart/Tundra Bks.

—The Cunning Man. 1996. (*0-14-771176-2*); 478p. pap. 13.95 (*0-14-024830-7*, Viking) Penguin Group (USA) Inc.

—The Cunning Man. unabr. ed. 1996. audio 97.00 (*0-7887-0294-7*, 94487E7) Recorded Bks., LLC.

—The Cunning Man. 1995. 480p. 23.95 o.p. (*0-670-85911-7*, Viking) Viking Penguin.

DeFelice, Cynthia C. The Apprenticeship of Lucas Whitaker, RS. 1996. 160p. (YA). (gr. 5). 16.00 (*0-374-34669-0*, Farrar, Straus & Giroux (BYR)) Farrar, Straus & Giroux.

—The Apprenticeship of Lucas Whitaker. 1998. 160p. (J). (gr. 3-7). pap. 5.99 (*0-380-72920-2*, Harper Trophy) HarperCollins Children's Bk. Group.

Dego, Giuliano. Doctor Max: A Novel. 1997. 768p. pap. 24.95 (*0-88268-201-6*) Station Hill Pr.

Delbanco, Nicholas. In the Name of Mercy. 320p. 1995. 21.45 o.p. (*0-446-51711-9*); 1998. reprint ed. pap. 12.99 (*0-446-67364-1*) Warner Bks., Inc.

Delinsky, Barbara. Straight from the Heart. (Men Made in America Ser.). 1993. mass mkt. (*0-373-45157-1*, 1-45157-4); 1986. mass mkt. (*0-373-25198-X*) Harlequin Enterprises, Ltd. (Harlequin Bks.).

—Straight from the Heart. l.t. ed. 2001. 328p. 29.95 (*0-7862-3098-3*) Thorndike Pr.

Doherty, P. C. Dove Amongst the Hawks. l.t. ed. 2001. (Linford Mystery Large Print Ser.). 280p. pap. 19.99 o.p. (*0-7089-5997-0*, Ulverscroft) Thorpe, F. A. Pubs. GBR. *Dist:* Ulverscroft Large Print Bks., Ltd., Ulverscroft Large Print Canada, Ltd.

Dooling, Richard. Critical Care. 288p. 1993. mass mkt. 4.99 (*0-380-71759-X*, Avon Bks.); 1992. 20.00 o.p. (*0-688-10926-8*, Morrow, William & Co.) Morrow/Avon.

—Critical Care. 1996. 256p. pap. 12.00 (*0-312-14304-4*) Picador.

—Critical Care. unabr. ed. 1994. audio 70.00 (*1-55690-665-X*, 92135E7) Recorded Bks., LLC.

—Critical Care Movieed. 1996. pap. 12.00 o.s.i (*0-312-17943-X*) Picador.

Doyle, Arthur Conan. The Man from Archangel: And Other Tales of Adventure. 1977. (Short Story Index Reprint Ser.). 19.95 (*0-8369-3189-0*) Ayer Co. Pubs., Inc.

—The Man from Archangel: And Other Tales of Adventure. 2001. 260p. per. 24.95 (*1-58963-601-5*) Fredonia Bks.

—The Stark Munro Letters. (Illus.). reprint ed. 44.50 (*0-404-61840-5*) AMS Pr., Inc.

—The Stark Munro Letters. reprint ed. lib. bdg. 98.00 (*0-7426-2696-2*) Classic Bks.

—The Stark Munro Letters. 1982. (Conan Doyle Centennial Ser.). (Illus.). 224p. 28.00 (*0-934468-46-X*) Gaslight Pubns.

Duncker, Patricia. The Doctor. 2000. 384p. 24.00 (*0-06-019601-7*, Ecco) HarperTrade.

Eberhart, Mignon G. Glass Slipper. l.t. ed. 1998. (Romance Ser.). 319p. 27.95 (*0-7838-0143-2*) Thorndike Pr.

Elizondo, Salvador. Farabeuf: The Chronicle of an Instant. Incledon, John, tr. 1992. (Library of World Literature in Translation: Vol. 27). (SPA.). 125p. text 15.00 (*0-8240-0459-0*) Garland Publishing, Inc.

—Farabeuf, o la Cronica de un Instante. 1981. (SPA.). 183p. 8.00 o.s.i (*84-85859-18-9*, 2005) Ediciones del Norte.

Engel, Howard. Mr. Doyle & Dr. Bell: A Victorian Mystery. 2003. 214p. 24.95 (*1-58567-417-6*) Overlook Pr., The.

Faulkner, Colleen. Tempting Zack Vol. 65. 2000. (Zebra Bouquet Ser.). 256p. mass mkt. 3.99 o.s.i (*0-8217-6700-3*, Zebra Bks.) Kensington Publishing Corp.

Fitzgerald, Penelope. The Gate of Angels. 1993. 352p. pap. 9.95 o.p. (*0-88184-960-X*, Carroll & Graf Pubs.) Avalon Publishing Group.

—The Gate of Angels. 1991. 176p. 19.00 o.s.i (*0-385-42150-8*) Doubleday Publishing.

—The Gate of Angels. l.t. ed. 1992. (Ulverscroft Large Print Ser.). 288p. 29.99 o.p. (*0-7089-2572-3*, Ulverscroft) Thorpe, F. A. Pubs. GBR. *Dist:* Ulverscroft Large Print Bks., Ltd., Ulverscroft Large Print Canada, Ltd.

Flaubert, Gustave. Madame Bovary. 1965. (Airmont Classics Ser.). (YA). (gr. 11 up). mass mkt. 2.50 o.p. (*0-8049-0089-2*, CL-89) Airmont Publishing Co., Inc.

—Madame Bovary. Bair, Lowell, tr. 1982. (Bantam Classics Ser.). 448p. mass mkt. 5.95 (*0-553-21341-5*); (gr. 9-12). mass mkt. 2.50 o.s.i (*0-553-21101-3*) Bantam Bks. (Bantam Classics).

—Madame Bovary. 1985. (Barron's Book Notes Ser.). (Illus.). 122p. (YA). (gr. 10-12). pap. 3.95 (*0-8120-3524-0*) Barron's Educational Series, Inc.

—Madame Bovary. unabr. ed. (FRE.). pap. 7.95 (*2-87714-130-6*) Bookking International FRA. *Dist:* Distribooks, Inc.

—Madame Bovary. 1983. (Illus.). 320p. reprint ed. lib. bdg. 27.95 (*0-89966-324-9*) Buccaneer Bks., Inc.

—Madame Bovary. (Early Best Sellers Ser.). reprint ed. lib. bdg. 48.00 (*0-7426-1025-X*); 2001. (Illus.). pap. text 28.00 (*0-7426-6025-7*) Classic Bks.

—Madame Bovary. Marmur, Mildred, tr. 1997. (New York Public Library Collector's Edition Ser.). (Illus.). 384p. 18.50 (*0-385-48719-3*) Doubleday Publishing.

—Madame Bovary. unabr. ed. 1996. (Thrift Editions Ser.). 256p. reprint ed. pap. 2.50 (*0-486-29257-6*) Dover Pubns., Inc.

—Madame Bovary. Aveling, Eleanor Marx, tr. 2004. (Barnes & Noble Classics Ser.). 400p. pap. 5.95 (*1-59308-052-2*) Fine Communications.

—Madame Bovary. (FRE.). 11.25 (*2-08-070464-8*, GF0086E) Flammarion et Cie FRA. *Dist:* Continental Bk. Co., Inc.

—Madame Bovary. Gothot-Mesch, ed. 1961. (FRE.). pap. 11.95 (*0-8288-9748-4*, 2266033581) French & European Pubns., Inc.

—Madame Bovary. Steegmuller, Francis, tr. l.t. ed. 1993. 499p. lib. bdg. 20.95 o.p. (*0-8161-5680-8*, Macmillan Reference USA) Gale Group.

—Madame Bovary. l.t. ed. 1999. (SPA.). 512p. 32.50 (*84-397-0569-7*) Grijalbo Mondadori, S.A.-Junior ESP. *Dist:* Continental Bk. Co., Inc.

—Madame Bovary. l.t. ed. 2000. 544p. pap. 22.00 (*0-06-095695-X*, HarperCollins) HarperTrade.

—Madame Bovary, 001. Bree, Germaine, ed. Lawrence, Merloyd, tr. 1969. (C). pap. 15.16 o.p. (*0-395-05210-6*, Riverside Editions) Houghton Mifflin Co.

—Madame Bovary. 2002. 336p. 26.99 (*1-4043-1578-0*); per. 21.99 (*1-4043-1579-9*) IndyPublish.com.

—Madame Bovary. Steegmuller, Francis, tr. 1991. (Vintage Bks.). (Illus.). 432p. pap. 12.00 (*0-679-73636-0*, Vintage) Knopf Publishing Group.

—Madame Bovary. Steegmuller, Francis, tr. 1993. (Everyman's Library). (Illus.). 368p. 17.00 (*0-679-42031-2*) Knopf, Alfred A. Inc.

—Madame Bovary. 2000. 7.95 (*3-89508-252-X*, 520219) Konemann.

—Madame Bovary. Hardy, Thomas, ed. 1999. (Cloth Bound Pocket Ser.). (Illus.). 7.95 (*3-8290-3006-1*) Konemann.

—Madame Bovary. (FRE.). pap. 8.95 (*2-253-00486-3*, LP0088E) Librairie Generale Francaise, LGF FRA. *Dist:* Continental Bk. Co., Inc.

—Madame Bovary. 1982. 396p. (C). pap. 11.25 (*0-07-554378-8*, McGraw-Hill Humanities, Social Sciences & World Languages) McGraw-Hill Higher Education.

—Madame Bovary. 1972. (FRE.). (C). pap. 13.95 (*0-8442-1758-1*, VF1758-1) McGraw-Hill/Contemporary.

—Madame Bovary. Marmur, Mildred, tr. from FRE. 2001. 408p. mass mkt. 5.95 (*0-451-52820-4*, Signet Classics) NAL.

—Madame Bovary. 1970. mass mkt. 0.60 o.p. (*0-451-50511-5*, Signet Classics); 1970. mass mkt. 0.50 o.p. (*0-451-50234-5*, Signet Classics); 1964. mass mkt. 1.50 o.p. (*0-451-51008-9*, Signet Classics); 1964. mass mkt. 2.75 o.p. (*0-451-51487-4*, Signet Classics); 1964. mass mkt. 2.50 o.p. (*0-451-51914-0*, Signet Classics); 1964. mass mkt. 0.95 o.p. (*0-451-50692-8*, Signet Classics); 1964. mass mkt. 0.75 o.p. (*0-451-50592-1*, Signet Classics); 1964. mass mkt. 2.75 o.p. (*0-451-52240-0*); 1964. mass mkt. 1.75 o.p. (*0-451-51214-6*, Signet Classics); 1964. mass mkt. 1.95 o.p. (*0-451-51681-8*, Signet Classics); 1964. mass mkt. 2.25 o.p. (*0-451-51365-7*, Signet Classics); 1964. mass mkt. 2.25 o.p. (*0-451-51805-5*, Signet Classics) NAL.

—Madame Bovary. Marmur, Mildred, tr. 1964. (Illus.). 400p. mass mkt. 5.95 o.s.i (*0-451-52387-3*, Signet Classics) NAL.

—Madame Bovary. l.t. ed. 2001. 519p. 26.00 (*1-58287-634-7*) North Bks.

—Madame Bovary. (C). pap. 15.75 (*0-393-94860-9*); 1965. (Illus.). xvi, 462p. pap. text 10.50 (*0-393-09608-4*, 9608) Norton, W. W. & Co., Inc.

—Madame Bovary. De Man, Paul, ed. & tr. by. 2nd ed. 2004. pap. (*0-393-97917-2*) Norton, W. W. & Co., Inc.

—Madame Bovary. Mauldon, Margaret, tr. 2004. (Oxford World's Classics Hardcovers Ser.). 384p. 26.00 (*0-19-280549-5*) Oxford Univ. Pr., Inc.

—Madame Bovary. 1999. (Oxford World's Classics Ser.). 400p. 15.00 (*0-19-210025-4*) Oxford Univ. Pr., Inc.

—Madame Bovary. Cave, Terence, ed. 1989. (Oxford World's Classics Ser.). 390p. pap. 6.95 o.p. (*0-19-281564-4*) Oxford Univ. Pr., Inc.

—Madame Bovary. abr. ed. 1992. (Classics on Cassette). audio 15.95 (*0-453-00784-8*) Penguin/HighBridge.

—Madame Bovary. (FRE.). pap. 11.95 (*2-266-08314-7*) Presses Pocket FRA. *Dist:* Distribooks, Inc.

—Madame Bovary. Steegmuller, Francis, tr. 1992. 476p. 16.95 o.s.i (*0-679-60013-2*) Random Hse., Inc.

—Madame Bovary. Steegmuller, Francis, tr. & intro. by. 1952. 396p. 3.95 o.s.i (*0-394-60028-2*, T17) Random Hse., Inc.

—Madame Bovary. Brombert, Victor, ed. 1985. (ENG & FRE.). 440p. 6.95 (*0-88332-467-9*) Schoenhof's Foreign Bks., Inc.

—Madame Bovary. 1976. (Folio Ser.: No. 804). (FRE.). pap. 10.95 (*2-07-036804-1*) Schoenhof's Foreign Bks., Inc.

—Madame Bovary. 2003. 28.95 (*0-7862-5602-8*) Thorndike Pr.

—Madame Bovary. 1964. 12.00 (*0-606-00911-6*) Turtleback Bks.

—Madame Bovary. 2002. 384p. pap. 10.00 (*0-14-044912-4*, Penguin Classics) Viking Penguin.

—Madame Bovary. Wall, Geoffrey, tr. & intro. by. 1993. (Penguin Classics Ser.). (Illus.). 320p. pap. 10.00 o.s.i (*0-14-044526-9*, Penguin Classics) Viking Penguin.

—Madame Bovary. Russell, Alan, tr. 1951. (Penguin Classics Ser.). 368p. pap. 3.95 o.p. (*0-14-044015-1*, Penguin Classics) Viking Penguin.

—Madame Bovary. 1998. (Classics Library). (Illus.). 288p. pap. 3.95 (*1-85326-078-9*, 0789WW) Wordsworth Editions, Ltd. GBR. *Dist:* Casemate Pubs. & Bk. Distributors, LLC.

—Madame Bovary. 2000. (SPA.). 420p. pap. 18.95 (*1-58348-813-8*) iUniverse, Inc.

—Madame Bovary Level 4. (FRE.). 7.25 (*2-09-031993-3*, CL9933E) Cle International FRA. *Dist:* Continental Bk. Co., Inc.

—Madame Bovary Level 4. 1998. (Oxford World's Classics Ser.). 400p. pap. 8.95 (*0-19-283399-5*) Oxford Univ. Pr., Inc.

Flaubert, Gustave, et al. Madame Bovary. 1998. E-Book 8.35 (*0-585-36395-1*) netLibrary, Inc.

Fortune, Gwendoline Y. Growing up Nigger Rich. 2002. 256p. 22.00 (*1-56554-963-5*) Pelican Publishing Co., Inc.

Foster, Bennett. Trigger Vengeance. l.t. ed. 2001. 223p. 21.95 (*1-57490-365-9*, Sagebrush Large Print Westerns) Beeler, Thomas T. Publisher.

Frandsen, Karen G. I'd Rather Get a Spanking Than Go to the Doctor. 1987. (Childhood Fantasies & Fears Ser.). (Illus.). 32p. (J). (ps-3). mass mkt. 3.95 o.p. (*0-516-43498-5*, Children's Pr.) Scholastic Library Publishing.

Freeman, Austin R. For the Defence: Dr. Thorndyke. l.t. ed. 1992. pap. 14.95 o.p. (*0-7927-1062-2*) BBC Audiobooks America.

Freeman, R. Austin. The Best Dr. Thorndyke Detective Stories. Bleiler, Everett F., ed. 1973. 274p. pap. 4.95 o.p. (*0-486-20388-3*) Dover Pubns., Inc.

—John Thorndyke's Cases. 1976. lib. bdg. 12.95 o.s.i (*0-89968-169-7*, Lightyear Pr.) Buccaneer Bks., Inc.

—John Thorndyke's Cases. 2000. (Illus.). 250p. pap. 9.95 (*0-7551-0365-3*) House of Stratus, Inc. GBR. *Dist:* Midpoint Trade Bks., Inc.

—Mr. Pottermack's Oversight. 1985. (Detective Stories Ser.). 352p. reprint ed. pap. 5.95 o.p. (*0-486-24780-5*) Dover Pubns., Inc.

—The Red Thumb Mark. 1986. 305p. mass mkt. 3.95 o.p. (*0-88184-240-0*, Carroll & Graf Pubs.) Avalon Publishing Group.

—The Red Thumb Mark. 1986. 320p. reprint ed. pap. 6.95 (*0-486-25210-8*) Dover Pubns., Inc.

—The Red Thumb Mark. 2001. 230p. pap. 9.95 (*0-7551-0374-2*) House of Stratus, Inc. GBR. *Dist:* Midpoint Trade Bks., Inc.

—The Stoneware Monkey. 1987. (Mystery Classics Ser.). 224p. reprint ed. pap. 6.95 o.p. (*0-486-25471-2*) Dover Pubns., Inc.

Frost, Mark. The List of Seven. 1993. 368p. 20.00 o.p. (*0-688-12245-0*, Morrow, William & Co.) Morrow/Avon.

—The List of Seven. abr. ed. 1993. audio 16.95 o.p. (*1-55800-840-3*) NewStar Media, Inc.

—The List of Seven. 1994. (Super Sound Buy, Dove Ser.). 8.99 o.p. (*0-7871-0238-5*) Penguin Group (USA) Inc.

—The List of 7. 1994. 416p. mass mkt. 5.99 (*0-380-72019-1*, Avon Bks.) Morrow/Avon.

Gaffney, Patricia. Sweet Everlasting. 384p. 2001. mass mkt. 6.99 (*0-451-20290-2*); 1993. mass mkt. 4.99 o.s.i (*0-451-40375-4*, Topaz) NAL.

—Sweet Everlasting. l.t. ed. 2001. (Americana Ser.). 608p. 30.95 (*0-7862-3319-2*); 581p. (*0-7862-3318-4*) Thorndike Pr.

Gansky, Alton L. By My Hands: A Novel. l.t. ed. 2001. (Christian Mystery Ser.). 505 psp. 23.95 (*0-7862-3245-5*) Thorndike Pr.

Garrison, Paul. Fire & Ice. 1999. 384p. mass mkt. 6.99 (*0-380-79436-5*, Eos); 1998. 400p. mass mkt. 15.95 (*0-380-97566-1*, Avon Bks.) Morrow/Avon.

—Fire & Ice. abr. ed. 1998. 25.00 incl. audio (*0-7871-1015-9*, Dove Audio) NewStar Media, Inc.

Giles, Janice H. Tara's Healing. 1976. 22.95 (*0-8488-0503-8*) Amereon, Ltd.

—Tara's Healing. l.t. ed. 1986. (General Ser.). 313p. 16.95 o.p. (*0-8161-4050-2*, Macmillan Reference USA) Gale Group.

—Tara's Healing. 1994. 256p. 28.00 o.p. (*0-8131-1886-7*); pap. 17.00 (*0-8131-0832-2*) Univ. Pr. of Kentucky.

Giles, Janice Holt. Act of Contrition. 2001. 240p. 25.00 (*0-8131-2172-8*) Univ. Pr. of Kentucky.

Gold, Becky. Centrum's Phil & Lil Go to the Doctor. 2002. (Illus.). 24p. (J). mass mkt. 3.50 (*0-689-85153-7*, Simon Spotlight/Nickelodeon) Simon & Schuster Children's Publishing.

Goldberg, Marshall. A Deadly Operation: A Novel of Medical Espionage. 1996. 240p. pap. 14.95 (*0-8023-1310-8*) Dufour Editions, Inc.

—Intelligence. 1996. 240p. pap. 14.95 (*0-8023-1311-6*) Dufour Editions, Inc.

Gordon, Noah. The Physician. 1987. 640p. mass mkt. 6.99 o.s.i (*0-449-21426-5*, Fawcett) Ballantine Bks.

—The Physician. 1986. 624p. 18.45 o.p. (*0-671-47748-X*, Simon & Schuster) Simon & Schuster.

—The Physician. 2002. 720p. pap. 8.95 (*0-7515-0389-4*) Warner Bks. GBR. *Dist:* Trafalgar Square.

—Shaman. 1992. 528p. 23.00 o.p. (*0-525-93554-1*, Dutton) Dutton/Plume.

—Shaman. 1993. pap. o.p. (*0-451-17929-3*); 576p. mass mkt. 6.99 o.s.i (*0-451-17701-0*) NAL. (Signet Bks.).

—Shaman. 2002. 652p. pap. 8.95 (*0-7515-0082-8*) Warner Bks. GBR. *Dist:* Trafalgar Square.

Gray, Alasdair. Poor Things. 2002. (British Literature Ser.). (Illus.). 319p. reprint ed. pap. 13.50 (*1-56478-307-3*) Dalkey Archive Pr.

—Poor Things: Episodes from the Early Life of Archibald McCandless M.D., Scottish Public Health Officer. 320p. 3.98 o.p. (*0-8317-3686-0*) Smithmark Pubs., Inc.

Gray, Alasdair, ed. Poor Things: Episodes from the Early Life of Archibald McCandless M.D., Scottish Public Health Officer. 1994. 336p. pap. 10.95 o.s.i (*0-15-600068-7*, Harvest Bks.); 1993. xiv, 317p. 21.95 o.s.i (*0-15-173076-8*) Harcourt Trade Pubs.

Green, Carmen. Doctor, Doctor. 2002. 28p. mass mkt. 6.99 (*1-58314-327-0*) Kensington Publishing Corp.

Gregory, Susanna. A Wicked Deed. 2003. (Illus.). 506p. pap. 7.95 (*0-7515-2544-8*) Warner Bks. GBR. *Dist:* Trafalgar Square.

Griffin, Nicholas. The House of Sight & Shadow. 2001. E-Book 10.00 (*1-58945-860-5*) Adobe Systems, Inc.

Grippando, James M. Found Money. l.t. ed. 2001. (Softcover Ser.). 466p. pap. 23.95 o.p. (*1-58724-069-6*, Wheeler Publishing, Inc.) Gale Group.

Grondahl, Jens Christian. Lucca. Born, Anne, tr. 336p. 2004. pap. 14.00 (*0-15-602961-8*, Harvest Bks.); 2003. 26.00 (*0-15-100594-X*) Harcourt Trade Pubs.

Guterson, David. East of the Mountains. 2001. 279p. 25.00 (*0-7881-9642-1*) DIANE Publishing Co.

—East of the Mountains. 2000. 304p. pap. 14.00 o.s.i (*0-15-601104-2*, Harvest Bks.) Harcourt Trade Pubs.

—East of the Mountains. 2003. (Illus.). 304p. pap. 13.00 (*1-4000-3265-2*, Vintage) Knopf Publishing Group.

Hallberg, Lynnette. Enchanted Evening. l.t. ed. 2001. 203p. pap. 22.95 (*0-7838-9474-0*) Thorndike Pr.

Hamilton, Andrew. A Taste of His Own Medicine. 1993. 160p. pap. 7.99 o.p. (*0-89107-755-3*) Crossway Bks.

Hannah, Barry. Ray. 1987. 12p. pap. 5.95 o.p. (*0-14-010515-8*, Penguin Bks.) Viking Penguin.
Hansen, Brooks. The Chess Garden: Or, the Twilight Letters of Gustav Uyterhoeven. 1996. (Illus.). 480p. reprint ed. 16.00 (*1-57322-563-0*, Riverhead Trade (Paperbacks)) Berkley Publishing Group.
—The Chess Garden: Or, the Twilight Letters of Gustav Uyterhoeven. 1995. (Illus.). 496p. 23.00 o.p. (*0-374-16015-5*) Farrar, Straus & Giroux.
—Chess Garden Readers. 1995. pap. (*0-374-99817-5*) Farrar, Straus & Giroux.
—Perlman's Ordeal. 1999. (Illus.). 400p. 24.00 o.p. (*0-374-23078-1*) Farrar, Straus & Giroux.
Hansen, Jennie L. Coming Home: A Novel. 1998. pap. 12.95 (*1-57734-288-7*, 01113437) Covenant Communications, Inc.
Harbouri, Petrie. The Brothers Carburi. 2002. 311p. (*0-7475-5342-4*) Bloomsbury Pr.
—The Brothers Carburi. 2003. 320p. pap. 12.00 (*0-7475-5708-X*) Bloomsbury Publishing, Ltd. GBR. *Dist:* Trafalgar Square.
Harington, Donald. Butterfly Weed. 1996. 384p. 24.00 o.s.i (*0-15-100164-2*); pap. 19.00 (*0-15-600219-1*, Harvest Bks.) Harcourt Trade Pubs.
Harris, Marilyn. Hatter Fox. 1986. 256p. mass mkt. 5.99 o.s.i (*0-345-33157-5*); 1985. mass mkt. 2.95 o.s.i (*0-345-32821-3*); 1982. mass mkt. 2.75 o.p. (*0-345-30026-2*) Ballantine Bks.
—Hatter Fox. 1974. 288p. pap. 1.95 o.p. (*0-553-11540-5*, Y11540-5) Bantam Bks.
—Hatter Fox. 1973. 12.95 o.s.i (*0-394-48514-9*) Random Hse., Inc.
Hathaway, Robin. The Doctor & the Dead Man's Chest. 2001. (Illus.). 352p. 24.95 (*0-312-26956-0*) St. Martin's Pr.
—The Doctor Digs a Grave. 272p. 1998. 22.95 (*0-312-18568-5*, Saint Martin's Minotaur); Vol. 1. 2nd ed. 1999. mass mkt. 5.99 (*0-312-96703-9*, St. Martin's Paperbacks) St. Martin's Pr.
—Doctor Makes a Dollhouse Call: Doctor Fenimore Mystery. 2000. (Doctor Fenimore Mysteries Ser.). 272p. 23.95 (*0-312-24192-5*, Saint Martin's Minotaur) St. Martin's Pr.
—Scarecrow. l.t. ed. 2003. (Mystery Ser.). 27.95 (*1-57490-510-4*) Beeler, Thomas T. Publisher.
—Scarecrow. Date not set. pap. (*0-312-30852-3*, Saint Martin's Griffin); mass mkt. (*0-312-98656-4*, St. Martin's Paperbacks) St. Martin's Pr.
—Scarecrow: A Mystery. 2003. 224p. 23.95 (*0-312-30851-5*, Saint Martin's Minotaur) St. Martin's Pr.
Hearn, Lafcadio. Chita: A Memory of Last Island. LaBarre, Delia, ed. 2003. 128p. 20.00 (*1-57806-558-5*, A Banner Bk.) Univ. Pr. of Mississippi.
Heath, Roy A. The Shadow Bride. 1995. 428p. 24.95 (*0-89255-213-1*) Persea Bks., Inc.
Hedge, Tricia, ed. Jekyll & Hyde. 1991. (Illus.). 80p. pap. text 5.95 o.p. (*0-19-421661-6*) Oxford Univ. Pr., Inc.
Hernon, Peter. The Kindling Effect. 1997. pap. 5.99 (*0-380-72634-3*, Avon Bks.) Morrow/Avon.
Hogan, Judy. The Shade. McClelland, Lucille A., ed. 1997. (Illus.). 391p. pap. 16.95 (*0-9652673-0-X*) Black Oaks Publishing.
Howard, Linda. Bluebird Winter. l.t. ed. 2002. 29.95 (*0-7862-4005-9*) Thorndike Pr.
—The Touch of Fire. 1997. 336p. mass mkt. 7.99 (*0-671-01972-4*, Pocket) Simon & Schuster.
—The Touch of Fire. Zion, Claire, ed. 1992. 336p. mass mkt. 5.99 (*0-671-72858-X*, Pocket) Simon & Schuster.
—The Touch of Fire. l.t. ed. 2001. (Famous Authors Ser.). 479p. 28.95 (*0-7862-2846-6*) Thorndike Pr.
Howard, Sara. Fantasy Man. 2001. (Romance Ser.). 256p. mass mkt. 4.99 o.p. (*0-8217-6793-3*) Kensington Publishing Corp.
Hudson, Jeffery, pseud. A Case of Need. 1993. 320p. 18.95 o.p. (*0-525-93802-8*, Dutton) Dutton/Plume.
—A Case of Need. l.t. ed. 1994. 19.95 o.p. (*1-56895-052-7*, Wheeler Publishing, Inc.) Gale Group.
Huyler, Frank. The Laws of Invisible Things. 2004. 320p. 24.00 (*0-8050-7330-2*) Holt, Henry & Co.
Iles, Greg. The Footprints of God. 2004. 560p. mass mkt. 7.99 (*0-7434-5414-6*, Pocket Star); 2003. 480p. 25.95 (*0-7432-3469-3*, Scribner) Simon & Schuster.
—The Footprints of God. l.t. ed. 2004. 711p. pap. 13.95 (*1-59413-025-6*, Large Print Pr.) Thorndike Pr.
—24 Hours. abr. ed. 2000. audio 24.95 o.p. (*1-56740-929-6*, 2196, Nova Audio Bks.); audio 73.25 (*1-56740-735-8*, 2195, Unabridged Library Editions); audio 32.95 (*1-56740-387-5*, 2194, Brilliance Audio Unabridged) Brilliance Audio.
—24 Hours. 2000. 335p. 24.95 o.s.i (*0-399-14624-5*) Penguin Group (USA) Inc.
Irving, John. The Cider House Rules. 1999. mass mkt. 7.99 (*0-345-91638-7*); 1999. 7.99 (*0-345-91557-7*); 1999. pap. 12.95 (*0-345-91558-5*); 1994. 608p. mass mkt. 7.99 (*0-345-38765-1*, Ballantine Bks.); 1997. 576p. reprint ed. pap. 14.95 (*0-345-41794-1*, Ballantine Bks.) Ballantine Bks.
—The Cider House Rules. 608p. 1991. mass mkt. 2.99 o.s.i (*0-553-19648-0*); 1986. mass mkt. 5.95 o.s.i (*0-553-25800-1*) Bantam Bks.
—The Cider House Rules. 1985. 640p. 18.95 o.p. (*0-688-03036-X*, Morrow, William & Co.) Morrow/Avon.
—The Cider House Rules. 1999. (Modern Library Ser.). 592p. 21.95 (*0-679-60335-2*) Random Hse., Inc.
—The Cider House Rules. 1999. 144p. 10.95 (*0-7868-8523-8*) Talk Miramax Bks.
—The Cider House Rules. l.t. ed. (Basic Ser.). 2001. 28.95 (*0-7862-2675-7*); 2000. 1064p. 30.95 (*0-7862-2674-9*) Thorndike Pr.
—The Cider House Rules. 1993. 14.04 (*0-606-20389-3*) Turtleback Bks.
Jacobson, Alan. False Accusations. 1999. 407p. 23.00 (*0-671-02678-X*, Atria); 2000. (Illus.). 448p. reprint ed. pap. 6.99 (*0-671-02679-8*, Pocket) Simon & Schuster.
Jewett, Sarah Orne. A Country Doctor, Set. unabr. ed. 1992. audio 41.95 (*1-55685-233-9*) Audio Bk. Contractors, Inc.
—A Country Doctor. 1999. (Bantam Classics Ser.). 288p. mass mkt. 4.95 (*0-553-21498-5*) Bantam Bks.
—A Country Doctor. 1986. 288p. pap. 11.95 o.p. (*0-452-00805-0*, Meridian Bks.) NAL.
—A Country Doctor. 1984. (Illus.). 371p. reprint ed. 25.00 o.p. (*0-89725-048-6*, 1261) Picton Pr.
—A Country Doctor. 1988. (Collected Works of Sarah Orne Jewett). reprint ed. lib. bdg. 59.00 (*0-7812-1306-1*) Reprint Services Corp.
—A Country Doctor. reprint ed. 59.00 (*0-403-03191-5*) Somerset Pubs., Inc.
Jin, Ha. Waiting. 2001. E-Book 11.50 (*1-58945-644-0*) Adobe Systems, Inc.
—Waiting. l.t. ed. 2000. 374p. 29.95 (*1-56895-885-4*, Wheeler Publishing, Inc.) Gale Group.
—Waiting. 2001. E-Book 11.50 (*0-375-72695-0*) Random Hse., Inc.
—Waiting. 2000. 19.05 (*0-606-21850-5*) Turtleback Bks.
—Waiting: A Novel. (Vintage International Ser.). 320p. 2000. pap. 13.00 (*0-375-70641-0*, Vintage); 1999. 24.00 (*0-375-40653-0*, Pantheon) Knopf Publishing Group.
Johnson, Margaret. Riches of the Heart. 1995. 192p. 18.95 o.s.i (*0-8034-9144-1*, Avalon Bks.) Bouregy, Thomas & Co., Inc.
Jones, Dylan. Thicker Than Water. 1994. 208p. 18.95 o.p. (*0-312-10558-4*, Saint Martin's Minotaur) St. Martin's Pr.
Jordan, Oakley. Death's Parallel. 2002. 406p. pap. 16.95 (*1-56825-078-9*) Rainbow Bks., Inc.
Kahn, James. The Echo Vector. 1988. 240p. 15.95 o.p. (*0-312-01023-0*); Vol. 1. 1989. pap. 3.95 o.p. (*0-312-91049-5*, St. Martin's Paperbacks) St. Martin's Pr.
Katz, Robert I. Surgical Risk: A Kurtz & Barent Mystery. 2002. pap. 12.95 (*1-930008-05-8*) Willowgate Pr.
Katz, William. Facemaker. 1988. 256p. text 16.95 o.p. (*0-07-033553-2*) McGraw-Hill Cos., The.
—Facemaker. 1989. 256p. mass mkt. 4.50 (*0-380-70685-7*, Avon Bks.) Morrow/Avon.
Kellerman, Jonathan. Dr. Death. 2001. 448p. reprint ed. mass mkt. 7.99 (*0-345-41388-1*, Ballantine Bks.) Ballantine Bks.
—Dr. Death. l.t. ed. 2000. 592p. 26.95 (*0-375-43079-2*) Random Hse. Large Print.
Kilby, Joan. Child of Her Dreams. 2002. (Harlequin Superromance Ser.: No. 1076). 304p. mass mkt. (*0-373-71076-3*, Harlequin Bks.) Harlequin Enterprises, Ltd.
Klass, Perri. The Mystery of Breathing: A Novel. 2004. 288p. tchr. ed. 24.00 (*0-618-10961-7*) Houghton Mifflin Co.
Kramsky, Jerry. Dr. Jekyll & Mr. Hyde. Darlington, Adeline, tr. from ITA. 2002. (Illus.). 64p. 15.95 (*1-56163-330-5*, Comics Lit) NBM Publishing Co.
Kraus, Harry L., Jr. Lethal Mercy. 1997. 384p. pap. 12.99 (*0-89107-921-1*) Crossway Bks.
—The Stain. 1997. 424p. pap. 12.99 (*0-89107-972-6*) Crossway Bks.
Kraus, Harry L. The Stain. 1998. (Christian Fiction Ser.). 568p. 23.95 (*0-7862-1510-0*, Five Star) Gale Group.
Kraus, Harry Lee. For the Rest of My Life. 2004. pap. 12.99 (*0-310-24978-3*) Zondervan.
Lacy, Al. One More Sunrise. 2004. pap. (*1-59052-308-3*) Multnomah Pubs., Inc.
Larsen, Margie, et al. Barney Goes to the Doctor. 1997. (Barney's Go to Ser.). (Illus.). 24p. (J). (ps). mass mkt. 3.50 (*1-57064-074-2*) Lyrick Publishing.
Lewis, Henry C. Odd Leaves from the Life of a Louisiana Swamp Doctor. 1985. reprint ed. lib. bdg. 18.75 o.p. (*0-8398-1160-8*) Irvington Pubs.
—Odd Leaves from the Life of a Louisiana Swamp Doctor. 1997. (Library of Southern Civilization). (Illus.). 240p. 24.95 (*0-8071-2185-1*); pap. 12.95 (*0-8071-2167-3*) Louisiana State Univ. Pr.
Lewis, Sinclair. Main Street. E-Book 3.95 (*0-594-05716-7*) 1873 Pr.
—Main Street. 1976. 25.95 (*0-8488-0828-2*) Amereon, Ltd.
—Main Street. 1996. 496p. pap. 10.95 (*0-7867-0325-3*, Carroll & Graf Pubs.) Avalon Publishing Group.
—Main Street. 1996. 544p. mass mkt. 5.95 (*0-553-21451-9*) Bantam Bks.
—Main Street. 1984. 297p. reprint ed. lib. bdg. 31.95 (*0-89966-495-4*) Buccaneer Bks., Inc.
—Main Street. reprint ed. lib. bdg. 48.00 (*0-7426-1369-0*); 2001. 451p. pap. 28.00 (*0-7426-5673-X*); 2001. pap. text 28.00 (*0-7426-6369-8*); 1998. 451p. lib. bdg. 108.00 (*1-58201-673-9*) Classic Bks.
—Main Street. unabr. ed. 1999. (Dover Thrift Editions Ser.). iv, 400p. pap. text 2.50 (*0-486-40655-5*) Dover Pubns., Inc.
—Main Street. 2003. (Barnes & Noble Classics Ser.). 576p. pap. 5.95 (*1-59308-036-0*) Fine Communications.
—Main Street. 1989. (Modern Classic Ser.). 451p. 15.95 o.s.i (*0-15-155547-8*) Harcourt Trade Pubs.
—Main Street. l.t. ed. 497p. pap. 37.12 (*0-7583-1456-6*); 621p. pap. 44.14 (*0-7583-1457-4*); 851p. pap. 62.17 (*0-7583-1458-2*); 1089p. pap. 74.20 (*0-7583-1459-0*); 1394p. pap. 88.64 (*0-7583-1460-4*); 1714p. pap. 111.80 (*0-7583-1461-2*); 2109p. pap. 127.07 (*0-7583-1462-0*); 2446p. pap. 149.71 (*0-7583-1463-9*); 1089p. lib. bdg. 86.20 (*0-7583-1451-5*); 2446p. lib. bdg. 180.60 (*0-7583-1455-8*); 851p. lib. bdg. 74.17 (*0-7583-1450-7*); 1394p. lib. bdg. 100.64 (*0-7583-1452-3*); 1714p. lib. bdg. 129.80 (*0-7583-1453-1*); 2109p. lib. bdg. 149.57 (*0-7583-1454-X*); 497p. lib. bdg. 43.12 (*0-7583-1448-5*); 621p. lib. bdg. 50.14 (*0-7583-1449-3*) Huge Print Pr.
—Main Street. 2002. 472p. 28.99 (*1-4043-1584-5*); per. 23.99 (*1-4043-1585-3*) IndyPublish.com.
—Main Street. 1999. 518p. pap. 9.95 o.p. (*1-930128-08-8*, JNMedia Bks.) JNMedia, Inc.
—Main Street. (*0-451-52742-9*); mass mkt. 0.95 o.p. (*0-451-02005-7*, Signet Bks.); 1970. mass mkt. 0.75 o.p. (*0-451-50093-8*, Signet Classics); 1970. mass mkt. 1.25 o.p. (*0-451-50500-X*, Signet Classics); 1970. mass mkt. 0.95 o.p. (*0-451-50352-X*, Signet Classics); 1961. mass mkt. 2.50 o.p. (*0-451-51392-4*, Signet Classics); 1961. mass mkt. 1.50 o.p. (*0-451-50753-3*, Signet Classics); 1961. mass mkt. 1.75 o.p. (*0-451-50875-0*, Signet Classics); 1961. mass mkt. 2.25 o.p. (*0-451-51140-9*, Signet Classics); 1961. 448p. mass mkt. 5.95 o.s.i (*0-451-52461-6*, Signet Classics); 1961. mass mkt. 3.95 o.p. (*0-451-51898-5*, Signet Classics); 1961. mass mkt. 3.50 o.p. (*0-451-51831-4*, Signet Classics); 1961. 440p. mass mkt. 4.50 o.p. (*0-451-52147-1*, Signet Classics); 1961. mass mkt. 2.95 o.p. (*0-451-51536-6*, Signet Classics); 1961. mass mkt. 3.50 o.p. (*0-451-51712-1*, Signet Classics); 1998. 440p. mass mkt. 5.95 (*0-451-52682-1*, Signet Bks.) NAL.
—Main Street. 2001. 510p. 25.00 (*1-58287-154-X*); 650p. lib. bdg. 26.00 (*1-58287-637-1*) North Bks.
—Main Street. 1996. (Literary Classics). 459p. pap. 10.00 (*1-57392-048-7*) Prometheus Bks., Pubs.
—Main Street. 2000. E-Book 4.95 (*0-679-64167-X*, Modern Library) Random House Adult Trade Publishing Group.
—Main Street. 1999. (Modern Library Ser.). 448p. pap. 9.95 o.s.i (*0-375-75314-1*) Random Hse., Inc.
—Main Street. E-Book 5.00 (*0-7410-0558-1*) SoftBook Pr.
—Main Street. 1920. 12.00 (*0-606-01015-7*) Turtleback Bks.
—Main Street. 1995. (Twentieth Century Classics Ser.). 448p. pap. 11.00 (*0-14-018901-7*, Penguin Classics) Viking Penguin.
—Main Street. 1999. E-Book 5.99 (*0-8220-7126-6*, Cliff Notes) Wiley, John & Sons, Inc.
—Sinclair Lewis: Main Street & Babbitt. Hersey, John, ed. 1992. (Library of America: Vol. 59). 898p. 40.00 (*0-940450-61-5*) Library of America, The.
Lewis, Sinclair & Hersey, John. Main Street & Babbitt. 1992. E-Book 40.00 (*0-585-20170-6*) netLibrary, Inc.
Liles, Maurine W. Willer & the Piney Woods Doctor. 1995. (Illus.). 112p. (J). (gr. 6-7). 15.95 (*1-57168-058-6*) Eakin Pr.
Ludlum, Robert & Lynds, Gayle. The Hades Factor. E-Book 15.95 (*0-312-27882-9*); 2001. 432p. mass mkt. 7.50 (*0-312-97305-5*, St. Martin's Paperbacks); 2001. E-Book 7.50 (*0-312-27158-1*); 2000. E-Book 15.95 (*0-312-27768-7*); 2000. xiii, 432p. pap. 15.95 o.p. (*0-312-26437-2*, Saint Martin's Griffin) St. Martin's Pr.
—The Hades Factor. l.t. ed. 2000. (Americana Ser.). 703p. 30.95 (*0-7862-2682-X*); 28.95 (*0-7862-2683-8*) Thorndike Pr.
Lynch, Patrick. Omega. 1997. 384p. 23.95 o.s.i (*0-525-94327-7*) Dutton/Plume.
—Omega. 1998. 432p. mass mkt. 6.99 o.s.i (*0-451-19323-7*, Signet Bks.) NAL.
Martin, Valerie. Mary Reilly. 1990. 272p. 18.95 o.s.i (*0-385-24968-3*) Doubleday Publishing.
Martini, Steve. The Jury. 2001. 448p. 25.95 o.p. (*0-399-14672-5*) Putnam Publishing Group, The.
—The Jury. l.t. ed. 2002. 416p. pap. 14.95 (*0-7862-2953-5*); 2001. 494p. 32.95 (*0-7862-2954-3*) Thorndike Pr.
Massad, Stewart. Doctors & Other Casualties. 1993. 336p. 18.45 o.p. (*0-446-51683-X*) Warner Bks., Inc.
Masters, Pricilla. Disturbing Ground. 2002. 288p. 24.95 (*0-7490-0582-3*) Allison & Busby, Ltd. GBR. *Dist:* International Publishers Marketing.
Masters, Priscilla. Disturbing Ground. 2003. (General Ser.). lib. bdg. 24.95 (*0-7862-4745-2*) Thorndike Pr.
Maugham, W. Somerset. Of Human Bondage. l.t. ed. 1998. 375p. text 39.95 (*1-56000-500-9*) Transaction Pubs.
—Of Human Bondage. 1992. (Twentieth Century Classics Ser.). 640p. pap. 11.95 (*0-14-018522-4*, Penguin Classics) Viking Penguin.
Mayer, Mercer. Doctor Critter. 1987. (J). 3.95 o.p. (*0-671-61147-X*, Atheneum) Simon & Schuster Children's Publishing.
Mays, James A. Mercy is King: A Novel. 2001. 300p. pap. 14.95 (*1-881524-87-6*) Milligan Bks.
—Trapped: A Novel. 2001. 300p. pap. 14.95 (*1-881524-86-8*) Milligan Bks.
McGrath, Patrick. Dr. Haggard's Disease. 1994. (Vintage Contemporaries Ser.). 192p. pap. 12.00 (*0-679-75261-7*) Random Hse., Inc.
—Dr. Haggard's Disease. 1993. 192p. 20.00 o.p. (*0-671-72733-8*, Simon & Schuster) Simon & Schuster.
McKenna, Lindsay. Protecting His Own. 2002. (Silhouette Intimate Moments Ser.). 256p. mass mkt. (*0-373-27255-3*, Silhouette) Harlequin Enterprises, Ltd.
McWilliam, Candia. A Case of Knives. 1988. 266p. 17.95 o.p. (*0-688-07912-1*, Morrow, William & Co.) Morrow/Avon.
Melnyczuk, Askold. Ambassador of the Dead. 288p. 2001. text 25.00 o.p. (*1-58243-132-9*); 2002. reprint ed. pap. text 15.00 (*1-58243-251-1*) Basic Bks. (Counterpoint Pr.).
Memmi, Albert. The Scorpion, or the Imaginary Confession. Levieux, Eleanor, tr. 1986. (Folio Ser.: No. 1715). (FRE.). 270p. pap. 10.95 (*2-07-037715-6*) Schoenhof's Foreign Bks., Inc.
Michener, James A. Recessional. 1995. 544p. mass mkt. 7.99 (*0-449-22345-0*, Fawcett) Ballantine Bks.
—Recessional. l.t. ed. 1994. 640p. 24.00 o.s.i (*0-679-75691-4*) Random Hse. Large Print.
Morgan, Kathleen. Child of Promise. 2002. (Brides of Culdee Creek Ser.: Bk. 4). 304p. (gr. 13 up). pap. 11.99 (*0-8007-5761-0*) Revell, Fleming H. Co.
Morris, Lynn & Morris, Gilbert. Island of the Innocent. 2000. 395p. 24.95 (*0-7862-2442-8*, Five Star) Gale Group.
Murray, John. A Few Short Notes on Tropical Butterflies: Stories. 288p. 2004. pap. 12.95 (*0-06-050929-5*, Perennial); 2003. 24.95 (*0-06-050928-7*, HarperCollins) HarperTrade.
Nichols, Frank Reed. The Knell. 2000. 151p. 22.95 (*0-923687-54-8*) Celo Valley Bks.
Nigam, Sanjay. The Transplanted Man. 2003. 368p. pap. 13.95 (*0-06-051215-6*, Perennial) HarperTrade.
—The Transplanted Man. 2002. 368p. 24.95 (*0-688-16819-1*, Morrow, William & Co.) Morrow/Avon.
Noble, Diane. Kingdom Come. l.t. ed. 2001. 257p. 24.95 (*0-7862-3461-X*) Thorndike Pr.
Ogburn, Martha D. Progeny. 1999. 288p. pap. 10.99 (*0-8054-1889-X*) Broadman & Holman Pubs.
Oldknow, Antony, ed. Four Short Novels: Carmilla, the Strange Case of Dr. Jekyll & Mr. Hyde, the Sign of the Four, & the Snows of Kilimanjaro. 1998. 295p. pap. text 18.00 (*1-881604-32-2*) Scopcraeft Pr.
Oliver, Jim. Wings in the Snow. 1998. 288p. pap. 12.95 (*1-55583-462-0*, Alyson Bks.) Alyson Pubns.
Organick, Avrum B. Blessings. 1999. iii, 250p. pap. 13.50 (*0-9671068-0-X*); 2nd ed. 2000. 270p. 22.95 (*0-9671068-2-6*); 2nd rev. ed. 2000. 270p. pap. 14.50 (*0-9671068-1-8*) Red Lake Pr.
Oxenbury, Helen. The Checkup. 1994. (Out & About Bks.). (Illus.). 240p. (J). (ps-1). pap. 3.99 o.p. (*0-14-055275-8*, Puffin Bks.) Penguin Putnam Bks. for Young Readers.
Palmer, Michael. Michael Palmer: Three Complete Novels. 1996. 784p. 13.99 (*0-517-14959-1*) Random Hse. Value Publishing.
—Miracle Cure. 1998. 416p. 23.95 o.s.i (*0-553-10523-X*); 1999. 448p. reprint ed. mass mkt. 7.50 (*0-553-57662-3*) Bantam Bks.
—Miracle Cure. unabr. ed. 1998. audio 64.00 (*0-7366-4158-0*, 4661) Books on Tape, Inc.
—Miracle Cure. l.t. ed. 1998. 27.95 o.p. (*1-56895-612-6*, Wheeler Publishing, Inc.) Gale Group.

Occupations

—Miracle Cure. abr. ed. 1998. audio 23.95 (*0-553-47816-8*); audio compact disk 29.95 (*0-553-45591-5*, ) Random Hse. Audio Publishing Group. (RH Audio).

—Miracle Cure. unabr. ed. 1998. audio 78.00 (*0-7887-1897-5*, 95319E7) Recorded Bks., LLC.

—Silent Treatment. 1996. 480p. reprint ed. mass mkt. 7.50 (*0-553-57221-0*) Bantam Bks.

—Silent Treatment. l.t. ed. (Core Collection). 632p. 1996. 23.95 (*0-7838-1405-4*); 1995. 26.95 o.p. (*0-7838-1406-2*) Gale Group. (Macmillan Reference USA).

—Silent Treatment. abr. ed. 1995. audio 16.99 o.s.i (*0-553-47345-X*, RH Audio) Random Hse. Audio Publishing Group.

—Silent Treatment, unabr. ed. audio 85.00 (*0-7887-0268-8*, 94477E7) Recorded Bks., LLC.

Parker, F. M. Blood & Dust. l.t. ed. 2001. 19.95 o.p. (*1-58724-089-0*, Wheeler Publishing, Inc.) Gale Group.

—Blood & Dust. 2000. 384p. mass mkt. 5.99 o.s.i (*0-7860-1152-1*, Pinnacle Bks.) Kensington Publishing Corp.

Pashman, Susan. The Speed of Light. 1997. 207p. 24.00 (*1-877946-86-9*) Permanent Pr., The.

Patterson, James. The Jericho Commandment & See How They Run. 1981. mass mkt. 2.50 o.s.i (*0-345-29241-3*) Ballantine Bks.

—See How They Run. l.t. ed. 1997. 26.95 o.p. (*1-56895-480-8*, Wheeler Publishing, Inc.) Gale Group.

—See How They Run. 1997. mass mkt. (*0-316-69382-0*) Little Brown & Co.

—See How They Run. 1997. 336p. reprint ed. mass mkt. 7.99 (*0-446-60392-9*) Warner Bks., Inc.

Peak, John. Mortal Judgments. E-Book 23.95 (*0-312-26461-5*); 1999. 352p. 23.95 o.p. (*0-312-19837-X*) St. Martin's Pr.

Penna, Richard. Yielding Ice about to Melt. 2003. 192p. 14.95 (*0-8023-1339-6*) Dufour Editions, Inc.

Petty, Kate. Going to the Doctor. 1987. (First Timers Ser.). (Illus.). 24p. (J). (gr. 1-3). mass mkt. 10.40 o.p. (*0-531-17069-1*, Watts, Franklin) Scholastic Library Publishing.

Pomidor, Bill. Anatomy of a Murder. 1996. (Cal & Plato Marley Mystery Ser.). 272p. mass mkt. 5.50 o.s.i (*0-451-18417-3*, Signet Bks.) NAL.

—Mind over Murder. 1998. (Cal & Plato Marley Mystery Ser.). 288p. mass mkt. 5.99 o.s.i (*0-451-19216-8*, Signet Bks.) NAL.

—Murder by Prescription. 1995. (Cal & Plato Marley Ser.). 288p. mass mkt. 4.99 o.s.i (*0-451-18416-5*, Signet Bks.) NAL.

—Skeletons in the Closet. 1997. (Cal & Plato Marley Mystery Ser.). 288p. mass mkt. 5.50 o.s.i (*0-451-18418-1*, Signet Bks.) NAL.

—Ten Little Medicine Men. 1998. (Cal & Plato Marley Mystery Ser.). 288p. mass mkt. 5.99 o.s.i (*0-451-19214-1*, Signet Bks.) NAL.

Randall, Rona. The Doctor Falls in Love. l.t. ed. 235p. 2001. (*0-7540-4289-8*); 2001. (*0-7540-4290-1*); 2000. pap. 20.95 (*0-7838-9191-1*) Gale Group. (Macmillan Reference USA).

Rawlings, William. The Lazard Legacy. 2003. 24.95 (*1-891799-23-1*) Harbor Hse.

Reece, Colleen L. Nurse Autumn's Secret Love. l.t. ed. 2001. 237p. 23.95 (*0-7862-3137-8*); (*0-7540-4457-2*) Thorndike Pr.

Reeves, Joan. Just One Look. 2003. 167p. 25.95 (*0-7862-5477-7*, Five Star) Gale Group.

Richards, Emilie. A Classic Encounter. 1998. (Men at Work Ser.: Vol. 33). per. (*0-373-81045-8*); 1988. mass mkt. (*0-373-09456-6*) Harlequin Enterprises, Ltd. (Harlequin Bks.).

Richmond, Grace. The Doctor's Secret. l.t. ed. 1994. 19.95 o.p. (*0-7927-1911-5*); pap. 17.95 o.p. (*0-7927-1910-7*) BBC Audiobooks America.

Roe, Caroline. An Antidote for Avarice. 1999. (Prime Crime Mysteries Ser.: 3). 288p. mass mkt. 6.50 o.s.i (*0-425-17260-0*, Prime Crime) Berkley Publishing Group.

—Cure for a Charlatan. 1999. (Chronicles of Issac of Girona Ser.: 2). 272p. mass mkt. 6.50 (*0-425-16734-8*, Prime Crime) Berkley Publishing Group.

—A Draught for a Dead Man. 336p. 2003. mass mkt. 6.50 (*0-425-19308-X*); 2002. (Illus.). 22.95 (*0-425-18648-2*, Prime Crime) Berkley Publishing Group.

—Remedy for Treason. 1998. (Chronicles of Issac of Girona Ser.: Vol. 1). 272p. mass mkt. 5.99 o.s.i (*0-425-16295-8*, Prime Crime) Berkley Publishing Group.

—Solace for a Sinner. 2000. (Isaac of Gerona Ser.). 288p. mass mkt. 6.50 o.s.i (*0-425-17776-9*, Prime Crime) Berkley Publishing Group.

Rosen, Norma. At the Center: A Novel. 1996. (Library of Modern Jewish Literature). 340p. reprint ed. pap. 17.95 (*0-8156-0428-9*, ROACP) Syracuse Univ. Pr.

Rubens, Bernice. A Solitary Grief. 1992. 240p. 23.95 o.p. (*1-85619-057-9*) Trafalgar Square.

Russell, Sheldon. Requiem at Dawn. 2000. (Illus.). 416p. mass mkt. 5.99 o.s.i (*0-7860-1103-3*, Pinnacle Bks.) Kensington Publishing Corp.

Savage, Les, Jr. Coffin Gap. 1999. 224p. mass mkt. 4.50 (*0-8439-4632-6*, Leisure Bks.) Dorchester Publishing Co., Inc.

—Coffin Gap. l.t. ed. 1997. (Western Ser.). 212p. 18.95 (*0-7862-0740-X*, Five Star) Gale Group.

—Coffin Gap. l.t. ed. 1998. (Western Ser.). 312p. 20.95 (*0-7862-0763-9*) Thorndike Pr.

Scarry, Richard. Dr. Doctor. 1988. (Golden Easy Readers Ser.: Level 2). (Illus.). 40p. (J). (ps-3). o.p. (*0-307-11654-9*, Golden Bks.) Random Hse. Children's Bks.

Segal, Erich. Prizes. 1996. 512p. mass mkt. 6.99 o.s.i (*0-8041-1427-7*, Ivy Bks.) Ballantine Bks.

—Prizes. l.t. ed. 1995. 27.95 (*1-56895-228-7*, Wheeler Publishing, Inc.) Gale Group.

—Prizes. abr. ed. 1995. 24.95 o.p. (*0-7871-0429-9*) NewStar Media, Inc.

Seifert, Elizabeth. Army Doctor. 1973. reprint ed. lib. bdg. 22.95 (*0-88411-006-0*) Amereon, Ltd.

—A Certain Dr. French. 1973. reprint ed. lib. bdg. 24.95 (*0-88411-008-7*) Amereon, Ltd.

—The Doctor Disagrees. 1974. reprint ed. lib. bdg. 23.95 (*0-88411-028-1*) Amereon, Ltd.

—A Doctor for Blue Jay Cove. 1973. reprint ed. lib. bdg. 25.95 (*0-88411-016-8*) Amereon, Ltd.

—A Doctor in the Family. 1974. reprint ed. lib. bdg. 22.95 (*0-88411-032-X*) Amereon, Ltd.

—The Doctor Makes a Choice. 1974. reprint ed. lib. bdg. 23.95 (*0-88411-044-3*) Amereon, Ltd.

—Doctor of Mercy. 1973. reprint ed. lib. bdg. 23.95 (*0-88411-025-7*) Amereon, Ltd.

—Doctor on Trial. 1974. reprint ed. lib. bdg. 24.95 (*0-88411-041-9*) Amereon, Ltd.

—Doctor Tuck. l.t. ed. 1998. (Candlelight Romance Ser.). 303p. 21.95 (*0-7862-1538-0*) Thorndike Pr.

—Doctor with a Mission. reprint ed. lib. bdg. 23.95 (*0-88411-034-6*) Amereon, Ltd.

—The Doctor's Bride. 1974. reprint ed. lib. bdg. 23.95 (*0-88411-043-5*) Amereon, Ltd.

—The Doctor's Daughter. l.t. ed. 1997. (Candlelights Ser.). 293p. lib. bdg. 19.95 o.p. (*0-7862-1250-0*) Thorndike Pr.

—The Doctor's Promise. l.t. ed. 2000. (Romance Ser.). 312p. 27.95 (*0-7862-2491-6*) Thorndike Pr.

—Dr. Ellison's Decision. Date not set. reprint ed. lib. bdg. 21.95 (*0-88411-011-7*, Aeonian Pr.) Amereon, Ltd.

—Dr. Woodward's Ambition. 1973. reprint ed. lib. bdg. 21.95 (*0-88411-012-5*) Amereon, Ltd.

—Hillbilly Doctor. 1973. reprint ed. lib. bdg. 22.95 (*0-88411-004-4*) Amereon, Ltd.

—Hospital Zone. 1973. reprint ed. lib. bdg. 26.95 (*0-88411-020-6*) Amereon, Ltd.

—Katie's Young Doctor. 1974. reprint ed. lib. bdg. 23.95 (*0-88411-050-8*) Amereon, Ltd.

—The New Doctor. 1974. reprint ed. lib. bdg. 24.95 (*0-88411-038-9*) Amereon, Ltd.

—Old Doc. 1973. 244p. reprint ed. lib. bdg. 22.95 (*0-88411-014-1*) Amereon, Ltd.

—Pay the Doctor. 1974. reprint ed. lib. bdg. 20.95 (*0-88411-055-9*) Amereon, Ltd.

—The Rival Doctors. 1974. reprint ed. lib. bdg. 22.95 (*0-88411-056-7*) Amereon, Ltd.

—The Strange Loyalty of Dr. Carlisle. 1973. reprint ed. lib. bdg. 24.95 (*0-88411-026-5*) Amereon, Ltd.

—Surgeon in Charge. 1973. reprint ed. lib. bdg. 22.95 (*0-88411-007-9*) Amereon, Ltd.

—Take Three Doctors. 1973. reprint ed. lib. bdg. 21.95 (*0-88411-018-4*) Amereon, Ltd.

—Thus Doctor Mallory. 1973. reprint ed. lib. bdg. 24.95 (*0-88411-003-6*) Amereon, Ltd.

—Thus Doctor Mallory. l.t. ed. 1997. (Romance-Hall Ser.). 375p. lib. bdg. 24.95 o.p. (*0-7838-8303-X*, Macmillan Reference USA) Gale Group.

—To Wed a Doctor. 1974. reprint ed. lib. bdg. 23.95 (*0-88411-057-5*) Amereon, Ltd.

—Two Doctors & a Girl. 1999. 304p. (*0-7540-3676-6*); (*0-7540-3675-8*) BBC Audiobooks America.

—Two Doctors & a Girl. 1978. mass mkt. 1.50 o.p. (*0-451-08118-8*, W8118, Signet Bks.) NAL.

—Two Doctors & a Girl. l.t. ed. 1999. (Candlelight Romance Ser.). 304p. 21.95 o.p. (*0-7862-1763-4*) Thorndike Pr.

—The Two Faces of Dr. Collier. 23.95 (*0-89190-937-0*) Amereon, Ltd.

—The Two Faces of Dr. Collier. 1974. mass mkt. 1.25 o.p. (*0-451-06534-4*); mass mkt. 0.95 o.p. (*0-451-05799-6*) NAL. (Signet Bks.).

—The Two Faces of Dr. Collier. l.t. ed. 2000. (Candlelight Romance Ser.). 352p. 21.95 (*0-7862-2590-4*); (*0-7540-4197-2*) Thorndike Pr.

—The Two Faces of Dr. Collier: The Doctor's Reputation. 1980. mass mkt. 1.95 o.p. (*0-451-09469-7*, J9469, Signet Bks.) NAL.

—Young Doctor Galahad. 1973. reprint ed. lib. bdg. 25.95 (*0-88411-001-X*) Amereon, Ltd.

Selzer, Richard. The Doctor Stories. 1998. viii, 389p. 25.00 o.p. (*0-312-18687-8*) Picador.

—Rituals of Surgery. 1974. 224p. 8.95 o.p. (*0-06-127760-6*) HarperCollins Pubs.

—Rituals of Surgery. 1987. 208p. pap. 6.95 o.p. (*0-688-06490-6*, Quill) HarperTrade.

—Rituals of Surgery. 2001. 208p. pap. text 18.95 (*0-87013-576-7*) Michigan State Univ. Pr.

—Rituals of Surgery. 1980. pap. 3.95 o.p. (*0-671-25340-9*, Touchstone) Simon & Schuster.

Shainberg, Lawrence. Memories of Amnesia. 1988. 219p. 16.95 o.s.i (*0-945167-00-8*) British American Publishing, Ltd.

Sharma, Prem. Mandalay's Child: A Novel. 1999. 392p. pap. 12.00 (*1-880404-20-6*) Bookwrights Pr.

Shepard, Steve. Murder of Crows: A Thriller. 1996. 272p. 23.95 o.p. (*0-89141-598-X*, Presidio Pr.) Ballantine Bks.

Shobin, David. The Cure. 2001. 341p. 24.95 (*0-312-26686-3*); 2002. 352p. reprint ed. mass mkt. 6.99 (*0-312-97920-7*, St. Martin's Paperbacks) St. Martin's Pr.

Shulman, Neil B. & Fleming, Sibley. Under the Backyard Sky. 1995. (Illus.). 32p. (J). (gr. 1-4). 13.95 o.p. (*1-56145-093-6*) Peachtree Pubs., Ltd.

Slaughter, Frank G. Spencer Brade, M. D. 1975. 375p. reprint ed. lib. bdg. 26.95 (*0-89190-287-2*, River-city Pr.) Amereon, Ltd.

Slaughter, Karin. A Faint Cold Fear. 2003. mass mkt. 7.99 (*0-06-053405-2*, Morrow, William & Co.) Morrow/Avon.

Smithers, David W. Dicken's Doctors. 1979. 68.00 o.p. (*0-08-023386-4*) Pergamon Pr. Reprint GBR. *Dist:* Franklin Bk. Co., Inc.

Soderberg, Hjalmar. Doctor Glas: A Novel. 2002. 160p. pap. 12.00 (*0-385-72267-2*, Anchor) Knopf Publishing Group.

Sommers, Tish. Big Bird Goes to the Doctor. 1986. (Sesame Street Growing-Up Bks.). (Illus.). 32p. (J). (ps). o.p. (*0-307-12019-8*, Golden Bks.) Random Hse. Children's Bks.

Southwick, Teresa. Sky Full of Promise. 2002. (Silhouette Romance Ser.). 192p. mass mkt. 3.99 o.s.i (*0-373-19624-5*, Silhouette) Harlequin Enterprises, Ltd. CAN. *Dist:* Simon & Schuster.

Stansfield, Anita. Where the Heart Leads. 2001. 246p. 14.95 (*1-57734-848-6*) Covenant Communications.

Steel, Danielle. Freddie & the Doctor. 1992. (Illus.). 32p. (J). (gr. 1-3). pap. 2.99 o.s.i (*0-440-40575-0*, Yearling) Random Hse. Children's Bks.

Steig, William. Doctor De Soto. 1990. (J). 11.10 (*0-606-03228-2*) Turtleback Bks.

Stein, Michael. The White Life. 1999. 184p. pap. text 16.00 o.s.i (*1-57962-025-6*); 172p. 24.00 o.p. (*1-57962-022-1*) Permanent Pr., The.

Stern, Tom. Gold Fever. 2000. 296p. 21.95 (*0-9703056-0-5*) A E I/TITAN.

Stevenson, Robert Louis. Dr. Jekyll & Mr. Hyde. Date not set. pap. text (*0-17-556567-8*) Addison-Wesley Longman, Inc.

—Dr. Jekyll & Mr. Hyde. (Illus.). lib. bdg. 19.95 (*0-88411-994-7*, Aeonian Pr.) Amereon, Ltd.

—Dr. Jekyll & Mr. Hyde. 1994. (Illustrated Classics Collection). 64p. pap. 4.95 (*0-7854-0664-6*, 40337); pap. 3.60 o.p. (*1-56103-420-7*) American Guidance Service, Inc.

—Dr. Jekyll & Mr. Hyde. 1985. (gr. 7 up). pap. 1.25 o.p. (*0-553-15402-8*); 1982. 128p. mass mkt. 3.95 (*0-553-21277-X*, Bantam Classics) Bantam Bks.

—Dr. Jekyll & Mr. Hyde. 1990. (Illus.). 48p. 3.75 o.s.i (*0-425-12025-2*, Classics Illustrated) Berkley Publishing Group.

—Dr. Jekyll & Mr. Hyde. Danahay, Martin A., ed. 1999. (Literary Texts Ser.). 325p. pap. (*1-55111-245-0*) Broadview Pr.

—Dr. Jekyll & Mr. Hyde. 1990. reprint ed. lib. bdg. 16.95 (*0-89968-552-8*) Buccaneer Bks., Inc.

—Dr. Jekyll & Mr. Hyde. 1991. (Vintage Bks.). 112p. pap. 8.00 (*0-679-73476-7*, Vintage) Knopf Publishing Group.

—Dr. Jekyll & Mr. Hyde. 1992. (Everyman's Library). 272p. 17.00 (*0-679-40538-0*) McKay, David Co., Inc.

—Dr. Jekyll & Mr. Hyde. 1987. mass mkt. 2.25 o.p. (*0-451-52138-2*); 128p. mass mkt. 3.95 o.p. (*0-451-52393-8*, Signet Classics) NAL.

—Dr. Jekyll & Mr. Hyde. 1999. E-Book 3.99 incl. cd-rom (*1-891595-92-X*) Quiet Vision Publishing.

—Dr. Jekyll & Mr. Hyde. 1987. (Running Press Classics Ser.). 63p. pap. 2.95 o.p. (*0-89471-491-0*); lib. bdg. 12.90 o.p. (*0-89471-492-9*) Running Pr. Bk. Pubs.

—Dr. Jekyll & Mr. Hyde. Shefter, Harry, ed. 1980. (Enriched Classics Ser.). 176p. mass mkt. 1.95 o.s.i (*0-671-48957-7*, Pocket) Simon & Schuster.

—Dr. Jekyll & Mr. Hyde. 1998. 135p. text 27.95 (*1-56000-517-3*) Transaction Pubs.

—Dr. Jekyll & Mr. Hyde. (Stepping Stone Adventures Ser.). 2000. 10.04 (*0-606-19893-8*); 1985. 10.00 (*0-606-02457-3*) Turtleback Bks.

—Dr. Jekyll & Mr. Hyde. 1997. (Classics Library). 256p. pap. 3.95 (*1-85326-061-4*, 0614WW) Wordsworth Editions, Ltd. GBR. *Dist:* Casemate Pubs. & Bk. Distributors, LLC.

—Dr. Jekyll & Mr. Hyde & Other Stories. E-Book 5.00 (*0-7607-1297-2*) Barnes & Noble, Inc.

—Dr. Jekyll & Mr. Hyde & Other Stories. 1982. (Oxford Progressive English Readers Ser.). (Illus.). pap. 4.95 o.p. (*0-19-581056-2*) Oxford Univ. Pr., Inc.

—Dr. Jekyll & Mr. Hyde & Other Stories. 1994. (Literary Classics Ser.). 221p. (YA). text 5.98 o.p. (*1-56138-474-7*, Courage Bks.) Running Pr. Bk. Pubs.

—Dr. Jekyll & Mr. Hyde & Other Stories. Calder, Jenni, ed. 1981. (English Library). pap. 2.95 o.p. (*0-14-005776-5*) Viking Penguin.

—Dr. Jekyll & Mr. Hyde & Other Stories. Calder, Jenni, ed. & intro. by. 1980. (Penguin English Library). 304p. pap. 6.95 o.s.i (*0-14-043117-9*, Penguin Classics) Viking Penguin.

—Dr. Jekyll & Mr. Hyde & Weir of Hermiston. Letley, Emma, ed. & intro. by. 1987. (Oxford World's Classics Ser.). 256p. pap. 5.95 o.p. (*0-19-281740-X*) Oxford Univ. Pr., Inc.

—Dr. Jekyll & Mr. Hyde Readalong. 1994. (Illustrated Classics Collection). 64p. pap. 14.95 incl. audio (*0-7854-0705-7*, 40339) American Guidance Service, Inc.

—El Extrano Casa de Dr. Jekyll y Mister Hyde. Teresa Agnes, ed. Heller, Rudolf, tr. 1979. Orig. Title: Dr. Jekyll & Mr. Hyde. (SPA., Illus.). 64p. stu. ed. 1.50 (*0-88301-567-6*); pap. text 3.95 (*0-88301-447-5*) Pendulum Pr., Inc.

—The Strange Case of Dr. Jekyll & Mr. Hyde. Wolfson, Susan J. & Qualls, Barry V., eds. 2000. 170p. (C). pap. text 8.95 (*1-58390-010-1*, Copley Editions) Copley Publishing Group, Inc.

—The Strange Case of Dr. Jekyll & Mr. Hyde. 1991. (Dover Thrift Editions Ser.). 64p. pap. 1.00 (*0-486-26688-5*) Dover Pubns., Inc.

—The Strange Case of Dr. Jekyll & Mr. Hyde, Level 5. 2000. (C). pap. 7.93 (*0-582-42745-2*) Longman Publishing Group.

—The Strange Case of Dr. Jekyll & Mr. Hyde. 1999. Bk. 1. E-Book 1.95 (*1-58515-237-4*); Bk. 2. E-Book 1.95 (*1-58515-238-2*) MesaView, Inc.

—The Strange Case of Dr. Jekyll & Mr. Hyde. Seely, John, ed. 1995. (Thornes Classic Novels Ser.). (Illus.). 195p. pap. 14.95 (*0-7487-1829-X*) Nelson Thornes GBR. *Dist:* Trans-Atlantic Pubns., Inc.

—The Strange Case of Dr. Jekyll & Mr. Hyde. Letley, Emma, ed. & intro. by. 1998. (Oxford World's Classics Ser.). 272p. pap. 6.95 (*0-19-283431-2*) Oxford Univ. Pr., Inc.

—The Strange Case of Dr. Jekyll & Mr. Hyde. 2nd ed. 1993. (Illus.). 110p. pap. text 5.95 (*0-19-585429-2*) Oxford Univ. Pr., Inc.

—The Strange Case of Dr. Jekyll & Mr. Hyde. 1996. (Classic Ser.). 96p. pap. 0.95 o.p. (*0-14-600177-X*) Penguin Group (USA) Inc.

—The Strange Case of Dr. Jekyll & Mr. Hyde. Qualls, Barry V., ed. & intro. by. 1995. 144p. mass mkt. 3.99 (*0-671-53210-3*, Pocket) Simon & Schuster.

—The Strange Case of Dr. Jekyll & Mr. Hyde. unabr. ed. 1996. 16.95 incl. audio (*1-883049-69-5*, 394107, Commuters Library) Sound Room Pubs., Inc.

—The Strange Case of Dr. Jekyll & Mr. Hyde. 1996. 272p. reprint ed. pap. 6.95 (*0-460-87792-5*, Everyman's Classic Library in Paperback) Tuttle Publishing.

—The Strange Case of Dr. Jekyll & Mr. Hyde. 1990. (Illus.). 164p. pap. 10.00 (*0-8032-9240-6*, Bison Bks.); reprint ed. 25.00 o.p. (*0-8032-4212-3*) Univ. of Nebraska Pr.

—The Strange Case of Dr. Jekyll & Mr. Hyde. 1999. 110p. reprint ed. pap. 8.95 (*1-57002-097-3*) University Publishing Hse., Inc.

—The Strange Case of Dr. Jekyll & Mr. Hyde & Other Stories. 2001. per. 14.00 (*1-891355-88-0*) Blue Unicorn Editions.

—The Strange Case of Dr. Jekyll & Mr. Hyde & Other Stories. 2003. (Barnes & Noble Classics Ser.). 304p. mass mkt. 3.95 (*1-59308-054-9*) Fine Communications.

—The Strange Case of Dr. Jekyll & Mr. Hyde & Other Stories. 1998. (Cloth Bound Pocket Ser.). 240p. 7.95 (*3-89508-079-9*, 521294) Konemann.

—The Strange Case of Dr. Jekyll & Mr. Hyde & Other Stories. 1963. (Illus.). 8.00 o.p. (*0-399-20040-1*) Putnam Publishing Group, The.

—The Strange Case of Dr. Jekyll & Mr. Hyde & Other Stories. 1994. xx, 252p. reprint ed. pap. text 6.95 o.p. (*0-460-87197-8*, Everyman's Classic Library in Paperback) Tuttle Publishing.

—The Works of Robert Louis Stevenson: Treasure Island, Kidnapped, The Strange Case of Dr. Jekyll & Mr. Hyde. 1995. (Classic Bonded Leather Ser.). 800p. (YA). 24.95 o.p. (*0-681-10373-6*) Borders Pr.

Strawn, Kathy. Matthew's Dad Is a Missionary. 1988. (Illus.). 32p. (Orig.). (J). (gr. 1-3). pap. text 2.95 o.p. (*0-936625-38-4*, W887107) Woman's Missionary Union.

Tallis, Raymond. Absence. 192p. 2000. pap. 15.95 (*1-902881-16-8*); 1999. 19.95 (*1-902881-00-1*) Toby Pr.

Tennant, Emma. Two Women of London: The Strange Case of Ms. Jekyll & Mrs. Hyde. 1992. 121p. (Orig.). pap. 6.95 o.p. (*0-571-14330-X*) Faber & Faber, Inc.

Thacker, Cathy Gillen. My Secret Wife. 2002. (Harlequin American Romance Ser.). 256p. mass mkt. o.s.i (*0-373-16945-0*, Harlequin Bks.) Harlequin Enterprises, Ltd.

Thomas, Donald. Jekyll, Alias Hyde: A Variation. 1988. 224p. 15.95 o.p. (*0-312-02592-0*, Saint Martin's Minotaur) St. Martin's Pr.

Thomas, William H. Learning from Hannah: Secrets for a Life Worth Living. 1999. (Illus.). x, 227p. 21.95 (*1-889242-09-8*) VanderWyk & Burnham.

Tyler, Royall. The Algerine Captive: Or, the Life & Adventures of Doctor Updike Underhill [Pseud] Six Years a Prisoner among the Algerines . . . 2002. (Modern Library Classics). (Illus.). 304p. pap. 13.95 (*0-375-76034-2*) Random Hse., Inc.

—The Algerine Captive: Or, the Life & Adventures of Doctor Updike Underhill [Pseud] Six Years a Prisoner among the Algerines . . . Cook, Donald L., ed. 1970. pap. 19.95 (*0-8084-0049-5*) Rowman & Littlefield Pubs., Inc.

—The Algerine Captive: Or, the Life & Adventures of Doctor Updike Underhill [Pseud] Six Years a Prisoner among the Algerines . . . 1967. reprint ed. 50.00 (*0-8201-1046-9*) Scholars' Facsimiles & Reprints.

Vernon, Claire. The Doctor Had a Double. l.t. ed. 2002. 183p. pap. 23.95 (*0-7862-3938-7*) Gale Group.

—The Doctor Was a Sailor. l.t. ed. 1994. 20.95 o.p. (*0-7927-1993-X*); pap. 18.95 o.p. (*0-7927-1992-1*) BBC Audiobooks America.

—The Doctor Went A'roaming. l.t. ed. 1999. (*0-7540-3633-2*) BBC Audiobooks America.

—The Doctor Who Forgot. l.t. ed. 2000. (G. K. Hall Nightingale Ser.). 220p. pap. 20.95 (*0-7838-9192-X*); (*0-7540-4293-6*) Gale Group. (Macmillan Reference USA).

—New Life for the Doctor. l.t. ed. 1993. 19.95 o.p. (*0-7927-1636-1*); pap. 17.95 o.p. (*0-7927-1635-3*) BBC Audiobooks America.

Vernon, Claire, contrib. by. The Doctor Went A'roaming. 1999. pap. (*0-7540-3634-0*) BBC Audiobooks America.

Vincent, L. M. Pas de Death. 1994. 256p. 20.95 o.p. (*0-312-10521-5*, Saint Martin's Minotaur) St. Martin's Pr.

Vine, Barbara, pseud. The Blood Doctor. 2003. 384p. pap. 13.00 (*1-4000-3252-0*, Vintage) Knopf Publishing Group.

Voeller, Sydell. Her Sister's Keeper. 1994. 192p. 18.95 o.s.i (*0-8034-9063-1*, Avalon Bks.) Bouregy, Thomas & Co., Inc.

—Her Sister's Keeper. 2001. E-Book 5.00 (*0-7599-0223-2*) Hard Shell Word Factory.

—Her Sister's Keeper. l.t. ed. 2001. (Candlelight Ser.). 190p. 22.95 (*0-7862-3626-4*) Thorndike Pr.

Vogt, Esther Loewen. The Splendid Vista. 1989. 184p. pap. 5.95 o.p. (*0-8361-3485-0*) Herald Pr.

—The Splendid Vista. l.t. ed. 2000. (Christian Fiction Ser.). 262p. 24.95 o.p. (*0-7862-2799-0*) Thorndike Pr.

Walters, Minette. Acid Row. 2002. (Illus.). 384p. 24.95 (*0-399-14862-0*) Penguin Group (USA) Inc.

—Acid Row. l.t. ed. 2002. (Core Collection). 488p. 29.95 (*0-7862-4635-9*) Thorndike Pr.

Watkins, Graham. Virus. 1995. 413p. (YA). 25.00 o.p. (*0-7867-0194-3*, Carroll & Graf Pubs.) Avalon Publishing Group.

—Virus. 1996. 438p. mass mkt. 5.99 o.s.i (*0-312-96003-4*, St. Martin's Paperbacks) St. Martin's Pr.

Webb, Debra. The Doctor Wore Boots. 2002. (Harlequin American Romance Ser.). 256p. mass mkt. o.s.i (*0-373-16948-5*, Harlequin Bks.) Harlequin Enterprises, Ltd.

White, Stephen. Cold Case. 2000. (Illus.). 368p. 24.95 (*0-525-94526-1*, Dutton) Dutton/Plume.

—Cold Case. 2001. 432p. mass mkt. 7.99 (*0-451-20155-8*, Signet Bks.) NAL.

—Cold Case. l.t. ed. 2000. (Mystery Ser.). 623p. 29.95 (*0-7862-2530-0*) Thorndike Pr.

—Private Practices. unabr. collector's ed. 1993. (Alan Gregory Ser.). audio 80.00 (*0-7366-2592-5*, 3337) Books on Tape, Inc.

—Private Practices. 1994. 432p. mass mkt. 7.99 (*0-451-40431-9*, Signet Bks.) NAL.

—Private Practices. 1993. 432p. 20.00 o.p. (*0-670-84673-2*, Viking) Viking Penguin.

—Privileged Information. unabr. collector's ed. 1992. (Alan Gregory Ser.). audio 72.00 (*0-7366-2262-4*, 3050) Books on Tape, Inc.

—Privileged Information. 2001. 384p. mass mkt. 6.99 (*0-7860-1356-7*, Pinnacle Bks.); 1999. 383p. mass mkt. 5.99 o.s.i (*0-7860-0624-2*); 1992. 384p. reprint ed. mass mkt. 5.99 o.s.i (*0-8217-3951-4*, Zebra Bks.) Kensington Publishing Corp.

—Privileged Information. 1991. 368p. 19.95 o.p. (*0-670-83765-2*) Viking Penguin.

Wilhelm, Kate. Clear & Convincing Proof. l.t. ed. 2003. 417p. 28.95 (*0-7862-6011-4*) Gale Group.

—Clear & Convincing Proof. 2003. 352p. (*1-55166-697-9*, Mira Bks.) Harlequin Enterprises, Ltd.

Williams, Gerard. Dr. Mortimer & the Aldgate Mystery. 2001. 224p. 22.95 (*0-312-26920-X*, Saint Martin's Minotaur) St. Martin's Pr.

Williams, William Carlos. The Doctor Stories. Coles, Robert, ed. 1984. 160p. 14.50 o.p. (*0-8112-0925-3*); pap. 10.95 (*0-8112-0926-1*, NDP585) New Directions Publishing Corp.

Wilson, F. Paul. Deep As the Marrow. 1997. 352p. 24.95 o.p. (*0-312-86264-4*, Forge Bks.) Doherty, Tom Assocs., LLC.

—The Fifth Harmonic: A Novel. 2003. 304p. 22.95 (*1-57174-386-3*) Hampton Roads Publishing Co., Inc.

Wilson, Hunter. In My Father's House. 1973. 288p. 18.95 o.p. (*0-8018-4337-5*) Johns Hopkins Univ. Pr.

Winckler, Martin. The Case of Doctor Sachs: A Novel. Asher, Linda, tr. from FRE. Orig. Title: La Maladie du Sachs. 432p. 2001. pap. 15.95 (*1-58322-261-8*); 2000. 27.95 (*1-58322-056-9*) Seven Stories Pr.

Wiseman, Bernard. Doctor Duck & Nurse Swan. 1984. (Illus.). 32p. (J). (ps-1). 9.95 o.p. (*0-525-44095-X*, Dutton) Dutton/Plume.

Wodehouse, P. G. Wodehouse Is the Best Medicine. 1992. 22.95 o.p. (*1-55882-128-7*) International Polygonics, Ltd.

Wolf, Leonard, ed. The Essential Dr. Jekyll & Mr. Hyde: The Definitive, Annotated Edition of Robert Louis Stevenson's Classic Novel. annot. ed. 1995. (Essentials Ser.). (Illus.). 304p. (Orig.). pap. 14.95 o.p. (*0-452-26969-5*, Plume) Dutton/Plume.

Yglesias, Rafael, Jr. Dr. Neruda's Cure for Evil. 1996. 704p. 24.95 o.p. (*0-446-52005-5*) Warner Bks., Inc.

Ziefert, Harriet. Dr. Cat. 1989. (Hello Reading! Ser.). (Illus.). 32p. (J). (ps-3). pap. 3.50 o.p. (*0-14-050985-2*) Penguin Putnam Bks. for Young Readers.

Ziefert, Harriet & Mandel, Suzy. Dr. Cat. 1995. (Easy-to-Read Bks.: Level 2, Red). (Illus.). 32p. (J). (gr. k-3). pap. 3.25 o.s.i (*0-14-037467-1*, Puffin Bks.) Penguin Putnam Bks. for Young Readers.

Zimmerman, R. D. Mindscream. 1989. 288p. 17.95 o.p. (*1-55611-137-1*) Fine, Donald I. Bks.

—Mindscream. 1990. mass mkt. 3.95 o.s.i (*0-8217-3099-1*, Zebra Bks.) Kensington Publishing Corp.

—Mindscream. 1991. 3.99 o.p. (*0-517-07483-4*) Random Hse. Value Publishing.

**POLICEWOMEN—FICTION**

Adler, Warren. American Quartet: A Fiona FitzGerald Mystery. 1982. 13.95 o.p. (*0-87795-365-1*, Morrow, William & Co.) Morrow/Avon.

—American Sextet: A Fiona FitzGerald Mystery. 1983. 256p. 13.95 o.p. (*0-87795-414-3*, Morrow, William & Co.) Morrow/Avon.

—Immaculate Deception: A Fiona FitzGerald Mystery. 1991. 18.95 o.p. (*1-55611-229-7*) Fine, Donald I. Bks.

—Immaculate Deception: A Fiona FitzGerald Mystery. 1992. 288p. mass mkt. 3.99 o.s.i (*0-8217-3935-2*, Zebra Bks.) Kensington Publishing Corp.

—Senator Love: A Fiona FitzGerald Mystery. 1991. 18.95 o.p. (*1-55611-244-0*) Fine, Donald I. Bks.

—Senator Love: A Fiona FitzGerald Mystery. 1992. 256p. reprint ed. mass mkt. 3.99 o.s.i (*0-8217-3998-0*, Zebra Bks.) Kensington Publishing Corp.

—The Ties That Bind: A Fiona FitzGerald Mystery. 1994. 224p. 19.95 o.p. (*1-55611-395-1*) Fine, Donald I. Bks.

—The Ties That Bind: A Fiona FitzGerald Mystery. 2001. E-Book 6.95 (*1-931304-20-3*); E-Book 6.95 (*1-931304-44-0*) Stonehouse Pr.

—The Ties That Bind: A Fiona FitzGerald Mystery. 2001. 0272p. 26.95 (*1-59006-020-2*) Stonehouse Pubns.

—The Witch of Watergate: A Fiona FitzGerald Mystery. 1992. 256p. 19.95 o.p. (*1-55611-296-3*) Fine, Donald I. Bks.

Allen, Kate. Give My Secrets Back: An Alison Kaine Mystery. 1995. 200p. (Orig.). pap. 9.95 (*0-934678-64-2*) New Victoria Pubs., Inc.

—Takes One to Know One: An Alison Kaine Mystery. 1996. 200p. (Orig.). pap. 10.95 (*0-934678-74-X*) New Victoria Pubs., Inc.

—Tell Me What You Like: An Alison Kaine Mystery. 1993. 219p. (Orig.). pap. 11.95 (*0-934678-48-0*) New Victoria Pubs., Inc.

Amato, Angela & Sharkey, Joe. Lady Gold. 1999. 384p. mass mkt. 6.99 (*0-312-96765-9*, St. Martin's Paperbacks); 1999. E-Book 23.95 (*0-312-20726-3*); 1998. 354p. 23.95 (*0-312-18541-3*) St. Martin's Pr.

Amis, Martin. Night Train. 1997. 149p. (*0-224-05018-4*) Cape, Jonathan Ltd. GBR. *Dist:* National Geographic Society, Trafalgar Square.

—Night Train. l.t. ed. 1998. 26.95 o.p. (*1-56895-570-7*, Wheeler Publishing, Inc.) Gale Group.

—Night Train. 1999. 176p. pap. 12.00 (*0-375-70114-1*, Vintage) Knopf Publishing Group.

—Night Train. abr. ed. 1998. audio 25.00 (*0-7871-1724-2*, 395703, Dove Audio) NewStar Media, Inc.

Angus, John. The Monster Squad. 1994. 304p. 20.95 o.p. (*0-312-11319-6*, Saint Martin's Minotaur) St. Martin's Pr.

Bailey, Jo. Bagged. 1991. 336p. 19.95 o.p. (*0-312-06296-6*, Saint Martin's Minotaur) St. Martin's Pr.

—Erased. 1996. 256p. 21.95 o.p. (*0-312-14330-3*, Saint Martin's Minotaur) St. Martin's Pr.

—Recycled. 1993. 18.95 (*0-312-08879-5*); 256p. 19.95 o.p. (*0-312-09901-0*) St. Martin's Pr. (Saint Martin's Minotaur).

Bannister, Jo. A Bleeding of Innocents. 1999. 304p. (*0-7540-3481-X*); pap. (*0-7540-3482-8*) BBC Audiobooks America.

—A Bleeding of Innocents. 1997. (WWL Mystery Ser.: No. 241). per. (*0-373-26241-8*, 1-26241-9, Worldwide Library) Harlequin Enterprises, Ltd.

—A Bleeding of Innocents. unabr. ed. 1998. audio 69.95 (*1-872672-97-3*) Magna Story Sound GBR. *Dist:* Ulverscroft Large Print Bks., Ltd.

—A Bleeding of Innocents. 1993. 224p. 18.95 o.p. (*0-312-09750-6*, Saint Martin's Minotaur) St. Martin's Pr.

—A Bleeding of Innocents. l.t. ed. 1998. (General Ser.). 304p. pap. 24.95 (*0-7862-1610-7*) Thorndike Pr.

—Broken Lines. 2000. (Castlemere Mystery Ser.). 272p. per. (*0-373-26338-4*, Harlequin Bks.) Harlequin Enterprises, Ltd.

—Broken Lines. 1999. 304p. 22.95 (*0-312-19842-6*, Saint Martin's Minotaur) St. Martin's Pr.

—Broken Lines. l.t. ed. 1999. (General Ser.). 336p. pap. 23.95 (*0-7862-1682-4*) Thorndike Pr.

—Changelings. 2002. (WWL Mystery Ser.: No. 410). mass mkt. (*0-373-26410-0*, 1-26410-0, Worldwide Library) Harlequin Enterprises, Ltd.

—Changelings. 2000. 374p. (*0-333-90189-4*) Macmillan Pr.

—Changelings. l.t. ed. 2001. (Magna Large Print Ser.). 368p. (*0-7505-1761-1*) Magna Large Print Bks. GBR. *Dist:* Ulverscroft Large Print Canada, Ltd.

—Changelings. 2000. 384p. 23.95 (*0-312-26567-0*, Saint Martin's Minotaur) St. Martin's Pr.

—Charisma. 1997. per. (*0-373-26253-1*, 1-26253-4, Worldwide Library) Harlequin Enterprises, Ltd.

—Charisma. 1994. 208p. 18.95 o.p. (*0-312-11252-1*, Saint Martin's Minotaur) St. Martin's Pr.

—The Hireling's Tale. 1999. 316p. 23.95 (*0-312-24400-2*, Saint Martin's Minotaur) St. Martin's Pr.

—The Hireling's Tale. l.t. ed. 1999. (General Ser.). 352p. pap. 22.95 (*0-7862-2163-1*) Thorndike Pr.

—No Birds Sing. 1998. (WWL Mystery Ser.). per. (*0-373-26283-3*, 1-26283-1, Worldwide Library) Harlequin Enterprises, Ltd.

—No Birds Sing. 1996. 240p. 21.95 (*0-312-14382-6*, Saint Martin's Minotaur) St. Martin's Pr.

—No Birds Sing. l.t. ed. 1997. (Ulverscroft Large Print Ser.). 464p. 29.99 o.p. (*0-7089-3732-2*, Ulverscroft) Thorpe, F. A. Pubs. GBR. *Dist:* Ulverscroft Large Print Bks., Ltd., Ulverscroft Large Print Canada, Ltd.

—A Taste for Burning. 1997. (Castlemere Mystery Ser.). per. (*0-373-26259-0*, 1-26259-1, Worldwide Library) Harlequin Enterprises, Ltd.

—A Taste for Burning. 1995. 208p. 19.95 o.p. (*0-312-13191-7*, Saint Martin's Minotaur) St. Martin's Pr.

Barnes, Trevor. Midsummer Night's Killing: A Mystery Introducing Scotland Yard's Blanche Hampton. 1992. 18.00 o.p. (*0-688-11047-9*, Morrow, William & Co.) Morrow/Avon.

—A Pound of Flesh. 1993. 20.00 o.p. (*0-688-11048-7*, Morrow, William & Co.) Morrow/Avon.

Blanchard, Alice. Darkness Peering. 2000. 336p. mass mkt. 6.99 (*0-553-58129-5*) Bantam Bks.

—Darkness Peering. l.t. ed. 2000. 26.95 o.p. (*1-56895-829-3*, Wheeler Publishing, Inc.) Gale Group.

Bland, Eleanor Taylor. Dead Time. 1993. 304p. mass mkt. 4.99 o.s.i (*0-451-40427-0*, Signet Bks.) NAL.

—Dead Time: A Marti MacAlister Mystery. 1992. 224p. 17.95 o.p. (*0-312-07053-5*, Saint Martin's Minotaur) St. Martin's Pr.

—Done Wrong. 1996. mass mkt. 5.99 (*0-312-95794-7*, St. Martin's Paperbacks); 1995. 216p. 20.95 o.p. (*0-312-13053-8*, Saint Martin's Minotaur) St. Martin's Pr.

—Gone Quiet. 1995. 336p. mass mkt. 4.99 o.s.i (*0-451-18267-7*, Signet Bks.) NAL.

—Gone Quiet: A Marti MacAlister Mystery. 1994. 224p. 19.95 o.p. (*0-312-11018-9*, Saint Martin's Minotaur) St. Martin's Pr.

—Keep Still. l.t. ed. 1996. (G. K. Hall Mystery Ser.). 316p. 21.95 o.p. (*0-7838-1931-5*, Macmillan Reference USA) Gale Group.

—Keep Still. 1996. 224p. 20.95 o.p. (*0-312-14318-4*, Saint Martin's Minotaur); Vol. 1. 1998. 240p. mass mkt. 5.99 (*0-312-96172-3*, St. Martin's Paperbacks) St. Martin's Pr.

—Scream in Silence: A Marti MacAlister Mystery. 2000. 290p. 23.95 (*0-312-20378-0*, Saint Martin's Minotaur) St. Martin's Pr.

—See No Evil. (Marti MacAlister Ser.). 288p. 1999. mass mkt. 5.99 (*0-312-96818-3*, St. Martin's Paperbacks); 1998. 22.95 o.p. (*0-312-16910-8*, Saint Martin's Minotaur) St. Martin's Pr.

—Slow Burn: A Marti MacAlister Mystery. 1993. 224p. 17.95 (*0-312-09237-7*, Saint Martin's Minotaur) St. Martin's Pr.

—Tell No Tales: A Marti MacAlister Mystery. l.t. ed. 1999. (Wheeler Large Print Book Ser.). 352p. pap. 23.95 (*1-56895-756-4*, Wheeler Publishing, Inc.) Gale Group.

—Tell No Tales: A Marti MacAlister Mystery. (Marti MacAlister Ser.). 2000. 288p. mass mkt. 5.99 (*0-312-97113-3*, St. Martin's Paperbacks); 1999. vii, 264p. 22.95 o.p. (*0-312-20067-6*, Saint Martin's Minotaur) St. Martin's Pr.

—Whispers in the Dark. l.t. ed. 2002. 28.95 o.p. (*1-58724-187-0*, Wheeler Publishing, Inc.) Gale Group.

Booth, Stephen. Blind to the Bones. 2003. 432p. 25.00 (*0-7432-3796-X*, Scribner) Simon & Schuster.

—Blood on the Tongue. 2003. (Illus.). 512p. mass mkt. 7.50 (*0-7434-5783-8*, Pocket); 2002. 400p. 25.00 (*0-7432-3618-1*, Scribner) Simon & Schuster.

Cannon, Taffy. Open Season on Lawyers: A Novel of Suspense. 2002. 13.95 (*1-880284-51-0*) Daniel, John & Co., Pubs.

Charles, Paul. The Ballad of Sean & Wilko. 2000. (Inspector Christy Kennedy Mystery Ser.: No. 4). 284p. 31.00 (*1-899344-58-6*); 283p. pap. 15.95 (*1-899344-57-8*) Do-Not Pr., The GBR. *Dist:* Dufour Editions, Inc.

—The Ballad of Sean & Wilko. 2000. 283p. (*1-902602-02-1*) New Island Bks. IRL. *Dist:* Dufour Editions, Inc.

—Fountain of Sorrow. 1999. 230p. 31.00 (*1-899344-38-1*); pap. 14.95 (*1-899344-39-X*) Do-Not Pr., The GBR. *Dist:* Dufour Editions, Inc.

—Last Boat to Camden Town: An Inspector Christy Kennedy Mystery. 1998. (Illus.). 168p. pap. 15.95 (*1-899344-30-6*); 34.95 (*1-899344-29-2*) Do-Not Pr., The GBR. *Dist:* Dufour Editions, Inc.

Clare, Baxter. Cry Havoc: A Detective Franco Mystery. 2003. 256p. pap. 12.95 (*1-931513-31-7*) Bella Bks., Inc.

Clausen, Lowen. Second Watch. 2003. 384p. mass mkt. 6.99 (*0-451-20819-6*, Signet Bks.) NAL.

—Second Watch. 2003. 365p. text 25.99 (*0-9725811-0-3*) Silo Pr.

Cook, Stephen. Dead Fit. 1993. 189p. 16.95 o.p. (*0-312-08756-X*, Saint Martin's Minotaur) St. Martin's Pr.

—One Dead Tory. 1994. (Detective Sergeant Judy Best Novel Ser.). 224p. reprint ed. 20.00 o.p. (*0-88150-302-9*) Countryman Pr.

Cornwell, Patricia. Isle of Dogs. l.t. ed. 2001. 663p. (*0-7540-1701-X*); (*0-7540-9101-5*) BBC Audiobooks America.

—Isle of Dogs. 2002. mass mkt. 7.99 (*0-425-18676-8*); 432p. reprint ed. mass mkt. 7.99 (*0-425-18290-8*) Berkley Publishing Group.

—Isle of Dogs. 2001. 368p. 26.95 (*0-399-14739-X*, Riverhead Bks. (Hardcovers)) Penguin Group (USA) Inc.

—Isle of Dogs. l.t. ed. 2002. 13.95 (*1-4104-0004-2*, Large Print Pr.); 2001. 663p. 29.95 (*0-7862-3359-1*); 2001. 663p. 32.95 (*0-7862-3358-3*) Thorndike Pr.

Crais, Robert. Demolition Angel. 2001. 400p. mass mkt. 6.99 (*0-345-43448-X*, Ballantine Bks.) Ballantine Bks.

—Demolition Angel. l.t. ed. 2000. (Wheeler Large Print Book Ser.). 474p. 29.95 (*1-56895-921-4*, Wheeler Publishing, Inc.) Gale Group.

Crombie, Deborah. All Shall Be Well. 1995. 272p. mass mkt. 6.99 (*0-425-14771-1*) Berkley Publishing Group.

—All Shall Be Well. 2004. 288p. mass mkt. 6.99 (*0-06-053439-7*, Avon Bks.) Morrow/Avon.

—All Shall Be Well: A Superintendent Duncan Kincaid - Sergeant Gemma James Mystery. 1994. 256p. text 20.00 (*0-684-19654-9*, Macmillan Reference USA) Gale Group.

—And Justice There Is None. 2002. E-Book 19.50 (*0-553-89707-1*) Bantam Bks.

—And Justice There Is None. 2003. 416p. mass mkt. 6.99 (*0-553-57930-4*); 2002. 336p. 23.95 (*0-553-10973-1*) Bantam Bks.

—And Justice There Is None. l.t. ed. 2003. 29.95 (*1-58724-400-4*, Wheeler Publishing, Inc.) Gale Group.

—Dreaming of the Bones. 1998. 416p. mass mkt. 6.99 (*0-553-57931-2*) Bantam Bks.

—Dreaming of the Bones. l.t. ed. 2000. pap. 25.95 (*1-56895-899-4*, Wheeler Publishing, Inc.) Gale Group.

—Dreaming of the Bones. l.t. ed. 1998. (Magna Large Print Ser.). 480p. o.p. (*0-7505-1315-2*) Magna Large Print Bks. GBR. *Dist:* Ulverscroft Large Print Canada, Ltd.

—Dreaming of the Bones. 1997. 350p. 21.50 (*0-684-80141-8*); 21.50 (*0-684-84720-5*) Simon & Schuster. (Scribner).

Occupations

—A Finer End. l.t. ed. 2001. (Illus.). 526p. 30.95 (0-7862-3581-0) Thorndike Pr.
—Kissed a Sad Goodbye. 1999. 336p. 23.95 o.s.i (0-553-10943-X) Bantam Bks.
—Kissed a Sad Goodbye. l.t. ed. 1999. (Large Print Book Ser.). pap. 24.95 (1-56895-731-9, Wheeler Publishing, Inc.) Gale Group.
—Kissed a Sad Goodbye. unabr. ed. 1999. audio 87.00 (0-7887-3751-1, 95869E7) Recorded Bks., LLC.
—Leave the Grave Green. 1996. 304p. mass mkt. 6.50 (0-425-15308-8) Berkley Publishing Group.
—Leave the Grave Green. l.t. ed. 2000. pap. 23.95 (1-56895-846-3, Wheeler Publishing, Inc.) Gale Group.
—Leave the Grave Green. l.t. ed. 1997. (Magna Large Print Ser.). 400p. (0-7505-1114-1) Magna Large Print Bks. GBR. *Dist:* Ulverscroft Large Print Canada, Ltd.
—Leave the Grave Green. 1995. 224p. 20.00 o.p. (0-684-19770-7, Scribner) Simon & Schuster.
—Mourn Not Your Dead. 1997. 304p. reprint ed. mass mkt. 6.99 (0-425-15778-4, Prime Crime) Berkley Publishing Group.
—Mourn Not Your Dead. l.t. ed. 1997. (Magna Large Print Ser.). 412p. (0-7505-1175-3) Magna Large Print Bks. GBR. *Dist:* Ulverscroft Large Print Canada, Ltd.
—Mourn Not Your Dead: A Duncan Kincaid/Gemma James Crime Novel. l.t. ed. 1996. 25.95 (1-56895-367-4, Wheeler Publishing, Inc.) Gale Group.
—Mourn Not Your Dead: A Duncan Kincaid/Gemma James Crime Novel. 1996. 288p. 21.00 o.p. (0-684-80131-0, Scribner) Simon & Schuster.
—A Share in Death: A Mystery Introducing Superintendent Duncan Kincaid & Sergeant Gemma James. 1994. 208p. reprint ed. mass mkt. 6.50 (0-425-14197-7, Prime Crime) Berkley Publishing Group.
—A Share in Death: A Mystery Introducing Superintendent Duncan Kincaid & Sergeant Gemma James. l.t. ed. 1995. (Magna Large Print Ser.). 259p. (0-7505-0833-7) Magna Large Print Bks. GBR. *Dist:* Ulverscroft Large Print Canada, Ltd.
—A Share in Death: A Mystery Introducing Superintendent Duncan Kincaid & Sergeant Gemma James. 1993. 256p. 20.00 o.p. (0-684-19527-5, Scribner) Simon & Schuster.
D'Amato, Barbara. Authorized Personnel Only. 2000. 352p. 24.95 (0-312-86564-3, Forge Bks.) Doherty, Tom Assocs., LLC.
—Killer.app. 350p. 1997. mass mkt. 5.99 (0-8125-5391-8); 1996. 22.95 o.p. (0-312-85991-0) Doherty, Tom Assocs., LLC. (Forge Bks.).
D'Arnuk, Nanisi B. Outside In: A Cameron Andrews Mystery. 1996. 200p. (Orig.). pap. 10.95 (0-934678-75-8) New Victoria Pubs., Inc.
Dold, Gaylord. Schedule 2, Vol. 1. 1996. 256p. text 21.95 o.p. (0-312-14730-9, Saint Martin's Minotaur) St. Martin's Pr.
Duncan, Patrick Sheane. A Private War. 2002. 368p. 24.95 o.s.i (0-399-14885-X, Putnam & Grosset) Penguin Group (USA) Inc.
Dunlap, Susan. As a Favor. 1991. 208p. mass mkt. 5.99 o.s.i (0-440-20999-4) Dell Publishing.
—As a Favor. 1984. 192p. 12.95 o.p. (0-312-05594-3) St. Martin's Pr.
—Cop Out. unabr. ed. 1997. audio 44.95 (0-7861-1192-5, 1949) Blackstone Audio Bks., Inc.
—Cop Out. 1998. (Jill Smith Mystery Ser.). 352p. mass mkt. 5.99 o.s.i (0-440-22479-9) Dell Publishing.
—Cop Out: A Jill Smith Mystery. 1997. 304p. 20.95 o.s.i (0-385-31600-3, Delacorte Pr.) Dell Publishing.
—Death & Taxes. l.t. ed. 1992. 24.95 o.p. (0-7927-1329-X); pap. 20.95 o.p. (0-7927-1328-1) BBC Audiobooks America.
—Diamond in the Buff. 1991. 192p. mass mkt. 5.50 o.s.i (0-440-20788-6) Dell Publishing.
—Diamond in the Buff. 1990. 176p. 14.95 o.p. (0-312-03814-3, Saint Martin's Minotaur) St. Martin's Pr.
—A Dinner to Die For. 1989. 240p. mass mkt. 5.99 o.s.i (0-440-20495-X) Dell Publishing.
—A Dinner to Die For. 1987. 224p. 15.95 o.p. (0-312-01019-2, Saint Martin's Minotaur) St. Martin's Pr.
—Karma. 1991. 240p. pap. 15.00 o.s.i (0-440-61365-5); mass mkt. 5.99 o.s.i (0-440-20982-X) Dell Publishing.
—Karma. 1991. reprint ed. 18.95 o.p. (0-7278-4229-3) Severn Hse. Pubs., Ltd.
—Not Exactly a Brahmin. 1991. 240p. mass mkt. 4.99 o.s.i (0-440-20998-6) Dell Publishing.
—Not Exactly a Brahmin. 1985. (Jill Smith Mystery Ser.). 192p. 12.95 o.p. (0-312-57947-0) St. Martin's Pr.
—Sudden Exposure. unabr. ed. 1998. audio 44.95 Blackstone Audio Bks., Inc.
—Sudden Exposure. 1997. 320p. pap. 19.00 o.s.i (0-440-61350-7); mass mkt. 5.50 o.s.i (0-440-21563-3) Dell Publishing.
—Sudden Exposure. abr. ed. 1996. (Jill Smith Mystery Ser.). audio 16.99 (0-88646-408-0, 7408) Durkin Hayes Publishing Ltd.
—Time Expired. l.t. ed. 1994. 24.95 o.p. (0-7927-1779-1); pap. 22.95 o.p. (0-7927-1778-3) BBC Audiobooks America.
—Time Expired. 1994. (Jill Smith Mystery Ser.). 304p. mass mkt. 5.99 o.s.i (0-440-21683-4) Dell Publishing.
—Too Close to the Edge. 1989. 224p. reprint ed. mass mkt. 5.50 o.s.i (0-440-20356-2) Dell Publishing.
—Too Close to the Edge. 1987. 240p. 14.95 o.p. (0-312-00198-3) St. Martin's Pr.
Eddy, Paul. Flint. l.t. ed. 2001. 520p. 28.95 (1-58724-029-7, Wheeler Publishing, Inc.) Gale Group.
—Flint. 2001. 432p. reprint ed. mass mkt. 6.99 o.s.i (0-451-40995-7, Onyx) NAL.
—Flint. 2000. 320p. 24.95 o.s.i (0-399-14653-9) Penguin Group (USA) Inc.
—Flint's Law. 2002. 352p. 24.95 o.s.i (0-399-14838-8) Penguin Group (USA) Inc.
Fiske, Dorsey. Raptor. 2000. 220p. 22.95 (0-312-87263-1, Forge Bks.) Doherty, Tom Assocs., LLC.
Forrest, Katherine V. Amateur City. 1984. (Kate Delafield Mystery Ser.: Vol. 1). 224p. pap. 11.95 (0-930044-55-X) Naiad Pr., Inc.
—Apparition Alley. (Kate Delafield Mystery Ser.). 256p. 1997. 21.95 o.s.i (0-425-15966-3); 1998. reprint ed. mass mkt. 5.99 o.s.i (0-425-16632-5) Berkley Publishing Group. (Prime Crime).
—The Beverly Malibu. (Kate Delafield Mystery Ser.). 1989. 16.95 o.p. (0-941483-47-9); 1991. 288p. reprint ed. pap. 11.95 (0-941483-48-7) Naiad Pr., Inc.
—Flashpoint. 256p. 1995. pap. 10.95 o.p. (1-56280-079-5); 1994. 22.95 (1-56280-043-4) Naiad Pr., Inc.
—Liberty Square: A Kate Delafield Mystery. (Kate Delafield Mystery Ser.). 256p. 2000. pap. 13.00 o.s.i (0-425-17675-4); 1997. mass mkt. 5.99 o.s.i (0-425-15899-3); 1996. 21.95 o.s.i (0-425-15467-X) Berkley Publishing Group. (Prime Crime).
—Murder at the Nightwood Bar. 1987. (Kate Delafield Mystery Ser.: Vol. 2). 240p. pap. 11.95 o.p. (0-930044-92-4) Naiad Pr., Inc.
—Murder by Tradition. 288p. 1991. text 18.95 o.p. (0-941483-89-4); 1993. (Kate Delafield Mystery Ser.: Vol. 4). reprint ed. pap. 11.95 (1-56280-002-7) Naiad Pr., Inc.
—Sleeping Bones: A Kate Delafield Mystery. (Kate Delafield Mystery Ser.). 272p. 1999. 21.95 o.s.i (0-425-17029-2); 2000. reprint ed. pap. 13.00 (0-425-17484-0, Prime Crime) Berkley Publishing Group.
Fox, Zachary Alan. All Fall Down. 1997. 480p. mass mkt. 5.99 o.s.i (0-7860-0450-9, Pinnacle Bks.); 384p. 22.00 o.p. (1-57566-139-X, Kensington Bks.) Kensington Publishing Corp.
Gardner, John. Bottled Spider. 29.99 (0-7278-7200-1); 2002. 384p. 26.99 (0-7278-5829-7) Severn Hse. Pubs., Ltd.
Garrison, Leslie Ann. Mental Graffiti: Tall Tales Trilogy. l.t. ed. 1999. (Tall Tales Ser.: No. 2). E-Book 24.95 incl. cd-rom (1-929077-27-0, Books OnScreen) PageFree Publishing, Inc.
—Sniper's Candy: Tall Tales Trilogy. l.t. ed. 2000. (Tall Tales Ser.: No. 3). E-Book 24.95 incl. cd-rom (1-929077-28-9, Books OnScreen) PageFree Publishing, Inc.
—Visions of Murder: Tall Tales Trilogy. l.t. ed. 1999. (Tall Tales Ser.). E-Book 14.99 incl. cd-rom (1-929077-26-2, Books OnScreen) PageFree Publishing, Inc.
Gilpatrick, Noreen. Shadow of Death. 1995. 400p. 19.95 o.s.i (0-89296-515-0); 1993. 384p. 17.95 (0-89296-514-2) Mysterious Pr.
Glass, Leslie. Burning Time. 1995. (April Woo Suspense Novels Ser.). 464p. mass mkt. 7.50 (0-553-56172-3) Bantam Bks.
—Hanging Time. 1996. (April Woo Suspense Novels Ser.). 448p. mass mkt. 7.50 (0-553-57191-5) Bantam Bks.
—Judging Time. 1998. (April Woo Suspense Novels Ser.). 320p. 24.95 o.p. (0-525-94404-4) Dutton/Plume.
—Judging Time. 1999. (April Woo Suspense Novels Ser.). 400p. mass mkt. 6.99 (0-451-19550-7, Signet Bks.) NAL.
—Loving Time. 1997. (April Woo Suspense Novels Ser.). 432p. reprint ed. mass mkt. 6.99 (0-553-57209-1) Bantam Bks.
—Stealing Time. 1999. (April Woo Suspense Novels Ser.). 320p. 24.95 o.p. (0-525-94460-5) Dutton/Plume.
—Stealing Time. 2000. (April Woo Suspense Novels Ser.). 400p. reprint ed. mass mkt. 6.99 (0-451-19965-0, Signet Bks.) NAL.
—Tracking Time: An April Woo Suspense Novel. 2000. (April Woo Suspense Novels Ser.). 336p. 23.95 o.s.i (0-525-94469-9) Dutton/Plume.
Gough, Laurence. Death on a No. 8 Hook. 2001. (Willows & Parker Mystery Ser.). 232p. mass mkt. 7.95 (0-7710-3533-0) McClelland & Stewart/Tundra Bks.
—The Goldfish Bowl. 2001. (Willows & Parker Mystery Ser.). 216p. mass mkt. 7.95 (0-7710-3532-2) McClelland & Stewart/Tundra Bks.
—The Goldfish Bowl. 1988. 192p. 13.95 o.p. (0-312-01434-1, Saint Martin's Minotaur) St. Martin's Pr.
—The Goldfish Bowl. 1990. 192p. pap. 3.95 o.p. (0-14-011596-X, Penguin Bks.) Viking Penguin.
—Heartbreaker. 1996. (Willows & Parker Mystery Ser.). 272p. mass mkt. 5.99 (0-7710-3447-4) McClelland & Stewart/Tundra Bks.
—Heartbreaker: A Willows & Parker Mystery. 1996. 272p. 22.95 o.p. (0-7710-3438-5) McClelland & Stewart/Tundra Bks.
—Hot Shots. 2002. 224p. mass mkt. 6.95 (0-7710-3545-4) McClelland & Stewart/Tundra Bks.
—Hot Shots. 1991. (Crime Monthly Ser.). 192p. pap. 4.95 o.p. (0-14-015488-4, Penguin Bks.) Penguin Group (USA) Inc.
—Hot Shots. 1990. 192p. 16.95 o.p. (0-670-83014-3) Viking Penguin.
—Karaoke Rap. 1998. (Willows & Parker Mystery Ser.). 368p. 20.95 o.p. (0-7710-3403-2) McClelland & Stewart/Tundra Bks.
—Killers. 1995. 256p. pap. 8.95 o.p. (0-575-05782-3) Gollancz, Victor GBR. *Dist:* Trafalgar Square.
—Killers. 1993. o.p. (0-7710-3439-3) McClelland & Stewart/Tundra Bks.
—Memory Lane. 1997. (Willows & Parker Mystery Ser.). 304p. mass mkt. 5.95 (0-7710-3404-0) McClelland & Stewart/Tundra Bks.
—Memory Lane: A Willows & Parker Mystery. 1997. 296p. 24.95 o.p. (0-7710-3437-7) McClelland & Stewart/Tundra Bks.
—Serious Crimes. 2002. 256p. mass mkt. 6.95 (0-7710-3546-2) McClelland & Stewart/Tundra Bks.
—Serious Crimes. 1999. pap. (0-670-83675-3) Viking Penguin.
—Shutterbug. 1999. (Willows & Parker Mystery Ser.). 288p. mass mkt. 7.95 (0-7710-3429-6) McClelland & Stewart/Tundra Bks.
—Shutterbug: A Willows & Parker Mystery. 1998. (Willows & Parker Mystery Ser.: Bk. 11). 288p. 20.95 o.p. (0-7710-3531-4) McClelland & Stewart/Tundra Bks.
—Silent Knives. 1988. 192p. 13.95 o.p. (0-312-01747-2, Saint Martin's Minotaur) St. Martin's Pr.
—Silent Knives. 1990. 192p. pap. 3.95 o.p. (0-14-012189-7, Penguin Bks.) Viking Penguin.
Grape, Jan. Austin City Blues. l.t. ed. 2001. (Five Star First Edition Mystery Ser.). 224p. 23.95 (0-7862-3014-2) Thorndike Pr.
Griffith, Nicola. The Blue Place: A Novel of Suspense. 1999. 320p. pap. 13.00 (0-380-79088-2, Perennial) HarperTrade.
—The Blue Place: A Novel of Suspense. 1998. 320p. pap. 23.00 (0-380-97446-0, Avon Bks.) Morrow/Avon.
Gross, Ken. Full Blown Rage. 1995. 288p. 21.00 o.p. (0-312-85757-8, Forge Bks.) Doherty, Tom Assocs., LLC.
Gruenfeld, Lee. Irreparable Harm. 388p. 4.98 o.p. (0-8317-7883-0) Smithmark Pubs., Inc.
—Irreparable Harm. 1994. 432p. mass mkt. 5.99 o.s.i (0-446-60059-8); 1993. 400p. 18.95 o.s.i (0-446-51713-5) Warner Bks., Inc.
Hall, James W. Body Language. 1999. E-Book 24.95 o.s.i (0-312-20761-1); 1998. 352p. 24.95 (0-312-19243-6) St. Martin's Pr.
—Body Language. l.t. ed. 1998. (Americana Ser.). 527p. 28.95 (0-7862-1686-7) Thorndike Pr.
—Off the Chart. 2003. (Illus.). audio compact disk 30.00 (1-55927-825-0); pap. 25.95 incl. audio (1-55927-883-8) Audio Renaissance.
—Off the Chart. 2003. 8p. 69.95 (0-7927-2890-4); 10p. pap. 94.95 (0-7927-2891-2) BBC Audiobooks America.
—Off the Chart. E-Book 20.95 (0-312-71013-5) St. Martin's Pr.
—Off the Chart. l.t. ed. 2003. 586p. 30.95 (0-7862-5796-2, Large Print Pr.) Thorndike Pr.
Handler, David. The Bright Silver Star. Date not set. pap. (0-312-30715-2, Saint Martin's Griffin); Date not set. mass mkt. (0-312-99461-3, St. Martin's Paperbacks); Date not set. mass mkt. (0-312-99620-9, St. Martin's Paperbacks); mass mkt. (0-312-98578-9, St. Martin's Paperbacks); E-Book (0-312-70566-2); 2003. 320p. 24.95 (0-312-30714-4, Saint Martin's Minotaur) St. Martin's Pr.
—The Cold Blue Blood. 2002. 320p. mass mkt. 6.50 (0-312-98610-6, St. Martin's Paperbacks); 2001. 304p. 23.95 (0-312-28003-3, Saint Martin's Minotaur) St. Martin's Pr.
—The Hot Pink Farmhouse. Date not set. mass mkt. (0-312-98579-7, St. Martin's Paperbacks); E-Book 17.95 (0-312-70893-9); 2002. 336p. 23.95 (0-312-28015-7, Saint Martin's Minotaur) St. Martin's Pr.
Harkness, Lucy. The Happy Pigs. 2001. 160p. pap. 16.95 (0-85640-656-2) Blackstaff Pr., The IRL. *Dist:* Dufour Editions, Inc.
—The Happy Pigs. 2002. 256p. 23.95 (0-312-28286-9) St. Martin's Pr.
Hess, Joan. Madness in Maggody. 1992. (Arly Hanks Mystery Ser.). 240p. mass mkt. 5.99 o.s.i (0-451-40299-5, Onyx) NAL.
—Madness in Maggody. 1990. 16.95 o.p. (0-312-05465-3, Saint Martin's Minotaur) St. Martin's Pr.
—Maggody & the Moonbeams. 2001. 256p. 23.00 (0-7432-0229-5, Simon & Schuster) Simon & Schuster.
—Maggody in Manhattan. 1992. (Arly Hanks Mystery Ser.). 272p. 18.00 o.p. (0-525-93519-3, Dutton) Dutton/Plume.
—Maggody in Manhattan. 1993. (Arly Hanks Mystery Ser.). 256p. reprint ed. mass mkt. 5.50 o.s.i (0-451-40376-2, Onyx) NAL.
—The Maggody Militia. 1997. (Arly Hanks Mystery Ser.). 320p. 21.95 o.s.i (0-525-94236-X) Dutton/Plume.
—The Maggody Militia. 1998. (Arly Hanks Mystery Ser.). 224p. mass mkt. 5.99 o.s.i (0-451-40726-1, Onyx) NAL.
—Malice in Maggody. 1991. (Arly Hanks Mystery Ser.). 240p. mass mkt. 5.99 o.s.i (0-451-40236-7, Onyx) NAL.
—Martians in Maggody. 1994. (Arly Hanks Mystery Ser.). 256p. 18.95 o.s.i (0-525-93840-0) Dutton/Plume.
—Martians in Maggody. 1995. (Arly Hanks Mystery Ser.). 304p. mass mkt. 5.50 o.s.i (0-451-40592-7, Onyx) NAL.
—Miracles in Maggody. unabr. ed. 1999. audio 39.95 Blackstone Audio Bks., Inc.
—Miracles in Maggody. 1995. (Arly Hanks Mystery Ser.). 288p. 20.95 o.p. (0-525-94051-0, Dutton) Dutton/Plume.
—Miracles in Maggody. 1996. (Arly Hanks Mystery Ser.). 288p. mass mkt. 5.99 o.s.i (0-451-40656-7) NAL.
—Mischief in Maggody. 1991. (Arly Hanks Mystery Ser.). 256p. mass mkt. 5.99 o.s.i (0-451-40253-7, Onyx) NAL.
—Mischief in Maggody. 1988. 176p. 14.95 o.p. (0-312-01792-8, Saint Martin's Minotaur) St. Martin's Pr.
—Misery Loves Maggody. 1999. 288p. 22.00 (0-684-84562-8, Simon & Schuster); 2000. (Illus.). 304p. reprint ed. pap. 6.99 (0-671-01684-9, Pocket) Simon & Schuster.
—Mortal Remains in Maggody. 1991. (Arly Hanks Mystery Ser.). 304p. 18.95 o.p. (0-525-93368-9, Dutton) Dutton/Plume.
—Mortal Remains in Maggody. 1992. (Arly Hanks Mystery Ser.). 272p. mass mkt. 4.50 o.s.i (0-451-40326-6, Onyx) NAL.
—Much Ado in Maggody. 1991. (Arly Hanks Mystery Ser.). 256p. mass mkt. 5.99 o.s.i (0-451-40268-5, Onyx) NAL.
—Much Ado in Maggody. 1989. 15.95 o.p. (0-312-02952-7, Saint Martin's Minotaur) St. Martin's Pr.
—Murder@Maggody.com. l.t. ed. 2000. (Wheeler Large Print Book Ser.). 312p. pap. 24.95 (1-56895-886-2, Wheeler Publishing, Inc.) Gale Group.
—Murder@Maggody.com. 2000. 256p. 22.00 o.s.i (0-684-84563-6, Simon & Schuster); 2001. (Illus.). 304p. reprint ed. mass mkt. 6.99 (0-671-01685-7, Pocket) Simon & Schuster.
—O Little Town of Maggody. 1993. (Arly Hanks Mystery Ser.). 256p. 19.00 o.p. (0-525-93654-8, Dutton) Dutton/Plume.
—O Little Town of Maggody. abr. ed. 1994. (Arly Hanks Mystery Ser.). audio 16.00 o.p. (0-453-00871-2, Penguin AudioBooks) HighBridge Co.
—O Little Town of Maggody. 1994. (Arly Hanks Mystery Ser.). 256p. mass mkt. 4.50 o.s.i (0-451-40457-2, Onyx) NAL.
Hightower, Lynn S. Eyeshot. 1996. 368p. 23.00 o.p. (0-06-017649-0) HarperCollins Pubs.
—Eyeshot. 1997. 368p. mass mkt. 6.50 o.p. (0-06-109609-1, HarperTorch) Morrow/Avon.
—Flashpoint. 1995. 352p. 22.00 o.p. (0-06-017648-2) HarperTrade.
—Flashpoint. 1996. 448p. mass mkt. 6.50 o.s.i (0-06-109456-0, HarperTorch) Morrow/Avon.
—No Good Deed. unabr. ed. 1998. audio 44.95 (0-7861-1438-X, 2324) Blackstone Audio Bks., Inc.
—No Good Deed. 1998. (Sonora Blair Mysteries Ser.). 400p. mass mkt. 6.50 (0-440-22531-0); 336p. 22.95 o.s.i (0-385-32359-X, Delacorte Pr.) Dell Publishing.
Hite, Molly. Breach of Immunity. 256p. 1994. pap. 8.95 o.p. (0-312-10434-0, Saint Martin's Griffin); 1991. 18.95 o.p. (0-312-06893-X, Saint Martin's Minotaur) St. Martin's Pr.
Hoag, Tami. A Thin Dark Line. 1998. 608p. reprint ed. mass mkt. 7.99 (0-553-57188-5) Bantam Bks.
—A Thin Dark Line. 2002. pap. incl. audio (0-7435-2754-2) Encore Performance Publishing.
—A Thin Dark Line. l.t. ed. 1997. (Large Print Book Ser.). 26.95 o.p. (1-56895-450-6, Wheeler Publishing, Inc.) Gale Group.
—A Thin Dark Line. unabr. ed. 1997. audio 117.00 (0-7887-1766-9, 95244E7) Recorded Bks., LLC.

—A Thin Dark Line. abr. ed. 1997. audio 23.00 (*0-671-57477-9*, 495077, Simon & Schuster Audioworks) Simon & Schuster Audio.

Hooper, Kay. Out of the Shadows. 2000. (Shadows Trilogy Ser.). 368p. mass mkt. 7.50 (*0-553-57695-X*) Bantam Bks.

—Out of the Shadows. l.t. ed. 504p. 2002. pap. 28.95 (*0-7862-3060-6*); 2001. 31.95 (*0-7862-3059-2*) Thorndike Pr.

Jance, J. A. Dead to Rights. (Joanna Brady Mystery Ser.). 2003. 384p. mass mkt. 7.50 (*0-380-72432-4*); 1996. 373p. mass mkt. 22.00 o.p. (*0-380-97394-4*) Morrow/Avon. (Avon Bks.).

—Desert Heat. l.t. ed. 2001. 269p. 26.95 (*1-57490-371-3*, Beeler Large Print Bks.) Beeler, Thomas T. Publisher.

—Desert Heat. 1993. (Joanna Brady Mystery Ser.). 384p. mass mkt. 7.50 (*0-380-76545-4*, Avon Bks.) Morrow/Avon.

—Devil's Claw. l.t. ed. 2000. (Wheeler Softcover Ser.). 449p. 25.95 (*1-56895-140-X*, Wheeler Publishing, Inc.) Gale Group.

—Devil's Claw. 2001. (Joanna Brady Mystery Ser.). 416p. mass mkt. 7.50 (*0-380-79249-4*) HarperCollins Pubs.

—Devil's Claw. 2000. (Joanna Brady Mystery Ser.). 384p. 24.00 (*0-380-97501-7*, Morrow, William & Co.) Morrow/Avon.

—Exit Wounds: A Novel of Suspense. l.t. ed. 2003. 480p. pap. 24.95 (*0-06-054549-6*, HarperLarge-Print) HarperTrade.

—Exit Wounds: A Novel of Suspense. 2003. 384p. 24.95 (*0-380-97731-1*, Morrow, William & Co.) Morrow/Avon.

—Paradise Lost. 2001. E-Book 7.99 (*0-06-001044-4*) HarperCollins Pubs.

—Paradise Lost. l.t. ed. 2001. 448p. pap. 25.00 (*0-06-621403-3*) HarperTrade.

—Paradise Lost. (Joanna Brady Mystery Ser.). 2002. 432p. mass mkt. 7.99 (*0-380-80469-7*, Avon Bks.); 2001. 384p. 25.00 (*0-380-97729-X*, Morrow, William & Co.) Morrow/Avon.

—Partner in Crime. 2002. E-Book 19.95 (*0-06-009828-7*); E-Book 19.95 (*0-06-009826-0*); E-Book 19.95 (*0-06-009825-2*) HarperCollins General Bks. Group. (PerfectBound).

—Partner in Crime. l.t. ed. 2002. 512p. pap. 24.95 (*0-06-009393-5*, HarperLargePrint) HarperTrade.

—Partner in Crime. 2003. 400p. mass mkt. 7.99 (*0-380-80470-0*); 2002. 384p. 24.95 (*0-380-97730-3*); 2002. 384p. 24.95 (*0-380-97730-3*) Morrow/Avon. (Morrow, William & Co.).

—Sheriff Brady, Vol. 5. 1924. o.s.i (*0-688-13822-5*, Morrow, William & Co.) Morrow/Avon.

—Shoot, Don't Shoot. l.t. ed. 1998. (Large Print Book Ser.). 25.95 (*1-56895-517-0*, Wheeler Publishing, Inc.) Gale Group.

—Shoot, Don't Shoot. (Joanna Brady Mystery Ser.). 1996. 384p. mass mkt. 7.99 (*0-380-76548-9*, Avon Bks.); 1995. 320p. (YA). 21.00 o.p. (*0-688-13821-7*, Morrow, William & Co.) Morrow/Avon.

—Tombstone Courage. (Joanna Brady Mystery Ser.). 1995. 416p. mass mkt. 7.99 (*0-380-76546-2*, Avon Bks.); 1994. 300p. 20.00 o.p. (*0-688-13247-2*, Morrow, William & Co.) Morrow/Avon.

—Tombstone Courage. l.t. ed. 2001. (Joanna Brady Mystery Ser.). 496p. 28.95 (*0-7862-3115-7*) Thorndike Pr.

Keating, H. R. F. A Detective under Fire. l.t. ed. 2003. (Magna Large Print Ser.). 320p. (*0-7505-2072-8*) Magna Large Print Bks. GBR. *Dist:* Ulverscroft Large Print Canada, Ltd.

—A Detective under Fire. Date not set. pap. (*0-312-31658-5*); mass mkt. (*0-312-99057-X*) St. Martin's Pr. (St. Martin's Paperbacks).

—The Hard Detective. l.t. ed. 2000. (G. K. Hall Nightingale Ser.). 263p. pap. 20.95 (*0-7838-9256-X*); (*0-7540-4297-9*); (*0-7540-4298-7*) Gale Group. (Macmillan Reference USA).

—The Hard Detective. 2000. 236p. 21.95 o.p. (*0-312-24648-X*, Saint Martin's Minotaur) St. Martin's Pr.

Keegan, Alex. Cuckoo: A Caz Flood Mystery. 1995. 410p. 23.95 o.p. (*0-312-13043-0*, Saint Martin's Minotaur) St. Martin's Pr.

Kerr, Philip. A Philosophical Investigation. 1995. 384p. mass mkt. 8.99 o.s.i (*0-7704-2592-5*) Bantam Bks.

—A Philosophical Investigation. 1994. 336p. pap. 14.00 o.s.i (*0-452-27140-1*, Plume) Dutton/Plume.

—A Philosophical Investigation. 1993. 329p. 20.00 o.p. (*0-374-23176-1*) Farrar, Straus & Giroux.

Killough, Lee. Bridling Chaos. rev. ed. 1998. 624p. pap. 19.00 (*0-9658345-3-0*) Meisha Merlin Publishing, Inc.

—The Doppelganger Gambit. 1979. mass mkt. 1.95 o.s.i (*0-345-28267-1*) Ballantine Bks.

—Dragon's Teeth. 1990. mass mkt. 4.95 o.s.i (*0-445-20906-2*) Warner Bks., Inc.

—Spider Play. 1986. pap. 3.50 o.s.i (*0-445-20273-4*) Warner Bks., Inc.

King, Laurie R. A Grave Talent. 1995. 368p. mass mkt. 6.99 (*0-553-57399-3*, Crimeline) Bantam Bks.

—A Grave Talent. unabr. ed. 1996. (Kate Martinelli Mystery Ser.: Vol. 1). audio 85.00 (*0-7887-0395-1*, 94587E7) Recorded Bks., LLC.

—A Grave Talent. 1993. 310p. 19.95 (*0-312-08804-3*, Saint Martin's Minotaur) St. Martin's Pr.

—Night Work. 2000. (Kate Martinelli Mysteries Ser.). 416p. mass mkt. 6.99 (*0-553-57825-1*) Bantam Bks.

—To Play the Fool. 1996. 320p. mass mkt. 6.99 (*0-553-57455-8*, Crimeline) Bantam Bks.

—To Play the Fool. unabr. ed. 1996. (Kate Martinelli Mystery Ser.: Vol. 2). audio 60.00 (*0-7887-0406-0*, 94598E7); audio Recorded Bks., LLC.

—To Play the Fool. 1995. 260p. 21.00 o.p. (*0-312-11907-0*, Saint Martin's Minotaur) St. Martin's Pr.

—With Child. 1997. 320p. mass mkt. 6.99 (*0-553-57458-2*) Bantam Bks.

—With Child. unabr. ed. 1996. (Kate Martinelli Mystery Ser.: Vol. 3). audio 70.00 (*0-7887-0579-2*, 94757E7) Recorded Bks., LLC.

—With Child. 1996. 275p. 21.95 o.p. (*0-312-14077-0*, Saint Martin's Minotaur) St. Martin's Pr.

—With Child. l.t. ed. 1998. (Ulverscroft Large Print Ser.). 528p. 29.99 (*0-7089-3904-X*, Ulverscroft) Thorpe, F. A. Pubs. GBR. *Dist:* Ulverscroft Large Print Bks., Ltd., Ulverscroft Large Print Canada, Ltd.

Kitt, Sandra. Close Encounters. l.t. ed. 2000. (G. K. Hall Core Ser.). 432p. 27.95 (*0-7838-9271-3*, Macmillan Reference USA) Gale Group.

—Close Encounters. 2000. 368p. mass mkt. 6.99 (*0-451-20048-9*, Signet Bks.) NAL.

Konrath, J. A. Whiskey Sour: A Jack Daniels Mystery. unabr. ed. 2004. audio 69.25 (*1-59355-487-7*, 5113, Brilliance Audio Unabridged Lib Ed); audio 27.95 (*1-59355-486-9*, 5111, Brilliance Audio Unabridged); audio compact disk 82.25 (*1-59355-489-3*, 5115, Brilliance Audio on CD Unabridged Lib Ed); audio compact disk 29.95 (*1-59355-488-5*, 5114, Brilliance Audio on CD Unabridged) Brilliance Audio.

—Whiskey Sour: A Jack Daniels Mystery. 2004. 23.95 (*1-4013-0087-1*) Hyperion Pr.

Krich, Rochelle Majer. Angel of Death. 1994. 384p. 27.00 (*0-89296-508-8*) Mysterious Pr.

—Angel of Death. 372p. pap. 4.98 o.p. (*0-7651-0305-2*) Smithmark Pubs., Inc.

—Angel of Death. 1996. 368p. mass mkt. 5.99 o.s.i (*0-446-40311-3*) Warner Bks., Inc.

—Blood Money: A Mystery. 2000. 352p. mass mkt. 6.99 (*0-380-78954-X*); 1999. 341p. 23.00 (*0-380-97379-0*) Morrow/Avon. (Avon Bks.).

—Dead Air: A Jessie Drake Mystery. 2001. 416p. mass mkt. 6.99 (*0-380-80701-7*); 2000. 304p. 23.00 (*0-380-97769-9*) Morrow/Avon. (Avon Bks.).

—Fair Game. 1994. 320p. mass mkt. 5.50 o.s.i (*0-446-40310-5*) Warner Bks., Inc.

Lake, M. D. Amends for Murder. l.t. ed. 1991. pap. 15.95 o.p. (*0-7927-0801-6*, AS0288) BBC Audiobooks America.

—Amends for Murder. 1989. pap. 4.99 (*0-380-75865-2*, Avon Bks.) Morrow/Avon.

—Cold Comfort. 1990. pap. 5.99 (*0-380-76032-0*, Avon Bks.) Morrow/Avon.

—Flirting with Death. 1996. (Orig.). pap. 5.99 o.p. (*0-380-77522-0*, Avon Bks.) Morrow/Avon.

—A Gift for Murder. 1992. (Peggy O'Neill Mystery Ser.). 256p. mass mkt. 5.50 (*0-380-76855-0*, Avon Bks.) Morrow/Avon.

—Grave Choices: A Peggy O'Neill Mystery. 1995. pap. 5.99 o.p. (*0-380-77521-2*, Avon Bks.) Morrow/Avon.

—Midsummer Malice. 1997. (Peggy O'Neill Mystery Ser.). pap. 5.99 o.p. (*0-380-78759-8*, Avon Bks.) Morrow/Avon.

—Murder by Mail. 1993. (Orig.). pap. 5.99 o.p. (*0-380-76856-9*, Avon Bks.) Morrow/Avon.

—Once upon a Crime. 1995. (Peggy O'Neill Mystery Ser.). (Orig.). pap. 5.50 (*0-380-77520-4*, Avon Bks.) Morrow/Avon.

—Poisoned Ivy. 1992. (Peggy O'Neill Mystery Ser.). 256p. pap. 5.50 (*0-380-76573-X*, Avon Bks.) Morrow/Avon.

Land, Jon. Blood Diamonds. E-Book 25.95 (*0-312-70604-9*, Tor Bks.); 2002. 384p. 25.95 (*0-7653-0226-8*, Forge Bks.); 2003. 416p. reprint ed. mass mkt. 7.99 (*0-7653-4148-4*, Forge Bks.) Doherty, Tom Assocs., LLC.

—Keepers of the Gate. Date not set. (*0-312-87830-3*); 2001. 320p. 25.95 (*0-312-85655-5*) Doherty, Tom Assocs., LLC. (Forge Bks.).

—The Pillars of Solomon. 2000. 438p. mass mkt. 6.99 (*0-8125-6672-6*); 1999. (Illus.). 352p. 24.95 (*0-312-86819-7*) Doherty, Tom Assocs., LLC. (Forge Bks.).

—A Walk in the Darkness. 2000. 352p. 25.95 (*0-312-87265-8*, Forge Bks.) Doherty, Tom Assocs., LLC.

—The Walls of Jericho. 1998. 480p. mass mkt. 6.99 (*0-8125-6456-1*, Tor Bks.); 1997. 304p. 23.95 (*0-312-86267-9*, Forge Bks.) Doherty, Tom Assocs., LLC.

—The Walls of Jericho. abr. ed. 1997. audio 17.00 (*1-56876-066-3*) Soundlines Entertainment, Inc.

Lewis, Catherine. Dry Fire: A Novel. 1996. 288p. 21.00 (*0-393-03835-1*) Norton, W. W. & Co., Inc.

Longworth, Gay. Dead Alone: A Mystery. 2003. 336p. 24.95 (*0-312-31061-7*, Saint Martin's Minotaur) St. Martin's Pr.

Lovesey, Peter. The House Sitter. 2003. 304p. 25.00 (*1-56947-326-9*) Soho Pr., Inc.

—The House Sitter. l.t. ed. 2003. (Peter Diamond Mystery Ser.). 560p. 28.95 (*0-7862-5807-1*) Thorndike Pr.

Lupoff, Richard A. The Bessie Blue Killer: A Hobart Lindsey - Marvia Plum Mystery. 1994. 304p. 20.95 o.p. (*0-312-10425-1*, Saint Martin's Minotaur) St. Martin's Pr.

—The Classic Car Killer. 1992. 288p. (Orig.). mass mkt. 4.99 o.s.i (*0-553-29607-8*) Bantam Bks.

—The Comic Book Killer. 1989. mass mkt. 3.95 o.s.i (*0-553-27781-2*) Bantam Bks.

—The Cover Girl Killer: A Hobart Lindsey - Marvia Plum Mystery. 1995. 224p. 21.95 o.p. (*0-312-13455-X*, Saint Martin's Minotaur) St. Martin's Pr.

—The Radio Red Killer. 1997. (Marvia Plum Mystery Ser.). 268p. text 22.95 o.p. (*0-312-17181-1*, Saint Martin's Minotaur) St. Martin's Pr.

—The Sepia Siren Killer. 1994. (Hobart Lidsey-Mariva Plum Mystery Ser.). 304p. 20.95 o.p. (*0-312-11332-3*, Saint Martin's Minotaur) St. Martin's Pr.

—The Silver Chariot Killer. 1996. 192p. text 21.95 o.p. (*0-312-14736-8*, Saint Martin's Minotaur) St. Martin's Pr.

Maitland, Barry. Babel. 2003. (Illus.). 288p. 24.95 (*1-55970-668-6*) Arcade Publishing, Inc.

—The Malcontenta. 2000. 348p. 24.95 (*1-55970-527-2*) Arcade Publishing, Inc.

Maron, Margaret. Baby Doll Games. 1988. 224p. mass mkt. 3.50 o.s.i (*0-553-27281-0*) Bantam Bks.

—Baby Doll Games. 1995. (Sigrid Harald Mystery Ser.). 224p. mass mkt. 5.99 o.s.i (*0-446-40418-7*) Warner Bks., Inc.

—Bloody Kin. 1992. 224p. mass mkt. 4.50 o.s.i (*0-553-29514-4*) Bantam Bks.

—Bloody Kin. 1985. (Crime Club Ser.). 192p. 12.95 o.p. (*0-385-23231-4*) Doubleday Publishing.

—Bloody Kin. 1995. 224p. mass mkt. 5.99 (*0-446-40416-0*) Warner Bks., Inc.

—Corpus Christmas. 1990. 224p. mass mkt. 3.95 o.s.i (*0-553-27410-4*) Bantam Bks.

—Death in Blue Folders. 1992. (Crime Line Ser.). 224p. mass mkt. 4.50 o.s.i (*0-553-29498-9*) Bantam Bks.

—Death in Blue Folders. l.t. ed. 1992. (Mystery Ser.). 400p. 29.99 o.p. (*0-7089-2665-7*, Ulverscroft) Thorpe, F. A. Pubs. GBR. *Dist:* Ulverscroft Large Print Bks., Ltd., Ulverscroft Large Print Canada, Ltd.

—Death of a Butterfly. 1991. 192p. mass mkt. 3.99 o.s.i (*0-553-29121-1*) Bantam Bks.

—Death of a Butterfly. 1984. (Crime Club Ser.). 192p. 11.95 o.p. (*0-385-19554-0*) Doubleday Publishing.

—Death of a Butterfly. l.t. ed. 1991. (Ulverscroft Large Print Ser.). 29.99 o.p. (*0-7089-2465-4*, Ulverscroft) Thorpe, F. A. Pubs. GBR. *Dist:* Ulverscroft Large Print Bks., Ltd., Ulverscroft Large Print Canada, Ltd.

—Fugitive Colors. 1995. 272p. 18.95 o.s.i (*0-89296-567-3*) Mysterious Pr.

—Fugitive Colors. 260p. pap. 3.98 o.p. (*0-7651-0363-X*) Smithmark Pubs., Inc.

—Fugitive Colors. 1996. (Sigrid Harald Mystery Ser.). 256p. mass mkt. 5.99 (*0-446-40393-8*) Warner Bks., Inc.

—One Coffee With. 1988. mass mkt. 3.50 o.s.i (*0-553-27479-1*) Bantam Bks.

—One Coffee With. l.t. ed. 1991. (Ulverscroft Large Print Ser.). 29.99 o.p. (*0-7089-2433-6*, Ulverscroft) Thorpe, F. A. Pubs. GBR. *Dist:* Ulverscroft Large Print Bks., Ltd., Ulverscroft Large Print Canada, Ltd.

—One Coffee With. 1995. (Sigrid Harald Mystery Ser.). 192p. mass mkt. 5.99 o.s.i (*0-446-40415-2*) Warner Bks., Inc.

—Past Imperfect. 1992. 256p. mass mkt. 4.99 o.s.i (*0-553-29546-2*) Bantam Bks.

—Past Imperfect. 1991. 192p. 14.95 o.s.i (*0-385-41364-5*) Doubleday Publishing.

—The Right Jack. 1987. 224p. mass mkt. 3.50 o.s.i (*0-553-26859-7*) Bantam Bks.

—The Right Jack. l.t. ed. 1992. (Mystery Ser.). 480p. 29.99 o.p. (*0-7089-2730-0*, Ulverscroft) Thorpe, F. A. Pubs. GBR. *Dist:* Ulverscroft Large Print Bks., Ltd., Ulverscroft Large Print Canada, Ltd.

—The Right Jack. 1995. (Sigrid Harald Mystery Ser.). 224p. mass mkt. 5.99 o.s.i (*0-446-40417-9*) Warner Bks., Inc.

Martin, Lee. Bird in a Cage. 1996. per. (*0-373-26225-6*, 1-26225-2, Worldwide Library) Harlequin Enterprises, Ltd.

—Bird in a Cage. 1995. 240p. 20.95 o.p. (*0-312-13028-7*, Saint Martin's Minotaur) St. Martin's Pr.

—A Conspiracy of Strangers. 1986. 208p. 13.95 o.p. (*0-312-16433-5*) St. Martin's Pr.

—The Day that Dusty Died. 1994. 304p. 20.95 o.p. (*0-312-09779-4*, Saint Martin's Minotaur) St. Martin's Pr.

—Death Warmed Over. 1991. mass mkt. (*0-373-26065-2*, Harlequin Bks.) Harlequin Enterprises, Ltd.

—Death Warmed Over. 1988. 224p. 15.95 o.p. (*0-312-02221-2*, Saint Martin's Minotaur) St. Martin's Pr.

—Deficit Ending. 1992. (Mystery Ser.: No. 101). mass mkt. (*0-373-26101-2*, Harlequin Bks.) Harlequin Enterprises, Ltd.

—Deficit Ending. 1990. 208p. 15.95 o.p. (*0-312-03813-5*, Saint Martin's Minotaur) St. Martin's Pr.

—Genealogy of Murder. 1997. (WWL Mystery Ser.: No. 239). per. (*0-373-26239-6*, 1-26239-3, Worldwide Library) Harlequin Enterprises, Ltd.

—Genealogy of Murder. 1996. 240p. 22.95 o.p. (*0-312-13975-6*, Saint Martin's Minotaur) St. Martin's Pr.

—Hacker. 1993. (WWL Mystery Ser.). per. (*0-373-26135-7*, 1-26135-3, Harlequin Bks.) Harlequin Enterprises, Ltd.

—Hacker: A Deb Ralston Mystery. 1992. 192p. 16.95 o.p. (*0-312-06990-1*, Saint Martin's Minotaur) St. Martin's Pr.

—Hal's Own Murder Case. 1991. mass mkt. (*0-373-26087-3*, Harlequin Bks.) Harlequin Enterprises, Ltd.

—Hal's Own Murder Case. 1989. 14.95 o.p. (*0-312-02925-X*, Saint Martin's Minotaur) St. Martin's Pr.

—Inherited Murder. 1994. (Deb Ralston Mystery Ser.). 304p. 19.95 o.p. (*0-312-11415-X*, Saint Martin's Minotaur) St. Martin's Pr.

—The Mensa Murders. 1993. mass mkt. (*0-373-26115-2*, 1-26115-5, Harlequin Bks.) Harlequin Enterprises, Ltd.

—The Mensa Murders. 1990. 192p. 15.95 o.p. (*0-312-05126-3*, Saint Martin's Minotaur) St. Martin's Pr.

—Murder at the Blue Owl. 1990. mass mkt. (*0-373-26054-7*, Harlequin Bks.) Harlequin Enterprises, Ltd.

—Murder at the Blue Owl. 1988. 208p. 14.95 o.p. (*0-312-01795-2*) St. Martin's Pr.

—Too Sane a Murder. 1984. 192p. 12.95 o.p. (*0-312-80901-8*) St. Martin's Pr.

Mathews, Francine. Death in a Cold Hard Light. 1999. (Indigo Ser.). 352p. reprint ed. mass mkt. 5.99 (*0-553-57625-9*) Bantam Bks.

—Death in a Cold Hard Light. unabr. collector's ed. 1998. (Merry Folger Ser.). audio 64.00 (*0-7366-4262-5*, 4761) Books on Tape, Inc.

—Death in a Mood Indigo. 1998. 352p. mass mkt. 5.99 (*0-553-57624-0*) Bantam Bks.

—Death in a Mood Indigo. unabr. collector's ed. 1997. (Merry Folger Ser.). audio 64.00 (*0-7366-4006-1*, 4504) Books on Tape, Inc.

—Death in Rough Water. unabr. collector's ed. 1997. (Merry Folger Ser.: Vol. 2). audio 56.00 (*0-7366-3631-5*, 4292) Books on Tape, Inc.

—Death in Rough Water: A Merry Folger Mystery. 1996. 288p. mass mkt. 5.50 (*0-380-72335-2*, Avon Bks.); 1995. 320p. 22.00 o.p. (*0-688-13473-4*, Morrow, William & Co.) Morrow/Avon.

—Death in the Off-Season. unabr. collector's ed. 1997. (Merry Folger Ser.: Vol. 1). audio 64.00 (*0-7366-3600-5*, 4255) Books on Tape, Inc.

—Death in the Off-Season. 1995. 352p. mass mkt. 4.99 (*0-380-72334-4*, Avon Bks.); 1994. 318p. 23.00 o.p. (*0-688-13443-2*, Morrow, William & Co.) Morrow/Avon.

McAllester, Melanie. The Lessons. 1994. 240p. pap. 9.95 (*0-933216-99-8*) Spinsters Ink Bks.

McBain, Ed, pseud. Driving Lessons. 2000. 80p. 12.95 (*0-7867-0805-0*, Carroll & Graf Pubs.) Avalon Publishing Group.

McBain, Ed, pseud & Hunter, Evan. Candyland: A Novel in Two Parts. l.t. ed. 2001. (Wheeler Large Print Book Ser.). 374p. 30.95 (*1-58724-094-7*, Wheeler Publishing, Inc.) Gale Group.

—Candyland: A Novel in Two Parts. 2001. 304p. 25.00 (*0-7432-1316-5*, Simon & Schuster); (Illus.). 368p. reprint ed. pap. 7.99 (*0-7434-1904-9*, Pocket) Simon & Schuster.

McCall, Thomas. Beyond Ice, Beyond Death. 1995. 304p. (J). 21.95 (*0-7868-6022-7*) Hyperion Pr.

—A Wide & Capable Revenge: A Nora Callum Mystery. 1993. 272p. 19.95 o.p. (*1-56282-864-9*) Hyperion Pr.

McDermid, Val. The Mermaids Singing. 1997. 480p. mass mkt. 6.50 o.p. (*0-06-101175-4*); 1996. 288p. mass mkt. 22.00 o.p. (*0-06-101174-6*) Morrow/Avon. (HarperTorch).

—The Wire in the Blood. unabr. ed. 1998. audio 94.95 (*0-7531-0350-8*, 980504) ISIS Audio Bks. GBR. *Dist:* Ulverscroft Large Print Bks., Ltd.

—The Wire in the Blood. ltd. ed. 1998. xii, 372p. 50.00 (*1-890208-21-3*) Poisoned Pen Pr.

—The Wire in the Blood. 2002. 528p. mass mkt. 6.99 (*0-312-98365-4*, St. Martin's Paperbacks) St. Martin's Pr.

McDonald, Cherokee P. Summer's Reason. 1994. 256p. 19.95 o.p. (*1-55611-409-5*) Fine, Donald I. Bks.

McGown, Jill. Death in the Family. 2004. 336p. mass mkt. 6.99 (*0-345-45849-4*, Fawcett); 2003. 320p. 22.95 (*0-345-45848-6*, Ballantine Bks.) Ballantine Bks.
—Death in the Family. l.t. ed. 2003. 30.45 (*0-7862-5380-0*) Thorndike Pr.
—Gone to Her Death. 1991. mass mkt. 4.99 (*0-449-21966-6*, Fawcett) Ballantine Bks.
—Gone to Her Death. l.t. ed. 1991. (General Ser.). 330p. lib. bdg. 22.95 o.p. (*0-8161-5094-X*, Macmillan Reference USA) Gale Group.
—Gone to Her Death. 1989. 256p. 16.95 o.p. (*0-312-03839-9*, Saint Martin's Minotaur) St. Martin's Pr.
—Murder . . . Now & Then. 1993. 304p. 20.95 o.p. (*0-312-10006-X*, Saint Martin's Minotaur) St. Martin's Pr.
—Murder at the Old Vicarage. 1991. (Mysteries Around the World Promotion Ser.). 256p. mass mkt. 6.50 (*0-449-21819-8*, Ivy Bks.) Ballantine Bks.
—Murder at the Old Vicarage. l.t. ed. 1990. (General Ser.). 348p. lib. bdg. 18.95 o.p. (*0-8161-4838-4*, Macmillan Reference USA) Gale Group.
—Murder at the Old Vicarage. 1988. 256p. 16.95 o.p. (*0-312-02615-3*, Saint Martin's Minotaur) St. Martin's Pr.
—Murder... Now & Then. 1995. (Mysteries Around the World Promotion). mass mkt. 5.99 o.s.i (*0-449-22311-6*, Fawcett) Ballantine Bks.
—Murder... Now & Then. 1993. 407p. pap. 13.95 (*0-330-33243-0*) Pan Bks. Ltd. GBR. *Dist:* Trans-Atlantic Pubns., Inc.
—The Murders of Mrs. Austin & Mrs. Beale. 1993. 256p. reprint ed. mass mkt. 6.50 (*0-449-22162-8*, Fawcett) Ballantine Bks.
—The Murders of Mrs. Austin & Mrs. Beale. 1991. 224p. 17.95 o.p. (*0-312-06422-5*, Saint Martin's Minotaur) St. Martin's Pr.
—The Other Woman. 1994. mass mkt. 5.99 (*0-449-22272-1*, Fawcett) Ballantine Bks.
—The Other Woman. l.t. ed. 1997. 477p. (*0-7505-1065-X*) Magna Large Print Bks. GBR. *Dist:* Ulverscroft Large Print Bks., Ltd.
—The Other Woman. 1993. 236p. 17.95 o.p. (*0-312-08868-X*, Saint Martin's Minotaur) St. Martin's Pr.
—A Perfect Match. 1990. 192p. mass mkt. 6.50 (*0-449-21820-1*, Fawcett) Ballantine Bks.
—A Perfect Match. 1983. 192p. 11.95 o.p. (*0-312-60069-0*) St. Martin's Pr.
—Scene of Crime. l.t. ed. 2001. 391p. 29.95 (*0-7862-3647-7*) Thorndike Pr.
McKevett, G. A. Bitter Sweets. 1996. 304p. 18.95 o.p. (*1-57566-032-6*) Kensington Publishing Corp.
McNab, Claire. Body Guard. 1994. (Detective Inspector Carol Ashton Mysteries Ser.: Vol. 6). 224p. pap. 11.95 (*1-56280-073-6*) Naiad Pr., Inc.
—Chain Letter: A Carol Ashton Mystery. 1997. (Detective Inspector Carol Ashton Mysteries Ser.: Vol. 9). 224p. (Orig.). pap. 11.95 (*1-56280-181-3*) Naiad Pr., Inc.
—Cop Out. 1991. (Detective Inspector Carol Ashton Mysteries Ser.: Vol. 4). 224p. (Orig.). pap. 10.95 (*0-941483-84-3*) Naiad Pr., Inc.
—Dead Certain. 1992. (Detective Inspector Carol Ashton Mysteries Ser.: No. 5). 224p. pap. 11.95 (*1-56280-027-2*) Naiad Pr., Inc.
—Death Club: A Detective Inspector Carol Ashton Mystery. 2001. 215p. pap. 11.95 (*1-56280-267-4*) Naiad Pr., Inc.
—Death down Under. 1990. (Detective Inspector Carol Ashton Mysteries Ser.: Vol. 3). 240p. pap. 11.95 (*0-941483-39-8*) Naiad Pr., Inc.
—Double Bluff. 1995. (Detective Inspector Carol Ashton Mysteries Ser.: Vol. 7). 192p. pap. 12.95 (*1-56280-096-5*) Naiad Pr., Inc.
—Fatal Reunion. 1989. (Detective Inspector Carol Ashton Mysteries Ser.: Vol. 2). 224p. pap. 11.95 (*0-941483-40-1*) Naiad Pr., Inc.
—Inner Circle: A Carol Ashton Mystery. 1996. (Detective Inspector Carol Ashton Mysteries Ser.: Vol. 8). 256p. pap. 11.95 (*1-56280-135-X*) Naiad Pr., Inc.
—Lessons in Murder. 1988. (Detective Inspector Carol Ashton Mysteries Ser.: Vol. 1). 216p. pap. 11.95 (*0-941483-14-2*) Naiad Pr., Inc.
—Past Due: A Detective Inspector Carol Ashton Mystery. 1998. (Detective Inspector Carol Ashton Mysteries Ser.: No. 10). 224p. pap. 11.95 (*1-56280-217-8*) Naiad Pr., Inc.
—Under Suspicion. 2000. (Detective Inspector Carol Ashton Mysteries Ser.). 204p. pap. 11.95 (*1-56280-261-5*) Naiad Pr., Inc.
McNaught, Judith. Night Whispers. l.t. ed. (Wheeler Press Paperback Ser.). 2000. 11.95 (*1-56895-968-0*); 1999. 27.95 o.p. (*1-56895-647-9*) Gale Group. (Wheeler Publishing, Inc.).
—Night Whispers. 1999. (Illus.). 464p. pap. 7.99 (*0-671-52574-3*, Pocket); 1998. mass mkt. 7.99 (*0-671-02834-0*, Pocket); 1998. (Illus.). 400p. 24.00 o.s.i (*0-671-00085-3*, Atria) Simon & Schuster.
—Night Whispers. 2001. audio 9.98 (*0-7435-0863-7*); audio 9.98 (*0-7435-0863-7*) Simon & Schuster Audio. (Simon & Schuster Audioworks).
Melville, Jennie. Dead Again: A Charmian Daniels Mystery. l.t. ed. 2000. 281p. (*0-7540-4212-X*); (*0-7540-4213-8*) Gale Group. (Macmillan Reference USA).
—Dead Again: A Charmian Daniels Mystery. l.t. ed. 2000. (Nightingale Ser.). 281p. pap. 20.95 (*0-7838-9099-0*) Thorndike Pr.
—Dead Set: A Charmian Daniels Mystery. 1995. (WWL Mystery Ser.). 252p. per. (*0-373-26174-8*, 1-26174-2, Harlequin Bks.) Harlequin Enterprises, Ltd.
—Dead Set: A Charmian Daniels Mystery. 1992. 17.95 (*0-312-08757-8*, Saint Martin's Minotaur) St. Martin's Pr.
—Death in the Family. 1995. 277p. 21.00 (*0-312-11772-8*, Saint Martin's Minotaur) St. Martin's Pr.
—A Different Kind of Summer. l.t. ed. 1993. 18.95 o.p. (*0-7451-6437-4*); 1992. audio 39.95 (*0-7451-2401-1*, CD 002) BBC Audiobooks America.
—A Different Kind of Summer. (Black Dagger Crime Ser.). 12.95 o.p. (*0-86220-800-9*, BD005) Chivers Pr. GBR. *Dist:* BBC Audiobooks America.
—Footsteps in the Blood. pap. 15.95 (*0-312-29187-6*, Saint Martin's Griffin); 1993. 192p. 17.95 (*0-312-09813-8*, Saint Martin's Minotaur) St. Martin's Pr.
—Making Good Blood. 1990. 15.95 o.p. (*0-312-04344-9*, Saint Martin's Minotaur) St. Martin's Pr.
—The Morbid Kitchen. 208p. 1996. 20.95 (*0-312-14681-7*, Saint Martin's Minotaur); 1995. per. 15.95 (*0-312-29172-8*, Saint Martin's Griffin) St. Martin's Pr.
—Murder Has a Pretty Face. 1991. reprint ed. per. (*0-373-26079-2*, Harlequin Bks.) Harlequin Enterprises, Ltd.
—Murder Has a Pretty Face. l.t. ed. 1996. (Magna Large Print Ser.). 400p. 29.99 (*0-7505-1047-1*) Magna Large Print Bks. GBR. *Dist:* Ulverscroft Large Print Bks., Ltd., Ulverscroft Large Print Canada, Ltd.
—Murder Has a Pretty Face. 1989. 256p. 16.95 o.p. (*0-312-03405-9*, Saint Martin's Minotaur) St. Martin's Pr.
—Murder in the Garden. 1991. 2.99 o.p. (*0-517-07814-7*) Random Hse. Value Publishing.
—Murder in the Garden. pap. 15.95 (*0-312-29185-X*, Saint Martin's Griffin); 1990. 224p. 15.95 (*0-312-03895-X*, Saint Martin's Minotaur) St. Martin's Pr.
—Revengeful Death. l.t. ed. 1998. (Magna Large Print Ser.). 272p. (*0-7505-1232-6*) Magna Large Print Bks. GBR. *Dist:* Ulverscroft Large Print Canada, Ltd.
—Tarot's Tower. 1979. mass mkt. 1.75 o.s.i (*0-449-24001-0*, Fawcett) Ballantine Bks.
—Tarot's Tower. 1978. 8.95 o.s.i (*0-671-22905-2*, Simon & Schuster) Simon & Schuster.
—Whoever Has the Heart. 218p. 3.95 o.p. (*0-8317-5152-5*) Smithmark Pubs., Inc.
—Whoever Has the Heart. 1994. 224p. 19.95 (*0-312-11099-5*, Saint Martin's Minotaur) St. Martin's Pr.
—Windsor Red. pap. 9.95 (*1-902002-01-6*) CT Publishing GBR. *Dist:* Trafalgar Square.
—Windsor Red. 1990. mass mkt. (*0-373-26051-2*, Harlequin Bks.) Harlequin Enterprises, Ltd.
—Windsor Red. 1988. 256p. 16.95 o.p. (*0-312-01846-0*, Saint Martin's Minotaur) St. Martin's Pr.
—Witching Murder. 1991. (Lythway Adult Ser.). 280p. 20.50 o.p. (*0-7451-1374-5*) Chivers Pr. GBR. *Dist:* BBC Audiobooks America.
—Witching Murder. pap. 15.95 (*0-312-29186-8*, Saint Martin's Griffin); 1991. 15.95 (*0-312-05999-X*, Saint Martin's Minotaur) St. Martin's Pr.
Meredith, Marilyn. Deadly Omen. 1999. (Tempe Crabtree Mystery Ser.). 230p. pap. 7.95 (*1-891940-03-1*) Golden Eagle Pr.
—Deadly Omen. 2001. E-Book 5.50 (*0-7599-0296-8*) Hard Shell Word Factory.
Micklebury, Penny. Keeping Secrets. 1994. 240p. pap. 9.95 o.p. (*1-56280-052-3*) Naiad Pr., Inc.
—Night Songs. 1995. 224p. pap. 10.95 o.p. (*1-56280-097-3*) Naiad Pr., Inc.
Monsour, Theresa. Clean Cut. 2004. 368p. mass mkt. 7.99 (*0-515-13705-7*, Jove) Berkley Publishing Group.
—Clean Cut. 2003. 304p. 23.95 (*0-399-14968-6*) Putnam Publishing Group, The.
—Road Kill. 2004. 320p. 24.95 (*0-399-15156-7*) Putnam Publishing Group, The.
Moore, Laurie. The Lady Godiva Murder. 2002. (Five Star First Edition Mystery Ser.). 327p. 25.95 (*0-7862-4827-0*, Five Star) Gale Group.
Morell, Mary. Final Rest. 1993. 250p. pap. 9.95 o.p. (*0-933216-94-7*) Spinsters Ink Bks.
Morice, Anne. Dead on Cue. 1985. 208p. 12.95 o.p. (*0-312-18519-7*) St. Martin's Pr.
—Death & the Dutiful Daughter. l.t. ed. 1986. (Nightingale Ser.). 288p. 10.95 o.p. (*0-8161-3866-4*, Macmillan Reference USA) Gale Group.
—Death in the Round. 1981. (Crime Monthly Ser.). 192p. pap. 2.95 o.p. (*0-14-005997-0*, Penguin Bks.) Viking Penguin.
—Design for Dying. unabr. ed. 1991. (Audio Ser.). audio 39.95 (*0-7451-6174-X*, CAT 4070) BBC Audiobooks America.
—Design for Dying. 1988. 192p. 14.95 o.p. (*0-312-01759-6*, Saint Martin's Minotaur) St. Martin's Pr.
—Fatal Charm. l.t. ed. 1990. (Nightingale Ser.). 276p. pap. 13.95 o.p. (*0-8161-4925-9*, Macmillan Reference USA) Gale Group.
—Hollow Vengeance. 1982. 196p. 10.95 o.p. (*0-312-38834-9*) St. Martin's Pr.
—Murder by Proxy. 1978. 7.95 o.p. (*0-312-55292-0*) St. Martin's Pr.
—Murder Post-Dated. 1986. 208p. mass mkt. 2.95 o.s.i (*0-553-25652-1*) Bantam Bks.
—Murder Post-Dated. l.t. ed. 1985. (Nightingale Ser.). 396p. pap. 11.95 o.p. (*0-8161-3769-2*, Macmillan Reference USA) Gale Group.
—Nursery Tea & Poison, Vol. 1. 1975. 6.95 o.p. (*0-312-58030-4*) St. Martin's Pr.
—Planning for Murder. l.t. ed. 1991. (Nightingale Ser.). 267p. pap. 14.95 o.p. (*0-8161-5246-2*, Macmillan Reference USA) Gale Group.
—Publish & Be Killed. l.t. ed. 1988. (Nightingale Ser.). 294p. 12.95 o.p. (*0-8161-4394-3*, Macmillan Reference USA) Gale Group.
—Publish & Be Killed. 1986. 192p. 12.95 o.p. (*0-312-00178-9*) St. Martin's Pr.
—Scared to Death. 1978. (Mystery Bookshelf Selection Ser.). pap. 2.95 o.p. (*0-312-70044-X*, Saint Martin's Griffin) St. Martin's Pr.
—Sleep of Death. 1982. 176p. 10.95 o.p. (*0-312-72863-8*) St. Martin's Pr.
—Treble Exposure. l.t. ed. 1988. (Nightingale Ser.). 312p. 12.95 o.p. (*0-8161-4622-5*, Macmillan Reference USA) Gale Group.
O'Connell, Carol. Crime School. 2003. 416p. mass mkt. 7.99 (*0-515-13535-6*, Jove) Berkley Publishing Group.
—Crime School. l.t. ed. 2003. 30.95 (*1-58724-376-8*, Wheeler Publishing, Inc.) Gale Group.
—Crime School. 2002. 352p. 24.95 o.s.i (*0-399-14928-7*, Putnam & Grosset) Putnam Publishing Group, The.
—Killing Critics. 1997. (Kathleen Mallory Novels Ser.). 400p. mass mkt. 7.99 (*0-515-12086-3*, Jove) Berkley Publishing Group.
—Killing Critics. abr. ed. (Kathleen Mallory Mystery Ser.). 1997. audio 7.99 o.p. (*1-56740-170-8*, 667, Paperback Nova Audio Bks.); 1996. audio 16.95 o.p. (*1-56100-894-X*, 1260, Nova Audio Bks.); 1996. 11p. audio 73.25 o.p. (*1-56100-316-6*, 917); 1996. audio 23.95 o.p. (*1-56100-691-2*, 152, Bookcassette) Brilliance Audio.
—Killing Critics. l.t. ed. 1996. (G. K. Hall Mystery Ser.). 534p. 25.95 o.p. (*0-7838-1903-X*, Macmillan Reference USA) Gale Group.
—Killing Critics. 1996. 304p. 23.95 o.s.i (*0-399-14168-5*, G. P. Putnam's Sons) Penguin Group (USA) Inc.
—Mallory's Oracle. l.t. ed. 1995. (Large Print Ser.). 330p. lib. bdg. 25.95 (*1-57490-024-2*, Beeler Large Print Bks.) Beeler, Thomas T. Publisher.
—Mallory's Oracle. 1995. (Kathleen Mallory Novels Ser.). 336p. mass mkt. 7.99 (*0-515-11647-5*, Jove) Berkley Publishing Group.
—Mallory's Oracle. 1994. 288p. 21.95 o.p. (*0-399-13975-3*, G. P. Putnam's Sons) Penguin Group (USA) Inc.
—Mallory's Oracle. abr. ed. 1996. audio 8.99 o.s.i (*0-679-45593-0*, RH Audio) Random Hse. Audio Publishing Group.
—Mallory's Oracle. 4.98 o.p. (*0-7651-0181-5*) Smithmark Pubs., Inc.
—The Man Who Cast Two Shadows. 1996. (Kathleen Mallory Novels Ser.). 336p. mass mkt. 7.99 (*0-515-11890-7*, Jove) Berkley Publishing Group.
—The Man Who Cast Two Shadows. l.t. ed. 1995. pap. 20.95 o.p. (*1-56895-258-9*, Wheeler Publishing, Inc.) Gale Group.
—The Man Who Cast Two Shadows. abr. ed. 1998. 8.99 o.s.i incl. audio (*0-375-40328-0*) Knopf, Alfred A. Inc.
—The Man Who Cast Two Shadows. 1995. 23.95 o.p. (*0-399-14064-6*, G. P. Putnam's Sons) Penguin Group (USA) Inc.
—Shell Game. 1999. (James Bond Adventure Ser.). 374p. 24.95 o.p. (*0-399-14495-1*, G. P. Putnam's Sons) Penguin Group (USA) Inc.
—The Shell Game. 2000. (Kathleen Mallory Novels Ser.). 416p. mass mkt. 7.50 (*0-425-17603-7*) Berkley Publishing Group.
—Shell Game, unabr. ed. 1999. (Chivers Sound Library American Collections). audio 96.95 (*0-7927-2347-3*, CSL 236, Chivers Sound Library) BBC Audiobooks America.
—Shell Game. l.t. ed. 2001. (Wheeler Large Print Book Ser.). 547p. pap. 23.95 (*1-58724-008-4*, Wheeler Publishing, Inc.) Gale Group.
—Stone Angel. 1998. (Kathleen Mallory Novels Ser.). 400p. mass mkt. 7.99 (*0-515-12298-X*, Jove) Berkley Publishing Group.
—Stone Angel. abr. ed. (Kathleen Mallory Mystery Ser.). 1998. audio 7.99 o.p. (*1-56740-255-0*, 705, Paperback Nova Audio Bks.); 1997. audio 16.95 o.p. (*1-56100-935-0*, 1382, Nova Audio Bks.); 1997. audio 73.25 o.p. (*1-56100-824-9*, 1059, Unabridged Library Editions); 1997. audio 23.95 (*1-56100-749-8*, 278, Bookcassette) Brilliance Audio.
—Stone Angel. l.t. ed. 1997. 24.95 o.p. (*1-56895-507-3*, Wheeler Publishing, Inc.) Gale Group.
—Stone Angel. 1997. 341p. 24.95 o.s.i (*0-399-14234-7*, G. P. Putnam's Sons) Penguin Group (USA) Inc.
O'Connell, Catherine. Skins. 1993. 215p. 20.00 o.p. (*1-55611-343-9*) Fine, Donald I. Bks.
O'Donnell, Lillian. Blue Death. 1998. 224p. 22.95 o.p. (*0-399-14367-X*) Penguin Group (USA) Inc.
—Casual Affairs. 1987. mass mkt. 2.95 o.s.i (*0-449-21064-2*, Fawcett) Ballantine Bks.
—Casual Affairs. 1985. 240p. 16.95 o.p. (*0-399-13100-0*) Putnam Publishing Group, The.
—The Children's Zoo. 1982. mass mkt. 3.50 o.s.i (*0-449-24498-9*, Fawcett) Ballantine Bks.
—Cop Without a Shield. 1984. 256p. mass mkt. 2.95 o.s.i (*0-449-20534-7*, Fawcett) Ballantine Bks.
—Cop Without a Shield. 1983. 256p. 13.95 o.p. (*0-399-12872-7*, G. P. Putnam's Sons) Penguin Putnam Bks. for Young Readers.
—A Good Night to Kill. 1989. 224p. mass mkt. 4.99 o.s.i (*0-449-21706-X*, Fawcett) Ballantine Bks.
—A Good Night to Kill. 1989. 256p. 17.95 o.p. (*0-399-13403-4*, G. P. Putnam's Sons) Penguin Putnam Bks. for Young Readers.
—Ladykiller. 1985. 240p. mass mkt. 2.95 o.s.i (*0-449-20744-7*, Fawcett) Ballantine Bks.
—Leisure Dying. 1976. 6.95 o.p. (*0-399-11741-5*) Putnam Publishing Group, The.
—Lockout. 1995. (Norah Mulcahaney Ser.). mass mkt. 5.99 o.s.i (*0-449-22329-9*, Fawcett) Ballantine Bks.
—Lockout. 1994. 240p. 19.95 o.p. (*0-399-13921-4*, G. P. Putnam's Sons) Penguin Group (USA) Inc.
—No Business Being a Cop. 1987. mass mkt. 2.95 o.s.i (*0-449-21322-6*); 1980. mass mkt. 1.95 o.p. (*0-449-24219-6*) Ballantine Bks. (Fawcett).
—No Business Being a Cop. 1979. 8.95 o.p. (*0-399-12276-1*) Putnam Publishing Group, The.
—The Other Side of the Door. 1988. mass mkt. 2.95 o.s.i (*0-449-21598-9*, Fawcett) Ballantine Bks.
—The Other Side of the Door. 1988. 240p. 17.95 o.p. (*0-399-13316-X*, G. P. Putnam's Sons) Penguin Putnam Bks. for Young Readers.
—A Private Crime. 1992. mass mkt. 3.99 o.s.i (*0-449-21989-5*, Fawcett) Ballantine Bks.
—A Private Crime. l.t. ed. 1992. (General Ser.). 333p. lib. bdg. 21.95 o.p. (*0-8161-5277-2*, Macmillan Reference USA) Gale Group.
—A Private Crime. 1991. 240p. 19.95 o.p. (*0-399-13585-5*, G. P. Putnam's Sons) Penguin Group (USA) Inc.
—Pushover. 1993. mass mkt. 4.99 o.s.i (*0-449-22152-0*, Fawcett) Ballantine Bks.
—Pushover. 1992. 240p. 19.95 o.p. (*0-399-13674-6*, G. P. Putnam's Sons) Penguin Group (USA) Inc.
Ormerod, Roger. The Second Jeopardy. 1988. (Crime Club Ser.). 12.95 o.s.i (*0-385-24613-7*) Doubleday Publishing.
—The Second Jeopardy. l.t. ed. 2001. (General Ser.). 313p. pap. 22.95 o.p. (*0-7862-2986-1*); (*0-7540-4346-0*); (*0-7540-4347-9*) Thorndike Pr.
Parker, T. Jefferson. Black Water. 2002. lib. bdg. 29.95 (*1-58547-255-7*, Platinum) Ctr. Point Large Print.
—Black Water. 2002. 352p. 23.95 (*0-7868-6804-X*) Hyperion Pr.
Paul, Barbara. The Apostrophe Thief. 1994. mass mkt. (*0-373-26155-1*, 1-26155-1, Harlequin Bks.) Harlequin Enterprises, Ltd.
—The Apostrophe Thief: A Mystery with Marian Larch. 1993. 256p. 20.00 o.p. (*0-684-19553-4*, Macmillan Reference USA) Gale Group.
—Fare Play. 1995. 256p. 20.00 (*0-684-19715-4*, Scribner) Simon & Schuster.
—Fare Play. l.t. ed. 1997. (Ulverscroft Large Print Ser.). 400p. 31.50 o.p. (*0-7089-3690-3*, Ulverscroft) Thorpe, F. A. Pubs. GBR. *Dist:* Ulverscroft Large Print Bks., Ltd., Ulverscroft Large Print Canada, Ltd.
—Fare Play: A Mystery with Marian Larch. l.t. ed. 1995. 314p. pap. 20.95 o.p. (*0-7838-1413-5*, Macmillan Reference USA) Gale Group.
—Full Frontal Murder. 1998. (WWL Mystery Ser.). per. (*0-373-26284-1*, 1-26284-9, Worldwide Library) Harlequin Enterprises, Ltd.
—Full Frontal Murder, Bk. 2. 1997. (Full Frontal Murder Ser.: Vol. 2). 256p. 20.50 (*0-684-19716-2*, Scribner) Simon & Schuster.
—Full Frontal Murder: A Mystery with Marian Larch. l.t. ed. 1998. (Mystery Ser.). 319p. 27.95 (*0-7838-8363-3*) Thorndike Pr.
—The Renewable Virgin. 1986. (Mystery Ser.). 192p. mass mkt. 2.95 o.s.i (*0-553-26234-3*) Bantam Bks.
—Renewable Virgin. l.t. ed. 1985. (Nightingale Ser.). 360p. 9.95 o.p. (*0-8161-3888-5*, Macmillan Reference USA) Gale Group.
—Renewable Virgin. 1985. 12.95 o.p. (*0-684-18300-5*, Scribner) Simon & Schuster.

Occupations

—You Have the Right to Remain Silent. 1993. (Mystery Ser.). mass mkt. (*0-373-26132-2*, 1-26132-0, Harlequin Bks.) Harlequin Enterprises, Ltd.

—You Have the Right to Remain Silent, unabr. ed. 1993. audio 51.00 (*1-55690-836-9*, 93204E7) Recorded Bks., LLC.

—You Have the Right to Remain Silent: A Mystery with Marian Larch. 1992. 256p. 20.00 o.s.i (*0-684-19380-9*, Scribner) Simon & Schuster.

Pears, Iain. The Bernini Bust. 1994. 192p. 19.95 o.s.i (*0-15-111830-2*) Harcourt Trade Pubs.

—The Immaculate Deception. 2000. 224p. 25.00 o.s.i (*0-7432-1257-6*, Scribner); 2001. 272p. reprint ed. mass mkt. 7.99 (*0-7434-2208-2*, Pocket) Simon & Schuster.

—The Immaculate Deception. l.t. ed. 2001. (Thorndike Basic Ser.). 333p. 28.95 (*0-7862-3257-9*) Thorndike Pr.

—The Last Judgement. 2002. 336p. pap. 13.00 (*0-425-18647-4*) Berkley Publishing Group.

—The Titian Committee. 2002. 272p. pap. 12.00 (*0-425-18500-1*); 1999. 240p. reprint ed. pap. 6.50 (*0-425-16895-6*, Prime Crime) Berkley Publishing Group.

—The Titian Committee. 1993. 189p. 19.95 (*0-15-190472-3*) Harcourt Trade Pubs.

Perry, Anne. Seven Dials. 2004. 352p. mass mkt. 7.50 (*0-345-44008-0*); 2003. 352p. 25.95 (*0-345-44007-2*, Ballantine Bks.); 2003. E-Book 17.85 (*0-345-46352-8*, Ballantine Bks.) Ballantine Bks.

—Seven Dials. 2003. (Basic Ser.). 552p. 32.95 (*0-7862-5210-3*) Thorndike Pr.

Phillips, Clyde. Sacrifice. 2003. 320p. 24.95 (*0-06-621237-5*, Morrow, William & Co.) Morrow/Avon.

Price, Richard. Samaritan. 2003. 400p. 25.00 (*0-375-41115-1*) Knopf, Alfred A. Inc.

—Samaritan. l.t. ed. 2003. 30.95 (*0-7862-5428-9*) Thorndike Pr.

Quest, Erica. Model Murder. l.t. ed. 1992. 18.95 o.p. (*0-7451-8408-1*) BBC Audiobooks America.

Ramthun, Bonnie. Earthquake Games. 2001. 352p. mass mkt. 6.99 o.s.i (*0-515-13177-6*, Jove) Berkley Publishing Group.

—Earthquake Games. 2000. 304p. 24.95 o.s.i (*0-399-14666-0*) Penguin Group (USA) Inc.

Rathbone, Julian. Accidents Will Happen. 1997. (Mask Noir Ser.). 256p. pap. text (*1-85242-312-9*) Serpent's Tail Ltd.

—Accidents Will Happen. 296p. 26.00 (*0-7278-5619-7*) Severn Hse. Pubs., Ltd.

—The Brandenburg Concerto. 1998. (Mask Noir Ser.). 224p. pap. (*1-85242-525-3*) Serpent's Tail Ltd.

—The Brandenburg Concerto. 256p. 25.99 (*0-7278-5716-9*) Severn Hse. Pubs., Ltd.

Robb, J. D., pseud. Ceremony in Death. 1997. 336p. mass mkt. 7.99 (*0-425-15762-8*) Berkley Publishing Group.

—Conspiracy in Death. 1999. 400p. mass mkt. 7.99 (*0-425-16813-1*) Berkley Publishing Group.

—Divided in Death. 2004. 448p. 23.95 (*0-399-15154-0*, Putnam & Grosset) Putnam Publishing Group, The.

—Glory in Death. 1995. 320p. mass mkt. 7.99 (*0-425-15098-4*) Berkley Publishing Group.

—Glory in Death. 2004. 320p. reprint ed. 19.95 (*0-399-15158-3*) Putnam Publishing Group, The.

—Holiday in Death. 1998. 336p. mass mkt. 7.99 (*0-425-16371-7*) Berkley Publishing Group.

—Imitation in Death. 2003. 352p. mass mkt. 7.99 (*0-425-19158-3*) Berkley Publishing Group.

—Immortal in Death. 1996. 320p. mass mkt. 7.99 (*0-425-15378-9*) Berkley Publishing Group.

—Immortal in Death. 2004. 288p. reprint ed. 19.95 (*0-399-15159-1*) Putnam Publishing Group, The.

—Judgment in Death. 2000. 368p. mass mkt. 7.99 (*0-425-17630-4*) Berkley Publishing Group.

—Judgment in Death. l.t. ed. 2002. (Core Ser.). 472p. pap. 30.95 (*0-7838-9335-3*) Gale Group.

—Judgment in Death. l.t. ed. 2001. (Core Ser.). 472p. 32.95 (*0-7838-9334-5*) Thorndike Pr.

—Loyalty in Death. 1999. 368p. mass mkt. 7.99 (*0-425-17140-X*) Berkley Publishing Group.

—Una Muerte Desnuda. 1999. (SPA.). 368p. 19.95 (*84-01-46800-0*) Lectorum Pubns., Inc.

—Naked in Death. 1995. 320p. mass mkt. 7.99 (*0-425-14829-7*) Berkley Publishing Group.

—Naked in Death. l.t. ed. 2000. (Americana Ser.). 445p. 29.95 (*0-7862-2415-0*) Thorndike Pr.

—Rapture in Death. 1996. 320p. mass mkt. 7.99 (*0-425-15518-8*) Berkley Publishing Group.

—Vengeance in Death. 1997. 384p. mass mkt. 7.99 (*0-425-16039-4*) Berkley Publishing Group.

—Witness in Death. 2000. 368p. mass mkt. 7.99 (*0-425-17363-1*) Berkley Publishing Group.

—Witness in Death. l.t. ed. 2001. 28.95 (*0-7862-2716-8*); 2000. 547p. 30.95 (*0-7862-2715-X*) Thorndike Pr.

Robb, J. D., pseud, et al. Silent Night. 1998. 352p. mass mkt. 7.50 (*0-515-12385-4*, Jove) Berkley Publishing Group.

Roberts, Carey. Pray God to Die: A Detective Anne Fitzhugh Mystery. 1993. 384p. 21.00 o.p. (*0-684-19562-3*, Scribner) Simon & Schuster.

Roberts, Nora. Heaven & Earth. l.t. ed. 2002. 32.95 (*0-7838-9618-2*) Gale Group.

—Heaven & Earth. l.t. ed. 2002. 424p. pap. 29.95 (*0-7838-9621-2*) Thorndike Pr.

—Night Shield. 2000. (Silhouette Intimate Moments Ser.: Vol. 1027). 256p. mass mkt. (*0-373-27097-6*, 1-27097-4, Silhouette) Harlequin Enterprises, Ltd.

—Night Shield. l.t. ed. 2001. (Thorndike Americana Ser.). 288p. 31.95 (*0-7862-3050-9*); (*0-7540-4455-6*); (*0-7540-4454-8*) Thorndike Pr.

—Remember When. 2004. 512p. mass mkt. 7.99 (*0-425-19547-3*) Berkley Publishing Group.

Roberts, Nora & Robb, J. D. Remember When. 2003. 448p. 25.95 (*0-399-15106-0*, Putnam & Grosset) Putnam Publishing Group, The.

—Remember When. l.t. ed. 2004. 544p. pap. 14.95 (*1-59413-022-1*); 2003. 729p. 32.95 (*0-7862-5695-8*) Thorndike Pr. (Large Print Pr.).

Rosenberg, Nancy Taylor. Abuse of Power. unabr. ed. 1997. audio 72.00 (*0-913369-73-X*, 4326) Books on Tape, Inc.

—Abuse of Power. 1997. 336p. 23.95 o.p. (*0-525-93768-4*) Dutton/Plume.

—Abuse of Power. l.t. ed. 1997. 448p. mass mkt. 7.99 (*0-451-18006-2*, Signet Bks.) NAL.

—Abuse of Power, unabr. ed. 1997. audio 78.00 (*0-7887-0916-X*, 94957E7) Recorded Bks., LLC.

—Abuse of Power. abr. ed. 1997. 3p. audio 16.95 o.s.i (*0-14-086507-1*, Penguin AudioBooks) Viking Penguin.

Santlofer, Jonathan. The Death Artist: A Novel of Suspense. 2003. 448p. mass mkt. 7.50 (*0-06-000442-8*, HarperTorch); 2002. 352p. 24.95 (*0-06-000441-X*, Morrow, William & Co.) Morrow/Avon.

Schermerhorn, James. Night of the Cat. 1993. 224p. 18.95 o.p. (*0-312-09887-1*, Saint Martin's Minotaur) St. Martin's Pr.

See, Lisa. Dragon Bones: A Novel. 2003. 368p. 24.95 (*0-679-46320-8*) Random Hse., Inc.

Shah, Diane K. High Heel Blue. 1997. 318p. 22.50 (*0-684-81431-5*, Simon & Schuster) Simon & Schuster.

Silva, Linda K. Tropical Storm. 1996. 245p. pap. 11.99 (*1-883061-14-8*) Rising Tide Pr.

Slaughter, Karin. Blindsighted: A Novel. 2001. 320p. 25.00 (*0-688-17457-4*, Morrow, William & Co.) Morrow/Avon.

—Kisscut. 2003. E-Book 7.99 (*0-06-057880-7*); E-Book 7.99 (*0-06-057883-1*); E-Book 7.99 (*0-06-057881-5*); E-Book 7.99 (*0-06-057882-3*) HarperCollins Pubs.

—Kisscut. 2003. 448p. mass mkt. 7.99 (*0-06-053404-4*, HarperTorch) Morrow/Avon.

Smith, Joan. Don't Leave Me This Way. 1991. mass mkt. 5.99 o.s.i (*0-449-21964-X*, Fawcett) Ballantine Bks.

—Don't Leave Me This Way. 1991. 288p. 18.95 o.s.i (*0-684-19233-0*, Macmillan Reference USA) Gale Group.

—Full Stop. (Loretta Lawson Mystery Ser.). 1997. 262p. mass mkt. 5.99 o.s.i (*0-449-22300-0*); 1996. 288p. 21.00 o.s.i (*0-449-91048-2*) Ballantine Bks. (Fawcett).

—A Masculine Ending. 1989. 224p. mass mkt. 5.99 o.s.i (*0-449-21688-8*, Fawcett) Ballantine Bks.

—A Masculine Ending. 1988. 186p. 15.95 o.s.i (*0-684-18938-0*, Macmillan Reference USA) Gale Group.

—What Men Say. 1995. mass mkt. 5.99 o.s.i (*0-449-22297-7*, Fawcett) Ballantine Bks.

—What Men Say: A Loretta Lawson Mystery. 1994. 224p. 20.00 o.s.i (*0-449-90920-4*, Fawcett) Ballantine Bks.

—Why Aren't They Screaming? 1990. 224p. mass mkt. 4.99 o.s.i (*0-449-21777-9*, Fawcett) Ballantine Bks.

—Why Aren't They Screaming? 1989. 208p. 16.95 o.s.i (*0-684-19028-1*, Scribner) Simon & Schuster.

Smith, Julie. The Axeman's Jazz. 1992. (Skip Langdon Novel Ser.). 368p. mass mkt. 6.99 (*0-8041-0954-0*, Ivy Bks.) Ballantine Bks.

—The Axeman's Jazz. 1991. 384p. 19.95 o.p. (*0-312-06295-8*, Saint Martin's Minotaur) St. Martin's Pr.

—Crescent City Kill. (Skip Langdon Novel Ser.). 1998. 368p. mass mkt. 6.50 o.s.i (*0-8041-1397-1*, Ivy Bks.); 1997. 326p. 4.99 o.s.i (*0-449-91000-8*, Fawcett) Ballantine Bks.

—House of Blues. 1996. (Skip Langdon Novel Ser.). 352p. reprint ed. mass mkt. 6.99 o.s.i (*0-8041-1342-4*, Ivy Bks.) Ballantine Bks.

—Jazz Funeral. 1994. (Skip Langdon Novel Ser.). 368p. mass mkt. 5.99 o.s.i (*0-8041-1252-5*, Ivy Bks.) Ballantine Bks.

—The Kindness of Strangers. 1997. (Skip Langdon Novel Ser.). mass mkt. 5.99 o.s.i (*0-8041-1273-8*, Ivy Bks.) Ballantine Bks.

—New Orleans Beat: A Skip Langdon Mystery. 1995. (Skip Langdon Novel Ser.). 368p. mass mkt. 6.50 o.s.i (*0-8041-1336-X*, Ivy Bks.) Ballantine Bks.

—New Orleans Mourning. 1990. (Skip Langdon Novel Ser.). 352p. mass mkt. 6.99 (*0-8041-0738-6*, Ivy Bks.) Ballantine Bks.

—New Orleans Mourning, unabr. ed. 1999. (Skip Langdon Mysteries Ser. ). audio 87.00 (*0-7887-3480-6*, 95775E7) Recorded Bks., LLC.

—New Orleans Mourning. 1990. 384p. 17.95 o.p. (*0-312-03892-5*, Saint Martin's Minotaur) St. Martin's Pr.

—82 Desire. (Skip Langdon Novel Ser.). 1999. 352p. mass mkt. 6.99 (*0-8041-1699-7*, Ivy Bks.); 1998. 320p. 24.00 o.s.i (*0-449-00060-5*, Fawcett) Ballantine Bks.

—82 Desire. l.t. ed. 1999. (Large Print Book Ser.). pap. 24.95 (*1-56895-628-2*, Wheeler Publishing, Inc.) Gale Group.

Stewart, Edward. Mortal Grace. 1995. 560p. mass mkt. 6.50 o.s.i (*0-440-21697-4*) Dell Publishing.

Thurlo, Aimee & Thurlo, David. Bad Medicine. 1997. (Ella Clah Novel Ser.). 384p. 23.95 (*0-312-86328-4*, Forge Bks.) Doherty, Tom Assocs., LLC.

—Changing Woman. E-Book 24.95 (*0-312-70549-2*, Tor Bks.); 2nd ed. 2002. 384p. 24.95 (*0-312-87059-0*, CPHC0654, Forge Bks.) Doherty, Tom Assocs., LLC.

—Enemy Way. (Ella Clah Novel Ser.: No. 4). 1999. 352p. mass mkt. 6.99 (*0-8125-6459-6*); 1998. 350p. 23.95 (*0-312-85520-6*) Doherty, Tom Assocs., LLC. (Forge Bks.).

—Plant Them Deep. mass mkt. (*0-7653-4398-3*); 2003. 336p. 24.95 (*0-7653-0478-3*) Doherty, Tom Assocs., LLC. (Forge Bks.).

Tooley, S. D. Nothing Else Matters. 2000. (Sam Casey Mystery Ser.). 288p. 22.95 (*0-9666021-2-9*) Full Moon Publishing.

—When the Dead Speak. 2000. (Sam Casey Mystery Ser.). 304p. pap. 6.50 (*0-9666021-3-7*) Full Moon Publishing.

—When the Dead Speak. Roerden, Chris, ed. 1999. (Sam Casey Mystery Ser.). 304p. 21.95 (*0-9666021-0-2*) Full Moon Publishing.

Uhnak, Dorothy. The Bait. 1976. pap. 1.95 o.s.i (*0-671-82326-4*, Pocket) Simon & Schuster.

—The Ledger. 1977. pap. 1.95 o.s.i (*0-671-82328-0*, Pocket) Simon & Schuster.

Victor, Cynthia. Only You. l.t. ed. 2000. 463p. 28.95 (*1-57490-322-5*, Beeler Large Print Bks.) Beeler, Thomas T. Publisher.

—Only You. 1995. 416p. mass mkt. 5.99 o.s.i (*0-451-40606-0*, Onyx) NAL.

—Only You. 1994. 416p. 19.95 o.p. (*0-670-84981-2*, Viking) Viking Penguin.

Villatoro, Marcos M. Minos: A Romilia Chacon Mystery. 2003. 320p. 24.95 (*1-932112-13-8*) Justin, Charles & Co. Pubs.

Weir, Charlene. A Cold Christmas. 2002. (WWL Mystery Ser.: No. 439). 256p. mass mkt. (*0-373-26439-9*, Worldwide Library) Harlequin Enterprises, Ltd.

—A Cold Christmas. 2001. 272p. 23.95 (*0-312-26931-5*, Saint Martin's Minotaur) St. Martin's Pr.

—Consider the Crows. 1995. (WWL Mystery Ser.). 251p. per. (*0-373-26172-1*, 1-26172-6, Harlequin Bks.) Harlequin Enterprises, Ltd.

—Consider the Crows. 1993. 272p. 19.95 o.p. (*0-312-09772-7*, Saint Martin's Minotaur) St. Martin's Pr.

—Family Practice. 1997. (Susan Wren Mystery Ser.). 301p. per. (*0-373-26236-1*, 0-26236-0, Worldwide Library) Harlequin Enterprises, Ltd.

—Family Practice. 1995. 320p. 22.95 (*0-312-13492-4*, Saint Martin's Minotaur) St. Martin's Pr.

—Murder Take Two. pap. 16.95 o.p. (*0-312-30029-8*, Saint Martin's Griffin); pap. 15.95 (*0-312-29193-0*, Saint Martin's Griffin); 1998. 336p. 23.95 (*0-312-18136-1*, Saint Martin's Minotaur) St. Martin's Pr.

—The Winter Widow. 1993. per. (*0-373-26128-4*, 1-26128-8, Harlequin Bks.) Harlequin Enterprises, Ltd.

—The Winter Widow. 1992. 256p. 18.95 o.p. (*0-312-07009-8*, Saint Martin's Minotaur) St. Martin's Pr.

Weis, Margaret & Baldwin, David. Dark Heart. 1998. (Dragon's Disciples Ser.: Vol. 1). 352p. 23.00 o.s.i (*0-06-105298-1*) HarperCollins Pubs.

—Dark Heart. 1999. (Dragon's Disciples Ser.: Vol. 1). 448p. mass mkt. 5.99 (*0-06-105791-6*, Eos) Morrow/Avon.

Williams, Arthur. Missing at Tenoclock. 1994. 216p. 19.95 (*0-8027-3185-6*) Walker & Co.

Wilson, Charles. When First We Deceive. 1994. 272p. 19.95 o.p. (*0-7867-0058-0*, Carroll & Graf Pubs.) Avalon Publishing Group.

—When First We Deceive. 1998. 272p. reprint ed. mass mkt. 4.50 (*0-8439-4401-3*, Leisure Bks.) Dorchester Publishing Co., Inc.

—When We First Deceive. 1998. E-Book 9.95 (*0-585-28456-3*) netLibrary, Inc.

Wishnia, K. J. A. 23 Shades of Black. 1997. pap. text 7.95 o.p. (*0-9656814-1-6*) Imaginary Pr., The.

—23 Shades of Black. 1998. (Filomena Buscarsela Mysteries Ser.). 304p. mass mkt. 6.99 o.s.i (*0-451-19748-8*, Signet Bks.) NAL.

—23 Shades of Black. 1998. 13.04 (*0-606-15828-6*) Turtleback Bks.

Wolfe, Susan. The Last Billable Hour. 1989. 240p. 15.95 o.p. (*0-312-02566-1*, Saint Martin's Minotaur) St. Martin's Pr.

Woods, Paula L. Inner City Blues: A Charlotte Justice Novel. 1999. 316p. 23.95 (*0-393-04680-X*) Norton, W. W. & Co., Inc.

Woods, Stuart. Blood Orchid. l.t. ed. 2003. 32.95 (*1-58724-395-4*, Wheeler Publishing, Inc.) Gale Group.

—Blood Orchid. 2003. 368p. reprint ed. mass mkt. 7.99 (*0-451-20881-1*, Signet Bks.) NAL.

—Blood Orchid. 2002. (Holly Barker Ser.: No. 3). 304p. 25.95 o.s.i (*0-399-14929-5*); 4p. 24.95 incl. audio (*0-399-14953-8*, Putnam Berkley Audio) Putnam Publishing Group, The.

—Orchid Blues. 2002. 400p. reprint ed. mass mkt. 7.99 (*0-451-20671-1*, Signet Bks.) NAL.

—Orchid Blues. 2001. 350p. 24.95 o.s.i (*0-399-14777-2*) Penguin Group (USA) Inc.

—Orchid Blues. l.t. ed. 2003. (Paperback Bestsellers Ser.). pap. 29.95 (*0-7838-9747-2*) Thorndike Pr.

Wren, M. K. Neely Jones: The Medusa Pool. 1999. 313p. 24.95 (*0-312-24223-9*, Saint Martin's Minotaur) St. Martin's Pr.

Yapalater, Karin. An Hour to Kill. 2003. 288p. 23.95 (*0-688-16599-0*, Morrow, William & Co.) Morrow/Avon.

York, Kieran. Timber City Masks: A Royce Madison Mystery. 1993. 230p. (Orig.). pap. 9.95 o.p. (*1-879427-13-3*) 3rd Side Pr., Inc.

Zachary, Hugh. Munday. 2003. 288p. pap. 13.95 (*1-4104-0134-0*, Five Star Trade); 318p. 25.95 (*0-7862-4323-6*, Five Star) Gale Group.

## POLITICIANS—FICTION

Achebe, Chinua. A Man of the People. 1981. 160p. pap. 10.95 (*0-385-08616-4*) Doubleday Publishing.

Adams, Kelly. The Silent Heart, No. 461. 1989. 2.50 o.s.i (*0-425-11544-5*) Berkley Publishing Group.

—The Silent Heart. l.t. ed. 2001. 240p. pap. 23.95 (*0-7838-9504-6*); (*0-7540-4583-8*); (*0-7540-4584-6*) Gale Group. (Macmillan Reference USA).

Amis, Martin. The Information. ltd. ed. 1995. 150.00 o.s.i (*0-517-70155-3*, Harmony) Crown Publishing Group.

—The Information. 1996. 384p. pap. 14.00 (*0-679-73573-9*, Vintage) Knopf Publishing Group.

Anonymous. Primary Colors: A Novel of Politics. 1998. 13.04 (*0-606-15920-7*) Turtleback Bks.

—Primary Colors: A Novel of Politics. 1998. mass mkt. 6.99 (*0-446-78840-6*); 1996. 528p. reprint ed. mass mkt. 6.99 o.s.i (*0-446-60427-5*) Warner Bks., Inc.

Antrim, Donald. Elect Mr. Robinson for a Better World. 1993. 192p. 20.00 o.p. (*0-670-85139-6*, Viking) Viking Penguin.

—Elect Mr. Robinson for a Better World: A Novel. 2001. 192p. pap. 12.00 (*0-375-72503-2*, Vintage) Knopf Publishing Group.

Barnard, Robert. A Murder in Mayfair. l.t. ed. 2003. 260p. pap. 22.95 o.s.i (*1-59058-081-8*) Poisoned Pen Pr.

—A Murder in Mayfair. 2000. (Illus.). 272p. (YA). 23.00 o.s.i (*0-684-86445-2*, Scribner) Simon & Schuster.

—A Murder in Mayfair. l.t. ed. 2000. (Basic Ser.). 379p. 27.95 (*0-7862-2656-0*); (*0-7540-4229-4*); (*0-7540-4230-8*) Thorndike Pr.

—Touched by the Dead. 2000. 223p. mass mkt. (*0-00-651326-3*) HarperCollins Pubs.

—Touched by the Dead. unabr. ed. 2000. audio 69.95 (*1-86042-712-X*, 2712X) Soundings, Ltd. GBR. *Dist:* Ulverscroft Large Print Bks., Ltd.

Barnes, Julian. The Porcupine. 1993. 160p. pap. 11.00 (*0-679-74482-7*, Vintage) Knopf Publishing Group.

Bell, James Scott. Final Witness. l.t. ed. 2003. 684p. 26.95 (*0-7862-5551-X*) Thorndike Pr.

Buckley, Christopher. The White House Mess. l.t. ed. 1987. 373p. 18.95 o.p. (*0-8161-4194-0*, Macmillan Reference USA) Gale Group.

Burke, James Lee. Lay down My Sword & Shield. Date not set. lib. bdg. 24.95 (*0-8488-1779-6*) Amereon, Ltd.

—Lay down My Sword & Shield. 1989. 272p. reprint ed. pap. 8.95 o.p. (*0-88150-150-6*) Countryman Pr.

—Lay down My Sword & Shield. 1999. 389p. mass mkt. 6.50 (*0-7868-8950-0*); 1995. 240p. (J). pap. 10.95 o.p. (*0-7868-8039-2*) Hyperion Pr.

Campbell, Robert. Pigeon Pie. l.t. ed. 1999. (Cloak & Dagger Ser.). 301p. 29.95 (*0-7862-1528-3*) Thorndike Pr.

Compton, David. The Acolyte. 1996. 400p. 22.50 (*0-684-80430-1*, Simon & Schuster) Simon & Schuster.

Crawford, F. Marion. An American Politician. 2000. 252p. E-Book 3.95 (*0-594-04578-9*) 1873 Pr.

—An American Politician. (BCL Ser. I). reprint ed. 29.50 (*0-404-01828-9*) AMS Pr., Inc.

—An American Politician. collector's ed. 2002. (Illus.). im. lthr. 38.85 (*1-4115-1190-5*); pap. 19.95 (*1-4115-0454-2*); 25.95 (*1-4115-0820-3*); pap. 17.95 (*1-4115-0227-2*) Polyglot Pr., Inc.

—An American Politician. 1967. 8.00 (*0-403-00034-3*) Scholarly Pr., Inc.

Crosland, Susan. Dangerous Games. 1993. 3.99 o.p. (*0-517-09793-1*) Random Hse. Value Publishing.

Date, S. V. Black Sunshine. 2002. 24.95 o.s.i (*0-399-14946-5*) Putnam Publishing Group, The.

Delahaye, Michael. Stalking-Horse. 1988. 288p. 17.95 o.s.i (*0-684-18942-9*, Scribner) Simon & Schuster.

Diamond, Diana. The Babysitter. 2001. 313p. 23.95 (*0-312-28047-5*) St. Martin's Pr.

Dickson, Gordon R. The Other. 1994. 384p. 22.95 o.p. (*0-312-85198-7*, Tor Bks.) Doherty, Tom Assocs., LLC.

Disraeli, Benjamin. Coningsby: Or, the New Generation. Smith, Sheila M., ed. 1982. (Oxford World's Classics Ser.). pap. 6.95 o.p. (*0-19-281580-6*) Oxford Univ. Pr., Inc.

Dominic, R. B. The Attending Physician. 1980. (Harper Novel of Suspense Ser.). o.p. (*0-06-011073-2*) HarperCollins Pubs.

—Unexpected Developments. 1983. 225p. 11.95 o.p. (*0-312-83278-8*) St. Martin's Pr.

Ferrell, Keith. Passing Judgement. 1996. 352p. 24.95 o.p. (*0-312-86173-7*, Forge Bks.) Doherty, Tom Assocs., LLC.

Flynn, Vince. Term Limits. 1997. ix, 363p. 24.00 (*0-9658510-0-1*) Cloak & Dagger Pr., Inc.

—Term Limits. (*0-671-02539-2*, Atria); 2001. 656p. E-Book 9.99 (*0-7434-4923-1*, Atria); 1999. (Illus.). 656p. mass mkt. 7.99 (*0-671-02318-7*, Pocket Star); 1998. 416p. 23.00 (*0-671-02317-9*, Atria) Simon & Schuster.

—Term Limits. abr. ed. 1998. 24.00 incl. audio (*0-671-58225-9*, Simon & Schuster Audioworks) Simon & Schuster Audio.

—Term Limits. 1999. 13.04 (*0-606-19064-3*) Turtleback Bks.

Forrest, Richard. A Child's Garden of Death. 1982. (Scene of the Crime Ser.: No. 44). pap. 2.25 o.p. (*0-440-11325-3*) Dell Publishing.

—A Child's Garden of Death. 1977. pap. 1.50 o.p. (*0-671-80924-5*, Pocket) Simon & Schuster.

—The Death at Yew Corner. 1984. 176p. pap. 2.95 o.p. (*0-440-11782-8*) Dell Publishing.

—The Death at Yew Corner. 1981. (Rinehart Suspense Novel Ser.). 228p. o.p. (*0-03-053386-4*) Holt, Henry & Co.

—The Death in the Willows. 1979. (Rinehart Suspense Novel Ser.). 228p. o.p. (*0-03-049296-3*) Holt, Henry & Co.

—Death on the Mississippi. 1989. 224p. 15.95 o.p. (*0-312-03323-0*, Saint Martin's Minotaur) St. Martin's Pr.

—Death Through the Looking Glass. 1979. pap. 1.75 o.s.i (*0-671-82157-1*, Pocket) Simon & Schuster.

—Death under the Lilacs. 1985. 208p. 13.95 o.p. (*0-312-18878-1*) St. Martin's Pr.

—Pied Piper of Death: A Lyon & Bea Wentworth Mystery. 1997. 240p. 21.95 o.p. (*0-312-15292-2*, Saint Martin's Minotaur) St. Martin's Pr.

Ghose, Zulfikar. A Different World. 318p. 1986. pap. 9.95 o.s.i (*0-87951-207-5*); 1985. 22.50 (*0-87951-982-7*) Overlook Pr., The.

Glickman, James. Sounding the Waters. l.t. ed. 1997. (Niagara Large Print Ser.). 433p. 29.50 o.p. (*0-7089-5859-1*, Linford) Thorpe, F. A. Pubs. GBR. *Dist:* Ulverscroft Large Print Bks., Ltd.

Harington, Donald. Thirteen Albatrosses: Or, Falling off the Mountain. 2002. 432p. 26.00 o.s.i (*0-8050-6855-4*) Holt, Henry & Co.

Higgins, George V. A Change of Gravity. 1997. 464p. 25.00 o.s.i (*0-8050-4815-4*) Holt, Henry & Co.

Hoag, Tami. Mismatch. l.t. ed. 2002. 267p. 29.95 (*0-7862-3488-1*) Gale Group.

—Mismatch. l.t. ed. 2002. 275p. 29.95 (*0-7540-4793-8*); (*0-7540-4792-X*) Thorndike Pr.

Hughes, Spenser. The Lambda Conspiracy: A Novel. 1993. pap. 10.99 o.p. (*0-8024-4738-4*) Moody Pr.

Jones, Solomon. Pipe Dream: A Novel. 2001. 368p. pap. 13.95 (*0-375-75660-4*, Villard Bks.) Random House Adult Trade Publishing Group.

Just, Ward. Jack Gance. 1989. 17.95 o.p. (*0-395-49337-4*) Houghton Mifflin Co.

Kennedy, William. Roscoe. l.t. ed. 2002. 563p. 30.95 (*0-7862-4038-5*) Gale Group.

—Roscoe. 2002. 306p. pap. 14.00 (*0-14-200173-2*) Penguin Group (USA) Inc.

—Roscoe. 2002. 304p. 24.95 o.s.i (*0-670-03029-5*, Viking) Viking Penguin.

Koch, Edward I. Murder at City Hall. 1995. 208p. mass mkt. 19.95 o.p. (*0-8217-5087-9*, Zebra Bks.) Kensington Publishing Corp.

—Murder on Broadway. 1997. 320p. mass mkt. 5.99 o.s.i (*1-57566-186-1*) Kensington Publishing Corp.

—Murder on 34th Street. 1998. 288p. mass mkt. 5.99 o.s.i (*1-57566-355-4*); 1997. 192p. 19.95 o.s.i (*1-57566-232-9*) Kensington Publishing Corp.

—The Senator Must Die. 1998. 224p. 22.00 o.s.i (*1-57566-325-2*, Kensington Bks.) Kensington Publishing Corp.

Koch, Edward I. & Resnicow, Herbert. Murder at City Hall. 1996. 224p. mass mkt. 5.99 o.s.i (*1-57566-053-9*) Kensington Publishing Corp.

Koch, Edward I. & Staub, Wendy Corsi. Murder on Broadway. 1996. 192p. 19.95 o.s.i (*1-57566-049-0*) Kensington Publishing Corp.

Lind, Michael. Powertown: A Novel. 1996. 79p. 23.00 o.p. (*0-06-017510-9*) HarperCollins Pubs.

Margolin, Phillip. The Undertaker's Widow. 1999. 336p. reprint ed. mass mkt. 7.99 (*0-553-58088-4*) Bantam Bks.

—The Undertaker's Widow. unabr. ed. 1998. audio 48.00 (*0-7366-4219-6*, 4717) Books on Tape, Inc.

—The Undertaker's Widow. unabr. ed. 1998. audio 29.95 o.s.i (*0-553-50218-2*, 751090, RH Audio) Random Hse. Audio Publishing Group.

—The Undertaker's Widow. l.t. ed. 2000. (Charnwood Large Print Ser.). 392p. (*0-7089-9146-7*, Ulverscroft) Thorpe, F. A. Pubs. GBR. *Dist:* Ulverscroft Large Print Bks., Ltd., Ulverscroft Large Print Canada, Ltd.

McCabe, Patrick. Call Me the Breeze. 2003. 352p. 24.95 (*0-06-052388-3*, HarperCollins) HarperTrade.

Meredith, George. The Tragic Comedians. 2000. 252p. pap. 9.95 (*0-594-01759-9*); E-Book 3.95 (*0-594-02639-3*) 1873 Pr.

Mikulski, Barbara & Oates, Marylouise. Capitol Offense. abr. ed. 1997. audio 7.99 o.p. (*1-56740-184-8*, 632, Paperback Nova Audio Bks.); 1996. audio 16.95 o.p. (*1-56100-903-2*, 820, Nova Audio Bks.); 1996. audio 23.95 o.p. (*1-56100-693-9*, 58, Bookcassette); 1996. audio 73.25 o.p. (*1-56100-318-2*, 1149, Unabridged Library Editions) Brilliance Audio.

—Capitol Offense. 1996. 320p. 23.95 o.s.i (*0-525-94214-9*) Dutton/Plume.

—Capitol Offense. 1997. 416p. mass mkt. 6.99 o.s.i (*0-451-19032-7*, Signet Bks.) NAL.

—Capitol Venture. 1997. 320p. 24.95 o.p. (*0-525-94277-7*) Dutton/Plume.

—Capitol Venture. 1999. 384p. mass mkt. 6.99 o.s.i (*0-451-19183-8*) NAL.

Mortimer, John. Paradise Postponed. l.t. ed. 1987. 555p. 18.95 o.p. (*0-8161-4247-5*, Macmillan Reference USA) Gale Group.

—Paradise Postponed. 1986. 384p. pap. 12.95 (*0-14-009864-X*, Penguin Bks.) Penguin Group (USA) Inc.

—Paradise Postponed. 1986. 400p. 17.95 o.p. (*0-670-80094-5*); 448p. reprint ed. pap. 11.95 o.s.i (*0-14-006928-3*) Viking Penguin.

—The Rapstone Chronicles: Paradise Postponed & Titmuss Regained. 1993. 704p. pap. 14.00 o.p. (*0-14-017595-4*, Penguin Bks.) Penguin Group (USA) Inc.

—The Sound of Trumpets. unabr. ed. 2000. (Leslie Titmuss Trilogy Ser.: Bk. 3). audio 59.95 (*0-7540-0315-9*, CAB 1738) Chivers Audio Bks. GBR. *Dist:* BBC Audiobooks America.

—The Sound of Trumpets. l.t. ed. 1999. (Core Ser.). 359p. 27.95 (*0-7838-8716-7*, Macmillan Reference USA) Gale Group.

—The Sound of Trumpets. 1999. 288p. pap. 12.95 o.s.i (*0-14-028851-1*) Penguin Group (USA) Inc.

—The Sound of Trumpets. 1999. (Rapstone Chronicles Ser.). 256p. 23.95 o.p. (*0-670-87861-8*) Viking Penguin.

—Titmuss Regained. l.t. ed. 1992. pap. 15.95 o.p. (*0-7927-0666-8*); 1991. 17.95 o.p. (*0-7927-0665-X*, E0007) BBC Audiobooks America.

—Titmuss Regained. l.t. ed. 1992. 70.95 o.p. (*0-8161-3213-5*, Macmillan Reference USA) Gale Group.

—Titmuss Regained. 1991. 288p. pap. 12.95 o.s.i (*0-14-014921-X*, Penguin Bks.) Penguin Group (USA) Inc.

—Titmuss Regained. 1990. 288p. 19.95 o.p. (*0-670-82333-3*, Viking) Viking Penguin.

—Titmuss Regained: Movie-TV Tie-In. 1992. 272p. pap. 10.00 o.p. (*0-14-017185-1*, Penguin Bks.) Penguin Group (USA) Inc.

Naipaul, V. S. The Mimic Men: A Novel. 1985. pap. 5.95 o.s.i (*0-394-73232-4*, Vintage) Knopf Publishing Group.

O'Brien, Tim. In the Lake of the Woods. 1994. 320p. tchr. ed. 21.95 o.p. (*0-395-48889-3*) Houghton Mifflin Co.

—In the Lake of the Woods. 1996. o.p. (*0-14-771179-7*); 1995. 320p. pap. 14.00 (*0-14-025094-8*, Penguin Bks.) Penguin Group (USA) Inc.

O'Connor, Edward. The Last Hurrah. Date not set. 437p. 28.95 (*0-8488-2373-7*) Amereon, Ltd.

O'Connor, Edwin. The Last Hurrah. 1970. pap. 2.95 o.p. (*0-553-14088-4*, G14088-4) Bantam Bks.

—The Last Hurrah. 1998. pap. 14.00 (*0-316-19092-6*, Back Bay); 1985. 427p. reprint ed. pap. 14.95 o.p. (*0-316-62659-7*) Little Brown & Co.

Parker, T. Jefferson. Silent Joe. l.t. ed. 2001. 501p. lib. bdg. 28.95 (*1-58547-125-9*) Ctr. Point Large Print.

—Silent Joe. 2001. vii, 341p. 23.95 (*0-7868-6728-0*); 2003. 400p. reprint ed. mass mkt. 7.99 (*0-7868-9003-7*) Hyperion Pr.

Peterson, Tracie. Shadows of the Canyon. 2002. (Desert Roses Ser.: Bk. 1). 368p. pap. 12.99 (*0-7642-2517-0*) Bethany Hse. Pubs.

—Shadows of the Canyon. l.t. ed. 2003. 482p. 26.95 (*0-7862-5784-9*) Gale Group.

Renek, Morris. Bread & Circus. 1987. 352p. 18.95 o.s.i (*1-55584-070-1*) Grove/Atlantic, Inc.

Richardson, Doug. Dark Horse. abr. ed. 1997. audio 16.95 o.p. (*1-56100-907-5*, 1169, Nova Audio Bks.); audio 89.25 o.p. (*1-56100-323-9*, 854, Unabridged Library Editions); audio 25.95 o.p. (*1-56100-698-X*, 82, Bookcassette) Brilliance Audio.

Richardson, Douglas. Dark Horse. 1997. 384p. 24.00 o.p. (*0-380-97314-6*, Avon Bks.) Morrow/Avon.

Sauter, Eric. Backfire. 1992. (Patrick Paige Ser.). 336p. 19.00 o.p. (*0-525-93483-9*, Dutton) Dutton/Plume.

Spencer, Elizabeth. The Voice at the Back Door. 1994. (Voices of the South Ser.). vii, 392p. pap. 17.95 (*0-8071-1927-X*) Louisiana State Univ. Pr.

Tarvin, Al. Chelsea & Sally. Haycox, Bobbi & Wordsmiths Unlimited Staff, eds. 1997. (Chelsea Ser.: No. 4). 280p. pap. 12.95 (*0-9643250-4-7*) CJH Enterprises.

—Chelsea & the Lords. 1999. (Chelsea Ser.: No. 5). 300p. pap. 12.95 (*0-9643250-5-5*) CJH Enterprises.

—Run, Chelsea, Run, Vol. 3. Haycox, Bobbi & CJH Enterprises Staff, eds. 1996. (Chelsea Ser.: Vol. 5). 260p. pap. 12.95 (*0-9643250-3-9*) CJH Enterprises.

Tindall, Gillian. The Journey of Martin Nadaud: A Life & Turbulent Times. 2000. (Illus.). 320p. 23.95 (*0-312-26185-3*) St. Martin's Pr.

Tolkien, Simon. Final Witness: A Novel. 2002. 304p. 24.95 (*0-375-50882-1*) Random Hse., Inc.

Warren, Robert Penn. All the King's Men. 15.95 (*0-8488-1504-1*) Amereon, Ltd.

—All the King's Men. 1981. 350p. reprint ed. lib. bdg. 35.95 (*0-89966-290-0*) Buccaneer Bks., Inc.

—All the King's Men. 1961. per. 6.50 (*0-8222-0018-X*) Dramatists Play Service, Inc.

—All the King's Men. Polk, Noel, ed. 656p. 2002. pap. 15.00 (*0-15-601295-2*, Harvest Bks.); 2001. 30.00 (*0-15-100610-5*) Harcourt Trade Pubs.

—All the King's Men. (HBJ Book Ser.). 1990. 540p. 19.00 (*0-15-104772-3*); 1983. 438p. pap. 11.00 o.s.i (*0-15-604762-4*, Harvest Bks.); 2nd anniv. ed. 1996. 456p. pap. 14.00 (*0-15-600480-1*, Harvest Bks.) Harcourt Trade Pubs.

—All the King's Men. 2nd ed. 1996. 20.05 (*0-606-00317-7*) Turtleback Bks.

—All the King's Men Play. 1960. 15.95 o.s.i (*0-394-40502-1*) Random Hse., Inc.

Weiss, Phillip. Cock-a-Doodle-Doo. 1995. 256p. 21.00 o.p. (*0-374-12515-5*) Farrar, Straus & Giroux.

—Cock-A-Doodle-Doo. 1996. 304p. pap. 12.95 o.p. (*0-312-14100-9*, Saint Martin's Griffin) St. Martin's Pr.

Yglesias, Jose. Double Double. 2000. (Pioneer Ser.). 200p. pap. 12.95 (*1-55885-272-7*) Arte Publico Pr.

—Double Double. 1974. reprint ed. pap. 8.95 o.p. (*0-89197-737-6*) Irvington Pubs.

## PRESIDENTS—FICTION

Alexander, Lawrence. The Strenuous Life. 1991. 304p. pap. 4.99 (*1-56129-236-2*) Knightsbridge Publishing.

Allan, Clarke. The First Man to Be First Lady. 1999. 309p. pap. 17.95 (*0-7414-0157-6*) Buy Bks. on the Web.Com.

Archer, Jeffrey. Shall We Tell the President? 1985. 228p. mass mkt. 3.95 o.s.i (*0-449-20806-0*); 1983. mass mkt. 3.50 o.s.i (*0-449-20320-4*); 1982. mass mkt. 2.95 o.s.i (*0-449-20065-5*); 1982. mass mkt. 2.95 o.s.i (*0-449-23686-2*) Ballantine Bks. (Fawcett).

—Shall We Tell the President? l.t. ed. 1987. 415p. 17.95 o.p. (*0-8161-4311-0*, Macmillan Reference USA) Gale Group.

—Shall We Tell the President? 1999. 336p. mass mkt. 6.99 (*0-06-101370-6*) HarperCollins Pubs.

—Shall We Tell the President? 1987. 288p. mass mkt. 5.50 (*0-671-63305-8*, Pocket) Simon & Schuster.

—Shall We Tell the President? 1977. 8.95 o.p. (*0-670-63934-6*) Viking Penguin.

Baldacci, David. Absolute Power. 1996. 528p. reprint ed. mass mkt. 7.99 (*0-446-60358-9*) Warner Bks., Inc.

Baruth, Philip E. The X President. 2003. 384p. pap. 11.95 (*0-553-80294-1*); E-Book (*0-553-89811-6*) Bantam Bks.

Bly, Stephen A. The Senator's Other Daughter. 2001. (Belles of Lordsburg Ser.: Vol. 1). 236p. pap. 10.99 (*1-58134-236-5*) Crossway Bks.

—The Senator's Other Daughter. l.t. ed. 2002. 420p. (Belles of Lordsburg Ser.: No. 1). pap. 16.95 (*1-4104-0035-2*, Walker Large Print); 26.95 (*0-7862-4026-1*) Gale Group.

Bowen, Marjorie. The Soldier of Virginia: A Novel on George Washington. 1997. pap. 12.90 (*0-921100-99-X*) Inheritance Pubns.

Braver, Adam. Mr. Lincoln's Wars: A Novel in Thirteen Stories. 2003. 320p. 23.95 (*0-06-008118-X*, Morrow, William & Co.) Morrow/Avon.

Brown, Dan. Deception Point. 2003. 576p. 17.95 (*0-7434-9030-4*, Atria); 2002. E-Book 9.99 (*0-7434-7543-7*, Atria); 2001. 384p. 25.00 o.s.i (*0-671-02737-9*, Atria); 2002. 576p. reprint ed. mass mkt. 7.99 (*0-671-02738-7*, Pocket) Simon & Schuster.

Brown, William Wells. Clotelle: Or, the Colored Heroine. 1977. (Black Heritage Library Collection). 11.95 (*0-8369-8517-6*) Ayer Co. Pubs., Inc.

—Clotelle: Or, the Colored Heroine. Wills, Susan, ed. rev. ed. 1998. (Illus.). 116p. (C). pap. 19.95 (*1-58112-899-1*) Dissertation.com.

—Clotelle: The Coloured Heroine. 1999. E-Book 2.49 (*1-58627-252-7*) Electric Umbrella Publishing.

Carr, Caleb. Killing Time: A Novel of the Future. E-Book 20.95 (*1-58945-534-7*) Adobe Systems, Inc.

—Killing Time: A Novel of the Future. l.t. ed. 2000. 368p. 25.95 (*0-375-43076-8*) Random Hse. Large Print.

—Killing Time: A Novel of the Future. 2001. E-Book 20.95 (*0-375-50648-9*) Random Hse., Inc.

Dick, Philip K. The Simulacra. 1976. 1.50 o.p. (*0-441-76701-X*) Ace Bks.

—The Simulacra. 2002. 224p. pap. 12.00 (*0-375-71926-1*, Vintage) Knopf Publishing Group.

Enright, Anne. The Pleasure of Eliza Lynch. 2003. 256p. 23.00 (*0-87113-868-9*, Atlantic Monthly Pr.) Grove/Atlantic, Inc.

Feldman, Ellen. Lucy: A Novel. 2003. 288p. 24.95 (*0-393-05153-6*) Norton, W. W. & Co., Inc.

Francis, Dick. Banker. 1998. pap. 6.99 (*0-449-45809-1*, Fawcett); 1986. 352p. mass mkt. 6.99 (*0-449-21199-1*, Fawcett); 1985. mass mkt. 4.50 o.p. (*0-449-21034-0*, Fawcett); 1984. mass mkt. 3.95 o.s.i (*0-449-20262-3*, Fawcett); 1984. mass mkt. 2.75 o.s.i (*0-449-20568-1*) Ballantine Bks.

—Banker. 1983. 14.95 o.p. (*0-399-12778-X*, G. P. Putnam's Sons) Penguin Putnam Bks. for Young Readers.

Frey, Stephen. The Legacy. 1998. 304p. 24.95 o.p. (*0-525-94207-6*) Dutton/Plume.

—The Legacy. l.t. ed. 1998. pap. 25.95 (*1-56895-664-9*, Wheeler Publishing, Inc.) Gale Group.

—The Legacy. 1999. 384p. reprint ed. mass mkt. 7.99 (*0-451-19015-7*, Onyx) NAL.

Galster, Michael & Sullivan, Michael. Blood Trail: A Novel. 1998. 312p. 19.95 (*0-915463-84-9*) Jameson Bks., Inc.

Green, Tim. The Fourth Perimeter. l.t. ed. 2002. 413p. 31.95 (*0-7862-3880-1*) Gale Group.

—The Fourth Perimeter. l.t. ed. 2003. 469p. 13.95 (*0-7862-3881-X*) Thorndike Pr.

—The Fourth Perimeter. 2003. 400p. mass mkt. 6.99 (*0-446-61251-0*); 2002. 352p. 24.95 o.p. (*0-446-52785-8*) Warner Bks., Inc.

Herman, Richard. The Last Phoenix. 2003. 496p. mass mkt. 7.99 (*0-06-103181-X*, HarperTorch); 2002. 448p. 25.95 (*0-06-620976-5*, Morrow, William & Co.) Morrow/Avon.

Higgins, Jack. Edge of Danger. 2001. 304p. 25.95 o.s.i (*0-399-14701-2*) Penguin Group (USA) Inc.

—Edge of Danger. l.t. ed. 2001. 341p. 29.95 (*0-7862-3171-8*); 32.95 (*0-7862-3170-X*); (*0-7540-1608-0*); (*0-7540-2464-4*) Thorndike Pr.

Hodges, La Merle. Presidents Marshal. 1991. (Unknown Marshal Ser.). 199p. pap. 13.95 (*1-58500-203-8*) 1stBooks Library.

Jeffers, H. Paul. The Adventure of the Stalwart Companions. 1978. 7.95 o.p. (*0-06-012248-X*) HarperCollins Pubs.

Karr, Kathleen. Dwight D. Eisenhower: Letters from a New Jersey Schoolgirl. 2002. (Dear Mr. President Ser.). (Illus.). 128p. (YA). 9.95 (*1-58837-007-0*) Winslow Pr.

Leithauser, Brad. The Friends of Freeland. unabr. collector's ed. 1997. Pt. 1. audio 72.00 (*0-7366-4003-7*, 4502-A); Pt. 2. audio 56.00 (*0-7366-4004-5*, 4502-B) Books on Tape, Inc.

—The Friends of Freeland. 1998. 528p. pap. 14.00 (*0-679-77270-7*, Vintage) Knopf Publishing Group.

Martin, William. Citizen Washington. 2000. 680p. mass mkt. 7.99 (*0-446-60785-1*); 1999. 583p. 27.00 o.p. (*0-446-52172-8*) Warner Bks., Inc.

Nyznyk, Darryl. The Third Term. 1997. 354p. 24.95 (*0-9656513-4-7*) Cross Dove Publishing Co., Inc.

Patterson, Richard North. Balance of Power. 2004. 640p. mass mkt. 7.99 (*0-345-45018-3*); 2003. 624p. 27.95 (*0-345-45017-5*, Ballantine Bks.); 2003. E-Book 9.99 (*0-345-46988-7*, Ballantine Bks.) Ballantine Bks.

—Balance of Power. unabr. ed. 2003. audio 44.95 (*0-7393-0130-6*, Listening Library) Random Hse. Audio Publishing Group.

—Balance of Power. l.t. ed. 2003. 992p. 29.95 (*0-375-43208-6*) Random Hse. Large Print.

—No Safe Place. abr. ed. 1998. audio compact disk 27.50 o.s.i (*0-375-40305-1*, RH Audio) Random Hse. Audio Publishing Group.

Reilly, Matthew. Area 7. E-Book 18.95 (*0-312-70417-8*); 2003. 512p. mass mkt. 6.99 (*0-312-98322-0*, St. Martin's Paperbacks); 2002. (Illus.). 400p. 24.95 (*0-312-26685-5*) St. Martin's Pr.

—Area 7. l.t. ed. 2002. (Adventure Ser.). 839p. 29.95 (*0-7862-4350-3*) Thorndike Pr.

Roth, Philip. Our Gang. 2001. 224p. pap. 12.00 (*0-375-72684-5*, Vintage) Knopf Publishing Group.

—Our Gang. 1971. 7.95 o.p. (*0-394-47886-X*) Random Hse., Inc.

Roussel, Peter. Ruffled Flourishes: A Novel. 2002. 280p. pap. 24.95 (*1-57168-537-5*, Eakin Pr.) Eakin Pr.
Saint, David A. The Winnowing. 1998. xiv, 331p. 24.95 (*0-9662818-0-2*) Topsail Pr., Inc.
Sandlin, Tim. Honey, Don't. 2003. 368p. 24.95 (*0-399-14998-8*, Putnam & Grosset) Putnam Publishing Group, The.
Sargent, Dave & Sargent, Pat. Popcorn (Blue Corn) Work Hard #47. 2001. (Saddle Up Ser.). 36p. (J). pap. 6.95 (*1-56763-660-8*); lib. bdg. 22.60 (*1-56763-659-4*) Ozark Publishing.
Schorr, Mark. Bully! 1985. 192p. 12.95 o.p. (*0-312-10798-6*) St. Martin's Pr.
Shafferman, Barbara. The President's Astrologer. Hill, Connie, ed. 1998. (Illus.). 384p. pap. 12.95 o.p. (*1-56718-674-2*, K674) Llewellyn Pubns.
Sir Oliver Mockery. Hollow Victory. 1998. 71p. (Orig.). pap. 9.95 o.p. (*1-57197-077-0*) Pentland Pr., Inc.
Stone, Irving. The President's Lady. 1968. mass mkt. 2.95 o.p. (*0-451-12824-9*); mass mkt. 1.25 o.p. (*0-451-06379-1*); mass mkt. 1.95 o.p. (*0-451-07919-1*); mass mkt. 2.50 o.p. (*0-451-09595-2*); mass mkt. 0.95 o.p. (*0-451-03373-6*); mass mkt. 1.75 o.p. (*0-451-07274-X*); mass mkt. 0.95 o.p. (*0-451-05191-2*) NAL. (Signet Bks.).
—The President's Lady. 1996. 288p. pap. 14.95 (*1-55853-431-8*) Rutledge Hill Pr.
Tarloff, Erik. Face-Time. 2000. 256p. reprint ed. pap. 12.95 (*0-671-03978-4*, Pocket) Simon & Schuster.
Uris, Leon. A God in Ruins. 1999. 483p. 26.00 (*0-06-018377-2*); 656p. pap. 27.50 (*0-06-093304-6*) HarperCollins Pubs.
—A God in Ruins. Set. abr. ed. 1999. audio 25.00 (*0-694-52040-3*, HarperAudio) HarperTrade.
—A God in Ruins. 2000. 528p. mass mkt. 7.99 (*0-06-109793-4*, Avon Bks.) Morrow/Avon.
Vidal, Gore. Empire. 1988. 480p. mass mkt. 6.99 o.s.i (*0-345-35472-9*) Ballantine Bks.
—Empire. 2000. (International Ser.). 496p. pap. 16.00 (*0-375-70874-X*, Vintage) Knopf Publishing Group.
—Empire. 1989. 3.99 o.p. (*0-517-68969-3*) Random Hse. Value Publishing.
—Empire. ltd. ed. 1987. 512p. 100.00 o.p. (*0-394-56127-9*) Random Hse., Inc.
Wells Brown, William. Clotelle: Or, the Colored Heroine. 2000. per. 12.50 (*1-58396-520-3*) Blue Unicorn Editions.
Wilson, F. Paul. Deep As the Marrow. 1997. 352p. 24.95 o.p. (*0-312-86264-4*, Forge Bks.) Doherty, Tom Assocs., LLC.
Womack, Jack. Going, Going, Gone. 224p. 2002. pap. 13.00 (*0-8021-3866-7*, Grove Pr.); 2001. 24.00 o.p. (*0-8021-1685-X*) Grove/Atlantic, Inc.
Zelman, Aaron S. & Smith, L. Neil. Hope: How Would You Feel If You No Longer Feared Your Government...? vii, 440p. pap. 14.95 (*0-9642304-5-3*) Jews For The Preservation of Firearms Ownership, Inc.


## PRESIDENTS—UNITED STATES—FICTION


Baldacci, David. Absolute Power. 1996. 480p. 22.95 o.p. (*0-446-51996-0*) Warner Bks., Inc.
Beinhart, Larry. American Hero. 1994. mass mkt. 6.99 (*0-345-91246-2*); reprint ed. mass mkt. 6.99 (*0-345-36663-8*) Ballantine Bks.
Bowen, Marjorie. The Soldier of Virginia: A Novel on George Washington. 1997. pap. 12.90 (*0-921100-99-X*) Inheritance Pubns.
Brown, William Wells. Clotel or the President's Daughter: A Narrative of Slave Life in the United States. 1969. (American Negro). reprint ed. 27.95 (*0-405-01853-3*) Ayer Co. Pubs., Inc.
—Clotel or the President's Daughter: A Narrative of Slave Life in the United States. 2000. (Bedford Cultural Editions Ser.). (Illus.). xv, 527p. pap. text 8.50 (*0-312-15265-5*) Bedford/Saint Martin's.
—Clotel or the President's Daughter: A Narrative of Slave Life in the United States. 1985. (Muckrakers Ser.). reprint ed. pap. text 6.50 o.p. (*0-89197-701-5*); lib. bdg. 19.95 o.p. (*0-8398-0176-9*) Irvington Pubs.
—Clotel or the President's Daughter: A Narrative of Slave Life in the United States. 2000. (Bedford Cultural Editions Ser.). (Illus.). xv, 527p. 45.00 o.p. (*0-312-22758-2*) Palgrave Macmillan.
—Clotel or the President's Daughter: A Narrative of Slave Life in the United States. 2001. (Modern Library Classics). 256p. pap. 10.95 (*0-679-78323-7*, Modern Library) Random House Adult Trade Publishing Group.
—Clotel or the President's Daughter: A Narrative of Slave Life in the United States. 1996. (American History Through Literature Ser.). 216p. (C). 76.95 (*1-56324-803-4*); (Illus.). pap. 22.95 (*1-56324-804-2*) Sharpe, M.E. Inc.
Chase-Riboud, Barbara. Sally Hemings: A Novel. 1994. 416p. reprint ed. pap. 12.00 o.s.i (*0-345-38971-9*) Ballantine Bks.
—Sally Hemings: A Novel. 1992. 300p. reprint ed. lib. bdg. 37.95 (*0-89966-915-8*) Buccaneer Bks., Inc.
—Sally Hemings: A Novel. 1980. 416p. mass mkt. 4.95 (*0-380-48686-5*, Avon Bks.) Morrow/Avon.
—Sally Hemings: A Novel. 2000. 368p. pap. 14.95 (*0-312-24704-4*, Saint Martin's Griffin) St. Martin's Pr.
—Sally Hemings: A Novel. 1979. 12.95 o.p. (*0-670-61605-2*) Viking Penguin.
Cook, Paul. Siege at the White House. 2001. 191p. pap. 20.99 (*0-7388-4550-7*); E-Book 8.00 (*0-7388-9833-3*) Xlibris Corp.
Davis, Kent L. Abraham Lincoln: A Most Humble Instrument in the Hands of the Almighty. 1998. (Illus.). 900p. lib. bdg. 89.00 o.p. (*1-888106-87-5*, Agreka) Agreka Bks., LLC.
—Abraham Lincoln: A Most Humble Instrument in the Hands of the Almighty. 2002. 898p. pap. 24.95 (*0-9719091-0-5*) Smile Awhile Enterprises.
Ehrlich, Ev. Big Government. 1999. 304p. pap. 14.00 o.s.i (*0-446-67555-5*) Warner Bks., Inc.
—Grant Speaks. 416p. 2000. (Illus.). 25.95 (*0-446-52387-9*); 2001. reprint ed. pap. 13.95 o.s.i (*0-446-67655-1*) Warner Bks., Inc.
Flynn, Vince. Transfer of Power. 2001. 416p. E-Book 9.99 (*0-7434-4924-X*, Atria); 1999. (Illus.). 395p. pap. 24.00 (*0-671-02319-5*, Atria); 2000. (Illus.). 592p. reprint ed. mass mkt. 7.99 (*0-671-02320-9*, Pocket Star) Simon & Schuster.
—Transfer of Power. l.t. ed. 2004. 751p. 29.95 (*0-7862-5872-1*) Thorndike Pr.
Gifford, Thomas. Saints Rest. 1997. 448p. mass mkt. 6.99 o.s.i (*0-553-57226-1*) Bantam Bks.
—Saint's Rest. 1997. 448p. pap. 23.00 (*0-553-76269-9*, Crimeline) Bantam Bks.
Gold, Glen David. Carter Beats the Devil: A Novel. 2003. mass mkt. 7.99 (*0-7868-9004-5*); 2002. 496p. pap. 14.95 (*0-7868-8632-3*); 2001. 496p. E-Book 14.95 (*0-7868-7020-6*); 2001. 496p. E-Book 14.95 (*0-7868-7018-4*); 2001. 496p. E-Book 14.95 (*0-7868-7017-6*); 2001. 496p. E-Book 14.95 (*0-7868-7021-4*); 2001. 496p. E-Book 14.95 (*0-7868-7019-2*); 2001. (Illus.). 496p. 24.95 (*0-7868-6734-5*) Hyperion Pr.
Henrick, Richard P. Nightwatch. 1999. 336p. 23.00 (*0-380-97423-1*, Avon Bks.) Morrow/Avon.
Higgins, Jack. The President's Daughter. 2003. 320p. pap. 14.95 (*0-425-19294-6*); 1998. 320p. mass mkt. 7.99 (*0-425-16341-5*); 1998. mass mkt. 6.99 (*0-425-16542-6*) Berkley Publishing Group.
—The President's Daughter. l.t. ed. 1997. (Large Print Book Ser.). 26.95 o.p. (*1-56895-495-6*, Wheeler Publishing, Inc.) Gale Group.
—The President's Daughter. abr. ed. 1997. 25.00 o.p. (*0-7871-1358-1*, 695116); 35.00 o.p. (*0-7871-1458-8*, 895269) NewStar Media, Inc.
—The President's Daughter. 1997. 320p. 23.95 o.s.i (*0-399-14239-8*, G. P. Putnam's Sons) Penguin Group (USA) Inc.
Kilian, Michael. Major Washington. 1998. 349p. 25.95 (*0-312-18131-0*) St. Martin's Pr.
Leib, Franklin Allen. Behold a Pale Horse. 2000. 303p. 23.95 (*0-312-89064-8*, Forge Bks.) Doherty, Tom Assocs., LLC.
MacKinnon, Douglas. First Victim. 1997. 320p. 19.95 (*0-87131-824-5*) Evans, M. & Co., Inc.
Manning, Anne. Presidential Liaison. 2000. 227p. E-Book 3.99 (*1-58608-098-9*) New Concepts Publishing.
Nance, John J. Headwind. 2001. 400p. 24.95 o.s.i (*0-399-14713-6*) Penguin Group (USA) Inc.
—Headwind. l.t. ed. (Americana Ser.). 645p. 2002. 28.95 (*0-7862-3075-4*); 2001. 31.95 (*0-7862-3066-5*) Thorndike Pr.
Nevin, David. Eagle's Cry. 2001. 608p. reprint ed. mass mkt. 7.99 (*0-8125-2472-1*, Forge Bks.) Doherty, Tom Assocs., LLC.
—The Eagle's Cry: A Novel of the Louisianna Purchase. 2000. 448p. 25.95 (*0-312-85511-7*, Forge Bks.) Doherty, Tom Assocs., LLC.
Reginald, R. & Elliot, Jeffrey M. If J. F. K. Had Lived: A Political Scenario. 1982. (Borgo Political Scenarios Ser.: Vol. 1). 64p. pap. 13.00 (*0-89370-255-2*); lib. bdg. 23.00 o.p. (*0-89370-155-6*) Millefleurs.
Safire, William. Freedom: A Novel of Abraham Lincoln & the Civil War. 1988. mass mkt. 7.99 (*0-380-70584-2*, Avon Bks.) Morrow/Avon.
Salomone, William G. Madam President. 2000. 319p. pap. 12.95 (*1-58721-812-7*) 1stBooks Library.
Sheldon, Sidney. The Best Laid Plans. 1997. 375p. 25.00 (*0-688-14911-1*); 1997. 400.00 (*0-688-15642-8*); 1997. 464p. 28.00 (*0-688-15624-X*); 1924. o.s.i (*0-688-15923-0*) Morrow/Avon. (Morrow, William & Co.).
—The Best Laid Plans. unabr. ed. 1997. 35.00 o.p. (*0-7871-1472-3*, 895983);Set. 18.00 o.p. (*0-7871-1471-5*, 395982) NewStar Media, Inc.
—The Best Laid Plans. 1998. 384p. mass mkt. 7.99 (*0-446-60408-9*) Warner Bks., Inc.
Sir Oliver Mockery. Hollow Victory. 1998. 71p. (Orig.). pap. 9.95 o.p. (*1-57197-077-0*) Pentland Pr., Inc.
Sisman, Robyn. Special Relationship. 1995. 336p. 22.95 o.s.i (*0-525-93872-9*) Dutton/Plume.
Stewart, Mariah. The President's Daughter. 2002. 400p. mass mkt. 6.99 (*0-345-44739-5*, Ivy Bks.) Ballantine Bks.
Stone, Irving. The President's Lady. 1968. mass mkt. 1.75 o.p. (*0-451-07274-X*); mass mkt. 2.50 o.p. (*0-451-09595-2*); mass mkt. 2.95 o.p. (*0-451-12824-9*); mass mkt. 0.95 o.p. (*0-451-03373-6*); mass mkt. 1.95 o.p. (*0-451-07919-1*); mass mkt. 0.95 o.p. (*0-451-05191-2*); mass mkt. 1.25 o.p. (*0-451-06379-1*) NAL. (Signet Bks.).
—The President's Lady. 1996. 288p. pap. 14.95 (*1-55853-431-8*) Rutledge Hill Pr.
Thompson, Julian F., intro. The Great Novels of Anthony Trollope. 1995. 912p. pap. 10.95 o.p. (*0-7867-0182-X*, Carroll & Graf Pubs.) Avalon Publishing Group.
Thor, Brad. The Lions of Lucerne. 2002. 432p. 25.00 (*0-7434-3673-3*, Atria); (Illus.). 544p. reprint ed. pap. 6.99 (*0-7434-3674-1*, Pocket Star) Simon & Schuster.
—The Lions of Lucerne. abr. ed. 2002. audio 26.00 (*0-7435-2103-X*); audio compact disk 30.00 (*0-7435-2104-8*) Simon & Schuster Audio. (Simon & Schuster Audioworks).
Updike, John. Memories of the Ford Administration. 1996. 384p. pap. 14.00 (*0-449-91211-6*, Fawcett) Ballantine Bks.
Vidal, Gore. Lincoln: A Novel. 1988. mass mkt. 4.95 o.p. (*0-345-00885-5*); 1988. mass mkt. 4.95 o.p. (*0-345-00790-5*); 1985. 672p. mass mkt. 6.99 o.s.i (*0-345-31221-X*) Ballantine Bks.
—Lincoln: A Novel, Pt. 2. unabr. ed. 1993. (American Chronicles Ser.: Vol. 1). (Illus.). audio 80.00 Books on Tape, Inc.
—Lincoln: A Novel. 1995. reprint ed. lib. bdg. 37.95 (*1-56849-626-5*) Buccaneer Bks., Inc.
—Lincoln: A Novel. 2000. (Ace's Exambusters Ser.). 672p. pap. 16.00 (*0-375-70876-6*, Vintage) Knopf Publishing Group.
—Lincoln: A Novel. abr. ed. 1985. audio 16.00 o.s.i (*0-394-55043-9*, RH Audio) Random Hse. Audio Publishing Group.
—Lincoln: A Novel. 1998. 21.00 o.s.i (*0-679-60284-4*); 1993. 768p. 25.00 o.s.i (*0-679-60048-5*); 1984. 657p. 75.00 o.p. (*0-394-53889-7*) Random Hse., Inc.
Wilson, F. Paul. Deep As the Marrow. 1997. 352p. 24.95 o.p. (*0-312-86264-4*, Forge Bks.) Doherty, Tom Assocs., LLC.


## PRIVATE INVESTIGATORS—FICTION


Abramo, J. L. Catching Water in a Net. l.t. ed. 2002. 367p. 28.95 (*0-7862-3996-4*) Gale Group.
—Catching Water in a Net: A Mystery. 2001. 224p. 22.95 (*0-312-28232-X*, Saint Martin's Minotaur) St. Martin's Pr.
—Clutching at Straws. mass mkt. (*0-312-98655-6*, St. Martin's Paperbacks); 2003. 240p. 22.95 (*0-312-30849-3*, Saint Martin's Minotaur) St. Martin's Pr.
—Clutching at Straws. l.t. ed. 2003. 400p. 28.95 (*0-7862-5824-1*) Thorndike Pr.
Acker, Kathy. Rip-Off Red, Girl Detective & the Burning Bombing of America. 2002. 208p. pap. 14.00 (*0-8021-3920-5*, Grove Pr.) Grove/Atlantic, Inc.
Adams, Douglas. Dirk Gently's Holistic Detective Agency. unabr. ed. 1997. 25.00 o.p. (*0-7871-1107-4*, 695351) NewStar Media, Inc.
—Dirk Gently's Holistic Detective Agency. 1990. 4.99 o.s.i (*0-517-02337-7*) Random Hse. Value Publishing.
—Dirk Gently's Holistic Detective Agency. 1991. 320p. mass mkt. 6.99 (*0-671-74672-3*, Pocket); 1989. 320p. mass mkt. 4.95 o.s.i (*0-671-69267-4*, Pocket); 1987. (Illus.). 264p. bds. 14.70 o.p. (*0-671-62582-9*, Simon & Schuster) Simon & Schuster.
—Dirk Gently's Holistic Detective Agency. abr. ed. 1987. audio 14.95 (*0-671-64724-5*, Simon & Schuster Audioworks) Simon & Schuster Audio.
—Dirk Gently's Holistic Detective Agency. 1987. 12.09 o.p. (*0-606-03771-3*) Turtleback Bks.
—The Long Dark Tea-Time of the Soul. 1991. 320p. mass mkt. 7.99 (*0-671-74251-5*, Pocket); 1990. 320p. mass mkt. 4.95 o.s.i (*0-671-69404-9*, Pocket); 1989. 17.95 o.p. (*0-671-62583-7*, Simon & Schuster) Simon & Schuster.
—The Long Dark Tea-Time of the Soul. 1988. 13.04 (*0-606-01764-X*) Turtleback Bks.
—The Salmon of Doubt: Hitchhiking the Galaxy One Last Time. 2003. 336p. pap. 13.95 (*0-345-46095-2*) Ballantine Bks.
—The Salmon of Doubt: Hitchhiking the Galaxy One Last Time. 2002. 336p. 24.00 (*1-4000-4508-8*, Harmony) Crown Publishing Group.
—The Salmon of Doubt: Hitchhiking the Galaxy One Last Time. abr. ed. 1997. pap. 24.95 o.s.i incl. audio (*0-7871-0401-9*, NewStar Pr.) NewStar Media, Inc.
—The Salmon of Doubt: Hitchhiking the Galaxy One Last Time. 1995. o.p. (*0-517-70117-0*) Random Hse., Inc.
—Two Complete Novels. 1994. 608p. 5.99 o.s.i (*0-517-11912-9*) Random Hse. Value Publishing.
Adams, Harold. The Barbed Wire Noose. l.t. ed. 1991. pap. 10.95 o.p. (*0-7927-0073-2*, C0125) BBC Audiobooks America.
—The Barbed Wire Noose. 192p. 1988. pap. 3.95 o.p. (*0-445-40727-1*); 1987. 15.45 (*0-89296-250-X*) Mysterious Pr.
—The Fourth Widow. 208p. 1987. pap. 3.50 o.p. (*0-445-40581-3*); 1986. 15.95 (*0-89296-231-3*) Mysterious Pr.
—The Man Who Met the Train. (Carl Wilcox Mystery Ser.: No. 7). 240p. 1989. pap. 3.95 o.p. (*0-445-40810-3*); 1988. 15.95 (*0-89296-251-8*) Mysterious Pr.
—The Man Who Missed the Party. l.t. ed. 1992. 18.95 o.p. (*0-7451-8330-1*); pap. 16.95 o.p. (*0-7927-1017-7*) BBC Audiobooks America.
—The Man Who Missed the Party. 1990. 192p. mass mkt. 4.95 o.s.i (*0-445-40885-5*, Mysterious Pr. Paperback Bks.) Warner Bks., Inc.
—The Man Who Missed the Party: A Carol Wilcox Mystery. 1989. 192p. 16.95 (*0-89296-252-6*) Mysterious Pr.
—The Missing Moon. 1983. 256p. mass mkt. 2.50 o.s.i (*0-441-53401-5*) Ace Bks.
—The Missing Moon. l.t. ed. 1991. 17.95 o.p. (*0-7451-9761-2*, C0076); 1990. pap. 15.95 o.p. (*0-7927-0216-6*, C0224) BBC Audiobooks America.
—The Missing Moon. 1988. 256p. mass mkt. 3.95 o.s.i (*0-445-40629-1*, Mysterious Pr. Paperback Bks.) Warner Bks., Inc.
—Murder. 1981. 256p. 2.50 o.s.i (*0-441-54706-0*) Ace Bks.
—Murder. l.t. ed. 1991. pap. 8.95 o.p. (*1-55504-839-0*, 102); 1989. 16.95 o.p. (*0-7451-9459-1*, 340) BBC Audiobooks America.
—Murder. 1988. 224p. mass mkt. 3.95 o.s.i (*0-445-40627-5*, Mysterious Pr. Paperback Bks.) Warner Bks., Inc.
—The Naked Liar. 1986. 15.95 o.p. (*0-89296-126-0*) Mysterious Pr.
—The Naked Liar. 1986. mass mkt. 3.95 o.s.i (*0-445-40126-5*, Mysterious Pr. Paperback Bks.) Warner Bks., Inc.
—A Perfectly Proper Murder: A Carl Wilcox Mystery. 1993. 18.95 (*0-8027-3237-2*) Walker & Co.
—A Way with Widows. l.t. ed. 1995. (Nightingale Ser.). 219p. pap. 17.95 (*0-7838-1144-6*, Macmillan Reference USA) Gale Group.
—A Way with Widows. (Carl Wilcox Mystery Ser.). 1999. 156p. pap. 7.95 (*0-8027-7574-8*); 1994. 142p. 18.95 (*0-8027-3190-2*) Walker & Co.
—When Rich Men Die. 1987. 240p. 16.95 o.s.i (*0-385-24005-8*) Doubleday Publishing.
—When Rich Men Die. l.t. ed. 1988. (Mainstream Ser.). 377p. reprint ed. lib. bdg. 19.95 o.p. (*1-55736-085-5*) ISIS Large Print Bks. GBR. *Dist:* Transaction Pubs.
—When Rich Men Die. 1988. 256p. pap. 3.50 (*0-380-70539-7*, Avon Bks.) Morrow/Avon.
Adams, Jane. Like Angels Falling. l.t. ed. 2002. 320p. pap. 24.95 (*0-7862-3691-4*) Gale Group.
Adler, Elizabeth A. All or Nothing. 2000. 368p. mass mkt. 6.99 (*0-440-23496-4*, Dell Bks.) Dell Publishing.
—All or Nothing. l.t. ed. 1999. 27.95 (*1-56895-825-0*, Wheeler Publishing, Inc.) Gale Group.
Aguilera, Carolina Garcia. One Hot Summer. 2003. 304p. pap. 12.95 (*0-06-000981-0*, Rayo) HarperTrade.
Albert, Neil. An Appointment in May: A Dave Garrett Mystery. 1996. (Dave Garrett Mystery Ser.). 288p. 20.95 (*0-8027-3279-8*) Walker & Co.
—Burning March. 1994. (Dave Garrett Mystery Ser.). 256p. 18.95 o.p. (*0-525-93718-8*, Dutton) Dutton/Plume.
—Burning March. 1995. (Dave Garrett Mystery Ser.). 256p. mass mkt. 4.50 o.s.i (*0-451-17860-2*, Signet Bks.) NAL.
—Cruel April: A Dave Garrett Mystery. 1995. (Dave Garrett Mystery Ser.). 272p. 19.95 o.s.i (*0-525-93719-6*, Dutton) Dutton/Plume.
—Cruel April: A Dave Garrett Mystery. 1996. (Dave Garrett Mystery Ser.). 272p. mass mkt. 5.50 o.s.i (*0-451-17861-0*, Signet Bks.) NAL.
—Cruel April: A Dave Garrett Mystery. l.t. ed. 1996. (Niagara Large Print Ser.). 336p. 29.50 o.p. (*0-7089-5826-5*, Ulverscroft) Thorpe, F. A. Pubs. GBR. *Dist:* Ulverscroft Large Print Bks., Ltd.
—The February Trouble: A Dave Garrett Mystery. 1994. (Dave Garrett Mystery Ser.). 256p. mass mkt. 3.99 o.s.i (*0-451-40417-3*, Signet Bks.) NAL.
—The February Trouble: A Dave Garrett Mystery. 1992. 235p. 19.95 (*0-8027-1244-4*) Walker & Co.
—The January Corpse. 1993. (Dave Garrett Mystery Ser.). 256p. mass mkt. 3.99 o.s.i (*0-451-40377-0*) NAL.
—The January Corpse. 1991. 192p. 18.95 (*0-8027-3206-2*) Walker & Co.
—Tangled June: A Dave Garrett Mystery. 1997. (Dave Garrett Mystery Ser.). 246p. 20.95 (*0-8027-3305-0*) Walker & Co.
Alder, Elizabeth A. All or Nothing. E-Book 6.99 (*1-930161-75-1*) Adobe Systems, Inc.

Allen, Conrad. Murder on the Caronia: A Mystery Featuring George Porter Dillman & Genevieve Masefield. 2003. 336p. 24.95 (0-312-28091-2, Saint Martin's Minotaur) St. Martin's Pr.

Allingham, Margery, et al. Canine Crimes. Mason, Cynthia, ed. 1993. 240p. (Orig.). mass mkt. 4.50 o.s.i (0-515-11250-X, Jove) Berkley Publishing Group.

Anaya, Rudolfo A. Rio Grande Fall. 1997. 352p. mass mkt. 6.99 (0-446-60486-0); 1996. 368p. 23.00 o.p. (0-446-51844-1) Warner Bks., Inc.

—Shaman Winter. 2000. 432p. mass mkt. 7.50 (0-446-60801-7); 1999. (Illus.). 374p. 30.00 o.p. (0-446-52374-7) Warner Bks., Inc.

—Zia Summer. 1996. 13.04 (0-606-17163-0) Turtleback Bks.

—Zia Summer. 1996. 368p. mass mkt. 7.50 (0-446-60316-3); 1995. 400p. (YA). 21.95 o.p. (0-446-51843-3) Warner Bks., Inc.

Ashwood-Collins, Anna. Red Roses for a Dead Trucker. E-Book 5.95 (0-9712538-2-X); 2002. 210p. pap. 16.95 (0-9712538-4-6) Pendulum Pr.

Atkins, Ace. Dark End of the Street. 2004. 416p. mass mkt. 7.50 (0-06-000461-4, HarperTorch); 2002. 336p. 23.95 (0-06-000460-6, Morrow, William & Co.) Morrow/Avon.

Babcock, Richard. Bow's Boy: A Novel. 2003. 336p. pap. 14.00 (0-7432-2728-X, Scribner) Simon & Schuster.

Babula, William. According to St. John. 2000. (Jeremiah St. John Detective Ser.: Vol. 2). 240p. pap. 12.95 (1-58345-501-9) Domhan Bks.

—St. John & the Seven Veils. 2000. (Jeremiah St. John Detective Ser.: Vol. 3). 208p. pap. 12.95 (1-58345-506-X) Domhan Bks.

—St. John's Baptism. 2000. (Jeremiah St. John Detective Ser.: Vol. 1). 260p. pap. 12.95 (1-58345-496-9) Domhan Bks.

—St. John's Bestiary. 2000. (Jeremiah St. John Detective Ser.: Vol. 4). 264p. pap. 12.95 (1-58345-511-6) Domhan Bks.

—St. John's Bestiary. 1994. 264p. 19.95 o.p. (1-885173-01-6) Write Way Publishing.

Baker, John. Poet in the Gutter. 1996. 240p. 21.95 o.p. (0-312-14393-1, Saint Martin's Minotaur) St. Martin's Pr.

Baldacci, David. Saving Faith. l.t. ed. 1999. pap. 25.00 o.p. (0-7838-8700-0, Macmillan Reference USA) Gale Group.

—Saving Faith. l.t. ed. 576p. 2000. pap. 13.95 (0-375-72798-1); 1999. 26.95 (0-375-40866-5) Random Hse. Large Print.

—Saving Faith. 2000. 528p. E-Book 7.95 (0-446-92262-5); 2000. E-Book 7.95 (0-446-93135-7, Warner Vision); 2000. 528p. E-Book 7.95 (0-446-92868-2); 2000. 528p. E-Book 7.95 (0-446-96096-9); 2000. 528p. E-Book 7.95 (0-446-92401-6); 1999. 464p. 26.95 (0-446-52577-4); 1999. 464p. mass mkt. 16.00 (0-446-67647-0); 2000. 528p. reprint ed. mass mkt. 7.99 (0-446-60889-0) Warner Bks., Inc.

Bannister, Jo. Echoes of Lies. 2001. 320p. 23.95 (0-312-28432-2, Saint Martin's Minotaur) St. Martin's Pr.

—True Witness. l.t. ed. 2003. (Magna Large Print Ser.). 416p. (0-7505-2013-2) Magna Large Print Bks. GBR. *Dist:* Ulverscroft Large Print Canada, Ltd.

—True Witness. Date not set. pap. (0-312-30818-3, Saint Martin's Griffin); mass mkt. (0-312-98645-9, St. Martin's Paperbacks); E-Book 23.95 (0-312-70924-2); 2002. 304p. 23.95 (0-312-30817-5, Saint Martin's Minotaur) St. Martin's Pr.

Banville, Vincent. Cannon Law. 2002. 300p. pap. 14.95 (1-902602-61-7) New Island Bks. IRL. *Dist:* Dufour Editions, Inc.

Barnao, Jack. Hammerlocke. 1987. 256p. 3.50 o.s.i (0-441-31609-3, Diamond Bks.) Berkley Publishing Group.

—Hammerlocke. 1986. 240p. 13.95 o.s.i (0-684-18683-7, Macmillan Reference USA) Gale Group.

—Lockestep. 1989. 3.50 (1-55773-159-4, Diamond Bks.) Berkley Publishing Group.

—Lockestep. 1988. (John Locke Mystery Ser.). 240p. 15.95 o.s.i (0-684-18782-5, Macmillan Reference USA) Gale Group.

—Lockestep. 186p. 2002. pap. 6.99 (0-7592-1432-8); 2002. E-Book 6.99 (0-7592-1430-1); 2002. E-Book 6.99 (0-7592-1429-8); 2001. E-Book 6.99 (0-7592-1428-X) ereads.com.

—Timelocke: A John Locke Mystery. 1991. 256p. 18.95 o.s.i (0-684-19298-5, Scribner) Simon & Schuster.

Barnes, Linda. Cold Case. 1998. 496p. mass mkt. 5.99 o.s.i (0-440-21226-X, Dell Bks.) Dell Publishing.

—Cold Case. l.t. ed. 1997. (Large Print Book Ser.). 27.95 (1-56895-427-1, Wheeler Publishing, Inc.) Gale Group.

—Coyote. 1991. 304p. mass mkt. 5.99 o.s.i (0-440-21089-5) Dell Publishing.

—Coyote. l.t. ed. 1991. (General Ser.). 332p. lib. bdg. 20.95 (0-8161-5197-0, Macmillan Reference USA) Gale Group.

—Coyote. unabr. ed. 1994. audio. (Carlotta Carlyle Mysteries Ser. : No. 3). audio 44.00 (0-7887-0036-7, 94235E7) Recorded Bks., LLC.

—Flashpoint. l.t. ed. 2000. (Wheeler Large Print Book Ser.). 354p. 26.95 (1-56895-856-0, Wheeler Publishing, Inc.) Gale Group.

—Flashpoint. 2001. 432p. mass mkt. 6.99 (0-7868-8948-9); 1999. 288p. 22.95 (0-7868-6317-X) Hyperion Pr.

—Hardware. 1996. 400p. mass mkt. 5.99 o.s.i (0-440-21223-5) Dell Publishing.

—Hardware. unabr. ed. 2000. (Carlotta Carlyle Mysteries Ser. : No. 6). audio 70.00 (0-7887-0262-9, 94471E7) Recorded Bks., LLC.

—The Snake Tattoo. 1990. 208p. mass mkt. 5.99 o.s.i (0-449-21759-0, Fawcett) Ballantine Bks.

—The Snake Tattoo. l.t. ed. 1990. (General Ser.). 350p. lib. bdg. 19.95 o.p. (0-8161-4866-X, Macmillan Reference USA) Gale Group.

—The Snake Tattoo. unabr. ed. 1993. (Carlotta Carlyle Mysteries Ser. : No. 2). audio 44.00 (1-55690-923-3, 93419E7) Recorded Bks., LLC.

—The Snake Tattoo. 2004. 320p. mass mkt. 6.99 (0-312-99355-2, St. Martin's Paperbacks); 1989. 288p. 17.95 o.p. (0-312-02643-9) St. Martin's Pr.

—Snapshot. 1994. 400p. mass mkt. 5.99 o.s.i (0-440-21220-0) Dell Publishing.

—Snapshot. l.t. ed. 1994. (Magna Large Print Ser.). 530p. (0-7505-0706-3) Magna Large Print Bks. GBR. *Dist:* Ulverscroft Large Print Canada, Ltd.

—Snapshot. unabr. ed. 1994. (Carlotta Carlyle Mysteries Ser. : No. 5). audio 70.00 (1-55690-969-1, 94112E7) Recorded Bks., LLC.

—Steel Guitar. 1992. 272p. pap. 19.00 o.s.i (0-440-61399-X); mass mkt. 5.99 o.s.i (0-440-21268-5) Dell Publishing.

—Steel Guitar. unabr. ed. 1993. (Carlotta Carlyle Mysteries Ser. : No. 4). audio 44.00 (1-55690-787-7, 93102E7) Recorded Bks., LLC.

—A Trouble of Fools. 1988. mass mkt. 5.99 o.s.i (0-449-21640-3, Fawcett) Ballantine Bks.

—A Trouble of Fools. l.t. ed. 1989. (General Ser.). 370p. lib. bdg. 19.95 o.p. (0-8161-4714-0, Macmillan Reference USA) Gale Group.

—A Trouble of Fools. 2001. 224p. mass mkt. 4.50 (0-7868-8953-5) Hyperion Pr.

—A Trouble of Fools. unabr. ed. 2000. (Carlotta Carlyle Mysteries Ser. : No. 1). audio 51.00 (1-55690-834-2, 93202E7) Recorded Bks., LLC.

—A Trouble of Fools. 1987. 228p. 15.95 o.p. (0-312-01100-8) St. Martin's Pr.

Barre, Richard. Bearing Secrets: A Wil Hardesty Mystery. 1998. (Wil Hardesty Ser.: Vol. 2). 288p. reprint ed. mass mkt. 5.99 o.s.i (0-425-16641-4) Berkley Publishing Group.

—Bearing Secrets: A Wil Hardesty Mystery. 1996. (Wil Hardesty Ser.). 312p. 22.95 (0-8027-3280-1) Walker & Co.

—Blackheart Highway. (Wil Hardesty Ser.: Vol. 4). 2000. 326p. mass mkt. 6.99 o.s.i (0-425-17467-0); 1999. 336p. 21.95 o.s.i (0-425-16903-0, Prime Crime) Berkley Publishing Group.

—Burning Moon: A Wil Hardesty Novel. 2003. (Illus.). 330p. 25.95 (1-59266-011-8) Capra Pr.

—The Ghosts of Morning: A Will Hardesty Mystery. 1998. 336p. 21.95 o.s.i (0-425-16300-8); 1999. 320p. reprint ed. mass mkt. 6.50 o.s.i (0-425-16931-6, Prime Crime) Berkley Publishing Group.

—The Innocents. 1997. (Wil Hardesty Ser.: Vol. 1). 288p. mass mkt. 6.50 o.s.i (0-425-16109-9, Prime Crime) Berkley Publishing Group.

—The Innocents. 1995. 332p. 19.95 (0-8027-3261-5) Walker & Co.

Beck, K. K. Amateur Night: A Jane Da Silva Mystery. 1993. 288p. 18.95 (0-89296-480-4) Mysterious Pr.

—Amateur Night: A Jane Da Silva Mystery. 1994. 256p. mass mkt. 5.50 o.s.i (0-446-40145-5) Warner Bks., Inc.

—Cold Smoked: A Jane Da Silva Mystery. 1995. 320p. 18.95 o.s.i (0-89296-537-1) Mysterious Pr.

—Cold Smoked: A Jane Da Silva Mystery. 1996. (Jane da Silva Mystery Ser.). 240p. mass mkt. 5.99 (0-446-40351-2) Warner Bks., Inc.

—Electric City: A Jane Da Silva Mystery. 1994. 304p. 18.95 o.s.i (0-89296-536-3) Mysterious Pr.

—Electric City: A Jane Da Silva Mystery. 1995. 224p. mass mkt. 5.50 (0-446-40350-4) Warner Bks., Inc.

—A Hopeless Case. 1992. 18.95 o.p. (0-89296-479-0) Mysterious Pr.

—A Hopeless Case. 1993. 272p. mass mkt. 4.99 o.s.i (0-446-40144-7) Warner Bks., Inc.

Beinhart, Larry. Foreign Exchange. 1992. mass mkt. 5.99 o.s.i (0-345-36665-4) Ballantine Bks.

—No One Rides for Free. 1993. mass mkt. 4.99 o.s.i (0-345-37294-8) Ballantine Bks.

—No One Rides for Free. 1987. 240p. pap. 3.95 (0-380-70283-5, Avon Bks.); 1986. 256p. 16.95 o.p. (0-688-06057-9, Morrow, William & Co.) Morrow/Avon.

—You Get What You Pay For. 1989. 368p. mass mkt. 4.95 o.s.i (0-345-36406-6) Ballantine Bks.

—You Get What You Pay For. 1988. 356p. 18.95 o.p. (0-688-06613-5, Morrow, William & Co.) Morrow/Avon.

Benjamin, Carol Lea. The Dog Who Knew Too Much: A Rachel Alexander & Dash Mystery. 1998. (Rachel Alexander & Dash Mystery Ser.: Vol. 2). 272p. reprint ed. mass mkt. 5.99 o.s.i (0-440-22637-6) Dell Publishing.

—The Dog Who Knew Too Much: A Rachel Alexander & Dash Mystery. 1997. (Rachel Alexander & Dash Mystery Ser.). 256p. 21.95 (0-8027-3312-3) Walker & Co.

—A Hell of a Dog. 1998. (Rachel Alexander & Dash Mystery Ser.). (Illus.). 276p. 22.95 (0-8027-3325-5) Walker & Co.

—A Hell of a Dog: A Rachel Alexander & Dash Mystery. 1999. (Rachel Alexander & Dash Mystery Ser.). 320p. mass mkt. 5.99 (0-440-22548-5) Dell Publishing.

—Lady Vanishes. 1999. (Rachel Alexander & Dash Mystery Ser.). 264p. 23.95 (0-8027-3335-2) Walker & Co.

—The Long Good Boy: A Rachel Alexander & Dash Mystery. 2001. 240p. 23.95 (0-8027-3364-6) Walker & Co.

—This Dog for Hire: A Rachel Alexander & Dash Mystery. 1997. (Rachel Alexander & Dash Mystery Ser.: Vol. 1). 304p. mass mkt. 6.50 (0-440-22520-5) Dell Publishing.

—This Dog for Hire: A Rachel Alexander & Dash Mystery. l.t. ed. 2002. 346p. 28.95 o.p. (0-7862-4191-8) Thorndike Pr.

—This Dog for Hire: A Rachel Alexander & Dash Mystery. 1996. (Rachel Alexander & Dash Mystery Ser.). 224p. 20.95 (0-8027-3292-5) Walker & Co.

Benjamin, Carol Lea & Sallis, James. The Long-Legged Fly: A Lew Griffin Novel. 2001. 200p. pap. 8.95 (0-8027-7620-5) Walker & Co.

Berger, Arthur A. Durkheim Is Dead! Sherlock Holmes Is Introduced to Social Theory. 2003. 200p. pap. 24.95 (0-7591-0298-8) AltaMira Pr.

Berger, Arthur Asa. Durkheim Is Dead! A Sherlock Holmes Mystery of Social Theory. 2003. (Illus.). 272p. 19.95 (0-7591-0300-3); 200p. pap. 70.00 o.s.i (0-7591-0299-6) AltaMira Pr.

Bergman, Andrew. Tender is Levine: A Jack Levine Mystery. 2001. 289p. 23.95 (0-312-26205-1, Saint Martin's Minotaur) St. Martin's Pr.

Berlinski, David. The Body Shop: An Aaron Asherfeld Mystery. 1996. 208p. text 20.95 o.p. (0-312-13935-7, Saint Martin's Minotaur) St. Martin's Pr.

—Less than Meets the Eye: An Aaron Asherfield Mystery. 1994. (Aaron Asherfeld Mystery Ser.). 208p. 18.95 o.p. (0-312-11298-X, Saint Martin's Minotaur) St. Martin's Pr.

—Less Than Meets the Eye: An Aaron Asherfield Mystery. 1994. 240p. 19.95 (0-312-10611-4, Saint Martin's Minotaur) St. Martin's Pr.

Birmingham, Ruth. Atlanta Graves. 1998. (Sunny Childs Mysteries Ser.). 288p. mass mkt. 5.99 o.s.i (0-425-16267-2) Berkley Publishing Group.

—Fulton County Blues. 1999. (Fulton County Blues Ser.: Vol. 2). 288p. mass mkt. 5.99 o.s.i (0-425-16697-X, Prime Crime) Berkley Publishing Group.

—Fulton County Blues. 2000. 12.04 (0-606-19296-4) Turtleback Bks.

—Sweet Georgia. 2000. (Sunny Childs Mysteries Ser.). 320p. mass mkt. 5.99 o.s.i (0-425-17671-1, Prime Crime) Berkley Publishing Group.

Black, Cara. Murder in Belleville: An Aimee Leduc Investigation. 2000. (Aimee Leduc Investigation Ser.). (Illus.). 341p. 23.00 (1-56947-211-4) Soho Pr., Inc.

—Murder in the Marais. 1999. (Aimee Leduc Investigation Ser.). 354p. 22.00 (1-56947-159-2) Soho Pr., Inc.

—Murder in the Marais: An Aimee Leduc Investigation. 2000. (Illus.). 360p. pap. 13.00 (1-56947-212-2) Soho Pr., Inc.

—Murder in the Sentier. (Illus.). 2003. 336p. pap. 13.00 (1-56947-331-5); 2002. 304p. 24.00 (1-56947-278-5) Soho Pr., Inc.

Black, Michael A. A Killing Frost. 2003. 270p. pap. 13.95 (1-4104-0131-6, Five Star Trade); 2002. 287p. 24.95 (0-7862-4309-0, Five Star) Gale Group.

Blanc, Nero. The Crossword Murder. 320p. 2000. mass mkt. 5.99 (0-425-17701-7); 1999. pap. 13.00 (0-425-16977-4, Prime Crime) Berkley Publishing Group.

—A Crossworder's Holiday. 208p. 2003. pap. 13.00 (0-425-19260-1); 2002. 22.95 (0-425-18733-0) Berkley Publishing Group. (Prime Crime).

—Two Down: A New Crossword Murder Mystery with Crosswords included. 2000. (Illus.). 304p. pap. 13.00 (0-425-17510-3, Prime Crime) Berkley Publishing Group.

Block, Lawrence. Chip Harrison Scores Again. 1997. (Chip Harrison Mysteries Ser.). 256p. mass mkt. 5.99 o.s.i (0-451-18797-0, Signet Bks.) NAL.

—Coward's Kiss. 1996. 160p. mass mkt. 3.95 (0-7867-0334-2, Carroll & Graf Pubs.) Avalon Publishing Group.

—Coward's Kiss. 1987. 160p. reprint ed. pap. 4.95 o.p. (0-88150-085-2) Countryman Pr.

—Coward's Kiss. 1999. (Mystery Ser.). 184p. pap. 19.95 (0-7862-2075-9, Five Star) Gale Group.

—Coward's Kiss. 2003. 224p. mass mkt. 4.99 (0-7434-5899-0) ibooks, Inc.

—A Dance at the Slaughterhouse. (Matthew Scudder Mystery Ser.: No. 9). 2000. 304p. pap. 13.00 (0-380-81373-4, Avon Bks.); 1991. 304p. 19.00 o.p. (0-688-10349-9, Morrow, William & Co.); 1992. 384p. reprint ed. mass mkt. 7.50 (0-380-71374-8, Avon Bks.) Morrow/Avon.

—A Dance at the Slaughterhouse. l.t. ed. 2000. (Matthew Scudder Mystery Ser.: No. 9). 468p. 28.95 (0-7862-2983-7) Thorndike Pr.

—The Devil Knows You're Dead. (Matthew Scudder Mystery Ser.: No. 11). 1999. 288p. pap. 12.50 (0-380-80759-9, Avon Bks.); 1993. 316p. 20.00 o.p. (0-688-12192-6, Morrow, William & Co.); 1994. 384p. reprint ed. mass mkt. 7.50 (0-380-72023-X, Avon Bks.) Morrow/Avon.

—The Devil Knows You're Dead. l.t. ed. 2001. (Matthew Scudder Mystery Ser.: No. 11). 503p. 30.95 (0-7862-3109-2); (0-7540-1578-5); (0-7540-2440-7) Thorndike Pr.

—Eight Million Ways to Die. 1986. (Matthew Scudder Mystery Ser.: No. 5). mass mkt. 3.50 o.s.i (0-515-08840-4); 1984. (Matthew Scudder Mystery Ser.: No. 5). 304p. mass mkt. 3.95 o.s.i (0-515-08090-X); 1983. mass mkt. 3.50 o.s.i (0-515-07257-5); 1983. mass mkt. 3.50 o.s.i (0-515-07537-X) Berkley Publishing Group. (Jove).

—Eight Million Ways to Die. l.t. ed. 2000. (Matthew Scudder Mystery Ser.: No. 5). 410p. pap. 24.95 (1-56895-939-7, Wheeler Publishing, Inc.) Gale Group.

—Eight Million Ways to Die. (Matthew Scudder Mystery Ser.: No. 5). 1982. 13.50 o.p. (0-87795-405-4, Morrow, William & Co.); 1993. 384p. reprint ed. mass mkt. 7.50 (0-380-71573-2, Avon Bks.) Morrow/Avon.

—Even the Wicked. (Matthew Scudder Mystery Ser.: No. 13). 1997. 328p. 23.00 (0-688-14181-1, Morrow, William & Co.); 1998. 400p. mass mkt. 7.50 (0-380-72534-7, Avon Bks.) Morrow/Avon.

—Everybody Dies. (Matthew Scudder Mystery Ser.: No. 14). 1999. 384p. mass mkt. 6.99 (0-380-72535-5, Avon Bks.); 1998. 336p. 25.00 o.p. (0-688-14182-X, Morrow, William & Co.) Morrow/Avon.

—Everybody Dies. l.t. ed. 1999. (Matthew Scudder Mystery Ser.: No. 14). 461p. 29.95 (0-7862-1706-5) Thorndike Pr.

—Hope to Die. l.t. ed. 2001. 480p. pap. 25.00 (0-06-621400-9) HarperCollins Pubs.

—Hope to Die. abr. ed. 2001. 32p. (ps-2). audio 25.95 (0-694-52604-5, HarperAudio) HarperTrade.

—Hope to Die. 2002. 400p. mass mkt. 7.99 (0-06-103097-X); 2001. 336p. 25.00 (0-06-019832-X) Morrow/Avon. (Morrow, William & Co.).

—In the Midst of Death. l.t. ed. 1991. (Matthew Scudder Mystery Ser.: No. 2). pap. 15.95 o.p. (0-7927-0601-3, AS0192); 17.95 o.p. (0-7451-8095-7, AH0156) BBC Audiobooks America.

—In the Midst of Death. 1989. (Matthew Scudder Mystery Ser.: No. 3). 192p. mass mkt. 3.50 o.s.i (0-515-08684-3); 1984. mass mkt. 2.95 o.s.i (0-515-08098-5); 1983. mass mkt. 2.95 o.s.i (0-515-07430-6); 1982. mass mkt. 2.75 o.s.i (0-515-06731-8) Berkley Publishing Group. (Jove).

—In the Midst of Death. 1976. (Matthew Scudder Mystery Ser.: No. 3). pap. 1.25 o.p. (0-440-14037-4) Dell Publishing.

—In the Midst of Death. 2002. E-Book 7.50 (0-06-052098-1); E-Book 7.50 (0-06-052094-9); E-Book 7.50 (0-06-052097-3); E-Book 7.50 (0-06-052096-5) HarperCollins General Bks. Group. (PerfectBound).

—In the Midst of Death. 1992. (Matthew Scudder Mystery Ser.: No. 3). 272p. mass mkt. 7.50 (0-380-76362-1, Avon Bks.) Morrow/Avon.

—A Long Line of Dead Men. (Matthew Scudder Mystery Ser.: No. 12). 1999. 304p. pap. 12.50 (0-380-80604-5, Avon Bks.); 1996. 368p. mass mkt. 7.50 (0-380-72024-8, Avon Bks.); 1994. 20.00 o.p. (0-688-12193-4, Morrow, William & Co.) Morrow/Avon.

—Make Out with Murder. unabr. ed. 1999. (Chip Harrison Mystery Ser.). audio 39.95 (0-7927-2291-4, CSL180, Chivers Sound Library) BBC Audiobooks America.

—Make Out with Murder. 1997. (Chip Harrison Mystery Ser.). 240p. mass mkt. 5.99 o.s.i (0-451-18798-9, Signet Bks.) NAL.

—No Score. unabr. ed. 2000. (Chip Harrison Mystery Ser.: Bk. 1). audio 54.95 (0-7927-2262-0, CSL 151) Chivers Audio Bks. GBR. *Dist:* BBC Audiobooks America.

Occupations

—No Score. 1996. (Chip Harrison Mystery Ser.). 277p. mass mkt. 5.50 o.s.i (*0-451-18796-2*, Signet Bks.) NAL.
—Out on the Cutting Edge. l.t. ed. 1995. (Matthew Scudder Mystery Ser.: No. 7). 330p. pap. 19.95 o.p. (*0-7838-1177-2*, Macmillan Reference USA) Gale Group.
—Out on the Cutting Edge. l.t. ed. 1995. (Magna Large Print Ser.). 348p. o.p. (*0-7505-0761-6*) Magna Large Print Bks. GBR. *Dist:* Ulverscroft Large Print Canada, Ltd.
—Out on the Cutting Edge. (Matthew Scudder Mystery Ser.: No. 7). 1989. 256p. 17.95 o.p. (*0-688-09069-9*, Morrow, William & Co.); 1990. 352p. reprint ed. mass mkt. 6.99 (*0-380-70993-7*, Avon Bks.) Morrow/Avon.
—The Sins of the Fathers. l.t. ed. 1990. (Matthew Scudder Mystery Ser.: No. 1). 17.95 o.p. (*0-7451-9866-X*, C0616); pap. 15.95 o.p. (*0-7927-0317-0*, C0810) BBC Audiobooks America.
—The Sins of the Fathers. mass mkt. 2.95 o.s.i (*0-515-08685-1*); 1988. (Matthew Scudder Mystery Ser.: No. 1). mass mkt. 3.50 o.s.i (*0-515-09831-0*); 1984. mass mkt. 2.95 o.s.i (*0-515-08157-4*); 1983. mass mkt. 2.95 o.s.i (*0-515-07516-7*); 1982. mass mkt. 2.75 o.s.i (*0-515-06729-6*) Berkley Publishing Group. (Jove).
—The Sins of the Fathers. 2002. E-Book 7.50 (*0-06-052108-2*); E-Book 7.50 (*0-06-052104-X*); E-Book 7.50 (*0-06-052105-8*); E-Book 7.50 (*0-06-052103-1*) HarperCollins General Bks. Group. (PerfectBound).
—A Stab in the Dark. 1989. (Matthew Scudder Mystery Ser.: No. 4). 192p. mass mkt. 3.50 o.s.i (*0-515-09885-X*); 1985. mass mkt. 2.95 o.s.i (*0-515-08635-5*); 1984. mass mkt. 2.95 o.s.i (*0-515-08158-2*); 1983. mass mkt. 2.95 o.s.i (*0-515-07399-7*); 1982. mass mkt. 2.75 o.s.i (*0-515-06717-2*) Berkley Publishing Group. (Jove).
—A Stab in the Dark. 2002. E-Book 7.50 (*0-06-052092-2*); E-Book 7.50 (*0-06-052091-4*); E-Book 7.50 (*0-06-052090-6*); E-Book 7.50 (*0-06-052093-0*) HarperCollins General Bks. Group. (PerfectBound).
—A Stab in the Dark. (Matthew Scudder Mystery Ser.: No. 4). 1981. 192p. 10.95 o.p. (*0-87795-340-6*, Morrow, William & Co.); 2002. 304p. reprint ed. mass mkt. 7.50 (*0-380-71574-0*, Avon Bks.) Morrow/Avon.
—A Ticket to the Boneyard. l.t. ed. (Matthew Scudder Mystery Ser.: No. 8). 1992. pap. 21.95 o.p. (*0-7927-1089-4*, CS0293); 1991. 23.95 o.p. (*0-7927-1088-6*, CH0221) BBC Audiobooks America.
—A Ticket to the Boneyard. l.t. ed. 1995. (Magna Large Print Ser.). 404p. (*0-7505-0911-2*) Magna Large Print Bks. GBR. *Dist:* Ulverscroft Large Print Canada, Ltd.
—A Ticket to the Boneyard. (Matthew Scudder Mystery Ser.: No. 8). 1990. 270p. 18.95 o.p. (*0-688-09070-2*, Morrow, William & Co.); 1991. 384p. reprint ed. mass mkt. 7.50 (*0-380-70994-5*, Avon Bks.) Morrow/Avon.
—Time to Murder & Create. 1984. (Matthew Scudder Mystery Ser.: No. 2). 192p. mass mkt. 3.50 o.s.i (*0-515-08159-0*, Jove) Berkley Publishing Group.
—Time to Murder & Create. l.t. ed. 1985. (Matthew Scudder Mystery Ser.: No. 2). 12.50 o.p. (*0-8166-0137-2*, Macmillan Reference USA) Gale Group.
—Time to Murder & Create. 1991. (Matthew Scudder Mystery Ser.: No. 2). 304p. mass mkt. 7.50 (*0-380-76365-6*, Avon Bks.) Morrow/Avon.
—The Topless Tulip Caper: A Chip Harrison Mystery, unabr. ed. 1999. (Chip Harrison Mystery Ser.). audio 39.95 (*0-7927-2303-1*, CSL192, Chivers Sound Library) BBC Audiobooks America.
—A Walk among the Tombstones. l.t. ed. 1993. (Matthew Scudder Mystery Ser.: No. 10). 431p. lib. bdg. 22.95 (*0-8161-5759-6*, Macmillan Reference USA) Gale Group.
—A Walk among the Tombstones. (Matthew Scudder Mystery Ser.: No. 10). 2000. 304p. pap. 12.50 (*0-380-81118-9*, Avon Bks.); 1992. 309p. 17.00 o.p. (*0-688-10350-2*, Morrow, William & Co.); 1993. 384p. reprint ed. mass mkt. 7.50 (*0-380-71375-6*, Avon Bks.) Morrow/Avon.
—A Walk among the Tombstones. 4.98 o.p. (*0-8317-8575-6*) Smithmark Pubs., Inc.
—When the Sacred Ginmill Closes. (Matthew Scudder Mystery Ser.: No. 6). 1990. mass mkt. 4.99 o.s.i (*0-515-10278-4*, Jove); 1987. 272p. 3.95 o.s.i (*0-441-88097-5*, Diamond Bks.) Berkley Publishing Group.
—When the Sacred Ginmill Closes. l.t. ed. 1987. (Matthew Scudder Mystery Ser.: No. 6). 361p. lib. bdg. 20.95 o.p. (*0-8161-4244-0*, Macmillan Reference USA) Gale Group.
—When the Sacred Ginmill Closes. 2002. E-Book 7.50 (*0-06-052101-5*); E-Book 7.50 (*0-06-052099-X*); E-Book 7.50 (*0-06-052100-7*); E-Book 7.50 (*0-06-052102-3*) HarperCollins General Bks. Group. (PerfectBound).
—When the Sacred Ginmill Closes. (Matthew Scudder Mystery Ser.: No. 6). 1997. 384p. mass mkt. 7.50 (*0-380-72825-7*, Avon Bks.); 1986. 15.95 o.p. (*0-87795-774-6*, Morrow, William & Co.) Morrow/Avon.
Bonansinga, Jay. Head Case. 1998. 318p. 23.00 (*0-684-82514-7*); 23.00 (*0-684-84931-3*) Simon & Schuster. (Simon & Schuster).
—Head Case. l.t. ed. 1998. (Core Ser.). 480p. 28.95 (*0-7838-0168-8*) Thorndike Pr.
Borton, D. B. Five Alarm Fire. 1996. 240p. mass mkt. 5.99 o.s.i (*0-425-15338-X*, Prime Crime) Berkley Publishing Group.
—Four Elements of Murder. 1995. 256p. (Orig.). mass mkt. 5.99 o.s.i (*0-425-14722-3*, Prime Crime) Berkley Publishing Group.
—One for the Money. 1993. 208p. 4.50 o.s.i (*1-55773-869-6*) Ace Bks.
—One for the Money. 1993. 208p. mass mkt. 4.99 o.s.i (*0-425-15328-2*) Berkley Publishing Group.
—Six Feet Under. 1997. 240p. mass mkt. 5.99 o.s.i (*0-425-15700-8*, Prime Crime) Berkley Publishing Group.
—Three Is a Crowd. 1994. 240p. (Orig.). mass mkt. 4.99 o.s.i (*0-425-14327-9*, Prime Crime) Berkley Publishing Group.
—Two Points for Murder. 1993. mass mkt. 4.99 o.s.i (*0-425-13947-6*) Berkley Publishing Group.
Bowen, Rhys. For the Love of Mike. Date not set. pap. (*0-312-31301-2*, St. Martin's Paperbacks); Date not set. mass mkt. (*0-312-99466-4*, St. Martin's Paperbacks); 2003. 320p. 23.95 (*0-312-31300-4*, Saint Martin's Minotaur) St. Martin's Pr.
Boyle, Alistair. Bluebeard's Last Stand: A Gil Yates Private Investigator Novel. 1998. (Gil Yates Private Investigator Ser.). 155p. 20.00 (*1-888310-45-6*) Knoll, Allen A. Pubs.
—The Con: A Gil Yates Private Investigator Novel. 1996. 222p. 19.95 (*0-9627297-9-5*) Knoll, Allen A. Pubs.
—The Missing Link: A Gil Yates Private Investigator Novel. 1995. 224p. 19.95 (*0-9627297-3-6*) Knoll, Allen A. Pubs.
—Ship Shapely: A Gil Yates Private Investigator Novel. 1999. 228p. 20.00 (*1-888310-99-5*) Knoll, Allen A. Pubs.
—The Unholy Ghost: A Gil Yates Private Investigator Novel. 2003. (Gil Yates Private Investigator Ser.: 7). 271p. 23.00 (*1-888310-67-7*) Knoll, Allen A. Pubs.
Bradbury, Ray. Let's All Kill Constance. 2003. pap. 13.95 (*0-06-051585-6*); 224p. 23.95 (*0-06-051584-8*) HarperCollins Pubs.
—Let's All Kill Constance. 2004. 256p. mass mkt. 7.50 (*0-06-056178-5*, Avon Bks.) Morrow/Avon.
—Let's All Kill Constance. l.t. ed. 2003. (Core Ser.). 28.95 (*0-7862-5523-4*) Thorndike Pr.
Braithwaite, Kent. The Wonderland Murders. 2000. 324p. pap. 14.95 (*1-891929-33-X*) Four Seasons Pubs.
Brewer, Steve. Baby Face. 2000. (Bubba Mabry Mystery Ser.). 256p. mass mkt. 5.95 (*1-890768-20-0*, Intrigue Pr.) Corvus Publishing.
—Baby Face. 1995. (Illus.). 256p. (J). mass mkt. 5.50 (*0-671-74735-5*, Pocket) Simon & Schuster.
—Dirty Pool. 2003. (WWL Mystery Ser.: No. 462). 272p. mass mkt. (*0-373-26462-3*, Worldwide Library) Harlequin Enterprises, Ltd.
—Dirty Pool. 1999. 272p. 23.95 o.p. (*0-312-20203-2*, Saint Martin's Minotaur) St. Martin's Pr.
—Lonely Street. unabr. ed. 1999. (Bubba Mabry Mystery Ser.). audio 39.95 (*1-55686-867-7*) Books in Motion.
—Lonely Street. 1999. (Bubba Mabry Mystery Ser.: No. 1). 256p. mass mkt. 5.95 (*1-890768-19-7*, Intrigue Pr.) Corvus Publishing.
—Lonely Street. Grad, Doug, ed. 1994. 224p. mass mkt. 4.99 (*0-671-74734-7*, Pocket) Simon & Schuster.
—Shaky Ground. 2003. (WWL Mystery Ser.: No. 454). 256p. mass mkt. (*0-373-26454-2*, Worldwide Library) Harlequin Enterprises, Ltd.
—Shaky Ground. 1997. 233p. 22.95 o.p. (*0-312-15652-9*, Saint Martin's Minotaur) St. Martin's Pr.
—Witchy Woman. 1996. 208p. 21.95 o.p. (*0-312-14076-2*, Saint Martin's Minotaur) St. Martin's Pr.
—Witchy Woman: A Bubba Mabry P. I. Mystery. 1999. (Bubba Mabry Mystery Ser.). 256p. reprint ed. mass mkt. 5.95 (*1-890768-13-8*, Intrigue Pr.) Corvus Publishing.
Brod, D. C. Masquerade in Blue. 1991. 208p. 19.95 (*0-8027-5792-8*) Walker & Co.
Brown, Fredric. Fabulous Clipjoint. 1986. 192p. pap. 8.95 o.p. (*0-87923-597-7*) Godine, David R. Pub.
—Hunter & Hunted Pt. One: The Ed & Am Hunter Novels. 2002. 640p. 29.99 (*0-9718185-0-9*) Stewart Masters Publishing, Ltd.
—Hunter & Hunted Pt. One: The Ed & Am Hunter Stories. ltd. ed. 2002. 640p. 79.99 (*0-9718185-1-7*) Stewart Masters Publishing, Ltd.
Bruen, Ken. The Guards: A Novel. 304p. 2004. pap. 12.95 (*0-312-32027-2*, Saint Martin's Griffin); 2003. 23.95 (*0-312-30355-6*, Saint Martin's Minotaur) St. Martin's Pr.
—The Killing of the Tinkers. Date not set. (*0-312-30357-2*); 2004. 256p. 22.95 (*0-312-30411-0*) St. Martin's Pr. (Saint Martin's Minotaur).
Bukowski, Charles. Pulp. deluxe ed. 1994. 200p. 40.00 o.p. (*0-87685-928-7*, Black Sparrow Pr.) Godine, David R. Pub.
—Pulp. 1998. reprint ed. 202p. 25.00 (*0-87685-927-9*); 208p. pap. 15.00 (*0-87685-926-0*) HarperCollins Pubs.
Burke, James Lee. Bitterroot: A Novel. 2001. 336p. 25.00 (*0-7432-0483-2*, Simon & Schuster) Simon & Schuster.
—Bitterroot: A Novel. l.t. ed. 2001. 560p. 25.00 o.s.i (*0-7432-1402-1*, Simon & Schuster) Simon & Schuster.
Calder, James. About Face. 2003. (Silicon Valley Ser.). 224p. pap. 11.95 (*0-8118-3680-0*) Chronicle Bks. LLC.
Calloway, Kate. Fifth Wheel: A Cassidy James Mystery. 1998. (Cassidy James Mysteries Ser.: No. 5). 256p. pap. 11.95 (*1-56280-218-6*) Naiad Pr., Inc.
—First Impressions: A Cassidy James Mystery. 1996. (Cassidy James Mysteries Ser.). 208p. (Orig.). pap. 11.95 (*1-56280-133-3*) Naiad Pr., Inc.
—Fourth Down: A Cassidy James Mystery. 1998. (Cassidy James Mysteries Ser.). 240p. (Orig.). pap. 11.95 (*1-56280-193-7*) Naiad Pr., Inc.
—Second Fiddle: A Cassidy James Mystery. 1996. (Cassidy James Mysteries Ser.). 224p. (Orig.). pap. 11.95 (*1-56280-161-9*) Naiad Pr., Inc.
—Seventh Heaven: A Cassidy James Mystery. 1999. (Cassidy James Mysteries Ser.). 230p. pap. 11.95 (*1-56280-262-3*) Naiad Pr., Inc.
—Sixth Sense: A Cassidy James Mystery. 1999. (Cassidy James Mysteries Ser.). 215p. pap. 11.95 (*1-56280-228-3*) Naiad Pr., Inc.
—Third Degree: A Cassidy James Mystery. 1997. (Cassidy James Mysteries Ser.). 256p. (Orig.). pap. 11.95 (*1-56280-185-6*) Naiad Pr., Inc.
Campbell, Robert. Alice in La-La Land. 1999. 232p. pap. 17.95 (*1-58444-024-4*) Disc-Us Bks., Inc.
—Alice in La-La Land. Chelius, Jane, ed. 1990. mass mkt. 4.95 (*0-671-73343-5*, Pocket) Simon & Schuster.
—Alice in La-La Land. 1987. 256p. 16.45 o.p. (*0-671-64483-1*, Simon & Schuster) Simon & Schuster.
—In La-La Land We Trust. 2000. E-Book 19.95 incl. cd-rom (*1-58444-076-7*); 1999. 230p. pap. 17.95 (*1-58444-051-1*) Disc-Us Bks., Inc.
—In La-La Land We Trust. 1986. 15.45 o.p. (*0-89296-170-8*) Mysterious Pr.
—In La-La Land We Trust. 1987. mass mkt. 4.95 o.p. (*0-445-40596-1*, Mysterious Pr. Paperback Bks.) Warner Bks., Inc.
—The La-La Land Quartet: Contains 4 Titles- Alice in La-La Land, in La-La Land We Trust, Sweet La-La Land, & Wizard of La-La Land. 2000. E-Book 24.95 incl. cd-rom (*1-58444-083-X*) Disc-Us Bks., Inc.
—Sweet La-La Land. 2000. E-Book 16.95 incl. cd-rom (*1-58444-075-9*); 1999. 232p. pap. 17.95 (*1-58444-050-3*) Disc-Us Bks., Inc.
—Sweet La-La Land. 1990. 18.95 o.p. (*0-671-64484-X*, Simon & Schuster) Simon & Schuster.
—Sweet La-La Land. Chelius, Jane, ed. 1991. 320p. reprint ed. mass mkt. 4.99 (*0-671-73236-6*, Pocket) Simon & Schuster.
—The Wizard of La-La Land. 1999. 244p. pap. 17.95 (*1-58444-052-X*) Disc-Us Bks., Inc.
—The Wizard of La-La Land. Chelius, Jane, ed. 1995. 288p. 20.00 o.p. (*0-671-70321-8*, Atria) Simon & Schuster.
Carlon, Patricia. Death by Demonstration. 192p. 2002. pap. 12.00 (*1-56947-257-2*); 2001. 22.00 (*1-56947-246-7*) Soho Pr., Inc.
—The Souvenir. 1996. 183p. pap. 12.00 (*1-56947-065-0*); 20.00 (*1-56947-048-0*) Soho Pr., Inc.
—The Souvenir. 2000. E-Book 12.95 (*1-86254-541-3*) Wakefield Pr. Pty, Ltd. AUS. *Dist:* BHB International, Inc.
Carter, Janice. The Real Allie Newman. 2002. (Harlequin Superromance Ser.: No. 1079). 304p. mass mkt. (*0-373-71079-8*, Harlequin Bks.) Harlequin Enterprises, Ltd.
Case, John. The Eighth Day. E-Book (*0-345-45872-9*); 2002. 384p. 25.95 (*0-345-43309-2*) Ballantine Bks.
—The Eighth Day. 2003. (Basic Ser.). 29.95 (*0-7862-5130-1*) Thorndike Pr.
Cebulash, Mel. Dirty Money. 1993. 3.95 (*1-56420-002-7*) New Readers Pr.
—Dirty Money: A Sully Gomez Mystery. 1993. (J). audio 10.95 (*1-56420-003-5*) New Readers Pr.
—Knockout Punch: A Sully Gomez Mystery. 1993. audio 9.95 o.p. (*1-56420-009-4*); 3.95 o.p. (*1-56420-008-6*) New Readers Pr.
—Set to Explode: A Sully Gomez Mystery. 1993. 3.95 o.p. (*1-56420-004-3*) New Readers Pr.
—Set to Explode: A/Sully Gomez Mystery. 1993. (J). audio 10.00 o.p. (*1-56420-005-1*) New Readers Pr.
—A Sucker for Redheads: A Sully Gomez Mystery. 1993. audio 9.95 o.p. (*1-56420-007-8*); 3.95 o.p. (*1-56420-006-X*) New Readers Pr.
Chambers, Peter. Lady, This Is Murder. 2000. 21.95 (*0-7540-8573-2*, Black Dagger) BBC Audiobooks America.
—Lady, This Is Murder. l.t. ed. 2000. (G. K. Hall Nightingale Ser.). 242p. pap. 20.95 (*0-7838-9257-8*); (*0-7540-4295-2*); (*0-7540-4296-0*) Gale Group. (Macmillan Reference USA).
—The Vanishing Holes Murders. l.t. ed. 2001. 201p. pap. 23.95 (*0-7838-9570-4*) Thorndike Pr.
—The Vanishing Holes Murders. l.t. ed. 1996. (Linford Mystery Library). 304p. pap. 17.99 o.p. (*0-7089-7942-4*, Linford) Thorpe, F. A. Pubs. GBR. *Dist:* Ulverscroft Large Print Bks., Ltd., Ulverscroft Large Print Canada, Ltd.
Chandler, Raymond. Adieu, Ma Jolie. 1988. Orig. Title: Farewell, My Lovely. (FRE.). 301p. pap. 11.95 (*0-7859-2102-8*, 2070380793) French & European Pubns., Inc.
—The Adventures of Philip Marlowe, Vol. 1. collector's ed. 1999. 34.98 incl. audio Radio Spirits, Inc.
—The Big Sleep. deluxe ltd. ed. 1986. (Illus.). 250p. 425.00 o.p. (*0-910457-09-3*) Arion Pr.
—The Big Sleep. 1975. 224p. mass mkt. 1.50 o.s.i (*0-345-24565-2*); 1973. mass mkt. 0.95 o.s.i (*0-345-22201-6*) Ballantine Bks.
—The Big Sleep. 1986. (Mystery Ser.). mass mkt. 9.95 o.p. (*0-553-06513-0*) Bantam Bks.
—The Big Sleep. 1994. reprint ed. lib. bdg. 29.95 o.p. (*1-56849-261-8*) Buccaneer Bks., Inc.
—The Big Sleep. l.t. ed. 2002. 232p. lib. bdg. 27.95 (*1-58547-164-X*) Ctr. Point Large Print.
—The Big Sleep. abr. ed. audio 15.95 o.p. (*0-88646-007-7*, 7009) Durkin Hayes Publishing Ltd.
—The Big Sleep. 1989. (Illus.). 256p. reprint ed. 22.95 o.p. (*0-86547-402-8*, North Point Pr.) Farrar, Straus & Giroux.
—The Big Sleep. Garrett, George P. et al, eds. 1989. (Film Scripts Ser.). reprint ed. pap. 19.95 (*0-89197-677-9*) Irvington Pubs.
—The Big Sleep. 1992. pap. 9.00 (*0-394-23906-7*); 1988. 240p. reprint ed. pap. 12.00 (*0-394-75828-5*) Knopf Publishing Group. (Vintage).
—The Big Sleep. abr. ed. 1993. 16.95 o.p. (*1-55800-690-7*); audio 29.95 o.p. (*1-55800-848-9*, 752391) NewStar Media, Inc.
—The Big Sleep. 1992. pap. 9.00 o.p. (*0-679-74091-0*); 1978. pap. 3.95 o.p. (*0-394-72631-6*) Random Hse., Inc.
—The Big Sleep. 2002. (Best Mysteries of All Time Ser.). 261p. (*0-7621-8880-4*, Impress) Scriptorium Pr., The.
—The Big Sleep. 1995. 288p. reprint ed. 35.00 (*1-883402-16-6*, Scribner) Simon & Schuster.
—The Big Sleep & Farewell, My Lovely. 1995. (Modern Library Ser.). 544p. 18.95 (*0-679-60140-6*) Random Hse., Inc.
—The Big Sleep & The High Window. abr. ed. 1999. audio 16.85 (*0-563-55892-X*) BBC Bk. Publishing GBR. *Dist:* Ulverscroft Large Print Bks., Ltd.
—La Dame du Lac. 1988. Orig. Title: Lady of the Lake. (FRE.). 258p. pap. 10.95 (*0-7859-2088-9*, 2070379434) French & European Pubns., Inc.
—Farewell, My Lovely. 1983. 256p. mass mkt. 2.25 o.s.i (*0-345-31528-6*, Ballantine Bks.); 1973. mass mkt. 0.95 o.s.i (*0-345-22202-4*) Ballantine Bks.
—Farewell, My Lovely. 1992. pap. 10.00 (*0-394-23907-5*); 1988. 304p. reprint ed. pap. 12.00 (*0-394-75827-7*) Knopf Publishing Group. (Vintage).
—Farewell, My Lovely. abr. ed. 1993. 16.95 o.p. (*1-55800-672-9*); audio 29.95 o.p. (*1-55800-769-5*) NewStar Media, Inc.
—Farewell, My Lovely. 1986. audio 14.95 o.p. (*0-394-55466-3*); 1985. audio 16.00 o.p. (*0-394-55048-X*) Random Hse. Audio Publishing Group. (RH Audio).
—Farewell, My Lovely. 1992. pap. 10.00 (*0-679-74090-2*); 1976. pap. 3.95 o.p. (*0-394-72138-1*) Random Hse., Inc.
—Farewell, My Lovely & The Lady in the Lake. abr. ed. 1999. audio 16.85 (*0-563-55897-0*) BBC Bk. Publishing GBR. *Dist:* Ulverscroft Large Print Bks., Ltd.
—La Grande Fenetre. 1989. Orig. Title: High Window. (FRE.). 276p. pap. 10.95 (*0-7859-2236-9*, 207038103X) French & European Pubns., Inc.
—Le Grande Sommeil. 1987. Orig. Title: Big Sleep. (FRE.). 252p. pap. 10.95 (*0-7859-2071-4*, 2070378659) French & European Pubns., Inc.
—The High Window. 1971. mass mkt. 0.95 o.s.i (*0-345-22203-2*) Ballantine Bks.
—The High Window. l.t. ed. 23.95 (*1-85695-367-X*) ISIS Large Print Bks. GBR. *Dist:* Transaction Pubs.
—The High Window. 1992. pap. 10.00 (*0-394-23908-3*); 1976. pap. 3.95 o.p. (*0-394-72141-1*); 1988. 272p. reprint ed. pap. 12.00 (*0-394-75826-9*) Knopf Publishing Group. (Vintage).

—The High Window. abr. ed. 1993. audio 15.95 o.p. (*1-55800-091-7*, 40290, Dove Audio) NewStar Media, Inc.

—Killer in the Rain. 1987. mass mkt. 3.95 o.s.i (*0-345-35185-1*); 1986. mass mkt. 2.95 o.s.i (*0-345-34195-3*); 1984. mass mkt. 2.50 o.s.i (*0-345-32020-4*); 1980. mass mkt. 2.25 o.s.i (*0-345-28858-0*); 1977. mass mkt. 1.95 o.s.i (*0-345-25728-6*) Ballantine Bks.

—Killer in the Rain & Other Stories. abr. ed. 1996. 24.95 o.p. (*0-7871-0555-4*, 693446) NewStar Media, Inc.

—The Lady in the Lake. Date not set. lib. bdg. 20.95 (*0-8488-2136-X*) Amereon, Ltd.

—The Lady in the Lake. 1976. (Crime Fiction Ser.). reprint ed. lib. bdg. 21.00 o.p. (*0-8240-2358-7*) Garland Publishing, Inc.

—The Lady in the Lake. l.t. ed. 23.95 (*1-85695-362-9*) ISIS Large Print Bks. GBR. *Dist:* Transaction Pubs.

—The Lady in the Lake. 1992. pap. 10.00 (*0-394-23909-1*); 1988. 272p. pap. 12.00 (*0-394-75825-0*); 1976. pap. 3.95 o.p. (*0-394-72145-4*) Knopf Publishing Group. (Vintage).

—The Lady in the Lake. abr. ed. 1993. audio 8.99 o.p. (*1-55800-916-7*); audio 15.95 o.p. (*1-55800-069-0*, 40240) NewStar Media, Inc. (Dove Audio).

—The Lady in the Lake. 1992. pap. 10.00 (*0-679-74088-0*) Random Hse., Inc.

—The Lady in the Lake. 1994. 288p. 35.00 (*1-883402-94-8*, Scribner) Simon & Schuster.

—Later Novels & Other Writings: The Lady in the Lake; The Little Sister; The Long Goodbye; Playback; Double Indemnity; Essays & Letters. MacShane, Frank, ed. 1995. 1088p. 35.00 (*1-883011-08-6*) Library of America, The.

—The Little Sister. l.t. ed. 1993. 21.95 o.p. (*0-7927-1654-X*); pap. 19.95 o.p. (*0-7927-1653-1*); audio 54.95 (*0-7451-5823-4*, CAB 057) BBC Audiobooks America.

—The Little Sister. 1985. mass mkt. 2.95 o.s.i (*0-345-32217-7*); 1983. mass mkt. 2.25 o.s.i (*0-345-31643-6*); 1977. mass mkt. 1.95 o.s.i (*0-345-25727-8*) Ballantine Bks.

—The Little Sister. 1988. (Vintage Crime Ser.). 256p. pap. 12.00 (*0-394-75767-X*, Vintage) Knopf Publishing Group.

—The Little Sister. abr. ed. 1993. pap. 15.95 o.p. incl. audio (*1-55800-082-8*, 40270) NewStar Media, Inc.

—The Little Sister. 1994. 256p. 35.00 (*1-883402-79-4*, Scribner) Simon & Schuster.

—The Little Sister. unabr. ed. 1983. (J). audio 49.95 o.p. (*0-8161-9777-6*) Thorndike Pr.

—The Long Goodbye. 1987. mass mkt. 3.95 o.s.i (*0-345-34938-5*); 1985. mass mkt. 2.95 o.s.i (*0-345-32132-4*); 1982. mass mkt. 2.50 o.s.i (*0-345-30582-5*); 1980. mass mkt. 2.25 o.s.i (*0-345-28859-9*); 1977. mass mkt. 1.95 o.s.i (*0-345-25734-0*) Ballantine Bks.

—The Long Goodbye. 1992. pap. 10.00 (*0-394-23910-5*); 1988. 384p. pap. 13.00 (*0-394-75768-8*) Knopf Publishing Group. (Vintage).

—The Long Goodbye. abr. ed. 1993. audio 15.95 o.p. (*1-55800-002-X*, 40010, Dove Audio) NewStar Media, Inc.

—The Long Goodbye. 1992. pap. 10.00 (*0-679-74087-2*) Random Hse., Inc.

—The Long Goodbye & The Little Sister. abr. ed. 1999. audio 16.85 (*0-563-55803-2*) BBC Bk. Publishing GBR. *Dist:* Ulverscroft Large Print Bks., Ltd.

—Midnight Raymond Chandler, 001. 1971. 10.25 o.p. (*0-395-13152-9*) Houghton Mifflin Co.

—Philip Marlowe. 1999. (Illus.). 416p. pap. 16.00 (*0-671-03890-7*) ibooks, Inc.

—Playback. 1987. mass mkt. 2.95 o.s.i (*0-345-32226-6*); 1987. mass mkt. 3.95 o.s.i (*0-345-34933-4*); 1984. mass mkt. 2.50 o.s.i (*0-345-31961-3*); 1980. mass mkt. 2.25 o.s.i (*0-345-28857-2*); 1976. mass mkt. 1.50 o.s.i (*0-345-25169-5*) Ballantine Bks.

—Playback. l.t. ed. 2001. (Dales Large Print Ser.). 240p. pap. 20.99 (*1-84262-094-0*) Dales Large Print Bks. GBR. *Dist:* Ulverscroft Large Print Bks., Ltd., Ulverscroft Large Print Canada, Ltd.

—Playback. 1988. (Vintage Crime Ser.). 176p. pap. 11.00 (*0-394-75766-1*, Vintage) Knopf Publishing Group.

—Playback. unabr. ed. 1993. pap. 24.95 o.p. (*1-55800-270-7*) NewStar Media, Inc.

—Raymond Chandler: Four Complete Philip Marlowe Novels. 1986. 8.99 o.s.i (*0-517-61811-7*) Random Hse. Value Publishing.

—Stories & Early Novels: Pulp Stories; The Big Sleep; Farewell, My Lovely; The High Window. MacShane, Frank, ed. 1995. 1216p. 35.00 (*1-883011-07-8*) Library of America, The.

—Trouble Is My Business. 1987. mass mkt. 3.95 o.s.i (*0-345-35494-X*); 1984. mass mkt. 2.50 o.s.i (*0-345-32021-2*); 1980. mass mkt. 2.25 o.s.i (*0-345-28862-9*) Ballantine Bks.

—Trouble Is My Business. 1992. pap. 9.00 (*0-394-23911-3*); 1988. 224p. pap. 12.00 (*0-394-75764-5*) Knopf Publishing Group. (Vintage).

—Trouble Is My Business. unabr. ed. 1993. audio 15.95 o.p. (*1-55800-090-9*, 40320, Dove Audio) NewStar Media, Inc.

—Trouble Is My Business. 1992. pap. 9.00 (*0-679-74086-4*) Random Hse., Inc.

—Un Tueur sous la Pluie. 1988. Orig. Title: Killer in the Rain. (FRE.). 245p. pap. 10.95 (*0-7859-2082-X*, 2070379108) French & European Pubns., Inc.

Chandler, Raymond & Parker, Robert B. Farewell, My Lovely & Poodle Springs. abr. ed. 1993. audio 17.95 (*1-55800-778-4*, Dove Audio) NewStar Media, Inc.

—Poodle Springs. 1990. (J). mass mkt. 7.50 o.s.i (*0-425-12343-X*) Berkley Publishing Group.

—Poodle Springs. abr. ed. 1993. audio 14.95 o.p. (*1-55800-168-9*, Dove Audio) NewStar Media, Inc.

—Poodle Springs. 1989. 18.95 o.p. (*0-399-13482-4*, G. P. Putnam's Sons) Penguin Putnam Bks. for Young Readers.

Chang, Leonard. Over the Shoulder. 2001. 400p. 26.00 (*0-06-019839-7*, Ecco) HarperTrade.

—Underkill: An Allen Choice Novel. 2003. 336p. 24.95 (*0-312-30843-4*, Saint Martin's Minotaur) St. Martin's Pr.

Chesbro, George C. An Affair of Sorcerers. 3rd ed. 1999. 352p. reprint ed. pap. 16.99 (*0-9674503-9-X*) Apache Beach Pubns.

—An Affair of Sorcerers. 1988. mass mkt. 3.50 o.s.i (*0-440-20047-4*) Dell Publishing.

—An Affair of Sorcerers. 1980. mass mkt. 2.25 o.p. (*0-451-09243-0*, E9243, Signet Bks.) NAL.

—An Affair of Sorcerers. 1979. 9.95 o.s.i (*0-671-24625-9*, Simon & Schuster) Simon & Schuster.

—The Beasts of Valhalla. 3rd ed. 1999. 336p. reprint ed. pap. 16.99 (*0-9674503-3-0*) Apache Beach Pubns.

—The Beasts of Valhalla. 1987. mass mkt. 3.95 o.s.i (*0-440-10484-X*) Dell Publishing.

—The Beasts of Valhalla. 1985. 352p. 15.95 o.s.i (*0-689-11516-4*, Scribner) Simon & Schuster.

—Bleeding in the Eye of a Brainstorm: A Mongo Mystery. 1995. 224p. 21.00 (*0-684-81495-1*, Simon & Schuster); 21.00 (*1-883402-67-0*, Scribner) Simon & Schuster.

—City of Whispering Stone. 3rd ed. 1999. 236p. reprint ed. pap. 16.99 (*0-9674503-1-4*) Apache Beach Pubns.

—City of Whispering Stone. 1988. pap. 3.50 o.s.i (*0-440-11259-1*) Dell Publishing.

—City of Whispering Stone. 1979. mass mkt. 1.95 o.p. (*0-451-08812-3*, J8812, Signet Bks.) NAL.

—City of Whispering Stone. 1978. 9.95 o.s.i (*0-671-24003-X*, Simon & Schuster) Simon & Schuster.

—The Cold Smell of Sacred Stone. 3rd ed. 1999. 304p. reprint ed. pap. 16.99 (*0-9674503-2-2*) Apache Beach Pubns.

—The Cold Smell of Sacred Stone. 1989. 304p. reprint ed. mass mkt. 4.50 o.s.i (*0-440-20394-5*) Dell Publishing.

—The Cold Smell of Sacred Stone. 1988. 320p. 16.95 o.s.i (*0-689-11913-5*, Scribner) Simon & Schuster.

—Dark Chant in a Crimson Key. 3rd ed. 1999. 224p. reprint ed. pap. 16.99 (*0-9674503-8-1*) Apache Beach Pubns.

—Dark Chant in a Crimson Key. 1992. 224p. 18.95 o.p. (*0-89296-463-4*) Mysterious Pr.

—Dark Chant in a Crimson Key. 1993. 224p. mass mkt. 5.99 o.p. (*0-446-40333-4*, Mysterious Pr. Paperback Bks.) Warner Bks., Inc.

—Dream of a Falling Eagle. 2002. 212p. per. 16.99 (*1-930253-14-1*) Apache Beach Pubns.

—The Fear in Yesterday's Rings. 3rd ed. 1999. 224p. reprint ed. pap. 16.99 (*0-9674503-5-7*) Apache Beach Pubns.

—The Fear in Yesterday's Rings. 1991. 18.95 o.p. (*0-89296-396-4*) Mysterious Pr.

—The Fear in Yesterday's Rings. abr. ed. 1991. audio 16.00 o.s.i Random Hse. Audio Publishing Group.

—The Fear in Yesterday's Rings. 1992. 224p. mass mkt. 4.99 (*0-446-40102-1*, Mysterious Pr. Paperback Bks.) Warner Bks., Inc.

—In the House of Secret Enemies. 1990. 240p. 18.95 o.p. (*0-89296-395-6*) Mysterious Pr.

—In the House of Secret Enemies. 1992. 240p. mass mkt. 4.99 o.p. (*0-446-40043-2*) Warner Bks., Inc.

—An Incident at Bloodtide. 3rd ed. 2000. 208p. reprint ed. 16.99 (*1-930253-00-1*) Apache Beach Pubns.

—An Incident at Bloodtide. 1993. 208p. 18.95 (*0-89296-464-2*) Mysterious Pr.

—An Incident at Bloodtide. 1994. 256p. mass mkt. 5.50 (*0-446-40054-8*, Mysterious Pr. Paperback Bks.) Warner Bks., Inc.

—The Language of Cannibals. 3rd ed. 1999. 208p. reprint ed. pap. 16.99 (*0-9674503-6-5*) Apache Beach Pubns.

—The Language of Cannibals. 1990. 208p. 18.95 o.p. (*0-89296-394-8*) Mysterious Pr.

—The Language of Cannibals. 1991. mass mkt. 4.95 o.p. (*0-446-40003-3*, Mysterious Pr. Paperback Bks.) Warner Bks., Inc.

—Second Horseman Out of Eden. 3rd ed. 1999. 256p. reprint ed. pap. 16.99 (*0-9674503-4-9*) Apache Beach Pubns.

—Second Horseman Out of Eden. 1989. 18.95 o.s.i (*0-689-11979-8*, Scribner) Simon & Schuster.

—Second Horseman Out of Eden. 1990. 256p. reprint ed. mass mkt. 4.95 (*0-445-40862-6*, Mysterious Pr. Paperback Bks.) Warner Bks., Inc.

—Shadow of a Broken Man. 3rd ed. 1999. 260p. reprint ed. pap. 16.99 (*0-9674503-7-3*) Apache Beach Pubns.

—Shadow of a Broken Man. 1987. mass mkt. 3.50 o.s.i (*0-440-17761-8*) Dell Publishing.

—Shadow of a Broken Man. 1983. mass mkt. 2.50 o.p. (*0-451-12013-2*, Signet Bks.) NAL.

—Shadow of a Broken Man. 1977. 7.95 o.p. (*0-671-22696-7*, Simon & Schuster) Simon & Schuster.

—Two Songs This Archangel Sings. 3rd ed. 1999. 256p. reprint ed. pap. 16.99 (*0-9674503-0-6*) Apache Beach Pubns.

—Two Songs This Archangel Sings. 1988. mass mkt. 3.95 o.s.i (*0-440-20105-5*) Dell Publishing.

—Two Songs This Archangel Sings. 1986. 320p. 14.95 o.p. (*0-689-11659-4*, Scribner) Simon & Schuster.

Chesney, Marion. Snobbery with Violence: A Mystery. 2003. 224p. 22.95 (*0-312-30451-X*, Saint Martin's Minotaur) St. Martin's Pr.

Child, Lee. Die Trying. 1999. 448p. reprint ed. mass mkt. 7.99 (*0-515-12502-4*, Jove) Berkley Publishing Group.

—Die Trying. 1998. 384p. 23.95 o.s.i (*0-399-14379-3*, G. P. Putnam's Sons) Penguin Group (USA) Inc.

—Echo Burning. l.t. ed. 2001. 510p. lib. bdg. 29.95 (*1-58547-135-6*) Ctr. Point Large Print.

—Echo Burning. 2001. (Illus.). 384p. 24.95 o.p. (*0-399-14726-8*) Penguin Group (USA) Inc.

—Killing Floor. 1998. 432p. mass mkt. 7.99 (*0-515-12344-7*, Jove) Berkley Publishing Group.

—Killing Floor. abr. ed. 2004. (Jack Reacher Ser.). audio compact disk 14.99 (*1-59355-558-X*, 5182, Brilliance Audio on CD Value Priced); audio 29.95 (*1-59355-557-1*, 5183, Brilliance Audio Unabridged) Brilliance Audio.

—Killing Floor. l.t. ed. 1998. pap. 23.95 (*1-56895-690-8*, Wheeler Publishing, Inc.) Gale Group.

—Killing Floor. 1997. 368p. 23.95 o.p. (*0-399-14253-3*, G. P. Putnam's Sons) Penguin Group (USA) Inc.

—Running Blind. abr. ed. 2000. audio 24.95 o.p. (*1-56740-906-7*, 2100, Nova Audio Bks.); audio 32.95 (*1-56740-362-X*, 2099); audio 73.25 (*1-56740-729-3*, 2101, Unabridged Library Editions) Brilliance Audio.

—Running Blind. 2000. (Jack Reacher Ser.). 360p. 18.95 o.s.i (*0-399-14623-7*) Penguin Group (USA) Inc.

—Tripwire. 2000. 432p. mass mkt. 7.99 (*0-515-12863-5*, Jove) Berkley Publishing Group.

—Tripwire. l.t. ed. 2000. (Wheeler Softcover Ser.). pap. 25.95 (*1-56895-912-5*, Wheeler Publishing, Inc.) Gale Group.

—Tripwire. 1999. 343p. 23.95 o.p. (*0-399-14467-6*, G. P. Putnam's Sons) Penguin Group (USA) Inc.

Churchill, Jill. The House of Seven Mabels: A Jane Jeffry Mystery. 2002. 240p. 23.95 (*0-380-97736-2*, Morrow, William & Co.) Morrow/Avon.

Clark, Carol Higgins. Decked: A Regan Reilly Mystery. 1993. (Super Sound Buy, Dove Ser.). 8.99 o.p. (*1-55800-804-7*); audio 16.95 o.p. (*1-55800-575-7*, Dove Audio) NewStar Media, Inc.

—Decked: A Regan Reilly Mystery. 1999. 288p. mass mkt. 4.50 o.s.i (*0-446-60777-0*); 1993. 288p. mass mkt. 7.99 (*0-446-36470-3*); 1992. 230p. 17.95 (*0-446-51549-3*) Warner Bks., Inc.

—Fleeced: A Regan Reilly Mystery. 2001. 272p. 22.00 (*0-7432-0581-2*); 320p. 22.00 (*0-7432-1661-X*) Simon & Schuster. (Scribner).

—Fleeced: A Regan Reilly Mystery. 1999. 272p. 22.00 (*0-446-52292-9*) Warner Bks., Inc.

—Iced. 1996. o.s.i (*0-316-87854-5*) Little Brown & Co.

—Iced. unabr. ed. 1995. 29.95 o.p. (*0-7871-0575-9*);Set. audio 17.95 o.p. (*0-7871-0220-2*, 392963) NewStar Media, Inc.

—Iced. 1999. 320p. mass mkt. 4.50 (*0-446-60778-9*); 1996. 320p. mass mkt. 7.99 (*0-446-60198-5*); 1995. 272p. 28.00 (*0-446-51764-X*) Warner Bks., Inc.

—Popped: A Regan Reilly Mystery. 2003. 288p. 23.00 (*0-7432-4937-2*, Scribner) Simon & Schuster.

—Snagged. l.t. ed. 1994. 22.95 o.p. (*0-7927-1915-8*); pap. 20.95 o.p. (*0-7927-1914-X*) BBC Audiobooks America.

—Snagged. abr. ed. 1993. (Regan Reilly Mystery Ser.). audio 16.95 o.p. (*1-55800-787-3*, 391606) NewStar Media, Inc.

—Snagged. 1994. 320p. mass mkt. 7.99 (*0-446-60076-8*); 1993. 227p. 28.00 (*0-446-51548-5*) Warner Bks., Inc.

—Twanged. l.t. ed. 1998. (Basic Ser.). 389p. 29.95 (*0-7862-1417-1*) Thorndike Pr.

—Twanged. 1999. 336p. mass mkt. 7.50 (*0-446-60536-0*); 1998. 272p. 28.00 (*0-446-51763-1*) Warner Bks., Inc.

Clark, Jack. Westerfield's Chain: A Mystery. 2002. 304p. 24.95 (*0-312-28960-X*, Saint Martin's Minotaur) St. Martin's Pr.

Clark, Mary Higgins, et al. Great Mysteries, Great Writers. abr. ed. 1994. audio 24.95 o.p. (*0-7871-0047-1*, 692220, Dove Audio) NewStar Media, Inc.

Cody, Liza. Backhand. 1992. 288p. mass mkt. 4.99 o.s.i (*0-553-29627-2*); mass mkt. 5.99 o.s.i (*0-7704-2531-3*) Bantam Bks.

—Backhand. unabr. ed. 1993. (Anna Lee Mystery Ser.: Vol. 6). audio 60.00 (*1-55690-808-3*, 93117E7) Recorded Bks., LLC.

—Backhand: An Anna Lee Mystery. 1992. 288p. 18.50 o.s.i (*0-385-42231-8*) Doubleday Publishing.

—Bad Company. 1983. 260p. 11.95 o.p. (*0-684-17760-9*, Macmillan Reference USA) Gale Group.

—Bad Company. 1992. pap. o.p. (*0-09-982120-6*) Hutchinson GBR. *Dist:* Random Hse. of Canada, Ltd.

—Bad Company. unabr. ed. 2000. audio compact disk 64.95 (*0-7531-0906-9*, 109069); 1997. audio 54.95 (*1-85695-740-3*, 940506) ISIS Audio Bks. GBR. *Dist:* Ulverscroft Large Print Bks., Ltd.

—Bad Company. 1984. 288p. mass mkt. 2.95 o.s.i (*0-446-30738-6*) Warner Bks., Inc.

—Dupe. 1992. mass mkt. 4.99 o.s.i (*0-7704-2439-2*); 256p. mass mkt. 4.99 o.s.i (*0-553-29641-8*) Bantam Bks.

—Dupe. 1981. 252p. 10.95 o.s.i (*0-684-17153-8*, Macmillan Reference USA) Gale Group.

—Dupe. 1992. pap. o.p. (*0-09-982110-9*) Hutchinson GBR. *Dist:* Random Hse. of Canada, Ltd.

—Dupe. 1984. mass mkt. 2.95 o.s.i (*0-446-30527-8*) Warner Bks., Inc.

—Head Case. l.t. ed. 1992. 18.95 o.p. (*0-7451-8282-8*, AH0274); pap. 16.95 o.p. (*0-7927-0951-9*, AS0310) BBC Audiobooks America.

—Head Case. 1989. 192p. reprint ed. mass mkt. 3.95 o.s.i (*0-553-27645-X*) Bantam Bks.

—Head Case. unabr. ed. 1997. audio 54.95 (*1-85695-745-4*, 940201) ISIS Audio Bks. GBR. *Dist:* Ulverscroft Large Print Bks., Ltd.

—Head Case: An Anna Lee Mystery. 1986. 196p. 13.95 o.s.i (*0-684-18586-5*, Macmillan Reference USA) Gale Group.

—Stalker. 1986. 208p. mass mkt. 3.50 o.s.i (*0-446-32807-3*) Warner Bks., Inc.

—The Stalker. 1989. mass mkt. 1.95 o.s.i (*0-553-18503-9*) Bantam Bks.

—Stalker: A Mystery. 1985. 168p. 11.95 o.s.i (*0-684-18234-3*, Scribner) Simon & Schuster.

—Under Contract. 1990. 208p. mass mkt. 3.95 o.s.i (*0-553-28345-6*) Bantam Bks.

—Under Contract. unabr. ed. 1993. (Anna Lee Mystery Ser.: Vol. 5). audio 51.00 (*1-55690-929-2*, 93425E7) Recorded Bks., LLC.

—Under Contract: An Anna Lee Mystery. 1987. 16.95 o.p. (*0-684-18780-9*, Scribner) Simon & Schuster.

Coggins, Mark. The Immortal Game. 1999. (Illus.). 310p. 25.00 (*0-918395-17-8*) Poltroon Pr.

Colbert, Curt. Sayonaraville. 2003. 14.95 (*0-9724412-1-2*) UglyTown.

Coleman, Reed Farrel. Redemption Street: A Moe Prager Mystery. 2004. 256p. 22.95 (*0-670-03291-3*, Viking) Viking Penguin.

Collins, Max Allan. Blood & Thunder. Landt, Fran, ed. abr. ed. 1999. audio 16.95 (*1-882071-57-3*) B&B Audio, Inc.

—Blood & Thunder, Set. unabr. ed. 1997. audio 69.95 (*0-7887-2211-6*, CSL 100, Chivers Sound Library) BBC Audiobooks America.

—Blood & Thunder. 1999. 320p. reprint ed. text 22.00 (*0-7881-6601-8*) DIANE Publishing Co.

—Blood & Thunder. 1995. 336p. 21.95 o.s.i (*0-525-93759-5*, Dutton) Dutton/Plume.

—Blood & Thunder. 1996. 368p. mass mkt. 5.99 o.s.i (*0-451-17976-5*, Signet Bks.) NAL.

—Carnal Hours. abr. ed. 1999. audio 16.95 (*1-882071-71-9*) B&B Audio, Inc.

—Carnal Hours. 1994. (Nathan Heller Ser.). 336p. 20.95 o.p. (*0-525-93758-7*) Dutton/Plume.

—Carnal Hours. 1995. (Nathan Heller Ser.). 400p. mass mkt. 5.99 o.s.i (*0-451-17975-7*, Signet Bks.) NAL.

—Chicago Confidential. 2002. 304p. 22.95 (*0-451-20650-9*) NAL.

—Damned in Paradise. 1996. (Nathan Heller Ser.). 320p. 23.95 o.p. (*0-525-94225-4*) Dutton/Plume.

—Damned in Paradise. 1998. (Nathan Heller Ser.: Vol. 8). 320p. mass mkt. 5.99 o.s.i (*0-451-19104-8*, Signet Bks.) NAL.

—Damned in Paradise. unabr. ed. 1997. audio 70.00 (*0-7887-0855-4*, 95001E7) Recorded Bks., LLC.

—Dying in the Post-War World: A Nathan Heller Casebook. 1991. (Nate Heller Ser.). 280p. 19.95 o.p. (*0-88150-210-3*) Countryman Pr.

—Dying in the Post-War World: A Nathan Heller Casebook. 1993. 3.99 o.p. (*0-517-10403-2*) Random Hse. Value Publishing.
—Flying Blind. 1998. (Nathan Heller Ser.). 304p. 24.95 o.p. (*0-525-94311-0*) Dutton/Plume.
—Flying Blind. 1999. 384p. mass mkt. 5.99 o.s.i (*0-451-19262-1*) NAL.
—Kisses of Death: A Nathan Heller Casebook. 2001. (Illus.). 208p. pap. (*1-885941-56-0*); 223p. o.p. (*1-885941-55-2*) Crippen & Landru, Pubs.
—Majic Man. 1999. 304p. 23.95 o.p. (*0-525-94515-6*) Dutton/Plume.
—Majic Man. 2000. (Nathan Heller Ser.). 384p. mass mkt. 5.99 o.s.i (*0-451-19945-6*, Signet Bks.) NAL.
—Majic Man. l.t. ed. 2000. (Basic Ser.). 527p. 28.95 (*0-7862-2529-7*) Thorndike Pr.
—The Million Dollar Wound. 1987. 320p. reprint ed. pap. 3.95 o.p. (*0-8125-0159-4*, Tor Bks.) Doherty, Tom Assocs., LLC.
—The Million Dollar Wound. 1986. (Illus.). 400p. 16.95 o.p. (*0-312-53252-0*) St. Martin's Pr.
—The Million Dollar Wound. 2003. (Illus.). 352p. mass mkt. 6.99 (*0-7434-7463-5*) ibooks, Inc.
—Neon Mirage. 1991. 288p. mass mkt. 4.99 o.s.i (*0-553-28548-3*) Bantam Bks.
—Neon Mirage. 1988. (Illus.). 384p. 18.95 o.p. (*0-312-01484-8*, Saint Martin's Minotaur) St. Martin's Pr.
—Stolen Away: A Novel of the Lindbergh Kidnapping. 528p. 1992. mass mkt. 5.99 o.s.i (*0-553-29614-0*); 1991. 22.50 o.s.i (*0-553-07133-5*) Bantam Bks.
—True Crime. 1986. 384p. reprint ed. pap. 3.95 o.p. (*0-8125-0152-7*, Tor Bks.) Doherty, Tom Assocs., LLC.
—True Crime. 1984. 15.95 o.p. (*0-312-82045-3*) St. Martin's Pr.
—True Crime. 2003. (Illus.). 368p. mass mkt. 6.99 (*0-7434-5900-8*) ibooks, Inc.
—True Detective. 1986. 384p. reprint ed. pap. 3.95 o.p. (*0-8125-0150-0*, Tor Bks.) Doherty, Tom Assocs., LLC.
—True Detective. 1983. (Illus.). 368p. 14.95 o.p. (*0-312-82051-8*) St. Martin's Pr.
Collins, Michael. The Blood-Red Dream. l.t. ed. 1991. 17.95 o.p. (*0-7451-8144-9*, AH0180); pap. 15.95 o.p. (*0-7927-0664-1*, AS0216) BBC Audiobooks America.
—The Cadillac Cowboy. 1995. 288p. 20.95 o.p. (*1-55611-461-3*) Fine, Donald I. Bks.
—Cassandra in Red. 1992. 256p. 19.95 o.p. (*1-55611-316-1*) Fine, Donald I. Bks.
—Castrato. 1991. 416p. reprint ed. pap. 4.99 (*0-8439-3131-0*) Dorchester Publishing Co., Inc.
—Castrato. 1989. 288p. 17.95 o.p. (*1-55611-113-4*) Fine, Donald I. Bks.
—Chasing Eights. 1992. 400p. reprint ed. pap. 4.99 (*0-8439-3274-0*) Dorchester Publishing Co., Inc.
—Chasing Eights. 1990. 18.95 o.p. (*1-55611-145-2*) Fine, Donald I. Bks.
—Crime, Punishment - & Resurrection. 1992. 272p. 19.95 o.p. (*1-55611-295-5*) Fine, Donald I. Bks.
—Freak. 1990. mass mkt. (*0-373-26050-4*, Harlequin Bks.) Harlequin Enterprises, Ltd.
—The Irishman's Horse. 1991. 18.95 o.p. (*1-55611-185-1*) Fine, Donald I. Bks.
—Minnesota Strip. 1987. 264p. 17.95 o.p. (*1-55611-032-4*) Fine, Donald I. Bks.
—Minnesota Strip. 1988. pap. (*0-373-97093-5*, Harlequin Bks.) Harlequin Enterprises, Ltd.
—Red Rosa. 1988. 264p. 17.95 o.p. (*1-55611-052-9*) Fine, Donald I. Bks.
—Red Rosa. 1989. 304p. reprint ed. mass mkt. (*0-373-97099-4*, Harlequin Bks.) Harlequin Enterprises, Ltd.
—Silent Scream. 1989. mass mkt. (*0-373-28000-9*, Harlequin Bks.) Harlequin Enterprises, Ltd.
—The Slasher. 1989. mass mkt. (*0-373-27999-X*, Harlequin Bks.) Harlequin Enterprises, Ltd.
Connelly, Michael. A Darkness More Than Night. 2001. 432p. 25.95 o.p. (*0-316-15407-5*); 400p. E-Book 14.95 (*0-7595-0067-3*); 400p. E-Book 14.95 (*0-7595-9076-1*); 400p. E-Book 14.95 (*0-7595-4069-1*) Little Brown & Co.
—A Darkness More Than Night. l.t. ed. 608p. 2002. 30.95 (*0-7862-2821-0*); 2001. 31.95 (*0-7862-2820-2*) Thorndike Pr.
—A Darkness More Than Night. deluxe ltd. ed. 2000. 150.00 (*1-890885-10-X*) Trice, B.E. Publishing.
—A Darkness More Than Night. 2002. 488p. reprint ed. mass mkt. 7.99 (*0-446-66790-0*) Warner Bks., Inc.
Connolly, John. The Killing Kind. 2001. (Illus.). 388p. pap. (*0-340-77121-6*) Hodder & Stoughton, Ltd. GBR. *Dist:* Trafalgar Square.
—The Killing Kind. 2002. 384p. 25.00 (*0-7434-5334-4*, Atria) Simon & Schuster.
—The White Road. 2004. (Illus.). 528p. mass mkt. 25.00 (*0-7434-5639-4*, Pocket); 2003. 400p. 25.00 (*0-7434-5638-6*, Atria); 2003. E-Book 19.99 (*0-7434-6263-7*, Atria) Simon & Schuster.
Conrad, Linda. Desperado Dad. 2002. (Silhouette Desire Ser.: No. 1458). 192p. mass mkt. (*0-373-76458-8*, Silhouette) Harlequin Enterprises, Ltd.
Cook, Bruce. Death As a Career Move. 1992. 272p. 18.95 o.p. (*0-312-06946-4*, Saint Martin's Minotaur) St. Martin's Pr.
—Mexican Standoff. 1988. 256p. 16.95 o.p. (*0-531-15089-5*, Watts, Franklin) Scholastic Library Publishing.
—Mexican Standoff. 1990. mass mkt. 3.95 (*0-312-92114-4*, St. Martin's Paperbacks) St. Martin's Pr.
—Rough Cut. 1992. 2.99 o.p. (*0-517-09052-X*) Random Hse. Value Publishing.
—Rough Cut. 1990. 240p. 16.95 o.p. (*0-312-05149-2*, Saint Martin's Minotaur) St. Martin's Pr.
—The Sidewalk Hilton. 1994. 320p. 21.95 o.p. (*0-312-11062-6*, Saint Martin's Minotaur) St. Martin's Pr.
Cook, Glen. Bitter Gold Hearts. 1990. (Garrett Files Ser.). 256p. reprint ed. mass mkt. 3.95 o.p. (*0-451-45072-8*, ROC) NAL.
—Cold Copper Tears. 1988. (Garrett Files Ser.). 256p. mass mkt. 3.50 o.p. (*0-451-15773-7*, ROC) NAL.
—Deadly Quicksilver Lies. 1994. (Garrett Files Ser.). 352p. (Orig.). mass mkt. 4.99 o.s.i (*0-451-45305-0*, ROC) NAL.
—Dread Brass Shadows. 1990. (Garrett Files Ser.). 256p. mass mkt. 5.50 o.s.i (*0-451-45008-6*, ROC) NAL.
—Faded Steel Heat. 1999. (Garrett Files Ser.). 368p. mass mkt. 6.99 o.s.i (*0-451-45479-0*, ROC) NAL.
—Old Tin Sorrows. 1989. (Glen Garrett Files Ser.). 256p. mass mkt. 3.99 o.s.i (*0-451-45157-0*, ROC) NAL.
—Petty Pewter Gods. 1995. (Garrett Files Ser.). 304p. mass mkt. 5.99 o.s.i (*0-451-45478-2*, ROC) NAL.
—Red Iron Nights. 1991. (Garrett Files Ser.). 272p. (Orig.). mass mkt. 5.50 o.s.i (*0-451-45108-2*, ROC) NAL.
—Sweet Silver Blues. 1990. (Garrett Files Ser.). 256p. reprint ed. mass mkt. 5.50 o.s.i (*0-451-45070-1*, ROC) NAL.
Copper, Basil. Bad Scene. l.t. ed. 2000. (G. K. Hall Nightingale Ser.). 217p. pap. 20.95 (*0-7838-8997-6*, Macmillan Reference USA) Gale Group.
—Bad Scene. l.t. ed. 1991. (Linford Mystery Large Print Ser.). pap. 17.99 o.p. (*0-7089-7021-4*, Ulverscroft) Thorpe, F. A. Pubs. GBR. *Dist:* Ulverscroft Large Print Bks., Ltd., Ulverscroft Large Print Canada, Ltd.
—The Breaking Point. l.t. ed. 1995. (Linford Mystery Large Print Ser.). 320p. pap. 17.99 o.p. (*0-7089-7805-3*, Linford) Thorpe, F. A. Pubs. GBR. *Dist:* Ulverscroft Large Print Bks., Ltd., Ulverscroft Large Print Canada, Ltd.
—The Caligari Complex. l.t. ed. 1999. (Linford Mystery Large Print Ser.). 304p. pap. 18.99 (*0-7089-5504-5*, Linford) Thorpe, F. A. Pubs. GBR. *Dist:* Ulverscroft Large Print Bks., Ltd., Ulverscroft Large Print Canada, Ltd.
—Crack in the Sidewalk. l.t. ed. 1997. (Linford Mystery Library). 320p. pap. 17.99 o.p. (*0-7089-5065-5*, Linford) Thorpe, F. A. Pubs. GBR. *Dist:* Ulverscroft Large Print Bks., Ltd., Ulverscroft Large Print Canada, Ltd.
—The Dark Mirror. (Black Dagger Crime Ser.). 16.50 o.p. (*0-86220-796-7*, BD001, Black Dagger) BBC Audiobooks America.
—The Dark Mirror. l.t. ed. 1997. (Linford Mystery Library). 416p. pap. 17.99 o.p. (*0-7089-5101-5*, Linford) Thorpe, F. A. Pubs. GBR. *Dist:* Ulverscroft Large Print Bks., Ltd., Ulverscroft Large Print Canada, Ltd.
—Dead File. l.t. ed. 1991. (Linford Mystery Large Print Ser.). pap. 17.99 o.p. (*0-7089-7001-X*, Ulverscroft) Thorpe, F. A. Pubs. GBR. *Dist:* Ulverscroft Large Print Bks., Ltd., Ulverscroft Large Print Canada, Ltd.
—Death Squad. l.t. ed. 1999. (Linford Mystery Large Print Ser.). 304p. pap. 18.99 (*0-7089-5460-X*, Linford) Thorpe, F. A. Pubs. GBR. *Dist:* Ulverscroft Large Print Bks., Ltd., Ulverscroft Large Print Canada, Ltd.
—Die Now, Live Later. l.t. ed. 1993. (Linford Mystery Library). 336p. pap. 17.99 o.p. (*0-7089-7341-8*, Ulverscroft) Thorpe, F. A. Pubs. GBR. *Dist:* Ulverscroft Large Print Bks., Ltd., Ulverscroft Large Print Canada, Ltd.
—Don't Bleed on Me. l.t. ed. 1991. (Linford Mystery Library). pap. 17.99 o.p. (*0-7089-7081-8*, Ulverscroft) Thorpe, F. A. Pubs. GBR. *Dist:* Ulverscroft Large Print Bks., Ltd., Ulverscroft Large Print Canada, Ltd.
—The Dossier of Solar Pons. 1987. (Academy Book Ser.). 278p. pap. 7.95 (*0-89733-252-0*) Academy Chicago Pubs., Ltd.
—Exploits of Solar Pons. 1993. (Illus.). 256p. (C). 25.00 (*1-878252-11-9*); 45.00 (*1-878252-14-3*) Fedogan & Bremer.
—The Far Horizon. 2001. 219p. (*0-7540-4399-1*); (*0-7540-4400-9*) Gale Group. (Macmillan Reference USA).
—The Far Horizon. l.t. ed. 2001. (G. K. Hall Nightingale Ser.). 219p. pap. 23.95 (*0-7838-9327-2*) Thorndike Pr.
—The Far Horizon. l.t. ed. 1993. (Linford Mystery Library). 336p. pap. 17.99 o.p. (*0-7089-7378-7*, Ulverscroft) Thorpe, F. A. Pubs. GBR. *Dist:* Ulverscroft Large Print Bks., Ltd., Ulverscroft Large Print Canada, Ltd.
—Feedback. l.t. ed. 2001. 225p. pap. 23.95 (*0-7838-9592-5*) Thorndike Pr.
—Feedback. l.t. ed. 1991. (Linford Mystery Library). pap. 17.99 o.p. (*0-7089-7129-6*, Ulverscroft) Thorpe, F. A. Pubs. GBR. *Dist:* Ulverscroft Large Print Bks., Ltd., Ulverscroft Large Print Canada, Ltd.
—The Further Adventures of Solar Pons. 1987. (Academy Book Ser.). 256p. pap. 7.95 (*0-89733-273-3*) Academy Chicago Pubs., Ltd.
—A Good Place to Die. l.t. ed. 1989. (Linford Mystery Library). pap. 17.99 o.p. (*0-7089-6742-6*, Ulverscroft) Thorpe, F. A. Pubs. GBR. *Dist:* Ulverscroft Large Print Bks., Ltd., Ulverscroft Large Print Canada, Ltd.
—A Great Year for Dying. l.t. ed. 1993. (Linford Mystery Library). 352p. pap. 17.99 o.p. (*0-7089-7349-3*, Ulverscroft) Thorpe, F. A. Pubs. GBR. *Dist:* Ulverscroft Large Print Bks., Ltd., Ulverscroft Large Print Canada, Ltd.
—The High Wall. l.t. ed. 1987. (Linford Mystery Library). 304p. pap. 17.99 o.p. (*0-7089-6455-9*, Linford) Thorpe, F. A. Pubs. GBR. *Dist:* Ulverscroft Large Print Bks., Ltd., Ulverscroft Large Print Canada, Ltd.
—Impact. l.t. ed. 1997. (Linford Mystery Library). 320p. pap. 17.99 o.p. (*0-7089-5070-1*, Linford) Thorpe, F. A. Pubs. GBR. *Dist:* Ulverscroft Large Print Bks., Ltd., Ulverscroft Large Print Canada, Ltd.
—The Lonely Place. l.t. ed. 1997. (Linford Mystery Library). 304p. pap. 17.99 o.p. (*0-7089-5060-4*, Ulverscroft) Thorpe, F. A. Pubs. GBR. *Dist:* Ulverscroft Large Print Bks., Ltd., Ulverscroft Large Print Canada, Ltd.
—The Long Rest. l.t. ed. 1994. 221p. lib. bdg. 16.95 (*0-8161-7421-0*, Macmillan Reference USA) Gale Group.
—The Marble Orchard. l.t. ed. 1998. (Linford Mystery Large Print Ser.). 256p. pap. 17.99 (*0-7089-5265-8*, Linford) Thorpe, F. A. Pubs. GBR. *Dist:* Ulverscroft Large Print Bks., Ltd., Ulverscroft Large Print Canada, Ltd.
—Night Frost. l.t. ed. 1996. (Linford Mystery Library). 368p. pap. 17.99 o.p. (*0-7089-7868-1*, Linford) Thorpe, F. A. Pubs. GBR. *Dist:* Ulverscroft Large Print Bks., Ltd., Ulverscroft Large Print Canada, Ltd.
—No Letters from the Grave. l.t. ed. 1998. (Linford Mystery Library). 240p. pap. 17.99 (*0-7089-5223-2*, Linford) Thorpe, F. A. Pubs. GBR. *Dist:* Ulverscroft Large Print Bks., Ltd., Ulverscroft Large Print Canada, Ltd.
—Print-Out. l.t. ed. 1993. (Dales Mystery Ser.). 246p. pap. 19.99 o.p. (*1-85389-380-3*) Dales Large Print Bks. GBR. *Dist:* Ulverscroft Large Print Bks., Ltd., Ulverscroft Large Print Canada, Ltd.
—Print-Out. l.t. ed. 1996. (Linford Mystery Library). 304p. pap. 17.99 o.p. (*0-7089-7861-4*, Linford) Thorpe, F. A. Pubs. GBR. *Dist:* Ulverscroft Large Print Bks., Ltd., Ulverscroft Large Print Canada, Ltd.
—A Quiet Room in Hell. l.t. ed. 1998. (Linford Mystery Large Print Ser.). 288p. pap. 17.99 (*0-7089-5294-1*, Linford) Thorpe, F. A. Pubs. GBR. *Dist:* Ulverscroft Large Print Bks., Ltd., Ulverscroft Large Print Canada, Ltd.
—The Recollections of Solar Pons. 1995. 25.00 (*1-878252-20-8*); 75.00 (*1-878252-21-6*) Fedogan & Bremer.
—Ricochet. l.t. ed. 1993. (Linford Mystery Library). 304p. pap. 17.99 o.p. (*0-7089-7382-5*, Linford) Thorpe, F. A. Pubs. GBR. *Dist:* Ulverscroft Large Print Bks., Ltd., Ulverscroft Large Print Canada, Ltd.
—Scratch on the Dark. 2002. 192p. 21.95 (*0-7540-8610-0*, Black Dagger) BBC Audiobooks America.
—Scratch on the Dark. l.t. ed. 2000. (Linford Mystery Large Print Ser.). 264p. pap. 18.99 (*0-7089-5767-6*, Ulverscroft) Thorpe, F. A. Pubs. GBR. *Dist:* Ulverscroft Large Print Bks., Ltd., Ulverscroft Large Print Canada, Ltd.
—The Secret Files of Solar Pons. 1979. (Solar Pons Ser.: No. 10). pap. 1.95 o.p. (*0-523-40656-8*, Pinnacle Bks.) Kensington Publishing Corp.
—Shock-Wave. l.t. ed. 1994. (Linford Mystery Library). 320p. pap. 17.99 o.p. (*0-7089-7629-8*, Linford) Thorpe, F. A. Pubs. GBR. *Dist:* Ulverscroft Large Print Bks., Ltd., Ulverscroft Large Print Canada, Ltd.
—Strong-Arm. l.t. ed. 1989. (Linford Mystery Library). 319p. pap. 17.99 o.p. (*0-7089-6629-2*, Linford) Thorpe, F. A. Pubs. GBR. *Dist:* Ulverscroft Large Print Bks., Ltd., Ulverscroft Large Print Canada, Ltd.
—Tight Corner. l.t. ed. 1994. (Linford Mystery Library). 304p. pap. 17.99 o.p. (*0-7089-7564-X*, Linford) Thorpe, F. A. Pubs. GBR. *Dist:* Ulverscroft Large Print Bks., Ltd., Ulverscroft Large Print Canada, Ltd.
—Trigger-Man. l.t. ed. 1994. (Linford Mystery Library). 320p. pap. 17.99 o.p. (*0-7089-7561-5*, Linford) Thorpe, F. A. Pubs. GBR. *Dist:* Ulverscroft Large Print Bks., Ltd., Ulverscroft Large Print Canada, Ltd.
—A Voice from the Dead. l.t. ed. 1998. (Linford Mystery Large Print Ser.). 304p. pap. 17.99 (*0-7089-5287-9*, Linford) Thorpe, F. A. Pubs. GBR. *Dist:* Ulverscroft Large Print Bks., Ltd., Ulverscroft Large Print Canada, Ltd.
—The Year of the Dragon. l.t. ed. 1991. (Linford Mystery Library). pap. 17.99 o.p. (*0-7089-7077-X*, Linford) Thorpe, F. A. Pubs. GBR. *Dist:* Ulverscroft Large Print Bks., Ltd., Ulverscroft Large Print Canada, Ltd.
Cormany, Michael. Lost Daughter. 1991. 224p. reprint ed. pap. 3.50 (*0-8439-3063-2*) Dorchester Publishing Co., Inc.
—Polaroid Man. 1993. 240p. reprint ed. pap. 3.99 (*0-8439-3542-1*) Dorchester Publishing Co., Inc.
—Red Winter. 1991. 224p. (Orig.). reprint ed. pap. 3.50 (*0-8439-3142-6*) Dorchester Publishing Co., Inc.
—Red Winter. 1991. (Orig.). 2.99 o.p. (*0-517-06332-8*) Random Hse. Value Publishing.
—Rich or Dead. 1991. 208p. reprint ed. pap. 3.50 (*0-8439-3186-8*) Dorchester Publishing Co., Inc.
Corris, Peter. Beware of the Dog. 1994. 288p. mass mkt. 4.99 o.s.i (*0-440-21753-9*) Dell Publishing.
—The Big Drop & Other Cliff Hardy Stories. 1988. 208p. mass mkt. 3.50 o.s.i (*0-449-13228-5*, Fawcett) Ballantine Bks.
—Deal Me Out. l.t. ed. 1991. 11.95 o.p. (*0-947072-56-X*, C0376); pap. 17.95 o.p. (*1-86340-123-7*, AUS058) BBC Audiobooks America.
—Deal Me Out. 1987. mass mkt. 2.95 o.s.i (*0-449-13229-3*, Fawcett) Ballantine Bks.
—The Dying Trade. 1986. 256p. mass mkt. 2.95 o.s.i (*0-449-13030-4*, Fawcett) Ballantine Bks.
—The Empty Beach. l.t. ed. 1988. pap. 9.95 o.p. (*1-86340-081-8*) BBC Audiobooks America.
—The Empty Beach. 1986. mass mkt. 2.95 o.s.i (*0-449-13029-0*, Fawcett) Ballantine Bks.
—The Greenwich Apartments. 1986. 173p. pap. (*0-04-820030-1*) Allen & Unwin Pty., Ltd. AUS. *Dist:* Paul & Co. Pubs. Consortium, Inc.
—The Greenwich Apartments. 1988. mass mkt. 3.50 o.s.i (*0-449-14514-X*, Fawcett) Ballantine Bks.
—Heroin Annie. l.t. ed. 1990. pap. 9.95 o.p. (*1-86340-071-0*); 1988. lib. bdg. 15.95 o.p. (*0-947072-17-9*) BBC Audiobooks America.
—Heroine Annie & Other Cliff Hardy Stories. 1987. 256p. mass mkt. 2.95 o.s.i (*0-449-13031-2*, Fawcett) Ballantine Bks.
—The January Zone. l.t. ed. 1991. 21.95 o.p. (*1-86340-200-4*, AUH082); 12.95 o.p. (*0-7451-9609-8*, AUS150) BBC Audiobooks America.
—The January Zone. 1988. mass mkt. 3.50 o.s.i (*0-449-14513-1*, Fawcett) Ballantine Bks.
—Make Me Rich. 1987. 192p. mass mkt. 2.95 o.s.i (*0-449-13021-5*, Fawcett) Ballantine Bks.
—Man in the Shadows, Vol. 5. 1991. (Spanish Bit Saga). 176p. mass mkt. 3.99 o.s.i (*0-553-29087-8*) Bantam Bks.
—The Marvellous Boy. 1986. mass mkt. 2.95 o.s.i (*0-449-13028-2*, Fawcett) Ballantine Bks.
—Matrimonial Causes: A Cliff Hardy Mystery. 1994. 288p. mass mkt. 4.99 o.s.i (*0-440-21747-4*) Dell Publishing.
—O'Fear. 1991. 208p. 15.00 o.s.i (*0-385-42119-2*) Doubleday Publishing.
—Wet Graves. unabr. ed. 2001. audio (*1-86442-312-9*, 590376) Bolinda Publishing Pty, Ltd.
—Wet Graves. 1995. 288p. mass mkt. 4.99 o.s.i (*0-440-21750-4*) Dell Publishing.
—White Meat. 1986. mass mkt. 2.95 o.s.i (*0-449-13027-4*, Fawcett) Ballantine Bks.
Coulter, Catherine. Beyond Eden. 1992. 368p. 20.00 o.p. (*0-525-93397-2*, Dutton) Dutton/Plume.
—Beyond Eden. l.t. ed. 1998. 25.95 o.p. (*1-56895-658-4*, Wheeler Publishing, Inc.) Gale Group.
—Beyond Eden. 448p. 1993. mass mkt. 7.50 o.s.i (*0-451-40339-8*, Onyx); 2000. reprint ed. mass mkt. 7.99 (*0-451-20231-7*, Signet Bks.) NAL.
Craig, Philip R. A Beautiful Place to Die: A Martha's Vineyard Mystery. 1991. 224p. mass mkt. 6.99 (*0-380-71155-9*, Avon Bks.) Morrow/Avon.
—A Case of Vineyard Poison. 1996. 224p. mass mkt. 5.99 (*0-380-72679-3*, Avon Bks.) Morrow/Avon.
—A Case of Vineyard Poison: A Martha's Vineyard Mystery. 1995. 253p. 20.00 o.p. (*0-684-19616-6*, Scribner) Simon & Schuster.
—Cliff Hanger: A Martha's Vineyard Mystery. 1993. 256p. 20.00 o.p. (*0-684-19552-6*, Macmillan Reference USA) Gale Group.
—Cliff Hanger: A Martha's Vineyard Mystery. 1994. 224p. mass mkt. 4.99 (*0-380-72240-2*, Avon Bks.) Morrow/Avon.

—A Deadly Vineyard Holiday. 1998. (Martha's Vineyard Mysteries Ser.). 240p. mass mkt. 6.50 (0-380-73110-X, Avon Bks.) Morrow/Avon.
—A Deadly Vineyard Holiday: A Martha's Vineyard Mystery. 1997. 282p. 20.50 (0-684-19718-9, Scribner) Simon & Schuster.
—A Deadly Vineyard Holiday: A Martha's Vineyard Mystery. l.t. ed. 1997. (Core Ser.). 344p. lib. bdg. 26.95 (0-7838-8278-5) Thorndike Pr.
—Death on a Vineyard Beach. 1997. 224p. mass mkt. 6.50 (0-380-72873-7, Avon Bks.) Morrow/Avon.
—Death on a Vineyard Beach: A Martha's Vineyard Mystery. 1996. 288p. 21.00 o.p. (0-684-19717-0, Scribner) Simon & Schuster.
—The Double Minded Men: A Martha's Vineyard Mystery. 1992. (Martha's Vineyard Mystery Ser.: No. 3). 256p. text 20.00 (0-684-19396-5, Macmillan Reference USA) Gale Group.
—The Double Minded Men: A Martha's Vineyard Mystery. 1993. 256p. pap. 4.99 (0-380-71973-8, Avon Bks.) Morrow/Avon.
—Off Season. 1996. (Martha's Vineyard Ser.: No. 5). 224p. mass mkt. 5.99 (0-380-72588-6, Avon Bks.) Morrow/Avon.
—Off Season: A Martha's Vineyard Mystery. 1994. 256p. 20.00 (0-684-19617-4, Macmillan Reference USA) Gale Group.
—A Shoot on Martha's Vineyard. 1999. (Martha's Vineyard Mysteries Ser.). 256p. mass mkt. 5.99 (0-380-73201-7, Avon Bks.) Morrow/Avon.
—Shoot on Martha's Vineyard: A Martha's Vineyard Mystery. 1998. (Martha's Vineyard Mysteries Ser.). 288p. 22.00 (0-684-83454-5, Scribner) Simon & Schuster.
—A Shoot on Martha's Vineyard: A Martha's Vineyard Mystery. l.t. ed. 1999. (Mystery Ser.). 427p. 27.95 (0-7862-1614-X) Thorndike Pr.
—Vineyard Blues: A Martha's Vineyard Mystery. 2001. 224p. mass mkt. 5.99 (0-380-81859-0, Avon Bks.) Morrow/Avon.
—Vineyard Blues: A Martha's Vineyard Mystery. 2000. (Martha's Vineyard Mysteries Ser.). (Illus.). 224p. 23.00 o.s.i (0-684-83455-3, Scribner) Simon & Schuster.
—Vineyard Blues: A Martha's Vineyard Mystery. l.t. ed. 2000. (Mystery Ser.). (Illus.). 339p. 29.95 (0-7862-2591-2) Thorndike Pr.
—Vineyard Enigma: A Martha Vineyard Mystery. 2002. (Illus.). 256p. 24.00 (0-7432-0523-5, Scribner) Simon & Schuster.
—A Vineyard Killing: A Martha's Vineyard Mystery. 2003. (Illus.). 240p. 24.00 (0-7432-0524-3, Scribner) Simon & Schuster.
—Vineyard Shadows: A Martha's Vineyard Mystery. 2002. 256p. mass mkt. 6.50 (0-380-82099-4) Morrow/Avon.
—Vineyard Shadows: A Martha's Vineyard Mystery. l.t. ed. 2001. 334p. 29.95 (0-7862-3646-9) Thorndike Pr.
—The Woman Who Walked into the Sea: A Martha's Vineyard Mystery. 1993. 224p. reprint ed. mass mkt. 4.99 (0-380-71536-8, Avon Bks.) Morrow/Avon.
—The Woman Who Walked into the Sea: A Martha's Vineyard Mystery. 1991. 224p. 17.95 o.s.i (0-684-19228-4, Scribner) Simon & Schuster.
Craig, Philip R. & Tapply, William G. First Light. l.t. ed. 2002. 443p. 29.95 (0-7862-4185-3) Gale Group.
—First Light: The First Ever Brady Coyne/J. W. Jackson Novel. 2002. 352p. E-Book 24.00 (0-7432-3484-7); 24.00 (0-7432-2208-3) Simon & Schuster. (Scribner).
Crais, Robert. The Devil's Cantina. 1999. 288p. 22.95 (0-7868-6355-2) Hyperion Pr.
—Free Fall. 1994. (Elvis Cole Mystery Ser.). mass mkt. 4.99 o.s.i (0-553-56831-0, Crimeline); 304p. mass mkt. 6.99 (0-553-56509-5) Bantam Bks.
—Indigo Slam. 2003. (Elvis Cole Mystery Ser.). 320p. mass mkt. 7.99 (0-345-43564-8, Ballantine Bks.) Ballantine Bks.
—Indigo Slam. unabr. ed. 1997. (Elvis Cole Mystery Ser.). audio 48.00 (0-7366-3833-4, 4553) Books on Tape, Inc.
—Indigo Slam. abr. ed. (Elvis Cole Mystery Ser.). 2000. audio 7.99 o.s.i (1-58788-097-0, 2352, Paperback Nova Audio Bks.); 1998. audio 7.99 o.s.i (1-56740-252-6, 2379, Nova Audio Bks.); 1997. audio 16.95 o.p. (1-56100-977-6, 1236, Nova Audio Bks.); 1997. audio 16.95 o.p.; 1997. audio 23.95 (1-56100-752-8, 144, Bookcassette); 1997. audio 57.25 (1-56100-827-3, 907, Unabridged Library Editions) Brilliance Audio.
—Indigo Slam. (Elvis Cole Mystery Ser.). 1999. 384p. mass mkt. 5.99 (0-7868-8929-2); 1997. 304p. 22.95 (0-7868-6261-0) Hyperion Pr.
—L. A. Requiem. 2000. (Elvis Cole Mystery Ser.). 416p. mass mkt. 6.99 (0-345-43447-1, Ballantine Bks.) Ballantine Bks.
—L. A. Requiem. l.t. ed. 2000. (Elvis Cole Mystery Ser.). 538p. 27.95 (1-56895-881-1, Wheeler Publishing, Inc.) Gale Group.
—L. A. Requiem, Set. abr. ed. 1999. (Elvis Cole Mystery Ser.). audio 25.00 Highsmith Inc.
—L. A. Requiem. abr. ed. 1999. (Elvis Cole Mystery Ser.). audio 25.00 (0-553-52648-0, RH Audio) Random Hse. Audio Publishing Group.
—Lullaby Town. (Elvis Cole Mystery Ser.). 1993. 352p. mass mkt. 6.99 (0-553-29951-4); 1992. 304p. 20.00 o.s.i (0-553-08197-7) Bantam Bks.
—The Monkey's Raincoat. (Elvis Cole Mystery Ser.). 1987. 208p. mass mkt. 2.95 o.s.i (0-553-26336-6); 1992. 224p. reprint ed. mass mkt. 7.50 (0-553-27585-2) Bantam Bks.
—Stalking the Angel. 1992. (Elvis Cole Mystery Ser.). 288p. mass mkt. 7.50 (0-553-28644-7) Bantam Bks.
—Sunset Express. unabr. ed. 1997. (Elvis Cole Mystery Ser.). audio 56.00 (0-913369-89-6, 4389) Books on Tape, Inc.
—Sunset Express. abr. ed. (Elvis Cole Mystery Ser.). 1997. audio 7.99 o.p. (1-56740-166-X, 707, Nova Audio Bks.); 1996. audio 16.95 o.p. (1-56100-905-9, 1066, Nova Audio Bks.); 1996. audio 57.25 o.p. (1-56100-320-4, 1065, Unabridged Library Editions); 1996. audio 23.95 o.p. (1-56100-695-5, 284, Bookcassette) Brilliance Audio.
—Sunset Express. (Elvis Cole Mystery Ser.). 1996. 288p. 21.95 o.p. (0-7868-6096-0); 2002. 416p. reprint ed. mass mkt. 6.99 (0-7868-8915-2) Hyperion Pr.
—Sunset Express. l.t. ed. 2001. (Elvis Cole Mystery Ser.). 288p. 28.95 (0-7862-3401-6); 485p. (0-7540-1644-7) Thorndike Pr.
—Voodoo River. (Elvis Cole Mystery Ser.). 1995. 304p. 21.95 (0-7868-6076-6); 2003. 416p. reprint ed. mass mkt. 7.99 (0-7868-8905-5) Hyperion Pr.
Crider, Bill. Dead on the Island. unabr. ed. 1995. audio 17.00 (1-883268-19-2) Spellbinders, Inc.
—Dead on the Island. 1991. 193p. 18.95 (0-8027-5787-1) Walker & Co.
—Gator Kill. Haywood, Richard, ed. unabr. ed. 1995. (Truman Smith Trilogy Ser.). audio 17.00 (1-883268-27-3) Spellbinders, Inc.
—Gator Kill: A Truman Smith. 1992. 202p. 18.95 (0-8027-3213-5) Walker & Co.
—Murder Takes a Break: A Truman Smith Mystery. 1997. (Truman Smith Mystery Ser.). 246p. 21.95 (0-8027-3308-5) Walker & Co.
—The Prairie Chicken Kill: A Truman Smith Mystery. 1996. (Truman Smith Mystery Ser.). 216p. 20.95 (0-8027-3282-8) Walker & Co.
—When Old Men Die. abr. ed. 1997. audio 17.00 (1-883268-33-8) Spellbinders, Inc.
—When Old Men Die. 1994. 192p. 19.95 (0-8027-3195-3) Walker & Co.
Crumley, James. Bordersnakes. 1997. 288p. mass mkt. 6.50 (0-446-60448-8); 1996. 336p. 22.00 o.p. (0-89296-573-8) Warner Bks., Inc.
—Dancing Bear. unabr. ed. 1997. audio 48.00 (0-7366-3819-9, 4487) Books on Tape, Inc.
—Dancing Bear. 1984. (Vintage Contemporaries Ser.). 240p. pap. 13.00 (0-394-72576-X, Vintage) Knopf Publishing Group.
—Dancing Bear. 1983. 256p. 12.95 o.p. (0-394-52195-1) Random Hse., Inc.
—The Final Country. l.t. ed. 2003. 25.95 (1-58724-412-8, Wheeler Publishing, Inc.) Gale Group.
—The Final Country. 2001. 320p. 24.95 (0-89296-666-1) Mysterious Pr.
—The Final Country. 2002. 320p. pap. 12.95 (0-446-67964-X, Mysterious Pr. Paperback Bks.) Warner Bks., Inc.
—The Last Good Kiss. 1992. audio 13.95 (1-55644-375-7, 12021) American Audio Prose Library, Inc.
—The Last Good Kiss. 1988. (Vintage Contemporaries Ser.). 256p. pap. 11.95 (0-394-75989-3, Vintage) Knopf Publishing Group.
—The Last Good Kiss. 1978. 8.95 o.p. (0-394-41946-4) Random Hse., Inc.
—The Last Good Kiss. 1983. mass mkt. 3.50 o.s.i (0-671-49889-4, Pocket) Simon & Schuster.
—The Mexican Tree Duck. unabr. ed. 1997. audio 48.00 (0-7366-3820-2, 4488) Books on Tape, Inc.
—The Mexican Tree Duck. 1993. 256p. 19.95 (0-89296-391-3) Mysterious Pr.
—The Mexican Tree Duck. 1994. 272p. mass mkt. 5.99 (0-446-40407-1); 2001. 256p. reprint ed. pap. 11.95 (0-446-67791-4) Warner Bks., Inc.
—The Wrong Case. 1985. (Vintage Contemporaries Ser.). 288p. pap. 12.00 (0-394-73558-7) Random Hse., Inc.
Cunningham, E. V., pseud. The Case of the Angry Actress. 1984. 192p. pap. 2.95 o.p. (0-440-11093-9) Dell Publishing.
—The Case of the Kidnapped Angel. 192p. 1983. (Masao Masuto Mystery Ser.: No. 5). pap. 2.95 o.p. (0-440-11224-9); 1982. 12.95 o.s.i (0-385-28118-8, Delacorte Pr.) Dell Publishing.
—The Case of the Kidnapped Angel. l.t. ed. 1983. 216p. pap. 7.95 o.p. (0-8161-3471-5, Macmillan Reference USA) Gale Group.
—The Case of the Murdered MacKenzie. 1984. (Masao Masuto Mystery Ser.). 192p. 11.95 o.s.i (0-385-29337-2, Delacorte Pr.) Dell Publishing.
—The Case of the Murdered MacKenzie. l.t. ed. 1985. (Nightingale Ser.). 386p. 9.95 o.p. (0-8161-3771-4, Macmillan Reference USA) Gale Group.
—The Case of the One-Penny Orange. l.t. ed. 1982. (Nightingale Ser.). lib. bdg. 11.95 o.p. (0-8161-3334-4, Macmillan Reference USA) Gale Group.
—The Case of the One-Penny Orange. 1982. (Masao Masuto Mystery Ser.). 176p. pap. o.p. (0-03-059858-3, Owl Bks.) Holt, Henry & Co.
—The Case of the Poisoned Eclairs. 1980. pap. 2.25 o.p. (0-440-11256-7) Dell Publishing.
—The Case of the Poisoned Eclairs. 1982. (Nightingale Ser.). pap. 9.95 o.p. (0-8161-3333-6, Macmillan Reference USA) Gale Group.
—The Case of the Poisoned Eclairs. 1979. o.p. (0-03-044721-6) Holt, Henry & Co.
—The Case of the Russian Diplomat. 1979. 1.75 o.s.i (0-515-04881-X, 04881-X, Jove) Berkley Publishing Group.
—The Case of the Russian Diplomat. (Masao Masuto Mystery Ser.). 1982. 176p. pap. o.p. (0-03-059857-5, Owl Bks.); 1978. o.p. (0-03-022456-X) Holt, Henry & Co.
—The Case of the Sliding Pool. 1983. pap. 2.95 o.p. (0-440-12092-6); 1981. 10.95 o.s.i (0-440-01114-0, Delacorte Pr.) Dell Publishing.
—The Case of the Sliding Pool. 1982. (Nightingale Ser.). pap. 9.95 o.p. (0-8161-3348-4, Macmillan Reference USA) Gale Group.
Cutler, Stan. Best Performance by a Patsy. 1991. (Goodman-Bradley Mystery Ser.). 352p. 18.95 o.p. (0-525-93317-4) Dutton/Plume.
—Best Performance by a Patsy. 1993. (Goodman-Bradley Mystery Ser.). 336p. mass mkt. 4.50 o.p. (0-451-40359-2, Onyx) NAL.
—The Face on the Cutting Room Floor. 1991. 320p. 18.95 o.p. (0-525-93381-6, Dutton) Dutton/Plume.
—The Face on the Cutting Room Floor. 1993. (Goodman-Bradley Mystery Ser.). 272p. mass mkt. 4.50 o.s.i (0-451-40394-0, Signet Bks.) NAL.
—Rough Cut. 1994. 336p. (Orig.). mass mkt. 4.99 o.s.i (0-451-18253-7) NAL.
—Shot on Location. 1993. (Goodman-Bradley Mystery Ser.). 352p. 19.00 o.p. (0-525-93576-2) Dutton/Plume.
—Shot on Location. 1994. (Goodman-Bradley Mystery Ser.). 336p. mass mkt. 4.99 o.p. (0-451-40391-6, Signet Bks.) NAL.
Darty, Peggy. Spirits. 1998. (Palisades Pure Romance Ser.). 252p. pap. 9.99 o.s.i (1-57673-460-9) Multnomah Pubs., Inc.
Davis, Kenn. Acts of Homicide. 1989. 224p. mass mkt. 3.50 o.s.i (0-449-13351-6, Fawcett) Ballantine Bks.
—As October Dies. 1987. 240p. mass mkt. 2.95 o.s.i (0-449-13097-5, Fawcett) Ballantine Bks.
—Blood of Poets. 1990. 208p. (Orig.). mass mkt. 3.95 o.s.i (0-449-13352-4, Fawcett) Ballantine Bks.
—Melting Point. 1986. 256p. (Orig.). mass mkt. 2.95 o.s.i (0-449-12901-2, Fawcett) Ballantine Bks.
—Nijinsky Is Dead. 1987. 240p. mass mkt. 2.95 o.s.i (0-449-13096-7, Fawcett) Ballantine Bks.
—Words Can Kill. 1984. (Orig.). mass mkt. 2.50 o.s.i (0-449-12667-6, Fawcett) Ballantine Bks.
Davis, Lindsey. The Accusers. 2004. (0-89296-811-7) Mysterious Pr.
—A Body in the Bath House. 2002. 368p. 24.95 (0-89296-771-4) Mysterious Pr.
—A Body in the Bath House. 2003. 368p. pap. 12.95 (0-446-69170-4, Mysterious Pr. Paperback Bks.) Warner Bks., Inc.
—One Virgin Too Many. 2000. E-Book 14.95 (0-7595-6032-3); 368p. E-Book 14.95 (0-7595-0032-0); E-Book 14.95 (0-7595-4032-2); 368p. E-Book 14.95 (0-7595-8033-2); 368p. E-Book 14.95 (0-7595-9037-0); (Illus.). 356p. 23.95 (0-89296-716-1) Mysterious Pr.
—One Virgin Too Many. 2001. 368p. reprint ed. pap. 12.95 (0-446-67769-8) Warner Bks., Inc.
—Two for the Lions. 2000. E-Book 4.95 (0-7595-6030-7); 464p. E-Book 4.95 (0-7595-4030-6); 464p. E-Book 4.95 (0-7595-0030-4); 464p. E-Book 4.95 (0-7595-9035-4) Mysterious Pr.
—Two for the Lions. 2000. (Marcus Didius Falco Mystery Ser.). 464p. mass mkt. 6.99 (0-446-60902-1); E-Book 4.95 (0-7595-8031-6) Warner Bks., Inc.
Dawson, Janet. A Credible Threat. 1996. 256p. 21.00 o.p. (0-449-90977-8, Fawcett) Ballantine Bks.
Derleth, August. The Final Adventures of Solar Pons. 1998. (August Derleth Library ). 240p. 28.00 (1-55246-012-6) Battered Silicon Dispatch Box, The.
—The Return of Solar Pons. 1975. (Solar Pons Ser.: No. 6). 288p. pap. 1.50 o.p. (0-523-23650-6, Pinnacle Bks.) Kensington Publishing Corp.
—Solar Pons: The Chronicles of Solar Pons, No. 1. 1973. 8.95 o.p. (0-87054-005-X, Mycroft & Moran) Arkham Hse. Pubs.
—The Solar Pons Omnibus Edition, 2 Vols., Set. Copper, Basil, ed. 1982. (Illus.). 39.95 o.p. (0-87054-006-8, Mycroft & Moran) Arkham Hse. Pubs.
Dewhurst, Eileen. Double Act. l.t. ed. 2001. (Magna Large Print Ser.). 320p. 31.99 (0-7505-1601-1) Magna Large Print Bks. GBR. Dist: Ulverscroft Large Print Bks., Ltd., Ulverscroft Large Print Canada, Ltd.
—Double Act. 2000. 218p. 26.00 (0-7278-5533-6) Severn Hse. Pubs., Ltd.
—Easeful Death. 2002. 224p. 25.99 (0-7278-5906-4) Severn Hse. Pubs., Ltd.
Dickinson, David. Death & the Jubilee. 2003. 352p. 24.00 (0-7867-1110-8, Carroll & Graf Pubs.) Avalon Publishing Group.
—Death of an Old Master. 2004. 272p. 24.00 (0-7867-1306-2, Carroll & Graf Pubs.) Avalon Publishing Group.
Dobyns, Stephen. Saratoga Backtalk. unabr. collector's ed. 1995. audio 36.00 (0-7366-2969-6, 3660) Books on Tape, Inc.
—Saratoga Backtalk. l.t. ed. 1995. (Large Print Bks.). pap. 21.95 o.p. (1-56895-089-6, Wheeler Publishing, Inc.) Gale Group.
—Saratoga Backtalk. 1994. 221p. 19.95 o.p. (0-393-03659-6) Norton, W. W. & Co., Inc.
—Saratoga Backtalk. 1995. (Charlie Bradshaw Mystery Ser.). 224p. pap. 5.99 o.s.i (0-14-024708-4, Penguin Bks.) Penguin Group (USA) Inc.
—Saratoga Bestiary. unabr. collector's ed. 1994. audio 42.00 (0-7366-2792-8, 3507) Books on Tape, Inc.
—Saratoga Bestiary. (Charlie Bradshaw Mystery Ser.). 1990. 304p. pap. 4.50 o.p. (0-14-010613-8, Penguin Bks.); 1988. 272p. 16.95 o.p. (0-670-82024-5) Viking Penguin.
—Saratoga Fleshpot. unabr. collector's ed. 1996. audio 36.00 (0-7366-3356-1, 4007) Books on Tape, Inc.
—Saratoga Fleshpot. 1995. 220p. 21.00 (0-393-03805-X) Norton, W. W. & Co., Inc.
—Saratoga Fleshpot. 1996. (Charlie Bradshaw Mystery Ser.). 224p. pap. 5.95 o.p. (0-14-025535-4, Penguin Bks.) Penguin Group (USA) Inc.
—Saratoga Haunting. unabr. collector's ed. 1994. audio 36.00 (0-7366-2836-3, 3544) Books on Tape, Inc.
—Saratoga Haunting. 1994. (Charlie Bradshaw Mystery Ser.). 224p. pap. 6.95 o.p. (0-14-017162-2, Penguin Bks.) Penguin Group (USA) Inc.
—Saratoga Haunting. 1993. (Charlie Bradshaw Mystery Ser.). 224p. 19.00 o.p. (0-670-84581-7, Viking) Viking Penguin.
—Saratoga Headhunter. unabr. collector's ed. 1994. audio 36.00 (0-7366-2754-5, 3477) Books on Tape, Inc.
—Saratoga Headhunter. 1991. (Charlie Bradshaw Mystery Ser.). 224p. pap. 4.95 o.p. (0-14-015606-2, Penguin Bks.) Penguin Group (USA) Inc.
—Saratoga Headhunter. (Crime Monthly Ser.). 1986. pap. 3.50 o.p. (0-14-007772-3, Penguin Bks.); 1985. 13.95 o.p. (0-670-80488-6) Viking Penguin.
—Saratoga Hexameter. unabr. collector's ed. 1994. audio 48.00 (0-7366-2890-8, 3590) Books on Tape, Inc.
—Saratoga Hexameter. l.t. ed. 1991. (General Ser.). 391p. lib. bdg. 20.95 (0-8161-5133-4, Macmillan Reference USA) Gale Group.
—Saratoga Hexameter. 1991. (Crime Monthly Ser.). 256p. pap. 4.95 o.p. (0-14-011691-5, Penguin Bks.) Penguin Group (USA) Inc.
—Saratoga Hexameter. 1990. (Charlie Bradshaw Mystery Ser.). 256p. 16.95 o.p. (0-670-82568-9, Viking) Viking Penguin.
—Saratoga Longshot. unabr. collector's ed. 1994. audio 36.00 (0-7366-2698-0, 3432) Books on Tape, Inc.
—Saratoga Longshot. 1987. (Charlie Bradshaw Mystery Ser.). 256p. pap. 3.95 o.p. (0-14-009627-2, Penguin Bks.) Viking Penguin.
—Saratoga Snapper. unabr. collector's ed. 1994. audio 42.00 (0-7366-2793-6, 3508) Books on Tape, Inc.
—Saratoga Snapper. l.t. ed. 1988. 329p. 17.95 o.p. (0-8161-4348-X, Macmillan Reference USA) Gale Group.
—Saratoga Snapper. (Charlie Bradshaw Mystery Ser.). 1987. 272p. pap. 3.95 o.p. (0-14-008812-1, Penguin Bks.); 1986. 288p. 15.95 o.p. (0-670-81059-2) Viking Penguin.
—Saratoga Strongbox. l.t. ed. 2000. pap. 23.95 (1-56895-848-X, Wheeler Publishing, Inc.) Gale Group.
—Saratoga Strongbox. 1999. (Charlie Bradshaw Mysteries Ser.). 224p. pap. 5.99 o.s.i (0-14-028012-X) Penguin Group (USA) Inc.
—Saratoga Strongbox. 1998. (Charlie Bradshaw Mysteries Ser.). 208p. 21.95 o.p. (0-670-87692-5) Viking Penguin.
—Saratoga Swimmer. unabr. collector's ed. 1994. audio 36.00 (0-7366-2753-7, 3476) Books on Tape, Inc.
—Saratoga Swimmer. 1981. 12.95 o.p. (0-689-11193-2, Scribner) Simon & Schuster.
—Saratoga Swimmer. 1983. (Charlie Bradshaw Mystery Ser.). 224p. pap. 5.95 o.p. (0-14-006357-9, Penguin Bks.) Viking Penguin.

—Saratoga Trifecta. 1995. (Charlie Bradshaw Mystery Ser.). 544p. pap. 24.00 o.s.i (*0-14-025196-0*, Penguin Bks.) Penguin Group (USA) Inc.
Dold, Gaylord. Samedi's Backpack: Mitch Robert's Mystery. 2001. 313p. 23.95 (*0-312-26643-X*, Saint Martin's Minotaur) St. Martin's Pr.
Donaldson, Stephen R. The Man Who Killed His Brother. 2002. (Illus.). 256p. 24.95 (*0-7653-0203-9*, Forge Bks.) Doherty, Tom Assocs., LLC.
Doolittle, Jerome. Head Lock. Grose, Bill, ed. 1993. 272p. 20.00 (*0-671-79978-9*, Atria) Simon & Schuster.
—Head Lock. 1900. per. 4.99 (*0-671-50288-3*, Pocket) Simon & Schuster.
—Head Lock. 262p. 3.98 o.p. (*0-8317-2353-X*) Smithmark Pubs., Inc.
Douglas, Carole Nelson. Chapel Noir. 2001. 480p. 25.95 (*0-312-85493-5*, Forge Bks.) Doherty, Tom Assocs., LLC.
—Femme Fatale. Date not set. mass mkt. (*0-7653-4595-1*); 2003. 554p. 25.95 (*0-7653-0682-4*) Doherty, Tom Assocs., LLC. (Forge Bks.).
Douglas, Lauren W. The Always Anonymous Beast. 1987. (Caitlin Reece Mysteries Ser.). 224p. pap. 8.95 o.p. (*0-941483-04-5*) Naiad Pr., Inc.
—The Daughters of Artemis. 1991. (Caitlin Reece Mystery Ser.). 240p. (Orig.). pap. 9.95 (*0-941483-95-9*) Naiad Pr., Inc.
—Goblin Market. 1993. (Caitlin Reece Mysteries Ser.: No. 5). 224p. pap. 10.95 (*1-56280-047-7*) Naiad Pr., Inc.
—Ninth Life. 1990. (Caitlin Reece Mysteries Ser.). 256p. pap. 9.95 (*0-941483-50-9*) Naiad Pr., Inc.
—A Rage of Maidens: Sixth Caitlin Reece Mystery. 1994. (Caitlin Reece Mysteries Ser.). 224p. pap. 10.95 (*1-56280-068-X*) Naiad Pr., Inc.
—A Tiger's Heart. 1992. (Caitlin Reece Mysteries Ser.: No. 4). 240p. pap. 9.95 (*1-56280-018-3*) Naiad Pr., Inc.
Doyle, Arthur Conan. The Case-Book of Sherlock Holmes. 1986. mass mkt. 3.50 o.p. (*0-425-10194-0*); 1984. mass mkt. 2.50 o.s.i (*0-425-07175-8*) Berkley Publishing Group.
—The Case-Book of Sherlock Holmes. 2001. vi, 296p. pap. 8.95 (*0-7551-0647-4*) House of Stratus, Inc. GBR. *Dist:* Midpoint Trade Bks., Inc.
—The Case-Book of Sherlock Holmes. Robson, W. W., ed. (Oxford World's Classics Ser.). 336p. 2000. pap. 10.00 (*0-19-283917-9*); 1993. (C). 13.95 o.p. (*0-19-212311-4*, 14608) Oxford Univ. Pr., Inc.
—The Case-Book of Sherlock Holmes. Robson, W. W., ed. & intro. by. 1995. (Oxford Sherlock Holmes Ser.). 334p. reprint ed. pap. 6.95 o.p. (*0-19-282374-4*) Oxford Univ. Pr., Inc.
—The Case-Book of Sherlock Holmes. 1999. 353p. E-Book 3.99 incl. cd-rom (*1-57646-185-8*) Quiet Vision Publishing.
—The Case-Book of Sherlock Holmes, Vol. 1. abr. ed. 1998. (BBC Radio Presents Ser.). 355p. 16.99 o.s.i incl. audio (*0-553-47904-0*, RH Audio) Random Hse. Audio Publishing Group.
—The Case-Book of Sherlock Holmes. l.t. ed. 1967. 12.00 o.p. (*0-85456-590-6*, Ulverscroft) Thorpe, F. A. Pubs. GBR. *Dist:* Ulverscroft Large Print Bks., Ltd.
—The Case-Book of Sherlock Holmes. unabr. ed. 2000. audio 14.95 (*0-00-105478-3*) Trafalgar Square.
—The Case-Book of Sherlock Holmes. 1998. (Classics Library). 400p. pap. 3.95 (*1-85326-070-3*, 0703WW) Wordsworth Editions, Ltd. GBR. *Dist:* Casemate Pubs. & Bk. Distributors, LLC.
—The Doings of Raffles Haw. 1977. (Short Story Index Reprint Ser.). 16.95 (*0-8369-3249-8*) Ayer Co. Pubs., Inc.
—The Doings of Raffles Haw. (Collected Works of Sir Arthur Conan Doyle). 2001. 199p. pap. text 28.00 (*0-7426-7686-2*); reprint ed. lib. bdg. 98.00 (*0-7426-2686-5*) Classic Bks.
—The Doings of Raffles Haw. 2002. 144p. per. 29.95 (*1-58963-866-2*) Fredonia Bks.
—The Doings of Raffles Haw. 1981. (Conan Doyle Centennial Ser.). (Illus.). 157p. 28.00 (*0-934468-43-5*) Gaslight Pubns.
—The Doings of Raffles Haw. 1986. 256p. 15.00 o.p. (*0-947898-37-9*) Periodicals Service Co.
—The Final Adventures of Sherlock Holmes. 2002. (Illus.). 251p. 27.50 (*0-7090-6738-0*) Hale, Robert Ltd. GBR. *Dist:* Trafalgar Square.
—The Firm of Girdlestone. (Collected Works of Sir Arthur Conan Doyle). 2001. 381p. pap. text 28.00 (*0-7426-7682-X*); reprint ed. lib. bdg. 98.00 (*0-7426-2682-2*) Classic Bks.
—The Firm of Girdlestone. 2001. (Illus.). 380p. per. 24.95 (*1-58963-392-X*) Fredonia Bks.
—The Firm of Girdlestone. 1981. (Conan Doyle Centennial Ser.). (Illus.). 364p. 16.95 o.p. (*0-934468-42-7*) Gaslight Pubns.
—His Last Bow: Some Reminiscences of Sherlock Holmes. Date not set. (Heritage Literary Ser.). pap. text 31.50 (*0-582-34914-1*) Addison-Wesley Longman, Ltd. GBR. *Dist:* Trans-Atlantic Pubns., Inc.
—His Last Bow: Some Reminiscences of Sherlock Holmes. 1987. mass mkt. 2.50 o.p. (*0-425-10491-5*); 1986. mass mkt. 2.50 o.s.i (*0-425-09579-7*); 1984. mass mkt. 2.50 o.s.i (*0-425-07502-8*); 1981. mass mkt. 1.95 o.s.i (*0-425-04870-5*); 1980. mass mkt. 1.75 o.s.i (*0-425-04534-X*); 1978. mass mkt. 1.50 o.s.i (*0-425-04003-8*); 1976. mass mkt. 1.25 o.s.i (*0-425-03129-2*); 1974. mass mkt. 0.95 o.s.i (*0-425-02804-6*) Berkley Publishing Group.
—His Last Bow: Some Reminiscences of Sherlock Holmes. 1990. reprint ed. lib. bdg. 18.95 o.p. (*0-89966-666-3*) Buccaneer Bks., Inc.
—His Last Bow: Some Reminiscences of Sherlock Holmes. reprint ed. lib. bdg. 98.00 (*0-7426-2735-7*); 2001. 212p. pap. text 28.00 (*0-7426-7735-4*) Classic Bks.
—His Last Bow: Some Reminiscences of Sherlock Holmes. 2001. v, 236p. pap. 8.95 (*0-7551-0646-6*) House of Stratus, Inc. GBR. *Dist:* Midpoint Trade Bks., Inc.
—His Last Bow: Some Reminiscences of Sherlock Holmes. Edwards, Owen D., ed. 1993. (Oxford Sherlock Holmes Ser.). 302p. (C). 13.95 o.p. (*0-19-212315-7*) Oxford Univ. Pr., Inc.
—His Last Bow: Some Reminiscences of Sherlock Holmes. Edwards, Owen D., ed. & intro. by. 1995. (Oxford World's Classics Ser.). 304p. reprint ed. pap. 6.95 o.p. (*0-19-282381-7*) Oxford Univ. Pr., Inc.
—His Last Bow: Some Reminiscences of Sherlock Holmes. 1993. 208p. pap. 6.95 o.p. (*0-14-005709-9*) Penguin Group (USA) Inc.
—His Last Bow: Some Reminiscences of Sherlock Holmes. collector's ed. 2002. (Illus.). im. lthr. 38.85 (*1-4115-1256-1*); pap. 19.95 (*1-4115-0526-3*); 25.95 (*1-4115-0884-X*); pap. 17.95 (*1-4115-0315-5*) Polyglot Pr., Inc.
—His Last Bow: Some Reminiscences of Sherlock Holmes. 2001. E-Book 2.95 (*1-58882-433-0*) PublishingOnline.
—His Last Bow: Some Reminiscences of Sherlock Holmes. 1999. 292p. E-Book 3.99 incl. cd-rom (*1-57646-183-1*) Quiet Vision Publishing.
—His Last Bow: Some Reminiscences of Sherlock Holmes. l.t. ed. 1977. (Ulverscroft Large Print Ser.). 29.99 o.p. (*0-7089-0076-3*, Ulverscroft) Thorpe, F. A. Pubs. GBR. *Dist:* Ulverscroft Large Print Bks., Ltd., Ulverscroft Large Print Canada, Ltd.
—The Hound of the Baskervilles. 1976. 19.95 (*0-8488-1286-7*) Amereon, Ltd.
—The Hound of the Baskervilles. 1994. (Illustrated Classics Collection). 64p. pap. 4.95 (*0-7854-0696-4*, 40450); pap. 3.60 o.p. (*1-56103-528-9*) American Guidance Service, Inc.
—The Hound of the Baskervilles. ltd. ed. 1985. (Illus.). 200p. 300.00 o.p. (*0-910457-06-9*) Arion Pr.
—The Hound of the Baskervilles. 1987. 192p. mass mkt. 6.50 (*0-345-35052-9*) Ballantine Bks.
—The Hound of the Baskervilles. Bennett, S. A., ed. 1992. (Adventures of Sherlock Holmes Ser.). (Illus.). 64p. pap. (*0-944099-17-3*) Bill Barry's Compass Bks.
—The Hound of the Baskervilles. 1986. lib. bdg. 19.95 (*0-89966-229-3*) Buccaneer Bks., Inc.
—The Hound of the Baskervilles. reprint ed. lib. bdg. 98.00 (*0-7426-2707-1*); lib. bdg. 48.00 (*0-7426-1122-1*) Classic Bks.
—The Hound of the Baskervilles. adapted ed. 1977. per. 6.50 (*0-8222-0536-X*) Dramatists Play Service, Inc.
—The Hound of the Baskervilles. (Illus.). 208p. 1988. pap. 10.95 o.p. (*0-86547-264-5*, North Point Pr.); 1986. 17.50 o.p. (*0-86547-263-7*) Farrar, Straus & Giroux.
—The Hound of the Baskervilles. 1976. (Crime Fiction Ser). reprint ed. lib. bdg. 21.00 o.p. (*0-8240-2364-1*) Garland Publishing, Inc.
—The Hound of the Baskervilles. 1975. (Illus.). 4.95 o.p. (*0-8052-3602-3*); pap. 2.95 o.p. (*0-8052-0505-5*) Knopf Publishing Group. (Schocken).
—The Hound of the Baskervilles. Goodenough, Simon, ed. 1984. (Illus.). 192p. pap. o.p. (*0-316-32002-1*) Little Brown & Co.
—The Hound of the Baskervilles. Eyre, A. G., ed. 2000. (Longman Simplified English Ser.). 72p. pap. text 5.95 o.p. (*0-582-52910-7*, 73976) Longman Publishing Group.
—The Hound of the Baskervilles. 1997. pap. 3.95 (*0-89375-410-2*); 1986. mass mkt. 2.50 o.p. (*0-451-52221-4*); 100th anniv. ed. 2001. 256p. mass mkt. 4.95 (*0-451-52801-8*) NAL.
—The Hound of the Baskervilles. Robson, W. W., ed. 1993. (Oxford Sherlock Holmes Ser.). 232p. (C). 13.95 o.p. (*0-19-212310-6*, 8954) Oxford Univ. Pr., Inc.
—The Hound of the Baskervilles. Robson, W. W., ed. & intro. by. (Oxford World's Classics Ser.). 232p. reprint ed. 1998. pap. 8.95 (*0-19-283519-X*); 1995. pap. 6.95 o.p. (*0-19-282377-9*) Oxford Univ. Pr., Inc.
—The Hound of the Baskervilles. 1981. (Sherlock Holmes Ser.). 176p. (C). pap. 5.95 (*0-14-000111-5*, Penguin Bks.) Penguin Group (USA) Inc.
—The Hound of the Baskervilles. 1996. (Sherlock Holmes Ser.). (Illus.). 120p. 9.98 (*1-879582-15-5*) Platinum Pr., Inc.
—The Hound of the Baskervilles. 1986. 11.00 (*0-606-01869-7*) Turtleback Bks.
—The Memoirs of Sherlock Holmes. 1986. mass mkt. 2.50 o.s.i (*0-425-09576-2*); 1984. mass mkt. 2.50 o.s.i (*0-425-07315-7*); 1976. mass mkt. 1.75 o.s.i (*0-425-04400-9*) Berkley Publishing Group.
—The Memoirs of Sherlock Holmes. 1982. reprint ed. lib. bdg. 21.95 o.p. (*0-89966-428-8*) Buccaneer Bks., Inc.
—The Memoirs of Sherlock Holmes. reprint ed. lib. bdg. 98.00 (*0-7426-2692-X*); 2001. (Collected Works of Sir Arthur Conan Doyle: Vol. 6). pap. text 28.00 (*0-7426-7692-7*) Classic Bks.
—The Memoirs of Sherlock Holmes. 2001. (Illus.). 300p. pap. 8.95 (*0-7551-0644-X*) House of Stratus, Inc. GBR. *Dist:* Midpoint Trade Bks., Inc.
—The Memoirs of Sherlock Holmes. 2002. 240p. 18.99 (*1-4043-1910-7*); per. 13.99 (*1-4043-1911-5*) IndyPublish.com.
—The Memoirs of Sherlock Holmes. 1976. (Illus.). 176p. 5.95 o.p. (*0-8052-3622-8*, Schocken) Knopf Publishing Group.
—The Memoirs of Sherlock Holmes. E-Book 2.95 (*1-57799-810-3*) Logos Research Systems, Inc.
—The Memoirs of Sherlock Holmes. l.t. ed. (Large Print Ser.). reprint ed. 1986. 421p. lib. bdg. 26.00 (*0-939495-31-7*); 1998. 270p. lib. bdg. 25.00 (*1-58287-049-7*) North Bks.
—The Memoirs of Sherlock Holmes. Roden, Christopher, ed. (Oxford World's Classics Ser.). 2000. 384p. pap. 9.95 (*0-19-283811-3*); 1993. 378p. (C). 13.95 o.p. (*0-19-212309-2*) Oxford Univ. Pr., Inc.
—The Memoirs of Sherlock Holmes. Roden, Christopher, ed. & intro. by. 1995. (Oxford World's Classics Ser.). 378p. reprint ed. pap. 6.95 o.p. (*0-19-282375-2*) Oxford Univ. Pr., Inc.
—The Memoirs of Sherlock Holmes. 1996. (Sherlock Holmes Ser.). (Illus.). 160p. 9.98 (*1-879582-14-7*) Platinum Pr., Inc.
—The Memoirs of Sherlock Holmes. collector's ed. 2002. (Illus.). im. lthr. 38.85 (*1-4115-1248-0*); pap. 19.95 (*1-4115-0518-2*); 25.95 (*1-4115-0886-6*); pap. 19.95 (*1-4115-0314-7*) Polyglot Pr., Inc.
—The Memoirs of Sherlock Holmes. 1999. 375p. E-Book 3.99 incl. cd-rom (*1-57646-178-5*) Quiet Vision Publishing.
—The Memoirs of Sherlock Holmes. 1994. audio 15.95 o.s.i (*0-553-74577-8*); 1994. audio 15.95 o.s.i (*0-553-74612-X*); 1993. audio 12.79 o.s.i (*0-553-74550-6*); 1993. audio 15.95 o.s.i (*0-553-70054-5*); Vols. 1-3. 1997. 29.95 o.s.i incl. audio (*0-553-47954-7*) Random Hse. Audio Publishing Group. (RH Audio).
—The Memoirs of Sherlock Holmes. l.t. ed. 1966. (Ulverscroft Large Print Ser.). 29.99 o.p. (*0-85456-573-6*, Ulverscroft) Thorpe, F. A. Pubs. GBR. *Dist:* Ulverscroft Large Print Bks., Ltd., Ulverscroft Large Print Canada, Ltd.
—The Memoirs of Sherlock Holmes. 2001. (Classics of Mystery & Suspense Ser.). 318p. (*1-58279-190-2*) Trident Pr. International.
—The Memoirs of Sherlock Holmes. 1951. 256p. pap. 3.95 o.p. (*0-14-000785-7*, Penguin Bks.) Viking Penguin.
—The Memoirs of Sherlock Holmes. 2001. 230p. pap. 12.95 (*0-595-01467-4*) iUniverse, Inc.
—The Original Illustrated Strand Sherlock Holmes: The Complete Facsimile Edition. 2000. (Illus.). 1126p. reprint ed. pap. text 25.00 (*0-7881-9173-X*) DIANE Publishing Co.
—The Return of Sherlock Holmes. Date not set. (Heritage Literary Ser.). pap. text 31.50 (*0-582-34913-3*) Addison-Wesley Longman, Ltd. GBR. *Dist:* Trans-Atlantic Pubns., Inc.
—The Return of Sherlock Holmes. 1985. 320p. mass mkt. 2.95 o.s.i (*0-345-32713-6*) Ballantine Bks.
—The Return of Sherlock Holmes. 1986. 320p. mass mkt. 2.95 o.p. (*0-425-10151-7*); 1986. mass mkt. 2.50 o.s.i (*0-425-09578-9*); 1985. mass mkt. 2.50 o.s.i (*0-425-08005-6*); 1983. mass mkt. 2.50 o.s.i (*0-425-07125-1*); 1982. mass mkt. 2.25 o.s.i (*0-425-04871-3*); 1979. mass mkt. 1.75 o.s.i (*0-425-04536-6*); 1978. mass mkt. 1.50 o.s.i (*0-425-04071-2*); 1976. mass mkt. 1.25 o.s.i (*0-425-03334-1*); 1973. mass mkt. 0.75 o.p. (*0-425-02353-2*) Berkley Publishing Group.
—The Return of Sherlock Holmes. reprint ed. lib. bdg. 98.00 (*0-7426-2711-X*) Classic Bks.
—The Return of Sherlock Holmes. E-Book 2.49 (*0-7574-0391-3*) Electric Umbrella Publishing.
—The Return of Sherlock Holmes. 1975. (Illus.). 5.95 o.p. (*0-8052-3603-1*); pap. 2.95 o.p. (*0-8052-0506-3*) Knopf Publishing Group. (Schocken).
—The Return of Sherlock Holmes. E-Book 2.95 (*1-57799-838-3*) Logos Research Systems, Inc.
—The Return of Sherlock Holmes. (English As a Second Language Bk.). 1981. pap. 5.95 o.p. (*0-582-52411-3*); Level 3. 2001. pap. 7.66 (*0-582-42697-9*) Longman Publishing Group.
—The Return of Sherlock Holmes. 1987. (Illus.). 320p. 25.00 o.p. (*0-89296-248-8*) Mysterious Pr.
—The Return of Sherlock Holmes. 2003. (Twelve-Point Ser.). lib. bdg. 25.00 (*1-58287-207-4*); lib. bdg. 26.00 (*1-58287-691-6*) North Bks.
—The Return of Sherlock Holmes. Green, Richard Lancelyn, ed. 1993. (Sherlock Holmes Ser.). 474p. (C). 13.95 o.p. (*0-19-212317-3*, 8952) Oxford Univ. Pr., Inc.
—The Return of Sherlock Holmes. Green, Richard Lancelyn, ed. & intro. by. 1995. (Oxford World's Classics Ser.). 456p. reprint ed. pap. 5.95 o.p. (*0-19-282376-0*) Oxford Univ. Pr., Inc.
—The Return of Sherlock Holmes. 1996. (Sherlock Holmes Ser.). (Illus.). 200p. 9.98 (*1-879582-13-9*) Platinum Pr., Inc.
—The Return of Sherlock Holmes. 1999. 482p. E-Book 3.99 incl. cd-rom (*1-57646-179-3*) Quiet Vision Publishing.
—The Return of Sherlock Holmes. l.t. ed. 1967. (Ulverscroft Large Print Ser.). 29.99 o.p. (*0-85456-574-4*, Ulverscroft) Thorpe, F. A. Pubs. GBR. *Dist:* Ulverscroft Large Print Bks., Ltd., Ulverscroft Large Print Canada, Ltd.
—The Return of Sherlock Holmes. 1987. 192p. pap. 3.50 o.p. (*0-14-010026-1*); 1982. 336p. pap. 5.95 o.p. (*0-14-005708-0*) Viking Penguin. (Penguin Bks.).
—The Return of Sherlock Holmes. 1997. (Classics Library). 320p. pap. 3.95 (*1-85326-058-4*, 0584WW) Wordsworth Editions, Ltd. GBR. *Dist:* Combined Publishing.
—The Return of Sherlock Holmes: The Oxford Sherlock Holmes. 1999. (Oxford World's Classics Ser.). pap. text 5.95 (*0-19-283761-3*) Oxford Univ. Pr., Inc.
—Sherlock Holmes: Selected Stories. Date not set. lib. bdg. 29.95 (*0-8488-1672-2*) Amereon, Ltd.
—Sherlock Holmes: Selected Stories. Roberts, S. C., ed. & intro. by. 1998. (Oxford World's Classics Ser.). 464p. pap. 10.95 (*0-19-283537-8*) Oxford Univ. Pr., Inc.
—Sherlock Holmes: Selected Stories. 1982. (Oxford World's Classics Ser.). 460p. pap. 7.95 o.p. (*0-19-281530-X*) Oxford Univ. Pr., Inc.
—Sherlock Holmes: The Complete Novels & Stories, Vol. II. 1986. (Bantam Classics Ser.). 768p. reprint ed. mass mkt. 6.95 (*0-553-21242-7*) Bantam Dell Publishing Group.
—Sherlock Holmes: The Complete Novels & Stories. 1986. 12.55 (*0-606-03127-8*) Turtleback Bks.
—Sherlock Holmes Reader. 1975. 3.95 o.s.i (*0-425-03010-5*) Berkley Publishing Group.
—A Study in Scarlet & The Sign of the Four. 1986. mass mkt. 2.50 o.s.i (*0-425-09577-0*); 1983. mass mkt. 2.25 o.s.i (*0-425-05209-5*); 1978. mass mkt. 1.75 o.s.i (*0-425-04117-4*); 1975. mass mkt. 1.25 o.s.i (*0-425-02838-0*) Berkley Publishing Group.
—A Study in Scarlet & The Sign of the Four. 2003. (Dover Thrift Editions Ser.). 208p. 2.50 (*0-486-43166-5*) Dover Pubns., Inc.
Driver, Lee. The Good Die Twice. (Chase Dagger Mystery Ser.). 2000. 304p. pap. 6.50 (*0-9666021-5-3*); 1999. 315p. 21.95 o.p. (*0-9666021-1-0*) Full Moon Publishing.
Dunlap, Susan. High Fall. 1995. (Kiernan O'Shaugnessy Mystery Ser.). 320p. mass mkt. 5.99 o.s.i (*0-440-21560-9*) Dell Publishing.
—High Fall. l.t. ed. 1995. (Large Print Bks.). pap. 20.95 (*1-56895-093-4*, Wheeler Publishing, Inc.) Gale Group.
—No Immunity: A Kiernan O'Shaughnessy Mystery. 1999. (Kiernan O'Shaugnessy Mystery Ser.). 352p. mass mkt. 5.99 o.s.i (*0-440-22480-2*) Dell Publishing.
—No Immunity: A Kiernan O'Shaughnessy Mystery. l.t. ed. 1999. pap. 23.95 (*1-56895-782-3*, Wheeler Publishing, Inc.) Gale Group.
—Pious Deception. 1990. 256p. mass mkt. 5.99 o.s.i (*0-440-20746-0*) Dell Publishing.
—Rogue Wave. 1992. 272p. mass mkt. 5.99 o.s.i (*0-440-21197-2*) Dell Publishing.
—Rogue Wave. 1994. 3.99 o.p. (*0-517-13047-5*) Random Hse. Value Publishing.
Dunlop, Barbara. Next to Nothing! 2002. (Harlequin Temptation Ser.). 224p. mass mkt. (*0-373-69101-7*, Harlequin Bks.) Harlequin Enterprises, Ltd.
Dunlop, Susan, et al. Crime's Leading Ladies. unabr. ed. 1995. 3p. audio 16.99 (*0-88646-376-9*, 390575) Durkin Hayes Publishing Ltd.
Dunn, Alan. Payback: A Mystery. 2003. 320p. 24.95 (*0-312-31099-4*) St. Martin's Pr.
Eichler, Selma. Murder Can Kill Your Social Life. 1994. (Desiree Shapiro Mystery Ser.). 256p. mass mkt. 5.99 (*0-451-18139-5*, Signet Bks.) NAL.
—Murder Can Kill Your Social Life. l.t. ed. 2001. 388p. 28.95 (*0-7862-3473-3*) Thorndike Pr.

—Murder Can Ruin Your Looks. 1995. (Desiree Shapiro Mystery Ser.: 2). 272p. (Orig.). mass mkt. 5.99 (*0-451-18384-3*, Signet Bks.) NAL.
—Murder Can Singe Your Old Flame. 1999. (Desiree Shapiro Mystery Ser.). 256p. mass mkt. 5.99 (*0-451-19218-4*, Signet Bks.) NAL.
—Murder Can Singe Your Old Flame: A Desiree Shapiro Mystery. l.t. ed. 2001. (Thorndike Mystery Ser.). 397p. 28.95 o.p. (*0-7862-3191-2*) Thorndike Pr.
—Murder Can Spoil Your Appetite. 2000. (Desiree Shapiro Mystery Ser.). 272p. mass mkt. 5.99 (*0-451-19958-8*, Signet Bks.) NAL.
—Murder Can Spook Your Cat: A Desiree Shapiro Mystery. 1998. (Desiree Shapiro Mystery Ser.). 272p. mass mkt. 5.99 (*0-451-19217-6*, Signet Bks.) NAL.
—Murder Can Stunt Your Growth. 1996. (Desiree Shapiro Mystery Ser.). 272p. mass mkt. 5.99 (*0-451-18514-5*, Signet Bks.) NAL.
—Murder Can Wreck a Reunion. 1997. (Desiree Shapiro Mystery Ser.). 272p. mass mkt. 5.99 (*0-451-18521-8*, Signet Bks.) NAL.
Ellroy, James. Brown's Requiem. 1998. 256p. pap. 13.00 (*0-380-73177-0*); 1981. pap. 4.99 (*0-380-78741-5*) Morrow/Avon. (Avon Bks.).
Elrod, P. N. A Chill in the Blood. (Vampire Files Ser.: Vol. 7). 336p. 1998. 20.95 o.s.i (*0-441-00501-2*); 1999. reprint ed. mass mkt. 6.50 o.s.i (*0-441-00627-2*) Ace Bks.
—Cold Streets. 2003. 384p. mass mkt. 6.99 (*0-441-01103-9*); (Vampire Files Ser.: Bk. 9). 22.95 (*0-441-01009-1*) Ace Bks.
—Dark Sleep. (Vampire Files Ser.: Vol. 8). 368p. 2000. mass mkt. 6.99 (*0-441-00723-6*); 1999. 21.95 o.s.i (*0-441-00591-8*) Ace Bks.
—Lady Crymsyn: A Novel of the Vampire Files. 2000. (Vampire Files Ser.: Vol. 9). (Illus.). 416p. 22.95 o.s.i (*0-441-00724-4*) Ace Bks.
—Vampire Files: Blood Art. 1991. (Vampire Files Ser.: Vol. 4). 208p. mass mkt. 5.99 o.s.i (*0-441-85945-3*) Ace Bks.
—Vampire Files: Blood on the Water. 1992. (Vampire Files Ser.: Vol. 6). 208p. mass mkt. 5.99 o.s.i (*0-441-85947-X*) Ace Bks.
—Vampire Files: Fire in the Blood. 1991. (Vampire Files Ser.: Vol. 5). mass mkt. 5.99 o.s.i (*0-441-85946-1*) Ace Bks.
—Vampire Files No. 01: Bloodlist. 1990. (Vampire Files Ser.). 208p. mass mkt. 6.50 o.s.i (*0-441-06795-6*) Ace Bks.
—Vampire Files No. 2: Lifeblood. 1990. (Vampire Files Ser.: Vol. 2). 208p. mass mkt. 5.99 o.s.i (*0-441-84776-5*) Ace Bks.
—Vampire Files No. 3: Bloodcircle. 1990. (Vampire Files Ser.: Vol. 3). mass mkt. 5.99 o.s.i (*0-441-06717-4*) Ace Bks.
Emerson, Earl. Catfish Cafe. 1999. 304p. mass mkt. 6.99 (*0-345-42212-0*); 1998. 272p. 22.00 o.p. (*0-345-42202-3*) Ballantine Bks.
—Deception Pass. 1998. (Thomas Black Mysteries Ser.). 304p. mass mkt. 6.99 (*0-345-40069-0*) Ballantine Bks.
—Deviant Behavior. 1990. (Thomas Black Mysteries Ser.). 224p. mass mkt. 6.50 (*0-345-36028-1*) Ballantine Bks.
—Deviant Behavior. 1988. 256p. 17.95 o.p. (*0-688-08335-8*, Morrow, William & Co.) Morrow/Avon.
—Fat Tuesday. 1988. (Thomas Black Mysteries Ser.). 288p. mass mkt. 6.99 (*0-345-35223-8*) Ballantine Bks.
—Fat Tuesday. 1987. 288p. 16.95 o.p. (*0-688-06770-0*, Morrow, William & Co.) Morrow/Avon.
—The Million-Dollar Tattoo. 1997. (Thomas Black Mysteries Ser.). 304p. mass mkt. 5.99 (*0-345-40067-4*) Ballantine Bks.
—The Million-Dollar Tattoo. unabr. ed. 1997. (Thomas Black Mystery Ser.: Vol. 9). audio 51.00 (*0-7887-0813-9*, 94963E7) Recorded Bks., LLC.
—Nervous Laughter. 1998. mass mkt. 3.99 o.s.i (*0-345-42945-1*); 1997. 288p. mass mkt. 6.50 (*0-345-41407-1*) Ballantine Bks.
—Nervous Laughter. 1986. mass mkt. 4.99 (*0-380-89906-X*, Avon Bks.) Morrow/Avon.
—The Portland Laugher. 1995. (Thomas Black Mysteries Ser.). 352p. mass mkt. 6.50 (*0-345-39782-7*) Ballantine Bks.
—Poverty Bay. 1998. mass mkt. 3.99 o.s.i (*0-345-42944-3*); 1997. 320p. mass mkt. 6.99 (*0-345-41406-3*) Ballantine Bks.
—Poverty Bay. 1985. 256p. mass mkt. 4.99 (*0-380-89647-8*, Avon Bks.) Morrow/Avon.
—Poverty Bay. unabr. ed. 1994. (Thomas Black Mystery Ser.: Vol. 2). audio 51.00 (*1-55690-980-2*, 94119E7) Recorded Bks., LLC.
—The Rainy City. 1998. mass mkt. 3.99 o.s.i (*0-345-42943-5*); 1997. 288p. mass mkt. 6.99 (*0-345-41405-5*) Ballantine Bks.
—The Rainy City. 1985. (Thomas Black Ser.). 240p. mass mkt. 4.99 (*0-380-89517-X*, Avon Bks.) Morrow/Avon.
—The Rainy City. unabr. ed. 1992. (Thomas Black Mystery Ser.: Vol. 1). audio 51.00 (*1-55690-723-0*, 92218E7) Recorded Bks., LLC.
—The Vanishing Smile. (Thomas Black Mysteries Ser.). 1996. 320p. mass mkt. 6.99 (*0-345-40453-X*); 1995. 272p. 21.00 o.s.i (*0-345-38486-5*) Ballantine Bks.
—Yellow Dog Party: A Thomas Black Mystery. 1992. (Thomas Black Mysteries Ser.). 256p. mass mkt. 6.99 (*0-345-37716-8*) Ballantine Bks.
—Yellow Dog Party: A Thomas Black Mystery. 1991. 288p. 19.00 o.p. (*0-688-09635-2*, Morrow, William & Co.) Morrow/Avon.
Engel, Howard. A City Called July. 1988. 39.50 o.p. (*0-14-778233-3*) Penguin Group (USA) Inc.
—A City Called July. 1986. 256p. 15.95 o.p. (*0-312-13986-1*) St. Martin's Pr.
—A City Called July. l.t. ed. 1989. (Ulverscroft Large Print Ser.). 481p. 29.99 o.p. (*0-7089-1957-X*, Ulverscroft) Thorpe, F. A. Pubs. GBR. *Dist:* Ulverscroft Large Print Bks., Ltd., Ulverscroft Large Print Canada, Ltd.
—A City Called July. 1988. 228p. pap. 3.95 o.p. (*0-14-010454-2*, Penguin Bks.) Viking Penguin.
—Getting Away with Murder. 1998. (Benny Cooperman Mystery Ser.). 248p. 22.95 (*0-87951-829-4*) Overlook Pr., The.
—Murder on Location. 1986. 35.00 o.p. (*0-14-779206-1*) Penguin Group (USA) Inc.
—Murder on Location. 1985. 222p. 12.95 o.p. (*0-312-55314-5*) St. Martin's Pr.
—Murder on Location. 1986. (Crime Monthly Ser.). 222p. pap. 3.50 o.p. (*0-14-007742-1*, Penguin Bks.) Viking Penguin.
—Murder Sees the Light: A Benny Cooperman Mystery. 1985. 256p. 13.95 o.p. (*0-312-55324-2*) St. Martin's Pr.
—Murder Sees the Light: A Benny Cooperman Mystery. l.t. ed. 1988. (Ulverscroft Large Print Ser.). 432p. 29.99 o.p. (*0-7089-1911-1*, Ulverscroft) Thorpe, F. A. Pubs. GBR. *Dist:* Ulverscroft Large Print Bks., Ltd., Ulverscroft Large Print Canada, Ltd.
—Murder Sees the Light: A Benny Cooperman Mystery. 1986. 240p. pap. 3.50 o.p. (*0-14-008975-6*, Penguin Bks.) Viking Penguin.
—The Ransom Game. 1984. 218p. 11.95 o.p. (*0-312-66383-8*) St. Martin's Pr.
—The Ransom Game. l.t. ed. 1989. (Ulverscroft Large Print Ser.). 29.99 o.p. (*0-7089-2052-7*, Ulverscroft) Thorpe, F. A. Pubs. GBR. *Dist:* Ulverscroft Large Print Bks., Ltd., Ulverscroft Large Print Canada, Ltd.
—The Ransom Game. 1986. (Crime Monthly Ser.). 224p. pap. 3.95 o.p. (*0-14-007741-3*, Penguin Bks.) Viking Penguin.
—The Suicide Murders. l.t. ed. 1987. pap. 13.95 o.p. (*1-55504-257-0*) BBC Audiobooks America.
—The Suicide Murders. 1984. 200p. 11.95 o.p. (*0-312-77527-X*) St. Martin's Pr.
—The Suicide Murders. 1985. (Crime Ser.). 208p. pap. 3.95 o.p. (*0-14-007740-5*, Penguin Bks.) Viking Penguin.
—There Was an Old Woman. 2000. (Benny Cooperman Mystery Ser.). 262p. 24.95 (*1-58567-044-8*) Overlook Pr., The.
—A Victim Must Be Found: A Benny Cooperman Mystery. l.t. ed. 1989. 383p. lib. bdg. 17.95 o.p. (*1-85057-734-X*, Macmillan Reference USA) Gale Group.
—A Victim Must Be Found: A Benny Cooperman Mystery. 1988. 288p. 16.95 o.p. (*0-312-02315-4*, Saint Martin's Minotaur) St. Martin's Pr.
—A Victim Must Be Found: A Benny Cooperman Mystery. 1990. 288p. pap. 3.95 o.p. (*0-14-011205-7*, Penguin Bks.) Viking Penguin.
Estleman, Loren D. Angel Eyes. 1986. mass mkt. 3.95 o.s.i (*0-449-21134-7*, Fawcett) Ballantine Bks.
—Angel Eyes. 1981. 11.95 o.p. (*0-395-31558-1*) Houghton Mifflin Co.
—Angel Eyes. 1984. 256p. pap. 2.75 o.p. (*0-523-42185-0*, Pinnacle Bks.) Kensington Publishing Corp.
—Angel Eyes. 2000. (Amos Walker Mysteries Ser.). 256p. reprint ed. pap. 14.00 (*0-671-03900-8*) ibooks, Inc.
—Downriver. 1989. mass mkt. 3.95 o.s.i (*0-449-21623-3*, Fawcett) Ballantine Bks.
—Downriver, 001. 1988. 192p. 15.95 o.p. (*0-395-41073-8*) Houghton Mifflin Co.
—Every Brilliant Eye. 1987. mass mkt. 4.95 o.s.i (*0-449-21137-1*, Fawcett) Ballantine Bks.
—Every Brilliant Eye. unabr. ed. 1986. (Amos Walker Ser.). audio 19.95 o.p. (*0-930435-26-5*, 378, Bookcassette) Brilliance Audio.
—Every Brilliant Eye. Howe, J. C., ed. unabr. ed. 1986. (Amos Walker Ser.). audio 57.25 o.p. (*1-56100-021-3*, 560) Brilliance Audio.
—Every Brilliant Eye, 001. 1986. 264p. 15.95 o.p. (*0-395-39428-7*) Houghton Mifflin Co.
—General Murders: Ten Amos Walker Mysteries. 1989. 192p. mass mkt. 3.95 o.s.i (*0-449-21696-9*, Fawcett) Ballantine Bks.
—General Murders: Ten Amos Walker Mysteries, 001. 1988. 256p. 16.95 o.p. (*0-395-41071-1*) Houghton Mifflin Co.
—General Murders: Ten Amos Walker Mysteries. l.t. ed. 1992. (Ulverscroft Large Print Ser.). 432p. 29.99 o.p. (*0-7089-2622-3*, Ulverscroft) Thorpe, F. A. Pubs. GBR. *Dist:* Ulverscroft Large Print Bks., Ltd., Ulverscroft Large Print Canada, Ltd.
—The Glass Highway. 1987. mass mkt. 3.95 o.s.i (*0-449-21136-3*, Fawcett) Ballantine Bks.
—The Glass Highway. unabr. ed. 1986. (Amos Walker Ser.). audio 57.25 o.p. (*1-56100-019-1*, 561) Brilliance Audio.
—The Glass Highway, 001. 1983. (Amos Walker Mysteries Ser.). 179p. 13.95 o.p. (*0-395-34636-3*) Houghton Mifflin Co.
—The Glass Highway. 1984. 224p. pap. 2.95 o.p. (*0-523-42263-6*, Pinnacle Bks.) Kensington Publishing Corp.
—The Glass Highway. E-Book 9.99 (*1-58824-389-3*); 2000. 240p. pap. 14.00 (*0-7434-0729-6*) ibooks, Inc.
—The Hours of the Virgin. abr. ed. 1999. (Amos Walker Ser.). audio 17.95 o.p. (*1-56740-847-8*, 1743, Nova Audio Bks.); 7p. audio 24.95 (*1-56740-437-5*, 1741, Bookcassette); audio 57.25 (*1-56740-663-7*, 1742, Unabridged Library Editions) Brilliance Audio.
—The Hours of the Virgin. 1999. (Amos Walker Mysteries Ser.). 288p. 23.00 (*0-89296-683-1*) Mysterious Pr.
—The Hours of the Virgin. 2000. 336p. (gr. 8 up). mass mkt. 6.99 (*0-446-60868-8*) Warner Bks., Inc.
—Lady Yesterday. 1988. 224p. mass mkt. 3.95 o.s.i (*0-449-21467-2*, Fawcett) Ballantine Bks.
—Lady Yesterday, 001. 1987. 15.95 o.p. (*0-395-41072-X*) Houghton Mifflin Co.
—The Midnight Man. 1987. mass mkt. 4.95 o.s.i (*0-449-21135-5*, Fawcett) Ballantine Bks.
—The Midnight Man. unabr. ed. 1986. (Amos Walker Ser.). audio 19.95 o.p. (*0-930435-18-4*, 370); audio 57.25 o.p. (*1-56100-013-2*, 552) Brilliance Audio.
—The Midnight Man, 001. 1982. 230p. 12.95 o.p. (*0-395-32204-9*) Houghton Mifflin Co.
—The Midnight Man. 1984. (Amos Walker Mysteries Ser.). 256p. pap. 2.95 o.p. (*0-523-42186-9*, Pinnacle Bks.) Kensington Publishing Corp.
—The Midnight Man. 2000. (Amos Walker Mysteries Ser.). 288p. pap. 14.00 (*0-7434-0002-X*) ibooks, Inc.
—Motor City Blue. 1986. mass mkt. 4.95 o.s.i (*0-449-21133-9*, Fawcett) Ballantine Bks.
—Motor City Blue, 001. 1980. 9.95 o.p. (*0-395-29447-9*) Houghton Mifflin Co.
—Never Street. abr. ed. (Amos Walker Mysteries Ser.). 1998. audio 7.99 o.p. (*1-56740-245-3*, 684, Paperback Nova Audio Bks.); 1997. audio 16.95 o.p. (*1-56100-934-2*, 1311, Nova Audio Bks.); 1997. audio 57.25 o.p. (*1-56100-823-0*, 961, Unabridged Library Editions); 1997. audio 23.95 o.p. (*1-56100-748-X*, 192, Bookcassette) Brilliance Audio.
—Never Street. l.t. ed. 1999. (Magna Large Print Ser.). 432p. (*0-7505-1448-5*) Magna Large Print Bks. GBR. *Dist:* Ulverscroft Large Print Canada, Ltd.
—Never Street. 1998. mass mkt. (*0-446-40483-7*, Mysterious Pr. Paperback Bks.); 1998. 352p. mass mkt. 6.99 (*0-446-60596-4*); 1997. 352p. 23.00 o.p. (*0-89296-633-5*) Warner Bks., Inc.
—Peeper. l.t. ed. 1991. 17.95 o.p. (*0-7451-8203-8*, AH0239); pap. 15.95 o.p. (*0-7927-0751-6*, AS0275) BBC Audiobooks America.
—Peeper. 1990. 224p. reprint ed. mass mkt. 4.99 o.s.i (*0-553-28605-6*) Bantam Bks.
—Poison Blonde: An Amos Walker Novel. 2003. (Amos Walker Ser.). 272p. 24.95 (*0-7653-0447-3*, Forge Bks.) Doherty, Tom Assocs., LLC.
—Silent Thunder. 1990. 224p. mass mkt. 4.95 o.s.i (*0-449-21854-6*, Fawcett) Ballantine Bks.
—Silent Thunder. l.t. ed. 1990. (Large Print Bks.). 286p. lib. bdg. 18.95 o.p. (*0-8161-4976-3*, Macmillan Reference USA) Gale Group.
—Silent Thunder, 001. 1989. 224p. 16.95 o.p. (*0-395-41074-6*) Houghton Mifflin Co.
—Silent Thunder. 2003. 240p. mass mkt. 6.99 (*0-7434-7480-5*) ibooks, Inc.
—Sinister Heights. 2002. lib. bdg. 29.95 (*1-58547-223-9*, Premier) Ctr. Point Large Print.
—Sinister Heights. 2002. 272p. 24.95 (*0-89296-738-2*) Mysterious Pr.
—A Smile on the Face of the Tiger. l.t. ed. 2001. (Large Print Book Ser.). 311p. 28.95 (*1-58724-024-6*, Wheeler Publishing, Inc.) Gale Group.
—A Smile on the Face of the Tiger. 2000. E-Book 14.95 (*0-446-93125-X*); 304p. E-Book 14.95 (*0-446-92250-1*); 304p. E-Book 14.95 (*0-446-92366-4*); 304p. 24.95 o.p. (*0-89296-706-4*) Mysterious Pr.
—A Smile on the Face of the Tiger. 2000. 304p. E-Book 14.95 (*0-446-92858-5*); E-Book 14.95 (*0-446-96087-X*); E-Book 14.95 (*0-446-91368-5*) Warner Bks., Inc.
—Sugartown. l.t. ed. 1985. lib. bdg. 16.95 o.p. (*0-89340-931-6*, 159) BBC Audiobooks America.
—Sugartown. l.t. ed. 1985. mass mkt. 4.99 o.s.i (*0-449-20998-9*, Fawcett) Ballantine Bks.
—Sugartown. unabr. ed. 1986. (Amos Walker Ser.). audio 15.95 o.p. (*0-930435-25-7*, 380, Bookcassette); audio 57.25 o.p. (*1-56100-020-5*, 562) Brilliance Audio.
—Sugartown. 1984. 220p. 13.95 o.p. (*0-395-36449-3*) Houghton Mifflin Co.
—Sugartown. 1984. 220p. 25.00 (*0-89366-256-9*) Ultramarine Publishing Co., Inc.
—Sugartown. E-Book 9.99 (*1-58824-394-X*); 2001. 256p. pap. 14.00 (*0-7434-1293-1*) ibooks, Inc.
—Sweet Women Lie. 1991. mass mkt. 4.99 o.s.i (*0-449-21944-5*, Fawcett) Ballantine Bks.
—Sweet Women Lie. 1990. (Amos Walker Mysteries Ser.). 208p. 18.95 o.p. (*0-395-53767-3*) Houghton Mifflin Co.
—The Witchfinder. abr. ed. (Amos Walker Mysteries Ser.). 1999. audio 7.99 o.s.i (*1-56740-292-5*, 1753, Paperback Nova Audio Bks.); 1998. audio 24.95 (*1-56740-052-3*, 7, Bookcassette); 1998. audio 57.25 (*1-56740-581-9*, 1101, Unabridged Library Editions); Set. 1998. audio 17.95 o.p. (*1-56740-778-1*, 440, Nova Audio Bks.) Brilliance Audio.
—The Witchfinder. 1998. (Amos Walker Mysteries Ser.). 320p. 23.00 o.p. (*0-89296-663-7*) Mysterious Pr.
—The Witchfinder. l.t. ed. 1998. (Cloak & Dagger Ser.). 408p. 27.95 (*0-7862-1509-7*) Thorndike Pr.
—The Witchfinder. l.t. ed. 2000. (Ulverscroft Large Print Ser.). 416p. 31.99 (*0-7089-4252-0*, Ulverscroft) Thorpe, F. A. Pubs. GBR. *Dist:* Ulverscroft Large Print Bks., Ltd., Ulverscroft Large Print Canada, Ltd.
—The Witchfinder. 1999. E-Book 4.95 (*0-446-92328-1*) Time Warner Bk. Group.
—The Witchfinder. 1999. 320p. mass mkt. 6.50 (*0-446-60760-6*); E-Book 4.95 (*0-446-91300-6*) Warner Bks., Inc.
Evans, Liz. Don't Mess with Mrs. In-Between. 2002. 406p. mass mkt. 7.95 (*0-7528-4297-8*) Trafalgar Square.
Faherty, Terence. Come Back Dead. 1997. 336p. 22.00 o.p. (*0-684-83084-1*, Simon & Schuster) Simon & Schuster.
—Kill Me Again: A Scott Elliott Mystery. 1996. 304p. 22.00 o.p. (*0-684-82688-7*, Simon & Schuster) Simon & Schuster.
—Raise the Devil. 2000. (Scott Elliott Mysteries Ser.). 264p. 23.95 (*0-312-26640-5*, Saint Martin's Minotaur) St. Martin's Pr.
Farmer, Philip Jose. Nothing Burns in Hell. 1999. 287p. mass mkt. 6.99 (*0-8125-6495-2*, Tor Bks.); 1998. 288p. 22.95 o.p. (*0-312-86470-1*, Forge Bks.) Doherty, Tom Assocs., LLC.
Fenady, Andrew J. A Night in Beverly Hills. 2003. 257p. 25.95 (*1-59414-068-5*, Five Star) Gale Group.
Fesperman, Dan. The Small Boat of Great Sorrows: A Novel. 2003. 307p. (*1-4000-3047-1*); 320p. 24.00 (*0-375-41472-X*) Knopf, Alfred A. Inc.
Fiffer, Sharon. The Wrong Stuff. Date not set. pap. (*0-312-31415-9*, St. Martin's Paperbacks); 2003. 320p. 24.95 (*0-312-31414-0*, Saint Martin's Minotaur) St. Martin's Pr.
Ford, G. M. The Bum's Rush. 1998. (Leo Waterman Mysteries Ser.). 320p. mass mkt. 5.99 (*0-380-72763-3*, Avon Bks.) Morrow/Avon.
—The Bum's Rush. 1997. (Leo Waterman Mysteries Ser.). 246p. 22.95 (*0-8027-3299-2*) Walker & Co.
—Cast in Stone. 1997. (Leo Waterman Mysteries Ser.). 304p. mass mkt. 5.99 (*0-380-72762-5*, Avon Bks.) Morrow/Avon.
—Cast in Stone. 1996. (Leo Waterman Mysteries Ser.). 288p. 21.95 (*0-8027-3267-4*) Walker & Co.
—The Deader the Better. (Leo Waterman Mysteries Ser.). 352p. 2000. 22.00 (*0-380-97723-0*); 2001. reprint ed. mass mkt. 6.99 (*0-380-80420-4*, Avon Bks.) Morrow/Avon.
—The Last Ditch. (Leo Waterman Mysteries Ser.). 2000. 320p. mass mkt. 5.99 (*0-380-79369-5*); 1999. 288p. 22.00 (*0-380-97557-2*) Morrow/Avon. (Avon Bks.).
—Slow Burn. (Leo Waterman Mysteries Ser.). 1999. 304p. mass mkt. 5.99 (*0-380-79367-9*); 1998. 288p. 20.00 (*0-380-97556-4*) Morrow/Avon. (Avon Bks.).
—Who in Hell Is Wanda Fuca? 1996. (Leo Waterman Mysteries Ser.). 320p. mass mkt. 5.99 (*0-380-72761-7*, Avon Bks.) Morrow/Avon.
—Who in Hell Is Wanda Fuca? 1995. 244p. 21.95 (*0-8027-3255-0*) Walker & Co.
Forrest, Katherine V. Murder by Tradition: A Kate Delafield Mystery. 2003. (Kate Delafield Mystery Ser.). 280p. pap. 12.95 (*1-55583-719-0*, Alyson Bks.) Alyson Pubns.
Francis, Dick. Come to Grief. 1996. 384p. mass mkt. 6.99 (*0-515-11952-0*, Jove) Berkley Publishing Group.

—Come to Grief. 1995. o.p. (0-399-19295-6); 320p. 23.95 o.p. (0-399-14082-4, G. P. Putnam's Sons) Penguin Group (USA) Inc.
—Come to Grief. abr. ed. 1999. pap. 9.98 incl. audio (0-671-04422-2, Simon & Schuster Audioworks) Simon & Schuster Audio.
—Come to Grief. l.t. ed. 1996. (Paperback Bestsellers Ser.). 402p. pap. 26.95 (0-7838-1509-3) Thorndike Pr.
—Come to Grief: International Edition. 1996. 6.99 o.s.i (0-515-11937-7, Jove) Berkley Publishing Group.
—Come to Grief: International Edition. l.t. ed. 1995. (Core Collection). 402p. 29.95 (0-7838-1508-5) Thorndike Pr.
—Reflex. 1981. 288p. 11.95 o.p. (0-399-12598-1) Putnam Publishing Group, The.
—Slay Ride. l.t. ed. 1993. 19.95 o.p. (0-7927-1431-8); pap. o.p. (0-7927-1430-X); 54.95 incl. audio (0-7451-5956-7) BBC Audiobooks America.
—Slay Ride. 1987. 272p. reprint ed. mass mkt. 5.95 o.s.i (0-449-21271-8, Fawcett) Ballantine Bks.
—Slay Ride. unabr. ed. 1991. audio 42.00 (0-7366-2081-8, 2886) Books on Tape, Inc.
—Slay Ride. 1984. mass mkt. 3.50 (0-671-50731-1); 1983. mass mkt. 2.95 (0-671-47021-3) Simon & Schuster. (Pocket).
—Slay Ride. l.t. ed. 1975. o.p. (0-85456-337-7, Ulverscroft) Thorpe, F. A. Pubs.
—Whip Hand. unabr. ed. 1989. audio 64.95 o.s.i (0-8161-9460-2) BBC Audiobooks America.
—Whip Hand. 1996. pap. 5.99 (0-449-45617-X); 1987. mass mkt. 5.99 o.s.i (0-449-21274-2) Ballantine Bks. (Fawcett).
—Whip Hand. 1999. 304p. mass mkt. 6.99 (0-515-12504-0, Jove) Berkley Publishing Group.
—Whip Hand. unabr. ed. 2000. (Sid Halley Adventure Ser.: Bk. 2). audio 59.95; 1993. audio 69.95 (0-7451-5960-5, CAB 358) Chivers Audio Bks. GBR. *Dist:* BBC Audiobooks America.
—Whip Hand. l.t. ed. 1995. 376p. 21.95 (0-8161-5785-5, Macmillan Reference USA) Gale Group.
—Whip Hand. 2001. (Best Mysteries of All Time Ser.). 288p. (0-7621-8871-5, IM Pr.) Reader's Digest Assn., Inc., The.
—Whip Hand. unabr. ed. 1991. audio 51.00 (1-55690-560-2, 91109E7) Recorded Bks., LLC.
—Whip Hand. 1982. 336p. mass mkt. 3.50 o.s.i (0-671-46404-3, Pocket) Simon & Schuster.
—Whip Hand. 1984. audio o.s.i. audio 39.95 o.s.i (0-8161-9785-7, 91109) Thorndike Pr.
—Whip Hand. l.t. ed. 1980. (Ulverscroft Large Print Ser.). 459p. o.p. (0-7089-0542-0, Ulverscroft) Thorpe, F. A. Pubs. GBR. *Dist:* Ulverscroft Large Print Canada, Ltd.
—Whip Hand. abr. ed. 1996. audio 16.95 o.s.i (0-14-086223-4, Penguin AudioBooks) Viking Penguin.
Frankel, Valerie. A Body to Die For. 1995. 240p. mass mkt. 5.50 (0-671-79520-1, Pocket) Simon & Schuster.
—A Deadline for Murder. Wells, Leslie, ed. 1991. 304p. (Orig.). bds. 3.95 (0-671-73021-5, Pocket) Simon & Schuster.
—Murder on Wheels. Isaacson, Dana, ed. 1992. 224p. (Orig.). mass mkt. 4.50 (0-671-73195-5, Pocket) Simon & Schuster.
—Prime Time for Murder. 1994. 256p. mass mkt. 4.99 (0-671-79519-8, Pocket) Simon & Schuster.
Friedman, Kinky. Armadillos & Old Lace. 1995. 256p. mass mkt. 7.50 (0-553-57447-7) Bantam Bks.
—Armadillos & Old Lace. 1994. 240p. 21.00 (0-671-86923-X, Simon & Schuster) Simon & Schuster.
—Blast from the Past. abr. ed. 2002. audio 17.95 (1-56511-593-7) HighBridge Co.
—Blast from the Past. 1999. 256p. pap. 15.00 (0-345-41630-9) Random Hse., Inc.
—Blast from the Past. 1998. 256p. 23.00 (0-684-80379-8, Simon & Schuster) Simon & Schuster.
—Blast from the Past. abr. ed. 1998. audio 17.95 (1-55935-282-5, 282-5BK) Soundelux Audio Publishing.
—A Case of Lone Star. 1988. mass mkt. 3.95 o.p. (0-425-11185-7) Berkley Publishing Group.
—A Case of Lone Star. 1987. 204p. 14.95 o.p. (0-688-06410-8, Morrow, William & Co.) Morrow/Avon.
—Elvis, Jesus & Coca Cola. 1994. 272p. mass mkt. 6.99 (0-553-56891-4) Bantam Bks.
—Elvis, Jesus & Coca Cola. 1993. 304p. 20.00 o.p. (0-671-86922-1, Simon & Schuster) Simon & Schuster.
—Frequent Flyer. 1990. mass mkt. 6.50 o.s.i (0-425-12345-6) Berkley Publishing Group.
—Frequent Flyer. 1989. 204p. 16.95 o.p. (0-688-08166-5, Morrow, William & Co.) Morrow/Avon.
—God Bless John Wayne. 1996. 256p. mass mkt. 6.99 (0-553-57633-X) Bantam Bks.
—God Bless John Wayne. 1995. 253p. 22.00 o.p. (0-684-81051-4, Simon & Schuster) Simon & Schuster.
—Greenwich Killing Time: A Thrilling Murder Mystery. 1987. 240p. mass mkt. 3.95 o.p. (0-425-10497-4) Berkley Publishing Group.
—Greenwich Killing Time: A Thrilling Murder Mystery. 1986. 13.95 o.p. (0-688-06409-4, Morrow, William & Co.) Morrow/Avon.
—The Love Song of J. Edgar Hoover. abr. ed. 1996. audio 16.95 (1-55927-412-3) Audio Renaissance.
—The Love Song of J. Edgar Hoover. 1998. mass mkt. o.p. (0-345-41510-8); 1997. 240p. pap. 12.95 (0-345-41509-4) Ballantine Bks.
—The Love Song of J. Edgar Hoover. l.t. ed. 1996. pap. 23.95 (1-56895-394-1, Wheeler Publishing, Inc.) Gale Group.
—The Love Song of J. Edgar Hoover. 1996. 23.00 (0-684-80377-1, Simon & Schuster) Simon & Schuster.
—Meanwhile Back at the Ranch. 2003. (Illus.). 272p. mass mkt. 6.99 (0-671-04745-0, Pocket Star) Simon & Schuster.
—The Mile High Club. 224p. 2000. 23.00 o.s.i (0-684-86486-X, Simon & Schuster); 2001. reprint ed. pap. 13.00 (0-671-04743-4, Pocket) Simon & Schuster.
—Musical Chairs. 1991. 288p. 18.95 o.p. (0-688-09148-2, Morrow, William & Co.) Morrow/Avon.
—Musical Chairs. 1993. 3.99 o.p. (0-517-10872-0) Random Hse. Value Publishing.
—Roadkill. abr. ed. 1997. audio 16.95 o.p. (1-55927-456-5) Audio Renaissance.
—Roadkill. 1998. 256p. pap. 12.95 (0-345-41632-5) Ballantine Bks.
—Roadkill. unabr. ed. 1998. audio 32.00 (0-7366-4130-0, 4633) Books on Tape, Inc.
—Roadkill. 1997. 256p. 23.00 o.p. (0-684-80378-X, Simon & Schuster) Simon & Schuster.
—Spanking Watson. 224p. 2000. pap. 12.95 (0-671-04742-6, Pocket); 1999. 23.00 (0-684-86531-9, Simon & Schuster); 1999. 23.00 o.s.i (0-684-85061-3, Simon & Schuster) Simon & Schuster.
—When the Cat's Away. 1989. mass mkt. 3.95 o.p. (0-425-11830-4) Berkley Publishing Group.
—When the Cat's Away. 1988. 224p. 16.95 o.p. (0-688-07555-X, Morrow, William & Co.) Morrow/Avon.
—When the Cat's Away. 1991. 3.99 o.p. (0-517-07564-4) Random Hse. Value Publishing.
Frost, Mark. The Six Messiahs. 1996. pap. 6.99 (0-380-72229-1, Avon Bks.); 1995. 448p. 23.00 o.p. (0-688-13092-5, Morrow, William & Co.) Morrow/Avon.
—The Six Messiahs. abr. ed. 1995. 24.95 o.p. (0-7871-0399-3) NewStar Media, Inc.
Fuller, Dean. Death of a Critic: An Alex Grismolet Mystery. 1996. 304p. 21.95 o.p. (0-316-29601-5) Little Brown & Co.
—Death of a Critic Vol. 1: An Alex Grismolet Mystery. 1996. 21.95 (0-316-92601-9) Little Brown & Co.
Fusilli, Jim. Closing Time. 2001. 320p. 23.95 o.s.i (0-399-14793-4) Penguin Group (USA) Inc.
—Tribeca Blues. 2003. 288p. 24.95 (0-399-15088-9) Putnam Publishing Group, The.
—A Well-Known Secret. 2003. 320p. mass mkt. 6.99 (0-425-19280-6, Prime Crime) Berkley Publishing Group.
—A Well-Known Secret. 2002. 304p. 23.95 (0-399-14931-7, Putnam & Grosset) Putnam Publishing Group, The.
Gale Group Staff, contrib. by. Don't Lie to Me. l.t. ed. 2001. (Five Star Mystery Ser.). 200p. 24.95 (0-7862-3011-8) Thorndike Pr.
Garcia-Aguilera, Carolina. Bitter Sugar. 2001. (Lupe Solano Mystery Ser.). 336p. 24.00 (0-380-97781-8, Morrow, William & Co.) Morrow/Avon.
—Bloody Secrets. 1999. 336p. reprint ed. mass mkt. 6.50 o.s.i (0-425-16779-8, Prime Crime) Berkley Publishing Group.
—Bloody Secrets. 1998. 274p. 23.95 o.p. (0-399-14386-6, G. P. Putnam's Sons) Penguin Group (USA) Inc.
—Bloody Shame: A Lupe Solano Mystery. 1998. 320p. mass mkt. 6.50 o.s.i (0-425-16140-4, Prime Crime) Berkley Publishing Group.
—Bloody Shame: A Lupe Solano Mystery. 1997. 288p. 22.95 o.p. (0-399-14256-8, G. P. Putnam's Sons) Penguin Group (USA) Inc.
—Bloody Waters: A Lupe Solano Mystery. 1997. (Lupo Solano Mystery Ser.). 304p. mass mkt. 5.99 o.s.i (0-425-15670-2, Prime Crime) Berkley Publishing Group.
—Bloody Waters: A Lupe Solano Mystery. 1996. 256p. 21.95 o.p. (0-399-14157-X, G. P. Putnam's Sons) Penguin Group (USA) Inc.
—A Miracle in Paradise. (Lupe Solano Mystery Ser.). 2000. 352p. mass mkt. 5.99 o.s.i (0-380-80738-6); 1999. viii, 277p. 23.00 (0-380-97779-6) Morrow/Avon. (Avon Bks.).
Garcia, Eric. Anonymous Rex: A Detective Story. 2001. 336p. pap. 12.95 o.s.i (0-425-17821-8); 2003. 368p. reprint ed. mass mkt. 6.99 (0-425-18888-4, Prime Crime) Berkley Publishing Group.
—Anonymous Rex: A Detective Story. 2001. (GER.). 384p. pap. 19.00 o.s.i (3-89480-087-9) Prisma Verlag GmbH DEU. *Dist:* Random Hse. of Canada, Ltd.
—Anonymous Rex: A Detective Story. 1999. 23.00 (0-676-79523-4); 384p. 23.00 o.s.i (0-375-50326-9) Random House Adult Trade Publishing Group. (Villard Bks.).
—Anonymous Rex: A Detective Story. 2002. (GER.). 384p. pap. 19.00 (1-4000-3974-6); 1999. (0-375-75508-X) Random Hse., Inc.
—Casual Rex: A Detective Story. 2001. E-Book 19.50 (1-58945-782-X) Adobe Systems, Inc.
—Casual Rex: A Detective Story. 2002. 352p. pap. 12.95 (0-425-18339-4) Berkley Publishing Group.
—Casual Rex: A Detective Story. 2001. E-Book 19.50 (0-375-50666-7, Villard Bks.) Random House Adult Trade Publishing Group.
—Hot & Sweaty Rex: A Mystery. 2004. 352p. 24.95 (0-375-50523-7, Villard Bks.) Random House Adult Trade Publishing Group.
Gault, William C. Cat & Mouse. 1988. 176p. 12.95 o.p. (0-312-01398-1, Saint Martin's Minotaur) St. Martin's Pr.
—The Chicano War. 1986. 192p. 14.95 o.p. (0-8027-5640-9) Walker & Co.
—Come Die with Me. 1987. 188p. 2.95 o.s.i (0-441-11539-X, Diamond Bks.) Berkley Publishing Group.
—County Kill. 1988. 2.95 (1-55773-017-2, Diamond Bks.) Berkley Publishing Group.
—Day of the Ram. 1988. 2.95 (1-55773-091-1, Diamond Bks.) Berkley Publishing Group.
—Dead Hero. 1988. 2.95 (1-55773-037-7, Diamond Bks.) Berkley Publishing Group.
—Dead Pigeon. 1992. (Mystery Scene Bk.). 160p. pap. 3.95 o.p. (0-88184-839-5, Carroll & Graf Pubs.) Avalon Publishing Group.
—Dead Seed. l.t. ed. 1987. pap. 13.95 o.p. (1-55504-039-X) BBC Audiobooks America.
—Dead Seed. 1985. 12.95 o.p. (0-8027-5604-2) Walker & Co.
—Death in Donegal Bay. 1984. 192p. 12.95 o.p. (0-8027-5591-7) Walker & Co.
—Murder in the Raw. 1988. 2.95 (1-55773-061-X, Diamond Bks.) Berkley Publishing Group.
Geason, Susan. Dogfish. 1993. 208p. (Orig.). pap. 9.95 o.p. (1-86373-088-5) Allen & Unwin Pty., Ltd. AUS. *Dist:* Independent Pubs. Group.
—Sharkbait. 1994. 176p. pap. 9.95 o.p. (1-86373-632-8) Independent Pubs. Group.
—Shaved Fish. 1993. 168p. (Orig.). pap. 9.95 o.p. (0-04-442274-1) Allen & Unwin Pty., Ltd. AUS. *Dist:* Independent Pubs. Group.
Gibson, Maggie. The First Holy Chameleon. 2002. 317p. pap. (0-575-40323-3) Weidenfeld & Nicolson, Ltd. GBR. *Dist:* Trafalgar Square.
Gibson, William. Pattern Recognition. 2003. 368p. 25.95 (0-399-14986-4, Putnam & Grosset) Putnam Publishing Group, The.
—Pattern Recognition. 2004. 368p. pap. 14.00 (0-425-19293-8) Berkley Publishing Group.
Gilbert, Anthony. The Black Stage. unabr. ed. 1989. (C). audio 54.95 (0-7451-5982-6) BBC Audiobooks America.
—The Black Stage. (Black Dagger Crime Ser.). 232p. 12.95 o.p. (0-86220-727-4) Chivers Pr. GBR. *Dist:* BBC Audiobooks America.
—Death Takes a Wife. l.t. ed. 1991. pap. 16.95 o.p. (0-7927-0515-7, CS0114) BBC Audiobooks America.
—The Mouse Who Wouldn't Play Ball. l.t. ed. 1991. pap. 16.95 o.p. (0-7927-0711-7, CS0247) BBC Audiobooks America.
—Murder Comes Home. l.t. ed. 1992. pap. 14.95 o.p. (0-7927-1067-3) BBC Audiobooks America.
—A Nice Little Killing. l.t. ed. 1991. pap. 10.95 o.p. (0-7927-0146-1, C0102) BBC Audiobooks America.
—Passenger to Nowhere. l.t. ed. 1990. pap. 16.95 o.p. (0-7927-0161-5, C0253) BBC Audiobooks America.
—Snake in the Grass. (Black Dagger Crime Ser.). 1993. 192p. 16.50 o.p. (0-7451-8616-5, Black Dagger); 1994. 18.95 o.p. (0-7451-6459-5) BBC Audiobooks America.
Goldsborough, Robert. The Bloodied Ivy. 1989. 208p. mass mkt. 4.99 o.s.i (0-553-27816-9) Bantam Bks.
—Death on a Deadline. 1988. mass mkt. 4.95 o.s.i (0-553-27024-9) Bantam Bks.
—Fade to Black. 1991. 256p. mass mkt. 4.99 o.s.i (0-553-29264-1) Bantam Bks.
—The Missing Chapter. 1993. 240p. 19.95 o.s.i (0-553-07241-2) Bantam Bks.
—The Missing Chapter: A Nero Wolfe Mystery. 1994. 272p. mass mkt. 4.99 o.s.i (0-553-56874-4) Bantam Bks.
—Murder in E Minor. 1987. 224p. (Orig.). mass mkt. 3.50 o.s.i (0-553-26120-7); mass mkt. 3.95 o.s.i (0-553-27938-6) Bantam Bks.
—Silver Spire. 1993. (Crime Line Ser.). 256p. mass mkt. 4.99 o.s.i (0-553-56387-4) Bantam Bks.
Gores, Joe. Contract Null & Void. 1996. 82p. 21.95 o.s.i (0-89296-592-4) Mysterious Pr.
—Contract Null & Void. 1997. (Dka File Novel Ser.). 336p. mass mkt. 6.50 o.s.i (0-446-40447-0) Warner Bks., Inc.
—Dead Man, set. unabr. ed. 1995. audio 69.95 (0-7862-9974-6, CSL 083) BBC Audiobooks America.
—Dead Man. 1993. 272p. 18.95 (0-89296-541-X) Mysterious Pr.
—Dead Man. 1994. 272p. mass mkt. 5.50 o.s.i (0-446-40391-1) Warner Bks., Inc.
—Dead Skip. 1981. mass mkt. 2.25 o.s.i (0-345-29206-5); 1974. mass mkt. 1.25 o.p. (0-345-24129-0) Ballantine Bks.
—Dead Skip. 1992. 208p. reprint ed. mass mkt. 4.99 o.s.i (0-446-40312-1, Mysterious Pr. Paperback Bks.) Warner Bks., Inc.
—Final Notice. 1992. 208p. reprint ed. mass mkt. 4.99 (0-446-40314-8, Mysterious Pr. Paperback Bks.) Warner Bks., Inc.
—Gone, No Forwarding. 1981. mass mkt. 2.25 o.s.i (0-345-29208-1) Ballantine Bks.
—Gone, No Forwarding. 1993. 224p. mass mkt. 5.50 o.s.i (0-446-40315-6) Warner Bks., Inc.
—32 Cadillacs. 1992. 352p. 18.95 (0-89296-298-4) Mysterious Pr.
—32 Cadillacs. 1993. 352p. mass mkt. 5.99 o.s.i (0-446-40360-1) Warner Bks., Inc.
Gorman, Ed. Save the Last Dance for Me. l.t. ed. 2002. (Mystery Ser.). 335p. 29.95 (0-7862-4398-8) Thorndike Pr.
—Wake up Little Susie: A Sam McCain Mystery. l.t. ed. 2000. (Mystery Ser.). 337p. 29.95 (0-7862-2464-9) Thorndike Pr.
—Will You Still Love Me Tomorrow? 2002. 208p. reprint ed. mass mkt. 5.99 (0-425-18716-0, Prime Crime) Berkley Publishing Group.
Goulart, Ron. Elementary My Dear Groucho. 1999. 261p. (J). 23.95 (0-312-20892-8, Saint Martin's Minotaur) St. Martin's Pr.
—Groucho Marx: Master Detective. 1998. 262p. (YA). 22.95 o.p. (0-312-18106-X, Saint Martin's Minotaur) St. Martin's Pr.
—Groucho Marx, Private Eye. 1999. 263p. 23.95 (0-312-19895-7, Saint Martin's Minotaur) St. Martin's Pr.
Grafton, Sue. A Is for Alibi. 1987. mass mkt. 3.50 o.s.i (0-553-26563-6); 224p. mass mkt. 7.99 (0-553-27991-2) Bantam Bks.
— A Is for Alibi, unabr. collector's ed. 1993. (Kinsey Millhone Mystery Ser.). audio 48.00 (0-7366-2455-4, 3219) Books on Tape, Inc.
— A Is for Alibi. 1994. (Kinsey Millhone Mystery Ser.). reprint ed. lib. bdg. 29.95 o.p. (1-56849-284-7) Buccaneer Bks., Inc.
— A Is for Alibi. l.t. ed. 1991. (Kinsey Millhone Mystery Ser.). 354p. 20.95 o.p. (0-8161-5144-X, Macmillan Reference USA) Gale Group.
— A Is for Alibi. 1982. (Kinsey Millhone Mystery Ser.). 256p. o.p. (0-03-059048-5); 288p. 27.00 (0-8050-1334-2) Holt, Henry & Co.
— A Is for Alibi. 1984. (Kinsey Millhone Mystery Ser.). 192p. mass mkt. 2.75 o.p. (0-451-12862-1) NAL.
— A Is for Alibi, Set. abr. ed. 1990. (Kinsey Millhone Mystery Ser.). audio 18.00 o.s.i (0-394-57977-1, 390310, RH Audio) Random Hse. Audio Publishing Group.
— A Is for Alibi. 2001. (Kinsey Millhone Mystery Ser.). 285p. (0-7621-8860-X) Reader's Digest Assn., Inc., The.
— A Is for Alibi. l.t. ed. 1988. (Kinsey Millhone Mystery Ser.). 432p. 15.95 o.p. (0-7089-1744-5, Ulverscroft) Thorpe, F. A. Pubs. GBR. *Dist:* Ulverscroft Large Print Bks., Ltd.
—B Is for Burglar. 1986. (Kinsey Millhone Mystery Ser.). 224p. mass mkt. 7.99 (0-553-28034-1); mass mkt. 3.50 o.s.i (0-553-26061-8) Bantam Bks.
—B Is for Burglar. 1994. (Kinsey Millhone Mystery Ser.). reprint ed. lib. bdg. 29.95 (1-56849-283-9) Buccaneer Bks., Inc.
—B Is for Burglar. l.t. ed. 1991. (Kinsey Millhone Mystery Ser.). 20.95 o.p. (0-8161-5145-8, Macmillan Reference USA) Gale Group.
—B Is for Burglar. 1985. (Kinsey Millhone Mystery Ser.). 240p. 27.00 (0-8050-1632-5) Holt, Henry & Co.
—B Is for Burglar. l.t. ed. 1988. (Kinsey Millhone Mystery Ser.). 448p. 17.95 o.p. (0-7089-1786-0, Ulverscroft) Thorpe, F. A. Pubs. GBR. *Dist:* Ulverscroft Large Print Bks., Ltd.
—C Is for Corpse. 1987. mass mkt. 3.50 o.s.i (0-553-26468-0); 224p. mass mkt. 7.99 (0-553-28036-8) Bantam Bks.
—C Is for Corpse. 1986. (Kinsey Millhone Mystery Ser.). 256p. 19.95 o.p. (0-03-001888-9); 258p. 27.00 (0-8050-2818-8) Holt, Henry & Co.
—C Is for Corpse. l.t. ed. 1991. (Kinsey Millhone Mystery Ser.). 371p. pap. 22.95 (0-8161-5146-6) Thorndike Pr.
—C Is for Corpse. l.t. ed. 1988. (Kinsey Millhone Mystery Ser.). 432p. 15.95 o.p. (0-7089-1898-0, Ulverscroft) Thorpe, F. A. Pubs. GBR. *Dist:* Ulverscroft Large Print Bks., Ltd.

—D Is for Deadbeat. 1988. (Kinsey Millhone Mystery Ser.). 256p. reprint ed. mass mkt. 7.99 (*0-553-27163-6*) Bantam Bks.

—D Is for Deadbeat. unabr. collector's ed. 1993. (Kinsey Millhone Mystery Ser.). audio 42.00 (*0-7366-2568-2*, 3317) Books on Tape, Inc.

—D Is for Deadbeat. l.t. ed. 1992. (Kinsey Millhone Mystery Ser.). 345p. 16.95 o.p. (*0-8161-5147-4*, Macmillan Reference USA) Gale Group.

—D Is for Deadbeat, Set. abr. ed. 1993. (Kinsey Millhone Mystery Ser.). audio 18.00 (*0-679-40354-X*, 390596, RH Audio) Random Hse. Audio Publishing Group.

—D Is for Deadbeat. l.t. ed. 1990. (Kinsey Millhone Mystery Ser.). 18.95 o.p. (*0-7089-2118-3*, Ulverscroft) Thorpe, F. A. Pubs. GBR. *Dist:* Ulverscroft Large Print Bks., Ltd.

—E Is for Evidence. 1989. (Kinsey Millhone Mystery Ser.). 208p. mass mkt. 7.99 (*0-553-27955-6*) Bantam Bks.

—E Is for Evidence. unabr. collector's ed. 1994. (Kinsey Millhone Mystery Ser.). audio 42.00 (*0-7366-2615-8*, 3357) Books on Tape, Inc.

—E Is for Evidence. l.t. ed. 1989. (Kinsey Millhone Mystery Ser.). 319p. 20.95 o.p. (*0-8161-4715-9*, Macmillan Reference USA) Gale Group.

—E Is for Evidence. 1988. (Kinsey Millhone Mystery Ser.). 240p. 27.00 (*0-8050-0459-9*) Holt, Henry & Co.

—E Is for Evidence. abr. ed. 1989. (Kinsey Millhone Mystery Ser.). audio 18.00 (*0-394-57982-8*, 390695, RH Audio) Random Hse. Audio Publishing Group.

—F Is for Fugitive. 1990. (Kinsey Millhone Mystery Ser.). 352p. mass mkt. 7.99 (*0-553-28478-9*) Bantam Bks.

—F Is for Fugitive. unabr. collector's ed. 1994. (Kinsey Millhone Mystery Ser.). audio 48.00 (*0-7366-2620-4*, 3360) Books on Tape, Inc.

—F Is for Fugitive. l.t. ed. 1990. (Kinsey Millhone Mystery Ser.). 368p. 21.95 (*0-8161-4901-1*, Macmillan Reference USA) Gale Group.

—F Is for Fugitive. 1989. (Kinsey Millhone Mystery Ser.). 272p. 25.00 (*0-8050-0460-2*) Holt, Henry & Co.

—F Is for Fugitive. abr. ed. 1989. (Kinsey Millhone Mystery Ser.). audio 18.00 (*0-394-57983-6*, 390742); audio 17.00 (*0-394-58173-3*) Random Hse. Audio Publishing Group. (RH Audio).

—G Is for Gumshoe. (Kinsey Millhone Mystery Ser.). 1997. pap. 12.95 o.s.i (*0-449-00062-1*); 1995. mass mkt. 6.99 o.p. (*0-449-45491-6*); 1993. mass mkt. 5.99 o.p. (*0-449-45161-5*); 1991. pap. 6.99 (*0-449-45764-8*); 1991. 352p. mass mkt. 7.99 (*0-449-21936-4*) Ballantine Bks. (Fawcett).

—G Is for Gumshoe. unabr. collector's ed. 1994. (Kinsey Millhone Mystery Ser.). audio 48.00 (*0-7366-2679-4*, 3415) Books on Tape, Inc.

—G Is for Gumshoe. l.t. ed. 1991. (Kinsey Millhone Mystery Ser.). 355p. 20.95 o.p. (*0-8161-5090-7*, Macmillan Reference USA) Gale Group.

—G Is for Gumshoe. 1990. (Kinsey Millhone Mystery Ser.). 272p. 27.00 (*0-8050-0461-0*) Holt, Henry & Co.

—G Is for Gumshoe. abr. ed. 1990. (Kinsey Millhone Mystery Ser.). audio 16.00 o.p. (*0-394-58632-8*);Set. audio 18.00 (*0-394-58563-1*, 390833) Random Hse. Audio Publishing Group. (RH Audio).

—G Is for Gumshoe. l.t. ed. 1991. (Kinsey Millhone Mystery Ser.). 355p. pap. 22.95 o.p. (*0-8161-5091-5*) Thorndike Pr.

—H Is for Homicide. (Kinsey Millhone Mystery Ser.). 1997. pap. 11.00 o.s.i (*0-449-00063-X*); 1995. mass mkt. 6.99 o.p. (*0-449-45492-4*); 1993. mass mkt. 5.99 o.p. (*0-449-45162-3*); 1992. pap. 6.99 (*0-449-45765-6*); 1992. 304p. mass mkt. 7.99 (*0-449-21946-1*) Ballantine Bks. (Fawcett).

—H Is for Homicide. unabr. collector's ed. 1994. (Kinsey Millhone Mystery Ser.). audio 48.00 (*0-7366-2728-6*, 3458) Books on Tape, Inc.

—H Is for Homicide. l.t. ed. 1992. (Kinsey Millhone Mystery Ser.). 390p. 16.95 o.p. (*0-8161-5281-0*, Macmillan Reference USA) Gale Group.

—H Is for Homicide. (Kinsey Millhone Mystery Ser.). 1991. 272p. 25.00 (*0-8050-1084-X*); 1992. 390p. lib. bdg. 20.95 (*0-8161-5280-2*) Holt, Henry & Co.

—H Is for Homicide, Set. abr. ed. 1991. (Kinsey Millhone Mystery Ser.). 18.00 incl. audio (*0-394-58698-0*, 390890, RH Audio) Random Hse. Audio Publishing Group.

—I Is for Innocent. (Kinsey Millhone Mystery Ser.). 1997. 304p. pap. 12.95 (*0-449-00064-8*); 1995. mass mkt. 6.99 o.p. (*0-449-45493-2*); 1994. mass mkt. 5.99 o.p. (*0-449-45335-9*); 1993. pap. 6.99 (*0-449-45766-4*); 1993. 352p. mass mkt. 7.99 (*0-449-22151-2*) Ballantine Bks. (Fawcett).

—I Is for Innocent. unabr. ed. 1993. (Kinsey Millhone Mystery Ser.). audio 56.00 (*0-7366-2433-3*, 3198) Books on Tape, Inc.

—I Is for Innocent. l.t. ed. 1994. (Kinsey Millhone Mystery Ser.). 373p. 16.95 o.p. (*0-8161-5538-0*, Macmillan Reference USA) Gale Group.

—I Is for Innocent. 1992. (Kinsey Millhone Mystery Ser.). 272p. 27.00 (*0-8050-1085-8*) Holt, Henry & Co.

—I Is for Innocent. abr. ed. 1992. (Kinsey Millhone Mystery Ser.). audio 18.00 (*0-679-41115-1*, 390946, RH Audio) Random Hse. Audio Publishing Group.

—I Is for Innocent. l.t. ed. 1993. (Kinsey Millhone Mystery Ser.). 373p. 24.95 (*0-8161-5537-2*) Thorndike Pr.

—J Is for Judgment. (Kinsey Millhone Mystery Ser.). 1997. pap. 11.00 o.s.i (*0-449-00065-6*); 1995. mass mkt. 6.99 o.p. (*0-449-45495-9*); 1994. pap. 6.99 (*0-449-45767-2*); 1994. 384p. mass mkt. 7.99 (*0-449-22148-2*) Ballantine Bks. (Fawcett).

—J Is for Judgment. unabr. ed. 1994. (Kinsey Millhone Mystery Ser.). audio 56.00 (*0-7366-2736-7*, 3463) Books on Tape, Inc.

—J Is for Judgment. l.t. ed. 1993. (Kinsey Millhone Mystery Ser.). lib. bdg. 23.95 o.p. (*0-8161-5750-2*, Macmillan Reference USA) Gale Group.

—J Is for Judgment. 1993. (Kinsey Millhone Mystery Ser.). 304p. 27.00 (*0-8050-1935-9*) Holt, Henry & Co.

—J Is for Judgment, Set. abr. ed. 1993. (Kinsey Millhone Mystery Ser.). audio 18.00 (*0-679-41368-5*, 390993, RH Audio) Random Hse. Audio Publishing Group.

—J Is for Judgment. l.t. ed. 1994. (Kinsey Millhone Mystery Ser.). 410p. pap. 20.95 (*0-8161-5751-0*) Thorndike Pr.

—K Is for Killer. (Kinsey Millhone Mystery Ser.). 1997. pap. 11.00 o.s.i (*0-449-00066-4*); 1995. pap. 6.99 (*0-449-45768-0*); 1995. 320p. mass mkt. 7.99 (*0-449-22150-4*) Ballantine Bks. (Fawcett).

—K Is for Killer. unabr. ed. 1995. (Kinsey Millhone Mystery Ser.). audio 56.00 (*0-7366-3043-0*, 3725) Books on Tape, Inc.

—K Is for Killer. l.t. ed. 1994. (Kinsey Millhone Mystery Ser.). 26.95 o.p. (*1-56895-101-9*, Wheeler Publishing, Inc.) Gale Group.

—K Is for Killer. 1994. (Kinsey Millhone Mystery Ser.). 304p. 27.00 (*0-8050-1936-7*) Holt, Henry & Co.

—Kinsey Millhone Mystery Series Boxed Set: G Is for Gumshoe; H Is for Homicide; I Is for Innocent, 3 vols. 1993. (Kinsey Millhone Mystery Ser.). 23.97 o.s.i (*0-449-22262-4*, Fawcett) Ballantine Bks.

—L Is for Lawless. (Kinsey Millhone Mystery Ser.). 1997. pap. 11.00 o.s.i (*0-449-00067-2*); 1996. pap. 6.99 (*0-449-45769-9*); 1996. 336p. mass mkt. 7.99 (*0-449-22149-0*) Ballantine Bks. (Fawcett).

—L Is for Lawless. unabr. ed. 1996. (Kinsey Millhone Mystery Ser.). audio 56.00 (*0-7366-3305-7*, 3959) Books on Tape, Inc.

—L Is for Lawless. 1995. (Kinsey Millhone Mystery Ser.). 304p. 24.00 (*0-8050-1937-5*) Holt, Henry & Co.

—L Is for Lawless, Set. abr. ed. 1995. (Kinsey Millhone Mystery Ser.). audio 18.00 (*0-679-42462-8*, 393143, RH Audio) Random Hse. Audio Publishing Group.

—L Is for Lawless. 1997. (Kinsey Millhone Mystery Ser.). 5.98 o.p. (*0-7651-0722-8*) Smithmark Pubs., Inc.

—L Is for Lawless. l.t. ed. (Kinsey Millhone Mystery Ser.). 384p. 1996. pap. 26.95 (*0-7838-1383-X*); 1995. 29.95 (*0-7838-1382-1*) Thorndike Pr.

—M Is for Malice. 1997. (Kinsey Millhone Mystery Ser.). 352p. mass mkt. 7.99 (*0-449-22360-4*, Fawcett) Ballantine Bks.

—M Is for Malice. unabr. collector's ed. 1997. (Kinsey Millhone Mystery Ser.). audio 56.00 (*0-913369-70-5*, 4322) Books on Tape, Inc.

—M Is for Malice. 1996. (Kinsey Millhone Mystery Ser.). (Illus.). 304p. 27.00 (*0-8050-3637-7*) Holt, Henry & Co.

—M Is for Malice. l.t. ed. 1997. (Kinsey Millhone Mystery Ser.). 458p. pap. 27.95 (*0-7838-1834-3*); lib. bdg. 29.95 (*0-7838-1833-5*) Thorndike Pr.

—N Is for Noose. 1999. (Kinsey Millhone Mystery Ser.). mass mkt. (*0-449-00457-0*); 336p. mass mkt. 7.99 (*0-449-22361-2*) Ballantine Bks. (Fawcett).

—N Is for Noose. unabr. ed. 1998. (Kinsey Millhone Mystery Ser.). audio 56.00 (*0-7366-4141-6*, 4645) Books on Tape, Inc.

—N Is for Noose, unabr. ed. 1999. (Kinsey Millhone Mystery Ser.). audio 39.95 Highsmith Inc.

—N Is for Noose. 1998. (Kinsey Millhone Mystery Ser.). 320p. 25.00 (*0-8050-3650-4*) Holt, Henry & Co.

—N Is for Noose. abr. ed. 2002. audio compact disk 25.95 (*0-553-71339-6*); 1998. audio 24.00 (*0-375-40289-6*, 495734); 1998. audio 34.95 (*0-375-40326-4*, AD37D) Random Hse. Audio Publishing Group. (RH Audio).

—N Is for Noose. l.t. ed. (Kinsey Millhone Mystery Ser.). 455p. 1999. pap. 27.95 (*0-7862-1297-7*); 1998. 30.95 (*0-7862-1296-9*) Thorndike Pr.

—O Is for Outlaw. 2001. (Kinsey Millhone Mystery Ser.). 368p. mass mkt. 7.99 (*0-449-00378-7*, Ballantine Bks.) Ballantine Bks.

—O Is for Outlaw. 1999. (Kinsey Millhone Mystery Ser.). 336p. 26.00 (*0-8050-5955-5*) Holt, Henry & Co.

—O Is for Outlaw. l.t. ed. (Kinsey Millhone Mystery Ser.). 534p. 2000. 28.95 (*0-7862-2045-7*); 1999. 31.95 (*0-7862-2044-9*) Thorndike Pr.

—P Is for Peril. 2001. (Kinsey Millhone Mystery Ser.). 304p. 26.95 (*0-399-14719-5*, Wood, Marian Bks.) Penguin Group (USA) Inc.

—P Is for Peril. l.t. ed. 2001. (Kinsey Millhone Mystery Ser.). 352p. 33.95 (*0-7862-2931-4*) Thorndike Pr.

—Q Is for Quarry. 2002. 400p. 26.95 (*0-399-14915-5*) Putnam Publishing Group, The.

—Q Is for Quarry. pap. o.p. (*0-7862-4369-4*); 2002. 640p. 33.95 (*0-7862-4370-8*) Thorndike Pr.

Graham, Heather. Dying to Have Her. l.t. ed. 2001. (Wheeler Large Print Book Ser.). 428p. 29.95 (*1-58724-085-8*, Wheeler Publishing, Inc.) Gale Group.

Grant-Adamson, Lesley. Too Many Questions. 1993. mass mkt. 4.50 o.s.i (*0-449-22104-0*, Fawcett) Ballantine Bks.

—Too Many Questions. 1991. 15.95 o.p. (*0-312-05434-3*, Saint Martin's Minotaur) St. Martin's Pr.

Grant, Linda. Blind Trust. 1991. (Catherine Sayler Mystery Ser.). mass mkt. 5.99 o.s.i (*0-8041-0791-2*, Ivy Bks.) Ballantine Bks.

—Blind Trust. 1990. 224p. 18.95 o.s.i (*0-684-19165-2*, Macmillan Reference USA) Gale Group.

—Lethal Genes. 1997. mass mkt. 5.99 o.s.i (*0-8041-1558-3*, Ivy Bks.) Ballantine Bks.

—Lethal Genes. 1996. 256p. 21.00 (*0-684-82653-4*, Scribner) Simon & Schuster.

—Love nor Money: An Inspector Catherine Sayler. 1992. (Northern California Mysteries Ser.). mass mkt. 4.50 o.s.i (*0-8041-0947-8*, Ivy Bks.) Ballantine Bks.

—Love nor Money: An Inspector Catherine Sayler. 1991. 288p. 19.95 o.s.i (*0-684-19379-5*, Macmillan Reference USA) Gale Group.

—Random Access Murder: The First Catherine Sayler Mystery. 1998. (Catherine Sayler Mystery Ser.: No. 1). 192p. reprint ed. mass mkt. 5.50 o.p. (*1-890768-09-X*, Intrigue Pr.) Corvus Publishing.

—Random Access Murder: The First Catherine Sayler Mystery. 1988. 192p. pap. 2.95 (*0-380-75534-3*, Avon Bks.) Morrow/Avon.

—Vampire Bytes: A Crime Novel with Catherine Sayler. 1999. mass mkt. 5.99 o.s.i (*0-8041-1862-0*, Ivy Bks.) Ballantine Bks.

—Vampire Bytes: A Crime Novel with Catherine Sayler. 1998. (Crime Novels Ser.). 288p. 22.00 (*0-684-82675-5*, Scribner) Simon & Schuster.

—A Woman's Place. 1995. (Catherine Sayler Mystery Ser.). mass mkt. 5.50 o.s.i (*0-8041-1327-0*, Ivy Bks.) Ballantine Bks.

—A Woman's Place. 1994. 288p. 20.00 o.p. (*0-684-19631-X*, Scribner) Simon & Schuster.

Grape, Jan. Found Dead in Texas. 2002. (Five Star First Edition Mystery Ser.). 233p. 25.95 (*0-7862-4841-6*, Five Star) Gale Group.

Green, Christine. Deadly Echo: A Kate Kunsella Mystery. 2002. 256p. 25.99 (*0-7278-5916-1*) Severn Hse. Pubs., Ltd.

Greenleaf, Stephen. Beyond Blame. 1986. pap. o.s.i (*0-345-00733-6*); mass mkt. 4.99 o.s.i (*0-345-33670-4*) Ballantine Bks.

—Blood Type: The New John Marshall Tanner Mystery. 1993. 304p. mass mkt. 4.99 o.s.i (*0-553-56106-5*) Bantam Bks.

—Blood Type: The New John Marshall Tanner Mystery. 1992. 304p. 20.00 o.p. (*0-688-11268-4*, Morrow, William & Co.) Morrow/Avon.

—Book Case: A John Marshall Tanner Mystery. 1991. 352p. mass mkt. 4.99 o.s.i (*0-553-29061-4*) Bantam Bks.

—Book Case: A John Marshall Tanner Mystery. 1991. 19.95 o.p. (*0-688-07669-6*, Morrow, William & Co.) Morrow/Avon.

—Death Bed. 1982. mass mkt. 2.50 o.s.i (*0-345-30189-7*) Ballantine Bks.

—Death Bed. 1991. 304p. mass mkt. 4.99 o.s.i (*0-553-29348-6*) Bantam Bks.

—Death Bed. 1980. 320p. 10.95 o.p. (*0-385-27139-5*) Doubleday Publishing.

—Death Bed. 1980. 306p. (J). o.p. (*0-8037-1701-6*, Dial Bks. for Young Readers) Penguin Putnam Bks. for Young Readers.

—The Death Bed. 1985. mass mkt. 2.95 o.s.i (*0-345-32742-X*) Ballantine Bks.

—Ellipsis: A John Marshall Tanner Novel. 2001. E-Book 24.00 (*1-58945-174-0*) Adobe Systems, Inc.

—Ellipsis: A John Marshall Tanner Novel. 2000. (John Marshall Tanner Mysteries Ser.). 272p. 24.00 o.s.i (*0-684-84955-0*); E-Book 24.00 (*0-7432-1075-1*) Simon & Schuster. (Scribner).

—False Conception: A John Marshall Tanner Novel. (John Marshall Tanner Mysteries Ser.). 1997. 336p. pap. 5.99 (*0-671-00794-7*, Pocket); 1994. 320p. 22.00 (*1-883402-87-5*, Scribner) Simon & Schuster.

—Fatal Obsession. 1985. mass mkt. 2.95 o.s.i (*0-345-33287-3*); 1984. mass mkt. 2.50 o.s.i (*0-345-31485-9*) Ballantine Bks.

—Fatal Obsession. 1991. 256p. mass mkt. 4.99 o.s.i (*0-553-29350-8*) Bantam Bks.

—Fatal Obsession. 1983. 264p. 14.95 o.p. (*0-385-27886-1*) Doubleday Publishing.

—Flesh Wounds: A John Marshall Tanner Mystery. (John Marshall Tanner Mysteries Ser.). 1997. 288p. per. 5.99 (*0-671-00795-5*, Pocket); 1996. 318p. 22.00 (*0-684-81583-4*, Scribner) Simon & Schuster.

—Grave Error. 1982. 240p. mass mkt. 2.50 o.s.i (*0-345-30188-9*) Ballantine Bks.

—Grave Error. 1991. 272p. mass mkt. 4.99 o.s.i (*0-553-29347-8*) Bantam Bks.

—Grave Error. 1985. 8.95 o.p. (*0-385-27058-5*) Doubleday Publishing.

—Past Tense. 1997. (John Marshall Tanner Mysteries Ser.). 352p. 22.00 (*0-684-83249-6*, Scribner) Simon & Schuster.

—Southern Cross: A John Marshall Tanner Novel. 1995. 320p. mass mkt. 4.99 o.s.i (*0-553-56817-5*) Bantam Bks.

—Southern Cross: A John Marshall Tanner Novel. 1993. 320p. 20.00 o.p. (*0-688-12772-X*, Morrow, William & Co.) Morrow/Avon.

—State's Evidence. 1985. 288p. mass mkt. 2.95 o.s.i (*0-345-32534-6*); 1983. mass mkt. 2.50 o.s.i (*0-345-30869-7*) Ballantine Bks.

—State's Evidence. 1991. 320p. mass mkt. 4.99 o.s.i (*0-553-29349-4*) Bantam Bks.

—State's Evidence. 1982. 320p. 15.95 o.p. (*0-385-27236-7*) Doubleday Publishing.

—Strawberry Sunday: A John Marshall Tanner Novel, 2000. audio 44.95 (*0-7861-1574-2*, P2403) Blackstone Audio Bks., Inc.

—Strawberry Sunday: A John Marshall Tanner Novel. 1999. 288p. 23.00 o.p. (*0-684-84954-2*, Scribner) Simon & Schuster.

—Strawberry Sunday: A John Marshall Tanner Novel. l.t. ed. 1999. (Americana Ser.). 439p. 27.95 (*0-7862-1951-3*) Thorndike Pr.

—Toll Call. 1988. mass mkt. 4.99 o.s.i (*0-345-35349-8*) Ballantine Bks.

Greenwood, Kerry. Flying Too High. 1992. mass mkt. 3.99 o.s.i (*0-449-14777-0*, Fawcett) Ballantine Bks.

—Murder on the Ballarat Train. 1993. (Orig.). mass mkt. 4.50 o.s.i (*0-449-14832-7*, Fawcett) Ballantine Bks.

Grey, Dorien. The Good Cop: A Dick Hardesty Mystery. 2002. per. 15.95 (*1-879194-75-9*) GLB Pubs.

—The Hired Man: A Dick Hardesty Mystery. 2002. 274p. per. (*1-879194-76-7*) GLB Pubs.

—The 9th Man: A Gay Mystery. 2001. (Dick Hardesty Series). 155p. pap. 14.95 (*1-879194-88-0*) GLB Pubs.

Haddam, Jane. Conspiracy Theory: A Gregor Demarkian Novel. 2003. 288p. 24.95 (*0-312-27188-3*) St. Martin's Pr.

Haines, Carolyn. Splintered Bones. 2003. 384p. mass mkt. 5.99 (*0-440-23721-1*); 2002. 320p. 23.95 (*0-385-33590-3*, Delacorte Pr.) Dell Publishing.

—Splintered Bones. l.t. ed. 2003. 496p. 25.95 (*0-375-43248-5*) Random Hse. Large Print.

Hall, David A. Return Trip Ticket. 1992. 176p. 16.95 o.p. (*0-312-08283-5*, Saint Martin's Minotaur) St. Martin's Pr.

Hall, Linda. Steal Away. 2003. (Teri Blake-Addison Mystery Series, Book One Ser.). 290p. pap. 11.99 (*1-59052-072-6*) Multnomah Pubs., Inc.

Hall, Parnell. Actor. 1993. 288p. 19.95 (*0-89296-520-7*) Mysterious Pr.

—Actor. 1994. 304p. mass mkt. 5.50 (*0-446-40364-4*, Mysterious Pr. Paperback Bks.) Warner Bks., Inc.

—Blackmail. 1994. 288p. 19.95 o.p. (*0-89296-521-5*) Mysterious Pr.

—Blackmail. 1995. 304p. mass mkt. 5.99 o.s.i (*0-446-40365-2*) Warner Bks., Inc.

—Client. 1990. 18.95 o.p. (*1-55611-169-X*) Fine, Donald I. Bks.

—Client. 1991. 272p. mass mkt. 4.50 o.p. (*0-451-40249-9*, Onyx) NAL.

—Detective. 1987. 300p. 17.95 o.p. (*1-55611-026-X*) Fine, Donald I. Bks.

—Detective. 1988. 256p. mass mkt. 3.95 o.p. (*0-451-40070-4*, Onyx) NAL.

—Favor. 1988. 17.95 o.p. (*1-55611-096-0*) Fine, Donald I. Bks.

—Favor. 1989. mass mkt. 3.95 o.p. (*0-451-40161-1*, 035, Onyx) NAL.

—Favor. 2002. 186p. pap. 6.99 (*0-7592-1854-4*); E-Book 6.99 (*0-7592-1851-X*); E-Book 6.99 (*0-7592-1849-8*); E-Book 6.99 (*0-7592-1850-1*) ereads.com.

—Juror. 1990. 18.95 o.p. (*1-55611-230-0*) Fine, Donald I. Bks.

—Juror. 1992. 304p. mass mkt. 4.99 o.p. (*0-451-40316-9*, Onyx) NAL.

—Movie. 1995. 82p. 19.95 o.p. (*0-89296-569-X*) Mysterious Pr.

—Movie. 1996. 288p. mass mkt. 5.99 (*0-446-40395-4*) Warner Bks., Inc.
—Murder. 1988. 256p. 17.95 o.s.i (*1-55611-058-8*) Fine, Donald I. Bks.
—Murder. 2002. 256p. reprint ed. pap. 13.95 (*1-58754-111-4*, Olmstead Pr.) Moyer Bell.
—Murder. 1989. mass mkt. 3.95 o.p. (*0-451-40110-7*, Onyx) NAL.
—Murder. E-Book 6.99 (*0-7592-1545-6*) ereads.com.
—Scam. 1998. 336p. pap. 6.50 (*0-446-40469-1*, Mysterious Pr. Paperback Bks.) Warner Bks., Inc.
—Scam: A Stanley Hastings Mystery. l.t. ed. 1997. (Americana Ser.). 463p. 26.95 (*0-7862-1210-1*) Thorndike Pr.
—Scam: A Stanley Hastings Mystery. 1997. 320p. 21.50 o.p. (*0-89296-623-8*) Warner Bks., Inc.
—Shot. 1993. 320p. mass mkt. 4.99 o.p. (*0-451-40354-1*, Onyx) NAL.
—Shot: A Stanley Hastings Novel of Suspense. 1991. 18.95 o.p. (*1-55611-239-4*) Fine, Donald I. Bks.
—Strangler. 1989. 304p. 16.95 o.p. (*1-55611-125-8*) Fine, Donald I. Bks.
—Strangler. 1990. mass mkt. 4.50 o.p. (*0-451-40217-0*, Onyx) NAL.
—Suspense: A Stanley Hastings Mystery Novel. 1998. 320p. 23.00 o.p. (*0-89296-624-6*) Mysterious Pr.
—Trial. 1996. 82p. 21.95 o.s.i (*0-89296-570-3*) Mysterious Pr.
—Trial. 1997. 288p. mass mkt. 5.99 (*0-446-40396-2*) Warner Bks., Inc.
Hamilton, Laurell K. A Caress of Twilight. 2003. 368p. mass mkt. 7.50 (*0-345-42342-9*, Fawcett); 2002. 336p. 23.95 o.s.i (*0-345-43527-3*) Ballantine Bks.
—A Kiss of Shadows. E-Book 18.50 (*1-58945-526-6*) Adobe Systems, Inc.
—A Kiss of Shadows. 2002. 480p. mass mkt. 6.99 (*0-345-42340-2*); 2001. E-Book 6.99 (*0-345-44688-7*) Ballantine Bks. (Ballantine Bks.).
—A Kiss of Shadows. l.t. ed. 2001. (Wheeler Large Print Book Ser.). 637p. 26.95 (*1-58724-014-9*, Wheeler Publishing, Inc.) Gale Group.
—Seduced by Moonlight. 2004. 336p. 23.95 (*0-345-44356-X*) Ballantine Bks.
Hamilton, Steve. Blood Is the Sky: An Alex McKnight Mystery. 2003. 304p. 21.95 (*0-312-30115-4*, Saint Martin's Minotaur) St. Martin's Pr.
—A Cold Day in Paradise. l.t. ed. 2001. 354p. lib. bdg. 28.95 (*1-58547-136-4*) Ctr. Point Large Print.
—A Cold Day in Paradise. (Alex McKnight Mysteries Ser.). 2000. 320p. mass mkt. 6.99 (*0-312-96919-8*, St. Martin's Paperbacks); 1998. 288p. 22.95 (*0-312-19248-7*, Saint Martin's Minotaur) St. Martin's Pr.
—A Cold Day in Paradise: A Mystery, Set. unabr. ed. 1999. (Chivers Sound Library American Collections). audio 54.95 (*0-7927-2326-0*, CSL 215, Chivers Sound Library) BBC Audiobooks America.
—North of Nowhere: An Alex McKnight Mystery. 2003. 352p. mass mkt. 6.99 (*0-312-98381-6*, St. Martin's Paperbacks); 2002. 288p. 23.95 (*0-312-26897-1*, Saint Martin's Minotaur) St. Martin's Pr.
Hammett, Dashiell. The Continental Op. Marcus, Steven, ed. 1992. pap. 10.00 (*0-394-23902-4*); 1989. 352p. pap. 13.00 (*0-679-72258-0*) Knopf Publishing Group. (Vintage).
—The Continental Op. Marcus, Steven, ed. 1992. pap. 10.00 (*0-679-74095-3*) Random Hse., Inc.
—The Dain Curse. Date not set. 150p. 18.95 (*0-8488-2429-6*); 1976. 21.95 (*0-8488-1039-2*) Amereon, Ltd.
—The Dain Curse. unabr. ed. 1980. audio 42.00 (*0-7366-0264-X*, 1259) Books on Tape, Inc.
—The Dain Curse. unabr. ed. 1996. audio 54.95 (*1-85695-717-9*, 941101) ISIS Audio Bks. GBR. *Dist:* Ulverscroft Large Print Bks., Ltd.
—The Dain Curse. 1989. 240p. pap. 12.00 (*0-679-72260-2*); 1978. pap. 1.50 o.p. (*0-394-72624-3*) Knopf Publishing Group. (Vintage).
—The Dain Curse. 1972. pap. 3.95 o.p. (*0-394-71827-5*) Random Hse., Inc.
—The Maltese Falcon. l.t. ed. 2001. 217p. 28.95 (*0-7838-9459-7*, Macmillan Reference USA) Gale Group.
—The Maltese Falcon. 2001. (Best Mysteries of All Time Ser.). 271p. (*0-7621-8867-7*, IM Pr.) Reader's Digest Assn., Inc., The.
—Red Harvest. Date not set. 143p. 18.95 (*0-8488-2348-6*) Amereon, Ltd.
—Red Harvest. unabr. ed. 1996. audio 42.00 (*0-7366-3442-8*, 4086) Books on Tape, Inc.
—Red Harvest. unabr. ed. 2000. audio compact disk 64.95 (*0-7531-0705-8*, 107058); 1996. audio 54.95 (*1-85695-707-1*, 940903) ISIS Audio Bks. GBR. *Dist:* Ulverscroft Large Print Bks., Ltd.
—Red Harvest. 1992. pap. 9.00 (*0-394-23904-0*); 1989. 224p. pap. 11.00 (*0-679-72261-0*) Knopf Publishing Group. (Vintage).
—Red Harvest. 1992. pap. 9.00 (*0-679-74093-7*); 1972. pap. 3.95 o.p. (*0-394-71828-3*) Random Hse., Inc.
—Red Harvest. 1994. 209p. 35.00 (*1-883402-95-6*, Scribner) Simon & Schuster.
Hardwick, Michael & Hardwick, Mollie. The Private Life of Sherlock Holmes. 1993. 200p. 25.00 (*0-86025-277-9*) Henry, Ian Pubns. GBR. *Dist:* Empire Publishing Service.
Hardwick, Phil. Conspiracy in Corinth, 8 vols., Vol. 7. 1999. (Mississippi Mysteries Ser.: Vol. 7). (Illus.). 120p. pap. 5.00 (*1-893062-11-2*) Quail Ridge Pr., Inc.
—Newcomer in New Albany. 1999. (Mississippi Mysteries Ser.: Vol. 4). (Illus.). 127p. pap. 5.00 (*1-893062-06-6*) Quail Ridge Pr., Inc.
Hart, Ellen. Immaculate Midnight: A Jane Lawless Mystery. E-Book 24.95 (*0-312-70728-2*); 2003. 336p. pap. 13.95 (*0-312-31365-9*, Saint Martin's Griffin); 2002. 384p. 24.95 (*0-312-26676-6*, Saint Martin's Minotaur) St. Martin's Pr.
Harvey, Clay. A Whisper of Black. 1997. 240p. 23.95 o.s.i (*0-399-14232-0*, G. P. Putnam's Sons) Penguin Group (USA) Inc.
—Whisper of Black. 1998. 320p. mass mkt. 6.99 o.s.i (*0-425-16450-0*) Berkley Publishing Group.
—A Whisper of Black. l.t. ed. 1998. (Charnwood Large Print Ser.). 336p. 29.99 o.p. (*0-7089-9016-9*, Ulverscroft) Thorpe, F. A. Pubs. GBR. *Dist:* Ulverscroft Large Print Bks., Ltd., Ulverscroft Large Print Canada, Ltd.
Hayes, Teddy. Dead by Popular Demand. 2003. 240p. pap. 10.95 (*1-902934-02-4*) X Pr., The GBR. *Dist:* National Bk. Network.
Haywood, Gar Anthony. All the Lucky Ones Are Dead: An Aaron Gunner Mystery. 2000. 240p. 23.95 o.s.i (*0-399-14540-0*, G. P. Putnam's Sons) Penguin Group (USA) Inc.
—Fear of the Dark. 1988. 192p. 13.95 o.p. (*0-312-01796-0*, Saint Martin's Minotaur) St. Martin's Pr.
—Fear of the Dark. 1990. 192p. pap. 3.95 o.p. (*0-14-013153-1*, Penguin Bks.) Viking Penguin.
—It's Not a Pretty Sight: An Aaron Gunner Mystery. 1998. 256p. mass mkt. 5.99 o.s.i (*0-425-16196-X*, Prime Crime) Berkley Publishing Group.
—It's Not a Pretty Sight: An Aaron Gunner Mystery. 1996. 240p. 22.95 o.p. (*0-399-14132-4*, G. P. Putnam's Sons) Penguin Group (USA) Inc.
—Not Long for This World. 1991. (Crime Monthly Ser.). 272p. pap. 4.95 o.p. (*0-14-015265-2*, Penguin Bks.) Penguin Group (USA) Inc.
—Not Long for This World. 1990. 17.95 o.p. (*0-312-04398-8*, Saint Martin's Minotaur) St. Martin's Pr.
—When Last Seen Alive. 1999. 256p. mass mkt. 5.99 o.s.i (*0-425-17027-6*) Berkley Publishing Group.
—When Last Seen Alive. 1997. 240p. 22.95 o.p. (*0-399-14303-3*, G. P. Putnam's Sons) Penguin Group (USA) Inc.
—You Can Die Trying. 1993. 224p. 17.95 o.p. (*0-312-09425-6*, Saint Martin's Minotaur) St. Martin's Pr.
—You Can Die Trying: An Aaron Gunner Mystery. 1994. (Crime Ser.). 224p. reprint ed. pap. 5.95 o.p. (*0-14-023946-4*, Penguin Bks.) Penguin Group (USA) Inc.
Healy, Jeremiah. Act of God. Chelius, Jane, ed. 1994. 352p. 20.00 (*0-671-79558-9*, Atria) Simon & Schuster.
—Blunt Darts. l.t. ed. 1985. lib. bdg. 16.95 o.p. (*0-89340-918-9*, 482) BBC Audiobooks America.
—Blunt Darts. Chelius, Jane, ed. 1991. 192p. reprint ed. mass mkt. 5.50 (*0-671-73742-2*, Pocket) Simon & Schuster.
—Blunt Darts. 1984. 192p. 12.95 o.s.i (*0-8027-5570-4*) Walker & Co.
—Blunt Darts. 1986. 192p. mass mkt. 3.50 o.s.i (*0-445-20210-6*) Warner Bks., Inc.
—Foursome. 1993. 352p. 20.00 (*0-671-79556-2*, Atria) Simon & Schuster.
—Foursome. Chelius, Jane, ed. 1994. 352p. reprint ed. mass mkt. 5.99 (*0-671-79557-0*, Pocket) Simon & Schuster.
—Invasion of Privacy. (John Francis Cuddy Mystery Ser.). 1997. 320p. pap. 5.99 (*0-671-89874-4*, Pocket); 1996. 352p. 21.00 o.p. (*0-671-89876-0*, Atria) Simon & Schuster.
—The Only Good Lawyer. (John Francis Cuddy Mystery Ser.). 1998. 304p. 23.00 o.s.i (*0-671-00953-2*, Atria); 1999. (Illus.). 400p. reprint ed. pap. 6.99 (*0-671-00954-0*, Pocket) Simon & Schuster.
—Rescue. 1996. 384p. pap. 5.99 (*0-671-89875-2*, Pocket) Simon & Schuster.
—Rescue. Chelius, Jane, ed. 1995. 368p. 20.00 o.p. (*0-671-89877-9*, Atria) Simon & Schuster.
—Right to Die. Chelius, Jane, ed. 1991. 256p. 18.95 o.p. (*0-671-70809-0*, Atria); 1992. 288p. reprint ed. mass mkt. 5.99 (*0-671-70810-4*, Pocket) Simon & Schuster.
—Shallow Graves. Chelius, Jane, ed. 1992. 288p. 19.00 (*0-671-70811-2*, Atria) Simon & Schuster.
—So Like Sleep. 1987. 256p. 15.95 o.p. (*0-06-015693-7*) HarperTrade.
—So Like Sleep. 1991. mass mkt. 4.50 (*0-671-74328-7*, Pocket) Simon & Schuster.
—Spiral: A John Frances Cuddy Mystery. (John Francis Cuddy Mystery Ser.). 1999. 368p. 23.00 o.s.i (*0-671-00955-9*, Atria); 2000. 400p. reprint ed. pap. 6.99 (*0-671-00956-7*, Pocket) Simon & Schuster.
—The Staked Goat. 1986. 224p. 14.95 o.p. (*0-06-015515-9*) HarperTrade.
—The Staked Goat. 1991. 320p. mass mkt. 5.99 (*0-671-74284-1*, Pocket) Simon & Schuster.
—Swan Dive. 1991. mass mkt. 5.99 (*0-671-74329-5*); 1989. mass mkt. 3.95 (*0-671-67185-5*) Simon & Schuster. (Pocket).
—Swan Dive: A Novel of Suspense. 1988. 224p. 16.95 o.p. (*0-06-015921-9*) HarperTrade.
—Yesterday's News: A Novel of Suspense. l.t. ed. 1990. 19.95 o.p. (*0-7927-0586-6*, C0581); pap. 17.95 o.p. (*0-7927-0587-4*) BBC Audiobooks America.
—Yesterday's News: A Novel of Suspense. 1989. 16.95 o.p. (*0-06-015922-7*) HarperTrade.
—Yesterday's News: A Novel of Suspense. Chelius, Jane, ed. 1990. 256p. reprint ed. mass mkt. 5.50 (*0-671-69584-3*, Pocket) Simon & Schuster.
Hegwood, Martin. Big Easy Backroad. E-Book 22.95 (*0-312-26441-0*); 2000. 256p. mass mkt. 5.99 (*0-312-97141-9*, St. Martin's Paperbacks); 3rd ed. 1999. 247p. 22.95 (*0-312-20277-6*, Saint Martin's Minotaur) St. Martin's Pr.
—Green-Eyed Hurricane. 2001. 304p. mass mkt. 6.50 (*0-312-97975-4*, St. Martin's Paperbacks); 2000. 272p. 23.95 (*0-312-20919-3*, Saint Martin's Minotaur) St. Martin's Pr.
—The Green-Eyed Hurricane. E-Book 23.95 (*0-312-27579-X*) St. Martin's Pr.
—Jackpot Bay: A Novel. 2002. 272p. 23.95 (*0-312-28096-3*, Saint Martin's Minotaur) St. Martin's Pr.
—Massacre Island. 2001. (Illus.). 288p. 23.95 (*0-312-28095-5*, Saint Martin's Minotaur) St. Martin's Pr.
Hill, Reginald. Blood Sympathy. 1996. (WWL Mystery Ser.). per. (*0-373-26210-8*, 1-26210-4, Worldwide Library) Harlequin Enterprises, Ltd.
—Blood Sympathy. 1994. 224p. 19.95 o.p. (*0-312-11249-1*, Saint Martin's Minotaur) St. Martin's Pr.
—Blood Sympathy. l.t. ed. 1995. (Ulverscroft Large Print Ser.). 464p. 29.99 o.p. (*0-7089-3368-8*, Ulverscroft) Thorpe, F. A. Pubs. GBR. *Dist:* Ulverscroft Large Print Bks., Ltd., Ulverscroft Large Print Canada, Ltd.
—Born Guilty. 1996. mass mkt. (*0-373-26226-4*, 1-26226-0, Worldwide Library) Harlequin Enterprises, Ltd.
—Born Guilty. unabr. ed. 1998. audio 69.95 (*1-85903-234-6*) Magna Story Sound GBR. *Dist:* Ulverscroft Large Print Bks., Ltd.
—Born Guilty. 1995. 240p. 20.95 o.p. (*0-312-13032-5*, Saint Martin's Minotaur) St. Martin's Pr.
—Born Guilty. l.t. ed. 1996. (Ulverscroft Large Print Ser.). 416p. 29.99 o.p. (*0-7089-3571-0*, Ulverscroft) Thorpe, F. A. Pubs. GBR. *Dist:* Ulverscroft Large Print Bks., Ltd., Ulverscroft Large Print Canada, Ltd.
—Killing the Lawyers. 1998. per. (*0-373-26298-1*, 1-26298-9, Mira Bks.) Harlequin Enterprises, Ltd.
—Killing the Lawyers. unabr. ed. 1998. audio 83.95 (*1-85903-235-4*) Magna Story Sound GBR. *Dist:* Ulverscroft Large Print Bks., Ltd.
—Killing the Lawyers. 1997. (Joe Sixsmith Mysteries Ser.). 336p. 23.95 o.p. (*0-312-16877-2*, Saint Martin's Minotaur) St. Martin's Pr.
—Singing the Sadness. 2001. (WWL Mystery Ser.: No. 371). 251p. mass mkt. (*0-373-26371-6*, 1-26371-4, Worldwide Library) Harlequin Enterprises, Ltd.
—Singing the Sadness. 2nd ed. 1999. 352p. 23.95 (*0-312-24238-7*, Saint Martin's Minotaur) St. Martin's Pr.
—Singing the Sadness. l.t. ed. 2000. (Charnwood Large Print Ser.). 392p. 31.99 (*0-7089-9143-2*, Ulverscroft) Thorpe, F. A. Pubs. GBR. *Dist:* Ulverscroft Large Print Bks., Ltd., Ulverscroft Large Print Canada, Ltd.
Howe, Melodie J. Beauty Dies. 1996. (Crime Ser.). 272p. pap. 5.95 o.s.i (*0-14-023565-5*) Penguin Group (USA) Inc.
—Beauty Dies: A Claire Conrad - Maggie Hill Mystery. 1994. 272p. 19.95 o.p. (*0-670-85449-2*, Viking) Viking Penguin.
Hoyt, Richard. Bigfoot. 1995. 246p. pap. text 4.99 (*0-8125-1948-5*, Forge Bks.); 1992. 224p. 17.95 o.p. (*0-312-85278-9*, Tor Bks.) Doherty, Tom Assocs., LLC.
—Decoys: A John Denson Mystery. 1980. 204p. 8.95 o.p. (*0-87131-330-8*) Evans, M. & Co., Inc.
—Decoys: A John Denson Mystery. 1984. (Crime Ser.). 208p. pap. 3.95 o.p. (*0-14-007217-9*, Penguin Bks.) Viking Penguin.
—Fish Story. 1987. 288p. reprint ed. pap. 3.95 o.p. (*0-8125-0491-7*, Tor Bks.) Doherty, Tom Assocs., LLC.
—Fish Story. 1985. (Mystery Ser.). 224p. 13.95 o.p. (*0-670-31672-5*) Viking Penguin.
—Siskiyou. 1984. 304p. (Orig.). pap. 3.50 o.p. (*0-8125-0487-9*, Tor Bks.) Doherty, Tom Assocs., LLC.
—Snake Eyes. (John Denson Mystery Ser.). 1996. 250p. mass mkt. 5.99 (*0-8125-5072-2*); 1995. 256p. 27.95 o.p. (*0-312-85805-1*) Doherty, Tom Assocs., LLC. (Forge Bks.).
—Thirty for a Harry: A John Denson Mystery. l.t. ed. 1991. 8.95 o.p. (*0-7451-9624-1*, 5043); pap. 10.95 o.p. (*0-7927-0024-4*, 647) BBC Audiobooks America.
—Thirty for a Harry: A John Denson Mystery. 1981. 192p. 8.95 o.p. (*0-87131-357-X*) Evans, M. & Co., Inc.
—Thirty for a Harry: A John Denson Mystery. 1984. (Crime Monthly Ser.). 192p. pap. 3.95 o.p. (*0-14-007216-0*, Penguin Bks.) Viking Penguin.
—Whoo? 2000. 224p. mass mkt. 5.99 (*0-8125-1276-6*, Forge Bks.); 1991. 17.95 o.p. (*0-312-85149-9*, Tor Bks.) Doherty, Tom Assocs., LLC.
Huff, Tanya. Blood Debt. 1997. (Victory Nelson Ser.). 336p. mass mkt. 6.99 (*0-88677-739-9*) DAW Bks., Inc.
—Blood Lines, Bk. 3. 1993. (Daw Book Collectors Ser.: Vol. 901). 272p. (Orig.). mass mkt. 5.99 o.s.i (*0-88677-530-2*) DAW Bks., Inc.
—Blood Pact. 1993. (Daw Book Collectors Ser.: Vol. 931). 336p. mass mkt. 5.99 o.s.i (*0-88677-582-5*) DAW Bks., Inc.
—Blood Price. 1991. (Daw Book Collectors Ser.: Vol. 850). 272p. (Orig.). mass mkt. 6.99 (*0-88677-471-3*) DAW Bks., Inc.
—Blood Trail. 1992. (Victor Nelson Investigator Ser.: Vol. 3). 304p. (Orig.). mass mkt. 6.99 (*0-88677-502-7*) DAW Bks., Inc.
Hunt, E. Howard. Islamorada. 1995. 240p. 20.95 o.s.i (*1-55611-438-9*) Fine, Donald I. Bks.
—Ixtapa. 1994. (Jack Novak Ser.). 224p. 19.95 o.p. (*1-55611-404-4*) Fine, Donald I. Bks.
—Izmir: A Jack Novak Adventure. 1996. (Jack Novak Adventure Ser.). 240p. 21.95 o.p. (*1-55611-474-5*) Fine, Donald I. Bks.
—Sonora. 2000. 315p. 23.95 (*0-312-87205-4*, Forge Bks.) Doherty, Tom Assocs., LLC.
—Sonora. 1999. pap. 24.95 (*1-55611-535-0*) Fine, Donald I. Bks.
Hunter, Stephen. Pale Horse Coming. 2003. 608p. pap. 7.99 (*0-671-03546-0*, Pocket); 2001. 496p. 25.00 (*0-684-86361-8*, Simon & Schuster); 2002. 624p. mass mkt. 7.99 (*0-7434-4382-9*, Pocket) Simon & Schuster.
—Pale Horse Coming. l.t. ed. 825p. 2003. 13.95 (*0-7862-3949-2*); 2002. 28.95 (*0-7862-3950-6*) Thorndike Pr.
Irvine, Robert. The Angels' Share. Isaacson, Dana, ed. 1990. 224p. reprint ed. bds. 3.95 (*0-671-69494-4*, Pocket) Simon & Schuster.
—The Angels' Share. 1989. 15.95 o.p. (*0-312-02862-8*, Saint Martin's Minotaur) St. Martin's Pr.
—Baptism for the Dead. 1990. 256p. mass mkt. 3.95 (*0-671-69495-2*, Pocket) Simon & Schuster.
—Called Home. 1991. 17.95 o.p. (*0-312-05829-2*, Saint Martin's Minotaur) St. Martin's Pr.
—Gone to Glory. Isaacson, Dana, ed. 1991. 224p. reprint ed. mass mkt. 3.95 (*0-671-72799-0*, Pocket) Simon & Schuster.
—Gone to Glory. 1990. 16.95 o.p. (*0-312-04321-X*, Saint Martin's Minotaur) St. Martin's Pr.
—The Great Reminder. 1993. 224p. 17.95 o.p. (*0-312-09302-0*, Saint Martin's Minotaur) St. Martin's Pr.
—The Hosanna Shout. 1994. 240p. 19.95 o.p. (*0-312-11418-4*, Saint Martin's Minotaur) St. Martin's Pr.
—Pillar of Fire: A Moroni Traveler Mystery. 1995. 272p. 21.95 o.p. (*0-312-13588-2*, Saint Martin's Minotaur) St. Martin's Pr.
—The Spoken Word. 1992. 224p. 17.95 o.p. (*0-312-07841-2*, Saint Martin's Minotaur) St. Martin's Pr.
Ishiguro, Kazuo. When We Were Orphans. E-Book 19.95 (*1-58945-537-1*) Adobe Systems, Inc.
—When We Were Orphans. 2001. 352p. reprint ed. pap. 14.00 (*0-375-72440-0*, Vintage) Knopf Publishing Group.
—When We Were Orphans. 2000. 352p. 25.00 (*0-375-41054-6*) Knopf, Alfred A. Inc.
—When We Were Orphans. 2001. E-Book 12.50 (*0-375-41265-4*) Random Hse., Inc.
Jackson, Hialeah. The Alligator's Farewell. 1998. (Annabelle Hardy Mystery Ser.: No. 1). 368p. mass mkt. 5.99 o.s.i (*0-440-22660-0*) Dell Publishing.
—Farewell, Conch Republic. 1999. 368p. mass mkt. 5.99 o.s.i (*0-440-22663-5*) Dell Publishing.
Jacobs, Nancy B. The Silver Scalpel. 1993. (Devon McDonald Ser.). 240p. 21.95 o.p. (*0-399-13834-X*, G. P. Putnam's Sons) Penguin Group (USA) Inc.
—A Slash of Scarlet. 1992. 240p. 19.95 o.p. (*0-399-13733-5*, G. P. Putnam's Sons) Penguin Group (USA) Inc.
—A Slash of Scarlet. Rubenstein, Julie, ed. 1993. 256p. reprint ed. mass mkt. 4.99 (*0-671-86504-8*, Pocket) Simon & Schuster.
—The Turquoise Tattoo. 1992. 256p. reprint ed. mass mkt. 4.99 (*0-671-75535-8*, Pocket) Simon & Schuster.

—The Turquoise Tattoo: A Devon MacDonald Mystery. 1991. 240p. 19.95 o.p. (0-399-13551-0, G. P. Putnam's Sons) Penguin Group (USA) Inc.

James, P. D. The Skull Beneath the Skin. unabr. ed. 1994. audio 88.00 (0-7366-2647-6, 3384) Books on Tape, Inc.

—The Skull Beneath the Skin. unabr. ed. 2000. (Cordelia Gray Mystery Ser.: Bk. 2). audio 69.95 (0-7451-6838-8, CAB 330) Chivers Audio Bks. GBR. *Dist:* BBC Audiobooks America.

—The Skull Beneath the Skin. l.t. ed. (Wheeler Large Print Book Ser.). 2001. 517p. 29.95 (1-58724-122-6, Wheeler Publishing, Inc.); 1983. 571p. 18.95 o.p. (0-8161-3508-8, Macmillan Reference USA); 1983. 9.95 o.p. (0-8161-3569-X, Macmillan Reference USA) Gale Group.

—The Skull Beneath the Skin. 1988. mass mkt. 4.95 (0-446-35272-1) Little Brown & Co.

—The Skull Beneath the Skin, Set. abr. ed. 1994. audio 15.99 o.s.i (0-553-47223-2, 391595, RH Audio) Random Hse. Audio Publishing Group.

—The Skull Beneath the Skin. (Classics Ser.). 2001. 352p. 25.00 (0-7432-2205-9, Scribner); 2001. 448p. pap. 12.00 (0-7432-1956-2, Touchstone); 1982. 352p. 13.95 o.s.i (0-684-17773-0, Scribner) Simon & Schuster.

—The Skull Beneath the Skin. 2001. 18.05 (0-606-22452-1) Turtleback Bks.

—The Skull Beneath the Skin. 1988. 432p. mass mkt. 7.99 o.p. (0-446-35372-8) Warner Bks., Inc.

—An Unsuitable Job for a Woman. unabr. ed. 2000. (Cordelia Gray Mystery Ser.: Bk. 1). audio 49.95 (0-7451-6064-6, CAB 180) Chivers Audio Bks. GBR. *Dist:* BBC Audiobooks America.

—An Unsuitable Job for a Woman. 1980. (General Ser.). lib. bdg. 13.95 o.p. (0-8161-6788-5, Macmillan Reference USA) Gale Group.

—An Unsuitable Job for a Woman. unabr. ed. 1992. audio 51.00 (1-55690-737-0, 92110E7) Recorded Bks., LLC.

—An Unsuitable Job for a Woman. 2001. (Classic Ser.). 208p. 25.00 (0-7432-2204-0, Scribner); 256p. pap. 12.00 (0-7432-1955-4, Touchstone); 320p. 25.00 o.p. (0-7432-2492-2, Scribner) Simon & Schuster.

—An Unsuitable Job for a Woman. 1988. 288p. reprint ed. mass mkt. 6.99 o.p. (0-446-31517-6) Warner Bks., Inc.

Jardine, Quintin. Poisoned Cherries. 2003. 256p. 28.00 (0-7472-7177-1); 2002. 352p. pap. 8.95 (0-7472-6472-4) Headline Bk. Publishing, Ltd. GBR. *Dist:* Trafalgar Square.

Jeffers, H. Paul. The Adventure of the Stalwart Companions. 1978. 7.95 o.p. (0-06-012248-X) HarperCollins Pubs.

—Rubout at the Onyx. 1987. mass mkt. 2.95 o.s.i (0-345-34676-9) Ballantine Bks.

—Rubout at the Onyx. 1981. (Joan Kahn Bk.). 192p. 10.95 o.p. (0-89919-046-4) Houghton Mifflin Co.

—Rubout at the Onyx. l.t. ed. 2001. (Paperback Ser.). 264p. 24.95 (0-7838-9330-2) Thorndike Pr.

Jennings, Maureen. Except the Dying. 1997. 288p. 23.95 (0-312-16829-2, 737113, Saint Martin's Minotaur) St. Martin's Pr.

—Except the Dying: A Mystery. 1999. 336p. mass mkt. 5.99 (0-06-109739-X, HarperTorch) Morrow/Avon.

—Let Loose the Dogs: A Mystery. Date not set. pap. (0-312-30752-7, Saint Martin's Griffin); E-Book (0-312-70575-1); 2003. 320p. 24.95 (0-312-30751-9, Saint Martin's Minotaur) St. Martin's Pr.

—Under the Dragon's Tail. 1999. 304p. mass mkt. 5.99 (0-06-109740-3, HarperTorch) Morrow/Avon.

—Under the Dragon's Tail. 1998. 256p. 21.95 o.p. (0-312-19348-3, Saint Martin's Minotaur) St. Martin's Pr.

Johnston. Blood Tree. 2003. 434p. mass mkt. (0-340-71706-8) New English Library, Ltd.

Jones, Douglas C. A Spider for Loco Shoat. 1997. 320p. 25.00 o.s.i (0-8050-4849-9) Holt, Henry & Co.

Kaminsky, Stuart M. Bullet for a Star. unabr. ed. 1994. audio 23.95 (0-7861-0731-6, 1482) Blackstone Audio Bks., Inc.

—Bullet for a Star. 1985. (Toby Peters Mystery Ser.). pap. 3.95 o.p. (0-89296-147-3) Mysterious Pr.

—Bullet for a Star. 1977. (Toby Peters Mystery Ser.). 188p. 7.95 o.p. (0-312-10797-8) St. Martin's Pr.

—Bullet for a Star. 1991. (Toby Peters Mystery Ser.). 192p. mass mkt. 4.99 (0-446-40061-0, Mysterious Pr. Paperback Bks.) Warner Bks., Inc.

—Buried Caesars. l.t. ed. 1991. (Toby Peters Mystery Ser.). 281p. 18.95 o.p. (0-7927-0490-8); pap. 16.95 o.p. (0-7927-0491-6, C0783) BBC Audiobooks America.

—Buried Caesars. 1989. (Toby Peters Mystery Ser.). 192p. 15.45 o.p. (0-89296-374-3) Mysterious Pr.

—Buried Caesars. unabr. ed. 1997. (Toby Peters Mystery Ser.: Vol. 14). audio 44.00 (0-7887-0401-X, 94593E7) Recorded Bks., LLC.

—Buried Caesars. 1990. (Toby Peters Mystery Ser.). 192p. mass mkt. 4.50 (0-445-40878-2, Mysterious Pr. Paperback Bks.) Warner Bks., Inc.

—Catch a Falling Clown. 1981. (Toby Peters Mystery Ser.). 182p. 10.95 o.p. (0-312-12377-9) St. Martin's Pr.

—Catch a Falling Clown. 1984. (Toby Peters Mystery Ser.). 182p. reprint ed. pap. 3.95 o.p. (0-14-007022-2, Penguin Bks.) Viking Penguin.

—Dancing in the Dark. unabr. ed. 1996. (Toby Peters Mystery Ser.). 30p. audio 39.95 (0-7861-0961-0, 754074) Blackstone Audio Bks., Inc.

—Dancing in the Dark. 1996. (Toby Peters Mystery Ser.). 228p. 19.95 o.s.i (0-89296-528-2) Mysterious Pr.

—Dancing in the Dark. unabr. ed. audio. 1996. (Toby Peters Mystery Ser.: Vol. 19). audio 44.00 (0-7887-0621-7, 94795E7) Recorded Bks., LLC.

—Dancing in the Dark. 1997. (Toby Peters Mystery Ser.). 224p. mass mkt. 5.99 o.p. (0-446-40337-7) Warner Bks., Inc.

—The Devil Met a Lady. unabr. ed. 1995. audio 39.95 (0-7861-0881-9, 1536) Blackstone Audio Bks., Inc.

—The Devil Met a Lady. 1993. (Toby Peters Mystery Ser.). 208p. 18.95 (0-89296-436-7) Mysterious Pr.

—The Devil Met a Lady. 1995. (Toby Peters Mystery Ser.). 208p. mass mkt. 5.50 (0-446-40423-3, Mysterious Pr. Paperback Bks.) Warner Bks., Inc.

—The Devil Met a Lady. 2000. (Toby Peters Mysteries Ser.). 240p. pap. 12.00 (0-7434-0004-6) ibooks, Inc.

—Devil on My Doorstep. 1998. (Rockford Files: Vol. 2). 304p. 22.95 (0-312-86444-2, Forge Bks.) Doherty, Tom Assocs., LLC.

—Down for the Count. l.t. ed. 1986. (Toby Peters Mystery Ser.). 307p. 11.95 o.p. (0-8161-4000-6, Macmillan Reference USA) Gale Group.

—Down for the Count. 1985. (Toby Peters Mystery Ser.). 192p. 12.95 o.p. (0-312-21862-1) St. Martin's Pr.

—Down for the Count. 1990. (Toby Peters Mystery Ser.). mass mkt. 4.50 o.s.i (0-445-40908-8, Mysterious Pr. Paperback Bks.) Warner Bks., Inc.

—The Fala Factor. 1985. (Toby Peters Mystery Ser.). pap. 3.95 o.p. (0-89296-148-1) Mysterious Pr.

—The Fala Factor. 1984. (Toby Peters Mystery Ser.). 174p. 11.95 o.p. (0-312-27967-1) St. Martin's Pr.

—The Fala Factor. 1993. (Toby Peters Mystery Ser.). 224p. mass mkt. 4.99 (0-446-40065-3, Mysterious Pr. Paperback Bks.) Warner Bks., Inc.

—A Fatal Glass of Beer. unabr. ed. 1998. (Toby Peters Mystery Ser.). audio 29.95 (0-7861-1465-7); audio 44.95 (0-7861-1346-4, 1766) Blackstone Audio Bks., Inc.

—A Fatal Glass of Beer, Set. unabr. ed. 1999. audio 44.95 Highsmith Inc.

—A Fatal Glass of Beer. 1997. (Toby Peters Mystery Ser.). (ACE.). 256p. 21.50 o.p. (0-89296-630-0) Mysterious Pr.

—A Fatal Glass of Beer. unabr. ed. 1997. (Toby Peters Mystery Ser.: Vol. 20). audio 51.00 (0-7887-0650-0, 94827E7) Recorded Bks., LLC.

—A Few Minutes Past Midnight. l.t. ed. 2002. 347p. 29.95 (0-7862-4118-7) Gale Group.

—The Green Bottle. unabr. ed. 1999. audio 69.95 (0-7927-2300-7, CSL189, Chivers Sound Library) BBC Audiobooks America.

—The Green Bottle. (Rockford Files: Vol. 1). 320p. 1996. 22.95 (0-312-86229-6); 1999. mass mkt. 5.99 (0-8125-7105-3) Doherty, Tom Assocs., LLC. (Forge Bks.).

—The Green Bottle. l.t. ed. 1998. (Americana Ser.). 437p. 28.95 (0-7862-1521-6) Thorndike Pr.

—He Done Her Wrong. unabr. ed. 1998. audio 39.95 (0-7861-1280-8, 2175) Blackstone Audio Bks., Inc.

—He Done Her Wrong. 1984. (Toby Peters Mystery Ser.). reprint ed. pap. 3.95 o.p. (0-89296-095-7) Mysterious Pr.

—He Done Her Wrong. 1983. (Toby Peters Mystery Ser.). 168p. 10.95 o.p. (0-312-36491-1) St. Martin's Pr.

—He Done Her Wrong. 1995. (Toby Peters Mystery Ser.). 208p. mass mkt. 5.50 (0-446-40191-9, Mysterious Pr. Paperback Bks.) Warner Bks., Inc.

—High Midnight. unabr. ed. 1995. audio 32.95 (0-7861-0765-0, 1614) Blackstone Audio Bks., Inc.

—High Midnight. 1984. (Toby Peters Mystery Ser.). reprint ed. pap. 3.95 o.p. (0-89296-091-4) Mysterious Pr.

—High Midnight. 1981. (Toby Peters Mystery Ser.). 188p. 9.95 o.p. (0-312-37234-5) St. Martin's Pr.

—The Howard Hughes Affair. 1980. (Toby Peters Mystery Ser.). 192p. 2.25 o.s.i (0-441-34462-3) Ace Bks.

—The Howard Hughes Affair. unabr. ed. 1999. audio 32.95 (0-7861-1397-9, 1570); 1995. audio 32.95 (0-7861-0668-9, 1570) Blackstone Audio Bks., Inc.

—The Howard Hughes Affair. 1979. (Toby Peters Mystery Ser.). 207p. 8.95 o.p. (0-312-39617-1) St. Martin's Pr.

—The Howard Hughes Affair. 1990. (Toby Peters Mystery Ser.). 224p. mass mkt. 4.95 o.s.i (0-445-40905-3, Mysterious Pr. Paperback Bks.) Warner Bks., Inc.

—The Man Who Shot Lewis Vance. unabr. ed. 1998. audio 5.99 (0-88646-963-5, PAC-7963) Durkin Hayes Publishing Ltd.

—The Man Who Shot Lewis Vance. 1986. (Toby Peters Mystery Ser.). 224p. 14.95 o.p. (0-312-51394-1) St. Martin's Pr.

—The Man Who Shot Lewis Vance. 1990. (Toby Peters Mystery Ser.). 208p. mass mkt. 4.50 o.s.i (0-445-40909-6, Mysterious Pr. Paperback Bks.) Warner Bks., Inc.

—The Melting Clock. l.t. ed. 1992. (Toby Peters Mystery Ser.). 260p. 19.95 o.p. (0-7927-1280-3); pap. 17.95 o.p. (0-7927-1281-1) BBC Audiobooks America.

—The Melting Clock. unabr. ed. 1998. (Toby Peters Mystery Ser.). audio 32.95 (0-7861-1468-1, 2227) Blackstone Audio Bks., Inc.

—The Melting Clock. 1991. (Toby Peters Mystery Ser.). 192p. 17.45 o.p. (0-89296-435-9) Mysterious Pr.

—The Melting Clock. 1993. (Toby Peters Mystery Ser.). 208p. mass mkt. 4.99 (0-446-40304-0, Mysterious Pr. Paperback Bks.) Warner Bks., Inc.

—Murder on the Yellow Brick Road. unabr. ed. 1994. audio 23.95 (0-7861-0785-5, 1511) Blackstone Audio Bks., Inc.

—Murder on the Yellow Brick Road. 1978. (Toby Peters Mystery Ser.). 197p. 7.95 o.p. (0-312-55318-8) St. Martin's Pr.

—Murder on the Yellow Brick Road. 1979. (Toby Peters Mystery Ser.). 208p. pap. 3.95 o.p. (0-14-005124-4, Penguin Bks.) Viking Penguin.

—Murder on the Yellow Brick Road. 2000. (Toby Peters Mysteries Ser.). 192p. pap. 12.00 (0-7434-0000-3) ibooks, Inc.

—Never Cross a Vampire. unabr. ed. 2000. audio compact disk 48.00 (0-7861-9943-1, z2256); 1999. audio compact disk 24.95 (0-7861-1461-4); 1998. audio 32.95 (0-7861-1353-7, 2256) Blackstone Audio Bks., Inc.

—Never Cross a Vampire, unabr. ed. 1999. audio 32.95 Highsmith Inc.

—Never Cross a Vampire. 1984. (Toby Peters Mystery Ser.). reprint ed. pap. 3.95 o.s.i (0-89296-087-6) Mysterious Pr.

—Never Cross a Vampire. 1980. (Toby Peters Mystery Ser.). 182p. 8.95 o.p. (0-312-56471-6) St. Martin's Pr.

—Never Cross a Vampire. 1995. (Toby Peters Mystery Ser.). 192p. mass mkt. 5.50 (0-446-40190-0, Mysterious Pr. Paperback Bks.) Warner Bks., Inc.

—Never Cross a Vampire. 2000. 224p. pap. 12.00 (0-7434-0713-X) ibooks, Inc.

—Poor Butterfly. unabr. ed. 1996. audio 32.95 (0-7861-1018-X, 1796) Blackstone Audio Bks., Inc.

—Poor Butterfly. 1990. (Toby Peters Mystery Ser.). 179p. 17.95 o.p. (0-89296-411-1) Mysterious Pr.

—Poor Butterfly. unabr. ed. 1997. (Toby Peters Mystery Ser.: Vol. 15). audio 35.00 (0-7887-0833-3, 94978E7) Recorded Bks., LLC.

—Poor Butterfly. 1991. (Toby Peters Mystery Ser.). mass mkt. 4.95 o.s.i (0-446-40011-4) Warner Bks., Inc.

—Retribution. mass mkt. 6.99 (0-8125-4036-0); 2001. 272p. 24.95 (0-312-87452-9) Doherty, Tom Assocs., LLC. (Forge Bks.).

—The Rockford Files: Devil on My Doorstep. unabr. ed. 2000. audio 49.95 (0-7927-2313-9, CSL 202) Chivers Audio Bks. GBR. *Dist:* BBC Audiobooks America.

—Smart Moves, unabr. ed. 1997. audio 39.95 (0-7861-1167-4, 1934) Blackstone Audio Bks., Inc.

—Smart Moves. 1987. (Toby Peters Mystery Ser.). 272p. 15.95 o.p. (0-312-00190-8) St. Martin's Pr.

—Smart Moves. 1996. (Toby Peters Mystery Ser.). 224p. reprint ed. mass mkt. 5.99 o.p. (0-446-40438-1, Mysterious Pr. Paperback Bks.) Warner Bks., Inc.

—Think Fast, Mr. Peters. 1996. (Toby Peters Mystery Ser.). 224p. mass mkt. 5.99 (0-446-40440-3, Mysterious Pr. Paperback Bks.) Warner Bks., Inc.

—To Catch a Spy. 2002. 240p. 24.00 (0-7867-1023-3, Carroll & Graf Pubs.) Avalon Publishing Group.

—Tomorrow Is Another Day. 1995. (Toby Peters Mystery Ser.). 208p. 18.95 o.s.i (0-89296-527-4) Mysterious Pr.

—Tomorrow Is Another Day. unabr. ed. 1995. (Toby Peters Mystery Ser.: Vol. 18). audio 51.00 (0-7887-0354-4, 94546E7) Recorded Bks., LLC.

—Tomorrow Is Another Day. 1996. (Toby Peters Mystery Ser.). 224p. mass mkt. 5.99 (0-446-40336-9, Mysterious Pr. Paperback Bks.) Warner Bks., Inc.

—You Bet Your Life. 1979. (Toby Peters Mystery Ser.). 215p. 8.95 o.p. (0-312-89662-X) St. Martin's Pr.

—You Bet Your Life. 1990. (Toby Peters Mystery Ser.). 224p. mass mkt. 4.95 o.s.i (0-445-40906-1, Mysterious Pr. Paperback Bks.) Warner Bks., Inc.

Katz, Jon. Death by Station Wagon. 1994. (Suburban Detective Mysteries Ser.). 336p. mass mkt. 5.99 o.s.i (0-553-29881-X) Bantam Bks.

—Death Row: A Suburban Detective Mystery. 1999. 288p. mass mkt. 5.99 o.s.i (0-553-57816-2) Bantam Bks.

—The Family Stalker. 1995. 336p. mass mkt. 5.50 o.s.i (0-553-56954-6) Bantam Bks.

—The Family Stalker: A Suburban Detective Mystery. 1994. 320p. 18.95 o.s.i (0-385-46903-9) Doubleday Publishing.

—The Fathers' Club. 1997. (Suburban Detective Mysteries Ser.). 272p. mass mkt. 5.99 o.s.i (0-553-57536-8) Bantam Bks.

—The Fathers' Club. l.t. ed. 1997. (Large Print Bks.). 24.95 (1-56895-406-9, Wheeler Publishing, Inc.) Gale Group.

—The Last Housewife. 1996. 384p. mass mkt. 5.99 o.s.i (0-553-56793-4) Bantam Bks.

—The Last Housewife. 1995. 19.95 (0-385-47743-0) Doubleday Publishing.

—The Last Housewife. l.t. ed. 1995. (Niagara Large Print Ser.). 467p. 29.50 o.p. (0-7089-5811-7, Ulverscroft) Thorpe, F. A. Pubs. GBR. *Dist:* Ulverscroft Large Print Bks., Ltd.

Katz, Michael J. The Big Freeze. 1991. 256p. 21.95 o.p. (0-399-13558-8, G. P. Putnam's Sons) Penguin Group (USA) Inc.

—Last Dance in Redondo Beach. 1989. 256p. 17.95 o.p. (0-399-13445-X, G. P. Putnam's Sons) Penguin Putnam Bks. for Young Readers.

—Last Dance in Redondo Beach. 1990. 288p. bds. 3.95 (0-671-67913-9, Pocket) Simon & Schuster.

—Murder off the Glass. 1987. 16.95 o.p. (0-8027-5667-0) Walker & Co.

Keannealy, Jerry. Vintage Polo. 1993. 256p. 19.95 o.p. (0-312-09932-0, Saint Martin's Minotaur) St. Martin's Pr.

Kearney, Susan. Royal Pursuit. 2002. (Harlequin Intrigue Ser.: No. 690). 256p. mass mkt. o.s.i (0-373-22690-X, Harlequin Bks.) Harlequin Enterprises, Ltd.

Kelley, Norman. A Phat Death: A Nina Halligan Mystery. 2003. 260p. pap. 14.95 (1-888451-48-3) Akashic Bks.

Kelly, Jack. Mobtown. 2003. 320p. mass mkt. 7.99 (0-7868-8981-0); 2002. pap. 13.95 (0-7868-8532-7); 2002. 288p. 23.95 (0-7868-6615-2) Hyperion Pr.

Kemprecos, Paul. Bluefin Blues: An Aristotle "Soc" Socarides Mystery. 1997. 224p. 20.95 o.p. (0-312-16787-3, Saint Martin's Minotaur) St. Martin's Pr.

—Cool Blue Tomb. 1991. 288p. mass mkt. 4.50 o.s.i (0-553-28881-4) Bantam Bks.

—Death in Deep Water. 1993. 336p. mass mkt. 4.99 o.s.i (0-553-29735-X) Bantam Bks.

—Death in Deep Water: An Aristotle "Soc" Socraides Mystery. 1992. 368p. 16.50 o.s.i (0-385-42379-9) Doubleday Publishing.

—A Feeding Frenzy. 1994. 336p. mass mkt. 4.99 o.s.i (0-553-56774-8) Bantam Bks.

—Mayflower Murder. 1996. 22.95 (0-312-14852-6, Saint Martin's Minotaur) St. Martin's Pr.

—Neptune's Eye. 1991. 320p. mass mkt. 4.50 o.s.i (0-553-29353-2) Bantam Bks.

Kendrick, Stephen. Night Watch: A Long-Lost Adventure in Which Sherlock Holmes Meets Father Brown. 2001. (Illus.). 272p. 23.00 (0-375-40367-1, Pantheon) Knopf Publishing Group.

Kennealy, Jerry. All That Glitters: A Nick Polo Mystery. 1996. 240p. 21.95 o.p. (0-312-15049-0, Saint Martin's Minotaur) St. Martin's Pr.

—Beggar's Choice. 1994. 256p. 20.95 o.p. (0-312-11478-8, Saint Martin's Minotaur) St. Martin's Pr.

—Green with Envy: A Nick Polo Mystery. 1991. 240p. 17.95 o.p. (0-312-06572-8, Saint Martin's Minotaur) St. Martin's Pr.

—Polo, Anyone? 1988. 224p. 15.95 o.p. (0-312-01491-0, Saint Martin's Minotaur) St. Martin's Pr.

—Polo in the Rough. 1989. 14.95 o.p. (0-312-02964-0, Saint Martin's Minotaur) St. Martin's Pr.

—Polo Solo. 1988. pap. 2.95 o.p. (0-312-91074-6, St. Martin's Paperbacks); 1987. 192p. 13.95 o.p. (0-312-00671-3) St. Martin's Pr.

—Polo's Ponies. 1988. 176p. 14.95 o.p. (0-312-02267-0, Saint Martin's Minotaur) St. Martin's Pr.

—Polo's Wild Card. 1992. 1.99 o.p. (0-517-08490-2) Random Hse. Value Publishing.

—Polo's Wild Card. 1990. 15.95 o.p. (0-312-04437-2, Saint Martin's Minotaur) St. Martin's Pr.

—Special Delivery: A Case for Nick Polo. 1992. 224p. 17.95 o.p. (0-312-08304-1, Saint Martin's Minotaur) St. Martin's Pr.

Kerr, Philip. Berlin Noir: March Violets - The Pale Criminal - A German Requiem. 1994. (Penguin Crime/Mystery Ser.). 848p. 15.95 (0-14-023170-6) Viking Penguin.

—A German Requiem. 1993. (Crime Ser.). 320p. pap. 4.95 o.p. (0-14-017561-X, Penguin Bks.) Penguin Group (USA) Inc.

—A German Requiem. 1991. 320p. 19.95 o.p. (0-670-83516-1, Viking) Viking Penguin.

—March Violets. (Crime Ser.). 256p. 1990. pap. 4.95 o.p. (0-14-011466-1, Penguin Bks.); 1989. 17.95 o.p. (0-670-82431-3) Viking Penguin.

—The Pale Criminal. 1991. (Crime Monthly Ser.). 288p. reprint ed. pap. 4.95 o.p. (*0-14-015393-4*, Penguin Bks.) Penguin Group (USA) Inc.
—The Pale Criminal. 1990. 288p. 18.95 o.p. (*0-670-82433-X*) Viking Penguin.
Kijewski, Karen. Alley Kat Blues. 1996. (Kat Colorado Mysteries Ser.). 384p. mass mkt. 6.99 (*0-553-57315-2*, Crimeline) Bantam Bks.
—Alley Kat Blues. 1995. 22.95 o.s.i (*0-385-46852-0*) Doubleday Publishing.
—Copy Kat. 1990. (Kat Colorado Mysteries Ser.). 400p. mass mkt. 6.99 (*0-553-29883-6*) Bantam Bks.
—Honky Tonk Kat. 1997. (Kat Colorado Mysteries Ser.). 368p. mass mkt. 6.99 o.s.i (*0-425-15860-8*) Berkley Publishing Group.
—Honky Tonk Kat. 1996. viii, 323p. 22.95 o.s.i (*0-399-14133-2*, G. P. Putnam's Sons) Penguin Group (USA) Inc.
—Honky Tonk Kat. 22.95 o.s.i (*0-399-14424-2*) Putnam Publishing Group, The.
—Honky Tonk Kat. abr. ed. 1996. (Kat Colorado Mysteries Ser.). 5p. audio 23.00 (*1-56876-059-0*) Soundlines Entertainment, Inc.
—Kat Scratch Fever. 1998. (Kat Colorado Mysteries Ser.). 368p. mass mkt. 6.99 o.s.i (*0-425-16339-3*) Berkley Publishing Group.
—Kat Scratch Fever. 1997. 323p. 22.95 o.p. (*0-399-14245-2*) Penguin Group (USA) Inc.
—Katapult. 1992. (Kat Colorado Mysteries Ser.). 288p. reprint ed. mass mkt. 6.99 (*0-380-71486-8*, Avon Bks.) Morrow/Avon.
—Katapult. 1990. 244p. 16.95 o.p. (*0-312-04679-0*, Saint Martin's Minotaur) St. Martin's Pr.
—Kat's Cradle. 1997. (Kat Colorado Mysteries Ser.). 320p. mass mkt. 6.99 (*0-553-29391-5*) Bantam Bks.
—Katwalk. 1990. (Kat Colorado Mysteries Ser.). 240p. reprint ed. mass mkt. 6.99 (*0-380-71187-7*, Avon Bks.) Morrow/Avon.
—Katwalk. 1989. 232p. 16.95 o.p. (*0-312-02969-1*, Saint Martin's Minotaur) St. Martin's Pr.
—Stray Kat Waltz. 1999. (Kat Colorado Mysteries Ser.). 352p. reprint ed. pap. 6.99 o.s.i (*0-425-16988-X*) Berkley Publishing Group.
—Stray Kat Waltz. 1998. (Kat Colorado Mysteries Ser. ). 311p. 22.95 o.s.i (*0-399-14368-8*, G. P. Putnam's Sons) Penguin Group (USA) Inc.
—Wild Kat. 1994. (Kat Colorado Mysteries Ser.). 400p. mass mkt. 6.99 (*0-553-56877-9*) Bantam Bks.
King, Laurie R. Justice Hall. 2002. 352p. 23.95 (*0-553-11113-2*) Bantam Bks.
Klavan, Andrew. Dynamite Road. Date not set. mass mkt. (*0-7653-4694-X*); 2003. 320p. 25.95 (*0-7653-0785-5*) Doherty, Tom Assocs., LLC. (Forge Bks.).
Knief, Charles. Diamond Head. (John Caine Mysteries Ser.). 1998. 240p. mass mkt. 6.50 (*0-312-96547-8*, St. Martin's Paperbacks); 1996. 256p. 21.95 o.p. (*0-312-14558-6*, Saint Martin's Minotaur) St. Martin's Pr.
—Emerald Flash. (John Caine Mysteries Ser.). 2000. 304p. mass mkt. 5.99 (*0-312-97058-7*, St. Martin's Paperbacks); 1999. 292p. 23.95 (*0-312-19866-3*, Saint Martin's Minotaur) St. Martin's Pr.
—Sand Dollars. (John Caine Mysteries Ser.). 1999. 304p. mass mkt. 5.99 (*0-312-96682-2*, St. Martin's Paperbacks); 1998. 336p. 23.95 (*0-312-18170-1*, 874700, Saint Martin's Minotaur) St. Martin's Pr.
—Silversword. mass mkt. (*0-312-98025-6*, St. Martin's Paperbacks); 2001. 400p. 24.95 (*0-312-27302-9*, Saint Martin's Minotaur) St. Martin's Pr.
Komo, Dolores. Clio Browne: Private Investigator. 1988. (WomanSleuth Mystery Ser.). 200p. pap. 6.95 o.p. (*0-89594-320-4*); lib. bdg. 22.95 o.p. (*0-89594-321-2*) Crossing Pr., Inc., The.
Krentz, Jayne Ann. Light in Shadow. 2003. 384p. mass mkt. 7.99 (*0-515-13618-2*, Jove) Berkley Publishing Group.
—Light in Shadow. 2003. 543p. pap. 13.95 (*1-4104-0164-2*, Wheeler Publishing, Inc.) Gale Group.
—Light in Shadow. 2002. 384p. 24.95 (*0-399-14938-4*, Putnam & Grosset) Putnam Publishing Group, The.
—Light in Shadow: A Whispering Spring Novel. l.t. ed. 2003. (Basic Ser.). 32.95 (*0-7862-5033-X*) Thorndike Pr.
—Sharp Edges. l.t. ed. 1998. 26.95 (*1-56895-549-9*, Wheeler Publishing, Inc.) Gale Group.
—Sharp Edges. 1998. (Illus.). 400p. mass mkt. 7.50 (*0-671-52409-7*, Pocket Star); 320p. 24.00 (*0-671-52310-4*, Atria) Simon & Schuster.
—Sharp Edges. abr. ed. 1998. audio 18.00 o.s.i (*0-671-57613-5*, 395615, Simon & Schuster Audioworks) Simon & Schuster Audio.
—Truth or Dare. 2003. 24.95 (*0-399-14999-6*) Putnam Publishing Group, The.
Krueger, William Kent. Blood Hollow. 2004. (*0-7434-8867-9*, Atria); pap. (*0-7434-4587-2*, Pocket Star) Simon & Schuster.
—Boundary Waters. (Cork O'Connor Mysteries Ser.). 1999. 336p. 23.00 (*0-671-01698-9*, Atria); 2000. 416p. reprint ed. mass mkt. 6.99 (*0-671-01699-7*, Pocket Star) Simon & Schuster.
—Iron Lake: A Cork O'Connor Mystery. 1999. (Illus.). 464p. mass mkt. 6.99 (*0-671-01697-0*, Pocket Star); 1998. E-Book 23.00 (*0-671-03690-4*, Atria); 1998. (Cork O'Connor Mysteries Ser.: Vol. 1). 320p. 23.00 (*0-671-01696-2*, Atria) Simon & Schuster.
—Iron Lake: A Cork O'Connor Mystery. l.t. ed. 2001. 584p. 29.95 (*0-7862-3174-2*) Thorndike Pr.
—Purgatory Ridge: A Cork O'Connor Mystery. 2001. (Illus.). 368p. 23.95 (*0-671-04753-1*, Atria); 2002. 448p. reprint ed. mass mkt. 6.99 (*0-671-04754-X*, Pocket Star) Simon & Schuster.
—Purgatory Ridge: A Cork O'Connor Mystery. l.t. ed. 2001. (Americana Ser.). 627p. 30.95 (*0-7862-3213-7*) Thorndike Pr.
Kurland, Michael, ed. My Sherlock Holmes: Untold Stories of the Great Detective. 2004. 384p. pap. 14.95 (*0-312-32595-9*); 2003. 368p. 24.95 (*0-312-28093-9*) St. Martin's Pr.
La Plante, Lynda. Cold Blood. 1999. 480p. mass mkt. 6.99 o.s.i (*0-515-12479-6*, Jove) Berkley Publishing Group.
—Cold Blood. unabr. ed. 2000. (Lorraine Page Mystery Ser.). audio 89.95 (*0-7451-8782-X*, CAB 1417) Chivers Audio Bks. GBR. *Dist:* BBC Audiobooks America.
—Cold Heart. unabr. ed. 1998. audio 84.95 (*0-7540-0213-6*, CAB 1636) BBC Audiobooks America.
—Cold Shoulder. 1997. 464p. mass mkt. 6.99 o.s.i (*0-515-12128-2*, Jove) Berkley Publishing Group.
—Cold Shoulder. unabr. ed. 2000. (Lorraine Page Mystery Ser.). audio 79.95 (*0-7451-6511-7*, CAB 1127) Chivers Audio Bks. GBR. *Dist:* BBC Audiobooks America.
Labovitz, Trudy. Ordinary Justice: A Zoe Kergulin Mystery. 1999. 248p. pap. 12.00 (*1-883523-31-1*) Spinsters Ink Bks.
Land, Jon. The Blue Widows. Date not set. mass mkt. (*0-7653-4526-9*); 2003. 384p. 24.95 (*0-7653-0599-2*) Doherty, Tom Assocs., LLC. (Forge Bks.).
Lardo, Vincent. McNally's Chance. l.t. ed. (Paperback Bestsellers Ser.). 2003. 416p. pap. 13.95 (*0-7862-3361-3*); 2001. 447p. 31.95 (*0-7862-3360-5*); 2001. 416p. (*0-7540-1697-8*) Thorndike Pr.
—McNally's Folly. l.t. ed. 431p. 2001. pap. 29.95 (*0-7862-2644-7*); 2000. (*0-7540-1532-7*) Thorndike Pr.
Lardo, Vincent & Sanders, Lawrence. McNally's Alibi. 2003. 304p. mass mkt. 7.99 (*0-425-19119-2*) Berkley Publishing Group.
—McNally's Chance. 2001. 320p. 24.95 o.p. (*0-399-14732-2*) Penguin Group (USA) Inc.
Larsgaard, Chris. The Heir Hunter. 2001. 448p. mass mkt. 6.99 (*0-440-23462-X*) Dell Publishing.
Lawrence, Martha C. Aquarius Descending. (Elizabeth Chase Mysteries Ser.). 2000. 320p. mass mkt. 5.99 (*0-312-97284-9*, St. Martin's Paperbacks); 1998. 304p. 23.95 o.p. (*0-312-19829-9*, Saint Martin's Minotaur) St. Martin's Pr.
—Aquarius Descending Newsletter Kit. Date not set. pap. (*0-312-20695-X*, Saint Martin's Griffin) St. Martin's Pr.
—Ashes of Aries. 2001. 256p. 23.95 (*0-312-20299-7*, Saint Martin's Minotaur) St. Martin's Pr.
—The Cold Heart of Capricorn. 240p. 1996. text 21.95 o.p. (*0-312-14569-1*, Saint Martin's Minotaur); Vol. 1. 1998. mass mkt. 5.99 o.s.i (*0-312-96294-0*, St. Martin's Paperbacks) St. Martin's Pr.
—Murder in Scorpio. 1996. 227p. mass mkt. 5.50 (*0-312-95984-2*, St. Martin's Paperbacks); 1995. 256p. 21.95 (*0-312-13567-X*, Saint Martin's Minotaur) St. Martin's Pr.
—Pisces Rising. 2000. 254p. 23.95 o.p. (*0-312-20298-9*, Saint Martin's Minotaur) St. Martin's Pr.
Leahey, Michael. Broken Machines. 2000. 294p. 23.95 (*0-312-26130-6*, Saint Martin's Minotaur) St. Martin's Pr.
Lee, Wendi. Crazy Like a Fox: An Angela Matelli Mystery. 2002. 240p. 22.95 (*0-312-26139-X*, Saint Martin's Minotaur) St. Martin's Pr.
—Deadbeat. 2000. 256p. mass mkt. (*0-373-26339-2*, Harlequin Bks.) Harlequin Enterprises, Ltd.
—Deadbeat. 1999. (Angela Matelli Mysteries Ser.). 256p. 22.95 o.p. (*0-312-16812-8*, Saint Martin's Minotaur) St. Martin's Pr.
—The Good Daughter. 1996. pap. 4.99 (*0-312-95696-7*, St. Martin's Paperbacks); 1994. 224p. 19.95 o.p. (*0-312-11259-9*, Saint Martin's Minotaur) St. Martin's Pr.
—He Who Dies. 2001. (WWL Mystery Ser.: No. 386). 252p. mass mkt. (*0-373-26386-4*, Worldwide Library) Harlequin Enterprises, Ltd.
—He Who Dies. E-Book 5.99 (*0-312-27437-8*) St. Martin's Pr.
—He Who Dies: An Angela Matelli Mystery. 2000. (Angela Matelli Mysteries Ser.). 247p. 23.95 (*0-312-20894-4*, Saint Martin's Minotaur) St. Martin's Pr.
—Missing Eden. 1999. per. (*0-373-26301-5*, Harlequin Bks.) Harlequin Enterprises, Ltd.
—Missing Eden. 1996. 240p. 21.95 o.p. (*0-312-14370-2*, Saint Martin's Minotaur) St. Martin's Pr.
Lehane, Dennis. Darkness, Take My Hand. 1996. 320p. 24.00 (*0-688-14380-6*, Morrow, William & Co.) Morrow/Avon.
—A Drink Before the War. 2003. 300p. pap. 14.00 (*0-15-602902-2*, Harvest Bks.); 1994. 288p. 22.95 (*0-15-100093-X*) Harcourt Trade Pubs.
—A Drink Before the War. 1996. 320p. mass mkt. 7.99 (*0-380-72623-8*, Avon Bks.) Morrow/Avon.
—A Drink Before the War. 336p. (*0-7278-5537-9*) Severn Hse. Pubs., Ltd.
—Gone, Baby, Gone. abr. ed. 1999. audio 7.99 o.s.i (*1-56740-305-0*, 1869, Paperback Nova Audio Bks.); 1998. audio 17.95 o.p. (*1-56740-783-8*, 450, Nova Audio Bks.); 1998. audio 26.95 (*1-56740-058-2*, 18, Bookcassette); 1998. audio 73.25 (*1-56740-587-8*, 881, Unabridged Library Editions) Brilliance Audio.
—Gone, Baby, Gone. 1999. 448p. mass mkt. 7.99 (*0-380-73035-9*, Avon Bks.); 1998. 256p. 24.00 (*0-688-15332-1*, Morrow, William & Co.) Morrow/Avon.
—Prayers for Rain. 2000. 416p. mass mkt. 7.99 (*0-380-73036-7*); 1999. 352p. 25.00 (*0-688-15333-X*, Morrow, William & Co.); 1999. 352p. 25.00 (*0-688-15333-X*, Morrow, William & Co.) Morrow/Avon.
—Prayers for Rain. l.t. ed. 1999. (Core Ser.). 570p. 29.95 (*0-7838-8786-8*) Thorndike Pr.
—Sacred. abr. ed. 1998. audio 7.99 o.p. (*1-56740-238-0*, 1650, Nova Audio Bks.); 1997. audio 16.95 o.p. (*1-56100-979-2*, 505, Nova Audio Bks.); 1997. audio 73.25 o.p. (*1-56100-829-X*, 1022, Unabridged Library Editions); 1997. audio 23.95 (*1-56100-754-4*, 244, Bookcassette) Brilliance Audio.
—Sacred. 1998. 400p. mass mkt. 7.99 (*0-380-72629-7*, Avon Bks.); 1997. 256p. 23.00 (*0-688-14381-4*, Morrow, William & Co.) Morrow/Avon.
Lescroart, John. Rasputin's Revenge. 1988. 288p. reprint ed. pap. 3.50 (*0-8439-2671-6*) Dorchester Publishing Co., Inc.
—Rasputin's Revenge. 2003. 288p. pap. 14.00 (*0-451-20981-8*) NAL.
—Rasputin's Revenge: The Further Startling Adventures of Auguste Lupa—Son of Holmes. 1987. 288p. 17.95 o.s.i (*1-55611-011-1*) Fine, Donald I. Bks.
—Son of Holmes. l.t. ed. 1991. 19.95 o.p. (*0-7927-0735-4*, CH018); pap. 17.95 o.p. (*0-7927-0736-2*, CS0122) BBC Audiobooks America.
—Son of Holmes. 1987. 256p. reprint ed. pap. 3.25 o.s.i (*0-8439-2461-6*) Dorchester Publishing Co., Inc.
—Son of Holmes. 1986. 223p. 15.95 o.s.i (*0-917657-64-0*) Fine, Donald I. Bks.
—Son of Holmes. 2003. 256p. pap. 14.00 (*0-451-20875-7*) NAL.
—Son of Holmes & Rasputin's Revenge: The Early Works of John T. Lescroart. 1995. 544p. pap. 16.95 o.s.i (*1-55611-437-0*) Fine, Donald I. Bks.
Leslie, John. Blue Moon. 1998. (Gideon Lowry Mystery Ser.: Vol. 4). 256p. 23.00 o.s.i (*0-671-53514-5*, Atria) Simon & Schuster.
—Killing Me Softly. Grose, Bill, ed. (Orig.). 1995. 272p. mass mkt. 5.50 (*0-671-86421-1*, Pocket); 1994. 256p. 20.00 (*0-671-86420-3*, Atria) Simon & Schuster.
—Love for Sale. 1997. (Gideon Lowry Mystery Ser.). 272p. pap. 6.50 (*0-671-51126-2*, Pocket) Simon & Schuster.
—Love for Sale: A Gideon Lowry Mystery. 1997. 272p. 22.00 (*0-671-51127-0*, Atria) Simon & Schuster.
—Night & Day. 256p. 2002. pap. 17.95 (*0-7434-7025-7*); 1996. mass mkt. 5.99 (*0-671-86423-8*) Simon & Schuster. (Pocket).
—Night & Day: A Gideon Lowry Mystery. Grose, William, ed. 1995. 256p. (Orig.). pap. 20.00 o.p. (*0-671-86422-X*, Atria) Simon & Schuster.
Lethem, Jonathan. Gun with Occasional Music. 2003. 288p. pap. 14.00 (*0-15-602897-2*, 53586160) Harcourt Trade Pubs.
—Motherless Brooklyn. 1999. 320p. 23.95 o.s.i (*0-385-49183-2*) Doubleday Publishing.
—Motherless Brooklyn. l.t. ed. 2000. (Basic Ser.). 492p. 30.95 (*0-7862-2695-1*) Thorndike Pr.
—Motherless Brooklyn. 2000. 19.05 (*0-606-21849-1*) Turtleback Bks.
—Motherless Brooklyn: A Novel. 2000. (Vintage Contemporaries Ser.). 336p. pap. 13.00 (*0-375-72483-4*, Vintage) Knopf Publishing Group.
Levitt, J. R. Carnivores. 1990. 256p. mass mkt. 3.95 o.p. (*0-451-16845-3*, Signet Bks.) NAL.
—Carnivores. 1989. 208p. 15.95 o.p. (*0-312-02553-X*, Saint Martin's Minotaur) St. Martin's Pr.
—Ten of Swords. 1991. 15.95 o.p. (*0-312-05386-X*, Saint Martin's Minotaur) St. Martin's Pr.
Lewin, Michael Z. And Baby Will Fall. l.t. ed. 1989. 304 p. pap. (*1-55504-755-6*) BBC Audiobooks America.
—And Baby Will Fall. 1990. mass mkt. (*0-373-26042-3*, Harlequin Bks.) Harlequin Enterprises, Ltd.
—And Baby Will Fall. 1988. 224p. 16.95 o.p. (*0-688-06880-4*, Morrow, William & Co.) Morrow/Avon.
—Ask the Right Question. 1979. 1.75 o.p. (*0-425-04027-5*) Berkley Publishing Group.
—Ask the Right Question. 1984. 192p. reprint ed. mass mkt. 3.50 o.p. (*0-06-080711-3*, P 711) HarperCollins Pubs.
—Ask the Right Question. 1991. mass mkt. 4.95 o.s.i (*0-446-40021-1*, Mysterious Pr. Paperback Bks.) Warner Bks., Inc.
—Called by a Panther. 1991. 17.95 o.p. (*0-89296-439-1*) Mysterious Pr.
—Called by a Panther. 1992. 272p. mass mkt. 4.99 o.s.i (*0-446-40159-5*) Warner Bks., Inc.
—The Enemies Within. 1979. mass mkt. 1.75 o.p. (*0-425-04029-1*) Berkley Publishing Group.
—Enemies Within. 1991. mass mkt. 4.95 o.s.i (*0-446-40024-6*, Mysterious Pr. Paperback Bks.) Warner Bks., Inc.
—The Enemies Within. 1984. 240p. reprint ed. mass mkt. 3.50 o.p. (*0-06-080712-1*, P 712, Perennial) HarperTrade.
—Family Business: A Novel of Detection. 1995. (Lunghi Family Mystery Ser.). 176p. reprint ed. 20.00 o.p. (*0-88150-348-7*, Foul Play) Norton, W. W. & Co., Inc.
—Missing Woman. 1982. mass mkt. 2.25 o.p. (*0-425-05391-1*) Berkley Publishing Group.
—Missing Woman. 1985. 224p. reprint ed. mass mkt. 3.50 o.p. (*0-06-080709-1*, P 709, Perennial) HarperTrade.
—Missing Woman. 1981. 224p. 10.95 o.p. (*0-394-50007-5*, Knopf Bks. for Young Readers) Random Hse. Children's Bks.
—Missing Woman. 1991. mass mkt. 4.99 (*0-446-40026-2*, Mysterious Pr. Paperback Bks.) Warner Bks., Inc.
—Out of Season. 1985. (Albert Samson Novel Ser.). 256p. reprint ed. mass mkt. 3.50 o.p. (*0-06-080774-1*, P 774, Perennial) HarperTrade.
—Out of Season. 1984. (Albert Samson, Private Eye Ser.). 256p. 12.95 o.p. (*0-688-03903-0*, Morrow, William & Co.) Morrow/Avon.
—Out of Season. 1991. mass mkt. 4.99 o.s.i (*0-446-40027-0*, Mysterious Pr. Paperback Bks.) Warner Bks., Inc.
—The Silent Salesman. 1981. mass mkt. 2.25 o.p. (*0-425-04031-3*) Berkley Publishing Group.
—The Silent Salesman. 1985. 272p. mass mkt. 3.50 o.p. (*0-06-080736-9*, P 736, Perennial) HarperTrade.
—The Silent Salesman. 1978. 7.95 o.p. (*0-394-40433-5*, Knopf Bks. for Young Readers) Random Hse. Children's Bks.
—The Silent Salesman. 1991. mass mkt. 4.99 o.s.i (*0-446-40025-4*, Mysterious Pr. Paperback Bks.) Warner Bks., Inc.
—Underdog. 1993. 272p. 18.95 (*0-89296-440-5*) Mysterious Pr.
—Underdog. 1995. 256p. mass mkt. 5.50 (*0-446-40436-5*, Mysterious Pr. Paperback Bks.) Warner Bks., Inc.
—Way We Die Now. 1991. mass mkt. 4.95 o.s.i (*0-446-40023-8*, Mysterious Pr. Paperback Bks.) Warner Bks., Inc.
—The Way We Die Now. 1979. 1.75 o.p. (*0-425-04028-3*) Berkley Publishing Group.
—The Way We Die Now. 1984. 224p. reprint ed. mass mkt. 3.50 o.p. (*0-06-080710-5*, P 710) HarperCollins Pubs.
Lewis, Roy. A Kind of Transaction: An Eric Ward Novel. l.t. ed. 1993. 296p. 15.95 o.p. (*0-7451-1679-5*, Macmillan Reference USA) Gale Group.
Lipinski, Thomas. Death in the Steel City. 2000. (Carroll Dorsey Mystery Ser.: Vol. 4). 224p. mass mkt. 5.99 (*0-380-79432-2*, Avon Bks.) Morrow/Avon.
—The Fall-Down Artist. 1994. (Carroll Dorsey Mystery Ser.). 304p. 20.95 o.p. (*0-312-10461-8*, Saint Martin's Minotaur) St. Martin's Pr.
—Picture of Her Tombstone. 1998. (Carroll Dorsey Mystery Ser.: 2). mass mkt. 5.99 (*0-380-73024-3*, Avon Bks.) Morrow/Avon.
—Picture of Her Tombstone. 1996. 240p. 21.95 (*0-312-14390-7*, Saint Martin's Minotaur) St. Martin's Pr.
—Steel City Confessions. 1999. (Carroll Dorsey Mystery Ser.: Vol. 3). 224p. mass mkt. 5.99 (*0-380-79431-4*, Avon Bks.) Morrow/Avon.
Lippman, Laura. Baltimore Blues. 1997. 304p. mass mkt. 6.99 (*0-380-78875-6*, Avon Bks.) Morrow/Avon.
—Butcher's Hill. 1998. (Tess Monaghan Mysteries Ser.: Vol. 3). 288p. mass mkt. 5.99 (*0-380-79846-8*, Avon Bks.) Morrow/Avon.
—Charm City. l.t. ed. 2002. (Wheeler Large Print Book Ser.). 27.95 (*1-58724-214-1*, Wheeler Publishing, Inc.) Gale Group.

—Charm City. 1997. (Tess Monaghan Mysteries Ser.: Vol. 2). 304p. mass mkt. 6.99 (*0-380-78876-4*, Avon Bks.) Morrow/Avon.

—In Big Trouble. 1999. (Tess Monaghan Mysteries Ser.). 352p. mass mkt. 6.99 (*0-380-79847-6*, Avon Bks.) Morrow/Avon.

—The Last Place. 2003. 432p. mass mkt. 7.50 (*0-380-81024-7*, Avon Bks.); 2002. 352p. 23.95 (*0-380-97819-9*, Morrow, William & Co.) Morrow/Avon.

—The Sugar House. 2000. (Tess Monaghan Mysteries Ser.). 320p. 24.00 (*0-380-97817-2*, Morrow, William & Co.) Morrow/Avon.

—The Sugar House: A Tess Monaghan Mystery. 2001. 384p. mass mkt. 6.99 (*0-380-81022-0*, Avon Bks.) Morrow/Avon.

—The Sugar House: A Tess Monaghan Mystery. l.t. ed. 2001. (Thorndike Americana Ser.). 483p. 28.95 (*0-7862-3288-9*) Thorndike Pr.

Liss, David. A Conspiracy of Paper. E-Book 19.95 (*1-58945-562-2*) Adobe Systems, Inc.

—A Conspiracy of Paper. 2001. (Reader's Circle Ser.). 464p. pap. 14.95 (*0-8041-1912-0*, Ballantine Bks.) Ballantine Bks.

—A Conspiracy of Paper. 2000. E-Book 19.95 (*0-375-50504-0*) Random Hse., Inc.

—A Conspiracy of Paper. l.t. ed. 2000. (Basic Ser.). 781p. pap. 28.95 (*0-7862-2665-X*) Thorndike Pr.

—A Spectacle of Corruption. 2004. audio 97.25 (*1-59355-655-1*); audio 24.95 (*1-59355-658-6*, 5283); audio compact disk 26.95 (*1-59355-656-X*, 5281); audio compact disk 26.95 (*1-59355-656-X*, 5281); audio 34.95 (*1-59355-654-3*, 5279) Brilliance Audio.

—A Spectacle of Corruption. 2004. 400p. 24.95 (*0-375-50855-4*) Random Hse., Inc.

Lochte, Dick. Blue Bayou. 1993. (Southern Mysteries Ser.). mass mkt. 4.99 o.s.i (*0-8041-1145-6*, Ivy Bks.) Ballantine Bks.

—Blue Bayou. 1992. 304p. 20.00 o.p. (*0-671-74711-8*, Simon & Schuster) Simon & Schuster.

—Laughing Dog. 1988. (Leo Bloodworth-Serendipity Dahlquist Mystery Ser.: Bk. 2). 272p. 17.95 o.p. (*0-87795-941-2*, Morrow, William & Co.) Morrow/Avon.

—Laughing Dog. 1989. 400p. reprint ed. mass mkt. 3.95 o.s.i (*0-446-35724-3*) Warner Bks., Inc.

—Lucky Dog & Other Tales of Murder. 2000. (Five Star Mystery Ser.). 207p. 20.95 (*0-7862-2688-9*, Five Star) Gale Group.

—The Neon Smile. 1996. mass mkt. 5.99 o.s.i (*0-8041-1405-6*, Ivy Bks.) Ballantine Bks.

—The Neon Smile. 1995. (Illus.). 304p. 21.00 (*0-671-74712-6*, Simon & Schuster) Simon & Schuster.

—Sleeping Dog. 1985. 288p. 15.95 o.p. (*0-87795-738-X*, Morrow, William & Co.) Morrow/Avon.

—Sleeping Dog. 2001. (Missing Mystery Ser.: Vol. 29). 292p. pap. 14.95 (*1-890208-51-5*) Poisoned Pen Pr.

—Sleeping Dog. 1986. 288p. mass mkt. 3.95 o.s.i (*0-446-32661-5*) Warner Bks., Inc.

Lordon, Randye. East of Nice. 2002. 288p. pap. 13.95 (*0-312-28714-3*, Saint Martin's Griffin) St. Martin's Pr.

—East of Niece. 2001. (Sydney Sloane Mystery Ser.). 288p. 23.95 (*0-312-27114-X*, Saint Martin's Minotaur) St. Martin's Pr.

Love, William F. Bishop's Revenge: A Bishop Regan & Davey Goldman Myster. 1993. 276p. 20.00 o.p. (*1-55611-351-X*) Fine, Donald I. Bks.

—Bloody Ten. 1992. 19.95 o.p. (*1-55611-275-0*) Fine, Donald I. Bks.

—Bloody Ten. 1994. mass mkt. (*0-373-26140-3*, Harlequin Bks.) Harlequin Enterprises, Ltd.

—The Chartreuse Clue. 1990. 18.95 o.p. (*1-55611-211-4*) Fine, Donald I. Bks.

—The Chartreuse Clue. 1991. 352p. reprint ed. mass mkt. 5.50 o.p. (*0-451-40273-1*, Onyx) NAL.

—The Fundamentals of Murder. 1991. 18.95 o.p. (*1-55611-233-5*) Fine, Donald I. Bks.

—The Ruby-Red Clue. 1992. Orig. Title: The Fundamentals of Murder. 288p. mass mkt. 4.99 o.s.i (*0-451-40329-0*, Onyx) NAL.

Lupica, Mike. Dead Air. 1987. 288p. mass mkt. 3.95 o.s.i (*0-345-30813-1*) Ballantine Bks.

—Extra Credits. 1990. mass mkt. 3.95 o.s.i (*0-345-36029-X*) Ballantine Bks.

—Limited Partner. 1991. mass mkt. 3.99 o.s.i (*0-345-37237-9*, Ballantine Bks.) Ballantine Bks.

Lutz, John. Blood Fire. 1991. 17.95 o.p. (*0-8050-0969-8*) Holt, Henry & Co.

—Blood Fire. 1992. (Fred Carver Mystery Ser.). 224p. reprint ed. mass mkt. 3.99 (*0-380-71446-9*, Avon Bks.) Morrow/Avon.

—Burn: A Fred Carver Mystery. 1995. (Henry Holt Mystery Ser.). 278p. 22.50 o.p. (*0-8050-3480-3*) Holt, Henry & Co.

—Buyer Beware. 1992. (Mystery Scene Bk.). 192p. pap. 3.95 o.p. (*0-88184-840-9*, Carroll & Graf Pubs.) Avalon Publishing Group.

—Buyer Beware. l.t. ed. 1988. pap. 17.95 o.p. (*1-55504-671-1*); lib. bdg. 19.95 o.p. (*1-55504-690-8*) BBC Audiobooks America.

—Buyer Beware. 1976. 6.95 o.p. (*0-399-11811-X*) Putnam Publishing Group, The.

—Dancer's Debt. 1988. 256p. 16.95 o.p. (*0-312-00028-6*) St. Martin's Pr.

—Death by Jury: An Alo Nudger Mystery. 1995. 352p. 23.95 o.p. (*0-312-13613-7*, Saint Martin's Minotaur) St. Martin's Pr.

—Diamond Eyes. 1990. 224p. 15.95 o.p. (*0-312-05074-7*, Saint Martin's Minotaur) St. Martin's Pr.

—Flame. unabr. ed. 1990. audio 57.25 o.p. (*1-56100-050-7*, 1197, Unabridged Library Editions); Set. audio 19.95 o.p. (*0-930435-56-7*, 344, Bookcassette) Brilliance Audio.

—Flame. 1996. 88p. pap. 5.95 o.p. (*0-8050-4567-8*, Owl Bks.) Holt, Henry & Co.

—Flame. 1991. 272p. pap. 3.95 (*0-380-71070-6*, Avon Bks.) Morrow/Avon.

—Hot: A Fred Carver Mystery. 1992. 288p. 18.95 o.p. (*0-8050-1584-1*) Holt, Henry & Co.

—Hot: A Fred Carver Mystery. 1993. 256p. mass mkt. 4.99 (*0-380-71447-7*, Avon Bks.) Morrow/Avon.

—Kiss. unabr. ed. 1990. audio 57.25 o.p. (*1-56100-056-6*, 920, Unabridged Library Editions); audio 19.95 o.p. (*0-930435-62-1*, 2030, Bookcassette) Brilliance Audio.

—Kiss. (Fred Carver Mystery Ser.). 1996. 88p. pap. 5.95 o.p. (*0-8050-4566-X*, Owl Bks.); 1988. 17.95 o.p. (*0-8050-0412-2*) Holt, Henry & Co.

—Kiss. 1990. 272p. pap. 3.95 (*0-380-70934-1*, Avon Bks.) Morrow/Avon.

—Lightning: A Fred Carver Mystery. unabr. ed. 1996. (P. I. Fred Carver Mystery Ser.). audio 48.00 (*0-7366-3519-X*, 4156) Books on Tape, Inc.

—Lightning: A Fred Carver Mystery. 1996. 88p. 22.50 o.p. (*0-8050-4379-9*) Holt, Henry & Co.

—Nightlines: The First Alo Nudger Mystery. 1987. 352p. pap. 3.95 o.p. (*0-8125-0648-0*, Tor Bks.) Doherty, Tom Assocs., LLC.

—Nightlines: The First Alo Nudger Mystery. 1984. 13.95 o.p. (*0-312-57324-3*) St. Martin's Pr.

—Oops! l.t. ed. 1998. (Large Print Book Ser.). pap. 23.95 o.p. (*1-56895-653-3*, Wheeler Publishing, Inc.) Gale Group.

—Oops! 1997. 304p. 22.95 o.p. (*0-312-18152-3*, Saint Martin's Minotaur) St. Martin's Pr.

—Ride the Lightning. 1990. mass mkt. 3.95 (*0-8125-0642-1*, Tor Bks.) Doherty, Tom Assocs., LLC.

—Ride the Lightning. 1987. 256p. 15.95 o.p. (*0-312-00182-7*) St. Martin's Pr.

—The Right to Sing the Blues. 1988. 256p. pap. 2.95 o.p. (*0-8125-0646-4*, Tor Bks.) Doherty, Tom Assocs., LLC.

—The Right to Sing the Blues. 1985. 256p. 14.95 o.p. (*0-312-68235-2*) St. Martin's Pr.

—The Right to Sing the Blues. E-Book 9.99 (*1-58824-387-7*); 2001. 256p. pap. 14.00 (*0-7434-1288-5*) ibooks, Inc.

—Scorcher. unabr. ed. 1990. audio 57.25 o.p. (*1-56100-060-4*, 1030, Unabridged Library Editions); audio 19.95 o.p. (*0-930435-66-4*, 252, Bookcassette) Brilliance Audio.

—Scorcher. 272p. 1995. pap. 5.95 o.p. (*0-8050-3829-9*, Owl Bks.); 1987. 16.95 o.p. (*0-8050-0411-4*) Holt, Henry & Co.

—Scorcher. 1988. 256p. pap. 3.95 (*0-380-70526-5*, Avon Bks.) Morrow/Avon.

—Spark: A Fred Carver Mystery. 1993. 288p. 19.95 o.p. (*0-8050-1993-6*) Holt, Henry & Co.

—Thicker Than Blood: An Alo Nudger Mystery, Set. unabr. ed. 1999. audio 54.95 (*0-7927-2314-7*, CSL203, Chivers Sound Library) BBC Audiobooks America.

—Thicker Than Blood: An Alo Nudger Mystery. 1993. 272p. 19.95 o.p. (*0-312-09922-3*, Saint Martin's Minotaur) St. Martin's Pr.

—Time Exposure. 1990. 2.99 o.p. (*0-517-05936-3*) Random Hse. Value Publishing.

—Time Exposure. 1989. 16.95 o.p. (*0-312-02990-X*, Saint Martin's Minotaur) St. Martin's Pr.

—Torch. 1994. (Henry Holt Mystery Ser.). 290p. 22.00 o.p. (*0-8050-2610-X*) Holt, Henry & Co.

—Tropical Heat. l.t. ed. 1991. 21.95 o.p. (*1-55504-579-0*); pap. 6.95 o.p. (*1-55504-550-2*, 456) BBC Audiobooks America.

—Tropical Heat. unabr. ed. 1989. (P. I. Fred Carver Mystery Ser.). audio 19.95 o.p. (*0-930435-53-2*, 359, Bookcassette); audio 57.25 o.p. (*1-56100-047-7*, 1107, Unabridged Library Editions) Brilliance Audio.

—Tropical Heat. 1995. 252p. pap. 5.95 o.p. (*0-8050-3828-0*, Owl Bks.); 1986. 224p. o.p. (*0-03-006958-0*) Holt, Henry & Co.

—Tropical Heat. 1987. 256p. pap. 3.95 (*0-380-70309-2*, Avon Bks.) Morrow/Avon.

Lyons. Castles Burning. 1981. mass mkt. 2.50 (*0-671-41864-5*, Pocket) Simon & Schuster.

Lyons, Arthur. All God's Children. 1976. mass mkt. 1.50 o.s.i (*0-345-25020-6*) Ballantine Bks.

—All God's Children. 1982. 224p. pap. o.p. (*0-03-060394-3*, Owl Bks.) Holt, Henry & Co.

—At the Hands of Another. 240p. 1986. pap. o.p. (*0-03-008533-0*, Owl Bks.); 1983. o.p. (*0-03-059616-5*) Holt, Henry & Co.

—Castles Burning. 1982. (Rinehart Suspense Novel Ser.). 224p. pap. o.p. (*0-03-062417-7*, Owl Bks.) Holt, Henry & Co.

—The Dead Are Discreet. 1983. 224p. pap. o.p. (*0-03-060393-5*, Owl Bks.) Holt, Henry & Co.

—Dead Ringer. 1983. 240p. pap. o.p. (*0-03-060396-X*, Owl Bks.) Holt, Henry & Co.

—False Pretenses. 1994. 240p. 18.95 o.s.i (*0-89296-220-8*) Mysterious Pr.

—False Pretenses. 1995. 224p. mass mkt. 5.50 o.s.i (*0-446-40422-5*) Warner Bks., Inc.

—Fast Fade: A Jacob Asch Mystery. 1987. 224p. 15.45 (*0-89296-216-X*) Mysterious Pr.

—Fast Fade: A Jacob Asch Mystery. 1988. 208p. mass mkt. 3.95 o.s.i (*0-445-40703-4*, Mysterious Pr. Paperback Bks.) Warner Bks., Inc.

—Hard Trade. 264p. 1983. pap. o.p. (*0-03-063333-8*, Owl Bks.); 1981. o.p. (*0-03-053621-9*) Holt, Henry & Co.

—The Killing Floor. 1982. pap. o.p. (*0-03-060397-8*, Owl Bks.) Holt, Henry & Co.

—Other People's Money. 1989. 213p. 17.95 o.s.i (*0-89296-218-6*) Mysterious Pr.

—Other People's Money. 1990. 224p. mass mkt. 4.95 o.s.i (*0-445-40903-7*, Mysterious Pr. Paperback Bks.) Warner Bks., Inc.

—Three with a Bullet. 240p. 1986. pap. 3.95 o.p. (*0-03-008539-X*, Owl Bks.); 1985. o.p. (*0-03-059617-3*) Holt, Henry & Co.

MacDonald, John D. Bright Orange for the Shroud. (Travis McGee Novel Ser.). 1987. 224p. mass mkt. 5.99 o.s.i (*0-449-13358-3*, Fawcett); 1996. reprint ed. mass mkt. 5.99 (*0-449-45615-3*, Fawcett); 1996. 352p. reprint ed. mass mkt. 6.99 (*0-449-22444-9*, Ballantine Bks.) Ballantine Bks.

—Bright Orange for the Shroud. unabr. collector's ed. 1978. (Travis McGee Ser.: No. 6). audio 48.00 (*0-7366-0174-0*, 1176) Books on Tape, Inc.

—Bright Orange for the Shroud. l.t. ed. 1985. 14.95 o.p. (*0-8161-3979-2*, Macmillan Reference USA) Gale Group.

—Cinnamon Skin. (Travis McGee Novel Ser.). 1996. 336p. mass mkt. 7.50 (*0-449-22484-8*); 1986. 288p. mass mkt. 5.95 o.s.i (*0-449-12873-3*) Ballantine Bks. (Fawcett).

—Cinnamon Skin. unabr. collector's ed. 1982. (Travis McGee Ser.: No. 20). audio 48.00 (*0-7366-0689-0*, 1649) Books on Tape, Inc.

—Cinnamon Skin. 1983. (General Ser.). lib. bdg. 14.95 o.p. (*0-8161-3504-5*, Macmillan Reference USA) Gale Group.

—Cinnamon Skin. 1982. 288p. o.p. (*0-06-014990-6*) HarperCollins Pubs.

—Cinnamon Skin. abr. ed. 2000. (Travis McGee Ser.). audio 9.99 (*0-375-41014-7*, RH Audio) Random Hse. Audio Publishing Group.

—Cinnamon Skin. 1990. 3.99 o.p. (*0-517-05439-6*) Random Hse. Value Publishing.

—The Damned. 1985. (Travis McGee Novel Ser.). mass mkt. 3.95 o.s.i (*0-449-12887-3*, Fawcett) Ballantine Bks.

—Darker Than Amber. 1997. mass mkt. 5.99 (*0-449-45637-4*); 1996. 320p. mass mkt. 6.99 (*0-449-22446-5*); 1987. 192p. mass mkt. 5.99 o.s.i (*0-449-13339-7*); 1984. 192p. mass mkt. 2.95 o.p. (*0-449-12752-4*) Ballantine Bks. (Fawcett).

—Darker Than Amber. l.t. ed. 1988. (General Ser.). 319p. 16.95 o.p. (*0-8161-4008-1*, Macmillan Reference USA) Gale Group.

—A Deadly Shade of Gold. (Travis McGee Novel Ser.). 1996. 448p. mass mkt. 6.99 (*0-449-22442-2*); 1987. 288p. mass mkt. 5.99 o.s.i (*0-449-13313-3*) Ballantine Bks. (Fawcett).

—A Deadly Shade of Gold. unabr. collector's ed. 1978. (Travis McGee Ser.: No. 5). audio 64.00 (*0-7366-0106-6*, 1114) Books on Tape, Inc.

—A Deadly Shade of Gold. l.t. ed. 1987. 447p. 16.95 o.p. (*0-8161-4004-9*, Macmillan Reference USA) Gale Group.

—The Deep Blue Goodbye. 1995. 320p. mass mkt. 6.99 (*0-449-22383-3*); 1986. 256p. mass mkt. 4.95 o.s.i (*0-449-13252-8*); 1984. mass mkt. 2.95 o.p. (*0-449-12673-0*) Ballantine Bks. (Fawcett).

—The Deep Blue Goodbye. l.t. ed. 1984. (General Ser.). 296p. 12.95 o.p. (*0-8161-3626-2*); 8.95 o.p. (*0-8161-3740-4*) Gale Group. (Macmillan Reference USA).

—The Dreadful Lemon Sky. (Travis McGee Novel Ser.). 1996. 320p. mass mkt. 6.99 (*0-449-22479-1*); 1987. 272p. mass mkt. 5.99 o.s.i (*0-449-13404-0*); 1985. 272p. mass mkt. 3.50 o.p. (*0-449-12964-0*) Ballantine Bks. (Fawcett).

—Dress Her in Indigo. 1997. pap. text 5.99 (*0-449-45716-8*); 1996. 336p. mass mkt. 7.50 (*0-449-22462-7*); 1987. 256p. mass mkt. 5.99 o.s.i (*0-449-13293-5*); 1985. mass mkt. 3.50 o.p. (*0-449-12984-5*) Ballantine Bks. (Fawcett).

—Dress Her in Indigo. unabr. collector's ed. 1980. (Travis McGee Ser.: No. 11). audio 56.00 (*0-7366-0243-7*, 1239) Books on Tape, Inc.

—Dress Her in Indigo. l.t. ed. 1985. (General Ser.). 360p. 13.95 o.p. (*0-8161-3822-2*); 9.95 o.p. (*0-8161-3820-6*) Gale Group. (Macmillan Reference USA).

—The Empty Copper Sea. 21.95 (*0-89190-778-5*) Amereon, Ltd.

—The Empty Copper Sea. 1996. 320p. mass mkt. 7.50 (*0-449-22480-5*); 1987. 256p. mass mkt. 4.99 o.s.i (*0-449-13333-8*); 1985. mass mkt. 3.50 o.p. (*0-449-12913-6*) Ballantine Bks. (Fawcett).

—The Empty Copper Sea. unabr. collector's ed. 1979. (Travis McGee Ser.: No. 17). audio 48.00 (*0-7366-0331-X*, 1318) Books on Tape, Inc.

—The Empty Copper Sea. 1979. lib. bdg. 13.50 o.p. (*0-8161-6702-8*, Macmillan Reference USA) Gale Group.

—The Empty Copper Sea. abr. ed. 1987. audio 15.95 o.s.i (*0-394-56085-X*, RH Audio) Random Hse. Audio Publishing Group.

—Five Complete Travis McGee Novels. 1988. 8.99 o.s.i (*0-517-47671-1*) Random Hse. Value Publishing.

—Free Fall in Crimson. 1996. 320p. mass mkt. 7.50 (*0-449-22482-1*); 1987. 288p. mass mkt. 4.95 o.s.i (*0-449-13253-6*); 1985. 288p. mass mkt. 3.50 o.p. (*0-449-12894-6*) Ballantine Bks. (Fawcett).

—Free Fall in Crimson. unabr. collector's ed. 1981. (Travis McGee Ser.: No. 19). audio 48.00 (*0-7366-0632-7*, 1593) Books on Tape, Inc.

—Free Fall in Crimson. l.t. ed. 1981. 13.50 o.p. (*0-8161-3272-0*, Macmillan Reference USA) Gale Group.

—Free Fall in Crimson. 1981. 224p. 15.00 o.p. (*0-06-014833-0*) HarperTrade.

—Free Fall in Crimson. 1992. audio 16.00 o.s.i (*0-394-55989-4*, RH Audio) Random Hse. Audio Publishing Group.

—The Girl in the Plain Brown Wrapper. 1997. mass mkt. 5.99 (*0-449-45715-X*); 1996. 352p. mass mkt. 7.50 (*0-449-22461-9*); 1987. 256p. mass mkt. 5.99 o.s.i (*0-449-13341-9*); 1985. mass mkt. 3.50 o.p. (*0-449-12915-2*) Ballantine Bks. (Fawcett).

—The Girl in the Plain Brown Wrapper. unabr. collector's ed. 1984. (Travis McGee Ser.: No. 10). audio 56.00 (*0-7366-0704-8*, 1667) Books on Tape, Inc.

—The Girl in the Plain Brown Wrapper. l.t. ed. 1984. (General Ser.). lib. bdg. 12.95 o.p. (*0-8161-3627-0*, Macmillan Reference USA) Gale Group.

—The Green Ripper. 21.95 (*0-89190-779-3*) Amereon, Ltd.

—The Green Ripper. (Travis McGee Novel Ser.). 1996. 320p. mass mkt. 7.50 (*0-449-22481-3*); 1987. 288p. mass mkt. 5.99 o.s.i (*0-449-13246-3*); 1985. 228p. mass mkt. 3.50 o.p. (*0-449-13042-8*) Ballantine Bks. (Fawcett).

—The Green Ripper. unabr. collector's ed. 1980. (Travis McGee Ser.: No. 18). audio 42.00 (*0-7366-0474-X*, 1449) Books on Tape, Inc.

—The Green Ripper. 1980. (General Ser.). lib. bdg. 12.95 o.p. (*0-8161-3023-X*, Macmillan Reference USA) Gale Group.

—The Green Ripper. 1979. 15.00 o.p. (*0-397-01362-0*) HarperCollins Pubs.

—The Green Ripper. abr. ed. (Travis McGee Ser.). 1994. audio 8.99 o.s.i (*0-679-43407-0*); 1991. audio 16.00 o.p. (*0-394-55988-6*); Set. 2000. audio 9.99 o.s.i (*0-375-41581-5*) Random Hse. Audio Publishing Group. (RH Audio).

—The Lonely Silver Rain. 1996. 320p. mass mkt. 7.50 (*0-449-22485-6*); 1986. 256p. mass mkt. 5.95 o.s.i (*0-449-12509-2*) Ballantine Bks. (Fawcett).

—The Lonely Silver Rain. unabr. collector's ed. 1986. (Travis McGee Ser.: No. 21). audio 42.00 (*0-7366-0476-6*, 1451) Books on Tape, Inc.

—The Long Lavender Look. (Travis McGee Novel Ser.). 1998. mass mkt. 5.99 (*0-449-45717-6*); 1996. 352p. mass mkt. 6.99 (*0-449-22474-0*); 1987. 256p. mass mkt. 4.95 o.s.i (*0-449-13334-6*) Ballantine Bks. (Fawcett).

—The Long Lavender Look. unabr. collector's ed. 1984. (Travis McGee Ser.: No. 12). audio 48.00 (*0-7366-0705-6*, 1668) Books on Tape, Inc.

—The Long Lavender Look. l.t. ed. 1986. (General Ser.). 363p. 15.95 o.p. (*0-8161-4007-3*, Macmillan Reference USA) Gale Group.

—The Long Lavender Look. abr. ed. (Travis McGee Ser.). 1994. audio 8.99 o.s.i (*0-679-43406-2*); 1990. audio 15.95 o.p. (*0-394-55982-7*) Random Hse. Audio Publishing Group. (RH Audio).

—Nightmare in Pink. (Travis McGee Novel Ser.). 1995. 304p. mass mkt. 6.99 (*0-449-22414-7*); 1987. 144p. mass mkt. 4.95 o.s.i (*0-449-13312-5*) Ballantine Bks. (Fawcett).

—Nightmare in Pink. unabr. collector's ed. 1983. (Travis McGee Ser.: No. 2). audio 36.00 (*0-7366-0700-5*, 1663) Books on Tape, Inc.

—Nightmare in Pink. 1976. (Adult Ser.). reprint ed. lib. bdg. 9.95 o.p. (*0-8161-6382-0*, Macmillan Reference USA) Gale Group.

—One Fearful Yellow Eye. 1997. mass mkt. 5.99 (*0-449-45639-0*); 1996. 336p. mass mkt. 7.50 (*0-449-22458-9*); 1987. 244p. mass mkt. 4.95 o.s.i (*0-449-13292-7*); 1985. mass mkt. 3.50 o.p. (*0-449-12933-0*) Ballantine Bks. (Fawcett).

—One Fearful Yellow Eye. 1983. (General Ser.). lib. bdg. 14.95 o.p. (*0-8161-3380-8*, Macmillan Reference USA) Gale Group.

—Pale Gray for Guilt. 1997. mass mkt. 5.99 (*0-449-45721-4*); 1996. 320p. mass mkt. 6.99 (*0-449-22460-0*); 1987. 224p. mass mkt. 5.99 o.s.i (*0-449-13331-1*); 1985. mass mkt. 3.95 o.p. (*0-449-12897-0*) Ballantine Bks. (Fawcett).

—Pale Gray for Guilt. unabr. collector's ed. 1984. (Travis McGee Ser.: No. 9). audio 48.00 (*0-7366-0703-X*, 1666) Books on Tape, Inc.

—Pale Gray for Guilt. l.t. ed. 1986. (Large Print Bks.). 357p. lib. bdg. 15.95 o.p. (*0-8161-4006-5*, Macmillan Reference USA) Gale Group.

—A Purple Place for Dying. 1995. 320p. mass mkt. 7.50 (*0-449-22438-4*); 1987. 160p. mass mkt. 5.99 o.s.i (*0-449-13336-2*); 1980. mass mkt. 2.25 o.p. (*0-449-14219-1*) Ballantine Bks. (Fawcett).

—A Purple Place for Dying. unabr. collector's ed. 1977. (Travis McGee Ser.: No. 3). audio 36.00 (*0-7366-0052-3*, 1064) Books on Tape, Inc.

—A Purple Place for Dying. l.t. ed. 1984. (General Ser.). 312p. 9.95 o.p. (*0-8161-3690-4*); lib. bdg. 13.95 o.p. (*0-8161-3625-4*) Gale Group. (Macmillan Reference USA).

—A Purple Place for Dying. 1976. 15.00 o.p. (*0-397-01166-0*) HarperCollins Pubs.

—The Quick Red Fox. 1996. mass mkt. 5.99 (*0-449-45613-7*); 1995. 320p. mass mkt. 7.50 (*0-449-22440-6*); 1987. 160p. mass mkt. 4.95 o.s.i (*0-449-13403-2*); 1981. mass mkt. 2.50 o.p. (*0-449-14264-7*) Ballantine Bks. (Fawcett).

—The Quick Red Fox. l.t. ed. 1993. 12.95 o.p. (*0-8161-3382-4*, Macmillan Reference USA) Gale Group.

—The Scarlet Ruse. 1996. 352p. mass mkt. 7.50 (*0-449-22477-5*); 1987. 320p. mass mkt. 4.95 o.s.i (*0-449-13247-1*); 1985. mass mkt. 3.50 o.p. (*0-449-13040-1*) Ballantine Bks. (Fawcett).

—The Scarlet Ruse. unabr. collector's ed. 1985. (Travis McGee Ser.: No. 14). audio 48.00 (*0-7366-0707-2*, 1670) Books on Tape, Inc.

—The Scarlet Ruse. 1980. (General Ser.). lib. bdg. 13.95 o.p. (*0-8161-3118-X*, Macmillan Reference USA) Gale Group.

—The Scarlet Ruse. abr. ed. 1994. (Travis McGee Ser.). audio 8.99 o.s.i (*0-679-43405-4*, RH Audio) Random Hse. Audio Publishing Group.

—A Tan & Sandy Silence. (Travis McGee Novel Ser.). 1996. 336p. mass mkt. 7.50 (*0-449-22476-7*, Fawcett); 1986. 256p. mass mkt. 4.95 o.s.i (*0-449-13250-1*, Fawcett); 1985. 256p. mass mkt. 3.50 o.p. (*0-449-12969-1*, Fawcett); 1984. mass mkt. 2.95 o.p. (*0-449-12707-9*); 1983. mass mkt. 2.95 o.p. (*0-449-12677-3*); 1982. mass mkt. 2.75 o.p. (*0-449-12404-5*); 1981. mass mkt. 2.50 o.p. (*0-449-14220-5*); 1978. mass mkt. 1.75 o.p. (*0-449-13635-3*) Ballantine Bks.

—A Tan & Sandy Silence. unabr. collector's ed. 1984. (Travis McGee Ser.: No. 13). audio 48.00 (*0-7366-0706-4*, 1669) Books on Tape, Inc.

—A Tan & Sandy Silence. l.t. ed. 1982. 360p. lib. bdg. 13.95 o.p. (*0-8161-3381-6*, Macmillan Reference USA) Gale Group.

—A Tan & Sandy Silence. abr. ed. 1994. audio 8.99 o.s.i (*0-679-43408-9*); 1993. audio 16.00 o.p. (*0-394-55983-5*) Random Hse. Audio Publishing Group. (RH Audio).

—The Turquoise Lament. 1996. 320p. mass mkt. 6.99 (*0-449-22478-3*); 1987. 256p. mass mkt. 5.99 o.s.i (*0-449-13249-8*); 1982. 256p. mass mkt. 2.95 o.p. (*0-449-14200-0*) Ballantine Bks. (Fawcett).

—The Turquoise Lament. unabr. collector's ed. 1983. (Travis McGee Ser.: No. 15). audio 48.00 (*0-7366-0708-0*, 1671) Books on Tape, Inc.

—The Turquoise Lament. l.t. ed. 1982. lib. bdg. 13.95 o.p. (*0-8161-3383-2*, Macmillan Reference USA) Gale Group.

—The Turquoise Lament. 1973. 15.00 (*0-397-00987-9*, Lippincott) Lippincott Williams & Wilkins.

—The Turquoise Lament. abr. ed. 1991. (Travis McGee Ser.). audio 16.00 o.s.i (*0-394-55985-1*, RH Audio) Random Hse. Audio Publishing Group.

MacDonald, Ross, pseud. The Drowning Pool. 1975. (Lew Archer Mystery Ser.). 224p. pap. 2.75 o.p. (*0-553-24135-4*) Bantam Bks.

—The Drowning Pool. l.t. ed. 2002. pap. 25.95 (*0-7838-9783-9*) Gale Group.

—The Drowning Pool. Barzun, Jacques & Taylor, Wendell H., eds. 1976. (Lew Archer Mystery Ser.). reprint ed. lib. bdg. 21.00 o.p. (*0-8240-2382-X*) Garland Publishing, Inc.

—The Drowning Pool. 1996. (Lew Archer Mystery Ser.). 256p. pap. 12.00 (*0-679-76806-8*) Random Hse., Inc.

—The Drowning Pool. 1993. (Lew Archer Mystery Ser.). 224p. mass mkt. 4.99 o.s.i (*0-446-35889-4*) Warner Bks., Inc.

MacGregor, T. J. Blue Pearl. 1994. 384p. 21.95 (*0-7868-6061-8*) Hyperion Pr.

—Dark Fields. 9999. 4.95 o.p. (*0-345-22756-5*); 1986. mass mkt. 5.99 o.s.i (*0-345-33756-5*) Ballantine Bks.

—Death Flats. 1991. (Florida Mysteries Ser.). (Orig.). mass mkt. 4.99 o.s.i (*0-345-35768-X*) Ballantine Bks.

—Death Sweet. 1988. 384p. mass mkt. 4.99 o.s.i (*0-345-33753-0*) Ballantine Bks.

—Kill Flash. 1987. pap. 3.95 o.p. (*0-345-00751-4*); mass mkt. 4.99 o.s.i (*0-345-33754-9*) Ballantine Bks.

—Kin Dread. 1990. 320p. (Orig.). mass mkt. 4.95 o.s.i (*0-345-35766-3*) Ballantine Bks.

—Mistress of the Bones. 1995. 352p. 21.95 (*0-7868-6106-1*) Hyperion Pr.

—On Ice. 1989. mass mkt. 4.99 o.s.i (*0-345-35045-6*) Ballantine Bks.

—Spree. 1992. (Florida Mysteries Ser.). (Orig.). mass mkt. 4.99 o.s.i (*0-345-37346-4*) Ballantine Bks.

—Storm Surge. 1993. 336p. (YA). 19.95 o.p. (*1-56282-789-8*) Hyperion Pr.

Maiman, Jaye. Baby, It's Cold: A Robin Miller Mystery. 1997. (Robin Miller Mysteries Ser.: Vol. 5). 256p. pap. 10.95 o.p. (*1-56280-156-2*); 1996. 288p. 19.95 (*1-56280-141-4*) Naiad Pr., Inc.

—Crazy for Loving. 1992. (Robin Miller Mysteries Ser.: No. 2). 320p. pap. 11.95 (*1-56280-025-6*) Naiad Pr., Inc.

—Every Time We Say Goodbye. 1999. (Robin Miller Mysteries Ser.: No. 7). 250p. pap. 11.95 (*1-56280-248-8*) Naiad Pr., Inc.

—I Left My Heart. 1991. (Robin Miller Mysteries Ser.: Vol. 1). 320p. pap. 11.95 o.p. (*0-941483-72-X*) Naiad Pr., Inc.

—Old Black Magic: A Robin Miller Mystery. 1997. (Robin Miller Mysteries Ser.: Vol. 6). 288p. pap. 11.95 o.p. (*1-56280-175-9*) Naiad Pr., Inc.

—Someone to Watch. 1995. (Robin Miller Mysteries Ser.: Vol. 4). 288p. pap. 10.95 (*1-56280-095-7*) Naiad Pr., Inc.

—Under My Skin. 1993. (Robin Miller Mysteries Ser.: No. 3). 336p. pap. 11.95 (*1-56280-049-3*) Naiad Pr., Inc.

Maness, Larry. Nantucket Revenge: A Jake Eaton Mystery. 1995. 208p. 19.95 o.s.i (*0-89141-566-1*, Presidio Pr.) Ballantine Bks.

—A Once Perfect Place: A Jake Eaton Mystery. 1996. 208p. 19.95 o.s.i (*0-89141-567-X*, Presidio Pr.) Ballantine Bks.

—Strangler: A Jake Eaton Mystery. 1998. 192p. 19.95 o.p. (*0-89141-568-8*, Presidio Pr.) Ballantine Bks.

Marcy, Jean. Cemetery Murders: A Meg Darcy Mystery. 1997. 200p. pap. 10.95 (*0-934678-83-9*) New Victoria Pubs., Inc.

—Dead & Blonde: A Meg Darcy Mystery. 1998. (Meg Darcy Mysteries Ser.: No. 2). 227p. pap. 10.95 (*0-934678-98-7*) New Victoria Pubs., Inc.

—Mommy Deadest: A Meg Darcy Mystery. 2000. (Meg Darcy Mysteries Ser.). 224p. pap. 11.95 (*1-892281-12-0*) New Victoria Pubs., Inc.

Martin, Paula K. & Weinstein, Joel. Project Sabotage: A Sir Mortimer Business Mystery. 2001. (Illus.). 259p. pap. 16.95 (*0-9701496-0-3*) MartinTate L.L.C.

Mathews, Francine. The Secret Agent. 2003. 528p. mass mkt. 6.99 (*0-553-58153-8*); 2002. (Illus.). 416p. 23.95 (*0-553-10913-8*) Bantam Bks.

Maxwell, A. E. Art of Survival. 1993. 336p. mass mkt. 4.99 o.p. (*0-06-104115-7*, HarperTorch) Morrow/Avon.

—The Art of Survival. 1990. mass mkt. 4.50 o.s.i (*0-553-28479-7*) Bantam Bks.

—Frog & the Scorpion. 1986. 264p. 16.95 o.p. (*0-385-19260-6*) Doubleday Publishing.

—The Frog & the Scorpion. 1987. 224p. mass mkt. 3.50 o.s.i (*0-553-26876-7*) Bantam Bks.

—The Frog & the Scorpion. 1993. 320p. mass mkt. 4.99 o.p. (*0-06-104113-0*, HarperTorch) Morrow/Avon.

—Gatsby's Vineyard. 1988. 240p. mass mkt. 3.50 o.s.i (*0-553-27409-0*) Bantam Bks.

—Gatsby's Vineyard. 1987. 240p. 15.95 o.s.i (*0-385-23712-X*) Doubleday Publishing.

—Gatsby's Vineyard. 1993. 320p. mass mkt. 4.99 o.p. (*0-06-104112-2*, HarperTorch) Morrow/Avon.

—The Golden Empire. 1979. (Orig.). mass mkt. 2.50 o.s.i (*0-449-14267-1*, Fawcett) Ballantine Bks.

—Just Another Day in Paradise. 1986. mass mkt. 2.95 o.s.i (*0-553-25789-7*) Bantam Bks.

—Just Another Day in Paradise. 1985. 240p. 14.95 o.p. (*0-385-19259-2*) Doubleday Publishing.

—Just Another Day in Paradise. 1993. 304p. mass mkt. 4.99 o.p. (*0-06-104114-9*, HarperTorch) Morrow/Avon.

—Just Enough Light to Kill. 1989. mass mkt. 3.95 o.s.i (*0-553-28213-1*) Bantam Bks.

—Just Enough Light to Kill. 1993. 336p. mass mkt. 4.99 o.s.i (*0-06-104111-4*, HarperTorch) Morrow/Avon.

—The King of Nothing. 1994. 320p. mass mkt. 5.50 o.p. (*0-06-104230-7*, HarperTorch) Morrow/Avon.

—Money Burns. 1993. 368p. mass mkt. 5.50 o.p. (*0-06-104123-8*, HarperTorch) Morrow/Avon.

—Money Burns. 1993. 3.99 o.p. (*0-517-10621-3*) Random Hse. Value Publishing.

—Murder Hurts. 1995. 352p. mass mkt. 4.99 o.p. (*0-06-104318-4*, HarperTorch) Morrow/Avon.

—Redwood Empire. (Harlequin Historicals Ser.). 1995. 440p. per. (*0-373-28867-0*, 1-28867-9); 1987. 416p. mass mkt. (*0-373-97049-8*) Harlequin Enterprises, Ltd. (Harlequin Bks.).

McCafferty, Taylor. Bed Bugs. Chelius, Jane, ed. 1993. 256p. (Orig.). mass mkt. 5.50 (*0-671-75468-8*, Pocket) Simon & Schuster.

—Hanky Panky. 1995. 256p. mass mkt. 5.50 (*0-671-51049-5*, Pocket) Simon & Schuster.

—Pet Peeves. Chelius, Jane, ed. 1990. 224p. (Orig.). mass mkt. 4.99 (*0-671-72802-4*, Pocket) Simon & Schuster.

—Ruffled Feathers. Chelius, Jane, ed. 1992. 224p. (Orig.). mass mkt. 4.50 (*0-671-72803-2*, Pocket) Simon & Schuster.

—Thin Skins. 1994. 256p. mass mkt. 4.99 (*0-671-79977-0*, Pocket) Simon & Schuster.

McCall, Wendell. Aim for the Heart. l.t. ed. 2002. 224p. lib. bdg. 28.95 (*1-58547-142-9*) Ctr. Point Large Print.

—Concerto in Dead Flat. l.t. ed. 2002. lib. bdg. 28.95 (*1-58547-157-7*, Premier) Ctr. Point Large Print.

—Concerto in Dead Flat. 2000. pap. 12.95 (*1-890208-52-3*); 1999. 277p. 23.95 (*1-890208-18-3*) Poisoned Pen Pr.

—Dead Aim. l.t. ed. 2001. 400p. lib. bdg. 28.95 (*1-58547-141-0*); 319p. (*1-74030-542-6*) Ctr. Point Large Print.

—Dead Aim. 1990. 272p. reprint ed. mass mkt. 3.95 o.s.i (*0-440-20510-7*) Dell Publishing.

—Dead Aim. 1999. (Chris Klick Mysteries Ser.: Vol. 11). 250p. pap. 14.95 (*1-890208-20-5*) Poisoned Pen Pr.

—Dead Aim. 1991. 2.99 o.p. (*0-517-07670-5*) Random Hse. Value Publishing.

—Dead Aim. 1988. 272p. 16.95 o.p. (*0-312-02184-4*, Saint Martin's Minotaur) St. Martin's Pr.

McCarver, Sam. The Case of the 2nd Seance: A John Darnell Mystery. l.t. ed. 2001. 344p. 27.95 (*0-7862-3331-1*) Thorndike Pr.

McClendon, Lise. Sweet & Lowdown: A Dorie Lennox Mystery. 2002. 288p. 23.95 (*0-312-28689-9*, Saint Martin's Minotaur) St. Martin's Pr.

McDermid, Val. Blue Genes: A Kate Brannigan Mystery. l.t. ed. 1997. (G. K. Hall Mystery Ser.). 358p. lib. bdg. 24.95 o.p. (*0-7838-8141-X*, Macmillan Reference USA) Gale Group.

—Blue Genes: A Kate Brannigan Mystery. 1997. 304p. 21.50 (*0-684-83398-0*, Scribner) Simon & Schuster.

—Blue Genes: A Kate Brannigan Mystery. unabr. ed. 2000. audio 54.95 (*0-7531-0620-5*, 990703); 8p. audio compact disk 64.95 (*0-7531-0899-2*, 108992) Ulverscroft Large Print Bks., Ltd.

—Clean Break. 2002. 12.95 (*1-883523-51-6*) Spinsters Ink Bks.

—Clean Break: A Kate Brannigan Mystery. 1996. 288p. mass mkt. 4.99 o.p. (*0-06-104393-1*, HarperTorch) Morrow/Avon.

—Clean Break: A Kate Brannigan Mystery. 1995. 288p. 20.00 o.s.i (*0-684-80461-1*, Scribner) Simon & Schuster.

—Crack Down. 1994. 288p. 20.00 (*0-684-19756-1*, Macmillan Reference USA) Gale Group.

—Crack Down. 1996. 256p. mass mkt. 4.99 o.s.i (*0-06-104394-X*) HarperCollins Pubs.

—Crack Down. 2002. 12.95 (*1-883523-50-8*) Spinsters Ink Bks.

—Dead Beat. 1993. 207p. 16.95 o.p. (*0-312-08754-3*, Saint Martin's Minotaur) St. Martin's Pr.

—Dead Beat. l.t. ed. 1997. pap. 20.95 o.p. (*0-7862-0929-1*) Thorndike Pr.

—Kickback. 1993. 192p. 17.95 o.p. (*0-312-09836-7*, Saint Martin's Minotaur) St. Martin's Pr.

Mcdonald, Gregory. Carioca Fletch. unabr. ed. 1989. audio 42.00 (*0-7366-1538-5*, 2408) Books on Tape, Inc.

—Carioca Fletch. 2002. (Illus.). 192p. pap. 12.00 (*0-375-71347-6*) Random Hse., Inc.

—Carioca Fletch. 1988. 288p. mass mkt. 4.99 o.s.i (*0-446-34899-6*) Warner Bks., Inc.

—Confess, Fletch. unabr. ed. 1988. audio 42.00 (*0-7366-1323-4*, 2227) Books on Tape, Inc.

—Confess, Fletch. 1976. 272p. mass mkt. 4.99 (*0-380-00814-9*, Avon Bks.) Morrow/Avon.

—Fletch. unabr. ed. 1988. audio 36.00 (*0-7366-1352-8*, 2253) Books on Tape, Inc.

—Fletch. 1976. 256p. mass mkt. 4.99 (*0-380-00645-6*, Avon Bks.) Morrow/Avon.

—Fletch & the Man Who. unabr. ed. 1988. audio 42.00 (*0-7366-1380-3*, 2273) Books on Tape, Inc.

—Fletch & the Man Who. l.t. ed. 1988. (General Ser.). 352p. pap. 17.95 o.p. (*0-8161-4654-3*, Macmillan Reference USA) Gale Group.

—Fletch & the Man Who. 1988. 288p. mass mkt. 4.99 o.s.i (*0-446-35560-7*) Warner Bks., Inc.

—Fletch & the Widow Bradley. unabr. ed. 1988. audio 36.00 (*0-7366-1418-4*, 2304) Books on Tape, Inc.

—Fletch & the Widow Bradley. 2000. E-Book (*1-930351-09-7*) FairHillBooks.com.

—Fletch & the Widow Bradley. 1982. (General Ser.). 11.95 o.p. (*0-8161-3377-8*, Macmillan Reference USA) Gale Group.

—Fletch & the Widow Bradley. 2002. (Vintage Crime/Black Lizard Ser.). 160p. pap. 11.00 (*0-375-71351-4*) Knopf, Alfred A. Inc.

—Fletch & the Widow Bradley. 1989. mass mkt. 4.99 o.s.i (*0-446-35997-1*) Warner Bks., Inc.

—The Fletch Chronicle Vol. 1: Fletch Won; Fletch, Too; Fletch & the Widow Bradley. 1989. 8.99 o.p. (*0-517-00308-2*) Random Hse. Value Publishing.

—The Fletch Chronicle Vol. 2: Fletch; Carioca Fletch; Confess, Fletch. 1989. 8.99 o.p. (*0-517-00307-4*) Random Hse. Value Publishing.

—The Fletch Chronicle Vol. 3: Fletch's Fortune; Fletch's Moxie; Fletch & the Man Who. 1989. 8.99 o.p. (*0-517-00309-0*) Random Hse. Value Publishing.

—Fletch Reflected. 1995. 288p. mass mkt. 6.50 o.s.i (*0-515-11676-9*, Jove) Berkley Publishing Group.

—Fletch Reflected. unabr. ed. 1996. audio 36.00 (*0-7366-3287-5*, 3942) Books on Tape, Inc.

—Fletch Reflected. 1994. 240p. 21.95 o.p. (*0-399-13983-4*, G. P. Putnam's Sons) Penguin Group (USA) Inc.

—Fletch Reflected. 224p. 4.98 o.p. (*0-7651-0180-7*) Smithmark Pubs., Inc.

—Fletch, Too. 2000. E-Book (*1-930351-06-2*) FairHillBooks.com.

—Fletch, Too. 2002. 256p. pap. 12.00 (*0-375-71353-0*, Vintage) Knopf Publishing Group.

—Fletch, Too. 1987. o.s.i (*0-446-51326-1*); mass mkt. 4.99 o.s.i (*0-446-34614-4*) Warner Bks., Inc.

—Fletch, Too. unabr. ed. 1989. audio 36.00 (*0-7366-1492-3*, 2368) Books on Tape, Inc.

—Fletch Won. unabr. ed. 1988. audio 42.00 (*0-7366-1452-4*, 2334) Books on Tape, Inc.

—Fletch Won. 2002. (Vintage Crime/Black Lizard Ser.). 272p. pap. 12.00 (*0-375-71352-2*) Knopf, Alfred A. Inc.

—Fletch Won. 272p. 1986. mass mkt. 4.99 o.s.i (*0-446-34095-2*); 1985. 14.45 o.p. (*0-446-51325-3*) Warner Bks., Inc.

—Fletch's Fortune. unabr. ed. 1988. audio 36.00 (*0-7366-1398-6*, 2287) Books on Tape, Inc.

—Fletch's Fortune. 1988. pap. 4.99 (*0-380-37978-3*, Avon Bks.) Morrow/Avon.

—Fletch's Moxie. unabr. ed. 1988. audio 42.00 (*0-7366-1442-7*, 2325) Books on Tape, Inc.

—Fletch's Moxie. 2000. E-Book (*1-930351-08-9*) FairHillBooks.com.

—Fletch's Moxie. 1989. 288p. mass mkt. 4.99 o.s.i (*0-446-35976-9*) Warner Bks., Inc.

—Son of Fletch. 1994. 272p. mass mkt. 5.99 o.s.i (*0-515-11470-7*, Jove) Berkley Publishing Group.

—Son of Fletch. 1993. 240p. 19.95 o.p. (*0-399-13831-5*, G. P. Putnam's Sons) Penguin Group (USA) Inc.

—Son of Fletch. 4.98 o.s.i (*0-8317-6523-2*) Smithmark Pubs., Inc.

McGarrity, Michael. The Judas Judge. abr. ed. 2000. (Kevin Kerney Novels Ser.). audio 25.00 o.s.i (*0-7435-0627-8*, Simon & Schuster Audioworks) Simon & Schuster Audio.

—The Judas Judge: A Kevin Kerney Novel. 2000. (Kevin Kerney Novels Ser.). 288p. 23.95 o.s.i (*0-525-94547-4*, Dutton) Dutton/Plume.

—Mexican Hat. l.t. ed. 2001. (Illus.). 302p. 26.95 (*1-57490-379-9*, Beeler Large Print Bks.) Beeler, Thomas T. Publisher.

—Mexican Hat. unabr. ed. 1998. (Kevin Kerney Mystery Ser.: Vol. 2). audio 51.00 (*0-7887-1892-4*, 95314E7) Recorded Bks., LLC.

—Mexican Hat. 1998. (Kevin Kerney Novels Ser.). (Illus.). 336p. mass mkt. 6.50 (*0-671-00253-8*, Pocket Star) Simon & Schuster.

—The Mexican Hat: A Novel. 1997. 304p. 22.95 (*0-393-04063-1*) Norton, W. W. & Co., Inc.

—Tularosa. l.t. ed. 1996. pap. 23.95 (*1-56895-372-0*, Wheeler Publishing, Inc.) Gale Group.

—Tularosa. 1996. 304p. 25.00 (*0-393-03922-6*) Norton, W. W. & Co., Inc.

—Tularosa. 1998. 3.99 (*0-671-02373-X*, Pocket); 1997. (Illus.). 336p. mass mkt. 6.99 (*0-671-00252-X*, Pocket Star) Simon & Schuster.

McInerny, Ralph. Celt & Pepper: A Mystery Set at the University of Notre Dame. 2002. 240p. 22.95 (*0-312-29117-5*, Saint Martin's Minotaur) St. Martin's Pr.

—Celt & Pepper: A Mystery Set at the University of Notre Dame. 2003. 28.95 (*0-7862-5179-4*) Thorndike Pr.

—Emerald Aisle: A Mystery Set at the University of Notre Dame. 2002. E-Book 23.95 (*1-59061-743-6*) Adobe Systems, Inc.

Occupations

—Emerald Aisle: A Mystery Set at the University of Notre Dame. l.t. ed. 2002. 344p. 28.95 (*0-7862-4345-7*) Gale Group.
—Emerald Aisle: A Mystery Set at the University of Notre Dame. mass mkt. (*0-312-98277-1*, St. Martin's Paperbacks); E-Book 23.95 (*0-312-70326-0*); 2001. 288p. 22.95 (*0-312-26938-2*, Saint Martin's Minotaur) St. Martin's Pr.
—Irish Coffee. Date not set. pap. (*0-312-30902-3*, Saint Martin's Griffin); mass mkt. (*0-312-98691-2*, St. Martin's Paperbacks); 2003. 288p. 23.95 (*0-312-30901-5*, Saint Martin's Minotaur) St. Martin's Pr.
—Irish Tenure: A Mystery Set at the University of Notre Dame. 2000. 263p. mass mkt. 5.99 (*0-312-97320-9*, St. Martin's Paperbacks); 1999. 246p. 22.95 o.p. (*0-312-20345-4*, Saint Martin's Minotaur) St. Martin's Pr.
—Irish Tenure: A Mystery Set at the University of Notre Dame. l.t. ed. 2000. (Basic Ser.). 336p. 28.95 (*0-7862-2667-6*) Thorndike Pr.
McKenna, Bridget. Caught Dead. 1995. 240p. (Orig.). mass mkt. 4.99 o.s.i (*0-425-14493-3*, Prime Crime) Berkley Publishing Group.
—Dead Ahead. 1994. 208p. (Orig.). mass mkt. 4.50 o.s.i (*0-425-14300-7*, Prime Crime) Berkley Publishing Group.
—Murder Beach. 1993. 208p. (Orig.). 4.50 o.p. (*1-55773-967-6*, Diamond Bks.) Ace Bks.
McKevett, G. A. Bitter Sweets. 304p. 1997. mass mkt. 5.50 o.s.i (*1-57566-169-1*); 1996. 18.95 o.p. (*1-57566-032-6*) Kensington Publishing Corp.
—Cooked Goose. 1999. 320p. mass mkt. 6.50 (*0-7582-0205-9*); 1999. 32p. mass mkt. 5.99 (*1-57566-479-8*); 1998. (Illus.). 304p. 20.00 o.s.i (*1-57566-359-7*) Kensington Publishing Corp.
—Death by Chocolate: A Savannah Reid Mystery. 2003. 256p. 22.00 (*1-57566-712-6*) Kensington Publishing Corp.
—Death by Chocolate: A Savannah Reid Mystery. l.t. ed. 2003. (Paperback Ser.). 25.95 (*0-7862-5324-X*) Thorndike Pr.
—Just Desserts. (Savannah Reid Mystery Ser.). 1996. 320p. mass mkt. 4.99 o.s.i (*1-57566-037-7*); 1995. mass mkt. 16.95 o.s.i (*0-8217-4924-2*) Kensington Publishing Corp.
—Killer Calories. (Savannah Reid Mystery Ser.). 2000. 320p. mass mkt. 5.99 (*1-57566-521-2*, Kensington Bks.); 1998. 320p. mass mkt. 5.99 o.s.i (*1-57566-298-1*); 1997. 304p. 18.95 o.s.i (*1-57566-163-2*) Kensington Publishing Corp.
—Sugar & Spite. (Savannah Reid Mystery Ser.). 2001. 34p. mass mkt. 5.99 (*1-57566-637-5*); 2000. 288p. 20.00 o.s.i (*1-57566-493-3*) Kensington Publishing Corp.
—Sugar & Spite. l.t. ed. 2003. (Savannah Reid Mystery Ser.). 397p. pap. 24.95 (*0-7862-5890-X*) Thorndike Pr.
Meadows, Lee E. Silent Conspiracy. 2002. (Lincoln Keller Mystery Ser.). pap. 16.95 (*1-928623-06-9*) Proctor Pubns.
—Silent Conspiracy: A Lincoln Keller Mystery. 1997. 270p. 24.95 o.p. (*1-882792-38-6*) Proctor Pubns.
—Silent Suspicion: A Lincoln Keller Mystery. 2000. (Lincoln Keller Mystery Ser.). 437p. 24.95 (*1-882792-93-9*) Proctor Pubns.
Michaels, Kasey. Too Good to Be True. l.t. ed. 2002. (Wheeler Large Print Book Ser.). 27.95 (*1-58724-213-3*, Wheeler Publishing, Inc.) Gale Group.
—Too Good to Be True. 2001. 384p. mass mkt. 6.50 (*0-8217-6774-7*, Zebra Bks.) Kensington Publishing Corp.
Michaels, Melisa. Cold Iron. E-Book 5.99 (*1-58787-097-5*) Electric Umbrella Publishing.
—Cold Iron. 1997. 368p. mass mkt. 5.99 o.s.i (*0-451-45654-8*, ROC) NAL.
—Sister to the Rain. E-Book 5.99 (*1-58787-099-1*) Electric Umbrella Publishing.
—Sister to the Rain. 1998. 320p. mass mkt. 5.99 o.s.i (*0-451-45730-7*, ROC) NAL.
Miller, Janice. The Jade Crucible. 1995. 324p. pap. 10.99 o.p. (*0-7852-7706-4*) Nelson, Thomas Inc.
—Plum Blossoms: Alexis Albright—Private Investigator. 1994. pap. 10.99 o.p. (*0-7852-8208-4*) Nelson, Thomas Inc.
Millett, Larry. The Disappearance of Sherlock Holmes: A Mystery Featuring Shadwell Rafferty. 2002. 352p. 23.95 o.s.i (*0-670-03140-2*, Viking) Viking Penguin.
—Sherlock Holmes & the Red Demon. 2001. (Sherlock Holmes Mysteries Ser.). (Illus.). 336p. pap. 5.99 (*0-14-029644-1*) Penguin Group (USA) Inc.
—Sherlock Holmes & the Rune Stone Mystery: From the American Chronicles of John H. Watson, M.D. 2000. (Sherlock Holmes Mysteries Ser.). 368p. pap. 5.99 (*0-14-029645-X*) Penguin Group (USA) Inc.
—Sherlock Holmes & the Rune Stone Mystery: From the American Chronicles of John H. Watson, M.D. 1999. (Sherlock Holmes Ser.). (Illus.). 317p. (J). 23.95 o.s.i (*0-670-88821-4*, Viking) Viking Penguin.
—Sherlock Holmes & the Secret Alliance. 2002. 336p. mass mkt. 6.99 (*0-14-200155-4*) Penguin Group (USA) Inc.
—Sherlock Holmes & the Secret Alliance. 2001. 336p. 24.95 o.s.i (*0-670-03015-5*, Viking) Viking Penguin.
Millhiser, Marlys. Rampant Reaper. E-Book 23.95 (*0-312-70742-8*) St. Martin's Pr.
—The Rampant Reaper. 2003. (WWL Mystery Ser.: No. 478). 288p. mass mkt. (*0-373-26478-X*, Worldwide Library) Harlequin Enterprises, Ltd.
—The Rampant Reaper: A Charlie Greene Mystery. 2002. 288p. 23.95 (*0-312-29096-9*, Saint Martin's Minotaur) St. Martin's Pr.
Mitchell, James C. Lovers Crossing. Date not set. pap. (*0-312-31531-7*, St. Martin's Paperbacks); 2003. 304p. 23.95 (*0-312-31530-9*, Saint Martin's Minotaur) St. Martin's Pr.
Montalban, Manuel Vazquez. The Angst-Ridden Executive. Emery, Ed, tr. from SPA. 1990. (Masks Noir Ser.). 240p. pap. o.p. (*1-85242-159-2*) Serpent's Tail Ltd.
—The Buenos Aires Quintet. 2003. 252p. pap. 15.00 (*1-85242-640-3*) Serpent's Tail Ltd. GBR. *Dist:* Consortium Bk. Sales & Distribution.
—Murder in the Central Committee. 1985. 203p. 13.95 o.p. (*0-89733-125-7*) Academy Chicago Pubs., Ltd.
—Murder in the Central Committee. Camiller, Patrick, tr. from SPA. 1999. 203p. (*1-85242-731-0*) Gallery Pr.
—Murder in the Central Committee. 1997. (Mask Noir Ser.). 224p. pap. text (*1-85242-131-2*) Serpent's Tail Ltd.
—Off Side. 2001. 278p. (Orig.). pap. 13.00 (*1-85242-742-6*) Serpent's Tail Ltd. GBR. *Dist:* Consortium Bk. Sales & Distribution.
—Olympic Death. 2000. (Mask Noir Ser.). 207p. pap. o.p. (*1-85242-257-2*) Serpent's Tail Ltd.
—Southern Seas. 2000. 214p. pap. (*1-85242-700-0*) Serpent's Tail Ltd.
—Southern Seas. Camiller, Patrick, tr. from SPA. 1990. 224p. pap. o.p. (*1-85242-132-0*) Serpent's Tail Ltd.
—Southern Seas. 1990. pap. 9.95 o.p. (*0-7453-0204-1*) Westview Pr.
Monteleone, Thomas F. Eyes of the Virgin. 2002. 304p. 24.95 (*0-312-87874-5*, Forge Bks.) Doherty, Tom Assocs., LLC.
Montgomery, Ian A. Dead Duck: A Jud Carson Mystery. Spafford, Jacalyn A., ed. 1993. 120p. (Orig.). pap. 9.95 (*1-890538-15-9*) Rhiannon Pubns.
Mooney, Chris. Deviant Ways. 2000. 384p. 24.95 (*0-671-04059-6*, Atria) Simon & Schuster.
Morgan, Robert. All Things under the Moon. 1994. 224p. (Orig.). mass mkt. 4.99 o.p. (*0-425-14302-3*, Prime Crime) Berkley Publishing Group.
—The Only Thing to Fear. 1994. 256p. mass mkt. 4.99 o.s.i (*0-425-14468-2*, Prime Crime) Berkley Publishing Group.
—Some Things Come Back. 1995. 256p. (Orig.). mass mkt. 4.99 o.s.i (*0-425-14690-1*, Prime Crime) Berkley Publishing Group.
—Some Things Never Die. 1993. 208p. (Orig.). 3.99 o.p. (*1-55773-887-4*, Diamond Bks.) Ace Bks.
—Thing That Darkness Hides. 1993. 4.50 o.p. (*1-55773-960-9*, Diamond Bks.) Ace Bks.
—Things That Are Not There. 1992. 208p. (Orig.). 3.99 o.p. (*1-55773-827-0*, Diamond Bks.) Ace Bks.
Morris, Gilbert. And Then There Were Two. l.t. ed. 2002. 431p. pap. 16.95 (*1-4104-0015-8*, Walker Large Print) Gale Group.
—And Then There Were Two. l.t. ed. 2001. (Dani Ross Mysteries Ser.). 463p. 24.95 o.p. (*0-7862-3088-6*) Thorndike Pr.
—Four of a Kind: A Dani Ross Mystery. l.t. ed. 2001. (Christian Mystery Ser.). 426p. 24.95 (*0-7862-3545-4*) Thorndike Pr.
—One by One. 2000. (Dani Ross Mysteries Ser.). Orig. Title: Guilt by Association. 286p. reprint ed. pap. 12.99 (*1-58134-192-X*) Crossway Bks.
—One by One. l.t. ed. 2002. Orig. Title: Guilt by Association. 490p. pap. 16.95 (*1-4104-0025-5*, Walker Large Print) Gale Group.
—One by One. l.t. ed. 2001. (Christian Mystery Ser.). Orig. Title: Guilt by Association. 467p. 24.95 (*0-7862-3087-8*) Thorndike Pr.
Morwood, Carolyn. A Simple Death. 2002. 186p. pap. 13.95 (*0-7043-4727-X*) Women's Pr., Ltd., The GBR. *Dist:* Trafalgar Square.
Muller, Marcia. Ask the Cards a Question. unabr. ed. 1996. (Sharon McCone Ser.). audio 36.00 (*0-7366-3454-1*, 4098) Books on Tape, Inc.
—Ask the Cards a Question: A Sharon McCone Mystery. l.t. ed. 1996. 239p. pap. 19.95 o.p. (*0-7838-1480-1*, Macmillan Reference USA) Gale Group.
—Ask the Cards a Question: A Sharon McCone Mystery. 1982. 168p. 10.95 o.p. (*0-312-05653-2*) St. Martin's Pr.
—Ask the Cards a Question: A Sharon McCone Mystery. 1990. 224p. reprint ed. mass mkt. 6.99 (*0-445-40849-9*) Warner Bks., Inc.
—Both Ends of the Night. unabr. ed. 1997. (Sharon McCone Ser.). audio 48.00 (*0-7366-3802-4*, 4473) Books on Tape, Inc.
—Both Ends of the Night. abr. ed. (Sharon Mccone Ser.). 1998. audio 7.99 o.p. (*1-56740-250-X*, 629, Paperback Nova Audio Bks.); 1997. audio 16.95 o.p. (*1-56100-985-7*, 1137); 1997. audio 73.25 o.p. (*1-56100-834-6*, 814, Unabridged Library Editions); 1997. audio 23.95 (*1-56100-759-5*, 51, Bookcassette) Brilliance Audio.
—Both Ends of the Night. l.t. ed. 1997. (Wheeler Large Print Book Ser.). pap. 24.95 (*1-56895-463-8*, Wheeler Publishing, Inc.) Gale Group.
—Both Ends of the Night. 1997. 368p. 22.50 o.p. (*0-89296-622-X*) Mysterious Pr.
—Both Ends of the Night. 1998. (Sharon McCone Mysteries Ser.). 384p. reprint ed. mass mkt. 6.99 (*0-446-60550-6*) Warner Bks., Inc.
—The Broken Promise Land. unabr. ed. 1996. (Sharon McCone Ser.). audio 64.00 (*0-7366-3383-9*, 4033) Books on Tape, Inc.
—The Broken Promise Land. abr. ed. (Sharon Mccone Ser.). 1997. audio 7.99 o.p. (*1-56740-177-5*, 630, Paperback Nova Audio Bks.); 1996. audio 16.95 o.p. (*1-56100-956-3*, 817, Nova Audio Bks.); 1996. audio 23.95 o.p. (*1-56100-718-8*, 53, Bookcassette); 1996. audio 73.25 o.p. (*1-56100-343-3*, 816, Unabridged Library Editions) Brilliance Audio.
—The Broken Promise Land. 1996. 82p. 22.95 o.s.i (*0-89296-621-1*) Mysterious Pr.
—The Broken Promise Land. 1997. (Sharon McCone Mysteries Ser.). 400p. reprint ed. mass mkt. 6.50 (*0-446-60410-0*) Warner Bks., Inc.
—The Cheshire Cat's Eye: A Sharon McCone Mystery. unabr. ed. 1996. (Sharon McCone Ser.). audio 36.00 (*0-7366-3490-8*, 4130) Books on Tape, Inc.
—The Cheshire Cat's Eye: A Sharon McCone Mystery. l.t. ed. 1988. (Nightingale Ser.). 278p. pap. 12.95 o.p. (*0-8161-4396-X*, Macmillan Reference USA) Gale Group.
—The Cheshire Cat's Eye: A Sharon McCone Mystery. 1983. 160p. 10.95 o.p. (*0-312-13175-5*) St. Martin's Pr.
—The Cheshire Cat's Eye: A Sharon McCone Mystery. 1990. 224p. reprint ed. mass mkt. 6.99 (*0-445-40850-2*) Warner Bks., Inc.
—Edwin of the Iron Shoes. 1993. (Black Dagger Crime Ser.). 184p. 16.50 o.p. (*0-7451-8617-3*, Black Dagger) BBC Audiobooks America.
—Edwin of the Iron Shoes. unabr. ed. 1996. (Sharon McCone Ser.). audio 36.00 (*0-7366-3408-8*, 4054) Books on Tape, Inc.
—Edwin of the Iron Shoes. 1977. (McKay-Washburn Mystery Ser.). 7.95 o.p. (*0-679-50782-5*) McKay, David Co., Inc.
—Edwin of the Iron Shoes. 1978. (Crime Ser.). pap. 1.95 o.p. (*0-14-004915-0*, Penguin Bks.) Viking Penguin.
—Edwin of the Iron Shoes. 1990. 224p. reprint ed. mass mkt. 6.99 (*0-445-40902-9*) Warner Bks., Inc.
—Eye of the Storm. unabr. ed. 1998. (Sharon McCone Ser.). audio 56.00 (*0-7366-4135-1*, 4640) Books on Tape, Inc.
—Eye of the Storm. 1988. 15.95 o.p. (*0-89296-269-0*) Mysterious Pr.
—Eye of the Storm. 1989. 256p. reprint ed. mass mkt. 6.99 o.s.i (*0-445-40625-9*) Warner Bks., Inc.
—Games to Keep the Dark Away: A Sharon McCone Mystery. unabr. ed. 1997. (Sharon McCone Ser.). audio 36.00 (*0-7366-3566-1*, 4212) Books on Tape, Inc.
—Games to Keep the Dark Away: A Sharon McCone Mystery. l.t. ed. 1986. (Nightingale Ser.). 278p. 11.95 o.p. (*0-8161-3903-2*, Macmillan Reference USA) Gale Group.
—Games to Keep the Dark Away: A Sharon McCone Mystery. 2003. 320p. pap. 14.95 (*0-312-31620-8*, L. A. Weekly Bks.) St. Martin's Pr.
—Games to Keep the Dark Away: A Sharon McCone Mystery. 1990. reprint ed. mass mkt. 6.99 (*0-445-40851-0*) Warner Bks., Inc.
—Leave a Message for Willie: A Sharon McCone Mystery. unabr. ed. 1997. (Sharon McCone Ser.). audio 42.00 (*0-7366-3779-6*, 4452) Books on Tape, Inc.
—Leave a Message for Willie: A Sharon McCone Mystery. l.t. ed. 1995. 266p. pap. 20.95 o.p. (*0-7838-1481-X*, Macmillan Reference USA) Gale Group.
—Leave a Message for Willie: A Sharon McCone Mystery. 1984. 192p. 11.95 o.p. (*0-312-47728-7*) St. Martin's Pr.
—Leave a Message for Willie: A Sharon McCone Mystery. 1990. 224p. reprint ed. mass mkt. 6.99 (*0-445-40900-2*) Warner Bks., Inc.
—Listen to the Silence. l.t. ed. 2000. (Wheeler Large Print Book Ser.). 328p. 28.95 o.p. (*1-56895-908-7*, Wheeler Publishing, Inc.) Gale Group.
—Listen to the Silence. 2000. 304p. 23.95 (*0-89296-689-0*) Mysterious Pr.
—McCone & Friends. 2000. 202p. (Illus.). (J). pap. 16.00 (*1-885941-38-2*); 40.00 o.p. (*1-885941-37-4*) Crippen & Landru, Pubs.
—Pennies on a Dead Woman's Eyes. 1992. 304p. 18.95 (*0-89296-454-5*) Mysterious Pr.
—Pennies on a Dead Woman's Eyes. 1993. 366p. reprint ed. mass mkt. 6.99 (*0-446-40033-5*) Warner Bks., Inc.
—The Shape of Dread. unabr. ed. 1999. audio 48.00 (*0-7366-4455-5*, 4900) Books on Tape, Inc.
—The Shape of Dread. 1989. 16.95 o.p. (*0-89296-271-2*) Mysterious Pr.
—The Shape of Dread. 1990. 288p. reprint ed. mass mkt. 6.99 (*0-445-40916-9*) Warner Bks., Inc.
—There's Nothing to Be Afraid Of. unabr. ed. 1997. (Sharon McCone Ser.). audio 48.00 (*0-7366-3780-X*, 4453) Books on Tape, Inc.
—There's Nothing to Be Afraid Of. 1985. 256p. 14.95 o.p. (*0-312-79955-1*) St. Martin's Pr.
—There's Nothing to Be Afraid Of. 1990. 224p. reprint ed. mass mkt. 6.99 o.s.i (*0-445-40901-0*) Warner Bks., Inc.
—There's Something in a Sunday: A Sharon McCone Mystery. unabr. ed. 1998. (Sharon McCone Ser.). audio 48.00 (*0-7366-4136-X*, 4641) Books on Tape, Inc.
—There's Something in a Sunday: A Sharon McCone Mystery. 1989. 15.95 o.p. (*0-89296-270-4*) Mysterious Pr.
—There's Something in a Sunday: A Sharon McCone Mystery. 1990. 224p. reprint ed. mass mkt. 6.99 (*0-445-40865-0*) Warner Bks., Inc.
—Till the Butchers Cut Him Down: A Sharon McCone Mystery. 1994. 352p. 18.95 o.s.i (*0-89296-455-3*) Mysterious Pr.
—Till the Butchers Cut Him Down: A Sharon McCone Mystery. 1995. pap. (*0-446-40034-3*, Mysterious Pr. Paperback Bks.); 336p. reprint ed. mass mkt. 5.99 (*0-446-60302-3*) Warner Bks., Inc.
—Trophies & Dead Things: A Sharon McCowe Mystery. unabr. ed. 1999. audio 48.00 Books on Tape, Inc.
—Trophies & Dead Things: A Sharon McCowe Mystery. l.t. ed. 1991. (General Ser.). 379p. lib. bdg. 19.95 o.p. (*0-8161-5134-2*, Macmillan Reference USA) Gale Group.
—Trophies & Dead Things: A Sharon McCowe Mystery. 1990. 272p. 16.95 o.p. (*0-89296-417-0*) Mysterious Pr.
—Trophies & Dead Things: A Sharon McCowe Mystery. 1991. 272p. reprint ed. mass mkt. 5.99 o.s.i (*0-446-40039-4*) Warner Bks., Inc.
—A Walk Through the Fire. 1999. 362p. 23.00 o.s.i (*0-89296-688-2*) Mysterious Pr.
—Where Echoes Live. 1991. 17.95 o.p. (*0-89296-418-9*) Mysterious Pr.
—Where Echoes Live. 1992. 368p. reprint ed. mass mkt. 6.99 (*0-446-40161-7*) Warner Bks., Inc.
—While Other People Sleep. unabr. ed. 1999. (Sharon McCone Ser.). audio 48.00 (*0-7366-4318-4*, 4790) Books on Tape, Inc.
—While Other People Sleep. unabr. ed. 1998. (Sharon McCone Ser.). audio 25.95 (*1-56740-061-2*, 1, Bookcassette); audio 57.25 (*1-56740-590-8*, 1095, Unabridged Library Editions);Set. audio 17.95 o.p. (*1-56740-786-2*, 448, Nova Audio Bks.) Brilliance Audio.
—While Other People Sleep. 1998. (Sharon McCone Mysteries Ser.). 344p. 23.00 o.p. (*0-89296-650-5*) Mysterious Pr.
—While Other People Sleep. l.t. ed. 1998. (Mystery Ser.). 432p. 28.95 o.p. (*0-7862-1615-8*) Thorndike Pr.
—While Other People Sleep. 1999. 304p. reprint ed. mass mkt. 6.99 (*0-446-60721-5*) Warner Bks., Inc.
—A Wild & Lonely Place: A Sharon McCone Mystery. unabr. ed. 2000. (Sharon McCone Ser.: 16). audio 48.00 Books on Tape, Inc.
—A Wild & Lonely Place: A Sharon McCone Mystery. 1995. 300p. 19.95 o.s.i (*0-89296-526-6*) Mysterious Pr.
—A Wild & Lonely Place: A Sharon McCone Mystery. 1996. 336p. reprint ed. mass mkt. 6.99 (*0-446-60328-7*) Warner Bks., Inc.
—Wolf in the Shadows. 1993. 368p. 18.95 (*0-89296-525-8*) Mysterious Pr.
—Wolf in the Shadows. 1994. 384p. reprint ed. mass mkt. 5.50 (*0-446-40383-0*) Warner Bks., Inc.
Muller, Marcia & Pronzini, Bill. Double. unabr. ed. 1997. audio 64.00 (*0-7366-3710-9*, 4394) Books on Tape, Inc.
—Double. 1984. 288p. 13.95 o.p. (*0-312-21807-9*) St. Martin's Pr.
—Double. 1995. 288p. reprint ed. mass mkt. 5.50 o.s.i (*0-446-40413-6*) Warner Bks., Inc.
Munger, Katy. Bad to the Bone. 2000. (Casey Jones Mysteries Ser.). 288p. mass mkt. 6.50 (*0-380-80064-0*, Avon Bks.) Morrow/Avon.
—Legwork. 1997. (Casey Jones Mysteries Ser.). 224p. mass mkt. 5.99 (*0-380-79136-6*, Avon Bks.) Morrow/Avon.

—Money to Burn. 1999. (Casey Jones Mysteries Ser.). 320p. mass mkt. 6.50 (*0-380-80063-2*, Avon Bks.) Morrow/Avon.
—Out of Time. 1998. (Casey Jones Mysteries Ser.). 272p. mass mkt. 6.50 (*0-380-79138-2*, Avon Bks.) Morrow/Avon.
Murphy, Haughton. Murder for Lunch. 1987. mass mkt. 2.95 o.s.i (*0-449-21276-9*, Fawcett) Ballantine Bks.
—Murder for Lunch. 1986. 240p. 14.70 o.p. (*0-671-60628-X*, Simon & Schuster) Simon & Schuster.
—Murder for Lunch. l.t. ed. 1990. (Ulverscroft Large Print Ser.). 29.99 o.p. (*0-7089-2225-2*, Ulverscroft) Thorpe, F. A. Pubs. GBR. *Dist:* Ulverscroft Large Print Bks., Ltd., Ulverscroft Large Print Canada, Ltd.
—Murder Keeps a Secret. 1990. 240p. mass mkt. 4.99 o.s.i (*0-449-21788-4*, Fawcett) Ballantine Bks.
—Murder Keeps a Secret. 1989. 16.95 o.p. (*0-671-66981-8*, Simon & Schuster) Simon & Schuster.
—Murder Saves Face. 1992. reprint ed. mass mkt. 3.99 o.s.i (*0-449-22065-6*, Fawcett) Ballantine Bks.
—Murder Saves Face. 1991. 288p. 18.95 o.p. (*0-671-70663-2*, Simon & Schuster) Simon & Schuster.
—Murder Takes a Partner. 1987. 288p. reprint ed. mass mkt. 3.50 o.s.i (*0-449-21434-6*, Fawcett) Ballantine Bks.
—Murder Takes a Partner. 1987. 240p. 15.45 o.p. (*0-671-63422-4*, Simon & Schuster) Simon & Schuster.
—Murder Takes a Partner. l.t. ed. 1990. (Ulverscroft Large Print Ser.). 29.99 o.p. (*0-7089-2158-2*, Ulverscroft) Thorpe, F. A. Pubs. GBR. *Dist:* Ulverscroft Large Print Bks., Ltd., Ulverscroft Large Print Canada, Ltd.
—Murder Times Two. 1990. 17.95 o.p. (*0-671-66982-6*, Simon & Schuster) Simon & Schuster.
—Murder Times Two: A Ruben Frost Mystery. 1991. 256p. mass mkt. 3.95 o.s.i (*0-449-21947-X*, Fawcett) Ballantine Bks.
—Murders & Acquisitions. 1989. mass mkt. 3.95 o.s.i (*0-449-21643-8*, Fawcett) Ballantine Bks.
—Murders & Acquisitions. 1988. 224p. 16.45 o.p. (*0-671-63735-5*, Simon & Schuster) Simon & Schuster.
—A Very Venetian Murder. 1993. mass mkt. 4.50 o.s.i (*0-449-22066-4*, Fawcett) Ballantine Bks.
—A Very Venetian Murder. 1992. 256p. 19.00 o.p. (*0-671-70664-0*, Simon & Schuster) Simon & Schuster.
Murray, Donna Huston. Farewell Performance: A Ginger Barnes Main Line Mystery. 2000. (Ginger Barnes Main Line Mysteries Ser.). 272p. mass mkt. 5.99 (*0-312-97456-6*, St. Martin's Paperbacks) St. Martin's Pr.
—Final Arrangements. 1996. (Ginger Barnes Main Line Mysteries Ser.). 290p. pap. text 5.99 (*0-312-95765-3*, St. Martin's Paperbacks) St. Martin's Pr.
—The Main Line Is Murder. 1995. (Ginger Barnes Main Line Mysteries Ser.). 294p. mass mkt. 5.99 (*0-312-95637-1*, St. Martin's Paperbacks) St. Martin's Pr.
—School of Hard Knocks: A Dead Letter Mystery. 1997. (Ginger Barnes Main Line Mysteries Ser.). 288p. mass mkt. 5.99 (*0-312-96104-9*, St. Martin's Paperbacks) St. Martin's Pr.
—A Score to Settle. 1999. (Ginger Barnes Main Line Mysteries Ser.). 288p. mass mkt. 5.99 (*0-312-96951-1*, St. Martin's Paperbacks) St. Martin's Pr.
Murray, Lynne. At Large. 2002. 288p. mass mkt. 6.50 (*0-312-98004-3*, St. Martin's Paperbacks); 2001. 260p. 23.95 (*0-312-28029-7*, Saint Martin's Minotaur); 2001. 287.40 (*0-312-28026-2*, Saint Martin's Minotaur) St. Martin's Pr.
—A Ton of Trouble. mass mkt. (*0-312-98467-7*, St. Martin's Paperbacks); E-Book 21.95 (*0-312-70744-4*); 2002. 160p. 22.95 (*0-312-30077-8*, Saint Martin's Minotaur) St. Martin's Pr.
Nebel, Frederick. The Adventures of Cardigan. 1988. (Dime Detective Bk.). 208p. 9.95 o.p. (*0-89296-950-4*) Mysterious Pr.
Nelscott, Kris. A Dangerous Road. 2001. 336p. mass mkt. 6.50 (*0-312-97643-7*, St. Martin's Paperbacks); 2000. 325p. 24.95 (*0-312-26264-7*, Saint Martin's Minotaur) St. Martin's Pr.
—Smoke-Filled Rooms: Smokey Dalton Novel. 2001. 320p. 24.95 (*0-312-26265-5*, Saint Martin's Minotaur) St. Martin's Pr.
—Stone Cribs. E-Book 18.95 (*0-312-71111-5*); 2004. 320p. 24.95 (*0-312-28784-4*, Saint Martin's Minotaur) St. Martin's Pr.
—Thin Walls: A Smokey Dalton Novel. 2002. 320p. 24.95 (*0-312-28783-6*, Saint Martin's Minotaur) St. Martin's Pr.
Nevins, Francis M. Into the Same River Twice. 1996. 224p. 21.00 o.p. (*0-7867-0314-8*, Carroll & Graf Pubs.) Avalon Publishing Group.
—Into the Same River Twice. 2000. 228p. pap. 14.95 (*0-595-00001-0*, Authors Choice Pr.) iUniverse, Inc.
Norbu, Jamyang. Sherlock Holmes - The Missing Years: The Adventures of the Great Detective in India & Tibet. 2001. 288p. 23.95 (*1-58234-132-X*) Bloomsbury Publishing.
O'Callaghan, Maxine. Death Is Forever. l.t. ed. 1999. (Five Star Mystery Ser.). 205p. 19.95 o.p. (*0-7862-1729-4*, Five Star) Gale Group.
—Down for the Count: A Delilah West Novel. 1998. (WWL Mystery Ser.: No. 294). per. (*0-373-26294-9*, 0-26294-9, Worldwide Library) Harlequin Enterprises, Ltd.
—Down for the Count: A Delilah West Novel. 1997. (Delilah West Mystery Ser.: Vol. 60). 240p. 20.95 (*0-312-16820-9*, Saint Martin's Minotaur) St. Martin's Pr.
—Down for the Count: A Delilah West Novel. l.t. ed. 1998. (Mystery Ser.). 307p. 26.95 (*0-7838-8404-4*) Thorndike Pr.
—Hit & Run. 1991. pap. 3.95 o.p. (*0-312-92440-2*, St. Martin's Paperbacks); 1989. 192p. 14.95 o.p. (*0-312-02584-X*, Saint Martin's Minotaur) St. Martin's Pr.
—Set-Up: A Delilah West Mystery. 1994. mass mkt. (*0-373-26144-6*, Harlequin Bks.) Harlequin Enterprises, Ltd.
—Set-Up: A Delilah West Mystery. 1991. 208p. 18.95 o.p. (*0-312-06462-4*, Saint Martin's Minotaur) St. Martin's Pr.
—Trade-Off. 1996. (Mystery Ser.). per. (*0-373-26191-8*, 1-26191-6, Worldwide Library) Harlequin Enterprises, Ltd.
—Trade-Off. 1994. 224p. 19.95 o.p. (*0-312-11081-2*, Saint Martin's Minotaur) St. Martin's Pr.
O'Donnell, Lillian. The Goddess Affair. 1997. mass mkt. 5.99 o.s.i (*0-449-28805-6*, Fawcett) Ballantine Bks.
—The Goddess Affair. l.t. ed. 1997. (Large Print Book Ser.). 25.95 o.p. (*1-56895-461-1*, Wheeler Publishing, Inc.) Gale Group.
—The Goddess Affair. 1996. 240p. 21.95 o.p. (*0-399-14183-9*, G. P. Putnam's Sons) Penguin Group (USA) Inc.
—The Raggedy Man. 1997. (Norah Mulcahaney Ser.). mass mkt. 5.99 o.s.i (*0-449-22428-7*, Fawcett) Ballantine Bks.
—The Raggedy Man. 1995. 240p. 19.95 o.p. (*0-399-14019-0*, G. P. Putnam's Sons) Penguin Group (USA) Inc.
—Used to Kill. 1994. mass mkt. 4.99 o.s.i (*0-449-22249-7*, Fawcett) Ballantine Bks.
—Used to Kill. 1993. 240p. 19.95 o.p. (*0-399-13782-3*, G. P. Putnam's Sons) Penguin Group (USA) Inc.
—A Wreath for the Bride. 1991. 224p. mass mkt. 4.99 o.s.i (*0-449-21867-8*, Fawcett) Ballantine Bks.
—A Wreath for the Bride. 1990. 240p. 18.95 o.p. (*0-399-13478-6*, G. P. Putnam's Sons) Penguin Putnam Bks. for Young Readers.
—A Wreath for the Bride. 1992. 2.99 o.p. (*0-517-07978-X*) Random Hse. Value Publishing.
Oliver, Maria-Antonia. Antipodes. McNerney, Kathleen, tr. from SPA. 1989. (International Women's Crime Ser.). 224p. (Orig.). reprint ed. pap. 8.95 o.p. (*0-931188-82-2*, Seal Pr.) Avalon Publishing Group.
—Study in Lilac. McNerney, Kathleen, tr. from CAT. 1987. (International Women's Crime Ser.). 161p. pap. 16.95 o.p. (*0-931188-53-9*); pap. 8.95 o.p. (*0-931188-52-0*) Avalon Publishing Group. (Seal Pr.).
O'Marie, Carol Anne. The Corporal Works of Murder. 2002. (Sister Mary Helen Mystery Ser.). 208p. 22.95 (*0-312-20917-7*, Saint Martin's Minotaur) St. Martin's Pr.
Overholser, Stephen. Molly & the Railroad Tycoon. l.t. ed. 2001. (Thorndike Western Ser.). 269p. 23.95 (*0-7862-3240-4*); (*0-7540-4529-3*); (*0-7540-4530-7*) Thorndike Pr.
—Molly on the Outlaw Trail. l.t. ed. 1999. (Paperback Ser.: Vol. 1). 224p. pap. 23.95 (*0-7838-8615-2*) Thorndike Pr.
Paretsky, Sara. At the Old Swimming Hole. abr. ed. 1999. audio 5.99 Durkin Hayes Publishing Ltd.
—Bitter Medicine. 1988. 272p. mass mkt. 6.99 o.s.i (*0-345-34722-6*) Ballantine Bks.
—Bitter Medicine. 1993. audio compact disk 56.00 (*0-7366-7125-0*) Books on Tape, Inc.
—Bitter Medicine. 1999. 352p. mass mkt. 7.50 (*0-440-23476-X*) Dell Publishing.
—Bitter Medicine. l.t. ed. 1989. 352p. 19.95 o.p. (*0-8161-4467-2*, Macmillan Reference USA) Gale Group.
—Bitter Medicine. 1987. 320p. 17.95 o.p. (*0-688-06448-5*, Morrow, William & Co.) Morrow/Avon.
—Blacklist. 2003. (V. I. Warshawski Novel Ser.). 448p. 24.95 (*0-399-15085-4*) Putnam Publishing Group, The.
—Blood Shot. unabr. ed. 1993. (V. I. Warshawski Ser.). audio 56.00 (*0-7366-2328-0*, 3108) Books on Tape, Inc.
—Blood Shot. 1989. (V.I. Warshawski Novels Ser.). 384p. mass mkt. 7.99 (*0-440-20420-8*) Dell Publishing.
—Blood Shot. l.t. ed. 1989. (General Ser.). 20.95 o.p. (*0-8161-4775-2*, Macmillan Reference USA) Gale Group.
—Blood Shot. abr. ed. 1990. audio 14.95 o.s.i (*0-553-45215-0*, RH Audio) Random Hse. Audio Publishing Group.
—Blood Shot. unabr. ed. 1993. (V. I. Warshawski Mystery Ser.: Vol. 1). audio 70.00 (*1-55690-899-7*, 93341E7) Recorded Bks., LLC.
—Burn Marks. unabr. ed. 1992. (V. I. Warshawski Ser.). audio 64.00 (*0-7366-2168-7*, 2967) Books on Tape, Inc.
—Burn Marks. 1991. (V.I. Warshawski Novels Ser.). 416p. mass mkt. 7.99 (*0-440-20845-9*) Dell Publishing.
—Burn Marks. l.t. ed. 1990. (Large Print Bks.). 533p. lib. bdg. 21.95 o.p. (*0-8161-5004-4*, Macmillan Reference USA) Gale Group.
—Burn Marks. abr. ed. 1990. audio 14.95 o.s.i (*0-553-45208-8*, RH Audio) Random Hse. Audio Publishing Group.
—Deadlock. l.t. ed. 1985. lib. bdg. 13.95 o.p. (*0-89340-898-0*, 842) BBC Audiobooks America.
—Deadlock. 1984. 272p. mass mkt. 5.95 o.s.i (*0-345-31954-0*) Ballantine Bks.
—Deadlock. 1992. (V.I. Warshawski Novels Ser.). 320p. mass mkt. 6.99 (*0-440-21332-0*) Dell Publishing.
—Deadlock. 1984. 264p. 14.95 o.p. (*0-385-27933-7*) Doubleday Publishing.
—Deadlock. l.t. ed. 1993. (General Ser.). 271p. pap. 18.95 o.p. (*0-8161-5562-3*); lib. bdg. 20.95 o.p. (*0-8161-5561-5*) Gale Group. (Macmillan Reference USA).
—Guardian Angel. unabr. ed. 1992. (V. I. Warshawski Ser.). audio 72.00 (*0-7366-2203-9*, 2998) Books on Tape, Inc.
—Guardian Angel. 1993. 432p. mass mkt. 7.99 (*0-440-21399-1*) Dell Publishing.
—Guardian Angel. l.t. ed. 1992. (General Ser.). 544p. 18.95 o.p. (*0-8161-5542-9*); lib. bdg. 21.95 o.p. (*0-8161-5541-0*) Gale Group. (Macmillan Reference USA).
—Guardian Angel. 1992. audio 15.95 o.s.i (*0-553-74558-1*); audio 16.99 o.s.i (*0-553-47035-3*) Random Hse. Audio Publishing Group. (RH Audio).
—Guardian Angel. 1993. 5.99 o.p. (*0-517-10926-3*) Random Hse. Value Publishing.
—Guardian Angel. unabr. ed. 1992. (V. I. Warshawski Mystery Ser.: Vol. 7). audio 85.00 (*1-55690-669-2*, 92233E7) Recorded Bks., LLC.
—Guardian Angel. 1992. (Audio Books Ser.). 69.95 o.p. incl. audio (*0-7838-8000-6*) Thorndike Pr.
—Guardian Angel: International Edition. 1992. 432p. mass mkt. 5.50 o.s.i (*0-440-29522-X*) Dell Publishing.
—Hard Time. (V.I. Warshawski Novels Ser.). 2000. 512p. mass mkt. 7.99 (*0-440-22470-5*, Delta); 1999. 400p. 24.95 (*0-385-31363-2*, Delacorte Pr.) Dell Publishing.
—Hard Time. l.t. ed. 1999. pap. 24.95 o.p. (*0-7838-8696-9*, Macmillan Reference USA) Gale Group.
—Hard Time. l.t. ed. 2000. 656p. pap. 13.95 (*0-375-70780-8*) Random Hse. Large Print.
—Hard Time. 2000. 13.04 (*0-606-18985-8*) Turtleback Bks.
—Indemnity Only. 1985. 224p. mass mkt. 4.95 o.s.i (*0-345-33634-8*); 1983. mass mkt. 2.50 o.s.i (*0-345-30684-8*) Ballantine Bks.
—Indemnity Only. unabr. ed. 1992. (V. I. Warshawski Ser.). audio 48.00 (*0-7366-2282-9*, 3069) Books on Tape, Inc.
—Indemnity Only. 1991. (V.I. Warshawski Novels Ser.). 336p. mass mkt. 6.99 (*0-440-21069-0*) Dell Publishing.
—Indemnity Only. 1982. 14.95 o.p. (*0-385-27213-8*) Doubleday Publishing.
—Indemnity Only. (Nightingale Ser.). 1982. pap. 9.95 o.p. (*0-8161-3439-1*); 1992. 381p. lib. bdg. 20.95 (*0-8161-5455-4*) Gale Group. (Macmillan Reference USA).
—Indemnity Only. abr. ed. 1991. audio 15.99 o.s.i (*0-553-45271-1*, RH Audio) Random Hse. Audio Publishing Group.
—Indemnity Only. l.t. ed. 1992. (Novels Ser.). 381p. pap. 20.95 (*0-8161-5456-2*) Thorndike Pr.
—Killing Orders. l.t. ed. 1986. lib. bdg. 17.95 o.p. (*1-55504-024-1*) BBC Audiobooks America.
—Killing Orders. 1988. pap. o.p. (*0-345-00730-1*); 1986. 288p. mass mkt. 5.95 o.s.i (*0-345-32777-2*) Ballantine Bks.
—Killing Orders. unabr. collector's ed. 1993. (V. I. Warshawski Ser.). audio 48.00 (*0-7366-2391-4*, 3162) Books on Tape, Inc.
—Killing Orders. 1993. 352p. mass mkt. 7.99 (*0-440-21528-5*, Dell Bks.) Dell Publishing.
—Sara Paretsky, 3 vols., Set. 1992. pap. 14.85 o.s.i (*0-440-36046-3*) Dell Publishing.
—Sara Paretsky: Three Complete Novels. 1995. 704p. 13.99 o.s.i (*0-517-14801-3*) Random Hse., Inc.
—The Sara Paretsky Value Collection: Indemnity Only, Blood Shots, & Burn Marks. abr. ed. 2000. audio 29.95 (*0-553-52724-X*, RH Audio) Random Hse. Audio Publishing Group.
—Settled Score. abr. ed. 1998. audio 4.99 (*0-88646-964-3*, 7964) Durkin Hayes Publishing Ltd.
—Skin Deep & Other Stories. unabr. ed. 1994. (V. I. Warshawski Mystery Ser.). audio 16.99 (*0-88646-373-4*, 391592) Durkin Hayes Publishing Ltd.
—Strung Out. unabr. ed. 1997. audio 4.99 (*0-88646-940-6*, 7940) Durkin Hayes Publishing Ltd.
—Three-Dot Po. unabr. ed. 1994. audio 8.95 o.p. (*1-879371-80-4*, 30030) Publishing Mills, Inc., The.
—Total Recall. 2002. 544p. mass mkt. 7.99 (*0-440-22471-3*) Dell Publishing.
—Tunnel Vision. unabr. ed. 1994. (V. I. Warshawski Ser.). audio 80.00 (*0-7366-2842-8*, 3550) Books on Tape, Inc.
—Tunnel Vision. (V.I. Warshawski Novels Ser.). 1995. 480p. mass mkt. 7.50 (*0-440-21752-0*); 1995. E-Book 6.99 (*0-440-33393-8*); 1994. 736p. 26.95 o.s.i (*0-385-31307-1*, Delacorte Pr.) Dell Publishing.
—Tunnel Vision. l.t. ed. 1994. (Large Print Bks.). pap. 22.95 o.p. (*1-56895-084-5*, Wheeler Publishing, Inc.) Gale Group.
—Tunnel Vision. abr. ed. 1993. (V.I. Warshawski Novels Ser.). audio 24.95 o.p. (*1-55800-975-2*, 692333) NewStar Media, Inc.
—Windy City Blues. unabr. ed. 1996. (V. I. Warshawski Ser.). audio 48.00 (*0-7366-3243-3*, 3902) Books on Tape, Inc.
—Windy City Blues. 1996. (V.I. Warshawski Novels Ser.). 352p. mass mkt. 7.99 (*0-440-21873-X*) Dell Publishing.
—Windy City Blues. 1996. pap. 6.99 (*0-440-29546-7*) Doubleday Publishing.
—Windy City Blues. unabr. ed. 1995. (V. I. Warshawski Mystery Ser.). 24.95 o.p. (*0-7871-0478-7*, 693248) NewStar Media, Inc.
—Windy City Blues. l.t. ed. 1996. (Paperback Bestsellers Ser.). 336p. pap. 24.95 (*0-7838-1562-X*); 26.95 (*0-7838-1561-1*) Thorndike Pr.
—A Woman's Eye. 1992. 464p. reprint ed. mass mkt. 6.99 (*0-440-21335-5*) Dell Publishing.
—A Woman's Eye. 1993. 5.99 o.p. (*0-517-11187-X*) Random Hse. Value Publishing.
—Women on the Case: 26 Original Stories by the Best Women Crime Writers of Our Times. 1997. 464p. mass mkt. 7.50 (*0-440-22325-3*) Dell Publishing.
Paretsky, Sara, ed. Beastly Tales. 1995. (Select Sound, Dove Ser.). 4.99 o.p. (*0-7871-0326-8*); 4.99 o.p. (*0-7871-0311-X*) Penguin Group (USA) Inc.
—Beastly Tales. 1989. 17.95 o.p. (*0-922066-14-0*) Wynwood.
Paretsky, Sara, intro. A Woman's Eye. l.t. ed. 1992. (General Ser.). 569p. lib. bdg. 21.95 o.p. (*0-8161-5457-0*, Macmillan Reference USA) Gale Group.
Paretsky, Sara & McCrumb, Sharyn. Lily & the Sockeyes & Happiness Is a Dead Poet. unabr. ed. 1994. audio 4.99 (*0-88646-725-X*) Durkin Hayes Publishing Ltd.
Parker, Robert B. Back Story. 2003. (Spencer Mystery Ser.). 304p. 24.95 (*0-399-14977-5*) Putnam Publishing Group, The.
—Family Honor. 2000. (Sunny Randall Ser.). 338p. mass mkt. 7.50 (*0-425-17706-8*) Berkley Publishing Group.
—Family Honor. l.t. ed. (Wheeler Press Paperback Ser.). 2000. 10.95 (*1-56895-977-X*); 1999. 27.95 (*1-56895-788-2*) Gale Group. (Wheeler Publishing, Inc.).
—Family Honor, Set. abr. ed. 1999. audio 18.00 Highsmith Inc.
—Family Honor. 1999. audio 30.00 (*0-7871-2354-4*); audio compact disk 36.00 (*0-7871-2369-2*); audio 18.00 (*0-7871-2355-2*, Dove Audio); audio 30.00 NewStar Media, Inc.
—Family Honor. l.t. ed. 1999. (Sunny Randall Ser.). 322p. 22.95 o.p. (*0-399-14566-4*, G. P. Putnam's Sons) Penguin Group (USA) Inc.
—Hugger Mugger. 2001. (Spenser Mystery Ser.: Bk. 27). 336p. reprint ed. mass mkt. 7.99 (*0-425-17955-9*) Berkley Publishing Group.
—Hugger Mugger. unabr. ed. 2000. audio 34.95 (*0-7366-4915-8*, 5222) Books on Tape, Inc.
—Hugger Mugger. l.t. ed. 2000. (Spenser Mystery Ser.). 309p. 27.95 (*1-56895-865-X*, Wheeler Publishing, Inc.) Gale Group.
—Hugger Mugger. 2000. (Spenser Mystery Ser.). 320p. 23.95 o.s.i (*0-399-14587-7*) Penguin Group (USA) Inc.
—Hugger Mugger. unabr. ed. 2000. (Spenser Mystery Ser.). audio 29.95 (*0-553-50246-8*); audio compact disk 34.99 (*0-553-45673-3*) Random Hse. Audio Publishing Group. (RH Audio).
—Hush Money. 2000. (Spenser Mystery Ser.). 336p. pap. 7.99 (*0-425-17401-8*) Berkley Publishing Group.
—Hush Money. l.t. ed. 1999. (Spenser Mystery Ser.). 27.95 (*1-56895-739-4*, Wheeler Publishing, Inc.) Gale Group.

—Hush Money. unabr. ed. 1999. (Spenser Mystery Ser.). audio 30.00 (*0-7871-1870-2*, 890100) NewStar Media, Inc.

—Hush Money. 1999. (Spenser Mystery Ser.). 336p. 22.95 o.p. (*0-399-14458-7*) Penguin Group (USA) Inc.

—Hush Money. 2000. 13.55 (*0-606-20394-X*); 13.55 (*0-606-20098-3*) Turtleback Bks.

—Mortal Stakes. 2002. (Best Mysteries of All Time Ser.). 288p. (*0-7621-8875-8*, Impress) Scriptorium Pr., The.

—Perchance to Dream. 1993. 288p. mass mkt. 6.99 o.s.i (*0-425-13131-9*) Berkley Publishing Group.

—Perchance to Dream. unabr. ed. 1994. (Spenser Ser.). audio 30.00 (*0-7366-2694-8*, 3428) Books on Tape, Inc.

—Perchance to Dream. abr. ed. 1993. 15.95 o.p. (*1-55800-291-X*, 41250) NewStar Media, Inc.

—Perchance to Dream. 1991. (Spenser Thriller Ser.). 272p. 19.95 o.p. (*0-399-13580-4*, G. P. Putnam's Sons) Penguin Group (USA) Inc.

—Perish Twice. 2001. 352p. reprint ed. mass mkt. 7.99 (*0-425-18215-0*) Berkley Publishing Group.

—Perish Twice. l.t. ed. (Wheeler Press Paperback Ser.). 2001. 12.95 (*1-56895-180-9*); 2000. 279p. 28.95 (*1-56895-992-3*) Gale Group. (Wheeler Publishing, Inc.).

—Perish Twice. 2000. 320p. 23.95 o.s.i (*0-399-14668-7*) Penguin Group (USA) Inc.

—Potshot. l.t. ed. 2001. 359p. (*0-7540-1661-7*); (*0-7540-9075-2*) BBC Audiobooks America.

—Potshot. 2002. 352p. reprint ed. mass mkt. 7.99 (*0-425-18288-6*) Berkley Publishing Group.

—Potshot. 2001. (Spenser Ser.). 294p. 23.95 o.p. (*0-399-14710-1*) Penguin Group (USA) Inc.

—Potshot. l.t. ed. (Paperback Bestsellers Ser.). 2002. 359p. pap. 29.95 (*0-7862-3237-4*); 2001. 407p. 32.95 (*0-7862-3232-3*) Thorndike Pr.

—Shrink Rap. 2003. 352p. mass mkt. 7.99 (*0-515-13620-4*, Jove) Berkley Publishing Group.

—Shrink Rap. 2002. 320p. 24.95 o.s.i (*0-399-14930-9*, Putnam & Grosset) Putnam Publishing Group, The.

—Sudden Mischief. l.t. ed. 1998. (Spenser Mystery Ser.). 27.95 (*1-56895-569-3*, Wheeler Publishing, Inc.) Gale Group.

—Sudden Mischief. 1998. 22.95 o.s.i (*0-399-14696-2*); 304p. 22.95 o.p. incl. audio (*0-399-14370-X*, G. P. Putnam's Sons); 304p. 22.95 o.p. incl. audio (*0-399-14370-X*, G. P. Putnam's Sons) Penguin Group (USA) Inc.

—Widow's Walk. 2002. 320p. 24.95 o.s.i (*0-399-14845-0*) Putnam Publishing Group, The.

Parker, Robert B. & Chandler, Raymond. Poodle Springs & Pastime. abr. ed. 1999. audio 25.00 (*0-7871-1894-X*, Dove Audio) NewStar Media, Inc.

Parker, Robert B. & Cohen, Stan. Sudden Mischief. 1999. (Spenser Mystery Ser.). 306p. reprint ed. pap. 7.99 (*0-425-16828-X*) Berkley Publishing Group.

Parrish, P. J. Paint It Black. 2002. 416p. mass mkt. 6.99 (*0-7860-1419-9*, Pinnacle Bks.) Kensington Publishing Corp.

Patterson, James. Cradle & All. l.t. ed. 2000. (Large Print Book Ser.). 305p. 31.95 (*1-56895-879-X*, Wheeler Publishing, Inc.) Gale Group.

—Cradle & All. 2000. 368p. 25.95 o.p. (*0-316-69061-9*) Little Brown & Co.

—Cradle & All. 2001. 384p. reprint ed. mass mkt. 7.99 (*0-446-60940-4*) Warner Bks., Inc.

Pelecanos, George P. Hard Revolution. 2004. 384p. 24.95 (*0-316-60897-1*) Little Brown & Co.

—Hard Revolution. abr. ed. 2004. audio 25.98 (*1-58621-600-7*); audio compact disk 31.98 (*1-58621-601-5*) Time Warner AudioBooks.

—Hell to Pay. 2002. E-Book 14.95 (*0-7595-8686-1*); 352p. 24.95 o.p. (*0-316-69506-8*) Little Brown & Co.

—Hell to Pay. l.t. ed. 2003. 536p. 30.45 (*0-7862-5615-X*) Thorndike Pr.

—Hell to Pay. 2003. 416p. mass mkt. 6.99 (*0-446-61132-8*) Warner Bks., Inc.

—Right As Rain. 2001. 336p. 24.95 (*0-316-69526-2*) Little Brown & Co.

—Right As Rain. l.t. ed. 2003. 525p. 30.45 (*0-7862-5609-5*) Thorndike Pr.

—Right As Rain. 2002. 384p. reprint ed. mass mkt. 6.99 (*0-446-61079-8*) Warner Bks., Inc.

Pendleton, Don. Copp for Hire. 1987. 272p. 16.95 o.p. (*1-55611-064-2*) Fine, Donald I. Bks.

—Copp in Deep. 1989. 252p. 17.95 o.p. (*1-55611-141-X*) Fine, Donald I. Bks.

—Copp in Deep. 1991. 256p. mass mkt. 4.50 o.p. (*0-06-100248-8*, HarperTorch) Morrow/Avon.

—Copp in Shock. 1992. 256p. 19.95 o.p. (*1-55611-287-4*) Fine, Donald I. Bks.

—Copp in Shock. 1993. 256p. mass mkt. 4.99 o.p. (*0-06-100459-6*, HarperTorch) Morrow/Avon.

—Copp in the Dark. l.t. ed. 1991. 19.95 o.p. (*0-7927-0982-9*, CH0157); pap. 17.95 o.p. (*0-7927-0983-7*, CS0256) BBC Audiobooks America.

—Copp in the Dark. 1990. (Joe Copp Ser.: No. 4). 18.95 o.p. (*1-55611-210-6*) Fine, Donald I. Bks.

—Copp in the Dark. 1992. 256p. mass mkt. 4.99 o.p. (*0-06-100347-6*, HarperTorch) Morrow/Avon.

—Copp on Fire. 1988. 16.95 o.p. (*1-55611-088-X*) Fine, Donald I. Bks.

—Copp on Fire. 1990. 256p. mass mkt. 4.50 o.p. (*0-06-100036-1*, HarperTorch) Morrow/Avon.

—Copp on Ice. 1991. 18.95 o.p. (*1-55611-235-1*) Fine, Donald I. Bks.

—Copp on Ice. 1992. 240p. mass mkt. 4.99 o.p. (*0-06-100458-8*, HarperTorch) Morrow/Avon.

Perry, Anne. Death of a Stranger. 2003. 352p. mass mkt. 7.50 (*0-345-44006-4*); 2002. 352p. 25.95 (*0-345-44005-6*, Ballantine Bks.); 2002. E-Book 18.00 (*0-345-45865-6*, Ballantine Bks.) Ballantine Bks.

—Death of a Stranger. l.t. ed. 2003. (Basic Ser.). 570p. 32.95 (*0-7862-4939-0*) Thorndike Pr.

—Funeral in Blue. 2001. 352p. 25.00 (*0-345-44001-3*, Ballantine Bks.) Ballantine Bks.

—Funeral in Blue. l.t. ed. 2002. (Basic Ser.). 574p. 30.95 (*0-7862-3640-X*) Gale Group.

—Slaves of Obsession. l.t. ed. 2000. (Large Print Bks.). 482p. 27.95 (*1-56895-945-1*, Wheeler Publishing, Inc.) Gale Group.

Phillips, Gary. Only the Wicked. 2000. 342p. 24.95 (*1-885173-64-4*) Write Way Publishing.

Pierce, David M. Angels in Heaven. 1992. 240p. 17.95 o.p. (*0-89296-483-9*) Mysterious Pr.

—Angels in Heaven. 1993. 208p. mass mkt. 4.99 (*0-446-40163-3*, Mysterious Pr. Paperback Bks.) Warner Bks., Inc.

—As She Rides By. 1996. 224p. 20.95 o.p. (*0-312-13924-1*, Saint Martin's Minotaur) St. Martin's Pr.

—Down in the Valley. 1990. 224p. pap. 4.95 o.p. (*0-14-011411-4*, Penguin Bks.) Viking Penguin.

—Hear the Wind Blow, Dear. 1990. 192p. pap. 4.95 o.p. (*0-14-011413-0*, Penguin Bks.) Viking Penguin.

—Roses Love Sunshine. 1990. 240p. pap. 4.95 o.p. (*0-14-011414-9*, Penguin Bks.) Viking Penguin.

—Write Me a Letter. 1993. 272p. 18.95 (*0-89296-484-7*) Mysterious Pr.

Pincus, Elizabeth. The Hangdog Hustle. 1995. (Neil Fury Ser.). 205p. (Orig.). pap. 9.95 (*1-883523-05-2*) Spinsters Ink Bks.

—The Solitary Twist. 1993. (Neil Fury Ser.). 225p. (Orig.). pap. 9.95 (*0-933216-93-9*) Spinsters Ink Bks.

—The Two Bit Tango. 1992. (Neil Fury Ser.). (Illus.). 193p. (Orig.). pap. 9.95 (*0-933216-88-2*) Spinsters Ink Bks.

Pirie, David. The Patient's Eyes Murder Rooms: The Dark Beginnings of Sherlock Holmes. 2002. (Illus.). 252p. 23.95 (*0-312-29095-0*, Saint Martin's Minotaur) St. Martin's Pr.

Pronzini, Bill. Bindlestiff. 1983. 208p. 11.95 o.p. (*0-312-07864-1*) St. Martin's Pr.

—Bleeders. l.t. ed. 2002. 352p. 30.45 (*0-7862-4119-5*) Gale Group.

—Blowback. 1983. 149p. reprint ed. pap. 4.95 o.p. (*0-88150-034-8*) Countryman Pr.

—Blowback. 1977. 6.95 o.p. (*0-394-40793-8*) Random Hse., Inc.

—Bones. l.t. ed. 1991. 21.95 o.p. (*0-7927-0937-3*, CH0147); pap. 19.95 o.p. (*0-7927-0938-1*, CS0244) BBC Audiobooks America.

—Bones. 1985. (Nameless Detective Ser.). 224p. 12.95 o.p. (*0-312-08769-1*, 087691) St. Martin's Pr.

—Boobytrap: A "Nameless Detective" Mystery. 1998. (Nameless Detective Mystery Ser.). 256p. 23.00 (*0-7867-0505-1*, Carroll & Graf Pubs.) Avalon Publishing Group.

—Boobytrap: A "Nameless Detective" Mystery. unabr. ed. 1999. ("Nameless Detective" Mystery Ser.). audio 54.95 (*0-7927-2269-8*, CSL158, Chivers Sound Library) BBC Audiobooks America.

—Boobytrap: A "Nameless Detective" Mystery. l.t. ed. 1999. (Mystery Ser.). 317p. 28.95 (*0-7862-1718-9*) Thorndike Pr.

—Breakdown. l.t. ed. 1992. 19.95 o.p. (*0-7927-1050-9*); pap. 17.95 o.p. (*0-7927-1051-7*) BBC Audiobooks America.

—Breakdown. 1991. 256p. mass mkt. 4.50 o.s.i (*0-440-21157-3*) Dell Publishing.

—Crazybone: A "Nameless Detective" Mystery. l.t. ed. 2000. (Mystery Ser.). 317p. 29.95 (*0-7862-2694-3*) Thorndike Pr.

—Deadfall. 1986. 272p. 15.95 o.p. (*0-312-18525-1*) St. Martin's Pr.

—Demons: A "Nameless Detective" Mystery. 1994. 288p. mass mkt. 4.99 o.s.i (*0-440-21118-2*) Dell Publishing.

—Demons: A "Nameless Detective" Mystery. l.t. ed. 1994. 65.95 o.p. (*0-7862-9982-7*, Macmillan Reference USA) Gale Group.

—Dragonfire: A "Nameless Detective" Mystery. 1982. 208p. 10.95 o.p. (*0-312-21893-1*) St. Martin's Pr.

—Epitaphs: A "Nameless Detective" Mystery. 1993. 304p. mass mkt. 4.99 o.s.i (*0-440-21117-4*); 1992. 240p. 19.00 o.s.i (*0-385-30504-4*, Delacorte Pr.) Dell Publishing.

—Hoodwink: A "Nameless Detective" Mystery. l.t. ed. 1990. pap. 17.95 o.p. (*0-7927-0193-3*, C0242) BBC Audiobooks America.

—Hoodwink: A "Nameless Detective" Mystery. 1981. 238p. 10.95 o.p. (*0-312-38969-8*) St. Martin's Pr.

—Illusions: A "Nameless Detective" Mystery. 1997. 256p. 23.00 o.p. (*0-7867-0403-9*, Carroll & Graf Pubs.) Avalon Publishing Group.

—Illusions: A "Nameless Detective" Mystery. unabr. ed. 2000. (Nameless Detective Mystery Ser.). audio 49.95 (*0-7927-2234-5*, CSL 123) Chivers Audio Bks. GBR. *Dist:* BBC Audiobooks America.

—Illusions: A "Nameless Detective" Mystery. 1999. 254p. lib. bdg. 26.95 (*0-7351-0222-8*) Replica Bks.

—Jackpot. 1990. 240p. reprint ed. mass mkt. 3.95 o.s.i (*0-440-20821-1*) Dell Publishing.

—Jackpot. l.t. ed. 1991. (General Ser.). 342p. lib. bdg. 20.95 (*0-8161-5037-0*, Macmillan Reference USA) Gale Group.

—Labyrinth. 2001. 186p. pap. 12.95 (*1-931755-01-9*) Mystery Vault, Inc.

—Labyrinth. 1980. 8.95 o.p. (*0-312-46352-9*) St. Martin's Pr.

—The Nameless Detective: Dragonfire-Bindlestiff. 1990. pap. 5.95 (*1-877961-15-9*) Knightsbridge Publishing.

—The Nameless Detective: Hoodwink & Scattershot. 1990. 560p. reprint ed. pap. 5.95 (*1-877961-94-9*) Knightsbridge Publishing.

—The Nameless Detective: Labyrinth & Bones. 1990. 560p. pap. 5.95 (*1-877961-92-2*) Knightsbridge Publishing.

—Nightshades: A "Nameless Detective" Mystery. 1984. 208p. 11.95 o.p. (*0-312-57338-3*) St. Martin's Pr.

—Quarry: A "Nameless Detective" Mystery. l.t. ed. 1992. 22.95 o.p. (*0-7927-1392-3*); pap. 20.95 o.p. (*0-7927-1391-5*) BBC Audiobooks America.

—Quarry: A "Nameless Detective" Mystery. 1992. 224p. mass mkt. 4.99 o.s.i (*0-440-21116-6*) Dell Publishing.

—Quicksilver: A "Nameless Detective" Mystery. 1984. 192p. 11.95 o.p. (*0-312-66081-2*) St. Martin's Pr.

—Scattershot: A "Nameless Detective" Mystery. l.t. ed. 1989. 18.95 o.p. (*1-55504-833-1*, 296) BBC Audiobooks America.

—Scattershot: A "Nameless Detective" Mystery. 1983. 176p. pap. 5.95 o.p. (*0-312-70047-4*, Saint Martin's Griffin) St. Martin's Pr.

—Sentinels: A "Nameless Detective" Mystery. 1996. 288p. 20.00 (*0-7867-0311-3*); 2002. 224p. reprint ed. pap. 11.00 (*0-7867-1014-4*) Avalon Publishing Group. (Carroll & Graf Pubs.).

—Sentinels: A "Nameless Detective" Mystery. l.t. ed. 1996. lib. bdg. 23.95 (*1-57490-074-9*, Beeler Large Print Bks.) Beeler, Thomas T. Publisher.

—Shackles: A "Nameless Detective" Mystery. 1988. 272p. 16.95 o.p. (*0-312-01818-5*, Saint Martin's Minotaur) St. Martin's Pr.

—The Snatch. 1984. (Nameless Detective Mystery Ser.). reprint ed. pap. 4.95 o.p. (*0-88150-021-6*) Countryman Pr.

—Spook. 2003. (Mystery Ser.). 366p. 30.95 (*0-7862-5307-X*) Thorndike Pr.

—Spook: A Nameless Detective Novel. 2002. 224p. 25.00 (*0-7867-1086-1*, Carroll & Graf Pubs.) Avalon Publishing Group.

—Undercurrent. 1984. 213p. pap. 4.95 o.p. (*0-88150-033-X*) Countryman Pr.

—The Vanished. 1984. (Nameless Detective Mystery Ser.). reprint ed. pap. 4.95 o.p. (*0-88150-022-4*) Countryman Pr.

—The Vanished. 1974. pap. 0.95 o.p. (*0-671-77714-9*, Pocket) Simon & Schuster.

—The Vanished. l.t. ed. 1999. (G. K. Hall Nightingale Ser.). 236p. pap. 20.95 (*0-7838-8766-3*) Thorndike Pr.

Pronzini, Bill & Wilcox, Collin. Two-Spot. 1993. 272p. mass mkt. 12.95 (*0-7867-0042-4*, Carroll & Graf Pubs.) Avalon Publishing Group.

—Two-Spot. 1978. 8.95 o.p. (*0-399-12129-3*) Putnam Publishing Group, The.

Pryor, Josh. Monkey in the Middle. 2003. 288p. 24.00 (*0-7867-1173-6*, Carroll & Graf Pubs.) Avalon Publishing Group.

Pye, Michael. Taking Lives. 2004. 304p. pap. 13.00 (*1-4000-7573-4*, Vintage) Knopf Publishing Group.

—Taking Lives. l.t. ed. 1999. (Basic Ser.). 535p. 27.95 (*0-7862-2096-1*) Thorndike Pr.

Queen, Ellery. The King Is Dead. l.t. ed. 2000. (G. K. Hall Paperback Ser.). 328p. pap. 23.95 (*0-7838-9282-9*, Macmillan Reference USA) Gale Group.

—The King Is Dead. 1994. (Ellery Queen Mystery Ser.). 224p. reprint ed. pap. 8.00 o.p. (*0-06-097605-5*, Perennial) HarperTrade.

—The King Is Dead. mass mkt. 0.25 o.p. (*0-451-00629-1*); 1977. mass mkt. 1.25 o.p. (*0-451-07361-4*); 1972. mass mkt. 0.95 o.p. (*0-451-05290-0*) NAL. (Signet Bks.).

—A Study in Terror. l.t. ed. 2001. 192p. pap. 24.95 (*0-7838-9485-6*); (*0-7540-4586-2*) Gale Group. (Macmillan Reference USA).

Quick, Amanda, pseud. Slightly Shady. l.t. ed. 2001. (Large Print Book Ser.). 391p. 31.95 (*1-58724-026-2*, Wheeler Publishing, Inc.) Gale Group.

Raleigh, Michael. A Body in Belmont Harbor. 1993. 277p. 17.95 o.p. (*0-312-08707-1*, Saint Martin's Minotaur) St. Martin's Pr.

—A Body in Belmont Harbor. 2000. (Paul Whelan Mystery Ser.). 292p. pap. 15.95 (*0-595-09340-X*) iUniverse, Inc.

—Death in Uptown. 2000. (Paul Whelan Mystery Ser.). 256p. pap. 14.95 (*0-595-09341-8*) iUniverse, Inc.

—Death in Uptown: A Paul Whelan Mystery. 1991. 17.95 o.p. (*0-312-05849-7*, Saint Martin's Minotaur) St. Martin's Pr.

—Killer on Argyle Street. 2000. (Paul Whelan Mystery Ser.). 256p. pap. 14.95 (*0-595-09343-4*) iUniverse, Inc.

—Killer on Argyle Street: A Chicago Mystery Featuring Paul Whelan. 1995. 298p. 21.95 o.p. (*0-312-13532-7*, Saint Martin's Minotaur) St. Martin's Pr.

—The Maxwell Street Blues. 1994. 280p. 20.95 o.p. (*0-312-11394-3*, Saint Martin's Minotaur) St. Martin's Pr.

—The Maxwell Street Blues. 2000. (Paul Whelan Mystery Ser.). 288p. pap. 15.95 (*0-595-09342-6*) iUniverse, Inc.

—The Riverview Murders. 1997. 213p. 21.95 o.p. (*0-312-15641-3*, Saint Martin's Minotaur) St. Martin's Pr.

Ramos, Manuel. Moony's Road to Hell. 2002. 208p. 19.95 (*0-8263-2949-7*) Univ. of New Mexico Pr.

Rand, Naomi R. Stealing for a Living. 2003. 256p. 23.95 (*0-06-019936-9*) HarperCollins Pubs.

Randisi, Robert J. The Dead of Brooklyn: A Nick Delvecchio Mystery. pap. 12.95 (*1-931755-19-1*) Mystery Vault, Inc.

—The Dead of Brooklyn: A Nick Delvecchio Mystery. 1991. 272p. 18.95 o.p. (*0-312-06330-X*, Saint Martin's Minotaur) St. Martin's Pr.

—The Dead of Brooklyn: A Nick Delvecchio Mystery. l.t. ed. 2002. (Mystery Ser.). 341p. 28.95 (*0-7862-4399-6*) Thorndike Pr.

—Delvecchio's Brooklyn: A Short Story Collection. l.t. ed. 2001. 207p. 23.95 (*0-7862-3044-4*, Five Star) Gale Group.

—Eye in the Ring. 1986. 256p. pap. 2.75 o.p. (*0-380-81455-2*, 81455-2, Avon Bks.) Morrow/Avon.

—Full Contact: A Miles Jacoby Mystery. l.t. ed. 1988. pap. 14.95 o.p. (*1-55504-699-1*, 827) BBC Audiobooks America.

—Full Contact: A Miles Jacoby Mystery. 2000. mass mkt. 2.95 (*0-380-69984-2*, Avon Bks.) Morrow/Avon.

—Full Contact: A Miles Jacoby Mystery. 1984. 256p. 13.95 o.p. (*0-312-30966-X*) St. Martin's Pr.

—Hard Look: A Miles Jacoby Mystery. 1993. (Miles Jacoby Mystery Ser.). 252p. 21.00 o.s.i (*0-8027-1251-7*) Walker & Co.

—No Exit from Brooklyn: A Nick Delvecchio Mystery. 1989. mass mkt. 3.95 (*0-8125-0825-4*, Tor Bks.) Doherty, Tom Assocs., LLC.

—No Exit from Brooklyn: A Nick Delvecchio Mystery. l.t. ed. 2002. (Mystery Ser.). 408p. 28.95 o.p. (*0-7862-3886-0*) Gale Group.

—No Exit from Brooklyn: A Nick Delvecchio Mystery. 2001. 277p. reprint ed. pap. 12.95 (*1-931755-13-2*) Mystery Vault, Inc.

—No Exit from Brooklyn: A Nick Delvecchio Mystery. 1987. 288p. 16.95 o.p. (*0-312-00169-X*) St. Martin's Pr.

—Separate Cases. 1990. 192p. 18.95 (*0-8027-5723-5*) Walker & Co.

—Stand-Up: A Miles Jacoby Mystery. 1994. 246p. 20.95 o.p. (*0-8027-3196-1*) Walker & Co.

—The Steinway Collection. 1986. 272p. pap. 2.75 o.p. (*0-380-85175-X*, 85175, Avon Bks.) Morrow/Avon.

Rathbone, Julian. Homage. 2002. 215p. pap. 9.95 (*0-7490-0567-X*) Allison & Busby, Ltd. GBR. *Dist:* International Publishers Marketing.

Redmann, J. M. Death by the Riverside. 1990. 256p. (Orig.). pap. 9.95 o.p. (*0-934678-27-8*) New Victoria Pubs., Inc.

—Death of Jocasta. 1992. 288p. (Orig.). pap. 10.95 o.p. (*0-934678-39-1*) New Victoria Pubs., Inc.

—The Intersection of Law & Desire. 1997. mass mkt. 5.99 (*0-380-72819-2*, Avon Bks.) Morrow/Avon.

—The Intersection of Law & Desire. 1995. 336p. 22.00 o.p. (*0-393-03793-2*) Norton, W. W. & Co., Inc.

—Lost Daughters: A Micky Knight Mystery. 1999. (Mickey Knight Mystery Ser.). 320p. text 24.95 o.p. (*0-393-04028-3*) Norton, W. W. & Co., Inc.

Riccardi, Theodore. The Oriental Casebook of Sherlock Holmes. 2003. 320p. 23.95 (*1-4000-6065-6*) Random House Adult Trade Publishing Group.

Rickards, John. Winter's End. mass mkt. (*0-312-98795-1*, St. Martin's Paperbacks); 2003. 304p. 23.95 (*0-312-31097-8*) St. Martin's Pr.

Ripley, W. L. Dreamsicle. unabr. ed. 1993. 57.25 o.p. incl. audio (*1-56100-149-X*, 1189, Unabridged Library Editions); audio 21.95 o.p. (*1-56100-516-9*, 341, Bookcassette) Brilliance Audio.
—Dreamsicle. 1993. 267p. 19.95 o.p. (*0-316-74726-2*) Little Brown & Co.
—Electric Country Roulette: A Wyatt Storme Mystery. 1996. 88p. 25.00 o.p. (*0-8050-3792-6*) Holt, Henry & Co.
—Storme Front. 1995. 340p. 22.50 o.p. (*0-8050-3601-6*) Holt, Henry & Co.
Roat, Ronald C. Close Softly the Doors. (Stuart Mallory Mystery Ser.). 1993. 148p. pap. 12.95 (*0-934257-96-5*); 2nd ed. 1991. 160p. 18.95 (*0-934257-48-5*) Story Line Pr.
—High Walk. 1996. (Stuart Mallory Mystery Ser.). 288p. 17.95 (*1-885266-16-2*) Story Line Pr.
—A Still & Icy Silence. 1993. (Stuart Mallory Mystery Ser.). 303p. 21.95 (*0-934257-94-9*) Story Line Pr.
Roberts, David. Bones of the Buried. 2001. 352p. 22.00 (*0-7867-0908-1*, Carroll & Graf Pubs.) Avalon Publishing Group.
Roberts, Gillian. Time & Trouble. 1999. 336p. mass mkt. 5.99 (*0-312-96996-1*, St. Martin's Paperbacks); 1998. 384p. 24.95 (*0-312-18673-8*, Saint Martin's Minotaur) St. Martin's Pr.
—Whatever Doesn't Kill You: An Emma Howe & Billie August Mystery. 2001. 312p. 23.95 (*0-312-26269-8*, Saint Martin's Minotaur) St. Martin's Pr.
Roberts, John Maddox. Desperate Highways. 1997. 304p. 23.95 o.p. (*0-312-17176-5*, Saint Martin's Minotaur) St. Martin's Pr.
—Ghosts of Saigon. 1996. 288p. 21.95 o.p. (*0-312-14345-1*, Saint Martin's Minotaur) St. Martin's Pr.
—The Tribune's Curse. 2003. (SPQR Ser.: No. VII). (Illus.). 224p. 22.95 o.s.i (*0-312-30488-9*, Saint Martin's Minotaur) St. Martin's Pr.
—A Typical American Town. 1994. 256p. 20.95 o.p. (*0-312-11359-5*, Saint Martin's Minotaur) St. Martin's Pr.
—A Typical American Town. l.t. ed. 1996. (Ulverscroft Large Print Ser.). 480p. 29.99 o.p. (*0-7089-3507-9*, Ulverscroft) Thorpe, F. A. Pubs. GBR. *Dist:* Ulverscroft Large Print Bks., Ltd., Ulverscroft Large Print Canada, Ltd.
Roberts, Les. The Best-Kept Secret. (Milan Jacovich Mysteries Ser.). 2000. 311p. mass mkt. 5.99 (*0-312-97126-5*, St. Martin's Paperbacks); 1999. 308p. 23.95 (*0-312-20499-X*, Saint Martin's Minotaur) St. Martin's Pr.
—A Carrot for the Donkey: A Saxon Mystery. 1989. 256p. 16.95 o.p. (*0-312-02554-8*, Saint Martin's Minotaur) St. Martin's Pr.
—The Cleveland Connection. (Milan Jacovich Mysteries Ser.). 1997. 336p. mass mkt. 5.99 o.s.i (*0-312-96218-5*, St. Martin's Paperbacks); 1993. 294p. 19.95 (*0-312-08746-2*, Saint Martin's Minotaur) St. Martin's Pr.
—Cleveland Local. 1998. (Milan Jacovich Mysteries Ser.). 288p. mass mkt. 5.99 (*0-312-96678-4*, St. Martin's Paperbacks) St. Martin's Pr.
—The Cleveland Local. 1997. (Milan Jacovich Mysteries Ser.). 288p. 22.95 o.p. (*0-312-16801-2*, Saint Martin's Minotaur) St. Martin's Pr.
—Collision Bend. (Milan Jacovich Mysteries Ser.). 1997. 288p. mass mkt. 5.99 (*0-312-96399-8*, St. Martin's Paperbacks); 1996. 320p. 22.95 o.p. (*0-312-14570-5*, Saint Martin's Minotaur) St. Martin's Pr.
—Deep Shaker. 1992. mass mkt. 3.99 (*0-312-92795-9*, St. Martin's Paperbacks); 1991. 17.95 o.p. (*0-312-05855-1*, Saint Martin's Minotaur) St. Martin's Pr.
—The Duke of Cleveland: A Milan Jacovich Mystery. 1995. 272p. 21.95 o.p. (*0-312-13473-8*, Saint Martin's Minotaur) St. Martin's Pr.
—The Dutch. l.t. ed. 2002. 28.95 (*0-7862-4096-2*) Gale Group.
—The Dutch. mass mkt. (*0-312-98028-0*, St. Martin's Paperbacks); 2001. 293p. 23.95 (*0-312-26579-4*, Saint Martin's Minotaur) St. Martin's Pr.
—Full Cleveland. 1990. mass mkt. 3.95 (*0-312-92345-7*, St. Martin's Paperbacks); 1989. 224p. 15.95 o.p. (*0-312-03349-4*, Saint Martin's Minotaur) St. Martin's Pr.
—The Indian Sign. E-Book 23.95 (*0-312-27594-3*); 2001. 304p. mass mkt. 6.50 (*0-312-97646-1*, St. Martin's Paperbacks); 2000. 274p. 23.95 (*0-312-25217-X*, Saint Martin's Minotaur) St. Martin's Pr.
—An Infinite Number of Monkeys. 1988. mass mkt. 2.95 (*0-312-91095-9*, St. Martin's Paperbacks); 1987. 176p. 12.95 o.p. (*0-312-00610-1*) St. Martin's Pr.
—Irish Sports Pages. mass mkt. (*0-312-98380-8*, St. Martin's Paperbacks); 2002. 304p. 23.95 (*0-312-28661-9*, Saint Martin's Minotaur) St. Martin's Pr.
—The Lake Effect: A Milan Jacovich Mystery. 1994. 352p. 21.95 (*0-312-11537-7*, Saint Martin's Minotaur) St. Martin's Pr.
—The Lemon Chicken Jones. 1993. 288p. 20.95 o.p. (*0-312-10490-1*, Saint Martin's Minotaur) St. Martin's Pr.
—Not Enough Horses. 1988. 224p. mass mkt. 3.50 o.p. (*0-312-91225-0*, St. Martin's Paperbacks); 256p. 15.95 o.p. (*0-312-01485-6*, Saint Martin's Minotaur) St. Martin's Pr.
—Pepper Pike. (Milan Jacovich Mysteries Ser.). 1988. 240p. 15.95 o.p. (*0-312-02266-2*, Saint Martin's Minotaur); Vol. 1. 1990. 232p. mass mkt. 5.99 o.s.i (*0-312-92213-2*, St. Martin's Paperbacks) St. Martin's Pr.
—Seeing the Elephant. 1992. 352p. 18.95 o.p. (*0-312-07081-0*, Saint Martin's Minotaur) St. Martin's Pr.
—A Shoot in Cleveland. (Milan Jacovich Mysteries Ser.). 1999. 336p. mass mkt. 5.99 (*0-312-96694-6*, St. Martin's Paperbacks); 1999. E-Book 5.99 o.s.i (*0-312-20742-5*); 1998. 368p. 23.95 o.p. (*0-312-18663-0*, Saint Martin's Minotaur) St. Martin's Pr.
—Snake Oil. 1990. 17.95 o.p. (*0-312-04424-0*, Saint Martin's Minotaur) St. Martin's Pr.
Roberts, Lora. The Affair of the Incognito Tenant: A Mystery with Sherlock Holmes. 2003. 264p. pap. 13.95 (*1-880284-67-7*) Daniel, John & Co., Pubs.
Robinson, Spider. Callahan's Lady. 1990. mass mkt. 4.99 o.s.i (*0-441-09072-9*); 11th ed. 1989. 16.95 o.p. (*0-441-09073-7*) Ace Bks.
—Callahan's Lady. 2001. 320p. pap. 6.99 (*0-671-31831-4*) Baen Bks.
—Lady Slings the Booze. 272p. 1993. mass mkt. 5.99 o.s.i (*0-441-46929-9*); 1992. 18.95 o.p. (*0-441-46928-0*) Ace Bks.
Roby, Kinley. Death in a Hammock. 2003. 266p. 25.95 (*0-7862-5396-7*, Five Star) Gale Group.
Roddy, Lee. Days of Deception. 1998. (Pinkerton Lady Chronicles Ser.: 1). 320p. (*1-56476-686-1*) Cook Communications Ministries.
—Days of Deception. l.t. ed. 2002. (Pinkerton Lady Chronicles: No. 1). 477p. pap. 16.95 (*1-4104-0018-2*, Walker Large Print) Gale Group.
—Days of Deception. l.t. ed. 2001. (Pinkerton Lady Chronicles Ser.). 477p. 23.95 (*0-7862-3186-6*) Thorndike Pr.
—Tomorrow's Promise. l.t. ed. 2001. (Christian Mystery Ser.). 465p. 23.95 (*0-7862-3207-2*) Thorndike Pr.
—Yesterday's Shadows. (Pinkerton Lady Chronicles Ser.: 2). 320p. pap. 10.99 (*1-56476-635-7*); 335p. pap. 10.99 (*1-56476-687-X*) Cook Communications Ministries.
—Yesterday's Shadows. l.t. ed. 2002. (Pinkerton Lady Chronicles: No. 2). 470p. pap. 16.95 (*1-4104-0037-9*, Walker Large Print) Gale Group.
—Yesterday's Shadows. l.t. ed. 2001. (Pinkerton Lady Chronicles Ser.). 467p. 23.95 (*0-7862-3208-0*) Thorndike Pr.
Rosen, Richard D. Fadeaway. 1986. 256p. 15.95 o.p. (*0-06-015599-X*) HarperTrade.
—Fadeaway. 1987. mass mkt. 3.95 o.p. (*0-451-40046-1*); 288p. mass mkt. 3.95 o.p. (*0-451-40148-4*) NAL. (Onyx).
—Saturday Night Dead. 1989. mass mkt. 3.95 o.p. (*0-451-40134-4*, Onyx) NAL.
—Saturday Night Dead. 1988. 28p. 16.95 o.p. (*0-670-81977-8*) Viking Penguin.
—Strike Three, You're Dead. l.t. ed. 1986. 19.95 o.p. (*1-55504-143-4*) BBC Audiobooks America.
—Strike Three, You're Dead. 1986. 256p. mass mkt. 3.95 o.p. (*0-451-40142-5*, Onyx); mass mkt. 2.95 o.p. (*0-451-14233-0*, Signet Bks.) NAL.
—Strike Three, You're Dead. 1984. 192p. 12.95 o.s.i (*0-8027-5587-9*) Walker & Co.
—World of Hurt. 1994. 264p. 20.95 (*0-8027-3251-8*) Walker & Co.
Ross, Clarissa. Out of the Fog. l.t. ed. 2002. 268p. 27.95 (*0-7862-4037-7*) Gale Group.
Rowland, Laura Joh. Bundori. 1997. 432p. mass mkt. 6.99 (*0-06-101197-5*, HarperTorch) Morrow/Avon.
—The Concubine's Tattoo. 2000. 384p. mass mkt. 6.99 (*0-312-96922-8*, St. Martin's Paperbacks); 1999. E-Book 6.50 (*0-312-24607-2*); 1998. 336p. 23.95 o.p. (*0-312-19252-5*, Saint Martin's Minotaur) St. Martin's Pr.
—The Samurai's Wife. 2000. 203p. 23.95 (*0-312-20325-X*, Saint Martin's Minotaur) St. Martin's Pr.
—Shinju. Date not set. 384p. mass mkt. (*0-06-101035-9*); 1996. 448p. mass mkt. 6.99 (*0-06-100950-4*) Morrow/Avon. (HarperTorch).
—The Way of the Traitor. 1998. 384p. mass mkt. 6.99 (*0-06-101090-1*) HarperCollins Pubs.
Rozan, S. J. A Bitter Feast. 1998. 320p. 23.95 o.p. (*0-312-19259-2*, Saint Martin's Minotaur); 1999. 336p. reprint ed. mass mkt. 5.99 (*0-312-97011-0*, St. Martin's Paperbacks) St. Martin's Pr.
—A Bitter Feast. l.t. ed. 1999. (Mystery Ser.). 519p. 27.95 (*0-7862-1773-1*) Thorndike Pr.
—A Bitter Feast: A Bill Smith-Lydia Chin Mystery. unabr. ed. 1999. audio 69.95 (*0-7927-2280-9*, CSL169, Chivers Sound Library) BBC Audiobooks America.
—Concourse: A Bill Smith-Lydia Chin Mystery. unabr. ed. 1998. audio 69.95 (*0-7927-2245-0*, CSL134, Chivers Sound Library) BBC Audiobooks America.
—Concourse: A Bill Smith-Lydia Chin Mystery. 3rd ed. 1996. (Lydia Chin, Bill Smith Mystery Ser.: Vol. 2). 291p. mass mkt. 6.50 (*0-312-95944-3*, St. Martin's Paperbacks) St. Martin's Pr.
—Reflecting the Sky. 2001. 312p. 24.95 (*0-312-24427-4*, Saint Martin's Minotaur); 2002. 384p. reprint ed. mass mkt. 6.50 (*0-312-98134-1*, St. Martin's Paperbacks) St. Martin's Pr.
—Winter & Night. E-Book 18.95 (*0-312-70434-8*); 2003. 400p. mass mkt. 6.99 (*0-312-98668-8*, St. Martin's Paperbacks); 2002. 304p. 24.95 (*0-312-24555-6*, Saint Martin's Minotaur) St. Martin's Pr.
Rucker, Lance. Intimate Falls: A Brandon Drake Novel. 2001. (Brandon Drake Mysteries). 405p. pap. (*0-9688274-0-3*) Lochenlode Publishing.
Russell, Alan. Political Suicide: A Novel. 2003. 336p. 24.95 (*0-312-31418-3*, Saint Martin's Minotaur) St. Martin's Pr.
Russell, Jay S. Burning Bright. 1998. 288p. 23.95 o.p. (*0-312-18545-6*) St. Martin's Pr.
—Celestial Dogs. 1997. 272p. 22.95 o.p. (*0-312-15076-8*, Saint Martin's Minotaur) St. Martin's Pr.
Sallis, James. Ghost of a Flea: A Lew Griffin Novel. 2002. 252p. 23.95 (*0-8027-3369-7*) Walker & Co.
Sand, Richard. Hands of Vengeance. 2003. pap. 15.95 (*1-930754-36-1*, Durban Hse.) Durban Hse. Publishing Co., Inc.
Sanders, Lawrence. McNally's Caper. 1995. (Archy McNally Mystery Ser.). 352p. mass mkt. 7.99 (*0-425-14530-1*) Berkley Publishing Group.
—McNally's Caper. l.t. ed. 384p. reprint ed. 1995. pap. 18.95 o.p. (*0-8161-5975-0*); 1994. lib. bdg. 24.95 (*0-8161-5974-2*) Gale Group. (Macmillan Reference USA).
—McNally's Caper. l.t. ed. 1995. (Magna Large Print Ser.). 403p. o.p. (*0-7505-0837-X*) Magna Large Print Bks. GBR. *Dist:* Ulverscroft Large Print Canada, Ltd.
—McNally's Caper. 1994. 320p. 22.95 o.p. (*0-399-13919-2*, G. P. Putnam's Sons) Penguin Group (USA) Inc.
—McNally's Dilemma. 2000. (Archy McNally Mystery Ser.). 336p. mass mkt. 7.99 (*0-425-17536-7*) Berkley Publishing Group.
—McNally's Dilemma. 1999. 320p. 24.95 o.s.i (*0-399-14490-0*) Penguin Group (USA) Inc.
—McNally's Dilemma. l.t. ed. (Thorndike/G. K. Hall Paperback Bestsellers Ser.). 2000. 407p. 28.95 (*0-7862-2247-6*); 1999. 432p. 31.95 (*0-7862-2246-8*) Thorndike Pr.
—McNally's Gamble. 1998. (Archy McNally Mystery Ser.). 368p. mass mkt. 7.50 (*0-425-16259-1*) Berkley Publishing Group.
—McNally's Gamble. l.t. ed. 1997. 26.95 o.p. (*1-56895-487-5*, Wheeler Publishing, Inc.) Gale Group.
—McNally's Gamble. 1997. 307p. 24.95 o.s.i (*0-399-14248-7*, G. P. Putnam's Sons) Penguin Group (USA) Inc.
—McNally's Gamble. 24.95 o.s.i (*0-399-14560-5*) Putnam Publishing Group, The.
—McNally's Gamble. 1998. audio 9.98 (*0-671-58153-8*); 1997. audio 18.00 (*0-671-53793-8*, 394532) Simon & Schuster Audio. (Simon & Schuster Audioworks).
—McNally's Luck. 1993. (Archy McNally Mystery Ser.). 336p. mass mkt. 7.99 (*0-425-13745-7*) Berkley Publishing Group.
—McNally's Luck. l.t. ed. (G. K. Hall Large Print Book Ser.). 350p. 1994. pap. 19.95 o.p. (*0-8161-5678-6*); 1993. 24.95 (*0-8161-5677-8*) Gale Group. (Macmillan Reference USA).
—McNally's Luck. l.t. ed. 1994. (Magna Large Print Ser.). 406p. o.p. (*0-7505-0679-2*) Magna Large Print Bks. GBR. *Dist:* Ulverscroft Large Print Canada, Ltd.
—McNally's Luck. 1992. 320p. 22.95 o.p. (*0-399-13762-9*, G. P. Putnam's Sons) Penguin Group (USA) Inc.
—McNally's Luck. 1994. 5.99 o.p. (*0-517-12590-0*) Random Hse. Value Publishing.
—McNally's Puzzle. l.t. ed. 1997. (Archy McNally Mystery Ser.). 352p. mass mkt. 7.99 (*0-425-15746-6*) Berkley Publishing Group.
—McNally's Puzzle. l.t. ed. 1996. 26.95 o.p. (*0-7838-1712-6*, Macmillan Reference USA) Gale Group.
—McNally's Puzzle. 1996. 320p. 24.95 o.p. (*0-399-14135-9*, G. P. Putnam's Sons) Penguin Group (USA) Inc.
—McNally's Puzzle, abr. ed. 1996. (Archy McNally Mystery Ser.). audio 18.00 (*0-671-53792-X*, 393484, Simon & Schuster Audioworks) Simon & Schuster Audio.
—McNally's Puzzle. l.t. ed. 1997. (Paperback Bestsellers Ser.). pap. 26.95 (*0-7838-1713-4*) Thorndike Pr.
—McNally's Risk. 1994. (Archy McNally Mystery Ser.). 336p. reprint ed. pap. 7.99 (*0-425-14286-8*) Berkley Publishing Group.
—McNally's Risk. l.t. ed. 1993. 322p. 26.95 o.p. (*1-56895-042-X*, Wheeler Publishing, Inc.) Gale Group.
—McNally's Risk. l.t. ed. 1994. (Magna Large Print Ser.). 420p. (*0-7505-0680-6*) Magna Large Print Bks. GBR. *Dist:* Ulverscroft Large Print Canada, Ltd.
—McNally's Risk. 1993. 320p. 22.95 o.p. (*0-399-13816-1*, G. P. Putnam's Sons) Penguin Group (USA) Inc.
—McNally's Risk, abr. ed. 1993. (Archy McNally Mystery Ser.). audio 17.00 (*0-671-79743-3*, 391159, Simon & Schuster Audioworks) Simon & Schuster Audio.
—McNally's Secret. 1993. (Archy McNally Mystery Ser.). 352p. pap. 7.99 (*0-425-13572-1*) Berkley Publishing Group.
—McNally's Secret. l.t. ed. 1993. (General Ser.). 381p. pap. 17.95 o.p. (*0-8161-5540-2*); lib. bdg. 22.95 o.p. (*0-8161-5539-9*) Gale Group. (Macmillan Reference USA).
—McNally's Secret. 1992. 320p. 21.95 o.p. (*0-399-13675-4*, G. P. Putnam's Sons) Penguin Group (USA) Inc.
—McNally's Secret. abr. ed. 1992. (Archy McNally Mystery Ser.). audio 17.00 (*0-671-74472-0*, 391160, Simon & Schuster Audioworks) Simon & Schuster Audio.
—McNally's Trial. 1996. (Archy McNally Mystery Ser.). 352p. pap. 7.99 (*0-425-14755-X*) Berkley Publishing Group.
—McNally's Trial. l.t. ed. 1995. (Large Print Bks.). 26.95 o.p. (*1-56895-208-2*, Wheeler Publishing, Inc.) Gale Group.
—McNally's Trial. 1995. 309p. 23.95 o.p. (*0-399-14006-9*) Penguin Group (USA) Inc.
—McNally's Trial. 1999. pap. 12.98 (*0-671-04455-9*, Simon & Schuster Audioworks) Simon & Schuster Audio.
—Three Complete Novels: McNally's Caper; McNally's Trial; McNally's Puzzle. 1998. 800p. 12.98 o.p. (*0-399-14435-8*, G. P. Putnam's Sons) Penguin Group (USA) Inc.
—Three Complete Novels: McNally's Secret; McNally's Luck; McNally's Risk. 1997. 576p. 12.98 o.p. (*0-399-14307-6*, G. P. Putnam's Sons) Penguin Group (USA) Inc.
—The Timothy Files. 1988. mass mkt. 7.50 (*0-425-10924-0*) Berkley Publishing Group.
—The Timothy Files. l.t. ed. 1988. (General Ser.). 508p. 19.95 o.p. (*0-8161-4479-6*, Macmillan Reference USA) Gale Group.
—The Timothy Files. 1987. 384p. 18.95 o.p. (*0-399-13261-9*, G. P. Putnam's Sons) Penguin Putnam Bks. for Young Readers.
—Timothy's Game. 1989. 352p. mass mkt. 7.50 (*0-425-11641-7*) Berkley Publishing Group.
—Timothy's Game. l.t. ed. 1989. (General Ser.). 468p. lib. bdg. 19.95 o.p. (*0-8161-4757-4*, Macmillan Reference USA) Gale Group.
—Timothy's Game. 1988. 384p. 18.95 o.p. (*0-399-13368-2*, G. P. Putnam's Sons) Penguin Putnam Bks. for Young Readers.
—Timothy's Game. abr. ed. 1988. audio 14.95 (*0-671-67015-8*, Simon & Schuster Audioworks) Simon & Schuster Audio.
Sanders, Lawrence & Lardo, Vincent. McNally's Folly. 2000. (Archy McNally Ser.). 320p. 24.95 o.s.i (*0-399-14618-0*) Penguin Group (USA) Inc.
Sanders, William. Blood Autumn. 1995. 272p. 21.00 o.p. (*0-312-11755-8*, Saint Martin's Minotaur) St. Martin's Pr.
—A Death on 66: A Taggart Roper Mystery. 1993. 256p. 20.95 o.p. (*0-312-10452-9*, Saint Martin's Minotaur) St. Martin's Pr.
—The Next Victim. 1993. 240p. 17.95 o.p. (*0-312-08861-2*, Saint Martin's Minotaur) St. Martin's Pr.
Sanderson, Jim. Safe Delivery. 2000. 224p. 21.95 (*0-8263-2191-7*) Univ. of New Mexico Pr.
Sandford, John. Mortal Prey. l.t. ed. 2003. 559p. pap. 14.95 (*0-7862-4367-8*) Thorndike Pr.
Sandford, John, pseud. Chosen Prey. 2002. 400p. mass mkt. 7.99 (*0-425-18287-8*) Berkley Publishing Group.
—Chosen Prey. l.t. ed. 2002. 477p. pap. 13.95 (*0-7838-9589-5*, Wheeler Publishing, Inc.) Gale Group.
—Chosen Prey. 2001. 416p. 26.95 o.s.i (*0-399-14728-4*) Penguin Group (USA) Inc.
—Chosen Prey. l.t. ed. 2001. 480p. 32.95 (*0-7838-9588-7*) Thorndike Pr.
—Easy Prey. 2001. 400p. reprint ed. mass mkt. 7.99 (*0-425-17876-5*) Berkley Publishing Group.
—Easy Prey. 2000. (Prey Ser.). 384p. 25.95 o.s.i (*0-399-14613-X*) Penguin Group (USA) Inc.
—Easy Prey. l.t. ed. (Core Ser.). 519p. 2001. pap. 29.95 (*0-7838-9073-7*); 2000. 31.95 (*0-7838-9074-5*) Thorndike Pr.
—Eyes of Prey. 1992. 368p. mass mkt. 7.99 (*0-425-13204-8*) Berkley Publishing Group.
—Eyes of Prey. 1991. 320p. 19.95 o.s.i (*0-399-13629-0*, G. P. Putnam's Sons) Penguin Group (USA) Inc.
—Eyes of Prey. 19.95 o.s.i (*0-399-13846-3*) Putnam Publishing Group, The.

Occupations

—John Sandford - Three Complete Novels: Mind Prey; Sudden Prey; Secret Prey. 2000. 752p. 14.98 (*0-399-14651-2*) Penguin Group (USA) Inc.
—Mind Prey. 1996. 368p. mass mkt. 7.99 (*0-425-15289-8*) Berkley Publishing Group.
—Mind Prey. l.t. ed. 1995. 25.95 o.p. (*1-56895-233-3*, Wheeler Publishing, Inc.) Gale Group.
—Mind Prey. 1995. 323p. 23.95 o.p. (*0-399-14009-3*, G. P. Putnam's Sons); o.p. (*0-399-19275-1*) Penguin Group (USA) Inc.
—Mind Prey. 23.95 o.s.i (*0-399-14291-6*) Putnam Publishing Group, The.
—Mortal Prey. 2002. 416p. 26.95 o.s.i (*0-399-14863-9*) Penguin Group (USA) Inc.
—Naked Prey. 2003. 368p. 26.95 (*0-399-15043-9*) Penguin Group (USA) Inc.
—Naked Prey. l.t. ed. 2003. 460p. 32.95 (*0-7862-5569-2*) Thorndike Pr.
—Night Prey. 1995. 416p. mass mkt. 7.99 (*0-425-14641-3*) Berkley Publishing Group.
—Night Prey. l.t. ed. 1994. pap. 21.95 o.p. (*1-56895-075-6*, Wheeler Publishing, Inc.) Gale Group.
—Night Prey. 1994. 320p. 22.95 o.p. (*0-399-13914-1*, G. P. Putnam's Sons) Penguin Group (USA) Inc.
—Night Prey. 22.95 o.s.i (*0-399-14176-6*) Putnam Publishing Group, The.
—Night Prey. unabr. ed. 1995. (Prey Ser.: No. 6). audio 70.00 (*0-7887-0192-4*, 94416E7) Recorded Bks., LLC.
—Night Prey, abr. ed. 1999. audio 17.00 (*0-671-51174-2*, 391266, Simon & Schuster Audioworks) Simon & Schuster Audio.
—Rules of Prey. 368p. 2003. pap. 10.00 (*0-425-19519-8*); 1990. mass mkt. 7.99 (*0-425-12163-1*) Berkley Publishing Group.
—Rules of Prey. 16.95 (*0-399-13635-5*) Penguin Group (USA) Inc.
—Rules of Prey. 1989. 320p. 16.95 o.s.i (*0-399-13465-4*, G. P. Putnam's Sons) Penguin Putnam Bks. for Young Readers.
—Rules of Prey. 2002. E-Book 7.99 (*0-7865-2677-7*) Penguin Putnam, Inc E-Books.
—Secret Prey. 1999. 400p. reprint ed. mass mkt. 7.99 (*0-425-16829-8*) Berkley Publishing Group.
—Secret Prey. l.t. ed. 1998. 27.95 (*1-56895-673-8*, Wheeler Publishing, Inc.) Gale Group.
—Secret Prey. 1998. 384p. 24.95 o.p. (*0-399-14382-3*, G. P. Putnam's Sons) Penguin Group (USA) Inc.
—Shadow Prey. 1991. 368p. mass mkt. 7.99 (*0-425-12606-4*) Berkley Publishing Group.
—Shadow Prey. abr. ed. audio 15.95 o.p. (*1-55994-419-6*, 326323, HarperAudio) HarperTrade.
—Shadow Prey. abr. ed. 2000. 3p. audio 7.95 (*1-57815-054-X*, 1036, Media Bks. Audio Publishing) Media Bks., L. L. C.
—Shadow Prey. 1990. 352p. 18.95 o.p. (*0-399-13543-X*, G. P. Putnam's Sons) Penguin Putnam Bks. for Young Readers.
—Shadow Prey. 18.95 o.s.i (*0-399-13750-5*) Putnam Publishing Group, The.
—Silent Prey. 1993. 384p. mass mkt. 7.99 (*0-425-13756-2*) Berkley Publishing Group.
—Silent Prey. 1992. 320p. 21.95 o.p. (*0-399-13742-4*, G. P. Putnam's Sons) Penguin Group (USA) Inc.
—Silent Prey. 21.95 o.s.i (*0-399-13905-2*) Putnam Publishing Group, The.
—Silent Prey, unabr. ed. 1993. (Prey Ser.: No. 4). audio 67.00 (*1-55690-918-7*, 93414K8) Recorded Bks., LLC.
—Sudden Prey. 1997. 400p. mass mkt. 7.99 (*0-425-15753-9*) Berkley Publishing Group.
—Sudden Prey. 23.95 (*0-399-14428-5*); 1996. 320p. 23.95 o.s.i (*0-399-14138-3*, G. P. Putnam's Sons) Penguin Group (USA) Inc.
—Sudden Prey. l.t. ed. 1996. (Core Ser.). 516p. 28.95 (*0-7838-1832-7*) Thorndike Pr.
—Winter Prey. 1994. 352p. mass mkt. 7.99 (*0-425-14123-3*) Berkley Publishing Group.
—Winter Prey. 1994. lib. bdg. 18.95 o.p. (*0-8161-5833-9*); 1993. 464p. lib. bdg. 24.95 (*0-8161-5832-0*) Gale Group. (Macmillan Reference USA).
—Winter Prey. abr. ed. 2000. audio 9.99 (*0-694-52325-9*, HarperAudio) HarperTrade.
—Winter Prey. 1993. 320p. 21.95 o.p. (*0-399-13815-3*, G. P. Putnam's Sons) Penguin Group (USA) Inc.
—Winter Prey. 21.95 o.s.i (*0-399-14071-9*) Putnam Publishing Group, The.
—Winter Prey, unabr. ed. 1995. (Prey Ser.: No. 5). audio 78.00 (*0-7887-0255-6*, 94464E7) Recorded Bks., LLC.
Santangello, Elena. Hang My Head & Cry. 2001. 322p. 24.95 (*0-312-26939-0*, Saint Martin's Minotaur) St. Martin's Pr.
Satterthwait, Walter. Accustomed to the Dark. 1998. (WWL Mystery Ser.). per. (*0-373-26263-9*, 1-26263-3, Worldwide Library) Harlequin Enterprises, Ltd.
—Accustomed to the Dark. 1996. 256p. 21.95 o.p. (*0-312-14535-7*, Saint Martin's Minotaur) St. Martin's Pr.
—At Ease with the Dead. 1993. per. (*0-373-83266-4*, 1-83266-6); 1991. mass mkt. (*0-373-26072-5*) Harlequin Enterprises, Ltd. (Harlequin Bks.).
—At Ease with the Dead. 1990. 16.95 o.p. (*0-312-04260-4*, Saint Martin's Minotaur) St. Martin's Pr.
—At Ease with the Dead: A Joshua Croft Mystery. 2002. 256p. pap. 13.95 (*0-8263-2970-5*) Univ. of New Mexico Pr.
—Escapade. 1996. 355p. mass mkt. 5.99 (*0-312-95920-6*, St. Martin's Paperbacks); 1995. 336p. 22.95 o.p. (*0-312-13068-6*, Saint Martin's Minotaur) St. Martin's Pr.
—A Flower in the Desert. 1993. (WWL Mystery Ser.). per. (*0-373-26134-9*, 1-26134-6, Harlequin Bks.) Harlequin Enterprises, Ltd.
—A Flower in the Desert. 1992. 240p. 17.95 o.p. (*0-312-07751-3*, Saint Martin's Minotaur) St. Martin's Pr.
—A Flower in the Desert: A Joshua Croft Mystery. 2003. 256p. pap. 13.95 (*0-8263-3203-X*); pap. 13.95 (*0-8263-2914-4*) Univ. of New Mexico Pr.
—The Hanged Man: A Joshua Croft Mystery. 1995. (WWL Mystery Ser.). 250p. per. (*0-373-26173-X*, 1-26173-4, Harlequin Bks.) Harlequin Enterprises, Ltd.
—The Hanged Man: A Joshua Croft Mystery. 1993. 256p. 19.95 o.p. (*0-312-09827-8*, Saint Martin's Minotaur) St. Martin's Pr.
—The Hanged Man: A Joshua Croft Mystery. 2003. 258p. pap. 13.95 (*0-8263-3365-6*) Univ. of New Mexico Pr.
—Masquerade. 1999. 336p. mass mkt. 5.99 (*0-312-96989-9*, St. Martin's Paperbacks); Vol. 1. 1998. (Masquerade Ser.: Vol. 1). 272p. 22.95 (*0-312-18629-0*, Saint Martin's Minotaur) St. Martin's Pr.
—Wall of Glass. 1993. per. (*0-373-83265-6*, 1-83265-8); 1989. mass mkt. (*0-373-26032-6*) Harlequin Enterprises, Ltd. (Harlequin Bks.).
—Wall of Glass. 1988. 256p. 16.95 o.p. (*0-312-01530-5*, Saint Martin's Minotaur) St. Martin's Pr.
—Wall of Glass: A Joshua Croft Mystery. 2002. 250p. pap. 13.95 (*0-8263-2887-3*) Univ. of New Mexico Pr.
Sayers, Dorothy L. Dorothy L. Sayers: The Complete Stories. 2002. 816p. pap. 17.95 (*0-06-008461-8*, Perennial) HarperTrade.
—Strong Poison. 1974. mass mkt. 0.75 o.p. (*0-451-05748-1*); mass mkt. 0.60 o.p. (*0-451-03264-0*) NAL. (Signet Bks.).
—Strong Poison. 2001. (Best Mysteries of All Time Ser.). 320p. (*0-7621-8865-0*, IM Pr.) Reader's Digest Assn., Inc., The.
Schutz, Benjamin M. All the Old Bargains. 1987. 208p. mass mkt. 2.95 o.s.i (*0-553-26335-8*) Bantam Bks.
—All the Old Bargains. 1985. (Leo Haggerty Thriller Ser.). 208p. 13.95 o.p. (*0-312-94014-9*) Bluejay Bks.
—Embrace the Wolf. (Mystery Ser.). 208p. 1990. mass mkt. 2.25 o.s.i (*0-553-18508-X*); 1986. mass mkt. 2.95 o.s.i (*0-553-26106-1*) Bantam Bks.
—Embrace the Wolf. 1985. (Leo Haggerty Thriller Ser.). 208p. 13.95 o.p. (*0-312-94137-4*) Bluejay Bks.
—A Fistful of Empty. 1999. pap. 4.95 (*0-14-012890-5*); 1991. 208p. 17.95 o.p. (*0-670-83111-5*) Viking Penguin.
—Mexico Is Forever. 1994. 256p. 18.95 o.p. (*0-312-10502-9*, Saint Martin's Minotaur) St. Martin's Pr.
—Mexico Is Forever. 1999. pap. 3.95 (*0-14-012891-3*, Viking) Viking Penguin.
—A Tax in Blood. 1989. mass mkt. 3.95 o.s.i (*0-553-28291-3*) Bantam Bks.
—A Tax in Blood. 1987. (Leo Haggerty Thriller Ser.). 288p. 14.95 o.p. (*0-312-94421-7*, Tor Bks.) Doherty, Tom Assocs., LLC.
—The Things We Do for Love. 1990. mass mkt. 3.95 o.s.i (*0-553-28489-4*) Bantam Bks.
—The Things We Do for Love. 1989. 224p. 16.95 o.s.i (*0-684-18990-9*, Scribner) Simon & Schuster.
Scoppettone, Sandra. Everything You Have Is Mine. 1992. (Lauren Laurano Mystery Ser.). 320p. mass mkt. 6.99 o.s.i (*0-345-37682-X*) Ballantine Bks.
—Everything You Have Is Mine. 1991. 261p. 19.95 o.p. (*0-316-77646-7*) Little Brown & Co.
—Gonna Take a Homicidal Journey: A Lauren Laurano Mystery. 1999. (Lauren Laurano Mystery Ser.). 288p. mass mkt. 6.99 (*0-345-43118-9*) Ballantine Bks.
—Gonna Take a Homicidal Journey: A Lauren Laurano Mystery. 1998. 240p. (gr. 8). 22.95 o.p. (*0-316-77665-3*) Little Brown & Co.
—I'll Be Leaving You Always: A Lauren Laurano Mystery. 1994. 288p. mass mkt. 6.50 (*0-345-38269-2*) Ballantine Bks.
—I'll Be Leaving You Always: A Lauren Laurano Mystery. 1993. 251p. 19.95 o.p. (*0-316-77647-5*) Little Brown & Co.
—Let's Face the Music & Die: A Lauren Laurano Mystery. 1997. (Lauren Laurano Mystery Ser.). 320p. mass mkt. 6.50 (*0-345-41225-7*) Ballantine Bks.
—Let's Face the Music & Die: A Lauren Laurano Mystery. 1996. 249p. 21.95 o.p. (*0-316-77664-5*) Little Brown & Co.
—My Sweet Untraceable You. 1995. 320p. mass mkt. 6.50 o.s.i (*0-345-39162-4*) Ballantine Bks.
—My Sweet Untraceable You. 1994. 275p. 19.95 o.p. (*0-316-77648-3*) Little Brown & Co.
Scott, Phillip. Gay Resort Murder Shock. 2003. 320p. pap. 13.95 (*1-55583-757-3*) Alyson Pubns.
Searls, Hank. The Adventures of Mike Blair. 1988. (Dime Detective Bk.). 224p. 8.95 o.p. (*0-89296-918-0*) Mysterious Pr.
Senuta, Michael. Second Thoughts about Sherlock Holmes. 2002. (Illus.). 32p. (YA). (gr. 4-12). pap. 8.00 (*0-934468-55-9*) Gaslight Pubns.
Seranella, Barbara. Unfinished Business: A Munch Mancini Crime Novel. 2001. 272p. 24.00 (*0-7432-1266-5*, Scribner) Simon & Schuster.
Shannon, John. The Concrete River. 1998. (Jack Liffey Mystery Ser.). 240p. reprint ed. mass mkt. 5.99 o.s.i (*0-425-16193-5*, Prime Crime) Berkley Publishing Group.
—The Concrete River. 1996. 192p. pap. 12.00 o.p. (*0-9639050-5-8*, West Coast Crime) Blue Heron Publishing.
—The Cracked Earth. 1999. (Jack Liffey Mystery Ser.). 288p. mass mkt. 5.99 o.s.i (*0-425-16732-1*) Berkley Publishing Group.
—The Poison Sky. 2000. (Jack Liffey Mystery Ser.). 241p. mass mkt. 5.99 o.s.i (*0-425-17424-7*, Prime Crime) Berkley Publishing Group.
Shayne, Maggie B. Kiss of the Shadow Man. 1994. (Shadows Ser.). mass mkt. (*0-373-27038-0*, 1-27038-8, Harlequin Bks.) Harlequin Enterprises, Ltd.
Sheckley, Robert. The Alternative Detective. 256p. 1997. pap. 13.95 o.p. (*0-312-85381-5*); 1993. 19.95 o.p. (*0-312-85023-9*) Doherty, Tom Assocs., LLC. (Forge Bks.).
—Draconian New York. 224p. 1997. pap. 12.95 (*0-312-86359-4*); 1996. 20.95 o.p. (*0-312-85130-8*) Doherty, Tom Assocs., LLC. (Forge Bks.).
—Soma Blues. 224p. 1998. pap. 13.95 (*0-312-86579-1*); 1997. 20.95 o.p. (*0-312-86273-3*) Doherty, Tom Assocs., LLC. (Forge Bks.).
Shelton, Connie. Reunions Can Be Murder. 2003. (WWL Mystery Ser.: No. 475). 256p. mass mkt. (*0-373-26475-5*, Worldwide Library) Harlequin Enterprises, Ltd.
—Reunions Can Be Murder: The Seventh Charlie Parker Mystery. 2002. (The Charlie Parker Mystery Ser.: No. 7). 255p. 23.95 (*1-890768-46-4*, Intrigue Pr.) Corvus Publishing.
Sherman, David J. The Dark Side. 2002. 348p. pap. 12.95 o.p. (*1-892343-26-6*, Oak Tree Pr.) Oak Tree Publishing.
—The Dark Side: A Jack Murphy Novel. 2002. 352p. per. 14.95 (*1-932306-51-X*) Bloody Mist Pr.
Shone, Anna. Mr. Donaghue Investigates. 1997. per. (*0-373-26238-8*, 0-26238-6, Worldwide Library) Harlequin Enterprises, Ltd.
—Mr. Donaghue Investigates. 1995. 256p. 21.95 o.p. (*0-312-13127-5*, Saint Martin's Minotaur) St. Martin's Pr.
—Secrets in Stone. 1996. 208p. 21.95 (*0-312-14043-6*, Saint Martin's Minotaur) St. Martin's Pr.
—Secrets in Stones. 1997. 48p. per. (*0-373-26247-7*, 1-26247-6, Worldwide Library) Harlequin Enterprises, Ltd.
Short, Sharon G. The Death We Share. 1995. mass mkt. 5.99 o.s.i (*0-449-14916-1*, Fawcett) Ballantine Bks.
—Past Pretense. 1994. (Orig.). mass mkt. 4.99 o.s.i (*0-449-14915-3*, Fawcett) Ballantine Bks.
Short, Sharon Gwyn. Angel's Bidding. 1993. (Midwest Mysteries Ser.). mass mkt. 4.99 o.s.i (*0-449-14873-4*, Fawcett) Ballantine Bks.
Shott, James R. Bathsheba: People of the Promise, Bk. 8. l.t. ed. 2003. (Christian Fiction Ser.). 26.95 (*0-7862-4534-4*) Thorndike Pr.
Shuman, M. K. Caesar Clue. 1990. 16.95 o.p. (*0-312-04275-2*, Saint Martin's Minotaur) St. Martin's Pr.
—Deep Kill. 1993. 2.99 o.p. (*0-517-09907-1*) Random Hse. Value Publishing.
—Deep Kill. 1991. 16.95 o.p. (*0-312-05854-3*, Saint Martin's Minotaur) St. Martin's Pr.
—The Last Man to Die: A Micah Dunn Mystery. 1992. 240p. 17.95 o.p. (*0-312-07858-7*, Saint Martin's Minotaur) St. Martin's Pr.
—The Maya Stone Murders. 1989. 256p. 16.95 o.p. (*0-312-02608-0*, Saint Martin's Minotaur) St. Martin's Pr.
Siegel, James. Epitaph. l.t. ed. 2003. (Large Print Ser.). 29.95 (*1-57490-484-1*, Beeler Large Print Bks.) Beeler, Thomas T. Publisher.
—Epitaph. 2003. 320p. pap. 12.95 (*0-446-67870-8*, Mysterious Pr. Paperback Bks.) Warner Bks., Inc.
Simmons, Dan. Hard Freeze: A Joe Kurtz Novel. 2002. 304p. 24.95 (*0-312-27854-3*, Saint Martin's Minotaur) St. Martin's Pr.
Simon, Roger L. The Big Fix. 1924. o.s.i (*1-55710-050-0*, Morrow, William & Co.) Morrow/Avon.
—The Big Fix. 1978. pap. 1.95 o.p. (*0-671-82010-9*, Pocket) Simon & Schuster.
—The Big Fix. 1986. 208p. mass mkt. 3.50 o.s.i (*0-446-30043-8*) Warner Bks., Inc.
—The Big Fix. 2000. (Moses Wine Mystery Ser.). (Illus.). 192p. reprint ed. pap. 14.00 (*0-671-03906-7*) ibooks, Inc.
—California Roll. 1986. 208p. mass mkt. 3.50 o.s.i (*0-446-32965-7*) Warner Bks., Inc.
—The Lost Coast. 1997. 79p. 22.50 o.p. (*0-06-017707-1*) HarperTrade.
—The Lost Coast. 272p. 2003. mass mkt. 6.99 (*0-7434-5913-X*); 2000. reprint ed. pap. 14.00 (*0-671-03904-0*) ibooks, Inc.
—Peking Duck. 1987. 256p. mass mkt. 3.95 (*0-446-34932-1*) Warner Bks., Inc.
—Peking Duck. 2002. E-Book 9.99 (*1-58824-340-0*); 2000. 304p. pap. 14.00 (*0-7434-0716-4*) ibooks, Inc.
—Raising the Dead: A Moses Wine Mystery. 1989. 240p. mass mkt. 4.95 (*0-446-34822-8*) Warner Bks., Inc.
—The Straight Man. 1987. 240p. mass mkt. 3.95 (*0-446-34389-7*) Warner Bks., Inc.
—Wild Turkey: A Moses Wine Mystery. 1986. 240p. mass mkt. 3.50 o.s.i (*0-446-30044-6*) Warner Bks., Inc.
—Wild Turkey: A Moses Wine Mystery. 2000. (Moses Wine Mysteries Ser.). 208p. pap. 14.00 (*0-7434-0012-7*) ibooks, Inc.
Slovo, Gillian. Death Comes Staccato. 1988. 12.95 o.s.i (*0-385-24609-9*) Doubleday Publishing.
Smith, Alexander McCall. The Full Cupboard of Life. 2004. 208p. 19.95 (*0-375-42218-8*, Pantheon) Knopf Publishing Group.
—The Kalahari Typing School for Men. l.t. ed. 2003. lib. bdg. 29.95 (*1-58547-331-6*, Platinum) Ctr. Point Large Print.
—The Kalahari Typing School for Men. 192p. 2004. pap. 11.95 (*1-4000-3180-X*, Anchor); 2003. 19.95 (*0-375-42217-X*, Pantheon) Knopf Publishing Group.
—The Kalahari Typing School for Men. 2003. 192p. 32.95 (*0-676-97568-2*) Knopf, Alfred A. Inc.
—The Kalahari Typing School for Men. audio 24.99 (*1-4025-4178-3*); audio compact disk 29.99 (*1-4025-4706-4*) Recorded Bks., LLC.
—The No. 1 Ladies' Detective Agency. l.t. ed. 2003. lib. bdg. 29.95 (*1-58547-328-6*, Platinum) Ctr. Point Large Print.
—The No. 1 Ladies' Detective Agency. 2003. 240p. pap. 11.95 (*1-4000-3477-9*, Anchor) Knopf Publishing Group.
—The No. 1 Ladies' Detective Agency. 2001. 202p. pap. 12.95 o.p. (*0-7486-6252-9*) Polygon GBR. *Dist:* AK Pr. Distribution.
—The No. 1 Ladies' Detective Agency. 2002. 240p. pap. 11.95 o.s.i (*1-4000-3134-6*, Knopf Bks. for Young Readers) Random Hse. Children's Bks.
—The No. 1 Ladies' Detective Agency. audio compact disk 29.99 (*1-4025-4535-5*) Recorded Bks., LLC.
—Tears of the Giraffe. 2002. 240p. pap. 11.95 (*1-4000-3135-4*, Knopf Bks. for Young Readers) Random Hse. Children's Bks.
—Tears of the Giraffe. audio 24.99 (*1-4025-4177-5*); audio compact disk 29.99 (*1-4025-4705-6*) Recorded Bks., LLC.
Smith, L. Neil. The Probability Broach. 1979. mass mkt. 1.95 o.s.i (*0-345-28593-X*, Del Rey) Ballantine Bks.
—The Probability Broach. 1996. 305p. pap. text 6.99 (*0-8125-3875-7*, Tor Bks.); 2001. 320p. reprint ed. pap. 15.95 (*0-7653-0153-9*, Orb Bks.) Doherty, Tom Assocs., LLC.
Solomita, Stephen. Damaged Goods: A Stanley Moodrow Novel. 1996. 384p. 22.00 o.p. (*0-684-81584-2*, Scribner) Simon & Schuster.
Spillane, Mickey. Body Lovers. l.t. ed. 1999. (Mike Hammer Ser.). 248p. pap. 24.95 (*0-7838-8540-7*) Thorndike Pr.
—The Hammer Strikes Again: Five Complete Mike Hammer Novels. 1989. 784p. 9.99 o.s.i (*0-517-67578-1*) Random Hse. Value Publishing.
—The Killing Man. 1989. (Mike Hammer Ser.). 17.95 o.p. (*0-525-24827-7*, Dutton) Dutton/Plume.
—The Killing Man. l.t. ed. 1993. (Mike Hammer Ser.). 363p. lib. bdg. 19.95 o.p. (*0-8161-5552-6*, Macmillan Reference USA) Gale Group.
—The Killing Man. 1990. (Mike Hammer Ser.). 320p. mass mkt. 4.95 o.p. (*0-451-16784-8*, Signet Bks.) NAL.
—The Killing Man. 1992. 2.99 o.p. (*0-517-07997-6*) Random Hse. Value Publishing.
—Kiss Me Deadly. 1953. mass mkt. 2.95 o.p. (*0-451-13602-0*); reprint ed. mass mkt. 3.95 o.p. (*0-451-16593-4*) NAL. (Signet Bks.).
—One Lonely Night. l.t. ed. 1994. (Mike Hammer Ser.). o.p. (*0-7927-2105-5*); pap. o.p. (*0-7927-2104-7*) BBC Audiobooks America.
—One Lonely Night. unabr. ed. 1991. (Mike Hammer Ser.). audio 48.00 (*0-7366-2020-6*, 2836) Books on Tape, Inc.

Occupations

—One Lonely Night. l.t. ed. 1996. 21.95 (*0-7838-1229-9*, Macmillan Reference USA) Gale Group.

—One Lonely Night. 1951. (Mike Hammer Ser.). mass mkt. 3.50 o.p. (*0-451-15349-9*); mass mkt. 2.95 o.p. (*0-451-13710-8*, Signet Bks.); mass mkt. 3.95 o.p. (*0-451-16597-7*, AE2165, Signet Bks.) NAL.

—One Lonely Night. abr. ed. 1991. (Mike Hammer Ser.). audio 15.95 (*0-671-72605-6*, 326314, Simon & Schuster Audioworks) Simon & Schuster Audio.

—The Snake. (Mike Hammer Ser.). 19.95 (*0-89190-837-4*) Amereon, Ltd.

—The Snake. 1999. (Mike Hammer Ser.). 240p. (*0-7540-3617-0*) BBC Audiobooks America.

—The Snake. l.t. ed. 1999. (Mike Hammer Ser.). 240p. pap. (*0-7540-3618-9*, Macmillan Reference USA) Gale Group.

—The Snake. 1964. (Mike Hammer Ser.). 160p. mass mkt. 3.95 o.p. (*0-451-13715-9*, AE2209, Signet Bks.) NAL.

—The Snake. l.t. ed. 1998. (Mike Hammer Ser.). 240p. pap. 23.95 (*0-7838-0412-1*) Thorndike Pr.

—Survival— Zero! l.t. ed. 1999. (Mike Hammer Ser.). 264p. (*0-7540-3955-2*, Macmillan Reference USA) Gale Group.

—Survival-Zero. 1971. (Mike Hammer Ser.). 160p. mass mkt. 4.50 o.p. (*0-451-13704-3*, Signet Bks.) NAL.

—Survival Zero! l.t. ed. 1999. (Mike Hammer Ser.). 264p. pap. 24.95 (*0-7838-8735-3*) Wiley, John & Sons, Inc.

—The Twisted Thing. l.t. ed. 1994. (Mike Hammer Ser.). lib. bdg. 17.95 (*0-8161-5557-7*, Macmillan Reference USA) Gale Group.

—Vengeance Is Mine. 1951. (Mike Hammer Ser.). mass mkt. 2.95 o.p. (*0-451-14687-5*) NAL.

Staalesen, Gunnar. The Writing on Wall. Sutcliffe, Hal, tr. from NOR. 2003. (Eurocrime Ser.). 256p. pap. 16.00 (*1-900850-58-3*) Arcadia Bks. GBR. *Dist:* Consortium Bk. Sales & Distribution.

Stabenow, Dana. Blood Will Tell: A Kate Shugak Mystery. 1997. (Kate Shugak Mystery Ser.). 256p. mass mkt. 6.99 (*0-425-15798-9*) Berkley Publishing Group.

—Blood Will Tell: A Kate Shugak Mystery. 1996. (Kate Shugak Mystery Ser.). 256p. 21.95 o.p. (*0-399-14124-3*, G. P. Putnam's Sons) Penguin Group (USA) Inc.

—Breakup: A Kate Shugak Mystery. 1998. (Kate Shugak Mysteries Ser.). 256p. mass mkt. 6.99 (*0-425-16261-3*) Berkley Publishing Group.

—Breakup: A Kate Shugak Mystery. 1997. (Kate Shugak Mystery Ser.). 256p. 21.95 o.s.i (*0-399-14250-9*, G. P. Putnam's Sons) Penguin Group (USA) Inc.

—A Cold-Blooded Business: A Kate Shugak Mystery. 1995. (Kate Shugak Mystery Ser.). 240p. (Orig.). mass mkt. 6.99 (*0-425-15849-7*, Prime Crime) Berkley Publishing Group.

—Cold-Blooded Business: A Kate Shugak Mystery. 1994. (Kate Shugak Mysteries Ser.). 231p. (Orig.). 17.95 o.s.i (*0-425-14173-X*) Berkley Publishing Group.

—A Cold Day for Murder. unabr. ed. 1999. audio 24.95 (*0-7366-4423-7*, 4830) Books on Tape, Inc.

—A Cold Day for Murder: A Kate Shugak Mystery. l.t. ed. 2001. 189p. 26.95 (*1-57490-355-1*, Beeler Large Print Bks.) Beeler, Thomas T. Publisher.

—A Cold Day for Murder: A Kate Shugak Mystery. 1992. (Kate Shugak Mystery Ser.). 208p. mass mkt. 6.99 (*0-425-13301-X*) Berkley Publishing Group.

—Dead in the Water: A Kate Shugak Mystery. 1993. (Kate Shugak Mysteries Ser.). 224p. mass mkt. 6.99 (*0-425-13749-X*) Berkley Publishing Group.

—A Fatal Thaw. unabr. collector's ed. 1999. (Kate Shugak Mystery Ser.). audio 40.00 (*0-7366-4459-8*, 4904) Books on Tape, Inc.

—A Fatal Thaw: A Kate Shugak Mystery. 1993. (Kate Shugak Mystery Ser.). 208p. mass mkt. 6.99 (*0-425-13577-2*) Berkley Publishing Group.

—A Fine & Bitter Snow: A Kate Shugak Novel. 2002. 304p. 24.95 (*0-312-20548-1*, Saint Martin's Minotaur) St. Martin's Pr.

—A Grave Denied: A Kate Shugak Novel. 2003. 304p. 24.95 (*0-312-30681-4*, Saint Martin's Minotaur) St. Martin's Pr.

—Hunter's Moon. unabr. collector's ed. 1999. audio 40.00 (*0-7366-4635-3*, 5007) Books on Tape, Inc.

—Hunter's Moon: A Kate Shugak Mystery. 1999. (Prime Crime Mysteries Ser.). 256p. reprint ed. mass mkt. 6.99 (*0-425-17259-7*, Prime Crime) Berkley Publishing Group.

—Hunter's Moon: A Kate Shugak Mystery. 1999. (Kate Shugak Mystery Ser.). 260p. 23.95 o.s.i (*0-399-14468-4*) Penguin Group (USA) Inc.

—Killing Grounds. 1999. (Kate Shugak Mysteries Ser.). 256p. reprint ed. mass mkt. 6.99 (*0-425-16773-9*, Prime Crime) Berkley Publishing Group.

—Killing Grounds. 1999. 12.04 (*0-606-16389-1*) Turtleback Bks.

—The Killing Grounds: A Kate Shugak Mystery. 1998. (Kate Shugak Mystery Ser.). 273p. 22.95 o.p. (*0-399-14356-4*, G. P. Putnam's Sons) Penguin Group (USA) Inc.

—Midnight Come Again. l.t. ed. 2001. (Large Print Book Ser.). 351p. pap. 23.95 o.p. (*1-58724-031-9*, Wheeler Publishing, Inc.) Gale Group.

—Midnight Come Again. E-Book 23.95 (*0-312-27415-7*); 2001. 320p. reprint ed. mass mkt. 6.99 (*0-312-97876-6*, St. Martin's Paperbacks) St. Martin's Pr.

—Midnight Come Again: A Kate Shugak Novel. 2000. (Kate Shugak Mysteries Ser.). 291p. 23.95 o.p. (*0-312-20596-1*, Saint Martin's Minotaur) St. Martin's Pr.

—Play with Fire: A Kate Shugak Mystery. (Kate Shugak Mystery Ser.). 1996. 320p. mass mkt. 6.99 (*0-425-15254-5*); 1995. 288p. 19.95 o.p. (*0-425-14717-7*, Prime Crime) Berkley Publishing Group.

Staincliffe, Cath. Stone Cold Red Hot. (Sal Kilkenny Myerstery Ser.). 2002. 263p. pap. 9.95 (*0-7490-0522-X*); 2001. 254p. 24.95 (*0-7490-0515-7*) Allison & Busby, Ltd. GBR. *Dist:* International Publishers Marketing.

—Stone Cold Red Hot. l.t. ed. 2002. (Magna Large Print Ser.). 320p. 32.50 (*0-7505-1875-8*) Magna Large Print Bks. GBR. *Dist:* Ulverscroft Large Print Bks., Ltd., Ulverscroft Large Print Canada, Ltd.

Stevenson, Richard. Chain of Fools. 1996. 208p. 20.95 o.p. (*0-312-14563-2*, Saint Martin's Minotaur) St. Martin's Pr.

—Chain of Fools: A Donald Strachey Mystery. 1997. (Donald Strachey Mystery Ser.). 192p. pap. 11.95 (*0-312-16796-2*, Saint Martin's Griffin) St. Martin's Pr.

—Death Trick. 190p. reprint ed. 1983. pap. 6.95 o.p. (*0-932870-27-9*); 2nd ed. 1996. pap. 9.95 o.p. (*1-55583-387-X*) Alyson Pubns.

—Death Trick. 1981. 224p. 10.95 o.p. (*0-312-18876-5*) St. Martin's Pr.

—Death Trick: A Murder Mystery. 2003. 199p. pap. 15.95 (*1-56023-470-9*, Southern Tier Editions) Haworth Pr., Inc., The.

—Ice Blues. 1987. 224p. mass mkt. 3.95 o.p. (*0-14-009403-2*, Penguin Bks.) Viking Penguin.

—Ice Blues: A Donald Strachey Mystery. 1995. 224p. pap. 8.95 (*0-312-13517-3*, Saint Martin's Griffin); 1986. 256p. 15.95 o.p. (*0-312-40379-8*) St. Martin's Pr.

—On the Other Hand, Death. 1995. 216p. 8.95 (*0-312-11871-6*, Saint Martin's Griffin) St. Martin's Pr.

—On the Other Hand, Death. 1985. (Crime Monthly Ser.). 224p. pap. 3.95 o.p. (*0-14-008319-7*, Penguin Bks.) Viking Penguin.

—On the Other Hand, Death: A Donald Strachey Mystery. 1984. 224p. 12.95 o.p. (*0-312-58458-X*) St. Martin's Pr.

—A Shock to the System: A Donald Strachey Mystery. 192p. 1996. pap. 9.95 (*0-312-14732-5*, Saint Martin's Griffin); 1995. 19.95 o.p. (*0-312-13610-2*, Saint Martin's Minotaur) St. Martin's Pr.

—Strachey's Folly. (Donald Strachey Mystery Ser.). 1999. 224p. pap. 11.95 (*0-312-24328-6*, Saint Martin's Griffin); 1998. 216p. 22.95 o.p. (*0-312-18669-X*, Saint Martin's Minotaur) St. Martin's Pr.

—Third Man Out: A Donald Strachey Mystery. pap. 15.95 (*0-312-30214-2*, Saint Martin's Griffin); 1993. pap. 8.95 (*0-312-08906-6*, Saint Martin's Griffin); 1992. 224p. 17.95 o.p. (*0-312-07110-8*, Saint Martin's Minotaur) St. Martin's Pr.

—Tongue Tied: A Donald Strachey Mystery. 2003. 224p. 22.95 (*0-312-30974-0*, Saint Martin's Minotaur) St. Martin's Pr.

Stone, Michael. A Long Reach. 1998. (Streeter Mystery Ser.). 240p. pap. 5.99 o.s.i (*0-14-024703-3*) Penguin Group (USA) Inc.

—A Long Reach. l.t. ed. 1997. (Niagara Large Print Ser.). 320p. 29.50 o.p. (*0-7089-5875-3*, Ulverscroft) Thorpe, F. A. Pubs. GBR. *Dist:* Ulverscroft Large Print Bks., Ltd.

—A Long Reach. 1997. (Streeter Mystery Ser.). 240p. 20.95 o.s.i (*0-670-86166-9*) Viking Penguin.

—The Low End of Nowhere: A Streeter Mystery. 1997. (Viking Mystery Suspense Ser.). 240p. pap. 5.95 o.s.i (*0-14-024694-0*) Penguin Group (USA) Inc.

—The Low End of Nowhere: A Streeter Mystery. l.t. ed. 1997. (Niagara Large Print Ser.). 290p. 29.50 o.p. (*0-7089-5863-X*, Linford) Thorpe, F. A. Pubs. GBR. *Dist:* Ulverscroft Large Print Bks., Ltd.

—The Low End of Nowhere: A Streeter Mystery. 1996. (Streeter Mystery Ser.). 240p. 20.95 o.p. (*0-670-86154-5*) Viking Penguin.

—Token of Remorse. 1998. (Streeter Mystery Ser.). 256p. 22.95 o.p. (*0-670-87774-3*) Viking Penguin.

—Token of Remorse: A Streeter Mystery. 1999. (Streeter Mystery Ser.). 256p. pap. 5.99 (*0-14-027546-0*, Puffin Bks.) Penguin Group (USA) Inc.

—Totally Dead. 2000. (Streeter Mystery Ser.). 240p. pap. 5.99 o.s.i (*0-14-028598-9*, Penguin Bks.) Penguin Group (USA) Inc.

—Totally Dead. 1999. (Streeter Mystery Ser.). 256p. 22.95 o.s.i (*0-670-88208-9*, Viking) Viking Penguin.

Stout, Rex. And Be a Villain. 1994. 256p. mass mkt. 5.99 (*0-553-23931-7*) Bantam Bks.

—And Four to Go. 1992. 240p. mass mkt. 5.99 (*0-553-24985-1*) Bantam Bks.

—And Four to Go. unabr. collector's ed. 1997. (Nero Wolfe Ser.). audio 42.00 (*0-7366-4059-2*, 4570) Books on Tape, Inc.

—And Four to Go. 1958. 2.95 o.p. (*0-670-12285-8*) Viking Penguin.

—Bad for Business. 1995. (Orig.). 240p. pap. 15.00 (*0-553-76302-4*); 176p. reprint ed. mass mkt. 4.99 (*0-553-25810-9*) Bantam Bks.

—Before Midnight. 1995. 224p. pap. 15.00 (*0-553-76304-0*); 1981. 160p. pap. 2.25 o.p. (*0-553-14797-8*) Bantam Bks.

—Before Midnight. unabr. collector's ed. 1995. (Nero Wolfe Ser.). audio 36.00 (*0-7366-3166-6*, 3836) Books on Tape, Inc.

—Before Midnight. l.t. ed. 1994. 267p. lib. bdg. 15.95 o.p. (*0-8161-5985-8*, Macmillan Reference USA) Gale Group.

—Before Midnight. 1955. 2.75 o.p. (*0-670-15525-X*) Viking Penguin.

—Bitter End: A Nero Wolfe Mystery. unabr. ed. 1997. audio 4.99 (*0-88646-941-4*, 7941) Durkin Hayes Publishing Ltd.

—The Black Mountain. unabr. ed. 2001. (Nero Wolfe Mystery Ser.). audio 29.95 (*1-57270-039-4*, N61039u, Audio Editions Bks. on Cassette) Audio Partners Publishing Corp.

—The Black Mountain. 1988. 224p. mass mkt. 3.50 o.s.i (*0-553-27291-8*) Bantam Bks.

—The Black Mountain. unabr. collector's ed. 1995. (Nero Wolfe Ser.). audio 42.00 (*0-7366-3167-4*, 3837) Books on Tape, Inc.

—The Black Mountain. 1954. 2.75 o.p. (*0-670-17258-8*) Viking Penguin.

—Black Orchids. 1992. 208p. mass mkt. 5.99 (*0-553-25719-6*) Bantam Bks.

—Black Orchids. unabr. collector's ed. 1994. (Nero Wolfe Ser.). audio 42.00 (*0-7366-2797-9*, 3512) Books on Tape, Inc.

—Black Orchids. abr. ed. 1996. (Paperback Audio Ser.). audio 9.99 (*0-88646-889-2*, 7889) Durkin Hayes Publishing Ltd.

—Black Orchids. 1982. (Reader's Request Ser.). lib. bdg. 13.95 o.p. (*0-8161-3289-5*, Macmillan Reference USA) Gale Group.

—The Broken Vase. 1995. (Mystery Ser.). 160p. (Orig.). mass mkt. 4.99 o.s.i (*0-553-25632-7*) Bantam Bks.

—The Broken Vase. 1976. (Orig.). pap. 1.25 o.s.i (*0-515-04065-7*, Jove) Berkley Publishing Group.

—The Broken Vase. l.t. ed. 1988. (Nightingale Ser.). 284p. (Orig.). pap. 11.95 o.p. (*0-8161-4392-7*, Macmillan Reference USA) Gale Group.

—Champagne for One: A Nero Wolfe Mystery. 1995. 224p. mass mkt. 5.99 (*0-553-24438-8*); 1980. 160p. pap. 1.95 o.p. (*0-553-13657-7*) Bantam Bks.

—Champagne for One: A Nero Wolfe Mystery. unabr. collector's ed. 1996. (Nero Wolfe Ser.). audio 36.00 (*0-7366-3345-6*, 3995) Books on Tape, Inc.

—Champagne for One: A Nero Wolfe Mystery. abr. ed. 1998. (Nero Wolfe Mysteries Ser.). audio 16.99 (*0-88646-456-0*, 7456) Durkin Hayes Publishing Ltd.

—Champagne for One: A Nero Wolfe Mystery. l.t. ed. 1987. (Nightingale Ser.). 302p. 11.95 o.p. (*0-8161-4282-3*, Macmillan Reference USA) Gale Group.

—The Cop-Killer: A Nero Wolfe Mystery. unabr. ed. 1994. audio 4.99 (*0-88646-705-5*) Durkin Hayes Publishing Ltd.

—Curtains for Three. 240p. 1995. pap. 15.00 (*0-553-76294-X*); 1994. mass mkt. 4.99 (*0-553-24498-1*) Bantam Bks.

—Curtains for Three. unabr. collector's ed. 1997. (Nero Wolfe Ser.). audio 42.00 (*0-7366-3747-8*, 4422) Books on Tape, Inc.

—Death of a Doxy. unabr. collector's ed. 1998. (Nero Wolfe Ser.). audio 36.00 (*0-7366-4044-4*, 4543) Books on Tape, Inc.

—Death of a Doxy. l.t. ed. 1996. (Nightingale Ser.). 208p. pap. 17.95 o.p. (*0-7838-1573-5*, Macmillan Reference USA) Gale Group.

—Death of a Doxy. 1966. 3.75 o.p. (*0-670-26126-2*) Viking Penguin.

—Death of a Dude: A Nero Wolfe Novel. 1990. 160p. pap. 3.95 o.s.i (*0-553-27422-8*); Vol. 1. 1994. (Death of a Dude Ser.: Vol. 1). 208p. mass mkt. 4.99 (*0-553-24730-1*) Bantam Bks.

—Death of a Dude: A Nero Wolfe Novel, Set. unabr. ed. 1994. audio 32.95 (*0-7861-0793-6*, 1533) Blackstone Audio Bks., Inc.

—Death of a Dude: A Nero Wolfe Novel. l.t. ed. 1999. (Mystery Ser.). 271p. 27.95 (*0-7862-1904-1*) Thorndike Pr.

—Death Times Three. 1995. 254p. pap. 15.00 (*0-553-76305-9*); 1994. 256p. mass mkt. 4.99 o.s.i (*0-553-27828-2*); 1991. mass mkt. 2.99 o.s.i (*0-553-19646-4*); 1985. 240p. mass mkt. 3.50 (*0-553-25425-1*) Bantam Bks.

—Death Times Three, Set. unabr. ed. 1995. audio 32.95 (*0-7861-0701-4*, 1578) Blackstone Audio Bks., Inc.

—The Doorbell Rang. 1992. 192p. mass mkt. 5.99 (*0-553-23721-7*) Bantam Bks.

—The Doorbell Rang. audio 19.95 (*0-7861-1394-4*); 1994. audio 23.95 (*0-7861-0775-8*, 1503) Blackstone Audio Bks., Inc.

—The Doorbell Rang. abr. ed. (Nero Wolfe Mystery Ser.). 2000. audio 19.99 (*0-88646-561-3*, DHA-6561); 1997. audio (*0-88646-443-9*, 7443) Durkin Hayes Publishing Ltd.

—The Doorbell Rang. l.t. ed. 1985. (Nightingale Ser.). 227p. 9.95 o.p. (*0-8161-3795-1*, Macmillan Reference USA) Gale Group.

—The Doorbell Rang. 2000. (Best Mysteries of All Time Ser.). 207p. (*0-7621-8857-X*) Reader's Digest Assn., Inc., The.

—The Doorbell Rang. 1968. 9.95 o.p. (*0-670-28021-6*, LT4); 1965. 3.50 o.p. (*0-670-27993-5*) Viking Penguin.

—Double for Death. 1995. (Orig.). 272p. pap. 19.00 (*0-553-76300-8*); 192p. mass mkt. 4.99 (*0-553-26059-6*) Bantam Bks.

—Eeny Meeny Murder Mo: A Nero Wolfe Mystery. abr. ed. 1999. (Nero Wolfe Ser.). audio 5.99 o.p. Brilliance Audio.

—Eeny Meeny Murder Mo: A Nero Wolfe Mystery. unabr. ed. 1999. audio 5.99 (*0-88646-992-9*, PAC-7992) Durkin Hayes Publishing Ltd.

—A Family Affair. 1993. 208p. mass mkt. 4.99 o.s.i (*0-553-24122-2*) Bantam Bks.

—A Family Affair. l.t. ed. 1978. lib. bdg. 9.95 o.p. (*0-8161-6561-0*, Macmillan Reference USA) Gale Group.

—A Family Affair. 1975. 152p. 9.95 o.p. (*0-670-30611-8*) Viking Penguin.

—The Father Hunt. 208p. 1995. pap. 15.00 (*0-553-76297-4*); Vol. 1. 1991. mass mkt. 3.95 (*0-553-24728-X*) Bantam Bks.

—The Father Hunt. 1983. (Nightingale Ser.). 240p. pap. 9.95 o.p. (*0-8161-3548-7*, Macmillan Reference USA) Gale Group.

—The Father Hunt. 1968. 4.50 o.p. (*0-670-30945-1*) Viking Penguin.

—Fer-de-Lance. Date not set. 304p. 23.95 (*0-8488-2403-2*) Amereon, Ltd.

—Fer-de-Lance. unabr. ed. 1997. (Nero Wolfe Mystery Ser.). audio 29.95 (*1-57270-035-1*, N61035u, Audio Editions Mystery Masters) Audio Partners Publishing Corp.

—Fer-de-Lance. 1997. 304p. mass mkt. 5.99 (*0-553-27819-3*); 1992. pap. 2.50 o.s.i (*0-553-23033-6*); 1984. mass mkt. 2.95 o.s.i (*0-553-24918-5*) Bantam Bks.

—Fer-de-Lance. unabr. collector's ed. 1994. (Nero Wolfe Ser.). audio 48.00 (*0-7366-2621-2*, 3361) Books on Tape, Inc.

—Fer-de-Lance. 1994. 320p. reprint ed. 35.00 (*1-883402-17-4*, Scribner) Simon & Schuster.

—The Final Deduction: A Nero Wolfe Novel. 1999. 261p. (*0-7540-3706-1*) BBC Audiobooks America.

—The Final Deduction: A Nero Wolfe Novel. 1992. 144p. mass mkt. 4.99 (*0-553-25254-2*) Bantam Bks.

—The Final Deduction: A Nero Wolfe Novel. unabr. collector's ed. 1996. (Nero Wolfe Ser.). audio 36.00 (*0-7366-3413-4*, 4059) Books on Tape, Inc.

—The Final Deduction: A Nero Wolfe Novel. l.t. ed. 1999. (Mystery Ser.). 261p. 26.95 (*0-7862-1771-5*) Thorndike Pr.

—Five of a Kind: The Third Nero Wolfe Omnibus. 1980. (Short Story Index Reprint Ser.). reprint ed. 37.95 (*0-8369-4136-5*) Ayer Co. Pubs., Inc.

—Frame-up for Murder. unabr. ed. 1997. audio 4.99 (*0-88646-931-7*, 7931) Durkin Hayes Publishing Ltd.

—Gambit. 1985. 160p. mass mkt. 2.95 o.s.i (*0-553-25172-4*) Bantam Bks.

—Gambit. unabr. collector's ed. 1996. (Nero Wolfe Ser.). audio 36.00 (*0-7366-3415-0*, 4061) Books on Tape, Inc.

—Gambit. l.t. ed. 1997. (Nightingale Ser.). 18.95 o.p. (*0-7838-1571-9*, Macmillan Reference USA) Gale Group.

—Gambit. 1962. 3.50 o.p. (*0-670-33376-X*) Viking Penguin.

—The Golden Spiders. unabr. ed. 1997. (Nero Wolfe Mystery Ser.). audio 29.95 (*1-57270-038-6*, N61038u, Audio Editions Mystery Masters) Audio Partners Publishing Corp.

—The Golden Spiders. 1984. 160p. pap. 2.50 o.p. (*0-553-23995-3*) Bantam Bks.

—The Golden Spiders. unabr. collector's ed. 1995. (Nero Wolfe Ser.). audio 42.00 (*0-7366-3132-1*, 3807) Books on Tape, Inc.

Occupations

—The Golden Spiders. l.t. ed. 1996. (Nightingale Ser.). pap. 17.95 (*0-7838-1572-7*, Macmillan Reference USA) Gale Group.

—The Golden Spiders. 1953. 2.50 o.p. (*0-670-34452-4*) Viking Penguin.

—The Great Legend. 1997. 288p. mass mkt. 4.95 (*0-7867-0443-8*, Carroll & Graf Pubs.) Avalon Publishing Group.

—The Hand in the Glove. 1992. 256p. mass mkt. 4.99 o.s.i (*0-553-22857-9*) Bantam Bks.

—Hand in the Glove. l.t. ed. 1986. (Nightingale Ser.). 384p. 10.95 o.p. (*0-8161-3964-4*, Macmillan Reference USA) Gale Group.

—Her Forbidden Knight. 256p. 2000. mass mkt. 5.95 (*0-7867-0729-1*); 1997. mass mkt. 4.95 o.p. (*0-7867-0444-6*) Avalon Publishing Group. (Carroll & Graf Pubs.).

—Her Forbidden Knight. 1998. 256p. 24.00 o.p. (*0-7278-5369-4*) Severn Hse. Pubs., Ltd.

—Homicide Trinity. 1993. 224p. mass mkt. 5.99 (*0-553-23446-3*) Bantam Bks.

—Homicide Trinity. unabr. collector's ed. 1999. (Nero Wolfe Ser.). audio 64.00 (*0-7366-4062-2*, 4573) Books on Tape, Inc.

—Homicide Trinity. 1962. 2.95 o.p. (*0-670-37758-9*) Viking Penguin.

—If Death Ever Slept. 208p. 1995. pap. 15.00 (*0-553-76296-6*); 1992. mass mkt. 4.99 (*0-553-23649-0*) Bantam Bks.

—If Death Ever Slept. abr. l.t. ed. 1989. 274p. 13.95 o.p. (*0-8161-4794-9*, Macmillan Reference USA) Gale Group.

—In the Best of Families. 1995. 272p. mass mkt. 5.99 (*0-553-27776-6*); 1980. pap. 2.50 o.p. (*0-553-24375-6*) Bantam Bks.

—Invitation to Murder. unabr. ed. 1996. (Paperback Audio Ser.). audio 9.99 (*0-88646-883-3*, 7883) Durkin Hayes Publishing Ltd.

—Justice Ends at Home & Other Stories. 1977. 8.95 o.p. (*0-670-41105-1*) Viking Penguin.

—The League of Frightened Men. unabr. ed. 1999. (Nero Wolfe Mystery Ser.). audio 29.95 (*1-57270-037-8*, N61037u) Audio Partners Publishing Corp.

—The League of Frightened Men. 320p. 1995. pap. 19.00 (*0-553-76298-2*); 1992. mass mkt. 4.99 (*0-553-25933-4*) Bantam Bks.

—The League of Frightened Men. 1979. 1.75 o.p. (*0-515-05116-0*, Jove) Berkley Publishing Group.

—The League of Frightened Men. unabr. collector's ed. 1994. (Nero Wolfe Ser.). audio 56.00 (*0-7366-2631-X*, 3370) Books on Tape, Inc.

—The League of Frightened Men. abr. ed. 1996. audio 16.99 (*0-88646-418-8*) Durkin Hayes Publishing Ltd.

—The League of Frightened Men. 1981. (Reader's Request Ser.). lib. bdg. 14.50 o.p. (*0-8161-3225-9*, Macmillan Reference USA) Gale Group.

—Might As Well Be Dead. 1980. 160p. pap. 1.95 o.p. (*0-553-14447-2*) Bantam Bks.

—Might as Well Be Dead. 1995. 224p. pap. 15.00 (*0-553-76303-2*) Bantam Bks.

—Might As Well Be Dead, Vol. 1. 1992. 224p. mass mkt. 4.99 (*0-553-24729-8*) Bantam Bks.

—Might As Well Be Dead. unabr. collector's ed. 1996. (Nero Wolfe Ser.). audio 42.00 (*0-7366-3225-5*, 3886) Books on Tape, Inc.

—Might As Well Be Dead. l.t. ed. 1997. (Nightingale Ser.). 262p. lib. bdg. 18.95 (*0-7838-1570-0*) Thorndike Pr.

—More Deaths Than One: A Nero Wolfe Mystery. l.t. ed. 1993. (Nightingale Ser.). 304p. reprint ed. pap. 16.95 o.p. (*0-8161-5757-X*, Macmillan Reference USA) Gale Group.

—The Mother Hunt. 1993. 224p. mass mkt. 5.99 (*0-553-24737-9*) Bantam Bks.

—The Mother Hunt. unabr. collector's ed. 1996. (Nero Wolfe Ser.). audio 36.00 (*0-7366-3523-8*, 4160) Books on Tape, Inc.

—The Mother Hunt. 1963. 3.50 o.p. (*0-670-49015-6*) Viking Penguin.

—The Mountain Cat Murders. 1993. 272p. mass mkt. 4.99 o.s.i (*0-553-25879-6*); 1982. 176p. pap. 2.50 o.p. (*0-553-20826-8*) Bantam Bks.

—Murder by the Book. 1995. 256p. pap. 19.00 (*0-553-76311-3*); 1985. mass mkt. 2.95 o.s.i (*0-553-24884-7*) Bantam Bks.

—Murder by the Book. unabr. collector's ed. 1995. (Nero Wolfe Ser.). audio 48.00 (*0-7366-3103-8*, 3779) Books on Tape, Inc.

—Murder by the Book. l.t. ed. 1996. 301p. 21.95 o.p. (*0-7838-1568-9*, Macmillan Reference USA) Gale Group.

—Murder by the Book. 1951. 2.50 o.p. (*0-670-49547-6*) Viking Penguin.

—Nero Wolfe: And Be a Villain. l.t. ed. 1988. 19.95 o.p. (*1-55504-643-6*); pap. 17.95 o.p. (*1-55504-644-4*) BBC Audiobooks America.

—Nero Wolfe Omnibus. lib. bdg. 26.95 (*0-8488-1893-8*) Amereon, Ltd.

—Not Quite Dead Enough. 1992. 208p. mass mkt. 5.99 (*0-553-26109-6*) Bantam Bks.

—Not Quite Dead Enough. unabr. collector's ed. 1994. (Nero Wolfe Ser.). audio 36.00 (*0-7366-2828-2*, 3536) Books on Tape, Inc.

—Not Quite Dead Enough. 1994. reprint ed. lib. bdg. 27.95 (*1-56849-341-X*) Buccaneer Bks., Inc.

—Not Quite Dead Enough. unabr. ed. 1994. audio 4.99 (*0-88646-727-6*) Durkin Hayes Publishing Ltd.

—An Officer & a Lady & Other Stories. 2000. 192p. mass mkt. 5.95 (*0-7867-0764-X*, Carroll & Graf Pubs.) Avalon Publishing Group.

—Over My Dead Body. 20.95 (*0-89190-341-0*) Amereon, Ltd.

—Over My Dead Body. unabr. ed. 2001. (Nero Wolfe Mystery Ser.). audio 29.95 (*1-57270-062-9*, N61062u, Audio Editions Bks. on Cassette) Audio Partners Publishing Corp.

—Over My Dead Body. 1993. (Crime Line Ser.). 272p. mass mkt. 5.99 (*0-553-23116-2*) Bantam Bks.

—Over My Dead Body. unabr. collector's ed. 1994. (Nero Wolfe Ser.). audio 48.00 (*0-7366-2747-2*, 3472) Books on Tape, Inc.

—Over My Dead Body. l.t. ed. 1982. lib. bdg. 13.95 o.p. (*0-8161-3288-7*, Macmillan Reference USA) Gale Group.

—Please Pass the Guilt. 1995. 176p. pap. 15.00 (*0-553-76308-3*); 1993. 192p. mass mkt. 4.99 (*0-553-23854-X*) Bantam Bks.

—Please Pass the Guilt. unabr. collector's ed. 1999. (Nero Wolfe Ser.). audio 32.00 (*0-7366-4456-3*, 4901) Books on Tape, Inc.

—Please Pass the Guilt. 1979. pap. 10.95 o.p. (*0-8161-6737-0*, Macmillan Reference USA) Gale Group.

—Plot It Yourself. unabr. ed. 2002. audio 24.95 (*1-57270-301-6*) Audio Partners Publishing Corp.

—Plot It Yourself. 1989. pap. 3.50 o.s.i (*0-553-27849-5*); 1985. 176p. mass mkt. 4.99 o.s.i (*0-553-25363-8*) Bantam Bks.

—Plot It Yourself. unabr. collector's ed. 1996. (Nero Wolfe Ser.). audio 36.00 (*0-7366-3354-5*, 4005) Books on Tape, Inc.

—Plot It Yourself. l.t. ed. 1984. (Nightingale Ser.). 248p. 8.95 o.p. (*0-8161-3547-9*, Macmillan Reference USA) Gale Group.

—Plot It Yourself. 1959. 2.95 o.p. (*0-670-56144-4*) Viking Penguin.

—The President Vanishes. 1982. 272p. pap. 2.50 o.p. (*0-553-22665-7*) Bantam Bks.

—Prisoner's Base. 1992. 224p. mass mkt. 5.99 (*0-553-24269-5*) Bantam Bks.

—Prisoner's Base. unabr. collector's ed. 1995. (Nero Wolfe Ser.). audio 42.00 (*0-7366-3137-2*, 3812) Books on Tape, Inc.

—Prisoner's Base. 1952. 2.50 o.p. (*0-670-57839-8*) Viking Penguin.

—A Prize for Princes. 1994. 256p. mass mkt. 4.95 o.p. (*0-7867-0104-8*, Carroll & Graf Pubs.) Avalon Publishing Group.

—A Prize for Princes. 1999. 312p. 26.00 (*0-7278-2277-2*) Severn Hse. Pubs., Ltd.

—The Red Box. unabr. ed. 1997. audio 29.95 (*1-57270-053-X*, N61053u, Audio Editions Bks. on Cassette) Audio Partners Publishing Corp.

—The Red Box. 1992. (Crime Line Ser.). 272p. mass mkt. 4.99 o.s.i (*0-553-24919-3*) Bantam Bks.

—The Red Box. 1979. 1.75 o.s.i (*0-515-05117-9*, Jove) Berkley Publishing Group.

—The Red Box. unabr. collector's ed. 1994. (Nero Wolfe Ser.). audio 48.00 (*0-7366-2697-2*, 3431) Books on Tape, Inc.

—The Red Box. abr. ed. 1995. audio 16.99 (*0-88646-377-7*, LFP 7377) Durkin Hayes Publishing Ltd.

—The Red Box. 1981. (Reader's Request Ser.). lib. bdg. 13.50 o.p. (*0-8161-3223-2*, Macmillan Reference USA) Gale Group.

—Red Threads. 1995. 272p. pap. 19.00 (*0-553-76299-0*); mass mkt. 4.99 (*0-553-22530-8*, Crimeline) Bantam Bks.

—A Right to Die? 1991. 208p. mass mkt. 5.99 (*0-553-24032-3*) Bantam Bks.

—A Right to Die? l.t. ed. 1996. (G. K. Hall Mystery Ser.). 224p. lib. bdg. 21.95 o.p. (*0-7838-1569-7*, Macmillan Reference USA) Gale Group.

—A Right to Die. unabr. collector's ed. 1997. (Nero Wolfe Ser.). audio 36.00 (*0-7366-3531-9*, 4170) Books on Tape, Inc.

—Royal Flush. 1965. 3.95 o.p. (*0-670-60934-X*) Viking Penguin.

—The Rubber Band. unabr. ed. 1997. (Nero Wolfe Mystery Ser.). audio 29.95 (*1-57270-052-1*, N61052u, Audio Editions Mystery Masters) Audio Partners Publishing Corp.

—The Rubber Band. 1995. 208p. pap. 15.00 (*0-553-76309-1*); 1982. 192p. mass mkt. 2.95 (*0-553-25550-9*) Bantam Bks.

—The Rubber Band. 1979. 1.75 o.s.i (*0-515-04867-4*, Jove) Berkley Publishing Group.

—The Rubber Band. unabr. collector's ed. 1994. (Nero Wolfe Ser.). audio 48.00 (*0-7366-2695-6*, 3429) Books on Tape, Inc.

—The Rubber Band. 1981. (Reader's Request Ser.). lib. bdg. 12.95 o.p. (*0-8161-3224-0*, Macmillan Reference USA) Gale Group.

—The Second Confession. unabr. ed. 2000. (Nero Wolfe Mystery Ser.). audio 29.95 (*1-57270-132-3*, N61132u, Audio Editions Mystery Masters) Audio Partners Publishing Corp.

—The Second Confession. 1995. 256p. mass mkt. 5.99 (*0-553-24594-5*) Bantam Bks.

—The Second Confession. unabr. collector's ed. 1995. (Nero Wolfe Ser.). audio 48.00 (*0-7366-3070-8*, 3752) Books on Tape, Inc.

—The Second Confession. l.t. ed. 1992. (Nightingale Series Large Print Bks.). 311p. pap. 15.95 (*0-8161-5202-0*, Macmillan Reference USA) Gale Group.

—The Silent Speaker. 1994. (Crime Line Ser.). 288p. mass mkt. 5.99 (*0-553-23497-8*) Bantam Bks.

—The Silent Speaker. unabr. collector's ed. 1994. (Nero Wolfe Ser.). audio 48.00 (*0-7366-2837-1*, 3545) Books on Tape, Inc.

—The Silent Speaker. l.t. ed. 2002. 350p. 29.45 (*0-7862-4195-0*) Thorndike Pr.

—Some Buried Caesar. 20.95 (*0-89190-340-2*) Amereon, Ltd.

—Some Buried Caesar. 1990. (Nero Wolfe Ser.). 288p. mass mkt. 5.99 (*0-553-25464-2*) Bantam Bks.

—Some Buried Caesar. 1982. (Reader's Request Ser.). 13.95 o.p. (*0-8161-3286-0*, Macmillan Reference USA) Gale Group.

—Some Buried Caeser. 1979. 1.75 o.s.i (*0-515-05118-7*, Jove) Berkley Publishing Group.

—The Sound of Murder. 1986. (Mystery Ser.). 192p. pap. 2.95 o.p. (*0-553-26148-7*) Bantam Bks.

—The Sound of Murder. 1979. 1.75 o.s.i (*0-515-05281-7*, Jove) Berkley Publishing Group.

—Target Practice. 1998. 320p. mass mkt. 5.95 (*0-7867-0496-9*, Carroll & Graf Pubs.) Avalon Publishing Group.

—Target Practice. l.t. ed. 1998. (Mystery Ser.). 424p. 28.95 (*0-7838-0178-5*) Thorndike Pr.

—This Won't Kill You. unabr. ed. 1998. audio 5.99 (*0-88646-865-5*, PAC-7865) Durkin Hayes Publishing Ltd.

—Three Aces. 1971. 8.95 o.p. (*0-670-70622-1*) Viking Penguin.

—Three at Wolfe's Door. 1995. 240p. mass mkt. 5.99 (*0-553-23803-5*, Crimeline) Bantam Bks.

—Three at Wolfe's Door. unabr. collector's ed. 1997. (Nero Wolfe Ser.). audio 48.00 (*0-7366-4060-6*, 4571) Books on Tape, Inc.

—Three for the Chair. 1985. 240p. mass mkt. 5.99 (*0-553-24813-8*) Bantam Bks.

—Three for the Chair. unabr. collector's ed. 1997. (Nero Wolfe Ser.). audio 42.00 (*0-7366-3750-8*, 4425) Books on Tape, Inc.

—Three for the Chair. 1957. 2.95 o.p. (*0-670-70779-1*) Viking Penguin.

—Three Men Out. 1991. 224p. mass mkt. 3.99 o.s.i (*0-553-24547-3*) Bantam Bks.

—Three Men Out. l.t. ed. 1990. (Nightingale Ser.). 296p. lib. bdg. 13.95 o.p. (*0-8161-4793-0*, Macmillan Reference USA) Gale Group.

—Three Men Out. 1954. 2.50 o.p. (*0-670-70846-1*) Viking Penguin.

—Three Trumps. 1973. 6.95 o.p. (*0-670-71031-8*) Viking Penguin.

—Three Witnesses. 1981. 224p. mass mkt. 5.99 (*0-553-24959-2*) Bantam Bks.

—Three Witnesses. unabr. collector's ed. 1997. (Nero Wolfe Ser.). audio 42.00 (*0-7366-3751-6*, 4426) Books on Tape, Inc.

—Three Witnesses. 1956. 2.75 o.p. (*0-670-71080-6*) Viking Penguin.

—Too Many Clients. 1955. 192p. mass mkt. 2.95 o.s.i (*0-553-25423-5*) Bantam Bks.

—Too Many Clients. unabr. collector's ed. 1996. (Nero Wolfe Ser.). audio 36.00 (*0-7366-3400-2*, 4047) Books on Tape, Inc.

—Too Many Clients. 1983. (Nightingale Ser.). 241p. pap. 9.95 o.p. (*0-8161-3549-5*, Macmillan Reference USA) Gale Group.

—Too Many Clients. 1960. 2.95 o.p. (*0-670-72010-0*) Viking Penguin.

—Too Many Cooks. 1995. 208p. pap. 15.00 (*0-553-76306-7*); 1988. 256p. mass mkt. 3.50 (*0-553-27290-X*) Bantam Bks.

—Too Many Cooks. l.t. ed. 1985. (Nightingale Ser.). 397p. 10.95 o.p. (*0-8161-3868-0*, Macmillan Reference USA) Gale Group.

—Too Many Cooks. 1976. (Crime Fiction Ser.). reprint ed. lib. bdg. 21.00 o.p. (*0-8240-2394-3*) Garland Publishing, Inc.

—Too Many Women: A Nero Wolfe Mystery. unabr. ed. 1999. audio 29.95 (*1-57270-104-8*, N61104u, Audio Editions Mystery Masters) Audio Partners Publishing Corp.

—Too Many Women: A Nero Wolfe Mystery. l.t. ed. 1999. 355p. (*0-7540-3882-3*); pap. (*0-7540-3883-1*) BBC Audiobooks America.

—Too Many Women: A Nero Wolfe Mystery. unabr. collector's ed. 1995. (Nero Wolfe Ser.). audio 48.00 (*0-7366-3045-7*, 3727) Books on Tape, Inc.

—Too Many Women: A Nero Wolfe Mystery. l.t. ed. 1999. (Mystery Ser.). 355p. 26.95 o.p. (*0-7862-2049-X*) Thorndike Pr.

—Trio for Blunt Instruments. 1979. pap. 1.75 o.p. (*0-553-13232-6*) Bantam Bks.

—Trio for Blunt Instruments. unabr. collector's ed. 1997. (Nero Wolfe Ser.). audio 48.00 (*0-7366-4061-4*, 4572) Books on Tape, Inc.

—Triple Jeopardy. 1995. 192p. pap. 15.00 (*0-553-76307-5*); 1993. 256p. mass mkt. 4.99 (*0-553-23591-5*) Bantam Bks.

—Triple Jeopardy. 1952. 2.50 o.p. (*0-670-73109-9*) Viking Penguin.

—Trouble in Triplicate. unabr. collector's ed. 1996. (Nero Wolfe Ser.). audio 48.00 (*0-7366-3268-9*, 3925) Books on Tape, Inc.

—Trouble in Triplicate. 1949. 2.50 o.p. (*0-670-73241-9*) Viking Penguin.

—Under the Andes. 1994. 290p. mass mkt. 4.95 (*0-7867-0179-X*, Carroll & Graf Pubs.) Avalon Publishing Group.

—Under the Andes. unabr. ed. 1997. audio 49.95 (*0-7861-1187-9*, 1947) Blackstone Audio Bks., Inc.

—Under the Andes. E-Book 2.95 (*1-57799-901-0*) Logos Research Systems, Inc.

—Under the Andes. 1985. 15.95 o.p. (*0-89296-119-8*) Mysterious Pr.

—Under the Andes. 1986. 312p. reprint ed. mass mkt. 3.50 (*0-445-40507-4*, Mysterious Pr. Paperback Bks.) Warner Bks., Inc.

—Where There's a Will. unabr. ed. 1999. (Nero Wolfe Mystery Ser.). audio 29.95 (*1-57270-096-3*, N61096u, Audio Editions Mystery Masters) Audio Partners Publishing Corp.

—Where There's a Will. l.t. ed. (Nero Wolfe Mystery Ser.). 1992. pap. 20.95 o.p. (*0-7927-1138-6*, CS0304); 1991. 22.95 o.p. (*0-7927-1137-8*, CH0233) BBC Audiobooks America.

—Where There's a Will. 256p. 1995. pap. 15.00 (*0-553-76301-6*); 1992. mass mkt. 4.99 (*0-553-29591-8*) Bantam Bks.

—Where There's a Will. unabr. collector's ed. 1994. (Nero Wolfe Ser.). audio 42.00 (*0-7366-2766-9*, 3487) Books on Tape, Inc.

—Where There's a Will. 1982. (Reader's Request Ser.). 13.95 o.p. (*0-8161-3287-9*, Macmillan Reference USA) Gale Group.

—Where There's a Will. 1941. pap. 1.50 o.p. (*0-380-01620-6*, 39529, Avon Bks.) Morrow/Avon.

Stout, Rex, contrib. by. Death of a Dude: A Nero Wolfe Novel. 1999. (*0-7540-3797-5*); (*0-7540-3798-3*) BBC Audiobooks America.

—The Final Deduction: A Nero Wolfe Novel. (*0-7540-3705-3*) BBC Audiobooks America.

Straley, John. Cold Water Burning. 2001. 224p. mass mkt. 6.50 (*0-553-58076-0*) Bantam Bks.

Summers, Cara. Short, Sweet & Sexy. 2002. (Harlequin Temptation Ser.). 216p. mass mkt. (*0-373-69100-9*, Harlequin Bks.) Harlequin Enterprises, Ltd.

Swanson, Doug J. Big Town. 1995. 288p. mass mkt. 4.50 o.p. (*0-06-109213-4*, HarperTorch) Morrow/Avon.

—Big Town: A Novel of Suspense. 1994. 224p. 18.00 o.p. (*0-06-017749-7*) HarperTrade.

—Dreamboat. 1996. 256p. mass mkt. 4.99 o.p. (*0-06-109214-2*) HarperCollins Pubs.

—Umbrella Man. 1999. (Jack Flippo Mysteries Ser.: Vol. 4). 273p. 23.95 o.p. (*0-399-14503-6*, G. P. Putnam's Sons) Penguin Group (USA) Inc.

—96 Tears. 1996. 208p. 22.50 o.p. (*0-06-017511-7*) HarperCollins Pubs.

Swift, Graham. The Light of Day. 2003. 336p. 24.00 (*0-375-41549-1*) Knopf, Alfred A. Inc.

Taibo, Paco Ignacio, II. An Easy Thing. 2002. (Missing Mystery Ser.: Vol. 49). 240p. pap. 14.95 o.s.i (*1-59058-006-0*) Poisoned Pen Pr.

—An Easy Thing. Neuman, William I., tr. 1990. 240p. 16.95 o.p. (*0-670-82462-3*, Viking) Viking Penguin.

—An Easy Thing. 1990. (Crime Ser.). 240p. reprint ed. pap. 4.50 o.p. (*0-14-011523-4*, Penguin Bks.) Viking Penguin.

—Frontera Dreams: A Hector Balascoran Shayne Detective Novel. Verner, William K., tr. from SPA. 2002. (Illus.). 120p. pap. 13.95 (*0-938317-58-X*) Cinco Puntos Pr.

—No Happy Ending. Neuman, William I., tr. 1993. 192p. 17.95 (*0-89296-517-7*) Mysterious Pr.

—No Happy Ending. 2003. 254p. pap. 14.95 o.s.i (*1-59058-038-9*) Poisoned Pen Pr.

—No Happy Ending. Neuman, William I., tr. 1994. 192p. mass mkt. 5.50 (*0-446-40329-6*, Mysterious Pr. Paperback Bks.) Warner Bks., Inc.

—Return to the Same City. Dail, Laura, tr. from SPA. 1996. Tr. of Regreso a la Misma Ciudad y Bajo la Lluvia. 192p. 25.00 (*0-89296-590-8*) Mysterious Pr.

—Return to the Same City. Dail, Laura, tr. 1997. Tr. of Regreso a la Misma Ciudad y Bajo la Lluvia. 176p. mass mkt. 5.99 (*0-446-40520-5*) Warner Bks., Inc.

—Some Clouds. Neuman, William I., tr. 1993. (Crime Ser.). 176p. pap. 9.00 o.p. (*0-14-014896-5*, Penguin Bks.) Penguin Group (USA) Inc.

—Some Clouds. 2002. 250p. pap. 14.95 o.s.i (*1-59058-032-X*) Poisoned Pen Pr.

—Some Clouds. Neuman, William I., tr. from SPA. 1992. 176p. 19.00 o.p. (*0-670-83825-X*, Viking) Viking Penguin.

Taylor, Elizabeth Atwood. The Cable Car Murder. 1988. 240p. reprint ed. mass mkt. 4.99 o.s.i (*0-8041-0281-3*, Ivy Bks.) Ballantine Bks.

—The Cable Car Murder. (Fingerprint Mysteries Ser.). 224p. 1983. pap. 5.95 o.p. (*0-312-11312-9*, Saint Martin's Griffin); 1981. 11.95 o.p. (*0-312-11311-0*) St. Martin's Pr.

—The Cable Car Murders. l.t. ed. 1982. 412p. reprint ed. 12.95 o.p. (*0-89621-360-9*) Thorndike Pr.

—Murder at Vassar. 1988. mass mkt. 4.95 o.s.i (*0-8041-0212-0*, Ivy Bks.) Ballantine Bks.

—Murder at Vassar. 1987. 256p. 15.95 o.p. (*0-312-00160-6*) St. Martin's Pr.

—The Northwest Murders. 1992. 288p. 18.95 o.p. (*0-312-07753-X*, Saint Martin's Minotaur) St. Martin's Pr.

Taylor, Jean. The Last of Her Lies: A Maggie Garrett Mystery. 1996. 238p. (Orig.). pap. 10.95 (*1-878067-75-3*, Seal Pr.) Avalon Publishing Group.

—We Know Where You Live. 1995. 240p. pap. 9.95 (*1-878067-62-1*, Seal Pr.) Avalon Publishing Group.

Taylor, Phoebe Atwood. Banbury Bog. 1978. reprint ed. lib. bdg. 16.95 o.p. (*0-89966-247-1*) Buccaneer Bks., Inc.

—Banbury Bog. 1987. (Asey Mayo Cape Cod Mystery Ser.). 176p. reprint ed. pap. 5.95 (*0-88150-090-9*, Foul Play) Norton, W. W. & Co., Inc.

—The Deadly Sunshade. l.t. ed. 1992. 19.95 o.p. (*0-7927-1318-4*); pap. 17.95 o.p. (*0-7927-1317-6*) BBC Audiobooks America.

—The Deadly Sunshade. 1989. (Asey Mayo Cape Cod Mystery Ser.). 300p. reprint ed. pap. 6.00 o.p. (*0-88150-136-0*) Countryman Pr.

—Death Lights a Candle. 1989. (Asey Mayo Cape Cod Mystery Ser.). 304p. reprint ed. pap. 7.95 (*0-88150-145-X*, Foul Play) Norton, W. W. & Co., Inc.

—Deathblow Hill. 1993. (Asey Mayo Cape Cod Mystery Ser.). 286p. pap. 6.50 (*0-88150-262-6*, Foul Play) Norton, W. W. & Co., Inc.

—Diplomatic Corpse. 1989. (Asey Mayo Cape Cod Mystery Ser.). 244p. reprint ed. pap. 5.95 o.p. (*0-88150-146-8*) Countryman Pr.

—Figure Away. 1979. (Foul Play Press Bks.). reprint ed. pap. 4.50 o.p. (*0-914378-48-1*) Countryman Pr.

—Figure Away. 1991. (Asey Mayo Cape Cod Mystery Ser.). 286p. reprint ed. pap. 5.95 o.p. (*0-88150-206-5*, Foul Play) Norton, W. W. & Co., Inc.

—Going, Going, Gone. 21.95 (*0-8488-1201-8*) Amereon, Ltd.

—Murder at the New York World's Fair. 1987. 265p. reprint ed. pap. 8.95 o.p. (*0-88150-095-X*) Countryman Pr.

—The Mystery of the Cape Cod Players. 1987. (Asey Mayo Cape Cod Mystyery Ser.). 272p. reprint ed. pap. 6.00 o.p. (*0-88150-091-7*) Countryman Pr.

—The Mystery of the Cape Cod Tavern. 1985. (Asey Mayo Cape Cod Mystery Ser.). 288p. pap. 7.95 (*0-88150-047-X*, Foul Play) Norton, W. W. & Co., Inc.

—Octagon House. 1983. pap. 4.50 o.p. (*0-914378-47-3*) Countryman Pr.

—Octagon House. 1991. (Asey Mayo Cape Cod Mystery Ser.). 296p. pap. 6.95 (*0-88150-194-8*, Foul Play) Norton, W. W. & Co., Inc.

—Octagon House. 1999. lib. bdg. 22.95 (*1-56723-139-X*, 148) Yestermorrow, Inc.

—Proof of the Pudding. 1979. (Foul Play Press Bks.). reprint ed. pap. 4.95 o.p. (*0-914378-55-4*) Countryman Pr.

—Proof of the Pudding. 1991. 192p. pap. 6.00 (*0-88150-193-X*, Foul Play) Norton, W. W. & Co., Inc.

—Punch with Care. 21.95 (*0-8488-1202-6*) Amereon, Ltd.

—Punch with Care. 1992. (Asey Mayo Cape Cod Mystery Ser.). 224p. pap. 7.95 (*0-88150-229-4*, Foul Play) Norton, W. W. & Co., Inc.

—The Six Iron Spiders. 1979. (Foul Play Press Bks.). reprint ed. pap. 4.95 o.p. (*0-914378-53-8*) Countryman Pr.

—The Six Iron Spiders. 1992. (Asey Mayo Cape Cod Mystery Ser.). 288p. pap. 6.95 (*0-88150-230-8*, Foul Play) Norton, W. W. & Co., Inc.

—The Tinkling Symbol. 1993. (Asey Mayo Cape Cod Mystery Ser.). 288p. pap. 7.95 (*0-88150-263-4*, Foul Play) Norton, W. W. & Co., Inc.

Thompson, Christian. That Which Doesn't Kill You. 2002. 254p. pap. 24.95 (*0-7490-0553-X*) Allison & Busby, Ltd. GBR. *Dist:* International Publishers Marketing.

Thrasher, L. L. Cat's Paw, Incorporated. 1995. (Brown Bag Mystery Line Ser.). 616p. 3.00 o.p. (*0-933031-41-6*) Council Oak Bks.

—Dogsbody, Inc. 1999. 288p. 22.95 o.p. (*1-885173-65-2*) Write Way Publishing.

Truluck, Bob. Street Level. E-Book 22.95 (*0-312-27616-8*); 2000. 218p. 22.95 (*0-312-26626-X*, Saint Martin's Minotaur) St. Martin's Pr.

Tyler, Lee. The Case of the Missing Links. 1999. 190p. pap. 10.95 (*1-56474-302-0*) Fithian Pr.

—The Teed-Off Ghost: A Hawai'ian Golf Mystery. 2002. 192p. pap. 12.95 (*1-56474-389-6*) Fithian Pr.

Upton, Robert. Dead on the Stick. 256p. 1987. pap. 3.50 o.p. (*0-14-007601-8*, Penguin Bks.); 1986. 15.95 o.p. (*0-670-80331-6*) Viking Penguin.

—The Faberge Egg. 1988. 208p. 16.95 o.p. (*0-525-24692-4*, Dutton) Dutton/Plume.

—Fade Out. 1984. (Amos McGuffin Mystery Ser.). 13.95 o.p. (*0-670-30469-7*) Viking Penguin.

—Fade Out: An Amos McGuffin Mystery. 1986. 192p. pap. 3.95 o.p. (*0-14-008312-X*, Penguin Bks.) Viking Penguin.

—A Golden Fleecing. 1979. 10.95 o.p. (*0-312-33730-2*) St. Martin's Pr.

—A Killing in Real Estate: An Amos McGuffin Mystery. 1990. 192p. 17.95 o.p. (*0-525-24927-3*, Dutton) Dutton/Plume.

—Who'd Want to Kill Old George? 1982. 224p. pap. 2.50 o.p. (*0-523-41537-0*, Pinnacle Bks.) Kensington Publishing Corp.

—Who'd Want to Kill Old George? 1976. 7.95 o.p. (*0-399-11867-5*) Putnam Publishing Group, The.

Vachss, Andrew. Blossom. 2001. E-Book 11.50 (*1-59061-234-5*) Adobe Systems, Inc.

—Blossom. 1991. 320p. mass mkt. 5.95 o.s.i (*0-8041-0751-3*, Ivy Bks.) Ballantine Bks.

—Blossom. 1996. 272p. pap. 13.00 (*0-679-77261-8*) McKay, David Co., Inc.

—Blue Belle. 2001. E-Book 11.00 (*1-59061-228-0*) Adobe Systems, Inc.

—Blue Belle. 1994. lib. bdg. 24.95 o.p. (*1-56849-463-7*) Buccaneer Bks., Inc.

—Blue Belle. 1990. 336p. mass mkt. 4.95 o.p. (*0-451-16290-0*, Signet Bks.) NAL.

—Blue Belle. 1995. 352p. pap. 13.00 (*0-679-76168-3*) Random Hse., Inc.

—Choice of Evil: A Burke Novel. 2001. E-Book 11.50 (*1-59061-222-1*) Adobe Systems, Inc.

—Choice of Evil: A Burke Novel. 2000. (Crime - Black Lizard Ser.). 336p. pap. 13.00 (*0-375-70662-3*, Vintage) Knopf Publishing Group.

—Choice of Evil: A Burke Novel. 1999. (Burke Novels Ser.). 305p. 23.00 o.s.i (*0-375-40647-6*) Knopf, Alfred A. Inc.

—Choice of Evil: A Burke Novel. 2001. E-Book 7.99 (*0-375-71913-X*) Random Hse., Inc.

—Down Here: A Burke Novel. 2004. 304p. 19.95 (*1-4000-4173-2*, Knopf) Knopf Publishing Group.

—Down in the Zero. 2001. E-Book 11.00 (*1-59061-229-9*) Adobe Systems, Inc.

—Down in the Zero. 1995. pap. 7.00 o.s.i (*0-679-76087-3*); 272p. pap. 12.00 (*0-679-76066-0*) Random Hse., Inc.

—False Allegations: A Burke Novel. 2001. E-Book 11.00 (*1-59061-235-3*) Adobe Systems, Inc.

—False Allegations: A Burke Novel. 1997. 240p. pap. 12.00 (*0-679-77293-6*, Vintage) Knopf Publishing Group.

—Flood: A Burke Novel. 2002. E-Book 11.50 (*1-59061-886-6*) Adobe Systems, Inc.

—Flood: A Burke Novel. 1994. lib. bdg. 24.95 o.p. (*1-56849-465-3*) Buccaneer Bks., Inc.

—Flood: A Burke Novel. 1985. 341p. 17.95 o.s.i (*0-917657-43-8*) Fine, Donald I. Bks.

—Flood: A Burke Novel. 1986. mass mkt. 5.99 (*0-671-61905-5*, Pocket) Simon & Schuster.

—Footsteps of the Hawk. 2001. E-Book 11.00 (*1-59061-233-7*) Adobe Systems, Inc.

—Footsteps of the Hawk. 1996. 256p. pap. 12.00 (*0-679-76663-4*) Random Hse., Inc.

—Hard Candy. 2001. E-Book 11.00 (*1-59061-230-2*) Adobe Systems, Inc.

—Hard Candy. 1994. lib. bdg. 24.95 o.p. (*1-56849-464-5*) Buccaneer Bks., Inc.

—Hard Candy. 1990. mass mkt. 4.95 o.p. (*0-451-16690-6*, Signet Bks.) NAL.

—Hard Candy. 1990. 4.99 o.p. (*0-517-05629-1*) Random Hse. Value Publishing.

—Hard Candy. 1995. 256p. pap. 12.00 (*0-679-76169-1*) Random Hse., Inc.

—Pain Management: A Burke Novel. 2001. E-Book 19.00 (*1-59061-376-7*) Adobe Systems, Inc.

—Pain Management: A Burke Novel. 2002. 336p. pap. 13.00 (*0-375-72647-0*) Random Hse., Inc.

—Sacrifice. 2001. E-Book 11.00 (*1-59061-231-0*) Adobe Systems, Inc.

—Sacrifice. 1992. mass mkt. 5.99 o.s.i (*0-8041-0919-2*, Ivy Bks.) Ballantine Bks.

—Sacrifice. 1992. 4.99 o.p. (*0-517-09513-0*) Random Hse. Value Publishing.

—Sacrifice. 1996. 288p. pap. 12.00 (*0-679-76410-0*) Random Hse., Inc.

—Safe House: A Burke Novel. 2001. E-Book 11.00 (*1-59061-225-6*) Adobe Systems, Inc.

—Safe House: A Burke Novel. 1999. 320p. pap. 12.00 (*0-375-70074-9*, Vintage) Knopf Publishing Group.

—Safe House: A Burke Novel. 2001. E-Book 7.99 (*0-375-71912-1*) Random Hse., Inc.

—Strega. 2001. E-Book 11.00 (*1-59061-232-9*) Adobe Systems, Inc.

—Strega. 1991. mass mkt. 5.99 o.s.i (*0-8041-0925-7*, Ivy Bks.) Ballantine Bks.

—Strega. 1987. 293p. 18.95 o.s.i (*0-394-55937-1*) Knopf, Alfred A. Inc.

—Strega. 1988. mass mkt. 4.50 o.p. (*0-451-15179-8*, Signet Bks.) NAL.

—Strega. 1988. 3.99 o.p. (*0-517-68183-8*) Random Hse. Value Publishing.

—Strega. 1996. 304p. pap. 12.00 (*0-679-76409-7*) Random Hse., Inc.

Valin, Jonathan. Day of Wrath. 1994. 320p. mass mkt. 4.99 o.s.i (*0-440-21041-0*) Dell Publishing.

—Day of Wrath. 1983. (Harry Stoner Mystery Ser.). 256p. pap. 3.50 (*0-380-63917-3*, Avon Bks.) Morrow/Avon.

—Dead Letter. 1994. 320p. mass mkt. 4.99 o.s.i (*0-440-21038-0*) Dell Publishing.

—Dead Letter. 1983. (Harry Stoner Mystery Ser.). 224p. pap. 3.50 (*0-380-61366-2*, Avon Bks.) Morrow/Avon.

—Extenuating Circumstances. 1989. 15.95 o.s.i (*0-440-50110-5*, Delacorte Pr.); 1989. 240p. 15.95 o.s.i (*0-385-29683-5*, Delacorte Pr.); 1990. 256p. reprint ed. mass mkt. 3.95 o.s.i (*0-440-20630-8*) Dell Publishing.

—Final Notice. 1994. 320p. mass mkt. 4.99 o.s.i (*0-440-21032-1*) Dell Publishing.

—Final Notice. 1982. (Harry Stoner Mystery Ser.). 192p. pap. 3.50 (*0-380-57893-X*, Avon Bks.) Morrow/Avon.

—Fire Lake. 1989. 272p. (YA). reprint ed. mass mkt. 4.99 o.s.i (*0-440-20145-4*) Dell Publishing.

—Fire Lake: A Harry Stoner Novel. 1987. 264p. 14.95 o.s.i (*0-385-29589-8*, Delacorte Pr.) Dell Publishing.

—Life's Work. 1987. 256p. reprint ed. mass mkt. 4.99 o.s.i (*0-440-14790-5*) Dell Publishing.

—Life's Work: A Harry Stoner Novel. 1986. 240p. 14.95 o.s.i (*0-385-29503-0*, Delacorte Pr.) Dell Publishing.

—The Lime Pit. 1994. 320p. mass mkt. 4.99 o.s.i (*0-440-21029-1*) Dell Publishing.

—The Lime Pit. 1983. (Harry Stoner Mystery Ser.). 208p. pap. 3.50 (*0-380-55442-9*, Avon Bks.) Morrow/Avon.

—The Music Lovers: A Harry Stoner Mystery. 1994. 304p. mass mkt. 4.99 o.s.i (*0-440-21686-9*) Dell Publishing.

—Natural Causes. 1994. 384p. mass mkt. 4.99 o.s.i (*0-440-21035-6*) Dell Publishing.

—Natural Causes. 1984. (Harry Stoner Mystery Ser.). 304p. pap. 2.95 o.p. (*0-380-68247-8*, 68247, Avon Bks.) Morrow/Avon.

—Second Chance: A Harry Stoner Mystery. 288p. 1992. mass mkt. 4.99 o.s.i (*0-440-21222-7*); 1991. 18.00 o.s.i (*0-385-29912-5*, Delacorte Pr.) Dell Publishing.

Valtos, William M. La Magdalena. 2002. (Theo Nikonos Mystery Ser.). 408p. pap. 15.95 (*1-57174-278-6*) Hampton Roads Publishing Co., Inc.

Van Dine, S. S. The Benson Murder Case. reprint ed. lib. bdg. 24.95 (*0-89190-511-1*, Rivercity Pr.) Amereon, Ltd.

—The Benson Murder Case. 1983. 256p. pap. 3.95 o.s.i (*0-684-17976-8*, Macmillan Reference USA) Gale Group.

—The Bishop Murder Case. reprint ed. lib. bdg. 25.95 (*0-89190-512-X*, Rivercity Pr.) Amereon, Ltd.

—The Bishop Murder Case. 1983. 256p. pap. 3.95 o.s.i (*0-684-17977-6*, Macmillan Reference USA) Gale Group.

—The Bishop Murder Case. l.t. ed. 1984. (Philo Vance Mystery Ser.). 453p. reprint ed. 14.95 o.p. (*0-89621-501-6*) Thorndike Pr.

—The Canary Murder Case. reprint ed. lib. bdg. 25.95 (*0-89190-513-8*, Rivercity Pr.) Amereon, Ltd.

—The Canary Murder Case. 1979. pap. 2.25 o.s.i (*0-684-16404-3*, Macmillan Reference USA) Gale Group.

—The Casino Murder Case. 1985. 312p. pap. 3.95 o.p. (*0-684-18503-2*, Macmillan Reference USA) Gale Group.

—The Dragon Murder Case: A Philo Vance Mystery. 1994. 336p. 35.00 (*1-883402-21-2*, Scribner) Simon & Schuster.

—Gracie Allen Murder Case: A Philo Vance Story. 21.95 (*0-8488-0850-9*) Amereon, Ltd.

—Gracie Allen Murder Case: A Philo Vance Story. 1994. 336p. reprint ed. pap. 6.95 (*1-883402-09-3*, Scribner) Simon & Schuster.

—The Greene Murder Case. reprint ed. lib. bdg. 27.95 (*0-89190-514-6*, Rivercity Pr.) Amereon, Ltd.

—The Greene Murder Case. 1980. pap. 2.95 o.s.i (*0-684-16734-4*, Scribner Paper Fiction) Simon & Schuster.

—The Kennel Murder Case: A Philo Vance Mystery. 1984. 312p. pap. 3.95 o.s.i (*0-684-18248-3*, Macmillan Reference USA) Gale Group.

—The Kidnap Murder Case: A Philo Vance Story. 1994. 320p. reprint ed. pap. 7.95 o.s.i (*1-883402-93-X*, Scribner) Simon & Schuster.

—The Scarab Murder Case. 1984. (Philo Vance Mystery Ser.). pap. 4.50 o.s.i (*0-684-18159-2*, Scribner Paper Fiction) Simon & Schuster.

—The Winter Murder Case: A Philo Vance Story. 1993. 196p. pap. 6.95 o.s.i (*1-883402-08-5*, Scribner) Simon & Schuster.

Ventura, Michael. The Death of Frank Sinatra: A Novel. 1996. 320p. 22.50 o.p. (*0-8050-3738-1*) Holt, Henry & Co.

—The Death of Frank Sinatra: A Novel. 1997. (Dead Letter Mysteries Ser.). 320p. mass mkt. 5.99 (*0-312-96474-9*, St. Martin's Paperbacks) St. Martin's Pr.

Wait, Lea. Shadows at the Fair: An Antique Print Mystery. (Illus.). 272p. 2003. mass mkt. 6.99 (*0-7434-5620-3*, Pocket); 2002. 24.00 (*0-7432-2553-8*, Scribner) Simon & Schuster.

—Shadows at the Fair: An Antique Print Mystery. 2003. (Americana Ser.). 28.95 (*0-7862-5003-8*) Thorndike Pr.

Waldman, Ayelet. A Playdate with Death. 2003. (Mommy-Track Mysteries Ser.: No. 3). 240p. mass mkt. 6.99 (*0-425-19104-4*, Prime Crime) Berkley Publishing Group.

Wallace, Patricia. August Nights. (Five Star First Edition Mystery Ser.). 2002. 274p. 25.95 (*0-7862-4180-2*, Five Star); 2003. 259p. pap. 13.95 (*1-4104-0125-1*, Five Star Trade) Gale Group.

Watson, John H. Sherlock Holmes & the Red Demon. Millett, Larry, ed. & intro. by. 1996. (Illus.). 336p. 22.95 (*0-670-87039-0*, Viking) Viking Penguin.

Weiner, Ellis. Drop Dead, My Lovely. 2004. 288p. 23.95 (*0-451-21117-0*) NAL.

Wesley, Valerie Wilson. Devil's Gonna Get Him. 1996. (Tamara Hayle Mystery Ser.: Vol. 2). 288p. mass mkt. 6.99 (*0-380-72492-8*, Avon Bks.) Morrow/Avon.

—Devil's Gonna Get Him. 1995. 212p. 19.95 o.p. (*0-399-14027-1*, G. P. Putnam's Sons) Penguin Group (USA) Inc.

—Easier to Kill. l.t. ed. 1999. pap. 23.95 o.p. (*1-56895-704-1*, Wheeler Publishing, Inc.) Gale Group.

—Easier to Kill. 1999. (Tamara Hayle Mystery Ser.). 304p. mass mkt. 6.99 (*0-380-72910-5*, Avon Bks.) Morrow/Avon.

—Easier to Kill. 1998. (Tamara Hayle Mystery Ser.: Vol. 5). 193p. 23.95 o.p. (*0-399-14445-5*) Penguin Group (USA) Inc.

—The Hiding Place. 1998. (Tamara Hayle Mystery Ser.). 288p. mass mkt. 6.99 (*0-380-72909-1*, Avon Bks.) Morrow/Avon.

—No Hiding Place. unabr. ed. 1998. audio 40.00 (*0-7366-4214-5*, 4712) Books on Tape, Inc.

—No Hiding Place: A Tamara Hayle Mystery. 1997. 207p. 21.95 o.s.i (*0-399-14318-1*, G. P. Putnam's Sons) Penguin Group (USA) Inc.

—When Death Comes Stealin. 1995. (Tamara Hayle Mystery Ser.: Vol. 1). 320p. reprint ed. mass mkt. 6.99 (*0-380-72491-X*, Avon Bks.) Morrow/Avon.

—When Death Comes Stealing. 1994. 224p. 19.95 o.p. (*0-399-13949-4*, G. P. Putnam's Sons) Penguin Group (USA) Inc.

—Where Evil Sleeps. unabr. ed. 1998. audio 40.00 (*0-7366-4120-3*, 4624) Books on Tape, Inc.

—Where Evil Sleeps. 1997. 288p. mass mkt. 6.50 (*0-380-72908-3*, Avon Bks.) Morrow/Avon.

—Where Evil Sleeps. 1996. 224p. 21.95 o.p. (*0-399-14145-6*, G. P. Putnam's Sons) Penguin Group (USA) Inc.

Wessel, John. Kiss It Goodbye: A Novel. 2002. 336p. E-Book 24.00 (*0-7432-2605-4*, Simon & Schuster) Simon & Schuster.

West, Charles G. The Sacred Disc. 2000. (San Joaquin Mysteries Ser.). 192p. pap. 12.95 (*0-9664520-4-6*); E-Book 7.00 (*1-930486-04-9*) Salvo Pr.

Whitelaw, Stella. Spin & Die. 2002. 256p. 25.99 (*0-7278-5831-9*); 28.99 (*0-7278-7193-5*) Severn Hse. Pubs., Ltd.

Wilcox, Collin. Bernhardt's Edge. 1991. pap. 3.95 o.p. (*0-8125-1148-4*); 1988. 320p. 17.95 o.p. (*0-312-93076-3*) Doherty, Tom Assocs., LLC. (Tor Bks.).

—Except for the Bones. 1991. 288p. 18.95 o.p. (*0-312-93162-X*, Tor Bks.) Doherty, Tom Assocs., LLC.

—Find Her a Grave. 1993. 288p. 19.95 o.p. (*0-312-85244-4*, Forge Bks.) Doherty, Tom Assocs., LLC.

—Silent Witness. 1992. mass mkt. 3.99 (*0-8125-1149-2*); 1990. 17.95 o.p. (*0-312-93161-1*) Doherty, Tom Assocs., LLC. (Tor Bks.).

Wilhelm, Kate. The Casebook of Constance & Charlie. Vol. 1. 1999. 614p. pap. 18.95 (*0-312-24501-7*); Vol. 2. 2000. 595p. pap. 16.95 (*0-312-25378-8*) St. Martin's Pr. (Saint Martin's Griffin).

—The Dark Door. 1993. 352p. pap. 4.50 (*0-8439-3416-6*) Dorchester Publishing Co., Inc.

—The Dark Door. 1988. 256p. 16.95 o.p. (*0-312-02182-8*) St. Martin's Pr.

—A Flush of Shadows: Five Short Novels. 1996. mass mkt. 5.99 o.s.i (*0-449-22434-1*, Fawcett) Ballantine Bks.

—A Flush of Shadows: Five Short Novels. 1995. 352p. 22.95 o.p. (*0-312-13075-9*, Saint Martin's Minotaur) St. Martin's Pr.

—Hamlet Trap: A Charlie Meiklejohn & Constance Leidl Mystery. 1988. mass mkt. 4.50 (*0-312-91125-4*, St. Martin's Paperbacks) St. Martin's Pr.

—The Hamlet Trap: A Constance & Charlie Meiklejohn Mystery. 1987. 240p. 15.95 o.p. (*0-312-94000-9*, Saint Martin's Minotaur) St. Martin's Pr.

—Seven Kinds of Death. 1994. 256p. reprint ed. pap. 4.50 (*0-8439-3570-7*) Dorchester Publishing Co., Inc.

—Seven Kinds of Death. 1992. 256p. 18.95 o.p. (*0-312-08290-8*, Saint Martin's Minotaur) St. Martin's Pr.

—Smart House. l.t. ed. 1991. 16.95 o.p. (*0-7451-9790-6*, C0300); pap. 15.95 o.p. (*0-7927-0255-7*, C0434) BBC Audiobooks America.

—Smart House. 1991. 272p. reprint ed. pap. 3.95 (*0-8439-3043-8*) Dorchester Publishing Co., Inc.

—Smart House: A Charlie Meiklejohn-Constance Leidl Mystery. 1989. 272p. 16.95 o.p. (*0-312-02642-0*, Saint Martin's Minotaur) St. Martin's Pr.

—Sweet, Sweet Poison. 1991. 272p. reprint ed. pap. 3.99 (*0-8439-3163-9*) Dorchester Publishing Co., Inc.

—Sweet, Sweet Poison. 1990. 16.95 o.p. (*0-312-04433-X*, Saint Martin's Minotaur) St. Martin's Pr.

Wiltse, David. Blown Away. l.t. ed. 1997. 368p. mass mkt. 6.50 o.s.i (*0-425-15971-X*) Berkley Publishing Group.

—Blown Away. l.t. ed. 1997. (G. K. Hall Core Ser.). 469p. lib. bdg. 26.95 (*0-7838-2009-7*, Macmillan Reference USA) Gale Group.

—Blown Away. 1996. 352p. 24.95 o.s.i (*0-399-14208-8*, G. P. Putnam's Sons) Penguin Group (USA) Inc.

—Blown Away: A John Becker Thriller. abr. ed. 1997. audio 17.00 (*1-56876-063-9*) Soundlines Entertainment, Inc.

Wiltz, Chris. A Diamond Before You Die. (Neal Rafferty Mystery Ser.). 208p. 1988. mass mkt. 3.95 o.s.i (*0-445-40536-8*); 1987. 15.95 o.p. (*0-89296-192-9*) Mysterious Pr.

—A Diamond Before You Die. l.t. ed. 1990. (Ulverscroft Large Print Ser.). 29.99 o.p. (*0-7089-2194-9*, Ulverscroft) Thorpe, F. A. Pubs. GBR. *Dist:* Ulverscroft Large Print Bks., Ltd., Ulverscroft Large Print Canada, Ltd.

—The Emerald Lizard: A Neal Rafferty Mystery. 1991. 224p. 17.95 o.p. (*0-525-24945-1*, Dutton) Dutton/Plume.

—The Killing Circle. l.t. ed. 1991. 8.95 o.p. (*0-7451-9395-1*, 1599); 1988. pap. 14.95 o.p. (*1-55504-628-2*, 333) BBC Audiobooks America.

—The Killing Circle. 1985. pap. 2.95 o.p. (*0-523-41933-3*, Pinnacle Bks.) Kensington Publishing Corp.

Wings, Mary. She Came by the Book. (Mistery Ser.). 272p. 1996. 21.95 o.p. (*0-425-15147-6*, Prime Crime); 1996. pap. 10.00 o.p. (*0-425-15144-1*); 1997. reprint ed. mass mkt. 5.99 o.s.i (*0-425-15697-4*, Prime Crime) Berkley Publishing Group.

—She Came in a Flash. 1990. 24p. pap. 10.00 o.p. (*0-452-26384-0*, Plume) Dutton/Plume.

—She Came in a Flash. 1989. 208p. 17.95 o.p. (*0-453-00648-5*) NAL.

—She Came in Drag. 1999. (Emma Victor Mysteries Ser.). 352p. mass mkt. 6.50 o.s.i (*0-425-16935-9*) Berkley Publishing Group.

—She Came to the Castro. (Emma Victor Mysteries Ser.). 272p. 1998. mass mkt. 5.99 o.s.i (*0-425-16222-2*); 1997. 21.95 o.s.i (*0-425-15629-X*) Berkley Publishing Group. (Prime Crime).

—She Came Too Late. 1987. (WomanSleuth Mystery Ser.). 208p. reprint ed. 20.95 o.p. (*0-89594-244-5*); pap. 7.95 o.p. (*0-89594-243-7*) Crossing Pr., Inc., The.

—She Came Too Late: An Emma Victor Mystery. 2000. (Emma Victor Mysteries Ser.: No. 1). 263p. reprint ed. pap. 10.95 o.p. (*1-55583-547-3*, Alyson Bks.) Alyson Pubns.

Winslow, Don. Cool Breeze on the Underground. 1991. 17.95 o.p. (*0-312-05407-6*, Saint Martin's Minotaur) St. Martin's Pr.

—A Long Walk up the Water Slide. (Neal Carey Mysteries Ser.). 1998. 277p. mass mkt. 5.99 (*0-312-96617-2*, St. Martin's Paperbacks); 1994. 256p. 20.95 o.p. (*0-312-11389-7*, Saint Martin's Minotaur) St. Martin's Pr.

—The Trail to Buddha's Mirror. 384p. 1992. 21.95 o.p. (*0-312-07099-3*, Saint Martin's Minotaur); Vol. 1. 1997. mass mkt. 5.99 (*0-312-96309-2*, St. Martin's Paperbacks) St. Martin's Pr.

—Way down on the High Lonely. 1998. (Dead Letter Mysteries Ser.). 288p. mass mkt. 5.99 (*0-312-96422-6*, St. Martin's Paperbacks) St. Martin's Pr.

—Way down on the High Lonely: A Neal Carey Mystery. 1993. 288p. 19.95 o.p. (*0-312-09934-7*, Saint Martin's Minotaur) St. Martin's Pr.

—While Drowning in the Desert. 1998. (Neal Carey Mysteries Ser.). 224p. mass mkt. 5.99 (*0-312-96118-9*, St. Martin's Paperbacks) St. Martin's Pr.

—While Drowning in the Desert: A Neal Carey Mystery. 1996. 192p. 20.95 o.p. (*0-312-14446-6*, Saint Martin's Minotaur) St. Martin's Pr.

Winspear, Jacqueline. Maisie Dobbs. l.t. ed. 2004. lib. bdg. 28.95 (*1-58547-406-1*, Platinum) Ctr. Point Large Print.

—Maisie Dobbs. 2003. 336p. 24.00 (*1-56947-330-7*) Soho Pr., Inc.

Wishnia, K. J. A. Red House. 2002. E-Book 23.95 (*1-59061-727-4*) Adobe Systems, Inc.

—Red House. 2002. 288p. mass mkt. 6.50 (*0-312-98500-2*, St. Martin's Paperbacks) St. Martin's Pr.

—Red House: A Filomena Buscarsela Mystery. 2001. 288p. 23.95 (*0-312-28182-X*, Saint Martin's Minotaur) St. Martin's Pr.

Witten, Matt. Strange Bedfellows: A Jacob Burns Mystery. 2000. (Jacob Burns Mysteries Ser.). 240p. mass mkt. 6.50 o.s.i (*0-451-20159-0*) NAL.

—Strange Bedfellows: A Jacob Burns Mystery. l.t. ed. 2001. (Thorndike Mystery Ser.). 352p. 27.95 (*0-7862-3214-5*) Thorndike Pr.

Womack, Steven. Chain of Fools. (Harry James Denton Mysteries Ser.). 320p. 1996. mass mkt. 6.50 (*0-345-39687-1*); 1995. pap. 19.00 (*0-345-46187-8*, Ballantine Bks.) Ballantine Bks.

—Chain of Fools. l.t. ed. 1997. (Ulverscroft Large Print Ser.). 544p. 29.99 (*0-7089-3730-6*, Ulverscroft) Thorpe, F. A. Pubs. GBR. *Dist:* Ulverscroft Large Print Bks., Ltd., Ulverscroft Large Print Canada, Ltd.

—Dead Folks' Blues. 272p. 1995. pap. 19.00 (*0-345-46186-X*, Ballantine Bks.); 1992. mass mkt. 5.99 o.s.i (*0-345-37674-9*) Ballantine Bks.

—Dead Folks' Blues. Haywood, Richard, ed. abr. ed. 1995. (Harry Denton Trilogy Ser.). audio 17.00 (*1-883268-25-7*) Spellbinders, Inc.

—Dirty Money. 2000. 320p. pap. 19.00 (*0-345-46190-8*, Ballantine Bks.); mass mkt. 6.50 (*0-345-41448-9*, Fawcett) Ballantine Bks.

—Murder Manual. 1998. (Harry James Denton Mysteries Ser.). 336p. mass mkt. 5.99 (*0-345-41447-0*); pap. 19.00 (*0-345-46189-4*, Ballantine Bks.) Ballantine Bks.

—Torch Town Boogie. 288p. 1995. pap. 19.00 (*0-345-46317-X*); 1993. mass mkt. 6.50 o.s.i (*0-345-38010-X*) Ballantine Bks.

—Torch Town Boogie. abr. ed. 1997. audio 17.00 (*1-883268-32-X*) Spellbinders, Inc.

—Torch Town Boogie. l.t. ed. 1996. (Ulverscroft Large Print Ser.). 480p. 29.99 o.p. (*0-7089-3600-8*, Ulverscroft) Thorpe, F. A. Pubs. GBR. *Dist:* Ulverscroft Large Print Bks., Ltd., Ulverscroft Large Print Canada, Ltd.

—Way Past Dead. 1995. 352p. pap. 19.00 (*0-345-46188-6*, Ballantine Bks.); 272p. mass mkt. 6.50 (*0-345-39043-1*) Ballantine Bks.

—Way Past Dead. abr. ed. 1997. audio 17.00 (*1-883268-30-3*) Spellbinders, Inc.

Woods, Stuart. Cold Paradise. l.t. ed. 2001. 523p. 32.95 (*0-7838-9470-8*, Macmillan Reference USA) Gale Group.

—Cold Paradise. 2002. 432p. reprint ed. mass mkt. 7.99 (*0-451-20562-6*, Signet Bks.) NAL.

—Cold Paradise. 2001. 352p. 24.95 o.p. (*0-399-14736-5*) Penguin Group (USA) Inc.

—Cold Paradise. l.t. ed. 2002. (Paperback Bestsellers Ser.). 440p. pap. 29.95 (*0-7838-9471-6*) Thorndike Pr.

—Dirty Work. l.t. ed. (Stone Barrington Ser.). 436p. 28.95 (*1-58724-440-3*, Wheeler Publishing, Inc.) Gale Group.

—Dirty Work. 2003. 368p. mass mkt. 7.99 (*0-451-21015-8*, Signet Bks.) NAL.

—Dirty Work. 2003. (Stone Barrington Ser.). 336p. 25.95 (*0-399-14982-1*) Penguin Group (USA) Inc.

—Dirty Work. abr. ed. 2003. (Stone Barrington Ser.). audio 25.95 (*0-399-14994-5*, Putnam Berkley Audio) Putnam Publishing Group, The.

—The Short Forever. l.t. ed. 2002. (Wheeler Large Print Book Ser.). 29.95 (*1-58724-215-X*, Wheeler Publishing, Inc.) Gale Group.

—The Short Forever. 2003. 368p. reprint ed. mass mkt. 7.99 (*0-451-20808-0*, Signet Bks.) NAL.

—The Short Forever. 2002. 336p. 24.95 o.s.i (*0-399-14868-X*) Putnam Publishing Group, The.

Wright, Eric. Death of a Sunday Writer. 1996. 224p. text 21.00 (*0-88150-377-0*) Norton, W. W. & Co., Inc.

—Death on the Rocks: A Lucy Trimble Mystery. 1999. 240p. 15.95 (*0-312-20525-2*, Saint Martin's Minotaur) St. Martin's Pr.

—Death on the Rocks: A Lucy Trimble Mystery. l.t. ed. 1999. (Mystery Ser.). 343p. 27.95 (*0-7862-2205-0*) Thorndike Pr.

York, Rebecca. Killing Moon. 2003. 352p. mass mkt. 5.99 (*0-425-19071-4*) Berkley Publishing Group.

Zackel, Fred. Cinderella After Midnight. 1980. 11.95 o.p. (*0-698-10990-2*) Putnam Publishing Group, The.

—Cocaine & Blue Eyes. 1983. 320p. mass mkt. 2.95 o.p. (*0-425-06241-4*) Berkley Publishing Group.

—Cocaine & Blue Eyes. 1978. 8.95 o.p. (*0-698-10934-1*) Putnam Publishing Group, The.

Zaremba, Eve. Beyond Hope. 1990. 184p. pap. 11.95 (*0-921299-02-8*) Second Story Pr. CAN. *Dist:* SCB Distributors.

—The Butterfly Effect: A Helen Keremos Detective Novel. 1994. 332p. pap. 9.95 (*0-929005-56-2*) Second Story Pr. CAN. *Dist:* SCB Distributors.

—Uneasy Lies: A Helen Keremos Mystery. 1994. 255p. pap. 11.95 (*0-929005-17-1*) Second Story Pr. CAN. *Dist:* LPC/InBook.

—White Noise: A Helen Keremos Mystery Novel. 1997. 248p. pap. 9.95 (*0-929005-97-X*) Second Story Pr. CAN. *Dist:* SCB Distributors.

—Work for a Million. (NFS Canada Ser.). 200p. pap. 11.95 o.p. (*0-921299-00-1*) Second Story Pr. CAN. *Dist:* SCB Distributors.

Zukowski, Sharon. Dancing in the Dark. 1994. (Mystery Ser.). mass mkt. (*0-373-26148-9*, 1-26148-6, Harlequin Bks.) Harlequin Enterprises, Ltd.

—Dancing in the Dark. 1992. 224p. 17.95 o.p. (*0-312-08174-X*, Saint Martin's Minotaur) St. Martin's Pr.

—The Hour of the Knife. 1993. (Mystery Ser.). mass mkt. (*0-373-26123-3*, 1-26123-9, Harlequin Bks.) Harlequin Enterprises, Ltd.

—The Hour of the Knife. 1991. 208p. 17.95 o.p. (*0-312-06372-5*, Saint Martin's Minotaur) St. Martin's Pr.

—Jungleland. 1999. pap. 22.95 (*0-525-93917-2*); 1997. 384p. mass mkt. 5.99 o.s.i (*0-451-19253-2*, Signet Bks.) NAL.

—Leap of Faith. 240p. pap. 3.98 o.p. (*0-7651-0402-4*) Smithmark Pubs., Inc.

—Leap of Faith: A Blaine Stewart Mystery. 1994. (Blaine Stewart Mystery Ser.). 256p. 18.95 o.p. (*0-525-93897-4*, Dutton) Dutton/Plume.

—Leap of Faith: A Blaine Stewart Mystery. 1995. (Blaine Stewart Mystery Ser.). 256p. mass mkt. 4.99 o.s.i (*0-451-18273-1*, Signet Bks.) NAL.

—Prelude to Death: A Blaine Stewart Mystery. 1996. (Blaine Stewart Mystery Ser.). 256p. 20.95 o.p. (*0-525-94079-0*, Dutton) Dutton/Plume.

—Prelude to Death: A Blaine Stewart Mystery. 1997. (Blaine Stewart Mystery Ser.). 272p. mass mkt. 5.50 o.s.i (*0-451-18272-3*) NAL.

### PSYCHOTHERAPISTS—FICTION

Allred, Tara C. Sanders' Starfish. 2003. pap. 15.95 (*1-55517-701-8*, Bonneville Bks.) Cedar Fort, Inc./CFI Distribution.

Andrews, Donna. Crouching Buzzard, Leaping Loon. 2003. 304p. 23.95 (*0-312-27731-8*, Saint Martin's Minotaur) St. Martin's Pr.

Holmes, Oliver Wendell. Psychiatric Novels of Oliver Wendell Holmes. 1946. 274p. (YA). reprint ed. pap. text 28.00 (*1-4047-6969-2*) Classic Textbooks.

—Psychiatric Novels of Oliver Wendell Holmes. 2nd abr. ed. 1971. reprint ed. 77.00 o.s.i (*0-8371-6142-8*, HOPN, Greenwood Pr.) Greenwood Publishing Group, Inc.

—Psychiatric Novels of Oliver Wendell Holmes. 1993. (BCL1-PS American Literature Ser.). 274p. reprint ed. lib. bdg. 79.00 (*0-7812-6969-5*) Reprint Services Corp.

Kates, Erica, ed. On the Couch: Great American Stories about Therapy. 1997. 224p. 23.00 o.p. (*0-87113-662-7*, Atlantic Monthly Pr.); 1999. 400p. reprint ed. pap. 14.00 (*0-87113-740-2*) Grove/Atlantic, Inc.

Katzenbach, John. The Analyst. 2002. E-Book 20.00 (*1-59061-776-2*) Adobe Systems, Inc.

—The Analyst. 2003. 512p. mass mkt. 7.99 (*0-345-42627-4*); 2002. 432p. 25.00 (*0-345-42626-6*) Ballantine Bks. (Ballantine Bks.).

—The Analyst. l.t. ed. 2002. 793p. 30.95 (*0-7862-4339-2*) Gale Group.

Matthews, Alex. Death's Domain: Sixth Cassidy McCabe Mystery. 2001. 320p. 23.95 (*1-890768-37-5*, Intrigue Pr.) Corvus Publishing.

Parker, Gary E. Dark Road to Daylight. 1997. 256p. pap. 12.99 (*0-7852-7785-4*) Nelson, Thomas Inc.

Sedgwick, John. The Education of Mrs. Bemis. 2002. 400p. 24.95 (*0-06-019565-7*) HarperCollins Pubs.

—The Education of Mrs. Bemis: A Novel. 2003. 400p. pap. 13.95 (*0-06-051259-8*, Perennial) HarperTrade.

Shange, Ntozake. Liliane: Resurrection of the Daughter. 1995. 304p. pap. 12.00 (*0-312-13559-9*) Picador.

—Liliane: Resurrection of the Daughter. 1994. 224p. 18.95 o.p. (*0-312-11310-2*) St. Martin's Pr.

Talley, Marcia. Unbreathed Memories. l.t. ed. 2002. 26.95 (*1-57490-396-9*) Beeler, Thomas T. Publisher.

—Unbreathed Memories. 2000. (Hannah Ives Mysteries Ser.). 288p. mass mkt. 5.99 (*0-440-23518-9*) Dell Publishing.

Yalom, Irvin D. Momma & the Meaning of Life: Tales of Psychotherapy. 1999. 256p. text 24.00 (*0-465-04386-0*) Basic Bks.

—Momma & the Meaning of Life: Tales of Psychotherapy. 2000. 272p. reprint ed. pap. 14.00 (*0-06-095838-3*, Perennial) HarperTrade.

### PUBLISHERS AND PUBLISHING—FICTION

Engelhardt, Tom. The Last Days of Publishing: A Novel. 2003. 224p. 24.95 (*1-55849-402-2*) Univ. of Massachusetts Pr.

Grimes, Martha. Foul Matter. l.t. ed. 2004. lib. bdg. 29.95 (*1-58547-389-8*, Platinum) Ctr. Point Large Print.

—Foul Matter. 2003. 384p. 25.95 (*0-670-03259-X*, Viking) Viking Penguin.

Gutteridge, Rene. Ghost Writer. l.t. ed. 2002. 619p. 25.95 (*0-7862-4266-3*) Gale Group.

Henley, John A. The Buchmans: A Novel. l.t. ed. 2001. (Five Star Western Ser.). 248p. 22.95 (*0-7862-2385-5*, Five Star) Gale Group.

Maguire, Elizabeth. Thinner, Blonder, Whiter. 2004. 336p. pap. 14.00 (*0-7867-1299-6*); 2002. 320p. 25.00 (*0-7867-1019-5*) Avalon Publishing Group. (Carroll & Graf Pubs.).

Mallon, James. Magazine. 2000. 278p. 22.95 o.p. (*1-57197-181-5*) Pentland Pr., Inc.

Messina, Lynn. Fashionistas. 2003. 288p. pap. (*0-373-25025-8*, Red Dress Ink) Harlequin Enterprises, Ltd.

Mylnowski, Sarah. Fishbowl. 2002. 368p. pap. (*0-373-25020-7*, Red Dress Ink) Harlequin Enterprises, Ltd.

Shubin, Seymour. A Matter of Fear. 2002. (Five Star First Edition Mystery Ser.). 216p. 24.95 (*0-7862-4310-4*, Five Star) Gale Group.

—A Matter of Fear. 2002. 236p. pap. 19.95 (*0-9718758-0-4*) Koenisha Pubns.

Vincenzi, Penny. No Angel: A Novel. 2003. 626p. 26.95 (*1-58567-481-8*) Overlook Pr., The.

Weisberger, Lauren. The Devil Wears Prada: A Novel. 2004. 368p. pap. 13.95 (*0-7679-1476-7*) Broadway Bks.

—The Devil Wears Prada: A Novel. 2003. 368p. 21.95 (*0-385-50926-X*) Doubleday Publishing.

—The Devil Wears Prada: A Novel. l.t. ed. 2003. 712p. 29.95 (*0-7862-5575-7*) Thorndike Pr.

## R

### RABBIS—FICTION

Appel, Allen. High Holiday Sutra. 1997. 192p. (Orig.). pap. 13.95 (*1-56689-065-9*) Coffee Hse. Pr.

Chefitz, Mitchell. The Thirty-Third Hour: A Novel. 2002. 320p. 24.95 (*0-312-27758-X*, Saint Martin's Minotaur); 2003. 288p. reprint ed. pap. 13.95 (*0-312-30323-8*, Saint Martin's Griffin) St. Martin's Pr.

Cheuse, Alan. The Grandmother's Club. 1985. 15.95 o.p. (*0-918222-67-2*) Applewood Bks.

—The Grandmother's Club. 1986. 326p. 18.95 o.p. (*0-87905-253-8*) Smith, Gibbs Pub.

—The Grandmother's Club. 1994. 348p. reprint ed. pap. 10.95 (*0-87074-374-0*) Southern Methodist Univ. Pr.

—The Grandmother's Club. 1988. 336p. pap. 6.95 o.p. (*0-14-010484-4*, Penguin Bks.) Viking Penguin.

Fast, Howard. The Outsider. 1985. 320p. mass mkt. 3.95 o.s.i (*0-440-16778-7*) Dell Publishing.

—The Outsider. l.t. ed. 1984. (Special Editions Ser.). 17.95 o.p. (*0-8161-3760-9*, Macmillan Reference USA) Gale Group.

—The Outsider, 001. 1984. 311p. 15.95 o.p. (*0-395-36101-X*) Houghton Mifflin Co.

Kahn, Sharon. Fax Me a Bagel: A Ruby the Rabbi's Wife Mystery. 2001. 272p. mass mkt. 5.99 (*0-425-18046-8*) Berkley Publishing Group.

—Fax Me a Bagel: A Ruby the Rabbi's Wife Mystery. 1998. (Ruby, the Rabbi's Wife Mysteries Ser.). 256p. 22.00 (*0-684-84737-X*); 22.00 (*0-684-85498-8*) Simon & Schuster. (Scribner).

—Never Nosh a Matzo Ball: A Ruby the Rabbi's Wife Mystery. 2000. 304p. 22.00 o.s.i (*0-684-84738-8*, Scribner) Simon & Schuster.

Kane, Andrew. Rabbi, Rabbi. 1995. 306p. 22.95 o.p. (*0-312-11879-1*) St. Martin's Pr.

Kemelman, Harry. The Day the Rabbi Resigned. l.t. ed. 1993. (Large Print Mystery Ser.). 345p. 24.95 o.p. (*0-7927-1414-8*); pap. 19.95 o.p. (*0-7927-1413-X*) BBC Audiobooks America.

—The Day the Rabbi Resigned. 1992. mass mkt. 5.99 o.s.i (*0-449-21908-9*); 273p. 20.00 o.s.i (*0-449-90681-7*) Ballantine Bks. (Fawcett).

—The Day the Rabbi Resigned. 2004. 288p. mass mkt. 6.99 (*0-7434-7979-3*) ibooks, Inc.

—Friday the Rabbi Slept Late. 1993. pap. o.p. (*0-449-45127-5*); 1986. mass mkt. 5.99 o.s.i (*0-449-21180-0*) Ballantine Bks. (Fawcett).

—Friday the Rabbi Slept Late. l.t. ed. 1983. (General Ser.). 339p. lib. bdg. 13.95 o.p. (*0-8161-3537-1*, Macmillan Reference USA) Gale Group.

—Monday the Rabbi Took Off. 1988. mass mkt. o.s.i (*0-449-20785-4*); 1986. 288p. mass mkt. 5.99 o.s.i (*0-449-21001-4*, Fawcett); 1981. mass mkt. 2.50 o.s.i (*0-449-23872-5*, Fawcett) Ballantine Bks.

—Monday the Rabbi Took Off. 1972. 316p. 5.95 o.p. (*0-399-10550-6*) Putnam Publishing Group, The.
—Monday the Rabbi Took Off. 2002. 368p. pap. 6.99 (*0-7434-5271-2*) ibooks, Inc.
—One Fine Day the Rabbi Bought a Cross. 1988. (Boston Mysteries Ser.). mass mkt. 5.99 o.s.i (*0-449-20687-4*, Fawcett) Ballantine Bks.
—One Fine Day the Rabbi Bought a Cross. l.t. ed. 1988. (Large Print Bks.). 353p. 18.95 o.p. (*0-8161-4347-1*, Macmillan Reference USA) Gale Group.
—One Fine Day the Rabbi Bought a Cross. 1987. 234p. 15.95 o.p. (*0-688-05631-8*, Morrow, William & Co.) Morrow/Avon.
—One Fine Day the Rabbi Bought a Cross. 1990. 3.99 o.p. (*0-517-05752-2*) Random Hse. Value Publishing.
—One Fine Day the Rabbi Bought a Cross. 2003. 320p. pap. 6.99 (*0-7434-7478-3*) ibooks, Inc.
—Saturday the Rabbi Went Hungry. 1987. 224p. mass mkt. 5.99 o.s.i (*0-449-21392-7*, Fawcett) Ballantine Bks.
—Saturday the Rabbi Went Hungry. 1988. 4.95 o.s.i (*0-517-01307-X*) Crown Publishing Group.
—Saturday the Rabbi Went Hungry. l.t. ed. 1983. 14.95 o.p. (*0-8161-3531-2*, Macmillan Reference USA) Gale Group.
—Someday the Rabbi Will Leave. 1986. 288p. mass mkt. 5.99 o.s.i (*0-449-20945-8*, Fawcett) Ballantine Bks.
—Someday the Rabbi Will Leave. 1985. 264p. 15.95 o.p. (*0-688-04174-4*, Morrow, William & Co.) Morrow/Avon.
—Someday the Rabbi Will Leave. 2003. 288p. pap. 6.99 (*0-7434-5911-3*) ibooks, Inc.
—Sunday the Rabbi Stayed Home. Date not set. mass mkt. (*0-449-20784-6*); 1985. 224p. mass mkt. 5.99 o.s.i (*0-449-21000-6*) Ballantine Bks. (Fawcett).
—Sunday the Rabbi Stayed Home. l.t. ed. 1977. (General Ser.). 420p. lib. bdg. 11.95 o.p. (*0-8161-6499-1*, Macmillan Reference USA) Gale Group.
—Sunday the Rabbi Stayed Home. 2002. (Rabbi Small Mystery Ser.). (Illus.). 304p. pap. 6.99 (*0-7434-5238-0*) ibooks, Inc.
—That Day the Rabbi Left Town. (Rabbi Small Mystery Ser.). 1997. 263p. mass mkt. 5.99 o.s.i (*0-449-22570-4*); 1996. 256p. 22.00 o.s.i (*0-449-91002-4*); 1996. 233p. lib. bdg. 22.95 (*1-57490-040-4*) Ballantine Bks. (Fawcett).
—Thursday the Rabbi Walked Out. 1986. mass mkt. 5.99 o.s.i (*0-449-21157-6*, Fawcett) Ballantine Bks.
—Thursday the Rabbi Walked Out. 2003. 256p. mass mkt. 6.99 (*0-7434-5860-5*) ibooks, Inc.
—Tuesday the Rabbi Saw Red. 1986. (Rabbi Ser.). mass mkt. 5.99 o.s.i (*0-449-21321-8*, Fawcett) Ballantine Bks.
—Tuesday the Rabbi Saw Red. 1974. (Adult Ser.). 508p. reprint ed. lib. bdg. 11.95 o.p. (*0-8161-6230-1*, Macmillan Reference USA) Gale Group.
—Tuesday the Rabbi Saw Red. 2003. 352p. pap. 6.99 (*0-7434-4534-1*) ibooks, Inc.
—Wednesday the Rabbi Got Wet. 1986. (Rabbi Ser.). mass mkt. 5.99 o.s.i (*0-449-21328-5*, Fawcett) Ballantine Bks.
Kossoff, David. A Small Town Is a World. 1979. 8.95 o.p. (*0-312-72985-5*) St. Martin's Pr.
Lerman, Rhoda. God's Ear: A Novel. 1988. 320p. 19.95 o.s.i (*0-8050-0413-0*) Holt, Henry & Co.
—God's Ear: A Novel. 1996. (Library of Modern Jewish Literature). 309p. reprint ed. pap. 17.95 (*0-8156-0427-0*, LEGEP) Syracuse Univ. Pr.
Leviant, Curt. The Man Who Thought He Was Messiah. 1990. 226p. 9.95 (*0-8276-0371-1*) Jewish Pubn. Society.
Millman, M. C. Juggling Act. 2003. 224p. (J). 17.95 (*0-910818-28-2*) Judaica Pr., Inc., The.
Potok, Chaim. The Promise. 1997. 384p. pap. 12.95 (*0-449-00116-4*); 1985. 384p. mass mkt. 7.99 (*0-449-20910-5*); 1982. mass mkt. 3.25 o.p. (*0-449-20076-0*) Ballantine Bks. (Fawcett).
—The Promise. l.t. ed. 1998. (Perennial Bestsellers Ser.). 512p. 26.95 (*0-7838-0256-0*) Thorndike Pr.
Schreiber, Mordecai. The Rabbi & the Nun: A Love Story. 1991. 253p. 18.95 (*0-88400-150-4*, Shengold Bks.) Schreiber Publishing, Inc.
Telushkin, Joseph. An Eye for an Eye. 1992. 288p. mass mkt. 4.99 o.s.i (*0-553-29620-5*) Bantam Bks.
—An Eye for an Eye. 1991. 272p. 15.00 o.s.i (*0-385-42116-8*) Doubleday Publishing.
Wasserman, Mira. Too Much of a Good Thing. 2003. (Illus.). (J). 6.95 (*1-58013-066-6*); lib. bdg. 14.95 (*1-58013-082-8*) Kar-Ben Publishing.
Wiesel, Elie, ed. The Golem: The Story of a Legend. Borchardt, Anne, tr. 1983. (Illus.). 105p. 12.50 o.p. (*0-671-45483-8*); 50.00 o.p. (*0-671-49624-7*) Summit Bks.

**REAL ESTATE AGENTS—FICTION**

Clark, Mary Higgins. Pretend You Don't See Her. unabr. ed. 1997. audio 48.00 (*0-7366-3711-7*, 4395) Books on Tape, Inc.
—Pretend You Don't See Her. 2000. E-Book 9.95 (*0-7432-0625-8*, Simon & Schuster); 1998. 320p. pap. 7.99 (*0-671-86715-6*, Pocket); 1997. 320p. 25.00 (*0-684-81039-5*, Simon & Schuster); 1997. 480p. 25.00 (*0-684-83416-2*, Simon & Schuster) Simon & Schuster.
—Pretend You Don't See Her. abr. ed. 1997. audio 18.00 (*0-671-57521-X*, 395160); audio compact disk 20.00 (*0-671-55715-7*) Simon & Schuster Audio. (Simon & Schuster Audioworks).
—Pretend You Don't See Her. 1998. 14.04 (*0-606-13721-1*) Turtleback Bks.
Lee, Barbara. Dead Man's Fingers. 1999. (Chesapeake Bay Mysteries Ser.). 276p. 22.95 o.p. (*0-312-20524-4*, Saint Martin's Minotaur) St. Martin's Pr.
—Death in Still Waters: A Chesapeake Bay Mystery. 1996. 226p. pap. text 5.50 (*0-312-95780-7*, St. Martin's Paperbacks); 1995. 240p. 20.95 o.p. (*0-312-13048-1*, Saint Martin's Minotaur) St. Martin's Pr.
—Final Closing. 1999. (WWL Mystery Ser.: No. 304). per. (*0-373-26304-X*, 1-26304-5, Worldwide Library) Harlequin Enterprises, Ltd.
—Final Closing: An Eve Elliot Mystery. 1997. (Eve Elliot Mystery Ser.). 304p. 22.95 o.p. (*0-312-16762-8*, Saint Martin's Minotaur) St. Martin's Pr.
Lewis, Beverly. The Redemption of Sarah Cain. 2000. (Heritage of Lancaster County Ser.). 320p. 16.99 (*0-7642-2388-7*); 320p. pap. 12.99 (*0-7642-2329-1*); 1p. pap. 15.99 o.p. (*0-7642-2389-5*); 384p. pap. 15.99 o.p. (*0-7642-2390-9*) Bethany Hse. Pubs.
—The Redemption of Sarah Cain. l.t. ed. 2001. (Thorndike Press Large Print Christian Romance Ser.). 384p. 25.95 (*0-7862-3113-0*) Thorndike Pr.
McClellan, Tierney. Closing Statement: A Schuyler Ridgway Mystery. 1995. 304p. (Orig.). mass mkt. 4.99 o.s.i (*0-451-18464-5*, Signet Bks.) NAL.
—Heir Condition. 1995. 256p. (Orig.). mass mkt. 5.50 o.s.i (*0-451-18144-1*, Signet Bks.) NAL.
—Killing in Real Estate. 1996. (Schuyler Ridgway Mystery Ser.). 256p. mass mkt. 5.50 o.s.i (*0-451-18765-2*) NAL.
—Two-Story Frame. 1997. (Schuyler Ridgway Mystery Ser.). 256p. mass mkt. 5.99 o.s.i (*0-451-19197-8*, Signet Bks.) NAL.
Smiley, Jane. Good Faith. 2004. 432p. pap. 13.95 (*0-385-72105-6*, Anchor) Knopf Publishing Group.
—Good Faith. 2003. 432p. 26.00 (*0-375-41217-4*) Knopf, Alfred A. Inc.
—Good Faith. l.t. ed. 2003. 691p. 28.00 (*0-375-43277-9*) Random Hse. Large Print.
—Good Faith. audio compact disk 49.99 (*1-4025-3635-6*) Recorded Bks., LLC.

# S

**SAMURAI—FICTION**

Furutani, Dale. Death at the Crossroads: A Samurai Mystery. 1999. audio 24.95 (*0-7366-4703-1*) Books on Tape, Inc.
—Death at the Crossroads: A Samurai Mystery. 1998. 256p. 22.00 (*0-688-15817-X*, Morrow, William & Co.) Morrow/Avon.
—Jade Palace Vendetta: A Samurai Mystery. 1999. (Samurai Mysteries Ser.). 222p. 23.00 (*0-688-15818-8*, Morrow, William & Co.) Morrow/Avon.
—Kill the Shogun. 2000. (Samurai Mysteries Ser.). 240p. 23.00 o.s.i (*0-688-15819-6*, Morrow, William & Co.) Morrow/Avon.
—Kill the Shogun: A Samurai Mystery. l.t. ed. 2001. (Thorndike Mystery Ser.). 327p. 27.95 (*0-7862-3190-4*) Thorndike Pr.
Oji, Hiroi. Samurai Crusader: Sunrise over Shanghai. 1997. (Viz Graphic Novel Ser.). (Illus.). 240p. pap. 16.95 (*1-56931-236-2*, Viz Comics) Viz Communications, Inc.
Rowland, Laura Joh. Bundori. 1997. 432p. mass mkt. 6.99 (*0-06-101197-5*, HarperTorch) Morrow/Avon.
—The Concubine's Tattoo. 2000. 384p. mass mkt. 6.99 (*0-312-96922-8*, St. Martin's Paperbacks); 1999. E-Book 6.50 (*0-312-24607-2*); 1998. 336p. 23.95 o.p. (*0-312-19252-5*, Saint Martin's Minotaur) St. Martin's Pr.
—The Dragon King's Palace: A Novel. 2003. 336p. 24.95 (*0-312-28266-4*, Saint Martin's Minotaur) St. Martin's Pr.
—The Pillow Book of Lady Wisteria. 2002. (Illus.). 256p. 24.95 (*0-312-28262-1*, Saint Martin's Minotaur); 2003. 368p. reprint ed. mass mkt. 6.99 (*0-312-98378-6*, St. Martin's Paperbacks) St. Martin's Pr.
—The Samurai's Wife. 2000. 203p. 23.95 (*0-312-20325-X*, Saint Martin's Minotaur) St. Martin's Pr.
—Shinju. Date not set. 384p. mass mkt. (*0-06-101035-9*); 1996. 448p. mass mkt. 6.99 (*0-06-100950-4*) Morrow/Avon. (HarperTorch).
—The Way of the Traitor. 1998. 384p. mass mkt. 6.99 (*0-06-101090-1*) HarperCollins Pubs.
Schaeffer, Susan Fromberg. Snow Fox. 2004. 448p. text 24.95 (*0-393-05814-X*) Norton, W. W. & Co., Inc.
Toda, Katsumi. Shadow of the Ninja. 1982. (Illus.). 118p. (Orig.). pap. 8.95 o.s.i (*0-86568-036-1*, 513) Unique Pubns.

**SCIENTISTS—FICTION**

Archer, Geoffrey. Skydancer. unabr. ed. 2000. 8p. audio 69.95 (*0-7540-0475-9*, CAB1898) BBC Audiobooks America.
—Skydancer. 1989. mass mkt. 4.95 o.p. (*0-8125-0025-3*, Tor Bks.) Doherty, Tom Assocs., LLC.
—Skydancer. l.t. ed. 1999. (Mystery Ser.). 424p. 26.95 (*0-7862-2226-3*); (*0-7540-2282-X*); (*0-7540-1377-4*) Thorndike Pr.
Banville, John. The Newton Letter. 1987. 96p. pap. 10.95 (*1-56792-096-9*); 12.95 o.p. (*0-87923-638-8*); pap. 9.95 o.p. (*0-87923-771-6*) Godine, David R. Pub.
—The Newton Letter. 1991. pap. 8.99 (*0-446-39283-9*) Warner Bks., Inc.
Bell, James Scott. The Darwin Conspiracy: The Confessions of Sir Max Busby. 2002. 288p. pap. 12.99 (*0-8054-2500-4*) Broadman & Holman Pubs.
Billing, Graham. Forbush & the Penguins. 1995. 168p. (Orig.). pap. 24.95 (*0-908812-40-X*) Canterbury Univ. Pr. NZL. *Dist:* Accents Pubns. Service, Inc.
Bishop, Nic, illus. The Tarantula Scientist. 2004. 80p. (J). (gr. 4-6). 18.00 (*0-618-14799-3*) Houghton Mifflin Co.
Braver, Gary. Elixir. 2000. 352p. 25.95 (*0-312-87308-5*, Forge Bks.); 2001. 448p. reprint ed. mass mkt. 7.99 (*0-8125-7591-1*, Tor Bks.) Doherty, Tom Assocs., LLC.
Brown, Dan. Deception Point. 2003. 576p. 17.95 (*0-7434-9030-4*, Atria); 2002. E-Book 9.99 (*0-7434-7543-7*, Atria); 2001. 384p. 25.00 o.s.i (*0-671-02737-9*, Atria); 2002. 576p. reprint ed. mass mkt. 7.99 (*0-671-02738-7*, Pocket) Simon & Schuster.
Butler, Robert Olen. Countrymen of Bones. 1985. 256p. mass mkt. 2.95 o.s.i (*0-345-32118-9*) Ballantine Bks.
—Countrymen of Bones. 1994. 25.00 o.p. (*0-8050-3202-9*); 224p. pap. 11.00 o.s.i (*0-8050-3142-1*, Owl Bks.) Holt, Henry & Co.
Cook, Robin. Acceptable Risk. abr. ed. 1995. audio 22.95 (*1-55927-321-6*, 692138) Audio Renaissance.
—Acceptable Risk. 1996. 400p. pap. 7.99 (*0-425-15186-7*) Berkley Publishing Group.
—Acceptable Risk. unabr. ed. 1995. audio 80.00 (*0-7366-3038-4*, 3720) Books on Tape, Inc.
—Acceptable Risk. l.t. ed. 1995. 26.95 o.p. (*1-56895-173-6*, Wheeler Publishing, Inc.) Gale Group.
—Acceptable Risk. 2001. 23.95 (*0-399-14275-4*); 1995. 432p. 23.95 o.s.i (*0-399-13971-0*, G. P. Putnam's Sons) Penguin Group (USA) Inc.
—Acceptable Risk. 406p. pap. 6.98 o.p. (*0-7651-0427-X*) Smithmark Pubs., Inc.
Craven, Wes. Fountain Society. 1999. 352p. 25.00 o.s.i (*0-684-84660-8*, Simon & Schuster); 2000. 464p. reprint ed. mass mkt. 6.99 (*0-671-01724-1*, Pocket) Simon & Schuster.
—Fountain Society. abr. ed. 1999. audio 25.00 (*0-671-58258-5*, Simon & Schuster Audioworks) Simon & Schuster Audio.
—Fountain Society. l.t. ed. 1999. (Basic Ser.). 589p. 27.95 (*0-7862-2270-0*) Thorndike Pr.
Delfosse, Pierre. A Lie for the Truth. 2000. 264p. pap. 21.99 (*0-7388-1545-4*); text 31.99 (*0-7388-1544-6*) Xlibris Corp.
Djerassi, Carl. The Bourbaki Gambit. 1996. 256p. pap. 12.95 (*0-14-025485-4*, Viking) Penguin Group (USA) Inc.
—The Bourbaki Gambit. 1994. 240p. (C). 19.95 (*0-8203-1652-0*) Univ. of Georgia Pr.
—Menachem's Seed: A Novel. 1998. 224p. pap. 12.95 (*0-14-027794-3*) Penguin Group (USA) Inc.
—Menachem's Seed: A Novel. 1997. 216p. 21.95 (*0-8203-1925-2*) Univ. of Georgia Pr.
Doss, James D. The Shaman Sings. 1994. 272p. 3000.00 o.p. (*0-312-10547-9*, Saint Martin's Minotaur) St. Martin's Pr.
—Shaman Sings. 1995. (Shaman Mysteries Ser.). 256p. mass mkt. 6.99 (*0-380-72496-0*, Avon Bks.) Morrow/Avon.
Doyle, Arthur Conan. The Lost World. 1989. 320p. pap. 12.00 (*0-89733-331-4*) Academy Chicago Pubs., Ltd.
—The Lost World. 1992. pap. text (*0-17-556535-X*) Addison-Wesley Longman, Inc.
—The Lost World. 1976. 21.95 (*0-8488-0990-4*) Amereon, Ltd.
—The Lost World. 1977. (J). (gr. 10 up). 0.95 o.s.i (*0-425-03514-X*) Berkley Publishing Group.
—The Lost World. unabr. ed. 1989. audio 39.95 (*1-55686-294-6*, 294) Books in Motion.
—The Lost World. 1988. lib. bdg. 18.95 (*0-89966-233-1*) Buccaneer Bks., Inc.
—The Lost World. 248p. 1997. mass mkt. 4.99 (*0-8125-6483-9*, Tor Classics); 1993. mass mkt. 4.99 o.s.i (*0-8125-3468-9*, Tor Bks.) Doherty, Tom Assocs., LLC.
—The Lost World. 1998. (Thrift Editions Ser.). 176p. pap. 2.00 (*0-486-40060-3*) Dover Pubns., Inc.
—The Lost World. l.t. ed. 1998. (Large Print Heritage Ser.). 340p. lib. bdg. 31.95 (*1-58118-034-9*, 22017) LRS.
—The Lost World. Matthews, Sarah, ed. 1996. (Thornes Classic Novels Ser.). (Illus.). 243p. pap. 16.95 (*0-7487-2481-8*) Nelson Thornes GBR. *Dist:* Trans-Atlantic Pubns., Inc.
—The Lost World. 1999. (Twelve-Point Ser.). lib. bdg. 25.00 (*1-58287-112-4*) North Bks.
—The Lost World. Duncan, Ian, ed. 1998. (Oxford World's Classics Ser.). 768p. pap. 9.95 (*0-19-283352-9*) Oxford Univ. Pr., Inc.
—The Lost World. Duncan, Ian & Trotter, David, eds. 1995. (Oxford Popular Fiction Ser.). 216p. pap. 7.95 o.p. (*0-19-283186-0*) Oxford Univ. Pr., Inc.
—The Lost World. unabr. ed. 2003. (YA). audio compact disk 20.00 (*1-4001-5086-8*) Tantor Media, Inc.
—The Lost World. 1998. (Classics Library). 480p. pap. 3.95 (*1-85326-245-5*, 2455WW) Wordsworth Editions, Ltd. GBR. *Dist:* Casemate Pubs. & Bk. Distributors, LLC.
Doyle, Arthur Conan, et al. The Annotated Lost World. 1996. (Illus.). 288p. 34.95 (*0-938501-23-2*) Wessex Pr.
Farnsworth, Clyde. Shadow Wars. 1998. 352p. 24.95 o.p. (*1-55611-518-0*) Fine, Donald I. Bks.
Feehan, Christine. Shadow Game. 2003. 352p. mass mkt. 6.99 (*0-515-13596-8*, Jove) Berkley Publishing Group.
—Shadow Game. l.t. ed. 2003. 553p. 29.95 (*0-7862-5924-8*, Large Print Pr.) Thorndike Pr.
Fitzgerald, Penelope. The Gates of Angels. unabr. ed. 2000. audio 32.95 Blackstone Audio Bks., Inc.
Follett, Ken. Code to Zero. 2000. 368p. 26.95 o.s.i (*0-525-94563-6*); 2000. E-Book 26.95 (*0-525-94612-8*, Dutton); 2015. audio 24.95 o.s.i (*0-525-94588-1*) Dutton/Plume.
—Code to Zero. l.t. ed. (Wheeler Press Paperback Ser.). 2001. 12.95 (*1-56895-183-3*); 2000. xii, 187p. 31.95 (*1-56895-133-7*) Gale Group. (Wheeler Publishing, Inc.).
—Code to Zero. 2001. pap. 7.99 (*0-451-20409-3*); 480p. reprint ed. mass mkt. 7.99 (*0-451-20453-0*) NAL. (Signet Bks.).
—Code to Zero. 2002. E-Book 7.99 (*0-7865-2613-0*) Penguin Putnam, Inc E-Books.
Francis, Dick. Twice Shy. 1997. mass mkt. 5.99 (*0-449-45728-1*, Fawcett); 1986. 352p. mass mkt. 5.99 o.s.i (*0-449-21314-5*, Fawcett); 1986. mass mkt. 4.50 o.p. (*0-449-21035-9*, Fawcett); 1985. mass mkt. o.s.i (*0-449-20756-0*); 1983. mass mkt. 3.50 o.p. (*0-449-20053-1*, Fawcett) Ballantine Bks.
—Twice Shy. 2003. 304p. mass mkt. 6.99 (*0-515-13488-0*, Jove) Berkley Publishing Group.
—Twice Shy. l.t. ed. 1982. 458p. lib. bdg. 14.95 o.p. (*0-8161-3445-6*, Macmillan Reference USA) Gale Group.
—Twice Shy. 1982. 13.95 o.s.i (*0-399-12707-0*) Putnam Publishing Group, The.
Frayn, Michael. A Landing on the Sun: A Novel. 2003. 272p. pap. 14.00 (*0-312-42190-7*) Picador.
Gitlin, Todd. The Murder of Albert Einstein. 1994. 352p. pap. 8.95 o.s.i (*0-553-37366-8*) Bantam Bks.
—The Murder of Albert Einstein. 1992. 25.00 o.p. (*0-374-21617-7*) Farrar, Straus & Giroux.
Goldstein, Rebecca. Properties of Light. 2001. 256p. reprint ed. pap. 13.00 (*0-618-15459-0*, Mariner Bks.) Houghton Mifflin Co. Trade & Reference Div.
—Properties of Light: A Novel of Love, Betrayal, & Quantum Physics. 2000. 224p. tchr. ed. 23.00 (*0-395-98659-1*) Houghton Mifflin Co.
Grace, Tom. Quantum. 2000. 384p. 24.95 o.s.i (*0-446-52410-7*) Warner Bks., Inc.
Grunwald, Lisa. The Theory of Everything. 1992. 352p. reprint ed. pap. 18.99 (*0-446-39368-1*) Warner Bks., Inc.
Jagose, Annamarie. Lulu: A Romance. 1998. 208p. (*0-86473-332-1*) Victoria Univ. Pr.
Kay, Jeremy. The Secret Laboratory Journals of Dr. Victor Frankenstein. (Illus.). 1998. 208p. pap. 17.95 (*0-87951-867-7*); 1996. 176p. 29.95 (*0-87951-511-2*) Overlook Pr., The.
Krentz, Jayne Ann. Absolutely, Positively. unabr. ed. 1996. audio 64.00 (*0-7366-3436-3*, 104621) Books on Tape, Inc.
—Absolutely, Positively. l.t. ed. 1996. 25.95 (*1-56895-286-4*, Wheeler Publishing, Inc.) Gale Group.
—Absolutely, Positively. 384p. 2003. mass mkt. 5.99 (*0-7434-6737-X*); 1997. pap. 7.99 (*0-671-77873-0*) Simon & Schuster. (Pocket).
—Absolutely, Positively. Zion, Claire, ed. 1996. 352p. 23.00 o.p. (*0-671-55170-1*, Atria) Simon & Schuster.

—Absolutely, Positively, abr. ed. 1997. audio 17.00 (*0-671-88653-3*, 394827, Simon & Schuster Audioworks) Simon & Schuster Audio.

Lethem, Jonathan. As She Climbed Across the Table. 1998. 224p. pap. 13.00 (*0-375-70012-9*, Vintage) Knopf Publishing Group.

Lichtenstein, Alice. The Genius of the World. 2000. (Illus.). 272p. pap. 13.00 o.p. (*1-58195-018-7*, Zoland Bks., Inc.) Steerforth Pr.

Lightman, Alan P. Einstein's Dreams. unabr. ed. 1994. audio 24.95 (*0-7366-2673-5*, 3410) Books on Tape, Inc.

—Einstein's Dreams. 1993. (Illus.). 192p. 23.00 (*0-679-41646-3*, Pantheon) Knopf Publishing Group.

—Einstein's Dreams. unabr. ed. 1993. (Limited Edition, Dove Ser.). audio compact disk 39.95 o.p. (*1-55800-854-3*); audio 16.95 o.p. (*1-55800-837-3*) NewStar Media, Inc.

—Einstein's Dreams. 1994. (Illus.). 179p. pap. 11.95 (*0-446-67011-1*) Warner Bks., Inc.

Loring, Emilie Baker. A Candle in Her Heart. 1976. reprint ed. lib. bdg. 22.95 (*0-88411-353-1*) Amereon, Ltd.

—A Candle in Her Heart. 1980. 224p. pap. 1.75 o.p. (*0-553-13484-1*) Bantam Bks.

Maccabee, Bruce. Abduction in My Life: A Novel of Alien Encounters. Crissey, Brian, ed. 2001. 15.00 (*1-893183-28-9*); 272p. per. 15.00 (*0-926524-54-2*, 556) Granite Publishing, LLC. (Wild Flower Pr.).

Mallon, Thomas. Two Moons: A Novel. 2001. (Harvest Book Ser.). (Illus.). 368p. reprint ed. pap. 14.00 (*0-15-601082-8*, Harvest Bks.) Harcourt Trade Pubs.

Masiel, David. 2182 kHz. l.t. ed. 2002. 28.95 (*0-7862-4475-5*) Thorndike Pr.

—2182 kHz: A Novel. 2002. 304p. 22.95 (*0-375-50606-3*) Random Hse., Inc.

McAllister, V. A. The Mosquito War. 2001. 320p. 25.95 (*0-312-87870-2*, Forge Bks.) Doherty, Tom Assocs., LLC.

McMahon, Thomas. Loving Little Egypt. 1988. 288p. pap. 6.95 o.p. (*0-14-009331-1*, Penguin Bks.); 1987. 320p. 16.95 o.p. (*0-670-81228-5*) Viking Penguin.

Mosley, Nicholas. Hopeful Monsters: A Novel. 551p. 2000. pap. 14.95 (*1-56478-242-5*); 1991. 21.95 o.p. (*0-916583-85-6*) Dalkey Archive Pr.

—Hopeful Monsters: A Novel. 1993. pap. 15.00 o.s.i (*0-679-73929-7*, Vintage) Knopf Publishing Group.

Murray, John. A Few Short Notes on Tropical Butterflies: Stories. 288p. 2004. pap. 12.95 (*0-06-050929-5*, Perennial); 2003. 24.95 (*0-06-050928-7*, HarperCollins) HarperTrade.

Oltion, Jerry. The Getaway Special. 400p. 2003. pap. 15.95 (*0-312-87778-1*); 2001. 26.95 (*0-312-87777-3*) Doherty, Tom Assocs., LLC. (Tor Bks.).

Powers, Richard. The Gold Bug Variations. 1991. 696p. 25.00 o.p. (*0-688-09891-6*, Morrow, William & Co.) Morrow/Avon.

—Gold Bug Variations. 1992. 640p. pap. 16.00 (*0-06-097500-8*, Perennial) HarperTrade.

Preuss, Paul. Core: A Novel. 1994. 400p. mass mkt. 5.99 (*0-380-71182-6*, Avon Bks.); 1993. 23.00 o.p. (*0-688-09662-X*, Morrow, William & Co.) Morrow/Avon.

Ralles, H. J. Darok 9. 2002. 229p. (YA). pap. 9.95 (*1-929976-10-0*) Top Pubns., Ltd.

Rosner, Elizabeth. The Speed of Light. 2003. 272p. pap. 12.95 (*0-345-44225-3*); 2001. 256p. 23.95 (*0-345-44224-5*) Ballantine Bks. (Ballantine Bks.).

—The Speed of Light. l.t. ed. 2002. 398p. 28.95 (*0-7862-4041-5*) Gale Group.

Ryan, Richard. Funnelweb. 1997. 339p. (*0-7329-0888-4*) Macmillan Education Australia.

Ryman, Geoff. Lust. Orig. Title: Lust, or, No harm done. Date not set. pap. (*0-312-31212-1*, St. Martin's Paperbacks); Date not set. mass mkt. (*0-312-98855-9*, St. Martin's Paperbacks); 2003. 400p. 25.95 (*0-312-31211-3*) St. Martin's Pr.

Sabbagh, Karl. A Rum Affair: A True Story of Botanical Fraud. 2000. (Illus.). viii, 276p. 24.00 o.p. (*0-374-25282-3*) Farrar, Straus & Giroux.

Scott, Holden. Skeptic. E-Book 6.99 (*0-312-26468-2*); 2000. 400p. mass mkt. 6.99 (*0-312-96928-7*, St. Martin's Paperbacks); 1999. 322p. 24.95 o.p. (*0-312-19334-3*) St. Martin's Pr.

Sealy, I. Allan. The Brainfever Bird. 2003. 200p. (*0-330-41205-1*) Picador.

Segal, Erich. Prizes. 1996. 512p. mass mkt. 6.99 o.s.i (*0-8041-1427-7*, Ivy Bks.) Ballantine Bks.

—Prizes. l.t. ed. 1995. 27.95 (*1-56895-228-7*, Wheeler Publishing, Inc.) Gale Group.

—Prizes. abr. ed. 1995. 24.95 o.p. (*0-7871-0429-9*) NewStar Media, Inc.

Shelley, Mary Wollstonecraft. Frankenstein. 2000. (SPA.). 320p. 8.95 (*84-406-1953-7*) B Ediciones S.A. ESP. *Dist:* Distribooks, Inc.

—Frankenstein. E-Book (*0-7607-1308-1*) Barnes & Noble, Inc.

—Frankenstein. 2001. per. 14.00 (*1-891355-53-8*); per. 15.50 (*1-58396-220-4*) Blue Unicorn Editions.

—Frankenstein. 1997. (Cambridge Literature Ser.). audio 14.95 o.p. (*0-521-59793-5*) Cambridge Univ. Pr.

—Frankenstein. 1999. (Bloom's Reviews Comprehensive Research & Study Guides). 72p. pap. 4.95 (*0-7910-4121-2*) Chelsea Hse. Pubs.

—Frankenstein. l.t. ed. 1998. 343p. pap. 19.95 (*1-58855-029-X*) Cyber Classics, Inc.

—Frankenstein. 1988. mass mkt. 4.95 (*0-938819-80-1*, Aerie) Doherty, Tom Assocs., LLC.

—Frankenstein. l.t. unabr. ed. 2001. (Large Print Classics Ser.). xv, 283p. pap. 9.95 (*0-486-41562-7*) Dover Pubns., Inc.

—Frankenstein. 2003. (Barnes & Noble Classics Ser.). 288p. pap. 3.95 (*1-59308-005-0*) Fine Communications.

—Frankenstein. l.t. ed. 2001. 315p. 27.95 (*0-7838-9622-0*, Hall, G. K. & Co.) Gale Group.

—Frankenstein. 2003. pap. 6.50 (*1-59456-236-9*) GreatUNpublished.com.

—Frankenstein. 1965. mass mkt. 1.50 o.p. (*0-451-51132-8*); mass mkt. 0.95 o.p. (*0-451-50839-4*); mass mkt. 0.75 o.p. (*0-451-50695-2*); mass mkt. 0.50 o.p. (*0-451-50329-5*); mass mkt. 1.25 o.p. (*0-451-50975-7*); mass mkt. 0.60 o.p. (*0-451-50618-9*) NAL. (Signet Classics).

—Frankenstein. (C). pap. (*0-393-97938-5*) Norton, W. W. & Co., Inc.

—Frankenstein. 2003. (Penguin Classics Ser.). 336p. pap. 8.00 (*0-14-143947-5*) Penguin Group (USA) Inc.

—Frankenstein. 1995. (SPA.). 304p. (*84-01-46253-3*) Plaza & Janés Editories, S.A.

—Frankenstein. (FRE.). pap. 10.95 (*2-266-00354-2*) Presses Pocket FRA. *Dist:* Distribooks, Inc.

—Frankenstein. 2004. 304p. mass mkt. 3.95 (*0-7434-8758-3*, Pocket) Simon & Schuster.

—Frankenstein: Or, the Modern Prometheus. 2001. (Oxford World's Classics Ser.). 224p. 15.00 (*0-19-514901-7*) Oxford Univ. Pr., Inc.

Shelley, Mary Wollstonecraft & Wells, H. G. Making Humans: Complete Texts with Introduction, Historical Contexts, Critical Essays. Wilt, Judith, ed. 2003. (New Riverside Editions Ser.). (Illus.). viii, 359p. 8.76 (*0-618-08489-4*) Houghton Mifflin Co.

Shimoda, Todd A. The Fourth Treasure. 2002. (Illus.). 368p. 24.95 (*0-385-50352-0*, Talese, Nan A.) Doubleday Publishing.

Shimoda, Todd A. & Shimoda, L. J. C. The Fourth Treasure. 2002. (Illus.). 349p. E-Book 22.50 (*0-385-50561-2*, Talese, Nan A.) Doubleday Publishing.

Stephenson, Neal. Quicksilver. 2003. (Baroque Cycle: Vol. 1). 944p. 27.95 (*0-380-97742-7*, Morrow, William & Co.) Morrow/Avon.

Vernon, John. The Great Unknown. 2001. 352p. tchr. ed. 24.00 (*0-618-10940-4*) Houghton Mifflin Co.

Voien, Steven. Black Leopard. 1997. 287p. 23.00 o.s.i (*0-679-44702-4*) Random Hse., Inc.

Wells, H. G. The Invisible Man. 3rd ed. 1992. (Longman Simplified English Ser.). (Illus.). 78p. pap. text 5.95 o.p. (*0-582-53697-9*) Addison-Wesley Longman, Inc.

—The Invisible Man. 1964. (Airmont Classics Ser.). (YA). (gr. 8 up). mass mkt. 2.95 o.p. (*0-8049-0040-X*, CL-40) Airmont Publishing Co., Inc.

—The Invisible Man. 19.95 (*0-89190-423-9*) Amereon, Ltd.

—The Invisible Man. 1994. (Illustrated Classics Collection). 64p. pap. 3.60 o.p. (*1-56103-488-6*) American Guidance Service, Inc.

—The Invisible Man. 1984. 144p. mass mkt. 2.25 o.s.i (*0-553-21155-2*); 1983. 160p. mass mkt. 4.95 (*0-553-21353-9*, Bantam Classics); 1983. mass mkt. 1.95 o.s.i (*0-553-21207-9*); 1983. 160p. mass mkt. 2.50 o.s.i (*0-553-21253-2*, Bantam Classics) Bantam Bks.

—The Invisible Man. 1981. 279p. reprint ed. lib. bdg. 14.00 o.s.i (*0-8376-0457-5*) Bentley Pubs.

—The Invisible Man. 1991. (Illus.). 3.95 (*0-425-12663-3*); 1982. 1.95 o.s.i (*0-425-05352-0*); 1980. 1.75 o.s.i (*0-425-04728-8*); 1978. 1.50 o.s.i (*0-425-04069-0*); 1976. 1.25 o.s.i (*0-425-03438-0*); 1975. 0.75 o.s.i (*0-425-02989-1*); 1968. 0.60 o.p. (*0-425-02124-6*) Berkley Publishing Group.

—The Invisible Man. 1982. reprint ed. lib. bdg. 21.95 (*0-89966-377-X*) Buccaneer Bks., Inc.

—The Invisible Man. l.t. ed. 2000. 314p. pap. 19.95 (*1-58855-000-1*) Cyber Classics, Inc.

—The Invisible Man. 1988. mass mkt. 4.95 (*1-55902-001-6*, Aerie) Doherty, Tom Assocs., LLC.

—The Invisible Man. 1992. (Thrift Editions Ser.). 112p. reprint ed. pap. 1.00 (*0-486-27071-8*) Dover Pubns., Inc.

—The Invisible Man. l.t. ed. 717p. pap. 57.00 (*0-7583-3303-X*); 140p. pap. 15.00 (*0-7583-3296-3*); 618p. pap. 50.00 (*0-7583-3302-1*); 502p. pap. 43.00 (*0-7583-3301-3*); 409p. pap. 36.00 (*0-7583-3300-5*); 319p. pap. 29.00 (*0-7583-3299-8*); 249p. pap. 23.00 (*0-7583-3298-X*); 182p. pap. 18.00 (*0-7583-3297-1*); 618p. lib. bdg. 56.00 (*0-7583-3294-7*); 140p. lib. bdg. 21.00 (*0-7583-3288-2*); 717p. lib. bdg. 63.00 (*0-7583-3295-5*); 182p. lib. bdg. 24.00 (*0-7583-3289-0*); 502p. lib. bdg. 49.00 (*0-7583-3293-9*); 249p. lib. bdg. 29.00 (*0-7583-3290-4*); 319p. lib. bdg. 35.00 (*0-7583-3291-2*); 409p. lib. bdg. 42.00 (*0-7583-3292-0*) Huge Print Pr.

—The Invisible Man. l.t. ed. 2000. (LRS Large Print Heritage Ser.). 238p. (YA). (gr. 6-12). lib. bdg. 28.95 (*1-58118-077-2*, 23671) LRS.

—The Invisible Man. Lake, David et al, eds. 1996. (Oxford World's Classics Ser.). 208p. (C). pap. 6.95 o.p. (*0-19-283195-X*) Oxford Univ. Pr., Inc.

—The Invisible Man. 2000. 120p. pap. 10.99 (*1-57646-278-1*); 2000. 120p. lib. bdg. 24.99 (*1-57646-529-2*); 1999. E-Book 3.99 o.p. incl. cd-rom (*1-57646-051-7*) Quiet Vision Publishing.

—The Invisible Man. 2002. (Modern Library Classics). 192p. pap. 5.95 (*0-8129-6645-7*) Random House Adult Trade Publishing Group.

—The Invisible Man. l.t. ed. 1996. (Large Print Perennial Bestseller Ser.). 220p. 21.95 (*0-7838-1545-X*) Thorndike Pr.

—The Invisible Man. Daly, Macdonald, ed. rev. ed. 1995. (Everyman Paperback Classics Ser.). 320p. (C). pap. 5.95 (*0-460-87628-7*, Everyman's Classic Library in Paperback) Tuttle Publishing.

—The Invisible Man. unabr. ed. 1997. 175p. reprint ed. pap. 14.95 o.p. (*1-57002-052-3*) University Publishing Hse., Inc.

Weston, Martha. The Dinosaurs Meet Dr. Clock: A Holiday House Reader. 2002. (Reader Level 1 Ser.). (Illus.). 32p. (J). (ps-3). tchr. ed. 14.95 (*0-8234-1661-5*) Holiday Hse., Inc.

White, Randy Wayne. Captiva. 1997. 336p. reprint ed. mass mkt. 6.99 (*0-425-15854-3*, Prime Crime) Berkley Publishing Group.

—Captiva. 1996. 256p. 21.95 o.s.i (*0-399-14140-5*, G. P. Putnam's Sons) Penguin Group (USA) Inc.

—The Heat Islands. (Doc Ford Novel Ser.). 1993. 307p. mass mkt. 6.99 (*0-312-92977-3*, St. Martin's Paperbacks); 1992. 336p. 19.95 (*0-312-06993-6*, Saint Martin's Minotaur) St. Martin's Pr.

—The Man Who Invented Florida. 1993. 288p. 20.95 o.p. (*0-312-09866-9*, Saint Martin's Minotaur); 1997. 294p. reprint ed. pap. 6.99 (*0-312-95398-4*, St. Martin's Paperbacks) St. Martin's Pr.

—The Mangrove Coast. 1999. (Prime Crime Mysteries Ser.). 336p. reprint ed. mass mkt. 6.99 (*0-425-17194-9*, Prime Crime) Berkley Publishing Group.

—The Mangrove Coast. 1998. 256p. 22.95 o.p. (*0-399-14372-6*, G. P. Putnam's Sons) Penguin Group (USA) Inc.

—North of Havana. 1998. 272p. mass mkt. 6.99 (*0-425-16294-X*, Prime Crime) Berkley Publishing Group.

—North of Havana. 1997. 256p. 22.95 o.p. (*0-399-14242-8*, G. P. Putnam's Sons) Penguin Group (USA) Inc.

—Sanibel Flats. 320p. 1990. 17.95 (*0-312-03926-3*, Saint Martin's Minotaur); 1991. reprint ed. mass mkt. 6.99 (*0-312-92602-2*, St. Martin's Paperbacks) St. Martin's Pr.

—Ten Thousand Islands. l.t. ed. 2001. xiv, 331p. 29.95 (*1-58724-110-2*, Wheeler Publishing, Inc.) Gale Group.

—Ten Thousand Islands. 2000. xvi, 320p. 23.95 o.s.i (*0-399-14620-2*) Penguin Group (USA) Inc.

Wolfson, Susan J. Frankenstein: A Cultural Edition. 2002. (Longman Cultural Edition Ser.). 384p. pap. 16.00 (*0-321-09698-3*) Longman Publishing Group.

Wyle, Dirk. Biotechnology Is Murder: A Ben Candidi Mystery. 2000. 271p. pap. 14.95 (*1-56825-045-2*, 045-2) Rainbow Bks., Inc.

—Pharmacology Is Murder: A Novel. 1998. 388p. pap. 16.95 (*1-56825-038-X*, 038X) Rainbow Bks., Inc.

# T

## TEACHERS—FICTION

Abrahams, Peter. The Tutor. 2003. 384p. mass mkt. 7.50 (*0-345-43941-4*); 2002. 368p. 25.95 (*0-345-43938-4*) Ballantine Bks.

—The Tutor. l.t. ed. 2003. lib. bdg. 29.95 (*1-58547-270-0*, Platinum) Ctr. Point Large Print.

Alers, Rochelle. Summer Magic. 1999. (Arabesque Ser.). 252p. mass mkt. 4.99 (*1-58314-012-3*) Kensington Publishing Corp.

Antrim, Donald. Elect Mr. Robinson for a Better World. 1993. 192p. 20.00 o.p. (*0-670-85139-6*, Viking) Viking Penguin.

—Elect Mr. Robinson for a Better World: A Novel. 2001. 192p. pap. 12.00 (*0-375-72503-2*, Vintage) Knopf Publishing Group.

Auster, Paul. Timbuktu. 1999. 192p. 22.00 o.s.i (*0-8050-5407-3*) Holt, Henry & Co.

—Timbuktu. 2000. 192p. pap. 11.00 (*0-312-26399-6*); mass mkt. 7.99 o.s.i (*0-312-97528-7*) Picador.

Averill, Thomas Fox. The Slow Air of Ewan MacPherson. 2003. 272p. pap. 13.00 (*0-425-19081-1*, BlueHen Bks.) Putnam Publishing Group, The.

Baldwin, Lydia W. A Yankee School-Teacher in Virginia. 1977. (Black Heritage Library Collection). reprint ed. 22.95 (*0-8369-8959-7*) Ayer Co. Pubs., Inc.

Ballard, Elizabeth. The Bracelet. 2003. (Illus.). 32p. 9.95 (*1-58685-050-4*) Smith, Gibbs Pub.

Barr, Marleen S. Oy Pioneer! 2003. (Library of American Fiction). 19.95 (*0-299-18910-4*) Univ. of Wisconsin Pr.

Baxter, Charles. Saul & Patsy: A Novel. 2003. 336p. 24.00 (*0-375-41029-5*, Pantheon) Knopf Publishing Group.

Berenson, Laurien. Dog Eat Dog: A Melanie Travis Mystery. (Melanie Travis Mystery Ser.). 1997. 336p. mass mkt. 5.99 (*1-57566-227-2*); 1996. 352p. 18.95 o.s.i (*1-57566-103-9*) Kensington Publishing Corp.

—Hair of the Dog: A Melanie Travis Mystery. (Melanie Travis Mystery Ser.). 1998. 336p. mass mkt. 5.99 (*1-57566-356-2*); 1997. 320p. 18.95 o.s.i (*1-57566-222-1*) Kensington Publishing Corp.

—Hush Puppy. (Melanie Travis Mystery Ser.). 2000. 32p. mass mkt. 5.99 (*1-57566-600-6*); 1999. 304p. 20.00 o.s.i (*1-57566-469-0*, Kensington Bks.) Kensington Publishing Corp.

—A Pedigree to Die For: A Melanie Travis Mystery. l.t. ed. 1995. 347p. pap. 20.95 o.p. (*0-7838-1446-1*, Macmillan Reference USA) Gale Group.

—A Pedigree to Die For: A Melanie Travis Mystery, 1. 1998. mass mkt. 5.99 (*1-57566-374-0*); 1997. 288p. pap. 9.95 o.s.i (*1-57566-125-X*); 1996. mass mkt. 4.99 o.p. (*0-8217-5227-8*); 1996. 288p. mass mkt. 4.99 o.s.i (*1-57566-003-2*); 1995. 304p. mass mkt. 16.95 o.p. (*0-8217-4827-0*, Zebra Bks.) Kensington Publishing Corp.

—Underdog: A Melanie Travis Mystery. 1996. 336p. mass mkt. 4.99 o.s.i (*1-57566-108-X*); 320p. 18.95 o.s.i (*1-57566-011-3*); mass mkt. 16.95 o.s.i (*0-8217-5224-3*) Kensington Publishing Corp.

—Watchdog. (Melanie Travis Mystery Ser.). 1999. 320p. mass mkt. 5.99 (*1-57566-472-0*, Kensington Bks.); 1998. 314p. (J). (gr. 10 up). 20.00 o.s.i (*1-57566-350-3*) Kensington Publishing Corp.

Bessey, Sian Ann. Cover of Darkness. 2002. (Illus.). 230p. 14.95 (*1-57734-985-7*) Covenant Communications.

Beverley, Jo. An Unwilling Bride. 2000. 352p. mass mkt. 6.99 (*0-8217-6724-0*); 1994. mass mkt. 3.99 o.s.i (*0-8217-4475-5*); 1992. mass mkt. 3.99 o.s.i (*0-8217-3669-8*, Zebra Bks.) Kensington Publishing Corp.

—An Unwilling Bride. l.t. ed. 2001. (Thorndike Press Large Print Romance Ser.). 581p. 28.95 (*0-7862-3334-6*) Thorndike Pr.

Binchy, Maeve. Evening Class. 2001. E-Book 7.99 (*1-58945-902-4*) Adobe Systems, Inc.

—Evening Class. unabr. ed. 1998. audio 96.95 o.p. (*0-7540-0000-1*, CAB 1423) BBC Audiobooks America.

—Evening Class. 1998. 544p. mass mkt. 7.99 (*0-440-22320-2*, 25456916, Dell Bks.); 1997. pap. 6.99 (*0-440-29550-5*) Dell Publishing.

—Evening Class. abr. ed. 1997. audio 24.95 (*0-553-47765-X*, 695019); audio compact disk 29.95 o.s.i (*0-553-45554-0*) Random Hse. Audio Publishing Group. (RH Audio).

—Evening Class. 1999. E-Book 7.50 (*0-440-33414-4*) Random Hse., Inc.

—Evening Class. unabr. ed. 2000. audio 95.00 (*0-7887-3999-9*, H1076K8, Clipper Audio) Recorded Bks., LLC.

—Evening Class. l.t. ed. (Paperback Bestsellers Ser.). 661p. 1998. pap. 27.95 (*0-7838-8113-4*); 1997. 29.95 (*0-7838-8112-6*) Thorndike Pr.

Blacklock, Dianne. Call Waiting: A Novel. 2003. 384p. 24.95 (*0-312-30348-3*) St. Martin's Pr.

Blanchard, Jay S. & Casanova, Ursula, eds. Modern Fiction about School Teaching: An Anthology. 1995. 352p. pap. 34.00 o.p. (*0-205-15250-3*) Allyn & Bacon, Inc.

Blauner, Peter. Man of the Hour. 1999. 432p. 24.00 o.p. (*0-316-03817-2*) Little Brown & Co.

—The Man of the Hour. 2000. 496p. mass mkt. 7.99 o.s.i (*0-446-60541-7*) Warner Bks., Inc.

Bohjalian, Chris. Trans-Sister Radio. E-Book 12.50 (*1-58945-533-9*) Adobe Systems, Inc.

—Trans-Sister Radio. 2001. 368p. reprint ed. pap. 14.00 (*0-375-70517-1*, Vintage) Knopf Publishing Group.

—Trans-Sister Radio. 2001. E-Book 12.50 (*0-609-50408-8*) Random Hse., Inc.

Borthwick, J. S. Bodies of Water. 1991. 287p. mass mkt. 5.99 (*0-312-92603-0*, St. Martin's Paperbacks); 1990. 17.95 o.p. (*0-312-04269-8*, Saint Martin's Minotaur) St. Martin's Pr.

—The Bridled Groom: A Dead Letter Mystery. 1995. 336p. mass mkt. 6.50 (*0-312-95505-7*, St. Martin's Paperbacks) St. Martin's Pr.

—The Bridled Groom: A Mystery. 1994. 304p. 20.95 o.p. (*0-312-10435-9*, Saint Martin's Minotaur) St. Martin's Pr.

—The Case of the Hook-Billed Kites. 1982. 256p. 12.95 o.p. (*0-312-12335-3*) St. Martin's Pr.

—The Case of the Hook-Billed Kites. 1983. 256p. pap. 3.95 o.p. (0-14-006785-X, Penguin Bks.) Viking Penguin.
—Coup de Grace. 2000. (Illus.). x, 335p. 24.95 (0-312-25313-3, Saint Martin's Minotaur) St. Martin's Pr.
—Coupe de Grace. 2001. (Sarah Deane Mysteries Ser.). 352p. mass mkt. 6.50 (0-312-97449-3, St. Martin's Paperbacks) St. Martin's Pr.
—The Down-East Murders. 1991. 296p. mass mkt. 6.50 (0-312-92606-5, St. Martin's Paperbacks) St. Martin's Pr.
—The Down-East Murders: A Mystery Set on the Coast of Maine. 1985. 288p. 14.95 o.p. (0-312-21855-9) St. Martin's Pr.
—Dude on Arrival: A Christmas Mystery. 1992. 306p. mass mkt. 6.50 (0-312-92955-2, St. Martin's Paperbacks); 1991. 320p. 19.95 o.p. (0-312-06341-5, Saint Martin's Minotaur) St. Martin's Pr.
—The Garden Plot. (Dead Letter Mysteries Ser.). 1998. 336p. pap. 6.50 (0-312-96291-6, St. Martin's Paperbacks); 1997. 352p. 23.95 (0-312-15131-4, Saint Martin's Minotaur) St. Martin's Pr.
—My Body Lies over the Ocean. (Sarah Deane Mysteries Ser.). 304p. 2000. mass mkt. 6.50 (0-312-97040-4, St. Martin's Paperbacks); 1998. 22.95 o.p. (0-312-19991-0, Saint Martin's Minotaur) St. Martin's Pr.
—The Student Body. 1991. 293p. mass mkt. 6.50 (0-312-92605-7, St. Martin's Paperbacks); 1987. mass mkt. 3.50 o.s.i (0-312-90738-9, St. Martin's Paperbacks); 1986. 320p. 16.95 o.p. (0-312-76934-2) St. Martin's Pr.
Bronte, Charlotte. The Professor. (Modern Library Ser.). E-Book 4.95 (1-931208-19-0) Adobe Systems, Inc.
—The Professor, unabr. ed. audio 41.95 (1-55685-026-3, 1985) Audio Bk. Contractors, Inc.
—The Professor, Set. unabr. ed. 2000. audio 69.95 (0-7540-0420-1, CAB 1843, Sterling Audio Bks.) BBC Audiobooks America.
—The Professor. unabr. ed. 2000. audio 49.95 (0-7861-1752-4, 2556); audio compact disk 64.00 (0-7861-9899-0, z2556) Blackstone Audio Bks., Inc.
—The Professor, 2. reprint ed. lib. bdg. 196.00 (0-7426-2191-X); 2001. 283p. pap. text 56.00 (0-7426-7191-7) Classic Bks.
—The Professor. 1972. 5.95 o.p. (0-460-01417-X); 1954. 10.50 o.p. (0-460-00417-4) Dutton/Plume. (Dutton).
—The Professor. E-Book 2.49 (0-7574-0384-0) Electric Umbrella Publishing.
—The Professor. 1999. (Twelve-Point Ser.). 250p. lib. bdg. 25.00 (1-58287-095-0) North Bks.
—The Professor. Smith, Margaret & Rosengarten, Herbert, eds. (Oxford World's Classics Ser.). 1999. 336p. pap. 7.95 (0-19-283511-4); 1991. 336p. pap. 5.95 o.p. (0-19-282741-3); 1987. (Illus.). 390p. 110.00 o.p. (0-19-812694-8) Oxford Univ. Pr., Inc.
—The Professor. 2000. E-Book 4.95 (0-679-63999-3, Modern Library) Random House Adult Trade Publishing Group.
—The Professor. E-Book 5.00 (0-7410-0451-8) SoftBook Pr.
—The Professor. Glen, Heather, ed. & intro. by. 1989. (Classics Ser.). 320p. pap. 8.95 (0-14-043311-2, Penguin Classics) Viking Penguin.
—The Professor. abr. ed. 1997. audio 16.95 o.s.i (0-14-086392-3, Penguin AudioBooks) Viking Penguin.
—The Professor. 1998. (Classics Library). 215p. pap. 3.95 (1-85326-208-0, 2080WW) Wordsworth Editions, Ltd. GBR. *Dist:* Casemate Pubs. & Bk. Distributors, LLC.
—The Professor. 1997 Edition. 1997. 288p. 14.50 o.s.i (0-679-60273-9) Random Hse., Inc.
—The Professor & Emma: A Fragment. 1910. 272p. pap. 5.95 o.p. (0-460-02508-2, Everyman's Classic Library in Paperback) Tuttle Publishing.
Brookhouse, Christopher. A Selfish Woman: A Novel. 2001. 144p. 24.00 (1-57962-036-1) Permanent Pr., The.
Brown, Sandra. A Kiss Remembered. 2003. 224p. mass mkt. 6.99 (0-446-61261-8); 2002. 192p. 19.95 o.p. (0-446-52978-8) Warner Bks., Inc.
Bruce, Leo. A Bone & a Hank of Hair. 1985. (Carolus Deene Mystery Ser.). 192p. reprint ed. 20.00 o.p. (0-89733-176-1); pap. 5.95 o.s.i (0-89733-175-3) Academy Chicago Pubs., Ltd.
—Dead Man's Shoes. 1987. (Carolus Deene Mystery Ser.). 216p. pap. 7.95 (0-89733-271-7) Academy Chicago Pubs., Ltd.
—Death at Hallows End. 2003. 221p. 22.50 (0-89733-516-3) Academy Chicago Pubs., Ltd.
—Death at St Asprey's School. 1984. (Carolus Deene Mystery Ser.). 221p. 14.95 o.p. (0-89733-095-1); pap. 7.95 (0-89733-094-3) Academy Chicago Pubs., Ltd.
—Death in Albert Park. 1983. (Carolus Deene Mystery Ser.). 239p. reprint ed. pap. 7.95 (0-89733-073-0) Academy Chicago Pubs., Ltd.
—Death of a Commuter. 1988. (Carolus Deene Mystery Ser.). 192p. pap. 7.95 (0-89733-326-8) Academy Chicago Pubs., Ltd.
—Death on All Hallowe'en. 1988. (Carolus Deene Mystery Ser.). 176p. pap. 7.95 (0-89733-292-X) Academy Chicago Pubs., Ltd.
—Death with Blue Ribbon. 1994. (Carolus Deene Mystery Ser.). 176p. pap. 7.95 (0-89733-345-4) Academy Chicago Pubs., Ltd.
—Die All, Die Merrily. 1987. (Carolus Deene Mystery Ser.). 192p. pap. 7.95 (0-89733-253-9) Academy Chicago Pubs., Ltd.
—Furious Old Women. 1983. (Carolus Deene Mystery Ser.). 191p. reprint ed. pap. 7.95 (0-89733-084-6) Academy Chicago Pubs., Ltd.
—Furious Old Women. Barzun, Jacques & Taylor, W. H., eds. 1983. (Crime Fiction 1950-1975 Ser.). 191p. lib. bdg. 5.00 o.p. (0-8240-4976-4) Garland Publishing, Inc.
—Jack on the Gallows Tree. 1983. (Carolus Deene Mystery Ser.). 189p. 15.00 (0-89733-071-4); pap. 7.95 (0-89733-072-2) Academy Chicago Pubs., Ltd.
—Nothing Like Blood. 1986. 4.95 o.p. (0-89733-127-3); 1985. 192p. 15.00 (0-89733-128-1) Academy Chicago Pubs., Ltd.
—Our Jubilee Is Death. 1986. (Carolus Deene Mystery Ser.). 189p. pap. 7.95 (0-89733-229-6) Academy Chicago Pubs., Ltd.
—Such Is Death. (Carolus Deene Mystery Ser.). 192p. 1986. 15.00 (0-89733-159-1); 1985. pap. 7.95 (0-89733-160-5) Academy Chicago Pubs., Ltd.
Burns, Michael. Gemini. Hansen, Marge D., ed. 2001. (Illus.). 387p. 24.95 (0-9701862-4-X) Poncha Pr.
Callen, Paulette. Charity. 1998. 320p. reprint ed. mass mkt. 6.99 o.s.i (0-425-16516-7) Berkley Publishing Group.
—Charity. 1997. 308p. 21.50 (0-684-82942-8, Simon & Schuster) Simon & Schuster.
Carr, Caleb. Killing Time: A Novel of the Future. l.t. ed. 2000. 368p. 25.95 (0-375-43076-8) Random Hse. Large Print.
Carvic, Heron. Miss Seeton Draws the Line. l.t. ed. 1991. pap. 10.95 o.p. (0-7927-0097-X, C0003) BBC Audiobooks America.
—Miss Seeton Draws the Line. 1988. mass mkt. 4.50 o.s.i (0-425-11097-4) Berkley Publishing Group.
—Miss Seeton Sings. l.t. ed. 1991. 19.95 o.p. (0-7927-0690-0, CH008); pap. 17.95 o.p. (0-7927-0691-9, CS0110) BBC Audiobooks America.
—Miss Seeton Sings. Fowler, Kathy, ed. 1988. 208p. reprint ed. mass mkt. 4.50 o.s.i (0-425-10714-0) Berkley Publishing Group.
—Odds on Miss Seeton. l.t. ed. 1991. 18.95 o.p. (0-7927-0933-0, CH0145); pap. 19.95 o.p. (0-7927-0934-9, CS0242) BBC Audiobooks America.
—Odds on Miss Seeton. 1989. mass mkt. 4.50 o.s.i (0-425-11307-8) Berkley Publishing Group.
—Odds on Miss Seeton. 1981. 279p. reprint ed. lib. bdg. 16.95 o.p. (0-89966-307-9) Buccaneer Bks., Inc.
—Odds on Miss Seeton. 1975. (Harper Novel of Suspense Ser.). 160p. 7.95 o.p. (0-06-010654-9) HarperCollins Pubs.
—Picture Miss Seeton. (Black Dagger Crime Ser.). 1993. 176p. 16.50 o.p. (0-7451-8615-7, Black Dagger); 1991. 12.95 o.p. (0-7927-0041-4, 476) BBC Audiobooks America.
—Picture Miss Seeton. 1988. (Heron Carvic's Miss Seeton Ser.). mass mkt. 4.50 o.s.i (0-425-10929-1) Berkley Publishing Group.
—Witch Miss Seeton. l.t. ed. 1990. pap. 16.95 o.p. (0-7927-0428-2, C0486); 18.95 o.p. (0-7927-0427-4, C0258) BBC Audiobooks America.
—Witch Miss Seeton. 1988. 192p. mass mkt. 4.50 o.s.i (0-425-10713-2) Berkley Publishing Group.
Chappell, Fred. Brighten the Corner Where You Are. 1989. 15.95 o.p. (0-312-03297-8); 8th ed. 1990. 212p. reprint ed. pap. 11.95 (0-312-05057-7, CPB1110, Saint Martin's Griffin) St. Martin's Pr.
Charles, Hampton. Miss Seeton at the Helm. 1990. mass mkt. 3.99 o.s.i (0-425-12264-6) Berkley Publishing Group.
—Miss Seeton at the Helm. l.t. ed. 1998. (G. K. Hall Nightingale Ser.). pap. 18.95 o.p. (0-8161-5926-2, Macmillan Reference USA) Gale Group.
Cohen, Leah Hager. Heart, You Bully, You Punk: A Novel. 2003. 224p. 23.95 (0-670-03167-4, Viking) Viking Penguin.
Collins, Wilkie. The Woman in White. 2002. (Modern Library Classics). 704p. pap. 7.95 (0-375-75906-9, Modern Library) Random House Adult Trade Publishing Group.
—The Woman in White. 2003. (Classics Ser.). 720p. pap. 8.00 (0-14-143961-0, Penguin Classics) Viking Penguin.
Colman, Hila. Confession of a Storyteller. 1984. pap. (0-671-45659-8, Simon Pulse) Simon & Schuster Children's Publishing.
Coote, Cathy. Innocents. 2002. 256p. pap. 12.00 (0-8021-3927-2, Grove Pr.) Grove/Atlantic, Inc.
Corrick, Martin. The Navigation Log: A Novel. 2004. 304p. pap. 13.95 (0-375-76053-9, Random Hse. Trade Paperbacks) Random House Adult Trade Publishing Group.
—The Navigation Log: A Novel. 2003. 304p. 24.95 (0-375-50812-0) Random Hse., Inc.
Crane, Hamilton. Bonjour, Miss Seeton. (Heron Carvic's Miss Seeton Ser.). 272p. 1997. 21.95 o.s.i (0-425-15968-X, Prime Crime); 1998. reprint ed. mass mkt. 5.99 o.s.i (0-425-16534-5) Berkley Publishing Group.
—Miss Seeton by Moonlight. 1992. mass mkt. 4.50 o.s.i (0-425-13265-X) Berkley Publishing Group.
—Miss Seeton by Moonlight. l.t. ed. 2000. (Mystery Ser.). 347p. 27.95 o.p. (0-7862-2481-9); (0-7540-4140-9); (0-7540-4141-7) Thorndike Pr.
—Miss Seeton Cracks the Case. 1991. mass mkt. 4.99 o.s.i (0-425-12676-5) Berkley Publishing Group.
—Miss Seeton Cracks the Case. l.t. ed. 1999. (Thorndike Mystery Ser.). o.p. (0-7862-1766-9, Macmillan Reference USA) Gale Group.
—Miss Seeton Goes to Bat. l.t. ed. 1999. (Mystery Ser.). 365p. 27.95 (0-7862-2065-1); (0-7540-3898-X); (0-7540-3897-1) Thorndike Pr.
—Miss Seeton Paints the Town. 1991. mass mkt. 4.99 o.s.i (0-425-12848-2) Berkley Publishing Group.
—Miss Seeton Paints the Town. l.t. ed. 2000. (Mystery Ser.). 352p. 27.95 (0-7862-2339-1) Thorndike Pr.
—Miss Seeton Rocks the Cradle. 1992. 208p. mass mkt. 4.99 o.s.i (0-425-13400-8) Berkley Publishing Group.
—Miss Seeton Rocks the Cradle. l.t. ed. 2000. (Mystery Ser.). 386p. 27.95 (0-7862-2840-7) Thorndike Pr.
—Miss Seeton Rules. 272p. 1995. mass mkt. 4.99 o.s.i (0-425-15006-2); 1994. 18.95 o.p. (0-425-14354-6) Berkley Publishing Group. (Prime Crime).
—Miss Seeton Undercover. 1994. 272p. mass mkt. 4.99 o.s.i (0-425-14405-4); 17.95 o.p. (0-425-14137-3) Berkley Publishing Group.
—Miss Seeton's Finest Hour. 1999. (Heron Carvic's Miss Seeton Ser.). 272p. mass mkt. 5.99 o.s.i (0-425-17026-8, Prime Crime) Berkley Publishing Group.
—Sold to Miss Seeton. 1996. mass mkt. 5.99 o.s.i (0-425-15462-9); 1995. 272p. 19.95 o.p. (0-425-14936-6, Prime Crime) Berkley Publishing Group.
—Sweet Miss Seeton. (Heron Carvic's Miss Seeton Ser.). 1996. 272p. 21.95 o.p. (0-425-15471-8); 1997. 256p. reprint ed. mass mkt. 5.99 o.s.i (0-425-15962-0) Berkley Publishing Group. (Prime Crime).
Crane, Hamilton & Carvic, Heron. Miss Seeton Goes to Bat. 1993. 208p. mass mkt. 4.99 o.s.i (0-425-13576-4) Berkley Publishing Group.
Creech, Sharon. A Fine, Fine School. 2001. (Illus.). 32p. (J). (ps-3). lib. bdg. 16.89 (0-06-027737-8, Cotler, Joanna Bks.) HarperCollins Children's Bk. Group.
Cronin, Justin. Mary & O'Neil. 2002. 256p. pap. 11.95 (0-385-33359-5, Delta) Dell Publishing.
Cross, Amanda. Honest Doubt. l.t. ed. 2001. 299p. 29.95 (0-7862-3317-6) Thorndike Pr.
Crusie, Jennifer. Crazy for You. l.t. ed. 2000. (Wheeler Large Print Book Ser.). 408p. 26.95 (1-56895-853-6, Wheeler Publishing, Inc.) Gale Group.
—Crazy for You. 2004. mass mkt. 3.99 (0-312-93281-2); 2000. 336p. mass mkt. 7.50 (0-312-97112-5, St. Martin's Paperbacks); 1999. 336p. 24.95 o.p. (0-312-19849-3) St. Martin's Pr.
Dams, Jeanne M. The Body in the Transept. 1996. (Dorothy Martin Mystery Ser.). 224p. mass mkt. 5.99 (0-06-101133-9, HarperTorch) Morrow/Avon.
—The Body in the Transept: A Dorothy Martin Mystery. unabr. collector's ed. 1996. audio 42.00 (0-913369-23-3, 4174) Books on Tape, Inc.
—The Body in the Transept: A Dorothy Martin Mystery. 1995. 216p. 19.95 (0-8027-3275-5) Walker & Co.
—Holy Terror in the Hebrides. 1999. (Dorothy Martin Mystery Ser.: Vol. 3). 272p. mass mkt. 5.99 (0-06-101346-3, HarperTorch) Morrow/Avon.
—Holy Terror in the Hebrides: A Dorothy Martin Mystery, , unabr. collector's ed. 1999. audio 40.00 (0-7366-4296-X, 4789) Books on Tape, Inc.
—Holy Terror in the Hebrides: A Dorothy Martin Mystery. l.t. ed. 2000. (Thorndike Senior Lifestyle Ser.). 333p. 27.95 o.p. (0-7862-2407-X, Macmillan Reference USA) Gale Group.
—Holy Terror in the Hebrides: A Dorothy Martin Mystery. 1997. (Dorothy Martin Mystery Ser.). 224p. 21.95 (0-8027-3311-5) Walker & Co.
—Malice in Miniature. 2000. (Dorothy Martin Mystery Ser.). 272p. mass mkt. 5.99 (0-06-101345-5) HarperCollins Pubs.
—Malice in Miniature: A Dorothy Martin Mystery, , unabr. collector's ed. 1999. audio 40.00 (0-7366-4506-3, 4919) Books on Tape, Inc.
—Malice in Miniature: A Dorothy Martin Mystery. l.t. ed. 2001. (Senior Lifestyles Ser.). 344p. 28.95 (0-7862-2408-8) Thorndike Pr.
—Malice in Miniature: A Dorothy Martin Mystery. 1998. (Dorothy Martin Mystery Ser.). (Illus.). 220p. (gr. 8). 22.95 (0-8027-3322-0) Walker & Co.
—Trouble in the Town Hall. 1998. (Dorothy Martin Mystery Ser.). 256p. mass mkt. 5.99 (0-06-101132-0, HarperTorch) Morrow/Avon.
—Trouble in the Town Hall: A Dorothy Martin Mystery. unabr. collector's ed. 1997. audio 42.00 (0-7366-3834-2, 4554) Books on Tape, Inc.
—Trouble in the Town Hall: A Dorothy Martin Mystery. l.t. ed. 2000. (Thorndike Senior Lifestyle Ser.). 315p. 27.95 (0-7862-2406-1) Thorndike Pr.
—Trouble in the Town Hall: A Dorothy Martin Mystery. 1996. (Dorothy Martin Mystery Ser.). 256p. 20.95 (0-8027-3285-2) Walker & Co.
—The Victim in Victoria Station. l.t. ed. 2001. (Dorothy Martin Mystery Ser.). (Illus.). 295p. 27.95 (0-7862-2409-6) Thorndike Pr.
—The Victim in Victoria Station: A Dorothy Martin Mystery. 1999. (Dorothy Martin Mystery Ser.). (Illus.). 208p. 23.95 (0-8027-3337-9) Walker & Co.
Davis, Lennard J. The Sonnets: A Novel. vi, 163p. (C). 2002. pap. text 16.95 (0-7914-4978-5); 2001. E-Book 25.50 (0-7914-4977-7); 2001. E-Book 25.50 (0-7914-4977-7) State Univ. of New York Pr.
Dawson, Clarence. Desert Vendetta. 1993. 260p. pap. 12.95 o.p. (0-86534-205-9) Sunstone Pr.
Dexter, Kathleen. Fifth Life of the Catwoman. 1996. 244p. pap. 14.95 (0-9651770-0-9) Llano Pr.
Dibdin, Michael. Dirty Tricks. 2003. (Vintage Crime/Black Lizard Ser.). 256p. pap. 12.00 (0-375-70009-9, Vintage) Knopf Publishing Group.
—Dirty Tricks. Chelius, Jane, ed. 1992. 256p. reprint ed. mass mkt. 4.99 (0-671-69546-0, Pocket) Simon & Schuster.
—Dirty Tricks. 1991. 241p. pap. 18.00 (0-671-69545-2) Summit Bks.
Dixon, Carol. Roll Call. 1995. 270p. (Orig.). pap. text 3.00 (1-56722-138-6) Word Aflame Pr.
Dobson, Joanne. Cold & Pure & Very Dead. 2001. 304p. mass mkt. 6.99 (0-553-58002-7) Bantam Bks.
—Cold & Pure & Very Dead: A Karen Pelletier Mystery. 2000. 272p. 22.95 o.s.i (0-385-49340-1) Doubleday Publishing.
Doig, Ivan. Prairie Nocturne: A Novel. 2003. 384p. 26.00 (0-7432-0135-3, Scribner) Simon & Schuster.
Dowling, Gregory. Every Picture Tells a Story. 1991. 22.95 o.p. (0-312-05815-2, Saint Martin's Minotaur) St. Martin's Pr.
—A Nice Steady Job. 1994. 296p. 20.95 o.p. (0-312-11035-9, Saint Martin's Minotaur) St. Martin's Pr.
—See Naples & Kill. 1988. 256p. 15.95 o.p. (0-312-02277-8, Saint Martin's Minotaur) St. Martin's Pr.
Eggleston, Edward. The Hoosier School Master. 1984. (Library of Indiana Classics). (Illus.). 232p. reprint ed. 20.00 o.p. (0-253-32850-0) Indiana Univ. Pr.
—The Hoosier School Master. 1988. (Collected Works of Edward Eggleston). reprint ed. lib. bdg. 79.00 (0-7812-1172-7) Reprint Services Corp.
—The Hoosier School Master. 1871. reprint ed. 69.00 Somerset Pubs., Inc.
Erickson, Lynn. Searching for Sarah. 1999. 352p. mass mkt. 5.99 o.s.i (0-515-12699-3, Jove) Berkley Publishing Group.
Evanick, Marcia. Family First. 1996. 240p. mass mkt. 3.50 o.s.i (0-553-44468-9) Bantam Bks.
Everhart, Robert B. Flirting on the Margins: An Educational Novel. Noblit, George W. & Pink, William T., eds. 1998. (Understanding Education & Policy Ser.). 256p. (C). text 52.50 (1-57273-204-0); pap. text 23.95 (1-57273-205-9) Hampton Pr., Inc.
Falconer, Helen. Sky High. 2003. 224p. 24.95 (0-89255-301-4); pap. 12.95 (0-89255-304-9) Persea Bks., Inc.
Fitzgerald, Penelope. At Freddie's. 1985. 324p. 14.95 o.p. (0-87923-439-3) Godine, David R. Pub.
—At Freddie's. 1999. 160p. pap. 12.00 (0-395-95618-8, Mariner Bks.) Houghton Mifflin Co. Trade & Reference Div.
—At Freddie's. l.t. ed. 2000. 226p. (0-7540-4074-7); (0-7540-4075-5) Thorndike Pr.
Flake, Sharon G. The Skin I'm In. 1999. 192p. (J). pap. 7.99 (0-7868-1307-5) Hyperion Pr.
Foley, Michael. Getting Used to Not Being Remarkable. 1998. 312p. pap. 18.95 (0-85640-626-0) Blackstaff Pr., The IRL. *Dist:* Dufour Editions, Inc.
Forney, Melissa. To Shape a Life: A Tribute to Teachers. 2000. (Illus.). 28p. 9.95 (1-928961-03-7) Barker Creek Publishing, Inc.
Forster, E. M. The Longest Journey. 1997. 304p. mass mkt. 4.95 o.s.i (0-553-21455-1) Bantam Bks.
—The Longest Journey. 1989. reprint ed. lib. bdg. 27.95 (0-89966-632-9) Buccaneer Bks., Inc.
—The Longest Journey. reprint ed. lib. bdg. 98.00 (0-7426-3113-3); 2001. 320p. pap. text 28.00 (0-7426-8113-0) Classic Bks.
—The Longest Journey. text (0-7131-6421-2) Hodder Arnold GBR. *Dist:* Routledge.
—The Longest Journey. Heine, Elizabeth, ed. 1985. (Abinger Edition of E. M. Forster Ser.: Vol. 2). 400p. 69.50 (0-8419-5832-7) Holmes & Meier Pubs., Inc.

—The Longest Journey. 2002. 284p. 19.99 (*1-4043-1380-X*); per. 14.99 (*1-4043-1381-8*) IndyPublish-.com.
—The Longest Journey. 1993. 320p. pap. 13.00 (*0-679-74815-6*, Vintage) Knopf Publishing Group.
—The Longest Journey. 1962. pap. 9.00 o.p. (*0-394-70040-6*) Knopf, Alfred A. Inc.
—The Longest Journey. 1999. 330p. reprint ed. lib. bdg. 29.95 (*0-7351-0068-3*) Replica Bks.
Fourth Graders at Rio Bravo-Greeley Elementary School Staff. Where's Our Teacher? 1995. (Kids Are Authors Picture Bks.). (Illus.). 24p. 5.99 (*0-87406-742-1*) Darby Creek Publishing.
Fowles, John. The Magus. 1978. mass mkt. 2.50 o.s.i (*0-440-15162-7*); 1985. 672p. mass mkt. 7.99 (*0-440-35162-6*) Dell Publishing.
—The Magus. 2001. 656p. pap. 16.95 (*0-316-29619-8*, Back Bay); 1978. 19.95 o.s.i (*0-316-29092-0*) Little Brown & Co.
—The Magus. annuals 1998. (Modern Library Ser.). 736p. 23.95 o.s.i (*0-679-60283-6*) Random Hse., Inc.
—The Magus. 1997. 656p. (*0-09-974391-4*) Trafalgar Square.
Fox, Paula. Poor George: A Novel. 2001. 230p. pap. 13.00 (*0-393-32131-2*, Norton Paperbacks) Norton, W. W. & Co., Inc.
Fuchs, Jake. Death of a Prof: Nursery School Murders II. 2001. 255p. pap. 13.95 (*0-88739-335-7*) Creative Arts Bk. Co.
Fujisawa, Tohru. GTO Vol. 1: Great Teacher Onizuka. 2002. (Illus.). 192p. pap. 9.99 (*1-931514-93-3*, TPDV-1322);Vol. 2. 192p. (YA). pap. 9.99 (*1-931514-96-8*);Vol. 3. (YA). pap. 9.99 (*1-931514-49-6*) TOKYOPOP, Inc.
Gansky, Alton. Out of Time. 2003. 352p. pap. 12.99 (*0-310-24959-7*) Zondervan.
Garfield, Henry. Room 13. 2001. 320p. (YA). (gr. 7 up). pap. 5.99 (*0-689-84153-1*, Simon Pulse) Simon & Schuster Children's Publishing.
—Room 13. 1997. 320p. 23.95 o.p. (*0-312-15203-5*, Saint Martin's Minotaur) St. Martin's Pr.
Garner, Laura. Ain't Nobody's Bizness. 270p. 2003. pap. 13.95 (*1-4104-0102-2*, Five Star Trade); 2002. 25.95 (*0-7862-4109-8*, Five Star) Gale Group.
Garner, Lydi Tracee. Come What May. 2002. 28p. mass mkt. 5.99 (*1-58314-392-0*) Kensington Publishing Corp.
Garton, Ray. Seductions. 1984. 288p. pap. 3.50 o.p. (*0-523-42309-8*, Pinnacle Bks.) Kensington Publishing Corp.
Garton, Ray & Licina, Scott V. Seductions. 1999. (Illus.). 280p. reprint ed. 50.00 (*1-892284-17-0*); 195.00 o.p. (*1-892284-18-9*) Subterranean Pr.
Gilpin, T. G. Missing Daisy. 1995. 204p. 19.95 o.p. (*0-312-13564-5*, Saint Martin's Minotaur) St. Martin's Pr.
Gilroy, Jack. The Wisdom Box. 2002. 277p. pap. 14.00 (*1-58684-234-X*) Global Academic Publishing.
Hamilton, Jane. The Short History of a Prince: A Novel. l.t. ed. 1998. 496p. 23.00 o.p. (*0-7838-8343-9*, Macmillan Reference USA) Gale Group.
—The Short History of a Prince: A Novel. 1999. 368p. pap. 12.95 (*0-385-47948-4*, Knopf Bks. for Young Readers) Random Hse. Children's Bks.
Harington, Donald. Butterfly Weed. 1996. 384p. 24.00 o.s.i (*0-15-100164-2*); pap. 19.00 (*0-15-600219-1*, Harvest Bks.) Harcourt Trade Pubs.
Harrar, George. The Spinning Man. 352p. 2004. pap. 14.00 (*0-425-19374-8*); 2003. 24.95 (*0-399-14983-X*) Putnam Publishing Group, The. (BlueHen Bks.).
Hart, William. Never Fade Away: A Novel. 2002. 202p. pap. 12.95 (*1-56474-386-1*) Fithian Pr.
Hassler, Jon. Dear James. 1996. pap. 12.95 o.s.i (*0-345-41013-0*); 1994. 432p. mass mkt. 6.99 o.s.i (*0-345-37708-7*) Ballantine Bks.
—A Green Journey. 1996. 304p. pap. 12.95 (*0-345-41041-6*); 1993. mass mkt. 5.99 o.p. (*0-345-90023-5*); 1986. 304p. mass mkt. 5.99 o.s.i (*0-345-33372-1*) Ballantine Bks.
—A Green Journey. 1985. 320p. 15.95 o.p. (*0-688-03982-0*, Morrow, William & Co.) Morrow/Avon.
—Staggerford. 1997. pap. 12.00 o.s.i (*0-345-41824-7*); 1986. 304p. mass mkt. 6.99 (*0-345-33375-6*) Ballantine Bks.
—Staggerford. 1977. 8.95 o.p. (*0-689-10793-5*, Atheneum) Simon & Schuster Children's Publishing.
Hayes, Daniel. No Effect. 1994. 180p. 15.95 o.s.i (*0-87923-989-1*) Godine, David R. Pub.
—No Effect. 1995. 9.09 o.p. (*0-606-07954-8*) Turtleback Bks.
Hedden, Worth Tuttle. The Other Room. 2002. 274p. pap. 14.95 (*0-9624878-1-3*, 0-9624878-1-3) Paperback Rack Bks.
Heller, Jane. Name Dropping. 2001. 352p. mass mkt. 6.99 (*0-312-97833-2*, St. Martin's Paperbacks) St. Martin's Pr.
Heller, Zoe. What Was She Thinking? Notes on a Scandal. 2003. 272p. 23.00 o.s.i (*0-8050-7333-7*) Holt, Henry & Co.
Highbridge, Dianne. A Much Younger Man. 1999. 214p. pap. 11.00 (*1-56947-147-9*); 1998. 224p. 20.00 (*1-56947-114-2*) Soho Pr., Inc.
Hobbie, Douglas. Boomfell. 1993. 448p. pap. 10.95 o.p. (*0-8050-2663-0*, Owl Bks.); 1991. 288p. 19.95 o.p. (*0-8050-1534-5*) Holt, Henry & Co.
—Boomfell. 1994. 3.99 o.p. (*0-517-11417-8*) Random Hse. Value Publishing.
Hooper, Chloe. A Child's Book of True Crime. (Illus.). 240p. 2003. pap. 13.00 (*0-7432-2513-9*); 2002. 24.00 (*0-7432-2512-0*) Simon & Schuster. (Scribner).
Hornsby, Wendy. Half a Mind. 304p. 1991. mass mkt. 3.99 o.p. (*0-451-40245-6*, Onyx); 1990. 16.95 o.p. (*0-453-00710-4*) NAL.
—No Harm. 1989. (WWL Mystery Ser.: No. 30). mass mkt. (*0-373-26030-X*, Harlequin Bks.) Harlequin Enterprises, Ltd.
Humphreys, Emyr. The Gift of a Daughter. 2000. 240p. 22.00 (*1-85411-222-8*) Seren Bks. GBR. *Dist:* Dufour Editions, Inc.
Hury, Hadley. The Edge of the Gulf. 2003. 324p. 24.95 (*1-59058-083-4*) Poisoned Pen Pr.
Hyde, Catherine Ryan. Pay It Forward. E-Book 23.00 (*1-930161-23-9*) Adobe Systems, Inc.
—Pay It Forward. l.t. ed. 2000. (Wheeler Hardcover Ser.). 27.95 (*1-56895-960-5*, Wheeler Publishing, Inc.) Gale Group.
—Pay It Forward. 2000. E-Book 23.00 (*0-7432-0596-0*, Simon & Schuster); E-Book 23.00 (*0-7432-0389-5*, Simon & Schuster); (Illus.). 288p. 23.00 o.s.i (*0-684-86271-9*, Simon & Schuster); 320p. mass mkt. 7.99 (*0-7434-1202-8*, Pocket) Simon & Schuster.
—Pay It Forward. 2000. 14.04 (*0-606-21795-9*) Turtleback Bks.
Ireland, Ann. The Instructor: A Novel. 1997. 216p. text 23.00 o.p. (*0-88001-537-3*) HarperCollins Pubs.
James, Simon. Dear Mr. Blueberry. 1996. 12.14 (*0-606-09186-6*) Turtleback Bks.
Joe, Yolanda. My Fine Lady. 2004. 288p. 23.95 (*0-525-94808-2*, Dutton) Dutton/Plume.
John, Sally D. Surrender of the Heart. 1999. 224p. pap. 9.99 (*1-58134-047-8*) Crossway Bks.
—Surrender of the Heart. 2000. 252p. 23.95 (*0-7862-2711-7*, Five Star) Gale Group.
Johnston, Janet. Ellie Brader Hates Mr. G. 1995. 8.60 o.p. (*0-606-07478-3*) Turtleback Bks.
Kane, Andrea. No Way Out. l.t. ed. 2002. (Wheeler Large Print Book Ser.). pap. 23.95 (*1-58724-205-2*, Wheeler Publishing, Inc.) Gale Group.
—No Way Out. 2003. 464p. mass mkt. 5.99 o.s.i (*0-7434-6731-0*); 2001. 464p. pap. 6.99 (*0-7434-1275-3*); 2001. E-Book 6.99 (*0-7434-1880-8*) Simon & Schuster. (Pocket).
Kennedy, Ellen Edwards. Irregardless of Murder: A Miss Prentice Cozy Mystery. 2001. (Miss Prentice Cozy Mystery). 288p. pap. 14.00 (*0-9661879-7-0*) St Kitts Pr.
Kittle, Katrina. Traveling Light. l.t. ed. 2000. (G. K. Hall Core Ser.). 407p. 27.95 (*0-7838-9173-3*) Thorndike Pr.
—Traveling Light. 2000. 320p. 18.95 (*0-446-52480-8*); 2001. 336p. reprint ed. pap. 13.95 (*0-446-67694-2*) Warner Bks., Inc.
Knight, Michael. Divining Rod: A Novel. 1998. 256p. 23.95 o.p. (*0-525-94379-X*) Dutton/Plume.
Lapierre, Janet. Baby Mine: A Port Silva Mystery. 1999. (Port Silva Mysteries Ser.). (Illus.). 255p. pap. 12.95 (*1-880284-32-4*) Daniel, John & Co., Pubs.
—Children's Games. 1989. 16.95 o.s.i (*0-684-19064-8*, Macmillan Reference USA) Gale Group.
—Children's Games. 1990. mass mkt. (*0-373-26052-0*, Harlequin Bks.) Harlequin Enterprises, Ltd.
—Children's Games. 1990. pap. o.s.i (*1-85381-112-2*) Virago Pr., Ltd. GBR. *Dist:* Little Brown & Co.
—The Cruel Mother. 1991. reprint ed. per. (*0-373-26078-4*, Harlequin Bks.) Harlequin Enterprises, Ltd.
—The Cruel Mother: A Meg Halloran Mystery. 1990. 224p. 18.95 o.s.i (*0-684-19170-9*, Macmillan Reference USA) Gale Group.
—Grandmother's House. 1991. 288p. 19.95 o.s.i (*0-684-19382-5*, Macmillan Reference USA) Gale Group.
—Grandmother's House. 1993. (Mystery Ser.). per. (*0-373-26120-9*, 1-26120-5, Harlequin Bks.) Harlequin Enterprises, Ltd.
—The Unquiet Grave. 1987. 240p. 15.95 o.p. (*0-312-01102-4*, Saint Martin's Minotaur) St. Martin's Pr.
Latour, Jose. Outcast. 1999. 217p. pap. 13.95 o.p. (*1-888451-07-6*, AKB04) Akashic Bks.
—Outcast. 2001. 304p. 24.00 (*0-06-018488-4*, Morrow, William & Co.) Morrow/Avon.
Leavitt, David. Martin Bauman: Or, A Sure Thing. 2000. 352p. tchr. ed. 26.00 (*0-395-90243-6*); 2001. 387p. reprint ed. pap. 14.00 (*0-618-15451-5*) Houghton Mifflin Co. Trade & Reference Div. (Mariner Bks.).
Lewis, Sara. Second Draft of My Life. 2003. 320p. pap. 13.00 (*0-7434-3670-9*, Washington Square Pr.) Simon & Schuster.
—The Second Draft of My Life. 2002. 320p. 24.00 (*0-7434-3669-5*, Atria) Simon & Schuster.
Libera, Antoni. Madame. Kolakowska, Agniewska, tr. from POL. 2000. vi, 439p. 26.00 o.p. (*0-374-20006-8*) Farrar, Straus & Giroux.
Lightman, Alan P. Reunion. 2003. 240p. 22.00 (*0-375-42167-X*, Pantheon) Knopf Publishing Group.
Ludlum, Robert. The Paris Option. l.t. ed. 2003. lib. bdg. 29.95 (*1-58547-272-7*, Platinum) Ctr. Point Large Print.
Macgoye, Marjorie. Coming to Birth. 2000. (Women Writing Africa Ser.). 192p. 30.00 (*1-55861-253-X*) Feminist Pr. at The City Univ. of New York.
Macgoye, Marjorie Oludhe. Coming to Birth. 2000. (Women Writing Africa Ser.). 192p. pap. 11.95 (*1-55861-249-1*) Feminist Pr. at The City Univ. of New York.
Mandel, Sally. Out of the Blue. 2002. 304p. mass mkt. 6.99 (*0-345-42891-9*, Ballantine Bks.) Ballantine Bks.
—Out of the Blue. l.t. ed. 2000. (Americana Ser.). 420p. 26.95 o.p. (*0-7862-2551-3*) Thorndike Pr.
Markoe, Merrill. It's My F—ing Birthday: A Novel. 2002. 224p. pap. 11.95 (*0-8129-6724-0*); 21.95 (*0-375-50712-4*) Random House Adult Trade Publishing Group. (Villard Bks.).
Marquis, Christopher. A Hole in the Heart: A Novel. 2003. 320p. 24.95 (*0-312-30630-X*) St. Martin's Pr.
Marshall, Catherine. Christy. abr. ed. 1995. pap. 19.95 o.p. incl. audio (*1-55927-324-0*) Audio Renaissance.
—Christy. 1994. reprint ed. lib. bdg. 35.95 (*1-56849-309-6*) Buccaneer Bks., Inc.
—Christy. 1967. text 14.95 o.p. (*0-07-040605-7*) McGraw-Hill Cos., The.
—Christy. 1976. 512p. mass mkt. 6.99 (*0-380-00141-1*, Avon Bks.) Morrow/Avon.
—Christy. 1968. 348p. mass mkt. 4.50 o.p. (*0-8007-8008-6*); 1995. (Illus.). 160p. (J). (gr. 6-9). 10.99 o.p. (*0-8007-1708-2*) Revell, Fleming H. Co.
—Christy. 1968. 13.04 (*0-606-00470-X*) Turtleback Bks.
—Christy. 2001. 512p. pap. 12.99 (*0-310-24163-4*) Zondervan.
—Christy: The Collectors Edition. 2001. (Illus.). 480p. (gr. 13 up). 24.99 (*0-8007-9290-4*) Chosen Bks.
—Christy: The Collectors Edition. l.t. ed. 1987. 721p. 20.95 o.p. (*0-8161-4186-X*, Macmillan Reference USA) Gale Group.
—Christy: The Young Readers Edition. 2001. (Illus.). 160p. (J). (gr. 6-9). 9.99 (*0-8007-9293-9*) Chosen Bks.
—Christy Books. 1995. pap. 19.99 (*0-8499-3947-X*) W Publishing Group.
—Christy's Choice. 1996. (Christy Fiction Ser.: No. 6). 128p. (Orig.). (J). (gr. 4-8). mass mkt. 4.99 (*0-8499-3919-4*) Nelson, Tommy.
—The Macmillan International Film Encyclopedia. 4th ed. 2001. 1520p. reprint ed. pap. 12.99 (*0-333-90690-X*, HarperResource) HarperInformation.
McCarthy, Mary. The Groves of Academe. 1974. pap. 3.95 o.p. (*0-452-25084-6*, 25084, Plume) Dutton/Plume.
—The Groves of Academe. 1992. 312p. pap. 14.00 o.s.i (*0-15-637211-8*, Harvest Bks.); 1952. 320p. 9.50 o.s.i (*0-15-137331-0*) Harcourt Trade Pubs.
—The Groves of Academe. 1981. 240p. pap. 2.95 o.p. (*0-380-52522-4*, 52522-0, Avon Bks.) Morrow/Avon.
—The Groves of Academe. 2000. 330p. text 27.95 (*1-56000-455-X*) Transaction Pubs.
Meganck, Glenn. Big Deal at the Center of the Earth. 1999. (Illus.). 67p. (J). 11.99 (*1-892339-02-1*) Beachfront Publishing.
Menaker, Daniel. The Treatment. 1999. 288p. pap. 18.95 (*0-671-03263-1*, Pocket) Simon & Schuster.
Meuser, Mark. Class Encounters. 2000. 185p. 17.95 (*1-58141-015-8*) Rivercross Publishing, Inc.
Meyers, Harold B. Reservations. 1999. 287p. 24.95 (*0-87081-524-5*) Univ. Pr. of Colorado.
Middleton, Stanley. Toward the Sea. 1995. 217p. o.p. (*0-09-179158-8*) Random Hse. of Canada, Ltd. CAN. *Dist:* Random Hse., Inc.
—Toward the Sea. l.t. ed. 1997. (General Ser.). 352p. pap. 22.95 (*0-7862-1128-8*) Thorndike Pr.
Miller, Dan, et al, eds. Critical Paths: Blake & the Argument of Method. 1987. (Illus.). xii, 382p. (C). pap. text 27.95 (*0-8223-0792-8*) Duke Univ. Pr.
Narayan, R. K. The English Teacher. 1980. 184p. pap. 15.00 (*0-226-56835-0*); lib. bdg. 9.95 o.p. (*0-226-56834-2*) Univ. of Chicago Pr.
Neel, Janet. O Gentle Death. 2001. 240p. 22.95 (*0-312-28052-1*, Saint Martin's Minotaur) St. Martin's Pr.
Newton, Charles & Kauffman, Gretchen. A Disgrace to the Profession: A Novel. 2003. 360p. pap. 13.95 (*0-9721900-0-7*, DTTP) Myers Hse. LLC.
O'Neill, Anthony. The Lamplighter: A Novel. 2004. 432p. mass mkt. 7.99 (*0-7434-6427-3*, Pocket Star); 2003. 320p. 25.00 (*0-7432-4349-8*, Scribner) Simon & Schuster.
Paling, Chris. Morning All Day. 1997. 193p. (*0-224-04446-X*) Cape, Jonathan Ltd. GBR. *Dist:* National Geographic Society, Trafalgar Square.
Palmer, Stuart. A Murder on the Blackboard. 1988. (Mystery Ser.). 224p. mass mkt. 3.50 o.s.i (*0-553-26796-5*) Bantam Bks.
—Murder on the Blackboard. 1992. 186p. reprint ed. pap. 5.95 (*1-55882-124-4*, Library of Crime Classics) International Polygonics, Ltd.
—Murder on Wheels. 1992. 307p. pap. 6.95 o.p. (*1-55882-113-9*) International Polygonics, Ltd.
—The Penguin Pool Murder. 1987. 224p. mass mkt. 2.95 o.s.i (*0-553-26334-X*) Bantam Bks.
—The Penguin Pool Murder. 1990. 182p. reprint ed. pap. 7.95 (*1-55882-076-0*) International Polygonics, Ltd.
Palmer, Stuart & Rice, Craig. People vs. Withers & Malone. 1990. 254p. reprint ed. pap. 7.95 o.p. (*1-55882-077-9*) International Polygonics, Ltd.
Piazza, Tom. My Cold War. 2003. 272p. 24.95 (*0-06-053340-4*, ReganBooks) HarperTrade.
Picoult, Jodi. Salem Falls. 2001. 448p. 24.95 (*0-7434-1870-0*, Atria); 2001. 704p. 24.95 (*0-7434-2159-0*, Atria); 2002. 464p. reprint ed. pap. 14.00 (*0-7434-1871-9*, Washington Square Pr.); 2001. reprint ed. E-Book 24.95 (*0-7434-2279-1*, Atria) Simon & Schuster.
Plain, Belva. Fortune's Hand. unabr. ed. 2000. audio 69.95 (*0-7540-0415-5*, CAB 1838);Set. 8p. audio compact disk 99.95 (*0-7540-5324-5*, CCD 015) Chivers Audio Bks. GBR. *Dist:* BBC Audiobooks America.
—Fortune's Hand. 2000. 432p. mass mkt. 7.99 (*0-440-22641-4*); 1999. mass mkt. 7.99 (*0-440-29575-0*) Dell Publishing.
—Fortune's Hand, Set. abr. ed. 1999. audio 25.00 Highsmith Inc.
—Fortune's Hand. abr. ed. 1999. audio Random Hse. Audio Publishing Group.
—Fortune's Hand. l.t. ed. 2000. (Thorndike/G. K. Hall Paperback Bestsellers Ser.). 519p. pap. 30.95 (*0-7862-2013-9*) Thorndike Pr.
Powys, John Cowper. Wolf Solent. 614p. text 35.95 (*0-912568-09-7*) Colgate Univ. Pr.
—Wolf Solent. 1984. 640p. reprint ed. pap. 9.95 o.p. (*0-06-091163-8*, CN 1163, Perennial) HarperTrade.
—Wolf Solent. 1998. 636p. pap. 17.00 (*0-375-70307-1*, Vintage) Knopf Publishing Group.
—Wolf Solent, 2 vols., Set. 1971. reprint ed. 79.00 (*0-403-01159-0*) Scholarly Pr., Inc.
Price, Richard. Samaritan. 2003. 400p. 25.00 (*0-375-41115-1*) Knopf, Alfred A. Inc.
—Samaritan. l.t. ed. 2003. 30.95 (*0-7862-5428-9*) Thorndike Pr.
Pyper, Andrew. Lost Girls. 2001. 464p. reprint ed. mass mkt. 6.50 (*0-440-23546-4*) Dell Publishing.
Raney, Deborah. Kindred Bond. 1998. (Portraits Ser.). 288p. pap. 8.99 o.p. (*1-55661-999-5*) Bethany Hse. Pubs.
—Kindred Bond. l.t. ed. 2000. (Christian Fiction Ser.). 351p. 22.95 (*0-7862-2257-3*, Five Star) Gale Group.
Ransom, Candice F. The Spitball Class. MacDonald, Patricia, ed. 1994. 144p. (Orig.). pap. 2.99 (*0-671-72910-1*, Aladdin) Simon & Schuster Children's Publishing.
Reece, Colleen L. In Search of Twilight. l.t. ed. 1999. (Candlelights Ser.). 239p. 20.95 (*0-7862-1872-X*) Thorndike Pr.
Reed, Kelvin L. Rookie Year: Journey of a First-Year Teacher. 1999. 336p. 21.95 (*0-9667631-2-2*) Peralta Publishing Co.
Reuss, Frederick. The Wasties: A Novel. 2003. 240p. pap. 13.00 (*0-375-72504-0*, Vintage) Knopf Publishing Group.
—The Wasties: A Novel. 2002. 240p. 23.00 (*0-375-42071-1*) Knopf, Alfred A. Inc.
Roberts, Gillian. Adam & Evil. 2000. (Amanda Pepper Mysteries Ser.). 240p. mass mkt. 6.50 (*0-345-42935-4*, Ballantine Bks.) Ballantine Bks.
—Adam & Evil. l.t. ed. 2000. (Beeler Large Print Mystery Ser.). 260p. 26.95 (*1-57490-292-X*, Beeler Large Print Bks.) Beeler, Thomas T. Publisher.
—Adam & Evil. unabr. ed. 2000. (Amanda Pepper Mysteries Ser.: No. 9). audio 54.00 (*0-7887-4311-2*, 96107E7) Recorded Bks., LLC.
—The Bluest Blood: An Amanda Pepper Mystery. (Amanda Pepper Mysteries Ser.). 1999. 304p. mass mkt. 6.50 (*0-345-42315-1*); Vol. 8. 1998. 240p. 22.00 o.s.i (*0-345-40326-6*, Ballantine Bks.) Ballantine Bks.
—The Bluest Blood: An Amanda Pepper Mystery. l.t. ed. 2000. (Beeler Large Print Mystery Ser.). (Illus.). 261p. 25.95 (*1-57490-321-7*, Beeler Large Print Bks.) Beeler, Thomas T. Publisher.
—Caught Dead in Philadelphia. 1988. 208p. mass mkt. 6.50 (*0-345-35340-4*) Ballantine Bks.
—Caught Dead in Philadelphia. unabr. ed. 1993. (Amanda Pepper Mysteries Ser.: Vol. 1). audio 44.00 (*1-55690-900-4*, 93342E7) Recorded Bks., LLC.

—Caught Dead in Philadelphia: A Mystery Introducing Amanda Pepper. 1987. 224p. 16.95 o.s.i (*0-684-18809-0*, Macmillan Reference USA) Gale Group.
—How I Spent My Summer Vacation. 1995. 256p. mass mkt. 5.99 (*0-345-38594-2*); pap. 19.00 o.s.i (*0-345-46533-4*) Ballantine Bks.
—I'd Rather Be in Philadelphia. 1993. 240p. mass mkt. 5.99 (*0-345-37782-6*) Ballantine Bks.
—In the Dead of Summer. 288p. 1996. mass mkt. 5.99 (*0-345-40650-8*); 1995. pap. 19.00 o.s.i (*0-345-46534-2*, Ballantine Bks.) Ballantine Bks.
—The Mummer's Curse. unabr. ed. 1996. (Amanda Pepper Mysteries Ser.: Vol. 7). audio 51.00 (*0-7887-0667-5*, 94844E7) Recorded Bks., LLC.
—The Mummers' Curse, Vol. 7. 1997. (Amanda Pepper Mysteries Ser.). 288p. mass mkt. 5.99 (*0-345-40324-X*, Ballantine Bks.) Ballantine Bks.
—Philly Stakes. 1990. 208p. mass mkt. 5.99 (*0-345-36266-7*) Ballantine Bks.
—Philly Stakes. unabr. ed. 1994. (Amanda Pepper Mysteries Ser.: Vol. 2). audio 51.00 (*1-55690-994-2*, 94133E7) Recorded Bks., LLC.
—Philly Stakes. 1989. 240p. 17.95 o.s.i (*0-684-19071-0*, Scribner) Simon & Schuster.
—With Friends Like These... 1995. 272p. pap. 19.00 o.s.i (*0-345-46535-0*) Ballantine Bks.
Roberts, Gillian & Foster, Alan Dean. With Friends Like These... 1994. 272p. mass mkt. 5.99 (*0-345-37784-2*); 1993. 256p. 18.00 o.s.i (*0-345-37783-4*) Ballantine Bks.
Roberts, Russell. The Invisible Heart: An Economic Romance. 2001. 288p. 30.00 (*0-262-18210-6*) MIT Pr.
—The Invisible Heart: An Economic Romance. 2000. E-Book 22.95 (*0-585-38169-0*) netLibrary, Inc.
Robinson, D. H. 1999: Apocalypse Maybe. 1997. 256p. pap. 12.95 (*0-9658820-0-4*) Kalos Pr.
Rogers, Jane. Promised Lands. 1998. 376p. pap. 14.95 (*0-87951-866-9*); 1997. 388p. 24.95 (*0-87951-753-0*) Overlook Pr., The.
Roiphe, Anne R. If You Knew Me. 1993. 212p. 19.95 o.p. (*0-316-75430-7*) Little Brown & Co.
—If You Knew Me. 1995. 224p. pap. 15.99 (*0-446-67071-5*) Warner Bks., Inc.
Rosen, Gerald. Mahatma Gandhi in a Cadillac. 1995. 275p. (Orig.). 21.95 (*1-883319-35-8*) Frog, Ltd.
—Mahatma Gandhi in a Cadillac. 1995. 275p. (Orig.). pap. 12.95 (*1-883319-36-6*) North Atlantic Bks.
Rosen, Marion. Death by Education. 1993. 224p. 17.95 o.p. (*0-312-09268-7*, Saint Martin's Minotaur) St. Martin's Pr.
Sachs, Marilyn. A Summer's Lease. 1981. mass mkt. 1.75 o.s.i (*0-440-97787-8*) Dell Publishing.
Salzman, Mark. The Soloist. 1995. 304p. pap. 13.00 (*0-679-75926-3*, Vintage) Knopf Publishing Group.
—The Soloist. l.t. ed. 2000. 300p. 34.95 (*1-56000-446-0*) Transaction Pubs.
Sanders, Glenda. Home Again. 2001. (Five Star Romance Ser.). 163p. 26.95 (*0-7862-3128-9*, Five Star) Gale Group.
Sheridan, Mike. The Violent Child. 2001. 232p. 26.00 (*1-57962-035-3*) Permanent Pr., The.
Simanga, Michael. In the Shadow of the Son. 1999. 261p. 24.95 (*0-88378-206-5*); 1998. 24.95 o.p. (*0-88378-207-3*) Third World Press.
Singer, Shelley. Following Jane. 1993. (Barrett Lake Mystery Ser.). 256p. (Orig.). mass mkt. 4.50 o.s.i (*0-451-17523-9*, Signet Bks.) NAL.
—Interview with Mattie: A Barrett Lake Mystery. 1995. (Barrett Lake Mystery Ser.). 288p. mass mkt. 4.99 o.s.i (*0-451-18492-0*, Signet Bks.) NAL.
—Picture of David. 1993. (Barrett Lake Mystery Ser.: No. 2). 256p. (Orig.). mass mkt. 4.50 o.p. (*0-451-17699-5*, Signet Bks.) NAL.
Southgate, Martha. The Fall of Rome. 224p. 2003. mass mkt. 6.99 (*0-7434-8256-5*); 2002. 23.00 (*0-684-86500-9*); 2003. reprint ed. pap. 12.00 (*0-7432-2721-2*) Simon & Schuster. (Scribner).
Spark, Muriel. The Prime of Miss Jean Brodie. unabr. ed. 1991. audio 19.95 o.p. (*0-945353-61-8*, M30361, Audio Editions Bks. on Cassette) Audio Partners Publishing Corp.
—The Prime of Miss Jean Brodie. 1998. 31.95 (*1-56849-698-2*) Buccaneer Bks., Inc.
—The Prime of Miss Jean Brodie. 1984. 192p. pap. 6.95 o.p. (*0-452-26179-1*); pap. 9.00 o.p. (*0-452-26451-0*) Dutton/Plume. (Plume).
—The Prime of Miss Jean Brodie. l.t. ed. 2002. 219p. 28.95 (*0-7862-4349-X*) Gale Group.
—The Prime of Miss Jean Brodie. 2000. (*0-06-099587-4*) HarperCollins Pubs.
—The Prime of Miss Jean Brodie. (Perennial Classics Ser.). 1999. 160p. pap. 13.00 (*0-06-093173-6*); 1994. 192p. pap. 13.00 o.p. (*0-06-092398-9*) HarperTrade. (Perennial).
—The Prime of Miss Jean Brodie. 1994. 192p. lib. bdg. 29.00 o.p. (*0-8095-9144-8*) Millefleurs.
—The Prime of Miss Jean Brodie. 1984. pap. 6.95 o.p. (*0-452-25589-9*) NAL.
—The Prime of Miss Jean Brodie. l.t. ed. 1985. 164p. 14.95 o.p. (*1-85089-051-X*) Transaction Pubs.
Sparks, Nicholas. A Bend in the Road. 2001. 352p. 23.95 o.p. (*0-446-52778-5*) Warner Bks., Inc.
Spencer, LaVyrle. Years. 496p. 2003. pap. 10.00 (*0-425-19578-3*); 1986. mass mkt. 7.99 (*0-515-08489-1*, Jove) Berkley Publishing Group.
—Years. l.t. ed. 1994. (General Ser.). 18.95 (*0-8161-5763-4*); 669p. lib. bdg. 21.95 o.p. (*0-8161-5762-6*) Gale Group. (Macmillan Reference USA).
Starer, Robert. The Music Teacher. 1997. 208p. 23.95 (*0-87951-756-5*) Overlook Pr., The.
Stoks, Peggy. Romy's Walk. 2003. (Abounding Love Ser.: Bk. 2). 26.95 (*0-7862-4591-3*) Thorndike Pr.
—Romy's Walk. 2001. (Abounding Love Ser.: Vol. 2). (Illus.). 288p. pap. 9.99 (*0-8423-1943-3*) Tyndale Hse. Pubs.
Talton, Jon. Camelback Falls: A David Mapstone Mystery. 2003. 224p. 22.95 (*0-312-30404-8*, Saint Martin's Minotaur) St. Martin's Pr.
—Concrete Desert: David Mapstone Mystery. 2001. 212p. 22.95 (*0-312-26953-6*, Saint Martin's Minotaur) St. Martin's Pr.
Terry, Marshall. Angels Prostate Fall. 2001. 176p. 19.95 (*0-87074-463-1*) Southern Methodist Univ. Pr.
Thomson, Colin A. Klanty's Daughters. 1993. 181p. pap. 14.95 (*1-55059-065-0*) Temeron Bks., Inc.
Trow, M. J. Maxwell's House. 1995. 222p. 20.95 o.p. (*0-312-13123-2*, Saint Martin's Minotaur) St. Martin's Pr.
Upadhyay, Samrat. The Guru of Love: A Novel. 2004. 304p. pap. 13.00 (*0-618-38268-2*, Mariner Bks.) Houghton Mifflin Co. Trade & Reference Div.
Vogrin, Valerie. Shebang. 2004. (*1-57806-564-X*); (*1-57806-614-X*) Univ. Pr. of Mississippi.
Ward, Nick. No Te Comas a la Maestra. Fabiancic, Miriam, tr. 2001. (SPA., Illus.). (J). (gr. k-1). pap. 3.95 (*0-439-26363-8*, SO30706) Scholastic, Inc.
Wardell, Delores. Naomi's Place. 2000. 304p. pap. 14.95 (*0-929765-89-3*) Seven Locks Pr.
Waugh, Evelyn. Decline & Fall. 1993. (Everyman's Library). 224p. 17.00 (*0-679-42041-X*) Knopf, Alfred A. Inc.
—Decline & Fall. 1977. 15.95 (*0-316-92619-1*) Little Brown & Co.
Weeks-Pearson, Tony. Dodo. 1986. 14.95 o.p. (*0-948681-00-4*) Viking Penguin.
Wesselmann, Debbie Lee. Trutor & the Balloonist. 1997. 259p. 22.95 (*1-878448-74-9*) MacMurray & Beck, Inc.
Wheeler, Joe L., ed. Focus on the Family Presents Heart to Heart Stories for Teachers. 2003. (Illus.). 304p. 12.99 (*0-8423-5412-3*) Tyndale Hse. Pubs.
Wick, Lori. Donovan's Daughter. (Californians Ser.: Vol. 4). 2000. 312p. pap. 9.99 (*0-7369-0257-0*); 1994. pap. 9.99 o.p. (*1-56507-129-8*) Harvest Hse. Pubs.
—Donovan's Daughter. l.t. ed. 1999. (Christian Fiction Ser.). 411p. 25.95 (*0-7862-2147-X*) Thorndike Pr.
Williams, Nigel. Hatchett & Lycett: A Comedy of Love, Betrayal, & Murder. 2002. 288p. pap. (*0-670-91255-7*, Viking) Viking Penguin.
Witthuhn, Bill. Shotnick. Witthuhn, Margaret, ed. 2001. 238p. pap. 14.95 (*0-9707941-0-X*) White Hen & Co.
Wood, Jane Roberts. Dance a Little Longer, Vol. 3. unabr. ed. 1995. audio 51.00 (*0-7887-0396-X*, 94588E7) Recorded Bks., LLC.
—Dance a Little Longer. 3rd ed. 2000. (Lucinda Richards Trilogy Ser.: Vol. 3). iv, 211p. reprint ed. pap. 15.95 (*1-57441-080-6*) Univ. of North Texas Pr.
—A Place Called Sweet Shrub. 1991. 320p. pap. 10.00 o.s.i (*0-440-50305-1*, Dell Bks.) Dell Publishing.
—A Place Called Sweet Shrub, Set. unabr. ed. 1996. audio 67.00 Recorded Bks., LLC.
—A Place Called Sweet Shrub. 3rd ed. 2000. (Lucinda Richards Trilogy Ser.: Vol. 2). 286p. reprint ed. pap. 15.95 (*1-57441-079-2*) Univ. of North Texas Pr.
—The Train to Estelline. 1988. 240p. pap. 11.95 o.s.i (*0-385-31289-X*, Delta); reprint ed. pap. 10.00 o.s.i (*0-440-50033-8*, Laurel) Dell Publishing.
—The Train to Estelline. unabr. ed. 1995. audio 44.00 (*0-7887-0164-9*, 94389E7) Recorded Bks., LLC.
—The Train to Estelline. 1987. 240p. 19.95 (*0-936650-05-2*) Temple, Ellen C. Publishing, Inc.
—The Train to Estelline. 3rd ed. 2000. (Lucinda Richards Trilogy Ser.: Vol. 1). 209p. reprint ed. pap. 15.95 (*1-57441-078-4*) Univ. of North Texas Pr.
—The Train to Estelline. 1987. E-Book 19.95 (*0-585-16344-8*) netLibrary, Inc.
Wright, Richard B. Clara Callan: A Novel. 2002. 432p. 25.95 (*0-06-050606-7*) HarperCollins Pubs.
—Clara Callan: A Novel. 2003. 432p. pap. 13.95 (*0-06-050607-5*, Perennial) HarperTrade.
Yager, Fred & Yager, Jan. Untimely Death: A Novel. 1998. 308p. 24.95 (*1-889262-01-3*) Hannacroix Creek Bks., Inc.
York, Lynn. The Piano Teacher: A Novel of Swan's Knob. 2004. 304p. pap. 13.00 (*0-452-28477-5*, Plume) Dutton/Plume.

**TEXAS RANGERS—FICTION**

Bean, Frederic. The Hangman's Tree. 2000. 288p. mass mkt. 5.99 o.s.i (*0-553-58020-5*) Bantam Bks.
Brown, Will C. Think Fast Ranger. 1999. 191p. pap. 19.00 (*0-7540-8061-7*) BBC Audiobooks America.
—Think Fast, Ranger! l.t. ed. 1998. (Nightingale Ser.). 274p. pap. 20.95 (*0-7838-8378-1*) Thorndike Pr.
Cole, Jackson. The Death Riders. 1999. 167 p. (*0-7540-3651-0*); pap. (*0-7540-3652-9*) BBC Audiobooks America.
—The Death Riders. l.t. ed. 1999. (Nightingale Ser.). 176p. pap. 20.95 (*0-7838-0445-8*) Thorndike Pr.
—Fast Draw. l.t. ed. 2002. 180p. pap. 22.95 (*0-7862-3941-7*) Gale Group.
—Guns of Mist River: A Texas Ranger Novel. l.t. ed. 1999. (G. K. Hall Nightingale Ser.). 146p. pap. 19.95 (*0-7838-8648-9*, Macmillan Reference USA) Gale Group.
—Hell in Paradise. l.t. ed. 2001. 195p. pap. 22.95 (*0-7838-9566-6*) Thorndike Pr.
—Thunder Range: A Jim Hatfield Texas Ranger Western. l.t. ed. 1998. (Nightingale Ser.). 168p. pap. 20.95 (*0-7838-0244-7*) Thorndike Pr.
—Two-Gun Devil. l.t. ed. 2000. (G. K. Hall Nightingale Ser.). 208p. pap. 20.95 (*0-7838-8847-3*); (*0-7540-4015-1*) Gale Group. (Macmillan Reference USA).
Cook, Christopher. Robbers. 2000. 372p. 24.95 (*0-7867-0776-3*, Carroll & Graf Pubs.) Avalon Publishing Group.
—Robbers. 2002. 368p. pap. 14.00 (*0-425-18346-7*) Berkley Publishing Group.
Cord, Barry. Six Bullets Left. l.t. ed. 2001. 121p. pap. 23.95 (*0-7838-9507-0*, Macmillan Reference USA) Gale Group.
Cunningham, Eugene. Ranger Way. l.t. ed. 1998. (Large Print Western Ser.). 227 p. (*0-7540-3433-X*) BBC Audiobooks America.
—Ranger Way. l.t. ed. 1998. (Nightingale Ser.). 232p. pap. 20.95 (*0-7838-0243-9*) Thorndike Pr.
Foster, Bennett. The Mexican Saddle: A Western Story. 1999. (Western Ser.). 200p. 19.95 (*0-7862-1328-0*, Five Star); 245p. 20.00 (*0-7838-8397-8*, Macmillan Reference USA) Gale Group.
Grey, Zane. Rangers of the Lone Star. 1999. 320p. mass mkt. 4.99 (*0-8439-4556-7*, Leisure Bks.) Dorchester Publishing Co., Inc.
—Rangers of the Lone Star. 1999. E-Book 9.95 (*0-585-30678-8*) netLibrary, Inc.
—Shadow on the Trail. l.t. ed. 1987. 395p. 17.95 o.p. (*0-8161-4124-X*, Macmillan Reference USA) Gale Group.
—Shadow on the Trail. 1992. 352p. mass mkt. 3.99 o.p. (*0-06-100443-X*, HarperTorch) Morrow/Avon.
—Shadow on the Trail. 1982. mass mkt. 2.50 (*0-671-45644-X*, Pocket) Simon & Schuster.
—Shadow on the Trail. l.t. ed. 1994. (Western Ser.). 465p. lib. bdg. 22.95 (*0-7862-0074-X*) Thorndike Pr.
—Shadow on the Trail. l.t. ed. 1975. (Ulverscroft Large Print Ser.). 12.00 o.p. (*0-85456-332-6*, Ulverscroft) Thorpe, F. A. Pubs. GBR. *Dist:* Ulverscroft Large Print Bks., Ltd., Ulverscroft Large Print Canada, Ltd.
Kelton, Elmer. Badger Boy. E-Book 23.95 (*1-58945-577-0*) Adobe Systems, Inc.
—Badger Boy. pap. text 23.95 (*0-312-70067-9*, Tor Bks.); 2002. mass mkt. 5.99 (*0-8125-7750-7*, Forge Bks.); 2001. 272p. 23.95 (*0-312-87319-0*, Forge Bks.) Doherty, Tom Assocs., LLC.
—The Buckskin Line. l.t. ed. 2001. lib. bdg. 26.95 (*1-58547-112-7*) Ctr. Point Large Print.
—The Buckskin Line. 2000. 393p. mass mkt. 5.99 (*0-8125-4020-4*); 2nd ed. 1999. 287p. 22.95 (*0-312-86522-8*) Doherty, Tom Assocs., LLC. (Forge Bks.).
—The Buckskin Line. abr. ed. 1999. 25.00 incl. audio (*0-7871-2005-7*, Dove Audio) NewStar Media, Inc.
—The Buckskin Line. 2000. 12.04 (*0-606-19646-3*) Turtleback Bks.
—Lone Star Rising. 2003. (Texas Rangers Ser.). 704p. 25.95 (*0-7653-0891-6*, Tor Bks.) Doherty, Tom Assocs., LLC.
—The Way of the Coyote. 2001. 288p. 23.95 (*0-312-87318-2*, Forge Bks.) Doherty, Tom Assocs., LLC.
Kimmel, Fred N. Red River Ranger. l.t. ed. 2000. iv, 258p. pap. 19.95 (*0-9661115-4-0*) Zantanon Pr.
Matheson, Richard. The Gun Fight. 1993. (Evans Novel of the West Ser.). 196p. 16.95 o.p. (*0-87131-726-5*) Evans, M. & Co., Inc.
McMurtry, Larry. Comanche Moon. 2000. (Lonesome Dove Ser.: No. 2). 720p. pap. 16.00 (*0-684-85755-3*, Simon & Schuster); 1998. (Lonesome Dove Ser.: No. 2). 816p. pap. 7.99 (*0-671-02064-1*, Pocket); 1998. mass mkt. 6.99 (*0-671-02049-8*, Pocket); 1997. (Lonesome Dove Ser.: No. 2). 752p. 28.50 (*0-684-80754-8*, Simon & Schuster) Simon & Schuster.
—Comanche Moon. l.t. ed. 1999. (Paperback Bestsellers Ser.: No. 2). 921p. pap. 28.95 (*0-7862-1392-2*) Thorndike Pr.
—Comanche Moon. 1998. 14.04 (*0-606-16182-1*) Turtleback Bks.
—Dead Man's Walk. unabr. ed. 1996. audio 80.00 (*0-7366-3211-5*, 3874) Books on Tape, Inc.
—Dead Man's Walk. l.t. ed. (Lonesome Dove Ser.: No. 1). 1999. 800p. 27.95 o.p. (*0-7838-1510-7*); 1996. pap. 25.95 o.p. (*0-7838-1511-5*) Gale Group. (Macmillan Reference USA).
—Dead Man's Walk. (Lonesome Dove Ser.: No. 1). 2000. 464p. pap. 15.00 (*0-684-85754-5*, Simon & Schuster); 1995. 480p. 26.00 (*0-684-80753-X*, Simon & Schuster); 1996. 528p. pap. 7.99 (*0-671-00116-7*, Pocket) Simon & Schuster.
—Dead Man's Walk. unabr. ed. 1995. (Lonesome Dove Ser.: No. 1). audio 45.00 (*0-671-55169-8*, 113285, Simon & Schuster Audioworks) Simon & Schuster Audio.
—Dead Man's Walk. l.t. ed. 1998. (Lonesome Dove Ser.: No. 1). 5.98 o.p. (*0-7651-0771-6*) Smithmark Pubs., Inc.
—Dead Man's Walk. 2000. 21.05 (*0-606-20274-9*) Turtleback Bks.
Mills, Anita. Comanche Rose. 1996. 384p. mass mkt. 5.99 o.s.i (*0-451-40554-4*, Topaz) NAL.
Neggers, Carla. The Cabin. l.t. ed. 2002. 458p. 28.95 (*0-7862-4211-6*) Gale Group.
—The Cabin. 2002. 384p. mass mkt. (*1-55166-845-9*, Mira Bks.) Harlequin Enterprises, Ltd.
Potter, Patricia. Wanted. 1994. 448p. mass mkt. 5.50 o.s.i (*0-553-56600-8*) Bantam Bks.
—Wanted. l.t. ed. 1995. (Large Print Bks.). pap. 21.95 o.p. (*1-56895-125-6*, Wheeler Publishing, Inc.) Gale Group.
Rae Rao, Linda. The Eagle Stirs Her Nest. 1997. (Eagle Wings Ser.). 256p. (gr. 10). pap. 10.99 o.p. (*0-8007-5607-X*) Revell, Fleming H. Co.
Scott, Bradford. Dead Man's Trail: A Walt Slade Texas Ranger Western. l.t. ed. 2000. (G. K. Hall Nightingale Ser.). 151p. pap. 20.95 (*0-7838-8848-1*, Macmillan Reference USA) Gale Group.
—The Pecos Trail. l.t. ed. 2000. 153p. 20.95 (*1-57490-310-1*, Sagebrush Large Print Westerns) Beeler, Thomas T. Publisher.
Scott, Leslie. Tombstone Showdown. l.t. ed. 2001. 180p. pap. 22.95 (*0-7838-9419-8*) Thorndike Pr.
Smith, Bobbi. The Half Breed. 2001. (Secret Fires Ser.: Bk. 2). 400p. mass mkt. 5.99 (*0-8439-4853-1*, Leisure Bks.) Dorchester Publishing Co., Inc.
—The Half-Breed. l.t. ed. 2001. (Thorndike Press Large Print Romance Ser.). 373p. 28.95 o.p. (*0-7862-3584-5*) Thorndike Pr.
Tilman, G. Wayne. Zack Bodeway, Texas Ranger. 2001. 216p. pap. 14.95 (*1-928704-86-7*, Fusion Pr.) Authorlink.
Ward, Jonas. Buchanan Calls the Shots. (Buchanan Ser.). 1981. 144p. mass mkt. 1.95 o.s.i (*0-449-14210-8*, Fawcett); 1978. mass mkt. 1.25 o.s.i (*0-449-13760-0*) Ballantine Bks.
—Buchanan Calls the Shots. l.t. ed. 1990. (Linford Western Large Print Ser.). pap. 17.99 (*0-7089-6943-7*, Linford) Thorpe, F. A. Pubs. GBR. *Dist:* Ulverscroft Large Print Bks., Ltd., Ulverscroft Large Print Canada, Ltd.
—Buchanan Gets Mad. 1981. (Buchanan Ser.). mass mkt. 1.95 o.s.i (*0-449-14209-4*, Fawcett) Ballantine Bks.
—Buchanan Gets Mad. l.t. ed. 1996. (Western Ser.). 199p. 23.95 (*0-7838-1661-8*) Thorndike Pr.
—Buchanan on the Prod. (Buchanan Ser.). 1981. 144p. mass mkt. 1.95 o.s.i (*0-449-14107-1*, Fawcett); 1975. mass mkt. 1.25 o.s.i (*0-449-13472-5*) Ballantine Bks.
—Buchanan on the Prod. l.t. ed. 1985. (Linford Western Library). 304p. pap. 17.99 (*0-7089-6144-4*, Linford) Thorpe, F. A. Pubs. GBR. *Dist:* Ulverscroft Large Print Bks., Ltd., Ulverscroft Large Print Canada, Ltd.
—Buchanan on the Run. (Buchanan Ser.). 1981. mass mkt. 1.75 o.s.i (*0-449-14208-6*, Fawcett); 1975. mass mkt. 1.25 o.s.i (*0-449-13474-1*) Ballantine Bks.
—Buchanan Says No. (Buchanan Ser.). 1981. mass mkt. 1.95 o.s.i (*0-449-14164-0*, Fawcett); 1978. mass mkt. 1.25 o.s.i (*0-449-13862-3*); 1974. mass mkt. 0.95 o.s.i (*0-449-13022-3*) Ballantine Bks.
—Buchanan Says No. l.t. ed. 1985. (Linford Western Library). 256p. pap. 17.99 (*0-7089-6140-1*, Linford) Thorpe, F. A. Pubs. GBR. *Dist:* Ulverscroft Large Print Bks., Ltd., Ulverscroft Large Print Canada, Ltd.
—Buchanan Takes Over. 1981. mass mkt. 1.95 o.s.i (*0-449-14063-6*, Fawcett) Ballantine Bks.
—Buchanan Takes Over. l.t. ed. 1989. (Linford Western Large Print Ser.). pap. 17.99 (*0-7089-6772-8*, Linford) Thorpe, F. A. Pubs. GBR. *Dist:* Ulverscroft Large Print Bks., Ltd., Ulverscroft Large Print Canada, Ltd.
—Buchanan's Big Fight. 1981. mass mkt. 1.95 o.s.i (*0-449-14406-2*, Fawcett) Ballantine Bks.

—Buchanan's Big Fight. l.t. ed. 1990. (Linford Western Large Print Ser.). pap. 17.99 (*0-7089-6868-6*, Linford) Thorpe, F. A. Pubs. GBR. *Dist:* Ulverscroft Large Print Bks., Ltd., Ulverscroft Large Print Canada, Ltd.
—Buchanan's Big Showdown. 1981. (Buchanan Ser.). 176p. mass mkt. 1.95 o.s.i (*0-449-14109-8*, Fawcett) Ballantine Bks.
—Buchanan's Black Sheep. 1984. (Buchanan Ser.). 176p. mass mkt. 2.50 o.s.i (*0-449-12412-6*, Fawcett) Ballantine Bks.
—Buchanan's Black Sheep. l.t. ed. 1990. (Linford Western Large Print Ser.). pap. 17.99 (*0-7089-6938-0*, Linford) Thorpe, F. A. Pubs. GBR. *Dist:* Ulverscroft Large Print Bks., Ltd., Ulverscroft Large Print Canada, Ltd.
—Buchanan's Gamble. (Buchanan Ser.). 1981. mass mkt. 1.95 o.s.i (*0-449-14177-2*, Fawcett); 1975. mass mkt. 1.25 o.s.i (*0-449-13473-3*) Ballantine Bks.
—Buchanan's Gamble. l.t. ed. 1989. (Linford Western Library). 305p. pap. 17.99 (*0-7089-6683-7*, Linford) Thorpe, F. A. Pubs. GBR. *Dist:* Ulverscroft Large Print Bks., Ltd., Ulverscroft Large Print Canada, Ltd.
—Buchanan's Gun. 1982. (Buchanan Ser.). 160p. mass mkt. 1.95 o.s.i (*0-449-14211-6*, Fawcett) Ballantine Bks.
—Buchanan's Gun. l.t. ed. 1976. (Ulverscroft Large Print Ser.). 29.99 o.p. (*0-85456-437-3*, Ulverscroft) Thorpe, F. A. Pubs. GBR. *Dist:* Ulverscroft Large Print Bks., Ltd., Ulverscroft Large Print Canada, Ltd.
—Buchanan's Manhunt. 1981. mass mkt. 1.75 o.s.i (*0-449-14119-5*, Fawcett) Ballantine Bks.
—Buchanan's Manhunt. l.t. ed. 1989. (Linford Western Library). pap. 17.99 (*0-7089-6760-4*, Linford) Thorpe, F. A. Pubs. GBR. *Dist:* Ulverscroft Large Print Bks., Ltd., Ulverscroft Large Print Canada, Ltd.
—Buchanan's Range War. 1980. (Buchanan Ser.). 224p. mass mkt. 1.75 o.s.i (*0-449-14357-0*, Fawcett) Ballantine Bks.
—Buchanan's Range War. l.t. ed. 1987. (Linford Western Library). 240p. pap. 17.99 o.p. (*0-7089-6351-X*, Linford) Thorpe, F. A. Pubs. GBR. *Dist:* Ulverscroft Large Print Bks., Ltd., Ulverscroft Large Print Canada, Ltd.
—Buchanan's Revenge. 1982. (Buchanan Ser.). 144p. mass mkt. 2.25 o.s.i (*0-449-12361-8*, Fawcett) Ballantine Bks.
—Buchanan's Revenge. l.t. ed. 1996. (G. K. Hall Western Ser.). 227p. 21.95 (*0-7838-1877-7*) Thorndike Pr.
—Buchanan's Revenge. l.t. ed. 1985. (Ulverscroft Large Print Ser.). 496p. 29.99 o.p. (*0-7089-1291-5*, Ulverscroft) Thorpe, F. A. Pubs. GBR. *Dist:* Ulverscroft Large Print Bks., Ltd., Ulverscroft Large Print Canada, Ltd.
—Buchanan's Showdown. 1976. mass mkt. 1.25 o.s.i (*0-449-13553-5*) Ballantine Bks.
—Buchanan's Siege. 1982. 160p. mass mkt. 2.25 o.s.i (*0-449-14086-5*, Fawcett) Ballantine Bks.
—Buchanan's Siege. l.t. ed. 1990. (Linford Western Library). pap. 17.99 (*0-7089-6804-X*, Linford) Thorpe, F. A. Pubs. GBR. *Dist:* Ulverscroft Large Print Bks., Ltd., Ulverscroft Large Print Canada, Ltd.
—Buchanan's Stage Line. 1986. (Buchanan Ser.). 176p. mass mkt. 2.50 o.s.i (*0-449-12847-4*, Fawcett) Ballantine Bks.
—Buchanan's Stage Line. l.t. ed. 1987. (Linford Western Library). 272p. pap. 17.99 o.p. (*0-7089-6427-3*, Linford) Thorpe, F. A. Pubs. GBR. *Dist:* Ulverscroft Large Print Bks., Ltd., Ulverscroft Large Print Canada, Ltd.
—Buchanan's Stolen Railway. 1979. (Buchanan Ser.). mass mkt. 1.75 o.s.i (*0-449-13977-8*, Fawcett) Ballantine Bks.
—Buchanan's Texas Treasure. 1982. (Buchanan Ser.). 160p. mass mkt. 2.25 o.s.i (*0-449-14175-6*, Fawcett) Ballantine Bks.
—Buchanan's Texas Treasure. l.t. ed. 1991. (Linford Western Large Print Ser.). pap. 17.99 (*0-7089-6960-7*, Ulverscroft) Thorpe, F. A. Pubs. GBR. *Dist:* Ulverscroft Large Print Bks., Ltd., Ulverscroft Large Print Canada, Ltd.
—Buchanan's War. (Buchanan Ser.). 1981. mass mkt. 1.95 o.s.i (*0-449-14137-3*, Fawcett); 1974. mass mkt. 0.95 o.s.i (*0-449-13025-8*) Ballantine Bks.
—Buchanan's War. l.t. ed. 1997. (G. K. Hall Western Ser.). 233p. lib. bdg. 20.95 (*0-7838-1878-5*) Thorndike Pr.
—Get Buchanan! 1979. (Buchanan Ser.). mass mkt. 1.50 o.s.i (*0-449-14062-8*, Fawcett) Ballantine Bks.
—Get Buchanan! l.t. ed. 1990. (Linford Western Library). pap. 17.99 o.p. (*0-7089-6811-2*, Ulverscroft) Thorpe, F. A. Pubs. GBR. *Dist:* Ulverscroft Large Print Bks., Ltd., Ulverscroft Large Print Canada, Ltd.
—The Name's Buchanan. (Buchanan Ser.). 1980. 128p. mass mkt. 1.75 o.s.i (*0-449-14135-7*, Fawcett); 1977. mass mkt. 1.25 o.s.i (*0-449-13858-5*) Ballantine Bks.
—The Name's Buchanan. l.t. ed. 1995. 204p. 18.95 (*0-7838-1471-2*, Macmillan Reference USA) Gale Group.
—Trap for Buchanan. 1979. (Buchanan Ser.). 144p. mass mkt. 1.50 o.s.i (*0-449-14082-2*, Fawcett) Ballantine Bks.
—Trap for Buchanan. l.t. ed. 1989. (Linford Western Library). 256p. pap. 17.99 (*0-7089-6715-9*, Linford) Thorpe, F. A. Pubs. GBR. *Dist:* Ulverscroft Large Print Bks., Ltd., Ulverscroft Large Print Canada, Ltd.
Wick, Lori. A Texas Sky. l.t. ed. 404p. 2002. (Yellow Rose Trilogy: No. 2). pap. 17.95 (*1-4104-0013-1*, Walker Large Print); 2001. 25.95 (*0-7862-2934-9*) Gale Group.
—A Texas Sky. 2000. (Yellow Rose Trilogy Ser.: Vol. 2). 288p. pap. 10.99 (*0-7369-0187-6*) Harvest Hse. Pubs.

## V

### VETERANS—FICTION

Bragg, Melvyn. The Son of War: A Novel. 2003. 432p. 25.95 (*1-55970-686-4*) Arcade Publishing, Inc.
Buckman, Daniel. The Names of Rivers. 2002. 197p. 21.00 (*1-888451-29-7*) Akashic Bks.
—The Names of Rivers. 2003. 208p. pap. 13.00 (*0-312-31460-4*) Picador.
—The Names of Rivers. Date not set. mass mkt. (*0-312-98981-4*, St. Martin's Paperbacks) St. Martin's Pr.
Burnard, Bonnie. A Good House: A Novel. 2000. 309p. 25.00 o.s.i (*0-8050-6495-8*) Holt, Henry & Co.
—A Good House: A Novel. 2001. 320p. pap. 14.00 (*0-312-42032-3*) Picador.
Caputo, Philip. Delcorso's Gallery. 1983. 374p. o.p. (*0-03-058277-6*) Holt, Henry & Co.
—DelCorso's Gallery. 2001. 368p. pap. 14.00 (*0-375-72509-1*, Vintage) Knopf Publishing Group.
—Delcorso's Gallery. 1991. 368p. reprint ed. pap. 11.00 (*0-06-098606-9*, Perennial) HarperTrade.
Crews, Harry. Celebration: A Novel. 1999. 272p. pap. 13.00 (*0-684-84810-4*, Touchstone); 1998. 256p. 22.50 (*0-684-83758-7*, Simon & Schuster) Simon & Schuster.
Croft, Barbara. Moon's Crossing. 2003. 208p. pap. 12.00 (*0-618-34153-6*, Mariner Bks.) Houghton Mifflin Co. Trade & Reference Div.
—Moon's Crossing. l.t. ed. 2003. 336p. 28.95 (*0-7862-5958-2*) Thorndike Pr.
Dailey, J. R. The Yellow Ribbon Snake. 2000. 144p. pap. 12.00 (*1-880284-37-5*) Daniel, John & Co., Pubs.
Gamble, Terry. The Water Dancers. 2003. 288p. 24.95 (*0-06-054266-7*, Morrow, William & Co.) Morrow/Avon.
Higgins, Jack. Toll for the Brave. 1979. pap. 1.75 o.s.i (*0-449-14105-5*, Fawcett); 1976. mass mkt. 1.50 o.s.i (*0-449-13496-2*) Ballantine Bks.
—Toll for the Brave. 1984. 224p. mass mkt. 4.99 o.p. (*0-451-13271-8*, Signet Bks.) NAL.
—Toll for the Brave. abr. ed. 1995. 16.95 o.p. (*0-7871-0033-1*, 391793) NewStar Media, Inc.
—Toll for the Brave. 1994. mass mkt. o.p. (*0-09-914000-4*) Random Hse. of Canada, Ltd. CAN. *Dist:* Random Hse., Inc.
Houston, James D. The Last Paradise. (Literature of the American West Ser.). 384p. 2000. pap. 17.95 (*0-8061-3290-6*); 1998. 24.95 (*0-8061-3033-4*) Univ. of Oklahoma Pr.
Maki, Alan. Written on Her Heart: A Novel. 2002. (Illus.). 160p. 14.99 (*0-8054-2488-1*) Broadman & Holman Pubs.
McCown, Clint. War Memorials. 2000. 220p. 23.95 (*1-55597-312-4*) Graywolf Pr.
—War Memorials. 2001. 240p. reprint ed. pap. 13.00 (*0-618-12847-6*, Mariner Bks.) Houghton Mifflin Co. Trade & Reference Div.
O'Nan, Stewart. The Names of the Dead. 1997. 416p. pap. 11.95 o.s.i (*0-14-026309-8*) Penguin Group (USA) Inc.
—A Prayer for the Dying: A Novel. l.t. ed. 2000. (Wheeler Large Print Book Ser.). 196p. 26.95 (*1-56895-841-2*, Wheeler Publishing, Inc.) Gale Group.
—A Prayer for the Dying: A Novel. 1999. 195p. 22.00 o.s.i (*0-8050-6147-9*) Holt, Henry & Co.
—A Prayer for the Dying: A Novel. 2000. 208p. pap. 13.00 (*0-312-25501-2*) Picador.
Parker, F. M. Blood & Dust. l.t. ed. 2001. 19.95 o.p. (*1-58724-089-0*, Wheeler Publishing, Inc.) Gale Group.
—Blood & Dust. 2000. 384p. mass mkt. 5.99 o.s.i (*0-7860-1152-1*, Pinnacle Bks.) Kensington Publishing Corp.
Pike, Arthur L. A River to Cross. 2001. 192p. pap. 17.50 o.s.i (*0-9578735-1-4*) International Specialized Bk. Services.
Powell, Mark. Prodigals: A Novel. 2002. 193p. 26.95 (*1-57233-189-5*) Univ. of Tennessee Pr.
Reyoung. Unbabbling. 1997. 256p. pap. 13.95 (*1-56478-164-X*) Dalkey Archive Pr.
Siler, Jenny. Easy Money. l.t. ed. 2001. (Softcover Ser.). 297p. pap. 23.95 (*1-58724-068-8*, Wheeler Publishing, Inc.) Gale Group.
—Easy Money. 1999. 272p. 24.00 o.s.i (*0-8050-6025-1*) Holt, Henry & Co.
—Easy Money. 2000. 352p. mass mkt. 6.99 (*0-312-97686-0*, St. Martin's Paperbacks) St. Martin's Pr.
Sinclair, Bertrand W., tr. Hidden Places. 2003. 251p. 24.95 (*1-57490-496-5*, Sagebrush Large Print Westerns) Beeler, Thomas T. Publisher.
Sutherland, Grant. The Consignment. 2004. 416p. mass mkt. 7.50 (*0-553-58331-X*); 2003. 368p. 23.95 (*0-553-80187-2*) Bantam Bks.
Thompson, Lee B. Addie. 2001. (Five Star First Edition Romance Ser.). 305p. 25.95 (*0-7862-3364-8*, Five Star) Gale Group.
Trumbo, Dalton. Johnny Got His Gun. Date not set. 255p. 22.95 (*0-8488-2411-3*) Amereon, Ltd.
—Johnny Got His Gun. 1984. 256p. mass mkt. 7.50 (*0-553-27432-5*) Bantam Bks.
—Johnny Got His Gun. 2000. (Underground Ser.). 332p. reprint ed. pap. 12.95 (*0-8065-1281-4*, Citadel Pr.) Kensington Publishing Corp.
—Johnny Got His Gun. 1970. 13.04 (*0-606-03683-0*) Turtleback Bks.
Yount, John. Toots in Solitude. 1985. 192p. pap. 5.95 o.p. (*0-312-80905-0*, Saint Martin's Griffin); 1983. 224p. 13.95 o.p. (*0-312-80904-2*) St. Martin's Pr.
—Toots in Solitude: A Novel. 1995. 200p. pap. 10.95 (*0-87074-384-8*) Southern Methodist Univ. Pr.

### VETERINARIANS—FICTION

Adamson, Lydia. Dr. Nightingale Seeks Greener Pastures: A Deirdre Quinn Nightingale Mystery. l.t. ed. 2001. 216p. 27.95 (*0-7862-3471-7*) Thorndike Pr.
Anderson, Laurie Halse. Homeless. 2000. (American Girl Wild at Heart Ser.: Bk. 2). (Illus.). 138p. (YA). 11.00 (*0-606-18359-0*) Turtleback Bks.
Coetzee, J. M. Disgrace. 2000. 224p. pap. 13.00 (*0-14-029640-9*) Penguin Group (USA) Inc.
—Disgrace. 1999. 224p. 23.95 o.s.i (*0-670-88731-5*, Viking) Viking Penguin.
—Disgrace. 2000. 608p. pap. (*0-09-928952-0*) Vintage UK GBR. *Dist:* Random Hse., Inc.
Crum, Laura. Breakaway. 2001. (Gail McCarthy Mysteries Ser.). 224p. 22.95 (*0-312-27181-6*, Saint Martin's Minotaur) St. Martin's Pr.
—Hayburner: A Gail McCarthy Mystery. 2003. 208p. 22.95 (*0-312-29047-0*, Saint Martin's Minotaur) St. Martin's Pr.
Eulo, Ken & Mauck, Joe. Claw. 1994. 22.00 o.s.i (*0-671-79963-0*, Simon & Schuster) Simon & Schuster.
—Claw. 320p. 3.98 o.p. (*0-7651-0133-5*) Smithmark Pubs., Inc.
—Claw. 1995. 319p. pap. text 5.50 (*0-312-95595-2*, St. Martin's Paperbacks) St. Martin's Pr.
Gould, Judith. A Moment in Time. 2001. 336p. 24.95 o.p. (*0-525-94607-1*, Dutton) Dutton/Plume.
—A Moment in Time. l.t. ed. 2002. (Large Print Book Ser.). 28.95 (*1-58724-162-5*, Wheeler Publishing, Inc.) Gale Group.
—A Moment in Time. 2002. 448p. reprint ed. mass mkt. 7.50 (*0-451-20653-3*, Signet Bks.) NAL.
Hendricks, Vicki. Sky Blues. Date not set. pap. (*0-312-30313-0*, Saint Martin's Griffin); E-Book 16.95 (*0-312-70431-3*); 2002. 224p. 22.95 (*0-312-28346-6*, Saint Martin's Minotaur) St. Martin's Pr.
Jensen, Liz. Ark Baby. 288p. 1999. 13.95 (*0-87951-729-8*); 1998. 24.95 (*0-87951-833-2*) Overlook Pr., The.
Keller, Janet. Necessary Risks. 1994. 192p. mass mkt. 5.99 o.s.i (*0-553-56784-5*) Bantam Bks.
Miller, Sue. While I Was Gone. 2002. 352p. mass mkt. 7.99 (*0-345-42074-8*); 2000. 304p. pap. 14.00 (*0-345-44328-4*); 2000. 304p. pap. 12.95 o.s.i (*0-345-43500-1*) Ballantine Bks.
—While I Was Gone. l.t. ed. 1999. 30.00 o.p. (*0-7838-8481-8*, Macmillan Reference USA) Gale Group.
—While I Was Gone. l.t. ed. 1999. 448p. 24.00 o.s.i (*0-375-70571-6*) Knopf, Alfred A. Inc.
—While I Was Gone. abr. ed. 2000. audio 25.95 (*0-375-41664-1*); 2000. audio compact disk 29.95 (*0-375-41665-X*); 1999. audio 24.00 o.s.i (*0-375-40563-1*, 691584) Random Hse. Audio Publishing Group. (RH Audio).
—While I Was Gone. l.t. ed. 2000. 448p. pap. 12.95 o.s.i (*0-375-72801-5*) Random Hse. Large Print.
—While I Was Gone. 2000. (Oprah's Book Club Ser.). 288p. 24.00 (*0-375-41178-X*) Random Hse., Inc.
—While I Was Gone. 2000. 19.00 (*0-606-22790-3*) Turtleback Bks.
North, Hailey. Tangled up in Love. 2002. 384p. mass mkt. 5.99 (*0-380-82069-2*) HarperCollins Pubs.
O'Donohoe, Nick. The Healing of Crossroads. 1996. 336p. mass mkt. 5.99 o.s.i (*0-441-00391-5*) Ace Bks.
—The Magic & the Healing. 1994. 352p. (Orig.). mass mkt. 4.99 o.s.i (*0-441-00053-3*) Ace Bks.
—Under the Healing Sun. 1995. 352p. (Orig.). mass mkt. 4.99 o.s.i (*0-441-00180-7*) Ace Bks.
Plimpton, George. Pet Peeves: Or Whatever Happened to Doctor Rawff? 2000. (Illus.). 80p. 16.95 (*0-87113-820-4*, Atlantic Monthly Pr.) Grove/Atlantic, Inc.
Roberts, Lillian. Almost Human. 1998. mass mkt. 5.99 o.s.i (*0-449-00228-4*, Fawcett) Ballantine Bks.
—The Hand That Feeds You. 1997. mass mkt. 5.50 o.s.i (*0-449-14986-2*, Fawcett) Ballantine Bks.
—Riding for a Fall. 1996. (Veterinarian Mystery Ser.). mass mkt. 5.50 o.s.i (*0-449-14985-4*, Fawcett) Ballantine Bks.
Stuart, Dee. Deadly Legacy. 1996. 352p. mass mkt. 4.99 o.s.i (*0-8217-5316-9*) Kensington Publishing Corp.

## W

### WOMEN ANTHROPOLOGISTS—FICTION

Arnold, Margot, pseud. The Cape Cod Caper. 1982. (Murder Mystery Ser.). 192p. 2.50 (*0-86721-206-3*, Jove) Berkley Publishing Group.
—The Cape Cod Caper. 1988. (Penny Spring & Sir Toby Glendower Mystery Ser.). 192p. pap. 7.95 (*0-88150-116-6*, Foul Play) Norton, W. W. & Co., Inc.
—The Cape Cod Conundrum. (Penny Spring & Sir Toby Glendower Mystery Ser.). 224p. 1992. text 20.00 o.p. (*0-88150-244-8*); 1994. reprint ed. pap. 7.95 (*0-88150-293-6*) Norton, W. W. & Co., Inc. (Foul Play).
—The Catacomb Conspiracy. 1992. (Penny Spring & Sir Toby Glendower Mystery Ser.). 260p. 18.95 o.p. (*0-88150-208-1*) Countryman Pr.
—The Catacomb Conspiracy. 1993. (Penny Spring & Sir Toby Glendower Mystery Ser.). 240p. pap. 7.95 (*0-88150-255-3*, Foul Play) Norton, W. W. & Co., Inc.
—Death of a Voodoo Doll. 1989. 220p. reprint ed. pap. 7.95 (*0-88150-132-8*, Foul Play) Norton, W. W. & Co., Inc.
—Death on the Dragon's Tongue. 1982. 224p. 2.50 (*0-86721-150-4*, Jove) Berkley Publishing Group.
—Death on the Dragon's Tongue. 1990. (Penny Spring & Sir Toby Glendower Mystery Ser.). 224p. reprint ed. pap. 7.95 (*0-88150-158-1*, Foul Play) Norton, W. W. & Co., Inc.
—Dirge for a Dorset Druid. (Penny Spring & Sir Toby Glendower Mystery Ser.). 240p. 1995. pap. 7.95 (*0-88150-334-7*); 1993. 20.00 (*0-88150-266-9*) Norton, W. W. & Co., Inc. (Foul Play).
—Exit Actors, Dying. 1982. 176p. 2.50 (*0-86721-181-4*, Jove) Berkley Publishing Group.
—Exit Actors, Dying. 1988. (Penny Spring & Sir Toby Glendower Mystery Ser.). 176p. reprint ed. pap. 7.95 (*0-88150-115-8*, Foul Play) Norton, W. W. & Co., Inc.
—Lament for a Lady Laird. 1982. 224p. 2.50 (*0-86721-132-6*, Jove) Berkley Publishing Group.
—Lament for a Lady Laird. 1990. (Penny Spring & Sir Toby Glendower Mystery Ser.). 224p. reprint ed. pap. 7.95 (*0-88150-159-X*, Foul Play) Norton, W. W. & Co., Inc.
—The Menehune Murders. 1989. (Penny Spring & Sir Toby Glendower Mystery Ser.). 240p. 17.95 o.p. (*0-88150-149-2*) Countryman Pr.
—The Menehune Murders. 1991. (Penny Spring & Sir Toby Glendower Mystery Ser.). 260p. pap. 7.95 (*0-88150-196-4*, Foul Play) Norton, W. W. & Co., Inc.
—The Midas Murders. 1995. (Penny Spring & Sir Toby Glendower Mystery Ser.). 224p. 20.00 (*0-88150-340-1*, Foul Play) Norton, W. W. & Co., Inc.
—The Midas Murders: A Penny Spring & Sir Toby Glendower Mystery. 1997. (Penny Spring & Sir Toby Glendower Mystery Ser.). 224p. pap. 7.95 (*0-88150-394-0*) Norton, W. W. & Co., Inc.
—Toby's Folly. 1990. 256p. 18.95 o.p. (*0-88150-177-8*) Countryman Pr.
—Toby's Folly. 1992. (Penny Spring & Sir Toby Glendower Mystery Ser.). 256p. pap. 7.95 (*0-88150-228-6*, Foul Play) Norton, W. W. & Co., Inc.
—Zadok's Treasure. 1982. 192p. 2.50 (*0-86721-228-4*, Jove) Berkley Publishing Group.
—Zadok's Treasure. 1989. (Penny Spring & Sir Toby Glendower Mystery Ser.). 192p. reprint ed. pap. 7.95 (*0-88150-133-6*, Foul Play) Norton, W. W. & Co., Inc.

Lively, Penelope. Spiderweb. l.t. ed. 240p. 2000. pap. 21.99 (*0-7531-6057-9*); 1999. 32.50 (*0-7531-5996-1*, 159961) ISIS Large Print Bks. GBR. *Dist:* Ulverscroft Large Print Bks., Ltd., Ulverscroft Large Print Canada, Ltd.

—Spiderweb. unabr. ed. 2000. audio 54.95 (*1-86042-512-7*, 25127) Soundings, Ltd. GBR. *Dist:* Ulverscroft Large Print Bks., Ltd.

—Spiderweb: A Novel. 1999. 224p. o.s.i (*0-06-019233-X*, HarperFlamingo) HarperCollins Pubs. Canada, Ltd.

—Spiderweb: A Novel. 2000. 224p. pap. 13.00 (*0-06-092972-3*, Perennial) HarperTrade.

Reichs, Kathy. Grave Secrets. 2003. mass mkt. (*0-7434-5738-2*, Pocket Star); 2002. 336p. 25.00 o.s.i (*0-7432-4414-1*, Scribner); 2002. (Illus.). 336p. 25.00 (*0-684-85973-4*, Scribner); 2002. 624p. 25.00 (*0-7432-3364-6*, Scribner) Simon & Schuster.

—Grave Secrets. l.t. ed. 2002. (Core Collection). 516p. 32.95 (*0-7862-4664-2*) Thorndike Pr.

**WOMEN ARCHAEOLOGISTS—FICTION**

Bergren, Lisa Tawn. Chosen. 1996. (Palisades Pure Romance Ser.). 294p. pap. 9.99 o.p. (*0-88070-768-2*, Palisades) Multnomah Pubs., Inc.

—The Chosen. 2001. (Full Circle Ser.). 288p. pap. 9.95 (*1-57856-467-0*) WaterBrook Pr.

Bosse, Malcolm. Stranger at the Gate. 1991. 4.99 o.p. (*0-517-07520-2*) Random Hse. Value Publishing.

—Stranger at the Gate. 1989. 19.95 o.p. (*0-671-66785-8*, Simon & Schuster) Simon & Schuster.

Carter, Elizabeth E. Valley of the Kings: A Novel of Tutankhamun. 1977. 7.95 o.p. (*0-525-22777-6*, Dutton) Dutton/Plume.

Castle, Jayne, pseud. After Dark. 2000. 336p. mass mkt. 6.99 (*0-515-12902-X*, Jove) Berkley Publishing Group.

—After Dark. l.t. ed. 2001. (Romance Ser.). 352p. 28.95 (*1-58724-071-8*, Wheeler Publishing, Inc.) Gale Group.

Clapsaddle-Counts, Ruth. Four Corners. 1998. 200p. 19.95 (*1-57197-079-7*) Pentland Pr., Inc.

Cole, Michael. A King's Ransom. 2003. 198p. pap. 14.95 (*1-55517-691-7*, 76917, Bonneville Bks.) Cedar Fort, Inc./CFI Distribution.

Connor, Beverly. Dressed to Die: A Lindsay Chamberlain Novel. 1998. (Lindsay Chamberlain Mysteries Ser.). 320p. 20.95 (*1-888952-89-X*) Cumberland Hse. Publishing.

—Questionable Remains. 1997. (Lindsay Chamberlain Mysteries Ser.). 288p. 20.95 (*1-888952-53-9*) Cumberland Hse. Publishing.

—Questionable Remains. 2001. (WWL Mystery Ser.: No. 385). 248p. mass mkt. (*0-373-26385-6*, 1-26385-4, Worldwide Library) Harlequin Enterprises, Ltd.

—A Rumor of Bones. 1996. (Lindsay Chamberlain Mysteries Ser.: Vol. 1). (Illus.). 254p. 20.95 o.p. (*1-888952-08-3*) Cumberland Hse. Publishing.

—Skeleton Crew. 1999. (Lindsay Chamberlain Mysteries Ser.: Vol. 3). (Illus.). 352p. 20.95 (*1-58182-042-9*, Cumberland Hearthside) Cumberland Hse. Publishing.

Coomer, Joe. Beachcombing for a Shipwrecked God. 1995. 304p. 22.95 (*1-55597-228-4*) Graywolf Pr.

—Beachcombing for a Shipwrecked God. 1997. 256p. pap. 12.00 (*0-684-82440-X*, Touchstone) Simon & Schuster.

Davis, Val. The Return of the Spanish Lady. 2001. 307p. 22.95 (*0-312-26224-8*, Saint Martin's Minotaur) St. Martin's Pr.

—Track of the Scorpion. 1997. (Nicolette Scott Mystery Ser.). 336p. mass mkt. 5.50 o.s.i (*0-553-57728-X*) Bantam Bks.

—Track of the Scorpion. 1996. 320p. 22.95 (*0-312-14437-7*) St. Martin's Pr.

—Wake of the Hornet. 2000. 304p. mass mkt. 5.99 o.s.i (*0-553-57804-9*) Bantam Bks.

Gear, Kathleen O'Neal & Gear, W. Michael. The Summoning God. (Illus.). 366p. pap. 15.95 (*0-312-87639-4*, Forge Bks.); 2000. (Anasazia Mysteries Ser.: Vol. 2). (Illus.). 352p. 25.95 (*0-312-86532-5*, Forge Bks.); 2001. (Anasazi Ser.). 576p. reprint ed. mass mkt. 7.99 (*0-8125-4034-4*, Tor Bks.) Doherty, Tom Assocs., LLC.

—The Visitant. (Anasazia Mysteries Ser.: Vol. 1). (Illus.). 2000. 501p. mass mkt. 6.99 (*0-8125-4033-6*, Tor Bks.); 1999. 364p. 19.95 (*0-312-86531-7*, Forge Bks.) Doherty, Tom Assocs., LLC.

Gentry, Christine. Mesozoic Murder. 2003. 300p. 24.95 o.s.i (*1-59058-048-6*); 500p. pap. 22.95 o.s.i (*1-59058-086-9*) Poisoned Pen Pr.

Hamilton, Lyn. The African Quest: An Archaeological Mystery. 2001. (Archaeological Mystery Ser.). (Illus.). 304p. 21.95 o.s.i (*0-425-17806-4*) Berkley Publishing Group.

—The Celtic Riddle. 2000. 304p. mass mkt. 6.50 (*0-425-17775-0*, Prime Crime) Berkley Publishing Group.

—The Celtic Riddle: An Archaeological Mystery. 2000. 296p. 21.95 o.s.i (*0-425-17235-X*, Prime Crime) Berkley Publishing Group.

—The Etruscan Chimera. 2003. 304p. mass mkt. 6.50 (*0-425-18908-2*, Prime Crime) Berkley Publishing Group.

—The Maltese Goddess: An Archaeological Mystery. 1998. (Archaeological Mystery Ser.). 256p. mass mkt. 6.50 (*0-425-16240-0*, Prime Crime) Berkley Publishing Group.

—The Moche Warrior: An Archaeological Mystery. (Archaeological Mystery Ser.). 336p. 1999. 21.95 o.s.i (*0-425-16809-3*); 2000. reprint ed. mass mkt. 6.50 (*0-425-17308-9*) Berkley Publishing Group. (Prime Crime).

—The Xibalba Murders: An Archeological Mystery. 1997. (Archaeological Mystery Ser.). 304p. mass mkt. 6.50 (*0-425-15722-9*, Prime Crime) Berkley Publishing Group.

Hannah, Kristin. The Enchantment. 416p. (Orig.). 2003. mass mkt. (*0-345-46564-4*); 1992. mass mkt. 3.99 (*0-449-14773-8*, Fawcett) Ballantine Bks.

—The Enchantment. l.t. ed. 1997. (Wheeler Large Print Book Ser.). (Orig.). 24.95 (*1-56895-448-4*, Wheeler Publishing, Inc.) Gale Group.

Illinik, C. J. The Tablets of Ararat. 2002. 352p. 12.99 (*0-8254-2908-0*) Kregel Pubns.

James, Peter. Prophecy. 1994. 288p. 20.95 o.p. (*0-312-10526-6*) St. Martin's Pr.

Knief, Charles. Silversword. mass mkt. (*0-312-98025-6*, St. Martin's Paperbacks); 2001. 400p. 24.95 (*0-312-27302-9*, Saint Martin's Minotaur) St. Martin's Pr.

La Tourrette, Jacqueline. The Pompeii Scroll. 1975. 256p. pap. 7.95 o.p. (*0-440-06091-5*, Delacorte Pr.) Dell Publishing.

—Shadows in Umbria. 1979. 9.95 o.p. (*0-399-12182-X*) Putnam Publishing Group, The.

Lee, Rachel. When I Wake. l.t. ed. 2000. (Wheeler Large Print Book Ser.). 416p. pap. 25.95 (*1-56895-996-6*, Wheeler Publishing, Inc.) Gale Group.

—When I Wake. 2000. 400p. E-Book 4.95 (*0-7595-9031-1*); 400p. E-Book 4.95 (*0-7595-4019-5*); 400p. E-Book 4.95 (*0-7595-0019-3*); 400p. E-Book 4.95 (*0-7595-8020-0*); 384p. reprint ed. mass mkt. 6.99 (*0-446-60655-3*, Warner Romance) Warner Bks., Inc.

McClain, Florence W. & Wagner, Mcclain. Visions of Murder. 1995. 336p. pap. 5.99 (*1-56718-452-9*) Llewellyn Pubns.

McKay, Claudia. Twist of Lime: A Lynn Evans Mystery. 1997. (Lynn Evans Mystery Ser.). 166p. pap. 10.95 (*0-934678-88-X*) New Victoria Pubs., Inc.

Ni Dhuibhne, Eilis. The Bray House. 1989. (Orig.). (C). pap. (*0-946211-96-5*) Attic Pr.

Peters, Elizabeth, pseud. The Ape Who Guards the Balance. l.t. ed. 1999. (Amelia Peabody Mystery Ser.: No. 10). 26.95 (*1-56895-597-9*, Wheeler Publishing, Inc.) Gale Group.

—The Ape Who Guards the Balance. 2002. E-Book 7.50 (*0-06-052324-7*); E-Book 7.50 (*0-06-052323-9*); E-Book 7.50 (*0-06-052322-0*); E-Book 7.50 (*0-06-052325-5*) HarperCollins General Bks. Group. (PerfectBound).

—The Ape Who Guards the Balance. (Amelia Peabody Mystery Ser.: No. 10). 1999. 464p. (gr. 8 up). mass mkt. 7.50 (*0-380-79856-5*); 1998. 384p. 24.00 (*0-380-97657-9*) Morrow/Avon. (Avon Bks.).

—Crocodile on the Sandbank. 1978. (Amelia Peabody Mystery Ser.: No. 1). mass mkt. 1.75 o.s.i (*0-449-23713-3*, Fawcett) Ballantine Bks.

—Crocodile on the Sandbank. 1988. (Amelia Peabody Mystery Ser.: No. 1). reprint ed. pap. 3.95 o.p. (*0-89296-072-8*) Mysterious Pr.

—Crocodile on the Sandbank. unabr. ed. 1990. (Amelia Peabody Mystery Ser.: No. 1). (YA). audio 60.00 (*1-55690-127-5*, 90085E7) Recorded Bks., LLC.

—Crocodile on the Sandbank. 1988. (Amelia Peabody Mystery Ser.). 272p. reprint ed. mass mkt. 7.50 (*0-445-40651-8*) Warner Bks., Inc.

—The Curse of the Pharaohs. l.t. ed. 1993. (Amelia Peabody Mystery Ser.). 14.95 o.p. (*0-8161-3274-7*, Macmillan Reference USA) Gale Group.

—The Curse of the Pharaohs. unabr. ed. 1990. (Amelia Peabody Mystery Ser.: Vol. 2). (YA). (gr. 10). audio 70.00 (*1-55690-130-5*, 90095E7) Recorded Bks., LLC.

—The Curse of the Pharaohs. 1988. (Amelia Peabody Mystery Ser.). 304p. reprint ed. mass mkt. 7.50 (*0-445-40648-8*) Warner Bks., Inc.

—The Deeds of the Disturber. l.t. ed. 1989. (Amelia Peabody Mystery Ser.: No. 5). 512p. 20.95 o.p. (*0-8161-4694-2*, Macmillan Reference USA) Gale Group.

—The Deeds of the Disturber. 2000. (Amelia Peabody Mystery Ser.: No. 5). 400p. mass mkt. 7.50 (*0-380-73195-9*, Avon Bks.) Morrow/Avon.

—The Deeds of the Disturber. unabr. ed. 1993. (Amelia Peabody Mystery Ser.: No. 5). audio 85.00 (*1-55690-942-X*, 93438E7) Recorded Bks., LLC.

—The Deeds of the Disturber. 1988. (Amelia Peabody Mystery Ser.: No. 5). 320p. 16.95 o.s.i (*0-689-11907-0*, Scribner) Simon & Schuster.

—The Deeds of the Disturber. 1989. (Amelia Peabody Mystery Ser.: No. 5). 304p. mass mkt. 5.99 (*0-446-35333-7*) Warner Bks., Inc.

—The Falcon at the Portal. l.t. ed. 1999. (Amelia Peabody Mystery Ser.: No. 11). 27.95 (*1-56895-765-3*, Wheeler Publishing, Inc.) Gale Group.

—The Falcon at the Portal. 2002. (Amelia Peabody Mystery Ser.). E-Book 7.50 (*0-06-621027-5*); E-Book 7.50 (*0-06-050440-4*); E-Book 7.50 (*0-06-018905-3*); E-Book 7.50 (*0-06-621028-3*) HarperCollins General Bks. Group. (PerfectBound).

—The Falcon at the Portal. (Amelia Peabody Mystery Ser.: No. 11). 2000. 464p. mass mkt. 7.50 (*0-380-79857-3*, Avon Bks.); 1999. 384p. (gr. 8). 24.00 (*0-380-97658-7*, Morrow, William & Co.) Morrow/Avon.

—The Falcon at the Portal. abr. ed. 1999. (Amelia Peabody Mystery Ser.: No. 11). audio 26.95 (*0-7871-1924-5*, Dove Audio) NewStar Media, Inc.

—The Falcon at the Portal. unabr. ed. (Amelia Peabody Mystery Ser.: No. 11). 2000. audio compact disk 119.00 (*0-7887-4206-X*, C1135E7); 1999. audio 96.00 (*0-7887-3744-9*, 95650E7) Recorded Bks., LLC.

—The Falcon at the Portal. 2000. (Amelia Peabody Mystery Ser.: No. 11). 13.04 (*0-606-18956-4*) Turtleback Bks.

—The Golden One: A Novel of Suspense. 2002. E-Book 19.95 (*0-06-009892-9*); E-Book 19.95 (*0-06-009840-6*) HarperCollins General Bks. Group. (PerfectBound).

—The Golden One: A Novel of Suspense. 2002. E-Book 19.95 (*0-06-009841-4*); E-Book 19.95 (*0-06-009842-2*) HarperCollins Pubs.

—The Golden One: A Novel of Suspense. l.t. ed. 2002. 688p. 25.95 (*0-06-009386-2*, HarperLargePrint) HarperTrade.

—The Golden One: A Novel of Suspense. 2003. 512p. mass mkt. 7.50 (*0-380-81715-2*, Avon Bks.); 2002. 448p. 25.95 (*0-380-97885-7*, Morrow, William & Co.) Morrow/Avon.

—He Shall Thunder in the Sky. 2001. (Amelia Peabody Mystery Ser.: Bk. 12). 512p. mass mkt. 7.50 (*0-380-79858-1*, Avon Bks.); 2000. (Amelia Peabody Mystery Ser.: Bk. 12). (Illus.). 416p. 25.00 (*0-380-97659-5*, Morrow, William & Co.); 2000. (*0-380-29962-3*) Morrow/Avon.

—He Shall Thunder in the Sky. l.t. ed. (Illus.). 728p. 2001. (Amelia Peabody Mystery Ser.: Bk. 12). pap. 29.95 (*0-7862-2828-8*); 2000. (Amelia Peabody Mystery Ser.: Bk. 12). 31.95 (*0-7862-2827-X*); 2000. (*0-7540-1498-3*) Thorndike Pr.

—The Hippopotamus Pool. l.t. ed. 1996. (Amelia Peabody Mystery Ser.: No. 8). 571p. lib. bdg. 24.95 o.p. (*0-7838-1726-6*, Macmillan Reference USA) Gale Group.

—The Hippopotamus Pool. unabr. ed. 2000. (Amelia Peabody Mystery Ser.: No. 8). (J). audio 85.00 (*0-7887-0607-1*, 94617E7) Recorded Bks., LLC.

—The Hippopotamus Pool. abr. ed. 1996. (Amelia Peabody Mystery Ser.: No. 8). audio 21.95 o.p. (*1-55935-207-8*) Soundelux Audio Publishing.

—The Hippopotamus Pool. (Amelia Peabody Mystery Ser.: No. 8). 1996. 82p. 22.95 o.s.i (*0-446-51833-6*); 1997. 448p. reprint ed. mass mkt. 7.50 (*0-446-60398-8*) Warner Bks., Inc.

—The Last Camel Died at Noon. l.t. ed. 1992. (Amelia Peabody Mystery Ser.: No. 6). 576p. pap. 24.95 (*0-8161-5358-2*); 574p. lib. bdg. 21.95 o.p. (*0-8161-5357-4*) Gale Group. (Macmillan Reference USA).

—The Last Camel Died at Noon. unabr. ed. 1991. (Amelia Peabody Mystery Ser.: No. 6). audio 91.00 (*1-55690-300-6*, 91318E7) Recorded Bks., LLC.

—The Last Camel Died at Noon. 1992. 448p. mass mkt. 7.50 (*0-446-36338-3*); 1991. (Amelia Peabody Mystery Ser.: No. 6). 18.95 o.p. (*0-446-51483-7*) Warner Bks., Inc.

—Lion in the Valley. 1990. (Amelia Peabody Mystery Ser.: No. 4). 320p. reprint ed. mass mkt. 4.99 o.p. (*0-8125-1242-1*, Tor Bks.) Doherty, Tom Assocs., LLC.

—Lion in the Valley. 1999. (Amelia Peabody Mystery Ser.: No. 4). 384p. mass mkt. 7.50 (*0-380-73119-3*, Avon Bks.) Morrow/Avon.

—Lion in the Valley. 1986. (Amelia Peabody Mystery Ser.: No. 4). 288p. 14.95 o.p. (*0-689-11619-5*, Scribner) Simon & Schuster.

—Lord of the Silent. l.t. ed. 2001. 704p. pap. 25.00 (*0-06-620961-7*) HarperCollins Pubs.

—Lord of the Silent. 2002. 496p. mass mkt. 7.50 (*0-380-81714-4*); 2001. (Illus.). 416p. 25.00 (*0-380-97884-9*, Morrow, William & Co.) Morrow/Avon.

—The Mummy Case. (Amelia Peabody Mystery Ser.: No. 3). 1994. mass mkt. 4.50 (*0-8125-3214-7*); 1992. mass mkt. 3.99 o.s.i (*0-8125-2031-9*); 1988. pap. 3.95 o.s.i (*0-8125-0793-2*); 1986. pap. 3.50 o.s.i (*0-8125-0760-6*) Doherty, Tom Assocs., LLC. (Tor Bks.).

—The Mummy Case. l.t. ed. 1985. (Amelia Peabody Mystery Ser.: No. 3). 450p. pap. 17.95 o.p. (*0-8161-3934-2*, Macmillan Reference USA) Gale Group.

—The Mummy Case. unabr. ed. 1991. (Amelia Peabody Mystery Ser.: No. 3). audio 78.00 (*1-55690-631-5*, 91420E7) Recorded Bks., LLC.

—The Mummy Case. 1995. (Amelia Peabody Mystery Ser.). 336p. reprint ed. mass mkt. 7.50 (*0-446-60193-4*) Warner Bks., Inc.

—Seeing a Large Cat. unabr. ed. 1997. (Amelia Peabody Mystery Ser.: No. 9). audio 90.00 (*0-7887-1297-7*, 95131E7) Recorded Bks., LLC.

—Seeing a Large Cat. (Amelia Peabody Mystery Ser.: No. 9). 1997. 416p. 24.00 o.p. (*0-446-51834-4*); 1998. 432p. reprint ed. mass mkt. 7.50 (*0-446-60557-3*) Warner Bks., Inc.

—The Snake, the Crocodile & the Dog. l.t. ed. (Amelia Peabody Mystery Ser.: No. 7). 555p. 1994. pap. 17.95 (*0-8161-5682-4*); 1993. 24.95 (*0-8161-5681-6*) Gale Group. (Macmillan Reference USA).

—The Snake, the Crocodile & the Dog. unabr. ed. 1992. (Amelia Peabody Mystery Ser.: No. 7). audio 91.00 (*1-55690-783-4*, 92422E7) Recorded Bks., LLC.

—The Snake, the Crocodile & the Dog. (Amelia Peabody Mystery Ser.: No. 7). 1992. 340p. 28.00 (*0-446-51585-X*); 1994. 448p. reprint ed. mass mkt. 7.50 (*0-446-36478-9*) Warner Bks., Inc.

Pfaff, Eugene E., Jr. & Causey, Michael. Uwharrie. 1993. 256p. 19.95 (*0-936389-30-3*) Tudor Pubs., Inc.

Preston, Douglas J. & Child, Lincoln. The Cabinet of Curiosities. 2003. 656p. mass mkt. 7.99 (*0-446-61123-9*); 2002. 480p. 25.95 (*0-446-53022-0*) Warner Bks., Inc.

—Thunderhead. 1999. 496p. 32.00 (*0-446-52337-2*); 2000. 560p. reprint ed. mass mkt. 7.50 (*0-446-60837-8*) Warner Bks., Inc.

Roberts, Nora. Birthright. 2004. 512p. mass mkt. 7.99 (*0-515-13711-1*, Jove) Berkley Publishing Group.

—Birthright. 2003. 480p. 25.95 (*0-399-14984-8*) Putnam Publishing Group, The.

—Birthright. l.t. ed. 2004. 741p. pap. 13.95 (*1-59413-026-4*, Large Print Pr.); 2003. 32.95 (*0-7862-5359-2*) Thorndike Pr.

Strauss, Victoria. Guardian of the Hills. 1995. (Illus.). 240p. (J). (gr. 7 up). 15.00 o.s.i (*0-688-06998-3*, Morrow, William & Co.) Morrow/Avon.

Walker, Jim. In Search of Eden. 2003. 350p. pap. 12.99 (*1-58229-313-9*) Howard Publishing Co.

Wood, Barbara. The Prophetess. abr. ed. 1997. audio 7.99 o.p. (*1-56740-167-8*, 690, Paperback Nova Audio Bks.); 1996. audio 16.95 o.p. (*1-56100-904-0*, 1350, Nova Audio Bks.); 1996. audio 89.25 o.p. (*1-56100-319-0*, 995, Unabridged Library Editions); 1996. audio 25.95 o.p. (*1-56100-694-7*, 222, Bookcassette) Brilliance Audio.

—The Prophetess. 1996. 400p. 23.95 o.p. (*0-316-81652-3*) Little Brown & Co.

—The Prophetess. 1997. 496p. reprint ed. mass mkt. 6.99 o.s.i (*0-446-60380-5*) Warner Bks., Inc.

**WOMEN ARTISTS—FICTION**

Adams, Henry. Esther: A Novel. 1997. (Literary Classics). 310p. pap. 11.00 (*1-57392-132-7*) Prometheus Bks., Pubs.

—Esther: A Novel. 1989. (Works of Henry Adams). reprint ed. lib. bdg. 79.00 (*0-7812-1439-4*) Reprint Services Corp.

—Esther: A Novel. 1976. reprint ed. 36.00 o.p. (*0-403-05725-6*) Scholarly Pr., Inc.

—Esther: A Novel. Spiller, Robert E., ed. 1976. reprint ed. lib. bdg. 50.00 (*0-8201-1187-2*) Scholars' Facsimiles & Reprints.

—Esther: A Novel. MacFarlane, Lisa, ed. & intro. by. 1999. (Classics Ser.). 256p. pap. 9.95 (*0-14-044754-7*, Penguin Classics) Viking Penguin.

Alameddine, Rabih. I, the Divine: A Novel in First Chapters. 2001. 288p. 23.95 (*0-393-04209-X*); 2002. 320p. reprint ed. pap. 13.95 (*0-393-32356-0*) Norton, W. W. & Co., Inc.

Amidon, Stephen. The Primitive. 1995. 272p. 23.00 o.p. (*0-88001-411-3*) HarperCollins Pubs.

Banks, L. A. Minion: A Vampire Huntress Legend. 2003. (Vampire Huntress Legend Ser.: Bk. 1). 288p. pap. 12.95 (*0-312-31680-1*, Saint Martin's Griffin) St. Martin's Pr.

Battrick, Elizabeth. Beatrix Potter's Tale. l.t. ed. 1998. (Ulverscroft Large Print Ser.). 432p. 29.99 (*0-7089-3891-4*, Ulverscroft) Thorpe, F. A. Pubs. GBR. *Dist:* Ulverscroft Large Print Bks., Ltd., Ulverscroft Large Print Canada, Ltd.

Bolitho, Janie. Framed in Cornwall. 2001. 192p. pap. 10.95 (*0-7490-0590-4*) Allison & Busby, Ltd. GBR. *Dist:* International Publishers Marketing.

—Framed in Cornwall. l.t. ed. 1999. (Dales Large Print Ser.). 368p. pap. o.p. (*1-85389-932-1*) Dales Large Print Bks. GBR. *Dist:* Ulverscroft Large Print Canada, Ltd.

—Snapped in Cornwall. 2000. 208p. mass mkt. 9.95 (*0-7490-0469-X*, London Hse.) Allison & Busby, Ltd. GBR. *Dist:* International Publishers Marketing.

Occupations

Braverman, Kate. The Incantation of Frida K. 2003. 240p. reprint ed. pap. 11.95 (*1-58322-571-4*) Seven Stories Pr.

Cato, Nancy. All the Rivers Run. 1984. 640p. mass mkt. 3.95 o.p. (*0-451-12535-5*, AE2535); 1982. mass mkt. 3.50 o.p. (*0-451-11345-4*); 1979. mass mkt. 2.95 o.p. (*0-451-08693-7*) NAL. (Signet Bks.).

—All the Rivers Run. 1978. 10.95 o.p. (*0-312-02021-X*) St. Martin's Pr.

—All the Rivers Run. l.t. ed. 1987. Vol. 2, Pt. 1. 752p. 15.95 o.p. (*0-7089-8432-0*); Vol. 2, Pt. 2. 416p. 15.95 o.p. (*0-7089-8433-9*) Thorpe, F. A. Pubs. GBR. (Charnwood). *Dist:* Ulverscroft Large Print Bks., Ltd.

Corby, Jane. Riverwood. l.t. ed. 1994. 18.95 o.p. (*0-7927-1970-0*); pap. 16.95 o.p. (*0-7927-1969-7*) BBC Audiobooks America.

—The Shadow & the Fear. l.t. ed. 1994. 18.95 o.p. (*0-7927-1815-1*); pap. 17.95 o.p. (*0-7927-1814-3*) BBC Audiobooks America.

Crone, Moira. A Period of Confinement. 1987. 304p. reprint ed. pap. 6.95 o.p. (*0-06-097108-8*, PL 7108, Perennial) HarperTrade.

—A Period of Confinement. 1986. 336p. 19.95 o.p. (*0-399-13136-1*, G. P. Putnam's Sons) Penguin Putnam Bks. for Young Readers.

De Lint, Charles. Memory & Dream. 1995. 448p. mass mkt. 6.99 (*0-8125-3407-7*); 1994. 400p. 22.95 o.p. (*0-312-85572-9*) Doherty, Tom Assocs., LLC. (Tor Bks.).

—The Onion Girl. E-Book 27.95 (*0-312-70303-1*); 2001. 508p. 27.95 (*0-312-87397-2*); 2002. 512p. reprint ed. pap. 14.95 (*0-7653-0381-7*) Doherty, Tom Assocs., LLC. (Tor Bks.).

Delinsky, Barbara. Coast Road. l.t. ed. 1998. (Large Print Book Ser.). 26.95 o.p. (*1-56895-666-5*, Wheeler Publishing, Inc.) Gale Group.

—Coast Road. 2003. 480p. mass mkt. 5.99 (*0-7434-6717-5*, Pocket); 1999. E-Book 24.00 (*0-684-86788-5*, Simon & Schuster); 1998. 480p. pap. 7.99 (*0-671-02604-6*, Pocket); 1998. 368p. (gr. 10 up). 24.00 o.s.i (*0-684-84576-8*, Simon & Schuster); 1998. 365p. (*0-684-85575-5*, Simon & Schuster); 1999. 480p. reprint ed. mass mkt. 7.99 (*0-671-02766-2*, Pocket) Simon & Schuster.

—Secret of the Stone. 1999. 256p. mass mkt. (*1-55166-489-5*, Mira Bks.); 1992. per. (*0-373-83251-6*, 1-83251-8, Harlequin Bks.); 1985. mass mkt. (*0-373-25165-3*, Harlequin Bks.) Harlequin Enterprises, Ltd.

Diehl, Margaret. Me & You. 1993. 2.99 o.p. (*0-517-10835-6*) Random Hse. Value Publishing.

—Me & You. Rosenman, Jane, ed. 1991. 272p. reprint ed. pap. (*0-671-70991-7*, Washington Square Pr.) Simon & Schuster.

—Me & You. 1990. 265p. 18.95 o.p. (*0-939149-31-1*) Soho Pr., Inc.

Enright, Rosemary. Isobel. 1995. mass mkt. 5.99 o.s.i (*0-8041-1314-9*, Ivy Bks.) Ballantine Bks.

—Isobel. 1994. 464p. 23.95 o.p. (*0-312-11063-4*) St. Martin's Pr.

Evans, Richard Paul. The Last Promise. 2002. 304p. 22.95 (*0-525-94696-9*) Dutton/Plume.

—The Last Promise. l.t. ed. 2003. (Wheeler Romance Ser.). 32.95 (*1-58724-375-X*, Wheeler Publishing, Inc.) Gale Group.

—The Last Promise. 2003. mass mkt. 6.99 (*0-451-41092-0*); 320p. mass mkt. 6.99 (*0-451-21101-4*) NAL. (Signet Bks.).

Fiedler, Jacqueline. Sketches with Wolves. 2001. 384p. pap. 6.99 (*0-671-01560-5*, Pocket) Simon & Schuster.

—Tiger's Palette. 1998. (Caroline Canfield Mystery Ser.). pap. 5.99 (*0-671-01559-1*, Pocket) Simon & Schuster.

Gemmell, Nikki. Alice Springs. 2000. 272p. pap. 12.95 o.s.i (*0-14-028642-X*, Penguin Bks.) Penguin Group (USA) Inc.

—Alice Springs. 1999. 256p. 23.95 o.p. (*0-670-88347-6*) Viking Penguin.

Godwin, Gail. Violet Clay. 1986. (Contemporary American Fiction Ser.). 336p. pap. 9.95 o.p. (*0-14-008220-4*, Penguin Bks.) Viking Penguin.

Gordon, Mary. Spending: A Utopian Divertimento. 304p. 1999. pap. 13.00 (*0-684-85204-7*); 1998. 24.00 (*0-684-83945-8*) Simon & Schuster. (Scribner).

—Spending: A Utopian Divertimento. 1999. 18.00 (*0-671-57994-0*, Simon & Schuster Audioworks) Simon & Schuster Audio.

Heitzmann, Kristen. A Rush of Wings. 2003. 384p. pap. 12.99 (*0-7642-2606-1*) Bethany Hse. Pubs.

Henderson, Lauren. Black Rubber Dress. E-Book 11.50 (*1-58945-549-5*) Adobe Systems, Inc.

—Black Rubber Dress. 1999. E-Book 11.50 (*0-609-60715-4*) Random Hse., Inc.

—Black Rubber Dress: A Sam Jones Novel. 1999. 304p. pap. 12.95 (*0-609-80438-3*, Three Rivers Pr.) Crown Publishing Group.

—Chained! 2000. 249p. (*0-09-180045-5*) Hutchinson, Fred Cancer Research Ctr.

—Chained! 2000. 256p. pap. o.p. (*0-09-180050-1*) Random Hse. of Canada, Ltd. CAN. *Dist:* Random Hse., Inc.

—Chained! A Novel. 2002. 336p. pap. 12.95 (*0-609-80865-6*, Three Rivers Pr.) Crown Publishing Group.

—Freeze My Margarita. E-Book 11.50 (*1-58945-594-0*) Adobe Systems, Inc.

—Freeze My Margarita. 2000. E-Book 11.50 (*0-609-60882-7*, Crown); 22.00 (*0-609-60744-8*); 288p. pap. 12.95 (*0-609-80487-1*, Crown) Crown Publishing Group.

—Freeze My Margarita: A Sam Jones Novel. 2000. 320p. pap. 13.00 (*0-609-80684-X*, Three Rivers Pr.) Crown Publishing Group.

Hitchcock, Jane S. Trick of the Eye. l.t. ed. 1993. 23.95 o.p. (*0-7927-1482-2*); pap. 21.95 o.p. (*0-7927-1481-4*) BBC Audiobooks America.

—Trick of the Eye. 1992. 288p. 19.00 o.p. (*0-525-93529-0*, Dutton) Dutton/Plume.

—Trick of the Eye. 1993. 256p. pap. o.p. (*0-451-17480-1*); 368p. mass mkt. 5.50 o.s.i (*0-451-17673-1*) NAL. (Signet Bks.).

Howard, Linda. Now You See Her. 1998. 336p. 23.00 o.s.i (*0-671-56882-5*, Atria); 1999. 368p. reprint ed. mass mkt. 7.99 (*0-671-03405-7*, Pocket) Simon & Schuster.

—Now You See Her. abr. ed. 1998. 18.00 (*0-671-58261-5*, Simon & Schuster Audioworks) Simon & Schuster Audio.

—Now You See Her. l.t. ed. 1999. (Paperback Bestsellers Ser.). 456p. pap. 27.95 (*0-7862-1728-6*); 28.95 o.p. (*0-7862-1727-8*) Thorndike Pr.

Johansen, Iris. The Face of Deception, Set. unabr. ed. 1999. (Eve Duncan Mystery Ser.: Vol. 1). audio 69.95 (*0-7927-2329-5*, CSL 218, Chivers Sound Library) BBC Audiobooks America.

—The Face of Deception. 1999. 480p. mass mkt. 7.50 (*0-553-57802-2*) Broadway Bks.

—The Face of Deception. l.t. ed. 1999. 454p. 27.95 (*1-56895-633-9*, Wheeler Publishing, Inc.) Gale Group.

—The Face of Deception. abr. ed. 1998. audio 25.00 (*0-553-52542-5*, 696036); audio compact disk 29.95 o.s.i (*0-553-45617-2*) Random Hse. Audio Publishing Group. (RH Audio).

—The Killing Game, unabr. ed. 2000. (Eve Duncan Mystery Ser.: Vol. 2). audio 69.95 (*0-7927-2338-4*, CSL 227, Chivers Sound Library) BBC Audiobooks America.

—The Killing Game. 2000. 384p. mass mkt. 7.50 (*0-553-58155-4*) Bantam Bks.

—The Killing Game. l.t. ed. 2000. (Thorndike/G. K. Hall Paperback Bestsellers Ser.). 443p. pap. 29.95 (*0-7838-8852-X*); 463p. 31.95 (*0-7838-8851-1*) Gale Group. (Macmillan Reference USA).

—The Killing Game. abr. ed. 1999. audio 25.00 Highsmith Inc.

King, Joan. Sarah M. Peale: America's First Woman Artist. 1987. (Illus.). 18.95 (*0-8283-1999-5*) Branden Bks.

Knight, Kathryn L. Dark Swan. 1996. (WWL Mystery Ser.). per. (*0-373-26203-5*, 1-26203-9, Worldwide Library) Harlequin Enterprises, Ltd.

—Dark Swan. 1994. 224p. 19.95 o.p. (*0-312-10961-X*, Saint Martin's Minotaur) St. Martin's Pr.

—Mortal Words. 1990. 17.95 o.p. (*0-671-68446-9*, Simon & Schuster) Simon & Schuster.

—Mortal Words. Chelius, Jane, ed. 1991. 352p. reprint ed. mass mkt. 4.50 (*0-671-68449-3*, Pocket) Simon & Schuster.

—Trace Elements. 1986. 15.95 o.p. (*0-393-02333-8*) Norton, W. W. & Co., Inc.

—Trace Elements. 1987. mass mkt. 3.50 (*0-671-64089-5*, Pocket) Simon & Schuster.

Lennox, Judith. The Italian Garden. 1993. 480p. 24.95 o.p. (*0-312-09810-3*) St. Martin's Pr.

Lynnford, Janet. Spellbound Summer. 2002. 368p. mass mkt. 5.99 o.s.i (*0-451-41052-1*) NAL.

Mapson, Jo-Ann. Blue Rodeo: A Novel. 1995. 336p. pap. 13.00 (*0-06-092635-X*, Perennial); 1994. 352p. 22.00 o.p. (*0-06-016944-3*) HarperTrade.

Matthews, Patricia. Rendezvous at Midnight. 2002. 25.95 (*0-7862-3698-1*, Five Star) Gale Group.

McKinnon, Karen. Narcissus Ascending. 2002. 224p. 21.00 (*0-312-29058-6*) Picador.

—Narcissus Ascending: A Novel. 2003. 224p. pap. 13.00 (*0-312-31218-0*) Picador.

Mori, Kyoko. Stone Field, True Arrow: A Novel. 2000. 288p. 24.00 o.s.i (*0-8050-4080-3*, Metropolitan Bks.) Holt, Henry & Co.

—Stone Field, True Arrow: A Novel. 2001. 288p. pap. 13.00 (*0-312-42042-0*) Picador.

Mujica, Bárbara. Frida. 2001. (Illus.). 320p. 26.95 (*1-58567-074-X*) Overlook Pr., The.

Popovac, Gwynn. Wet Paint, 001. 1986. 19.95 o.p. (*0-395-38222-X*) Houghton Mifflin Co.

Rae, Catherine M. The Hidden Cove. l.t. ed. 2000. 268p. lib. bdg. 27.95 (*1-58547-035-X*) Ctr. Point Large Print.

—The Hidden Cove. 1999. 183p. reprint ed. text 20.00 (*0-7881-6634-4*) DIANE Publishing Co.

—The Hidden Cove. 1995. 192p. 19.95 o.p. (*0-312-13511-4*) St. Martin's Pr.

Riley, Judith M. The Serpent Garden. 1997. 480p. pap. 13.95 o.s.i (*0-14-025880-9*) Penguin Group (USA) Inc.

—The Serpent Garden. 1996. (Illus.). 480p. 24.95 o.p. (*0-670-86661-X*) Viking Penguin.

Roberts, Sherry. Maud's House. 216p. 1995. pap. 11.00 (*0-918949-28-9*); 1994. 18.00 (*0-918949-32-7*) Roberts, Sherry.

Schoemperlen, Diane. In the Language of Love: A Novel in 100 Chapters. 1996. 368p. 23.95 o.p. (*0-670-86517-6*, Viking) Viking Penguin.

Shange, Ntozake. Liliane: Resurrection of the Daughter. 1995. 304p. pap. 12.00 (*0-312-13559-9*) Picador.

—Liliane: Resurrection of the Daughter. 1994. 224p. 18.95 o.p. (*0-312-11310-2*) St. Martin's Pr.

Traxler, Patricia. Blood. 2001. 352p. 24.95 (*0-312-27484-X*, Saint Martin's Minotaur) St. Martin's Pr.

—Blood: A Novel. 2002. 368p. pap. 13.95 (*0-312-30401-3*, Saint Martin's Griffin) St. Martin's Pr.

Tuten, Frederic. The Green Hour. 2003. (Illus.). 256p. 24.95 (*0-393-05105-6*); 272p. pap. 13.95 (*0-393-32533-4*) Norton, W. W. & Co., Inc.

Villanueva, Alma L. The Ultraviolet Sky. 1988. 379p. 28.00 (*0-916950-85-9*) Bilingual Pr./Editorial Bilingue.

—The Ultraviolet Sky. 1993. 384p. pap. 9.00 o.s.i (*0-385-42014-5*) Doubleday Publishing.

Wadley, Margot. The Gripping Beast. 2002. 208p. mass mkt. 6.50 (*0-312-97960-6*, St. Martin's Paperbacks) St. Martin's Pr.

—Gripping Beast. E-Book 21.95 (*0-312-70139-X*) St. Martin's Pr.

—The Gripping Beast: An Orkney Mystery. 2001. 200p. 21.95 (*0-312-27254-5*, Saint Martin's Minotaur) St. Martin's Pr.

Ward, Just S. Ambition & Love. 1994. 277p. 22.95 o.p. (*0-395-68196-0*) Houghton Mifflin Co.

Wilson, Susan. Beauty. l.t. ed. 1996. 24.95 (*1-56895-368-2*, Wheeler Publishing, Inc.) Gale Group.

Woodiwiss, Kathleen E. The Elusive Flame. abr. ed. 1999. audio 7.99 o.s.i (*1-56740-316-6*, 1866, Paperback Nova Audio Bks.); 1998. audio 39.95 (*1-56740-407-3*, 1492, Brilliance Audio Unabridged); 1998. 16p. audio 89.25 (*1-56740-605-X*, 1632, Unabridged Library Editions) Brilliance Audio.

—The Elusive Flame. l.t. ed. 1998. (Large Print Book Ser.). 27.95 o.p. (*1-56895-692-4*, Wheeler Publishing, Inc.) Gale Group.

—The Elusive Flame. 1999. 496p. mass mkt. 7.50 (*0-380-80786-6*); 1998. 432p. pap. 14.00 o.p. (*0-380-76655-8*) Morrow/Avon. (Avon Bks.).

Woolson, Constance F. Women Artists, Women Exiles: "Miss Grief" & Other Stories. Weimer, Joan M., ed. 1988. (American Women Writers Ser.). 350p. (Orig.). (C). text 42.00 (*0-8135-1347-2*); pap. text 17.00 (*0-8135-1348-0*) Rutgers Univ. Pr.

**WOMEN JOURNALISTS—FICTION**

Adler, Elizabeth A. Now or Never. l.t. ed. 1997. 448p. mass mkt. 6.99 (*0-440-22464-0*) Dell Publishing.

Aiken, Ginny. Lark. 2000. (Bellamy's Blossoms Ser.: No. 2). 320p. pap. 9.99 (*0-8423-3560-9*) Tyndale Hse. Pubs.

Albright, Letha. Daredevil's Apprentice. 2002. (Viv Powers Mystery Ser.). 255p. pap. 12.95 (*0-9705049-4-2*) Avocet Pr., Inc.

—Tulsa Time. 2000. (Dark Oak Mysteries Ser.). 220p. pap. 11.95 (*1-892343-12-6*) Oak Tree Publishing.

Alers, Rochelle. Private Passions. 2001. (Arabesque Ser.). 256p. mass mkt. 5.99 (*1-58314-151-0*) BET Bks.

Allen, Tricia. A Well-Respected Dead Man. 2003. (Five Star First Edition Mystery Ser.). 319p. 25.95 (*0-7862-5441-6*, Five Star) Gale Group.

Amos, Diane. Getting Personal. 2004. 323p. pap. 13.95 (*1-4104-0195-2*, Five Star Trade); 2003. 325p. 26.95 (*0-7862-5169-7*, Five Star) Gale Group.

Anderson, Linda. The Secrets of Sadie Maynard. 1999. (Illus.). 480p. pap. 6.50 (*0-671-02768-9*, Pocket) Simon & Schuster.

Anthony, Evelyn. Exposure. l.t. ed. 1994. 486p. lib. bdg. 23.95 (*0-8161-7429-6*, Macmillan Reference USA) Gale Group.

—Exposure. 1994. 288p. 22.00 o.p. (*0-06-017774-8*) HarperTrade.

Atwood, Margaret. Bodily Harm. 1995. 304p. pap. 10.95 o.s.i (*0-553-37789-2*); 1983. mass mkt. 4.50 o.p. (*0-553-23289-4*); 1983. mass mkt. 4.50 o.s.i (*0-553-26969-0*); 1983. 304p. mass mkt. 6.50 o.s.i (*0-553-27455-4*) Bantam Bks.

—Bodily Harm. 2002. lib. bdg. 27.95 (*1-58547-236-0*, Premier) Ctr. Point Large Print.

—Bodily Harm. 1998. 304p. pap. 12.95 (*0-385-49107-7*) Doubleday Publishing.

—Bodily Harm. 1982. 45.00 (*0-671-44153-1*) Ultramarine Publishing Co., Inc.

Bates, Karen Grigsby. Plain Brown Wrapper: An Alex Powell Novel. 2001. 336p. pap. 13.00 (*0-380-80890-0*, Avon Bks.) Morrow/Avon.

Bedell, Geraldine. Party Tricks. 1998. 288p. 22.95 o.p. (*0-312-18154-X*, Saint Martin's Minotaur) St. Martin's Pr.

Begley, Louis. Shipwreck. 2003. 256p. 23.00 (*1-4000-4098-1*) Knopf, Alfred A. Inc.

Belsky, R. G. Loverboy. 1998. mass mkt. 6.50 (*0-380-79068-8*); 1997. 313p. mass mkt. 23.00 (*0-380-97439-8*) Morrow/Avon. (Avon Bks.).

Bickmore, Barbara. Distant Star. 1993. (Illus.). 544p. (Orig.). pap. 10.00 o.s.i (*0-345-36109-1*) Ballantine Bks.

Blackstock, Terri. Presumption of Guilt. l.t. ed. 1999. (Christian Mystery Ser.). 453p. 25.95 (*0-7862-1959-9*) Thorndike Pr.

—Presumption of Guilt. 1997. (Sun Coast Chronicles Ser.). 304p. pap. 12.99 (*0-310-20018-0*); audio 14.99 (*0-310-21085-2*) Zondervan.

Bolton, Clyde. Turn Left on Green: A Novel of Stock Car Racing. 2002. 200p. 24.95 (*1-57966-027-4*) River City Publishing.

Bowman, Elizabeth A. White Chocolate. 1999. 375p. mass mkt. 6.99 (*0-8125-7181-9*); 1998. 352p. 23.95 o.p. (*0-312-86306-3*) Doherty, Tom Assocs., LLC. (Forge Bks.).

Bradford, Barbara Taylor. Dangerous to Know. unabr. ed. 1996. audio 56.00 (*0-7366-3209-3*, 3872) Books on Tape, Inc.

—Dangerous to Know. 1995. 514p. 24.00 o.p. (*0-06-017722-5*); audio 22.50 o.p. (*0-694-51554-X*, HarperAudio) HarperTrade.

—Dangerous to Know. 1996. 400p. mass mkt. 7.99 (*0-06-109208-8*, HarperTorch) Morrow/Avon.

—Dangerous to Know. l.t. ed. (Paperback Bestsellers Ser.). 431p. 1996. pap. 25.95 (*0-7838-1364-3*); 1995. 28.95 (*0-7838-1363-5*) Thorndike Pr.

—Where You Belong. 2000. 464p. mass mkt. 7.99 (*0-440-23515-4*) Dell Publishing.

—Where You Belong. abr. ed. 2000. audio 25.00 (*0-553-52603-0*); audio compact disk 29.95 (*0-553-45674-1*) Random Hse. Audio Publishing Group. (RH Audio).

—Where You Belong. l.t. ed. 2000. 528p. pap. 13.95 (*0-375-72797-3*); 24.95 (*0-375-40974-2*) Random Hse. Large Print.

Brandeis, Robin. She Scoops to Conquer. 2002. 212p. 12.95 (*1-892281-18-X*); pap. 11.95 (*1-892281-17-1*) New Victoria Pubs., Inc.

Brown, Sandra. The Standoff. l.t. ed. 2001. 352p. pap. 12.95 (*0-375-72804-X*); 2000. 336p. 19.95 (*0-375-43054-7*) Random Hse. Large Print.

—The Standoff. 2001. 272p. E-Book 4.95 (*0-446-96028-4*); 2000. 224p. 19.95 (*0-446-52701-7*) Warner Bks., Inc.

—Sweet Anger. l.t. ed. (Paperback Bestsellers Ser.). 2001. 354p. 28.95 (*0-7862-2293-X*); 2000. 375p. 30.95 (*0-7862-2292-1*) Thorndike Pr.

—Sweet Anger. 1999. 320p. reprint ed. mass mkt. 6.99 (*0-446-60308-2*) Warner Bks., Inc.

Buchanan, Edna. Act of Betrayal. unabr. collector's ed. 1996. (Britt Montero Ser.). audio 56.00 (*0-7366-3306-5*, 3960) Books on Tape, Inc.

—Act of Betrayal. abr. ed. (Britt Montero Mystery Ser.). 1997. 3p. audio 7.99 o.p. (*1-56740-148-1*, 617, Paperback Nova Audio Bks.); 1996. audio 17.95 o.p. (*1-56100-868-0*, 454, Nova Audio Bks.); 1996. 7p. audio 57.25 o.p. (*1-56100-296-8*, 786, Unabridged Library Editions); 1996. audio 23.95 o.p. (*1-56100-671-8*, 24, Bookcassette) Brilliance Audio.

—Act of Betrayal, Set. unabr. ed. 1999. audio 57.25 Highsmith Inc.

—Act of Betrayal. 1997. 448p. mass mkt. 5.99 (*0-7868-8923-3*); 1996. 320p. 21.95 o.p. (*0-7868-6098-7*) Hyperion Pr.

—Act of Betrayal. unabr. ed. 2000. (Britt Montero Mystery Ser.: Vol. 4). audio 60.00 (*0-7887-0488-5*, 94681E7) Recorded Bks., LLC.

—Contents under Pressure. unabr. collector's ed. 1993. (Britt Montero Ser.). audio 56.00 (*0-7366-2378-7*, 3150) Books on Tape, Inc.

—Contents under Pressure. 1992. 304p. (YA). 21.95 o.p. (*1-56282-932-7*) Hyperion Pr.

—Contents under Pressure. 1994. (Britt Montero Mysteries Ser.). 368p. mass mkt. 6.99 (*0-380-72260-7*, Avon Bks.) Morrow/Avon.

—Contents under Pressure. l.t. ed. 472p. pap. 2.99 o.s.i (*0-7669-1026-1*) World Pubns., Inc.

—Garden of Evil. (Britt Montero Mysteries Ser.). 2000. 320p. mass mkt. 6.99 (*0-380-79841-7*); 1999. 319p. 24.00 (*0-380-97654-4*) Morrow/Avon. (Avon Bks.).

—Garden of Evil. l.t. ed. 2000. (Mystery Ser.). 437p. 29.95 (*0-7862-2331-6*) Thorndike Pr.

—The Ice Maiden. l.t. ed. 2003. lib. bdg. 29.95 (*1-58547-309-X*, Platinum) Ctr. Point Large Print.

—The Ice Maiden. 2003. 320p. mass mkt. 7.50 (*0-380-72834-6*, Avon Bks.); 2002. 304p. 23.95 (*0-380-97332-4*, Morrow, William & Co.) Morrow/Avon.

—Margin of Error. l.t. ed. 1998. pap. 24.95 (*1-56895-563-4*, Wheeler Publishing, Inc.) Gale Group.

—Margin of Error. 1997. 304p. 22.95 o.p. (*0-7868-6232-7*); 1998. 384p. reprint ed. mass mkt. 5.99 (*0-7868-8931-4*) Hyperion Pr.

—Margin of Error. l.t. ed. 2000. (Ulverscroft Large Print Ser.). 488p. (*0-7089-4189-3*, Ulverscroft) Thorpe, F. A. Pubs. GBR. *Dist:* Ulverscroft Large Print Bks., Ltd., Ulverscroft Large Print Canada, Ltd.
—Miami, It's Murder. unabr. collector's ed. 1994. (Britt Montero Ser.). audio 48.00 (*0-7366-2740-5*, 3466) Books on Tape, Inc.
—Miami, It's Murder. unabr. ed. 1994. audio 57.25 o.p. (*1-56100-175-9*, 941, Unabridged Library Editions); audio 21.95 o.p. (*1-56100-548-7*, 175, Bookcassette) Brilliance Audio.
—Miami, It's Murder. abr. ed. audio 17.00 o.p. (*1-55994-794-2*, CPN 2383, HarperAudio) Harper-Trade.
—Suitable for Framing. unabr. collector's ed. 1995. (Britt Montero Ser.). audio 56.00 (*0-7366-3072-4*, 3754) Books on Tape, Inc.
—Suitable for Framing. abr. ed. 1995. audio 16.95 o.p. (*1-56100-401-4*, 1383, Nova Audio Bks.); audio 23.95 o.p. (*1-56100-609-2*, 281, Bookcassette); 9p. audio 57.25 o.p. (*1-56100-234-8*, 1062, Unabridged Library Editions) Brilliance Audio.
—Suitable for Framing. l.t. ed. 1995. 25.95 o.p. (*1-56895-210-4*, Wheeler Publishing, Inc.) Gale Group.
—Suitable for Framing. 1996. 368p. mass mkt. 4.99 (*0-7868-8901-2*); 1995. 256p. 21.95 (*0-7868-6047-2*) Hyperion Pr.
—Suitable for Framing. abr. ed. 2000. audio 7.95 (*1-57815-028-0*, 1033, Media Bks. Audio Publishing) Media Bks., L. L. C.
—Suitable for Framing. unabr. ed. 2000. (Britt Montero Mystery Ser.: Vol. 3). audio 60.00 (*0-7887-0296-3*, 94489E7) Recorded Bks., LLC.
—You Only Die Twice. l.t. ed. 2001. 396p. lib. bdg. 27.95 (*1-58547-124-0*) Ctr. Point Large Print.
—You Only Die Twice. 2002. 368p. mass mkt. 6.99 (*0-380-79842-5*) Morrow/Avon.
Burke, Jan. Bones: An Irene Kelly Novel. l.t. ed. 2000. (Wheeler Large Print Book Ser.). 561p. pap. 25.95 (*1-56895-940-0*, Wheeler Publishing, Inc.) Gale Group.
—Bones: An Irene Kelly Novel. 2001. 448p. mass mkt. 6.99 (*0-451-20247-3*, Signet Bks.) NAL.
—Bones: An Irene Kelly Novel. 1999. (Irene Kelly Mystery Ser.: No. 7). 384p. 23.00 o.s.i (*0-684-85551-8*, Simon & Schuster) Simon & Schuster.
—Dear Irene, An Irene Kelly Novel. 1996. pap. 5.50 (*0-380-72556-8*, Avon Bks.) Morrow/Avon.
—Dear Irene, An Irene Kelly Novel. 1995. 288p. 20.00 o.s.i (*0-671-78216-9*, Simon & Schuster) Simon & Schuster.
—Flight: A Novel of Suspense. l.t. ed. 2001. 601p. 28.95 o.p. (*1-58724-051-3*, Wheeler Publishing, Inc.) Gale Group.
—Goodnight, Irene: An Irene Kelly Novel. 1994. (Irene Kelly Mystery Ser.). 256p. pap. 5.99 (*0-380-72279-8*, Avon Bks.) Morrow/Avon.
—Goodnight, Irene: An Irene Kelly Novel. 1993. 18.00 o.p. (*0-671-78200-2*, Simon & Schuster) Simon & Schuster.
—Goodnight, Irene: An Irene Kelly Novel. l.t. ed. 1995. (Ulverscroft Large Print Ser.). 528p. 29.99 o.p. (*0-7089-3287-8*, Ulverscroft) Thorpe, F. A. Pubs. GBR. *Dist:* Ulverscroft Large Print Bks., Ltd., Ulverscroft Large Print Canada, Ltd.
—Hocus: An Irene Kelly Novel. l.t. ed. 1997. lib. bdg. 24.95 (*1-57490-106-0*, Beeler Large Print Bks.) Beeler, Thomas T. Publisher.
—Hocus: An Irene Kelly Novel. 1998. (Irene Kelly Mystery Ser.). 480p. mass mkt. 6.99 o.p. (*0-06-104439-3*) HarperCollins Pubs.
—Hocus: An Irene Kelly Novel. 1997. 336p. 22.00 (*0-684-80344-5*); 22.00 (*0-684-00492-5*) Simon & Schuster. (Simon & Schuster).
—Liar: An Irene Kelly Mystery. 1999. (Irene Kelly Mystery Ser.). 400p. mass mkt. 7.50 (*0-06-104440-7*) HarperCollins Pubs.
—Liar: An Irene Kelly Mystery. 1998. (Irene Kelly Mystery Ser.). 352p. 23.00 (*0-684-80345-3*, Simon & Schuster) Simon & Schuster.
—Remember Me, Irene: An Irene Kelly Novel. 1997. 352p. mass mkt. 5.50 o.s.i (*0-06-104438-5*, HarperTorch) Morrow/Avon.
—Remember Me, Irene: An Irene Kelly Novel. 1996. 304p. 21.00 o.p. (*0-684-80343-7*, Simon & Schuster) Simon & Schuster.
—Sweet Dreams, Irene: An Irene Kelly Novel. 1995. pap. 4.99 (*0-380-72350-6*, Avon Bks.) Morrow/Avon.
—Sweet Dreams, Irene: An Irene Kelly Novel. 1994. 287p. 18.00 (*0-671-78210-X*, Simon & Schuster) Simon & Schuster.
Cail, Carol. If Two of Them Are Dead. 1996. 224p. 15.95 (*0-312-14361-3*, Saint Martin's Minotaur) St. Martin's Pr.
—Unsafe Keeping. 1996. 304p. mass mkt. 5.50 o.s.i (*0-440-22298-2*) Dell Publishing.
—Unsafe Keeping. pap. (*0-312-30031-X*, Saint Martin's Griffin); pap. 15.95 (*0-312-29194-9*, Saint Martin's Griffin); 1995. 218p. 15.95 (*0-312-13198-4*, Saint Martin's Minotaur) St. Martin's Pr.
—Who Was Sylvia? 1999. (Maxey Burnell Mystery Ser.). 180p. pap. text 16.99 (*1-886199-04-3*, Madison Publishing Co.) Deadly Alibi Pr., Ltd.
Carlson, Melody. Someone to Belong To. 2001. (Whispering Pines Ser.: Vol. 3). (Illus.). 311p. pap. 9.99 o.p. (*0-7369-0064-0*) Harvest Hse. Pubs.
Carter, Raphael. The Fortunate Fall. 1999. 13.95 (*0-312-87079-5*); 1997. 288p. pap. 13.95 (*0-312-86327-6*); 1996. 288p. 21.95 o.p. (*0-312-86034-X*) Doherty, Tom Assocs., LLC. (Tor Bks.).
Carver, Caroline. Blood Junction. 2002. 336p. 24.95 (*0-89296-770-6*) Mysterious Pr.
—Blood Junction. 2003. (Basic Ser.). 28.95 (*0-7862-5058-5*) Thorndike Pr.
—Blood Junction. 2003. 400p. mass mkt. 6.99 (*0-446-61319-3*) Warner Bks., Inc.
Cashdan, Linda. Special Interests. 1990. 18.95 o.p. (*0-312-04426-7*) St. Martin's Pr.
Chace, Susan. Intimacy. 1990. 180p. pap. 7.95 o.p. (*0-452-26375-1*, Plume) Dutton/Plume.
—Intimacy. 1988. 176p. 14.95 o.s.i (*0-394-57030-8*) Random Hse., Inc.
Chappell, Helen. Dead Duck. 1997. (Sam & Hollis Mystery Ser.). mass mkt. 5.50 o.s.i (*0-449-15001-1*, Fawcett) Ballantine Bks.
—Dead Duck. l.t. ed. 2000. (Beeler Large Print Mystery Ser.). 231p. 25.95 (*1-57490-320-9*, Beeler Large Print Bks.) Beeler, Thomas T. Publisher.
—Giving up the Ghost. l.t. ed. 2001. (Beeler Large Print Mystery Ser.). 188p. 25.95 (*1-57490-350-0*, Beeler Large Print Bks.) Beeler, Thomas T. Publisher.
—Giving up the Ghost: A Sam & Hollis Mystery. 1999. (Sam & Hollis Mystery Ser.). 256p. mass mkt. 5.99 o.s.i (*0-440-22575-2*) Dell Publishing.
Charbonneau, Eileen. Waltzing in Ragtime. 1997. 399p. mass mkt. 6.99 (*0-8125-4468-4*); 1996. 480p. 26.95 o.p. (*0-312-86180-X*) Doherty, Tom Assocs., LLC. (Forge Bks.).
Chase, Elaine Raco. Double Occupancy. 1982. (Candlelight Regency Romance Ser.: No. 56). pap. 2.25 o.p. (*0-440-11732-1*) Dell Publishing.
—Double Occupancy. l.t. ed. 2002. 244p. 27.95 (*0-7862-4034-2*) Gale Group.
Cherrington, John. Vancouver at the Dawn. 1997. (Illus.). 208p. pap. (*1-55017-157-7*) Harbour Publishing Co., Ltd.
Claire, Edie. Never Preach Past Noon. 2000. (Leigh Koslow Mysteries Ser.). 272p. mass mkt. 5.99 (*0-451-20144-2*, Signet Bks.) NAL.
—Never Preach Past Noon: A Leigh Koslow Mystery. l.t. ed. 2001. (Thorndike Mystery Ser.). 392p. 28.95 (*0-7862-3177-7*) Thorndike Pr.
Clark, Mary Higgins. We'll Meet Again. 2000. E-Book 9.95 (*1-930161-67-0*) Adobe Systems, Inc.
—We'll Meet Again. 1999. E-Book 9.95 (*0-684-85767-7*, Simon & Schuster); 1999. 320p. 25.00 (*0-684-83597-5*, Simon & Schuster); 2005. 320p. pap. 12.00 (*0-7432-6133-X*, Simon & Schuster); 1999. 480p. 25.00 (*0-684-86211-5*, Simon & Schuster); 2000. (Illus.). 384p. reprint ed. mass mkt. 7.99 (*0-671-00456-5*, Pocket) Simon & Schuster.
—We'll Meet Again. 2000. 14.04 (*0-606-17764-7*) Turtleback Bks.
Clark, Mary Jane. Close to You. 2001. 336p. 24.95 (*0-312-26266-3*) St. Martin's Pr.
—Do You Want to Know a Secret? 1999. 320p. mass mkt. 6.99 (*0-312-96924-4*, St. Martin's Paperbacks); 1998. 304p. 23.95 o.p. (*0-312-19260-6*) St. Martin's Pr.
—Do You Want to Know a Secret? l.t. ed. 1999. (Core Ser.). 400p. 29.95 (*0-7838-8530-X*) Thorndike Pr.
—Let Me Whisper in Your Ear. l.t. ed. 2000. (G. K. Hall Core Ser.). 347p. 31.95 (*0-7838-9284-5*, Macmillan Reference USA) Gale Group.
—Let Me Whisper in Your Ear. E-Book 22.95 (*0-312-27611-7*); 2000. 304p. 23.95 o.p. (*0-312-26191-8*); 2001. 336p. reprint ed. mass mkt. 6.99 (*0-312-97743-3*, St. Martin's Paperbacks) St. Martin's Pr.
Clarke, Hope C. Best Seller. 2003. 15.00 (*1-929279-02-7*) A New Hope Publishing.
Coleman, Evelyn. What a Woman's Gotta Do. 1999. 400p. mass mkt. 6.99 (*0-440-23500-6*) Dell Publishing.
—What a Woman's Gotta Do. 1998. 320p. 23.00 (*0-684-83175-9*, Simon & Schuster) Simon & Schuster.
Coleridge, Nicholas. With Friends Like These. 1997. 384p. 24.95 (*0-312-17066-1*) St. Martin's Pr.
Collins, Jackie. Lethal Seduction. 2003. E-Book 26.00 (*0-7432-1112-X*); 2000. 480p. 26.00 (*0-684-85031-1*) Simon & Schuster. (Simon & Schuster).
—Lethal Seduction. l.t. ed. 2001. 720p. 32.50 o.p. (*0-7432-0425-5*) Thorpe, F. A. Pubs. GBR. *Dist:* Ulverscroft Large Print Bks., Ltd.
Conant, Susan. Animal Appetite: A Dog Lover's Mystery. 1998. (Dog Lover's Mysteries Ser.). 304p. reprint ed. mass mkt. 5.99 o.s.i (*0-553-57186-9*, Crimeline) Bantam Bks.
—Animal Appetite: A Dog Lover's Mystery. 1997. 288p. 21.95 o.s.i (*0-385-47725-2*) Doubleday Publishing.
—The Barker Street Regulars: A Dog Lover's Mystery. 1999. (Dog Lover's Mysteries Ser.). 288p. mass mkt. 6.99 (*0-553-57655-0*) Bantam Bks.
—The Barker Street Regulars: A Dog Lover's Mystery. l.t. ed. 1998. (Large Print Book Ser.). pap. 23.95 (*1-56895-609-6*, Wheeler Publishing, Inc.) Gale Group.
—Bite of Death. 1991. 4.50 (*1-55773-490-9*) Ace Bks.
—Bite of Death. 1994. mass mkt. 5.99 o.s.i (*0-425-14542-5*) Berkley Publishing Group.
—Black Ribbon: A Dog Lover's Mystery. 1995. (Dog Lover's Mysteries Ser.). 288p. reprint ed. mass mkt. 5.99 o.s.i (*0-553-29875-5*, Crimeline) Bantam Bks.
—Bloodlines. 1993. (Dog Lover's Mysteries Ser.). 272p. mass mkt. 5.99 (*0-553-29886-0*) Bantam Bks.
—Creature Discomforts. 2001. (Dog Lover's Mysteries Ser.). 224p. mass mkt. 6.99 (*0-553-58059-0*, Spectra) Bantam Bks.
—Creature Discomforts: A Dog Lover's Mystery. l.t. ed. 2001. (Beeler Large Print Mystery Ser.). 228p. 25.95 (*1-57490-360-8*, Beeler Large Print Bks.) Beeler, Thomas T. Publisher.
—Creature Discomforts: A Dog Lover's Mystery. 2000. 256p. 22.95 o.s.i (*0-385-49446-7*) Doubleday Publishing.
—Dead & Doggone. 2003. (Mystery Ser.). 27.95 (*1-57490-466-3*) Beeler, Thomas T. Publisher.
—Dead & Doggone. 1990. mass mkt. 5.99 o.s.i (*0-425-14429-1*, Prime Crime) Berkley Publishing Group.
—Evil Breeding. 2000. (Dog Lover's Mysteries Ser.). 224p. reprint ed. mass mkt. 6.99 (*0-553-58052-3*) Bantam Bks.
—Gone to the Dogs: A Dog Lover's Mystery. 1992. (Dog Lover's Mysteries Ser.). 272p. mass mkt. 5.99 (*0-553-29734-1*) Bantam Bks.
—Gone to the Dogs: A Dog Lover's Mystery. l.t. ed. 2003. (Mystery Ser.). 27.95 (*1-57490-488-4*, Beeler Large Print Bks.) Beeler, Thomas T. Publisher.
—Gone to the Dogs: A Dog Lover's Mystery. 1992. 224p. 16.50 o.s.i (*0-385-42378-0*) Doubleday Publishing.
—New Leash on Death. 1990. 4.50 (*1-55773-385-6*) Berkley Publishing Group.
—A New Leash on Death. 1994. 192p. mass mkt. 5.99 (*0-425-14622-7*) Berkley Publishing Group.
—Paws Before Dying. 1991. 4.50 (*1-55773-550-6*) Ace Bks.
—Paws Before Dying. 1991. mass mkt. 5.99 o.s.i (*0-425-14430-5*) Berkley Publishing Group.
—Ruffly Speaking: A Dog Lover's Mystery. 1994. (Dog Lover's Mysteries Ser.). 304p. mass mkt. 6.99 (*0-553-29484-9*) Bantam Bks.
—Stud Rites: A Dog Lover's Mystery. 1997. (Dog Lover's Mysteries Ser.). 272p. mass mkt. 5.99 o.s.i (*0-553-57300-4*, Crimeline) Bantam Bks.
Cook, Ann Turner. Shadow over Cedar Key: A Brandy O'Bannon Mystery. 2003. 258p. pap. 16.95 (*0-595-27843-4*) iUniverse, Inc.
Daheim, Mary R. The Alpine Advocate. 1992. (Emma Lord Mysteries Ser.). 240p. mass mkt. 6.99 (*0-345-37672-2*) Ballantine Bks.
—The Alpine Betrayal. 1993. (Emma Lord Mysteries Ser.). 240p. mass mkt. 6.99 (*0-345-37937-3*) Ballantine Bks.
—The Alpine Christmas. 1993. (Emma Lord Mysteries Ser.). 272p. mass mkt. 6.99 (*0-345-38270-6*) Ballantine Bks.
—The Alpine Decoy. 1994. (Emma Lord Mysteries Ser.). 256p. mass mkt. 6.99 (*0-345-38841-0*) Ballantine Bks.
—The Alpine Escape. 1995. (Emma Lord Mysteries Ser.). 288p. (Orig.). mass mkt. 6.99 (*0-345-38842-9*) Ballantine Bks.
—The Alpine Fury. 1995. 320p. (Orig.). mass mkt. 6.99 (*0-345-38843-7*) Ballantine Bks.
—The Alpine Gamble. 1996. (Emma Lord Mysteries Ser.). 304p. mass mkt. 6.99 (*0-345-39641-3*) Ballantine Bks.
—The Alpine Gamble. l.t. ed. 1999. (Beeler Large Print Mystery Ser.). (*1-57490-210-5*, Beeler Large Print Bks.) Beeler, Thomas T. Publisher.
—The Alpine Hero. 1996. (Emma Lord Mysteries Ser.). 320p. mass mkt. 6.99 (*0-345-39642-1*) Ballantine Bks.
—The Alpine Hero. l.t. ed. 1999. (Beeler Large Print Mystery Ser.). 25.95 (*1-57490-203-2*, Beeler Large Print Bks.) Beeler, Thomas T. Publisher.
—The Alpine Icon. 1997. (Emma Lord Mysteries Ser.). 336p. mass mkt. 6.99 (*0-345-39643-X*) Ballantine Bks.
—The Alpine Icon. l.t. ed. 1998. 353p. 24.95 (*1-57490-138-9*, Beeler Large Print Bks.) Beeler, Thomas T. Publisher.
—The Alpine Journey. 1998. (Emma Lord Mysteries Ser.). 320p. mass mkt. 6.99 (*0-345-39644-8*) Ballantine Bks.
—The Alpine Kindred. l.t. ed. 2004. 448p. 25.95 (*0-375-43253-1*) Random Hse. Large Print.
—The Alpine Kindred: An Emma Lord Mystery. 1998. (Emma Lord Mysteries Ser.). 320p. mass mkt. 6.99 (*0-345-42122-1*) Ballantine Bks.
—The Alpine Legacy. 1999. (Emma Lord Mysteries Ser.). 320p. mass mkt. 6.99 (*0-345-42123-X*, Ballantine Bks.) Ballantine Bks.
—The Alpine Nemesis. 2001. (Emma Lord Mystery Ser.). 320p. mass mkt. 6.99 (*0-345-42125-6*) Ballantine Bks.
D'Amato, Barbara. Hard Bargain: A Cat Marsala Mystery. 1999. (Cat Marsala Ser.). 288p. mass mkt. 5.99 o.s.i (*0-425-16898-0*) Berkley Publishing Group.
—Hard Bargain: A Cat Marsala Mystery. 1997. (Illus.). 288p. 21.00 o.s.i (*0-684-83353-0*, Scribner) Simon & Schuster.
—Hard Case: A Cat Marsala Mystery. 1995. 240p. mass mkt. 4.99 o.s.i (*0-425-15009-7*, Prime Crime) Berkley Publishing Group.
—Hard Case: A Cat Marsala Mystery. 1994. 288p. 20.00 o.p. (*0-684-19686-7*, Macmillan Reference USA) Gale Group.
—Hard Christmas: A Cat Marsala Mystery. 1996. 288p. mass mkt. 5.99 o.s.i (*0-425-15465-3*, Prime Crime) Berkley Publishing Group.
—Hard Christmas: A Cat Marsala Mystery. 1995. 288p. 20.00 (*0-684-19687-5*, Scribner) Simon & Schuster.
—Hard Evidence: A Cat Marsala Mystery. 2000. (Cat Marsala Mysteries Ser.). (Illus.). 255p. mass mkt. 6.50 o.s.i (*0-425-17412-3*, Prime Crime) Berkley Publishing Group.
—Hard Evidence: A Cat Marsala Mystery. l.t. ed. 2000. (Wheeler Large Print Bks.). (Illus.). 247p. pap. 23.95 (*1-56895-861-7*, Wheeler Publishing, Inc.) Gale Group.
—Hard Luck: A Cat Marsala Mystery. 1992. 224p. text 20.00 (*0-684-19408-2*, Macmillan Reference USA) Gale Group.
—Hard Luck: A Cat Marsala Mystery. 1993. (Mystery Ser.). per. (*0-373-26124-1*, 1-26124-7, Harlequin Bks.) Harlequin Enterprises, Ltd.
—Hard Tack: A Cat Marsala Mystery. 1991. 224p. 18.95 o.s.i (*0-684-19299-3*, Macmillan Reference USA) Gale Group.
—Hard Tack: A Cat Marsala Mystery. 1992. (WWL Mystery Ser.: No. 97). per. (*0-373-26097-0*, 1-26097-5, Harlequin Bks.) Harlequin Enterprises, Ltd.
—Hard Women: A Cat Marsala Mystery. 1993. 256p. 20.00 o.p. (*0-684-19564-X*, Macmillan Reference USA) Gale Group.
—Hard Women: A Cat Marsala Mystery. 1994. per. (*0-373-26150-0*, 1-26150-2, Harlequin Bks.) Harlequin Enterprises, Ltd.
—Hardball. 2003. 224p. pap. 13.00 (*1-932325-01-8*) Crum Creek Pr.
—Hardball. 1990. 224p. 17.95 o.s.i (*0-684-19140-7*, Macmillan Reference USA) Gale Group.
—Hardball. 1993. (Illus.). per. (*0-373-83302-4*, 1-83302-9); 1991. mass mkt. (*0-373-26066-0*) Harlequin Enterprises, Ltd. (Harlequin Bks.).
Daniel, David. White Rabbit: A Mystery. 2003. 368p. 25.95 (*0-312-30429-3*, Saint Martin's Minotaur) St. Martin's Pr.
Danks, Denise. Baby Love. 2003. 245p. pap. (*0-575-06843-4*); 256p. mass mkt. (*0-7528-4803-8*) Orion Publishing Group, Ltd. GBR. *Dist:* Trafalgar Square.
—Better off Dead. 2002. 184p. pap. 7.95 (*0-7528-4379-6*) Trafalgar Square.
—Fame Grabber. 2003. 192p. mass mkt. 7.95 (*0-7528-4398-2*) Orion Publishing Group, Ltd. GBR. *Dist:* Trafalgar Square.
—Fame Grabber. 1992. 187p. 16.95 o.p. (*0-312-08786-1*, Saint Martin's Minotaur) St. Martin's Pr.
—Phreak. 2002. 240p. pap. 7.95 (*0-7528-4377-X*) Trafalgar Square.
—The Pizza House Crash. 2002. 260p. pap. 7.95 (*0-7528-4378-8*) Trafalgar Square.
—Wink a Hopeful Eye. 2003. 224p. mass mkt. 7.95 (*0-7528-4397-4*) Orion Publishing Group, Ltd. GBR. *Dist:* Trafalgar Square.
—Wink a Hopeful Eye. 1994. 224p. 19.95 o.p. (*0-312-11355-2*, Saint Martin's Minotaur) St. Martin's Pr.
Davidson, Sara. Cowboy: A Love Story. l.t. ed. 1999. 26.95 (*1-56895-758-0*, Wheeler Publishing, Inc.) Gale Group.
—Cowboy: A Love Story. 288p. 2000. pap. 13.00 (*0-06-093135-3*, Perennial); 1999. 24.00 (*0-06-099582-3*, HarperCollins); 1999. 24.00 o.p. (*0-06-019326-3*, HarperCollins) HarperTrade.
Davis, Jill A. Girls' Poker Night. 2002. 240p. 23.95 o.s.i (*0-375-50514-8*); E-Book 19.00 (*1-58836-225-6*) Random Hse., Inc.
Delinsky, Barbara. Shades of Grace. l.t. ed. 1996. 535p. 25.95 o.p. (*0-7838-1642-1*, Macmillan Reference USA) Gale Group.
—Shades of Grace. 1995. 368p. 22.00 o.p. (*0-06-017781-0*) HarperCollins Pubs.
—Shades of Grace. 1997. 464p. mass mkt. 6.99 (*0-06-109282-7*, HarperTorch) Morrow/Avon.

Occupations

Dempsey, Diana. Falling Star. 2002. 416p. (Orig.). mass mkt. 6.99 (*0-451-41035-1*, Onyx) NAL.

DesErmia, Helen. Shadow People: A Novel. 1995. 10.99 o.p. (*0-7852-7920-2*); o.p. (*0-7852-4956-7*) Nelson, Thomas Inc.

Didion, Joan. The Last Thing He Wanted. 1997. 240p. pap. 12.00 (*0-679-75285-4*, Vintage) Knopf Publishing Group.

—The Last Thing He Wanted. 1996. 227p. 23.00 o.s.i (*0-679-43331-7*) Knopf, Alfred A. Inc.

Doss, James D. The Shaman Sings. 1994. 272p. 3000.00 o.p. (*0-312-10547-9*, Saint Martin's Minotaur) St. Martin's Pr.

—Shaman Sings. 1995. (Shaman Mysteries Ser.). 256p. mass mkt. 6.99 (*0-380-72496-0*, Avon Bks.) Morrow/Avon.

Doughty, Louise. An English Murder. 2000. 240p. 23.00 (*0-7867-0757-7*, Carroll & Graf Pubs.) Avalon Publishing Group.

—An English Murder. 2001. 240p. reprint ed. mass mkt. 6.50 (*0-440-23687-8*) Dell Publishing.

—An English Murder: A Mystery. l.t. ed. 2000. (Mystery Ser.). 269p. 26.95 (*0-7862-2836-9*) Thorndike Pr.

Drury, Joan M. Closed in Silence. 1998. (Tyler Jones Feminist Mystery Ser.: No. 3). 224p. pap. 10.95 (*1-883523-29-X*) Spinsters Ink Bks.

—The Other Side of Silence. 1993. 256p. pap. 9.95 (*0-933216-92-0*) Spinsters Ink Bks.

—Silent Words. 1996. 224p. pap. 10.95 (*1-883523-13-3*) Spinsters Ink Bks.

Du Plessix Gray, Francine. Lovers & Tyrants. 1988. pap. 7.95 (*0-393-30547-3*) Norton, W. W. & Co., Inc.

—Lovers & Tyrants. 1976. 8.95 o.s.i (*0-671-22338-0*, Simon & Schuster) Simon & Schuster.

Due, Tananarive. My Soul to Keep. 1997. 352p. 24.00 o.p. (*0-06-018742-5*) HarperCollins Pubs.

—My Soul to Keep. 1998. 352p. pap. 15.95 (*0-06-105366-X*, Eos) Morrow/Avon.

Dunn, Carol. The Case of the Murdered Muckaker. 2002. 256p. 23.95 (*0-312-27284-7*, Saint Martin's Minotaur) St. Martin's Pr.

Dunn, Carola. Damsel in Distress: A Daisy Dalrymple Mystery. 2002. (Daisy Dalrymple Mystery Ser.). 256p. mass mkt. 5.99 (*1-57566-754-1*, Kensington Bks.) Kensington Publishing Corp.

—Damsel in Distress: A Daisy Dalrymple Mystery. 1997. (Daisy Dalrymple Mysteries Ser.). 234p. 21.95 o.p. (*0-312-16806-3*, Saint Martin's Minotaur) St. Martin's Pr.

—Dead in the Water. 2002. 256p. mass mkt. 5.99 (*1-57566-756-8*, Kensington Bks.) Kensington Publishing Corp.

—Dead in the Water. 1998. (Daisy Dalrymple Mysteries Ser.). 256p. 22.95 o.p. (*0-312-19181-2*, Saint Martin's Minotaur) St. Martin's Pr.

—Death at Wentwater Court. 2000. (Daisy Dalrymple Mysteries Ser.). (Illus.). 256p. (J). mass mkt. 5.99 (*1-57566-750-9*) Kensington Publishing Corp.

—Death at Wentwater Court. 1994. 240p. 19.95 o.p. (*0-312-11030-8*, Saint Martin's Minotaur) St. Martin's Pr.

—Murder on the Flying Scotsman. 1996. (Daisy Dalrymple Mysteries Ser.). 240p. 21.95 (*0-312-15175-6*, Saint Martin's Minotaur) St. Martin's Pr.

—Rattle His Bones: A Daisy Dalrymple Mystery. 2003. 256p. mass mkt. 5.99 (*0-7582-0168-0*) Kensington Publishing Corp.

—Rattle His Bones: A Daisy Dalrymple Mystery. 2000. (Daisy Dalrymple Mysteries Ser.). (Illus.). 243p. 22.95 (*0-312-20572-4*, Saint Martin's Minotaur) St. Martin's Pr.

—Rattle His Bones: A Daisy Dalrymple Mystery. l.t. ed. 2000. (Mystery Ser.). (Illus.). 355p. 26.95 (*0-7862-2913-6*) Thorndike Pr.

—Requiem for a Mezzo. 2001. 256p. mass mkt. 5.99 (*1-57566-752-5*, Kensington Bks.) Kensington Publishing Corp.

—Requiem for a Mezzo: A Daisy Dalrymple Mystery. 1996. (Daisy Dalrymple Mysteries Ser.). 240p. 20.95 (*0-312-14036-3*, Saint Martin's Minotaur) St. Martin's Pr.

—Requiem for a Mezzo: A Daisy Dalrymple Mystery. l.t. ed. 1996. 285p. pap. 23.95 (*0-7838-1857-2*) Thorndike Pr.

—Styx & Stones: A Daisy Dalrymple Mystery. 2nd ed. 1999. (Daisy Dalrymple Mysteries Ser.). 240p. 22.95 (*0-312-20592-9*, Saint Martin's Minotaur) St. Martin's Pr.

—To Davy Jones Below: A Daisy Dalrymple Mystery. 2003. mass mkt. 5.99 (*0-7582-0169-9*) Kensington Publishing Corp.

—To Davy Jones Below: A Daisy Dalrymple Mystery. 2001. (Daisy Dalrymple Mysteries Ser.). 256p. 22.95 (*0-312-26669-3*, Saint Martin's Minotaur) St. Martin's Pr.

—The Winter Garden Mystery. l.t. ed. 1995. 326p. 23.95 o.p. (*0-7838-1487-9*, Macmillan Reference USA) Gale Group.

—The Winter Garden Mystery. 2001. (Daisy Dalrymple Mysteries Ser.). 256p. mass mkt. 5.99 (*1-57566-751-7*, Kensington Bks.) Kensington Publishing Corp.

—The Winter Garden Mystery. 1995. (Daisy Dalrymple Mysteries Ser.). 224p. 21.95 o.p. (*0-312-13217-4*, Saint Martin's Minotaur) St. Martin's Pr.

Eagle, Kathleen. You Never Can Tell. l.t. ed. 2001. 400p. 25.00 o.p. (*0-06-620960-9*) HarperCollins Pubs.

—You Never Can Tell. 2002. 384p. mass mkt. 6.99 (*0-380-81015-8*); 2001. 320p. 24.00 (*0-380-97816-4*) Morrow/Avon. (Morrow, William & Co.).

Edwards, Louis. N: A Romantic Mystery. 240p. 1998. pap. 12.95 o.s.i (*0-452-27788-4*, Plume); 1997. 22.95 o.p. (*0-525-94182-7*) Dutton/Plume.

Ellis, Alice Thomas. Unexplained Laughter. 2002. pap. 15.95 (*1-888173-53-X*) Akadine Pr., The.

—Unexplained Laughter. 1987. 160p. 14.95 o.p. (*0-06-015722-4*) HarperTrade.

Elm, Joanna. Delusion. 1999. 374p. mass mkt. 6.99 (*0-8125-6480-4*, Tor Bks.); 1997. 384p. 23.95 (*0-312-86064-1*, Forge Bks.) Doherty, Tom Assocs., LLC.

English, Brenda H. Corruption of Faith. 1997. 272p. mass mkt. 5.99 o.s.i (*0-425-16091-2*, Prime Crime) Berkley Publishing Group.

—Corruption of Justice. 1999. 272p. mass mkt. 5.99 o.s.i (*0-425-16811-5*, Prime Crime) Berkley Publishing Group.

—Corruption of Power. 1998. (Sutton McPhee Mystery Ser.). 288p. mass mkt. 5.99 o.s.i (*0-425-16398-9*, Prime Crime) Berkley Publishing Group.

Ephron, Delia. Big City Eyes. 2001. 256p. reprint ed. pap. 12.95 (*0-345-44345-4*, Ballantine Bks.) Ballantine Bks.

—Big City Eyes. 2000. 256p. 23.95 o.s.i (*0-399-14391-2*) Penguin Group (USA) Inc.

—Big City Eyes. l.t. ed. 2001. (Thorndike Americana Ser.). 339p. 30.95 (*0-7862-3175-0*) Thorndike Pr.

Evanovich, Janet. Full Speed. l.t. ed. 2003. 563p. pap. 14.95 (*0-375-43284-1*, Random House Large Print) Random Hse. Large Print.

Evanovich, Janet & Hughes, Charlotte. Full Speed. 2003. 352p. mass mkt. 7.99 (*0-312-98329-8*, St. Martin's Paperbacks) St. Martin's Pr.

Fast, Howard. An Independent Woman. 1997. 340p. 25.00 (*0-15-100271-1*) Harcourt Trade Pubs.

Feldman, Ellen. Rearview Mirror. 1996. 384p. mass mkt. 5.99 o.s.i (*0-440-21516-1*) Dell Publishing.

Fell, Doris Elaine. Always in September. 1993. (Seasons of Intrigue Ser.: Vol. 1). 288p. pap. 9.99 o.p. (*0-89107-760-X*) Crossway Bks.

Ferrars, E. X. Answer Came There None. l.t. ed. 1994. (Magna Large Print Ser.). 300p. o.p. (*0-7505-0685-7*) Magna Large Print Bks. GBR. *Dist:* Ulverscroft Large Print Canada, Ltd.

Fielding, Liz. His Desert Rose. 2000. (Harlequin Romance Ser.: Vol. 3618). mass mkt. (*0-373-03618-3*, 1-03618-5); (Harlequin Large Print Ser.: Vol. 464). mass mkt. (*0-373-15864-5*) Harlequin Enterprises, Ltd. (Harlequin Bks.).

Fletcher, Jessica & Bain, Donald. Murder in a Minor Key: A Murder, She Wrote Mystery. l.t. ed. 2003. 366p. pap. 24.45 (*0-7862-5357-6*) Thorndike Pr.

Flock, Elizabeth. But Inside I'm Screaming. 2003. 320p. pap. (*1-55166-727-4*, Mira Bks.) Harlequin Enterprises, Ltd.

Forbes, Leslie. Bombay Ice. 1999. 416p. reprint ed. pap. 13.95 (*0-553-38047-8*) Bantam Bks.

—Bombay Ice. unabr. ed. 1998. audio 76.95 (*0-7861-1430-4*, 2316) Blackstone Audio Bks., Inc.

—Bombay Ice. 1998. (*0-374-90777-3*); 400p. 24.00 o.p. (*0-374-11530-3*) Farrar, Straus & Giroux.

—Bombay Ice. abr. ed. 1998. 3p. audio 17.95 (*1-55935-277-9*) Soundelux Audio Publishing.

—Bombay Ice. (GER.). pap. (*3-548-24703-2*) Ullstein-Taschenbuch-Verlag DEU. *Dist:* International Bk. Import Service, Inc.

Foster, B. J. Bayou Shadows. 2000. 267p. 21.95 (*0-9675884-5-6*) Cresent Hse. Publishing.

Fox, Kathryn. The Seduction. 2002. 34p. mass mkt. 5.99 o.s.i (*0-8217-7243-0*) Kensington Publishing Corp.

Frome, Shelly. Lilac Moon: A Mystery! Gosline, Sheldon, ed. l.t. ed. 2003. (Illus.). 343p. text 22.95 (*0-9719496-5-4*) Shangri-La Pubns.

Galgoczi, Erzsebet. Another Love. Rieder, Ines & Newman, Felice, trs. from GER. 1991. 160p. 24.95 o.p. (*0-939416-52-2*); pap. 8.95 o.p. (*0-939416-51-4*) Cleis Pr.

Garland, Ardella. Details at Ten. E-Book 21.00 (*1-58945-169-4*) Adobe Systems, Inc.

—Details at Ten: A Georgia Barnett Mystery. 2000. 208p. 21.00 o.s.i (*0-684-87375-3*, Simon & Schuster) Simon & Schuster.

Garrett, Annie. Angel Flying Too Close to the Ground. l.t. ed. 1996. (Large Print Bks.). pap. 22.95 (*1-56895-382-8*, Wheeler Publishing, Inc.) Gale Group.

—Angel Flying Too Close to the Ground. 1997. 208p. mass mkt. 5.99 (*0-312-96012-3*, St. Martin's Paperbacks) St. Martin's Pr.

—Angel Flying Too Close to the Ground: A Love Story. 1996. 192p. 17.95 o.p. (*0-312-13920-9*) St. Martin's Pr.

—Because I Wanted You. l.t. ed. 1997. lib. bdg. 21.95 (*1-57490-105-2*, Beeler Large Print Bks.) Beeler, Thomas T. Publisher.

—Because I Wanted You. 1998. (Because I Wanted You Ser.: Vol. 1). 240p. pap. 5.99 (*0-312-96659-8*, St. Martin's Paperbacks); 1997. 226p. 18.95 (*0-312-15427-5*); 1997. 18.95 (*0-312-15473-9*) St. Martin's Pr.

Gilchrist, Ellen. Sarah Conley: A Novel. 1997. 272p. (gr. 8). 23.95 o.p. (*0-316-31477-3*) Little Brown & Co.

Gitlin, Todd. The Murder of Albert Einstein. 1994. 352p. pap. 8.95 o.s.i (*0-553-37366-8*) Bantam Bks.

—The Murder of Albert Einstein. 1992. 25.00 o.p. (*0-374-21617-7*) Farrar, Straus & Giroux.

Glen, Alison. Showcase: A Charlotte Sams Mystery. 1992. 206p. 19.00 o.s.i (*0-671-74573-5*, Simon & Schuster) Simon & Schuster.

—Trunk Show. 1995. 238p. 20.00 (*0-671-79115-X*, Simon & Schuster) Simon & Schuster.

Goldstein, Lisa. Dark Cities Underground. 2000. 252p. pap. 13.95 (*0-312-86827-8*); 2nd ed. 1999. 256p. 22.95 (*0-312-86828-6*) Doherty, Tom Assocs., LLC. (Tor Bks.).

Grant-Adamson, Lesley. Curse the Darkness. 1990. 19.95 o.p. (*0-312-04291-4*, Saint Martin's Minotaur) St. Martin's Pr.

—Death on Widow's Walk. 1985. 224p. 13.95 o.p. (*0-684-18318-8*, Macmillan Reference USA) Gale Group.

—The Face of Death. 1987. 288p. mass mkt. 2.95 o.s.i (*0-449-21210-6*, Fawcett) Ballantine Bks.

—The Face of Death. 1986. 304p. 14.95 o.s.i (*0-684-18588-1*, Macmillan Reference USA) Gale Group.

—The Face of Death. l.t. ed. 1987. (Ulverscroft Large Print Ser.). 560p. 29.99 o.p. (*0-7089-1684-8*, Ulverscroft) Thorpe, F. A. Pubs. GBR. *Dist:* Ulverscroft Large Print Bks., Ltd., Ulverscroft Large Print Canada, Ltd.

—The Face of Death, Set. 1987. audio 54.95 o.p. (*1-85496-106-3*, US0127) Ulverscroft Audio (U.S.A.).

—Guilty Knowledge. 1988. 272p. 16.95 o.p. (*0-312-01438-4*, Saint Martin's Minotaur) St. Martin's Pr.

—Wild Justice. 1988. 224p. 14.95 o.p. (*0-312-01845-2*, Saint Martin's Minotaur) St. Martin's Pr.

Gray, Etha. Sweet Daddy Red. Gray, Etha & Farley, Carrie, eds. 2003. 114p. pap. 14.95 (*1-879940-13-2*) Concepts 'N' Publishing.

Gray, Francine D. Lovers & Tyrants. 1977. (gr. 10 up). pap. 2.25 o.p. (*0-671-82446-5*, Pocket) Simon & Schuster.

Gray, Francine du Plessix. Lovers & Tyrants. 1982. 320p. 3.50 (*0-86721-126-1*) Berkley Publishing Group.

Groom, Winston. Such a Pretty, Pretty Girl. l.t. ed. 1999. 30.00 o.p. (*0-7838-8485-0*, Macmillan Reference USA) Gale Group.

—Such a Pretty, Pretty Girl. abr. ed. 1999. audio 24.00 o.s.i (*0-375-40588-7*, 494172, RH Audio) Random Hse. Audio Publishing Group.

Gross, Ken. A High Pressure System. 1993. 320p. 20.95 o.p. (*0-312-85444-7*, Forge Bks.) Doherty, Tom Assocs., LLC.

Haddock, Lisa. Edited Out. 1994. (Carmen Ramirez Mystery Ser.: Vol. 1). 224p. pap. 9.95 (*1-56280-077-9*) Naiad Pr., Inc.

—Final Cut. 1995. (Carmen Ramirez Mystery Ser.: Vol. 2). 224p. pap. 10.95 o.p. (*1-56280-088-4*) Naiad Pr., Inc.

Hall, Patricia. The Dead of Winter. 1996. (Yorkshire Mystery Ser.). 21.95 o.p. (*0-312-15148-9*, Saint Martin's Minotaur) St. Martin's Pr.

—Dead on Arrival. l.t. ed. 2000. (Dales Large Print Ser.). 400p. pap. (*1-84262-012-6*) Dales Large Print Bks. GBR. *Dist:* Ulverscroft Large Print Canada, Ltd.

—Dead on Arrival. 2001. (Yorkshire Mystery Ser.). 224p. 22.95 (*0-312-26572-7*, Saint Martin's Minotaur) St. Martin's Pr.

—Death by Election. l.t. ed. 1994. (Dales Large Print Ser.). 418p. pap. o.p. (*1-85389-519-9*) Dales Large Print Bks. GBR. *Dist:* Ulverscroft Large Print Canada, Ltd.

—Death by Election. 1994. (Yorkshire Mystery Ser.). 256p. 20.95 o.p. (*0-312-11461-3*, Saint Martin's Minotaur) St. Martin's Pr.

—Deep Freeze. l.t. ed. 2002. (Magna Large Print Ser.). 416p. (*0-7505-1880-4*) Magna Large Print Bks. GBR. *Dist:* Ulverscroft Large Print Canada, Ltd.

—Deep Freeze: A Yorkshire Mystery. 2003. (Yorkshire Mystery Ser.). 272p. 23.95 (*0-312-28212-5*, Saint Martin's Minotaur) St. Martin's Pr.

—Dying Fall. l.t. ed. 1995. (Dales Large Print Ser.). 432p. pap. o.p. (*1-85389-561-X*) Dales Large Print Bks. GBR. *Dist:* Ulverscroft Large Print Canada, Ltd.

—Dying Fall. 1996. 248p. mass mkt. o.s.i (*0-7515-1204-4*) Little Brown & Co.

—Dying Fall. 1995. (Yorkshire Mystery Ser.). 248p. 21.95 o.p. (*0-312-13477-0*, Saint Martin's Minotaur) St. Martin's Pr.

—In the Bleak Midwinter. 1997. 250p. mass mkt. o.s.i (*0-7515-1712-7*); 1995. 256p. o.s.i (*0-316-91279-4*) Little Brown & Co.

—The Italian Girl. 2000. 208p. 21.95 (*0-312-26489-5*, Saint Martin's Minotaur) St. Martin's Pr.

—Perils of the Night. 1998. (Yorkshire Mystery Ser.). 224p. 22.95 (*0-312-19996-1*, Saint Martin's Minotaur) St. Martin's Pr.

Hamilton, Denise. The Jasmine Trade: A Novel of Suspense Introducing Eve Diamond. 2001. 288p. 24.00 (*0-7432-1269-X*); E-Book 9.99 (*0-7432-1477-3*) Simon & Schuster. (Scribner).

—Sugar Skull: An Eve Diamond Novel. 2004. (Illus.). 400p. mass mkt. 6.99 (*0-7434-8221-2*, Pocket Star); 2003. 304p. 25.00 (*0-7432-4539-3*, Scribner); 2003. 304p. 25.00 (*0-7432-4784-1*, Scribner) Simon & Schuster.

Handberg, Ron. Cry Vengeance. 1995. 464p. mass mkt. 6.50 o.s.i (*0-06-100840-0*, HarperTorch) Morrow/Avon.

Harayda, Janice. The Accidental Bride. 304p. 2000. pap. 13.95 (*0-312-26281-7*, Saint Martin's Griffin); 3rd ed. 1999. 22.95 o.p. (*0-312-20357-8*) St. Martin's Pr.

Harrod-Eagles, Cynthia. Blood Sinister. l.t. ed. 2001. (Magna Large Print Ser.). 384p. (*0-7505-1599-6*) Magna Large Print Bks. GBR. *Dist:* Ulverscroft Large Print Canada, Ltd.

—Blood Sinister. E-Book 23.95 (*0-312-70251-5*); 2001. 308p. 23.95 (*0-312-27485-8*, Saint Martin's Minotaur) St. Martin's Pr.

Hart, Carolyn G. Dead Man's Island. 1994. 352p. mass mkt. 6.99 (*0-553-56607-5*) Bantam Bks.

—Dead Man's Island. unabr. ed. 1997. (Henrie O Mysteries Ser.). audio 48.00 (*0-7366-3837-7*, 4557) Books on Tape, Inc.

—Dead Man's Island. l.t. ed. 1994. (G. K. Hall Mystery Ser.). 355p. lib. bdg. 23.95 o.p. (*0-8161-5874-6*, Macmillan Reference USA) Gale Group.

—Death in Lovers' Lane. unabr. ed. 1998. (Henrie O Mysteries Ser.). audio 48.00 (*0-7366-4168-8*, 4670) Books on Tape, Inc.

—Death in Lovers' Lane. l.t. ed. 1997. (Wheeler Large Print Book Ser.). 25.95 (*1-56895-467-0*, Wheeler Publishing, Inc.) Gale Group.

—Death in Lovers' Lane. 1997. 288p. mass mkt. 20.00 o.p. (*0-380-97413-4*); 1998. 320p. reprint ed. mass mkt. 6.50 (*0-380-79002-5*) Morrow/Avon. (Avon Bks.).

—Death in Paradise. unabr. ed. 1998. (Henrie O Mysteries Ser.). audio 48.00 (*0-7366-4263-3*, 4762) Books on Tape, Inc.

—Death in Paradise. 1999. 304p. mass mkt. 6.50 (*0-380-79003-3*); 1998. 288p. 20.00 (*0-380-97414-2*) Morrow/Avon. (Avon Bks.).

—Death in Paradise, Set. abr. ed. 1998. audio 18.00 (*0-7871-1704-8*, Dove Audio) NewStar Media, Inc.

—Death in Paradise. l.t. ed. 2000. (Mystery Ser.). 415p. 29.95 (*0-7862-2679-X*) Thorndike Pr.

—Death on the River Walk. l.t. ed. 2000. (Large Print Book Ser.). pap. 23.95 (*1-56895-822-6*, Wheeler Publishing, Inc.) Gale Group.

—Death on the River Walk. 2000. 336p. mass mkt. 6.99 (*0-380-79005-X*); 1999. 256p. 22.00 (*0-380-97415-0*) Morrow/Avon. (Avon Bks.).

—Letter from Home. 2003. 272p. 22.95 (*0-425-19179-6*, Prime Crime) Berkley Publishing Group.

—Resort to Murder. 2001. 304p. 24.00 (*0-380-97773-7*, Morrow, William & Co.) Morrow/Avon.

—Resort to Murder. l.t. ed. 2001. 456p. 29.95 (*0-7862-3490-3*) Thorndike Pr.

—Scandal in Fair Haven. 1995. 352p. mass mkt. 6.99 (*0-553-56537-0*) Bantam Bks.

—Scandal in Fair Haven. unabr. ed. 1998. (Henrie O Mysteries Ser.). audio 56.00 (*0-7366-4144-0*, 4648) Books on Tape, Inc.

—Scandal in Fair Haven. l.t. ed. 1994. 414p. lib. bdg. 20.95 o.p. (*0-8161-7406-7*, Macmillan Reference USA) Gale Group.

Hayter, Sparkle. The Chelsea Girl Murders. 2000. (Robin Hudson Mysteries Ser.). 240p. 23.00 (*0-688-15518-9*, Morrow, William & Co.) Morrow/Avon.

—The Last Manly Man. 1999. (Robin Hudson Mysteries Ser.). 256p. reprint ed. pap. 9.95 o.s.i (*0-688-16972-4*, Quill) HarperTrade.

—The Last Manly Man: A Robin Hudson Mystery. 1998. (Robin Hudson Mysteries Ser.). 256p. 22.00 (*0-688-15517-0*, Morrow, William & Co.) Morrow/Avon.

—Nice Girls Finish Last. 1997. (Viking Mystery Suspense Ser.). 256p. pap. 5.95 (*0-14-024516-2*) Penguin Group (USA) Inc.

—Nice Girls Finish Last: A Robin Hudson Mystery. 1996. (Robin Hudson Mystery Ser.). 256p. 20.95 o.p. (*0-670-86039-5*) Viking Penguin.

—What's a Girl Gotta Do? 1995. (Robin Hudson Mystery Ser.). 288p. pap. 6.99 (*0-14-024481-6*, Penguin Bks.) Penguin Group (USA) Inc.
—What's a Girl Gotta Do? 1994. 270p. 19.95 o.p. (*1-56947-000-6*) Soho Pr., Inc.
Hazo, Samuel J. Stills. 1989. 17.95 o.s.i (*0-689-12058-3*, Scribner) Simon & Schuster.
—Stills: A Novel. 1998. 192p. pap. 16.95 (*0-8156-0537-4*) Syracuse Univ. Pr.
Heidish, Marcy. Deadline. 1991. 16.95 o.p. (*0-312-06012-2*, Saint Martin's Minotaur) St. Martin's Pr.
Heller, Jean. Handyman. 1995. 316p. 23.95 o.p. (*0-312-85818-3*, Forge Bks.) Doherty, Tom Assocs., LLC.
Hicks, Barbara Jean. China Doll. l.t. ed. 1999. (Christian Fiction Ser.). 332p. 23.95 o.p. (*0-7862-2155-0*) Thorndike Pr.
Hicks, Barbara Jean, et al. China Doll. 1998. (Palisades Pure Romance Ser.). 266p. pap. 9.99 o.p. (*1-57673-262-2*, Palisades) Multnomah Pubs., Inc.
Hoag, Tami. Still Waters. 1992. 464p. mass mkt. 7.99 (*0-553-29272-2*) Bantam Bks.
Holmes, Rupert. Where the Truth Lies. 2003. 400p. 24.95 (*0-679-45220-6*); E-Book 17.50 (*1-58836-328-7*) Random Hse., Inc.
Howard, Linda. An Independent Wife. abr. ed. 1999. audio 7.99 (*1-55204-175-1*, MIR-1175) Durkin Hayes Publishing Ltd.
—An Independent Wife. (Mira Bks.). 1999. 248p. mass mkt. (*1-55166-500-X*, Harlequin Bks.); 1994. mass mkt. (*0-373-48293-0*, 5-48293-0, Mira Bks.); 1987. pap. (*0-373-04604-9*, Harlequin Bks.) Harlequin Enterprises, Ltd.
—An Independent Wife. l.t. ed. 2000. (Basic Ser.). 282p. 28.95 (*0-7862-2606-4*) Thorndike Pr.
Howard, Tracie. Why Sleeping Dogs Lie. 2003. 288p. pap. 12.95 (*0-451-20977-X*) NAL.
Huges, Charlotte. Valley of the Shadow. 1998. mass mkt. 5.99 (*0-380-78454-8*, Avon Bks.) Morrow/Avon.
Hunt, David, pseud. The Magician's Tale. 1998. 416p. reprint ed. mass mkt. 7.50 o.s.i (*0-425-16482-9*) Berkley Publishing Group.
—The Magician's Tale. 1997. 416p. 24.95 o.s.i (*0-399-14260-6*, G. P. Putnam's Sons) Penguin Group (USA) Inc.
—Trick of Light. 1999. 416p. reprint ed. mass mkt. 7.50 o.s.i (*0-425-17035-7*) Berkley Publishing Group.
—Trick of Light. 1998. 400p. 24.95 o.p. (*0-399-14393-9*, G. P. Putnam's Sons) Penguin Group (USA) Inc.
Hyde, Bill. Bodie Gone: A Novel of Suspense. 2001. (First Fiction Ser.). 256p. 26.95 (*0-86534-317-9*) Sunstone Pr.
Hyde, Eleanor. Animal Instincts. 1996. 230p. mass mkt. 5.50 o.s.i (*0-449-14941-2*, Fawcett) Ballantine Bks.
—In Murder We Trust. 1995. mass mkt. 5.50 o.s.i (*0-449-14942-0*, Fawcett) Ballantine Bks.
Jacobs, Nancy Baker. Star Struck: A Quinn Collins Mystery. 2002. (Five Star First Edition Mystery Ser.). 327p. 25.95 (*0-7862-4171-3*, Five Star) Gale Group.
Jaffe, Jody. Chestnut Mare, Beware. 1997. mass mkt. 5.99 o.s.i (*0-8041-1552-4*, Ivy Bks.); 1996. 288p. 21.00 o.s.i (*0-449-90998-0*, Fawcett) Ballantine Bks.
—Chestnut Mare, Beware. unabr. collector's ed. 1997. audio 64.00 (*0-7366-3599-8*, 4250) Books on Tape, Inc.
—Horse of a Different Killer. 1996. mass mkt. 5.99 o.s.i (*0-8041-1472-2*, Ivy Bks.); 1995. 288p. 21.00 o.s.i (*0-449-90997-2*) Ballantine Bks.
—Horse of a Different Killer. unabr. collector's ed. 1997. audio 48.00 (*0-913369-53-5*, 4265) Books on Tape, Inc.
—In Colt Blood. 1999. mass mkt. 5.99 o.s.i (*0-8041-1711-X*, Ivy Bks.) Ballantine Bks.
—In Colt Blood. collector's ed. 1999. audio 56.00 (*0-7366-4787-2*, 5134) Books on Tape, Inc.
Johansen, Iris. And Then You Die. 1998. 352p. mass mkt. 7.50 (*0-553-57998-3*) Bantam Bks.
—And Then You Die. l.t. ed. 1998. (Romance Ser.). 448p. 28.95 (*0-7862-1310-8*) Thorndike Pr.
Jorgensen, Christine T. Dead on Her Feet. 1999. (Stella the Stargazer Mystery Ser.). 256p. 23.95 (*0-8027-3334-4*) Walker & Co.
Kadow, Jeannine. Burnout. 1999. 384p. 23.95 o.p. (*0-525-94464-8*) Dutton/Plume.
—Burnout. 2000. 432p. reprint ed. mass mkt. 6.99 o.s.i (*0-451-19823-9*) NAL.
Kallen, Lucille. C. B. Greenfield: No Lady in the House. 1984. 208p. mass mkt. 3.95 o.s.i (*0-345-32396-3*) Ballantine Bks.
—C. B. Greenfield: No Lady in the House. 1982. 12.95 o.p. (*0-671-43240-0*, Simon & Schuster) Simon & Schuster.
—C. B. Greenfield: No Lady in the House. l.t. ed. 1982. 374p. reprint ed. 10.95 o.p. (*0-89621-365-X*) Thorndike Pr.
—C. B. Greenfield: The Piano Bird. 1985. 224p. mass mkt. 3.95 o.s.i (*0-345-31118-3*, Ballantine Bks.) Ballantine Bks.
—C. B. Greenfield: The Piano Bird. 1984. 175p. 13.95 o.p. (*0-394-53081-0*) Random Hse., Inc.
—C. B. Greenfield: The Tanglewood Murder. 1985. mass mkt. 3.95 o.s.i (*0-345-33143-5*) Ballantine Bks.
—Introducing C. B. Greenfield. 1985. 208p. mass mkt. 3.95 o.s.i (*0-345-33426-4*); 1984. mass mkt. 2.50 o.p. (*0-345-32159-6*) Ballantine Bks.
—Introducing C. B. Greenfield. l.t. ed. 1980. 363p. reprint ed. 11.95 o.p. (*0-89621-260-2*) Thorndike Pr.
Kallmaker, Karin. Making Up for Lost Time. 1998. 288p. (Orig.). pap. 11.95 (*1-56280-196-1*) Naiad Pr., Inc.
Katz, William. Facemaker. 1988. 256p. text 16.95 o.p. (*0-07-033553-2*) McGraw-Hill Cos., The.
—Facemaker. 1989. 256p. mass mkt. 4.50 (*0-380-70685-7*, Avon Bks.) Morrow/Avon.
Keats, Jonathan. The Pathology of Lies. 1999. 288p. pap. 14.00 (*0-446-67445-1*) Warner Bks., Inc.
Kennett, Shirley. Burning Rose. 2003. 232p. pap. 13.95 (*1-4104-0106-5*, Five Star Trade); 2002. 228p. 24.95 (*0-7862-3661-2*, Five Star) Gale Group.
Knox-Mawer, June. The Shadow of Wings. 1997. 321p. 26.00 o.p. (*0-297-81567-9*) Weidenfeld & Nicolson, Ltd. GBR. *Dist:* Trafalgar Square.
Krich, Rochelle Majer. Dream House. 2003. 400p. 24.95 (*0-345-44972-X*, Ballantine Bks.) Ballantine Bks.
Landis, Catherine E. Some Days There's Pie. 2002. (Illus.). 304p. 23.95 (*0-312-28384-9*) St. Martin's Pr.
—Some Days There's Pie. l.t. ed. 2002. 28.95 (*0-7862-4598-0*) Thorndike Pr.
—Some Days There's Pie: A Novel. 2003. 304p. reprint ed. pap. 12.95 (*0-312-30929-5*, Saint Martin's Griffin) St. Martin's Pr.
Lange, Kelly. Dead File. 2003. 320p. 24.95 (*0-89296-751-X*) Mysterious Pr.
—Dead File. 2004. mass mkt. (*0-446-61387-8*) Warner Bks., Inc.
Larson, Ellen. The Hatch & Brood of Time. 1999. (NJ Mysteries Ser.: Vol. 1). 304p. pap. 14.95 (*0-9669877-0-5*) Savvy Pr.
Laurence, Janet. Death at the Table. l.t. ed. 1997. (Paperback Ser.). 360p. lib. bdg. 21.95 (*0-7838-8255-6*, Macmillan Reference USA) Gale Group.
—Death at the Table. 1999. (Mystery Ser.: Bk. 316). per. (*0-373-26316-3*, 1-26316-9, Worldwide Library) Harlequin Enterprises, Ltd.
—Death at the Table. l.t. ed. 1997. 224p. 20.95 o.p. (*0-312-15105-5*, Saint Martin's Minotaur) St. Martin's Pr.
Leland, Mary. Approaching Priests. 1992. 224p. 23.95 o.p. (*1-85619-065-X*) Trafalgar Square.
Lette, Kathy. Nip 'N' Tuck. 2004. 272p. pap. 13.00 (*0-7434-5687-4*, Washington Square Pr.) Simon & Schuster.
—Nip 'n' Tuck. 2001. xi, 255p. (*0-330-36288-7*) Picador.
Lewis, Fiona. Between Men: A Novel. 1995. 304p. 21.00 o.p. (*0-87113-586-8*, Atlantic Monthly Pr.) Grove/Atlantic, Inc.
Little, Benilde. Good Hair. 1996. 240p. 22.00 (*0-684-80176-0*, Simon & Schuster) Simon & Schuster.
—Good Hair: A Novel. 2003. 240p. pap. 12.00 (*0-684-83557-6*, Free Pr.) Simon & Schuster.
Lively, Penelope. Cleopatra's Sister. l.t. ed. 1993. 23.95 o.p. (*1-56895-039-X*, Wheeler Publishing, Inc.) Gale Group.
Logue, Mary. Still Explosion. 248p. 1994. pap. 9.95 o.p. (*1-878067-48-6*); 1993. text 18.95 o.p. (*1-878067-29-X*) Avalon Publishing Group. (Seal Pr.).
MacDonald, Janice. The Man on the Cliff. 2002. (Harlequin Superromance Ser.: No. 1077). mass mkt. (*0-373-71077-1*, Harlequin Bks.) Harlequin Enterprises, Ltd.
MacDonald, Shari. Diamonds. 1996. (Palisades Pure Romance Ser.). 238p. pap. 9.99 o.s.i (*0-88070-982-0*, Palisades) Multnomah Pubs., Inc.
MacDonnell, Julia. A Year of Favor: A Novel. 1994. 330p. 25.00 o.p. (*0-688-12546-8*, Morrow, William & Co.) Morrow/Avon.
Margolis, Sue. Apocalipstick. 2003. 320p. pap. 11.95 (*0-385-33656-X*, Delta) Dell Publishing.
Marklund, Liza. The Bomber. von Hofsten, Kajsa, tr. 2001. 336p. 24.95 (*0-7434-1783-6*, Atria) Simon & Schuster.
—The Bomber. reprint ed. 2002. 448p. mass mkt. 6.99 (*0-7434-1784-4*, Pocket); 2001. E-Book 24.95 (*0-7434-1785-2*, Atria) Simon & Schuster.
Maxted, Anna. Getting over It. 2001. 416p. pap. 14.00 (*0-06-098824-X*); 2000. 288p. 25.00 (*0-06-039320-3*) HarperTrade. (ReganBooks).
McConnell, Vicki P. The Burnton Widows: A Nyla Wade Mystery. 1984. (Nyla Wade Mystery Ser.). (Illus.). 240p. pap. 7.95 o.p. (*0-930044-52-5*) Naiad Pr., Inc.
—Double Daughter. 1988. 216p. pap. 8.95 o.p. (*0-941483-26-6*) Naiad Pr., Inc.
—Mrs. Porter's Letter. 1982. (Nyla Wade Ser.). 224p. pap. 7.95 o.p. (*0-930044-29-0*) Naiad Pr., Inc.
McDermid, Val. Booked for Murder. 2nd ed. 2000. (Lindsay Gordon Mystery Ser.). 260p. pap. 12.00 (*1-883523-37-0*) Spinsters Ink Bks.
—Common Murder. 2nd ed. 1995. 264p. pap. 10.95 (*1-883523-08-7*) Spinsters Ink Bks.
—Common Murder. l.t. ed. 2001. 286p. 32.50 (*0-7531-6538-4*) Thorpe, F. A. Pubs. GBR. *Dist:* Ulverscroft Large Print Bks., Ltd., Ulverscroft Large Print Canada, Ltd.
—Conferences Are Murder: A Lindsay Gordon Mystery. 1999. (Lindsay Gordon Mystery Ser.: Vol. 4). (Illus.). 264p. pap. 12.00 (*1-883523-30-3*) Spinsters Ink Bks.
—Deadline for Murder: A Lindsay Gordon Mystery. 2nd ed. 1997. (Kate Brannigan Mystery Ser.). 264p. (Orig.). pap. 10.95 (*1-883523-17-6*) Spinsters Ink Bks.
—Final Edition. l.t. ed. 2001. 288p. 32.50 (*0-7531-6540-6*) Thorpe, F. A. Pubs. GBR. *Dist:* Ulverscroft Large Print Bks., Ltd., Ulverscroft Large Print Canada, Ltd.
—A Place of Execution. l.t. ed. 2001. (Large Print Book Ser.). 659p. 29.95 (*1-58724-125-0*, Wheeler Publishing, Inc.) Gale Group.
—A Place of Execution. 2000. 403p. 24.95 (*0-312-26632-4*, Saint Martin's Minotaur); 2001. 480p. reprint ed. mass mkt. 6.99 (*0-312-97953-3*, St. Martin's Paperbacks) St. Martin's Pr.
—Report for Murder. l.t. ed. 2001. (Magna Large Print Ser.). 400p. 32.50 (*0-7505-1699-2*) Magna Large Print Bks. GBR. *Dist:* Ulverscroft Large Print Bks., Ltd., Ulverscroft Large Print Canada, Ltd.
—Report for Murder. 224p. 25.00 (*0-7278-5554-9*) Severn Hse. Pubs., Ltd.
—Report for Murder. 2nd ed. 1998. 264p. pap. 10.95 (*1-883523-24-9*) Spinsters Ink Bks.
—Report for Murder. 1989. 208p. 16.95 o.p. (*0-312-03888-7*, Saint Martin's Minotaur) St. Martin's Pr.
McGarry, Jean. Gallagher's Travels. 1997. (Poetry & Fiction Ser.). 224p. 28.00 (*0-8018-5634-5*) Johns Hopkins Univ. Pr.
McKay, Claudia. The Kali Connection. 1994. 190p. (Orig.). pap. 9.95 (*0-934678-54-5*) New Victoria Pubs., Inc.
—Twist of Lime: A Lynn Evans Mystery. 1997. (Lynn Evans Mystery Ser.). 166p. pap. 10.95 (*0-934678-88-X*) New Victoria Pubs., Inc.
McKitterick, Molly. Murder in a Mayonnaise Jar. 1993. 224p. 17.95 o.p. (*0-312-09346-2*, Saint Martin's Minotaur) St. Martin's Pr.
McLarin, Kim. Taming It Down: A Novel. 1998. 320p. 24.00 (*0-688-15516-2*, Morrow, William & Co.) Morrow/Avon.
McNeill, Elisabeth. Hot News. 2003. 288p. 25.99 (*0-7278-5939-0*) Severn Hse. Pubs., Ltd.
McPhee, Jenny. The Center of Things. 2002. 272p. pap. 13.95 (*0-345-44765-4*, Ballantine Bks.) Ballantine Bks.
—The Center of Things. 2001. 256p. 22.95 (*0-385-50077-7*) Doubleday Publishing.
Meier, Leslie. Father's Day Murder. 2004. 256p. mass mkt. 6.50 (*1-57566-835-1*, Kensington Bks.) Kensington Publishing Corp.
—Father's Day Murder. l.t. ed. 2003. (Lucy Stone Mystery Ser.). 307p. 28.95 (*0-7862-5617-6*) Thorndike Pr.
Meriwether, Louise. Shadow Dancing. 2000. 304p. pap. 12.95 (*0-345-42595-2*, One World/Ballantine) Ballantine Bks.
Miller, Carlene. Reporter on the Run: A Lexy Hyatt Mystery. 2001. (Lexy Hyatt Mysteries Ser.). 200p. pap. 11.95 (*1-892281-14-7*) New Victoria Pubs., Inc.
Miscione, Lisa. The Darkness Gathers: A Novel. 2003. 304p. 23.95 (*0-312-28359-8*, Saint Martin's Minotaur) St. Martin's Pr.
Morris, Gilbert. Flying Cavalier. 1999. (House of Winslow Ser.: Vol. 23). 320p. pap. 11.99 (*0-7642-2115-9*) Bethany Hse. Pubs.
Nathan, Melissa. Pride, Prejudice & Jasmin Field. 2001. 280p. pap. 6.50 (*0-06-107233-8*) HarperCollins Pubs.
—Pride, Prejudice, & Jasmine Field: A Novel. 2001. 288p. pap. 14.00 (*0-06-018495-7*, Avon Bks.) Morrow/Avon.
Nessen, Ron. Knight & Day. audio 24.95 (*0-7861-1399-5*) Blackstone Audio Bks., Inc.
—Knight & Day. 1996. 256p. mass mkt. 5.99 (*0-8125-5053-6*, Forge Bks.) Doherty, Tom Assocs., LLC.
—Press Corpse. 1997. (Knight & Day Mysteries Ser.). 215p. pap. 5.99 (*0-8125-6793-5*, Forge Bks.) Doherty, Tom Assocs., LLC.
Nessen, Ron & Neuman, Johanna. Death with Honors. unabr. ed. 1999. (Knight & Day Mystery Ser.: Vol. 3). audio 29.95 (*0-7861-1534-3*);Pt. 3. audio 44.95 (*0-7861-1484-3*, 2336) Blackstone Audio Bks., Inc.
—Death with Honors, No. 3. 1998. (Knight & Day Mysteries Ser.). 288p. 22.95 o.p. (*0-312-85594-X*, Forge Bks.) Doherty, Tom Assocs., LLC.
—Knight & Day. unabr. ed. 1996. audio 32.95 (*0-7861-1009-0*, 1788) Blackstone Audio Bks., Inc.
—Knight & Day. 1995. 256p. 21.95 o.p. (*0-312-85588-5*, Forge Bks.) Doherty, Tom Assocs., LLC.
—Press Corpse. unabr. ed. 2000. audio 27.95 (*0-7861-1545-9*); 1999. audio 39.95 Blackstone Audio Bks., Inc.
—Press Corpse. 1996. 256p. 21.95 o.p. (*0-312-85592-3*, Forge Bks.) Doherty, Tom Assocs., LLC.
O'Brien, Meg. Eagles Die Too: A Jessica James Mystery. 1992. 256p. 16.50 o.s.i (*0-385-42265-2*) Doubleday Publishing.
—Salmon in the Soup. 1990. 256p. (Orig.). mass mkt. 3.95 o.s.i (*0-553-28617-X*) Bantam Bks.
—Thin Ice. 1994. 416p. mass mkt. 4.99 o.s.i (*0-553-56962-7*) Bantam Bks.
Orde, Lewis. The Proprietor's Daughter. 1988. 18.95 (*0-316-67340-4*) Little Brown & Co.
Osborn, David. Murder in the Napa Valley. unabr. ed. 1993. audio 30.00 (*0-7366-2534-8*, 3286) Books on Tape, Inc.
—Murder in the Napa Valley. 1995. 224p. mass mkt. 4.99 o.s.i (*0-8217-4844-0*, Zebra Bks.) Kensington Publishing Corp.
—Murder in the Napa Valley. 2000. 176p. pap. 12.95 (*0-7432-1294-0*, Simon & Schuster) Simon & Schuster.
—Murder in the Napa Valley: A Margaret Barlow Mystery. 1993. 224p. 19.00 (*0-671-70487-7*, Simon & Schuster) Simon & Schuster.
—Murder on Martha's Vineyard. unabr. ed. 1992. audio 42.00 (*0-7366-2188-1*, 2983) Books on Tape, Inc.
—Murder on the Chesapeake. unabr. ed. 1993. audio 36.00 (*0-7366-2437-6*, 3202) Books on Tape, Inc.
—Murder on the Chesapeake. 2000. 208p. pap. 19.00 (*0-7432-1271-1*); 1992. 320p. 19.00 o.s.i (*0-671-70486-9*) Simon & Schuster. (Simon & Schuster).
—Murder on the Chesapeake: A Margaret Barlow Mystery. 1993. 304p. mass mkt. 3.99 o.s.i (*0-8217-4165-9*, Zebra Bks.) Kensington Publishing Corp.
Palmer, Diana. Roomful of Roses. 2000. 248p. mass mkt. (*1-55166-641-3*, Harlequin Bks.); 1997. per. (*1-55166-418-6*, 1-66418-4, Mira Bks.) Harlequin Enterprises, Ltd.
—Roomful of Roses. l.t. ed. 2000. (Romance Ser.). 215p. 27.95 (*0-7862-2613-7*); (*0-7540-4358-4*); (*0-7540-4359-2*) Thorndike Pr.
Papa, Ariella. On the Verge. 2002. 304p. pap. (*0-373-25017-7*, Red Dress Ink) Harlequin Enterprises, Ltd.
Peart, Jane. Undaunted Spirit. l.t. ed. 2002. (Westward Dreams Ser.). 350p. 25.95 (*0-7862-3127-0*) Gale Group.
—Undaunted Spirit. 1999. (Westward Dreams Ser.: Vol. 5). 240p. pap. 9.99 (*0-310-22012-2*) Zondervan.
Pella, Judith & Peterson, Tracie. Ties That Bind. 2000. (Ribbons West Ser.: Vol. 3). 288p. pap. 12.99 (*0-7642-2073-X*) Bethany Hse. Pubs.
Pence, Joanne. Cook in Time. 1999. (Angie Amalfi Mysteries Ser.). 352p. mass mkt. 6.99 (*0-06-104454-7*) HarperCollins Pubs.
—Cooking Most Deadly. 1996. (Angie Amalfi Mysteries Ser.). 256p. mass mkt. 6.50 (*0-06-104395-8*, HarperTorch) Morrow/Avon.
—Cooking up Trouble. 1995. (Angie Amalfi Mysteries Ser.). 320p. mass mkt. 6.99 (*0-06-108200-7*, HarperTorch) Morrow/Avon.
—Cook's Night Out. 1998. (Angie Amalfi Mysteries Ser.). 304p. mass mkt. 5.99 (*0-06-104396-6*) HarperCollins Pubs.
—Cooks Overboard. 1998. (Angie Amalfi Mysteries Ser.: Vol. 6). 304p. mass mkt. 5.99 (*0-06-104453-9*, HarperTorch) Morrow/Avon.
—Something's Cooking. 650th ed. 1993. (Angie Amalfi Mysteries Ser.). 336p. mass mkt. 6.50 (*0-06-108096-9*, HarperTorch) Morrow/Avon.
—Too Many Cooks. 1994. (Angie Amalfi Mysteries Ser.). 352p. mass mkt. 6.50 (*0-06-108199-X*, HarperTorch) Morrow/Avon.
Peterson, Audrey. Murder in Burgundy. 1989. mass mkt. 3.95 o.s.i (*0-671-65737-2*, Pocket) Simon & Schuster.
—Nocturne Murder. 1987. 14.95 o.p. (*0-87795-862-9*, Morrow, William & Co.) Morrow/Avon.
—Nocturne Murder. 1989. 2.99 o.p. (*0-517-69456-5*) Random Hse. Value Publishing.
Peterson, Tracie. Framed. 1998. (Portraits Ser.). 240p. pap. 8.99 o.p. (*1-55661-992-8*) Bethany Hse. Pubs.
—Framed. l.t. ed. 2000. (Christian Mystery Ser.). 367p. 24.95 (*0-7862-2696-X*) Thorndike Pr.
Phillips, Michael. Into the Long Dark Night. 1992. (Journals of Corrie Belle Hollister: Vol. 6). 304p. pap. 10.99 o.p. (*1-55661-300-8*) Bethany Hse. Pubs.
—Land of the Brave & the Free. 1993. (Journals of Corrie Belle Hollister: Vol. 7). 320p. (J). (gr. 4-7). pap. 10.99 o.p. (*1-55661-308-3*) Bethany Hse. Pubs.
Phillips, Michael & Pella, Judith. Sea to Shining Sea. 1992. (Journals of Corrie Belle Hollister: Vol. 5). 320p. (J). pap. 10.99 o.p. (*1-55661-227-3*) Bethany Hse. Pubs.

Pickard, Nancy. Ring of Truth. 2001. (Marie Lightfoot Mysteries Ser.). 23.95 (*0-7434-1205-2*); reprint ed. E-Book 23.95 (*0-7434-1805-0*) Simon & Schuster. (Atria).

—The Whole Truth. (Marie Lightfoot Mysteries Ser.). E-Book 22.95 (*1-58945-297-6*) Adobe Systems, Inc.

—The Whole Truth. (Marie Lightfoot Mysteries Ser.). 2000. 272p. 22.95 o.s.i (*0-671-88795-5*, Atria); 2001. reprint ed. E-Book 22.95 (*0-7434-1804-2*, Atria); 2001. (Illus.). 368p. reprint ed. mass mkt. 6.99 o.s.i (*0-671-88794-7*, Pocket) Simon & Schuster.

—The Whole Truth. l.t. ed. 2000. (Marie Lightfoot Mysteries Ser.). 439p. 29.95 (*0-7862-2577-7*) Thorndike Pr.

Porter, Anna. Hidden Agenda. 1986. 280p. 14.95 o.p. (*0-525-24427-1*, Dutton) Dutton/Plume.

—Mortal Sins. 1988. 288p. 17.95 o.p. (*0-453-00616-7*) NAL.

Price, Richard. Freedomland. 1999. 736p. mass mkt. 7.99 (*0-440-22644-9*) Dell Publishing.

Prose, Francine. Bigfoot Dreams. 1998. 288p. pap. 12.00 (*0-8050-4860-X*, Owl Bks.) Holt, Henry & Co.

—Bigfoot Dreams. 1986. 16.95 o.p. (*0-394-54976-7*, Pantheon) Knopf Publishing Group.

—Bigfoot Dreams. 1987. 288p. pap. 6.95 o.p. (*0-14-009837-2*, Penguin Bks.) Viking Penguin.

Quine, Roger. Susie Goes to the Devil. 2003. 240p. mass mkt. 8.95 (*1-903931-34-7*) Chimera Pubns. GBR. *Dist:* Client Distribution Services.

Quinn, Sally. Happy Endings. l.t. ed. 1992. 24.95 o.p. (*0-7927-1378-8*); pap. 21.95 o.p. (*0-7927-1377-X*) BBC Audiobooks America.

—Happy Endings. 1991. 544p. 22.00 o.p. (*0-671-64941-8*, Simon & Schuster) Simon & Schuster.

Racina, Thom. Hidden Agenda. 1998. 368p. 24.95 o.p. (*0-525-94031-6*) Dutton/Plume.

—Hidden Agenda. 1999. 368p. reprint ed. mass mkt. 6.99 o.s.i (*0-451-18600-1*) NAL.

—Snow Angel. 1996. 304p. 23.95 o.s.i (*0-525-94030-8*) Dutton/Plume.

—Snow Angel. 1997. 416p. mass mkt. 6.99 (*0-451-18599-4*, Signet Bks.) NAL.

Rawlings, Ellen. Deadly Harvest. 1997. mass mkt. 5.99 o.s.i (*0-449-14987-0*, Fawcett) Ballantine Bks.

—The Murder Lover. 1996. mass mkt. 5.99 o.s.i (*0-449-14988-9*, Fawcett) Ballantine Bks.

Reid, Van. Mollie Peer: Or the Underground Adventures of the Moosepath League. 2000. 368p. pap. 14.00 (*0-14-029185-7*) Penguin Group (USA) Inc.

—Mollie Peer: Or the Underground Adventures of the Moosepath League. 1999. 416p. 24.95 o.p. (*0-670-88633-5*, Viking) Viking Penguin.

Roberts, Nora. Partners. 1992. (NR Flowers Ser.: No. 21). per. (*0-373-51021-7*, 5-51021-9); 1985. pap. (*0-373-07094-2*) Harlequin Enterprises, Ltd. (Harlequin Bks.).

—Partners. l.t. ed. 2001. (Famous Authors Ser.). 320p. 30.95 (*0-7862-2612-9*) Thorndike Pr.

Robitaille, Julie. Iced. 1994. (Kit Powell Mystery Ser.). 224p. 19.95 o.p. (*0-312-11434-6*, Saint Martin's Minotaur) St. Martin's Pr.

—Jinx. (Brown Bag Mystery Line Ser.). 1995. 358p. 3.00 o.p. (*0-933031-58-0*); 1992. 14.95 o.p. (*0-933031-44-0*) Council Oak Bks.

Roper, Gayle G. Caught in a Bind. 2000. (Amhearst Mystery Ser.). 320p. pap. 10.99 (*0-310-21850-0*) Zondervan.

—Caught in the Act. 2000. (Five Star Christian Fiction Ser.). 311p. 24.95 (*0-7862-2776-1*, Five Star) Gale Group.

—Caught in the Act? 1998. (Amhearst Mystery Ser.: 2). 272p. pap. 10.99 (*0-310-21909-4*) Zondervan.

—Caught in the Middle. 1997. (Amhearst Mystery Ser.: Vol. 1). 240p. pap. 10.99 (*0-310-20995-1*) Zondervan.

Rose, M. J. Lip Service. 1998. 285p. pap. 12.95 o.p. (*0-9664332-0-3*) Pigeonhole Pr.

—Lip Service. 2000. E-Book 18.00 (*0-7434-1253-2*, Pocket); 1999. 320p. 18.00 o.s.i (*0-671-04131-2*, Atria); 2000. 320p. reprint ed. pap. 13.00 (*0-671-04132-0*, Atria) Simon & Schuster.

Rubino, Jane. Cheat the Devil. 1998. 352p. 24.95 (*1-885173-56-3*) Write Way Publishing.

—Death of a DJ. 1997. 224p. mass mkt. 4.99 o.p. (*0-06-104433-4*, HarperTorch) Morrow/Avon.

—Death of a DJ. 1995. 225p. 20.95 (*1-885173-09-1*) Write Way Publishing.

—Fruitcake. 1997. 384p. 24.95 (*1-885173-29-6*) Write Way Publishing.

—Plot Twist. 2000. 400p. 24.95 (*1-885173-80-6*) Write Way Publishing.

Ryan, Richard. Funnelweb. 1997. 339p. (*0-7329-0888-4*) Macmillan Education Australia.

Salvatore, Diane. Love, Zena Beth. 1992. 224p. 18.95 o.p. (*1-56280-015-9*) Naiad Pr., Inc.

Sandford, John, pseud. The Night Crew. 1998. 368p. mass mkt. 7.99 (*0-425-16338-5*) Berkley Publishing Group.

—The Night Crew. l.t. ed. 1997. 25.95 o.p. (*1-56895-497-2*, Wheeler Publishing, Inc.) Gale Group.

—The Night Crew. 1997. 368p. 23.95 o.s.i (*0-399-14237-1*, G. P. Putnam's Sons) Penguin Group (USA) Inc.

—The Night Crew. 23.95 o.s.i (*0-399-14552-4*) Putnam Publishing Group, The.

Sandstrom, Eve K. Homicide Report. 1998. 368p. mass mkt. 5.99 o.s.i (*0-451-19034-3*, Onyx) NAL.

—The Smoking Gun: A Nell Matthews Mystery. 2000. (Neil Matthews Mysteries Ser.). 240p. mass mkt. 5.99 o.s.i (*0-451-19976-6*, Signet Bks.) NAL.

—The Smoking Gun: A Nell Matthews Mystery. l.t. ed. 2000. (Mystery Ser.). 365p. 26.95 (*0-7862-2977-2*) Thorndike Pr.

—Violence Beat. 1997. 384p. mass mkt. 5.99 o.s.i (*0-451-19033-5*, Signet Bks.) NAL.

Saul, John. Black Lightning. Grey, Linda, ed. 1996. 448p. mass mkt. 7.99 (*0-449-22504-6*, Fawcett) Ballantine Bks.

Schulenburg, Marnie. Murder off the Record. 1998. 304p. 23.95 o.p. (*1-885173-50-4*) Write Way Publishing.

Scott, Barbara & Younce, Carrie. Secrets of the Gathering Darkness. 1996. 288p. pap. 11.99 o.p. (*0-7852-7776-5*) Nelson, Thomas Inc.

—Sedona Storm. 1993. 10.99 o.p. (*0-7852-8266-1*) Nelson, Thomas Inc.

Shah, Diane K. Dying Cheek to Cheek. 1992. 464p. 18.50 o.s.i (*0-385-42250-4*) Doubleday Publishing.

Shames, Laurence. Mangrove Squeeze. abr. ed. 1998. audio 16.95 (*1-55927-485-9*) Audio Renaissance.

—Mangrove Squeeze. 1999. 352p. mass mkt. 6.99 (*0-345-43306-8*) Ballantine Bks.

—Mangrove Squeeze. unabr. collector's ed. 1998. audio 56.00 (*0-7366-4261-7*, 4760) Books on Tape, Inc.

—Mangrove Squeeze. 1998. 320p. 22.95 o.p. (*0-7868-6301-3*); mass mkt. 5.99 (*0-7868-8945-4*) Hyperion Pr.

—Mangrove Squeeze, unabr. ed. 1998. audio 60.00 (*0-7887-2037-6*, 95401E7) Recorded Bks., LLC.

Shankman, Sarah. Digging up Momma. (Samantha Adams Mystery Ser.). 1998. 288p. 22.00 (*0-671-89753-5*, Atria); 1999. 336p. reprint ed. mass mkt. 6.50 (*0-671-89752-7*, Pocket) Simon & Schuster.

—First Kill All the Lawyers. 1991. mass mkt. 5.99 (*0-671-74893-9*); 1988. 224p. mass mkt. 3.50 (*0-671-64529-3*) Simon & Schuster. (Pocket).

—He Was Her Man. Chelius, Jane, ed. 288p. 1993. 20.00 (*0-671-77553-7*, Atria); 1994. reprint ed. mass mkt. 5.50 (*0-671-77563-4*, Pocket) Simon & Schuster.

—Impersonal Attractions. 1985. 272p. 14.95 o.p. (*0-312-40997-4*) St. Martin's Pr.

—The King Is Dead. Chelius, Jane, ed. 1992. 288p. 20.00 (*0-671-73459-8*, Atria); 1993. 320p. reprint ed. mass mkt. 5.99 (*0-671-73460-1*, Pocket) Simon & Schuster.

—Now Let's Talk of Graves. Chelius, Jane, ed. 1990. 304p. 18.95 o.p. (*0-671-68456-6*, Atria); 1991. 320p. reprint ed. mass mkt. 5.99 (*0-671-68457-4*, Pocket) Simon & Schuster.

—She Walks in Beauty. l.t. ed. 1993. (General Ser.). 484p. 20.95 o.p. (*0-8161-5478-3*, Macmillan Reference USA) Gale Group.

—She Walks in Beauty. 1991. 320p. 20.00 (*0-671-73657-4*, Atria) Simon & Schuster.

—She Walks in Beauty. Chelius, Jane, ed. 1992. 352p. reprint ed. mass mkt. 5.99 (*0-671-73658-2*, Pocket) Simon & Schuster.

Sheldon, Sidney. The Sky Is Falling. 2000. 336p. pap. 16.00 (*0-06-018523-6*) HarperCollins Pubs.

—The Sky Is Falling. 2000. 336p. 26.00 (*0-06-019834-6*, Morrow, William & Co.); 400p. pap. 26.00 (*0-06-019912-1*) Morrow/Avon.

—The Sky Is Falling. 2001. 416p. mass mkt. 7.99 (*0-446-61017-8*) Warner Bks., Inc.

Sherrill, Martha. My Last Movie Star: A Novel of Hollywood. 2004. 384p. pap. 13.95 (*0-375-75949-2*, Random Hse. Trade Paperbacks) Random House Adult Trade Publishing Group.

—My Last Movie Star: A Novel of Hollywood. 2003. 368p. 23.95 (*0-375-50769-8*) Random Hse., Inc.

Shreve, Anita. Strange Fits of Passion. l.t. ed. 2000. 350p. lib. bdg. 25.95 (*1-58547-045-7*) Ctr. Point Large Print.

—Strange Fits of Passion. (Harvest Book Ser.). 1999. 352p. pap. 13.00 (*0-15-600710-X*, Harvest Bks.); 1991. 336p. 18.95 (*0-15-185760-1*) Harcourt Trade Pubs.

—Strange Fits of Passion. 1992. 384p. mass mkt. 5.99 o.s.i (*0-451-40300-2*, Onyx) NAL.

Sibley, Celestine. Ah, Sweet Mystery: A Kate Mulcay Novel of Suspense. 1991. 224p. 19.00 o.p. (*0-06-016304-6*) HarperTrade.

—Ah, Sweet Mystery: A Kate Mulcay Novel of Suspense. 1992. 272p. mass mkt. 4.50 o.p. (*0-06-109083-2*, HarperTorch) Morrow/Avon.

—Dire Happenings at Scratch Ankle: A Kate Mulcay Mystery. 1993. 224p. 19.00 o.p. (*0-06-017703-9*) HarperTrade.

—Dire Happenings at Scratch Ankle: A Kate Mulcay Mystery. 1994. 224p. mass mkt. 4.50 o.p. (*0-06-109050-6*, HarperTorch) Morrow/Avon.

—A Plague of Kinfolks: A Kate Mulcay Mystery. 1996. 224p. mass mkt. 4.99 o.s.i (*0-06-109049-2*); 1995. 208p. 20.00 o.p. (*0-06-017704-7*) HarperCollins Pubs.

—Straight As an Arrow: A Kate Mulcay Mystery. 1992. 256p. 19.00 o.p. (*0-06-016305-4*) HarperTrade.

—Straight As an Arrow: A Kate Mulcay Mystery. 1994. 224p. mass mkt. 4.50 o.p. (*0-06-109190-1*, HarperTorch) Morrow/Avon.

Siddons, Anne Rivers. Downtown. 1994. 352p. 288.00 o.p. (*0-06-017602-4*) HarperCollins Pubs.

—Downtown. 1994. 352p. 24.00 o.p. (*0-06-017934-1*); Set. 1999. audio (*1-55994-732-2*, 692189, Harper-Audio) HarperTrade.

—Downtown. 1995. 512p. mass mkt. 7.99 (*0-06-109968-6*, HarperTorch) Morrow/Avon.

—Downtown. unabr. ed. 1994. audio 97.00 (*0-7887-0062-6*, 94318E7) Recorded Bks., LLC.

—Downtown. 374p. 6.98 o.p. (*0-7651-0027-4*) Smithmark Pubs., Inc.

—Downtown. l.t. ed. (Paperback Bestsellers Ser.). 647p. 1995. 22.95 (*0-8161-7411-3*); 1994. lib. bdg. 27.95 (*0-8161-7410-5*) Thorndike Pr.

Sims, Elizabeth. Damn Straight. 2003. (Lillian Byrd Crime Story Ser.). 280p. pap. 13.95 (*1-55583-786-7*) Alyson Pubns.

Smith, Taylor. Random Acts. abr. ed. 1998. audio 7.99 (*1-55204-154-9*) Durkin Hayes Publishing Ltd.

—Random Acts. 1998. (Mira Bks.). 441p. mass mkt. (*1-55166-431-3*, 1-66431-7, Mira Bks.) Harlequin Enterprises, Ltd.

Sohn, Amy. Run Catch Kiss: A Gratifying Novel. 256p. 2000. pap. 12.00 (*0-684-86753-2*); 1999. 23.00 (*0-684-85302-7*) Simon & Schuster. (Simon & Schuster).

Steel, Danielle. Bittersweet. 2000. 448p. mass mkt. 7.99 (*0-440-22484-5*); 1999. 384p. 26.95 (*0-385-31957-6*, Delacorte Pr.); 1999. 384p. 200.00 (*0-385-33388-9*, Delacorte Pr.) Dell Publishing.

—Bittersweet. l.t. ed. 2004. 576p. 24.95 (*0-375-43321-X*) Random Hse. Large Print.

—Journey. 2001. 368p. mass mkt. 7.99 (*0-440-23702-5*); 2000. 336p. 200.00 (*0-385-33304-8*, Delacorte Pr.); 2000. 336p. 26.95 (*0-385-31687-9*, Delacorte Pr.) Dell Publishing.

—Journey. abr. unabr. ed. 2000. audio compact disk 29.95 (*0-553-71219-5*); audio 39.95 (*0-553-50260-3*) Random Hse. Audio Publishing Group. (RH Audio).

—Journey. l.t. ed. 464p. 2001. pap. 13.95 (*0-375-72807-4*); 2000. 26.95 (*0-375-43080-6*) Random Hse. Large Print.

—Message from Nam. l.t. ed. 1990. 672p. 24.95 o.s.i (*0-385-30136-7*); 408p. 21.95 (*0-385-29907-9*) Bantam Doubleday Dell Large Print Group, Inc. (Delacorte Large Type).

—Message from Nam. 1991. 432p. mass mkt. 7.99 (*0-440-20941-2*); 1990. 408p. 125.00 (*0-385-30137-5*, Delacorte Pr.) Dell Publishing.

—Message from Nam. l.t. ed. 1993. pap. 19.95 o.p. (*0-8161-5794-4*, Macmillan Reference USA) Gale Group.

—Message from Nam. abr. ed. 1994. audio 16.99 (*0-553-45281-9*, RH Audio) Random Hse. Audio Publishing Group.

Stein, Triss. Digging up Death: A Kay Engles Mystery. 1999. (WWL Mystery Ser.: Bk. 310). per. (*0-373-26310-4*, 1-26310-2, Harlequin Bks.) Harlequin Enterprises, Ltd.

—Digging up Death: A Kay Engles Mystery. 1998. (Kay Engles Mystery Ser.). 204p. 22.95 (*0-8027-3319-0*) Walker & Co.

—Murder at the Class Reunion. 1995. 253p. per. (*0-373-26181-0*, 1-26181-7, Harlequin Bks.) Harlequin Enterprises, Ltd.

—Murder at the Class Reunion. 1993. 205p. 19.95 (*0-8027-3232-1*) Walker & Co.

Stewart, Ed. Doomsday Flight. 1995. 475p. pap. 11.99 (*1-56476-482-6*, 6-3482) Cook Communications Ministries.

—Millennium's Dawn. 1994. 480p. pap. 11.99 o.p. (*1-56476-345-5*, 6-3345) Cook Communications Ministries.

—Millennium's Eve. 1993. 448p. pap. 12.99 (*1-56476-133-9*, 6-3133) Cook Communications Ministries.

Stewart, Leah. Body of a Girl. 2000. 320p. 23.95 (*0-670-89164-9*, Viking) Viking Penguin.

Strohmeyer, Sarah. Bubbles Ablaze: A Mystery. 2003. 256p. 23.95 (*0-525-94738-8*, Dutton) Dutton/Plume.

—Bubbles in Trouble. 2002. 288p. 22.95 o.s.i (*0-525-94649-7*, Dutton) Dutton/Plume.

Sumner, Mark. The Monster of Minnesota. 1997. (News from the Edge Ser.: Vol. 1). 208p. mass mkt. 6.50 o.s.i (*0-441-00459-8*) Ace Bks.

Sumner, Mark. News from the Edge. 1999. (News from the Edge Ser.). 208p. mass mkt. 6.50 o.s.i (*0-441-00628-0*) Ace Bks.

—News from the Edge: Insanity, Illinois, No. 2. 1998. 208p. mass mkt. 6.50 o.s.i (*0-441-00511-X*) Ace Bks.

Thoene, Bodie. The Twilight of Courage. 1999. 324p. pap. text 9.97 (*0-7852-6923-1*) Nelson, Thomas Pubs.

Thoene, Bodie & Thoene, Brock. The Twilight of Courage. 1995. 528p. pap. 12.99 (*0-7852-7596-7*); 1994. 524p. 22.99 o.p. (*0-7852-8196-7*) Nelson, Thomas Inc.

Thompson, Vicki Lewis. Truly, Madly, Deeply. 2002. (Harlequin Blaze Ser.). mass mkt. (*0-373-79056-2*, Harlequin Bks.) Harlequin Enterprises, Ltd.

Tyre, Peg. In the Midnight Hour. 1996. 272p. mass mkt. 5.99 (*0-380-72811-7*, Avon Bks.) Morrow/Avon.

Van Wormer, Laura. The Bad Witness. 2003. 448p. mass mkt. (*1-55166-739-8*); 2002. 304p. (*1-55166-952-8*) Harlequin Enterprises, Ltd. (Mira Bks.).

—Expose. 1999. 384p. (*1-55166-526-3*, Mira Bks.) Harlequin Enterprises, Ltd.

Vidal, Gore. The Golden Age: A Novel. 2001. 480p. reprint ed. pap. 15.00 (*0-375-72481-8*, Vintage) Knopf Publishing Group.

—The Golden Age: A Novel. abr. ed. 2000. audio compact disk 29.95 (*0-553-71214-4*); audio 39.95 (*0-553-50265-4*) Random Hse. Audio Publishing Group. (RH Audio).

—The Golden Age: A Novel. l.t. ed. 2000. 720p. 27.50 (*0-375-43082-2*) Random Hse. Large Print.

Viets, Elaine. Back Stab: A Francesca Vierling Mystery. 1997. (Francesca Vierling Mystery Ser.). 320p. mass mkt. 5.99 o.s.i (*0-440-22431-4*) Dell Publishing.

—Doc in the Box: A Francesca Vierling Mystery. 2000. (Francesca Vierling Mystery Ser.). 256p. mass mkt. 5.99 o.s.i (*0-440-23620-7*) Bantam Dell Publishing Group.

—The Pink Flamingo Murders: A Francesca Vierling Mystery. 1999. 272p. mass mkt. 5.99 o.s.i (*0-440-22445-4*) Dell Publishing.

—The Pink Flamingo Murders: A Francesca Vierling Mystery. 1999. 272p. pap. 19.00 (*0-440-61351-5*) Random Hse., Inc.

—Rubout: A Francesca Vierling Mystery. 1998. (Francesca Vierling Mystery Ser.). 320p. mass mkt. 5.99 o.s.i (*0-440-22444-6*) Dell Publishing.

—Rubout: A Francesca Vierling Mystery. 1998. 320p. pap. 19.00 (*0-440-61348-5*) Random Hse., Inc.

Walker, Mary Willis. All the Dead Lie Down. unabr. ed. 1998. audio 64.00 (*0-7366-4220-X*, 4718) Books on Tape, Inc.

—All the Dead Lie Down. l.t. ed. 1998. (Large Print Bks.). 26.95 (*1-56895-669-X*, Wheeler Publishing, Inc.) Gale Group.

—All the Dead Lie Down, unabr. ed. 1998. audio 78.00 (*0-7887-2166-6*, 95462E7) Recorded Bks., LLC.

—The Red Scream. 1995. 416p. mass mkt. 6.99 (*0-553-57172-9*, Crimeline) Bantam Bks.

—The Red Scream. unabr. ed. 1996. audio 64.00 (*0-7366-3381-2*, 4031) Books on Tape, Inc.

—The Red Scream. 1994. 19.95 o.s.i (*0-385-46858-X*) Doubleday Publishing.

—The Red Scream, unabr. ed. 1996. audio 85.00 (*0-7887-0468-0*, 94661E7) Recorded Bks., LLC.

—The Red Scream. l.t. ed. 1997. (Niagara Large Print Ser.). 524p. 29.50 o.p. (*0-7089-5814-1*, Ulverscroft) Thorpe, F. A. Pubs. GBR. *Dist:* Ulverscroft Large Print Bks., Ltd., Ulverscroft Large Print Canada, Ltd.

—Under the Beetle's Cellar. 1996. 368p. reprint ed. mass mkt. 6.50 (*0-553-57173-7*, Crimeline) Bantam Bks.

—Under the Beetle's Cellar. unabr. ed. 1996. audio 64.00 (*0-7366-3382-0*, 4032) Books on Tape, Inc.

—Under the Beetle's Cellar. l.t. ed. 1996. pap. 22.95 o.p. (*1-56895-313-5*, Wheeler Publishing, Inc.) Gale Group.

—Under the Beetle's Cellar. unabr. ed. audio 75.00 (*0-7887-0515-6*, 94709E7); 1999. audio compact disk 99.00 (*0-7887-3410-5*, C1016E7) Recorded Bks., LLC.

Walters, Minette. The Sculptress. l.t. ed. 1994. (Magna Large Print Ser.). 488p. 29.99 o.p. (*0-7505-0625-3*) Magna Large Print Bks. GBR. *Dist:* Ulverscroft Large Print Bks., Ltd., Ulverscroft Large Print Canada, Ltd.

—The Sculptress. 1993. (Illus.). 308p. 21.95 o.p. (*0-312-09909-6*, Saint Martin's Minotaur); Vol. 1. 1994. mass mkt. 7.99 (*0-312-95361-5*, St. Martin's Paperbacks) St. Martin's Pr.

Ware, Ciji. Midnight on Julia Street. 1999. 470p. mass mkt. 6.99 (*0-449-00187-3*, Fawcett) Ballantine Bks.

Warner, Penny. Dead Body Language. 1997. (Connor Westphal Mystery Ser.). 288p. mass mkt. 5.50 o.s.i (*0-553-57586-4*, Crimeline) Bantam Bks.

—A Quiet Undertaking. 2000. 272p. mass mkt. 5.50 o.s.i (*0-553-57965-7*) Bantam Bks.

—Right to Remain Silent. 1998. 288p. mass mkt. 5.50 o.s.i (*0-553-57962-2*, Crimeline) Bantam Bks.

—Sign of Foul Play: A Connor Westphal Mystery. 1997. (Connor Westphal Mystery Ser.). 288p. mass mkt. 5.50 o.s.i (*0-553-57587-2*, Crimeline) Bantam Bks.

Waterhouse, Jane. Dead Letter. 2000. 320p. mass mkt. 5.99 o.s.i (*0-425-17779-3*) Berkley Publishing Group.

—Dead Letter. l.t. ed. 2000. (Large Print Bks.). pap. 25.95 (*1-56895-953-2*, Wheeler Publishing, Inc.) Gale Group.

—Dead Letter. 1998. 304p. 23.95 o.p. (*0-399-14436-6*) Penguin Group (USA) Inc.

—Graven Images. 1997. 320p. mass mkt. 5.99 o.s.i (*0-425-15673-7*, Prime Crime) Berkley Publishing Group.

—Graven Images. 1995. 352p. 23.95 o.s.i (*0-399-14080-8*, G. P. Putnam's Sons) Penguin Group (USA) Inc.

—Shadow Walk. 1999. (Prime Crime Mysteries Ser.). 320p. reprint ed. mass mkt. 5.99 o.s.i (*0-425-16946-4*, Prime Crime) Berkley Publishing Group.

—Shadow Walk. 1997. 320p. 23.95 o.p. (*0-399-14305-X*, G. P. Putnam's Sons) Penguin Group (USA) Inc.

Webb, Cynthia. No Daughter of the South. 1997. 200p. (Orig.). pap. 10.95 (*0-934678-82-0*) New Victoria Pubs., Inc.

Weiner, Jennifer. Good in Bed. 2006. 432p. mass mkt. (*0-7434-7549-6*, Pocket Star); 2002. 400p. pap. 14.00 (*0-7434-1817-4*, Washington Square Pr.); 2001. 384p. 24.95 (*0-7434-1816-6*, Atria); 2001. reprint ed. E-Book 24.95 (*0-7434-1818-2*, Atria) Simon & Schuster.

—Good in Bed. l.t. ed. 2001. (Large Print Women's Fiction Ser.). 689p. 29.95 (*0-7862-3644-2*) Thorndike Pr.

Wetlaufer, Suzy. Judgement Call: A Novel. 1992. 20.00 o.p. (*0-688-10930-6*, Morrow, William & Co.) Morrow/Avon.

White, Kate. A Body to Die For. l.t. ed. 2003. 460p. 30.95 (*0-7862-5767-9*) Thorndike Pr.

—A Body to Die For. 2004. 400p. mass mkt. 6.99 (*0-446-61385-1*); 2003. 304p. 23.95 (*0-446-53148-0*) Warner Bks., Inc.

—If Looks Could Kill. l.t. ed. 2002. (Core Collection). 470p. 28.95 o.p. (*0-7862-4497-6*) Thorndike Pr.

—If Looks Could Kill. (Bailey Wiggins Mystery Ser.). 2002. 336p. 22.95 o.p. (*0-446-53023-9*); 2003. 416p. reprint ed. mass mkt. 6.99 (*0-446-61257-X*) Warner Bks., Inc.

Wilson, John. The Disappearance of Lyndsey Barratt. 1998. 400p. 24.00 (*0-688-15280-5*, Morrow, William & Co.) Morrow/Avon.

Wolff, Isabel. Making Minty Malone. 1999. 433p. (*0-00-651340-9*) HarperCollins Pubs.

—Making Minty Malone. 2000. 432p. mass mkt. 6.99 (*0-451-40925-6*, Onyx) NAL.

Wood, N. Lee. Looking for the Mahdi. 1996. 304p. pap. 12.00 o.p. (*0-441-00298-6*) Ace Bks.

Woods, Sherryl. Bank on It. 2000. 235p. 26.95 (*0-7351-0306-2*); pap. 16.95 (*0-7351-0307-0*) Replica Bks.

—Bank on It. 1993. 240p. mass mkt. 4.99 o.s.i (*0-446-36404-5*) Warner Bks., Inc.

—Body & Soul. 2000. 254p. 26.95 (*0-7351-0310-0*); pap. 16.95 (*0-7351-0311-9*) Replica Bks.

—Body & Soul. 1990. 19.00 o.p. (*0-7278-4111-4*) Severn Hse. Pubs., Ltd.

—Body & Soul. 1994. 256p. mass mkt. 5.50 o.s.i (*0-446-60155-1*, Mysterious Pr. Paperback Bks.); 1989. 3.95 (*0-445-20900-3*) Warner Bks., Inc.

—Deadly Obsession. 2000. 236p. 26.95 (*0-7351-0314-3*); pap. 16.95 (*0-7351-0315-1*) Replica Bks.

—Deadly Obsession. 1995. 256p. mass mkt. 5.50 (*0-446-60091-1*) Warner Bks., Inc.

—Hide & Seek. unabr. collector's ed. 1994. audio 36.00 (*0-7366-2778-2*, 3497) Books on Tape, Inc.

—Hide & Seek. 2000. 339p. 28.95 (*0-7351-0304-6*); pap. 18.95 (*0-7351-0305-4*) Replica Bks.

—Hide & Seek. 1993. 240p. mass mkt. 4.99 o.s.i (*0-446-36405-3*) Warner Bks., Inc.

—Reckless. 2000. 240p. 26.95 (*0-7351-0312-7*); 235p. pap. 16.95 (*0-7351-0313-5*) Replica Bks.

—Reckless. 1990. reprint ed. 18.00 o.p. (*0-7278-4048-7*) Severn Hse. Pubs., Ltd.

—Reckless. 1993. 240p. mass mkt. 4.99 o.s.i (*0-446-36549-1*); 1989. pap. 3.95 (*0-445-20819-8*) Warner Bks., Inc.

—Stolen Moments. 2000. 253p. 26.95 (*0-7351-0300-3*); pap. 16.95 (*0-7351-0301-1*) Replica Bks.

—Stolen Moments. 1991. reprint ed. 18.95 o.p. (*0-7278-4174-2*) Severn Hse. Pubs., Ltd.

—Stolen Moments. 1995. 256p. mass mkt. 5.99 o.s.i (*0-446-60163-2*); 1990. mass mkt. 4.95 (*0-445-21010-9*, Mysterious Pr. Paperback Bks.) Warner Bks., Inc.

—Ties That Bind. 2000. 255p. 26.95 (*0-7351-0308-9*); 16.95 (*0-7351-0309-7*) Replica Bks.

—Ties That Bind. 1991. 256p. reprint ed. 19.00 o.p. (*0-7278-4245-5*) Severn Hse. Pubs., Ltd.

—Ties That Bind. 1991. 256p. mass mkt. 4.99 (*0-446-36117-8*) Warner Bks., Inc.

—Wages of Sin. 1999. 254p. pap. 16.95 (*0-7351-0322-4*); reprint ed. 26.95 o.p. (*0-7351-0071-3*) Replica Bks.

—Wages of Sin. 1994. 272p. mass mkt. 5.50 (*0-446-60088-1*) Warner Bks., Inc.

—White Lightning. 2000. 316p. 28.95 (*0-7351-0302-X*); pap. 18.95 (*0-7351-0303-8*) Replica Bks.

—White Lightning. 1995. 320p. mass mkt. 5.99 o.p. (*0-446-60090-3*) Warner Bks., Inc.

### WOMEN JUDGES—FICTION

Coughlin, William Jeremiah. Her Honor. 1994. lib. bdg. 39.95 (*1-56849-405-X*) Buccaneer Bks., Inc.

—Her Honor. l.t. ed. 1990. (Magna Large Print Ser.). 555p. o.p. (*1-85057-671-8*) Magna Large Print Bks. GBR. *Dist:* Ulverscroft Large Print Canada, Ltd.

—Her Honor. 1988. 352p. mass mkt. 5.99 o.p. (*0-451-40083-6*, Signet Bks.); 1987. 17.95 o.p. (*0-453-00532-2*) NAL.

Dunmore, Helen. Your Blue-Eyed Boy. 288p. 1999. pap. 13.00 (*0-316-19747-5*, Back Bay); 1998. (YA). (gr. 8 up). 23.95 o.p. (*0-316-19738-6*) Little Brown & Co.

Gotlieb, Phyllis. Flesh & Gold. 1999. 13.95 (*0-312-87110-4*); 1999. 286p. pap. 13.95 (*0-312-86830-8*); 1998. 288p. 23.95 (*0-312-86523-6*) Doherty, Tom Assocs., LLC. (Tor Bks.).

Harrington, William. Partners. 1980. 352p. 12.45 o.p. (*0-87223-586-6*) Putnam Publishing Group, The.

Madame Justice. 2000. (Andy Ser.: No. 3). 336p. (C). mass mkt. 7.99 (*0-9673506-4-6*) Trent Martin Pubns.

Maron, Margaret. Bootlegger's Daughter. 1992. 272p. 18.95 (*0-89296-445-6*) Mysterious Pr.

—Bootlegger's Daughter. audio o.p. National Humanities Ctr.

—Bootlegger's Daughter. unabr. ed. 1994. (Deborah Knott Mystery Ser.: Vol. 1). audio 60.00 (*0-7887-0086-3*, 94326E7) Recorded Bks., LLC.

—Bootlegger's Daughter. l.t. ed. 2000. (Mystery Ser.). 426p. 29.95 o.p. (*0-7862-2327-8*) Thorndike Pr.

—Bootlegger's Daughter. 1993. 272p. reprint ed. mass mkt. 6.99 (*0-446-40323-7*) Warner Bks., Inc.

—Home Fires: A Deborah Knott Mystery. 1998. (Deborah Knott Mysteries Ser.: Vol. 6). 245p. 22.00 o.p. (*0-89296-655-6*) Mysterious Pr.

—Home Fires: A Deborah Knott Mystery. unabr. ed. 1999. (Deborah Knott Mystery Ser.: Vol. 6). audio 46.00 (*0-7887-3212-9*, 95726E7) Recorded Bks., LLC.

—Home Fires: A Deborah Knott Mystery. 2000. 288p. reprint ed. mass mkt. 6.50 (*0-446-60810-6*) Warner Bks., Inc.

—Killer Market. 1997. 288p. 22.00 o.p. (*0-89296-654-8*) Mysterious Pr.

—Killer Market. unabr. ed. 2000. (Deborah Knott Ser.: Vol. 5). audio 51.00 (*0-7887-2944-6*, 95724E7) Recorded Bks., LLC.

—Killer Market. l.t. ed. 1998. (*0-7540-3329-5*); (*0-7540-3330-9*) Thorndike Pr.

—Killer Market. 1999. 304p. reprint ed. mass mkt. 6.99 (*0-446-60619-7*) Warner Bks., Inc.

—Shooting at Loons. l.t. ed. 1994. pap. 19.95 o.p. (*1-56895-083-7*, Wheeler Publishing, Inc.) Gale Group.

—Shooting at Loons. 1994. 240p. 18.95 (*0-89296-447-2*) Mysterious Pr.

—Shooting at Loons. 1995. 256p. reprint ed. mass mkt. 6.99 (*0-446-40424-1*) Warner Bks., Inc.

—Southern Discomfort. Bk. II. 1993. 256p. 17.95 (*0-89296-446-4*) Mysterious Pr.

—Southern Discomfort. unabr. ed. 1994. (Deborah Knott Mystery Ser.: Vol. 2). audio 51.00 (*0-7887-0032-4*, 94231E7) Recorded Bks., LLC.

—Southern Discomfort. l.t. ed. 2000. (Mystery Ser.). 351p. 29.95 (*0-7862-2330-8*) Thorndike Pr.

—Southern Discomfort. 1994. 224p. reprint ed. mass mkt. 6.99 (*0-446-40080-7*) Warner Bks., Inc.

—Storm Track. 2000. (Deborah Knott Mysteries Ser.). 272p. 22.95 (*0-89296-656-4*) Mysterious Pr.

—Storm Track. l.t. ed. 2000. (Mystery Ser.). 349p. 29.95 (*0-7862-2465-7*) Thorndike Pr.

—Up Jumps the Devil. unabr. ed. 2000. (Deborah Knott Mystery Ser.: Vol. 4). audio 51.00 (*0-7887-1310-8*, 95152E7) Recorded Bks., LLC.

—Up Jumps the Devil. 1996. 256p. 20.00 o.s.i (*0-89296-568-1*); 1997. 304p. reprint ed. mass mkt. 6.99 (*0-446-60406-2*) Warner Bks., Inc.

Porter, Joyce. A Meddler & Her Murder. 1992. 176p. pap. 7.95 o.p. (*0-89733-328-4*); pap. 7.95 (*0-89733-322-5*) Academy Chicago Pubs., Ltd.

Riehl, Gene. Quantico Rules: A Novel. 2003. 304p. 24.95 (*0-312-31051-X*) St. Martin's Pr.

Rosenberg, Nancy Taylor. Interest of Justice. unabr. ed. 1996. audio 80.00 (*0-913369-20-9*, 4169) Books on Tape, Inc.

—Interest of Justice. l.t. ed. 1993. 384p. 21.00 o.p. (*0-525-93680-7*, Dutton) Dutton/Plume.

—Interest of Justice. l.t. ed. 1993. 26.95 (*1-56895-047-0*, Wheeler Publishing, Inc.) Gale Group.

—Interest of Justice. 1994. 448p. mass mkt. 7.99 o.s.i (*0-451-18021-6*, Signet Bks.) NAL.

—Interest of Justice. abr. ed. 1993. (Classics on Cassette). 2p. audio 16.00 o.p. (*0-453-00855-0*) Penguin/HighBridge.

—Interest of Justice. 5.98 o.s.i (*0-8317-2670-9*) Smithmark Pubs., Inc.

Thayer, Nancy. Custody. l.t. ed. 2002. (Basic Ser.). 605p. 30.95 (*0-7862-3907-7*) Gale Group.

—Custody. E-Book 23.95 (*0-312-70324-4*); 2001. 320p. 24.95 (*0-312-27734-2*) St. Martin's Pr.

Trackler, Richard. The Roll-Call Vote. 2001. 300p. pap. 17.95 (*1-57197-277-3*) Pentland Pr., Inc.

Turow, Scott. The Burden of Proof. 1990. audio 8.95 American Audio Prose Library, Inc.

—The Burden of Proof. unabr. collector's ed. 1990. audio 96.00 (*0-7366-1786-8*, 2623) Books on Tape, Inc.

—The Burden of Proof. 1990. 640p. 30.00 (*0-374-11734-9*); 367.20 o.p. (*0-374-11735-7*); E-Book 22.95 (*0-374-70093-1*); 640p. E-Book 9.95 o.p. (*0-374-70091-5*); E-Book 22.92 (*0-374-70092-3*) Farrar, Straus & Giroux.

—The Burden of Proof. l.t. ed. 1991. (General Ser.). 690p. 14.95 o.p. (*0-8161-5125-3*); 14.95 o.p. (*0-8161-5132-6*) Gale Group. (Macmillan Reference USA).

—The Burden of Proof. abr. ed. 1990. audio 17.00 (*0-671-70743-4*, Simon & Schuster Audioworks) Simon & Schuster Audio.

—The Burden of Proof. reprint ed. 2000. 608p. pap. 14.95 (*0-446-67712-4*); 1991. 576p. mass mkt. 7.99 (*0-446-36058-9*) Warner Bks., Inc.

—The Laws of Our Fathers. 1996. 817p. 26.95 (*0-374-18423-2*) Farrar, Straus & Giroux.

—The Laws of Our Fathers. l.t. ed. (Paperback Bestsellers Ser.). 931p. 1997. pap. 26.95 (*0-7838-1946-3*); 1996. 29.95 (*0-7838-1945-5*) Thorndike Pr.

—The Laws of Our Fathers. 1997. 832p. reprint ed. mass mkt. 7.99 (*0-446-60440-2*) Warner Bks., Inc.

Wallach, Anne T. Trials. 1996. 382p. 24.95 o.s.i (*0-525-94091-X*) Dutton/Plume.

—Trials. 1998. 416p. mass mkt. 6.99 o.s.i (*0-451-18741-5*, Signet Bks.) NAL.

Wilhelm, Kate. Justice for Some. 1994. (Northwest Mysteries Ser.). mass mkt. 5.99 o.s.i (*0-449-22247-0*, Fawcett) Ballantine Bks.

—Justice for Some. 1993. 272p. 18.95 o.p. (*0-312-09319-5*, Saint Martin's Minotaur) St. Martin's Pr.

Williams, Billy Dee. Twilight. Date not set. E-Book (*0-312-70749-5*, Tor Bks.) Doherty, Tom Assocs., LLC.

Williams, Billy Dee & Bowman, Elizabeth Atkins. Twilight. 2002. 432p. 25.95 (*0-312-87909-1*, Forge Bks.) Doherty, Tom Assocs., LLC.

### WOMEN LAWYERS—FICTION

Abbott, Cameron. An Inexpressible State of Grace. 2003. 17.95 (*1-56023-469-5*, Harrington Park Pr.) Haworth Pr., Inc., The.

Adams, Jenoyne. Resurrecting Mingus: A Novel. 2001. 256p. 23.00 (*0-684-87352-4*, Free Pr.) Simon & Schuster.

Adler, Elizabeth A. All or Nothing. 2000. 368p. mass mkt. 6.99 (*0-440-23496-4*, Dell Bks.) Dell Publishing.

—All or Nothing. l.t. ed. 1999. 27.95 (*1-56895-825-0*, Wheeler Publishing, Inc.) Gale Group.

Alder, Elizabeth A. All or Nothing. E-Book 6.99 (*1-930161-75-1*) Adobe Systems, Inc.

Alers, Rochelle. Just Before Dawn. 2000. (Arabesque Ser.). 256p. mass mkt. 5.99 (*1-58314-103-0*, Arabesque) BET Bks.

Barrett, Margaret & Dennis, Charles. Given the Evidence. 1999. 400p. reprint ed. mass mkt. 6.50 o.s.i (*0-671-00154-X*, Pocket) Simon & Schuster.

Barrett, Margaret, et al. Given the Evidence. 1998. 320p. 23.00 (*0-671-00153-1*, Atria) Simon & Schuster.

Bell, James S. Circumstantial Evidence. 1997. 480p. pap. 13.99 o.p. (*0-8054-6359-3*) Broadman & Holman Pubs.

Bell, James Scott. A Greater Glory. 2003. (Trials of Kit Shannon Ser.). 304p. pap. 12.99 (*0-7642-2645-2*) Bethany Hse. Pubs.

—A Higher Justice. 2003. (Trials of Kit Shannon Ser.). 304p. pap. 12.99 (*0-7642-2646-0*) Bethany Hse. Pubs.

Berne, Suzanne. A Perfect Arrangement: A Novel. 2001. 301p. tchr. ed. 23.95 (*1-56512-261-5*, Shannon Ravenel Bks.) Algonquin Bks. of Chapel Hill.

—A Perfect Arrangement: A Novel. 2002. 320p. pap. 13.00 (*0-452-28322-1*, Plume) Dutton/Plume.

Bernhardt, William. The Midnight Before Christmas: A Holiday Thriller. 1999. 240p. mass mkt. 5.99 (*0-345-42811-0*) Ballantine Bks.

Bickmore, Barbara. Beyond the Promise. l.t. ed. 1997. 25.95 (*1-57490-129-X*, Beeler Large Print Bks.) Beeler, Thomas T. Publisher.

—Beyond the Promise. 1998. 480p. mass mkt. 6.99 o.s.i (*1-57566-329-5*); 1997. 384p. 23.00 o.s.i (*1-57566-220-5*) Kensington Publishing Corp.

Biehl, Michael. Doctored Evidence: A Suspense Novel. 2003. 320p. mass mkt. 6.99 (*0-425-19311-X*) Berkley Publishing Group.

—Doctored Evidence: A Suspense Novel. 2002. 278p. pap. 24.95 (*1-882593-55-3*); 2003. 272p. reprint ed. pap. (*1-882593-70-7*) Bridge Works Publishing Co., Inc.

Blackstock, Terri. Evidence of Mercy. l.t. ed. 1998. (Christian Fiction Ser.). 527p. 24.95 (*0-7862-1402-3*) Thorndike Pr.

—Evidence of Mercy. 1995. (Sun Coast Chronicles Ser.: Bk. 1). 352p. pap. 12.99 (*0-310-20015-6*) Zondervan.

—Line of Duty. 2003. (Newpointe 911 Ser.: Bk. 5). 384p. pap. 12.99 (*0-310-25064-1*) Zondervan.

Brandon, Jay. Defiance County. 1997. 288p. pap. 6.99 (*0-671-53655-9*, Pocket); 1996. 384p. 23.00 o.p. (*0-671-53654-0*, Atria) Simon & Schuster.

Brown, Sandra. Best Kept Secrets. 1991. reprint ed. 19.95 o.p. (*0-7278-4136-X*) Severn Hse. Pubs., Ltd.

—Best Kept Secrets. 135.60 (*0-446-17428-9*); 2003. 480p. 16.95 (*0-446-53328-9*); 1989. 432p. reprint ed. mass mkt. 7.99 (*0-446-35393-0*) Warner Bks., Inc.

—The Witness. abr. ed. 1995. 17.95 o.p. (*0-7871-0296-2*, 392959); 39.95 o.p. (*0-7871-0298-9*, 102973) NewStar Media, Inc.

—The Witness. 1995. 432p. 21.95 o.s.i (*0-446-51631-7*); 1996. 448p. reprint ed. mass mkt. 7.99 (*0-446-60330-9*) Warner Bks., Inc.

Burke, Alafair. Judgment Calls: A Mystery. 2003. 352p. 23.00 (*0-8050-7386-8*) Holt, Henry & Co.

Cameron, Sue. Love, Sex & Murder. 1996. 368p. 23.95 o.s.i (*0-446-51852-2*) Warner Bks., Inc.

Cannon, Taffy. Class Reunions Are Murder. 9999. mass mkt. o.p. (*0-449-14951-X*); 1996. mass mkt. 5.50 o.s.i (*0-449-22389-2*) Ballantine Bks. (Fawcett).

—A Pocketful of Karma. 1993. 256p. 19.95 o.p. (*0-88184-906-5*, Carroll & Graf Pubs.) Avalon Publishing Group.

—A Pocketful of Karma. 1995. mass mkt. 5.50 o.s.i (*0-449-22388-4*, Fawcett) Ballantine Bks.

—Tangled Roots. 1995. 320p. 19.95 o.p. (*0-7867-0137-4*, Carroll & Graf Pubs.) Avalon Publishing Group.

—Tangled Roots. Date not set. mass mkt. (*0-449-14950-1*); 1995. mass mkt. 5.99 o.s.i (*0-449-22390-6*) Ballantine Bks. (Fawcett).

Charles, Kate. A Drink of Deadly Wine. 1993. (Book of Psalms Mysteries Ser.). 304p. mass mkt. 5.99 o.s.i (*0-446-40194-3*) Warner Bks., Inc.

Chastain, Thomas. The Prosecutor: A Novel. 1992. 288p. 20.00 o.p. (*0-688-10088-0*, Morrow, William & Co.) Morrow/Avon.

Clark, Mary Higgins. Let Me Call You Sweetheart. 2000. E-Book 9.95 (*0-7432-0623-1*, Simon & Schuster); 1996. 320p. pap. 7.99 (*0-671-56817-5*, Pocket); 1995. 26.00 o.s.i (*0-684-80395-X*, Simon & Schuster) Simon & Schuster.

—Let Me Call You Sweetheart. abr. ed. 1995. audio 18.00 (*0-671-52128-4*, 393021, Simon & Schuster Audioworks) Simon & Schuster Audio.

—Let Me Call You Sweetheart. 1996. 14.04 (*0-606-09540-3*) Turtleback Bks.

Close, Ellis. The Best Defense. 1999. 432p. mass mkt. 6.99 o.s.i (*0-06-093087-X*); 1998. 272p. 24.00 (*0-06-017496-X*) HarperCollins Pubs.

Coel, Margaret. The Shadow Dancer. 2002. 304p. 22.95 (*0-425-18640-7*, Prime Crime) Berkley Publishing Group.

—The Shadow Dancer. l.t. ed. 2003. lib. bdg. 28.95 (*1-58547-284-0*, Platinum) Ctr. Point Large Print.

—The Story Teller. 1999. (Arapaho Indian Mysteries Ser.). 256p. reprint ed. mass mkt. 6.50 (*0-425-17025-X*, Prime Crime) Berkley Publishing Group.

Coletta, Phyllis. Big Bad-Ass Book of Shots. 2004. 700p. pap. text 9.95 (*0-7624-1901-6*) Running Pr. Bk. Pubs.

Collins, Tess. The Law of Revenge. 9999. mass mkt. o.p. (*0-345-41484-5*); 1997. (*0-449-91075-X*, Fawcett); 1997. mass mkt. 6.99 (*0-449-22534-8*, Fawcett); 1997. mass mkt. 5.99 o.s.i (*0-8041-1684-9*, Ivy Bks.) Ballantine Bks.

—The Law of Revenge. l.t. ed. 1997. (Niagara Large Print Ser.). 416p. 29.50 o.p. (*0-7089-5888-5*, Ulverscroft) Thorpe, F. A. Pubs. GBR. *Dist:* Ulverscroft Large Print Bks., Ltd.

—The Law of the Dead. 1999. mass mkt. 6.99 o.s.i (*0-8041-1795-0*, Ivy Bks.) Ballantine Bks.

Condon, Richard. The Venerable Bead: A Deadly Serious Novel. pap. 14.95 (*0-312-31277-6*, Saint Martin's Griffin); 1992. 304p. 21.95 o.p. (*0-312-08331-9*) St. Martin's Pr.

Cooper, Natasha. Bitter Herbs. l.t. ed. 1995. (Ulverscroft Large Print Ser.). 528p. 29.99 o.p. (*0-7089-3291-6*, Ulverscroft) Thorpe, F. A. Pubs. GBR. *Dist:* Ulverscroft Large Print Bks., Ltd., Ulverscroft Large Print Canada, Ltd.

—Bloody Roses. 1993. 256p. 20.00 o.s.i (*0-517-59022-0*, Crown) Crown Publishing Group.

—A Common Death. l.t. ed. 1991. (Ulverscroft Large Print Ser.). Orig. Title: Festering Lillies. 29.99 o.p. (0-7089-2458-1, Ulverscroft) Thorpe, F. A. Pubs. GBR. Dist: Ulverscroft Large Print Bks., Ltd., Ulverscroft Large Print Canada, Ltd.

—Creeping Ivy. 1999. 342p. 23.95 o.p. (0-312-20520-1, Saint Martin's Minotaur) St. Martin's Pr.

—Creeping Ivy. l.t. ed. 1999. (Ulverscroft Large Print Ser.). 376p. 31.99 o.p. (0-7089-4144-3, Ulverscroft) Thorpe, F. A. Pubs. GBR. Dist: Ulverscroft Large Print Bks., Ltd., Ulverscroft Large Print Canada, Ltd.

—The Drowning Pool. 1998. (WWL Mystery Ser.). per. (0-373-26271-X, 1-26271-6, Worldwide Library) Harlequin Enterprises, Ltd.

—The Drowning Pool: A Willow King Mystery. 1997. (Willow King Mysteries Ser.). 240p. 21.95 (0-312-15130-6, Saint Martin's Minotaur) St. Martin's Pr.

—Fault Lines. 2000. 346p. 23.95 (0-312-25316-8, Saint Martin's Minotaur) St. Martin's Pr.

—Fault Lines. l.t. ed. 2000. (Ulverscroft Large Print Ser.). 480p. 31.99 (0-7089-4276-8, Ulverscroft) Thorpe, F. A. Pubs. GBR. Dist: Ulverscroft Large Print Bks., Ltd., Ulverscroft Large Print Canada, Ltd.

—Poison Flowers. unabr. ed. 1998. audio 83.95 (1-85903-128-5) Magna Story Sound GBR. Dist: Ulverscroft Large Print Bks., Ltd.

—Poison Flowers. 1993. 3.99 o.p. (0-517-09845-8) Random Hse. Value Publishing.

—Poison Flowers. l.t. ed. 1992. (Mystery Ser.). 544p. 29.99 o.p. (0-7089-2726-2, Ulverscroft) Thorpe, F. A. Pubs. GBR. Dist: Ulverscroft Large Print Bks., Ltd., Ulverscroft Large Print Canada, Ltd.

—Rotten Apples. 1997. (WWL Mystery Ser.: No. 244). per. (0-373-26244-2, 1-26244-3, Worldwide Library) Harlequin Enterprises, Ltd.

—Rotten Apples. unabr. ed. 1998. audio 76.95 (1-85903-141-2) Magna Story Sound GBR. Dist: Ulverscroft Large Print Bks., Ltd.

—Rotten Apples. 1995. 288p. 21.95 o.p. (0-312-13161-5, Saint Martin's Minotaur) St. Martin's Pr.

—Sour Grapes. 1999. (WWL Mystery Ser.: Vol. 319). pap. (0-373-26319-8, Worldwide Library) Harlequin Enterprises, Ltd.

—Sour Grapes. 1998. (Willow King Mysteries Ser.). 304p. 22.95 (0-312-18666-5, Saint Martin's Minotaur) St. Martin's Pr.

Cooper, Natasha & Myers, Tanya. Festering Lillies. unabr. ed. 1996. audio 69.95 o.p. (1-85903-111-0, 31110) Magna Story Sound GBR. Dist: Ulverscroft Large Print Bks., Ltd.

Creighton, Kathleen. The Black Sheep's Baby. 2002. (Silhouette Intimate Moments Ser.). 256p. mass mkt. (0-373-27231-6, Silhouette) Harlequin Enterprises, Ltd.

Devane, Terry. Juror Number Eleven: A Novel. 2003. 336p. mass mkt. 6.99 (0-425-19066-8) Berkley Publishing Group.

—Juror Number Eleven: A Novel. 2002. 320p. 24.95 o.s.i (0-399-14886-8) Penguin Group (USA) Inc.

—A Stain upon the Robe. 2004. 352p. mass mkt. 6.99 (0-425-19742-5) Berkley Publishing Group.

—A Stain upon the Robe. 2003. 304p. 24.95 (0-399-15108-7) Putnam Publishing Group, The.

—Uncommon Justice. 2002. 352p. reprint ed. mass mkt. 6.99 (0-425-18424-2) Berkley Publishing Group.

—Uncommon Justice. 2001. 240p. 24.95 o.p. (0-399-14717-9) Penguin Group (USA) Inc.

Dixon, Louisa. Next to Last Chance. 1998. 345p. 24.95 (1-885478-39-9) Genesis Pr., Inc.

Donovan, Kate. Stolen Kisses. 2001. (Romances Ser.). 219p. 25.95 (0-7862-3340-0, Five Star) Gale Group.

Downing, Sybil. Fire in the Hole. (Women's West Ser.). 1998. 239p. pap. 16.95 (0-87081-515-6); 1996. 248p. 22.50 o.p. (0-87081-380-3) Univ. Pr. of Colorado.

—Fire in the Hole. 1996. E-Book 12.95 (0-585-02261-5) netLibrary, Inc.

Fairstein, Linda. Cold Hit. l.t. ed. 2000. (Wheeler Large Print Book Ser.). 469p. 27.95 (1-56895-816-1, Wheeler Publishing, Inc.) Gale Group.

—Cold Hit. (Alexandra Cooper Mysteries Ser.). 2003. (Illus.). 464p. pap. 7.99 (0-671-01955-4, Pocket); 2002. 416p. E-Book (0-7432-3006-X, Scribner); 1999. 416p. 25.00 o.s.i (0-684-84846-5, Scribner); 2000. 416p. reprint ed. 7.99 (0-671-04212-2, Pocket) Simon & Schuster.

—Cold Hit. abr. ed. 1999. (Alexandra Cooper Ser.). audio 24.00 (0-671-04550-4, Simon & Schuster Audioworks) Simon & Schuster Audio.

—The Dead-House. 2001. E-Book 25.00 (1-59061-256-6) Adobe Systems, Inc.

—The Dead-House. 2003. 528p. mass mkt. 7.99 (0-671-01954-6, Pocket); 2001. (Illus.). 416p. 25.00 (0-684-84904-6, Scribner); 2001. 416p. E-Book 25.00 (0-7432-3007-8, Scribner); 2001. 560p. 25.00 (0-7432-2403-5, Scribner) Simon & Schuster.

—The Dead-House. abr. ed. 2001. audio 26.00 (0-7435-0902-1); audio compact disk 30.00 (0-7435-0903-X) Simon & Schuster Audio. (Simon & Schuster Audioworks).

—Final Jeopardy. 1998. 336p. mass mkt. 3.99 (0-671-02487-6, Pocket); 1997. (Illus.). 336p. pap. 7.99 (0-671-01012-3, Pocket); 1996. 400p. 22.50 o.p. (0-684-81489-7, Scribner); 1996. 23.00 o.p. (0-684-00314-7, Scribner) Simon & Schuster.

—The Kills. 2004. 400p. 25.00 (0-7432-2355-1); 2003. 624p. 25.00 (0-7432-5380-9) Simon & Schuster. (Scribner).

—Likely to Die. (Alexandra Cooper Mysteries Ser.). 1998. (Illus.). 448p. mass mkt. 7.99 (0-671-01493-5, Pocket); 1997. 400p. 24.00 (0-684-81488-9, Scribner) Simon & Schuster.

Felding, Joy. Tell Me No Secrets. 4.98 o.p. (0-8317-8649-3) Smithmark Pubs., Inc.

Fielding, Joy. Tell Me No Secrets. l.t. ed. 1994. 23.95 o.p. (0-7927-1895-X); 24.95 o.p. (0-7927-1896-8) BBC Audiobooks America.

—Tell Me No Secrets. l.t. ed. 1994. (Magna Large Print Ser.). 595p. o.p. (0-7505-0681-4) Magna Large Print Bks. GBR. Dist: Ulverscroft Large Print Canada, Ltd.

—Tell Me No Secrets. 1994. 416p. mass mkt. 5.99 (0-380-72122-8, Avon Bks.); 1993. 352p. 20.00 o.p. (0-688-08868-6, Morrow, William & Co.) Morrow/Avon.

Finder, Joseph. High Crimes. 1999. 400p. mass mkt. 7.99 (0-380-72880-X, Avon Bks.); 1998. 352p. 24.95 (0-688-14962-6, Morrow, William & Co.) Morrow/Avon.

—High Crimes. l.t. ed. 2000. (Charnwood Large Print Ser.). 440p. (0-7089-9128-9, Ulverscroft) Thorpe, F. A. Pubs. GBR. Dist: Ulverscroft Large Print Bks., Ltd., Ulverscroft Large Print Canada, Ltd.

—High Crimes. 1999. 13.04 (0-606-19265-4) Turtleback Bks.

Forster, R. A. Character Witness. 1997. 304p. mass mkt. 5.99 o.s.i (0-7860-0378-2, Pinnacle Bks.) Kensington Publishing Corp.

Fyfield, Frances. A Clear Conscience. unabr. ed. 1995. audio 69.95 (0-7451-6547-8, CAB 1163) BBC Audiobooks America.

—A Clear Conscience. 1996. (Helen West Mystery Ser.). mass mkt. 5.99 o.s.i (0-345-38508-X) Ballantine Bks.

—A Clear Conscience. unabr. ed. 2000. (West & Bailey Mystery Ser.). audio 59.95 Chivers Audio Bks. GBR. Dist: BBC Audiobooks America.

—A Clear Conscience. deluxe ed. 1995. 20.00 (0-676-50224-5, Pantheon) Knopf Publishing Group.

—A Clear Conscience. 2001. 272p. mass mkt. 6.99 (0-14-028251-3) Penguin Group (USA) Inc.

—A Clear Conscience. 1995. o.p. (0-676-50194-X) Random Hse., Inc.

—Deep Sleep. unabr. ed. 1996. (Prosecutor Helen West Mysteries Ser.). audio 54.95 (0-7451-4144-7, CAB827) BBC Audiobooks America.

—Deep Sleep. Chelius, Jane, ed. 240p. 1993. mass mkt. 4.99 o.p. (0-671-73547-0, Pocket); 1992. 18.00 o.p. (0-671-73546-2, Atria) Simon & Schuster.

—Not That Kind of Place. 1990. 224p. 17.95 o.p. (0-671-67666-0, Atria) Simon & Schuster.

—Not That Kind of Place. Chelius, Jane, ed. 1991. 256p. reprint ed. mass mkt. 5.50 (0-671-73945-X, Pocket) Simon & Schuster.

—Perfectly Pure & Good. 1995. (Mysteries Around the World Promotion Ser.). mass mkt. 5.99 o.s.i (0-345-38279-X, Ivy Bks.) Ballantine Bks.

—Perfectly Pure & Good. 1994. 224p. 20.00 o.s.i (0-679-42665-5, Pantheon) Knopf Publishing Group.

—Perfectly Pure & Good. l.t. ed. 1995. (Magna Large Print Ser.). 359p. o.p. (0-7505-0797-7) Magna Large Print Bks. GBR. Dist: Ulverscroft Large Print Canada, Ltd.

—Perfectly Pure & Good. 2000. 256p. pap. 5.99 (0-14-029195-4) Penguin Group (USA) Inc.

—A Question of Guilt. unabr. ed. 1993. (Prosecutor Helen West Mysteries Ser.). audio 69.95 (0-7451-5972-9, CAB 602) BBC Audiobooks America.

—A Question of Guilt. unabr. ed. 2000. (West & Bailey Mystery Ser.). audio 59.95 Chivers Audio Bks. GBR. Dist: BBC Audiobooks America.

—A Question of Guilt. 1990. 288p. mass mkt. 4.99 (0-671-67665-2, Pocket); 1989. 16.95 o.p. (0-671-67664-4, Atria) Simon & Schuster.

—A Question of Guilt. 1991. (Audio Books Ser.). audio 69.95 o.p. (0-8161-9227-8) Thorndike Pr.

—Shadow Play. l.t. ed. 1994. 22.95 o.p. (0-7927-1828-3); pap. 20.95 o.p. (0-7927-1827-5) BBC Audiobooks America.

—Shadow Play. 1994. mass mkt. 5.99 o.s.i (0-345-38507-1) Ballantine Bks.

—Shadow Play. 1999. 288p. pap. 5.99 (0-14-028683-7, Penguin Bks.) Penguin Group (USA) Inc.

—Shadows on the Mirror. Chelius, Jane, ed. 1991. 17.95 o.p. (0-671-70161-4, Atria); 1992. 224p. reprint ed. mass mkt. 4.50 (0-671-70162-2, Pocket) Simon & Schuster.

—Trial by Fire. l.t. ed. 1992. 18.95 o.p. (0-7927-1200-5); pap. 16.95 o.p. (0-7927-1174-2) BBC Audiobooks America.

—Without Consent. unabr. ed. 1997. (West & Bailey Mystery Ser.). audio 59.95 (0-7451-6799-3, CAB 1415) Chivers Audio Bks. GBR. Dist: BBC Audiobooks America.

—Without Consent. 1998. 272p. mass mkt. 5.99 (0-14-027477-4) Penguin Group (USA) Inc.

—Without Consent. l.t. ed. 1998. (Mystery Ser.). 325p. 26.95 (0-7838-8437-0) Thorndike Pr.

—Without Consent. 1997. (Helen West Mystery Ser.). 224p. 21.95 o.p. (0-670-87682-8) Viking Penguin.

Gaylord, Louise. Anacacho: An Allie Armington Mystery. 2002. 288p. 21.95 (0-9720227-0-8) Little Moose Pr.

Geary, Nancy Whitman. Misfortune. 2001. 504p. 28.95 (1-58724-066-1, Wheeler Publishing, Inc.) Gale Group.

—Misfortune. 2001. 368p. 23.95 o.p. (0-446-52753-X) Warner Bks., Inc.

Godwin, Gail. Glass People. 1996. 224p. pap. 15.00 (0-345-38990-5) Ballantine Bks.

—Glass People. 1986. (Contemporary American Fiction Ser.). 224p. pap. 6.95 o.p. (0-14-008222-0, Penguin Bks.) Viking Penguin.

Gordimer, Nadine. None to Accompany Me. 1996. (0-14-771180-0); 1995. 336p. pap. 15.00 o.s.i (0-14-025039-5, Penguin Bks.) Penguin Group (USA) Inc.

Grayson, Kristine. Utterly Charming. l.t. ed. 2000. (Five Star Romance Ser.). 289p. 26.95 (0-7862-2761-3, Five Star) Gale Group.

—Utterly Charming. 2000. 352p. mass mkt. 5.99 o.s.i (0-8217-6473-X); 319p. mass mkt. 5.99 o.s.i (0-8217-6472-1) Kensington Publishing Corp.

Green, Tim. The Letter of the Law. l.t. ed. 2000. (Wheeler Large Print Book Ser.). 341p. 28.95 (1-56895-956-7, Wheeler Publishing, Inc.) Gale Group.

—The Letter of the Law. 352p. 2000. E-Book 14.95 (0-7595-0027-4); 2000. E-Book 14.95 (0-7595-9027-3); 2000. E-Book 14.95 (0-7595-8027-8); 2000. 24.95 o.p. (0-446-52299-6); 2001. reprint ed. mass mkt. 7.99 (0-446-60995-1) Warner Bks., Inc.

—The Red Zone. abr. ed. 1998. audio 17.98 (1-57042-594-9) Time Warner AudioBooks.

—The Red Zone. 1999. 384p. mass mkt. 7.50 (0-446-60756-8); 1998. 325p. 24.00 o.p. (0-446-52298-8) Warner Bks., Inc.

Gruenfeld, Lee. The Expert. 1998. 464p. 24.95 o.p. (0-525-94406-0) Dutton/Plume.

—The Expert, 1 vol. 1999. 512p. reprint ed. mass mkt. 6.99 o.s.i (0-451-18807-1, Onyx) NAL.

Gutman, Amy. Equivocal Death: A Novel. 2001. 368p. 24.95 o.p. (0-316-38195-0) Little Brown & Co.

Hager, Jean. Ravenmocker. 1992. 272p. 17.95 (0-89296-493-6) Mysterious Pr.

—Ravenmocker. 1994. 256p. reprint ed. mass mkt. 5.99 o.s.i (0-446-40107-2) Warner Bks., Inc.

—The Redbird's Cry. l.t. ed. 1994. 357p. pap. 18.95 (0-8161-7402-4, Macmillan Reference USA) Gale Group.

—The Redbird's Cry. 1994. 288p. 18.95 (0-89296-494-4) Mysterious Pr.

—The Redbird's Cry. 1995. 256p. reprint ed. mass mkt. 5.50 (0-446-40106-4) Warner Bks., Inc.

—Seven Black Stones. 1995. (Molly Bearpaw Ser.). 304p. 18.95 o.s.i (0-89296-565-7) Mysterious Pr.

—Seven Black Stones. 1996. 256p. reprint ed. mass mkt. 5.99 (0-446-40386-5) Warner Bks., Inc.

—The Spirit Caller. 1997. 272p. 21.50 o.p. (0-89296-640-8) Mysterious Pr.

—The Spirit Caller. 1998. mass mkt. (0-446-40488-8, Mysterious Pr. Paperback Bks.); 320p. mass mkt. 6.99 (0-446-60595-6) Warner Bks., Inc.

Hallberg, Lynnette. Enchanted Evening. l.t. ed. 2001. 203p. pap. 22.95 (0-7838-9474-0) Thorndike Pr.

Haran, Maeve. It Takes Two. 1996. 560p. mass mkt. 6.50 o.p. (0-06-100882-6) HarperCollins Pubs.

Harper, Karen. The Dark Road Home. l.t. ed. 1998. 26.95 (1-57490-135-4, Beeler Large Print Bks.) Beeler, Thomas T. Publisher.

—The Dark Road Home. 1996. 448p. mass mkt. 5.99 o.s.i (0-451-18725-3) NAL.

Hartzmark, Gini. A Bitter Business. (Kate Millholland Novel Ser.). 1997. 340p. mass mkt. 5.99 o.s.i (0-8041-1241-X, Ivy Bks.); 1995. 320p. 4.99 o.s.i (0-449-90989-1, Fawcett) Ballantine Bks.

—Dead Certain. 2000. (Kate Millholland Novel Ser.). 320p. mass mkt. 6.50 o.s.i (0-8041-1900-7, Ivy Bks.) Ballantine Bks.

—Fatal Reaction. 1998. (Kate Millholland Novel Ser.). 352p. mass mkt. 6.50 o.s.i (0-8041-1743-8, Ivy Bks.) Ballantine Bks.

—Final Option. 1994. (Midwest Mysteries Ser.). (Orig.). mass mkt. 5.99 o.s.i (0-8041-1227-4, Ivy Bks.) Ballantine Bks.

—Principal Defense. 1992. (Midwest Mysteries Ser.). mass mkt. 5.99 o.s.i (0-8041-1074-3, Ivy Bks.) Ballantine Bks.

—Rough Trade. 1999. 293p. mass mkt. 6.50 (0-8041-1829-9, Ivy Bks.) Ballantine Bks.

Hill, Linda. Treasured Past. 2000. 189p. pap. 11.95 (1-56280-263-1) Naiad Pr., Inc.

Hinze, Vicki. Duplicity. 1999. 370p. mass mkt. 5.99 o.p. (0-312-96894-9, St. Martin's Paperbacks) St. Martin's Pr.

Hoag, Tami. Cry Wolf. 1997. 560p. mass mkt. 7.99 (0-553-56160-X) Bantam Bks.

—Guilty As Sin. 1997. 624p. mass mkt. 7.99 (0-553-56452-8) Bantam Bks.

—Guilty As Sin. l.t. ed. 1996. 825p. 25.95 o.p. (0-7838-1821-1, Macmillan Reference USA) Gale Group.

Hoffman, Jilliane P. Retribution. 2004. 432p. 24.95 (0-399-15127-3, Putnam & Grosset); 2003. 224.55 (0-399-19767-2) Putnam Publishing Group, The.

Isaacs, Susan. Lily White. 1996. 480p. 25.00 o.p. (0-06-017607-5) HarperCollins Pubs.

—Lily White. l.t. ed. 1997. 656p. mass mkt. 7.99 (0-06-109309-2, HarperTorch) Morrow/Avon.

—Lily White. l.t. ed. (Paperback Bestsellers Ser.). 738p. 1997. pap. 27.95 (0-7862-0829-5); 1996. 28.95 o.p. (0-7862-0828-7) Thorndike Pr.

Jackson, Lisa. The McCaffertys: Slade. 2002. (Silhouette Special Edition Ser.). 256p. mass mkt. (0-373-24480-0, Silhouette) Harlequin Enterprises, Ltd.

Jacobs, Jonnie. Cold Justice. 2003. 480p. mass mkt. 6.99 (0-7860-1543-8, Pinnacle Bks.); 2002. 34p. 23.00 (1-57566-827-0, Kensington Bks.) Kensington Publishing Corp.

—Evidence of Guilt. (Kali O'Brien Mystery Ser.). 1998. 384p. mass mkt. 5.99 (1-57566-279-5); 1997. 368p. 18.95 o.p. (1-57566-141-1) Kensington Publishing Corp. (Kensington Bks.).

—Intent to Harm. 2003. 352p. 22.00 (1-57566-829-7, Kensington Bks.) Kensington Publishing Corp.

—Motion to Dismiss. (Kali O'Brien Mystery Ser.). 2000. 400p. mass mkt. 5.99 (1-57566-543-3); 1999. 304p. 22.00 (1-57566-395-3) Kensington Publishing Corp.

—Motion to Dismiss. 2002. 284p. per. 17.95 (0-7592-1227-9) ereads.com.

—Shadow of Doubt. (Kali O'Brien Mystery Ser.). 1997. 308p. mass mkt. 5.50 o.s.i (1-57566-146-2, Kensington Bks.); 1996. 304p. pap. 18.95 o.p. (1-57566-017-2); 1996. mass mkt. 18.95 o.s.i (0-8217-5254-5) Kensington Publishing Corp.

Joe, Yolanda. The Hatwearer's Lesson. l.t. ed. 2003. lib. bdg. 28.95 (1-58547-339-1, Platinum) Ctr. Point Large Print.

—The Hatwearer's Lesson. 2003. 288p. 23.95 (0-525-94716-7) Dutton/Plume.

Kahn, Michael A. Death Benefits: A Rachel Gold Mystery. 1992. (Rachel Gold Mystery Ser.). 320p. 19.00 o.p. (0-525-93456-1, Dutton) Dutton/Plume.

—Death Benefits: A Rachel Gold Mystery. 1994. (Rachel Gold Mystery Ser.). 320p. mass mkt. 4.99 o.s.i (0-451-17687-1, Signet Bks.) NAL.

—Due Diligence. 1996. (Rachel Gold Mystery Ser.). 400p. mass mkt. 5.99 o.s.i (0-451-17970-6, Signet Bks.) NAL.

—Due Dilligence: A Rachel Gold Mystery. 1995. (Rachel Gold Mystery Ser.). 336p. 20.95 o.s.i (0-525-93743-9, Dutton) Dutton/Plume.

—Firm Ambitions. 1995. 320p. mass mkt. 5.99 o.s.i (0-451-17961-7, Onyx) NAL.

—Firm Ambitions: A Rachel Gold Mystery. 1994. (Rachel Gold Mystery Ser.). 320p. 18.95 o.p. (0-525-93742-0, Dutton) Dutton/Plume.

—Sheer Gall. 1996. (Rachel Gold Mystery Ser.). 320p. 23.95 o.s.i (0-525-94188-6) Dutton/Plume.

—Sheer Gall. 1998. (Rachel Gold Mystery Ser.). 368p. mass mkt. 5.99 o.s.i (0-451-40733-4, Onyx) NAL.

—Trophy Widow. E-Book 25.95 (0-312-70732-0, Tor Bks.); 2002. 432p. 25.95 (0-7653-0218-7, Forge Bks.) Doherty, Tom Assocs., LLC.

Kane, Stephanie. Blind Spot. 2000. 336p. mass mkt. 5.99 (0-553-58175-9) Bantam Bks.

Kaufelt, David A. The Fat Boy Murders. 1993. 240p. 20.00 (0-671-76092-0, Atria) Simon & Schuster.

—The Fat Boy Murders. Grose, Bill, ed. 1994. 256p. reprint ed. mass mkt. 5.50 (0-671-76093-9, Pocket) Simon & Schuster.

—The Fat Boy Murders. 230p. 3.98 o.p. (0-8317-2355-6) Smithmark Pubs., Inc.

—The Ruthless Realtor Murders: A Wyn Lewis Mystery. 1998. per. 6.50 (0-671-51148-3, Pocket); 1997. 240p. 22.00 o.s.i (0-671-51147-5, Atria) Simon & Schuster.

—The Winter Women Murders. 1995. 256p. mass mkt. 5.50 (0-671-76095-5, Pocket) Simon & Schuster.

—The Winter Women Murders: A Wyn Lewis Mystery. Grose, Bill, ed. 1994. 224p. 20.00 o.p. (0-671-76094-7, Atria) Simon & Schuster.

Kazantzis, Judith. Of Love & Terror. 2002. 340p. pap. 17.99 (0-86356-316-3) I.B.Tauris & Co., Ltd. GBR. Dist: Holtzbrinck Pubs., Palgrave Macmillan.

Kelly, Lelia. False Witness. 2000. 416p. mass mkt. 6.99 o.s.i (0-7860-1193-9); 312p. 23.00 o.s.i (1-57566-490-9, Kensington Bks.) Kensington Publishing Corp.

—Presumption of Guilt. 1998. 352p. mass mkt. 5.99 (*0-7860-0584-X*, Pinnacle Bks.); 224p. 22.95 o.s.i (*1-57566-249-3*) Kensington Publishing Corp.

Korelitz, Jean H. A Jury of Her Peers. l.t. ed. 1996. 25.95 (*1-56895-386-0*, Wheeler Publishing, Inc.) Gale Group.

—A Jury of Her Peers. 1997. 448p. mass mkt. 5.99 o.s.i (*0-451-18871-3*, Signet Bks.) NAL.

Korelitz, Jean Hanff. The Sabbathday River. 1999. 512p. 25.00 o.p. (*0-374-25323-4*); 1999. E-Book 25.00 (*0-374-70005-2*); 1998. pap. (*0-374-97008-4*) Farrar, Straus & Giroux.

Kress, Nancy. Beggars in Spain. E-Book 3.49 (*1-930936-40-0*) Fictionwise, Inc.

—Beggars in Spain. 1994. 448p. mass mkt. 7.50 (*0-380-71877-4*, Eos); 1993. 438p. 23.00 (*0-688-12189-6*, Morrow, William & Co.) Morrow/Avon.

Krich, Rochelle Majer. Speak No Evil. 1996. 82p. 21.95 o.p. (*0-89296-584-3*) Mysterious Pr.

—Speak No Evil. 1997. 384p. mass mkt. 6.50 o.p. (*0-446-40505-1*) Warner Bks., Inc.

Lambert, Mercedes. Dogtown: A Whitney Logan Mystery. 1991. (Whitney Logan Mystery Ser.). 272p. 18.95 o.p. (*0-670-83479-3*) Viking Penguin.

—Soultown: A Whitney Logan Mystery. 1996. (Whitney Logan Mystery Ser.). 256p. 21.95 o.s.i (*0-670-86684-9*, Viking) Viking Penguin.

Latt, Mimi. Powers of Attorney. 1993. 512p. 23.00 o.p. (*0-671-78708-X*, Simon & Schuster) Simon & Schuster.

—Powers of Attorney. Rubenstein, Julie, ed. 1994. 544p. reprint ed. mass mkt. 6.99 (*0-671-86916-7*, Pocket) Simon & Schuster.

—Pursuit of Justice. l.t. ed. 1998. (Large Print Bks.). pap. 24.95 (*1-56895-589-8*, Wheeler Publishing, Inc.) Gale Group.

—Pursuit of Justice. 1999. (Illus.). 480p. mass mkt. 6.99 o.s.i (*0-671-03411-1*, Pocket); 1998. 384p. 23.00 (*0-684-81184-7*, Simon & Schuster) Simon & Schuster.

Le Carré, John. The Constant Gardener. E-Book 9.99 (*1-58945-504-5*) Adobe Systems, Inc.

—The Constant Gardener. 2001. 496p. 7.99 (*0-7434-2855-2*, Pocket); 2000. 496p. 28.00 o.s.i (*0-7432-1505-2*, Scribner); 2001. 576p. reprint ed. mass mkt. 7.99 (*0-7434-2291-0*, Pocket) Simon & Schuster.

—The Constant Gardener. E-Book 9.99 (*0-7410-0341-4*) SoftBook Pr.

—The Constant Gardener. l.t. ed. 2001. 704p. 32.50 o.p. (*0-7432-1556-7*) Thorpe, F. A. Pubs. GBR. *Dist:* Ulverscroft Large Print Bks., Ltd.

Lysaught, Brian. Eye of the Beholder. 1995. 320p. 21.50 o.p. (*0-684-80078-0*, Simon & Schuster) Simon & Schuster.

MacDougal, Bonnie. Angle of Impact. 1998. mass mkt. 6.99 o.s.i (*0-345-41446-2*) Ballantine Bks.

—Angle of Impact. abr. ed. 1999. audio 7.99 o.s.i (*1-56740-290-9*, 1747, Nova Audio Bks.); 1998. audio 17.95 o.p. (*1-56740-773-0*, 458, Nova Audio Bks.); 1998. audio 26.95 (*1-56100-799-4*, 34, Bookcassette); 1998. audio 73.25 (*1-56740-833-8*, 798, Unabridged Library Editions) Brilliance Audio.

Margolin, Phillip. After Dark. 1996. 384p. mass mkt. 7.99 (*0-553-56908-2*) Bantam Bks.

—After Dark. l.t. ed. 1995. (Large Print Bks.). 24.95 o.p. (*1-56895-240-6*, Wheeler Publishing, Inc.) Gale Group.

—Ties That Bind. l.t. ed. 2003. 544p. pap. 25.95 (*0-06-053326-9*, HarperLargePrint) HarperTrade.

—Wild Justice. 2002. E-Book 7.99 (*0-06-621026-7*); 2002. E-Book 7.99 (*0-06-621025-9*); 2001. mass mkt. 186.37 o.s.i (*0-06-008372-7*); 2001. E-Book 7.99 (*0-06-018919-3*); 2000. 464p. pap. 26.00 (*0-06-019913-X*) HarperCollins Pubs.

—Wild Justice. 2000. 384p. 26.00 (*0-06-019624-6*, HarperCollins) HarperTrade.

Marlowe, Toby. Beyond a Reasonable Doubt. 1997. 352p. mass mkt. 5.99 o.s.i (*0-7860-0429-0*, Pinnacle Bks.) Kensington Publishing Corp.

Maron, Margaret. Bootlegger's Daughter. 1992. 272p. 18.95 (*0-89296-445-6*) Mysterious Pr.

—Bootlegger's Daughter. 1993. 272p. reprint ed. mass mkt. 6.99 (*0-446-40323-7*) Warner Bks., Inc.

—Home Fires: A Deborah Knott Mystery. l.t. ed. 1999. (Mystery Ser.). 325p. 29.95 (*0-7862-1620-4*) Thorndike Pr.

—Southern Discomfort, Bk. II. 1993. 256p. 17.95 (*0-89296-446-4*) Mysterious Pr.

—Southern Discomfort. l.t. ed. 2000. (Mystery Ser.). 351p. 29.95 (*0-7862-2330-8*) Thorndike Pr.

—Southern Discomfort. 1994. 224p. reprint ed. mass mkt. 6.99 (*0-446-40080-7*) Warner Bks., Inc.

Martini, Steve. Critical Mass. 1999. reprint ed. 384p. mass mkt. 7.99 (*0-515-12648-9*); 7.99 (*0-515-12583-0*) Berkley Publishing Group. (Jove).

—Critical Mass. l.t. ed. 1998. 28.95 (*1-56895-668-1*, Wheeler Publishing, Inc.) Gale Group.

—Critical Mass. 1998. 448p. 25.95 o.p. (*0-399-14362-9*) Penguin Group (USA) Inc.

—The List. 1997. 438p. 24.95 o.p. (*0-399-14261-4*, G. P. Putnam's Sons) Penguin Group (USA) Inc.

—The List. l.t. ed. (Core Ser.). 586p. 1999. 30.95 (*0-7838-8089-8*); 1998. pap. 27.95 (*0-7838-8090-1*) Thorndike Pr.

Matera, Lia. Designer Crimes: A Laura Di Palma Mystery. (Laura Di Palma Mystery Ser.). 1996. 288p. pap. 6.50 (*0-671-00196-5*, Pocket); 1995. 240p. 21.00 o.s.i (*0-684-80312-7*, Simon & Schuster) Simon & Schuster.

—Face Value: A Laura Di Palma Mystery. (Laura Di Palma Ser.). 1995. o.s.i (*0-684-88840-8*, Pocket); 1995. (Illus.). 272p. mass mkt. 5.99 (*0-671-88840-4*, Pocket); 1994. 221p. 20.00 (*0-671-74197-7*, Simon & Schuster) Simon & Schuster.

—The Good Fight. 1991. (Laura Di Palma Ser.). mass mkt. 5.99 o.s.i (*0-345-37107-0*, Ballantine Bks.) Ballantine Bks.

—The Good Fight. 1990. 17.95 o.p. (*0-671-68561-9*, Simon & Schuster) Simon & Schuster.

—A Hard Bargain. 1993. (Laura Di Palma Ser.). mass mkt. 5.99 o.s.i (*0-345-38059-2*) Ballantine Bks.

—A Hard Bargain. 1992. 224p. 19.00 o.p. (*0-671-74196-9*, Simon & Schuster) Simon & Schuster.

—Havana Twist: A Willa Jansson Mystery. abr. ed. 1998. (Willa Jansson Mystery Ser.). 3p. audio 18.00 (*0-7871-1735-8*, Dove Audio) NewStar Media, Inc.

—Havana Twist: A Willa Jansson Mystery. (Willa Jansson Mystery Ser.). 1999. 352p. pap. 6.99 o.s.i (*0-671-00421-2*, Pocket); 1998. 256p. 22.00 (*0-684-83470-7*, Simon & Schuster) Simon & Schuster.

—Hidden Agenda. 1992. (Willa Jansson Ser.). mass mkt. 5.99 o.s.i (*0-345-37128-3*, Ballantine Bks.) Ballantine Bks.

—Hidden Agenda. 1988. mass mkt. 3.50 o.s.i (*0-553-27721-9*) Bantam Bks.

—Last Chants. (Willa Jansson Mystery Ser.). 1997. 320p. pap. 5.99 (*0-671-88096-9*, Pocket); 1996. 240p. 21.00 (*0-684-81085-9*, Simon & Schuster) Simon & Schuster.

—Prior Convictions. 1992. (Northern California Mysteries Ser.). mass mkt. 5.99 o.s.i (*0-345-37445-2*) Ballantine Bks.

—Prior Convictions. 1991. 224p. 17.95 o.p. (*0-671-68560-0*, Simon & Schuster) Simon & Schuster.

—Radical Departure. 1991. (Laura Di Palma Ser.). 224p. (Orig.). mass mkt. 5.99 o.s.i (*0-345-37126-7*) Ballantine Bks.

—A Radical Departure. 1988. mass mkt. 3.50 o.s.i (*0-553-27072-9*) Bantam Bks.

—The Smart Money. 1991. 192p. (Orig.). mass mkt. 5.99 o.s.i (*0-345-37127-5*) Ballantine Bks.

—The Smart Money. 1988. 208p. (Orig.). mass mkt. 3.50 o.s.i (*0-553-27268-3*) Bantam Bks.

—Star Witness. (Willa Jansson Mystery Ser.). 1998. 336p. pap. 6.50 (*0-671-00420-4*, Pocket); 1997. 240p. 21.50 (*0-684-83469-3*, Simon & Schuster) Simon & Schuster.

—Where Lawyers Fear to Tread. 1991. (Willa Jansson Ser.). mass mkt. 5.99 o.s.i (*0-345-37125-9*) Ballantine Bks.

—Where Lawyers Fear to Tread. 1987. mass mkt. 3.50 o.s.i (*0-553-27588-7*) Bantam Bks.

—Where Lawyers Fear to Tread. 1999. (Mystery Ser.). 209p. 20.95 o.p. (*0-7862-1814-2*, Five Star) Gale Group.

Matturro, Claire Hamner. Skinny-Dipping. 2004. (*0-06-056705-8*, Morrow, William & Co.) Morrow/Avon.

McCann, Timmothy B. Until... 1999. 272p. pap. 12.00 (*0-380-80579-0*, Avon Bks.) Morrow/Avon.

McGuire, Christine. Until Judgment Day. 2003. 368p. mass mkt. 6.99 (*0-7434-2230-9*, Pocket) Simon & Schuster.

McKemmish, Jan. Only Lawyers Dancing. 1993. 192p. reprint ed. lib. bdg. 24.95 o.p. (*0-939416-70-0*); pap. 9.95 o.p. (*0-939416-69-7*) Cleis Pr.

McKinney, Meagan. A Man to Slay Dragons. 1996. 416p. mass mkt. 5.99 o.s.i (*0-8217-5345-2*, Zebra Bks.); 384p. pap. 21.95 o.p. (*1-57566-009-1*) Kensington Publishing Corp.

McKinzie, Clinton. Trial by Ice & Fire. 2004. 400p. mass mkt. 6.99 (*0-440-23727-0*, Dell Bks.); 2003. 320p. 21.95 (*0-385-33735-3*, Delacorte Pr.) Dell Publishing.

—Trial by Ice & Fire. l.t. ed. 2003. 559p. 29.95 (*0-7862-6064-5*) Gale Group.

Michael, Judith, pseud. Sleeping Beauty. l.t. ed. 1992. (General Ser.). 832p. lib. bdg. 23.95 o.p. (*0-8161-5490-2*); 16.95 o.p. (*0-8161-5491-0*) Gale Group. (Macmillan Reference USA).

—Sleeping Beauty. 1994. 640p. mass mkt. 7.99 o.s.i (*0-671-89959-7*, Pocket); 1991. 560p. 22.00 o.p. (*0-671-64893-4*, Simon & Schuster) Simon & Schuster.

—Sleeping Beauty. Grose, Bill, ed. 1992. 640p. reprint ed. mass mkt. 5.99 (*0-671-78252-5*, Pocket) Simon & Schuster.

Mickelbury, Penny. One Must Wait. 1998. 256p. 22.00 (*0-684-83741-2*, Simon & Schuster) Simon & Schuster.

—One Must Wait. 1999. 304p. mass mkt. 6.50 (*0-312-97186-9*, St. Martin's Paperbacks) St. Martin's Pr.

—Paradise Interrupted. 2001. 288p. 23.00 (*0-684-85991-2*, Simon & Schuster) Simon & Schuster.

—The Step Between. 240p. 2002. pap. 17.95 (*0-7432-4636-5*); 2000. 22.00 (*0-684-85990-4*) Simon & Schuster. (Simon & Schuster).

—Where to Choose. 1999. 256p. 22.00 (*0-684-83742-0*, Simon & Schuster) Simon & Schuster.

—Where to Choose. 2001. 240p. reprint ed. mass mkt. 6.50 (*0-312-97708-5*, 20-3261, St. Martin's Paperbacks) St. Martin's Pr.

Mitchard, Jacquelyn. The Most Wanted. l.t. ed. 1998. (Large Print Bks.). 407p. 27.95 (*1-56895-605-3*, Wheeler Publishing, Inc.) Gale Group.

—The Most Wanted. 1999. 416p. reprint ed. mass mkt. 7.99 o.s.i (*0-451-19685-6*, Signet Bks.) NAL.

—The Most Wanted. 1998. 448p. (gr. 9). 24.95 o.s.i (*0-670-87884-7*, Viking) Viking Penguin.

Mittman, Stephanie. The Courtship. 1997. 400p. mass mkt. 5.99 o.s.i (*0-440-22181-1*) Dell Publishing.

O'Shaughnessy, Perri. Acts of Malice. abr. ed. 1999. audio 17.95 o.p. (*1-56740-852-4*, 1759, Nova Audio Bks.); audio 73.25 (*1-56740-668-8*, 1758, Unabridged Library Editions); audio 26.95 (*1-56740-442-1*, 1757, Bookcassette) Brilliance Audio.

—Acts of Malice. 2000. 480p. mass mkt. 7.99 (*0-440-22581-7*) Dell Publishing.

—Acts of Malice. l.t. ed. 1999. 503p. 27.95 (*1-56895-766-1*, Wheeler Publishing, Inc.) Gale Group.

—Acts of Malice, Set. abr. ed. 1999. audio 17.95. audio 73.25 Highsmith Inc.

—Breach of Promise. 1999. 560p. mass mkt. 7.99 (*0-440-22473-X*) Broadway Bks.

—Breach of Promise. l.t. ed. 1999. pap. 23.95 (*1-56895-808-0*, Wheeler Publishing, Inc.) Gale Group.

—Invasion of Privacy. 1997. 544p. mass mkt. 7.99 (*0-440-22069-6*) Dell Publishing.

—Motion to Suppress. 1996. 480p. mass mkt. 7.99 (*0-440-22068-8*) Dell Publishing.

—Motion to Suppress. l.t. ed. 1999. pap. 24.95 (*1-56895-755-6*, Wheeler Publishing, Inc.) Gale Group.

—Move to Strike. 2001. 512p. reprint ed. mass mkt. 7.99 (*0-440-22582-5*) Dell Publishing.

—Move to Strike. l.t. ed. 2000. (Wheeler Large Print Book Ser.). 540p. 27.95 (*1-56895-988-5*, Wheeler Publishing, Inc.) Gale Group.

—Obstruction of Justice. abr. ed. 1998. audio 7.99 o.s.i (*1-56740-240-2*, 1333, Paperback Nova Audio Bks.); 1997. audio 16.95 o.p. (*1-56740-753-6*, 498, Nova Audio Bks.); 1997. audio 89.25 (*1-56740-553-3*, 969, Unabridged Library Editions); 1997. audio 25.95 (*1-56100-774-9*, 201, Bookcassette) Brilliance Audio.

—Obstruction of Justice. 1998. 512p. reprint ed. mass mkt. 7.99 (*0-440-22472-1*) Dell Publishing.

—Obstruction of Justice. 1997. 400p. 23.95 o.s.i (*0-385-31870-7*) Doubleday Publishing.

—Obstruction of Justice. l.t. ed. 2000. 27.95 (*1-56895-845-5*, Wheeler Publishing, Inc.) Gale Group.

—Obstruction of Justice. unabr. ed. 1999. audio 89.25 Highsmith Inc.

—Writ of Execution. l.t. ed. 2001. 665p. 29.95 o.p. (*0-7862-3511-X*) Thorndike Pr.

Parker, Barbara. Suspicion of Betrayal. 1999. 352p. 23.95 o.s.i (*0-525-94468-0*, Dutton Studio) Dutton/Plume.

—Suspicion of Betrayal. 2000. 432p. mass mkt. 6.99 (*0-451-19838-7*, Signet Bks.) NAL.

—Suspicion of Betrayal. l.t. ed. 1999. (Mystery Ser.). 568p. 29.95 (*0-7862-2000-7*) Thorndike Pr.

—Suspicion of Deceit. 1998. 368p. 23.95 o.p. (*0-525-94401-X*) Dutton/Plume.

—Suspicion of Deceit. 1999. 432p. reprint ed. mass mkt. 6.99 (*0-451-19549-3*, Signet Bks.) NAL.

—Suspicion of Deceit. unabr. ed. 1998. audio 78.00 (*0-7887-3572-1*, 95937E7) Recorded Bks., LLC.

—Suspicion of Deceit. l.t. ed. 1998. (Cloak & Dagger Ser.). 615p. 26.95 o.p. (*0-7862-1460-0*) Thorndike Pr.

—Suspicion of Guilt. 1995. 400p. 22.95 o.p. (*0-525-93769-2*, Dutton) Dutton/Plume.

—Suspicion of Guilt. l.t. ed. 1995. 26.95 (*1-56895-232-5*, Wheeler Publishing, Inc.) Gale Group.

—Suspicion of Guilt. 1996. 432p. mass mkt. 6.99 (*0-451-17703-7*, Signet Bks.) NAL.

—Suspicion of Guilt, unabr. ed. 1995. audio 91.00 (*0-7887-0353-6*, 94545E7) Recorded Bks., LLC.

—Suspicion of Innocence. 1994. 352p. 20.95 o.p. (*0-525-93744-7*); 20.95 (*0-525-93747-1*) Dutton/Plume. (Dutton).

—Suspicion of Innocence. 1994. 448p. mass mkt. 6.99 (*0-451-17340-6*, Signet Bks.) NAL.

—Suspicion of Innocence, unabr. ed. 1994. audio 85.00 (*0-7887-0024-3*, 94223E7) Recorded Bks., LLC.

—Suspicion of Innocence. 344p. 4.98 o.p. (*0-8317-4569-X*) Smithmark Pubs., Inc.

—Suspicion of Malice. 2000. 352p. 22.95 o.s.i (*0-525-94542-3*) Dutton/Plume.

—Suspicion of Malice. 2001. 432p. reprint ed. mass mkt. 6.99 (*0-451-20125-6*, Signet Bks.) NAL.

—Suspicion of Malice. l.t. ed. 2000. (Mystery Ser.). 565p. 29.95 (*0-7862-2655-2*) Thorndike Pr.

—Suspicion of Vengeance. 2001. 368p. 23.95 o.s.i (*0-525-94601-2*, Dutton) Dutton/Plume.

—Suspicion of Vengeance. l.t. ed. 2002. 30.95 (*0-7862-3751-1*) Gale Group.

—Suspicion of Vengeance. 2003. 448p. reprint ed. mass mkt. 7.50 (*0-451-20451-4*, Signet Bks.) NAL.

Patterson, Richard North. Degree of Guilt. unabr. collector's ed. 1994. audio 104.00 (*0-7366-2612-3*, 3354) Books on Tape, Inc.

—Degree of Guilt. unabr. ed. 1993. audio 16.00 o.s.i (*0-679-42131-9*); Set. 1994. audio 8.99 o.s.i (*0-679-43409-7*) Random Hse. Audio Publishing Group. (RH Audio).

—Eyes of a Child. 1997. pap. 12.00 o.s.i (*0-345-41813-1*) Ballantine Bks.

—The Final Judgment. 1998. pap. 7.99 (*0-345-91462-7*); 1996. 512p. mass mkt. 7.99 o.s.i (*0-345-40761-X*) Ballantine Bks.

—The Final Judgment. 1996. mass mkt. o.s.i (*0-345-40498-X*) Ballantine Bks. of Canada.

—The Final Judgment. l.t. ed. 1995. 640p. 25.95 o.p. (*0-7838-1581-6*, Macmillan Reference USA) Gale Group.

—The Final Judgment. 1995. 400p. 25.00 o.s.i (*0-679-42989-1*) Knopf, Alfred A. Inc.

—The Final Judgment, Set. abr. ed. 1998. audio 8.99 o.s.i (*0-375-40299-3*); 1995. audio 18.00 o.s.i (*0-679-44765-2*, 393153) Random Hse. Audio Publishing Group. (RH Audio).

—The Final Judgment: A Novel. l.t. ed. 1995. 640p. pap. 25.00 (*0-679-76666-9*) Random Hse. Large Print.

Peak, John. Mortal Judgments. E-Book 23.95 (*0-312-26461-5*); 1999. 352p. 23.95 o.p. (*0-312-19837-X*) St. Martin's Pr.

Peterson, Tracie & Bell, James Scott. Angel of Mercy. 2002. (Shannon Family Saga Ser.: Vol. 3). 384p. pap. 12.99 (*0-7642-2420-4*) Bethany Hse. Pubs.

Picoult, Jodi. A Perfect Match. 2002. 368p. 25.00 (*0-7434-1872-7*, Atria) Simon & Schuster.

—Perfect Match: A Novel. 2002. E-Book 9.99 (*0-7434-2280-5*, Atria) Simon & Schuster.

Piesman, Marissa. Alternate Sides. 1996. 304p. mass mkt. 5.50 o.s.i (*0-440-22240-0*) Dell Publishing.

—Close Quarters. 1995. 304p. mass mkt. 4.99 o.s.i (*0-440-21162-X*) Dell Publishing.

—Heading Uptown: A Nina Fischman Mystery. l.t. ed. 1993. 21.95 o.p. (*0-7927-1658-2*); pap. 19.95 o.p. (*0-7927-1657-4*) BBC Audiobooks America.

—Heading Uptown: A Nina Fischman Mystery. 1994. 320p. mass mkt. 5.50 o.s.i (*0-440-21161-1*) Dell Publishing.

—Personal Effects. Chelius, Jane, ed. 1991. 224p. (Orig.). mass mkt. 4.50 (*0-671-74275-2*, Pocket) Simon & Schuster.

—Survival Instincts. 1997. (Nina Fischman Mystery Ser.). 224p. mass mkt. 5.99 o.s.i (*0-440-22453-5*, Dell Bks.) Dell Publishing.

—Unorthodox Practices. 1989. 224p. mass mkt. 4.99 (*0-671-67315-7*, Pocket) Simon & Schuster.

Podrug, Junius. Presumed Guilty. 1998. 576p. mass mkt. 6.99 (*0-8125-5507-4*); 1997. 384p. 24.95 (*0-312-86242-3*) Doherty, Tom Assocs., LLC. (Forge Bks.).

Robson, Ruthann. Another Mother. 272p. 1996. pap. 10.95 o.p. (*0-312-14542-X*, Saint Martin's Griffin); 1995. 21.95 o.p. (*0-312-13431-2*) St. Martin's Pr.

Rogers, Chris. Bitch Factor. 1998. 336p. mass mkt. 5.99 (*0-553-58001-9*) Bantam Bks.

—The Rage Factor. 2000. 400p. mass mkt. 5.99 (*0-553-58070-1*) Bantam Bks.

Rosenberg, Nancy Taylor. Buried Evidence. 2000. 359p. 24.95 (*0-7868-6619-5*) Disney Pr.

—Buried Evidence. 2002. E-Book 5.95 (*0-7868-6986-0*); 2003. 368p. reprint ed. mass mkt. 7.99 (*0-7868-8983-7*) Hyperion Pr.

—Buried Evidence. l.t. ed. 2000. (Americana Ser.). 575p. 30.95 (*0-7862-2924-1*) Thorndike Pr.

—Conflict of Interest. 2002. 320p. 24.95 (*0-7868-6620-9*) Hyperion Pr.

—Conflict of Interest. l.t. ed. 2002. (Americana Ser.). 475p. 31.95 (*0-7862-4226-4*); 28.95 (*0-7862-4227-2*) Thorndike Pr.

—Mitigating Circumstances. l.t. ed. 1994. 21.95 o.p. (*0-7927-1753-8*); pap. 21.95 o.p. (*0-7927-1752-X*) BBC Audiobooks America.

—Mitigating Circumstances. unabr. ed. 1996. audio 72.00 (*0-7366-3476-2*, 4119) Books on Tape, Inc.

—Mitigating Circumstances. 1993. 368p. 21.00 o.p. (*0-525-93587-8*) Dutton/Plume.

—Mitigating Circumstances. 1993. 448p. mass mkt. 7.99 o.s.i (*0-451-17672-3*, Signet Bks.) NAL.

—Mitigating Circumstances. abr. ed. 1993. audio 16.00 o.p. (*0-453-00817-8*) Penguin/HighBridge.

—Mitigating Circumstances, unabr. ed. 1997. audio 78.00 (*0-7887-0822-8*, 94972E7) Recorded Bks., LLC.

—Trial by Fire. unabr. ed. 1996. audio 64.00 (*0-7366-3433-9*, 4077) Books on Tape, Inc.

—Trial by Fire. 1996. 352p. 22.95 o.p. (*0-525-93767-6*) Dutton/Plume.
—Trial by Fire. l.t. ed. 1996. (Large Print Bks.). 27.95 (*1-56895-305-4*, Wheeler Publishing, Inc.) Gale Group.
—Trial by Fire. 1996. 448p. mass mkt. 7.99 (*0-451-18005-4*, Signet Bks.) NAL.
—Trial by Fire, unabr. ed. audio 78.00 (*0-7887-0521-0*, 94716E7) Recorded Bks., LLC.
—Trial by Fire. abr. ed. 1996. audio 16.95 o.s.i (*0-14-086200-5*, Penguin AudioBooks) Viking Penguin.
Ross, JoAnn. Homeplace. 1999. (Illus.). 416p. pap. 6.99 (*0-671-02706-9*, Pocket) Simon & Schuster.
Rotstein, Nancy-Gay. Shattering Glass. 1996. 352p. 22.00 o.p. (*0-374-26223-3*) Farrar, Straus & Giroux.
Rudman, Anne Beane, et al. Given the Crime. 1998. 336p. pap. 6.50 (*0-671-00152-3*, Pocket); 320p. 22.00 (*0-671-00151-5*, Atria) Simon & Schuster.
Schanker, D. R. A Criminal Appeal. 2000. 352p. mass mkt. 5.99 o.s.i (*0-440-23581-2*) Dell Publishing.
—A Criminal Appeal. 1998. 288p. 23.95 (*0-312-19253-3*, Saint Martin's Minotaur) St. Martin's Pr.
—Natural Law. 2001. 242p. 22.95 (*0-312-26684-7*, Saint Martin's Minotaur) St. Martin's Pr.
Scottoline, Lisa. Courting Trouble. 2002. 320p. 25.95 (*0-06-018514-7*) HarperCollins Pubs.
—Courting Trouble. l.t. ed. 2002. 496p. 25.95 (*0-06-008193-7*, HarperLargePrint) HarperTrade.
—Courting Trouble. 2003. 432p. mass mkt. 7.99 (*0-06-103141-0*, HarperTorch) Morrow/Avon.
—Everywhere That Mary Went. l.t. ed. 2000. (Wheeler Large Print Book Ser.). 350p. 25.95 o.p. (*1-56895-854-4*, Wheeler Publishing, Inc.) Gale Group.
—Everywhere That Mary Went. 2003. 352p. pap. 11.95 (*0-06-054047-8*, Perennial) HarperTrade.
—Everywhere That Mary Went. 1993. 368p. mass mkt. 7.99 (*0-06-104293-5*, HarperTorch) Morrow/Avon.
—Final Appeal. l.t. ed. 1997. (Large Print Book Ser.). 25.95 (*1-56895-489-1*, Wheeler Publishing, Inc.) Gale Group.
—Final Appeal. 2003. 336p. pap. 11.95 (*0-06-053955-0*, Perennial) HarperTrade.
—Final Appeal. 1994. 352p. mass mkt. 7.99 (*0-06-104294-3*, HarperTorch) Morrow/Avon.
—Legal Tender. l.t. ed. 1997. (Large Print Bks.). pap. 24.95 (*1-56895-413-1*, Wheeler Publishing, Inc.) Gale Group.
—Legal Tender. 1997. 464p. mass mkt. 7.99 (*0-06-109412-9*); 1996. 304p. 23.00 o.p. (*0-06-017658-X*) HarperCollins Pubs.
—Mistaken Identity. 1999. 496p. 24.00 o.s.i (*0-06-018747-6*); 608p. mass mkt. 7.99 o.p. (*0-06-101419-2*) HarperCollins Pubs.
—Mistaken Identity. 2000. 592p. mass mkt. 7.99 (*0-06-109611-3*, HarperTorch) Morrow/Avon.
—Mistaken Identity. l.t. ed. (Thorndike/G. K. Hall Paperback Bestsellers Ser.). 704p. 2000. pap. 27.95 (*0-7862-1976-9*); 1999. 30.95 (*0-7862-1975-0*) Thorndike Pr.
—Mistaken Identity. 2000. 13.55 (*0-606-17714-0*) Turtleback Bks.
—Moment of Truth. 2000. 358p. 25.00 (*0-06-019609-2*); 544p. pap. 25.00 (*0-06-095611-9*) HarperCollins Pubs.
—Moment of Truth. abr. ed. 2000. audio 25.00 (*0-694-52310-0*); audio 39.95 (*0-694-52305-4*) HarperTrade. (HarperAudio).
—Moment of Truth. 2001. 448p. mass mkt. 7.50 (*0-06-103059-7*, HarperTorch) Morrow/Avon.
—Moment of Truth. unabr. ed. 1999. audio 75.00 (*0-7887-4152-7*, 96182E7) Recorded Bks., LLC.
—Rough Justice. l.t. ed. 1998. (Large Print Book Ser.). 26.95 o.p. (*1-56895-521-9*, Wheeler Publishing, Inc.) Gale Group.
—Rough Justice. 1998. 480p. mass mkt. 7.99 (*0-06-109610-5*); 1997. 352p. 24.00 o.s.i (*0-06-018746-8*) HarperCollins Pubs.
—Running from the Law. l.t. ed. 1996. 24.95 o.p. (*1-56895-319-4*, Wheeler Publishing, Inc.) Gale Group.
—Running from the Law. 1996. 464p. mass mkt. 7.99 (*0-06-109411-0*) HarperCollins Pubs.
—Running from the Law. 1995. 320p. 20.00 o.p. (*0-06-017659-8*) HarperTrade.
—The Vendetta Defense. 2001. 403p. E-Book 19.95 (*0-06-621323-1*); 400p. 25.00 (*0-06-018507-4*) HarperCollins Pubs.
Sheldon, Sidney. Rage of Angels. 1980. 504p. 18.95 (*0-688-03687-2*, Morrow, William & Co.) Morrow/Avon.
Sloan, Susan R. Act of God. 2003. 608p. mass mkt. 7.99 (*0-446-61260-X*); 2002. 544p. 24.95 o.p. (*0-446-52451-4*) Warner Bks., Inc.
Smith, Janet L. Practice to Deceive. 1993. (Northwest Mysteries Ser.). mass mkt. 4.99 o.s.i (*0-8041-0978-8*, Ivy Bks.) Ballantine Bks.
—Sea of Troubles. 1991. 224p. mass mkt. 4.99 o.s.i (*0-8041-0759-9*, Ivy Bks.) Ballantine Bks.
—Sea of Troubles. 1990. 197p. pap. 8.95 o.p. (*0-9602676-9-7*, Perseverance Pr.) Daniel, John & Co., Pubs.
—Sea of Troubles. 1990. 200p. (C). reprint ed. lib. bdg. 29.00 o.p. (*0-8095-4208-0*) Millefleurs.
—A Vintage Murder. 1995. mass mkt. 5.99 o.s.i (*0-8041-1385-8*, Ivy Bks.); 1994. 240p. 20.00 o.s.i (*0-449-90871-2*, Fawcett) Ballantine Bks.
Smith, Julie. Dead in the Water. (Orig.). 1993. pap. 4.99 o.p. (*0-8041-9804-7*); 1991. mass mkt. 4.99 o.s.i (*0-8041-0855-2*) Ballantine Bks. (Ivy Bks.).
—Death Turns a Trick. 1993. pap. 3.99 o.p. (*0-8041-9805-5*); 1992. reprint ed. mass mkt. 5.99 o.s.i (*0-8041-0856-0*) Ballantine Bks. (Ivy Bks.).
—Other People's Skeletons. 1995. 240p. pap. 15.00 (*0-345-47164-4*); 1994. pap. 4.99 o.p. (*0-8041-9820-9*, Ivy Bks.); 1993. mass mkt. 5.99 o.s.i (*0-8041-1086-7*, Ivy Bks.) Ballantine Bks.
—Other People's Skeletons. 1999. (Mystery Ser.). 232p. 20.95 (*0-7862-1953-X*, Five Star) Gale Group.
—The Sourdough Wars. 1993. pap. 4.99 o.p. (*0-8041-9807-1*); 1992. mass mkt. 5.99 o.s.i (*0-8041-0929-X*) Ballantine Bks. (Ivy Bks.).
—Tourist Trap. 1993. pap. 4.99 o.p. (*0-8041-9806-3*); 1992. mass mkt. 5.99 o.s.i (*0-8041-0930-3*) Ballantine Bks. (Ivy Bks.).
—Tourist Trap. 1986. 240p. 15.45 o.p. (*0-89296-162-7*) Mysterious Pr.
—Tourist Trap. 1987. 240p. mass mkt. 3.95 o.s.i (*0-445-40640-2*, Mysterious Pr. Paperback Bks.) Warner Bks., Inc.
Sorrells, Walter. Will to Murder. 1996. 304p. (Orig.). mass mkt. 5.50 (*0-380-78020-8*, Avon Bks.) Morrow/Avon.
Sprague, Gretchen. Death in Good Company. 1999. (WWL Mystery Ser.: No. 303). mass mkt. (*0-373-26303-1*, 1-26303-7, Worldwide Library) Harlequin Enterprises, Ltd.
—Death in Good Company. 1997. 224p. 21.95 o.p. (*0-312-16813-6*, Saint Martin's Minotaur) St. Martin's Pr.
—Death in Good Company. l.t. ed. 1998. (Basic Ser.). 335p. 28.95 (*0-7862-1345-0*) Thorndike Pr.
—Maquette for Murder. 2001. (WWL Mystery Ser.: No. 378). 251p. mass mkt. (*0-373-26378-3*, Worldwide Library) Harlequin Enterprises, Ltd.
—Maquette for Murder. E-Book 5.99 (*0-312-27355-X*); 2000. 240p. 22.95 (*0-312-19920-1*, Saint Martin's Minotaur) St. Martin's Pr.
Steel, Danielle. Lightning. 1996. 464p. pap. 7.99 (*0-440-22150-1*); 1995. 408p. 24.95 (*0-385-31192-3*, Delacorte Pr.); 1995. 408p. 200.00 (*0-385-31488-4*, Delacorte Pr.) Dell Publishing.
—Lightning. 1996. mass mkt. 8.99 o.s.i (*0-440-22292-3*) Doubleday Publishing.
—Lightning. 1995. audio 24.98 o.s.i (*0-553-74681-2*); audio 24.95 (*0-553-47364-6*, 692955) Random Hse. Audio Publishing Group. (RH Audio).
Stevenson, William. Boobytrap. 1987. (Illus.). 312p. 17.95 o.s.i (*0-385-23492-9*) Doubleday Publishing.
Stone, Katherine. Happy Endings. 1995. 384p. mass mkt. 5.99 o.s.i (*0-8217-4856-4*); 1994. 368p. mass mkt. 15.95 o.p. (*0-8217-4646-4*) Kensington Publishing Corp. (Zebra Bks.).
Summers, Cara. Short, Sweet & Sexy. 2002. (Harlequin Temptation Ser.). 216p. mass mkt. (*0-373-69100-9*, Harlequin Bks.) Harlequin Enterprises, Ltd.
Tanenbaum, Robert K. Act of Revenge. l.t. ed. 2001. (Large Print Book Ser.). 575p. 28.95 (*1-58724-025-4*, Wheeler Publishing, Inc.) Gale Group.
—Act of Revenge. 1999. 416p. o.p. (*0-06-019218-6*, HarperFlamingo) HarperCollins Pubs. Canada, Ltd.
—Act of Revenge. 2000. 544p. mass mkt. 7.50 (*0-06-109730-6*, HarperTorch) Morrow/Avon.
—Corruption of Blood. unabr. ed. 1998. (Butch Karp Mystery Ser.). audio 80.00 (*0-7366-4045-2*, 4544) Books on Tape, Inc.
—Corruption of Blood. 1996. 416p. mass mkt. 7.99 (*0-451-18196-4*, Signet Bks.) NAL.
—Depraved Indifference. 1990. 400p. reprint ed. mass mkt. 7.99 (*0-451-16842-9*, Signet Bks.) NAL.
—Falsely Accused. unabr. ed. 1998. (Butch Karp Mystery Ser.). audio 56.00 (*0-7366-4026-6*, 452511.95) Books on Tape, Inc.
—Falsely Accused. 1996. 320p. 23.95 o.s.i (*0-525-94168-1*) Dutton/Plume.
—Immoral Certainty. unabr. ed. 1997. (Butch Karp Mystery Ser.). audio 64.00 (*0-7366-3689-7*, 4368) Books on Tape, Inc.
—Immoral Certainty. 1992. 400p. reprint ed. mass mkt. 7.99 (*0-451-17186-1*, Signet Bks.) NAL.
—Irresistible Impulse. unabr. ed. 1998. (Butch Karp Mystery Ser.). audio 64.00 (*0-7366-4134-3*, 4639) Books on Tape, Inc.
—Irresistible Impulse. 1998. 445p. mass mkt. 6.99 (*0-451-19261-3*, Signet Bks.) NAL.
—Justice Denied. unabr. ed. 1997. (Butch Karp Mystery Ser.). audio 64.00 (*0-7366-3688-9*, 4367) Books on Tape, Inc.
—Justice Denied. abr. ed. 1994. pap. 16.00 o.p. incl. audio (*0-453-00903-4*, 25024-33894) Penguin/HighBridge.
—Material Witness. unabr. ed. 1997. (Butch Karp Mystery Ser.). audio 64.00 (*0-7366-3687-0*, 4366) Books on Tape, Inc.
—Material Witness. 1994. 416p. mass mkt. 7.99 (*0-451-18020-8*, Signet Bks.) NAL.
—No Lesser Plea. 1988. 368p. reprint ed. mass mkt. 7.99 (*0-451-15496-7*, Signet Bks.) NAL.
—No Lesser Plea. 1987. 17.95 o.p. (*0-531-09783-8*, Watts, Franklin) Scholastic Library Publishing.
—Reckless Endangerment. unabr. ed. 1999. (Butch Karp Mystery Ser.). audio 88.00 (*0-7366-4351-6*, 4828) Books on Tape, Inc.
—Reckless Endangerment. abr. ed. 1998. audio 17.95 o.p. (*1-56740-784-6*, 443, Nova Audio Bks.); audio 26.95 (*1-56740-059-0*, 10, Bookcassette); audio 73.25 o.p. (*1-56740-588-6*, 1001) Brilliance Audio.
—Reckless Endangerment. 1998. 352p. 23.95 o.p. (*0-525-94347-1*) Dutton/Plume.
—Reckless Endangerment. 1999. 448p. reprint ed. mass mkt. 7.99 (*0-451-19328-8*, Signet Bks.) NAL.
—Reversible Error. unabr. ed. 1997. (Butch Karp Mystery Ser.). audio 56.00 (*0-7366-3686-2*, 4365) Books on Tape, Inc.
—Reversible Error. 1993. 448p. reprint ed. mass mkt. 7.99 (*0-451-17519-0*, Signet Bks.) NAL.
—True Justice. 2000. 384p. 24.95 o.s.i (*0-7434-0589-7*, Atria); 2001. (Illus.). 464p. reprint ed. mass mkt. 7.99 (*0-7434-0590-0*, Pocket) Simon & Schuster.
—True Justice. l.t. ed. 2001. (Thorndike Mystery Ser.). 681p. 30.95 (*0-7862-3032-0*) Thorndike Pr.
Tarvin, Al. Chelsea & Sally. Haycox, Bobbi & Wordsmiths Unlimited Staff, eds. 1997. (Chelsea Ser.: No. 4). 280p. pap. 12.95 (*0-9643250-4-7*) CJH Enterprises.
—Chelsea & the Lords. 1999. (Chelsea Ser.: No. 5). 300p. pap. 12.95 (*0-9643250-5-5*) CJH Enterprises.
—Chelsea, Chelsea. Ausley, Lisa, ed. rev. ed. (Chelsea Ser.: No. 1). 233p. 1996. reprint ed. pap. 12.95 (*0-9643250-6-3*); Vol. 1. 1994. (Illus.). pap. 12.95 o.p. (*0-9643250-0-4*) CJH Enterprises.
—Chelsea, the Final Chapter. 2nd rev. ed. 1997. (Chelsea Ser.: No. 5). 305p. reprint ed. pap. 12.95 o.p. (*0-9643250-7-1*); (Illus.). pap. 12.95 (*0-9643250-1-2*) CJH Enterprises.
—Run, Chelsea, Run, Vol. 3. Haycox, Bobbi & CJH Enterprises Staff, eds. 1996. (Chelsea Ser.: Vol. 5). 260p. pap. 12.95 (*0-9643250-3-9*) CJH Enterprises.
Underwood, Michael. A Compelling Case. 1994. audio 49.95 (*1-85496-592-1*, 65921); Set. 1999. audio 39.95 Soundings, Ltd. GBR. *Dist:* Ulverscroft Large Print Bks., Ltd., ISIS Publishing.
—A Compelling Case. 1989. 14.95 o.p. (*0-312-02887-3*, Saint Martin's Minotaur) St. Martin's Pr.
—A Compelling Case. l.t. ed. 1991. (Ulverscroft Large Print Ser.). 29.99 (*0-7089-2381-X*, Ulverscroft) Thorpe, F. A. Pubs. GBR. *Dist:* Ulverscroft Large Print Bks., Ltd., Ulverscroft Large Print Canada, Ltd.
—Crime upon Crime. 1980. 224p. 9.95 o.p. (*0-312-17204-4*) St. Martin's Pr.
—A Dangerous Business. 1991. 15.95 o.p. (*0-312-05842-X*, Saint Martin's Minotaur) St. Martin's Pr.
—A Dangerous Business. l.t. ed. 1993. (Mystery Ser.). 368p. 29.99 o.p. (*0-7089-2923-0*, Ulverscroft) Thorpe, F. A. Pubs. GBR. *Dist:* Ulverscroft Large Print Bks., Ltd., Ulverscroft Large Print Canada, Ltd.
—Death at Deepwood Grange. 1986. 192p. 12.95 o.p. (*0-312-18604-5*) St. Martin's Pr.
—Death at Deepwood Grange. 1993. (Audio Books Ser.). 39.95 o.p. incl. audio (*0-7838-8012-X*) Thorndike Pr.
—Death at Deepwood Grange. l.t. ed. 1987. (Ulverscroft Large Print Ser.). 336p. 29.99 o.p. (*0-7089-1673-2*, Ulverscroft) Thorpe, F. A. Pubs. GBR. *Dist:* Ulverscroft Large Print Bks., Ltd., Ulverscroft Large Print Canada, Ltd.
—Death in Camera. l.t. ed. 1985. (Nightingale Ser.). 288p. 10.95 o.p. (*0-8161-3811-7*, Macmillan Reference USA) Gale Group.
—Death in Camera. 1984. 192p. 11.95 o.p. (*0-312-18612-6*) St. Martin's Pr.
—Double Jeopardy. 1981. 224p. 9.95 o.p. (*0-312-21814-1*) St. Martin's Pr.
—Double Jeopardy. l.t. ed. 1982. (Ulverscroft Large Print Ser.). 336p. 29.99 o.p. (*0-7089-0885-3*, Ulverscroft) Thorpe, F. A. Pubs. GBR. *Dist:* Ulverscroft Large Print Bks., Ltd., Ulverscroft Large Print Canada, Ltd.
—Dual Enigma. 1988. 192p. 15.95 o.p. (*0-312-02197-6*, Saint Martin's Minotaur) St. Martin's Pr.
—Dual Enigma. l.t. ed. 1990. (Ulverscroft Large Print Ser.). 29.99 o.p. (*0-7089-2263-5*, Ulverscroft) Thorpe, F. A. Pubs. GBR. *Dist:* Ulverscroft Large Print Bks., Ltd., Ulverscroft Large Print Canada, Ltd.
—Goddess of Death. 1982. 224p. 10.95 o.p. (*0-312-33056-1*) St. Martin's Pr.
—Guilty Conscience. 1999. audio 54.95 Soundings, Ltd. GBR. *Dist:* Ulverscroft Large Print Bks., Ltd.
—Guilty Conscience. 1993. 208p. 18.95 o.p. (*0-312-09824-3*, Saint Martin's Minotaur) St. Martin's Pr.
—Guilty Conscience. l.t. ed. 1994. (Ulverscroft Large Print Ser.). 432p. 29.99 o.p. (*0-7089-3103-0*, Ulverscroft) Thorpe, F. A. Pubs. GBR. *Dist:* Ulverscroft Large Print Bks., Ltd., Ulverscroft Large Print Canada, Ltd.
—The Hidden Man. 1999. audio 49.95 Soundings, Ltd. GBR. *Dist:* Ulverscroft Large Print Bks., Ltd.
—The Hidden Man. 1985. 196p. 10.95 o.p. (*0-312-37196-9*) St. Martin's Pr.
—The Hidden Man. l.t. ed. 1986. (Ulverscroft Large Print Ser.). 352p. 29.99 o.p. (*0-7089-1536-1*, Ulverscroft) Thorpe, F. A. Pubs. GBR. *Dist:* Ulverscroft Large Print Bks., Ltd., Ulverscroft Large Print Canada, Ltd.
—The Injudicious Judge. unabr. ed. 1993. audio 49.95 (*1-85496-682-0*, 66820) Soundings, Ltd. GBR. *Dist:* Ulverscroft Large Print Bks., Ltd.
—The Injudicious Judge. 1988. 224p. 15.95 o.p. (*0-312-01447-3*, Saint Martin's Minotaur) St. Martin's Pr.
—The Injudicious Judge. l.t. ed. 1989. (Ulverscroft Large Print Ser.). 29.99 o.p. (*0-7089-2083-7*, Ulverscroft) Thorpe, F. A. Pubs. GBR. *Dist:* Ulverscroft Large Print Bks., Ltd., Ulverscroft Large Print Canada, Ltd.
—A Party to Murder. unabr. ed. 1993. audio 49.95 (*1-85496-667-7*, 66677) Soundings, Ltd. GBR. *Dist:* Ulverscroft Large Print Bks., Ltd.
—A Party to Murder. 1984. 200p. 10.95 o.p. (*0-312-59768-1*) St. Martin's Pr.
—A Party to Murder. l.t. ed. 1985. (Ulverscroft Large Print Ser.). 320p. 12.50 o.p. (*0-7089-1246-X*, Ulverscroft) Thorpe, F. A. Pubs. GBR. *Dist:* Ulverscroft Large Print Bks., Ltd., Ulverscroft Large Print Canada, Ltd.
—Rosa's Dilemma. 1992. 1.99 o.p. (*0-517-08491-0*) Random Hse. Value Publishing.
—Rosa's Dilemma. 1990. 15.95 o.p. (*0-312-04416-X*, Saint Martin's Minotaur) St. Martin's Pr.
—Rosa's Dilemma. l.t. ed. 1992. (Romance Ser.). 368p. 29.99 o.p. (*0-7089-2780-7*, Ulverscroft) Thorpe, F. A. Pubs. GBR. *Dist:* Ulverscroft Large Print Bks., Ltd., Ulverscroft Large Print Canada, Ltd.
—The Seeds of Murder. 1992. 224p. 17.95 o.p. (*0-312-07800-5*, Saint Martin's Minotaur) St. Martin's Pr.
—The Seeds of Murder. l.t. ed. 1993. (Mystery Ser.). 416p. 29.99 o.p. (*0-7089-2979-6*, Ulverscroft) Thorpe, F. A. Pubs. GBR. *Dist:* Ulverscroft Large Print Bks., Ltd., Ulverscroft Large Print Canada, Ltd.
—The Uninvited Corpse. unabr. ed. 1993. 49.95 incl. audio (*1-85496-712-6*, 67126) Soundings, Ltd. GBR. *Dist:* Ulverscroft Large Print Bks., Ltd.
—The Uninvited Corpse. 1987. 224p. 15.95 o.p. (*0-312-00023-5*) St. Martin's Pr.
—The Uninvited Corpse. l.t. ed. 1988. 336p. 17.95 o.p. (*0-7089-1889-1*, Ulverscroft) Thorpe, F. A. Pubs. GBR. *Dist:* Ulverscroft Large Print Bks., Ltd.
Van Gieson, Judith. Ditch Rider: A Neil Hamel Mystery. (Neil Hamel Mystery Ser.). 240p. 1999. mass mkt. 5.99 (*0-06-109515-X*); 1998. 23.00 (*0-06-017513-3*) HarperCollins Pubs.
—Hotshots. 1996. (Neil Hamel Mystery Ser.). 256p. 22.00 o.p. (*0-06-017512-5*) HarperCollins Pubs.
—The Lies That Bind: A Neil Hamel Mystery. 1994. 304p. mass mkt. 4.99 o.p. (*0-06-109051-4*) HarperCollins Pubs.
—The Lies That Bind: A Neil Hamel Mystery. 1993. 256p. 20.00 o.p. (*0-06-017705-5*) HarperTrade.
—North of the Border: A Neil Hamel Mystery. 1993. 176p. mass mkt. 4.99 (*0-671-76967-7*, Pocket) Simon & Schuster.
—North of the Border: A Neil Hamel Mystery. 2002. 178p. pap. 13.95 (*0-8263-2886-5*) Univ. of New Mexico Pr.
—North of the Border: A Neil Hamel Mystery. 1988. 16.95 o.p. (*0-8027-5706-5*) Walker & Co.
—The Other Side of Death. 1991. 224p. 18.95 o.p. (*0-06-016581-2*) HarperTrade.
—The Other Side of Death. 2003. 224p. pap. 13.95 (*0-8263-3207-2*) Univ. of New Mexico Pr.
—Parrot Blues. 1995. 256p. 20.00 o.p. (*0-06-017706-3*) HarperTrade.
—Parrot Blues. 1995. 272p. mass mkt. 4.99 o.p. (*0-06-109048-4*, HarperTorch) Morrow/Avon.
—Raptor. 1990. 17.95 o.p. (*0-06-016167-1*) HarperTrade.
—Raptor. Isaacson, Dana, ed. 1991. 256p. reprint ed. mass mkt. 4.99 (*0-671-73243-9*, Pocket) Simon & Schuster.
—Raptor. 2002. 252p. pap. 13.95 (*0-8263-2974-8*) Univ. of New Mexico Pr.
—The Wolf Path: A Neil Hamel Mystery. 1992. 224p. 19.00 o.p. (*0-06-016804-8*) HarperTrade.
—The Wolf Path: A Neil Hamel Mystery. 1993. 256p. mass mkt. 4.50 o.p. (*0-06-109139-1*, HarperTorch) Morrow/Avon.
Vargas Llosa, Mario. The Feast of the Goat. Grossman, Edith, tr. from SPA. 2001. Tr. of Fiesta del Chivo. 416p. 25.00 (*0-374-15476-7*) Farrar, Straus & Giroux.

—The Feast of the Goat. 2002. Tr. of Fiesta del Chivo. 416p. pap. 14.00 (*0-312-42027-7*) Picador.
—The Feast of the Goat: International Edition. 2002. mass mkt. 7.99 (*0-312-98706-4*) Picador.
Warren, Nancy. Whisper. 2002. (Harlequin Blaze Ser.). mass mkt. (*0-373-79051-1*, Harlequin Bks.) Harlequin Enterprises, Ltd.
Wheat, Carolyn. Dead Man's Thoughts. 1995. 240p. mass mkt. 4.99 o.p. (*0-425-14933-1*) Berkley Publishing Group.
—Dead Man's Thoughts. 1983. 256p. 14.95 o.p. (*0-312-18501-4*) St. Martin's Pr.
—Fresh Kills. 240p. (Orig.). 1996. mass mkt. 5.50 o.s.i (*0-425-15276-6*); 1995. 19.95 o.p. (*0-425-14785-1*, Prime Crime); 1995. pap. 9.00 o.p. (*0-425-14920-X*, Prime Crime) Berkley Publishing Group.
—Mean Streak. (Cass Jameson Legal Mysteries Ser.). 240p. 1997. mass mkt. 5.99 o.s.i (*0-425-15577-3*); 1996. 19.95 o.p. (*0-425-15317-7*) Berkley Publishing Group. (Prime Crime).
—Sworn to Defend. (Cass Jameson Legal Mysteries Ser.). 320p. 1998. 22.95 o.s.i (*0-425-16303-2*); 1999. reprint ed. mass mkt. 5.99 o.s.i (*0-425-16932-4*) Berkley Publishing Group. (Prime Crime).
—Troubled Waters. (Cass Jameson Legal Mysteries Ser.). 1998. 256p. mass mkt. 5.99 o.s.i (*0-425-16380-6*); 1997. 240p. 21.95 o.s.i (*0-425-15784-9*) Berkley Publishing Group. (Prime Crime).
—Troubled Waters. 1998. 12.04 (*0-606-15743-3*) Turtleback Bks.
—Where Nobody Dies. 1988. 240p. mass mkt. 3.50 o.s.i (*0-553-27369-8*) Bantam Bks.
—Where Nobody Dies. 1996. (Cass Jameson Legal Mysteries Ser.). 272p. mass mkt. 5.99 o.s.i (*0-425-15408-4*, Prime Crime) Berkley Publishing Group.
—Where Nobody Dies. 1986. 288p. 15.95 o.p. (*0-312-86700-X*) St. Martin's Pr.
Whelan, Hilary. A Shoulder to Die On. 1995. 192p. 18.95 o.p. (*0-312-11889-9*, Saint Martin's Minotaur) St. Martin's Pr.
White, Stephen. The Program. abr. ed. 2001. audio 24.95 o.s.i (*1-58788-359-7*, 2545, Nova Audio Bks.); audio 34.95 (*1-58788-357-0*, 2543, Brilliance Audio Unabridged); audio 87.25 (*1-58788-358-9*, 2544) Brilliance Audio.
—The Program. l.t. ed. 2002. pap. 28.95 (*0-7862-3412-1*) Thorndike Pr.
Wilhelm, Kate. Best Defense. 1995. mass mkt. 6.99 o.s.i (*0-449-22314-0*, Fawcett) Ballantine Bks.
—Best Defense. 1994. 352p. 21.95 o.p. (*0-312-10937-7*) St. Martin's Pr.
—Death Qualified. 1992. (Northwest Mysteries Ser.). mass mkt. 5.99 o.s.i (*0-449-22155-5*, Fawcett) Ballantine Bks.
—Death Qualified. 1991. 22.95 o.p. (*0-312-05853-5*) St. Martin's Pr.
—Defense for the Devil. 2000. 448p. mass mkt. (*1-55166-628-6*, 1-66628-8, Mira Bks.) Harlequin Enterprises, Ltd.
—Defense for the Devil. E-Book 24.95 (*0-312-26451-8*); 1999. 400p. 24.95 o.p. (*0-312-19854-X*) St. Martin's Pr.
—Desperate Measures. 2001. 384p. 24.95 (*0-312-27663-X*, Saint Martin's Minotaur) St. Martin's Pr.
—Malice Prepense. 1996. 368p. text 24.95 o.p. (*0-312-14364-8*) St. Martin's Pr.
—No Defense. l.t. ed. 2003. (Large Print Ser.). 29.95 (*1-57490-503-1*) Beeler, Thomas T. Publisher.
—No Defense. 2001. 448p. mass mkt. (*1-55166-785-1*, 1-66785-6, Mira Bks.) Harlequin Enterprises, Ltd.
—No Defense. 2000. 376p. 24.95 (*0-312-20953-3*) St. Martin's Pr.
Williams, Nicola. Without Prejudice. 1998. 256p. 21.95 o.p. (*0-312-18683-5*, Saint Martin's Minotaur) St. Martin's Pr.
Wyrick, E. L. Power in the Blood. 1996. 336p. 22.95 o.p. (*0-312-13590-4*, Saint Martin's Minotaur) St. Martin's Pr.
—A Strange & Bitter Crop. 1994. 304p. 20.95 o.p. (*0-312-11075-8*, Saint Martin's Minotaur) St. Martin's Pr.


**WOMEN PHYSICIANS—FICTION**


Alder, Elizabeth. A Summer in Tuscany. 2002. (Illus.). 304p. 23.95 o.s.i (*0-312-26996-X*) St. Martin's Pr.
Alexander, Hannah. Silent Pledge. 2000. 352p. pap. 11.99 (*0-7642-2444-1*) Bethany Hse. Pubs.
Allingham, Margery. The Patient at Peacocks Hall. 20.95 (*0-89190-165-5*) Amereon, Ltd.
—The Patient at Peacocks Hall. l.t. ed. 2000. (G. K. Hall Nightingale Ser.). 156p. pap. 20.95 (*0-7838-8966-6*, Macmillan Reference USA) Gale Group.
Alter, Judy. Mattie. 1997. 192p. reprint ed. mass mkt. 3.99 (*0-8439-4156-1*, Leisure Bks.) Dorchester Publishing Co., Inc.
—Mattie. 1988. (Double D Western Ser.). 192p. pap. 12.95 o.s.i (*0-385-24167-4*) Doubleday Publishing.
Bannister, Jo. Gilgamesh. unabr. ed. 1998. audio 63.95 o.p. (*1-85903-013-0*) Magna Story Sound GBR. *Dist:* Ulverscroft Large Print Bks., Ltd.
—The Going down of the Sun. 1989. 12.95 o.s.i (*0-385-26451-8*) Doubleday Publishing.
—Striving with Gods. 1984. (Crime Club Ser.). 192p. 11.95 o.p. (*0-385-19482-X*) Doubleday Publishing.
Barker, Margaret. Reluctant Partners. l.t. ed. 2001. (Mills & Boon Large Print Ser.). 288p. 27.99 (*0-263-17147-7*) Harlequin Mills & Boon, Ltd. GBR. *Dist:* Ulverscroft Large Print Bks., Ltd., Ulverscroft Large Print Canada, Ltd.
Benson, Ann. The Burning Road. 2000. 720p. mass mkt. 6.50 (*0-440-22591-4*) Dell Publishing.
—The Plague Tales. 1998. 688p. mass mkt. 6.99 (*0-440-22510-8*) Dell Publishing.
Bohjalian, Chris. The Law of Similars. 1999. E-Book 11.50 (*0-609-60629-8*) Crown Publishing Group.
—The Law of Similars. l.t. ed. 1999. (Large Print Book Ser.). 27.95 (*1-56895-723-8*, Wheeler Publishing, Inc.) Gale Group.
—The Law of Similars. 2000. 336p. pap. 13.00 (*0-679-77147-6*, Vintage) Knopf Publishing Group.
Brand, Moses. Joe's Trial. 2000. 484p. 16.95 (*0-942520-12-2*) Distributors, The.
Breznik, Melitta. Night Duty. Theobold, Roslyn, tr. from GER. 1999. 131p. pap. 12.00 o.p. (*1-883642-85-X*) Steerforth Pr.
Brockmann, Suzanne. The Unsung Hero. 2003. 416p. mass mkt. 3.99 o.s.i (*0-345-46339-0*); mass mkt. (*0-345-46561-X*) Ballantine Bks. (Ivy Bks.).
—The Unsung Hero. l.t. ed. 2001. (Softcover Ser.). 533p. 23.95 (*1-58724-067-X*, Wheeler Publishing, Inc.) Gale Group.
Brown, Sandra. The Crush. l.t. ed. 2003. 662p. pap. 13.95 (*1-4104-0160-X*, Wheeler Publishing, Inc.) Gale Group.
—The Crush. 2002. 32.95 (*0-7862-4347-3*) Thorndike Pr.
—The Crush. 480p. 2003. mass mkt. 7.99 (*0-446-61305-3*); 2002. 26.95 (*0-446-52704-1*) Warner Bks., Inc.
Campbell, Phyllis. Come Home, My Heart. l.t. ed. 2001. (Candlelight Ser.). 207p. 22.95 (*0-7862-3627-2*) Thorndike Pr.
Carr, Robyn. Down By The River. 2003. 384p. mass mkt. (*1-55166-704-5*, Mira Bks.) Harlequin Enterprises, Ltd.
Christofferson, April. Clinical Trial. 2000. 333p. 24.95 o.p. (*0-312-86899-5*); 2001. 464p. reprint ed. mass mkt. 7.99 (*0-8125-7468-0*) Doherty, Tom Assocs., LLC. (Forge Bks.).
Clark, Beverly. Yesterday Is Gone. 1997. 293p. mass mkt. 10.95 (*1-885478-12-7*, Indigo) Genesis Pr., Inc.
Connor, Bernadette Y. The Parcel Express Murders. 2002. 239p. 22.00 (*0-9715838-0-3*); pap. 13.00 (*0-9715838-1-1*) Bee Con Bks.
Cook, Robin. Outbreak. 1988. 352p. mass mkt. 7.99 (*0-425-10687-X*) Berkley Publishing Group.
—Outbreak. unabr. ed. 1993. audio 48.00 (*0-7366-2348-5*, 3126) Books on Tape, Inc.
—Outbreak. l.t. ed. 1987. (General Ser.). 383p. 19.95 o.p. (*0-8161-4316-1*, Macmillan Reference USA) Gale Group.
—Outbreak. 1987. 368p. 17.95 o.p. (*0-399-13187-6*) Putnam Publishing Group, The.
—Outbreak. 1988. 14.04 (*0-606-00934-5*) Turtleback Bks.
—Vital Signs. 1992. 352p. pap. 7.99 (*0-425-13176-9*) Berkley Publishing Group.
—Vital Signs. unabr. ed. 1991. audio 72.00 (*0-7366-1964-X*, 2785) Books on Tape, Inc.
—Vital Signs. 1994. reprint ed. lib. bdg. 32.95 (*1-56849-267-7*) Buccaneer Bks., Inc.
—Vital Signs. l.t. ed. 1991. 560p. pap. 16.95 o.p. (*0-8161-5304-3*); lib. bdg. 22.95 o.p. (*0-8161-5303-5*) Gale Group. (Macmillan Reference USA).
—Vital Signs. 1991. 400p. 21.95 o.p. (*0-399-13575-8*, G. P. Putnam's Sons) Penguin Group (USA) Inc.
—Vital Signs. abr. ed. 1991. audio 15.95 (*0-671-72972-1*, Simon & Schuster Audioworks) Simon & Schuster Audio.
—Vital Signs. 1992. 14.04 (*0-606-00935-3*) Turtleback Bks.
Cooke, John Peyton. Haven: A Novel of Anxiety. 1996. 480p. 22.95 o.s.i (*0-89296-610-6*) Mysterious Pr.
—Haven: A Novel of Anxiety. 1998. mass mkt. (*0-446-40465-9*, Mysterious Pr. Paperback Bks.) Warner Bks., Inc.
Cordy, Michael. Crime Zero: A Novel. 1999. viii, 414p. 25.00 (*0-688-15509-X*, Morrow, William & Co.) Morrow/Avon.
Cornwell, Patricia. The Scarpetta Collection Vol. I: Postmortem & Body of Evidence. 2003. 640p. 26.95 (*0-7432-5580-1*, Scribner) Simon & Schuster.
—The Scarpetta Collection Vol. II: All That Remains & Cruel & Unusual. 2003. 672p. 26.95 (*0-7432-5581-X*, Scribner) Simon & Schuster.
Cuthbert, Margaret. The Silent Cradle. 1999. 496p. mass mkt. 6.99 (*0-671-01514-1*, Pocket); 1998. 368p. 23.00 o.s.i (*0-671-01513-3*, Atria) Simon & Schuster.
—The Silent Cradle. abr. ed. 1998. audio 18.00 (*0-671-58064-7*, 393598, Simon & Schuster Audioworks) Simon & Schuster Audio.
—The Silent Cradle. abr. ed. 1999. audio 16.85 (*0-671-01116-2*) Ulverscroft Audio (U.S.A.).
Dantz, William R. Nine Levels Down. 1999. 312p. mass mkt. 6.99 (*0-8125-2416-0*); 1995. 288p. 21.95 o.p. (*0-312-85483-8*) Doherty, Tom Assocs., LLC. (Forge Bks.).
Donaldson, Don J. In the Blood. 2001. 352p. mass mkt. 6.99 o.s.i (*0-425-17878-1*) Berkley Publishing Group.
English, Doris. A Healing Love. 1999. (Steeple Hill Love Inspired Ser.: Bk. 60). per. (*0-373-87060-4*, 1-87060-9, Harlequin Bks.) Harlequin Enterprises, Ltd.
Francis, Suzette. Rules for a Pretty Woman. 2003. 320p. pap. 13.95 (*0-06-053542-3*, Avon Bks.) Morrow/Avon.
Gansky, Alton. Marked for Mercy. l.t. ed. 2001. (Ridgeline Mystery Ser.). 411p. 24.95 (*0-7862-3205-6*) Thorndike Pr.
—A Small Dose of Murder, No. 4. (Ridgeline Mysteries Ser.: Vol. 2). 323p. pap. 12.99 (*1-56476-679-9*) Cook Communications Ministries.
—A Small Dose of Murder. l.t. ed. 2001. (Ridgeline Mystery Ser.). 402p. 24.95 (*0-7862-3204-8*) Thorndike Pr.
Gash, Jonathan. Different Women Dancing. l.t. ed. 1997. (Large Print Book Ser.). pap. 23.95 o.p. (*1-56895-512-X*, Wheeler Publishing, Inc.) Gale Group.
—Different Women Dancing. 1998. 304p. pap. 5.99 o.s.i (*0-14-026411-6*) Penguin Group (USA) Inc.
—Different Women Dancing. 1997. 320p. 21.95 o.s.i (*0-670-87369-1*) Viking Penguin.
—Prey Dancing. l.t. ed. 1999. (Dr. Clare Burtonall Mysteries Ser.). pap. 24.95 (*1-56895-626-6*, Wheeler Publishing, Inc.) Gale Group.
—Prey Dancing. 1999. (Dr. Clare Burtonall Mysteries Ser.). 288p. pap. 5.99 o.s.i (*0-14-028016-2*, Penguin Bks.) Penguin Group (USA) Inc.
—Prey Dancing. 1998. (Dr. Clare Burtonall Mysteries Ser.). 288p. 21.95 o.p. (*0-670-87764-6*) Viking Penguin.
Gerritsen, Tess. Harvest. unabr. ed. 1999. audio compact disk 96.00 (*0-7887-3716-3*, C1073E7); 1997. audio 80.00 (*0-7887-0790-6*, 94940E7) Recorded Bks., LLC.
—Harvest. 1997. (Illus.). 368p. mass mkt. 7.99 (*0-671-55302-X*, Pocket); 1996. 352p. 22.00 (*0-671-55301-1*, Atria) Simon & Schuster.
—Harvest. 2003. audio 9.95 (*0-7435-3286-4*, Encore); 1996. audio 18.00 o.s.i (*0-671-57067-6*, 394242, Simon & Schuster Audioworks) Simon & Schuster Audio.
—Harvest Export. 1997. per. 6.99 (*0-671-01370-X*, Pocket) Simon & Schuster.
—Life Support. l.t. ed. 1998. 26.95 (*1-56895-561-8*, Wheeler Publishing, Inc.) Gale Group.
—Life Support. 1998. (Illus.). 400p. mass mkt. 7.99 (*0-671-55304-6*, Pocket); 1997. 336p. 23.00 (*0-671-55303-8*, Atria) Simon & Schuster.
—Under the Knife. 2000. 256p. mass mkt. (*1-55166-611-1*, 1-66611-4, Mira Bks.); 1990. (Harlequin Intrigue Ser.: No. 136). (Illus.). 253p. pap. (*0-373-22136-3*, Harlequin Bks.) Harlequin Enterprises, Ltd.
—Under the Knife. l.t. ed. 2001. (Thorndike Famous Authors Ser.). 376p. 29.95 (*0-7862-3133-5*) Thorndike Pr.
Gerritsen, Tess, et al. Suspense & Adventure: Under the Knife; Adam's Story; Return to Yesterday; Everything but Time; Marriage, Diamond Style. 2001. (Harlequin Special Releases Ser.: No. 4). 266p. mass mkt. (*0-373-83495-0*, 1-83495-1, Harlequin Bks.) Harlequin Enterprises, Ltd.
Gibbons, Kaye. Charms for the Easy Life. unabr. ed. 2000. audio 54.95 (*0-7927-2352-X*, CSL 241, Chivers Sound Library) BBC Audiobooks America.
—Charms for the Easy Life. l.t. ed. 1993. 23.95 o.p. (*1-56895-030-6*, Wheeler Publishing, Inc.) Gale Group.
—Charms for the Easy Life. 1995. 256p. pap. 12.95 (*0-380-72557-6*); 1994. 304p. mass mkt. 7.99 (*0-380-72270-4*) Morrow/Avon. (Avon Bks.).
—Charms for the Easy Life. 1993. 256p. 19.95 o.s.i (*0-399-13791-2*) Penguin Group (USA) Inc.
—Charms for the Easy Life. Set. abr. ed. 1999. audio 17.00 (*0-671-88535-9*, 390510, Simon & Schuster Audioworks) Simon & Schuster Audio.
—Charms for the Easy Life. 1993. 13.04 (*0-606-07154-7*) Turtleback Bks.
Glass, Joseph. Blood: A Susan Shader Novel. 2000. (Susan Shader Novels Ser.). 400p. 24.00 (*0-684-85963-7*, Simon & Schuster) Simon & Schuster.
Gordon, Abigail. The Elusive Doctor. l.t. ed. 2001. (Mills & Boon Large Print Ser.). 288p. 27.99 (*0-263-16851-4*) Harlequin Mills & Boon, Ltd. GBR. *Dist:* Ulverscroft Large Print Bks., Ltd., Ulverscroft Large Print Canada, Ltd.
—Finger on the Pulse. l.t. ed. 2001. (Mills & Boon Large Print Ser.). 288p. 27.99 (*0-263-16829-8*) Harlequin Mills & Boon, Ltd. GBR. *Dist:* Ulverscroft Large Print Bks., Ltd., Ulverscroft Large Print Canada, Ltd.
Gordon, Noah. Matters of Choice. 1996. 368p. 24.95 o.p. (*0-525-94080-4*, Dutton) Dutton/Plume.
—Matters of Choice. 1997. 448p. mass mkt. 6.99 o.s.i (*0-451-18726-1*, Signet Bks.); 1996. pap. 12.95 (*0-452-27635-7*) NAL.
Grace, C. L. A Maze of Murders: A Medieval Mystery Featuring Kathryn Swinbrooke. 2003. 256p. 23.95 (*0-312-29016-0*, Saint Martin's Minotaur) St. Martin's Pr.
—Saintly Murders: A Medieval Mystery. 2001. 256p. 23.95 (*0-312-26993-5*, Saint Martin's Minotaur) St. Martin's Pr.
Greer, Robert. Heat Shock: A Novel. 2003. 320p. 24.95 (*0-89296-753-6*) Mysterious Pr.
Hornby, Nick. How to Be Good. 2002. 320p. pap. 13.00 (*1-57322-932-6*, Riverhead Trade (Paperbacks)) Berkley Publishing Group.
—How to Be Good. 2001. 320p. 24.95 o.s.i (*1-57322-193-7*, Riverhead Bks. (Hardcovers)) Putnam Publishing Group, The.
Horowitz, Renee B. Deadly Rx. 2001. 172p. per. 13.75 (*0-7433-0363-6*) Clocktower Bks.
—Deadly Rx. 1997. mass mkt. 5.50 (*0-380-78620-6*, Avon Bks.) Morrow/Avon.
—Rx for Murder. 2001. 160p. per. 13.50 (*0-7433-0116-1*) Clocktower Bks.
—Rx for Murder. 1997. mass mkt. 5.50 (*0-380-78619-2*, Avon Bks.) Morrow/Avon.
Klass, Perri. Love & Modern Medicine: Stories. 2001. 240p. pap. 13.00 (*0-618-10960-9*, Mariner Bks.) Houghton Mifflin Co. Trade & Reference Div.
Kraus, Harry Lee. Could I Have This Dance? 2002. 416p. pap. 12.99 (*0-310-24089-1*) Zondervan.
Kraus, Jim & Kraus, Terri. The Promise: A Novel. 2001. (Circle of Destiny Ser.). 416p. pap. 10.99 o.p. (*0-8423-1837-2*) Tyndale Hse. Pubs.
Krich, Rochelle Majer. Fertile Ground: A Mystery. 1999. mass mkt. 6.99 (*0-380-78953-1*); 1998. 352p. mass mkt. 22.00 (*0-380-97378-2*) Morrow/Avon. (Avon Bks.).
Land, Jon. Fires of Midnight. 1996. 361p. pap. text 6.99 (*0-8125-5252-0*); 1995. 320p. 22.95 o.p. (*0-312-85971-6*) Doherty, Tom Assocs., LLC. (Forge Bks.).
Landreth, Marsha. A Clinic for Murder. 1993. (Dr. Sam Turner Mystery Ser.). 212p. 19.95 o.s.i (*0-8027-3241-0*) Walker & Co.
—The Holiday Murders. l.t. ed. 1999. (Paperback Ser.). 328p. 24.95 (*0-7838-8827-9*) Thorndike Pr.
—The Holiday Murders. 1992. 243p. 19.95 o.s.i (*0-8027-1246-0*) Walker & Co.
—Vial Murders. 1994. (Doctor Samantha Turner Mystery Ser.). 224p. 19.95 (*0-8027-3199-6*) Walker & Co.
LeBeau, Sinclair. Glory of Love. 1997. 191p. mass mkt. 10.95 (*1-885478-19-4*, Indigo) Genesis Pr., Inc.
Lee, Mark. The Canal House. 2003. 368p. tchr. ed. 23.95 (*1-56512-379-4*, 72379) Algonquin Bks. of Chapel Hill.
—The Canal House. 2004. 368p. pap. 14.00 (*0-15-602954-5*, Harvest Bks.) Harcourt Trade Pubs.
Lipman, Elinor. The Pursuit of Alice Thrift. 2004. 288p. pap. 12.95 (*0-375-72459-1*, Vintage) Knopf Publishing Group.
—The Pursuit of Alice Thrift: A Novel. 2003. 288p. 23.95 (*0-679-46313-5*) Random Hse., Inc.
Lynn, Mary E. The Tavera Legacy. 1993. 448p. 24.95 o.p. (*0-312-93136-0*, Forge Bks.) Doherty, Tom Assocs., LLC.
Lyon, George Ella. With a Hammer for My Heart. 1997. (Illus.). 224p. (J). pap. 21.95 o.p. (*0-7894-2460-6*) Dorling Kindersley Publishing, Inc.
—With a Hammer for My Heart. 1999. 224p. reprint ed. pap. 12.00 (*0-380-73217-3*, Avon Bks.) Morrow/Avon.
McCrery, Nigel. Silent Witness. pap. (*0-312-30022-0*, Saint Martin's Griffin); 2001. 324p. per. 15.95 (*0-312-29197-3*, Dunne, Thomas Bks.); 1998. 320p. 23.95 (*0-312-18178-7*, Saint Martin's Minotaur) St. Martin's Pr.
—Silent Witness. l.t. ed. 1999. (Charnwood Large Print Ser.). 344p. 31.99 o.p. (*0-7089-9116-5*, Ulverscroft) Thorpe, F. A. Pubs. GBR. *Dist:* Ulverscroft Large Print Bks., Ltd., Ulverscroft Large Print Canada, Ltd.
—The Spider's Web. 1999. 320p. 22.95 o.p. (*0-312-20017-X*, Saint Martin's Minotaur) St. Martin's Pr.
—Strange Screams of Death. l.t. ed. 2001. (Charnwood Large Print Ser.). 408p. 32.50 (*0-7089-9191-2*) Ulverscroft Large Print Bks., Ltd.
Michaels, Fern. Sara's Song. 1998. mass mkt. 7.99 (*0-8217-7671-1*, Zebra Bks.); 416p. mass mkt. 7.50 (*0-8217-7480-8*) Kensington Publishing Corp.
Mina, Denise. Sanctum. 2004. 24.95 (*0-316-73592-2*) Little Brown & Co.

Morris, Lynn & Morris, Gilbert. Cheney Duvall, M. D. Series, Vols. 1-3. 1995. (Cheney Duvall, M. D. Ser.). pap. 29.99 o.p. (*1-55661-798-4*, 252798) Bethany Hse. Pubs.

—A City Not Forsaken. 1995. (Cheney Duvall, M. D. Ser.: Bk. 3). 336p. pap. 11.99 (*1-55661-424-1*) Bethany Hse. Pubs.

—A City Not Forsaken. 2000. (Christian Fiction Ser.: Bk. 3). 312p. 23.95 (*0-7862-2227-1*, Five Star); 1997. (Inspirational Ser.). 498p. lib. bdg. 23.95 (*0-7838-2025-9*, Macmillan Reference USA) Gale Group.

—Driven with the Wind. 2000. (Cheney Duvall, M. D. Ser.: 8). (Illus.). 320p. pap. 11.99 (*1-55661-699-6*) Bethany Hse. Pubs.

—Driven with the Wind. 2002. (Five Star Christian Fiction Ser.). 376p. 24.95 (*0-7862-4790-8*, Five Star) Gale Group.

—In the Twilight, in the Evening, 6. 1997. (Cheney Duvall, M. D. Ser.: Vol. 6). 320p. pap. 11.99 (*1-55661-427-6*) Bethany Hse. Pubs.

—In the Twilight, in the Evening. 1998. 23.95 (*0-7862-1365-5*, Five Star) Gale Group.

—Island of the Innocent. 1998. (Cheney Duvall, M. D. Ser.: Bk. 7). 320p. pap. 11.99 (*1-55661-698-8*) Bethany Hse. Pubs.

—The Secret Place of Thunder. 1996. (Cheney Duvall, M. D. Ser.: No. 5). 336p. pap. 11.99 (*1-55661-426-8*) Bethany Hse. Pubs.

—The Secret Place of Thunder. l.t. ed. 1998. (Cheney Duvall, M. D. Ser.: Vol. 5). 393p. 24.95 (*0-7862-1514-3*) Thorndike Pr.

—Shadow of the Mountains. 1994. (Cheney Duvall, M. D. Ser.: No. 2). 336p. pap. 11.99 (*1-55661-423-3*) Bethany Hse. Pubs.

—Shadow of the Mountains. (Christian Fiction Ser.). 1999. 23.95 (*0-7862-2089-9*, Five Star); 1995. 481p. 21.95 (*0-7838-1489-5*, Macmillan Reference USA) Gale Group.

—The Stars for a Light. 1994. (Cheney Duvall, M. D. Ser.: Bk. 1). 320p. pap. 11.99 (*1-55661-422-5*) Bethany Hse. Pubs.

—The Stars for a Light. 1999. (Christian Fiction Ser.: Vol. 1). (Illus.). 344p. 23.95 (*0-7862-1828-2*, Five Star); 1995. 355p. 21.95 o.p. (*0-7838-1376-7*, Macmillan Reference USA) Gale Group.

—Toward the Sunrising. 1996. (Cheney Duvall, M. D. Ser.: Vol. 4). 368p. pap. 11.99 (*1-55661-425-X*) Bethany Hse. Pubs.

—Toward the Sunrising. 1998. (Cheney Duvall, M. D. Ser.: Vol. 4). 362p. 23.95 (*0-7862-1436-8*, Five Star) Gale Group.

—Where Two Seas Met. l.t. ed. 2001. (Cheney Duvall, M. D. Ser.). 480p. pap. 17.99 (*0-7642-2610-X*) Bethany Hse. Pubs.

—Where Two Seas Met Bk #1. 2001. (Cheney Duvall, M. D. Ser.). 320p. pap. 12.99 (*1-55661-437-3*) Bethany Hse. Pubs.

Nessen, Ron & Neuman, Johanna. Knight & Day. 1995. 256p. 21.95 o.p. (*0-312-85588-5*, Forge Bks.) Doherty, Tom Assocs., LLC.

Palmer, Michael. Critical Judgment. 1997. 464p. mass mkt. 6.99 o.s.i (*0-553-84015-0*); 1998. 480p. reprint ed. mass mkt. 7.50 (*0-553-57408-6*) Bantam Bks.

—Critical Judgment. unabr. ed. 1997. audio 80.00 (*0-913369-35-7*, 4206) Books on Tape, Inc.

—Critical Judgment. l.t. ed. 1996. (Core Collection). 605p. 27.95 (*0-7838-1940-4*) Thorndike Pr.

—Natural Causes. 1994. 496p. mass mkt. 7.50 (*0-553-56876-0*) Bantam Bks.

—Natural Causes. abr. ed. 2000. audio 9.99 (*0-553-52727-4*, RH Audio) Random Hse. Audio Publishing Group.

—Natural Causes. unabr. ed. 1994. audio audio 91.00 (*0-7887-0085-5*, 94325E7) Recorded Bks., LLC.

Parsons, Julie. Mary, Mary. 1998. viii, 376p. (*1-86059-080-2*) Town Hse. IRL. *Dist:* Rinehart, Roberts Pubs.

—Mary, Mary: A Novel. 1999. 304p. 23.00 (*0-684-85324-8*, Simon & Schuster) Simon & Schuster.

Parsons, Julie & Simon and Schuster Staff. Mary, Mary. 2000. 336p. mass mkt. 6.99 (*0-06-103049-X*) HarperCollins Pubs.

Paul, Paula. Half a Mind to Murder. 2003. 208p. mass mkt. 5.99 (*0-425-19282-2*, Prime Crime) Berkley Publishing Group.

Ramsay, Eileen. Butterflies in December. 1996. 346p. mass mkt. o.s.i (*0-7515-1649-X*); 1995. 352p. o.s.i (*0-316-91422-3*) Little Brown & Co.

—Butterflies in December. l.t. ed. 1998. (Magna Large Print Ser.). 438p. (*0-7505-1223-7*) Magna Large Print Bks. GBR. *Dist:* Ulverscroft Large Print Canada, Ltd.

Reasoner, J. L. Healer's Calling. 1996. 352p. mass mkt. 5.99 o.s.i (*0-425-15487-4*) Berkley Publishing Group.

Riefe, Barbara. Amelia Dale Archer Story. 1998. 304p. (YA). (gr. 8 up). 22.95 o.p. (*0-312-86077-3*, Forge Bks.) Doherty, Tom Assocs., LLC.

Robinson, Leah Ruth. Blood Run. 1999. 352p. mass mkt. 6.99 (*0-380-79113-7*, Avon Bks.) Morrow/Avon.

—Blood Run. 1989. mass mkt. 4.50 o.p. (*0-451-40143-3*, Onyx); 1988. 17.95 o.p. (*0-453-00611-6*) NAL.

—Unnatural Causes. 1999. 384p. 24.00 (*0-380-97459-2*, Avon Bks.) Morrow/Avon.

Robinson, Leah Ruth, photos by. First Cut. 1997. 368p. mass mkt. 24.00 o.p. (*0-380-97458-4*); 1998. reprint ed. mass mkt. 6.99 (*0-380-79124-2*) Morrow/Avon. (Avon Bks.).

Roe, C. F. Bad Blood. l.t. ed. 1993. (Magna Large Print Ser.). 366p. (*0-7505-0486-2*) Magna Large Print Bks. GBR. *Dist:* Ulverscroft Large Print Canada, Ltd.

—A Bonny Case of Murder: Dr. Jean Montrose Mystery. 1994. (Dr. Jean Montrose Mystery Ser.). 256p. (Orig.). mass mkt. 3.99 o.s.i (*0-451-18067-4*) NAL.

—A Classy Touch of Murder. 1993. (Dr. Jean Montrose Mystery Ser.: No. 3). 256p. mass mkt. 5.99 o.s.i (*0-451-17713-4*, Signet Bks.) NAL.

—A Classy Touch of Murder. 256p. 24.00 (*0-7278-5183-7*) Severn Hse. Pubs., Ltd.

—Death by Fire. l.t. ed. 1992. (Magna Large Print Ser.). 345p. (*0-7505-0128-6*) Magna Large Print Bks. GBR. *Dist:* Ulverscroft Large Print Canada, Ltd.

—A Fiery Hint of Murder. 1993. (Dr. Jean Montrose Mystery Ser.: No. 2). 256p. reprint ed. mass mkt. 5.50 o.s.i (*0-451-17606-5*, Signet Bks.) NAL.

—The Hidden Cause of Murder. 1996. (Dr. Jean Montrose Mystery Ser.). 256p. mass mkt. 5.50 o.s.i (*0-451-18633-8*, Signet Bks.) NAL.

—A Nasty Bit of Murder. 1992. (Dr. Jean Montrose Mystery Ser.). 288p. mass mkt. 5.50 o.s.i (*0-451-17468-2*, Signet Bks.) NAL.

—A Relative Act of Murder. 1995. (Dr. Jean Montrose Mystery Ser.). 256p. (Orig.). mass mkt. 5.50 o.s.i (*0-451-18183-2*, Signet Bks.) NAL.

—Tangled Knot of Murder. 1996. (Dr. Jean Montrose Mystery Ser.). 256p. mass mkt. 5.50 o.s.i (*0-451-19079-3*, Signet Bks.) NAL.

—A Torrid Piece of Murder: A Dr. Jean Montrose Mystery. 1994. (Dr. Jean Montrose Mystery Ser.). 256p. (Orig.). mass mkt. 5.50 o.s.i (*0-451-18182-4*, Signet Bks.) NAL.

Sandoz, Mari. Miss Morissa: Doctor of the Gold Trail. 1980. 249p. reprint ed. pap. 13.95 (*0-8032-9118-3*, Bison Bks.) Univ. of Nebraska Pr.

Scholefield, Alan. Burn Out. 1995. 346p. 22.95 o.p. (*0-312-13035-X*, Saint Martin's Minotaur) St. Martin's Pr.

Seifert, Elizabeth. Miss Doctor. 1973. lib. bdg. 23.95 (*0-88411-024-9*) Amereon, Ltd.

Sheldon, Sidney. Nothing Lasts Forever. 1994. 398p. 23.00 o.p. (*0-688-08491-5*, Morrow, William & Co.) Morrow/Avon.

Shreve, Susan Richards. The Visiting Physician. l.t. ed. 1996. (Large Print Bks.). 25.95 o.p. (*1-56895-369-0*, Wheeler Publishing, Inc.) Gale Group.

Slaughter, Karin. A Faint Cold Fear. abr. ed. 2003. audio 25.95 (*0-06-051468-X*, HarperAudio) HarperTrade.

—Kisscut. 2003. E-Book 7.99 (*0-06-057880-7*); E-Book 7.99 (*0-06-057881-5*); E-Book 7.99 (*0-06-057883-1*); E-Book 7.99 (*0-06-057882-3*) HarperCollins Pubs.

—Kisscut. 2003. 448p. mass mkt. 7.99 (*0-06-053404-4*, HarperTorch) Morrow/Avon.

Soule, Maris. Lyon's Pride. 1993. (Harlequin Romance Ser.). pap. (*0-373-08930-9*, 5-08930-5, Silhouette) Harlequin Enterprises, Ltd.

Spruill, Steven. My Soul to Take. l.t. ed. 1994. o.p. (*0-7927-2093-8*); pap. o.p. (*0-7927-2092-X*) BBC Audiobooks America.

—My Soul to Take. 1994. 304p. 22.00 o.p. (*0-312-09879-0*); Vol. 1. 1995. (My Soul to Take Ser.: Vol. 1). 295p. mass mkt. 5.50 (*0-312-95253-8*, St. Martin's Paperbacks) St. Martin's Pr.

—Rulers of Darkness. 1995. 357p. 22.95 o.p. (*0-312-13163-1*); Vol. 1. 1998. (Rulers of Darkness Ser.: Vol. 1). 352p. mass mkt. 6.50 (*0-312-95668-1*, St. Martin's Paperbacks) St. Martin's Pr.

Steinbach, Meredith. Zara. 1996. 277p. pap. 15.95 (*0-8101-5059-X*, TriQuarterly Bks.) Northwestern Univ. Pr.

Stephens, Kay. Sign of the Moon. 1999. 373p. (*0-7540-2192-0*); (*0-7540-1263-8*) BBC Audiobooks America.

—Sign of the Moon. 1998. 256p. 24.00 o.p. (*0-7278-5268-X*) Severn Hse. Pubs., Ltd.

—Sign of the Moon. l.t. ed. 1999. (Romance Ser.). 375p. 25.95 (*0-7862-1783-9*) Thorndike Pr.

Stone, Katharine. Thief of Hearts. 1999. 416p. 23.00 o.p. (*0-446-52181-7*) Warner Bks., Inc.

Stone, Katherine. Katherine Stone: A New Collection of Three Complete Novels. 1995. 752p. 6.99 o.s.i (*0-517-11840-8*) Random Hse. Value Publishing.

—Thief of Hearts. 2000. 448p. E-Book 4.95 (*0-446-92329-X*) Time Warner Bk. Group.

—Thief of Hearts. 2000. E-Book 4.95 (*0-446-91275-1*) Warner Bks., Inc.

—A Thief of Hearts. 2000. 448p. mass mkt. 7.50 (*0-446-60829-7*) Warner Bks., Inc.

Warren, Linda. Cowboy at the Crossroads. 2002. (Harlequin Superromance Ser.: No. 1075). 297p. mass mkt. (*0-373-71075-5*, Harlequin Bks.) Harlequin Enterprises, Ltd.

Wilson, F. Paul. Implant. 1996. 437p. mass mkt. 6.99 (*0-8125-4470-6*); 1995. 352p. 23.95 o.p. (*0-312-89034-6*) Doherty, Tom Assocs., LLC. (Forge Bks.).

Wood, Barbara. Vital Signs. l.t. ed. 1985. (General Ser.). 683p. 18.95 o.p. (*0-8161-3928-8*, Macmillan Reference USA) Gale Group.

—Vital Signs. 1986. mass mkt. 2.95 o.p. (*0-451-15454-1*, Signet Bks.) NAL.

### WOMEN SCIENTISTS—FICTION

Card, Orson Scott & Kidd, Kathryn H. Lovelock. 1995. 300p. pap. text 5.99 (*0-8125-1805-5*); 1994. 288p. 21.95 o.p. (*0-312-85732-2*) Doherty, Tom Assocs., LLC. (Tor Bks.).

Charbonneau, Louis. White Harvest. 1994. 288p. 21.00 o.p. (*1-55611-362-5*) Fine, Donald I. Bks.

—White Harvest. l.t. ed. 1997. (Ulverscroft Large Print Ser.). 576p. 31.50 (*0-7089-3681-4*, Ulverscroft) Thorpe, F. A. Pubs. GBR. *Dist:* Ulverscroft Large Print Bks., Ltd., Ulverscroft Large Print Canada, Ltd.

Collins, Helen. Mutagenesis. 1994. 320p. mass mkt. 4.99 o.p. (*0-8125-2163-3*); 1993. 352p. 22.95 o.p. (*0-312-85387-4*) Doherty, Tom Assocs., LLC. (Tor Bks.).

Cussler, Clive & Kemprecos, Paul. Blue Gold: A Novel from the NUMA Files. (NUMA Files Ser.: Vol. 2). 2000. (Illus.). 400p. pap. 16.00 (*0-671-78546-X*); 2001. 416p. reprint ed. mass mkt. 7.99 (*0-7434-1822-0*) Simon & Schuster. (Pocket).

Girard, Paula Tanner. The Seventh Sister. 2001. (Five Star Romance Ser.). 219p. 25.95 (*0-7862-3503-9*, Five Star) Gale Group.

Long, Jeff. Year Zero. 2002. 416p. 25.00 (*0-7434-0611-7*); E-Book 6.99 (*0-7434-8231-X*) Simon & Schuster. (Atria).

McAuley, Paul. The Secret of Life. 416p. 2001. 25.95 (*0-7653-0080-X*); 2002. reprint ed. mass mkt. 7.99 (*0-7653-4193-X*) Doherty, Tom Assocs., LLC. (Tor Bks.).

McGrail, Anna. Mrs. Einstein: A Novel. 1998. 320p. 24.95 (*0-393-04611-7*) Norton, W. W. & Co., Inc.

Minichino, Camille. The Boric Acid Murder. 2002. (Gloria Lamerino Mystery Ser.). 288p. 23.95 (*0-312-28502-7*, Saint Martin's Minotaur) St. Martin's Pr.

—The Boric Acid Murder. 2002. (Senior Lifestyles Ser.). 28.95 (*0-7862-4810-6*) Thorndike Pr.

Nova, Craig. The Universal Donor. 1997. 288p. tchr. ed. 23.00 o.p. (*0-395-70938-5*) Houghton Mifflin Co.

—The Universal Donor. 1998. (Norton Paperback Fiction Ser.). 256p. pap. 13.00 (*0-393-31845-1*, Norton Paperbacks) Norton, W. W. & Co., Inc.

Roiphe, Anne R. If You Knew Me. 1993. 212p. 19.95 o.p. (*0-316-75430-7*) Little Brown & Co.

—If You Knew Me. 1995. 224p. pap. 15.99 (*0-446-67071-5*) Warner Bks., Inc.

Rothenberg, Rebecca. The Bulrush Murders: A Botanical Mystery. 1991. 240p. 18.95 o.p. (*0-88184-749-6*, Carroll & Graf Pubs.) Avalon Publishing Group.

—The Bulrush Murders: A Botanical Mystery. 1994. 256p. mass mkt. 5.99 o.s.i (*0-446-40404-7*) Warner Bks., Inc.

—The Dandelion Murders. 1994. 304p. 18.95 o.s.i (*0-89296-561-4*) Mysterious Pr.

—The Dandelion Murders. 1995. 272p. mass mkt. 5.50 (*0-446-40378-4*, Mysterious Pr. Paperback Bks.) Warner Bks., Inc.

—The Shy Tulip Murders. 1996. 336p. 21.95 o.s.i (*0-89296-607-6*) Mysterious Pr.

—The Shy Tulip Murders. 1997. 304p. mass mkt. 5.99 (*0-446-40462-4*, Mysterious Pr. Paperback Bks.) Warner Bks., Inc.

Welt, Elly. Berlin Wild. 1988. 400p. mass mkt. 4.50 o.p. (*0-451-40028-3*, Onyx) NAL.

—Berlin Wild. 1986. 384p. 17.95 o.p. (*0-670-80925-X*) Viking Penguin.

Zettel, Sarah. The Quiet Invasion. 2000. 384p. 23.95 (*0-446-52489-1*) Mysterious Pr.

# RELATIONSHIPS

## B

### BROTHERS—FICTION

Adams, Jessica. Tom, Dick & Debbie Harry. 2002. 304p. 23.95 (*0-312-29062-4*) St. Martin's Pr.

Aellen, Richard. Redeye. 1989. mass mkt. 4.95 o.s.i (*0-553-28282-4*) Bantam Bks.

—Redeye. 1988. 352p. 18.95 o.p. (*1-55611-082-0*) Fine, Donald I. Bks.

Alder, Douglas D. Sons of Bear Lake: A Novel. 2002. 259p. pap. 16.95 (*1-55517-667-4*, Salt Pr.) Cedar Fort, Inc./CFI Distribution.

Archer, Jeffrey. Sons of Fortune. 2003. 544p. mass mkt. 7.99 o.s.i (*0-312-99353-6*, St. Martin's Paperbacks); mass mkt. 7.99 (*0-312-99380-3*, St. Martin's Paperbacks); 400p. 27.95 (*0-312-31319-5*) St. Martin's Pr.

—Sons of Fortune. l.t. ed. 2003. 32.95 (*0-7862-5462-9*) Thorndike Pr.

Auch, Mary Jane. Monster Brother. 1994. (Illus.). 32p. (J). (ps-3). tchr. ed. 15.95 (*0-8234-1095-1*) Holiday Hse., Inc.

Axinn, Donald E. The Ego Makers: A Novel. 1998. 320p. 23.95 (*1-55970-336-9*) Arcade Publishing, Inc.

Bailey, Eleanor. Marlene Dietrich Lived Here. 439p. pap. 11.95 (*0-552-99863-X*) Corgi Bks. Ltd. GBR. *Dist:* Trafalgar Square.

—Marlene Dietrich Lived Here. 2002. 359p. (*0-385-60120-4*) Doubleday Publishing.

Baldwin, James. Just above My Head. 2000. 592p. pap. 11.95 (*0-385-33456-7*); 1980. mass mkt. 5.95 o.s.i (*0-440-14777-8*); 1980. 560p. mass mkt. 6.99 o.s.i (*0-440-20599-9*) Dell Publishing.

—Just above My Head. 1979. 608p. 12.95 o.p. (*0-385-27074-7*) Doubleday Publishing.

Banks, Russell. Affliction. 1990. 368p. pap. 13.00 (*0-06-092007-6*, Perennial); 1989. 320p. 18.95 o.p. (*0-06-016142-6*) HarperTrade.

—Affliction. 1991. 2.99 o.p. (*0-517-06406-5*) Random Hse. Value Publishing.

—Continental Drift. 1986. 432p. mass mkt. 5.99 o.s.i (*0-345-33021-8*) Ballantine Bks.

—Continental Drift. (Perennial Classics Ser.). 2000. 432p. pap. 15.00 (*0-06-095673-9*, Perennial); 1994. (Illus.). 384p. pap. 13.50 (*0-06-092574-4*); 1985. 416p. 17.95 o.p. (*0-06-015383-0*) HarperTrade.

—Gegenstroemung. 2003. (GER.). 508p. pap. 27.00 (*1-4000-5511-3*) Random Hse. Information Group.

Barnes, Kim. Finding Caruso. 2004. 320p. pap. 14.00 (*0-425-19393-4*) Berkley Publishing Group.

—Finding Caruso. 2003. 320p. 23.95 (*0-399-14967-8*) Putnam Publishing Group, The.

Barthelme, Frederick. The Brothers: A Novel. 2001. 272p. pap. text 14.00 (*1-58243-130-2*, Counterpoint Pr.) Basic Bks.

—The Brothers: A Novel. 1994. 272p. reprint ed. pap. 10.95 o.p. (*0-14-013209-0*, Penguin Bks.) Penguin Group (USA) Inc.

—The Brothers: A Novel. 1993. 272p. 21.00 o.p. (*0-670-83242-1*, Viking) Viking Penguin.

Basu, Jay. The Stars Can Wait: A Novel. 2002. 192p. 21.00 o.s.i (*0-8050-6887-2*) Holt, Henry & Co.

—The Stars Can Wait: A Novel. 2003. 192p. pap. 12.00 (*0-312-42115-X*) Picador.

Bennett, James W. Plunking Reggie Jackson. 2001. (Illus.). 208p. (J). (gr. 7-12). 16.00 (*0-689-83137-4*, Simon & Schuster Children's Publishing) Simon & Schuster Children's Publishing.

Benoit, Brent. All Saints' Day. 2002. (Sewanee Writers' Ser.). 345p. 26.95 (*1-58567-312-9*) Overlook Pr., The.

Blackburn, Thomas Wakefield. Compadneros. l.t. ed. 2001. (G. K. Hall Paperback Ser.). 245p. pap. 23.95 (*0-7838-9415-5*, Macmillan Reference USA) Gale Group.

Bledsoe, Lucy Jane. This Wild Silence: A Novel. 2003. 272p. pap. 13.95 (*1-55583-773-5*) Alyson Pubns.

Blume, Judy. A Box of Fudge: Fudge-a-Mania; Otherwise Known as Sheila the Great; Tales of a Fourth Grade Nothing; Superfudge, 4 vols. 2000. (gr. 4-7). 19.96 (*0-440-79920-1*, Dell Books for Young Readers) Random Hse. Children's Bks.

—Fudge-a-Mania. 2002. (Illus.). (J). 13.40 (*0-7587-0013-X*) Book Wholesalers, Inc.

—Fudge-a-Mania. (Illus.). 160p. 2003. pap. 5.99 (*0-14-230230-9*, Puffin Bks.); 2002. (J). 15.99 (*0-525-46927-3*, Dutton Children's Bks.) Penguin Putnam Bks. for Young Readers.

—Pure Fudge, 4 vols., Set. 2002. (J). 47.97 o.p. (*0-525-47121-9*, Dutton Children's Bks.) Penguin Putnam Bks. for Young Readers.

Bouncing off the Moon. Date not set. pap. (*0-7653-0292-6*, Tor Bks.) Doherty, Tom Assocs., LLC.

Bowering, Marilyn. Visible Worlds. 1999. 304p. pap. 13.00 o.s.i (*0-06-092926-X*) HarperCollins Pubs.

—Visible Worlds. 1998. 304p. o.s.i (*0-06-019148-1*, HarperFlamingo) HarperCollins Pubs. Canada, Ltd.

Boyne, Walter J. Dawn over Kitty Hawk: A Novel of the Wright Brothers. 2003. 400p. 24.95 (*0-7653-0471-6*, 52996964, Forge Bks.) Doherty, Tom Assocs., LLC.

Bransford, Stephen. The Last Photograph: A Story of Brothers. 1995. 12.99 o.p. (*0-7852-8011-1*) Nelson, Thomas Inc.

Brink, Carol Ryrie. Snow in the River. 1993. (Reprint Ser.). 308p. reprint ed. pap. 19.95 (*0-87422-097-1*) Washington State Univ. Pr.

Brossard, Chandler. The Bold Saboteurs. 4th ed. 2001. 362p. reprint ed. pap. 15.00 (*1-928746-18-7*) Herodias.

Brown, James. Final Performance. 1988. 320p. 18.95 o.p. (*0-688-06842-1*, Morrow, William & Co.) Morrow/Avon.

Buckman, Daniel. The Names of Rivers. 2002. 197p. 21.00 (*1-888451-29-7*) Akashic Bks.

—The Names of Rivers. 2003. 208p. pap. 13.00 (*0-312-31460-4*) Picador.

—The Names of Rivers. Date not set. mass mkt. (*0-312-98981-4*, St. Martin's Paperbacks) St. Martin's Pr.

Buechner, Frederick. The Storm. 208p. 2002. pap. 13.95 (*0-06-061145-6*); 1998. 18.00 (*0-06-061144-8*) HarperSanFrancisco.

—The Storm. l.t. ed. 1999. (Inspirational Ser.). 223p. 25.95 (*0-7838-8605-5*) Thorndike Pr.

Bunn, T. Davis. Gibraltar Passage. l.t. ed. 1994. (Rendezvous with Destiny Ser.: No. 2). 192p. pap. 8.99 o.p. (*1-55661-380-6*) Bethany Hse. Pubs.

Burton, Philip. You, My Brother. 1973. 10.95 o.p. (*0-394-48478-9*) Random Hse., Inc.

Campbell, Ramsey. The Last Voice They Hear. 1999. 384p. pap. 6.99 (*0-8125-4194-4*, Tor Bks.) Doherty, Tom Assocs., LLC.

—The Last Voice They Hear. 1998. 6.99 (*0-312-87078-7*) St. Martin's Pr.

Campbell, Ramsey & Robbins, Harold. The Last Voice They Hear. 1998. 384p. 24.95 o.p. (*0-312-86611-9*, Forge Bks.) Doherty, Tom Assocs., LLC.

Carillo, Charles. My Ride with Gus. 256p. 1997. pap. 5.99 (*0-671-53569-2*, Pocket Star); 1996. 22.00 (*0-671-53568-4*, Atria) Simon & Schuster.

Carlson, Richard. Men & Other Mammals. 2002. 290p. pap. 13.00 (*0-7868-8861-X*) Hyperion Pr.

Carroll, James. The City Below. 1996. 432p. pap. 14.00 (*0-395-82522-9*); 1994. 422p. 22.95 o.s.i (*0-395-59070-1*) Houghton Mifflin Co.

Christensen, Lars Saabye. The Half Brother. 2004. 26.00 (*1-55970-715-1*) Arcade Publishing, Inc.

Coben, Harlan. Gone for Good. 2003. 432p. mass mkt. 6.99 (*0-440-23673-8*); 2002. mass mkt. 6.99 (*0-440-29604-8*); 2002. 352p. 23.95 (*0-385-33558-X*, Delacorte Pr.) Dell Publishing.

—Gone for Good. l.t. ed. 2002. (Wheeler Hardcover Ser.). 29.95 (*1-58724-227-3*, Wheeler Publishing, Inc.) Gale Group.

—Gone for Good. abr. ed. 2002. audio compact disk 29.95 (*0-553-71298-5*, RH Audio) Random Hse. Audio Publishing Group.

—Gone for Good. l.t. ed. 2003. (Paperback Bestsellers Ser.). pap. 13.95 (*1-4104-0087-5*) Thorndike Pr.

Coe, Christopher. I Look Divine. 1987. 128p. 12.95 (*0-89919-530-X*) Houghton Mifflin Co.

—I Look Divine. 1988. (Contemporaries Ser.). pap. 8.00 o.s.i (*0-394-75995-8*, Vintage) Knopf Publishing Group.

Cohen, Matt. The Bookseller. 1996. 256p. 22.95 o.p. (*0-312-14288-9*) St. Martin's Pr.

Collins, Max Allan. Saving Private Ryan. l.t. ed. 2001. 248p. lib. bdg. 27.95 (*1-58547-126-7*) Ctr. Point Large Print.

—Saving Private Ryan. 1998. 319p. mass mkt. 6.50 o.s.i (*0-451-19727-5*, Signet Bks.) NAL.

Collins, Michael. The Resurrectionists. 2002. 304p. 24.00 (*0-7432-2904-5*, Scribner) Simon & Schuster.

Conroy, Jack. A World to Win. 2000. (Radical Novel Reconsidered Ser.). xxxv, 348p. reprint ed. pap. text 17.95 (*0-252-06927-7*) Univ. of Illinois Pr.

Cook, Thomas H. Places in the Dark. 2001. 304p. reprint ed. mass mkt. 6.50 (*0-553-58067-1*, Spectra) Bantam Bks.

—Places in the Dark. l.t. ed. 2000. (Americana Ser.). 373p. 28.95 (*0-7862-2556-4*) Thorndike Pr.

Cookson, Catherine. House of Men. l.t. ed. 2002. lib. bdg. 29.95 (*1-58547-070-8*, Platinum) Ctr. Point Large Print.

—House of Men. 2000. pap. 10.95 (*0-552-14088-0*) Transworld Publishers Ltd. GBR. *Dist:* Trafalgar Square.

Cooper, Susan. Green Boy. 2002. (Illus.). 208p. (J). (gr. 4-6). 16.00 (*0-689-84751-3*, McElderry, Margaret K.) Simon & Schuster Children's Publishing.

Cord, Barry. The Gun-Shy Kid. 1979. reprint ed. pap. 1.25 o.s.i (*0-505-51379-X*) Dorchester Publishing Co., Inc.

Corrick, Martin. The Navigation Log: A Novel. 2004. 304p. pap. 13.95 (*0-375-76053-9*, Random Hse. Trade Paperbacks) Random House Adult Trade Publishing Group.

—The Navigation Log: A Novel. 2003. 304p. 24.95 (*0-375-50812-0*) Random Hse., Inc.

Crosswell, Jack. Murder of a Brother. 2001. 256p. 18.95 (*1-57197-265-X*) Pentland Pr., Inc.

D'Amato, Barbara. Good Cop, Bad Cop. 1999. 304p. mass mkt. 6.99 (*0-8125-9014-7*); 1998. 320p. 22.95 o.p. (*0-312-86562-7*) Doherty, Tom Assocs., LLC. (Forge Bks.).

Dangor, Achmat. Kafka's Curse: A Novel. 240p. 2000. pap. 12.00 o.s.i (*0-375-70462-0*, Vintage); 1999. 22.00 o.s.i (*0-375-40510-0*, Pantheon) Knopf Publishing Group.

Date, S. V. Black Sunshine. 2002. 24.95 o.s.i (*0-399-14946-5*) Putnam Publishing Group, The.

Davis, Christopher. Dog Horse Rat. 1999. pap. (*0-14-011731-8*); 1990. 272p. 17.95 o.p. (*0-670-82580-8*) Viking Penguin. (Viking).

—Dog Horse Rat. 2000. 252p. pap. 15.95 (*0-595-09198-9*, Backinprint.com) iUniverse, Inc.

De Graaf, Anne. Where the Fire Burns. 1995. 17.04 (*0-606-18975-0*) Turtleback Bks.

—Where the Fire Burns: A Novel. 1997. (Hidden Harvest Ser.: Vol. 2). 352p. pap. 10.99 o.p. (*1-55661-619-8*) Bethany Hse. Pubs.

Deveraux, Jude. The Blessing. l.t. ed. 1999. 27.95 (*1-56895-629-0*, Wheeler Publishing, Inc.) Gale Group.

—The Blessing. 1999. 336p. pap. 7.99 (*0-671-89109-X*, Pocket Star); 1998. 320p. 20.00 o.s.i (*0-671-89108-1*, Atria) Simon & Schuster.

Dickey, Eric Jerome. Thieves' Paradise: A Novel. 2002. 320p. 19.95 (*0-525-94663-2*, Dutton) Dutton/Plume.

Dostoyevsky, Fyodor. The Brothers Karamazov. 1966. (Airmont Classics Ser.). (C). (gr. 11 up). mass mkt. 3.95 o.p. (*0-8049-0128-7*, CL-128) Airmont Publishing Co., Inc.

—The Brothers Karamazov. 1976. 38.95 (*0-8488-0797-9*) Amereon, Ltd.

—The Brothers Karamazov. MacAndrew, Andrew R., tr. 1984. (Bantam Classics Ser.). 1072p. reprint ed. mass mkt. 7.99 (*0-553-21216-8*) Bantam Dell Publishing Group.

—The Brothers Karamazov. 1983. 595p. reprint ed. lib. bdg. 45.95 (*0-89966-315-X*) Buccaneer Bks., Inc.

—The Brothers Karamazov. Van der Eng, Jan & Meijer, Jan M., eds. 1971. text (*90-279-1758-2*) De Gruyter, Walter Inc.

—The Brothers Karamazov. Volokhonsky, Larissa & Pevear, Richard, trs. 1991. (Vintage Bks.). 832p. pap. 17.00 o.s.i (*0-679-72925-9*, Vintage) Knopf Publishing Group.

—The Brothers Karamazov, Vol. 722. 1955. (Russian Library). pap. 5.95 o.p. (*0-394-70722-2*, V722, Vintage) Knopf Publishing Group.

—The Brothers Karamazov. Pevear, Richard & Volokhonsky, Larissa, trs. 1992. (Everyman's Library: Vol. 70). 848p. 20.00 (*0-679-41003-1*) Knopf, Alfred A. Inc.

—The Brothers Karamazov. Garnett, Constance, tr. 1950. (Modern Library College Editions Ser.). 940p. (C). pap. 11.25 (*0-07-553575-0*, T12, McGraw-Hill Humanities, Social Sciences & World Languages) McGraw-Hill Higher Education.

—The Brothers Karamazov. Komroff-Hill, Manuel, ed. 1986. 704p. mass mkt. 7.95 o.s.i (*0-451-52388-1*, CE1464, Signet Classics) NAL.

—The Brothers Karamazov. Matlaw, Ralph E., ed. 1976. (Critical Editions Ser.). 1000p. (C). o.p. (*0-393-04426-2*); pap. text 13.00 (*0-393-09214-3*) Norton, W. W. & Co., Inc.

—The Brothers Karamazov. Garnett, Constance, tr. 1977. 822p. 17.00 o.s.i (*0-394-60415-6*) Random Hse., Inc.

—The Brothers Karamazov. McDuff, David, tr. & intro. by. 1993. (Penguin Classics Ser.). 960p. 14.00 (*0-14-044527-7*, Penguin Classics) Viking Penguin.

—The Brothers Karamazov. 1982. (Penguin Classics Ser.). 944p. pap. 6.95 o.p. (*0-14-044416-5*, Penguin Classics) Viking Penguin.

—The Brothers Karamazov, 2 vols. Magarshack, David, tr. 1958. (Penguin Classics Ser.). 1. 408p. pap. 3.50 o.p. (*0-14-044078-X*); 2. 544p. pap. 4.95 o.p. (*0-14-044079-8*) Viking Penguin. (Penguin Bks.).

—The Brothers Karamazov: A Novel in Four Parts with Epilogue. Pevear, Richard & Volokhonsky, Larissa, trs. from RUS. 1990. 832p. 40.00 o.s.i (*0-86547-422-2*, North Point Pr.) Farrar, Straus & Giroux.

Douglass, Sara. Enchanter. pap. (*0-312-87889-3*); 2002. mass mkt. 7.99 (*0-7653-4196-4*) Doherty, Tom Assocs., LLC. (Tor Bks.).

DuBois, Brendan. Betrayed. pap. (*0-312-31019-6*, St. Martin's Paperbacks); mass mkt. (*0-312-98757-9*, St. Martin's Paperbacks); 2003. 304p. 24.95 (*0-312-31018-8*, Saint Martin's Minotaur) St. Martin's Pr.

Eagle, Kathleen. Night Falls Like Silk. l.t. ed. 2004. lib. bdg. 29.95 (*1-58547-390-1*, Platinum) Ctr. Point Large Print.

—Night Falls Like Silk. 2003. 272p. 24.95 (*0-06-621470-X*, Morrow, William & Co.) Morrow/Avon.

Edwards, Michelle, et al. What's That Noise? 2002. (Illus.). 32p. (J). (gr. k-2). 15.99 (*0-7636-1350-9*) Candlewick Pr.

Enger, Leif. Peace Like a River. l.t. ed. 2002. (Wheeler Large Print Book Ser.). 28.95 (*1-58724-212-5*, Wheeler Publishing, Inc.) Gale Group.

—Peace Like a River. 320p. 2002. pap. 13.00 (*0-8021-3925-6*, Grove Pr.); 2001. 24.00 (*0-87113-795-X*, Atlantic Monthly Pr.) Grove/Atlantic, Inc.

Estes, Eleanor. The Moffat Museum. 1989. 272p. (J). (gr. k-6). pap. 3.25 o.s.i (*0-440-40201-8*, Yearling) Random Hse. Children's Bks.

—The Moffat Museum. 2001. (J). 12.05 (*0-606-20805-4*) Turtleback Bks.

—The Moffats. 2001. (J). 12.05 (*0-606-20806-2*) Turtleback Bks.

Fergusson, Bruce C. The Piper's Sons. 1999. 352p. 24.95 o.p. (*0-525-94431-1*) Dutton/Plume.

—The Piper's Sons. 1999. 432p. reprint ed. mass mkt. 6.99 o.s.i (*0-451-40875-6*, Signet Bks.) NAL.

Ferrars, E. X. Thy Brother Death. 1993. 17.00 o.s.i (*0-385-48092-X*) Doubleday Publishing.

—Thy Brother Death. l.t. ed. 1994. (Ulverscroft Large Print Ser.). 336p. 29.99 o.p. (*0-7089-3202-9*, Ulverscroft) Thorpe, F. A. Pubs. GBR. *Dist:* Ulverscroft Large Print Bks., Ltd., Ulverscroft Large Print Canada, Ltd.

Fletcher, Ralph J. Tommy Trouble & the Magic Marble. 2002. 64p. mass mkt. 3.99 (*0-439-34048-9*) Scholastic, Inc.

Flynn, T. T. Two Faces West. 1998. 192p. 17.50 (*0-7540-8029-3*, Gunsmoke); 1993. 18.95 o.p. (*0-7927-1853-4*); 1993. pap. 16.95 o.p. (*0-7927-1852-6*) BBC Audiobooks America.

Folsom, Allan. Day of Confession. l.t. ed. 1999. 27.95 (*1-56895-648-7*, Wheeler Publishing, Inc.) Gale Group.

—Day of Confession. 1998. 576p. (gr. 8). 25.00 (*0-316-28755-5*) Little Brown & Co.

—Day of Confession. 1999. 688p. mass mkt. 7.99 (*0-446-60453-4*) Warner Bks., Inc.

Francis, H. E. The Invisible Country. 2003. 533p. 29.95 (*1-929490-06-2*) Beil, Frederic C. Pub., Inc.

Frey, Stephen. Trust Fund. E-Book 19.95 (*1-58945-513-4*) Adobe Systems, Inc.

—Trust Fund. 2001. E-Book 6.99 (*0-345-44714-X*) Random Hse., Inc.

—Trust Fund. l.t. ed. 2001. 496p. 30.95 (*0-7862-3168-8*) Thorndike Pr.

Friedman, Mark. Columbus Slaughters Braves: A Novel. 2001. (Illus.). 224p. tchr. ed. 23.00 (*0-618-02520-0*, Mariner Bks.) Houghton Mifflin Co. Trade & Reference Div.

Garwood, Julie. The Clayborne Brides: The Rose Trilogy. l.t. ed. 1998. (Large Print Bks.). 26.95 o.p. (*1-56895-515-4*, Wheeler Publishing, Inc.) Gale Group.

Gerrold, David. Bouncing off the Moon. 2002. 384p. pap. 6.99 o.s.i (*0-8125-8973-4*); 2001. 288p. 22.95 (*0-312-87841-9*) Doherty, Tom Assocs., LLC. (Tor Bks.).

Goodman, Jo. My Reckless Heart. l.t. ed. 2001. (Thorne Brothers Trilogy Ser.). (Illus.). 456p. 26.95 (*0-7862-2947-0*, Five Star) Gale Group.

—My Reckless Heart. 1998. 448p. mass mkt. 5.99 o.s.i (*0-8217-5843-8*, Zebra Bks.) Kensington Publishing Corp.

—With All My Heart. 2001. (Thorne Brothers Trilogy Ser.). (Illus.). 473p. (J). 26.95 (*0-7862-2959-4*, Five Star) Gale Group.

—With All My Heart, 1. 1999. 429p. mass mkt. 5.99 o.s.i (*0-8217-6145-5*) Kensington Publishing Corp.

Gottlieb, Eli. The Boy Who Went Away. 1998. 224p. reprint ed. pap. 10.95 o.s.i (*0-553-37927-5*) Bantam Bks.

—The Boy Who Went Away. 1996. 208p. 21.95 (*0-312-15070-9*) St. Martin's Pr.

Guest, Judith. Ordinary People. 1986. 256p. mass mkt. 5.95 o.s.i (*0-345-33505-8*); 1982. mass mkt. 2.95 o.s.i (*0-345-30734-8*); 1980. mass mkt. 2.75 o.p. (*0-345-29132-8*); 1977. mass mkt. 2.75 o.p. (*0-345-25755-3*) Ballantine Bks.

—Ordinary People. 1983. 5.60 (*0-87129-500-8*, O39) Dramatic Publishing Co.

—Ordinary People. 1981. (General Ser.). lib. bdg. 12.95 o.p. (*0-8161-3207-0*, Macmillan Reference USA) Gale Group.

—Ordinary People. 1982. 15.00 (*0-606-10277-9*) Turtleback Bks.

—Ordinary People. 1982. 272p. 11.00 (*0-14-006517-2*); 1976. 288p. (YA). 12.95 o.p. (*0-670-52831-5*) Viking Penguin.

Hamill, Dennis. House on Fire. 1996. 368p. 22.00 o.p. (*0-87113-614-7*, Atlantic Monthly Pr.) Grove/Atlantic, Inc.

—House on Fire. 1998. 400p. pap. 6.99 (*0-671-00350-X*, Pocket) Simon & Schuster.

Handke, Peter. Repetition. Manheim, Ralph, tr. from GER. 1988. 225p. 18.95 o.s.i (*0-374-24934-2*) Farrar, Straus & Giroux.

Harbouri, Petrie. The Brothers Carburi. 2002. 311p. (*0-7475-5342-4*) Bloomsbury Pr.

—The Brothers Carburi. 2003. 320p. pap. 12.00 (*0-7475-5708-X*) Bloomsbury Publishing, Ltd. GBR. *Dist:* Trafalgar Square.

Harris, Mark. Speed. 1990. 285p. 19.95 o.p. (*1-55611-180-0*) Fine, Donald I. Bks.

—Speed. l.t. ed. 1991. (General Ser.). 431p. lib. bdg. 21.95 (*0-8161-5208-X*, Macmillan Reference USA) Gale Group.

—Speed. 1998. 285p. pap. 15.00 (*0-8032-7314-2*, HARSPX) Univ. of Nebraska Pr.

—Speed. 1991. mass mkt. 5.99 (*0-446-36211-5*) Warner Bks., Inc.

Hatoum, Milton. The Brothers. Gledson, John, tr. from POR. 2002. 240p. 23.00 (*0-374-14118-5*) Farrar, Straus & Giroux.

Henry, Steve. Nobody Asked Me! 2001. (Illus.). 32p. (J). (ps-k). 14.95 (*0-688-17865-0*); lib. bdg. 14.89 (*0-688-17866-9*) HarperCollins Children's Bk. Group.

Higgins, Jack. Flight of Eagles. 1999. 336p. reprint ed. mass mkt. 7.99 (*0-425-16968-5*) Berkley Publishing Group.

—Flight of Eagles. l.t. ed. 1998. 28.95 o.p. (*1-56895-655-X*, Wheeler Publishing, Inc.) Gale Group.

—Flight of Eagles. 1998. 328p. 24.95 o.p. (*0-399-14376-9*, G. P. Putnam's Sons) Penguin Group (USA) Inc.

—Midnight Runner. 2003. 304p. mass mkt. 7.99 (*0-425-18941-4*) Berkley Publishing Group.

—Midnight Runner. 2002. 288p. 25.95 o.s.i (*0-399-14833-7*, Riverhead Bks. (Hardcovers)) Penguin Group (USA) Inc.

—Midnight Runner. l.t. ed. 13.95 (*1-4104-0090-5*, Large Print Pr.); 2003. 449p. 13.95 (*0-7862-4107-1*); 2002. 449p. 32.95 (*0-7862-4106-3*) Thorndike Pr.

Higgs, Liz Curtis. Thorn in My Heart. 2003. (Illus.). 496p. pap. 13.99 (*1-57856-512-X*) WaterBrook Pr.

Hijuelos, Oscar. The Mambo Kings Play Songs of Love. 1989. 384p. 18.95 o.s.i (*0-374-20125-0*) Farrar, Straus & Giroux.

—The Mambo Kings Play Songs of Love. (Perennial Classics Ser.). 2004. 464p. pap. 14.00 (*0-06-095545-7*); 1994. 416p. pap. 13.00 (*0-06-097327-7*); 1992. 416p. reprint ed. pap. 12.00 o.p. (*0-06-097451-6*) HarperTrade. (Perennial).

—Los Reyes del Mambo Tocan Canciones de Amor. 1996. (SPA.). 560p. pap. 14.00 (*0-06-095214-8*, HC12648, Perennial) HarperTrade.

Hill, Susan. Stuart at the Fun House. 2001. (I Can Read Bks.). (Illus.). (J). 10.10 (*0-606-21470-4*) Turtleback Bks.

Idstrom, Annika. My Brother Sebastian. Tate, Joan, tr. from FIN. 1991. 130p. (Orig.). pap. 21.00 (*1-85610-002-2*) Forest Bks. GBR. *Dist:* Dufour Editions, Inc.

Inchbald, Elizabeth. Nature & Art. 2002. 168p. 93.99 (*1-4043-2128-4*); per. 88.99 (*1-4043-2129-2*) IndyPublish.com.

—Nature & Art. 1994. (Revolution & Romanticism, 1789-1834 Ser.). 203p. (*1-85477-170-1*) Woodstock Books.

James, Eloisa. Enchanting Pleasures. 2001. 352p. 21.95 o.s.i (*0-385-33362-5*, Delacorte Pr.); 2002. 432p. reprint ed. mass mkt. 6.50 (*0-440-23458-1*) Dell Publishing.

James, Russell. Count Me Out. 368p. 1998. pap. 10.00 (*0-393-31832-X*, Foul Play); 1997. 22.95 o.p. (*0-88150-384-3*) Norton, W. W. & Co., Inc.

Janigian, Aris. Bloodvine. 2003. 296p. 21.95 (*1-890771-63-5*) Heyday Bks.

Jennings, Sharon. The Bye-Bye Pie. ed. 2000. (J). (gr. 2). spiral bd. (*0-616-01684-0*) Canadian National Institute for the Blind/Institut National Canadien pour les Aveugles.

—The Bye-Bye Pie. 2002. (Illus.). 32p. (J). (ps-k). pap. (*1-55041-785-1*) Fitzhenry & Whiteside, Ltd.

Jewell, Lisa. A Friend of the Family: A Novel. 2003. 336p. 23.95 (*0-525-94734-5*, Plume) Dutton/Plume.

Johnson, R. M. The Harris Family. 2001. 352p. 23.00 (*0-7432-1600-8*); 2002. 368p. reprint ed. pap. 14.00 (*0-7434-2302-X*) Simon & Schuster. (Simon & Schuster).

Johnston, Tony. That Summer. 2002. (Illus.). 32p. (J). (gr. 1-4). 16.00 (*0-15-201585-X*) Harcourt Children's Bks.

Joji Tsubota. Children in the Wind. Epp, Robert, tr. 1991. 180p. 22.50 (*0-7103-0393-9*, A5365) Routledge.

Jonell, Lynne. It's My Birthday, Too! 2001. (Illus.). (J). 12.14 (*0-606-21256-6*) Turtleback Bks.

Keegan, Christopher. Ride into Yesterday. 1992. 137p. 18.95 o.p. (*0-8027-4132-0*) Walker & Co.

Keillor, Garrison. WLT: A Radio Romance. l.t. ed. 412p. 1993. pap. 18.95 o.p. (*0-7927-1305-2*); 1992. 21.95 o.p. (*0-7927-1306-0*) BBC Audiobooks America.

—WLT: A Radio Romance. 1992. 416p. reprint ed. pap. 14.00 (*0-14-010380-5*, Penguin Bks.) Penguin Group (USA) Inc.

—WLT: A Radio Romance. 1991. 416p. 21.95 o.p. (*0-670-81857-7*); 1992. 256p. 125.00 o.s.i (*0-670-84265-6*) Viking Penguin. (Viking).

Kertes, Joseph. Boardwalk. 1998. 220p. pap. 16.95 (*1-55022-340-2*) ECW Pr. CAN. *Dist:* LPC Group.



For book reviews, descriptive annotations, tables of contents, cover images, author biographies & additional information, updated daily, subscribe to **www.booksinprint.com** 521

Kihlman, Christer. The Blue Mother. 1990. (Modern Scandinavian Literature in Translation Ser.). 315p. reprint ed. pap. 97.70 (0-608-02383-3, 206302500004) Bks. on Demand.

—The Blue Mother. Tate, Joan, tr. from FIN. 1990. (Modern Scandinavian Literature in Translation Ser.). vi, 308p. text 29.95 o.p. (0-8032-2721-3); pap. 11.95 o.p. (0-8032-7769-5, Bison Bks.) Univ. of Nebraska Pr.

Kingsley, Johanna. Treasures. 1992. 4.99 o.p. (0-517-08868-1) Random Hse. Value Publishing.

—Treasures. 1991. mass mkt. 5.99 (0-446-36123-2); 1990. 19.95 o.p. (0-446-51450-0) Warner Bks., Inc.

Klempner, Joseph T. Change of Course. 1998. 144p. 18.95 (0-312-18563-4) St. Martin's Pr.

Koontz, Dean. By the Light of the Moon. 2003. 496p. mass mkt. 7.99 (0-553-58276-3); 2002. 448p. 26.95 (0-553-80143-0, Spectra) Bantam Bks.

Kraft, Erik P. Lenny & Mel. (Ready-for-Chapters Ser.). (Illus.). 64p. (J). 2003. pap. 3.99 (0-689-85891-4, Aladdin); 2002. (gr. 2-5). 15.00 (0-689-84173-6, Simon & Schuster Children's Publishing) Simon & Schuster Children's Publishing.

Kristof, Agota. The Third Lie. Romano, Marc, tr. from FRE. 1996. 144p. 20.00 o.p. (0-8021-1583-7, Grove Pr.) Grove/Atlantic, Inc.

Kurata, Phillip. The Reluctant Agent. 2001. 248p. (0-931846-61-7) Washington Writers' Publishing Hse.

Lamb, Wally. I Know This Much Is True. l.t. ed. 1998. 949 p. 29.95 (1-57490-164-8) Beeler, Thomas T. Publisher.

—I Know This Much Is True. 2003. 912p. mass mkt. 7.99 (0-06-109764-0); 2000. (0-06-039280-0); 1998. 912p. pap. 16.00 o.s.i (0-06-109812-4) HarperCollins Pubs.

—I Know This Much Is True. 1999. 912p. pap. 16.00 (0-06-098756-1, ReganBooks); 1998. 912p. 27.50 (0-06-039162-6, ReganBooks); 1998. audio 25.00 (0-694-51940-5, 695741, HarperAudio) HarperTrade.

—I Know This Much Is True. unabr. ed. 1999. audio 177.00 (0-7887-2491-6, 95566E7) Recorded Bks., LLC.

Lanham, Edwin. The Stricklands: A Novel. 2nd ed. 2002. 336p. 19.95 (0-8061-3419-4) Univ. of Oklahoma Pr.

Lennon, J. Robert. The Funnies. 2000. (Illus.). 336p. 13.00 (1-57322-781-1, Riverhead Trade (Paperbacks)) Berkley Publishing Group.

—The Funnies. 1999. 320p. 23.95 o.s.i (1-57322-126-0, Riverhead Bks. (Hardcovers)) Putnam Publishing Group, The.

—On the Night Plain: A Novel. 2001. 256p. 23.00 (0-8050-6722-1) Holt, Henry & Co.

—On the Night Plain: A Novel. 2002. 256p. pap. 13.00 (0-312-42086-2) Picador.

Ligon, Susan. There's a Brand-New Baby in the House and... I'm the Big Brother. 2002. 48p. (J). (ps-k). 17.99 (0-8499-7791-6) Nelson, Tommy.

Loriga, Ray. My Brother's Gun: A Novel of Disposable Lives, Immediate Fame, & a Big Black Automatic. Cordero, Kristina, tr. 1997. 128p. 18.95 (0-312-16947-7) St. Martin's Pr.

Louis, Adrian C. Skins. 2002. 320p. reprint ed. pap. 18.00 (0-944024-44-0) Ellis Pr., The.

Ludlum, Robert. The Apocalypse Watch. 1996. 768p. mass mkt. 7.99 (0-553-56957-0); mass mkt. 7.50 o.s.i (0-553-84005-3) Bantam Bks.

—The Apocalypse Watch. l.t. ed. 1995. 28.95 o.p. (1-56895-238-4, Wheeler Publishing, Inc.) Gale Group.

—The Gemini Contenders. 1989. 416p. mass mkt. 7.99 (0-553-28209-3); 432p. mass mkt. 3.99 o.s.i (0-553-19945-5) Bantam Bks.

—The Gemini Contenders. 1977. mass mkt. 3.50 o.s.i (0-440-12859-5) Dell Publishing.

—The Gemini Contenders. 1976. 8.95 o.p. (0-385-27273-1) Doubleday Publishing.

—The Gemini Contenders. l.t. ed. 1988. (General Ser.). 595p. 21.95 o.p. (0-8161-4447-8, Macmillan Reference USA) Gale Group.

Lysaght, Brian. Last Dance of the Viper. 2001. 464p. 27.95 (0-7653-0062-1, Forge Bks.) Doherty, Tom Assocs., LLC.

Maclean, Norman F. A River Runs Through It & Other Stories. 1976. xviii, 422 p. (0-8161-6398-7); 1993. 310p. 16.95 o.p. (0-8161-5735-9) Gale Group. (Macmillan Reference USA).

—A River Runs Through It & Other Stories. Peters, Sally, ed. 1992. 256p. reprint ed. mass mkt. 6.99 (0-671-77697-5, Pocket) Simon & Schuster.

—A River Runs Through It & Other Stories. 2001. 232p. 20.00 o.s.i (0-226-50055-1); 1983. (Illus.). 128p. (C). 50.00 o.s.i (0-226-50059-4) Univ. of Chicago Pr.

—A River Runs Through It & Other Stories: Anniversity Edition. 25th ed. 2001. 232p. pap. 11.00 o.s.i (0-226-50057-8, P821); 1983. (Illus.). 128p. (C). 25.00 o.s.i (0-226-50058-6) Univ. of Chicago Pr.

MacLeod, Alistair. No Great Mischief. 2001. (Vintage International Ser.). 304p. pap. 13.00 (0-375-72665-9, Vintage) Knopf Publishing Group.

—No Great Mischief. 2000. (Illus.). 283p. 23.95 o.p. (0-393-04970-1) Norton, W. W. & Co., Inc.

Mahy, Margaret, et al. Los Siete Hermanos Chinos. 2003. (Mariposa Ser.). (SPA., Illus.). 40p. (J). (gr. 3-5). pap. 5.99 (0-590-48131-2, SO6414, Scholastic en Espanola) Scholastic, Inc.

McCrum, Robert. Suspicion: A Novel. 1997. 256p. 23.00 o.p. (0-393-04046-1) Norton, W. W. & Co., Inc.

McFarland, Dennis. The Music Room. l.t. ed. 1991. (General Ser.). 381p. 21.95 o.p. (0-8161-5131-8, Macmillan Reference USA) Gale Group.

—The Music Room. 1990. 275p. 19.95 o.p. (0-395-54417-3) Houghton Mifflin Co.

—The Music Room. 1991. 288p. reprint ed. pap. 12.00 o.p. (0-380-71456-6, Avon Bks.) Morrow/Avon.

—The Music Room. 2001. pap. (0-312-27744-X); 288p. pap. 13.00 (0-312-27470-X) Picador.

McGinley, Patrick. The Devil's Diary. 1988. 256p. 16.95 o.p. (0-312-02193-3) St. Martin's Pr.

McGregor, Elizabeth. The Ice Child. 2001. (Illus.). 400p. 24.95 o.p. (0-525-94567-9, Dutton) Dutton/Plume.

—The Ice Child. l.t. ed. 2001. (Wheeler Large Print Book Ser.). (Illus.). 540p. 29.95 o.p. (1-58724-109-9, Wheeler Publishing, Inc.) Gale Group.

—The Ice Child. 2002. pap. 6.99 (0-451-20539-1, Signet Bks.); 448p. reprint ed. mass mkt. 7.99 (0-451-41061-0, Onyx) NAL.

McInerny, Ralph. The Book of Kills: A Mystery Set at the University of Notre Dame. E-Book 23.95 (0-312-27604-4); 2000. 275p. 23.95 o.p. (0-312-20346-2, Saint Martin's Minotaur); 2001. 288p. reprint ed. mass mkt. 6.50 o.s.i (0-312-97922-3, St. Martin's Paperbacks) St. Martin's Pr.

—The Book of Kills: A Mystery Set at the University of Notre Dame. 2001. (Basic Ser.). 375p. 28.95 o.p. (0-7862-3642-6) Thorndike Pr.

—Lack of the Irish: A Mystery Set at the University of Notre Dame. (Notre Dame Mystery Ser.). 1999. 240p. mass mkt. 5.99 (0-312-96927-9, St. Martin's Paperbacks); 1998. 224p. 21.95 o.p. (0-312-19294-0, Saint Martin's Minotaur) St. Martin's Pr.

—On This Rockne: A Notre Dame Mystery. (Notre Dame Mystery Ser.). 1998. 320p. pap. 5.99 (0-312-96738-1, St. Martin's Paperbacks); 1997. 224p. 20.95 o.p. (0-312-17054-8, 749186, Saint Martin's Minotaur) St. Martin's Pr.

McKinney, Meagan. Gentle from the Night. l.t. ed. 1998. 397p. 25.95 (1-57490-136-2, Beeler Large Print Bks.) Beeler, Thomas T. Publisher.

—Gentle from the Night. 1997. 352p. mass mkt. 5.99 o.s.i (0-8217-5803-9, Zebra Bks.); 1997. 352p. 21.95 o.s.i (1-57566-136-5); 1995. 384p. mass mkt. 18.95 o.p. (0-8217-4825-4) Kensington Publishing Corp.

Meltzer, Brad. The Millionaires. abr. ed. 2002. audio 24.98 (1-58621-204-4); audio 29.98 (1-58621-205-2); audio 39.98 (1-58621-206-0) Time Warner AudioBooks.

—The Millionaires. 2002. 496p. 25.95 (0-446-52729-7); 656p. 25.95 (0-446-52995-8); 544p. reprint ed. mass mkt. 7.99 (0-446-61192-1) Warner Bks., Inc.

Memmi, Albert. The Scorpion, or the Imaginary Confession. Levieux, Eleanor, tr. 1986. (Folio Ser.: No. 1715). (FRE.). 270p. pap. 10.95 (2-07-037715-6) Schoenhof's Foreign Bks., Inc.

Meno, Joe. Tender As Hellfire. E-Book 22.95 (0-312-26852-1); 1999. 244p. 22.95 (0-312-20051-X) St. Martin's Pr.

Mills, Scott. Trenches. 2002. 176p. pap. 14.95 (1-891830-28-7) Top Shelf Productions.

Miner, W. Lawrence, Jr. A Journey into the Fourth Dimension: The Lasting Legacy of Derek Saul. Dailey, Christopher, ed. 2000. 207p. pap. 12.00 (1-928992-01-3, 549) Agents of Change.

Mittman, Stephanie. The Courtship. 1997. 400p. mass mkt. 5.99 o.s.i (0-440-22181-1) Dell Publishing.

Monteilh, Marissa. Hot Boyz. 2004. 352p. pap. 13.95 (0-06-059094-7, Avon Bks.) Morrow/Avon.

Morgan, Robert. This Rock. 2001. 336p. tchr. ed. 24.95 (1-56512-303-4) Algonquin Bks. of Chapel Hill.

—This Rock. l.t. ed. 2002. (Wheeler Large Print Book Ser.). 29.95 (1-58724-168-4, Wheeler Publishing, Inc.) Gale Group.

—This Rock. unabr. ed. 2002. audio 85.00 (0-7887-9807-3) Recorded Bks., LLC.

—This Rock: A Novel. 2002. 336p. reprint ed. pap. 14.00 (0-7432-2579-1, Touchstone) Simon & Schuster.

Morley, John D. The Anatomy Lesson. 1996. 184p. pap. o.s.i (0-349-10721-1) Little Brown & Co.

Myrer, Anton. A Green Desire. 2001. 576p. pap. 15.95 (0-06-093463-8, Perennial) HarperTrade.

—A Green Desire. 1983. 720p. pap. 3.95 (0-380-61580-0, Avon Bks.) Morrow/Avon.

—A Green Desire. 1982. 528p. 14.95 o.p. (0-399-12630-9) Putnam Publishing Group, The.

O'Brien, Flann. The Hard Life. 2nd ed. 179p. reprint ed. 1996. pap. 11.95 (1-56478-141-0); 1994. pap. 9.95 o.p. (1-56478-042-2) Dalkey Archive Pr.

—The Hard Life. 1977. pap. 3.50 o.p. (0-14-004517-1, Penguin Bks.) Viking Penguin.

O'Brien, Tim. Northern Lights. 1999. 368p. pap. 14.95 (0-7679-0441-9) Broadway Bks.

—Northern Lights. 1975. 320p. 8.95 o.s.i (0-440-06664-6, Delacorte Pr.) Dell Publishing.

O'Donovan, Siofra. Malinski. 2002. 214p. pap. 16.95 (1-901866-51-3); pap. 16.95 (1-901866-69-6) Lilliput Pr., Ltd., The IRL. *Dist:* Dufour Editions, Inc.

Ortese, Anna M. The Iguana. Martin, Henry, tr. from ITA. 1988. Tr. of Iguana. 208p. 14.95 (0-914232-87-8); pap. 9.00 (0-914232-95-9) McPherson & Co.

Overholser, Stephen. Double-Cross: A Western Story. l.t. ed. 2002. 354p. 25.95 (0-7862-2388-X); 2001. 256p. 23.95 (0-7862-2387-1, Five Star) Gale Group.

Owen, Howard. Answers to Lucky. 1996. 224p. 22.00 o.p. (0-06-017312-2) HarperCollins Pubs.

—Answers to Lucky: A Novel. 1997. 224p. pap. 12.00 (0-06-092809-3, Perennial) HarperTrade.

Owens, Janis. My Brother Michael. 1997. 304p. 18.95 (1-56164-124-3) Pineapple Pr., Inc.

—Myra Sims. 1999. 480p. 22.95 (1-56164-177-4) Pineapple Pr., Inc.

Patterson, James. The Beach House. 2002. 368p. pap. 16.00 (0-446-67938-0) Warner Bks., Inc.

Patterson, James & de Jonge, Peter. The Beach House. 2002. 368p. 26.95 (0-316-96968-0); 464p. 26.95 o.p. (0-316-73374-1) Little Brown & Co.

—The Beach House. 2003. 384p. reprint ed. mass mkt. 7.99 (0-446-61254-5) Warner Bks., Inc.

Phillips, Carly. The Bachelor. l.t. ed. 2002. 29.95 (1-58724-329-6, Wheeler Publishing, Inc.) Gale Group.

—The Bachelor. 2003. 320p. pap. 12.95 (0-446-69250-6); 2002. 336p. reprint ed. mass mkt. 5.99 (0-446-61054-2, Warner Romance) Warner Bks., Inc.

—The Heartbreaker. l.t. ed. 2003. 385p. 31.95 (1-58724-517-5, Wheeler Publishing, Inc.) Gale Group.

—The Heartbreaker. 2004. mass mkt. 6.99 (0-446-61056-9); 2003. 288p. 16.95 (0-446-51152-8) Warner Bks., Inc.

Pratt, James Michael. Ticket Home. 2002. 352p. mass mkt. 6.99 (0-312-97989-4, St. Martin's Paperbacks); 2001. 356p. 23.95 (0-312-26633-2) St. Martin's Pr.

Price, Richard. Clockers. 2001. 608p. pap. 14.95 (0-06-093498-0, Perennial) HarperTrade.

Putney, Mary Jo. The Wild Child. 2000. 384p. mass mkt. 6.99 (0-449-00584-4, Ballantine Bks.) Ballantine Bks.

—The Wild Child. l.t. ed. 1999. (Large Print Book Ser.). 28.95 (1-56895-791-2, Wheeler Publishing, Inc.) Gale Group.

Puzo, Mario. Fools Die. 1979. mass mkt. 4.50 o.p. (0-451-14145-8); mass mkt. 3.95 o.p. (0-451-13149-5); mass mkt. 3.50 o.p. (0-451-08881-6); 544p. mass mkt. 7.99 (0-451-16019-3) NAL. (Signet Bks.).

—Fools Die. 1978. 12.50 o.p. (0-399-12244-3) Putnam Publishing Group, The.

Randall, Stephen. The Other Side of Mulholland. 2001. 277p. 23.95 (0-312-26216-7, L. A. Weekly Bks.) St. Martin's Pr.

Rathbun, Bill. Whatever Happened to Professor Coyote? A Journey to the Heart of the Handgame. 1999. (Illus.). 320p. 25.00 (0-9631242-3-4); 250p. pap. 15.95 (0-9631242-4-2); 250p. cd-rom 10.95 (0-9631242-5-0) Yerba Buena Pr.

Reece, Colleen L. Honor Bound. 1983. 176p. 3.95 o.p. (0-8024-0153-8) Moody Pr.

—Honor Bound. l.t. ed. 2001. 101p. 24.95 (0-7862-3443-1) Thorndike Pr.

Reiken, Frederick. The Odd Sea. 1999. 224p. pap. 10.95 (0-385-33338-2, Delta) Dell Publishing.

—The Odd Sea. 1998. 208p. 22.00 (0-15-100360-2) Harcourt Trade Pubs.

Reinhold, Margaret. Mr. Porter & the Brothers Jones. 2001. 160p. 24.00 (1-57962-031-0) Permanent Pr., The.

Richardson, Bill. Bachelor Brothers' Bed & Breakfast. l.t. ed. 1997. 21.95 (1-57490-131-1, Beeler Large Print Bks.) Beeler, Thomas T. Publisher.

—Bachelor Brothers' Bed & Breakfast Pillow Book. 1998. 208p. pap. 10.95 (0-312-19440-4, Saint Martin's Griffin); 1997. 18.95 (0-312-16779-2); 1997. 384p. pap. 11.95 (0-312-17183-8, Saint Martin's Griffin); 1996. 160p. 18.95 (0-312-14546-2) St. Martin's Pr.

Roberts, Cynthia S. The Fox-Red Hills. 1993. 23.95 o.p. (0-312-08784-5) St. Martin's Pr.

Roberts, Nora. Sea Swept. 1998. (Chesapeake Bay Ser.: Bk. 1). 352p. mass mkt. 7.99 (0-515-12184-3, Jove) Berkley Publishing Group.

—Sea Swept. l.t. ed. 1998. (Chesapeake Bay Ser.: Bk. 1). 503p. 29.95 (0-7862-1433-3) Thorndike Pr.

—The Stanislaski Brothers: Mikhail & Alex. l.t. ed. 2001. (Thorndike Press Large Print Americana Ser.). 653p. 31.95 (0-7862-3276-5) Thorndike Pr.

Robinson, Eden. Monkey Beach: A Novel. 2002. (Illus.). 384p. pap. 13.00 (0-618-21905-6, Mariner Bks.) Houghton Mifflin Co. Trade & Reference Div.

Root, Phyllis. What Baby Wants. 2002. (Illus.). (J). 23.40 (0-7587-3955-9) Book Wholesalers, Inc.

—What Baby Wants. 2001. (J). 12.14 (0-606-21514-X) Turtleback Bks.

Russell, Paul. War Against the Animals: A Novel. 2003. 320p. 24.95 (0-312-20935-5) St. Martin's Pr.

Scofield, Sandra J. Beyond Deserving. 1992. (Contemporary Fiction Ser.). 320p. pap. 11.95 o.p. (0-452-26907-5, Plume) Dutton/Plume.

—Beyond Deserving. 1991. 310p. 28.00 (1-877946-07-9) Permanent Pr., The.

Seidler, Tor. Brothers below Zero. (Illus.). 144p. (J). 2003. (gr. 5 up). pap. 5.99 (0-06-440936-8, Harper Trophy); 2002. (gr. 3 up). 14.95 (0-06-029179-6, Geringer, Laura Bk.); 2002. (gr. 5 up). lib. bdg. 14.89 (0-06-029180-X, Geringer, Laura Bk.) HarperCollins Children's Bk. Group.

Sernovitz, Gary. Great American Plain. 2001. 240p. 23.00 o.s.i (0-8050-6777-9) Holt, Henry & Co.

—Great American Plain: A Novel. 2002. 240p. pap. 13.00 (0-312-42107-9) Picador.

Smith, Cotton. Behold a Red Horse. 2001. 320p. mass mkt. 4.99 (0-8439-4894-9, Leisure Bks.) Dorchester Publishing Co., Inc.

Smith, Jerry. Deadman's Throttle. 1998. (Jason Street Mysteries Ser.). 191p. pap. 12.95 (1-884313-13-2, DT) Whitehorse Pr.

Smith, Wilbur. The Blue Horizon. 2003. 624p. 27.95 (0-312-27824-1) St. Martin's Pr.

—Monsoon. 2000. 864p. mass mkt. 7.99 (0-312-97154-0, St. Martin's Paperbacks); 1999. 544p. 26.95 (0-312-20339-X) St. Martin's Pr.

Snider, Clifton. Wrestling with Angels: A Tale of Two Brothers. 2002. 249p. pap. 21.99 (1-4010-3073-4); text 31.99 (1-4010-5536-2); E-Book 8.00 (1-4010-3074-2) Xlibris Corp.

Spragg, Mark. The Fruit of Stone: A Novel. 2003. 336p. reprint ed. pap. 14.00 (1-57322-993-8, Riverhead Trade (Paperbacks)) Berkley Publishing Group.

Stallone, Sylvester. Paradise Alley. 1978. 1.95 o.p. (0-425-03811-4); 1977. (Illus.). 8.95 o.p. (0-399-12080-7) Berkley Publishing Group.

Stevenson, Robert Louis. The Master of Ballantrae. 2003. 160p. pap. 2.00 (0-486-42685-8) Dover Pubns., Inc.

—The Master of Ballantrae & Weir of Hermiston. 1992. (Everyman's Library). xlix, 373p. 17.00 (0-679-41744-3) Knopf, Alfred A. Inc.

—The Master of Ballantrae & Weir of Hermiston. 318p. 1994. pap. 6.95 o.p. (0-460-87226-5); 1925. pap. 5.95 o.p. (0-460-11764-5) Tuttle Publishing. (Everyman's Classic Library in Paperback).

Stickland, Caroline. An Ancient Hope. l.t. ed. 1994. 392p. lib. bdg. 21.95 (0-8161-7469-5, Macmillan Reference USA) Gale Group.

—An Ancient Hope. 1994. 272p. 20.95 o.p. (0-312-10929-6) St. Martin's Pr.

Tartt, Donna. The Little Friend. 2003. 640p. pap. 14.95 (1-4000-3169-9); 2002. 576p. 26.00 (0-679-43938-2) Knopf Publishing Group. (Vintage).

Theroux, Marcel. The Confessions of Mycroft Holmes: A Paper Chase. 2001. (Illus.). 224p. 23.00 o.s.i (0-15-100647-4); 2002. 228p. reprint ed. pap. 14.00 (0-15-600743-6, Harvest Bks.) Harcourt Trade Pubs.

Thornburg, Newton. Eve's Men. 1999. 277p. mass mkt. 6.99 (0-8125-8419-8); 1998. 288p. 22.95 (0-312-86399-3) Doherty, Tom Assocs., LLC. (Forge Bks.).

Turteltaub, H. N. Over the Wine-Dark Sea. 2001. E-Book 25.95 (1-59061-136-5) Adobe Systems, Inc.

—Over the Wine-Dark Sea. 2002. mass mkt. 6.99 (0-7653-4451-3, Tor Bks.) Doherty, Tom Assocs., LLC.

Tyler, Anne. Saint Maybe. 1996. 352p. pap. 14.00 (0-449-91160-8); 1992. 384p. mass mkt. 7.99 (0-8041-0874-9, Ivy Bks.) Ballantine Bks.

—Saint Maybe. abr. ed. 1991. 16.00 o.s.i incl. audio (0-679-40634-4, 391507, RH Audio) Random Hse. Audio Publishing Group.

—Saint Maybe. 1996. 18.05 (0-606-12503-5) Turtleback Bks.

Wallace, Rich. Restless: A Ghost's Story. 2003. 176p. (YA). 15.99 (0-670-03605-6, Viking) Viking Penguin.

Weltner, Peter. How the Body Prays. 1999. 260p. 23.95 (1-55597-288-8) Graywolf Pr.

White, Michael C. A Brother's Blood: A Novel. 1996. 336p. 22.50 o.p. (0-06-018667-4) HarperCollins Pubs.

—A Brother's Blood: A Novel. 1997. 336p. pap. 13.00 (0-06-092859-X, Perennial) HarperTrade.

Wieland, Mitch. Willy Slater's Lane. 1996. 176p. pap. 12.95 (*0-87074-409-7*) Southern Methodist Univ. Pr.
—Willy Slater's Lane: A Novel. 1996. 176p. 22.50 o.p. (*0-87074-408-9*) Southern Methodist Univ. Pr.
Wilber, Peggy M. What Digby Dug Up. (Godprints Early Readers Ser.). (Illus.). 32p. (J). (gr. k-2). pap. 5.99 (*0-7814-3724-5*) Cook Communications Ministries.
Wilkinson, Sylvia. On the 7th Day God Created the Chevrolet. 1993. 424p. 18.95 o.p. (*0-945575-13-0*) Algonquin Bks. of Chapel Hill.
Willard, Dale. My Son, My Brother, My Friend: A Novel in Letters. 2nd rev. ed. 2002. 101p. pap. 8.95 (*0-940895-17-X*) Cornerstone Pr. Chicago.
Willard, Dale C. My Son, My Brother, My Friend. 1978. pap. 3.95 o.p. (*0-87784-651-0*) InterVarsity Pr.
Williams, William G. The Coal King Slaves: A Coal Miner's Story. 2002. (Illus.). 208p. pap. 14.95 (*1-57249-319-4*, Burd Street Pr.) White Mane Publishing Co., Inc.
Wisler, G. Clifton. The Wetherbys. 1992. mass mkt. 4.99 o.s.i (*0-449-14830-0*, Fawcett) Ballantine Bks.
—The Wetherbys. l.t. ed. 2000. 22.95 o.p. (*1-56895-835-8*, Wheeler Publishing, Inc.) Gale Group.
Zusak, Markus. Getting the Girl. 2003. (YA). 261p. (*0-439-38950-X*); 263p. pap. 16.95 (*0-439-38949-6*) Scholastic, Inc. (Levine, Arthur A. Bks.).

**BROTHERS AND SISTERS—FICTION**

Abish, Walter. How German Is It=Wie Deutsch Ist Es. 1982. 195p. text 15.25 o.p. (*0-85635-396-5*) Brill Academic Pubs., Inc.
Agee, Jonis. Strange Angels. 1994. 79p. pap. 12.50 o.p. (*0-06-097589-X*) HarperCollins Pubs.
—Strange Angels. 1993. 384p. 21.95 o.p. (*0-395-60835-X*) Houghton Mifflin Co.
—Strange Angels. 2000. 416p. pap. 13.95 (*0-14-029186-5*) Penguin Group (USA) Inc.
Ansay, A. Manette. Sister. 1997. 240p. pap. 13.00 (*0-380-72976-8*, Perennial) HarperTrade.
—Sister. 1996. 224p. 24.00 o.p. (*0-688-14449-7*, Morrow, William & Co.) Morrow/Avon.
Antrim, Donald. The Hundred Brothers. 1998. (Vintage Contemporaries Ser.). 208p. pap. 12.00 (*0-679-76942-0*) Crown Publishing Group.
—The Hundred Brothers. 1997. 206p. 21.00 o.s.i (*0-517-70310-6*) Random Hse. Value Publishing.
Appelfeld, Aharon. Unto the Soul. Green, Jeffery M., tr. 1998. pap. 13.00 o.s.i (*0-8052-1097-0*, Schocken) Knopf Publishing Group.
Asher, Sandy. Things Are Seldom What They Seem. 1983. 144p. (J). (gr. 7). pap. 11.95 (*0-385-29250-3*, Delacorte Pr.) Dell Publishing.
Askew, Rilla. The Mercy Seat. 1998. 448p. pap. 13.95 (*0-14-026515-5*) Penguin Group (USA) Inc.
—The Mercy Seat. 1997. 448p. 23.95 o.p. (*0-670-87467-1*) Viking Penguin.
Asprin, Robert L. E.Godz. 2003. 288p. 17.00 (*0-7434-3605-9*) Baen Bks.
Barbash, Tom. The Last Good Chance: A Novel. 448p. 2003. pap. 15.00 (*0-312-42267-9*); 2002. 24.00 (*0-312-28796-8*) Picador.
Beattie, Ann. The Doctor's House: A Novel. l.t. ed. 2002. 336p. lib. bdg. 29.95 (*1-58547-199-2*, Platinum) Ctr. Point Large Print.
—The Doctor's House: A Novel. 288p. 2002. 24.00 (*0-7432-1264-9*); 2002. E-Book 24.00 (*0-7432-1466-8*); 2003. reprint ed. pap. 13.00 (*0-7432-3501-0*) Simon & Schuster. (Scribner).
Bellows, Nathaniel. On This Day: A Novel. 2003. 272p. 24.95 (*0-06-051211-3*) HarperCollins Pubs.
—On This Day: A Novel. 2004. 288p. pap. 12.95 (*0-06-051212-1*, Perennial) HarperTrade.
Binder, Mark. The Brothers Schlemiel - A Serialized Novel Via Email: A Tale of Twins from Chelm. 2000. (Brothers Schlemiel Ser.). E-Book 19.95 (*0-9702642-0-8*) Light Pubns.
Bingham, Linda S. All Roads Lead Home. 2003. 24.95 (*1-57168-774-2*, Eakin Pr.) Eakin Pr.
Blincoe, Nicholas. White Mice. 2002. 247p. pap. 17.95 (*0-340-75046-4*) Hodder & Stoughton, Ltd. GBR. *Dist:* Trafalgar Square.
Boswell, James. The Sower's Seeds. 2002. 360p. pap. 14.95 (*0-9717806-0-9*) Fourth Lloyd Productions.
Bradford, Barbara Taylor. Barbara Taylor Bradford: Three Complete Novels. 1992. 1040p. 14.99 (*0-517-08470-8*) Random Hse. Value Publishing.
Bradshaw, Rita. The Twisted Cord. l.t. ed. 2000. (Magna Large Print Ser.). 496p. 31.99 (*0-7505-1535-X*) Magna Large Print Bks. GBR. *Dist:* Ulverscroft Large Print Bks., Ltd., Ulverscroft Large Print Canada, Ltd.
—The Twisted Cord. 1999. 432p. 26.00 (*0-7278-2223-3*) Severn Hse. Pubs., Ltd.
Brown, Laurene Krasny. Rex & Lilly Playtime. (Rex & Lilly Ser.). (Illus.). 32p. (J). (ps-1). 1997. pap. 3.95 (*0-316-11110-4*); 1995. 12.95 o.p. (*0-316-11386-7*) Little Brown & Co.
—Rex & Lilly Playtime. 1997. (Rex & Lilly Ser.). (Illus.). 32p. (J). (ps-1). 10.10 (*0-606-11794-6*) Turtleback Bks.
Cameron, Anne. Wedding Cakes, Rats & Rodeo Queens. 1995. 296p. pap. o.p. (*0-00-647958-8*) HarperCollins Pubs. Canada, Ltd.
Card, Orson Scott. Ender's Game. Date not set. mass mkt. (*0-7655-5070-9*, Tor Bks.); 2000. (Ender Ser.: Bk. 1). 349p. mass mkt. 3.99 o.p. (*0-8125-8904-1*, Tor Bks.); 1994. (Ender Ser.: Bk. 1). 384p. mass mkt. 6.99 (*0-8125-2358-X*, Tor Bks.); 1992. (Ender Ser.: Bk. 1). 256p. pap. 13.95 (*0-312-85323-8*, Tor Bks.); 1991. (Ender Ser.: Bk. 1). 368p. reprint ed. mass mkt. 4.95 o.s.i (*0-8125-1349-5*, Tor Bks.); 1987. (Ender Ser.: Bk. 1). pap. 3.95 o.s.i (*0-8125-3355-0*, Tor Bks.); ltd. ed. 1992. (Ender Ser.: Bk. 1). 256p. 200.00 (*0-312-85402-1*, Tor Bks.); 2002. 324p. (J). reprint ed. mass mkt. 5.99 (*0-7653-4229-4*, Starscape); 1991. (Ender Ser.: Bk. 1). 368p. reprint ed. mass mkt. 4.99 o.s.i (*0-8125-1911-6*, Tor Bks.); rev. ed. 1994. (Ender Ser.: Bk. 1). 384p. pap. 6.99 (*0-8125-5070-6*, Tor Bks.); 4th rev. ed. 1985. (Ender Ser.: Bk. 1). 226p. 24.95 (*0-312-93208-1*, Tor Bks.) Doherty, Tom Assocs., LLC.
—Ender's Game. 1985. (Ender Ser.: Bk. 1). 13.04 (*0-606-04043-9*) Turtleback Bks.
Cather, Willa. O, Pioneers. 2004. 240p. mass mkt. 4.95 (*0-451-52919-7*, Signet Classics) NAL.
Churchill, Jill. Love for Sale: A Grace & Favor Mystery. 2004. 272p. mass mkt. 6.99 (*0-06-103122-4*, Avon Bks.); 2003. 224p. 23.95 (*0-06-019942-3*, Morrow, William & Co.) Morrow/Avon.
—Someone to Watch over Me: A Grace & Favor Mystery. l.t. ed. 2002. 309p. 28.95 (*0-7862-4356-2*) Gale Group.
—Someone to Watch over Me: A Grace & Favor Mystery. 2002. 272p. mass mkt. 6.99 (*0-06-103123-2*, Avon Bks.); 2001. 240p. 24.00 (*0-06-019941-5*, Morrow, William & Co.) Morrow/Avon.
Clark, Mary Higgins. Daddy's Little Girl. 2002. 304p. 26.00 (*0-7432-0604-5*, Simon & Schuster) Simon & Schuster.
Clarke, Judith. Friend of My Heart. 1994. 148p. pap. 12.95 (*0-7022-2699-8*) Univ. of Queensland Pr. AUS. *Dist:* International Specialized Bk. Services.
Colegate, Isabel. Winter Journey. l.t. ed. 2001. (Senior Lifestyles Ser.). 323p. 28.95 (*0-7862-3374-5*) Thorndike Pr.
—A Winter Journey. 2002. 208p. reprint ed. pap. text 14.00 (*1-58243-250-3*, Counterpoint Pr.) Basic Bks.
Conroy, Pat. The Prince of Tides. l.t. ed. 1993. pap. 21.95 o.p. (*0-7927-1358-3*); 1992. 24.95 o.p. (*0-7927-1359-1*) BBC Audiobooks America.
—The Prince of Tides. 1987. 672p. mass mkt. 7.99 (*0-553-26888-0*) Bantam Bks.
—The Prince of Tides, 001. 1986. 576p. tchr. ed. 30.00 (*0-395-35300-9*) Houghton Mifflin Co.
—The Prince of Tides. 2002. E-Book 8.99 (*0-7953-0100-6*) RosettaBooks.
—The Prince of Tides. 1991. 14.04 (*0-606-03895-7*) Turtleback Bks.
Craft, Mary Beth. Golden Grove. 1999. 183p. 16.95 (*1-885478-97-6*) Genesis Pr., Inc.
Darby, Catherine. Sabre's Child. l.t. ed. 2001. 233p. pap. 22.95 (*0-7862-3194-7*); (*0-7540-4414-9*); (*0-7540-4415-7*) Thorndike Pr.
Desai, Anita. Fasting, Feasting. 2000. 240p. pap. 13.00 (*0-618-06582-2*, Mariner Bks.) Houghton Mifflin Co. Trade & Reference Div.
—Fasting, Feasting. 1999. 227p. (*0-7011-6894-3*) Random Hse. of Canada, Ltd. CAN. *Dist:* Random Hse., Inc.
—Fasting, Feasting. l.t. ed. 2000. (Basic Ser.). 323p. 27.95 (*0-7862-2638-2*); (*0-7540-4239-1*); (*0-7540-4240-5*) Thorndike Pr.
Dodd, Susan. No Earthly Notion. 224p. 1987. pap. 6.95 o.p. (*0-14-008531-9*, Penguin Bks.); 1986. 15.95 o.p. (*0-670-80913-6*) Viking Penguin.
Duberstein, Larry. The Mt. Monadnock Blues. 2003. 26.00 (*1-57962-093-0*) Permanent Pr., The.
Dunmore, Helen. A Spell of Winter. l.t. ed. 2001. 312p. 28.95 (*0-7838-9530-5*, Macmillan Reference USA) Gale Group.
—A Spell of Winter. 320p. 2002. pap. 13.00 (*0-8021-3876-4*); 2001. 24.00 o.p. (*0-87113-782-8*) Grove/Atlantic, Inc.
—A Spell of Winter. 1999. pap. (*0-316-19794-7*) Little Brown & Co.
Eisenberg, Nora. The War at Home. 2002. 217p. pap. 14.95 (*0-9679520-4-2*) Leapfrog Pr.
Eliot, George. The Mill on the Floss. 1976. 30.95 (*0-8488-0483-X*) Amereon, Ltd.
—The Mill on the Floss. 1987. (Classics Ser.). 496p. mass mkt. 4.50 o.s.i (*0-553-21319-9*, Bantam Classics) Bantam Bks.
—The Mill on the Floss. reprint ed. Pt. 1. 2001. 404p. pap. text 28.00 (*0-7426-5072-3*); Pt. 1. 1999. (Writings of George Eliot Ser.: Vol. 5). 404p. lib. bdg. (*1-58201-072-2*); Pt. 2. 2001. 400p. pap. text 28.00 (*0-7426-5073-1*); Pt. 2. 1999. (Writings of George Eliot Ser.: Vol. 6). 400p. lib. bdg. 88.00 (*1-58201-073-0*) Classic Bks.
—The Mill on the Floss. 2003. (Dover Thrift Editions Ser.). 416p. 3.50 (*0-486-42680-7*) Dover Pubns., Inc.
—The Mill on the Floss. 1972. 3.95 o.p. (*0-460-01325-4*); 1956. 10.50 o.p. (*0-460-00325-9*) Dutton/Plume. (Dutton).
—The Mill on the Floss. 1994. 96p. pap. 16.95 (*1-85459-276-9*, M88) Hern, Nick Bks. GBR. *Dist:* Theatre Communications Group, Inc.
—The Mill on the Floss. 1992. 640p. 20.00 (*0-679-41726-5*) Knopf, Alfred A. Inc.
—The Mill on the Floss. 1998. (Cloth Bound Pocket Ser.). 240p. 7.95 (*3-89508-461-1*, 520049) Konemann.
—The Mill on the Floss. Cairns, Peter, ed. 1988. pap. 5.72 (*0-582-33169-2*, 72063) Longman Publishing Group.
—The Mill on the Floss. 2002. 560p. mass mkt. 5.95 (*0-451-52826-3*, Signet Classics); 1968. mass mkt. 0.95 o.p. (*0-451-50438-0*, Signet Classics); 1968. mass mkt. 0.75 o.p. (*0-451-50278-7*, Signet Classics); 1965. mass mkt. 3.50 o.p. (*0-451-51543-9*); 1965. mass mkt. 1.95 o.p. (*0-451-51055-0*, Signet Classics); 1965. mass mkt. 1.50 o.p. (*0-451-50892-0*, Signet Classics); 1965. mass mkt. 1.25 o.p. (*0-451-50672-3*, Signet Classics); 1965. 560p. mass mkt. 5.95 o.s.i (*0-451-52396-2*); 1965. mass mkt. 3.95 o.p. (*0-451-51922-1*, CE1543, Signet Classics); 1965. mass mkt. 2.95 o.p. (*0-451-51472-6*, Signet Classics) NAL.
—The Mill on the Floss. 2003. (Twelve-Point Ser.). lib. bdg. 27.00 (*1-58287-240-6*); lib. bdg. 28.00 (*1-58287-724-6*) North Bks.
—The Mill on the Floss. Haight, Gordon S., ed. (Oxford World's Classics Ser.). 1998. 576p. pap. 8.95 (*0-19-283364-2*); 1982. 550p. pap. 5.95 o.p. (*0-19-281567-9*); 1980. (Illus.). 516p. (C). text 130.00 o.p. (*0-19-812560-7*); 2nd ed. 1997. 566p. pap. 5.95 o.p. (*0-19-282488-0*) Oxford Univ. Pr., Inc.
—The Mill on the Floss. 2001. (Modern Library Classics). 656p. pap. 8.95 (*0-375-75783-X*, Modern Library) Random House Adult Trade Publishing Group.
—The Mill on the Floss. Shuttleworth, Sally, ed. 1991. (English Texts Ser.). 450p. (C). pap. 19.95 o.p. (*0-415-01316-X*, A6066) Routledge.
—The Mill on the Floss. 1991. (Pocket Classics Ser.). 512p. reprint ed. pap. 4.50 o.p. (*0-7509-0012-1*) Sutton Publishing, Ltd. GBR. *Dist:* International Publishers Marketing.
—The Mill on the Floss. 2000. (Signature Classics Ser.). 486p. 24.95 (*1-58279-088-4*); lib. bdg. 29.95 (*1-58279-083-3*) Trident Pr. International.
—The Mill on the Floss. 1981. 12.00 (*0-606-03858-2*) Turtleback Bks.
—The Mill on the Floss. Skilton, David, ed. 1993. 492p. pap. 6.95 o.p. (*0-460-87286-9*, Everyman's Classic Library in Paperback) Tuttle Publishing.
—The Mill on the Floss. 1992. 506p. pap. 6.95 o.p. (*0-460-87109-9*, Everyman's Classic Library in Paperback) Tuttle Publishing.
—The Mill on the Floss. 2003. 704p. pap. 9.00 (*0-14-143962-9*, Penguin Classics) Viking Penguin.
—The Mill on the Floss. Byatt, A. S., ed. 1980. (Penguin Classics Ser.). 696p. 8.95 (*0-14-043120-9*, Penguin Classics) Viking Penguin.
—The Mill on the Floss. 1995. (Wordsworth Collection). 512p. pap. 3.95 (*1-85326-074-6*, 0746WW) Wordsworth Editions, Ltd. GBR. *Dist:* Casemate Pubs. & Bk. Distributors, LLC.
Eliot, George & Haight, Gordon Sherman. The Mill on the Floss. 1980. E-Book 8.35 (*0-585-36085-5*) netLibrary, Inc.
Emmons, Cai. His Mother's Son. 2003. 376p. 25.00 (*0-15-100734-9*) Harcourt Trade Pubs.
Even, Aaron Roy. Bloodroot. 2000. 261p. 22.95 (*0-312-26561-1*) St. Martin's Pr.
Fante, John. The Road to Los Angeles. 1992. 167p. o.p. (*0-87685-651-2*, Black Sparrow Pr.) Godine, David R. Pub.
—The Road to Los Angeles. 1995. reprint ed. 288p. 20.00 (*0-87685-650-4*); 168p. pap. 14.00 (*0-87685-649-0*) HarperCollins Pubs.
Feldhake, Susan C. Joy in the Morning. 1994. (Enduring Faith Ser.: Vol. 6). 208p. pap. 9.99 o.p. (*0-310-47941-X*) Zondervan.
Fell, Doris Elaine. Betrayal in Paris. 2003. 350p. pap. 12.99 (*1-58229-314-7*) Howard Publishing Co.
Fine, Africa. Becoming Maren. 2003. 26.95 (*1-59414-081-2*, Five Star) Gale Group.
Flanagan, Mary. Adele. 1997. 245p. (*0-7475-3332-6*) Bloomsbury Publishing, Ltd.
—Adele: A Novel. 1997. 304p. 22.00 (*0-393-04547-1*) Norton, W. W. & Co., Inc.
Fleutiaux, Pierrette. We Are Eternal: A Novel. Leggett, Jeremy, tr. 1994. ix, 565p. 24.95 o.p. (*0-316-28617-6*) Little Brown & Co.
Foos, Laurie. Bingo under the Crucifix: A Novel. 2002. 190p. pap. 14.00 (*1-56689-133-7*) Coffee Hse. Pr.
Forbes, Edith. Nowle's Passing. 1997. 272p. pap. 12.00 (*1-878067-99-0*); 1996. 266p. 21.95 o.p. (*1-878067-72-9*) Avalon Publishing Group. (Seal Pr.).
Forsyth, Moira. Waiting for Lindsay. 2001. 288p. 23.95 (*0-312-27873-X*) St. Martin's Pr.
Fromm, Pete. How All This Started. 2001. 320p. pap. 14.00 (*0-312-27697-4*); 2000. 305p. 23.00 o.s.i (*0-312-20933-9*) Picador.
Gardner, John. October Light. 1983. mass mkt. 3.95 o.s.i (*0-345-31550-2*); 1977. mass mkt. 2.50 o.p. (*0-345-27193-9*) Ballantine Bks.
—October Light. 1986. pap. 6.95 o.s.i (*0-394-74058-0*); 1989. reprint ed. pap. 15.00 o.s.i (*0-679-72133-9*) Knopf Publishing Group. (Vintage).
Genberg, Ira. Reckless Homicide. 1998. (Reckless Homicide Ser.: Vol. 1). 384p. mass mkt. 6.99 (*0-312-96679-2*, St. Martin's Paperbacks); 1997. 304p. 23.95 (*0-312-17974-X*); 1997. E-Book 6.99 o.s.i (*0-312-20739-5*) St. Martin's Pr.
Gibb, Camilla. The Petty Details of So-and-So's Life. 2003. 336p. pap. 13.95 (*0-385-65803-6*) Doubleday Publishing.
Gilmore-Scott, Monique. Ties That Bind: Way down Deep. 1998. 249p. pap. 13.95 (*0-9664355-0-8*) Writing Minds.
Goudge, Elizabeth. Green Dolphin Street. 2001. 576p. 33.95 (*0-8488-2770-8*) Amereon, Ltd.
—Green Dolphin Street. 2000. 512p. 38.95 (*0-89966-113-0*) Buccaneer Bks., Inc.
Grahame, Kenneth. Dream Days. 2001. (Company of Books Ser.). (Illus.). 163p. (YA). 22.95 (*1-58579-018-4*, Common Reader Editions) Akadine Pr., The.
—Dream Days. 1985. (Illus.). (J). (gr. 4 up). 14.95 o.p. (*0-8253-0281-1*) Beaufort Bks., Inc.
—Dream Days. 2000. E-Book 2.49 (*1-58744-147-0*) Electric Umbrella Publishing.
—Dream Days. 1976. (Classics of Children's Literature, 1621-1932: Vol. 62). (Illus.). (J). reprint ed. lib. bdg. 46.00 o.p. (*0-8240-2311-0*) Garland Publishing, Inc.
—Dream Days. 1975. (Illus.). mass mkt. 4.95 o.p. (*0-380-00288-4*, 23994, Avon Bks.) Morrow/Avon.
—Dream Days. 1993. (Illus.). 240p. (YA). (gr. 5 up). 18.95 o.s.i (*0-89815-546-0*) Ten Speed Pr.
—The Golden Age. 2001. (Company of Books Ser.). (Illus.). 174p. (YA). (gr. 5 up). 22.95 (*1-58579-019-2*, Common Reader Editions) Akadine Pr., The.
—The Golden Age. 1985. (Illus.). 288p. (J). (gr. 4 up). reprint ed. 14.95 o.p. (*0-8253-0331-1*) Beaufort Bks., Inc.
—The Golden Age. 1976. (Classics of Children's Literature, 1621-1932: Vol. 59). (Illus.). (J). reprint ed. lib. bdg. 46.00 o.p. (*0-8240-2308-0*) Garland Publishing, Inc.
—The Golden Age. 1975. (Illus.). mass mkt. 4.95 o.p. (*0-380-00289-2*, 23986, Avon Bks.) Morrow/Avon.
—The Golden Age. mass mkt. 0.75 o.p. (*0-451-50207-8*, Signet Classics) NAL.
—The Golden Age. (Ebook Classic Ser.). E-Book 5.00 (*0-7410-1093-3*) SoftBook Pr.
—The Golden Age. 1993. (Illus.). 264p. (YA). (gr. 5 up). 18.95 o.s.i (*0-89815-545-2*) Ten Speed Pr.
Green, Terence M. Shadow of Ashland. 2000. 223p. pap. 13.95 (*0-312-87301-8*, Forge Bks.); 1997. 223p. mass mkt. 5.99 (*0-8125-5526-0*, Tor Bks.); 1996. 224p. 17.95 o.p. (*0-312-85958-9*, Forge Bks.) Doherty, Tom Assocs., LLC.
Gross, Gwendolen. Getting Out: A Novel. 2002. 304p. 24.00 (*0-8050-6834-1*) Holt, Henry & Co.
Gunn, Kirsty. Rain. 1996. 104p. reprint ed. pap. 11.00 (*0-8021-3447-5*, Grove Pr.) Grove/Atlantic, Inc.
—Rain: A Novel. 1994. 128p. pap. 15.00 o.p. (*0-87113-592-2*, Atlantic Monthly Pr.) Grove/Atlantic, Inc.
Guymon, Shannon. Justifiable Means. 2003. 188p. pap. 13.95 (*1-55517-677-1*, 76771, Bonneville Bks.) Cedar Fort, Inc./CFI Distribution.
Haien, Jeannett. The All of It. 1988. 160p. reprint ed. pap. 12.00 (*0-06-097147-9*, PL-7147, Perennial) HarperTrade.
Haien, Jeannette. All of It. 1986. 160p. 14.95 o.p. (*0-87923-623-X*) Godine, David R. Pub.
Hall, Sands. Catching Heaven. E-Book 12.50 (*1-930161-77-8*) Adobe Systems, Inc.
Hansen, Jennie L. Abandoned: A Novel. 2002. (Illus.). 262p. 14.95 (*1-59156-070-5*) Covenant Communications.
Hanson, Rick. Spare Parts. 1995. 256p. mass mkt. 4.99 (*0-8217-0156-8*, Zebra Bks.); 1995. 256p. mass mkt. 4.99 o.s.i (*0-7860-0156-9*, Pinnacle Bks.); 1994. 288p. mass mkt. 20.00 o.s.i (*0-8217-4738-X*, Zebra Bks.) Kensington Publishing Corp.
Hardy, Edward. Geyser Life: A Novel. 1996. 288p. 21.95 (*1-882593-16-2*) Bridge Works Publishing Co., Inc.
Hart, Josephine. The Reconstructionist. l.t. ed. 2002. 256p. pap. 24.95 (*0-7862-3726-0*) Gale Group.
—The Reconstructionist. 2001. 288p. 26.95 (*1-58567-170-3*) Overlook Pr., The.
Heinlein, Robert A. Podkayne of Mars. 1987. mass mkt. 3.95 o.s.i (*0-441-67402-X*) Ace Bks.
—Podkayne of Mars. 1995. 288p. pap. 5.99 (*0-671-87671-6*); 1993. 256p. reprint ed. pap. 10.00 (*0-671-72179-8*) Baen Bks.

—Podkayne of Mars. 1983. 2.50 o.s.i (*0-425-06826-9*); 1982. 2.25 o.s.i (*0-425-05713-5*); 1979. 1.75 o.s.i (*0-425-04236-7*); 1976. 1.25 o.s.i (*0-425-03153-5*); 1976. 1.50 o.s.i (*0-425-03434-8*); 1971. 0.95 o.p. (*0-425-02073-8*) Berkley Publishing Group.

—Podkayne of Mars. 1963. 7.95 o.p. (*0-399-10642-1*) Putnam Publishing Group, The.

—Podkayne of Mars. 1999. lib. bdg. 20.95 (*1-56723-164-0*) Yestermorrow, Inc.

Hershon, Joanna. Swimming. l.t. ed. 2001. 552p. 28.95 (*0-7862-3368-0*) Thorndike Pr.

Holland, Cecelia. The Soul Thief. E-Book 24.95 (*0-312-70605-7*, Tor Bks.); 2004. 304p. pap. 14.95 (*0-312-86997-5*, Forge Bks.); 2002. 304p. 24.95 o.s.i (*0-312-84885-4*, Forge Bks.) Doherty, Tom Assocs., LLC.

Hughes, Glyn. Bronte. 1996. 432p. 24.95 o.p. (*0-312-14816-X*) St. Martin's Pr.

—Bronte. 2000. 431p. 27.95 (*0-593-03549-6*) Transworld Publishers Ltd. GBR. *Dist:* Trafalgar Square.

Hyde, Catherine R. Funerals for Horses. 1997. (Emerging Writers Ser.). 256p. 19.95 (*0-9653524-3-9*) Russian Hill Pr.

James, Henry. The Turn of the Screw. E-Book 2.49 (*1-58627-970-X*) Electric Umbrella Publishing.

Jefferson, Blanche. So Strong This Bond. 1995. pap. 11.95 (*0-935016-35-X*) Zinn Publishing Group.

Jha, Raj Kamal. The Blue Bedspread. 2001. (Harvest Book Ser.). 240p. reprint ed. pap. 13.00 (*0-15-601088-7*, Harvest Bks.) Harcourt Trade Pubs.

—The Blue Bedspread: A Novel. 1999. 228p. 16.95 (*0-330-37385-4*) Picador GBR. *Dist:* Trans-Atlantic Pubns., Inc.

Johnson, Greg. Sticky Kisses. 2001. 324p. 24.95 o.p. (*1-55583-637-2*) Alyson Pubns.

Johnson, Greg, told to. Sticky Kisses: A Novel. 2002. 328p. pap. 13.95 (*1-55583-770-0*) Alyson Pubns.

Jooste, Pamela. Like Water in Wild Places. 2000. 270p. Doubleday Publishing.

—Like Water in Wild Places. 2003. 315p. pap. 12.00 (*0-552-99867-2*) Transworld Publishers Ltd. GBR. *Dist:* Trafalgar Square.

Kihn, Greg. Shade of Pale. 256p. 1998. pap. 5.99 (*0-8125-5109-5*, Tor Bks.); 1997. 21.95 (*0-312-86046-3*, Forge Bks.) Doherty, Tom Assocs., LLC.

Kittle, Katrina. Traveling Light. l.t. ed. 2000. (G. K. Hall Core Ser.). 407p. 27.95 (*0-7838-9173-3*) Thorndike Pr.

—Traveling Light. 2000. 320p. 18.95 (*0-446-52480-8*); 2001. 336p. reprint ed. pap. 13.95 (*0-446-67694-2*) Warner Bks., Inc.

Koontz, Dean. The Bad Place. 1990. 432p. mass mkt. 7.99 (*0-425-12434-7*) Berkley Publishing Group.

—The Bad Place. l.t. ed. 1991. (Magna Large Print Ser.). 612p. o.p. (*0-7505-0103-0*) Magna Large Print Bks. GBR. *Dist:* Ulverscroft Large Print Canada, Ltd.

—The Bad Place. 2001. 19.95 (*0-399-13703-3*) Penguin Group (USA) Inc.

—The Bad Place. 1990. 384p. 19.95 o.p. (*0-399-13498-0*); 75.00 o.p. (*0-399-13510-3*) Penguin Putnam Bks. for Young Readers. (G. P. Putnam's Sons).

—The Bad Place. 1990. 14.04 (*0-606-00936-1*) Turtleback Bks.

Lawson, Mary. Crow Lake: A Novel. 304p. 2003. pap. 12.95 (*0-385-33613-6*, Delta); 2002. 23.95 o.s.i (*0-385-33611-X*, Dial Bks.) Dell Publishing.

Leland, Christopher T. The Professor of Aesthetics. 1994. 160p. 18.95 o.p. (*0-944072-37-2*, Zoland Bks., Inc.) Steerforth Pr.

Leon, Bonnie. Where Freedom Grows. 1998. (Sowers Triology Ser.: Vol. 1). 300p. pap. 12.99 (*0-8054-1272-7*) Broadman & Holman Pubs.

Lessing, Doris. Mara & Dann: An Adventure. 1998. 416p. o.p. (*0-06-018294-6*, HarperFlamingo) HarperCollins Pubs. Canada, Ltd.

—Mara & Dann: An Adventure. 2000. 416p. pap. 14.00 (*0-06-093056-X*, Perennial) HarperTrade.

Levy, Deborah. Billy & Girl. 1996. 185p. text (*0-7475-2835-7*) Bloomsbury Publishing, Ltd. GBR. *Dist:* AMACOM.

—Billy & Girl. 1998. (British Literature Ser.). 192p. pap. 13.95 (*1-56478-202-6*) Dalkey Archive Pr.

Lipman, Elinor. The Dearly Departed. 2001. E-Book 8.95 (*1-58945-947-4*) Adobe Systems, Inc.

—The Dearly Departed. 2002. 288p. pap. 13.00 (*0-375-72458-3*, Vintage) Knopf Publishing Group.

—The Dearly Departed: A Novel. 2001. E-Book 19.00 (*1-58836-013-X*) Random Hse., Inc.

Littell, John S. Carvel, the Christmas Cat. 2003. 208p. 14.95 (*1-4022-0048-X*, Sourcebooks Landmark) Sourcebooks, Inc.

Lively, Penelope. Passing On. 224p. 1990. 17.95 o.p. (*0-8021-1155-6*); 1999. reprint ed. pap. 12.00 (*0-8021-3626-5*, Grove Pr.) Grove/Atlantic, Inc.

—Passing On. 1991. 224p. reprint ed. pap. 12.00 o.s.i (*0-06-097370-6*, Perennial) HarperTrade.

—Passing On. l.t. ed. 1990. 342p. 19.95 (*1-85089-329-2*) ISIS Large Print Bks. GBR. *Dist:* Transaction Pubs.

Long, Goldberry M. Juniper Tree Burning. 2002. 464p. pap. 14.00 (*0-7432-2211-3*, Simon & Schuster) Simon & Schuster.

Loring, Emilie Baker. Behind the Cloud. reprint ed. lib. bdg. 19.95 (*0-88411-367-1*) Amereon, Ltd.

—Behind the Cloud. 1981. 208p. pap. 1.95 o.p. (*0-553-14295-X*) Bantam Bks.

—Behind the Cloud. l.t. ed. 1999. 30.00 o.p. (*0-7862-1754-5*, Macmillan Reference USA) Gale Group.

Mackay, Shena. Dunedin. 1993. 296p. reprint ed. 21.95 o.p. (*1-55921-093-1*) Moyer Bell.

Mackay, Shena. Dunedin. 1994. pap. 5.95 o.p. (*1-55921-119-9*) Moyer Bell.

Maddox, Muriel. Myra's Daughters: A Contemporary Novel. 2001. 280p. 22.95 (*0-86534-323-3*) Sunstone Pr.

Mahon, Annette. Just Friends. 1998. (Avalon Romances Ser.). 192p. lib. bdg. 18.95 (*0-8034-9317-7*, Avalon Bks.) Bouregy, Thomas & Co., Inc.

Major, Marcus. Four Guys & Trouble. 2001. 272p. 23.95 o.p. (*0-525-94568-7*, Dutton) Dutton/Plume.

—Four Guys & Trouble. 2002. 384p. mass mkt. 6.99 (*0-451-41017-3*, Onyx) NAL.

Maristed, Kai. Out after Dark: A Novel. 1993. 328p. 28.00 (*1-877946-30-3*) Permanent Pr., The.

Martin, LaJoyce. The Mistress of Magnolia Manor. 2003. 168p. pap. 9.99 (*1-56722-620-5*) Word Aflame Pr.

McCarthy, Cormac. Outer Dark. 1970. mass mkt. 0.95 o.s.i (*0-345-22105-2*) Ballantine Bks.

—Outer Dark. 1984. 242p. reprint ed. pap. 7.50 o.p. (*0-88001-064-9*) HarperCollins Pubs.

—Outer Dark. 1993. 256p. pap. 13.00 (*0-679-72873-2*, Vintage) Knopf Publishing Group.

—Outer Dark. 1994. 26.25 (*0-8446-6749-8*) Smith, Peter Pub., Inc.

McCullough, Sharon Pierce. Bunbun, the Middle One. 2001. (Illus.). 24p. (J). (ps-k). 14.99 (*1-84148-325-7*) Barefoot Bks., Inc.

McDermid, Terry Z. Matters of the Heart. 1999. 182p. 18.95 (*0-8034-9373-8*, Avalon Bks.) Bouregy, Thomas & Co., Inc.

McFarland, Dennis. School for the Blind. 1995. 272p. mass mkt. 6.99 o.s.i (*0-8041-1350-5*, Ivy Bks.) Ballantine Bks.

—School for the Blind. 1994. 304p. 21.95 o.p. (*0-395-64497-6*) Houghton Mifflin Co.

McGiffen, Steve. Tennant's Rock. 2001. 224p. 23.95 (*0-312-26657-X*) St. Martin's Pr.

McGovern, Cammie. The Art of Seeing. 2002. 288p. 24.00 (*0-7432-2835-9*, Scribner) Simon & Schuster.

Miller, Calvin. Wind. 2000. (Illus.). 160p. 12.99 (*0-7642-2362-3*) Bethany Hse. Pubs.

Millner, Denene & Chiles, Nick. In Love & War. 2003. 352p. 23.95 (*0-525-94709-4*) Dutton/Plume.

—In Love & War. 2004. 352p. pap. 14.00 (*0-451-21115-4*) NAL.

Minot, George. The Blue Bowl. 2004. 384p. 24.00 (*0-394-57348-X*) Knopf, Alfred A. Inc.

Mitchard, Jacquelyn. A Theory of Relativity. 2002. 416p. mass mkt. 7.99 (*0-06-103199-2*); 2001. 368p. 26.00 (*0-06-621023-2*); 2001. E-Book 7.99 (*0-06-001068-1*) HarperCollins Pubs.

—A Theory of Relativity. l.t. ed. 2001. 624p. pap. 26.00 (*0-06-621060-7*, HarperLargePrint) HarperTrade.

Mockler, Karen. After Moses. 2003. 212p. 23.00 (*1-931561-37-0*) MacAdam/Cage Publishing, Inc.

Monfredo, Grace Miriam. Children of Cain. 2002. (Illus.). 352p. 22.95 (*0-425-18641-5*, Prime Crime) Berkley Publishing Group.

Morgan, Marlo. Message from Forever: A Novel of Aboriginal Wisdom. 1998. 336p. 24.00 o.s.i (*0-06-019107-4*, HarperCollins) HarperTrade.

Morgan, Mary. The House at the Edge of the Jungle. 1998. 206p. 21.95 (*0-312-19898-1*, Saint Martin's Minotaur) St. Martin's Pr.

—House at the Edge of the Jungle. E-Book 21.95 (*0-312-26834-3*) St. Martin's Pr.

Morris, Gilbert. The Fiery Ring. 2002. (House of Winslow Ser.: Bk. 28). (Illus.). 320p. pap. 11.99 (*0-7642-2622-3*) Bethany Hse. Pubs.

Morris, Gilbert & Ferguson, J. Landon. The Silver Thread. 2000. (Chronicles of the Golden Frontier Ser.: Bk. 4). 316p. pap. 11.99 (*1-58134-212-8*) Crossway Bks.

Morris, Mary. The Waiting Room. 1990. 288p. pap. 8.95 o.p. (*0-14-013344-5*, Penguin Bks.) Viking Penguin.

Nagy, Gloria. The Beauty. 2001. 290p. 26.95 (*1-58567-149-5*) Overlook Pr., The.

Neihart, Ben. Burning Girl. 2000. 256p. pap. 13.00 (*0-688-17689-5*); 1999. 245p. 24.00 (*0-688-15691-6*) Morrow/Avon. (Morrow, William & Co.).

Newman, Sandra. The Only Good Thing Anyone Has Ever Done. 2003. 400p. 24.95 (*0-06-051498-1*) HarperCollins Pubs.

Nicholson, Joy. The Tribes of Palos Verdes. 224p. 1997. 19.95 o.p. (*0-312-15677-4*); 3rd ed. 1998. pap. 11.95 (*0-312-19532-X*, CPB1114, Saint Martin's Griffin) St. Martin's Pr.

Noon, Jeff. Vurt. 2000. (SPA.). 336p. pap. 10.47 (*84-397-0538-7*) AIMS International Bks., Inc.

—Vurt, Vol. 1. 1996. (Vurt Ser.: Vol. 1). 384p. pap. 14.95 (*0-312-14144-0*, Saint Martin's Griffin) St. Martin's Pr.

Oates, Joyce Carol. Angel of Light. 1981. 440p. 15.50 o.p. (*0-525-05483-9*, 01505-450, Dutton) Dutton/Plume.

—Angel of Light. 1982. 608p. mass mkt. 3.95 o.s.i (*0-446-30189-2*) Warner Bks., Inc.

O'Brien, Edna. Wild Decembers: A Novel. 2000. 256p. 24.00 (*0-618-04567-8*) Houghton Mifflin Co.

—Wild Decembers: A Novel. 2001. 272p. pap. 13.00 (*0-618-12691-0*, Mariner Bks.) Houghton Mifflin Co. Trade & Reference Div.

—Wild Decembers: A Novel. l.t. ed. 2000. (Core Ser.). 358p. pap. 27.95 (*0-7838-9072-9*) Thorndike Pr.

O'Dell, Tawni. Back Roads. 2004. 432p. pap. 14.00 (*0-451-21245-2*); 2001. 416p. mass mkt. 7.99 (*0-451-20234-1*, Signet Bks.) NAL.

—Back Roads. l.t. ed. 511p. 2001. 28.95 o.p. (*0-7862-2762-1*); 2000. 30.95 (*0-7862-2754-0*) Thorndike Pr.

—Back Roads. 2000. 338p. 24.95 o.s.i (*0-670-89418-4*, Penguin Bks.); 1999. 352p. 24.95 o.s.i (*0-670-88760-9*) Viking Penguin.

Oke, Janette. Beyond the Gathering Storm. 2000. 256p. pap. 11.99 (*0-7642-2400-X*); 256p. text 16.99 o.p. (*0-7642-2401-8*); 368p. pap. 16.99 (*0-7642-2403-4*) Bethany Hse. Pubs.

—Beyond the Gathering Storm. l.t. ed. 2000. (Christian Fiction Ser.). 357p. 26.95 o.p. (*0-7862-2942-X*) Thorndike Pr.

Palmer, Catherine. The Happy Room. 2003. (Large Print Softcover Ser.). 441p. pap. 16.95 (*1-4104-0074-3*); 27.95 (*0-7862-4849-1*) Thorndike Pr.

—The Happy Room. 368p. 2003. pap. 12.99 (*0-8423-5422-0*); 2002. 19.99 (*0-8423-5421-2*) Tyndale Hse. Pubs.

Parker, Michael. Towns Without Rivers. 2001. 368p. 25.00 (*0-380-97860-1*, Morrow, William & Co.) Morrow/Avon.

Parrish, Patt. Escape the Past. l.t. ed. 1999. (Candlelight Romance Ser.). 256p. 19.95 (*0-7862-2028-7*) Thorndike Pr.

—Escape the Past. l.t. ed. 1985. 192p. 13.95 o.s.i (*0-8027-0825-0*) Walker & Co.

Peale, Cynthia. The White Crow. 2003. 336p. mass mkt. 6.50 (*0-440-23566-9*) Dell Publishing.

—The White Crow. 2002. 336p. 24.95 (*0-385-49638-9*) Doubleday Publishing.

Penley, Gary. Jubal. 2003. 272p. 23.00 (*1-58980-129-6*) Pelican Publishing Co., Inc.

Phillips, Michael. My Father's World. 1996. (Journals of Corrie Belle Hollister: No. 1). 288p. text 14.99 o.p. (*1-55661-905-7*) Bethany Hse. Pubs.

Phillips, Michael & Pella, Judith. My Father's World. 1990. (Journals of Corrie Belle Hollister: No. 1). 288p. pap. 10.99 o.p. (*1-55661-104-8*) Bethany Hse. Pubs.

—My Father's World. l.t. ed. 1994. 366p. lib. bdg. 20.95 (*0-8161-5994-7*, Macmillan Reference USA) Gale Group.

Phillips, Michael R. & Pella, Judith. My Father's World. 2000. 300p. 24.95 o.p. (*0-7862-2871-7*, Five Star) Gale Group.

Plain, Belva. Treasures. 1993. 528p. mass mkt. 7.99 (*0-440-21400-9*) Dell Publishing.

—Treasures. l.t. ed. 1993. pap. 19.95 o.p. (*0-8161-5803-7*, Macmillan Reference USA) Gale Group.

—Treasures. 1992. audio 12.79 o.s.i (*0-553-70024-3*, RH Audio) Random Hse. Audio Publishing Group.

Raczymow, Henri. Writing the Book of Esther. Katz, Dori, tr. from FRE. 1995. (French Expressions Ser.). 220p. 24.00 (*0-8419-1335-8*) Holmes & Meier Pubs., Inc.

Relling, William, Jr. The Criminalist. 2003. 368p. mass mkt. 6.99 (*0-8439-5278-4*, Leisure Bks.) Dorchester Publishing Co., Inc.

Ricci, Nino. Where She Has Gone. 336p. 1999. pap. 13.00 o.s.i (*0-312-20681-X*); 1998. 25.00 o.p. (*0-312-18700-9*) Picador.

Rice, Ben. Pobby & Dingan. E-Book 14.50 (*1-58945-535-5*) Adobe Systems, Inc.

—Pobby & Dingan. 2003. 112p. reprint ed. pap. 10.00 (*1-4000-3188-5*, Vintage) Knopf Publishing Group.

—Pobby & Dingan. 2000. (Illus.). 112p. 18.00 (*0-375-41127-5*) Knopf, Alfred A. Inc.

—Pobby & Dingan. 2001. E-Book 14.50 (*0-375-41261-1*) Random Hse., Inc.

Roberts, Nora. Three Fates. 2003. 496p. mass mkt. 7.99 (*0-515-13506-2*, Jove) Berkley Publishing Group.

—Three Fates. l.t. ed. 2002. 742p. 32.95 (*0-7862-3835-6*) Gale Group.

—Three Fates. 2002. 432p. 25.95 o.s.i (*0-399-14840-X*) Penguin Group (USA) Inc.

—Three Fates. l.t. ed. 2003. 733p. pap. 14.95 (*1-4104-0098-0*, Large Print Pr.); 2002. pap. 29.95 (*0-7862-3839-9*) Thorndike Pr.

—Time & Again. l.t. ed. 2002. 662p. 31.95 (*0-7862-3983-2*) Gale Group.

—Time & Again. l.t. ed. 2002. pap. 28.95 (*0-7862-3992-1*) Thorndike Pr.

Robinson, Eden. Monkey Beach. 2000. 384p. 24.00 (*0-618-10168-3*) Houghton Mifflin Co.

—Monkey Beach. 2000. 384p. (*0-676-97075-3*) Knopf, Alfred A. Inc.

Rogers, Jane. Island. 2001. (Illus.). 238p. reprint ed. pap. 13.00 (*0-618-13931-1*, Mariner Bks.) Houghton Mifflin Co. Trade & Reference Div.

—Island. 2000. 261p. 25.95 (*1-58567-076-6*) Overlook Pr., The.

Roorbach, Bill. The Smallest Color. 336p. 2001. text 25.00 o.p. (*1-58243-152-3*); 2002. reprint ed. pap. text 15.00 (*1-58243-252-X*) Basic Bks. (Counterpoint Pr.).

Rose, Heather. White Heart. 1999. 320p. (*1-86359-126-5*) Transworld Pubs.

Rosner, Elizabeth. The Speed of Light. 2003. 272p. pap. 12.95 (*0-345-44225-3*); 2001. 256p. 23.95 (*0-345-44224-5*) Ballantine Bks. (Ballantine Bks.).

—The Speed of Light. l.t. ed. 2002. 398p. 28.95 (*0-7862-4041-5*) Gale Group.

Ruffell, Ann. Blood Brother. 1980. (Julia MacRae Blackbird Bks.). 160p. (J). (gr. 7 up). lib. bdg. 8.90 o.p. (*0-531-04177-8*, Watts, Franklin) Scholastic Library Publishing.

Salinger, J. D. Franny & Zooey. 1981. mass mkt. 2.95 o.s.i (*0-553-20348-7*); 208p. mass mkt. 3.95 o.s.i (*0-553-26973-9*, Bantam Classics) Bantam Bks.

—Franny & Zooey. (FRE.). pap. 15.50 (*2-02-013327-X*) Editions du Seuil FRA. *Dist:* Distribooks, Inc.

—Franny & Zooey. 2001. (Illus.). 208p. pap. 13.95 (*0-316-76902-9*, Back Bay); 1961. 201p. 24.95 (*0-316-76954-1*); 1991. 208p. reprint ed. mass mkt. 5.99 (*0-316-76949-5*) Little Brown & Co.

Scott, Sophfronia. All I Need to Get By. 2004. 320p. pap. 13.95 (*0-312-31856-1*, Saint Martin's Griffin) St. Martin's Pr.

Shands, Linda. A Time to Search. 1995. (Seasons Remembered Ser.: Vol. 3). 180p. (Orig.). pap. 9.99 o.p. (*0-8308-1933-9*, 1933) InterVarsity Pr.

Shapiro, Dani. Family History. 288p. 2004. pap. 13.00 (*1-4000-3211-3*); 2003. 23.00 (*0-375-41547-5*) Knopf, Alfred A. Inc.

—Family History. l.t. ed. 2003. 460p. 25.00 (*0-375-43279-5*) Random Hse. Large Print.

Shreve, Susan Richards. Plum & Jaggers. l.t. ed. 2000. (Wheeler Hardcover Ser.). 297p. 25.95 (*1-56895-137-X*, Wheeler Publishing, Inc.) Gale Group.

—Plum & Jaggers. 2001. 240p. pap. 13.00 o.p. (*0-312-42025-0*) Picador.

—Plum & Jaggers: A Novel. 2000. 228p. 21.00 o.p. (*0-374-23462-0*) Farrar, Straus & Giroux.

Smith, Charlie. Shine Hawk. 1988. 368p. 17.95 o.s.i (*0-945167-01-6*) British American Publishing, Ltd.

—Shine Hawk. 1990. 384p. reprint ed. pap. (*0-671-68498-1*, Washington Square Pr.) Simon & Schuster.

—Shine Hawk: A Novel by Charlie Smith. 1998. 384p. pap. 16.95 (*0-8203-1997-X*) Univ. of Georgia Pr.

Snelling, Lauraine. Daughter of Twin Oaks. 2000. (Secret Refuge Ser.: Vol. 1). 288p. pap. 11.99 (*1-55661-839-5*) Bethany Hse. Pubs.

—Daughter of Twin Oaks. 2001. 350p. 24.95 o.p. (*0-7862-3684-1*, Five Star) Gale Group.

Stead, C. K. Sister Hollywood. 1994. pap. 13.00 (*0-00-271218-0*) HarperCollins Pubs.

—Sister Hollywood. 1989. 220p. o.p. (*0-00-223479-3*) HarperSanFrancisco.

—Sister Hollywood. 1991. 2.99 o.p. (*0-517-07830-9*) Random Hse. Value Publishing.

—Sister Hollywood. 1990. 15.95 o.p. (*0-312-04423-2*) St. Martin's Pr.

—Sister Hollywood. l.t. ed. 1991. (Ulverscroft Large Print Ser.). 29.99 o.p. (*0-7089-2507-3*, Ulverscroft) Thorpe, F. A. Pubs. GBR. *Dist:* Ulverscroft Large Print Bks., Ltd., Ulverscroft Large Print Canada, Ltd.

Stout, Janis. Home Truth. 1993. 3.49 o.p. (*0-517-10834-8*) Random Hse. Value Publishing.

—Home Truth. 1992. 256p. 19.95 o.p. (*0-939149-66-4*) Soho Pr., Inc.

Summers, Judith. Dear Sister. 1985. 256p. 14.95 o.p. (*0-312-18544-8*) St. Martin's Pr.

Thayer, Nancy. An Act of Love. l.t. ed. 1998. 26.95 (*1-56895-540-5*, Wheeler Publishing, Inc.) Gale Group.

—An Act of Love. 1999. (Act of Love Ser.: Vol. 1). 308p. pap. 6.99 (*0-312-96535-4*, St. Martin's Paperbacks); 1997. 256p. 22.95 o.p. (*0-312-15471-2*) St. Martin's Pr.

Thon, Melanie Rae. Sweet Hearts. 2001. (Illus.). 256p. tchr. ed. 23.00 (*0-395-78589-8*, Mariner Bks.) Houghton Mifflin Co. Trade & Reference Div.

Urquhart, Jane. The Stone Carvers. 2003. 400p. pap. 14.00 (*0-14-200358-1*) Penguin Group (USA) Inc.

—The Stone Carvers. 2002. 400p. 25.95 (*0-670-03044-9*, Viking) Viking Penguin.

Valentine, Jane. Sevenoaks. 2001. pap. 17.95 (*0-595-18094-9*) iUniverse, Inc.

Vandermeer, Jeff. Veniss Underground. 2003. 188p. pap. 15.00 (*1-894815-64-5*) Prime.

Vesaas, Tarjei. Birds. Stoverud, Torbjorn & Barnes, Michael, trs. 1996. 28.00 (*0-7206-0701-9*) Owen, Peter Ltd. GBR. *Dist:* Dufour Editions, Inc.

—The Birds. Barnes, Michael & Stoverud, Torbjorn, trs. from NOR. 2002. (Peter Owen Modern Classics Ser.). 234p. pap. 18.95 (*0-7206-1143-1*) Owen, Peter Ltd. GBR. *Dist:* Dufour Editions, Inc.

—The Birds. Stoverud, Torbjorn & Barnes, Michael, trs. from NOR. 1995. 224p. pap. 24.00 (*0-7206-0952-6*) Owen, Peter Ltd. GBR. *Dist:* Dufour Editions, Inc.

Ware, Linda J. God, Why Is She the Way She Is? 1979. (J). (gr. 3-6). pap. 1.00 o.p. (*0-570-03621-6*, 39-1063) Concordia Publishing Hse.

Whitney, P. This Is Graceanne's Book. 1999. 304p. 22.95 (*0-312-20597-X*) St. Martin's Pr.

Willett, Marcia. Holding On. 1999. (Illus.). 308p. text (*0-7472-2184-7*) Headline Bk. Publishing, Ltd. GBR. *Dist:* Trafalgar Square.

Yamanaka, Lois-Ann. Blu's Hanging. 1997. 288p. 22.00 o.s.i (*0-374-11499-4*) Farrar, Straus & Giroux.

—Blu's Hanging. 1998. 272p. pap. 12.95 (*0-380-73139-8*, Perennial) HarperTrade.

Zafris, Nancy. The Metal Shredders. 2002. 320p. 24.95 o.s.i (*0-399-14922-8*, BlueHen Bks.) Putnam Publishing Group, The.

Zimmerman, R. D. Red Trance. 1995. 320p. mass mkt. 4.99 o.s.i (*0-440-21763-6*) Dell Publishing.

—Red Trance. 1994. 237p. 20.00 o.p. (*0-688-13030-5*, Morrow, William & Co.) Morrow/Avon.

## D

### DATING (SOCIAL CUSTOMS)—FICTION

Blackston, Ray. Flabbergasted: A Novel. 2003. 336p. 22.99 (*0-8007-1837-2*); 333p. 22.99 (*0-8007-6569-9*) Revell, Fleming H. Co.

Broussard, Meredith. The Dictionary of Failed Relationships: 26 Tales of Love Gone Wrong. 2003. 320p. pap. 11.00 (*0-609-81009-X*, Three Rivers Pr.) Crown Publishing Group.

Bushnell, Candace. 4 Blondes. 2001. 256p. pap. 12.00 (*0-8021-3825-X*, Grove Pr.); 2000. 245p. 24.00 (*0-87113-819-0*, Atlantic Monthly Pr.) Grove/Atlantic, Inc.

—4 Blondes. 2002. 384p. mass mkt. 7.99 (*0-451-20389-5*, Signet Bks.) NAL.

—4 Blondes. l.t. ed. 2001. 445p. 31.95 (*0-7862-3151-3*) Thorndike Pr.

Cach, Lisa. Dating Without Novocaine. 2002. 288p. pap. (*0-373-25014-2*, Red Dress Ink) Harlequin Enterprises, Ltd.

Chamberlin, Holly. Living Single. 2004. 352p. mass mkt. 6.99 (*0-7582-0144-3*, Kensington Bks.) Kensington Publishing Corp.

Dearie, John. Love & Other Recreational Sports: A Novel. 2003. 240p. text 23.95 (*0-670-03219-0*, Viking) Viking Penguin.

Green, Jane. Straight Talking. 2003. 320p. pap. 11.95 (*0-7679-1559-3*) Broadway Bks.

Hayden, Paul. Last Wave. 2003. 208p. pap. 11.95 (*0-7434-6472-9*, MTV) Simon & Schuster.

Jackson, Edwardo. Neva Hafta: A Novel. 368p. 2003. pap. 13.95 (*0-375-75774-0*); 2002. 22.95 (*0-375-50637-3*, Villard Bks.) Random House Adult Trade Publishing Group.

Kizis, Deanna. How to Meet Cute Boys: A Novel. 2003. (Illus.). 272p. 21.95 (*0-446-53072-7*) Warner Bks., Inc.

Markoe, Merrill. It's My F—ing Birthday: A Novel. 2002. 224p. pap. 11.95 (*0-8129-6724-0*); 21.95 (*0-375-50712-4*) Random House Adult Trade Publishing Group. (Villard Bks.).

Maxted, Anna. Behaving Like Adults. 2003. 400p. 24.95 (*0-06-009667-5*, ReganBooks) HarperTrade.

Mlynowski, Sarah. Milkrun. 2003. 352p. mass mkt. (*0-373-25035-5*); 2001. 288p. pap. (*0-373-25012-6*) Harlequin Enterprises, Ltd. (Red Dress Ink).

O'Connell, Jennifer. Bachelorette #1. 2003. 256p. pap. 12.95 (*0-451-21098-0*) NAL.

Owens, Michael T. Pick-Up Lines: A Novel. Cadet, Guichard, ed. 2003. (YA). (gr. 11 up). pap. 15.00 (*0-9718191-5-7*, 212-591-6465) La Caille Nous Publishing Co.

Robinson, Chet Kelly. No More Mr. Nice Guy: A Love Story. 2002. 288p. pap. 13.95 (*0-375-76047-4*, Villard Bks.) Random House Adult Trade Publishing Group.

Senate, Melissa. See Jane Date. 2003. 352p. mass mkt. (*0-373-25027-4*); 2001. 283p. pap. (*0-373-25011-8*, 1-25011-7) Harlequin Enterprises, Ltd. (Red Dress Ink).

Steel, Danielle. Dating Game: A Novel. 2004. 464p. mass mkt. 7.99 (*0-440-24075-1*); 2003. 384p. 200.00 (*0-385-33691-8*, Delacorte Pr.); 2003. 384p. 26.95 (*0-385-33631-4*, Delacorte Pr.) Dell Publishing.

—Dating Game: A Novel. l.t. ed. 2004. 576p. pap. 14.95 (*0-375-43312-0*) Random Hse. Large Print.

## F

### FATHERS AND DAUGHTERS—FICTION

Abu-Jaber, Diana. Arabian Jazz: A Novel. 2003. 384p. pap. 14.95 (*0-393-32422-2*) Norton, W. W. & Co., Inc.

Adler, C. S. Daddy's Climbing Tree. 1993. 144p. (J). (gr. 4-6). tchr. ed. 15.00 (*0-395-63032-0*, Clarion Bks.) Houghton Mifflin Co. Trade & Reference Div.

Agell, Charlotte. I Wear Long Green Hair in Summer. 1994. (Illus.). 32p. (J). (ps-4). 7.95 (*0-88448-113-1*) Tilbury Hse. Pubs.

Aks, Patricia. A Friend for Keeps. 1989. 144p. mass mkt. 2.95 o.s.i (*0-449-70296-0*, Fawcett) Ballantine Bks.

—Lisa's Choice. 1985. 160p. (Orig.). mass mkt. 2.25 o.s.i (*0-449-70097-6*, Fawcett) Ballantine Bks.

Alcock, Vivien. The Sylvia Game. 1997. 224p. (YA). (gr. 7-7). pap. 4.95 o.s.i (*0-395-81650-5*) Houghton Mifflin Co.

Allen, Suzanne. Almost Starring Dad. 1990. (Scrambled Eggs Ser.: No. 2). (J). (gr. 4-7). mass mkt. 2.75 o.p. (*0-425-12218-2*) Berkley Publishing Group.

Allyn, Doug. Icewater Mansions. 1995. 247p. 21.00 o.p. (*0-312-11829-5*, Saint Martin's Minotaur) St. Martin's Pr.

Anderson, Joan. Sally's Submarine. 1995. (Illus.). 32p. (J). (gr. k up). 15.00 o.p. (*0-688-12690-1*); lib. bdg. 14.93 o.p. (*0-688-12691-X*) Morrow/Avon. (Morrow, William & Co.).

Anderson, Launi K. Janey's Own. 1997. (Latter-Day Daughters Ser.). (J). pap. o.p. (*1-57345-319-6*, Cinnamon Tree) Deseret Bk. Co.

Andrews, V. C. Heaven. unabr. ed. 1990. (Casteel Ser.). audio 80.00 (*0-7366-1736-1*, 2576) Books on Tape, Inc.

—Heaven. l.t. ed. 1986. (General Ser.). 588p. 19.95 o.p. (*0-8161-4078-2*); 10.95 o.p. (*0-8161-4079-0*) Gale Group. (Macmillan Reference USA).

—Heaven. unabr. ed. 1995. audio 84.95 (*1-85695-865-5*, 940904) ISIS Audio Bks. GBR. *Dist:* Ulverscroft Large Print Bks., Ltd.

—Heaven. 1997. 464p. mass mkt. 3.99 (*0-671-01005-0*, Pocket) Simon & Schuster.

—Heaven. Marrow, Linda, ed. 1990. (Casteel Ser.). 448p. mass mkt. 7.99 (*0-671-72944-6*, Pocket) Simon & Schuster.

—Heaven. 1985. 16.45 o.s.i (*0-671-60536-4*, Simon & Schuster) Simon & Schuster.

—Heaven. 1985. 14.04 (*0-606-00660-5*) Turtleback Bks.

Angell, Judie. Yours Truly: A Novel. 1993. 192p. (YA). (gr. 7 up). mass mkt. 15.95 o.p. (*0-531-05472-1*); mass mkt. 15.99 o.p. (*0-531-08622-4*) Scholastic, Inc. (Orchard Bks.).

Arditti, Michael. Pagan's Father. 2000. 416p. pap. 14.00 (*1-56947-183-5*); 1996. 436p. 24.00 o.p. (*1-56947-062-6*) Soho Pr., Inc.

Attoe, David. Lion at the Door: A Novel. 1989. 240p. 17.95 (*0-316-05800-9*) Little Brown & Co.

Atwood, Margaret. Surfacing. 1987. 240p. mass mkt. 5.99 o.s.i (*0-449-21375-7*, Fawcett) Ballantine Bks.

—Surfacing. 1995. 208p. pap. 10.95 o.s.i (*0-553-37780-9*) Bantam Bks.

—Surfacing. 1998. 208p. pap. 12.95 (*0-385-49105-0*) Doubleday Publishing.

—Surfacing. 1997. 200p. mass mkt. 6.95 (*0-7710-9899-5*) McClelland & Stewart/Tundra Bks.

—Surfacing. 1983. 224p. pap. 3.50 o.p. (*0-446-31107-3*) Warner Bks., Inc.

Ayres, Katherine. Family Tree. 1996. 144p. (J). (gr. 3-7). 15.95 o.s.i (*0-385-32227-5*, Delacorte Pr.) Dell Publishing.

—Family Tree. 1997. (Yearling Ser.). 176p. (gr. 3-7). pap. text 4.50 (*0-440-41193-9*, Dell Books for Young Readers) Random Hse. Children's Bks.

Babb, Sanora. The Lost Traveler. 1995. 314p. pap. 10.95 (*0-8263-1568-2*) Univ. of New Mexico Pr.

—The Lost Traveler. 1995. E-Book 10.95 (*0-585-24077-9*) netLibrary, Inc.

Bail, Murray. Eucalyptus: A Novel. 1998. 272p. 23.00 o.p. (*0-374-14857-0*) Farrar, Straus & Giroux.

—Eucalyptus: A Novel. 1999. (Harvest Book Ser.). 264p. pap. 13.00 (*0-15-600781-9*, Harvest Bks.) Harcourt Trade Pubs.

Ballard, Robin. Gracie. 1993. (Illus.). 24p. (J). (ps up). 14.00 o.p. (*0-688-11806-2*); lib. bdg. 13.93 o.p. (*0-688-11807-0*) HarperCollins Children's Bk. Group. (Greenwillow Bks.).

Balzac, Honoré de. Le Pere Goriot. Raffel, Burton, tr. 1994. (Critical Editions Ser.). (FRE.). 29.95 o.p. (*0-393-03620-0*) Norton, W. W. & Co., Inc.

Barker, Jane Valentine. Mari: A Novel. 1997. (Women's West Ser.: No. 2). 200p. 19.95 (*0-87081-452-4*) Univ. Pr. of Colorado.

—Mari: A Novel. 1997. E-Book 19.95 (*0-585-02195-3*) netLibrary, Inc.

Barrientos, Tanya Maria. Family Resemblance. 2003. 272p. pap. 12.95 (*0-451-20872-2*) NAL.

Barrows, Allison. The Artist's Model. 1996. (Illus.). 32p. (J). (ps-3). lib. bdg. 15.95 o.s.i (*0-87614-948-4*, Carolrhoda Bks.) Lerner Publishing Group.

Bates, Betty. Call Me Friday the Thirteenth. 1983. (Illus.). 112p. (J). (gr. 3-6). 9.95 o.p. (*0-8234-0498-6*) Holiday Hse., Inc.

—Call Me Friday the Thirteenth. 1985. (Illus.). 112p. (J). (gr. 3-7). pap. 2.50 o.s.i (*0-440-40984-5*, Laurel Leaf) Random Hse. Children's Bks.

Battle-Lavert, Gwendolyn. Off to School. 1995. (Illus.). 32p. (J). (ps-3). 15.95 (*0-8234-1185-0*) Holiday Hse., Inc.

Bausch, Richard. Mr. Field's Daughter. 1989. 18.95 o.p. (*0-671-64051-8*, Simon & Schuster) Simon & Schuster.

Begley, Louis. About Schmidt. 1997. (Ballantine Reader's Circle Ser.). 304p. pap. 13.95 (*0-449-91116-0*, Fawcett) Ballantine Bks.

—About Schmidt, 5 cass. 2002. audio 29.99 (*0-7887-9027-7*, 00494); 1997. audio 51.00 (*0-7887-0876-7*, 95011E7) Recorded Bks., LLC.

Belden, Wilanne Schneider. Mind-Find. 1988. 191p. (YA). (gr. 7 up). 14.95 (*0-15-254270-1*) Harcourt Trade Pubs.

Benjamin, Carol Lea. The Wicked Stepdog. 1982. (Illus.). 128p. (J). (gr. 3-7). lib. bdg. 11.89 o.p. (*0-690-04171-3*) HarperCollins Children's Bk. Group.

—The Wicked Stepdog. 1986. 128p. (YA). (gr. 5 up). mass mkt. 2.50 (*0-380-70089-1*, Avon Bks.) Morrow/Avon.

Bennett, Cherie. The Fall of the the Perfect Girl. 1993. (Surviving Sixteen Ser.: No. 2). 224p. (J). (gr. 7 up). pap. 3.50 o.p. (*0-14-036319-X*, Puffin Bks.) Penguin Putnam Bks. for Young Readers.

—On the Edge. 1994. (Wild Hearts Ser.). 208p. (J). (gr. 3-6). pap. 3.50 (*0-671-88781-5*, Simon Pulse) Simon & Schuster Children's Publishing.

—Sunset Embrace. 1993. 224p. mass mkt. 3.99 o.s.i (*0-425-13840-2*) Berkley Publishing Group.

—Sunset Stranger: It's a Strange World. 1994. 224p. (Orig.). (YA). mass mkt. 3.99 o.s.i (*0-425-14129-2*) Berkley Publishing Group.

Berg, Elizabeth. Durable Goods. l.t. ed. 2000. 248p. lib. bdg. 25.95 (*1-58547-049-X*) Ctr. Point Large Print.

—Durable Goods. 1997. pap. 6.99 (*0-380-72884-2*); 1999. 208p. reprint ed. pap. 13.00 o.s.i (*0-380-72308-5*) Morrow/Avon. (Avon Bks.).

Bergland, Martha. Idle Curiosity. 1997. 225p. 22.95 (*1-55597-257-8*) Graywolf Pr.

Berkeley, Sara. Shadowing Hannah. 2000. 288p. pap. 15.95 (*1-902602-04-8*) New Island Bks. IRL. *Dist:* Dufour Editions, Inc.

Berman, Sharon L. With a Face Like Mine. 1981. 160p. 8.95 o.p. (*0-87777-062-X*, Dutton) Dutton/Plume.

Best, Cari. Getting Used to Harry. 1996. (Illus.). 32p. (J). (ps-3). pap. 15.95 o.p. (*0-531-09494-4*); lib. bdg. 16.99 (*0-531-08794-8*) Scholastic, Inc. (Orchard Bks.).

—Taxi! Taxi! 1994. (Illus.). (J). 14.95 o.p. (*0-316-09259-2*) Little Brown & Co.

—Taxi! Taxi! 1997. (Illus.). 32p. (J). (ps-3). mass mkt. 6.95 o.p. (*0-531-07084-0*, Orchard Bks.) Scholastic, Inc.

Blair, L. E. Problem Dad. 1993. (Girl Talk Ser.: No. 22). (Illus.). 128p. (J). (ps-3). pap. 2.95 o.s.i (*0-307-22022-2*, 22022, Golden Bks.) Random Hse. Children's Bks.

Blanchard, Alice. Darkness Peering. 2000. 336p. mass mkt. 6.99 (*0-553-58129-5*) Bantam Bks.

—Darkness Peering. l.t. ed. 2000. 26.95 o.p. (*1-56895-829-3*, Wheeler Publishing, Inc.) Gale Group.

Bly, Stephen A. The Senator's Other Daughter. 2001. (Belles of Lordsburg Ser.: Vol. 1). 236p. pap. 10.99 (*1-58134-236-5*) Crossway Bks.

—The Senator's Other Daughter. l.t. ed. 2002. 420p. (Belles of Lordsburg Ser.: No. 1). pap. 16.95 (*1-4104-0035-2*, Walker Large Print); 26.95 (*0-7862-4026-1*) Gale Group.

Bograd, Larry. Los Alamos Light, RS. 1983. 168p. (YA). (gr. 7 up). 12.95 o.p. (*0-374-34656-9*, Farrar, Straus & Giroux (BYR)) Farrar, Straus & Giroux.

Bond, Nancy. Truth to Tell. 1994. 336p. (YA). (gr. 7 up). 17.95 (*0-689-50601-5*, McElderry, Margaret K.) Simon & Schuster Children's Publishing.

Bosworth, Sheila. Slow Poison. 1993. mass mkt. 4.99 o.s.i (*0-8041-1124-3*, Ivy Bks.) Ballantine Bks.

—Slow Poison. 1998. (Voices of the South Ser.). 336p. pap. 17.95 (*0-8071-2278-5*) Louisiana State Univ. Pr.

Box, C. J. Open Season. 2002. 304p. reprint ed. mass mkt. 6.50 (*0-425-18546-X*, Prime Crime) Berkley Publishing Group.

—Open Season. 2002. lib. bdg. 28.95 (*1-58547-248-4*, Premier) Ctr. Point Large Print.

—Open Season. 2001. 304p. 23.95 (*0-399-14748-9*) Penguin Group (USA) Inc.

Boyt, Susie. The Characters of Love. 1997. 192p. 19.95 o.p. (*0-297-81766-3*) Weidenfeld & Nicolson, Ltd. GBR. *Dist:* Trafalgar Square.

Braddon, M. E. Eleanor's Victory. 1996. (Pocket Classics Ser.). 416p. pap. 12.95 (*0-7509-1118-2*) Sutton Publishing, Ltd. GBR. *Dist:* International Publishers Marketing.

Brand, Max. Dan Barry's Daughter. 1976. reprint ed. lib. bdg. 25.95 (*0-88411-516-X*) Amereon, Ltd.

Breznik, Melitta. Night Duty. Theobold, Roslyn, tr. from GER. 1999. 131p. pap. 12.00 o.p. (*1-883642-85-X*) Steerforth Pr.

Brillhart, Julie. When Daddy Came to School. 1995. (Illus.). 24p. (J). (ps-3). lib. bdg. 13.95 (*0-8075-8878-4*) Whitman, Albert & Co.

Brockmeier, Kevin. The Truth about Celia: A Novel. 2003. 240p. 22.00 (*0-375-42135-1*, Pantheon) Knopf Publishing Group.

Brooks, Bruce. Midnight Hour Encores. (Trophy Keypoint Bks.). (gr. 7 up). 1988. (Illus.). 272p. (J). pap. 6.99 (*0-06-447021-0*, Harper Trophy); 1986. 288p. (YA). lib. bdg. 14.89 o.p. (*0-06-020710-8*) HarperCollins Children's Bk. Group.

Brown, John G. Decorations in a Ruined Cemetery. 1994. 19.95 o.p. (*0-395-67025-X*) Houghton Mifflin Co.

—Decorations in a Ruined Cemetery. 1995. 256p. pap. 12.00 o.p. (*0-380-72447-2*, Avon Bks.) Morrow/Avon.

Brown, John Gregory. Decorations in a Ruined Cemetery. 2001. 256p. reprint ed. pap. 13.00 (*0-618-15452-3*, Mariner Bks.) Houghton Mifflin Co. Trade & Reference Div.

Bryant, Bonnie. Horse Wise. 1990. (Saddle Club Ser.: No. 11). 144p. (J). (gr. 4-6). pap. 3.99 o.p. (*0-553-15805-8*) Bantam Bks.

—Horse Wise. 1990. (Saddle Club Ser.: No. 11). (J). (gr. 4-6). 9.09 o.p. (*0-606-03650-4*) Turtleback Bks.

Bryant, Sally S. Here's Juggins. 1996. (Illus.). 176p. (J). (gr. 4-7). 19.95 (*0-945980-62-0*) North Country Pr.

Buckley, Helen E. Someday with My Father. 1985. (Illus.). 32p. (J). (ps-3). lib. bdg. 12.89 o.p. (*0-06-020878-3*) HarperCollins Children's Bk. Group.

Budhos, Marina. The Professor of Light. 1999. 254p. 23.95 o.p. (*0-399-14473-0*, G. P. Putnam's Sons) Penguin Group (USA) Inc.

—The Professor of Light. 2000. 19.50 (*81-86939-08-3*) RST Indiaink Publishing IND. *Dist:* South Asia Bks.

Bunting, Eve. In the Haunted House. (Illus.). 32p. (J). (ps-ps). 1994. pap. 5.95 (*0-395-69942-8*); 1990. tchr. ed. 14.95 o.p. (*0-395-51589-0*) Houghton Mifflin Co. Trade & Reference Div. (Clarion Bks.).

—In the Haunted House. 1990. 12.10 (*0-606-07701-4*) Turtleback Bks.

—A Perfect Father's Day. 1993. (Illus.). 32p. (J). (ps-3). pap. 5.95 (*0-395-66416-0*, Clarion Bks.) Houghton Mifflin Co. Trade & Reference Div.

—A Perfect Father's Day. Giblin, James C., ed. 1991. (Illus.). 32p. (J). (ps-3). 13.95 o.p. (*0-395-52590-X*, Clarion Bks.) Houghton Mifflin Co. Trade & Reference Div.

Burgess, Anthony. The Pianoplayers. 1986. 256p. 16.95 o.p. (*0-87795-832-7*, Morrow, William & Co.) Morrow/Avon.

—The Pianoplayers. 1987. pap. 4.95 (*0-671-63792-4*, Washington Square Pr.) Simon & Schuster.

Burnham, Sophy. Buccaneer. 1977. (Illus.). (J). (gr. 5-8). 7.95 o.p. (*0-7232-6147-4*, Warne, Frederick) Penguin Putnam Bks. for Young Readers.

Burns, Eric. The Autograph: A Modern Fable of a Father & Daughter. 1997. (Illus.). 69p. 19.00 (*1-57392-167-X*) Prometheus Bks., Pubs.

Burstein, Fred. Anna's Rain. 1990. (Illus.). 32p. (J). (ps-1). 14.95 o.p. (*0-531-05827-1*); mass mkt. 14.99 o.p. (*0-531-08427-2*) Scholastic, Inc. (Orchard Bks.).

Busser, Marianne & Schroder, Ron. On the Road with Poppa Whopper. (Illus.). 64p. (J). 1997. (gr. 1-4). pap. 5.95 (*1-55858-776-4*); 1945. (gr. 2-4). 13.95 o.p. (*1-55858-373-4*); 1945. (gr. 2-4). 14.50 o.p. (*1-55858-374-2*) North-South Bks., Inc.

Butler, Charles. The Darkling. 1998. 176p. (YA). (gr. 7-12). 16.00 (*0-689-81796-7*, 870383, McElderry, Margaret K.) Simon & Schuster Children's Publishing.

Byatt, A. S. The Shadow of the Sun. 1993. (Harvest Book Ser.). 324p. pap. 14.00 (*0-15-681416-1*, Harvest Bks.) Harcourt Trade Pubs.

Byrd, Elizabeth. I'll Get By. 1981. 204p. (J). (gr. 7). 9.95 o.p. (*0-670-39134-4*) Viking Penguin.

Caines, Jeannette F. Daddy. 1977. (Illus.). 32p. (J). (gr. k-3). lib. bdg. 12.89 o.p. (*0-06-020924-0*) HarperCollins Children's Bk. Group.

Caisley, Raewyn. Hannah & Her Dad. 1994. (Voyages Ser.). (Illus.). (J). 4.25 (*0-383-03787-5*) SRA/McGraw-Hill.

Caldwell, Bo. The Distant Land of My Father. 2002. (Harvest Book Ser.). (Illus.). 400p. pap. 14.00 (*0-15-602713-5*, Harvest Bks.) Harcourt Trade Pubs.

—The Distant Land of My Father: A Novel of Shanghai. 2001. (Illus.). 384p. 23.95 (*0-8118-3240-6*) Chronicle Bks. LLC.

—The Distant Land of My Father: A Novel of Shanghai. l.t. ed. 2003. (Charnwood Large Print Ser.). 496p. 32.50 (*0-7089-9446-6*) Thorpe, F. A. Pubs. GBR. *Dist:* Ulverscroft Large Print Bks., Ltd., Ulverscroft Large Print Canada, Ltd.

Calvert, Patricia. Glennis, Before & After. 1996. 160p. (J). (gr. 4-7). 16.00 (*0-689-80641-8*, Atheneum) Simon & Schuster Children's Publishing.

Cameron, Carey. Daddy Boy. 1989. 377p. 15.95 o.p. (*0-912697-84-9*) Algonquin Bks. of Chapel Hill.

Campbell, Louisa & Taylor, Bridget S. Phoebe's Fabulous Father. 1996. (Illus.). 32p. (J). (ps-3). 14.00 (*0-15-200996-5*) Harcourt Trade Pubs.

Campbell, Ramsey. Nazareth Hill. 1997. 384p. 23.95 o.p. (*0-312-86344-6*, Forge Bks.) Doherty, Tom Assocs., LLC.

Cannell, Stephen J. Runaway Heart. abr. ed. 2003. (Illus.). audio 25.95 (*1-55927-902-8*); audio 25.95 (*1-55927-902-8*); audio compact disk 32.00 (*1-55927-903-6*) Audio Renaissance.

—Runaway Heart. l.t. ed. 2003. 517p. 28.95 (*1-58724-515-9*, Wheeler Publishing, Inc.) Gale Group.

—Runaway Heart. Date not set. mass mkt. (*0-312-99718-3*, St. Martin's Paperbacks); E-Book 18.95 (*0-312-71056-9*); 2003. (Illus.). 400p. 24.95 (*0-312-30426-9*) St. Martin's Pr.

Cannon, Bettie. A Bellsong for Sarah Raines. 1987. 192p. (YA). (gr. 7 up). text 14.95 o.s.i (*0-684-18839-2*, Atheneum) Simon & Schuster Children's Publishing.

Carlstrom, Nancy White. Goodbye Geese. 1991. (Illus.). 32p. (J). (ps-3). 14.95 o.p. (*0-399-21832-7*, Philomel) Penguin Putnam Bks. for Young Readers.

Carpenter, William. A Keeper of Sheep. 340p. 1994. 21.95 (*1-57131-000-2*); 1996. reprint ed. pap. 13.95 (*1-57131-007-X*) Milkweed Editions.

Carr, Jan & Martin, Ann M. The Baby-Sitters Club: The Movie Keepsake. 1995. (Baby-Sitters Club Ser.). 48p. (J). (gr. 2-5). pap. 12.95 (*0-590-60405-8*) Scholastic, Inc.

Carris, Joan D. The Revolt of Ten-X. 1980. (J). (gr. 4-6). 7.95 o.p. (*0-15-266462-9*) Harcourt Children's Bks.

Carter, Alden R. Dancing on Dark Water. 1994. 144p. (YA). (gr. 7-9). pap. 3.25 (*0-590-45600-8*) Scholastic, Inc.

—Dancing on Dark Water. 1990. (Point Ser.). (J). 8.35 o.p. (*0-606-05799-4*) Turtleback Bks.

—Robodad. 1990. 144p. (YA). 14.95 o.s.i (*0-399-22191-3*, G. P. Putnam's Sons) Penguin Putnam Bks. for Young Readers.

Catalanotto, Peter. The Painter. 1996. (Illus.). 32p. (J). (ps-3). pap. 15.95 (*0-531-09465-0*); lib. bdg. 16.99 (*0-531-08765-4*) Scholastic, Inc. (Orchard Bks.).

Caudle, Neil. Voices from Home. 1992. mass mkt. 4.99 o.s.i (*0-345-36870-3*) Ballantine Bks.

—Voices from Home. 1989. 304p. 19.95 o.s.i (*0-399-13421-2*, G. P. Putnam's Sons) Penguin Putnam Bks. for Young Readers.

Cazet, Denys. Born in the Gravy. (Illus.). 32p. (J). (ps-1). 1997. mass mkt. 5.95 (*0-531-07096-4*); 1993. mass mkt. 15.99 o.p. (*0-531-08638-0*); 1993. pap. 15.95 (*0-531-05488-8*) Scholastic, Inc. (Orchard Bks.).

Cebulash, Mel. Carly & Co, No. 1. 1989. 144p. mass mkt. 2.95 o.s.i (*0-449-14555-7*, Fawcett) Ballantine Bks.

Chaikin, Linda L. Desert Rose. 2003. (Illus.). 350p. pap. 10.99 (*0-7369-1234-7*) Harvest Hse. Pubs.

Chambers, John W. Marisol y Magdelena, Bk. 1. 1998. (J). 15.00 (*0-689-81024-5*, Simon & Schuster Children's Publishing) Simon & Schuster Children's Publishing.

Chaplan, Roberta. Tell Me a Story, Paint Me the Sun: When a Girl Feels Ignored by Her Father. 1991. (Illus.). 48p. (J). (gr. 3-6). pap. 8.95 o.p. (*0-945354-24-X*) American Psychological Assn.

Charbonnet, Gabrielle. Molly's Heart. 1995. (Princess Ser.: No. 1). 128p. (J). (gr. 3-7). mass mkt. 3.50 (*0-590-22287-2*) Scholastic, Inc.

Chardiet, Bernice. I Help Daddy. 1994. (Lift-the-Flap Bks.). (Illus.). 16p. (J). (ps-1). pap. 4.99 o.s.i (*0-14-054999-4*) Penguin Putnam Bks. for Young Readers.

Christiansen, C. B. A Small Pleasure. 1988. 144p. (YA). (gr. 7 up). 13.95 (*0-689-31369-1*, Atheneum) Simon & Schuster Children's Publishing.

Clark, Jack. Westerfield's Chain: A Mystery. 2002. 304p. 24.95 (*0-312-28960-X*, Saint Martin's Minotaur) St. Martin's Pr.

Clayton, Meg Waite. The Language of Light. Date not set. pap. (*0-312-31803-0*, St. Martin's Paperbacks); Date not set. mass mkt. (*0-312-99126-6*, St. Martin's Paperbacks); 2003. 352p. 24.95 (*0-312-31801-4*) St. Martin's Pr.

Cleary, Beverly. Ramona y Su Padre. 1996. (SPA.). 160p. (J). (gr. 4-7). 8.95 o.p. (*84-239-2770-9*) Lectorum Pubns., Inc.

Coetzee, J. M. Disgrace. 2000. 224p. pap. 13.00 (*0-14-029640-9*) Penguin Group (USA) Inc.

—Disgrace. 1999. 224p. 23.95 o.s.i (*0-670-88731-5*, Viking) Viking Penguin.

—Disgrace. 2000. 608p. pap. (*0-09-928952-0*) Vintage UK GBR. *Dist:* Random Hse., Inc.

Cohen, Leah Hager. Heart, You Bully, You Punk: A Novel. 2003. 224p. 23.95 (*0-670-03167-4*, Viking) Viking Penguin.

Cohlene, Terri. Ribbons for Mikele. 2003. (Illus.). 32p. (J). lib. bdg. 16.89 (*0-688-13094-1*, Morrow, William & Co.) Morrow/Avon.

—Won't Papa Be Surprised! 2003. (Illus.). 32p. (J). 15.99 (*0-688-13093-3*, Morrow, William & Co.) Morrow/Avon.

Collins, Brandilyn. Capture the Wind for Me. 2003. (Bradleyville Ser.). 352p. pap. 12.99 (*0-310-24243-6*) Zon Bks.

Collins, Wilkie. The Legacy of Cain. 1993. (Pocket Classics Ser.). pap. 10.95 o.s.i (*0-7509-0453-4*) Sutton Publishing.

Colman, Hila. Weekend Sisters. 1988. (J). (gr. 6 up). mass mkt. 2.95 o.s.i (*0-449-70206-5*, Fawcett) Ballantine Bks.

—What's the Matter with the Dobsons? 1982. (J). (gr. 5-7). pap. (*0-671-43143-9*, Simon Pulse) Simon & Schuster Children's Publishing.

Compton, Ralph. Death Rides a Chestnut Mare. 1999. (Signet Historical Fiction Ser.). 320p. mass mkt. 5.99 (*0-451-19761-5*, Signet Bks.) NAL.

—Death Rides a Chestnut Mare. l.t. ed. 2002. (Western Ser.). 437p. 25.95 (*0-7862-4182-9*) Thorndike Pr.

Conkie, Heather. Sara's Homecoming. 1993. (Road to Avonlea Ser.: No. 12). 128p. (J). (gr. 4-7). pap. 3.99 o.s.i (*0-553-48038-3*) Bantam Bks.

Conroy, Pat. Beach Music. 1996. (Illus.). 816p. reprint ed. mass mkt. 7.99 (*0-553-57457-4*) Bantam Bks.

—Beach Music. 1995. 640p. 32.50 (*0-385-41304-1*, Talese, Nan A.); 628p. 200.00 o.s.i (*0-385-47590-X*) Doubleday Publishing.

—Beach Music. 628p. pap. 8.98 o.p. (*0-7651-0633-7*) Smithmark Pubs., Inc.

—Beach Music. 1996. 14.04 (*0-606-11096-8*) Turtleback Bks.

Cookson, Catherine. The Parson's Daughter. l.t. ed. 1988. 594p. 21.95 o.p. (*0-8161-4389-7*, Macmillan Reference USA) Gale Group.

—The Parson's Daughter. 1987. 19.45 o.p. (*0-671-63293-0*) Summit Bks.

—The Upstart. 1999. per. (*1-55166-527-1*, Mira Bks.) Harlequin Enterprises, Ltd.

—The Upstart. 1998. 352p. 23.00 (*0-684-84315-3*, Simon & Schuster) Simon & Schuster.

—The Upstart. l.t. ed. 1998. (Basic Ser.). 539p. 29.95 (*0-7862-1401-5*) Thorndike Pr.

—The Upstart. 1997. 480p. mass mkt. 10.95 (*0-552-14037-6*) Transworld Publishers Ltd. GBR. *Dist:* Trafalgar Square.

Coombs, Karen Mueller. Samantha Gill, Belly Dancer. 1989. 128p. (J). pap. 2.75 (*0-380-75737-0*, Avon Bks.) Morrow/Avon.

Cooney, Linda A. Freshman Rivals. 1991. (Freshman Dorm Ser.: No. 12). 224p. (YA). mass mkt. 3.50 o.p. (*0-06-106122-0*, HarperTorch) Morrow/Avon.

Cooper, J. California. In Search of Satisfaction. 1994. 21.95 o.s.i (*0-385-46785-0*); 1995. 368p. reprint ed. pap. 13.00 (*0-385-46786-9*) Doubleday Publishing.

Cornelius, Patricia. My Sister Jill: A Novel. 2003. 224p. 23.95 (*0-312-31228-8*) St. Martin's Pr.

Covington, Dennis. Lasso the Moon. 1996. 208p. (YA). (gr. 7 up). mass mkt. 4.50 o.s.i (*0-440-22013-0*, Laurel Leaf); (J). 20.95 (*0-385-30991-0*, Dell Books for Young Readers) Random Hse. Children's Bks.

—Lasso the Moon. 1996. 9.60 o.p. (*0-606-09526-8*) Turtleback Bks.

Coyle, Neva. Close to a Father's Heart. 1996. (Summerwind Ser.: Vol. 3). 256p. pap. 8.99 o.p. (*1-55661-548-5*) Bethany Hse. Pubs.

—Close to a Father's Heart. l.t. ed. 2001. 300p. 23.95 (*0-7862-2936-5*, Five Star) Gale Group.

—Inside the Private Hedge. 1996. (Summerwind Ser.: Vol. 2). 256p. (Orig.). pap. 8.99 o.p. (*1-55661-547-7*) Bethany Hse. Pubs.

Craig, Peter. Sweetheart Cons. 2004. 23.95 (*1-4013-0044-8*) Hyperion Pr.

Crompton, Anne E. The Rainbow Pony. 1995. 128p. (J). (gr. 4-7). pap. 3.99 (*0-671-51121-1*, Aladdin) Simon & Schuster Children's Publishing.

—The Wildflower Pony. 1996. 128p. (J). (gr. 3-6). per. 3.99 (*0-671-51120-3*, Aladdin) Simon & Schuster Children's Publishing.

Cross, Gillian. Born of the Sun. 1984. (Illus.). 240p. (YA). (gr. 7-12). tchr. ed. 11.95 o.p. (*0-8234-0528-1*) Holiday Hse., Inc.

—Born of the Sun. 1987. (J). (gr. k-12). mass mkt. 2.95 o.s.i (*0-440-90710-1*, Laurel Leaf) Random Hse. Children's Bks.

Cummings, Pat. Carousel. 1994. (Illus.). 32p. (J). (ps-3). 14.95 (*0-02-725512-3*, Simon & Schuster Children's Publishing) Simon & Schuster Children's Publishing.

D'Anard, Elizabeth. Cinderella Summer. 1992. (Changes Romance Ser.: No. 5). 240p. (YA). (gr. 7 up). mass mkt. 3.50 o.p. (*0-06-106776-8*, HarperTorch) Morrow/Avon.

Darcy, Emma. Bride of His Choice. 2000. (Harlequin Presents Ser.: No. 2080). per. (*0-373-12080-X*, 1-12080-7, Harlequin Bks.) Harlequin Enterprises, Ltd.

—Bride of His Choice. l.t. ed. 2000. (Harlequin I Romance Ser.). 288p. 22.95 (*0-263-16484-5*) Thorndike Pr.

Daugharty, Janice. Necessary Lies. 1995. 176p. 20.00 o.p. (*0-06-017177-4*) HarperCollins Pubs.

Day, Dianne. Beacon Street Mourning: A Fremont Jones Mystery. 2001. 304p. mass mkt. 5.99 (*0-553-58061-2*) Bantam Bks.

de Paola, Tomie. The Days of the Blackbird: A Tale of Northern Italy. 1997. (Illus.). 32p. (J). (ps-3). 16.99 (*0-399-22929-9*, G. P. Putnam's Sons) Penguin Group (USA) Inc.

De Pressense, Domitille. Natalie: The Spanking. 1990. (Illus.). 28p. (J). (ps-1). pap. 0.30 o.p. (*0-8120-4506-8*) Barron's Educational Series, Inc.

Delton, Judy. Walk on a Snowy Night. 1982. (Illus.). 32p. (J). (gr. k-3). lib. bdg. 12.89 o.p. (*0-06-021593-3*) HarperCollins Children's Bk. Group.

Deutermann, P. T. Darkside: A Novel. 2002. (Illus.). 352p. 24.95 (*0-312-28120-X*) St. Martin's Pr.

—Hunting Season. 2001. 402p. 24.95 (*0-312-26979-X*) St. Martin's Pr.

DiFonte, Ugo. The Foodtaster. Elbling, Peter, tr. from ITA. 2002. 284p. 28.00 (*1-57962-047-7*) Permanent Pr., The.

Dodd, Christina. Scandalous Again. l.t. ed. 2003. 369p. 30.95 (*1-58724-482-9*, Wheeler Publishing, Inc.) Gale Group.

—Scandalous Again. 2003. 384p. mass mkt. 6.99 (*0-06-009265-3*, Avon Bks.) Morrow/Avon.

Doucet, Sharon Arms. Back Before Dark. 2004. 272p. pap. 12.95 (*0-451-21104-9*) NAL.

Douglas, Eileen. Rachel & the Upside down Heart. 1990. (Illus.). 32p. (J). 6.95 o.p. (*0-8431-2734-1*, Price Stern Sloan) Penguin Putnam Bks. for Young Readers.

Douglass, Barbara. Sizzle Wheels. 1981. (Illus.). 174p. (J). (gr. 3-6). 9.95 o.p. (*0-664-32680-3*) Westminster John Knox Pr.

Dubosarsky, Ursula. High Hopes. 1991. 120p. (YA). (gr. 5-9). 12.95 o.p. (*0-670-83560-9*, Viking Children's Bks.) Penguin Putnam Bks. for Young Readers.

Dunne, John Gregory. Dutch Shea, Jr. 1982. 16.50 o.p. (*0-671-41292-2*, Simon & Schuster) Simon & Schuster.

Dupasquier, Philippe. Dear Daddy... 1985. (Illus.). 32p. (J). (ps-2). lib. bdg. 12.95 o.p. (*0-02-733170-9*, Simon & Schuster Children's Publishing) Simon & Schuster Children's Publishing.

Dwyer, Kelly. Self-Portrait with Ghosts. 2000. 272p. mass mkt. 6.99 o.s.i (*0-425-17696-7*) Berkley Publishing Group.

—Self-Portrait with Ghosts. 1999. 320p. 23.95 o.p. (*0-399-14440-4*, G. P. Putnam's Sons) Penguin Group (USA) Inc.

Earls, Nick. Perfect Skin. 2001. 368p. 24.95 (*0-312-28056-4*) St. Martin's Pr.

—Perfect Skin. 2000. 353p. (*0-670-89104-5*) Viking.

—Perfect Skin: A Novel. 2002. 368p. pap. 13.95 (*0-312-30303-3*, Saint Martin's Griffin) St. Martin's Pr.

Eicher, Terry & Geller, Jesse D., eds. Fathers & Daughters: Portraits in Fiction. 1990. 352p. 16.95 o.p. (*0-453-00727-9*) NAL.

Eidson, Tom. The Last Ride. 1995. 352p. mass mkt. 6.99 o.s.i (*0-515-11741-2*, Jove) Berkley Publishing Group.

—The Last Ride. l.t. ed. 1995. (Large Print Bks.). 23.95 (*1-56895-241-4*, Wheeler Publishing, Inc.) Gale Group.

—The Last Ride. 1995. 21.95 o.p. (*0-399-14057-3*, G. P. Putnam's Sons) Penguin Group (USA) Inc.

Eisenberg, Nora. Just the Way You Want Me: A Novel. 2003. 220p. pap. 14.95 (*0-9679520-8-5*) Leapfrog Pr.

Ekberg, Susan. The Trust Walk. 1995. (Illus.). 32p. (J). (gr. k-5). 17.95 (*0-9630419-6-7*) Spiritseeker Publishing, Inc.

Elbling, Peter. The Food Taster: A Novel. 2003. 272p. reprint ed. pap. 13.00 (*0-452-28434-1*, Plume) Dutton/Plume.

Eliot, George. Silas Marner. Acclaim Comics Staff, ed. 1997. (Classics Illustrated Study Guides). (Illus.). mass mkt. 4.99 (*1-57840-050-3*) Acclaim Bks.

—Silas Marner. 1994. pap. text 39.50 (*0-582-23662-2*) Addison-Wesley Longman, Ltd. GBR. *Dist:* Trans-Atlantic Pubns., Inc.

—Silas Marner. unabr. ed. 1963. (Classics Ser.). mass mkt. 2.50 o.p. (*0-8049-0014-0*, CL-14) Airmont Publishing Co., Inc.

—Silas Marner. 20.95 (*0-88411-275-6*) Amereon, Ltd.

—Silas Marner. l.t. ed. 1992. pap. 19.95 o.p. (*0-7927-1093-2*, CSO295); 1991. 21.95 o.p. (*0-7927-1092-4*, CH0223) BBC Audiobooks America.

—Silas Marner. 1981. 192p. pap. 1.95 o.s.i (*0-553-21048-3*); mass mkt. 3.95 (*0-553-21229-X*) Bantam Bks. (Bantam Classics).

—Silas Marner. Seely, Elizabeth & Seely, John, eds. 1999. (Classic Novels Ser.). 256p. pap. 8.95 (*0-7641-1150-7*) Barron's Educational Series, Inc.

—Silas Marner. 1987. 188p. reprint ed. lib. bdg. 21.95 (*0-89966-621-3*) Buccaneer Bks., Inc.

—Silas Marner. 1997. (Cambridge Literature Ser.). audio compact disk 18.95 o.p. (*0-521-59805-2*) Cambridge Univ. Pr.

—Silas Marner. Bousted, Mary, ed. 1995. (Literature Ser.). (Illus.). 256p. pap. text 9.95 (*0-521-48572-X*) Cambridge Univ. Pr.

—Silas Marner. (Early Best Sellers Ser.). reprint ed. lib. bdg. 48.00 (*0-7426-1022-5*); 2001. (Illus.). pap. text 28.00 (*0-7426-6022-2*) Classic Bks.

—Silas Marner. unabr. ed. 1996. (Thrift Editions Ser.). 160p. reprint ed. pap. 1.50 (*0-486-29246-0*) Dover Pubns., Inc.

—Silas Marner. 1972. 2.95 o.p. (*0-460-01121-9*); 1958. 10.50 o.p. (*0-460-00121-3*) Dutton/Plume. (Dutton).

—Silas Marner. E-Book 2.49 (*0-7574-3509-2*) Electric Umbrella Publishing.

—Silas Marner. 1980. (FRE.). pap. 11.95 (*0-7859-2434-5*, 2070371913) French & European Pubns., Inc.

—Silas Marner. l.t. ed. 2002. (Perennial Bestseller Ser.). 304p. 28.95 (*0-7838-9756-1*) Gale Group.

—Silas Marner. Clay, N. L., ed. 1986. (Guide Novel Ser.). pap. text 3.95 o.p. (*0-435-16280-2*) Heinemann.

—Silas Marner. 2000. (HRW Library). 220p. 17.90 (*0-03-056459-X*) Holt, Rinehart & Winston.

—Silas Marner. l.t. ed. 190p. pap. 19.76 (*0-7583-2312-3*); 693p. pap. 52.27 (*0-7583-2317-4*); 242p. pap. 22.70 (*0-7583-2313-1*); 852p. pap. 67.81 (*0-7583-2318-2*); 1006p. pap. 77.39 (*0-7583-2319-0*); 334p. pap. 28.44 (*0-7583-2314-X*); 433p. pap. 35.33 (*0-7583-2315-8*); 561p. pap. 43.59 (*0-7583-2316-6*); 242p. lib. bdg. 28.70 (*0-7583-2305-0*); 334p. lib. bdg. 34.44 (*0-7583-2306-9*); 852p. lib. bdg. 81.01 (*0-7583-2310-7*); 190p. lib. bdg. 25.76 (*0-7583-2304-2*); 1006p. lib. bdg. 89.39 (*0-7583-2311-5*); 693p. lib. bdg. 58.27 (*0-7583-2309-3*); 433p. lib. bdg. 41.33 (*0-7583-2307-7*); 561p. lib. bdg. 49.59 (*0-7583-2308-5*) Huge Print Pr.

—Silas Marner. l.t. unabr. ed. 1992. (Isis Large Print Bks.). 196p. 29.99 (*1-85089-538-4*, 895384) ISIS Large Print Bks. GBR. *Dist:* Ulverscroft Large Print Bks., Ltd., Ulverscroft Large Print Canada, Ltd.

—Silas Marner. 1993. (Everyman's Library). 240p. 17.00 (*0-679-42030-4*) Knopf, Alfred A. Inc.

—Silas Marner. E-Book 1.95 (*1-57799-883-9*) Logos Research Systems, Inc.

—Silas Marner. 2nd rev. ed. 1996. pap. text 5.90 o.s.i (*0-582-27531-8*); Level 3. 2000. pap. 7.66 (*0-582-41640-X*) Longman Publishing Group.

—Silas Marner. (Signet Classics). 1999. 208p. mass mkt. 3.95 (*0-451-52721-6*, Signet Classics); 1997. pap. 2.95 (*0-89375-996-1*); 1960. mass mkt. 0.50 o.p. (*0-451-50021-0*, Signet Classics); 1960. mass mkt. 0.75 o.p. (*0-451-50733-9*, Signet Classics); 1960. mass mkt. 0.95 o.p. (*0-451-50999-4*, Signet Classics); 1960. mass mkt. 1.25 o.p. (*0-451-51238-3*, Signet Classics); 1960. mass mkt. 1.95 o.p. (*0-451-51591-9*, Signet Classics); 1960. mass mkt. 1.75 o.p. (*0-451-51678-8*, Signet Classics); 1960. mass mkt. 1.95 o.p. (*0-451-51945-0*, Signet Classics); 1960. 192p. mass mkt. 1.95 o.p. (*0-451-52108-0*, Signet Classics); 1960. 192p. mass mkt. 3.95 o.s.i (*0-451-52427-6*, Signet Classics); 1960. mass mkt. 1.75 o.p. (*0-451-51418-1*, Signet Classics); 1960. mass mkt. 0.60 o.p. (*0-451-50644-8*, Signet Classics) NAL.

—Silas Marner. Seely, Elizabeth, ed. 1995. (Thornes Classic Novels Ser.). (Illus.). 247p. pap. 15.95 (*0-7487-1831-1*) Nelson Thornes GBR. *Dist:* Trans-Atlantic Pubns., Inc.

—Silas Marner. l.t. ed. 1998. (Large Print Ser.). reprint ed. 347p. lib. bdg. 26.00 (*0-939495-66-X*); 207p. lib. bdg. 25.00 (*1-58287-085-3*) North Bks.

—Silas Marner. Cave, Terence, ed. & intro. by. (Oxford World's Classics Ser.). 1998. 232p. pap. 6.95 (*0-19-283458-4*); 1996. 250p. pap. 4.95 o.p. (*0-19-283210-7*) Oxford Univ. Pr., Inc.

—Silas Marner. 1995. (Illus.). 94p. pap. text 5.95 (*0-19-586311-9*) Oxford Univ. Pr., Inc.

—Silas Marner. Hedge, Tricia, ed. 1995. (Illus.). 80p. pap. text 5.95 o.p. (*0-19-422708-1*) Oxford Univ. Pr., Inc.

—Silas Marner. 1986. (World's Best Reading Ser.). (Illus.). 208p. 12.95 o.p. (0-89577-248-5) Reader's Digest Assn., Inc., The.

—Silas Marner. 2001. 189p. E-Book 4.00 (1-929670-73-7) Renaissance E Bks.

—Silas Marner. E-Book 5.00 (0-7410-0430-5) SoftBook Pr.

—Silas Marner. 1986. (Bantam Classics Ser.). 10.00 (0-606-02467-0) Turtleback Bks.

—Silas Marner. Smith, Anne, ed. 1993. 256p. pap. 4.95 (0-460-87263-X, Everyman's Classic Library in Paperback) Tuttle Publishing.

—Silas Marner. 1998. 7.95 (81-85944-82-2) UBS Pubs. Distributions, Ltd. IND. *Dist:* South Asia Bks.

—Silas Marner. 2003. 240p. pap. 7.00 (0-14-143975-0, Penguin Classics) Viking Penguin.

—Silas Marner. Carroll, David, ed. 1997. (Penguin Classics Ser.). 240p. 6.95 (0-14-043480-1, Penguin Classics) Viking Penguin.

—Silas Marner. Leavis, Q. D., ed. 1968. (English Library). 272p. pap. 6.95 o.p. (0-14-043030-X, Penguin Classics) Viking Penguin.

—Silas Marner. 1999. E-Book 5.99 (0-8220-7190-8, Cliff Notes) Wiley, John & Sons, Inc.

—Silas Marner. 1998. (Classics Library). 176p. pap. 3.95 (1-85326-221-8, 2218WW) Wordsworth Editions, Ltd. GBR. *Dist:* Casemate Pubs. & Bk. Distributors, LLC.

—Silas Marner: The Weaver of Raveloe. 2001. (Modern Library Classics). 240p. pap. 6.95 (0-375-75749-X, Modern Library) Random House Adult Trade Publishing Group.

—Silas Marner, Brother Jacob. 400p. reprint ed. 2001. pap. text 28.00 (0-7426-5074-X); 1999. (Writings of George Eliot Ser.: Vol. 7). lib. bdg. 88.00 (1-58201-074-9) Classic Bks.

—Silas Marner, Brother Jacob, & The Lifted Veil. Mudford, Peter, ed. rev. ed. 1996. (Everyman Paperback Classics Ser.). 348p. (C). pap. 6.95 (0-460-87568-X, Everyman's Classic Library in Paperback) Tuttle Publishing.

Elkins, Aaron. Turncoat: A Novel of Suspense. 2002. 304p. 24.95 (0-06-019770-6, Morrow, William & Co.) Morrow/Avon.

Ernaux, Annie. A Man's Place. 1993. 112p. pap. 15.00 o.s.i (0-345-37895-4) Ballantine Bks.

—A Man's Place. 1992. 99p. 15.95 o.p. (0-941423-75-1) Four Walls Eight Windows.

—A Man's Place. Leslie, Tanya, tr. 1992. 99p. 15.95 (1-888363-19-3) Seven Stories Pr.

Ewing, Barbara. The Trespass: A Novel. 2003. 416p. 24.95 (0-312-31420-5) St. Martin's Pr.

Farris, John. Sacrifice. 1995. 379p. pap. text 5.99 (0-8125-0956-0); 1994. 320p. 15.50 o.p. (0-312-85067-0) Doherty, Tom Assocs., LLC. (Tor Bks.).

Feibleman, Peter S. The Daughters of Necessity. 1999. (Voices of the South Ser.). 318p. pap. 15.95 (0-8071-2388-9) Louisiana State Univ. Pr.

Felder, Deborah G. Changing Times. 1998. (Treasured Horses Ser.: Vol. 5). (Illus.). (J). (gr. 3-7). mass mkt. 4.50 (0-590-31657-5) Scholastic, Inc.

Fell, Doris Elaine. Before Winter Comes. 1994. (Seasons of Intrigue Ser.: Vol. 2). 320p. pap. 9.99 o.p. (0-89107-815-0) Crossway Bks.

Ferber, Elizabeth. Soon Found, Soon Lost. 1994. 18.95 (1-882611-02-0); pap. 11.95 (1-882611-03-9) Yardbird Bks.

Ferris, Jean. Relative Strangers, RS. 1993. 240p. (YA). 16.00 o.p. (0-374-36243-2, Farrar, Straus & Giroux (BYR)) Farrar, Straus & Giroux.

Feuer, Elizabeth. Lost Summer, RS. 1995. 192p. (J). (gr. 7 up). 16.00 o.p. (0-374-31020-3, Farrar, Straus & Giroux (BYR)) Farrar, Straus & Giroux.

—Lost Summer. 1997. (J). (gr. 3-7). pap. 3.99 o.p. (0-380-72732-3, Avon Bks.) Morrow/Avon.

—Paper Doll, RS. (Aerial Fiction Ser.). 192p. 1994. (J). (gr. 7 up). pap. 3.95 o.p. (0-374-45724-7, Aerial); 1990. 13.95 o.p. (0-374-35736-6, Farrar, Straus & Giroux (BYR)) Farrar, Straus & Giroux.

Fforde, Jasper. The Eyre Affair. l.t. ed. 2002. 576p. 28.95 (0-7862-4293-0) Gale Group.

—The Eyre Affair. 2003. 384p. pap. 14.00 (0-14-200180-5) Penguin Group (USA) Inc.

—The Eyre Affair. 2002. 272p. 23.95 (0-670-03064-3, Viking) Viking Penguin.

Fine, Anne. Summer House Loon. 1979. (J). (gr. 6 up). o.p. (0-690-03933-6) HarperCollins Children's Bk. Group.

Finger, Anne. Bone Truth. 1994. 192p. (Orig.). pap. 11.95 (1-56689-028-4) Coffee Hse. Pr.

Flagg, Fannie. Coming Attractions. l.t. ed. 1983. 14.95 o.p. (0-8161-3294-1, Macmillan Reference USA) Gale Group.

—Daisy Fay & the Miracle Man, Set. abr. ed. 1992. (Illus.). pap. 16.00 o.s.i incl. audio (0-679-41025-2, RH Audio) Random Hse. Audio Publishing Group.

—Daisy Fay & the Miracle Man. l.t. ed. 1993. pap. 18.00 o.s.i (0-679-74947-0) Random Hse. Large Print.

—Daisy Fay & the Miracle Man. 1992. 320p. reprint ed. pap. 13.95 (0-446-39452-1) Warner Bks., Inc.

Flanagan, Richard. The Sound of One Hand Clapping. 432p. 2001. pap. 12.00 (0-8021-3784-9); 2000. 24.00 o.p. (0-87113-802-6, Atlantic Monthly Pr.) Grove/Atlantic, Inc.

—The Sound of One Hand Clapping. 1997. 422p. (0-7329-0896-5) Macmillan Education Australia.

Fleischman, Paul. Rear-View Mirror. 1986. (Charlotte Zolotow Bk.). 128p. (YA). (gr. 7 up). 12.95 o.s.i (0-06-021866-5); lib. bdg. 12.89 o.p. (0-06-021867-3) HarperCollins Children's Bk. Group.

Franklin, Yelena. A Bowl of Sour Cherries. 1998. (New American Voices Ser.: Vol. 2). 242p. pap. text 14.00 (1-877727-81-4) White Pine Pr.

French, Marilyn. Our Father. 1996. mass mkt. 6.99 (0-345-91020-6, Fawcett); 1995. 448p. mass mkt. 6.99 o.s.i (0-345-38490-3) Ballantine Bks.

—Our Father: A Novel. 1994. 450p. 22.95 o.p. (0-316-29390-3) Little Brown & Co.

Freymann-Weyr, Garret. When I Was Older. 2002. 176p. (J). pap. 5.99 (0-14-230093-4, Puffin Bks.) Penguin Putnam Bks. for Young Readers.

Friedman, Bruce J. A Father's Kisses. 1996. 258p. 22.95 o.p. (1-55611-499-0) Fine, Donald I. Bks.

Furgerson, Celesta. Sculptured in Twilight. 1999. 202p. pap. 12.00 (0-9679875-0-4) River Bend Pr., Inc.

Fusilli, Jim. Closing Time. 2002. 320p. reprint ed. mass mkt. 6.50 (0-425-18712-8) Berkley Publishing Group.

—Closing Time. 2001. 320p. 23.95 o.s.i (0-399-14793-4) Penguin Group (USA) Inc.

Gabaldon, Diana, et al. Fathers & Daughters. 2000. 320p. mass mkt. 5.99 o.s.i (0-451-20016-0, Signet Bks.) NAL.

—Fathers & Daughters. Morgan, Jill, ed. 1999. (Illus.). 240p. 14.95 o.s.i (0-451-19695-3, Signet Bks.) NAL.

Gaddis, William. Agape Agape. 2003. 128p. pap. 13.00 (0-14-243763-8, Penguin Classics) Viking Penguin.

Gaddis, William, frwd. Agape, Agape. 2002. 128p. 23.95 o.s.i (0-670-03131-3, Viking) Viking Penguin.

Galbraith, Kathryn O. Holding Onto Sunday. 1995. (Illus.). 48p. (J). (gr. 1-4). mass mkt. 14.00 o.s.i (0-689-50623-6, McElderry, Margaret K.) Simon & Schuster Children's Publishing.

Garcia, Eric. Matchstick Men: A Novel of Petty Crimes. 2002. 240p. 22.95 (0-375-50522-9, Villard Bks.) Random House Adult Trade Publishing Group.

Gardner, Lisa. The Next Accident. l.t. ed. 2001. 560p. 30.95 (0-7862-3494-6); 30.95 (0-7862-3495-4) Thorndike Pr.

Garlock, Dorothy. High on a Hill. l.t. ed. 2002. lib. bdg. 29.95 (1-58547-221-2, Platinum) Ctr. Point Large Print.

—High on a Hill. 2002. 400p. 21.95 o.p. (0-446-52946-X); 416p. reprint ed. mass mkt. 6.99 (0-446-61209-X) Warner Bks., Inc.

Garrison, Paul. The Ripple Effect: A Novel of Suspense. 2004. pap. (0-06-008170-8, Morrow, William & Co.) Morrow/Avon.

Gemmell, Nikki. Alice Springs. 2000. 272p. pap. 12.95 o.s.i (0-14-028642-X, Penguin Bks.) Penguin Group (USA) Inc.

—Alice Springs. 1999. 256p. 23.95 o.p. (0-670-88347-6) Viking Penguin.

Geringer, Laura. Silverpoint. 1991. (Charlotte Zolotow Bk.). 160p. (YA). (gr. 5 up). 13.95 o.p. (0-06-023849-6); (Illus.). lib. bdg. 13.89 (0-06-023850-X) HarperCollins Children's Bk. Group.

Gilchrist, Ellen. Net of Jewels. 1993. 360p. pap. 12.95 o.p. (0-316-31432-3); 1992. 21.95 o.p. (0-316-31424-2) Little Brown & Co.

Gill, William. Fortune's Child: A Novel. 1993. 400p. 22.00 o.p. (0-06-016954-0) HarperTrade.

Girard, Linda W. At Daddy's on Saturdays. Levine, Abby, ed. 1987. (Albert Whitman Concept Bks.). (Illus.). 32p. (J). (ps-3). pap. 6.95 (0-8075-0473-4); lib. bdg. 14.95 o.p. (0-8075-0475-0) Whitman, Albert & Co.

Gleitzman, Morris. Blabber Mouth. 1995. 144p. (J). (gr. 3 up). 11.00 (0-15-200369-X) Harcourt Children's Bks.

—Blabber Mouth. 1995. 160p. (J). (gr. 3 up). pap. 5.00 o.s.i (0-15-200370-3) Harcourt Trade Pubs.

—Sticky Beak. 1995. 144p. (J). (gr. 3 up). pap. 5.00 (0-15-200367-3, Harcourt Paperbacks) Harcourt Children's Bks.

Godden, Rumer. The Peacock Spring. 1976. 286p. (YA). 10.95 o.p. (0-670-54558-9) Viking Penguin.

Godfrey, Martyn N. The Great Science Fair Disaster. 1992. (J). mass mkt. 2.95 o.p. (0-590-44081-0, Scholastic Paperbacks) Scholastic, Inc.

Godwin, Gail. Father Melancholy's Daughter. 1997. 416p. reprint ed. pap. 13.95 (0-380-72986-5, Perennial) HarperTrade.

—Father Melancholy's Daughter. 1992. pap. 5.99 (0-380-70314-9, Avon Bks.); 1991. 512p. 21.95 o.p. (0-688-06531-7, Morrow, William & Co.) Morrow/Avon.

Gold, Herbert. Daughter Mine. E-Book 23.95 (0-312-27576-5) St. Martin's Pr.

Goldstein, Rebecca. Late Summer Passion of a Woman of Mind. 1989. 256p. 18.95 o.s.i (0-374-18406-2) Farrar, Straus & Giroux.

—Late Summer Passion of a Woman of Mind. 1990. pap. 8.95 o.s.i (0-679-72823-6, Vintage) Knopf Publishing Group.

Goodman, Joan Elizabeth. Songs from Home. 1994. 224p. (YA). (gr. 5 up). pap. 4.95 (0-15-203591-5); (Illus.). 10.95 o.s.i (0-15-203590-7) Harcourt Trade Pubs.

—Songs from Home. 1994. 10.10 o.p. (0-606-09875-5) Turtleback Bks.

Goodwin, Stephen. Breaking Her Fall. 416p. 2004. pap. (0-15-602969-3, Harvest Bks.); 2003. 24.00 (0-15-100806-X) Harcourt Trade Pubs.

Gordimer, Nadine. Burger's Daughter. 2015. 10.95 o.p. (0-670-19475-1); 1980. 368p. 13.95 (0-14-005593-2) Viking Penguin.

Gordon, Neil. The Gun Runner's Daughter. 2000. 416p. reprint ed. mass mkt. 6.99 o.s.i (0-553-58211-9) Bantam Bks.

Goudge, Eileen. Blessing in Disguise. 1994. 576p. 22.95 o.s.i (0-670-84961-8, Viking) Viking Penguin.

Grambling, Lois G. Daddy Will Be There. 1998. (Illus.). 24p. (J). (ps-3). 15.99 (0-688-14983-9, Greenwillow Bks.) HarperCollins Children's Bk. Group.

Green, Tim. The Fifth Angel. 384p. 2004. mass mkt. 6.99 (0-446-61377-0, Warner Vision); 2003. 24.95 (0-446-53085-9) Warner Bks., Inc.

—The First 48. 2004. 336p. 24.95 (0-446-53144-8) Warner Bks., Inc.

Greenberg, Melanie H. My Father's Luncheonette. 1991. (Illus.). 2p. (J). (ps-2). 12.95 o.p. (0-525-44725-3, Dutton Children's Bks.) Penguin Putnam Bks. for Young Readers.

Greene, Constance C. Nora: Maybe a Ghost Story. 1993. (Illus.). 208p. (J). (gr. 4-7). 10.95 (0-15-277696-6); 48p. (YA). (gr. 5-9). pap. 4.95 o.s.i (0-15-276895-5) Harcourt Children's Bks. (Gulliver Bks.).

Greenwood, Pamela D. I Found Mouse. 1994. (Illus.). 48p. (J). (ps). tchr. ed. 14.95 o.p. (0-395-65478-5) Houghton Mifflin Co.

Greer, Bonnie. Hanging by Her Teeth. 1995. (Ninety's Title Ser.). 176p. (Orig.). pap. (1-85242-185-1) Serpent's Tail Ltd.

Grenville, Kate. Albion's Story. 384p. 1994. 21.95 (0-15-100122-7); 1996. reprint ed. pap. 13.00 (0-15-600241-8, Harvest Bks.) Harcourt Trade Pubs.

Griffin, Peni R. Vikki Vanishes. 1995. 160p. (J). (gr. 7 up). pap. 15.00 (0-689-80028-2, McElderry, Margaret K.) Simon & Schuster Children's Publishing.

Griffiths, John. The Presidential Archives. 1996. 384p. 23.00 (0-7867-0316-4, Carroll & Graf Pubs.) Avalon Publishing Group.

Guccione, Leslie D. Nobody Listens to Me. 1991. 176p. (J). (gr. 3-7). mass mkt. 2.95 o.p. (0-590-43106-4, Scholastic Paperbacks) Scholastic, Inc.

Haddix, Margaret Peterson. Don't You Dare Read This, Mrs. Dunphrey. 1996. 112p. (YA). (gr. 7 up). 16.99 (0-689-80097-5, Simon & Schuster Children's Publishing) Simon & Schuster Children's Publishing.

Hahn, Mary Downing. Following the Mystery Man. 1988. 192p. (J). (gr. 4-8). 13.95 o.p. (0-89919-680-2, Clarion Bks.) Houghton Mifflin Co. Trade & Reference Div.

—Following the Mystery Man. 1989. 192p. (J). (gr. 4-7). reprint ed. pap. 4.99 (0-380-70677-6, Avon Bks.) Morrow/Avon.

—Following the Mystery Man. 1988. (J). 11.04 (0-606-04225-3) Turtleback Bks.

Haig, Kathryn. Apple Blossom Time. 1998. 464p. 26.95 o.p. (0-312-18313-5) St. Martin's Pr.

—Apple Blossom Time. 2000. 458p. pap. 9.95 (0-552-14537-8) Transworld Publishers Ltd. GBR. *Dist:* Trafalgar Square.

Hall, Brian. The Saskiad. 1997. 380p. tchr. ed. 23.95 o.p. (0-395-82754-X) Houghton Mifflin Co.

Hall, Lynn. Denison's Daughter. 1983. 128p. (YA). (gr. 7 up). 10.95 o.s.i (0-684-17955-5, Macmillan Reference USA) Gale Group.

—Flyaway. 1987. 128p. (YA). (gr. 7 up). 12.95 o.s.i (0-684-18888-0, Atheneum) Simon & Schuster Children's Publishing.

Hamilton, Gail. Nothing Endures but Change. 1993. (Road to Avonlea Ser.: No. 11). 128p. (J). (gr. 4-7). pap. 3.99 o.p. (0-553-48037-5) Bantam Bks.

Hamilton, Morse. Effie's House. 1990. 224p. (J). (gr. 7 up). 13.95 o.p. (0-688-09307-8, Greenwillow Bks.) HarperCollins Children's Bk. Group.

Hamilton, Ruth. Nest of Sorrows. 2000. (J). pap. 10.95 (0-552-13755-3) Transworld Publishers Ltd. GBR. *Dist:* Trafalgar Square.

Hamilton, Virginia. Plain City. (J). 2003. 208p. (gr. 4-7). mass mkt. 5.99 (0-590-47365-4, Scholastic Paperbacks); 1993. 176p. (gr. 3-7). pap. 13.95 (0-590-47364-6) Scholastic, Inc.

Hammer, Charles. Me, the Beef & the Bum, RS. 1984. 181p. (YA). (gr. 5 up). 15.00 o.p. (0-374-34903-7, Farrar, Straus & Giroux (BYR)) Farrar, Straus & Giroux.

Hansen, Jennie L. Beyond Summer Dreams. 2001. 282p. 14.95 (1-57734-889-3) Covenant Communications.

Harbottle, Philip. Dynamite's Daughter. l.t. ed. 2001. (Dales Large Print Ser.). 224p. pap. 21.99 (1-84262-128-9) Dales Large Print Bks. GBR. *Dist:* Ulverscroft Large Print Bks., Ltd., Ulverscroft Large Print Canada, Ltd.

Hardy, Thomas. The Life & Death of the Mayor of Casterbridge: A Story of a Man of Character. 1962. 12.00 (0-606-01055-6) Turtleback Bks.

—The Mayor of Casterbridge. 8.97 (0-673-58355-4); 1991. pap. text (0-17-556573-2) Addison-Wesley Longman, Inc.

—The Mayor of Casterbridge. 1994. pap. text 34.60 (0-582-22586-8) Addison-Wesley Longman, Ltd. GBR. *Dist:* Trans-Atlantic Pubns., Inc.

—The Mayor of Casterbridge. 1965. (Airmont Classics Ser.). mass mkt. 1.95 o.p. (0-8049-0063-9, CL-63) Airmont Publishing Co., Inc.

—The Mayor of Casterbridge. reprint ed. lib. bdg. 25.95 (0-88411-560-7) Amereon, Ltd.

—The Mayor of Casterbridge. 1981. (Bantam Classics Ser.). 336p. mass mkt. 5.99 (0-553-21024-6, Bantam Classics) Bantam Bks.

—The Mayor of Casterbridge. Page, Norman, ed. 1997. (Literary Texts Ser.). 411p. (C). pap. (1-55111-122-5) Broadview Pr.

—The Mayor of Casterbridge. 1990. 326p. reprint ed. lib. bdg. 24.95 (0-89966-719-8) Buccaneer Bks., Inc.

—The Mayor of Casterbridge, 2. reprint ed. lib. bdg. 196.00 (0-7426-2792-6) Classic Bks.

—The Mayor of Casterbridge. E-Book 2.49 (1-58627-417-1) Electric Umbrella Publishing.

—The Mayor of Casterbridge, 001. Heilman, Robert B., ed. 1962. (gr. 9 up). pap. 16.36 (0-395-05158-4, Riverside Editions) Houghton Mifflin Co.

—The Mayor of Casterbridge. l.t. ed. 335p. pap. 27.96 (0-7583-1488-4); 423p. pap. 32.94 (0-7583-1489-2); 583p. pap. 40.73 (0-7583-1490-6); 969p. pap. 69.29 (0-7583-1492-2); 1469p. pap. 92.92 (0-7583-1494-9); 750p. pap. 50.07 (0-7583-1491-4); 1734p. pap. 112.29 (0-7583-1495-7); 1196p. pap. 81.06 (0-7583-1493-0); 1196p. lib. bdg. 93.06 (0-7583-1485-X); 969p. lib. bdg. 81.29 (0-7583-1484-1); 583p. lib. bdg. 46.73 (0-7583-1482-5); 423p. lib. bdg. 38.94 (0-7583-1481-7); 335p. lib. bdg. 33.96 (0-7583-1480-9); 1469p. lib. bdg. 104.92 (0-7583-1486-8); 1734p. lib. bdg. 130.29 (0-7583-1487-6); 750p. lib. bdg. 56.07 (0-7583-1483-3) Huge Print Pr.

—The Mayor of Casterbridge. 2002. 336p. 96.99 (1-4043-1836-4); per. 91.99 (1-4043-1837-2) IndyPublish.com.

—The Mayor of Casterbridge. 1993. (Everyman's Library). 17.00 (0-679-42035-5) Knopf, Alfred A. Inc.

—The Mayor of Casterbridge. l.t. ed. 2000. (LRS Large Print Heritage Ser.). 579p. (YA). (gr. 6-12). lib. bdg. 35.95 (1-58118-075-6, 23667) LRS.

—The Mayor of Casterbridge. Adams, Richard, ed. 1988. (Study Texts Ser.). pap. text 4.29 (0-582-33171-4, 72064) Longman Publishing Group.

—The Mayor of Casterbridge. (Classics Ser.). 1999. (Illus.). 384p. mass mkt. 5.95 (0-451-52735-6, Signet Classics); 1962. 336p. mass mkt. 5.95 o.s.i (0-451-52519-1, Signet Classics); 1962. mass mkt. 2.25 o.p. (0-451-52305-9, Signet Classics); 1962. mass mkt. 1.95 o.p. (0-451-51230-8) NAL.

—The Mayor of Casterbridge. l.t. ed. reprint ed. 1997. 468p. lib. bdg. 26.00 (0-939495-14-7); 1998. 265p. lib. bdg. 25.00 (1-58287-048-9) North Bks.

—The Mayor of Casterbridge. Robinson, James K., ed. 1977. (Critical Editions Ser.). (Illus.). 14.95 o.p. (0-393-04459-9); 436p. (C). pap. text 10.50 o.p. (0-393-09174-0) Norton, W. W. & Co., Inc.

—The Mayor of Casterbridge. 2nd ed. 2000. (Critical Editions Ser.). (Illus.). xvii, 461p. pap. 11.00 (0-393-97498-7, Norton Paperbacks) Norton, W. W. & Co., Inc.

—The Mayor of Casterbridge. 1999. (YA). 9.95 (1-56137-350-8) Novel Units, Inc.

—The Mayor of Casterbridge. Kramer, Dale, ed. & intro. by. 1998. (Oxford World's Classics Ser.). (Illus.). 464p. pap. 7.95 (0-19-283441-X) Oxford Univ. Pr., Inc.

—The Mayor of Casterbridge. (Oxford World's Classics Ser.). (Illus.). 1987. 456p. pap. 5.95 o.p. (0-19-281728-0); 2nd ed. 1993. 126p. pap. text 5.95 (0-19-585118-8) Oxford Univ. Pr., Inc.

—The Mayor of Casterbridge. 2003. o.p. (0-333-16892-5) Pan Macmillan.

—The Mayor of Casterbridge. 2001. E-Book 2.25 (1-58882-538-8) PublishingOnline.

—The Mayor of Casterbridge. 2002. (Paperback Classics Ser.). (Illus.). 416p. pap. 7.95 (0-375-76006-7, Modern Library) Random House Adult Trade Publishing Group.

—The Mayor of Casterbridge. 1984. (gr. 11-12). mass mkt. 1.75 o.s.i (*0-671-41524-7*, Pocket) Simon & Schuster.

—The Mayor of Casterbridge. (Ebook Classic Ser.). E-Book 5.00 (*0-7410-0449-6*) SoftBook Pr.

—The Mayor of Casterbridge. 1977. (Hardy New Wessex Editions Ser.). pap. 2.95 o.p. (*0-312-52326-2*, Saint Martin's Griffin) St. Martin's Pr.

—The Mayor of Casterbridge. l.t. ed. 1998. (Perennial Bestsellers Ser.). 512p. 27.95 (*0-7838-0351-6*) Thorndike Pr.

—The Mayor of Casterbridge. l.t. ed. 1982. 13.95 o.p. (*0-7089-8021-X*, Charnwood) Thorpe, F. A. Pubs. GBR. *Dist:* Ulverscroft Large Print Bks., Ltd.

—The Mayor of Casterbridge. l.t. ed. 1998. 492p. text 29.95 (*1-56000-518-1*) Transaction Pubs.

—The Mayor of Casterbridge. Norris, Pamela, ed. 1993. 448p. pap. 4.95 (*0-460-87279-6*, Everyman's Classic Library in Paperback) Tuttle Publishing.

—The Mayor of Casterbridge. 2000. 11.95 (*81-85944-99-7*) UBS Pubs. Distributions, Ltd. IND. *Dist:* South Asia Bks.

—The Mayor of Casterbridge. Wilson, Keith, ed. & intro. by. 1998. (Penguin Classics Ser.). (Illus.). 448p. 7.95 (*0-14-043513-1*, Penguin Classics) Viking Penguin.

—The Mayor of Casterbridge. Seymour-Smith, Martin, ed. 1978. (English Library). 448p. pap. 7.95 o.s.i (*0-14-043125-X*, Penguin Classics) Viking Penguin.

—The Mayor of Casterbridge. 1999. E-Book 5.99 (*0-8220-7127-4*, Cliff Notes) Wiley, John & Sons, Inc.

—The Mayor of Casterbridge. 1998. (Classics Library). 352p. pap. 3.95 (*1-85326-098-3*, 0983WW) Wordsworth Editions, Ltd. GBR. *Dist:* Casemate Pubs. & Bk. Distributors, LLC.

—The Mayor of Casterbridge: Digital Reprint of 1922 Harper & Brothers Edition. Exams Unlimited, Inc. Staff, ed. 2001. 391p. (C). reprint ed. cd-rom 6.95 (*1-885343-92-2*) Exams Unlimited, Inc.

—The Mayor of Casterbridge: The Life & Death of a Man of Character. 2001. (Collected Works of Thomas Hardy). reprint ed. pap. text 56.00 (*0-7426-7792-3*) Classic Bks.

Hardy, Thomas & Moody, Rick. The Mayor of Casterbridge. 2001. (Oxford World's Classics Ser.). 464p. 18.00 (*0-19-514810-X*) Oxford Univ. Pr., Inc.

Harper, Jo & Harper, Josephine. Prairie Dog Pioneers. 2000. (SPA., Illus.). 48p. (J). (ps-3). 16.95 (*1-890515-10-8*) Turtle Bks.

Harris, Lisa. Boxes. 2000. (Bright Hill Press Chapbook Award Ser.). 32p. pap. 6.00 (*1-892471-03-5*) Bright Hill Pr.

Hart, Virginia. A Rocky Romance. 1998. 192p. 18.95 (*0-8034-9325-8*, Avalon Bks.) Bouregy, Thomas & Co., Inc.

Hatcher, Robin Lee. Dear Lady. 1997. 368p. mass mkt. 5.99 o.p. (*0-06-108687-8*) HarperCollins Pubs.

—Dear Lady. 2000. (Coming to America Bk.: No. 1). 304p. pap. 10.99 (*0-310-23083-7*) Zondervan.

Hawkes, John. Travesty. 1976. 128p. 5.95 o.p. (*0-8112-0597-5*) New Directions Publishing Corp.

Hawks, Robert. This Stranger, My Father. 1988. 228p. (J). (gr. 5-9). 13.95 o.p. (*0-395-44089-0*) Houghton Mifflin Co.

—This Stranger, My Father. 1990. 240p. (J). (gr. 4). mass mkt. 2.95 (*0-380-70739-X*, Avon Bks.) Morrow/Avon.

Haynes, Betsy. Great Dad Disaster. 1994. 8.60 o.p. (*0-606-06426-5*) Turtleback Bks.

—The Great Dad Disaster. 1994. 176p. (J). (gr. 4-7). pap. 3.50 o.s.i (*0-553-48169-X*) Bantam Bks.

Haynes, Mary. Catch the Sea. 1990. 176p. pap. 3.95 o.p. (*0-14-034369-5*, Puffin Bks.) Penguin Putnam Bks. for Young Readers.

—Catch the Sea. 1989. 176p. (J). (gr. 4 up). lib. bdg. 13.95 o.p. (*0-02-743451-6*, Simon & Schuster Children's Publishing) Simon & Schuster Children's Publishing.

Hearn, Lafcadio. Chita: A Memory of Last Island. LaBarre, Delia, ed. 2003. 128p. 20.00 (*1-57806-558-5*, A Banner Bk.) Univ. Pr. of Mississippi.

Hegi, Ursula. Salt Dancers. 1997. 240p. pap. 12.00 (*0-684-84482-6*, Touchstone); 1996. pap. (*0-684-00289-2*, Scribner Paper Fiction); 1996. 240p. per. 11.00 (*0-684-82530-9*, Scribner Paper Fiction); 1995. 240p. 22.00 (*0-684-80209-0*, Simon & Schuster) Simon & Schuster.

Henkes, Kevin. Protecting Marie. 1995. (Illus.). 208p. (J). (gr. 3 up). 16.99 (*0-688-13958-2*, Greenwillow Bks.) HarperCollins Children's Bk. Group.

—Protecting Marie. 1996. (Illus.). 208p. (YA). (gr. 5-9). pap. 5.99 (*0-14-038320-4*) Penguin Putnam Bks. for Young Readers.

Hermes, Patricia. Calling Me Home. 1998. (Avon Camelot Bks.). 144p. (J). (gr. 4-7). 15.00 (*0-380-97451-7*, Eos) Morrow/Avon.

—Calling Me Home. 1999. (Illus.). (J). 10.04 (*0-606-17961-5*) Turtleback Bks.

—Fly Away Home: The Novelization & Story Behind the Film. novel ed. 1996. (Medallion Edition Ser.). (Illus.). 160p. (J). pap. 6.95 (*1-55704-303-5*) Newmarket Pr.

—A Solitary Secret. 1985. 135p. (J). (gr. 6 up). 11.95 o.p. (*0-15-277190-5*) Harcourt Children's Bks.

—Take Care of My Girl: A Novel. 1992. (J). 15.95 o.p. (*0-316-35913-0*) Little Brown & Co.

—When Snow Lay Soft on the Mountains. 1996. (Illus.). 32p. (J). (ps-3). 15.95 o.p. (*0-316-36005-8*) Little Brown & Co.

Hesse, Karen. Sable. 96p. (YA). 1994. (gr. 2 up). 15.95 (*0-8050-2416-6*); ERS. 1998. (Illus.). (gr. 4 up). pap. 7.95 (*0-8050-5772-2*) Holt, Henry & Co. (Holt, Henry & Co. Bks. For Young Readers).

Hickman, Patricia. The Touch. 2002. (Illus.). 192p. 12.99 (*0-8423-4017-3*) Tyndale Hse. Pubs.

Higgins, Pamela L. Up & down the Mountain: Helping Children Cope with Parental Alcoholism. 1994. (Illus.). 36p. (J). (ps-3). mass mkt. 8.95 (*0-88282-133-4*) New Horizon Pr. Pubs., Inc.

Hines, Anna Grossnickle. Sky All Around. 1989. (Illus.). 32p. (J). (gr. 4-7). 13.95 o.p. (*0-89919-801-5*) Clarion IND. *Dist:* Houghton Mifflin Co.

Hoffman, Alice. Local Girls. 2000. 208p. pap. 12.95 (*0-425-17434-4*) Berkley Publishing Group.

—Local Girls. 1999. 197p. 22.95 o.s.i (*0-399-14507-9*) Penguin Group (USA) Inc.

—Local Girls. l.t. ed. 1999. (Americana Ser.). 208p. 29.95 (*0-7862-2009-0*) Thorndike Pr.

—Local Girls. 2000. 19.00 (*0-606-20422-9*) Turtleback Bks.

Holland, Isabelle. Hitchhike. 1987. mass mkt. 2.75 o.s.i (*0-449-70272-3*, Fawcett) Ballantine Bks.

—Hitchhike. 1977. (YA). (gr. 5-9). 12.95 (*0-397-31751-4*) HarperCollins Children's Bk. Group.

—Jennie Kiss'd Me. 1985. 208p. (Orig.). mass mkt. 2.25 o.s.i (*0-449-70065-8*, Fawcett) Ballantine Bks.

Hopper, Nancy J. Carrie's Games. 1989. 128p. (YA). (gr. 7 up). pap. 2.50 (*0-380-70538-9*, Avon Bks.) Morrow/Avon.

—Carrie's Games. 1987. 144p. (J). (gr. 7 up). 12.95 o.p. (*0-525-67186-2*, Dutton Children's Bks.) Penguin Putnam Bks. for Young Readers.

Horowitz, Ruth. Bat Time. 1991. (Illus.). 32p. (J). (ps-2). lib. bdg. 13.95 o.p. (*0-02-744541-0*, Simon & Schuster Children's Publishing) Simon & Schuster Children's Publishing.

Howard, Ellen. Gillyflower. 1986. 128p. (J). (gr. 4-8). 13.95 o.p. (*0-689-31274-1*, Atheneum) Simon & Schuster Children's Publishing.

—Gilly's Secret. 1993. Orig. Title: Gillyflower. 128p. (J). (gr. 3-7). reprint ed. pap. 3.95 o.s.i (*0-689-71746-6*, Aladdin) Simon & Schuster Children's Publishing.

Howard, Linda. A Game of Chance. 2002. 308p. mass mkt. (*0-373-48493-3*); 2000. (Silhouette Intimate Moments Ser.: Vol. 1021). 249p. mass mkt. (*0-373-27091-7*, 1-27091-7) Harlequin Enterprises, Ltd. (Silhouette).

—A Game of Chance. l.t. ed. 2001. (Americana Ser.). 341p. 31.95 o.p. (*0-7862-3025-8*) Thorndike Pr.

Hurwitz, Gregg. The Kill Clause: A Novel. 2003. 400p. 24.95 (*0-06-053038-3*); 388p. pap. 7.50 (*0-06-053039-1*) Morrow/Avon. (Morrow, William & Co.).

Irvine, Alexander C. A Scattering of Jades. E-Book 25.95 (*0-312-70730-4*); 2002. 448p. 25.95 (*0-7653-0116-4*) Doherty, Tom Assocs., LLC. (Tor Bks.).

Ishiguro, Kazuo. An Artist of the Floating World. 1989. (Vintage International Ser.). 208p. pap. 12.00 (*0-679-72266-1*, Vintage) Knopf Publishing Group.

—An Artist of the Floating World. 1986. 208p. 15.95 o.p. (*0-399-13119-1*) Putnam Publishing Group, The.

—An Artist of the Floating World. 2000. 26.50 (*0-8446-7123-1*) Smith, Peter Pub., Inc.

—An Artist of the Floating World. l.t. ed. 2001. 262p. pap. 25.95 (*0-7862-3565-9*); 280p. (*0-7540-4619-2*); 280p. (*0-7540-4620-6*) Thorndike Pr.

Jackson, Loretta & Britton, Vickie. Arctic Legacy. 1997. 192p. lib. bdg. 18.95 (*0-8034-9359-2*, Avalon Bks.) Bouregy, Thomas & Co., Inc.

Jacobs, Barbara. The Dead Leaves: A Novel. Unger, David, tr. from SPA. 1993. 126p. pap. 10.95 (*1-880684-08-X*) Curbstone Pr.

James, Henry. The Golden Bowl. unabr. ed. 2000. mass mkt. 5.99 (*0-8125-6510-X*, Tor Classics) Doherty, Tom Assocs., LLC.

—The Golden Bowl. 1992. (Everyman's Library). 640p. 20.00 (*0-679-41733-8*) Knopf, Alfred A. Inc.

—The Portrait of a Lady: Complete Text with Introduction, Historical Contexts. Cohn, Jan, ed. 2001. (New Riverside Editions Ser.). viii, 619p. 12.36 (*0-618-10735-5*) Houghton Mifflin Co.

James, Maddie. Falling for Grace. l.t. ed. 2002. (Thorndike Romance Ser.). 290p. 28.95 (*0-7862-3909-3*) Gale Group.

—Falling for Grace. 2000. (Zebra Bouquet Ser.: Vol. 55). 256p. mass mkt. 3.99 o.p. (*0-8217-6651-1*, Zebra Bks.) Kensington Publishing Corp.

James, Russell. Count Me Out. 368p. 1998. pap. 10.00 (*0-393-31832-X*, Foul Play); 1997. 22.95 o.p. (*0-88150-384-3*) Norton, W. W. & Co., Inc.

Javernick, Ellen. Where's Brooke? (Rookie Readers Ser.). (Illus.). 32p. (J). 1993. (gr. 1-2). pap. 4.95 o.p. (*0-516-42012-7*); 1992. (ps-2). mass mkt. 14.60 o.p. (*0-516-02012-9*) Scholastic Library Publishing. (Children's Pr.).

Jensen, Kathryn. Pocket Change. 1991. 192p. (YA). (gr. 7 up). pap. 2.95 o.p. (*0-590-43419-5*, Scholastic Paperbacks) Scholastic, Inc.

—Pocket Change. 1989. 176p. (YA). (gr. 7 up). text 14.95 o.s.i (*0-02-747731-2*, Simon & Schuster Children's Publishing) Simon & Schuster Children's Publishing.

Joe, Yolanda. My Fine Lady. 2004. 288p. 23.95 (*0-525-94808-2*, Dutton) Dutton/Plume.

Johansson, Alice Nicole. Lila on the Loose! 1996. (Unicorn Club Ser.: No. 14). 144p. (J). (gr. 3-7). pap. 3.50 o.p. (*0-553-48400-1*, Dell Books for Young Readers) Random Hse. Children's Bks.

Johnson, Norma. Gabriel's Girl. 1984. mass mkt. 2.25 o.s.i (*0-449-70104-2*, Fawcett) Ballantine Bks.

Johnston, Jennifer. The Invisible Worm. 1993. 192p. 19.95 o.p. (*0-88184-950-2*, Carroll & Graf Pubs.) Avalon Publishing Group.

—The Invisible Worm. 1998. 192p. o.p. (*1-85619-041-2*) Random Hse. of Canada, Ltd. CAN. *Dist:* Random Hse., Inc.

Johnston, Norma. Gabriel's Girl. 1983. 192p. (J). (gr. 5-9). 12.95 o.p. (*0-689-30989-9*, Atheneum) Simon & Schuster Children's Publishing.

Jolin, Dominique. It's Not Fair! 1996. (Illus.). 24p. (J). (ps-3). 14.95 (*0-89594-780-3*) Crossing Pr., Inc., The.

Jones, Adrienne. The Beckoner. 1980. 256p. (YA). (gr. 7 up). lib. bdg. 12.89 o.p. (*0-06-023060-6*) HarperCollins Children's Bk. Group.

Jones, Robin D. No Shakespeare Allowed. 1989. 176p. (J). (gr. 6-9). lib. bdg. 14.95 o.s.i (*0-689-31488-4*, Atheneum) Simon & Schuster Children's Publishing.

Jordan, Jennifer L. Existing Solutions. 1993. 176p. pap. 9.95 (*0-9634075-1-1*) Our Power Pr.

Jose, Nicholas. The Rose Crossing. 1996. 288p. 22.95 (*0-87951-673-9*) Overlook Pr., The.

Joyce, Graham. Smoking Poppy. 288p. 2003. pap. 14.00 (*0-671-03940-7*, Washington Square Pr.); 2002. 23.00 (*0-671-03939-3*, Atria) Simon & Schuster.

Joyce, James. Eveline. 1990. (Short Story Library). (Illus.). 32p. (YA). (gr. 5 up). lib. bdg. 13.95 o.p. (*0-88682-308-0*, Creative Education) Creative Co., The.

Kafka, Carol. Mirror Mirror. 2000. 402p. pap. 14.95 (*0-929093-06-2*, Taylor Productions) GRM Assocs.

Kaniuk, Yoram. His Daughter. Simckes, Seymour, tr. from HEB. 1989. 293p. (C). text 17.50 (*0-8076-1215-4*) Braziller, George Inc.

Kaplan, Johanna. O My America! A Novel. 1980. 286p. o.p. (*0-06-012289-7*) HarperCollins Pubs.

—O My America! A Novel. 1981. pap. 3.50 o.p. (*0-380-56515-3*, 56515, Avon Bks.) Morrow/Avon.

—O My America! A Novel. 1995. (Library of Modern Jewish Literature). 286p. pap. 17.95 (*0-8156-0328-2*) Syracuse Univ. Pr.

Kaufman, Schuyler. Death in Grandfather's Shadow: A Murder Mystery. 2001. 237p. (*1-887905-20-0*) Parkway Pubs., Inc.

Keene, Carolyn. A Mind of Her Own. Greenberg, Ann, ed. 1991. (River Heights Ser.: No. 14). 160p. (Orig.). (YA). (gr. 6 up). pap. 2.99 (*0-671-73117-3*, Simon Pulse) Simon & Schuster Children's Publishing.

Kellerman, Faye. Stalker: A Peter Decker & Rina Lazarus Novel. l.t. ed. 2000. 624p. pap. 25.00 (*0-06-019729-3*, HarperLargePrint) HarperTrade.

—Stalker: A Peter Decker & Rina Lazarus Novel. 2000. 416p. 25.00 (*0-688-15613-4*, Morrow, William & Co.) Morrow/Avon.

Kemper, Marjorie. Until That Good Day: A Novel. 2003. 320p. 24.95 (*0-312-29079-9*) St. Martin's Pr.

Kennedy, A. L. Everything You Need. 1999. 568p. (*0-224-04433-8*) Random Hse. UK, Ltd.

—Everything You Need: A Novel. 2002. 560p. pap. 14.00 (*0-375-70747-6*, Vintage) Knopf Publishing Group.

Khan, Adib. Seasonal Adjustments. 1995. 240p. pap. 11.95 (*1-86373-652-2*) Allen & Unwin Pty., Ltd. AUS. *Dist:* Paul & Co. Pubs. Consortium, Inc.

Kidd, Nina. June Mountain Secret. 1991. (Illus.). 32p. (J). (gr. k-3). lib. bdg. 14.89 o.p. (*0-06-023168-8*) HarperCollins Children's Bk. Group.

Kim, Patti. Cab Called Reliable. 1997. 156p. 18.95 o.p. (*0-312-15489-5*) St. Martin's Pr.

Kincaid, Jamaica. Mr. Potter. 2002. 144p. 20.00 (*0-374-21494-8*) Farrar, Straus & Giroux.

Kingman, Lee. The Refiner's Fire, 001. 1981. (J). (gr. 7 up). 8.95 o.p. (*0-395-31606-5*) Houghton Mifflin Co.

Klass, Sheila S. Next Stop: Nowhere. 1995. (Illus.). 176p. (YA). (gr. 7-9). pap. 14.95 (*0-590-46686-0*) Scholastic, Inc.

Klein, Norma. Now That I Know. 1989. 176p. (YA). mass mkt. 2.95 o.s.i (*0-553-28115-1*) Bantam Bks.

—Older Men. 1988. 192p. (YA). mass mkt. 3.50 o.s.i (*0-449-70261-8*, Fawcett) Ballantine Bks.

—Older Men. 1987. 240p. (YA). (gr. 7 up). 15.95 o.p. (*0-8037-0178-0*, Dial Bks. for Young Readers) Penguin Putnam Bks. for Young Readers.

Klempner, Joseph T. Irreparable Damage. E-Book 24.95 (*0-312-70676-6*); 2002. 272p. 24.95 (*0-312-28303-2*) St. Martin's Pr.

Knoedler, Michael. Callie's Way Home. 1991. (Destination Ser.). 160p. (YA). (gr. 6-12). pap. 3.95 o.p. (*0-89486-729-6*, 5116A) Hazelden Publishing & Educational Services.

Knox, Elizabeth. Black Oxen. 2001. 448p. 25.00 o.p. (*0-374-11405-6*) Farrar, Straus & Giroux.

—Black Oxen. 2002. 448p. pap. 14.00 (*0-312-42049-8*) Picador.

Komaiko, Leah. Just My Dad & Me. 1995. (Illus.). 32p. (J). lib. bdg. 15.89 (*0-06-024574-3*); 15.95 o.p. (*0-06-024573-5*) HarperCollins Children's Bk. Group. (Harper Festival).

Kraus, Harry Lee. Could I Have This Dance? 2002. 416p. pap. 12.99 (*0-310-24089-1*) Zondervan.

—For the Rest of My Life. 2004. pap. 12.99 (*0-310-24978-3*) Zondervan.

Krieger, Ellen & Haddix, Margaret Peterson. Don't You Dare Read This, Mrs. Dunphrey. 1997. 112p. (YA). (gr. 7-11). mass mkt. 4.99 (*0-689-81543-3*, Simon Pulse) Simon & Schuster Children's Publishing.

Krisher, Trudy B. Kinship. 1997. 304p. (YA). (gr. 7). 15.95 o.s.i (*0-385-32272-0*, Delacorte Pr.) Dell Publishing.

Lakin, Pat. Hurricane! 2000. (Our World Ser.). (Illus.). 32p. (J). (gr. k-4). 22.90 (*0-7613-1616-7*) Millbrook Pr., Inc.

Lasky, Kathryn. Beyond the Divide. 1986. (YA). (gr. 7 up). mass mkt. 3.25 o.s.i (*0-440-91021-8*, Laurel Leaf) Random Hse. Children's Bks.

—Beyond the Divide. (gr. 7 up). 1995. 304p. (J). pap. 4.99 (*0-689-80163-7*, Simon Pulse); 1983. 264p. (YA). lib. bdg. 17.00 (*0-02-751670-9*, Simon & Schuster Children's Publishing) Simon & Schuster Children's Publishing.

Lawrence, D. H. You Touched Me. 1982. (Short Story Library). (Illus.). 32p. (YA). (gr. 5 up). lib. bdg. 13.95 o.p. (*0-87191-894-3*, 1072-3, Creative Education) Creative Co., The.

Lee, Harper. To Kill a Mockingbird. 1991. 300p. reprint ed. lib. bdg. 22.95 (*0-89966-858-5*) Buccaneer Bks., Inc.

—To Kill a Mockingbird. 1970. 80p. pap. 5.95 (*0-87129-920-8*, T91) Dramatic Publishing Co.

—To Kill a Mockingbird. l.t. ed. 1992. (General Ser.). 430p. lib. bdg. 16.95 o.p. (*0-8161-5241-1*, Macmillan Reference USA) Gale Group.

—To Kill a Mockingbird. (Perennial Classics Ser.). 336p. 2002. pap. 11.95 (*0-06-093546-4*, Perennial); 35th anniv. ed. 1995. 18.00 (*0-06-017322-X*) HarperTrade.

—To Kill a Mockingbird. 1961. 23.00 (*0-397-00151-7*, Lippincott) Lippincott Williams & Wilkins.

—To Kill a Mockingbird. 1969. 312p. (*0-7710-5234-0*) McClelland & Stewart.

—To Kill a Mockingbird. l.t. ed. 1976. 12.00 o.p. (*0-85456-572-8*, Ulverscroft) Thorpe, F. A. Pubs. GBR. *Dist:* Ulverscroft Large Print Bks., Ltd.

Leitch, Patricia. Show Jumper Wanted. 1997. (Horseshoes Ser.: Vol. 5). 112p. (J). (gr. 3-7). pap. 3.95 o.p. (*0-06-440638-5*, Harper Trophy) HarperCollins Children's Bk. Group.

L'Engle, Madeleine. Certain Women. 1992. 351p. 21.00 o.p. (*0-374-12025-0*) Farrar, Straus & Giroux.

—Certain Women. 1993. 368p. pap. 15.00 (*0-06-065207-1*) HarperSanFrancisco.

Leonard, Marcia. The Tin Can Man. 1998. (Real Kids Readers Ser.: 1). (Illus.). 32p. (J). (ps-1). pap. 4.99 (*0-7613-2037-7*) Millbrook Pr., Inc.

Levandoski, Rob. Fresh Eggs: An American Fable. 2002. 280p. 26.00 (*1-57962-048-5*) Permanent Pr., The.

Levy, Marilyn. Remember to Remember Me. 1988. (J). (gr. 5 up). mass mkt. 2.95 o.s.i (*0-449-70278-2*, Fawcett) Ballantine Bks.

—Touching. 1988. (J). (gr. 6 up). mass mkt. 3.50 o.s.i (*0-449-70267-7*, Fawcett) Ballantine Bks.

Lewis, Thomas P. Frida's Office Day. 1989. (I Can Read Bks.). (Illus.). 64p. (J). (ps-3). 11.95 (*0-06-023843-7*) HarperCollins Children's Bk. Group.

Linton, John. Vermillion Cliffs: A Tale of Triumph over Fear. 2003. (Illus.). 350p. pap. 19.95 (*1-55517-702-6*, 77026, Bonneville Bks.) Cedar Fort, Inc./CFI Distribution.

Linz, Cathie. Daddy in Dress Blues. 2000. (Silhouette Romance Ser.: Vol. 1470). 185p. mass mkt. (*0-373-19470-6*, 1-19470-3, Harlequin Bks.) Harlequin Enterprises, Ltd.

—Daddy in Dress Blues. l.t. ed. 2001. (Basic Ser.). (Illus.). 224p. 28.95 (*0-7862-3056-8*) Thorndike Pr.

Lisle, Janet Taylor. Gold Dust Letters. 1996. 128p. (J). (gr. 4-7). pap. 3.99 o.s.i (*0-380-72516-9*, Harper Trophy) HarperCollins Children's Bk. Group.
—The Gold Dust Letters. 1994. (Investigators of the Unknown Ser.: Vol. 1). 128p. (J). (gr. 4-7). pap. 15.95 (*0-531-06830-7*); lib. bdg. 16.99 (*0-531-08680-1*) Scholastic, Inc. (Orchard Bks.).
Littleton, Mark. Danger on Midnight Trail. 1994. mass mkt. 3.99 o.p. (*1-56507-246-4*) Harvest Hse. Pubs.
—Secrets of Moonlight Mountain. 1993. (J). mass mkt. 3.99 o.p. (*0-89081-960-2*) Harvest Hse. Pubs.
Lively, Penelope. The Road to Lichfield. 224p. 1991. 17.95 o.p. (*0-8021-1134-3*); 1999. reprint ed. pap. 12.00 (*0-8021-3625-7*, Grove Pr.) Grove/Atlantic, Inc.
—The Road to Lichfield. 1992. 224p. reprint ed. pap. 12.00 o.p. (*0-06-097461-3*, Perennial) HarperTrade.
Locker, Thomas. Miranda's Smile. (J). 2000. (Illus.). pap. 4.99 (*0-14-055669-9*, Puffin Bks.); 1994. 32p. 15.89 o.s.i (*0-8037-1689-3*, Dial Bks. for Young Readers); 1994. 32p. 15.99 o.s.i (*0-8037-1688-5*, Dial Bks. for Young Readers) Penguin Putnam Bks. for Young Readers.
Lowery, Linda. Laurie Tells. 1994. (Illus.). (J). (gr. 3-6). lib. bdg. 19.95 (*0-87614-790-2*, Carolrhoda Bks.) Lerner Publishing Group.
Lutters, Valerie A. The Haunting of Julie Unger. 1977. (J). (gr. 4-6). 1.79 o.p. (*0-689-30590-7*, Atheneum) Simon & Schuster Children's Publishing.
Lutzeier, Elizabeth. The Wall. 1992. 160p. (J). (gr. 5-9). 14.95 o.p. (*0-8234-0987-2*) Holiday Hse., Inc.
Lyons, Genevieve. Alice's Awakening. l.t. ed. 2000. 248p. (*0-7540-4205-7*, Macmillan Reference USA) Gale Group.
—Alice's Awakening. 224p. 26.00 (*0-7278-5506-9*) Severn Hse. Pubs., Ltd.
—Alice's Awakening. l.t. ed. 2000. (Nightingale Ser.). 248p. pap. 20.95 (*0-7838-9109-1*) Thorndike Pr.
Lyons, Pam. Tug of Love. 1986. (Heartlines Ser.: No. 7). (Orig.). (J). (gr. 6 up). mass mkt. 2.50 o.s.i (*0-440-98818-7*, Laurel Leaf) Random Hse. Children's Bks.
Maccarone, Grace. I Shop with My Daddy. 1998. (Hello Reader! Ser.). (Illus.). (J). (ps-1). mass mkt. 3.99 (*0-590-50196-8*) Scholastic, Inc.
MacDonald, George. George MacDonald: The Parish Papers: Edited for Today's Readers. Hamilton, Dan, ed. 1997. 500p. 14.99 (*1-56476-618-7*) Cook Communications Ministries.
—The Vicar's Daughter. 1985. 216p. 5.95 o.p. (*0-89693-330-X*) Cook Communications Ministries.
MacDonald, Malcolm. Kernow & Daughter. 1996. 400p. 23.95 o.p. (*0-312-13995-0*) St. Martin's Pr.
MacInnes, Mairi. Quondam Wives. Novel. 1993. 128p. 19.95 o.p. (*0-8071-1810-9*) Louisiana State Univ. Pr.
MacKenzie, Henry. Julia de Roubigne, Vol. 4. 1976. reprint ed. 30.00 (*0-404-04094-2*) AMS Pr., Inc.
—Julia de Roubigne. 2000. 192p. pap. 16.95 (*1-86232-047-0*) Tuckwell Pr. Ltd. GBR. *Dist:* General Distribution Services, Inc.
Mahoney, Mary R. The Hurry-Up Summer. 1987. 192p. 13.95 o.s.i (*0-399-21430-5*, G. P. Putnam's Sons) Penguin Putnam Bks. for Young Readers.
Mahy, Margaret. The Catalogue of the Universe. l.t. ed. 1987. (J). (gr. 7 up). 13.95 o.p. (*0-7451-0449-5*, Galaxy Children's Large Print) BBC Audiobooks America.
—The Catalogue of the Universe. 1994. 192p. (YA). (gr. 7 up). pap. 3.99 o.s.i (*0-14-036600-8*, Puffin Bks.) Penguin Putnam Bks. for Young Readers.
Mandelbaum, Pili. You Be Me, I'll Be You. 1990. Tr. of Noire Comme le Cafe, Blanc Comme la Lune. (Illus.). 40p. (J). (ps-3). 13.95 o.p. (*0-916291-27-8*) Kane/Miller Bk. Pubs.
Mandrell, Louise & Collins, Ace. Best Man for the Job: A Story about the Meaning of Father's Day. 1993. (Illus.). 32p. (J). (gr. 1-4). 12.95 o.p. (*1-56530-039-4*) Summit Publishing Group - Legacy Bks.
Manfredi, Renee. Where Love Leaves Us. 1994. (Iowa Short Fiction Award Ser.). 158p. 11.50 (*0-87745-444-2*); E-Book 20.00 (*1-58729-138-X*) Univ. of Iowa Pr.
Manushkin, Fran. Lulu's Mixed-Up Movie. 1995. (Angel Corners Ser.: No. 3). 96p. (J). (gr. 4-7). pap. 3.99 o.p. (*0-14-037200-8*, Puffin Bks.) Penguin Putnam Bks. for Young Readers.
Marino, Anne N. The Collapsible World. 2000. 171p. 22.95 (*0-393-04909-4*) Norton, W. W. & Co., Inc.
Marino, Jan. For the Love of Pete. 1994. (J). (gr. 4 up). pap. 3.50 (*0-380-72281-X*, Avon Bks.) Morrow/Avon.
—For the Love of Pete: A Novel. 1993. (J). 14.95 o.p. (*0-316-54627-5*) Little Brown & Co.
—Searching for Atticus. 1997. 256p. (YA). (gr. 7 up). 16.00 (*0-689-80066-5*, Simon & Schuster Children's Publishing) Simon & Schuster Children's Publishing.
Marks, Alan. Thief's Daughter, RS. 1994. (Illus.). 48p. (J). (gr. 1-4). 11.00 o.p. (*0-374-37481-3*, Farrar, Straus & Giroux (BYR)) Farrar, Straus & Giroux.
Martin, Bill, Jr. & Archambault, John. White Dynamite & Curly Kidd, ERS. 1989. (Illus.). 32p. (J). (ps-3). pap. 6.95 (*0-8050-1018-1*, Holt, Henry & Co. Bks. For Young Readers) Holt, Henry & Co.
Martin, Stephen H. The Mt. Pelee Redemption: A Metalphysical Mystery. 1998. 224p. pap. 12.95 (*1-57174-116-X*) Hampton Roads Publishing Co., Inc.
Martinusen, Cindy McCormick. North of Tomorrow. 2002. 416p. pap. 10.99 (*0-8423-5237-6*) Tyndale Hse. Pubs.
Maso, Carole. Art Lover. 1995. 256p. pap. 14.00 (*0-88001-410-5*, Ecco) HarperTrade.
—The Art Lover: A Novel. 1990. (Illus.). 256p. 18.95 o.p. (*0-86547-427-3*, North Point Pr.) Farrar, Straus & Giroux.
Mayer, Mercer. Shibumi & the Kitemaker. (Illus.). 48p. 2003. pap. 5.95 (*0-7614-5145-5*); 1999. (J). 18.95 (*0-7614-5054-8*, Cavendish Children's Bks.) Cavendish, Marshall Corp.
Maynard, Joyce. The Usual Rules. E-Book 24.95 (*0-312-70971-4*) St. Martin's Pr.
—The Usual Rules. l.t. ed. 2003. 542p. 29.95 (*0-7862-5548-X*) Thorndike Pr.
—The Usual Rules: A Novel. 2004. 400p. pap. 13.95 (*0-312-28369-5*); 2003. 320p. 24.95 (*0-312-24261-1*) St. Martin's Pr.
Mazer, Norma Fox. D, My Name Is Danita. 1991. 176p. (J). (gr. 4-6). 13.95 (*0-590-43655-4*) Scholastic, Inc.
—D, My Name is Danita. 1994. 176p. (J). (gr. 4-6). mass mkt. 3.25 o.p. (*0-590-43656-2*) Scholastic, Inc.
McClintock, Barbara. The Fantastic Drawings of Danielle. (Illus.). 32p. (J). (ps-3). 2004. pap. 5.95 (*0-618-43230-2*); 1996. tchr. ed. 17.00 o.p. (*0-395-73980-2*) Houghton Mifflin Co.
McConnochie, Mardi. Coldwater. 2002. 320p. pap. 14.95 (*0-345-44812-X*, Ballantine Bks.) Ballantine Bks.
McCully, Emily Arnold. Popcorn at the Palace. 1997. (Illus.). 40p. (J). (gr. k-3). 16.00 (*0-15-277699-0*) Harcourt Children's Bks.
McDaniel, Lurlene. Until Angels Close My Eyes. 1998. 256p. (YA). (gr. 7-12). mass mkt. 4.99 (*0-553-57115-X*, Starfire) Random Hse. Children's Bks.
—When Happily Ever after Ends. 1992. (Bantam Starfire Bks.). 176p. (YA). (gr. 7 up). mass mkt. 4.99 (*0-553-29056-8*) Bantam Bks.
McDonald, Megan. The Bridge to Nowhere. 1993. 160p. (YA). (gr. 7 up). pap. 15.95 (*0-531-05478-0*); (J). (ps-3). lib. bdg. 16.99 (*0-531-08628-3*) Scholastic, Inc. (Orchard Bks.).
McFadden, Bernice L. The Warmest December. 2001. 256p. 22.95 o.s.i (*0-525-94564-4*) Dutton/Plume.
—The Warmest December. l.t. ed. 2001. 208p. 29.95 (*0-7862-3439-3*) Thorndike Pr.
McFann, Jane. One More Chance. 1988. 192p. (YA). (gr. 6 up). pap. 2.50 o.p. (*0-380-75466-5*, Avon Bks.) Morrow/Avon.
McGinnis, Lila S. If Daddy Only Knew Me. 1995. (Albert Whitman Concept Bks.). (Illus.). 32p. (J). (ps-3). lib. bdg. 14.95 o.p. (*0-8075-3537-0*) Whitman, Albert & Co.
McGrail, Anna. Mrs. Einstein: A Novel. 1998. 320p. 24.95 (*0-393-04611-7*) Norton, W. W. & Co., Inc.
McKelvey, Douglas Kaine. The Angel Knew Papa & the Dog. 1996. 96p. (J). (gr. 3-7). 14.95 o.s.i (*0-399-23042-4*, Philomel) Penguin Putnam Bks. for Young Readers.
McKinty, Adrian. Orange Rhymes with Everything. 1997. 295p. 23.00 o.p. (*0-688-14432-2*, Morrow, William & Co.) Morrow/Avon.
McMurtry, Larry. Some Can Whistle. l.t. ed. 1990. (General Ser.). 399p. 13.95 o.p. (*0-8161-5010-9*); lib. bdg. 20.95 o.p. (*0-8161-4987-9*) Gale Group. (Macmillan Reference USA).
—Some Can Whistle. 1989. 19.95 o.p. (*0-671-64267-7*, Simon & Schuster) Simon & Schuster.
—Some Can Whistle. Grose, William, ed. 1990. 384p. reprint ed. mass mkt. 6.99 (*0-671-72213-1*, Pocket) Simon & Schuster.
McMurtry, Larry & Prichard, Michael. Some Can Whistle. unabr. collector's ed. 1990. audio 56.00 (*0-7366-1803-1*, 2640) Books on Tape, Inc.
McNab, Nan. Victoria's Market. 1994. (Illus.). 32p. (J). (ps-3). 14.95 o.p. (*1-86373-235-7*); pap. 6.95 o.p. (*1-86373-383-3*) Independent Pubs. Group.
McPhail, David M. Farm Morning. D'Andrade, Diane, ed. 1991. (Illus.). 32p. (J). (ps-3). pap. 7.00 (*0-15-227300-X*, Voyager Bks./Libros Viajeros) Harcourt Children's Bks.
McPhee, Martha. Gorgeous Lies: A Novel. 2002. 336p. 25.00 (*0-15-100613-X*) Harcourt Trade Pubs.
Mead, Alice. Crossing the Starlight Bridge. 128p. (J). (gr. 4-7). 1995. pap. 4.50 (*0-689-80105-X*, Aladdin); 1994. lib. bdg. 15.00 (*0-02-765950-X*, Simon & Schuster Children's Publishing) Simon & Schuster Children's Publishing.
—Crossing the Starlight Bridge. 1995. 10.00 (*0-606-07403-1*) Turtleback Bks.
Meyer, Carolyn. Wild Rover. 1989. 208p. (YA). (gr. 7 up). lib. bdg. 14.95 o.s.i (*0-689-50475-6*, McElderry, Margaret K.) Simon & Schuster Children's Publishing.
Modiano, Patrick. Catherine Certitude. Rodarmor, William, tr. from FRE. 2001. (Illus.). 64p. (YA). (gr. 4 up). reprint ed. 17.95 (*0-87923-959-X*) Godine, David R. Pub.
Mones, Nicole. Lost in Translation. 1999. 384p. pap. 13.95 (*0-385-31944-4*, Delta) Dell Publishing.
Moranville, Sharelle Byars. Over the River, ERS. 2002. 192p. (YA). (gr. 4-9). 16.95 (*0-8050-7049-4*, Holt, Henry & Co. Bks. For Young Readers) Holt, Henry & Co.
Morgenroth, Barbara. Ride a Proud Horse. 1978. (J). (gr. 6-9). 8.95 o.p. (*0-689-30624-5*, Atheneum) Simon & Schuster Children's Publishing.
Mori, Kyoko. Stone Field, True Arrow: A Novel. 2000. 288p. 24.00 o.s.i (*0-8050-4080-3*, Metropolitan Bks.) Holt, Henry & Co.
—Stone Field, True Arrow: A Novel. 2001. 288p. pap. 13.00 (*0-312-42042-0*) Picador.
Morris, Mary McGarry. Fiona Range. l.t. ed. 2000. 28.95 (*1-56895-882-X*, Wheeler Publishing, Inc.) Gale Group.
—Fiona Range. 2000. 400p. 24.95 o.s.i (*0-670-89156-8*, Viking); 2001. 432p. reprint ed. 14.00 (*0-14-100184-4*) Viking Penguin.
Moulton, Deborah. Summer Girl. 1992. 128p. (J). (gr. 5-9). 15.00 o.p. (*0-8037-1153-0*, Dial Bks. for Young Readers) Penguin Putnam Bks. for Young Readers.
Mulford, Philippa Greene. Emily Smiley Sings the Blues, Vol. 3. 1998. (Emily Smiley Ser.: Vol. 3). (J). (gr. 2-6). mass mkt. 3.99 (*0-8125-6352-2*, Tor Bks.) Doherty, Tom Assocs., LLC.
Munsch, Robert. Get Me Another One! 1992. 32p. pap. 4.95 o.s.i (*0-385-25337-0*) Doubleday Publishing.
—Where Is Gah-Ning? 2003. (Illus.). 32p. (J). (ps-2). pap. 4.95 (*1-55037-982-8*); lib. bdg. 14.95 (*1-55037-983-6*) Annick Pr., Ltd. CAN. *Dist:* Firefly Bks., Ltd.
Munsil, Janet. Donde Hay Humo. 2003. (Hablemos Ser.). (SPA., Illus.). 24p. (J). (gr. 1 up). pap. 5.95 (*1-55037-968-2*) Annick Pr., Ltd. CAN. *Dist:* Firefly Bks., Ltd., Lectorum Pubns., Inc.
Murphy, Claire Rudolf. To the Summit. 1998. 208p. pap. 3.99 (*0-380-79537-X*, Avon Bks.) Morrow/Avon.
—To the Summit. 1992. 160p. (YA). (gr. 7 up). 15.00 o.p. (*0-525-67383-0*, Dutton Children's Bks.) Penguin Putnam Bks. for Young Readers.
—To the Summit. 1998. (J). 9.09 o.p. (*0-606-13853-6*) Turtleback Bks.
Murphy, Jill. Worlds Apart. 1989. 144p. (J). (gr. 3-7). 13.95 o.p. (*0-399-21566-2*, G. P. Putnam's Sons) Penguin Putnam Bks. for Young Readers.
Murray, Earl. South of Eden. 2001. mass mkt. 5.99 (*0-8125-7515-6*); 2001. 304p. mass mkt. 5.99 (*0-8125-7172-X*); 2000. 320p. 23.95 (*0-312-86923-1*) Doherty, Tom Assocs., LLC. (Forge Bks.).
Murray, Marguerite. The Sea Bears. 1984. 168p. (J). (gr. 4-9). 10.95 o.s.i (*0-689-31050-1*, Atheneum) Simon & Schuster Children's Publishing.
Nelson, Theresa. The Twenty-Five Cent Miracle. 224p. 1986. (YA). (gr. 7 up). lib. bdg. 14.95 o.s.i (*0-02-724370-2*, Simon & Schuster Children's Publishing); 1989. (J). (gr. 4-7). reprint ed. pap. 3.95 o.s.i (*0-689-71326-6*, Aladdin) Simon & Schuster Children's Publishing.
Neufeld, John. Sunday Father. 1977. (Signet Young Adult Mystery Ser.). 160p. (J). (gr. 6). mass mkt. 1.50 o.p. (*0-451-07292-8*, W7292, Signet Vista) NAL.
Newman, Shirlee Petkin. Isabella: A Wish for Miguel, Peru, 1820. 1997. (Girlhood Journeys Ser.: No. 1). (Illus.). 72p. (J). (gr. 2-6). pap. 5.99 (*0-689-81572-7*, Aladdin) Simon & Schuster Children's Publishing.
Nixon, Joan Lowery. And Maggie Makes Three. 1986. 128p. (J). (gr. 3-7). 12.95 (*0-15-250355-2*) Harcourt Children's Bks.
—Maggie Forevermore. 1987. 112p. (J). (gr. 3-7). 13.95 (*0-15-250345-5*) Harcourt Trade Pubs.
—Maggie Forevermore. 1989. 112p. (J). (gr. k-6). pap. 2.75 o.s.i (*0-440-40211-5*, Yearling) Random Hse. Children's Bks.
—Maggie, Too. 1987. 112p. (J). (gr. k-6). pap. 2.50 o.s.i (*0-440-45288-0*, Yearling) Random Hse. Children's Bks.
North, Darian. Thief of Souls. 1997. 368p. 23.95 o.p. (*0-525-94200-9*) Dutton/Plume.
—Thief of Souls. 1998. 432p. mass mkt. 6.99 o.s.i (*0-451-18896-9*, Signet Bks.) NAL.
Oates, Joyce Carol. A Garden of Earthly Delights: A Novel. rev. ed. 2003. (Modern Library 20th Century Rediscovery). 432p. pap. 13.95 (*0-8129-6834-4*, Modern Library) Random House Adult Trade Publishing Group.
—Man Crazy: A Novel. 1997. 288p. 23.95 o.p. (*0-525-94232-7*, Abrahams, William Bks.) Dutton/Plume.
—Man Crazy: A Novel. l.t. ed. 1998. (Basic Ser.). 307p. 28.95 (*0-7862-1273-X*) Thorndike Pr.
O'Brien, Edna. Down by the River. 1998. 272p. pap. 12.95 (*0-452-27877-5*, Plume) Dutton/Plume.
—Down by the River. 1997. 256p. 23.00 o.p. (*0-374-14327-7*) Farrar, Straus & Giroux.
O'Connor, Joseph. The Salesman. 400p. 2000. pap. 14.00 (*0-312-20431-0*); 1999. (Illus.). 24.00 o.p. (*0-312-19998-8*) Picador.
O'Dell, Scott. The Spanish Smile. 1983. 160p. mass mkt. 4.50 o.s.i (*0-449-70094-1*, Fawcett) Ballantine Bks.
—The Spanish Smile, 001. 1982. (J). (gr. 7 up). 13.95 o.p. (*0-395-32867-5*) Houghton Mifflin Co.
Odenbach, Ginny & Osborn, Linda. Feather. Yarnaught, Paula, ed. 1995. (Illus.). 88p. (Orig.). (J). (gr. 3-8). pap. 4.50 (*1-885101-14-7*) Writers Pr., Inc.
O'Donnell, Mary King. Quincie Bolliver. 2001. (Double Mountain Bks.). xvi, 425p. pap. text 19.95 (*0-89672-449-2*, Double Mountain Bks.) Texas Tech Univ. Pr.
Oke, Janette. The Matchmakers. 1997. 144p. text 12.99 o.p. (*0-7642-2002-0*); pap. 12.99 o.p. (*0-7642-2020-9*) Bethany Hse. Pubs.
—The Matchmakers. l.t. ed. 2001. (Illus.). 197p. 25.95 (*0-7862-3256-0*); (*0-7540-4523-4*); (*0-7540-4524-2*) Thorndike Pr.
Oliver, Jim. Wings in the Snow. 1998. 288p. pap. 12.95 (*1-55583-462-0*, Alyson Bks.) Alyson Pubns.
Oneal, Zibby. In Summer Light. 1986. 160p. (YA). (gr. 6 up). mass mkt. 3.50 o.s.i (*0-553-25940-7*) Bantam Bks.
—In Summer Light. 1985. 16p. (J). (gr. 7 up). 12.95 o.p. (*0-670-80784-2*, Viking Children's Bks.) Penguin Putnam Bks. for Young Readers.
Orr, Wendy. Nim's Island. 2001. (Illus.). 128p. (gr. 3-7). lib. bdg. 16.99 o.s.i (*0-375-91123-5*, Knopf Bks. for Young Readers) Random Hse. Children's Bks.
Osborne, Mary Pope. Love Always, Blue. 1983. 192p. (J). (gr. 6 up). 12.95 o.p. (*0-8037-0031-8*, 01258-370, Dial Bks. for Young Readers) Penguin Putnam Bks. for Young Readers.
Palmer, Catherine. Hide & Seek. 2001. (HeartQuest Ser.: Vol. 2). (Illus.). 288p. pap. 9.99 (*0-8423-1165-3*) Tyndale Hse. Pubs.
—Love's Proof. 2003. (HeartQuest Ser.). 336p. pap. 9.99 (*0-8423-7032-3*) Tyndale Hse. Pubs.
Parker, Al. Murder in Detroit. 2000. 185p. pap. 11.95 (*1-56315-260-6*) SterlingHouse Pubs., Inc.
Pascal, Francine, creator. Out of Reach. 1988. (Sweet Valley High Ser.: No. 50). 160p. (YA). (gr. 7 up). mass mkt. 2.95 o.s.i (*0-553-27596-8*) Bantam Bks.
—Second Chance. l.t. ed. 1989. (Sweet Valley High Ser.: No. 53). 133p. (YA). (gr. 7 up). reprint ed. 9.50 o.p. (*1-55905-008-X*); lib. bdg. 10.50 o.p. (*1-55905-018-7*) Grey Castle Pr.
Pascoe, Judy. Our Father Who Art in a Tree: A Novel. 2004. 208p. pap. 10.95 (*0-375-75987-5*, Random Hse. Trade Paperbacks) Random House Adult Trade Publishing Group.
—Our Father Who Art in a Tree: A Novel. 2003. 208p. 19.95 (*0-375-50799-X*) Random Hse., Inc.
Pate, Alexs D. Finding Makeba. 1996. 256p. 21.95 o.p. (*0-399-14200-2*, G. P. Putnam's Sons) Penguin Group (USA) Inc.
Peck, Richard. Through a Brief Darkness. 1997. 144p. (J). pap. 3.99 o.s.i (*0-14-038557-6*) Penguin Putnam Bks. for Young Readers.
—Through a Brief Darkness. 1997. (J). 9.09 o.p. (*0-606-11986-8*) Turtleback Bks.
—Unfinished Portrait of Jessica. 176p. (J). 1993. mass mkt. 3.99 o.s.i (*0-440-21886-1*); 1991. 15.00 o.s.i (*0-385-30500-1*, Delacorte Pr.) Dell Publishing.
Perez-Mercado, Mary Margaret. Splat! 1999. (Rookie Readers Ser.). (Illus.). 24p. (J). (gr. k-1). lib. bdg. 16.00 (*0-516-21615-5*, Children's Pr.) Scholastic Library Publishing.
Peters, Lisa W. Meg & Dad Discover Treasure in the Air, ERS. 1995. (Illus.). 88p. (J). (gr. k-3). 15.95 o.p. (*0-8050-2418-2*, Holt, Henry & Co. Bks. For Young Readers) Holt, Henry & Co.
Pfeffer, Susan Beth. Most Precious Blood. 1993. 176p. (YA). mass mkt. 3.99 o.s.i (*0-553-56128-6*) Bantam Bks.
Phillips, Michael. The Eleventh Hour. 2000. (Secret of the Rose Ser.). 496p. mass mkt. 6.99 (*0-8423-4289-3*, Living Bks.); 1994. (Secret of the Rose Ser.: No. 1). 504p. 8.99 o.p. (*0-8423-3932-9*); 1993. (Secret of the Rose Ser.: Vol. 1). 504p. pap. 8.99 (*0-8423-3933-7*) Tyndale Hse. Pubs.
—A Rose Remembered. (Secret of the Rose Ser.: Vol. 2). 2001. 528p. mass mkt. 7.99 (*0-8423-4291-5*, Living Bks.); 1994. 576p. pap. 11.99 o.p. (*0-8423-5929-X*) Tyndale Hse. Pubs.
Pitt, Jane. Secret Hearts. 1986. (Heartlines Ser.: No. 2). (Orig.). (J). (gr. 6 up). mass mkt. 2.50 o.s.i (*0-440-97722-3*, Laurel Leaf) Random Hse. Children's Bks.
Polland, Madeleine A. No Price Too High. 1984. 312p. 17.95 o.s.i (*0-385-29338-0*, Delacorte Pr.) Dell Publishing.

—No Price Too High. l.t. ed. 1985. (Charnwood Romance Ser.). 576p. 29.99 o.p. (*0-7089-8290-5*, Charnwood) Thorpe, F. A. Pubs. GBR. *Dist:* Ulverscroft Large Print Bks., Ltd., Ulverscroft Large Print Canada, Ltd.

Presser, Arlynn. Second to None. 1994. 224p. mass mkt. 3.50 o.s.i (*0-8217-4514-X*, Zebra Bks.) Kensington Publishing Corp.

Pronzini, Bill. In an Evil Time. l.t. ed. 2001. 400p. 29.95 (*0-7862-3648-5*) Thorndike Pr.

—In an Evil Time. 2002. reprint ed. pap. 8.95 (*0-8027-7629-9*) Walker & Co.

Quin-Harkin, Janet. Lovebirds: International Edition. 1994. (YA). pap. 3.50 (*0-553-24181-8*) Bantam Bks.

Raffel, Dawn. Carrying the Body: A Novel. 2002. 144p. 18.00 (*0-7432-2863-4*, Scribner) Simon & Schuster.

Raymond, Patrick. The Maple Moon. 1992. 104p. (YA). (gr. 7-9). 17.95 o.p. (*0-09-174389-3*) Hutchinson GBR. *Dist:* Trafalgar Square.

Raynor, Mary, illus. Thank You for the Tadpole. 1988. (Share-a-Story Bks.). (J). (gr. k-2). 8.95 o.s.i (*0-385-29604-5*, Delacorte Pr.) Dell Publishing.

Ready, Ann C. Her Father's Daughter. 1981. 192p. (Orig.). (J). (gr. 6-12). 1.95 o.s.i (*0-448-14688-6*) Ace Bks.

Reding, Jaclyn. White Mist. l.t. ed. 2001. (G. K. Hall Core Ser.). 367p. 28.95 (*0-7838-9428-7*, Macmillan Reference USA) Gale Group.

Reid, Barbara. Zoe's Snowy Day. 1991. 12p. (J). pap. 3.95 o.p. (*0-590-44714-9*) Scholastic, Inc.

—Zoe's Windy Day. 1991. (Board Bk.). 12p. (J). pap. 3.95 o.p. (*0-590-44712-2*) Scholastic, Inc.

Reid, Paul Carey. Swimming in the Starry River. 1994. 384p. (J). 19.95 (*0-7868-6005-7*) Hyperion Pr.

—Swimming in the Starry River. 1995. 384p. (J). pap. 11.95 (*0-312-14136-X*, Saint Martin's Griffin) St. Martin's Pr.

Reisfeld, Randi. He's Not What You Think. 1997. (Love Stories Ser.). 192p. (YA). (gr. 7-12). mass mkt. 3.99 o.s.i (*0-553-57077-3*) Bantam Bks.

Rhodes, Judy C. The Hunter's Heart. 1993. 160p. (J). (gr. 4-7). text 14.95 o.p. (*0-02-775935-0*, Simon & Schuster Children's Publishing) Simon & Schuster Children's Publishing.

Rice, Eve. Swim! 1996. (Illus.). 24p. (J). (ps-3). 15.00 o.s.i (*0-688-14274-5*); lib. bdg. 14.93 o.p. (*0-688-14275-3*) HarperCollins Children's Bk. Group. (Greenwillow Bks.).

Ridley, William J. The Summit Sojourners. 2002. 208p. 23.95 (*0-87839-184-3*) North Star Pr. of St. Cloud.

Riecken, Nancy. Today Is the Day. 1996. (Illus.). 32p. (J). (ps-3). 14.95 o.p. (*0-395-73917-9*) Houghton Mifflin Co.

Rinald, Ann. But in the Fall I'm Leaving. 1986. 224p. pap. 2.50 o.p. (*0-380-70138-3*, Avon Bks.) Morrow/Avon.

Rinaldi, Ann. But in the Fall I'm Leaving. 1985. 224p. (YA). (gr. 7 up). 12.95 o.p. (*0-8234-0560-5*) Holiday Hse., Inc.

Roberts, Michele. Impossible Saints. 1998. 320p. o.p. (*0-88001-597-7*, Ecco) HarperTrade.

Roberts, Nora. Island of Flowers. 1992. (NR Flowers Ser.: No. 10). per. (*0-373-51010-1*, 5-51010-2, Harlequin Bks.) Harlequin Enterprises, Ltd.

—Island of Flowers. l.t. ed. 2002. (Core Collection). 167p. 31.95 (*0-7862-4218-3*) Thorndike Pr.

Robinson, Fay. Pizza Soup. 1993. (Bear & Alligator Tales Ser.). (Illus.). 32p. (J). (ps-2). lib. bdg. 17.70 o.p. (*0-516-02373-X*); mass mkt. 3.95 o.p. (*0-516-42373-8*) Scholastic Library Publishing. (Children's Pr.).

Rockwell, Anne F. Ducklings & Pollywogs. 1994. (Illus.). 32p. (J). (ps-2). pap. 14.95 (*0-02-777452-X*, Simon & Schuster Children's Publishing) Simon & Schuster Children's Publishing.

Rodowsky, Colby. Sydney, Herself, RS. 1993. 192p. (YA). (gr. 7 up). pap. 5.95 (*0-374-47390-0*, Sunburst) Farrar, Straus & Giroux.

Rojany, Lisa. Casper: Junior Novelization. 1995. (Illus.). (J). (gr. 2 up). 3.95 o.s.i (*0-8431-3854-8*, Price Stern Sloan) Penguin Putnam Bks. for Young Readers.

Rooke, Leon. The Fall of Gravity: A Novel. 2000. 271p. tchr. ed. (*0-919028-36-5*) Allen, Thomas & Son, Ltd.

Root, Phyllis. Contrary Bear. 1996. (Illus.). 32p. (J). (ps-1). 13.95 o.s.i (*0-06-025085-2*); lib. bdg. 13.89 o.s.i (*0-06-025086-0*) HarperCollins Children's Bk. Group.

Rose, Joel. Kill Kill Faster Faster. 1998. 224p. pap. 11.95 o.s.i (*0-14-027329-8*) Penguin Group (USA) Inc.

Ross, Marilyn. Message from a Ghost. l.t. ed. 2001. 295p. 26.95 (*0-7862-3336-2*) Thorndike Pr.

Rossi, Agnes. The Houseguest. 2000. 304p. reprint ed. 13.00 o.s.i (*0-452-28197-0*, Plume) Dutton/Plume.

—The Houseguest: A Novel. l.t. ed. 2000. (Americana Ser.). 504p. 28.95 (*0-7862-2547-5*) Thorndike Pr.

Rossner, Judith. His Little Women. 1990. 19.95 o.p. (*0-671-64858-6*, Simon & Schuster) Simon & Schuster.

—His Little Women. Rubenstein, Julie, ed. 1991. 448p. reprint ed. mass mkt. 5.95 (*0-671-70124-X*, Pocket) Simon & Schuster.

Roth, Philip. When She Was Good. 1995. 320p. pap. 13.00 (*0-679-75925-5*, Vintage) Knopf Publishing Group.

—When She Was Good. 1985. (Fiction Ser.). 320p. pap. 5.95 o.p. (*0-14-007676-X*, Penguin Bks.) Viking Penguin.

Rue, Nancy N. Janis Project. 1988. 224p. (YA). (gr. 9-12). pap. 7.95 o.p. (*0-89107-486-4*) Crossway Bks.

Russo, Richard. Empire Falls. unabr. ed. 2001. audio 42.95 (*0-694-52559-6*, HarperAudio) HarperTrade.

—Empire Falls. 2002. 496p. pap. 14.95 (*0-375-72640-3*, Vintage) Knopf Publishing Group.

—Empire Falls. 2001. 496p. 25.95 (*0-679-43247-7*) Knopf, Alfred A. Inc.

—Empire Falls. unabr. ed. 2001. audio 122.00 (*0-7887-8928-7*) Recorded Bks., LLC.

—Empire Falls. l.t. ed. 2001. (Thorndike Press Large Print Americana Ser.). 902p. 30.95 (*0-7862-3651-5*) Thorndike Pr.

Ryan, Mary. Hope. mass mkt. (*0-312-98744-7*, St. Martin's Paperbacks) St. Martin's Pr.

—Hope: A Novel. 2003. 480p. 27.95 (*0-312-30970-8*) St. Martin's Pr.

Ryder, Joanne. My Father's Hands. 1994. (Illus.). 32p. (J). (ps-3). 16.99 (*0-688-09189-X*) HarperCollins Children's Bk. Group.

—My Father's Hands. 1994. (Illus.). 32p. (YA). (ps up). lib. bdg. 15.93 (*0-688-09190-3*, Morrow, William & Co.) Morrow/Avon.

Sachs, Marilyn. Ghosts in the Family. 1995. 176p. (J). (gr. 3-6). 15.99 o.s.i (*0-525-45421-7*, Dutton Children's Bks.) Penguin Putnam Bks. for Young Readers.

Samson, Polly. Out of the Picture. 2002. 256p. (Orig.). pap. 12.00 (*1-86049-864-7*) Virago Pr., Ltd. GBR. *Dist:* Trafalgar Square.

Schulte, Elaine L. Tricia's Got Trouble. 1993. (Twelve Candles Club Ser.: Vol. 4). 128p. (J). (gr. 3-7). pap. 5.99 o.p. (*1-55661-253-2*) Bethany Hse. Pubs.

Schultz, Marion. Who Needs Glamour Anyway? 1988. 144p. (YA). (gr. 7 up). mass mkt. 2.75 o.s.i (*0-449-70255-3*, Fawcett) Ballantine Bks.

Segal, Elaine. She Loves You: A Curious Tale Concerning a Miraculous Intervention. 1997. (Illus.). 64p. 16.45 (*0-684-83895-8*, Simon & Schuster) Simon & Schuster.

Shannon, George. Dancing the Breeze. 1991. (Illus.). 32p. (J). (ps-1). lib. bdg. 13.95 o.p. (*0-02-782190-0*, Simon & Schuster Children's Publishing) Simon & Schuster Children's Publishing.

Sharma, Akhil. An Obedient Father. 2000. 282p. 23.00 o.p. (*0-374-10501-4*) Farrar, Straus & Giroux.

—An Obedient Father. 2001. 300p. pap. 13.00 (*0-15-601203-0*, Harvest Bks.) Harcourt Trade Pubs.

Sharratt, Nick. Look What I Found! 1992. (Illus.). 32p. (J). (ps). 9.95 o.p. (*1-56402-017-7*) Candlewick Pr.

Shawhan, Dorothy. Lizzie. 1995. 352p. 20.00 (*1-56352-227-6*) Longstreet Pr., Inc.

Shea, Suzanne Strempek. Hoopi Shoopi Donna. 1996. 368p. 22.00 o.p. (*0-671-53544-7*, Atria) Simon & Schuster.

Sheldon, Sidney. Morning, Noon & Night. 1995. 398p. 24.00 (*0-688-08492-3*, Morrow, William & Co.) Morrow/Avon.

Showers, Paul. Los Sonidos a Mi Alrededor. Marcuse, Aida E., tr. 1996. (SPA., Illus.). 32p. (J). (ps-2). 16.95 o.s.i (*0-06-026228-1*); pap. 6.95 (*0-06-443418-4*, HC2028) HarperCollins Children's Bk. Group.

Shreve, Anita. Fortune's Rocks. 1999. 320p. (gr. 8). 24.95 o.p. (*0-316-78101-0*); 2001. 480p. reprint ed. pap. 13.95 (*0-316-67810-4*, Back Bay) Little Brown & Co.

—Fortune's Rocks. l.t. ed. 1999. 688p. 24.95 (*0-375-43052-0*) Random Hse. Large Print.

Shreve, Susan Richards. The Goalie. 96p. (J). (gr. 3 up). 1998. pap. 4.50 o.p. (*0-688-15858-7*); 1996. 15.00 o.p. (*0-688-14379-2*) Morrow/Avon. (Morrow, William & Co.).

Shulman, Neil B. & Fleming, Sibley. Under the Backyard Sky. 1995. (Illus.). 32p. (J). (gr. 1-4). 13.95 o.p. (*1-56145-093-6*) Peachtree Pubs., Ltd.

Shyer, Marlene Fanta. Two Daughters. 2002. 32p. mass mkt. 6.99 o.s.i (*0-7582-0037-4*) Kensington Publishing Corp.

—Two Daughters. l.t. ed. 2002. (Women's Fiction Ser.). 28.95 (*0-7862-4409-7*) Thorndike Pr.

Simon, Lisa. The Dude of My Dreams. 1995. (Full House Stephanie Ser.: No. 10). 144p. (J). (gr. 4-6). pap. 3.99 (*0-671-52274-4*, Simon Spotlight) Simon & Schuster Children's Publishing.

Simpson, Mona. The Lost Father. 1993. (Vintage Contemporaries Ser.). 528p. pap. 14.00 (*0-679-73303-5*, Vintage) Knopf Publishing Group.

—A Regular Guy. 1997. pap. 13.00 (*0-679-77271-5*); 1996. 372p. 25.00 o.s.i (*0-679-45091-2*) McKay, David Co., Inc.

Singer, Reanne S. The Storm's Crossing: A Young Girl's Triumph over a Terrible Secret. 1993. 176p. (YA). 13.95 (*0-925190-62-4*) Fairview Pr.

Singleton, Linda Joy. Stand up & Cheer! 1996. (Cheer Squad Ser.: No. 3). 144p. (Orig.). (YA). (gr. 6-8). pap. 3.99 o.p. (*0-380-78440-8*, Avon Bks.) Morrow/Avon.

Skloot, Floyd. Summer Blue: A Novel. 2004. 218p. 18.95 (*0-934257-08-6*) Story Line Pr.

Skolsky, Mindy Warshaw. Hannah & the Best Father on Route 9W. 1982. (Illus.). 128p. (J). (gr. 3-6). lib. bdg. 12.89 o.p. (*0-06-025744-X*) HarperCollins Children's Bk. Group.

Slater, Teddy. Junior Gymnasts. 1996. (Junior Gymnasts Ser.: No. 5). (J). mass mkt. 3.99 (*0-590-95987-5*) Scholastic, Inc.

Slepian, Jan. Back to Before. 1993. 192p. (J). (gr. 5-9). 14.95 o.p. (*0-399-22011-9*, Philomel) Penguin Putnam Bks. for Young Readers.

—Back to Before. 1994. 144p. (J). (gr. 4-6). pap. 3.25 (*0-590-48459-1*) Scholastic, Inc.

—Back to Before. 1993. 8.35 o.p. (*0-606-06219-X*) Turtleback Bks.

Smiley, Jane. At Paradise Gate. 16th l.t. ed. 2001. 271p. lib. bdg. 27.95 (*1-58547-073-2*) Ctr. Point Large Print.

—At Paradise Gate. 224p. 1998. pap. 12.00 (*0-684-85223-3*); 1993. pap. 11.00 (*0-671-88533-2*) Simon & Schuster. (Touchstone).

—A Thousand Acres. 1997. mass mkt. 9.50 (*0-8041-9717-2*); 1996. 416p. mass mkt. 7.99 o.s.i (*0-8041-1576-1*) Ballantine Bks. (Ivy Bks.).

—A Thousand Acres. 1991. 371p. 25.00 o.s.i (*0-394-57773-6*) Knopf, Alfred A. Inc.

—A Thousand Acres. 1992. 18.05 (*0-606-20075-4*) Turtleback Bks.

Smith, Florence B. In Search of Katlan. 2000. 200p. pap. 8.00 (*1-893463-35-4*) Prickly Pr.

Smurthwaite, Donald S. A Wise, Blue Autumn: A Novel about Fathers, Daughters & Remembering. 2001. 151p. pap. 12.95 (*1-57345-922-4*, SKU 4132192, Bookcraft, Inc.) Deseret Bk. Co.

Snelling, Lauraine. Hawaiian Sunrise. l.t. ed. 2001. (Thorndike Press Large Print Christian Romance Ser.). 429p. 24.95 (*0-7862-3284-6*) Thorndike Pr.

—Hawaiian Sunrise: A Novel. 1999. 288p. pap. 9.99 (*1-55661-991-X*) Bethany Hse. Pubs.

—Out of the Blue. 1996. (High Hurdles Ser.: No. 4). 176p. (YA). (gr. 6-9). pap. 5.99 (*1-55661-508-6*) Bethany Hse. Pubs.

—Out of the Mist. 1993. (Golden Filly Ser.: No. 7). 160p. (J). (gr. 4-7). pap. 5.99 (*1-55661-338-5*) Bethany Hse. Pubs.

—Shadow over San Mateo. 1993. (Golden Filly Ser.: Vol. 6). 160p. (Orig.). (J). (gr. 4-7). pap. 5.99 (*1-55661-292-3*) Bethany Hse. Pubs.

Spanidou, Irini. God's Snake. 1998. 256p. pap. 13.00 (*0-375-70286-5*, Vintage) Knopf Publishing Group.

—God's Snake. 1986. 15.95 o.p. (*0-393-02320-6*) Norton, W. W. & Co., Inc.

—God's Snake. 1987. 256p. pap. 6.95 o.p. (*0-14-010360-0*, Penguin Bks.) Viking Penguin.

Spelman, Cornelia Maude. After Charlotte's Mom Died. 1996. (Illus.). 24p. (J). (gr. k-4). lib. bdg. 13.95 (*0-8075-0196-4*) Whitman, Albert & Co.

Stahl, Hilda. Sendi Lee Mason & the Big Mistake. 1991. (Growing up Adventure Ser.). 128p. (J). (gr. 1-4). pap. 4.99 o.p. (*0-89107-613-1*) Crossway Bks.

Stallsmith, Audrey. Rosemary for Remembrance. 1998. (Thyme Will Tell Mysteries Ser.: Vol. 1). 304p. pap. 6.95 o.s.i (*1-57856-040-3*) WaterBrook Pr.

Stallwood, Veronica. Deathspell. l.t. ed. 1994. 21.95 o.p. (*0-7927-1989-1*); pap. 19.95 o.p. (*0-7927-1988-3*) BBC Audiobooks America.

—Deathspell. 1992. 224p. text 20.00 (*0-684-19517-8*, Macmillan Reference USA) Gale Group.

Stanley, Sanna. Monkey Sunday: Story from a Village in Zaire, RS. 1998. (Illus.). 32p. (J). (gr. k-3). 16.00 o.p. (*0-374-35018-3*, Farrar, Straus & Giroux (BYR)) Farrar, Straus & Giroux.

Staples, Donna. Arena Beach. 1993. (YA). tchr. ed. 14.95 o.p. (*0-395-65366-5*) Houghton Mifflin Co.

Strachan, Ian. The Soutar Retrospective. 1987. 176p. (J). 13.95 o.p. (*0-19-271464-3*) Oxford Univ. Pr., Inc.

Strasser, Todd. Hey Dad, Get a Life! 1996. 160p. (J). (gr. 4-7). tchr. ed. 15.95 (*0-8234-1278-4*) Holiday Hse., Inc.

Streeter, Edward. Father of the Bride. 1993. reprint ed. lib. bdg. 21.95 (*1-56849-136-0*) Buccaneer Bks., Inc.

—Father of the Bride. adapted ed. 1951. per. 6.50 (*0-8222-0390-1*) Dramatists Play Service, Inc.

—Father of the Bride. anniv. ed. 1999. (Simon & Schuster Classic Editions). (Illus.). 240p. 23.00 (*0-684-86354-5*, Simon & Schuster) Simon & Schuster.

Stretton, Barbara. The Truth of the Matter. 1984. 256p. (J). reprint ed. (*0-399-21147-0*) Putnam Publishing Group, The.

—The Truth of the Matter. 1983. 256p. (J). (gr. 7-12). 10.95 o.p. (*0-394-86144-2*, Knopf Bks. for Young Readers) Random Hse. Children's Bks.

Stuart, Alexander H. The War Zone. 1990. 224p. pap. 8.95 o.s.i (*0-553-34878-7*) Bantam Bks.

Sucher, Cheryl P. The Rescue of Memory. 1997. 288p. 23.00 o.s.i (*0-684-81462-5*, Scribner) Simon & Schuster.

Susann, Jacqueline. Once Is Not Enough. 1998. 480p. pap. 14.00 (*0-8021-3545-5*); 1997. o.p. (*0-8021-3537-4*) Grove/Atlantic, Inc. (Grove Pr.).

—Once Is Not Enough. 1973. 7.95 o.p. (*0-688-00156-4*, Morrow, William & Co.) Morrow/Avon.

Swift, Graham. Out of This World. 1993. 207p. pap. 11.00 (*0-679-74032-5*) McKay, David Co., Inc.

—Out of This World. 1988. 208p. 16.95 o.p. (*0-671-65827-1*, Simon & Schuster) Simon & Schuster.

—The Sweet-Shop Owner. 1993. 221p. pap. 10.00 (*0-679-73980-7*, Vintage) Knopf Publishing Group.

Tallent, Elizabeth. Museum Pieces. 1986. 240p. pap. 7.95 o.p. (*0-03-008003-7*, Owl Bks.) Holt, Henry & Co.

—Museum Pieces. Goerner, Lee, ed. 1985. 206p. 14.95 o.s.i (*0-394-53928-1*) Knopf, Alfred A. Inc.

Tang, Peusner, et al. Sing for Your Father, Su Phan. 1999. (Illus.). 112p. (J). (gr. 4-7). pap. text 4.50 o.p. (*0-440-41538-1*) Dell Publishing.

Taylor, Theodore. Sweet Friday Island. 1994. 192p. (YA). (gr. 7 up). 10.95 (*0-15-200009-7*); pap. 6.00 (*0-15-200012-7*, Harcourt Paperbacks) Harcourt Children's Bks.

—Sweet Friday Island. 1994. 10.10 o.p. (*0-606-06777-9*) Turtleback Bks.

Thayer, Steve. Moon over Lake Elmo. 2001. 256p. pap. 10.95 o.s.i (*0-451-20373-9*) NAL.

Thesman, Jean. The Last April Dancers. 1987. 224p. (YA). (gr. 7 up). 13.95 o.p. (*0-395-43024-0*) Houghton Mifflin Co.

—The Last April Dancers. 1989. 224p. (YA). (gr. 7 up). pap. 2.75 (*0-380-70614-8*, Avon Bks.) Morrow/Avon.

—The Storyteller's Daughter. 1997. 192p. (YA). (gr. 7-9). tchr. ed. 16.00 (*0-395-80978-9*) Houghton Mifflin Co.

—The Storyteller's Daughter. 1999. 192p. (J). (gr. 5-9). pap. 4.99 o.s.i (*0-14-130314-X*, Puffin Bks.) Penguin Putnam Bks. for Young Readers.

Thomas, D. M. Eating Pavlova. 1995. 240p. pap. 10.95 (*0-7867-0270-2*); 1994. 231p. 21.00 o.p. (*0-7867-0142-0*) Avalon Publishing Group. (Carroll & Graf Pubs.).

Thomas, Ianthe. Eliza's Daddy. 1976. (Let Me Read Ser.). (Illus.). (J). (gr. 1-5). 4.95 o.p. (*0-15-225400-5*) Harcourt Children's Bks.

Thomas, Jane Resh. Daddy Doesn't Have to Be a Giant Anymore. 1996. (Illus.). 48p. (J). (gr. k-3). tchr. ed. 14.95 o.p. (*0-395-69427-2*, Clarion Bks.) Houghton Mifflin Co. Trade & Reference Div.

Thomas, Linda. Daddy's Not-So-Little Girl. Clancy, Lisa, ed. 1995. (Full House Stephanie Ser.: No. 7). 128p. (J). (gr. 4-6). pap. 3.99 (*0-671-89860-4*, Simon Spotlight) Simon & Schuster Children's Publishing.

Thomas, Sue. Water. 240p. 1995. pap. 11.95 (*0-87951-600-3*); 1994. 21.95 (*0-87951-532-5*) Overlook Pr., The.

Thomson, Colin A. Klanty's Daughters. 1993. 181p. pap. 14.95 (*1-55059-065-0*) Temeron Bks., Inc.

Thornburg, Newton. A Man's Game. 1997. 300p. mass mkt. 6.99 (*0-8125-5374-8*); 1996. 304p. 22.95 o.p. (*0-312-85923-6*) Doherty, Tom Assocs., LLC. (Forge Bks.).

Tiffany, Grace. My Father Had a Daughter: Judith Shakespeare's Tale. 2003. 304p. 21.95 (*0-425-19003-X*) Berkley Publishing Group.

Toombs, Jane. The Restless Obsession. 2000. (Five Star Romance Ser.). 227p. pap. 26.95 (*0-7862-2632-3*, Five Star) Gale Group.

Trott, Susan. Divorcing Daddy. 1992. 208p. 18.95 o.p. (*0-88184-754-2*, Carroll & Graf Pubs.) Avalon Publishing Group.

Tubach, Sally Patterson. Memoirs of a Terrorist. 1996. (SUNY Series, The Margins of Literature). 174p. (C). pap. text 19.95 (*0-7914-3006-5*); text 20.50 (*0-7914-3005-7*) State Univ. of New York Pr.

Valentine, Johnny. The Daddy Machine. 1992. (Illus.). 48p. (Orig.). (J). (gr. k-4). pap. 6.95 o.p. (*1-55583-107-9*, Alyson Wonderland) Alyson Pubns.

Vargas Llosa, Mario. The Feast of the Goat. Grossman, Edith, tr. from SPA. 2001. Tr. of Fiesta del Chivo. 416p. 25.00 (*0-374-15476-7*) Farrar, Straus & Giroux.

—The Feast of the Goat. 2002. Tr. of Fiesta del Chivo. 416p. pap. 14.00 (*0-312-42027-7*) Picador.

—The Feast of the Goat: International Edition. 2002. mass mkt. 7.99 (*0-312-98706-4*) Picador.

Victor, Cynthia. The Sisters. l.t. ed. 1999. (Wheeler Large Print Bks.). 27.95 (*1-56895-646-0*, Wheeler Publishing, Inc.) Gale Group.

—The Sisters, 1 vol. 1999. 352p. mass mkt. 6.99 o.s.i (*0-451-40866-7*) NAL.

Vigna, Judith. Daddy's New Baby. Fay, Ann, ed. 1982. (Albert Whitman Concept Bks.). (Illus.). 32p. (J). (ps-3). lib. bdg. 11.95 o.p. (*0-8075-1435-7*) Whitman, Albert & Co.
—I Live with Daddy. 1997. 32p. (J). (gr. 1-4). lib. bdg. 14.95 (*0-8075-3512-5*) Whitman, Albert & Co.
Vine, Barbara, pseud. The Chimney Sweeper's Boy. unabr. collector's ed. 1998. audio 72.00 (*0-7366-4533-0*, 4719) Books on Tape, Inc.
—The Chimney Sweeper's Boy. l.t. ed. 1998. 24.00 o.p. (*0-7838-0156-4*, Macmillan Reference USA) Gale Group.
—The Chimney Sweeper's Boy. unabr. ed. 1998. audio 91.00 (*0-7887-2171-2*, 95467E7) Recorded Bks., LLC.
—The Chimney Sweeper's Boy. 1999. per. (*0-671-03430-8*); 352p. pap. 14.95 (*0-671-03429-4*) Simon & Schuster. (Pocket).
—The Chimney Sweeper's Boy. 1999. 20.05 (*0-606-19048-1*) Turtleback Bks.
—The Chimney Sweeper's Boy. 1998. 352p. text o.p. (*0-670-87927-4*, Viking) Viking Penguin.
Vine, Barbara, pseud, contrib. by. The Chimney Sweeper's Boy. 1998. (*0-670-87937-1*) Viking Penguin.
Vreeland, Susan. Girl in Hyacinth Blue. 1999. 242p. 17.50 (*1-878448-90-0*); 150p. 17.50 o.p. MacMurray & Beck, Inc.
—Girl in Hyacinth Blue. 2000. (Illus.). 256p. pap. 13.00 (*0-14-029628-X*) Penguin Group (USA) Inc.
—Girl in Hyacinth Blue. l.t. ed. 2000. (Basic Ser.). 227p. 28.95 (*0-7862-2440-1*) Thorndike Pr.
—Girl in Hyacinth Blue. 2000. 17.05 (*0-606-20671-X*) Turtleback Bks.
Walker, Alice. By the Light of My Father's Smile. 1999. mass mkt. (*0-345-43455-2*, Ballantine Bks.); 256p. pap. 13.95 (*0-345-42606-1*) Ballantine Bks.
—By the Light of My Father's Smile. 1998. 222p. 22.95 o.s.i (*0-375-50152-5*) Random Hse., Inc.
—By the Light of My Father's Smile. 1999. (Illus.). 20.00 (*0-606-17985-2*) Turtleback Bks.
Wall, Kathryn R. Perdition House: A Bay Tanner Mystery. 2003. 368p. 24.95 (*0-312-31385-3*, Saint Martin's Minotaur) St. Martin's Pr.
Wallace, John. Little Bean. 1996. (Illus.). 24p. (J). (ps-k). 10.95 o.p. (*0-694-00853-2*, Harper Festival) HarperCollins Children's Bk. Group.
Wallace, Rangeley. No Defense. 1997. 272p. mass mkt. 5.99 (*0-312-96169-3*, St. Martin's Paperbacks); 1995. 256p. 21.95 o.p. (*0-312-13571-8*) St. Martin's Pr.
Wardlaw, Lee. Don't Look Back. 1993. (Orig.). (J). pap. 3.50 (*0-380-76419-9*, Avon Bks.) Morrow/Avon.
Weller, Anthony. The Garden of the Peacocks. 1996. 288p. 22.95 o.p. (*1-56924-763-3*, Marlowe & Co.) Avalon Publishing Group.
Wendel, Tim. Castro's Curveball. 2000. 304p. pap. 12.95 (*0-345-43474-9*) Ballantine Bks.
—Castro's Curveball. 1999. audio 27.95 (*0-7861-1700-1*); 2000. audio compact disk 56.00 (*0-7861-9938-5*, z2383); 1999. audio 44.95 (*0-7861-1553-X*, 2383) Blackstone Audio Bks., Inc.
Wendt, Albert. Ola. 1995. 352p. pap. 16.95 (*0-8248-1585-8*) Univ. of Hawaii Pr.
Wenner, Kate. Setting Fires. 2001. 352p. reprint ed. pap. 13.00 (*0-425-18210-X*) Berkley Publishing Group.
—Setting Fires. 2000. 304p. 24.00 o.s.i (*0-684-83748-X*, Scribner) Simon & Schuster.
Westall, Robert. A Place to Hide. 1994. 208p. (YA). (gr. 5 up). 13.95 (*0-590-47748-X*) Scholastic, Inc.
Whalen, Clara W. Rowhani. 1995. 240p. 20.95 o.p. (*1-56167-234-3*) Noble Hse.
Whitehouse, Melissa. The Care & Training of Parents. 1995. 64p. (J). pap. 6.00 (*1-56002-499-2*, University Editions) Aegina Pr., Inc.
Wick, Lori. A Song for Silas. 204p. 1996. (Place Called Home Ser.: Vol. 2). pap. 8.99 (*1-56507-589-7*); 1990. pap. 6.99 o.s.i (*0-89081-839-8*) Harvest Hse. Pubs.
—A Song for Silas. l.t. ed. 2000. (Christian Romance Ser.). (Illus.). 270p. 25.95 (*0-7862-2728-1*) Thorndike Pr.
Wieland, Liza. Bombshell. 2001. 272p. 19.95 (*0-87074-462-3*) Southern Methodist Univ. Pr.
Wiggins, VeraLee. LeeAnne, the Disposable Kid. 1994. (J). (gr. 7-10). pap. 5.99 o.p. (*0-8280-0791-8*) Review & Herald Publishing Assn.
Wiggs, Susan. The You I Never Knew. l.t. ed. 2001. 667p. 29.95 (*0-7862-3448-2*) Thorndike Pr.
—The You I Never Knew. 2001. 528p. reprint ed. mass mkt. 6.99 (*0-446-60872-6*) Warner Bks., Inc.
Wilensky, Amy S. 24/7. 1997. (Love Stories Ser.). 192p. (YA). (gr. 7-12). mass mkt. 4.50 o.s.i (*0-553-57074-9*, Dell Books for Young Readers) Random Hse. Children's Bks.
Wilentz, Amy. Martyrs' Crossing. 2001. 320p. 24.00 (*0-684-85436-8*, Simon & Schuster) Simon & Schuster.
Wilhelm, Kate. The Deepest Water. 2000. 279p. 23.95 o.p. (*0-312-26143-8*, Saint Martin's Minotaur) St. Martin's Pr.
Williams, Carol Lynch. Sarah's Quest. 1995. (Latter-Day Daughters Ser.). (J). pap. 4.95 (*1-56236-504-5*) Aspen Bks.
Williams, Joy. State of Grace. 1990. pap. 12.00 (*0-679-72619-5*, Vintage) Knopf Publishing Group.
Wimmer, Dick. The Irish Wine Trilogy. 2001. 320p. 13.00 (*0-14-100059-7*) Viking Penguin.
Winter, Jenny. Coolcat Alley. 1997. (*0-7981-3675-8*) Human & Rousseau.
Wolfe, Elle. Lonely Heart. 1990. (YA). mass mkt. 1.79 (*0-8125-1004-6*, Tor Bks.) Doherty, Tom Assocs., LLC.
Wolitzer, Meg. The Dream Book. 1986. 160p. (J). (gr. 5 up). 11.95 o.p. (*0-688-05148-0*, Greenwillow Bks.) HarperCollins Children's Bk. Group.
—The Dream Book. 1987. 160p. (J). (gr. 3-7). pap. 2.50 (*0-380-70356-4*, Avon Bks.) Morrow/Avon.
Wolverton, Linda. Running Before the Wind. 1987. (J). (gr. 6 up). 13.95 o.p. (*0-395-42116-0*) Houghton Mifflin Co.
Wright, Barbara. Easy Money: A Novel. 1995. 402p. 18.95 o.p. (*0-945575-63-7*) Algonquin Bks. of Chapel Hill.
Wright, Ronald. Henderson's Spear: A Novel. 2002. 368p. 25.00 (*0-8050-6996-8*) Holt, Henry & Co.
Yamanaka, Lois-Ann. Father of the Four Passages. 2001. 288p. 23.00 (*0-374-15387-6*) Farrar, Straus & Giroux.
Yates, Dan. Angels to the Rescue. 1997. (J). pap. 11.95 (*1-57734-210-0*, 01113267) Covenant Communications, Inc.
Yezierska, Anzia. Bread Givers. 3rd ed. 2002. (Illus.). 336p. (C). pap. 8.95 (*0-89255-290-5*) Persea Bks., Inc.
—Bread Givers: A Struggle Between a Father of the Old World & a Daughter of the New World. 25th ed. 1975. 320p. (C). pap. 8.95 (*0-89255-014-7*) Persea Bks., Inc.
Yolen, Jane. All Those Secrets of the World. (J). (ps-3). 1993. 32p. pap. 5.95 o.p. (*0-316-96895-1*); 1991. 14.95 o.p. (*0-316-96891-9*) Little Brown & Co.
—All Those Secrets of the World. 1991. 12.10 (*0-606-05113-9*) Turtleback Bks.
—The Stone Silences. 1984. 128p. (J). (gr. 7 up). 10.95 o.s.i (*0-399-20971-9*, Philomel) Penguin Putnam Bks. for Young Readers.
Yorke, Margaret. Almost the Truth. 1995. 294p. mass mkt. o.s.i (*0-7515-1216-8*) Little Brown & Co.
—Almost the Truth. 1995. (Cloak & Dagger Ser.). 278p. 18.95 o.p. (*0-89296-582-7*) Mysterious Pr.
—Almost the Truth. 1996. 240p. mass mkt. 5.99 o.s.i (*0-446-40479-9*) Warner Bks., Inc.
Zach, Cheryl. Dear Diary No. 1: Runaway. 1995. (Archive Ser.). 240p. (Orig.). mass mkt. 4.50 o.s.i (*0-425-15047-X*) Berkley Publishing Group.
Zahava, Irene, ed. My Father's Daughter: Stories by Women. 1990. 275p. (Orig.). 20.95 o.p. (*0-89594-424-3*) Crossing Pr., Inc., The.
Zambreno, Mary Frances. Fire Bird. 2001. (Voyage of the Basset Ser.: Vol. 5). 192p. (J). (gr. 3-7). pap. 3.99 o.s.i (*0-375-81109-5*, Random Hse. Bks. for Young Readers) Random Hse. Children's Bks.
Zei, Alki. The Sound of the Dragon's Feet. Fenton, Edward, tr. 1979. (J). (gr. 5-7). 8.50 o.p. (*0-525-39712-4*, Dutton) Dutton/Plume.

### FATHERS AND SONS—FICTION

Abani, Chris. GraceLand. 2004. 336p. 24.00 (*0-374-16589-0*) Farrar, Straus & Giroux.
Alphin, Elaine Marie. Picture Perfect. 2003. (Illus.). 244p. (J). 15.95 (*0-8225-0535-5*, Carolrhoda Bks.) Lerner Publishing Group.
Amsden, David. Important Things That Don't Matter. 2004. 272p. pap. 12.95 (*0-06-051389-6*, Morrow, William & Co.) Morrow/Avon.
—Important Things That Don't Matter: A Novel. 2003. 272p. 24.95 (*0-06-051388-8*, Morrow, William & Co.) Morrow/Avon.
Anderson, Glenn L. The Doomsday Factor. 1987. 160p. 11.98 (*0-88290-319-5*) Horizon Pubs. & Distributors, Inc.
Anderson, Sherwood. Windy McPherson's Son. E-Book 3.95 (*0-594-06379-5*); 2000. 252p. pap. 9.95 (*0-594-06378-7*) 1873 Pr.
—Windy McPherson's Son. (Collected Works of Sherwood Anderson). 347p. reprint ed. 2001. (Illus.). pap. text 28.00 (*0-7426-5508-3*); 1998. lib. bdg. 98.00 (*1-58201-508-2*) Classic Bks.
—Windy McPherson's Son. 1965. (Chicago in Fiction Ser.). reprint ed. pap. 2.45 o.s.i (*0-226-01905-5*, P250) Univ. of Chicago Pr.
—Windy McPherson's Son. 1993. (Prairie State Bks.). 392p. pap. 17.95 (*0-252-06357-0*) Univ. of Illinois Pr.
Andreasen, Dan. With a Little Help from Daddy. 2002. (Illus.). 32p. (J). 15.95 (*0-689-84565-0*, McElderry, Margaret K.) Simon & Schuster Children's Publishing.
Anthony, Ronald. The Forever Year. 2003. 320p. 24.95 (*0-7653-0405-8*, Forge Bks.) Doherty, Tom Assocs., LLC.
Averill, Thomas Fox. The Slow Air of Ewan MacPherson. 2003. 272p. pap. 13.00 (*0-425-19081-1*, BlueHen Bks.) Putnam Publishing Group, The.
Baker, Keith. Inheritance. l.t. ed. 1998. (Ulverscroft Large Print Ser.). 608p. 29.99 (*0-7089-3890-6*, Ulverscroft) Thorpe, F. A. Pubs. GBR. *Dist:* Ulverscroft Large Print Bks., Ltd., Ulverscroft Large Print Canada, Ltd.
—Inheritance: A Novel. 1998. 288p. 24.00 (*0-688-15321-6*, Morrow, William & Co.) Morrow/Avon.
Barbieri, Elaine. The Wild One. 2001. (Secret Fires Ser.: Bk. 1). 400p. mass mkt. 5.99 (*0-8439-4826-4*, Leisure Bks.) Dorchester Publishing Co., Inc.
—The Wild One. l.t. ed. 2001. (Romance Ser.: Vol. 1). 393p. 28.95 o.p. (*0-7862-3592-6*) Thorndike Pr.
Barkley, Brad. Money Love. 2000. 320p. 24.95 (*0-393-04929-9*) Norton, W. W. & Co., Inc.
Bausch, Robert. On the Way Home. 2000. (Voices of the South Ser.). 224p. pap. 15.95 (*0-8071-2638-1*) Louisiana State Univ. Pr.
—On the Way Home. 1983. 240p. pap. 3.50 (*0-380-63131-8*, 63131-8, Avon Bks.) Morrow/Avon.
—On the Way Home. 1982. 260p. 13.95 o.p. (*0-312-58459-8*) St. Martin's Pr.
Becker, Geoffrey. Bluestown. pap. 15.95 (*0-312-30456-0*, Saint Martin's Griffin); 1997. pap. 11.95 o.p. (*0-312-15481-X*, Saint Martin's Griffin); 1996. 280p. 21.95 o.p. (*0-312-14223-4*) St. Martin's Pr.
Bell, Madison Smartt. Anything Goes: A Novel. 2002. 320p. 24.00 (*0-375-42125-4*, Pantheon) Knopf Publishing Group.
Bennett, Arnold. Clayhanger. 1976. (Fiction Ser.). 528p. pap. 5.95 o.p. (*0-14-000997-3*, Penguin Bks.) Viking Penguin.
Bergen, David. See the Child: A Novel. 2002. 240p. 23.00 (*0-7432-2925-8*, Simon & Schuster) Simon & Schuster.
Bergren, Lisa Tawn. The Bridge. 2002. 256p. pap. 9.99 (*1-57856-536-7*) Random Hse., Inc.
—The Bridge. 2000. 256p. 10.95 (*1-57856-272-4*) WaterBrook Pr.
Blackburn, Julia. The Book of Color. 1996. 192p. pap. 15.00 (*0-679-75837-2*) Random Hse., Inc.
Blair, Clarence. Compadre. 2001. 212p. pap. 19.95 (*0-7596-0802-4*) 1stBooks Library.
Bromell, Henry. Little America. 2001. E-Book 19.00 (*1-59061-173-X*) Adobe Systems, Inc.
—Little America. 2002. 416p. pap. 14.00 (*0-375-71891-5*, Vintage) Knopf Publishing Group.
Brook, Rhidian. The Testimony of Taliesin Jones. 2001. 208p. pap. 13.00 (*0-14-200157-0*) Penguin Group (USA) Inc.
Brossard, Chandler. The Bold Saboteurs. 4th ed. 2001. 362p. reprint ed. pap. 15.00 (*1-928746-18-7*) Herodias.
Brown, Larry. Father & Son. 1996. 360p. tchr. ed. 22.95 (*1-56512-014-0*) Algonquin Bks. of Chapel Hill.
—Father & Son. 1997. 352p. pap. 14.00 (*0-8050-5303-4*, Owl Bks.) Holt, Henry & Co.
—Father & Son. l.t. ed. 1998. (Niagara Large Print Ser.). 422p. 29.50 o.p. (*0-7089-5867-2*, Ulverscroft) Thorpe, F. A. Pubs. GBR. *Dist:* Ulverscroft Large Print Bks., Ltd., Ulverscroft Large Print Canada, Ltd.
Buckman, Daniel. Morning Dark. 2003. 224p. 22.95 (*0-312-31462-0*) St. Martin's Pr.
—The Names of Rivers. 2002. 197p. 21.00 (*1-888451-29-7*) Akashic Bks.
—The Names of Rivers. 2003. 208p. pap. 13.00 (*0-312-31460-4*) Picador.
—The Names of Rivers. Date not set. mass mkt. (*0-312-98981-4*, St. Martin's Paperbacks) St. Martin's Pr.
Buechner, Frederick. The Storm. 208p. 2002. pap. 13.95 (*0-06-061145-6*); 1998. 18.00 (*0-06-061144-8*) HarperSanFrancisco.
—The Storm. l.t. ed. 1999. (Inspirational Ser.). 223p. 25.95 (*0-7838-8605-5*) Thorndike Pr.
Cairns, Al. Nothing Sacred. 1998. 320p. mass mkt. 6.99 (*0-7704-2766-9*) Bantam Bks.
Cameron, Stella. Finding Ian. l.t. ed. 2001. 400p. 30.95 (*0-7838-9457-0*, Macmillan Reference USA) Gale Group.
—Finding Ian. 2002. 336p. mass mkt. 6.99 (*0-8217-7082-9*); 2001. 34p. 22.00 o.s.i (*1-57566-713-4*) Kensington Publishing Corp.
Campbell, Ramsey. Pact of the Fathers. 2003. 416p. mass mkt. 6.99 (*0-7653-4353-3*, Tor Bks.); 2001. 432p. 26.95 (*0-312-87869-9*, Forge Bks.) Doherty, Tom Assocs., LLC.
Carroll, James. Secret Father. l.t. ed. 2003. 626p. 29.95 (*0-7862-6051-3*) Gale Group.
—Secret Father. 2003. 352p. tchr. ed. 25.00 (*0-618-15284-9*) Houghton Mifflin Co.
Carter, Stephen L. The Emperor of Ocean Park: A Novel. 2003. 672p. reprint ed. pap. 14.00 (*0-375-71292-5*, Vintage) Knopf Publishing Group.
—The Emperor of Ocean Park: A Novel. 2002. 672p. 26.95 (*0-375-41363-4*) Knopf, Alfred A. Inc.
—The Emperor of Ocean Park: A Novel. l.t. ed. 2002. 1152p. 26.95 (*0-375-43165-9*) Random Hse. Large Print.
Cartwright, Gene. I Never Played Catch with My Father. Ortman, Lisa, ed. 3rd ed. 1996. 384p. 23.95 (*0-9649756-0-2*) Falcon Creek Publishing Co.
Cheatham, Tony M. Father's Footsteps. Morton, Randolph B. & Cadet, Guichard, eds. 2002. 300p. pap. 15.00 (*0-9718191-1-4*) La Caille Nous Publishing Co.
Childress, Mark. Gone for Good. 1999. (Ballantine Reader's Circle Ser.). 400p. pap. 12.95 (*0-345-41453-5*) Ballantine Bks.
Clancy, Tom. The Teeth of the Tiger. 2003. 448p. 27.95 (*0-399-15079-X*); 640p. 150.00 (*0-399-15136-2*) Putnam Publishing Group, The.
Clarke, Brock. The Ordinary White Boy. 272p. text o.s.i (*0-15-100733-0*); 2002. pap. 13.00 (*0-15-602709-7*, Harvest Bks.); 2001. 24.00 o.s.i (*0-15-100810-8*, Harvest Bks.) Harcourt Trade Pubs.
Coburn, Walt. Law Rides the Range. 2002. 128p. 19.00 (*0-7540-8137-0*); 1991. pap. 6.95 o.p. (*1-55504-761-0*, 992) BBC Audiobooks America.
—Law Rides the Range. l.t. ed. 2002. 250p. pap. 24.95 (*0-7862-4062-8*) Gale Group.
—Law Rides the Range. l.t. ed. 1992. (Linford Western Library). 352p. pap. 17.99 (*0-7089-7245-4*, Linford) Thorpe, F. A. Pubs. GBR. *Dist:* Ulverscroft Large Print Bks., Ltd., Ulverscroft Large Print Canada, Ltd.
Collins, Max Allan. Road to Perdition. 2002. 256p. mass mkt. 6.99 (*0-451-41029-7*) Penguin Group (USA) Inc.
Collins, Michael. The Resurrectionists. 2002. 304p. 24.00 (*0-7432-2904-5*, Scribner) Simon & Schuster.
Collins, Wilkie. Armadale. 1999. (Works of Wilkie Collins: Vol. 8). reprint ed. Pt. 1. 579p. lib. bdg. 98.00 (*1-58201-029-3*); Pt. 2. 575p. lib. bdg. 98.00 (*1-58201-030-7*) Classic Bks.
—Armadale. 1977. (Illus.). 597p. pap. 9.95 o.p. (*0-486-23429-0*) Dover Pubns., Inc.
—Armadale. Peters, Catharine, ed. 1999. (Oxford World's Classics Ser.). 880p. pap. 12.95 (*0-19-283467-3*) Oxford Univ. Pr., Inc.
—Armadale. Peters, Catherine, ed. 1990. (Oxford World's Classics Ser.). (Illus.). 716p. pap. 11.95 o.p. (*0-19-281802-3*) Oxford Univ. Pr., Inc.
—Armadale, 2 vols., Set. 1988. reprint ed. lib. bdg. 150.00 (*0-7812-0752-5*) Reprint Services Corp.
—Armadale, 2 vols., Set. 1972. (Illus.). reprint ed. 69.00 (*0-403-00433-0*) Scholarly Pr., Inc.
—Armadale. Sutherland, John, ed. & intro. by. 1995. (Classics Ser.). 752p. 11.95 (*0-14-043411-9*, Penguin Classics) Viking Penguin.
Cook, Thomas. A Mortal Memory. 1994. 320p. mass mkt. 6.50 (*0-553-56532-X*) Bantam Bks.
Cook, Thomas H. Mortal Memory. l.t. ed. 1993. 89.95 o.p. incl. audio (*0-7862-9999-1*, Macmillan Reference USA) Gale Group.
Cookson, Catherine. The Upstart. unabr. ed. 1997. 11p. audio 89.95 o.p. (*1-86042-137-7*) Beeler, Thomas T. Publisher.
Covington, Vicki. Night Ride Home: A Novel. 2001. (Literature & the Religious Spirit Ser.: Vol. 2). ix, 242p. pap. 11.95 (*0-918954-78-9*) Baylor Univ. Pr.
Coyne, Tom. A Gentleman's Game. l.t. ed. 2001. 352p. 25.00 (*0-06-620996-X*, HarperLargePrint) HarperTrade.
—A Gentleman's Game: A Novel. 2001. 224p. 24.00 o.p. (*0-87113-791-7*, Atlantic Monthly Pr.); 2002. 272p. reprint ed. pap. 13.00 (*0-8021-3890-X*, Grove Pr.) Grove/Atlantic, Inc.
—A Gentleman's Game: A Novel. unabr. ed. 2001. audio 34.95 (*0-694-52522-7*, H227, HarperAudio) HarperTrade.
Crews, Harry. All We Need of Hell: A Novel. 1988. 162p. reprint ed. pap. 6.95 o.p. (*0-06-091460-2*, PL-1460, Perennial) HarperTrade.
Crummey, Michael. River Thieves: A Novel. 2002. 432p. pap. (*0-385-65817-6*, Anchor Canada) Doubleday Canada, Ltd. CAN. *Dist:* Random Hse., Inc.
—River Thieves: A Novel. 2002. (Illus.). 352p. 24.00 (*0-618-14531-1*) Houghton Mifflin Co.
—River Thieves: A Novel. 2003. 352p. pap. 13.00 (*0-618-34071-8*, Mariner Bks.) Houghton Mifflin Co. Trade & Reference Div.
D'Angelo, Edward. The Lies That Bind. 2001. 336p. 24.00 (*0-688-17493-0*, Morrow, William & Co.) Morrow/Avon.
Deb, Siddartha. The Point of Return: A Novel. 2003. 320p. 24.95 (*0-06-050151-0*, Ecco) HarperTrade.
Deb, Siddhartha. The Point of Return. 2004. 320p. pap. 13.95 (*0-06-050153-7*) HarperTrade.
Delffs, Dudley J. Forgiving August. 1993. 254p. (Orig.). pap. 10.00 o.p. (*0-89109-747-3*) Pinon Pr.
Demogorgon. 2004. pap. (*0-7653-0662-X*, Forge Bks.) Doherty, Tom Assocs., LLC.
Dohrmann, Bernhard. Diamond Heart: My Father's Stories: an Adult Fairy Tale. 1997. (*1-890465-40-2*) LSA Publishing.

Relationships

Doig, Ivan. Mountain Time, abr. ed. 1999. 25.00 incl. audio (*0-7871-2016-2*, Dove Audio) NewStar Media, Inc.

—Mountain Time. 320p. 2000. pap. 13.00 (*0-684-86569-6*); 1999. 25.00 o.s.i (*0-684-83295-X*) Simon & Schuster. (Scribner).

—Mountain Time. l.t. ed. 1999. (Americana Ser.). 487p. 29.95 (*0-7862-2216-6*) Thorndike Pr.

Dorfman, Ariel. The Nanny & the Iceberg. 1999. 353p. 25.00 o.p. (*0-374-21898-6*) Farrar, Straus & Giroux.

—The Nanny & the Iceberg. 2003. 272p. 14.95 (*1-58322-567-6*) Seven Stories Pr.

Doster, Stephen. Lord Baltimore. 2002. (Salem Selections Ser.). 360p. 22.95 (*0-89587-264-1*) Blair, John F. Pub.

Dostoyevsky, Fyodor. The Brothers Karamazov. 1966. (Airmont Classics Ser.). (C). (gr. 11 up). mass mkt. 3.95 o.p. (*0-8049-0128-7*, CL-128) Airmont Publishing Co., Inc.

—The Brothers Karamazov. 1976. 38.95 (*0-8488-0797-9*) Amereon, Ltd.

—The Brothers Karamazov. MacAndrew, Andrew R., tr. 1984. (Bantam Classics Ser.). 1072p. reprint ed. mass mkt. 7.99 (*0-553-21216-8*) Bantam Dell Publishing Group.

—The Brothers Karamazov. unabr. ed. 1999. (World Classic Literature Ser.). (RUS.). pap. 10.95 (*2-87714-268-X*) Bookking International FRA. *Dist:* Distribooks, Inc.

—The Brothers Karamazov. 1983. 595p. reprint ed. lib. bdg. 45.95 (*0-89966-315-X*) Buccaneer Bks., Inc.

—The Brothers Karamazov. Van der Eng, Jan & Meijer, Jan M., eds. 1971. text (*90-279-1758-2*) De Gruyter, Walter Inc.

—The Brothers Karamazov. Pevear, Richard & Volokhonsky, Larissa, trs. from RUS. 2002. 816p. pap. 17.00 (*0-374-52837-3*) Farrar, Straus & Giroux.

—The Brothers Karamazov. Volokhonsky, Larissa & Pevear, Richard, trs. 1991. (Vintage Bks.). 832p. pap. 17.00 o.s.i (*0-679-72925-9*, Vintage) Knopf Publishing Group.

—The Brothers Karamazov, Vol. 722. 1955. (Russian Library). pap. 5.95 o.p. (*0-394-70722-2*, V722, Vintage) Knopf Publishing Group.

—The Brothers Karamazov. Pevear, Richard & Volokhonsky, Larissa, trs. 1992. (Everyman's Library: Vol. 70). 848p. 20.00 (*0-679-41003-1*) Knopf, Alfred A. Inc.

—The Brothers Karamazov. Garnett, Constance, tr. 1950. (Modern Library College Editions Ser.). 940p. (C). pap. 11.25 (*0-07-553575-0*, T12, McGraw-Hill Humanities, Social Sciences & World Languages) McGraw-Hill Higher Education.

—The Brothers Karamazov. mass mkt. 0.75 o.p. (*0-451-01488-X*, Signet Bks.) NAL.

—The Brothers Karamazov. Komroff, Manuel, ed. Garnett, Constance, tr. from RUS. 1999. (Signet Classics). 752p. mass mkt. 8.95 (*0-451-52734-8*, Signet Bks.) NAL.

—The Brothers Karamazov. 1986. mass mkt. 3.50 o.p. (*0-451-52090-4*); mass mkt. 3.95 o.p. (*0-451-52243-5*) NAL. (Signet Classics).

—The Brothers Karamazov. Komroff-Hill, Manuel, ed. 1986. 704p. mass mkt. 7.95 o.s.i (*0-451-52388-1*, CE1464, Signet Classics) NAL.

—The Brothers Karamazov. 1971. mass mkt. 0.75 o.p. (*0-451-50033-4*); 1971. mass mkt. 0.95 o.p. (*0-451-50490-9*); 1958. mass mkt. 1.25 o.p. (*0-451-50665-0*); 1958. mass mkt. 1.50 o.p. (*0-451-50915-3*); 1958. mass mkt. 1.95 o.p. (*0-451-51154-9*); 1958. mass mkt. 2.50 o.p. (*0-451-51336-3*); 1958. mass mkt. 2.75 o.p. (*0-451-51464-5*) NAL. (Signet Classics).

—The Brothers Karamazov. 2002. (C). pap. text 38.75 (*0-393-94168-X*) Norton, W. W. & Co., Inc.

—The Brothers Karamazov. Matlaw, Ralph E., ed. 1976. (Critical Editions Ser.). 1000p. (C). o.p. (*0-393-04426-2*); pap. text 13.00 (*0-393-09214-3*) Norton, W. W. & Co., Inc.

—The Brothers Karamazov. Avsey, Ignat, tr. from RUS. 1994. (Oxford World's Classics Ser.). (Illus.). 1,050p. pap. 8.95 o.p. (*0-19-282664-6*) Oxford Univ. Pr., Inc.

—The Brothers Karamazov. 2nd ed. text, stu. ed. (*0-13-716879-9*) Prentice Hall (Schl. Div.).

—The Brothers Karamazov. annuals 1996. (Modern Library Ser.). 912p. 21.00 (*0-679-60181-3*) Random Hse., Inc.

—The Brothers Karamazov. Garnett, Constance, tr. 1977. 822p. 17.00 o.s.i (*0-394-60415-6*) Random Hse., Inc.

—The Brothers Karamazov. 1970. 13.00 (*0-606-02916-8*) Turtleback Bks.

—The Brothers Karamazov. Carey, John, ed. 2003. (Classics Ser.). 960p. pap. 14.00 (*0-14-044924-8*, Penguin Classics) Viking Penguin.

—The Brothers Karamazov. McDuff, David, tr. & intro. by. 1993. (Penguin Classics Ser.). 960p. 14.00 (*0-14-044527-7*, Penguin Classics) Viking Penguin.

—The Brothers Karamazov. 1982. (Penguin Classics Ser.). 944p. pap. 6.95 o.p. (*0-14-044416-5*, Penguin Classics) Viking Penguin.

—The Brothers Karamazov, 2 vols. Magarshack, David, tr. 1958. (Penguin Classics Ser.). 1. 408p. pap. 3.50 o.p. (*0-14-044078-X*); 2. 544p. pap. 4.95 o.p. (*0-14-044079-8*) Viking Penguin. (Penguin Bks.).

—The Brothers Karamazov: A Dramatization. 1995. per. 6.50 (*0-8222-1425-3*) Dramatists Play Service, Inc.

—The Brothers Karamazov: A Novel in Four Parts with Epilogue. Pevear, Richard & Volokhonsky, Larissa, trs. from RUS. 1990. 832p. 40.00 o.s.i (*0-86547-422-2*, North Point Pr.) Farrar, Straus & Giroux.

Ducker, Bruce. Lead Us Not into Penn Station. 1994. 224p. 24.00 (*1-877946-36-2*) Permanent Pr., The.

—Lead Us Not into Penn Station. 1994. 172p. per. 15.95 (*0-7592-4164-3*) ereads.com.

Dyja, Tom. Meet John Trow. 2002. (Illus.). 336p. 24.95 (*0-670-03099-6*, Viking) Viking Penguin.

Ellis, Ron. Cogan's Woods. 2001. 166p. 19.95 (*0-87108-915-7*) Pruett Publishing Co.

Enger, Leif. Peace Like a River. l.t. ed. 2002. (Wheeler Large Print Book Ser.). 28.95 (*1-58724-212-5*, Wheeler Publishing, Inc.) Gale Group.

—Peace Like a River. 320p. 2002. pap. 13.00 (*0-8021-3925-6*, Grove Pr.); 2001. 24.00 (*0-87113-795-X*, Atlantic Monthly Pr.) Grove/Atlantic, Inc.

Estleman, Loren D. Thunder City: A Novel of Detroit. 2001. 245p. mass mkt. 6.99 (*0-8125-4538-9*); 1999. 256p. 22.95 (*0-312-86369-1*) Doherty, Tom Assocs., LLC. (Forge Bks.).

—Thunder City: A Novel of Detroit. l.t. ed. 2000. (G. K. Hall Core Ser.). 327p. 28.95 (*0-7838-9030-3*, Macmillan Reference USA) Gale Group.

Evans, Shirlee. Winds of Promise. l.t. ed. 1999. (Inspirational Ser.). 163p. 25.95 (*0-7838-8673-X*, Macmillan Reference USA) Gale Group.

—Winds of Promise. 1990. 224p. pap. 7.99 (*0-8361-3506-7*) Herald Pr.

Faulkner, William. The Unvanquished. (Vintage International Ser.). 1991. 272p. pap. 12.95 (*0-679-73652-2*); Vol. 351. 1966. (Illus.). pap. 8.00 o.p. (*0-394-70351-0*, V351) Knopf Publishing Group. (Vintage).

Fergusson, Bruce C. The Piper's Sons. 1999. 352p. 24.95 o.p. (*0-525-94431-1*) Dutton/Plume.

—The Piper's Sons. 1999. 432p. reprint ed. mass mkt. 6.99 o.s.i (*0-451-40875-6*, Signet Bks.) NAL.

Figueredo, D. H. Un Mundo Nuevo. 2000. (SPA.). 13.10 (*0-606-19833-4*); 13.10 (*0-606-19834-2*) Turtleback Bks.

Ford, Richard. Independence Day. 1996. 464p. pap. 14.00 (*0-679-73518-6*, Vintage) Knopf Publishing Group.

—Independence Day. 1995. 464p. 29.95 (*0-679-49265-8*) Knopf, Alfred A. Inc.

—Independence Day. deluxe ltd. num. ed. 1995. 451p. 125.00 (*0-9631925-2-3*) Trice, B.E. Publishing.

Fortune, Lawrence. Beyond the Silence. 2001. 50p. pap. 9.95 (*1-57197-242-0*) Pentland Pr., Inc.

Freeborn, Richard & Turgenev, Ivan. Fathers & Sons. 1998. E-Book 9.40 (*0-585-35312-3*) netLibrary, Inc.

Freedman, J. F. Fallen Idols. 2003. 432p. 19.95 (*0-446-53189-8*) Warner Bks., Inc.

Friel, Brian. Fathers & Sons. 1988. 104p. pap. 7.95 o.p. (*0-571-15079-9*) Faber & Faber, Inc.

Fuqua, Jonathon Scott. The Re-Appearance of Sam Webber. 1999. 240p. 23.95 (*1-890862-02-9*) Bancroft Pr.

Gaines, Ernest J. In My Father's House. l.t. ed. 1993. 12.50 o.p. (*0-8161-6648-X*, Macmillan Reference USA) Gale Group.

—In My Father's House. 1978. 13.95 o.s.i (*0-394-47938-6*) Knopf, Alfred A. Inc.

—In My Father's House. 1983. 224p. reprint ed. pap. 6.95 o.p. (*0-393-30124-9*) Norton, W. W. & Co., Inc.

—In My Father's House. 1992. (Vintage Contemporaries Ser.). 224p. pap. 11.95 (*0-679-72791-4*) Random Hse., Inc.

Gantos, Jack. Joey Pigza Loses Control. RS. 2000. (J). E-Book 4.95 (*0-374-70039-7*); (J). E-Book 4.95 (*0-374-70040-0*); E-Book 4.95 o.p. (*0-374-70041-9*); 208p. (J). (gr. 4-7). 16.00 (*0-374-39989-1*) Farrar, Straus & Giroux. (Farrar, Straus & Giroux (BYR)).

—Joey Pigza Loses Control. abr. unabr. ed. 2000. audio 22.00 (*0-8072-6161-0*); (J). (gr. 4-8). audio 30.00 (*0-8072-8725-3*); (J). (gr. 5 up). audio 30.00 (*0-8072-8728-8*, YA248CX) Random Hse. Audio Publishing Group. (Listening Library).

Gaston, Bill. The Good Body. 2000. ix, 166p. (*1-896951-21-X*) Cormorant Bks.

—The Good Body. 288p. 2002. pap. 13.95 (*0-06-098887-8*); 2001. 25.00 (*0-06-039411-0*) HarperTrade. (ReganBooks).

Gautreau, Norman G. Sea Room. 314p. 2003. pap. 12.50 (*1-931561-38-9*); 2002. pap. 25.00 (*1-931561-07-9*) MacAdam/Cage Publishing, Inc.

Gerrold, David. The Martian Child. 2002. 192p. 21.95 (*0-7653-0311-6*, Forge Bks.) Doherty, Tom Assocs., LLC.

—The Martian Child: A Novel about a Single Father Adopting a Son. 2003. 192p. reprint ed. pap. 12.95 (*0-7653-0602-6*, Tor Bks.) Doherty, Tom Assocs., LLC.

Gill, Judy. Catherine's Image. l.t. ed. 2003. 234p. 24.95 (*0-7862-5079-8*) Thorndike Pr.

Gitlin, Todd. Sacrifice: A Novel. 1999. 256p. 23.00 o.s.i (*0-8050-6032-4*, Metropolitan Bks.) Holt, Henry & Co.

Glass, Julia. Three Junes: A Novel. l.t. ed. 2003. (Romance Ser.). 28.95 (*1-58724-379-2*, Wheeler Publishing, Inc.) Gale Group.

—Three Junes: A Novel. 368p. 2002. 25.00 (*0-375-42144-0*, Pantheon); 2003. reprint ed. pap. 14.00 (*0-385-72142-0*, Anchor) Knopf Publishing Group.

—Three Junes: A Novel. 2002. 368p. 25.00 (*0-375-42241-2*) Knopf, Alfred A. Inc.

Goddard, Robert. Out of the Sun. 1997. 410p. mass mkt. (*0-552-14224-7*); 1996. 333p. o.s.i (*0-593-03614-X*) Bantam Bks. (Corgi).

—Out of the Sun. 352p. 1998. pap. 13.00 o.s.i (*0-8050-5836-2*, Owl Bks.); 1997. 25.00 o.s.i (*0-8050-5109-0*) Holt, Henry & Co.

—Out of the Sun. l.t. ed. 1997. (Charnwood Large Print Ser.). 496p. 29.99 o.p. (*0-7089-8967-5*, Ulverscroft) Thorpe, F. A. Pubs. GBR. *Dist:* Ulverscroft Large Print Bks., Ltd., Ulverscroft Large Print Canada, Ltd.

Golding, Michael. Benjamin's Gift. 2001. 320p. E-Book 9.95 (*0-446-92330-3*) Time Warner Bk. Group.

—Benjamin's Gift. 2001. 320p. E-Book 9.95 (*0-446-92060-6*); 2001. 320p. E-Book 9.95 (*0-7595-9138-5*); 2001. 320p. E-Book 9.95 (*0-446-96042-X*); 2000. 320p. pap. 12.95 (*0-446-67571-7*); 1999. E-Book 9.95 (*0-446-91302-2*); 1999. 320p. 25.00 (*0-446-52110-8*) Warner Bks., Inc.

Gordimer, Nadine. The House Gun. 1998. 294p. 24.00 (*0-374-17307-9*) Farrar, Straus & Giroux.

—The House Gun. l.t. ed. 1998. 26.95 o.p. (*1-56895-615-0*, Wheeler Publishing, Inc.) Gale Group.

—The House Gun. 1999. 304p. 14.00 (*0-14-027820-6*) Viking Penguin.

Gornick, Lisa. A Private Sorcery. 2002. 384p. tchr. ed. 23.95 (*1-56512-341-7*) Algonquin Bks. of Chapel Hill.

Green, Tim. The Fourth Perimeter. l.t. ed. 2002. 413p. 31.95 (*0-7862-3880-1*) Gale Group.

—The Fourth Perimeter. l.t. ed. 2003. 469p. 13.95 (*0-7862-3881-X*) Thorndike Pr.

—The Fourth Perimeter. abr. ed. 2002. audio 24.98 (*1-58621-207-9*) Time Warner AudioBooks.

—The Fourth Perimeter. 2003. 400p. mass mkt. 6.99 (*0-446-61251-0*); 2002. 352p. 24.95 o.p. (*0-446-52785-8*) Warner Bks., Inc.

Greene, A. C. They Are Ruining Ibiza: A Novella. 1998. 123p. 21.95 (*1-57441-042-3*) Univ. of North Texas Pr.

Gregory, Kay. His Father's Wife. l.t. ed. 2001. (G.K. Hall Large Print Romance Ser.). 385p. 26.95 (*0-7838-9631-X*, Hall, G. K. & Co.) Gale Group.

—His Father's Wife. 1997. (Scarlet Ser.). 400p. mass mkt. 3.99 (*1-85487-959-6*) Scarlet Bks. GBR. *Dist:* London Bridge.

Groom, Winston. Gump & Co. l.t. ed. 1996. (Wheeler Large Print Bks.). pap. 24.95 (*1-56895-293-7*, Wheeler Publishing, Inc.) Gale Group.

—Gump & Co. 1996. 256p. mass mkt. 6.99 (*0-671-52264-7*, Pocket); 1995. 256p. 22.00 o.p. (*0-671-52170-5*, Atria); 1995. per. 6.99 (*0-671-56307-6*, Pocket) Simon & Schuster.

—Gump & Co., Set. abr. ed. 1995. 18.00 incl. audio (*0-671-53680-X*, 393274, Simon & Schuster Audioworks) Simon & Schuster Audio.

—Gump & Co. 1997. 1.98 o.p. (*0-7651-0699-X*) Smithmark Pubs., Inc.

Gross, Gwendolen. Field Guide. 2002. (Illus.). 288p. reprint ed. pap. 14.00 (*0-15-600766-5*, Harvest Bks.) Harcourt Trade Pubs.

—Field Guide: A Novel. 2001. (Harvest Book Ser.). (Illus.). 275p. 23.00 o.s.i (*0-8050-6492-3*) Holt, Henry & Co.

Hamill, Pete. The Gift. 1974. mass mkt. 1.50 o.p. (*0-345-24276-9*) Ballantine Bks.

—The Gift. 1979. 111p. pap. 1.95 o.p. (*0-553-13541-4*) Bantam Bks.

—The Gift. 1973. 4.95 o.p. (*0-394-47338-8*) Random Hse., Inc.

Hansen, Ron. Atticus. 256p. 1997. pap. 13.00 (*0-06-092786-0*, Perennial); 1996. 22.00 o.p. (*0-06-018217-2*) HarperTrade.

—Atticus. unabr. ed. 1997. audio 44.00 (*0-7887-0943-7*, 95076E7) Recorded Bks., LLC.

Harmon, A. G. A House All Stilled: A Novel. 2002. 248p. 29.95 (*1-57233-202-6*) Univ. of Tennessee Pr.

Harrison, William. The Blood Latitudes. 2000. 280p. 25.00 (*1-878448-97-8*) MacMurray & Beck, Inc.

Hatcher, Robin Lee. The Shepherd's Voice: A Novel. 2003. 289p. 25.95 (*0-7862-4936-6*, Five Star) Gale Group.

Hauptman, William. Storm Season. 2001. (Southwestern Writers Collection). (Illus.). 318p. (C). pap. 21.95 (*0-292-73453-0*) Univ. of Texas Pr.

—The Storm Season. 1993. 336p. mass mkt. 5.99 o.s.i (*0-553-56386-6*) Bantam Bks.

Hauser, Marianne. Shootout with Father. 2002. 100p. pap. 11.95 (*1-57366-100-7*) Fiction Collective Two, Inc.

Hazelgrove, William E. Tobacco Sticks. 1997. 352p. reprint ed. mass mkt. 5.99 o.s.i (*0-553-57559-7*) Bantam Bks.

—Tobacco Sticks. 1995. 308p. 18.95 (*0-9630052-8-6*) Pantonne Pr., Inc.

Hedges, Peter. An Ocean in Iowa: A Novel. 1998. 248p. (J). 22.95 (*0-7868-6404-4*) Hyperion Pr.

—An Ocean in Iowa: A Novel. 1999. 256p. pap. 11.00 (*0-684-85970-X*, Touchstone) Simon & Schuster.

Hijuelos, Oscar. Mr. Ives' Christmas. 1996. 256p. pap. 78.00 o.p. (*0-06-092774-7*); 1995. 272p. 19.00 o.p. (*0-06-017131-6*) HarperCollins Pubs.

—Mr. Ives' Christmas. 1996. 256p. pap. 13.95 (*0-06-092754-2*, Perennial) HarperTrade.

Holwitz, Peter. Stick Kid. 2004. 40p. (J). 13.99 (*0-399-24163-9*, Philomel) Penguin Putnam Bks. for Young Readers.

Hosseini, Khaled. The Kite Runner. 2004. 384p. pap. 14.00 (*1-59448-000-1*, Riverhead Trade (Paperbacks)) Berkley Publishing Group.

Hunter, Travis E. The Hearts of Men: A Novel. 2001. 288p. pap. 13.95 (*0-375-75709-0*, Villard Bks.) Random House Adult Trade Publishing Group.

Huntington, Geoffrey. Sorcerers of the Nightwing. 2002. (Ravenscliff Ser.: Bk. 1). (Illus.). 288p. 17.95 (*0-06-001425-3*, ReganBooks) HarperTrade.

Jackson, Brian Keith. Walking Through Mirrors. 1999. 272p. pap. 14.00 (*0-671-56894-9*, Washington Square Pr.); 1998. 258p. 23.00 (*0-671-56893-0*, Atria) Simon & Schuster.

—Walking Through Mirrors. 1999. 20.05 (*0-606-19129-1*) Turtleback Bks.

James, Peter. Prophecy. 1994. 288p. 20.95 o.p. (*0-312-10526-6*) St. Martin's Pr.

Johnson, R. M. Father Found. 2000. 384p. 23.00 (*0-684-84471-0*); 2001. 400p. reprint ed. pap. 13.95 (*0-7434-1246-X*) Simon & Schuster. (Simon & Schuster).

—The Harris Men. 336p. 1999. 23.00 o.s.i (*0-684-84470-2*); 2000. reprint ed. pap. 12.95 (*0-7434-0059-3*) Simon & Schuster. (Simon & Schuster).

Johnson, Wayne. The Devil You Know: A Novel. 2004. 400p. 23.00 (*0-609-60964-5*) Crown Publishing Group.

Jordan, Neil. Nightlines. 1995. 192p. 21.00 (*0-679-44438-6*) Random Hse., Inc.

Joyce, Graham. Indigo. 272p. 2001. pap. 14.00 (*0-671-03938-5*, Washington Square Pr.); 2000. 23.95 (*0-671-03937-7*, Atria) Simon & Schuster.

Judd, Alan. Legacy. 2003. 256p. 24.00 (*0-375-41484-3*) Knopf, Alfred A. Inc.

Kafka-Gibbons, Paul. Dupont Circle: A Novel. 2001. 256p. tchr. ed. 24.00 (*0-395-86932-3*) Houghton Mifflin Co.

—Dupont Circle: A Novel. 2002. 256p. pap. 13.00 (*0-618-21918-8*, Mariner Bks.) Houghton Mifflin Co. Trade & Reference Div.

Keating, H. R. F. The Soft Detective. 1998. 272p. 22.95 o.p. (*0-312-19335-1*, Saint Martin's Minotaur) St. Martin's Pr.

—The Soft Detective. l.t. ed. 1998. (Mystery Ser.). 343p. 26.95 (*0-7862-1565-8*) Thorndike Pr.

Kimball, Michael. Green Girls: A Novel of Suspense. 2002. 384p. 24.95 (*0-06-008737-4*, Morrow, William & Co.) Morrow/Avon.

King, Jonathon. Shadow Men. unabr. ed. 2004. (Max Freeman Ser.). audio 27.95 (*1-59355-306-4*, 4918, Brilliance Audio Unabridged); audio 69.25 (*1-59355-307-2*, 4919, Brilliance Audio Unabridged Lib Ed); audio compact disk 29.95 (*1-59355-308-0*, 4920, Brilliance Audio on CD Unabridged); audio compact disk 82.25 (*1-59355-309-9*, 4921, Brilliance Audio on CD Unabridged Lib Ed) Brilliance Audio.

—Shadow Men. 2004. 288p. 23.95 (*0-525-94807-4*, Dutton) Dutton/Plume.

Kokoros, Jim. The Rich Part of Life. 2001. 327p. 24.95 (*0-312-27479-3*) St. Martin's Pr.

Koss, Amy Goldman. A Stranger in Dadland. Hornik, Lauri, ed. 2001. (Illus.). 128p. (J). (gr. 5 up). 16.99 (*0-8037-2563-9*, Dial Bks. for Young Readers) Penguin Putnam Bks. for Young Readers.

Kowalski, William. Eddie's Bastard: A Novel. 1999. viii, 367p. 24.00 (*0-06-019355-7*) HarperCollins Pubs.

—Eddie's Bastard: A Novel. 2000. 384p. pap. 14.00 (*0-06-109825-6*, Perennial) HarperTrade.

Kroll, Morton. Old Caper, Youngblood. 292p. E-Book 5.00 (*1-929939-05-1*) PublishingOnline.

LaBate, Jim. Mickey Mantle Day in Amsterdam: Another Novella by Jim LaBate. 1999. (Illus.). 61p. (YA). (gr. 7-12). pap. 7.95 (*0-9662100-7-7*) Mohawk River Pr.

Lasser, Scott. Battle Creek: A Novel. 2000. 288p. pap. 14.00 (*0-688-17763-8*, Perennial) HarperTrade.

—Battle Creek: A Novel. 1999. 265p. 24.00 o.p. (*0-688-16785-3*, Morrow, William & Co.) Morrow/Avon.

Lawlor, Laurie. Old Crump: The True Story of a Trip West. 2002. (Illus.). 32p. (J). (gr. 2-4). tchr. ed. 16.95 (*0-8234-1608-9*) Holiday Hse., Inc.

Le Carré, John. Single & Single. l.t. ed. (Wheeler Press Paperback Ser.). 2000. 11.95 (*1-56895-969-9*); 1999. 28.95 (*1-56895-748-3*) Gale Group. (Wheeler Publishing, Inc.).

—Single & Single. 1999. (SPA.). 352p. (*84-01-01220-1*) Plaza & Janés Editories, S.A.

—Single & Single. 2000. (SPA.). pap. 13.95 (*84-01-01350-X*) Plaza & Janés Editories, S.A. ESP. *Dist:* Distribooks, Inc.

—Single & Single. 1999. 352p. 26.00 o.s.i (*0-684-86305-7*, Scribner); 1999. (Illus.). 352p. 26.00 o.s.i (*0-684-85926-2*, Scribner); 2003. 368p. reprint ed. pap. 14.00 (*0-7434-5806-0*, Scribner); 2000. 400p. reprint ed. mass mkt. 7.99 (*0-671-02797-2*, Pocket) Simon & Schuster.

Lees, Stuart. The Lucky Sovereign. 2002. (Illus.). (J). (gr. 3-5). 15.95 (*1-57091-488-5*, Talewinds) Charlesbridge Publishing, Inc.

Lees, Stuart, illus. The Lucky Sovereign. 2002. (J). pap. (*1-57091-489-3*, Talewinds) Charlesbridge Publishing, Inc.

Leighton, Lee. Beyond the Pass. 1997. 155p. 17.50 (*0-7451-4700-3*, Gunsmoke) BBC Audiobooks America.

—Beyond the Pass. 1982. mass mkt. 1.95 o.s.i (*0-345-29219-7*) Ballantine Bks.

—Beyond the Pass. l.t. ed. 2000. 255p. (*0-7540-4307-X*); (*0-7540-4308-8*) Gale Group. (Macmillan Reference USA).

—Beyond the Pass. l.t. ed. 2000. (Nightingale Ser.). 255p. 20.95 (*0-7838-9177-6*) Thorndike Pr.

Lennon, J. Robert. The Funnies. 2000. (Illus.). 336p. 13.00 (*1-57322-781-1*, Riverhead Trade (Paperbacks)) Berkley Publishing Group.

—The Funnies. 1999. 320p. 23.95 o.s.i (*1-57322-126-0*, Riverhead Bks. (Hardcovers)) Putnam Publishing Group, The.

Lerman, Rhoda. God's Ear: A Novel. 1988. 320p. 19.95 o.s.i (*0-8050-0413-0*) Holt, Henry & Co.

—God's Ear: A Novel. 1996. (Library of Modern Jewish Literature). 309p. reprint ed. pap. 17.95 (*0-8156-0427-0*, LEGEP) Syracuse Univ. Pr.

Lewis, Jim. The King Is Dead: A Novel. 2003. 272p. 24.00 (*0-375-41417-7*) Knopf, Alfred A. Inc.

Lindsay, James. Brutal Music: A Novel. 2002. 22.50 (*0-87074-471-2*) Southern Methodist Univ. Pr.

London, Jonathan. Froggy Bakes a Cake. 2000. (Reading Railroad Bks.). (Illus.). 32p. (J). (ps-3). mass mkt. 3.49 (*0-448-42153-4*, Grosset & Dunlap) Penguin Putnam Bks. for Young Readers.

—Froggy Bakes a Cake. 2000. (Illus.). (J). 9.64 (*0-606-21801-7*) Turtleback Bks.

Lupica, Mike. Wild Pitch. 2003. 352p. mass mkt. 7.99 (*0-425-19204-0*) Berkley Publishing Group.

—Wild Pitch. 2002. 352p. 24.95 (*0-399-14927-9*, Putnam & Grosset) Putnam Publishing Group, The.

Lysaght, Brian. Last Dance of the Viper. 2001. 464p. 27.95 (*0-7653-0062-1*, Forge Bks.) Doherty, Tom Assocs., LLC.

Maclean, Norman F. A River Runs Through It. 1979. 17.05 (*0-606-19234-4*) Turtleback Bks.

—A River Runs Through It. 1989. (Illus.). vi, 168p. 27.50 (*0-226-50060-8*) Univ. of Chicago Pr.

—A River Runs Through It & Other Stories. 1976. xviii, 422 p. (*0-8161-6398-7*); 1993. 310p. 16.95 o.p. (*0-8161-5735-9*) Gale Group. (Macmillan Reference USA).

—A River Runs Through It & Other Stories. abr. unabr. ed. 2000. audio 24.95 (*1-56511-362-4*) HighBridge Co.

—A River Runs Through It & Other Stories. Peters, Sally, ed. 1992. 256p. reprint ed. mass mkt. 6.99 (*0-671-77697-5*, Pocket) Simon & Schuster.

—A River Runs Through It & Other Stories. 2001. 232p. 20.00 o.s.i (*0-226-50055-1*); 1983. (Illus.). 128p. (C). 50.00 o.s.i (*0-226-50059-4*) Univ. of Chicago Pr.

—A River Runs Through It & Other Stories: Anniversity Edition. 25th ed. 2001. 232p. pap. 11.00 o.s.i (*0-226-50057-8*, P821); 1983. (Illus.). 128p. (C). 25.00 o.s.i (*0-226-50058-6*) Univ. of Chicago Pr.

Malloy, Brian. Year of Ice. 2003. 272p. pap. 12.95 (*0-312-31369-1*, Saint Martin's Griffin) St. Martin's Pr.

Manguel, Alberto. Fathers & Sons: An Anthology. 1998. 291p. pap. 15.95 o.p. (*0-8118-1630-3*) Chronicle Bks. LLC.

Manley, Frank. The Cockfighter. 1998. 224p. 19.95 (*1-56689-073-X*) Coffee Hse. Pr.

—The Cockfighter. 1999. 208p. pap. 11.95 o.s.i (*0-385-49420-3*) Doubleday Publishing.

Many, Paul. My Life, Take Two. 2000. 192p. (YA). (gr. 6 up). 16.95 (*0-8027-8708-8*) Walker & Co.

Marion, Stephen. Hollow Ground: A Novel. 2002. 320p. tchr. ed. 23.95 (*1-56512-323-9*) Algonquin Bks. of Chapel Hill.

—Hollow Ground: A Novel. 2003. 320p. pap. 14.00 (*0-312-42235-0*) Picador.

Mathews, Francine. The Secret Agent. 2003. 528p. mass mkt. 6.99 (*0-553-58153-8*); 2002. (Illus.). 416p. 23.95 (*0-553-10913-8*) Bantam Bks.

Maxwell, Robin. The Queen's Bastard. 1999. 448p. 24.95 (*1-55970-475-6*) Arcade Publishing, Inc.

—The Queen's Bastard. 2000. 448p. pap. 13.00 (*0-684-85760-X*, Touchstone) Simon & Schuster.

McCusker, Paul. The Faded Flower. 2001. 144p. 12.99 (*0-310-23554-5*) Zondervan.

McDonough, Yona Zeldis. The Four Temperaments. 2002. 320p. 23.95 (*0-385-50361-X*) Doubleday Publishing.

McGhee, Alison. Was It Beautiful? A Novel. 256p. 2004. pap. 13.00 (*1-4000-5154-1*, Three Rivers Pr.); 2003. 23.00 (*0-609-60978-5*) Crown Publishing Group.

McMillan, Rosalyn. The Flip Side of Sin. 2000. 352p. 24.00 o.s.i (*0-684-86287-5*, Simon & Schuster); 2001. 432p. reprint ed. pap. 6.99 (*0-671-03435-9*, Pocket) Simon & Schuster.

Meador, D. J. His Father's House. 1994. 384p. (YA). (gr. 10-12). 25.00 (*1-56554-032-8*) Pelican Publishing Co., Inc.

Michaels, Lisa. Grand Ambition: A Novel. l.t. ed. 2001. 275p. 26.95 (*1-57490-374-8*, Beeler Large Print Bks.) Beeler, Thomas T. Publisher.

—Grand Ambition: A Novel. 288p. 2002. pap. 13.95 (*0-393-32295-5*); 2001. (Illus.). 23.95 (*0-393-05047-5*) Norton, W. W. & Co., Inc.

Miller, Christopher. Simon Silber: Works for Solo Piano. 2002. 240p. tchr. ed. 23.00 (*0-618-14336-X*) Houghton Mifflin Co.

Milofsky, David. Playing from Memory. 1982. 304p. pap. 2.95 o.p. (*0-380-57166-8*, 57166-8, Avon Bks.) Morrow/Avon.

—Playing from Memory. 1981. 12.95 o.p. (*0-671-25252-6*, Simon & Schuster) Simon & Schuster.

—Playing from Memory. 1999. 270p. reprint ed. pap. 14.95 (*0-87081-526-1*) Univ. Pr. of Colorado.

Mitchell, David. Number 9 Dream. 2001. E-Book 19.95 (*1-58836-215-9*) Random Hse., Inc.

—Number 9 Dream: A Novel. 2003. 416p. pap. 13.95 (*0-8129-6692-9*) Random House Adult Trade Publishing Group.

Moggach, Deborah. Driving in the Dark. l.t. ed. 2002. (General Ser.). 240p. pap. 25.95 (*0-7862-4257-4*) Thorndike Pr.

Mooney, Robert. Father of the Man: A Novel. 2002. 240p. 23.00 (*0-375-42204-8*, Pantheon) Knopf Publishing Group.

Moore, John L. The Breaking of Ezra Riley. rev. ed. 2000. 784p. pap. 14.99 (*0-8054-2331-1*) Broadman & Holman Pubs.

—The Breaking of Ezra Riley. 1986. (Illus.). 226p. pap. 8.50 o.p. (*0-937959-03-0*, Falcon) Globe Pequot Pr., The.

—The Breaking of Ezra Riley. 1990. 287p. pap. 9.99 o.p. (*0-7459-1882-4*) Lion Publishing.

—The Breaking of Ezra Riley. 1994. 10.99 o.p. (*0-8407-6760-9*) Nelson, Thomas Inc.

Morris, Scott M. Waiting for April: A Novel. 2003. 352p. tchr. ed. 24.95 (*1-56512-370-0*, 72370) Algonquin Bks. of Chapel Hill.

Mutabaruka, Mustafa. Seed. 2002. (Illus.). 275p. pap. 14.95 (*1-888451-31-9*) Akashic Bks.

Nolan, Peggy. The Spy Who Came in from the Sea. 2000. 129p. (J). (gr. 5-9). 14.95 (*1-56164-186-3*) Pineapple Pr., Inc.

Oe, Kenzaburo. Rouse up O Young Men of the New Age! 2002. 240p. 24.00 o.p. (*0-8021-1710-4*, Grove Pr.) Grove/Atlantic, Inc.

Owen, Howard. The Rail. 2002. 256p. 25.00 (*1-57962-043-4*) Permanent Pr., The.

Oz, Amos. The Same Sea. De Lange, Nicholas, tr. 2002. Tr. of Oto Ha-yam. 216p. pap. 13.00 (*0-15-601312-6*, Harvest Bks.) Harcourt Trade Pubs.

—The Same Sea. De Lange, Nicholas R. M., tr. from HEB. 2001. Tr. of Oto Ha-yam. 208p. 24.00 (*0-15-100572-9*) Harcourt Trade Pubs.

Palmer, Catherine. Fatal Harvest. 2003. (Fatal Harvest Ser.). 352p. pap. 12.99 (*0-8423-7548-1*) Tyndale Hse. Pubs.

Papandreou, Nicholas. A Crowded Heart. 192p. 1999. pap. 12.00 o.s.i (*0-312-20400-0*); 1998. 21.00 o.p. (*0-312-18685-1*) Picador.

Parekh, Sameer. Stealing the Ambassador. 288p. 2002. 23.00 (*0-7432-1429-3*); 2003. reprint ed. pap. 13.00 (*0-7432-1430-7*) Simon & Schuster. (Free Pr.).

Parker, Robert B. All Our Yesterdays. 1995. 480p. mass mkt. 7.50 (*0-440-22146-3*); 1994. 528p. 27.95 o.s.i (*0-385-31374-8*, Delacorte Pr.) Dell Publishing.

Parker, T. Jefferson. Silent Joe. l.t. ed. 2001. 501p. lib. bdg. 28.95 (*1-58547-125-9*) Ctr. Point Large Print.

—Silent Joe. 2001. vii, 341p. 23.95 (*0-7868-6728-0*); 2003. 400p. reprint ed. mass mkt. 7.99 (*0-7868-9003-7*) Hyperion Pr.

Parks, Tim. Destiny. 2000. 248p. 24.95 (*1-55970-517-5*); 2001. 256p. reprint ed. pap. 12.95 (*1-55970-575-2*) Arcade Publishing, Inc.

—Destiny. 1999. 248p. (*0-436-22088-1*) Secker, Martin & Warburg, Ltd.

Parsons, Tony. Man & Boy: A Novel. l.t. ed. 2002. 346p. pap. 25.95 (*0-7862-3724-4*) Gale Group.

—Man & Boy: A Novel. 2002. 368p. pap. 12.00 (*0-7432-2508-2*, Touchstone) Simon & Schuster.

—Man & Boy: A Novel. 2001. (Illus.). 368p. text 21.00 o.p. (*1-57071-725-7*) Sourcebooks, Inc.

Patchett, Ann. Taft. 1999. 272p. pap. 13.00 o.s.i (*0-345-43353-X*, Ballantine Bks.); 1995. mass mkt. 5.99 o.s.i (*0-8041-1388-2*, Ivy Bks.) Ballantine Bks.

—Taft. 2003. 256p. pap. 12.95 (*0-06-054076-1*, Perennial) HarperTrade.

—Taft. 1994. 288p. 21.95 o.p. (*0-395-69461-2*) Houghton Mifflin Co.

Patino, Ernesto. In the Shadow of a Stranger. 2002. 224p. 27.50 (*0-7090-6871-9*) Hale, Robert Ltd. GBR. *Dist:* Trafalgar Square.

Perabo, Susan. The Broken Places. 2001. 224p. E-Book 23.00 (*0-7432-1325-4*); 2002. 256p. reprint ed. pap. 12.00 (*0-7432-2315-2*) Simon & Schuster. (Simon & Schuster).

—The Broken Places: A Novel. 2001. (Illus.). 256p. 23.00 (*0-684-86234-4*, Simon & Schuster) Simon & Schuster.

Perry, S. D. The Rising Son. 2003. (Star Trek Deep Space Nine Ser.). 336p. pap. 6.99 (*0-7434-4838-3*, Star Trek) Simon & Schuster.

Philbrick, W. R. Young Man & the Sea. 2004. (J). 16.95 (*0-439-36829-4*, Blue Sky Pr., The) Scholastic, Inc.

Phillips, Thomas Hal. Red Midnight. 2002. 256p. 28.00 (*1-57806-474-0*) Univ. Pr. of Mississippi.

Pontiggia, Giuseppe. Born Twice. 2003. 208p. pap. 13.00 (*0-375-72768-X*, Vintage) Knopf Publishing Group.

Potok, Chaim. The Chosen. (Ballantine Reader's Circle Ser.). 1996. 304p. pap. 13.95 (*0-449-91154-3*); 1987. 304p. mass mkt. 6.99 (*0-449-21344-7*); 1985. mass mkt. 3.50 o.p. (*0-449-20962-8*); 1982. mass mkt. 2.95 o.p. (*0-449-20334-4*) Ballantine Bks. (Fawcett).

—The Chosen. 1994. reprint ed. lib. bdg. 35.95 (*1-56849-319-3*) Buccaneer Bks., Inc.

—The Chosen. 25th anniv. ed. 1992. 30.00 o.s.i (*0-679-40222-5*) Knopf, Alfred A. Inc.

—The Chosen. 1967. 9.95 o.p. (*0-671-13674-7*, Simon & Schuster) Simon & Schuster.

—The Chosen. l.t. ed. 1998. (Perennial Bestsellers Ser.). 413p. 27.95 (*0-7838-8450-8*) Thorndike Pr.

—The Chosen. 1976. 13.04 (*0-606-00469-6*) Turtleback Bks.

Pratt, James Michael. Paradise Bay. E-Book 23.95 (*0-312-70638-3*); 2003. 352p. mass mkt. 6.99 (*0-312-98674-2*, St. Martin's Paperbacks); 2002. 304p. 23.95 (*0-312-26634-0*) St. Martin's Pr.

Pritchett, V. S. Dead Man Leading. 1984. (Twentieth Century Classics Ser.). 224p. pap. 6.95 o.p. (*0-19-281469-9*) Oxford Univ. Pr., Inc.

Quammen, David. Blood Line: Stories of Fathers & Sons. 1987. (Short Fiction Ser.). 192p. pap. 8.00 o.p. (*1-55597-100-8*) Graywolf Pr.

—Blood Line: Stories of Fathers & Sons. 2000. 192p. reprint ed. pap. 14.00 (*1-55566-272-2*) Johnson Bks.

Queen, Ellery. A Fine & Private Place. l.t. ed. 2002. (Paperback Ser.). 257p. 24.95 o.p. (*0-7838-9759-6*) Gale Group.

—A Fine & Private Place. 1976. mass mkt. 1.25 o.p. (*0-451-07183-2*); 1972. mass mkt. 0.95 o.p. (*0-451-04978-0*) NAL. (Signet Bks.).

—The House of Brass. l.t. ed. 2001. 278p. pap. 24.95 (*0-7838-9598-4*, Macmillan Reference USA) Gale Group.

Quin, Ann. Berg. 2001. 168p. reprint ed. pap. 11.95 (*1-56478-302-2*) Dalkey Archive Pr.

Rathbone, Julian. Blame Hitler. 288p. (*0-575-06284-3*) Gollancz, Victor.

—Blame Hitler. 288p. mass mkt. 10.95 (*0-575-40094-3*) Gollancz, Victor GBR. *Dist:* Trafalgar Square.

—Blame Hitler. l.t. ed. 1998. 24.95 (*0-7531-5582-6*) ISIS Large Print Bks. GBR. *Dist:* Transaction Pubs.

Reisig, Michael. The Old Man's Letters. 1999. 110p. pap. 5.99 (*0-9651240-4-5*); 2nd l.t. rev. ed. 2000. 192p. per. 8.95 (*0-9651240-6-1*) Clear Creek Pr.

Rhode, William. Paperback Orginal: When the Travelling Ends, & the Drugs Wear Off, the Writing Must Begin. 2003. 464p. pap. 14.00 o.p. (*1-57322-980-6*, Riverhead Trade (Paperbacks)) Berkley Publishing Group.

Rice, Luanne. Summer Light. 2002. 496p. reprint ed. mass mkt. 7.50 (*0-553-58265-8*) Bantam Bks.

—Summer Light. l.t. ed. 2001. 525p. lib. bdg. 29.95 (*1-58547-144-5*) Ctr. Point Large Print.

Richman, Alyson. The Mask Carver's Son. 384p. 2001. pap. 14.95 (*1-58234-129-X*); 2000. 23.95 (*1-58234-063-3*) Bloomsbury Publishing.

Rochelle, Warren G. The Wild Boy. 2001. 270p. 22.95 (*1-930846-04-5*) Golden Gryphon Pr.

Rolens, Sharon. What Else but Home: A Novel. 2003. 336p. 23.95 (*1-882593-75-8*) Bridge Works Publishing Co., Inc.

Rouaud, Jean. Of Illustrious Men. Wright, Barbara, tr. from FRE. 160p. 1995. pap. 10.95 (*1-55970-319-9*); 1994. 19.95 (*1-55970-265-6*) Arcade Publishing, Inc.

Rushdie, Salman. Haroun & the Sea of Stories. l.t. ed. 1991. (J). (gr. 1-8). 14.95 o.p. (*0-7451-1428-8*, Galaxy Children's Large Print) BBC Audiobooks America.

—Haroun & the Sea of Stories. 1999. 96p. pap. 13.00 (*0-571-19693-4*) Faber & Faber, Inc.

—Haroun & the Sea of Stories. 1999. pap. 4.99 (*0-14-037636-4*); 1991. 224p. (J). 18.95 (*0-670-83804-7*); 1991. 204p. (J). reprint ed. 14.00 (*0-14-015737-9*, Penguin Bks.) Viking Penguin.

Russell, Alan. Shame. 1998. 304p. 23.00 (*0-684-81527-3*); 23.00 (*0-684-85189-X*) Simon & Schuster. (Simon & Schuster).

Rutman, Leo. Thy Father's Son: A Novel. 2002. 352p. 24.95 (*0-312-29061-6*) St. Martin's Pr.

Rylant, Cynthia. Henry & Mudge & the Funny Lunch. 2004. (Henry & Mudge Ser.). (Illus.). 40p. (J). (gr. k-3). 14.95 (*0-689-81178-0*, Simon & Schuster Children's Publishing) Simon & Schuster Children's Publishing.

Salmon, Elon. When There Were Heroes. 2003. 256p. pap. 13.95 (*1-899235-59-0*) Lewis, Dewi Publishing GBR. *Dist:* Consortium Bk. Sales & Distribution.

Savage, Les, Jr. Last of the Breed. l.t. ed. 2001. (Paperback Ser.). 269p. 23.95 (*0-7838-9342-6*) Thorndike Pr.

Shalev, Meir. Four Meals. Harshav, Barbara, tr. from HEB. 2002. 336p. pap. 14.00 (*1-84195-114-5*) Canongate Bks. GBR. *Dist:* Grove/Atlantic, Inc., Publishers Group West.

Sher, Ira. Gentlemen of Space: A Novel. 304p. 2004. pap. 13.00 (*0-7432-4219-X*); 2003. 23.00 (*0-7432-4218-1*) Simon & Schuster. (Free Pr.).

Shipton, Jonathan. How to Be a Happy Hippo. 1999. (Illus.). 32p. (J). (ps-2). 14.95 (*1-888444-61-4*) Little Tiger Pr.

—How to Be a Happy Hippo. 2001. 32p. pap. 5.95 (*1-58925-357-4*, Tiger Tales) ME Media LLC.

Silver, Jim. Kill Zone: A Novel. 1999. 320p. 23.00 (*0-684-84289-0*, Simon & Schuster) Simon & Schuster.

Sima, Carol Ann. The Mermaid That Came Between Them. 2002. 288p. 24.95 (*1-56689-124-8*) Coffee Hse. Pr.

Simmons, Charles. Salt Water. 1998. 192p. 19.95 o.p. (*0-8118-2182-X*) Chronicle Bks. LLC.

—Salt Water. 1999. 176p. pap. 12.00 (*0-671-03567-3*, Pocket) Simon & Schuster.

Slavitt, David R. Aspects of the Novel: A Novel. 2003. 192p. 20.00 (*0-945774-56-7*) Catbird Pr.

Smith, Bobbi. The Half Breed. 2001. (Secret Fires Ser.: Bk. 2). 400p. mass mkt. 5.99 (*0-8439-4853-1*, Leisure Bks.) Dorchester Publishing Co., Inc.

—The Half-Breed. l.t. ed. 2001. (Thorndike Press Large Print Romance Ser.). 373p. 28.95 o.p. (*0-7862-3584-5*) Thorndike Pr.

Spencer, Scott. The Rich Man's Table. 1999. 272p. reprint ed. pap. 12.95 o.s.i (*0-425-16945-6*) Berkley Publishing Group.

Stark, Stephen. The Second Son. Rosenman, Jane, ed. 1994. 432p. reprint ed. pap. o.p. (*0-671-87119-6*, Washington Square Pr.) Simon & Schuster.

—Second Son: A Novel. 1992. 288p. 22.50 o.p. (*0-8050-1943-X*) Holt, Henry & Co.

Stein, Michael. The White Life. 1999. 184p. pap. text 16.00 o.s.i (*1-57962-025-6*); 172p. 24.00 o.p. (*1-57962-022-1*) Permanent Pr., The.

Steinbeck, John. East of Eden. (Steinbeck's Centennial Ser.). 2002. 608p. pap. 16.00 (*0-14-200065-5*); 1970. pap. 3.95 o.p. (*0-670-00278-X*) Penguin Group (USA) Inc.

Stephens, Michael. The Brooklyn Book of the Dead. 1994. 228p. 19.95 o.p. (*1-56478-037-6*) Dalkey Archive Pr.

Stern, Richard. Father's Words. 1986. 14.95 o.p. (*0-87795-791-6*, Morrow, William & Co.) Morrow/Avon.

Stevenson, Robert Louis. Weir of Hermiston. Kerrigan, Catherine, ed. 1996. xxxvi, 178p. 51.00 (*0-7486-0473-1*) Edinburgh Univ. Pr. GBR. *Dist:* Columbia Univ. Pr.

—Weir of Hermiston. Miller, Karl, ed. 1997. (Penguin Classics Ser.). 176p. pap. 9.95 o.p. (*0-14-043560-3*) Viking Penguin.

—Weir of Hermiston: An Unfinished Romance. 1977. (Short Story Index Reprint Ser.). reprint ed. 19.95 (*0-8369-3861-5*) Ayer Co. Pubs., Inc.

—Weir of Hermiston: And Other Stories. Binding, Paul, ed. & intro. by. 1980. (English Library). 320p. pap. 10.95 o.s.i (*0-14-043138-1*, Penguin Classics) Viking Penguin.

Straub, Peter. Mr. X. 1999. 512p. 25.95 o.s.i (*0-679-40138-5*) Random Hse., Inc.

Strohm, Craig. Comeback: A Novel. 2001. 16.95 (*1-57733-096-X*) Pelican Publishing Co., Inc.

Stutzman, Ervin R. Tobias of the Amish: A True Story of Tangled Strands in Faith, Family & Community. 2001. 352p. (Illus.). pap. 15.99 (*0-8361-9170-6*); 22.99 (*0-8361-9190-0*) Herald Pr.

Tarpley, Natasha. Bippity Bop Barbershop. 2002. (Illus.). 32p. (J). (gr. k-3). 15.95 (*0-316-52284-8*) Little Brown Children's Bks.

Taylor, D. J. The Comedy Man. 2002. 352p. pap. 9.95 (*0-7156-3157-8*) Duckworth, Gerald & Co., Ltd. GBR. *Dist:* International Publishers Marketing.

Trollope, Anthony. Mr. Scarborough's Family, 3. reprint ed. lib. bdg. 294.00 (*0-7426-2496-X*); 2001. pap. text 84.00 (*0-7426-7496-7*) Classic Bks.

—Mr. Scarborough's Family. Harvey, Geoffrey, ed. 1989. (Oxford World's Classics Ser.). 672p. pap. 9.95 o.p. (*0-19-281808-2*) Oxford Univ. Pr., Inc.

Troy, Judy. From the Black Hills. 1999. 300p. pap. 19.00 (*0-8129-9173-7*) Random Hse., Inc.

—From the Black Hills. l.t. ed. 1999. (Americana Ser.). 341p. 27.95 (*0-7862-2213-1*) Thorndike Pr.

—From the Black Hills: A Novel. 1999. 284p. 23.95 o.s.i (*0-375-50230-0*) Random Hse., Inc.

Turgenev, Ivan. Fathers & Sons. 2002. (World Digital Library). E-Book 3.95 (*0-594-08428-8*) 1873 Pr.

—Fathers & Sons. Garnett, Constance, tr. 1967. (Airmont Classics Ser.). mass mkt. 1.95 o.p. (*0-8049-0129-5*, CL-129) Airmont Publishing Co., Inc.

—Fathers & Sons. 20.95 (*0-88411-444-9*) Amereon, Ltd.

—Fathers & Sons. 1982. 224p. mass mkt. 1.95 o.s.i (*0-553-21089-0*, Bantam Classics) Bantam Bks.

—Fathers & Sons. Makanowitzky, Barbara, tr. from RUS. 1982. (Classics Ser.). 224p. mass mkt. 3.95 o.s.i (*0-553-21259-1*, Bantam Classics) Bantam Bks.

—Fathers & Sons. unabr. ed. 1999. (World Classic Literature Ser.). (RUS.). pap. 8.95 (*2-87714-262-0*) Bookking International FRA. *Dist:* Distribooks, Inc.

—Fathers & Sons. 1987. 206p. reprint ed. lib. bdg. 19.95 (*0-89966-578-0*) Buccaneer Bks., Inc.

—Fathers & Sons. 1965. (*0-521-06656-5*) Cambridge Univ. Pr.

—Fathers & Sons. 1999. (Cloth Bound Pocket Ser.). 240p. 7.95 (*3-89508-456-5*, 520003) Konemann.

—Fathers & Sons. Guerney, Bernard G., tr. 1950. (Modern Library College Editions Ser.). (C). pap. text 8.25 o.p. (*0-07-553634-X*, T38) McGraw-Hill Cos., The.

—Fathers & Sons. mass mkt. 0.50 o.p. (*0-451-01066-3*, Signet Bks.); 1968. mass mkt. 0.60 o.p. (*0-451-50399-6*, Signet Classics); 1968. mass mkt. 0.50 o.p. (*0-451-50050-4*, Signet Classics); 1961. 320p. mass mkt. 5.95 o.s.i (*0-451-52383-0*); 1961. mass mkt. 0.75 o.p. (*0-451-50816-5*, Signet Classics); 1961. mass mkt. 0.95 o.p. (*0-451-50972-2*, Signet Classics); 1961. mass mkt. 1.25 o.p. (*0-451-51058-5*, Signet Classics); 1961. mass mkt. 1.95 o.p. (*0-451-51500-5*, Signet Classics); 1961. mass mkt. 2.25 o.p. (*0-451-51915-9*, Signet Classics) NAL.

—Fathers & Sons. Reavey, George, tr. 1961. 208p. mass mkt. 6.95 (*0-451-52382-2*, Signet Classics) NAL.

—Fathers & Sons. l.t. ed. 1996. 450p. lib. bdg. 26.00 (*0-939495-92-9*); 1998. 235p. reprint ed. lib. bdg. 25.00 (*1-58287-029-2*) North Bks.

—Fathers & Sons. Katz, Michael R., ed. & tr. by. 1995. (Critical Editions Ser.). 343p. (C). pap. text 8.00 (*0-393-96752-2*) Norton, W. W. & Co., Inc.

—Fathers & Sons. Katz, Michael R., tr. 1993. 288p. 25.00 (*0-393-03559-X*) Norton, W. W. & Co., Inc.

—Fathers & Sons. 1966. (C). pap. o.p. (*0-393-09652-1*) Norton, W. W. & Co., Inc.

—Fathers & Sons. Matlaw, Ralph E., ed. & tr. by. 2nd ed. 1989. (Critical Editions Ser.). 345p. (C). pap. o.p. (*0-393-95795-0*) Norton, W. W. & Co., Inc.

—Fathers & Sons. Freeborn, Richard, tr. from RUS. 2000. (Oxford World's Classics Ser.: Vol. 17). 256p. 13.00 o.p. (*0-19-210040-8*) Oxford Univ. Pr., Inc.

—Fathers & Sons. Freeborn, Richard, tr. & intro. by. 1998. (Oxford World's Classics Ser.). 296p. pap. 8.95 (*0-19-283392-8*) Oxford Univ. Pr., Inc.

—Fathers & Sons. Freeborn, Richard, ed. & tr. by. 1991. (Oxford World's Classics Ser.). 294p. pap. 5.95 o.p. (*0-19-282256-X*) Oxford Univ. Pr., Inc.

—Fathers & Sons. 2001. (Modern Library Classics). 256p. pap. 10.95 (*0-375-75839-9*, Modern Library) Random House Adult Trade Publishing Group.

—Fathers & Sons. Edmonds, Rosemary, tr. from RUS. 1965. (Classics Ser.). 304p. pap. 11.00 (*0-14-044147-6*, Penguin Classics) Viking Penguin.

—Fathers & Sons. 1997. (Classics Library). 208p. pap. 3.95 (*1-85326-286-2*, 2862WW) Wordsworth Editions, Ltd. GBR. *Dist:* Combined Publishing.

Turgenev, Ivan & Garnett, Constance B. Fathers & Sons. 1998. (Thrift Editions Ser.). 176p. pap. 2.50 (*0-486-40073-5*) Dover Pubns., Inc.

Tuten, Frederic. Tallien: A Brief Romance. 1994. 152p. pap. 13.95 o.p. (*0-7145-2990-7*) Boyars, Marion Pubs., Inc.

—Tallien: A Brief Romance. 1988. 230p. 17.95 o.p. (*0-374-27249-2*) Farrar, Straus & Giroux.

Tyree, Omar R. Single Mom: A Novel. (Illus.). 400p. 1999. pap. 13.00 (*0-684-85593-3*); 1998. 24.00 (*0-684-85592-5*) Simon & Schuster. (Simon & Schuster).

Van Leeuwen, Jean. Hannah of Fairfield. Fogelman, Phyllis, ed. 1999. (Pioneer Daughters Ser.: No. 1). (Illus.). 96p. (J). (gr. 2-5). 14.89 (*0-8037-2336-9*, Dial Bks. for Young Readers) Penguin Putnam Bks. for Young Readers.

van Loon, Karel. A Father's Affair. Garrett, Sam, tr. 2003. 208p. 23.00 (*1-84195-421-7*) Canongate Bks. GBR. *Dist:* Grove/Atlantic, Inc.

Walker, George F. Nothing Sacred. 1988. (Illus.). 98p. pap. 11.95 (*0-88910-331-3*) Consortium Bk. Sales & Distribution.

Wallace, Daniel. Big Fish. l.t. ed. 2001. (Basic Ser.). 208p. 29.95 (*0-7862-3043-6*) Thorndike Pr.

—Big Fish. 2003. 208p. pap. 12.00 (*0-14-200427-8*, Penguin Bks.) Viking Penguin.

—Big Fish: A Novel of Mythic Proportions. 1998. 180p. tchr. ed. 17.95 (*1-56512-217-8*) Algonquin Bks. of Chapel Hill.

—Big Fish: A Novel of Mythic Proportions. 1999. 192p. pap. 10.95 (*0-14-028277-7*) Penguin Group (USA) Inc.

Watt, Alan. Diamond Dogs. 2000. 256p. 23.95 o.p. (*0-316-92581-0*); 256p. E-Book 14.95 (*0-446-92255-2*); 256p. E-Book 14.95 (*0-446-91361-8*); E-Book 14.95 (*0-446-93128-4*); 256p. E-Book 14.95 (*0-446-92365-6*) Little Brown & Co.

—Diamond Dogs. 2001. 256p. pap. 13.95 (*0-446-67784-1*); 2000. 256p. E-Book 14.95 (*0-446-92857-7*); 2000. E-Book 14.95 (*0-446-96086-1*) Warner Bks., Inc.

Weesner, Theodore. The Car Thief. 2001. 370p. pap. 13.00 (*0-8021-3763-6*, Grove Pr.) Grove/Atlantic, Inc.

—The Car Thief. 1987. (Vintage Contemporaries Ser.). pap. 6.95 o.s.i (*0-394-74097-1*, Vintage) Knopf Publishing Group.

Wells, Ken. Logan's Storm: A Novel. 2003. 304p. pap. 12.95 (*0-375-76067-9*) Random House Adult Trade Publishing Group.

—Logan's Storm: A Novel. 2002. 304p. 21.95 (*0-375-50525-3*) Random Hse., Inc.

—Meely LaBauve: A Novel. 2001. 272p. pap. 11.95 (*0-375-75816-X*); 2000. 256p. 19.95 o.s.i (*0-375-50311-0*) Random Hse., Inc.

—Meely LaBauve: A Novel. l.t. ed. 2001. (Americana Ser.). 309p. 28.95 (*0-7862-3023-1*) Thorndike Pr.

West, John Foster. Time Was. 2002. 307p. 20.00 (*1-887905-66-9*) Parkway Pubs., Inc.

Willard, Tom. The Stone Ponies. 320p. 2001. (Black Sabre Chronicles Ser.). mass mkt. 6.99 (*0-8125-6478-2*); 2000. (Black Sabre Chronicles Ser.: No. 4). 24.95 o.p. (*0-312-85763-2*) Doherty, Tom Assocs., LLC. (Forge Bks.).

Williams, Mark London. Danger Boy: Ancient Fire, No. 1. 2004. 224p. (J). 9.99 (*0-7636-2152-8*) Candlewick Pr.

Williams, Niall. The Fall of Light. l.t. ed. 2002. 509p. 27.95 (*0-7862-3945-X*) Gale Group.

—The Fall of Light. 2003. (Illus.). 384p. pap. 13.95 (*0-446-67987-9*); 2002. 320p. 24.95 o.p. (*0-446-52840-4*) Warner Bks., Inc.

Williams, William G. The Coal King Slaves: A Coal Miner's Story. 2002. (Illus.). 208p. pap. 14.95 (*1-57249-319-4*, Burd Street Pr.) White Mane Publishing Co., Inc.

Wilson, Angus. Anglo-Saxon Attitudes. 1963. mass mkt. 0.75 o.p. (*0-451-50151-9*, Signet Classics) NAL.

—Anglo-Saxon Attitudes. 1960. pap. 1.85 o.p. (*0-670-00062-0*) Penguin Group (USA) Inc.

—Anglo-Saxon Attitudes. 1996. 352p. pap. 14.95 o.p. (*0-312-14275-7*, Saint Martin's Griffin) St. Martin's Pr.

—Anglo-Saxon Attitudes. 1978. 352p. pap. 4.95 o.p. (*0-14-001311-3*, Penguin Bks.); 1956. 4.50 o.p. (*0-670-12635-7*) Viking Penguin.

Wood, James. The Book Against God: A Novel. 2003. 272p. 24.00 o.s.i (*0-374-11538-9*) Farrar, Straus & Giroux.

—The Book Against God: A Novel. Date not set. pap. (*0-312-42251-2*) Picador.

Worku, Daniachew. The Thirteenth Sun: A Novel. 2000. pap. 16.95 (*1-56902-123-6*); 184p. 49.95 (*1-56902-122-8*) Red Sea Pr.

Yates, Dan. Lack of Evidence: A Novel. 2003. 195p. (*1-59156-206-6*) Covenant Communications.

Yorgason, Blaine M. Gabriel's Well. 2000. 160p. 15.95 (*1-57345-641-1*, Shadow Mountain) Deseret Bk. Co.

**FRIENDSHIP—FICTION**

Ada, Alma Flor. Friend Frog. 2000. (Illus.). 32p. (J). (ps-3). 16.00 (*0-15-201522-1*) Harcourt Children's Bks.

Aiken, Joan & Austen, Jane. Emma Watson: The Watsons Completed. l.t. ed. 1997. 25.95 (*1-56895-441-7*, Wheeler Publishing, Inc.) Gale Group.

—Emma Watson: The Watsons Completed. 1996. 224p. 20.95 o.p. (*0-312-14593-4*) St. Martin's Pr.

All by Myself. 1976. o.p. (*0-86112-040-X*) Brimax Bks., Ltd.

Anderson, Dillon. I & Claudie. 2000. (Double Mountain Bks.). (Illus.). vii, 247p. 15.95 (*0-89672-429-8*) Texas Tech Univ. Pr.

Andrews, V. C. Falling Stars. 2001. 400p. 25.00 (*0-671-03986-5*, Atria); E-Book 7.99 (*0-7434-2168-X*, Pocket); (Illus.). 416p. pap. 7.99 (*0-671-03987-3*, Pocket) Simon & Schuster.

—Falling Stars. l.t. ed. 2002. 403p. 30.95 (*0-7838-9753-7*) Thorndike Pr.

Appollo, Annette. The Last One Home. 2000. 400p. mass mkt. 6.99 o.s.i (*0-06-109721-7*); 1999. 288p. 24.00 o.s.i (*0-06-019208-9*) HarperCollins Pubs.

—The Last One Home. l.t. ed. 1999. (Thorndike Senior Lifestyle Ser.). 464p. pap. 26.95 (*0-7862-2069-4*) Thorndike Pr.

Arnold, Marilyn. The Classmates. 2003. 292p. pap. 17.95 (*1-55517-707-7*, 77077, Bonneville Bks.) Cedar Fort, Inc./CFI Distribution.

Ashbery, John & Schuyler, James. A Nest of Ninnies. 1997. 192p. 21.00 o.p. (*0-88001-523-3*) Harper-Collins Pubs.

Ashcom, Robert L. Winter Run. 2002. 240p. tchr. ed. 19.95 (*1-56512-328-X*, 72328) Algonquin Bks. of Chapel Hill.

Ashley, Renee. Someplace Like This. 2003. 192p. 26.00 (*1-57962-090-6*) Permanent Pr., The.

Atwood, Margaret. Oryx & Crake. 2003. 400p. 26.00 (*0-385-50385-7*, Talese, Nan A.); E-Book 12.00 (*0-385-51088-8*) Doubleday Publishing.

—Oryx & Crake. 2004. 400p. pap. 14.00 (*0-385-72167-6*, Anchor) Knopf Publishing Group.

—Oryx & Crake. 2003. 392p. (*0-7710-0868-6*) McClelland & Stewart/Tundra Bks.

—Oryx & Crake. l.t. ed. 2003. 592p. 28.00 (*0-375-43212-4*) Random Hse. Large Print.

—The Robber Bride. l.t. ed. 1993. 880p. 27.00 o.s.i (*0-385-47216-1*, Bantam Large Type) Bantam Doubleday Dell Large Print Group, Inc.

Austin, Lynn. Fire by Night. 2003. (Refiners Fire Ser.). 432p. pap. 12.99 (*1-55661-443-8*) Bethany Hse. Pubs.

B Small Publishing Staff. My Friends. 1999. (Illus.). 24p. pap. (*1-874735-50-6*) B Small Publishing.

Babcock, Richard. Bow's Boy: A Novel. 2003. 336p. pap. 14.00 (*0-7432-2728-X*, Scribner) Simon & Schuster.

Bacon, Margaret. The Ewe Lamb. l.t. ed. 2000. (Magna Large Print Ser.). 432p. 31.99 (*0-7505-1589-9*) Magna Large Print Bks. GBR. *Dist:* Ulverscroft Large Print Bks., Ltd., Ulverscroft Large Print Canada, Ltd.

—The Ewe Lamb. 2000. 284p. 26.00 (*0-7278-5435-6*) Severn Hse. Pubs., Ltd.

Barker, Nicola. Behindlings: A Novel. 544p. 2003. pap. 13.95 (*0-06-093362-3*); 2002. 27.95 (*0-06-018569-4*) HarperTrade. (Ecco).

Barrientos, Tanya Maria. Frontera Street: A Novel. 2002. 272p. pap. 12.95 (*0-451-20635-5*) NAL.

Barrowcliffe, Mark. Infidelity for First Time Fathers. 2002. 337p. 24.95 (*0-312-29146-9*) St. Martin's Pr.

Bathurst, Bella. Special. 2003. 320p. pap. 12.00 (*0-618-26327-6*, Mariner Bks.) Houghton Mifflin Co. Trade & Reference Div.

Battle, Lois. The Florabama Ladies' Auxiliary & Sewing Circle. l.t. ed. 2001. 358p. 30.95 (*0-7862-3305-2*) Thorndike Pr.

—The Florabama Ladies' Auxiliary & Sewing Circle. 2001. 352p. 24.95 o.s.i (*0-670-89469-9*, Viking) Viking Penguin.

Baumbich, Charlene. Dearest Dorothy, Slow down, You're Wearing Us Out! 2004. 256p. pap. 10.95 (*0-14-200418-9*) Penguin Group (USA) Inc.

Baumbich, Charlene Ann. Dearest Dorothy, Slow down, You're Wearing Us Out! l.t. ed. 2003. 383p. 26.95 (*0-7862-5559-5*) Thorndike Pr.

Beagle, Peter S. A Dance for Emilia. l.t. ed. 2001. (G. K. Hall Large Print Book Ser.). 96p. 26.95 o.p. (*0-7838-9501-1*, Macmillan Reference USA) Gale Group.

—A Dance for Emilia. 2000. 96p. 14.95 o.s.i (*0-451-45800-1*, ROC) NAL.

Berg, Elizabeth. Talk Before Sleep. 1995. 304p. mass mkt. 6.50 o.s.i (*0-440-22109-9*) Dell Publishing.

—Talk Before Sleep. 1997. 224p. pap. 13.95 (*0-385-31878-2*) Doubleday Publishing.

—Talk Before Sleep. abr. ed. 2001. audio 9.99 (*0-553-70197-5*, RH Audio) Random Hse. Audio Publishing Group.

Bernardo, Jose Raul. Las Sabias Mujeres de la Habana. 2002. (SPA.). 384p. pap. 13.95 (*0-06-093616-9*, Rayo) HarperTrade.

—The Wise Women of Havana. 2002. 336p. 24.95 (*0-06-621123-9*, Rayo) HarperTrade.

Berry, Carmen Renee & Traeder, Tamara. Girlfriends. l.t. ed. 1999. (Americana Ser.). 304p. 27.95 (*0-7862-1969-6*) Thorndike Pr.

Binchy, Maeve. Circle of Friends. 1991. 608p. mass mkt. 5.99 o.s.i (*0-440-20996-X*); 1991. 608p. mass mkt. 7.99 (*0-440-21126-3*, 2766354); 1990. 576p. 19.95 o.s.i (*0-440-29400-2*) Dell Publishing.

—Circle of Friends. l.t. ed. 1991. (General Ser.). 755p. 22.95 o.p. (*0-8161-5207-1*, Macmillan Reference USA) Gale Group.

—Circle of Friends. 1999. (*0-7621-0252-7*) Reader's Digest Assn., Inc., The.

—Light a Penny Candle. 1992. 600p. mass mkt. (*0-09-919651-4*) Arrow Bks., Ltd. GBR. *Dist:* Random Hse. of Canada, Ltd.

—Light a Penny Candle. l.t. ed. 1991. (General Ser.). 772p. 16.95 o.p. (*0-8161-5067-2*); lib. bdg. 16.95 o.p. (*0-8161-5066-4*) Gale Group. (Macmillan Reference USA).

—Light a Penny Candle. 1997. 592p. mass mkt. 7.50 o.s.i (*0-451-19202-8*, Signet Bks.) NAL.

—Light a Penny Candle. 1983. 540p. 17.75 o.p. (*0-670-42827-2*) Viking Penguin.

—Scarlet Feather. 2001. 528p. 25.95 o.s.i (*0-525-94593-8*, Dutton) Dutton/Plume.

—Scarlet Feather. 2001. 560p. mass mkt. 7.99 (*0-451-20446-8*, Signet Bks.) NAL.

—Scarlet Feather. l.t. ed. 2001. 912p. 25.95 (*0-375-43106-3*) Random Hse. Large Print.

—Tara Road. l.t. ed. 1999. 743p. (*0-7540-2212-9*) BBC Audiobooks America.

—Tara Road. 2000. 656p. mass mkt. 7.99 (*0-440-23559-6*); 1999. 512p. 24.95 o.s.i (*0-385-33395-1*, Delacorte Pr.) Dell Publishing.

—Tara Road. l.t. ed. (Paperback Bestsellers Ser.). 743p. 2000. pap. 28.95 (*0-7862-1837-1*); 1999. 31.95 (*0-7862-1836-3*) Thorndike Pr.

—Tara Road. 2000. 14.04 (*0-606-18987-4*) Turtleback Bks.

Binchy, Maeve, contrib. by. Tara Road. (*0-7540-1282-4*) BBC Audiobooks America.

Black, Jim. River Season: A Novel. 2003. 208p. 23.95 (*0-670-03227-1*, Viking) Viking Penguin.

Blacklock, Dianne. Call Waiting: A Novel. 2003. 384p. 24.95 (*0-312-30348-3*) St. Martin's Pr.

Blake, Cindy. Girl Talk. 2002. 224p. 25.99 (*0-7278-5905-6*) Severn Hse. Pubs., Ltd.

Bloom, Rebecca. Girl Anatomy: A Novel. 2003. 272p. pap. 12.95 (*0-06-093680-0*, Perennial) Harper-Trade.

—Girl Anatomy: A Novel. 2002. 272p. 24.95 (*0-06-621257-X*, Morrow, William & Co.) Morrow/Avon.

Bluh, Bonnie. The Eleanor Roosevelt Girls. 1999. 225p. pap. 12.00 (*0-9664820-1-8*) LyreBird Bks., Inc.

Blume, Judy. Summer Sisters: A Novel. 2003. 416p. pap. 13.95 (*0-385-33766-3*, Delta) Dell Publishing.

Bouldrey, Brian. The Boom Economy: Or, Scenes from Clerical Life. 2003. ix, 283p. 24.95 (*0-299-18900-7*, Terrace Bks.) Univ. of Wisconsin Pr.

Bowker, David. The Death You Deserve: A Novel. 2003. 256p. pap. 12.95 (*0-312-31178-8*, Saint Martin's Griffin) St. Martin's Pr.

Bradford, Barbara Taylor. A Sudden Change of Heart. 1999. mass mkt. (*0-440-29567-X*); 400p. mass mkt. 7.99 (*0-440-23514-6*) Dell Publishing.

—A Sudden Change of Heart. l.t. ed. 1999. 11.95 (*1-56895-965-6*); 29.95 o.p. (*1-56895-735-1*) Gale Group. (Wheeler Publishing, Inc.).

—A Sudden Change of Heart. l.t. ed. 2000. (Charnwood Large Print Ser.). 440p. o.p. (*0-7089-9134-3*, Ulverscroft) Thorpe, F. A. Pubs. GBR. *Dist:* Ulverscroft Large Print Bks., Ltd., Ulverscroft Large Print Canada, Ltd.

—The Triumph of Katie Byrne. l.t. ed. 2001. 496p. 24.95 (*0-375-43097-0*) Random Hse. Large Print.

Bram, Christopher. Lives of the Circus Animals: A Novel. 2003. 352p. 24.95 (*0-06-054253-5*); pap. 13.95 (*0-06-054254-3*) HarperCollins Pubs.

Brashares, Ann. The Second Summer of the Sisterhood. l.t. ed. 2003. 379p. 25.95 (*0-7862-5545-5*) Thorndike Pr.

Brett, Simon. The Torso in the Town. 2003. 352p. mass mkt. 6.99 (*0-425-19212-1*, Prime Crime) Berkley Publishing Group.

—The Torso in the Town. l.t. ed. 2002. (Core Collection). 381p. 28.95 o.p. (*0-7862-4674-X*) Thorndike Pr.

Bright, Vonette Z. & Moser, Nancy. 'Round the Corner. 2003. (Sister Circle Ser.). 300p. pap. 12.99 (*0-8423-7190-7*) Tyndale Hse. Pubs.

Brockett, Deborah A. Stained Glass Rose. 2002. 143p. pap. 14.95 (*1-890437-61-1*) Western Reflections Publishing Co.

Brookhouse, Christopher. Passing Game. 2000. 160p. 19.95 (*0-9665798-2-8*) Safe Harbor Bks.

Brookner, Anita. Brief Lives. l.t. ed. 2000. 312p. lib. bdg. 27.95 (*1-58547-018-X*) Ctr. Point Large Print.
—Brief Lives. 1992. (Vintage Contemporaries Ser.). 272p. pap. 13.00 (*0-679-73733-2*, Vintage) Knopf Publishing Group.
—The Rules of Engagement. 2003. 288p. 23.95 (*1-4000-6165-2*, Random House) Random House Adult Trade Publishing Group.
Brooks, Martha. Two Moons in August. 1998. 160p. (YA). (gr. 7-12). pap. text 4.95 (*0-88899-170-3*) Groundwood Bks. CAN. *Dist:* Publishers Group West.
Brouwer, Sigmund. Dr. Drabble's Remarkable Underwater Breathing Pills. rev. ed. 1994. (Doctor Drabble Ser.: Bk. 1). (Illus.). 32p. (J). (gr. 1-5). pap. text 3.99 o.p. (*0-8499-3659-4*) W Publishing Group.
Brown, Parry A. The Shirt Off His Back. 1998. 244p. pap. 14.95 (*0-9666503-0-1*) ShanKrys Publishing, Inc.
—The Shirt off His Back. E-Book 11.00 (*1-58945-615-7*) Adobe Systems, Inc.
—The Shirt off His Back. 2001. E-Book 11.00 (*0-375-50654-3*) Random Hse., Inc.
—The Shirt off His Back: A Novel. 2001. 256p. pap. 13.95 (*0-375-75659-0*, Villard Bks.) Random House Adult Trade Publishing Group.
Brownstein, Gabriel. The Curious Case of Benjamin Button, Apt. 3W. 2003. 224p. pap. 13.95 (*0-393-32478-8*); 2002. 192p. 23.95 (*0-393-05151-X*) Norton, W. W. & Co., Inc.
Bruns, Donn. Barbados Heat. Date not set. mass mkt. (*0-312-99459-1*, St. Martin's Paperbacks); 2003. 320p. 24.95 (*0-312-30492-7*) St. Martin's Pr.
Buckley, William F., Jr. Brothers No More. l.t. ed. 1996. pap. 22.95 o.p. (*1-56895-283-X*, Wheeler Publishing, Inc.) Gale Group.
Buckley, William F., Jr. & Hodges, Candace. Brothers No More. 1996. (Harvest Book Ser.). 304p. pap. 12.00 (*0-15-600476-3*) Harcourt Trade Pubs.
Bunn, Curtis. Baggage Check. 2000. 21.95 (*1-886433-47-X*) A & B Distributors & Pubs. Group.
Burley, Charlotte & LeFlore, Lyah. Cosmopolitan Girls. 2004. 272p. pap. 11.95 (*0-7679-1567-4*) Broadway Bks.
Butler, Tajuana. The Night Before Thirty: A Novel. 2003. 240p. 19.95 (*1-4000-6020-6*, Villard Bks.) Random House Adult Trade Publishing Group.
—Sorority Sisters: A Novel. 2001. 240p. pap. 12.95 (*0-375-75758-9*, Villard Bks.) Random House Adult Trade Publishing Group.
Campbell, Alexandra. That Dangerous Age. l.t. ed. 2003. (Magna Large Print Ser.). 512p. (*0-7505-2067-1*) Magna Large Print Bks. GBR. *Dist:* Ulverscroft Large Print Canada, Ltd.
—That Dangerous Age. 2002. 400p. pap. (*0-14-100643-9*) Penguin Group (USA) Inc.
Campbell, Drusilla. Wildwood. 2003. 352p. pap. 15.00 (*0-7582-0293-8*) Kensington Publishing Corp.
Canizares, Susan. Tedd & Huggly. 1999. (Learning Center Emergent Readers Ser.). (J). 3.25 (*0-439-04610-6*) Scholastic, Inc.
Cantor, Jay. Great Neck: A Novel. 720p. 2004. pap. 15.00 (*0-375-71339-5*); 2003. 27.95 (*0-375-41394-4*) Knopf, Alfred A. Inc.
Carlstrom, Nancy White. The Way to Wyatt's House. 2000. (Illus.). 32p. (J). (gr. k-3). lib. bdg. 16.85 (*0-8027-8742-8*) Walker & Co.
Carter, Reg. The Ex-factor: The Wrath of Carmen Hunt. collector's ed. 2003. 204p. per. 19.95 o.p. (*0-9676268-3-8*) BraZen.
Cave, Dorothy. Song on a Blue Guitar: A Novel. 2002. 190p. pap. 18.95 (*0-86534-349-7*) Sunstone Pr.
Center for Learning Network Staff. Tara Road/the Return Journey: Curriculum Unit —Novel Series— Grades 9-12. 1999. (Novel Ser.). 65p. (YA). (gr. 9-12). tchr. ed., spiral bd. 18.95 (*1-56077-636-6*) Ctr. for Learning, The.
Chaviano, Diana. El Hombre, la Hembra y el Hambre. 1997. (Autores Espanoles E Iberoamericanos Ser.).Tr. of Man, Woman, Hunger. (SPA., Illus.). 312p. 24.95 (*84-08-02530-9*) GeoPlaneta, Editorial, S. A. ESP. *Dist:* Lectorum Pubns., Inc.
Cheska, Anna. Drop Dead Gorgeous. 2002. 384p. 24.95 (*0-312-30040-9*) St. Martin's Pr.
Chevalier, Tracy. Falling Angels: A Novel. 2002. 336p. pap. 13.00 (*0-452-28320-5*, Plume); 2001. 324p. 24.95 o.s.i (*0-525-94581-4*, Dutton) Dutton/Plume.
Chevigny, Bell G. Chloe & Olivia. 1990. 368p. 18.95 o.p. (*0-8021-1182-3*) Grove/Atlantic, Inc.
Chiaverini, Jennifer. The Cross-Country Quilters: An Elm Creek Quilts Novel. 2002. 368p. pap. 13.00 (*0-452-28308-6*, Plume) Dutton/Plume.
—The Cross-Country Quilters: An Elm Creek Quilts Novel. l.t. ed. 2001. 495p. 29.95 (*0-7838-9559-3*, Macmillan Reference USA) Gale Group.
—The Cross-Country Quilters: An Elm Creek Quilts Novel. 2001. 368p. 21.00 (*0-7432-0257-0*, Simon & Schuster) Simon & Schuster.
—The Quilter's Apprentice: A Novel. 2000. 272p. pap. 13.00 (*0-452-28172-5*, Plume) Dutton/Plume.
—The Quilter's Apprentice: A Novel. 1999. 272p. 18.00 (*0-684-84972-0*, Simon & Schuster) Simon & Schuster.
—Round Robin: An Elm Creek Quilts Novel. 2001. 304p. pap. 13.00 (*0-452-28227-6*, Plume) Dutton/Plume.
—Round Robin: An Elm Creek Quilts Novel. l.t. ed. 2000. (Large Print Bks.). 420p. pap. 24.95 (*1-56895-952-4*, Wheeler Publishing, Inc.) Gale Group.
—Round Robin: An Elm Creek Quilts Novel. 2000. 336p. 20.00 (*0-684-86892-X*, Simon & Schuster) Simon & Schuster.
—The Runaway Quilt: An Elm Creek Quilts Novel. 2003. 336p. reprint ed. pap. 13.00 (*0-452-28398-1*, Plume) Dutton/Plume.
—The Runaway Quilt: An Elm Creek Quilts Novel. 2002. (Illus.). 336p. 21.00 (*0-7432-2226-1*, Simon & Schuster) Simon & Schuster.
—The Runaway Quilt: An Elm Creek Quilts Novel. l.t. ed. 2002. (Core Ser.). 29.95 (*0-7862-4472-0*) Thorndike Pr.
Child, Maureen. Some Kind of Wonderful. 2004. 352p. mass mkt. 5.99 (*0-312-98727-7*, St. Martin's Paperbacks) St. Martin's Pr.
Clements, Marcelle. Midsummer. 304p. 2004. pap. (*0-15-602965-0*, Harvest Bks.); 2003. 24.00 (*0-15-100836-1*) Harcourt Trade Pubs.
Coburn, Randy Sue. Remembering Jody. 1999. 322p. 22.95 (*0-7867-0566-3*, Carroll & Graf Pubs.) Avalon Publishing Group.
Coe, Jonathan. The Rotters' Club. 2003. 432p. pap. 14.00 (*0-375-71312-3*, Vintage) Knopf Publishing Group.
—The Rotters' Club. 2001. 405p. (*0-670-89252-1*, Viking) Viking Penguin.
Colgan, Jenny. Amanda's Wedding. 288p. 2001. 23.95 o.p. (*0-446-52647-9*); 2001. E-Book 14.95 (*0-7595-4144-2*); 2001. E-Book 14.95 (*0-7595-8146-0*); 2001. E-Book 14.95 (*0-7595-6142-7*); 2001. E-Book 14.95 (*0-7595-0142-4*); 2001. E-Book 14.95 (*0-7595-9162-8*); 2002. reprint ed. pap. 13.95 (*0-446-67811-2*) Warner Bks., Inc.
—Talking to Addison. 320p. 2003. pap. 13.95 (*0-446-69015-5*); 2002. 23.95 o.p. (*0-446-52661-4*) Warner Bks., Inc.
Comfort, Louise. Lily's Busy Day. 2003. (Fairy Phones Ser.). (Illus.). 10p. (J). bds. 4.95 (*0-7641-5692-6*) Barron's Educational Series, Inc.
Conly, Jane Leslie. What Happened on Planet Kid, ERS. 2000. 216p. (J). (gr. 5-9). 16.95 (*0-8050-6065-0*, Holt, Henry & Co. Bks. For Young Readers) Holt, Henry & Co.
Copeland, Lori. A Case of Bad Taste. 2003. (Morning Shade Mystery Ser.). 304p. pap. 12.99 (*0-8423-7115-X*) Tyndale Hse. Pubs.
Copeland, Sheila. A Chocolate Affair. 288p. mass mkt. 6.99 (*1-58314-441-2*, Arabesque); 2001. 240p. pap. 15.00 (*1-58314-234-7*, Sepia) BET Bks.
Croskery, Beverly F. Shamir, the White Elephant: A Rain Forest Adventure. 1997. (Illus.). 128p. (J). (gr. 3-6). 14.95 (*0-9657619-4-0*) Bell-Forsythe Publishing Co.
Cunningham, Michael. A Home at the End of the World. 352p. audio compact disk 39.95 (*1-55927-990-7*) Audio Renaissance.
—A Home at the End of the World. l.t. ed. 2003. 536p. 29.95 (*0-7862-5745-8*, Large Print Pr.) Thorndike Pr.
—A Home at the End of the World: A Novel. 1995. mass mkt. 6.99 o.s.i (*0-553-57550-3*); 1992. 480p. pap. 6.99 o.s.i (*0-553-55002-0*) Bantam Bks.
—A Home at the End of the World: A Novel. 1990. 18.95 o.s.i (*0-374-17250-1*) Farrar, Straus & Giroux.
—A Home at the End of the World: A Novel. 1998. 352p. pap. 14.00 (*0-312-20231-8*) Picador.
Dallas, Sandra. Buster Midnight's Cafe. l.t. ed. 2004. lib. bdg. 27.95 (*1-58547-381-2*, Premier) Ctr. Point Large Print.
—Buster Midnight's Cafe. 1991. 288p. pap. 8.99 o.s.i (*0-440-50382-5*) Dell Publishing.
—Buster Midnight's Cafe. 1998. 224p. reprint ed. pap. 12.95 (*0-312-18062-4*, NPB 0241, Saint Martin's Griffin) St. Martin's Pr.
—The Chili Queen: A Novel. l.t. ed. 2003. lib. bdg. 29.95 (*1-58547-265-4*, Platinum) Ctr. Point Large Print.
—The Chili Queen: A Novel. E-Book 16.95 (*0-312-70782-7*); 2003. 304p. pap. 13.95 (*0-312-32026-4*, Saint Martin's Griffin); 2002. 304p. 22.95 (*0-312-30349-1*) St. Martin's Pr.
Dart, Iris Rainer. Some Kind of Miracle. l.t. ed. 2003. 448p. pap. 24.95 (*0-06-057003-2*, HarperLarge-Print); audio 25.95 (*0-06-056940-9*, HarperAudio) HarperTrade.
—Some Kind of Miracle. 2003. 304p. 24.95 (*0-06-620953-6*, Morrow, William & Co.) Morrow/Avon.
Davis, Gloria. In December. 2003. (*0-936389-93-1*) Tudor Pubs., Inc.
De Beer, Hans. Kleiner Eisbar, Kennst du Den Weg? 1998. Tr. of Little Polar Bear, Take Me Home!. (GER.). (J). 15.95 (*3-314-00757-4*) North-South Bks., Inc.
de Brunhoff, Laurent. Babar Raconte le Meilleur Ami des Elephants. (Babar Ser.). (FRE., Illus.). 48p. (J). (ps-3). 19.95 (*0-7859-8823-8*) French & European Pubns., Inc.
Deaner, Janice. Notes on Extinction. 256p. 2001. 25.95 o.s.i (*0-525-94415-X*); 2003. reprint ed. pap. 14.00 (*0-452-27974-7*, Plume) Dutton/Plume.
DeBerry, Virginia. Trying to Sleep in the Bed You Made. 1996. 384p. 24.95 (*0-312-15233-7*) St. Martin's Pr.
DeFord, Frank. An American Summer: A Novel. 2002. 256p. 24.00 (*1-57071-992-6*, Sourcebooks Landmark) Sourcebooks, Inc.
Delinsky, Barbara. The Woman Next Door: A Novel. 2001. 368p. 25.00 (*0-7432-0469-7*, Simon & Schuster) Simon & Schuster.
—The Woman Next Door: A Novel. l.t. ed. 2002. 504p. 14.95 (*0-7862-3512-8*); 2001. 541p. 32.95 (*0-7862-3510-1*) Thorndike Pr.
Devlin, Martina. Three Wise Men. 2000. 437p. pap. (*0-00-651458-8*) HarperCollins Pubs.
D'Haene, Elise. Licking Our Wounds. 1997. 208p. 24.00 (*1-877946-81-8*) Permanent Pr., The.
Diamant, Anita. Good Harbor: A Novel. l.t. ed. 2001. 31.95 (*1-58724-140-4*, Wheeler Publishing, Inc.) Gale Group.
—Good Harbor: A Novel. 256p. 2002. E-Book (*0-7432-2976-2*); 2001. 25.00 (*0-7432-2532-5*); 2002. reprint ed. pap. 13.00 (*0-7432-2572-4*) Simon & Schuster. (Scribner).
Diamond, Rickey G. Second Sight. 2002. pap. 14.95 (*0-934971-80-3*) Calyx Bks.
—Second Sight: A Novel. 1999. 272p. 24.00 o.s.i (*0-06-019203-8*) HarperCollins Pubs.
Diamond, Sarah. The Beach Road. 2003. 304p. mass mkt. 11.00 (*0-7528-4329-X*); 2002. 256p. pap. 17.95 (*0-7528-3843-1*) Orion Publishing Group, Ltd. GBR. *Dist:* Trafalgar Square.
Dickens, Charles. The Pickwick Papers. 1968. (Classics Ser.). mass mkt. 2.95 o.p. (*0-8049-0191-0*, CL-191) Airmont Publishing Co., Inc.
—The Pickwick Papers. 1983. 784p. mass mkt. 6.99 (*0-553-21123-4*, Bantam Classics) Bantam Bks.
—The Pickwick Papers. 2000. 700p. per. 25.00 (*1-58396-005-8*) Blue Unicorn Editions.
—The Pickwick Papers. 1983. 495p. reprint ed. lib. bdg. 49.95 (*0-89966-314-1*) Buccaneer Bks., Inc.
—The Pickwick Papers. 1998. (Illus.). 925p. pap. text 5.99 (*0-8125-6719-6*, Tor Classics) Doherty, Tom Assocs., LLC.
—The Pickwick Papers. 1972. 5.50 o.p. (*0-460-01235-5*); 1954. 15.50 o.p. (*0-460-00235-X*) Dutton/Plume. (Dutton).
—The Pickwick Papers. 1991. (Complete Novels of Charles Dickens Ser.). (Illus.). 916p. (C). pap. 5.50 o.p. (*0-7493-0753-6*, A0529) Heinemann.
—The Pickwick Papers. l.t. ed. 888p. pap. 68.26 (*0-7583-3664-0*); 1154p. pap. 78.29 (*0-7583-3665-9*); 1582p. pap. 104.35 (*0-7583-3666-7*); 2024p. pap. 126.02 (*0-7583-3667-5*); 4547p. pap. 265.18 (*0-7583-3671-3*); 2591p. pap. 160.03 (*0-7583-3668-3*); 3187p. pap. 195.33 (*0-7583-3669-1*); 3920p. pap. 230.83 (*0-7583-3670-5*); 2024p. lib. bdg. 145.22 (*0-7583-3659-4*); 2591p. lib. bdg. 188.06 (*0-7583-3660-8*); 3187p. lib. bdg. 232.41 (*0-7583-3661-6*); 4547p. lib. bdg. 329.77 (*0-7583-3663-2*); 3920p. lib. bdg. 283.81 (*0-7583-3662-4*); 888p. lib. bdg. 80.26 (*0-7583-3656-X*); 1582p. lib. bdg. 122.35 (*0-7583-3658-6*); 1154p. lib. bdg. 90.29 (*0-7583-3657-8*) Huge Print Pr.
—The Pickwick Papers. l.t. unabr. ed. 1991. (Isis Large Print Bks.: Vol. 1). 450p. 29.99 (*1-85089-464-7*, 894647);Vol. 2. 540p. 24.95 (*1-85089-514-7*, 895147) ISIS Large Print Bks. GBR. *Dist:* Ulverscroft Large Print Bks., Ltd., Ulverscroft Large Print Canada, Ltd., Transaction Pubs., Ulverscroft Large Print Canada, Ltd.
—The Pickwick Papers. E-Book 1.95 (*1-57799-939-8*) Logos Research Systems, Inc.
—The Pickwick Papers. 1968. mass mkt. 1.25 o.p. (*0-451-50443-7*); 1968. mass mkt. 0.95 o.p. (*0-451-50200-0*); 1964. mass mkt. 2.25 o.p. (*0-451-51135-2*); 1964. mass mkt. 2.95 o.p. (*0-451-51413-0*); 1964. mass mkt. 3.95 o.p. (*0-451-51620-6*); 1964. 888p. mass mkt. 6.95 o.s.i (*0-451-51756-3*, CE1756); 1964. mass mkt. 1.95 o.p. (*0-451-50950-1*) NAL. (Signet Classics).
—The Pickwick Papers. Kinsley, James, ed. & intro. by. (Oxford World's Classics Ser.). (Illus.). 1998. 786p. pap. 10.95 (*0-19-283457-6*); 1988. 772p. pap. 6.95 o.p. (*0-19-281775-2*) Oxford Univ. Pr., Inc.
—The Pickwick Papers. Kinsley, James, ed. 1986. (Clarendon Dickens Ser.). (Illus.). 1,002p. text 149.00 o.p. (*0-19-812631-X*) Oxford Univ. Pr., Inc.
—The Pickwick Papers. 1999. 1378p. E-Book 3.99 incl. audio compact disk (*1-57646-106-8*) Quiet Vision Publishing.
—The Pickwick Papers. 2003. (Illus.). 816p. pap. 10.95 (*0-8129-6727-5*, Modern Library) Random House Adult Trade Publishing Group.
—The Pickwick Papers. E-Book 5.00 (*0-7410-1421-1*) SoftBook Pr.
—The Pickwick Papers, 2 vols. 2000. (Signature Classics Ser.). (Illus.). 872p. (*1-58279-066-3*); (*1-58279-072-8*) Trident Pr. International.
—The Pickwick Papers. 1964. 13.00 (*0-606-00941-8*) Turtleback Bks.
—The Pickwick Papers. Andrews, Malcolm, ed. 1998. (Everyman Paperback Classics Ser.). (Illus.). 960p. pap. 5.95 (*0-460-87664-3*, Everyman's Classic Library in Paperback) Tuttle Publishing.
—The Pickwick Papers. Patten, Robert L., ed. 1973. (Penguin English Library). (Illus.). 960p. pap. 9.95 o.s.i (*0-14-043078-4*, Penguin Classics) Viking Penguin.
—The Pickwick Papers. 1999. E-Book 3.95 (*0-8220-7163-0*); E-Book 3.95 (*0-8220-7163-0*) Wiley, John & Sons, Inc. (Cliff Notes).
—The Pickwick Papers. (Wordsworth Collection). 784p. pap. 3.95 (*1-85326-052-5*, 0525WW) Wordsworth Editions, Ltd. GBR. *Dist:* Casemate Pubs. & Bk. Distributors, LLC.
—The Posthumous Papers of the Pickwick Club. Boz, ed. 2001. (Collected Works of Charles Dickens). (Illus.). reprint ed. pap. text 28.00 (*0-7426-7303-0*) Classic Bks.
—The Posthumous Papers of the Pickwick Club. 1999. (Everyman's Library). 976p. 23.00 (*0-375-40548-8*) Knopf, Alfred A. Inc.
—The Posthumous Papers of the Pickwick Club. 1987. (Illus.). 826p. 17.95 (*0-19-254501-9*) Oxford Univ. Pr., Inc.
—The Posthumous Papers of the Pickwick Club. 2000. (Classics Ser.). (Illus.). 848p. pap. 11.00 (*0-14-043611-1*, Penguin Classics) Viking Penguin.
—The Posthumous Papers of the Pickwick Club: Digital Reprint of 1885 Philadelphia: J. B. Lippincott & Co. Edition. Exams Unlimited, Inc. Staff, ed. 2001. (Illus.). 1100p. (C). reprint ed. cd-rom 9.25 (*1-885343-50-7*) Exams Unlimited, Inc.
Dickins, Barry. The House of the Lord. 1999. 209p. (*1-86330-562-9*, Vintage) Knopf Publishing Group.
Dickson, Athol. They Shall See God: A Novel. 2002. (Moving Fiction Ser.). 464p. pap. 11.99 (*0-8423-5292-9*) Tyndale Hse. Pubs.
Dorner, Marjorie. Seasons of Sun & Rain. 2000. 360p. 23.95 (*1-57131-027-4*); reprint ed. pap. 14.95 (*1-57131-033-9*) Milkweed Editions.
—Seasons of Sun & Rain. l.t. ed. 2000. (Thorndike Senior Lifestyle Ser.). 512p. 26.95 (*0-7862-2414-2*) Thorndike Pr.
Drabble, Margaret. The Seven Sisters. 320p. 2003. pap. 14.00 (*0-15-602875-1*); 2002. 25.00 (*0-15-100740-3*) Harcourt Trade Pubs.
—The Seven Sisters. 2003. 320p. pap. (*0-7710-2905-5*) McClelland & Stewart.
Dunmore, Helen. Mourning Ruby. 2004. 23.95 (*0-399-15148-6*) Putnam Publishing Group, The.
Durstewitz, Jeff & Williams, Ruth. Younger Than That Now: A Shared Passage from the Sixties. 2001. 352p. pap. 13.95 (*0-553-38048-6*) Bantam Bks.
Earls, Nick. Two to Go: A Novel. 2003. 368p. pap. 14.95 (*0-312-28472-1*, Saint Martin's Griffin) St. Martin's Pr.
Edgerton, Dale. Goneaway Road. 2003. 320p. pap. 17.95 (*1-56023-434-2*); 39.95 (*1-56023-433-4*) Haworth Pr., Inc., The. (Southern Tier Editions).
Ellis, Alice Thomas. The Summer House: A Trilogy. 2001. (Common Reader Edition Ser.). 360p. reprint ed. pap. 19.95 (*1-58579-028-1*) Akadine Pr., The.
—The Summer House: A Trilogy. 1993. 352p. pap. 11.95 o.p. (*0-14-023876-X*, Penguin Bks.) Penguin Group (USA) Inc.
Evans, Max. Now & Forever: A Novel of Love & Betrayal Reincarnate. 2003. 176p. 21.95 (*0-8263-3318-4*) Univ. of New Mexico Pr.
Evans, Penelope. The Last Girl. 1997. (Last Girl Ser.: Vol. 1). 256p. mass mkt. 5.99 (*0-312-96315-7*, St. Martin's Paperbacks); 1995. 240p. text 21.95 o.p. (*0-312-13998-5*) St. Martin's Pr.
—The Last Girl. 2000. pap. 10.95 (*0-552-99602-5*) Transworld Publishers Ltd. GBR. *Dist:* Trafalgar Square.
Fagan, Cary. Animals Waltz. 1996. 288p. 21.95 (*0-312-13921-7*) St. Martin's Pr.
Fast, Howard. Greenwich. 2002. 240p. reprint ed. mass mkt. 6.99 (*0-515-13346-9*, Jove) Berkley Publishing Group.
—Greenwich. 2000. 304p. 25.00 o.s.i (*0-15-100620-2*) Harcourt Trade Pubs.
—Greenwich. l.t. ed. 2002. (General Ser.). 320p. pap. 24.95 (*0-7862-4229-9*) Thorndike Pr.

Fielding, Joy. Grand Avenue. 2001. 400p. 25.00 (*0-7434-0707-5*, Atria); 2001. 400p. 25.00 (*0-7434-4845-6*, Atria); 2001. 400p. 25.00 (*0-7434-4836-7*, Atria); 2002. 528p. pap. 25.00 (*0-7434-6667-5*, Pocket); 2001. 528p. 25.00 (*0-7434-2269-4*, Atria); 2002. (Illus.). 560p. reprint ed. mass mkt. 7.99 (*0-7434-0708-3*, Pocket Star) Simon & Schuster.

Fischer, John. Saint Ben with the Saints' & Angels' Song, 2 vols. 2001. (Saint Ben Ser.). 480p. pap. 10.99 (*0-7642-2522-7*) Bethany Hse. Pubs.

Fiske, Dorsey. Raptor. 2000. 220p. 22.95 (*0-312-87263-1*, Forge Bks.) Doherty, Tom Assocs., LLC.

Fox, Mem. Wilfrid Gordon McDonald Partridge: Big Book. 1995. (Illus.). 32p. (J). (ps-3). 19.95 (*0-916291-56-1*) Kane/Miller Bk. Pubs.

Frayn, Michael. Spies: A Novel. 2002. 288p. 23.00 o.s.i (*0-8050-7058-3*, Metropolitan Bks.) Holt, Henry & Co.

—Spies: A Novel. 2003. 272p. pap. 13.00 (*0-312-42117-6*) Picador.

—Spies: A Novel. l.t. ed. (General Ser.). 25.95 (*0-7862-4480-1*) Thorndike Pr.

Fredriksson, Marianne. Simon's Family: A Novel of Mothers & Sons. 2000. 368p. pap. 14.00 (*0-345-43630-X*) Ballantine Bks.

—Two Women: A Novel of Friendship. l.t. ed. 2001. 304p. 30.95 o.p. (*0-7838-9469-4*, Macmillan Reference USA) Gale Group.

Funny Friends. 1997. (Big Comfy Couch Digest Ser.). (Illus.). 32p. (J). (ps-1). pap. (*0-7666-0011-4*, Honey Bear Bks.) Modern Publishing.

Gaffney, Patricia. The Saving Graces. l.t. ed. 2001. 12.95 (*1-56895-975-3*); 1999. 27.95 (*1-56895-785-8*) Gale Group. (Wheeler Publishing, Inc.).

—The Saving Graces. 2000. pap. (*0-06-099592-0*); 2000. 528p. mass mkt. 7.99 (*0-06-109710-1*); 1999. 400p. 24.00 (*0-06-019192-9*) HarperCollins Pubs.

—The Saving Graces. 2004. 400p. pap. 12.95 (*0-06-059832-8*, Perennial) HarperTrade.

Ga'g, Wanda. Snippy & Snappy. 1998. (Wanda Ga'g Classic Collection). (Illus.). 48p. (J). (ps-3). 9.98 (*0-7651-0861-5*) Smithmark Pubs., Inc.

Gage, Elizabeth. The Hourglass. 1999. 304p. mass mkt. (*1-55166-546-8*, 1-66546-2); 240p. pap. (*1-55166-503-4*, 1-66503-3) Harlequin Enterprises, Ltd. (Mira Bks.).

Gardner, Katy. Losing Gemma: A Novel. 2002. 368p. pap. 13.00 (*1-57322-933-4*, Riverhead Bks. (Hardcovers)) Putnam Publishing Group, The.

Gibbon, Maureen. Swimming Sweet Arrow: A Novel. 2000. 352p. (YA). (gr. 8). 21.95 o.p. (*0-316-30599-5*) Little Brown & Co.

Gierach, John. Death, Taxes, & Leaky Waders: A John Gierach Fly-Fishing Treasury. 2000. (Illus.). 416p. 25.00 (*0-684-86858-X*, Simon & Schuster) Simon & Schuster.

Gire, Ken. Kim's Diary. 97p. (J). (gr. 3-7). pap. 4.99 (*0-7814-3427-0*) Cook Communications Ministries.

Glaister, Lesley. Now You See Me. 2001. 288p. (*0-7475-5206-1*) Bloomsbury Pr.

Goldsher, Alan. Jam. 2002. 272p. 26.00 (*1-57962-040-X*) Permanent Pr., The.

Goldsmith, Olivia. Bad Boy. 2001. 336p. 24.95 o.s.i (*0-525-94558-X*) Dutton/Plume.

—Bad Boy. l.t. ed. 2000. (Wheeler Romance Ser.). 417p. 26.95 (*1-56895-143-4*, Wheeler Publishing, Inc.) Gale Group.

—Pen Pals. 2002. (Illus.). 368p. 24.95 o.s.i (*0-525-94644-6*, Dutton) Dutton/Plume.

—Pen Pals. 2002. 432p. reprint ed. mass mkt. 7.99 (*0-451-20667-3*, Signet Bks.) NAL.

—Pen Pals. l.t. ed. 2002. (Basic Ser.). 716p. 29.95 (*0-7862-4206-X*) Thorndike Pr.

Graham, Laurie. The Future Homemakers of America. l.t. ed. 2003. (Core Ser.). 468p. 28.95 (*0-7862-4930-7*) Thorndike Pr.

—The Future Homemakers of America. 2002. 400p. reprint ed. pap. 14.00 (*0-446-67936-4*) Warner Bks., Inc.

Graves, Sarah. Unhinged: A Home Repair Is Homicide Mystery. 2003. 368p. mass mkt. 6.50 (*0-553-58227-5*); 272p. 19.95 (*0-553-80229-1*) Bantam Bks.

Green, Allison. Half-Moon Scar. E-Book 22.95 (*0-312-27593-5*); 2000. viii, 227p. 22.95 (*0-312-26170-5*) St. Martin's Pr.

Green, Carmen. Atlanta Live. 2003. 288p. pap. 15.00 (*1-58314-293-2*) BET Bks.

Green, Jane. Bookends: A Novel. 2002. 368p. 21.00 (*0-7679-0780-9*) Broadway Bks.

Greene, Thomas Christopher. Mirror Lake. 2003. 224p. 22.00 (*0-7432-4427-3*, Simon & Schuster) Simon & Schuster.

Greenwood, Tammy. Undressing the Moon. 2003. 256p. pap. 13.95 (*0-312-30327-0*, Saint Martin's Griffin) St. Martin's Pr.

Greenwood, Tammy, ed. Undressing the Moon. 2002. 256p. 23.95 (*0-312-28473-X*) St. Martin's Pr.

Gregson, Rebecca. Eggshell Days. pap. (*0-312-31042-0*, St. Martin's Paperbacks); mass mkt. (*0-312-98769-2*, St. Martin's Paperbacks); 2003. 320p. 24.95 (*0-312-31041-2*) St. Martin's Pr.

Gunn, Robin Jones. Sisterchicks Do the Hula. 2004. pap. (*1-59052-226-5*) Multnomah Pubs., Inc.

Gutcheon, Beth Richardson. Five Fortunes: A Novel. 416p. 1999. pap. 13.95 (*0-06-092995-2*, Perennial); 1998. 24.00 o.s.i (*0-06-017679-2*, HarperCollins) HarperTrade.

Halaby, Laila. West of the Jordan: A Novel. 2003. (Bluestreak Ser.). 240p. pap. 14.00 (*0-8070-8359-3*) Beacon Pr.

Hale, Keith. Cody. (Orig.). 1987. 190p. pap. 6.95 o.p. (*1-55583-105-2*); 1994. 191p. reprint ed. pap. 5.95 o.p. (*1-55583-601-1*) Alyson Pubns.

Hall, Linda. Chat Room. 2003. (Teri Blake-Addision Mystery Series, Book 2 Ser.). 290p. pap. 11.99 (*1-59052-200-1*) Multnomah Pubs., Inc.

Hamill, Pete. Snow in August. 2001. 17.95 (*1-56511-626-7*) HighBridge Co.

—Snow in August. 1997. 304p. 23.95 o.p. (*0-316-34094-4*) Little Brown & Co.

—Snow in August. l.t. ed. (Thorndike/G. K. Hall Paperback Bestsellers Ser.). 507p. 1998. pap. 25.95 o.p. (*0-7862-1222-5*); 1997. 28.95 (*0-7862-1221-7*) Thorndike Pr.

—Snow in August. 1999. 20.05 (*0-606-20074-6*) Turtleback Bks.

—Snow in August. reprint ed. 1999. 384p. pap. 14.00 (*0-446-67525-3*); 1998. 400p. mass mkt. 7.99 (*0-446-60625-1*) Warner Bks., Inc.

Hammond, Diane Coplin. Going to Bend: A Novel. 2004. 304p. 23.95 (*0-385-50943-X*) Doubleday Publishing.

Hammond, Gerald. Into the Blue. l.t. ed. 2001. (Magna Large Print Ser.). 304p. 32.50 (*0-7505-1608-9*) Magna Large Print Bks. GBR. *Dist:* Ulverscroft Large Print Bks., Ltd., Ulverscroft Large Print Canada, Ltd.

—Into the Blue. 2000. 224p. 25.00 (*0-7278-5509-3*) Severn Hse. Pubs., Ltd.

Hannah, Sophie. The Superpower of Love. 2003. 440p. pap. 14.00 (*1-56947-320-X*); 2002. 336p. 25.00 (*1-56947-281-5*) Soho Pr., Inc.

Harris, E. Lynn. If This World Were Mine. 1998. 336p. pap. 13.00 (*0-385-48656-1*, Knopf Bks. for Young Readers) Random Hse. Children's Bks.

—If This World Were Mine. l.t. ed. 2003. 525p. 29.95 (*0-7862-5895-0*) Thorndike Pr.

Harte, Kelly. Guilty Feet. 2003. (Red Dress Ink Ser.: No. 16). 320p. pap. (*0-373-25026-6*, Red Dress Ink) Harlequin Enterprises, Ltd.

Hassler, Jon. The Staggerford Flood. 2003. 208p. pap. 13.00 (*0-452-28462-7*, Plume) Dutton/Plume.

—The Staggerford Flood. 2002. 208p. 24.95 (*0-670-03125-9*, Viking) Viking Penguin.

Hay, Elizabeth. Small Change. 2001. 256p. pap. text 14.50 (*1-58243-167-1*, Counterpoint Pr.) Basic Bks.

Hayes, Hunter. A Pair Like No Otha' A Novel. 2002. 384p. pap. 13.95 (*0-380-81485-4*, Avon Bks.) Morrow/Avon.

Haynes, Melinda Rucker. Mother of Pearl. l.t. ed. 2000. (Thorndike/G. K. Hall Paperback Bestsellers Ser.). 760p. 30.00 (*0-7862-2182-8*, Macmillan Reference USA) Gale Group.

—Mother of Pearl. 1999. 445p. 23.95 (*0-7868-6485-0*); 448p. 23.95 (*0-7868-6627-6*) Hyperion Pr.

—Mother of Pearl. reprint ed. 2001. 512p. pap. 7.99 (*0-7434-3103-0*, Pocket); 2000. 496p. pap. 13.95 (*0-671-77467-0*, Washington Square Pr.) Simon & Schuster.

—Mother of Pearl. l.t. ed. 1999. (Basic Ser.). 760p. 31.95 (*0-7862-2181-X*) Thorndike Pr.

—Mother of Pearl. 2000. 20.00 (*0-606-19128-3*) Turtleback Bks.

Hecht, Julie. The Unprofessionals. 2003. 23.95 (*0-06-053247-5*) HarperCollins Pubs.

—The Unprofessionals: A Novel. 2003. 240p. 23.95 (*1-4000-6174-1*) Random Hse., Inc.

Heller, Zoe. What Was She Thinking? Notes on a Scandal. 2003. 272p. 23.00 o.s.i (*0-8050-7333-7*) Holt, Henry & Co.

Hemingway, Ernest. Elements of Literature: The Old Man & the Sea. 1989. pap. text, stu. ed. 15.33 (*0-03-023452-2*) Holt, Rinehart & Winston.

—The Old Man & the Sea. 128p. 1979. (Illus.). pap. 3.50 o.s.i (*0-684-16326-8*); 1977. 30.00 (*0-684-15363-7*); 1977. text 6.95 o.s.i (*0-684-51528-8*); 1950. 14.00 (*0-684-10245-5*); 1950. pap. 6.95 o.s.i (*0-684-71805-7*) Gale Group. (Macmillan Reference USA).

—The Old Man & the Sea. 1990. 10.92 (*0-02-635123-4*) Glencoe/McGraw-Hill.

—The Old Man & the Sea. o.p. (*0-582-78224-4*) Moonbeam Pubns., Inc.

—The Old Man & the Sea. l.t. ed. reprint ed. 10.00 (*0-89064-252-4*) National Assn. for Visually Handicapped.

—The Old Man & the Sea. 1952. text, stu. ed. 25.20 o.p. (*0-02-352990-3*, Macmillan College) Prentice Hall PTR.

—The Old Man & the Sea. (Scribner Classics). 1996. (Illus.). 96p. 20.00 (*0-684-83049-3*); 1995. 128p. pap. 10.00 (*0-684-80122-1*) Simon & Schuster. (Scribner).

—The Old Man & the Sea. l.t. ed. 1994. 113p. lib. bdg. 21.95 (*0-8161-5970-X*) Thorndike Pr.

—The Old Man & the Sea. 1995. 16.05 (*0-606-00201-4*) Turtleback Bks.

Hemingway, Ernest & Prentice-Hall Staff. The Old Man & the Sea. 2nd ed. text, stu. ed. (*0-13-717273-7*) Prentice Hall (Schl. Div.).

Hemphill, Paul. Nobody's Hero: A Novel. 2002. 336p. 25.95 (*1-57966-029-0*) River City Publishing.

Hensley, Dennis. Misadventures in the (213) 1999. 304p. pap. 15.00 (*0-688-17128-1*, Perennial) HarperTrade.

—Misadventures in the (213) 1998. 304p. 24.00 (*0-688-15452-2*, Morrow, William & Co.) Morrow/Avon.

—Misadventures in the (213), abr. ed. 1999. audio 18.00 (*1-57511-063-6*) Publishing Mills, Inc., The.

Hesser, Terry Spencer. Kissing Doorknobs. l.t. ed. 2000. (Young Adult Ser.). 211p. (J). 21.95 (*0-7862-2190-9*) Thorndike Pr.

Hill, Donna. An Ordinary Woman: A Novel. 2002. 320p. 23.95 (*0-312-28191-9*) St. Martin's Pr.

Hilmon, Darrious. Five Dimes: A Novel. 2003. 256p. pap. 12.95 (*0-451-20869-2*) NAL.

Hilton, Joni. That's What Friends Are For: A Novel. 1997. 300p. pap. 9.95 (*1-57734-111-2*, 01112791) Covenant Communications, Inc.

Hinton, J. Lynne. Forever Friends. 2004. 213p. pap. 12.95 (*0-06-251749-X*) HarperSanFrancisco.

—Forever Friends: A Novel. 2003. 224p. 21.95 (*0-06-251748-1*) HarperSanFrancisco.

Hinton, Lynne. Friendship Cake. l.t. ed. 2001. lib. bdg. 27.95 (*1-58547-153-4*) Ctr. Point Large Print.

—Friendship Cake. 2000. 224p. 20.00 (*0-688-17147-8*) HarperCollins Pubs.

—Friendship Cake. 2001. 336p. mass mkt. 7.50 o.s.i (*0-380-82014-5*) Morrow/Avon.

—Friendship Cake: A Novel. 2002. 240p. pap. 11.95 (*0-06-251731-7*) HarperSanFrancisco.

—Garden of Faith: A Novel. l.t. ed. 2002. lib. bdg. 28.95 (*1-58547-251-4*, Platinum) Ctr. Point Large Print.

—Garden of Faith: A Novel. 2002. 224p. 20.95 (*0-06-251746-5*) HarperSanFrancisco.

—Hope Springs: A Novel. 2003. 240p. pap. 13.95 (*0-06-251747-3*) HarperSanFrancisco.

Hoffman, Alice. Fortune's Daughter. 1986. 272p. mass mkt. 5.99 o.s.i (*0-449-20976-8*, Fawcett) Ballantine Bks.

—Fortune's Daughter. 1999. 320p. pap. 13.00 (*0-425-16870-0*) Berkley Publishing Group.

—Fortune's Daughter. l.t. ed. 2000. (G. K. Hall Core Ser.). 338p. 30.95 (*0-7838-9026-5*, Macmillan Reference USA) Gale Group.

—Fortune's Daughter. 1985. 272p. 15.95 o.p. (*0-399-13056-X*, G. P. Putnam's Sons) Penguin Putnam Bks. for Young Readers.

—Local Girls. 1999. 197p. 22.95 o.s.i (*0-399-14507-9*) Penguin Group (USA) Inc.

—Local Girls. l.t. ed. 2000. (Thorndike/G. K. Hall Paperback Bestsellers Ser.). 208p. pap. 28.95 (*0-7862-2010-4*) Thorndike Pr.

Hoffman, William. Blood & Guile. 2000. 256p. 24.00 (*0-06-019794-3*) HarperCollins Pubs.

—Blood & Guile. l.t. ed. 2001. (Thorndike Mystery Ser.). 357p. 29.95 (*0-7862-3172-6*) Thorndike Pr.

Hollander, David. L. I. E. E-Book 18.50 (*1-58945-595-9*) Adobe Systems, Inc.

—L. I. E. 2001. E-Book 11.50 (*0-375-50641-1*) Random Hse., Inc.

Holt, Tom. Lucia Triumphant. 2004. (Lucia Ser.). 224p. pap. 12.95 (*1-55921-310-8*) Moyer Bell.

Hoover, Jerald LeVon. My Friend, My Hero. 2001. (*1-886433-77-1*) A & B Distributors & Pubs. Group.

Hosseini, Khaled. The Kite Runner. 2004. 384p. pap. 14.00 (*1-59448-000-1*, Riverhead Trade (Paperbacks)) Berkley Publishing Group.

—The Kite Runner. 384p. 2004. pap. (*0-385-66007-3*, Anchor Canada); 2003. (*0-385-66006-5*) Doubleday Canada, Ltd. CAN. *Dist:* Random Hse., Inc.

—The Kite Runner. 2003. 336p. 24.95 (*1-57322-245-3*, Riverhead Bks. (Hardcovers)) Putnam Publishing Group, The.

Howard, Tracie & Carter, Danita. Talk of the Town. 2002. 304p. pap. 12.95 (*0-451-20703-3*) NAL.

Hucker, Hazel. Trials of Friendship. 1998. 293p. pap. text o.s.i (*0-7515-1825-5*) Little Brown & Co.

—Trials of Friendship. 1997. 268p. 22.95 o.p. (*0-312-17051-3*) St. Martin's Pr.

Hudson-Smith, Linda. Ladies in Waiting. 2002. 288p. pap. 15.00 (*1-58314-295-9*, New Spirit) BET Bks.

Humphreys, Helen. Leaving Earth. 1998. 224p. 22.00 o.s.i (*0-8050-5957-1*, Metropolitan Bks.) Holt, Henry & Co.

—Leaving Earth. 2000. 256p. pap. 13.00 (*0-312-25500-4*) Picador.

Hustvedt, Siri. What I Loved: A Novel. 2003. 384p. 25.00 (*0-8050-7170-9*) Holt, Henry & Co.

—What I Loved: A Novel. 2004. 384p. pap. 14.00 (*0-312-42119-2*); 2003. mass mkt. 7.99 (*0-312-99387-0*) Picador.

Hutton, Carol. Eternal Journey. 2000. 149p. E-Book 14.95 (*0-7595-8018-9*); 149p. E-Book 14.95 (*0-7595-0018-5*); 149p. E-Book 14.95 (*0-7595-9018-4*); (Illus.). 160p. 19.95 o.p. (*0-446-52657-6*) Warner Bks., Inc.

—The Eternal Journey. 2001. 160p. reprint ed. pap. 12.95 (*0-446-67731-0*) Warner Bks., Inc.

Hylton, Sara. Melissa. l.t. ed. 493p. (*0-7505-1019-6*) Magna Large Print Bks. GBR. *Dist:* Ulverscroft Large Print Bks., Ltd.

—Melissa. 1996. 304p. 22.95 (*0-312-14677-9*) St. Martin's Pr.

Inclan, Jessica Barksdale. The Matter of Grace. 2004. 320p. mass mkt. 6.99 (*0-451-21185-5*, Signet Bks.) NAL.

—The Matter of Grace. 2002. 272p. pap. 12.95 (*0-451-20575-8*) Penguin Group (USA) Inc.

Irving, John. A Prayer for Owen Meany. 1999. 7.99 (*0-345-91555-0*); 1990. 640p. mass mkt. 7.99 (*0-345-36179-2*, Ballantine Bks.); 1989. mass mkt. 4.95 o.s.i (*0-345-36352-3*); 1997. 560p. reprint ed. pap. 14.95 (*0-345-41797-6*, Ballantine Bks.) Ballantine Bks.

—A Prayer for Owen Meany. 1990. (GER.). 864p. (*3-257-01850-9*) Diogenes Verlag AG CHE. *Dist:* International Bk. Import Service, Inc.

—A Prayer for Owen Meany. 2002. (Illus.). 672p. 22.95 (*0-679-64259-5*, Modern Library) Random House Adult Trade Publishing Group.

—A Prayer for Owen Meany. 1990. 14.04 (*0-606-16249-6*) Turtleback Bks.

Jackson, Brenda. Perfect Timing. 2004. 304p. mass mkt. 6.99 (*0-7582-0029-3*, Kensington Bks.); 2003. 304p. pap. 15.00 (*0-7582-0011-0*); 2002. 34p. 24.00 o.s.i (*1-57566-921-8*, Kensington Bks.) Kensington Publishing Corp.

—The Savvy Sistahs. Date not set. (*0-312-31511-2*); 2003. 320p. pap. 13.95 o.s.i (*0-312-31512-0*, Saint Martin's Griffin) St. Martin's Pr.

—Ties That Bind: A Novel. 2002. 368p. pap. 13.95 (*0-312-30611-3*, Saint Martin's Griffin) St. Martin's Pr.

Jackson, Neta. The Yada Yada Prayer Group. 2003. 400p. 13.99 (*1-59145-074-8*) Integrity Pubs.

Jaffe, Rona. The Room-Mating Season. 2003. 9p. 79.95 (*0-7927-2878-5*); 10p. pap. 94.95 (*0-7927-2879-3*) BBC Audiobooks America.

—The Room-Mating Season. 2003. 384p. 24.95 (*0-525-94713-2*, Dutton) Dutton/Plume.

—The Room-Mating Season. 2004. 448p. mass mkt. (*0-7783-2031-6*, Mira Bks.) Harlequin Enterprises, Ltd.

—The Room-Mating Season. l.t. ed. 2003. (Women's Fiction Ser.). 29.95 (*0-7862-5544-7*) Thorndike Pr.

Jaro, Benita Kane. The Door in the Wall. 2002. (Illus.). xi, 207p. pap. 19.95 (*0-86516-534-3*) Bolchazy-Carducci Pubs.

Jaro, Benita Kane, contrib. by. The Door in the Wall. 2002. (Illus.). pap. 19.95 (*0-86516-533-5*) Bolchazy-Carducci Pubs.

Jennings, Patrick. Putnam & Pennyroyal. 1999. (Illus.). 192p. (J). (gr. 2-5). pap. 15.95 (*0-439-07965-9*) Scholastic, Inc.

Johnson-Hodge, Margaret. Some Sunday. 2003. 320p. mass mkt. 6.99 (*0-7582-0026-9*, Kensington Bks.); 2002. 32p. pap. 15.00 (*0-7582-0003-X*); 2001. 32p. 24.00 o.s.i (*1-57566-916-1*, Dafina) Kensington Publishing Corp.

—Some Sunday. l.t. ed. 2002. (African American Ser.). 562p. 29.95 (*0-7862-3870-4*) Thorndike Pr.

Johnson, Julia. Freckle Juice. 1998. (Literature Unit Ser.). (Illus.). 48p. (gr. 3-5). pap., tchr. ed. 7.99 (*1-57690-345-1*, TCA2345) Teacher Created Materials, Inc.

Jones, Susanna. The Earthquake Bird. 2001. 224p. 22.45 o.p. (*0-89296-742-0*) Mysterious Pr.

—The Earthquake Bird. l.t. ed. 2002. 236p. 28.95 (*0-7862-4136-5*) Thorndike Pr.

—The Earthquake Bird. 2003. 224p. pap. 12.95 (*0-446-67975-5*, Mysterious Pr. Paperback Bks.) Warner Bks., Inc.

Jooste, Pamela. Frieda & Min. 2001. 348p. pap. 13.00 (*0-552-99758-7*) Transworld Publishers Ltd. GBR. *Dist:* Trafalgar Square.

Jordan, Penny. Now or Never. 2003. 448p. mass mkt. (*1-55166-671-5*, Mira Bks.) Harlequin Enterprises, Ltd.

Joseph, Mark. The Wild Card: A Novel. 2001. 293p. 24.95 (*0-312-26120-9*) St. Martin's Pr.

Josseini, Khaled. Kite Runner. l.t. ed. 2003. lib. bdg. 29.95 (*1-58547-363-4*, Platinum) Ctr. Point Large Print.

Kagan, Elaine. The Girls. 1995. mass mkt. 6.99 o.s.i (*0-345-39351-1*) Ballantine Bks.

—The Girls: A Novel. 1994. 307p. 23.00 o.s.i (*0-679-43395-3*) Knopf, Alfred A. Inc.

Kasischke, Laura. The Life Before Her Eyes. 2002. 288p. pap. 13.00 (*0-15-602712-7*, Harvest Bks.); 24.00 (*0-15-100888-4*) Harcourt Trade Pubs.

Kear, Cynthia. Searching for Grace. 1998. 24.95 (*0-947993-75-4*) Malvern Publishing Co., Ltd. GBR. *Dist:* British Bk. Co., Inc.

Kelly, Cathy. Someone Like You: A Novel. 2001. 480p. 24.95 o.p. (*0-525-94605-5*) Dutton/Plume.

—Someone Like You: A Novel. 2000. viii, 581p. (*1-85371-904-8*) Poolbeg Pr.

Kelly, Susan S. Even Now. l.t. ed. 2001. (Thorndike Press Large Print Women's Fiction Ser.). 358p. 28.95 (*0-7862-3677-9*) Thorndike Pr.

—Even Now. 2001. 288p. 22.95 o.p. (*0-446-52762-9*) Warner Bks., Inc.

Kent, Susan & Davis, Sandra. All or Nothing: A Novel. Maitland, Jeffrey, ed. 2001. 238p. pap. 17.95 (*1-85776-544-3*) Book Guild, Ltd. GBR. *Dist:* Trans-Atlantic Pubns., Inc.

Keyes, Marian. Last Chance Saloon. 2003. 528p. pap. 13.95 (*0-06-008624-6*, Perennial) HarperTrade.

—Last Chance Saloon. 2002. 544p. mass mkt. 7.99 (*0-380-82029-3*); 2001. 384p. 25.00 (*0-688-18072-8*, Morrow, William & Co.) Morrow/Avon.

—Last Chance Saloon. 1999. 505p. (*1-85371-965-X*) Poolbeg Pr. IRL. *Dist:* Dufour Editions, Inc.

—Lucy Sullivan Is Getting Married. 2002. 624p. pap. 13.95 (*0-06-009037-5*, Perennial) HarperTrade.

—Lucy Sullivan Is Getting Married. 1996. 740p. pap. 12.95 (*1-85371-615-4*) Poolbeg Pr. IRL. *Dist:* Dufour Editions, Inc.

Knowles, John. A Separate Peace. 1990. mass mkt. o.s.i (*0-553-54007-6*); 1984. 208p. mass mkt. 5.99 o.s.i (*0-553-28041-4*) Bantam Bks.

—A Separate Peace. 1975. 12.04 (*0-606-01345-8*) Turtleback Bks.

Kondoleon, Harry. Diary of a Lost Boy. 1995. 224p. 10.00 o.s.i (*1-57322-504-5*, Riverhead Trade (Paperbacks)) Berkley Publishing Group.

Koontz, Dean. False Memory. 2000. 784p. mass mkt. o.s.i (*0-553-58367-0*); 784p. mass mkt. 7.99 (*0-553-58022-1*); mass mkt. (*0-553-84028-2*) Bantam Bks.

—False Memory. l.t. ed. 2000. 864p. pap. 14.95 (*0-375-72790-6*); 592p. 26.95 (*0-375-40970-X*) Random Hse. Large Print.

Koppelman, Susan. Women's Friendships: A Collection of Short Stories. 1991. E-Book 15.95 (*0-585-16933-0*) netLibrary, Inc.

Koppelman, Susan, intro. Women's Friendships: A Collection of Short Stories. 1991. 352p. 32.50 (*0-8061-2376-1*); pap. 15.95 (*0-8061-2386-9*) Univ. of Oklahoma Pr.

Koretsky, J. Lea. Wall of Darkness. 2002. 119p. pap. 14.95 (*1-58790-020-3*) Regent Pr.

Kowalski, William. The Adventures of Flash Jackson: A Novel. 2003. 320p. 24.95 (*0-06-621136-0*) HarperCollins Pubs.

—The Adventures of Flash Jackson: A Novel. 2004. 336p. pap. 13.95 (*0-06-093624-X*, Perennial) HarperTrade.

Kraus, Joanna H. Sunday Gold. 2003. 110p. 9.95 (*1-932162-19-4*) Benoy Publishing.

—Sunday Gold. 1998. 53p. pap. 5.60 (*0-87129-867-8*, SC6) Dramatic Publishing Co.

Lambright, Evelyn Slim. The Justus Girls. 2001. 368p. 24.00 (*0-06-018476-0*) HarperCollins Pubs.

Lamott, Anne. Blue Shoe. 2003. 336p. pap. 14.00 (*1-57322-342-5*, Riverhead Trade (Paperbacks)) Berkley Publishing Group.

—Blue Shoe. l.t. ed. 2002. (Wheeler Hardcover Ser.). 430p. 31.95 (*1-58724-362-8*, Wheeler Publishing, Inc.) Gale Group.

—Blue Shoe. 2002. 304p. 24.95 (*1-57322-226-7*, Riverhead Bks. (Hardcovers)) Putnam Publishing Group, The.

Lanchester, John. Fragrant Harbor. 2003. 352p. pap. 14.00 (*0-14-200337-9*) Penguin Group (USA) Inc.

Landvick, Lorna. Your Oasis on Flame Lake. 2003. 322p. 30.95 (*1-57490-500-7*, Beeler Large Print Bks.) Beeler, Thomas T. Publisher.

Landvik, Lorna. Angry Housewives Eating Bon Bons. 2004. 432p. pap. 13.95 (*0-345-44282-2*) Ballantine Bks.

—Angry Housewives Eating Bon Bons. l.t. ed. 2003. 30.95 (*0-7862-5406-8*) Thorndike Pr.

Lang, Jefferson. "Who's Laughing Now?" 2001. pap. 21.95 (*0-595-17621-6*) iUniverse, Inc.

Lansdale, Joe R. A Fine Dark Line. l.t. ed. 2003. 31.95 (*1-58724-419-5*, Wheeler Publishing, Inc.) Gale Group.

—A Fine Dark Line. 2003. 320p. 24.95 (*0-89296-729-3*) Mysterious Pr.

—A Fine Dark Line. 2003. 320p. pap. 12.95 (*0-446-69167-4*, Mysterious Pr. Paperback Bks.) Warner Bks., Inc.

Laser, Michael. Old Buddy, Old Pal. 1999. 160p. 24.00 (*1-57962-021-3*) Permanent Pr., The.

Lawrence, D. H. The Rainbow & Women in Love. Beynon, Richard, ed. 2003. (Readers' Guides to Essential Criticism Ser.). 192p. pap. 14.99 o.s.i (*1-874166-69-2*) Palgrave Macmillan.

—Women in Love. E-Book 4.95 (*1-931208-66-2*) Adobe Systems, Inc.

—Women in Love. 30.95 (*0-89190-612-6*) Amereon, Ltd.

—Women in Love. 1996. 560p. reprint ed. mass mkt. 4.95 (*0-553-21454-3*, Bantam Classics) Bantam Bks.

—Women in Love. E-Book 5.00 (*0-7607-1338-3*) Barnes & Noble, Inc.

—Women in Love. 1984. 421p. reprint ed. lib. bdg. 27.95 (*0-89966-496-2*) Buccaneer Bks., Inc.

—Women in Love. Farmer, David H. et al, eds. 1987. (Cambridge Edition of the Works of D. H. Lawrence). (Illus.). 706p. 115.00 o.p. (*0-521-23565-0*); 705p. pap. 55.00 (*0-521-28041-9*) Cambridge Univ. Pr.

—Women in Love. reprint ed. lib. bdg. 98.00 (*0-7426-3142-7*); 2001. 548p. pap. text 28.00 (*0-7426-8142-4*) Classic Bks.

—Women in Love. 2002. (Thrift Editions Ser.). 400p. pap. 3.50 (*0-486-42458-8*) Dover Pubns., Inc.

—Women in Love. 1992. 20.00 (*0-679-41326-X*, Everyman's Library) Knopf Publishing Group.

—Women in Love. 1992. (Everyman's Library). 20.00 (*0-679-40995-5*) Knopf, Alfred A. Inc.

—Women in Love. 1995. 544p. mass mkt. 6.95 (*0-451-52591-4*, Signet Bks.) NAL.

—Women in Love. 2002. (Twelve-Point Ser.). lib. bdg. 25.00 (*1-58287-180-9*); 722p. lib. bdg. 28.00 (*1-58287-663-0*) North Bks.

—Women in Love. Bradshaw, David, ed. 1998. (Oxford World's Classics Ser.). 576p. pap. 9.95 (*0-19-282995-5*) Oxford Univ. Pr., Inc.

—Women in Love. (Penguin Great Books of the 20th Century Ser.). 2000. (Illus.). 512p. pap. 12.95 o.s.i (*0-14-028337-4*); 1960. pap. 2.75 o.p. (*0-670-00065-5*) Penguin Group (USA) Inc.

—Women in Love. 2000. E-Book 4.95 (*0-679-64166-1*); 576p. pap. 8.95 (*0-375-75488-1*) Random House Adult Trade Publishing Group. (Modern Library).

—Women in Love. 1978. 6.95 o.s.i (*0-394-60442-3*) Random Hse., Inc.

—Women in Love. l.t. ed. 1982. (Charnwood Large Print Ser.). 769p. 29.99 o.p. (*0-7089-8049-X*, Ulverscroft) Thorpe, F. A. Pubs. GBR. *Dist:* Ulverscroft Large Print Bks., Ltd., Ulverscroft Large Print Canada, Ltd.

—Women in Love. 1998. 15.00 (*0-606-21001-6*) Turtleback Bks.

—Women in Love. Farmer, David H. et al, eds. 1995. (Twentieth Century Classics Ser.). (Illus.). 592p. 10.95 (*0-14-018816-9*, Penguin Classics) Viking Penguin.

—Women in Love. 1990. 608p. pap. 8.95 o.p. (*0-14-018221-7*, Penguin Bks.); 1989. 464p. 18.95 o.p. (*0-670-82585-9*) Viking Penguin.

—Women in Love. Ross, Charles L., ed. 1982. (English Library). 608p. pap. 4.95 o.p. (*0-14-043156-X*, Penguin Classics) Viking Penguin.

—Women in Love. 1976. 496p. pap. 7.95 o.p. (*0-14-004260-1*, Penguin Bks.) Viking Penguin.

—Women in Love. 1995. (Classics Ser.). 464p. pap. 3.95 (*1-85326-007-X*, 007XWW) Wordsworth Editions, Ltd. GBR. *Dist:* Casemate Pubs. & Bk. Distributors, LLC.

Lawrence, Rae. Jacqueline Susann's Shadow of the Dolls. 2001. 320p. 22.00 o.s.i (*0-609-60585-2*) Crown Publishing Group.

—Jacqueline Susann's Shadow of the Dolls. 2002. 368p. mass mkt. 7.99 o.s.i (*0-7582-0272-5*) Kensington Publishing Corp.

Lebrecht, Norman. The Song of Names. 2004. 320p. pap. 14.00 (*1-4000-3489-2*) Knopf Publishing Group.

Lehrer, James. Flying Crows: A Novel. 2004. 256p. 23.95 (*1-4000-6197-0*) Random Hse., Inc.

Lehrer, Kate. Out of Eden. l.t. ed. 1997. (Niagara Large Print Ser.). 548p. 29.50 o.p. (*0-7089-5869-9*, Ulverscroft) Thorpe, F. A. Pubs. GBR. *Dist:* Ulverscroft Large Print Bks., Ltd.

—Out of Eden: A Novel. 2003. ix, 342p. pap. 16.95 (*1-931868-33-6*) Capital Bks., Inc.

Leigh, Wendy. The Secret Letters of Marilyn Monroe & Jacqueline Kennedy. 2003. 288p. 24.95 (*0-312-30368-8*) St. Martin's Pr.

—The Secret Letters of Marilyn Monroe & Jacqueline Kennedy. l.t. ed. 2003. (Women's Fiction Ser.). 28.95 (*0-7862-5546-3*) Thorndike Pr.

Lentricchia, Frank. Lucchesi & the Whale. Fish, Stanley & Jameson, Fredric, eds. 2003. 128p. pap. 16.95 (*0-8223-3171-3*) Duke Univ. Pr.

—Lucchesi & the Whale. 2001. (Post-Contemporary Interventions Ser.). 104p. pap. 24.95 (*0-8223-2654-X*) Duke Univ. Pr.

Lethem, Jonathan. The Fortress of Solitude: A Novel. 2003. 528p. 26.00 (*0-385-50069-6*) Doubleday Publishing.

—The Fortress of Solitude: A Novel. l.t. ed. 2003. 824p. 31.95 (*0-7862-5996-5*) Gale Group.

Levinson, Barry. Sixty-Six. 2003. 288p. 24.00 (*0-7679-1533-X*) Broadway Bks.

Levithan, David. Boy Meets Boy. 2003. 192p. (gr. 7). (J). 15.95 (*0-375-82400-6*); lib. bdg. 17.99 (*0-375-92400-0*, Knopf Bks. for Young Readers) Random Hse. Children's Bks.

Lewis, Beverly. Hide Behind the Moon. 1998. (Summerhill Secrets Ser.: Vol. 8). 144p. (J). (gr. 6-9). pap. 5.99 (*1-55661-874-3*) Bethany Hse. Pubs.

Lionni, Leo. Nadarin. 1998. (SPA., Illus.). 32p. (J). (ps-3). 7.95 (*84-264-4650-7*, LUM6507) Lectorum Pubns., Inc.

Longhi, Jon. Wake up & Smell the Beer. 2003. 160p. pap. 13.95 (*0-916397-83-1*) Manic D Pr.

Lurie, Alison. The Last Resort. 1998. 336p. 22.00 o.s.i (*0-8050-5866-4*) Holt, Henry & Co.

Lurie, Alison, contrib. by. The Last Resort. 1998. 254p. (*0-7011-6713-0*) Chatto & Windus.

MacFarlane, Bud, Jr. Conceived Without Sin. 1997. 608p. pap. text 3.99 (*0-9646316-1-X*) St. Jude Media.

Mackay, Shena. The Orchard on Fire. l.t. unabr. ed. 2000. 288p. 32.50 (*0-7531-6026-9*, 160269) ISIS Large Print Bks. GBR. *Dist:* Ulverscroft Large Print Bks., Ltd.

—The Orchard on Fire. 1996. 215p. 19.95 (*1-55921-175-X*) Moyer Bell.

MacLaverty, Bernard. The Anatomy School. 368p. 2003. 14.95 (*0-393-32457-5*); 2002. 25.95 (*0-393-05052-1*) Norton, W. W. & Co., Inc.

—The Anatomy School. 2002. 368p. pap. (*0-676-97445-7*, Vintage) Random Hse. of Canada, Ltd. CAN. *Dist:* Random Hse., Inc.

Macomber, Debbie. Between Friends: A Novel. 2003. 416p. mass mkt. (*1-55166-674-X*); 2002. 384p. (*1-55166-905-6*, 1-66905-0) Harlequin Enterprises, Ltd. (Mira Bks.).

—Thursdays at Eight. 2001. 304p. (*1-55166-811-4*, Mira Bks.) Harlequin Enterprises, Ltd.

Major, Marcus. Four Guys & Trouble. 2001. 272p. 23.95 o.p. (*0-525-94568-7*, Dutton) Dutton/Plume.

—Four Guys & Trouble. 2002. 384p. mass mkt. 6.99 (*0-451-41017-3*, Onyx) NAL.

Malone, Michael. The Last Noel. 304p. 2003. pap. 14.00 (*1-4022-0147-8*); 2002. 18.00 (*1-4022-0012-9*) Sourcebooks, Inc. (Sourcebooks Landmark).

Manuel, Lynn. The Cherry Pit Princess. 1997. (Illus.). 160p. (J). (gr. 4-7). pap. 5.95 (*1-55050-118-6*) Coteau Bks. CAN. *Dist:* General Distribution Services, Inc.

—The Cherry Pit Princess. 1997. 12.00 (*0-606-19012-0*) Turtleback Bks.

Mapson, Jo-Ann. Along Came Mary. 2003. 368p. 24.00 (*0-7432-2461-2*); E-Book 24.00 (*0-7432-3878-8*) Simon & Schuster. (Simon & Schuster).

—Along Came Mary. l.t. ed. 2003. 30.95 (*1-58724-414-4*, Wheeler Publishing, Inc.) Gale Group.

—Along Came Mary: A Bad Girl Creek Novel. 2004. 384p. pap. 13.00 (*0-7432-2462-0*, Simon & Schuster) Simon & Schuster.

—Bad Girl Creek. 2002. 384p. pap. 13.00 (*0-7432-1771-3*, Simon & Schuster) Simon & Schuster.

—Bad Girl Creek: A Novel. l.t. ed. 2001. 529p. 29.95 o.p. (*1-58724-126-9*, Wheeler Publishing, Inc.) Gale Group.

—Bad Girl Creek: A Novel. 2001. 384p. 24.00 (*0-7432-0256-2*, Simon & Schuster) Simon & Schuster.

Martel, John. Billy Strobe. 2001. 400p. 25.95 o.p. (*0-525-94618-7*, Dutton) Dutton/Plume.

—Billy Strobe. 2002. 544p. reprint ed. mass mkt. 7.99 (*0-451-20668-1*, Signet Bks.) NAL.

Martin, Ann M. A Corner of the Universe. 2002. 208p. (J). (gr. 5-8). pap. 15.95 (*0-439-38880-5*, Scholastic Pr.) Scholastic, Inc.

Martin, J. Wallis. A Likeness in Stone. 1998. 288p. 22.95 (*0-312-18626-6*) St. Martin's Pr.

—A Likeness in Stone. l.t. ed. 1998. (Mystery Ser.). 376p. 26.95 (*0-7862-1684-0*) Thorndike Pr.

—A Likeness in Stone. l.t. ed. 1998. (Ulverscroft Large Print Ser.). 448p. 29.99 o.p. (*0-7089-3895-7*, Ulverscroft) Thorpe, F. A. Pubs. GBR. *Dist:* Ulverscroft Large Print Bks., Ltd., Ulverscroft Large Print Canada, Ltd.

Martin, Joe. Fire in the Rock. 2003. 272p. pap. 13.95 (*0-345-45691-2*, Ballantine Bks.) Ballantine Bks.

—Fire in the Rock. 2001. 300p. 21.95 (*0-9708972-1-9*) Novello Festival Pr.

Martin, Julia Wallis. A Likeness in Stone. 1999. 282p. mass mkt. 6.50 (*0-312-97077-3*, St. Martin's Paperbacks) St. Martin's Pr.

Martin, S. R. Talk to Me. 1999. (Insomniacs Ser.: No. 3). (Illus.). 80p. (YA). (gr. 7-12). mass mkt. 2.99 (*0-590-69142-2*) Scholastic, Inc.

Martinez, Nina Marie. Caramba! A Tale Told in Turns of the Card. 2004. (Illus.). 384p. 24.95 (*0-375-41375-8*) Knopf, Alfred A. Inc.

Mason, J. D. And on the Eighth Day She Rested: A Novel. 2003. 288p. pap. 13.95 (*0-312-30989-9*, Saint Martin's Griffin) St. Martin's Pr.

Matalon, Ronit. Bliss: A Novel. Cohen, Jessica, tr. from HEB. 2003. 272p. 23.00 (*0-8050-6602-0*, Metropolitan Bks.) Holt, Henry & Co.

Matthews, Carole. Bare Necessity. 2003. 384p. pap. 13.95 (*0-06-053214-9*, Avon Bks.) Morrow/Avon.

Mattison, Alice. Hilda & Pearl. 2001. 304p. pap. 13.00 (*0-06-093693-2*, Perennial) HarperTrade.

—Hilda & Pearl. 1995. 288p. 22.00 o.p. (*0-688-13127-1*, Morrow, William & Co.) Morrow/Avon.

McAfee, Carol. Walk among Birches. 2002. 288p. 22.00 o.p. (*1-57071-908-X*, Sourcebooks Landmark) Sourcebooks, Inc.

McComas, Paul. Unplugged: A Novel. 2002. 272p. pap. 14.95 (*1-880284-60-X*) Daniel, John & Co., Pubs.

McCracken, Elizabeth. Niagara Falls All over Again. 2002. 320p. pap. 12.95 (*0-385-33648-9*); E-Book 11.50 (*0-440-33391-1*) Dell Publishing. (Delta).

—Niagara Falls All over Again. l.t. ed. 2002. 490p. 27.95 (*1-58724-155-2*, Wheeler Publishing, Inc.) Gale Group.

McCullers, Carson. The Heart Is a Lonely Hunter. 1999. mass mkt. (*0-553-23911-2*); 1999. mass mkt. (*0-553-22698-3*); 1994. mass mkt. 6.99 (*0-553-54173-0*); 1983. 320p. mass mkt. 6.50 (*0-553-26963-1*, Bantam Classics); 1983. (YA). (gr. 10-12). mass mkt. 3.50 o.s.i (*0-553-25481-2*) Bantam Bks.

—The Heart Is a Lonely Hunter. 1994. lib. bdg. 19.95 (*1-56849-462-9*) Buccaneer Bks., Inc.

—The Heart Is a Lonely Hunter, 001. 9999. 18.95 o.p. (*0-395-07978-0*) Houghton Mifflin Co.

—The Heart Is a Lonely Hunter. 2000. 320p. pap. 12.00 (*0-618-08474-6*, Mariner Bks.) Houghton Mifflin Co. Trade & Reference Div.

—The Heart Is a Lonely Hunter. mass mkt. 0.25 o.p. (*0-451-00596-1*, Signet Bks.) NAL.

—The Heart Is a Lonely Hunter. 1993. (Modern Library Ser.). 448p. 18.95 (*0-679-42474-1*, Modern Library) Random House Adult Trade Publishing Group.

—The Heart Is a Lonely Hunter. l.t. ed. 1999. (Perennial Bestsellers Ser.). 474p. 27.95 (*0-7838-8773-6*) Thorndike Pr.

—The Heart Is a Lonely Hunter. 1953. 12.04 (*0-606-00786-5*) Turtleback Bks.

McDermid, Val. The Distant Echo. Date not set. mass mkt. (*0-312-99483-4*, St. Martin's Paperbacks); 2003. 384p. 24.95 o.s.i (*0-312-30199-5*, Saint Martin's Minotaur) St. Martin's Pr.

McDonell, J. M. Half Crazy: A Novel, Vol. 1. 1995. 258p. 19.95 (*0-316-55560-6*) Little Brown & Co.

—Half Crazy: A Novel. 2000. 310p. pap. 12.95 (*1-893224-04-X*, New Millennium Pr.) New Millennium Entertainment.

McFadden, Bernice L. Sugar. 240p. 2000. 22.95 (*0-525-94531-8*, Dutton); 2001. reprint ed. pap. 13.00 (*0-452-28220-9*, Plume) Dutton/Plume.

—Sugar. l.t. ed. 2002. (African American Ser.). 386p. 28.95 (*0-7862-3871-2*) Thorndike Pr.

—Sugar. 2001. 19.05 (*0-606-20932-8*) Turtleback Bks.

—This Bitter Earth. 2002. 288p. pap. 13.00 (*0-452-28381-7*, Plume); 23.95 o.s.i (*0-525-94636-5*, Dutton) Dutton/Plume.

—This Bitter Earth. l.t. ed. 2002. (African American Ser.). 420p. 29.95 (*0-7862-3882-8*) Thorndike Pr.

McGhee, Alison. Shadow Baby: Today Show Book Club Edition. 2003. 256p. pap. 14.00 (*0-312-42377-2*) Picador.

McInerney, Jay. The Last of the Savages. 1997. 288p. pap. 13.00 (*0-679-74952-7*, Vintage) Knopf Publishing Group.

McKenna, Marita C. The Magdelen. 2002. 352p. pap. 14.95 (*0-7653-0513-5*, Forge Bks.) Doherty, Tom Assocs., LLC.

McKinnon, Karen. Narcissus Ascending: A Novel. 2003. 224p. pap. 13.00 (*0-312-31218-0*) Picador.

McMillan, Terry. Waiting to Exhale. l.t. ed. 1993. (General Ser.). 600p. pap. 17.95 (*0-8161-5618-2*); lib. bdg. 23.95 o.p. (*0-8161-5617-4*) Gale Group. (Macmillan Reference USA).

—Waiting to Exhale. 1996. 155p. per. 20.97 (*0-671-85153-5*); 1993. 416p. mass mkt. 6.50 (*0-671-86417-3*); 1992. 264.00 o.p. (*0-670-77972-5*); 1995. 416p. reprint ed. mass mkt. 7.99 (*0-671-53745-8*) Simon & Schuster. (Pocket).

—Waiting to Exhale. Rosenman, Jane, ed. 1994. 416p. reprint ed. pap. 14.00 (*0-671-50148-8*, Washington Square Pr.) Simon & Schuster.

—Waiting to Exhale. 1992. 416p. 22.95 (*0-670-83980-9*, Viking) Viking Penguin.

Medina, C. C. A Little Love. 2001. 432p. mass mkt. 7.50 o.s.i (*0-446-60976-5*) Warner Bks., Inc.

Medlicott, Joan. The Gardens of Covington. 2001. E-Book 23.95 (*1-58945-793-5*) Adobe Systems, Inc.

—The Gardens of Covington. l.t. ed. 2001. (Illus.). 451p. 28.95 o.p. (*1-58724-081-5*, Wheeler Publishing, Inc.) Gale Group.

—The Gardens of Covington. 2001. (Illus.). 326p. 23.95 (*0-312-27555-2*) St. Martin's Pr.

—Ladies of Covington Send Their Love. 2000. 326p. 24.95 (*0-312-25329-X*) St. Martin's Pr.

—The Ladies of Covington Send Their Love. 2000. E-Book 6.99 (*0-312-27387-8*) St. Martin's Pr.

—The Ladies of Covington Send Their Love. l.t. ed. 2000. (Americana Ser.). 624p. 26.95 (*0-7862-2976-4*) Thorndike Pr.

—Untitled Ladies of Covington. 320p. No. 1. 2004. mass mkt. 6.99 (*0-7434-7037-0*, Pocket Star); No. 2. 2005. mass mkt. (*0-7434-7041-9*, Pocket); No. 3. 2006. mass mkt. (*0-7434-7045-1*, Pocket); Vol. 2. 2004. 24.00 (*0-7434-7039-7*, Atria); Vol. 3. 2005. 24.00 (*0-7434-7043-5*, Atria) Simon & Schuster.

Mitchard, Jacquelyn. The Most Wanted. l.t. ed. 1998. (Large Print Bks.). 407p. 27.95 (*1-56895-605-3*, Wheeler Publishing, Inc.) Gale Group.

—The Most Wanted. 1999. 416p. reprint ed. mass mkt. 7.99 o.s.i (*0-451-19685-6*, Signet Bks.) NAL.

—The Most Wanted. 1998. 448p. (gr. 9). 24.95 o.s.i (*0-670-87884-7*, Viking) Viking Penguin.

Mitchell, Sharon. Near Perfect. 2001. 336p. 23.95 o.s.i (*0-525-94621-7*, Dutton) Dutton/Plume.

—Near Perfect. 2002. 352p. reprint ed. mass mkt. 6.99 o.s.i (*0-451-20689-4*, Signet Bks.) NAL.

—Near Perfect. l.t. ed. 2002. (African American Ser.). 572p. 29.95 (*0-7862-3865-8*) Thorndike Pr.

—Nothing but the Rent. 1999. 352p. mass mkt. 6.99 (*0-451-19260-5*, Signet Bks.) NAL.

Monroe, Mary. Gonna Lay down My Burdens. 2003. 320p. pap. 15.00 (*0-7582-0001-3*); 2002. 288p. 24.00 (*1-57566-911-0*) Kensington Publishing Corp.

Montgomery, L. M. Anne of Green Gables. 2001. 276p. 25.99 (*1-58827-584-1*); per. 20.99 (*1-58827-585-X*) IndyPublish.com.

—Anne of Green Gables. Stemach, Jerry, ed. 2000. text 65.00 incl. audio, cd-rom (*1-58702-311-3*); text 50.00 (*1-58702-502-7*) Johnston, Don Inc.

—Anne of Green Gables. 2003. 320p. mass mkt. 4.95 (*0-451-52882-4*, Signet Classics) NAL.

—Anne of Green Gables. (Illustrated Junior Library Ser.). 2000. 9.99 o.s.i (*0-448-42432-0*); 1970. 6.95 o.p. (*0-448-02545-0*) Penguin Putnam Bks. for Young Readers. (Grosset & Dunlap).

—Anne of Green Gables. E-Book 5.00 (*0-7410-0400-3*) SoftBook Pr.

Moody, Martha. Best Friends: A Novel. 2002. 496p. pap. 14.00 (*1-57322-935-0*, Riverhead Trade (Paperbacks)) Berkley Publishing Group.

—Best Friends: A Novel. 2001. 400p. 26.95 o.p. (*1-57322-188-0*, Riverhead Bks. (Hardcovers)) Putnam Publishing Group, The.

Moore, Alison. Synonym for Love. 1996. 256p. pap. 10.95 o.p. (*0-452-27622-5*, Plume) Dutton/Plume.

—Synonym for Love. 1995. 256p. text 19.95 (*1-56279-074-9*) Mercury Hse.

Moritsugu, Kim. Old Flames. 1999. 212p. 17.95 (*0-88984-203-5*) Porcupine's Quill, Inc. CAN. *Dist:* Univ. of Toronto Pr.

Morris, Mary. Acts of God. 2000. 256p. 23.00 (*0-312-24663-3*) Picador.

Moyes, Jojo. Windfallen. 2004. 512p. mass mkt. 7.50 (*0-06-001291-9*, HarperTorch); 2003. 400p. 24.95 (*0-06-001290-0*, Morrow, William & Co.) Morrow/Avon.

Myerson, Julie. Something Might Happen. 2003. 336p. 23.95 (*0-316-77984-9*) Little Brown & Co.

Nattel, Lilian. The Singing Fire. 2004. 352p. (*0-676-97600-X*) Knopf Canada CAN. *Dist:* Random Hse. of Canada, Ltd., Random Hse., Inc.

Neihart, Ben. Burning Girl. 2000. 256p. pap. 13.00 (*0-688-17689-5*); 1999. 245p. 24.00 (*0-688-15691-6*) Morrow/Avon. (Morrow, William & Co.).

Nersesian, Arthur. Dogrun. 2000. (Illus.). 272p. pap. 12.95 (*0-671-77542-1*, MTV) Simon & Schuster.

Newberry, Clare Turlay. Babette. 1999. (Clare Newberry Classics Ser.). (Illus.). 32p. (J). (ps-3). 9.98 (*0-7651-0950-6*) Smithmark Pubs., Inc.

Nunes, Rachel Ann. Ariana: A Novel: a Gift Most Precious. 2003. 221p. pap. 14.95 (*1-55517-646-1*, 76461) Cedar Fort, Inc./CFI Distribution.

Nunez, Sigrid. For Rouenna. 2001. 208p. 22.00 o.p. (*0-374-25430-3*) Farrar, Straus & Giroux.

—For Rouenna. l.t. ed. 2001. 273p. 27.95 (*1-58724-217-6*, Wheeler Publishing, Inc.) Gale Group.

—For Rouenna: A Novel. 2002. 240p. pap. 13.00 (*0-312-42063-3*) Picador.

O'Brien, Keith. Between Friends. 2000. 208p. pap. 13.95 (*0-9679394-4-5*) Global Learning Systems, LLC.

O'Brien, Tim. July, July: A Novel. 2002. 336p. tchr. ed. 26.00 (*0-618-03969-4*) Houghton Mifflin Co.

O'Conner, Varley. A Company of Three. 2003. 320p. 24.95 (*1-56512-373-5*) Algonquin Bks. of Chapel Hill.

O'Hanlon, Ardal. Knick Knack Paddy Whack. 2001. 256p. reprint ed. pap. 13.00 (*0-15-601353-3*, Harvest Bks.) Harcourt Trade Pubs.

—Knick Knack Paddy Whack: A Novel. 2000. (Illus.). 244p. 23.00 o.s.i (*0-8050-6330-7*) Holt, Henry & Co.

Ojikutu, Bayo. 47th Street Black: A Novel. 2003. 432p. pap. 12.95 (*0-609-80847-8*, Crown) Crown Publishing Group.

Oke, Janette. A Searching Heart. l.t. ed. 1999. (Prairie Legacy Ser.: Vol. 2). 312p. (*0-7540-3614-6*) BBC Audiobooks America.

—A Searching Heart. 1998. (Prairie Legacy Ser.: Bk. 2). 256p. text 16.99 o.s.i (*0-7642-2140-X*); 256p. pap. 12.99 (*0-7642-2139-6*); 352p. pap. 16.99 o.p. (*0-7642-2142-6*) Bethany Hse. Pubs.

—A Searching Heart. l.t. ed. 1999. (Prairie Legacy Ser.: Vol. 2). 312p. 27.95 (*0-7838-0404-0*) Thorndike Pr.

Oke, Janette, contrib. by. A Searching Heart. (*0-7540-3613-8*) BBC Audiobooks America.

Oke, Janette & Bunn, T. Davis. Return to Harmony. 1996. 224p. text 15.99 o.p. (*1-55661-901-4*); 288p. pap. 12.99 o.p. (*1-55661-902-2*); 224p. pap. 10.99 o.p. (*1-55661-878-6*) Bethany Hse. Pubs.

—Return to Harmony. l.t. ed. 1997. (Inspirational Ser.). 273p. lib. bdg. 24.95 (*0-7838-8220-3*, Macmillan Reference USA) Gale Group.

O'Nan, Stewart. A Prayer for the Dying: A Novel. l.t. ed. 2000. (Wheeler Large Print Book Ser.). 196p. 26.95 (*1-56895-841-2*, Wheeler Publishing, Inc.) Gale Group.

—A Prayer for the Dying: A Novel. 1999. 195p. 22.00 o.s.i (*0-8050-6147-9*) Holt, Henry & Co.

—A Prayer for the Dying: A Novel. 2000. 208p. pap. 13.00 (*0-312-25501-2*) Picador.

O'Neill, Jamie. At Swim, Two Boys. 2002. E-Book 28.00 (*1-4014-9977-5*) Barnes & Noble Digital.

—At Swim, Two Boys. 2003. 576p. pap. 15.00 (*0-7432-2295-4*); 2002. E-Book 28.00 (*0-7432-4187-8*); 2002. 576p. 28.00 (*0-7432-2294-6*); 2001. 643p. (*0-7432-0712-2*); 2001. 643p. pap. (*0-7432-0713-0*) Simon & Schuster. (Scribner).

Palliser, Charles. The Unburied. 1999. 400p. 24.00 (*0-374-28035-5*) Farrar, Straus & Giroux.

—The Unburied. 2000. 432p. reprint ed. pap. 13.95 (*0-7434-1051-3*, Washington Square Pr.) Simon & Schuster.

—The Unburied. l.t. ed. 2000. (Basic Ser.). 655p. 29.95 (*0-7862-2543-2*) Thorndike Pr.

Paraskevas, Betty. Hoppy & Joe. 1999. (Illus.). 32p. (J). (ps-3). 16.00 (*0-689-82199-9*, Simon & Schuster Children's Publishing) Simon & Schuster Children's Publishing.

Parr, Todd. The Best Friend's Book. 2000. (Illus.). 24p. (J). (ps-3). 5.95 (*0-316-69201-8*) Little Brown & Co.

Pascal, Francine, creator. Got a Problem? 1999. (Sweet Valley Junior High Ser.: No. 11). 160p. (gr. 3-7). pap. text 4.50 o.s.i (*0-553-48669-1*, Sweet Valley) Random Hse. Children's Bks.

Patterson, James. 1st to Die. 2001. 432p. 26.95 o.p. (*0-316-66600-9*) Little Brown & Co.

—1st to Die. l.t. ed. 2001. 464p. 32.95 (*0-7862-3291-9*); pap. 29.95 (*0-7862-3292-7*); (*0-7540-2486-5*); (*0-7540-1631-5*) Thorndike Pr.

—1st to Die. 2001. E-Book 4.95 (*0-7595-8434-6*) Time Warner Bk. Group.

—1st to Die. 2001. 432p. pap. 16.00 (*0-446-67842-2*); 2002. 488p. reprint ed. mass mkt. 7.99 (*0-446-61003-8*) Warner Bks., Inc.

—1st to Die. 2001. E-Book 4.95 (*0-7595-6427-2*) ereads.com.

Patterson, Richard North. The Outside Man. 1997. pap. 12.00 o.s.i (*0-345-41815-8*); 1995. mass mkt. 6.99 o.p. (*0-345-90514-8*); 1985. mass mkt. 2.95 o.s.i (*0-345-32533-8*, Ballantine Bks.); 1982. 320p. mass mkt. 7.99 (*0-345-30020-3*) Ballantine Bks.

—The Outside Man. l.t. ed. 2000. (Wheeler Large Print Book Ser.). 324p. 29.95 o.p. (*1-56895-907-9*, Wheeler Publishing, Inc.) Gale Group.

—The Outside Man. 1981. 252p. 11.95 o.p. (*0-316-69362-6*) Little Brown & Co.

Pearce, Jonathan. Buds: A Story about Friendship. 2003. 154p. per. 12.95 (*1-59411-006-9*) Writers' Collective, The.

Pearson, T. R. True Cross. 2003. 272p. 24.95 (*0-670-03238-7*, Viking) Viking Penguin.

Peart, Jane. Homeward the Seeking Heart. 1990. (Orphan Train West Ser.). 192p. (gr. 10 up). pap. 7.99 o.p. (*0-8007-5374-7*) Revell, Fleming H. Co.

—Homeward the Seeking Heart. l.t. ed. 2000. (Christian Fiction Ser.). 291p. (YA). 24.95 (*0-7862-2531-9*) Thorndike Pr.

Pete, Eric E. Someone's in the Kitchen. 2002. 243p. pap. 15.00 (*0-9704995-1-5*) E-fect Publishing.

Peterson, John. The Littles & Their Amazing New Friend. 1999. (Littles Ser.). (Illus.). 102p. (J). (gr. 1-5). mass mkt. 3.99 (*0-590-87612-0*) Scholastic, Inc.

Pfister, Marcus. Flocon et Cache-Noisette. 1998. Tr. of Hopper's Treetop Adventure. (FRE., Illus.). 15.95 (*3-314-21021-3*) North-South Bks., Inc.

—Mats und die Wundersteine. 1998. Tr. of Milo & the Magical Stones. (GER., Illus.). (J). 18.95 (*3-314-00780-9*) North-South Bks., Inc.

Phillips, Michael. Angels Watching over Me. 2002. (Shenandoah Sisters Ser.: Bk. 1). 320p. 16.99 (*0-7642-2705-X*); pap. 12.99 (*0-7642-2700-9*) Bethany Hse. Pubs.

—A Day to Pick Your Own Cotton. 2003. (Shenandoah Sisters Ser.). 320p. 17.99 (*0-7642-2706-8*); pap. 12.99 (*0-7642-2701-7*) Bethany Hse. Pubs.

Plain, Belva. Looking Back. 2002. 400p. reprint ed. mass mkt. 7.99 (*0-440-23577-4*) Dell Publishing.

—Looking Back. l.t. ed. 2001. 496p. 25.95 (*0-375-43098-9*) Random Hse. Large Print.

Plass, Adrian. Ghosts: The Story of a Reunion. 2003. 206p. pap. 11.99 (*0-551-03110-7*); 224p. pap. 10.99 (*0-310-24917-1*) Zondervan.

Powell, Jacqueline. Anyone Who Has a Heart. 2003. 352p. 23.95 (*0-446-53174-X*) Warner Bks., Inc.

Preston, John. Franny, the Queen of Provincetown. 1983. 96p. pap. 4.95 o.p. (*0-932870-31-7*) Alyson Pubns.

—Franny, the Queen of Provincetown. 1995. 112p. pap. 8.95 o.p. (*0-312-14106-8*, Saint Martin's Griffin) St. Martin's Pr.

Price, Reynolds. The Tongues of Angels. 1991. 244p. mass mkt. 5.99 o.s.i (*0-345-37102-X*, Ballantine Bks.) Ballantine Bks.

—The Tongues of Angels. 2000. 208p. pap. 11.00 (*0-7432-0221-X*, Scribner) Simon & Schuster.

Purcell, Deirdre. Marble Gardens. l.t. ed. 2003. (Charnwood Large Print Ser.). 544p. 32.50 (*0-7089-4826-X*) Thorpe, F. A. Pubs. GBR. *Dist:* Ulverscroft Large Print Bks., Ltd., Ulverscroft Large Print Canada, Ltd.

Pye, Frances. Sharing Sean: A Novel. 2004. 480p. (*0-06-054556-9*, Morrow, William & Co.) Morrow/Avon.

Pym, Barbara. Jane & Prudence. 1990. 22p. pap. 10.00 o.p. (*0-452-26895-8*, Plume); 1981. 13.95 o.p. (*0-525-13640-1*, Dutton) Dutton/Plume.

—Jane & Prudence. l.t. ed. 1985. (General Ser.). 384p. 15.95 o.p. (*0-8161-3861-3*, Macmillan Reference USA) Gale Group.

—Jane & Prudence. 1982. mass mkt. 3.50 o.p. (*0-06-080594-3*, P 594); 1987. 224p. reprint ed. pap. 6.95 o.p. (*0-06-097101-0*, PL 7101) HarperTrade. (Perennial).

—Jane & Prudence. 1999. 256p. pap. 12.95 (*1-55921-226-8*) Moyer Bell.

—Jane & Prudence. 1990. 22p. pap. 8.95 o.p. (*0-525-48570-8*, Obelisk) NAL.

—No Fond Return of Love. 2003. 256p. reprint ed. pap. 12.95 (*1-55921-306-X*) Moyer Bell.

Rayyan, Omar, illus. Lilacs, Lotuses & Ladybugs. 1997. (*0-7802-8033-4*) Wright Group, The.

Reeve, Clara. The School for Widows. Casler, Jeanine M., ed. 2002. 384p. 60.00 (*0-87413-804-3*) Univ. of Delaware Pr.

Renault, Mary. The Last of the Wine. 2nd ed. 2001. (Vintage Bks.). (Illus.). 400p. pap. 14.00 (*0-375-72681-0*, Vintage) Knopf Publishing Group.

Revoyr, Nina. The Necessary Hunger. 1997. 368p. 22.50 (*0-684-83234-8*, Simon & Schuster) Simon & Schuster.

—The Necessary Hunger. 1998. 368p. pap. 14.95 (*0-312-18142-6*, Saint Martin's Griffin) St. Martin's Pr.

Rice, Christopher. A Density of Souls. 2001. 288p. pap. 13.00 (*0-7868-8646-3*); 2000. 274p. 23.95 (*0-7868-6646-2*) Talk Miramax Bks.

Richmond, Michelle. Dream of the Blue Room. 2003. 297p. 23.00 (*1-931561-24-9*) MacAdam/Cage Publishing, Inc.

Riggs, Bob. My Best Defense. 1996. 208p. (Orig.). (J). (gr. 4-9). pap. 5.95 (*1-886747-01-6*) Ward Hill Pr.

Rivera, Beatriz. Playing with Light. 2000. 245p. pap. 12.95 (*1-55885-310-3*) Arte Publico Pr.

Rivera, Rick P. Stars Always Shine. 2001. 192p. pap. 15.00 (*1-931010-03-X*) Bilingual Pr./Editorial Bilingue.

Roberts, Nora. Carolina Moon. 2001. 480p. reprint ed. mass mkt. 7.99 (*0-515-13038-9*, Jove) Berkley Publishing Group.

—Carolina Moon. 2000. 448p. 24.95 o.p. (*0-399-14592-3*) Penguin Group (USA) Inc.

—Carolina Moon. 2002. 24.95 o.s.i (*0-399-15030-7*) Putnam Publishing Group, The.

—Carolina Moon. l.t. ed. 2000. (Basic Ser.). 712p. 31.95 (*0-7862-2287-5*) Thorndike Pr.

Robinson, C. Kelly. Between Brothers: A Novel. 2001. 384p. pap. 13.95 (*0-375-75772-4*); 256p. pap. 13.95 (*0-676-90055-0*) Random House Adult Trade Publishing Group. (Villard Bks.).

Rodriguez, Abraham. The Buddha Book. 2001. 304p. pap. 14.00 (*0-312-26299-X*) Picador.

Rogers, Jacqueline. Best Friends Sleep Over. 2000. (Illus.). 32p. (YA). (ps-4). mass mkt. 5.99 (*0-439-19994-8*) Scholastic, Inc.

Rosenfeld, Arthur. A Cure for Gravity. 2001. 384p. mass mkt. 6.99 (*0-8125-6566-5*); 2000. 269p. 23.95 (*0-312-87455-3*) Doherty, Tom Assocs., LLC. (Forge Bks.).

Rowan, Paula S. Rick & Rocky. 2000. (Illus.). 32p. (J). (ps-1). 12.95 (*0-7683-2175-1*) CEDCO Publishing.

Roy, Jacqueline. The Fat Lady Sings. 2002. 184p. pap. 14.95 (*0-7043-4711-3*); 2001. 288p. pap. 16.95 (*0-7043-4647-8*) Women's Pr., Ltd., The GBR. *Dist:* Trafalgar Square.

Rudner, Rita. Tickled Pink. abr. ed. 2004. audio compact disk 14.99 (*1-59355-666-7*, 5285) Brilliance Audio.

—Tickled Pink. 2001. 320p. 25.00 (*0-7434-4261-X*); E-Book 25.00 (*0-7434-5135-X*) Simon & Schuster. (Atria).

—Tickled Pink: A Comic Novel. l.t. ed. 2002. 486p. 29.95 (*0-7862-4074-1*) Gale Group.

—Tickled Pink: A Comic Novel. 2002. 320p. reprint ed. pap. 14.00 (*0-7434-4262-8*, Washington Square Pr.) Simon & Schuster.

Rylant, Cynthia. Henry & Mudge under the Yellow Moon. 1998. (Henry & Mudge Ser.). (Illus.). (J). (gr. k-3). pap., tchr. ed. 29.95 incl. audio (*0-87499-447-0*); pap. 15.95 incl. audio (*0-87499-445-4*) Live Oak Media.

—Thimbleberry Stories. 2000. (Thimbleberry Collection: Vol. 1). (Illus.). 64p. (J). (gr. k-3). 15.00 (*0-15-201081-5*) Harcourt Children's Bks.

Saxton, Judith A. Harvest Moon. 1996. 536p. 26.95 o.p. (*0-312-15138-1*) St. Martin's Pr.

Schine, Cathleen. The Evolution of Jane. unabr. ed. 1998. audio 24.95 (*1-56740-087-6*, 1484, Bookcassette); audio 57.25 (*1-56740-616-5*, 1485, Unabridged Library Editions) Brilliance Audio.

—The Evolution of Jane. 1999. 224p. pap. 12.95 (*0-452-28120-2*, Plume) Dutton/Plume.

—The Evolution of Jane. 1998. 256p. tchr. ed. 24.00 o.s.i (*0-395-82657-8*) Houghton Mifflin Co.

Schwarz, Christina. All Is Vanity. 2003. 400p. pap. 14.95 (*0-345-43911-2*, Ballantine Bks.) Ballantine Bks.

—All Is Vanity: A Novel. 2002. 384p. 24.95 (*0-385-49972-8*) Doubleday Publishing.

—All Is Vanity: A Novel. l.t. ed. 2003. (Basic Ser.). 488p. 30.95 (*0-7862-4933-1*) Thorndike Pr.

Scragg, Leah, ed. John Lyly Euphues: Anatomy of Wit & 'Euphues & His England' 2003. (Revels Plays Companions Library). (Illus.). 400p. 74.95 o.s.i (*0-7190-6458-9*) Manchester Univ. Pr. GBR. *Dist:* Holtzbrinck Pubs.

Segal, Susan. Aria: A Novel. 2003. 352p. reprint ed. pap. 14.00 (*0-425-18997-X*) Berkley Publishing Group.

—Aria: Novel. 2001. 23.95 (*1-882593-45-6*) Bridge Works Publishing Co., Inc.

Selway, Martina, illus. Wish You Were Here. 1994. 32p. (J). (ps-3). (*1-59093-045-2*); per. (*1-59093-046-0*) Warehousing & Fulfillment Specialists, LLC (WFS, LLC). (Eager Minds Pr.).

Settle, Cheryl Hicks. You've Heard of Abraham, Now Meet Floyd, 1. 1997. pap. 3.99 (*1-57988-156-4*) Sanctuary Bks.

Shamsie, Kamila. Kartography. 2002. (Illus.). 352p. pap. (*0-7475-5730-6*) Bloomsbury Pr.

—Kartography. 320p. 2004. pap. (*0-15-602973-1*, Harvest Bks.); 2003. 24.00 (*0-15-101010-2*) Harcourt Trade Pubs.

—Kartography. 2002. 343p. (*0-19-579833-3*) Oxford Univ. Pr., Inc.

Sharing Good Times. 1997. (Big Comfy Couch Coloring & Activity Ser.). (Illus.). 32p. (J). (ps-1). pap. (*0-7666-0008-4*, Honey Bear Bks.) Modern Publishing.

Shay, Kathryn, et al. The Lipstick Chronicles. 2003. 448p. pap. 13.00 (*0-425-19175-3*) Berkley Publishing Group.

Siddons, Anne Rivers. Islands. 2004. 384p. 24.95 (*0-06-621111-5*); 2003. E-Book 19.95 (*0-06-057677-4*); 2003. E-Book 19.95 (*0-06-057674-X*); 2003. E-Book 19.95 (*0-06-057676-6*); 2003. E-Book 19.95 (*0-06-057675-8*); 2004. audio compact disk 29.95 (*0-06-055458-4*) HarperCollins Pubs.

—Islands. l.t. ed. 2004. 512p. pap. 24.95 (*0-06-054545-3*, HarperLargePrint) HarperTrade.

—Outer Banks. 416p. 2003. pap. 11.95 (*0-06-053806-6*, Perennial); 1991. 19.95 o.p. (*0-06-016249-X*) HarperTrade.

—Outer Banks. 1992. 576p. mass mkt. 7.99 (*0-06-109973-2*, HarperTorch) Morrow/Avon.

Sijie, Dai. Balzac & the Little Chinese Seamstress: A Novel. 2002. Tr. of Balzac et la Petite Tailleuse Chinoise. 192p. pap. 10.00 (*0-385-72220-6*, Anchor Bible) Doubleday Publishing.

—Balzac & the Little Chinese Seamstress: A Novel. Rilke, Ina, tr. from FRE. 2001. Tr. of Balzac et la Petite Tailleuse Chinoise. 208p. 18.00 (*0-375-41309-X*) Knopf, Alfred A. Inc.

Simpson, Mona. Off Keck Road. E-Book 15.95 (*1-58945-518-5*) Adobe Systems, Inc.

—Off Keck Road. 2001. E-Book 10.00 (*0-375-41263-8*) Random Hse., Inc.

—Off Keck Road. l.t. ed. 2001. (Thorndike Press Large Print Women's Fiction Ser.). 229p. (*0-7862-3242-0*) Thorndike Pr.

—Off Keck Road: A Novella. 2001. 176p. reprint ed. pap. 11.00 (*0-375-70906-1*, Vintage) Knopf Publishing Group.

Singleton, Elyse. This Side of the Sky. 2003. 336p. pap. 14.00 (*0-425-19312-8*); 2002. 304p. 24.95 o.s.i (*0-399-14920-1*) Putnam Publishing Group, The. (BlueHen Bks.).

Skalski, Ken, photos by. You're My Friend. 1996. (Puzzle Place Board Bks.). (Illus.). 16p. (J). (ps). 4.50 o.s.i (*0-448-41296-9*, Grosset & Dunlap) Penguin Putnam Bks. for Young Readers.
Smith, Andrea. Friday Nights at Honeybee's. 2003. 320p. 22.95 (*0-385-33428-1*, Dial Bks.) Dell Publishing.
Smith, Brad. All Hat: A Novel. 2003. 320p. 24.00 (*0-8050-7217-9*) Holt, Henry & Co.
—All Hat: A Novel. 2004. 320p. pap. 14.00 (*0-312-42317-9*) Picador.
Smith, Carol. Friends for Life. 480p. 2001. pap. 4.95 (*0-446-52004-7*); 1997. mass mkt. 6.50 (*0-446-60445-3*) Warner Bks., Inc.
Smith, Charlie. Shine Hawk. 1988. 368p. 17.95 o.s.i (*0-945167-01-6*) British American Publishing, Ltd.
—Shine Hawk. 1990. 384p. reprint ed. pap. (*0-671-68498-1*, Washington Square Pr.) Simon & Schuster.
—Shine Hawk: A Novel by Charlie Smith. 1998. 384p. pap. 16.95 (*0-8203-1997-X*) Univ. of Georgia Pr.
Smith, Lee. The Last Girls: A Novel. (Illus.). 2003. 384p. 24.95 (*1-56512-405-7*); 2002. 400p. tchr. ed. 24.95 (*1-56512-363-8*, 72363) Algonquin Bks. of Chapel Hill.
—The Last Girls: A Novel. 2003. 432p. pap. 14.95 (*0-345-46495-8*) Ballantine Bks.
—The Last Girls: A Novel. l.t. ed. 2002. 30.95 (*0-7862-4734-7*) Thorndike Pr.
Smith, Thea. She Let Herself Go. l.t. ed. 2002. (Five Star First Edition Women's Fiction Ser.). 365p. 25.95 (*0-7862-3704-X*, Five Star) Gale Group.
Smith, Zadie. White Teeth. E-Book 19.95 (*1-58945-566-5*) Adobe Systems, Inc.
—White Teeth. l.t. ed. 2000. 717p. 28.95 o.p. (*1-56895-950-8*, Wheeler Publishing, Inc.) Gale Group.
—White Teeth. 2001. E-Book 19.95 (*0-375-50561-X*) Random Hse., Inc.
—White Teeth: A Novel. 2001. (International Ser.). 464p. reprint ed. pap. 14.00 (*0-375-70386-1*, Vintage) Knopf Publishing Group.
—White Teeth: A Novel. 2000. (Illus.). 464p. 24.95 (*0-375-50185-1*) Random Hse., Inc.
Snyder, Don J. Winter Dreams: A Novel. 2004. 256p. 23.95 (*0-385-50850-6*) Doubleday Publishing.
Steinbeck, John. Of Mice & Men. (Steinbeck's Centennial Ser.). 2002. 112p. pap. 11.00 (*0-14-200067-1*); 1963. pap. 1.45 o.p. (*0-670-00125-2*) Penguin Group (USA) Inc.
Stoberock, Johanna. City of Ghosts: A Novel. 2003. 256p. 23.95 (*0-393-05172-2*) Norton, W. W. & Co., Inc.
Stone, Katherine. Roommates. 1997. (Romance Ser.). 477p. lib. bdg. 26.95 (*0-7862-1207-1*, Five Star) Gale Group.
—Roommates. 1996. mass mkt. 6.99 o.s.i (*0-8217-5206-5*); 1987. mass mkt. 4.95 o.s.i (*0-8217-3355-9*); 1987. mass mkt. 4.50 o.p. (*0-8217-2156-9*) Kensington Publishing Corp. (Zebra Bks.).
—Star Light, Star Bright. l.t. ed. 2002. 393p. 30.95 (*0-7862-4207-8*) Gale Group.
—Star Light, Star Bright. 2002. 384p. (*1-55166-875-0*, Mira Bks.) Harlequin Enterprises, Ltd.
Stonich, Sarah. These Granite Islands: A Novel. 2001. 320p. 24.95 o.p. (*0-316-81583-7*) Little Brown & Co.
—These Granite Islands: A Novel. l.t. ed. 2001. (Thorndike Press Large Print Women's Fiction Ser.). 440p. 29.95 (*0-7862-3313-3*) Thorndike Pr.
—Three Granite Islands: A Novel. 2002. 336p. reprint ed. pap. 13.95 (*0-316-81558-6*, Back Bay) Little Brown & Co.
Stratton-Porter, Gene. At the Foot of the Rainbow. 1976. reprint ed. lib. bdg. 22.95 (*0-89190-941-9*, Rivercity Pr.) Amereon, Ltd.
—At the Foot of the Rainbow. 2000. per. 12.50 (*1-58396-458-4*) Blue Unicorn Editions.
—At the Foot of the Rainbow. 1990. reprint ed. lib. bdg. 27.95 (*0-89968-543-9*) Buccaneer Bks., Inc.
—At the Foot of the Rainbow. E-Book 2.49 (*1-58627-575-5*) Electric Umbrella Publishing.
—At the Foot of the Rainbow. (Library of Indiana Classics). (Illus.). 1999. 252p. pap. 11.95 (*0-253-21244-8*); 1998. 272p. 24.95 (*0-253-33467-5*) Indiana Univ. Pr.
—At the Foot of the Rainbow. 2001. 168p. 23.99 (*1-58827-642-2*); per. 18.99 (*1-58827-643-0*) IndyPublish.com.
—At the Foot of the Rainbow. l.t. ed. 2003. 165p. E-Book 2.99 (*1-932681-35-3*) NuVision Pubns.
Stroby, Wallace. The Barbed-Wire Kiss: A Novel. 2003. 368p. 24.95 (*0-312-30034-4*, Saint Martin's Minotaur) St. Martin's Pr.
Summers, Bre. Tainted Waters: A Book about Friendship, Love & New Beginnings. 2000. 270p. pap. 12.00 (*0-9677037-4-3*) Demme Publishing Group.
Susann, Jacqueline. Valley of the Dolls. unabr. ed. 2000. audio 29.95 (*0-929071-50-6*) B&B Audio, Inc.
—Valley of the Dolls. 1981. 512p. pap. 3.95 o.p. (*0-553-24286-5*) Bantam Bks.
—Valley of the Dolls. 1997. 448p. reprint ed. pap. 12.00 (*0-8021-3519-6*, Grove Pr.) Grove/Atlantic, Inc.
—Valley of the Dolls. abr. ed. 1993. pap. 15.95 o.p. incl. audio (*1-55800-059-3*, 40190) NewStar Media, Inc.
—Valley of the Dolls. 1991. (Newmarket Home Library). 448p. reprint ed. 5.95 o.p. (*0-937858-02-1*) Newmarket Pr.
Tan, Hwee Hwee. Foreign Bodies. 1999. 278p. 24.00 (*0-89255-236-0*) Persea Bks., Inc.
—Foreign Bodies. 2000. 304p. pap. 12.95 (*0-671-04170-3*, Washington Square Pr.) Simon & Schuster.
Tatlock, Ann. I'll Watch the Moon. 2003. 400p. pap. 12.99 (*0-7642-2764-5*) Bethany Hse. Pubs.
Toksvig, S. Flying under Bridges. 2001. 310p. (*0-316-85635-5*) Little Brown & Co.
Torres, Maruja. Un Calor Tan Cercano. 1998. (SPA., Illus.). 272p. 11.95 (*84-204-2990-2*) Alfaguara, Ediciones, S.A.- Grupo Santillana ESP. *Dist:* Santillana USA Publishing Co., Inc.
Townsend, Anne. Flashcard, No. 1: Faun & the Naughtiest Pig - Boy from Mindoro. 1988. (J). pap. 8.95 o.p. (*0-85363-131-X*) OMF Bks.
Traxler, Patricia. Blood. 2001. 352p. 24.95 (*0-312-27484-X*, Saint Martin's Minotaur) St. Martin's Pr.
—Blood: A Novel. 2002. 368p. pap. 13.95 (*0-312-30401-3*, Saint Martin's Griffin) St. Martin's Pr.
Trobaugh, Augusta. River Jordan. 2004. 272p. 23.95 (*0-525-94755-8*, Dutton) Dutton/Plume.
Trollope, Joanna. The Best of Friends. 2002. 320p. reprint ed. pap. 13.00 (*0-425-18317-3*) Berkley Publishing Group.
—Girl from the South. 2003. 352p. pap. 14.00 (*0-425-19350-0*) Berkley Publishing Group.
—Girl from the South. 2002. 304p. 24.95 (*0-670-03097-X*, Viking) Viking Penguin.
Troubaugh, Augusta. Swan Place. 2004. 304p. pap. 13.00 (*0-452-28414-7*, Plume) Dutton/Plume.
Tyau, Kathleen. Makai. 2000. (Bluestreak Ser.). 296p. pap. 14.00 (*0-8070-8345-3*) Beacon Pr.
—Makai. 1999. 256p. 24.00 o.p. (*0-374-20000-9*) Farrar, Straus & Giroux.
Tyree, Omar R. Just Say No! A Novel. 2001. (Illus.). 496p. 24.00 (*0-684-87293-5*, Simon & Schuster) Simon & Schuster.
Uhlman, Fred. Reunion. 112p. 1997. pap. 10.00 (*0-374-52515-3*); 1977. 6.95 o.p. (*0-374-24951-2*) Farrar, Straus & Giroux.
Uppal, Priscila. The Divine Economy of Salvation. 2002. 416p. 24.95 (*1-56512-365-4*, 72365) Algonquin Bks. of Chapel Hill.
—The Divine Economy of Salvation. 2003. 416p. pap. (*0-385-65805-2*, Anchor Canada) Doubleday Canada, Ltd. CAN. *Dist:* Random Hse., Inc.
Vickers, Salley. Instances of the Number 3. 2002. E-Book 15.00 (*0-374-70400-7*); E-Book 15.00 o.p. (*0-374-70401-5*); E-Book 15.00 (*0-374-70398-1*); E-Book 15.00 (*0-374-70402-3*); E-Book (*0-374-70403-1*); 320p. 23.00 (*0-374-17702-3*) Farrar, Straus & Giroux.
—Instances of the Number 3. l.t. ed. 2002. (Core Collection). 375p. 30.95 (*0-7862-4492-5*) Thorndike Pr.
—Instances of the Number 3: A Novel. 2003. (Illus.). 320p. pap. 14.00 (*0-312-42112-5*) Picador.
Voss, Louise. To Be Someone: A Novel. 2001. 400p. 23.00 o.s.i (*0-609-60892-4*, Crown) Crown Publishing Group.
Wall, Judith Henry. The Girlfriends Club: A Novel. 2003. 416p. mass mkt. 6.99 (*0-7434-6511-3*, Pocket); 2002. 320p. 23.00 (*0-684-87387-7*, Simon & Schuster) Simon & Schuster.
—The Girlfriends Club: A Novel. l.t. ed. 2002. 29.95 (*0-7862-4553-0*) Thorndike Pr.
Wall, William. Alice Falling. 2000. 208p. 23.95 (*0-393-05001-7*) Norton, W. W. & Co., Inc.
Walsh, Lawrence & Walsh, Suella. They Would Never Be Friends. 1996. 158p. (J). lib. bdg. o.p. (*0-88092-159-5*) Royal Fireworks Publishing Co.
Walton, Jo. The Prize in the Game. 2002. (Illus.). 256p. 25.95 (*0-7653-0263-2*, Tor Bks.) Doherty, Tom Assocs., LLC.
Warner, Alan. The Sopranos. 2000. (Harvest Book Ser.). 336p. pap. 14.00 (*0-15-601201-4*, Harvest Bks.) Harcourt Trade Pubs.
Wartski, Maureen C. My Name Is Nobody. 1988. 15.95 (*0-8027-6770-2*) Walker & Co.
Weber, Katherine. Objects in Mirror Are Closer Than They Appear. 1996. 272p. pap. 12.00 (*0-312-14383-4*) Picador.
Weigelt, Udo. The Sandman. James, J. Alison, tr. from GER. 2003. (Illus.). 32p. (J). (gr. k-3). 15.95 (*0-7358-1789-8*) North-South Bks., Inc.
Wells, Rebecca. Divine Secrets of the Ya-Ya Sisterhood. l.t. ed. 2002. 12.95 (*1-56895-199-X*); 1998. 27.95 o.p. (*1-56895-621-5*, Wheeler Publishing, Inc.) Gale Group.
—Divine Secrets of the Ya-Ya Sisterhood. 2002. 480p. mass mkt. 7.99 (*0-06-000810-5*); 1996. 368p. 24.00 (*0-06-017328-9*); 1998. 256p. 22.00 (*0-06-019345-X*) HarperCollins Pubs.
—Divine Secrets of the Ya-Ya Sisterhood. 2000. 368p. mass mkt. 7.99 (*0-06-101507-5*, HarperTorch) Morrow/Avon.
—Divine Secrets of the Ya-Ya Sisterhood: A Novel. 1997. 368p. pap. 14.00 (*0-06-092833-6*, Perennial) HarperTrade.
—Divine Secrets of the Ya-Ya Sisterhood: A Novel. 2002. 480p. mass mkt. 7.99 (*0-06-050225-8*) Morrow/Avon.
—Les Divins Secrets des Petits Ya Ya. 2000. Tr. of Divine Secrets of the Ya Ya Sisterhood. (FRE.). pap. 12.95 (*2-266-09548-X*) Presses Pocket FRA. *Dist:* Distribooks, Inc.
—The Ya-Ya Boxed Set: Divine Secrets of the Ya-Ya Sisterhood & Little Altars Everywhere, 2 bks. 1999. 608p. pap. 27.00 (*0-06-093205-8*, Perennial) HarperTrade.
Welsh, Irvine. Glue. 2001. ix, 469p. pap. 14.95 (*0-393-32215-7*) Norton, W. W. & Co., Inc.
Westermann, John. High Crimes. 2001. 208p. pap. 12.00 (*1-56947-244-0*); 1988. 234p. 15.95 (*0-939149-15-X*) Soho Pr., Inc.
Whiteford, Merry. If Wishes Were Horses: A Novel. 2003. 256p. 23.95 (*0-312-30188-X*) St. Martin's Pr.
Wickham, Madeleine. Cocktails for Three. 2000. (Illus.). 300p. 13.00 (*0-552-99834-6*) Corgi Bks. Ltd. GBR. *Dist:* Trafalgar Square.
—Cocktails for Three. l.t. ed. 2002. (Women's Fiction Ser.). 28.95 (*0-7862-3906-9*) Gale Group.
—Cocktails for Three. Date not set. E-Book 23.95 (*0-312-70151-9*); 2002. 304p. mass mkt. 6.50 (*0-312-98499-5*, St. Martin's Paperbacks); 2001. 304p. 23.95 (*0-312-28192-7*) St. Martin's Pr.
Wilder, Staci. For Such a Time As This. 2003. pap. 10.99 (*1-56722-632-9*) Word Aflame Pr.
William, Kate. Taking Sides. 1986. (Sweet Valley High Ser.: No. 31). (YA). (gr. 7 up). 8.35 o.p. (*0-606-03146-4*) Turtleback Bks.
Williams, Alicia. The Scarecrow, the Lion & the Tinman: A Novelette about Forbidden Friendships. 1996. ix, 127p. (Orig.). pap. 11.00 (*1-889316-00-8*) Ecrivez!.
Williams, Joy. The Quick & the Dead. 2002. (Vintage Contemporaries Ser.). 320p. pap. 13.00 (*0-375-72764-7*, Vintage) Knopf Publishing Group.
Wills, Geoffrey. A Friend for Frances. 1986. (Care Bear Ser.). (J). pap. 11.95 o.p. (*0-516-09002-X*, Children's Pr.) Scholastic Library Publishing.
Witting, Amy. Marias War. 1998. 254p. text (*0-670-88312-3*) Viking.
Wittlinger, Ellen. What's in a Name. 2001. (Illus.). 192p. (YA). mass mkt. 4.99 (*0-689-84532-4*, Simon Pulse) Simon & Schuster Children's Publishing.
Wolitzer, Meg. Surrender, Dorothy. 1999. 224p. 22.00 (*0-684-84844-9*); 2000. 240p. reprint ed. pap. 12.95 (*0-671-04254-8*) Simon & Schuster. (Scribner).
Woodhouse, Sarah. My Summer with Julia. 2000. 256p. 23.95 (*0-312-26622-7*) St. Martin's Pr.
—My Summer with Julia. l.t. ed. 2001. (Thorndike General Ser.). 261p. 24.95 (*0-7862-3028-2*) Thorndike Pr.
Woodruff, Nancy. Someone Else's Child. E-Book 23.00 (*1-58945-250-X*) Adobe Systems, Inc.
—Someone Else's Child. 2000. 256p. 23.00 (*0-684-86507-6*, Simon & Schuster) Simon & Schuster.
Ziefert, Harriet & Boon, Emilie. Little Hippo's New Friend. 1998. (Little Hippo Ser.). (Illus.). (J). (ps). (*0-7894-3105-X*) Dorling Kindersley Publishing, Inc.
Zinsser, Anne. Pirates on Our River. 1998. (Illus.). (J). (gr. 3-5). pap. 5.95 (*0-933951-77-9*) Locust Hill Pr.

# G

## GAY MEN—FICTION

Ackerley, Joe R. We Think the World of You. 1981. 190p. pap. 5.95 o.p. (*0-916870-36-7*) Creative Arts Bk. Co.
—We Think the World of You. 2000. (New York Review Books Classics Ser.). 211p. pap. 12.95 (*0-940322-26-9*) New York Review of Bks., Inc., The.
—We Think the World of You. 1988. pap. 12.95 o.p. (*0-14-011554-4*) Penguin Group (USA) Inc.
—We Think the World of You. 1989. pap. 7.95 o.s.i (*0-671-67811-6*, Simon & Schuster) Simon & Schuster.
Alameddine, Rabih. Koolaids: The Art of War. 256p. 1999. pap. 13.00 (*0-312-20658-5*); 1998. 23.00 (*0-312-18693-2*) Picador.
—Koolaids: The Art of War, a Novel. 2000. 245p. reprint ed. 23.00 (*0-7881-9338-4*) DIANE Publishing Co.
Alumit, Noel. Letters to Montgomery Clift. 2003. 288p. pap. 13.95 (*1-55583-815-4*) Alyson Pubns.
—Letters to Montgomery Clift. 2002. 244p. 25.00 (*1-931561-02-8*) MacAdam/Cage Publishing, Inc.
Argiri, Laura. The God in Flight. 1996. 496p. pap. 22.00 o.s.i (*0-14-025413-7*, Penguin Bks.) Penguin Group (USA) Inc.
Arnott, Jake. The Long Firm. 2001. 343p. reprint ed. 25.00 (*1-56947-169-X*) Soho Pr., Inc.
Ashley, Leonard R. N. What I Know about You: 100 Lesbian & Gay New York Voices. 2002. 313p. pap. 22.99 (*1-4010-3173-0*) Xlibris Corp.
Baker, James Robert. Testosterone: A Novel. viii, 200p. 2001. pap. 12.95 (*1-55583-714-X*); 2000. 22.95 o.p. (*1-55583-567-8*, Alyson Bks.) Alyson Pubns.
—Tim & Pete: A Novel. 2001. 256p. pap. 12.95 (*1-55583-566-X*, Alyson Bks.) Alyson Pubns.
Barker, Pat. The Eye in the Door, Vol. 2. unabr. ed. 2001. audio 59.95 (*0-7451-2765-7*, SAB 129) Chivers Audio Bks. GBR. *Dist:* BBC Audiobooks America.
—The Eye in the Door. 288p. 1995. pap. 14.00 (*0-452-27272-6*, Abrahams, William Bks.); 1994. 20.95 o.p. (*0-525-93808-7*, Dutton) Dutton/Plume.
—The Eye in the Door. l.t. ed. 1996. 25.95 o.p. (*1-56895-350-X*, Wheeler Publishing, Inc.) Gale Group.
—The Eye in the Door. unabr. ed. 1997. audio 51.00 (*0-7887-0819-8*, 94969E7) Recorded Bks., LLC.
Bean, Joseph, ed. Horsemen: Leathersex Short Fiction. 1997. 189p. pap. 14.95 (*0-943595-69-X*) Leyland Pubns.
Beck, Timothy. He's the One. 2003. 368p. pap. 14.00 (*0-7582-0324-1*, Kensington Bks.); 352p. 23.00 (*0-7582-0323-3*) Kensington Publishing Corp.
Bergman, David. Men on Men 7: Best New Gay Fiction. 1998. (Men on Men Ser.). 320p. pap. 13.95 o.s.i (*0-452-27734-5*, Plume) Dutton/Plume.
Bergman, David, ed. Men on Men: Best New Gay Fiction, Vol. 6. 1996. (Men on Men Ser.). 368p. pap. 12.95 o.s.i (*0-452-27708-6*, Plume) Dutton/Plume.
—Men on Men 5: Best New Gay Fiction. 1994. (Men on Men Ser.). 352p. pap. 13.95 o.s.i (*0-452-27244-0*, Plume) Dutton/Plume.
Bergman, David & Woelz, Karl, eds. Men on Men 2000: Best New Gay Fiction for the Millennium. 2000. 350p. pap. 12.95 o.s.i (*0-452-28082-6*, Plume) Dutton/Plume.
Bookbinder, Bernie. Out at the Old Ball Game: A Novel. 1995. 347p. 21.95 o.s.i (*1-882593-09-X*); 2002. 262p. reprint ed. pap. 13.95 (*1-882593-56-1*) Bridge Works Publishing Co., Inc.
Bouldrey, Brian. Best American Gay Fiction, Vol. 2. 2nd ed. 1997. 320p. 29.95 o.p. (*0-316-10298-9*) Little Brown & Co.
—Best American Gay Fiction, 1996. 1996. 336p. reprint ed. pap. 19.99 (*0-316-10317-9*) Little Brown & Co.
—The Boom Economy: Or, Scenes from Clerical Life. 2003. ix, 283p. 24.95 (*0-299-18900-7*, Terrace Bks.) Univ. of Wisconsin Pr.
—Love, the Magician. (Gay Men's Fiction Ser.). 2003. 190p. pap. 19.95 (*1-56023-994-8*, Southern Tier Editions); 2000. viii, 189p. (C). 49.95 (*1-56023-993-X*, Harrington Park Pr.) Haworth Pr., Inc., The.
Bouldrey, Brian, ed. Best American Gay Fiction. 1998. mass mkt. 15.00 (*0-316-19077-2*); Vol. 2. 1997. (Best American Gay Fiction Ser.: Vol. 2). 336p. pap. 19.99 (*0-316-10299-7*); Vol. 3. 1998. 304p. pap. 15.00 (*0-316-10236-9*) Little Brown & Co.
Boulter, Amanda. Around the Houses. 2002. 192p. pap. 14.00 (*1-85242-697-7*) Serpent's Tail Ltd. GBR. *Dist:* Consortium Bk. Sales & Distribution.
Bowes, Richard. Minions of the Moon. 320p. 2000. pap. 13.95 (*0-312-87228-3*); 1998. (Illus.). 23.95 (*0-312-86566-X*) Doherty, Tom Assocs., LLC. (Tor Bks.).
Boyd, Randy. Uprising: The Suspense Thriller. 1998. 335p. pap. 11.95 (*0-9665333-7-2*, 966-001) West Beach Bks.
Boyle, Dan. Huddle. 2003. 244p. pap. 16.95 (*1-56023-459-8*, Southern Tier Editions) Haworth Pr., Inc., The.
Bram, Christopher. Gossip. 352p. 1998. pap. 13.95 o.s.i (*0-452-27338-2*, Plume); 1997. 23.95 o.p. (*0-525-93914-8*) Dutton/Plume.
Brown, Dave. Bristlecone Peak. 1998. (Legend of the Golden Feather Ser.: Vol. 1). 320p. pap. 14.95 (*1-878406-13-2*) Parker Distributing.
Brown, David E. Home to Kentucky. 1999. (Legend of the Golden Feather Ser.: Vol. 3). 300p. pap. 14.95 (*1-878406-22-1*) Parker Distributing.
—The Protectors. 1998. (Legend of the Golden Feather Ser.: Vol. 2). 270p. pap. 14.95 (*1-878406-20-5*) Parker Distributing.
Burnett, Allison. Christopher: A Tale of Seduction. 2003. 272p. (Orig.). pap. 13.95 (*0-7679-1333-7*) Broadway Bks.
Burton, Peter, ed. The Mammoth Book of Gay Short Stories. 1997. (Mammoth Bks.). 512p. pap. 10.95 (*0-7867-0430-6*, Carroll & Graf Pubs.) Avalon Publishing Group.
Busch, Charles. Whores of Lost Atlantis: A Novel. 1993. 304p. 21.95 o.p. (*1-56282-780-4*) Hyperion Pr.

Carbado, Devon W., et al, eds. Black Like Us: A Century of Lesbian, Gay & Bisexual African American Fiction. 2002. 575p. pap. 24.95 (*1-57344-108-2*) Cleis Pr.

Cashorali, Peter. Gay Fairy & Folk Tales: More Traditional Stories Retold for Gay Men. 1997. 176p. 19.95 (*0-571-19926-7*) Faber & Faber, Inc.

Christian, M., ed. Dirty Words: Provocative Erotica. 2001. xx, 183p. pap. 14.95 o.p. (*1-55583-563-5*, Alyson Bks.) Alyson Pubns.

Christian, M. & Sheppard, Simon, eds. Roughed Up: More Tales of Gay Men, Sex, & Power. 2003. 240p. pap. 14.95 (*1-55583-720-4*) Alyson Pubns.

Cole, C. Bard. Briefly Told Lives. 2002. (Illus.). 224p. pap. 13.95 (*0-312-27690-7*, Saint Martin's Griffin); 2000. xi, 205p. 22.95 (*0-312-25351-6*) St. Martin's Pr.

Cooke, John Peyton. The Chimney Sweeper. 1995. 320p. 21.95 o.s.i (*0-89296-523-1*) Mysterious Pr.

—The Chimney Sweeper. 1996. 288p. mass mkt. 5.99 (*0-446-40388-1*) Warner Bks., Inc.

—Torsos. 1994. 368p. 19.95 o.s.i (*0-89296-522-3*) Mysterious Pr.

—Torsos. 1995. 352p. mass mkt. 5.99 o.s.i (*0-446-40454-3*) Warner Bks., Inc.

Cooper, Dennis. Guide. 1997. 160p. 22.00 o.p. (*0-8021-1608-6*, Grove Pr.) Grove/Atlantic, Inc.

Cooper, Steven. With You in Spirit. 2003. 280p. pap. 13.95 (*1-55583-783-2*) Alyson Pubns.

Corlett, William. Now & Then. 2nd ed. 1998. 300p. reprint ed. pap. 11.95 o.p. (*1-55583-424-8*) Alyson Pubns.

—Now & Then. 1996. 346p. pap. o.s.i (*0-349-10775-0*); 1995. 352p. pap. o.s.i (*0-349-10646-0*) Little Brown & Co.

Corn, Alfred Dewitt. Part of His Story. 1997. 264p. 24.00 (*0-922811-29-6*) Mid-List Pr.

Craft, Michael. Boy Toy: A Mark Manning Mystery. 2001. (Mark Manning Mystery Ser.). 272p. 23.95 (*0-312-26917-X*) St. Martin's Pr.

Craig, Michael D. The Ice Sculptures: A Novel of Hollywood. 2004. pap. (*1-56023-481-4*, Southern Tier Editions) Haworth Pr., Inc., The.

Cunningham, Michael. A Home at the End of the World. 352p. audio compact disk 39.95 (*1-55927-990-7*) Audio Renaissance.

—A Home at the End of the World. l.t. ed. 2003. 536p. 29.95 (*0-7862-5745-8*, Large Print Pr.) Thorndike Pr.

—A Home at the End of the World: A Novel. 1995. mass mkt. 6.99 o.s.i (*0-553-57550-3*); 1992. 480p. pap. 6.99 o.s.i (*0-553-55002-0*) Bantam Bks.

—A Home at the End of the World: A Novel. 1990. 18.95 o.s.i (*0-374-17250-1*) Farrar, Straus & Giroux.

—A Home at the End of the World: A Novel. 1998. 352p. pap. 14.00 (*0-312-20231-8*) Picador.

Currier, Jameson. Dancing on the Moon: Short Stories about AIDS. 1994. 208p. pap. 9.95 o.p. (*0-14-017272-6*, Penguin Bks.) Penguin Group (USA) Inc.

Curtis, Craig. Fabulous Hell: A Novel. unabr. ed. 2000. 239p. pap. 12.95 o.p. (*1-55583-479-5*, Alyson Bks.) Alyson Pubns.

Darieck, Scott. Traitor to the Race. 1996. 224p. pap. 10.95 o.p. (*0-452-27335-8*, Plume) Dutton/Plume.

Dessaix, Robert. Night Letters: A Journey Through Switzerland & Italy. 1999. 276p. pap. 13.00 o.s.i (*0-312-19939-2*) Picador.

—Night Letters: A Journey Through Switzerland & Italy. 1997. 276p. 22.95 (*0-312-16950-7*) St. Martin's Pr.

Dietz, Ulysses G. Desmond: A Novel about Love & the Modern Vampire. 1998. 300p. pap. 13.95 o.p. (*1-55583-470-1*) Alyson Pubns.

Dowell, Coleman. Island People. 1996. 309p. reprint ed. pap. 12.95 (*1-56478-093-7*) Dalkey Archive Pr.

—Island People. 1976. 320p. 12.50 o.p. (*0-8112-0604-1*) New Directions Publishing Corp.

Drake, Robert, et al, eds. Circa 2000: Gay Fiction at the Millennium. 2000. xi, 331p. pap. 14.95 o.p. (*1-55583-517-1*, Alyson Bks.) Alyson Pubns.

Drinnan, Neal. Glove Puppet. 1999. 256p. pap. 12.95 (*0-312-24444-4*, Saint Martin's Griffin); 1998. 236p. 22.95 (*0-312-19271-1*) St. Martin's Pr.

Duberstein, Larry. The Mt. Monadnock Blues. 2003. 26.00 (*1-57962-093-0*) Permanent Pr., The.

Duncker, Patricia. Hallucinating Foucault. 2nd ed. 1996. 192p. 21.00 o.p. (*0-88001-499-7*, Ecco) HarperTrade.

—Hallucinating Foucault. 1998. 192p. pap. 12.00 (*0-375-70185-0*, Vintage) Knopf Publishing Group.

Dunford, Warren. Making a Killing. 2001. 325p. pap. 13.95 (*1-55583-657-7*) Alyson Pubns.

—Soon to Be a Major Motion Picture: A Novel. 2000. 255p. pap. 12.95 (*1-55583-582-1*, Alyson Bks.) Alyson Pubns.

Edgerton, Dale. Goneaway Road. 2003. 320p. pap. 17.95 (*1-56023-434-2*); 39.95 (*1-56023-433-4*) Haworth Pr., Inc., The. (Southern Tier Editions).

Ely, Stanley E. Perfect Mondays. E-Book 9.95 (*1-891305-87-5*); 2002. 271p. pap. 15.95 (*1-891305-62-X*) Painted Leaf Pr.

Erich, John & Grant, Jesse, eds. Friction 2: Best Gay Erotic Stories. 1999. viii, 429p. pap. 14.95 (*1-55583-482-5*) Alyson Pubns.

Ford, Michael Thomas. Looking for It: A Novel. 2004. 23.00 (*0-7582-0407-8*) Kensington Publishing Corp.

Foxxe, Austin & Grant, Jesse, eds. Friction 6: Best Gay Erotic Fiction. 2003. 386p. pap. 15.95 (*1-55583-768-9*) Alyson Pubns.

Fritscher, Jack. Jacked: The Beast of Jack Fritscher. 2002. 232p. pap. 14.95 (*1-55583-746-8*) Alyson Pubns.

Gadol, Peter. Light at Dusk. 2000. 288p. 24.00 (*0-312-20336-5*) Picador.

Gale, Patrick. Tree Surgery for Beginners. 1999. (Illus.). 275p. 25.00 (*0-571-19958-5*) Faber & Faber, Inc.

Gambone, Philip. Beijing. 2003. viii, 312p. 26.95 (*0-299-18490-0*) Univ. of Wisconsin Pr.

Garber, Eric & Gomez, Jewelle, eds. Swords of the Rainbow. 1996. 352p. pap. text 11.95 o.p. (*1-55583-266-0*) Alyson Pubns.

Geary, Joseph. Spiral: A Novel. 2003. 368p. 24.95 (*0-375-42223-4*) Random Hse., Inc.

Gladstone, Jim, ed. The Big Book of Misunderstanding. 2003. 242p. 27.95 (*1-56023-383-4*); 2002. 300p. pap. 17.95 (*1-56023-382-6*) Haworth Pr., Inc., The. (Harrington Park Pr.).

Glass, Julia. Three Junes: A Novel. l.t. ed. 2003. (Romance Ser.). 28.95 (*1-58724-379-2*, Wheeler Publishing, Inc.) Gale Group.

—Three Junes: A Novel. 368p. 2002. 25.00 (*0-375-42144-0*, Pantheon); 2003. reprint ed. pap. 14.00 (*0-385-72142-0*, Anchor) Knopf Publishing Group.

—Three Junes: A Novel. 2002. 368p. 25.00 (*0-375-42241-2*) Knopf, Alfred A. Inc.

Gooch, Brad. The Golden Age of Promiscuity. 1996. 303p. 24.00 o.s.i (*0-679-44708-3*) Knopf, Alfred A. Inc.

—The Golden Age of Promiscuity. 1992. mass mkt. 7.95 (*1-56333-550-6*, Hard Candy) Masquerade Bks., Inc.

Grant, Jesse, ed. Best of Friction: The First Five Years. 2002. 416p. pap. 15.95 (*1-55583-761-1*) Alyson Pubns.

—Friction 4: Best Gay Erotic Fiction. 2001. 294p. pap. 14.95 o.p. (*1-55583-593-7*, Alyson Bks.) Alyson Pubns.

—Men for All Seasons: Stories of Sports & Sex. 2000. (Illus.). 251p. pap. 12.95 (*1-55583-562-7*, Alyson Bks.) Alyson Pubns.

Grant, Jesse & Foxxe, Austin, eds. Friction 3: Best Gay Erotic Fiction. 1999. 407p. pap. 14.95 (*1-55583-535-X*, Alyson Bks.) Alyson Pubns.

Griffith, Nicola. Bending the Landscape: Horror. 2003. 332p. pap. 15.95 (*1-58567-372-2*) Overlook Pr., The.

Griffith, Nicola & Pagel, Stephen, eds. Bending the Landscape: Horror. 2001. 384p. 28.95 (*1-58567-116-9*) Overlook Pr., The.

Grimsley, Jim. Boulevard. 2002. 304p. tchr. ed. 23.95 (*1-56512-251-8*) Algonquin Bks. of Chapel Hill.

Grubisic, Brett Josef, ed. Contra/Diction: New Queer Male Fiction. 1998. 225p. pap. 15.95 (*1-55152-056-7*) Arsenal Pulp Pr., Ltd. CAN. *Dist:* LPC Group.

Guerra, Erasmo. Between Dances: A Novel. 2000. 224p. pap. 15.00 (*1-891305-23-9*) Painted Leaf Pr.

Guibert, Herve. To the Friend Who Did Not Save My Life. Coverdale, Linda, tr. from FRE. 1991. 272p. text 18.95 (*0-689-12120-2*) Central Bureau voor Schimmelcultures NLD. *Dist:* Lubrecht & Cramer, Ltd.

—To the Friend Who Did Not Save My Life. Coverdale, Linda, tr. from FRE. 1994. (High Risk Ser.). 240p. reprint ed. pap. (*1-85242-328-5*) Serpent's Tail Ltd.

Guinan, Doug. California Screaming: A Novel. 1999. 208p. reprint ed. pap. 12.95 (*1-55583-539-2*) Alyson Pubns.

—California Screaming: A Novel. 1998. 304p. 24.00 (*0-684-84936-4*, Simon & Schuster) Simon & Schuster.

Gurganus, Allan. Plays Well with Others. unabr. collector's ed. 1998. audio 96.00 (*0-7366-4206-4*, 4702) Books on Tape, Inc.

—Plays Well with Others. 1999. 368p. pap. 14.00 (*0-375-70203-2*, Vintage) Knopf Publishing Group.

—Plays Well with Others. 1997. 336p. 25.00 o.p. (*0-394-58914-9*) Knopf, Alfred A. Inc.

—Plays Well with Others. abr. ed. 1997. audio 18.00 o.s.i (*0-679-46055-1*, RH Audio) Random Hse. Audio Publishing Group.

Haig, Brian. Mortal Allies. (Wheeler Hardcover Ser.). 28.95 (*1-58724-294-X*, Wheeler Publishing, Inc.) Gale Group.

—Mortal Allies. 2002. 496p. 24.95 (*0-446-53026-3*); 2003. 608p. reprint ed. mass mkt. 6.99 (*0-446-61258-8*) Warner Bks., Inc.

Hansen, Joseph. The Boy Who Was Buried This Morning. 1991. 192p. reprint ed. pap. 5.95 o.p. (*0-452-26617-3*, Plume) Dutton/Plume.

—The Boy Who Was Buried This Morning. 1990. 176p. 16.95 o.p. (*0-670-83324-X*) Viking Penguin.

—Country of Old Men: The Last Dave Brandstetter Mystery. 1992. 192p. pap. 7.00 o.p. (*0-452-26805-2*, Plume) Dutton/Plume.

—Country of Old Men: The Last Dave Brandstetter Mystery. 1991. 192p. 17.95 o.p. (*0-670-83826-8*) Viking Penguin.

—Death Claims. 1980. 88p. pap. 5.95 o.p. (*0-8050-0622-2*); pap. 3.95 o.p. (*0-03-057484-6*) Holt, Henry & Co. (Owl Bks.).

—Death Claims. 192p. pap. 9.95 o.p. (*1-874061-62-9*) Oldcastle Bks., Ltd. GBR. *Dist:* Trafalgar Square.

—Early Graves. 1987. 208p. 15.95 o.p. (*0-89296-249-6*) Mysterious Pr.

—Early Graves. 1988. 208p. mass mkt. 3.95 o.s.i (*0-445-40735-2*, Mysterious Pr. Paperback Bks.) Warner Bks., Inc.

—Fadeout. 2000. (Dave Brandstetter Mysteries Ser.). 256p. reprint ed. pap. 11.95 o.p. (*1-55583-552-X*, Alyson Bks.) Alyson Pubns.

—Fadeout. unabr. ed. 1995. (Dave Brandstetter Mystery Ser.: No. 1). audio 24.95 (*1-888348-01-1*, HCB201) Hall Closet Bk. Co.

—Fadeout. 1980. 88p. pap. 5.95 o.p. (*0-8050-1054-8*);Vol. 1. pap. 3.95 o.p. (*0-03-057486-2*) Holt, Henry & Co. (Owl Bks.).

—Gravedigger. 1985. pap. o.p. (*0-03-003682-8*, Owl Bks.); 1985. 192p. pap. 5.95 o.p. (*0-8050-0196-4*, Owl Bks.); 1982. o.p. (*0-03-056063-2*) Holt, Henry & Co.

—The Little Dog Laughed: A Dave Brandstetter Mystery. 1987. 192p. pap. 5.95 o.p. (*0-8050-0627-3*, Owl Bks.); 1986. 15.95 o.p. (*0-8050-0083-6*) Holt, Henry & Co.

—The Man Everybody Was Afraid Of. 1981. pap. o.p. (*0-03-059894-X*, Owl Bks.); 1981. 192p. pap. 5.95 o.p. (*0-8050-0723-7*, Owl Bks.); 1978. 192p. o.p. (*0-03-042376-7*) Holt, Henry & Co.

—The Man Everybody Was Afraid Of. 192p. pap. 9.95 o.p. (*1-874061-66-1*) Oldcastle Bks., Ltd. GBR. *Dist:* Trafalgar Square.

—Nightwork. 1985. (Dave Brandsetter Mystery Ser.). 88p. pap. 5.95 o.p. (*0-8050-1055-6*); pap. 3.95 o.p. (*0-03-003679-8*) Holt, Henry & Co. (Owl Bks.).

—Obedience. 1988. 208p. 16.95 (*0-89296-296-8*) Mysterious Pr.

—Obedience. 1989. mass mkt. 4.95 (*0-445-40844-8*, Mysterious Pr. Paperback Bks.) Warner Bks., Inc.

—Skinflick. 1980. 192p. pap. o.p. (*0-03-057641-5*, Owl Bks.); 1980. 89p. pap. 5.95 o.p. (*0-8050-0197-2*, Owl Bks.); 1979. 192p. o.p. (*0-03-048931-8*) Holt, Henry & Co.

—Troublemaker: A Dave Brandstetter Mystery. 2002. 176p. pap. 12.95 (*1-55583-710-7*) Alyson Pubns.

—Troublemaker: A Dave Brandstetter Mystery. 1981. pap. 3.95 o.p. (*0-03-057487-0*); 1988. 89p. reprint ed. pap. 5.95 o.p. (*0-8050-0812-8*) Holt, Henry & Co. (Owl Bks.).

Hardy, James E. Back 2 Back: An Anthology Featuring the Best-Sellers: B-Boy Blues & 2nd Time Around, 2 vols., Set. 1997. 530p. reprint ed. 22.95 o.p. (*1-55583-420-5*) Alyson Pubns.

—If Only for One Nite. 1998. 208p. pap. 12.95 (*1-55583-467-1*); 1997. 185p. 17.95 (*1-55583-373-X*) Alyson Pubns.

—The 2nd Time Around. 1996. 288p. pap. 12.95 (*1-55583-372-1*) Alyson Pubns.

Hartnett, P. Call Me. 1997. (Stonewall Inn Editions Ser.). 192p. pap. 11.95 (*0-312-18063-2*, Saint Martin's Griffin) St. Martin's Pr.

Hartnett, P. -P. Call Me. 1997. 184p. (Orig.). pap. 16.95 (*1-901072-00-2*) Pulp Faction GBR. *Dist:* AK Pr. Distribution.

Healey, Trebor. Through It Came Bright Colors. 2003. 252p. 34.95 (*1-56023-451-2*, Southern Tier Editions) Haworth Pr., Inc., The.

Healey, Trebor, ed. Through It Came Bright Colors. 2003. (Illus.). 252p. pap. 19.95 (*1-56023-452-0*, Southern Tier Editions) Haworth Pr., Inc., The.

Herren, Greg, ed. Full Body Contact: Sexy, Sweaty Men of Sport. 2002. 256p. pap. 14.95 (*1-55583-725-5*) Alyson Pubns.

—Shadows of the Night: Queer Tales of the Uncanny & Unusual. 2004. 211p. pap. text 16.95 (*1-56023-394-X*, Harrington Park Pr.) Haworth Pr., Inc., The.

Hill, Stan. The Love You Leave Behind. 2000. Bk. 1. 528p. pap. 26.99 (*0-7388-1811-9*); Bk. 1. 528p. text 36.99 (*0-7388-1810-0*); Bk. 2. 478p. pap. 24.99 (*0-7388-1813-5*); Bk. 2. 478p. text 34.99 (*0-7388-1812-7*) Xlibris Corp.

Holleran, Andrew. Beauty of Men. 1997. 288p. pap. 12.95 o.s.i (*0-452-27774-4*, Plume) Dutton/Plume.

—The Beauty of Men, Vol. 1. 1996. 272p. 24.00 o.p. (*0-688-04857-9*, Morrow, William & Co.) Morrow/Avon.

—In September, the Light Changes: The Stories of Andrew Holleran. 2000. 320p. pap. 12.95 (*0-452-28171-7*, Plume) Dutton/Plume.

—In September, the Light Changes: The Stories of Andrew Holleran. 1999. 304p. (J). 23.95 (*0-7868-6518-0*) Hyperion Pr.

—In September the Light Changes: The Stories of Andrew Holleran. 1999. 306p. 23.95 (*0-7868-6461-3*) Hyperion Pr.

Hollinghurst, Alan. The Spell. 1998. 257p. o.p. (*0-7011-6519-7*) Random Hse. of Canada, Ltd. CAN. *Dist:* Random Hse., Inc.

—The Spell. 2000. 272p. 12.95 (*0-14-028637-3*); 1999. 288p. 24.95 o.p. (*0-670-88356-5*) Viking Penguin.

House, Richard. Bruiser. 1997. (High Risk Ser.). 254p. pap. o.p. (*1-85242-437-0*) Serpent's Tail Ltd.

—Uninvited. 2002. 224p. reprint ed. pap. 15.00 (*1-85242-438-9*) Serpent's Tail Ltd. GBR. *Dist:* Consortium Bk. Sales & Distribution.

Hunter, Fred. The Chicken Asylum. 2001. 272p. 23.95 (*0-312-27117-4*, Saint Martin's Minotaur) St. Martin's Pr.

Huxley, Michael, ed. Fantasies Made Flesh. 2002. 432p. per. 15.95 (*1-891855-30-1*) Florida Literary Foundation.

—Saints & Sinners: An Anthology. 2003. 360p. pap. 15.95 (*1-891855-25-5*, STARbooks Pr.) Florida Literary Foundation.

Isherwood, Christopher. The Memorial: Portrait of a Family. 1988. (Michael di Capua Bks.). 288p. pap. 8.95 o.s.i (*0-374-52067-4*) Farrar, Straus & Giroux.

—The Memorial: Portrait of a Family. 294p. reprint ed. lib. bdg. 32.00 (*0-8371-3544-3*) Irvington Pubs.

—The Memorial: Portrait of a Family. 1977. pap. 2.25 o.p. (*0-380-01814-4*, 53983-7, Avon Bks.) Morrow/Avon.

—The Memorial: Portrait of a Family. 1999. 296p. reprint ed. pap. 15.95 (*0-8166-3369-X*) Univ. of Minnesota Pr.

Itiel, Joseph. Escort Tales: The Trophy Boy & Other Stories. 2003. 124p. 24.95 (*1-56023-391-5*); pap. 12.95 (*1-56023-392-3*) Haworth Pr., Inc., The. (Harrington Park Pr.).

Iversen, Cap. Silver Saddles. 1993. (Dakota Ser.: No. 2). 222p. pap. 7.95 o.p. (*1-55583-213-X*) Alyson Pubns.

Jensen, Michael. Frontiers. 2000. 320p. reprint ed. pap. 14.95 (*0-671-02721-2*, Pocket) Simon & Schuster.

Johnson, Greg, told to. Sticky Kisses: A Novel. 2002. 328p. pap. 13.95 (*1-55583-770-0*) Alyson Pubns.

Jones, Simmons. Show Me the Way to Go Home. 1991. 336p. 19.95 o.p. (*0-945575-41-6*) Algonquin Bks. of Chapel Hill.

—Show Me the Way to Go Home. 1993. (Stonewall Inn Editions Ser.). 336p. pap. 9.95 (*0-312-09387-X*, Saint Martin's Griffin) St. Martin's Pr.

Kafka-Gibbons, Paul. Dupont Circle: A Novel. 2001. 256p. tchr. ed. 24.00 (*0-395-86932-3*) Houghton Mifflin Co.

—Dupont Circle: A Novel. 2002. 256p. pap. 13.00 (*0-618-21918-8*, Mariner Bks.) Houghton Mifflin Co. Trade & Reference Div.

Kenry, Chris. Can't Buy Me Love. 2002. 336p. pap. 14.00 (*1-57566-846-7*); 2001. 34p. 23.00 (*1-57566-845-9*) Kensington Publishing Corp.

Kerr, Peg. The Wild Swans. 2001. 464p. mass mkt. 6.99 (*0-446-60847-5*) Warner Bks., Inc.

Killian, Kevin. Little Men. 1996. 128p. pap. text 12.95 (*1-889097-01-2*) Hard Pr. Editions.

Kimmel, Michael S., ed. Love Letters Between a Certain Late Nobleman & the Famous Mr. Wilson. 1990. (Journal of Homosexuality Ser.: No. 19, No. 2). (Illus.). 124p. pap. text 19.95 (*0-918393-69-8*, Harrington Park Pr.); text 3.95 (*0-86656-985-5*) Haworth Pr., Inc., The.

King, Atticus. Pretense . . . of Innocence. 1996. 256p. (Orig.). pap. 12.95 (*1-56184-081-5*) New Falcon Pubns.

Kirby, Robert. Curbside Boys. 2002. (Illus.). 150p. pap. 10.95 (*1-57344-154-6*) Cleis Pr.

Kittle, Katrina. Traveling Light. l.t. ed. 2000. (G. K. Hall Core Ser.). 407p. 27.95 (*0-7838-9173-3*) Thorndike Pr.

—Traveling Light. 2000. 320p. 18.95 (*0-446-52480-8*); 2001. 336p. reprint ed. pap. 13.95 (*0-446-67694-2*) Warner Bks., Inc.

Kondoleon, Harry. Diary of a Lost Boy. 1995. 224p. 10.00 o.s.i (*1-57322-504-5*, Riverhead Trade (Paperbacks)) Berkley Publishing Group.

Kramer, Larry. Faggots. 1987. pap. 7.95 o.p. (*0-452-25997-5*); 384p. pap. 8.95 o.p. (*0-452-26204-6*); 384p. pap. 12.95 o.s.i (*0-452-26396-4*) Dutton/Plume. (Plume).

—Faggots. 2000. xvi, 363p. reprint ed. pap. 14.00 (*0-8021-3691-5*, Grove Pr.) Grove/Atlantic, Inc.

—Faggots. 1978. 10.95 o.p. (*0-394-41095-5*) Random Hse., Inc.

—Faggots. 1984. 384p. mass mkt. 3.95 o.p. (*0-446-32059-5*) Warner Bks., Inc.

Kranz, Rachel. Leaps of Faith. 2000. 565p. 25.00 o.p. (*0-374-18444-5*) Farrar, Straus & Giroux.

Kroll, Gerry & Goss, Fred, eds. Up All Hours: Scorching Tales of Sex Around the Clock. 1998. 256p. pap. 12.95 o.p. (*1-55583-402-7*) Alyson Pubns.

Kvaale, Tom. Turkish Meat: An Erotic Novel. 1997. 160p. pap. 14.95 (*0-943595-66-5*) Leyland Pubns.

Labonte, Richard, ed. Best Gay Erotica, 2003. 2003. 250p. 14.95 (*1-57344-162-7*) Cleis Pr.

Labonte, Richard & Sadownick, Douglas, eds. Best Gay Erotica 1997. 1997. (Best Gay Erotica Ser.: Vol. 2). 200p. pap. 14.95 o.p. (*1-57344-067-1*) Cleis Pr.

Lane, Joel. The Blue Mask. 2003. 224p. pap. 15.00 (*1-85242-688-8*) Serpent's Tail Ltd. GBR. *Dist:* Consortium Bk. Sales & Distribution.

Lassell, Michael. Certain Ecstasies: Bedtime Stories. 1999. pap. text 15.00 (*1-891305-12-3*) Painted Leaf Pr.

Laurents, David, ed. Stocking Stuffers: Gay Erotic Holiday Stories. 2002. 160p. pap. 12.00 (*1-885865-42-2*) Circlet Pr., Inc.

Leavitt, David. Martin Bauman: Or, A Sure Thing. 2000. 352p. tchr. ed. 26.00 (*0-395-90243-6*); 2001. 387p. reprint ed. pap. 14.00 (*0-618-15451-5*) Houghton Mifflin Co. Trade & Reference Div. (Mariner Bks.).

Leddick, David. The Handsomest Man in the World. 2004. 199p. pap. text 17.95 (*1-56023-458-X*, Southern Tier Editions) Haworth Pr., Inc., The.

Lemon, Brendan. Last Night: A Novel. 2003. 248p. pap. 13.95 (*1-55583-801-4*, Alyson Bks.) Alyson Pubns.

Lennon, Tom. Crazy Love. 1999. 240p. (*0-86278-560-X*) O'Brien Pr., Ltd., The.

Leventhal, Stan. Barbie in Bondage. 1996. (Orig.). mass mkt. 6.95 (*1-56333-415-1*, Hard Candy) Masquerade Bks., Inc.

—Skydiving on Christopher Street. 1995. 225p. (Orig.). mass mkt. 6.95 (*1-56333-287-6*, Hard Candy) Masquerade Bks., Inc.

Levithan, David. Boy Meets Boy. 2003. 192p. (gr. 7). (J). 15.95 (*0-375-82400-6*); lib. bdg. 17.99 (*0-375-92400-0*, Knopf Bks. for Young Readers) Random Hse. Children's Bks.

Leyland, Winston. Meatmen: An Anthology of Gay Male Comics. 2000. (Anthology of Gay Male Comics Ser.: Vol. 24). (Illus.). 160p. pap. text 17.95 (*0-943595-77-0*) Leyland Pubns.

—Meatmen Vol. 2: An Anthology of Gay Male Comics. 1996. 192p. pap. text 16.95 (*0-943595-04-5*) Leyland Pubns.

—Meatmen Vol. 23: An Anthology of Gay Male Comics. 1999. 160p. pap. 16.95 (*0-943595-76-2*) Leyland Pubns.

Leyland, Winston, ed. Meatmen: An Anthology of Gay Male Comics, Vol. 15. 1993. (Illus.). 160p. pap. 17.95 (*0-943595-38-X*) Leyland Pubns.

—Meatmen Vol. 1: An Anthology of Gay Male Comics. 2nd ed. 1996. (Meatmen Ser.). (Illus.). 192p. reprint ed. pap. 16.95 (*0-917342-23-2*) Leyland Pubns.

—Meatmen Vol. 3: An Anthology of Gay Male Comics. 2nd ed. 1990. (Illus.). 160p. reprint ed. pap. 14.95 o.p. (*0-943595-10-X*) Leyland Pubns.

—Meatmen Vol. 4: An Anthology of Gay Male Comics. 1988. (Illus.). 160p. pap. 14.95 o.p. (*0-943595-12-6*) Leyland Pubns.

—Meatmen Vol. 5: An Anthology of Gay Male Comics. 1989. (Illus.). pap. 14.95 o.p. (*0-943595-15-0*) Leyland Pubns.

—Meatmen Vol. 6: An Anthology of Gay Male Comics. 1989. (Illus.). pap. 17.95 (*0-943595-20-7*) Leyland Pubns.

—Meatmen Vol. 7: An Anthology of Gay Male Comics. 1990. (Illus.). pap. 13.95 o.p. (*0-943595-22-3*) Leyland Pubns.

—Meatmen Vol. 8: An Anthology of Gay Male Comics. 1990. (Illus.). pap. 13.95 o.p. (*0-943595-23-1*) Leyland Pubns.

—Meatmen Vol. 9: An Anthology of Gay Male Comics. 1990. (Illus.). pap. 14.95 o.p. (*0-943595-24-X*) Leyland Pubns.

—Meatmen Vol. 10: An Anthology of Gay Male Comics. 1991. (Illus.). pap. 17.95 (*0-943595-27-4*) Leyland Pubns.

—Meatmen Vol. 11: An Anthology of Gay Male Comics. 1991. (Illus.). pap. 17.95 (*0-943595-28-2*) Leyland Pubns.

—Meatmen Vol. 12: An Anthology of Gay Male Comics. 1991. (Illus.). pap. 17.95 (*0-943595-29-0*) Leyland Pubns.

—Meatmen Vol. 13: An Anthology of Gay Male Comics. 1992. (Illus.). 160p. pap. 15.95 o.p. (*0-943595-31-2*) Leyland Pubns.

—Meatmen Vol. 14: An Anthology of Gay Male Comics. 1993. (Illus.). 160p. pap. 17.95 (*0-943595-35-5*) Leyland Pubns.

—Meatmen Vol. 16: An Anthology of Gay Male Comics. 1995. (Illus.). 160p. pap. 17.95 (*0-943595-44-4*) Leyland Pubns.

—Meatmen Vol. 17: An Anthology of Gay Male Comics. 1995. (Illus.). 160p. pap. 16.95 (*0-943595-50-9*) Leyland Pubns.

—Meatmen Vol. 18: An Anthology of Gay Male Comics. 1996. (Illus.). 160p. pap. 16.95 (*0-943595-53-3*) Leyland Pubns.

—Meatmen Vol. 19: An Anthology of Gay Male Comics. 1996. 160p. pap. text 16.95 (*0-943595-60-6*) Leyland Pubns.

—Meatmen Vol. 20: An Anthology of Gay Male Comics. 20th ed. 1997. (Illus.). 160p. pap. 16.95 (*0-943595-63-0*) Leyland Pubns.

—Meatmen Vol. 21: An Anthology of Gay Male Comics. 1997. (Illus.). 160p. pap. 16.95 (*0-943595-68-1*) Leyland Pubns.

—Meatmen Vol. 22: An Anthology of Gay Male Comics. 1998. (Illus.). 160p. pap. 16.95 (*0-943595-75-4*) Leyland Pubns.

—Meatmen Vol. 25: An Anthology of Gay Male Comics. 2002. (Illus.). 160p. pap. 17.95 (*0-943595-86-X*) Leyland Pubns.

Manrique, Jaime. Twilight at the Equator: A Novel. 1997. 224p. 23.95 o.s.i (*0-571-19901-1*) Faber & Faber, Inc.

—Twilight at the Equator: A Novel. 1997. pap. 18.00 (*1-891305-18-2*) Painted Leaf Pr.

—Twilight at the Equator: A Novel. 2003. 198p. pap. 15.95 (*0-299-18774-8*) Univ. of Wisconsin Pr.

March, R.J. Looking for Trouble: And Other Stories. 1999. xi, 372p. pap. 12.95 (*1-55583-455-8*) Alyson Pubns.

McCauley, Stephen. True Enough: A Novel. 2002. 320p. pap. 14.00 (*0-7434-4403-5*, Washington Square Pr.) Simon & Schuster.

McConnell, David. The Firebrat. 2003. 246p. 22.00 (*0-929435-71-0*) AttaGirl Pr.

McDonell, J. M. Half Crazy: A Novel, Vol. 1. 1995. 258p. 19.95 (*0-316-55560-6*) Little Brown & Co.

—Half Crazy: A Novel. 2000. 310p. pap. 12.95 (*1-893224-04-X*, New Millennium Pr.) New Millennium Entertainment.

McEwan, Ian. Enduring Love. unabr. ed. 2000. audio 59.95 (*0-7540-0200-4*, CAB 1623) Chivers Audio Bks. GBR. *Dist:* BBC Audiobooks America.

—Enduring Love. 1998. 272p. 23.95 o.s.i (*0-385-49112-3*, Talese, Nan A.) Doubleday Publishing.

—Enduring Love, Set. abr. ed. 1997. audio 24.95 (*1-57511-040-7*) Publishing Mills, Inc., The.

—Enduring Love. 1998. 272p. pap. 13.00 (*0-385-49414-9*, Knopf Bks. for Young Readers) Random Hse. Children's Bks.

—Enduring Love. unabr. ed. 1998. audio 51.00 (*0-7887-2176-3*, 95472E7) Recorded Bks., LLC.

—Enduring Love. l.t. ed. 1998. (Basic Ser.). 395p. 29.95 (*0-7862-1447-3*) Thorndike Pr.

—Enduring Love. abr. ed. 1999. audio 16.85 (*0-00-105565-8*) Ulverscroft Audio (U.S.A.).

Meeker, Richard. Better Angel. 1987. 284p. reprint ed. pap. 6.95 o.p. (*1-55583-116-8*) Alyson Pubns.

—Better Angel. 2000. 250p. reprint ed. pap. 14.95 (*1-883938-63-5*) Dry Bones Pr.

Merlis, Mark. An Arrow's Flight. 1999. 376p. pap. 13.95 (*0-312-24288-3*, Saint Martin's Griffin); 1998. 384p. 24.95 o.p. (*0-312-18675-4*) St. Martin's Pr.

—Man about Town. 2003. 368p. 24.95 (*0-00-715611-1*, Fourth Estate) HarperTrade.

Merrick, Gordon. An Idol for Others. 1998. 400p. pap. 14.95 o.p. (*1-55583-295-4*) Alyson Pubns.

—An Idol for Others. 1977. pap. 3.95 o.p. (*0-380-00971-4*, 84756-6, Avon Bks.) Morrow/Avon.

—Now Let's Talk about Music. 1997. 256p. reprint ed. pap. 12.95 o.p. (*1-55583-293-8*) Alyson Pubns.

—Now Let's Talk about Music. 1981. 432p. mass mkt. 4.95 o.p. (*0-380-77867-X*, 60055-2, Avon Bks.) Morrow/Avon.

—The Quirk. 1998. 400p. reprint ed. pap. 12.95 o.p. (*1-55583-294-6*, Alyson Bks.) Alyson Pubns.

—The Quirk. 1978. pap. 3.95 o.p. (*0-380-38992-4*, 84970-4, Avon Bks.) Morrow/Avon.

Merrick, Gordon & Hulse, Charles. The Good Life. 1997. 350p. (Orig.). pap. 14.95 o.p. (*1-55583-298-9*) Alyson Pubns.

Michaels, Grant. Body to Dye For. 1991. (Stonewall Inn Editions Ser.: Vol. 1). 241p. pap. 11.95 (*0-312-05825-X*, Saint Martin's Griffin); 1990. 17.95 o.p. (*0-312-04273-6*, Saint Martin's Minotaur) St. Martin's Pr.

—Dead As a Doornail. (Stan Kraychik Mystery Ser.). 256p. 1999. pap. 12.95 (*0-312-20644-5*, Saint Martin's Griffin); 1998. 22.95 o.p. (*0-312-18077-2*, Saint Martin's Minotaur) St. Martin's Pr.

—Dead on Your Feet. 256p. 1993. 12.99 o.p. (*0-312-09781-6*, Saint Martin's Minotaur); 4th ed. 1994. (Stonewall Inn Editions Ser.: Vol. 1). pap. 11.95 (*0-312-11457-5*, Saint Martin's Griffin) St. Martin's Pr.

—Love You to Death. (Stonewall Inn Editions Ser.). 1993. 10.95 (*0-312-08841-8*, Saint Martin's Griffin); 1992. 256p. 18.95 (*0-312-07027-6*, Saint Martin's Minotaur) St. Martin's Pr.

—Mask for a Diva. 1996. 304p. pap. 10.95 (*0-312-14120-3*, Saint Martin's Griffin); 1994. 272p. 20.95 o.p. (*0-312-11462-1*, Saint Martin's Minotaur) St. Martin's Pr.

—Time to Check Out: A Stan Kraychik Mystery. 1996. 272p. 21.95 o.p. (*0-312-14434-2*, Saint Martin's Minotaur); 1997. 256p. reprint ed. pap. 12.95 (*0-312-15673-1*, NPB 0273, Saint Martin's Griffin) St. Martin's Pr.

Monette, Paul. Taking Care of Mrs. Carroll. 1978. 8.95 o.p. (*0-316-57821-5*) Little Brown & Co.

—Taking Care of Mrs. Carroll. 1979. pap. 2.75 o.p. (*0-380-45161-1*, 45161-1, Avon Bks.) Morrow/Avon.

—Taking Care of Mrs. Carroll. 1988. (Stonewall Inn Editions Ser.). 288p. pap. 12.95 (*0-312-01515-1*, Saint Martin's Griffin) St. Martin's Pr.

Moore, Marshall. The Concrete Sky. 2003. 274p. pap. 17.95 (*1-56023-436-9*); 273p. 44.95 (*1-56023-435-0*) Haworth Pr., Inc., The. (Southern Tier Editions).

Mordden, Ethan. I've a Feeling We're Not in Kansas Anymore. 1996. (Stonewall Inn Editions Ser.: Vol. 1). 208p. pap. 9.95 (*0-312-14112-2*, Saint Martin's Griffin) St. Martin's Pr.

—Some Men Are Lookers. 1997. 352p. 23.95 (*0-312-15660-X*) St. Martin's Pr.

—Some Men Are Lookers: New Stories in the Buddies Cycle. 1999. E-Book 13.95 (*0-312-20743-3*) St. Martin's Pr.

—Venice Adriana. (Stonewall Inn Editions Ser.). 1999. 324p. pap. 13.95 (*0-312-20680-1*, Saint Martin's Griffin); 1998. 304p. 23.95 o.p. (*0-312-18202-3*) St. Martin's Pr.

Morgan, Christopher. Muscle-Bound: And Other Stories. 2002. 348p. pap. 14.95 (*1-55583-651-8*) Alyson Pubns.

Murdoch, Iris. 20th Century Bell. 2001. (Penguin Twentieth-Century Classics Ser.). 320p. pap. 15.00 (*0-14-118669-0*) Viking Penguin.

Murphy, Timothy. Getting off Clean. (Stonewall Inn Editions Ser.). 1998. 336p. pap. 13.95 (*0-312-18720-3*, Saint Martin's Griffin); 1997. 272p. 23.95 (*0-312-15132-2*) St. Martin's Pr.

Nava, Michael. The Hidden Law. 2003. (Henry Rios Mystery Ser.). 232p. pap. 12.95 (*1-55583-778-6*, Alyson Bks.) Alyson Pubns.

—Howtown. 2003. (Henry Rios Mystery Ser.). 232p. pap. 12.95 (*1-55583-779-4*, Advocate Bks.) Alyson Pubns.

—Rag & Bone: A Henry Rios Novel. 2001. 304p. 24.95 o.s.i (*0-399-14708-X*) Penguin Group (USA) Inc.

Nelson, Casey. Nothing Gold Can Stay. 2000. 212p. pap. 12.95 o.p. (*1-55583-492-2*, Alyson Bks.) Alyson Pubns.

Nissen, Axel, ed. & intro. The Romantic Friendship Reader: Love Stories Between Men in Victorian America. 2003. 312p. text 55.00 (*1-55553-591-7*); pap. text 22.50 (*1-55553-590-9*) Northeastern Univ. Pr.

O'Donnell, Mark. Getting over Homer. 1997. 208p. pap. 11.00 (*0-679-78122-6*, Vintage) Knopf Publishing Group.

Oliver, Jim. Wings in the Snow. 1998. 288p. pap. 12.95 (*1-55583-462-0*, Alyson Bks.) Alyson Pubns.

Olshan, Joseph. In Clara's Hands. 2003. 305p. 26.00 (*0-7475-5497-8*); 2002. 320p. pap. 12.00 (*0-7475-5704-7*) Bloomsbury Publishing, Ltd. GBR. *Dist:* Trafalgar Square.

Ortleb, Charles. Iron Peter: A Year in the Mythopoetic Life of New York City. 1998. 150p. pap. 13.00 (*0-9663454-0-1*) Rubicon Media.

Outland, Orland. Different People: A Novel. 2003. 336p. pap. 13.95 (*1-55583-826-X*); 256p. 23.95 o.p. (*1-55583-763-8*, Alyson Bks.) Alyson Pubns.

Owens, Durrell. The Song of a Manchild. 2004. 293p. pap. 19.95 (*1-56023-480-6*, Harrington Park Pr.) Haworth Pr., Inc., The.

Parker, Canaan. Sky Daddy. 1997. 250p. pap. 10.95 o.p. (*1-55583-398-5*) Alyson Pubns.

Patrick, John, ed. Beautiful Boys. 2nd ed. 2002. 528p. per. 15.95 (*1-891855-33-6*) Florida Literary Foundation.

—Boys on the Prowl. 2000. (Illus.). 500p. pap. 14.95 (*1-891855-06-9*, STARbooks Pr.) Florida Literary Foundation.

—Taboo! 2nd ed. 2002. 648p. per. 15.95 (*1-891855-34-4*) Florida Literary Foundation.

—Tarnished Angels. 1992. 192p. (Orig.). pap. 1.95 o.p. (*1-877978-33-7*, STARbooks Pr.) Florida Literary Foundation.

Patrick, John & Butler, John, eds. Wild & Willing. 2002. 380p. per. 14.95 (*1-891855-16-6*) Florida Literary Foundation.

Phillips, Edward O. Buried on Sunday: A Geoffrey Chadwick Novel. 2000. 240p. pap. 11.99 (*1-896332-12-9*) Riverbank, Pr., The CAN. *Dist:* General Distribution Services, Inc.

—Buried on Sunday: A Geoffrey Chadwick Novel. 1988. 192p. 13.95 o.p. (*0-312-01742-1*, Saint Martin's Minotaur) St. Martin's Pr.

—Sunday's Child: A Geoffry Chadwick Novel. 2000. 280p. pap. 11.99 (*1-896332-07-2*) Riverbank, Pr., The CAN. *Dist:* General Distribution Services, Inc.

—Sunday's Child: A Geoffry Chadwick Novel. (Stonewall Inn Editions Ser.). 240p. 1988. pap. 7.95 o.p. (*0-312-02294-8*, Saint Martin's Griffin); 1987. 15.95 o.p. (*0-312-01097-4*) St. Martin's Pr.

Picano, Felice. A House on the Ocean, a House on the Bay. 2003. 270p. 17.95 (*1-56023-440-7*, Southern Tier Editions) Haworth Pr., Inc., The.

—Looking Glass Lives: A Novel. 1998. (Illus.). 240p. pap. 12.95 (*1-55583-481-7*) Alyson Pubns.

—The Lure: A Novel. 2002. 344p. pap. 14.95 (*1-55583-699-2*) Alyson Pubns.

—Men Who Loved Me. 2003. 303p. 19.95 (*1-56023-442-3*, Southern Tier Editions) Haworth Pr., Inc., The.

—The New York Years: Stories. 2000. 223p. pap. 12.95 (*1-55583-522-8*, Alyson Bks.) Alyson Pubns.

Pierce, David M. Elf Child. Pierce, David M., ed. 2003. 259p. pap. 19.95 (*1-56023-428-8*) Haworth Pr., Inc., The.

Posey, Ernest. Hormone Pirates of Xenobia & Dream Studs of Kama Loka. 1996. 256p. pap. 11.95 o.p. (*1-55583-385-3*) Alyson Pubns.

Powell, Patricia. A Small Gathering of Bones. 2003. 144p. pap. 13.00 (*0-8070-8367-4*) Beacon Pr.

Preston, John. Franny, the Queen of Provincetown. 1983. 96p. pap. 4.95 o.p. (*0-932870-31-7*) Alyson Pubns.

—Franny, the Queen of Provincetown. 1995. 112p. pap. 8.95 o.p. (*0-312-14106-8*, Saint Martin's Griffin) St. Martin's Pr.

—Journals of a Master: Entertainment for a Master & the Love of a Master. 1997. 311p. (Orig.). pap. 12.95 o.p. (*1-55583-401-9*) Alyson Pubns.

Quinn, Jay. Rebel Yell 2: More Stories of Contemporary Southern Gay Men. 2002. 288p. (C). pap. 17.95 (*1-56023-159-9*, Southern Tier Editions) Haworth Pr., Inc., The.

Quinn, Jay, ed. Rebel Yell 2: More Stories of Contemporary Southern Gay Men. 2002. 278p. (C). lib. bdg. 29.95 (*1-56023-158-0*, Southern Tier Editions) Haworth Pr., Inc., The.

Raphael, Frederic. A Double Life. 2000. 374p. 24.00 (*0-945774-46-X*) Catbird Pr.

Raphael, Lev. Death of a Constant Lover. 2000. (Nick Hoffman Mystery Ser.). 288p. pap. 12.95 (*0-312-26496-8*, Saint Martin's Griffin) St. Martin's Pr.

—Death of a Constant Lover. 1999. (Nick Hoffman Mystery Ser.). 288p. 22.95 (*0-8027-3326-3*) Walker & Co.

—The Edith Wharton Murders: A Nick Hoffman Mystery. (Stonewall Inn Editions Ser.). 1998. 240p. pap. 11.95 (*0-312-19863-9*, Saint Martin's Griffin); 1997. 208p. 21.95 o.p. (*0-312-15519-0*, Saint Martin's Minotaur) St. Martin's Pr.

—Let's Get Criminal. 1996. 240p. 20.95 o.p. (*0-312-13999-3*, Saint Martin's Minotaur); 2nd ed. 1997. 244p. pap. 11.95 (*0-312-15160-8*, Saint Martin's Griffin) St. Martin's Pr.

—Little Miss Evil: A Nick Hoffman Mystery. 2000. (Nick Hoffman Mystery Ser.). 184p. 23.95 (*0-8027-3342-5*) Walker & Co.

Reidinger, Paul. The City Kid. 2001. (Southern Tier Ser.). 250p. (C). 39.95 (*1-56023-168-8*, Harrington Park Pr.); pap. 16.95 (*1-56023-169-6*, Southern Tier Editions) Haworth Pr., Inc., The.

Reinhart, Robert C. The Consequence of Sex. 2003. 248p. pap. 14.95 (*1-55583-772-7*, Alyson Bks.) Alyson Pubns.

Renault, Mary. The Charioteer. 2003. 352p. pap. 14.00 (*0-375-71418-9*, Vintage); 1983. pap. 6.95 o.s.i (*0-394-71480-6*, Pantheon) Knopf Publishing Group.

—Charioteer. 1994. (Harvest Book Ser.). 348p. pap. 10.95 o.s.i (*0-15-616768-9*, Harvest Bks.) Harcourt Trade Pubs.

—The Charioteer. unabr. ed. 1988. audio 85.00 (*1-55690-097-X*, 88760E7) Recorded Bks., LLC.

Rettenmund, Matthew. Blind Items. 288p. 2000. pap. 13.95 (*0-312-26295-7*, Saint Martin's Griffin); 1998. 22.95 (*0-312-19242-8*) St. Martin's Pr.

Ridgway, Keith. The Long Falling. 1999. 306p. pap. 13.00 (*0-395-95782-6*); 1998. 320p. 22.00 o.p. (*0-395-90530-3*) Houghton Mifflin Co.

Ridout, James W. The Man Pilot. 2003. 366p. pap. 17.95 (*1-56023-460-1*, Southern Tier Editions) Haworth Pr., Inc., The.

Rizzo, Cindy, et al, eds. All the Ways Home: Parenting & Children in the Lesbian & Gay Communities - A Collection of Short Fiction. 1995. 200p. 19.95 (*0-934678-68-5*); pap. 10.95 (*0-934678-65-0*) New Victoria Pubs., Inc.

Roberts, Byrd. Commonwealth Chronicles: Short Stories of Virginia. 2002. per. 14.95 (*1-879194-74-0*) GLB Pubs.

Rodi, Robert. Bitch Goddess: A Novel. 2002. 320p. pap. 13.00 (*0-452-28310-8*, Plume) Dutton/Plume.

—Drag Queen. 272p. 1996. pap. 12.95 o.s.i (*0-452-27344-7*, Plume); 1995. 21.95 o.p. (*0-525-93925-3*, Dutton) Dutton/Plume.

—Fag Hag. (Plume Fiction Ser.). 304p. 1993. pap. 14.00 (*0-452-26940-7*, Plume); 1992. 20.00 o.p. (*0-525-93406-5*, Dutton) Dutton/Plume.

Rooney, William. Rooney's Shorts. 2000. 137p. (C). 39.95 (*1-56023-954-9*); 137p. (C). pap. 14.95 (*1-56023-150-5*); 138p. pap. 14.95 (*0-7890-0719-3*) Haworth Pr., Inc., The. (Harrington Park Pr.).

Roszak, Theodore. The Blizzard. 2001. (*1-58195-107-8*, Zoland Bks., Inc.) Steerforth Pr.

—The Devil & Daniel Silverman. 2003. 348p. pap. 15.95 (*0-9679520-7-7*) Leapfrog Pr.

Rowe, Michael. Brothers of the Night: Tales of Men, Blood & Immortality. 1997. 180p. pap. 14.95 o.p. (1-57344-025-6) Cleis Pr.
Rowe, Michael, ed. Queer Fear: Gay Horror Fiction. 2000. 256p. pap. 16.95 (1-55152-084-2) Arsenal Pulp Pr., Ltd. CAN. Dist: Consortium Bk. Sales & Distribution.
—Queer Fear II: Gay Horror Fiction. 2002. (Illus.). 304p. pap. 17.95 (1-55152-122-9) Arsenal Pulp Pr., Ltd. CAN. Dist: Consortium Bk. Sales & Distribution.
Ruff, Shawn, ed. Go the Way Your Blood Beats: An Anthology of Gay & Lesbian Literary Writings by African Americans. 1996. 480p. pap. 16.95 o.p. (0-8050-4437-X, Owl Bks.) Holt, Henry & Co.
Ruff, Shawn S. Go the Way Your Blood Beats. 1996. 480p. 30.00 o.p. (0-8050-4736-0) Holt, Henry & Co.
Sarkessian, Juliet, ed. Trio Sonata: A Novel. 2002. (Gay Men's Fiction Ser.). 200p. 24.95 (1-56023-401-6); pap. 14.95 (1-56023-402-4) Haworth Pr., Inc., The. (Harrington Park Pr.).
Schiefelbein, Michael. Vampire Thrall: A Novel. 2003. 224p. pap. 13.95 (1-55583-728-X) Alyson Pubns.
Schimel, Lawrence. His Tongue. 2001. 161p. pap. 14.95 (1-58394-049-9) Frog, Ltd.
Schimel, Lawrence, ed. The Mammoth Book of Gay Erotica. 1998. (Mammoth Bks.). 544p. pap. 10.95 (0-7867-0476-4, Carroll & Graf Pubs.) Avalon Publishing Group.
Schulman, Sarah. Rat Bohemia. 240p. 1996. pap. 10.95 o.p. (0-452-27182-7, Plume); 1995. 19.95 o.p. (0-525-93790-0, Dutton) Dutton/Plume.
Scott, Darieck. Traitor to the Race. 1995. 224p. 20.95 o.p. (0-525-93912-1) Dutton/Plume.
Scott, Phillip. Gay Resort Murder Shock. 2003. 320p. pap. 13.95 (1-55583-757-3) Alyson Pubns.
Self, Will. Dorian. 2004. 288p. pap. 13.00 (0-8021-4047-5, Grove Pr.) Grove/Atlantic, Inc.
Self, Will & Wilde, Oscar. Dorian: An Imitation. 2003. 288p. 23.00 (0-8021-1729-5, Grove Pr.) Grove/Atlantic, Inc.
Selvadurai, Shyam. Cinnamon Gardens. 2000. (Harvest Book Ser.). 368p. pap. 14.00 (0-15-601328-2, Harvest Bks.) Harcourt Trade Pubs.
—Cinnamon Gardens. 1999. 400p. 23.95 (0-7868-6473-7) Hyperion Pr.
—Funny Boy: A Novel in Six Stories. 1998. (Between the Covers Collection). audio (0-86492-262-0) Goose Lane Editions.
—Funny Boy: A Novel in Six Stories. 1997. (Harvest Book Ser.). 320p. pap. 13.00 (0-15-600500-X, Harvest Bks.) Harcourt Trade Pubs.
—Funny Boy: A Novel in Six Stories. 1996. 320p. 23.00 o.p. (0-688-14595-7, Morrow, William & Co.) Morrow/Avon.
Sheppard, Simon. Hotter Than Hell: And Other Stories. 2001. 264p. pap. 14.95 (1-55583-596-1, Alyson Bks.) Alyson Pubns.
Sibley, William Jack. Any Kind of Luck. 2002. 288p. pap. 14.00 (0-7582-0255-5) Kensington Publishing Corp.
Skee, Mickey. F. U. Majoring in Carnal Knowledge. 2002. 272p. pap. 14.95 (1-55583-649-6) Alyson Pubns.
Snider, Clifton. Wrestling with Angels: A Tale of Two Brothers. 2002. 249p. pap. 21.99 (1-4010-3073-4); text 31.99 (1-4010-5536-2); E-Book 8.00 (1-4010-3074-2) Xlibris Corp.
Solomon, Andrew. A Stone Boat. 1996. 256p. pap. 13.00 (0-452-27498-2, Plume) Dutton/Plume.
—A Stone Boat. 1994. 288p. 22.95 o.p. (0-571-17240-7) Faber & Faber, Inc.
Stambolian, George. Men on Men: Best New Gay Fiction. 1986. (Men on Men Ser.). 384p. pap. 13.95 o.p. (0-452-25882-0, Plume) Dutton/Plume.
—Men on Men Four: Best New Gay Fiction. 1988. (Men on Men Ser.). pap. 9.95 o.p. (0-452-26143-0) NAL.
—Men on Men 3: Best New Gay Fiction. 1990. (Men on Men Ser.). 38p. 21.95 o.p. (0-525-24905-2); pap. 10.95 (0-525-26514-7) Dutton/Plume. (Dutton).
Stambolian, George, ed. Men on Men Four: Best New Gay Fiction. 1992. (Men on Men Ser.). 416p. 25.00 o.p. (0-525-93504-5, Dutton) Dutton/Plume.
—Men on Men 4: Best New Gay Fiction. 1992. (Men on Men Ser.). 416p. pap. 12.95 o.p. (0-452-26856-7, Dutton) Dutton/Plume.
Stambolian, George, ed. & intro. Men on Men 2: Best New Gay Fiction. 1988. (Men on Men Ser.). 384p. pap. 12.00 o.p. (0-452-26402-2, Plume) Dutton/Plume.
Stambolian, George, intro. Men on Men: Best New Gay Fiction, No. 3. 1990. (Men on Men Ser.). 384p. pap. 12.95 o.p. (0-452-26514-2, Plume) Dutton/Plume.
Stevens, David. Waters of Babylon: A Novel about Lawrence after Arabia. 2000. 320p. 24.00 o.s.i (0-684-86210-7, Simon & Schuster) Simon & Schuster.
Stevenson, Richard. Death Trick: A Murder Mystery. 2003. 199p. pap. 15.95 (1-56023-470-9, Southern Tier Editions) Haworth Pr., Inc., The.
—Tongue Tied: A Donald Strachey Mystery. 2003. 224p. 22.95 (0-312-30974-0, Saint Martin's Minotaur) St. Martin's Pr.
Storandt, William. The Summer They Came: A Novel. 2002. 272p. pap. 12.95 (0-375-75909-3, Villard Bks.) Random House Adult Trade Publishing Group.
Suresha, Ron Jackson. Bearotica: Hot, Hairy, Heavy Fiction. 2002. 288p. pap. 15.95 (1-55583-577-5) Alyson Pubns.
Sycamore, Matt Bernstein. Pulling Taffy. 2003. 224p. pap. 16.95 (0-9710846-3-7) Suspect Thoughts Pr.
Tan, Cecilia, ed. & intro. Blood Kiss: Vampire Erotica. 1994. 138p. (Orig.). pap. 9.95 (1-885865-00-7) Circlet Pr., Inc.
Tapon, Philippe. Parisian from Kansas. (William Abrahams Book Ser.). 336p. 1998. pap. 13.95 o.s.i (0-452-27735-3, Plume); 1997. 23.95 o.s.i (0-525-94239-4) Dutton/Plume.
Taylor, Robert. The Innocent: A Novel. 1997. 256p. (Orig.). pap. 14.95 (1-56474-230-X) Fithian Pr.
Thompson, M. A. Wolfchild. 2000. 108p. pap. 20.99 (0-7388-3229-4) Xlibris Corp.
Tien-Wen, Chu. Notes of a Desolate Man. 1999. (Modern Chinese Literature from Taiwan Ser.). viii, 169p. text 22.00 (0-231-11608-X) Columbia Univ. Pr.
—Notes of a Desolate Man. Goldblatt, Howard & Lin, Sylvia Li-Chun, trs. 2000. 184p. reprint ed. pap. 15.95 (0-231-11609-8) Columbia Univ. Pr.
Toibin, Colm. The Story of the Night. 1998. 304p. pap. 13.00 (0-8050-5825-7, Owl Bks.); 1997. 312p. 23.00 o.s.i (0-8050-5211-9) Holt, Henry & Co.
—The Story of the Night. 1997. 320p. pap. 19.99 (0-7710-8556-7) McClelland & Stewart/Tundra Bks.
Trevelyan, Julie K. & Brassart, Scott, eds. The Ghost of Carmen Miranda: And Other Spooky Gay & Lesbian Tales. 1998. 300p. pap. 11.95 o.p. (1-55583-488-4) Alyson Pubns.
Truong, Monique. The Book of Salt. 2003. 272p. tchr. ed. 24.00 (0-618-30400-2) Houghton Mifflin Co.
Van Wagoner, Robert H. Dancing Naked: A Novel. 1999. 369p. 20.95 (1-56085-130-9) Signature Bks., Inc.
Vickery, Bob. Cock Tales: Erotic Short Stories. 1997. pap. text 14.95 (0-943595-65-7) Leyland Pubns.
—Cocksure: Erotic Fiction. 2002. 240p. pap. 14.95 (1-55583-739-5) Alyson Pubns.
Virga, Vincent. Vadriel Vail. 2001. 382p. pap. 14.95 (1-55583-583-X) Alyson Pubns.
Welsh, Louise. The Cutting Room. 304p. 2004. pap. (1-84195-474-8); 2003. (1-84195-383-0) Canongate Bks.
—The Cutting Room. 2002. 304p. 24.00 (1-84195-280-X) Canongate Bks. GBR. Dist: Grove/Atlantic, Inc.
Whyte, Christopher. Gay Decameron. 1999. 352p. mass mkt. 10.95 (0-575-40121-4); 1998. 346p. 27.00 (0-575-06505-2) Gollancz, Victor GBR. Dist: Trafalgar Square.
Wilde, Oscar. Teleny. 1992. mass mkt. 4.95 o.s.i (1-56333-020-2, Badboy) Masquerade Bks., Inc.
—Teleny. 1999. 200p. pap. 14.95 (1-902852-00-1) Prowler/GMP GBR. Dist: LPC/InBook.
—Teleny. 1984. 192p. mass mkt. 3.95 o.s.i (0-446-30791-2) Warner Bks., Inc.
—Teleny. 1984. 184p. reprint ed. pap. 14.95 (0-917342-33-X); lib. bdg. 25.00 (0-917342-32-1) Gay Sunshine Pr., Inc.
Wilhoit, Stephen W. A Brief Guide to Writing from Readings. 2nd ed. 2001. (Illus.). x, 305p. pap. 21.95 (0-8223-2589-6) Duke Univ. Pr.
Willis, Paul, ed. Sex Buddies: Erotic Stories about Sex Without Strings. 2003. 274p. pap. 14.95 (1-55583-756-5) Alyson Pubns.
Wilson, John Morgan. Blind Eye: A Benjamin Justice Novel. 2003. 288p. 23.95 (0-312-30919-8, Saint Martin's Minotaur) St. Martin's Pr.
—Justice at Risk: A Benjamin Justice Mystery. 2000. (Benjamin Justice Mystery Ser.). 368p. mass mkt. 6.50 (0-553-57860-X) Bantam Bks.
—Justice at Risk: A Benjamin Justice Mystery. 1999. (Benjamin Justice Mystery Ser.). 304p. 22.95 o.s.i (0-385-49116-6) Doubleday Publishing.
—Revision of Justice: A Benjamin Justice Mystery. 1999. (Benjamin Justice Mystery Ser.). 416p. mass mkt. 5.99 (0-553-57533-3) Bantam Bks.
—Simple Justice: A Benjamin Justice Mystery. 1997. (Benjamin Justice Mystery Ser.). 304p. mass mkt. 6.50 o.s.i (0-553-57532-5) Bantam Bks.
—Simple Justice: A Benjamin Justice Mystery. 1996. 256p. 21.00 o.s.i (0-385-48234-5) Doubleday Publishing.
Zimmerman, R. D. Closet: A Todd Mills Mystery. 1995. 320p. mass mkt. 4.99 o.s.i (0-440-21869-1) Dell Publishing.
—Closet: A Todd Mills Mystery. 1997. 304p. pap. 10.95 o.s.i (0-385-32004-3) Doubleday Publishing.
—Innuendo. 2000. (Todd Mills Mysteries Ser.). 320p. pap. 11.95 (0-385-31926-6, Dial Bks.) Dell Publishing.
—Outburst: A Todd Mills Mystery. 1999. (Illus.). 304p. pap. 19.00 (0-385-31923-1, Delacorte Pr.) Dell Publishing.
—Tribe. 1996. 288p. mass mkt. 5.50 o.s.i (0-440-21870-5) Dell Publishing.
—Tribe: A Todd Mills Mystery. 1997. 272p. pap. 10.95 o.s.i (0-385-32002-7) Doubleday Publishing.
Zubro, Mark Richard. Another Dead Teenager. 1995. 194p. 19.95 o.p. (0-312-13024-4, Saint Martin's Minotaur) St. Martin's Pr.
—Are You Nuts? (Tom & Scott Mystery Ser.). 256p. 1999. pap. 12.95 (0-312-20634-8, Saint Martin's Griffin); 1998. 21.95 (0-312-18528-6, Saint Martin's Minotaur) St. Martin's Pr.
—Drop Dead. (Paul Turner Mystery Ser.). 2000. 256p. pap. 12.95 (0-312-26314-7, Saint Martin's Griffin); 1999. 245p. 22.95 (0-312-20532-5, Saint Martin's Minotaur) St. Martin's Pr.
—An Echo of Death: A Tom & Scott Mystery. (Tom & Scott Mystery Ser.). 1995. 208p. pap. 11.95 (0-312-13480-0, Saint Martin's Griffin); 1994. 192p. 18.95 o.p. (0-312-11268-8, Saint Martin's Minotaur) St. Martin's Pr.
—Here Comes the Corpse. 2002. (Tom & Scott Mystery Ser.: No. 9). 256p. 23.95 (0-312-28098-X, Saint Martin's Minotaur) St. Martin's Pr.
—One Dead Drag Queen. E-Book 22.95 (0-312-27586-2); 2001. 256p. pap. 12.95 (0-312-27702-4, Saint Martin's Griffin); 2000. 256p. 22.95 o.s.i (0-312-20937-1, Saint Martin's Minotaur) St. Martin's Pr.
—Political Poison: A Paul Turner Mystery. (Paul Turner Mystery Ser.). 1994. 208p. pap. 11.95 (0-312-11044-8, Saint Martin's Griffin); 1993. 192p. 10.99 o.p. (0-312-09364-0, Saint Martin's Minotaur) St. Martin's Pr.
—The Principal Cause of Death. (Tom & Scott Mystery Ser.). 1993. 192p. pap. 11.95 (0-312-09896-0, Saint Martin's Griffin); 1992. 208p. 11.99 o.p. (0-312-07767-X, Saint Martin's Minotaur) St. Martin's Pr.
—Rust on the Razor. (Tom & Scott Mystery Ser.). 224p. 1997. pap. 11.95 (0-312-15644-8, Saint Martin's Griffin); 1996. text 20.95 o.p. (0-312-14404-0, Saint Martin's Minotaur) St. Martin's Pr.
—A Simple Suburban Murder. (Stonewall Inn Editions Ser.). 1990. 6.50 o.p. (0-312-03887-9, Saint Martin's Minotaur); 1990. 224p. pap. 8.95 (0-312-03933-6, Saint Martin's Griffin); 1989. 224p. 15.95 o.p. (0-312-02640-4, Saint Martin's Minotaur) St. Martin's Pr.
—Sorry Now? 1991. 208p. 11.99 o.p. (0-312-06470-5, Saint Martin's Minotaur); 3rd ed. 1992. 192p. pap. 10.95 (0-312-08299-1, Saint Martin's Griffin) St. Martin's Pr.
—The Truth Can Get You Killed. (Stonewall Inn Editions Ser.). 224p. 1998. pap. 11.95 (0-312-18765-3, Saint Martin's Griffin); 1997. 21.95 (0-312-15679-0, Saint Martin's Minotaur) St. Martin's Pr.
—Why Isn't Becky Twitchell Dead? 1970. 208p. 15.00 o.p. (0-312-03955-7) Palgrave Macmillan.
—Why Isn't Becky Twitchell Dead? 1991. (Stonewall Inn Editions Ser.). 189p. pap. 12.95 (0-312-05996-5, Saint Martin's Griffin) St. Martin's Pr.

### GRANDPARENTS—FICTION

Andrews, V. C. Honey. 2002. E-Book 4.99 (1-4014-9985-6) Barnes & Noble Digital.
—Honey. l.t. ed. 2002. 168p. 29.95 (0-7838-9752-9) Gale Group.
Badami, Anita Rau. The Hero's Walk. 2001. 359p. 23.95 (1-56512-312-3) Algonquin Bks. of Chapel Hill.
Bauer, Tricia. Boondocking: A Novel. 1997. 21.95 (1-882593-19-7) Bridge Works Publishing Co., Inc.
—Boondocking: A Novel. 1999. 240p. pap. 11.95 (0-312-19839-6, Saint Martin's Griffin) St. Martin's Pr.
Bell, Nancy. Biggie & the Devil Diet. E-Book 16.95 (0-312-70885-8) St. Martin's Pr.
—Biggie & the Devil Diet. 2003. (Mystery Ser.). 30.95 (0-7862-4831-9) Thorndike Pr.
—Biggie & the Devil Diet: A Mystery. 2002. (Biggie Ser.). 224p. 22.95 (0-312-30184-7, Saint Martin's Minotaur) St. Martin's Pr.
Berger, Jason. Forested Moments. 2002. 137p. (1-888725-79-6); 124p. per. 14.95 (1-888725-73-7) Science & Humanities Pr. (BeachHouse Bks.).
Bowden, Susan. Bitter Harvest. l.t. ed. 2001. 361p. 26.95 (1-57490-373-X, Beeler Large Print Bks.) Beeler, Thomas T. Publisher.
—Bitter Harvest. 2001. 352p. mass mkt. 6.99 o.s.i (0-451-20237-6) NAL.
Brennan, Maeve. The Visitor. 2001. 96p. pap. text 10.00 (1-58243-161-2, Counterpoint Pr.) Basic Bks.
—Visitor. 2000. 96p. text 16.95 o.p. (1-58243-083-7, Counterpoint Pr.) Basic Bks.
Cisneros, Sandra. Caramelo. 2003. 464p. pap. 13.95 (0-679-74258-1, Vintage); (SPA.). 496p. pap. 13.95 (1-4000-3099-4, Vintage); 464p. 24.00 (1-4000-4150-3) Knopf Publishing Group.
—Caramelo. 2002. 464p. 24.00 (0-679-43554-9) Knopf, Alfred A. Inc.
—Caramelo. 2002. (SPA.). 496p. 24.00 (0-375-41509-2) Random Hse., Inc.
—Caramelo. 2003. (Spanish Language Ser.). (SPA.). 28.95 (0-7862-5124-7); 30.95 (0-7862-5138-7) Thorndike Pr.
Clarke, Judith. Friend of My Heart. 1994. 148p. pap. 12.95 (0-7022-2699-8) Univ. of Queensland Pr. AUS. Dist: International Specialized Bk. Services.
Coleman, Jane Candia. The Italian Quartet. 2001. (Five Star First Edition Women's Fiction Ser.). 197p. 25.95 (0-7862-3379-6, Five Star) Gale Group.
Devereaux, Robert. A Flight of Storks & Angels. 2003. 317p. 25.95 (1-59414-058-8, Five Star) Gale Group.
Dickens, Charles. The Old Curiosity Shop. 2001. (Classics Ser.). xxxiv, 608p. pap. (0-14-043742-8, Penguin Classics) Viking Penguin.
Duncan, Pamela. Moon Women. 2002. 336p. pap. 12.95 (0-385-33521-0, Delta) Dell Publishing.
Foer, Jonathan Safran. Everything Is Illuminated: A Novel. 2003. 288p. pap. 13.95 (0-06-052970-9, Perennial) HarperTrade.
—Everything Is Illuminated: A Novel. 2002. (Illus.). 288p. tchr. ed. 24.00 (0-618-17387-0) Houghton Mifflin Co.
Francis, Dorothy Brenner. Keys to Love. l.t. ed. 2002. 185p. 26.95 (0-7862-4036-9) Gale Group.
Gardam, Jane. Faith Fox. 2003. 416p. 25.00 (0-7867-1221-X) Avalon Publishing Group.
—Faith Fox. 1997. 410p. pap. o.s.i (0-349-10823-4) Little Brown & Co.
Gebler, Carlo. The Eleventh Summer. 1985. 160p. 13.95 o.p. (0-525-24331-3, Abrahams, William Bks.) Dutton/Plume.
—The Eleventh Summer. 1990. pap. 7.95 o.p. (0-671-67779-9, Fireside) Simon & Schuster.
Graves, Lonnie. Aunt Millipus & Her Will. 2002. 17.95 (1-57168-720-3, Eakin Pr.) Eakin Pr.
Griffin, Frank James. Till the Tide Comes In. 2003. (0-945582-90-0) Down The Shore Publishing.
Harmon, A. G. A House All Stilled: A Novel. 2002. 248p. 29.95 (1-57233-202-6) Univ. of Tennessee Pr.
Hirsch, Harvey. Grandma's Lost Gift: A Christmas Story. 1994. Orig. Title: The Creche of Krakow. (Illus.). 56p. pap. 7.95 (0-929613-00-7, 100GLG) Cobblestone Pr.
Hopkins, Lila. Weave Me a Song: A Novel: a Chronicle of Family Devotion, a Story of Love, Betrayal, Forgiveness & Reunion. 2002. 229p. 19.95 (0-9713045-7-2) High Country Pubs., Ltd.
Hoyt, Richard. Old Soldiers Sometimes Lie. E-Book 19.95 (0-312-70863-7, Tor Bks.); 2002. 432p. 25.95 (0-7653-0331-0, Forge Bks.) Doherty, Tom Assocs., LLC.
Inclan, Jessica Barksdale. When You Go Away: A Novel. 2003. 256p. pap. 12.95 (0-451-20787-4) NAL.
Johnson, Guy. Echoes of a Distant Summer: A Novel. 2002. 688p. 24.95 (0-375-50567-9) Random Hse., Inc.
Kraft, Eric. Herb 'n' Lorna. 1995. 320p. pap. 13.00 (0-312-13509-2) Picador.
—Herb 'n' Lorna: A Novel. 1989. pap. 8.95 o.p. (0-525-48513-9, Obelisk) NAL.
Loring, Emilie Baker. High of Heart, No. 30. 1981. 224p. pap. 1.95 o.p. (0-553-20112-3) Bantam Bks.
Lowell, Elizabeth. Die in Plain Sight: A Novel of Suspense. 2003. 400p. 24.95 (0-06-050412-9, Morrow, William & Co.) Morrow/Avon.
Martinusen, Cindy McCormick. North of Tomorrow. 2002. 416p. pap. 10.99 (0-8423-5237-6) Tyndale Hse. Pubs.
Matott, Justin. When Did I Meet You Grandpa? 2000. (Illus.). 32p. (J). (gr. 1-7). 16.95 (1-889191-14-0) Clove Pubns.
McNeil, Jean. Hunting down Home. 1999. 240p. 16.00 (1-57131-026-6) Milkweed Editions.
Mickle, Shelley F. The Queen of October. (Front Porch Paperback Ser.). 1992. 320p. tchr. ed. 8.95 (1-56512-003-5, 72003); 1989. 308p. 15.95 o.p. (0-945575-21-1) Algonquin Bks. of Chapel Hill.
Miller, Sue. The World Below. 2001. E-Book 20.00 (1-59061-312-0) Adobe Systems, Inc.
—The World Below. 2001. 288p. 25.00 (0-375-41094-5) Knopf, Alfred A. Inc.
—The World Below. unabr. ed. 2001. audio 34.95 (0-375-41993-4); audio compact disk 39.95 (0-375-41994-2) Random Hse. Audio Publishing Group. (RH Audio).
—The World Below. l.t. ed. 2001. 448p. 25.00 (0-375-43131-4) Random Hse. Large Print.
—The World Below. 2002. 304p. pap. 13.95 (0-345-44076-5) Random Hse., Inc.

Mitchard, Jacquelyn. A Theory of Relativity. 2002. 416p. mass mkt. 7.99 (*0-06-103199-2*); 2001. 368p. 26.00 (*0-06-621023-2*); 2001. E-Book 7.99 (*0-06-001068-1*) HarperCollins Pubs.

—A Theory of Relativity. l.t. ed. 2001. 624p. pap. 26.00 (*0-06-621060-7*, HarperLargePrint) HarperTrade.

Moriarty, Laura. The Center of Everything: A Novel. 2003. 304p. 22.95 (*1-4013-0031-6*) Hyperion Pr.

—The Center of Everything: A Novel. l.t. ed. 2003. 610p. 30.95 (*0-7862-5563-3*) Thorndike Pr.

—People in General. 2004. pap. 14.00 (*0-7868-8845-8*) Hyperion Pr.

Myers, Bill. When the Last Leaf Falls. l.t. ed. 2002. (Inspirational Ser.). 169p. 27.95 (*0-7862-4610-3*) Thorndike Pr.

—When the Last Leaf Falls. 2001. 144p. 12.99 (*0-310-23091-8*) Zondervan.

Oke, Janette. Like Gold Refined. 2000. (Prairie Legacy Ser.: Vol. 4). 1p. pap. 15.99 o.p. (*0-7642-2164-7*); 256p. text 15.99 o.p. (*0-7642-2162-0*); 256p. pap. 12.99 (*0-7642-2161-2*); 368p. pap. 16.99 (*0-7642-2163-9*) Bethany Hse. Pubs.

—Like Gold Refined. l.t. ed. 2000. (G. K. Hall Inspirational Ser.). (Illus.). 312p. 27.95 (*0-7838-9184-9*, Macmillan Reference USA) Gale Group.

Pierce, Todd. The Australia Stories. 2003. 223p. 20.00 (*1-931561-28-1*) MacAdam/Cage Publishing, Inc.

Poitier-Henderson, Beverly. Nana. 2001. 136p. pap. 10.95 o.p. (*0-595-17730-1*, Writers Club Pr.) iUniverse, Inc.

Poli, Judi. Smile, & Give Your Face a Holiday. 2002. 108p. pap. 10.99 (*1-59160-001-4*) Xulon Pr., Inc.

Roberts, Nora. The MacGregor Brides. l.t. ed. 2002. (Wheeler Large Print Book Ser.). 28.95 (*1-58724-191-9*, Wheeler Publishing, Inc.) Gale Group.

—The MacGregor Brides. 384p. 2002. mass mkt. (*0-373-21847-8*); 1997. per. (*0-373-48350-3*) Harlequin Enterprises, Ltd. (Harlequin Bks.).

Rolens, Sharon. Worthy's Town: A Novel. 2000. 230p. 22.95 (*1-882593-35-9*); 2002. 288p. reprint ed. pap. 13.95 (*1-882593-57-X*) Bridge Works Publishing Co., Inc.

—Worthy's Town: A Novel. l.t. ed. 2001. 343p. 28.95 (*0-7862-3376-1*) Thorndike Pr.

Scott, Joanna. Make Believe. 2001. (Illus.). 272p. reprint ed. pap. 13.95 (*0-316-77666-1*, Back Bay) Little Brown & Co.

—Make Believe: A Novel. l.t. ed. 2000. (G. K. Hall Core Ser.). 343p. 28.95 (*0-7838-9086-9*, Macmillan Reference USA) Gale Group.

—Make Believe: A Novel. 2000. 272p. 23.95 o.p. (*0-316-77616-5*) Little Brown & Co.

Seiffert, Rachel. The Dark Room: A Novel. 2002. 288p. pap. 13.00 (*0-375-72632-2*) Knopf, Alfred A. Inc.

Sethi, Robbie Clipper. Fifty-Fifty: A Novel in Many Voices. 2003. (Illus.). 217p. 24.95 (*0-929306-24-4*) Silicon Pr.

Stegner, Wallace. Angle of Repose. 1981. mass mkt. 2.95 o.p. (*0-449-23796-6*); 1985. 512p. reprint ed. mass mkt. 5.95 o.s.i (*0-449-20988-1*) Ballantine Bks. (Fawcett).

—Angle of Repose. unabr. collector's ed. 1996. Pt. 1. audio 72.00 (*0-7366-3281-6*, 3937 A); Pt. 2. audio 80.00 (*0-7366-3282-4*, 3937-B) Books on Tape, Inc.

—Angle of Repose. 1971. 12.95 o.p. (*0-385-07882-X*) Doubleday Publishing.

—Angle of Repose. 1998. (*0-14-771245-9*); 1997. (*0-14-771219-X*); 1992. 512p. pap. 13.95 (*0-14-016930-X*, Penguin Bks.) Penguin Group (USA) Inc.

—Angle of Repose. 1996. 9.99 o.p. (*0-517-18489-3*) Random Hse. Value Publishing.

—Angle of Repose. 2000. (Modern Library Ser.). 656p. 23.95 o.s.i (*0-679-60338-7*) Random Hse., Inc.

—Angle of Repose. 2000. 21.05 (*0-606-21897-1*) Turtleback Bks.

—Angle of Repose. 2000. (Classics Ser.). 512p. 15.00 (*0-14-118547-3*, Penguin Classics) Viking Penguin.

Stephens, C. A. Sailing on the Ice: And Other Stories from the Old Squire's Farm. 1996. (Illus.). 377p. pap. 17.98 (*1-55853-862-3*) Rutledge Hill Pr.

—Stories from the Old Squire's Farm. 2001. 420p. pap. 17.98 (*1-55853-959-X*) Rutledge Hill Pr.

—Stories from the Old Squire's Farm. Waugh, Eric J. & Waugh, Charles, eds. 1995. 288p. 18.95 o.p. (*1-55853-334-6*) Rutledge Hill Pr.

Tarlton, John S. The Cost of Doing Business: A Novel. 2001. 272p. 22.95 (*1-882593-42-1*); 2003. 406p. reprint ed. pap. 15.95 (*1-882593-72-3*) Bridge Works Publishing Co., Inc.

VanDenburgh, Jane. Failure to Zigzag. 1989. 336p. 16.95 o.p. (*0-86547-356-0*, North Point Pr.) Farrar, Straus & Giroux.

—Failure to Zigzag. 1990. pap. 8.95 (*0-380-71019-6*, Avon Bks.) Morrow/Avon.

—Failure to Zigzag: A Novel. 2000. 336p. pap. text 14.00 (*1-58243-076-4*, Counterpoint Pr.) Basic Bks.

Vea, Alfredo, Jr. La Maravilla. 320p. 1994. pap. 13.95 (*0-452-27160-6*, Plume); 1993. 21.00 o.p. (*0-525-93588-6*) Dutton/Plume.

Walker, Alice. The Third Life of Grange Copeland. Bernard, Andre, ed. 2003. 328p. pap. 14.00 (*0-15-602836-0*, Harvest Bks.) Harcourt Trade Pubs.

Watson, Sterling. Sweet Dream Baby. 2002. 320p. 22.00 (*1-4022-0017-X*, Sourcebooks Landmark) Sourcebooks, Inc.

Weld, William F. Stillwater: A Novel. l.t. ed. 2002. 275p. 28.95 (*0-7862-4170-5*) Gale Group.

—Stillwater: A Novel. 2002. 240p. 23.00 (*0-7432-0598-7*); E-Book 9.99 (*0-7432-1770-5*) Simon & Schuster. (Simon & Schuster).

Whack, Rita Coburn. Meant to Be: A Novel. 2002. 320p. pap. 11.95 (*0-375-75809-7*, Villard Bks.) Random House Adult Trade Publishing Group.

Wheeler, Joe L., ed. Stories for Grandparents. 2002. (Heart to Heart Ser.). (Illus.). 288p. 12.99 (*0-8423-5379-8*) Tyndale Hse. Pubs.

Whitfield, Eric T. The Job. 2001. 114p. pap. (*1-888725-68-0*); pap. (*1-888725-69-9*) Science & Humanities Pr. (BeachHouse Bks.).

Wilhelm, Kate. Skeletons. 2002. 304p. 24.95 (*0-312-30075-1*, Saint Martin's Minotaur) St. Martin's Pr.

# L

## LESBIANS—FICTION

Abbott, Cameron. An Inexpressible State of Grace. 2003. 17.95 (*1-56023-469-5*, Harrington Park Pr.) Haworth Pr., Inc., The.

Adams, Laura & Kallmaker, Karin. Seeds of Fire. 2002. (Tunnel of Light Trilogy: Bk. 2). 274p. pap. 12.95 (*1-931513-19-8*) Bella Bks., Inc.

Advocate. The Story of Me. 2000. 125p. pap. 9.95 (*0-595-13744-X*, Writers Club Pr.) iUniverse, Inc.

Albarella, Joan. Agenda for Murder: A Nikki Barnes Mystery. 1998. 223p. pap. 11.99 (*1-883061-20-2*) Rising Tide Pr.

—Called to Kill: A Nikki Barnes Mystery. 2000. 213p. pap. 12.00 (*1-883061-28-8*) Rising Tide Pr.

—Close to You: A Nikki Barnes Mystery. 2003. 222p. pap. 14.95 (*0-595-27303-3*, Mystery & Suspense Pr.) iUniverse, Inc.

Allen, Kate. I Knew You Would Call. 1995. 202p. (Orig.). pap. 10.95 (*0-934678-70-7*) New Victoria Pubs., Inc.

Anshaw, Carol. Lucky in the Corner. 2002. 256p. tchr. ed. 23.00 (*0-395-94040-0*) Houghton Mifflin Co.

Arnold, Madelyn. Year of Full Moons. 2000. 498p. 25.95 (*0-312-19965-1*) St. Martin's Pr.

Arnold, Madelyn M. On Ships at Sea. (Stonewall Inn Editions Ser.). 1993. pap. 9.95 (*0-312-08867-1*, Saint Martin's Griffin); 1991. 256p. 18.95 o.p. (*0-312-06463-2*) St. Martin's Pr.

Ashley, Leonard R. N. What I Know about You: 100 Lesbian & Gay New York Voices. 2002. 313p. pap. 22.99 (*1-4010-3173-0*) Xlibris Corp.

Bailey, Auden. Drifting at the Bottom of the World. 2002. 288p. pap. 12.95 (*1-931513-17-1*) Bella Bks., Inc.

Barr, Nevada. Bittersweet. 1999. 368p. pap. 13.95 (*0-380-79950-2*) Morrow/Avon.

—Bittersweet. 1989. 344p. reprint ed. pap. 9.95 o.p. (*0-933216-64-5*) Spinsters Ink Bks.

Bechdel, Alison. Dykes & Sundry Other Carbon-Based Life-Forms to Watch Out For. 2003. (Illus.). 128p. pap. 13.95 (*1-55583-828-6*, Alyson Bks.) Alyson Pubns.

Bennett, Saxon. Talk of the Town. 2003. 220p. pap. 12.95 (*1-931513-18-X*) Bella Bks., Inc.

Bikis, Gwendolyn. Your Loving Arms. 2002. 247p. (C). 27.95 (*1-56023-220-X*); pap. 17.95 (*1-56023-221-8*) Haworth Pr., Inc., The. (Alice Street Editions).

Blackman, Marci. Po Man's Child: A Novel. 1999. 240p. pap. 12.95 (*0-916397-59-9*) Manic D Pr.

Boock, Paula. Dare Truth or Promise. 1999. 208p. (YA). (gr. 7-12). tchr. ed. 15.00 (*0-395-97117-9*) Houghton Mifflin Co.

Brady, Maureen. Ginger's Fire. 2003. 174p. pap. 14.95 (*1-56023-444-X*); 39.95 (*1-56023-443-1*) Haworth Pr., Inc., The. (Alice Street Editions).

Brand, Dionne. In Another Place, Not Here. 1997. 256p. 24.00 o.p. (*0-8021-1622-1*); 247p. 24.00 o.p. (*0-8021-1615-9*) Grove/Atlantic, Inc. (Grove Pr.).

Bridgforth, Sharon. Bull-Jean Stories. 1998. 111p. pap. 12.00 (*0-9656659-1-7*) RedBone Pr.

Broussard, Meredith. The Dictionary of Failed Relationships: 26 Tales of Love Gone Wrong. 2003. 320p. pap. 11.00 (*0-609-81009-X*, Three Rivers Pr.) Crown Publishing Group.

Brown, Angela. Best Lesbian Love Stories. 2003. 280p. pap. 14.95 (*1-55583-765-4*) Alyson Pubns.

Brown, Rita Mae. Venus Envy. 1994. 400p. mass mkt. 7.50 (*0-553-56497-8*) Bantam Bks.

Brownrigg, Sylvia. Pages for You. 2001. vii, 263p. 22.00 o.p. (*0-374-22859-0*); E-Book 22.00 (*0-374-70207-1*) Farrar, Straus & Giroux.

—Pages for You. 2002. 272p. pap. 13.00 (*0-312-42004-8*) Picador.

—Pages for You Microsoft Reader. 2001. E-Book 22.00 (*0-374-70210-1*) Farrar, Straus & Giroux.

Bryher, Winifred. Bryher: Two Novels. 2000. (Living Out Ser.). xli, 289p. 50.00 (*0-299-16770-4*); pap. 19.95 (*0-299-16774-7*) Univ. of Wisconsin Pr.

Bufford, Bridget. Minus One: A Twelve-Step Journey. 2003. 274p. pap. text 17.95 (*1-56023-468-7*, Alice Street Editions) Haworth Pr., Inc., The.

Calhoun, Jackie. Off Season. 2000. 220p. pap. 12.95 (*0-9677753-0-2*) Bella Bks., Inc.

Carbado, Devon W., et al, eds. Black Like Us: A Century of Lesbian, Gay & Bisexual African American Fiction. 2002. 575p. pap. 24.95 (*1-57344-108-2*) Cleis Pr.

Chadwick, Cynn. Cat Rising: A Novel. 2002. 244p. 27.95 (*1-56023-407-5*); pap. 17.95 (*1-56023-408-3*) Haworth Pr., Inc., The. (Alice Street Editions).

—Girls with Hammers. 2004. 19.95 (*1-56023-475-X*, Harrington Park Pr.) Haworth Pr., Inc., The.

Christian, M. Speaking Parts: Provocative Lesbian Erotica. 2002. 208p. pap. 13.95 (*1-55583-700-X*) Alyson Pubns.

Christian, Paula. Twilight Girls: Two Unforgettable Classics from the Golden Age of Lesbian Pulp Fiction. 2003. 34p. pap. 15.00 (*0-7582-0313-6*) Kensington Publishing Corp.

Clarke, Caro. The Wolf Ticket: A Novel. 1998. 216p. pap. 12.95 (*1-56341-098-2*); lib. bdg. 24.95 (*1-56341-099-0*) Firebrand Bks.

Conn, Nicole. She Walks in Beauty. 2002. 320p. pap. 14.95 (*1-56280-269-0*) Naiad Pr., Inc.

Cooney, Ellen. The White Palazzo. 2002. 219p. pap. 14.00 (*1-56689-134-5*) Coffee Hse. Pr.

Darling, Julia. Crocodile Soup: A Novel. 2000. 352p. 25.00 (*0-06-019602-5*, Ecco) HarperTrade.

Davis, Kaye. Devil's Leg Crossing. 1997. (Maris Middleton Mysteries Ser.). 240p. pap. 11.95 o.p. (*1-56280-158-9*) Naiad Pr., Inc.

—Possessions: A Maris Middleton Mystery. 1998. (Maris Middleton Mysteries Ser.). 240p. (Orig.). pap. 11.95 (*1-56280-192-9*) Naiad Pr., Inc.

—Shattered Illusions: A Maris Middleton Mystery. 1999. (Maris Middleton Mysteries Ser.: No. 4). 240p. pap. 11.95 (*1-56280-252-6*) Naiad Pr., Inc.

—Until the End: A Maris Middleton Mystery. 1999. (Maris Middleton Mysteries Ser.: No. 3). 224p. pap. 11.95 (*1-56280-222-4*) Naiad Pr., Inc.

De la Pena, Terri. Margins: A Novel. 2000. (Djuna Bks.). 336p. pap. 12.95 (*1-58005-039-5*, Seal Pr.) Avalon Publishing Group.

Dean, Elizabeth. Between Girlfriends. 256p. 2004. pap. 15.00 (*0-7582-0365-9*, Kensington Bks.); 2003. 23.00 (*0-7582-0364-0*) Kensington Publishing Corp.

DeLynn, Jane. Don Juan in the Village: A Novel. 2003. pap. 21.95 (*0-299-19004-8*) Univ. of Wisconsin Pr.

Denison, Lyn. Dream Lover. 2004. 224p. reprint ed. pap. 12.95 (*1-931513-96-1*) Bella Bks., Inc.

—Dream Lover. 1997. 240p. pap. 11.95 o.p. (*1-56280-173-2*) Naiad Pr., Inc.

D'Haene, Elise. Licking Our Wounds. 1997. 208p. 24.00 (*1-877946-81-8*) Permanent Pr., The.

Donoghue, Emma. Stir-Fry. 256p. 1995. pap. 11.00 o.p. (*0-06-092624-4*, Perennial); 1994. 20.00 o.p. (*0-06-017109-X*) HarperTrade.

—Stir-Fry: A Novel. 2001. 240p. pap. 12.95 o.p. (*1-55583-723-9*, Alyson Bks.) Alyson Pubns.

Douglas, Lauren W. The Always Anonymous Beast. 1987. (Caitlin Reece Mysteries Ser.). 224p. pap. 8.95 o.p. (*0-941483-04-5*) Naiad Pr., Inc.

—The Daughters of Artemis. 1991. (Caitlin Reece Mystery Ser.). 240p. (Orig.). pap. 9.95 (*0-941483-95-9*) Naiad Pr., Inc.

—Goblin Market. 1993. (Caitlin Reece Mysteries Ser.: No. 5). 224p. pap. 10.95 (*1-56280-047-7*) Naiad Pr., Inc.

—Ninth Life. 1990. (Caitlin Reece Mysteries Ser.). 256p. pap. 9.95 (*0-941483-50-9*) Naiad Pr., Inc.

—A Rage of Maidens: Sixth Caitlin Reece Mystery. 1994. (Caitlin Reece Mysteries Ser.). 224p. pap. 10.95 (*1-56280-068-X*) Naiad Pr., Inc.

—A Tiger's Heart. 1992. (Caitlin Reece Mysteries Ser.: No. 4). 240p. pap. 9.95 (*1-56280-018-3*) Naiad Pr., Inc.

Dreher, Sarah. Bad Company: A Stoner McTavish Mystery. 1995. 235p. pap. 10.95 (*0-934678-66-9*); trans. 19.95 (*0-934678-67-7*) New Victoria Pubs., Inc.

—A Captive in Time. 1990. (Stoner McTavish Mystery Ser.). 256p. (Orig.). pap. 10.95 (*0-934678-22-7*) New Victoria Pubs., Inc.

—Gray Magic. 1987. (Stoner McTavish Mystery Ser.). 282p. (Orig.). pap. 9.95 (*0-934678-11-1*) New Victoria Pubs., Inc.

—Otherworld. 1993. (Stoner McTavish Mystery Ser.). 256p. (Orig.). pap. 10.95 (*0-934678-44-8*) New Victoria Pubs., Inc.

—Solitaire & Brahms. 1997. 292p. pap. 12.95 (*0-934678-85-5*) New Victoria Pubs., Inc.

—Something Shady. 1986. (Stoner McTavish Mystery Ser.). 272p. pap. 8.95 (*0-934678-07-3*) New Victoria Pubs., Inc.

—Stoner McTavish. 1985. (Stoner McTavish Mystery Ser.). 200p. pap. 9.95 (*0-934678-06-5*) New Victoria Pubs., Inc.

Drury, Joan M. Closed in Silence. 1998. (Tyler Jones Feminist Mystery Ser.: No. 3). 224p. pap. 10.95 (*1-883523-29-X*) Spinsters Ink Bks.

—The Other Side of Silence. 1993. 256p. pap. 9.95 (*0-933216-92-0*) Spinsters Ink Bks.

—Silent Words. 1996. 224p. pap. 10.95 (*1-883523-13-3*) Spinsters Ink Bks.

Flagg, Fannie. Fried Green Tomatoes at the Whistle Stop Cafe. 1998. pap. 11.00 (*0-449-45860-1*); 1997. 432p. pap. 14.95 (*0-449-91135-7*) Ballantine Bks. (Fawcett).

—Fried Green Tomatoes at the Whistle Stop Cafe. 1989. 420p. 7.95 o.p. (*0-07-021257-0*) McGraw-Hill Cos., The.

—Fried Green Tomatoes at the Whistle Stop Cafe. l.t. ed. 1993. 528p. pap. 18.00 (*0-679-74495-9*) Random Hse. Large Print.

—Fried Green Tomatoes at the Whistle Stop Cafe. 1987. 416p. 25.00 o.s.i (*0-394-56152-X*) Random Hse., Inc.

—Fried Green Tomatoes at the Whistle Stop Cafe. 1999. (*0-7621-0253-5*) Reader's Digest Assn., Inc., The.

—Fried Green Tomatoes at the Whistle Stop Cafe. 2000. (Illus.). (J). 13.55 (*0-606-17986-0*); 1997. 16.10 o.p. (*0-606-12298-2*) Turtleback Bks.

—Fried Green Tomatoes at the Whistle Stop Cafe: A Novel. 2002. 416p. 23.00 (*0-375-50841-4*) Random Hse., Inc.

—Fried Green Tomatoes at the Whistlestop Cafe. 2000. 416p. mass mkt. 7.99 (*0-8041-1561-3*, Ballantine Bks.) Ballantine Bks.

Fleming, Anne. Pool Hopping: And Other Stories. 1999. 222p. pap. (*1-896095-18-6*, Polestar Book Pubs.) Raincoast Bk. Distribution.

Forrest, Katherine V. Amateur City. 1984. (Kate Delafield Mystery Ser.: Vol. 1). 224p. pap. 11.95 (*0-930044-55-X*) Naiad Pr., Inc.

—Amateur City: A Kate Delafield Mystery. 2003. (Kate Delafield Mystery Ser.). 216p. pap. 12.95 (*1-55583-718-2*) Alyson Pubns.

—Apparition Alley. (Kate Delafield Mystery Ser.). 256p. 1997. 21.95 o.s.i (*0-425-15966-3*); 1998. reprint ed. mass mkt. 5.99 o.s.i (*0-425-16632-5*) Berkley Publishing Group. (Prime Crime).

—The Beverly Malibu. (Kate Delafield Mystery Ser.). 1989. 16.95 o.p. (*0-941483-47-9*); 1991. 288p. reprint ed. pap. 11.95 (*0-941483-48-7*) Naiad Pr., Inc.

—The Beverly Malibu: A Kate Delafield Mystery. 2003. (Kate Delafield Mystery Ser.). 280p. pap. 12.95 (*1-55583-716-6*, Alyson Bks.) Alyson Pubns.

—Curious Wine: A Novel. 2002. 200p. pap. 12.95 (*1-55583-661-5*) Alyson Pubns.

—Daughters of an Amber Noon: A Novel. 2002. 232p. pap. 13.95 (*1-55583-663-1*) Alyson Pubns.

—Flashpoint. 256p. 1995. pap. 10.95 o.p. (*1-56280-079-5*); 1994. 22.95 (*1-56280-043-4*) Naiad Pr., Inc.

—Liberty Square: A Kate Delafield Mystery. (Kate Delafield Mystery Ser.). 256p. 2000. pap. 13.00 o.s.i (*0-425-17675-4*); 1997. mass mkt. 5.99 o.s.i (*0-425-15899-3*); 1996. 21.95 o.s.i (*0-425-15467-X*) Berkley Publishing Group. (Prime Crime).

—Murder at the Nightwood Bar. 1987. (Kate Delafield Mystery Ser.: Vol. 2). 240p. pap. 11.95 o.p. (*0-930044-92-4*) Naiad Pr., Inc.

—Murder by Tradition. 288p. 1991. text 18.95 o.p. (*0-941483-89-4*); 1993. (Kate Delafield Mystery Ser.: Vol. 4). reprint ed. pap. 11.95 (*1-56280-002-7*) Naiad Pr., Inc.

—Murder by Tradition: A Kate Delafield Mystery. 2003. (Kate Delafield Mystery Ser.). 280p. pap. 12.95 (*1-55583-719-0*, Alyson Bks.) Alyson Pubns.

—Sleeping Bones: A Kate Delafield Mystery. (Kate Delafield Mystery Ser.). 272p. 1999. 21.95 o.s.i (*0-425-17029-2*); 2000. reprint ed. pap. 13.00 (*0-425-17484-0*, Prime Crime) Berkley Publishing Group.

Foster, Nicole, ed. Electric: Best Lesbian Erotic Fiction. 1999. x, 313p. pap. 12.95 (*1-55583-500-7*) Alyson Pubns.

—Electric 2: Best Lesbian Erotic Fiction. 2003. 296p. pap. 13.95 (*1-55583-796-4*) Alyson Pubns.

Fox, Astrid. The Fox Tales. 2002. pap. 13.95 (*1-873741-79-0*) Millivres Bks. GBR. *Dist:* Consortium Bk. Sales & Distribution.

Fritchley, Alma. Chicken Feed. 138p. pap. 11.95 (*0-7043-4692-3*); 1999. 222p. pap. 13.95 (*0-7043-4570-6*) Women's Pr., Ltd., The GBR. *Dist:* Trafalgar Square.

—Chicken Out. 2000. (Letty Campbell Mystery Ser.: No. 3). 164p. pap. 13.95 (*0-7043-4619-2*) Women's Pr., Ltd., The GBR. *Dist:* Trafalgar Square.

—Chicken Run: A Letty Campbell Mystery. 1998. 136p. pap. 13.95 (0-7043-4515-3) Women's Pr., Ltd., The GBR. Dist: Trafalgar Square.
Galgoczi, Erzsebet. Another Love. Rieder, Ines & Newman, Felice, trs. from GER. 1991. 160p. 24.95 o.p. (0-939416-52-2); pap. 8.95 o.p. (0-939416-51-4) Cleis Pr.
Garber, Eric & Gomez, Jewelle, eds. Swords of the Rainbow. 1996. 352p. pap. text 11.95 o.p. (1-55583-266-0) Alyson Pubns.
Grier, Barbara & Cassidy, Christine, eds. The Very Thought of You: Erotic Love Stories. 1999. 275p. pap. 14.95 (1-56280-250-X) Naiad Pr., Inc.
Griffith, Nicola. Bending the Landscape: Horror. 2003. 332p. pap. 15.95 (1-58567-372-2) Overlook Pr., The.
—The Blue Place: A Novel of Suspense. 1999. 320p. pap. 13.00 (0-380-79088-2, Perennial) Harper-Trade.
—The Blue Place: A Novel of Suspense. 1998. 320p. pap. 23.00 (0-380-97446-0, Avon Bks.) Morrow/Avon.
Griffith, Nicola & Pagel, Stephen, eds. Bending the Landscape: Horror. 2001. 384p. 28.95 (1-58567-116-9) Overlook Pr., The.
Henley, Patricia. In the River Sweet: A Novel. 2002. 304p. 24.00 (0-375-42127-0, Pantheon) Knopf Publishing Group.
Herren, Greg, ed. Shadows of the Night: Queer Tales of the Uncanny & Unusual. 2004. 211p. pap. text 16.95 (1-56023-394-X, Harrington Park Pr.) Haworth Pr., Inc., The.
Hucklenbroich, Frankie. A Crystal Diary: A Novel. 1997. 240p. lib. bdg. 26.95 (1-56341-083-4) Firebrand Bks.
Jacovsky, Marilyn. Irregulars. 1999. 160p. pap. 16.00 (1-57962-018-3) Permanent Pr., The.
Johnson, Barbara. Bad Moon Rising: A Colleen Fitzgerald Mystery. 1998. (Colleen Fitzgerald Mysteries Ser.). 224p. pap. 11.95 (1-56280-211-9) Naiad Pr., Inc.
—The Beach Affair. 1995. (Colleen Fitzgerald Mysteries Ser.). 224p. pap. 10.95 (1-56280-090-6) Naiad Pr., Inc.
Kallmaker, Karin. Frosting on the Cake. 2003. 288p. reprint ed. pap. 12.95 (1-931513-40-6) Bella Bks., Inc.
—Frosting on the Cake. 2001. 260p. pap. 11.95 (1-56280-266-6) Naiad Pr., Inc.
—Substitute for Love. 2004. 288p. reprint ed. pap. 12.95 (1-931513-62-7) Bella Bks., Inc.
—Substitute for Love. 2002. 288p. pap. 12.95 (1-56280-265-8) Naiad Pr., Inc.
Kear, Cynthia. Searching for Grace. 1998. 24.95 (0-947993-75-4) Malvern Publishing Co., Ltd. GBR. Dist: British Bk. Co., Inc.
Keesey, Pam, ed. Daughters of Darkness: Lesbian Vampire Stories. 250p. 1993. 24.95 o.p. (0-939416-77-8); 1993. pap. 9.95 o.p. (0-939416-78-6); 2nd ed. 1998. pap. 14.95 (1-57344-076-0) Cleis Pr.
Kieran. Sugar with Spice. 1989. 176p. (Orig.). pap. 8.95 o.p. (0-934411-24-7, Banned Bks.) Edward-William Publishing Co.
Lee, Diana. A Taste for Blood. 2003. 370p. pap. 19.95 (1-56023-461-X, Alice Street Editions) Haworth Pr., Inc., The.
Lemus, Felicia Luna. The Trace Elements of Random Tea Parties. 2003. 256p. 23.00 (0-374-27856-3) Farrar, Straus & Giroux.
Litherland, Donna. The Green Lanai. Davidson, E. Beth, ed. 2002. (Illus.). 191p. (0-9607888-6-7) Barney Pr.
Lordon, Randye. East of Niece. 2001. (Sydney Sloane Mystery Ser.). 288p. 23.95 (0-312-27114-X, Saint Martin's Minotaur) St. Martin's Pr.
Lowell, Jax P. Mothers. 336p. 1996. pap. 13.95 (0-312-14373-7, Saint Martin's Griffin); 1995. 22.95 o.p. (0-312-13126-7) St. Martin's Pr.
MacLean, Judy. Rosemary & Juliet. 2004. 265p. pap. text 17.95 (1-56023-483-0, Alice Street Editions) Haworth Pr., Inc., The.
Maddison, Lauren. Death by Prophecy: A Connor Hawthorne Mystery. 2002. (Connor Hawthorne Mystery Ser.). 408p. pap. 14.95 (1-55583-764-6) Alyson Pubns.
Maiman, Jaye. Baby, It's Cold: A Robin Miller Mystery. 1997. (Robin Miller Mysteries Ser.: Vol. 5). 256p. pap. 10.95 o.p. (1-56280-156-2); 1996. 288p. 19.95 (1-56280-141-4) Naiad Pr., Inc.
—Crazy for Loving. 1992. (Robin Miller Mysteries Ser.: No. 2). 320p. pap. 11.95 (1-56280-025-6) Naiad Pr., Inc.
—Every Time We Say Goodbye. 1999. (Robin Miller Mysteries Ser.: No. 7). 250p. pap. 11.95 (1-56280-248-8) Naiad Pr., Inc.
—I Left My Heart. 1991. (Robin Miller Mysteries Ser.: Vol. 1). 320p. pap. 11.95 o.p. (0-941483-72-X) Naiad Pr., Inc.
—Old Black Magic: A Robin Miller Mystery. 1997. (Robin Miller Mysteries Ser.: Vol. 6). 288p. pap. 11.95 o.p. (1-56280-175-9) Naiad Pr., Inc.
—Someone to Watch. 1995. (Robin Miller Mysteries Ser.: Vol. 4). 288p. pap. 10.95 (1-56280-095-7) Naiad Pr., Inc.
—Under My Skin. 1993. (Robin Miller Mysteries Ser.: No. 3). 336p. pap. 11.95 (1-56280-049-3) Naiad Pr., Inc.
Maney, Mabel. Kiss the Girls & Make Them Spy: An Original Jane Bond Parody. 2001. 288p. pap. 14.00 (0-380-80310-0, HarperEntertainment) Morrow/Avon.
Manning, Rosemary. The Chinese Garden. 2000. 192p. pap. 12.95 (1-55861-216-5); 208p. 29.00 (1-55861-215-7) Feminist Pr. at The City Univ. of New York.
Manthorne, Jackie. The Deadly Reunion. 1995. 252p. pap. 10.95 (0-921881-32-0) Ragweed Pr. CAN. Dist: General Distribution Services, Inc.
Marcy, Jean. Cemetery Murders: A Meg Darcy Mystery. 1997. 200p. pap. 10.95 (0-934678-83-9) New Victoria Pubs., Inc.
—Dead & Blonde: A Meg Darcy Mystery. 1998. (Meg Darcy Mysteries Ser.: No. 2). 227p. pap. 10.95 (0-934678-98-7) New Victoria Pubs., Inc.
—Mommy Deadest: A Meg Darcy Mystery. 2000. (Meg Darcy Mysteries Ser.). 224p. pap. 11.95 (1-892281-12-0) New Victoria Pubs., Inc.
Marks, Tinker. Theoretically Dead. 2001. 200p. pap. 11.95 (1-892281-16-3) New Victoria Pubs., Inc.
Martin, Marianne K. Legacy of Love. rev. ed. 2003. 220p. pap. 12.95 (1-931513-15-5) Bella Bks., Inc.
—Legacy of Love. 1997. 240p. pap. 11.95 (1-56280-184-8) Naiad Pr., Inc.
Maso, Carole. The American Woman in the Chinese Hat. 1994. 200p. 19.95 (1-56478-045-7) Dalkey Archive Pr.
—The American Woman in the Chinese Hat. 1995. 224p. pap. 13.00 o.s.i (0-452-27507-5, Plume) Dutton/Plume.
McClune, Lindsay, ed. On Our Backs: The Best Erotic Fiction. 2001. xx, 248p. pap. 14.95 (1-55583-652-6, Alyson Bks.) Alyson Pubns.
McConaughy, V. Till There Was You. 2003. 220p. pap. 13.95 (0-9742005-0-6) Heart Wings Publishing.
McConnell, Vicki P. The Burnton Widows: A Nyla Wade Mystery. 1984. (Nyla Wade Mystery Ser.). (Illus.). 240p. pap. 7.95 o.p. (0-930044-52-5) Naiad Pr., Inc.
—Double Daughter. 1988. 216p. pap. 8.95 o.p. (0-941483-26-6) Naiad Pr., Inc.
—Mrs. Porter's Letter. 1982. (Nyla Wade Ser.). 224p. pap. 7.95 o.p. (0-930044-29-0) Naiad Pr., Inc.
McDermid, Val. Booked for Murder. 2nd ed. 2000. (Lindsay Gordon Mystery Ser.). 260p. pap. 12.00 (1-883523-37-0) Spinsters Ink Bks.
—Common Murder. l.t. ed. 2001. 286p. 32.50 (0-7531-6538-4) Thorpe, F. A. Pubs. GBR. Dist: Ulverscroft Large Print Bks., Ltd., Ulverscroft Large Print Canada, Ltd.
—Conferences Are Murder: A Lindsay Gordon Mystery. 1999. (Lindsay Gordon Mystery Ser.: Vol. 4). (Illus.). 264p. pap. 12.00 (1-883523-30-3) Spinsters Ink Bks.
—Deadline for Murder: A Lindsay Gordon Mystery. 2nd ed. 1997. (Kate Brannigan Mystery Ser.). 264p. (Orig.). pap. 10.95 (1-883523-17-6) Spinsters Ink Bks.
—Final Edition. l.t. ed. 2001. 288p. 32.50 (0-7531-6540-6) Thorpe, F. A. Pubs. GBR. Dist: Ulverscroft Large Print Bks., Ltd., Ulverscroft Large Print Canada, Ltd.
—Report for Murder. l.t. ed. 2001. (Magna Large Print Ser.). 400p. 32.50 (0-7505-1699-2) Magna Large Print Bks. GBR. Dist: Ulverscroft Large Print Bks., Ltd., Ulverscroft Large Print Canada, Ltd.
—Report for Murder. 224p. 25.00 (0-7278-5554-9) Severn Hse. Pubs., Ltd.
—Report for Murder. 2nd ed. 1998. 264p. pap. 10.95 (1-883523-24-9) Spinsters Ink Bks.
—Report for Murder. 1989. 208p. 16.95 o.p. (0-312-03888-7, Saint Martin's Minotaur) St. Martin's Pr.
McKay, Claudia. The Kali Connection. 1994. 190p. (Orig.). pap. 9.95 (0-934678-54-5) New Victoria Pubs., Inc.
McNab, Claire. Body Guard. 1994. (Detective Inspector Carol Ashton Mysteries Ser.: Vol. 6). 224p. pap. 11.95 (1-56280-073-6) Naiad Pr., Inc.
—Chain Letter: A Carol Ashton Mystery. 1997. (Detective Inspector Carol Ashton Mysteries Ser.: Vol. 9). 224p. (Orig.). pap. 11.95 (1-56280-181-3) Naiad Pr., Inc.
—Cop Out. 1991. (Detective Inspector Carol Ashton Mysteries Ser.: Vol. 4). 224p. (Orig.). pap. 10.95 (0-941483-84-3) Naiad Pr., Inc.
—Dead Certain. 1992. (Detective Inspector Carol Ashton Mysteries Ser.: No. 5). 224p. pap. 11.95 (1-56280-027-2) Naiad Pr., Inc.
—Death Club: A Detective Inspector Carol Ashton Mystery. 2001. 215p. pap. 11.95 (1-56280-267-4) Naiad Pr., Inc.
—Death down Under. 1990. (Detective Inspector Carol Ashton Mysteries Ser.: Vol. 3). 240p. pap. 11.95 (0-941483-39-8) Naiad Pr., Inc.
—Double Bluff. 1995. (Detective Inspector Carol Ashton Mysteries Ser.: Vol. 7). 192p. pap. 12.95 (1-56280-096-5) Naiad Pr., Inc.
—Fatal Reunion. 1989. (Detective Inspector Carol Ashton Mysteries Ser.: Vol. 2). 224p. pap. 11.95 (0-941483-40-1) Naiad Pr., Inc.
—Inner Circle: A Carol Ashton Mystery. 1996. (Detective Inspector Carol Ashton Mysteries Ser.: Vol. 8). 256p. pap. 11.95 (1-56280-135-X) Naiad Pr., Inc.
—Lessons in Murder. 1988. (Detective Inspector Carol Ashton Mysteries Ser.: Vol. 1). 216p. pap. 11.95 (0-941483-14-2) Naiad Pr., Inc.
—Murder Undercover: A Denise Cleever Thriller. 1999. (Denise Cleever Thrillers Ser.). 240p. pap. 12.95 (1-56280-259-3) Naiad Pr., Inc.
—Out of Sight: A Denise Cleever Thriller. 2002. (Denise Cleever Thrillers Ser.: No. 3). 240p. pap. 12.95 (1-56280-268-2) Naiad Pr., Inc.
—Past Due: A Detective Inspector Carol Ashton Mystery. 1998. (Detective Inspector Carol Ashton Mysteries Ser.: No. 10). 224p. pap. 11.95 (1-56280-217-8) Naiad Pr., Inc.
—Set Up. 1999. (Detective Inspector Carol Ashton Mysteries Ser.: Vol. 11). 202p. pap. 11.95 (1-56280-255-0) Naiad Pr., Inc.
—Under Suspicion. 2000. (Detective Inspector Carol Ashton Mysteries Ser.). 204p. pap. 11.95 (1-56280-261-5) Naiad Pr., Inc.
Meyerding, Jane. Everywhere House. 1994. 256p. (Orig.). pap. 9.95 (0-934678-42-1) New Victoria Pubs., Inc.
Michaels, Joanne. Nun in the Closet. 1994. 200p. (Orig.). pap. 9.95 (0-934678-43-X) New Victoria Pubs., Inc.
Mildon, Marsha. Stalking the Goddess Ship. 1999. 210p. pap. 10.95 (1-892281-02-3) New Victoria Pubs., Inc.
Miller, Carlene. Reporter on the Run: A Lexy Hyatt Mystery. 2001. (Lexy Hyatt Mysteries Ser.). 200p. pap. 11.95 (1-892281-14-7) New Victoria Pubs., Inc.
Miller, Martha. Dispatch to Death: A Mystery. 2003. 220p. 12.95 (1-892281-20-1) New Victoria Pubs., Inc.
Moore, Madeline. As You Desire. 1993. 180p. (Orig.). pap. 9.95 (0-933216-95-5) Spinsters Ink Bks.
Morris, Sandra A. By the Sea Shore: A Jess Shore Mystery. 2000. 219p. pap. 12.00 (1-883061-32-6) Rising Tide Pr.
Muller, Marcia. Cyanide Wells. 2003. (Illus.). 304p. 24.95 (0-89296-781-1) Mysterious Pr.
—Cyanide Wells. l.t. ed. 2003. 432p. 30.95 (0-7862-5837-3) Thorndike Pr.
—Cyanide Wells. 2004. mass mkt. (0-446-61421-1) Warner Bks., Inc.
Newman, Leslea. The Best Short Stories of Leslea Newman. 2003. 304p. pap. 14.95 (1-55583-775-1) Alyson Pubns.
—Heather Has Two Mommies: Tenth Anniversary Edition. (Illus.). 32p. (J). (ps-3). 2nd anniv. ed. 2004. 18.95 o.p. (1-55583-570-8, Alyson Wonderland); 10th anniv. ed. 2000. pap. 10.95 (1-55583-543-0, Alyson Bks.) Alyson Pubns.
—Out of the Closet & Nothing to Wear. 1997. 232p. (Orig.). pap. 10.95 o.p. (1-55583-415-9) Alyson Pubns.
Pincus, Elizabeth. The Hangdog Hustle. 1995. (Neil Fury Ser.). 205p. (Orig.). pap. 9.95 (1-883523-05-2) Spinsters Ink Bks.
—The Solitary Twist. 1993. (Neil Fury Ser.). 225p. (Orig.). pap. 9.95 (0-933216-93-9) Spinsters Ink Bks.
—The Two Bit Tango. 1992. (Neil Fury Ser.). (Illus.). 193p. (Orig.). pap. 9.95 (0-933216-88-2) Spinsters Ink Bks.
Redmann, J. M. Death by the Riverside. 1990. 256p. (Orig.). pap. 9.95 o.p. (0-934678-27-8) New Victoria Pubs., Inc.
—Death of Jocasta. 1992. 288p. (Orig.). pap. 10.95 o.p. (0-934678-39-1) New Victoria Pubs., Inc.
—The Intersection of Law & Desire. 1997. mass mkt. 5.99 (0-380-72819-2, Avon Bks.) Morrow/Avon.
—The Intersection of Law & Desire. 1995. 336p. 22.00 o.p. (0-393-03793-2) Norton, W. W. & Co., Inc.
—Lost Daughters: A Micky Knight Mystery. 1999. (Mickey Knight Mystery Ser.). 320p. text 24.95 o.p. (0-393-04028-3) Norton, W. W. & Co., Inc.
Reed, Valerie, ed. A Woman's Touch: New Lesbian Love Stories. 2003. 272p. pap. 13.95 (1-55583-794-8) Alyson Pubns.
Richardson, Tracey. Last Rites: A Stevie Houston Mystery. 1997. (Stevie Houston Mysteries Ser.). 176p. pap. 11.95 (1-56280-164-3) Naiad Pr., Inc.
Rivers, Diana. Clouds of War. 2002. (Hadra Archives Ser.: Bk. 595). 220p. pap. 12.95 (1-931513-12-0) Bella Bks., Inc.
Rizzo, Cindy, et al, eds. All the Ways Home: Parenting & Children in the Lesbian & Gay Communities - A Collection of Short Fiction. 1995. 200p. 19.95 (0-934678-68-5); pap. 10.95 (0-934678-65-0) New Victoria Pubs., Inc.
Robson, Ruthann. The Struggle for Happiness. E-Book 13.95 (0-312-27395-9); 2001. 240p. pap. 13.95 (0-312-27329-0, Saint Martin's Griffin); 2000. 228p. 22.95 (0-312-25219-6) St. Martin's Pr.
Rowe, Michael, ed. Queer Fear: Gay Horror Fiction. 2000. 256p. pap. 16.95 (1-55152-084-2) Arsenal Pulp Pr., Ltd. CAN. Dist: Consortium Bk. Sales & Distribution.
—Queer Fear II: Gay Horror Fiction. 2002. (Illus.). 304p. pap. 17.95 (1-55152-122-9) Arsenal Pulp Pr., Ltd. CAN. Dist: Consortium Bk. Sales & Distribution.
Ruff, Shawn, ed. Go the Way Your Blood Beats: An Anthology of Gay & Lesbian Literary Writings by African Americans. 1996. 480p. pap. 16.95 o.p. (0-8050-4437-X, Owl Bks.) Holt, Henry & Co.
Ruff, Shawn S. Go the Way Your Blood Beats. 1996. 480p. 30.00 o.p. (0-8050-4736-0) Holt, Henry & Co.
Saum, Karen. I Never Read Thoreau. 1996. 200p. (Orig.). pap. 10.95 (0-934678-76-6) New Victoria Pubs., Inc.
Schiano, Rita. Sweet Bitter Love. unabr. ed. 1996. 214p. pap. 10.99 (1-883061-15-6) Rising Tide Pr.
Schmidt, Carol. Cabin Fever. 1995. (Laney Samms Mysteries Ser.). 224p. pap. 10.95 (1-56280-098-1) Naiad Pr., Inc.
—Silverlake Heat. 1993. 224p. pap. 9.95 o.p. (1-56280-031-0) Naiad Pr., Inc.
—Sweet Cherry Wine. 1994. (Laney Samms Mysteries Ser.). 272p. pap. 9.95 (1-56280-063-9) Naiad Pr., Inc.
Schmidt, Heidi Jon. The Bride of Catastrophe. 2003. 400p. 24.00 (0-312-28177-3) Picador.
Schulman, Sarah. Rat Bohemia. 240p. 1996. pap. 10.95 o.p. (0-452-27182-7, Plume); 1995. 19.95 o.p. (0-525-93790-0, Dutton) Dutton/Plume.
Scoppettone, Sandra. Everything You Have Is Mine. 1992. (Lauren Laurano Mystery Ser.). 320p. mass mkt. 6.99 o.s.i (0-345-37682-X) Ballantine Bks.
—Everything You Have Is Mine. 1991. 261p. 19.95 o.p. (0-316-77646-7) Little Brown & Co.
—Gonna Take a Homicidal Journey: A Lauren Laurano Mystery. 1999. (Lauren Laurano Mystery Ser.). 288p. mass mkt. 6.99 (0-345-43118-9) Ballantine Bks.
—Gonna Take a Homicidal Journey: A Lauren Laurano Mystery. 1998. 240p. (gr. 8). 22.95 o.p. (0-316-77665-3) Little Brown & Co.
—I'll Be Leaving You Always: A Lauren Laurano Mystery. 1994. 288p. mass mkt. 6.50 (0-345-38269-2) Ballantine Bks.
—I'll Be Leaving You Always: A Lauren Laurano Mystery. 1993. 251p. 19.95 o.p. (0-316-77647-5) Little Brown & Co.
—Let's Face the Music & Die: A Lauren Laurano Mystery. 1997. (Lauren Laurano Mystery Ser.). 320p. mass mkt. 6.50 (0-345-41225-7) Ballantine Bks.
—Let's Face the Music & Die: A Lauren Laurano Mystery. 1996. 249p. 21.95 o.p. (0-316-77664-5) Little Brown & Co.
—My Sweet Untraceable You. 1995. 320p. mass mkt. 6.50 o.s.i (0-345-39162-4) Ballantine Bks.
—My Sweet Untraceable You. 1994. 275p. 19.95 o.p. (0-316-77648-3) Little Brown & Co.
Silva, Linda K. Tropical Storm. 1996. 245p. pap. 11.99 (1-883061-14-8) Rising Tide Pr.
Silvera, Makeda. The Heart Does Not Bend. 2003. 272p. pap. 12.95 (0-679-31187-4) Knopf, Alfred A. Inc.
Sims, Elizabeth. Damn Straight. 2003. (Lillian Byrd Crime Story Ser.). 280p. pap. 13.95 (1-55583-786-7) Alyson Pubns.
Smith, Mitchell. Daydreams. 1987. 464p. 17.95 o.p. (0-07-059082-6) McGraw-Hill Cos., The.
—Daydreams. 1988. 448p. mass mkt. 5.99 o.s.i (0-451-40089-5, Onyx) NAL.
Starhawk. Walking to Mercury. 496p. 1997. 23.95 o.s.i (0-553-10233-8); 1998. reprint ed. pap. 23.00 (0-553-37839-2) Bantam Bks.
Stelboum, Judith P. Past Perfect. 2003. 270p. pap. 19.95 (1-56023-201-3); 2000. 257p. 49.95 (1-56023-200-5, Harrington Park Pr.) Haworth Pr., Inc., The.
Stevens, Tracey. Chalice of the Goddess. Snowden, Susan, ed. 2003. 313p. (YA). per. 19.99 (0-9719628-4-7) Amazing Dreams Publishing.
Stewart, Jean. Emerald City Blues. 1996. 228p. pap. 11.99 (1-883061-09-1) Rising Tide Pr.
Stinson, Susan. Fat Girl Dances with Rocks. 1994. 180p. pap. 10.95 (1-883523-02-8) Spinsters Ink Bks.
Sumner, Penny. Crosswords: The 2nd Victoria Cross Mystery. 1994. 256p. pap. 9.95 (1-56280-064-7) Naiad Pr., Inc.
—The End of April. 1992. (Victoria Cross Mystery Ser.). 256p. pap. 8.95 o.p. (1-56280-007-8) Naiad Pr., Inc.
Surkis, Alisa & Nolan, Monica. The Big Book of Lesbian Horse Stories. 2002. 288p. pap. 14.00 (0-7582-0254-7) Kensington Publishing Corp.

Tan, Cecilia, ed. A Taste of Midnight: Vampire Erotica. 2000. (Erotic Vampire Ser.: Vol. 4). 224p. pap. 14.95 (*1-885865-23-6*) Circlet Pr., Inc.
Tan, Cecilia, ed. & intro. Blood Kiss: Vampire Erotica. 1994. 138p. (Orig.). pap. 9.95 (*1-885865-00-7*) Circlet Pr., Inc.
Taormino, Tristan, ed. Best Lesbian Erotica, 2003. 2003. 250p. pap. 14.95 (*1-57344-161-9*) Cleis Pr.
Taormino, Tristan & Gomez, Jewelle, eds. Best Lesbian Erotica 1997. 1997. (Best Lesbian Erotica Ser.: Vol. 2). 200p. pap. 14.95 o.p. (*1-57344-065-5*) Cleis Pr.
Taylor, Valerie. The Girls in 3-B. 2003. (Femmes Fatales Ser.). 208p. pap. 13.95 (*1-55861-456-7*); lib. bdg. 14.95 (*1-55861-462-1*) Feminist Pr. at The City Univ. of New York.
Tea, Michelle. Valencia. 2000. 202p. pap. 13.00 (*1-58005-035-2*, Seal Pr.) Avalon Publishing Group.
Tell, Dorothy. The Hallelujah Murders. 1991. (Poppy Dillworth Mystery Ser.). 176p. pap. 8.95 (*0-941483-88-6*) Naiad Pr., Inc.
—Murder at Red Rook Ranch. 1990. 224p. pap. 8.95 (*0-941483-80-0*) Naiad Pr., Inc.
—Wilderness Trek. 1990. 160p. pap. 8.95 o.p. (*0-941483-60-6*) Naiad Pr., Inc.
Trevelyan, Julie K. & Brassart, Scott, eds. The Ghost of Carmen Miranda: And Other Spooky Gay & Lesbian Tales. 1998. 300p. pap. 11.95 o.p. (*1-55583-488-4*) Alyson Pubns.
Tulchinsky, Karen X., ed. Hot & Bothered: Short Short Fiction on Lesbian Desire. 1998. 224p. pap. 14.95 (*1-55152-051-6*) Arsenal Pulp Pr., Ltd. CAN. *Dist:* LPC Group.
—Hot & Bothered 2: Short Short Fiction on Lesbian Desire. 1999. (Illus.). 249p. pap. 14.95 (*1-55152-068-0*) Arsenal Pulp Pr., Ltd. CAN. *Dist:* LPC Group.
—Hot & Bothered 3: Short Short Fiction on Lesbian Desire. 2001. (Illus.). 230p. pap. 15.95 (*1-55152-102-4*) Arsenal Pulp Pr., Ltd. CAN. *Dist:* Consortium Bk. Sales & Distribution.
—Hot & Bothered 4: Short Short Fiction on Lesbian Desire. 2003. 240p. pap. 15.95 (*1-55152-145-8*) Arsenal Pulp Pr., Ltd. CAN. *Dist:* Consortium Bk. Sales & Distribution.
Van Dyke, Annette. Hooded Murder: A Jessie Batelle Mystery. 1996. 208p. pap. 10.95 o.p. (*1-56280-134-1*) Naiad Pr., Inc.
Wadsworth, Ann. Light, Coming Back. 2001. 320p. 24.95 (*1-55583-633-X*) Alyson Pubns.
—Light, Coming Back: A Novel. 2002. 344p. pap. 13.95 (*1-55583-767-0*) Alyson Pubns.
Warren, Patricia N. Billy's Boy: Sequel to The Front Runner & Harlan's Race. 1997. (Illus.). 324p. 24.95 (*0-9641099-4-8*) Wildcat Pr.
Watts, Julia. Finding H. F. 2004. 165p. (YA). (gr. 7 up). pap. 12.95 (*1-55583-622-4*) Alyson Pubns.
Webb, Cynthia. No Daughter of the South. 1997. 200p. (Orig.). pap. 10.95 (*0-934678-82-0*) New Victoria Pubs., Inc.
Wells, Jess, ed. Lip Service: Alluring New Lesbian Erotica. 1999. viii, 272p. pap. 12.95 (*1-55583-503-1*) Alyson Pubns.
—Love Shook My Heart 2: Lesbian Love Stories. 2001. 290p. pap. 14.95 (*1-55583-617-8*) Alyson Pubns.
West, Gabrielle. Time of Grace. 2002. 272p. pap. 13.95 (*0-86327-863-9*) Wolfhound Pr. IRL. *Dist:* Interlink Publishing Group, Inc.
Wilson, Barbara. Salt Water & Other Stories. 1999. 249p. pap. 12.95 o.p. (*1-55583-486-8*) Alyson Pubns.
Wings, Mary. Divine Victim. 256p. 1994. pap. 10.95 o.p. (*0-452-27210-6*, Plume); 1993. 20.00 o.p. (*0-525-93626-2*, Dutton) Dutton/Plume.
—She Came by the Book. (Mistery Ser.). 272p. 1996. 21.95 o.p. (*0-425-15147-6*); 1997. reprint ed. mass mkt. 5.99 o.s.i (*0-425-15697-4*) Berkley Publishing Group. (Prime Crime).
—She Came in a Flash. 1990. 24p. pap. 10.00 o.p. (*0-452-26384-0*, Plume) Dutton/Plume.
—She Came in a Flash. 1989. 208p. 17.95 o.p. (*0-453-00648-5*) NAL.
—She Came in Drag. 1999. (Emma Victor Mysteries Ser.). 352p. mass mkt. 6.50 o.s.i (*0-425-16935-9*) Berkley Publishing Group.
—She Came to the Castro. (Emma Victor Mysteries Ser.). 272p. 1998. mass mkt. 5.99 o.s.i (*0-425-16222-2*); 1997. 21.95 o.s.i (*0-425-15629-X*) Berkley Publishing Group. (Prime Crime).
—She Came Too Late. 1987. (WomanSleuth Mystery Ser.). 208p. reprint ed. 20.95 o.p. (*0-89594-244-5*); pap. 7.95 o.p. (*0-89594-243-7*) Crossing Pr., Inc., The.
—She Came Too Late: An Emma Victor Mystery. 2000. (Emma Victor Mysteries Ser.: No. 1). 263p. reprint ed. pap. 10.95 o.p. (*1-55583-547-3*, Alyson Bks.) Alyson Pubns.
Winsloe, Christa. The Child Manuela: The Novel of Maedchen in Uniform. (Homosexuality Ser.). reprint ed. 1989. pap. 22.95 (*0-88143-104-4*); 1975. 28.95 (*0-405-07377-1*) Ayer Co. Pubs., Inc.
—The Child Manuela: The Novel of Maedchen in Uniform. 1994. o.s.i (*1-85381-745-7*) Random Hse., Inc.
Winterson, Jeanette. Oranges Are Not the Only Fruit. 1997. 192p. 12.00 (*0-8021-3516-1*) Grove/Atlantic, Inc.
—Oranges Are Not the Only Fruit. Fisketjon, Gary, ed. 1995. (Fiction Ser.). 90p. reprint ed. pap. 12.00 o.p. (*0-87113-163-3*, Grove Pr.) Grove/Atlantic, Inc.
Wolverton, Terry & Drake, Robert, eds. Circa 2000: Lesbian Fiction at the Millennium. 2000. 352p. pap. 14.95 o.p. (*1-55583-518-X*, Alyson Bks.) Alyson Pubns.
—Hers 3: Brilliant New Fiction by Lesbian Writers. 1999. xiv, 270p. pap. 15.00 (*0-571-19962-3*) Faber & Faber, Inc.
York, Rachel. Chasing Lightning: The Amorous Adventures of Scarlett Faye. 2003. 384p. pap. 15.00 (*0-7582-0368-3*) Kensington Publishing Corp.
—Chasing Lightning: The Amorous Adventures of Scarlett Faye. 2001. 465p. pap. 16.00 o.p. (*0-7388-5176-0*); text 25.00 o.p. (*0-7388-5175-2*) Xlibris Corp.
Young, Laura Dehart. Forever & the Night. 2001. 224p. pap. 11.95 (*1-931513-00-7*) Bella Bks., Inc.
Zahava, Irene, ed. Speaking for Ourselves: Short Stories by Jewish Lesbians. 1990. 150p. pap. 8.95 o.p. (*0-89594-428-6*); lib. bdg. 23.95 o.p. (*0-89594-429-4*) Crossing Pr., Inc., The.
Zaremba, Eve. Beyond Hope. 1990. 184p. pap. 11.95 (*0-921299-02-8*) Second Story Pr. CAN. *Dist:* SCB Distributors.
—The Butterfly Effect: A Helen Keremos Detective Novel. 1994. 332p. pap. 9.95 (*0-929005-56-2*) Second Story Pr. CAN. *Dist:* SCB Distributors.
—White Noise: A Helen Keremos Mystery Novel. 1997. 248p. pap. 9.95 (*0-929005-97-X*) Second Story Pr. CAN. *Dist:* SCB Distributors.
Zschokke, Magdalena. Salt Rock Mysteries. 2000. 208p. pap. 11.95 (*1-892281-07-4*) New Victoria Pubs., Inc.

# M

## MAN-WOMAN RELATIONSHIPS—FICTION

Abbey, Edward. Black Sun: A Novel. lib. bdg. 19.95 (*0-8488-0900-9*) Amereon, Ltd.
—Black Sun: A Novel. 1991. reprint ed. lib. bdg. 21.95 (*1-56849-082-8*) Buccaneer Bks., Inc.
—Black Sun: A Novel. 2003. 176p. pap. 15.00 (*1-55566-286-2*) Johnson Bks.
—Black Sun: A Novel. reprint ed. 1990. 168p. lib. bdg. 29.00 o.p. (*0-8095-4064-9*); 1988. 160p. (C). lib. bdg. 19.95 o.p. (*0-8095-4028-2*) Millefleurs.
—Black Sun: A Novel. 1982. 160p. pap. 5.99 (*0-380-58503-0*, Avon Bks.) Morrow/Avon.
Ackerman, Karl. The Patron Saint of Unmarried Women. 1995. pap. 9.95 o.p. (*0-312-13142-9*, Saint Martin's Griffin); 1994. 304p. 20.95 o.p. (*0-312-11037-5*) St. Martin's Pr.
Adams, Alice. Rich Rewards. 1981. (Contemporary American Fiction Ser.). 205p. pap. 6.95 o.p. (*0-14-005918-0*, Penguin Bks.) Viking Penguin.
Adams, Glenda. Longleg. 1992. 339p. pap. 9.95 (*0-943433-09-6*) Cane Hill Pr.
Adams, Henry. Esther: A Novel. 1997. (Literary Classics). 310p. pap. 11.00 (*1-57392-132-7*) Prometheus Bks., Pubs.
—Esther: A Novel. 1989. (Works of Henry Adams). reprint ed. lib. bdg. 79.00 (*0-7812-1439-4*) Reprint Services Corp.
—Esther: A Novel. 1976. reprint ed. 36.00 o.p. (*0-403-05725-6*) Scholarly Pr., Inc.
—Esther: A Novel. Spiller, Robert E., ed. 1976. reprint ed. lib. bdg. 50.00 (*0-8201-1187-2*) Scholars' Facsimiles & Reprints.
—Esther: A Novel. MacFarlane, Lisa, ed. & intro. by. 1999. (Classics Ser.). 256p. pap. 9.95 (*0-14-044754-7*, Penguin Classics) Viking Penguin.
Adams, Pepper. The Bachelor Cure. l.t. ed. 1995. 200p. per. 20.95 o.p. (*0-7838-1488-7*, Macmillan Reference USA) Gale Group.
Adler, Elizabeth A. Peach. l.t. ed. 1993. 24.95 o.p. (*1-56895-036-5*, Wheeler Publishing, Inc.) Gale Group.
Agee, Jonis. South of Resurrection. 1998. 368p. pap. 12.95 (*0-14-024172-8*) Penguin Group (USA) Inc.
—South of Resurrection. 1997. 360p. 24.95 o.p. (*0-670-85809-9*) Viking Penguin.
Ahern, Cecelia. PS, I Love You. 2004. pap. 14.00 (*1-4013-9885-5*) Hyperion Pr.
Aidoo, Ama Ata. Changes: A Love Story. 1993. (Women Writing Africa Ser.). 208p. 35.00 (*1-55861-064-2*); pap. 15.95 (*1-55861-065-0*) Feminist Pr. at The City Univ. of New York.
Alcorn, Alfred. The Long Run of Myles Mayberry. 1999. (Illus.). 240p. pap. 13.00 o.p. (*1-58195-001-2*, Zoland Bks., Inc.) Steerforth Pr.
Alcott, Louisa May. Behind a Mask: The Unknown Thrillers of Louisa May Alcott. Stern, Madeleine B., ed. & afterword by by. Date not set. lib. bdg. 22.95 (*0-88411-096-6*, Aeonian Pr.) Amereon, Ltd.
—Behind a Mask: The Unknown Thrillers of Louisa May Alcott. Stern, Madeleine B., ed. & afterword by by. 1997. 320p. reprint ed. pap. 13.95 (*0-688-15132-9*, Quill) HarperTrade.
—Behind a Mask: The Unknown Thrillers of Louisa May Alcott, Vol. 1. Stern, Madeleine B., ed. & afterword by by. 1995. 23.00 (*0-688-00338-9*, Morrow, William & Co.) Morrow/Avon.
—A Double Life: Newly Discovered Thrillers of Louisa May Alcott. Stern, Madeleine B. et al, eds. 1988. 17.95 o.s.i (*0-316-03101-1*) Little Brown & Co.
—Freaks of Genius: Unknown Thrillers of Louisa May Alcott. Shealy, Daniel et al, eds. 1991. (Contributions to the Study of Popular Culture Ser.: No. 28). 256p. 67.95 (*0-313-27627-7*, SKE, Greenwood Pr.) Greenwood Publishing Group, Inc.
—From Jo March's Attic: Stories of Intrigue & Suspense. Stern, Madeleine B. & Shealy, Daniel, eds. 1993. (Illus.). 160p. text 24.95 (*1-55553-177-6*) Northeastern Univ. Pr.
—A Long Fatal Love Chase. l.t. ed. 1996. 368p. mass mkt. 6.99 (*0-440-22301-6*) Dell Publishing.
—A Long Fatal Love Chase. l.t. ed. 1997. (Thorndike/G. K. Hall Paperback Bestsellers Ser.). 356p. pap. 25.95 (*0-7862-0623-3*) Thorndike Pr.
—The Lost Stories of Louisa May Alcott. Shealy, Daniel, ed. 2000. 166p. pap. 12.00 (*0-8065-1654-2*, Citadel Pr.) Kensington Publishing Corp.
—Louisa May Alcott Unmasked: Collected Thrillers. Stern, Madeleine B., ed. & intro. by. 1995. (Illus.). 780p. text 55.00 (*1-55553-225-X*); 754p. pap. text 24.95 (*1-55553-226-8*) Northeastern Univ. Pr.
—Modern Magic. Stern, Madeleine B., ed. & intro. by. Date not set. lib. bdg. 23.95 (*0-8488-1881-4*) Amereon, Ltd.
—A Modern Mephistopheles. 2000. 252p. pap. 9.95 (*0-594-04555-X*); E-Book 3.95 (*0-594-04558-4*) 1873 Pr.
—A Modern Mephistopheles. 1995. 240p. reprint ed. pap. 15.00 (*0-553-37795-7*, Bantam Classics) Bantam Bks.
—A Modern Mephistopheles. 1987. 437p. (C). pap. text 17.95 o.s.i (*0-275-92780-6*, B2780, Praeger Pubs.) Greenwood Publishing Group, Inc.
—A Modern Mephistopheles. 1989. (Works of Louisa May Alcott). reprint ed. lib. bdg. 79.00 (*0-7812-1636-2*) Reprint Services Corp.
—A Modern Mephistopheles: And, Taming a Tartar. Stern, Madeleine B., ed. & intro. by. 1987. 437p. 72.95 o.s.i (*0-275-92754-7*, C2754, Praeger Pubs.) Greenwood Publishing Group, Inc.
—Plots & Counterplots: More Unknown Thrillers of Louisa May Alcott. Stern, Madeleine B., ed. & intro. by. 1976. (Illus.). 320p. 9.95 o.p. (*0-688-03046-7*, Morrow, William & Co.) Morrow/Avon.
Allegretto, Michael. Shadow House. 1994. 304p. 19.95 o.p. (*0-7867-0070-X*, Carroll & Graf Pubs.) Avalon Publishing Group.
Allen, Charlotte Vale. Illusions. 1987. 320p. 16.95 o.p. (*0-689-11891-0*, Scribner) Simon & Schuster.
Almond, Steve. My Life in Heavy Metal. 2002. 224p. 23.00 (*0-8021-1630-2*, Grove Pr.) Grove/Atlantic, Inc.
—My Life in Heavy Metal: Stories. 2003. 224p. pap. 12.00 (*0-8021-4013-0*) Grove/Atlantic, Inc.
Alpert, Cathryn. Rocket City. 1996. (Vintage Contemporaries Ser.). 368p. pap. 13.00 (*0-679-77016-X*, Vintage) Knopf Publishing Group.
—Rocket City. 1995. 347p. 22.95 o.p. (*1-878448-62-5*) MacMurray & Beck, Inc.
Amis, Kingsley. Difficulties with Girls. 1991. 3.99 o.p. (*0-517-06319-0*) Random Hse. Value Publishing.
—Difficulties with Girls. 1989. 304p. 18.95 o.p. (*0-671-67582-6*) Summit Bks.
—Jake's Thing. 1980. 288p. pap. 7.95 o.p. (*0-14-005096-5*, Penguin Bks.); 1979. 11.95 o.p. (*0-670-40471-3*) Viking Penguin.
—Stanley & the Women. 1988. 256p. reprint ed. pap. 6.95 o.p. (*0-06-097145-2*, PL-7145, Perennial) HarperTrade.
—Stanley & the Women. 1985. 256p. 14.70 o.p. (*0-671-60317-5*) Summit Bks.
Amis, Martin. The Rachel Papers. 1992. 240p. pap. 12.00 (*0-679-73458-9*, Vintage) Knopf Publishing Group.
—Success. 1989. 224p. 7.95 o.s.i (*0-517-57206-0*, Harmony) Crown Publishing Group.
—Success. unabr. ed. 1999. audio 54.95 (*0-7531-0289-7*, 970908) ISIS Audio Bks. GBR. *Dist:* Ulverscroft Large Print Bks., Ltd.
—Success. 1991. 224p. pap. 12.00 (*0-679-73448-1*, Vintage) Knopf Publishing Group.
Andersdatter, Karla. The Doorway. 3rd ed. 2004. per. (*0-935430-25-3*) In Between Bks.
—The Doorway. 1990. 275p. 17.95 (*0-911051-50-3*) Plain View Pr.
Andrews, V. C. All That Glitters. l.t. ed. 2000. 26.95 (*1-56895-236-8*, Wheeler Publishing, Inc.) Gale Group.
—All That Glitters. 1995. (Landry Ser.). 352p. mass mkt. 7.99 (*0-671-87319-9*, Pocket) Simon & Schuster.
—All That Glitters. Marrow, Linda, ed. 1995. 352p. 23.00 o.p. (*0-671-87574-4*, Atria) Simon & Schuster.
—Tarnished Gold. l.t. ed. 2000. (Large Print Bks.). 26.95 o.p. (*1-56895-338-0*, Wheeler Publishing, Inc.) Gale Group.
Anthony, Piers & Lackey, Mercedes. If I Pay Thee Not in Gold. 1993. 416p. (YA). 20.00 (*0-671-72175-5*) Baen Bks.
Anthony, Ray. All Woman. 2003. 240p. pap. 10.95 (*1-902934-06-7*) X Pr., The GBR. *Dist:* National Bk. Network.
Antoni, Brian. Paradise Overdose. 1997. 256p. reprint ed. pap. 12.00 (*0-8021-3487-4*, Grove Pr.) Grove/Atlantic, Inc.
—Paradise Overdose. 1994. 320p. 21.00 (*0-671-88426-3*, Simon & Schuster) Simon & Schuster.
Arensberg, Ann. Group Sex. 1986. 15.95 o.s.i (*0-394-55310-1*) Knopf, Alfred A. Inc.
—Group Sex: A Romantic Comedy. 1987. mass mkt. 5.95 o.s.i (*0-671-64362-2*, Pocket) Simon & Schuster.
Argers, Helen. The Gilded Lily. 1998. 320p. 23.95 (*0-312-18571-5*) St. Martin's Pr.
—Gilded Lily. 1998. 320p. (*0-312-13976-4*) St. Martin's Pr.
—Noblesse Oblige. l.t. ed. 1995. 424p. reprint ed. lib. bdg. 22.95 (*0-7838-1230-2*, Macmillan Reference USA) Gale Group.
—Noblesse Oblige. 1994. 320p. 21.95 o.p. (*0-312-11324-2*) St. Martin's Pr.
Arkham, Candice. Forbidden Yearnings. l.t. ed. 1994. 19.95 o.p. (*0-7927-1901-8*); pap. 17.95 o.p. (*0-7927-1900-X*) BBC Audiobooks America.
Arnoldi, Katie. Chemical Pink. 2002. 272p. reprint ed. pap. 13.95 (*0-312-87891-5*, Forge Bks.) Doherty, Tom Assocs., LLC.
Asher, Jane. Trying to Get Out. 2002. 296p. (*0-00-225902-8*) HarperCollins Pubs.
Ashour, Linda P. Sweet Remedy. 1999. 335p. reprint ed. text 23.00 (*0-7881-6624-7*) DIANE Publishing Co.
—Sweet Remedy. 1996. 336p. 23.00 (*0-684-81833-7*, Simon & Schuster) Simon & Schuster.
Atwood, Margaret. The Edible Woman. 1995. 320p. pap. 10.95 o.s.i (*0-553-37792-2*); 1991. 304p. mass mkt. 5.99 o.s.i (*0-553-29699-X*); 1984. mass mkt. 3.95 o.s.i (*0-7704-1811-2*); 1984. 304p. mass mkt. 7.99 o.s.i (*0-7704-2301-9*) Bantam Bks.
—The Edible Woman. 1998. 336p. pap. 12.95 (*0-385-49106-9*) Doubleday Publishing.
—The Edible Woman. 1989. 288p. mass mkt. 4.95 (*0-446-31498-6*) Warner Bks., Inc.
—The Handmaid's Tale. 1996. pap. 11.00 o.s.i (*0-449-91153-5*); 1986. 408p. mass mkt. 6.99 o.s.i (*0-449-21260-2*); 1986. mass mkt. 5.95 o.p. (*0-449-44829-0*) Ballantine Bks. (Fawcett).
—The Handmaid's Tale. 1986. 304p. mass mkt. 8.99 o.s.i (*0-7704-2263-2*) Bantam Bks.
—The Handmaid's Tale. l.t. ed. 1987. 484p. 12.95 o.p. (*0-8161-4171-1*); 18.95 o.p. (*0-8161-4172-X*) Gale Group. (Macmillan Reference USA).
—The Handmaid's Tale, 001. 1986. 240p. 16.95 o.p. (*0-395-40425-8*) Houghton Mifflin Co.
—The Handmaid's Tale. 1998. 320p. pap. 13.95 (*0-385-49081-X*, Knopf Bks. for Young Readers) Random Hse. Children's Bks.
—The Handmaid's Tale. 1988. 4.99 o.p. (*0-517-67174-3*) Random Hse. Value Publishing.
—The Handmaid's Tale. 1998. (Illus.). 19.00 (*0-606-18124-5*); 1985. 12.09 o.p. (*0-606-03797-7*) Turtleback Bks.
—Life Before Man. 1987. 384p. mass mkt. 5.99 o.s.i (*0-449-21377-3*, Fawcett) Ballantine Bks.
—Life Before Man. 1995. 368p. pap. 10.95 o.s.i (*0-553-37782-5*); 1984. 304p. mass mkt. 5.95 o.s.i (*0-7704-2029-X*) Bantam Bks.
—Life Before Man. 1998. 384p. pap. 13.00 (*0-385-49110-7*) Doubleday Publishing.
—Life Before Man. 1980. 11.95 o.p. (*0-671-25115-5*, Simon & Schuster) Simon & Schuster.
—Life Before Man. 1984. 304p. mass mkt. 3.95 o.s.i (*0-446-31331-9*) Warner Bks., Inc.
August, Elizabeth. A Wedding for Emily Smytheshire. 1993. (Harlequin Romance Ser.). per. (*0-373-08953-8*, 5-08953-7, Silhouette) Harlequin Enterprises, Ltd.
Austen, Jane. Persuasion. Date not set. 122p. 17.95 (*0-8488-2542-X*) Amereon, Ltd.
—Persuasion. 1984. (Bantam Classics Ser.). 240p. mass mkt. 4.95 (*0-553-21137-4*, Bantam Classics) Bantam Bks.
—Persuasion. Bree, Linda, ed. 1998. (Literary Texts Ser.). (Illus.). 306p. pap. (*1-55111-131-4*) Broadview Pr.

—Persuasion. 1986. 240p. reprint ed. lib. bdg. 18.95 (*0-89966-538-1*) Buccaneer Bks., Inc.

—Persuasion. 1999. 256p. pap. 3.99 (*0-8125-6588-6*, Tor Classics) Doherty, Tom Assocs., LLC.

—Persuasion. 1997. 224p. reprint ed. pap. text 2.00 (*0-486-29555-9*) Dover Pubns., Inc.

—Persuasion. E-Book 2.49 (*1-929120-78-8*) Electric Umbrella Publishing.

—Persuasion. Clay, N. L., ed. 1986. (Guide Novel Ser.). pap. text 4.50 o.p. (*0-435-16040-0*) Heinemann.

—Persuasion. 1998. (Cloth Bound Pocket Ser.). 350p. 7.95 (*3-8290-0901-1*, 520664) Konemann.

—Persuasion. l.t. ed. 1998. (Large Print Heritage Ser.). 371p. lib. bdg. 34.95 (*1-58118-027-6*, 22023) LRS.

—Persuasion. 1992. (Everyman's Library). 304p. 15.00 (*0-679-40986-6*) McKay, David Co., Inc.

—Persuasion. 1996. pap., tchr. ed. (*0-451-52661-9*, Signet Classics); 1996. 288p. mass mkt. 4.95 (*0-451-52638-4*); 1964. 256p. mass mkt. 4.95 o.p. (*0-451-52289-3*, Signet Classics) NAL.

—Persuasion. l.t. ed. reprint ed. 1996. 405p. lib. bdg. 26.00 (*0-939495-04-X*); 1998. 243p. lib. bdg. 25.00 (*1-58287-055-1*) North Bks.

—Persuasion. Spacks, Patricia M., ed. 1994. (Critical Editions Ser.). 316p. (C). pap. text 7.00 (*0-393-96018-8*) Norton, W. W. & Co., Inc.

—Persuasion. Davie, John, ed. (Oxford World's Classics Ser.). 1998. 304p. pap. 4.95 (*0-19-283361-8*); 1990. 302p. pap. 4.50 o.p. (*0-19-282759-6*) Oxford Univ. Pr., Inc.

—Persuasion. Davie, John N., ed. 1981. (Oxford World's Classics Ser.). pap. 2.95 o.p. (*0-19-281546-6*) Oxford Univ. Pr., Inc.

—Persuasion. 1999. (Jane Austen Works). 200p. E-Book 3.99 incl. audio compact disk (*1-57646-148-3*) Quiet Vision Publishing.

—Persuasion. annuals 1995. (Modern Library Ser.). 192p. 14.95 o.s.i (*0-679-60191-0*, Modern Library) Random House Adult Trade Publishing Group.

—Persuasion. 1988. (Zodiac Press Ser.). 248p. o.p. (*0-7011-1235-2*) Random Hse. of Canada, Ltd. CAN. *Dist:* Random Hse., Inc.

—Persuasion. 1995. 15.00 o.s.i (*0-676-50518-X*); 1989. o.s.i (*1-85381-099-1*) Random Hse., Inc.

—Persuasion. l.t. ed. 1990. (Charnwood Large Print Ser.). 389p. 29.99 (*0-7089-8534-3*, Charnwood) Thorpe, F. A. Pubs. GBR. *Dist:* Ulverscroft Large Print Bks., Ltd., Ulverscroft Large Print Canada, Ltd.

—Persuasion. 1999. 9.04 (*0-606-18650-6*); 1984. 11.00 (*0-606-02200-7*) Turtleback Bks.

—Persuasion. Beer, Gillian, ed. & intro. by. 1999. (Penguin Classics Ser.). 272p. (C). 5.95 (*0-14-043467-4*) Viking Penguin.

—Persuasion. Harding, D. W., ed. 1967. (Penguin Classics Ser.). 400p. (C). pap. 5.95 o.s.i (*0-14-043005-9*) Viking Penguin.

—Persuasion. abr. ed. 1996. 4p. pap. 23.95 o.s.i incl. audio (*0-14-086058-4*, 693419, Penguin AudioBooks) Viking Penguin.

—Persuasion. 1998. (Classics Library). 192p. pap. 3.95 (*1-85326-056-8*, 0568WW) Wordsworth Editions, Ltd. GBR. *Dist:* Casemate Pubs. & Bk. Distributors, LLC.

—Persuasion: Penguin Reader Level 2. 1998. pap. 7.00 (*0-14-081527-9*) Longman Publishing Group.

Baer, Judy, et al. Reunited. 1998. (HeartQuest Anthologies Ser.). 400p. pap. 9.99 o.p. (*0-8423-0868-7*) Tyndale Hse. Pubs.

Baker, Brenda J. The Maleness of God. 1999. 282p. pap. (*1-55050-158-5*) Coteau Bks.

Baker-Kline, Christina. Desire Lines: A Novel. 1999. 320p. 24.00 (*0-688-15107-8*, Morrow, William & Co.) Morrow/Avon.

Baker, Nicholson. Vox: A Novel. 1993. 176p. pap. 11.00 (*0-679-74211-5*) Random Hse., Inc.

Baldwin, Faith. Arizona Star. 1976. reprint ed. lib. bdg. 24.95 (*0-88411-601-8*) Amereon, Ltd.

—The Office Wife. 1976. reprint ed. lib. bdg. 23.95 (*0-88411-603-4*) Amereon, Ltd.

Bank, Melissa. The Girls' Guide to Hunting & Fishing. unabr. ed. 1999. (Chivers Sound Library American Collections). audio 54.95 (*0-7927-2331-7*, CSL 220, Chivers Sound Library) BBC Audiobooks America.

—The Girls' Guide to Hunting & Fishing. unabr. ed. 2000. audio compact disk 64.95 (*0-7540-5328-8*, CCD 019) Chivers Audio Bks. GBR. *Dist:* BBC Audiobooks America.

—The Girls' Guide to Hunting & Fishing. l.t. ed. (Bestsellers Ser.). 2000. 325p. 27.95 (*0-7862-2169-0*); 1999. (Illus.). 325p. 30.95 (*0-7862-2168-2*); 1999. (*0-7540-1360-X*); 1999. (*0-7540-2269-2*) Thorndike Pr.

—The Girls' Guide to Hunting & Fishing. 2000. 19.00 (*0-606-19483-5*) Turtleback Bks.

—The Girls' Guide to Hunting & Fishing. 2000. (Illus.). 288p. (YA). 12.95 (*0-14-029324-8*); 1999. 288p. 23.95 (*0-670-88300-X*); 1999. 2p. audio 24.95 o.s.i (*0-14-180028-3*, Penguin AudioBooks) Viking Penguin.

Banks, Iain M. A Song of Stone. 1999. 288p. per. 12.00 (*0-684-85536-4*); 1998. 23.00 (*0-684-85725-1*); 1998. 288p. 23.00 (*0-684-85353-1*) Simon & Schuster. (Simon & Schuster).

—Song of Stone. 1997. 280p. pap. o.s.i (*0-316-64172-3*) Little Brown & Co.

—Walking on Glass, 001. 1986. 239p. 15.95 o.p. (*0-395-40048-1*) Houghton Mifflin Co.

Barlow, Linda. Leaves of Fortune. 1990. 560p. reprint ed. mass mkt. 4.95 o.s.i (*0-440-20471-2*) Dell Publishing.

Barrowcliffe, Mark. Infidelity for First Time Fathers. 2002. 337p. 24.95 (*0-312-29146-9*) St. Martin's Pr.

Barry, Maxine. Dark Desire. 1998. 388p. text 19.95 (*1-85487-547-7*); 400p. mass mkt. 3.99 (*1-85487-566-3*) Scarlet Bks. GBR. *Dist:* London Bridge.

Barthelme, Frederick. Painted Desert: A Novel. 1995. 256p. 22.95 o.s.i (*0-670-86469-2*, Viking) Viking Penguin.

—Two Against One. 1988. 270p. 17.95 o.p. (*1-55584-214-3*) Grove/Atlantic, Inc.

Bass, Rick. Platte River. 1994. 145p. 19.95 o.p. (*0-395-68080-8*) Houghton Mifflin Co.

Bates, H. E. Feast of July. 1995. pap. 15.00 (*0-679-76501-8*, Vintage) Knopf Publishing Group.

—Love for Lydia. l.t. ed. 1993. 24.95 o.p. (*0-7927-1783-X*); pap. 22.95 o.p. (*0-7927-1782-1*) BBC Audiobooks America.

Bauer, Tricia. Hollywood & Hardwood: A Novel. 1999. 272p. 22.95 (*1-882593-26-X*) Bridge Works Publishing Co., Inc.

Bausch, Richard. Wives & Lovers. 2004. 272p. pap. 12.95 (*0-06-057183-7*, Perennial) HarperTrade.

Bean, Henry. False Match. 1982. 13.50 o.p. (*0-671-44251-1*, Simon & Schuster) Simon & Schuster.

Beattie, Ann. Chilly Scenes of Winter. 1991. (Vintage Contemporaries Ser.). 288p. pap. 13.00 (*0-679-73234-9*, Vintage) Knopf Publishing Group.

—Chilly Scenes of Winter. 1985. mass mkt. 3.95 o.s.i (*0-446-31343-2*) Warner Bks., Inc.

—Distortions. 1991. (Vintage Contemporaries Ser.). 288p. pap. 13.00 (*0-679-73235-7*, Vintage) Knopf Publishing Group.

—Falling in Place. 1981. pap. 2.50 o.p. (*0-445-04650-3*, Fawcett) Ballantine Bks.

—Falling in Place. (Vintage Contemporaries Ser.). 1991. 342p. pap. 19.00 (*0-679-73192-X*); 1980. 10.95 o.p. (*0-394-50323-6*) Random Hse., Inc.

Beauford, Fred. The Womanizer. unabr. ed. 2000. 250p. pap. 21.99 (*1-929188-01-3*) Morton Bks.

Beaven, Derek. Acts of Mutiny. 288p. 2001. pap. 13.00 o.s.i (*0-312-24121-6*); 2000. 24.00 (*0-312-24100-3*) Picador.

Beckett, Samuel. Dream of Fair to Middling Women. Date not set. (*0-7145-4212-1*); 1996. 252p. pap. 15.95 (*0-7145-4213-X*) Riverrun Pr., Inc.

—Endgame. 1993. 264p. 21.95 (*1-55970-217-6*) Arcade Publishing, Inc.

—Endgame. Beckett, Samuel, tr. from FRE. 1958. pap. 3.95 o.p. (*0-394-17208-6*, E96) Grove/Atlantic, Inc.

—Endgame: Production Notebook. rev. ed. 1993. (Theatrical Notebooks of Samuel Beckett Ser.: Vol. 2). Tr. of Fin de Partie. (ENG & FRE.). 256p. 75.00 (*0-8021-1089-4*, Grove Pr.) Grove/Atlantic, Inc.

Benabib, Kim. Obscene Bodies: A Novel. 1996. 256p. 22.00 o.p. (*0-06-017437-4*) HarperCollins Pubs.

Benard, Cheryl. Turning on the Girls. 2001. 312p. 23.00 o.p. (*0-374-28178-5*) Farrar, Straus & Giroux.

—Turning on the Girls. 2002. 320p. reprint ed. pap. 14.00 (*0-7434-4291-1*, Washington Square Pr.) Simon & Schuster.

Berger, John. G. 1992. (Vintage International Ser.). 336p. pap. 15.00 (*0-679-73654-9*, Vintage) Knopf Publishing Group.

—G. A Novel. 1991. pap. 11.00 o.p. (*0-394-73654-0*, Pantheon) Knopf Publishing Group.

—To the Wedding: A Novel. 1995. 192p. 22.00 o.s.i (*0-679-43981-1*, Pantheon) Knopf Publishing Group.

Berger, Thomas. Reinhart's Women. 1981. 13.95 o.s.i (*0-385-28857-3*, Delacorte Pr.) Dell Publishing.

—Reinhart's Women, Vol. 1. 1989. pap. 8.95 o.s.i (*0-316-11601-7*) Little Brown & Co.

—Sneaky People. 1990. pap. 10.95 o.s.i (*0-316-09222-3*) Little Brown & Co.

Bergren, Lisa T. Refuge. 1994. 336p. pap. 8.99 o.p. (*0-88070-621-X*, Multnomah Bks.) Multnomah Pubs., Inc.

Bergren, Lisa Tawn. Refuge. 1995. 336p. pap. 9.99 o.p. (*0-88070-875-1*, Palisades) Multnomah Pubs., Inc.

—Refuge. 2001. (Full Circle Ser.). 320p. pap. 10.99 (*1-57856-468-9*) WaterBrook Pr.

Bernheim, Emmanuele. Sa Femme: Or the Other Woman. 1995. 128p. pap. 9.95 o.p. (*0-14-024178-7*) Penguin Group (USA) Inc.

Berry, Venise. So Good. 1996. 288p. 21.95 o.p. (*0-525-93885-0*, Dutton) Dutton/Plume.

Bickmore, Barbara. Beyond the Promise. l.t. ed. 1997. 25.95 (*1-57490-129-X*, Beeler Large Print Bks.) Beeler, Thomas T. Publisher.

—Beyond the Promise. 1998. 480p. mass mkt. 6.99 o.s.i (*1-57566-329-5*); 1997. 384p. 23.00 o.s.i (*1-57566-220-5*) Kensington Publishing Corp.

—Deep in the Heart. l.t. ed. 1996. lib. bdg. 24.95 (*1-57490-067-6*, Beeler Large Print Bks.) Beeler, Thomas T. Publisher.

—Deep in the Heart. 1997. 448p. mass mkt. 5.99 o.s.i (*1-57566-225-6*); 1996. 358p. 22.95 o.s.i (*1-57566-039-3*) Kensington Publishing Corp.

Billington, Rachel. Occasion of Sin. 1983. 320p. 14.50 o.p. (*0-671-45938-4*) Summit Bks.

—Theo & Matilda: A Novel. 1991. 352p. 21.95 o.p. (*0-06-016483-2*) HarperTrade.

Bingham, Charlotte. Belgravia. l.t. ed. 2000. (Magna Large Print Ser.). 416p. (*0-7505-1515-5*) Magna Large Print Bks. GBR. *Dist:* Ulverscroft Large Print Canada, Ltd.

—Belgravia. 2000. pap. 6.95 (*0-553-40427-X*) Transworld Publishers Ltd. GBR. *Dist:* Trafalgar Square.

Binstock, R. C. The Soldier. 1996. 288p. 24.00 o.p. (*1-56947-059-6*) Soho Pr., Inc.

—Tree of Heaven. 1996. 220p. pap. 12.00 (*1-56947-069-3*); 1995. 212p. 22.00 (*1-56947-038-3*) Soho Pr., Inc.

Bishop, Michael. Ancient of Days. 1995. 354p. pap. 13.95 (*0-312-89027-3*); 1986. 416p. reprint ed. mass mkt. 3.95 (*0-8125-3197-3*) Doherty, Tom Assocs., LLC. (Tor Bks.).

—Ancient of Days. 1985. 310p. 16.95 o.p. (*0-87795-724-X*, Morrow, William & Co.) Morrow/Avon.

Blackstock, Terri. When Dreams Cross. 1997. (Second Chances Ser.: Vol. 2). 240p. pap. 10.99 (*0-310-20709-6*) Zondervan.

Blackwell, Lawana. Like a River Glorious. 1995. (Victorian Serenade: No. 1). 334p. pap. 8.99 (*0-8423-7954-1*) Tyndale Hse. Pubs.

Blair, Cynthia. Once More with Feeling. 1996. mass mkt. 5.99 o.s.i (*0-345-38638-8*) Ballantine Bks.

Blake, Cindy. Second Wives. 2000. 432p. mass mkt. 6.99 (*0-312-97121-4*, St. Martin's Paperbacks); 2000. mass mkt. (*0-312-97568-6*); 1999. 336p. 24.95 o.p. (*0-312-19328-9*) St. Martin's Pr.

Blake, Jennifer. Shameless. 1997. mass mkt. 5.99 o.s.i (*0-449-15002-X*, Fawcett) Ballantine Bks.

Blake, Jennifer, et al. Purrfect Romance. l.t. ed. 1996. (Large Print Bks.). pap. 23.95 (*1-56895-284-8*, Wheeler Publishing, Inc.) Gale Group.

Blanchot, Maurice. Awaiting Oblivion. Gregg, John, tr. 1997. (French Modernist Library Ser.). 87p. text 40.00 (*0-8032-1257-7*) Univ. of Nebraska Pr.

—Awaiting Oblivion. 1997. (French Modernist Library Ser.). 87p. pap. 15.00 (*0-8032-6157-8*, Bison Bks.) Univ. of Nebraska Pr.

Bogner, Norman. The Madonna Complex. 2000. 352p. 25.95 o.p. (*0-312-87519-3*, Forge Bks.) Doherty, Tom Assocs., LLC.

Bonner, Cindy. Looking after Lily. 1999. 336p. tchr. ed. 18.95 (*1-56512-045-0*) Algonquin Bks. of Chapel Hill.

—Looking after Lily. l.t. ed. 1994. 22.95 o.p. (*0-7927-2076-8*); pap. 21.95 o.p. (*0-7927-2075-X*) BBC Audiobooks America.

—Looking after Lily. 1995. 320p. mass mkt. 4.99 o.s.i (*0-451-40587-0*, Signet Bks.) NAL.

—The Passion of Dellie O'Barr. 1996. 362p. tchr. ed. 18.95 (*1-56512-103-1*, 72103) Algonquin Bks. of Chapel Hill.

—Right from Wrong: A Novel. 1999. 336p. tchr. ed. 19.95 (*1-56512-104-X*, 72104) Algonquin Bks. of Chapel Hill.

—Right from Wrong: A Novel. l.t. ed. 1999. (Basic Ser.). 472p. 28.95 (*0-7862-1990-4*) Thorndike Pr.

Booth, Pat. Marry Me. l.t. ed. 1996. (G. K. Hall Core Ser.). 528p. lib. bdg. 25.95 (*0-7838-1865-3*, Macmillan Reference USA) Gale Group.

—Marry Me. 1997. 384p. mass mkt. 5.99 o.s.i (*1-57566-191-8*) Kensington Publishing Corp.

—Marry Me: A Novel. 1996. 343p. 22.95 o.p. (*0-316-10256-3*) Little Brown & Co.

—Pat Booth: Three Complete Novels. 1994. 928p. 6.99 o.s.i (*0-517-10065-7*) Random Hse. Value Publishing.

Borthwick, J. S. Bodies of Water. 1991. 287p. mass mkt. 5.99 (*0-312-92603-0*, St. Martin's Paperbacks); 1990. 17.95 o.p. (*0-312-04269-8*, Saint Martin's Minotaur) St. Martin's Pr.

—The Bridled Groom: A Mystery. 1994. 304p. 20.95 o.p. (*0-312-10435-9*, Saint Martin's Minotaur) St. Martin's Pr.

—The Case of the Hook-Billed Kites. 1982. 256p. 12.95 o.p. (*0-312-12335-3*) St. Martin's Pr.

—The Case of the Hook-Billed Kites. 1983. 256p. pap. 3.95 o.p. (*0-14-006785-X*, Penguin Bks.) Viking Penguin.

—Dude on Arrival: A Christmas Mystery. 1992. 306p. mass mkt. 6.50 (*0-312-92955-2*, St. Martin's Paperbacks); 1991. 320p. 19.95 o.p. (*0-312-06341-5*, Saint Martin's Minotaur) St. Martin's Pr.

Bosworth, Sheila. Almost Innocent. 1996. (Voices of the South Ser.). 268p. (C). pap. 16.95 (*0-8071-2066-9*) Louisiana State Univ. Pr.

—Almost Innocent. 1984. 320p. 16.45 o.p. (*0-671-50365-0*, Simon & Schuster) Simon & Schuster.

—Almost Innocent. 1986. (Contemporary American Fiction Ser.). 272p. pap. 6.95 o.p. (*0-14-008443-6*, Penguin Bks.) Viking Penguin.

Bower, B. M. Chip, of the Flying U. 1999. 256p. 19.00 (*0-7540-8066-8*, Gunsmoke) BBC Audiobooks America.

—Chip, of the Flying U. 1975. lib. bdg. 16.95 o.p. (*0-89966-012-6*) Buccaneer Bks., Inc.

—Chip, of the Flying U. l.t. ed. 2003. lib. bdg. 26.95 (*1-58547-343-X*, Western) Ctr. Point Large Print.

—Chip, of the Flying U. 1995. (Illus.). 264p. pap. 8.95 (*0-8032-6121-7*, Bison Bks.) Univ. of Nebraska Pr.

—Lonesome Land. 1975. lib. bdg. 16.95 o.p. (*0-89966-022-3*) Buccaneer Bks., Inc.

—Lonesome Land. 1997. (Illus.). 326p. pap. 13.95 (*0-8032-6134-9*, Bison Bks.) Univ. of Nebraska Pr.

Bowman, Elizabeth A. White Chocolate. 1999. 375p. mass mkt. 6.99 (*0-8125-7181-9*); 1998. 352p. 23.95 o.p. (*0-312-86306-3*) Doherty, Tom Assocs., LLC. (Forge Bks.).

Bowman, Jeanne. Doomed to Hate. l.t. ed. 1994. 18.95 o.p. (*0-7927-1987-5*); pap. 17.95 o.p. (*0-7927-1986-7*) BBC Audiobooks America.

Braddon, Mary Elizabeth. Aurora Floyd. Nemesvari, Richard & Surridge, Lisa, eds. 1998. (Literary Texts Ser.). (Illus.). 635p. pap. (*1-55111-123-3*) Broadview Pr.

—Aurora Floyd. 1999. (Oxford World's Classics Ser.). 498p. pap. 12.95 (*0-19-283727-3*) Oxford Univ. Pr., Inc.

—Aurora Floyd. Edwards, P. D., ed. 1996. (Oxford World's Classics Ser.). 500p. pap. 12.95 o.p. (*0-19-282402-3*) Oxford Univ. Pr., Inc.

—Aurora Floyd. 1987. o.s.i (*0-86068-510-1*) Random Hse., Inc.

Bradford, Barbara Taylor. Everything to Gain. l.t. ed. 1994. 26.95 o.p. (*1-56895-152-3*, Wheeler Publishing, Inc.) Gale Group.

—Everything to Gain. 1994. 352p. 24.00 o.p. (*0-06-017723-3*) HarperCollins Pubs.

—Love in Another Town. unabr. ed. 1996. audio 30.00 (*0-7366-3257-3*, 3914) Books on Tape, Inc.

—Love in Another Town. 1995. 224p. 225.00 o.p. (*0-06-017684-9*) HarperCollins Pubs.

—Love in Another Town. abr. ed. 1995. audio 17.00 o.s.i (*0-694-51598-1*, 393244, HarperAudio) HarperTrade.

—Love in Another Town. 1996. 240p. mass mkt. 5.99 (*0-06-109209-6*, HarperTorch) Morrow/Avon.

—Love in Another Town. 182p. pap. 3.98 o.p. (*0-7651-0528-4*) Smithmark Pubs., Inc.

—Love in Another Town. l.t. ed. 1996. (Paperback Bestsellers Ser.). 208p. pap. 24.95 (*0-7838-1560-3*); 26.95 (*0-7838-1559-X*) Thorndike Pr.

—Power of a Woman. 1997. 352p. 25.00 o.p. (*0-06-018268-7*) HarperCollins Pubs.

—Power of a Woman. 1998. 432p. mass mkt. 7.50 (*0-06-109440-4*, HarperTorch) Morrow/Avon.

—Power of a Woman. l.t. ed. (Paperback Bestsellers Ser.). 464p. 1999. pap. 28.95 (*0-7862-1224-1*); 1998. 31.95 (*0-7862-1223-3*) Thorndike Pr.

Braine, John. Waiting for Sheila. 1977. 9.95 o.p. (*0-416-00571-3*, NO. 0183) Routledge.

Brandewyne, Rebecca. The Jacaranda Tree. 1996. (Illus.). 384p. reprint ed. 24.00 (*0-7278-4857-7*) Severn Hse. Pubs., Ltd.

Brenna, Duff. The Altar of the Body: A Novel. 2002. 336p. pap. 13.00 (*0-312-26914-5*) Picador.

Briscoe, Connie. Sisters & Lovers. 416p. 1996. pap. 13.95 (*0-345-40969-8*); 1995. mass mkt. 6.99 (*0-8041-1334-3*, Ivy Bks.) Ballantine Bks.

—Sisters & Lovers. 1994. 352p. 22.00 o.p. (*0-06-017116-2*) HarperTrade.

—Sisters & Lovers. l.t. ed. 1997. (Niagara Large Print Ser.). 437p. 29.50 o.p. (*0-7089-5805-2*, Ulverscroft) Thorpe, F. A. Pubs. GBR. *Dist:* Ulverscroft Large Print Bks., Ltd., Ulverscroft Large Print Canada, Ltd.

Bronte, Charlotte. Jane Eyre. (World Digital Library). 2002. E-Book 3.95 (*0-594-08278-1*); 2000. 252p. E-Book 9.95 (*0-594-06663-8*) 1873 Pr.

—Jane Eyre. 8.97 (*0-673-58353-8*); 1997. pap. text o.p. (*0-17-556627-5*) Addison-Wesley Longman, Inc.

—Jane Eyre. (Modern Library Ser.). E-Book 4.95 (*1-931208-17-4*) Adobe Systems, Inc.

—Jane Eyre. 1963. mass mkt. 4.95 (*0-8049-0017-5*, CL-17) Airmont Publishing Co., Inc.

—Jane Eyre. Date not set. lib. bdg. 28.95 (*0-8488-1269-7*) Amereon, Ltd.

—Jane Eyre. l.t. ed. 1997. 741p. pap. 24.95 (*1-55701-207-5*) BNI Pubns., Inc.

—Jane Eyre. 1983. (Bantam Classics Ser.). 528p. reprint ed. mass mkt. 4.95 (*0-553-21140-4*) Bantam Dell Publishing Group.

—Jane Eyre. 1996. (Case Studies in Contemporary Criticism). 696p. pap. text 8.50 (*0-312-09545-7*) Bedford/Saint Martin's.

—Jane Eyre. Kendrick, Walter, ed. 1980. (Macdonald Classics Ser.). 508p. (C). 19.95 (*0-8464-1070-2*) Beekman Pubs., Inc.
—Jane Eyre. 2000. 6.98 (*0-681-99485-1*, 50885537) Borders Pr.
—Jane Eyre. Nemesvari, Richard, ed. 1999. (Literary Texts Ser.). 680p. pap. (*1-55111-180-2*) Broadview Pr.
—Jane Eyre. 1984. 599p. reprint ed. lib. bdg. 27.95 (*0-89966-493-8*) Buccaneer Bks., Inc.
—Jane Eyre. 1997. (Cambridge Literature Ser.). audio compact disk 22.95 o.p. (*0-521-59796-X*) Cambridge Univ. Pr.
—Jane Eyre. Cockcroft, Susan, ed. 1996. (Cambridge Literature Ser.). (Illus.). 528p. pap. text 11.95 o.p. (*0-521-56865-X*) Cambridge Univ. Pr.
—Jane Eyre, 3. reprint ed. lib. bdg. 294.00 (*0-7426-2188-X*); 2001. pap. text 84.00 (*0-7426-7188-7*) Classic Bks.
—Jane Eyre. 1998. 480p. pap. 14.95 incl. disk (*1-55701-233-4*); 1997. 741p. pap. 24.95 (*1-58855-021-4*) Cyber Classics, Inc.
—Jane Eyre. 1994. 488p. pap. text 3.99 (*0-8125-2337-7*, Tor Classics) Doherty, Tom Assocs., LLC.
—Jane Eyre. 1997. (New York Public Library Collector's Edition Ser.). 576p. 18.50 o.s.i (*0-385-48717-7*) Doubleday Publishing.
—Jane Eyre. 2002. (Thrift Editions Ser.). (Illus.). 448p. pap. 3.50 (*0-486-42449-9*) Dover Pubns., Inc.
—Jane Eyre. 1972. 2.95 o.p. (*0-460-01287-8*, Dutton) Dutton/Plume.
—Jane Eyre. E-Book 2.49 (*1-58627-105-9*) Electric Umbrella Publishing.
—Jane Eyre. Luaces, Juan G., tr. 7th ed. 1991. (Nueva Austral Ser.: No. 59). (SPA., Illus.). 488p. 19.95 (*84-239-1859-9*) Elliot's Bks.
—Jane Eyre. 2003. (Barnes & Noble Classics Ser.). 608p. pap. 4.95 (*1-59308-007-7*) Fine Communications.
—Jane Eyre. 2002. (Classics for Young Readers Ser.). (SPA.). (*84-392-0935-5*, EV30620) Gaviota Ediciones ESP. *Dist:* Lectorum Pubns., Inc.
—Jane Eyre. 6th ed. 1998. (Clasicos Universales Ser.: Vol. 5). (SPA., Illus.). 375p. pap. (*84-08-01725-X*) GeoPlaneta, Editorial, S. A.
—Jane Eyre. (HRW Library). 2000. 581p. 17.90 (*0-03-095764-8*); 1997. text 8.25 (*0-03-051488-6*) Holt, Rinehart & Winston.
—Jane Eyre. l.t. ed. 661p. pap. 46.42 (*0-7583-1185-0*); 525p. pap. 38.72 (*0-7583-1184-2*); 912p. pap. 64.90 (*0-7583-1186-9*); 1172p. pap. 77.48 (*0-7583-1187-7*); 1515p. pap. 100.58 (*0-7583-1188-5*); 1868p. pap. 116.43 (*0-7583-1189-3*); 2704p. pap. 155.70 (*0-7583-1191-5*); 2171p. pap. 132.40 (*0-7583-1190-7*); 2171p. lib. bdg. 152.77 (*0-7583-1182-6*); 1515p. lib. bdg. 118.98 (*0-7583-1180-X*); 525p. lib. bdg. 44.72 (*0-7583-1176-1*); 661p. lib. bdg. 52.42 (*0-7583-1177-X*); 1172p. lib. bdg. 89.48 (*0-7583-1179-6*); 1868p. lib. bdg. 137.16 (*0-7583-1181-8*); 912p. lib. bdg. 76.90 (*0-7583-1178-8*); 2704p. lib. bdg. 193.87 (*0-7583-1183-4*) Huge Print Pr.
—Jane Eyre. 1996. (Illus.). 466p. pap. 12.95 o.p. (*0-7868-8118-6*) Hyperion Pr.
—Jane Eyre. 2002. 500p. 29.99 (*1-4043-1064-9*); per. 24.99 (*1-4043-1065-7*) IndyPublish.com.
—Jane Eyre. Ba'Albaki, Munir, tr. (ARA.). 200p. pap. 14.95 (*0-86685-755-9*) International Bk. Ctr., Inc.
—Jane Eyre. 1998. (Cloth Bound Pocket Ser.). 240p. 7.95 (*3-89508-259-7*, 520184) Konemann.
—Jane Eyre. E-Book 2.95 (*1-57799-817-0*) Logos Research Systems, Inc.
—Jane Eyre. Ballantine, Cecil, ed. 1986. (Illus.). 32p. pap. text o.p. (*0-582-33152-8*) Longman Publishing Group.
—Jane Eyre. (English As a Second Language Bk.). 1981. pap. text 5.95 o.p. (*0-582-53843-2*, 74218); 2nd rev. ed. 1996. pap. text 5.90 o.s.i (*0-582-27511-3*); Level 3. 2000. (C). pap. 7.66 (*0-582-41780-5*); Level 5. 2000. (C). pap. 7.66 (*0-582-41932-8*) Longman Publishing Group.
—Jane Eyre. E-Book 1.95 (*1-58515-060-6*) MesaView, Inc.
—Jane Eyre. (Signet Classics). 1997. 480p. (C). mass mkt. 4.95 (*0-451-52655-4*); 1968. mass mkt. 0.60 o.p. (*0-451-50449-6*, Signet Classics); 1968. mass mkt. 0.50 o.p. (*0-451-50011-3*, Signet Classics); 1960. mass mkt. 1.25 o.p. (*0-451-51013-5*, Signet Classics); 1960. mass mkt. 1.75 o.p. (*0-451-51556-0*, Signet Classics); 1960. 464p. mass mkt. 4.95 o.s.i (*0-451-52332-6*, Signet Classics); 1960. mass mkt. 2.25 o.p. (*0-451-51465-3*, Signet Classics); 1960. mass mkt. 1.75 o.p. (*0-451-51347-9*, Signet Classics); 1960. mass mkt. 1.50 o.p. (*0-451-51117-4*, Signet Classics); 1960. mass mkt. 0.95 o.p. (*0-451-50871-8*, Signet Classics); 1960. mass mkt. 1.95 o.p. (*0-451-51884-5*); 1960. mass mkt. 0.75 o.p. (*0-451-50726-6*, Signet Classics) NAL.
—Jane Eyre. Schorer, Mark, ed. 1977. (Gotham Library Ser.). 429p. 12.50 o.p. (*0-8147-7780-5*); pap. 5.50 o.p. (*0-8147-7781-3*) New York Univ. Pr.
—Jane Eyre. 1998. 550p. reprint ed. lib. bdg. 25.00 (*1-58287-089-6*) North Bks.
—Jane Eyre. 2nd ed. 1997. (C). pap. text 16.50 o.p. (*0-393-98367-6*) Norton, W. W. & Co., Inc.
—Jane Eyre. Dunn, Richard J., ed. 2nd ed. 1987. 24.95 o.p. (*0-393-02424-5*) Norton, W. W. & Co., Inc.
—Jane Eyre. 3rd ed. 2002. (C). pap. text 11.50 (*0-393-94110-8*); pap. text 16.00 (*0-393-94097-7*) Norton, W. W. & Co., Inc.
—Jane Eyre. 2000. (Oxford World's Classics Ser.). 544p. 15.00 o.p. (*0-19-210042-4*) Oxford Univ. Pr., Inc.
—Jane Eyre. Smith, Margaret, ed. & intro. by. 1998. (Oxford World's Classics Ser.). 532p. pap. 6.95 o.p. (*0-19-283356-1*) Oxford Univ. Pr., Inc.
—Jane Eyre. Smith, Margaret, ed. 1980. 518p. pap. 5.95 o.p. (*0-19-281513-X*) Oxford Univ. Pr., Inc.
—Jane Eyre. Jack, Jane & Smith, Margaret, eds. 1969. (Clarendon Edition of the Novels of the Brontes). 72.00 o.p. (*0-19-811490-7*) Oxford Univ. Pr., Inc.
—Jane Eyre. Smith, Margaret, ed. 2nd ed. 2001. (Oxford World's Classics Ser.). 542p. pap. 6.95 (*0-19-283965-9*) Oxford Univ. Pr., Inc.
—Jane Eyre. Newman, Beth, ed. 1996. (Case Studies in Contemporary Criticism). 592p. 55.00 (*0-312-12795-2*) Palgrave Macmillan.
—Jane Eyre. 2001. (Embellished Manuscripts). 160p. 14.95 (*1-55156-199-9*) Paperblank Bk. Co.
—Jane Eyre. 2000. (Illustrated Junior Library Ser.). 9.99 o.p. (*0-448-42439-8*, Grosset & Dunlap) Penguin Putnam Bks. for Young Readers.
—Jane Eyre. 2001. pap. (*1-57646-269-2*) Quiet Vision Publishing.
—Jane Eyre. 2000. (Modern Library Classics). 752p. pap. 7.95 (*0-679-78332-6*); E-Book 4.95 (*0-679-64118-1*) Random House Adult Trade Publishing Group. (Modern Library).
—Jane Eyre. annuals (Modern Library Ser.). 1993. 704p. 19.95 (*0-679-42472-5*); 1992. o.s.i (*1-85381-137-8*); 1928. 3.95 o.s.i (*0-394-60064-9*) Random Hse., Inc.
—Jane Eyre. 1984. (Illus.). 480p. 12.95 o.p. (*0-89577-200-0*) Reader's Digest Assn., Inc., The.
—Jane Eyre. (Courage Unabridged Classics Ser.). 1997. 336p. pap. 6.00 o.p. (*0-7624-0547-3*, Courage Bks.); 1991. 336p. text 5.98 o.p. (*1-56138-022-9*, Courage Bks.); 1988. pap. 4.95 o.p. (*0-89471-631-X*) Running Pr. Bk. Pubs.
—Jane Eyre. 2000. E-Book 2.95 (*1-58853-014-0*) Sensory Publishing, Inc.
—Jane Eyre. (Enriched Classics Ser.). 1997. 576p. pap. 5.99 (*0-671-01479-X*, Pocket); 1994. 3.95 o.p. (*0-671-00602-9*) Simon & Schuster.
—Jane Eyre. 1996. (Classic Library). 12.98 o.p. (*0-7651-9981-5*) Smithmark Pubs., Inc.
—Jane Eyre. 1996. 592p. pap. text 14.95 o.p. (*0-312-14202-1*) St. Martin's Pr.
—Jane Eyre. l.t. ed. 1994. 689p. lib. bdg. 23.95 (*0-7838-1135-7*) Thorndike Pr.
—Jane Eyre. l.t. ed. 1997. (Charnwood Large Print Ser.). 740p. 29.99 (*0-7089-8015-5*, Ulverscroft) Thorpe, F. A. Pubs. GBR. *Dist:* Ulverscroft Large Print Bks., Ltd., Ulverscroft Large Print Canada, Ltd.
—Jane Eyre. abr. ed. 2000. mass mkt. 11.95 incl. audio (*1-85998-487-8*) Trafalgar Square.
—Jane Eyre. 2000. (Signature Classics Ser.). 436p. 24.95 (*1-58279-068-X*); lib. bdg. 29.95 (*1-58279-074-4*) Trident Pr. International.
—Jane Eyre. 1998. 19.00 (*0-606-16071-X*); 1981. 11.00 (*0-606-13533-2*); 1960. 11.00 (*0-606-00892-6*) Turtleback Bks.
—Jane Eyre. 1998. xlv, 530p. pap. 6.95 (*0-460-87596-5*); 1991. 474p. pap. 6.95 o.p. (*0-460-87085-8*) Tuttle Publishing. (Everyman's Classic Library in Paperback).
—Jane Eyre. 1999. 9.50 (*81-85944-80-6*) UBS Pubs. Distributions, Ltd. IND. *Dist:* South Asia Bks.
—Jane Eyre. Mason, Michael, ed. & intro. by. (Classics Ser.). 2003. 576p. 8.00 (*0-14-243720-4*); 1996. 560p. pap. 7.95 o.s.i (*0-14-043400-3*) Viking Penguin. (Penguin Classics).
—Jane Eyre. Leavis, Q. D., ed. 1966. 496p. pap. 5.95 o.p. (*0-14-043011-3*, Penguin Classics) Viking Penguin.
—Jane Eyre. 1999. E-Book 5.99 (*0-8220-7104-5*, Cliff Notes) Wiley, John & Sons, Inc.
—Jane Eyre. 1997. (Classics Library). 448p. pap. 3.95 (*1-85326-020-7*, 0207WW) Wordsworth Editions, Ltd. GBR. *Dist:* Casemate Pubs. & Bk. Distributors, LLC.
—Jane Eyre: Critical Edition. 2nd ed. (Critical Editions Ser.). (C). pap. text 38.50 (*0-393-99008-7*); 1999. pap. text 28.00 o.p. (*0-393-98061-8*) Norton, W. W. & Co., Inc.
—Jane Eyre: Critical Edition. Dunn, Richard J., ed. 2nd ed. 1987. (Critical Editions Ser.). 497p. (C). pap. text 10.00 o.p. (*0-393-95589-3*, 95589) Norton, W. W. & Co., Inc.
—Jane Eyre: Critical Edition. 3rd ed. (Critical Editions Ser.). 2001. (C). pap. text 29.00 (*0-393-94427-1*); 2000. xiv, 321p. pap. 8.00 (*0-393-97542-8*, Norton Paperbacks) Norton, W. W. & Co., Inc.
—Jane Eyre Authoritive Text. 1971. (C). pap. o.p. (*0-393-09966-0*) Norton, W. W. & Co., Inc.
—Villette, Set. 1990. audio 83.95 (*1-55685-171-5*) Audio Bk. Contractors, Inc.
—Villette. 1986. (Bantam Classics Ser.). 512p. mass mkt. 5.95 (*0-553-21243-5*) Bantam Bks.
—Villette. 1974. reprint ed. 9.95 o.p. (*0-460-00351-8*) Biblio Distribution.
—Villette. unabr. ed. 1997. audio 89.95 (*0-7861-1104-6*, 1871) Blackstone Audio Bks., Inc.
—Villette. 1992. reprint ed. lib. bdg. 24.95 (*0-89966-998-0*) Buccaneer Bks., Inc.
—Villette. audio HarperTrade.
—Villette. l.t. unabr. ed. 1991. (Isis Large Print Bks.). 601p. 29.99 o.p. (*1-85089-449-3*, 894493) ISIS Large Print Bks. GBR. *Dist:* Ulverscroft Large Print Bks., Ltd., Ulverscroft Large Print Canada, Ltd.
—Villette. 1992. 256p. 20.00 (*0-679-40988-2*) McKay, David Co., Inc.
—Villette. 1987. 496p. mass mkt. 5.95 o.s.i (*0-451-52083-1*, Signet Classics) NAL.
—Villette. 1999. (Twelve-Point Ser.). lib. bdg. 25.00 (*1-58287-114-0*) North Bks.
—Villette. Smith, Margaret & Rosengarten, Herbert, eds. (Oxford World's Classics Ser.). 698p. 1998. pap. 9.95 o.p. (*0-19-283433-9*); 1990. pap. 6.95 o.p. (*0-19-281836-8*) Oxford Univ. Pr., Inc.
—Villette. Rosengarten, Herbert & Smith, Margaret, eds. 1985. (Illus.). 824p. 160.00 o.p. (*0-19-812597-6*) Oxford Univ. Pr., Inc.
—Villette. 1968. (Oxford World's Classics Ser.). 16.95 o.p. (*0-19-250047-3*) Oxford Univ. Pr., Inc.
—Villette. Smith, Margaret & Rosengarten, Herbert, eds. 2nd ed. 2001. (Oxford World's Classics Ser.). 592p. pap. 10.95 (*0-19-283964-0*) Oxford Univ. Pr., Inc.
—Villette. Nestor, Pauline, ed. 1992. (New Casebooks Ser.). 184p. 45.00 o.p. (*0-312-07909-5*) Palgrave Macmillan.
—Villette. 2000. E-Book 4.95 (*0-679-64008-8*); 1997. 608p. 18.50 o.s.i (*0-679-60274-7*) Random House Adult Trade Publishing Group. (Modern Library).
—Villette. 1994. o.s.i (*1-85381-136-X*) Random Hse., Inc.
—Villette. Kemp, Sandra, ed. 1993. 576p. pap. 5.95 o.p. (*0-460-87247-8*, Everyman's Classic Library in Paperback) Tuttle Publishing.
—Villette. 1909. 529p. pap. 5.95 o.p. (*0-460-11351-8*, Everyman's Classic Library in Paperback) Tuttle Publishing.
—Villette. Tillotson, Geoffrey & Hawes, Donald, eds. 1978. (Riverside Editions). reprint ed. 26.25 o.p. (*0-8357-0347-9*, ST-00024) University Microfilms, Inc.
—Villette. Lilly, Mark, ed. 1980. (Classics Ser.). 624p. pap. 10.95 (*0-14-043118-7*, Penguin Classics) Viking Penguin.
—Villette. abr. ed. 1995. (Classics on Audio Ser.). pap. 16.95 o.s.i incl. audio (*0-14-086076-2*) Viking Penguin.
Bronte, Charlotte & Everyman's Library Staff. Jane Eyre. 1991. (Everyman's Library: Vol. 10). 326p. 20.00 (*0-679-40582-8*) Random Hse., Inc.
Bronte, Charlotte & Johnson, Diane. Jane Eyre. 1997. (Modern Library Ser.). 704p. 19.00 o.s.i (*0-679-60269-0*, Modern Library) Random House Adult Trade Publishing Group.
Bronte, Emily. Wuthering Heights. 2000. 252p. E-Book 9.95 (*0-594-04088-4*) 1873 Pr.
—Wuthering Heights. 1991. pap. text (*0-17-556575-9*) Addison-Wesley Longman, Inc.
—Wuthering Heights. 2001. E-Book 4.95 (*1-931208-21-2*) Adobe Systems, Inc.
—Wuthering Heights. unabr. ed. 1963. (Classics Ser.). mass mkt. 4.95 (*0-8049-0011-6*, CL-11) Airmont Publishing Co., Inc.
—Wuthering Heights. Date not set. 320p. 24.95 (*0-8488-2218-8*) Amereon, Ltd.
—Wuthering Heights. 1997. 386p. pap. 14.95 incl. disk (*1-55701-238-5*); 506p. pap. 22.95 (*1-55701-208-3*) BNI Pubns., Inc.
—Wuthering Heights. 1983. mass mkt. o.s.i (*0-553-19633-2*); mass mkt. 1.95 o.s.i (*0-553-21141-2*) Bantam Bks.
—Wuthering Heights. 1983. (Bantam Classics Ser.). 336p. reprint ed. mass mkt. 4.95 (*0-553-21258-3*) Bantam Dell Publishing Group.
—Wuthering Heights. Seely, Elizabeth & Seely, John, eds. 1999. (Classic Novels ). 368p. pap. 8.95 (*0-7641-1148-5*) Barron's Educational Series, Inc.
—Wuthering Heights. Murfin, Ross C. & Peterson, Linda H., eds. 1991. (Case Studies in Contemporary Criticism). 467p. (C). pap. text 8.50 (*0-312-03547-0*) Bedford/Saint Martin's.
—Wuthering Heights. 2nd ed. 2003. pap. text 8.50 (*0-312-25686-8*) Bedford/Saint Martin's.
—Wuthering Heights. Kendrick, Walter, ed. 1990. (Classics Ser.). 400p. (C). 19.95 (*0-8464-1072-9*) Beekman Pubs., Inc.
—Wuthering Heights. 1988. 360p. 40.00 o.p. (*0-913720-31-3*) Beil, Frederic C. Pub., Inc.
—Wuthering Heights. 1990. (Illus.). 3.75 o.s.i (*0-425-12259-X*, Classics Illustrated) Berkley Publishing Group.
—Wuthering Heights. per. 14.50 (*1-58396-669-2*) Blue Unicorn Editions.
—Wuthering Heights. 2002. pap. 4.95 (*1-59109-024-5*) Booksurge, LLC.
—Wuthering Heights. 2000. 6.98 (*0-681-99570-X*, 50885620) Borders Pr.
—Wuthering Heights. 1986. 320p. reprint ed. lib. bdg. 25.95 (*0-89966-520-9*) Buccaneer Bks., Inc.
—Wuthering Heights. 1997. (Cambridge Literature Ser.). audio 16.95 o.p. (*0-521-59798-6*) Cambridge Univ. Pr.
—Wuthering Heights. Hoyes, Richard, ed. 1997. (Cambridge Literature Ser.). (Illus.). 416p. pap. text 11.95 o.p. (*0-521-58949-5*) Cambridge Univ. Pr.
—Wuthering Heights. reprint ed. lib. bdg. 98.00 (*0-7426-2197-9*); 2001. (Illus.). 385p. pap. text 28.00 (*0-7426-7197-6*) Classic Bks.
—Wuthering Heights. 1986. o.s.i (*0-517-62145-2*); xxxi, 431p. 2.99 o.s.i (*0-517-60612-7*) Crown Publishing Group.
—Wuthering Heights. l.t. ed. 1997. 506p. pap. 22.95 (*1-58855-022-2*) Cyber Classics, Inc.
—Wuthering Heights. 1961. pap. 2.25 o.s.i (*0-440-39728-6*, Laurel) Dell Publishing.
—Wuthering Heights. 1989. 224p. mass mkt. 3.99 (*0-8125-0516-6*, Tor Classics); 1989. mass mkt. 3.25 o.s.i (*0-8125-0517-4*, Tor Classics); 1988. mass mkt. 4.95 (*0-938819-83-6*, Aerie); 1988. mass mkt. 2.25 (*0-938819-52-6*, Aerie) Doherty, Tom Assocs., LLC.
—Wuthering Heights. unabr. ed. 1996. (Thrift Editions Ser.). 256p. reprint ed. pap. 2.50 (*0-486-29256-8*) Dover Pubns., Inc.
—Wuthering Heights. 1972. 2.50 o.p. (*0-460-01243-6*); 1955. 12.95 o.p. (*0-460-00243-0*) Dutton/Plume. (Dutton).
—Wuthering Heights. E-Book 1.95 (*1-58627-104-0*) Electric Umbrella Publishing.
—Wuthering Heights. 2003. (Barnes & Noble Classics Ser.). 368p. mass mkt. 4.95 (*1-59308-044-1*) Fine Communications.
—Wuthering Heights. 2001. 240p. pap. 16.95 o.p. (*1-929925-57-3*) FirstPublish.
—Wuthering Heights. 1990. 10.92 (*0-02-635143-9*) Glencoe/McGraw-Hill.
—Wuthering Heights. l.t. ed. 2000. 464p. pap. 22.00 (*0-06-095570-8*) HarperCollins Pubs.
—Wuthering Heights. Clay, N. L., ed. 1986. (Guide Novel Ser.). pap. text 4.50 o.p. (*0-435-16100-8*) Heinemann.
—Wuthering Heights. 1979. (Blackie Chosen Classics Ser.). 320p. 3.95 o.p. (*0-216-88523-X*) Hippocrene Bks., Inc.
—Wuthering Heights. 1997. text 8.25 (*0-03-051489-4*) Holt, Rinehart & Winston.
—Wuthering Heights. Pritchett, V. S., ed. 1956. (YA). pap. 16.36 (*0-395-05102-9*, Riverside Editions) Houghton Mifflin Co.
—Wuthering Heights. l.t. ed. 1426p. pap. 84.35 (*0-7583-2934-2*); 939p. pap. 62.39 (*0-7583-2932-6*); 1159p. pap. 72.96 (*0-7583-2933-4*); 322p. pap. 24.22 (*0-7583-2928-8*); 725p. pap. 44.33 (*0-7583-2931-8*); 563p. pap. 35.94 (*0-7583-2930-X*); 407p. pap. 28.95 (*0-7583-2929-6*); 1680p. pap. 101.81 (*0-7583-2935-0*); 1426p. lib. bdg. 100.73 (*0-7583-2926-1*); 1159p. lib. bdg. 87.00 (*0-7583-2925-3*); 725p. lib. bdg. 50.99 (*0-7583-2923-7*); 939p. lib. bdg. 75.66 (*0-7583-2924-5*); 563p. lib. bdg. 42.65 (*0-7583-2922-9*); 407p. lib. bdg. 34.95 (*0-7583-2921-0*); 1680p. lib. bdg. 127.48 (*0-7583-2927-X*); 322p. lib. bdg. 30.22 (*0-7583-2920-2*) Huge Print Pr.
—Wuthering Heights. l.t. ed. 1992. (Clear Type Classics Ser.). 418p. 22.95 o.p. (*1-85695-310-6*) ISIS Large Print Bks. GBR. *Dist:* Transaction Pubs.
—Wuthering Heights. 1999. 348p. pap. 9.95 o.p. (*1-930128-12-6*, JNMedia Bks.) JNMedia, Inc.
—Wuthering Heights. 1977. pap. 1.95 o.p. (*0-523-40126-4*, Pinnacle Bks.) Kensington Publishing Corp.
—Wuthering Heights. 1998. (Cloth Bound Pocket Ser.). 240p. 7.95 (*3-89508-208-2*, 520082) Konemann.
—Wuthering Heights. l.t. ed. 1997. (Large Print Heritage Ser.). 536p. lib. bdg. 35.95 (*1-58118-003-9*, 21964) LRS.
—Wuthering Heights. 1996. (Longman Fiction Ser.). pap. text 5.90 o.s.i (*0-582-27495-8*) Longman Publishing Group.
—Wuthering Heights. Blatchford, Roy, ed. 1993. (Literature Ser.). pap. 5.95 (*0-582-07782-6*, TG7655) Longman Publishing Group.
—Wuthering Heights. 1993. (Fiction Ser.). pap. text 6.50 (*0-582-09672-3*, 79835) Longman Publishing Group.
—Wuthering Heights. E-Book 1.95 (*1-58515-093-2*) MesaView, Inc.

—Wuthering Heights. 2004. 336p. mass mkt. 4.95 (*0-451-52925-1*, Signet Classics); 1993. 328p. mass mkt. o.p. (*0-451-52583-3*, Signet Classics); 1979. o.p.; 1959. mass mkt. 1.50 o.p. (*0-451-51179-4*, Signet Classics); 1959. mass mkt. 1.25 o.p. (*0-451-51020-8*, Signet Classics); 1959. mass mkt. 0.95 o.p. (*0-451-50874-2*, Signet Classics); 1959. mass mkt. 1.75 o.p. (*0-451-51240-5*, Signet Classics); 1959. mass mkt. 1.75 o.p. (*0-451-51650-8*, Signet Classics); 1959. mass mkt. 1.95 o.p. (*0-451-51958-2*, Signet Classics); 1959. mass mkt. 0.75 o.p. (*0-451-50750-9*, Signet Classics); 1959. mass mkt. 1.95 o.p. (*0-451-51388-6*, Signet Classics); 1959. mass mkt. 2.25 o.p. (*0-451-52119-6*); 1959. mass mkt. 0.60 o.p. (*0-451-50610-3*, Signet Classics); 1959. mass mkt. 0.50 o.p. (*0-451-50010-5*, Signet Classics); 1959. 336p. reprint ed. mass mkt. 4.95 (*0-451-52338-5*) NAL.

—Wuthering Heights. 1997. (Thornes Classic Novels Ser.). (Illus.). 354p. pap. 16.95 (*0-7487-2978-X*) Nelson Thornes GBR. *Dist:* Trans-Atlantic Pubns., Inc.

—Wuthering Heights. l.t. ed. (Large Print Ser.). 1992. 566p. lib. bdg. 26.00 (*0-939495-28-7*); 1998. 350p. reprint ed. lib. bdg. 25.00 (*1-58287-083-7*) North Bks.

—Wuthering Heights. Sale, William M., Jr., ed. 1972. (C). pap. o.p. (*0-393-09400-6*) Norton, W. W. & Co., Inc.

—Wuthering Heights. 2nd ed. 2002. (Norton Critical Edition Ser.). 416p. pap. 12.10 (*0-393-97889-3*) Norton, W. W. & Co., Inc.

—Wuthering Heights. 1999. (Oxford World's Classics Ser.). 384p. 15.50 (*0-19-210027-0*) Oxford Univ. Pr., Inc.

—Wuthering Heights. Stoneman, Patsy & Jack, Ian, eds. 1998. (Oxford World's Classics Ser.). (Illus.). 432p. pap. 5.95 (*0-19-283354-5*) Oxford Univ. Pr., Inc.

—Wuthering Heights. Jack, Ian, ed. 1981. (Oxford World's Classics Ser.). (C). pap. 4.50 o.p. (*0-19-281543-1*) Oxford Univ. Pr., Inc.

—Wuthering Heights. Marsden, Hilda & Jack, Ian, eds. 1976. (Clarendon Edition of the Novels of the Brontes). 65.00 o.p. (*0-19-812511-9*) Oxford Univ. Pr., Inc.

—Wuthering Heights. Stoneman, Patsy, ed. 1993. (New Casebooks Ser.). 208p. 49.95 o.p. (*0-312-09689-5*) Palgrave Macmillan.

—Wuthering Heights. Peterson, Linda H., ed. 1992. text 39.95 o.p. (*0-312-06523-X*) Palgrave Macmillan.

—Wuthering Heights. 1997. (*0-14-771199-1*) Penguin Group (USA) Inc.

—Wuthering Heights. 1999. pap. 2.99 o.p. (*0-14-130547-9*); 1990. 352p. pap. 3.99 o.p. (*0-14-035113-2*) Penguin Putnam Bks. for Young Readers. (Puffin Bks.).

—Wuthering Heights. abr. ed. 1993. (Classics on Cassette). 16.00 incl. audio (*0-453-00819-4*) Penguin/HighBridge.

—Wuthering Heights. 2000. pap. (*1-57646-268-4*); 1999. 200p. E-Book 3.99 incl. audio compact disk (*1-57646-161-0*) Quiet Vision Publishing.

—Wuthering Heights. (Classics Ser.). 2000. 464p. pap. 6.95 (*0-375-75644-2*); 2000. E-Book 4.95 (*0-679-64000-2*); 1994. 448p. 17.95 o.s.i (*0-679-60135-X*) Random House Adult Trade Publishing Group. (Modern Library).

—Wuthering Heights. 1987. 9.99 o.s.i (*0-517-64301-4*) Random Hse. Value Publishing.

—Wuthering Heights. 1991. (Everyman's Library: Vol. 2). 544p. 17.00 (*0-679-40543-7*); 1990. o.s.i (*1-85381-138-6*); 1978. (Illus.). 400p. 12.95 o.s.i (*0-394-60458-X*); 1950. (Modern Library College Editions Ser.). pap. text 4.00 o.p. (*0-394-30904-9*, T4) Random Hse., Inc.

—Wuthering Heights. 1982. (Illus.). 303p. 12.95 o.p. (*0-89577-159-4*) Reader's Digest Assn., Inc., The.

—Wuthering Heights. Glen, Heather, ed. 1996. (English Texts Ser.). 400p. (C). pap. 20.99 o.p. (*0-415-00667-8*) Routledge.

—Wuthering Heights. (Courage Unabridged Classics Ser.). 1998. 256p. pap. 6.00 o.p. (*0-7624-0559-7*, Courage Bks.); 1991. 248p. text 5.98 o.p. (*1-56138-035-0*, Courage Bks.); 1986. 256p. pap. 4.95 o.p. (*0-89471-480-5*); 1986. 256p. lib. bdg. 12.90 o.p. (*0-89471-481-3*) Running Pr. Bk. Pubs.

—Wuthering Heights. 1992. 416p. mass mkt. 3.50 o.p. (*0-590-46030-7*, Scholastic Paperbacks) Scholastic, Inc.

—Wuthering Heights. 2000. E-Book 2.95 (*1-58853-026-4*) Sensory Publishing, Inc.

—Wuthering Heights. 2004. 400p. mass mkt. 4.95 (*0-7434-8764-8*, Pocket); 2003. 336p. pap. 4.99 (*0-7434-8507-6*, MTV) Simon & Schuster.

—Wuthering Heights. Peters, Sally, ed. 1992. 352p. mass mkt. 4.99 (*0-671-79022-6*, Pocket) Simon & Schuster.

—Wuthering Heights. 1997. (Enriched Classics Ser.). 400p. reprint ed. mass mkt. 5.99 (*0-671-01480-3*, Pocket) Simon & Schuster.

—Wuthering Heights. 1930. 25.00 (*0-689-83079-3*, Atheneum) Simon & Schuster Children's Publishing.

—Wuthering Heights. (Ebook Classic Ser.). E-Book 5.00 (*0-7410-0464-X*) SoftBook Pr.

—Wuthering Heights. 1996. pap. text 15.95 o.p. (*0-312-13826-1*) St. Martin's Pr.

—Wuthering Heights. l.t. ed. 2000. (Perennial Bestsellers Ser.). 492p. 27.95 (*0-7838-9062-1*) Thorndike Pr.

—Wuthering Heights. l.t. ed. 1997. (Charnwood Large Print Ser.). 551p. 29.99 (*0-7089-8950-0*, Ulverscroft) Thorpe, F. A. Pubs. GBR. *Dist:* Ulverscroft Large Print Bks., Ltd., Ulverscroft Large Print Canada, Ltd.

—Wuthering Heights. l.t. ed. 1998. 440p. text 29.95 (*1-56000-527-0*) Transaction Pubs.

—Wuthering Heights. 1999. (Signature Classics Ser.). (Illus.). 384p. 24.95 (*1-58279-033-7*); 29.95 (*1-58279-045-0*) Trident Pr. International.

—Wuthering Heights. 1989. 9.04 (*0-606-18662-X*); 1981. 11.00 (*0-606-13932-X*); 1959. 11.00 (*0-606-01582-5*) Turtleback Bks.

—Wuthering Heights. unabr. ed. 1997. 230p. reprint ed. pap. 14.95 o.p. (*1-57002-048-5*) University Publishing Hse., Inc.

—Wuthering Heights. 2002. (Penguin Classics Ser.). (Illus.). 416p. pap. 7.00 (*0-14-143955-6*, Penguin Classics) Viking Penguin.

—Wuthering Heights. Nestor, Pauline, ed. 1996. (Penguin Classics Ser.). 400p. (C). pap. 6.95 o.s.i (*0-14-043418-6*) Viking Penguin.

—Wuthering Heights. Daiches, David, ed. 1990. (English Library). 384p. pap. 5.95 o.p. (*0-14-043001-6*, Penguin Classics) Viking Penguin.

—Wuthering Heights. 2000. text 6.00 (*0-8220-7231-9*, Cliff Notes) Wiley, John & Sons, Inc.

—Wuthering Heights. 1997. (Classics Library). 272p. pap. 3.95 (*1-85326-001-0*, 0010WW) Wordsworth Editions, Ltd. GBR. *Dist:* Casemate Pubs. & Bk. Distributors, LLC.

—Wuthering Heights: Complete Text with Introduction, Contexts, Critical Essays. Hoeveler, Diane Long, ed. 2002. (New Riverside Edtions Ser.). (Illus.). viii, 456p. pap. 8.76 (*0-618-08486-X*) Houghton Mifflin Co.

—Wuthering Heights: Norton Critical Edition. Sale, William M., Jr. & Dunn, Richard J., eds. 3rd rev. ed. 1990. (Critical Editions Ser.). 396p. pap. text (*0-393-95760-8*) Norton, W. W. & Co., Inc.

—Wuthering Heights: Study Text. Adams, Richard & Cookson, Linda, eds. 1989. (Study Texts Ser.). (Illus.). 338p. pap. text 5.95 o.p. (*0-582-33098-X*, TG7232) Longman Publishing Group.

—Wuthering Heights: 1818 Version. Jack, Ian, ed. 2nd ed. 1995. (Oxford World's Classics Ser.). 428p. pap. 4.95 o.p. (*0-19-282350-7*) Oxford Univ. Pr., Inc.

—Wuthering Heights & Poems. Drabble, Margaret, ed. 1993. 432p. pap. 4.95 o.p. (*0-460-87311-3*, Everyman's Classic Library in Paperback) Tuttle Publishing.

—Wuthering Heights & Poems. 1991. 403p. pap. 5.95 o.p. (*0-460-87036-X*, Everyman's Classic Library in Paperback) Tuttle Publishing.

—Wuthering Heights with Connections. 2000. (HRW Library). 399p. 17.90 (*0-03-095770-2*) Holt, Rinehart & Winston.

Bronte, Emily, et al. Wuthering Heights. 1998. E-Book 6.25 (*0-585-35916-4*) netLibrary, Inc.

Brookner, Anita. The Debut. 1981. 11.95 o.p. (*0-671-42626-5*, Simon & Schuster) Simon & Schuster.

—Incidents in the Rue Laugier. l.t. ed. 1996. 25.95 (*1-56895-301-1*, Wheeler Publishing, Inc.) Gale Group.

—Incidents in the Rue Laugier. unabr. ed. 2001. audio 54.95 (*1-85695-232-0*, 951002) ISIS Audio Bks. GBR. *Dist:* Ulverscroft Large Print Bks., Ltd.

—Incidents in the Rue Laugier. 1997. 240p. pap. 13.00 (*0-679-76512-3*, Vintage) Knopf Publishing Group.

—Lewis Percy. l.t. ed. 1991. (General Ser.). 357p. pap. 20.95 o.p. (*0-8161-5074-5*, Macmillan Reference USA) Gale Group.

—Lewis Percy. 1991. (Vintage Contemporaries Ser.). 272p. pap. 14.00 (*0-679-72944-5*, Vintage) Knopf Publishing Group.

—Lewis Percy. 1991. 3.99 o.p. (*0-517-07930-5*) Random Hse. Value Publishing.

—The Misalliance. 1988. 192p. reprint ed. pap. 11.00 o.p. (*0-06-097134-7*, PL-7134, Perennial) Harper-Trade.

—The Misalliance. 1987. 192p. 14.95 o.s.i (*0-394-55340-3*, Pantheon) Knopf Publishing Group.

—Providence. 1994. (Vintage Contemporaries Ser.). 192p. pap. 13.00 (*0-679-73814-2*) Knopf, Alfred A. Inc.

—The Rules of Engagement. 2003. 288p. 23.95 (*1-4000-6165-2*, Random House) Random House Adult Trade Publishing Group.

—Undue Influence. l.t. ed. 2000. (G. K. Hall Core Ser.). 306p. 29.95 (*0-7838-9001-X*, Macmillan Reference USA) Gale Group.

—Undue Influence. 2001. 240p. pap. 12.00 (*0-375-70734-4*, Vintage) Knopf Publishing Group.

Broughton, Rhoda. Cometh up As a Flower: An Autobiography. 1993. (Pocket Classics Ser.). x, 285p. 8.00 o.p. (*0-7509-0448-8*) Sutton Publishing, Ltd. GBR. *Dist:* International Publishers Marketing.

—Cometh up as a Flower: An Autobiography, 2 vols., 1 bk. reprint ed. 44.50 (*0-404-61794-8*) AMS Pr., Inc.

Broussard, Meredith. The Dictionary of Failed Relationships: 26 Tales of Love Gone Wrong. 2003. 320p. pap. 11.00 (*0-609-81009-X*, Three Rivers Pr.) Crown Publishing Group.

Brown, Carrie. Lamb in Love. 1999. 348p. tchr. ed. 21.95 (*1-56512-203-8*, 72203) Algonquin Bks. of Chapel Hill.

Brown, Karen. A Hard Dry Road. 2003. 171p. 26.95 (*0-7862-5337-1*, Five Star) Gale Group.

Brown, Sandra. Adam's Fall. l.t. ed. 1994. 23.95 o.p. (*1-56895-068-3*, Wheeler Publishing, Inc.) Gale Group.

—Breakfast in Bed. 1991. 192p. mass mkt. 2.75 o.s.i (*0-553-21623-6*); 1996. 240p. mass mkt. 7.50 (*0-553-57158-3*) Bantam Bks.

—Breakfast in Bed. l.t. ed. 1996. (Large Print Bks.). 25.95 o.p. (*1-56895-307-0*, Wheeler Publishing, Inc.) Gale Group.

—Breakfast in Bed. abr. ed. 1995. audio 16.99 o.s.i (*0-553-47432-4*, RH Audio) Random Hse. Audio Publishing Group.

—Breakfast in Bed. unabr. ed. 1997. audio 35.00 (*0-7887-0845-7*, 94991E7) Recorded Bks., LLC.

—Charade. abr. ed. 1993. audio 16.95 o.p. (*0-7871-0015-3*, 390507, Dove Audio); 1994. 39.95 o.p. (*0-7871-0101-X*, 112717) NewStar Media, Inc.

—Charade. 1994. 416p. 21.95 o.s.i (*0-446-51656-2*); 1995. 496p. reprint ed. mass mkt. 7.99 (*0-446-60185-3*) Warner Bks., Inc.

Brownrigg, Sylvia. The Metaphysical Touch. 24.00 o.p. (*0-374-20873-5*); 1999. 390p. 24.00 o.s.i (*0-374-19965-5*) Farrar, Straus & Giroux.

—The Metaphysical Touch. 2000. 400p. pap. 15.00 (*0-312-26357-0*) Picador.

Bryers, Paul. Coming First. 1988. 252p. pap. 7.95 o.p. (*0-87113-224-9*) Grove/Atlantic, Inc.

Buchan, Elizabeth. Perfect Love. 2003. 448p. pap. 13.95 (*0-312-32464-2*, Saint Martin's Griffin); 1999. 256p. 24.95 o.p. (*0-312-20568-6*) St. Martin's Pr.

Bunn, T. Davis. Gibraltar Passage. l.t. ed. 1994. (Rendezvous with Destiny Ser.: No. 2). 192p. pap. 8.99 o.p. (*1-55661-380-6*) Bethany Hse. Pubs.

Burdett, John. A Personal History of Thirst: A Psychological Thriller in the Tradition of Damage. 1996. 320p. 23.00 o.p. (*0-688-14399-7*, Morrow, William & Co.) Morrow/Avon.

Busch, Frederick. Harry & Catherine. 1991. 304p. pap. 10.00 o.s.i (*0-679-73076-1*, Vintage) Knopf Publishing Group.

Bush, Catherine. The Rules of Engagement. 2002. pap. 24.00 (*0-374-52870-5*); 2000. 302p. 24.00 o.s.i (*0-374-25280-7*) Farrar, Straus & Giroux.

Bushnell, Candace. 4 Blondes. 2001. 256p. pap. 12.00 (*0-8021-3825-X*, Grove Pr.); 2000. 245p. 24.00 (*0-87113-819-0*, Atlantic Monthly Pr.) Grove/Atlantic, Inc.

—4 Blondes. 2002. 384p. mass mkt. 7.99 (*0-451-20389-5*, Signet Bks.) NAL.

—4 Blondes. l.t. ed. 445p. 2002. pap. 28.95 (*0-7862-3152-1*); 2001. 31.95 (*0-7862-3151-3*) Thorndike Pr.

Butler, Robert Olen. The Alleys of Eden. 1983. 256p. mass mkt. 2.95 o.s.i (*0-345-30774-7*) Ballantine Bks.

—The Alleys of Eden. 1994. 256p. 25.00 o.p. (*0-8050-3199-5*); pap. 11.00 o.s.i (*0-8050-3141-3*, Owl Bks.) Holt, Henry & Co.

—Countrymen of Bones. 1985. 256p. mass mkt. 2.95 o.s.i (*0-345-32118-9*) Ballantine Bks.

—Countrymen of Bones. 1994. 25.00 o.p. (*0-8050-3202-9*); 224p. pap. 11.00 o.s.i (*0-8050-3142-1*, Owl Bks.) Holt, Henry & Co.

—Sun Dogs. 1985. 240p. mass mkt. 2.95 o.s.i (*0-345-32125-1*) Ballantine Bks.

—Sun Dogs. 1994. 25.00 o.p. (*0-8050-3201-0*); 218p. pap. 11.00 o.s.i (*0-8050-3143-X*, Owl Bks.) Holt, Henry & Co.

—Sun Dogs. 1982. 250p. 12.95 o.p. (*0-8180-0636-6*) Horizon Pr.

—They Whisper. 1994. 352p. 22.50 o.p. (*0-8050-1985-5*) Holt, Henry & Co.

Butler, Robert Olen & Nemeroy, Howard. The Alleys of Eden. 1981. 12.95 o.p. (*0-8180-0631-5*) Horizon Pr.

Byatt, A. S. Possession: A Romance. 1991. (International Ser.). 576p. reprint ed. pap. 14.00 (*0-679-73590-9*, Vintage) Knopf Publishing Group.

Cain, James M. The Postman Always Rings Twice. 20.95 (*0-89190-815-3*) Amereon, Ltd.

—The Postman Always Rings Twice. 1981. 457p. reprint ed. lib. bdg. 27.95 (*0-89968-234-0*, Lightyear Pr.) Buccaneer Bks., Inc.

—The Postman Always Rings Twice. 1992. pap. 8.00 (*0-394-23899-0*); 1989. 128p. pap. 10.00 (*0-679-72325-0*) Knopf Publishing Group. (Vintage).

—The Postman Always Rings Twice. 1993. 4.99 o.p. (*0-517-10682-5*) Random Hse. Value Publishing.

—The Postman Always Rings Twice. 1992. pap. 8.00 (*0-679-74097-X*) Random Hse., Inc.

—The Postman Always Rings Twice. 1995. 200p. reprint ed. 35.00 (*1-883402-18-2*, Scribner) Simon & Schuster.

Campion, Anna & Campion, Jane. Holy Smoke: A Novel. 1999. (Illus.). 272p. pap. 14.00 (*0-7868-8563-7*); 259p. 22.95 (*0-7868-6349-8*) Hyperion Pr.

Campion, Jane & Pullinger, Kate. The Piano: A Novel. 1994. 218p. (J). 17.95 o.p. (*0-7868-6121-5*) Hyperion Pr.

Canter, MacKenzie. The Indictment. 1994. 256p. 21.00 o.p. (*0-7867-0073-4*, Carroll & Graf Pubs.) Avalon Publishing Group.

Canty, Kevin. Nine Below Zero. 2000. (Contemporaries Ser.). 384p. pap. 13.00 (*0-375-70799-9*, Vintage) Knopf Publishing Group.

Carlson, Melody. Heartland Skies, No. 1. 1998. (Heartland Skies Ser.: Vol. 1). 252p. pap. 9.99 o.p. (*1-57673-264-9*, Palisades) Multnomah Pubs., Inc.

Cartland, Barbara. Barbara Cartland's Etiquette for Love & Romance. l.t. ed. 1986. lib. bdg. 13.95 o.p. (*0-7451-0282-4*, Macmillan Reference USA) Gale Group.

—Five Complete Novels: Moon Over Eden, No Time for Love, The Incredible Honeymoon, Kiss the Moonlight, A Kiss in Rome. 1993. (Five Complete Novels Ser.). 13.99 o.s.i (*0-517-09299-9*) Random Hse. Value Publishing.

—Five Complete Novels of Dukes & Their Ladies. 1995. (Wings Bestsellers Ser.). 672p. 13.99 o.s.i (*0-517-14679-7*) Random Hse., Inc.

—Three Complete Novels of Dukes & Their Ladies: Never Laugh at Love, The Disgraceful Duke, A Touch of Love. 1996. 448p. 7.99 o.s.i (*0-517-15046-8*) Random Hse. Value Publishing.

—Three Complete Novels of Earls & Their Ladies. 1996. 432p. 7.99 o.s.i (*0-517-14772-6*) Crown Publishing Group.

—Three Complete Novels of Royalty & Romance. 1995. 432p. 7.99 o.s.i (*0-517-14678-9*) Crown Publishing Group.

Casey, John. An American Romance. 1977. 9.95 o.p. (*0-689-10770-6*, Atheneum) Simon & Schuster Children's Publishing.

Cassity, Martin M., Jr. Fifty-Nine Front Street. 1993. pap. 13.95 (*1-881399-09-5*) Beaver Pond Publishing & Printing, Inc.

Castillo, Ana. The Mixquiahuala Letters & Sapogonia. 1994. 368p. pap. 13.00 (*0-385-47080-0*) Doubleday Publishing.

—Sapogonia. 1990. 320p. 27.00 (*0-916950-95-6*); pap. 17.00 (*0-916950-96-4*) Bilingual Pr./Editorial Bilingue.

Cawood, Chris. 1998: The Year of the Beast. Seale, Gaynell, ed. 1996. 312p. (Orig.). pap. 12.95 (*0-9642231-9-8*) Magnolia Hill Pr.

Cecala, Kathy. Secret Vow. 1997. 192p. 19.95 o.p. (*0-525-94290-4*) Dutton/Plume.

—Secret Vow. 1998. 288p. mass mkt. 6.99 o.s.i (*0-451-19227-3*, Onyx) NAL.

Chadwick, Elizabeth. The Conquest. 1997. 568p. pap. text o.s.i (*0-7515-1177-3*) Little Brown & Co.

—The Conquest. 1997. 464p. 25.95 (*0-312-15497-6*) St. Martin's Pr.

—Conquest. 1996. 458p. o.s.i (*0-316-91222-0*) Little Brown & Co.

Chalmers, Benita R. When Love Calls. 1998. 192p. (Orig.). pap. 6.99 (*0-9669658-0-9*) Poole & Smith Publishing.

Chamberlain, Diane. Reflection. 1996. 384p. 24.00 o.p. (*0-06-017652-0*) HarperCollins Pubs.

—Reflection. 1997. 416p. mass mkt. 5.99 o.s.i (*0-06-109396-3*, HarperTorch) Morrow/Avon.

Chance, Megan. A Season in Eden. 1999. 352p. mass mkt. 5.99 (*0-06-108705-X*) HarperCollins Pubs.

—A Season in Eden. l.t. ed. 2000. (Americana Ser.). 443p. 29.95 (*0-7862-2477-0*) Thorndike Pr.

Chapman, R. W., ed. The Oxford Illustrated Jane Austen, 6 vols. 3rd ed. Incl. Vol. I. Sense & Sensibility. 3rd ed. Austen, Jane. 446p. 20.00 (*0-19-254701-1*); Vol. III. Joseph Andrews. 3rd ed. Fielding, Henry. 584p. 20.00 (*0-19-254703-8*); Vol. IV. Emma. 3rd ed. Austen, Jane. 536p. 20.00 (*0-19-254704-6*); Vol. V. Northanger Abbey. 3rd ed. Austen, Jane. 348p. 20.00 (*0-19-254705-4*); Vol. VI. Minor Works. Austen, Jane. 486p. 20.00 (*0-19-254706-2*); reprint ed. (Oxford Illustrated Austen Ser.). (Illus.). 3184p. 1988. 95.00 (*0-19-254707-0*) Oxford Univ. Pr., Inc.

Charbonneau, Eileen. Waltzing in Ragtime. 1997. 399p. mass mkt. 6.99 (*0-8125-4468-4*); 1996. 480p. 26.95 o.p. (*0-312-86180-X*) Doherty, Tom Assocs., LLC. (Forge Bks.).

Charles, Caroline. Laird of Drumm. l.t. ed. 1996. 235p. pap. 20.95 o.p. (*0-7838-1896-3*, Macmillan Reference USA) Gale Group.

Charnas, Suzy McKee. The Furies. 1995. 399p. pap. text 6.99 (*0-8125-4819-1*, Tor Bks.); 1994. 383 p. 22.95 o.p. (*0-312-85717-9*, Tor Bks.); 2001. 320p. reprint ed. pap. 14.95 (*0-312-86606-2*, Orb Bks.) Doherty, Tom Assocs., LLC.

Chavez, Denise. Loving Pedro Infante. 2001. 325p. 24.00 (*0-374-19411-4*) Farrar, Straus & Giroux.

—Loving Pedro Infante. 2002. 336p. pap. 13.00 (*0-7434-4573-2*, Washington Square Pr.) Simon & Schuster.

Chesney, Marion. Sir Philip's Folly. l.t. ed. 1994. (Poor Relation Ser.: Vol. 4). 223p. lib. bdg. 17.95 (*0-8161-7414-8*, Macmillan Reference USA) Gale Group.

—Sir Philip's Folly. 1993. (Poor Relation Ser.: Vol. 4). 160p. 17.95 o.p. (*0-312-09912-6*) St. Martin's Pr.

Clapsaddle-Counts, Ruth. Four Corners. 1998. 200p. 19.95 (*1-57197-079-7*) Pentland Pr., Inc.

Clark, Catherine C. The Saturday Treat. 1993. 384p. 22.95 o.p. (*0-312-09908-8*) St. Martin's Pr.

Clarke, Lindsay. Alice's Masque. 1994. 246p. o.p. (*0-224-03287-9*) Random Hse. UK, Ltd.

Clive, Caroline A. Paul Ferroll. 1997. (Oxford Popular Fiction Ser.). 236p. pap. 9.95 o.p. (*0-19-283247-6*) Oxford Univ. Pr., Inc.

—Paul Ferroll. 2002. 244p. pap. 18.95 (*1-59224-848-9*); lib. bdg. 29.95 (*1-59224-849-7*) Wildside Pr.

—Paul Ferroll: A Tale. reprint ed. 44.50 (*0-404-61821-9*) AMS Pr., Inc.

Cockington, James. When the Man in the Gold Mustang Met the Girl from the Pink Pussycat. 1997. (*0-09-183389-2*) Trafalgar Square.

Coffman, Elaine. Someone Like You. 1998. 345p. mass mkt. 5.99 o.s.i (*0-449-15006-2*, Fawcett) Ballantine Bks.

—Someone Like You. l.t. ed. 1998. pap. 24.95 (*1-56895-543-X*, Wheeler Publishing, Inc.) Gale Group.

Cohen, Richard. Say You Want Me. 1988. 268p. 17.95 (*0-939149-12-5*) Soho Pr., Inc.

Cohn, Paul D. Shelee & Me: Journeys of Intimate Discovery. 1996. 392p. pap. 11.95 (*0-9645876-3-7*) Burns-Cole Pubs.

Collard, Cyril. Savage Nights. 1995. 240p. pap. 11.95 (*0-87951-580-5*) Overlook Pr., The.

—Savage Nights. Rodarmor, William, tr. 1994. 240p. 18.95 (*0-87951-534-1*) Overlook Pr., The.

Collier, G. K. The Gamester. 1994. 21.95 o.p. (*0-312-11277-7*) St. Martin's Pr.

Collignon, Rick. Perdido. 1997. 224p. 19.50 (*1-878448-76-5*) MacMurray & Beck, Inc.

Collin, Richard O. Contessa. 1994. 496p. 25.95 o.p. (*0-312-09773-5*) St. Martin's Pr.

Collins, Jackie. American Star. l.t. ed. 1993. 27.95 o.p. (*1-56895-025-X*, Wheeler Publishing, Inc.) Gale Group.

—American Star. 1993. 472p. 23.00 o.p. (*0-671-66625-8*, Simon & Schuster) Simon & Schuster.

—Thrill! l.t. ed. 1998. (Large Print Book Ser.). 27.95 (*1-56895-601-0*, Wheeler Publishing, Inc.) Gale Group.

—Thrill! 1998. 544p. mass mkt. 7.99 (*0-671-02094-3*, Pocket); 480p. 25.00 (*0-684-85029-X*, Simon & Schuster) Simon & Schuster.

Collins, Lynne. Change of Heart. l.t. ed. 1993. 18.95 o.p. (*0-7927-1686-8*); pap. 16.95 o.p. (*0-7927-1685-X*) BBC Audiobooks America.

—Duel for the Doctor. l.t. ed. 1994. 18.95 o.p. (*0-7927-1926-3*); pap. 16.95 o.p. (*0-7927-1925-5*) BBC Audiobooks America.

Collins, Warwick. The Rationalist. 1994. 251p. 21.00 o.s.i (*0-671-86939-6*, Simon & Schuster) Simon & Schuster.

Colwin, Laurie. Another Marvelous Thing. 1994. 144p. pap. 11.00 (*0-06-097650-0*) HarperTrade.

Comfort, Bonnie. Denial. 1996. pap. 5.99 (*0-380-72716-1*, Avon Bks.) Morrow/Avon.

—Denial. 1995. 302p. 22.00 o.p. (*0-671-89696-2*, Simon & Schuster) Simon & Schuster.

Conley, Robert J. Mountain Windsong: A Novel of the Trail of Tears. 1995. 224p. pap. 11.95 (*0-8061-2746-5*); 1992. 240p. 19.95 o.p. (*0-8061-2452-0*) Univ. of Oklahoma Pr.

—Mountain Windsong: A Novel of the Trail of Tears. 1995. E-Book 11.95 (*0-585-14947-X*) netLibrary, Inc.

Conrad, Joseph. Victory: An Island Tale. (Collected Works of Joseph Conrad). 2001. pap. text 28.00 (*0-7426-7668-4*); reprint ed. lib. bdg. 98.00 (*0-7426-2668-7*) Classic Bks.

—Victory: An Island Tale. 1971. 352p. pap. 9.95 o.s.i (*0-385-09314-4*) Doubleday Publishing.

—Victory: An Island Tale. abr. ed. audio (*0-00-104969-0*) HarperCollins Pubs. Ltd.

—Victory: An Island Tale. 1995. 300p. (J). pap. 9.95 (*0-7868-8142-9*) Hyperion Pr.

—Victory: An Island Tale. 1998. (Everyman's Library). 464p. 20.00 (*0-375-40047-8*) Knopf, Alfred A. Inc.

—Victory: An Island Tale. Batchelor, John, ed. 1996. (Oxford World's Classics Ser.). (Illus.). 472p. (C). pap. 5.95 o.p. (*0-19-281708-6*) Oxford Univ. Pr., Inc.

—Victory: An Island Tale. Mallios, Peter, ed. 2003. (Modern Library Classics). (Illus.). 432p. pap. 9.95 (*0-375-75908-5*, Modern Library) Random House Adult Trade Publishing Group.

—Victory: An Island Tale. 1998. (Classics Library). pap. 3.95 (*1-85326-256-0*, 2560WW) Wordsworth Editions, Ltd. GBR. *Dist:* Combined Publishing.

Conran, Shirley. Shirley Conran: Three Complete Novels. 1994. 1024p. 6.99 o.s.i (*0-517-10073-8*) Random Hse. Value Publishing.

Constable, George. Where You Are. 1996. 336p. 21.95 o.s.i (*0-385-48438-0*) Doubleday Publishing.

Constant, Jan. MacKenzie's Woman. l.t. ed. 1993. 269p. lib. bdg. 15.95 (*0-8161-5842-8*, Macmillan Reference USA) Gale Group.

Cook, Paul M. Sally, Sally, Sally, Sally. 2002. 78p. 19.95 (*0-615-12048-2*) PMC Bks. & Music.

Cook, Thomas H. The Chatham School Affair. 1997. 336p. mass mkt. 6.99 (*0-553-57193-1*) Bantam Bks.

Cooley, Martha. The Archivist. 336p. 1999. pap. 13.00 (*0-316-15846-1*, Back Bay); 1998. (YA). (gr. 8 up). 22.95 o.p. (*0-316-15872-0*) Little Brown & Co.

Coover, Robert. Spanking the Maid. deluxe ltd. ed. 1981. 125.00 (*0-89723-024-8*); 75.00 (*0-89723-023-X*) Bruccoli Clark Layman, Inc.

—Spanking the Maid. 1998. 112p. pap. 11.00 (*0-8021-3540-4*); 1982. 96p. pap. 4.95 o.p. (*0-394-17971-4*) Grove/Atlantic, Inc. (Grove Pr.).

Copeland, Lori. Promise Me Tomorrow. (Orig.). 1998. mass mkt. o.s.i (*0-449-00505-4*); 1993. mass mkt. 5.99 o.s.i (*0-449-14752-5*, Fawcett) Ballantine Bks.

—Promise Me Tomorrow. l.t. ed. 1994. (Orig.). 22.95 o.p. (*1-56895-064-0*, Wheeler Publishing, Inc.) Gale Group.

Coulter, Catherine. The Hellion Bride. 1992. (Bride Trilogy Ser.: Vol. 2). 384p. mass mkt. 7.99 (*0-515-10974-6*, Jove) Berkley Publishing Group.

—The Hellion Bride. l.t. ed. 1996. 456p. 25.95 o.p. (*0-7838-1294-9*, Macmillan Reference USA) Gale Group.

—The Hellion Bride. l.t. ed. 1995. (Magna Large Print Ser.). 500p. o.p. (*0-7505-0764-0*) Magna Large Print Bks. GBR. *Dist:* Ulverscroft Large Print Canada, Ltd.

—The Hellion Bride. abr. ed. 1992. (Bride Trilogy Ser.: Bk. 2). 3p. audio 15.95 (*1-879371-22-7*, 40090) Publishing Mills, Inc., The.

—Lord of Falcon Ridge. l.t. ed. 1995. (Large Print Bks.). (Orig.). pap. 20.95 o.p. (*1-56895-253-8*, Wheeler Publishing, Inc.) Gale Group.

—Lord of Hawkfell Island. l.t. ed. 1995. (Large Print Bks.). pap. 20.95 o.p. (*1-56895-235-X*, Wheeler Publishing, Inc.) Gale Group.

—Lord of Raven's Peak. l.t. ed. 1995. (Large Print Bks.). (Orig.). 23.95 o.p. (*1-56895-223-6*, Wheeler Publishing, Inc.) Gale Group.

—The Wyndham Legacy. l.t. ed. 1994. 602p. 23.95 o.p. (*0-8161-5941-6*, Macmillan Reference USA) Gale Group.

—The Wyndham Legacy. 1994. 304p. 19.95 o.p. (*0-399-13878-1*, G. P. Putnam's Sons) Penguin Group (USA) Inc.

Cowan, Andrew. Common Ground. 1997. 256p. 22.00 o.s.i (*0-15-100265-7*) Harcourt Trade Pubs.

Cowasjee, Saros. The Assistant Professor. 1996. 160p. pap. 13.95 (*0-920661-50-5*) TSAR Pubns. CAN. *Dist:* LPC/InBook.

Crane, Teresa. Strange Are the Ways. 570p. 4.98 o.p. (*0-8317-4637-8*) Smithmark Pubs., Inc.

—Strange Are the Ways. 1993. 576p. 25.95 o.p. (*0-312-09919-3*) St. Martin's Pr.

Crawford, Dianna & Laity, Sally. The Gathering Dawn. 1994. (Freedom's Holy Light Ser.: Vol. 2). 367p. 10.99 o.p. (*0-8423-1303-6*) Tyndale Hse. Pubs.

—The Kindled Flame. 1994. (Freedom's Holy Light Ser.: Vol. 2). 320p. pap. 10.99 o.p. (*0-8423-1336-2*) Tyndale Hse. Pubs.

Crow, Donna Fletcher. Where Love Begins. 2nd ed. 1995. (Cambridge Chronicles: Vol. 3). 224p. reprint ed. pap. 9.99 o.p. (*0-89107-808-8*) Crossway Bks.

—Where Love Begins. l.t. ed. 1997. (Christian Fiction Ser.). 319p. 23.95 (*0-7862-1231-4*) Thorndike Pr.

Crusie, Jennifer. Tell Me Lies. l.t. ed. 1998. 26.95 o.p. (*1-56895-568-5*, Wheeler Publishing, Inc.) Gale Group.

—Tell Me Lies. 2004. mass mkt. 3.99 (*0-312-93282-0*); 1999. (Tell Me Lies Ser.: Vol. 1). 368p. mass mkt. 7.50 (*0-312-96680-6*, St. Martin's Paperbacks); 1998. 322p. 24.95 o.p. (*0-312-17940-5*) St. Martin's Pr.

Cumyn, Richard. The Limit of Delta Y over Delta X. 1994. 190p. pap. (*0-86492-176-4*) Goose Lane Editions.

Cunningham, Michael. The Hours. E-Book 13.00 (*0-374-91952-6*); 2003. E-Book 9.00 (*0-374-70468-6*); 1998. 230p. 23.00 (*0-374-17289-7*); 1998. E-Book 23.00 o.p. (*0-374-70011-7*); 1998. E-Book 9.00 o.p. (*0-374-70006-0*); 1998. E-Book 9.00 (*0-374-70009-5*); 1998. E-Book 9.00 (*0-374-70016-8*); 1998. pap. o.s.i (*0-374-93947-0*) Farrar, Straus & Giroux.

—The Hours. 240p. 2000. pap. 13.00 (*0-312-24302-2*); 2002. pap. 13.00 (*0-312-30506-0*) Picador.

—The Hours. l.t. ed. (Paperback Bestsellers Ser.). 2000. 253p. pap. 30.00 (*0-7838-8714-0*); 1999. 250p. pap. 30.95 (*0-7838-8715-9*) Thorndike Pr.

—The Hours. 2000. 19.05 (*0-606-19100-3*) Turtleback Bks.

Dailey, Janet. Legacies. 1995. 400p. 22.95 o.s.i (*0-316-17205-7*) Little Brown & Co.

—The Proud & the Free. l.t. ed. 1995. 647p. 26.95 o.p. (*1-56895-167-1*, Wheeler Publishing, Inc.) Gale Group.

—The Proud & the Free. 1994. 322p. 22.95 o.p. (*0-316-17165-4*) Little Brown & Co.

—The Proud & the Free. unabr. ed. 1994. 49.95 o.p. (*0-7871-0008-0*);Set. 24.95 o.p. (*0-7871-0007-2*) NewStar Media, Inc.

—The Proud & the Free. 1995. 400p. mass mkt. 6.99 o.s.i (*0-446-60208-6*) Warner Bks., Inc.

—Riding High. 1994. (Janet Dailey's Love Scenes Ser.). pap. 4.75 (*1-56420-098-1*) New Readers Pr.

D'Alpuget, Blanche. White Eye. 1994. 254p. pap. 22.00 (*0-671-62005-3*, Simon & Schuster) Simon & Schuster.

Danvers, Dennis. Time & Time Again. 1994. 304p. 22.00 (*0-671-78800-0*, Simon & Schuster) Simon & Schuster.

Darcy, Emma. Dark Heritage. l.t. ed. 1995. 194p. 21.95 o.p. (*0-7838-1236-1*, Macmillan Reference USA) Gale Group.

—The Wedding. l.t. ed. 1996. (G. K. Hall Romance Ser.). 210p. 22.95 o.p. (*0-7838-1241-8*); 217 p. (*0-7451-4883-2*) Gale Group. (Macmillan Reference USA).

—The Wedding. 1992. (Harlequin Presents Ser.: No. 463). per. (*0-373-11463-X*, 1-11463-6, Harlequin Bks.) Harlequin Enterprises, Ltd.

Daugharty, Janice. Dark of the Moon. Howle, Jane, ed. 1994. 275p. 19.00 (*1-880909-17-0*) Baskerville Pubs., Inc.

—Dark of the Moon: A Novel. 1995. 288p. pap. 12.00 o.s.i (*0-06-097655-1*, Perennial) HarperTrade.

David, Lawrence. Need. 1996. 355p. mass mkt. 6.99 (*0-312-95922-2*, St. Martin's Paperbacks) St. Martin's Pr.

Davidson, Sara. Cowboy: A Love Story. l.t. ed. 1999. 26.95 (*1-56895-758-0*, Wheeler Publishing, Inc.) Gale Group.

—Cowboy: A Love Story. 288p. 2000. pap. 13.00 (*0-06-093135-3*, Perennial); 1999. 24.00 (*0-06-099582-3*, HarperCollins); 1999. 24.00 o.p. (*0-06-019326-3*, HarperCollins) HarperTrade.

Davies, Andrew. B. Monkey. 1998. 224p. (J). pap. 11.95 (*0-7868-8249-2*) Hyperion Pr.

Davies, June W. Storm Before Sunrise. 1993. 574p. 24.95 o.p. (*0-312-10552-5*) St. Martin's Pr.

Davies, Rhys. Ram with Red Horns. 1997. 180p. pap. 16.95 (*1-85411-165-5*) Seren Bks. GBR. *Dist:* Dufour Editions, Inc.

Davis, Claire. Winter Range. E-Book 23.00 (*0-312-27169-7*); 2001. 272p. pap. 13.00 (*0-312-28425-X*); 2000. 262p. 23.00 o.p. (*0-312-26140-3*) Picador.

Davis, Lydia. The End of the Story. 1995. 192p. 20.00 o.p. (*0-374-14831-7*) Farrar, Straus & Giroux.

De Botton, Alain. Kiss & Tell. 1997. 272p. pap. 13.00 (*0-312-15561-1*); 1996. 208p. 22.00 o.p. (*0-312-14282-X*) Picador.

—The Romantic Movement. 1996. 336p. pap. 14.00 (*0-312-14403-2*) Picador.

—The Romantic Movement: Sex, Shopping & the Novel. 1995. (Illus.). 326p. 23.00 o.p. (*0-312-13159-3*) Picador.

De Graaf, Anne. Where the Fire Burns. 1995. 17.04 (*0-606-18975-0*) Turtleback Bks.

—Where the Fire Burns: A Novel. 1997. (Hidden Harvest Ser.: Vol. 2). 352p. pap. 10.99 o.p. (*1-55661-619-8*) Bethany Hse. Pubs.

De La Fayette, Marie-Madeleine. La Princesse de Cleves. unabr. ed. (FRE.). pap. 7.95 (*2-87714-160-8*) Bookking International FRA. *Dist:* Distribooks, Inc.

—La Princesse de Cleves. 1958. (Folio Ser.: No. 778). pap. 9.95 (*2-07-036778-9*) Schoenhof's Foreign Bks., Inc.

—La Princesse de Cleves. audio Spoken Arts, Inc.

De Lafayette, Madame. The Princesse de Cleves. Mitfod, Nancy, tr. from FRE. 1978. (Penguin Classics Ser.). pap. 5.95 o.p. (*0-14-044337-1*) Viking Penguin.

—La Princesse de Cleves, Set. 1991. (FRE.). audio 38.95 Olivia & Hill Pr., The.

—The Princesse de Cleves: The Princesse de Montpensier, The Comtesse de Tende. Cave, Terence, ed. & tr. by. 1992. (Oxford World's Classics Ser.). 272p. pap. 8.95 o.p. (*0-19-282687-5*) Oxford Univ. Pr., Inc.

—The Princesse de Cleves: The Princesse de Montpensier; The Comtesse de Tende. 1999. (Oxford World's Classics Ser.). 288p. pap. 10.95 (*0-19-283726-5*) Oxford Univ. Pr., Inc.

De Lafayette, Madame, et al. The Princesse de Cleves. Buss, Robin, tr. & intro. by. 8th ed. 1992. (Classics Ser.). 192p. pap. 10.95 (*0-14-044587-0*, Penguin Classics) Viking Penguin.

DeJarnett, Don Patrick. I Cry But I Shed No Tears. 2000. 136p. pap. 17.95 (*1-56167-587-3*) American Literary Pr., Inc.

DeLillo, Don. The Body Artist. 128p. 2001. mass mkt. 7.99 (*0-7432-2280-6*); 2001. 22.00 (*0-7432-0395-X*); 2001. 22.00 (*0-7432-1564-8*); 2002. reprint ed. pap. 12.00 (*0-7432-0396-8*) Simon & Schuster. (Scribner).

—The Body Artist. l.t. ed. 2001. 160p. 32.50 o.p. (*0-7432-1221-5*) Thorpe, F. A. Pubs. GBR. *Dist:* Ulverscroft Large Print Bks., Ltd.

DeMille, Nelson. Spencerville. 1994. 464p. 23.95 o.p. (*0-446-51505-1*); 1995. 656p. reprint ed. mass mkt. 7.99 (*0-446-60245-0*) Warner Bks., Inc.

Desai, Anita. Journey to Ithaca. 1995. 320p. 23.00 o.s.i (*0-679-43900-5*) Knopf, Alfred A. Inc.

—Journey to Ithaca. 1996. 336p. pap. 15.00 o.s.i (*0-14-025818-3*) Penguin Group (USA) Inc.

Deval, Jacqueline. Reckless Appetites: A Culinary Romance. 1993. 288p. text 21.00 o.p. (*0-88001-322-2*) HarperCollins Pubs.

Dickey, Eric Jerome. Cheaters. 1999. 224p. 24.95 o.s.i (*0-525-94386-2*) Dutton/Plume.

—Cheaters. 2000. 448p. mass mkt. 7.50 (*0-451-19407-1*, Signet Bks.) NAL.

—Milk in My Coffee. 1998. 304p. 23.95 o.s.i (*0-525-94385-4*, Dutton Children's Bks.) Dutton/Plume.

—Milk in My Coffee. 1999. 384p. reprint ed. mass mkt. 7.50 (*0-451-19406-3*, Signet Bks.) NAL.

—Naughty or Nice. 2003. 176p. 17.95 (*0-525-94776-0*, Dutton) Dutton/Plume.

Dickinson, Peter. The Yellow Room Conspiracy. 1994. 272p. 18.95 o.s.i (*0-89296-556-8*) Mysterious Pr.

—The Yellow Room Conspiracy. 1995. 256p. mass mkt. 5.99 (*0-446-40373-3*) Warner Bks., Inc.

Dilke, Annabel. Present from the Past. 1994. 240p. 23.95 (*0-233-98800-9*) Andre Deutsch GBR. *Dist:* Trafalgar Square, Trans-Atlantic Pubns., Inc.

Doctorow, E. L. Loon Lake. 1988. 320p. mass mkt. 5.95 o.s.i (*0-449-21603-9*, Fawcett) Ballantine Bks.

—Loon Lake. 1981. 304p. pap. 3.50 o.s.i (*0-553-20027-5*) Bantam Bks.

—Loon Lake. 1996. 272p. reprint ed. pap. 14.00 (*0-452-27568-7*, Plume) Dutton/Plume.

—Loon Lake. 1992. pap. 11.00 o.s.i (*0-679-73625-5*, Vintage) Knopf Publishing Group.

—Loon Lake. 1980. 35.00 o.p. (*0-394-51176-X*) Random Hse., Inc.

Dolan, Charlotte L. Fallen Angel. l.t. ed. 1994. 302p. lib. bdg. 20.95 (*0-8161-5947-5*, Macmillan Reference USA) Gale Group.

Donnelly, Jane. No Place to Run. l.t. ed. 1994. 18.95 o.p. (*0-7927-2154-3*) BBC Audiobooks America.

—No Place to Run. 1988. pap. (*0-373-02906-3*, Harlequin Bks.) Harlequin Enterprises, Ltd.

Douglas, Kirk. Last Tango in Brooklyn. l.t. ed. 1994. 392p. lib. bdg. 24.95 (*0-8161-7465-2*, Macmillan Reference USA) Gale Group.

—Last Tango in Brooklyn. 352p. 1995. mass mkt. 6.50 o.s.i (*0-446-60201-9*); 1994. 30.00 (*0-446-51695-3*) Warner Bks., Inc.

Drabble, Margaret. The Millstone. 1984. 144p. pap. 6.95 o.p. (*0-452-25976-2*); 192p. pap. 9.00 o.p. (*0-452-26456-1*); pap. 5.95 o.p. (*0-452-25516-3*); (Illus.). 144p. pap. 7.95 o.p. (*0-452-26126-0*) Dutton/Plume. (Plume).

—The Millstone. 1998. (Harvest Book Ser.). 192p. pap. 12.00 (*0-15-600619-7*, Harvest Bks.) Harcourt Trade Pubs.

—The Waterfall. 1986. pap. 6.95 o.p. (*0-452-25825-1*); pap. 7.95 o.p. (*0-452-26017-5*); 30p. pap. 10.00 o.p. (*0-452-26192-9*) Dutton/Plume. (Plume).

—The Waterfall. l.t. ed. 1987. (Mainstream Ser.). 350p. reprint ed. 15.95 o.p. (*1-85089-138-9*) ISIS Large Print Bks. GBR. *Dist:* Transaction Pubs.

Dreiser, Theodore. An American Tragedy. Date not set. pap. text (*0-17-557044-2*) Addison-Wesley Longman, Inc.

—An American Tragedy. Date not set. 832p. 38.95 (*0-8488-2253-6*) Amereon, Ltd.

—An American Tragedy. 1978. 874 p. reprint ed. lib. bdg. 32.00 (*0-8376-0424-9*) Bentley Pubs.

—An American Tragedy. 1990. reprint ed. lib. bdg. 54.95 (*0-89966-709-0*) Buccaneer Bks., Inc.

—An American Tragedy. (Collected Works of Theodore Dreiser). 349p. reprint ed. 2001. (Illus.). pap. text 28.00 (*0-7426-5614-4*); 1998. lib. bdg. 98.00 (*1-58201-614-3*) Classic Bks.

—An American Tragedy. 1999. 17.95 (*0-8085-0951-9*) Econo-Clad Bks.

—An American Tragedy. 2003. (Library of America: Vol. 140). 972p. 40.00 (*1-931082-31-6*) Library of America, The.

—An American Tragedy. mass mkt. 0.25 o.p. (*0-451-00755-7*, Signet Bks.); 2000. 880p. mass mkt. 9.95 (*0-451-52770-4*, Signet Classics); 1964. mass mkt. 1.50 o.p. (*0-451-50619-7*, Signet Classics); 1964. mass mkt. 1.95 o.p. (*0-451-50938-2*, Signet Classics); 1964. mass mkt. 1.25 o.p. (*0-451-50365-1*, Signet Classics); 1964. mass mkt. 3.50 o.p. (*0-451-51563-3*, Signet Classics); 1964. mass mkt. 3.95 o.p. (*0-451-51696-6*, Signet Classics); 1964. mass mkt. 4.50 o.p. (*0-451-52043-2*, Signet Classics); 1964. mass mkt. 0.95 o.p. (*0-451-50235-3*, Signet Classics); 1964. 880p. mass mkt. 9.95 o.s.i (*0-451-52465-9*, Signet Classics); 1964. 832p. mass mkt. 4.95 o.p. (*0-451-52204-4*, Signet Classics); 1964. mass mkt. 2.50 o.p. (*0-451-51276-6*, Signet Classics) NAL.

—An American Tragedy. 2002. E-Book 5.24 (*0-7953-0792-6*) RosettaBooks.

—An American Tragedy. 1964. 16.00 (*0-606-00332-0*) Turtleback Bks.

—Jennie Gerhardt. West, James L. W., III, ed. & intro. by. 1994. (Twentieth Century Classics Ser.). 464p. pap. 14.00 o.s.i (*0-14-018710-3*, Penguin Classics) Viking Penguin.

Drury, Tom. The End of Vandalism. 1994. 321p. 21.95 o.p. (*0-395-62151-8*) Houghton Mifflin Co.

—The End of Vandalism: A Novel. 1995. 336p. pap. 12.95 o.s.i (*0-449-90982-4*, Fawcett) Ballantine Bks.

Dubus, Andre. Dancing after Hours: Stories. 1997. 256p. pap. 12.00 (*0-679-75114-9*, Vintage) Knopf Publishing Group.

—Dancing after Hours: Stories. 1996. 240p. 23.00 o.s.i (*0-679-43107-1*) Knopf, Alfred A. Inc.

—Voices from the Moon: A Novel. 1985. 128p. 6.95 o.s.i (*0-517-55846-7*, Crown) Crown Publishing Group.

—Voices from the Moon: A Novel. 1984. 160p. 12.95 (*0-87923-532-2*) Godine, David R. Pub.

Duhrssen, Alfred. Difficult Women: A Novel. 2000. 281p. 15.95 (*1-886157-25-1*, Wallaroo Bks.) BkMk Pr. of the Univ. of Missouri-Kansas City.

Dunmore, Helen. Mourning Ruby. 2004. 23.95 (*0-399-15148-6*) Putnam Publishing Group, The.

Durrell, Lawrence. Clea. unabr. ed. 1994. (Alexandria Quartet Ser.: Vol. IV). audio 64.00 (*0-7366-2808-8*, 3522) Books on Tape, Inc.

—Clea. 1961. (Alexandria Quartet Ser.). pap. 6.25 o.p. (*0-525-47083-2*, Plume) Dutton/Plume.

—Clea. abr. ed. (Alexandria Quartet Ser.: Vol. IV). 1996. audio 17.98 (*962-634-566-7*, NA306614); 1995. audio compact disk 19.98 (*962-634-066-5*, NA306612) Naxos of America, Inc. (Naxos AudioBooks).

—Clea. 2002. (SPA.). 344p. mass mkt. 9.95 (*1-4000-0032-7*) Random Hse., Inc.

—Clea, Vol. 4. 1981. 288p. mass mkt. 3.95 o.s.i (*0-671-45103-0*, Pocket) Simon & Schuster.

—Clea. l.t. ed. 2000. (Perennial Bestsellers Ser.). 381p. 25.95 (*0-7838-8975-5*) Thorndike Pr.

—Clea. 1991. (Alexandria Quartet Ser.). 287p. reprint ed. 14.00 (*0-14-015322-5*) Viking Penguin.

Eagle, Kathleen. The Last True Cowboy. 1999. 400p. mass mkt. 6.50 (*0-380-78492-0*); 1998. 211p. 20.00 (*0-380-97522-X*) Morrow/Avon. (Avon Bks.).

Eisner, William. The Sevigne Letters. Putnam, Jeff, ed. 1994. 201p. 18.00 (*1-880909-27-8*) Baskerville Pubs., Inc.

Eliot, George. Adam Bede. 1976. (Airmont Classics Ser.). mass mkt. 1.95 o.p. (*0-8049-0103-1*, CL 103) Airmont Publishing Co., Inc.

—Adam Bede. 1976. 29.95 (*0-8488-0481-3*) Amereon, Ltd.

—Adam Bede. 2000. Vol. 2. per. (*1-891355-21-X*); Vol.1. per. 14.00 (*1-891355-20-1*) Blue Unicorn Editions.

—Adam Bede. reprint ed. 1992. lib. bdg. 27.95 (*0-89968-276-6*, Lightyear Pr.); 1977. 466p. lib. bdg. 27.95 o.s.i (*0-89966-265-X*) Buccaneer Bks., Inc.

—Adam Bede. reprint ed. Pt. 1. 2001. (Writings of George Eliot Ser.: Vol. 3). 420p. pap. text 28.00 (*0-7426-5070-7*); Pt. 1. 1999. (Writings of George Eliot Ser.: Vol. 3). 420p. lib. bdg. 88.00 (*1-58201-070-6*); Pt. 2. 2001. 364p. pap. text 28.00 (*0-7426-5071-5*); Pt. 2. 1999. (Writings of George Eliot Ser.: Vol. 4). 364p. lib. bdg. 88.00 (*1-58201-071-4*) Classic Bks.

—Adam Bede. E-Book 2.49 (*1-58744-086-5*) Electric Umbrella Publishing.

—Adam Bede. 1973. (Collins Classics Ser.). 478p. (*0-00-424521-0*) HarperSanFrancisco.

—Adam Bede. Paterson, John, ed. 1968. pap. 13.16 o.p. (*0-395-05204-1*, Riverside Editions) Houghton Mifflin Co.

—Adam Bede, 3 vols. l.t. ed. 2000. 1891p. 138.36 (*0-7583-0005-0*); 1538p. 120.93 (*0-7583-0004-2*); 1201p. 91.44 (*0-7583-0003-4*); 938p. 78.54 (*0-7583-0002-6*); 2326p. 174.41 (*0-7583-0006-9*); 2698p. 193.58 (*0-7583-0007-7*); 548p. 46.02 (*0-7583-0000-X*); 685p. 53.78 (*0-7583-0001-8*); 1891p. pap. 119.19 (*0-7583-0013-1*); 2326p. pap. 143.57 (*0-7583-0014-X*); 2698p. pap. 159.27 (*0-7583-0015-8*); 1538p. pap. 102.93 (*0-7583-0012-3*); 685p. pap. 47.78 (*0-7583-0009-3*); 548p. pap. 40.02 (*0-7583-0008-5*); 1201p. pap. 79.44 (*0-7583-0011-5*); 938p. pap. 66.54 (*0-7583-0010-7*) Huge Print Pr.

—Adam Bede. 2001. 516p. 29.99 (*1-58827-312-1*); per. 24.99 (*1-58827-313-X*) IndyPublish.com.

—Adam Bede. 1999. (Cloth Bound Pocket Ser.). 7.95 (*3-8290-3005-3*, 521122) Konemann.

—Adam Bede. E-Book 1.95 (*1-57799-953-3*) Logos Research Systems, Inc.

—Adam Bede. 1992. (Everyman's Library: Vol. 59 0). 20.00 (*0-679-40991-2*) McKay, David Co., Inc.

—Adam Bede. 1969. mass mkt. 0.75 o.p. (*0-451-50076-8*, Signet Classics); 1969. mass mkt. 0.95 o.p. (*0-451-50483-6*, Signet Classics); 1961. mass mkt. 1.75 o.p. (*0-451-51015-1*, Signet Classics); 1961. mass mkt. 2.95 o.p. (*0-451-51578-1*, Signet Classics); 1961. mass mkt. 4.50 o.p. (*0-451-52110-2*); 1961. mass mkt. 3.50 o.p. (*0-451-51848-9*); 1961. mass mkt. 4.95 o.p. (*0-451-52256-7*, Signet Classics); 1961. mass mkt. 1.95 o.p. (*0-451-51342-8*, Signet Classics); 1961. mass mkt. 1.50 o.p. (*0-451-50790-8*, Signet Classics); 1961. 512p. mass mkt. 6.95 (*0-451-52527-2*, Signet Classics) NAL.

—Adam Bede. 2001. (Twelve-Point Ser.). lib. bdg. 27.00 (*1-58287-138-8*) North Bks.

—Adam Bede. Martin, Carol A., ed. 2001. (Clarendon Edition of the Novels of George Eliot Ser.). (Illus.). 688p. text 165.00 (*0-19-812595-X*) Oxford Univ. Pr., Inc.

—Adam Bede. (Oxford World's Classics Ser.). 1998. 656p. pap. 8.95 (*0-19-283495-9*); 1996. 646p. (C). pap. 5.95 o.p. (*0-19-283166-6*) Oxford Univ. Pr., Inc.

—Adam Bede. 2002. (Modern Library Classics). 624p. pap. 8.95 (*0-375-75901-8*, Modern Library) Random House Adult Trade Publishing Group.

—Adam Bede. 2001. 549p. E-Book 4.00 (*1-929670-68-0*) Renaissance E Bks.

—Adam Bede. 1971. pap. 0.95 o.s.i (*0-671-47190-2*, Washington Square Pr.) Simon & Schuster.

—Adam Bede. (Ebook Classic Ser.). E-Book 5.00 (*0-7410-1117-4*) SoftBook Pr.

—Adam Bede. 1985. 15.00 (*0-606-17254-8*) Turtleback Bks.

—Adam Bede. 1994. 528p. pap. 5.50 o.p. (*0-460-87461-6*, Everyman's Classic Library in Paperback) Tuttle Publishing.

—Adam Bede. Gill, Stephen, ed. 1980. (Classics Ser.). 608p. 8.95 (*0-14-043121-7*, Penguin Classics) Viking Penguin.

—Adam Bede. 1972. 4.95 o.p. (*0-460-01027-1*) Viking Penguin.

—Adam Bede. 1999. E-Book 5.99 (*0-8220-7250-5*, Cliff Notes) Wiley, John & Sons, Inc.

—Felix Holt, the Radical. unabr. ed. 1998. audio 71.95 (*1-55685-563-X*) Audio Bk. Contractors, Inc.

—Felix Holt, the Radical. Baker, William & Womack, Kenneth, eds. 2000. (Literary Texts Ser.). (Illus.). 700p. pap. (*1-55111-228-0*) Broadview Pr.

—Felix Holt, the Radical. (Writings of George Eliot Ser.: Vol. 10). 400p. reprint ed. Pt. 1. 2001. pap. text 28.00 (*0-7426-5077-4*); Pt. 1. 1999. lib. bdg. 88.00 (*1-58201-077-3*); Pt. 2. 2001. pap. text 28.00 (*0-7426-5078-2*); Pt. 2. 1999. lib. bdg. 88.00 (*1-58201-078-1*) Classic Bks.

—Felix Holt, the Radical. l.t. ed. 1991. (Large Print Bks.). 537p. 24.95 (*1-85089-579-1*) ISIS Large Print Bks. GBR. *Dist:* Transaction Pubs., Ulverscroft Large Print Canada, Ltd.

—Felix Holt, the Radical. 1970. (Norton Library, N517). xxi, 487 p. (J). (*0-393-00517-8*) Norton, W. W. & Co., Inc.

—Felix Holt, the Radical. 1998. (Oxford World's Classics Ser.). 432p. pap. 12.95 (*0-19-283821-0*) Oxford Univ. Pr., Inc.

—Felix Holt, the Radical. Thompson, Fred C., ed. 1988. (Oxford World's Classics Ser.). 430p. pap. 7.95 o.p. (*0-19-281781-7*) Oxford Univ. Pr., Inc.

—Felix Holt, the Radical. Thomson, Fred C., ed. 1981. (Clarendon Edition of the Novels of George Eliot Ser.). (Illus.). 464p. text 137.00 (*0-19-812561-5*) Oxford Univ. Pr., Inc.

—Felix Holt, the Radical. 1997. (Everyman Paperback Classics Ser.). 320p. pap. 6.95 o.p. (*0-460-87687-2*, Everyman's Classic Library in Paperback) Tuttle Publishing.

—Felix Holt, the Radical. Coveney, Peter, ed. 1973. (English Library). 688p. pap. 6.95 o.p. (*0-14-043084-9*, Penguin Classics) Viking Penguin.

—Felix Holt, the Radical. Mugglestone, Lynda, ed. & intro. by. 140th ed. 1995. (Classics Ser.). 592p. pap. 14.00 (*0-14-043435-6*, Penguin Classics) Viking Penguin.

Elkin, Stanley. Mrs. Ted Bliss. 2002. (American Literature Ser.). 294p. reprint ed. pap. 14.95 (*1-56478-322-7*) Dalkey Archive Pr.

—Mrs. Ted Bliss. l.t. ed. 1996. pap. 22.95 o.p. (*1-56895-314-3*, Wheeler Publishing, Inc.) Gale Group.

—Mrs. Ted Bliss. 1995. 304p. 22.95 (*0-7868-6104-5*) Hyperion Pr.

—Mrs. Ted Bliss. 1996. pap. 12.00 (*0-380-72896-6*, Avon Bks.) Morrow/Avon.

—Mrs. Ted Bliss. unabr. ed. 1997. audio 78.00 (*0-7887-1073-7*, 95086E7) Recorded Bks., LLC.

Ellis, Alice Thomas. The Summer House: A Trilogy. 2001. (Common Reader Edition Ser.). 360p. reprint ed. pap. 19.95 (*1-58579-028-1*) Akadine Pr., The.

—The Summer House: A Trilogy. 1993. 352p. pap. 11.95 o.p. (*0-14-023876-X*, Penguin Bks.) Penguin Group (USA) Inc.

Ellis, Trey. Home Repairs: A Novel. 1993. 256p. 21.00 o.p. (*0-671-76924-3*, Simon & Schuster) Simon & Schuster.

Emecheta, Buchi. Kehinde. 1994. (African Writers Ser.). 160p. pap. 13.95 (*0-435-90985-1*, 90985) Heinemann.

Erdrich, Louise. The Bingo Palace. l.t. ed. 1994. 25.95 o.p. (*1-56895-073-X*, Wheeler Publishing, Inc.) Gale Group.

—The Bingo Palace. 288p. 1995. pap. 78.00 o.p. (*0-06-092614-7*); 1994. 207.00 o.p. (*0-06-017102-2*) HarperCollins Pubs.

—The Bingo Palace. 288p. 1995. pap. 13.00 (*0-06-092585-X*, Perennial); 1994. 23.00 o.p. (*0-06-017080-8*) HarperTrade.

Ernaux, Annie. Simple Passion. 1994. 80p. reprint ed. pap. 8.50 o.s.i (*0-345-38254-4*) Ballantine Bks.

—Simple Passion. 1993. 80p. 15.00 o.p. (*1-56858-003-7*) Four Walls Eight Windows.

—Simple Passion. Leslie, Tanya, tr. from FRE. 1993. 72p. 14.95 (*1-888363-26-6*) Seven Stories Pr.

—A Simple Passion. Leslie, Tanya, tr. from FRE. 2003. 72p. reprint ed. pap. 8.95 (*1-58322-574-9*) Seven Stories Pr.

Evans, Nicholas. The Horse Whisperer. 1995. (Illus.). 416p. 24.95 (*0-385-31523-6*, Delacorte Pr.) Dell Publishing.

—The Horse Whisperer. 1996. 7.50 (*0-440-29545-9*) Doubleday Publishing.

—The Horse Whisperer. l.t. ed. 1995. (Basic Ser.). 618p. 27.95 o.p. (*0-7862-0498-2*) Thorndike Pr.

—The Horse Whisperer. 1996. 14.04 (*0-606-10213-2*) Turtleback Bks.

Fante, John. Ask the Dust. 1996. reprint ed. 165p. 25.00 (*0-87685-444-7*); 168p. pap. 15.00 (*0-87685-443-9*) HarperCollins Pubs.

Faschinger, Lilian. Magdalena the Sinner: A Novel. 1997. 320p. 24.00 o.s.i (*0-06-018653-4*) HarperCollins Pubs.

Fast, Howard. Redemption. 1999. 288p. 24.00 o.s.i (*0-15-100455-2*) Harcourt Trade Pubs.

Fauset, Jessie Redmon. The Chinaberry Tree: A Novel of American Life. reprint ed. 29.50 (*0-404-00256-0*) AMS Pr., Inc.

—The Chinaberry Tree: A Novel of American Life. 36.95 (*0-405-18503-0*) Ayer Co. Pubs., Inc.

—The Chinaberry Tree: A Novel of American Life. 1995. (African American Women Writers, 1910-1940 Ser.). 341p. 25.00 o.s.i (*0-8161-1627-X*, Macmillan Reference USA) Gale Group.

—The Chinaberry Tree: A Novel of American Life. 1969. 341p. reprint ed. 60.00 o.s.i (*0-8371-1919-7*, FAC&) Greenwood Publishing Group, Inc.

Faust, Ron. When She Was Bad. 1994. 320p. 22.95 o.p. (*0-312-85164-2*, Forge Bks.) Doherty, Tom Assocs., LLC.

Feather, Jane. Valentine. 1995. 448p. mass mkt. 6.50 (*0-553-56470-6*) Bantam Bks.

—Valentine. (Romance Ser.). 1996. lib. bdg. 24.95 (*0-7862-0860-0*, Five Star); 1995. 24.95 (*1-56895-162-0*, Wheeler Publishing, Inc.) Gale Group.

—Virtue. 1993. 448p. mass mkt. 6.50 (*0-553-56054-9*) Bantam Bks.

—Virtue. l.t. ed. 1993. 549p. lib. bdg. 21.95 (*0-8161-5871-1*, Macmillan Reference USA) Gale Group.

Feldman, Ellen. Lucy. 2004. 304p. pap. 13.95 (*0-393-32510-5*) Norton, W. W. & Co., Inc.

Fields, Jennie. Crossing Brooklyn Ferry: A Novel. 2002. 384p. pap. 12.95 (*0-06-009943-7*, Perennial) HarperTrade.

—Crossing Brooklyn Ferry: A Novel. 1998. mass mkt. 6.99 (*0-380-73168-1*, Avon Bks.); 1997. 288p. 23.00 (*0-688-14589-2*, Morrow, William & Co.) Morrow/Avon.

—Crossing Brooklyn Ferry: A Novel. l.t. ed. 1998. (Charnwood Large Print Ser.). 512p. 29.99 o.p. (*0-7089-9004-5*, Ulverscroft) Thorpe, F. A. Pubs. GBR. *Dist:* Ulverscroft Large Print Bks., Ltd., Ulverscroft Large Print Canada, Ltd.

—Lily Beach. 1993. 416p. 21.00 o.p. (*0-689-12176-8*, Scribner) Simon & Schuster.

—Lily Beach. 1994. 291p. pap. 15.99 (*0-446-67038-3*) Warner Bks., Inc.

Filipacchi, Amanda. Vapor. 1999. 320p. 22.95 (*0-7867-0617-1*, Carroll & Graf Pubs.) Avalon Publishing Group.

—Vapor: A Novel. 2003. 320p. pap. 14.00 (*0-7867-1129-9*, Carroll & Graf Pubs.) Avalon Publishing Group.

Fisher, Vardis. Mountain Man. 1976. reprint ed. lib. bdg. 24.95 (*0-89190-832-3*, Rivercity Pr.) Amereon, Ltd.

—Mountain Man. 1993. reprint ed. lib. bdg. 27.95 (*1-56849-196-4*) Buccaneer Bks., Inc.

—Mountain Man. 1990. 320p. (YA). (gr. 10 up). mass mkt. 4.95 (*0-671-73907-7*, Pocket) Simon & Schuster.

—Mountain Man. 1977. 384p. 12.95 o.p. (*0-918522-52-8*) Univ. of Idaho Pr.

Fitzgerald, F. Scott. F. Scott Fitzgerald: The Love of The Last Tycoon. Bruccoli, Matthew J., ed. 1993. (Works of F. Scott Fitzgerald). (Illus.). 448p. 45.00 (*0-521-40231-X*) Cambridge Univ. Pr.

—The Great Gatsby. (Scribner Classics). 1996. 176p. 25.00 (*0-684-83042-6*, Scribner); 1992. pap. 6.00 o.s.i (*0-02-019882-5*, Scribner Paper Fiction) Simon & Schuster.

—The Great Gatsby. l.t. ed. 1995. 203p. 21.95 (*0-7838-1222-1*) Thorndike Pr.

—The Great Gatsby. l.t. ed. 1999. 240p. 24.95 (*1-56000-490-8*) Transaction Pubs.

—The Love of the Last Tycoon. 1995. 17.05 (*0-606-20777-5*) Turtleback Bks.

Fletcher, Stephanie D. E-Mail: A Love Story. 1996. 256p. 21.95 o.p. (*1-55611-477-X*) Fine, Donald I. Bks.

Fleutiaux, Pierrette. We Are Eternal: A Novel. Leggett, Jeremy, tr. 1994. ix, 565p. 24.95 o.p. (*0-316-28617-6*) Little Brown & Co.

Flusfeder, D. L. Man Kills Woman. 1993. 358p. 21.00 o.p. (*0-374-20162-5*) Farrar, Straus & Giroux.

Follett, Ken. A Place Called Freedom. 1998. pap. 6.99 (*0-449-45861-X*, Fawcett); 1996. 464p. mass mkt. 7.99 (*0-449-22515-1*, Fawcett); 1996. mass mkt. (*0-449-22517-8*, Ballantine Bks.) Ballantine Bks.

—A Place Called Freedom. l.t. ed. 1995. 672p. 25.00 o.p. (*0-7838-1590-5*, Macmillan Reference USA) Gale Group.

—A Place Called Freedom. l.t. ed. 1995. 672p. 25.00 o.p. (*0-679-76509-3*) Random Hse. Large Print.

Ford, Elaine. Monkey Bay. 256p. 1990. pap. 7.95 o.p. (*0-14-012057-2*, Penguin Bks.); 1989. 17.95 o.p. (*0-670-82752-5*) Viking Penguin.

Ford, Ford Madox. Ladies Whose Bright Eyes: A Romance. 1987. 363p. pap. 9.50 o.p. (*0-88001-088-6*) HarperCollins Pubs.

Ford, Richard. A Multitude of Sins: Stories. 304p. 2003. pap. 13.00 (*0-375-72656-X*); 2002. 25.00 (*0-375-41212-3*) Knopf, Alfred A. Inc.

Forester, C. S. The African Queen. 1977. 136p. reprint ed. lib. bdg. 21.95 (*0-89244-065-1*, Queens Hse., Inc.) Amereon, Ltd.

—The African Queen. reprint ed. 1992. 316p. lib. bdg. 21.95 o.p. (*0-89966-903-4*); 1990. lib. bdg. 18.95 o.p. (*0-89968-508-0*) Buccaneer Bks., Inc.

—The African Queen. 1984. 256p. reprint ed. pap. 13.95 (*0-316-28910-8*, Back Bay) Little Brown & Co.

—The African Queen. 1940. 3.95 o.s.i (*0-394-60102-5*) Random Hse., Inc.

—The African Queen. l.t. ed. 1994. 260p. lib. bdg. 21.95 (*0-8161-7459-8*) Thorndike Pr.

Forster, E. M. Howard's End. Date not set. lib. bdg. 27.95 (*0-8488-1664-1*) Amereon, Ltd.

—Howard's End. 1985. (Bantam Classics Ser.). 288p. mass mkt. 4.99 (*0-553-21208-7*) Bantam Bks.

—Howard's End. 2002. (Thrift Editions Ser.). (Illus.). 256p. pap. 3.00 (*0-486-42454-5*) Dover Pubns., Inc.

—Howard's End. Stallybrass, Oliver, ed. 1978. (Abinger Edition of E. M. Forster Ser.). 276p. text 29.50 o.p. (*0-8419-5806-8*) Holmes & Meier Pubs., Inc.

—Howard's End. 2002. 344p. 96.99 (*1-4043-0824-5*); per. 91.99 (*1-4043-0825-3*) IndyPublish.com.

—Howard's End. 1954. pap. 4.95 o.p. (*0-394-70007-4*, Vintage) Knopf Publishing Group.

—Howard's End. (Signet Classics). 1998. 288p. mass mkt. 4.95 o.s.i (*0-451-52717-8*, Signet Classics); 1992. 288p. mass mkt. 4.99 o.s.i (*0-451-17429-1*, Signet Bks.); 1986. 464p. mass mkt. 6.95 (*0-451-52141-2*, Signet Classics) NAL.

—Howard's End. 1999. (Twelve-Point Ser.). 330p. lib. bdg. 25.00 (*1-58287-100-0*) North Bks.

—Howard's End. 2001. E-Book 4.95 (*0-679-64145-9*, Modern Library) Random House Adult Trade Publishing Group.

—Howard's End. 1991. (Everyman's Library: Vol. 25). 400p. 19.00 (*0-679-40668-9*) Random Hse., Inc.

—Howard's End. 1997. pap. text 17.95 o.p. (*0-312-15464-X*) St. Martin's Pr.

—Howard's End. 2000. (Classics Ser.). (Illus.). 352p. 11.00 (*0-14-118213-X*, Penguin Classics) Viking Penguin.

—Howards End. 2003. (Barnes & Noble Classics Ser.). 368p. pap. 6.95 (*1-59308-022-0*) Fine Communications.

—Howards End. 1989. (Vintage International Ser.). 368p. pap. 10.00 (0-679-72255-6, Vintage) Knopf Publishing Group.
—Howards End. annuals 1999. (Modern Library Ser.). 368p. pap. 9.95 (0-375-75376-1, Modern Library) Random House Adult Trade Publishing Group.
—Howard's End. 1981. 391p. reprint ed. lib. bdg. 25.95 (0-89966-301-X) Buccaneer Bks., Inc.
—Howard's End. reprint ed. lib. bdg. 98.00 (0-7426-3108-7); 2001. pap. text 28.00 (0-7426-8108-4) Classic Bks.
—Howard's End. l.t. ed. 1993. (General Ser.). 474p. 22.95 o.p. (0-8161-5652-2, Macmillan Reference USA) Gale Group.
—Howard's End. l.t. ed. 1999. 457p. lib. bdg. 26.00 (0-939495-74-0) North Bks.
—Howard's End: Case Studies. 1996. (Case Studies in Contemporary Criticism). 512p. 49.95 (0-312-16292-8) Palgrave Macmillan.
—Howard's End & Other Stories. 1997. (Giant Courage Classics Ser.). 444p. text 8.98 o.p. (0-7624-0176-1, Courage Bks.) Running Pr. Bk. Pubs.
Foss, Rich. Jonas & Sally: A Novel. 332p. 2000. pap. 11.95 (1-56148-305-2); 1994. 19.95 (1-56148-128-9) Good Bks.
Fowles, John. The French Lieutenant's Woman. 1994. reprint ed. lib. bdg. 32.95 (1-56849-280-4) Buccaneer Bks., Inc.
—The French Lieutenant's Woman. 1998. pap. 13.95 (0-316-18989-8, Back Bay); 1969. 467p. 29.95 o.p. (0-316-29099-8); Vol. 1. 1998. 480p. pap. 14.95 (0-316-29116-1) Little Brown & Co.
—The French Lieutenant's Woman. 1981. mass mkt. 3.50 o.p. (0-451-11095-1, Signet Bks.); 1981. mass mkt. 3.95 o.p. (0-451-13598-9, Signet Bks.); 1981. 368p. mass mkt. 6.99 o.s.i (0-451-16375-3); 1971. mass mkt. 1.50 o.p. (0-451-04479-7, Signet Bks.); 1970. mass mkt. 2.50 o.p. (0-451-08535-3, Signet Bks.); 1970. mass mkt. 1.75 o.p. (0-451-06484-4, Signet Bks.); 1970. mass mkt. 2.25 o.p. (0-451-08066-1, Signet Bks.); 1970. mass mkt. 2.95 o.p. (0-451-09003-9, Signet Bks.) NAL.
Fremlin, Celia. Possession. 1985. 158p. reprint ed. pap. 7.95 (0-89733-169-9) Academy Chicago Pubs., Ltd.
French, Marilyn. The Bleeding Heart. 1980. 12.95 o.p. (0-671-44784-X) Summit Bks.
French, Nicci. Killing Me Softly: A Novel of Obsession. 1999. (0-07-862220-4) McGraw-Hill Cos., The.
—Killing Me Softly: A Novel of Obsession. 1999. 320p. 24.00 (0-89296-697-1) Mysterious Pr.
—Killing Me Softly: A Novel of Obsession. l.t. ed. 1999. (Basic Ser.). 488p. 28.95 (0-7862-2220-4) Thorndike Pr.
—Killing Me Softly: A Novel of Obsession. movie tie-in ed. 2000. 400p. reprint ed. mass mkt. 7.50 (0-446-60838-6) Warner Bks., Inc.
Friedmann, Patty. Eleanor Rushing: A Novel. 288p. 2000. pap. text 14.00 (1-58243-077-2); 1999. text 23.00 o.p. (1-58243-003-9) Basic Bks. (Counterpoint Pr.).
A Fulfilling & Meaningful Sexual Endeavor: The Total Pillage of Eddie Smock. 2000. (Illus.). 160p. mass mkt. 9.95 (0-9678222-0-3) Mooney, Dave.
Futterman, Enid. Bittersweet Journey: A Modestly Erotic Novel of Love, Longing & Chocolate. 1998. (Illus.). 96p. 22.95 o.p. (0-670-87694-1) Viking Penguin.
Gaddis, Peggy. Second Chance at Love. l.t. ed. 1993. 18.95 o.p. (0-7927-1791-0); pap. 17.95 o.p. (0-7927-1790-2) BBC Audiobooks America.
Garcia, Lionel G. To a Widow with Children. 1994. 238p. 19.95 (1-55885-069-4) Arte Publico Pr.
Garcia Ponce, Juan. The House on the Beach: A Novel. Vargas, Margarita & Bruce-Novoa, Juan, trs. from SPA. 1994. (Texas Pan American Ser.). (Illus.). 224p. (Orig.). (C). 30.00 o.p. (0-292-72763-1); pap. 15.95 o.p. (0-292-72764-X) Univ. of Texas Pr.
Garcia Márquez, Gabriel. Of Love & Other Demons. 1996. (0-14-771138-X) Penguin Group (USA) Inc.
—Of Love & Other Demons. Grossman, Edith, tr. 1996. (Penguin Great Books of the 20th Century Ser.). 160p. 13.00 (0-14-025636-9) Viking Penguin.
Gardner, Lynn. Emeralds & Espionage. 1995. 252p. pap. 10.95 (1-55503-771-2, 01111825) Covenant Communications, Inc.
Garlock, Dorothy. Almost Eden. l.t. ed. 1996. 24.95 o.p. (0-7838-1638-3, Macmillan Reference USA) Gale Group.
—Almost Eden. 1995. 336p. reprint ed. mass mkt. 6.99 (0-446-36372-3) Warner Bks., Inc.
—The Listening Sky. l.t. ed. 1996. 25.95 o.p. (1-56895-317-8, Wheeler Publishing, Inc.) Gale Group.
—Tenderness. l.t. ed. 1993. 434p. lib. bdg. 20.95 o.p. (0-8161-5851-7, Macmillan Reference USA) Gale Group.
—Tenderness. 384p. 1998. mass mkt. 3.99 (0-446-60685-5); 1993. mass mkt. 6.99 (0-446-36370-7) Warner Bks., Inc.
—Wild Sweet Wilderness. 1989. 394p. mass mkt. 5.99 (0-445-20678-0) Warner Bks., Inc.
Garwood, Julie. The Clayborne Brides: One Pink Rose, One White Rose, One Red Rose. 1998. (Clayborne Brides Ser.). 464p. pap. 7.99 (0-671-02177-X, Pocket) Simon & Schuster.
—The Clayborne Brides: The Rose Trilogy. l.t. ed. 1998. (Large Print Bks.). 26.95 o.p. (1-56895-515-4, Wheeler Publishing, Inc.) Gale Group.
—The Lion's Lady. l.t. ed. 1994. 498p. pap. 17.95 (0-8161-5388-4); lib. bdg. 23.95 o.p. (0-8161-5387-6) Gale Group. (Macmillan Reference USA).
—The Lion's Lady. Marrow, Linda, ed. 1991. 384p. mass mkt. 7.99 (0-671-73783-X, Pocket) Simon & Schuster.
—The Lion's Lady. 1990. mass mkt. 4.95 (0-671-72699-4, Pocket) Simon & Schuster.
Gaskell, Elizabeth. Sylvia's Lovers, 3. reprint ed. lib. bdg. 294.00 (0-7426-2368-8); 2001. pap. text 84.00 (0-7426-7368-5) Classic Bks.
—Sylvia's Lovers. 1964. 15.50 o.p. (0-460-00524-3, Dutton) Dutton/Plume.
—Sylvia's Lovers. 2001. (Twelve-Point Ser.). 450p. lib. bdg. 25.00 (1-58287-167-1); 681p. lib. bdg. 28.00 (1-58287-650-9) North Bks.
—Sylvia's Lovers. (Oxford World's Classics Ser.). 560p. 2000. pap. 11.95 (0-19-283731-1); 1982. pap. 9.95 o.p. (0-19-281571-7) Oxford Univ. Pr., Inc.
—Sylvia's Lovers. Handley, Graham & Henry, Nancy, eds. 1989. (Everyman Paperback Classics Ser.). 592p. pap. 8.95 (0-460-87783-6, Everyman's Classic Library in Paperback) Tuttle Publishing.
—Sylvia's Lovers. Foster, Shirley, ed. & intro. by. 1997. (Penguin Classics Ser.). 528p. pap. 11.95 o.p. (0-14-043422-4, Penguin Classics) Viking Penguin.
Gault, Rebecca. Into the Blue. l.t. ed. 2001. (Romance Ser.). 272p. 25.95 (0-7862-2929-2, Five Star) Gale Group.
Gear, W. Michael. People of the Sea, Vol. 1. 1958. 425p. 22.95 o.p. (0-312-93122-0, Tor Bks.) Doherty, Tom Assocs., LLC.
Gee, Maggie. Christopher & Alexandra. 1992. 19.95 o.p. (0-395-60484-2) Houghton Mifflin Co.
George, Nelson. Show & Tell: A Novel. 2001. 224p. pap. 12.00 (0-7432-0443-3); E-Book 9.99 (0-7432-1225-8) Simon & Schuster. (Touchstone).
—Urban Romance. 1998. mass mkt. 5.99 (0-345-42685-1) Ballantine Bks.
—Urban Romance. 1994. 286p. reprint ed. pap. 12.98 (1-879360-36-5) Noble Pr., Inc., The.
—Urban Romance: A Novel of New York in the '80s. 1994. 288p. 24.95 o.p. (0-399-13865-X, G. P. Putnam's Sons) Penguin Group (USA) Inc.
Gerard, Robert V. Lady from Atlantis. 1995. 256p. pap. 12.95 (1-880666-21-9) Oughten Hse. Foundation, Inc.
Gifford, Barry. Wild at Heart. 1990. 172p. 15.95 o.p. (0-8021-1181-5) Grove/Atlantic, Inc.
—Wild at Heart. 1990. pap. 8.95 o.s.i (0-679-73439-2, Vintage) Knopf Publishing Group.
—The Wild Life of Sailor & Lula. 1996. 320p. reprint ed. pap. 13.00 (0-8021-3454-8, Grove Pr.) Grove/Atlantic, Inc.
—The Wild Life of Sailor & Lula. pap. 17.95 (0-86241-804-6) Payback Pr. GBR. *Dist:* AK Pr. Distribution.
Gilchrist, Ellen. Sarah Conley: A Novel. 1997. 272p. (gr. 8). 23.95 o.p. (0-316-31477-3) Little Brown & Co.
—Starcarbon: A Meditation on Love. 1994. 306p. 22.95 o.p. (0-316-31327-0) Little Brown & Co.
Gill, Elizabeth. The Road to Berry Edge. l.t. ed. 1997. (Romance Ser.). 380p. lib. bdg. 25.95 (0-7838-8302-1) Thorndike Pr.
Gillmore, Inez H. Angel Island. Reginald, R. & Melville, Douglas, eds. 1978. (Lost Race & Adult Fantasy Ser.). (Illus.). reprint ed. lib. bdg. 36.95 (0-405-10979-2) Ayer Co. Pubs., Inc.
—Angel Island. 1988. 288p. pap. 8.95 o.p. (0-452-26200-3, Plume) Dutton/Plume.
Glasgow, Ellen. The Sheltered Life. 24.95 (0-88411-646-8) Amereon, Ltd.
—The Sheltered Life. 1985. 408p. reprint ed. pap. 23.00 (0-15-681690-3, Harvest Bks.) Harcourt Trade Pubs.
—The Sheltered Life. 1994. 352p. (C). pap. 14.95 (0-8139-1514-7) Univ. Pr. of Virginia.
Godwin, Gail. The Good Husband. 1995. 496p. pap. 13.95 (0-345-39645-6) Ballantine Bks.
—The Good Husband. l.t. ed. 1994. (Large Print Bks.). 620p. pap. 24.95 (1-56895-086-1, Wheeler Publishing, Inc.) Gale Group.
—The Odd Woman. 1995. 436p. pap. 19.00 (0-345-38991-3) Ballantine Bks.
—The Odd Woman. 1976. 1.95 o.p. (0-425-03167-5) Berkley Publishing Group.
—The Odd Woman. 1985. (Contemporary American Fiction Ser.). 432p. pap. 8.95 o.p. (0-14-008221-2, Penguin Bks.) Viking Penguin.
—The Odd Woman. 1983. 432p. mass mkt. 3.95 o.p. (0-446-30569-3, 305693) Warner Bks., Inc.
Gold, Herbert. A Girl of Forty. 1986. 254p. 16.95 o.s.i (0-917657-63-2) Fine, Donald I. Bks.
Goldsmith, Olivia. Pen Pals. 2002. (Illus.). 368p. 24.95 o.s.i (0-525-94644-6, Dutton) Dutton/Plume.
—Pen Pals. 2002. 432p. reprint ed. mass mkt. 7.99 (0-451-20667-3, Signet Bks.) NAL.
—Pen Pals. l.t. ed. 2002. (Basic Ser.). 716p. 29.95 (0-7862-4206-X) Thorndike Pr.
—Switcheroo. l.t. ed. 1998. (Large Print Book Ser.). 26.95 (1-56895-680-0, Wheeler Publishing, Inc.) Gale Group.
—Switcheroo. 1998. 272p. 23.00 (0-06-017568-0) HarperCollins Pubs.
—Switcheroo, Set. abr. ed. 1998. audio 22.00 o.s.i (0-694-51868-9, 695730, HarperAudio) HarperTrade.
—Switcheroo: A Novel. 1999. 400p. mass mkt. 6.99 (0-06-109765-9, HarperTorch) Morrow/Avon.
Goodis, David. The Blonde on the Street Corner. 1997. (Midnight Classics Ser.). 155p. (Orig.). reprint ed. pap. (1-85242-447-8) Serpent's Tail Ltd.
Goodwin, Karen. Bad Advice: A Novel. 2002. 288p. 22.95 (0-8118-3692-4) Chronicle Bks. LLC.
Goodwin, Karin. Sleeping with Random Beasts. 1998. 256p. 22.95 o.p. (0-8118-1989-2) Chronicle Bks. LLC.
Goodwin, Suzanne. The Difference. 1995. 384p. 22.95 o.p. (0-312-13051-1) St. Martin's Pr.
—Sheer Chance. 1997. 288p. 22.95 o.p. (0-312-15654-5) St. Martin's Pr.
Goold, G. P., ed. Callirhoe: Love Story in Syracuse. 1995. (Loeb Classical Library: Vol. 481). 400p. text 21.50 (0-674-99530-9, L481) Harvard Univ. Pr.
Gordimer, Nadine. My Son's Story. 1990. 277p. 19.95 o.s.i (0-374-21751-3) Farrar, Straus & Giroux.
—My Son's Story. 1991. 292p. reprint ed. 12.95 (0-14-015975-4) Viking Penguin.
—None to Accompany Me. 1996. (0-14-771180-0); 1995. 336p. pap. 15.00 o.s.i (0-14-025039-5, Penguin Bks.) Penguin Group (USA) Inc.
Gordon, Helen Heightsman. Voice of the Vanquished: The Story of the Slave Marina & Hernan Cortes. 1996. 475p. pap. 15.00 (1-56002-530-1) Anacade International.
Gostin, Jennifer. Peregrine's Rest. 1996. 256p. 26.00 (1-877946-74-5) Permanent Pr., The.
Goudge, Eileen. Garden of Lies. l.t. ed. 1990. (Magna Large Print Ser.). 820p. o.p. (1-85057-837-0) Magna Large Print Bks. GBR. *Dist:* Ulverscroft Large Print Canada, Ltd.
—Garden of Lies. 1989. 544p. 19.95 o.p. (0-670-82458-5) Viking Penguin.
—One Last Dance. l.t. ed. 1999. 29.95 (0-7862-2005-8, Macmillan Reference USA) Gale Group.
—One Last Dance. l.t. ed. 2001. (Magna Large Print Ser.). 576p. (0-7505-1750-6) Magna Large Print Bks. GBR. *Dist:* Ulverscroft Large Print Canada, Ltd.
—One Last Dance. 2000. 448p. mass mkt. 7.99 (0-451-19948-0, Signet Bks.) NAL.
—One Last Dance. 1999. 398p. 24.95 o.p. (0-670-88575-4) Viking Penguin.
Gould, Judith. My Second Love. 1997. 464p. 25.95 o.p. (0-525-93930-X) Dutton/Plume.
Gould, Sandra. Faradays Popcorn Factory. 2000. 2888p. pap. 13.95 (0-312-25385-0, Saint Martin's Griffin) St. Martin's Pr.
Gould, Sandra Lee. Faraday's Popcorn Factory. 1999. 23.95 o.s.i (0-312-20780-8); 1998. 288p. 23.95 o.p. (0-312-18578-2) St. Martin's Pr.
Graham, Heather. Heather Graham: Three Complete Novels. 1994. 832p. 13.99 o.s.i (0-517-10171-8) Random Hse. Value Publishing.
Grant-Adamson, Lesley. Wish You Were Here. 1996. 176p. 19.95 o.p. (0-312-14075-4, Saint Martin's Minotaur) St. Martin's Pr.
Greeley, Andrew M. Summer at the Lake. 1997. 412p. 24.95 (0-312-86082-X, Forge Bks.) Doherty, Tom Assocs., LLC.
—Summer at the Lake. l.t. ed. 1998. 25.95 o.p. (1-56895-559-6, Wheeler Publishing, Inc.) Gale Group.
—Wages of Sin. 1993. mass mkt. 6.99 o.s.i (0-515-11222-4, Jove) Berkley Publishing Group.
—Wages of Sin. 1992. 352p. 21.95 o.p. (0-399-13752-1, G. P. Putnam's Sons) Penguin Group (USA) Inc.
Green, Jane. Jemima J. A Novel about Ugly Ducklings & Swans. 2001. 384p. reprint ed. pap. 11.95 (0-7679-0518-0) Broadway Bks.
Greenberg, Joanne. Of Such Small Differences. 1988. 18.95 o.p. (0-8050-0902-7) Holt, Henry & Co.
Greenwood, T. Breathing Water. 1999. 276p. 23.95 o.p. (0-312-20283-0); 2000. 288p. reprint ed. pap. 13.95 (0-312-26289-2, NPB 0264, Saint Martin's Griffin) St. Martin's Pr.
Greer, Andrew Sean. The Confessions of Max Tivoli. 2004. 272p. 23.00 (0-374-12871-5) Farrar, Straus & Giroux.
Gregory, Kay. The Love Game. l.t. ed. 2001. (Romance Ser.). 272p. 25.95 (0-7862-3036-3, Five Star) Gale Group.
Gregory, Philippa. A Respectable Trade. l.t. ed. 1995. 682p. 26.95 o.p. (0-7838-1477-1, Macmillan Reference USA) Gale Group.
—A Respectable Trade. 1995. 512p. 25.00 o.p. (0-06-017663-6) HarperCollins Pubs.
—A Respectable Trade. 1996. 480p. mass mkt. 5.99 o.p. (0-06-109433-1, HarperTorch) Morrow/Avon.
Grondahl, Jens Christian. Lucca. Born, Anne, tr. 336p. 2004. pap. 14.00 (0-15-602961-8, Harvest Bks.); 2003. 26.00 (0-15-100594-X) Harcourt Trade Pubs.
Grumbach, Doris. The Book of Knowledge: A Novel. 1995. 256p. 22.00 o.p. (0-393-03770-3) Norton, W. W. & Co., Inc.
Guerard, Albert J. & Escandon, Maria A. Suspended Sentences. 1999. 136p. (Orig.). pap. 12.00 (1-880284-30-8) Daniel, John & Co., Pubs.
Gunn, Robin Jones. Secrets. 1999. (Christian Fiction Ser.). 248p. pap. 23.95 (0-7862-1948-3, Five Star) Gale Group.
—Secrets, 8 vols. 2003. (Glenbrooke Ser.: Vol. 1). 287p. pap. 10.99 (1-57673-420-X); Bk. 1. 1994. (Palisades Pure Romance Ser.). 263p. pap. 9.99 o.s.i (0-88070-721-6, Palisades) Multnomah Pubs., Inc.
Guy, Rosa. My Love, My Friend: Or the Pleasant Girl. 1985. 128p. 12.95 o.p. (0-03-000507-8) Holt, Henry & Co.
—My Love, My Friend or the Peasant Girl. 1990. 128p. pap. 9.95 o.p. (0-8050-1659-7, Owl Bks.) Holt, Henry & Co.
Haddock, K. S. The Patricidal Bedside Companion. 1994. 208p. (Orig.). pap. 12.95 o.p. (0-312-10522-3, Saint Martin's Griffin) St. Martin's Pr.
Haddrill, Marilyn & Holmes, Doris. Sting of the Scorpion. 1994. 216p. (Orig.). pap. 9.95 (0-9623682-9-6) Arroyo Pr.
Hagan, Patricia. Orchids in Moonlight. l.t. ed. 1994. 22.95 o.p. (1-56895-059-4, Wheeler Publishing, Inc.) Gale Group.
—Orchids in Moonlight. 1993. 384p. mass mkt. 5.50 o.p. (0-06-108038-1, HarperTorch) Morrow/Avon.
Haines, Carolyn. Touched. 1996. 384p. 23.95 o.s.i (0-525-94160-6, Dutton) Dutton/Plume.
Hairston, Alex. If Only You Knew. 2004. 240p. pap. 14.00 (1-58314-395-5, Sepia) BET Bks.
Haley, Susan. Getting Married in Buffalo Jump. 1987. 256p. 17.95 o.p. (0-525-24528-6, 01646-490, Dutton) Dutton/Plume.
Hall, Barbara. Better Place. 1994. 287p. 21.00 (0-671-78422-6, Simon & Schuster) Simon & Schuster.
Hall, Sands. Catching Heaven. E-Book 12.50 (1-930161-77-8) Adobe Systems, Inc.
Hamill, Dennis. House on Fire. 1996. 368p. 22.00 o.p. (0-87113-614-7, Atlantic Monthly Pr.) Grove/Atlantic, Inc.
—House on Fire. 1998. 400p. pap. 6.99 (0-671-00350-X, Pocket) Simon & Schuster.
Hamill, Pete. Loving Women. 2003. mass mkt. 6.99 o.p. (0-7582-0678-X, Kensington Bks.); 2003. mass mkt. 6.99 (0-7860-1638-8, Pinnacle Bks.); 1990. mass mkt. 5.50 o.s.i (1-55817-385-4, Pinnacle Bks.) Kensington Publishing Corp.
Hamilton, Jane. Disobedience: A Novel. 2001. 288p. pap. 13.00 (0-385-72046-7, Knopf Bks. for Young Readers) Random Hse. Children's Bks.
—Disobedience: A Novel. l.t. ed. 2001. (Thorndike Basic Ser.). 463p. 31.95 (0-7862-3159-9); pap. 29.95 (0-7862-3158-0) Thorndike Pr.
Hansen, Derek. Sole Survivor. 1999. (Illus.). 432p. 25.00 o.s.i (0-684-85407-4, Simon & Schuster) Simon & Schuster.
—Sole Survivor: A Novel. 2000. 432p. pap. 14.00 (0-684-86325-1, Simon & Schuster) Simon & Schuster.
Hansen, Jennie. Run Away Home. 1997. pap. 11.95 (1-57734-208-9, 01113240) Covenant Communications, Inc.
—When Tomorrow Comes: A Novel. 1994. pap. 11.95 (1-55503-725-9, 019403) Covenant Communications, Inc.
Hanyen, Jim. All the Way Home. 1995. 230p. 10.75 o.p. (1-880664-06-2) E. M. Productions.
Hardy, Barbara. London Lovers. 1996. 208p. 29.95 (0-7206-0964-X) Owen, Peter Ltd. GBR. *Dist:* Dufour Editions, Inc.
Hardy, Robin. Padre: A Novel. 1994. 288p. (Orig.). pap. 10.00 o.p. (0-89109-799-6) NavPress Publishing Group.
Harrison, Colin. Bodies Electric. l.t. ed. 1994. pap. 24.95 o.p. (0-7927-1994-8) BBC Audiobooks America.
—Bodies Electric. 1994. pap. 5.99 o.p. (0-380-72310-7, Avon Bks.) Morrow/Avon.
Hart, Christopher. Rescue Me! 2001. 272p. pap. (0-571-20625-5) Faber & Faber, Inc.
Hartley, L. P. The Go-Between. 1997. (Twentieth Century Classics Ser.). 336p. pap. 13.95 o.p. (0-14-018852-5, Penguin Classics) Viking Penguin.

Hauptmann, Gaby. In Search of an Impotent Man. 2000. 320p. 24.00 o.s.i (*0-06-019603-3*) HarperCollins Pubs.

Havens, Virginia. Roxey's Choice: A Novel. 1994. pap. 9.95 o.p. (*1-55503-712-7*) Covenant Communications, Inc.

Hawkes, John. The Blood Oranges. 1972. 9.95 o.p. (*0-8112-0285-2*); pap. 12.95 (*0-8112-0061-2*, NDP338) New Directions Publishing Corp.

—The Blood Oranges. 1998. 288p. pap. 11.95 o.s.i (*0-14-026734-4*) Penguin Group (USA) Inc.

—Death, Sleep & the Traveler. 1975. 192p. pap. 9.95 (*0-8112-0569-X*, NDP393) New Directions Publishing Corp.

Hawkesworth, John. In My Lady's Chamber. 1980. (Reader's Request Ser.). lib. bdg. 11.95 o.p. (*0-8161-6795-8*, Macmillan Reference USA) Gale Group.

Hays, Mary. Memoirs of Emma Courtney. Brooks, Marilyn L., ed. 2000. (Literary Texts Ser.). 340p. (*1-55111-314-7*) Broadview Pr.

—Memoirs of Emma Courtney. Brooks, Marilyn, ed. 2000. (Literary Texts Ser.). 340p. pap. (*1-55111-155-1*) Broadview Pr.

—Memoirs of Emma Courtney. 1974. (Feminist Controversy in England, 1788-1810 Ser.). lib. bdg. 121.00 o.p. (*0-8240-0870-7*) Garland Publishing, Inc.

—Memoirs of Emma Courtney. Ty, Eleanor, ed. (Oxford World's Classics Ser.). 2001. 272p. pap. 12.95 (*0-19-283729-X*); 1996. 266p. (C). pap. 11.95 o.p. (*0-19-282306-X*) Oxford Univ. Pr., Inc.

Hays, Mary & Brooks, Marilyn L. Memoirs of Emma Courtney. 2000. E-Book 24.95 (*0-585-23649-6*) netLibrary, Inc.

Hazzard, Shirley. The Evening of the Holiday. 1988. 144p. pap. 6.95 o.p. (*0-14-010451-8*, Penguin Bks.) Viking Penguin.

Heliodorus. An Ethiopian Romance. Hadas, Moses, tr. 1976. reprint ed. lib. bdg. 24.75 o.p. (*0-8371-9085-1*, HEER, Greenwood Pr.) Greenwood Publishing Group, Inc.

—An Ethiopian Romance. (Illus.). (C). pap. text (*0-472-08559-X*) Univ. of Michigan Pr.

—An Ethiopian Romance. Hadas, Moses, tr. from GEC. & intro. by. 1999. 277p. pap. 19.95 (*0-8122-1672-5*) Univ. of Pennsylvania Pr.

Hemingway, Ernest. The Garden of Eden. unabr. collector's ed. 1990. audio 48.00 (*0-7366-1822-8*, 2658) Books on Tape, Inc.

—The Garden of Eden. 1987. 251p. pap. 9.95 o.s.i (*0-684-18871-6*); 1986. 250p. 18.95 o.s.i (*0-684-18693-4*); 1987. 300p. 19.95 o.p. (*0-8161-4152-5*); 1987. 300p. 11.95 o.p. (*0-8161-4153-3*) Gale Group. (Macmillan Reference USA).

—The Garden of Eden. 1995. 256p. pap. 12.00 (*0-684-80452-2*, Scribner) Simon & Schuster.

Hendrie, Laura. Remember Me: A Novel. l.t. ed. 2000. (Americana Ser.). 624p. 29.95 (*0-7862-2453-3*) Thorndike Pr.

Heyward, Du Bose & Heyward, Dorothy. Porgy. 1980. (American Drama Ser.). Dell Publishing.

Heyward, DuBose. Porgy. Date not set. reprint ed. lib. bdg. 20.95 (*0-89190-684-3*, American Reprint Co.) Amereon, Ltd.

—Porgy. 1991. 196p. reprint ed. lib. bdg. 18.95 (*0-89966-768-6*) Buccaneer Bks., Inc.

—Porgy. 2nd ed. (Illus.). 192p. reprint ed. pap. 20.00 o.p. (*0-937684-22-8*, P23.H1587PO) Tradd Street Pr.

—Porgy. 2001. (Banner Bks.). 208p. reprint ed. pap. 18.00 (*1-57806-356-6*) Univ. Pr. of Mississippi.

Heyward, Dubose & Heyward, Dorothy. Porgy: A Gullah Version. Geraty, Virginia M., tr. & intro. by. 1990. 129p. pap. 8.95 (*0-941711-11-0*) Wyrick & Co.

Hillmer, Timothy. The Hookmen. 1996. 256p. pap. 11.00 (*0-684-81386-6*, Touchstone) Simon & Schuster.

—The Hookmen. 1994. 280p. 22.50 o.p. (*0-87081-348-X*) Univ. Pr. of Colorado.

Hiscox, Edward T. The Hiscox Standard Baptist Manual. 1965. pap. 10.00 (*0-8170-0340-1*) Judson Pr.

Hobbie, Douglas. This Time Last Year. 1998. 336p. 23.00 o.s.i (*0-8050-5492-8*) Holt, Henry & Co.

Hoffman, Alice. Here on Earth. 2015. 336p. mass mkt. 7.50 o.s.i (*0-425-16430-6*); 1998. 304p. pap. 13.00 (*0-425-16731-3*); 1999. 336p. reprint ed. mass mkt. 7.99 (*0-425-16969-3*) Berkley Publishing Group.

—Here on Earth. 2001. 23.95 o.s.i (*0-399-14901-5*); 1997. 304p. 23.95 o.p. (*0-399-14313-0*, G. P. Putnam's Sons) Penguin Group (USA) Inc.

—Here on Earth. 1999. 14.04 (*0-606-16392-1*) Turtleback Bks.

Hoffman, Jill. Jilted. 1993. 320p. 20.00 o.p. (*0-671-79518-X*, Simon & Schuster) Simon & Schuster.

Holmes, Clare F. The Academy of Love. l.t. ed. 1993. 236p. lib. bdg. 15.95 (*0-8161-5841-X*, Macmillan Reference USA) Gale Group.

—The Burning Quest. l.t. ed. 1994. 270p. lib. bdg. 16.95 (*0-8161-5843-6*, Macmillan Reference USA) Gale Group.

Hornby, Nick. About a Boy. l.t. ed. 1998. 424p. (*0-7540-1206-9*) BBC Audiobooks America.

—About a Boy. movie tie-in ed. 320p. 2002. pap. 12.95 (*1-57322-957-1*); 1999. reprint ed. pap. 12.95 (*1-57322-733-1*) Berkley Publishing Group. (Riverhead Trade (Paperbacks)).

—About a Boy. 2002. pap. (*1-57322-961-X*) Penguin Group (USA) Inc.

—About a Boy. 1998. 288p. 22.95 o.s.i (*1-57322-087-6*, Riverhead Bks. (Hardcovers)) Putnam Publishing Group, The.

—About a Boy. l.t. ed. 1998. (Basic Ser.). 424p. 28.95 (*0-7862-1606-9*) Thorndike Pr.

—High Fidelity. 336p. 2000. pap. 14.00 (*1-57322-821-4*); 1996. pap. 14.00 (*1-57322-551-7*) Berkley Publishing Group. (Riverhead Trade (Paperbacks)).

—High Fidelity. 1995. 304p. 21.95 o.p. (*1-57322-016-7*, Riverhead Bks. (Hardcovers)) Putnam Publishing Group, The.

Hornby, Nick, contrib. by. High Fidelity. abr. ed. 1998. audio 17.95 o.p. (*1-57322-102-3*) Putnam Publishing Group, The.

Howatch, Susan. Ultimate Prizes. 1990. mass mkt. 5.95 o.s.i (*0-449-21913-5*) Ballantine Bks.

—Ultimate Prizes. l.t. ed. 1990. (General Ser.). 668p. 21.95 o.p. (*0-8161-4994-1*, Macmillan Reference USA) Gale Group.

—Ultimate Prizes. 1991. 4.99 o.p. (*0-517-06772-2*) Random Hse. Value Publishing.

Hucker, Hazel. Cousin Susannah. 1996. 384p. 23.95 (*0-312-13950-0*) St. Martin's Pr.

—A Dangerous Happiness. 1996. pap. o.s.i (*0-7515-1625-2*); o.s.i (*0-7515-1648-1*) Little Brown & Co.

—A Dangerous Happiness. 1996. 272p. 21.95 (*0-312-14307-9*) St. Martin's Pr.

—A Dangerous Happiness. l.t. ed. 1996. (Ulverscroft Large Print Ser.). 560p. 29.99 o.p. (*0-7089-3487-0*, Ulverscroft) Thorpe, F. A. Pubs. GBR. *Dist:* Ulverscroft Large Print Bks., Ltd., Ulverscroft Large Print Canada, Ltd.

Hudson, William Henry. Green Mansions: A Romance of the Tropical Forest. reprint ed. 35.00 (*0-404-03402-0*) AMS Pr., Inc.

—Green Mansions: A Romance of the Tropical Forest. Date not set. lib. bdg. 23.95 (*0-8488-2146-7*) Amereon, Ltd.

—Green Mansions: A Romance of the Tropical Forest. Baxter, Beth, ed. abr. ed. 1993. audio 12.95 (*1-882071-06-9*, 008) B&B Audio, Inc.

—Green Mansions: A Romance of the Tropical Forest. 1989. audio 49.95 (*1-55686-293-8*, 293) Books in Motion.

—Green Mansions: A Romance of the Tropical Forest. unabr. collector's ed. 1982. audio 48.00 (*0-7366-3862-8*, 9069) Books on Tape, Inc.

—Green Mansions: A Romance of the Tropical Forest. 1982. reprint ed. lib. bdg. 25.95 (*0-89966-374-5*) Buccaneer Bks., Inc.

—Green Mansions: A Romance of the Tropical Forest. 2001. (Collected Works of W. H. Hudson ). reprint ed. pap. text 28.00 (*0-7426-8540-3*) Classic Bks.

—Green Mansions: A Romance of the Tropical Forest. 1989. 320p. pap. 8.95 (*0-486-25993-5*) Dover Pubns., Inc.

—Green Mansions: A Romance of the Tropical Forest. abr. ed. 1977. audio 12.95 o.p. (*0-694-50302-9*, SWC 1561, Caedmon) HarperTrade.

—Green Mansions: A Romance of the Tropical Forest. unabr. ed. 1982. audio 29.00 Jimcin Recordings.

—Green Mansions: A Romance of the Tropical Forest. l.t. ed. (Large Print Ser.). reprint ed. 1992. 410p. lib. bdg. 26.00 (*0-939495-40-6*); 1998. 245p. lib. bdg. 25.00 (*1-58287-032-2*) North Bks.

—Green Mansions: A Romance of the Tropical Forest. Duncan, Ian, ed. 1998. (Oxford World's Classics Ser.). 240p. pap. 9.95 (*0-19-283288-3*) Oxford Univ. Pr., Inc.

—Green Mansions: A Romance of the Tropical Forest. 1999. E-Book 3.99 incl. cd-rom (*1-891595-90-3*) Quiet Vision Publishing.

—Green Mansions: A Romance of the Tropical Forest. E-Book 5.00 (*0-7410-0873-4*) SoftBook Pr.

—Green Mansions: A Romance of the Tropical Forest. 1999. E-Book 5.99 (*0-8220-7269-6*, Cliff Notes) Wiley, John & Sons, Inc.

Hunt, Angela Elwell. The Troubadour's Quest. 1994. (Theyn Chronicles Ser.: Vol. 2). 395p. pap. 9.99 o.p. (*0-8423-1287-0*) Tyndale Hse. Pubs.

Hunter, Evan. Criminal Conversation. reprint ed. 2002. 480p. pap. 6.99 (*0-7434-2154-X*); 2001. E-Book 6.99 (*0-7434-2155-8*) Simon & Schuster. (Pocket).

—Criminal Conversation. 1995. 384p. mass mkt. 6.50 (*0-446-36513-0*, Warner Vision); 1994. 400p. 21.95 o.s.i (*0-446-51755-0*) Warner Bks., Inc.

—Privileged Conversation. unabr. ed. 1996. audio 48.00 (*0-7366-3425-8*, 4070) Books on Tape, Inc.

—Privileged Conversation. Set. abr. ed. 1996. audio 21.95 (*1-55935-195-0*, 693519) Soundelux Audio Publishing.

—Privileged Conversation. 1997. 336p. mass mkt. 6.99 (*0-446-60382-1*); 1996. 82p. 22.95 o.s.i (*0-446-52028-4*) Warner Bks., Inc.

Hunter, Travis E. The Hearts of Men: A Novel. 2000. 260p. pap. 12.00 (*0-9675546-7-5*) Jimrose Publishing Co.

Huth, Angela. Invitation to the Married Life: A Novel. 1992. 304p. 19.95 o.p. (*0-8021-1465-2*) Grove/Atlantic, Inc.

Huysmans, J. K. Marthe. Putnam, Samuel, tr. from FRE. 1992. (El-E-Phant Bks.: No. 1). 120p. (Orig.). (C). pap. 10.95 o.p. (*1-55713-138-4*) Sun & Moon Pr.

Hyde, Catherine Ryan. Pay It Forward. E-Book 23.00 (*1-930161-23-9*) Adobe Systems, Inc.

—Pay It Forward. l.t. ed. 2000. (Wheeler Hardcover Ser.). 27.95 (*1-56895-960-5*, Wheeler Publishing, Inc.) Gale Group.

—Pay It Forward. 2000. E-Book 23.00 (*0-7432-0596-0*, Simon & Schuster); E-Book 23.00 (*0-7432-0389-5*, Simon & Schuster); (Illus.). 288p. 23.00 o.s.i (*0-684-86271-9*, Simon & Schuster); 320p. mass mkt. 7.99 (*0-7434-1202-8*, Pocket) Simon & Schuster.

—Pay It Forward. 2000. 14.04 (*0-606-21795-9*) Turtleback Bks.

Ibbotson, Eva. The Morning Gift. 1993. 336p. 19.95 o.p. (*0-312-09338-1*) St. Martin's Pr.

Irving, John. The 158-Pound Marriage. 1997. 176p. pap. 13.95 (*0-345-41796-8*); 1990. 256p. mass mkt. 6.99 (*0-345-36743-X*) Ballantine Bks.

—The 158-Pound Marriage. 1982. mass mkt. 3.95 (*0-671-46811-1*, Pocket) Simon & Schuster.

Jackson, Edwardo. Ever After: A Novel. 1999. 300p. pap. 13.95 o.p. (*1-58348-545-7*) iUniverse, Inc.

James, Henry. The American. 1968. (Airmont Classics Ser.). mass mkt. 2.95 o.p. (*0-8049-0176-7*, CL 176) Airmont Publishing Co., Inc.

—The American. 1976. 22.95 (*0-8488-0756-1*) Amereon, Ltd.

—The American. 2001. per. 14.00 (*1-891355-32-5*) Blue Unicorn Editions.

—The American. 1990. 336p. reprint ed. lib. bdg. 28.95 (*0-89966-697-3*) Buccaneer Bks., Inc.

—The American. reprint ed. pap. 75.00 (*1-4047-3446-5*); 1877. pap. text 28.00 (*1-4047-3370-1*) Classic Textbooks.

—The American. 1999. E-Book 2.49 (*1-58627-978-5*) Electric Umbrella Publishing.

—The American. Bruccoli, Matthew J. & Pearce, R. H., eds. 1962. (C). pap. 16.36 (*0-395-05163-0*, Riverside Editions) Houghton Mifflin Co.

—The American. l.t. ed. 1875p. pap. 120.17 (*0-7583-0175-8*); 1616p. pap. 107.93 (*0-7583-0174-X*); 1314p. pap. 87.15 (*0-7583-0173-1*); 1068p. pap. 74.47 (*0-7583-0172-3*); 835p. pap. 62.39 (*0-7583-0171-5*); 652p. pap. 44.33 (*0-7583-0170-7*); 476p. pap. 35.94 (*0-7583-0169-3*); 381p. pap. 30.56 (*0-7583-0168-5*); 1068p. lib. bdg. 86.47 (*0-7583-0164-2*); 652p. lib. bdg. 50.33 (*0-7583-0162-6*); 381p. lib. bdg. 36.56 (*0-7583-0160-X*); 476p. lib. bdg. 41.94 (*0-7583-0161-8*); 835p. lib. bdg. 74.39 (*0-7583-0163-4*); 1314p. lib. bdg. 99.15 (*0-7583-0165-0*); 1616p. lib. bdg. 125.93 (*0-7583-0166-9*); 1875p. lib. bdg. 138.17 (*0-7583-0167-7*) Huge Print Pr.

—The American. 1976. (Novels & Tales of Henry James Ser.: Vol. 2). xxii, 539p. reprint ed. lib. bdg. 45.00 (*0-678-02802-8*) Kelley, Augustus M. Pubs.

—The American. 2000. (Vintage Bks.). 384p. pap. 13.00 (*0-375-72611-X*, Vintage) Knopf Publishing Group.

—The American. 1965. 336p. mass mkt. 7.95 (*0-451-52517-5*); mass mkt. 4.50 o.p. (*0-451-52241-9*, Signet Classics) NAL.

—The American. 2001. (Twelve-Point Ser.). 402p. lib. bdg. 25.00 (*1-58287-148-5*); 508p. 26.00 (*1-58287-631-2*) North Bks.

—The American. Tuttleton, James W., ed. 1978. (Critical Editions Ser.). 14.95 o.p. (*0-393-04476-9*); 496p. (C). pap. text 10.50 (*0-393-09091-4*) Norton, W. W. & Co., Inc.

—The American. Poole, Adrian, ed. & intro. by. 1999. (Oxford World's Classics Ser.). 448p. pap. 10.95 (*0-19-283322-7*) Oxford Univ. Pr., Inc.

—The American. 2001. E-Book 2.95 (*1-58882-619-8*) PublishingOnline.

—The American. 1999. 544p. pap. 22.95 (*0-7351-0195-7*); lib. bdg. 32.95 (*0-7351-0174-4*) Replica Bks.

—The American. 1992. (Notable American Authors Ser.). reprint ed. lib. bdg. 75.00 (*0-7812-3370-4*); lib. bdg. 75.00 (*0-7812-3446-8*) Reprint Services Corp.

—The American. (Ebook Classic Ser.). E-Book 5.00 (*0-7410-0466-6*) SoftBook Pr.

—The American. Bradbury, Malcolm, ed. 1989. (Everyman Paperback Classics Ser.). 416p. pap. 8.95 (*0-460-87657-0*, Everyman's Classic Library in Paperback) Tuttle Publishing.

—The American. Spengemann, William C., ed. 1981. (American Library). 480p. pap. 4.95 o.p. (*0-14-039009-X*, Penguin Classics) Viking Penguin.

—The American. Spengemann, William C., ed. & intro. by. 1981. (Classics Ser.). 480p. pap. 11.95 (*0-14-039082-0*, Penguin Classics) Viking Penguin.

—The Sacred Fount. 2000. 252p. E-Book 9.95 (*0-594-05443-5*) 1873 Pr.

—The Sacred Fount. 2000. audio 35.95 (*1-55685-605-9*) Audio Bk. Contractors, Inc.

—The Sacred Fount. 1979. reprint ed. pap. 4.95 o.p. (*0-394-17081-4*, B418, Grove Pr.) Grove/Atlantic, Inc.

—The Sacred Fount. 1995. (Revived Modern Classic Ser.: Vol. 790). 236p. pap. 11.95 (*0-8112-1279-3*, NDP790) New Directions Publishing Corp.

—The Sacred Fount. 1992. (Notable American Authors Ser.). reprint ed. lib. bdg. 75.00 (*0-7812-3428-X*) Reprint Services Corp.

—The Sacred Fount. Lyon, John, ed. & intro. by. 1995. (Penguin Classics Ser.). 240p. pap. 10.95 o.p. (*0-14-043350-3*, Penguin Classics) Viking Penguin.

James, Henry & Poole, Adrian. The American. 1999. E-Book 11.50 (*0-585-38492-4*) netLibrary, Inc.

James, Kelvin C. A Fling with a Demon Lover: A Novel. 1996. 79p. 22.00 o.p. (*0-06-017350-5*) HarperCollins Pubs.

Japrisot, Sebastien. A Very Long Engagement. Coverdale, Linda, tr. from FRE. 1994. Tr. of Long Dimanche de Finacailles. 336p. pap. 14.00 (*0-452-27297-1*, Plume) Dutton/Plume.

—A Very Long Engagement. 1993. Tr. of Long Dimanche de Finacailles. 327p. 23.00 o.p. (*0-374-28335-4*) Farrar, Straus & Giroux.

Jardin, Alexandre. Fanfan. (FRE.). pap. 13.95 (*2-07-038513-2*) Gallimard, Editions FRA. *Dist:* Distribooks, Inc.

—Fanfan. 1994. 176p. 18.95 o.p. (*0-312-10981-4*) St. Martin's Pr.

Jin, Ha. Waiting. 2001. E-Book 11.50 (*1-58945-644-0*) Adobe Systems, Inc.

—Waiting. l.t. ed. 2000. 374p. 29.95 (*1-56895-885-4*, Wheeler Publishing, Inc.) Gale Group.

—Waiting. 2001. E-Book 11.50 (*0-375-72695-0*) Random Hse., Inc.

—Waiting. 2000. 19.05 (*0-606-21850-5*) Turtleback Bks.

—Waiting: A Novel. (Vintage International Ser.). 320p. 2000. pap. 13.00 (*0-375-70641-0*, Vintage); 1999. 24.00 (*0-375-40653-0*, Pantheon) Knopf Publishing Group.

Joe, Yolanda. He Say, She Say. 1996. 272p. 21.95 o.s.i (*0-385-48507-7*) Doubleday Publishing.

—He Say, She Say. l.t. ed. 1997. (Niagara Large Print Ser.). 332p. 29.50 o.p. (*0-7089-5871-0*, Ulverscroft) Thorpe, F. A. Pubs. GBR. *Dist:* Ulverscroft Large Print Bks., Ltd.

—He Say, She Say. 1998. 304p. mass mkt. 6.99 (*0-446-60570-0*) Warner Bks., Inc.

Johnson, Darlene. Dream in Color. 2000. 400p. pap. 14.95 (*0-9679745-0-X*) Brandywine Publishing.

Johnson, Denis. The Stars at Noon. 1995. 192p. pap. 12.00 (*0-06-097610-1*, Perennial) HarperTrade.

Johnson, Greg. Pagan Babies. 1994. (Plume Contemporary Fiction Ser.). 320p. pap. 11.95 o.p. (*0-452-27132-0*, Plume) Dutton/Plume.

Johnson, Janine. One Love: An Unbelievable Journey. 1998. E-Book 5.50 o.p. (*1-892745-12-7*) Petals of Life Publishing.

Jolley, Elizabeth. Cabin Fever: A Novel. 1991. 224p. 19.95 o.p. (*0-06-016622-3*) HarperTrade.

—The Sugar Mother. 1988. 192p. 16.95 o.p. (*0-06-015940-5*) HarperTrade.

Jones, Gayl. Eva's Man. 1987. (Black Women Writers Ser.). 177p. reprint ed. pap. 12.00 (*0-8070-6319-3*) Beacon Pr.

—The Healing. 1999. (Blue Streak). 296p. pap. 12.00 (*0-8070-6325-8*) Beacon Pr.

—The Healing. Atwan, Helene, ed. 1998. 336p. 23.00 o.p. (*0-8070-6314-2*) Beacon Pr.

—The Healing. l.t. ed. 1998. (Americana Ser.). 488p. 28.95 (*0-7862-1504-6*) Thorndike Pr.

Jong, Erica. How to Save Your Own Life. 1977. 8.95 o.p. (*0-03-017726-X*) Holt, Henry & Co.

—Parachutes & Kisses. 1984. 405p. 16.95 o.p. (*0-453-00466-0*) NAL.

Josipovici, Gabriel. In a Hotel Garden. 1995. 160p. (Orig.). pap. 9.95 (*0-8112-1291-2*, NDP801) New Directions Publishing Corp.

Kachtick, Keith. Hungry Ghost. 2004. pap. (*0-06-052391-3*, Perennial) HarperTrade.

Kagan, Elaine. The Girls: A Novel. 1994. 307p. 23.00 o.s.i (*0-679-43395-3*) Knopf, Alfred A. Inc.

Kane, Andrew. Rabbi, Rabbi. 1995. 306p. 22.95 o.p. (*0-312-11879-1*) St. Martin's Pr.

Kane, Kathleen. Small Treasures. 1993. (Homespun Ser.). 336p. 4.99 o.p. (*1-55773-866-1*, Diamond Bks.) Ace Bks.

Kaplan, Hester. The Edge of Marriage. 2001. 192p. pap. 12.95 (*0-393-32144-4*, Norton Paperbacks) Norton, W. W. & Co., Inc.

Kapur, Manju. Difficult Daughters. 1998. 262 p. (*0-14-027862-1*) Viking Penguin.

Kaufman, Daniel. To Be a Man: Visions of Self, Views from Within. 1994. 192p. 20.00 (*0-671-88107-8*, Simon & Schuster) Simon & Schuster.

Keane, John B. Letters of a Love-Hungry Farmer. 1993. 96p. 10.95 o.p. (*0-312-09862-6*) St. Martin's Pr.

Kennedy, A. L. Original Bliss: A Novel. 2000. 224p. pap. 12.00 (*0-375-70278-4*, Vintage) Knopf Publishing Group.

—Original Bliss: A Novel. 1999. 224p. 21.00 o.s.i (*0-375-40272-1*) Knopf, Alfred A. Inc.

Kercheval, Jesse L. The Museum of Happiness. 1993. 276p. 22.95 o.s.i (*0-571-19821-X*) Faber & Faber, Inc.

Kessler, Alfred. The Eighth Day of the Week. 2000. 185p. pap. 16.00 (*1-929355-00-9*) Pleasure Boat Studio: A Literary Pr.

Keyes, Marian. Last Chance Saloon. 2003. 528p. pap. 13.95 (*0-06-008624-6*, Perennial) HarperTrade.

—Last Chance Saloon. 2002. 544p. mass mkt. 7.99 (*0-380-82029-3*); 2001. 384p. 25.00 (*0-688-18072-8*, Morrow, William & Co.) Morrow/Avon.

—Last Chance Saloon. 1999. 505p. (*1-85371-965-X*) Poolbeg Pr. IRL. *Dist:* Dufour Editions, Inc.

—Rachel's Holiday. 2001. 528p. mass mkt. 6.99 (*0-380-81768-3*, Avon Bks.); 2000. 576p. 25.00 (*0-688-18071-X*, Morrow, William & Co.) Morrow/Avon.

—Rachel's Holiday. 1998. (*1-85371-896-3*) Poolbeg Pr. IRL. *Dist:* Dufour Editions, Inc.

—Watermelon. 2002. 432p. pap. 13.95 (*0-06-009036-7*, Perennial) HarperTrade.

—Watermelon. 1999. 448p. mass mkt. 6.99 (*0-380-79609-0*); 1998. 432p. mass mkt. 15.95 (*0-380-97617-X*) Morrow/Avon. (Avon Bks.).

—Watermelon. 1995. 612p. pap. 11.95 (*1-85371-508-5*) Poolbeg Pr. IRL. *Dist:* Dufour Editions, Inc.

Kierkegaard, Soren. Diary of a Seducer. Hannay, Alastair, tr. from DAN. 2000. 240p. pap. 13.95 (*1-885586-05-1*) Turtle Point Pr.

Kilgo, James. Daughter of My People. 2000. 303p. reprint ed. pap. 13.95 o.s.i (*0-425-17266-X*) Berkley Publishing Group.

—Daughter of My People. 1998. 288p. 24.00 (*0-8203-2002-1*) Univ. of Georgia Pr.

Kimeldorf, Martin. Modem Man. 1999. (Illus.). 77p. E-Book 2.95 (*1-929939-20-5*) PublishingOnline.

King, Richard. Kindling Does for Firewood. 1997. 190p. (Orig.). pap. 11.95 (*1-86448-168-4*) Allen & Unwin Pty., Ltd. AUS. *Dist:* Independent Pubs. Group.

King, Tabitha. Caretakers. 1984. mass mkt. 3.95 o.p. (*0-451-13156-8*); 352p. mass mkt. 5.99 o.s.i (*0-451-16169-6*) NAL. (Signet Bks.).

—Pearl. 1988. 324p. 18.95 o.p. (*0-453-00626-4*) NAL.

—Survivor. 1997. 448p. 24.95 o.p. (*0-525-94241-6*) Dutton/Plume.

—Survivor. 1998. 496p. mass mkt. 7.99 o.p. (*0-451-19090-4*, Signet Bks.) NAL.

Kinney, Harrison. Thurber Country. 2003. (Illus.). 288p. 25.00 (*0-7432-3340-9*, Simon & Schuster) Simon & Schuster.

Klein, Norma. That's My Baby. 1988. (YA). (gr. 12 up). 16.95 o.p. (*0-670-81730-9*, Viking Children's Bks.) Penguin Putnam Bks. for Young Readers.

Kok, Marilyn. Glory. 1995. 294p. pap. 9.99 o.s.i (*0-88070-754-2*, Palisades) Multnomah Pubs., Inc.

Koppelman, Susan, ed. Women in the Trees: U. S. Women's Short Stories about Battering & Resistance, 1839-1994. 1996. 384p. pap. 16.00 o.p. (*0-8070-6777-6*) Beacon Pr.

Koppelman, Susan, ed. & intro. The Other Woman: Stories of Two Women & a Man. 1984. 384p. pap. 12.95 (*0-935312-25-0*) Feminist Pr. at The City Univ. of New York.

Krahn, Betina M. The Perfect Mistress. l.t. ed. 1995. pap. 21.95 o.p. (*1-56895-274-0*, Wheeler Publishing, Inc.) Gale Group.

Krantz, Judith. Judith Krantz: Three Complete Novels. 1994. 992p. 13.99 o.s.i (*0-517-10180-7*) Random Hse. Value Publishing.

—Lovers. 1995. 544p. mass mkt. 7.99 (*0-553-56135-9*) Bantam Bks.

—Lovers. unabr. ed. 1997. audio 99.95 (*1-85695-924-4*, 950304) ISIS Audio Bks. GBR. *Dist:* Ulverscroft Large Print Bks., Ltd.

—Lovers. abr. ed. 1995. audio 8.99 o.s.i (*0-679-44348-7*, 391115, RH Audio) Random Hse. Audio Publishing Group.

—Lovers. l.t. ed. Date not set. pap. 4.99 (*0-517-19680-8*) Random Hse. Large Print.

Krentz, Jayne Ann. Absolutely, Positively. unabr. ed. 1996. audio 64.00 (*0-7366-3436-3*, 104621) Books on Tape, Inc.

—Absolutely, Positively. l.t. ed. 1996. 25.95 (*1-56895-286-4*, Wheeler Publishing, Inc.) Gale Group.

—Absolutely, Positively. 384p. 2003. mass mkt. 5.99 (*0-7434-6737-X*); 1997. pap. 7.99 (*0-671-77873-0*) Simon & Schuster. (Pocket).

—Absolutely, Positively. Zion, Claire, ed. 1996. 352p. 23.00 o.p. (*0-671-55170-1*, Atria) Simon & Schuster.

—Absolutely, Positively, abr. ed. 1997. audio 17.00 (*0-671-88653-3*, 394827, Simon & Schuster Audioworks) Simon & Schuster Audio.

—Gift of Fire. l.t. ed. 1994. 22.95 o.p. (*0-7927-1954-9*); pap. o.p. (*0-7927-1953-0*) BBC Audiobooks America.

—Gift of Fire. 1992. 352p. reprint ed. 20.00 o.p. (*0-7278-4354-0*) Severn Hse. Pubs., Ltd.

—Gift of Gold. l.t. ed. 1994. pap. 22.95 o.p. (*0-7927-1885-2*); 23.95 o.p. (*0-7927-1886-0*) BBC Audiobooks America.

—Gift of Gold. unabr. collector's ed. 1996. audio 72.00 (*0-7366-3445-2*, 4089) Books on Tape, Inc.

—Gift of Gold. 1997. (Romance Ser.). 407p. lib. bdg. 24.95 (*0-7862-0910-0*, Five Star) Gale Group.

—Gift of Gold. 384p. 1993. mass mkt. 7.99 (*0-446-36381-2*); 1988. mass mkt. 4.95 (*0-445-20658-6*) Warner Bks., Inc.

—Trust Me. l.t. ed. 1995. (Large Print Bks.). 25.95 o.p. (*1-56895-204-X*, Wheeler Publishing, Inc.) Gale Group.

—Trust Me. 1998. per. 6.99 (*0-671-01969-4*); 1995. 368p. mass mkt. 7.99 (*0-671-51692-2*) Simon & Schuster. (Pocket).

—Trust Me. Zion, Claire, ed. 1995. 320p. 22.00 o.p. (*0-671-51691-4*, Atria) Simon & Schuster.

—Trust Me. 2001. audio 9.98 o.s.i (*0-671-04437-0*); Set. 1995. audio 17.00 (*0-671-88652-5*, 391817) Simon & Schuster Audio. (Simon & Schuster Audioworks).

Kritlow, William. Driving Lessons: A Novel. 1993. pap. 10.99 o.p. (*0-7852-8214-9*) Nelson, Thomas Inc.

Krysl, Marilyn. How to Accommodate Men: Stories. 1998. 195p. pap. 13.95 (*1-56689-076-4*) Coffee Hse. Pr.

Kundera, Milan. Identity. l.t. ed. 1999. (General Ser.). 168p. 30.00 o.p. (*0-7862-1818-5*, Macmillan Reference USA) Gale Group.

—Identity. Asher, Linda, tr. from FRE. 1998. 176p. 23.00 o.s.i (*0-06-017564-8*) HarperCollins Pubs.

—Identity. aut. ed. 1998. 240p. pap. 23.00 (*0-06-019278-X*) HarperCollins Pubs.

—Identity. Asher, Linda, tr. from FRE. 1999. 176p. pap. 13.00 (*0-06-093031-4*, Perennial) HarperTrade.

Kupfer, Fern. Love Lies. 1994. 271p. 21.00 o.s.i (*0-671-87534-5*, Simon & Schuster) Simon & Schuster.

Kureishi, Hanif. Intimacy. 1999. 128p. 16.00 (*0-684-85275-6*, Scribner) Simon & Schuster.

—Intimacy & Midnight All Day: A Novel & Stories. 2001. 336p. pap. 13.00 (*0-7432-1714-4*, Scribner) Simon & Schuster.

—Midnight All Day. 1999. 217p. (*0-571-19456-7*) Faber & Faber, Inc.

Lacey, Rick. Cat Fever. 1994. 24.95 (*0-9642466-0-0*) Karson Publishing.

Lacy, Al. Season of Valor: Gettysburg, 8 vols., Vol. 6. 2003. (Battles of Destiny Ser.: No. 6). 294p. pap. 9.99 (*0-88070-865-4*, Multnomah Bks.) Multnomah Pubs., Inc.

Lafayette, Marie J. The Princess of Cleves. 1977. 210p. reprint ed. 38.50 o.s.i (*0-8371-9729-5*, LAFPC, Greenwood Pr.) Greenwood Publishing Group, Inc.

Laity, Sally & Crawford, Dianna. The Tempering Blaze. 1995. (Freedom's Holy Light Ser.: Vol. 3). 393p. pap. 10.99 o.p. (*0-8423-6902-3*) Tyndale Hse. Pubs.

Lake, Amy. The Earl's Wife. l.t. ed. 2001. (First Edition Romance Ser.). 285p. 26.95 (*0-7862-3035-5*, Five Star) Gale Group.

Lamb, Caroline P. Glenarvon, 3 vols., Set. 3rd ed. reprint ed. 97.50 (*0-404-56767-3*) AMS Pr., Inc.

—Glenarvon, 3 vols. in 1. 1972. 272p. reprint ed. 50.00 (*0-8201-1093-0*) Scholars' Facsimiles & Reprints.

—Glenarvon. 2003. 264p. reprint ed. (*1-85477-132-9*) Woodstock Books.

Lambkin, David. The Hanging Tree. 400p. 1998. pap. text 18.00 (*1-887178-71-6*); 1996. text 23.00 o.p. (*1-887178-19-8*) Basic Bks. (Counterpoint Pr.).

Landis, J. D. Lying in Bed: A Novel. 1995. 294p. tchr. ed. 19.95 (*1-56512-068-X*) Algonquin Bks. of Chapel Hill.

Lane, Simon. Still Life with Books: A Novel. 1993. 176p. 17.95 (*1-882593-02-2*) Bridge Works Publishing Co., Inc.

Lau, Evelyn. Other Women. 1996. 192p. 19.50 o.p. (*0-684-82457-4*, Simon & Schuster) Simon & Schuster.

Lawrence, D. H. D.H. Lawrence: Mr. Noon. Vasey, Lindeth, ed. 1984. (Cambridge Edition of the Works of D. H. Lawrence). (Illus.). 416p. 49.95 o.p. (*0-521-25251-2*) Cambridge Univ. Pr.

—Lady Chatterley's Lover. 1976. 20.95 (*0-8488-0559-3*) Amereon, Ltd.

—Lady Chatterley's Lover. abr. ed. audio 12.95 (*0-89926-156-6*, 844) Audio Bk. Co.

—Lady Chatterley's Lover, Kay, Marilyn, ed. abr. ed. 1986. audio 12.95 (*1-882071-10-7*, 012) B&B Audio, Inc.

—Lady Chatterley's Lover. 1983. (Classics Ser.). 384p. mass mkt. 2.95 o.s.i (*0-553-21272-9*, Bantam Classics) Bantam Bks.

—Lady Chatterley's Lover. Durrell, Lawrence, ed. 1983. (Bantam Classics Ser.). 384p. mass mkt. 4.95 (*0-553-21262-1*) Bantam Bks.

—Lady Chatterley's Lover. unabr. collector's ed. 1987. audio 72.00 (*0-7366-1127-4*, 2050) Books on Tape, Inc.

—Lady Chatterley's Lover. 1981. reprint ed. lib. bdg. 23.95 (*0-89966-375-3*) Buccaneer Bks., Inc.

—Lady Chatterley's Lover. abr. ed. audio 15.95 o.p. (*0-88646-044-1*, 7061) Durkin Hayes Publishing Ltd.

—Lady Chatterley's Lover. l.t. ed. 1993. (General Ser.). 474p. lib. bdg. 19.95 o.p. (*0-8161-5651-4*, Macmillan Reference USA) Gale Group.

—Lady Chatterley's Lover. 1993. 384p. pap. 12.00 (*0-8021-3334-7*, Grove Pr.); 1987. 384p. pap. 3.95 o.p. (*0-8021-3068-2*); 1969. pap. 3.95 o.p. (*0-394-62424-6*, B479) Grove/Atlantic, Inc.

—Lady Chatterley's Lover. abr. ed. 2000. audio 7.95 (*1-57815-121-X*, 1083, Media Bks. Audio Publishing) Media Bks., L. L. C.

—Lady Chatterley's Lover. 1959. mass mkt. 2.95 o.p. (*0-451-52247-8*); 304p. mass mkt. 5.95 o.p. (*0-451-52498-5*, CE1787) NAL. (Signet Classics).

—Lady Chatterley's Lover. 1986. 5.99 o.s.i (*0-517-38587-2*) Random Hse. Value Publishing.

—Lady Chatterley's Lover. (Modern Library Ser.). 1993. 560p. 17.95 o.s.i (*0-679-60065-5*); 1960. 3.95 o.s.i (*0-394-60148-3*) Random Hse., Inc.

—Lady Chatterley's Lover, unabr. ed. 1988. audio 78.00 (*1-55690-292-1*, 88100E7) Recorded Bks., LLC.

—Lady Chatterley's Lover. Squires, Michael, ed. & intro. by. 1995. (Twentieth Century Classics Ser.). 400p. 12.00 (*0-14-018786-3*, Penguin Classics) Viking Penguin.

—Lady Chatterley's Lover & a Propos of "Lady Chatterley's Lover" Squires, Michael, ed. 1993. (Cambridge Edition of the Works of D. H. Lawrence). (Illus.). 522p. 120.00 (*0-521-22266-4*) Cambridge Univ. Pr.

—Mr. Noon. Vasey, Lindeth, ed. 1987. (Cambridge Edition of the Works of D. H. Lawrence). (Illus.). 416p. pap. 40.00 (*0-521-27247-5*) Cambridge Univ. Pr.

—Mr. Noon. Vasey, Lindeth, ed. (Penguin Twentieth-Century Classics Ser.). (Illus.). 1997. 368p. pap. 21.00 (*0-14-018973-4*); 1985. 384p. 22.50 o.p. (*0-670-80818-0*) Viking Penguin.

LeBeau, Sinclair. Somebody's Someone. 1999. 162p. mass mkt. 8.95 (*1-885478-57-7*, Indigo) Genesis Pr., Inc.

Leebron, Fred G. Out West. 1997. (Harvest Book Ser.). 256p. pap. 12.00 o.s.i (*0-15-600546-8*, Harvest Bks.) Harcourt Trade Pubs.

—Out West: A Novel. 1996. 256p. 21.95 o.s.i (*0-385-48420-8*) Doubleday Publishing.

Lefcourt, Peter. Di & I: A Novel. 1995. 320p. pap. 72.00 o.p. (*0-06-097669-1*); pap. 12.00 o.p. (*0-06-097668-3*) HarperTrade. (Perennial).

—Eleven Karens. 2003. 240p. 24.00 (*0-684-87034-7*, Simon & Schuster) Simon & Schuster.

Leimbach, Marti. Love & Houses. 1997. 288p. 20.50 o.p. (*0-684-83670-X*, Simon & Schuster) Simon & Schuster.

Leland, Mary. Approaching Priests. 1992. 224p. 23.95 o.p. (*1-85619-065-X*) Trafalgar Square.

Lemann, Nancy. Lives of the Saints. Lish, Gordon, ed. 1985. 143p. 13.95 o.s.i (*0-394-54445-5*) Knopf, Alfred A. Inc.

—Lives of the Saints: Novel. 1997. (Voices of the South Ser.). 160p. pap. 13.95 (*0-8071-2162-2*) Louisiana State Univ. Pr.

Lennox, Judith. Some Old Lover's Ghost. 1999. 480p. reprint ed. pap. 14.00 (*0-688-17219-9*, Quill) HarperTrade.

—Some Old Lover's Ghost. 2000. 479p. 29.95 (*0-385-40675-4*); 571p. pap. 10.95 (*0-552-14333-2*) Transworld Publishers Ltd. GBR. *Dist:* Trafalgar Square.

Leonard, Hugh. Parnell & the Englishwoman. 1991. 256p. 19.95 o.s.i (*0-689-12127-X*, Scribner) Simon & Schuster.

Lette, Kathy. Girl's Night Out. 1989. 224p. 16.95 o.p. (*0-688-08511-3*, Morrow, William & Co.) Morrow/Avon.

Lewis, Eddie. Ray Had an Idea about Love. 1995. 240p. 21.00 o.s.i (*0-671-88762-9*, Simon & Schuster) Simon & Schuster.

Lewis, Fiona. Between Men: A Novel. 1995. 304p. 21.00 o.p. (*0-87113-586-8*, Atlantic Monthly Pr.) Grove/Atlantic, Inc.

Lewis, Jel D. The Perfect Lady. 1994. 200p. pap. 12.95 (*0-9639917-0-1*) Writer's Unlimited Publishing.

Liebrecht, Savyon. A Man & a Woman & a Man. Pomerantz, Marsha, tr. from HEB. 2001. 224p. 24.95 (*0-89255-266-2*) Persea Bks., Inc.

—A Man & a Woman & a Man: A Novel. Pomerantz, Marsha, tr. 2003. 256p. pap. 14.00 (*0-89255-297-2*) Persea Bks., Inc.

Lindsay, Paul. Harbour My Heart. l.t. ed. 1993. 18.95 o.p. (*0-7927-1805-4*); pap. 17.95 o.p. (*0-7927-1804-6*) BBC Audiobooks America.

Lindsey, David L. Animosity. l.t. ed. 2001. (Americana Ser.). 447p. 28.95 o.p. (*0-7862-3324-9*) Thorndike Pr.

—Animosity. 2001. 352p. 24.95 o.p. (*0-446-52791-2*) Warner Bks., Inc.

Linz, Cathie. Pride & Joy. 1985. (Candlelight Regency Romance Ser.: No. 313). pap. 1.95 o.p. (*0-440-16935-6*) Dell Publishing.

—Pride & Joy. 1998. (Romance Ser.). pap. text 24.95 (*0-7862-1494-5*, Five Star) Gale Group.

Lipman, Elinor. The Ladies' Man. l.t. ed. 2000. 26.95 (*1-56895-837-4*, Wheeler Publishing, Inc.) Gale Group.

—The Ladies' Man. 2000. (Contemporaries Ser.). 272p. pap. 13.00 (*0-375-70731-X*, Vintage) Knopf Publishing Group.

Lipman, Victoria. Leaving Alva. 1998. 192p. 22.00 (*0-684-83415-4*, Simon & Schuster) Simon & Schuster.

Lispector, Clarice. An Apprenticeship or The Book of Delights. Mazzara, Richard A. & Parris, Lorri A., trs. from POR. 1986. (Texas Pan American Ser.). 140p. text 18.95 (*0-292-79030-9*) Univ. of Texas Pr.

Lively, Penelope. Heat Wave: A Novel. l.t. ed. 1997. (Core Ser.). 335p. lib. bdg. 25.95 o.p. (*0-7838-1989-9*, Macmillan Reference USA) Gale Group.

—Heat Wave: A Novel. 1996. 224p. 22.00 o.p. (*0-06-017476-5*) HarperCollins Pubs.

Loewen, Paul. Butterfly. 1996. 288p. pap. 10.95 o.p. (*0-452-27583-0*, Plume) Dutton/Plume.

—Butterfly. 1988. 272p. 16.95 o.p. (*0-312-01395-7*) St. Martin's Pr.

Loos, Anita. But Gentlemen Marry Brunettes. 1994. 96p. pap. 7.95 o.p. (*0-14-018488-0*, Penguin Classics) Viking Penguin.

—Gentlemen Prefer Blondes. 1994. lib. bdg. 21.95 (*1-56849-512-9*) Buccaneer Bks., Inc.

—Gentlemen Prefer Blondes. 1958. 5.60 (*0-87129-412-5*, G13) Dramatic Publishing Co.

—Gentlemen Prefer Blondes. (Illus.). 1998. 216p. pap. 10.95 (*0-87140-170-3*); 1963. 5.95 o.p. (*0-87140-888-0*) Liveright Publishing Corp.

—Gentlemen Prefer Blondes. 1994. 160p. pap. 8.95 o.s.i (*0-14-018487-2*, Penguin Classics) Viking Penguin.

—Gentlemen Prefer Blondes & But Gentlemen Marry Brunettes: The Illuminating Diary of a Professional Lady. 1998. (Twentieth Century Classics Ser.). (Illus.). 352p. 12.95 (*0-14-118069-2*, Penguin Classics) Viking Penguin.

Lott, Bret. The Man Who Owned Vermont. 1999. 240p. pap. 12.00 (*0-671-03820-6*); 1988. 224p. pap. (*0-671-64587-0*) Simon & Schuster. (Washington Square Pr.).

—The Man Who Owned Vermont. 1987. 231p. 16.95 o.p. (*0-670-81582-9*) Viking Penguin.

—A Stranger's House. 1999. 256p. pap. 12.00 (*0-671-03822-2*); 1990. 272p. pap. (*0-671-68328-4*) Simon & Schuster. (Washington Square Pr.).

—A Stranger's House. 1988. 272p. 17.95 o.p. (*0-670-82246-9*) Viking Penguin.

Lott, Tim. The Love Secrets of Don Juan. 2003. 320p. text (*0-670-91269-7*, Viking) Viking Penguin.

Lowell, Elizabeth. Only His. l.t. ed. 1996. (Large Print Bks.). pap. 23.95 (*1-56895-292-9*, Wheeler Publishing, Inc.) Gale Group.

—Where the Heart Is. 2002. E-Book 6.99 (*0-06-050395-5*); E-Book 6.99 (*0-06-050396-3*); E-Book 6.99 (*0-06-050394-7*); E-Book 6.99 (*0-06-050393-9*) HarperCollins General Bks. Group. (PerfectBound).

Macdonald, Malcolm. To the End of Her Days. 1994. 384p. 23.95 o.p. (*0-312-11080-4*) St. Martin's Pr.

MacDonald, Shari. Forget-Me-Not. 1996. 274p. pap. 9.99 o.s.i (*0-88070-769-0*, Palisades) Multnomah Pubs., Inc.

Maitland, Sara. Ancestral Truths: A Novel. 1995. 88p. pap. 12.00 o.p. (*0-8050-3779-9*, Owl Bks.); 1994. 304p. 22.50 o.p. (*0-8050-2536-7*) Holt, Henry & Co.

Malecot, Andre. Eye on the Western Stars: A Novel. 1995. 176p. (Orig.). pap. 10.95 (*1-56474-113-3*) Fithian Pr.

Mallon, Thomas. Dewey Defeats Truman. 1997. 368p. pap. 14.00 (*0-312-18086-1*) Picador.

Malouf, Melissa. It Had to Be You: The Joan & Ernest Story. 1997. 176p. 25.00 (*1-888105-19-4*) Avisson Pr., Inc.

Manning, Olivia. The Wind Changes. 1991. (Modern Classics Ser.). 336p. (Orig.). pap. 8.95 o.p. (*0-14-016219-4*) Penguin Group (USA) Inc.

Mapson, Jo-Ann. Blue Rodeo: A Novel. 1995. 336p. pap. 13.00 (*0-06-092635-X*, Perennial); 1994. 352p. 22.00 o.p. (*0-06-016944-3*) HarperTrade.

—Hank & Chloe: A Novel. l.t. ed. 1993. 24.95 o.p. (*0-7927-1718-X*); pap. 22.95 o.p. (*0-7927-1699-X*) BBC Audiobooks America.

—Hank & Chloe: A Novel. 1993. 320p. 20.00 o.p. (*0-06-016943-5*) HarperTrade.

—The Wilder Sisters: A Novel. l.t. ed. 2000. 26.95 (*1-56895-866-8*, Wheeler Publishing, Inc.) Gale Group.
—The Wilder Sisters: A Novel. 1999. 384p. (J). 24.00 (*0-06-019116-3*) HarperCollins Pubs.
—The Wilder Sisters: A Novel. 2000. 384p. pap. 13.00 (*0-06-093107-8*, Perennial) HarperTrade.
Margolis, Sue. Neurotica. 2000. 336p. reprint ed. mass mkt. 6.50 o.s.i (*0-553-58106-6*) Bantam Bks.
—Neurotica. 2003. 336p. pap. 11.95 (*0-385-33757-4*, Delta); E-Book (*0-440-33461-6*) Dell Publishing.
Mark, Andrew, et al. Falling Bodies: Novel. 1999. 272p. 22.95 o.s.i (*0-399-14447-1*, G. P. Putnam's Sons) Penguin Group (USA) Inc.
Markson, David. Springer's Progress. 1990. 240p. reprint ed. pap. 9.95 o.p. (*0-916583-57-0*) Dalkey Archive Pr.
Marshall, Sybil. A Nest of Magpies. pap. 15.95 (*0-312-31070-6*, Saint Martin's Griffin); 1994. 476p. 24.95 (*0-312-11034-0*) St. Martin's Pr.
Martin, Catherine. The Silent Sea. Foxton, Rosemary, ed. 1996. 569p. pap. (*0-86840-373-3*) UNSW Pr.
Martin, David. The Crying Heart Tattoo. 1982. 352p. o.p. (*0-03-060488-5*) Holt, Henry & Co.
—The Crying Heart Tattoo: A Novel. 1994. 320p. pap. 12.95 o.p. (*0-8118-0777-0*) Chronicle Bks. LLC.
Martin, LaJoyce. Ordered Steps. 1996. (Path of Promise Ser.). 208p. pap. 9.99 (*1-56722-190-4*) Word Aflame Pr.
Martin, Steve. Shopgirl: A Novella. l.t. ed. 2001. (Wheeler Large Print Book Ser.). 151p. 28.95 (*1-58724-012-2*, Wheeler Publishing, Inc.) Gale Group.
—Shopgirl: A Novella. 2001. 112p. pap. 10.95 (*0-7868-8568-8*); 2001. 144p. E-Book 12.95 (*0-7868-7165-2*); 2001. 144p. E-Book 12.95 (*0-7868-7163-6*); 2001. 144p. E-Book 12.95 (*0-7868-7161-X*); 2001. 144p. E-Book 12.95 (*0-7868-7162-8*); 2001. 144p. E-Book 12.95 (*0-7868-7160-1*); 2000. (Illus.). 130p. 17.95 (*0-7868-6658-6*) Hyperion Pr.
Martin, Valerie. A Recent Martyr. 1987. 16.95 o.p. (*0-395-43613-3*) Houghton Mifflin Co.
—A Recent Martyr. 1989. pap. 7.95 o.s.i (*0-679-72158-4*, V158, Vintage) Knopf Publishing Group.
Martinez, Demetria. MotherTongue. 1994. (Orig.). 136p. 17.00 o.p. (*0-927534-42-8*); 121p. pap. 10.00 o.p. (*0-927534-43-6*) Bilingual Pr./Editorial Bilingue.
Maxwell, Evan. All the Winters That Have Been: A Novel. 1995. 192p. 15.00 o.p. (*0-06-017633-4*) HarperCollins Pubs.
Mazur, Grace Dane. Trespass. 2002. 300p. pap. 14.95 (*1-55597-364-7*) Graywolf Pr.
McCloy, Kristin. Some Girls. 272p. 1995. pap. 12.95 o.s.i (*0-452-27273-4*, Plume); 1994. 20.95 o.s.i (*0-525-93837-0*) Dutton/Plume.
McCourtney, Lorena. Betrayed. 1996. 290p. pap. 9.99 o.p. (*0-88070-756-9*, Palisades) Multnomah Pubs., Inc.
McCracken, Elizabeth. The Giant's House: A Romance. 1997. 304p. pap. 13.00 (*0-380-73020-0*, Avon Bks.) Morrow/Avon.
McCullough, Colleen. The Thorn Birds. 1998. lib. bdg. 11.95 (*1-56849-697-4*) Buccaneer Bks., Inc.
—The Thorn Birds. 1977. 19.95 o.p. (*0-06-012956-5*) HarperTrade.
—The Thorn Birds. 1978. 540p. mass mkt. 6.95 o.p. (*0-380-56390-8*, 56390-8); 704p. mass mkt. 7.99 (*0-380-01817-9*) Morrow/Avon. (Avon Bks.).
—The Thorn Birds. 1998. (Modern Classics Ser.). 704p. 9.99 o.s.i (*0-517-20165-8*) Random Hse. Value Publishing.
—The Thorn Birds. 1978. 13.04 (*0-606-01301-6*) Turtleback Bks.
—Tim. 1974. 256p. 15.95 o.p. (*0-06-012891-7*) HarperTrade.
—Tim; An Indecent Obsession; Missalonghi. 1999. 768p. 13.99 o.s.i (*0-517-20166-6*) Random Hse. Value Publishing.
McEwan, Ian. The Innocent. 1995. 288p. mass mkt. 6.99 o.s.i (*0-553-56554-0*); 1991. 320p. pap. 6.99 o.s.i (*0-553-55000-4*) Bantam Bks.
—The Innocent. 288p. 1998. pap. 14.00 (*0-385-49433-5*); 1990. 18.95 o.p. (*0-385-41370-X*) Doubleday Publishing.
McGahern, John. The Pornographer. 1979. 11.45 o.p. (*0-06-013021-0*) HarperCollins Pubs.
—The Pornographer. 1983. 256p. pap. 6.95 o.p. (*0-14-006489-3*, Penguin Bks.) Viking Penguin.
McGarry, Jean. Dream Date: Stories. 2002. (Johns Hopkins, Poetry & Fiction Ser.). 248p. pap. 16.95 (*0-8018-6937-4*) Johns Hopkins Univ. Pr.
McGrath, Patrick. Dr. Haggard's Disease. 1994. (Vintage Contemporaries Ser.). 192p. pap. 12.00 (*0-679-75261-7*) Random Hse., Inc.
—Dr. Haggard's Disease. 1993. 192p. 20.00 o.p. (*0-671-72733-8*, Simon & Schuster) Simon & Schuster.
McGuane, Thomas. Something to Be Desired. 1985. (Vintage Contemporaries Ser.). 192p. pap. 12.00 (*0-394-73156-5*, Vintage) Knopf Publishing Group.
—Something to Be Desired. 1984. 224p. 14.95 o.p. (*0-394-52873-5*) Random Hse., Inc.
McKeown, Barry. Ashes by Now. 1996. 330p. 18.95 o.p. (*0-944957-59-5*) Rivercross Publishing, Inc.
McKinney, Meagan. Fair Is the Rose. l.t. ed. 1993. 12.95 o.p. (*1-56895-031-4*, Wheeler Publishing, Inc.) Gale Group.
McKinnon, K. C. Dancing at the Harvest Moon. 1999. (Illus.). 248p. mass mkt. 6.50 o.s.i (*0-449-00527-5*, Fawcett) Ballantine Bks.
—Dancing at the Harvest Moon. l.t. ed. 1998. 25.95 o.p. (*1-56895-551-0*, Wheeler Publishing, Inc.) Gale Group.
McKinnon, Karen. Narcissus Ascending. 2002. 224p. 21.00 (*0-312-29058-6*) Picador.
—Narcissus Ascending: A Novel. 2003. 224p. pap. 13.00 (*0-312-31218-0*) Picador.
McMillan, Terry. Disappearing Acts. l.t. ed. 1993. 24.95 o.p. (*1-56895-033-0*, Wheeler Publishing, Inc.) Gale Group.
—Disappearing Acts. Rosenman, Jane, ed. 1993. 384p. mass mkt. 7.99 (*0-671-87200-1*, Pocket); 1990. 400p. reprint ed. pap. (*0-671-70843-0*, Washington Square Pr.) Simon & Schuster.
—Disappearing Acts. 1989. 448p. 26.95 (*0-670-82461-5*) Viking Penguin.
McMurtry, Larry. Cadillac Jack. 1995. reprint ed. lib. bdg. 27.95 o.p. (*1-56849-648-6*) Buccaneer Bks., Inc.
—Cadillac Jack. 2002. 400p. pap. 14.00 (*0-684-85383-3*, Simon & Schuster) Simon & Schuster.
—Cadillac Jack. Grose, Bill, ed. 1990. mass mkt. 7.99 (*0-671-73902-6*, Pocket) Simon & Schuster.
—Cadillac Jack. 1990. mass mkt. 4.95 (*0-671-70825-2*, Pocket); 1987. 400p. pap. 14.00 (*0-671-63720-7*, Simon & Schuster); 1985. pap. 8.95 o.s.i (*0-671-55541-3*, Touchstone); 1982. 416p. 75.00 o.p. (*0-671-45983-X*, Simon & Schuster) Simon & Schuster.
—Leaving Cheyenne. 1976. 22.95 (*0-8488-0373-6*) Amereon, Ltd.
—Leaving Cheyenne. unabr. collector's ed. 1983. audio 48.00 (*0-7366-0763-3*, 1720) Books on Tape, Inc.
—Leaving Cheyenne. unabr. ed. 1993. audio 70.00 (*1-55690-847-4*, 93214E7) Recorded Bks., LLC.
—Leaving Cheyenne. 304p. 2002. pap. 14.00 (*0-684-85387-6*); 1992. pap. 12.00 (*0-671-75490-4*) Simon & Schuster. (Simon & Schuster).
—Leaving Cheyenne. Grose, Bill, ed. 1992. 320p. reprint ed. mass mkt. 7.99 (*0-671-75380-0*, Pocket) Simon & Schuster.
—Leaving Cheyenne. 1986. (Southwest Landmark Ser.: No. 3). 312p. reprint ed. 15.95 o.p. (*0-89096-242-1*) Texas A&M Univ. Pr.
—Leaving Cheyenne. 1979. (Contemporary American Fiction Ser.). 256p. pap. 8.95 o.p. (*0-14-005221-6*, Penguin Bks.) Viking Penguin.
—Terms of Endearment. l.t. ed. 1984. (General Ser.). 18.95 o.p. (*0-8161-3708-0*, Macmillan Reference USA) Gale Group.
—Terms of Endearment. 1988. mass mkt. 4.50 o.p. (*0-451-15817-2*); 1983. mass mkt. 2.95 o.p. (*0-451-15778-8*); 1976. mass mkt. 1.95 o.p. (*0-451-07173-5*) NAL. (Signet Bks.).
—Terms of Endearment. 1999. 416p. pap. 13.00 (*0-684-85390-6*, Simon & Schuster) Simon & Schuster.
—Terms of Endearment. Grose, Bill, ed. 1992. 432p. mass mkt. 7.99 (*0-671-75872-1*, Pocket) Simon & Schuster.
—Terms of Endearment. 1989. 416p. pap. 11.00 (*0-671-68208-3*); 1975. 448p. 9.95 o.s.i (*0-671-22102-7*) Simon & Schuster. (Simon & Schuster).
McNaught, Judith. Perfect. Marrow, Linda, ed. 1993. 528p. 22.00 (*0-671-79552-X*, Atria); 1994. 704p. reprint ed. mass mkt. 7.99 (*0-671-79553-8*, Pocket) Simon & Schuster.
—Perfect. abr. ed. 1993. audio 17.00 (*0-671-86556-0*, 391361, Simon & Schuster Audioworks) Simon & Schuster Audio.
—Perfect. l.t. ed. 1993. (Romance Ser.). 1008p. lib. bdg. 26.95 (*1-56054-731-6*) Thorndike Pr.
—Remember When. 2003. 432p. mass mkt. 5.99 (*0-7434-6728-0*, Pocket); 1996. 400p. 24.00 (*0-671-52570-0*, Atria); 1997. 432p. reprint ed. mass mkt. 7.99 (*0-671-79555-4*, Pocket) Simon & Schuster.
—Remember When. l.t. ed. 1997. 704p. pap. 28.95 (*0-7862-0569-5*) Thorndike Pr.
—Tender Triumph. l.t. ed. 1993. 21.95 o.p. (*1-56895-013-6*, Wheeler Publishing, Inc.) Gale Group.
—Tender Triumph. 1990. mass mkt. 4.95 (*0-671-73514-4*, Pocket) Simon & Schuster.
—Until You. l.t. ed. 1994. 26.95 o.p. (*1-56895-160-4*, Wheeler Publishing, Inc.) Gale Group.
—Until You. 1994. 448p. 22.00 o.p. (*0-671-88059-4*, Atria) Simon & Schuster.
—Until You. Marrow, Linda, ed. 1995. 448p. reprint ed. mass mkt. 7.99 (*0-671-88060-8*, Pocket) Simon & Schuster.
—Whitney, My Love. l.t. ed. 1994. 25.95 o.p. (*1-56895-107-8*, Wheeler Publishing, Inc.) Gale Group.
Mda, Zakes. Ways of Dying. 1995. (Southern African Writing Ser.). 192p. (Orig.). pap. 10.95 o.p. (*0-19-571106-8*) Oxford Univ. Pr., Inc.
—Ways of Dying. 2002. 216p. (Orig.). pap. 13.00 (*0-312-42091-9*) Picador.
Medoff, Jillian. Good Girls Gone Bad. 2002. 304p. 24.95 (*0-06-621269-3*, Morrow, William & Co.) Morrow/Avon.
Medwed, Mameve. Mail. 1997. 336p. 23.00 o.p. (*0-446-52088-8*); 1998. 320p. reprint ed. pap. 12.95 (*0-446-67375-7*) Warner Bks., Inc.
Meredith, George. The Egoist. 1999. E-Book 1.95 (*1-58515-098-3*) MesaView, Inc.
—The Egoist. mass mkt. 0.75 o.p. (*0-451-50191-8*, Signet Classics); 1986. pap. 5.95 o.p. (*0-452-00820-4*, Meridian Bks.) NAL.
—The Egoist. Adams, Robert M., ed. 1979. (Critical Editions Ser.). (C). o.p. (*0-393-04431-9*); 561p. pap. text 12.00 (*0-393-09171-6*) Norton, W. W. & Co., Inc.
—The Egoist. 1968. (Oxford World's Classics Ser.). 12.95 o.p. (*0-19-250508-4*) Oxford Univ. Pr., Inc.
—The Egoist. Wilson, Angus, ed. 1979. (Penguin Classics Ser.). 608p. pap. 12.95 o.p. (*0-14-043034-2*, Penguin Classics) Viking Penguin.
—The Egoist. 448p. pap. 3.95 (*1-85326-266-8*) Wordsworth Editions, Ltd. GBR. *Dist:* Combined Publishing.
—The Egoist: A Comedy in Narrative. Harris, Margaret, ed. 1992. (Oxford World's Classics Ser.). 610p. pap. 9.95 o.p. (*0-19-281817-1*) Oxford Univ. Pr., Inc.
Metzger, Deena. What Dinah Thought. 1989. 384p. 19.95 o.p. (*0-670-82750-9*) Viking Penguin.
Michaels, Barbara, pseud. Houses of Stone. 1994. 400p. reprint ed. mass mkt. 7.50 o.s.i (*0-425-14306-6*) Berkley Publishing Group.
—Houses of Stone. 1993. 336p. 21.00 o.p. (*0-671-68949-5*, Simon & Schuster) Simon & Schuster.
—Houses of Stone. l.t. ed. (Paperback Bestsellers Ser.). 556p. 1995. 20.95 (*0-8161-5937-8*); 1994. lib. bdg. 25.95 (*0-8161-5936-X*) Thorndike Pr.
—Patriot's Dream. l.t. ed. 1995. pap. 21.95 o.p. (*0-7927-2020-2*); 1994. 22.95 o.p. (*0-7927-2021-0*) BBC Audiobooks America.
Michaels, Fern. Dear Emily. l.t. ed. 1995. (Large Print Bks.). 26.95 (*1-56895-254-6*, Wheeler Publishing, Inc.) Gale Group.
—Dear Emily. 2002. 448p. mass mkt. 7.50 (*0-8217-7316-X*); 2002. 448p. mass mkt. 7.99 (*0-8217-7670-3*, Zebra Bks.); 1996. 448p. mass mkt. 6.99 o.s.i (*0-8217-5676-1*, Zebra Bks.); 1995. 512p. mass mkt. 5.99 o.s.i (*0-8217-4952-8*, Zebra Bks.) Kensington Publishing Corp.
—Dear Emily. 1996. 448p. reprint ed. 22.00 (*0-7278-4802-X*) Severn Hse. Pubs., Ltd.
—Desperate Measures. 1996. 448p. mass mkt. 6.99 (*0-8041-1536-2*, Ivy Bks.) Ballantine Bks.
—Texas Fury. 1991. reprint ed. 21.95 o.p. (*0-7278-4269-2*) Severn Hse. Pubs., Ltd.
—What You Wish For. l.t. ed. 2000. (Romance Ser.). 431p. 27.95 o.p. (*1-56895-998-2*, Wheeler Publishing, Inc.) Gale Group.
—What You Wish For. 2000. 32p. 24.00 o.s.i (*1-57566-573-5*); 2001. 352p. reprint ed. mass mkt. 7.99 (*0-8217-6828-X*) Kensington Publishing Corp.
—Wish List. 1996. (Romances Ser.). lib. bdg. 24.95 (*0-7862-0851-1*, Five Star); 26.95 (*1-56895-336-4*, Wheeler Publishing, Inc.) Gale Group.
—Wish List. 352p. 2002. mass mkt. 7.50 (*0-8217-7363-1*); 1996. mass mkt. 6.99 o.s.i (*0-8217-5228-6*, Zebra Bks.) Kensington Publishing Corp.
Middleton, Stanley. Live & Learn. 1996. 248p. o.p. (*0-09-179220-7*) Random Hse. of Canada, Ltd. CAN. *Dist:* Random Hse., Inc.
Miller, Sue. The Good Mother. 1994. 320p. pap. 13.95 (*0-385-31243-1*, Delta); 1987. 464p. mass mkt. 6.99 o.s.i (*0-440-12938-9*) Dell Publishing.
—The Good Mother. l.t. ed. 1987. 485p. 12.95 o.p. (*0-8161-4170-3*); 18.95 o.p. (*0-8161-4169-X*) Gale Group. (Macmillan Reference USA).
—The Good Mother. 2002. 320p. pap. 12.95 (*0-06-050593-1*, Perennial); 1986. 310p. 17.95 o.p. (*0-06-015551-5*) HarperTrade.
—While I Was Gone. 2002. 352p. mass mkt. 7.99 (*0-345-42074-8*); 2000. 304p. pap. 14.00 (*0-345-44328-4*); 2000. 304p. pap. 12.95 o.s.i (*0-345-43500-1*) Ballantine Bks.
—While I Was Gone. l.t. ed. 1999. 30.00 o.p. (*0-7838-8481-8*, Macmillan Reference USA) Gale Group.
—While I Was Gone. l.t. ed. 1999. 448p. 24.00 o.s.i (*0-375-70571-6*) Knopf, Alfred A. Inc.
—While I Was Gone. abr. ed. 2000. audio 25.95 (*0-375-41664-1*); 2000. audio compact disk 29.95 (*0-375-41665-X*); 1999. audio 24.00 o.s.i (*0-375-40563-1*, 691584) Random Hse. Audio Publishing Group. (RH Audio).
—While I Was Gone. l.t. ed. 2000. 448p. pap. 12.95 o.s.i (*0-375-72801-5*) Random Hse. Large Print.
—While I Was Gone. 2000. (Oprah's Book Club Ser.). 288p. 24.00 (*0-375-41178-X*) Random Hse., Inc.
—While I Was Gone. 2000. 19.00 (*0-606-22790-3*) Turtleback Bks.
Millington, Mil. Things My Girlfriend & I Have Argued About: A Novel. 2003. 384p. pap. 12.95 (*0-8129-6666-X*, Villard Bks.) Random House Adult Trade Publishing Group.
Minger, Elda. The Dare. 2003. 320p. mass mkt. 6.99 (*0-425-19276-8*) Berkley Publishing Group.
Mirabelli, Eugene. The Language Nobody Speaks. 1999. 144p. 20.00 (*0-935891-02-1*) Spring Harbor Pr.
—The Language Nobody Speaks: A Novel. 1999. 139p. pap. 13.00 (*0-935891-03-X*) Spring Harbor Pr.
Mittermeyer, Helen. Under the Sign of Venus. 1993. 560p. 9.98 o.p. (*0-8317-9066-0*) Smithmark Pubs., Inc.
Moline, Karen. Lunch. 1994. 287p. 22.00 o.p. (*0-688-13320-7*, Morrow, William & Co.) Morrow/Avon.
Monroe, Debra. Newfangled: A Novel. 304p. 2000. pap. 12.00 (*0-684-85197-0*, Touchstone); 1998. 22.00 (*0-684-81905-8*, Simon & Schuster) Simon & Schuster.
Monroe, Mary. Gonna Lay down My Burdens. 2003. 320p. pap. 15.00 (*0-7582-0001-3*); 2002. 288p. 24.00 (*1-57566-911-0*) Kensington Publishing Corp.
Montagu, Lady Mary Wortley. Romance Writings. Grundy, Isobel, ed. 1996. 304p. (C). text 104.00 (*0-19-818319-4*, Clarendon Press) Oxford Univ. Pr., Inc.
Monti, Dean. The Sweep of the Second Hand. 2002. 336p. reprint ed. pap. 14.00 (*0-425-18625-3*) Berkley Publishing Group.
Morley, John D. Feast of Fools. 1994. ix, 443p. 23.95 o.p. (*0-312-11786-8*) St. Martin's Pr.
—The Feast of Fools. 1995. 464p. pap. 13.95 o.p. (*0-312-13493-2*, Saint Martin's Griffin) St. Martin's Pr.
Morrell, David. Extreme Denial. abr. ed. 1996. audio 24.95 o.p. (*0-7871-0582-1*) NewStar Media, Inc.
—Extreme Denial. 480p. 1996. 32.00 (*0-446-51962-6*); 1997. reprint ed. mass mkt. 7.50 (*0-446-60396-1*) Warner Bks., Inc.
Morris, Gilbert. Land of the Shadow. 1993. (Appomattox Saga Ser.: Vol. 4). 338p. pap. 8.99 o.p. (*0-8423-5742-4*) Tyndale Hse. Pubs.
—Out of the Whirlwind. 1994. (Appomattox Saga Ser.: No. 5). (Illus.). 316p. pap. 8.99 o.p. (*0-8423-1658-2*) Tyndale Hse. Pubs.
Morris, Gilbert & Ferguson, J. Landon. Unseen Riches. 1999. (Chronicles of the Golden Frontier Ser.: Bk. 2). 368p. pap. 11.99 (*1-58134-022-2*) Crossway Bks.
Morsi, Pamela. Marrying Stone. l.t. ed. 1995. 423p. pap. 20.95 o.p. (*0-7838-1415-1*, Macmillan Reference USA) Gale Group.
Mosley, Nicholas. Natalie Natalia. 2nd rev. ed. 1996. 278p. pap. 12.95 (*1-56478-086-4*) Dalkey Archive Pr.
Mount, Ferdinand. Fairness. 306p. 2001. 26.00 (*0-7867-0850-6*); 2002. reprint ed. pap. 13.00 (*0-7867-0992-8*) Avalon Publishing Group. (Carroll & Graf Pubs.).
Mrabet, Mohammed. Love with a Few Hairs. Bowles, Paul, tr. from ARA. 1986. 176p. reprint ed. pap. 8.95 (*0-87286-192-9*) City Lights Bks.
Murakami, Haruki. The Wind-Up Bird Chronicle. Rubin, Jay, tr. 1997. 640p. 25.95 o.s.i (*0-679-44669-9*) Knopf, Alfred A. Inc.
—The Wind-Up Bird Chronicle: A Novel. 1998. 624p. pap. 15.00 (*0-679-77543-9*, Vintage) Knopf Publishing Group.
Murphy, Barbara B. No Place to Run. l.t. ed. 1994. pap. 17.95 o.p. (*0-7927-2153-5*) BBC Audiobooks America.
Murray, Earl. In the Arms of the Sky. 2000. 304p. mass mkt. 6.99 (*0-8125-5143-5*); 1998. 301p. 22.95 (*0-312-86123-0*) Doherty, Tom Assocs., LLC. (Forge Bks.).
Myerson, Julie. Me & the Fat Man. 1999. 224p. o.p. (*0-88001-649-3*, Ecco) HarperTrade.
Narayan, Kirin. Love, Stars & All That. 1994. 320p. 20.00 (*0-671-79395-0*, Atria) Simon & Schuster.
Naumoff, Lawrence. A Plan for Women. 1999. 288p. (C). pap. 13.00 (*0-15-600452-6*, Harvest Bks.); 1997. 272p. 23.00 o.s.i (*0-15-100231-2*) Harcourt Trade Pubs.
—Taller Women: A Cautionary Tale. 1992. 304p. 21.95 o.s.i (*0-15-187991-5*) Harcourt Trade Pubs.
Nelson, Antonya. Talking in Bed. 1996. 275p. tchr. ed. 22.95 o.p. (*0-395-68678-4*) Houghton Mifflin Co.
—Talking in Bed. 1998. 288p. pap. 11.00 (*0-684-83800-1*, Scribner) Simon & Schuster.
Nelson-Weyh, Christie. Woodacre: A Novel. 1998. 258p. (*0-9654951-2-4*) Thumbprint Pr.
Newman, Frances. Dead Lovers are Faithful Lovers: A Novel by Frances Newman. 1994. (Brown Thrasher Bks.). 312p. reprint ed. pap. 17.95 (*0-8203-1588-5*) Univ. of Georgia Pr.

Newmann, Frances. Dead Lovers Are Faithful Lovers. 1977. (Rediscovered Fiction by American Women Ser.). lib. bdg. 33.95 (*0-405-10051-5*) Ayer Co. Pubs., Inc.

Nichols, John. Sterile Cuckoo. 1996. (Norton Paperback Fiction Ser.). 224p. reprint ed. pap. 13.00 (*0-393-31535-5*) Norton, W. W. & Co., Inc.

Nighbert, David F. Shutout. 1995. 307p. 21.95 o.p. (*0-312-11890-2*, Saint Martin's Minotaur) St. Martin's Pr.

Nova, Craig. The Book of Dreams. 1994. 336p. 22.95 o.p. (*0-395-63650-7*) Houghton Mifflin Co.

Novas, Himilce. Mangos, Bananas & Coconuts: A Cuban Love Story. 1996. 168p. 9.95 (*1-55885-092-9*) Arte Publico Pr.

Nuelle, Helen. Surrender to Love. l.t. ed. 1993. 19.95 o.p. (*0-7927-1688-4*); pap. 17.95 o.p. (*0-7927-1687-6*) BBC Audiobooks America.

Oakleaf, David, ed. Love in Excess or the Fatal Enquiry: Eliza Haywood. 1994. (Literary Texts Ser.). 240p. pap. (*1-55111-016-4*) Broadview Pr.

Oakley, Ann. The Men's Room. 1989. 18.95 o.s.i (*0-689-12050-8*, Scribner) Simon & Schuster.

Oates, Joyce Carol. Beasts. 2003. 160p. pap. 11.00 (*0-7867-1103-5*); 2002. 128p. 14.00 (*0-7867-0896-4*) Avalon Publishing Group. (Carroll & Graf Pubs.).

—Mysteries of Winterthurn. 1984. 482p. 16.95 o.p. (*0-525-24208-2*, Dutton) Dutton/Plume.

—You Must Remember This. 1987. 480p. 19.95 o.p. (*0-525-24545-6*, Abrahams, William Bks.) Dutton/Plume.

—You Must Remember This. 1988. 450p. reprint ed. pap. 13.00 o.p. (*0-06-097169-X*, PL-7169, Perennial) HarperTrade.

O'Brien, John. Stripper Lessons. 1997. 208p. pap. 12.00 (*0-8021-3507-2*, Grove Pr.) Grove/Atlantic, Inc.

Ogburn, Martha D. Progeny. 1999. 288p. pap. 10.99 (*0-8054-1889-X*) Broadman & Holman Pubs.

Okas, John. Routes. 1994. 225p. 26.00 (*1-877946-43-5*) Permanent Pr., The.

Oke, Janette. Seasons of the Heart, 4 vols. 1993. 576p. 12.99 (*0-88486-088-4*, Arrowood Pr.) BBS Publishing Corp.

Oliver, Julia. Goodbye to the Buttermilk Sky. 1995. 192p. pap. 10.95 o.p. (*0-452-27425-7*, Plume) Dutton/Plume.

—Goodbye to the Buttermilk Sky. 1994. 192p. 18.00 o.p. (*1-881320-18-9*, Black Belt Pr.) River City Publishing.

—Goodbye to the Buttermilk Sky. 2001. (Deep South Bks.). pap. text 16.95 (*0-8173-1145-9*) Univ. of Alabama Pr.

O'Neal, Charles. Three Wishes for Jamie. 1976. 22.95 (*0-8488-0184-9*) Amereon, Ltd.

—Three Wishes for Jamie. 1991. 256p. reprint ed. pap. 5.95 (*1-56129-066-1*) Knightsbridge Publishing.

—Three Wishes for Jamie. 1980. 256p. reprint ed. 26.00 (*0-933256-08-6*); pap. text 16.00 (*0-933256-09-4*) Second Chance Pr.

Ong, Anna. Amazon Dreams: A Woman's Quest to End the Struggle Between Men & Women. 2000. 320p. E-Book 8.00 (*0-7388-7360-8*) Xlibris Corp.

O'Reilly, Sean. Love & Sleep: A Romance. 2003. 13.00 (*0-7867-1235-X*, Carroll & Graf Pubs.) Avalon Publishing Group.

—Love & Sleep: A Romance. 2002. 208p. pap. (*0-571-20545-3*) Faber & Faber, Inc.

O'Rourke, Frank. Ellen & the Barber: Three Love Stories of the Thirties. 1999. E-Book 20.95 o.s.i (*0-312-24610-2*); 1998. 208p. 20.95 o.p. (*0-312-19263-0*) St. Martin's Pr.

Osborn, Carolyn. Warriors & Maidens. 1991. 188p. (C). 19.95 (*0-87565-084-8*) Texas Christian Univ. Pr.

Ouida. Under Two Flags, 3 vols., 2 bks. reprint ed. 84.50 (*0-404-62088-4*);1. o.p. (*0-404-62089-2*);Vol. 2. o.p. (*0-404-62090-6*) AMS Pr., Inc.

Palmen, Connie. The Laws. Huijing, Richard, tr. from DUT. 1993. 208p. 18.50 (*0-8076-1329-0*) Braziller, George Inc.

Palmer, Elizabeth. Flowering Judas. unabr. ed. 1997. audio 69.95 (*0-7540-0058-3*, CAB 1481) BBC Audiobooks America.

—Flowering Judas. 2000. 408p. mass mkt. (*1-55166-593-X*, 1-66593-4, Mira Bks.) Harlequin Enterprises, Ltd.

—Flowering Judas. 1997. 280p. 22.95 o.p. (*0-312-16843-8*) St. Martin's Pr.

—Flowering Judas. l.t. ed. 1998. (Core Ser.). 442p. 28.95 (*0-7838-8401-X*) Thorndike Pr.

—Old Money. 1996. 288p. 21.95 o.p. (*0-312-14020-7*) St. Martin's Pr.

Parent, Gail. A Sign of the Eighties. 1987. 320p. 17.95 o.p. (*0-399-13262-7*, G. P. Putnam's Sons) Penguin Putnam Bks. for Young Readers.

Parks, Tim. Europa. 1999. 272p. pap. 12.95 (*1-55970-506-X*) Arcade Publishing, Inc.

—Europa. 1997. 261p. (*0-436-20213-1*) Secker, Martin & Warburg, Ltd.

—Europa: A Novel. 1998. 272p. 23.95 (*1-55970-444-6*) Arcade Publishing, Inc.

—Loving Roger. 1987. 160p. 15.95 o.p. (*0-8021-0016-3*) Grove/Atlantic, Inc.

—Loving Roger. 1989. 160p. pap. 6.95 o.p. (*0-14-011459-9*, Penguin Bks.) Viking Penguin.

Parsons, Tony. Man & Wife. 2004. 368p. pap. 13.00 (*0-7432-3614-9*, Touchstone); 2003. 352p. 23.00 (*0-7434-5665-3*, Atria) Simon & Schuster.

Pascal, Francine, creator. Fight Fire with Fire. 1997. (Sweet Valley High Ser.: No. 137). 208p. (Orig.). (gr. 7 up). mass mkt. 3.99 o.s.i (*0-553-57071-4*, Dell Books for Young Readers) Random Hse. Children's Bks.

Paton, Alan. Too Late the Phalarope. 23.95 (*0-89190-392-5*) Amereon, Ltd.

—Too Late the Phalarope. unabr. collector's ed. 1982. audio 42.00 (*0-7366-0346-8*, 1332) Books on Tape, Inc.

—Too Late the Phalarope. 1996. 288p. pap. 13.00 (*0-684-81895-7*, Scribner); 1983. pap. 7.95 (*0-684-10455-5*); 1950. pap. 7.95 o.s.i (*0-684-71866-9*, Scribner Paper Fiction); 1985. 272p. reprint ed. pap. 5.95 o.s.i (*0-684-18500-8*, Scribner Paper Fiction) Simon & Schuster.

Paulson, Michael G. & Alvarez-Detrell, Tamara. Madame de la Fayette's The Princess of Cleves: A New Translation. 1994. 196p. (Orig.). 41.00 (*0-8191-9732-7*) Univ. Pr. of America.

Peart, Jane. Autumn Encore. 1993. (International Romance Ser.). 192p. (gr. 10). reprint ed. pap. 7.99 o.p. (*0-8007-5480-8*) Revell, Fleming H. Co.

Penn, W. S. The Absence of Angels: A Novel. 1995. (American Indian Literature & Critical Studies Ser.: Vol. 14). 272p. pap. 19.95 (*0-8061-2714-7*) Univ. of Oklahoma Pr.

Penn, William. The Absence of Angels. 1994. 274p. 28.00 (*1-877946-42-7*) Permanent Pr., The.

Perlman, Elliot. Three Dollars. 1999. 358p. 22.00 (*1-878448-88-9*) MacMurray & Beck, Inc.

Phillips, George. Black Tickets. 1979. 288p. pap. 11.95 o.s.i (*0-385-28088-2*, Delta) Dell Publishing.

Phillips, Jayne Anne. Black Tickets. 1989. mass mkt. 8.95 o.s.i (*0-440-55022-X*, Delta); 1982. mass mkt. 3.95 o.s.i (*0-440-30924-7*, Laurel); 1979. 8.95 o.s.i (*0-440-00708-9*, Delacorte Pr.) Dell Publishing.

—Black Tickets. 2001. 288p. pap. 13.00 (*0-375-72735-3*, Vintage) Knopf Publishing Group.

Phillips, Max. The Artist's Wife: A Novel. 2001. 272p. 23.00 o.s.i (*0-8050-6670-5*) Holt, Henry & Co.

—The Artist's Wife: A Novel. 2003. 256p. pap. 15.00 (*1-56649-273-4*) Welcome Rain Pubs.

—Snakebite Sonnet: A Novel. 1996. 320p. 22.95 o.p. (*0-316-70620-5*) Little Brown & Co.

Phillips, Michael. Home for My Heart. 1994. (Journals of Corrie Belle Hollister: Vol. 8). 320p. pap. 10.99 o.p. (*1-55661-440-3*) Bethany Hse. Pubs.

A Photo Marriage: Novel. 2000. 403p. pap. 12.95 (*0-9637101-7-6*); lib. bdg. 195.00 (*0-9637101-9-2*) Candlelight Pr.

Pilch, Jerzy. His Current Woman. Johnston, Bill, tr. from POL. 2002. 128p. pap. 15.95 (*0-8101-1918-8*, Hydra Bks.) Northwestern Univ. Pr.

Pilcher, Rosamunde. Wild Mountain Thyme. l.t. ed. 1994. 19.95 o.p. (*0-7927-1724-4*); pap. 17.95 o.p. (*0-7927-1723-6*) BBC Audiobooks America.

—Wild Mountain Thyme. 1989. 304p. reprint ed. mass mkt. 5.50 o.s.i (*0-440-20250-7*) Dell Publishing.

—Wild Mountain Thyme. 1996. mass mkt. 6.50 (*0-312-96123-5*, St. Martin's Paperbacks); 1979. 8.95 o.p. (*0-312-87981-4*) St. Martin's Pr.

Plain, Belva. After the Fire. 2001. 448p. reprint ed. mass mkt. 7.99 (*0-440-23574-X*) Dell Publishing.

—After the Fire. l.t. ed. 544p. 2001. pap. 13.95 (*0-375-72805-8*); 2000. 25.95 (*0-375-40976-9*) Random Hse. Large Print.

—Fortune's Hand. unabr. ed. 2000. audio 69.95 (*0-7540-0415-5*, CAB 1838);Set. 8p. audio compact disk 99.95 (*0-7540-5324-5*, CCD 015) Chivers Audio Bks. GBR. *Dist:* BBC Audiobooks America.

—Fortune's Hand. 2000. 432p. mass mkt. 7.99 (*0-440-22641-4*); 1999. mass mkt. 7.99 (*0-440-29575-0*) Dell Publishing.

—Fortune's Hand, Set. abr. ed. 1999. audio 25.00 Highsmith Inc.

—Fortune's Hand. abr. ed. 1999. audio Random Hse. Audio Publishing Group.

—Fortune's Hand. l.t. ed. 2000. (Thorndike/G. K. Hall Paperback Bestsellers Ser.). 519p. pap. 30.95 (*0-7862-2013-9*) Thorndike Pr.

—Fortune's Hand. 2000. (Illus.). 14.04 (*0-606-18103-2*) Turtleback Bks.

Plante, David. The Age of Terror. 1998. (Illus.). 224p. 24.95 o.p. (*0-312-19824-8*) St. Martin's Pr.

—The Age of Terror: Novel. 1999. 240p. pap. 13.95 (*0-312-25366-4*, Saint Martin's Griffin) St. Martin's Pr.

—Annunciation. 1994. 346p. 21.95 o.p. (*0-395-68091-3*) Houghton Mifflin Co.

Portis, Charles. The Dog of the South. 1999. 246p. 15.95 (*0-87951-931-2*) Overlook Pr., The.

Powell, Dawn. The Locusts Have No King. 1996. 286p. pap. 14.00 (*1-883642-42-6*) Steerforth Pr.

—The Locusts Have No King. 1990. 304p. reprint ed. pap. 9.95 o.s.i (*1-878274-00-7*) Yarrow Pr.

Powys, John Cowper. A Glastonbury Romance. 1987. 1120p. reprint ed. 35.00 (*0-87951-282-2*) Overlook Pr., The.

Price, Bruce D. Too Easy. 1994. 21.00 (*0-671-88673-8*, Simon & Schuster) Simon & Schuster.

Price, Eugenia. The Waiting Time. l.t. ed. 1998. (Waiting Time Ser.: Vol. 1). 352p. pap. 6.99 (*0-312-96506-0*, St. Martin's Paperbacks) St. Martin's Pr.

—The Waiting Time. l.t. ed. 1998. (Bestsellers Ser.). 547p. pap. 27.95 (*0-7862-1065-6*) Thorndike Pr.

Prior, Amy, ed. Strictly Casual: Women on Love. 2003. 256p. pap. 14.00 (*1-85242-687-X*) Serpent's Tail Ltd. GBR. *Dist:* Consortium Bk. Sales & Distribution.

Puig, Manuel. Heartbreak Tango: A Serial. 1987. pap. 7.95 o.p. (*0-525-48288-1*, Plume) Dutton/Plume.

—Heartbreak Tango: A Serial. Levine, Suzanne J., tr. 1975. pap. 2.45 o.p. (*0-525-47397-1*, Dutton) Dutton/Plume.

—Heartbreak Tango: A Serial. Levine, Suzanne J., tr. 1991. 22p. pap. 8.95 o.p. (*0-14-015346-2*, 0772-230, Penguin Bks.) Penguin Group (USA) Inc.

—Heartbreak Tango: A Serial. 1996. (Penguin Twentieth-Century Classics Ser.). 224p. pap. 11.95 o.s.i (*0-14-018997-1*, Viking) Viking Penguin.

Purcell, Trip. Sunset Beach. 1996. 320p. (Orig.). pap. 12.95 (*1-884570-47-X*) Research Triangle Publishing.

Pym, Barbara. Some Tame Gazelle. 1992. 256p. pap. 10.95 o.p. (*0-452-26919-9*, Plume); 1983. 252p. 13.95 o.p. (*0-525-24178-7*, Dutton) Dutton/Plume.

—Some Tame Gazelle. l.t. ed. 1984. (General Ser.). 14.95 o.p. (*0-8161-3639-4*, Macmillan Reference USA) Gale Group.

—Some Tame Gazelle. 1986. 256p. reprint ed. pap. 7.95 o.p. (*0-06-097042-1*, PL7042, Perennial) HarperTrade.

Quesinberry, Bonita M. Shades of the Rainbow. 1999. E-Book 4.95 (*1-930364-63-6*, Bookmice) McGraw Publishing, Inc.

Quick, Amanda, pseud. Desire. 1993. 400p. mass mkt. 7.50 (*0-553-56153-7*, Fanfare) Bantam Bks.

—Desire. l.t. ed. 1994. 25.95 o.p. (*1-56895-067-5*, Wheeler Publishing, Inc.) Gale Group.

—Surrender. l.t. ed. 1994. 25.95 (*1-56895-103-5*, Wheeler Publishing, Inc.) Gale Group.

—Surrender. l.t. ed. 1995. (Magna Large Print Ser.). 382p. o.p. (*0-7505-0842-6*) Magna Large Print Bks. GBR. *Dist:* Ulverscroft Large Print Canada, Ltd.

Quindlen, Anna. Black & Blue: A Novel. 2000. 288p. pap. 13.95 (*0-385-33313-7*, Delta); 1999. 384p. mass mkt. 7.99 (*0-440-22610-4*) Dell Publishing.

—Black & Blue: A Novel. l.t. ed. 1998. 27.95 o.p. (*1-56895-565-0*, Wheeler Publishing, Inc.) Gale Group.

—Black & Blue: A Novel, abr. ed. 1998. audio 24.00 (*0-375-40190-3*, RH Audio) Random Hse. Audio Publishing Group.

—Black & Blue: A Novel. 1998. 296p. 23.00 (*0-375-50051-0*) Random Hse., Inc.

—Black & Blue: A Novel. 1999. 13.55 (*0-606-16456-1*) Turtleback Bks.

Quindlen, Anna, contrib. by. Black & Blue: A Novel. 1998. (*0-679-43539-5*, Random Hse. Bks. for Young Readers) Random Hse. Children's Bks.

Radcliffe, Ann. Castles of Athlin & Dunbayne: A Highland Story. 1974. (Gothic Novels Ser.). reprint ed. 51.95 (*0-405-00808-2*) Ayer Co. Pubs., Inc.

—Castles of Athlin & Dunbayne: A Highland Story. Milbank, Alison, ed. 1995. (Oxford World's Classics Ser.). 146p. pap. 9.95 o.p. (*0-19-282357-4*) Oxford Univ. Pr., Inc.

—A Sicilian Romance. 1972. (Gothic Novels Ser.). reprint ed. 46.95 (*0-405-00809-0*) Ayer Co. Pubs., Inc.

—A Sicilian Romance. Milbank, Alison, ed. (Oxford World's Classics Ser.). 1999. 256p. pap. 10.95 (*0-19-283666-8*); 1993. 244p. (C). pap. 8.95 o.p. (*0-19-282212-8*) Oxford Univ. Pr., Inc.

—A Sicilian Romance, 1792, 2 vols. in 1. 2003. (Revolution & Romanticism Ser.). 498p. (*1-85477-190-6*) Woodstock Books.

Rand, Ayn. Anthem. 1953. (Classic Ser.). 105p. 12.95 (*0-87004-124-X*) Caxton Pr.

—Anthem. E-Book 4.95 (*1-57998-138-0*) Delphi Productions, Ltd.

—Anthem. Peikoff, Leonard, ed. & intro. by. 50th anniv. ed. 1999. 256p. pap. 13.95 (*0-452-28125-3*, Plume) Dutton/Plume.

—Anthem. 50th anniv. ed. 1995. 128p. 23.95 (*0-525-94015-4*, Dutton) Dutton/Plume.

—Anthem. 2000. E-Book 2.49 (*1-58744-164-0*) Electric Umbrella Publishing.

—Anthem. abr. unabr. ed. 2002. audio 18.95 (*1-56511-547-3*); audio compact disk 22.95 (*1-56511-548-1*) HighBridge Co.

—Anthem. E-Book 2.95 (*1-57799-813-8*); E-Book 2.95 (*1-57799-974-6*) Logos Research Systems, Inc.

—Anthem. 1969. mass mkt. 0.75 o.p. (*0-451-04063-5*); 1968. mass mkt. 0.50 o.p. (*0-451-01985-7*); 1968. mass mkt. 0.60 o.p. (*0-451-02809-0*); 1961. mass mkt. 3.50 o.p. (*0-451-15331-6*); 1961. mass mkt. 2.95 o.p. (*0-451-14086-9*); 1961. mass mkt. 3.95 o.p. (*0-451-15993-4*); 1961. mass mkt. 1.50 o.p. (*0-451-07846-2*); 1961. mass mkt. 1.75 o.p. (*0-451-11712-3*); 1961. mass mkt. 2.50 o.p. (*0-451-12737-4*); 1961. mass mkt. 0.95 o.p. (*0-451-04789-3*); 1961. mass mkt. 1.25 o.p. (*0-451-06594-8*); 1961. 256p. mass mkt. 9.99 o.s.i (*0-451-16683-3*); 50th anniv. ed. 1996. (Illus.). 272p. mass mkt. 7.99 (*0-451-19113-7*) NAL. (Signet Bks.).

—Anthem. (SparkNotes Literature Study Guides). 64-96p. pap., stu. ed. 4.95 (*1-58663-825-4*) Spark Publishing Group.

—Anthem. 50th ed. 1995. 14.04 (*0-606-00353-3*) Turtleback Bks.

—The Fountainhead. 752p. 2002. 39.95 (*0-452-28376-0*); 1994. pap. 20.00 (*0-452-27333-1*) Dutton/Plume. (Plume).

—The Fountainhead. 1996. 720p. mass mkt. 8.99 (*0-451-19115-3*, Signet Bks.); 1970. mass mkt. 1.50 o.p. (*0-451-04406-1*, Signet Bks.); 1968. mass mkt. 0.95 o.p. (*0-451-01995-4*, Signet Bks.); 1968. mass mkt. 1.25 o.p. (*0-451-03235-7*, Signet Bks.); 1968. mass mkt. 0.75 o.p. (*0-451-00934-7*, Signet Bks.); 1968. mass mkt. 0.75 o.p. (*0-451-01468-5*, Signet Bks.); 1952. mass mkt. 4.95 o.p. (*0-451-13319-6*, ROC); 1952. mass mkt. 3.95 o.p. (*0-451-12739-0*, Signet Bks.); 1952. mass mkt. 3.95 o.p. (*0-451-11810-3*, Signet Bks.); 1952. mass mkt. 3.50 o.p. (*0-451-09956-7*, Signet Bks.); 1952. mass mkt. 1.95 o.p. (*0-451-06400-3*, Signet Bks.); 1952. mass mkt. 2.25 o.p. (*0-451-06629-4*, Signet Bks.); 1952. mass mkt. 2.75 o.p. (*0-451-08415-2*, Signet Bks.); 1952. mass mkt. 2.95 o.p. (*0-451-09380-1*, Signet Bks.); 1952. mass mkt. 1.75 o.p. (*0-451-05954-9*, Signet Bks.); 1952. mass mkt. 2.50 o.p. (*0-451-07602-8*, Signet Bks.); 1952. mass mkt. 5.99 o.p. (*0-451-15823-7*, Signet Bks.); 50th anniv. ed. 1952. 704p. mass mkt. 7.99 o.p. (*0-451-17512-3*, Signet Bks.) NAL.

—The Fountainhead. Date not set. 15.00 (*0-672-50669-6*) Sams.

—The Fountainhead. 2000. (Scribner Classics). 752p. 50.00 (*0-684-86971-3*, Scribner) Simon & Schuster.

—The Fountainhead. 1993. 15.04 (*0-606-01752-6*) Turtleback Bks.

—We the Living. 1959. 19.95 o.p. (*0-394-45124-4*) Random Hse., Inc.

Raney, Deborah. In the Still of Night. l.t. ed. 1997. 240p. pap. 9.99 o.p. (*1-55661-667-8*) Bethany Hse. Pubs.

—In the Still of Night. l.t. ed. 1997. (Christian Fiction Ser.). 331p. 23.95 o.p. (*0-7862-1235-7*) Thorndike Pr.

Reade, Charles. "It Is Never Too Late to Mend" Proofs of Its Prison Revelations. 2001. (Complete Writings of Charles Reade). reprint ed. pap. text 28.00 (*0-7426-8732-5*) Classic Bks.

Rechy, John. Our Lady of Babylon: A Novel. 1996. 352p. 23.95 o.p. (*1-55970-335-0*) Arcade Publishing, Inc.

Redd, Louise. Playing the Bones. 1997. 256p. pap. 11.95 o.s.i (*0-452-27824-4*, Plume) Dutton/Plume.

—Playing the Bones: A Novel. 1996. 256p. 21.95 o.p. (*0-316-73511-6*) Little Brown & Co.

Redd, Mary Allen. The Dogwood Tree. 2003. 301p. pap. 12.00 (*0-9636548-4-5*) Cascade Bks.

—The World of Holly Prickle: For Women Who Have Worked for Men. 1993. 290p. (Orig.). pap. 10.00 (*0-9636548-0-2*) Cascade Bks.

Rees, Emlyn & Lloyd, Josie. Come Together: A Novel. 1999. 304p. 21.95 o.s.i (*0-375-50232-7*, Villard Bks.) Random House Adult Trade Publishing Group.

Reisfeld, Randi. An American Betty in Paris. 1996. (Clueless Ser.). 160p. (YA). (gr. 6 up). pap. 4.99 (*0-671-56869-8*, Simon Pulse) Simon & Schuster Children's Publishing.

Rentschler, L. A. Jitters: A Novel about Pre-Marital Stress. 1995. 288p. pap. 12.95 (*0-9640583-0-8*) White Willow Enterprises.

Rhys, Jean. Wide Sargasso Sea. 1992. (Norton Paperback Fiction Ser.). 190p. pap. 12.95 (*0-393-30880-4*) Norton, W. W. & Co., Inc.

Richards, Cinda. Dillon's Promise. l.t. ed. 1993. 19.95 o.p. (*0-7927-1630-2*); pap. 17.95 o.p. (*0-7927-1629-9*) BBC Audiobooks America.

Richards, David Adams. The Bay of Love & Sorrows. 2003. (Illus.). 320p. 24.95 (*1-55970-650-3*) Arcade Publishing, Inc.

—The Bay of Love & Sorrows. 2002. 320p. pap. (*0-385-66005-7*, Anchor Canada) Doubleday Canada, Ltd. CAN. *Dist:* Random Hse., Inc.

Richardson, Samuel. Pamela. Duncan-Eaves, T. C. & Kimpel, B. D., eds. 1971. (C). pap. 16.36 (*0-395-11152-8*, Riverside Editions) Houghton Mifflin Co.

Relationships

—Pamela. 1991. 453p. pap. 7.95 (*0-460-87064-5*, Everyman's Classic Library in Paperback) Tuttle Publishing.

Richler, Mordecai. Barney's Version. 1999. 368p. pap. 14.00 (*0-671-02846-4*, Washington Square Pr.) Simon & Schuster.

Ridgway, Rick. Three Squirt Dog. 1994. 176p. pap. 12.95 o.p. (*0-312-11079-0*, Saint Martin's Griffin) St. Martin's Pr.

Riefe, Barbara. The Woman Who Fell from the Sky. 1994. 336p. 22.95 o.p. (*0-312-85446-3*, Forge Bks.) Doherty, Tom Assocs., LLC.

Riley, Wilma. Cut-Out. 1993. 256p. pap. 12.95 (*1-55050-053-8*) Coteau Bks. CAN. *Dist:* General Distribution Services, Inc.

Rizzo, Kay D. She Said No: But He Crossed the Line Between Passion & Violence. 1994. 189p. pap. 10.99 o.p. (*0-8163-1179-X*) Pacific Pr. Publishing Assn.

—Sweet Strings of Love. 1994. (Chloe Celeste Chronicles Ser.: Vol. 3). 248p. pap. 9.99 (*0-8163-1221-4*) Pacific Pr. Publishing Assn.

Robards, Karen. Heartbreaker. l.t. ed. 1997. 20.00 (*0-7838-8092-8*, Macmillan Reference USA) Gale Group.

—Hunter's Moon. 1996. 448p. mass mkt. 7.99 (*0-440-21593-5*) Dell Publishing.

—Hunter's Moon. l.t. ed. 1996. 25.95 o.p. (*1-56895-296-1*, Wheeler Publishing, Inc.) Gale Group.

—Night Magic. l.t. ed. 1993. 21.95 o.p. (*0-7927-1873-9*) BBC Audiobooks America.

—One Summer. l.t. ed. 1994. pap. 21.95 o.p. (*0-7927-1608-6*); 1993. 23.95 o.p. (*0-7927-1609-4*) BBC Audiobooks America.

—The Senator's Wife. 1999. 448p. mass mkt. 7.99 (*0-440-21599-4*) Dell Publishing.

—The Senator's Wife. l.t. ed. 1998. (Large Print Book Ser.). 27.95 (*1-56895-584-7*, Wheeler Publishing, Inc.) Gale Group.

Roberts, Karen. Night Magic. l.t. ed. 1994. pap. 20.95 o.p. (*0-7927-1872-0*) BBC Audiobooks America.

Roberts, Nora. Irish Hearts: Irish Thoroughbred & Irish Rose, 2 bks. in 1. 2000. 512p. mass mkt. (*0-373-48400-3*, Harlequin Bks.) Harlequin Enterprises, Ltd.

—Irish Hearts: Irish Thoroughbred & Irish Rose. l.t. ed. 568p. 2001. pap. 28.95 (*0-7862-2967-5*); 2000. 30.95 (*0-7862-2966-7*) Thorndike Pr.

—Irish Rebel. 2002. 256p. mass mkt. (*0-373-23993-9*, Harlequin Bks.); 2000. (Silhouette Special Edition Ser.: Bk. 1328). 250p. per. (*0-373-24328-6*, 1-24328-6, Silhouette) Harlequin Enterprises, Ltd.

—Irish Rebel. l.t. ed. 2000. (Americana Ser.). 295p. 30.95 (*0-7862-2968-3*) Thorndike Pr.

—Private Scandals. 1993. 352p. 19.95 o.p. (*0-399-13828-5*, G. P. Putnam's Sons) Penguin Group (USA) Inc.

—Sweet Revenge. 1997. 400p. mass mkt. 7.50 (*0-553-27859-2*) Bantam Bks.

—Sweet Revenge. l.t. ed. 1998. (Large Print Book Ser.). 25.95 o.p. (*1-56895-531-6*, Wheeler Publishing, Inc.) Gale Group.

Robinson, Kathleen. Heaven's Only Daughter. l.t. ed. 1994. 476p. reprint ed. lib. bdg. 22.95 (*0-8161-5961-0*, Macmillan Reference USA) Gale Group.

—Heaven's Only Daughter. 1993. 368p. 21.95 o.p. (*0-312-09304-7*) St. Martin's Pr.

Robison, James. The Illustrator. 1988. 17.95 o.p. (*0-671-52724-X*) Summit Bks.

Rodgers, Joni. Crazy for Trying. 1999. pap. 13.00 (*1-878448-92-7*); 1996. 301p. 24.00 o.p. (*1-878448-73-0*) MacMurray & Beck, Inc.

—Sugar Land. 1999. 352p. pap. 12.00 (*1-883523-32-X*) Spinsters Ink Bks.

Rogan, Barbara. A Heartbeat Away. l.t. ed. 1994. 25.95 o.p. (*0-7927-1981-6*); pap. 24.95 o.p. (*0-7927-1980-8*) BBC Audiobooks America.

—A Heartbeat Away. 1993. 288p. 20.00 o.p. (*0-688-11582-9*, Morrow, William & Co.) Morrow/Avon.

Rose, Joel. Kill Kill Faster Faster. 1998. 224p. pap. 11.95 o.s.i (*0-14-027329-8*) Penguin Group (USA) Inc.

Rosenfeld, Lucinda. What She Saw... 2000. 304p. 23.95 o.s.i (*0-375-50375-7*) Random Hse., Inc.

—Why She Went Home: A Novel. 2004. 320p. 23.95 (*1-4000-6185-7*, Random House) Random House Adult Trade Publishing Group.

Ross, Dana Fuller, pseud. Yankee Rogue. l.t. ed. 1994. 22.95 o.p. (*1-56895-066-7*, Wheeler Publishing, Inc.) Gale Group.

Ross, John. Donald Winter, a Novel: A Failing Marriage. 2000. 254p. E-Book 8.00 (*0-7388-8417-0*) Xlibris Corp.

Rossi, Agnes. The Houseguest. 2000. 304p. reprint ed. 13.00 o.s.i (*0-452-28197-0*, Plume) Dutton/Plume.

—The Houseguest: A Novel. l.t. ed. 2000. (Americana Ser.). 504p. 28.95 (*0-7862-2547-5*) Thorndike Pr.

Rossner, Judith. Olivia: Or The Weight of the Past. l.t. ed. 1995. (Large Print Bks.). 24.95 (*1-56895-166-3*, Wheeler Publishing, Inc.) Gale Group.

Rowntree, Kathleen. Mr. Brightly's Evening Off. 1997. (Illus.). 270p. (J). (*0-385-40879-X*) Doubleday Publishing.

—Mr. Brightly's Evening Off. l.t. unabr. ed. 1998. 24.95 (*0-7531-5856-6*, 158566) ISIS Large Print Bks. GBR. *Dist:* ISIS Publishing.

—Mr. Brightly's Evening Off. 2000. 271p. (J). pap. 10.95 (*0-552-99733-1*) Transworld Publishers Ltd. GBR. *Dist:* Trafalgar Square.

Roy, Lucinda. Lady Moses: A Novel. 1998. 400p. 24.00 o.s.i (*0-06-018244-X*) HarperCollins Pubs.

—Lady Moses: A Novel. 1998. 400p. pap. 13.00 (*0-06-093084-5*, Perennial) HarperTrade.

Running Press Staff. The Gift of the Magi. 1999. (Miniature Editions Ser.). 96p. text 4.95 (*0-7624-1130-9*) Running Pr. Bk. Pubs.

Rush, Norman. Mating. 1993. 5.99 o.p. (*0-517-10972-7*) Random Hse. Value Publishing.

—Mating: A Novel. 1992. 496p. pap. 15.00 (*0-679-73709-X*, Vintage) Knopf Publishing Group.

Rushford, Patricia H. & James, Harrison. Secrets, Lies, & Alibis. 2003. 320p. 13.99 (*1-59145-081-0*) Integrity Pubs.

Russell, Jane. The Lord Had Something Better in Mind. 2000. E-Book (*1-930739-03-6*) Internet Book Co., Inc.

Ryan, Mary. Shadows from the Fire. 1995. 288p. 21.95 o.p. (*0-312-13168-2*) St. Martin's Pr.

—Summer's End. 1996. 352p. 23.95 o.p. (*0-312-14427-X*) St. Martin's Pr.

Ryan, Nan. Written in the Stars. 1992. 448p. mass mkt. 4.99 o.s.i (*0-440-21072-0*) Dell Publishing.

—Written in the Stars. 2003. 448p. mass mkt. 5.99 (*0-505-52510-0*, Love Spell) Dorchester Publishing Co., Inc.

Ryman, Rebecca. Olivia & Jai. 1990. 19.95 o.p. (*0-312-04146-2*) St. Martin's Pr.

Sallis, Susan. Choices. 2000. 411p. pap. 10.95 (*0-552-14549-1*) Transworld Publishers Ltd. GBR. *Dist:* Trafalgar Square.

Salter, James. A Sport & a Pastime. 1985. 192p. reprint ed. pap. 13.00 (*0-86547-210-6*, North Point Pr.) Farrar, Straus & Giroux.

—A Sport & a Pastime. 1995. (Modern Library Ser.). 196p. reprint ed. 14.95 o.s.i (*0-679-60156-2*) Random Hse., Inc.

—A Sport & a Pastime. 1980. (Contemporary American Fiction Ser.). pap. 3.50 o.p. (*0-14-005638-6*, Penguin Bks.) Viking Penguin.

Samson, Lisa. The Highlander & His Lady. 1994. pap. 9.99 o.s.i (*1-56507-206-5*) Harvest Hse. Pubs.

—The Warrior's Bride. 1997. (Abbey Ser.: No. 3). 400p. pap. 9.99 o.p. (*1-56507-636-2*) Harvest Hse. Pubs.

Sand, George. Horace. Rogow, Zack, tr. from FRE. 1995. (Illus.). 352p. pap. 15.95 (*1-56279-082-X*) Mercury Hse.

—Indiana. Ives, George B., tr. from FRE. 1992. (Illus.). 327p. reprint ed. pap. 16.95 (*0-915864-57-6*) Academy Chicago Pubs., Ltd.

—Indiana. lib. bdg. 23.95 (*0-8488-2024-X*) Amereon, Ltd.

—Indiana. Ives, G. B., tr. 1975. xxi, 327p. reprint ed. 21.50 o.p. (*0-86527-260-3*) Fertig, Howard Inc.

—Indiana. 1984. (FRE.). pap. 16.95 (*0-7859-2907-X*, 2070376044) French & European Pubns., Inc.

—Indiana. Hochman, Eleanor, tr. 1993. 272p. mass mkt. 5.95 o.s.i (*0-451-52572-8*, Signet Classics) NAL.

—Indiana. Schor, Naomi, ed. Raphael, Sylvia, tr. from FRE. 2001. (Oxford World's Classics Ser.). 320p. pap. 10.95 (*0-19-283797-4*) Oxford Univ. Pr., Inc.

—Indiana. Raphael, Silvia, tr. 1995. (Oxford World's Classics Ser.). 306p. (C). pap. 10.95 o.p. (*0-19-283075-9*) Oxford Univ. Pr., Inc.

—Indiana. (Folio Ser.: No. 1604). (FRE.). 13.95 (*2-07-037604-4*) Schoenhof's Foreign Bks., Inc.

—The Master Pipers. Lloyd, Rosemary, tr. 1994. (Oxford World's Classics Ser.). (Illus.). 356p. pap. 10.95 o.p. (*0-19-283097-X*) Oxford Univ. Pr., Inc.

Sandemose, Aksel. The Werewolf. Lannestock, Gustaf, tr. from NOR. 2nd ed. 2002. (Library of World Fiction). 394p. pap. 24.95 (*0-299-03744-4*) Univ. of Wisconsin Pr.

Saxton, Judith. Still Waters. 1998. 504p. 26.95 o.p. (*0-312-18185-X*) St. Martin's Pr.

Scanlan, Patricia. Francesca's Party. 2003. 512p. mass mkt. (*1-55166-746-0*, Mira Bks.) Harlequin Enterprises, Ltd.

—Francesca's Party. Date not set. (*0-312-30187-1*) St. Martin's Pr.

—Francesca's Party: A Novel. 2002. 464p. 24.95 (*0-312-30172-3*) St. Martin's Pr.

Schaeffer, Susan F. The Injured Party. 1987. pap. 3.95 o.p. (*0-312-90624-2*, St. Martin's Paperbacks); 1986. 304p. 16.95 o.p. (*0-312-41798-5*) St. Martin's Pr.

—The Madness of a Seduced Woman. 1991. 592p. pap. 16.95 o.s.i (*0-452-26709-9*, Plume) Dutton/Plume.

—The Madness of a Seduced Woman: A Novel. 1983. 560p. 16.95 o.p. (*0-525-24165-5*, 01646-490, Dutton) Dutton/Plume.

Schine, Cathleen. The Love Letter. 1999. pap. 12.95 o.s.i (*0-452-28141-5*); 1998. 272p. pap. 12.95 (*0-452-27948-8*) Dutton/Plume.

—The Love Letter. l.t. ed. 1995. 334p. 23.95 o.p. (*0-7838-1451-8*, Macmillan Reference USA) Gale Group.

—The Love Letter. 1995. 224p. tchr. ed. 19.95 o.p. (*0-395-68996-1*) Houghton Mifflin Co.

—The Love Letter. 1999. 362p. mass mkt. 6.99 o.s.i (*0-451-19867-0*); 1996. 368p. mass mkt. 6.99 o.s.i (*0-451-18847-0*) NAL. (Signet Bks.).

—To the Birdhouse. 1996. 288p. pap. 10.95 (*0-452-27662-4*, Plume) Dutton/Plume.

—To the Birdhouse. 1990. 17.95 o.s.i (*0-374-27828-8*) Farrar, Straus & Giroux.

Schmidt, Heidi Jon. The Bride of Catastrophe. 2003. 400p. 24.00 (*0-312-28177-3*) Picador.

Scott, Evelyn. Escapade. 1971. reprint ed. 39.00 o.p. (*0-403-01199-X*) Scholarly Pr., Inc.

—Escapade. exp. ed. 1995. 286p. (C). pap. 16.95 (*0-8139-1641-0*) Univ. Pr. of Virginia.

Serao, Mathilde. The Conquest of Rome. Caesar, Ann, ed. (Women's Classics Ser.). 250p. (C). 1993. pap. text 20.00 (*0-8147-7964-6*); 1992. text 55.00 (*0-8147-7955-7*) New York Univ. Pr.

Settle, Mary Lee. Charley Bland. 1991. 208p. pap. 8.95 o.p. (*0-88184-709-7*, Carroll & Graf Pubs.) Avalon Publishing Group.

—Charley Bland. 1989. 18.95 o.p. (*0-374-12078-1*) Farrar, Straus & Giroux.

—Charley Bland. 1996. (Mary Lee Settle Collection). 208p. pap. 12.95 (*1-57003-149-5*) Univ. of South Carolina Pr.

Seveigny, Genevieve. A Half-Dozen Eclairs: Travels in the Guise of Letters. 2002. (ENG, SPA & SWA.). 60p. (C). pap. 14.00 (*0-9641837-3-0*) Texture Pr.

Shannon, Ray. Firecracker. 2004. 320p. 23.95 (*0-399-15146-X*) Putnam Publishing Group, The.

Shapiro, Anna. Life & Love, Such As They Are. 1994. 240p. 21.00 (*0-671-87114-5*, Simon & Schuster) Simon & Schuster.

Shreve, Anita. Resistance. unabr. collector's ed. 1995. audio 48.00 (*0-7366-3121-6*, 3797) Books on Tape, Inc.

—Resistance. 1999. 222p. reprint ed. text 22.00 (*0-7881-6622-0*) DIANE Publishing Co.

—Resistance. 1998. pap. 13.00 (*0-316-19062-4*, Back Bay); 1995. 222p. 21.95 (*0-316-78999-2*); 1997. 256p. reprint ed. pap. 13.95 (*0-316-78984-4*, Back Bay) Little Brown & Co.

—Where or When. l.t. ed. 1993. 24.95 o.p. (*0-7927-1807-0*); 293p. pap. 22.95 o.p. (*0-7927-1806-2*) BBC Audiobooks America.

—Where or When. unabr. collector's ed. 1994. audio 42.00 (*0-7366-2759-6*, 3482) Books on Tape, Inc.

—Where or When. (Harvest Book Ser.). 252p. 1999. pap. 13.00 (*0-15-600652-9*, Harvest Bks.); 1993. 13.00 (*0-15-131461-6*) Harcourt Trade Pubs.

—Where or When. 1994. 304p. mass mkt. 5.99 o.s.i (*0-451-40478-5*, Signet Bks.) NAL.

—Where or When. abr. ed. 1994. audio 16.95 (*1-879371-54-5*, 40220) Publishing Mills, Inc., The.

Sibley, Holli. Ellie's Child. 2000. 74p. E-Book 3.95 (*1-930677-04-9*) London Circle Publishing.

Siddons, Anne Rivers. Downtown. 1994. 352p. 288.00 o.p. (*0-06-017602-4*) HarperCollins Pubs.

—Downtown. 1994. 352p. 24.00 o.p. (*0-06-017934-1*); Set. 1999. audio (*1-55994-732-2*, 692189, Harper-Audio) HarperTrade.

—Downtown. 1995. 512p. mass mkt. 7.99 (*0-06-109968-6*, HarperTorch) Morrow/Avon.

—Downtown. unabr. ed. 1994. audio 97.00 (*0-7887-0062-6*, 94318E7) Recorded Bks., LLC.

—Downtown. 374p. 6.98 o.p. (*0-7651-0027-4*) Smithmark Pubs., Inc.

—Downtown. l.t. ed. (Paperback Bestsellers Ser.). 647p. 1995. 22.95 (*0-8161-7411-3*); 1994. lib. bdg. 27.95 (*0-8161-7410-5*) Thorndike Pr.

Sigerson, Davitt. Faithful: A Novel. 2004. 224p. 23.95 (*0-385-51050-0*, Talese, Nan A.) Doubleday Publishing.

Skwiot, Rick. Sleeping with Pancho Villa. 1998. 176p. 19.95 (*0-87081-506-7*) Univ. Pr. of Colorado.

Small, Lass. Small Treasures. 1993. 560p. 9.98 o.p. (*0-8317-7866-0*) Smithmark Pubs., Inc.

Smart, Elizabeth. By Grand Central Station I Sat down & Wept. 1992. 240p. pap. 12.00 (*0-679-73804-5*, Vintage) Knopf Publishing Group.

Smart, William, ed. Women & Men & Women: An Anthology of Short Stories. 1975. pap. text 15.95 o.p. (*0-312-88725-6*) St. Martin's Pr.

Smith, Ron. What Men Know about Women. 1999. 240p. pap. 17.95 (*0-88982-183-6*) Oolichan Bks. CAN. *Dist:* General Distribution Services, Inc.

Smith, Rosamond, pseud. Soul-Mate. 1989. 256p. 17.95 o.p. (*0-525-24768-8*, Dutton) Dutton/Plume.

Snow, Penelope. Men Are a Joke. 1997. 96p. mass mkt. 5.99 o.s.i (*0-7860-0361-8*, Pinnacle Bks.) Kensington Publishing Corp.

Soard, Lori. Picking up Cowboys. 1999. 230p. E-Book 4.99 (*1-58365-040-7*, Timeless Romance) Sierra Raconteur Publishing.

Sollers, Philippe. Watteau in Venice. 1994. Orig. Title: Fete a Venise. 288p. text 22.00 (*0-684-19451-1*, Scribner) Simon & Schuster.

Sonnett, Sherry. Restraint. 1996. 320p. mass mkt. 5.99 o.s.i (*0-451-18642-7*, Signet Bks.) NAL.

Sonnett, Shery. Restraint. 1995. 319p. 21.00 (*0-671-87958-8*, Simon & Schuster) Simon & Schuster.

Spark, Muriel. Territorial Rights. 1984. 248p. pap. 6.95 o.p. (*0-399-50930-5*) Putnam Publishing Group, The.

Sparks, Nicholas. The Notebook. l.t. ed. 1996. (Basic Ser.). 268p. 27.95 o.p. (*0-7862-0821-X*) Thorndike Pr.

—The Notebook. 2000. 13.04 (*0-606-19126-7*) Turtleback Bks.

—The Notebook. 2000. 214p. E-Book 5.95 (*0-446-96105-1*); 2000. E-Book 5.95 (*0-446-93064-4*); 1999. 214p. E-Book 4.95 (*0-446-91459-2*); 1996. 224p. 20.00 (*0-446-52080-2*); 1999. 240p. reprint ed. pap. 12.95 (*0-446-67609-8*); 1998. 256p. reprint ed. mass mkt. 7.50 (*0-446-60523-9*) Warner Bks., Inc.

—The Notebook: Reading Group Guide. 2000. pap. (*0-446-79043-5*) Warner Bks., Inc.

Sparrow, Rose. Shoshoni Man: A Tale of Self-Discovery & Love. 1994. 13.95 (*1-885275-10-2*) Howie, C.J. Co.

Spatz, Gregory. No One but Us. 1995. 224p. (YA). tchr. ed. 17.95 (*1-56512-037-X*, 72037) Algonquin Bks. of Chapel Hill.

Spellman, Cathy Cash. The Playground of the Gods. 1996. 82p. 21.95 (*0-446-51701-1*) Warner Bks., Inc.

Spencer, Brent. The Lost Son. 1995. 288p. 19.95 (*1-55970-266-4*) Arcade Publishing, Inc.

Spencer, LaVyrle. Family Blessings. l.t. ed. 1994. 26.95 o.p. (*1-56895-061-6*, Wheeler Publishing, Inc.) Gale Group.

—Family Blessings. 1994. 384p. 22.95 o.p. (*0-399-13906-0*, G. P. Putnam's Sons) Penguin Group (USA) Inc.

—Years. 496p. 2003. pap. 10.00 (*0-425-19578-3*); 1986. mass mkt. 7.99 (*0-515-08489-1*, Jove) Berkley Publishing Group.

—Years. l.t. ed. 1994. (General Ser.). 18.95 (*0-8161-5763-4*); 669p. lib. bdg. 21.95 o.p. (*0-8161-5762-6*) Gale Group. (Macmillan Reference USA).

Spiegelman, Katia. Peculiar Politics: A Romantic Comedy. 1993. 240p. 21.95 o.p. (*0-7145-2952-4*) Boyars, Marion Pubs., Inc.

St. Aubin De Teran, Lisa. Nocturne. 1993. 224p. 19.95 o.p. (*0-312-09888-X*) St. Martin's Pr.

St. John, Madeleine. The Essence of the Thing. 240p. 1999. pap. text 11.95 (*0-7867-0679-1*); 1998. 22.00 (*0-7867-0560-4*) Avalon Publishing Group. (Carroll & Graf Pubs.).

Stahl, Hilda. The Women of Catawba. 1993. 240p. pap. 9.99 o.p. (*0-8407-5080-3*) Nelson, Thomas Inc.

Stansfield, Anita. First Love & Forever: A Novel. 1994. pap. 12.95 (*1-55503-714-3*, 019401) Covenant Communications, Inc.

—First Love, Second Chances: A Novel. 1995. pap. 12.95 (*1-55503-776-3*, 01111833) Covenant Communications, Inc.

Star, Nancy. Up Next. (May Morrison Mysteries Ser.). 1999. 368p. mass mkt. 6.50 (*0-671-00894-3*, Pocket Star); 1998. 352p. 23.00 (*0-671-00893-5*, Atria) Simon & Schuster.

Stark, Stephen. The Second Son. Rosenman, Jane, ed. 1994. 432p. reprint ed. pap. o.p. (*0-671-87119-6*, Washington Square Pr.) Simon & Schuster.

—Second Son: A Novel. 1992. 288p. 22.50 o.p. (*0-8050-1943-X*) Holt, Henry & Co.

Steel, Danielle. Bittersweet. 2000. 448p. mass mkt. 7.99 (*0-440-22484-5*); 1999. 384p. 26.95 (*0-385-31957-6*, Delacorte Pr.); 1999. 384p. 200.00 (*0-385-33388-9*, Delacorte Pr.) Dell Publishing.

—Bittersweet. l.t. ed. 2004. 576p. 24.95 (*0-375-43321-X*) Random Hse. Large Print.

—Journey. 2001. 368p. mass mkt. 7.99 (*0-440-23702-5*); 2000. 336p. 200.00 (*0-385-33304-8*, Delacorte Pr.); 2000. 336p. 26.95 (*0-385-31687-9*, Delacorte Pr.) Dell Publishing.

—Journey. abr. unabr. ed. 2000. audio compact disk 29.95 (*0-553-71219-5*); audio 39.95 (*0-553-50260-3*) Random Hse. Audio Publishing Group. (RH Audio).

—Journey. l.t. ed. 464p. 2001. pap. 13.95 (*0-375-72807-4*); 2000. 26.95 (*0-375-43080-6*) Random Hse. Large Print.

Stern, Amanda. The Long Haul. 2003. 128p. pap. 12.00 (*1-932360-06-9*) Soft Skull Pr., Inc.

Stevens, Susan. Ivory Innocence. l.t. ed. 1994. 19.95 o.p. (*0-7927-1838-0*); pap. 17.95 o.p. (*0-7927-1837-2*) BBC Audiobooks America.

Stewart, Michael. Compulsion. 1994. 384p. 23.00 o.p. (*0-06-017767-5*) HarperTrade.

Stokes, Penelope J. Home Fires Burning. 1996. (Faith on the Home Front Ser.: Vol. 1). 345p. pap. 8.99 o.p. (*0-8423-0851-2*) Tyndale Hse. Pubs.

Stone, Katherine. Katherine Stone: A New Collection of Three Complete Novels. 1995. 752p. 6.99 o.s.i (*0-517-11840-8*) Random Hse. Value Publishing.
—Katherine Stone: Thee Complete Novels. 1994. 752p. 6.99 o.s.i (*0-517-10115-7*) Random Hse. Value Publishing.
—Pearl Moon. 1996. mass mkt. 5.99 o.s.i (*0-449-22415-5*, Fawcett) Ballantine Bks.
—Pearl Moon. l.t. ed. (Large Print Bks.). 24.95 o.p. (*1-56895-165-5*, Wheeler Publishing, Inc.) Gale Group.
—Promises. l.t. ed. 1995. 23.95 o.p. (*0-7927-2018-0*); 1994. pap. 25.95 o.p. (*0-7927-2019-9*) BBC Audiobooks America.
Storey, Gail D. God's Country Club. 1999. 238p. reprint ed. pap. 12.95 (*0-89255-242-5*) Persea Bks., Inc.
—God's Country Club: A Novel. 1996. 224p. 22.95 (*0-89255-219-0*) Persea Bks., Inc.
Strom, Carolyn & Bernheim, Emmanuele. Sa Femme: Or the Other Woman. 1995. 128p. 14.95 o.p. (*0-670-85811-0*) Viking Penguin.
Stuart, Jesse H. Daughter of the Legend. Spurlock, John H., ed. 1994. (Illus.). 256p. (YA). (gr. 8 up). reprint ed. 22.00 (*0-945084-42-0*) Stuart, Jesse Foundation, The.
Sutherland, John, ed. Under Two Flags: A Story of the Household & the Desert. 1995. (Oxford Popular Fiction Ser.). 550p. pap. 12.95 o.p. (*0-19-282328-0*) Oxford Univ. Pr., Inc.
Svoboda, Terese. Cannibal. 1994. 138p. (C). 20.00 (*0-8147-8012-1*) New York Univ. Pr.
—Cannibal. 1994. E-Book 19.95 (*0-585-31629-5*) netLibrary, Inc.
Swann, E. L. Night Gardening. l.t. ed. 2000. (G. K. Hall Core Ser.). 256p. 28.95 (*0-7838-9036-2*, Macmillan Reference USA) Gale Group.
—Night Gardening. 2000. (Illus.). 208p. mass mkt. 6.50 o.s.i (*0-7868-8952-7*) Hyperion Pr.
—Night Gardening: A Novel. 1999. 215p. 16.95 (*0-7868-6498-2*) Hyperion Pr.
Swarthout, Glendon F. Pinch Me, I Must Be Dreaming. l.t. ed. 1995. 319p. pap. 20.95 o.p. (*0-7838-1416-X*, Macmillan Reference USA) Gale Group.
—Pinch Me, I Must Be Dreaming. 1994. 256p. 20.95 o.p. (*0-312-11383-8*) St. Martin's Pr.
Szczypiorski, Andrzej. Self-Portrait with Woman. Johnson, Bill, tr. 1996. 224p. 21.00 o.p. (*0-8021-1567-5*, Grove Pr.) Grove/Atlantic, Inc.
—Self-Portrait with Woman. Johnston, Bill, tr. from POL. 1997. 256p. reprint ed. pap. 12.00 (*0-8021-3488-2*, Grove Pr.) Grove/Atlantic, Inc.
Szeman, Sherri. The Kommandant's Mistress. 2000. 273p. pap. 13.95 (*1-55970-542-6*) Arcade Publishing, Inc.
—The Kommandant's Mistress. 1993. 224p. 17.50 o.p. (*0-06-017011-5*); 1994. 288p. reprint ed. pap. 12.50 o.p. (*0-06-092497-7*, Perennial) HarperTrade.
Tachihara, Masaaki. Wind & Stone: A Novel. Kohl, Stephen W., tr. from JPN. 1992. (Rock Spring Collection). (Illus.). 0159p. pap. 10.95 (*0-9628137-7-X*) Stone Bridge Pr.
Tarloff, Erik. Face-Time. 2000. 256p. reprint ed. pap. 12.95 (*0-671-03978-4*, Pocket) Simon & Schuster.
Taylor-Hall, Mary A. Come & Go, Molly Snow. 1996. 272p. pap. 11.00 o.p. (*0-380-72702-1*, Avon Bks.) Morrow/Avon.
—Come & Go, Molly Snow: A Novel. 1995. 256p. 21.00 (*0-393-03735-5*) Norton, W. W. & Co., Inc.
Taylor, Janelle. Destiny Mine. l.t. ed. 1995. 448p. lib. bdg. 21.95 o.p. (*0-7838-1208-6*, Macmillan Reference USA) Gale Group.
—Janelle Taylor: Promise Me Forever; Follow the Wind; Kiss of the Night Wind. 1993. 896p. 13.99 o.s.i (*0-517-10011-8*) Random Hse. Value Publishing.
—A New Collection of Three Complete Novels: Bittersweet Ecstasy, Forever Ecstasy & Savage Conguest. 1994. 13.99 o.s.i (*0-517-12205-7*) Random Hse. Value Publishing.
—Three Complete Western Love Stories. 1996. 13.99 o.s.i (*0-517-14924-9*) Random Hse. Value Publishing.
Taylor, Lucy. Dancing with Demons. deluxe ed. 1998. (Illus.). 300p. 45.00 (*1-891480-02-2*) Obsidian Bks., Etc.
Taylor, Valerie. The Girls in 3-B. 2003. (Femmes Fatales Ser.). 208p. pap. 13.95 (*1-55861-456-7*); lib. bdg. 14.95 (*1-55861-462-1*) Feminist Pr. at The City Univ. of New York.
Tennant, Emma. The Story of Sylvia & Ted: A Novel. 2001. (John MacRae Bks.). 192p. 22.00 (*0-8050-6675-6*) Holt, Henry & Co.
Tepper, Sheri S. The Gate to Women's Country. 1993. 336p. mass mkt. 7.50 (*0-553-28064-3*, Spectra) Bantam Bks.
—The Gate to Women's Country. 1988. 288p. 17.95 o.s.i (*0-385-24709-5*); o.s.i (*0-385-41688-1*) Doubleday Publishing.
Thaddeus, Eva. Steps of the Sun: A Novel. 1997. 244p. 21.95 (*0-918056-09-8*) Ariadne Pr.
Thayer, Nancy. My Dearest Friend. 1989. 384p. 18.95 o.s.i (*0-684-18856-2*, Macmillan Reference USA) Gale Group.
Thirkell, Angela. Love at All Ages. 2001. (Illus.). 336p. pap. 12.95 (*1-55921-297-7*) Moyer Bell.
Thomas, Abigail. Getting over Tom. 1994. 224p. 16.95 o.p. (*1-56512-024-8*) Algonquin Bks. of Chapel Hill.
—Getting over Tom: Stories. 1995. 224p. pap. 10.00 (*0-684-81347-5*, Touchstone) Simon & Schuster.
Thomas, Elizabeth Marshall. The Animal Wife. 1990. 320p. 19.95 o.p. (*0-395-52453-9*) Houghton Mifflin Co. Trade & Reference Div.
Thomas, Jacquelin. The Prodigal Husband. 2002. 288p. pap. 15.00 (*1-58314-254-1*, New Spirit) BET Bks.
Thomas, Rosie. The White Dove. 1986. 640p. 18.95 o.p. (*0-670-80013-9*) Viking Penguin.
Thompson, Kate. Down among the Gods. 1997. 281p. (*1-86049-349-1*) Virago Pr., Ltd.
Thurlo, Aimee & Thurlo, David. The Second Shadow. 1993. 384p. 21.95 o.p. (*0-312-85450-1*, Forge Bks.) Doherty, Tom Assocs., LLC.
Toibin, Colm. The South. 240p. 1991. 18.95 o.p. (*0-670-83870-5*, Viking); 1992. reprint ed. 13.00 (*0-14-014986-4*) Viking Penguin.
Toma, T. L. Border Dance. 1996. 344p. (Orig.). pap. 12.95 (*0-87074-401-1*) Southern Methodist Univ. Pr.
—Border Dance: A Novel. 1996. 344p. 22.50 (*0-87074-400-3*) Southern Methodist Univ. Pr.
Tong, Su. Raise the Red Lantern. 2004. 288p. pap. 12.95 (*0-06-059633-3*, Perennial) HarperTrade.
Topley, Donald. The Last Longship. 2001. 297p. pap. 15.95 (*1-58345-582-5*); 2000. 308p. 22.95 (*1-58345-630-9*) Domhan Bks.
Toteras, D. K. Rape of the Sleeping Woman: And the Practice of Hypnagogic Sex. 1995. 320p. (Orig.). pap. 14.95 (*0-9644122-0-9*) Nine Muses Pr.
Tozzi, Federigo. Ghisola. Wilhelm, James J., ed. Klopp, Charles, tr. from ITA. 1990. (Library of World Literature in Translation: Vol. 18). 160p. reprint ed. text 15.00 (*0-8240-3313-2*) Garland Publishing, Inc.
Trollope, Anthony. The Bertrams, 3 vols. Hall, N. John, ed. 1981. (Selected Works of Anthony Trollope). reprint ed. lib. bdg. 115.95 (*0-405-14130-0*) Ayer Co. Pubs., Inc.
—The Bertrams. 1986. 487p. reprint ed. pap. 9.95 o.p. (*0-486-25119-5*) Dover Pubns., Inc.
—The Bertrams. Harvey, Geoffrey, ed. 1991. (Oxford World's Classics Ser.). 628p. pap. 11.95 o.p. (*0-19-282645-X*) Oxford Univ. Pr., Inc.
—The Bertrams. 1993. (Trollope Ser.). 496p. pap. 8.95 o.p. (*0-14-043807-6*, Penguin Classics) Viking Penguin.
—An Eye for an Eye, 2 vols. Hall, N. John, ed. 1981. (Selected Works of Anthony Trollope). reprint ed. lib. bdg. 49.95 (*0-405-14169-6*) Ayer Co. Pubs., Inc.
—An Eye for an Eye, 2. reprint ed. lib. bdg. 196.00 (*0-7426-2481-1*) Classic Bks.
—An Eye for an Eye. Wolff, Robert L., ed. 1979. (Ireland Nineteenth Century Fiction Ser.: Vol. 56). 440p. lib. bdg. 101.00 o.p. (*0-8240-3505-4*) Garland Publishing, Inc.
—An Eye for an Eye. Sutherland, John, ed. 1992. (Oxford World's Classics Ser.). 250p. pap. 8.95 o.p. (*0-19-282910-6*) Oxford Univ. Pr., Inc.
—An Eye for an Eye. 1994. (Trollope Ser.). 448p. pap. 8.95 o.p. (*0-14-043840-8*, Penguin Classics) Viking Penguin.
—The Kellys & the O'Kellys. Wolff, Robert L., ed. 1979. (Ireland Nineteenth Century Fiction Ser.: Vol. 54). 888p. lib. bdg. 152.00 o.p. (*0-8240-3503-8*) Garland Publishing, Inc.
—The Kellys & the O'Kellys. 2003. (Twelve-Point Ser.). lib. bdg. 25.00 (*1-58287-264-3*); lib. bdg. 26.00 (*1-58287-748-3*) North Bks.
—Nina Balatka: The Story of a Maiden of Prague, 2 vols. Hall, N. John, ed. 1981. (Selected Works of Anthony Trollope). reprint ed. 55.95 (*0-405-14148-3*) Ayer Co. Pubs., Inc.
—Rachel Ray, 2 vols. Hall, N. John, ed. 1981. (Selected Works of Anthony Trollope). reprint ed. lib. bdg. 71.95 (*0-405-14140-8*) Ayer Co. Pubs., Inc.
—Rachel Ray. 1980. 391p. reprint ed. pap. 7.95 (*0-486-23930-6*) Dover Pubns., Inc.
—Rachel Ray. 1989. (Oxford World's Classics Ser.). 450p. pap. 9.95 o.p. (*0-19-281809-0*) Oxford Univ. Pr., Inc.
—Rachel Ray. Sutherland, John, ed. & intro. by. 1996. (Penguin Classics Ser.). 368p. pap. 9.95 o.p. (*0-14-043410-0*) Viking Penguin.
—La Vendee: An Historical Romance, 3 vols. Hall, N. John, ed. 1981. (Selected Works of Anthony Trollope). reprint ed. 115.95 (*0-405-14122-X*) Ayer Co. Pubs., Inc.
—La Vendee: An Historical Romance. McCormack, W. J., ed. 1994. (Oxford World's Classics Ser.). (Illus.). 500p. (C). pap. 10.95 o.p. (*0-19-282838-X*) Oxford Univ. Pr., Inc.
—La Vendee: An Historical Romance, 1850. 1993. (Trollope Ser.). 992p. pap. 9.95 o.p. (*0-14-043802-5*, Penguin Classics) Viking Penguin.
Trollope, Anthony & Sutherland, John. An Eye for an Eye. l.t. ed. 1998. (Perennial Bestsellers Ser.). 291p. 25.95 (*0-7838-8454-0*) Thorndike Pr.
Tsukiyama, Gail. The Samurai's Garden. 1995. text 18.95 o.p. (*0-312-11813-9*); 1996. 224p. reprint ed. pap. 12.95 (*0-312-14407-5*, NPB 0231, Saint Martin's Griffin) St. Martin's Pr.
Tyler, Anne. Celestial Navigation. l.t. ed. 1994. 366p. 24.95 o.p. (*0-7927-1977-8*); pap. 22.95 o.p. (*0-7927-1976-X*) BBC Audiobooks America.
—Celestial Navigation. 1996. 288p. pap. 13.95 (*0-449-91180-2*, Fawcett); 1992. 256p. mass mkt. 5.99 o.s.i (*0-8041-0888-9*, Ivy Bks.) Ballantine Bks.
—Celestial Navigation. mass mkt. 3.95 o.s.i (*0-425-08638-0*); 1986. 256p. mass mkt. 5.95 o.p. (*0-425-09840-0*); 1985. mass mkt. 3.95 o.s.i (*0-425-09142-2*); 1984. mass mkt. 3.50 o.s.i (*0-425-07013-1*) Berkley Publishing Group.
—Celestial Navigation. 1974. 7.95 o.p. (*0-394-49038-X*, Knopf Bks. for Young Readers) Random Hse. Children's Bks.
—Celestial Navigation. 1983. 256p. pap. 3.50 o.p. (*0-446-31169-3*) Warner Bks., Inc.
Upadhyay, Samrat. The Guru of Love: A Novel. 2004. 304p. pap. 13.00 (*0-618-38268-2*, Mariner Bks.) Houghton Mifflin Co. Trade & Reference Div.
Updike, John. S. 1988. 288p. 29.95 (*0-394-56835-4*) Knopf, Alfred A. Inc.
—Toward the End of Time. 1998. 352p. pap. 12.95 (*0-449-00041-9*, Fawcett); mass mkt. (*0-449-00305-1*, Ballantine Bks.) Ballantine Bks.
—Toward the End of Time. 1997. 334p. 25.00 (*0-375-40006-0*) Knopf, Alfred A. Inc.
Urquhart, Jane. The Whirlpool. reprint ed. 2000. 224p. pap. 16.95 (*1-56792-171-X*); 1989. 238p. 16.95 o.s.i (*0-87923-806-2*) Godine, David R. Pub.
—The Whirlpool. 1999. mass mkt. o.s.i (*0-7710-8656-3*) McClelland & Stewart/Tundra Bks.
VanDenburgh, Jane. The Physics of Sunset. 1999. 304p. 24.00 o.s.i (*0-679-42483-0*, Pantheon) Knopf Publishing Group.
Vernon, Claire. The Doctor Was a Sailor. l.t. ed. 1994. 20.95 o.p. (*0-7927-1993-X*); pap. 18.95 o.p. (*0-7927-1992-1*) BBC Audiobooks America.
Veryan, Patricia. Never Doubt I Love. 1996. mass mkt. 4.99 o.s.i (*0-449-22412-0*, Fawcett) Ballantine Bks.
—Never Doubt I Love. 1995. 21.95 o.p. (*0-312-11864-3*) St. Martin's Pr.
—A Shadow's Bliss. l.t. ed. 1994. 486p. lib. bdg. 22.95 o.p. (*0-8161-7481-4*, Macmillan Reference USA) Gale Group.
—A Shadow's Bliss. 1994. (Tales of the Jewelled Men Ser.: Vol. 4). 336p. 21.95 o.p. (*0-312-10543-6*) St. Martin's Pr.
Victor, Barbara. Coriander. 1994. mass mkt. 5.99 o.s.i (*0-345-38454-7*) Ballantine Bks.
—Coriander. 1993. 22.00 o.p. (*1-55611-353-6*) Fine, Donald I. Bks.
—Coriander. l.t. ed. 1996. 24.95 o.p. (*1-56895-281-3*, Wheeler Publishing, Inc.) Gale Group.
Victor, Cynthia. Only You. l.t. ed. 2000. 463p. 28.95 (*1-57490-322-5*, Beeler Large Print Bks.) Beeler, Thomas T. Publisher.
—Only You. 1995. 416p. mass mkt. 5.99 o.s.i (*0-451-40606-0*, Onyx) NAL.
—Only You. 1994. 416p. 19.95 o.p. (*0-670-84981-2*, Viking) Viking Penguin.
Villegas, Anna T. All We Know of Heaven. 1997. 208p. 19.95 o.p. (*0-312-14613-2*) St. Martin's Pr.
Viteritti, Laurette. The Jewel of the Lotus Flower. 2001. pap. 16.95 (*0-595-18251-8*) iUniverse, Inc.
Vizinczey, Stephen. In Praise of Older Women. 1971. mass mkt. 0.95 o.s.i (*0-345-21956-2*) Ballantine Bks.
—In Praise of Older Women. Brady, Upton B., ed. 1986. 181p. 12.95 o.p. (*0-87113-083-1*); pap. 6.95 o.p. (*0-87113-077-7*) Grove/Atlantic, Inc.
—In Praise of Older Women: The Amorous Recollections of A. V. rev. ed. 1990. (Phoenix Fiction Ser.). x, 192p. pap. 14.00 (*0-226-85886-3*) Univ. of Chicago Pr.
Volk, Toni. Maybe in Missoula. 1994. 280p. 22.00 o.p. (*1-56947-007-3*) Soho Pr., Inc.
Von Arnim, Elizabeth. Enchanted April. lib. bdg. 24.95 (*0-8488-1888-1*) Amereon, Ltd.
—Enchanted April. abr. ed. 1994. (Read-Along Ser.). pap. 29.99 incl. audio (*0-88646-836-1*, LSR 7347) Durkin Hayes Publishing Ltd.
—Enchanted April. 1993. 320p. mass mkt. 5.99 (*0-671-86864-0*, Pocket) Simon & Schuster.
—The Enchanted April, Set. unabr. ed. 1998. 35.95 incl. audio (*1-55685-519-2*) Audio Bk. Contractors, Inc.
—The Enchanted April. unabr. ed. 2000. audio compact disk 56.00 (*0-7861-9927-X*, z1428); 1994. audio 44.95 (*0-7861-0476-7*, 1428) Blackstone Audio Bks., Inc.
—The Enchanted April. unabr. ed. 2000. audio 49.95 (*0-7451-2757-6*, SAB 123) Chivers Audio Bks. GBR. *Dist:* BBC Audiobooks America.
—The Enchanted April, Set. unabr. ed. 1999. audio 44.95 Highsmith Inc.
—The Enchanted April. Ng, Donna, ed. 1995. 192p. reprint ed. pap. (*0-671-53614-1*, Washington Square Pr.) Simon & Schuster.
—The Enchanted April. 2001. (Modern Classics). 361p. reprint ed. 13.95 (*0-86068-517-9*) Virago Pr., Ltd. GBR. *Dist:* Trafalgar Square.
Wachtel, Chuck. The Gates: A Novel. 1994. 416p. 23.95 o.p. (*0-670-83886-1*, Viking) Viking Penguin.
Wagner, Geoffrey. A Singular Passion. 1994. 303p. 20.00 (*1-880909-22-7*) Baskerville Pubs., Inc.
Walker, Barbara G. Feminist Fairy Tales. 256p. 1997. pap. 13.95 (*0-06-251320-6*); 1995. (Illus.). 22.00 o.p. (*0-06-251319-2*) HarperSanFrancisco.
Waller, Robert James. Slow Waltz in Cedar Bend. unabr. ed. 1994. audio 30.00 o.p. Books on Tape, Inc.
—Slow Waltz in Cedar Bend. unabr. ed. 1993. audio 22.95 o.p. (*1-55800-876-4*, 592099); audio compact disk 59.95 o.p. (*1-55800-880-2*) NewStar Media, Inc.
—Slow Waltz in Cedar Bend. 1994. 227p. mass mkt. 4.99 o.s.i (*0-446-60164-0*); 1993. 200p. 25.00 (*0-446-51653-8*) Warner Bks., Inc.
—Slow Waltz in Cedar Bend & the Bridges of Madison County. 1993. audio 19.88 o.p. (*1-55800-927-2*, Dove Audio) NewStar Media, Inc.
Watkins, Paul. The Story of My Disappearance. 224p. 1999. pap. 11.00 (*0-312-20026-9*); 1998. 21.00 o.p. (*0-312-17995-2*) Picador.
—Story of My Disappearance. unabr. ed. 1998. audio 51.00 (*0-7887-2179-8*, 95475E7 ) Recorded Bks., LLC.
Watson, Larry. Laura. pap. (*0-671-03842-7*, Pocket); 2001. 352p. reprint ed. pap. 13.95 (*0-671-56776-4*, Washington Square Pr.) Simon & Schuster.
Watson, Richard. Niagara. 1993. 192p. 19.95 (*1-56689-006-3*) Coffee Hse. Pr.
Watts, Timothy. Steal Away. 1996. 272p. 22.00 (*1-56947-067-7*) Soho Pr., Inc.
Webb, Charles. New Cardiff. 2002. (Illus.). 368p. pap. 14.00 (*0-7434-4416-7*, Washington Square Pr.) Simon & Schuster.
Weesner, Theodore. Novemberfest. 1994. 384p. 24.00 o.s.i (*0-679-43099-7*) Knopf, Alfred A. Inc.
—Novemberfest. 1996. 397p. pap. 15.95 (*0-87451-766-4*, Hardscrabble Bks.) Univ. Pr. of New England.
Weiss, Daniel E. The Roaches Have No King. Silverberg, Ira, ed. 1994. 240p. (Orig.). pap. o.p. (*1-85242-326-9*) Serpent's Tail Ltd.
Wells, Dee. Jane. 1987. 288p. reprint ed. pap. 7.95 o.p. (*0-06-097078-2*, PL 7078, Perennial) HarperTrade.
Wells, Rosalie. The Mountains of Tomorrow. l.t. ed. 1994. 19.95 o.p. (*0-7927-1830-5*); pap. 17.95 o.p. (*0-7927-1829-1*) BBC Audiobooks America.
Welter, John. Night of the Avenging Blowfish: A Novel of Covert Operations, Love & Luncheon Meat. 1994. 304p. pap. 11.95 (*1-56512-050-7*) Algonquin Bks. of Chapel Hill.
Wesley, Mary. An Imaginative Experience. 1995. 376p. mass mkt. 10.95 o.p. (*0-552-99592-4*) Bantam Bks.
—An Imaginative Experience. unabr. ed. 2000. audio 49.95 (*0-7451-4383-0*, CAB 1067) Chivers Audio Bks. GBR. *Dist:* BBC Audiobooks America.
—An Imaginative Experience. 1996. 224p. pap. 10.95 o.s.i (*0-14-024749-1*, Penguin Bks.) Penguin Group (USA) Inc.
—An Imaginative Experience. l.t. ed. 1995. (Charnwood Large Print Ser.). 304p. 29.99 o.p. (*0-7089-8848-2*, Charnwood) Thorpe, F. A. Pubs. GBR. *Dist:* Ulverscroft Large Print Bks., Ltd., Ulverscroft Large Print Canada, Ltd.
—An Imaginative Experience. abr. ed. 1997. mass mkt. 16.95 incl. audio (*1-85998-022-8*) Trafalgar Square.
—An Imaginative Experience. 1995. 224p. 21.95 o.p. (*0-670-85649-5*, Viking) Viking Penguin.
—Not That Sort of Girl. (King Penguin Ser.). 1989. 320p. pap. 11.95 o.s.i (*0-14-010826-2*, Penguin Bks.); 1988. 17.95 o.p. (*0-670-82121-7*) Viking Penguin.
West, Morris. The Lovers. 1993. 304p. 22.00 o.s.i (*1-55611-370-6*) Fine, Donald I. Bks.
West, Paul. Life with Swan. 2001. 300p. pap. 15.95 (*1-58567-123-1*) Overlook Pr., The.
—Life with Swan. 1999. 304p. 24.00 (*0-684-84864-3*, Scribner) Simon & Schuster.
—Sporting with Amaryllis. 1996. 160p. 19.95 (*0-87951-666-6*) Overlook Pr., The.
Wharton, Edith. The Buccaneers. 2000. (Illus.). 414p. reprint ed. 16.00 (*0-7881-9371-6*) DIANE Publishing Co.
—The Buccaneers. Mainwaring, Marion, ed. l.t. ed. 1994. 26.95 (*1-56895-062-4*, Wheeler Publishing, Inc.) Gale Group.
—The Buccaneers. 1995. (Illus.). 448p. 15.95 o.p. (*0-670-86645-8*, Viking); 1969. pap. 3.50 o.p. (*0-14-044212-X*, Penguin Classics); 1994. 384p. reprint ed. 13.00 (*0-14-023202-8*) Viking Penguin.

—Ethan Frome. 20.95 (*0-89190-509-X*) Amereon, Ltd.
—Ethan Frome. E-Book 5.00 (*0-7607-1307-3*) Barnes & Noble, Inc.
—Ethan Frome. 2002. 110p. pap. 3.95 (*1-59109-098-9*) Booksurge, LLC.
—Ethan Frome. 1995. reprint ed. lib. bdg. 19.95 (*1-56849-636-2*) Buccaneer Bks., Inc.
—Ethan Frome. Peel, Edith, ed. 1999. (Literature Ser.). (Illus.). 172p. pap. text 11.95 (*0-521-64529-8*) Cambridge Univ. Pr.
—Ethan Frome. (Collected Works of Edith Wharton). 195p. 2001. pap. text 28.00 (*0-7426-5976-3*); 1998. reprint ed. lib. bdg. 88.00 (*1-58201-976-2*) Classic Bks.
—Ethan Frome. 1991. (Illus.). 96p. pap. 1.00 (*0-486-26690-7*) Dover Pubns., Inc.
—Ethan Frome. 1987. 192p. pap. 8.00 (*0-684-18906-2*); 1982. 192p. pap. 1.95 o.s.i (*0-684-17487-1*); 1977. 192p. 30.00 (*0-684-15326-2*); 1977. text 11.25 o.s.i (*0-684-51564-4*); 1977. pap. text (*0-684-51565-2*); 1910. pap. 5.95 o.s.i (*0-684-71927-4*, SL8) Gale Group. (Macmillan Reference USA).
—Ethan Frome. l.t. ed. 360p. pap. 32.97 (*0-7583-0846-9*); 420p. pap. 37.22 (*0-7583-0847-7*); 80p. pap. 13.16 (*0-7583-0840-X*); 294p. pap. 28.30 (*0-7583-0845-0*); 107p. pap. 15.07 (*0-7583-0841-8*); 240p. pap. 24.48 (*0-7583-0844-2*); 145p. pap. 17.76 (*0-7583-0842-6*); 187p. pap. 20.73 (*0-7583-0843-4*); 294p. lib. bdg. 39.55 (*0-7583-0837-X*); 240p. lib. bdg. 35.73 (*0-7583-0836-1*); 187p. lib. bdg. 31.98 (*0-7583-0835-3*); 360p. lib. bdg. 44.22 (*0-7583-0838-8*); 420p. lib. bdg. 48.47 (*0-7583-0839-6*); 80p. lib. bdg. 19.76 (*0-7583-0832-9*); 107p. lib. bdg. 23.06 (*0-7583-0833-7*); 145p. lib. bdg. 27.67 (*0-7583-0834-5*) Huge Print Pr.
—Ethan Frome. 1999. 110p. pap. 9.95 o.p. (*1-930128-05-3*, JNMedia Bks.) JNMedia, Inc.
—Ethan Frome. (Signet Classics). 2000. 176p. mass mkt. 4.95 (*0-451-52766-6*); 1996. pap., instr.'s gde. ed. (*0-451-16661-2*); 1992. 160p. mass mkt. 3.95 o.p. (*0-451-52580-9*); 1987. 160p. mass mkt. 4.95 o.s.i (*0-451-52227-3*); 1987. mass mkt. 2.50 o.p. (*0-451-52079-3*) NAL. (Signet Classics).
—Ethan Frome. 1991. 96p. (C). reprint ed. pap. text 2.75 (*0-914061-23-2*) Orchises Pr.
—Ethan Frome. Showalter, Elaine, ed. & intro. by. (Oxford World's Classics Ser.). 1998. 160p. pap. 7.95 (*0-19-283496-7*); 1996. 156p. pap. 6.95 o.p. (*0-19-282515-1*) Oxford Univ. Pr., Inc.
—Ethan Frome. 1911. 178p. text 9.50 o.s.i (*0-02-426690-6*, Macmillan College) Prentice Hall PTR.
—Ethan Frome. 1999. (Illus.). 182p. reprint ed. lib. bdg. 29.95 (*0-7351-0119-1*) Replica Bks.
—Ethan Frome. 1997. 160p. pap. 10.00 (*0-684-82591-0*, Scribner) Simon & Schuster.
—Ethan Frome. 1997. 16.05 (*0-606-00613-3*) Turtleback Bks.
—Ethan Frome. (Great Books of the 20th Century Ser.). 1994. 208p. 7.95 (*0-14-018736-7*); 1987. 224p. pap. 6.95 o.p. (*0-14-039058-8*) Viking Penguin. (Penguin Classics).
—Ethan Frome. 1993. 4.99 o.s.i (*1-85381-672-8*); 1991. 9.95 (*1-85381-228-5*) Virago Pr., Ltd. GBR. *Dist:* Random Hse. of Canada, Ltd., Trafalgar Square.
—Ethan Frome. 1999. E-Book 5.99 (*0-8220-7064-2*, Cliff Notes) Wiley, John & Sons, Inc.
—Ethan Frome. (Classics Library). 96p. pap. 3.95 (*1-84022-408-8*); 1998. pap. 3.95 (*1-85326-555-1*, 5551WW) Wordsworth Editions, Ltd. GBR. *Dist:* Combined Publishing.
—Ethan Frome: Authoritative Text, Backgrounds & Contexts, Criticism. Lauer, Kristin O. & Wolff, Cynthia G., eds. 1994. (Critical Editions Ser.). (C). pap. text 7.50 (*0-393-96635-6*) Norton, W. W. & Co., Inc.
—Ethan Frome & Other Short Fiction. 1987. (Classics Ser.). 256p. mass mkt. 5.50 (*0-553-21255-9*, Bantam Classics) Bantam Bks.
—Ethan Frome & Other Stories. 1996. 176p. text 5.98 o.p. (*1-56138-763-0*, Courage Bks.) Running Pr. Bk. Pubs.
—Ethan Frome & Summer. (Twelve-Point Ser.). 1998. lib. bdg. 25.00 (*1-58287-027-6*); 1993. 449p. reprint ed. lib. bdg. 26.00 (*0-939495-27-9*) North Bks.
—Ethan Frome & Summer. 2001. (Modern Library Classics). 304p. pap. 7.95 (*0-375-75728-7*, Modern Library) Random House Adult Trade Publishing Group.
—The Reef. 1998. (Collected Works of Edith Wharton). 366p. reprint ed. lib. bdg. 88.00 (*1-58201-991-6*) Classic Bks.
—The Reef. 2000. 304p. mass mkt. 4.99 (*0-380-81549-4*, Avon Bks.) Morrow/Avon.
—The Reef. Orgel, Stephen, ed. 1998. (Oxford World's Classics Ser.). 236p. pap. 9.95 o.p. (*0-19-282319-1*) Oxford Univ. Pr., Inc.
—The Reef. 1996. 336p. 16.00 (*0-679-44724-5*) Random Hse., Inc.
—The Reef. 1996. 336p. pap. 12.00 (*0-684-82444-2*, Scribner); 1984. 384p. pap. 9.95 o.s.i (*0-684-18249-1*, Scribner Paper Fiction); 1977. 384p. 20.00 (*0-684-15557-5*, Scribner) Simon & Schuster.
—The Reef. 1995. (Penguin Great Books of the 20th Century Ser.). 368p. pap. 10.95 o.s.i (*0-14-018731-6*, Penguin Classics) Viking Penguin.
—Summer. lib. bdg. 20.95 (*0-8488-1876-8*) Amereon, Ltd.
—Summer. 1993. 224p. mass mkt. 4.95 (*0-553-21422-5*) Bantam Bks.
—Summer. 1998. (Collected Works of Edith Wharton). 290p. reprint ed. lib. bdg. 88.00 (*1-58201-994-0*) Classic Bks.
—Summer. 1980. pap. 6.50 o.p. (*0-06-080507-2*, P 507, Perennial) HarperTrade.
—Summer. 1991. 318p. reprint ed. lib. bdg. 25.00 o.p. (*0-8095-9073-5*) Millefleurs.
—Summer. 1993. 216p. mass mkt. 4.95 (*0-451-52566-3*, Signet Classics) NAL.
—Summer. 1970. reprint ed. 59.00 (*0-403-00259-1*) Scholarly Pr., Inc.
—Summer. 1998. 256p. pap. 10.00 (*0-684-84258-0*, Scribner) Simon & Schuster.
—Summer. l.t. ed. 1996. (Perennial Bestsellers Ser.). lib. bdg. 22.95 (*0-7838-1831-9*) Thorndike Pr.
—Summer. 1993. (Great Books of the 20th Century Ser.). 224p. 9.95 (*0-14-018679-4*, Penguin Classics) Viking Penguin.
—Three Novels of Old New York: The House of Mirth; The Custom of the the Country; The Age of Innocence. 1997. (Penguin Twentieth-Century Classics Ser.). 992p. pap. 16.95 o.p. (*0-14-018984-X*) Viking Penguin.
Wharton, Edith & Mainwaring, Marion. The Buccaneers. abr. ed. 1993. (Classics on Cassette). 16.00 o.p. incl. audio (*0-453-00854-2*, 390454) Penguin/HighBridge.
—The Buccaneers. 1993. 416p. 22.00 o.p. (*0-670-85219-8*, Viking) Viking Penguin.
Wharton, Edith & Showalter, Elaine. Ethan Frome. 1996. E-Book 7.30 (*0-585-35118-X*) netLibrary, Inc.
Wheelis, Allen. The Way Things Are. Putnam, Jeff, ed. 1994. 181p. 18.00 (*1-880909-14-6*) Baskerville Pubs., Inc.
White, Franklin. Fed up with the Fanny. 304p. 2003. mass mkt. 6.99 (*0-7434-8240-9*); 1998. 23.00 (*0-684-84491-5*) Simon & Schuster. (Simon & Schuster).
Whitfield, Van. Beeperless Remote: A Guy, Some Girls & His Answering Machine: A Romantic Comedy. 1999. 288p. pap. 12.00 (*0-385-48934-X*) Doubleday Publishing.
Whitnell, Barbara. Charmed Circle. 1993. 352p. 21.95 o.p. (*0-312-10438-3*) St. Martin's Pr.
Wick, Lori. The Knight & the Dove. (Kensington Chronicles Ser.). 1995. 345p. pap. 9.99 (*1-56507-289-8*); 2nd ed. 2004. reprint ed. pap. 10.99 (*0-7369-1324-6*) Harvest Hse. Pubs.
—The Knight & the Dove. l.t. ed. 2001. (Kensington Chronicles Ser.). 543p. 28.95 (*0-7862-2955-1*) Thorndike Pr.
—Promise Me Tomorrow. 1997. (Rocky Mountain Memories Ser.: Vol. 4). 400p. pap. 10.99 (*1-56507-695-8*) Harvest Hse. Pubs.
—To Know Her by Name. l.t. ed. 1998. (Christian Fiction Ser.). 589p. 24.95 (*0-7862-1466-X*) Thorndike Pr.
—To Know Her by Name: A Novel. 1997. (Rocky Mountain Memories Ser.: Vol. 3). 300p. (Orig.). pap. 10.99 (*1-56507-574-9*) Harvest Hse. Pubs.
—Where the Wild Rose Blooms. 1996. (Rocky Mountain Memories Ser.: No. 1). pap. 10.99 (*1-56507-391-6*) Harvest Hse. Pubs.
—Where the Wild Rose Blooms. l.t. ed. 1998. (Christian Fiction Ser.). 543p. 24.95 o.p. (*0-7862-1525-9*) Thorndike Pr.
—Whispers of Moonlight. 1996. (Rocky Mountain Memories Ser.: Vol. 2). pap. 10.99 (*1-56507-483-1*) Harvest Hse. Pubs.
—Wings of the Morning. (Kensington Chronicles Ser.). 1994. 273p. pap. 9.99 (*1-56507-177-8*); 2nd ed. 2004. reprint ed. pap. 10.99 (*0-7369-1321-1*) Harvest Hse. Pubs.
—Wings of the Morning. l.t. ed. 2001. (Christian Fiction Ser.). 402p. 27.95 (*0-7862-2958-6*) Thorndike Pr.
Wiggins, Marianne. Eveless Eden. 1995. 337p. 23.00 o.p. (*0-06-016951-6*) HarperTrade.
Wilcox, James. Polite Sex: A Novel. 1991. 228p. 19.95 o.p. (*0-06-016356-9*); 1993. 288p. reprint ed. pap. 12.00 o.p. (*0-06-092165-X*, Perennial) HarperTrade.
—Polite Sex: A Novel. 1999. pap. (*0-316-94010-0*); 288p. pap. 13.00 (*0-316-94134-4*, Back Bay) Little Brown & Co.
Wilkins, Christopher. The Measure of Love. 2000. 208p. 21.00 (*0-7867-0758-5*, Carroll & Graf Pubs.) Avalon Publishing Group.
Williams, Niall. As It Is in Heaven. l.t. ed. 1999. (Basic Ser.). 488p. 29.95 (*0-7862-2282-4*) Thorndike Pr.
—As It Is in Heaven. abr. ed. 1999. audio 17.98 (*1-57042-703-8*) Time Warner AudioBooks.
—As It Is in Heaven. 1999. E-Book 9.95 (*0-446-91304-9*); 1999. 320p. 23.00 (*0-446-52548-0*); 2000. 336p. reprint ed. pap. 13.95 (*0-446-67601-2*) Warner Bks., Inc.
—Four Letters of Love. 1997. 352p. 23.00 o.p. (*0-374-15817-7*) Farrar, Straus & Giroux.
—Four Letters of Love. l.t. ed. 1997. (G. K. Hall Core Ser.). 371p. 26.95 (*0-7838-8297-1*) Thorndike Pr.
—Four Letters of Love. 1998. 288p. reprint ed. pap. 13.99 (*0-446-67493-1*) Warner Bks., Inc.
Williams, Susan D. Sunset Coast. 1995. 320p. pap. 11.99 o.p. (*0-89107-854-1*) Crossway Bks.
Williamson, Nicol. Ming's Kingdom. 1996. 246p. o.p. (*0-09-179222-3*) Random Hse. of Canada, Ltd. CAN. *Dist:* Random Hse., Inc.
Williamson, Penelope. The Passions of Emma. l.t. ed. 1998. (Large Print Book Ser.). 26.95 (*1-56895-526-X*, Wheeler Publishing, Inc.) Gale Group.
—The Passions of Emma. 1997. 432p. 19.50 o.p. (*0-446-52153-1*); 1998. 464p. reprint ed. mass mkt. 6.99 (*0-446-60597-2*) Warner Bks., Inc.
Wilson, Angus. Anglo-Saxon Attitudes. 1963. mass mkt. 0.75 o.p. (*0-451-50151-9*, Signet Classics) NAL.
—Anglo-Saxon Attitudes. 1960. pap. 1.85 o.p. (*0-670-00062-0*) Penguin Group (USA) Inc.
—Anglo-Saxon Attitudes. 1996. 352p. pap. 14.95 o.p. (*0-312-14275-7*, Saint Martin's Griffin) St. Martin's Pr.
—Anglo-Saxon Attitudes. 1978. 352p. pap. 4.95 o.p. (*0-14-001311-3*, Penguin Bks.); 1956. 4.50 o.p. (*0-670-12635-7*) Viking Penguin.
Wilson, Susan. Beauty. l.t. ed. 1996. 24.95 (*1-56895-368-2*, Wheeler Publishing, Inc.) Gale Group.
Wimberly, Clara. The Jeweled Heart of Rosemont Castle. l.t. ed. 1994. 391p. pap. 18.95 (*0-8161-7493-8*, Macmillan Reference USA) Gale Group.
—The Jeweled Heart of Rosemont Castle. 1992. 288p. mass mkt. 3.99 o.s.i (*0-8217-4000-8*, Zebra Bks.) Kensington Publishing Corp.
Wintering. Date not set. pap. (*0-312-28376-8*, Saint Martin's Griffin) St. Martin's Pr.
Winterson, Jeanette. The Passion. 1997. 176p. pap. 12.00 (*0-8021-3522-6*, Grove Pr.); 1988. 180p. 16.95 o.p. (*0-87113-183-8*) Grove/Atlantic, Inc.
—The Passion. 1990. (Vintage International Ser.). pap. 10.00 o.s.i (*0-679-72437-0*, Vintage) Knopf Publishing Group.
Wolcott, James. The Catsitters. 2001. 320p. 25.00 (*0-06-019414-6*) HarperCollins Pubs.
—The Catsitters. 2002. 320p. pap. 12.95 (*0-06-093218-X*, Perennial) HarperTrade.
Wolfe, Thomas. The Good Child's River. 1991. (H. Eugene & Lillian Youngs Lehman Ser.). (Illus.). xvi, 316p. (C). 24.95 (*0-8078-2002-4*) Univ. of North Carolina Pr.
Wood. Hungry Tide. 2000. 477p. pap. 9.95 (*0-552-14118-6*) Transworld Publishers Ltd. GBR. *Dist:* Trafalgar Square.
Woods, Stuart. Heat. 1994. 320p. 138.00 o.p. (*0-06-017623-7*, HarperCollins); 23.00 o.p. (*0-06-017776-4*) HarperTrade.
—Heat. 1995. 384p. mass mkt. 7.99 (*0-06-109358-0*, HarperTorch) Morrow/Avon.
Woodward, Lilian. Nurse to the Maharajah. l.t. ed. 1994. 19.95 o.p. (*0-7927-1817-8*); pap. 17.95 o.p. (*0-7927-1816-X*) BBC Audiobooks America.
Woolf, Virginia. Night & Day. reprint ed. lib. bdg. 98.00 (*0-7426-3271-7*); 2001. 538p. pap. text 28.00 (*0-7426-8271-4*) Classic Bks.
—Night & Day. 1999. E-Book 2.49 (*1-58627-475-9*) Electric Umbrella Publishing.
—Night & Day. 1973. (Harvest Book Ser.). 516p. reprint ed. pap. 16.00 o.s.i (*0-15-665600-0*, HB263, Harvest Bks.) Harcourt Trade Pubs.
—Night & Day. Raitt, Suzanne, ed. 1992. (Oxford World's Classics Ser.). 582p. pap. (*0-19-281842-2*) Oxford Univ. Pr., Inc.
—Night & Day. l.t. ed. 2000. 590p. 37.95 (*0-7658-0782-3*) Transaction Pubs.
—Night & Day. Briggs, Julia, ed. & intro. by. 1996. (Twentieth Century Classics Ser.). (Illus.). 496p. 13.95 (*0-14-018568-2*, Penguin Classics) Viking Penguin.
—The Voyage Out, Set. unabr. ed. 1991. (YA). (gr. 9 up). audio 59.95 (*1-55685-194-4*) Audio Bk. Contractors, Inc.
—The Voyage Out. 1991. 448p. mass mkt. 4.95 o.s.i (*0-553-21394-6*, Bantam Classics) Bantam Bks.
—The Voyage Out. unabr. ed. 1997. audio 69.95 (*0-7861-1163-1*, 1932);Set. audio 69.95 Blackstone Audio Bks., Inc.
—The Voyage Out. (Collected Works of Virginia Woolf). reprint ed. lib. bdg. 98.00 (*0-7426-3267-9*) Classic Bks.
—The Voyage Out. 1968. 384p. reprint ed. pap. 12.00 (*0-15-693625-9*, Harvest Bks.) Harcourt Trade Pubs.
—The Voyage Out. 1991. 432p. mass mkt. 4.95 o.s.i (*0-451-52555-8*, Signet Classics) NAL.
—The Voyage Out. Sage, Lorna, ed. (Oxford World's Classics Ser.). 2001. 496p. pap. 10.95 (*0-19-283711-7*); 1996. 482p. (C). pap. 8.95 o.p. (*0-19-281834-1*) Oxford Univ. Pr., Inc.
—The Voyage Out. 2000. (Modern Library Ser.). 528p. 17.95 o.s.i (*0-679-64028-2*) Random Hse., Inc.
—The Voyage Out. Wheare, Jane, ed. 1992. (Twentieth Century Classics Ser.). 400p. pap. 11.95 (*0-14-018563-1*, Penguin Classics) Viking Penguin.
Worby, Anne. High Hostage. l.t. ed. 1994. 19.95 o.p. (*0-7927-2026-1*); pap. 17.95 o.p. (*0-7927-2025-3*) BBC Audiobooks America.
Wyatt, Charles. Listening to Mozart. 1995. (John Simmons Short Fiction Award Ser.). 194p. 22.95 (*0-87745-524-4*); E-Book 22.95 (*1-58729-256-4*) Univ. of Iowa Pr.
Yamada, Amy. Trash: A Novel. Noma, Chikako & Bell, Susan, eds. Johnson, Sonya L., tr. 1995. 384p. 18.00 (*1-56836-018-5*) Kodansha America, Inc.
Ying, Hong. K: The Art of Love. 2002. 252p. pap. 14.95 (*0-7145-3072-7*) Boyars, Marion Pubs., Inc.
Yorgason, Blaine M. To Soar with the Eagle. 1993. 280p. o.p. (*0-87579-745-8*) Deseret Bk. Co.
Yorke, Christy. The Wishing Garden. 2000. 368p. mass mkt. 5.99 (*0-553-58036-1*) Bantam Bks.
Yount, John. Toots in Solitude. 1985. 192p. pap. 5.95 o.p. (*0-312-80905-0*, Saint Martin's Griffin); 1983. 224p. 13.95 o.p. (*0-312-80904-2*) St. Martin's Pr.
—Toots in Solitude: A Novel. 1995. 200p. pap. 10.95 (*0-87074-384-8*) Southern Methodist Univ. Pr.
Zahavi, Helen. Dirty Weekend: A Novel of Revenge. 1994. 188p. pap. 10.95 o.p. (*0-939416-85-9*) Cleis Pr.
—The Weekend. 1991. 17.95 o.p. (*1-55611-241-6*) Fine, Donald I. Bks.
Zigman, Laura. Animal Husbandry. abr. ed. 1997. audio 16.95 (*1-55927-489-1*) Audio Renaissance.
—Animal Husbandry. unabr. ed. 2000. audio 69.95 (*0-7927-2368-6*, CSL257, Chivers Sound Library) BBC Audiobooks America.
—Animal Husbandry. 1998. 320p. pap. 13.95 (*0-385-31903-7*, Delta) Dell Publishing.
—Animal Husbandry. l.t. ed. 1998. (Americana Ser.). 389p. 27.95 (*0-7862-1434-1*) Thorndike Pr.
—Her: A Novel. 2003. 224p. reprint ed. pap. 12.00 (*0-375-71322-0*, Anchor) Knopf Publishing Group.
Zola, Emile. Paris. Vizetelly, Ernest Alfred, tr. 1993. (Pocket Classics Ser.). pap. text 10.95 (*0-7509-0450-X*) Sutton Publishing.
Zollinger, Norman. Chapultepec. 1995. 384p. 24.95 o.p. (*0-312-85530-3*, Forge Bks.) Doherty, Tom Assocs., LLC.
—Not of War Only: A Novel of the Mexican Revolution. 1995. 597p. mass mkt. 5.99 (*0-8125-3013-6*); 1994. 416p. 22.95 o.p. (*0-312-85529-X*) Doherty, Tom Assocs., LLC. (Forge Bks.).

**MARRIAGE—FICTION**

Adams, Anna. Unexpected Marriage. 2001. (Harlequin Superromance Ser.: No. 1023). 299p. mass mkt. (*0-373-71023-2*, 1-71023-5, Harlequin Bks.) Harlequin Enterprises, Ltd.
Adamse, Michael. Anniversary: A Love Story. 1998. 250p. pap. 10.95 (*1-55874-542-4*) Health Communications, Inc.
Adler, C. S. Down by the River. 1983. (J). (gr. 7-10). pap. (*0-671-45288-6*, Simon Pulse) Simon & Schuster Children's Publishing.
Adler, Curtis. January Colours. 2004. 320p. pap. 10.00 (*0-684-02092-0*) Simon & Schuster, Ltd. GBR. *Dist:* Simon & Schuster, Inc.
Allman, Paul. The Knot. Rosen, Roger, ed. 1988. (Flipside Fiction Ser.). (YA). (gr. 7-12). lib. bdg. 12.95 o.p. (*0-8239-0776-7*) Rosen Publishing Group, Inc., The.
Alvarez, Alfred. Day of Atonement. 1993. 3.99 o.p. (*0-517-09789-3*) Random Hse. Value Publishing.
Ames, Mildred. Cassandra-Jamie. 1985. 144p. (J). (gr. 6-8). 12.95 o.s.i (*0-684-18472-9*, Macmillan Reference USA) Gale Group.
Anderson, Caroline. The Impetuous Bride. 2001. (Harlequin Romance Ser.: No. 3676). 192p. mass mkt. (*0-373-03676-0*, 1-03676-3, Harlequin Bks.) Harlequin Enterprises, Ltd.
Anderson, Patrick. Impetuous Bride. l.t. ed. 2001. (Nearlyweds Ser.). mass mkt. (*0-373-15922-6*, Harlequin Bks.) Harlequin Enterprises, Ltd.
Ansay, A. Manette. Midnight Champagne. 1999. 240p. 24.00 (*0-688-15244-9*, Morrow, William & Co.) Morrow/Avon.
—Midnight Champagne: A Novel. 2000. (Illus.). 240p. pap. 13.00 (*0-380-72975-X*, Perennial) HarperTrade.
Applegate, K. A. Bonfire. 1993. (Ocean City Ser.: No. 3). 256p. mass mkt. 3.50 o.p. (*0-06-106794-6*, HarperTorch) Morrow/Avon.
—Swept Away. 1995. (Ocean City Ser.: No. 8). 240p. (J). mass mkt. 3.99 o.p. (*0-06-106285-5*, HarperTorch) Morrow/Avon.

Archer, Catherine. Autumn's Bride. 2001. (Harlequin Historicals Ser.: No. 582). mass mkt. (*0-373-29182-5*, Harlequin Bks.) Harlequin Enterprises, Ltd.

Armstrong, Lindsay. By Marriage Divided. 2002. (Harlequin Presents Ser.: No. 2234). 184p. mass mkt. (*0-373-12234-9*, 1-12234-0, Harlequin Bks.) Harlequin Enterprises, Ltd.

—Un Marido Inesperado. 2001. (Harlequin Jazmin Ser.). (SPA.). 160p. pap. (*0-373-68005-8*, 1-68005-7, Harlequin Bks.) Harlequin Enterprises, Ltd.

—A Question of Marriage. 2001. (Harlequin Presents Ser.: No. 2208). 192p. mass mkt. (*0-373-12208-X*, Harlequin Bks.) Harlequin Enterprises, Ltd.

Ashley, Bernard. A Break in the Sun. 1980. (Illus.). 186p. (J). (gr. 6 up). 26.95 (*0-87599-230-7*) Phillips, S.G. Inc.

Bagley, Pat. Hana, the No-Cow Wife. 1993. (Illus.). (J). 12.95 (*0-87579-714-8*) Deseret Bk. Co.

Baird, Pat. Italian's Runaway Bride. 2001. mass mkt. (*0-373-12219-5*, Harlequin Bks.) Harlequin Enterprises, Ltd.

Baker, Candida. Women & Horses: Infidelity & Treachery in Both a Modern & an Ancient Tale of Foolish Lovers. 1992. 192p. 16.95 o.p. (*0-312-07127-2*) St. Martin's Pr.

Baker, Jennifer. For Better, for Worse. 1993. (First Comes Love Ser.). 308p. (YA). (gr. 7-9). mass mkt. 3.50 o.p. (*0-590-46314-4*) Scholastic, Inc.

—In Sickness & in Health. 1993. (First Comes Love Ser.). 308p. (YA). (gr. 7-9). mass mkt. 3.50 (*0-590-46315-2*) Scholastic, Inc.

—Till Death Do Us Part. 1993. (First Comes Love Ser.). 308p. (YA). (gr. 7-9). mass mkt. 3.50 o.p. (*0-590-46316-0*) Scholastic, Inc.

—To Have & to Hold. 1993. (First Comes Love Ser.). 308p. (YA). (gr. 7-9). mass mkt. 3.50 o.p. (*0-590-46313-6*) Scholastic, Inc.

Barasch, Lynne. The Reluctant Flower Girl. 2001. (Illus.). 40p. (J). (gr. k-3). lib. bdg. 14.89 (*0-06-028810-8*) HarperCollins Children's Bk. Group.

Barbaresi, Nina. Frog Went A-Courting. 1985. (Illus.). 32p. (Orig.). (J). (gr. k-3). pap. 2.50 o.p. (*0-590-33301-1*) Scholastic, Inc.

Barnes, Frances. Figaro. 1994. (Voyages Ser.). (Illus.). (J). (*0-383-03686-0*) SRA/McGraw-Hill.

Barthelme, Frederick. Natural Selection. 1991. (Contemporay American Fiction Ser.). 224p. pap. 8.95 o.p. (*0-14-012889-1*, Penguin Bks.) Penguin Group (USA) Inc.

Baumbach, Jonathan. Seven Wives: A Novel. 1994. 128p. 18.95 (*0-932511-86-4*); pap. 10.95 (*0-932511-87-2*) Fiction Collective Two, Inc.

Bausch, Richard. Violence. 1992. 19.95 o.p. (*0-395-59509-6*) Houghton Mifflin Co.

—Violence. 1993. (Contemporaries Ser.). pap. 13.00 o.s.i (*0-679-74379-0*, Vintage) Knopf Publishing Group.

Beck, Martine. Wedding of Brown Bear & White Bear, Vol. 1. 1990. (J). (ps-3). 12.95 o.p. (*0-316-08652-5*) Little Brown & Co.

Beckwith, Lillian. An Island Apart. 2001. 192p. pap. 9.95 (*0-7551-0284-3*) House of Stratus, Inc. GBR. *Dist:* Midpoint Trade Bks., Inc.

—An Island Apart. 1993. 176p. 18.95 o.p. (*0-312-10483-9*) St. Martin's Pr.

Benjamin, Carol Lea. The Wicked Stepdog. 1982. (Illus.). 128p. (J). (gr. 3-7). lib. bdg. 11.89 o.p. (*0-690-04171-3*) HarperCollins Children's Bk. Group.

—The Wicked Stepdog. 1986. 128p. (YA). (gr. 5 up). mass mkt. 2.50 (*0-380-70089-1*, Avon Bks.) Morrow/Avon.

Bennet, Bridget, ed. Ripples of Dissent: Women's Stories of Marriage from the 1890s. 1997. 384p. 45.00 (*0-460-87777-1*) Dent, J.M. & Sons GBR. *Dist:* Trafalgar Square.

Bennett, Cherie. Sunset Wedding. 1993. mass mkt. 3.99 o.s.i (*0-425-13982-4*) Berkley Publishing Group.

Bergland, Martha. Farm under a Lake. 1990. (Vintage Contemporaries Ser.). 208p. pap. 9.95 o.s.i (*0-679-73011-7*, Vintage) Knopf Publishing Group.

Beverley, Jo. An Arranged Marriage. 2000. (Romances Ser.). pap. 27.95 (*0-7862-2496-7*, Five Star) Gale Group.

Bianchin, Helen. Husband Test: Presents Passion. 2001. mass mkt. (*0-373-12218-7*, Harlequin Bks.) Harlequin Enterprises, Ltd.

Bingham, Sallie. Matron of Honor. 192p. 1994. 19.95 o.p. (*0-944072-38-0*); 1996. reprint ed. pap. 10.95 o.p. (*0-944072-63-1*) Steerforth Pr. (Zoland Bks., Inc.).

—Upstate. 1993. 176p. 21.95 o.p. (*1-877946-33-8*); 2nd ed. 128p. pap. 16.00 (*1-877946-50-8*) Permanent Pr., The.

Blayne, Sara. An Improper Bride. 2001. 352p. mass mkt. 5.99 o.s.i (*0-8217-6775-5*, Zebra Bks.) Kensington Publishing Corp.

Boll, Heinrich. And Never Said a Word. Vennewitz, Leila, tr. 1979. pap. text 5.95 o.p. (*0-07-006421-0*) McGraw-Hill Cos., The.

—And Never Said a Word. Vennewitz, Leila, tr. from GER. 1994. (European Classics Ser.). 204p. (C). 41.00 (*0-8101-1153-5*); pap. 10.95 (*0-8101-1147-0*) Northwestern Univ. Pr.

Bond, Nancy. Country of Broken Stone. 1986. pap. 12.95 o.s.i (*0-689-50163-3*, Atheneum) Simon & Schuster Children's Publishing.

Bothwell, Jean. Defiant Bride. 1969. (J). (gr. 7 up). 5.95 o.p. (*0-15-223090-4*) Harcourt Children's Bks.

Brand, Fiona. Marrying McCabe. 2001. (Silhouette Intimate Moments Ser.: No. 1099). 249p. mass mkt. (*0-373-27169-7*, 1-27169-1, Silhouette) Harlequin Enterprises, Ltd.

Bright, Susie. Marrying Marcus. 2001. (Virgin Bride Ser.). 192p. mass mkt. (*0-373-19558-3*, Harlequin Bks.) Harlequin Enterprises, Ltd.

Brookner, Anita. Lewis Percy. l.t. ed. 1991. (General Ser.). 357p. pap. 20.95 o.p. (*0-8161-5074-5*, Macmillan Reference USA) Gale Group.

—Lewis Percy. 1991. (Vintage Contemporaries Ser.). 272p. pap. 14.00 (*0-679-72944-5*, Vintage) Knopf Publishing Group.

—Lewis Percy. 1991. 3.99 o.p. (*0-517-07930-5*) Random Hse. Value Publishing.

Brown, Debra Lee. The Mackintosh Bride. 2001. (Harlequin Historicals Ser.: No. 576). mass mkt. (*0-373-29176-0*, 1-29176-4, Harlequin Bks.) Harlequin Enterprises, Ltd.

Browning, Dixie. The Millionaire's Pregnant Bride. 2002. (Silhouette Desire Ser.: No. 1420). mass mkt. (*0-373-76420-0*, 1-76420-8, Silhouette) Harlequin Enterprises, Ltd.

Buck, Pearl S. East Wind - West Wind. 1993. (Oriental Novels of Pearl S. Buck Ser.: Vol. 8). 272p. reprint ed. pap. 11.95 (*1-55921-086-9*) Moyer Bell.

Buehner, Caralyn. Fanny's Dream. (Illus.). 32p. 2003. pap. 6.99 (*0-14-250060-7*, Puffin Bks.); 1996. (J). 15.99 (*0-8037-1496-3*, Dial Bks. for Young Readers); 1996. (J). 14.89 o.p. (*0-8037-1497-1*, Dial Bks. for Young Readers) Penguin Putnam Bks. for Young Readers.

Burton, Mary. The Perfect Wife. 2002. (Harlequin Historicals Ser.: No. 614). 297p. mass mkt. (*0-373-29214-7*, 1-29214-3, Harlequin Bks.) Harlequin Enterprises, Ltd.

Cage, Patricia. The Gift of Life. 1994. (Heartbeats Ser.). 112p. (YA). (gr. 7 up). pap. 5.95 (*0-7910-2930-1*) Chelsea Hse. Pubs.

Cannam, Helen. The Reunion. 2003. 208p. 25.99 (*0-7278-5925-0*) Severn Hse. Pubs., Ltd.

Cargile, Phillip. Old Friends & Married People. 1998. 184p. pap. 13.95 (*0-9653711-0-7*) IP Bks.

Carmichael, C. J. A Second-Chance Proposal. 2002. (Harlequin Superromance Ser.: No. 1038). 296p. mass mkt. (*0-373-71038-0*, 1-71038-3, Harlequin Bks.) Harlequin Enterprises, Ltd.

Chaplin, Elizabeth. Hostage to Fortune. 1993. 272p. 17.95 (*0-89296-504-5*) Mysterious Pr.

Chastain, Sandra. The Mail Order Groom. 2002. 304p. mass mkt. 5.99 (*0-553-58050-7*) Bantam Bks.

Child, Maureen. Did You Say Twins? 2001. (Fortunes of Texas Ser.). (Illus.). 183p. mass mkt. (*0-373-76408-1*, Harlequin Bks.) Harlequin Enterprises, Ltd.

Christenberry. Triplet Secret Babies: Triplets, Quads, Quints. 2001. (Harlequin American Romance Ser.). mass mkt. (*0-373-16901-9*, Harlequin Bks.) Harlequin Enterprises, Ltd.

Christenberry, Judy. Least Likely to Wed. 2002. (Silhouette Romance Ser.: No. 1570). mass mkt. (*0-373-19570-2*, 1-19570-0, Silhouette) Harlequin Enterprises, Ltd.

Clark, Clara. Nellie Bishop. 2003. (Illus.). 128p. (gr. 7-12). pap. 12.95 o.s.i (*1-56397-642-0*) Boyds Mills Pr.

Clayton, Alana. A Devilish Husband. 2001. (Zebra Regency Romance Ser.). 256p. mass mkt. 4.99 o.s.i (*0-8217-7100-0*) Kensington Publishing Corp.

Cleary, Beverly. Sister of the Bride. 2003. (Cleary Reissue Ser.). (Illus.). 304p. (J). (gr. 5 up). pap. 5.99 (*0-06-053298-X*) HarperCollins Children's Bk. Group.

Colter, Cara. Wed by a Will. 2001. (Silhouette Romance Ser.: No. 1544). mass mkt. (*0-373-19544-3*, 1-19544-5, Silhouette) Harlequin Enterprises, Ltd.

Cone, Molly. Paul David Silverman Is a Father. 1983. (Skinny Bks.). (Illus.). 64p. (J). (gr. 2 up). 8.95 o.p. (*0-525-44050-X*, Dutton) Dutton/Plume.

Connell, Evan S. Mr. Bridge. l.t. ed. 1991. (Paperback Ser.). 436p. pap. 15.95 o.p. (*0-8161-5205-5*, Macmillan Reference USA) Gale Group.

—Mrs. Bridge. 1990. 246p. reprint ed. pap. 9.95 (*0-86547-056-1*, North Point Pr.) Farrar, Straus & Giroux.

—Mrs. Bridge. l.t. ed. 1991. pap. 15.95 o.p. (*0-8161-5206-3*, Macmillan Reference USA) Gale Group.

—Mrs. Bridge. 1963. pap. 1.65 o.p. (*0-670-00122-8*) Penguin Group (USA) Inc.

—Mrs. Bridge. 1959. 3.75 o.p. (*0-670-49448-8*) Viking Penguin.

Cooke, Elizabeth & Wharton, Edith. Zeena. 1996. 352p. 23.95 o.p. (*0-312-14775-9*) St. Martin's Pr.

Cooney, Linda A. Freshman Promises. 1992. (Freshman Dorm Ser.: No. 19). 240p. (YA). mass mkt. 3.99 o.p. (*0-06-106134-4*, HarperTorch) Morrow/Avon.

Cooper, Amy J. Aunt Abigail's Beau. 1992. (Road to Avonlea Ser.: No. 7). 112p. (J). (gr. 4-7). pap. 3.99 o.s.i (*0-553-48033-2*) Bantam Bks.

Cooper, Rand R. The Last to Go: A Family Chronicle. 1988. 304p. 16.95 (*0-15-148430-9*) Harcourt Trade Pubs.

Coulter, Catherine. Wild Star. l.t. ed. 2000. (Wheeler Large Print Book Ser.). 508p. 28.95 o.p. (*1-56895-915-X*, Wheeler Publishing, Inc.) Gale Group.

—Wild Star. 2002. 400p. mass mkt. 7.99 (*0-451-20639-8*, Signet Bks.); 1986. 464p. mass mkt. 7.99 o.s.i (*0-451-40447-5*, Onyx) NAL.

—Wild Star. 1994. reprint ed. lib. bdg. 22.00 (*0-7278-4687-6*) Severn Hse. Pubs., Ltd.

Cravens, Gwyneth. Gates of Paradise. 1990. 256p. 18.95 o.p. (*0-89919-981-X*) Houghton Mifflin Co.

Crook, Elizabeth. The Raven's Bride: A Novel of Eliza Allen & Sam Houston. 1993. (Southwest Life & Letters Ser.). 432p. reprint ed. pap. 12.95 (*0-87074-348-1*) Southern Methodist Univ. Pr.

Dailey, Janet. For Mike's Sake. 1988. mass mkt. (*0-373-89847-9*, Harlequin Bks.) Harlequin Enterprises, Ltd.

—For Mike's Sake. 1999. 132p. per. 19.95 (*0-7592-3811-1*) ereads.com.

Dalton, Emily. A Baby for Lord Roderick. 2002. (Harlequin American Romance Ser.: No. 926). 248p. mass mkt. (*0-373-16926-4*, 1-16926-7, Harlequin Bks.) Harlequin Enterprises, Ltd.

Darcy, Emma. The Arranged Marriage. 2002. (Harlequin Presents Ser.: No. 2253). 187p. mass mkt. (*0-373-12253-5*, 1-12253-0, Harlequin Bks.) Harlequin Enterprises, Ltd.

—The Arranged Marriage. l.t. ed. 2002. (Harlequin I Romance Ser.). 288p. 27.99 (*0-263-17360-7*) Harlequin Mills & Boon, Ltd. GBR. *Dist:* Thorndike Pr., Ulverscroft Large Print Bks., Ltd., Ulverscroft Large Print Canada, Ltd.

Davidson, Carolyn. A Convenient Wife. 2001. (Harlequin Historicals Ser.: No. 585). 304p. mass mkt. o.s.i (*0-373-29185-X*, 1-29185-5, Harlequin Bks.) Harlequin Enterprises, Ltd.

De Mejo, Oscar. The Tiny Visitor. 1982. (Illus.). 64p. (J). (gr. 4-8). 9.95 o.p. (*0-394-85256-7*, Pantheon) Knopf Publishing Group.

De Vere White, Terence. Johnnie Cross. 1983. 160p. 12.95 o.p. (*0-312-44463-X*) St. Martin's Pr.

Dean, Karen S. Between Dances: Maggie Adams' Eighteenth Summer. 1982. 176p. pap. 2.50 o.p. (*0-380-79285-0*, Avon Bks.) Morrow/Avon.

Denison, David. Wedding Deal. l.t. ed. 2001. mass mkt. (*0-373-15924-2*, Harlequin Bks.) Harlequin Enterprises, Ltd.

Denison, Janelle. The Wedding Deal. 2001. (Harlequin Romance Ser.: No. 3678). 192p. mass mkt. (*0-373-03678-7*, 1-03678-9, Harlequin Bks.) Harlequin Enterprises, Ltd.

Dlovu, Nandi. A Bride for the King. 1994. (Heartbeats Ser.). 112p. (YA). (gr. 7 up). pap. 5.95 (*0-7910-2936-0*) Chelsea Hse. Pubs.

Dodd, Christina. Scandalous Again. l.t. ed. 2003. 369p. 30.95 (*1-58724-482-9*, Wheeler Publishing, Inc.) Gale Group.

—Scandalous Again. 2003. 384p. mass mkt. 6.99 (*0-06-009265-3*, Avon Bks.) Morrow/Avon.

Douglas, Charlotte. Licensed to Marry. 2001. (Harlequin Intrigue Ser.: No. 638). 248p. mass mkt. (*0-373-22638-1*, 1-22638-0, Harlequin Bks.) Harlequin Enterprises, Ltd.

Drescher, Joan. My Mother's Getting Married. 1986. (Illus.). 32p. (J). (ps-3). 10.89 o.p. (*0-8037-0176-4*, Dial Bks. for Young Readers) Penguin Putnam Bks. for Young Readers.

Drew, Jennifer. One Bride Too Many/One Groom to Go. 2001. (Harlequin Duets Ser.: No. 59). 378p. mass mkt. (*0-373-44125-8*, 1-44125-2, Harlequin Bks.) Harlequin Enterprises, Ltd.

Driscoll, Jack. Lucky Man, Lucky Woman: A Love Story. 2000. (Norton Paperback Fiction Ser.). 272p. pap. 13.00 (*0-393-31945-8*) Norton, W. W. & Co., Inc.

—Lucky Man, Lucky Woman: A Love Story. 1999. (Editor's Book Award Ser.). 264p. 24.50 (*1-888889-08-X*) Pushcart Pr., The.

Drury, Tom. The End of Vandalism. 1994. 321p. 21.95 o.p. (*0-395-62151-8*) Houghton Mifflin Co.

—The End of Vandalism: A Novel. 1995. 336p. pap. 12.95 o.s.i (*0-449-90982-4*, Fawcett) Ballantine Bks.

Dufresne, John. Louisiana Power & Light. 1995. 320p. pap. 13.95 (*0-452-27502-4*, Plume) Dutton/Plume.

—Louisiana Power & Light. 1994. xi, 306p. 22.00 o.p. (*0-393-03648-0*) Norton, W. W. & Co., Inc.

Dundon, Susan. To My Ex-Husband. 1994. 255p. 20.00 o.p. (*0-688-12459-3*, Morrow, William & Co.) Morrow/Avon.

Eberhart, Mignon G. Melora. l.t. ed. 2000. (Romance Ser.). 330p. 27.95 (*0-7838-9150-4*) Thorndike Pr.

Eidus, Janice. Urban Bliss. 1998. 180p. reprint ed. pap. 9.95 (*0-87286-339-5*) City Lights Bks.

Emecheta, Buchi. The Moonlight Bride. 1983. 77p. (YA). (gr. 6-10). pap. 8.95 (*0-8076-1063-1*) Braziller, George Inc.

Emery, Anne. Stepfamily. 1980. 140p. (J). (gr. 5-7). 9.50 o.p. (*0-664-32660-9*) Westminster John Knox Pr.

Esdaile, Leslie, et al. After the Vows. 2001. (Indigo Love Stories Ser.). pap. 10.95 (*1-58571-047-4*, Indigo) Genesis Pr., Inc.

Evanick, Marcia. His Chosen Bride. 2002. 304p. mass mkt. o.s.i (*0-373-51181-7*, 1-51181-5, Harlequin Bks.); 1996. per. (*0-373-07717-3*, 1-07717-1, Silhouette) Harlequin Enterprises, Ltd.

Evans, Shirlee. A Life Apart: Sequel to a Life in Her Hands. 1990. 176p. (Orig.). pap. 6.99 (*0-8361-3536-9*) Herald Pr.

Ferguson, Jo Ann, et al. Mistletoe Kittens. 1999. (Zebra Regency Romance Ser.). 256p. mass mkt. 4.99 o.s.i (*0-8217-6303-2*, Zebra Bks.) Kensington Publishing Corp.

Fetzer, Amy J. Single Father Seeks... 2002. (Silhouette Desire Ser.: No. 1445). mass mkt. (*0-373-76445-6*, Silhouette) Harlequin Enterprises, Ltd.

Fielding, Liz. The Marriage Merger. 2002. (Harlequin Romance Ser.: No. 3704). mass mkt. (*0-373-03704-X*, 1-03704-3); 256p. mass mkt. (*0-373-15950-1*, 1-15950-8) Harlequin Enterprises, Ltd. (Harlequin Bks.).

—The Marriage Merger. 2002. (Harlequin II Romance Ser.). 24.95 (*0-263-17365-8*) Harlequin Mills & Boon, Ltd. GBR. *Dist:* Thorndike Pr.

Fields, Terri. Fifth-Grade Frankenstein. 1996. (J). (gr. 5-7). mass mkt. 3.50 (*0-590-62368-0*) Scholastic, Inc.

—Fifth-Grade Frankenstein. 1996. 9.55 (*0-606-11324-X*) Turtleback Bks.

Fitzhugh, Louise. Sport. 1979. 250p. (J). (gr. 4-6). pap. 8.95 o.s.i (*0-385-28908-1*, Delacorte Pr.) Dell Publishing.

—Sport. 1982. 224p. (YA). reprint ed. pap. 3.25 o.s.i (*0-440-48221-6*, Yearling) Random Hse. Children's Bks.

Fleischer, Leonore. Shadowlands. 1993. 272p. mass mkt. 4.99 o.s.i (*0-451-18105-0*, Signet Bks.) NAL.

Foley, Michael. Getting Used to Not Being Remarkable. 1998. 312p. pap. 18.95 (*0-85640-626-0*) Blackstaff Pr., The IRL. *Dist:* Dufour Editions, Inc.

Ford, Elaine. Life Designs. 1997. 192p. 22.95 o.p. (*0-944072-80-1*, Zoland Bks., Inc.) Steerforth Pr.

Foreman, James. The Pumpkin Shell. 1983. 160p. mass mkt. 1.95 o.s.i (*0-449-70054-2*, Fawcett) Ballantine Bks.

Forman, James D. The Pumpkin Shell, RS. 1981. 160p. (J). (gr. 7 up). 10.95 o.p. (*0-374-36159-2*, Farrar, Straus & Giroux (BYR)) Farrar, Straus & Giroux.

Forster, E. M. The Longest Journey. 1997. 304p. mass mkt. 4.95 o.s.i (*0-553-21455-1*) Bantam Bks.

—The Longest Journey. 1989. reprint ed. lib. bdg. 27.95 (*0-89966-632-9*) Buccaneer Bks., Inc.

—The Longest Journey. reprint ed. lib. bdg. 98.00 (*0-7426-3113-3*); 2001. 320p. pap. text 28.00 (*0-7426-8113-0*) Classic Bks.

—The Longest Journey. text (*0-7131-6421-2*) Hodder Arnold GBR. *Dist:* Routledge.

—The Longest Journey. Heine, Elizabeth, ed. 1985. (Abinger Edition of E. M. Forster Ser.: Vol. 2). 400p. 69.50 (*0-8419-5832-7*) Holmes & Meier Pubs., Inc.

—The Longest Journey. 2002. 284p. 19.99 (*1-4043-1380-X*); per. 14.99 (*1-4043-1381-8*) IndyPublish-.com.

—The Longest Journey. 1993. 320p. pap. 13.00 (*0-679-74815-6*, Vintage) Knopf Publishing Group.

—The Longest Journey. 1962. pap. 9.00 o.p. (*0-394-70040-6*) Knopf, Alfred A. Inc.

—The Longest Journey. 1999. 330p. reprint ed. lib. bdg. 29.95 (*0-7351-0068-3*) Replica Bks.

Fox, Susan. The Wife He Chose. 2001. (Harlequin Romance Ser.: No. 3668). 184p. mass mkt. (*0-373-03668-X*, 1-03668-0, Harlequin Bks.) Harlequin Enterprises, Ltd.

Gardner, Bonnie. Sgt. Billy's Bride. 2002. (Harlequin American Romance Ser.: No. 911). 256p. mass mkt. (*0-373-16911-6*, 1-16911-9, Harlequin Bks.) Harlequin Enterprises, Ltd.

Gardner, Hayley. Kidnapping His Bride. 2002. (Silhouette Romance Ser.: No. 1598). 192p. mass mkt. (*0-373-19598-2*, 1-19598-1, Silhouette) Harlequin Enterprises, Ltd.

Garwood, Julie. The Bride. l.t. ed. 1991. (General Ser.). 489p. 21.95 o.p. (*0-8161-5160-1*, Macmillan Reference USA) Gale Group.

—The Bride. 2002. 352p. 18.00 (*0-7434-5292-5*, Atria); 1996. 384p. mass mkt. 3.99 (*0-671-00351-8*, Pocket) Simon & Schuster.

—The Bride. Marrow, Linda, ed. 1991. 368p. mass mkt. 7.99 (*0-671-73779-1*, Pocket Star) Simon & Schuster.

—The Bride. 1990. mass mkt. 4.95 (*0-671-72697-8*, Pocket) Simon & Schuster.

Gedney, Mona K., et al. A Bride's Bouquet. 1997. 320p. mass mkt. 4.99 o.s.i (*0-8217-5649-4*) Kensington Publishing Corp.

George, Sara. The Journal of Mrs. Pepys: Portrait of a Marriage. 2000. 352p. pap. 11.95 (*0-312-26347-3*, Saint Martin's Griffin); 1999. 340p. 21.95 o.p. (*0-312-20554-6*) St. Martin's Pr.

Gerard, Cindy. The Bridal Arrangement. 2001. (Silhouette Desire Ser.: No. 1392). mass mkt. (*0-373-76392-1*, 1-76392-9, Silhouette) Harlequin Enterprises, Ltd.

Gilchrist, Ellen. Starcarbon: A Meditation on Love. 1994. 306p. 22.95 o.p. (*0-316-31327-0*) Little Brown & Co.

Glaister, Lesley. Limestone & Clay. 1994. 208p. 19.00 (*0-689-12199-7*, Scribner) Simon & Schuster.

Glass, Leslie. The Silent Bride. 2002. 400p. mass mkt. 6.99 (*0-451-41037-8*, Onyx) NAL.

Godwin, Gail. Evensong. 2000. (Ballantine Reader's Circle Ser.). 432p. pap. 14.00 (*0-345-43477-3*) Ballantine Bks.

—Evensong. l.t. ed. 1999. (Basic Ser.). 29.95 o.p. (*0-7862-2008-2*, Macmillan Reference USA) Gale Group.

—The Good Husband. 1995. 496p. pap. 13.95 (*0-345-39645-6*) Ballantine Bks.

—The Good Husband. l.t. ed. 1994. (Large Print Bks.). 620p. pap. 24.95 (*1-56895-086-1*, Wheeler Publishing, Inc.) Gale Group.

Goldsmith, Olivia. Young Wives. 2000. ix, 512p. 25.00 (*0-06-017553-2*); 784p. pap. 25.00 (*0-06-095563-5*) HarperCollins Pubs.

Gordon, Lucy. La Unica Esposa. 2001. (Harlequin Julia Ser.: No. 11). Tr. of Only Wife. (SPA.). 160p. pap. (*0-373-67011-7*, 1-67011-6, Harlequin Bks.) Harlequin Enterprises, Ltd.

Gordon, Neil. Stand in Bride. l.t. ed. 2001. mass mkt. (*0-373-15927-7*, Harlequin Bks.) Harlequin Enterprises, Ltd.

—Stand in Bride X-Mas. 2001. mass mkt. (*0-373-03681-7*, Harlequin Bks.) Harlequin Enterprises, Ltd.

Goudge, Eileen. Something Borrowed, Something Blue. 1988. (Super Seniors Ser.: No. 3). (J). (gr. k-12). mass mkt. 2.95 o.s.i (*0-440-20055-5*, Laurel Leaf) Random Hse. Children's Bks.

Gould, Judith. Rhapsody: A Love Story. 1999. 352p. 23.95 o.s.i (*0-525-94516-4*, Dutton) Dutton/Plume.

—Rhapsody: A Love Story. l.t. ed. 2000. (Wheeler Large Print Book Ser.). 548p. 26.95 (*1-56895-849-8*, Wheeler Publishing, Inc.) Gale Group.

—Rhapsody: A Love Story. 2000. 432p. mass mkt. 6.99 (*0-451-40933-7*, Onyx) NAL.

Graham, Heather. Heather Graham: Three Complete Novels. 1994. 832p. 13.99 o.s.i (*0-517-10171-8*) Random Hse. Value Publishing.

Green, Michael. Pregnant Bride. 2001. 256p. mass mkt. o.s.i (*0-373-24440-1*, Harlequin Bks.) Harlequin Enterprises, Ltd.

Green, Phyllis & Luks, Margaret. A New Mother for Martha. 1978. (Illus.). 32p. (J). (gr. k-3). 16.95 o.p. (*0-87705-330-8*, Kluwer Academic/Human Science Pr.) Kluwer Academic Pubs.

Greene, Constance C. Getting Nowhere. 1977. (J). 11.50 o.p. (*0-670-33762-5*) Viking Penguin.

Greenwood, Leigh. Undercover Honeymoon. 2002. (Silhouette Special Edition Ser.: No. 1452). 250p. mass mkt. (*0-373-24452-5*, 1-24452-4, Silhouette) Harlequin Enterprises, Ltd.

Gregory, Kay. Marry Me Stranger. 2000. (Five Star Romance Ser.). 307p. pap. 26.95 o.p. (*0-7862-2635-8*, Five Star) Gale Group.

Greyle, Katherine. Major Wyclyff's Campaign. 2001. 320p. mass mkt. 4.99 (*0-8439-4920-1*, Leisure Bks.) Dorchester Publishing Co., Inc.

Grondahl, Jens Christian. Silence in October. Born, Anne, tr. from DAN. 2001. 304p. 24.00 (*0-15-100399-8*) Harcourt Trade Pubs.

Gross, Ruth Belov. The Girl Who Wouldn't Get Married. 1984. (Illus.). 32p. (J). (ps-2). 9.95 o.s.i (*0-02-736900-5*, Simon & Schuster Children's Publishing) Simon & Schuster Children's Publishing.

Hale, Deborah. My Lord Protector. 1999. (Harlequin Historicals Ser.: No. 452). per. (*0-373-29052-7*, 1-29052-7, Harlequin Bks.) Harlequin Enterprises, Ltd.

Hannay, Barbara. The Wedding Countdown. 2000. (Harlequin Romance Ser.: Vol. 3613). mass mkt. (*0-373-03613-2*, 1-03613-6); (Harlequin Large Print Ser.: Vol. 459). mass mkt. (*0-373-15859-9*) Harlequin Enterprises, Ltd. (Harlequin Bks.).

Haran, Maeve. It Takes Two. 1996. 560p. mass mkt. 6.50 o.p. (*0-06-100882-6*) HarperCollins Pubs.

Harbison, Elizabeth. A Pregnant Proposal. 2001. (Silhouette Romance Ser.: No. 1553). mass mkt. (*0-373-19553-2*, 1-19553-6, Silhouette) Harlequin Enterprises, Ltd.

Hardy, Robin. Streiker the Killdeer. 1993. 8p. pap. 9.00 o.p. (*0-89109-763-5*, Discipleship Journal) NavPress Publishing Group.

Harrison, Kathryn. The Binding Chair: or A Visit from the Foot Emancipation Society. l.t. ed. 2000. (Compass Press Large Print Book Ser.). 419p. 26.95 (*1-56895-139-6*, Wheeler Publishing, Inc.) Gale Group.

—The Binding Chair: or A Visit from the Foot Emancipation Society. 2001. 336p. pap. 13.00 (*0-06-093442-5*, Perennial) HarperTrade.

Hart, Jessica. Assignment: Baby. l.t. ed. 2002. 288p. 24.95 (*0-263-17298-8*) Gale Group.

—Assignment: Baby. 2002. (Harlequin Romance Ser.: No. 3688). 186p. mass mkt. (*0-373-03688-4*, 1-03688-8, Harlequin Bks.) Harlequin Enterprises, Ltd.

Hart, Jillian. Bluebonnet Bride. 2001. (Harlequin Historicals Ser.: No. 586). 296p. mass mkt. (*0-373-29186-8*, 1-29186-3, Harlequin Bks.) Harlequin Enterprises, Ltd.

Hatcher, Robin Lee. Firstborn. l.t. ed. 2004. lib. bdg. 27.95 (*1-58547-393-6*, Premier) Ctr. Point Large Print.

—Firstborn. 336p. 2003. pap. 12.99 (*0-8423-5557-X*); 2002. 19.99 (*0-8423-4010-6*) Tyndale Hse. Pubs.

Head, Ann. Mr. & Mrs. Bo Jo Jones. 1968. (Illus.). 192p. (YA). (gr. 7 up). mass mkt. 4.99 (*0-451-16319-2*, Signet Bks.) NAL.

Heath, Roy A. The Armstrong Trilogy: From the Heat of Day, One Generation, Genetha. 1994. 552p. (Orig.). pap. 15.00 (*0-89255-199-2*) Persea Bks., Inc.

—From the Heat of the Day. 1980. 160p. 9.95 o.p. (*0-8052-8003-0*, Schocken) Knopf Publishing Group.

—From the Heat of the Day: A Novel. 1992. 160p. 19.95 o.p. (*0-89255-175-5*) Persea Bks., Inc.

Henkes, Kevin. Two under Par. 1987. (Illus.). 128p. (J). (gr. 2 up). pap. 15.95 (*0-688-06708-5*, Greenwillow Bks.) HarperCollins Children's Bk. Group.

Henley, Arthur. Lily & Joel: A Novel of Life, Love & AudioTapes. Powell, Judith L. & Fawcett, Yvonne, eds. 1992. 208p. (Orig.). 21.95 o.p. (*1-56087-052-4*); pap. 9.95 o.p. (*1-56087-051-6*) Top of the Mountain Publishing.

Hingle, Metsy. And the Winner Gets... Married. 2002. (Silhouette Desire Ser.: No. 1442). mass mkt. (*0-373-76442-1*, Silhouette) Harlequin Enterprises, Ltd.

Hobbie, Douglas. This Time Last Year. 1998. 336p. 23.00 o.s.i (*0-8050-5492-8*) Holt, Henry & Co.

Hoberman, Mary Ann. Mr. & Mrs. Muddle. 1988. (Illus.). 32p. (J). (gr. k-4). 13.95 o.p. (*0-316-36735-4*, Joy Street Bks.) Little Brown & Co.

Holland, Suellen. Hard Time in the Meantime. 1984. 160p. mass mkt. 2.25 o.p. (*0-451-12690-4*, Signet Vista) NAL.

Holt, Victoria. Paragon Revels. l.t. ed. 1994. 22.95 o.p. (*0-7927-1923-9*) BBC Audiobooks America.

—Paragon Revels. l.t. ed. 1972. (Ulverscroft Large Print Ser.). 12.00 o.p. (*0-85456-141-2*, Ulverscroft) Thorpe, F. A. Pubs. GBR. *Dist:* Ulverscroft Large Print Bks., Ltd., Ulverscroft Large Print Canada, Ltd.

Ireland, Liz. Husband Material. 2001. 352p. mass mkt. 5.99 (*0-8217-7115-9*) Kensington Publishing Corp.

James, Henry. The Golden Bowl. 1992. (Everyman's Library). 640p. 20.00 (*0-679-41733-8*) Knopf, Alfred A. Inc.

John, Laurie. Here Comes the Bride. 1996. (Sweet Valley University Ser.: No. 20). (YA). (gr. 7 up). 9.09 o.p. (*0-606-09942-5*) Turtleback Bks.

Johnson, Darlene. Dream in Color. 2000. 400p. pap. 14.95 (*0-9679745-0-X*) Brandywine Publishing.

Johnson, Joyce. In the Night Cafe. Rosenman, Jane, ed. 1990. 240p. reprint ed. pap. (*0-671-70111-8*, Washington Square Pr.) Simon & Schuster.

Johnston, Joan. Hawk's Way Bride: The Unforgiving Bride/The Headstrong Bride/The Disobedient Bride. 2001. (Silhouette Special Releases Ser.). 408p. mass mkt. (*0-373-48440-2*, Silhouette) Harlequin Enterprises, Ltd.

Jones, Annie. Cupid's Corner. l.t. ed. 2001. 239p. 23.95 (*0-7862-3093-2*, Five Star) Gale Group.

Jordan, Penny. The City-Girl Bride. 2002. (Harlequin Presents Ser.: No. 2229). 186p. mass mkt. (*0-373-12229-2*, 1-12229-0, Harlequin Bks.) Harlequin Enterprises, Ltd.

—The Marriage Demand. 2001. (Harlequin Presents Ser.: No. 2211). mass mkt. (*0-373-12211-X*, 1-12211-8, Harlequin Bks.) Harlequin Enterprises, Ltd.

—The Marriage Demand. l.t. ed. 2002. (Mills & Boon Large Print Ser.). 288p. 27.99 (*0-263-17260-0*) Harlequin Mills & Boon, Ltd. GBR. *Dist:* Thorndike Pr., Ulverscroft Large Print Bks., Ltd., Ulverscroft Large Print Canada, Ltd.

Joyce, James. The Boarding House. 1982. (Short Story Library). (Illus.). (J). lib. bdg. 13.95 o.p. (*0-87191-895-1*, 1066-2, Creative Education) Creative Co., The.

Just, Ward. The Translator. 1991. 313p. 21.95 o.p. (*0-395-57168-5*) Houghton Mifflin Co.

Keats, Ezra Jack. Louie's Search. (Illus.). 40p. (J). (ps-3). 1984. text 15.00 o.s.i (*0-02-749700-3*, Simon & Schuster Children's Publishing); 1989. reprint ed. mass mkt. 4.95 (*0-689-71354-1*, Aladdin) Simon & Schuster Children's Publishing.

Kennedy, William. The Flaming Corsage. unabr. collector's ed. 1996. audio 48.00 (*0-7366-3405-3*, 4051) Books on Tape, Inc.

—The Flaming Corsage. l.t. ed. 1997. (Large Print Bks.). 24.95 (*1-56895-397-6*, Wheeler Publishing, Inc.) Gale Group.

—The Flaming Corsage. 1997. 224p. pap. 11.95 (*0-14-024270-8*) Penguin Group (USA) Inc.

—The Flaming Corsage. 1996. 224p. 23.95 o.s.i (*0-670-85872-2*, Viking) Viking Penguin.

—The Flaming Corsage: Selections from the Novel. abr. ed. 1996. audio 18.95 o.p. (*0-14-086342-7*, Penguin AudioBooks) Viking Penguin.

King, Ruchama. Seven Blessings: A Novel. 2003. 256p. 23.95 (*0-312-30915-5*) St. Martin's Pr.

King, Stephen. Rose Madder. l.t. ed. 1995. 652p. 27.95 o.p. (*1-56895-261-9*, Wheeler Publishing, Inc.) Gale Group.

—Rose Madder. 1996. mass mkt. 7.50 (*0-451-18876-4*); 480p. mass mkt. 7.99 (*0-451-18636-2*) NAL. (Signet Bks.).

—Rose Madder. pap. 6.98 o.p. (*0-7651-0399-0*) Smithmark Pubs., Inc.

—Rose Madder. 1996. 14.04 (*0-606-09798-8*) Turtleback Bks.

—Rose Madder. 1995. (Illus.). 432p. 25.95 (*0-670-85869-2*, Viking); 16p. audio 59.95 o.s.i (*0-14-086158-0*) Viking Penguin.

King, Tabitha. The Book of Reuben. 1994. 368p. 22.95 o.p. (*0-525-93766-8*, Dutton) Dutton/Plume.

Kingsbury, Karen & Smalley, Gary. Redemption. 2002. (Redemption Ser.). 384p. pap. 12.99 (*0-8423-5622-3*); 19.99 (*0-8423-5523-5*) Tyndale Hse. Pubs.

Klein, Norma. Breaking Up. 1981. 176p. pap. 2.50 (*0-380-55830-0*, Avon Bks.) Morrow/Avon.

—Family Secrets. 1987. 224p. mass mkt. 3.99 o.s.i (*0-449-70195-6*, Fawcett) Ballantine Bks.

—Family Secrets. 1985. (Illus.). 272p. (YA). (gr. 8 up). 13.95 o.p. (*0-8037-0221-3*, Dial Bks. for Young Readers) Penguin Putnam Bks. for Young Readers.

Kleypas, Lisa. When Strangers Marry. l.t. ed. 2003. 29.95 (*1-58724-407-1*, Wheeler Publishing, Inc.) Gale Group.

—When Strangers Marry. 2002. 400p. mass mkt. 7.50 (*0-06-050736-5*, Avon Bks.) Morrow/Avon.

Koch, Irene Bonk. Divine Compass. 2003. 232p. pap. 19.95 (*1-59286-663-8*) PublishAmerica, Inc.

Kotzwinkle, William. Swimmer in the Secret Sea: Novella. 1994. 96p. 10.95 o.p. (*0-8118-0715-0*) Chronicle Bks. LLC.

LaHaye, Beverly & Blackstock, Terri. Times & Seasons. 2001. 371p. 16.99 (*0-310-23319-4*) Zondervan.

Laurens, Stephanie. All about Passion. 2001. 432p. mass mkt. 7.50 (*0-380-81202-9*) Morrow/Avon.

Law, Susan Kay. The Bad Man's Bride: Marrying Miss Bright. 2001. 384p. mass mkt. 5.99 (*0-380-81906-6*, Avon Bks.) Morrow/Avon.

—Wedding Story. 2003. 384p. mass mkt. 5.99 (*0-06-052518-5*, Avon Bks.) Morrow/Avon.

Lawrence, Kim. A Convenient Husband. 2001. (Harlequin Presents Ser.: No. 2209). mass mkt. (*0-373-12209-8*, Harlequin Bks.) Harlequin Enterprises, Ltd.

—The Prospective Wife. 2002. (Harlequin Presents Ser.: No. 2231). 185p. mass mkt. (*0-373-12231-4*, 1-12231-6, Harlequin Bks.) Harlequin Enterprises, Ltd.

Leclaire, Day. The Bride's Proposition. 2000. (Harlequin Romance Ser.: Vol. 3611). per. (*0-373-03611-6*, 1-03611-0); (Harlequin Large Print Ser.: Vol. 457). mass mkt. (*0-373-15857-2*) Harlequin Enterprises, Ltd. (Harlequin Bks.).

Lee, Linda Francis. The Wedding Diaries. 2003. 368p. mass mkt. 6.99 (*0-8041-1997-X*) Ballantine Bks.

Lee, Miranda. Fugitive Bride. 2001. (Harlequin Presents Ser.: No. 2212). 192p. mass mkt. o.s.i (*0-373-12212-8*, 1-12212-6, Harlequin Bks.) Harlequin Enterprises, Ltd.

—Matrimonio en Peligro. 2001. (Harlequin Bianca Ser.: No. 243). Tr. of Marriage in Peril. (SPA.). 160p. pap. (*0-373-33593-8*, 1-33593-4, Harlequin Bks.) Harlequin Enterprises, Ltd.

—El Matrimonio Tenia un Precio. 2002. (Harlequin Bianca Ser.: No. 289). Tr. of Marriage Had a Price. (SPA.). 160p. mass mkt. o.s.i (*0-373-33639-X*, 1-33639-5, Harlequin Bks.) Harlequin Enterprises, Ltd.

Leimbach, Marti. Love & Houses. 1997. 288p. 20.50 o.p. (*0-684-83670-X*, Simon & Schuster) Simon & Schuster.

Lerman, Rhoda. Animal Acts. 1994. 272p. 22.50 o.p. (*0-8050-1418-7*) Holt, Henry & Co.

Levine, Michael. Julia: Nothing Lasts Forever. 1998. (Party of Five: No. 4). 160p. (J). (gr. 3-6). pap. 4.50 (*0-671-01773-X*, Simon Pulse) Simon & Schuster Children's Publishing.

Lewis, Sara. The Answer Is Yes. 1998. 288p. (C). 23.00 o.s.i (*0-15-100326-2*) Harcourt Trade Pubs.

—The Answer Is Yes. l.t. ed. 1998. (Inspirational Ser.). 407p. 26.95 o.p. (*0-7838-0392-3*) Thorndike Pr.

—The Answer Is Yes: A Novel. 1999. (Harvest Book Ser.). 272p. pap. 13.00 (*0-15-600564-6*, Harvest Bks.) Harcourt Trade Pubs.

Lindbergh, Anne M. Dearly Beloved. 1991. 202p. reprint ed. lib. bdg. 37.95 (*0-89966-790-2*) Buccaneer Bks., Inc.

—Dearly Beloved. rev. ed. 2003. 208p. pap. 14.95 (*1-55652-490-0*) Chicago Review Pr., Inc.

—Dearly Beloved: A Theme & Variations. 1962. (Helen & Kurt Wolff Bk.). 7.95 o.s.i (*0-15-124070-1*) Harcourt Trade Pubs.

Lingard, Joan. Strangers in the House. 1983. 144p. (J). (gr. 7 up). 12.95 o.p. (*0-525-66912-4*, Dutton Children's Bks.) Penguin Putnam Bks. for Young Readers.

Linz, Cathie. A Prince at Last. 2002. (Silhouette Romance Ser.: No. 1594). mass mkt. (*0-373-19594-X*, 1-19594-0, Silhouette) Harlequin Enterprises, Ltd.

Lipman, Victoria. Leaving Alva. 1998. 192p. 22.00 (*0-684-83415-4*, Simon & Schuster) Simon & Schuster.

Litton, Josie. Dream of Me/Believe in Me. 2001. 816p. mass mkt. 5.99 (*0-553-58436-7*) Bantam Bks.

Logan, Leandra. Mariage dans la Jet-Set. 2001. (FRE.). (*0-373-38426-2*, Harlequin French) Harlequin Enterprises, Ltd.

Long, David. The Falling Boy. 1998. 256p. pap. 12.95 o.s.i (*0-452-27997-6*, Plume) Dutton/Plume.

—The Falling Boy. 1997. 288p. 22.00 o.s.i (*0-684-80034-9*, Scribner) Simon & Schuster.

Lott, Bret. Reed's Beach. 1999. 352p. pap. 14.00 (*0-671-03819-2*, Washington Square Pr.) Simon & Schuster.

—Reed's Beach. Rosenman, Jane, ed. 352p. 1993. 20.00 (*0-671-79238-5*, Atria); 1994. reprint ed. pap. (*0-671-79239-3*, Washington Square Pr.) Simon & Schuster.

—Reed's Beach. 342p. 4.98 o.p. (*0-8317-2824-8*) Smithmark Pubs., Inc.

Lovelace, Maud Hart. Betsy's Wedding. 1996. (Betsy-Tacy Ser.). (Illus.). 320p. (J). (gr. 3-7). pap. 6.95 (*0-06-440544-3*, Harper Trophy) HarperCollins Children's Bk. Group.

—Betsy's Wedding. 1996. 13.00 (*0-606-14163-4*) Turtleback Bks.

Lurie, Alison. The War Between the Tates. 1991. pap. 8.95 (*0-380-71135-4*, Avon Bks.) Morrow/Avon.

Lyle, Letcher L. Dark but Full of Diamonds. 1981. (YA). (gr. 12 up). 10.95 o.s.i (*0-698-20517-0*, Coward-McCann) Putnam Publishing Group, The.

MacDonald, Shari. A Match Made in Heaven. 2001. (Salinger Sisters Ser.: Vol. 3). 231p. 23.95 (*0-7862-3094-0*, Five Star) Gale Group.

MacKenzie, Henry. Julia de Roubigne, Vol. 4. 1976. reprint ed. 30.00 (*0-404-04094-2*) AMS Pr., Inc.

—Julia de Roubigne. 2000. 192p. pap. 16.95 (*1-86232-047-0*) Tuckwell Pr. Ltd. GBR. *Dist:* General Distribution Services, Inc.

Malamud, Bernard. Dubin's Lives. 2003. 376p. pap. 15.00 (*0-374-52882-9*); 1979. 362p. 10.00 o.p. (*0-374-14414-1*) Farrar, Straus & Giroux.

—Dubin's Lives. 1980. 432p. pap. 2.50 o.p. (*0-380-48413-7*, 48413-7, Avon Bks.) Morrow/Avon.

—Dubin's Lives. 1994. (Penguin Twentieth-Century Classics Ser.). 400p. pap. 10.95 o.s.i (*0-14-018760-X*, Penguin Classics) Viking Penguin.

Mallery, Susan & Child, Maureen. Shotgun Grooms: Lucas's Convenient Bride/Jackson's Mail-Order Bride. 2001. (Harlequin Historicals Ser.: No. 575). 298p. mass mkt. (*0-373-29175-2*, 1-29175-6, Harlequin Bks.) Harlequin Enterprises, Ltd.

Malone, Susan M. By the Book. 1993. 247p. 18.00 (*1-880909-00-6*) Baskerville Pubs., Inc.

Malouf, Melissa. It Had to Be You: The Joan & Ernest Story. 1997. 176p. 25.00 (*1-888105-19-4*) Avisson Pr., Inc.

Martin, Ann M. Bummer Summer. 1983. 160p. (J). (gr. 5-9). 14.95 o.p. (*0-8234-0483-8*) Holiday Hse., Inc.

—Bummer Summer. (J). (gr. 4-6). 1990. 160p. pap. 3.50 o.p. (*0-590-43622-8*); 1984. pap. 1.95 o.p. (*0-590-33139-6*) Scholastic, Inc.

Marton, Sandra. The Alvares Bride. 2001. (Harlequin Presents Ser.: No. 2202). mass mkt. (*0-373-12202-0*, 1-12202-7, Harlequin Bks.) Harlequin Enterprises, Ltd.

Maushart, Susan. Wifework: What Marriage Really Means for Women. 2003. 270p. pap. 14.95 (*1-58234-276-8*); 2002. 288p. 24.95 (*1-58234-202-4*) Bloomsbury Publishing.

McClymer, Kelly. The Infamous Bride. 2001. (Once Upon a Wedding Ser.). 32p. mass mkt. 5.99 o.s.i (*0-8217-7185-X*, Zebra Bks.) Kensington Publishing Corp.

McMahon, Barbara. The Marriage Test. 2001. (Harlequin Romance Ser.: No. 3669). 186p. mass mkt. (*0-373-03669-8*, 1-03669-8, Harlequin Bks.) Harlequin Enterprises, Ltd.

—Marrying Margot: Beaufort Brides. 2000. (Harlequin Romance Ser.: Vol. 3612). per. *(0-373-03612-4*, Harlequin Bks.) Harlequin Enterprises, Ltd.

Merritt, Jackie. Marked for Marriage. 2002. (Silhouette Special Edition Ser.: No. 1447). mass mkt. *(0-373-24447-9*, 1-24447-4, Silhouette) Harlequin Enterprises, Ltd.

Michaels, Fern. What You Wish For. l.t. ed. 2000. (Romance Ser.). 431p. 27.95 o.p. *(1-56895-998-2*, Wheeler Publishing, Inc.) Gale Group.

—What You Wish For. 2000. 32p. 24.00 o.s.i *(1-57566-573-5)*; 2001. 352p. reprint ed. mass mkt. 7.99 *(0-8217-6828-X)* Kensington Publishing Corp.

Michaels, Kasey, et al. The McCallum Quintuplets: Great Expectations; Delivered with a Kiss; And Babies Make Seven. 2002. (Harlequin American Romance Ser.: No. 909). 248p. mass mkt. *(0-373-16909-4*, 1-16909-3, Harlequin Bks.) Harlequin Enterprises, Ltd.

Michaels, Leigh. His Trophy Wife. 2001. (Harlequin Romance Ser.: No. 3672). 192p. mass mkt. o.s.i *(0-373-03672-8)*; 256p. mass mkt. o.s.i *(0-373-15918-8)* Harlequin Enterprises, Ltd. (Harlequin Bks.).

—His Trophy Wife. l.t. ed. (Harlequin Romance Ser.). 23.95 *(0-263-17251-1)* Harlequin Mills & Boon, Ltd. GBR. *Dist:* Thorndike Pr.

—Novia de Alquiler. 2001. (Harlequin Jazmin Ser.). (SPA.). 160p. pap. *(0-373-68006-6*, 1-68006-5, Harlequin Bks.) Harlequin Enterprises, Ltd.

Michaels, Leonard. Sylvia. 1992. 144p. 10.00 *(1-56279-029-3)* Mercury Hse.

Michel and Company Staff. Happy Ever After! 1994. (Illus.). 32p. 6.95 *(0-8362-4714-0)* Andrews McMeel Publishing.

Mikels, Jennifer. The Marriage Bargain. l.t. ed. 2001. (Thorndike Silhouette Romance Ser.). 280p. 23.95 o.p. *(0-373-04683-9)* Harlequin Mills & Boon, Ltd. GBR. *Dist:* Thorndike Pr.

Miklowitz, Gloria D. The Day the Senior Class Got Married. 1985. 160p. (J). (gr. 6 up). mass mkt. 2.75 o.s.i *(0-440-92096-5*, Laurel Leaf) Random Hse. Children's Bks.

Miles, Cassie. Wedding Captives. 2002. (Harlequin Intrigue Ser.: No. 649). 251p. mass mkt. *(0-373-22649-7*, 1-22649-7, Harlequin Bks.) Harlequin Enterprises, Ltd.

Miller, Linda Lael. Snowflakes on the Sea. (Mira Bks.). 1998. 256p. per. *(1-55166-428-3*, 1-66428-3, Mira Bks.); 1994. mass mkt. *(0-373-48303-1*, 5-48303-7, Silhouette); 1988. pap. *(0-373-04623-5*, Harlequin Bks.); 1984. mass mkt. *(0-373-50397-0*, Harlequin Bks.) Harlequin Enterprises, Ltd.

—Snowflakes on the Sea. l.t. ed. 2001. (Americana Ser.). 368p. 28.95 *(0-7862-2615-3)* Thorndike Pr.

Montgomery, L. M. At the Altar: Matrimonial Tales. 1995. 240p. (YA). (gr. 4-7). mass mkt. 5.50 o.s.i *(0-553-56748-9)* Bantam Bks.

Morimoto, Junko. The Mouse's Marriage. 1988. (Illus.). 32p. (J). (ps-1). pap. 4.99 o.s.i *(0-14-050678-0*, Puffin Bks.) Penguin Putnam Bks. for Young Readers.

Nagy, Gloria. Marriage: A Novel. 1995. 448p. 22.95 o.p. *(0-316-59675-2)* Little Brown & Co.

Native, A. Marita, or, the Folly of Love. Newell, Stephanie, ed. 2001. (African Sources for African History Ser.: Vol. 2). (Illus.). pap. 29.00 *(90-04-12186-2)* Brill Academic Pubs., Inc.

Neels, Anderson. Marrying a Doctor. l.t. ed. 2001. mass mkt. *(0-373-15920-X*, Harlequin Bks.) Harlequin Enterprises, Ltd.

—Marrying a Doctor: The Doctor's Girl & A Special Kind of Woman. 2001. (Harlequin Romance Ser.: No. 3674). mass mkt. *(0-373-03674-4*, Harlequin Bks.) Harlequin Enterprises, Ltd.

Neels, Betty & Fielding, Liz. The Engagement Effect: An Ordinary Girl; A Perfect Proposal. 2002. (Harlequin Romance Ser.: No. 3689). 186p. mass mkt. *(0-373-03689-2*, 1-03689-6, Harlequin Bks.) Harlequin Enterprises, Ltd.

Neff, James. Doctor's Instant Family. 2001. (Bachelors of Shotgun Ridge Ser.). mass mkt. *(0-373-16902-7*, Harlequin Bks.) Harlequin Enterprises, Ltd.

Neff, Mindy. In the Enemy's Embrace. 2002. (Harlequin American Romance Ser.: No. 925). 249p. mass mkt. *(0-373-16925-6*, 1-16925-9, Harlequin Bks.) Harlequin Enterprises, Ltd.

Nelson, Betty P. Uncertain April. 1994. 336p. 20.95 *(0-312-11084-7)*; 20.95 o.p. *(0-312-11086-3)* St. Martin's Pr.

Newman, Frances. Dead Lovers are Faithful Lovers: A Novel by Frances Newman. 1994. (Brown Thrasher Bks.). 312p. reprint ed. pap. 17.95 *(0-8203-1588-5)* Univ. of Georgia Pr.

Nichols, John. Conjugal Bliss: A Comedy of Marital Arts. 1994. 320p. 22.50 o.p. *(0-8050-2803-X)* Holt, Henry & Co.

Noonan, Roz & Stine, Megan. Julia: Everything Changes. 1997. (Party of Five: No. 2). 160p. (J). (gr. 3-6). pap. 3.99 *(0-671-01721-7*, Simon Pulse) Simon & Schuster Children's Publishing.

Norris, Frank. The Pit: A Story of Chicago. 1992. (BCL1-PS American Literature Ser.). 421p. reprint ed. lib. bdg. 99.00 *(0-7812-6813-3)* Reprint Services Corp.

—The Pit: A Story of Chicago. 1994. (Twentieth Century Classics Ser.). 416p. pap. 15.00 *(0-14-018758-8*, Penguin Classics) Viking Penguin.

Nostlinger, Christine. Marrying off Mother. Bell, Anthea, tr. 1982. 132p. (J). (gr. 4-6). 10.95 o.p. *(0-15-252138-0)* Harcourt Children's Bks.

Okimoto, Jean Davies. It's Just Too Much. 1982. (J). (gr. 5-8). pap. *(0-671-43492-6*, Simon Pulse) Simon & Schuster Children's Publishing.

Osborn, Kathy & Carey, Jacqueline. Wedding Pictures: A Novel. 1997. (Illus.). 154p. 22.95 o.p. *(0-8118-1109-3)* Chronicle Bks. LLC.

Pade. From Boss to Bridegroom. 2001. (Silhouette Special Edition Ser.: No. 9). mass mkt. *(0-373-38708-3*, Silhouette) Harlequin Enterprises, Ltd.

Palmer, Elizabeth. Old Money. 1996. 288p. 21.95 o.p. *(0-312-14020-7)* St. Martin's Pr.

—Scarlet Angel. 1998. per. *(1-55166-456-9*, Harlequin Bks.) Harlequin Enterprises, Ltd.

—Scarlet Angel. 3.98 o.p. *(0-8317-4618-1)* Smithmark Pubs., Inc.

—Scarlet Angel. 1993. 19.95 o.p. *(0-312-09917-7)* St. Martin's Pr.

Parker, Cam. Camp Off-the-Wall. 1987. 128p. (J). (gr. 3-7). pap. 2.50 *(0-380-75196-8*, Avon Bks.) Morrow/Avon.

—A Horse in New York. 1989. 144p. (Orig.). (J). (gr. 5 up). pap. 2.75 *(0-380-75704-4*, Avon Bks.) Morrow/Avon.

Parsons, Tony. Man & Wife. 2004. 368p. pap. 13.00 *(0-7432-3614-9*, Touchstone); 2003. 352p. 23.00 *(0-7434-5665-3*, Atria) Simon & Schuster.

Pascal, Francine, creator. Here Comes the Bride. 1996. (Sweet Valley University Ser.: No. 20). 240p. (gr. 7 up). mass mkt. 4.50 o.s.i *(0-553-56702-0)* Bantam Bks.

—A Married Woman. 1994. (Sweet Valley University Ser.: No. 5). 240p. (gr. 7 up). mass mkt. 4.50 *(0-553-56309-2)* Bantam Bks.

Paul, Gregory S. Prisoner Bride. 2001. mass mkt. *(0-373-29187-6*, Harlequin Bks.) Harlequin Enterprises, Ltd.

Peck, Dale. Law of Enclosures. 1996. 320p. 23.00 o.p. *(0-374-18419-4)* Farrar, Straus & Giroux.

—Law of Enclosures. 1997. (U Ser.). 320p. pap. 12.00 *(0-671-00347-X*, Washington Square Pr.) Simon & Schuster.

Pelletier, Cathie. A Marriage Made at Woodstock. Ng, Donna, ed. 1995. 288p. reprint ed. bds. *(0-671-51694-9*, Washington Square Pr.) Simon & Schuster.

Petersen, P. J. I Hate Weddings. 2000. (Illus.). 96p. (J). (gr. 2-5). 15.99 *(0-525-46327-5*, Dutton Children's Bks.) Penguin Putnam Bks. for Young Readers.

Pfeffer, Susan Beth. Starring Peter & Leigh. 1978. (J). 7.95 o.s.i *(0-440-08226-9*, Delacorte Pr.) Dell Publishing.

Phillips, Michael. Braxtons of Miracle Springs. 1996. (Journals of Corrie & Christopher). 272p. text 14.99 o.p. *(1-55661-904-9)*; pap. 10.99 o.p. *(1-55661-635-X)* Bethany Hse. Pubs.

Picoult, Jodi. Picture Perfect. 2002. 384p. pap. 13.95 *(0-425-18550-8)*; 1996. 432p. reprint ed. mass mkt. 6.50 o.s.i *(0-425-15411-4)* Berkley Publishing Group.

—Picture Perfect. 1995. 23.95 o.p. *(0-399-14040-9*, G. P. Putnam's Sons) Penguin Group (USA) Inc.

Pryor, Bonnie. Rats, Spiders & Love. 1986. (Illus.). 128p. (J). (gr. 4-6). 16.00 o.p. *(0-688-05867-1*, Morrow, William & Co.) Morrow/Avon.

—Rats, Spiders & Love. 1989. 128p. (J). (gr. k-6). pap. 2.75 o.s.i *(0-440-40138-0*, Yearling) Random Hse. Children's Bks.

Rachlin, Nahid. Married to a Stranger. 1993. 232p. pap. 12.95 *(0-87286-276-3)* City Lights Bks.

Ragen, Naomi. Jephte's Daughter. l.t. ed. 1990. (General Ser.). 538p. 21.95 o.p. *(0-8161-4826-0*, Macmillan Reference USA) Gale Group.

—Jephte's Daughter. 1990. 416p. 18.45 o.s.i *(0-446-51486-1)* Warner Bks., Inc.

Reid, Michelle. The Spanish Husband. l.t. ed. 2001. (Mills & Boon Large Print Ser.). 288p. 27.99 o.p. *(0-263-16761-5)* Harlequin Mills & Boon, Ltd. GBR. *Dist:* Thorndike Pr., Ulverscroft Large Print Bks., Ltd.

—The Unforgettable Husband. 2001. (Harlequin Presents Ser.: No. 2205). 192p. mass mkt. *(0-373-12205-5*, Harlequin Bks.) Harlequin Enterprises, Ltd.

—The Unforgettable Husband. l.t. ed. 2002. (Mills & Boon Large Print Ser.). 288p. 27.99 *(0-263-17253-8)* Harlequin Mills & Boon, Ltd. GBR. *Dist:* Thorndike Pr., Ulverscroft Large Print Bks., Ltd., Ulverscroft Large Print Canada, Ltd.

Rhodes, Pam. Letting Go. l.t. ed. 2003. (Ulverscroft Large Print Ser.). 440p. 32.50 *(0-7089-4797-2)* Thorpe, F. A. Pubs. GBR. *Dist:* Ulverscroft Large Print Bks., Ltd., Ulverscroft Large Print Canada, Ltd.

Richardson, Arleta. Grandma's Attic: Wedding Bells Ahead. (Grandma's Attic Ser.). 156p. (J). (gr. 3-7). pap. 6.99 *(0-7814-3292-8)* Cook Communications Ministries.

Richardson, Brenda L. Chesapeake Song. 371p. 1999. pap. 19.95 *(1-56743-040-6)*; 1994. pap. 10.95 *(1-56743-063-5)* HarperTrade. (Amistad Pr.).

—Chesapeake Song. 1996. 480p. mass mkt. 5.99 o.s.i *(0-7860-0304-9*, Pinnacle Bks.) Kensington Publishing Corp.

Riley, Mildred E. Love Always. 1997. 191p. pap. 10.95 *(1-885478-15-1)* Genesis Pr., Inc.

Rimmer, Christine. The Marriage Conspiracy. 2001. (Silhouette Special Edition Ser.: No. 1423). 256p. mass mkt. *(0-373-24423-1*, Silhouette) Harlequin Enterprises, Ltd.

Ritchie, Jo-Ann. Jonie & Her Soldier. Wheeler, Gerald, ed. 1985. 128p. (YA). (gr. 8 up). pap. 5.50 o.p. *(0-8280-0249-5)* Review & Herald Publishing Assn.

Rivers, Francine. The Scarlet Thread. l.t. ed. 2002. 651p. 26.95 *(0-7862-4363-5)* Gale Group.

—The Scarlet Thread. 2000. 416p. mass mkt. 6.99 *(0-8423-4271-0*, Living Bks.); 1997. (Illus.). 352p. pap. 12.99 *(0-8423-3568-4)* Tyndale Hse. Pubs.

Robards, Karen. Maggy's Child. l.t. ed. 1994. 25.95 o.p. *(1-56895-057-8*, Wheeler Publishing, Inc.) Gale Group.

Roberts, Nadine. Who Said Sweet Sixteen? 1983. mass mkt. 2.25 o.s.i *(0-449-70084-4*, Fawcett) Ballantine Bks.

Rolofson, Kristine. A Bride for Calder Brown. 2001. (Harlequin Temptation Ser.: No. 850). mass mkt. *(0-373-25950-6*, Harlequin Bks.) Harlequin Enterprises, Ltd.

Ross, Kathryn. Bride by Deception. l.t. ed. 2001. (Romance Ser.). 288p. 27.99 *(0-263-16762-3)* Harlequin Mills & Boon, Ltd. GBR. *Dist:* Thorndike Pr., Ulverscroft Large Print Bks., Ltd., Ulverscroft Large Print Canada, Ltd.

Roszel, Renee. Her Hired Husband. l.t. ed. 2002. 288p. 24.95 *(0-263-17290-2)* Gale Group.

—Her Hired Husband. l.t. ed. 2001. (Ready for Baby Ser.). mass mkt. *(0-373-15928-5*, Harlequin Bks.) Harlequin Enterprises, Ltd.

—Her Hired Husband: Ready for Baby. 2001. 192p. mass mkt. *(0-373-03682-5*, Harlequin Bks.) Harlequin Enterprises, Ltd.

Sanders, Dori. Clover. 1999. 196p. 17.95 *(0-945575-26-2*, 71526) Algonquin Bks. of Chapel Hill.

Sanders, Louis. The Englishman's Wife. 2003. 224p. pap. 14.00 *(1-85242-692-6)* Serpent's Tail Ltd. GBR. *Dist:* Consortium Bk. Sales & Distribution.

Schulze, Dallas. Substitute Wife. 2003. 384p. mass mkt. *(1-55166-677-4*, Mira Bks.) Harlequin Enterprises, Ltd.

Schwartz, Steven. Therapy: A Novel. 1995. 352p. pap. 12.95 o.p. *(0-452-27431-1*, Plume) Dutton/Plume.

—Therapy: A Novel. 1994. 352p. 22.95 o.s.i *(0-15-100062-X)* Harcourt Trade Pubs.

Scofield, Sandra J. Opal on Dry Ground. 1995. mass mkt. 5.99 o.s.i *(0-8041-1360-2*, Ivy Bks.) Ballantine Bks.

Scott, Amanda. Border Bride. 2001. 352p. mass mkt. 5.99 o.s.i *(0-8217-7000-4*, Zebra Bks.) Kensington Publishing Corp.

Shapiro, Jane. After Moondog. 1992. 22.95 o.s.i *(0-15-193096-1)* Harcourt Trade Pubs.

—After Moondog. 1993. 336p. reprint ed. pap. 13.99 o.s.i *(0-446-39526-9)* Warner Bks., Inc.

Shetterly, Caitlin, ed. Fault Lines: Stories of Divorce. 2001. 368p. 21.95 *(0-425-18161-8)* Berkley Publishing Group.

Singer, June F. Brilliant Divorces. 1993. 20.00 o.p. *(0-688-12001-6*, Morrow, William & Co.) Morrow/Avon.

Skibell, Joseph. The English Disease. 2003. 256p. tchr. ed. 23.95 *(1-56512-257-7*, 72257) Algonquin Bks. of Chapel Hill.

Small, David. Hoover's Bride. 1995. (Illus.). 32p. (J). (ps-4). 16.00 o.s.i *(0-517-59707-1)*; 17.99 o.s.i *(0-517-59708-X)* Random Hse. Children's Bks. (Random Hse. Bks. for Young Readers).

Smith, J. P. The Discovery of Light. 1992. 256p. 20.00 o.p. *(0-670-83903-5*, Viking) Viking Penguin.

Spencer, Judith. Millionaire's Marriage: Wedlocked. 2001. mass mkt. *(0-373-12220-9*, Harlequin Bks.) Harlequin Enterprises, Ltd.

Spicci, Joan. Beyond the Limit: The Dream of Sofya Kovalevskaya. 2002. 448p. 26.95 *(0-7653-0233-0*, Forge Bks.) Doherty, Tom Assocs., LLC.

St. John, Cheryl. The Gunslinger's Bride. 2001. (Harlequin Historicals Ser.: No. 577). 299p. mass mkt. *(0-373-29177-9*, 1-29177-2, Harlequin Bks.) Harlequin Enterprises, Ltd.

St. John, Madeleine. A Pure Clear Light. 2000. 240p. 22.00 *(0-7867-0756-9*, Carroll & Graf Pubs.) Avalon Publishing Group.

—A Pure Clear Light. 1996. 233p. *(1-85702-387-0)* Fourth Estate, Ltd.

Stahl, Hilda. The Makeshift Husband. 1993. (Prairie Ser.: Bk. 3). 172p. pap. 6.99 *(0-934998-48-5)* Evangel Publishing Hse.

Steel, Danielle. Journey. 2001. 368p. mass mkt. 7.99 *(0-440-23702-5)*; 2000. 336p. 200.00 *(0-385-33304-8*, Delacorte Pr.); 2000. 336p. 26.95 *(0-385-31687-9*, Delacorte Pr.) Dell Publishing.

—Journey. abr. unabr. ed. 2000. audio compact disk 29.95 *(0-553-71219-5)*; audio 39.95 *(0-553-50260-3)* Random Hse. Audio Publishing Group. (RH Audio).

—Journey. l.t. ed. 464p. 2001. pap. 13.95 *(0-375-72807-4)*; 2000. 26.95 *(0-375-43080-6)* Random Hse. Large Print.

—Lightning. 1996. 464p. pap. 7.99 *(0-440-22150-1)*; 1995. 408p. 24.95 *(0-385-31192-3*, Delacorte Pr.); 1995. 408p. 200.00 *(0-385-31488-4*, Delacorte Pr.) Dell Publishing.

—Lightning. 1996. mass mkt. 8.99 o.s.i *(0-440-22292-3)* Doubleday Publishing.

Steele, Jessica. A Suitable Husband. 2001. (Harlequin Romance Ser.: No. 3667). 184p. mass mkt. *(0-373-03667-1*, 1-03667-2, Harlequin Bks.) Harlequin Enterprises, Ltd.

—A Suitable Husband. l.t. ed. 2001. (Harlequin Romance Ser.). 288p. 27.99 *(0-263-17226-0)* Harlequin Mills & Boon, Ltd. GBR. *Dist:* Thorndike Pr., Ulverscroft Large Print Bks., Ltd., Ulverscroft Large Print Canada, Ltd.

Steele, Robert. Part Time Marriage. l.t. ed. 2001. mass mkt. *(0-373-15926-9*, Harlequin Bks.) Harlequin Enterprises, Ltd.

—Part Time Marriage: To Have & to Hold. 2001. mass mkt. *(0-373-03680-9*, Harlequin Bks.) Harlequin Enterprises, Ltd.

Sterling, Donna. Wife by Deception. 2001. (Harlequin Superromance Ser.: No. 1017). mass mkt. *(0-373-71017-8*, Harlequin Bks.) Harlequin Enterprises, Ltd.

Stine, R. L. Forbidden Secrets. 1996. (Fear Street Sagas: No. 3). 176p. (YA). (gr. 7 up). pap. 3.99 *(0-671-52954-4*, Simon Pulse) Simon & Schuster Children's Publishing.

Stirling, Jessica. The Workhouse Girl. unabr. ed. 1997. audio 110.95 *(0-7451-8786-2*, CAB 1421) BBC Audiobooks America.

—The Workhouse Girl. 1997. 472p. text 25.95 o.p. *(0-312-15698-7)* St. Martin's Pr.

—The Workhouse Girl. l.t. ed. 1998. (Romance Ser.). 616p. 28.95 *(0-7838-0124-6)* Thorndike Pr.

Struther. Mrs. Miniver. 1989. xxi, 153p. o.s.i *(1-85381-090-8)* Virago Pr., Ltd. GBR. *Dist:* Little Brown & Co.

Struther, Jan. Mrs. Miniver. 23.95 *(0-88411-677-8)* Amereon, Ltd.

—Mrs. Miniver. 1990. reprint ed. lib. bdg. 19.95 *(0-89968-554-4)* Buccaneer Bks., Inc.

—Mrs. Miniver. l.t. ed. 2001. 175p. 28.95 *(0-7838-9635-2*, Hall, G. K. & Co.) Gale Group.

—Mrs. Miniver. 1990. 162p. pap. 8.95 *(0-15-663140-7)*; 1966. pap. 0.50 o.p. *(0-15-663138-5)* Harcourt Trade Pubs. (Harvest Bks.).

—Mrs. Miniver. 1985. 320p. reprint ed. mass mkt. 3.95 o.p. *(0-06-080761-X*, P 761, Perennial) HarperTrade.

—Mrs. Miniver. l.t. ed. 1991. 145p. 21.95 o.p. *(1-85089-364-0)* ISIS Large Print Bks. GBR. *Dist:* Transaction Pubs.

Stuart, Sarah P. The Year Roger Wasn't Well: A Novel. 1994. 256p. 20.00 o.p. *(0-06-017079-4)* HarperTrade.

Sullivan, Walter. Time to Dance: A Novel. 1995. 195p. 22.95 *(0-8071-1985-7)* Louisiana State Univ. Pr.

Sutherland, William L. News from Fort God. 1993. (First Novel Ser.). 224p. pap. 12.00 o.p. *(0-922811-17-2)* Mid-List Pr.

Suzanne, Jamie. The Middle School Gets Married. 1993. (Sweet Valley Twins Ser.: No. 68). 144p. (J). (gr. 3-7). pap. 3.50 o.s.i *(0-553-48055-3)* Bantam Bks.

—The Middle School Gets Married. 1993. (Sweet Valley Twins Ser.: No. 68). (J). (gr. 3-7). 8.60 o.p. *(0-606-05648-3)* Turtleback Bks.

Swan, Sharon. Home Grown Husband. 2002. (Harlequin American Romance Ser.: No. 928). 251p. mass mkt. *(0-373-16928-0*, 1-16928-3, Harlequin Bks.) Harlequin Enterprises, Ltd.

Swanson, William, ed. Wives & Husbands: Twenty Short Stories about Marriage. 1989. mass mkt. 4.95 o.p. *(0-451-62733-4*, Mentor) NAL.

Talcott, Deanna. Marrying for a Mom. 2001. (Silhouette Romance Ser.: No. 1543). mass mkt. *(0-373-19543-5*, 1-19543-7, Silhouette) Harlequin Enterprises, Ltd.

Tallent, Elizabeth. Honey. 1994. 224p. pap. 12.00 *(0-679-75511-X*, Vintage) Knopf Publishing Group.

Tanneberg, Ward M. September Strike. 1994. (Ward Tanneberg Ser.: No. 1). pap. 11.99 *(1-56476-339-0*, 6-3339) Cook Communications Ministries.

Tayloe, Roberta L. I Married a Stranger: A Novel. 1994. 160p. (Orig.). pap. 9.95 *(1-56474-079-X)* Fithian Pr.

Templeton, Rosalyn A. Honky Tonk Cinderella. 2001. (How to Marry...Ser.). mass mkt. *(0-373-27190-5*, Harlequin Bks.) Harlequin Enterprises, Ltd.

Terris, Susan. No Scarlet Ribbons, RS. 1981. 154p. (J). (gr. 5 up). 14.00 o.p. (*0-374-35532-0*, Farrar, Straus & Giroux (BYR)) Farrar, Straus & Giroux.
—No Scarlet Ribbons. 1983. 160p. pap. 2.25 o.p. (*0-380-62844-9*, 62844-9, Avon Bks.) Morrow/Avon.
Thayer, Nancy. An Act of Love. l.t. ed. 1998. 26.95 (*1-56895-540-5*, Wheeler Publishing, Inc.) Gale Group.
—An Act of Love. 1999. (Act of Love Ser.: Vol. 1). 308p. pap. 6.99 (*0-312-96535-4*, St. Martin's Paperbacks); 1997. 256p. 22.95 o.p. (*0-312-15471-2*) St. Martin's Pr.
Thomas, Rosie. Other People's Marriages. 1994. 425p. 21.00 o.p. (*0-688-12962-5*, Morrow, William & Co.) Morrow/Avon.
Thompson, Jean. City Boy. 2004. 320p. 24.00 (*0-7432-4282-3*, Simon & Schuster) Simon & Schuster.
Tucker, Bonnie & Labrecque, Jennifer. A Rosey Little Christmas/Jingle Bell Bride? 2001. (Harlequin Duets Ser.: No. 64). mass mkt. (*0-373-44130-4*, 1-44130-2, Harlequin Bks.) Harlequin Enterprises, Ltd.
Turchi, Peter. The Girls Next Door. 1989. 320p. 18.95 o.p. (*0-453-00665-5*) NAL.
Updike, John. Rabbit, Run. 1983. 288p. mass mkt. 5.99 o.s.i (*0-449-20506-1*, Fawcett) Ballantine Bks.
Valtorta, Laura. Family Meal. 1993. 127p. (Orig.). pap. 9.95 (*0-932112-33-1*) Carolina Wren Pr.
VanDenburgh, Jane. Physics of Sunset. 2001. 304p. pap. text 15.00 (*1-58243-100-0*, Counterpoint Pr.) Basic Bks.
Vigna, Judith. Daddy's New Baby. Fay, Ann, ed. 1982. (Albert Whitman Concept Bks.). (Illus.). 32p. (J). (ps-3). lib. bdg. 11.95 o.p. (*0-8075-1435-7*) Whitman, Albert & Co.
Vogt, Esther Loewen. The Lonely Plains. 1993. (Heart for the Prairie Ser.: Bk. 2). 125p. (gr. 11-12). pap. 9.99 (*0-88965-100-0*, 0021000, Horizon Bks.) Christian Pubns., Inc.
—Song of the Prairie. 1995. 182p. (gr. 11-12). pap. 9.99 (*0-88965-109-4*, 0021094, Horizon Bks.) Christian Pubns., Inc.
—Song of the Prairie. l.t. ed. 1998. (Christian Fiction Ser.). 240p. 23.95 (*0-7862-1490-2*) Thorndike Pr.
Wade, Rebecca. An Innocent Mistress: Four Brides for Four Brothers. 2001. 384p. mass mkt. 5.99 o.s.i (*0-380-81619-9*, Avon Bks.) Morrow/Avon.
Walker, Mildred. The Body of a Young Man. 1997. 186p. pap. 9.00 (*0-8032-9787-4*, Bison Bks.) Univ. of Nebraska Pr.
Wallace, Carol M. The Wrong House. 1994. 320p. 21.95 o.p. (*0-312-10579-7*) St. Martin's Pr.
Webber, Meredith. Claimed: One Wife. l.t. ed. 2001. (Mills & Boon Large Print Ser.). 288p. 27.99 (*0-263-17148-5*) Harlequin Mills & Boon, Ltd. GBR. *Dist:* Ulverscroft Large Print Bks., Ltd., Ulverscroft Large Print Canada, Ltd.
Weber, Carl. Married Men. 2003. 48p. mass mkt. 6.99 (*0-7582-0303-9*); 2001. 384p. pap. 14.00 (*1-57566-696-0*) Kensington Publishing Corp.
The Wedding. 2001. 9.98 (*0-671-77510-3*, Simon & Schuster Audioworks) Simon & Schuster Audio.
Weldon, Fay. Puffball. 1990. 272p. pap. 8.95 o.p. (*0-14-013118-3*, Penguin Bks.) Viking Penguin.
—Trouble. 1993. 240p. 21.00 o.p. (*0-670-84148-X*, Viking) Viking Penguin.
—Worst Fears. 1996. 208p. 21.00 o.p. (*0-87113-635-X*, Atlantic Monthly Pr.) Grove/Atlantic, Inc.
Wesley, Mary. A Dubious Legacy. l.t. ed. 1992. pap. 17.95 o.p. (*0-7927-1356-7*); 19.95 o.p. (*0-7927-1357-5*) BBC Audiobooks America.
—A Dubious Legacy. 1992. 272p. 21.00 o.p. (*0-670-84672-4*, Viking) Viking Penguin.
Weston, Sophie. The Bridesmaid's Secret. 2002. (Harlequin Romance Ser.: No. 3687). 187p. mass mkt. (*0-373-03687-6*, 1-03687-0, Harlequin Bks.) Harlequin Enterprises, Ltd.
White, Edmund. The Married Man. 2001. 336p. pap. 14.00 (*0-679-78144-7*, Vintage) Knopf Publishing Group.
Whittenburg, Karen Toller. The C. E. O.'s Unplanned Proposal. 2002. (Harlequin American Romance Ser.: No. 910). 256p. mass mkt. (*0-373-16910-8*, 1-16910-1, Harlequin Bks.) Harlequin Enterprises, Ltd.
Wiggins, VeraLee. Julius Again: More Adventures with the Perfectly Pesky Pet Parrot. 1995. (Julius & Friends Ser.: No. 2). 94p. (J). (gr. 2 up). pap. 6.99 o.p. (*0-8163-1239-7*) Pacific Pr. Publishing Assn.
Wilkins, Gina F. Dateline Matrimony. 2001. (Silhouette Special Edition Ser.: No. 1424). 256p. mass mkt. (*0-373-24424-X*, Silhouette) Harlequin Enterprises, Ltd.
Wilks, Eileen. Jacob's Proposal. 2001. (Silhouette Desire Ser.: No. 1397). mass mkt. (*0-373-76397-2*, Silhouette) Harlequin Enterprises, Ltd.
Willey, Margaret. If Not for You. (Trophy Keypoint Bks.). 160p. (YA). (gr. 7 up). 1990. mass mkt. 3.25 (*0-06-447015-6*, Harper Trophy); 1988. 11.95 (*0-06-026494-2*); 1988. lib. bdg. 11.89 o.p. (*0-06-026499-3*) HarperCollins Children's Bk. Group.
Williams, Barbara. Mitzi & the Terrible Tyrannosaurus Rex. 1982. (Illus.). 112p. (J). (gr. 2-4). 10.95 o.p. (*0-525-45105-6*, 0966-290, Dutton) Dutton/Plume.
Williams, Dennis. Mail Order Brides. 2001. mass mkt. (*0-373-29189-2*, Harlequin Bks.) Harlequin Enterprises, Ltd.
—Merger by Matrimony. 2001. (9 to 5 Ser.). 192p. mass mkt. o.s.i (*0-373-12222-5*, Harlequin Bks.) Harlequin Enterprises, Ltd.
Wilson, Charles. When First We Deceive. 1994. 272p. 19.95 o.p. (*0-7867-0058-0*, Carroll & Graf Pubs.) Avalon Publishing Group.
—When First We Deceive. 1998. 272p. reprint ed. mass mkt. 4.50 (*0-8439-4401-3*, Leisure Bks.) Dorchester Publishing Co., Inc.
—When We First Deceive. 1998. E-Book 9.95 (*0-585-28456-3*) netLibrary, Inc.
Wilson, Gayle. Lady Sarah's Son. 1999. (Harlequin Historicals Ser.: No. 483). per. (*0-373-29083-7*, 1-29083-2, Harlequin Bks.) Harlequin Enterprises, Ltd.
Winn, Bonnie K. Substitute Father. 2001. (Harlequin Superromance Ser.: No. 1019). mass mkt. (*0-373-71019-4*, Harlequin Bks.) Harlequin Enterprises, Ltd.
Winters, Rebecca. His Majesty's Marriage, 2 vols. in 1. l.t. ed. 2002. 250p. mass mkt. (*0-373-15949-8*, 1-15949-0, Harlequin Bks.) Harlequin Enterprises, Ltd.
—His Majesty's Marriage. l.t. ed. 2002. (Harlequin 1 Ser.). 288p. 24.95 (*0-263-17356-9*) Harlequin Mills & Boon, Ltd. GBR. *Dist:* Thorndike Pr.
Winters, Rebecca & Gordon, Lucy. His Majesty's Marriage: The Prince's Choice/The King's Bride, 2 bks. in 1. 2002. (Harlequin Romance Ser.: No. 3703). mass mkt. (*0-373-03703-1*, 1-03703-5, Harlequin Bks.) Harlequin Enterprises, Ltd.
Winton, Tim. The Riders. l.t. ed. 1996. 392p. lib. bdg. 24.95 (*1-57490-036-6*) Beeler, Thomas T. Publisher.
—The Riders. 384p. 1996. pap. 12.00 (*0-684-82277-6*); 1995. 22.50 (*0-684-80296-1*) Simon & Schuster. (Scribner).
Wolf, Laura. Diary of a Mad Bride. 2002. 304p. pap. 10.95 (*0-385-33583-0*, Delta) Dell Publishing.
Wolitzer, Hilmer. Wish You Were Here, RS. 1986. 180p. (J). (gr. 4-7). pap. 3.45 o.p. (*0-374-48412-0*, Sunburst) Farrar, Straus & Giroux.
Wood, Phyllis A. Meet Me in the Park, Angie. 1983. 118p. (YA). (gr. 7-10). 11.95 o.p. (*0-664-32710-9*) Westminster John Knox Pr.
Woolrich, Cornell. The Bride Wore Black. reprint ed. lib. bdg. 20.95 (*0-88411-876-2*) Amereon, Ltd.
—The Bride Wore Black. 1984. 224p. mass mkt. 2.25 o.s.i (*0-345-30487-X*) Ballantine Bks.
—The Bride Wore Black. 1990. reprint ed. lib. bdg. 16.95 (*0-89968-562-5*) Buccaneer Bks., Inc.
—The Bride Wore Black. 1994. 35.00 (*1-883402-22-0*, Scribner) Simon & Schuster.
—The Bride Wore Black. 2001. 256p. pap. 12.00 (*0-7434-1316-4*) ibooks, Inc.
Zalben, Jane Breskin. Maybe It Will Rain Tomorrow, RS. 1983. 181p. (J). (gr. 7 up). 12.95 o.p. (*0-374-34878-2*, Farrar, Straus & Giroux (BYR)) Farrar, Straus & Giroux.

**MARRIED PEOPLE—FICTION**

Abrahams, Peter. A Perfect Crime. l.t. ed. 1999. (Core Ser.). 447p. 29.95 o.p. (*0-7838-8476-1*) Thorndike Pr.
Adamoli, Vida. Sons, Lovers, Etcetera. 1997. 250p. pap. 13.95 o.p. (*0-7472-5501-6*) Headline Bk. Publishing, Ltd. GBR. *Dist:* Trafalgar Square.
Adams, Alice. After the War. l.t. ed. 2001. (G. K. Hall Core Ser.). 367p. 31.95 (*0-7838-9392-2*, Macmillan Reference USA) Gale Group.
—After the War. 2001. 320p. reprint ed. pap. 14.00 (*0-7434-2222-8*, Washington Square Pr.) Simon & Schuster.
Adamse, Michael. Anniversary: A Love Story. 1998. 250p. pap. 10.95 (*1-55874-542-4*) Health Communications, Inc.
Adler, Warren. The Children of the Roses. 2004. (*1-4022-0197-4*) Sourcebooks, Inc.
Amiel, Joseph. Deeds. 1988. mass mkt. 4.95 o.s.i (*0-449-14522-0*, Fawcett) Ballantine Bks.
—Deeds. 1988. 484p. 19.95 o.s.i (*0-689-11862-7*, Scribner) Simon & Schuster.
Amis, Kingsley. Difficulties with Girls. 1991. 3.99 o.p. (*0-517-06319-0*) Random Hse. Value Publishing.
—Difficulties with Girls. 1989. 304p. 18.95 o.p. (*0-671-67582-6*) Summit Bks.
Aniebo, I. N. The Journey Within. 1978. (African Writers Ser.). pap. 7.95 o.p. (*0-435-90206-7*) Heinemann.
Ashley, Renee. Someplace Like This. 2003. 192p. 26.00 (*1-57962-090-6*) Permanent Pr., The.
Atwood, Margaret. Life Before Man. 1987. 384p. mass mkt. 5.99 o.s.i (*0-449-21377-3*, Fawcett) Ballantine Bks.
—Life Before Man. 1995. 368p. pap. 10.95 o.s.i (*0-553-37782-5*); 1984. 304p. mass mkt. 5.95 o.s.i (*0-7704-2029-X*) Bantam Bks.
—Life Before Man. 1998. 384p. pap. 13.00 (*0-385-49110-7*) Doubleday Publishing.
—Life Before Man. 1980. 11.95 o.p. (*0-671-25115-5*, Simon & Schuster) Simon & Schuster.
—Life Before Man. 1984. 304p. mass mkt. 3.95 o.s.i (*0-446-31331-9*) Warner Bks., Inc.
Auchincloss, Louis. Watchfires. 001. 1982. 368p. 13.95 o.p. (*0-395-31546-8*) Houghton Mifflin Co.
Ball, Karen. The Breaking Point. 2003. 400p. pap. 12.99 (*1-59052-033-5*) Multnomah Pubs., Inc.
Barfoot, Joan. Critical Injuries. 2002. 336p. text 25.00 (*1-58243-208-2*, Basic Civitas Bks.) Basic Bks.
—Critical Injuries. 2002. 336p. pap. 13.95 (*0-7043-4768-7*) Women's Pr., Ltd., The GBR. *Dist:* Trafalgar Square.
Barth, John. On with the Story: Stories. 1996. 272p. 23.95 o.p. (*0-316-08263-5*) Little Brown & Co.
—Sabbatical: A Romance. 1983. 366p. pap. 5.95 o.p. (*0-14-006619-5*); 1982. 352p. 14.95 o.p. (*0-399-12717-8*); 1982. 50.00 o.p. (*0-399-12723-2*) Putnam Publishing Group, The.
—Sabbatical: A Romance. 1996. 366p. reprint ed. pap. 12.95 (*1-56478-096-1*) Dalkey Archive Pr.
Barthelme, Frederick. Two Against One. 1988. 270p. 17.95 o.p. (*1-55584-214-3*) Grove/Atlantic, Inc.
Basch, Rachel. Degrees of Love. 1999. 368p. mass mkt. 6.50 (*0-06-101404-4*) HarperCollins Pubs.
—Degrees of Love. 1999. 12.55 (*0-606-16722-6*) Turtleback Bks.
—Degrees of Love: A Novel. 1998. 256p. text 23.95 (*0-393-04625-7*) Norton, W. W. & Co., Inc.
Baumbach, Jonathan. Chez Charlotte & Emily. 1979. 15.95 (*0-914590-56-1*); pap. 10.95 (*0-914590-57-X*) Fiction Collective Two, Inc.
Baxter, Charles. Saul & Patsy: A Novel. 2003. 336p. 24.00 (*0-375-41029-5*, Pantheon) Knopf Publishing Group.
Beattie, Ann. Another You. 1996. 336p. pap. 19.00 (*0-679-73464-3*, Vintage) Knopf Publishing Group.
—Another You. audio o.p. National Humanities Ctr.
Bebris, Carrie. Pride & Prescience. 2004. 288p. 21.95 (*0-7653-0508-9*, Forge Bks.) Doherty, Tom Assocs., LLC.
Bender, Carrie. Beyond Mist Blue Mountains. 2003. (Dora's Diary Ser.: Vol. 3). (Illus.). 163p. 8.99 (*0-8361-9165-X*) Herald Pr.
Bennett, Alan. The Clothes They Stood up In. 2001. E-Book 11.95 (*1-58945-614-9*) Adobe Systems, Inc.
—The Clothes They Stood up In. 1998. 112p. pap. 8.00 (*1-86197-090-0*) Profile Bks. Ltd. GBR. *Dist:* Renouf Publishing Co., Ltd.
—The Clothes They Stood up In. 2001. E-Book 13.50 (*0-375-50689-6*) Random Hse., Inc.
—The Clothes They Stood up In: And the Lady in the Van. 2002. 240p. pap. 9.95 (*0-8129-6965-0*) Random House Adult Trade Publishing Group.
—The Clothes They Stood up in And the Lady in the Van. 2002. 240p. pap. 9.95 (*0-8129-6643-0*) Random House Adult Trade Publishing Group.
Benson, Angela. Abiding Hope. 2003. 256p. mass mkt. 6.99 (*1-58314-323-8*, New Spirit) BET Bks.
—Abiding Hope. 2001. (HeartQuest Ser.). (Illus.). 256p. pap. 9.99 (*0-8423-1940-9*) Tyndale Hse. Pubs.
Berg, Elizabeth. Open House. 2000. 256p. 23.95 o.s.i (*0-375-50100-2*) Random Hse., Inc.
—Open House: A Novel. E-Book 19.50 (*1-58945-605-X*) Adobe Systems, Inc.
—Open House: A Novel. 2001. (Reader's Circle Ser.). 272p. reprint ed. pap. 14.95 (*0-345-43516-8*, Ballantine Bks.) Ballantine Bks.
—Open House: A Novel. l.t. ed. (Wheeler Press Paperback Ser.). 2001. 12.95 (*1-56895-181-7*); 2000. 271p. 28.95 (*1-56895-923-0*) Gale Group. (Wheeler Publishing, Inc.).
—Open House: A Novel. 2001. E-Book 19.50 (*0-375-50587-3*) Random Hse., Inc.
Bergland, Martha. A Farm under a Lake. 1989. 208p. 17.95 o.s.i (*1-55597-119-9*) Graywolf Pr.
Berry, Bertice. Jim & Louella's Homemade Heartfix Remedy. 2002. 224p. 22.95 (*0-385-50377-6*) Doubleday Publishing.
Bianchin, Helen. Dark Tyrant. l.t. ed. 1994. 18.95 o.p. (*0-7927-2152-7*); pap. 17.95 o.p. (*0-7927-2151-9*) BBC Audiobooks America.
—Dark Tyrant. 1984. mass mkt. (*0-373-10751-X*, Harlequin Bks.) Harlequin Enterprises, Ltd.
Biggs, Undra E. Backfield in Motion. Cadet, Guichard, ed. 2002. 288p. pap. 15.00 (*0-9718191-3-0*) La Caille Nous Publishing Co.
Bills, Greg. Fearful Symmetry. 336p. 1997. pap. 12.95 o.p. (*0-452-27574-1*, Plume); 1996. 23.95 o.s.i (*0-525-94081-2*, Dutton) Dutton/Plume.
Binchy, Maeve. Silver Wedding. 1990. 432p. reprint ed. mass mkt. 7.99 (*0-440-20777-0*) Dell Publishing.
—Silver Wedding. l.t. ed. 2001. 382p. 29.95 (*0-7862-3583-7*); 453p. (*0-7540-1708-7*); 453p. (*0-7540-9107-4*) Thorndike Pr.
—Silver Wedding. l.t. ed. 1989. o.p. (*0-7089-8522-X*, Charnwood) Thorpe, F. A. Pubs.
Blauner, Peter. The Last Good Day. 2003. 432p. 24.95 (*0-316-09873-6*) Little Brown & Co.
Bly, Stephen A. & Bly, Janet. Fox Island. 1996. (Hidden West Ser.: Vol. 1). 240p. pap. 10.99 o.p. (*0-89283-941-4*, Vine Bks.) Servant Pubns.
Bosse, Malcolm. Fire in Heaven: A Novel. 1986. 608p. 18.45 o.p. (*0-671-47080-9*, Simon & Schuster) Simon & Schuster.
Boylan, Clare. Beloved Stranger. 320p. 2001. text 24.00 o.p. (*1-58243-096-9*); 2002. reprint ed. pap. text 15.00 (*1-58243-224-4*) Basic Bks. (Counterpoint Pr.).
Boyle, Josephine. Holy Terror. 1995. 21.95 o.p. (*0-312-11824-4*, Saint Martin's Minotaur) St. Martin's Pr.
Boyle, T. Coraghessan. The Tortilla Curtain, Set. abr. ed. 1995. audio 16.95 (*1-55927-353-4*, 393174) Audio Renaissance.
—The Tortilla Curtain. unabr. ed. 1996. audio 80.00 (*0-7366-3300-6*, 3955) Books on Tape, Inc.
—The Tortilla Curtain. l.t. ed. 1996. 25.95 (*1-56895-287-2*, Wheeler Publishing, Inc.) Gale Group.
—The Tortilla Curtain. 1996. 368p. pap. 14.00 (*0-14-023828-X*) Penguin Group (USA) Inc.
—The Tortilla Curtain. unabr. ed. audio 85.00 (*0-7887-0457-5*, 94650E7) Recorded Bks., LLC.
—The Tortilla Curtain. 1995. 368p. 23.95 o.s.i (*0-670-85604-5*, Viking) Viking Penguin.
Brown, Rosellen. Tender Mercies. 1979. mass mkt. 2.25 o.s.i (*0-345-28499-2*) Ballantine Bks.
—Tender Mercies. l.t. ed. 2002. lib. bdg. 28.95 (*1-58547-192-5*, Premier) Ctr. Point Large Print.
—Tender Mercies. 1998. 288p. pap. 11.95 (*0-385-33332-3*); 1994. 368p. mass mkt. 5.99 o.s.i (*0-440-21696-6*) Dell Publishing.
—Tender Mercies. 1986. (Contemporary American Fiction Ser.). 272p. pap. 6.95 o.p. (*0-14-008579-3*, Penguin Bks.) Viking Penguin.
Burke, Jan. Flight: A Novel of Suspense. l.t. ed. 2001. 601p. 28.95 o.p. (*1-58724-051-3*, Wheeler Publishing, Inc.) Gale Group.
Busch, Frederick. A Memory of War. 2004. 368p. pap. 14.95 (*0-345-46051-0*) Ballantine Bks.
—A Memory of War. l.t. ed. 2003. lib. bdg. 28.95 (*1-58547-350-2*, Platinum) Ctr. Point Large Print.
—A Memory of War. 2003. 352p. 25.95 (*0-393-04978-7*) Norton, W. W. & Co., Inc.
Butler, Robert Olen. Wabash: A Novel. 1988. mass mkt. 3.95 o.s.i (*0-345-35211-4*) Ballantine Bks.
—Wabash: A Novel. 1994. 25.00 o.p. (*0-8050-3200-2*); 207p. pap. 11.00 o.s.i (*0-8050-3138-3*, Owl Bks.) Holt, Henry & Co.
Calisher, Hortense. Age: A Love Story. 1996. 124p. reprint ed. pap. 13.95 (*0-7145-3012-3*) Boyars, Marion Pubs., Inc.
—Age: A Love Story. 128p. 1989. pap. 8.95 o.p. (*1-55584-371-9*); 1987. 14.95 o.p. (*1-55584-132-5*) Grove/Atlantic, Inc.
Card, Orson Scott. Treasure Box. abr. ed. 1997. audio 7.99 o.p. (*1-56740-182-1*, 711, Paperback Nova Audio Bks.); audio 23.95 (*1-56100-717-X*, 297, Bookcassette); 5p. audio 57.25 o.p. (*1-56100-342-5*, 1085, Unabridged Library Editions) Brilliance Audio.
—Treasure Box. 1996. 320p. 24.00 o.p. (*0-06-017654-7*) HarperCollins Pubs.
—Treasure Box. 1997. 384p. mass mkt. 6.99 (*0-06-109398-X*, HarperTorch) Morrow/Avon.
—Treasure Box. 1997. 13.04 (*0-606-22211-1*) Turtleback Bks.
Carkeet, David. The Full Catastrophe. 1990. 18.95 o.p. (*0-671-64319-3*, Simon & Schuster) Simon & Schuster.
—The Full Catastrophe. Rosenman, Jane, ed. 1991. 324p. reprint ed. pap. (*0-671-73245-5*, Washington Square Pr.) Simon & Schuster.
Cather, Willa. Alexander's Bridge. 1977. reprint ed. lib. bdg. 19.95 (*0-89190-520-0*, Queens Hse., Inc.) Amereon, Ltd.
—Alexander's Bridge. 2001. per. 12.50 (*1-58396-412-6*); per. 15.50 (*1-58396-413-4*) Blue Unicorn Editions.
—Alexander's Bridge. 1990. reprint ed. lib. bdg. 16.95 (*0-89968-491-2*) Buccaneer Bks., Inc.
—Alexander's Bridge. (Collected Works of Willa Cather). 174p. reprint ed. 2001. pap. 28.00 (*0-7426-5566-0*); 1998. lib. bdg. 88.00 (*1-58201-566-X*) Classic Bks.
—Alexander's Bridge. 2002. (Thrift Editions Ser.). 160p. pap. 2.00 (*0-486-42450-2*) Dover Pubns., Inc.
—Alexander's Bridge. 1999. E-Book 2.49 (*1-58627-088-5*) Electric Umbrella Publishing.
—Alexander's Bridge. l.t. ed. 79p. pap. 13.58 (*0-7583-0120-0*); 273p. pap. 30.60 (*0-7583-0125-1*); 336p. pap. 35.67 (*0-7583-0126-X*); 222p. pap. 26.47 (*0-7583-0124-3*); 99p. pap. 14.60 (*0-7583-0121-9*); 136p. pap. 18.72 (*0-7583-0122-7*); 174p. pap. 22.55 (*0-7583-0123-5*); 390p. pap. 40.00 (*0-7583-0127-8*); 99p. lib. bdg. 20.60 (*0-7583-0113-8*); 136p. lib. bdg. 24.72 (*0-7583-0114-6*); 174p. lib. bdg. 29.66 (*0-7583-0115-4*); 222p. lib. bdg. 34.47

(*0-7583-0116-2*); 273p. lib. bdg. 38.09 (*0-7583-0117-0*); 79p. lib. bdg. 19.58 (*0-7583-0112-X*); 390p. lib. bdg. 46.34 (*0-7583-0119-7*); 336p. lib. bdg. 42.54 (*0-7583-0118-9*) Huge Print Pr.
—Alexander's Bridge. 2001. 128p. 22.99 (*1-58827-482-9*); per. 18.99 (*1-58827-483-7*) IndyPublish-.com.
—Alexander's Bridge, l.t. ed. 2001. 135p. lib. bdg. 24.95 net. (*1-58118-080-2*) LRS.
—Alexander's Bridge. 2001. (Twelve-Point Ser.). 205p. lib. bdg. 25.00 (*1-58287-168-X*); 309p. lib. bdg. 26.00 (*1-58287-651-7*) North Bks.
—Alexander's Bridge. Lindemann, Marilee, ed. & intro. by. 1997. (Oxford World's Classics Ser.). 152p. pap. 8.95 o.p. (*0-19-283214-X*) Oxford Univ. Pr., Inc.
—Alexander's Bridge. 1998. 112p. 22.00 (*0-684-81907-4*, Simon & Schuster) Simon & Schuster.
—Alexander's Bridge. (Ebook Classic Ser.). E-Book 5.00 (*0-7410-1301-0*) SoftBook Pr.
—Alexander's Bridge. 1977. 140p. reprint ed. pap. 9.95 (*0-8032-5863-1*, Bison Bks.) Univ. of Nebraska Pr.
—Alexander's Bridge. 1990. xxiii, 176p. pap. 12.00 o.s.i (*1-85381-163-7*) Virago Pr., Ltd. GBR. *Dist:* Trafalgar Square.
—Alexander's Bridge. l.t. ed. 2000. 201p. 16.99 (*1-930142-29-3*); pap. 9.99 (*1-930142-28-5*) Write Together Publishing.
Cather, Willa & O'Brien, Sharon. Alexander's Bridge. 1988. 216p. pap. 6.00 o.p. (*0-452-00875-1*, Meridian Bks.) NAL.
Chaplin, Elizabeth. Hostage to Fortune. l.t. ed. 2001. (Ulverscroft Large Print Ser.). 408p. 32.50 (*0-7089-4427-2*) Ulverscroft Large Print Bks., Ltd.
—Hostage to Fortune. 1994. 256p. mass mkt. 4.99 (*0-446-40306-7*, Mysterious Pr. Paperback Bks.) Warner Bks., Inc.
Cheek, Mavis. Parlour Games. 2003. (General Ser.). lib. bdg. 24.95 (*0-7862-4780-0*) Thorndike Pr.
Chesney, Marion. My Dear Duchess. l.t. ed. 1987. 224p. mass mkt. 3.99 o.s.i (*0-451-14960-2*, Signet Bks.) NAL.
—My Dear Duchess. l.t. ed. 2001. 301p. (*0-7862-3362-1*); (*0-7540-4553-6*); (*0-7540-4554-4*) Thorndike Pr.
Chraibi, Driss. Inspector Ali. McGlashlan, Lara, tr. from FRE. 1994. 143p. 26.00 (*0-89410-746-1*); pap. 12.95 (*0-89410-747-X*) Rienner, Lynne Pubs., Inc. (Three Continents).
Christie, Agatha. By the Pricking of My Thumbs. abr. ed. 2003. (Agatha Christie Audio Mystery Ser.). (Illus.). audio 12.95 (*1-55927-904-4*) Audio Renaissance.
Christopher Murray, Victoria. Temptation. 1997. 279p. pap. 12.95 o.p. (*1-881524-14-0*) Milligan Bks.
Churchman, Deborah. Cross a Dark Bridge: A Novel. 1996. 130p. 14.95 (*0-918056-08-X*) Ariadne Pr.
Ciresi, Rita. Remind Me Again Why I Married You. 2003. 320p. pap. 14.00 (*0-385-33585-7*, Delta); 304p. 23.95 (*0-385-33584-9*, Delacorte Pr.) Dell Publishing.
Clark, Mary Higgins. Mount Vernon Love Story. 2003. 272p. mass mkt. 6.99 (*0-7434-4894-4*, Pocket); 2002. E-Book 9.99 (*0-7432-0630-4*, Simon & Schuster); 2002. (Illus.). 224p. 22.00 (*0-7432-2987-8*, Simon & Schuster); 2002. 352p. 22.00 (*0-7432-3380-8*, Simon & Schuster); 2002. 224p. 22.00 (*0-7432-4304-8*, Simon & Schuster) Simon & Schuster.
—Mount Vernon Love Story. abr. ed. 2002. audio 26.00 (*0-7435-2288-5*); audio compact disk 30.00 (*0-7435-2287-7*) Simon & Schuster Audio. (Simon & Schuster Audioworks).
—Remember Me. 1997. reprint ed. lib. bdg. 15.95 (*1-56849-589-7*) Buccaneer Bks., Inc.
—Remember Me. 2000. E-Book 9.95 (*0-7432-0622-3*, Simon & Schuster); 1995. 352p. mass mkt. 7.99 (*0-671-86709-1*, Pocket); 1994. 304p. 23.50 o.s.i (*0-671-86708-3*, Simon & Schuster); 1994. 26.00 (*0-671-89468-4*, Simon & Schuster) Simon & Schuster.
—Remember Me. abr. ed. 1994. audio 18.00 (*0-671-88793-9*, 391464, Simon & Schuster Audioworks) Simon & Schuster Audio.
Collins, Wilkie. Man & Wife. (Works of Wilkie Collins: Vol. 3). reprint ed. Pt. 1. 2001. 574p. pap. text 28.00 (*0-7426-5024-3*); Pt. 1. 1999. 574p. lib. bdg. 98.00 (*1-58201-024-2*); Pt. 2. 2001. 615p. pap. text 28.00 (*0-7426-5025-1*); Pt. 2. 1999. 615p. lib. bdg. 98.00 (*1-58201-025-0*) Classic Bks.
—Man & Wife. 1983. (Illus.). 239p. reprint ed. pap. 5.95 o.p. (*0-486-24451-2*) Dover Pubns., Inc.
—Man & Wife. 2002. 696p. 32.99 (*1-4043-1608-6*); per. 27.99 (*1-4043-1609-4*) IndyPublish.com.
—Man & Wife. 1999. E-Book 1.95 (*1-58515-264-1*) MesaView, Inc.
—Man & Wife. Page, Norman, ed. & intro. by. 1999. (Oxford World's Classics Ser.). 688p. pap. 14.95 (*0-19-283696-X*) Oxford Univ. Pr., Inc.
—Man & Wife. Page, Norman, ed. 1995. (Oxford World's Classics Ser.). 682p. pap. 13.95 o.p. (*0-19-283146-1*) Oxford Univ. Pr., Inc.
Colwin, Laurie. Happy All the Time. 1979. (General Ser.). lib. bdg. 13.95 o.p. (*0-8161-6683-8*, Macmillan Reference USA) Gale Group.
—Happy All the Time. 2000. 224p. pap. 12.00 (*0-06-095532-5*); 1993. 528p. reprint ed. pap. 12.00 (*0-06-097564-4*) HarperTrade. (Perennial).
—Happy All the Time. 1983. mass mkt. 3.95 o.s.i (*0-671-49587-9*, Pocket) Simon & Schuster.
—Happy All the Time. 1985. 224p. pap. 8.95 o.p. (*0-14-007687-5*, Penguin Bks.) Viking Penguin.
Connell, Evan S. Mr. Bridge. reprint ed. 1990. 367p. pap. 9.95 o.s.i (*0-86547-054-5*); 1982. 384p. 35.00 o.p. (*0-86547-057-X*) Farrar, Straus & Giroux. (North Point Pr.).
—Mr. Bridge. 1977. pap. 2.50 o.p. (*0-671-82937-8*, Pocket) Simon & Schuster.
Connell, Vivian. The Chinese Room. 2003. 256p. pap. 12.00 (*1-56980-264-5*) Barricade Bks., Inc.
Craig, Alisa, pseud. A Dismal Thing to Do. 1986. (Crime Club Ser.). 192p. 12.95 o.p. (*0-385-23263-2*) Doubleday Publishing.
—Murder Goes Mumming. l.t. ed. 1982. 289p. reprint ed. 9.95 o.p. (*0-89621-354-4*) Thorndike Pr.
Crittenden, Danielle. Amanda Bright @ Home: A Novel. 2003. 336p. 23.95 (*0-446-53074-3*) Warner Bks., Inc.
—Amanda Bright@Home. l.t. ed. 2003. 456p. 28.95 (*0-7862-5685-0*) Thorndike Pr.
Cronin, Justin. Mary & O'Neil. 2002. 256p. pap. 11.95 (*0-385-33359-5*, Delta) Dell Publishing.
Cronley, Jay. Shoot. 1997. 154p. text 19.95 o.p. (*0-312-15655-3*) St. Martin's Pr.
Cuccio, Joan F. The Geometry of Love. 1997. 172p. 24.00 (*1-877946-82-6*) Permanent Pr., The.
Cumyn, Alan. Losing It. mass mkt. (*0-312-98569-X*, St. Martin's Paperbacks); E-Book (*0-312-70532-8*); 2003. 384p. 24.95 (*0-312-30691-1*) St. Martin's Pr.
Cutting, Mary S. Little Stories of Married Life. 1977. (Short Story Index Reprint Ser.). reprint ed. 19.95 (*0-8369-3796-1*) Ayer Co. Pubs., Inc.
Dailey, Janet. A Tradition of Pride: Mississippi. 1991. (Americana Ser.: No. 874). mass mkt. (*0-373-89874-6*); 1988. pap. (*0-373-21924-5*); 1987. (Americana Ser.: No. 24). pap. (*0-373-89824-X*) Harlequin Enterprises, Ltd. (Harlequin Bks.).
—A Tradition of Pride: Mississippi. l.t. ed. 2001. 224p. (Illus.). 28.95 (*0-7862-2699-4*); (*0-7540-4581-1*); (*0-7540-4582-X*) Thorndike Pr.
—A Tradition of Pride: Mississippi. E-Book 6.99 (*0-7592-0833-6*); 2001. 120p. pap. 12.95 (*0-7592-3798-0*) ereads.com.
Dangor, Achmat. Kafka's Curse: A Novel. 240p. 2000. pap. 12.00 o.s.i (*0-375-70462-0*, Vintage); 1999. 22.00 o.s.i (*0-375-40510-0*, Pantheon) Knopf Publishing Group.
—Kafka's Curse: A Novella & Three Other Stories. 1997. (Illus.). (*0-7957-0054-7*) Kwela Bks.
Dawson, Jill. Fred & Edie. l.t. ed. 2002. 324p. pap. 25.95 (*0-7862-3956-5*) Gale Group.
—Fred & Edie. 2001. 288p. 25.00 (*1-56649-222-X*) Welcome Rain Pubs.
—Fred & Edie: A Novel. 2002. 288p. pap. 13.00 (*0-618-19728-1*) Houghton Mifflin Co.
Delderfield, R. F. To Serve Them All My Days. 1972. 9.95 o.s.i (*0-671-21371-7*, Simon & Schuster) Simon & Schuster.
Delinsky, Barbara. The Woman Next Door: A Novel. 2001. E-Book 9.99 (*1-58945-935-0*) Adobe Systems, Inc.
—The Woman Next Door: A Novel. 2001. 368p. 25.00 (*0-7432-0469-7*); pap. 16.00 (*0-7432-2214-8*) Simon & Schuster. (Simon & Schuster).
—The Woman Next Door: A Novel. l.t. ed. 2002. 504p. 14.95 (*0-7862-3512-8*); 2001. 541p. 32.95 (*0-7862-3510-1*) Thorndike Pr.
Diamond, Diana. The Trophy Wife. l.t. ed. 2000. 26.95 (*1-57490-305-5*, Beeler Large Print Bks.) Beeler, Thomas T. Publisher.
—The Trophy Wife. 2000. 261p. 23.95 (*0-312-20600-3*) St. Martin's Pr.
Divakaruni, Chitra Banerjee. The Vine of Desire: A Novel. 2003. 384p. pap. 13.00 (*0-385-49730-X*, Anchor Canada) Doubleday Canada, Ltd. CAN. *Dist:* Random Hse., Inc.
Drabble, Margaret. The Realms of Gold. 1988. 384p. reprint ed. mass mkt. 5.99 o.s.i (*0-8041-0363-1*, Ivy Bks.) Ballantine Bks.
—The Realms of Gold. 1982. 368p. pap. 3.95 o.p. (*0-553-22603-7*) Bantam Bks.
Duberstein, Larry. The Alibi Breakfast. 1995. 229p. 22.00 (*1-877946-59-1*) Permanent Pr., The.
—The Alibi Breakfast. 2002. pap. 6.99 (*0-7592-4159-7*); E-Book 6.99 (*0-7592-4161-9*); E-Book 6.99 (*0-7592-4163-5*); E-Book 6.99 (*0-7592-4162-7*) ereads.com.
Ducker, Bruce. Marital Assets. 1993. 252p. 26.00 (*1-877946-26-5*) Permanent Pr., The.
Dunne, Catherine. In the Beginning. 1997. 288p. pap. o.p. (*0-224-04426-5*) Random Hse. UK, Ltd.
Durham, David Anthony. A Walk Through Darkness. l.t. ed. 2002. 28.95 (*1-58724-242-7*, Wheeler Publishing, Inc.) Gale Group.
—A Walk Through Darkness. 2003. 304p. reprint ed. pap. 13.00 (*0-385-72036-X*, Anchor) Knopf Publishing Group.
—A Walk Through Darkness: A Novel. 2002. 304p. 23.95 (*0-385-49925-6*) Doubleday Publishing.
Edgerton, Clyde. Raney. 1985. 240p. 16.95 (*0-912697-17-2*) Algonquin Bks. of Chapel Hill.
Edgerton, Clyde, et al. Pete & Shirley: The Great Tar Heel Novel. Perkins, David, ed. 1995. 116p. pap. 13.95 (*1-878086-49-9*) Down Home Pr.
Elliott, George P. Middlemarch. 2003. 912p. mass mkt. 6.95 (*0-451-52917-0*, Signet Classics) NAL.
Ephron, Nora. Heartburn. l.t. ed. 1983. 13.95 o.p. (*0-8161-3616-5*, Macmillan Reference USA) Gale Group.
Erdrich, Louise. The Master Butchers Singing Club. 2003. 400p. 25.95 (*0-06-620977-3*) HarperCollins Pubs.
—The Master Butchers Singing Club. 2004. 416p. pap. 13.95 (*0-06-093533-2*, Perennial); 2003. 704p. pap. 25.95 (*0-06-053327-7*, HarperLargePrint) Harper-Trade.
Evans, Elizabeth. Blue Hour: A Novel. 1994. 350p. 17.95 o.p. (*1-56512-018-3*) Algonquin Bks. of Chapel Hill.
Farber, Thomas. The Beholder: A Novel. 2002. 208p. 22.00 (*0-8050-6972-0*, Metropolitan Bks.) Holt, Henry & Co.
—The Beholder: A Novel. 2003. 208p. pap. 13.00 (*0-312-42182-6*) Picador.
Faulks, Sebastian. On Green Dolphin Street: A Novel. 2003. 368p. pap. 14.00 (*0-375-70456-6*, Vintage) Knopf Publishing Group.
—On Green Dolphin Street: A Novel. 2002. 368p. 24.95 (*0-375-50225-4*) Random Hse., Inc.
Ferrier, Susan. Marriage. Set. unabr. ed. 1994. (Orig.). audio 65.95 (*1-55685-322-X*) Audio Bk. Contractors, Inc.
—Marriage. Foltinek, Herbert, ed. & intro. by. 1986. (Oxford World's Classics Ser.). 528p. (Orig.). pap. 6.95 o.p. (*0-19-281743-4*) Oxford Univ. Pr., Inc.
—Marriage. 2nd ed. 1998. (Oxford World's Classics Ser.). 524p. (Orig.). pap. 10.95 o.p. (*0-19-282524-0*) Oxford Univ. Pr., Inc.
—Marriage. 1986. (Virago Modern Classics Ser.). 512p. (Orig.). pap. 6.95 o.p. (*0-14-016126-0*, Penguin Bks.) Viking Penguin.
Ferrier, Susan, et al. Marriage. Foltinek, Herbert, ed. 2nd ed. 2002. (Oxford World's Classics Ser.). 528p. (Orig.). pap. 10.95 (*0-19-283893-8*) Oxford Univ. Pr., Inc.
Fielding, Henry. Amelia. 1978. reprint ed. 16.95 o.p. (*0-460-10852-2*) Biblio Distribution.
—Amelia. (Complete Works of Henry Fielding: Vol. 6). Pt. 1. 2001. 320p. reprint ed. pap. text 28.00 (*0-7426-5099-5*); Pt. 1. 1999. 320p. reprint ed. lib. bdg. 88.00 (*1-58201-099-4*); Pt. 2. 2001. 342p. pap. text 28.00 (*0-7426-5100-2*); Pt. 2. 1999. 342p. reprint ed. lib. bdg. 88.00 (*1-58201-100-1*) Classic Bks.
—Amelia. 1902. (YA). reprint ed. pap. text 38.00 (*1-4047-7836-5*) Classic Textbooks.
—Amelia. 1978. 15.50 o.p. (*0-460-00852-8*, Dutton) Dutton/Plume.
—Amelia. Blewett, David, ed. & intro. by. 1987. (Penguin Classics Ser.). 608p. pap. 8.95 o.p. (*0-14-043229-9*, Penguin Classics) Viking Penguin.
—Amelia. Battestin, Martin C., ed. 1983. (Works of Henry Fielding Ser.). (Illus.). 693p. 50.00 o.p. (*0-8195-5084-1*); pap. 14.95 o.p. (*0-8195-6114-2*) Wesleyan Univ. Pr.
Fitzgerald, F. Scott. The Beautiful & Damned. 2002. (Dover Thrift Editions Ser.). 288p. pap. 3.00 (*0-486-42132-5*) Dover Pubns., Inc.
—The Beautiful & Damned. Margolies, Alan, ed. 1998. (Oxford World's Classics Ser.). 400p. pap. 8.95 (*0-19-283264-6*) Oxford Univ. Pr., Inc.
—The Beautiful & Damned. 2003. E-Book 9.99 (*0-7432-4730-2*); 1995. 464p. pap. 13.00 (*0-684-80155-8*) Simon & Schuster. (Scribner).
—The Beautiful & Damned. 1998. (Twentieth Century Classics Ser.). 448p. 10.00 (*0-14-118087-0*, Penguin Classics) Viking Penguin.
Fleming, Thomas J. The Wages of Fame. 1999. 688p. mass mkt. 6.99 (*0-8125-7182-7*); 1998. 461p. 26.95 (*0-312-86309-8*) Doherty, Tom Assocs., LLC. (Forge Bks.).
Ford, Ford Madox. The Good Soldier: A Tale of Passion. 1990. reprint ed. lib. bdg. 23.95 (*0-89966-669-8*) Buccaneer Bks., Inc.
—The Good Soldier: A Tale of Passion. 1998. 236p. pap. 12.95 (*1-85754-300-9*) Carcanet Pr., Ltd. GBR. *Dist:* Paul & Co. Pubs. Consortium, Inc.
—The Good Soldier: A Tale of Passion. 1980. 256p. reprint ed. lib. bdg. 24.50 o.p. (*0-374-92773-1*) Hippocrene Bks., Inc.
—The Good Soldier: A Tale of Passion. 2002. 180p. 23.99 (*1-4043-0588-2*); per. 19.99 (*1-4043-0589-0*) IndyPublish.com.
—The Good Soldier: A Tale of Passion. Schorer, Mark, tr. 1989. (Vintage International Ser.). 304p. pap. 12.00 (*0-679-72218-1*, Vintage) Knopf Publishing Group.
—The Good Soldier: A Tale of Passion. l.t. ed. 1995. 330p. lib. bdg. 26.00 (*0-939495-88-0*); 1998. 212p. reprint ed. lib. bdg. 25.00 (*1-58287-031-4*) North Bks.
—The Good Soldier: A Tale of Passion. Stannard, Martin, ed. 1995. (Critical Editions Ser.). 401p. (C). pap. text 9.00 (*0-393-96634-8*) Norton, W. W. & Co., Inc.
—The Good Soldier: A Tale of Passion. 1999. (Great Books of the 20th Century Ser.). (Illus.). 192p. pap. 13.00 (*0-14-028331-5*) Penguin Group (USA) Inc.
—The Good Soldier: A Tale of Passion. (Everyman's Library). 1991. 864p. 17.00 (*0-679-40665-4*); 1957. pap. 3.95 o.p. (*0-394-70045-7*) Random Hse., Inc.
—The Good Soldier: A Tale of Passion. 1992. 21.50 o.p. (*0-8446-6637-8*) Smith, Peter Pub., Inc.
—The Good Soldier: A Tale of Passion. 1990. (Penguin Twentieth-Century Classics Ser.). 240p. 13.00 (*0-14-018081-8*, Penguin Classics) Viking Penguin.
—The Good Soldier: A Tale of Passion. 1998. lib. bdg. 21.95 (*1-56723-040-7*) Yestermorrow, Inc.
Franzen, Jonathan. The Corrections: A Novel. 2001. 528p. 26.00 o.p. (*0-374-10012-8*); 576p. 26.00 (*0-374-12998-3*); E-Book 26.00 (*0-374-70187-3*); E-Book 26.00 (*0-374-70186-5*); E-Book 26.00 o.p. (*0-374-70185-7*); E-Book 9.00 (*0-374-70184-9*) Farrar, Straus & Giroux.
—The Corrections: A Novel. 2002. pap. (*0-312-42161-3*); 592p. pap. 15.00 (*0-312-42127-3*); mass mkt. 7.99 (*0-312-98429-4*) Picador.
—The Corrections: A Novel. l.t. ed. 2003. (Paperback Bestsellers Ser.). pap. 29.95 (*0-7838-9767-7*) Thorndike Pr.
Frayn, Michael. The Trick of It. 1991. 176p. pap. 8.95 o.p. (*0-14-012651-1*) Penguin Group (USA) Inc.
—The Trick of It. 1990. 176p. 17.95 o.p. (*0-670-82985-4*, Viking) Viking Penguin.
—The Trick of It: A Novel. 2002. 176p. pap. 12.00 (*0-312-42144-3*) Picador.
Frucht, Abby. Snap. 1988. 368p. 17.95 (*0-89919-501-6*) Houghton Mifflin Co.
Funderburk, Robert. Love & Glory. 1994. (Innocent Years Ser.: No. 1). 304p. pap. 8.99 o.p. (*1-55661-460-8*) Bethany Hse. Pubs.
—Love & Glory. l.t. ed. 2000. (Christian Fiction Ser.). 397p. 24.95 (*0-7862-2375-8*) Thorndike Pr.
Gaddis, William. Carpenter's Gothic. 1986. 272p. pap. 12.95 o.s.i (*0-14-008993-4*, Penguin Bks.); 1985. 256p. 16.95 o.p. (*0-670-69793-1*) Viking Penguin.
Gardner, Lynn. Pearls & Peril. 1996. pap. 10.95 (*1-55503-932-4*, 01112422) Covenant Communications, Inc.
Gautreaux, Tim. Next Step in the Dance. 352p. 1999. pap. 14.00 (*0-312-19936-8*); 1998. 23.00 o.p. (*0-312-18143-4*) Picador.
Gill, John. The Tenant. 1985. 160p. 16.95 o.p. (*0-89733-142-7*); pap. 7.95 o.p. (*0-89733-141-9*) Academy Chicago Pubs., Ltd.
Gilman, Charlotte Perkins. The Yellow Wallpaper. 1993. (J). o.p. (*0-88682-584-9*, Creative Education) Creative Co., The.
—The Yellow Wallpaper. 2nd rev. ed. 1996. 64p. pap. 5.95 (*1-55861-158-4*) Feminist Pr. at The City Univ. of New York.
—The Yellow Wallpaper & Other Stories. 2000. 252p. E-Book 3.95 (*0-594-04673-4*) 1873 Pr.
Godwin, Rebecca T. Private Parts. 1992. 18.95 o.p. (*1-56352-021-4*) Longstreet Pr., Inc.
Goldsmith, Olivia. Switcheroo. unabr. ed. 1998. audio 56.00 (*0-7366-4190-4*, 896064) Books on Tape, Inc.
—Switcheroo. l.t. ed. 1998. (Large Print Book Ser.). 26.95 (*1-56895-680-0*, Wheeler Publishing, Inc.) Gale Group.
—Switcheroo. 1998. 272p. 23.00 (*0-06-017568-0*) HarperCollins Pubs.
—Switcheroo, Set. abr. ed. 1998. audio 22.00 o.s.i (*0-694-51868-9*, 695730, HarperAudio) Harper-Trade.
—Switcheroo. unabr. ed. 1998. audio 60.00 (*0-7887-1977-7*, 95364E7) Recorded Bks., LLC.
—Switcheroo: A Novel. 1999. 400p. mass mkt. 6.99 (*0-06-109765-9*, HarperTorch) Morrow/Avon.
Goldstein, Rebecca. The Mind-Body Problem. 1983. 13.95 o.p. (*0-394-52474-8*) Random Hse., Inc.
Goodwin, Stephen. The Blood of Paradise. 1979. 8.95 o.p. (*0-525-06846-5*, Dutton) Dutton/Plume.
—The Blood of Paradise. 2000. (Virginia Bookshelf Ser.). xi, 242p. pap. 14.95 (*0-8139-1877-4*) Univ. Pr. of Virginia.
—Blood of Paradise. 1985. pap. 3.95 o.p. (*0-380-69890-0*, Avon Bks.) Morrow/Avon.
Gordimer, Nadine. The Pickup: A Novel. 2001. 224p. 24.00 (*0-374-23210-5*) Farrar, Straus & Giroux.
—The Pickup: A Novel. l.t. ed. 2002. 390p. 29.95 (*0-7862-3848-8*) Gale Group.
—The Pickup: A Novel. 2002. 288p. pap. 14.00 (*0-14-200142-2*) Penguin Group (USA) Inc.

Gordon, Caroline. Aleck Maury, Sportsman: A Novel. 1980. (Lost American Fiction Ser.). 308p. reprint ed. pap. 12.95 o.p. (*0-8093-0988-2*) Southern Illinois Univ. Pr.

—Aleck Maury, Sportsman: A Novel. 1996. xv, 287p. pap. 15.95 (*0-8203-1866-3*) Univ. of Georgia Pr.

Graham, Laurie. The Future Homemakers of America. l.t. ed. 2003. (Core Ser.). 468p. 28.95 (*0-7862-4930-7*) Thorndike Pr.

—The Future Homemakers of America. 2002. 400p. reprint ed. pap. 14.00 (*0-446-67936-4*) Warner Bks., Inc.

Grant, Tracy. Daughter of the Game. 496p. 2003. mass mkt. 6.99 (*0-06-103206-9*, HarperTorch); 2002. 24.95 (*0-06-621133-6*, Morrow, William & Co.) Morrow/Avon.

Greeley, Andrew M. Irish Stew: A Nuala Anne McGrail Novel. 2002. 304p. 25.95 (*0-312-87188-0*, Forge Bks.) Doherty, Tom Assocs., LLC.

—Irish Stew: A Nuala Anne McGrail Novel. l.t. ed. 2003. 25.95 (*1-58724-413-6*, Wheeler Publishing, Inc.) Gale Group.

Grenville, Kate. Albion's Story. 384p. 1994. 21.95 (*0-15-100122-7*); 1996. reprint ed. pap. 13.00 (*0-15-600241-8*, Harvest Bks.) Harcourt Trade Pubs.

Hadley, Tessa. Accidents in the Home: A Novel. 2002. 256p. 23.00 o.s.i (*0-8050-7064-8*) Holt, Henry & Co.

—Accidents in the Home: A Novel. 2003. 256p. pap. 14.00 (*0-312-42102-8*) Picador.

Haigh, Jennifer. Mrs. Kimble: A Novel. 2003. 400p. 24.95 (*0-06-050939-2*, Morrow, William & Co.) Morrow/Avon.

Hamilton, William. The Lap of Luxury. 1990. 300p. 17.95 o.p. (*0-87113-246-X*); pap. 8.95 (*0-87113-342-3*, Atlantic Monthly Pr.) Grove/Atlantic, Inc.

Hammett, Dashiell. The Thin Man. Date not set. (Thin Man Ser.). 137p. 18.95 (*0-8488-2438-5*) Amereon, Ltd.

—The Thin Man. (Thin Man Ser.). 1992. pap. 9.00 (*0-394-23905-9*); 1989. 208p. pap. 11.00 (*0-679-72263-7*) Knopf Publishing Group. (Vintage).

—The Thin Man. (Thin Man Ser.). 1992. pap. 9.00 (*0-679-74092-9*); 1972. pap. 2.95 o.p. (*0-394-71774-0*) Random Hse., Inc.

—The Thin Man. 1994. (Thin Man Ser.). 272p. 35.00 (*1-883402-70-0*, Scribner) Simon & Schuster.

—The Thin Man. l.t. ed. 2001. (Perennial Bestsellers Ser.). 269p. 28.95 (*0-7838-9460-0*) Thorndike Pr.

Hannah, Kristin. Angel Falls. l.t. ed. 2001. (Basic Ser.). 429p. pap. 28.95 (*0-7862-2499-1*) Thorndike Pr.

Haywood, Eliza. The History of Miss Betsy Thoughtless. Blouch, Christine, ed. 1998. (Literary Texts Ser.). 620p. (C). pap. (*1-55111-147-0*) Broadview Pr.

—The History of Miss Betsy Thoughtless, 4 vols. Paulson, Ronald, ed. 1979. (Novel 1720-1805 Ser.: Vol. 4). lib. bdg. 150.00 o.p. (*0-8240-3653-0*) Garland Publishing, Inc.

—The History of Miss Betsy Thoughtless. 1997. (Oxford World's Classics Ser.). (Illus.). 624p. pap. 14.95 o.p. (*0-19-282490-2*) Oxford Univ. Pr., Inc.

Heath, Roy A. The Shadow Bride. 1995. 428p. 24.95 (*0-89255-213-1*) Persea Bks., Inc.

Heller, Jane. The Secret Ingredient. l.t. ed. 2002. 523p. 30.95 (*0-7862-3916-6*) Gale Group.

—The Secret Ingredient. 2002. 336p. 24.95 (*0-312-26172-1*); 2003. 352p. reprint ed. mass mkt. 6.99 (*0-312-98673-4*, St. Martin's Paperbacks) St. Martin's Pr.

Heller, Keith. The Woman Who Knew Gandhi: A Novel. 2004. 224p. pap. 12.00 (*0-618-33545-5*) Houghton Mifflin Co. Trade & Reference Div.

Hemingway, Ernest. The Garden of Eden. unabr. collector's ed. 1990. audio 48.00 (*0-7366-1822-8*, 2658) Books on Tape, Inc.

—The Garden of Eden. 1987. 251p. pap. 9.95 o.s.i (*0-684-18871-6*); 1986. 250p. 18.95 o.s.i (*0-684-18693-4*); 1987. 300p. 19.95 o.p. (*0-8161-4152-5*); 1987. 300p. 11.95 o.p. (*0-8161-4153-3*) Gale Group. (Macmillan Reference USA).

—The Garden of Eden. 1995. 256p. pap. 12.00 (*0-684-80452-2*, Scribner) Simon & Schuster.

Henke, Roxanne. Becoming Olivia. 2004. (Coming Home to Brewster Ser.). pap. 11.99 (*0-7369-1149-9*) Harvest Hse. Pubs.

Hiaasen, Carl. Stormy Weather. l.t. ed. 1996. 26.95 (*1-56895-276-7*, Wheeler Publishing, Inc.) Gale Group.

—Stormy Weather. 1995. 352p. 24.00 o.s.i (*0-679-41982-9*) Knopf, Alfred A. Inc.

—Stormy Weather. reprint ed. 2001. 416p. pap. 14.95 (*0-446-67716-7*); 1996. 400p. mass mkt. 7.99 (*0-446-60342-2*) Warner Bks., Inc.

Highsmith, Patricia. A Suspension of Mercy. 2001. 235p. pap. 11.00 (*0-393-32197-5*) Norton, W. W. & Co., Inc.

—A Suspension of Mercy. 1982. 208p. pap. 3.95 o.p. (*0-14-003470-6*, Penguin Bks.) Viking Penguin.

Hill, Rebecca. Among Birches. 1986. 352p. 17.95 o.p. (*0-688-06165-6*, Morrow, William & Co.) Morrow/Avon.

—Among Birches. 1987. 320p. pap. 6.95 o.p. (*0-14-009852-6*, Penguin Bks.) Viking Penguin.

Hornby, Nick. How to Be Good. 2002. 320p. pap. 13.00 (*1-57322-932-6*, Riverhead Trade (Paperbacks)) Berkley Publishing Group.

—How to Be Good. 2001. 320p. 24.95 o.s.i (*1-57322-193-7*, Riverhead Bks. (Hardcovers)) Putnam Publishing Group, The.

Howells, William Dean. A Hazard of New Fortunes. 2002. (Modern Library Classics). 624p. pap. 13.95 (*0-375-75927-1*, Modern Library) Random House Adult Trade Publishing Group.

—A Modern Instance. unabr. ed. 1997. (J). (gr. 10 up). audio 65.95 (*1-55685-461-7*, 461-7) Audio Bk. Contractors, Inc.

—A Modern Instance. 1882. 255p. (YA). reprint ed. pap. text 28.00 (*1-4047-3235-7*) Classic Textbooks.

—A Modern Instance, 001. Gibson, W., ed. 1957. (YA). (gr. 9 up). pap. 13.16 o.p. (*0-395-05119-3*, Riverside Editions) Houghton Mifflin Co.

—A Modern Instance. 1977. (Selected Edition of W. D. Howells Ser.: Vol. 10). 608p. 20.00 o.p. (*0-253-33864-6*) Indiana Univ. Pr.

—A Modern Instance. mass mkt. 0.75 o.p. (*0-451-50249-3*, Signet Classics) NAL.

—A Modern Instance. 2003. (Twelve-Point Ser.). lib. bdg. 25.00 (*1-58287-220-1*); lib. bdg. 26.00 (*1-58287-704-1*) North Bks.

—A Modern Instance. 1992. (Notable American Authors Ser.). reprint ed. lib. bdg. 75.00 (*0-7812-3235-X*) Reprint Services Corp.

—A Modern Instance. l.t. ed. 1999. 524p. text 27.95 (*1-56000-487-8*) Transaction Pubs.

—A Modern Instance. 1984. (Classics Ser.). 480p. (C). 14.00 (*0-14-039027-8*, Penguin Classics) Viking Penguin.

Humphreys, Emyr. The Gift of a Daughter. 2000. 240p. 22.00 (*1-85411-222-8*) Seren Bks. GBR. *Dist:* Dufour Editions, Inc.

Hustvedt, Siri. What I Loved: A Novel. 2003. 384p. 25.00 (*0-8050-7170-9*) Holt, Henry & Co.

—What I Loved: A Novel. 2004. 384p. pap. 14.00 (*0-312-42119-2*); 2003. mass mkt. 7.99 (*0-312-99387-0*) Picador.

Huth, Angela. Invitation to the Married Life: A Novel. 1992. 304p. 19.95 o.p. (*0-8021-1465-2*) Grove/Atlantic, Inc.

Iakovou, Takis & Iakovou, Judy. Go Close Against the Enemy. 1999. (WWL Mystery Ser.: Bk. 314). 256p. per. (*0-373-26314-7*, 1-26314-4, Worldwide Library) Harlequin Enterprises, Ltd.

—Go Close Against the Enemy. 1998. 288p. 23.95 o.p. (*0-312-18587-1*, Saint Martin's Minotaur) St. Martin's Pr.

—So Dear to Wicked Men. 1998. (WWL Mystery Ser.). per. (*0-373-26277-9*, 1-26277-3, Worldwide Library) Harlequin Enterprises, Ltd.

—So Dear to Wicked Men, Vol. 1. 1996. (So Dear to Wicked Men Ser.: Vol. 1). 320p. 22.95 (*0-312-14740-6*, Saint Martin's Minotaur) St. Martin's Pr.

Irving, John. The 158-Pound Marriage. 1997. 176p. pap. 13.95 (*0-345-41796-8*); 1990. 256p. mass mkt. 6.99 (*0-345-36743-X*) Ballantine Bks.

—The 158-Pound Marriage. 1982. mass mkt. 3.95 (*0-671-46811-1*, Pocket) Simon & Schuster.

Isaacs, Susan. Almost Paradise. 1984. 500p. 16.95 o.p. (*0-06-015236-2*) HarperTrade.

Jackson, Brenda. Ties That Bind: A Novel. 2002. 368p. pap. 13.95 (*0-312-30611-3*, Saint Martin's Griffin) St. Martin's Pr.

Jacobs, Pat. Going Inland. Padayachee, Vishnu, ed. 2002. 216p. pap. 17.95 o.s.i (*1-86368-374-7*) Fremantle Arts Centre Pr. AUS. *Dist:* International Specialized Bk. Services.

—Going Inland. l.t. ed. 2000. (Ulverscroft Large Print Ser.). 320p. 31.99 (*0-7089-4282-2*, Ulverscroft) Thorpe, F. A. Pubs. GBR. *Dist:* Ulverscroft Large Print Bks., Ltd., Ulverscroft Large Print Canada, Ltd.

Jacobson, Alan. The Hunted. 2001. 416p. 24.95 (*0-671-02680-1*); reprint ed. E-Book 24.95 (*0-7434-2202-3*) Simon & Schuster. (Atria).

Jagose, Annamarie. Lulu: A Romance. 1998. 208p. (*0-86473-332-1*) Victoria Univ. Pr.

James, Henry. The Portrait of a Lady: Complete Text with Introduction, Historical Contexts. Cohn, Jan, ed. 2001. (New Riverside Editions Ser.). viii, 619p. 12.36 (*0-618-10735-5*) Houghton Mifflin Co.

—The Real Thing. 2000. 252p. E-Book 3.95 (*0-594-05606-3*) 1873 Pr.

—The Sacred Fount. 2000. 252p. E-Book 9.95 (*0-594-05443-5*) 1873 Pr.

—The Sacred Fount. 2000. audio 35.95 (*1-55685-605-9*) Audio Bk. Contractors, Inc.

—The Sacred Fount. 1979. reprint ed. pap. 4.95 o.p. (*0-394-17081-4*, B418, Grove Pr.) Grove/Atlantic, Inc.

—The Sacred Fount. 1995. (Revived Modern Classic Ser.: Vol. 790). 236p. pap. 11.95 (*0-8112-1279-3*, NDP790) New Directions Publishing Corp.

—The Sacred Fount. 1992. (Notable American Authors Ser.). reprint ed. lib. bdg. 75.00 (*0-7812-3428-X*) Reprint Services Corp.

—The Sacred Fount. Lyon, John, ed. & intro. by. 1995. (Penguin Classics Ser.). 240p. pap. 10.95 o.p. (*0-14-043350-3*, Penguin Classics) Viking Penguin.

James, Kay-Marie. Cooking for Harry: A Low-Carbohydrate Novel. 2004. 208p. 21.00 (*1-4000-4502-9*, Shaye Areheart Bks.) Crown Publishing Group.

Janowitz, Tama. A Cannibal in Manhattan. 1989. (Illus.). 256p. 3.99 o.p. (*0-517-56624-9*) Random Hse. Value Publishing.

Jones, Patricia. Red on a Rose: A Novel. 2001. 352p. (Orig.). pap. 14.00 (*0-380-81730-6*, Avon Bks.) Morrow/Avon.

Jones, Susanna. Water Lily. 2003. 224p. 23.95 (*0-89296-776-5*) Mysterious Pr.

—Water Lily. 2004. 224p. pap. 12.95 (*0-446-69168-2*, Mysterious Pr. Paperback Bks.) Warner Bks., Inc.

Jordan, Neil. The Dream of a Beast. 1989. 12.95 o.s.i (*0-394-57314-5*) Random Hse., Inc.

Joyce, James. Ulysses. 2001. (Modern Library Ser.). E-Book 9.95 (*1-931208-63-8*) Adobe Systems, Inc.

—Ulysses: A Reproduction of the 1922 First Edition. 2002. (Illus.). 736p. pap. 29.95 (*0-486-42444-8*) Dover Pubns., Inc.

Kelly, Susan S. Even Now. 2001. 288p. 22.95 o.p. (*0-446-52762-9*) Warner Bks., Inc.

Kennedy, William P. Dark Tide: A Novel of Suspense. l.t. ed. 1995. 535p. lib. bdg. 25.95 o.p. (*0-7838-1286-8*, Macmillan Reference USA) Gale Group.

—Dark Tide: A Novel of Suspense. 1996. 374p. pap. text 5.99 (*0-312-95776-9*, St. Martin's Paperbacks); 1995. 359p. 22.95 o.p. (*0-312-11768-X*) St. Martin's Pr.

Kenney, Susan. Sailing. l.t. ed. 1989. (General Ser.). 480p. 19.95 o.p. (*0-8161-4726-4*, Macmillan Reference USA) Gale Group.

—Sailing. 1989. 336p. pap. 8.95 o.p. (*0-14-009333-8*, Penguin Bks.); 1988. 318p. 18.95 o.p. (*0-670-81229-3*) Viking Penguin.

Kent, Gordon. Top Hook. 2003. 576p. mass mkt. 6.99 (*0-440-23749-1*, Dell Bks.); 2002. 480p. 24.95 (*0-385-33627-6*, Delacorte Pr.) Dell Publishing.

King-Scott, Jackie. The Allure. 2003. pap. 9.99 (*0-8024-1562-8*) Moody Pr.

Klavan, Andrew. Man & Wife: A Novel of Psychological Suspense. l.t. ed. 2002. lib. bdg. 28.95 (*1-58547-205-0*, Premier) Ctr. Point Large Print.

—Man & Wife: A Novel of Psychological Suspense. 304p. 2001. 24.95 (*0-7653-0215-2*); 2003. reprint ed. mass mkt. 6.99 (*0-7653-4137-9*) Doherty, Tom Assocs., LLC. (Forge Bks.).

Knight, Arthur Winfield. Blue Skies Falling. 2001. 224p. 22.95 (*0-312-87779-X*, Forge Bks.) Doherty, Tom Assocs., LLC.

Krentz, Jayne Ann. Between the Lines. 2000. 256p. mass mkt. (*1-55166-595-6*, 1-66595-8, Mira Bks.); 1993. mass mkt. (*0-373-83270-2*, 1-83270-8, Harlequin Bks.); 1986. mass mkt. (*0-373-25225-0*, Harlequin Bks.) Harlequin Enterprises, Ltd.

—Between the Lines. l.t. ed. 2002. (Thorndike Romance Ser.). 288p. 30.95 (*0-7862-4002-4*) Thorndike Pr.

—Truth or Dare. 2003. 24.95 (*0-399-14999-6*) Putnam Publishing Group, The.

—The Wedding Night. l.t. ed. 2002. 260p. 30.95 (*0-7862-4142-X*) Gale Group.

—The Wedding Night. 2001. 256p. mass mkt. (*1-55166-851-3*); 1991. (Harlequin Temptation Ser.: No. 365). mass mkt. (*0-373-25465-2*) Harlequin Enterprises, Ltd. (Harlequin Bks.).

Lange, Kelly. The Trophy Wife. 1995. 382p. 23.00 o.p. (*0-684-80191-4*, Simon & Schuster) Simon & Schuster.

Langley, Lee. Persistent Rumours. 304p. 1998. pap. 14.95 (*1-57131-014-2*); 1994. 21.95 (*1-57131-001-0*) Milkweed Editions.

Larrabee, Kathryn. An Everyday Savior. 2002. 288p. 24.95 (*1-56858-225-0*) Four Walls Eight Windows.

Law, Janice. The Night Bus. 352p. 2000. 24.95 o.s.i (*0-312-84882-X*); 2001. reprint ed. pap. 15.95 (*0-312-87599-1*) Doherty, Tom Assocs., LLC. (Forge Bks.).

Leavitt, Caroline. Coming Back to Me: A Novel. 2003. 320p. pap. 13.95 (*0-312-30554-0*, Saint Martin's Griffin) St. Martin's Pr.

Leavitt, David. The Lost Language of Cranes. 1997. 368p. pap. 12.00 o.p. (*0-395-87733-4*) Houghton Mifflin Co.

—The Lost Language of Cranes. 1988. 3.99 o.p. (*0-517-67347-9*) Random Hse. Value Publishing.

Leebron, Fred G. In the Middle of All This. 264p. 2004. pap. 13.00 (*0-15-602742-9*, Harvest Bks.); 2002. 24.00 (*0-15-100834-5*) Harcourt Trade Pubs.

Leith, Prue. Leaving Patrick. l.t. ed. 2000. (General Ser.). viii, 429p. pap. 23.95 (*0-7862-2419-3*) Thorndike Pr.

Leonard, Hugh. A Wild People: A Novel. 2002. 288p. 23.95 (*0-312-29029-2*) St. Martin's Pr.

Leroy, Margaret. Postcards from Berlin. 2003. 400p. 22.95 (*0-316-73813-1*) Little Brown & Co.

Lescroart, John. Nothing but the Truth. 1999. mass mkt. 7.99 (*0-440-29574-2*) Bantam Dell Publishing Group.

—Nothing but the Truth. 2000. mass mkt. 7.99 (*0-440-22664-3*); 448p. 24.95 o.s.i (*0-385-33353-6*, Delacorte Pr.) Dell Publishing.

—Nothing but the Truth. l.t. ed. 2000. 27.95 (*1-56895-813-7*, Wheeler Publishing, Inc.) Gale Group.

—Nothing but the Truth. 2001. 464p. mass mkt. 7.99 (*0-451-20285-6*) NAL.

—Nothing but the Truth. abr. ed. 2000. audio 25.95 (*0-553-52662-6*, RH Audio) Random Hse. Audio Publishing Group.

Lewis, Sinclair. Main Street. E-Book 3.95 (*0-594-05716-7*) 1873 Pr.

—Main Street. 1976. 25.95 (*0-8488-0828-2*) Amereon, Ltd.

—Main Street. 1996. 496p. pap. 10.95 (*0-7867-0325-3*, Carroll & Graf Pubs.) Avalon Publishing Group.

—Main Street. 1996. 544p. mass mkt. 5.95 (*0-553-21451-9*) Bantam Bks.

—Main Street. 1984. 297p. reprint ed. lib. bdg. 31.95 (*0-89966-495-4*) Buccaneer Bks., Inc.

—Main Street. reprint ed. lib. bdg. 48.00 (*0-7426-1369-0*); 2001. 451p. pap. 28.00 (*0-7426-5673-X*); 2001. pap. text 28.00 (*0-7426-6369-8*); 1998. 451p. lib. bdg. 108.00 (*1-58201-673-9*) Classic Bks.

—Main Street. unabr. ed. 1999. (Dover Thrift Editions Ser.). iv, 400p. pap. text 2.50 (*0-486-40655-5*) Dover Pubns., Inc.

—Main Street. 2003. (Barnes & Noble Classics Ser.). 576p. pap. 5.95 (*1-59308-036-0*) Fine Communications.

—Main Street. 1989. (Modern Classic Ser.). 451p. 15.95 o.s.i (*0-15-155547-8*) Harcourt Trade Pubs.

—Main Street. l.t. ed. 1394p. pap. 88.64 (*0-7583-1460-4*); 1714p. pap. 111.80 (*0-7583-1461-2*); 2109p. pap. 127.07 (*0-7583-1462-0*); 1089p. pap. 74.20 (*0-7583-1459-0*); 2446p. pap. 149.71 (*0-7583-1463-9*); 851p. pap. 62.17 (*0-7583-1458-2*); 621p. pap. 44.14 (*0-7583-1457-4*); 497p. pap. 37.12 (*0-7583-1456-6*); 2446p. lib. bdg. 180.60 (*0-7583-1455-8*); 2109p. lib. bdg. 149.57 (*0-7583-1454-X*); 1714p. lib. bdg. 129.80 (*0-7583-1453-1*); 1394p. lib. bdg. 100.64 (*0-7583-1452-3*); 1089p. lib. bdg. 86.20 (*0-7583-1451-5*); 851p. lib. bdg. 74.17 (*0-7583-1450-7*); 621p. lib. bdg. 50.14 (*0-7583-1449-3*); 497p. lib. bdg. 43.12 (*0-7583-1448-5*) Huge Print Pr.

—Main Street. 2002. 472p. 28.99 (*1-4043-1584-5*); per. 23.99 (*1-4043-1585-3*) IndyPublish.com.

—Main Street. 1999. 518p. pap. 9.95 o.p. (*1-930128-08-8*, JNMedia Bks.) JNMedia, Inc.

—Main Street. (*0-451-52742-9*); mass mkt. 0.95 o.p. (*0-451-02005-7*, Signet Bks.); 1970. mass mkt. 1.25 o.p. (*0-451-50500-X*, Signet Classics); 1970. mass mkt. 0.95 o.p. (*0-451-50352-X*, Signet Classics); 1970. mass mkt. 0.75 o.p. (*0-451-50093-8*, Signet Classics); 1961. 440p. mass mkt. 4.50 o.p. (*0-451-52147-1*, Signet Classics); 1961. mass mkt. 3.50 o.p. (*0-451-51831-4*, Signet Classics); 1961. mass mkt. 3.50 o.p. (*0-451-51712-1*, Signet Classics); 1961. mass mkt. 2.95 o.p. (*0-451-51536-6*, Signet Classics); 1961. mass mkt. 2.50 o.p. (*0-451-51392-4*, Signet Classics); 1961. mass mkt. 2.25 o.p. (*0-451-51140-9*, Signet Classics); 1961. mass mkt. 1.50 o.p. (*0-451-50753-3*, Signet Classics); 1961. 448p. mass mkt. 5.95 o.s.i (*0-451-52461-6*, Signet Classics); 1961. mass mkt. 1.75 o.p. (*0-451-50875-0*, Signet Classics); 1961. mass mkt. 3.95 o.p. (*0-451-51898-5*, Signet Classics); 1998. 440p. mass mkt. 5.95 (*0-451-52682-1*, Signet Bks.) NAL.

—Main Street. 2001. 510p. 25.00 (*1-58287-154-X*); 650p. lib. bdg. 26.00 (*1-58287-637-1*) North Bks.

—Main Street. 1996. (Literary Classics). 459p. pap. 10.00 (*1-57392-048-7*) Prometheus Bks., Pubs.

—Main Street. 2000. E-Book 4.95 (*0-679-64167-X*, Modern Library) Random House Adult Trade Publishing Group.

—Main Street. 1999. (Modern Library Ser.). 448p. pap. 9.95 o.s.i (*0-375-75314-1*) Random Hse., Inc.

—Main Street. E-Book 5.00 (*0-7410-0558-1*) SoftBook Pr.

—Main Street. 1920. 12.00 (*0-606-01015-7*) Turtleback Bks.

—Main Street. 1995. (Twentieth Century Classics Ser.). 448p. pap. 11.00 (*0-14-018901-7*, Penguin Classics) Viking Penguin.

—Main Street. 1999. E-Book 5.99 (*0-8220-7126-6*, Cliff Notes) Wiley, John & Sons, Inc.

—Sinclair Lewis: Main Street & Babbitt. Hersey, John, ed. 1992. (Library of America: Vol. 59). 898p. 40.00 (*0-940450-61-5*) Library of America, The.

Lewis, Sinclair & Hersey, John. Main Street & Babbitt. 1992. E-Book 40.00 (*0-585-20170-6*) netLibrary, Inc.

Livingston, Nancy. Two Sisters. 1994. 592p. 25.95 o.p. (*0-312-11346-3*) St. Martin's Pr.

Loh, Sandra Tsing. If You Lived Here, You'd Be Home by Now: A Novel. 1998. 240p. 13.00 o.s.i (*1-57322-695-5*, Riverhead Trade (Paperbacks)) Berkley Publishing Group.

—If You Lived Here, You'd Be Home by Now: A Novel. 1997. 224p. 23.95 o.p. (1-57322-068-X, Riverhead Bks. (Hardcovers)) Putnam Publishing Group, The.

London, Jack. The Valley of the Moon. unabr. ed. 1992. audio 64.95 (1-55686-434-5, 434) Books in Motion.

—The Valley of the Moon. 1998. (Collected Works of Jack London). 530p. reprint ed. lib. bdg. 118.00 (1-58201-748-4) Classic Bks.

—The Valley of the Moon. E-Book 1.95 (1-58515-165-3) MesaView, Inc.

—The Valley of the Moon. 1999. (California Fiction Ser.). 436p. pap. text 16.95 (0-520-21820-5) Univ. of California Pr.

Lordan, Beth. But Come Ye Back: A Novel. 2004. 288p. 23.95 (0-06-053036-7, Morrow, William & Co.) Morrow/Avon.

Lynn, Alison. One Man Missing. 2004. 224p. pap. 13.00 (0-7432-5026-5, Touchstone) Simon & Schuster.

Mackay, Shena. An Advent Calendar. 1997. 160p. 19.95 (1-55921-211-X) Moyer Bell.

Margolis, David. The Stepman. 1996. 192p. 24.00 (1-877946-76-1) Permanent Pr., The.

Marquis, Christopher. A Hole in the Heart: A Novel. 2003. 320p. 24.95 (0-312-30630-X) St. Martin's Pr.

Martin, Lou. Above the Slate: An Appalachian Love Story. 2002. 217p. 12.00 (1-931672-11-3) Stuart, Jesse Foundation, The.

Mason, Bobbie A. Spence & Lila. 1988. (Illus.). 96p. (YA). 12.95 o.p. (0-06-015911-1) HarperTrade.

Mason, Bobbie Ann. Spence & Lila. 1989. (Illus.). 176p. reprint ed. pap. 10.00 o.p. (0-06-091559-5, PL 1559, Perennial) HarperTrade.

—Spence & Lila: A Love Story. 1998. (Illus.). 176p. pap. 13.00 (0-88001-594-2, Ecco) HarperTrade.

Mason, Richard. The Drowning People. 1999. 352p. o.s.i (0-385-25830-5) Doubleday Canada, Ltd. CAN. *Dist:* Random Hse., Inc.

—The Drowning People. 1999. 288p. 24.00 o.p. (0-446-52524-3); 2000. 400p. reprint ed. mass mkt. 7.50 (0-446-60800-9) Warner Bks., Inc.

McCauley, Stephen. True Enough: A Novel. 2002. 320p. pap. 14.00 (0-7434-4403-5, Washington Square Pr.) Simon & Schuster.

McCullers, Carson. Reflections in a Golden Eye. 1990. 160p. mass mkt. 4.99 o.s.i (0-553-56968-6) Bantam Bks.

—Reflections in a Golden Eye. 2000. 182p. pap. 10.00 (0-618-08475-4, Mariner Bks.) Houghton Mifflin Co. Trade & Reference Div.

McInerney, Jay. Brightness Falls. 1993. (Vintage Contemporaries Ser.). 432p. pap. 14.00 (0-679-74532-7, Vintage) Knopf Publishing Group.

McKnight, Reginald. He Sleeps: A Novel. 2002. 224p. pap. 13.00 (0-312-42104-4) Picador.

McMurtry, Larry. Moving On, Pt. 1. unabr. collector's ed. 1992. audio 80.00 (0-7366-2185-7, 2981-A) Books on Tape, Inc.

—Moving On. Grose, Bill, ed. 1991. mass mkt. 7.99 (0-671-74408-9, Pocket) Simon & Schuster.

—Moving On. 800p. 1987. pap. 11.00 (0-671-63320-1, Touchstone); 1999. reprint ed. pap. 15.00 (0-684-85388-4, Simon & Schuster) Simon & Schuster.

Michaels, Fern. Desperate Measures. 1996. 448p. mass mkt. 6.99 (0-8041-1536-2, Ivy Bks.) Ballantine Bks.

Michaels, Lisa. Grand Ambition: A Novel. l.t. ed. 2001. 275p. 26.95 (1-57490-374-8, Beeler Large Print Bks.) Beeler, Thomas T. Publisher.

—Grand Ambition: A Novel. 288p. 2002. pap. 13.95 (0-393-32295-5); 2001. (Illus.). 23.95 (0-393-05047-5) Norton, W. W. & Co., Inc.

Middleton, Stanley. Valley of Decision. 1987. 232p. 15.95 (0-941533-08-5, New Amsterdam Bks) Dee, Ivan R. Pub.

Miller, Sue. The Distinguished Guest. 1995. 288p. 24.00 o.p. (0-06-017673-3) HarperCollins Pubs.

—The World Below. 2001. E-Book 20.00 (1-59061-312-0) Adobe Systems, Inc.

—The World Below. 2001. 288p. 25.00 (0-375-41094-5) Knopf, Alfred A. Inc.

—The World Below. unabr. ed. 2001. audio 34.95 (0-375-41993-4); audio compact disk 39.95 (0-375-41994-2) Random Hse. Audio Publishing Group. (RH Audio).

—The World Below. l.t. ed. 2001. 448p. 25.00 (0-375-43131-4) Random Hse. Large Print.

—The World Below. 2002. 304p. pap. 13.95 (0-345-44076-5) Random Hse., Inc.

Milofsky, David. Playing from Memory. 1982. 304p. pap. 2.95 o.p. (0-380-57166-8, 57166-8, Avon Bks.) Morrow/Avon.

—Playing from Memory. 1981. 12.95 o.p. (0-671-25252-6, Simon & Schuster) Simon & Schuster.

—Playing from Memory. 1999. 270p. reprint ed. pap. 14.95 (0-87081-526-1) Univ. Pr. of Colorado.

Minatra, MaryAnn. Before Night Falls. 1996. (Legacy of Honor Ser.: Vol. 1). 420p. pap. 10.99 o.s.i (1-56507-432-7) Harvest Hse. Pubs.

Moggach, Deborah. Close to Home. 1998. 249p. mass mkt. o.p. (0-7493-1229-7) Random Hse. of Canada, Ltd.

—Close to Home. l.t. ed. 2001. 273p. pap. 24.95 (0-7862-3485-7) Thorndike Pr.

Moore, Brian. Cold Heaven. 1997. 272p. reprint ed. pap. 12.95 o.s.i (0-452-27867-8, Plume) Dutton/Plume.

—Cold Heaven. 1983. o.p. (0-03-063257-9) Holt, Henry & Co.

Moran, Thomas. Anja the Liar. 2003. 336p. 25.95 (1-57322-260-7, Riverhead Bks. (Hardcovers)) Putnam Publishing Group, The.

Morgan, Robert. The Truest Pleasure. 1998. 334p. pap. 12.95 (1-56512-222-4); 1995. 336p. tchr. ed. 18.95 o.p. (1-56512-105-8, 72105) Algonquin Bks. of Chapel Hill.

—The Truest Pleasure. unabr. ed. 1999. audio 69.95 (0-7927-2298-1, CSL187, Chivers Sound Library) BBC Audiobooks America.

—The Truest Pleasure. abr. ed. 2000. 18.95 (1-56511-389-6) HighBridge Co.

Morrison, Toni. Tar Baby. 1987. pap. 8.95 o.p. (0-452-25258-X); 1987. 352p. pap. 7.95 o.p. (0-452-26012-4, Z5326); 1987. 320p. pap. 12.95 (0-452-26479-0); 1982. pap. 6.95 o.p. (0-452-25326-8) Dutton/Plume. (Plume).

—Tar Baby. 2004. 320p. pap. 13.00 (1-4000-3344-6, Vintage) Knopf Publishing Group.

—Tar Baby. 1981. 320p. 26.95 (0-394-42329-1) Knopf, Alfred A. Inc.

—Tar Baby. 1993. pap. 5.99 o.s.i (0-451-18238-3); 1983. mass mkt. 3.95 o.p. (0-451-12224-0); 1983. 272p. mass mkt. 5.99 o.p. (0-451-16639-6); 1983. 320p. mass mkt. 4.50 o.p. (0-451-15260-3) NAL. (Signet Bks.).

—Tar Baby. 1983. 19.00 (0-606-01962-6) Turtleback Bks.

Morrissy, Mary. Mother of Pearl: A Novel. 1995. 281p. 22.00 o.p. (0-684-19667-0, Scribner) Simon & Schuster.

Moyes, Patricia. Angel Death. 1982. (Henry Tibbett Mystery Ser.). 240p. pap. 5.95 o.s.i (0-8050-0505-6, Owl Bks.) Holt, Henry & Co.

—Angel Death. l.t. ed. 1982. (Henry Tibbett Mystery Ser.). 457p. 12.50 o.p. (0-7089-0746-6, Ulverscroft) Thorpe, F. A. Pubs. GBR. *Dist:* Ulverscroft Large Print Bks., Ltd., Ulverscroft Large Print Canada, Ltd.

—Black Girl, White Girl. unabr. ed. 1993. (Henry Tibbett Mystery Ser.). audio 36.00 (0-7366-2327-2, 3107) Books on Tape, Inc.

—Black Girl, White Girl. l.t. ed. 1991. (Henry Tibbett Mystery Ser.). 326p. lib. bdg. 19.95 o.p. (0-8161-5011-7, Macmillan Reference USA) Gale Group.

—Black Girl, White Girl. (Henry Tibbett Mystery Ser.). 224p. 1990. pap. 5.95 o.s.i (0-8050-1149-8, Owl Bks.); 1989. 15.95 o.p. (0-8050-1148-X) Holt, Henry & Co.

—Black Widower. unabr. ed. 1992. (Henry Tibbett Mystery Ser.). audio 42.00 (0-7366-2272-1, 3060) Books on Tape, Inc.

—Black Widower. 1985. (Henry Tibbett Mystery Ser.). 224p. pap. 5.95 o.s.i (0-8050-0243-X, Owl Bks.) Holt, Henry & Co.

—Black Widower. 1977. (Henry Tibbett Mystery Ser.). 224p. pap. 2.95 o.p. (0-14-004334-9, Penguin Bks.) Viking Penguin.

—The Coconut Killings. (Henry Tibbett Mystery Ser.). 1985. 224p. pap. 5.95 o.s.i (0-8050-0754-7, Owl Bks.); 1985. pap. o.p. (0-03-005608-X, Owl Bks.); 1977. o.p. (0-03-018481-9) Holt, Henry & Co.

—The Coconut Killings. 1979. (Henry Tibbett Mystery Ser.). pap. 1.95 o.p. (0-14-004593-7, Penguin Bks.) Viking Penguin.

—The Curious Affair of the Third Dog. unabr. ed. 1993. (Henry Tibbett Mystery Ser.). audio 44.95 (0-7861-0428-7, 1380) Blackstone Audio Bks., Inc.

—The Curious Affair of the Third Dog. 1986. (Henry Tibbett Mystery Ser.). 224p. pap. 5.95 o.s.i (0-8050-0503-X); pap. o.p. (0-03-009534-4) Holt, Henry & Co. (Owl Bks.).

—The Curious Affair of the Third Dog. 1976. (Henry Tibbett Mystery Ser.). 208p. pap. 1.95 o.p. (0-14-004027-7, Penguin Bks.) Viking Penguin.

—Death & the Dutch Uncle. 1983. (Henry Tibbett Mystery Ser.). 256p. pap. 5.95 o.s.i (0-8050-0506-4, Owl Bks.) Holt, Henry & Co.

—Death on the Agenda. 1984. (Henry Tibbett Mystery Ser.). 192p. pap. 5.95 o.s.i (0-8050-0507-2, Owl Bks.) Holt, Henry & Co.

—Down among the Dead Men. (Henry Tibbett Mystery Ser.). 18.50 o.p. (0-86220-823-8, BD022, Black Dagger); 1994. 18.95 o.p. (0-7451-6461-7) BBC Audiobooks America.

—Down among the Dead Men. 1982. (Henry Tibbett Mystery Ser.). 240p. pap. 2.50 o.p. (0-440-11627-9) Dell Publishing.

—Down among the Dead Men. 1986. (Henry Tibbett Mystery Ser.). 240p. pap. 5.95 o.s.i (0-8050-0117-4, Owl Bks.) Holt, Henry & Co.

—Falling Star. 1982. (Henry Tibbett Mystery Ser.). (Orig.). 256p. pap. 5.95 o.s.i (0-8050-0755-5); pap. o.p. (0-03-059784-6) Holt, Henry & Co. (Owl Bks.).

—Johnny under Ground. (Henry Tibbett Mystery Ser.). 18.50 o.p. (0-86220-789-4, C1029, Black Dagger); 1993. 18.95 o.p. (0-7451-6441-2); 1996. audio 54.95 (0-7451-2414-3, CDA015) BBC Audiobooks America.

—Johnny under Ground. 1983. (Henry Tibbett Mystery Ser.). pap. 2.95 o.p. (0-440-14211-3) Dell Publishing.

—Johnny under Ground. Barzun, Jacques & Taylor, W. H., eds. 1983. (Henry Tibbett Mystery Ser.). 253p. lib. bdg. 18.00 o.p. (0-8240-4987-X) Garland Publishing, Inc.

—Johnny under Ground: An Inspector Henry Tibbett Mystery. 1987. (Henry Tibbett Mystery Ser.). 256p. pap. 5.95 o.s.i (0-8050-0270-7, Owl Bks.) Holt, Henry & Co.

—Many Deadly Returns. unabr. ed. 1994. (Henry Tibbett Mystery Ser.). audio 49.95 (0-7861-0433-3, 1385) Blackstone Audio Bks., Inc.

—Many Deadly Returns. 1981. (Henry Tibbett Mystery Ser.). pap. 2.25 o.p. (0-440-16172-X) Dell Publishing.

—Many Deadly Returns: An Inspector Henry Tibbett Mystery. 1987. (Henry Tibbett Mystery Ser.). 256p. pap. 5.95 o.s.i (0-8050-0598-6, Owl Bks.) Holt, Henry & Co.

—Murder a la Mode. 1983. (Henry Tibbett Mystery Ser.). 224p. pap. 5.95 o.s.i (0-8050-0706-7, Owl Bks.) Holt, Henry & Co.

—Murder Fantastical. (Henry Tibbett Mystery Ser.). 189p. 12.95 o.p. (0-86220-722-3) Chivers Pr. GBR. *Dist:* BBC Audiobooks America.

—Murder Fantastical. 1984. (Henry Tibbett Mystery Ser.). 256p. pap. 5.95 o.s.i (0-8050-0504-8, Owl Bks.) Holt, Henry & Co.

—Night Ferry to Death. (Henry Tibbett Mystery Ser.). 192p. 1986. pap. 5.95 o.s.i (0-8050-0116-6, Owl Bks.); 1985. o.p. (0-03-004477-4) Holt, Henry & Co.

—Night Ferry to Death. l.t. ed. 1987. (Henry Tibbett Mystery Ser.). 336p. 29.99 o.p. (0-7089-1615-5, Ulverscroft) Thorpe, F. A. Pubs. GBR. *Dist:* Ulverscroft Large Print Bks., Ltd., Ulverscroft Large Print Canada, Ltd.

—Season of Snows & Sins. (Henry Tibbett Mystery Ser.). 1988. 224p. pap. 6.95 o.s.i (0-8050-0849-7); 1983. pap. o.p. (0-03-063542-X) Holt, Henry & Co. (Owl Bks.).

—A Six-Letter Word for Death. 1985. (Henry Tibbett Mystery Ser.). 256p. pap. 5.95 o.s.i (0-8050-0244-8, Owl Bks.) Holt, Henry & Co.

—A Six-Letter Word for Death. l.t. ed. 1984. (Henry Tibbett Mystery Ser.). 432p. 29.99 o.p. (0-7089-1163-3, Ulverscroft) Thorpe, F. A. Pubs. GBR. *Dist:* Ulverscroft Large Print Bks., Ltd., Ulverscroft Large Print Canada, Ltd.

—To Kill a Coconut. l.t. ed. 1981. (Ulverscroft Large Print Ser.). 336p. 29.99 o.p. (0-7089-0632-X, Ulverscroft) Thorpe, F. A. Pubs. GBR. *Dist:* Ulverscroft Large Print Bks., Ltd., Ulverscroft Large Print Canada, Ltd.

—Twice in a Blue Moon. (Henry Tibbett Mystery Ser.). 1994. pap. 5.95 o.s.i (0-8050-2948-6, Owl Bks.); 1993. 192p. 19.95 o.p. (0-8050-2823-4) Holt, Henry & Co.

—Who Is Simon Warwick? (Henry Tibbett Mystery Ser.). 1982. pap. o.p. (0-03-059783-8, Owl Bks.); 1982. 176p. pap. 5.95 o.s.i (0-8050-0719-9, Owl Bks.); 1979. 180p. o.p. (0-03-044726-7) Holt, Henry & Co.

Mukherjee, Bharati. Wife. 1992. reprint ed. mass mkt. 5.99 o.s.i (0-449-22098-2, Fawcett) Ballantine Bks.

—Wife, 001. 1975. 224p. 7.95 o.p. (0-395-20439-9) Houghton Mifflin Co.

—Wife. 1987. 224p. pap. 6.95 o.p. (0-14-009300-1, Penguin Bks.) Viking Penguin.

Murray, Victoria Christopher. Temptation. 2003. (African American Ser.). 28.95 (0-7862-5072-0) Thorndike Pr.

—Temptation. 2001. 400p. pap. 13.95 (0-446-67783-3); 2000. 368p. 19.95 o.p. (0-446-52792-0); 2000. 368p. E-Book 14.95 (0-446-92372-9); 2000. E-Book 14.95 (0-446-92864-X); 2000. 368p. E-Book 14.95 (0-446-96092-6); 2000. 368p. E-Book 14.95 (0-446-92263-3); 2000. 368p. E-Book 14.95 (0-446-91364-2); 2000. E-Book 14.95 (0-446-93136-5) Warner Bks., Inc.

Myerson, Julie. Something Might Happen. 2003. 336p. 23.95 (0-316-77984-9) Little Brown & Co.

Naumoff, Lawrence. The Night of the Weeping Women. 1989. 240p. mass mkt. 3.95 o.s.i (0-8041-0488-3, Ivy Bks.) Ballantine Bks.

—The Night of the Weeping Women. 1988. 252p. 16.95 o.p. (0-87113-187-0) Grove/Atlantic, Inc.

—The Night of the Weeping Women. 1997. (Harvest Book Ser.). 256p. pap. 11.00 (0-15-600364-3, Harvest Bks.) Harcourt Trade Pubs.

Neville, Jim. Swimming the Channel. 1994. 192p. 18.95 o.p. (0-312-11337-4) St. Martin's Pr.

Nicol, Margaret. Enemy of the Average. 1997. 622p. 25.00 (1-888310-60-X) Knoll, Allen A. Pubs.

Niffenegger, Audrey. The Time Traveler's Wife. 2004. 544p. pap. 14.00 (0-15-602943-X, Harvest Bks.) Harcourt Trade Pubs.

—The Time Traveler's Wife. 2003. 518p. 25.00 (1-931561-46-X) MacAdam/Cage Publishing, Inc.

—The Time Traveler's Wife: Today Show Book Club Edition. 2003. 518p. 25.00 (1-931561-64-8) MacAdam/Cage Publishing, Inc.

Nordberg, Bette. Pacific Hope. 2001. 384p. pap. 11.99 (0-7642-2397-6) Bethany Hse. Pubs.

Norris, Frank. McTeague. 2004. 272p. pap. 5.95 (0-486-43408-7) Dover Pubns., Inc.

—McTeague. 2003. 368p. mass mkt. 7.95 (0-451-52891-3); 1969. mass mkt. 0.60 o.p. (0-451-50201-9); 1969. mass mkt. 0.75 o.p. (0-451-50381-3); 1969. mass mkt. 0.95 o.p. (0-451-50479-8); 1964. mass mkt. 1.25 o.p. (0-451-50752-5); 1964. mass mkt. 1.50 o.p. (0-451-50957-9); 1964. mass mkt. 1.75 o.p. (0-451-51119-0); 1964. mass mkt. 1.95 o.p. (0-451-51303-7); 1964. mass mkt. 2.25 o.p. (0-451-51574-9); 1964. mass mkt. 2.50 o.p. (0-451-51790-3); 1964. mass mkt. 2.75 o.p. (0-451-51860-8); 1964. mass mkt. 2.95 o.p. (0-451-52049-1); 1964. mass mkt. 3.50 o.p. (0-451-52178-1) NAL. (Signet Classics).

—The Pit: A Story of Chicago. 1971. 432p. reprint ed. lib. bdg. 22.00 (0-8376-0407-9) Bentley Pubs.

—The Pit: A Story of Chicago. 1976. lib. bdg. 19.95 (0-89968-069-0, Lightyear Pr.) Buccaneer Bks., Inc.

—The Pit: A Story of Chicago. reprint ed. lib. bdg. 48.00 (0-7426-1189-2) Classic Bks.

—The Pit: A Story of Chicago. 1983. 7.50 o.p. (0-8446-0825-4) Smith, Peter Pub., Inc.

Oates, Joyce Carol. American Appetites. 1990. 352p. pap. 12.50 o.p. (0-06-097278-5, Perennial) HarperTrade.

—American Appetites. 1992. 4.99 o.p. (0-517-07979-8) Random Hse. Value Publishing.

O'Brien, Tim. In the Lake of the Woods. 1994. 320p. tchr. ed. 21.95 o.p. (0-395-48889-3) Houghton Mifflin Co.

—In the Lake of the Woods. 1996. o.p. (0-14-771179-7); 1995. 320p. pap. 14.00 (0-14-025094-8, Penguin Bks.) Penguin Group (USA) Inc.

O'Hara, John. Appointment in Samarra. (Modern Library Ser.). 1994. 364p. 14.95 o.s.i (0-679-60110-4); 1982. 256p. mass mkt. 10.00 o.s.i (0-394-71192-0); 1934. 3.00 o.p. (0-394-41542-6) Random Hse., Inc.

—Appointment in Samarra. 1993. reprint ed. lib. bdg. 89.00 (0-7812-5481-7) Reprint Services Corp.

—Appointment in Samarra. l.t. ed. 1998. (Perennial Bestsellers Ser.). 331p. 25.95 (0-7838-0376-1) Thorndike Pr.

Oke, Janette. A Quiet Strength. 1999. (Prairie Legacy Ser.: Vol. 3). 256p. text 16.99 o.p. (0-7642-2157-4) Bethany Hse. Pubs.

Olsen, Tillie. Tell Me a Riddle. 1988. pap. 7.95 o.s.i (0-440-55010-6, Delta); 1978. 8.95 o.s.i (0-440-08654-X, Delacorte Pr.); 1971. 128p. pap. 13.95 (0-385-29010-1, Delta) Dell Publishing.

—Tell Me a Riddle. Rosenfelt, Deborah S., ed. 1995. (Women Writers: Text & Contexts Ser.). 200p. (C). text 38.00 (0-8135-2136-X); pap. text 14.00 (0-8135-2137-8) Rutgers Univ. Pr.

—Tell Me a Riddle. 1984. 27.50 (0-8446-6090-6) Smith, Peter Pub., Inc.

Olsen, Tillie & Rosenfelt, Deborah Silverton. Tell Me a Riddle. 1995. E-Book 38.00 (0-585-00268-1) netLibrary, Inc.

O'Nan, Stewart. A World Away: A Novel. 352p. 1999. pap. 13.00 o.s.i (0-8050-5775-7, Owl Bks.); 1998. 23.00 o.s.i (0-8050-5774-9) Holt, Henry & Co.

—A World Away: A Novel. 2003. 352p. pap. 14.00 (0-312-42277-6) Picador.

Owen, Howard. Fat Lightning. 1996. 192p. pap. 11.00 o.p. (0-06-097676-4) HarperCollins Pubs.

—Fat Lightning. 1994. 181p. 24.00 (1-877946-41-9) Permanent Pr., The.

Oz, Amos. To Know a Woman. 1992. 272p. pap. 13.00 (0-15-690680-5, Harvest Bks.); 1991. 262p. 13.00 o.s.i (0-15-190499-5) Harcourt Trade Pubs.

—To Know a Woman. 262p. 4.98 o.p. (0-8317-7448-7) Smithmark Pubs., Inc.

Page, Patricia Margaret. Clean Start. 2002. 322p. 24.95 (0-89733-506-6) Academy Chicago Pubs., Ltd.

Palahniuk, Chuck. Diary: A Novel. 2003. 272p. 24.95 (0-385-50947-2) Doubleday Publishing.

Paling, Chris. Morning All Day. 1997. 193p. (0-224-04446-X) Cape, Jonathan Ltd. GBR. *Dist:* National Geographic Society, Trafalgar Square.

Palmer, Elizabeth. Plucking the Apple. l.t. ed. 1999. 396p. 27.95 (0-7838-8624-1, Macmillan Reference USA) Gale Group.

—Plucking the Apple. 1999. (Mira Bks.). 378p. mass mkt. (1-55166-493-3, 1-66493-7, Mira Bks.) Harlequin Enterprises, Ltd.

—Plucking the Apple. 1994. 272p. 20.95 o.p. (0-312-11326-9) St. Martin's Pr.

Palmer, Elizabeth, contrib. by. Plucking the Apple. 1999. (*0-7540-1300-6*) BBC Audiobooks America.

Pears, Iain. The Immaculate Deception. 2000. 224p. 25.00 o.s.i (*0-7432-1257-6*, Scribner); 2001. 272p. reprint ed. mass mkt. 7.99 (*0-7434-2208-2*, Pocket) Simon & Schuster.

—The Immaculate Deception. l.t. ed. 2001. (Thorndike Basic Ser.). 333p. 28.95 (*0-7862-3257-9*) Thorndike Pr.

Pellegrino, Charles R. Flying to Valhalla. 1993. 338p. 22.00 (*0-688-12506-9*, Morrow, William & Co.) Morrow/Avon.

Perdue, Tito. The New Austerities. 1993. 224p. 20.00 (*1-56145-086-3*) Peachtree Pubs., Ltd.

Pilcher, Rosamunde. Voices in Summer. l.t. ed. 1985. (Nightingale Ser.). 454p. 11.95 o.p. (*0-8161-3792-7*, Macmillan Reference USA) Gale Group.

—Voices in Summer. 1989. pap. 3.95 o.s.i (*0-312-91474-1*, St. Martin's Paperbacks); 1984. 288p. 13.95 o.p. (*0-312-85076-X*) St. Martin's Pr.

Plain, Belva. After the Fire. 2001. 448p. reprint ed. mass mkt. 7.99 (*0-440-23574-X*) Dell Publishing.

—After the Fire. l.t. ed. 544p. 2001. pap. 13.95 (*0-375-72805-8*); 2000. 25.95 (*0-375-40976-9*) Random Hse. Large Print.

—Promises. l.t. ed. (Paperback Bestsellers Ser.). 1997. 582p. pap. 27.95 (*0-7838-1841-6*); 1996. 512p. lib. bdg. 29.95 (*0-7838-1842-4*) Thorndike Pr.

Pousson, Martin. No Place, Louisiana. 2003. 272p. reprint ed. pap. 14.00 (*1-57322-976-8*, Riverhead Trade (Paperbacks)) Berkley Publishing Group.

—No Place, Louisiana. 2002. 240p. 24.95 o.s.i (*1-57322-200-3*); (*1-57322-199-6*) Putnam Publishing Group, The. (Riverhead Bks. (Hardcovers)).

Powell, Lawrence C. Eucalyptus Fair. 1992. 271p. 20.00 (*0-9632966-0-4*); 100.00 (*0-9632966-1-2*) Books West Southwest.

Premchand, Nirmala. Rai, Alok, tr. from HIN. 2001. 218p. pap. 15.95 (*0-19-565826-4*) Oxford Univ. Pr., Inc.

Price, Reynolds. Good Hearts. 1988. 352p. 18.95 o.s.i (*0-689-11973-9*, Scribner) Simon & Schuster.

Prince, Peter. Bubbles. 2000. 246p. (*0-7475-4917-6*) Bloomsbury Pr.

Pronzini, Bill & Muller. The Lighthouse: A Novel of Terror. 1987. pap. 3.95 o.p. (*0-312-90876-8*, St. Martin's Paperbacks) St. Martin's Pr.

Pronzini, Bill & Muller, Marcia. The Lighthouse: A Novel of Terror. 1992. (Mystery Scene Bk.). 304p. mass mkt. 4.50 (*0-88184-885-9*, Carroll & Graf Pubs.) Avalon Publishing Group.

—The Lighthouse: A Novel of Terror. l.t. ed. 2001. 390p. pap. 24.95 (*0-7838-9616-6*, Hall, G. K. & Co.) Gale Group.

—The Lighthouse: A Novel of Terror. 1986. 336p. 16.95 o.p. (*0-312-00150-9*) St. Martin's Pr.

Purdy, James. The Nephew. 1987. 176p. pap. 7.95 o.p. (*1-55584-085-X*) Grove/Atlantic, Inc.

—The Nephew. 1980. 152p. pap. 3.95 o.p. (*0-14-005670-X*, Penguin Bks.) Viking Penguin.

Pym, Barbara. A Glass of Blessings. l.t. ed. 1986. (General Ser.). 427p. 17.95 o.p. (*0-8161-3841-9*, Macmillan Reference USA) Gale Group.

—A Glass of Blessings. 1987. 272p. reprint ed. pap. 6.95 o.p. (*0-06-097074-X*, PL 7074, Perennial) HarperTrade.

Rambach, Peggy. Fighting Gravity: A Novel. 2001. 150p. pap. 19.00 (*1-58642-023-2*) Steerforth Pr.

Raney, Deborah. A Vow to Cherish. 1996. 240p. pap. 8.99 o.p. (*1-55661-666-X*) Bethany Hse. Pubs.

Rao, Raja. The Serpent & the Rope. 1988. 400p. pap. 9.95 o.s.i (*0-87951-243-1*); 1986. 408p. 22.50 (*0-87951-220-2*) Overlook Pr., The.

Ray, Jeanne. Step-Ball-Change: A Novel. 2002. 240p. 22.95 (*0-609-61003-1*, Shaye Areheart Bks.) Crown Publishing Group.

—Step-Ball-Change: A Novel. l.t. ed. 2002. (Core Collection). 284p. 31.95 (*0-7862-4371-6*) Thorndike Pr.

Reed, Kit. @ Expectations. 2000. 302p. 22.95 (*0-312-87486-3*); 2001. 304p. reprint ed. pap. 12.95 (*0-7653-0181-4*) Doherty, Tom Assocs., LLC. (Forge Bks.).

Rice, Luanne. Crazy in Love. 1989. 256p. mass mkt. 4.99 o.s.i (*0-449-21754-X*, Fawcett) Ballantine Bks.

—Crazy in Love. l.t. ed. 2001. 445p. 31.95 o.p. (*0-7838-9441-4*, Macmillan Reference USA) Gale Group.

—Crazy in Love. 1988. (Illus.). 320p. 18.95 o.p. (*0-670-82131-4*) Viking Penguin.

—Secrets of Paris. l.t. ed. 1992. (General Ser.). 393p. 20.95 o.p. (*0-8161-5329-9*, Macmillan Reference USA) Gale Group.

—Secrets of Paris. 1991. 336p. 19.95 o.p. (*0-670-82773-8*) Viking Penguin.

Ripley, Alexandra. From Fields of Gold. l.t. ed. 1995. 577p. lib. bdg. 24.95 o.p. (*0-7838-1237-X*, Macmillan Reference USA) Gale Group.

—From Fields of Gold. 1996. 464p. mass mkt. 6.50 (*0-446-60249-3*); 1994. 480p. 24.95 o.s.i (*0-446-51406-3*) Warner Bks., Inc.

Robbins, David L. Souls to Keep: A Novel. 1999. 272p. mass mkt. 6.50 o.s.i (*0-06-109791-8*); 1998. 320p. 23.00 o.s.i (*0-06-101300-5*) HarperCollins Pubs.

Robinson, Elisabeth. The True & Outstanding Adventures of the Hunt Sisters. 2004. (Illus.). 336p. 23.95 (*0-316-73502-7*) Little Brown & Co.

Roby, Kimberla Lawson. Behind Closed Doors. 1997. 244p. reprint ed. pap. 12.00 (*1-57478-005-0*) Black Classic Pr.

—Behind Closed Doors. 1997. x, 250p. pap. 12.00 (*0-9653470-4-4*) Lenox Pr.

—Casting the First Stone. 2000. x, 300p. 22.00 o.s.i (*1-57566-489-5*, Kensington Bks.); 2001. 32p. reprint ed. pap. 14.00 (*1-57566-633-2*) Kensington Publishing Corp.

Roiphe, Anne. Torch Song. 1977. 226p. 8.95 o.p. (*0-374-27848-2*) Farrar, Straus & Giroux.

Roper, Martin. Gone: A Novel. 2002. 256p. 23.00 o.s.i (*0-8050-6775-2*) Holt, Henry & Co.

—Gone: A Novel. 2003. 240p. pap. 13.00 (*0-312-42125-7*) Picador.

Ross, Dan. The Third Spectre. l.t. ed. 2001. (Thorndike Candlelight Romance Ser.). 223p. 22.95 (*0-7862-3281-1*) Thorndike Pr.

Roth, Philip. My Life as a Man. 1994. 352p. pap. 14.00 (*0-679-74827-X*, Vintage) Knopf Publishing Group.

—My Life as a Man. 1985. (Fiction Ser.). 352p. pap. 5.95 o.p. (*0-14-007680-8*, Penguin Bks.) Viking Penguin.

Saroyan, William. Boys & Girls Together: A Novel. 1995. 160p. pap. 10.00 (*1-56980-047-2*) Barricade Bks., Inc.

Sarton, May. The Bridge of Years. 1985. 352p. reprint ed. pap. 4.95 (*0-393-30239-3*) Norton, W. W. & Co., Inc.

—Kinds of Love. 1994. 352p. pap. 13.95 (*0-393-31101-5*); 1970. 12.95 o.p. (*0-393-08620-8*); 1980. 352p. reprint ed. pap. 5.95 o.p. (*0-393-00968-8*) Norton, W. W. & Co., Inc.

Scott, Kathleen. A Test of Love. 2002. 240p. pap. 9.99 (*0-8254-3664-8*) Kregel Pubns.

Segal, Harriet. The Skylark's Song: A Rich, Multi-Generational Family Saga. 1994. 512p. 23.95 o.p. (*1-55611-385-4*) Fine, Donald I. Bks.

Senstad, Susan Schwartz. Music for the Third Ear. 256p. 2002. pap. 13.00 (*0-312-28776-3*); 2001. 22.00 (*0-312-26621-9*) Picador.

Shand, Rosa. The Gravity of Sunlight. 2001. 256p. 24.00 (*1-56947-192-4*); reprint ed. pap. 13.00 (*1-56947-240-8*) Soho Pr., Inc.

Shands, Linda. Time to Embrace. 1995. (Seasons Remembered Ser.: Vol. 2). 232p. (Orig.). pap. 9.99 o.p. (*0-8308-1932-0*, 1932) InterVarsity Pr.

Shields, Carol. Happenstance. 1980. 224p. 12.95 o.p. (*0-07-092377-9*) McGraw-Hill Cos., The.

—Happenstance. 1994. pap. 10.95 (*0-14-771022-7*) NAL.

—Happenstance. 1994. 416p. pap. 14.00 (*0-14-017951-8*, Penguin Bks.) Penguin Group (USA) Inc.

Shields, Carol & Howard, Blanche. A Celibate Season. 1995. 200p. pap. 14.95 o.p. (*1-55050-024-4*) Coteau Bks. CAN. *Dist:* General Distribution Services, Inc.

—A Celibate Season. 1999. 240p. pap. 12.95 (*0-14-027511-8*) Penguin Group (USA) Inc.

Shreve, Anita. All He Ever Wanted. 2004. (Illus.). 336p. pap. 14.95 (*0-316-73573-6*, Back Bay); 2003. 320p. 25.95 (*0-316-78226-2*); 2003. 496p. 25.95 (*0-316-71112-8*) Little Brown & Co.

—The Last Time They Met. 2003. 336p. mass mkt. 7.99 (*0-316-71373-2*); 2001. 320p. E-Book 14.95 (*0-7595-4308-9*); 2001. 320p. E-Book 14.95 (*0-7595-9338-8*); 2001. 320p. E-Book 14.95 (*0-7595-6305-5*); 2001. 320p. E-Book 14.95 (*0-7595-8311-0*); 2001. 320p. E-Book 14.95 (*0-7595-0305-2*) Little Brown & Co.

—The Last Time They Met. Pietsch, Michael, ed. 2001. 320p. 24.95 o.p. (*0-316-78114-2*) Little Brown & Co.

—The Last Time They Met. 2002. 352p. reprint ed. pap. 13.95 (*0-316-78126-6*, Back Bay) Little Brown & Co.

—The Last Time They Met. l.t. ed. (Paperback Bestsellers Ser.). 2002. 475p. pap. 13.95 (*0-7862-3311-7*); 2002. 13.95 (*1-4104-0010-7*, Large Print Pr.); 2001. 496p. 31.95 (*0-7862-3310-9*); 2001. 475p. (*0-7540-1660-9*); 2001. 475p. (*0-7540-9074-4*) Thorndike Pr.

—Sea Glass. 2002. 416p. mass mkt. 7.99 (*0-316-70782-1*); 2002. 384p. 25.95 (*0-316-78081-2*); 2002. E-Book 14.95 (*0-7595-8693-4*); 2002. 512p. 25.95 (*0-316-73373-3*); 2003. 416p. reprint ed. pap. 14.95 (*0-316-08969-9*, Back Bay) Little Brown & Co.

Shyer, Marlene Fanta. Two Daughters. 2002. 32p. mass mkt. 6.99 o.s.i (*0-7582-0037-4*) Kensington Publishing Corp.

—Two Daughters. l.t. ed. 2002. (Women's Fiction Ser.). 28.95 (*0-7862-4409-7*) Thorndike Pr.

Simpson, Donna. Lady Delafont's Dilemma. 2002. (Five Star Romance Ser.). 264p. 25.95 (*0-7862-3911-5*, Five Star) Gale Group.

Simpson, Thomas W. The Fingerprints of Armless Mike. 1996. 390p. 19.95 o.p. (*0-446-51809-3*) Warner Bks., Inc.

Singh, Jacquelin. Home to India. 1997. 217p. 24.00 (*1-877946-85-0*) Permanent Pr., The.

Sleem, Patty. Second Time Around: Second Marriages & Their Spiritual Issues. 1995. 336p. 25.00 (*1-885288-00-X*); pap. 17.00 (*1-885288-05-0*) PREP Publishing.

Smith, Thea. She Let Herself Go. l.t. ed. 2002. (Five Star First Edition Women's Fiction Ser.). 365p. 25.95 (*0-7862-3704-X*, Five Star) Gale Group.

Solomon, Nina. Single Wife: A Novel. 2003. 336p. tchr. ed. 23.95 (*1-56512-382-4*, 72382) Algonquin Bks. of Chapel Hill.

Sorrentino, Gilbert. The Sky Changes. 1998. 160p. pap. 11.95 (*1-56478-183-6*) Dalkey Archive Pr.

—The Sky Changes. 1986. 160p. pap. 12.50 o.p. (*0-86547-243-2*, North Point Pr.) Farrar, Straus & Giroux.

Spark, Muriel. Reality & Dreams. 1997. 160p. 22.00 o.p. (*0-395-83811-8*) Houghton Mifflin Co.

Spencer, Elizabeth. The Night Travellers. 2002. (Voices of the South Ser.). 384p. pap. 17.95 (*0-8071-2792-2*) Louisiana State Univ. Pr.

—The Night Travellers. 1992. (Contemporary American Fiction Ser.). 384p. reprint ed. pap. 10.00 o.p. (*0-14-015281-4*, Penguin Bks.) Penguin Group (USA) Inc.

—The Night Travellers. 1991. 352p. 21.95 o.p. (*0-670-83915-9*) Viking Penguin.

Spencer, Nelsie. The Playgroup: A Novel. 2003. 352p. 24.95 (*0-312-31172-9*) St. Martin's Pr.

Stansfield, Anita. Now & Forever: A Novel. 1996. 304p. pap. 11.95 (*1-55503-910-3*, 01112236) Covenant Communications, Inc.

—To Love Again: A Sequel to Return to Love. 1998. pap. 12.95 (*1-57734-260-7*, 01113283) Covenant Communications, Inc.

Steel, Danielle. Family Album. 1985. 408p. 19.95 (*0-385-29392-5*, Delacorte Pr.) Dell Publishing.

—Family Album. l.t. ed. 1985. (Special Editions Ser.). 616p. 18.95 o.p. (*0-8161-3859-1*, Macmillan Reference USA) Gale Group.

—The Kiss. 2002. 448p. mass mkt. 7.99 (*0-440-23669-X*); 2001. 360p. 200.00 (*0-385-33589-X*, Delacorte Pr.); 2001. 360p. 26.95 (*0-385-33540-7*, Delacorte Pr.) Dell Publishing.

—The Kiss. l.t. ed. 544p. 2002. pap. 14.95 (*0-375-72817-1*); 2001. 26.95 (*0-375-43132-2*) Random Hse. Large Print.

Stegner, Wallace. Angle of Repose. 1981. mass mkt. 2.95 o.p. (*0-449-23796-6*); 1985. 512p. reprint ed. mass mkt. 5.95 o.s.i (*0-449-20988-1*) Ballantine Bks. (Fawcett).

—Angle of Repose. unabr. collector's ed. 1996. Pt. 1. audio 72.00 (*0-7366-3281-6*, 3937 A); Pt. 2. audio 80.00 (*0-7366-3282-4*, 3937-B) Books on Tape, Inc.

—Angle of Repose. 1971. 12.95 o.p. (*0-385-07882-X*) Doubleday Publishing.

—Angle of Repose. 1998. (*0-14-771245-9*); 1997. (*0-14-771219-X*); 1992. 512p. pap. 13.95 (*0-14-016930-X*, Penguin Bks.) Penguin Group (USA) Inc.

—Angle of Repose. 1996. 9.99 o.p. (*0-517-18489-3*) Random Hse. Value Publishing.

—Angle of Repose. 2000. (Modern Library Ser.). 656p. 23.95 o.s.i (*0-679-60338-7*) Random Hse., Inc.

—Angle of Repose. 2000. 21.05 (*0-606-21897-1*) Turtleback Bks.

—Angle of Repose. 2000. (Classics Ser.). 512p. 15.00 (*0-14-118547-3*, Penguin Classics) Viking Penguin.

—Crossing to Safety. 1997. 288p. 7.99 o.s.i (*0-517-18776-0*) Random Hse. Value Publishing.

—The Spectator Bird. 1976. 240p. 6.95 o.p. (*0-385-07890-0*) Doubleday Publishing.

—The Spectator Bird. 1977. (Spring Adult Ser.). lib. bdg. 11.50 o.p. (*0-8161-6443-6*, Macmillan Reference USA) Gale Group.

—The Spectator Bird. 1992. 24.25 (*0-8446-6607-6*) Smith, Peter Pub., Inc.

—The Spectator Bird. 1979. 214p. reprint ed. pap. 6.95 o.p. (*0-8032-9107-8*, Bison Bks.) Univ. of Nebraska Pr.

—The Spectator Bird. 1990. (Contemporary American Fiction Ser.). 224p. reprint ed. 14.00 (*0-14-013940-0*) Viking Penguin.

Stegner, Wallace, told to. Crossing to Safety. 1999. (*0-14-771373-0*) Penguin Group (USA) Inc.

Stonich, Sarah. These Granite Islands: A Novel. 2001. 320p. 24.95 o.p. (*0-316-81583-7*) Little Brown & Co.

Tallent, Elizabeth. Museum Pieces. 1986. 240p. pap. 7.95 o.p. (*0-03-008003-7*, Owl Bks.) Holt, Henry & Co.

—Museum Pieces. Goerner, Lee, ed. 1985. 206p. 14.95 o.s.i (*0-394-53928-1*) Knopf, Alfred A. Inc.

Tanenbaum, Robert K. True Justice. 2000. 384p. 24.95 o.s.i (*0-7434-0589-7*, Atria); 2001. (Illus.). 464p. reprint ed. mass mkt. 7.99 (*0-7434-0590-0*, Pocket) Simon & Schuster.

—True Justice. l.t. ed. 2001. (Thorndike Mystery Ser.). 681p. 30.95 (*0-7862-3032-0*) Thorndike Pr.

Taylor, Peter. A Woman of Means. 1983. 140p. 16.95 (*0-913720-44-5*) Beil, Frederic C. Pub., Inc.

—A Woman of Means. 1986. (Southern Writers Ser.). 128p. mass mkt. 3.95 (*0-380-70099-9*, Avon Bks.) Morrow/Avon.

—A Woman of Means. 1996. 144p. pap. 10.00 (*0-312-14448-2*) Picador.

Tefs, Wayne. Home Free. 1997. (Willow Island Trilogy Ser.). 224p. pap. 14.95 (*0-88801-217-9*) Turnstone Pr. CAN. *Dist:* General Distribution Services, Inc.

Tennant, Emma. Emma in Love: Jane Austen's Emma Continued. 229p. 1997. pap. 11.00 o.p. (*1-85702-663-2*); 1996. pap. (*1-85702-527-X*) Fourth Estate, Ltd. GBR. *Dist:* Trafalgar Square.

—Pemberley: Or Pride & Prejudice Continued. l.t. ed. 1995. (Charnwood Large Print Ser.). 272p. 29.99 o.p. (*0-7089-8826-1*, Charnwood) Thorpe, F. A. Pubs. GBR. *Dist:* Ulverscroft Large Print Bks., Ltd., Ulverscroft Large Print Canada, Ltd.

Tennant, Emma & Austen, Jane. Pemberley: Or Pride & Prejudice Continued. 1993. 184p. pap. 18.95 (*0-312-10793-5*) St. Martin's Pr.

—An Unequal Marriage: Or Pride & Prejudice Twenty Years Later. 1994. 224p. 18.95 o.p. (*0-312-11533-4*) St. Martin's Pr.

Thackeray, William Makepeace. Vanity Fair. 2001. (Modern Library Classics). 768p. pap. 7.95 (*0-375-75726-0*, Modern Library) Random House Adult Trade Publishing Group.

Thirkell, Angela M. Ankle Deep. lib. bdg. 20.95 (*0-8488-1879-2*) Amereon, Ltd.

Thomas, Abigail. An Actual Life. 1996. 252p. tchr. ed. 17.95 (*1-56512-133-3*, 72133) Algonquin Bks. of Chapel Hill.

—An Actual Life. 1997. 240p. pap. 14.95 (*0-684-83751-X*, Touchstone) Simon & Schuster.

Tilghman, Christopher. Mason's Retreat. Date not set. (*0-679-45240-0*) McKay, David Co., Inc.

—Mason's Retreat. 1997. 304p. pap. 13.00 o.p. (*0-312-15586-7*) Picador.

—Mason's Retreat. 1995. 290p. 22.00 o.s.i (*0-679-45143-9*) Random Hse., Inc.

Toteras, D. K. Rape of the Sleeping Woman: And the Practice of Hypnagogic Sex. 1995. 320p. (Orig.). pap. 14.95 (*0-9644122-0-9*) Nine Muses Pr.

Tremain, Rose. The Colour. 2003. (Illus.). 352p. 25.00 (*0-374-12605-4*); pap. (*0-374-91874-0*) Farrar, Straus & Giroux.

Trollope, Anthony. Is He Popenjoy?, 3. reprint ed. lib. bdg. 294.00 (*0-7426-2478-1*); 2001. pap. text 84.00 (*0-7426-7478-9*) Classic Bks.

—Is He Popenjoy? Sutherland, John, ed. 1986. (Oxford World's Classics Ser.). 690p. pap. 9.95 o.p. (*0-19-281716-7*) Oxford Univ. Pr., Inc.

—Is He Popenjoy? 1994. (Trollope Ser.). 656p. pap. 8.95 o.p. (*0-14-043839-4*, Penguin Classics) Viking Penguin.

—Kept in the Dark. 1978. (Illus.). pap. 3.95 o.p. (*0-486-23609-9*) Dover Pubns., Inc.

—Kept in the Dark. Pigman, G. W., III, ed. 1992. (Oxford World's Classics Ser.). 250p. pap. 9.95 o.p. (*0-19-282740-5*) Oxford Univ. Pr., Inc.

—Kept in the Dark. 1994. (Trollope Ser.). 512p. pap. 8.95 o.p. (*0-14-043847-5*, Penguin Classics) Viking Penguin.

Trollope, Joanna. Next of Kin. 2002. 352p. pap. 14.00 (*0-425-18474-9*) Berkley Publishing Group.

—Next of Kin. l.t. ed. 2001. (Thorndike Press Large Print Women's Fiction Ser.). 533p. 29.95 (*0-7862-3666-3*) Thorndike Pr.

—Next of Kin. 2001. 304p. 23.95 o.p. (*0-670-89999-2*, Viking) Viking Penguin.

Twain, Mark. Eve's Diary. 2001. 114p. lib. bdg. 25.99 (*1-57646-571-3*) Quiet Vision Publishing.

Tyler, Anne. The Amateur Marriage. 2004. 320p. 24.95 (*1-4000-4207-0*) Knopf Publishing Group.

—The Amateur Marriage. l.t. ed. 2004. 512p. 26.95 (*0-375-43336-8*) Random Hse. Large Print.

Upadhyay, Samrat. The Guru of Love. 2003. 304p. tchr. ed. 23.00 (*0-618-24727-0*) Houghton Mifflin Co. Trade & Reference Div.

Upchurch, Michael. Passive Intruder: A Novel. 1995. 352p. 23.00 o.p. (*0-393-03865-3*) Norton, W. W. & Co., Inc.

Updike, John. The Afterlife & Other Stories. 1994. 336p. 29.95 (*0-679-43583-2*) Knopf, Alfred A. Inc.

—Couples. 1996. 480p. pap. 14.95 (*0-449-91190-X*); 1982. mass mkt. 3.25 o.p. (*0-449-20041-8*); 1981. mass mkt. 2.95 o.p. (*0-449-24023-1*) Ballantine Bks. (Fawcett).

—Couples. 1968. 480p. 35.00 (*0-394-42066-7*) Knopf, Alfred A. Inc.

—Marry Me. 1996. 320p. pap. 13.95 (*0-449-91215-9*, Fawcett) Ballantine Bks.

—Marry Me. 1976. 22.95 (*0-394-40856-X*) Knopf, Alfred A. Inc.

—Too Far to Go. 1982. 256p. mass mkt. 7.50 (*0-449-20016-7*); 1980. mass mkt. 2.50 o.p. (*0-449-24002-9*) Ballantine Bks. (Fawcett).

Walker, David J. A Beer at a Bawdy House. E-Book 23.95 o.p. (*0-312-27340-1*); 2000. 307p. 23.95 (*0-312-25242-0*, Saint Martin's Minotaur) St. Martin's Pr.

—Ticket to Die For. 1998. (Wild Onion Ltd. Mysteries Ser.). 272p. 22.95 (*0-312-19345-9*, Saint Martin's Minotaur) St. Martin's Pr.

Wall, Michael. Women Laughing. 2001. (Oberon Modern Plays Ser.). 120p. pap. 16.95 (*1-84002-156-X*) Theatre Communications Group, Inc.

Wall, William. Alice Falling. 2000. 208p. 23.95 (*0-393-05001-7*) Norton, W. W. & Co., Inc.

Weale, Anne. All My Worldly Goods. 1989. 542p. 22.95 o.p. (*0-312-03965-4*) St. Martin's Pr.

Weldon, Fay. The Heart of the Country. 1992. 3.99 o.p. (*0-517-07995-X*) Random Hse. Value Publishing.

—The Heart of the Country. 208p. 1990. pap. 9.95 o.p. (*0-14-010397-X*, Penguin Bks.); 1988. 17.95 o.p. (*0-670-81875-5*) Viking Penguin.

—The Hearts & Lives of Men. 1989. 384p. reprint ed. mass mkt. 4.95 o.s.i (*0-440-20322-8*) Dell Publishing.

—The Hearts & Lives of Men. 1990. 4.99 o.p. (*0-517-03020-9*) Random Hse. Value Publishing.

—The Hearts & Lives of Men. 1988. 36p. 18.95 o.p. (*0-670-82098-9*) Viking Penguin.

Wendorf, Patricia. The Marriage Menders. l.t. ed. 2000. (G. K. Hall Romance Ser.). 535p. 27.95 (*0-7838-9021-4*, Macmillan Reference USA) Gale Group.

Wharton, Edith. Ethan Frome. 20.95 (*0-89190-509-X*) Amereon, Ltd.

—Ethan Frome. E-Book 5.00 (*0-7607-1307-3*) Barnes & Noble, Inc.

—Ethan Frome. 2002. 110p. pap. 3.95 (*1-59109-098-9*) Booksurge, LLC.

—Ethan Frome. 1995. reprint ed. lib. bdg. 19.95 (*1-56849-636-2*) Buccaneer Bks., Inc.

—Ethan Frome. Peel, Edith, ed. 1999. (Literature Ser.). (Illus.). 172p. pap. text 11.95 (*0-521-64529-8*) Cambridge Univ. Pr.

—Ethan Frome. (Collected Works of Edith Wharton). 195p. 2001. pap. text 28.00 (*0-7426-5976-3*); 1998. reprint ed. lib. bdg. 88.00 (*1-58201-976-2*) Classic Bks.

—Ethan Frome. 1991. (Illus.). 96p. pap. 1.00 (*0-486-26690-7*) Dover Pubns., Inc.

—Ethan Frome. 1987. 192p. pap. 8.00 (*0-684-18906-2*); 1982. 192p. pap. 1.95 o.s.i (*0-684-17487-1*); 1977. 192p. 30.00 (*0-684-15326-2*); 1977. text 11.25 o.s.i (*0-684-51564-4*); 1977. pap. text (*0-684-51565-2*); 1910. pap. 5.95 o.s.i (*0-684-71927-4*, SL8) Gale Group. (Macmillan Reference USA).

—Ethan Frome. l.t. ed. 360p. pap. 32.97 (*0-7583-0846-9*); 420p. pap. 37.22 (*0-7583-0847-7*); 80p. pap. 13.16 (*0-7583-0840-X*); 294p. pap. 28.04 (*0-7583-0845-0*); 107p. pap. 15.07 (*0-7583-0841-8*); 240p. pap. 24.48 (*0-7583-0844-2*); 145p. pap. 17.76 (*0-7583-0842-6*); 187p. pap. 20.73 (*0-7583-0843-4*); 294p. lib. bdg. 39.55 (*0-7583-0837-X*); 240p. lib. bdg. 35.73 (*0-7583-0836-1*); 187p. lib. bdg. 31.98 (*0-7583-0835-3*); 360p. lib. bdg. 44.22 (*0-7583-0838-8*); 420p. lib. bdg. 48.47 (*0-7583-0839-6*); 80p. lib. bdg. 19.76 (*0-7583-0832-9*); 107p. lib. bdg. 23.06 (*0-7583-0833-7*); 145p. lib. bdg. 27.67 (*0-7583-0834-5*) Huge Print Pr.

—Ethan Frome. 1999. 110p. pap. 9.95 o.p. (*1-930128-05-3*, JNMedia Bks.) JNMedia, Inc.

—Ethan Frome. (Signet Classics). 2000. 176p. mass mkt. 4.95 (*0-451-52766-6*); 1996. pap., instr.'s gde. ed. (*0-451-16661-2*); 1992. 160p. mass mkt. 3.95 o.p. (*0-451-52580-9*); 1987. 160p. mass mkt. 4.95 o.s.i (*0-451-52227-3*); 1987. mass mkt. 2.50 o.p. (*0-451-52079-3*) NAL. (Signet Classics).

—Ethan Frome. 1991. 96p. (C). reprint ed. pap. text 2.75 (*0-914061-23-2*) Orchises Pr.

—Ethan Frome. Showalter, Elaine, ed. & intro. by. (Oxford World's Classics Ser.). 1998. 160p. pap. 7.95 (*0-19-283496-7*); 1996. 156p. pap. 6.95 o.p. (*0-19-282515-1*) Oxford Univ. Pr., Inc.

—Ethan Frome. 1911. 178p. text 9.50 o.s.i (*0-02-426690-6*, Macmillan College) Prentice Hall PTR.

—Ethan Frome. 1999. (Illus.). 182p. reprint ed. lib. bdg. 29.95 (*0-7351-0119-1*) Replica Bks.

—Ethan Frome. 1997. 160p. pap. 10.00 (*0-684-82591-0*, Scribner) Simon & Schuster.

—Ethan Frome. 1997. 16.05 (*0-606-00613-3*) Turtleback Bks.

—Ethan Frome. (Great Books of the 20th Century Ser.). 1994. 208p. 7.95 (*0-14-018736-7*); 1987. 224p. pap. 6.95 o.p. (*0-14-039058-8*) Viking Penguin. (Penguin Classics).

—Ethan Frome. 1993. 4.99 o.s.i (*1-85381-672-8*); 1991. 9.95 (*1-85381-228-5*) Virago Pr., Ltd. GBR. *Dist:* Random Hse. of Canada, Ltd., Trafalgar Square.

—Ethan Frome. 1999. E-Book 5.99 (*0-8220-7064-2*, Cliff Notes) Wiley, John & Sons, Inc.

—Ethan Frome. (Classics Library). 96p. pap. 3.95 (*1-84022-408-8*); 1998. pap. 3.95 (*1-85326-555-1*, 5551WW) Wordsworth Editions, Ltd. GBR. *Dist:* Combined Publishing.

—Ethan Frome: Authoritative Text, Backgrounds & Contexts, Criticism. Lauer, Kristin O. & Wolff, Cynthia G., eds. 1994. (Critical Editions Ser.). (C). pap. text 7.50 (*0-393-96635-6*) Norton, W. W. & Co., Inc.

—Ethan Frome & Other Short Fiction. 1987. (Classics Ser.). 256p. mass mkt. 5.50 (*0-553-21255-9*, Bantam Classics) Bantam Bks.

—Ethan Frome & Other Stories. 1996. 176p. text 5.98 o.p. (*1-56138-763-0*, Courage Bks.) Running Pr. Bk. Pubs.

—Ethan Frome & Summer. (Twelve-Point Ser.). 1998. lib. bdg. 25.00 (*1-58287-027-6*); 1993. 449p. reprint ed. lib. bdg. 26.00 (*0-939495-27-9*) North Bks.

—Ethan Frome & Summer. 2001. (Modern Library Classics). 304p. pap. 7.95 (*0-375-75728-7*, Modern Library) Random House Adult Trade Publishing Group.

—The Glimpses of the Moon. 1994. 256p. 25.00 (*0-684-19693-X*); 364p. lib. bdg. 23.95 (*0-8161-7408-3*) Gale Group. (Macmillan Reference USA).

—The Glimpses of the Moon. 1996. 304p. pap. 11.00 (*0-684-82619-4*, Scribner) Simon & Schuster.

Wharton, Edith & Showalter, Elaine. Ethan Frome. 1996. E-Book 7.30 (*0-585-35118-X*) netLibrary, Inc.

White, Stephen. Blinded. 2004. 400p. 24.95 (*0-385-33620-9*, Delacorte Pr.) Dell Publishing.

Whitnell, Barbara. A Clear Blue Sky. 1995. 320p. 23.95 o.p. (*0-312-13945-4*) St. Martin's Pr.

Whitson, Stephanie Grace. Heart of the Sandhills. 2002. 288p. pap. 13.99 (*0-7852-6824-3*) Nelson, Thomas Inc.

Wick, Lori. Who Brings Forth the Wind? 1994. (Kensington Chronicles Ser.). 396p. pap. 9.99 (*1-56507-229-4*) Harvest Hse. Pubs.

—Who Brings Forth the Wind? l.t. ed. 2001. (Thorndike Christian Fiction Ser.). 568p. 26.95 (*0-7862-2957-8*) Thorndike Pr.

Wickham, Madeleine. The Tennis Party. 1996. 256p. text 22.95 o.p. (*0-312-14053-3*) St. Martin's Pr.

Wickham, Madeline. The Tennis Party. 1996. 256p. pap. 10.95 (*0-552-99639-4*) Transworld Publishers Ltd. GBR. *Dist:* Trafalgar Square.

Winterson, Jeanette. Written on the Body. 1994. 192p. pap. 12.00 (*0-679-74447-9*) Knopf, Alfred A. Inc.

Woiwode, Larry. What I'm Going to Do, I Think. 1970. mass mkt. 1.25 o.p. (*0-345-21916-3*) Ballantine Bks.

—What I'm Going to Do, I Think. 1969. 309p. 5.95 o.p. (*0-374-28792-9*) Farrar, Straus & Giroux.

—What I'm Going to Do, I Think. 1984. pap. 1.75 o.p. (*0-380-00837-8*, 31039-2, Avon Bks.) Morrow/Avon.

Wolitzer, Hilma. Silver. 1989. mass mkt. 4.95 o.s.i (*0-8041-0485-9*, Ivy Bks.) Ballantine Bks.

—Silver. 1988. 352p. 18.95 o.s.i (*0-374-26422-8*) Farrar, Straus & Giroux.

—Silver. l.t. ed. 1989. (General Ser.). 384p. pap. 13.95 o.p. (*0-8161-4933-X*); lib. bdg. 20.95 o.p. (*0-8161-4743-4*) Gale Group. (Macmillan Reference USA).

Woods, Stuart. Imperfect Strangers. l.t. ed. 1995. 26.95 o.p. (*1-56895-203-1*, Wheeler Publishing, Inc.) Gale Group.

—Imperfect Strangers. 1994. 320p. 23.00 o.p. (*0-06-017775-6*) HarperCollins Pubs.

—Imperfect Strangers. abr. ed. audio 17.00 o.p. (*1-55994-673-3*, CPN 2472, HarperAudio) HarperTrade.

—Imperfect Strangers. 1995. 368p. mass mkt. 7.99 (*0-06-109404-8*, HarperTorch) Morrow/Avon.

Woolf, Virginia. Mrs. Dalloway. 1990. 18.05 (*0-606-21562-X*) Turtleback Bks.

—To the Lighthouse. 24.95 (*0-88411-849-5*) Amereon, Ltd.

—To the Lighthouse. (HBJ Book Ser.). 1990. 236p. 18.00 (*0-15-190737-4*); 1989. 228p. pap. 12.00 (*0-15-690739-9*, Harvest Bks.); 1981. 209p. 17.95 o.p. (*0-15-190736-6*); 1964. pap. 5.95 o.p. (*0-15-690738-0*, Harvest Bks.) Harcourt Trade Pubs.

—To the Lighthouse. Drabble, Margaret, ed. 1992. (Oxford World's Classics Ser.). 328p. pap. (*0-19-281816-3*) Oxford Univ. Pr., Inc.

—To the Lighthouse. Kemp, Sandra, ed. 1995. (English Texts Ser.). 227p. (C). pap. 19.99 o.p. (*0-415-01663-0*, A7125) Routledge.

—To the Lighthouse. 1990. 18.80 o.p. (*0-8446-6210-0*) Smith, Peter Pub., Inc.

—To the Lighthouse. l.t. ed. 1997. (Perennial Ser.). 278p. 24.95 (*0-7838-8137-1*) Thorndike Pr.

—To the Lighthouse. Dick, Susan, ed. 1982. 366p. o.p. (*0-8020-5524-9*) Univ. of Toronto Pr.

Woolf, Virginia & Cather, Willa. O Pioneers! & Other Tales of the Praire: New York Public Library Collector's Edition. 1999. (New York Public Library Collector's Edition Ser.). (Illus.). 432p. 18.95 o.s.i (*0-385-48720-7*) Doubleday Publishing.

Woolf, Virginia & Everyman's Library Staff. To the Lighthouse. 1992. (Everyman's Library). 272p. 17.00 (*0-679-40537-2*) Knopf, Alfred A. Inc.

Wubbels, Lance. Keeper of the Harvest. 1995. (Gentle Hills Ser.: Bk. 3). 288p. pap. 10.99 o.p. (*1-55661-420-9*); 416p. pap. 15.99 o.p. (*1-55661-685-6*) Bethany Hse. Pubs.

Yates, Richard. Revolutionary Road. 1983. pap. 7.95 o.s.i (*0-385-29203-1*, Delta); 1983. pap. 7.95 o.s.i (*0-440-57428-5*, Delta); 1971. pap. 1.75 o.p. (*0-440-37412-X*) Dell Publishing.

—Revolutionary Road. 1971. 337p. reprint ed. 74.95 (*0-8371-6221-1*, YARR, Greenwood Pr.) Greenwood Publishing Group, Inc.

—Revolutionary Road. (Contemporaries Ser.). 1989. pap. 15.00 o.p. (*0-679-72191-6*); 2nd ed. 2000. 368p. pap. 14.00 (*0-375-70844-8*) Knopf Publishing Group. (Vintage).

—Young Hearts Crying. 1984. 354p. 16.95 o.s.i (*0-385-29269-4*, Delacorte Pr.) Dell Publishing.

Yorke, Margaret. The Price of Guilt. 2000. 336p. 24.95 (*0-312-25332-X*, Saint Martin's Minotaur) St. Martin's Pr.

—The Price of Guilt. l.t. ed. 2000. (Charnwood Large Print Ser.). 360p. 31.99 o.p. (*0-7089-9183-1*, Charnwood) Thorpe, F. A. Pubs. GBR. *Dist:* Ulverscroft Large Print Bks., Ltd., Ulverscroft Large Print Canada, Ltd.

—Serious Intent. 280p. 1996. mass mkt. o.s.i (*0-7515-1596-5*); 1995. o.s.i (*0-316-91280-8*) Little Brown & Co.

—Serious Intent. 1996. 82p. 21.95 o.s.i (*0-89296-583-5*) Mysterious Pr.

—Serious Intent. 1997. 288p. mass mkt. 5.99 (*0-446-40514-0*) Warner Bks., Inc.

**MOTHER AND CHILD—FICTION**

Albanese, Laurie Lico. Lynelle by the Sea. 240p. 2000. (Illus.). 22.95 o.p. (*0-525-94536-9*, Dutton); 2001. reprint ed. pap. 13.00 o.s.i (*0-452-28218-7*, Plume) Dutton/Plume.

—Lynelle by the Sea. l.t. ed. 2000. (Americana Ser.). 371p. 26.95 (*0-7862-2916-0*) Thorndike Pr.

Andrews, V. C. Cat. l.t. ed. 2000. (G. K. Hall Core Ser.). 170p. 28.95 (*0-7838-8805-8*, Macmillan Reference USA) Gale Group.

—Cat. 1999. (Wildflowers Ser.: No. 4). 160p. mass mkt. 3.99 o.s.i (*0-671-02803-0*, Pocket) Simon & Schuster.

—Cat. 1999. (Wildflower Ser.). 10.04 (*0-606-17530-X*) Turtleback Bks.

Badone, Ellen, ed. Religious Orthodoxy & Popular Faith in European Society. 1990. (Illus.). 226p. pap. text 22.00 (*0-691-02850-8*) Princeton Univ. Pr.

Banks, Lynne Reid. Alice-by-Accident. 2002. 144p. (J). (gr. 3-7). pap. 5.95 (*0-380-81560-5*) HarperCollins Children's Bk. Group.

Barbara, Diane & Donnier, Chris. Mom & Me. 2004. (Illus.). (J). 15.95 (*0-8109-4820-6*) Abrams, Harry N., Inc.

Barker, Raffaella. Hens Dancing: A Novel. 2001. E-Book 19.95 (*0-375-50685-3*) Random Hse., Inc.

—Summertime. 2003. 336p. reprint ed. pap. 14.00 (*0-385-72185-4*, Anchor) Knopf Publishing Group.

—Summertime: A Novel. 2002. 336p. 24.95 (*0-375-50387-0*) Random Hse., Inc.

Biggs, Undra E. Backfield in Motion. Cadet, Guichard, ed. 2002. 288p. pap. 15.00 (*0-9718191-3-0*) La Caille Nous Publishing Co.

Chamberlain, Diane. The Courage Tree. 2002. 416p. mass mkt. (*1-55166-869-6*, 1-66869-8); 2001. 384p. (*1-55166-799-1*, 1-66799-7) Harlequin Enterprises, Ltd. (Mira Bks.).

—The Escape Artist. 1998. 400p. mass mkt. 6.50 o.s.i (*0-06-109073-5*); 1997. 336p. 24.00 o.p. (*0-06-017651-2*) HarperCollins Pubs.

Chen, Ying. Ingratitude. Volk, Carol, tr. from FRE. 1998. 160p. 20.00 o.p. (*0-374-17554-3*) Farrar, Straus & Giroux.

Chen, Ying & Volk, Carol. Ingratitude. 1999. 154p. pap. text 14.95 (*0-520-22013-7*) Univ. of California Pr.

Chong, Kevin. Baroque-a-Nova. 2002. 224p. 23.95 o.s.i (*0-399-14825-6*) Penguin Group (USA) Inc.

Clark, Mary Higgins. Where Are the Children? E-Book 9.95 (*1-930161-68-9*) Adobe Systems, Inc.

—Where Are the Children? 2000. E-Book 9.95 (*0-7432-0611-8*); 1999. (Illus.). 272p. 25.00 (*0-684-86356-1*) Simon & Schuster. (Simon & Schuster).

Cope, Todd F. So Much for Christmas. 2003. 140p. pap. 10.95 (*1-55517-710-7*, 77107, Bonneville Bks.) Cedar Fort, Inc./CFI Distribution.

Crone, Moira. A Period of Confinement. 1987. 304p. reprint ed. pap. 6.95 o.p. (*0-06-097108-8*, PL 7108, Perennial) HarperTrade.

—A Period of Confinement. 1986. 336p. 19.95 o.p. (*0-399-13136-1*, G. P. Putnam's Sons) Penguin Putnam Bks. for Young Readers.

Daniell, Rosemary. The Hurricane Season: A Novel. 1992. 416p. 20.00 o.p. (*0-688-08860-0*, Morrow, William & Co.) Morrow/Avon.

Daugharty, Janice. Dark of the Moon. Howle, Jane, ed. 1994. 275p. 19.00 (*1-880909-17-0*) Baskerville Pubs., Inc.

—Dark of the Moon: A Novel. 1995. 288p. pap. 12.00 o.s.i (*0-06-097655-1*, Perennial) HarperTrade.

Denker, Henry. This Child Is Mine: A Novel. 1995. 330p. 23.00 o.p. (*0-688-14125-0*, Morrow, William & Co.) Morrow/Avon.

Deshpande, Shashi. Binding Vine. 2001. 256p. 23.95 (*1-55861-267-X*) Feminist Pr. at The City Univ. of New York.

Durrant, Sabine. Having It & Eating It. 2002. 272p. 23.95 o.s.i (*1-57322-215-1*, Riverhead Bks. (Hardcovers)) Putnam Publishing Group, The.

Easton, Patricia H. A Bridge to Hope. 1996. (Stafford Chronicles Ser.: Vol. 1). 280p. pap. 10.99 o.p. (*0-89283-950-3*, Vine Bks.) Servant Pubns.

Escandon, Maria Amparo. Esperanza's Box of Saints: A Novel. 1999. 256p. pap. 12.00 (*0-684-85614-X*, Touchstone) Simon & Schuster.

—Esperanza's Box of Saints: A Novel. 1999. 18.05 (*0-606-16079-5*) Turtleback Bks.

Evans, Shirlee. A Life Apart: Sequel to a Life in Her Hands. 1990. 176p. (Orig.). pap. 6.99 (*0-8361-3536-9*) Herald Pr.

Ferriss, Lucy. Nerves of the Heart: A Novel. 2002. 307p. 27.50 (*1-57233-185-2*) Univ. of Tennessee Pr.

Frucht, Abby. Are You Mine: A Novel. 1993. 293p. 19.95 o.p. (*0-8021-1539-X*) Grove/Atlantic, Inc.

—Polly's Ghost: A Novel. 2000. 368p. 25.00 o.s.i (*0-684-83589-4*, Scribner) Simon & Schuster.

—Polly's Ghost: A Novel. l.t. ed. 2000. (Basic Ser.). 624p. 28.95 (*0-7862-2564-5*) Thorndike Pr.

Fyfield, Frances. Undercurrents. 2001. 407p. (*0-7838-9480-5*, Macmillan Reference USA) Gale Group.

—Undercurrents. 2001. 278p. 23.95 o.p. (*0-670-89636-5*, Viking) Viking Penguin.

Grunwald, Lisa. New Year's Eve. 1998. 384p. pap. 13.99 (*0-446-67403-6*) Warner Bks., Inc.

Guest, Judith. Errands. 1997. 366p. mass mkt. 7.50 o.s.i (*0-345-40905-1*) Ballantine Bks.

Guymon, Shannon. Never Letting Go of Hope. 2001. vi, 170p. pap. (*1-55517-534-1*, Bonneville Bks.) Cedar Fort, Inc./CFI Distribution.

Hale, Veda Tebbs. Ragged Circle. 2002. 230p. pap. 15.95 (*1-55517-669-0*, 76690, Bonneville Bks.) Cedar Fort, Inc./CFI Distribution.

Harrison, Jim. Dalva. 1988. 18.95 o.p. (*0-525-24624-X*, Seymour Lawrence) NAL.

Hendry, Diana. Back Soon. 1995. 10.15 o.p. (*0-606-07254-3*) Turtleback Bks.

Hickman, Patricia. The Touch. 2002. (Illus.). 192p. 12.99 (*0-8423-4017-3*) Tyndale Hse. Pubs.

Hill, Kathleen. Still Waters in Niger. 2002. 205p. pap. 15.95 (*0-8101-5134-0*); 1999. 207p. 24.95 (*0-8101-5089-1*) Northwestern Univ. Pr. (TriQuarterly Bks.).

Hoffman, Alice. Fortune's Daughter. 1986. 272p. mass mkt. 5.99 o.s.i (*0-449-20976-8*, Fawcett) Ballantine Bks.

—Fortune's Daughter. 1999. 320p. pap. 13.00 (*0-425-16870-0*) Berkley Publishing Group.

—Fortune's Daughter. l.t. ed. 2000. (G. K. Hall Core Ser.). 338p. 30.95 (*0-7838-9026-5*, Macmillan Reference USA) Gale Group.

—Fortune's Daughter. 1985. 272p. 15.95 o.p. (*0-399-13056-X*, G. P. Putnam's Sons) Penguin Putnam Bks. for Young Readers.

Inclan, Jessica Barksdale. When You Go Away: A Novel. 2003. 256p. pap. 12.95 (*0-451-20787-4*) NAL.

Kenison, Katrina & Hirsch, Kathleen, eds. Mothers: Twenty Stories of Contemporary Motherhood. 1996. 352p. 22.00 o.p. (*0-86547-498-2*, North Point Pr.) Farrar, Straus & Giroux.

Kilpack, Josi S. Surrounded by Strangers: Choices Are Rarely Black & White. 2003. 280p. pap. 16.95 (*1-55517-679-8*, 76798, Bonneville Bks.) Cedar Fort, Inc./CFI Distribution.

Koppelman, Amy. A Mouthful of Air. 2003. 212p. 23.00 (*1-931561-30-3*) MacAdam/Cage Publishing, Inc.

Margolis, Seth J. Losing Isaiah. 1994. 400p. reprint ed. mass mkt. 5.99 o.s.i (*0-515-11539-8*, Jove) Berkley Publishing Group.

—Losing Isaiah. 1993. 384p. 22.95 o.p. (*1-56282-807-X*) Hyperion Pr.

Mda, Zakes. The Madonna of Excelsior. 2004. 272p. 23.00 (*0-374-20008-4*) Farrar, Straus & Giroux.

Miller, Sue. The Good Mother. 1994. 320p. pap. 13.95 (*0-385-31243-1*, Delta); 1987. 464p. mass mkt. 6.99 o.s.i (*0-440-12938-9*) Dell Publishing.

—The Good Mother. l.t. ed. 1987. 485p. 12.95 o.p. (*0-8161-4170-3*); 18.95 o.p. (*0-8161-4169-X*) Gale Group. (Macmillan Reference USA).

—The Good Mother. 2002. 320p. pap. 12.95 (*0-06-050593-1*, Perennial); 1986. 310p. 17.95 o.p. (*0-06-015551-5*) HarperTrade.

Moats, Lillian. Legacy of Shadows. 1999. (Illus.). 173p. 18.00 (*0-9669576-0-1*) Three Arts Pr.

Moses, Kate. Wintering: A Novel of Sylvia Plath. 2003. 336p. pap. 13.00 (*1-4000-3500-7*, Anchor) Knopf Publishing Group.

—Wintering: A Novel of Sylvia Plath. 2003. 272p. 23.95 o.s.i (*0-312-28375-X*) St. Martin's Pr.

Nattel, Lilian. The Theater of Consolation. 2005. 320p. pap. 14.00 (*0-7432-4967-4*); 2004. 336p. 25.00 (*0-7432-4966-6*) Simon & Schuster. (Scribner).

Nolan, Christopher. The Banyan Tree: A Novel. 2000. 374p. 25.95 (*1-55970-511-6*); 2001. 384p. reprint ed. pap. 13.95 (*1-55970-574-4*) Arcade Publishing, Inc.

—The Banyan Tree: A Novel. l.t. unabr. ed. 2000. 512p. 32.50 o.p. (*0-7531-6104-4*, 161044) ISIS Large Print Bks. GBR. *Dist:* Ulverscroft Large Print Bks., Ltd.

—The Banyan Tree: A Novel. 2002. 384p. reprint ed. pap. 13.00 (*0-385-72068-8*, Knopf Bks. for Young Readers) Random Hse. Children's Bks.

Oates, Joyce Carol. Expensive People. 1982. 256p. mass mkt. 2.95 o.s.i (*0-449-20012-4*, Fawcett) Ballantine Bks.

—Expensive People. 1990. 243p. reprint ed. pap. 10.95 (*0-86538-069-4*) Ontario Review Pr.

O'Brien, Edna. Time & Tide. 1992. 325p. 21.00 o.p. (*0-374-27776-1*) Farrar, Straus & Giroux.

—Time & Tide. 1993. 336p. mass mkt. 10.99 o.p. (*0-446-39510-2*) Warner Bks., Inc.

O'Carroll, Brendan. The Chisellers. 2000. 192p. pap. 11.95 (*0-452-28122-9*, Plume) Dutton/Plume.

—The Chisellers. l.t. ed. 2000. (G. K. Hall Core Ser.). 230p. 28.95 (*0-7838-9259-4*, Macmillan Reference USA) Gale Group.

—The Mammy. l.t. ed. 2000. 262p. lib. bdg. 26.95 (*1-58547-037-6*) Ctr. Point Large Print.

—The Mammy. 1999. 176p. pap. 11.95 (*0-452-28103-2*, Plume) Dutton/Plume.

—The Mammy. 1994. 174 p. (*0-86278-372-0*) O'Brien Pr., Ltd., The.

Pearson, Allison. I Don't Know How She Does It: The Life of Kate Reddy, Working Mother. l.t. ed. 2003. 31.95 (*1-58724-401-2*, Wheeler Publishing, Inc.) Gale Group.

—I Don't Know How She Does It: The Life of Kate Reddy, Working Mother. 2003. 352p. pap. 13.95 (*0-375-71375-1*) Knopf, Alfred A. Inc.

—I Don't Know How She Does It: The Life of Kate Reddy, Working Mother. 2002. 352p. 23.00 (*0-375-41405-3*) Random Hse., Inc.

Pesetsky, Bette. Midnight Sweets. 1989. 208p. mass mkt. 3.95 o.s.i (*0-8041-0533-2*, Ivy Bks.) Ballantine Bks.

—Midnight Sweets. 1988. 224p. 17.95 o.s.i (*0-689-12020-6*, Scribner) Simon & Schuster.

Picoult, Jodi. Keeping Faith: A Novel. 2000. 432p. pap. 13.95 (*0-688-17774-3*, Perennial) HarperTrade.

—Keeping Faith: A Novel. 1999. 422p. 24.00 (*0-688-16825-6*, Morrow, William & Co.) Morrow/Avon.

—Keeping Faith: A Novel. 2000. 19.05 (*0-606-21710-X*) Turtleback Bks.

Porter-Gaylord, Laurel. I Love My Mommy Because. 2004. 20p. bds. 6.99 (*0-525-47248-7*, Dutton Children's Bks.) Penguin Putnam Bks. for Young Readers.

Racine, David. Floating in a Most Peculiar Way. 1999. 230p. 24.00 (*0-9657639-3-5*) Van Neste Bks.

Roddie, Shen. Not Now, Mrs. Wolf. 2000. 12.10 (*0-606-19386-3*) Turtleback Bks.

Roth, Carol. Who Will Tuck Me in Tonight. 2003. 32p. (J). lib. bdg. 16.50 (*0-7358-1773-1*) North-South Bks., Inc.

Rotstein, Nancy-Gay. Shattering Glass. 1996. 352p. 22.00 o.p. (*0-374-26223-3*) Farrar, Straus & Giroux.

Schlein, Miriam. Always Right Now. 2004. 32p. (J). 15.99 (*0-06-052116-3*); lib. bdg. 16.89 (*0-06-052117-1*) HarperCollins Children's Bk. Group. (Greenwillow Bks.).

Schneider, Ursula W. The Cross-Eyed God. 1996. 160p. (Orig.). pap. 9.95 (*1-56002-558-1*, University Editions) Aegina Pr., Inc.

Schwartz, Lynne Sharon. Disturbances in the Field. 1983. 384p. 15.95 o.p. (*0-06-015202-8*) Harper-Trade.

Sexton, Linda G. Points of Light. 1988. 288p. 16.95 (*0-316-78200-9*) Little Brown & Co.

Sharp, Paula. The Woman Who Was Not All There. 1988. 17.95 o.p. (*0-06-015989-8*) HarperTrade.

Stephens, Martha. Children of the World: A Novel. 1994. 416p. (Orig.). pap. 22.50 (*0-87074-378-3*); pap. 10.95 (*0-87074-379-1*) Southern Methodist Univ. Pr.

Stirling, Jessica. Lantern for the Dark. l.t. ed. 1993. pap. 22.95 o.p. (*0-7927-1596-9*); 24.95 o.p. (*0-7927-1597-7*) BBC Audiobooks America.

—Lantern for the Dark. 1992. 368p. 19.95 o.p. (*0-312-07857-9*) St. Martin's Pr.

Texier, Catherine. Panic Blood. 1990. 352p. 18.95 o.p. (*0-670-83231-6*, Viking) Viking Penguin.

Weldon, Fay. The Heart of the Country. 1992. 3.99 o.p. (*0-517-07995-X*) Random Hse. Value Publishing.

—The Heart of the Country. 208p. 1990. pap. 9.95 o.p. (*0-14-010397-X*, Penguin Bks.); 1988. 17.95 o.p. (*0-670-81875-5*) Viking Penguin.

Wheeler, Joe L. Mom in My Heart. 1997. 159p. pap. 10.99 o.p. (*0-8423-0552-1*) Tyndale Hse. Pubs.

Whitney, Phyllis A. Feather on the Moon. l.t. ed. 1989. 368p. 21.95 o.p. (*0-8161-4686-1*); 13.95 o.p. (*0-8161-4687-X*) Gale Group. (Macmillan Reference USA).

Wickham, Madeleine. Swimming Pool Sunday. 1998. 304p. 22.95 o.p. (*0-312-18188-4*) St. Martin's Pr.

Wilson, Gayle. Lady Sarah's Son. 1999. (Harlequin Historicals Ser.: No. 483). per. (*0-373-29083-7*, 1-29083-2, Harlequin Bks.) Harlequin Enterprises, Ltd.

Wolitzer, Meg. Hidden Pictures, 001. 1986. 16.95 o.p. (*0-395-36002-1*) Houghton Mifflin Co.

Wright, Sarah E. This Child's Gonna Live. 1986. 304p. (C). reprint ed. pap. 10.95 o.p. (*0-935312-67-6*); 2nd ed. 2002. 320p. pap. 15.95 (*1-55861-397-8*) Feminist Pr. at The City Univ. of New York.

Yorke, Margaret. Criminal Damage. 1993. 256p. 17.95 (*0-89296-499-5*) Mysterious Pr.

Zaroulis, Nancy. Certain Kinds of Loving. 1986. 312p. 15.95 o.p. (*0-385-17549-3*) Doubleday Publishing.

—Certain Kinds of Loving. l.t. ed. 1988. 360p. 18.95 o.p. (*0-8161-4327-7*, Macmillan Reference USA) Gale Group.

## MOTHERS AND DAUGHTERS—FICTION

Abbey, Lynn. Out of Time. 2000. 320p. mass mkt. 6.50 (*0-441-00751-1*) Ace Bks.

Adams, Glenda. The Tempest of Clemenza: A Novel. 1996. 312p. 22.95 o.p. (*0-571-19897-X*) Faber & Faber, Inc.

Adeline Mowbray. 1986. pap. 9.95 o.p. (*0-86358-085-8*) Pandora Pr. GBR. *Dist:* HarperSanFrancisco.

Adler, Warren. Mourning Glory. l.t. ed. 2001. (Wheeler Large Print Book Ser.). 498p. 28.95 o.p. (*1-58724-115-3*, Wheeler Publishing, Inc.) Gale Group.

—Mourning Glory. 352p. 2002. mass mkt. 6.99 o.s.i (*0-7582-0044-7*); 2001. 23.00 o.s.i (*1-57566-898-X*) Kensington Publishing Corp.

—Mourning Glory. E-Book 9.95 (*1-59006-071-7*); E-Book 9.95 (*1-931304-23-8*) Stonehouse Pr., Inc.

Aiken, Joan. Lady Catherines Necklace. 2000. 172p. 21.95 (*0-312-24406-1*) St. Martin's Pr.

—Lady Catherine's Necklace. l.t. ed. 2000. (General Ser.). 230p. pap. 24.95 (*0-7862-2629-3*) Thorndike Pr.

Alberts, Laurie. Lost Daughters. 1999. 217p. text 26.95 (*0-87451-898-9*, Hardscrabble Bks.) Univ. Pr. of New England.

Alder, Elizabeth. A Summer in Tuscany. 2002. (Illus.). 304p. 23.95 o.s.i (*0-312-26996-X*) St. Martin's Pr.

Allen, Grant. The Woman Who Did. Windle, Sarah & Trotter, David, eds. 1995. (Oxford Popular Fiction Ser.). 148p. pap. 8.95 o.p. (*0-19-282312-4*) Oxford Univ. Pr., Inc.

Allen, Shirley S. Roxanna Britton. 2001. 388p. per. 16.00 (*1-884162-08-8*) Criterion Hse.

Allison, Dorothy. Cavedweller. abr. ed. 1998. audio 7.99 o.s.i (*1-56740-280-1*, 1681, Paperback Nova Audio Bks.); audio 17.95 o.p. (*1-56740-763-3*, 463, Nova Audio Bks.); audio 28.95 (*1-56100-788-9*, 60, Bookcassette); 15p. audio 89.25 (*1-56740-567-3*, 822, Unabridged Library Editions) Brilliance Audio.

—Cavedweller. 448p. 1999. pap. 13.95 (*0-452-27969-0*, Plume); 1998. 24.95 o.s.i (*0-525-94167-3*) Dutton/Plume.

—Cavedweller. l.t. ed. 1998. (Basic Ser.). 683p. 28.95 (*0-7862-1503-8*) Thorndike Pr.

Alther, Lisa. Kinflicks. 1996. 528p. pap. 13.95 o.p. (*0-452-27677-2*, Plume) Dutton/Plume.

—Kinflicks. 1977. mass mkt. 2.50 o.p. (*0-451-08445-4*); mass mkt. 3.50 o.p. (*0-451-11241-5*); mass mkt. 2.95 o.p. (*0-451-09474-3*); mass mkt. 2.75 o.p. (*0-451-08984-7*); mass mkt. 2.25 o.p. (*0-451-07390-8*); mass mkt. 3.95 o.p. (*0-451-11985-1*); 528p. reprint ed. mass mkt. 5.99 o.p. (*0-451-15685-4*) NAL. (Signet Bks.).

—Kinflicks. 1976. 8.95 o.p. (*0-394-49836-4*, Knopf Bks. for Young Readers) Random Hse. Children's Bks.

Alvarez, Julia. En el Nombre de Salome. 2002. Tr. of In the Name of Salome. (SPA.). 384p. pap. 14.00 (*0-375-72690-X*, Vintage) Knopf Publishing Group.

—In the Name of Salome. 2000. 357p. tchr. ed. 23.95 (*1-56512-276-3*, 72276) Algonquin Bks. of Chapel Hill.

Andrews, V. C. Cinnamon. l.t. ed. 2002. (Core Collection). 186p. 29.95 (*0-7838-9750-2*) Gale Group.

—The End of the Rainbow. 2002. (Hudson Ser.: No. 4). E-Book 7.99 (*1-59061-643-X*) Adobe Systems, Inc.

—The End of the Rainbow. 2001. (Hudson Ser.: Vol. 4). 384p. 24.95 (*0-671-03984-9*, Atria); E-Book 24.95 (*0-7434-2167-1*, Pocket); (Illus.). 384p. reprint ed. pap. 7.99 (*0-671-03985-7*, Pocket) Simon & Schuster.

—The End of the Rainbow. l.t. ed. 2001. 430p. 31.95 (*0-7838-9512-7*) Thorndike Pr.

—The End of the Rainbow. 2001. (Hudson Family Ser.). 14.04 (*0-606-20651-5*) Turtleback Bks.

—Ice. 2002. E-Book 4.99 (*1-4014-9962-7*) Barnes & Noble Digital.

—Ice. 2001. (Shooting Stars Ser.). (Illus.). 208p. pap. 4.99 (*0-671-03994-6*); reprint ed. E-Book 4.99 (*0-7434-2172-8*) Simon & Schuster. (Pocket).

—Unfinished Symphony. 1997. (Logan Ser.). 352p. 24.00 o.s.i (*0-671-53469-6*, Atria); 384p. mass mkt. 7.99 (*0-671-53473-4*, Pocket) Simon & Schuster.

—Unfinished Symphony. l.t. ed. 1998. (Core Ser.). 479p. 30.95 (*0-7838-8407-9*) Thorndike Pr.

—Unfinished Symphony. 1997. 14.04 (*0-606-13883-8*) Turtleback Bks.

Anshaw, Carol. Lucky in the Corner. 2002. 256p. tchr. ed. 23.00 (*0-395-94040-0*) Houghton Mifflin Co.

Askari, Brent. Not Ready for Prime Time. 1999. 234p. 24.95 (*0-7867-0648-1*, Carroll & Graf Pubs.) Avalon Publishing Group.

Atkinson, Kate. Emotionally Weird. (*0-312-28221-4*); 2001. 352p. pap. 23.00 (*0-312-27999-X*); 2000. 343p. 25.00 o.p. (*0-312-20324-1*) Picador.

Badami, Anita Rau. Tamarind Woman. 2002. 272p. 23.95 (*1-56512-335-2*) Algonquin Bks. of Chapel Hill.

—Tamarind Woman. 2004. 304p. pap. 13.95 (*0-345-46494-X*) Ballantine Bks.

Baggott, Julianna. Girl Talk. 2001. E-Book 23.95 (*0-7434-2143-4*, Atria); 2001. (Illus.). 256p. 23.95 (*0-7434-0082-8*, Atria); 2002. 272p. reprint ed. pap. 14.00 (*0-7434-0083-6*, Washington Square Pr.) Simon & Schuster.

Bailey, Eleanor. Idioglossia. 2003. 448p. pap. 13.00 (*0-552-99860-5*) Black Swan GBR. *Dist:* Trafalgar Square.

—Idioglossia. 2000. 381p. (*0-385-60114-X*) Doubleday Publishing.

Bailey-Williams, Nicole. A Little Piece of Sky. 2002. 176p. reprint ed. pap. 9.95 (*0-7679-1216-0*, Harlem Moon) Broadway Bks.

Bainbridge, Beryl. According to Queeney. 224p. 2001. 22.00 (*0-7867-0773-9*); 2002. reprint ed. pap. 12.00 (*0-7867-0982-0*) Avalon Publishing Group. (Carroll & Graf Pubs.).

—According to Queeney. l.t. ed. 2002. 242p. pap. 23.95 (*0-7862-3958-1*) Gale Group.

Bambola, Sylvia. Waters of Marah. 2004. 12.99 (*0-8024-7905-7*) Moody Pr.

Bandele, Asha. Daughter: A Novel. 2003. 272p. 23.00 (*0-7432-1184-7*, Scribner) Simon & Schuster.

Banks, T. J. Souleiado. 2002. (Five Star First Edition Women's Fiction Ser.). 268p. 25.95 (*0-7862-3703-1*, Five Star) Gale Group.

Barkhordar-Nahai, Gina. Moonlight on the Avenue of Faith. 2000. 400p. reprint ed. pap. 13.95 (*0-671-04283-1*, Washington Square Pr.) Simon & Schuster.

Bates, Roy. The Angel of Eleventh Avenue. 2002. 128p. 9.95 (*1-4022-0028-5*) Sourcebooks, Inc.

Bausch, Robert. The Gypsy Man. 2002. 512p. 25.00 (*0-15-100172-3*) Harcourt Trade Pubs.

Bedford, Sybille. Compass Error. 2001. 240p. pap. text 16.00 (*1-58243-159-0*, Counterpoint Pr.) Basic Bks.

Bell, Michele Ashman. Candle in the Window. 2001. 3.95 (*1-57734-904-0*) Covenant Communications.

Bender, Karen E. Like Normal People. l.t. ed. 2000. (G. K. Hall Core Ser.). 384p. 27.95 (*0-7838-9301-9*, Macmillan Reference USA) Gale Group.

—Like Normal People. 2000. 288p. tchr. ed. 23.00 (*0-395-94515-1*) Houghton Mifflin Co.

—Like Normal People. 2001. 288p. pap. 13.00 (*0-618-12692-9*, Mariner Bks.) Houghton Mifflin Co. Trade & Reference Div.

Berg, Elizabeth. What We Keep. l.t. ed. 1998. 26.95 (*1-56895-661-4*, Wheeler Publishing, Inc.) Gale Group.

—What We Keep: A Novel. 1999. (Ballantine Reader's Circle Ser.). 304p. pap. 14.00 (*0-345-42329-1*) Ballantine Bks.

—What We Keep: A Novel. 1998. 288p. 23.00 o.s.i (*0-375-50099-5*) Random Hse., Inc.

Berman, Sabina. Bubbeh. Labinger, Andrea G., tr. from SPA. 1998. (Discoveries Ser.). 96p. pap. 12.95 (*0-935480-93-5*) Latin American Literary Review Pr.

Bialosky, Jill. House under Snow. 2003. 264p. pap. 14.00 (*0-15-602746-1*, Harvest Bks.); 2002. 256p. 24.00 (*0-15-100685-7*) Harcourt Trade Pubs.

Billington, Rachel. Loving Attitudes. 1988. 224p. 15.95 o.p. (*0-688-07574-6*, Morrow, William & Co.) Morrow/Avon.

—Loving Attitudes. l.t. ed. 1989. (Ulverscroft Large Print Ser.). 473p. o.p. (*0-7089-1939-1*, Ulverscroft) Thorpe, F. A. Pubs. GBR. *Dist:* Ulverscroft Large Print Canada, Ltd.

Blackstock, Terri. Never Again Good-Bye. 1996. (Second Chances Ser.: No. 1). 240p. pap. 10.99 (*0-310-20707-X*) Zondervan.

—Never Again Goodbye. l.t. ed. 1999. (Christian Fiction Ser.). 312p. 24.95 (*0-7862-1675-1*) Thorndike Pr.

—Seaside: A Novella. l.t. ed. 2001. 137p. 26.95 (*0-7838-9511-9*, Macmillan Reference USA) Gale Group.

Block, Brett Ellen. The Grave of God's Daughter. 2004. 304p. 23.95 (*0-06-052504-5*, Morrow, William & Co.) Morrow/Avon.

Bockoven, Georgia. Disguised Blessing. l.t. ed. 2000. (Large Print Book Ser.). 379p. pap. 24.95 (*1-56895-913-3*, Wheeler Publishing, Inc.) Gale Group.

—Disguised Blessing. 2000. 400p. mass mkt. 6.50 (*0-06-103020-1*) HarperCollins Pubs.

Boyle, Kay. Process: A Novel. Spanier, Sandra Whipple, ed. & intro. by. 2002. (Illus.). 168p. 24.95 (*0-252-02668-3*) Univ. of Illinois Pr.

Bradford, Barbara Taylor. Power of a Woman. 1997. 352p. 25.00 o.p. (*0-06-018268-7*) HarperCollins Pubs.

—Power of a Woman. 1998. 432p. mass mkt. 7.50 (*0-06-109440-4*, HarperTorch) Morrow/Avon.

—Power of a Woman. l.t. ed. (Paperback Bestsellers Ser.). 464p. 1999. pap. 28.95 (*0-7862-1224-1*); 1998. 31.95 (*0-7862-1223-3*) Thorndike Pr.

Brady, Maureen. Folly. 1994. 224p. reprint ed. 35.00 (*1-55861-078-2*); pap. 12.95 (*1-55861-079-0*) Feminist Pr. at The City Univ. of New York.

—Folly: A Novel. 1982. 198p. 23.95 o.p. (*0-89594-091-4*); pap. 8.95 o.p. (*0-89594-090-6*) Crossing Pr., Inc., The.

Brandeis, Gayle. The Book of Dead Birds: A Novel. 2003. 256p. 23.95 (*0-06-052803-6*, HarperCollins) HarperTrade.

Brasfield, Lynette. Nature Lessons: A Novel. 2003. 288p. 23.95 (*0-312-31034-X*) St. Martin's Pr.

Brenna, Duff. The Altar of the Body. 2001. 336p. 24.00 (*0-312-26865-3*) Picador.

—The Altar of the Body: A Novel. 2002. 336p. pap. 13.00 (*0-312-26914-5*) Picador.

Brennan, Maeve. The Visitor. 2001. 96p. pap. text 10.00 (*1-58243-161-2*, Counterpoint Pr.) Basic Bks.

—Visitor. 2000. 96p. text 16.95 o.p. (*1-58243-083-7*, Counterpoint Pr.) Basic Bks.

Brookner, Anita. The Bay of Angels. E-Book 9.95 (*1-58945-826-5*) Adobe Systems, Inc.

—The Bay of Angels. 2002. 208p. pap. 12.00 (*0-375-72760-4*) Knopf, Alfred A. Inc.

—The Bay of Angels. E-Book 19.00 (*1-58836-006-7*) Random Hse., Inc.

—The Bay of Angels. 2001. (Thorndike Press Large Print Women's Fiction Ser.). 335p. 29.95 (*0-7862-3654-X*) Thorndike Pr.

—Fraud. (Vintage Contemporaries Ser.). 1994. 272p. pap. 13.00 (*0-679-74308-1*); 1994. mass mkt. o.s.i (*0-394-22272-5*); 1993. 262p. 21.00 o.s.i (*0-679-41606-4*) Random Hse., Inc.

—Undue Influence. l.t. ed. 2000. (G. K. Hall Core Ser.). 306p. 29.95 (*0-7838-9001-X*, Macmillan Reference USA) Gale Group.

—Undue Influence. 2001. 240p. pap. 12.00 (*0-375-70734-4*, Vintage) Knopf Publishing Group.

Brown, Rosellen. Half a Heart. l.t. ed. 2001. (Large Print Book Ser.). 575p. 29.95 (*1-58724-017-3*, Wheeler Publishing, Inc.) Gale Group.

—Half a Heart. 2001. 416p. pap. 14.00 (*0-312-27830-6*) Picador.

Bruckheimer, Linda. The Southern Belles of Honeysuckle Way. 2004. 336p. 24.95 (*0-525-94454-0*, Dutton) Dutton/Plume.

Bruneau, Carol. Purple for Sky. 2000. 407p. (*1-896951-24-4*) Cormorant Bks.

Bunting, Josiah, III. All Loves Excelling. 2002. 320p. reprint ed. pap. 14.00 (*0-425-18612-1*) Berkley Publishing Group.

—All Loves Excelling. 2001. 224p. 22.95 (*1-882593-40-5*) Bridge Works Publishing Co., Inc.

Burgess, Yvonne. Say a Little Mantra for Me. 2nd ed. 1995. (Ravan Writers Ser.). 166p. reprint ed. pap. text 12.95 (*0-86975-467-X*) Ravan Pr. ZMB. *Dist:* Ohio Univ. Pr.

Burke, Martyn. Ivory Joe. 303p. 2002. 24.91 (*1-58721-540-3*); 2000. pap. 17.10 (*1-58721-515-2*) 1stBooks Library.

Burns, Elizabeth. Tilt: Every Family Spins on Its Own Axis. 2003. 256p. 22.00 (*1-4022-0041-2*, Sourcebooks Landmark) Sourcebooks, Inc.

Burton, Rainelle. The Root Worker. 2001. 208p. 25.95 (*1-58567-140-1*) Overlook Pr., The.

—The Root Worker. 2002. 208p. reprint ed. pap. 13.00 (*0-14-200085-X*) Viking Penguin.

Bush, Catherine. Minus Time. 2nd ed. 1995. (High Risk Ser.). 320p. pap. (*1-85242-408-7*) Serpent's Tail Ltd.

—Minus Time: A Novel. 1993. 352p. 19.95 o.p. (*1-56282-881-9*) Hyperion Pr.

Butler, Tajuana. Hand-Me-Down Heartache: A Novel. 2003. 256p. pap. 11.95 (*0-8129-6833-6*); 2001. E-Book 18.00 (*1-58836-107-1*) Random House Adult Trade Publishing Group. (Villard Bks.).

Campbell, Bebe Moore. What You Owe Me. 2001. 400p. 25.95 o.p. (0-399-14784-5) Penguin Group (USA) Inc.
—What You Owe Me. 2002. (African American Ser.). 915p. 29.95 (0-7862-3875-5) Thorndike Pr.
Campbell, Bonnie Jo. Women & Other Animals: Stories. 1999. 208p. 27.50 (1-55849-219-4) Univ. of Massachusetts Pr.
Campbell, Drusilla. Edge of the Sky. 2004. 324p. pap. 15.00 (0-7582-0535-X, Kensington Bks.) Kensington Publishing Corp.
Carey, Lisa. The Mermaids Singing. 2001. 288p. pap. 13.00 (0-380-81559-1, Perennial) HarperTrade.
—The Mermaids Singing. 1998. 257p. (YA). 22.00 (0-380-97674-9, Avon Bks.) Morrow/Avon.
—Mermaids Singing. 1999. 352p. (gr. 8 up). mass mkt. 6.99 (0-380-79960-X, Avon Bks.) Morrow/Avon.
Cartland, Barbara. A Caretaker of Love. l.t. ed. 2001. (G. K. Hall Romance Ser.). 208p. 27.95 (0-7838-9461-9, Macmillan Reference USA) Gale Group.
Chaikin, Linda Lee. Tomorrow's Treasure. 2003. 400p. pap. 13.99 (1-57856-513-8) WaterBrook Pr.
Chepaitis, Barbara. These Dreams. 2003. 320p. pap. 13.00 (0-7434-3751-9, Washington Square Pr.); 2002. 320p. 24.00 (0-7434-3750-0, Atria); 2002. E-Book 9.99 (0-7434-3793-4, Atria) Simon & Schuster.
Chiaverini, Jennifer. Quilter's Legacy. 2004. 320p. pap. 13.00 (0-452-28467-8, Plume) Dutton/Plume.
Christie, Agatha. A Daughter's a Daughter & Other Novels. 2001. 576p. pap. 17.95 (0-312-27472-6, Saint Martin's Griffin) St. Martin's Pr.
Ciresi, Rita. Sometimes I Dream in Italian. 2001. 224p. pap. 12.95 (0-385-33494-X, Delta) Dell Publishing.
—Sometimes I Dream in Italian. l.t. ed. 2001. (Basic Ser.). 320p. 28.95 (0-7862-3080-0) Thorndike Pr.
Claire, Regi. The Beauty Room. 2002. 160p. pap. 12.95 (0-7486-6322-3) Polygon GBR. *Dist:* Interlink Publishing Group, Inc.
Clark, Catherine. Gilmore Girls. 2002. (Illus.). 160p. mass mkt. 5.99 (0-06-051023-4, HarperEntertainment) Morrow/Avon.
Clark, Mary Jane. Close to You. 2001. 336p. 24.95 (0-312-26266-3) St. Martin's Pr.
Cline, Rachel. What to Keep: A Novel. 2004. 304p. 23.95 (1-4000-6183-0) Random Hse., Inc.
Cohen, Anthea. Dream On. l.t. ed. 2000. (G. K. Hall Nightingale Ser.). 287p. pap. 20.95 (0-7838-9258-6); (0-7540-4299-5); (0-7540-4300-2) Gale Group. (Macmillan Reference USA).
Collins, Brandilyn. Color the Sidewalk for Me. 2002. 384p. pap. 12.99 (0-310-24242-8) Zondervan.
Collins, Joan. Star Quality. 2003. 368p. mass mkt. 6.99 (0-7868-9048-7) Hyperion Pr.
—Star Quality: A Novel. 2003. mass mkt. 7.99 (0-7868-9060-6); 2002. 368p. 23.95 (1-4013-0000-6); 2002. mass mkt. 7.99 (0-7868-9064-9) Hyperion Pr.
—Star Quality: A Novel. 2003. (Core Ser.). 32.95 (0-7862-4694-4) Thorndike Pr.
Cook, Karin. What Girls Learn: A Novel. 1998. 19.05 (0-606-15863-4) Turtleback Bks.
Coyle, Neva. Close to a Father's Heart. 1996. (Summerwind Ser.: Vol. 3). 256p. pap. 8.99 o.p. (1-55661-548-5) Bethany Hse. Pubs.
—Close to a Father's Heart. l.t. ed. 2001. 300p. 23.95 (0-7862-2936-5, Five Star) Gale Group.
Crawford, Dianna. Lady of the River. 2003. (HeartQuest Ser.). 352p. pap. 9.99 (0-8423-6011-5) Tyndale Hse. Pubs.
Craze, Galaxy. By the Shore. 2000. 240p. pap. 12.00 (0-8021-3687-7, Grove Pr.); 1999. 232p. 24.00 o.p. (0-87113-746-1, Atlantic Monthly Pr.) Grove/Atlantic, Inc.
—By the Shore. 2000. 18.05 (0-606-19408-8) Turtleback Bks.
Crowe, Carole. Waiting for Dolphins. 2003. 144p. (YA). pap. 9.95 (1-59078-073-6); (Illus.). (gr. 7-9). 16.95 (1-56397-847-4) Boyds Mills Pr.
Cruz, Angie. Soledad. 2001. 240p. 23.00 (0-7432-1201-0, Simon & Schuster) Simon & Schuster.
Darcy, Emma. Bride of His Choice. 2000. (Harlequin Presents Ser.: No. 2080). per. (0-373-12080-X, 1-12080-7, Harlequin Bks.) Harlequin Enterprises, Ltd.
—Bride of His Choice. l.t. ed. 2000. (Harlequin I Romance Ser.). 288p. 22.95 (0-263-16484-5) Thorndike Pr.
Darling, Julia. Crocodile Soup: A Novel. 2000. 352p. 25.00 (0-06-019602-5, Ecco) HarperTrade.
Darrieussecq, Marie. A Brief Stay with the Living. 2003. 272p. (0-571-21494-0) Faber & Faber, Inc.
David, Esther. The Walled City. 2002. (Library of Modern Jewish Literature). 204p. pap. 19.95 (0-8156-0750-4) Syracuse Univ. Pr.
Davison, Liam. The Betrayal. 1999. 273p. (0-670-88652-1, Viking) Viking Penguin.
Dorrell, Linda. Face to Face. 2002. 224p. (gr. 13 up). pap. 11.99 (0-8010-6425-2) Baker Bks.
Dorris, Michael. A Yellow Raft in Blue Water. 1987. 356p. 16.95 o.p. (0-8050-0045-3) Holt, Henry & Co.
—A Yellow Raft in Blue Water. 2001. pap., stu. ed., wbk. ed. (1-56137-934-4) Novel Units, Inc.
—A Yellow Raft in Blue Water. 1988. 384p. reprint ed. pap. 14.00 o.p. (0-446-38787-8) Warner Bks., Inc.
—A Yellow Raft in Blue Water: A Novel. 2003. 384p. pap. 14.00 (0-312-42185-0) Picador.
Douglas, Carole Nelson. Femme Fatale. Date not set. mass mkt. (0-7653-4595-1); 2003. 554p. 25.95 (0-7653-0682-4) Doherty, Tom Assocs., LLC. (Forge Bks.).
Drabble, Margaret. The Seven Sisters. 320p. 2003. pap. 14.00 (0-15-602875-1); 2002. 25.00 (0-15-100740-3) Harcourt Trade Pubs.
—The Seven Sisters. 2003. 320p. pap. (0-7710-2905-5) McClelland & Stewart.
Dufaux, Jean, et al. Dixie Road, Vol. 2. 2000. (Illus.). 48p. pap. 10.95 (1-56163-265-1) NBM Publishing Co.
Duncan, Pamela. Moon Women. 2002. 336p. pap. 12.95 (0-385-33521-0, Delta) Dell Publishing.
Durban, Pam. So Far Back. 272p. 2001. pap. 13.00 (0-312-28347-4); 2000. 23.00 o.s.i (0-312-26869-6) Picador.
—So Far Back. E-Book 23.00 (0-312-27168-9) St. Martin's Pr.
Eagle, Kathleen. Once upon a Wedding. 2003. 384p. mass mkt. 6.99 (0-06-103243-3, Avon Bks.); 2002. 304p. 24.95 (0-06-621472-6, Morrow, William & Co.) Morrow/Avon.
Elam, Patricia. Breathing Room. 2001. (Illus.). 352p. 24.95 (0-671-02842-1, Atria) Simon & Schuster.
Engel, Mary Potter. A Woman of Salt. 2001. 256p. text 24.00 (1-58243-156-6, Counterpoint Pr.) Basic Bks.
—A Woman of Salt. 2003. 256p. pap. text 17.00 (1-58243-249-X) Perseus Publishing.
Ephron, G. H. Addiction. 2001. 304p. 23.95 (0-312-26677-4, Saint Martin's Minotaur) St. Martin's Pr.
Esaki-Smith, Anna. Meeting Luciano. 1999. 252p. tchr. ed. 18.95 (1-56512-215-1, 72215) Algonquin Bks. of Chapel Hill.
—Meeting Luciano. 2000. 272p. pap. 12.00 (0-345-43682-2, Ballantine Bks.) Ballantine Bks.
Esquivel, Laura. The Law of Love. 1997. Tr. of Ley del Amor. (Illus.). 288p. pap. 18.95 (0-609-80127-9) Random Hse. Value Publishing.
Everson, Eva Marie & Chadwick, G. W. Shadow of Dreams: A Novel. 2001. 199p. pap. 10.99 (1-58660-143-1) Barbour Publishing, Inc.
Everson, Eva Marie & Chadwick, G. W. Francis. Shadow of Dreams. l.t. ed. 2003. (Christian Mystery Ser.). 28.95 (0-7862-4565-4) Thorndike Pr.
Fielding, Joy. The First Time. l.t. ed. 2001. (Wheeler Large Print Book Ser.). 510p. 29.95 o.p. (1-58724-057-2, Wheeler Publishing, Inc.) Gale Group.
—The First Time. 2003. (Illus.). 512p. mass mkt. 5.99 (0-7434-6714-0, Pocket Star); 2000. (Illus.). 400p. 24.95 (0-7434-0705-9, Atria); 1999. (0-7434-2268-6, Atria); 1999. 512p. mass mkt. 7.99 (0-7434-4636-4, Pocket); 2001. (Illus.). 512p. reprint ed. mass mkt. 7.99 (0-7434-0706-7, Pocket Star); 2001. 400p. reprint ed. mass mkt. 7.99 (0-7434-1724-0, Pocket) Simon & Schuster.
Fitch, Janet. White Oleander, Set. abr. ed. 1999. audio 24.98 Highsmith Inc.
—White Oleander. (Oprah's Book Club Selection Ser. ). 1999. pap. 7.99 (0-316-28508-0, Back Bay); 1999. 390p. (gr. 8). 24.95 (0-316-56932-1); 1999. 400p. 24.00 o.p. (0-316-28526-9); 2000. 464p. pap. 13.95 (0-316-28495-5, Back Bay) Little Brown & Co.
—White Oleander. unabr. ed. 1999. audio 96.00 (0-7887-3471-7, 95890E7); audio compact disk 112.00 (0-7887-3970-0, C1089E7) Recorded Bks., LLC.
—White Oleander. l.t. ed. 2002. 14.00 (1-4104-0081-6, Large Print Pr.); 2000. 613p. pap. 27.95 (0-7862-2166-6); 1999. 613p. 30.95 (0-7862-2095-3) Thorndike Pr.
—White Oleander. abr. ed. 1999. audio 24.98 (1-57042-821-2) Time Warner AudioBooks.
—White Oleander. 2000. 19.75 (0-606-19031-7) Turtleback Bks.
Fitzgerald, Penelope. Offshore. 1989. 150p. pap. 7.95 o.p. (0-88184-476-4, Carroll & Graf Pubs.) Avalon Publishing Group.
—Offshore. l.t. ed. 1994. 18.95 o.p. (0-7927-2028-8); pap. 17.95 o.p. (0-7927-2027-X) BBC Audiobooks America.
—Offshore. 1987. 15.95 o.p. (0-8050-0561-7) Holt, Henry & Co.
—Offshore. 1998. 144p. pap. 11.00 (0-395-47804-9) Houghton Mifflin Co.
—Offshore, Human Voices: The Beginning of Spring. 2003. 480p. 23.00 (1-4000-4125-2, Everyman's Library) Knopf Publishing Group.
Florey, Kitty Burns. Souvenir of Cold Springs. 2001. 320p. text 25.00 (1-58243-153-1, Counterpoint Pr.) Basic Bks.
—Souvenir of Cold Springs. 2003. 336p. pap. 14.00 (0-425-18840-X) Berkley Publishing Group.
Frank, Dorothea Benton. Plantation. 2004. 544p. pap. 13.95 (0-425-19418-3) Berkley Publishing Group.
Frankel, Valerie. The Not-So-Perfect Man. 2004. 368p. pap. 13.95 (0-06-053668-3, Avon Bks.) Morrow/Avon.
Freed, Lynn. House of Women. 2003. 240p. reprint ed. pap. 12.95 (0-316-09556-7, Back Bay) Little Brown & Co.
—House of Women: A Novel. 2002. 224p. 23.95 o.p. (0-316-66633-5) Little Brown & Co.
French, Wendy. Smothering. Date not set. mass mkt. (0-7653-4703-2); 2003. 304p. 23.95 (0-7653-0793-6) Doherty, Tom Assocs., LLC. (Forge Bks.).
Friesen, Gayle. Janey's Girl. (YA). (gr. 6 up). 2001. 224p. pap. 6.95 (1-55074-463-1); 1998. (Illus.). 316p. text (1-55074-461-5) Kids Can Pr., Ltd.
Fromm, Pete. As Cool As I Am: A Novel. 2003. 272p. 24.00 (0-312-30775-6) Picador.
Gaffney, Patricia. Circle of Three. l.t. ed. 2000. 608p. pap. 24.00 (0-06-019706-4) HarperCollins Pubs.
—Circle of Three. 2000. 432p. 24.00 (0-06-019375-1, HarperCollins) HarperTrade.
—Circle of Three: A Novel. 2001. 448p. mass mkt. 7.50 (0-06-109836-1, HarperTorch) Morrow/Avon.
Ganesan, Indira. The Journey. 2001. (Bluestreak Ser.). 176p. pap. 13.00 (0-8070-8353-4) Beacon Pr.
Garcia, Eric. Matchstick Men: A Novel of Petty Crimes. 2003. 240p. pap. 12.95 (0-8129-6821-2) Random House Adult Trade Publishing Group.
Garcia, Cristina. Dreaming in Cuban. 1999. pap. (0-345-91367-1, Ballantine Bks.); 1993. (SPA.). 256p. pap. 14.00 (0-345-38143-2, One World/ Ballantine) Ballantine Bks.
—Dreaming in Cuban. 1992. 20.00 o.s.i (0-679-40883-5) Knopf, Alfred A. Inc.
—Sonar en Cubano. 1994. (SPA.). 336p. pap. 12.95 (0-345-39139-X, RH9018, Ballantine Bks.) Ballantine Bks.
Garnett, Gale Z. Visible Amazement. 2001. (Illus.). 288p. 23.00 (0-684-87306-0, Simon & Schuster) Simon & Schuster.
Garrotto, A. J. Finding Isabella. 2000. (Tango 2 Romance Ser.). 270p. pap. 8.95 (1-58571-005-9) Genesis Pr., Inc.
Gershten, Donna M. Kissing the Virgin's Mouth. 2001. 240p. 23.00 (0-06-018567-8) HarperCollins Pubs.
Gertler, Stephanie. Drifting. 2003. 288p. 23.95 (0-525-94735-3, Dutton) Dutton/Plume.
—Drifting. 2004. 352p. mass mkt. 6.99 (0-451-21263-0, Signet Bks.) NAL.
Gibbons, Kaye. Sights Unseen. l.t. ed. 1995. 191p. 23.95 o.p. (0-7838-1485-2, Macmillan Reference USA) Gale Group.
—Sights Unseen. 1996. mass mkt. o.s.i (0-349-10759-9) Little Brown & Co.
—Sights Unseen. 1997. 224p. pap. 12.00 (0-380-72972-5); 1996. 240p. mass mkt. 6.99 (0-380-72681-5) Morrow/Avon. (Avon Bks.).
—Sights Unseen. 1995. 256p. 19.95 o.p. (0-399-13986-9, G. P. Putnam's Sons) Penguin Group (USA) Inc.
—Sights Unseen. abr. ed. 1995. audio 17.00 (0-671-88568-5, 393158, Simon & Schuster Audioworks) Simon & Schuster Audio.
Giroux, E. X. The Dying Room. 1993. 288p. 19.95 o.p. (0-312-09791-3, Saint Martin's Minotaur) St. Martin's Pr.
Goldstein, Rebecca. Mazel. 1996. 368p. pap. 12.95 o.s.i (0-14-023905-7, Penguin Bks.) Penguin Group (USA) Inc.
—Mazel. 2002. (Library of American Fiction). 368p. pap. 19.95 (0-299-18124-3) Univ. of Wisconsin Pr.
—Mazel. 1995. 368p. 23.95 o.s.i (0-670-85648-7, Viking) Viking Penguin.
Goodman, Carol. The Seduction of Water. 2003. 368p. 23.95 (0-345-45090-6, Ballantine Bks.) Ballantine Bks.
—The Seduction of Water. l.t. ed. 2003. 28.95 (1-58724-421-7, Wheeler Publishing, Inc.) Gale Group.
Goudge, Eileen. Stranger in Paradise. 2002. 432p. reprint ed. mass mkt. 7.99 (0-451-20577-4, Signet Bks.) NAL.
—Stranger in Paradise. l.t. ed. 2002. (Carson Spring Ser.: Bk. 1). 573p. pap. 13.95 (0-7862-3447-4); 2001. 586p. 31.95 (0-7862-3446-6) Thorndike Pr.
—Stranger in Paradise. 2001. (Carson Spring Ser.: Bk. 1). 384p. 24.95 o.s.i (0-670-89987-9, Viking) Viking Penguin.
—Taste of Honey. 2003. 432p. reprint ed. mass mkt. 7.99 (0-451-20734-3, Signet Bks.) NAL.
—Taste of Honey. l.t. ed. 2002. (Basic Ser.). 699p. 32.95 (0-7862-4562-X) Thorndike Pr.
—Taste of Honey. 2002. 336p. 24.95 o.s.i (0-670-03098-8, Viking) Viking Penguin.
—Thorns of Truth. l.t. ed. 1998. 27.95 (1-56895-659-2, Wheeler Publishing, Inc.) Gale Group.
—Thorns of Truth. 1999. 416p. reprint ed. mass mkt. 7.99 (0-451-18527-7, Signet Bks.) NAL.
—Thorns of Truth. 1998. 448p. 24.95 o.p. (0-670-87942-8, Viking) Viking Penguin.
Gould, Judith. The Greek Villa. 2003. 352p. 23.95 (0-451-21047-6) NAL.
Grau, Shirley Ann. Roadwalkers. 2003. (Voices of the South Ser.). 292p. 17.95 (0-8071-2913-5) Louisiana State Univ. Pr.
Graver, Elizabeth. The Honey Thief: A Novel. 2000. 272p. pap. 13.00 (0-15-601390-8, Harvest Bks.) Harcourt Trade Pubs.
—The Honey Thief: A Novel. 1999. 263p. 22.95 (0-7868-6282-3) Hyperion Pr.
—The Honey Thief: A Novel. l.t. ed. 1999. (Basic Ser.). 400p. 28.95 (0-7862-2256-5) Thorndike Pr.
Gupta, Sunetra. A Sin of Color: A Novel of Obsession. 2001. 288p. pap. 15.00 (1-57071-856-3, Sourcebooks Landmark) Sourcebooks, Inc.
Gutteridge, Rene. Troubled Waters. 2003. 400p. pap. 12.99 (0-7642-2644-4) Bethany Hse. Pubs.
Hadley, Tessa. Everything Will Be All Right. 2003. 320p. 24.00 (0-8050-7065-6) Holt, Henry & Co.
Haines, Lise. In My Sister's Country. 2002. 336p. 24.95 o.s.i (0-399-14857-4, Riverhead Bks. (Hardcovers)); 2003. 304p. reprint ed. pap. 13.00 (0-425-18862-0, BlueHen Bks.) Putnam Publishing Group, The.
Hannah, Kristin. Summer Island. 2002. 416p. mass mkt. 6.99 (0-345-44113-3) Ballantine Bks.
—Summer Island. l.t. ed. 2001. 368p. lib. bdg. 29.95 (1-58547-107-0); 367p. 17.97 (1-74030-498-5) Ctr. Point Large Print.
—Summer Island: A Novel. 2001. 336p. 21.00 o.s.i (0-609-60737-5, Crown) Crown Publishing Group.
Harper, M. A. The Worst Day of My Life, So Far: My Mother, Alzheimer's & Me. 2002. (Harvest Book Ser.). 288p. reprint ed. pap. 14.00 (0-15-600718-5, Harvest Bks.) Harcourt Trade Pubs.
—The Worst Day of My Life, So Far: My Mother, Alzheimer's & Me. 2001. (Illus.). 228p. (YA). 24.00 (1-892514-97-4) Hill Street Pr., LLC.
Harris, Joanne. Five Quarters of the Orange. l.t. ed. 2001. 420p. lib. bdg. 28.95 (1-58547-137-2) Ctr. Point Large Print.
—Five Quarters of the Orange. 2002. 320p. pap. 13.95 (0-06-095802-2, Perennial) HarperTrade.
—Five Quarters of the Orange. 2001. 320p. 25.00 (0-06-019813-3, Morrow, William & Co.) Morrow/ Avon.
Hassinger, Amy. Nina: Adolescence. 2003. 320p. 23.95 (0-399-15062-5, Putnam & Grosset) Putnam Publishing Group, The.
Hatcher, Robin Lee. Firstborn. l.t. ed. 2004. lib. bdg. 27.95 (1-58547-393-6, Premier) Ctr. Point Large Print.
—Firstborn. 336p. 2003. pap. 12.99 (0-8423-5557-X); 2002. 19.99 (0-8423-4010-6) Tyndale Hse. Pubs.
Haynes, David. All American Dream Dolls. 1999. (Harvest Book Ser.). 288p. pap. 12.00 (0-15-600572-7, Harvest Bks.) Harcourt Trade Pubs.
—All American Dream Dolls. 1997. 288p. 21.95 (1-57131-015-0) Milkweed Editions.
Hearon, Shelby. Ella in Bloom. l.t. ed. 2001. (Thorndike Press Large Print Women's Fiction Ser.). 336p. 29.95 (0-7862-3302-8) Thorndike Pr.
—Ella in Bloom: A Novel. 2002. 272p. reprint ed. 13.00 (0-14-200088-4) Viking Penguin.
—The Second Dune. 2003. (Texas Tradition Ser.: No. 33). 200p. pap. 17.95 (0-87565-273-5) Texas Christian Univ. Pr.
Heller, Jane. Lucky Stars. E-Book 24.95 (0-312-70995-1); 2004. 352p. mass mkt. 6.99 (0-312-99006-5, St. Martin's Paperbacks); 2003. 352p. 24.95 (0-312-28848-4) St. Martin's Pr.
Henderson, M. R. Victim. 2002. (Five Star First Edition Mystery Ser.). 250p. 24.95 (0-7862-3930-1, Five Star) Gale Group.
Hendricks, Judith R. Isabel's Daughter. 2004. 400p. pap. 13.95 (0-06-050347-5, Perennial) HarperTrade.
—Isabel's Daughter. 2003. 400p. 24.95 (0-06-050346-7, Morrow, William & Co.) Morrow/Avon.
Herbst, Josephine. Pity Is Not Enough. 1998. (Radical Novel Reconsidered Ser.). 400p. pap. text 18.95 (0-252-06652-9) Univ. of Illinois Pr.
Hicks, Barbara Jean. China Doll. l.t. ed. 1999. (Christian Fiction Ser.). 332p. 23.95 o.p. (0-7862-2155-0) Thorndike Pr.
Hicks, Barbara Jean, et al. China Doll. 1998. (Palisades Pure Romance Ser.). 266p. pap. 9.99 o.p. (1-57673-262-2, Palisades) Multnomah Pubs., Inc.
Hobhouse, Janet. The Furies. 1992. 304p. 22.50 o.s.i (0-385-24547-5); 1994. 240p. reprint ed. pap. 12.95 o.s.i (0-385-47054-1) Doubleday Publishing.
—The Furies. 2004. (New York Review Books Classics Ser.). 320p. pap. 14.00 (1-59017-085-7) New York Review of Bks., Inc., The.
Hoffman, Alice. Local Girls. 2000. 208p. pap. 12.95 (0-425-17434-4) Berkley Publishing Group.
—Local Girls. 1999. 197p. 22.95 o.s.i (0-399-14507-9) Penguin Group (USA) Inc.
—Local Girls. l.t. ed. (Thorndike/G. K. Hall Paperback Bestsellers Ser.). 208p. 2000. pap. 28.95 (0-7862-2010-4); 1999. 29.95 (0-7862-2009-0) Thorndike Pr.

—Local Girls. 2000. 19.00 (*0-606-20422-9*) Turtleback Bks.
—White Horses. 1999. 320p. pap. 12.95 (*0-425-17050-0*); 1993. 304p. mass mkt. 7.99 (*0-425-13980-8*); 1983. mass mkt. 3.50 o.s.i (*0-425-06325-9*) Berkley Publishing Group.
—White Horses. 1982. 256p. 12.95 o.p. (*0-399-12709-7*) Putnam Publishing Group, The.
—White Horses. l.t. ed. 2000. (Basic Ser.). 469p. 29.95 (*0-7862-2313-8*) Thorndike Pr.
Hoffman, Eva. The Secret. 2004. 272p. pap. 12.95 (*0-345-46536-9*) Ballantine Bks.
—The Secret. 2002. 272p. text 25.00 (*1-58648-150-9*) PublicAffairs.
Holman, Sheri. The Mammoth Cheese. l.t. ed. 2003. 726p. 28.95 (*0-7862-6066-1*) Gale Group.
—The Mammoth Cheese. 2003. 592p. 24.00 (*0-87113-900-6*, Atlantic Monthly Pr.) Grove/Atlantic, Inc.
Huff Fisk, Sarah. Found among the Fragments: A Story of Love & Courage. 1997. (Illus.). 320p. (Orig.). pap. 15.95 (*0-9655917-2-7*) Pinhook Publishing Co.
Hugo, Lynne & Villegas, Anna T. Baby's Breath: A Novel. 2000. 384p. 24.95 (*0-912184-13-2*) Synergistic Pr., Inc.
Hyde, Elisabeth. Crazy as Chocolate. 2002. 272p. 25.00 (*1-931561-03-6*) MacAdam/Cage Publishing, Inc.
Hyde, Elizabeth. Crazy as Chocolate. 2003. 272p. pap. 14.00 (*0-425-19246-6*) Berkley Publishing Group.
Jance, J. A. Paradise Lost. 2001. E-Book 7.99 (*0-06-001044-4*) HarperCollins Pubs.
—Paradise Lost. (Joanna Brady Mystery Ser.). 2002. 432p. mass mkt. 7.99 (*0-380-80469-7*, Avon Bks.); 2001. 384p. 25.00 (*0-380-97729-X*, Morrow, William & Co.) Morrow/Avon.
Jenny, Zoe. The Pollen Room: A Novel. 2000. 144p. pap. 10.00 o.s.i (*0-684-85459-7*, Simon & Schuster) Simon & Schuster.
—The Pollen Room: A Novel. Gaffney, Elizabeth, tr. from GER. 1999. 144p. 20.00 o.s.i (*0-684-85458-9*, Simon & Schuster) Simon & Schuster.
Jong, Erica. Inventing Memory: A Novel of Mothers & Daughters. 1997. 336p. 25.00 o.p. (*0-06-017943-0*) HarperTrade.
—Inventing Memory: A Novel of Mothers & Daughters. 1998. 384p. mass mkt. 6.99 (*0-06-109180-4*, HarperTorch) Morrow/Avon.
—Inventing Memory: A Novel of Mothers & Daughters. abr. ed. 1997. 25.00 o.p. (*0-7871-1457-X*) NewStar Media, Inc.
Kagan, Elaine. No Good-Byes. 2001. 400p. mass mkt. 7.50 (*0-06-101492-3*) HarperCollins Pubs.
—No Good-Byes. 2000. 279p. 24.00 (*0-688-15746-7*, Morrow, William & Co.) Morrow/Avon.
Kaplan, Hester. Kinship Theory: A Novel. 2002. 304p. pap. 13.95 (*0-316-50426-2*, Back Bay); 2001. 288p. 24.95 o.p. (*0-316-48211-0*) Little Brown & Co.
Kauffman, Janet. Collaborators. 1993. 144p. reprint ed. pap. 11.00 o.p. (*1-55597-185-7*) Graywolf Pr.
—Collaborators. 1987. 136p. pap. 5.95 o.p. (*0-14-009342-7*, Penguin Bks.) Viking Penguin.
Kazan, Frances. Halide's Gift: A Novel. 2002. 376p. pap. 12.95 (*0-375-75997-2*) Random House Adult Trade Publishing Group.
—Halide's Gift: A Novel. 2001. E-Book 19.95 (*1-58836-018-0*) Random Hse., Inc.
Kear, Cynthia. Searching for Grace. 1998. 24.95 (*0-947993-75-4*) Malvern Publishing Co., Ltd. GBR. *Dist:* British Bk. Co., Inc.
Kelby, N. M. Theatre of the Stars: A Novel of Physics & Memory. Date not set. 23.95 (*0-7868-6858-9*) Hyperion Pr.
Keller, Nora O. Comfort Woman. 1998. 224p. pap. 12.95 (*0-14-026335-7*) Penguin Group (USA) Inc.
—Comfort Woman. 1997. 224p. 21.95 o.s.i (*0-670-87269-5*, Viking) Viking Penguin.
Kelly, Theresa. Tomorrow I'll Miss You. 1999. (Aloha Cove Ser.: Vol. 3). (Illus.). 160p. (J). (gr. 8-12). pap. 6.00 (*0-570-05485-0*) Concordia Publishing Hse.
Keyes, Marian. Watermelon. 2002. 432p. pap. 13.95 (*0-06-009036-7*, Perennial) HarperTrade.
—Watermelon. 1999. 448p. mass mkt. 6.99 (*0-380-79609-0*); 1998. 432p. mass mkt. 15.95 (*0-380-97617-X*) Morrow/Avon. (Avon Bks.).
—Watermelon. 1995. 612p. pap. 11.95 (*1-85371-508-5*) Poolbeg Pr. IRL. *Dist:* Dufour Editions, Inc.
Kimhi, Alona. Weeping Susannah. 2002. 391p. pap. 14.00 (*1-86046-630-3*) Faber & Faber, Inc.
Kimmel, Haven. Rattlesnake Kite. 2004. 288p. 24.00 (*0-7432-4775-2*, Free Pr.) Simon & Schuster.
—Something Rising Light Swift. 2005. 288p. pap. 13.00 (*0-7432-4777-9*, Free Pr.) Simon & Schuster.
Kinkade, Thomas & Spencer, Katherine. Home Song: A Cape Light Novel. 384p. 2003. pap. 13.95 (*0-425-19183-4*); 2002. 23.95 (*0-425-18624-5*) Berkley Publishing Group.
Kirshenbaum, Binnie. An Almost Perfect Moment: A Novel. 2004. 288p. 23.95 (*0-06-052086-8*, Ecco) HarperTrade.
Koja, Kathe. The Blue Mirror, RS. 2004. (YA). 16.00 (*0-374-30849-7*, Farrar, Straus & Giroux (BYR)) Farrar, Straus & Giroux.
Koppelman, Susan, ed. Between Mothers & Daughters: Stories Across a Generation. 2003. (Women's Stories Project Ser.). 360p. pap. 16.95 (*1-55861-459-1*) Feminist Pr. at The City Univ. of New York.
Koppelman, Susan, ed. & intro. Between Mothers & Daughters: Stories Across a Generation. 1985. 336p. pap. 14.95 (*0-935312-26-9*) Feminist Pr. at The City Univ. of New York.
Krantz, Judith. The Jewels of Tessa Kent. 1999. 480p. mass mkt. 7.99 (*0-553-56137-5*) Bantam Bks.
—The Jewels of Tessa Kent. l.t. ed. 1998. 672p. 25.95 o.p. (*0-7838-0267-6*, Macmillan Reference USA) Gale Group.
—The Jewels of Tessa Kent. l.t. ed. 1998. 672p. 25.95 (*0-375-70421-3*) Random Hse. Large Print.
Krepismann, Charlotte. Inheritance: A Mixed Blessing. 1999. 192p. (Orig.). pap. 12.95 (*1-891571-04-4*) Easy Break, First Time Publishing.
Kuban, Karla. Marchlands: A Novel. 1999. 272p. pap. 12.00 o.s.i (*0-684-85444-9*, Scribner) Simon & Schuster.
Lamott, Anne. Blue Shoe. 2003. 336p. pap. 14.00 (*1-57322-342-5*, Riverhead Trade (Paperbacks)) Berkley Publishing Group.
—Blue Shoe. l.t. ed. 2002. (Wheeler Hardcover Ser.). 430p. 31.95 (*1-58724-362-8*, Wheeler Publishing, Inc.) Gale Group.
—Blue Shoe. 2002. 304p. 24.95 (*1-57322-226-7*, Riverhead Bks. (Hardcovers)) Putnam Publishing Group, The.
Landis, Jill Marie. Magnolia Creek. l.t. ed. 2002. (Core Collection). 490p. 30.95 (*0-7862-4665-0*) Thorndike Pr.
Lapierre, Janet. Old Enemies. 1993. 256p. text 20.00 (*0-684-19614-X*, Macmillan Reference USA) Gale Group.
Larson, Bob. Shock Talk: The Exorcist Files. 2001. xii, 241p. pap. 12.99 (*0-7852-7009-4*) Nelson, Thomas Pubs.
Le Guin, Ursula K. Searoad. 2004. 224p. pap. 13.95 (*1-59030-084-X*) Shambhala Pubns., Inc.
LeClaire, Anne D. Leaving Eden. 2003. 320p. pap. 13.95 (*0-345-44575-9*); 2002. 304p. 23.95 (*0-345-44574-0*) Ballantine Bks. (Ballantine Bks.).
—Leaving Eden. l.t. ed. 2003. (Women's Fiction Ser.). 341p. 29.95 (*0-7862-4871-8*) Gale Group.
Leroy, Margaret. Postcards from Berlin. 2003. 400p. 22.95 (*0-316-73813-1*) Little Brown & Co.
Lessing, Doris. The Sweetest Dream. 2002. E-Book 19.95 (*0-06-008494-4*); E-Book 19.95 (*0-06-050455-2*); E-Book 19.95 (*0-06-008492-8*); E-Book 19.95 (*0-06-008493-6*) HarperCollins General Bks. Group. (PerfectBound).
—The Sweetest Dream. 2002. 496p. 26.95 (*0-06-621334-7*) HarperCollins Pubs.
—The Sweetest Dream. 2003. 496p. pap. 13.95 (*0-06-093755-6*, Perennial) HarperTrade.
Levy, Justine. The Rendezvous: A Novel. Davis, Lydia, tr. 1999. 144p. pap. 11.00 (*0-684-84632-2*, Scribner Paper Fiction); 1997. 142p. 21.50 (*0-684-82579-1*, Scribner) Simon & Schuster.
Lewis, Beverly. The Sunroom. l.t. ed. 1998. (Inspirational Ser.). 176p. 25.95 (*0-7838-0281-1*) Thorndike Pr.
Lindsay, Taylor. The Madness of Maura McGee. l.t. ed. 1999. E-Book 24.95 incl. cd-rom (*1-929077-72-6*, Books OnScreen) PageFree Publishing, Inc.
Maddox, Muriel. Myra's Daughters: A Contemporary Novel. 2001. 280p. 22.95 (*0-86534-323-3*) Sunstone Pr.
Mandeville, Joyce. Careful Mistakes. 1996. 184p. o.s.i (*0-316-87899-5*) Little Brown & Co.
—Careful Mistakes: A Novel. 1997. 432p. 21.95 (*0-316-87999-1*) Little Brown & Co.
Manfredi, Renee. Above the Thunder. 2004. 24.00 (*1-931561-59-1*) MacAdam/Cage Publishing, Inc.
Manicka, Rani. The Rice Mother. 2003. 448p. 24.95 (*0-670-03192-5*, Viking) Viking Penguin.
Mantel, Hilary. Every Day Is Mother's Day. l.t. ed. 2001. (G. K. Hall Paperback Ser.). 307p. (gr. 4-7). pap. 24.95 (*0-7838-9458-9*); (*0-7540-4541-2*); (*0-7540-4540-4*) Gale Group. (Macmillan Reference USA).
—Every Day Is Mother's Day. 2000. 225p. pap. 13.00 (*0-8050-6272-6*, Owl Bks.) Holt, Henry & Co.
Marciano, Francesca. Casa Rossa. 352p. 2003. pap. 14.00 (*0-375-72637-3*, Vintage); 2002. 25.00 (*0-375-42123-8*, Pantheon) Knopf Publishing Group.
Markley, Elaine & Bergamot, Stella. Soul Song. 1998. x, 192p. 22.95 (*0-9664412-4-9*) Spirit Song Publishing.
Martin, Emer. More Bread or I'll Appear. 2000. 288p. pap. 12.00 (*0-385-72009-2*) Doubleday Publishing.
—More Bread or I'll Appear. 1999. 268p. tchr. ed. 23.00 (*0-395-91871-5*) Houghton Mifflin Co.
Mattison, Alice. Hilda & Pearl. 2001. 304p. pap. 13.00 (*0-06-093693-2*, Perennial) HarperTrade.
—Hilda & Pearl. 1995. 288p. 22.00 o.p. (*0-688-13127-1*, Morrow, William & Co.) Morrow/Avon.
McBride, Regina. The Land of Women. 2003. 256p. pap. 13.00 (*0-7432-2888-X*, Touchstone) Simon & Schuster.
—The Nature of Water & Air: A Novel. 2001. 320p. pap. 13.00 (*0-7432-0323-2*, Touchstone) Simon & Schuster.
McCabe, Patrick. Emerald Germs of Ireland. 2002. 336p. pap. 13.95 (*0-06-095678-X*, Perennial) HarperTrade.
McInerney, Merry. Dog People. 287p. 2000. pap. 14.95 (*0-312-87292-5*); 1998. 22.95 (*0-312-85699-7*) Doherty, Tom Assocs., LLC. (Forge Bks.).
McInerny, Ralph. Last Things. Date not set. pap. (*0-312-30900-7*, Saint Martin's Griffin); mass mkt. (*0-312-98690-4*, St. Martin's Paperbacks); 2003. 352p. 24.95 (*0-312-30899-X*, Saint Martin's Minotaur) St. Martin's Pr.
—Last Things. l.t. ed. 2003. (Father Dowling Mystery Ser.). 460p. 29.95 (*0-7862-5735-0*) Thorndike Pr.
McKinley, Tamara. Windflowers. l.t. ed. 2002. (Magna Large Print Ser.). 480p. 32.50 (*0-7505-1922-3*) Magna Large Print Bks. GBR. *Dist:* Ulverscroft Large Print Bks., Ltd., Ulverscroft Large Print Canada, Ltd.
—Windflowers. Date not set. pap. (*0-312-31434-5*); mass mkt. (*0-312-98961-X*) St. Martin's Pr. (St. Martin's Paperbacks).
—Windflowers: A Novel of Australia. 2002. 480p. 26.95 (*0-312-30750-0*) St. Martin's Pr.
McKoy-Hibbert, Erica. Mi Neva Know Sey. 2000. 167p. 12.95 (*1-930331-00-2*) Machibb Creations.
McMillan, Rosalyn. One Better. 2001. 384p. E-Book 4.95 (*0-446-92307-9*) Time Warner Bk. Group.
—One Better. 1999. E-Book 4.95 (*0-446-91289-1*); 1998. 400p. mass mkt. 7.99 (*0-446-60599-9*); 1997. 416p. 22.00 o.p. (*0-446-52242-2*) Warner Bks., Inc.
McMullan, Margaret. In My Mother's House. Date not set. mass mkt. (*0-312-99153-3*, St. Martin's Paperbacks); 2003. 272p. 23.95 (*0-312-31824-3*) St. Martin's Pr.
McMurtry, Larry. Terms of Endearment. l.t. ed. 1984. (General Ser.). 18.95 o.p. (*0-8161-3708-0*, Macmillan Reference USA) Gale Group.
—Terms of Endearment. 1988. mass mkt. 4.50 o.p. (*0-451-15817-2*); 1983. mass mkt. 2.95 o.p. (*0-451-15778-8*); 1976. mass mkt. 1.95 o.p. (*0-451-07173-5*) NAL. (Signet Bks.).
—Terms of Endearment. 1999. 416p. pap. 13.00 (*0-684-85390-6*, Simon & Schuster) Simon & Schuster.
—Terms of Endearment. Grose, Bill, ed. 1992. 432p. mass mkt. 7.99 (*0-671-75872-1*, Pocket) Simon & Schuster.
—Terms of Endearment. 1989. 416p. pap. 11.00 (*0-671-68208-3*); 1975. 448p. 9.95 o.s.i (*0-671-22102-7*) Simon & Schuster. (Simon & Schuster).
McPhee, Martha. Bright Angel Time. 256p. 2003. pap. 14.00 (*0-15-602934-0*); 1999. pap. 13.00 o.s.i (*0-15-600586-7*) Harcourt Trade Pubs. (Harvest Bks.).
Medwin, Thomas. Lady Singleton. 2000. (*0-8201-1529-0*) Scholars' Facsimiles & Reprints.
Menendez, Ana. Loving Che. 2003. 240p. 22.00 (*0-87113-908-1*) Grove/Atlantic, Inc.
Meyer, Carolyn. Brown Eyes Blue: A Novel. 2003. 352p. 23.95 (*1-882593-68-5*); 2004. 240p. reprint ed. pap. 15.95 (*1-882593-83-9*) Bridge Works Publishing Co., Inc.
Mickle, Shelley F. The Turning Hour. 2001. 260p. 24.95 (*0-913515-22-1*) River City Publishing.
Minatoya, Lydia Y. The Strangeness of Beauty. 1999. (Illus.). 384p. 23.00 (*0-684-85362-0*, Simon & Schuster) Simon & Schuster.
Monroe, Mary Alice. The Beach House. l.t. ed. 2002. (Basic Ser.). 652p. 28.95 (*0-7862-4738-X*) Thorndike Pr.
Mori, Kyoko. Stone Field, True Arrow: A Novel. 2000. 288p. 24.00 o.s.i (*0-8050-4080-3*, Metropolitan Bks.) Holt, Henry & Co.
—Stone Field, True Arrow: A Novel. 2001. 288p. pap. 13.00 (*0-312-42042-0*) Picador.
Moriarty, Laura. The Center of Everything: A Novel. 2003. 304p. 22.95 (*1-4013-0031-6*) Hyperion Pr.
—The Center of Everything: A Novel. l.t. ed. 2003. 610p. 30.95 (*0-7862-5563-3*) Thorndike Pr.
—People in General. 2004. pap. 14.00 (*0-7868-8845-8*) Hyperion Pr.
Morris, Wright. Plains Song: For Female Voices. 1991. 232p. reprint ed. pap. 10.95 o.s.i (*0-87923-835-6*) Godine, David R. Pub.
—Plains Song: For Female Voices. 1980. (Illus.). 12.95 o.p. (*0-06-013047-4*) HarperTrade.
—Plains Song: For Female Voices. 2000. (Illus.). 229p. pap. 14.00 (*0-8032-8267-2*, Bison Bks.) Univ. of Nebraska Pr.
—Plains Song: For Female Voices. 1981. (Contemporary American Fiction Ser.). 241p. pap. 6.95 o.p. (*0-14-005778-1*, Penguin Bks.) Viking Penguin.
Morrissey, Donna. Downhill Chance. 2003. (Illus.). 448p. pap. 14.00 (*0-618-18927-0*) Houghton Mifflin Co.
—Kit's Law. 2001. (Illus.). 384p. pap. 13.00 (*0-618-10927-7*, Mariner Bks.) Houghton Mifflin Co. Trade & Reference Div.
—Kit's Law. 1999. 383p. pap. (*0-670-88601-7*) Viking.
Morrissy, Mary. Mother of Pearl: A Novel. 1995. 281p. 22.00 o.p. (*0-684-19667-0*, Scribner) Simon & Schuster.
Mortman, Doris. Before & Again. Date not set. mass mkt. (*0-312-99476-1*, St. Martin's Paperbacks); 2003. 384p. 24.95 (*0-312-27557-9*) St. Martin's Pr.
Mueller, Marnie. My Mother's Island. 2002. 237p. 24.95 (*1-880684-82-9*) Curbstone Pr.
Nahai, Gina B. Moonlight on the Avenue of Faith. 1999. 384p. 24.00 o.s.i (*0-15-100388-2*) Harcourt Trade Pubs.
Nelson, Liza. Playing Botticelli. 2001. 288p. pap. 12.95 o.s.i (*0-425-17818-8*) Berkley Publishing Group.
Neri, Kris. Dem Bones' Revenge. 2003. (WWL Mystery Ser.: No. 466). 272p. mass mkt. (*0-373-26466-6*, Worldwide Library) Harlequin Enterprises, Ltd.
Newman, Nancy. Disturbing the Peace. 2002. 320p. pap. 13.95 (*0-380-79839-5*, Avon Bks.) Morrow/Avon.
Ng, Mei. Eating Chinese Food Naked. 1998. 256p. mass mkt. 14.00 (*0-671-01145-6*, Scribner) Simon & Schuster.
—Eating Chinese Food Naked. l.t. ed. 1998. (Core Ser.). 344p. 26.95 (*0-7838-0240-4*) Thorndike Pr.
—Eating Chinese Food Naked: A Novel. 1998. 224p. 20.50 (*0-684-81416-1*, Scribner) Simon & Schuster.
Nunes, Rachel Ann. Ariana: A Novel. 2003. 310p. pap. 16.95 (*1-55517-648-8*, 76488) Cedar Fort, Inc./CFI Distribution.
Oates, Joyce Carol. A Garden of Earthly Delights: A Novel. rev. ed. 2003. (Modern Library 20th Century Rediscovery). 432p. pap. 13.95 (*0-8129-6834-4*, Modern Library) Random House Adult Trade Publishing Group.
Offill, Jenny. Last Things. 1999. 272p. 23.00 o.p. (*0-374-18405-4*) Farrar, Straus & Giroux.
Oke, Janette. Like Gold Refined. 2000. (Prairie Legacy Ser.: Vol. 4). 1p. pap. 15.99 o.p. (*0-7642-2164-7*); 256p. text 15.99 o.p. (*0-7642-2162-0*); 256p. pap. 12.99 (*0-7642-2161-2*); 368p. pap. 16.99 (*0-7642-2163-9*) Bethany Hse. Pubs.
—Like Gold Refined. l.t. ed. 2000. (G. K. Hall Inspirational Ser.). (Illus.). 312p. 27.95 (*0-7838-9184-9*, Macmillan Reference USA) Gale Group.
Oldfield, Pamela. A Woman Alone. l.t. ed. 2001. 428p. (*0-7540-1569-6*); (*0-7540-2431-8*) Gale Group. (Macmillan Reference USA).
—A Woman Alone. l.t. ed. 2001. (G. K. Hall Romance Ser.). 428p. 26.95 (*0-7838-9364-7*) Thorndike Pr.
Pai, Helen. Gilmore Girls, Bk. 4. 2002. (Illus.). 176p. mass mkt. 5.99 (*0-06-050916-3*) HarperCollins Pubs.
Park, Christine, et al, eds. Close Company: Stories of Mothers & Daughters. 2000. 298p. 14.95 (*0-86068-888-7*) Virago Pr., Ltd. GBR. *Dist:* Trafalgar Square.
Parker, Gary. The Wedding Dress. 112p. (C). 12.99 (*0-7814-3700-8*) Cook Communications Ministries.
Parr, Delia. Home to Trinity. 2003. (Americana Ser.). 508p. 28.95 (*0-7862-5116-6*) Thorndike Pr.
—Home to Trinity: A Novel. 2003. 352p. 25.95 (*0-312-27098-4*) St. Martin's Pr.
—A Place Called Trinity. 2002. (Illus.). 304p. 24.95 (*0-312-28288-5*) St. Martin's Pr.
—A Place Called Trinity. l.t. ed. 2002. (Americana Ser.). 491p. 28.95 (*0-7862-4443-7*) Thorndike Pr.
—A Place Called Trinity: A Novel. 2003. 320p. reprint ed. pap. 12.95 (*0-312-31005-6*, Saint Martin's Griffin) St. Martin's Pr.
Paton Walsh, Jill. The Serpentine Cave. 1997. 224p. 20.95 (*0-312-16999-X*) St. Martin's Pr.
—The Serpentine Cave. l.t. ed. 1998. (Charnwood Large Print Ser.). 272p. 29.99 o.p. (*0-7089-9001-0*, Charnwood) Thorpe, F. A. Pubs. GBR. *Dist:* Ulverscroft Large Print Bks., Ltd., Ulverscroft Large Print Canada, Ltd.
Pearson, Carol Lynn. Will You Still Be My Daughter? 2000. (Fable for Our Times Ser.). (Illus.). 32p. 9.95 (*0-87905-959-1*) Smith, Gibbs Pub.
Pedersen, Laura. Going Away Party. 2001. (Illus.). 315p. 22.00 o.p. (*1-58654-010-6*) Story Line Pr.
Pettigrew, Dawn Karima. The Way We Make Sense: A Novel. 2002. 136p. pap. 11.95 (*1-879960-66-4*) Aunt Lute Bks.
Phillips, Caryl. The Final Passage. 1985. 208p. o.p. (*0-571-13437-8*) Faber & Faber Ltd.
—The Final Passage. 1985. 208p. pap. 8.95 o.p. (*0-571-13438-6*) Faber & Faber, Inc.
—The Final Passage. 1995. 208p. pap. 15.00 (*0-679-75931-X*, Vintage) Knopf Publishing Group.
—The Final Passage. 1990. 208p. pap. 7.95 o.p. (*0-14-012796-8*, Penguin Bks.) Viking Penguin.
Phillips, Delores. The Darkest Child: A Novel. 2004. 388p. 26.00 (*1-56947-345-5*) Soho Pr., Inc.

Phillips, Jayne Anne. MotherKind. 2001. 304p. pap. 13.00 (0-375-70192-3, Vintage) Knopf Publishing Group.
Pittman, Joseph. Tilting at Windmills. 2001. 304p. 21.95 (0-7434-0737-7, Atria) Simon & Schuster.
Plain, Belva. After the Fire. 2001. 448p. reprint ed. mass mkt. 7.99 (0-440-23574-X) Dell Publishing.
—After the Fire. l.t. ed. 544p. 2001. pap. 13.95 (0-375-72805-8); 2000. 25.95 (0-375-40976-9) Random Hse. Large Print.
Powell, Sophie. The Mushroom Man. 2004. 208p. pap. 14.00 (0-425-19413-2) Berkley Publishing Group.
—The Mushroom Man. 2003. 208p. 23.95 (0-399-14963-5, Putnam & Grosset) Putnam Publishing Group, The.
Prince, Althea. Loving This Man. 2002. 200p. pap. 15.95 (1-894663-06-3) Insomniac Pr. CAN. Dist: Strauss Consultants.
Pruett, Lynn. Ruby River. 2004. 288p. pap. 13.00 (0-8021-4039-4, Grove Pr.); 2002. 336p. 24.00 (0-87113-855-7, Atlantic Monthly Pr.) Grove/Atlantic, Inc.
—Ruby River. 2003. (Americana Ser.). 28.95 (0-7862-5144-1) Thorndike Pr.
Purdy, James. Gertrude of Stony Island Avenue. 1999. 192p. pap. 13.00 o.s.i (0-688-17226-1, Quill) HarperTrade.
—Gertrude of Stony Island Avenue. 1998. 144p. 19.95 (0-688-15901-X, Morrow, William & Co.) Morrow/Avon.
—Gertrude of Stony Island Avenue. 1996. 256p. 27.95 (0-7206-1011-7) Owen, Peter Ltd. GBR. Dist: Dufour Editions, Inc.
Quindlen, Anna. One True Thing. 1995. 400p. mass mkt. 6.99 (0-440-22103-X) Dell Publishing.
—One True Thing. 1997. 304p. pap. 14.00 (0-385-31920-7) Doubleday Publishing.
—One True Thing. l.t. ed. 1995. (Large Print Bks.). 26.95 (1-56895-168-X, Wheeler Publishing, Inc.) Gale Group.
—One True Thing. 1999. 9.98 (0-671-77616-9); 1998. 18.00 incl. audio (0-671-04333-1) Simon & Schuster Audio. (Simon & Schuster Audioworks).
Raeff, Anne. Clara Mondschein's Melancholia: A Novel. 2002. 258p. 25.00 (1-931561-16-8) MacAdam/Cage Publishing, Inc.
Rawlings, Marjorie Kinnan. Blood of My Blood. Meriwether, Anne Blythe, ed. 2002. 192p. 24.95 (0-8130-2443-9) Univ. Pr. of Florida.
Rax, Cydney. My Daughter's Boyfriend. 2004. 320p. 22.00 (1-4000-4920-2) Crown Publishing Group.
Ray, Jeanne. Step-Ball-Change. 2004. 320p. pap. 13.95 (0-451-21116-2) NAL.
Reid, Nicole Louise. In the Breeze of Passing Things. 2003. 22.00 (1-931561-42-7) MacAdam/Cage Publishing, Inc.
Rendell, Ruth. The Crocodile Bird, Set. abr. ed. 1993. audio 16.95 (1-55927-258-9, 390580) Audio Renaissance.
—The Crocodile Bird. 1997. 368p. mass mkt. 7.99 (0-7704-2598-4) Bantam Bks.
—The Crocodile Bird. unabr. collector's ed. 1994. audio 56.00 (0-7366-2670-0, 3407) Books on Tape, Inc.
—The Crocodile Bird. 1994. 384p. mass mkt. 6.99 (0-440-21865-9) Dell Publishing.
—The Crocodile Bird. 1993. 368p. 25.95 o.s.i (0-385-25429-6) Doubleday Publishing.
—The Crocodile Bird, unabr. ed. 1994. audio 78.00 (1-55690-944-6, 93440E7) Recorded Bks., LLC.
Reynolds, Clay. The Vigil. 1988. (Southwest Life & Letters Ser.). 232p. reprint ed. pap. 8.95 o.p. (0-87074-269-8) Southern Methodist Univ. Pr.
—The Vigil. 2001. (Illus.). 240p. pap. 17.95 (0-89672-457-3) Texas Tech Univ. Pr.
Rice, Luanne. Dream Country. 2002. 544p. mass mkt. 7.50 (0-553-58264-X) Bantam Bks.
—Dream Country. l.t. ed. 557p. 2002. pap. 29.95 (0-7838-9385-X); 2001. 32.95 (0-7838-9384-1) Gale Group. (Macmillan Reference USA).
—Follow the Stars Home. l.t. ed. 2000. (Large Print Book Ser.). 26.95 o.p. (1-56895-864-1, Wheeler Publishing, Inc.) Gale Group.
—Summer Light. 2002. 496p. reprint ed. mass mkt. 7.50 (0-553-58265-8) Bantam Bks.
—Summer Light. l.t. ed. 2001. 525p. lib. bdg. 29.95 (1-58547-144-5) Ctr. Point Large Print.
Riddle, Paxton. The Education of Ruby Loonfoot. (Five Star First Edition Women's Fiction Ser.). 2002. 340p. 25.95 (0-7862-4437-2, Five Star); 2003. 351p. pap. 13.95 (1-4104-0133-2, Five Star Trade) Gale Group.
—The Education of Ruby Loonfoot. l.t. ed. 2003. (Core Ser.). 28.95 (0-7862-5496-3) Thorndike Pr.
Rivers, Francine. The Last Sin Eater. l.t. ed. 2001. 472p. 27.95 (0-7862-3390-7) Thorndike Pr.
—The Last Sin Eater. 1999. 336p. pap. 12.99 (0-8423-3571-4) Tyndale Hse. Pubs.
—The Last Sin Eater: A Novel. 1998. 336p. 12.99 (0-8423-3570-6) Tyndale Hse. Pubs.
Robards, Karen. Ghost Moon. l.t. ed. 517p. 2001. pap. 28.95 (0-7838-9114-8); 2000. 30.95 (0-7838-9110-5) Gale Group. (Macmillan Reference USA).
Rogers, Jane. Island. 2001. (Illus.). 238p. reprint ed. pap. 13.00 (0-618-13931-1, Mariner Bks.) Houghton Mifflin Co. Trade & Reference Div.
—Island. 2000. 261p. 25.95 (1-58567-076-6) Overlook Pr., The.
Roper, Gayle G. Summer Shadows. 2003. (Seaside Seasons Ser.). 400p. pap. 11.99 (1-57673-969-4) Multnomah Pubs., Inc.
Rosario, Nelly. El Canto de Agua: A Novel. 2003. (SPA.). 272p. pap. 12.00 (1-4000-3004-8, Vintage) Knopf Publishing Group.
—Song of the Water Saints: A Novel. 2003. 256p. pap. 12.00 (0-375-72549-0, Vintage) Knopf Publishing Group.
—Song of the Water Saints: A Novel. Minton, Jenny, ed. 2002. 256p. 23.00 (0-375-42087-8, Pantheon) Knopf Publishing Group.
Rose, Marcia. Like Mother, Like Daughter. 1995. mass mkt. 6.99 o.s.i (0-345-37572-6) Ballantine Bks.
Rosenberg, Saralee. A Little Help from Above. 2003. 352p. pap. 13.95 (0-06-009620-9, Avon Bks.) Morrow/Avon.
Rossner, Judith. Olivia: Or The Weight of the Past. l.t. ed. 1995. (Large Print Bks.). 24.95 (1-56895-166-3, Wheeler Publishing, Inc.) Gale Group.
—Perfidia: A Novel. 1998. 384p. reprint ed. mass mkt. 7.50 o.s.i (0-440-22613-9) Dell Publishing.
Ryan, Teresa LeYung. Love Made of Heart. 2002. 304p. 23.00 (0-7582-0216-4) Kensington Publishing Corp.
Ryan, Teresa Loyung. Love Made of Heart. 2003. 320p. pap. 15.00 (0-7582-0217-2, Kensington Bks.) Kensington Publishing Corp.
Sagastizabal, Patricia. A Secret for Julia: A Novel. Zatz, Asa, tr. from SPA. 2001. 256p. 23.95 (0-393-05044-0) Norton, W. W. & Co., Inc.
Sager, Carole B. Extravagant Gestures. 1987. 288p. 3.95 o.s.i (0-441-22372-9) Ace Bks.
—Extravagant Gestures. 1985. 16.95 o.p. (0-87795-765-7, Morrow, William & Co.) Morrow/Avon.
Samson, Lisa. Women's Intuition. 2002. 400p. pap. 12.99 (1-57856-596-0) WaterBrook Pr.
Santiago, Esmeralda. America's Dream. 336p. 2002. pap. 12.95 (0-06-050884-1, Rayo); 1997. pap. 14.00 (0-06-092826-3, Perennial) HarperTrade.
—America's Dream: El Sueno de America. 1996. 79p. 23.00 o.p. (0-06-017279-7) HarperCollins Pubs.
Schine, Cathleen. She Is Me: A Novel. 2003. 272p. 23.95 (0-316-78609-8) Little Brown & Co.
Schulman, Audrey. A House Named Brazil. 2001. 320p. pap. 13.95 (0-380-80880-3, Perennial) HarperTrade.
—A House Named Brazil. 2000. (Illus.). 301p. 23.00 (0-380-97799-0, Morrow, William & Co.) Morrow/Avon.
Schwarz, Christina. Drowning Ruth: A Novel. 2001. (Reader's Circle Ser.). 368p. pap. 14.95 (0-345-43910-4, Ballantine Bks.) Ballantine Bks.
—Drowning Ruth: A Novel. 2000. 352p. 23.95 o.s.i (0-385-49971-X) Doubleday Publishing.
—Drowning Ruth: A Novel. l.t. ed. (Wheeler Press Paperback Ser.). 2001. pap. 12.95 (1-56895-179-5); 2000. 422p. 28.95 (1-56895-959-1) Gale Group. (Wheeler Publishing, Inc.).
—Drowning Ruth: A Novel. 2001. 20.05 (0-606-21165-9) Turtleback Bks.
Scofield, Sandra J. Opal on Dry Ground. 1995. mass mkt. 5.99 o.s.i (0-8041-1360-2, Ivy Bks.) Ballantine Bks.
—Plain Seeing. 1997. 320p. 24.00 o.s.i (0-06-017342-4) HarperCollins Pubs.
Seveigny, Genevieve. A Half-Dozen Eclairs: Travels in the Guise of Letters. 2002. (ENG, SPA & SWA.). 60p. (C). pap. 14.00 (0-9641837-3-0) Texture Pr.
Shange, Ntozake. Sassafrass, Cypress & Indigo. 2nd ed. 1996. 240p. pap. 13.00 (0-312-14091-6) Picador.
Sharp, Paula. I Loved You All. 2000. 370p. 23.95 (0-7868-6266-1) Hyperion Pr.
Sheepshanks, Mary. Picking up the Pieces. 1998. 304p. 23.95 o.p. (0-312-19997-X) St. Martin's Pr.
—Picking Up the Pieces. 1999. 336p. mass mkt. 5.99 (0-312-97037-4, St. Martin's Paperbacks) St. Martin's Pr.
Sheffield, Elisabeth. Gone. 2003. (Illus.). 258p. pap. 13.95 (1-57366-108-2) Fiction Collective Two, Inc.
Shepard, Karen. An Empire of Women. 2002. 272p. pap. 12.95 (0-425-18456-0) Berkley Publishing Group.
—An Empire of Women. l.t. ed. 2001. (Hardcover Ser.). 281p. 29.95 (1-58724-077-7, Wheeler Publishing, Inc.) Gale Group.
—An Empire of Women. 2000. 320p. 24.95 o.s.i (0-399-14667-9) Penguin Group (USA) Inc.
Shields, Carol. Unless: A Novel. 2003. 336p. pap. 13.95 (0-00-715461-5); 2002. (Illus.). 224p. 24.95 (0-00-714107-6) HarperTrade. (Fourth Estate).
—Unless: A Novel. l.t. ed. 2002. (Basic Ser.). 29.95 (0-7862-4599-9) Thorndike Pr.
Shimoda, Todd A. The Fourth Treasure. 2002. (Illus.). 368p. 24.95 (0-385-50352-0, Talese, Nan A.) Doubleday Publishing.
Shortridge, Jennie. Riding with the Queen. 2003. 352p. pap. 12.95 (0-451-21027-1) NAL.
Shyer, Marlene Fanta. Two Daughters. 2002. 32p. mass mkt. 6.99 o.s.i (0-7582-0037-4) Kensington Publishing Corp.
—Two Daughters. l.t. ed. 2002. (Women's Fiction Ser.). 28.95 (0-7862-4409-7) Thorndike Pr.
Simone, Nea A. Reaching Back. 2002. 272p. pap. 15.00 (1-58314-317-3, Sepia) BET Bks.
Simpson, Mona. Anywhere but Here. 1987. audio 13.95 (1-55644-195-9, 7071) American Audio Prose Library, Inc.
—Anywhere but Here. l.t. ed. 1999. 660p. 25.95 (1-57490-214-8, Beeler Large Print Bks.) Beeler, Thomas T. Publisher.
—Anywhere but Here. 1999. pap. 14.00 (0-676-58970-7); 1992. 544p. pap. 14.00 (0-679-73738-3); 1987. 416p. pap. 9.95 o.p. (0-394-75559-6) Knopf Publishing Group. (Vintage).
—Anywhere but Here. 1986. 18.95 o.s.i (0-394-55283-0) Knopf, Alfred A. Inc.
—Off Keck Road. E-Book 15.95 (1-58945-518-5) Adobe Systems, Inc.
—Off Keck Road. 2001. E-Book 10.00 (0-375-41263-8) Random Hse., Inc.
—Off Keck Road. l.t. ed. 2001. (Thorndike Press Large Print Women's Fiction Ser.). 229p. (0-7862-3242-0) Thorndike Pr.
—Off Keck Road: A Novella. 2001. 176p. reprint ed. pap. 11.00 (0-375-70906-1, Vintage) Knopf Publishing Group.
Smiley, Jane. At Paradise Gate. 16th l.t. ed. 2001. 271p. lib. bdg. 27.95 (1-58547-073-2) Ctr. Point Large Print.
—At Paradise Gate. 224p. 1998. pap. 12.00 (0-684-85223-3); 1993. pap. 11.00 (0-671-88533-2) Simon & Schuster. (Touchstone).
Smith, D. L. The Miracles of Santo Fico. 2003. 28.95 (0-7862-5243-X) Thorndike Pr.
—The Miracles of Santo Fico. 368p. 2004. pap. 16.00 (0-446-69036-8); 2003. 22.95 (0-446-53103-0) Warner Bks., Inc.
Solwitz, Sharon. Bloody Mary: A Novel. 2003. 224p. pap. 13.95 (1-889330-93-0) Sarabande Bks., Inc.
Spencer, Elizabeth. The Night Travellers. 2002. (Voices of the South Ser.). 384p. pap. 17.95 (0-8071-2792-2) Louisiana State Univ. Pr.
—The Night Travellers. 1992. (Contemporay American Fiction Ser.). 384p. reprint ed. pap. 10.00 o.p. (0-14-015281-4, Penguin Bks.) Penguin Group (USA) Inc.
—The Night Travellers. 1991. 352p. 21.95 o.p. (0-670-83915-9) Viking Penguin.
Stacy, Judith Minthorn. Betty Sweet Tells All. 2002. 256p. 22.95 (0-06-018485-X) HarperCollins Pubs.
—Betty Sweet Tells All. 2003. 256p. pap. 12.95 (0-06-053615-2, Perennial) HarperTrade.
Stansbury, Nicole. Places to Look for a Mother. 2002. 320p. 22.00 (0-7867-0978-2); 2003. 288p. reprint ed. pap. 13.00 (0-7867-1177-9) Avalon Publishing Group. (Carroll & Graf Pubs.).
Steinke, Rene. The Fires. 2000. 256p. pap. 13.00 (0-688-17584-8, Quill) HarperTrade.
—The Fires. 1999. 243p. 23.00 (0-688-16150-2, Morrow, William & Co.) Morrow/Avon.
Stern, Kathryn. Another Song about the King: A Novel. 2001. (Reader's Circle Ser.). 304p. pap. 14.00 (0-345-43319-X, Ballantine Bks.) Ballantine Bks.
Stewart, Kathleen. The Red Room. 1999. 315p. (1-86508-143-4) Allen & Unwin Pty., Ltd.
Stone, Sarah. The True Sources of the Nile. 2002. 304p. 23.95 (0-385-50301-6) Doubleday Publishing.
Straight, Susan. Highwire Moon: A Novel. 2001. (Illus.). 320p. tchr. ed. 24.00 (0-618-05614-9) Houghton Mifflin Co.
—Highwire Moon: A Novel. 2002. (Illus.). 320p. pap. 14.00 (0-385-72261-3, Anchor) Knopf Publishing Group.
Strout, Elizabeth. Amy & Isabelle. l.t. ed. 1999. 28.95 (1-56895-728-9, Wheeler Publishing, Inc.) Gale Group.
—Amy & Isabelle. 2000. 320p. pap. 13.00 (0-375-70519-8, Vintage) Knopf Publishing Group.
Szeman, Sherri. Only with the Heart: A Novel. 2000. 323p. 24.95 (1-55970-538-8); 2001. 336p. reprint ed. pap. 13.95 (1-55970-595-7) Arcade Publishing, Inc.
Tan, Amy. The Bonesetter's Daughter. 2003. 400p. pap. 14.95 (0-345-45737-4, Ballantine Bks.); 2002. 416p. mass mkt. o.s.i (0-345-45571-1); 2002. 416p. reprint ed. mass mkt. 7.99 (0-8041-1498-6, Ballantine Bks.) Ballantine Bks.
—The Bonesetter's Daughter. 2001. 400p. 25.95 o.s.i (0-399-14643-1); 150.00 (0-399-14685-7) Penguin Group (USA) Inc.
—The Bonesetter's Daughter. l.t. ed. 567p. 2002. pap. 29.95 (0-7862-2951-9); 2001. 32.95 (0-7862-2952-7); 2001. (0-7540-2453-9); 2001. (0-7540-1594-7) Thorndike Pr.
—The Joy Luck Club. 1996. mass mkt. 6.99 (0-8041-9896-9); 1990. 352p. mass mkt. 7.99 (0-8041-0630-4); 1989. mass mkt. 4.95 o.s.i (0-8041-0642-8) Ballantine Bks. (Ivy Bks.).
—The Joy Luck Club. (Modern Critical Interpretations Ser.). 176p. pap. 19.95 (0-7910-7117-0) Chelsea Hse. Pubs.
—The Joy Luck Club. 1991. (Vintage Contemporaries Ser.). (Illus.). 288p. pap. 12.95 (0-679-72768-X, Vintage) Knopf Publishing Group.
—The Joy Luck Club. 1989. 288p. 24.95 (0-399-13420-4) Penguin Group (USA) Inc.
—The Joy Luck Club. 2003. E-Book 8.99 (0-7953-1076-5) RosettaBooks.
—The Joy Luck Club. 1990. 14.04 (0-606-01172-2) Turtleback Bks.
Tanney, Katherine. Carousel of Progress. 2001. 272p. pap. 19.00 (0-8129-9254-7, Villard Bks.) Random House Adult Trade Publishing Group.
Tatlock, Ann. I'll Watch the Moon. 2003. 400p. pap. 12.99 (0-7642-2764-5) Bethany Hse. Pubs.
Thurlo, Aimee & Thurlo, David. Changing Woman. E-Book 24.95 (0-312-70549-2, Tor Bks.); 2nd ed. 2002. 384p. 24.95 (0-312-87059-0, CPHC0654, Forge Bks.) Doherty, Tom Assocs., LLC.
—Plant Them Deep. mass mkt. (0-7653-4398-3); 2003. 336p. 24.95 (0-7653-0478-3) Doherty, Tom Assocs., LLC. (Forge Bks.).
Toibin, Colm. The Blackwater Lightship. 1999. 272p. 16.95 o.p. (0-330-38985-8) Picador GBR. Dist: Trans-Atlantic Pubns., Inc.
—The Blackwater Lightship. 288p. 2000. 24.00 o.s.i (0-684-87389-3); 2001. reprint ed. pap. 13.00 (0-7432-0331-3) Simon & Schuster. (Scribner).
Trigiani, Adriana. Milk Glass Moon: A Big Stone Gap Novel. 2002. 272p. 24.95 (0-375-50618-7) Random Hse., Inc.
Tsukiyama, Gail. Dreaming Water. E-Book 23.95 (0-312-70692-8); 2002. 224p. 23.95 (0-312-20607-0); 2003. 240p. reprint ed. pap. 12.95 (0-312-31608-9, Saint Martin's Griffin) St. Martin's Pr.
—Dreaming Water. 2002. (Women's Fiction Ser.). 29.95 (0-7862-4797-5) Thorndike Pr.
Turtledove, Harry. In the Presence of Mine Enemies. 2003. 464p. pap. 24.95 (0-451-52902-2) NAL.
Tyler, Sandra. After Lydia. 1995. 306p. 22.00 (0-15-193111-9) Harcourt Trade Pubs.
Valentine, Jane. Sevenoaks. 2001. pap. 17.95 (0-595-18094-9) iUniverse, Inc.
Van Draanen, Wendelin. Sammy Keyes & the Hollywood Mummy. unabr. ed. 2001. (Sammy Keyes Ser.). (J). audio 23.95 (0-87499-799-2, OAK011) Live Oak Media.
—Sammy Keyes & the Hollywood Mummy. 2001. (Sammy Keyes Ser.). 272p. (gr. 5-8). text 15.95 (0-375-80266-5, Knopf Bks. for Young Readers) Random Hse. Children's Bks.
Victor, Cynthia. Relative Sins. l.t. ed. 2001. 520p. 28.95 (1-57490-339-X) Beeler, Thomas T. Publisher.
—Relative Sins. 1993. 464p. reprint ed. mass mkt. 5.99 o.s.i (0-451-17601-4, Onyx) NAL.
—Relative Sins. 1992. 464p. 17.95 o.p. (0-670-83884-5, Viking) Viking Penguin.
Vida, Vendela. And Now You Can Go. 2003. 208p. 19.95 (1-4000-4027-2) Knopf, Alfred A. Inc.
Viehl, S. L. Blade Dancer. 2004. 416p. mass mkt. 6.99 (0-451-45946-6); 2003. 320p. 22.95 (0-451-45926-1) NAL. (ROC).
Vine, Barbara, pseud. Asta's Book. 1994. pap. 23.95 o.p. (0-7927-1758-9); 491p. 24.95 o.p. (0-7927-1759-7) BBC Audiobooks America.
Waldman, Ayelet. Daughter's Keeper. 2003. 352p. 24.00 (1-4022-0096-X, Sourcebooks Landmark) Sourcebooks, Inc.
Wall, Judith Henry. My Mother's Daughter: A Novel. l.t. ed. 2001. 504p. 28.95 (1-57490-372-1, Beeler Large Print Bks.) Beeler, Thomas T. Publisher.
Wallen, Jacqueline. Sudden Loss of Serenity. 2004. 220p. 12.95 (1-892281-21-X) New Victoria Pubs., Inc.
Weidenweber, Sigrid. Escaping the Twilight. 2003. 226p. pap. 15.95 (0-9726535-5-4, 255-0091) Arnica Publishing, Inc.
Wells, Rebecca. Divine Secrets of the Ya-Ya Sisterhood. l.t. ed. 2002. 12.95 (1-56895-199-X); 1998. 27.95 o.p. (1-56895-621-5, Wheeler Publishing, Inc.) Gale Group.
—Divine Secrets of the Ya-Ya Sisterhood. 2002. 480p. mass mkt. 7.99 (0-06-000810-5); 1996. 368p. 24.00 (0-06-017328-9); 1998. 256p. 22.00 (0-06-019345-X) HarperCollins Pubs.
—Divine Secrets of the Ya-Ya Sisterhood. 2000. 368p. mass mkt. 7.99 (0-06-101507-5, HarperTorch) Morrow/Avon.
—Divine Secrets of the Ya-Ya Sisterhood: A Novel. 1997. 368p. pap. 14.00 (0-06-092833-6, Perennial) HarperTrade.
—Divine Secrets of the Ya-Ya Sisterhood: A Novel. 2002. 480p. mass mkt. 7.99 (0-06-050225-8) Morrow/Avon.

—Les Divins Secrets des Petits Ya Ya. 2000. Tr. of Divine Secrets of the Ya Ya Sisterhood. (FRE.). pap. 12.95 (*2-266-09548-X*) Presses Pocket FRA. *Dist:* Distribooks, Inc.

—The Ya-Ya Boxed Set: Divine Secrets of the Ya-Ya Sisterhood & Little Altars Everywhere, 2 bks. 1999. 608p. pap. 27.00 (*0-06-093205-8*, Perennial) HarperTrade.

Wendorf, Patricia. The Marriage Menders. l.t. ed. 2000. (G. K. Hall Romance Ser.). 535p. 27.95 (*0-7838-9021-4*, Macmillan Reference USA) Gale Group.

West, Rebecca. The Fountain Overflows. 2003. (New York Review Books Classics Ser.). 408p. pap. 16.95 (*1-59017-034-2*) New York Review of Bks., Inc., The.

Wexler, Merin. The Porno Girl: And Other Stories. 2003. 224p. 22.95 (*0-312-31057-9*) St. Martin's Pr.

Wharton, Edith. The Old Maid: The 'Fifties. 2003. 144p. pap. 10.95 (*0-8129-7002-0*, Modern Library) Random House Adult Trade Publishing Group.

Wheeler, Joe L. Mom in My Heart. 1997. 159p. pap. 10.99 o.p. (*0-8423-0552-1*) Tyndale Hse. Pubs.

Whitney, Phyllis A. Listen for the Whisperer. 23.95 (*0-8488-1222-0*) Amereon, Ltd.

—Listen for the Whisperer. 9999. pap. 5.99 o.p. (*0-449-45244-1*); 1995. 256p. pap. 19.00 (*0-345-46622-5*); 1982. mass mkt. 2.95 o.p. (*0-449-23156-9*) Ballantine Bks. (Fawcett).

—Listen for the Whisperer. 1972. 5.95 o.p. (*0-385-03354-0*) Doubleday Publishing.

—Listen for the Whisperer. l.t. ed. 2001. 400p. 29.95 (*0-7838-9546-1*, Macmillan Reference USA) Gale Group.

Willett, Marcia. A Summer in the Country. Date not set. mass mkt. (*0-312-99715-9*, St. Martin's Paperbacks); 2003. 320p. 24.95 (*0-312-28781-X*) St. Martin's Pr.

Willis, Sarah. A Good Distance. 2004. 320p. 22.95 (*0-425-19426-4*) Berkley Publishing Group.

Winthrop, Elizabeth. Promises. 2000. (Illus.). 32p. (J). (ps-3). tchr. ed. 16.00 (*0-395-82272-6*, Clarion Bks.) Houghton Mifflin Co. Trade & Reference Div.

Wood, Barbara. Sacred Ground. E-Book 24.95 (*1-59061-241-8*) Adobe Systems, Inc.

—Sacred Ground. 2001. 340p. 24.95 (*0-312-27537-4*) St. Martin's Pr.

Wood, Jane Roberts. Roseborough. l.t. ed. 2003. 377p. 29.95 (*0-7862-5658-3*) Thorndike Pr.

—Roseborough: A Novel. 2003. 290p. 23.95 (*0-525-94715-9*, Dutton) Dutton/Plume.

Yorke, Christy. The Wishing Garden. l.t. ed. 2000. (G. K. Hall Core Ser.). 439p. 27.95 (*0-7838-9302-7*, Macmillan Reference USA) Gale Group.

Yun, Mia. House of the Winds. 1998. (Emerging Voices Ser.). 256p. 22.95 (*1-56656-305-4*) Interlink Publishing Group, Inc.

—House of the Winds. 2000. 240p. pap. 12.95 (*0-14-029194-6*) Penguin Group (USA) Inc.

## MOTHERS AND SONS—FICTION

Alcala, Kathleen. Treasures in Heaven: A Novel. 2003. (Latino Voices Ser.). 224p. pap. 15.95 (*0-8101-2036-4*) Northwestern Univ. Pr.

Allen, Richard E. Ozzy on the Outside. 1991. 208p. (YA). mass mkt. 3.50 o.s.i (*0-440-20767-3*) Dell Publishing.

Andersen, E. Chuck. 18.95 (*0-8118-3920-6*) Chronicle Bks. LLC.

Asch, Frank. Bread & Honey. 1992. (Sunny Day Bks.). (Illus.). 48p. (J). (ps-2). 2.95 o.s.i (*0-448-40319-6*, Grosset & Dunlap) Penguin Putnam Bks. for Young Readers.

Ash, Frank. Bread & Honey. 1992. (Illus.). 42p. (J). (ps-3). lib. bdg. 18.60 o.p. (*0-8368-0880-0*) Stevens, Gareth Inc.

Auch, Mary Jane. Kidnapping Kevin Kowalski. 1990. 128p. (J). (gr. 4-6). 15.95 o.p. (*0-8234-0815-9*) Holiday Hse., Inc.

—Kidnapping Kevin Kowalski. 1992. 128p. (J). (gr. 3-7). pap. 2.95 o.p. (*0-590-44335-6*, Scholastic Paperbacks) Scholastic, Inc.

Auerbach, Jessica. Catch Your Breath. 1996. 256p. 23.95 o.p. (*0-399-14166-9*, G. P. Putnam's Sons) Penguin Group (USA) Inc.

Banks, Kate. Spider, Spider, RS. 1996. (Illus.). 32p. (J). (ps-3). 14.00 o.p. (*0-374-37151-2*, Farrar, Straus & Giroux (BYR)) Farrar, Straus & Giroux.

Baronian, Jean-Baptiste. I Love You with All My Heart. 1998. (Illus.). 32p. (J). (ps-1). 14.95 (*0-8118-2031-9*) Chronicle Bks. LLC.

Bates, Betty. It Must've Been the Fishsticks. 1983. 144p. (J). (gr. 5-7). pap. (*0-671-46540-6*, Simon Pulse) Simon & Schuster Children's Publishing.

Bauer, Douglas. The Book of Famous Iowans: A Novel. 256p. 1998. pap. 12.00 o.s.i (*0-8050-6002-2*, Owl Bks.); 1997. 25.00 o.s.i (*0-8050-4300-4*) Holt, Henry & Co.

Bauer, Marion Dane. A Question of Trust. (YA). (gr. 4 up). 1995. mass mkt. 2.99 o.p. (*0-590-47923-7*); 1994. 128p. pap. 14.95 o.p. (*0-590-47915-6*) Scholastic, Inc.

—A Question of Trust. 1994. (YA). (gr. 4 up). 8.09 o.p. (*0-606-08591-2*) Turtleback Bks.

Bedford, Deborah. A Rose by the Door. l.t. ed. 2002. (Wheeler Large Print Book Ser.). 28.95 (*1-58724-208-7*, Wheeler Publishing, Inc.) Gale Group.

—A Rose by the Door. 2001. 352p. pap. 11.95 (*0-446-67789-2*); E-Book 9.95 (*0-7595-9671-9*); E-Book 9.95 (*0-7595-8610-1*); E-Book 9.95 (*0-7595-4603-7*); E-Book 9.95 (*0-7595-6601-1*); E-Book 9.95 (*0-7595-0600-0*) Warner Bks., Inc.

Bennett, Jay. Sing Me a Death Song. 1990. 144p. (gr. 7 up). mass mkt. 6.50 (*0-449-70369-X*, Fawcett) Ballantine Bks.

—Sing Me a Death Song. 1990. (J). 12.95 o.p. (*0-531-15115-8*); 160p. (YA). (gr. 7-12). lib. bdg. 14.40 o.p. (*0-531-10853-8*) Scholastic Library Publishing. (Watts, Franklin).

Benson, Peter. Riptide. 1995. 218p. text 25.00 o.p. (*0-340-60659-2*) Hodder & Stoughton, Ltd. GBR. *Dist:* Lubrecht & Cramer, Ltd., Trafalgar Square.

Bills, Greg. Consider This Home. 1994. 318p. 21.00 (*0-671-79873-1*, Simon & Schuster) Simon & Schuster.

Blakeslee, Mermer. Same Blood. 1989. 16.95 o.p. (*0-395-48601-7*) Houghton Mifflin Co.

Blatchford, Claire H. Nick's Mission. 1995. (Lerner Mysteries Ser.). 156p. (J). (gr. 4-7). lib. bdg. 14.95 (*0-8225-0740-4*, Lerner Pubns.) Lerner Publishing Group.

Bobrick, Sam & Stein, Julie. Sheldon & Mrs. Levine: An Excruciatingly Painful Correspondence Between a Mother & Her Son. Lovka, Bob, ed. 1994. (Illus.). 48p. 14.95 o.p. (*0-8431-3668-5*, Price Stern Sloan) Penguin Putnam Bks. for Young Readers.

Bornstein, Ruth. Of Course a Goat. 1980. (Illus.). 32p. (J). (ps-3). lib. bdg. 12.89 o.p. (*0-06-020609-8*) HarperCollins Children's Bk. Group.

Bosquet, Alain. A Russian Mother. Bray, Barbara, tr. from FRE. 1996. (French Expressions Ser.). 284p. 26.00 (*0-8419-1329-3*) Holmes & Meier Pubs., Inc.

Bowering, Marilyn. To All Appearances a Lady. 1999. (*0-241-13001-8*, Elm Tree Bks.); 1999. pap. 8.95 (*0-14-013313-5*); 1990. 336p. 18.95 o.p. (*0-670-83340-1*) Viking Penguin.

Boyd, Jim. Companions of the Blest. 2002. 281p. 28.95 (*1-57168-734-3*); pap. 22.95 (*1-57168-733-5*) Eakin Pr. (Eakin Pr.).

Bradfield, Scott. History of Luminous Motion. 1996. 288p. pap. 13.00 o.p. (*0-312-14089-4*) Picador.

—The History of Luminous Motion. 1990. (Vintage Contemporaries Ser.). 288p. pap. 11.00 o.s.i (*0-679-72943-7*, Vintage) Knopf Publishing Group.

Broome, Errol. Rockhopper. 1995. (Illus.). 96p. (J). (gr. 4-7). pap. 6.95 o.p. (*1-86373-678-6*) Allen & Unwin Pty., Ltd. AUS. *Dist:* Independent Pubs. Group.

Broughton, T. Alan. Winter Journey. 1985. 10.95 o.p. (*0-525-23515-9*, Dutton) Dutton/Plume.

Campbell, Ramsey. Silent Children. 2000. 352p. reprint ed. 24.95 (*0-312-87056-6*, MHC 0149, Tor Bks.) Doherty, Tom Assocs., LLC.

Cazet, Denys. Are There Any Questions? 1992. (Illus.). 32p. (J). (ps-2). 15.95 o.p. (*0-531-05451-9*); mass mkt. 16.99 o.p. (*0-531-08601-1*) Scholastic, Inc. (Orchard Bks.).

Chardiet, Bernice. I Help Mommy. 1994. (Lift-the-Flap Bks.). (Illus.). 16p. (J). (ps-3). pap. 4.99 o.s.i (*0-14-054998-6*) Penguin Putnam Bks. for Young Readers.

Cheuse, Alan. The Grandmother's Club. 1994. 348p. reprint ed. pap. 10.95 (*0-87074-374-0*) Southern Methodist Univ. Pr.

Chevalier, Christa. Spence & the Mean Old Bear. Levine, Abby, ed. 1986. (Spence Bks.). (Illus.). 32p. (J). (ps-1). 13.95 o.p. (*0-8075-7572-0*) Whitman, Albert & Co.

—Spence Isn't Spence Anymore. Levine, Abby, ed. 1985. (Illus.). 32p. (J). (ps-1). 13.95 o.p. (*0-8075-7565-8*) Whitman, Albert & Co.

Clark, Eliza. Bite the Stars. 2002. 256p. pap. 13.00 (*1-931561-11-7*) MacAdam/Cage Publishing, Inc.

Clark, Katharine. Steal Away. 368p. 1999. mass mkt. 6.50 o.s.i (*0-449-00319-1*); 1998. 24.00 o.s.i (*0-449-00276-4*) Ballantine Bks. (Fawcett).

Clifford, Eth. I Never Wanted to be Famous, 001. 1986. (J). (gr. 3-5). 12.95 o.p. (*0-395-40420-7*) Houghton Mifflin Co.

Coleman, Jane Candia. Desperate Acts. 2001. (First Edition Romance Ser.). 305p. 25.95 (*0-7862-3210-2*, Five Star) Gale Group.

Collins, Joan. Infamous. 1996. 320p. 23.95 o.p. (*0-525-94129-0*, Dutton) Dutton/Plume.

Condon, Richard. The Manchurian Candidate. 1972. mass mkt. 1.25 o.p. (*0-451-05309-5*, Signet Bks.) NAL.

—The Manchurian Candidate. 320p. pap. 11.00 (*1-874061-08-4*) Oldcastle Bks., Ltd. GBR. *Dist:* Trafalgar Square.

—The Manchurian Candidate. movie tie-in ed. 2004. mass mkt. 6.99 (*0-7434-8297-2*, Pocket Star) Simon & Schuster.

Connelly, Michael. The Last Coyote. l.t. ed. 1995. (Large Print Bks.). pap. 24.95 (*1-56895-272-4*, Wheeler Publishing, Inc.) Gale Group.

Cookson, Catherine. The Invisible Cord. l.t. ed. 1994. pap. 21.95 o.p. (*0-7927-1877-1*); 22.95 o.p. (*0-7927-1878-X*) BBC Audiobooks America.

—My Beloved Son. 1993. 22.00 (*0-671-75865-9*, Simon & Schuster) Simon & Schuster.

Cooper, Steven. With You in Spirit. 2003. 280p. pap. 13.95 (*1-55583-783-2*) Alyson Pubns.

Cowen-Fletcher, Jane. Mama Zooms. 32p. (J). (ps-3). 1994. pap. 4.99 (*0-590-45775-6*); 1993. (Illus.). pap. 14.95 o.p. (*0-590-45774-8*) Scholastic, Inc.

Craig, Amanda. In a Dark Wood. 2002. 320p. 24.95 (*0-385-50262-1*, Talese, Nan A.) Doubleday Publishing.

—In a Dark Wood: A Novel. 2003. 320p. pap. 13.00 (*0-385-72117-X*) Doubleday Publishing.

—In a Dark Wood: A Novel. 2000. 276p. (*1-85702-682-9*) Fourth Estate, Ltd. GBR. *Dist:* Trafalgar Square.

Daly, Niki. Ben's Gingerbread Man. 1985. (Illus.). 24p. (J). (ps-1). 4.95 o.p. (*0-670-80806-7*, Viking Children's Bks.) Penguin Putnam Bks. for Young Readers.

Danielewski, Mark Z. The Whalestoe Letters. 2000. 86p. pap. 8.95 (*0-375-71441-3*, Pantheon) Knopf Publishing Group.

Dann, Patty. Sweet & Crazy. Date not set. pap. (*0-312-31667-4*, St. Martin's Paperbacks); mass mkt. (*0-312-99049-9*, St. Martin's Paperbacks); 2003. 208p. 22.95 (*0-312-31666-6*) St. Martin's Pr.

Dawson, Carol. The Mother-in-Law Diaries. 2000. 288p. reprint ed. pap. 17.95 (*0-671-04085-5*, Pocket) Simon & Schuster.

Defirenze, Rina. Mystery of the Mona Lisa: Leonardo Da Vinci's Greatest Painting. 1996. 354p. 22.95 o.p. (*0-8038-9381-7*) Hastings Hse. Daytrips Pubs.

Delton, Judy. My Mom Hates Me in January. 1977. (Albert Whitman Concept Bks.). (Illus.). (J). (gr. 1-3). lib. bdg. 12.95 o.p. (*0-8075-5356-5*) Whitman, Albert & Co.

DeMaria, Robert. The Satyr. 1992. 176p. 24.00 (*0-933256-78-7*) Second Chance Pr.

DeMarinis, Rick. The Year of the Zinc Penny. l.t. ed. 1990. (General Ser.). 288p. lib. bdg. 19.95 o.p. (*0-8161-5056-7*, Macmillan Reference USA) Gale Group.

—The Year of the Zinc Penny. 1990. 176p. reprint ed. pap. 9.00 o.p. (*0-06-097339-0*, Perennial) HarperTrade.

—The Year of the Zinc Penny. 1989. 17.95 o.p. (*0-393-02758-9*) Norton, W. W. & Co., Inc.

—The Year of the Zinc Penny. 1999. pap. 18.95 (*0-670-82575-1*) Viking Penguin.

DeWitt, Helen. The Last Samurai: A Novel. 2002. 544p. pap. 14.95 (*0-7868-8700-1*); 2000. viii, 530p. 24.95 (*0-7868-6668-3*) Talk Miramax Bks.

Dinardo, Jeffrey. Timothy & the Christmas Gift. 1989. (J). pap. 12.95 o.p. (*0-671-67959-7*, Simon & Schuster Children's Publishing) Simon & Schuster Children's Publishing.

Disney, Walter Elias. Very Best Mama: Peek-a-Pooh. 1997. 10p. (J). (ps-k). 6.98 o.s.i (*1-57082-525-4*) Mouse Works.

Dodd, Susan. Mamaw. 1990. 288p. mass mkt. 3.95 o.s.i (*0-345-36297-7*) Ballantine Bks.

—Mamaw. 1988. 368p. 18.95 o.p. (*0-670-82180-2*, Viking) Viking Penguin.

—Mamaw: A Novel of an Outlaw Mother. 1999. 368p. reprint ed. pap. 13.00 (*0-688-17001-3*, Quill) HarperTrade.

Dodge, Jim. Stone Junction. 1991. pap. 10.95 o.p. (*0-87113-454-3*, Atlantic Monthly Pr.); 1990. 19.95 o.p. (*0-87113-331-8*); 1998. 376p. reprint ed. pap. 12.00 (*0-8021-3585-4*, Grove Pr.) Grove/Atlantic, Inc.

Doherty, Berlie. Dear Nobody. 1994. 240p. (J). (gr. 7 up). pap. 5.95 (*0-688-12764-9*, Harper Trophy) HarperCollins Children's Bk. Group.

Dorflinger, Carolyn. Tomorrow Is Mom's Birthday. (Illus.). 32p. (J). (ps-3). 1996. pap. 5.95 (*1-879085-67-4*); 1994. 14.95 (*1-879085-84-4*) Charlesbridge Publishing, Inc. (Whispering Coyote).

Dorr, Roberta Kells. Honored. 2003. 96p. 10.99 (*0-8007-1817-8*) Revell, Fleming H. Co.

Dracup, Angela. The Placing. 1991. 192p. (YA). (gr. 8 up). 19.95 o.p. (*0-575-04890-5*) Gollancz, Victor GBR. *Dist:* Trafalgar Square.

Earley, Tony. Jim the Boy: A Novel. l.t. ed. 2000. (Wheeler Large Print Book Ser.). 227p. 27.95 (*1-56895-990-7*, Wheeler Publishing, Inc.) Gale Group.

—Jim the Boy: A Novel. Adams, Terry, ed. 2001. (Illus.). 256p. pap. 12.95 (*0-316-19895-1*, Back Bay); 2000. 240p. 23.95 (*0-316-19964-8*) Little Brown & Co.

Ellis, David. A Jury of One. 2004. 400p. 24.95 (*0-399-15149-4*) Putnam Publishing Group, The.

Emmons, Cai. His Mother's Son. 2003. 376p. 25.00 (*0-15-100734-9*) Harcourt Trade Pubs.

Evans, Richard Paul. The Last Promise. 2002. 304p. 22.95 (*0-525-94696-9*) Dutton/Plume.

—The Last Promise. l.t. ed. 2003. (Wheeler Romance Ser.). 32.95 (*1-58724-375-X*, Wheeler Publishing, Inc.) Gale Group.

—The Last Promise. 2003. mass mkt. 6.99 (*0-451-41092-0*); 320p. mass mkt. 6.99 (*0-451-21101-4*) NAL. (Signet Bks.).

Farmer, Patti. Bartholomew's Dream. 1994. (Illus.). 32p. (J). (ps-2). 12.95 o.p. (*0-8120-6403-8*); pap. 4.95 o.p. (*0-8120-1991-1*) Barron's Educational Series, Inc.

Farrell, Sue. To the Post Office with Mama. 1994. (Illus.). 24p. (J). (ps-k). pap. 4.95 (*1-55037-358-7*); lib. bdg. 15.95 (*1-55037-359-5*) Annick Pr., Ltd. CAN. *Dist:* Firefly Bks., Ltd.

—To the Post Office with Mama. ed. 1994. (J). (gr. 2). spiral bd. (*0-616-01636-0*) Canadian National Institute for the Blind/Institut National Canadien pour les Aveugles.

Feinstein, Elaine. Dark Inheritance. l.t. ed. 2001. 258p. pap. 22.95 (*0-7862-3566-7*); 274p. (*0-7540-4623-0*); 274p. (*0-7540-4624-9*) Thorndike Pr.

—Dark Inheritance. 2001. 154p. pap. 13.95 (*0-7043-4725-3*); 234p. pap. 16.95 (*0-7043-4671-0*) Women's Pr., Ltd., The GBR. *Dist:* Trafalgar Square.

Ferber, Edna. Personality Plus: Some Experiences of Emma McChesney & Her Son, Jock. 1977. (Short Story Index Reprint Ser.). (Illus.). reprint ed. 19.95 (*0-8369-3813-5*) Ayer Co. Pubs., Inc.

—Personality Plus: Some Experiences of Emma McChesney & Her Son, Jock. 2002. (Illus.). 176p. pap. 14.95 (*0-252-07087-9*) Univ. of Illinois Pr.

Findley, Timothy. The Piano Man's Daughter. 1996. 480p. 26.00 o.s.i (*0-517-70307-6*, Crown) Crown Publishing Group.

—The Piano Man's Daughter. 2002. 512p. pap. 14.95 (*0-06-093643-6*, Perennial) HarperTrade.

—Die Tochter des Klavierspielers. (GER.). 496p. pap. (*3-612-27808-8*) Econ-Verlag GmbH DEU. *Dist:* International Bk. Import Service, Inc.

Flagg, Fannie. Standing in the Rainbow: A Novel. 2003. 544p. mass mkt. 7.99 (*0-8041-1935-X*, Ballantine Bks.) Ballantine Bks.

—Standing in the Rainbow: A Novel. 2002. 512p. 25.95 (*0-679-42615-9*); 816p. 27.95 (*0-375-43172-1*) Random Hse., Inc.

Fleming, Susan. The Pig at Thirty-Seven Pinecrest Drive. 1981. (Illus.). 130p. (J). (gr. 3-5). 9.95 o.p. (*0-664-32676-5*) Westminster John Knox Pr.

Franklin, Kristine L. Nerd No More. 1996. (Illus.). 144p. (J). (gr. 4-7). 16.99 (*1-56402-674-4*) Candlewick Pr.

Gaeddert, LouAnn. The Kid with the Red Suspenders. 1983. (Illus.). 80p. (J). (gr. 2-4). 9.95 o.p. (*0-525-44046-1*, Dutton) Dutton/Plume.

Gatewood, Robert Payne. The Sound of the Trees: A Novel. 2002. 304p. 25.00 o.s.i (*0-8050-6802-3*) Holt, Henry & Co.

—The Sound of the Trees: A Novel. 2003. 304p. pap. 14.00 (*0-312-42188-5*) Picador.

Gibbon, Lewis G. Grey Granite. 1991. (Canongate Classic Ser.). 240p. pap. 9.95 o.p. (*0-86241-312-5*) Trafalgar Square.

—A Scots Quair: A Trilogy of Sunset Song, Cloud Howe & Grey Granite. 1987. 496p. (C). reprint ed. 16.95 o.p. (*0-8052-3661-9*, Schocken) Knopf Publishing Group.

Gifford, Barry. Wyoming. 2000. (Illus.). 129p. 21.95 (*1-55970-523-X*) Arcade Publishing, Inc.

—Wyoming. 2004. reprint ed. pap. 8.95 (*1-58322-636-2*) Seven Stories Pr.

Gilchrist, Guy. My Mom's Okay. 1991. (Mudpie Bks.). (Illus.). 24p. (J). (ps-3). 5.95 (*1-56288-088-8*) Checkerboard Pr., Inc.

Gove, Doris. One Rainy Night. 1994. (Illus.). 32p. (J). (gr. 2-5). 14.95 (*0-689-31800-6*, Atheneum) Simon & Schuster Children's Publishing.

Graver, Elizabeth. Night Light. 2004. 304p. 23.00 (*0-8050-6539-3*) Holt, Henry & Co.

Gray, Nigel. Little Pig's Tale. 1990. (Illus.). 32p. (J). (ps-2). 13.95 o.p. (*0-02-736942-0*, Simon & Schuster Children's Publishing) Simon & Schuster Children's Publishing.

Haggerty, Mary E. A Crack in the Wall. 1993. (ENG & SPA., Illus.). 32p. (J). (ps-5). 14.95 o.p. (*1-880000-03-2*, LLB032) Lee & Low Bks., Inc.

—Una Grieta en la Pared. González, Tomás, tr. from ENG. 1994. Tr. of A Crack in the Wall. (SPA., Illus.). 32p. (J). (gr. 3-5). 14.95 o.p. (*1-880000-09-1*) Lee & Low Bks., Inc.

Haggerty, Mary Elizabeth. Una Grieta en la Pared. González, Tomás, tr. from ENG. 1994. (SPA., Illus.). 32p. (J). (ps-5). pap. 6.95 (*1-880000-12-1*) Lee & Low Bks., Inc.

Hale, Irina. Small Big Bad Boy. 1991. 32p. (J). (ps-3). 11.95 o.p. (*0-670-83818-7*, Viking Children's Bks.) Penguin Putnam Bks. for Young Readers.

Hall, James W. Under Cover of Daylight. 1997. 352p. pap. 9.95 o.s.i (*0-385-31867-7*, Delta) Dell Publishing.

—Under Cover of Daylight. l.t. ed. 2001. (Large Print Book Ser.). 358p. 26.95 (*1-58724-028-9*, Wheeler Publishing, Inc.) Gale Group.

—Under Cover of Daylight. 2001. 272p. pap. 10.00 (*0-393-32125-8*); 1987. 16.95 o.p. (*0-393-02484-9*) Norton, W. W. & Co., Inc.

—Under Cover of Daylight. 1988. 384p. mass mkt. 6.50 o.s.i (*0-446-35231-4*) Warner Bks., Inc.

Hall, Kirsten. At the Carnival. 1996. (My First Hello Reader! Ser.). (Illus.). 32p. (J). (ps-3). 3.99 (*0-590-68994-0*, Cartwheel Bks.) Scholastic, Inc.

Halligan, Marion. The Golden Dress. 1999. 380p. (*0-14-027302-6*) Penguin Group (USA) Inc.

Halvorson, Marilyn. Let It Go. 1988. (YA). (gr. 5 up). mass mkt. 2.95 o.s.i (*0-440-20053-9*, Laurel Leaf) Random Hse. Children's Bks.

Hamilton, Dorothy. Joel's Other Mother. 1984. (Illus.). 120p. (J). (gr. 3-7). pap. 3.95 o.p. (*0-8361-3355-2*) Herald Pr.

Hamilton, Jane. Disobedience: A Novel. 2001. 288p. pap. 13.00 (*0-385-72046-7*, Knopf Bks. for Young Readers) Random Hse. Children's Bks.

—Disobedience: A Novel. l.t. ed. 2001. (Thorndike Basic Ser.). 463p. 31.95 (*0-7862-3159-9*); pap. 29.95 (*0-7862-3158-0*) Thorndike Pr.

Hancock, Marianne. Looking for Oliver: A Mother's Search for the Son She Gave up for Adoption. 2003. 240p. (C). pap. 19.95 (*1-84310-142-4*) Kingsley, Jessica Pubs. GBR. *Dist:* Taylor & Francis, Inc.

Hardie, Kerry. A Winter Marriage. 2002. 400p. 24.95 (*0-316-07622-8*) Little Brown & Co.

Hardy, Jon. Biker. 1987. 126p. (YA). (gr. 7 up). 13.95 o.p. (*0-19-271473-2*) Oxford Univ. Pr., Inc.

Hardy, Jules. Altered Land: A Novel. 2002. 336p. 24.95 (*1-55970-642-2*) Arcade Publishing, Inc.

Hawkes, Judith. My Soul to Keep. 1996. 336p. 23.95 o.p. (*0-525-93957-1*, Dutton) Dutton/Plume.

Hayner, Linda K. The Foundling. 1997. 352p. (YA). (gr. 10 up). pap. 9.95 (*0-89084-941-2*, 108951) Jones, Bob Univ. Pr.

Hearne, Betsy. Eli's Ghost. 1987. (Illus.). 112p. (J). (gr. 3-7). 13.95 (*0-689-50420-9*, McElderry, Margaret K.) Simon & Schuster Children's Publishing.

Heath, Roy A. The Shadow Bride. 1995. 428p. 24.95 (*0-89255-213-1*) Persea Bks., Inc.

Heiligman, Deborah. Into the Night. 1990. (Illus.). 32p. (J). (ps-1). 14.95 (*0-06-026381-4*); lib. bdg. 14.89 o.p. (*0-06-026382-2*) HarperCollins Children's Bk. Group.

Helmer, John. Mother Tongue. 2001. 272p. pap. 12.95 (*0-7043-8139-7*) Quartet Bks., Ltd. GBR. *Dist:* Interlink Publishing Group, Inc.

Hepinstall, Kathy. Prince of Lost Places. 2004. 256p. mass mkt. 6.99 (*0-425-19378-0*) Berkley Publishing Group.

—Prince of Lost Places. 2003. 228p. 28.95 (*1-58724-438-1*) Gale Group.

—Prince of Lost Places. 2003. 192p. 23.95 (*0-399-14936-8*) Putnam Publishing Group, The.

Herman, Charlotte. My Mother Didn't Kiss Me Goodnight. 1980. (Illus.). 32p. (J). (ps-3). 7.95 o.p. (*0-525-35495-6*, Dutton Children's Bks.) Penguin Putnam Bks. for Young Readers.

Herman, Hank. Above the Rim. 1997. (Super Hoops Ser.: No. 11). 96p. (gr. 4-6). pap. text 3.50 o.s.i (*0-553-48474-5*, Skylark) Random Hse. Children's Bks.

—Foul! 1997. (Super Hoops Ser.: No. 10). 96p. (gr. 4-6). pap. text 3.50 o.s.i (*0-553-48432-X*, Skylark) Random Hse. Children's Bks.

Hood, Susan. The Bestest Mom. 1998. (Rugrats Ser.). (Illus.). 32p. (J). (ps-2). pap. 5.99 (*0-689-82047-X*, Simon Spotlight/Nickelodeon) Simon & Schuster Children's Publishing.

Huff Fisk, Sarah. Found among the Fragments: A Story of Love & Courage. 1997. (Illus.). 320p. (Orig.). pap. 15.95 (*0-9655917-2-7*) Pinhook Publishing Co.

Huston, Bo. The Listener: A Novella & Four Stories. 1993. 176p. 17.95 o.p. (*0-312-09931-2*) St. Martin's Pr.

—The Listener: A Novella & Other Stories. 1994. 176p. pap. 5.99 o.p. (*0-312-11313-7*, Saint Martin's Griffin) St. Martin's Pr.

Hyde, Catherine Ryan. Pay It Forward. E-Book 23.00 (*1-930161-23-9*) Adobe Systems, Inc.

—Pay It Forward. l.t. ed. 2000. (Wheeler Hardcover Ser.). 27.95 (*1-56895-960-5*, Wheeler Publishing, Inc.) Gale Group.

—Pay It Forward. 2000. E-Book 23.00 (*0-7432-0596-0*, Simon & Schuster); E-Book 23.00 (*0-7432-0389-5*, Simon & Schuster); (Illus.). 288p. 23.00 o.s.i (*0-684-86271-9*, Simon & Schuster); 320p. mass mkt. 7.99 (*0-7434-1202-8*, Pocket) Simon & Schuster.

—Pay It Forward. 2000. 14.04 (*0-606-21795-9*) Turtleback Bks.

Ignatieff, Michael. Scar Tissue. 199p. 2000. pap. 18.00 (*0-374-52769-5*); 1994. 20.00 o.p. (*0-374-25428-1*) Farrar, Straus & Giroux.

Indiana, Gary. Depraved Indifference. 336p. 2003. pap. 12.95 (*0-06-095728-X*, Perennial); 2002. 24.95 (*0-06-019726-9*, HarperCollins) HarperTrade.

—Depraved Indifference. Date not set. pap. (*0-312-31642-9*, St. Martin's Paperbacks); mass mkt. (*0-312-99048-0*, St. Martin's Paperbacks); 2003. 336p. reprint ed. pap. 13.95 (*0-312-31641-0*, Saint Martin's Griffin) St. Martin's Pr.

Jackson, Edwardo. Neva Hafta: A Novel. 368p. 2003. pap. 13.95 (*0-375-75774-0*); 2002. 22.95 (*0-375-50637-3*, Villard Bks.) Random House Adult Trade Publishing Group.

James, Mary. The Shuteyes. (J). 1994. 376p. (gr. 4-7). pap. 3.25 (*0-590-45070-0*); 1993. 176p. (gr. 3-7). pap. 13.95 o.p. (*0-590-45069-7*) Scholastic, Inc.

Jewell, Lisa. A Friend of the Family: A Novel. 2003. 336p. 23.95 (*0-525-94734-5*, Plume) Dutton/Plume.

Jonell, Lynne. Mommy Go Away! 1997. (Illus.). 32p. (J). (ps-1). 12.99 (*0-399-23001-7*, G. P. Putnam's Sons) Penguin Group (USA) Inc.

Joosse, Barbara M. I Love You the Purplest. 1996. (Illus.). 32p. (J). (ps-3). 15.95 (*0-8118-0718-5*) Chronicle Bks. LLC.

—The Pitiful Life of Simon Schultz. 1991. 192p. (J). (gr. 5-9). lib. bdg. 13.89 (*0-06-022487-8*) HarperCollins Children's Bk. Group.

Joyce, Michael. Liam's Going. 2002. 208p. 22.00 (*0-929701-66-6*) McPherson & Co.

Kangas, Juli. Hello, Honey Bear. 1992. (Furry Pals Ser.). (Illus.). 12p. (J). (ps). 2.95 o.p. (*0-448-40141-X*, Grosset & Dunlap) Penguin Putnam Bks. for Young Readers.

Katz, Welwyn W. Out of the Dark. 1996. 192p. (J). (gr. 6-9). 16.00 (*0-689-80947-6*, McElderry, Margaret K.) Simon & Schuster Children's Publishing.

Kavanaugh, Michelle. Emerald Explosion. 1988. 200p. (YA). (gr. 9-12). lib. bdg. 11.95 o.p. (*0-910923-46-9*) Pineapple Pr., Inc.

Keller, Beverly. When Mother Got the Flu. 1984. (Illus.). 64p. (J). (gr. 1-4). 8.99 o.p. (*0-698-30743-7*, Coward-McCann) Putnam Publishing Group, The.

Kihlman, Christer. The Blue Mother. 1990. (Modern Scandinavian Literature in Translation Ser.). 315p. reprint ed. pap. 97.70 (*0-608-02383-3*, 206302500004) Bks. on Demand.

—The Blue Mother. Tate, Joan, tr. from FIN. 1990. (Modern Scandinavian Literature in Translation Ser.). vi, 308p. text 29.95 o.p. (*0-8032-2721-3*); pap. 11.95 o.p. (*0-8032-7769-5*, Bison Bks.) Univ. of Nebraska Pr.

King, Stephen. The Talisman. 1985. 12.60 o.p. (*0-606-02450-6*) Turtleback Bks.

—El Talisman. 2002. Orig. Title: The Talisman. (SPA.). 816p. 26.95 (*1-4000-0229-X*) Random Hse., Inc.

King, Stephen & Straub, Peter. The Talisman. 2001. 768p. mass mkt. 7.99 (*0-345-44488-4*, Ballantine Bks.) Ballantine Bks.

—The Talisman. 1987. 784p. mass mkt. 8.50 o.s.i (*0-425-10533-4*) Berkley Publishing Group.

—The Talisman. 1984. 672p. 35.00 (*0-670-69199-2*) Viking Penguin.

—El Talisman. 1998. Orig. Title: The Talisman. (SPA.). 212p. (*84-08-02430-2*) GeoPlaneta, Editorial, S. A.

Klevin, Jill R. Turtles Together Forever! 1982. (Illus.). 160p. (J). (gr. 4-6). pap. 9.95 o.s.i (*0-385-29045-4*, Delacorte Pr.) Dell Publishing.

Knight, Kathryn L. Dark Swan. 1994. 224p. 19.95 o.p. (*0-312-10961-X*, Saint Martin's Minotaur) St. Martin's Pr.

—Mortal Words. 1990. 17.95 o.p. (*0-671-68446-9*, Simon & Schuster) Simon & Schuster.

—Mumbo Jumbo. 1991. 17.95 o.p. (*0-671-68448-5*, Simon & Schuster) Simon & Schuster.

—Mumbo Jumbo. Chelius, Jane, ed. 1992. 224p. reprint ed. mass mkt. 4.99 (*0-671-68447-7*, Pocket) Simon & Schuster.

—Trace Elements. 1986. 15.95 o.p. (*0-393-02333-8*) Norton, W. W. & Co., Inc.

Koertge, Ronald. Confess-O-Rama. 1998. (Laurel-Leaf Bks.). 176p. (YA). (gr. 7-12). mass mkt. 4.50 o.s.i (*0-440-22713-5*, Laurel Leaf) Random Hse. Children's Bks.

—Confess-O-Rama. 1996. 176p. (YA). (gr. 7-12). pap. 16.95 (*0-531-09515-0*, Orchard Bks.) Scholastic, Inc.

—Tiger, Tiger, Burning Bright. 1995. 179p. (YA). (gr. 7 up). pap. 3.99 (*0-380-72474-X*, Avon Bks.) Morrow/Avon.

—Tiger, Tiger, Burning Bright. 1994. 192p. (YA). (gr. 7 up). pap. 17.95 (*0-531-06840-4*); mass mkt. 18.99 o.p. (*0-531-08690-9*) Scholastic, Inc. (Orchard Bks.).

—Where the Kissing Never Stops. 1988. (J). (gr. k-12). reprint ed. mass mkt. 2.95 o.s.i (*0-440-20167-5*) Dell Publishing.

—Where the Kissing Never Stops. 1986. 224p. (YA). (gr. 7 up). 14.95 o.p. (*0-316-50096-8*) Little Brown & Co.

—Where the Kissing Never Stops. 1993. 224p. (J). pap. 3.99 (*0-380-71796-4*, Avon Bks.) Morrow/Avon.

—Where the Kissing Never Stops. 1986. 9.09 o.p. (*0-606-02989-3*) Turtleback Bks.

Koontz, Dean. The Servants of Twilight. 1990. 432p. mass mkt. 7.99 (*0-425-12125-9*); 1988. 18.95 o.p. (*0-913165-24-7*) Berkley Publishing Group.

—The Servants of Twilight. l.t. ed. 1994. (Magna Large Print Ser.). 721p. o.p. (*0-7505-0637-7*) Magna Large Print Bks. GBR. *Dist:* Ulverscroft Large Print Canada, Ltd.

—The Servants of Twilight. 1996. (SPA.). 496p. (*84-01-49545-8*) Plaza & Janés Editories, S.A.

—The Servants of Twilight. l.t. ed. 2001. (Famous Authors Ser.). 765p. 29.95 (*0-7862-2866-0*) Thorndike Pr.

—The Servants of Twilight. 1984. 14.04 (*0-606-04537-6*) Turtleback Bks.

Kraft, Eric. Inflating a Dog: The Story of Ella's Lunch Launch. 2003. (Illus.). 256p. pap. 14.00 (*0-312-42221-0*); 2002. 336p. 25.00 (*0-312-28804-2*) Picador.

Kroetsch, Robert. The Man from the Creeks. 1998. 320p. o.s.i (*0-679-30917-9*) Random Hse. of Canada, Ltd. CAN. *Dist:* Random Hse., Inc.

Krosoczka, Jarrett J. Goodnight, Monkey Boy! 2001. (Illus.). 40p. (J). (ps). 14.95 (*0-375-81121-4*, Knopf Bks. for Young Readers) Random Hse. Children's Bks.

Kung, Dinah L. Left in the Care of: A Novel of Suspense. 1997. 272p. 23.00 o.p. (*0-7867-0494-2*, Carroll & Graf Pubs.) Avalon Publishing Group.

—Left in the Care Of: A Novel of Suspense. 1999. 270p. lib. bdg. 29.95 (*0-7351-0224-4*) Replica Bks.

LaHaye, Beverly & Blackstock, Terri. Times & Seasons. 2001. 371p. 16.99 (*0-310-23319-4*) Zondervan.

Landstrom, Lena. Will Goes to the Beach. Wiberg, Carla, tr. from SWE. 1995. (Illus.). 32p. (J). (ps-3). 13.00 (*91-29-62914-4*) R & S Bks. SWE. *Dist:* Holtzbrinck Pubs.

Landstrom, Olof & Landstrom, Lena. Will Goes to the Beach. Wiberg, Carla, tr. from SWE. 2001. (Illus.). 28p. (J). (ps-1). pap. 4.95 (*91-29-65305-3*) R & S Bks. SWE. *Dist:* Farrar, Straus & Giroux, Holtzbrinck Pubs.

Langley, Lee. Persistent Rumours. 304p. 1998. pap. 14.95 (*1-57131-014-2*); 1994. 21.95 (*1-57131-001-0*) Milkweed Editions.

Launko, Okniba. Ma'mi. 1995. (Junior African Writers Ser.). (Illus.). 80p. (J). (gr. 4-7). pap. 4.95 (*0-7910-3164-0*) Chelsea Hse. Pubs.

Lavin, Mary. The Story of the Widow's Son. 1993. (Creative Short Stories Ser.). 32p. (YA). (gr. 3-12). lib. bdg. 18.60 (*0-88682-500-8*, Creative Education) Creative Co., The.

Lawrence, D. H. Sons & Lovers. 1998. pap. text o.p. (*0-17-556631-3*); 1930. 124p. pap. text 5.95 (*0-582-52634-5*) Addison-Wesley Longman, Inc.

—Sons & Lovers. 1976. 23.95 (*0-8488-0561-5*) Amereon, Ltd.

—Sons & Lovers. 1985. (Classics Ser.). 432p. mass mkt. 5.95 (*0-553-21192-7*) Bantam Bks.

—Sons & Lovers. 1982. reprint ed. lib. bdg. 28.95 (*0-89966-400-8*) Buccaneer Bks., Inc.

—Sons & Lovers. Baron, Helen & Baron, Carl, eds. 1992. (Cambridge Edition of the Works of D. H. Lawrence). 466p. (C). 34.95 o.p. (*0-521-43221-9*); (Illus.). 757p. 125.00 o.p. (*0-521-24276-2*) Cambridge Univ. Pr.

—Sons & Lovers. 1988. (Study Texts Ser.). pap. text 5.95 (*0-582-33166-8*, 72062) Longman Publishing Group.

—Sons & Lovers. 1985. 416p. mass mkt. 5.95 (*0-451-51882-9*, Signet Classics) NAL.

—Sons & Lovers. 1998. (Twelve-Point Ser.). 463p. reprint ed. lib. bdg. 25.00 (*1-58287-072-1*) North Bks.

—Sons & Lovers. 1997. (Critical Editions Ser.). (C). pap. (*0-393-95758-6*, Norton Paperbacks) Norton, W. W. & Co., Inc.

—Sons & Lovers. Trotter, David, ed. & intro. by. 1998. (Oxford World's Classics Ser.). 528p. pap. 10.95 (*0-19-283860-1*) Oxford Univ. Pr., Inc.

—Sons & Lovers. (Modern Library Ser.). 1997. 616p. 18.50 o.s.i (*0-679-60268-2*); 1991. 432p. 17.00 (*0-679-40572-0*) Random Hse., Inc.

—Sons & Lovers. Baron, Helen & Baron, Carl, eds. 1995. (Twentieth Century Classics Ser.). 544p. 10.95 (*0-14-018832-0*, Penguin Classics) Viking Penguin.

—Sons & Lovers. 1989. 512p. pap. 8.95 o.p. (*0-14-018215-2*, 462, Penguin Classics); 1982. 512p. pap. 4.95 o.p. (*0-14-043154-3*, Penguin Bks.); 1976. 432p. pap. 6.95 o.p. (*0-14-004217-2*, Viking); 1913. 10.00 o.p. (*0-670-65764-6*) Viking Penguin.

—Sons & Lovers. 1997. (Classics Library). 400p. pap. 3.95 (*1-85326-047-9*, 0479WW) Wordsworth Editions, Ltd. GBR. *Dist:* Casemate Pubs. & Bk. Distributors, LLC.

—Sons & Lovers, Level 5. 2000. (Illus.). vi, 72p. pap. 7.93 (*0-582-41696-5*) Addison-Wesley Longman, Inc.

—Sons & Lovers: A Facsimile of the Manuscript. Schorer, Mark, ed. 1978. 200.00 o.p. (*0-520-03190-3*) Univ. of California Pr.

—Sons & Lovers: Text & Criticism. Moynahan, Julian, ed. 1977. (Critical Studies: No. 4). 640p. pap. 14.95 o.p. (*0-14-015504-X*, Viking) Viking Penguin.

Layefsky, Virginia. Impossible Things. 1998. (Accelerated Reader Bks. ). 208p. (J). (gr. 5-9). 14.95 (*0-7614-5038-6*, Cavendish Children's Bks.) Cavendish, Marshall Corp.

Learning about Love. 1986. (J). (ps-2). 10.95 o.p. (*0-516-02020-X*, Children's Pr.) Scholastic Library Publishing.

Lebrun, Claude. Good Morning, Little Brown Bear! (Little Brown Bear Ser.). (Illus.). (J). 1997. 16p. mass mkt. 3.95 o.p. (*0-516-17849-0*); 1996. mass mkt. 12.00 o.p. (*0-516-07849-6*) Scholastic Library Publishing. (Children's Pr.).

LeClaire, Anne D. Entering Normal. 2002. 336p. pap. 14.00 (*0-345-44573-2*, Ballantine Bks.) Ballantine Bks.

—Entering Normal. l.t. ed. 2001. (Women's Fiction Ser.). 582p. 29.95 (*0-7862-3567-5*) Thorndike Pr.

Lee, Huy Voun. In the Park, ERS. 1998. (Illus.). 32p. (J). (ps-3). 16.95 (*0-8050-4128-1*, Holt, Henry & Co. Bks. For Young Readers) Holt, Henry & Co.

Lee, Huy-Voun. In the Snow, ERS. 1995. (Illus.). (J). (ps-3). 15.95 o.s.i (*0-8050-3172-3*, Holt, Henry & Co. Bks. For Young Readers) Holt, Henry & Co.

LeRoy, J. T. The Heart Is Deceitful above All Things. 2002. 250p. pap. 13.95 (*1-58234-211-3*) Bloomsbury Publishing.

Levin, Ira. Son of Rosemary. 1997. 272p. 22.95 o.p. (*0-525-94374-9*) Dutton/Plume.

—Son of Rosemary. 1998. 320p. mass mkt. 6.99 o.s.i (*0-451-19472-1*, Onyx) NAL.

—Son of Rosemary: The Sequel to Rosemary's Baby. l.t. ed. 1998. (Basic Ser.). 301p. 28.95 (*0-7862-1272-1*) Thorndike Pr.

Levy, Marilyn. No Way Home. 1990. 160p. (YA). mass mkt. 3.95 o.s.i (*0-449-70326-6*, Fawcett) Ballantine Bks.

Lindgren, Barbro. The Wild Baby. Prelutsky, Jack, tr. from SWE. 1981. (Illus.). (J). (gr. k-3). lib. bdg. 15.93 o.p. (*0-688-00601-9*, Greenwillow Bks.) HarperCollins Children's Bk. Group.

—The Wild Baby Gets a Puppy: Swedish Edition. Prelutsky, Jack, tr. 1988. Orig. Title: Vilda bebin far en hund. (Illus.). 32p. (J). (ps-3). reprint ed. 12.95 o.p. (*0-688-06711-5*); lib. bdg. 12.88 o.p. (*0-688-06712-3*) HarperCollins Children's Bk. Group. (Greenwillow Bks.).

—The Wild Baby Goes to Sea. Prelutsky, Jack, tr. 1983. Tr. of Den Vilda Bebiresan. (Illus.). 24p. (J). (gr. k-3). lib. bdg. 12.88 o.p. (*0-688-01961-7*, Greenwillow Bks.) HarperCollins Children's Bk. Group.

Lipsky, David. The Art Fair. 1996. 224p. 22.50 o.s.i (*0-385-42610-0*) Doubleday Publishing.

Liu, Aimee E. Flash House. 2004. 472p. pap. 13.95 (*0-446-69121-6*); 2003. (Illus.). 464p. 24.95 (*0-446-53097-2*) Warner Bks., Inc.

London, Joan. Gilgamesh. 272p. 2004. pap. 13.00 (*0-8021-4121-8*); 2003. 23.00 (*0-8021-1741-4*) Grove/Atlantic, Inc. (Grove Pr.).

Lopez, Steve. Third & Indiana: A Novel. 1994. 336p. (J). 21.95 o.p. (*0-670-85676-2*, Viking) Viking Penguin.

Lowell, Jax P. Mothers. 336p. 1996. pap. 13.95 (*0-312-14373-7*, Saint Martin's Griffin); 1995. 22.95 o.p. (*0-312-13126-7*) St. Martin's Pr.

MacDonald, Patricia. Not Guilty. 2003. (Illus.). 464p. mass mkt. 7.50 (*0-7434-2356-9*, Pocket); 2002. 368p. 24.00 (*0-7434-2355-0*, Atria) Simon & Schuster.

Magona, Sindiwe. Mother to Mother. (Bluestreak Ser.). 216p. 2000. pap. 13.00 (*0-8070-0949-0*); 1999. 20.00 o.p. (*0-8070-0948-2*) Beacon Pr.

Magona, Sindiwe, et al, contrib. by. Mother to Mother. 1998. 210p. 22.00 (*0-86486-433-7*) Interlink Publishing Group, Inc.

Maguire, Gregory. Oasis. 1998. 170p. (J). (gr. 4-7). pap. 4.95 (*0-7868-1293-1*) Disney Pr.

—Oasis. 1996. 176p. (YA). (gr. 7-9). tchr. ed. 14.95 (*0-395-67019-5*, Clarion Bks.) Houghton Mifflin Co. Trade & Reference Div.

—Oasis. 1998. 11.00 (*0-606-15655-0*) Turtleback Bks.

Maillard, Keith. Hazard Zone: A Novel. 1996. 80p. (Orig.). pap. 14.00 o.p. (*0-00-224397-0*) HarperSanFrancisco.

Mann, Peggy. There Are Two Kinds of Terrible. 1979. (J). (gr. 5 up). pap. 1.50 o.p. (*0-380-45823-3*, 45823, Avon Bks.) Morrow/Avon.

Martin, C. L. The Blueberry Train. 1995. (Illus.). 32p. (J). (ps-3). 15.00 (*0-689-80304-4*, Atheneum) Simon & Schuster Children's Publishing.

Martin, LaJoyce. The Broken Bow. 1996. 192p. (Orig.). pap. 9.99 (*1-56722-139-4*, 1567221394) Word Aflame Pr.

—Two Scars Against One. 1995. 192p. (Orig.). pap. 9.99 (*1-56722-025-8*) Word Aflame Pr.

McCabe, Patrick. Emerald Germs of Ireland. 2001. 320p. 25.00 (*0-06-019678-5*) HarperCollins Pubs.

McFarland, Dennis. Singing Boy: A Novel. 2001. 320p. 25.00 o.s.i (*0-8050-6608-X*) Holt, Henry & Co.

—Singing Boy: A Novel. l.t. ed. 2001. 560p. 28.95 (*0-7862-3517-9*) Thorndike Pr.

McGregor, Elizabeth. The Ice Child. 2001. (Illus.). 400p. 24.95 o.p. (*0-525-94567-9*, Dutton) Dutton/ Plume.

—The Ice Child. l.t. ed. 2001. (Wheeler Large Print Book Ser.). (Illus.). 540p. 29.95 o.p. (*1-58724-109-9*, Wheeler Publishing, Inc.) Gale Group.

—The Ice Child. 2002. pap. 6.99 (*0-451-20539-1*, Signet Bks.); 448p. reprint ed. mass mkt. 7.99 (*0-451-41061-0*, Onyx) NAL.

McNeil, Gil. The Only Boy for Me. 2002. 276p. 23.95 (*1-58234-223-7*) Bloomsbury Publishing.

Melnyczuk, Askold. Ambassador of the Dead. 288p. 2001. text 25.00 o.p. (*1-58243-132-9*); 2002. reprint ed. pap. text 15.00 (*1-58243-251-1*) Basic Bks. (Counterpoint Pr.).

Mertz, Stephen. Night Wind. 2003. 277p. pap. 13.95 (*1-4104-0135-9*, Five Star Trade); 2002. 305p. 26.95 (*0-7862-4353-8*, Five Star) Gale Group.

—Night Wind. l.t. ed. 2003. 406p. pap. 24.95 (*0-7862-5503-X*) Thorndike Pr.

Miller, Andrew. Oxygen. 2003. 352p. pap. 14.00 (*0-15-602740-2*, Harvest Bks.); 2002. 336p. 24.00 (*0-15-100721-7*) Harcourt Trade Pubs.

Miller, Donald E. The Case for Liberal Christianity. 1981. 154p. 18.00 o.p. (*0-06-065753-7*) Harper-Collins Pubs.

Millet, Lydia. Omnivores. 1996. 224p. pap. 17.95 o.p. (*1-56512-089-2*, 72089) Algonquin Bks. of Chapel Hill.

Mills, Deanie F. Ordeal. 1997. 432p. 23.95 o.s.i (*0-525-94202-5*) Dutton/Plume.

Milton, Hilary. Tornado! 1983. (Single Title Ser.). 160p. (J). (gr. 4 up). lib. bdg. 12.90 o.p. (*0-531-04542-0*, Watts, Franklin) Scholastic Library Publishing.

Minarik, Else Holmelund. Little Bear. 1957. (I Can Read Bks.). (Illus.). 64p. (J). (gr. k-3). 15.99 (*0-06-024240-X*); lib. bdg. 16.89 (*0-06-024241-8*) HarperCollins Children's Bk. Group.

—Little Bear. 1978. (I Can Read Bks.). (Illus.). 64p. (J). (gr. k-3). pap. 3.99 (*0-06-444004-4*, Harper Trophy) HarperCollins Children's Bk. Group.

—Little Bear. 1978. (I Can Read Bks.). (J). (ps-1). 10.10 (*0-606-01530-2*) Turtleback Bks.

—Little Bear. unabr. ed. 1990. (I Can Read Bks.). (Illus.). 64p. (J). (gr. k-3). pap. 8.99 incl. audio (*1-55994-234-7*, HarperAudio) HarperTrade.

—Little Bear, Level 1. 1986. (I Can Read Bks.). (Illus.). 64p. (J). (ps-1). 5.98 o.p. incl. audio (*0-694-00113-9*, JC-068, Harper Trophy) Harper-Collins Children's Bk. Group.

—Little Bear, 3 bks., Set. 1992. (I Can Read Bks.). (Illus.). 160p. (J). (gr. k-3). pap. 11.97 (*0-06-444197-0*, Harper Trophy) HarperCollins Children's Bk. Group.

—Osito. 1995. (SPA., Illus.). 64p. (J). (ps-3). 11.95 (*84-204-3044-7*, AF1346) Alfaguara, Ediciones, S.A.- Grupo Santillana ESP. *Dist:* Lectorum Pubns., Inc., Santillana USA Publishing Co., Inc.

Mitcham, Judson. Sabbath Creek: A Novel. 2004. 22.95 (*0-8203-2577-5*) Univ. of Georgia Pr.

Moody, Rick. Purple America. 1998. pap. 13.95 (*0-316-19006-3*, Back Bay); 1997. 304p. (YA). (gr. 8 up). 23.95 o.p. (*0-316-57925-4*); 1998. 304p. reprint ed. pap. 13.95 (*0-316-55977-6*, Back Bay) Little Brown & Co.

Moore, George. Esther Waters. 1977. 377p. reprint ed. pap. 11.00 o.p. (*0-915864-53-3*) Academy Chicago Pubs., Ltd.

—Esther Waters. 1942. (Black & Gold Library). 7.95 o.p. (*0-87140-872-4*) Liveright Publishing Corp.

—Esther Waters. Skilton, David, ed. 1983. (Oxford World's Classics Ser.). 424p. pap. 9.95 o.p. (*0-19-281578-4*) Oxford Univ. Pr., Inc.

—Esther Waters. Laurie, Hilary, ed. 1993. 384p. pap. 9.95 (*0-460-87326-1*, Everyman's Classic Library in Paperback) Tuttle Publishing.

Moore, Ruth N. Danger in the Pines. 1983. 160p. (J). (gr. 4-9). text 7.95 o.p. (*0-8361-3313-7*) Herald Pr.

Morgan, Kathleen. Embrace the Dawn. 2002. 416p. pap. 12.99 (*0-8423-4097-1*) Tyndale Hse. Pubs.

Morris, Monique W. Too Beautiful for Words. 288p. 2002. pap. 11.95 (*0-06-093594-4*); 2001. 24.00 (*0-06-621105-0*) HarperTrade. (Amistad Pr.).

Morris, Winifred. Liar. 1996. 176p. (YA). (gr. 7 up). 15.95 (*0-8027-8461-5*) Walker & Co.

Mulrooney, Gretta. Araby. 1998. 182p. pap. (*0-00-225688-6*, HarperCollins) HarperTrade.

Murphy, Jill. The Last Noo-Noo. (Illus.). 32p. (J). (ps-k). 1998. bds. 5.99 o.s.i (*0-7636-0391-0*); 1995. 14.95 o.p. (*1-56402-581-0*) Candlewick Pr.

Murphy, Mary. I Like It When... 1997. (Illus.). 32p. (J). (ps). 11.95 (*0-15-200039-9*, Red Wagon Bks.) Harcourt Children's Bks.

Murr, Naeem. Genius of the Sea: A Novel. 2003. 304p. 23.00 (*0-7432-3795-1*, Free Pr.) Simon & Schuster.

Neitzel, Shirley. I'm Taking a Trip on My Train. 1999. (Illus.). 40p. (J). (ps-3). 15.95 (*0-688-15833-1*, Greenwillow Bks.) HarperCollins Children's Bk. Group.

Newman, Leslea. Saturday Is Pattyday. 1993. (Illus.). 24p. (J). (gr. 1-3). lib. bdg. 14.95 (*0-934678-52-9*); (ps-5). pap. 6.95 (*0-934678-51-0*) New Victoria Pubs., Inc.

—Saturday Is Pattyday. 1993. (Illus.). 24p. (J). pap. 5.95 (*0-88961-181-5*) Women's Pr. CAN. *Dist:* Univ. of Toronto Pr.

Nicholson, Joy. The Tribes of Palos Verdes. 224p. 1997. 19.95 o.p. (*0-312-15677-4*); 3rd ed. 1998. pap. 11.95 (*0-312-19532-X*, CPB1114, Saint Martin's Griffin) St. Martin's Pr.

Novak, Karen. Ordinary Monsters. 2003. 288p. pap. 13.95 (*1-58234-291-1*) Bloomsbury Publishing.

—Ordinary Monsters: A Novel. 2002. 288p. 24.95 (*1-58234-241-5*) Bloomsbury Publishing.

O'Brien, Anne Sibley. I Don't Want to Go, ERS. 1986. (Busy Day Board Bks.). (Illus.). 14p. (J). (ps-2). pap. 3.95 o.p. (*0-8050-0051-8*, Holt, Henry & Co. Bks. For Young Readers) Holt, Henry & Co.

O'Connor, Frank. My Oedipus Complex. 1986. (Creative's Classic Short Stories Ser.). (Illus.). 40p. (J). (gr. 4 up). lib. bdg. 13.95 o.p. (*0-88682-062-6*, 1078-2, Creative Education) Creative Co., The.

O'Grady, Timothy. Motherland. 1990. 240p. 19.95 o.p. (*0-8050-1230-3*) Holt, Henry & Co.

Oke, Janette. The Matchmakers. 1997. 144p. text 12.99 o.p. (*0-7642-2002-0*); pap. 12.99 o.p. (*0-7642-2020-9*) Bethany Hse. Pubs.

—The Matchmakers. l.t. ed. 2001. (Illus.). 197p. 25.95 (*0-7862-3256-0*); (*0-7540-4524-2*); (*0-7540-4523-4*) Thorndike Pr.

Palmer, Catherine. A Whisper of Danger. 2003. (Christian Mystery Ser.). 26.95 (*0-7862-4874-2*) Thorndike Pr.

—A Whisper of Danger. 2000. (Treasures of the Heart Ser.). (Illus.). 384p. pap. 9.99 (*0-8423-3886-1*) Tyndale Hse. Pubs.

Paris, Lena. Mom Is Single. 1980. (Social Values Ser.). (Illus.). 32p. (J). (gr. k-3). lib. bdg. 13.27 o.p. (*0-516-01477-3*, Children's Pr.) Scholastic Library Publishing.

Parkinson, Carolyn S. My Mommy Has Cancer. 1991. (Illus.). 20p. (J). (ps-4). pap. 8.95 (*0-9630287-0-7*) Solace Publishing, Inc.

Patterson, James. Suzanne's Diary for Nicholas. l.t. ed. 2001. 303p. 12.95 (*0-7862-3298-6*, Wheeler Publishing, Inc.) Gale Group.

—Suzanne's Diary for Nicholas. 2001. 272p. E-Book 14.95 (*0-7595-4491-3*); E-Book 14.95 (*0-7595-9558-5*); E-Book 14.95 (*0-7595-8496-6*); E-Book 14.95 (*0-7595-6488-4*); E-Book 14.95 (*0-7595-0488-1*) Little Brown & Co.

—Suzanne's Diary for Nicholas. Pietsch, Michael, ed. 2001. 272p. 22.95 o.p. (*0-316-96944-3*) Little Brown & Co.

—Suzanne's Diary for Nicholas. l.t. ed. 2002. 12.95 (*1-4104-0009-3*, Large Print Pr.); 2001. 319p. 32.95 (*0-7862-3297-8*); 2001. 303p. (*0-7540-9106-6*); 2001. 303p. 32.95 (*0-7540-1707-9*) Thorndike Pr.

—Suzanne's Diary for Nicholas. 2002. 272p. pap. 12.95 (*0-446-67959-3*); 304p. reprint ed. mass mkt. 7.50 (*0-446-61108-5*) Warner Bks., Inc.

Picoult, Jodi. A Perfect Match. 2002. 368p. 25.00 (*0-7434-1872-7*, Atria) Simon & Schuster.

—Perfect Match: A Novel. 2002. E-Book 9.99 (*0-7434-2280-5*, Atria) Simon & Schuster.

Porte, Barbara Ann. Harry's Mom. 1985. (Greenwillow Read-Alone Bks.). (Illus.). 48p. (J). (gr. 1-4). 13.95 o.p. (*0-688-04817-X*); lib. bdg. 15.93 o.p. (*0-688-04818-8*) HarperCollins Children's Bk. Group. (Greenwillow Bks.).

Porter-Gaylord, Laurel. I Love My Mommy Because... 1991. (Illus.). 24p. (J). (ps-3). 7.99 (*0-525-44625-7*, Dutton Children's Bks.) Penguin Putnam Bks. for Young Readers.

Powell, Randy. Tribute to Another Dead Rock Star, RS. 1999. 224p. (YA). (gr. 7-12). 17.00 (*0-374-37748-0*, Farrar, Straus & Giroux (BYR)) Farrar, Straus & Giroux.

—Tribute to Another Dead Rock Star. l.t. ed. 2000. (Young Adult Ser.). 224p. (J). 21.95 (*0-7862-2191-7*) Thorndike Pr.

Preston, Caroline, contrib. by. Lucy Crocker 2.0. 2001. 368p. pap. 14.00 o.s.i (*0-684-85450-3*, Scribner) Simon & Schuster.

Price, Reynolds. Noble Norfleet. 2003. 320p. pap. 13.00 (*0-7432-0418-2*); 2002. E-Book (*0-7432-3393-X*); 2002. (Illus.). 320p. 26.00 (*0-7432-0417-4*) Simon & Schuster. (Scribner).

Quindlen, Anna. Black & Blue: A Novel. 2000. 288p. pap. 13.95 (*0-385-33313-7*, Delta); 1999. 384p. mass mkt. 7.99 (*0-440-22610-4*) Dell Publishing.

—Black & Blue: A Novel. l.t. ed. 1998. 27.95 o.p. (*1-56895-565-0*, Wheeler Publishing, Inc.) Gale Group.

—Black & Blue: A Novel, abr. ed. 1998. audio 24.00 (*0-375-40190-3*, RH Audio) Random Hse. Audio Publishing Group.

—Black & Blue: A Novel. 1998. 296p. 23.00 (*0-375-50051-0*) Random Hse., Inc.

—Black & Blue: A Novel. 1999. 13.55 (*0-606-16456-1*) Turtleback Bks.

Quindlen, Anna, contrib. by. Black & Blue: A Novel. 1998. (*0-679-43539-5*, Random Hse. Bks. for Young Readers) Random Hse. Children's Bks.

Racina, Tom. The Madman's Diary. 2001. reprint ed. mass mkt. 6.99 (*0-451-40981-7*, Signet Bks.) NAL.

Radin, Ruth Y. All Joseph Wanted. 1991. (Illus.). 80p. (J). (gr. 4-7). 15.00 o.s.i (*0-02-775641-6*, Simon & Schuster Children's Publishing) Simon & Schuster Children's Publishing.

Redel, Victoria. Loverboy. 2001. 224p. 21.95 (*1-55597-322-1*) Graywolf Pr.

—Loverboy. 2002. 224p. reprint ed. pap. 13.00 (*0-15-600724-X*, Harvest Bks.) Harcourt Trade Pubs.

Richards, Elizabeth. Rescue. 1999. 276p. 22.00 (*0-671-02397-7*); 2000. 288p. reprint ed. pap. 12.95 o.s.i (*0-671-02398-5*) Simon & Schuster. (Atria).

—Rescue. 2000. 19.00 (*0-606-19502-5*) Turtleback Bks.

Ridgway, Keith. The Long Falling. 1999. 306p. pap. 13.00 (*0-395-95782-6*); 1998. 320p. 22.00 o.p. (*0-395-90530-3*) Houghton Mifflin Co.

Robards, Karen. Maggy's Child. l.t. ed. 1994. 25.95 o.p. (*1-56895-057-8*, Wheeler Publishing, Inc.) Gale Group.

Roberts, Laird. The Swan Hunter. 2002. 136p. pap. 12.95 (*1-55517-665-8*, Salt Pr.) Cedar Fort, Inc./CFI Distribution.

Roley, Brian Ascalon. The American Son: A Novel. 2001. 256p. pap. 13.00 (*0-393-32154-1*, Norton Paperbacks) Norton, W. W. & Co., Inc.

Roos, Stepehn. Silver Secrets. 1991. (Maple Street Kids Ser.). (Illus.). 96p. (J). (gr. 2-6). per. 1.50 o.p. (*0-89486-777-6*, T5171) Hazelden Publishing & Educational Services.

Roper, Gayle G. Spring Rain, 3 vols. 2003. (Seaside Seasons: Vol. 1). 352p. pap. 11.99 (*1-57673-638-5*) Multnomah Pubs., Inc.

Rosenberg, Liz. Monster Mama. (Illus.). 32p. (J). (ps-3). 1997. pap. 6.99 (*0-698-11429-9*, PaperStar); 1993. 16.99 (*0-399-21989-7*, Philomel) Penguin Putnam Bks. for Young Readers.

Rosselson, Leon. Where's My Mom? (Illus.). 32p. (J). (ps-k). 1996. bds. 5.99 o.p. (*1-56402-835-6*); 1994. 13.95 o.p. (*1-56402-392-3*) Candlewick Pr.

Rostler, William. It's Your Move. 1984. (Orig.). (J). (gr. 5 up). pap. (*0-671-54716-X*, Simon Pulse) Simon & Schuster Children's Publishing.

Roth, Philip. Portnoy's Complaint. 2002. 288p. 20.00 o.s.i (*0-375-50793-0*) Random Hse., Inc.

Roy, Ronald. I Am a Thief. 1982. (Illus.). 96p. (J). (gr. 5 up). 8.95 o.p. (*0-525-45114-5*, Dutton) Dutton/ Plume.

Rukstalis, Susan. How Many Steps Before the Queen? 1992. (Illus.). 32p. (J). (ps-4). 14.95 (*0-9628914-2-8*) Padakami Pr.

Rushdie, Salman. The Moor's Last Sigh. l.t. ed. 1996. 625p. 26.95 o.p. (*0-7838-1664-2*, Macmillan Reference USA) Gale Group.

—The Moor's Last Sigh. 448p. 1997. pap. 14.95 (*0-679-74466-5*); 1996. 25.00 o.s.i (*0-679-42049-5*) Knopf Publishing Group. (Pantheon).

Rushforth, Peter. Kindergarten. 1989. 208p. pap. 10.95 (*0-87923-701-5*) Godine, David R. Pub.

—Kindergarten. 1980. 8.95 o.p. (*0-394-50917-X*) Knopf, Alfred A. Inc.

—Kindergarten. 1983. pap. 2.95 o.p. (*0-380-56150-6*, 56150, Avon Bks.) Morrow/Avon.

Russo, Marisabina. Trade-in Mother. 1993. (Illus.). 32p. (J). (ps up). lib. bdg. 13.93 o.p. (*0-688-11417-2*, Greenwillow Bks.) HarperCollins Children's Bk. Group.

—Trade-In Mother. 1993. (Illus.). 32p. (J). (ps up). 14.00 o.s.i (*0-688-11416-4*, Greenwillow Bks.) HarperCollins Children's Bk. Group.

Ryan, Mary E. Alias. 1997. 176p. (YA). (gr. 7-12). 16.00 (*0-689-80789-9*, Simon & Schuster Children's Publishing) Simon & Schuster Children's Publishing.

Rylant, Cynthia. A Kindness. 1990. 128p. (J). reprint ed. mass mkt. 3.25 o.s.i (*0-440-20579-4*, Laurel Leaf) Random Hse. Children's Bks.

—A Kindness. 1988. 128p. (YA). (gr. 7 up). 15.95 o.p. (*0-531-05767-4*, Orchard Bks.) Scholastic, Inc.

Samson, Lisa. Love's Ransom. 1997. (Abbey Ser.). 350p. (Orig.). pap. 9.99 o.p. (*1-56507-529-3*) Harvest Hse. Pubs.

Sargent, Dave. Say You Love Me. Bowen, Debbie, ed. 1998. (Illus.). 31p. (J). (gr. k-6). pap. 6.00 (*1-56763-130-4*); lib. bdg. 17.25 o.p. (*1-56763-129-0*) Ozark Publishing.

Savitz, Harriet May. Swimmer. 1986. 96p. (Orig.). (J). (gr. 4-7). pap. 2.50 o.p. (*0-590-33946-X*, Scholastic Paperbacks) Scholastic, Inc.

Schopen, Bernard. The Desert Look. 1990. 256p. 17.95 (*0-89296-354-9*) Mysterious Pr.

—The Desert Look. 1995. (Western Literature Ser.). 272p. pap. 18.00 (*0-87417-259-4*) Univ. of Nevada Pr.

—The Desert Look. 1991. mass mkt. 4.95 o.s.i (*0-446-40009-2*, Mysterious Pr. Paperback Bks.) Warner Bks., Inc.

Schupack, Deborah. The Boy on the Bus. l.t. ed. 2003. (Basic Ser.). 28.95 (*0-7862-5573-0*) Thorndike Pr.

—The Boy on the Bus: A Novel. 2004. 256p. pap. 12.00 (*0-7432-4221-1*); 2003. 224p. 23.00 (*0-7432-4220-3*) Simon & Schuster. (Free Pr.).

Sebastian, Tim. Last Rights. unabr. ed. 1995. audio 69.95 (*0-7451-6495-1*, CAB 1111) BBC Audiobooks America.

—Last Rights. 1995. 272p. mass mkt. 5.50 (*0-380-71864-2*, Avon Bks.) Morrow/Avon.

—Last Rights: A Novel. l.t. ed. 1994. 402p. lib. bdg. 22.95 o.p. (*0-8161-7438-5*, Macmillan Reference USA) Gale Group.

Sebastian, Timothy. Last Rights. 1994. 270p. 22.00 o.p. (*0-688-11448-2*, Morrow, William & Co.) Morrow/ Avon.

Selby, Hubert, Jr. Requiem for a Dream. 2000. viii, 279p. pap. 14.95 (*1-56025-248-0*); 1988. 280p. (C). reprint ed. pap. 12.95 (*0-938410-56-3*); 1988. 304p. (C). reprint ed. lib. bdg. 20.00 o.p. (*0-938410-57-1*) Avalon Publishing Group. (Thunder's Mouth Pr.).

Settle, Mary Lee. Charley Bland. 1991. 208p. pap. 8.95 o.p. (*0-88184-709-7*, Carroll & Graf Pubs.) Avalon Publishing Group.

—Charley Bland. 1989. 18.95 o.p. (*0-374-12078-1*) Farrar, Straus & Giroux.

—Charley Bland. 1996. (Mary Lee Settle Collection). 208p. pap. 12.95 (*1-57003-149-5*) Univ. of South Carolina Pr.

Shalev, Meir. The Loves of Judith. Harshav, Barbara, tr. from HEB. 1999. 320p. o.p. (*0-88001-635-3*, Ecco) HarperTrade.

Sharmat, Marjorie Weinman. Hooray for Mother's Day! 1986. (Illus.). 32p. (J). (ps-3). 14.95 o.p. (*0-8234-0588-5*) Holiday Hse., Inc.

—My Mother Never Listens to Me. Tucker, Kathleen, ed. 1984. (Albert Whitman Concept Bks.). (Illus.). 32p. (J). (ps-3). 11.95 o.p. (*0-8075-5347-6*) Whitman, Albert & Co.

Shecter, Ben. The Discontented Mother. 1980. (Illus.). 32p. (J). (gr. k-3). 6.95 o.p. (*0-15-223574-4*) Harcourt Children's Bks.

Shepard, Elizabeth. H. 1995. 180p. 17.95 o.s.i (*0-670-85927-3*, Viking) Viking Penguin.

Sheridan, Mike. The Violent Child. 2001. 232p. 26.00 (*1-57962-035-3*) Permanent Pr., The.

Shriver, Lionel. We Need to Talk about Kevin: A Novel. 416p. 2004. pap. 14.95 (*1-58243-268-6*); 2003. text 25.00 (*1-58243-267-8*) Basic Bks. (Counterpoint Pr.).

—We Need to Talk about Kevin: A Novel. 2004. 416p. pap. 13.95 (*0-06-072448-X*, Perennial) Harper-Trade.

Smith, Deborah. Sweet Hush. 2003. 7p. audio compact disk 74.95 (*0-7927-2853-X*); 54.95 (*0-7927-2852-1*) BBC Audiobooks America.

—Sweet Hush. 2003. 336p. 23.95 (*0-316-80650-1*) Little Brown & Co.

—Sweet Hush. 2003. 433p. 30.95 (*0-7862-5449-1*) Thorndike Pr.

—Sweet Hush. 2004. 416p. mass mkt. 6.99 (*0-446-61140-9*) Warner Bks., Inc.

Smith, Doris B. Last Was Lloyd. 1990. 128p. (J). (gr. 3 up). pap. 3.95 o.p. (*0-14-034444-6*, Puffin Bks.) Penguin Putnam Bks. for Young Readers.

Snelling, Lauraine. Hawaiian Sunrise. l.t. ed. 2001. (Thorndike Press Large Print Christian Romance Ser.). 429p. 24.95 (*0-7862-3284-6*) Thorndike Pr.

—Hawaiian Sunrise: A Novel. 1999. 288p. pap. 9.99 (*1-55661-991-X*) Bethany Hse. Pubs.

Snyder, Carol. Ike & Mama & the Once-a-Year Suit. 1992. (Illus.). 48p. (J). (gr. 2-5). reprint ed. pap. 5.95 (*0-8276-0418-1*) Jewish Pubn. Society.

Solomon, Andrew. A Stone Boat. 1996. 256p. pap. 13.00 (*0-452-27498-2*, Plume) Dutton/Plume.

—A Stone Boat. 1994. 288p. 22.95 o.p. (*0-571-17240-7*) Faber & Faber, Inc.

Sondheimer, Ilse. The Boy Who Could Make His Mother Stop Yelling. 1982. (Illus.). 32p. (J). (ps-6). pap. 2.95 (*0-943156-01-7*); lib. bdg. 9.95 (*0-943156-00-9*) Rainbow Pr.

Spencer, Brent. The Lost Son. 1995. 288p. 19.95 (*1-55970-266-4*) Arcade Publishing, Inc.

Steel, Danielle. The House on Hope Street. 2000. 240p. 19.95 (*0-385-33306-4*, Delacorte Pr.) Dell Publishing.

—The House on Hope Street. l.t. ed. 2000. 336p. 19.95 (*0-375-43063-6*) Random Hse. Large Print.

—Johnny Angel. 2003. 192p. 19.95 (*0-385-33549-0*, Delacorte Pr.) Dell Publishing.

—Johnny Angel. l.t. ed. 272p. 2004. pap. 14.95 (*0-375-72826-0*); 2003. 21.95 (*0-375-43207-8*) Random Hse. Large Print.

Stein, Garth. Raven Stole the Moon. 1998. 336p. 22.00 (*0-671-00459-X*, Atria) Simon & Schuster.

Stevens, April. Angel Angel. l.t. ed. 1995. 269p. pap. 20.95 o.p. (*0-7838-1452-6*, Macmillan Reference USA) Gale Group.

—Angel Angel. 1995. 224p. 19.95 o.p. (0-670-85839-0, Viking) Viking Penguin.
Stevenson, Melody. The Life Stone of Singing Bird: A Novel. 1996. 176p. 19.95 o.p. (0-571-19886-4) Faber & Faber, Inc.
Strachan, Ian G. God's Angry Babies. unabr. ed. 1997. 296p. 35.00 (0-89410-828-X); pap. 16.95 (0-89410-829-8) Rienner, Lynne Pubs., Inc. (Three Continents).
Stranger, Joyce. The Call of the Sea. 2003. 192p. 25.99 (0-7278-5938-2) Severn Hse. Pubs., Ltd.
Sullivan, Walter. Sojourn of a Stranger. 2003. (Voices of the South Ser.). 316p. pap. 17.95 (0-8071-2917-8) Louisiana State Univ. Pr.
Tan, Amy. The Joy Luck Club. Andrews, Richard, ed. 1995. (Cambridge Literature Ser.). (Illus.). 336p. pap. text 11.95 (0-521-48562-2) Cambridge Univ. Pr.
—The Joy Luck Club & The Kitchen God's Wife. 1992. 15.98 o.s.i (0-8041-1052-2, Ivy Bks.) Ballantine Bks.
—The Kitchen God's Wife. 1996. mass mkt. 6.99 (0-8041-9897-7); 1992. 544p. mass mkt. 7.99 (0-8041-0753-X) Ballantine Bks. (Ivy Bks.).
—The Kitchen God's Wife. 1993. 432p. pap. 13.00 (0-679-74808-3, Vintage) Knopf Publishing Group.
—The Kitchen God's Wife. unabr. ed. 1993. audio 39.95 o.p. (0-7871-0018-8, Dove Audio); 39.95 o.p. (1-55800-434-3, 133134);Set. 15.95 o.p. (1-55800-266-9, 391032) NewStar Media, Inc.
—The Kitchen God's Wife. 1991. 320p. 22.95 o.p. (0-399-13578-2) Putnam Publishing Group, The.
—The Kitchen God's Wife. 1992. 14.04 (0-606-01177-3) Turtleback Bks.
Tarlton, John S. The Cost of Doing Business: A Novel. 2001. 272p. 22.95 (1-882593-42-1); 2003. 406p. reprint ed. pap. 15.95 (1-882593-72-3) Bridge Works Publishing Co., Inc.
Taylor, Alice. Across the River. 2000. 283p. (1-902011-13-9) Mount Eagle Pubns., Ltd.
—Across the River. 2001. 288p. 23.95 (0-312-27843-8) St. Martin's Pr.
Testa, Maria. Nine Candles. 1996. (Illus.). 32p. (J). (gr. 2-4). lib. bdg. 19.93 (0-87614-940-9, Carolrhoda Bks.) Lerner Publishing Group.
Tester, Victoria Edwards. Dying in the City of Flowers. 2003. (Five Star First Edition Women's Fiction Ser.). 197p. 26.95 (0-7862-4766-5, Five Star) Gale Group.
Thirkell, Angela. The Demon in the House. l.t. ed. 264p. 2003. pap. 21.99 (0-7531-6730-1); 2002. 32.50 (0-7531-6729-8) ISIS Large Print Bks. GBR. *Dist:* Ulverscroft Large Print Bks., Ltd., Ulverscroft Large Print Bks., Ltd., Ulverscroft Large Print Canada, Ltd.
Thirkell, Angela M. The Demon in the House: A Novel. 1996. 254p. pap. 12.95 (1-55921-159-8) Moyer Bell.
Tilghman, Christopher. Mason's Retreat. Date not set. (0-679-45240-0) McKay, David Co., Inc.
—Mason's Retreat. 1997. 304p. pap. 13.00 o.p. (0-312-15586-7) Picador.
—Mason's Retreat. 1995. 290p. 22.00 o.s.i (0-679-45143-9) Random Hse., Inc.
Toole, John Kennedy. A Confederacy of Dunces. 21.95 (0-8488-1207-7) Amereon, Ltd.
—A Confederacy of Dunces. 416p. 1982. pap. 4.50 o.s.i (0-394-17969-2, B-474); 20th anniv. ed. 1987. pap. 14.00 (0-8021-3020-8, Grove Pr.) Grove/Atlantic, Inc.
—A Confederacy of Dunces. 1980. 352p. 24.95 (0-8071-0657-7); 20th anniv. ed. 2000. 338p. 24.95 (0-8071-2606-3); 20th anniv. ltd. ed. 2000. (Illus.). 338p. 75.00 (0-8071-2607-1) Louisiana State Univ. Pr.
—A Confederacy of Dunces. 1994. 480p. 10.99 o.s.i (0-517-12270-7) Random Hse. Value Publishing.
—A Confederacy of Dunces. 1987. 18.00 (0-606-20071-1) Turtleback Bks.
Travolta, John. Propeller One-Way Night Coach: A Fable for all Ages. 1997. 96p. 14.00 o.p. (0-446-52257-0) Warner Bks., Inc.
Treichel, Hans-Ulrich. Lost: A Novel. 2000. (Vintage International Ser.). 144p. pap. 11.00 (0-375-70622-4, Vintage) Knopf Publishing Group.
Tremain, Rose. The Way I Found Her. Set. unabr. ed. 1999. audio 84.95 (0-7540-0343-4, CAB1766, Sterling Audio Bks.) BBC Audiobooks America.
—The Way I Found Her. l.t. ed. 1998. 24.95 (1-57490-165-6, Beeler Large Print Bks.) Beeler, Thomas T. Publisher.
—The Way I Found Her. 1998. 368p. 25.00 o.s.i (0-374-28666-3) Farrar, Straus & Giroux.
—The Way I Found Her. 1999. 368p. pap. 14.00 (0-671-03570-3, Washington Square Pr.) Simon & Schuster.
Tyler, Anne. The Clock Winder. 1996. (First Ballantine Books Trade Ed). 320p. pap. 14.95 (0-449-91179-9, Fawcett) Ballantine Bks.
—The Clock Winder. 1986. mass mkt. 3.95 o.s.i (0-425-09277-1); 1983. mass mkt. 3.50 o.s.i (0-425-06247-3) Berkley Publishing Group.
—The Clock Winder. abr. ed. 1993. audio 16.00 o.s.i (0-679-41502-5, RH Audio) Random Hse. Audio Publishing Group.
—The Clock Winder. 1972. 8.95 o.p. (0-394-47898-3, Knopf Bks. for Young Readers) Random Hse. Children's Bks.
Tyler, Linda W. Waiting for Mom. (Illus.). (J). (ps-2). 1989. 320p. pap. 3.95 o.p. (0-14-050652-7, Puffin Bks.); 1987. 12.95 o.p. (0-670-81408-3, Viking Children's Bks.) Penguin Putnam Bks. for Young Readers.
Tyree, Omar R. Single Mom: A Novel. (Illus.). 400p. 1999. pap. 13.00 (0-684-85593-3); 1998. 24.00 (0-684-85592-5) Simon & Schuster. (Simon & Schuster).
Ungerer, Tomi. No Kiss for Mother. 1993. 40p. (J). pap. 4.99 o.s.i (0-440-40886-5) Dell Publishing.
—No Kiss for Mother. 1998. (Illus.). 40p. (J). (ps-3). pap. text 5.95 (1-57098-208-2) Rinehart, Roberts Pubs.
Valentine, Jane. Sevenoaks. 2001. pap. 17.95 (0-595-18094-9) iUniverse, Inc.
Vidal, Gore. The Golden Age: A Novel. 2001. 480p. reprint ed. pap. 15.00 (0-375-72481-8, Vintage) Knopf Publishing Group.
—The Golden Age: A Novel. abr. ed. 2000. audio compact disk 29.95 (0-553-71214-4); audio 39.95 (0-553-50265-4) Random Hse. Audio Publishing Group. (RH Audio).
—The Golden Age: A Novel. l.t. ed. 2000. 720p. 27.50 (0-375-43082-2) Random Hse. Large Print.
Walters, Catherine. When Will It Be Spring? 1998. (Illus.). 32p. (J). (ps-2). 15.99 o.s.i (0-525-45881-6, Dutton Children's Bks.) Penguin Putnam Bks. for Young Readers.
Wardlaw, Lee. Operation Rhinoceros. 1992. (Illus.). 120p. (Orig.). (J). (gr. 3-6). pap. 3.50 (0-931093-14-7) Red Hen Pr.
Warner, Marina. The Leto Bundle. 2002. 384p. 26.00 (0-374-18548-4) Farrar, Straus & Giroux.
Watmough, David. The Mother's Glass. 1993. 320p. pap. o.p. (0-00-647399-7) HarperCollins Pubs. Canada, Ltd.
Weiss, Nicki. On a Hot, Hot Day. 1992. (Illus.). 32p. (J). (ps-1). 13.95 o.p. (0-399-22119-0, G. P. Putnam's Sons) Penguin Group (USA) Inc.
West, John Foster. Time Was. 2002. 307p. 20.00 (1-887905-66-9) Parkway Pubs., Inc.
Wheeler, Joe L. Mom in My Heart. 1997. 159p. pap. 10.99 o.p. (0-8423-0552-1) Tyndale Hse. Pubs.
Wheelis, Allen. The Life & Death of My Mother. 1991. 128p. 17.95 o.p. (0-393-03067-9) Norton, W. W. & Co., Inc.
Whelan, Gloria. The President's Mother. 1996. 250p. pap. 10.99 o.p. (0-89283-942-2) Servant Pubns.
White, Gill. Refuge. 2003. 339p. mass mkt. 8.95 (0-552-14886-5) Transworld Publishers Ltd. GBR. *Dist:* Trafalgar Square.
Wickens, Elaine. Anna Day & the O-Ring. 1994. (Illus.). 24p. (J). (gr. 2 up). pap. 6.95 o.p. (1-55583-252-0, Alyson Wonderland) Alyson Pubns.
Wilentz, Amy. Martyrs' Crossing. 2001. 320p. 24.00 (0-684-85436-8, Simon & Schuster) Simon & Schuster.
Wisler, G. Clifton. A Special Gift. 1983. (Voyager Ser.). 80p. pap. 3.50 o.p. (0-8010-9661-8) Baker Bks.
Wittenborn, Dirk. Fierce People. 2003. (Illus.). 352p. pap. 14.95 (1-58234-292-X); 2002. 304p. 24.95 (1-58234-242-3) Bloomsbury Publishing.
Wolf, Jake. And Then What? 1993. (Illus.). 32p. (J). (ps up). 14.00 o.p. (0-688-10285-9); 13.89 o.s.i (0-688-10286-7) HarperCollins Children's Bk. Group. (Greenwillow Bks.).
Woodson, Jacqueline. From the Notebooks of Melanin Sun. 160p. (gr. 7 up). 2003. (J). mass mkt. 5.99 (0-590-45881-7, Scholastic Paperbacks); 1995. (YA). pap. 14.95 o.p. (0-590-45880-9, Blue Sky Pr., The) Scholastic, Inc.
—From the Notebooks of Melanin Sun. 1997. (Point Signature Ser.). (J). 10.04 (0-606-11357-6) Turtleback Bks.
Yates, Madeleine. Mommy's Coming Back. 1988. (Illus.). (J). (gr. 2 up). ring bd. 0.50 o.p. (0-687-27152-5) Abingdon Pr.
Yorke, Christy. Magic Spells. 1999. 368p. mass mkt. 5.99 o.s.i (0-553-57842-1) Bantam Bks.
—Magic Spells. l.t. ed. 2000. (G. K. Hall Core Ser.). 477p. 27.95 (0-7838-9028-1) Thorndike Pr.
Zimelman, Nathan. If I Were Strong Enough. 1982. (Illus.). 32p. (J). (gr. k-3). pap. text 9.95 o.p. (0-687-18670-6) Abingdon Pr.
Zindel, Paul. I Love My Mother. 1975. (Illus.). 32p. (J). (gr. k-3). lib. bdg. 13.89 o.p. (0-06-026836-0) HarperCollins Children's Bk. Group.
Zolotow, Charlotte. The Quiet Mother & the Noisy Little Boy. 1989. (Charlotte Zolotow Bk.). (Illus.). 32p. (J). (ps-3). 13.00 (0-06-026978-2); lib. bdg. 12.89 o.p. (0-06-026979-0) HarperCollins Children's Bk. Group.
—The Seashore Book. (Trophy Picture Book Ser.). (Illus.). 32p. (J). (ps-3). 1994. pap. 6.99 (0-06-443364-1); 1992. 16.95 (0-06-020213-0); 1992. lib. bdg. 14.89 o.p. (0-06-020214-9) HarperCollins Children's Bk. Group.

## S

### SINGLE WOMEN—FICTION

Berg, Elizabeth. Never Change. 2002. 240p. pap. 13.00 (0-7434-1133-1, Washington Square Pr.); 2001. 224p. 23.95 (0-7434-1132-3, Atria); 2001. E-Book 23.95 (0-7434-2180-9, Pocket); 2001. 368p. 23.95 (0-7434-2309-7, Atria); 2001. 368p. pap. 23.95 (0-7434-4927-4, Pocket) Simon & Schuster.
Bushnell, Candace. 4 Blondes. 2001. 256p. pap. 12.00 (0-8021-3825-X, Grove Pr.); 2000. 245p. 24.00 (0-87113-819-0, Atlantic Monthly Pr.) Grove/Atlantic, Inc.
—4 Blondes. 2002. 384p. mass mkt. 7.99 (0-451-20389-5, Signet Bks.) NAL.
—4 Blondes. l.t. ed. 2001. 445p. 31.95 (0-7862-3151-3) Thorndike Pr.
Cabot, Meggin. The Boy Next Door. 2002. 384p. pap. 13.95 (0-06-009619-5, Avon Bks.) Morrow/Avon.
Carroll, Leslie. Temporary Insanity. 2004. pap. (0-06-056337-0, Avon Bks.) Morrow/Avon.
Casey, Maud. The Shape of Things to Come: A Novel. 2002. 272p. pap. 12.95 (0-06-008441-3, Perennial) HarperTrade.
—The Shape of Things to Come: A Novel. 2001. 272p. 24.00 (0-688-17695-X, Morrow, William & Co.) Morrow/Avon.
Caspary, Vera. Laura. 1977. 216p. reprint ed. lib. bdg. 23.95 (0-89244-066-X, Queens Hse., Inc.) Amereon, Ltd.
—Laura. 1993. reprint ed. lib. bdg. 29.95 (1-56849-193-X) Buccaneer Bks., Inc.
—Laura. 1955. per. 6.50 (0-8222-0646-3) Dramatists Play Service, Inc.
—Laura. 1981. 224p. mass mkt. 1.95 o.p. (0-380-00043-1, 51565-1, Avon Bks.) Morrow/Avon.
—Laura. 2002. (Best Mysteries of All Time Ser.). 262p. (0-7621-8876-6, Impress) Scriptorium Pr., The.
—Laura. E-Book 9.99 (1-58824-335-4) ibooks, Inc.
Checketts, Candie. Another Chance: A Novel. 2003. 330p. 14.95 (1-59156-181-7) Covenant Communications.
Chessman, Harriet Scott. Ohio Angels. 1999. 144p. 24.00 (1-57962-020-5) Permanent Pr., The.
—Ohio Angels: A Novel. 2002. 144p. 24.00 (1-58322-519-6) Seven Stories Pr.
Chessman, Harriet Scott, ed. Ohio Angels. 1999. 144p. pap. 16.00 (1-57962-071-X) Permanent Pr., The.
Daswani, Kavita. For Matrimonial Purposes. 2003. 288p. 23.95 (0-399-15070-6) Putnam Publishing Group, The.
Foxx, Nina. Going Buck Wild. 2004. pap. (0-06-056449-0, Avon Bks.) Morrow/Avon.
Gaskell, Whitney. Pushing 30. 2003. 352p. pap. 11.95 (0-553-38224-1); E-Book (0-553-89805-1) Bantam Bks.
Green, Jane. Jemima J. A Novel about Ugly Ducklings & Swans. 2001. (J). E-Book 15.95 (0-7679-0738-8); 384p. reprint ed. pap. 11.95 (0-7679-0518-0) Broadway Bks.
Haines, Carolyn. Splintered Bones. 2003. 384p. mass mkt. 5.99 (0-440-23721-1); 2002. 320p. 23.95 (0-385-33590-3, Delacorte Pr.) Dell Publishing.
—Splintered Bones. l.t. ed. 2003. 496p. 25.95 (0-375-43248-5) Random Hse. Large Print.
Holden, Wendy. Simply Divine. 2000. 304p. pap. 12.95 (0-452-28167-9, Plume) Dutton/Plume.
—Simply Divine. unabr. ed. 2001. audio compact disk 124.00 (0-7887-7169-8, C1422); 2000. audio 88.00 (0-7887-4858-0, 96427E7) Recorded Bks., LLC.
Hruby, Andes. The Trouble with Catherine. 2002. 288p. 23.95 o.s.i (0-525-94640-3, Dutton) Dutton/Plume.
Lang, Adele. Confessions of a Sociopathic Social Climber: The Katya Livingston Chronicles. Orig. Title: What Katya Did Next: Chronicles of a Sociopathic Social Climber. 196p. 2002. 22.95 (0-312-28811-5); 2003. reprint ed. pap. 12.95 (0-312-31361-6, Saint Martin's Griffin) St. Martin's Pr.
Matthews, Carole. Bare Necessity. 2003. 384p. pap. 13.95 (0-06-053214-9, Avon Bks.) Morrow/Avon.
McNeil, Gil. The Only Boy for Me. 2002. 276p. 23.95 (1-58234-223-7) Bloomsbury Publishing.
McPhee, Phoebe. The Alphabetical Hook-Up List R-Z. 2002. (Illus.). 224p. pap. 9.95 (0-7434-4844-8, MTV) Simon & Schuster.
Mlynowski, Sarah. Milkrun. 2003. 352p. mass mkt. (0-373-25035-5); 2001. 288p. pap. (0-373-25012-6) Harlequin Enterprises, Ltd. (Red Dress Ink).
Naylor, Clare. Catching Alice. 2000. 336p. pap. 14.00 (0-449-00557-7, Ballantine Bks.) Ballantine Bks.
Pastan, Rachel. This Side of Married. 2004. 272p. 23.95 (0-670-03306-5) Viking Penguin.
Plain, Belva. Looking Back. 2002. 400p. reprint ed. mass mkt. 7.99 (0-440-23577-4) Dell Publishing.
—Looking Back. l.t. ed. 2001. 496p. 25.95 (0-375-43098-9) Random Hse. Large Print.
Pye, Frances. Sharing Sean: A Novel. 2004. 480p. (0-06-054556-9, Morrow, William & Co.) Morrow/Avon.
Rawles, Nancy. Crawfish Dreams. 2004. 368p. pap. 13.00 (0-385-72213-3, Anchor) Knopf Publishing Group.
Rosenfeld, Lucinda. Why She Went Home: A Novel. 2004. 320p. 23.95 (1-4000-6185-7, Random House) Random House Adult Trade Publishing Group.
Rue, Nancy. Antonia's Choice: A Novel. 2003. 300p. pap. 11.99 (1-59052-076-9) Multnomah Pubs., Inc.
Schmais, Libby. The Essential Charlotte. 2003. 256p. 23.95 (0-312-31164-8) St. Martin's Pr.
Senate, Melissa. See Jane Date. 2003. 352p. mass mkt. (0-373-25027-4); 2001. 283p. pap. (0-373-25011-8, 1-25011-7) Harlequin Enterprises, Ltd. (Red Dress Ink).
Sohn, Amy. Sex & the City: Kiss & Tell. 160p. 2005. 50.00 (0-7434-6370-6); 2002. (Illus.). 40.00 (0-7434-5681-5) Simon & Schuster. (Pocket).
Urquhart, Jane. The Stone Carvers. 2003. 400p. pap. 14.00 (0-14-200358-1) Penguin Group (USA) Inc.
—The Stone Carvers. 2002. 400p. 25.95 (0-670-03044-9, Viking) Viking Penguin.
Weiner, Jennifer. Good in Bed. 2006. 432p. mass mkt. (0-7434-7549-6, Pocket Star); 2002. 400p. pap. 14.00 (0-7434-1817-4, Washington Square Pr.); 2001. 384p. 24.95 (0-7434-1816-6, Atria); 2001. reprint ed. E-Book 24.95 (0-7434-1818-2, Atria) Simon & Schuster.
—Good in Bed. abr. ed. 2003. audio 25.00 (0-7435-0846-7); audio compact disk 32.00 (0-7435-0847-5) Simon & Schuster Audio. (Simon & Schuster Audioworks).
—Good in Bed. l.t. ed. 2001. (Large Print Women's Fiction Ser.). 689p. 29.95 (0-7862-3644-2) Thorndike Pr.
Wharton, Edith. The Old Maid: The 'Fifties. 2003. 144p. pap. 10.95 (0-8129-7002-0, Modern Library) Random House Adult Trade Publishing Group.
Wolff, Isabel. The Trials of Tiffany Trott. 1999. 416p. mass mkt. 7.99 (0-451-40888-8, Onyx) NAL.
Young, Elizabeth. Asking for Trouble: A Novel. 2001. 416p. pap. 14.00 (0-380-81897-3, Avon Bks.) Morrow/Avon.
—Asking for Trouble: A Novel. 2000. (Illus.). 400p. o.p. (0-434-00944-X) Random Hse. of Canada, Ltd. CAN. *Dist:* Random Hse., Inc.

### SISTERS—FICTION

Abrahams, Peter. Crying Wolf. E-Book 19.95 (0-345-44260-1); 2001. 352p. mass mkt. 6.99 (0-345-43503-6, Fawcett) Ballantine Bks.
Alcott, Louisa May. Good Wives, Pt. II. 1995. (Children's Library). (Illus.). 352p. (J). 10.95 o.p. (0-681-10350-7) Borders Pr.
—Little Women. 2000. 252p. E-Book 9.95 (0-594-05582-2) 1873 Pr.
—Little Women. 1981. mass mkt. 2.50 o.s.i (0-441-05466-8) Ace Bks.
—Little Women. 1987. 608p. (gr. k-6). pap. text 4.99 o.s.i (0-440-44768-2) Dell Publishing.
—Little Women. 1994. 461p. mass mkt. 3.99 (0-8125-2333-4, Tor Classics) Doherty, Tom Assocs., LLC.
—Little Women. 1941. 93p. pap. 5.60 (0-87129-320-X, L27) Dramatic Publishing Co.
—Little Women. 1972. 2.95 o.p. (0-460-01248-7, Dutton) Dutton/Plume.
—Little Women. E-Book 2.49 (1-929120-48-6) Electric Umbrella Publishing.
—Little Women. 1997. pap. 5.50 (1-57514-326-7, 1051) Encore Performance Publishing.
—Little Women. (Focus on the Family Great Stories Ser.). 1999. (Illus.). 576p. (J). pap. 9.99 o.p. (1-56179-744-8); 1997. 15.99 o.p. (1-56179-552-6) Focus on the Family Publishing.
—Little Women. 1994. (Everyman's Library Children's Classics Ser.). 530p. (gr. 4 up). 14.95 (0-679-43642-1, Everyman's Library) Knopf Publishing Group.
—Little Women. 1988. (Knopf Book & Cassette Classics Ser.). (Illus.). 512p. (J). 18.95 o.s.i (0-394-56279-8) Knopf, Alfred A. Inc.
—Little Women. 1994. 512p. (J). (gr. 4-7). 19.95 (0-316-03107-0); 1994. 512p. (J). (gr. 4-7). pap. 9.99 (0-316-03105-4); 1968. (Illus.). 524p. (YA). (gr. 7 up). 19.95 (0-316-03095-3) Little Brown & Co.
—Little Women. E-Book 2.95 (1-57799-829-4) Logos Research Systems, Inc.
—Little Women. 1981. (English As a Second Language Bk.). pap. text 4.46 net. (0-582-53489-5, 74091) Longman Publishing Group.
—Little Women. 1998. (Little Brown Notebooks Ser.). (Illus.). 256p. 9.99 (1-897954-77-8) M Q Pubns. GBR. *Dist:* Independent Pubs. Group.

—Little Women. 1983. (Modern Library College Editions Ser.). 603p. (C). pap. 11.25 (*0-07-554389-3*, McGraw-Hill Humanities, Social Sciences & World Languages) McGraw-Hill Higher Education.

—Little Women. (J). E-Book 1.95 (*1-58515-196-3*) MesaView, Inc.

—Little Women. 1983. mass mkt. 3.50 o.p. (*0-451-52214-1*); 480p. (J). (gr. 3 up). mass mkt. 3.95 (*0-451-52341-5*, Signet Classics) NAL.

—Little Women. Alderson, Valerie, ed. & intro. by. (Oxford World's Classics Ser.). 1998. 530p. pap. 7.95 (*0-19-283434-7*); 1995. 526p. pap. 5.95 o.p. (*0-19-282765-0*) Oxford Univ. Pr., Inc.

—Little Women. 1982. (Oxford Graded Readers Ser.). (Illus.). 48p. (YA). (gr. 7-12). pap. text 3.25 o.p. (*0-19-421804-X*) Oxford Univ. Pr., Inc.

—Little Women. 1998. pap. 7.00 (*0-582-40194-1*) Pearson Education.

—Little Women. (Classics Ser.). 1995. (Illus.). 336p. (YA). (gr. 5 up). pap. 4.99 o.p. (*0-14-036668-7*); 1983. 304p. (J). (gr. 3-7). pap. 3.50 o.p. (*0-14-035008-X*, Puffin Bks.); 1981. (Illus.). (J). (gr. 4-6). 9.95 o.s.i (*0-448-11019-9*, Grosset & Dunlap); 1963. (Illus.). (J). (gr. 4-6). 3.95 o.p. (*0-448-05466-3*, Grosset & Dunlap) Penguin Putnam Bks. for Young Readers.

—Little Women. 1988. (Children's Classics Ser.). (Illus.). 400p. (J). (gr. 2 up). 12.99 o.s.i (*0-517-63489-9*) Random Hse. Value Publishing.

—Little Women. 1985. (Illus.). 432p. (J). (gr. 4-12). 12.95 o.p. (*0-89577-209-4*) Reader's Digest Assn., Inc., The.

—Little Women. 1995. (Literary Classics Giant Ser.). 688p. text 8.98 o.p. (*1-56138-566-2*, Courage Bks.) Running Pr. Bk. Pubs.

—Little Women. 1986. 256p. (J). (gr. 3-7). pap. 2.50 o.p. (*0-590-40498-9*, Scholastic Paperbacks) Scholastic, Inc.

—Little Women. 1994. 592p. mass mkt. 5.99 (*0-671-51764-3*, Pocket) Simon & Schuster.

—Little Women. Barish, Wendy, ed. 1982. (Illus.). 576p. (J). 15.95 o.p. (*0-671-44447-6*, Atheneum) Simon & Schuster Children's Publishing.

—Little Women. 1995. (Little Brown Notebook Ser.). (Illus.). 256p. 6.95 (*0-8069-3975-3*) Sterling Publishing Co., Inc.

—Little Women. (Bullseye Step into Classics Ser.). 1994. 10.04 (*0-606-09566-7*); 1962. 10.10 o.p. (*0-606-00974-4*) Turtleback Bks.

—Little Women. 1940. (J). 6.00 (*0-87602-150-X*) Anchorage Pr.

—Little Women. 1994. 144p. (YA). pap. 3.99 (*0-671-51902-6*, Aladdin) Simon & Schuster Children's Publishing.

—Little Women. 1983. (YA). (gr. 6 up). reprint ed. lib. bdg. 18.95 (*0-89966-408-3*) Buccaneer Bks., Inc.

—Little Women. (Early Best Sellers Ser.). reprint ed. lib. bdg. 48.00 (*0-7426-1003-9*) Classic Bks.

—Little Women. abr. ed. 1994. (J). (gr. 5-7). pap. 29.99 incl. audio (*0-88646-835-3*, LSR 7315) Durkin Hayes Publishing Ltd.

—Little Women, ERS. 1993. (Little Classics Ser.). (Illus.). 308p. (J). (gr. 4-8). 15.95 o.p. (*0-8050-2767-X*, Holt, Henry & Co. Bks. For Young Readers) Holt, Henry & Co.

—Little Women. l.t. ed. 298p. pap. 25.86 (*0-7583-1401-9*); 1145p. pap. 85.69 (*0-7583-1407-8*); 988p. pap. 76.39 (*0-7583-1406-X*); 806p. pap. 64.52 (*0-7583-1405-1*); 659p. pap. 49.05 (*0-7583-1404-3*); 515p. pap. 39.88 (*0-7583-1403-5*); 404p. pap. 32.23 (*0-7583-1402-7*); 238p. pap. 21.50 (*0-7583-1400-0*); 238p. lib. bdg. 27.50 (*0-7583-1392-6*); 1145p. lib. bdg. 97.69 (*0-7583-1399-3*); 988p. lib. bdg. 88.39 (*0-7583-1398-5*); 806p. lib. bdg. 78.69 (*0-7583-1397-7*); 659p. lib. bdg. 55.05 (*0-7583-1396-9*); 515p. lib. bdg. 45.88 (*0-7583-1395-0*); 404p. lib. bdg. 38.23 (*0-7583-1394-2*); 298p. lib. bdg. 31.86 (*0-7583-1393-4*) Huge Print Pr.

—Little Women. l.t. ed. 1998. 665p. lib. bdg. 28.00 (*0-939495-51-1*) North Bks.

—Little Women. deluxe l.t. ed. 1947. (Illustrated Junior Library Ser.). (Illus.). 288p. (J). (gr. 2 up). 19.99 (*0-448-06019-1*, Grosset & Dunlap) Penguin Putnam Bks. for Young Readers.

—Little Women. abr. ed. 1997. 2p. audio 16.95 o.s.i (*0-14-086146-7*); audio 16.95 o.s.i (*0-14-086146-7*) Viking Penguin.

—Little Women: Four Funny Sisters. Lindskoog, Kathryn, ed. 1991. (Young Reader's Library). (Illus.). (J). (gr. 3-7). pap. 12.99 o.p. (*0-88070-437-3*) Zonderkidz.

—Little Women Vol. 2: The Sisters Grow Up. Lindskoog, Kathryn, ed. 1991. (Illus.). (J). (gr. 3-7). pap. 4.99 o.p. (*0-88070-463-2*) Zonderkidz.

—Mujercitas. 1995. (SPA.). 304p. 13.50 (*84-01-00914-6*, PJ9396) Plaza & Janés Editories, S.A. ESP. *Dist:* Distribooks, Inc., Lectorum Pubns., Inc.

—Mujercitas. 2002. (SPA.). 304p. mass mkt. 7.95 (*1-4000-0080-7*) Random Hse., Inc.

Alcott, Louisa May & Golden Books Staff. Little Women. 1987. (Golden Classics Ser.). (Illus.). 128p. (J). (gr. 3-7). pap. 8.95 o.s.i (*0-307-17116-7*, Golden Bks.) Random Hse. Children's Bks.

Ali, Monica. Brick Lane: A Novel. l.t. ed. 2003. 676p. 30.95 (*0-7862-6018-1*) Gale Group.

—Brick Lane: A Novel. 2003. 384p. 25.00 (*0-7432-4330-7*); E-Book (*0-7432-4971-2*) Simon & Schuster. (Scribner).

Allen, Charlotte Vale. Claudia's Shadow. 1996. 399p. mass mkt. (*1-55166-177-2*, 1-66177-6); 304p. per. (*1-55166-245-0*, 1-66245-1) Harlequin Enterprises, Ltd. (Mira Bks.).

—Leftover Dreams. 1999. 596p. reprint ed. pap. 23.00 (*1-892738-29-5*) Island Nation Pr., LLC.

—Promises. 1991. 432p. mass mkt. 5.95 o.s.i (*0-8041-0664-9*, Ivy Bks.) Ballantine Bks.

—Promises. 1987. 464p. mass mkt. 4.50 o.p. (*0-425-10193-2*); 1984. mass mkt. 3.95 o.s.i (*0-425-07445-5*); 1983. mass mkt. 3.50 o.s.i (*0-425-06167-1*); 1982. mass mkt. 3.25 o.s.i (*0-425-05502-7*); 1981. mass mkt. 2.95 o.s.i (*0-425-04843-8*) Berkley Publishing Group.

—Promises. 1980. 11.95 o.p. (*0-525-18540-2*, Dutton) Dutton/Plume.

—Promises. 1980. 369p. reprint ed. pap. 20.00 (*1-892738-26-0*) Island Nation Pr., LLC.

Allfrey, P. Orchid House. 1987. o.s.i (*0-86068-242-0*) Random Hse., Inc.

Allfrey, Phyllis S. The Orchid House. 2nd ed. 1985. 235p. reprint ed. 20.00 o.s.i (*0-89410-433-0*); pap. 12.00 o.p. (*0-89410-434-9*) Rienner, Lynne Pubs., Inc. (Three Continents).

—The Orchid House. 1996. 250p. (C). pap. text 16.95 (*0-8135-2332-X*) Rutgers Univ. Pr.

—The Orchid House. l.t. ed. 1992. 320p. text 24.95 (*1-85089-599-6*) Transaction Pubs.

Ansa, Tina McElroy. Ugly Ways. 1993. 277p. 19.95 o.s.i (*0-15-192553-4*) Harcourt Trade Pubs.

—Ugly Ways: A Novel. 1995. (Harvest American Writing Ser.). 288p. pap. 14.00 (*0-15-600077-6*, Harvest Bks.) Harcourt Trade Pubs.

Aston, Elizabeth. Mr. Darcy's Daughters: A Novel. 2003. 368p. pap. 14.00 (*0-7432-4397-8*, Touchstone) Simon & Schuster.

Atwood, Margaret. The Blind Assassin. 2000. 544p. 26.00 (*0-385-47572-1*, Talese, Nan A.) Doubleday Publishing.

—The Blind Assassin. pap. (*0-385-72856-5*) Knopf Publishing Group.

—The Blind Assassin. 2001. 544p. pap. 14.95 (*0-385-72095-5*, Knopf Bks. for Young Readers) Random Hse. Children's Bks.

—The Blind Assassin. l.t. ed. 2000. 832p. 26.00 (*0-375-43085-7*) Random Hse. Large Print.

Austen, Jane. Jane Austen's Pride & Prejudice. Johnson, Claudia L. & Wolfson, Susan J., eds. 2002. (Longman Cultural Edition Ser.). 464p. pap. 16.00 (*0-321-10507-9*) Longman Publishing Group.

—Pride & Prejudice. 2000. 252p. E-Book 9.95 (*0-594-05313-7*) 1873 Pr.

—Pride & Prejudice. 1998. pap. 4.99 o.p. (*1-57840-200-X*) Acclaim Bks.

—Pride & Prejudice. 1997. pap. text o.p. (*0-17-556586-4*) Addison-Wesley Longman, Inc.

—Pride & Prejudice. unabr. ed. 1962. (Classics Ser.). mass mkt. 4.95 (*0-8049-0001-9*, CL-1) Airmont Publishing Co., Inc.

—Pride & Prejudice. Date not set. lib. bdg. 25.95 (*0-8488-0420-1*) Amereon, Ltd.

—Pride & Prejudice. 2001. 7.95 (*0-8010-1211-2*) Baker Bks.

—Pride & Prejudice. 1991. mass mkt. 4.95 (*0-553-54088-2*); 1983. mass mkt. 1.95 o.s.i (*0-553-21215-X*); 1983. 352p. reprint ed. mass mkt. 4.95 (*0-553-21310-5*, Bantam Classics) Bantam Bks.

—Pride & Prejudice. 1999. (Classic Novels ). 392p. pap. 8.95 (*0-7641-1147-7*) Barron's Educational Series, Inc.

—Pride & Prejudice. Kendrick, Walter, ed. 1980. (Mcdonald Classics Ser.). 410p. 19.95 (*0-8464-1071-0*) Beekman Pubs., Inc.

—Pride & Prejudice. 1988. lib. bdg. 19.95 (*0-89966-243-9*) Buccaneer Bks., Inc.

—Pride & Prejudice. 1997. (Cambridge Literature Ser.). audio 16.95 o.p. (*0-521-59792-7*); audio compact disk 22.95 o.p. (*0-521-59791-9*) Cambridge Univ. Pr.

—Pride & Prejudice. Bain, Richard, ed. 1996. (Literature Ser.). (Illus.). 384p. pap. text 11.95 o.p. (*0-521-57654-7*) Cambridge Univ. Pr.

—Pride & Prejudice, 3 Vols. reprint ed. lib. bdg. 294.00 (*0-7426-2071-9*); 2001. pap. text 84.00 (*0-7426-7071-6*) Classic Bks.

—Pride & Prejudice. 1994. 332p. mass mkt. 3.99 (*0-8125-2336-9*, Tor Classics) Doherty, Tom Assocs., LLC.

—Pride & Prejudice. unabr. ed. 1995. (Thrift Editions Ser.). 272p. pap. 2.50 (*0-486-28473-5*) Dover Pubns., Inc.

—Pride & Prejudice. 1942. 107p. pap. 5.60 (*0-87129-686-1*, P36) Dramatic Publishing Co.

—Pride & Prejudice. 1985. (Illus.). 352p. 20.00 o.p. (*0-525-18381-7*, Dutton) Dutton/Plume.

—Pride & Prejudice. 1980. (Reader's Request Ser.). lib. bdg. 13.95 o.p. (*0-8161-3076-0*, Macmillan Reference USA) Gale Group.

—Pride & Prejudice. l.t. ed. 1999. 480p. pap. 20.00 (*0-06-093325-9*) HarperCollins Pubs.

—Pride & Prejudice. Clay, N. L., ed. 1986. (Guide Novel Ser.). pap. text 4.50 o.p. (*0-435-16041-9*) Heinemann.

—Pride & Prejudice. 1997. pap. 8.25 (*0-03-051487-8*) Holt, Rinehart & Winston.

—Pride & Prejudice. Schorer, Mark, ed. 1956. pap. 16.36 (*0-395-05101-0*, Riverside Editions) Houghton Mifflin Co.

—Pride & Prejudice. l.t. ed. 1224p. pap. 85.50 (*0-7583-1942-8*); 995p. pap. 74.61 (*0-7583-1941-X*); 806p. pap. 63.79 (*0-7583-1940-1*); 623p. pap. 45.49 (*0-7583-1939-8*); 349p. pap. 29.76 (*0-7583-1937-1*); 484p. pap. 36.91 (*0-7583-1938-X*); 1444p. pap. 95.94 (*0-7583-1943-6*); 276p. pap. 24.62 (*0-7583-1936-3*); 995p. lib. bdg. 86.61 (*0-7583-1933-9*); 806p. lib. bdg. 75.79 (*0-7583-1932-0*); 623p. lib. bdg. 51.49 (*0-7583-1931-2*); 484p. lib. bdg. 42.91 (*0-7583-1930-4*); 349p. lib. bdg. 35.76 (*0-7583-1929-0*); 276p. lib. bdg. 30.62 (*0-7583-1928-2*); 1224p. lib. bdg. 97.50 (*0-7583-1934-7*); 1444p. lib. bdg. 107.94 (*0-7583-1935-5*) Huge Print Pr.

—Pride & Prejudice. 1991. 327p. (*1-85715-001-5*, Everyman's Library) Knopf Publishing Group.

—Pride & Prejudice. 1991. 416p. 17.00 (*0-679-40542-9*) Knopf, Alfred A. Inc.

—Pride & Prejudice. 1998. (Cloth Bound Pocket Ser.). 240p. 7.95 (*3-89508-207-4*, 521305) Konemann.

—Pride & Prejudice. l.t. ed. 1997. (Large Print Heritage Ser.). 560p. lib. bdg. 36.95 (*1-58118-009-8*, 21967) LRS.

—Pride & Prejudice. (Longman Fiction Ser.). 1997. pap. 9.07 (*0-582-27508-3*); 1993. pap. text 6.50 o.p. (*0-582-09674-X*, 79823) Longman Publishing Group.

—Pride & Prejudice. Adams, Richard, ed. 1983. (Study Texts Ser.). pap. text 5.95 (*0-582-33086-6*, 72039) Longman Publishing Group.

—Pride & Prejudice. 9999. o.p.; 1996. 336p. mass mkt. 4.95 (*0-451-52588-4*, Signet Classics); 1961. mass mkt. 0.50 o.p. (*0-451-50082-2*, Signet Classics); 1961. mass mkt. 1.75 o.p. (*0-451-51916-7*, Signet Classics); 1961. mass mkt. 0.60 o.p. (*0-451-50721-5*, Signet Classics); 1961. mass mkt. 0.75 o.p. (*0-451-50843-2*, Signet Classics); 1961. mass mkt. 0.95 o.p. (*0-451-50977-3*, Signet Classics); 1961. mass mkt. 1.25 o.p. (*0-451-51111-5*, Signet Classics); 1961. mass mkt. 1.50 o.p. (*0-451-51253-7*, Signet Classics); 1961. mass mkt. 1.75 o.p. (*0-451-51396-7*, Signet Classics); 1961. mass mkt. 1.95 o.p. (*0-451-51491-2*, Signet Classics); 1961. mass mkt. 1.50 o.p. (*0-451-51662-1*, Signet Classics); 1950. 336p. mass mkt. 3.95 o.p. (*0-451-52365-2*); 1950. mass mkt. 2.25 o.p. (*0-451-52226-5*, Signet Classics); 1950. mass mkt. 1.95 o.p. (*0-451-52075-0*, Signet Classics) NAL.

—Pride & Prejudice. Worrall, Andrew, ed. 1997. (Thornes Classic Novels Ser.). (Illus.). 376p. pap. 16.95 (*0-7487-2977-1*) Nelson Thornes GBR. *Dist:* Trans-Atlantic Pubns., Inc.

—Pride & Prejudice. abr. ed. 1996. 19.95 o.p. (*0-7871-0306-3*) NewStar Media, Inc.

—Pride & Prejudice. l.t. ed. 1998. 480p. lib. bdg. 26.00 (*0-939495-50-3*); 355p. reprint ed. lib. bdg. 25.00 (*1-58287-058-6*) North Bks.

—Pride & Prejudice. (C). pap. text (*0-393-99771-5*) Norton, W. W. & Co., Inc.

—Pride & Prejudice. Gray, Donald J., ed. 1966. (Critical Editions Ser.). 450p. (C). pap. o.p. (*0-393-09668-8*) Norton, W. W. & Co., Inc.

—Pride & Prejudice. 3rd ed. 2000. (Critical Editions Ser.). viii, 413p. (C). pap. 7.25 (*0-393-97604-1*, Norton Paperbacks) Norton, W. W. & Co., Inc.

—Pride & Prejudice. 1999. (Oxford World's Classics Ser.). 366p. 12.50 o.p. (*0-19-210026-2*) Oxford Univ. Pr., Inc.

—Pride & Prejudice. Kinsley, James, ed. 1998. (Oxford World's Classics Ser.). 410p. pap. 6.95 (*0-19-283355-3*) Oxford Univ. Pr., Inc.

—Pride & Prejudice. Hedge, Tricia, ed. 1995. (Illus.). 112p. pap. text 5.95 o.p. (*0-19-422710-3*) Oxford Univ. Pr., Inc.

—Pride & Prejudice. Kinsley, James, ed. 1990. (Oxford World's Classics Ser.). 390p. pap. 5.95 o.p. (*0-19-282760-X*) Oxford Univ. Pr., Inc.

—Pride & Prejudice. Kinsley, James & Bradbrook, F. W., eds. 1980. (Oxford World's Classics Ser.). pap. 2.25 o.p. (*0-19-281503-2*) Oxford Univ. Pr., Inc.

—Pride & Prejudice. 2nd ed. 1993. (Illus.). 126p. pap. text 5.95 (*0-19-585472-1*) Oxford Univ. Pr., Inc.

—Pride & Prejudice, Vol. II. Chapman, R. W., ed. 3rd ed. 1988. (Illus.). 432p. reprint ed. 21.50 (*0-19-254702-X*) Oxford Univ. Pr., Inc.

—Pride & Prejudice. 2000. 384p. pap. 2.99 o.s.i (*0-14-130930-X*) Penguin Putnam Bks. for Young Readers.

—Pride & Prejudice. 1996. 144p. pap. 20.00 (*81-209-0025-1*) Pitambar Publishing IND. *Dist:* State Mutual Bk. & Periodical Service, Ltd.

—Pride & Prejudice. collector's ed. 2002. (Illus.). im. lthr. 38.85 (*1-931927-42-1*); pap. 19.95 (*1-931927-43-X*); 25.95 (*1-931927-41-3*); pap. 17.95 (*1-931927-01-4*) Polyglot Pr., Inc.

—Pride & Prejudice. text (*0-13-981465-5*) Prentice Hall (Schl. Div.).

—Pride & Prejudice. (Jane Austen Works: Vol. 7). 2000. 280p. lib. bdg. 36.99 (*1-57646-350-8*); 2000. 280p. pap. 19.99 o.p. (*1-57646-267-6*); 1999. 200p. E-Book 3.99 incl. audio compact disk (*1-57646-150-5*); 2000. 518p. pap. 34.99 (*1-57646-351-6*) Quiet Vision Publishing.

—Pride & Prejudice. (Modern Library Ser.). 2000. E-Book 4.95 (*0-679-64112-2*); 2000. 320p. pap. 7.95 (*0-679-78326-1*); 1995. (Illus.). 304p. 14.95 (*0-679-60168-6*) Random House Adult Trade Publishing Group. (Modern Library).

—Pride & Prejudice. 1988. (Zodiac Press Ser.). 248p. o.p. (*0-7011-1236-0*) Random Hse. of Canada, Ltd. CAN. *Dist:* Random Hse., Inc.

—Pride & Prejudice. 1996. o.s.i (*0-679-60252-6*); 1989. o.s.i (*1-85381-097-5*); 1986. pap. 16.00 o.s.i incl. audio (*0-394-55731-X*) Random Hse., Inc.

—Pride & Prejudice. 1984. (Illus.). 368p. 25.00 o.p. (*0-89577-198-5*) Reader's Digest Assn., Inc., The.

—Pride & Prejudice. (Literary Classics Ser.). 368p. 2002. 9.00 o.p. (*0-7624-0550-3*); 1992. text 5.98 o.p. (*1-56138-171-3*, Courage Bks.) Running Pr. Bk. Pubs.

—Pride & Prejudice. 2000. 416p. mass mkt. 4.99 (*0-439-10135-2*) Scholastic, Inc.

—Pride & Prejudice. 2000. E-Book 2.95 (*1-58853-022-1*) Sensory Publishing, Inc.

—Pride & Prejudice. 400p. 2005. (Illus.). mass mkt. 4.99 (*0-7434-6748-5*); 2004. mass mkt. 4.95 (*0-7434-8759-1*) Simon & Schuster. (Pocket).

—Pride & Prejudice. Shefter, Harry, ed. 1985. (Enriched Classics Ser.). mass mkt. 2.50 o.p. (*0-671-41678-2*, Pocket) Simon & Schuster.

—Pride & Prejudice. 1982. 464p. mass mkt. 2.95 o.s.i (*0-671-44389-5*, Pocket) Simon & Schuster.

—Pride & Prejudice. 1996. (Classic Library). 12.98 o.p. (*0-7651-9980-7*) Smithmark Pubs., Inc.

—Pride & Prejudice. 2003. (Perennial Bestsellers Ser.). 28.95 (*0-7862-4964-1*) Thorndike Pr.

—Pride & Prejudice. l.t. ed. 1984. (Charnwood Large Print Ser.). 532p. 29.99 (*0-7089-8228-X*, Charnwood) Thorpe, F. A. Pubs. GBR. *Dist:* Ulverscroft Large Print Bks., Ltd., Ulverscroft Large Print Canada, Ltd.

—Pride & Prejudice. Daleski, H. M., ed. 2003. 456p. 9.95 (*1-59264-001-X*); pap. 7.95 (*1-59264-000-1*) Toby Pr.

—Pride & Prejudice. 1986. (Illus.). 352p. 25.95 o.p. (*0-7126-1011-1*) Trafalgar Square.

—Pride & Prejudice. 1999. (Signature Classics Ser.). (Illus.). 352p. 24.95 (*1-58279-032-9*); 29.95 (*1-58279-044-2*) Trident Pr. International.

—Pride & Prejudice. 1950. 11.00 (*0-606-01933-2*) Turtleback Bks.

—Pride & Prejudice. Norris, Pamela, ed. 1993. 384p. pap. 3.95 (*0-460-87212-5*, Everyman's Classic Library in Paperback) Tuttle Publishing.

—Pride & Prejudice. 1906. 352p. pap. 4.95 o.p. (*0-460-11022-5*, Everyman's Classic Library in Paperback) Tuttle Publishing.

—Pride & Prejudice. (Penguin Classics Ser.). 2002. 480p. pap. 8.00 (*0-14-143951-3*, Penguin Classics); 1997. 384p. pap. 7.95 o.s.i (*0-14-043426-7*, Penguin Classics); 1996. 400p. pap. 9.95 o.p. (*0-14-043596-4*) Viking Penguin.

—Pride & Prejudice. Tanner, Tony, ed. 1980. pap. 1.95 o.p. (*0-14-005774-9*) Viking Penguin.

—Pride & Prejudice. 1976. 2.95 o.p. (*0-460-01022-0*) Viking Penguin.

—Pride & Prejudice. Tanner, Tony, ed. 1972. (English Library). 400p. pap. 7.95 o.s.i (*0-14-043072-5*, Penguin Classics) Viking Penguin.

—Pride & Prejudice. 2000. text 6.00 (*0-8220-7172-X*); text 6.00 (*0-8220-7172-X*) Wiley, John & Sons, Inc. (Cliff Notes).

—Pride & Prejudice. 1997. (Classics Library). 288p. pap. 3.95 (*1-85326-000-2*, 0002WW) Wordsworth Editions, Ltd. GBR. *Dist:* Casemate Pubs. & Bk. Distributors, LLC.

—Pride & Prejudice. 1992. E-Book 8.98 (*0-585-25816-3*) netLibrary, Inc.

—Pride & Prejudice: An Authoritative Text. Gray, Donald J., ed. 2001. x, 219p. pap. (*0-393-10321-8*) Norton, W. W. & Co., Inc.

—Sense & Sensibility. (Modern Library Ser.). E-Book 4.95 (*1-931208-09-3*) Adobe Systems, Inc.

—Sense & Sensibility. unabr. ed. 1965. (Classics Ser.). (YA). (gr. 10 up). mass mkt. 2.50 o.p. (*0-8049-0058-2*, CL-58) Airmont Publishing Co., Inc.

—Sense & Sensibility. Date not set. 181p. 19.95 (*0-8488-2549-7*) Amereon, Ltd.

—Sense & Sensibility. 2001. 7.95 (*0-8010-1212-0*) Baker Bks.

—Sense & Sensibility. 1982. (Bantam Classics Ser.). 352p. (gr. 9-12). mass mkt. 4.95 (*0-553-21334-2*, Bantam Classics) Bantam Bks.

—Sense & Sensibility. 1996. 356p. (*0-7607-0043-5*); pap. (*0-7607-0045-1*) Barnes & Noble, Inc.

—Sense & Sensibility. 1981. 544p. (YA). reprint ed. lib. bdg. 18.95 (*0-89966-287-0*) Buccaneer Bks., Inc.

—Sense & Sensibility, 3 Vols. reprint ed. lib. bdg. 294.00 (*0-7426-2070-0*); 2001. pap. text 84.00 (*0-7426-7070-8*) Classic Bks.

—Sense & Sensibility. 1995. 342p. pap. text 2.99 (*0-8125-4312-2*, Tor Classics) Doherty, Tom Assocs., LLC.

—Sense & Sensibility. unabr. ed. 1996. (Thrift Editions Ser.). 272p. reprint ed. pap. text 2.00 (*0-486-29049-2*) Dover Pubns., Inc.

—Sense & Sensibility. 1998. (Cloth Bound Pocket Ser.). 240p. 7.95 (*3-89508-233-3*, 520181) Konemann.

—Sense & Sensibility. E-Book 2.95 (*1-57799-845-6*) Logos Research Systems, Inc.

—Sense & Sensibility. 1992. (Everyman's Library). 416p. 15.95 (*0-679-40987-4*) McKay, David Co., Inc.

—Sense & Sensibility. E-Book 1.95 (*1-58515-174-2*) MesaView, Inc.

—Sense & Sensibility. 1997. 320p. mass mkt. 4.95 (*0-451-52589-2*, Signet Classics); 1995. 320p. mass mkt. 5.99 o.s.i (*0-451-18790-3*, Signet Bks.); 1961. 320p. mass mkt. 3.95 o.s.i (*0-451-52419-5*, CE1826, Signet Classics); 1961. mass mkt. 2.95 o.p. (*0-451-52185-4*) NAL.

—Sense & Sensibility. l.t. ed. reprint ed. 1997. 465p. lib. bdg. 26.00 (*0-939495-09-0*); 1998. 363p. lib. bdg. 25.00 (*1-58287-070-5*) North Bks.

—Sense & Sensibility. 2001. pap., tchr. ed., wbk. ed. (*1-56137-897-6*) Novel Units, Inc.

—Sense & Sensibility. Kinsley, James, ed. (Oxford World's Classics Ser.). 1998. 400p. pap. 5.95 (*0-19-283358-8*); 1990. 398p. pap. 4.95 o.p. (*0-19-282761-8*) Oxford Univ. Pr., Inc.

—Sense & Sensibility. Kinsley, James & Lamont, Claire, eds. 1980. (Oxford World's Classics Ser.). pap. 2.95 o.p. (*0-19-281501-6*) Oxford Univ. Pr., Inc.

—Sense & Sensibility, Vol. I. Chapman, R. W., ed. 3rd ed. 1988. (Illus.). 446p. reprint ed. 20.00 (*0-19-254701-1*) Oxford Univ. Pr., Inc.

—Sense & Sensibility. abr. ed. 1996. (Illus.). 336p. (YA). (gr. 4-7). pap. 3.99 (*0-14-037850-2*, Puffin Bks.) Penguin Putnam Bks. for Young Readers.

—Sense & Sensibility. 2000. (Jane Austen Works: Vol. 6). 240p. lib. bdg. 33.99 (*1-57646-347-8*); pap. 18.99 o.p. (*1-57646-266-8*) Quiet Vision Publishing.

—Sense & Sensibility. (Paperback Classics Ser.). 2001. 304p. pap. 6.95 (*0-375-75673-6*); 1995. 288p. 14.95 (*0-679-60195-3*) Random House Adult Trade Publishing Group. (Modern Library).

—Sense & Sensibility. 1988. (Zodiac Press Ser.). 280p. o.p. (*0-7011-1237-9*) Random Hse. of Canada, Ltd. CAN. *Dist:* Random Hse., Inc.

—Sense & Sensibility. 1996. 380p. 17.00 (*0-676-50808-1*); 1989. o.s.i (*1-85381-098-3*) Random Hse., Inc.

—Sense & Sensibility. 1997. 9.00 o.p. (*0-7624-0566-X*); 1996. 352p. text 8.98 o.p. (*1-56138-705-3*, Courage Bks.) Running Pr. Bk. Pubs.

—Sense & Sensibility. 2000. E-Book 2.95 (*1-58853-007-8*) Sensory Publishing, Inc.

—Sense & Sensibility. E-Book 5.00 (*0-7410-0429-1*) SoftBook Pr.

—Sense & Sensibility. l.t. ed. 1985. (Charnwood Large Print Ser.). 501p. 29.99 (*0-7089-8246-8*, Charnwood) Thorpe, F. A. Pubs. GBR. *Dist:* Ulverscroft Large Print Bks., Ltd., Ulverscroft Large Print Canada, Ltd.

—Sense & Sensibility. 1983. 11.00 (*0-606-13771-8*); 1961. 11.00 (*0-606-00959-0*) Turtleback Bks.

—Sense & Sensibility. Todd, Janet, ed. 1989. (Paperback Classics). 416p. pap. 4.95 (*0-460-87914-6*, Everyman's Classic Library in Paperback) Tuttle Publishing.

—Sense & Sensibility. 1999. 10.95 (*81-7476-260-4*) UBS Pubs. Distributions, Ltd. IND. *Dist:* South Asia Bks.

—Sense & Sensibility. Ballaster, Ros, ed. & intro. by. 1996. (Penguin Classics Ser.). 368p. (C). 6.95 (*0-14-043425-9*) Viking Penguin.

—Sense & Sensibility. 1972. 3.95 o.p. (*0-460-01021-2*) Viking Penguin.

—Sense & Sensibility. Tanner, Tony, ed. 1969. (English Library). 400p. pap. 4.95 o.p. (*0-14-043047-4*, Penguin Classics) Viking Penguin.

—Sense & Sensibility. 1998. (Classics Library). 272p. pap. 3.95 (*1-85326-016-9*, 0169WW) Wordsworth Editions, Ltd. GBR. *Dist:* Casemate Pubs. & Bk. Distributors, LLC.

—Sense & Sensibility. 1996. E-Book 8.98 (*0-585-23463-9*) netLibrary, Inc.

Austen, Jane & Hemmant, Lynette. Pride & Prejudice. 1980. 14.95 o.p. (*0-437-24575-6*) Trafalgar Square.

Austen, Jane & Kinsley, James. Pride & Prejudice. 1990. E-Book 13.13 (*0-585-37761-8*) netLibrary, Inc.

Axelsson, Majgull. April Witch: A Novel. 2003. 432p. pap. 12.95 (*0-8129-6688-0*); 2002. 416p. 24.95 (*0-375-50517-2*, Villard Bks.) Random House Adult Trade Publishing Group.

Ballard, F. Mignon. An Angel to Die For. E-Book 22.95 (*0-312-27632-X*); 2000. 307p. 23.95 o.p. (*0-312-24174-7*, Saint Martin's Minotaur) St. Martin's Pr.

Ballard, Mignon F. An Angel to Die For. l.t. ed. 2001. (Beeler Large Print Mystery Ser.). 246p. 26.95 (*1-57490-337-3*, Beeler Large Print Bks.) Beeler, Thomas T. Publisher.

—An Angel to Die For. 2001. 208p. mass mkt. 5.99 o.s.i (*0-425-18208-8*) Berkley Publishing Group.

Barclay, Tessa. The Precious Gift. l.t. ed. 1998. (G. K. Hall Romance Ser.). 518p. pap. 24.95 o.p. (*0-7838-0271-4*, Macmillan Reference USA) Gale Group.

Barthelme, Frederick. Tracer. 2001. 128p. pap. text 13.00 (*1-58243-129-9*, Counterpoint Pr.) Basic Bks.

—Tracer. 1985. 104p. 13.70 o.p. (*0-671-54253-2*, Simon & Schuster) Simon & Schuster.

—Tracer. 1986. 128p. pap. 4.95 o.p. (*0-14-008969-1*, Penguin Bks.) Viking Penguin.

Bartolomeo, Christina. Cupid & Diana. 1998. (Illus.). 224p. 22.00 (*0-684-83977-6*, Scribner) Simon & Schuster.

—Cupid & Diana. l.t. ed. 1999. (Americana Ser.). 319p. 27.95 (*0-7862-1750-2*) Thorndike Pr.

—Cupid & Diana: A Novel. 1999. 224p. pap. 11.00 (*0-684-85622-0*, Scribner) Simon & Schuster.

Bawden, Nina. A Little Love, a Little Learning. 21.95 (*0-88411-122-9*) Amereon, Ltd.

—A Little Love, a Little Learning. l.t. unabr. ed. 1998. 304p. pap. 21.99 (*0-7531-5863-9*, 158639); 32.50 (*0-7531-5584-2*, 155842) ISIS Large Print Bks. GBR. *Dist:* Ulverscroft Large Print Bks., Ltd., Ulverscroft Large Print Canada, Ltd.

Berg, Elizabeth. Durable Goods. 2003. 224p. pap. 12.95 (*0-8129-6814-X*) Random House Adult Trade Publishing Group.

—What We Keep. l.t. ed. 1998. 26.95 (*1-56895-661-4*, Wheeler Publishing, Inc.) Gale Group.

—What We Keep: A Novel. 1999. (Ballantine Reader's Circle Ser.). 304p. pap. 14.00 (*0-345-42329-1*) Ballantine Bks.

—What We Keep: A Novel. 1998. 288p. 23.00 o.s.i (*0-375-50099-5*) Random Hse., Inc.

Berlin, Ellin. The Best of Families. 1978. pap. 1.95 o.s.i (*0-449-23541-6*, Fawcett) Ballantine Bks.

Bialosky, Jill. House under Snow. 2003. 264p. pap. 14.00 (*0-15-602746-1*, Harvest Bks.); 2002. 256p. 24.00 (*0-15-100685-7*) Harcourt Trade Pubs.

Bingham, Sallie. Matron of Honor. 192p. 1994. 19.95 o.p. (*0-944072-38-0*); 1996. reprint ed. pap. 10.95 o.p. (*0-944072-63-1*) Steerforth Pr. (Zoland Bks., Inc.).

—Small Victories. 1993. 312p. pap. 9.95 o.p. (*0-944072-25-9*); 20.95 o.p. (*0-944072-20-8*) Steerforth Pr. (Zoland Bks., Inc.).

Birch, Carol. Little Sister. 2001. 278p. pap. 13.00 (*1-86049-530-3*); 1998. 278p. o.s.i (*1-86049-267-3*); 1998. o.s.i (*1-86049-434-X*) Virago Pr., Ltd. GBR. *Dist:* Trafalgar Square, Little Brown & Co.

Blackstock, Terri. Seaside: A Novella. l.t. ed. 2001. 137p. 26.95 (*0-7838-9511-9*, Macmillan Reference USA) Gale Group.

—Seaside: A Novella. 2001. (Illus.). 128p. 12.99 (*0-310-23318-6*) Zondervan.

Blair, Kerry Lynn. The Heart Has Forever. 2000. 297p. pap. 13.95 (*1-57734-647-5*) Covenant Communications, Inc.

Blaylock, James P. Winter Tides. 352p. 1997. 21.95 o.s.i (*0-441-00444-X*); 1998. reprint ed. mass mkt. 6.50 o.s.i (*0-441-00575-6*) Ace Bks.

Bledsoe, Lucy Jane. This Wild Silence: A Novel. 2003. 272p. pap. 13.95 (*1-55583-773-5*) Alyson Pubns.

Bosworth, Sheila. Slow Poison. 1993. mass mkt. 4.99 o.s.i (*0-8041-1124-3*, Ivy Bks.) Ballantine Bks.

—Slow Poison. 1998. (Voices of the South Ser.). 336p. pap. 17.95 (*0-8071-2278-5*) Louisiana State Univ. Pr.

Bourne, Lesley-Anne. The Bubble Star. 1998. 184p. pap. 15.95 (*0-88984-199-3*) Porcupine's Quill, Inc. CAN. *Dist:* General Distribution Services, Inc.

Bowman, Elizabeth Atkins. A Dark Secret. 2001. 384p. mass mkt. 6.99 (*0-8125-7456-7*); 2000. 416p. 25.95 (*0-312-86806-5*) Doherty, Tom Assocs., LLC. (Forge Bks.).

Bright, Vonette & Moser, Nancy. Sister Circle Endcap Kit. 2003. (*0-8423-2618-9*) Tyndale Hse. Pubs.

Briscoe, Connie. Sisters & Lovers. 416p. 1996. pap. 13.95 (*0-345-40969-8*); 1995. mass mkt. 6.99 (*0-8041-1334-3*, Ivy Bks.) Ballantine Bks.

—Sisters & Lovers. 1994. 352p. 22.00 o.p. (*0-06-017116-2*) HarperTrade.

—Sisters & Lovers. l.t. ed. 1997. (Niagara Large Print Ser.). 437p. 29.50 o.p. (*0-7089-5805-2*, Ulverscroft) Thorpe, F. A. Pubs. GBR. *Dist:* Ulverscroft Large Print Bks., Ltd., Ulverscroft Large Print Canada, Ltd.

Briskin, Jacqueline. Too Much, Too Soon. 1986. 496p. mass mkt. 5.95 o.p. (*0-425-08783-2*); 1985. mass mkt. 3.95 o.s.i (*0-425-09156-2*) Berkley Publishing Group.

—Too Much, Too Soon. l.t. ed. 1986. (Special Editions Ser.). 760p. 19.95 o.p. (*0-8161-3984-9*); 11.95 o.p. (*0-8161-3987-3*) Gale Group. (Macmillan Reference USA).

—Too Much, Too Soon. 1985. 480p. 17.95 o.p. (*0-399-13071-3*, G. P. Putnam's Sons) Penguin Putnam Bks. for Young Readers.

Brookner, Anita. Falling Slowly. l.t. ed. 1998. 26.95 (*1-56895-700-9*, Wheeler Publishing, Inc.) Gale Group.

—Falling Slowly. 2000. 240p. pap. 12.00 (*0-375-70424-8*, Vintage) Knopf Publishing Group.

Broughton, Rhoda. Cometh up As a Flower: An Autobiography. 1993. (Pocket Classics Ser.). x, 285p. 8.00 o.p. (*0-7509-0448-8*) Sutton Publishing, Ltd. GBR. *Dist:* International Publishers Marketing.

—Cometh up as a Flower: An Autobiography, 2 vols., 1 bk. reprint ed. 44.50 (*0-404-61794-8*) AMS Pr., Inc.

Brown, Parry. Sittin' in the Front Pew: A Novel. 2002. 256p. pap. 13.95 (*0-375-75705-8*, Villard Bks.) Random House Adult Trade Publishing Group.

Brown, Rita Mae. Bingo. 1989. 384p. mass mkt. 6.50 o.s.i (*0-553-28220-4*); 1999. 288p. reprint ed. pap. 19.00 (*0-553-38040-0*) Bantam Bks.

Brown, Sandra. Seduction by Design. 1982. mass mkt. (*0-373-45833-9*, Harlequin Bks.) Harlequin Enterprises, Ltd.

—The Switch. l.t. ed. 2000. 691p. 29.95 (*0-7862-2560-2*); 31.95 (*0-7862-2559-9*) Thorndike Pr.

—The Switch. 2000. 600p. E-Book 14.95 (*0-446-92406-7*) Time Warner Bk. Group.

—The Switch. 2001. 600p. E-Book 14.95 (*0-446-91356-1*); 2001. 600p. E-Book 6.95 (*0-446-96100-0*); 2000. E-Book 14.95 (*0-446-93143-8*); 2000. 600p. E-Book 14.95 (*0-446-92269-2*); 2000. 600p. E-Book 14.95 (*0-446-92874-7*); 2000. 480p. 25.95 (*0-446-52703-3*); 2001. 576p. reprint ed. mass mkt. 7.99 (*0-446-60994-3*) Warner Bks., Inc.

Bruckheimer, Linda. The Southern Belles of Honeysuckle Way. 2004. 336p. 24.95 (*0-525-94454-0*, Dutton) Dutton/Plume.

Carey, Edward. Alva & Irva: The Twins Who Saved a City. (Illus.). 224p. 2004. pap. 13.00 (*0-15-602960-X*, Harvest Bks.); 2003. 24.00 (*0-15-100782-9*) Harcourt Trade Pubs.

Carter, Angela. Wise Children. 1992. 232p. 21.00 o.p. (*0-374-29133-0*) Farrar, Straus & Giroux.

—Wise Children. 1991. (*0-316-13053-2*) Little Brown & Co.

—Wise Children. 1993. 240p. pap. 12.95 (*0-14-017530-X*, Penguin Bks.) Penguin Group (USA) Inc.

Castillo, Ana. So Far from God: A Novel. 1994. 256p. pap. 14.00 (*0-452-27209-2*, Plume) Dutton/Plume.

—So Far from God: A Novel. 1993. 256p. 19.95 o.p. (*0-393-03490-9*) Norton, W. W. & Co., Inc.

—So Far from God: A Novel. 1994. 20.05 (*0-606-22208-1*) Turtleback Bks.

Chaikin, Linda L. Tuesday's Child. 2000. (Day to Remember Ser.: Bk. 2). (Illus.). 335p. pap. 10.99 o.p. (*0-7369-0068-3*) Harvest Hse. Pubs.

—Wednesday's Child. 2000. (Day to Remember Ser.). (Illus.). 443p. pap. 10.99 (*0-7369-0069-1*) Harvest Hse. Pubs.

Chappell, Helen. A Whole World of Trouble. 2003. (Illus.). 224p. 23.00 (*0-7432-1529-X*, Simon & Schuster) Simon & Schuster.

Cheska, Anna. Moving to the Country. 2001. 374p. 25.95 (*0-312-28132-3*) St. Martin's Pr.

Ciresi, Rita. Sometimes I Dream in Italian. 2001. 224p. pap. 12.95 (*0-385-33494-X*, Delta) Dell Publishing.

—Sometimes I Dream in Italian. l.t. ed. 2001. (Basic Ser.). 320p. 28.95 (*0-7862-3080-0*) Thorndike Pr.

Clair, Maxine. October Suite: A Novel. 2002. E-Book 19.00 (*1-59061-867-X*) Adobe Systems, Inc.

—October Suite: A Novel. 2002. 352p. pap. 12.95 (*0-375-76095-4*) Random House Adult Trade Publishing Group.

—October Suite: A Novel. 2001. E-Book 19.00 (*1-58836-059-8*) Random Hse., Inc.

—October Suite: A Novel. l.t. ed. 2002. (African American Ser.). 563p. 28.95 (*0-7862-4094-6*) Thorndike Pr.

Cohen, Leah Hager. Heat Lightning. 1998. pap. 12.00 o.p. (*0-380-72928-8*); 1997. 326p. 22.00 o.p. (*0-380-97468-1*) Morrow/Avon. (Avon Bks.).

Collins, Wilkie. No Name. (Works of Wilkie Collins: Vol. 12). 576p. reprint ed. Pt. 1. 1999. lib. bdg. 98.00 (*1-58201-033-1*); Pt.1. 2001. pap. text 28.00 (*0-7426-5033-2*) Classic Bks.

—No Name. 1978. (Illus.). reprint ed. pap. 9.95 o.p. (*0-486-23605-6*) Dover Pubns., Inc.

—No Name. 2002. Vol. 1. 328p. 96.99 (*1-4043-2184-5*); Vol. 1. 328p. per. 91.99 (*1-4043-2185-3*); Vol. 2. 436p. 98.99 (*1-4043-2186-1*); Vol. 2. 436p. per. 93.99 (*1-4043-2187-X*) IndyPublish.com.

—No Name. Blain, Virginia, ed. & intro. by. 1998. (Oxford World's Classics Ser.). (Illus.). 784p. pap. 11.95 (*0-19-283388-X*) Oxford Univ. Pr., Inc.

—No Name. 1987. (Oxford World's Classics Ser.). (Illus.). 590p. pap. 10.95 o.p. (*0-19-281648-9*) Oxford Univ. Pr., Inc.

—No Name. 1992. (BCL1-PR English Literature Ser.). 609p. reprint ed. lib. bdg. 109.00 (*0-7812-7503-2*) Reprint Services Corp.

—No Name. 1995. (Classics Ser.). 640p. pap. 14.00 (*0-14-043397-X*, Penguin Classics) Viking Penguin.

Cook, Karin. What Girls Learn: A Novel. 1997. 23.00 o.s.i (*0-679-44828-4*, Pantheon) Knopf Publishing Group.

—What Girls Learn: A Novel. 1998. 320p. pap. 13.00 (*0-679-76944-7*) Random Hse., Inc.

—What Girls Learn: A Novel. 1998. 19.05 (*0-606-15863-4*) Turtleback Bks.

Cooper, J. California. In Search of Satisfaction. 1994. 21.95 o.s.i (*0-385-46785-0*); 1995. 368p. reprint ed. pap. 13.00 (*0-385-46786-9*) Doubleday Publishing.

Cooper, Susan Rogers. Don't Drink the Water. 2000. (E. J. Pugh Mysteries Ser.). 192p. mass mkt. 5.99 o.s.i (*0-380-80533-2*, Avon Bks.) Morrow/Avon.

—Don't Drink the Water: An E. J. Pugh Mystery. l.t. ed. 2001. 192p. pap. 24.95 (*0-7838-9521-6*); 239p. (*0-7540-4631-1*); 239p. pap. (*0-7540-4632-X*) Gale Group. (Macmillan Reference USA).

Corbin, Steven. No Easy Place to Be. 1989. 19.95 o.p. (*0-671-65884-0*, Simon & Schuster) Simon & Schuster.

Coulter, Catherine. The Maze. 1998. 352p. mass mkt. 7.99 (*0-515-12249-1*, Jove) Berkley Publishing Group.

—The Maze. l.t. ed. 1998. (Large Print Book Ser.). 26.95 o.p. (*1-56895-578-2*, Wheeler Publishing, Inc.) Gale Group.

—The Maze. 1997. 384p. 19.95 o.s.i (*0-399-14264-9*, G. P. Putnam's Sons) Penguin Group (USA) Inc.

Cowell, Stephanie. Marrying Mozart: A Novel. 2004. 368p. 24.95 (*0-670-03268-9*, Viking) Viking Penguin.

Cowie, Vera. Fortunes. 1987. 512p. 18.95 o.p. (*0-525-24570-7*, Dutton) Dutton/Plume.

—Fortunes. 1988. 544p. mass mkt. 4.95 o.p. (*0-451-40094-1*, Onyx) NAL.

Cowley, Joy. Classical Music. 1999. 215p. (*0-14-028838-4*) Penguin Group (USA) Inc.

Crane, Cheri J. Sabrina & Kate. 2000. 281p. pap. 13.95 (*1-57734-660-2*) Covenant Communications, Inc.

Cross, Claire. Double Trouble. 2001. 352p. mass mkt. 6.99 (*0-515-13178-4*, Jove) Berkley Publishing Group.

Crusie, Jennifer. Welcome to Temptation. l.t. ed. 2000. (Wheeler Large Print Book Ser.). 479p. 28.95 (*1-56895-906-0*, Wheeler Publishing, Inc.) Gale Group.

—Welcome to Temptation. 2004. mass mkt. 3.99 (*0-312-93280-4*); 2000. 352p. 24.95 (*0-312-25294-3*); 2001. 416p. reprint ed. mass mkt. 7.50 (*0-312-97425-6*, St. Martin's Paperbacks) St. Martin's Pr.

Culleton, Beatrice. April Raintree. 2nd rev. ed. 1992. 193p. (gr. 7-12). pap. 18.00 (*1-895411-41-6*) Peguis Pubs., Ltd.

—In Search of April Raintree. 1992. 196p. (C). pap. 7.00 o.p. (*1-895411-46-7*) Peguis Pubs., Ltd.

Da Costa, Portia. Hotbed. 2002. 256p. mass mkt. (*0-352-33614-5*, Black Lace) Virgin Publishing Ltd.

Dagg, Jillian. Family Affairs. 1999. 183p. 18.95 (*0-8034-9385-1*, Avalon Bks.) Bouregy, Thomas & Co., Inc.

Davis, Kathryn. Labrador. 1988. 256p. 17.95 o.s.i (*0-374-18251-5*) Farrar, Straus & Giroux.

—Labrador. 2000. 240p. pap. 13.00 (*0-618-07542-9*, Mariner Bks.) Houghton Mifflin Co. Trade & Reference Div.

Dean, Pamela. Juniper, Gentian & Rosemary. 352p. 1999. (J). pap. 14.95 (*0-312-85970-8*); 1998. (YA). (gr. 10 up). 24.95 o.p. (*0-312-86004-8*) Doherty, Tom Assocs., LLC. (Tor Bks.).

DeBerry, Virginia & Grant, Donna. Far from the Tree. 2000. 352p. 24.95 (*0-312-20291-1*) St. Martin's Pr.

Delinsky, Barbara. For My Daughters. l.t. ed. 1994. 445p. lib. bdg. 23.95 o.p. (*0-8161-7403-2*, Macmillan Reference USA) Gale Group.

—For My Daughters. 1994. 288p. 20.00 o.p. (*0-06-017618-0*) HarperCollins Pubs.

—For My Daughters. 1995. 416p. mass mkt. 7.99 (*0-06-109280-0*, HarperTorch) Morrow/Avon.

Desai, Anita. Clear Light of Day. 1980. 183p. o.p. (*0-06-010984-X*) HarperCollins Pubs.

—Clear Light of Day. 2000. 192p. pap. 12.00 (*0-618-07451-1*, Mariner Bks.) Houghton Mifflin Co. Trade & Reference Div.

—Clear Light of Day. 1982. pap. 5.95 o.p. (*0-14-005860-5*) Penguin Group (USA) Inc.

—Clear Light of Day. 192p. 1989. pap. 12.95 o.p. (*0-14-010859-9*); 1986. pap. 6.95 o.p. (*0-14-008670-6*) Viking Penguin. (Penguin Bks.).

Diamond, Diana. The Good Sister. l.t. ed. 2003. 423p. 30.95 (*1-58724-505-1*, Wheeler Publishing, Inc.) Gale Group.

—The Good Sister. E-Book 24.95 (*0-312-70662-6*); 2002. 320p. 24.95 (*0-312-29165-5*); 2003. 352p. reprint ed. mass mkt. 6.99 (*0-312-98468-5*, St. Martin's Paperbacks) St. Martin's Pr.

Dickey, Eric Jerome. Sister, Sister. 1996. 256p. 23.95 (*0-525-94126-6*) Dutton/Plume.

—Sister, Sister. 1997. 368p. mass mkt. 7.50 (*0-451-18802-0*, Signet Bks.) NAL.

—Sister, Sister. 1997. 13.04 (*0-606-15705-0*) Turtleback Bks.

—Sister Sister. 2000. 256p. pap. 13.95 (*0-451-20101-9*, Signet Bks.) NAL.

Dodd, Susan. The Mourners' Bench: A Novel. l.t. ed. 1999. 26.95 (*1-56895-599-5*, Wheeler Publishing, Inc.) Gale Group.

—The Mourners' Bench: A Novel. 1999. 288p. reprint ed. pap. 13.00 (*0-688-16973-2*, Perennial) HarperTrade.

—The Mourners' Bench: A Novel. 1998. 288p. 24.00 (*0-688-15799-8*, Morrow, William & Co.) Morrow/Avon.

Donnelly, Nisa. The Love Songs of Phoenix Bay. (Stonewall Inn Editions Ser.). 1995. 320p. pap. 12.95 o.p. (*0-312-13561-0*, Saint Martin's Griffin); 1994. 304p. 13.99 o.p. (*0-312-11391-9*) St. Martin's Pr.

Drabble, Margaret. A Summer Bird-Cage. 1985. 192p. pap. 8.95 o.p. (*0-452-26050-7*); pap. 6.95 o.p. (*0-452-25761-1*); pap. 9.95 o.p. (*0-452-26472-3*) Dutton/Plume. (Plume).

Drechsler, Debbie. The Summer of Love. 2002. (Illus.). 144p. 24.95 o.p. (*1-896597-37-8*) Drawn & Quarterly Pubns. CAN. *Dist:* Chronicle Bks. LLC.

Duff, Gerald. Graveyard Working. 1994. 185p. 18.00 (*1-880909-15-4*) Baskerville Pubs., Inc.

Dunmore, Helen. Talking to the Dead. 304p. 1998. pap. 13.95 (*0-316-19645-2*); 1997. (gr. 8). 21.95 o.p. (*0-316-19741-6*) Little Brown & Co.

—Talking to the Dead. l.t. ed. 1997. (Core Ser.). 281p. lib. bdg. 27.95 (*0-7838-8329-3*) Thorndike Pr.

Dwyer, Kelly. Self-Portrait with Ghosts. 2000. 272p. mass mkt. 6.99 o.s.i (*0-425-17696-7*) Berkley Publishing Group.

—Self-Portrait with Ghosts. 1999. 320p. 23.95 o.p. (*0-399-14440-4*, G. P. Putnam's Sons) Penguin Group (USA) Inc.

Egan, Jennifer. The Invisible Circus. 1996. 352p. pap. 13.00 (*0-312-14090-8*) Picador.

Ellis, Virginia. The Wedding Dress. l.t. ed. 2002. (Women's Fiction Ser.). 321p. 29.95 (*0-7862-4705-3*) Thorndike Pr.

Eugenides, Jeffrey. The Virgin Suicides. 1993. 249p. 20.00 (*0-374-28438-5*) Farrar, Straus & Giroux.

—The Virgin Suicides. movie tie-in ed. 1994. 256p. reprint ed. pap. 12.95 (*0-446-67025-1*) Warner Bks., Inc.

Evans, Elizabeth. Rowing In Eden: A Novel. 2000. 352p. 25.00 (*0-06-019550-9*) HarperCollins Pubs.

—Rowing in Eden: A Novel. 2001. 352p. pap. 13.00 (*0-06-095470-1*, Perennial) HarperTrade.

Evans, Pamela. Town Belles. 1997. 474p. mass mkt. 13.95 (*0-7472-5166-5*) Headline Bk. Publishing, Ltd. GBR. *Dist:* Trafalgar Square.

—Town Belles. l.t. ed. 1997. (General Ser.). 544p. pap. 22.95 (*0-7862-1115-6*) Thorndike Pr.

Fairweather, Lori. Blood & Water: A Pacific Northwest Mystery. 1999. 321p. 24.00 (*0-688-16118-9*, Morrow, William & Co.) Morrow/Avon.

Ferrars, E. X. Ninth Life. 1992. 200p. reprint ed. 14.95 o.p. (*0-86220-832-7*, Black Dagger) BBC Audiobooks America.

—Ninth Life. l.t. ed. 2001. 265p. pap. 23.95 (*0-7838-9493-7*) Thorndike Pr.

Ferrier, Susan. Marriage. Foltinek, Herbert, ed. & intro. by. 1986. (Oxford World's Classics Ser.). 528p. (Orig.). pap. 6.95 o.p. (*0-19-281743-4*) Oxford Univ. Pr., Inc.

—Marriage. 2nd ed. 1998. (Oxford World's Classics Ser.). 524p. (Orig.). pap. 10.95 o.p. (*0-19-282524-0*) Oxford Univ. Pr., Inc.

—Marriage. 1986. (Virago Modern Classics Ser.). 512p. (Orig.). pap. 6.95 o.p. (*0-14-016126-0*, Penguin Bks.) Viking Penguin.

Ferrier, Susan, et al. Marriage. Foltinek, Herbert, ed. 2nd ed. 2002. (Oxford World's Classics Ser.). 528p. (Orig.). pap. 10.95 (*0-19-283893-8*) Oxford Univ. Pr., Inc.

Fleming, Julie Elaine. Moving Lila. E-Book 22.95 (*0-312-27533-1*); 2000. 212p. 22.95 (*0-312-24409-6*) St. Martin's Pr.

Flynt, Candace. Mother Love. 1988. 352p. pap. 7.95 o.p. (*0-452-26076-0*, Plume) Dutton/Plume.

—Mother Love. 1987. 84p. 17.95 o.s.i (*0-374-21374-7*) Farrar, Straus & Giroux.

—Mother Love. 2003. (Voices of the South Ser.). 360p. pap. 17.95 (*0-8071-2697-7*) Louisiana State Univ. Pr.

Forbes, Leslie. Bombay Ice. 1999. 416p. reprint ed. pap. 13.95 (*0-553-38047-8*) Bantam Bks.

—Bombay Ice. 1998. 400p. 24.00 o.p. (*0-374-11530-3*) Farrar, Straus & Giroux.

—Bombay Ice. (GER.). pap. (*3-548-24703-2*) Ullstein-Taschenbuch-Verlag DEU. *Dist:* International Bk. Import Service, Inc.

Forster, E. M. Howard's End: Authoritative Text, Textual Appendix, Backgrounds & Contexts, Criticism. Armstrong, Paul B., ed. 1998. (Critical Editions Ser.). (C). pap. text 14.20 (*0-393-97011-6*) Norton, W. W. & Co., Inc.

—Howard's End: Complete, Authoritative Text with Biographical & Historical Contexts, Critical History, & Essays from Five Contemporary Critical Perspectives. Duckworth, Alistair M., ed. 1996. (Case Studies in Contemporary Criticism). 499p. (C). pap. text 10.00 (*0-312-11182-7*) Bedford/Saint Martin's.

Fowlkes, L. A. Caught Up. 2003. (Illus.). 152p. per. 9.99 (*0-9723759-0-2*, 10) FowlkesBooks.

Frankel, Valerie. Smart vs. Pretty. 2001. 304p. mass mkt. 6.99 (*0-06-101478-8*, Avon Bks.) Morrow/Avon.

French, Marilyn. Our Father. 1996. mass mkt. 6.99 (*0-345-91020-6*, Fawcett); 1995. 448p. mass mkt. 6.99 o.s.i (*0-345-38490-3*) Ballantine Bks.

—Our Father: A Novel. 1994. 450p. 22.95 o.p. (*0-316-29390-3*) Little Brown & Co.

Garcia, Cristina. Las Hermanas Aguero. l.t. ed. 2002. Tr. of Aguero Sisters. (SPA.). 425p. 28.95 (*0-7862-4796-7*) Thorndike Pr.

George, Anne. Murder Carries a Torch. 2000. (Southern Sisters Mysteries Ser.). 272p. 23.00 (*0-380-97810-5*, Morrow, William & Co.) Morrow/Avon.

—Murder Carries a Torch: A Southern Sisters Mystery. l.t. ed. 2001. (Large Print Bks.). 274p. pap. 23.95 (*1-58724-127-7*, Wheeler Publishing, Inc.) Gale Group.

—Murder Carries a Torch: A Southern Sisters Mystery. 2001. 288p. mass mkt. 6.99 (*0-380-80938-9*, Avon Bks.) Morrow/Avon.

—Murder Gets a Life. l.t. ed. 2000. (Beeler Large Print Mystery Ser.). 234p. 26.95 (*1-57490-290-3*, Beeler Large Print Bks.) Beeler, Thomas T. Publisher.

—Murder Gets a Life: A Southern Sisters Mystery. (Southern Sisters Mysteries Ser.). 1999. 272p. mass mkt. 6.99 (*0-380-79366-0*); 1998. 256p. 20.00 o.p. (*0-380-97558-0*) Morrow/Avon. (Avon Bks.).

—Murder Makes Waves. l.t. ed. 2000. (Beeler Large Print Mystery Ser.). 246p. 26.95 (*1-57490-274-1*, Beeler Large Print Bks.) Beeler, Thomas T. Publisher.

—Murder Makes Waves. (Southern Sisters Mysteries Ser.). 1998. 272p. mass mkt. 6.99 (*0-380-78450-5*); 1997. 256p. 20.00 o.p. (*0-380-97527-0*) Morrow/Avon. (Avon Bks.).

—Murder on a Bad Hair Day. l.t. ed. 1999. (Beeler Large Print Mystery Ser.). 277p. 26.95 (*1-57490-238-5*, Beeler Large Print Bks.) Beeler, Thomas T. Publisher.

—Murder on a Bad Hair Day. 1996. (Southern Sisters Mysteries Ser.). 256p. mass mkt. 6.99 (*0-380-78087-9*, Avon Bks.) Morrow/Avon.

—Murder Runs in the Family. l.t. ed. 2000. (Beeler Large Print Mystery Ser.). 243p. 26.95 (*1-57490-258-X*, Beeler Large Print Bks.) Beeler, Thomas T. Publisher.

—Murder Runs in the Family. 1997. (Southern Sisters Mysteries Ser.). 288p. mass mkt. 6.99 (*0-380-78449-1*, Avon Bks.) Morrow/Avon.

—Murder Shoots the Bull. 2000. (Southern Sisters Mysteries Ser.). 272p. mass mkt. 6.99 (*0-380-80149-3*, Avon Bks.) Morrow/Avon.

—Murder Shoots the Bull: A Southern Sisters Mystery. l.t. ed. 1999. (*0-07-862222-0*) McGraw-Hill Cos., The.

—Murder Shoots the Bull: A Southern Sisters Mystery. 1999. (Southern Sisters Mysteries Ser.). 247p. 22.00 (*0-380-97688-9*, Avon Bks.) Morrow/Avon.

—Murder Shoots the Bull: A Southern Sisters Mystery. l.t. ed. 1999. (Americana Ser.). 358p. 26.95 (*0-7862-2222-0*) Thorndike Pr.

Gilchrist, Ellen. The Anna Papers. 1989. 277p. pap. 16.99 (*0-316-31320-3*) Little Brown & Co.

—The Anna Papers: A Novel. 1988. 192p. 16.95 o.s.i (*0-316-31316-5*) Little Brown & Co.

Glencoe McGraw-Hill Staff. Topics from the Restless, Bk. 1. unabr. ed. 1999. (Wordsworth Classics Ser.). (YA). (gr. 10 up). pap. 21.00 (*0-89061-116-5*, R1165WW) Jamestown.

Goldstein, Rebecca. The Dark Sister. 1993. 288p. pap. 12.95 o.p. (*0-14-017247-5*, Penguin Bks.) Penguin Group (USA) Inc.

—The Dark Sister. 2004. pap. (*0-299-19994-0*) Univ. of Wisconsin Pr.

—The Dark Sister. 1991. 288p. 19.95 o.p. (*0-670-83556-0*) Viking Penguin.

Goudge, Eileen. Such Devoted Sisters. 1992. pap. o.p. (*0-451-17216-7*); 624p. mass mkt. 7.99 (*0-451-17337-6*) NAL. (Signet Bks.).

—Such Devoted Sisters. 1992. 576p. 22.00 o.p. (*0-670-83954-X*, Viking) Viking Penguin.

Grayson, Emily. The Observatory. l.t. ed. 2001. 22p. lib. bdg. 25.95 (*1-58547-150-X*) Ctr. Point Large Print.

—The Observatory. 2000. 192p. 20.00 (*0-688-17439-6*, Morrow, William & Co.) Morrow/Avon.

—The Observatory: A Novel. 2001. 304p. mass mkt. 6.99 (*0-380-81762-4*) Morrow/Avon.

Greenwood, Ed. Silverfall: Stories of the Seven Sisters. 1999. (Forgotten Realms Ser.). (Illus.). 376p. pap. 14.95 (*0-7869-1365-7*) Wizards of the Coast.

Grindle, Lucretia W. The Nightspinners: A Novel. 2003. 304p. 23.95 (*0-375-50776-0*) Random Hse., Inc.

Grosvenor, Linda Dominique. Like Boogie on Tuesday. 2002. 448p. pap. 15.00 (*1-58314-260-6*, Sepia) BET Bks.

—Like Boogie on Tuesday. unabr. ed. 2000. 355p. pap. 14.95 o.p. (*0-9700102-1-4*) Sadorian Pubns.

Grosvenor, Shelia. Like Boogie on Tuesday. 2003. 448p. mass mkt. 6.99 (*1-58314-442-0*, Arabesque) BET Bks.

Grunwald, Lisa. New Year's Eve. l.t. ed. 1997. (Niagara Large Print Ser.). 416p. 29.50 o.p. (*0-7089-5876-1*, Ulverscroft) Thorpe, F. A. Pubs. GBR. *Dist:* Ulverscroft Large Print Bks., Ltd.

—New Year's Eve. 1998. 384p. pap. 13.99 (*0-446-67403-6*) Warner Bks., Inc.

Hall, Rachel Howzell. A Quiet Storm: A Novel. 2002. 256p. pap. 13.00 (*0-7432-2616-X*, Touchstone) Simon & Schuster.

Hall, Sands. Catching Heaven. 2001. (Reader's Circle Ser.). 400p. pap. 14.00 (*0-345-44000-5*, Ballantine Bks.) Ballantine Bks.

Hanauer, Cathi. My Sister's Bones. 1997. 272p. pap. 14.95 (*0-385-31704-2*) Doubleday Publishing.

Hart, Lenore. Waterwoman. 2003. 256p. reprint ed. pap. 14.00 (*0-425-19007-2*) Berkley Publishing Group.

Hay, Elizabeth. A Student of Weather. 2003. 384p. text 24.00 (*1-58243-123-X*, Counterpoint Pr.) Basic Bks.

—A Student of Weather. 2000. 376p. (*0-7710-3789-9*) McClelland & Stewart.

Haynes, David. All American Dream Dolls. 1999. (Harvest Book Ser.). 288p. pap. 12.00 (*0-15-600572-7*, Harvest Bks.) Harcourt Trade Pubs.

—All American Dream Dolls. 1997. 288p. 21.95 (*1-57131-015-0*) Milkweed Editions.

Hazzard, Shirley. The Transit of Venus. 1981. 368p. 3.95 o.p. (*0-425-07511-7*) Berkley Publishing Group.

—The Transit of Venus. 1990. 352p. pap. 13.95 (*0-14-010747-9*, Penguin Bks.) Penguin Group (USA) Inc.

—The Transit of Venus. 1980. 11.95 o.p. (*0-670-72426-2*) Viking Penguin.

Hegland, Jean. Into the Forest. 1998. 256p. pap. 13.95 (*0-553-37961-5*) Bantam Bks.

—Into the Forest. 1996. 208p. 25.95 o.p. (*0-934971-50-1*); pap. 13.95 o.p. (*0-934971-49-8*) Calyx Bks.

Hellenga, Robert R. The Fall of a Sparrow. 1998. 464p. 25.00 o.s.i (*0-684-85026-5*, Scribner) Simon & Schuster.

Hickman, Patricia. Katrina's Wings. 2002. (Five Star Christian Fiction Ser.). 375p. 24.95 (*0-7862-4750-9*, Five Star) Gale Group.

—Katrina's Wings: Miracles Happen in the Most Unexpected Places. 2000. 352p. pap. 10.95 (*1-57856-293-7*) WaterBrook Pr.

Higgs, Liz Curtis. Thorn in My Heart. 2003. (Illus.). 496p. pap. 13.99 (*1-57856-512-X*) WaterBrook Pr.

Hoffman, Alice. Local Girls. 2000. 208p. pap. 12.95 (*0-425-17434-4*) Berkley Publishing Group.

—Local Girls. 1999. 197p. 22.95 o.s.i (*0-399-14507-9*) Penguin Group (USA) Inc.

—Local Girls. l.t. ed. (Thorndike/G. K. Hall Paperback Bestsellers Ser.). 208p. 2000. pap. 28.95 (*0-7862-2010-4*); 1999. 29.95 (*0-7862-2009-0*) Thorndike Pr.

—Local Girls. 2000. 19.00 (*0-606-20422-9*) Turtleback Bks.

Holeman, Linda. Promise Song. 1997. 264p. (YA). (gr. 6-9). pap. 6.95 (*0-88776-387-1*) Tundra Bks. of Northern New York.

Hood, Ann. The Properties of Water. 1996. 288p. reprint ed. pap. 9.95 o.s.i (*0-553-37565-2*) Bantam Bks.

Hyde, Elizabeth. Crazy as Chocolate. 2003. 272p. pap. 14.00 (*0-425-19246-6*) Berkley Publishing Group.

Iles, Greg. Dead Sleep. 2002. 480p. reprint ed. mass mkt. 7.99 (*0-451-20652-5*, Signet Bks.) NAL.

—Dead Sleep. 2001. 352p. 19.95 o.p. (*0-399-14735-7*) Penguin Group (USA) Inc.

—Dead Sleep. l.t. ed. 12.95 (*1-4104-0053-0*, Large Print Pr.); 2003. 703p. pap. 12.95 (*0-7862-3681-7*); 2001. 681p. 30.95 (*0-7862-3682-5*) Thorndike Pr.

Inclan, Jessica Barksdale. Her Daughter's Eyes. 2003. 320p. mass mkt. 6.99 (*0-451-20564-2*, Signet Bks.); 2001. (Illus.). 224p. pap. 12.95 (*0-451-20282-1*) NAL.

—Her Daughter's Eyes. l.t. ed. 2001. (Women's Fiction Ser.). 240p. 28.95 (*0-7862-3472-5*) Thorndike Pr.

Jacobs, Nancy Baker. Double or Nothing. l.t. ed. 2001. (Five Star First Edition Mystery Ser.). 156p. 23.95 o.p. (*0-7862-3010-X*) Thorndike Pr.

James, Breggie. Sister Secrets. 1997. 432p. (Orig.). pap. 12.95 (*0-9659042-0-2*) BeeJay Enterprises.

Jansen, Sheila. Becky Ryan. 2002. 320p. 26.99 (*0-7278-5897-1*) Severn Hse. Pubs., Ltd.

Jewell, Lisa. One-Hit Wonder. 2002. 352p. 23.95 o.s.i (*0-525-94653-5*, Dutton) Dutton/Plume.

—One-Hit Wonder. 464p. (*0-7278-5910-2*) Severn Hse. Pubs., Ltd.

Jewsbury, Geraldine E. The Half Sisters. Wilkes, Joanne, ed. & intro. by. 1999. (Oxford World's Classics Ser.). 448p. pap. 12.95 (*0-19-283757-5*) Oxford Univ. Pr., Inc.

—The Half Sisters. Wilkes, Joanne, ed. 1994. (Oxford World's Classics Ser.). 442p. pap. 11.95 o.p. (*0-19-283114-3*) Oxford Univ. Pr., Inc.

—The Half-Sisters: A Tale, 2 vols., 1 bk. reprint ed. 44.50 (*0-404-61945-2*) AMS Pr., Inc.

Johansen, Iris. And Then You Die. 1998. 352p. mass mkt. 7.50 (*0-553-57998-3*) Bantam Bks.

—And Then You Die. l.t. ed. 1998. (Romance Ser.). 448p. 28.95 (*0-7862-1310-8*) Thorndike Pr.

Johnson, Diane. Le Divorce. (William Abrahams Book Ser.). 320p. 1998. pap. 14.00 (*0-452-27733-7*, Plume); 1997. 23.95 (*0-525-94238-6*); 2003. pap. 12.95 (*0-452-28448-1*, Plume) Dutton/Plume.

—Le Divorce. l.t. ed. 2004. 482p. pap. 25.95 (*1-58724-591-4*, Wheeler Publishing, Inc.) Gale Group.

Johnson, Shawne. Getting Our Breath Back: A Novel. 2002. 224p. 22.95 o.s.i (*0-525-94654-3*, Dutton) Dutton/Plume.

Jones, Annie. The Snowbirds. 2003. 336p. pap. 11.99 (*1-57673-623-7*) Multnomah Pubs., Inc.

—The Snowbirds. l.t. ed. 2003. 25.95 (*0-7862-5490-4*) Thorndike Pr.

Jones, Matthew F. Blind Pursuit. 1997. 256p. 22.00 o.p. (*0-374-11435-8*) Farrar, Straus & Giroux.

—Blind Pursuit. l.t. ed. 1997. (G. K. Hall Mystery Ser.). 301p. lib. bdg. 25.95 o.p. (*0-7838-8224-6*, Macmillan Reference USA) Gale Group.

Joyce, Brenda. Double Take. l.t. ed. 2003. 566p. 30.95 (*1-58724-497-7*, Wheeler Publishing, Inc.) Gale Group.

—Double Take. Date not set. mass mkt. (*0-312-99145-2*, St. Martin's Paperbacks); 2003. 384p. 24.95 (*0-312-28474-8*) St. Martin's Pr.

—House of Dreams. l.t. ed. 2001. (Large Print Book Ser.). 624p. 26.95 (*1-58724-036-X*, Wheeler Publishing, Inc.) Gale Group.

—House of Dreams. mass mkt. 3.99 (*0-312-99885-6*, St. Martin's Paperbacks); E-Book 23.95 (*0-312-27166-2*); 2001. 416p. mass mkt. 6.99 (*0-312-97740-9*, St. Martin's Paperbacks); 2000. 416p. 23.95 o.p. (*0-312-26247-7*) St. Martin's Pr.

Julavits, Heidi. The Effect of Living Backwards. 2003. 336p. 23.95 (*0-399-15049-8*) Putnam Publishing Group, The.

Kazan, Frances. Halide's Gift: A Novel. 2002. 376p. pap. 12.95 (*0-375-75997-2*) Random House Adult Trade Publishing Group.

—Halide's Gift: A Novel. 2001. E-Book 19.95 (*1-58836-018-0*) Random Hse., Inc.

Kear, Cynthia. Searching for Grace. 1998. 24.95 (*0-947993-75-4*) Malvern Publishing Co., Ltd. GBR. *Dist:* British Bk. Co., Inc.

Kelman, Judith. Summer of Storms. 2001. 304p. 24.95 o.p. (*0-399-14674-1*) Penguin Group (USA) Inc.

Keyser, Elizabeth Lennox & Alcott, Louisa May. Little Women. 1997. pap. 13.95 (*0-8057-3896-7*, Macmillan Reference USA) Gale Group.

Kidd, Sue Monk. The Secret Life of Bees: A Novel. l.t. ed. 2002. 474p. 29.95 (*0-7862-4306-6*) Gale Group.

—The Secret Life of Bees: A Novel. 2003. 336p. pap. 14.00 (*0-14-200174-0*) Penguin Group (USA) Inc.

—The Secret Life of Bees: A Novel. 2002. pap. 24.95 (*0-670-03237-9*); 320p. 24.95 (*0-670-89460-5*, Viking) Viking Penguin.

Kirchner, Bharti. Darjeeling. E-Book 24.95 (*0-312-70733-9*); 2002. 320p. 24.95 (*0-312-28642-2*) St. Martin's Pr.

Lambton, Anne. The Sisters. 1976. 1.95 o.p. (*0-425-03181-0*) Berkley Publishing Group.

Landvik, Lorna. Patty Jane's House of Curl. 1999. 304p. (J). mass mkt. 6.99 (*0-8041-1460-9*, Ivy Bks.) Ballantine Bks.

—Patty Jane's House of Curl. l.t. ed. 1998. (Niagara Large Print Ser.). 368p. 29.50 o.p. (*0-7089-5877-X*, Ulverscroft) Thorpe, F. A. Pubs. GBR. *Dist:* Ulverscroft Large Print Bks., Ltd., Ulverscroft Large Print Canada, Ltd.

—Patty Jane's House of Curl: A Novel. 1996. (Reader's Circle Ser.). 320p. pap. 14.00 (*0-449-91100-4*, Ballantine Bks.) Ballantine Bks.

—Patty Jane's House of Curl: A Novel. 1995. 256p. 19.95 o.s.i (*1-882593-12-X*) Bridge Works Publishing Co., Inc.

Larson, Elyse. The Hope Before Us. 2002. (Women of Valor Ser.: Vol. 3). 352p. pap. 12.99 (0-7642-2376-3) Bethany Hse. Pubs.
Lawrence, Carole. Looking for Mary Gabriel. E-Book 23.95 (0-312-70677-4); 2002. 320p. 23.95 (0-312-28541-8) St. Martin's Pr.
Lawrence, D. H. The Rainbow & Women in Love. Beynon, Richard, ed. 2003. (Readers' Guides to Essential Criticism Ser.). 192p. pap. 14.99 o.s.i (1-874166-69-2) Palgrave Macmillan.
—Women in Love. E-Book 4.95 (1-931208-66-2) Adobe Systems, Inc.
—Women in Love. 30.95 (0-89190-612-6) Amereon, Ltd.
—Women in Love. 1996. 560p. reprint ed. mass mkt. 4.95 (0-553-21454-3, Bantam Classics) Bantam Bks.
—Women in Love. E-Book 5.00 (0-7607-1338-3) Barnes & Noble, Inc.
—Women in Love. 1984. 421p. reprint ed. lib. bdg. 27.95 (0-89966-496-2) Buccaneer Bks., Inc.
—Women in Love. Farmer, David H. et al, eds. 1987. (Cambridge Edition of the Works of D. H. Lawrence). (Illus.). 706p. 115.00 o.p. (0-521-23565-0); 705p. pap. 55.00 (0-521-28041-9) Cambridge Univ. Pr.
—Women in Love. reprint ed. lib. bdg. 98.00 (0-7426-3142-7); 2001. 548p. pap. text 28.00 (0-7426-8142-4) Classic Bks.
—Women in Love. 2002. (Thrift Editions Ser.). 400p. pap. 3.50 (0-486-42458-8) Dover Pubns., Inc.
—Women in Love. 1992. 20.00 (0-679-41326-X, Everyman's Library) Knopf Publishing Group.
—Women in Love. 1992. (Everyman's Library). 20.00 (0-679-40995-5) Knopf, Alfred A. Inc.
—Women in Love. 1995. 544p. mass mkt. 6.95 (0-451-52591-4, Signet Bks.) NAL.
—Women in Love. 2002. (Twelve-Point Ser.). lib. bdg. 25.00 (1-58287-180-9); 722p. lib. bdg. 28.00 (1-58287-663-0) North Bks.
—Women in Love. Bradshaw, David, ed. 1998. (Oxford World's Classics Ser.). 576p. pap. 9.95 (0-19-282995-5) Oxford Univ. Pr., Inc.
—Women in Love. (Penguin Great Books of the 20th Century Ser.). 2000. (Illus.). 512p. pap. 12.95 o.s.i (0-14-028337-4); 1960. pap. 2.75 o.p. (0-670-00065-5) Penguin Group (USA) Inc.
—Women in Love. 2000. E-Book 4.95 (0-679-64166-1); 576p. pap. 8.95 (0-375-75488-1) Random House Adult Trade Publishing Group. (Modern Library).
—Women in Love. 1978. 6.95 o.s.i (0-394-60442-3) Random Hse., Inc.
—Women in Love. l.t. ed. 1982. (Charnwood Large Print Ser.). 769p. 29.99 o.p. (0-7089-8049-X, Ulverscroft) Thorpe, F. A. Pubs. GBR. *Dist:* Ulverscroft Large Print Bks., Ltd., Ulverscroft Large Print Canada, Ltd.
—Women in Love. 1998. 15.00 (0-606-21001-6) Turtleback Bks.
—Women in Love. Farmer, David H. et al, eds. 1995. (Twentieth Century Classics Ser.). (Illus.). 592p. 10.95 (0-14-018816-9, Penguin Classics) Viking Penguin.
—Women in Love. 1990. 608p. pap. 8.95 o.p. (0-14-018221-7, Penguin Bks.); 1989. 464p. 18.95 o.p. (0-670-82585-9) Viking Penguin.
—Women in Love. Ross, Charles L., ed. 1982. (English Library). 608p. pap. 4.95 o.p. (0-14-043156-X, Penguin Classics) Viking Penguin.
—Women in Love. 1976. 496p. pap. 7.95 o.p. (0-14-004260-1, Penguin Bks.) Viking Penguin.
—Women in Love. 1995. (Classics Ser.). 464p. pap. 3.95 (1-85326-007-X, 007XWW) Wordsworth Editions, Ltd. GBR. *Dist:* Casemate Pubs. & Bk. Distributors, LLC.
Leavitt, Caroline. Coming Back to Me. mass mkt. (0-312-97987-8, St. Martin's Paperbacks) St. Martin's Pr.
—Coming Back to Me: A Novel. 2003. 320p. pap. 13.95 (0-312-30554-0, Saint Martin's Griffin) St. Martin's Pr.
Lee, Helen E. Water Marked. 1999. 320p. 24.00 o.s.i (0-684-83843-5, Scribner) Simon & Schuster.
Lee, Helen Elaine. Water Marked: A Novel. 2001. 320p. reprint ed. pap. 13.00 (0-684-86573-4, Scribner) Simon & Schuster.
Lehmann, Rosamond. The Echoing Grove. 2003. 304p. pap. 13.95 (1-84408-036-6) Time Warner Bks. UK GBR. *Dist:* Trafalgar Square.
Leith, Prue. Sisters: A Novel. 2002. 304p. 23.95 (0-312-28779-8) St. Martin's Pr.
Lewis, Beverly. The Betrayal. 2003. (Abram's Daughters Ser.). 320p. 17.99 (0-7642-2807-2); 432p. pap. 16.99 (0-7642-2806-4); 320p. pap. 12.99 (0-7642-2331-3); audio 16.99 (0-7642-2808-0) Bethany Hse. Pubs.
—The Covenant. 2002. (Abram's Daughters Ser.: No. 1). 320p. 16.99 (0-7642-2717-3); 320p. pap. 12.99 (0-7642-2330-5); pap. 16.99 (0-7642-2719-X); 400p. pap. 16.99 (0-7642-2718-1) Bethany Hse. Pubs.
Lewis, Jim. Sister: A Novel. 1993. 216p. 20.00 o.p. (1-55597-178-4) Graywolf Pr.
Lewis, Susan. Stolen Beginnings. 1992. 672p. mass mkt. 5.50 o.p. (0-06-100441-3, HarperTorch) Morrow/Avon.
—Stolen Beginnings: A Novel. 1992. 576p. 22.00 o.p. (0-06-017966-X) HarperTrade.
Lively, Penelope. The Photograph. 2003. 240p. 24.95 (0-670-03205-0, Viking) Viking Penguin.
Livingston, Nancy. Two Sisters. 1994. 592p. 25.95 o.p. (0-312-11346-3) St. Martin's Pr.
Long, David. The Falling Boy. 1998. 256p. pap. 12.95 o.s.i (0-452-27997-6, Plume) Dutton/Plume.
—The Falling Boy. 1997. 288p. 22.00 o.s.i (0-684-80034-9, Scribner) Simon & Schuster.
Louard, Janette M. Mama's Girls. 2002. 240p. pap. 14.00 (1-58314-258-4, Sepia) BET Bks.
MacDonald, Ann-Marie. Fall on Your Knees: A Novel. 512p. 2002. pap. 14.00 (0-7432-3718-8, Touchstone); 1998. pap. 14.00 (0-684-83868-0, Touchstone); 1997. 23.00 (0-684-83320-4, Simon & Schuster) Simon & Schuster.
MacDonald, Shari. Love on the Run. 2000. 227p. 23.95 (0-7862-2708-7, Five Star) Gale Group.
—Love on the Run. 1998. (Salinger Sisters Ser.: Bk. 1). 256p. pap. 6.95 (1-57856-084-5) WaterBrook Pr.
Maitland, Barry. Marx Sisters. 2000. (Kathy & Brock Mysteries Ser.). 336p. pap. 6.99 (0-14-029176-8) Penguin Group (USA) Inc.
—The Marx Sisters: A Kathy Kolla & David Brock Mystery. 1999. (Kathy & Brock Mysteries Ser.). 314p. 23.95 (1-55970-474-8) Arcade Publishing, Inc.
Mapson, Jo-Ann. The Wilder Sisters: A Novel. l.t. ed. 2000. 26.95 (1-56895-866-8, Wheeler Publishing, Inc.) Gale Group.
—The Wilder Sisters: A Novel. 1999. 384p. (J). 24.00 (0-06-019116-3) HarperCollins Pubs.
—The Wilder Sisters: A Novel. 2000. 384p. pap. 13.00 (0-06-093107-8, Perennial) HarperTrade.
Maracle, Lee. Ravensong. 1994. 208p. pap. (0-88974-044-5, Press Gang Pubs.) Raincoast Bk. Distribution.
Marciano, Francesca. Casa Rossa. 352p. 2003. pap. 14.00 (0-375-72637-3, Vintage); 2002. 25.00 (0-375-42123-8, Pantheon) Knopf Publishing Group.
Marsh, Jean. The House of Eliott. 1994. 272p. 20.95 o.p. (0-312-10996-2) St. Martin's Pr.
Martella, Maureen. Maddy Goes to Hollywood. 1999. 391p. o.p. (0-434-00780-3) Random Hse. of Canada, Ltd. CAN. *Dist:* Random Hse., Inc.
Martin, Nancy. How to Murder a Millionaire. 2002. 272p. mass mkt. 6.50 (0-451-20724-6, Signet Bks.) NAL.
—How to Murder a Millionaire. 2003. (Mystery Ser.). 359p. 28.95 (0-7862-5391-6) Thorndike Pr.
Martinac, Paula, ed. The One You Call Sister: New Women's Fiction. 1989. 216p. (C). 24.95 o.p. (0-939416-30-1); pap. 9.95 o.p. (0-939416-31-X) Cleis Pr.
May, Julian. Blood Trillium. 1993. 480p. mass mkt. 5.99 o.s.i (0-553-56198-7) Bantam Bks.
McCafferty, Barbara Taylor. Double Dealer. 2000. (Bert & Nan Tatum Mystery Ser.). 250p. 20.00 o.s.i (1-57566-507-7, Kensington Bks.) Kensington Publishing Corp.
—Double Exposure. annuals 1998. (Bert & Nan Tatum Mystery Ser.). 320p. mass mkt. 5.99 o.s.i (1-57566-343-0) Kensington Publishing Corp.
—Double Murder. 1996. 288p. 18.95 o.s.i (1-57566-084-9, Kensington Bks.) Kensington Publishing Corp.
McCafferty, Barbara Taylor & Herald, Beverly Taylor. Double Date. (Partners in Crime Ser.). 2002. 288p. mass mkt. 5.99 (1-57566-732-0); 2001. 256p. 22.00 o.s.i (1-57566-639-1) Kensington Publishing Corp.
—Double Date. l.t. ed. 2001. 336p. 28.95 (0-7862-3326-5) Thorndike Pr.
—Double Dealer. 2000. 272p. mass mkt. 5.99 o.s.i (1-57566-642-1) Kensington Publishing Corp.
—Double Dealer. l.t. ed. 2000. (Mystery Ser.). 352p. 26.95 (0-7862-2835-0) Thorndike Pr.
—Double Exposure. annuals 1997. (Bert & Nan Tatum Mystery Ser.). 288p. 18.95 o.s.i (1-57566-207-8) Kensington Publishing Corp.
—Double Murder. 1997. (Bert & Nan Tatum Mystery Ser.). 288p. mass mkt. 5.50 (1-57566-212-4) Kensington Publishing Corp.
McConnochie, Mardi. Coldwater. 2002. 320p. pap. 14.95 (0-345-44812-X, Ballantine Bks.) Ballantine Bks.
McEwan, Ian. Atonement: A Novel. 2002. E-Book 12.00 (1-4014-4204-8) Barnes & Noble Digital.
—Atonement: A Novel. 368p. 2002. 26.00 (0-385-50395-4, Talese, Nan A.); 2003. reprint ed. pap. 14.00 (0-385-72179-X) Doubleday Publishing.
—Atonement: A Novel. l.t. ed. 2002. 624p. 29.95 (0-7862-3921-2) Gale Group.
—Atonement: A Novel. pap. (1-4000-3514-7) Knopf Publishing Group.
—Atonement: A Novel. unabr. ed. 2002. audio 34.99 (1-4025-1178-7, 01234) Recorded Bks., LLC.
McGlothin, Victor. What's a Woman to Do? 2003. 352p. 19.95 (0-312-28687-2) St. Martin's Pr.
McInerney, Merry. Dog People. 287p. 2000. pap. 14.95 (0-312-87292-5); 1998. 22.95 (0-312-85699-7) Doherty, Tom Assocs., LLC. (Forge Bks.).
McKay, Rena. Golden Echo. 2003. 180p. 25.95 (1-59414-017-0, Five Star) Gale Group.
—Golden Echo. 1985. mass mkt. (0-373-08347-5, Harlequin Bks.) Harlequin Enterprises, Ltd.
McPhee, Martha. Bright Angel Time. 256p. 2003. pap. 14.00 (0-15-602934-0); 1999. pap. 13.00 o.s.i (0-15-600586-7) Harcourt Trade Pubs. (Harvest Bks.).
Medoff, Jillian. Hunger Point. 1998. 544p. mass mkt. 6.99 o.s.i (0-06-101227-0, HarperTorch) Morrow/Avon.
—Hunger Point: A Novel. 2002. 384p. pap. 13.95 (0-06-098923-8) HarperCollins Pubs.
—Hunger Point: A Novel. 1997. 384p. 24.00 o.p. (0-06-039189-8, ReganBooks) HarperTrade.
Messud, Claire. When the World Was Steady. 270p. 1994. 19.95 (0-9645611-0-7); 1995. reprint ed. pap. 11.95 (0-9645611-3-1) Granta.
Michael, Judith, pseud. Deceptions. 1994. 528p. mass mkt. 7.99 (0-671-89954-6, Pocket) Simon & Schuster.
—Deceptions. Grose, Bill, ed. 1989. mass mkt. 6.50 o.s.i (0-671-69382-4, Pocket) Simon & Schuster.
—Deceptions. 1985. mass mkt. 4.50 (0-671-55773-4, Pocket); 1983. mass mkt. 3.95 o.s.i (0-671-46968-1, Pocket); 1982. 500p. 15.95 o.p. (0-671-42491-2, Simon & Schuster) Simon & Schuster.
—A Tangled Web. l.t. ed. 1995. (Large Print Bks.). 25.95 o.p. (1-56895-201-5, Wheeler Publishing, Inc.) Gale Group.
—A Tangled Web. Rubenstein, Julie, ed. 1995. mass mkt. 6.50 (0-671-52548-4, Pocket) Simon & Schuster.
—A Tangled Web. 1994. 464p. 23.00 (0-671-79879-0, Simon & Schuster); 1995. 592p. reprint ed. mass mkt. 7.99 (0-671-53288-X, Pocket) Simon & Schuster.
Michaels, Fern. The Guest List. 2000. (Five Star Romance Ser.). 398p. 27.95 (0-7862-2985-3, Five Star); 468p. 27.95 (1-56895-943-5, Wheeler Publishing, Inc.) Gale Group.
—The Guest List. 2002. mass mkt. 7.99 (0-8217-7602-9); 2000. 4p. mass mkt. 7.50 o.s.i (0-8217-6657-0, Zebra Bks.) Kensington Publishing Corp.
Miles, Cassie. Critic's Choice. l.t. ed. 2002. 217p. 27.95 (0-7862-4262-0) Gale Group.
Miller, Karen E. Quinones. I'm Telling. 240p. 2002. 21.00 (0-7432-1435-8); 2003. reprint ed. pap. 12.00 (0-7432-1436-6) Simon & Schuster. (Simon & Schuster).
Mitchell, Sara. Trial of the Innocent. 1995. (Shadowcatchers Ser.: Bk. 1). 336p. pap. 9.99 o.p. (1-55661-497-7) Bethany Hse. Pubs.
—Trial of the Innocent. l.t. ed. 2000. (Christian Mystery Ser.: Vol. 1). 479p. 24.95 (0-7862-2726-5) Thorndike Pr.
Moriarty, Liane. Three Wishes. 2004. 352p. (Orig.). 24.95 (0-06-058612-5) HarperCollins Pubs.
Mukherjee, Bharati. Desirable Daughters: A Novel. 2003. mass mkt. (0-7868-8976-4) Disney Pr.
—Desirable Daughters: A Novel. 2003. pap. 13.95 (0-7868-8515-7); 2002. 320p. 24.95 (0-7868-6598-9) Hyperion Pr.
Nirgad, Lia. As High As the Scooter Can Fly: A Novel. 2002. 188p. 23.95 (1-58567-313-7) Overlook Pr., The.
O'Brien, Meg. Thin Ice. 1994. 416p. mass mkt. 4.99 o.s.i (0-553-56962-7) Bantam Bks.
O'Connor, Kathleen Sheehan. Different Kinds of Loving. 2000. 346p. (1-902011-14-7) Mount Eagle Pubns., Ltd.
O'Connor, Sheila. Tokens of Grace: A Novella in Stories. 1990. (Illus.). 128p. pap. 9.95 (0-915943-47-6) Milkweed Editions.
Oke, Janette. The Birthright. ltd. ed. 2001. (Song of Acadia Ser.). 288p. pap. 10.99 o.p. (0-7642-8801-6) Bethany Hse. Pubs.
—The Bluebird & the Sparrow. 2003. (Classics for Girls Ser.). (Illus.). 176 p. (J). 9.99 (0-7642-2712-2); 1998. (Women of the West Ser.: Bk. 10). 288p. mass mkt. 5.99 o.p. (0-7642-2099-3, 202099); 1995. (Women of the West Ser.: Vol. 10). 256p. pap. 11.99 (1-55661-612-0); 1995. (Women of the West Ser.). 336p. (J). pap. 12.99 o.p. (1-55661-613-9) Bethany Hse. Pubs.
—The Bluebird & the Sparrow. l.t. ed. 1995. 305p. 22.95 (0-7838-1479-8, Macmillan Reference USA) Gale Group.
Oke, Janette & Bunn, T. Davis. The Beloved Land. 2002. (Song of Arcadia Ser.: No. 5). 288p. 16.99 (0-7642-2723-8); 288p. pap. 11.99 (0-7642-2722-X); pap. 15.99 (0-7642-2725-4); 432p. pap. 16.99 (0-7642-2724-6) Bethany Hse. Pubs.
—The Beloved Land. l.t. ed. 2003. (Song of Acadia Ser.). 494p. 28.95 (0-7862-5087-9) Thorndike Pr.
—The Birthright. 2001. (Song of Acadia Ser.). 288p. pap. 11.99 (0-7642-2229-5); 1p. pap. 15.99 o.p. (0-7642-2231-7); 288p. text 16.99 o.p. (0-7642-2230-9) Bethany Hse. Pubs.
Osborn, Karen. Patchwork. (American Ser.). 1992. 324p. pap. 8.95 (0-15-671365-9, Harvest Bks.); 1991. 309p. 19.95 o.s.i (0-15-171292-1) Harcourt Trade Pubs.
Palmer, Elizabeth. Golden Rule. 1998. 304p. 22.95 (0-312-19274-6) St. Martin's Pr.
—The Golden Rule. l.t. ed. 1998. 455 p. (0-7540-2148-3, Macmillan Reference USA) Gale Group.
—The Golden Rule. l.t. ed. 1998. (Core Ser.). 456p. 26.95 (0-7838-0347-8) Thorndike Pr.
Park, Frances. When My Sister Was Cleopatra Moon. 2000. 243p. 22.95 (0-7868-6647-0) Talk Miramax Bks.
Pastan, Rachel. This Side of Married. 2004. 272p. 23.95 (0-670-03306-5) Viking Penguin.
Pella, Judith. Somewhere a Song. 2002. (Daughters of Fortune Ser.). 432p. 18.99 (0-7642-2720-3); 432p. pap. 13.99 (0-7642-2422-0); 720p. pap. 18.99 (0-7642-2721-1) Bethany Hse. Pubs.
—Toward the Sunrise. 2003. (Daughters of Fortune Ser.). 720p. pap. 16.99 (0-7642-2845-5) Bethany Hse. Pubs.
—Written on the Wind. 2001. (Daughters of Fortune Ser.). 464p. pap. 13.99 (0-7642-2421-2); 464p. text 18.99 o.s.i (0-7642-2608-8); 720p. pap. 18.99 (0-7642-2609-6) Bethany Hse. Pubs.
Peterson, Tracie. A Slender Thread. 2000. 384p. pap. 12.99 (0-7642-2251-1) Bethany Hse. Pubs.
Phillips, Jayne Anne. Shelter. 2002. 336p. pap. 13.00 (0-375-72739-6) Random Hse., Inc.
Plain, Belva. Legacy of Silence. 1999. 432p. mass mkt. 7.99 (0-440-22640-6); mass mkt. 7.99 o.s.i (0-440-29557-2) Dell Publishing.
—Legacy of Silence. l.t. ed. (Paperback Bestsellers Ser.). 471p. 1999. pap. 27.95 (0-7862-1512-7); 1998. 30.95 (0-7862-1511-9) Thorndike Pr.
Powell, Dawn. My Home Is Far Away. 1995. 295p. pap. 14.00 (1-883642-43-4) Steerforth Pr.
Powell, Sophie. The Mushroom Man. 2004. 208p. pap. 14.00 (0-425-19413-2) Berkley Publishing Group.
—The Mushroom Man. 2003. 208p. 23.95 (0-399-14963-5, Putnam & Grosset) Putnam Publishing Group, The.
Prentice-Hall Staff. Pride & Prejudice. 2nd ed. text, stu. ed. (0-13-716978-7) Prentice Hall (Schl. Div.).
Puig, Manuel. Tropical Night Falling. Levine, Suzanne J., tr. 1993. 192p. pap. 8.95 o.p. (0-393-30908-8) Norton, W. W. & Co., Inc.
—Tropical Night Falling. Levine, Suzanne J., tr. 1991. 192p. 19.00 o.p. (0-671-67996-1, Simon & Schuster) Simon & Schuster.
Pym, Barbara. Some Tame Gazelle. 1992. 256p. pap. 10.95 o.p. (0-452-26919-9, Plume); 1983. 252p. 13.95 o.p. (0-525-24178-7, Dutton) Dutton/Plume.
—Some Tame Gazelle. l.t. ed. 1984. (General Ser.). 14.95 o.p. (0-8161-3639-4, Macmillan Reference USA) Gale Group.
—Some Tame Gazelle. 1984. 256p. reprint ed. pap. o.p. (0-06-080713-X, P 713) HarperCollins Pubs.
—Some Tame Gazelle. 1986. 256p. reprint ed. pap. 7.95 o.p. (0-06-097042-1, PL7042, Perennial) HarperTrade.
—Some Tame Gazelle. 1999. 252p. pap. 11.95 (1-55921-264-0) Moyer Bell.
—An Unsuitable Attachment. 1982. 224p. 13.95 o.p. (0-525-24117-5, Dutton) Dutton/Plume.
—An Unsuitable Attachment. 256p. 1983. mass mkt. o.p. (0-06-080653-2, P 653); 1986. reprint ed. pap. 7.95 o.p. (0-06-097055-3, PL/7055) HarperTrade. (Perennial).
Raffel, Dawn. Carrying the Body: A Novel. 2002. 144p. 18.00 (0-7432-2863-4, Scribner) Simon & Schuster.
Raife, Alexandra. The Way Home. 2003. 380p. pap. 13.00 (0-340-82237-6) Hodder & Stoughton, Ltd. GBR. *Dist:* Trafalgar Square.
—The Way Home. l.t. ed. 2003. (Charnwood Large Print Ser.). 432p. 32.50 (0-7089-4964-9) Thorpe, F. A. Pubs. GBR. *Dist:* Ulverscroft Large Print Bks., Ltd.
Random House Disney Staff. Cinderella. 2002. (Illus.). (J). 2.99 (0-7364-2076-2, RH/Disney) Random Hse. Children's Bks.
Raskin, Barbara. Current Affairs. 1991. 336p. mass mkt. 5.95 o.s.i (0-8041-0537-5, Ivy Bks.) Ballantine Bks.
Redwood, John H. The Old Settler. 1998. per. 6.50 (0-8222-1642-6) Dramatists Play Service, Inc.
Reece, Colleen L. In Search of Twilight. l.t. ed. 1999. (Candlelights Ser.). 239p. 20.95 (0-7862-1872-X) Thorndike Pr.
—Nurse Autumn's Secret Love. l.t. ed. 2001. 237p. 23.95 (0-7862-3137-8); (0-7540-4457-2) Thorndike Pr.
Reese, Laura. Topping from Below. abr. ed. 1997. audio 16.95 (1-882071-58-1) B&B Audio, Inc.

—Topping from Below. 1995. 368p. 22.95 o.p. (0-312-12000-1); 4th ed. 1996. 384p. pap. 13.95 (0-312-14435-0, CPB1157, Saint Martin's Griffin) St. Martin's Pr.

Reid, Nicole Louise. In the Breeze of Passing Things. 2003. 22.00 (1-931561-42-7) MacAdam/Cage Publishing, Inc.

Rice, Luanne. Blue Moon. 1994. 352p. mass mkt. 7.50 (0-553-56818-3) Bantam Bks.

—Blue Moon. 1993. 320p. 21.00 o.p. (0-670-84301-6, Viking) Viking Penguin.

—Safe Harbor. 2003. 432p. mass mkt. 7.50 (0-553-58395-6, Bantam); 2002. 352p. 22.95 (0-553-80218-6) Bantam Bks.

—Safe Harbor. l.t. ed. 2002. (Wheeler Large Print Book Ser.). 28.95 (1-58724-183-8, Wheeler Publishing, Inc.) Gale Group.

—Stone Heart. l.t. ed. 2001. 491p. 31.95 (0-7838-9440-6, Macmillan Reference USA) Gale Group.

—Stone Heart. 1990. 320p. 19.95 o.p. (0-670-83267-7, Viking) Viking Penguin.

Richards, Emilie. The Parting Glass. 2003. 464p. (1-55166-709-6, Mira Bks.) Harlequin Enterprises, Ltd.

Roberts, Nora. Brazen Virtue. 2002. 304p. mass mkt. 7.99 (0-553-27283-7, Spectra) Bantam Bks.

—Brazen Virtue. l.t. ed. 2001. 464p. 18.95 (0-375-43112-8) Random Hse. Large Print.

—Montana Sky. 1997. 480p. mass mkt. 7.99 (0-515-12061-8, Jove) Berkley Publishing Group.

—Montana Sky. 1996. 448p. 23.95 o.s.i (0-399-14122-7, G. P. Putnam's Sons) Penguin Group (USA) Inc.

—Montana Sky. 23.95 o.s.i (0-399-14426-9) Putnam Publishing Group, The.

—The Stanislaski Sisters: Natasha & Rachel. l.t. ed. 2001. (Americana Ser.). 667p. 31.95 (0-7862-3366-4) Thorndike Pr.

Robinson, Elisabeth. The True & Outstanding Adventures of the Hunt Sisters. 2004. (Illus.). 336p. 23.95 (0-316-73502-7) Little Brown & Co.

Rochlin, Harriet. On Her Way Home: A Novel. 2001. (Desert Dwellers Trilogy Ser.: No. 3). 270p. 21.95 (1-56474-666-6) Fithian Pr.

Rochow, Eugene George & Krahe, Eduard. Perkin, Kipping, Lapworth - Success Through Sisterhood: A Historical Novel. 2001. (Illus.). 161p. text 33.95 (3-540-41604-8) Springer-Verlag New York, Inc.

Roe, Jill. Angels Flying Slowly. l.t. ed. 1996. 270p. pap. 20.95 o.p. (0-7838-1820-3, Macmillan Reference USA) Gale Group.

—Angels Flying Slowly. 1995. 224p. 20.95 o.p. (0-312-13427-4) St. Martin's Pr.

Rosenberg, Saralee. A Little Help from Above. 2003. 352p. pap. 13.95 (0-06-009620-9, Avon Bks.) Morrow/Avon.

Ross, Marilyn. Message from a Ghost. l.t. ed. 2001. 295p. 26.95 (0-7862-3336-2); (0-7540-4542-0) Thorndike Pr.

Rossner, Judith. His Little Women. 1990. 19.95 o.p. (0-671-64858-6, Simon & Schuster) Simon & Schuster.

—His Little Women. Rubenstein, Julie, ed. 1991. 448p. reprint ed. mass mkt. 5.95 (0-671-70124-X, Pocket) Simon & Schuster.

Roy, Lucinda. The Hotel Alleluia: A Novel. 1999. 368p. 25.00 (0-06-019395-6) HarperCollins Pubs.

Rudnick, Paul. I'll Take It. 1990. 304p. mass mkt. 5.99 o.s.i (0-345-36225-X) Ballantine Bks.

—I'll Take It. 1991. 3.99 o.p. (0-517-06840-0) Random Hse. Value Publishing.

Ryan, James. Seeds of Doubt. 2002. 295p. 22.95 (1-86159-106-3) Orion Publishing Group, Ltd. GBR. Dist: Trafalgar Square.

Saunders, Kate. The Marrying Game: A Novel. 2003. 384p. 24.95 (0-312-31043-9) St. Martin's Pr.

Saxton, Judith A. First Love, Last Love. l.t. ed. 1993. (General Fiction Ser.). 762p. 29.99 o.p. (0-7505-0494-3) Magna Large Print Bks. GBR. Dist: Ulverscroft Large Print Bks., Ltd., Ulverscroft Large Print Canada, Ltd.

—First Love, Last Love. 1993. 22.95 o.p. (0-312-08779-9) St. Martin's Pr.

Schaeffer, Susan F. The Golden Rope. 1996. 480p. 25.00 o.s.i (0-394-58821-5) Random Hse., Inc.

Schaeffer, Susan Fromberg. Golden Rope. 1997. 384p. pap. 12.95 o.s.i (0-449-91284-1, Fawcett) Ballantine Bks.

Schaffert, Timothy. The Phantom Limbs of the Rollow Sisters. 2002. 240p. 23.95 o.s.i (0-399-14900-7, BlueHen Bks.) Putnam Publishing Group, The.

Schmais, Libby. The Perfect Elizabeth: A Tale of Two Sisters. E-Book 22.95 (0-312-27589-7); 2001. 240p. pap. 12.95 (0-312-27080-1, CPB1125, Saint Martin's Griffin); 2000. 228p. 22.95 o.p. (0-312-25225-0) St. Martin's Pr.

Schow, Vione I. Phay Vanneth: Dead or Alive? 2002. 180p. pap. 12.95 (1-55517-605-4, Bonneville Bks.) Cedar Fort, Inc./CFI Distribution.

Schwarz, Christina. Drowning Ruth: A Novel. 2001. (Reader's Circle Ser.). 368p. pap. 14.95 (0-345-43910-4, Ballantine Bks.) Ballantine Bks.

—Drowning Ruth: A Novel. 2000. 352p. 23.95 o.s.i (0-385-49971-X) Doubleday Publishing.

—Drowning Ruth: A Novel. l.t. ed. (Wheeler Press Paperback Ser.). 2001. pap. 12.95 (1-56895-179-5); 2000. 422p. 28.95 (1-56895-959-1) Gale Group. (Wheeler Publishing, Inc.).

Shange, Ntozake. Sassafrass, Cypress & Indigo. 2nd ed. 1996. 240p. pap. 13.00 (0-312-14091-6) Picador.

Shea, Christina. Moira's Crossing. 2001. (Illus.). 256p. pap. 12.95 (0-7434-1057-2, Pocket) Simon & Schuster.

—Moira's Crossing. 2000. 248p. 22.95 (0-312-20347-0); E-Book 12.95 (0-312-27345-2) St. Martin's Pr.

Shortridge, Jennie. Riding with the Queen. 2003. 352p. pap. 12.95 (0-451-21027-1) NAL.

Siddons, Anne Rivers. Fault Lines. 1995. 320p. 288.00 o.p. (0-06-017683-0) HarperCollins Pubs.

—Fault Lines. 1995. 320p. 24.00 o.p. (0-06-017614-8) HarperTrade.

—Fault Lines. 1996. 368p. mass mkt. 7.99 (0-06-109334-3, HarperTorch) Morrow/Avon.

—Fault Lines. l.t. ed. 1996. (Basic Ser.). 602p. 28.95 (0-7862-0570-9) Thorndike Pr.

Simons, Paullina. The Bronze Horseman. Date not set. E-Book 7.99 (0-06-000610-2); 2002. 658p. E-Book 7.99 (0-06-000608-0) HarperCollins Pubs.

—The Bronze Horseman. 2002. 912p. mass mkt. 7.99 (0-06-103112-7, Avon Bks.); 2001. (Illus.). 656p. 26.95 (0-06-019926-1, Morrow, William & Co.) Morrow/Avon.

—The Bronze Horseman: A Novel. unabr. ed. 2001. audio 29.95 (0-694-52553-7, HarperAudio) HarperTrade.

Smiley, Jane. At Paradise Gate. 16th l.t. ed. 2001. 271p. lib. bdg. 27.95 (1-58547-073-2) Ctr. Point Large Print.

—At Paradise Gate. 224p. 1998. pap. 12.00 (0-684-85223-3); 1993. pap. 11.00 (0-671-88533-2) Simon & Schuster. (Touchstone).

—A Thousand Acres. 1997. mass mkt. 9.50 (0-8041-9717-2, Ivy Bks.); 1996. 416p. mass mkt. 7.99 o.s.i (0-8041-1576-1, Ivy Bks.); 1992. 400p. pap. 14.95 o.s.i (0-449-90748-1, Fawcett) Ballantine Bks.

—A Thousand Acres. 1991. 371p. 25.00 o.s.i (0-394-57773-6) Knopf, Alfred A. Inc.

—A Thousand Acres. 1992. 18.05 (0-606-20075-4) Turtleback Bks.

Smith, Danyel. More Like Wrestling: A Novel. 304p. 2004. pap. 12.95 (0-609-80993-8, Three Rivers Pr.); 2003. 23.95 (1-4000-4644-0, Crown) Crown Publishing Group.

Smith, Deborah. When Venus Fell. 1999. 464p. mass mkt. 6.99 (0-553-56279-7) Bantam Bks.

Smith, Thea. She Let Herself Go. l.t. ed. 2002. (Five Star First Edition Women's Fiction Ser.). 365p. 25.95 (0-7862-3704-X, Five Star) Gale Group.

Snelling, Lauraine. Sisters of the Confederacy. 2000. (Secret Refuge Ser.: Vol. 2). (Illus.). 304p. pap. 11.99 (1-55661-840-9) Bethany Hse. Pubs.

—Sisters of the Confederacy. l.t. ed. 2002. 349p. 24.95 (0-7862-3685-X, Five Star) Gale Group.

Spencer, LaVyrle. Forgiving. 1992. 464p. mass mkt. 7.99 (0-515-10803-0, Jove) Berkley Publishing Group.

—Forgiving, Vol. 6. l.t. ed. 1992. (General Ser.). 654p. lib. bdg. 22.95 o.p. (0-8161-5306-X); 16.95 o.p. (0-8161-5307-8) Gale Group. (Macmillan Reference USA).

—Forgiving. 1991. 19.95 o.p. (0-399-03599-0, Morrow, William & Co.) Morrow/Avon.

—Forgiving, Set. abr. ed. 1993. 15.95 o.p. (1-55800-299-5, 41310) NewStar Media, Inc.

—Forgiving. 1991. 384p. 19.95 o.p. (0-399-13599-5, G. P. Putnam's Sons) Penguin Group (USA) Inc.

—Forgiving. 19.95 o.s.i (0-399-13847-1) Putnam Publishing Group, The.

Stahl, Maryanne. The Opposite Shore. 2003. 256p. pap. 12.95 (0-451-20866-8) NAL.

Steel, Danielle. Kaleidoscope. 2000. mass mkt. (0-440-23692-4); 1989. 432p. mass mkt. 7.99 (0-440-20192-6); 1987. 408p. 18.95 (0-385-29594-4, Delacorte Pr.) Dell Publishing.

—Kaleidoscope. 1987. 19.95 o.s.i (0-385-29606-1) Doubleday Publishing.

—Mirror Image. 1999. 560p. mass mkt. 7.99 (0-440-22477-2); 1998. 432p. 200.00 (0-385-33343-9, Delacorte Pr.); 1998. 752p. 31.95 o.s.i (0-385-33331-5, Delacorte Pr.) Dell Publishing.

—Mirror Image. l.t. ed. 1998. 432p. 26.95 (0-385-31509-0) Doubleday Publishing.

Stegner, Wallace. Remembering Laughter. 1996. 160p. pap. 13.00 (0-14-025240-1, Viking) Penguin Group (USA) Inc.

Stirling, Jessica. The Island Wife. 1998. 416p. 24.95 o.p. (0-312-19289-4) St. Martin's Pr.

—Sisters Three. Date not set. pap. (0-312-31432-9); mass mkt. (0-312-98959-8) St. Martin's Pr. (St. Martin's Paperbacks).

—The Sisters Three. 2002. 448p. 26.95 (0-312-30523-0) St. Martin's Pr.

—The Wind from the Hills. 1998. 442p. mass mkt. 13.95 (0-340-67197-1) Hodder & Stoughton, Ltd. GBR. Dist: Lubrecht & Cramer, Ltd., Trafalgar Square.

—The Wind from the Hills. 1999. 442p. 25.95 (0-312-24433-9) St. Martin's Pr.

Stone, Katherine. Katherine Stone: Thee Complete Novels. 1994. 752p. 6.99 o.s.i (0-517-10115-7) Random Hse. Value Publishing.

—Twins. 1997. (Romance Ser.). 464p. 24.95 (0-7862-0904-6, Five Star); 26.95 (1-56895-428-X, Wheeler Publishing, Inc.) Gale Group.

—Twins. 1996. 480p. mass mkt. 6.99 o.s.i (0-8217-5207-3); 1989. mass mkt. 4.95 o.s.i (0-8217-3492-X); 1989. mass mkt. 4.50 o.p. (0-8217-2646-3) Kensington Publishing Corp. (Zebra Bks.).

Summerfield, Lin. Never Walk Behind Me. l.t. ed. 1991. (Magna Large Print Ser.). 389p. o.p. (0-7505-0120-0) Magna Large Print Bks. GBR. Dist: Ulverscroft Large Print Canada, Ltd.

—Never Walk Behind Me. 1993. 214p. 19.95 o.s.i (0-8027-3223-2) Walker & Co.

Swan, Mary. The Deep & Other Stories. 2004. 240p. pap. 12.95 (0-8129-6650-3, Random Hse. Trade Paperbacks) Random House Adult Trade Publishing Group.

—The Deep & Other Stories. 2003. 240p. 23.95 (0-375-50851-1) Random Hse., Inc.

Taggart, Susan. Web of Intrigue. l.t. ed. 2001. (Christian Mystery Ser.). 419p. 23.95 (0-7862-3072-X) Thorndike Pr.

Taggart, Susan M. Web of Intrigue. 1998. (Portraits Ser.). 256p. pap. 8.99 o.p. (0-7642-2069-1, 212069) Bethany Hse. Pubs.

Tan, Amy. The Hundred Secret Senses. 1996. 416p. mass mkt. 7.99 (0-8041-1109-X); mass mkt. 6.99 o.s.i (0-8041-1502-8) Ballantine Bks. (Ivy Bks.).

—The Hundred Secret Senses. 2000. 358p. reprint ed. text 25.00 (0-7881-9204-3) DIANE Publishing Co.

—The Hundred Secret Senses. 1998. 368p. pap. 13.95 (0-375-70152-4, Vintage) Knopf Publishing Group.

—The Hundred Secret Senses. abr. ed. 1995. 24.95 o.p. (0-7871-0565-1, 693129); 39.95 o.p. (0-7871-0566-X, 103131) NewStar Media, Inc.

—The Hundred Secret Senses. 1995. 24.95 o.s.i (0-399-14775-6); 368p. 100.00 (0-399-14115-4) Penguin Group (USA) Inc.

—The Hundred Secret Senses. 1995. 368p. 24.95 o.p. (0-399-14114-6) Putnam Publishing Group, The.

—The Hundred Secret Senses. l.t. ed. 1996. (Paperback Bestsellers Ser.). 568p. pap. 26.95 (0-7862-0597-0); 28.95 (0-7862-0598-9) Thorndike Pr.

Tartt, Donna. The Little Friend. 2003. 640p. pap. 14.95 (1-4000-3169-9); 2002. 576p. 26.00 (0-679-43938-2) Knopf Publishing Group. (Vintage).

Trollope, Joanna. A Spanish Lover. 1994. 384p. pap. 12.95 (0-552-99549-5) Bantam Bks.

—A Spanish Lover. 1998. 368p. mass mkt. 6.99 (0-425-16234-6); 2001. 384p. reprint ed. pap. 14.00 (0-425-18170-7) Berkley Publishing Group.

Tucker, Lisa. The Song Reader. l.t. ed. 2003. 439p. 29.95 (0-7862-6014-9) Gale Group.

—The Song Reader. 2003. 320p. pap. 12.00 (0-7434-6445-1, Downtown Pr.) Simon & Schuster.

Upcher, Caroline. Grace & Favor. 368p. 2002. mass mkt. 6.99 o.s.i (1-57566-903-X); 2001. pap. 14.00 (1-57566-904-8) Kensington Publishing Corp.

Vera, Yvonne. The Stone Virgins. 192p. 2004. pap. 12.00 (0-374-52894-2); 2003. 18.00 (0-374-27008-2) Farrar, Straus & Giroux.

Vida, Nina. Between Sisters. abr. ed. 1996. 17.95 o.p. (0-7871-0658-5) NewStar Media, Inc.

Voeller, Sydell. Her Sister's Keeper. 1994. 192p. 18.95 o.s.i (0-8034-9063-1, Avalon Bks.) Bouregy, Thomas & Co., Inc.

—Her Sister's Keeper. 2001. E-Book 5.00 (0-7599-0223-2) Hard Shell Word Factory.

—Her Sister's Keeper. l.t. ed. 2001. (Candlelight Ser.). 190p. 22.95 (0-7862-3626-4) Thorndike Pr.

Wagman, Diana. Spontaneous. 2000. 261p. 23.95 (0-312-26234-5); 2001. 272p. reprint ed. pap. 13.95 (0-312-28349-0) St. Martin's Pr. (L. A. Weekly Bks.).

Walker, Alice. The Color Purple. Bernard, Andre, ed. 2003. 300p. pap. 14.00 (0-15-602835-2, Harvest Bks.) Harcourt Trade Pubs.

Wall, Judith Henry. Handsome Women. 1991. 576p. mass mkt. 5.99 o.p. (0-451-40258-8, Onyx) NAL.

—Handsome Women. 1990. 528p. 19.95 o.p. (0-670-82652-9, Viking) Viking Penguin.

—My Mother's Daughter. 2000. 432p. 25.00 (0-684-83766-8, Simon & Schuster) Simon & Schuster.

—My Mother's Daughter: A Novel. l.t. ed. 2001. 504p. 28.95 (1-57490-372-1, Beeler Large Print Bks.) Beeler, Thomas T. Publisher.

Wallace, Marilyn. The Seduction. 1994. 304p. mass mkt. 5.50 o.s.i (0-553-56840-X) Bantam Bks.

—The Seduction. l.t. ed. 1999. 255p. 25.95 (1-57490-175-3, Beeler Large Print Bks.) Beeler, Thomas T. Publisher.

—The Seduction. l.t. ed. 1997. (Ulverscroft Large Print Ser.). 432p. 31.50 o.p. (0-7089-3692-X, Ulverscroft) Thorpe, F. A. Pubs. GBR. Dist: Ulverscroft Large Print Bks., Ltd., Ulverscroft Large Print Canada, Ltd.

Weber, Carl. Baby Momma Drama. 2004. 328p. pap. 15.00 (0-7582-0013-7, Kensington Bks.); 2003. 320p. 24.00 (1-57566-908-0) Kensington Publishing Corp.

—Baby Momma Drama. l.t. ed. 2003. (African American Ser.). 29.95 (0-7862-5423-8) Thorndike Pr.

Weber, Janice. Devil's Food. 1996. 480p. 22.95 o.p. (0-446-51772-0) Warner Bks., Inc.

Weber, Katharine. The Little Women. 2003. 256p. 23.00 (0-374-18959-5) Farrar, Straus & Giroux.

Weiner, Jennifer. In Her Shoes. 2003. 448p. pap. 14.00 (0-7434-1820-4, Washington Square Pr.); 2002. 432p. 25.00 (0-7434-1819-0, Atria) Simon & Schuster.

—In Her Shoes. 2003. (Women's Fiction Ser.). 29.95 (0-7862-4942-0) Thorndike Pr.

West, Michael L. American Pie: A Novel. 1996. 79p. 24.00 o.p. (0-06-018357-8) HarperCollins Pubs.

—American Pie: A Novel. 1997. 336p. pap. 13.95 (0-06-098433-3, Perennial) HarperTrade.

Wheeler, Joe L., compiled by. Heart to Heart Stories for Sisters. 2002. (Focus on the Family Presents Ser.). (Illus.). 320p. 12.99 (0-8423-5378-X) Tyndale Hse. Pubs.

White, Stephen. Critical Conditions. l.t. ed. 2000. 27.95 (1-57490-280-6, Beeler Large Print Bks.) Beeler, Thomas T. Publisher.

—Critical Conditions. 1998. (Alan Gregory Ser.). 320p. 24.95 o.p. (0-525-94270-X) Dutton/Plume.

—Critical Conditions. 1999. (Alan Gregory Ser.). 416p. mass mkt. 7.99 (0-451-19170-6, Signet Bks.) NAL.

Wick, Lori. Pretense. 1998. 700p. pap. 12.99 (1-56507-945-0) Harvest Hse. Pubs.

Willett, Jincy. Winner of the National Book Award: A Novel of Fame, Honor, & Really Bad Weather. 2003. 336p. 23.95 (0-312-31181-8) St. Martin's Pr.

Williamson, Kristin. Treading on Dreams. 1998. (0-14-027932-6) Penguin Group (USA) Inc.

Witt, Lana. The Heart of a Thirsty Woman. 368p. 2000. pap. 13.95 o.s.i (0-671-01146-4); 1999. 23.00 o.s.i (0-684-84152-5) Simon & Schuster. (Scribner).

Wood, Monica. Secret Language: A Novel. 1992. 276p. 22.95 o.s.i (0-571-12948-X) Faber & Faber, Inc.

Wright, Richard B. Clara Callan: A Novel. 2002. 432p. 25.95 (0-06-050606-7) HarperCollins Pubs.

—Clara Callan: A Novel. 2003. 432p. pap. 13.95 (0-06-050607-5, Perennial) HarperTrade.

Wykham, Helen. Ribstone Pippins. 1996. 226p. (Orig.). pap. 14.95 (0-7145-3017-4) Boyars, Marion Pubs., Inc.

Yurk, Amy. The Language of Sisters. 2002. (Illus.). 256p. (Orig.). pap. 12.95 (0-451-20700-9) NAL.

## T

### TWINS—FICTION

Abrahams, Peter. Crying Wolf. E-Book 19.95 (0-345-44260-1); 2001. 352p. mass mkt. 6.99 (0-345-43503-6, Fawcett) Ballantine Bks.

Aellen, Richard. Redeye. 1989. mass mkt. 4.95 o.s.i (0-553-28282-4) Bantam Bks.

—Redeye. 1988. 352p. 18.95 o.p. (1-55611-082-0) Fine, Donald I. Bks.

Ambrose, David. Coincidence. 2002. 320p. 23.95 o.p. (0-446-52797-1) Warner Bks., Inc.

Anastas, Benjamin. An Underachiever's Diary. 1999. 160p. pap. 10.95 (0-380-73218-1, Perennial) HarperTrade.

Andrews, V. C. All That Glitters. l.t. ed. 2000. 26.95 (1-56895-236-8, Wheeler Publishing, Inc.) Gale Group.

—All That Glitters. Marrow, Linda, ed. 1995. 352p. 23.00 o.p. (0-671-87574-4, Atria) Simon & Schuster.

—Pearl in the Mist. l.t. ed. 1995. 555p. 19.95 o.p. (0-7838-1165-9); 514p. 24.95 (0-7838-1164-0) Gale Group. (Macmillan Reference USA).

—Pearl in the Mist. Marrow, Linda, ed. 1994. 384p. 23.00 (0-671-75937-X, Atria); mass mkt. 7.99 (0-671-75936-1, Pocket) Simon & Schuster.

—Pearl in the Mist. 1994. 14.04 (0-606-07067-2) Turtleback Bks.

Archer, Jeffrey. Sons of Fortune. 2003. 544p. mass mkt. 7.99 o.s.i (0-312-99353-6, St. Martin's Paperbacks); mass mkt. 7.99 (0-312-99380-3, St. Martin's Paperbacks); 400p. 27.95 (0-312-31319-5) St. Martin's Pr.

—Sons of Fortune. l.t. ed. 2003. 32.95 (0-7862-5462-9) Thorndike Pr.

Babson, Marian. The Cat Next Door. l.t. ed. 2002. (Mystery Ser.). 300p. 30.95 (0-7862-4552-2) Thorndike Pr.

Bar-Zohar, Michael. Brothers. 1993. 400p. 21.00 o.s.i (0-449-90511-X, Fawcett) Ballantine Bks.
Bar-Zohar, Michael & Hastings, Michael. Brothers. 1995. mass mkt. 5.99 o.s.i (0-449-14678-2, Fawcett) Ballantine Bks.
Blaylock, James P. Winter Tides. 352p. 1997. 21.95 o.s.i (0-441-00444-X); 1998. reprint ed. mass mkt. 6.50 o.s.i (0-441-00575-6) Ace Bks.
Bly, Stephen A. The Outlaw's Twin Sister. 2002. (Belles of Lordsburg Ser.: 3). 240p. pap. 10.99 (1-58134-359-0) Crossway Bks.
Bowering, Marilyn. Visible Worlds. 1999. 304p. pap. 13.00 o.s.i (0-06-092926-X) HarperCollins Pubs.
—Visible Worlds. 1998. 304p. o.s.i (0-06-019148-1, HarperFlamingo) HarperCollins Pubs. Canada, Ltd.
Brown, Sandra. The Switch. l.t. ed. 2000. 691p. 29.95 (0-7862-2560-2); 31.95 (0-7862-2559-9) Thorndike Pr.
—The Switch. 2000. 600p. E-Book 14.95 (0-446-92406-7) Time Warner Bk. Group.
—The Switch. 2001. 600p. E-Book 14.95 (0-446-91356-1); 2001. 600p. E-Book 6.95 (0-446-96100-0); 2000. 600p. E-Book 14.95 (0-446-92269-2); 2000. E-Book 14.95 (0-446-93143-8); 2000. 600p. E-Book 14.95 (0-446-92874-7); 2000. 480p. 25.95 (0-446-52703-3); 2001. 576p. reprint ed. mass mkt. 7.99 (0-446-60994-3) Warner Bks., Inc.
Bruckner, Pascal. The Divine Child: A Novel. Neugroschel, Joachim, tr. from FRE. 1994. 214p. 21.95 o.p. (0-316-11404-9) Little Brown & Co.
Carey, Edward. Alva & Irva: The Twins Who Saved a City. (Illus.). 224p. 2004. pap. 13.00 (0-15-602960-X, Harvest Bks.); 2003. 24.00 (0-15-100782-9) Harcourt Trade Pubs.
Carr, Philippa. We'll Meet Again. 1995. mass mkt. 5.99 o.s.i (0-449-14895-5, Fawcett) Ballantine Bks.
—We'll Meet Again. 1993. 368p. 22.95 o.p. (0-399-13805-6, G. P. Putnam's Sons) Penguin Group (USA) Inc.
Carter, Angela. Wise Children. 1992. 232p. 21.00 o.p. (0-374-29133-0) Farrar, Straus & Giroux.
—Wise Children. 1991. (0-316-13053-2) Little Brown & Co.
—Wise Children. 1993. 240p. pap. 12.95 (0-14-017530-X, Penguin Bks.) Penguin Group (USA) Inc.
Cave, Hugh B. Disciples of Dread. 384p. 1989. mass mkt. 4.95 (0-8125-1648-6); 1988. 17.95 o.p. (0-312-93101-8) Doherty, Tom Assocs., LLC. (Tor Bks.).
Chatwin, Bruce. On the Black Hill. 1984. 256p. pap. 14.00 (0-14-006896-1, Penguin Bks.) Penguin Group (USA) Inc.
—On the Black Hill. 1983. 256p. 14.75 o.p. (0-670-52492-1) Viking Penguin.
Chesney, Marion. A Governess of Distinction. 1992. mass mkt. 3.99 o.s.i (0-449-21994-1, Fawcett) Ballantine Bks.
—A Governess of Distinction. l.t. ed. 1999. (Paperback Ser.). 200p. pap. 23.95 (0-7838-8519-9) Thorndike Pr.
Churchman, Deborah. Cross a Dark Bridge: A Novel. 1996. 130p. 14.95 (0-918056-08-X) Ariadne Pr.
Cooley, Nicole. Judy Garland & Ginger Love. 2000. pap. 13.00 (0-06-098744-8) HarperCollins Pubs.
—Judy Garland & Ginger Love. 1998. 304p. 24.00 o.s.i (0-06-039251-7, ReganBooks) HarperTrade.
Corrick, Martin. The Navigation Log: A Novel. 2004. 304p. pap. 13.95 (0-375-76053-9, Random Hse. Trade Paperbacks) Random House Adult Trade Publishing Group.
—The Navigation Log: A Novel. 2003. 304p. 24.95 (0-375-50812-0) Random Hse., Inc.
Cross, Claire. Double Trouble. 2001. 352p. mass mkt. 6.99 (0-515-13178-4, Jove) Berkley Publishing Group.
Cussler, Clive. Trojan Odyssey: A Dirk Pitt Novel. 2003. (Dirk Pitt Adventure Ser.: No. 17). 496p. 27.95 (0-399-15080-3) Putnam Publishing Group, The.
Darcy, Emma. A Marriage Betrayed. 1999. (Harlequin Presents Ser.: Vol. 2069). mass mkt. (0-373-12069-9, Harlequin Bks.) Harlequin Enterprises, Ltd.
—A Marriage Betrayed. l.t. ed. 2000. (Harlequin I Romance Ser.). 22.95 (0-263-16406-3) Harlequin Mills & Boon, Ltd. GBR. *Dist:* Thorndike Pr.
de Loo, Tessa. The Twins. Levitt, Ruth, tr. from DUT. 2001. 356p. reprint ed. pap. 14.00 (1-56947-261-0) Soho Pr., Inc.
Douglas, Marion. The Doubtful Guests. 1993. 192p. pap. 7.99 o.p. (0-920501-92-3) Orca Bk. Pubs.
Duff, Gerald. That's All Right, Mama. 1995. 278p. 21.00 (1-880909-33-2) Baskerville Pubs., Inc.
El Saadawi, Nawal. The Circling Song. 1989. 128p. (C). o.p. (0-86232-816-0); pap. o.p. (0-86232-817-9) Zed Bks., Ltd.
Elliott, Scott. Coiled in the Heart. 2003. 304p. 23.95 (0-399-15038-2, Putnam & Grosset) Putnam Publishing Group, The.
Fairweather, Lori. Blood & Water: A Pacific Northwest Mystery. 1999. 321p. 24.00 (0-688-16118-9, Morrow, William & Co.) Morrow/Avon.
Follett, Ken. The Third Twin. 1998. pap. 7.99 (0-449-45862-8); 1997. pap. text 7.99 (0-449-45794-X); 1997. 480p. mass mkt. 7.99 (0-449-22742-1); 1997. mass mkt. 6.99 o.s.i (0-449-22761-8) Ballantine Bks. (Fawcett).
—The Third Twin. l.t. ed. 1996. 672p. pap. 25.95 o.p. (0-7838-1923-4) Random Hse. Large Print.
—The Third Twin. l.t. ed. 1996. (Large Print Ser.). 25.95 o.s.i (0-679-75897-6) Random Hse., Inc.
Francis, Dick. Break In. 1987. 384p. mass mkt. 5.99 o.s.i (0-449-20755-2, Fawcett) Ballantine Bks.
—Break In. l.t. ed. 1987. (General Ser.). 18.95 o.p. (0-8161-4161-4); pap. 11.95 o.p. (0-8161-4162-2) Gale Group. (Macmillan Reference USA).
—Break In. 2001. 17.95 (0-399-13685-1) Penguin Group (USA) Inc.
—Break In. 1986. 17.95 o.p. (0-399-13121-3, G. P. Putnam's Sons) Penguin Putnam Bks. for Young Readers.
Friedmann, Patty. Odds: A Novel. 2000. 272p. text 24.00 (1-58243-087-X, Counterpoint Pr.) Basic Bks.
George, Melanie. To Die For. 2002. 352p. mass mkt. 5.99 (0-8217-7121-3) Kensington Publishing Corp.
Grayson, Emily. The Observatory. l.t. ed. 2001. 22p. lib. bdg. 25.95 (1-58547-150-X) Ctr. Point Large Print.
—The Observatory. 2000. 192p. 20.00 (0-688-17439-6, Morrow, William & Co.) Morrow/Avon.
—The Observatory: A Novel. 2001. 304p. mass mkt. 6.99 (0-380-81762-4) Morrow/Avon.
Green, Angela. Cassandra's Disk. 2002. 240p. pap. 21.95 (0-7206-1144-X) Owen, Peter Ltd. GBR. *Dist:* Dufour Editions, Inc.
Grindle, Lucretia W. The Nightspinners: A Novel. 2003. 304p. 23.95 (0-375-50776-0) Random Hse., Inc.
Grindle, Lucretia Walsh. The Nightspinners. 2003. 7p. 59.95 (0-7927-2864-5); 9p. 89.95 (0-7927-2865-3) BBC Audiobooks America.
—The Nightspinners: A Novel. 2003. 304p. pap. 11.95 (0-375-75984-0, Random Hse. Trade Paperbacks) Random House Adult Trade Publishing Group.
Gruenfeld, Lee. The Halls of Justice. 1996. 448p. 24.95 o.p. (0-525-94130-4, Dutton) Dutton/Plume.
—The Halls of Justice. 1997. 480p. mass mkt. 6.99 o.s.i (0-451-18806-3, Onyx) NAL.
Grunwald, Lisa. New Year's Eve. l.t. ed. 1997. (Niagara Large Print Ser.). 416p. 29.50 o.p. (0-7089-5876-1, Ulverscroft) Thorpe, F. A. Pubs. GBR. *Dist:* Ulverscroft Large Print Bks., Ltd.
—New Year's Eve. 1998. 384p. pap. 13.99 (0-446-67403-6) Warner Bks., Inc.
Hemingway, Amanda. Poison Heart. 1990. 19.95 o.p. (0-671-70975-5, Simon & Schuster) Simon & Schuster.
Herman, Kathy. Vital Signs. 2002. (Baxter Ser.). 320p. pap. 11.99 (1-59052-040-8) Multnomah Pubs., Inc.
Higgins, Jack. Flight of Eagles. 1999. 336p. reprint ed. mass mkt. 7.99 (0-425-16968-5) Berkley Publishing Group.
—Flight of Eagles. l.t. ed. 1998. 28.95 o.p. (1-56895-655-X, Wheeler Publishing, Inc.) Gale Group.
—Flight of Eagles. 1998. 328p. 24.95 o.p. (0-399-14376-9, G. P. Putnam's Sons) Penguin Group (USA) Inc.
Hinton, Lynne. The Things I Know Best: A Novel. 16th l.t. ed. 2002. 184p. lib. bdg. 27.95 (1-58547-154-2) Ctr. Point Large Print.
—The Things I Know Best: A Novel. 2002. 304p. mass mkt. 7.50 (0-06-104101-7) HarperCollins Pubs.
—The Things I Know Best: A Novel. 176p. 2003. pap. 12.95 (0-06-251728-7); 2001. 20.00 (0-06-251727-9) HarperSanFrancisco.
Holland, Cecelia. The Soul Thief. E-Book 24.95 (0-312-70605-7, Tor Bks.); 2004. 304p. pap. 14.95 (0-312-86997-5, Forge Bks.); 2002. 304p. 24.95 o.s.i (0-312-84885-4, Forge Bks.) Doherty, Tom Assocs., LLC.
Jones, Matthew F. Blind Pursuit. 1997. 256p. 22.00 o.p. (0-374-11435-8) Farrar, Straus & Giroux.
—Blind Pursuit. l.t. ed. 1997. (G. K. Hall Mystery Ser.). 301p. lib. bdg. 25.95 o.p. (0-7838-8224-6, Macmillan Reference USA) Gale Group.
Joyce, Brenda. Double Take. l.t. ed. 2003. 566p. 30.95 (1-58724-497-7, Wheeler Publishing, Inc.) Gale Group.
—Double Take. Date not set. mass mkt. (0-312-99145-2, St. Martin's Paperbacks); 2003. 384p. 24.95 (0-312-28474-8) St. Martin's Pr.
Kelleher, Victor. Voices from the River. 1994. 213p. pap. 14.95 (0-7022-2358-1) Univ. of Queensland Pr. AUS. *Dist:* International Specialized Bk. Services.
Kristof, Agota. The Third Lie. Romano, Marc, tr. from FRE. 1996. 144p. 20.00 o.p. (0-8021-1583-7, Grove Pr.) Grove/Atlantic, Inc.
Kroll, Steven. Loose Tooth. 1984. (Illus.). 32p. (J). (ps-3). 13.95 o.p. (0-8234-0518-4) Holiday Hse., Inc.
—Loose Tooth. 1992. (Illus.). 32p. (J). (ps-3). mass mkt. 4.99 o.p. (0-590-45713-6) Scholastic, Inc.
—Loose Tooth. 1984. (J). 10.19 o.p. (0-606-02729-7) Turtleback Bks.
Lamb, Wally. I Know This Much Is True. l.t. ed. 1998. 949 p. 29.95 (1-57490-164-8) Beeler, Thomas T. Publisher.
—I Know This Much Is True. 2003. 912p. mass mkt. 7.99 (0-06-109764-0); 2000. (0-06-039280-0); 1998. 912p. pap. 16.00 o.s.i (0-06-109812-4) HarperCollins Pubs.
—I Know This Much Is True. 1999. 912p. pap. 16.00 (0-06-098756-1, ReganBooks); 1998. 912p. 27.50 (0-06-039162-6, ReganBooks); 1998. audio 25.00 (0-694-51940-5, 695741, HarperAudio) HarperTrade.
—I Know This Much Is True. unabr. ed. 1999. audio 177.00 (0-7887-2491-6, 95566E7) Recorded Bks., LLC.
Lindsey, Johanna. A Man to Call My Own. 2003. 352p. 25.00 (0-7434-5633-5, Atria) Simon & Schuster.
Lowenthal, Michael. The Same Embrace. 1999. 400p. pap. 12.95 (0-452-27975-5, Plume); 1998. 304p. 23.95 o.p. (0-525-94416-8, Dutton) Dutton/Plume.
Lynn, Elizabeth A. Dragon's Winter. 352p. 1998. 21.95 o.s.i (0-441-00502-0); 1999. reprint ed. mass mkt. 6.50 (0-441-00611-6) Ace Bks.
MacLean, Amanda. Everlasting. 1996. (Palisades Pure Romance Ser.). 316p. pap. 9.99 o.p. (0-88070-929-4, Palisades) Multnomah Pubs., Inc.
Macomber, Debbie. Sooner or Later. l.t. ed. 2000. (Wheeler Softcover Ser.). 346p. pap. 25.95 (1-56895-141-8, Wheeler Publishing, Inc.) Gale Group.
—Sooner or Later. 1998. 368p. mass mkt. 3.99 o.p. (0-06-104475-X) HarperCollins Pubs.
—Sooner or Later. 1996. 368p. mass mkt. 6.99 (0-06-108345-3, HarperTorch) Morrow/Avon.
Maney, Mabel. Kiss the Girls & Make Them Spy: An Original Jane Bond Parody. 2001. 288p. pap. 14.00 (0-380-80310-0, HarperEntertainment) Morrow/Avon.
McCafferty, Barbara Taylor. Double Dealer. 2000. (Bert & Nan Tatum Mystery Ser.). 250p. 20.00 o.s.i (1-57566-507-7, Kensington Bks.) Kensington Publishing Corp.
—Double Exposure. annuals 1998. (Bert & Nan Tatum Mystery Ser.). 320p. mass mkt. 5.99 o.s.i (1-57566-343-0) Kensington Publishing Corp.
—Double Murder. 1996. 288p. 18.95 o.s.i (1-57566-084-9, Kensington Bks.) Kensington Publishing Corp.
McCafferty, Barbara Taylor & Herald, Beverly Taylor. Double Date. (Partners in Crime Ser.). 2002. 288p. mass mkt. 5.99 (1-57566-732-0); 2001. 256p. 22.00 o.s.i (1-57566-639-1) Kensington Publishing Corp.
—Double Date. l.t. ed. 2001. 336p. 28.95 (0-7862-3326-5) Thorndike Pr.
—Double Dealer. 2000. 272p. mass mkt. 5.99 o.s.i (1-57566-642-1) Kensington Publishing Corp.
—Double Dealer. l.t. ed. 2000. (Mystery Ser.). 352p. 26.95 (0-7862-2835-0) Thorndike Pr.
—Double Exposure. annuals 1997. (Bert & Nan Tatum Mystery Ser.). 288p. 18.95 o.s.i (1-57566-207-8) Kensington Publishing Corp.
—Double Murder. 1997. (Bert & Nan Tatum Mystery Ser.). 288p. mass mkt. 5.50 (1-57566-212-4) Kensington Publishing Corp.
McCall, Dinah. Chase the Moon, 1. 1999. (Romance Ser.). 263p. 26.95 (0-7862-1784-7, Five Star); pap. 24.95 (1-56895-705-X, Wheeler Publishing, Inc.) Gale Group.
McCourtney, Lorena. Riptide: A Novel. 2002. (Julesburg Mysteries Ser.: Vol. 2). 336p. (gr. 13 up). pap. 12.99 (0-8007-5777-7) Revell, Fleming H. Co.
McGaughey, Neil. Best Money Murder Can Buy: A Stokes Moran Mystery. 1996. 256p. 21.00 (0-684-19761-8, Scribner) Simon & Schuster.
Michael, Judith, pseud. Deceptions. 1994. 528p. mass mkt. 7.99 (0-671-89954-6, Pocket) Simon & Schuster.
—Deceptions. Grose, Bill, ed. 1989. mass mkt. 6.50 o.s.i (0-671-69382-4, Pocket) Simon & Schuster.
—Deceptions. 1985. mass mkt. 4.50 (0-671-55773-4, Pocket); 1983. mass mkt. 3.95 o.s.i (0-671-46968-1, Pocket); 1982. 500p. 15.95 o.p. (0-671-42491-2, Simon & Schuster) Simon & Schuster.
—A Tangled Web. l.t. ed. 1995. (Large Print Bks.). 25.95 o.p. (1-56895-201-5, Wheeler Publishing, Inc.) Gale Group.
—A Tangled Web. Rubenstein, Julie, ed. 1995. mass mkt. 6.50 (0-671-52548-4, Pocket) Simon & Schuster.
—A Tangled Web. 1994. 464p. 23.00 (0-671-79879-0, Simon & Schuster); 1995. 592p. reprint ed. mass mkt. 7.99 (0-671-53288-X, Pocket) Simon & Schuster.
Miller, Linda Lael. Two Brothers: The Gunslinger. l.t. ed. 1999. 26.95 (1-56895-812-9, Wheeler Publishing, Inc.) Gale Group.
—Two Brothers: The Lawman. l.t. ed. 1999. 27.95 (1-56895-747-5, Wheeler Publishing, Inc.) Gale Group.
—Two Brothers: The Lawman & the Gunslinger. 1998. 320p. pap. 12.00 (0-671-00401-8); 2001. (Illus.). 432p. reprint ed. mass mkt. 7.99 (0-7434-1154-4) Simon & Schuster. (Pocket).
Morgan, Marlo. Message from Forever: A Novel of Aboriginal Wisdom. 1998. 336p. 24.00 o.s.i (0-06-019107-4, HarperCollins) HarperTrade.
Nassauer, Rudolph. Kramer's Goats. 1987. (Illus.). 188p. 24.95 (0-7206-0659-4) Owen, Peter Ltd. GBR. *Dist:* Dufour Editions, Inc.
Novas, Himilce. Mangos, Bananas & Coconuts: A Cuban Love Story. 1996. 168p. 9.95 (1-55885-092-9) Arte Publico Pr.
Ohio, Denise. Blue. 1993. 192p. 20.00 o.p. (0-929701-37-2); pap. 12.00 (0-929701-30-5) McPherson & Co.
Overholser, Stephen. Double-Cross: A Western Story. l.t. ed. 2002. 354p. 25.95 (0-7862-2388-X); 2001. 256p. 23.95 (0-7862-2387-1, Five Star) Gale Group.
Palmer, Joyce. Greenwichtown. 2001. 272p. 23.95 (0-312-26597-2) St. Martin's Pr.
—Greenwichtown: A Novel. 2002. 272p. pap. 14.95 (0-312-28321-0, Saint Martin's Griffin) St. Martin's Pr.
Peterson, Tracie. A Veiled Reflection. 2002. 317p. 24.95 (0-7862-3679-5, Five Star) Gale Group.
Pratt, James Michael. Ticket Home. l.t. ed. 2001. (Large Print Book Ser.). 399p. 28.95 (1-58724-004-1, Wheeler Publishing, Inc.) Gale Group.
—Ticket Home. 2002. 352p. mass mkt. 6.99 (0-312-97989-4, St. Martin's Paperbacks); 2001. 356p. 23.95 (0-312-26633-2) St. Martin's Pr.
Putney, Mary Jo. The Wild Child. 2000. 384p. mass mkt. 6.99 (0-449-00584-4, Ballantine Bks.) Ballantine Bks.
—The Wild Child. l.t. ed. 1999. (Large Print Book Ser.). 28.95 (1-56895-791-2, Wheeler Publishing, Inc.) Gale Group.
Reece, Colleen L. Nurse Autumn's Secret Love. l.t. ed. 2001. 237p. 23.95 (0-7862-3137-8); (0-7540-4457-2) Thorndike Pr.
Richardson, Bill. Bachelor Brothers' Bed & Breakfast. l.t. ed. 1997. 21.95 (1-57490-131-1, Beeler Large Print Bks.) Beeler, Thomas T. Publisher.
—Bachelor Brothers' Bed & Breakfast Pillow Book. 1998. 208p. pap. 10.95 (0-312-19440-4, Saint Martin's Griffin); 1997. 18.95 (0-312-16779-2); 1997. 384p. pap. 11.95 (0-312-17183-8, Saint Martin's Griffin); 1996. 160p. 18.95 (0-312-14546-2) St. Martin's Pr.
Roy, Arundhati. The God of Small Things. 1998. 336p. pap. 14.00 (0-06-097749-3, Perennial) HarperTrade.
—The God of Small Things. l.t. ed. 1997. (G. K. Hall Core Ser.). 471p. 26.95 (0-7838-8296-3) Thorndike Pr.
Roy, Arundhati, contrib. by. The God of Small Things. 1997. (81-86939-00-8) RST Indiaink Publishing.
Rubel, Nicole. Sam & Violet's Birthday Book. 1982. (Snuggle & Read Story Bks.). (Illus.). 32p. (Orig.). (J). (ps-3). pap. 1.95 o.p. (0-380-79095-5, 79095-5, Avon Bks.) Morrow/Avon.
Sala, Sharon. Chase the Moon. 1997. 352p. mass mkt. 6.99 (0-06-108445-X, 15477440, HarperTorch) Morrow/Avon.
Samson, Lisa. The Temptation of Aaron Campbell. 1996. (Highlanders Ser.). (Orig.). pap. 9.99 o.p. (1-56507-390-8) Harvest Hse. Pubs.
Schaeffer, Susan F. The Golden Rope. 1996. 480p. 25.00 o.s.i (0-394-58821-5) Random Hse., Inc.
Schaeffer, Susan Fromberg. Golden Rope. 1997. 384p. pap. 12.95 o.s.i (0-449-91284-1, Fawcett) Ballantine Bks.
Schow, Vione I. Phay Vanneth: Dead or Alive? 2002. 180p. pap. 12.95 (1-55517-605-4, Bonneville Bks.) Cedar Fort, Inc./CFI Distribution.
Scofield, Sandra J. Beyond Deserving. 1992. (Contemporary Fiction Ser.). 320p. pap. 11.95 o.p. (0-452-26907-5, Plume) Dutton/Plume.
—Beyond Deserving. 1991. 310p. 28.00 (1-877946-07-9) Permanent Pr., The.
Scottoline, Lisa. Mistaken Identity. 1999. 496p. 24.00 o.s.i (0-06-018747-6); 608p. mass mkt. 7.99 o.p. (0-06-101419-2) HarperCollins Pubs.
—Mistaken Identity. 2000. 592p. mass mkt. 7.99 (0-06-109611-3, HarperTorch) Morrow/Avon.
—Mistaken Identity. l.t. ed. (Thorndike/G. K. Hall Paperback Bestsellers Ser.). 704p. 2000. pap. 27.95 (0-7862-1976-9); 1999. 30.95 (0-7862-1975-0) Thorndike Pr.
—Mistaken Identity. 2000. 13.55 (0-606-17714-0) Turtleback Bks.
Slouka, Mark. God's Fool: A Novel. 2002. 288p. 24.00 (0-375-40216-0) Knopf, Alfred A. Inc.
Smith, Rosamond, pseud. Lives of the Twins. 1989. 208p. pap. 3.95 (0-380-70656-3, Avon Bks.) Morrow/Avon.
—Lives of the Twins. 1990. 2.99 o.p. (0-517-05960-6) Random Hse. Value Publishing.
—Lives of the Twins. 1987. 208p. 16.45 o.p. (0-671-64468-8, Simon & Schuster) Simon & Schuster.

—Starr Bright Will Be With You Soon. 2000. 272p. pap. 12.95 o.s.i (*0-452-28035-4*, Plume); 1999. 304p. 23.95 o.p. (*0-525-94452-4*, Dutton) Dutton/Plume.

Stansfield, Anita. Gables Against the Sky. 2000. 567p. pap. 14.95 (*1-57734-607-6*) Covenant Communications, Inc.

Steel, Danielle. Mirror Image. 1999. 560p. mass mkt. 7.99 (*0-440-22477-2*); 1998. 432p. 200.00 (*0-385-33343-9*, Delacorte Pr.); 1998. 752p. 31.95 o.s.i (*0-385-33331-5*, Delacorte Pr.) Dell Publishing.

—Mirror Image. l.t. ed. 1998. 432p. 26.95 (*0-385-31509-0*) Doubleday Publishing.

Stewart, Michael. Grace. 1989. 18.95 o.p. (*0-87113-305-9*) Grove/Atlantic, Inc.

—Grace. 1992. 400p. mass mkt. 5.50 o.p. (*0-06-100520-7*, HarperTorch) Morrow/Avon.

Stolz, Karen. Fanny & Sue: A Novel. 2004. 256p. pap. 13.00 (*0-7868-8605-6*) Hyperion Pr.

Stone, Katherine. Illusions. l.t. ed. 1994. 512p. reprint ed. lib. bdg. 20.95 o.p. (*0-8161-5946-7*, Macmillan Reference USA) Gale Group.

—Illusions. 1996. 418p. mass mkt. 6.99 (*0-8217-5247-2*, Zebra Bks.); 1994. 448p. mass mkt. 5.99 o.s.i (*0-8217-4617-0*); 1994. mass mkt. 18.95 o.s.i (*0-8217-4453-4*, Zebra Bks.) Kensington Publishing Corp.

—Thief of Hearts. 2000. 448p. E-Book 4.95 (*0-446-92329-X*) Time Warner Bk. Group.

—Thief of Hearts. 2000. E-Book 4.95 (*0-446-91275-1*) Warner Bks., Inc.

—A Thief of Hearts. 2000. 448p. mass mkt. 7.50 (*0-446-60829-7*) Warner Bks., Inc.

—Twins. 1997. (Romance Ser.). 464p. 24.95 (*0-7862-0904-6*, Five Star); 26.95 (*1-56895-428-X*, Wheeler Publishing, Inc.) Gale Group.

—Twins. 1996. 480p. mass mkt. 6.99 o.s.i (*0-8217-5207-3*); 1989. mass mkt. 4.95 o.s.i (*0-8217-3492-X*); 1989. mass mkt. 4.50 o.p. (*0-8217-2646-3*) Kensington Publishing Corp. (Zebra Bks.).

Strauss, Darin. Chang & Eng. 336p. 2001. pap. 13.00 (*0-452-28109-1*, Plume); 2000. 23.95 o.s.i (*0-525-94512-1*) Dutton/Plume.

—Chang & Eng. l.t. ed. 2000. (Hardcover Ser.). 478p. 25.95 (*1-56895-135-3*, Wheeler Publishing, Inc.) Gale Group.

—Chang & Eng. 2000. o.p. (*0-525-94551-2*) NAL.

—Chang & Eng. 2001. 19.05 (*0-606-22779-2*) Turtleback Bks.

Stryker, Dev. A Wilderness of Mirrors. 2000. (Amelia Pierce Mysteries Ser.). 320p. 24.95 o.s.i (*0-312-86441-8*, Forge Bks.) Doherty, Tom Assocs., LLC.

Sullivan, Mary. Stay. 2000. 183p. pap. 13.00 o.p. (*1-58195-025-X*, Zoland Bks., Inc.) Steerforth Pr.

Suyin, Han. The Enchantress. 1986. 304p. pap. 3.95 o.p. (*0-553-25151-1*); 1985. mass mkt. 3.50 (*0-553-17945-4*) Bantam Bks.

—Enchantress. l.t. ed. 1985. (General Ser.). 520p. 18.95 o.p. (*0-8161-3905-9*, Macmillan Reference USA) Gale Group.

Theroux, Paul. Half Moon Street. 1984. 14.95 o.p. (*0-395-36511-2*) Houghton Mifflin Co.

Thoene, Jake & Thoene, Luke. Heart of Allegiance: A Novel. 2003. pap. 9.99 (*0-7852-6383-7*); 1998. (Portraits of Destiny Ser.: Vol. 1). 420p. pap. 12.99 (*0-7852-7145-7*) Nelson, Thomas Inc.

Thompson, Alice. Justine. 240p. 1999. pap. text 13.00 (*1-58243-053-5*); 1998. 18.00 (*1-887178-65-1*) Basic Bks. (Counterpoint Pr.).

Trollope, Joanna. A Spanish Lover. 1994. 384p. pap. 12.95 (*0-552-99549-5*) Bantam Bks.

—A Spanish Lover. 1998. 368p. mass mkt. 6.99 (*0-425-16234-6*); 2001. 384p. reprint ed. pap. 14.00 (*0-425-18170-7*) Berkley Publishing Group.

Vernon, Claire. The Doctor Had a Double. l.t. ed. 2002. 183p. pap. 23.95 (*0-7862-3938-7*) Gale Group.

—The Dutiful Doctor. l.t. ed. 2002. (Nightingale Ser.). 23.95 (*0-7862-4252-3*) Thorndike Pr.

Weber, Janice. Devil's Food. 1996. 480p. 22.95 o.p. (*0-446-51772-0*) Warner Bks., Inc.

Weis, Margaret & Hickman, Tracy. The Dragonlance Legends. 1988. (Dragonlance Collector's Edition Ser.). 912p. 16.95 o.p. (*0-88038-610-X*) TSR, Inc.

—The Dragonlance Legends. 1988. (Dragonlance Collector's Edition Ser.). 912p. pap. 12.95 o.p. (*0-88038-653-3*) Wizards of the Coast.

Wilson, F. Paul & Costello, Matthew J. Mirage. l.t. ed. 1997. (Mystery-Hall Ser.). 530p. lib. bdg. 24.95 o.p. (*0-7838-2022-4*, Macmillan Reference USA) Gale Group.

—Mirage. 1996. 384p. 23.00 o.p. (*0-446-51976-6*, Aspect); 1997. 352p. mass mkt. 6.99 (*0-446-60473-9*) Warner Bks., Inc.

# W

## WIDOWERS—FICTION

Abresch, Peter. Bloody Bonsai. 1999. (WWL Mystery Ser.: No. 321). per. (*0-373-26321-X*, 1-26321-9, Worldwide Library) Harlequin Enterprises, Ltd.

—Bloody Bonsai. l.t. ed. 1999. (Thorndike Senior Lifestyle Ser.). 360p. 27.95 (*0-7862-1787-1*) Thorndike Pr.

—Bloody Bonsai. 1998. 240p. 21.95 (*1-885173-34-2*) Write Way Publishing.

—Killing Thyme. l.t. ed. 2002. 386p. pap. 25.95 (*0-7862-4336-8*) Gale Group.

—Killing Thyme. 2000. (James P. Dandy Elderhostel Mysteries Ser.). 256p. mass mkt. (*0-373-26356-2*, 1-26356-5, Harlequin Bks.) Harlequin Enterprises, Ltd.

—Killing Thyme. 1999. (Jim Dandy Elderhostel Mystery Ser.: No. 2). 279p. 23.95 (*1-885173-68-7*) Write Way Publishing.

Adler, Warren. Mourning Glory. l.t. ed. 2001. (Wheeler Large Print Book Ser.). 498p. 28.95 o.p. (*1-58724-115-3*, Wheeler Publishing, Inc.) Gale Group.

—Mourning Glory. 352p. 2002. mass mkt. 6.99 o.s.i (*0-7582-0044-7*); 2001. 23.00 o.s.i (*1-57566-898-X*) Kensington Publishing Corp.

—Mourning Glory. E-Book 9.95 (*1-59006-071-7*); E-Book 9.95 (*1-931304-23-8*) Stonehouse Pr., Inc.

Auster, Paul. The Book of Illusions: A Novel. 2002. 336p. 24.00 (*0-8050-5408-1*) Holt, Henry & Co.

—The Book of Illusions: A Novel. l.t. ed. 2003. (Americana Ser.). 453p. 29.95 (*0-7862-4868-8*) Thorndike Pr.

—The Book of Illusions: A Novel: International Edition. 2003. mass mkt. 7.99 (*0-312-99096-0*) Picador.

Auster, Paul, ed. The Book of Illusions: A Novel. 2003. 336p. pap. 14.00 (*0-312-42181-8*) Picador.

Barre, Richard. Bethany. 2003. 64p. 17.95 (*1-59266-038-X*) Capra Pr.

Bell, Michele Ashman. Candle in the Window. 2001. 3.95 (*1-57734-904-0*) Covenant Communications.

Brown, Sandra. Seduction by Design. l.t. ed. 256p. 2002. pap. 29.95 (*0-7862-3353-2*); 2001. 32.95 (*0-7862-3352-4*) Thorndike Pr.

—Seduction by Design. 2002. 240p. mass mkt. 6.99 (*0-446-60310-4*); 2001. (Illus.). 192p. 19.95 o.p. (*0-446-52767-X*) Warner Bks., Inc.

Buchwald, Art. Stella in Heaven: Almost a Novel. 2000. 144p. 23.95 o.s.i (*0-399-14642-3*) Penguin Group (USA) Inc.

—Stella in Heaven: Almost a Novel. l.t. ed. 2000. (Core Ser.). 165p. 31.95 (*0-7838-9308-6*) Thorndike Pr.

Carroll, James. Secret Father. l.t. ed. 2003. 626p. 29.95 (*0-7862-6051-3*) Gale Group.

—Secret Father. 2003. 352p. tchr. ed. 25.00 (*0-618-15284-9*) Houghton Mifflin Co.

Coben, Harlan. No Second Chance. 2003. 352p. 24.95 (*0-525-94729-9*, Dutton) Dutton/Plume.

Cohen, Paula Marantz. Jane Austen in Boca. l.t. ed. 2003. (Thorndike Press Large Print Women's Fiction Ser.). 388p. 28.95 (*0-7862-4973-0*) Thorndike Pr.

Collins, Brandilyn. Capture the Wind for Me. 2003. (Bradleyville Ser.). 352p. pap. 12.99 (*0-310-24243-6*) Zon Bks.

Cooley, Martha. The Archivist. 336p. 1999. pap. 13.00 (*0-316-15846-1*, Back Bay); 1998. (YA). (gr. 8 up). 22.95 o.p. (*0-316-15872-0*) Little Brown & Co.

Cote, Lyn. Lost in His Love. 2000. (Blessed Assurance Ser.: No. 2). 256p. pap. 12.99 (*0-8054-1968-3*) Broadman & Holman Pubs.

Crow, Donna Fletcher. All Things New. 1997. (Virtuous Heart Ser.: Vol. 1). 208p. pap. 11.99 (*0-8341-1674-X*) Beacon Hill Pr. of Kansas City.

—All Things New. 2003. 204p. 25.95 (*1-59414-084-7*, Five Star) Gale Group.

Darty, Peggy. Sundance. 1996. (Palisades Pure Romance Ser.). 252p. pap. 9.99 o.s.i (*0-88070-952-9*, Palisades) Multnomah Pubs., Inc.

Deveraux, Jude. Wild Orchids. 2003. 352p. 25.95 (*0-7434-3712-8*); 560p. 25.95 (*0-7434-6761-2*) Simon & Schuster. (Atria).

Dibdin, Michael. Thanksgiving. 2002. 192p. pap. 12.00 (*0-375-72607-1*, Vintage) Knopf Publishing Group.

—Thanksgiving. l.t. ed. 2001. 213p. pap. 24.95 (*0-7862-3308-7*); 190p. (*0-7540-4501-3*); 190p. (*0-7540-4502-1*) Thorndike Pr.

Elmore, Ronn. Mercy, Mercy Me. 2003. 304p. 22.95 (*0-446-52984-2*, Walk Worthy Pr.) Warner Bks., Inc.

Etteth, Ravi Shankar. The Tiger by the River. 2002. 270p. (*0-385-60363-0*) Doubleday Publishing.

Evans, Shirlee. Winds of Promise. l.t. ed. 1999. (Inspirational Ser.). 163p. 25.95 (*0-7838-8673-X*, Macmillan Reference USA) Gale Group.

—Winds of Promise. 1990. 224p. pap. 7.99 (*0-8361-3506-7*) Herald Pr.

Freedman, J. F. Fallen Idols. 2003. 432p. 19.95 (*0-446-53189-8*) Warner Bks., Inc.

Frey, Stephen. The Day Trader. 2002. E-Book 20.00 (*1-4014-9969-4*) Barnes & Noble Digital.

—The Day Trader. l.t. ed. 2002. 470p. 30.95 (*0-7838-9782-0*) Gale Group.

—The Day Trader: A Novel of Risk & Reward. 2002. 304p. 24.95 (*0-345-44324-1*, Ballantine Bks.) Ballantine Bks.

Gaiman, Neil. American Gods: A Novel. 2001. E-Book 19.95 (*0-06-001062-2*) HarperCollins Pubs.

—American Gods: A Novel. 2001. 480p. 26.00 (*0-380-97365-0*, Morrow, William & Co.) Morrow/Avon.

Handler, David. The Cold Blue Blood. 2002. 320p. mass mkt. 6.50 (*0-312-98610-6*, St. Martin's Paperbacks); 2001. 304p. 23.95 (*0-312-28003-3*, Saint Martin's Minotaur) St. Martin's Pr.

Hannah, Kristin. On Mystic Lake. 2004. 432p. pap. 13.95 (*0-345-47117-2*); 2000. 416p. mass mkt. 6.99 (*0-449-14967-6*, Ballantine Bks.) Ballantine Bks.

—On Mystic Lake. abr. ed. 2000. audio 7.99 (*1-56740-328-X*, 1954, Paperback Nova Audio Bks.); 1999. audio 17.95 o.p. (*1-56740-826-5*, 1604, Nova Audio Bks.); 1999. audio 39.95 (*1-56740-406-5*, 1602, Brilliance Audio Unabridged); 1999. 10p. audio 73.25 (*1-56740-634-3*, 1603, Unabridged Library Editions) Brilliance Audio.

—On Mystic Lake. l.t. ed. 1999. (Large Print Book Ser.). 27.95 (*1-56895-631-2*, Wheeler Publishing, Inc.) Gale Group.

—On Mystic Lake, abr. ed. 1999. audio 17.95 Highsmith Inc.

Hart, Josephine. Oblivion. 1997. 208p. pap. 10.95 o.s.i (*0-14-025318-1*) Penguin Group (USA) Inc.

—Oblivion. 1995. 208p. 19.95 o.p. (*0-670-86612-1*) Viking Penguin.

Hatcher, Robin Lee. Dear Lady. 1997. 368p. mass mkt. 5.99 o.p. (*0-06-108687-8*) HarperCollins Pubs.

—Dear Lady. 2000. (Coming to America Bk.: No. 1). 304p. pap. 10.99 (*0-310-23083-7*) Zondervan.

Johnson, Denis. The Name of the World. 2000. 144p. 22.00 (*0-06-019248-8*) HarperCollins Pubs.

—The Name of the World: A Novel. 2001. 144p. pap. 12.00 (*0-06-092965-0*, Perennial) HarperTrade.

Kaminsky, Stuart M. Retribution. mass mkt. 6.99 (*0-8125-4036-0*); 2001. 272p. 24.95 (*0-312-87452-9*) Doherty, Tom Assocs., LLC. (Forge Bks.).

Koontz, Dean. Sole Survivor. 1997. 416p. mass mkt. 7.99 o.s.i (*0-345-38437-7*); mass mkt. 6.99 (*0-345-41294-X*) Ballantine Bks.

—Sole Survivor. aut. ed. 1997. 25.95 o.s.i (*0-676-52202-5*) Random Hse., Inc.

Landis, Jill Marie. Summer Moon. 416p. 2002. mass mkt. 6.99 (*0-345-44040-4*); 2001. 15.95 (*0-345-44039-0*) Ballantine Bks. (Ballantine Bks.).

—Summer Moon. l.t. ed. 2001. 620p. 30.95 (*0-7862-3453-9*) Thorndike Pr.

Lish, Gordon. Epigraph. 1996. 176p. 22.00 (*1-56858-076-2*) Four Walls Eight Windows.

Lively, Penelope. The Photograph. 2003. 240p. 24.95 (*0-670-03205-0*, Viking) Viking Penguin.

Lyon, Annette. Lost Without You: A Novel. 2002. 201p. 14.95 (*1-59156-019-5*) Covenant Communications.

Miller, Linda Lael. Courting Susannah. 2000. 352p. mass mkt. 7.99 (*0-671-00400-X*, Pocket) Simon & Schuster.

—Courting Susannah. l.t. ed. 2001. (Thorndike Americana Ser.). 477p. 30.95 (*0-7862-3226-9*) Thorndike Pr.

Morris, Gilbert. Pilgrim Song. 2003. (House of Winslow Ser.). 320p. pap. 11.99 (*0-7642-2638-X*) Bethany Hse. Pubs.

Naylor, Phyllis Reynolds. After: A Novel. 2003. 384p. 25.00 (*1-56947-354-4*) Soho Pr., Inc.

Nunes, Rachel Ann. This Very Moment. 2001. 185p. 14.95 (*1-57734-934-2*) Covenant Communications.

Oke, Janette. The Matchmakers. 1997. 144p. text 12.99 o.p. (*0-7642-2002-0*); pap. 12.99 o.p. (*0-7642-2020-9*) Bethany Hse. Pubs.

—The Matchmakers. l.t. ed. 2001. (Illus.). 197p. 25.95 (*0-7862-3256-0*); (*0-7540-4523-4*); (*0-7540-4524-2*) Thorndike Pr.

Palmer, Catherine. Hide & Seek. 2001. (HeartQuest Ser.: Vol. 2). (Illus.). 288p. pap. 9.99 (*0-8423-1165-3*) Tyndale Hse. Pubs.

Parkhurst, Carolyn. The Dogs of Babel. 2004. 288p. pap. 15.00 (*0-316-77850-8*, Back Bay); 2003. 272p. (gr. 8 up). 21.95 (*0-316-16868-8*) Little Brown & Co.

—The Dogs of Babel. l.t. ed. 2003. 384p. 32.95 (*0-7862-5913-2*) Thorndike Pr.

Pearson, Ridley. Parallel Lies. l.t. ed. 480p. 2002. pap. 13.95 (*0-7838-9467-8*); 2001. 32.95 o.p. (*0-7838-9466-X*) Gale Group. (Macmillan Reference USA).

—Parallel Lies. 2001. 368p. E-Book 14.95 (*0-7868-7042-7*); 2001. 368p. E-Book 14.95 (*0-7868-7040-0*); 2001. 368p. E-Book 14.95 (*0-7868-7044-3*); 2001. 368p. E-Book 14.95 (*0-7868-7041-9*); 2001. 384p. 23.95 (*0-7868-6564-4*); 2001. E-Book 14.95 (*0-7868-7191-1*); 2003. 384p. reprint ed. mass mkt. 7.99 (*0-7868-8961-6*) Hyperion Pr.

Pilcher, Robin. An Ocean Apart. abr. ed. 1999. audio 25.00 (*0-7871-1867-2*, 698452, Dove Audio) NewStar Media, Inc.

—An Ocean Apart. 1999. 512p. mass mkt. 6.99 (*0-312-97184-2*, St. Martin's Paperbacks); 1998. 470p. 24.95 o.p. (*0-312-19995-3*) St. Martin's Pr.

—An Ocean Apart. l.t. ed. 1999. (Basic Ser.). 699p. 30.95 (*0-7862-1911-4*) Thorndike Pr.

Plass, Adrian. Ghosts: The Story of a Reunion. 2003. 206p. pap. 11.99 (*0-551-03110-7*); 224p. pap. 10.99 (*0-310-24917-1*) Zondervan.

Poulson, Clair. Conflict of Interest: A Novel. 2003. 296p. 14.95 (*1-59156-209-0*) Covenant Communications.

Reding, Jaclyn. White Mist. l.t. ed. 2001. (G. K. Hall Core Ser.). 367p. 28.95 (*0-7838-9428-7*, Macmillan Reference USA) Gale Group.

Rice, Luanne. The Secret Hour. 2004. 432p. mass mkt. 7.50 (*0-553-58401-4*); 2003. 352p. 22.95 (*0-553-80224-0*) Bantam Bks.

—The Secret Hour. 2003. (Core Ser.). 482p. 31.95 (*0-7862-5371-1*) Thorndike Pr.

Rossi, Agnes. The Houseguest. 2000. 304p. reprint ed. 13.00 o.s.i (*0-452-28197-0*, Plume) Dutton/Plume.

—The Houseguest: A Novel. l.t. ed. 2000. (Americana Ser.). 504p. 28.95 (*0-7862-2547-5*) Thorndike Pr.

Schumacher, Barrett. Fear Itself. 2002. 384p. 26.95 (*0-7653-0130-X*, Forge Bks.) Doherty, Tom Assocs., LLC.

Scott, Joanna. Fading, My Parmacheene Belle. 1996. 288p. pap. 14.00 o.p. (*0-8050-3972-4*, Owl Bks.) Holt, Henry & Co.

—Fading, My Parmacheene Belle. 1987. 17.45 (*0-89919-451-6*) Houghton Mifflin Co.

Searcy, David. Ordinary Horror. 2001. 224p. 24.95 o.p. (*0-670-89476-1*, Viking) Viking Penguin.

Smurthwaite, Donald. Letters by a Half-Moon. 2003. 142p. (*1-59038-175-0*) Deseret Bk. Co.

Sparks, Nicholas. A Bend in the Road. l.t. ed. 2001. 544p. 23.95 (*0-375-43083-0*) Random Hse. Large Print.

—A Bend in the Road. 2001. 352p. 23.95 o.p. (*0-446-52778-5*) Warner Bks., Inc.

—Message in a Bottle. l.t. ed. (Paperback Bestsellers Ser.). 464p. 1999. pap. 27.95 (*0-7862-1423-6*); 1998. 30.95 (*0-7862-1422-8*) Thorndike Pr.

—Message in a Bottle. 2000. 288p. E-Book 4.95 (*0-446-92352-4*) Time Warner Bk. Group.

—Message in a Bottle. 2000. 288p. E-Book 5.95 (*0-446-96104-3*); 2000. 214p. E-Book 5.95 (*0-446-96076-4*); 2000. 214p. E-Book 5.95 (*0-446-92009-6*); 2000. E-Book 5.95 (*0-446-93041-5*); 2000. 288p. E-Book 5.95 (*0-446-96021-7*); 2000. 288p. E-Book 4.95 (*0-446-91460-6*); 1998. 336p. 20.00 (*0-446-52356-9*); 1999. 352p. reprint ed. pap. 12.95 (*0-446-67607-1*); 1999. 384p. reprint ed. mass mkt. 7.50 (*0-446-60681-2*) Warner Bks., Inc.

Sparks, Nicholas & South, Nigel. Message in a Bottle. 1983. 192p. text 49.95 o.p. (*0-566-00621-9*) Ashgate Publishing Co.

Spencer, LaVyrle. Then Came Heaven. 368p. 2003. pap. 10.00 (*0-425-19576-7*); 1999. reprint ed. pap. 7.99 (*0-515-12462-1*, Jove) Berkley Publishing Group.

—Then Came Heaven. l.t. ed. 1998. (Large Print Book Ser.). 28.95 (*1-56895-535-9*, Wheeler Publishing, Inc.) Gale Group.

—Then Came Heaven. abr. ed. 1997. 18.00 o.p. (*0-7871-1676-9*, 395617) NewStar Media, Inc.

—Then Came Heaven. 1997. xiii, 332p. 24.95 o.p. (*0-399-14369-6*, G. P. Putnam's Sons); 24.95 o.s.i (*0-399-14699-7*) Penguin Group (USA) Inc.

—Then Came Heaven. l.t. ed. 2000. (Charnwood Large Print Ser.). 376p. (*0-7089-9139-4*, Ulverscroft) Thorpe, F. A. Pubs. GBR. *Dist:* Ulverscroft Large Print Bks., Ltd., Ulverscroft Large Print Canada, Ltd.

Stansfield, Anita. When Hearts Meet. 2001. (Illus.). 130p. 12.95 (*1-57734-855-9*) Covenant Communications.

Taylor, Andrew. Judgement of Strangers. pap. 14.95 (*0-312-28730-5*, Saint Martin's Griffin); 1998. (Roth Trilogy Ser.: Vol. 2). 304p. 22.95 o.p. (*0-312-19292-4*, Saint Martin's Minotaur) St. Martin's Pr.

Thayer, Cynthia. Certain Slant of Light. 2000. 259p. 23.95 (*0-312-26132-2*) St. Martin's Pr.

—A Certain Slant of Light. E-Book 23.95 (*0-312-27591-9*); 2001. 288p. pap. 12.95 (*0-312-27564-1*, Saint Martin's Griffin) St. Martin's Pr.

Thurlow, Kathy. Mrs. Love. 2001. (Five Star First Edition Romance Ser.). 247p. 25.95 (*0-7862-3385-0*, Five Star) Gale Group.

—Mrs. Love. 1999. E-Book 5.50 (*1-58200-268-1*); 248p. E-Book 5.50 (*1-58200-148-0*) Hard Shell Word Factory.

Wallant, Edward Lewis. The Human Season. 1973. 192p. reprint ed. pap. 1.65 o.p. (*0-15-642330-8*, Harvest Bks.) Harcourt Trade Pubs.

—The Human Season. 1998. (Library of Modern Jewish Literature). 181p. pap. text 16.95 (*0-8156-0560-9*) Syracuse Univ. Pr.

Wick, Lori. The Long Road Home. 1991. (Fireside Ser.). 224p. pap. 6.99 o.s.i (*0-89081-885-1*); 1997. (Place Called Home Ser.: Vol. 3). 192p. reprint ed. pap. 8.99 (*1-56507-590-0*) Harvest Hse. Pubs.

—The Long Road Home. l.t. ed. 2001. (Christian Romance Ser.). (Illus.). 288p. 25.95 o.p. (*0-7862-2956-X*) Thorndike Pr.

—Sophie's Heart. 1995. 425p. pap. 10.99 (*1-56507-311-8*); 2nd ed. 2003. reprint ed. mass mkt. 6.99 (*0-7369-1279-7*) Harvest Hse. Pubs.

—Sophie's Heart. l.t. ed. 1999. (Romance Ser.). 643p. 28.95 (*0-7838-0432-6*) Thorndike Pr.

Yehoshua, A. B. Five Seasons. 1990. 36p. pap. 9.95 o.p. (*0-525-48555-4*, Dutton) Dutton/Plume.

—Five Seasons. Date not set. pap. (*0-15-601089-5*, Harvest Bks.) Harcourt Trade Pubs.

**WIDOWS—FICTION**

Adams, Alice. Medicine Men. l.t. ed. 2000. 302p. lib. bdg. 28.95 (*1-58547-022-8*) Ctr. Point Large Print.

—Medicine Men, 000. 1997. 23.00 o.p. (*0-676-52928-3*) Random Hse., Inc.

—Medicine Men. 1998. 256p. pap. 14.00 (*0-671-02067-6*, Washington Square Pr.) Simon & Schuster.

Agee, Jonis. South of Resurrection. 1998. 368p. pap. 12.95 (*0-14-024172-8*) Penguin Group (USA) Inc.

—South of Resurrection. 1997. 360p. 24.95 o.p. (*0-670-85809-9*) Viking Penguin.

Ahern, Cecelia. P.S. I Love You. 2004. 23.95 (*1-4013-0090-1*) Hyperion Pr.

Alers, Rochelle. Gentle Yearning. 1998. (Indigo Love Stories Ser.). 213p. pap. 10.95 (*1-885478-24-0*) Genesis Pr., Inc.

Allingham, Margery. Safer Than Love. 17.95 (*0-89190-166-3*) Amereon, Ltd.

—Safer Than Love. l.t. ed. 2000. (Nightingale Ser.). 172p. pap. 21.95 (*0-7838-9096-6*) Thorndike Pr.

Atwood, Margaret. The Blind Assassin. 2000. 544p. 26.00 (*0-385-47572-1*, Talese, Nan A.) Doubleday Publishing.

—The Blind Assassin. pap. (*0-385-72856-5*) Knopf Publishing Group.

—The Blind Assassin. 2001. 544p. pap. 14.95 (*0-385-72095-5*, Knopf Bks. for Young Readers) Random Hse. Children's Bks.

—The Blind Assassin. l.t. ed. 2000. 832p. 26.00 (*0-375-43085-7*) Random Hse. Large Print.

Austin, Lynn N. Hidden Places. 2001. 432p. pap. 12.99 (*0-7642-2197-3*) Bethany Hse. Pubs.

Ballard, Mignon F. The War in Sallie's Station. 275p. 2003. pap. 13.95 (*1-4104-0117-0*, Five Star Trade); 2001. 25.95 (*0-7862-3377-X*, Five Star) Gale Group.

Barker, Pat. Mind to Kill. 2003. 272p. 23.00 (*0-374-20905-7*) Farrar, Straus & Giroux.

Barkley, Brad. Alison's Automotive Repair Manual: A Novel. 288p. 2004. pap. 13.95 (*0-312-32579-7*, Saint Martin's Griffin); 2003. (Illus.). 23.95 (*0-312-29138-8*) St. Martin's Pr.

Bell, Michele Ashman. Yesterday's Love. 2000. 14.95 (*1-57734-602-5*) Covenant Communications, Inc.

Benedict, Elizabeth. Almost. 2001. 256p. tchr. ed. 24.00 (*0-618-14332-7*) Houghton Mifflin Co.

Beresford-Howe, Constance. A Serious Widow. 1993. pap. (*0-7710-1103-2*) McClelland & Stewart/Tundra Bks.

Beverley, Jo. The Devil's Heiress. 2001. 384p. mass mkt. 6.99 (*0-451-20254-6*, Signet Bks.) NAL.

Blevins, Meredith. The Hummingbird Wizard. Date not set. mass mkt. (*0-7653-4683-4*, Forge Bks.); E-Book 18.95 (*0-312-71097-6*, Tor Bks.); 2003. (Illus.). 400p. 24.95 o.s.i (*0-7653-0769-3*, Forge Bks.) Doherty, Tom Assocs., LLC.

Bly, Stephen A. The General's Notorious Widow. 2001. (Belles of Lordsburg Ser.: Vol. 2). 240p. pap. 10.99 (*1-58134-280-2*) Crossway Bks.

—The General's Notorious Widow. l.t. ed. 2002. 397p. (Belles of Lordsburg Ser.: No. 2). pap. 16.95 (*1-4104-0033-6*, Walker Large Print); 26.95 (*0-7862-4023-7*) Gale Group.

Brett, Simon. Mrs. Pargeter's Package. 1991. 288p. 18.95 o.s.i (*0-684-19286-1*, Macmillan Reference USA) Gale Group.

—Mrs. Pargeter's Package. unabr. ed. 2001. audio 54.95 (*1-85089-648-8*, 91061); 1999. audio compact disk 59.95 (*0-7531-0711-2*, 107112) ISIS Audio Bks. GBR. *Dist:* Ulverscroft Large Print Bks., Ltd.

—Mrs. Pargeter's Package. l.t. ed. 1991. (Magna Large Print Ser.). 270p. o.p. (*0-7505-0130-8*) Magna Large Print Bks. GBR. *Dist:* Ulverscroft Large Print Canada, Ltd.

—Mrs. Pargeter's Package. 1992. 224p. mass mkt. 4.99 (*0-446-36204-2*) Warner Bks., Inc.

—Mrs. Pargeter's Plot. 1999. (WWL Mystery Ser.: No. 322). per. (*0-373-26322-8*, 1-26322-7, Worldwide Library) Harlequin Enterprises, Ltd.

—Mrs. Pargeter's Plot, unabr. ed. 2001. audio 49.95 (*0-7531-0103-3*, 961001); 2000. audio compact disk 59.95 (*0-7531-0904-2*, 109042) ISIS Audio Bks. GBR. *Dist:* Ulverscroft Large Print Bks., Ltd.

—Mrs. Pargeter's Plot. l.t. ed. 1998. (Magna Large Print Ser.). 320p. o.p. (*0-7505-1284-9*) Magna Large Print Bks. GBR. *Dist:* Ulverscroft Large Print Canada, Ltd.

—Mrs. Pargeter's Plot. 1998. (Mrs. Pargeter Mysteries Ser.). 256p. 22.00 (*0-684-83714-5*, Scribner) Simon & Schuster.

—Mrs. Pargeter's Plot. l.t. ed. 1998. (Mystery Ser.). 255p. 30.95 (*0-7838-0172-6*) Thorndike Pr.

—Mrs. Pargeter's Point of Honour. 2003. (Mystery Ser.). 28.95 (*1-57490-465-5*) Beeler, Thomas T. Publisher.

—Mrs. Pargeter's Point of Honour. 2000. (Mrs. Pargeter Mysteries Ser.). 256p. mass mkt. (*0-373-26361-9*, 1-26361-5, Worldwide Library) Harlequin Enterprises, Ltd.

—Mrs. Pargeter's Point of Honour, unabr. ed. 1999. audio 54.95 (*0-7531-0466-0*, 981201) ISIS Audio Bks. GBR. *Dist:* Ulverscroft Large Print Bks., Ltd.

—Mrs. Pargeter's Point of Honour. l.t. ed. 1999. (Magna Large Print Ser.). 320p. o.p. (*0-7505-1394-2*) Magna Large Print Bks. GBR. *Dist:* Ulverscroft Large Print Canada, Ltd.

—Mrs. Pargeter's Point of Honour. 272p. 2002. pap. 18.95 (*0-7432-4186-X*); 1999. 23.00 o.s.i (*0-684-86295-6*) Simon & Schuster. (Scribner).

—Mrs. Pargeter's Pound of Flesh. 1993. 224p. 20.00 o.p. (*0-684-19565-8*, Macmillan Reference USA) Gale Group.

—Mrs. Pargeter's Pound of Flesh. unabr. ed. 2001. audio 54.95 (*1-85695-571-0*, 93051) ISIS Audio Bks. GBR. *Dist:* Ulverscroft Large Print Bks., Ltd.

—Mrs. Pargeter's Pound of Flesh. l.t. ed. 1993. (Magna Large Print Ser.). 307p. (*0-7505-0579-6*) Magna Large Print Bks. GBR. *Dist:* Ulverscroft Large Print Canada, Ltd.

—Mrs. Pargeter's Pound of Flesh. 1994. (Crime Ser.). 208p. pap. 5.95 o.p. (*0-14-023485-3*, Penguin Bks.) Penguin Group (USA) Inc.

—Mrs., Presumed Dead. 1990. 256p. mass mkt. 3.95 o.s.i (*0-440-20552-2*) Dell Publishing.

—Mrs., Presumed Dead. 1989. 256p. 17.95 o.s.i (*0-684-18851-1*, Macmillan Reference USA) Gale Group.

—Mrs., Presumed Dead. unabr. ed. 2001. audio 54.95 (*1-85695-429-3*, 89042) ISIS Audio Bks. GBR. *Dist:* Ulverscroft Large Print Bks., Ltd.

—A Nice Class of Corpse. 1988. 224p. mass mkt. 3.50 o.s.i (*0-440-20113-6*) Dell Publishing.

—A Nice Class of Corpse. 1987. 196p. 14.95 o.p. (*0-684-18685-3*, Macmillan Reference USA) Gale Group.

—A Nice Class of Corpse. unabr. ed. 2001. audio 54.95 (*1-85089-755-7*, 87122) ISIS Audio Bks. GBR. *Dist:* Ulverscroft Large Print Bks., Ltd.

—A Nice Class of Corpse. l.t. ed. 1987. (Mainstream Ser.). 236p. reprint ed. lib. bdg. 17.95 o.p. (*1-85089-174-5*) ISIS Large Print Bks. GBR. *Dist:* Transaction Pubs.

Bright, Vonette Z. & Moser, Nancy. The Sister Circle. 2003. 352p. pap. 12.99 (*0-8423-7189-3*) Tyndale Hse. Pubs.

Brookner, Anita. The Bay of Angels. E-Book 9.95 (*1-58945-826-5*) Adobe Systems, Inc.

—The Bay of Angels. 2002. 208p. pap. 12.00 (*0-375-72760-4*) Knopf, Alfred A. Inc.

—The Bay of Angels. E-Book 19.00 (*1-58836-006-7*) Random Hse., Inc.

—The Bay of Angels. 2001. (Thorndike Press Large Print Women's Fiction Ser.). 335p. 29.95 (*0-7862-3654-X*) Thorndike Pr.

—Brief Lives. l.t. ed. 2000. 312p. lib. bdg. 27.95 (*1-58547-018-X*) Ctr. Point Large Print.

—Brief Lives. 1992. (Vintage Contemporaries Ser.). 272p. pap. 13.00 (*0-679-73733-2*, Vintage) Knopf Publishing Group.

—Brief Lives. 1993. 4.49 o.p. (*0-517-10943-3*) Random Hse. Value Publishing.

—Visitors. l.t. ed. 1998. 301p. (*0-7540-2099-1*) BBC Audiobooks America.

—Visitors. l.t. ed. 1998. (G. K. Hall Core Ser.). 305p. 27.95 o.p. (*0-7838-8444-3*, Macmillan Reference USA) Gale Group.

—Visitors. 1998. 256p. pap. 13.00 (*0-679-78147-1*, Vintage) Knopf Publishing Group.

—Visitors. 1997. 242p. 23.00 o.s.i (*0-679-45785-2*) Random Hse., Inc.

Brown, Sandra. Fanta C. 1997. 256p. mass mkt. 7.50 (*0-553-56274-6*); Vol. 216. 1987. 192p. mass mkt. 2.50 o.s.i (*0-553-21836-0*) Bantam Bks.

—Fanta C. abr. ed. 1993. 16.95 o.p. (*1-55800-733-4*) NewStar Media, Inc.

—Send No Flowers. 2000. 256p. mass mkt. 6.99 (*0-553-57601-1*); 1984. 192p. mass mkt. 2.25 o.s.i (*0-553-21659-7*) Bantam Bks.

—Send No Flowers. l.t. ed. (Wheeler Press Paperback Ser.). 2000. pap. 10.95 (*1-56895-974-5*); 1999. 27.95 (*1-56895-720-3*) Gale Group. (Wheeler Publishing, Inc.).

—Send No Flowers, abr. ed. 1999. audio 18.00 Highsmith Inc.

Buckley, Christopher. No Way to Treat a First Lady. 2002. 304p. 24.95 (*0-375-50734-5*) Random House Adult Trade Publishing Group.

—No Way to Treat a First Lady. 2002. E-Book 19.95 (*1-58836-257-4*) Random Hse., Inc.

—No Way to Treat a First Lady: A Novel. 2003. 304p. pap. 13.95 (*0-375-75875-5*, Random Hse. Trade Paperbacks) Random House Adult Trade Publishing Group.

—No Way to Treat a First Lady: A Novel. 2003. (Americana Ser.). 29.95 (*0-7862-5044-5*) Thorndike Pr.

Cameron, Kate. Under the Wolf's Head: The First Callista Bagley Gardening Mystery. 1999. 274p. 24.95 (*0-9661879-3-8*, SKP98-44) St Kitts Pr.

Cannon, Julie. Truelove & Homegrown Tomatoes. l.t. ed. 2001. (Thorndike Press Large Print Americana Ser.). 352p. 28.95 (*0-7862-3762-7*) Thorndike Pr.

—TrueLove & Homegrown Tomatoes: A Novel. 2001. 224p. 19.95 (*1-892514-87-7*) Hill Street Pr., LLC.

—Truelove Homegrown Tomatoes. 2003. 288p. pap. 13.00 (*0-7432-4588-1*, Touchstone) Simon & Schuster.

Carlon, Patricia. The Running Woman. 1998. 189p. pap. 12.00 (*1-56947-132-0*); 196p. 21.00 (*1-56947-110-X*) Soho Pr., Inc.

—The Running Woman. l.t. ed. 1998. (Mystery Ser.). 320p. 26.95 (*0-7862-1671-9*) Thorndike Pr.

Carlson, Melody. Shades of Light. 1998. (Palisades Pure Romance Ser.). 240p. pap. 9.99 o.p. (*1-57673-283-5*, Palisades) Multnomah Pubs., Inc.

Chamberlain, Diane. Reflection. 1996. 384p. 24.00 o.p. (*0-06-017652-0*) HarperCollins Pubs.

—Reflection. 1997. 416p. mass mkt. 5.99 o.s.i (*0-06-109396-3*, HarperTorch) Morrow/Avon.

Chappell, Helen. Dead Duck. 1997. (Sam & Hollis Mystery Ser.). mass mkt. 5.50 o.s.i (*0-449-15001-1*, Fawcett) Ballantine Bks.

—Dead Duck. l.t. ed. 2000. (Beeler Large Print Mystery Ser.). 231p. 25.95 (*1-57490-320-9*, Beeler Large Print Bks.) Beeler, Thomas T. Publisher.

—Giving up the Ghost. l.t. ed. 2001. (Beeler Large Print Mystery Ser.). 188p. 25.95 (*1-57490-350-0*, Beeler Large Print Bks.) Beeler, Thomas T. Publisher.

—Giving up the Ghost: A Sam & Hollis Mystery. 1999. (Sam & Hollis Mystery Ser.). 256p. mass mkt. 5.99 o.s.i (*0-440-22575-2*) Dell Publishing.

Cheska, Anna. Drop Dead Gorgeous. 2002. 384p. 24.95 (*0-312-30040-9*) St. Martin's Pr.

Clarkson, Ewan. The Flight of the Osprey. 1996. 192p. 19.95 o.p. (*0-312-13973-X*) St. Martin's Pr.

—The Flight of the Osprey. l.t. ed. 1996. (Large Print Ser.). 368p. 29.99 o.p. (*0-7089-3567-2*, Ulverscroft) Thorpe, F. A. Pubs. GBR. *Dist:* Ulverscroft Large Print Bks., Ltd., Ulverscroft Large Print Canada, Ltd.

Cleage, Pearl. I Wish I Had a Red Dress. l.t. ed. 2001. (Hardcover Ser.). 340p. 30.95 (*1-58724-062-9*, Wheeler Publishing, Inc.) Gale Group.

—I Wish I Had a Red Dress. 2001. 336p. 24.00 (*0-380-97733-8*, Morrow, William & Co.) Morrow/Avon.

Comfort, Barbara. The Cashmere Kid. (Tish McWhinny Mystery Ser.). 224p. 1994. pap. 6.95 (*0-88150-321-5*); 1993. text 18.00 o.p. (*0-88150-254-5*) Norton, W. W. & Co., Inc. (Foul Play).

—Elusive Quarry. (Tish McWhinny Mystery Ser.). 224p. 1996. pap. 7.50 (*0-88150-370-3*); 1995. 19.00 o.p. (*0-88150-332-0*) Norton, W. W. & Co., Inc. (Foul Play).

—Grave Consequences. (Vermont Village Murders Ser.). (Orig.). 1989. 233p. pap. 5.95 (*0-9608726-4-7*); 1994. 240p. reprint ed. pap. 6.00 o.p. (*0-88150-296-0*, Foul Play) Norton, W. W. & Co., Inc.

—A Pair for the Queen. 1999. 221p. pap. 7.95 (*0-393-31913-X*); 1998. (Tish McWhinny Mystery Ser.: Vol. 5). 192p. 22.00 (*0-393-04627-3*) Norton, W. W. & Co., Inc.

—Phoebe's Knee. (Tish McWhinny Mystery Ser.). (Orig.). 1994. 224p. pap. 7.95 (*0-88150-295-2*, Foul Play); 1986. 220p. pap. 3.95 (*0-9608726-3-9*) Norton, W. W. & Co., Inc.

Comfort, Barbara, contrib. by. A Pair for the Queen. l.t. ed. 1999. (Senior Lifestyles Ser.). 320p. o.p. (*0-7862-2297-2*) Thorndike Pr.

Coulter, Catherine. False Pretenses. l.t. ed. 1998. (Large Print Book Ser.). 26.95 (*1-56895-594-4*, Wheeler Publishing, Inc.) Gale Group.

—False Pretenses. 1988. 19.95 o.p. (*0-453-00641-8*); 1989. 352p. reprint ed. mass mkt. 7.50 o.s.i (*0-451-40127-1*, Onyx) NAL.

Curtis, Jack. Christmas in Calico: An American Fable. 1998. 192p. 14.95 (*0-87596-543-1*) Rodale Pr., Inc.

—Christmas in Calico: An American Fable. 1996. 220p. pap. text 8.95 (*0-9640537-1-3*) Monterey Publishing.

Cutler, Judith. Coming Alive. 224p. 25.00 (*0-7278-5616-2*) Severn Hse. Pubs., Ltd.

Dailey, Janet. The Widow & the Wastrel: Ohio. 1992. (Americana Ser.: No. 885). mass mkt. (*0-373-89885-1*); 1988. pap. (*0-373-21935-0*) Harlequin Enterprises, Ltd. (Harlequin Bks.).

—The Widow & the Wastrel: Ohio. l.t. ed. 2001. 231p. 29.95 (*0-7862-2746-X*); (*0-7540-4675-3*); (*0-7540-4676-1*) Thorndike Pr.

—The Widow & the Wastrel: Ohio. 124p. 2002. pap. 6.99 (*0-7592-3840-5*); 2002. E-Book 6.99 (*0-7592-0191-9*); 2002. E-Book 6.99 (*1-58586-473-0*); 2001. E-Book 6.99 (*0-7592-0934-0*) ereads.com.

Danner, Craig Joseph. Himalayan Dhaba: A Novel. 2001. 256p. 24.00 (*0-9706405-9-5*, HD134) Crispin/Hammer Pr.

—Himalayan Dhaba: A Novel. 2002. 23.95 o.s.i (*0-525-94690-X*); 2003. 320p. reprint ed. pap. 13.00 (*0-452-28387-6*, Plume) Dutton/Plume.

DeLillo, Don. The Body Artist. 128p. 2001. mass mkt. 7.99 (*0-7432-2280-6*); 2001. 22.00 (*0-7432-0395-X*); 2001. 22.00 (*0-7432-1564-8*); 2002. reprint ed. pap. 12.00 (*0-7432-0396-8*) Simon & Schuster. (Scribner).

—The Body Artist. l.t. ed. 2001. 160p. 32.50 o.p. (*0-7432-1221-5*) Thorpe, F. A. Pubs. GBR. *Dist:* Ulverscroft Large Print Bks., Ltd.

Delinsky, Barbara. The Woman Next Door: A Novel. 2001. E-Book 9.99 (*1-58945-935-0*) Adobe Systems, Inc.

—The Woman Next Door: A Novel. 2001. 368p. 25.00 (*0-7432-0469-7*); pap. 16.00 (*0-7432-2214-8*) Simon & Schuster. (Simon & Schuster).

—The Woman Next Door: A Novel. l.t. ed. 2002. 504p. 14.95 (*0-7862-3512-8*); 2001. 541p. 32.95 (*0-7862-3510-1*) Thorndike Pr.

Deveraux, Jude. The Blessing. l.t. ed. 1999. 27.95 (*1-56895-629-0*, Wheeler Publishing, Inc.) Gale Group.

—The Blessing. 1999. 336p. pap. 7.99 (*0-671-89109-X*, Pocket Star); 1998. 320p. 20.00 o.s.i (*0-671-89108-1*, Atria) Simon & Schuster.

Diamond, Diana. The Daughter-in-Law: A Novel. 2003. 304p. 24.95 (*0-312-31046-3*) St. Martin's Pr.

Dickinson, Peter. Some Deaths Before Dying. l.t. ed. 2000. (G. K. Hall Core Ser.). 366p. 28.95 (*0-7838-9016-8*, Macmillan Reference USA) Gale Group.

—Some Deaths Before Dying. 1999. 256p. 27.00 (*0-89296-696-3*) Mysterious Pr.

—Some Deaths Before Dying. 256p. (*0-7278-5670-7*) Severn Hse. Pubs., Ltd.

—Some Deaths Before Dying. 2000. 256p. pap. 13.95 o.s.i (*0-446-67612-8*) Warner Bks., Inc.

Earley, Tony. Jim the Boy: A Novel. l.t. ed. 2000. (Wheeler Large Print Book Ser.). 227p. 27.95 (*1-56895-990-7*, Wheeler Publishing, Inc.) Gale Group.

—Jim the Boy: A Novel. Adams, Terry, ed. 2001. (Illus.). 256p. pap. 12.95 (*0-316-19895-1*, Back Bay); 2000. 240p. 23.95 (*0-316-19964-8*) Little Brown & Co.

Estleman, Loren D. City of Widows. 1995. 254p. pap. text 5.99 (*0-8125-3538-3*); 1994. 256p. 20.95 o.p. (*0-312-85667-9*) Doherty, Tom Assocs., LLC. (Forge Bks.).

Fitzgerald, Penelope. The Bookshop. 1978. 118p. (*0-7156-1320-0*) Duckworth, Gerald & Co., Ltd.

—The Bookshop. l.t. ed. 1999. (General Ser.). 168p. pap. 21.95 o.p. (*0-7862-2167-4*); (*0-7540-3910-2*); (*0-7540-3909-9*) Thorndike Pr.

—The Bookshop: A Novel. 1997. 128p. pap. 11.00 (*0-395-86946-3*, Mariner Bks.) Houghton Mifflin Co. Trade & Reference Div.

Frame, Ronald. Permanent Violet. 2002. 160p. pap. 12.95 (*0-7486-6321-5*) Polygon GBR. *Dist:* Interlink Publishing Group, Inc.

Gaiman, Neil. American Gods: A Novel. 2003. 608p. pap. 14.95 (*0-06-055812-1*, Perennial) HarperTrade.

—American Gods: A Novel. 2002. 608p. mass mkt. 7.99 (*0-380-78903-5*) Morrow/Avon.

Giles, Janice Holt. Act of Contrition. 2001. 240p. 25.00 (*0-8131-2172-8*) Univ. Pr. of Kentucky.

Godwin, Gail. Evenings at Five. 2003. (Illus.). 128p. 14.95 (*0-345-46102-9*, Ballantine Bks.) Ballantine Bks.

Goudge, Eileen. Stranger in Paradise. 2002. 432p. reprint ed. mass mkt. 7.99 (*0-451-20577-4*, Signet Bks.) NAL.

—Stranger in Paradise. l.t. ed. 2002. (Carson Spring Ser.: Bk. 1). 573p. pap. 13.95 (*0-7862-3447-4*); 2001. 586p. 31.95 (*0-7862-3446-6*) Thorndike Pr.

—Stranger in Paradise. 2001. (Carson Spring Ser.: Bk. 1). 384p. 24.95 o.s.i (*0-670-89987-9*, Viking) Viking Penguin.

Gould, Judith. The Best Is Yet to Come: A Novel. 2002. 320p. 24.95 o.s.i (*0-525-94659-4*) NAL.

Goyer, Tricia. From Dust & Ashes: A Story of Liberation. 2003. 448p. pap. 12.99 (*0-8024-1554-7*) Moody Pr.

Graham, Brendan. Element of Fire. 2001. 356p. (*0-00-225977-X*) HarperCollins Pubs.

Graham, Heather. King of the Castle. 1995. 248p. per. (*1-55166-019-9*, Mira Bks.) Harlequin Enterprises, Ltd.

—Slow Burn. l.t. ed. 2002. (Wheeler Large Print Book Ser.). pap. 23.95 (*1-58724-190-0*, Wheeler Publishing, Inc.) Gale Group.

—Slow Burn. 2001. 384p. mass mkt. (*1-55166-864-5*, 1-99/97-9, Mira Bks.) Harlequin Enterprises, Ltd.

Greer, Ibby. Moving Day: A Season of Letters: A Novel. 2001. 169p. 24.95 (*1-55618-190-6*) Brunswick Publishing Corp.

Guest, Judith. Errands. 1997. 366p. mass mkt. 7.50 o.s.i (*0-345-40905-1*) Ballantine Bks.

Gurganus, Allan. Oldest Living Confederate Widow Tells All. 1996. 736p. pap. 15.00 o.s.i (*0-449-91169-1*, Fawcett); 1994. pap. 6.99 o.p. (*0-8041-9826-8*, Ivy Bks.); 1990. 912p. mass mkt. 6.99 o.s.i (*0-8041-0643-6*, Ivy Bks.) Ballantine Bks.

—Oldest Living Confederate Widow Tells All. 2001. 736p. reprint ed. pap. 16.00 (*0-375-72663-2*, Vintage) Knopf Publishing Group.

—Oldest Living Confederate Widow Tells All. 1992. 5.99 o.p. (*0-517-08827-4*); 1991. 5.99 o.p. (*0-517-06769-2*) Random Hse. Value Publishing.

Hall, Gregory. The Dark Backward. 1997. 416p. mass mkt. 5.99 o.s.i (*0-451-18850-0*, Signet Bks.) NAL.

—The Dark Backward. 1995. (Illus.). 416p. 22.95 o.p. (*0-670-86185-5*, Viking) Viking Penguin.

Harper, Karen. River of Sky. 1994. 416p. 21.95 o.p. (*0-525-93822-2*, Dutton) Dutton/Plume.

—River of Sky. 1995. 448p. mass mkt. 5.99 o.s.i (*0-451-18490-4*, Signet Bks.) NAL.

Harris, Joanne. Five Quarters of the Orange. l.t. ed. 2001. 420p. lib. bdg. 28.95 (*1-58547-137-2*) Ctr. Point Large Print.

—Five Quarters of the Orange. 2002. 320p. pap. 13.95 (*0-06-095802-2*, Perennial) HarperTrade.

—Five Quarters of the Orange. 2001. 320p. 25.00 (*0-06-019813-3*, Morrow, William & Co.) Morrow/Avon.

Hays, Mary. Learning to Drive. 2003. 320p. 23.00 (*1-4000-4780-3*) Crown Publishing Group.

Heckler, Jonellen. Circumstances Unknown. Grose, Bill, ed. 1993. 288p. 21.00 o.p. (*0-671-78056-5*, Atria); 1994. 336p. reprint ed. mass mkt. 5.99 (*0-671-78059-X*, Pocket) Simon & Schuster.

Heller, Jane. Lucky Stars. E-Book 24.95 (*0-312-70995-1*); 2004. 352p. mass mkt. 6.99 (*0-312-99006-5*, St. Martin's Paperbacks); 2003. 352p. 24.95 (*0-312-28848-4*) St. Martin's Pr.

Henderson, M. R. Victim. 2002. (Five Star First Edition Mystery Ser.). 250p. 24.95 (*0-7862-3930-1*, Five Star) Gale Group.

Howard, Linda. All That Glitters. (Mira Bks.). 1998. 248p. per. (*1-55166-432-1*, 1-66432-5, Mira Bks.); 1993. mass mkt. (*0-373-48270-1*, Silhouette) Harlequin Enterprises, Ltd.

—All That Glitters. l.t. ed. 2001. (Romance Ser.). 341p. 28.95 (*0-7862-2622-6*) Thorndike Pr.

Irving, John. A Widow for One Year: A Novel. 1999. mass mkt. (*0-345-43283-5*); 576p. pap. 14.95 (*0-345-42471-9*) Ballantine Bks. (Ballantine Bks.).

—A Widow for One Year: A Novel. l.t. ed. 1998. pap. 27.95 o.p. (*0-7838-0149-1*, Macmillan Reference USA) Gale Group.

—A Widow for One Year: A Novel. 2003. 576p. 19.95 (*0-8129-6857-3*, Modern Library) Random House Adult Trade Publishing Group.

—A Widow for One Year: A Novel. 1999. E-Book 13.50 (*0-375-50447-8*); 1998. 27.95 o.s.i (*0-676-57821-7*); 1998. pap. 27.95 o.s.i (*0-375-70289-X*) Random Hse., Inc.

—A Widow for One Year: A Novel. deluxe ltd. ed. 1998. (Illus.). 120.00 (*0-9664661-0-1*) Unicycle Pr., Inc.

Isaacs, Susan. Long Time No See. 2001. 368p. 26.00 (*0-06-019570-3*); 496p. pap. 26.00 (*0-06-621404-1*) HarperCollins Pubs.

Jackson, Hialeah. Farewell, Conch Republic. 1999. 368p. mass mkt. 5.99 o.s.i (*0-440-22663-5*) Dell Publishing.

James, Caryn. Glorie. 1999. 256p. pap. 12.95 o.s.i (*0-14-028154-1*, Puffin Bks.) Penguin Group (USA) Inc.

—Glorie. 1998. 240p. 24.00 o.p. (*0-944072-87-9*, Zoland Bks., Inc.) Steerforth Pr.

Joyce, Brenda. The Chase. 2003. 29.95 (*1-57490-482-5*, Beeler Large Print Bks.) Beeler, Thomas T. Publisher.

—The Chase. E-Book 24.95 (*0-312-70731-2*); 2002. 384p. 24.95 (*0-312-28449-7*); 2003. 480p. reprint ed. mass mkt. 6.99 (*0-312-98376-X*, St. Martin's Paperbacks) St. Martin's Pr.

Kahn, Sharon. Don't Cry for Me, Hot Pastrami: A Ruby, the Rabbi's Wife Mystery. 2001. 304p. 24.00 o.s.i (*0-684-87155-6*); E-Book 24.00 (*0-7432-1825-6*) Simon & Schuster. (Scribner).

—Don't Cry for Me, Hot Pastrami: A Ruby, the Rabbi's Wife Mystery. l.t. ed. 2001. (G.K. Hall Large Print Core Ser.). 339p. 27.95 o.p. (*0-7838-9679-4*) Thorndike Pr.

—Fax Me a Bagel: A Ruby the Rabbi's Wife Mystery. 2001. 272p. mass mkt. 5.99 (*0-425-18046-8*) Berkley Publishing Group.

—Fax Me a Bagel: A Ruby the Rabbi's Wife Mystery. 1998. (Ruby, the Rabbi's Wife Mysteries Ser.). 256p. 22.00 (*0-684-84737-X*); 22.00 (*0-684-85498-8*) Simon & Schuster. (Scribner).

—Which Big Giver Stole the Chopped Liver? 2004. 272p. 24.00 (*0-7432-4357-9*, Scribner) Simon & Schuster.

Kay, Terry. Taking Lottie Home. l.t. ed. 2001. (G. K. Hall Core Ser.). 379p. 30.95 (*0-7838-9399-X*, Macmillan Reference USA) Gale Group.

—Taking Lottie Home. 2001. 320p. pap. 13.00 (*0-06-093701-7*, Perennial) HarperTrade.

—Taking Lottie Home. 2000. viii, 294p. 25.00 (*0-688-17646-1*, Morrow, William & Co.) Morrow/Avon.

Kincaid, Nanci. Verbena. 2003. 368p. pap. 14.00 (*0-425-19171-0*, Berkley/Pacer) Berkley Publishing Group.

—Verbena: A Novel. 2002. 338p. tchr. ed. 24.95 (*1-56512-348-4*, Shannon Ravenel Bks.) Algonquin Bks. of Chapel Hill.

Kleypas, Lisa. Where Dreams Begin. l.t. ed. 2002. (Wheeler Large Print Book Ser.). 28.95 (*1-58724-192-7*, Wheeler Publishing, Inc.) Gale Group.

—Where Dreams Begin. 2000. 384p. mass mkt. 6.99 (*0-380-80231-7*, Avon Bks.) Morrow/Avon.

Lansdowne, Judith. Just in Time. 2003. (Zebra Historical Romance Ser.). 32p. mass mkt. 5.99 (*0-8217-7421-2*) Kensington Publishing Corp.

Lawrence, D. H. Quetzalcoatl. 1995. (Illus.). 333p. 30.00 o.p. (*0-933806-60-4*) Black Swan Bks., Ltd.

—Quetzalcoatl. Martz, Louis L., ed. & intro. by. 1998. (Paperbook Ser.: Vol. 864). 358p. pap. 14.95 (*0-8112-1385-4*, NDP864) New Directions Publishing Corp.

MacDonald, Patricia. Not Guilty. 2003. (Illus.). 464p. mass mkt. 7.50 (*0-7434-2356-9*, Pocket); 2002. 368p. 24.00 (*0-7434-2355-0*, Atria) Simon & Schuster.

Macomber, Debbie. For All My Tomorrows. 1996. 256p. per. (*1-55166-156-X*, 1-66156-0, Mira Bks.); 1989. (Silhouette Special Edition Ser.: No. 530). pap. (*0-373-09530-9*, Silhouette) Harlequin Enterprises, Ltd.

—For All My Tomorrows. l.t. ed. 2000. (Romance Ser.). 287p. pap. 28.95 (*0-7838-9048-6*) Thorndike Pr.

—The Playboy & the Widow. (Mira Bks.). 1996. 256p. per. (*1-55166-080-6*, 1-66080-2, Mira Bks.); 1988. pap. (*0-373-09482-5*, Harlequin Bks.) Harlequin Enterprises, Ltd.

Madden, David. The Suicide's Wife. 1979. pap. 1.95 o.p. (*0-380-47522-7*, 47522, Avon Bks.) Morrow/Avon.

Mallon, Thomas. Two Moons: A Novel. 2001. (Harvest Book Ser.). (Illus.). 368p. reprint ed. pap. 14.00 (*0-15-601082-8*, Harvest Bks.) Harcourt Trade Pubs.

Marquis, Christopher. A Hole in the Heart: A Novel. 2003. 320p. 24.95 (*0-312-30630-X*) St. Martin's Pr.

Martin, Sarah Beth. The One True Ocean. 2003. 320p. pap. 14.00 (*1-4022-0143-5*, Sourcebooks Landmark) Sourcebooks, Inc.

Mawer, Simon. The Fall. 2004. 400p. pap. 13.95 (*0-316-73559-0*, Back Bay); 2003. 384p. 24.95 (*0-316-09780-2*) Little Brown & Co.

McFarland, Dennis. Singing Boy: A Novel. 2001. 320p. 25.00 o.s.i (*0-8050-6608-X*) Holt, Henry & Co.

—Singing Boy: A Novel. l.t. ed. 2001. 560p. 28.95 (*0-7862-3517-9*) Thorndike Pr.

McGregor, Elizabeth. The Ice Child. 2001. (Illus.). 400p. 24.95 o.p. (*0-525-94567-9*, Dutton) Dutton/Plume.

—The Ice Child. l.t. ed. 2001. (Wheeler Large Print Book Ser.). (Illus.). 540p. 29.95 o.p. (*1-58724-109-9*, Wheeler Publishing, Inc.) Gale Group.

—The Ice Child. 2002. pap. 6.99 (*0-451-20539-1*, Signet Bks.); 448p. reprint ed. mass mkt. 7.99 (*0-451-41061-0*, Onyx) NAL.

McNeill, Elisabeth. Unforgettable. 288p. 25.99 (*0-7278-5761-4*); 29.99 (*0-7278-7209-5*) Severn Hse. Pubs., Ltd.

Michaels, Kasey. Someone to Love. l.t. ed. 2001. 495p. 27.95 (*0-7862-3491-1*) Thorndike Pr.

—Someone to Love. 2001. 368p. reprint ed. mass mkt. 6.99 (*0-446-60585-9*, Warner Romance) Warner Bks., Inc.

Mitchard, Jacquelyn. Twelve Times Blessed. 2003. 14p. pap. 110.95 (*0-7927-2882-3*); 17p. pap. 124.95 (*0-7927-2883-1*) BBC Audiobooks America.

—Twelve Times Blessed. 2003. (Illus.). 544p. 25.95 (*0-06-621475-0*, HarperCollins); 912p. pap. 25.95 (*0-06-053419-2*, HarperLargePrint); 640p. audio compact disk 29.95 (*0-06-053469-9*, HarperAudio) HarperTrade.

—Twelve Times Blessed. 2004. 624p. mass mkt. 7.99 (*0-06-103247-6*, HarperTorch) Morrow/Avon.

Mitchell, Sharon. Near Perfect. 2001. 336p. 23.95 o.s.i (*0-525-94621-7*, Dutton) Dutton/Plume.

—Near Perfect. 2002. 352p. reprint ed. mass mkt. 6.99 o.s.i (*0-451-20689-4*, Signet Bks.) NAL.

—Near Perfect. l.t. ed. 2002. (African American Ser.). 572p. 29.95 (*0-7862-3865-8*) Thorndike Pr.

Moisionier, Beatrice Culleton. Gatherings XI. 2001. (Gatherings Ser.). (Illus.). 320p. pap. 16.95 (*0-919441-98-X*) Theytus Bks., Ltd. CAN. *Dist:* Orca Bk. Pubs.

Moyer, Marsha. The Second Coming of Lucy Hatch. l.t. ed. 2003. lib. bdg. 28.95 (*1-58547-299-9*, Platinum) Ctr. Point Large Print.

—The Second Coming of Lucy Hatch. 2003. 320p. pap. 13.95 (*0-06-008166-X*); 2002. 304p. 24.95 (*0-06-008165-1*) Morrow/Avon. (Morrow, William & Co.).

Nehring, Radine Trees. A Valley to Die For. 2002. (Something to Die for Ser.). 284p. pap. 14.00 (*0-9661879-9-7*) St Kitts Pr.

Nolan, Christopher. The Banyan Tree: A Novel. 2000. 374p. 25.95 (*1-55970-511-6*); 2001. 384p. reprint ed. pap. 13.95 (*1-55970-574-4*) Arcade Publishing, Inc.

—The Banyan Tree: A Novel. l.t. unabr. ed. 2000. 512p. 32.50 o.p. (*0-7531-6104-4*, 161044) ISIS Large Print Bks. GBR. *Dist:* Ulverscroft Large Print Bks., Ltd.

—The Banyan Tree: A Novel. 2002. 384p. reprint ed. pap. 13.00 (*0-385-72068-8*, Knopf Bks. for Young Readers) Random Hse. Children's Bks.

Nunes, Rachel Ann. Twice in a Lifetime: A Novel. 2002. 330p. pap. 16.95 (*1-55517-626-7*) Cedar Fort, Inc./CFI Distribution.

O'Carroll, Brendan. The Mammy. l.t. ed. 2000. 262p. lib. bdg. 26.95 (*1-58547-037-6*) Ctr. Point Large Print.

—The Mammy. 1999. 176p. pap. 11.95 (*0-452-28103-2*, Plume) Dutton/Plume.

—The Mammy. 1994. 174 p. (*0-86278-372-0*) O'Brien Pr., Ltd., The.

Oke, Janette. The Matchmakers. 1997. 144p. text 12.99 o.p. (*0-7642-2002-0*); pap. 12.99 o.p. (*0-7642-2020-9*) Bethany Hse. Pubs.

—The Matchmakers. l.t. ed. 2001. (Illus.). 197p. 25.95 (*0-7862-3256-0*); (*0-7540-4523-4*); (*0-7540-4524-2*) Thorndike Pr.

Peterson, Tracie. Across the Years. 2002. (Desert Roses Ser.: Bk. 2). 384p. pap. 12.99 (*0-7642-2518-9*) Bethany Hse. Pubs.

—Across the Years. l.t. ed. 2004. (Desert Roses Ser.: No. 2). 458p. 27.95 (*0-7862-5780-6*) Thorndike Pr.

—Entangled. 1997. (Portraits Ser.). 256p. pap. 8.99 o.p. (*1-55661-936-7*) Bethany Hse. Pubs.

—Entangled. 2000. (Christian Fiction Ser.). 290p. 23.95 (*0-7862-2228-X*, Five Star) Gale Group.

Powell, Sophie. The Mushroom Man. 2004. 208p. pap. 14.00 (*0-425-19413-2*) Berkley Publishing Group.

—The Mushroom Man. 2003. 208p. 23.95 (*0-399-14963-5*, Putnam & Grosset) Putnam Publishing Group, The.

Pruett, Lynn. Ruby River. 2004. 288p. pap. 13.00 (*0-8021-4039-4*, Grove Pr.); 2002. 336p. 24.00 (*0-87113-855-7*, Atlantic Monthly Pr.) Grove/Atlantic, Inc.

—Ruby River. 2003. (Americana Ser.). 28.95 (*0-7862-5144-1*) Thorndike Pr.

Quick, Amanda, pseud. Wicked Widow. l.t. ed. 2001. pap. 29.95 (*0-7862-2598-X*); 2000. 453p. 31.95 (*0-7862-2596-3*) Thorndike Pr.

Raife, Alexandra. Among Friends. 2002. 410p. mass mkt. 9.95 (*0-340-79292-2*) Hodder & Stoughton, Ltd. GBR. *Dist:* Trafalgar Square.

Ray, Francis. I Know Who Holds Tomorrow. 2nd ed. 2002. 352p. pap. 13.95 (*0-312-30050-6*, CPB1181, Saint Martin's Griffin) St. Martin's Pr.

Rice, Pam. Coming to My Senses. 2002. (Five Star First Edition Romance Ser.). 265p. 25.95 (*0-7862-3034-7*, Five Star) Gale Group.

—Coming to My Senses. l.t. ed. 2003. 392p. 28.95 (*0-7862-6028-9*, Large Print Pr.) Thorndike Pr.

Rice, Patricia. Nobody's Angel. 2001. 352p. mass mkt. 6.99 (*0-449-00602-6*, Ivy Bks.) Ballantine Bks.

—Nobody's Angel. l.t. ed. 2001. (Thorndike Press Large Print Americana Ser.). 528p. 28.95 (*0-7862-3756-2*) Thorndike Pr.

Robinson, Roxana. Sweetwater: A Novel. 2003. 336p. 24.95 (*0-375-50916-X*) Random Hse., Inc.

—Sweetwater: A Novel. l.t. ed. 2003. 565p. 29.95 (*0-7862-5648-6*) Thorndike Pr.

Rosenberg, Nancy Taylor. Abuse of Power. unabr. ed. 1997. audio 72.00 (*0-913369-73-X*, 4326) Books on Tape, Inc.

—Abuse of Power. 1997. 336p. 23.95 o.p. (*0-525-93768-4*) Dutton/Plume.

—Abuse of Power. l.t. ed. 1997. 448p. mass mkt. 7.99 (*0-451-18006-2*, Signet Bks.) NAL.

—Abuse of Power. unabr. ed. 1997. audio 78.00 (*0-7887-0916-X*, 94957E7) Recorded Bks., LLC.

—Abuse of Power. abr. ed. 1997. 3p. audio 16.95 o.s.i (*0-14-086507-1*, Penguin AudioBooks) Viking Penguin.

Rosenblum, Robert. Afterlove. 2004. 352p. mass mkt. 7.99 (*0-451-41126-9*, Onyx); 2003. 320p. 22.95 (*0-451-20786-6*) NAL.

Ross, Ann B. Miss Julia Hits the Road. 2003. 7p. 59.95 (*0-7927-2872-6*); 9p. 89.95 (*0-7927-2873-4*) BBC Audiobooks America.

—Miss Julia Hits the Road. 2004. 352p. pap. 14.00 (*0-14-200404-9*) Penguin Group (USA) Inc.

—Miss Julia Hits the Road. l.t. ed. 2003. (Basic Ser.). 30.95 (*0-7862-5497-1*) Thorndike Pr.

—Miss Julia Hits the Road. 2003. 320p. 24.95 (*0-670-03207-7*, Viking) Viking Penguin.

—Miss Julia Speaks Her Mind: A Novel. 2000. 288p. pap. 13.00 (*0-688-17775-1*); 1999. 273p. 23.00 (*0-688-16788-8*, Morrow, William & Co.) Morrow/Avon.

—Miss Julia Speaks Her Mind: A Novel. l.t. ed. 1999. (Thorndike Senior Lifestyle Ser.). 393p. 27.95 (*0-7862-2255-7*) Thorndike Pr.

—Miss Julia Takes Over. 2002. 336p. reprint ed. pap. 14.00 (*0-14-200089-2*) Penguin Group (USA) Inc.

—Miss Julia Takes Over. l.t. ed. 2001. (Thorndike Press Large Print Senior Lifestyles Ser.). 482p. 28.95 (*0-7862-3515-2*) Thorndike Pr.

—Miss Julia Takes Over. 2001. 352p. 24.95 o.s.i (*0-670-91026-0*, Viking) Viking Penguin.

—Miss Julia Throws a Wedding. 2003. 336p. pap. 14.00 (*0-14-200271-2*) Penguin Group (USA) Inc.

—Miss Julia Throws a Wedding. l.t. ed. 2002. (Basic Ser.). 453p. 28.95 o.p. (*0-7862-4561-1*) Thorndike Pr.

—Miss Julia Throws a Wedding. 2002. 304p. text 24.95 (*0-670-03105-4*, Viking) Viking Penguin.

Rubens, Bernice. Birds of Passage. 1984. mass mkt. 3.95 o.s.i (*0-671-50282-4*, Pocket) Simon & Schuster.

—Birds of Passage. Silberman, J., ed. 1982. 224p. 12.95 o.p. (*0-671-44798-X*) Summit Bks.

Rutter, Joy. A Disturbing Presence. 2003. 232p. pap. 16.95 (*1-4137-0113-2*) PublishAmerica, Inc.

Sargent, Dave & Sargent, Pat. Dizzy (claybank) Have Courage #22. 2001. (Saddle Up Ser.). 36p. (J). lib. bdg. 22.60 (*1-56763-679-9*) Ozark Publishing.

Shreve, Anita. The Pilot's Wife. l.t. ed. 2001. pap. 11.95 (*1-56895-146-9*); 1998. 337p. 27.95 (*1-56895-686-X*) Gale Group. (Wheeler Publishing, Inc.).

—The Pilot's Wife. (Oprah's Book Club Selection Ser.). 2001. 320p. mass mkt. 7.99 (*0-316-78822-8*); 2000. 304p. pap. 7.99 (*0-316-78915-1*); 1999. 320p. pap. 13.95 (*0-316-78990-9*); 1999. 23.95 (*0-316-60194-2*); 1998. 304p. 23.95 o.p. (*0-316-78908-9*); 1999. 304p. reprint ed. pap. 13.95 (*0-316-60195-0*, Back Bay) Little Brown & Co.

—The Pilot's Wife. 1999. 19.75 (*0-606-19029-5*) Turtleback Bks.

Shreve, Porter. The Obituary Writer. 2000. 224p. pap. 12.00 (*0-395-98132-8*) Houghton Mifflin Co.

Siler, Jenny. Shot: A Novel. 2002. 256p. 24.00 (*0-8050-7203-9*) Holt, Henry & Co.

Smith, Deborah. Sweet Hush. 2003. 7p. audio compact disk 74.95 (*0-7927-2853-X*); 54.95 (*0-7927-2852-1*) BBC Audiobooks America.

—Sweet Hush. 2003. 336p. 23.95 (*0-316-80650-1*) Little Brown & Co.

—Sweet Hush. 2003. 433p. 30.95 (*0-7862-5449-1*) Thorndike Pr.

—Sweet Hush. 2004. 416p. mass mkt. 6.99 (*0-446-61140-9*) Warner Bks., Inc.

Sparks, Nicholas. The Guardian. 2003. 400p. 24.95 (*0-446-52779-3*); 720p. 24.95 (*0-446-53231-2*) Warner Bks., Inc.

Swann, E. L. Night Gardening. l.t. ed. 2000. (G. K. Hall Core Ser.). 256p. 28.95 (*0-7838-9036-2*, Macmillan Reference USA) Gale Group.

—Night Gardening. 2000. (Illus.). 208p. mass mkt. 6.50 o.s.i (*0-7868-8952-7*) Hyperion Pr.

—Night Gardening: A Novel. 1999. 215p. 16.95 (*0-7868-6498-2*) Hyperion Pr.

Tanner, Janet. Shadows of the Past. 2003. 288p. 26.99 (*0-7278-5926-9*) Severn Hse. Pubs., Ltd.

Thompson, Carlene. All Fall Down. 1993. pap. 4.99 (*0-380-77021-0*, Avon Bks.) Morrow/Avon.

—All Fall Down. 2002. mass mkt. (*0-312-98462-6*, St. Martin's Paperbacks) St. Martin's Pr.

Todd, Charles. A Fearsome Doubt: An Inspector Ian Rutledge Mystery. 2003. 384p. mass mkt. 6.99 (*0-553-58317-4*); 2002. 304p. 24.95 (*0-553-80180-5*); 2002. E-Book 19.99 (*0-553-89709-8*) Bantam Bks.

Towler, Katherine. Snow Island. 2003. 292p. 28.95 (*1-57490-492-2*, Beeler Large Print Bks.) Beeler, Thomas T. Publisher.

—Snow Island: A Novel. 2003. 304p. pap. 13.00 (*0-452-28390-6*) Dutton/Plume.

—Snow Island: A Novel. 2002. 287p. 25.00 (*1-931561-01-X*) MacAdam/Cage Publishing, Inc.

Tyler, Anne. Back When We Were Grownups. 2001. 288p. 25.00 (*0-375-41253-0*) Knopf, Alfred A. Inc.

—Back When We Were Grownups. l.t. ed. 2001. 416p. 25.00 (*0-375-43118-7*) Random Hse. Large Print.

Vickers, Salley. Instances of the Number 3. 2002. E-Book 15.00 (*0-374-70400-7*); E-Book 15.00 (*0-374-70398-1*); E-Book 15.00 o.p. (*0-374-70401-5*); E-Book 15.00 (*0-374-70402-3*); E-Book (*0-374-70403-1*); 320p. 23.00 (*0-374-17702-3*) Farrar, Straus & Giroux.

—Instances of the Number 3. l.t. ed. 2002. (Core Collection). 375p. 30.95 (*0-7862-4492-5*) Thorndike Pr.
—Instances of the Number 3: A Novel. 2003. (Illus.). 320p. pap. 14.00 (*0-312-42112-5*) Picador.
Vincent, Catherine. Invitation to Paradise. l.t. ed. 2003. 137p. pap. 23.95 (*0-7862-5459-9*) Thorndike Pr.
Wadham, Lucy. Lost. 2000. 320p. 24.95 (*0-7867-0785-2*, Carroll & Graf Pubs.) Avalon Publishing Group.
Wait, Lea. Stopping to Home. 2001. (Illus.). 160p. (J). (gr. 3-7). 16.00 (*0-689-83832-8*, McElderry, Margaret K.) Simon & Schuster Children's Publishing.
Wall, Kathryn R. Perdition House: A Bay Tanner Mystery. 2003. 368p. 24.95 (*0-312-31385-3*, Saint Martin's Minotaur) St. Martin's Pr.
West, Yvonne. Rosemary for Remembrance: A Novel. 1997. 192p. 19.95 (*1-56474-202-4*) Fithian Pr.
Willett, Marcia. A Week in Winter. E-Book 24.95 (*0-312-70651-0*); 2003. 416p. mass mkt. 6.99 (*0-312-98667-X*, St. Martin's Paperbacks); 2002. 352p. 24.95 (*0-312-28785-2*) St. Martin's Pr.
—A Week in Winter: A Novel. l.t. ed. 2002. 28.95 (*0-7862-4590-5*) Thorndike Pr.
Winston, Lolly. Good Grief. 2004. 18.00 (*0-446-53304-1*) Warner Bks., Inc.
Wood, Jane Roberts. Roseborough. l.t. ed. 2003. 377p. 29.95 (*0-7862-5658-3*) Thorndike Pr.
—Roseborough: A Novel. 2003. 290p. 23.95 (*0-525-94715-9*, Dutton) Dutton/Plume.
Wright, Bill. After You've Gone. 2004. 224p. pap. 12.00 (*0-7432-4640-3*, Touchstone) Simon & Schuster.

# SETTINGS

## A

### ACAPULCO (MEXICO)—FICTION

Chase, Elaine Raco. Double Occupancy. 1982. (Candlelight Regency Romance Ser.: No. 56). pap. 2.25 o.p. (*0-440-11732-1*) Dell Publishing.
—Double Occupancy. l.t. ed. 2002. 244p. 27.95 (*0-7862-4034-2*) Gale Group.
Hess, Joan. Closely Akin to Murder. 1996. (Claire Malloy Mystery Ser.). 240p. 21.95 o.s.i (*0-525-93911-3*, Dutton) Dutton/Plume.
—Closely Akin to Murder. 1997. (Claire Malloy Mysteries Ser.). 272p. mass mkt. 5.99 o.s.i (*0-451-40561-7*, Onyx) NAL.

### ADIRONDACK MOUNTAINS (N.Y.)—FICTION

Altsheler, Joseph A. The Rulers of the Lakes. 2000. 252p. E-Book 3.95 (*0-594-01819-6*) 1873 Pr.
—The Rulers of the Lakes. 25.95 (*0-8488-0906-8*) Amereon, Ltd.
—The Rulers of the Lakes. 1993. reprint ed. lib. bdg. 21.95 (*0-89968-565-X*) Buccaneer Bks., Inc.
Bacheller, Irving. Eben Holden: A Tale of the North Country. 1974. (BCL Ser.: No. I). 27.50 (*0-404-00439-3*) AMS Pr., Inc.
—Eben Holden: A Tale of the North Country. reprint ed. lib. bdg. 48.00 (*0-7426-1108-6*) Classic Bks.
—Eben Holden: A Tale of the North Country. 1903. 432p. (YA). reprint ed. pap. text 28.00 (*1-4047-6671-5*) Classic Textbooks.
—Eben Holden: A Tale of the North Country. 1992. (BCL1-PS American Literature Ser.). 432p. reprint ed. lib. bdg. 99.00 (*0-7812-6671-8*) Reprint Services Corp.
—Eben Holden: A Tale of the North Country. 1969. reprint ed. 16.00 (*0-403-00142-0*) Scholarly Pr., Inc.
—Eben Holden: A Tale of the North Country. 1998. (Classics Library). pap. 3.95 (*1-85326-573-X*, 573XWW) Wordsworth Editions, Ltd. GBR. *Dist:* Combined Publishing.
Briant, John H. Adirondack Detective. 2000. (Illus.). v, 266p. pap. 14.95 (*0-9648327-2-0*) Chalet Publishing.
—Adirondack Detective Returns. 2002. (Adirondack Detective Ser.: Vol. 2). 366p. pap. 14.95 (*0-9648327-3-9*) Chalet Publishing.
Bruchac, Joseph. Long River: A Novel. 1995. 312p. 19.95 (*1-55591-213-3*) Fulcrum Publishing.
—The Waters Between: A Novel of the Dawn Land. 1998. 310p. pap. 14.95 (*1-58465-015-X*); text 26.00 o.p. (*0-87451-881-4*) Univ. Pr. of New England. (Hardscrabble Bks.).
Crabbe, Richard Edward. The Empire of Shadows. 2003. 384p. 24.95 (*0-312-20614-3*) St. Martin's Pr.
Crosman, Coral. Eve of Innocence. 1984. 132p. (Orig.). pap. 6.25 (*0-913884-04-9*) Porphyrion Pr.
DeAndrea, William L. Killed on the Rocks. 1990. 240p. 17.95 o.p. (*0-89296-210-0*) Mysterious Pr.
—Killed on the Rocks. 1992. 2.99 o.p. (*0-517-08869-X*) Random Hse. Value Publishing.
—Killed on the Rocks. 1991. 240p. mass mkt. 4.99 (*0-446-40060-2*, Mysterious Pr. Paperback Bks.) Warner Bks., Inc.
Deming, Philander. Adirondack Stories. 1972. reprint ed. 39.50 (*0-8422-8038-3*) Irvington Pubs.
—The Best Adirondack Stories of Philander Deming. 1997. (Ne York Classics Ser.). (Illus.). 221p. 24.95 (*0-8156-0442-4*) Syracuse Univ. Pr.
Doctorow, E. L. Loon Lake. 1988. 320p. mass mkt. 5.95 o.s.i (*0-449-21603-9*, Fawcett) Ballantine Bks.
—Loon Lake. 1981. 304p. pap. 3.50 o.s.i (*0-553-20027-5*) Bantam Bks.
—Loon Lake. 1996. 272p. reprint ed. pap. 14.00 (*0-452-27568-7*, Plume) Dutton/Plume.
—Loon Lake. 1992. pap. 11.00 o.s.i (*0-679-73625-5*, Vintage) Knopf Publishing Group.
—Loon Lake. 1980. 35.00 o.p. (*0-394-51176-X*) Random Hse., Inc.
—Three Screenplays: Daniel, Ragtime, Loon Lake. Levine, Paul, ed. 2003. 480p. 36.95 (*0-8018-7201-4*) Johns Hopkins Univ. Pr.
Dreiser, Theodore. An American Tragedy. Date not set. pap. text (*0-17-557044-2*) Addison-Wesley Longman, Inc.
—An American Tragedy. Date not set. 832p. 38.95 (*0-8488-2253-6*) Amereon, Ltd.
—An American Tragedy. 1978. 874 p. reprint ed. lib. bdg. 32.00 (*0-8376-0424-9*) Bentley Pubs.
—An American Tragedy. 1990. reprint ed. lib. bdg. 54.95 (*0-89966-709-0*) Buccaneer Bks., Inc.
—An American Tragedy. (Collected Works of Theodore Dreiser). 349p. reprint ed. 2001. (Illus.). pap. text 28.00 (*0-7426-5614-4*); 1998. lib. bdg. 98.00 (*1-58201-614-3*) Classic Bks.
—An American Tragedy. 1999. 17.95 (*0-8085-0951-9*) Econo-Clad Bks.
—An American Tragedy. 2003. (Library of America: Vol. 140). 972p. 40.00 (*1-931082-31-6*) Library of America, The.
—An American Tragedy. mass mkt. 0.25 o.p. (*0-451-00755-7*, Signet Bks.); 2000. 880p. mass mkt. 9.95 (*0-451-52770-4*, Signet Classics); 1964. mass mkt. 1.50 o.p. (*0-451-50619-7*, Signet Classics); 1964. mass mkt. 1.95 o.p. (*0-451-50938-2*, Signet Classics); 1964. mass mkt. 1.25 o.p. (*0-451-50365-1*, Signet Classics); 1964. mass mkt. 3.50 o.p. (*0-451-51563-3*, Signet Classics); 1964. mass mkt. 3.95 o.p. (*0-451-51696-6*, Signet Classics); 1964. mass mkt. 4.50 o.p. (*0-451-52043-2*, Signet Classics); 1964. mass mkt. 0.95 o.p. (*0-451-50235-3*, Signet Classics); 1964. 880p. mass mkt. 9.95 o.s.i (*0-451-52465-9*, Signet Classics); 1964. 832p. mass mkt. 4.95 o.p. (*0-451-52204-4*, Signet Classics); 1964. mass mkt. 2.50 o.p. (*0-451-51276-6*, Signet Classics) NAL.
—An American Tragedy. 2002. E-Book 5.24 (*0-7953-0792-6*) RosettaBooks.
—An American Tragedy. 1964. 16.00 (*0-606-00332-0*) Turtleback Bks.
Fleming, Ian. The Spy Who Loved Me. 2003. 176p. pap. 13.00 (*0-14-200326-3*) Penguin Group (USA) Inc.
Freed, Brian M. An Adirondack Life. 2000. 386p. pap. 21.79 (*1-58721-066-5*) 1stBooks Library.
Frey, James N. Winter of the Wolves. 1992. 288p. 19.95 o.p. (*0-8050-1764-X*) Holt, Henry & Co.
—Winter of the Wolves. 1993. 320p. mass mkt. 4.50 o.p. (*0-06-104274-9*, HarperTorch) Morrow/Avon.
Goodman, Carol. The Lake of Dead Languages. 2003. 432p. pap. 13.95 (*0-345-45089-2*); 2002. 400p. 23.95 (*0-345-45088-4*) Ballantine Bks. (Ballantine Bks.).
—The Lake of Dead Languages. l.t. ed. 2002. 29.95 (*1-58724-244-3*, Wheeler Publishing, Inc.) Gale Group.
Hubbard, S. W. Take the Bait. 2003. 336p. mass mkt. 6.50 (*0-7434-6653-5*, Pocket) Simon & Schuster.
Kennedy, Ellen Edwards. Irregardless of Murder: A Miss Prentice Cozy Mystery. 2001. (Miss Prentice Cozy Mystery). 288p. pap. 14.00 (*0-9661879-7-0*) St Kitts Pr.
Lowe, William T. After the Summer People Leave: 12 Baffling Adirondack Mystery Stories. 1996. 252p. (Orig.). pap. 12.95 (*0-9632476-4-6*) Pinto Pr.
Martino, Terry DeFranco. A Town in a Home. 1999. 188p. pap. 11.95 (*1-56315-192-8*) SterlingHouse Pubs., Inc.
Neggers, Carla. The Cabin. l.t. ed. 2002. 458p. 28.95 (*0-7862-4211-6*) Gale Group.
—The Cabin. 2002. 384p. mass mkt. (*1-55166-845-9*, Mira Bks.) Harlequin Enterprises, Ltd.
Oates, Joyce Carol. Bellefleur. 1991. 592p. pap. 17.95 (*0-452-26794-3*, Plume); 1990. pap. 11.95 o.p. (*0-525-48567-8*); 1980. (C). 13.95 o.p. (*0-525-06302-1*, Dutton) Dutton/Plume.
—Bellefleur. 1987. pap. 9.95 o.p. (*0-525-48347-0*, Obelisk) NAL.
—Bellefleur. 1981. 688p. mass mkt. 4.50 o.s.i (*0-446-30732-7*) Warner Bks., Inc.
Rinehart, Mary Roberts. The Circular Staircase. Date not set. lib. bdg. 20.95 (*0-8488-2159-9*) Amereon, Ltd.
—The Circular Staircase. 1991. 368p. 4.95 o.p. (*0-88184-772-0*); 1985. 272p. pap. 3.50 o.p. (*0-88184-106-4*) Avalon Publishing Group. (Carroll & Graf Pubs.).
—The Circular Staircase. 1976. lib. bdg. 19.95 (*0-89968-181-6*, Lightyear Pr.) Buccaneer Bks., Inc.
—The Circular Staircase. E-Book 2.49 (*1-58627-657-3*) Electric Umbrella Publishing.
—The Circular Staircase. 1989. audio 32.00 Jimcin Recordings.
—The Circular Staircase. 1997. 288p. mass mkt. 5.50 o.s.i (*1-57566-180-2*); 1985. mass mkt. 3.50 o.p. (*0-8217-1723-5*, Zebra Bks.); 1985. mass mkt. 3.95 o.s.i (*0-8217-3528-4*, Zebra Bks.) Kensington Publishing Corp.
—Circular Staircase. 2004. 288p. mass mkt. 5.99 (*0-7582-0528-7*, Kensington Bks.) Kensington Publishing Corp.
—The Circular Staircase, Set. unabr. ed. 1989. audio 35.95 (*1-55685-151-0*) Audio Bk. Contractors, Inc.
—The Circular Staircase. unabr. ed. 1992. audio 44.95 (*0-7861-0619-0*, 2109) Blackstone Audio Bks., Inc.
—The Circular Staircase. unabr. ed. 1993. audio 39.95 (*1-55686-469-8*, 469) Books in Motion.
—The Circular Staircase. 1997. (Dover Mystery Classics Ser.). (Illus.). 160p. reprint ed. pap. text 2.00 (*0-486-29713-6*) Dover Pubns., Inc.
—The Circular Staircase. l.t. ed. 1980. lib. bdg. 13.95 o.p. (*0-8161-6641-2*, Macmillan Reference USA) Gale Group.
Roberts, J. R. Treasure Hunt. 2003. (Gunsmith Ser.: No. 255). 192p. mass mkt. 4.99 (*0-515-13494-5*, Jove) Berkley Publishing Group.
Robinson, Roxana. Sweetwater: A Novel. 2003. 336p. 24.95 (*0-375-50916-X*) Random Hse., Inc.
—Sweetwater: A Novel. l.t. ed. 2003. 565p. 29.95 (*0-7862-5648-6*) Thorndike Pr.
Sheffer, Roger. Lost River. 1988. (Illus.). 144p. (Orig.). pap. 14.95 (*0-935939-02-4*) Night Tree Pr.
Spencer-Fleming, Julia. A Fountain Filled with Blood. E-Book 23.95 (*0-312-71002-X*); 2004. mass mkt. 6.99 (*0-312-99543-1*, St. Martin's Paperbacks); 2003. 304p. 23.95 (*0-312-30410-2*, Saint Martin's Minotaur) St. Martin's Pr.
—In the Bleak Midwinter. E-Book 17.95 (*0-312-70446-1*); 2003. 384p. mass mkt. 6.99 (*0-312-98676-9*, St. Martin's Paperbacks); 2002. 272p. 23.95 (*0-312-28847-6*, Saint Martin's Minotaur) St. Martin's Pr.
—Out of the Deep I Cry. 2004. 304p. 23.95 (*0-312-31262-8*) St. Martin's Pr.
Wilcox, Stephen F. The Green Mosaic. 1994. 272p. 20.95 o.p. (*0-312-11428-1*, Saint Martin's Minotaur) St. Martin's Pr.
Wood, Bari. Doll's Eyes. 1994. 384p. mass mkt. 5.50 (*0-380-72097-3*, Avon Bks.); 1993. 303p. 20.00 o.p. (*0-688-12440-2*, Morrow, William & Co.) Morrow/Avon.

### AFGHANISTAN—FICTION

Bearden, Milton. Black Tulip. 2002. pap. 19.00 (*0-8129-9177-X*) Random House Adult Trade Publishing Group.
—The Black Tulip: A Novel of War in Afghanistan. 2002. 336p. pap. 12.95 (*0-375-76083-0*) Random House Adult Trade Publishing Group.
Blair, E. J. Do unto Others. 2002. 600p. 35.95 (*0-940121-75-1*) Cross Cultural Pubns., Inc.
Block, Lawrence. Here Comes a Hero. 1986. 176p. mass mkt. 2.95 o.s.i (*0-515-08686-X*); 1985. mass mkt. 2.95 o.s.i (*0-515-08420-4*) Berkley Publishing Group. (Jove).
Bolger, Daniel P. Feast of Bones. 1991. mass mkt. 4.99 o.s.i (*0-8041-0834-X*, Ivy Bks.); 1990. 19.95 o.p. (*0-89141-370-7*, Presidio Pr.) Ballantine Bks.
Bradshaw, Gillian. Horses of Heaven. 1992. 512p. mass mkt. 5.99 o.s.i (*0-553-29796-1*, Spectra) Bantam Bks.
—Horses of Heaven. 1991. 464p. 20.00 o.s.i (*0-385-41466-8*) Doubleday Publishing.
Drummond, Emma. Beyond All Frontiers. 1985. 448p. pap. 3.95 o.p. (*0-312-90077-5*, St. Martin's Paperbacks); 1983. 472p. 13.95 o.p. (*0-312-07773-4*) St. Martin's Pr.
Follett, Ken. Lie down with Lions. unabr. ed. 1986. audio 72.00 (*0-7366-0591-6*, 1558) Books on Tape, Inc.
—Lie down with Lions. unabr. ed. 2004. audio 29.95 (*1-59355-652-7*, 5277, Brilliance Audio Unabridged); 1986. audio 19.95 (*0-930435-20-6*, 161, Bookcassette); 1986. audio 73.25 (*1-56100-015-9*, 1265, Unabridged Library Editions) Brilliance Audio.
—Lie down with Lions. l.t. ed. 1986. 537p. 19.95 o.p. (*0-8161-4167-3*); 11.95 o.p. (*0-8161-4168-1*) Gale Group. (Macmillan Reference USA).
—Lie down with Lions. abr. ed. 2001. audio (*0-333-73529-3*) Macmillan U.K. GBR. *Dist:* Macmillan Publishing Co., Inc.
—Lie down with Lions. 1986. 333p. 18.95 o.p. (*0-688-05891-4*, Morrow, William & Co.) Morrow/Avon.
—Lie down with Lions. 2003. 320p. pap. 13.95 (*0-451-21046-8*); 1994. mass mkt. 5.99 (*0-451-18292-8*); 1986. 384p. mass mkt. 4.95 o.p. (*0-451-14642-5*, Signet Bks.); 1986. 384p. mass mkt. 7.99 (*0-451-16350-8*) NAL.
—Lie down with Lions. abr. ed. 1999. 14.95 incl. audio (*0-671-62147-5*, 391065, Simon & Schuster Audioworks) Simon & Schuster Audio.
Hensher, Philip. The Mulberry Empire. 2002. 496p. 26.00 (*0-375-41488-6*) Random Hse., Inc.
—The Mulberry Empire: A Novel. 2003. 496p. pap. 15.00 (*1-4000-3089-7*) Doubleday Publishing.
Hirsh, M. E. Kabul: A Novel. 2002. (Illus.). 464p. pap. 14.95 (*0-312-30173-1*, Saint Martin's Griffin) St. Martin's Pr.
Hosseini, Khaled. The Kite Runner. 2004. 384p. pap. 14.00 (*1-59448-000-1*, Riverhead Trade (Paperbacks)) Berkley Publishing Group.
—The Kite Runner. 384p. 2004. pap. (*0-385-66007-3*, Anchor Canada); 2003. (*0-385-66006-5*) Doubleday Canada, Ltd. CAN. *Dist:* Random Hse., Inc.
—The Kite Runner. 2003. 336p. 24.95 (*1-57322-245-3*, Riverhead Bks. (Hardcovers)) Putnam Publishing Group, The.
Josseini, Khaled. Kite Runner. l.t. ed. 2003. lib. bdg. 29.95 (*1-58547-363-4*, Platinum) Ctr. Point Large Print.
Khadra, Yasmina. The Swallows of Kabul: A Novel. Cullen, John, tr. from FRE. 2004. 208p. 18.95 (*0-385-51001-2*, Talese, Nan A.) Doubleday Publishing.
Kruse, John. The Hour of the Lily. 1987. 448p. 18.95 o.p. (*0-312-01129-6*) St. Martin's Pr.
Michener, James A. Caravans. 1986. mass mkt. 5.95 o.p. (*0-449-44521-6*); 1986. 448p. mass mkt. 7.99 (*0-449-21380-3*); 1985. mass mkt. 4.95 o.p. (*0-449-21051-0*); 1983. mass mkt. 3.95 o.p. (*0-449-20415-4*); 1983. mass mkt. 3.75 o.p. (*0-449-20285-2*) Ballantine Bks. (Fawcett).
—Caravans. l.t. ed. 1993. 16.95 o.p. (*0-8161-3261-5*, Macmillan Reference USA) Gale Group.
—Caravans. 2003. (Illus.). 352p. pap. 14.95 (*0-8129-6982-0*, Random Hse. Trade Paperbacks) Random House Adult Trade Publishing Group.
—Caravans. 1963. 29.95 o.s.i (*0-394-41849-2*) Random Hse., Inc.
Rahimi, Atiq. Earth & Ashes. Goknar, Erday, tr. from PER. 2002. 96p. 19.00 (*0-15-100698-9*) Harcourt Trade Pubs.
Shah, Idries. Kara Kush. 1991. 575p. 17.95 o.p. (*0-8128-3098-9*) Holt, Henry & Co.
—Kara Kush. 1986. 575p. mass mkt. 10.00 (*0-00-617402-7*, KAKU2) Octagon Pr., Ltd. GBR. *Dist:* ISHK.
—Kara Kush: A Novel of Afghanistan. 2002. 575p. 26.95 (*1-58567-321-8*) Overlook Pr., The.
White, Robin A. The Sword of Orion. 1996. mass mkt. 6.99 (*0-449-14953-6*); 1995. mass mkt. 5.99 o.s.i (*0-449-28709-2*) Ballantine Bks. (Fawcett).
—The Sword of Orion. 1993. 320p. 21.00 o.s.i (*0-517-58807-2*, Crown) Crown Publishing Group.
Wilson, Steven E. Winter in Kandahar. 2003. 464p. per. 14.95 (*0-9729480-0-7*) Hailey-Grey Bks.
Yermakov, Oleg. Afghan Tales. Romano, Marc, tr. 1993. 20.00 o.p. (*0-688-12394-5*, Morrow, William & Co.) Morrow/Avon.

### AFRICA—FICTION

Achebe, Chinua. Anthills of the Savannah. 1997. 224p. pap. 10.95 (*0-385-26045-8*) Doubleday Publishing.
Achebe, Chinua & Innes, Lynn, eds. Contemporary African Short Stories. 1992. (African Writers Ser.). (Illus.). 256p. (C). pap. 11.95 (*0-435-90566-X*, 90566, African Writers Series) Heinemann.
Agualusa, Jose Eduardo. Creole Nation. 2002. 288p. pap. 16.00 (*1-900850-61-3*) Arcadia Bks. GBR. *Dist:* Consortium Bk. Sales & Distribution.
Aidoo, Ama Ata. The Girl Who Can. 2003. (Caribbean Writers Seriesr Ser.). 112p. pap. 11.95 (*0-435-91013-2*) Heinemann.
Akare, Thomas. The Slums. 1981. (African Writers Ser.). 192p. (Orig.). (C). pap. 7.95 (*0-435-90241-5*, 90241) Heinemann.
Alcock, Gudrun. Dooley's Lion: A Junior Novel. 1985. (Illus.). 112p. (J). (gr. 4 up). 11.95 o.p. (*0-88045-066-5*) Stemmer Hse. Pubs., Inc.
Aldrich, Thomas Bailey. The Queen of Sheba. 2000. 252p. E-Book 3.95 (*0-594-04253-4*) 1873 Pr.
—The Queen of Sheba. 1989. (Works of Thomas Bailey Aldrich). reprint ed. lib. bdg. 79.00 (*0-7812-1673-7*) Reprint Services Corp.
Ameritonia Staff. Marathon Love. Holmes, Sarah, ed. 2000. 215p. pap. (*0-9701345-0-9*) Ameritonia Inspirations.
Andreas, Neshani. The Purple Violet of Oshaantu. 2001. (African Writers Ser.). 185p. pap. 14.95 (*0-435-91208-9*) Greenwood Publishing Group, Inc.
Awe, Olusola Isaac. The Beautiful Beast. 2000. 72p. (Orig.). pap. 8.95 (*1-56167-361-7*, Five Star Special Edition) American Literary Pr., Inc.

Settings

Awoonor, Kofi. This Earth, My Brother... 1972. (African Writers Ser.). 183p. (C). pap. 8.95 (*0-435-90108-7*, 90108) Heinemann.

Ba, Amadou Hampate. The Fortunes of Wangrin. Taylor, Aina Pavolini, tr. from FRE. 2000. 376p. pap. 17.95 (*0-253-21226-X*); lib. bdg. 39.95 (*0-253-33429-2*) Indiana Univ. Pr.

Badke, William B. Saluso's Game. 1996. (Ben Sylvester Mystery Ser.). 260p. pap. 9.99 o.p. (*0-88070-866-2*, Multnomah Bks.) Multnomah Pubs., Inc.

—Saluso's Game. l.t. ed. 2000. (Christian Mystery Ser.). 317p. 23.95 (*0-7862-2524-6*) Thorndike Pr.

Balewa, Alhaji S. Shaihu Umar: A Historical Novel about Slavery in Africa. Hisket, Mervin, tr. 1989. (Topics in World History Ser.). (Illus.). 144p. 18.95 (*1-55876-012-1*); 124p. pap. 9.95 (*1-55876-006-7*) Wiener, Markus Pubs., Inc.

Ballard, J. G. The Crystal World. unabr. ed. 1996. audio 39.95 (*0-7451-5768-8*, CAB260) BBC Audiobooks America.

—The Crystal World. 1988. 216p. pap. 14.00 (*0-374-52096-8*) Farrar, Straus & Giroux.

—The Crystal World. 1990. audio 39.95 o.p. (*0-8161-9629-X*) Thorndike Pr.

—The Day of Creation. 1988. 17.95 o.s.i (*0-374-13527-4*) Farrar, Straus & Giroux.

Barnes, Steven. Zulu Heart. 2004. 656p. mass mkt. 6.99 (*0-446-61195-6*); 2003. (Illus.). 480p. 24.95 (*0-446-53122-7*) Warner Bks., Inc. (Aspect).

Barnett, Jill. Sentimental Journey. 2002. 528p. pap. 6.99 (*0-671-03534-7*, Pocket Star); 2001. 448p. 24.95 (*0-671-03533-9*, Atria) Simon & Schuster.

—Sentimental Journey. l.t. ed. 2002. (Basic Ser.). 741p. 29.95 (*0-7862-3638-8*) Thorndike Pr.

Bauman, Christian. The Ice Beneath You: A Novel. 2002. 256p. pap. 13.00 (*0-7432-2784-0*, Touchstone) Simon & Schuster.

Becker, Walt William. Link. 1998. (Illus.). 384p. 25.00 (*0-688-15822-6*, Morrow, William & Co.) Morrow/Avon.

—The Link. 2000. 432p. mass mkt. 6.99 o.s.i (*0-380-73161-4*, Avon Bks.) Morrow/Avon.

Beguin, Rebecca. In Unlikely Places: Searching for Miss Poole. 1990. 200p. (Orig.). pap. 8.95 (*0-934678-25-1*) New Victoria Pubs., Inc.

Behn, Aphra. Oroonoko: The Royal Slave. 1997. (Critical Editions Ser.). (Illus.). v, 90p. pap. 8.95 (*0-393-31205-4*) Norton, W. W. & Co., Inc.

Bellow, Saul. Henderson the Rain King. abr. ed. 1986. audio 15.95 o.p. (*0-88646-159-6*, 71607) Durkin Hayes Publishing Ltd.

—Henderson the Rain King. 1976. pap. 2.50 o.p. (*0-380-00832-7*, 58313-5, Avon Bks.) Morrow/Avon.

—Henderson the Rain King. 1965. pap. 2.75 o.p. (*0-670-00170-8*) Penguin Group (USA) Inc.

—Henderson the Rain King. (Great Books of the 20th Century Ser.). 1996. 352p. 13.95 (*0-14-018942-4*, Penguin Classics); 1984. 352p. pap. 11.95 o.p. (*0-14-007269-1*, Penguin Bks.); 1965. pap. 4.95 o.p. (*0-14-004229-6*, Penguin Bks.); 1959. 12.95 o.p. (*0-670-36655-2*) Viking Penguin.

Bennett, Ronan. The Catastrophist. 1998. pap. (*0-7472-7310-3*) Review.

—The Catastrophist. 2000. 336p. pap. 13.00 (*0-684-87036-3*); 2000. E-Book 24.00 (*0-7432-1337-8*); 1999. (Illus.). 336p. 24.00 o.s.i (*0-684-86334-0*) Simon & Schuster. (Simon & Schuster).

Beti, Mongo. King Lazarus. Green, Peter, tr. from FRE. 1970. (African Writers Ser.). (Orig.). pap. 7.95 o.p. (*0-435-90077-3*) Heinemann.

—Lament for an African Pol. Bjornson, Richard, tr. from FRE. & intro. by. 1985. Tr. of Ruine Preque Cocasse d'un Polichinelle. 366p. pap. 10.00 o.s.i (*0-89410-305-9*, Three Continents) Rienner, Lynne Pubs., Inc.

—Perpetua & the Habit of Unhappiness. 1978. (African Writers Ser.). (C). pap. 10.95 o.p. (*0-435-90181-8*) Heinemann.

—The Story of the Madman: A Novel. Darnel, Elizabeth, tr. from FRE. 2001. pap. 16.95 (*0-8139-2049-3*) Univ. Pr. of Virginia.

Beti, Mongo & Darnel, Elizabeth. The Story of the Madman: A Novel. 2001. (Caribbean & African Literature Translated from French Ser.). 190p. 45.00 (*0-8139-2048-5*) Univ. Pr. of Virginia.

Bickmore, Barbara. East of the Sun. 1988. pap. 8.95 o.s.i (*0-345-34259-3*) Ballantine Bks.

Bizzio, Sergio. El Son de Africa. 1993. Tr. of African Sound. (SPA.). 152p. (YA). pap. 9.95 (*968-16-4043-8*, FC438) Fondo de Cultura Economica MEX. *Dist:* Continental Bk. Co., Inc.

Boateng, Yaw M. The Return. 1977. (African Writers Ser.: No. 186). viii, 120p. (Orig.). pap. text 6.00 o.p. (*0-435-90186-9*) Heinemann.

Bognomo, Joe Eoueme. Madoulina. 2003. (Illus.). 32p. (J). (ps-3). pap. 8.95 (*1-56397-822-9*) Boyds Mills Pr.

Borden, G. F. Easter Day, Nineteen Forty-One. 1987. 256p. 16.95 o.p. (*0-688-06538-4*, Morrow, William & Co.) Morrow/Avon.

Boyd, William. An Ice Cream War. 1999. 416p. pap. 15.00 (*0-375-70502-3*, Vintage) Knopf Publishing Group.

—An Ice-Cream War. 1992. 384p. reprint ed. pap. 10.00 (*0-380-71567-8*, Avon Bks.) Morrow/Avon.

—An Ice-Cream War: A Tale of the Empire. 1984. 432p. reprint ed. pap. 7.95 o.p. (*0-14-006571-7*, Penguin Bks.) Viking Penguin.

Boyle, T. Coraghessan. Water Music. 1981. 15.95 o.p. (*0-316-10467-1*) Little Brown & Co.

—Water Music. 1983. (Penguin Contemporary American Fiction Ser.). 480p. 13.95 (*0-14-006550-4*) Viking Penguin.

Branson, Kristen L. 15 Seconds. 2001. 136p. pap. 10.95 (*0-595-17738-7*) iUniverse, Inc.

Brink, André. The Other Side of Silence. 320p. 2004. pap. (*0-15-602964-2*, Harvest Bks.); 2003. 25.00 (*0-15-100770-5*) Harcourt Trade Pubs.

Brown, Steve. Rescue! 2003. 235p. per. 15.95 (*0-9712521-2-2*) Chick Springs Publishing.

Brunger, Scott. A Trade in Death: An Economics Mystery. 1993. 192p. (Orig.). pap. 7.95 (*0-377-00265-8*) Friendship Pr.

Bull, Bartle. The Devil's Oasis. 2001. (Illus.). 356p. 25.00 (*0-7867-0844-1*); 2002. 336p. reprint ed. pap. 14.00 (*0-7867-0990-1*) Avalon Publishing Group. (Carroll & Graf Pubs.).

Burroughs, Edgar Rice. The Beasts of Tarzan. 2000. 252p. E-Book 3.95 (*0-594-05518-0*) 1873 Pr.

—The Beasts of Tarzan. 1985. (Tarzan Ser.: No. 3). 160p. mass mkt. 4.99 o.s.i (*0-345-32433-1*, Del Rey); 1980. mass mkt. 1.95 o.p. (*0-345-29513-7*); 1979. mass mkt. 1.75 o.p. (*0-345-28324-4*); 1977. mass mkt. 1.50 o.p. (*0-345-25832-0*); 1975. mass mkt. 1.25 o.p. (*0-345-24161-4*) Ballantine Bks.

—The Beasts of Tarzan. rev. ed. 2000. 200p. per. 9.90 (*1-58396-013-9*) Blue Unicorn Editions.

—The Beasts of Tarzan, Bk. 3. unabr. ed. 1993. audio 39.95 (*1-55686-480-9*, 480) Books in Motion.

—The Beasts of Tarzan. E-Book 3.49 (*1-929120-13-3*) Electric Umbrella Publishing.

—The Beasts of Tarzan. 2002. 192p. 24.99 (*1-58827-834-4*); per. 19.99 (*1-58827-835-2*) IndyPublish.com.

—The Beasts of Tarzan. (Tarzan Ser.: No. 3). E-Book 1.95 (*1-57799-821-9*) Logos Research Systems, Inc.

—The Beasts of Tarzan. 1999. E-Book 1.95 (*1-58515-077-0*) MesaView, Inc.

—The Beasts of Tarzan. 2003. (Quiet Vision Classic Ser.). (Illus.). 210p. text 24.99 (*1-57646-658-2*); 2003. (Quiet Vision Classic Ser.). (Illus.). 210p. pap. 12.99 (*1-57646-641-8*); 2000. (Tarzan Ser.: Vol. 3). 144p. pap. 9.99 (*1-57646-236-6*); 2000. (Tarzan Ser.: Vol. 3). 144p. lib. bdg. 27.99 (*1-57646-474-1*); 2000. (Tarzan Ser.: Vol. 3). 270p. pap. 17.99 (*1-57646-475-X*); 2000. (Tarzan Ser.: Vol. 3). 270p. lib. bdg. 29.99 (*1-57646-476-8*) Quiet Vision Publishing.

—The Beasts of Tarzan. E-Book 5.00 (*0-7410-0833-5*) SoftBook Pr.

—The Beasts of Tarzan. 2002. 240p. lib. bdg. 29.95 (*1-58715-621-0*) Wildside Pr.

—The Jungle Tales of Tarzan. E-Book 3.95 (*0-594-06141-5*) 1873 Pr.

—The Jungle Tales of Tarzan. 1980. mass mkt. 1.95 o.p. (*0-345-29478-5*); 1975. mass mkt. 1.25 o.p. (*0-345-24164-9*); No. 6. 1986. 192p. mass mkt. 3.95 o.s.i (*0-345-34413-8*, Del Rey) Ballantine Bks.

—The Jungle Tales of Tarzan. l.t. ed. 2000. 350p. per. 15.50 (*1-58396-103-8*); 2001. 200p. per. 9.90 (*1-58396-007-4*) Blue Unicorn Editions.

—The Jungle Tales of Tarzan. E-Book 3.49 (*1-929120-18-4*) Electric Umbrella Publishing.

—The Jungle Tales of Tarzan. 2002. 184p. 93.99 (*1-4043-1154-8*); per. 89.99 (*1-4043-1155-6*) IndyPublish.com.

—The Jungle Tales of Tarzan. (Tarzan Ser.: No. 6). E-Book 1.95 (*1-57799-824-3*) Logos Research Systems, Inc.

—The Jungle Tales of Tarzan. 1999. E-Book 1.95 (*1-58515-079-7*) MesaView, Inc.

—The Jungle Tales of Tarzan. 2003. (Quiet Vision Classic Ser.). (Illus.). text 24.99 (*1-57646-661-2*); 2003. (Quiet Vision Classic Ser.). (Illus.). pap. 12.99 (*1-57646-646-9*); 2000. (Tarzan Ser.: Vol. 6). 140p. pap. 9.99 (*1-57646-237-4*); 2000. (Tarzan Ser.: Vol. 6). 140p. lib. bdg. 27.99 (*1-57646-483-0*); 1999. (Tarzan Ser.: Vol. 6). 344p. E-Book 3.99 o.p. incl. cd-rom (*1-891595-58-X*); 2000. (Tarzan Ser.: Vol. 6). 298p. pap. 19.99 (*1-57646-484-9*); 2000. (Tarzan Ser.: Vol. 6). 298p. lib. bdg. 31.99 (*1-57646-485-7*) Quiet Vision Publishing.

—The Jungle Tales of Tarzan. 2nd ed. 2002. 256p. lib. bdg. 29.95 (*1-59224-958-2*) Wildside Pr.

—The Return of Tarzan. Date not set. 221p. 21.95 (*0-8488-2223-4*) Amereon, Ltd.

—The Return of Tarzan. 1984. (Tarzan Ser.: Vol. 2). 224p. mass mkt. 5.99 (*0-345-31575-8*, Ballantine Bks.) Ballantine Bks.

—The Return of Tarzan. unabr. ed. 2000. audio 44.95 (*0-7861-1728-1*, 2531) Blackstone Audio Bks., Inc.

—The Return of Tarzan. rev. ed. 2000. 300p. per. 9.90 (*1-58396-021-X*) Blue Unicorn Editions.

—The Return of Tarzan, Bk. 2. unabr. ed. 1993. audio 39.95 (*1-55686-479-5*, 479) Books in Motion.

—The Return of Tarzan. E-Book 1.49 (*1-929120-22-2*) Electric Umbrella Publishing.

—The Return of Tarzan. (Tarzan Ser.: No. 2). E-Book 2.95 (*1-57799-820-0*) Logos Research Systems, Inc.

—The Return of Tarzan. 1999. E-Book 1.95 (*1-58515-080-0*) MesaView, Inc.

—The Return of Tarzan. (Tarzan Ser.: Vol. 2). 2000. 178p. pap. 9.99 (*1-57646-244-7*); 2000. 178p. lib. bdg. 29.99 (*1-57646-471-7*); 1999. 443p. E-Book 3.99 o.p. incl. cd-rom (*1-891595-54-7*); 2000. 370p. pap. 24.99 (*1-57646-472-5*); 2000. 370p. lib. bdg. 34.99 (*1-57646-473-3*) Quiet Vision Publishing.

—The Son of Tarzan. 2000. 252p. pap. 9.95 (*0-594-04535-5*); E-Book 3.95 (*0-594-04538-X*) 1873 Pr.

—The Son of Tarzan. 1986. (Tarzan Ser.: No. 4). 222p. mass mkt. 4.99 o.s.i (*0-345-33556-2*, Del Rey) Ballantine Bks.

—The Son of Tarzan. rev. ed. 2000. 300p. per. 9.90 (*1-58396-022-8*) Blue Unicorn Editions.

—The Son of Tarzan, Bk. 4. unabr. ed. 1993. audio 49.95 (*1-55686-481-7*, 481) Books in Motion.

—The Son of Tarzan. E-Book 1.49 (*1-929120-23-0*) Electric Umbrella Publishing.

—The Son of Tarzan. (Tarzan Ser.: No. 4). E-Book 1.95 (*1-57799-822-7*) Logos Research Systems, Inc.

—The Son of Tarzan. 1999. E-Book 1.95 (*1-58515-081-9*) MesaView, Inc.

—The Son of Tarzan. 2000. (Tarzan Ser.: Vol. 4). 184p. pap. 9.99 (*1-57646-245-5*); 154p. lib. bdg. 28.99 (*1-57646-477-6*); 388p. pap. 24.99 (*1-57646-478-4*); 388p. lib. bdg. 35.99 (*1-57646-479-2*) Quiet Vision Publishing.

—The Son of Tarzan. unabr. ed. 2002. audio compact disk 42.00 (*1-4001-0056-9*); audio compact disk 20.00 (*1-4001-5056-6*) Tantor Media, Inc.

—The Son of Tarzan. 1998. lib. bdg. 27.95 (*1-56723-026-1*) Yestermorrow, Inc.

—Tarzan: Jungle Stories. unabr. ed. 1995. audio 39.95 (*1-55686-591-0*) Books in Motion.

—Tarzan & the Ant Men. (Tarzan Ser.). 1980. mass mkt. 1.95 o.p. (*0-345-28997-8*); 1979. mass mkt. 1.75 o.p. (*0-345-27984-0*); 1976. mass mkt. 1.25 o.p. (*0-345-24169-X*); 1969. mass mkt. 0.50 o.p. (*0-345-21752-7*); No. 10. 1985. 190p. mass mkt. 3.99 o.s.i (*0-345-32393-9*, Del Rey) Ballantine Bks.

—Tarzan & the Castaways. 1987. mass mkt. 2.50 o.s.i (*0-345-35255-6*); 1985. mass mkt. 2.25 o.s.i (*0-345-33433-7*); 1979. mass mkt. 1.95 o.p. (*0-345-28615-4*); 1977. mass mkt. 1.75 o.p. (*0-345-25964-5*) Ballantine Bks.

—Tarzan & the Castaways. 1975. (Illus.). reprint ed. 14.95 o.p. (*0-940724-10-3*) Hunt, Paul.

—Tarzan & the City of Gold. (Tarzan Ser.). 1980. mass mkt. 1.75 o.p. (*0-345-28035-0*); 1975. mass mkt. 1.25 o.p. (*0-345-24486-9*); No. 16. 1980. mass mkt. 3.95 o.s.i (*0-345-28987-0*, Del Rey) Ballantine Bks.

—Tarzan & the Forbidden City. 1980. 176p. mass mkt. 4.50 o.s.i (*0-345-29106-9*, Del Rey); 1977. mass mkt. 1.75 o.p. (*0-345-25960-2*); 1975. mass mkt. 1.25 o.p. (*0-345-24976-3*) Ballantine Bks.

—Tarzan & the Foreign Legion. 1987. mass mkt. 3.99 o.s.i (*0-345-34750-1*, Del Rey); 1984. mass mkt. 2.25 o.p. (*0-345-32454-4*); 1980. mass mkt. 1.95 o.p. (*0-345-28981-1*); 1977. mass mkt. 1.75 o.p. (*0-345-25962-9*); 1975. mass mkt. 1.25 o.p. (*0-345-24978-X*) Ballantine Bks.

—Tarzan & the Golden Lion. (Tarzan Ser.). 1980. mass mkt. 1.95 o.p. (*0-345-28998-6*); 1978. mass mkt. 1.75 o.p. (*0-345-27983-2*); 1976. mass mkt. 1.25 o.p. (*0-345-24168-1*); No. 9. 1986. 192p. mass mkt. 3.99 o.s.i (*0-345-34237-2*, Del Rey) Ballantine Bks.

—Tarzan & the Jewels of Opar. 2000. 252p. pap. 9.95 (*0-594-04520-7*); E-Book 3.95 (*0-594-04523-1*) 1873 Pr.

—Tarzan & the Jewels of Opar. 1998. mass mkt. 5.99 (*0-345-91423-6*, Del Rey); 1980. mass mkt. 1.95 o.p. (*0-345-28917-X*); 1978. mass mkt. 1.75 o.p. (*0-345-27728-7*); 1977. mass mkt. 1.50 o.p. (*0-345-27277-3*); 1975. mass mkt. 1.25 o.p. (*0-345-24163-0*); No. 5. 1984. 158p. mass mkt. 5.99 o.s.i (*0-345-32161-8*, Del Rey) Ballantine Bks.

—Tarzan & the Jewels of Opar. 2000. 200p. per. 9.90 (*1-58396-010-4*); 2001. 350p. per. 15.50 (*1-58396-105-4*) Blue Unicorn Editions.

—Tarzan & the Jewels of Opar, Bk. 5. unabr. ed. 1994. audio 39.95 (*1-55686-495-7*) Books in Motion.

—Tarzan & the Jewels of Opar. E-Book 3.49 (*1-929120-20-6*) Electric Umbrella Publishing.

—Tarzan & the Jewels of Opar. (Tarzan Ser.: No. 5). E-Book 1.95 (*1-57799-823-5*) Logos Research Systems, Inc.

—Tarzan & the Jewels of Opar. 1999. E-Book 1.95 (*1-58515-084-3*) MesaView, Inc.

—Tarzan & the Jewels of Opar. 2003. (Illus.). 196p. text 24.99 (*1-57646-660-4*); 2003. (Illus.). 196p. pap. 12.99 (*1-57646-644-2*); 2000. (Tarzan Ser.: Vol. 5). 146p. pap. 9.99 (*1-57646-247-1*); 2000. (Tarzan Ser.: Vol. 5). 146p. lib. bdg. 27.99 (*1-57646-480-6*); 1999. (Tarzan Ser.: Vol. 5). 333p. E-Book 3.99 o.p. incl. cd-rom (*1-891595-57-1*); 2000. (Tarzan Ser.: Vol. 5). 280p. pap. 19.99 (*1-57646-481-4*); 2000. (Tarzan Ser.: Vol. 5). 280p. lib. bdg. 30.99 (*1-57646-482-2*) Quiet Vision Publishing.

—Tarzan & the Jewels of Opar. E-Book 5.00 (*0-7410-0800-9*) SoftBook Pr.

—Tarzan & the Jewels of Opar. 2002. 248p. lib. bdg. 29.95 (*1-59224-959-0*) Wildside Pr.

—Tarzan & the Leopard Men. 1986. (Tarzan Ser.: Vol. 18). mass mkt. 4.99 o.s.i (*0-345-33828-6*, Del Rey); 1979. mass mkt. 1.95 o.p. (*0-345-28687-1*); 1978. mass mkt. 1.75 o.p. (*0-345-27804-6*); 1975. mass mkt. 1.25 o.p. (*0-345-24488-5*) Ballantine Bks.

—Tarzan & the Lion Men. (Tarzan Ser.). 1978. mass mkt. 1.75 o.p. (*0-345-28008-3*); 1975. mass mkt. 1.25 o.p. (*0-345-24487-7*); No. 17. 1980. 192p. mass mkt. 2.95 o.s.i (*0-345-28988-9*, Del Rey) Ballantine Bks.

—Tarzan & the Lost Empire, No. 12. 1985. 190p. mass mkt. 3.95 o.s.i (*0-345-32957-0*, Del Rey) Ballantine Bks.

—Tarzan & the Madman No. 23. 1987. mass mkt. 3.95 o.s.i (*0-345-35037-5*, Del Rey); 1977. mass mkt. 1.75 o.s.i (*0-345-25963-7*) Ballantine Bks.

—Tarzan & the Madman No. 23. 1975. (Illus.). reprint ed. 60.00 o.p. (*0-940724-11-1*) Hunt, Paul.

—Tarzan & the Tarzan Twins. 1982. (Illus.). 14.95 o.p. (*0-940724-12-X*) Hunt, Paul.

—The Tarzan Collection, 3 vols. rev. ed. 2000. 1200p. per. 35.00 (*1-58396-009-0*) Blue Unicorn Editions.

—The Tarzan Collection. 1999. E-Book 8.99 incl. cd-rom (*1-57646-061-4*) Quiet Vision Publishing.

—Tarzan, Lion Man & Leopard Man. 1999. mass mkt. (*0-345-41754-2*, Del Rey) Ballantine Bks.

—Tarzan, Lord of the Jungle. 1980. mass mkt. 1.95 o.p. (*0-345-28986-2*); 1978. mass mkt. 1.75 o.p. (*0-345-27985-9*); No. 11. 1984. 190p. mass mkt. 4.99 o.s.i (*0-345-32455-2*, Del Rey) Ballantine Bks.

—Tarzan of the Apes. 22.95 (*0-8488-1257-3*) Amereon, Ltd.

—Tarzan of the Apes, unabr. ed. 1999. (YA). (gr. 5 up). audio 41.95 (*1-55685-633-4*) Audio Bk. Contractors, Inc.

—Tarzan of the Apes. abr. ed. 1999. audio 16.95 (*1-882071-43-3*) B&B Audio, Inc.

—Tarzan of the Apes. 1984. (Tarzan Ser.: Vol. 1). (Illus.). 288p. mass mkt. 6.99 (*0-345-31977-X*, Del Rey) Ballantine Bks.

—Tarzan of the Apes. unabr. ed. 1995. 9p. audio 44.95 (*0-7861-0673-5*, 1575) Blackstone Audio Bks., Inc.

—Tarzan of the Apes. rev. ed. 2000. 300p. per. 9.90 (*1-58396-011-2*) Blue Unicorn Editions.

—Tarzan of the Apes, Bk. 1. unabr. ed. 1993. audio 49.95 (*1-55686-477-9*, 477) Books in Motion.

—Tarzan of the Apes. unabr. collector's ed. 1993. (YA). (gr. 8 up). audio 48.00 (*0-7366-2596-8*, 3341) Books on Tape, Inc.

—Tarzan of the Apes. 1976. reprint ed. lib. bdg. 25.95 (*0-89966-046-0*) Buccaneer Bks., Inc.

—Tarzan of the Apes. 1999. (Tarzan of the Apes Ser.). 352p. mass mkt. 4.99 (*0-8125-7238-6*, Tor Bks.) Doherty, Tom Assocs., LLC.

—Tarzan of the Apes. 1997. (Thrift Editions Ser.). 224p. reprint ed. pap. text 2.00 (*0-486-29570-2*) Dover Pubns., Inc.

—Tarzan of the Apes. E-Book 3.49 (*1-929120-09-5*) Electric Umbrella Publishing.

—Tarzan of the Apes. unabr. ed. 1989. (YA). (gr. 6-10). audio 39.00 Jimcin Recordings.

—Tarzan of the Apes. E-Book 2.95 (*1-57799-819-7*) Logos Research Systems, Inc.

—Tarzan of the Apes. 1990. 228p. (YA). mass mkt. 4.95 (*0-451-52423-3*, Signet Classics) NAL.

—Tarzan of the Apes. abr. ed. (Ultimate Classics Ser.). 1994. audio 29.95 o.p. (*0-7871-0063-3*, Dove Audio); 1993. 16.95 o.p. (*1-55800-757-1*, 391741) NewStar Media, Inc.

—Tarzan of the Apes. (Tarzan Ser.: Vol. 1). 1999. 483p. E-Book 3.99 o.p. incl. cd-rom (*1-891595-53-9*); 2000. 378p. pap. 24.99 (*1-57646-469-5*); 2000. 378p. lib. bdg. 35.99 (*1-57646-470-9*) Quiet Vision Publishing.

—Tarzan of the Apes. 1998. 672p. 9.99 o.s.i (*0-517-18907-0*); 1988. xvi, 848p. 7.99 o.s.i (*0-517-65957-3*) Random Hse. Value Publishing.

—Tarzan of the Apes. l.t. ed. 1994. 381p. lib. bdg. 21.95 (*0-7838-1160-8*) Thorndike Pr.

—Tarzan of the Apes. 1963. 12.04 (*0-606-14346-7*) Turtleback Bks.

—Tarzan of the Apes. 1990. (Penguin Twentieth-Century Classics Ser.). 320p. 8.95 (*0-14-018464-3*, Penguin Classics) Viking Penguin.

—Tarzan the Invincible. 1987. 192p. mass mkt. 3.99 o.s.i (*0-345-35163-0*, Del Rey); 1980. mass mkt. 1.95 o.p. (*0-345-28989-7*); 1978. mass mkt. 1.25 o.p. (*0-345-24484-2*); 1978. mass mkt. 1.75 o.p. (*0-345-28055-5*); 1974. mass mkt. 0.95 o.p. (*0-345-21908-2*) Ballantine Bks.
—Tarzan the Magnificent. 1980. 200p. mass mkt. 3.95 o.s.i (*0-345-28980-3*, Del Rey); 1977. mass mkt. 1.75 o.p. (*0-345-25961-0*); 1975. mass mkt. 1.25 o.p. (*0-345-24977-1*) Ballantine Bks.
—Tarzan the Terrible. 1979. mass mkt. 1.95 o.p. (*0-345-28745-2*); 1978. mass mkt. 1.75 o.p. (*0-345-27982-4*); 1969. mass mkt. 0.50 o.p. (*0-345-21750-0*); No. 8. 1985. 190p. mass mkt. 3.99 o.s.i (*0-345-32392-0*, Del Rey) Ballantine Bks.
—Tarzan the Terrible. 2001. per. (*1-58396-255-7*); 2000. per. 9.90 (*1-58396-093-7*); 2001. per. (*1-58396-256-5*); 2001. per. 15.50 (*1-58396-179-8*) Blue Unicorn Editions.
—Tarzan the Terrible. E-Book 2.49 (*0-7574-0327-1*) Electric Umbrella Publishing.
—Tarzan the Terrible. 2003. (Illus.). 266p. text 24.99 (*1-57646-663-9*); 2003. (Illus.). 266p. pap. 12.99 (*1-57646-648-5*); 2000. (Tarzan Ser.: Vol. 8). 186p. pap. 9.99 (*1-57646-249-8*); 2000. (Tarzan Ser.: Vol. 8). 186p. lib. bdg. 30.99 (*1-57646-489-X*); 2000. (Tarzan Ser.: Vol. 8). 388p. lib. bdg. 34.99 (*1-57646-491-1*) Quiet Vision Publishing.
—Tarzan the Terrible. 2002. 284p. lib. bdg. 29.95 (*1-59224-960-4*) Wildside Pr.
—Tarzan the Triumphant. 1987. mass mkt. 2.50 o.s.i (*0-345-35274-2*); 1978. mass mkt. 1.75 o.p. (*0-345-28054-7*) Ballantine Bks.
—Tarzan the Untamed. 1979. mass mkt. 1.95 o.p. (*0-345-28868-8*); 1978. mass mkt. 1.75 o.p. (*0-345-27697-3*); 1971. mass mkt. 0.50 o.p. (*0-345-21749-7*); No. 7. 1984. 254p. mass mkt. 4.99 o.s.i (*0-345-32391-2*, Del Rey) Ballantine Bks.
—Tarzan the Untamed. 2000. 300p. per. 9.90 (*1-58396-012-0*); 2001. per. 15.50 (*1-58396-107-0*) Blue Unicorn Editions.
—Tarzan the Untamed. 1999. 96p. (YA). (gr. 7 up). pap. 11.95 (*1-56971-418-5*) Dark Horse Comics.
—Tarzan the Untamed. E-Book 1.49 (*1-929120-24-9*) Electric Umbrella Publishing.
—Tarzan the Untamed. (Tarzan Ser.: No. 7). E-Book 1.95 (*1-57799-825-1*) Logos Research Systems, Inc.
—Tarzan the Untamed. 2003. (Illus.). 294p. text 24.99 (*1-57646-662-0*); 2003. (Illus.). 294p. pap. 12.99 (*1-57646-647-7*); 2000. (Tarzan Ser.: Vol. 7). 206p. pap. 9.99 (*1-57646-248-X*); 2000. (Tarzan Ser.: Vol. 7). 206p. lib. bdg. 31.99 (*1-57646-486-5*); 1999. (Tarzan Ser.: Vol. 7). 510p. E-Book 3.99 o.p. incl. cd-rom (*1-891595-59-8*); 2000. (Tarzan Ser.: Vol. 7). 434p. pap. 29.99 (*1-57646-487-3*); 2000. (Tarzan Ser.: Vol. 7). 434p. lib. bdg. 38.99 (*1-57646-488-1*) Quiet Vision Publishing.
—Tarzan the Untamed. 2002. 236p. lib. bdg. 29.95 (*1-58715-311-4*) Wildside Pr.
—Tarzan Triumphant: And Tarzan & the City of Gold. 1997. (Tarzan Ser.). mass mkt. 6.99 o.s.i (*0-345-41641-4*, Del Rey) Ballantine Bks.
—Tarzan 2 in 1: Tarzan & the Golden Lion & Tarzan & the Ant Men, Vols. 9 and10. 1997. (Access to History Ser.). 426p. mass mkt. 5.99 o.s.i (*0-345-41348-2*, Del Rey) Ballantine Bks.
—Tarzan 2 in 1: Tarzan & the Jewels of Opar & Jungle Tales of Tarzan. 1996. (Tarzan Ser.). 340p. mass mkt. 5.99 o.s.i (*0-345-40831-4*) Ballantine Bks.
—Tarzan 2 in 1: Tarzan, Lord of the Jungle & Tarzan & the Lost Empire. 1997. (Tarzan the Classics Ser.). 406p. mass mkt. 5.99 o.s.i (*0-345-41347-4*, Del Rey) Ballantine Bks.
—Tarzan 2 in 1: Tarzan the Untamed & Tarzan the Terrible, Vol. 7 & 8. 1997. mass mkt. 5.99 o.s.i (*0-345-40832-2*, Del Rey) Ballantine Bks.
—Tarzan 2-in-1: The Beasts of Tarzan/The Son of Tarzan, 2 vols. in 1, Vols. 3-4. 1996. (Tarzan the Classics Ser.). 384p. mass mkt. 6.99 (*0-345-40830-6*, Del Rey) Ballantine Bks.
—Tarzan 3 in 1. 1996. mass mkt. o.s.i (*0-345-40647-8*) Ballantine Bks.
—Tarzan's Quest. 1999. mass mkt. (*0-345-41755-0*, Del Rey); 1977. mass mkt. 1.75 o.p. (*0-345-25959-9*) Ballantine Bks.
—Tarzan's Quest No. 19. 1980. 178p. mass mkt. 4.99 o.s.i (*0-345-29562-5*, Del Rey) Ballantine Bks.
Burroughs, Edgar Rice & Lansdale, Joe R. Tarzan: The Lost Adventures. 1997. (Tarzan Ser.). 272p. mass mkt. 5.99 o.s.i (*0-345-41273-7*, Del Rey) Ballantine Bks.
—Tarzan: The Lost Adventures. ltd. ed. 1996. (Illus.). 208p. (YA). (gr. 7 up). pap. 19.95 (*1-56971-083-X*) Dark Horse Comics.
—Terminator: The Tempest. ltd. ed. 1996. (Illus.). 208p. (YA). (gr. 7 up). 99.95 o.p. (*1-56971-128-3*) Dark Horse Comics.
Burroughs, Edgar Rice, et al. Tarzan: Le Monstre. 1998. (Illus.). 160p. (YA). (gr. 9 up). pap. 16.95 (*1-56971-296-4*) Dark Horse Comics.
—Tarzan of the Apes. 1999. 104p. (YA). (gr. 7 up). pap. 12.95 (*1-56971-416-9*) Dark Horse Comics.
Burroughs, William S. Ghost of Chance. 1995. (High Risk Ser.). (Illus.). 96p. (*1-85242-406-0*) Serpent's Tail Ltd.
—Ghost of Chance. 2002. (Illus.). 96p. pap. 11.00 (*1-85242-457-5*) Serpent's Tail Ltd. GBR. *Dist:* Consortium Bk. Sales & Distribution.
Calasso, Roberto. The Ruin of Kasch. Weaver, William & Sartarelli, Stephen, trs. 1996. Orig. Title: Rovina di Kasch. 400p. pap. 14.95 (*0-674-78029-9*) Harvard Univ. Pr.
—The Ruin of Kasch. Weaver, William & Sartorelli, Stephen, trs. from ITA. 1996. Orig. Title: Rovina di Kasch. 400p. pap. text 24.95 (*0-674-78026-4*, Belknap Pr.) Harvard Univ. Pr.
Canning, Victor. Black Flamingo. 2001. (Black Dagger Crime Ser.). 192p. 21.95 (*0-7540-8597-X*, Black Dagger) BBC Audiobooks America.
Carey, Robert D. & Furbay, John H. Freedom Ships: The Spectacular Epic of African Americans Who Dared to Find Their Freedom Long Before Emancipation. 1999. (Illus.). 358p. (Orig.). pap. 14.95 (*0-9669613-0-7*, 101) Af-Am Links Pr.
Carr, Caleb. Killing Time: A Novel of the Future. l.t. ed. 2000. 368p. 25.95 (*0-375-43076-8*) Random Hse. Large Print.
Casper, Claudia. The Reconstruction. 1998. pap. 12.95 (*0-312-18164-7*, Saint Martin's Griffin); 1996. 272p. 22.95 o.p. (*0-312-15199-3*) St. Martin's Pr.
Cheney-Coker, Syl. The Last Harmattan of Alusine Dunbar. 1990. (African Writers Ser.). 398p. (Orig.). (C). pap. 9.95 (*0-435-90572-4*, 90572) Heinemann.
Chinodya, Shimmer. Dew in the Morning. 2001. (African Writers Ser.). 218p. pap. 15.95 (*0-435-91206-2*) Heinemann.
Chraibi, Driss. The Mother Spring. Harter, Hugh A., tr. from FRE. 1982. 118p. 12.00 (*0-89410-401-2*); pap. 12.00 (*0-89410-402-0*) Rienner, Lynne Pubs., Inc. (Three Continents).
—The Simple Past. Harter, Hugh A., tr. 1990. 163p. pap. 11.95 o.s.i (*0-89410-400-4*); 1989. 123p. pap. 11.95 o.p. (*0-89410-399-7*) Rienner, Lynne Pubs., Inc. (Three Continents).
Christie, Agatha. Death on the Nile. unabr. ed. 2001. audio 29.95 (*1-57270-203-6*, N61203u, Audio Editions Mystery Masters) Audio Partners Publishing Corp.
—Death on the Nile. abr. ed. 2003. (Agatha Christie Audio Mystery Ser.). (Illus.). audio 12.95 (*1-55927-905-2*) Audio Renaissance.
—Death on the Nile. unabr. ed. 1997. (Hercule Poirot Mystery Ser.). audio 69.95 (*0-7451-5839-0*, CAB 601) BBC Audiobooks America.
—Death on the Nile. 1987. mass mkt. o.s.i (*0-553-16787-1*) Bantam Bks.
—Death on the Nile. 2000. (Hercule Poirot Mystery Ser.). 320p. mass mkt. 5.99 (*0-425-17373-9*); (Illus.). 307p. reprint ed. pap. 12.00 o.s.i (*0-425-17441-7*) Berkley Publishing Group.
—Death on the Nile. 1985. (Agatha Christie Ser.). 12.95 o.s.i (*0-396-08573-3*, G. P. Putnam's Sons) Penguin Putnam Bks. for Young Readers.
—Death on the Nile. l.t. ed. 1983. 480p. 12.50 o.p. (*0-85456-671-6*, Ulverscroft) Thorpe, F. A. Pubs. GBR. *Dist:* Ulverscroft Large Print Bks., Ltd.
—Death on the Nile. 2001. 12.04 (*0-606-21143-8*); 1992. 12.04 (*0-606-12248-6*) Turtleback Bks.
—Death on the Nile: BBC. abr. ed. 1997. (Hercule Poirot Mystery Ser.). audio 16.99 o.s.i (*0-553-47811-7*, RH Audio) Random Hse. Audio Publishing Group.
Clark, Don L. Sunday in Sudan. 2000. 19.95 (*1-58345-933-2*); pap. 13.95 (*1-58345-934-0*) Domhan Bks.
Cocks, Chris. Cyclone Blues. 2001. 294p. pap. 17.50 (*0-620-25438-6*) Covos-Day Bks. ZAF. *Dist:* BHB International, Inc.
Coetzee, J. M. Dusklands. 1985. (Fiction Ser.). 144p. pap. 9.95 o.p. (*0-14-007114-8*, Penguin Bks.) Viking Penguin.
—Waiting for the Barbarians. 1999. (Penguin Great Books of the 20th Century Ser.). (Illus.). 160p. pap. 14.00 (*0-14-028335-8*, Penguin Bks.) Penguin Group (USA) Inc.
—Waiting for the Barbarians. 1982. 160p. 14.00 (*0-14-006110-X*) Viking Penguin.
Conde, Maryse. A Season in Rihata. Philcox, Richard, tr. 1988. (Caribbean Writers Ser.). 192p. (Orig.). (C). pap. 9.95 (*0-435-98832-8*, 98832) Heinemann.
Conrad, Joseph. Heart of Darkness. unabr. ed. audio 23.80 Audio Bk. Co.
—Heart of Darkness. l.t. ed. 1998. 181p. pap. 19.95 (*1-55701-210-5*) BNI Pubns., Inc.
—Heart of Darkness. 1982. 128p. reprint ed. 12.50 (*0-8376-0458-3*) Bentley Pubs.
—Heart of Darkness. unabr. ed. 1994. audio 23.95 (*0-7861-0442-2*, 1394) Blackstone Audio Bks., Inc.
—Heart of Darkness. unabr. ed. 1987. audio 26.95 (*1-55686-232-6*) Books in Motion.
—Heart of Darkness. Goonetilleke, D. C. R A., ed. 1995. 280p. pap. (*1-55111-065-2*) Broadview Pr.
—Heart of Darkness. 1979. 8.50 o.p. (*0-460-00694-0*, Dutton) Dutton/Plume.
—Heart of Darkness. 2003. (Green Integer Bks.: Vol. 58). 160p. pap. 10.95 (*1-892295-49-0*) Green Integer.
—Heart of Darkness. 1972. audio 19.95 o.p. (*0-694-50399-1*, SWC 2043, Caedmon) HarperTrade.
—Heart of Darkness, Set. unabr. ed. 1999. audio 23.95 Highsmith Inc.
—Heart of Darkness. 1993. (Everyman's Library: Vol. 174). 144p. 15.00 (*0-679-42801-1*) Knopf, Alfred A. Inc.
—Heart of Darkness. 1999. (Cloth Bound Pocket Ser.). 7.95 (*3-8290-3003-7*, 521120) Konemann.
—Heart of Darkness. l.t. ed. 1997. (Large Print Heritage Ser.). 156p. lib. bdg. 26.95 (*1-58118-004-7*, 21963) LRS.
—Heart of Darkness. 1993. audio 32.00 (*1-56544-021-8*, 350010); audio Literate Ear, Inc.
—Heart of Darkness. unabr. ed. 1993. 19.95 o.p. (*1-55800-673-7*, 492058) NewStar Media, Inc.
—Heart of Darkness. Kimbrough, Robert, ed. rev. ed. 1972. (Critical Editions Ser.). (C). pap. o.p. (*0-393-09773-0*) Norton, W. W. & Co., Inc.
—Heart of Darkness. (Penguin Great Books of the 20th Century Ser.). 1999. 160p. pap. 10.00 (*0-14-028163-0*); 1994. 128p. pap. 3.95 o.p. (*0-14-024017-9*, Penguin Bks.) Penguin Group (USA) Inc.
—Heart of Darkness. abr. ed. 1994. (Classics on Cassette). pap. 16.00 o.s.i incl. audio (*0-453-00913-1*, 390908) Penguin/HighBridge.
—Heart of Darkness. 1999. E-Book 3.99 incl. cd-rom (*1-57646-005-3*) Quiet Vision Publishing.
—Heart of Darkness. 1958. pap. Random Hse., Inc.
—Heart of Darkness, Set. unabr. ed. audio 24.95 (*1-883049-78-4*, Commuters Library) Sound Room Pubs., Inc.
—Heart of Darkness. 1996. pap. text 13.95 o.p. (*0-312-13843-1*) St. Martin's Pr.
—Heart of Darkness. Murfin, Ross C., ed. 1989. 270p. (C). pap. text 7.95 o.s.i (*0-312-00761-2*) St. Martin's Pr.
—Heart of Darkness. 2nd ed. 1996. 304p. pap. text 14.95 o.p. (*0-312-14204-8*) St. Martin's Pr.
—Heart of Darkness. abr. ed. 1999. audio 14.95 (*0-00-105049-4*, Trafalgar Square Publishing) Trafalgar Square.
—Heart of Darkness. Watts, Cedric, ed. 1995. pap. 6.95 o.p. (*0-460-87292-3*, Everyman's Classic Library in Paperback) Tuttle Publishing.
—Heart of Darkness. (Penguin Great Books of the 20th Century Ser.). 1995. 224p. pap. 7.95 (*0-14-018652-2*); 1989. 128p. pap. 3.95 o.p. (*0-14-018090-7*) Viking Penguin. (Penguin Classics).
—Heart of Darkness. O'Prey, Paul, ed. 1984. (English Library). 128p. pap. 2.95 o.p. (*0-14-043168-3*, Penguin Classics) Viking Penguin.
—Heart of Darkness. 1998. (Classics Library). 240p. pap. 3.95 (*1-85326-240-4*, 2404WW) Wordsworth Editions, Ltd. GBR. *Dist:* Casemate Pubs. & Bk. Distributors, LLC.
—Heart of Darkness. 1998. lib. bdg. 18.95 (*1-56723-033-4*) Yestermorrow, Inc.
Conrad, Joseph & Goonetilleke, D. C. R A. Heart of Darkness. 2nd ed. 1999. (Literary Texts Ser.). 260p. pap. (*1-55111-307-4*) Broadview Pr.
Coplin, Keith. Croftons Fire. 2004. 288p. 21.95 (*0-399-15112-5*, G. P. Putnam's Sons) Penguin Putnam Bks. for Young Readers.
Courtemanche, Gil. A Sunday at the Pool in Kigali. Claxton, Patricia, tr. from FRE. 2003. 272p. 23.00 (*1-4000-4107-4*, Everyman's Library) Knopf Publishing Group.
Couto, Mia. Under the Frangipani. 2001. 160p. pap. 15.00 (*1-85242-729-9*) Serpent's Tail Ltd. GBR. *Dist:* Consortium Bk. Sales & Distribution.
Covey, Stephen R. The Lion King. 1994. (Little Golden Bks.). (Illus.). 24p. (J). (ps-2). bds. 2.99 (*0-307-30145-1*, 98136, Golden Bks.) Random Hse. Children's Bks.
Crichton, Michael. Congo.Tr. of Congo. 1997. pap. 12.00 o.s.i (*0-345-41893-X*); 1995. mass mkt. 6.99 o.p. (*0-345-90401-X*); 1992. mass mkt. 5.99 o.p. (*0-345-90230-0*); 1992. 336p. mass mkt. 7.99 o.s.i (*0-345-37849-0*) Ballantine Bks.
—Congo. 1993. Tr. of Congo. reprint ed. lib. bdg. 27.95 (*1-56849-126-3*) Buccaneer Bks., Inc.
—Congo. l.t. ed. 1981. Tr. of Congo. lib. bdg. 14.95 o.p. (*0-8161-3202-X*, Macmillan Reference USA) Gale Group.
—Congo.Tr. of Congo. 2003. 464p. mass mkt. 7.99 (*0-06-054183-0*); 1981. pap. 3.95 o.p. (*0-380-56176-X*, 69682-7) Morrow/Avon. (Avon Bks.).
—Congo. 1985. Tr. of Congo. (SPA.). 320p. 13.95 (*84-01-49234-3*) Plaza & Janés Editories, S.A. ESP. *Dist:* Distribooks, Inc.
—Congo, Set. abr. ed.Tr. of Congo. 1998. audio 8.99 o.s.i (*0-375-40297-7*); 1993. audio 17.00 o.s.i (*0-679-43113-6*, 390553) Random Hse. Audio Publishing Group. (RH Audio).
—Congo. l.t. ed. 1996. (Charnwood Large Print Ser.).Tr. of Congo. 480p. 29.99 (*0-7089-8912-8*, Charnwood) Thorpe, F. A. Pubs. GBR. *Dist:* Ulverscroft Large Print Bks., Ltd., Ulverscroft Large Print Canada, Ltd.
Dadie, Bernard B. The Black Cloth: A Collection of African Folk Tales. Hatch, Karen C., tr. from FRE. 1987. Tr. of Pagne Noir. 176p. pap. 17.95 (*0-87023-557-5*); lib. bdg. o.p. (*0-87023-556-7*) Univ. of Massachusetts Pr.
Dangarembga, Tsitsi. Nervous Conditions. 2002. 224p. 14.00 (*1-58005-063-8*); 2002. 210p. reprint ed. pap. 14.00 (*1-878067-77-X*); 1989. 204p. reprint ed. pap. 12.95 o.p. (*0-931188-74-1*) Avalon Publishing Group. (Seal Pr.).
Danze, Philip. Conjuring Maud. 2002. 192p. 23.00 (*0-9671851-3-0*) GreyCore Pr.
De Graaf, Anne. Into the Nevernight. 2003. (Negotiator Ser.: Bk. 1). (Illus.). 448p. pap. 12.99 (*0-8423-5289-5*) Tyndale Hse. Pubs.
De Grandsaigne, J. African Short Stories: An Anthology. 1985. 208p. text 29.95 o.p. (*0-312-01029-X*) Palgrave Macmillan.
Dekker, Ted. Thunder of Heaven. 2002. vii, 295p. pap. 13.99 (*0-8499-4292-6*) W Publishing Group.
Deveson, Anne. Lines in the Sand. 2000. 331p. (*0-670-89187-8*, Viking) Viking Penguin.
Dhillon, Polly. Kijabe: An African Historical Saga. 2000. (Illus.). vii, 307p. 10.95 (*1-885288-21-2*, 914-017) PREP Publishing.
Dickinson, Peter. Tefuga. l.t. ed. 1987. 464p. 20.95 o.p. (*1-55504-178-7*); pap. 18.95 o.p. (*1-55504-202-3*) BBC Audiobooks America.
Dikobe, Modikwe. The Marabi Dance. 1984. (African Writers Ser.). 128p. (C). pap. 8.95 (*0-435-90124-9*, 90124, African Writers Series) Heinemann.
Dipoko, M. S. Because of Women. 1969. (African Writers Ser.). 178p. (C). pap. 8.95 (*0-435-90057-9*, 90057) Heinemann.
Djoleto, Amu. The Strange Man. 1968. (African Writers Ser.). 279p. (C). pap. 9.95 (*0-435-90041-2*, 90041, African Writers Series) Heinemann.
Dongala, Emmanuel. The Fire of Origins. 2003. 256p. reprint ed. pap. 16.95 (*1-55652-492-7*, Hill, Lawrence Bks.) Chicago Review Pr., Inc.
—The Fire of Origins: A Novel. Corti, Lillian, tr. from FRE. 2000. 256p. 25.00 (*1-55652-420-X*, Hill, Lawrence Bks.) Chicago Review Pr., Inc.
—Little Boys Come from the Stars. Rejouis, Joel et al, trs. from FRE. 2001. 246p. 22.00 o.p. (*0-374-18496-8*) Farrar, Straus & Giroux.
—Little Boys Come from the Stars. 2002. 256p. pap. 12.00 (*0-385-72122-6*, Knopf Bks. for Young Readers) Random Hse. Children's Bks.
Dooling, Richard. White Man's Grave: A Novel. 1994. 356p. 22.00 o.p. (*0-374-28951-4*) Farrar, Straus & Giroux.
—White Man's Grave: A Novel. 1995. 400p. pap. 15.00 (*0-312-13214-X*) Picador.
Douglass, Keith. Bloodstorm. 2001. (SEAL Team Seven Ser.: Vol. 13). 272p. mass mkt. 5.99 o.s.i (*0-425-17881-1*) Berkley Publishing Group.
Downing, Henry F. The American Cavalryman: A Liberian Romance. reprint ed. 37.50 (*0-404-00148-3*) AMS Pr., Inc.
Doyle, Peter R. Ambushed in Africa. 1993. (Daring Adventure Ser.: Vol. 1). (J). (gr. 4). pap. 5.99 o.p. (*1-56179-142-3*) Focus on the Family Publishing.
Drew, Eileen. Blue Taxis: Stories about Africa. 1989. (Illus.). 160p. pap. 9.95 (*0-915943-41-7*) Milkweed Editions.
—The Ivory Crocodile. 1996. 288p. 21.95 (*1-56689-042-X*) Coffee Hse. Pr.
Dumile, Feni, illus. Tales from Southern Africa. 1973. (Perspectives on Southern Africa Ser.: No. 4). pap. 6.95 o.p. (*0-520-01911-3*) Univ. of California Pr.
Durant, Isadore. Death among the Fossils. 1999. pap. o.p. (*0-8263-1951-3*); 266p. 21.95 (*0-8263-1950-5*) Univ. of New Mexico Pr.
—Death among the Fossils. 1999. E-Book 21.95 (*0-585-18847-5*) netLibrary, Inc.
Eastlake, William. Jack Armstrong in Tangier & Other Escapes. 1984. 13.00 (*0-917453-01-8*); pap. 6.50 (*0-917453-02-6*); 20.00 o.p. (*0-917453-00-X*) Bamberger Bks.
Ebersohn, Wessel. Divide the Night. 1982. 224p. pap. 2.95 o.p. (*0-394-70810-5*, Vintage); 1981. 10.95 o.p. (*0-394-52076-9*, Pantheon) Knopf Publishing Group.
Echenique, Alfredo Bryce. La Amigdalitis de Tarzan. 2000. (SPA.). 319p. pap. 15.95 (*968-19-0562-8*) Aguilar Editorial MEX. *Dist:* Lectorum Pubns., Inc., Santillana USA Publishing Co., Inc.
Ekwensi, Cyprian O. Beautiful Feathers. 1971. (African Writers Ser.). 160p. pap. 7.95 o.p. (*0-435-90084-6*) Heinemann.
—Restless City & Christmas Gold. 1975. (African Writers Ser.). pap. text 6.50 o.p. (*0-435-90172-9*) Heinemann.
Farah, Nuruddin. From a Crooked Rib. 1970. (African Writers Ser.). pap. text 6.50 o.p. (*0-435-90080-3*) Heinemann.

—Sardines. 1992. (Variations on the Theme of an African Dictatorship Ser.). 272p. pap. 14.00 (*1-55597-161-X*) Graywolf Pr.

—Sweet & Sour Milk. 1980. (African Writers Ser.: No. 226). 237p. (Orig.). pap. text 6.50 o.p. (*0-435-90226-1*) Heinemann.

Farmer, Philip Jose. The Dark Heart of Time: A Tarzan Novel. 1999. 512p. mass mkt. 6.99 o.s.i (*0-345-42463-8*, Del Rey) Ballantine Bks.

Fielding, Helen. Cause Celeb. 2001. 23.95 (*0-330-33269-4*, Viking); 2001. 342p. 24.95 o.p. (*0-670-89450-8*, Viking); 2002. 352p. reprint ed. 13.00 (*0-14-200022-1*) Viking Penguin.

Fitzgerald, Penelope. The Golden Child. 1999. 192p. pap. 12.00 (*0-395-95619-6*) Houghton Mifflin Co.

—The Golden Child. l.t. ed. 2000. (General Ser.). xix, 231p. 23.95 (*0-7862-2809-1*); (Illus.). 266p. pap. 23.95 (*0-7862-2808-3*) Thorndike Pr.

—The Golden Child. l.t. ed. 2000. 266p. (*0-7540-4257-X*); (*0-7540-4258-8*) Thorndike Pr.

Fletcher, Inglis. Red Jasmine. 320p. reprint ed. lib. bdg. 23.95 (*0-89244-012-0*, Queens Hse., Inc.) Amereon, Ltd.

Forbath, Peter. The Last Hero. unabr. ed. 1999. Pt. I. audio 76.95 (*0-7861-1674-9*, 2502A); Pt. II. audio 56.95 (*0-7861-1713-3*, 2502B) Blackstone Audio Bks., Inc.

—The Last Hero. 1988. 800p. 21.95 o.p. (*0-671-24285-7*, Simon & Schuster) Simon & Schuster.

—The Last Hero. 1990. mass mkt. 12.95 (*0-446-39179-4*) Warner Bks., Inc.

Forester, C. S. The African Queen. 1977. 136p. reprint ed. lib. bdg. 21.95 (*0-89244-065-1*, Queens Hse., Inc.) Amereon, Ltd.

—The African Queen. unabr. collector's ed. 1980. audio 36.00 (*0-7366-0366-2*, 1350) Books on Tape, Inc.

—The African Queen. reprint ed. 1992. 316p. lib. bdg. 21.95 o.p. (*0-89966-903-4*); 1990. lib. bdg. 18.95 o.p. (*0-89968-508-0*) Buccaneer Bks., Inc.

—The African Queen. unabr. ed. 2000. audio 49.95 (*1-56054-966-1*, SAB 010) Chivers Audio Bks. GBR. *Dist:* BBC Audiobooks America.

—The African Queen. abr. ed. 1980. audio 15.95 o.p. (*0-88646-054-9*, TC-LFP 7072) Durkin Hayes Publishing Ltd.

—The African Queen. 1984. 256p. reprint ed. pap. 13.95 (*0-316-28910-8*, Back Bay) Little Brown & Co.

—The African Queen. 1940. 3.95 o.s.i (*0-394-60102-5*) Random Hse., Inc.

—The African Queen. l.t. ed. 1994. 260p. lib. bdg. 21.95 (*0-8161-7459-8*) Thorndike Pr.

Gary, Gabelhouse. Dreams of the N'Dorobo: Mystery, Murder, & Mysticism in the Shadows of Africa. 2004. 272p. 22.95 (*1-59228-066-8*, Lyons Pr.) Globe Pequot Pr., The.

Gellhorn, Martha E. The Weather in Africa: Three Novellas. 1993. (Eland Travel Fiction Ser.). 296p. reprint ed. pap. 14.95 o.p. (*0-87052-759-2*) Hippocrene Bks., Inc.

Gelman, Rita Golden. Professor Coconut & the Thief, ERS. 1977. (J). (gr. 1-5). o.p. (*0-03-016931-3*, Holt, Henry & Co. Bks. For Young Readers) Holt, Henry & Co.

Gifford, Thomas. Praetorian. 1994. 736p. mass mkt. 6.50 o.s.i (*0-553-56502-8*) Bantam Bks.

Gilman, Dorothy. Caravan. 1993. 256p. mass mkt. 6.99 (*0-449-22175-X*, Fawcett) Ballantine Bks.

—Caravan. unabr. ed. 1992. audio 60.00 (*1-55690-661-7*, 92326E7) Recorded Bks., LLC.

—Mrs. Pollifax & the Lion Killer. 1996. 224p. mass mkt. 6.99 (*0-449-15004-6*, Fawcett) Ballantine Bks.

—Mrs. Pollifax & the Lion Killer. l.t. ed. 1996. 320p. 21.00 o.p. (*0-7838-1677-4*, Macmillan Reference USA) Gale Group.

—Mrs. Pollifax & the Lion Killer. l.t. ed. 1996. 320p. pap. 21.00 o.s.i (*0-679-75872-0*) Random Hse. Large Print.

—Mrs. Pollifax on Safari. 1987. 224p. mass mkt. 6.99 (*0-449-21524-5*); 1985. mass mkt. 2.95 o.p. (*0-449-21011-1*) Ballantine Bks. (Fawcett).

—Mrs. Pollifax on Safari. 1977. 7.95 o.p. (*0-385-07506-5*) Doubleday Publishing.

Gordimer, Nadine. None to Accompany Me. unabr. ed. 1994. audio 23.95 o.p. (*1-56100-600-9*, 197, Bookcassette); audio 73.25 o.p. (*1-56100-225-9*, 965, Unabridged Library Editions) Brilliance Audio.

—None to Accompany Me. 1995. 336p. pap. 15.00 o.s.i (*0-14-025039-5*, Penguin Bks.) Penguin Group (USA) Inc.

—Six Feet of the Country. 1986. 112p. pap. 13.00 (*0-14-006559-8*, Penguin Bks.) Penguin Group (USA) Inc.

Gowdy, Barbara. The White Bone: A Novel. 1999. (Illus.). 330p. 23.00 o.s.i (*0-8050-6036-7*, Metropolitan Bks.) Holt, Henry & Co.

—The White Bone: A Novel. 2000. 336p. pap. 14.00 (*0-312-26412-7*) Picador.

Grabill, Larry, et al. Things Come Together: The African Carries the Torch. 2001. 148p. pap. 11.99 (*0-9717235-0-8*) Bibleline Pubns.

Gray, Stephen, ed. The Penguin Book of Southern African Stories. 1986. 336p. pap. 9.95 o.p. (*0-14-007239-X*, Penguin Bks.) Viking Penguin.

Green, Hubert. Magnolia, Magnolia, Where Are You? 2001. pap. text (*0-9720272-0-3*) Green, Hubert.

—Magnolia, Magnolia, Where Are You? 2003. 104p. pap. (*1-4120-0092-0*) Trafford Publishing.

Greene, Graham. The Heart of the Matter. l.t. ed. 1999. (Perennial Bestsellers Ser.). 413p. 26.95 (*0-7838-8570-9*) Thorndike Pr.

Grell, Mike. Sable. 2001. 384p. mass mkt. 6.99 (*0-8125-6550-9*, Tor Bks.); 2000. 352p. 24.95 o.s.i (*0-312-84872-2*, Forge Bks.) Doherty, Tom Assocs., LLC.

Gruber, Michael. Tropic of Night. 2003. 432p. 24.95 (*0-06-050954-6*) HarperCollins Pubs.

—Tropic of Night. 2004. 480p. mass mkt. 7.50 (*0-06-050955-4*, HarperTorch) Morrow/Avon.

Gurnah, Abdulrazak. By the Sea: A Novel. 2001. 256p. text 22.95 (*1-56584-658-3*) New Pr., The.

—Paradise. 256p. 1995. pap. 11.00 (*1-56584-163-8*); 1994. text 19.95 o.p. (*1-56584-162-X*) New Pr., The.

Hagerfors, Lennart. The Whales in Lake Tanganyika. Hollo, Anselm, tr. from SWE. 1989. 176p. 16.95 o.p. (*0-8021-1095-9*) Grove/Atlantic, Inc.

Haggard, H. Rider. Allan Quatermain, Being an Account of His Further Adventures & Discoveries in Company with Sir Henry Curtis, Bart., Commander John Good, R.N., & One Umslopogaas. Reginald, R. & Menville, Douglas A., eds. 1980. (Newcastle Forgotten Fantasy Library: Vol. 18). 278p. reprint ed. lib. bdg. 25.00 o.p. (*0-89370-517-9*) Millefleurs.

—Allan's Wife. 240p. 21.95 (*0-8488-2607-8*) Amereon, Ltd.

—Allan's Wife. 1980. (Forgotten Fantasy Library: Vol. 24). reprint ed. pap. 5.95 o.p. (*0-87877-123-9*, New Page Bks.) Career Pr., Inc.

—Allan's Wife. 2001. 128p. 23.99 (*1-58827-532-9*); per. 18.99 (*1-58827-533-7*) IndyPublish.com.

—Allan's Wife. 2002. 132p. per. 14.95 (*1-58715-710-1*) Wildside Pr.

—Allan's Wife: With Hunter Quatermain's Story, A Tale of Three Lions, & Long Odds. Reginald, R., ed. 1981. (Forgotten Fantasy Library: Vol. 24). 240p. lib. bdg. 27.00 o.p. (*0-89370-523-3*) Millefleurs.

—The Annotated She: A Critical Edition of H. Rider Haggard's Victorian Romance. 1991. (Illus.). 288p. 10.00 (*0-253-32072-0*) Indiana Univ. Pr.

—Ayesha: The Return of She. 1976. reprint ed. lib. bdg. 26.95 (*0-89190-701-7*, Rivercity Pr.) Amereon, Ltd.

—Ayesha: The Return of She. 1990. reprint ed. lib. bdg. 22.95 (*0-89968-512-9*) Buccaneer Bks., Inc.

—Ayesha: The Return of She. 1977. (Forgotten Fantasy Library: Vol. 14). 360p. reprint ed. pap. 5.95 o.p. (*0-87877-113-1*, New Page Bks.) Career Pr., Inc.

—Ayesha: The Return of She. 1978. (Illus.). 189p. reprint ed. pap. 7.95 (*0-486-23649-8*) Dover Pubns., Inc.

—Ayesha: The Return of She. 1971. 359p. reprint ed. spiral bd. 23.60 (*0-7873-1129-4*) Health Research.

—Ayesha: The Return of She. Reginald, R. & Menville, Douglas A., eds. 1980. (Newcastle Forgotten Fantasy Library: Vol. 14). 359p. reprint ed. lib. bdg. 19.95 o.p. (*0-89370-513-6*) Millefleurs.

—Ayesha: The Return of She. 1999. 320p. pap. 7.95 (*1-902058-04-6*) Pulp Fictions GBR. *Dist:* 7 Hills Bk. Distributors.

—The Classic Adventures: Sir H. Rider Haggard. 1986. (Illus.). 336p. 7.98 o.p. (*1-85079-043-4*) Sterling Publishing Co., Inc.

—H. Rider Haggard. 2003. cd-rom 19.00 (*0-931968-48-8*) B & R Samizdat Express.

—H. Rider Haggard. 1996. 9.99 o.s.i (*0-517-15056-5*) Random Hse. Value Publishing.

—King Solomon's Mines. Date not set. reprint ed. lib. bdg. 20.95 (*0-89190-703-3*, American Reprint Co.) Amereon, Ltd.

—King Solomon's Mines. Kay, Marilyn, ed. abr. ed. 1987. pap. 12.95 incl. audio (*1-882071-12-3*, 014) B&B Audio, Inc.

—King Solomon's Mines. unabr. ed. 2000. audio compact disk 56.00 (*0-7861-9882-6*, z2575); audio 44.95 (*0-7861-0610-7*, 2575) Blackstone Audio Bks., Inc.

—King Solomon's Mines. l.t. ed. 1986. (Mainstream Ser.). (Illus.). xi, 317p. 15.95 o.p. (*1-85089-063-3*) ISIS Large Print Bks. GBR. *Dist:* Transaction Pubs.

—King Solomon's Mines. 1989. audio 35.00 Jimcin Recordings.

—King Solomon's Mines. 1981. (English As a Second Language Bk.). pap. text 5.95 o.p. (*0-582-53502-6*, 74101) Longman Publishing Group.

—King Solomon's Mines. l.t. ed. (Large Print Ser.). 1992. 382p. lib. bdg. 26.00 (*0-939495-49-X*); 1998. 240p. reprint ed. lib. bdg. 25.00 (*1-58287-044-6*) North Bks.

—King Solomon's Mines. Butts, Dennis, ed. & intro. by. 1998. (Oxford World's Classics Ser.). (Illus.). 368p. pap. 9.95 (*0-19-283485-1*) Oxford Univ. Pr., Inc.

—King Solomon's Mines. Butts, Dennis, ed. 1990. (Oxford World's Classics Ser.). (Illus.). 366p. pap. 5.95 o.p. (*0-19-282204-7*) Oxford Univ. Pr., Inc.

—King Solomon's Mines. 1988. pap. 4.95 o.p. (*0-19-581013-9*) Oxford Univ. Pr., Inc.

—King Solomon's Mines, unabr. ed. 2001. audio 60.00 (*1-55690-845-8*, 93212E7) Recorded Bks., LLC.

—King Solomon's Mines. 1999. (Gateway Movie Classics Ser.). 382p. pap. 14.95 (*0-89526-329-7*, Gateway Editions) Regnery Publishing, Inc., An Eagle Publishing Co.

—King Solomon's Mines. 1998. (Children's Classics). 224p. pap. 3.95 (*1-85326-105-X*, 105XWW) Wordsworth Editions, Ltd. GBR. *Dist:* Advanced Global Distribution Services.

—She. 1967. (Airmont Classics Ser.). (gr. 8 up). mass mkt. 1.95 o.p. (*0-8049-0146-5*, CL-146) Airmont Publishing Co., Inc.

—She. 1976. reprint ed. lib. bdg. 23.95 (*0-89190-705-X*, Rivercity Pr.) Amereon, Ltd.

—She. 1978. (Del Rey Bk.). pap. 1.95 o.s.i (*0-345-27453-9*) Ballantine Bks.

—She. 1990. reprint ed. lib. bdg. 20.95 (*0-89968-514-5*) Buccaneer Bks., Inc.

—She. 1994. 352p. (YA). mass mkt. 5.95 o.s.i (*0-451-52584-1*, Signet Classics) NAL.

—She. 1991. (Oxford World's Classics Ser.). (Illus.). 380p. pap. 7.95 o.p. (*0-19-282767-7*, 6021) Oxford Univ. Pr., Inc.

—She. 1998. xvi, 246p. pap. text 7.95 (*1-902058-03-8*) Pulp Fictions GBR. *Dist:* 7 Hills Bk. Distributors.

—She. 1999. (Gateway Movie Classics Ser.). 382p. pap. 14.95 (*0-89526-328-9*, Gateway Editions) Regnery Publishing, Inc., An Eagle Publishing Co.

—She. 380p. pap. 4.00 o.p. (*1-85326-234-X*) Wordsworth Editions, Ltd. GBR. *Dist:* Casemate Pubs. & Bk. Distributors, LLC.

—She & Allan. reprint ed. lib. bdg. 25.95 (*0-89190-706-8*, Rivercity Pr.) Amereon, Ltd.

—She & Allan. 1978. (Del Rey Bk.). mass mkt. 1.95 o.s.i (*0-345-27449-0*) Ballantine Bks.

—She & Allan. 1975. (Forgotten Fantasy Library: Vol. 6). (Illus.). 302p. pap. 5.95 o.p. (*0-87877-105-0*, F-112, New Page Bks.) Career Pr., Inc.

—She & Allan. Reginald, R. & Menville, Douglas A., eds. 1980. (Forgotten Fantasy Library: Vol. 6). 303p. reprint ed. lib. bdg. 31.00 o.p. (*0-89370-505-5*) Millefleurs.

—She & Allan. 1999. 320p. pap. 7.95 (*1-902058-05-4*) Pulp Fictions GBR. *Dist:* 7 Hills Bk. Distributors.

—She & Allan. 2001. 408p. pap. 19.95 (*1-58715-422-6*) Wildside Pr.

—She, King Solomon's Mines & Allan Quartermain. 1951. 636p. pap. 12.95 (*0-486-20643-2*) Dover Pubns., Inc.

—Wisdom's Daughter: The Life & Love Story of She-Who-Must-Be-Obeyed. 24.95 (*0-89190-714-9*) Amereon, Ltd.

—Wisdom's Daughter: The Life & Love Story of She-Who-Must-Be-Obeyed. Reginald, R. & Melville, Douglas, eds. 1978. (Lost Race & Adult Fantasy Ser.). reprint ed. lib. bdg. 36.95 (*0-405-10983-0*) Ayer Co. Pubs., Inc.

—Wisdom's Daughter: The Life & Love Story of She-Who-Must-Be-Obeyed. 1978. (Del Rey Bk.). mass mkt. 1.95 o.s.i (*0-345-27428-8*) Ballantine Bks.

Harlech-Jones, Brian. A Small Space. E-Book (*1-84045-039-8*) Online Originals.

Harrison, William. The Blood Latitudes. 2000. 280p. 25.00 (*1-878448-97-8*) MacMurray & Beck, Inc.

Hausman, Gerald. Sitting on the Blue-Eyed Bear: Navajo Myths & Legends. 1976. (Illus.). 144p. (J). (gr. 7 up). 10.00 o.p. (*0-88208-061-X*, Hill, Lawrence Bks.) Chicago Review Pr., Inc.

Hemingway, Ernest. True at First Light: A Fictional Memoir. 2003. 320p. pap. 13.00 (*0-684-86572-6*, Scribner) Simon & Schuster.

—True at First Light: A Fictional Memoir. Hemingway, Patrick, ed. & intro. by. 1999. 320p. 26.00 (*0-684-84921-6*); (Illus.). 528p. 26.00 (*0-684-86448-7*) Simon & Schuster. (Scribner).

—True at First Light: A Fictional Memoir. unabr. ed. 1999. audio 45.00 o.s.i (*0-671-04448-6*, Simon & Schuster Audioworks) Simon & Schuster Audio.

Henty, G. A. The Dash for Khartoum: A Tale of the Nile Expedition. 2002. 406p. 29.95 (*1-59087-119-7*, GAH119); per. 19.95 (*1-59087-118-9*, GAH118) Althouse Pr.

—The Dash for Khartoum: A Tale of the Nile Expedition. collector's ed. 2002. (Illus.). im. lthr. 38.85 (*1-4115-1330-4*); pap. 19.95 (*1-4115-0589-1*); 25.95 (*1-4115-0926-9*); pap. 17.95 (*1-4115-0115-2*) Polyglot Pr., Inc.

—The Dash for Khartoum: A Tale of the Nile Expedition. 1999. (Illus.). 296p. pap. 13.99 (*0-88019-399-9*) Schmul Publishing Co., Inc.

Hershenow, Nicholas. The Road Builder. 2001. 520p. 25.95 o.p. (*0-399-14754-3*, BlueHen Bks.) Putnam Publishing Group, The.

Honwana, Luis B. We Killed Mangy-Dog & Other Mozambique Stories. 1969. (African Writers Ser.). 117p. (C). pap. 8.95 (*0-435-90060-9*, 90060) Heinemann.

Hopkinson, Nalo, ed. Mojo: Conjure Stories. 2003. 352p. pap. 13.95 (*0-446-67929-1*, Aspect) Warner Bks., Inc.

Hunter, Frederic. Africa, Africa! Fifteen Stories. 2000. 263p. 23.95 (*1-885942-17-6*); 264p. pap. 14.95 (*1-885942-18-4*) Cune Pr., LLC.

Huxley, Elspeth. The African Poison Murders. 1976. (Crime Fiction Ser.). reprint ed. lib. bdg. 21.00 o.p. (*0-8240-2377-3*) Garland Publishing, Inc.

—The African Poison Murders. 1989. 224p. pap. 3.95 o.p. (*0-14-011256-1*, Penguin Bks.); 1988. 22p. 16.95 o.p. (*0-670-82263-9*) Viking Penguin.

—Red Strangers. 2000. (Penguin Classics Ser.). 432p. pap. 15.00 o.s.i (*0-14-118205-9*, Penguin Bks.) Viking Penguin.

Ingalls, Rachel. Binstead's Safari. 1988. 15.45 o.p. (*0-671-63934-X*, Simon & Schuster); pap. 6.95 o.s.i (*0-671-65955-3*, Touchstone) Simon & Schuster.

Isegawa, Moses. Abyssinian Chronicles: A Novel. 2001. 480p. pap. 15.00 (*0-375-70577-5*) Random Hse., Inc.

Jackson-Opoku, Sandra. The River Where Blood Is Born. 1998. (Ballantine Reader's Circle Ser.). 432p. pap. 12.95 (*0-345-42476-X*) Ballantine Bks.

Jardin, Martine. Unorthodox Proposal. 2001. pap. (*1-59109-053-9*, PO 00003) Zumaya Pubns.

Jeal, Tim. For God & Glory. 1996. 448p. 25.00 o.p. (*0-688-11871-2*, Morrow, William & Co.) Morrow/Avon.

—The Missionary's Wife. 1997. 345p. (*0-316-88113-9*) Little Brown & Co.

Jeffers, Eugene. A Rumor of Distant Tribes. 1994. 256p. pap. 16.95 (*0-918056-06-3*) Ariadne Pr.

Johnson, Debra A. I Dreamed I Was a Big Baboon. 1994. (I Dreamed I Was Ser.). (J). lib. bdg. 21.95 (*1-56239-305-7*) ABDO Publishing Co.

Johnson, Lamont. Tarzan, collector's ed. 1997. 64p. pap. 59.98 o.p. incl. audio (*1-57019-239-1*, 4203) Radio Spirits, Inc.

Jones, Thom. Cold Snap: Stories. 1995. 228p. 19.95 o.p. (*0-316-47307-3*) Little Brown & Co.

Jumbam, Kenjo. The White Man of God. 1981. (African Writers Ser.). 151p. (Orig.). (C). pap. 8.95 (*0-435-90231-8*, 90231) Heinemann.

Kahiga, Samuel. The Girl from Abroad. 1974. (African Writers Ser.). pap. text 6.50 o.p. (*0-435-90158-3*) Heinemann.

Kai, Tara. Dar Es Salaam: A Novel. 2002. 640p. 24.95 (*1-882593-61-8*); 2004. 236p. reprint ed. pap. 15.95 (*1-882593-79-0*) Bridge Works Publishing Co., Inc.

Kane, Cheikh H. Ambiguous Adventure. Woods, Katherine, tr. 1972. (African Writers Ser.). 186p. (C). pap. 10.95 (*0-435-90119-2*, 90119, African Writers Series) Heinemann.

Katz, Naomi & Milton, Nancy D., eds. Fragment from a Lost Diary & Other Stories: Women of Asia, Africa & Latin America. 1975. pap. 8.95 o.p. (*0-8070-6385-1*, BP508) Beacon Pr.

Kayira, Legson. The Detainee. 1974. (African Writers Ser.). pap. 7.00 o.p. (*0-435-90162-1*) Heinemann.

Kelleher, Victor. The Traveller: Stories of 2 Continents. 1988. 218p. pap. 14.95 (*0-7022-2103-1*) Univ. of Queensland Pr. AUS. *Dist:* International Specialized Bk. Services.

Kelly, Clint. The Lost Kingdom. 1994. (YA). 10.99 o.p. (*0-8407-7822-8*) Nelson, Thomas Inc.

King, Francis. The Woman Who Was God. 1988. 18.95 o.p. (*1-55584-248-8*) Grove/Atlantic, Inc.

Kingsolver, Barbara. The Poisonwood Bible. unabr. ed. 1998. audio 44.95 (*1-56740-408-1*, 1498, Brilliance Audio Unabridged); 16p. audio 89.25 (*1-56740-610-6*, 1630, Unabridged Library Editions) Brilliance Audio.

—The Poisonwood Bible. l.t. ed. (Thorndike/G. K. Hall Paperback Bestsellers Ser.). 712p. 2000. pap. 27.95 (*0-7838-8468-0*); 1999. 29.95 o.p. (*0-7838-8467-2*) Gale Group. (Macmillan Reference USA).

—The Poisonwood Bible. (Oprah's Book Club Ser.). 560p. 2000. 26.00 (*0-06-018579-1*); 1998. 26.00 (*0-06-017540-0*) HarperCollins Pubs.

—The Poisonwood Bible. 2003. 672p. mass mkt. 7.99 (*0-06-051282-2*, HarperTorch) Morrow/Avon.

—The Poisonwood Bible. 1998. 20.05 (*0-606-19420-7*) Turtleback Bks.

—The Poisonwood Bible: A Novel. 1999. 560p. pap. 15.00 (*0-06-093053-5*, Perennial) HarperTrade.

Knip, Fred M. Robertson Lucas & the Road to Mongu. 2001. 481p. pap. 24.99 (*0-7388-5725-4*) Xlibris Corp.

Konadu, Asare. Ordained by the Oracle. 1969. (African Writers Ser.). (C). pap. 8.95 o.p. (*0-435-90055-2*) Heinemann.

Kosinski, Jerzy N. The Devil Tree. 2003. 206p. pap. 12.00 (*0-8021-3965-5*, Grove Pr.) Grove/Atlantic, Inc.

Kourouma, Ahmadou. Monnew. Poller, Nidra, tr. 272p. 1993. 25.00 (*1-56279-027-7*); 1994. reprint ed. pap. 13.95 (*1-56279-058-7*) Mercury Hse.

—The Suns of Independence. Adams, Adrian, tr. from FRE. 1982. 160p. (C). 17.50 o.p. (*0-8419-0626-2*, Africana Pub.) Holmes & Meier Pubs., Inc.

La Guma, Alex. In the Fog of the Season's End. 1973. 8.95 (*0-89388-058-2*) Okpaku Communications Corp.

Laing, Kojo. Woman of the Aeroplanes. 1990. 208p. 16.95 o.p. (*0-688-07941-5*, Morrow, William & Co.) Morrow/Avon.

Langley, Judy & Kikugawa, Wendy. Down African Roads. 1997. (Land Far Away Ser.). (Illus.). 32p. (J). (ps-k). per. 7.99 (*1-56309-218-2*, N978106, New Hope) Woman's Missionary Union.

LaValle, Victor D. The Ecstatic: A Novel. 2002. 288p. 22.95 (*0-609-61014-7*, Crown) Crown Publishing Group.

—The Ecstatic: A Novel. 2003. 288p. pap. 13.00 (*0-375-71331-X*, Vintage) Knopf Publishing Group.

Laye, Camara. Radiance of the King. 1989. (International Ser.). pap. 12.00 o.s.i (*0-679-72200-9*, Vintage) Knopf Publishing Group.

—The Radiance of the King. 2001. (New York Review Books Classics Ser.). xxiv, 279p. pap. 12.95 (*0-940322-58-7*) New York Review of Bks., Inc., The.

Leonard, Elmore. Pagan Babies. abr. ed. 2000. audio 25.95 o.s.i (*0-553-52751-7*, RH Audio) Random Hse. Audio Publishing Group.

—Pagan Babies. l.t. ed. 2000. 352p. 24.95 o.s.i (*0-375-43086-5*) Random Hse. Large Print.

Lessing. Proper Marriage. 1969. pap. 3.95 (*0-586-02116-7*) HarperCollins Pubs.

Lessing, Doris. African Stories. 1981. pap. 14.95 o.s.i (*0-671-42809-8*, Touchstone) Simon & Schuster.

—Martha Quest. 1991. (Children of Violence Ser.). 256p. pap. 11.00 o.p. (*0-452-26576-2*, Plume) Dutton/Plume.

—Martha Quest. 1995. (Children of Violence Ser.: Vol. 1). 240p. pap. 14.00 (*0-06-097666-7*, Perennial) HarperTrade.

—Martha Quest. 1995. 336p. lib. bdg. 35.00 o.p. (*0-8095-9169-3*) Millefleurs.

—Martha Quest. 1970. (Children of Violence Ser.). pap. 8.95 o.p. (*0-452-26124-4*) NAL.

—Martha Quest. 1970. (Children of Violence Ser.). pap. 2.95 o.p. (*0-452-25021-8*); pap. 3.95 o.p. (*0-452-25095-1*); pap. 4.95 o.p. (*0-452-25353-5*); pap. 5.95 o.p. (*0-452-25637-2*) Dutton/Plume. (Plume).

—Martha Quest. 2001. (Perennial Classics Ser.). 336p. pap. 14.00 (*0-06-095969-X*, Perennial) HarperTrade.

—Martha Quest. (Children of Violence Ser.). mass mkt. 0.75 o.p. (*0-451-02874-0*, Signet Bks.) NAL.

—Martha Quest: A Complete Novel from Doris Lessing's Masterwork, Children of Violence. 1970. (Children of Violence Ser.). pap. 6.95 o.p. (*0-452-25968-1*, Plume) Dutton/Plume.

—A Proper Marriage. 1991. 352p. pap. 8.95 o.p. (*0-452-26577-0*, Plume) Dutton/Plume.

—A Proper Marriage. 1995. 448p. lib. bdg. 35.00 o.p. (*0-8095-9170-7*) Millefleurs.

—A Proper Marriage: A Complete Novel from Doris Lessing's Masterwork, Children of Violence. 1970. pap. 7.95 o.p. (*0-452-25789-1*, Z5093, Plume) Dutton/Plume.

—A Proper Marriage: A Novel. 1995. (Children of Violence Ser.: Vol. 2). 448p. pap. 15.00 (*0-06-097663-2*, Perennial) HarperTrade.

Liking, Werewere. It Shall Be of Jasper & Coral & Love-Across-a-Hundred-Lives. de Jager, Marjolijn, tr. from FRE. 2000. xliii, 252p. 55.00 (*0-8139-1942-8*); pap. 17.50 (*0-8139-1943-6*) Univ. Pr. of Virginia.

Littlefair, Brian. Desert Burial: A Novel. 2002. (Illus.). 272p. 25.00 o.s.i (*0-8050-6723-X*) Holt, Henry & Co.

Liyong, Taban lo, contrib. by. Women in Folktales & Short Stories of Africa: An Anthology Collected & Edited. 1997. (Illus.). (*0-620-21465-1*) Kwagga Pubs.

Lomami-Tshibamba, Paul, et al. Ngando, Victoire de l'Amour, Le Mystere de l'Enfant Disparu. 1962. (B. E. Ser.: No. 28). (FRE.). 35.00 (*0-8115-2979-7*) Periodicals Service Co.

Lubega, Bonnie. The Outcasts. 1971. (African Writers Ser.). pap. text 5.00 o.p. (*0-435-90105-2*) Heinemann.

Lumry, Amanda & Harvitz, Laura. Alistair on Safari: Adventures at an African Game Reserve. 2001. (Illus.). 32p. (J). (gr. 5-7). 16.00 o.p. (*0-9662257-4-0*) Eaglemont Pr.

Maalouf, Amin. Leo Africanus. 1992. 272p. reprint ed. pap. 16.95 (*1-56131-022-0*, New Amsterdam Bks) Dee, Ivan R. Pub.

—Leo Africanus. 1989. 17.95 o.p. (*0-393-02630-2*) Norton, W. W. & Co., Inc.

Macauley, Dunstan L. D. Baa Salaka: Sacrificial Lamb. 2000. 269p. pap. 21.99 (*0-7388-1255-2*); text 31.99 (*0-7388-1254-4*) Xlibris Corp.

Malarkey, Tucker. An Obvious Enchantment: A Novel. 2001. E-Book 11.00 (*1-58836-102-0*) Random Hse., Inc.

Mann, Kenny. Yellow Dog Dreaming. (Illus.). 74p. 1996. pap. 15.00 (*1-887478-06-X*); 1995. 25.00 o.s.i (*1-887478-03-5*) Red Sea. (WiseAcre Bks.).

—Yellow Dog Dreaming. 2nd ed. 1995. (Illus.). 73p. reprint ed. 15.00 (*0-9657999-0-5*) rafiki Bks.

Mantel, Hilary. A Change of Climate. 1997. 336p. pap. 14.00 o.s.i (*0-8050-5205-4*, Owl Bks.) Holt, Henry & Co.

—A Change of Climate. 1994. 354p. 22.00 (*0-689-12201-2*, Scribner) Simon & Schuster.

Marechera, Dambudzo. Black Sunlight. 1988. (African Writers Ser.). 128p. (Orig.). (C). pap. 9.95 (*0-435-90237-7*, 90237) Heinemann.

Markham, Beryl. The Splendid Outcast: Beryl Markham's African Stories. 1987. 160p. 14.95 o.p. (*0-86547-301-3*, North Point Pr.) Farrar, Straus & Giroux.

Marryat, Frederick. The Mission, or Scenes in Africa. 1970. (Colonial Novel Ser.). (Illus.). 308p. reprint ed. 25.00 o.p. (*0-8419-0057-4*, Africana Pub.) Holmes & Meier Pubs., Inc.

Mason, A. E. W. The Four Feathers. reprint ed. lib. bdg. 22.95 (*0-88411-176-8*) Amereon, Ltd.

—The Four Feathers. 1987. 290p. pap. 3.95 o.p. (*0-88184-321-0*, Carroll & Graf Pubs.) Avalon Publishing Group.

—The Four Feathers. 1993. reprint ed. lib. bdg. 18.95 (*1-56849-211-1*) Buccaneer Bks., Inc.

—The Four Feathers. 2002. mass mkt. 5.99 (*0-7653-4614-1*, Tor Bks.) Doherty, Tom Assocs., LLC.

—The Four Feathers. 1977. reprint ed. pap. text 1.50 o.s.i (*0-505-51162-2*, 51162) Dorchester Publishing Co., Inc.

—The Four Feathers. l.t. ed. 2003. 24.95 (*1-58724-426-8*, Wheeler Publishing, Inc.) Gale Group.

—The Four Feathers. 1999. pap. 14.95 (*0-89526-263-0*) Regnery Publishing, Inc., An Eagle Publishing Co.

—The Four Feathers. 2002. E-Book 6.99 (*0-7434-5435-9*); 400p. reprint ed. pap. 6.99 (*0-7434-4821-9*) Simon & Schuster. (Pocket).

—The Four Feathers. Hoppenstand, Gary, ed. & intro. by. 2001. (Twentieth Century Classics Ser.). 304p. 12.00 (*0-14-218001-7*, Penguin Classics) Viking Penguin.

McAllister, Angela. The Honey Festival. 1999. (Illus.). (J). (gr. 1-8). pap. 13.99 (*0-8037-1240-5*, Dial Bks. for Young Readers) Penguin Putnam Bks. for Young Readers.

McBrier, Page. Beatrice's Goat. 2001. (Illus.). 40p. (J). (ps-3). 16.00 (*0-689-82460-2*, Atheneum) Simon & Schuster Children's Publishing.

McCormick, Wendy. Daddy, Will You Miss Me? 1999. (Illus.). 32p. (J). (ps-1). 16.00 (*0-689-81898-X*, Simon & Schuster Children's Publishing) Simon & Schuster Children's Publishing.

McKnight, Reginald. He Sleeps. 2001. 224p. 23.00 o.s.i (*0-8050-4828-6*) Holt, Henry & Co.

Meadows, David E. Joint Task Force: Liberia, Bk. 1. 2003. 320p. mass mkt. 6.99 (*0-425-19206-7*) Berkley Publishing Group.

Mendels, Ora. Mandela's Children. 1987. 16.95 o.p. (*0-316-54506-6*) Little Brown & Co.

Meyers, Margaret. Swimming in the Congo. 1995. 280p. pap. 13.95 (*1-57131-006-1*) Milkweed Editions.

Miljak, Ante. Eyes of the Owl. 1997. 185p. 19.95 o.p. (*1-56315-078-6*) SterlingHouse Pubs., Inc.

Miller, David L. Baby the Lost Legend. 1985. (J). (gr. 3 up). pap. 6.95 o.p. (*0-671-54091-2*, Simon & Schuster Children's Publishing) Simon & Schuster Children's Publishing.

Mofolo, Thomas. Chaka: An Historical Romance. Dutton, F. H., tr. 1970. (International African Institute Ser.). 26.00 o.p. (*0-19-724172-7*) Oxford Univ. Pr., Inc.

Mollel, Tololwa M. To Dinner, for Dinner. 2000. (Illus.). 32p. (J). (ps-3). tchr. ed. 16.95 (*0-8234-1527-9*) Holiday Hse., Inc.

Morris, Gilbert. The Final Adversary. 1992. (House of Winslow Ser.: Bk. 12). 304p. pap. 11.99 (*1-55661-261-3*) Bethany Hse. Pubs.

—White Hunter. 1999. (House of Winslow Ser.: Vol. 22). (Illus.). 320p. pap. 11.99 (*1-55661-909-X*) Bethany Hse. Pubs.

Morrow, Baker H. Horses Like the Wind & Other Stories of Africa. 2001. (Illus.). xi, 102p. 35.00 (*0-87081-626-8*) Univ. Pr. of Colorado.

—Horses Like the Wind, & Other Stories of Africa. 2001. (Illus.). xi, 102p. pap. (*0-87081-629-2*) Univ. Pr. of Colorado.

Mphahlele, Es'kia. Chirundu. 1979. 168p. (Orig.). pap. 7.95 o.p. (*0-88208-122-5*, Hill, Lawrence Bks.) Chicago Review Pr., Inc.

—Chirundu. 2nd ed. 1994. 172p. (Orig.). pap. text 14.95 (*0-86975-449-1*) Ravan Pr. ZMB. *Dist:* Ohio Univ. Pr.

—Modern African Stories. Komey, Ellis A., ed. 1966. 228p. pap. o.p. (*0-571-11217-X*) Faber & Faber Ltd.

Mudimbe, V. Y. The Rift. de Jager, Marjolijn, tr. 1993. (Emergent Literatures Ser.). 128p. 16.95 (*0-8166-2312-0*) Univ. of Minnesota Pr.

Mugo, Phoebe, ed. Lodu's Escape: And Other Stories from Africa. 1994. (Illus.). 64p. (Orig.). (J). (gr. 3-5). pap. 6.95 (*0-377-00269-0*) Friendship Pr.

Mulaisho, Dominic. The Tongue of the Dumb. 1971. (African Writers Ser.). pap. text 7.00 o.p. (*0-435-90098-6*) Heinemann.

Mungoshi, Charles. Waiting for the Rain. 1975. (African Writers Ser.). pap. text 7.00 o.p. (*0-435-90170-2*) Heinemann.

Munonye, John. Bridge to a Wedding. 1978. (African Writers Ser.). 228p. (C). pap. 8.95 o.p. (*0-435-90195-8*) Heinemann.

—A Dancer of Fortune. 1975. (African Writers Ser.). pap. text 6.50 o.p. (*0-435-90153-2*) Heinemann.

—Oil Man of Obange. 1971. (African Writers Ser.). 186p. (C). pap. 8.95 o.p. (*0-435-90094-3*, 90094) Heinemann.

—A Wreath for the Maidens. 1973. (African Writers Ser.). pap. text 7.00 o.p. (*0-435-90121-4*) Heinemann.

Mwangi, Meja. Carcase for Hounds. 1974. (African Writers Ser.). pap. text 6.50 o.p. (*0-435-90145-1*) Heinemann.

—Going down River Road. 1976. (African Writers Ser.). 215p. (C). pap. 8.95 (*0-435-90176-1*, 90176, African Writers Series) Heinemann.

—Kill Me Quick. 1973. (African Writers Ser.). 151p. (C). pap. 8.95 o.p. (*0-435-90143-5*) Heinemann.

Naipaul, V. S. A Bend in the River. 1989. (International Ser.). 288p. pap. 13.00 (*0-679-72202-5*, Vintage) Knopf Publishing Group.

—A Bend in the River. 1979. 13.95 o.s.i (*0-394-50573-5*) Knopf, Alfred A. Inc.

—A Bend in the River. 1980. pap. 5.95 o.p. (*0-394-74314-8*) Random Hse., Inc.

—A Bend in the River. 1992. 26.75 (*0-8446-6631-9*) Smith, Peter Pub., Inc.

—A Bend in the River. l.t. ed. 1999. (Perennial Bestsellers Ser.). 439p. 27.95 (*0-7838-8616-0*) Thorndike Pr.

—Half a Life. 2001. 224p. 24.00 (*0-375-40737-5*) Knopf, Alfred A. Inc.

—Half a Life: A Novel. 2002. 224p. pap. 13.00 (*0-375-70728-X*) Knopf, Alfred A. Inc.

—In a Free State. 1984. 256p. mass mkt. 10.00 o.s.i (*0-394-72205-1*, Vintage) Knopf Publishing Group.

—In a Free State. 1977. 256p. pap. 3.95 o.p. (*0-14-003711-X*, Penguin Bks.) Viking Penguin.

Naipaul, V. S. & Hardwick, Elizabeth. A Bend in the River. 1997. (Modern Library Ser.). 448p. 17.95 o.s.i (*0-679-60267-4*) Random Hse., Inc.

Native, A. Marita, or, the Folly of Love. Newell, Stephanie, ed. 2001. (African Sources for African History Ser.: Vol. 2). (Illus.). pap. 29.00 (*90-04-12186-2*) Brill Academic Pubs., Inc.

Ngugi wa Thiong'o. Secret Lives & Other Stories. 1975. 160p. 6.95 o.p. (*0-88208-058-X*, Hill, Lawrence Bks.) Chicago Review Pr., Inc.

—Secret Lives & Other Stories. 1992. 144p. (C). pap. 8.95 (*0-435-90150-8*, 90150) Heinemann.

Nwankwo, Nkem. Danda. 1970. (African Writers Ser.). pap. 7.95 o.p. (*0-435-90067-6*) Heinemann.

Nyamfukudza, S. Non-Believer's Journey. 1981. (African Writers Ser.). (Orig.). (C). pap. text 7.00 o.p. (*0-435-90233-4*) Heinemann.

Nzekwu, Onuora. Blade Among the Boys. 1972. (African Writers Ser.). pap. 7.95 o.p. (*0-435-90091-9*) Heinemann.

—Wand of Noble Wood. 1971. (African Writers Ser.). pap. 7.00 o.p. (*0-435-90085-4*) Heinemann.

Obradovic, Nadezda. Looking for a Rain God: An Anthology of Contemporary African Short Stories. 1990. pap. 9.95 o.s.i (*0-671-67177-4*, Fireside) Simon & Schuster.

Okara, Gabriel. The Voice. 1970. (C). pap. text 12.95 o.s.i (*0-8419-0015-9*, Africana Pub.) Holmes & Meier Pubs., Inc.

Okri, Ben. Songs of Enchantment. 304p. 1994. pap. 12.00 o.s.i (*0-385-47157-2*); 1993. 21.00 o.s.i (*0-385-47154-8*, Talese, Nan A.) Doubleday Publishing.

Olu, Easmon C. Bisi & the Golden Disc. 1990. (Illus.). 32p. (J). 13.95 (*0-940793-56-3*, Crocodile Bks.) Interlink Publishing Group, Inc.

Omotoso, Kole. The Combat. 1972. (African Writers Ser.). 88p. (C). pap. 8.95 o.p. (*0-435-90122-2*) Heinemann.

Osborne, Mary Pope. Lions at Lunchtime, No. 11. 1998. (Magic Tree House Ser.: No. 11). (Illus.). 96p. (J). (gr. k-3). lib. bdg. 11.99 (*0-679-98340-6*, Random Hse. Bks. for Young Readers) Random Hse. Children's Bks.

Ousmane, Sembene. God's Bits of Wood. 1996. 256p. pap. 13.95 (*0-435-90959-2*, African Writers Series); 1970. pap. 7.95 o.p. (*0-435-90063-3*) Heinemann.

—God's Bits of Wood. Price, Francis, tr. from FRE. 1987. (African Writers Ser.). 256p. (C). reprint ed. pap. 10.95 (*0-435-90892-8*, 90892) Heinemann.

Palangyo, P. Dying in the Sun. 1968. (African Writers Ser.). pap. text 6.50 o.p. (*0-435-90053-6*) Heinemann.

Palmer, Catherine. A Kiss of Adventure. 2000. (Treasures of the Heart Ser.). (Illus.). 384p. (J). pap. 7.99 (*0-8423-3884-5*) Tyndale Hse. Pubs.

—The Treasure of Timbuktu. 1997. (HeartQuest Ser.: No. 1). pap. 10.99 o.p. (*0-8423-5775-0*) Tyndale Hse. Pubs.

Peel, Colin D. Blood of Your Sisters. 1997. 192p. 20.95 o.p. (*0-312-15065-2*, Saint Martin's Minotaur) St. Martin's Pr.

—Blood of Your Sisters. l.t. ed. 1997. (Ulverscroft Large Print Ser.). 400p. 29.99 o.p. (*0-7089-3867-1*, Ulverscroft) Thorpe, F. A. Pubs. GBR. *Dist:* Ulverscroft Large Print Bks., Ltd., Ulverscroft Large Print Canada, Ltd.

Peteni, R. L. A Hill of Fools. 1976. (African Writers Ser.). 151p. (C). pap. 8.95 (*0-435-90178-8*, 90178, African Writers Series) Heinemann.

Philbrick, Rodman. Coffins. 320p. mass mkt. 6.99 (*0-8125-6651-3*, Tor Bks.); E-Book 23.95 (*0-312-70547-6*, Tor Bks.); 2002. 320p. 23.95 (*0-312-87273-9*, Forge Bks.) Doherty, Tom Assocs., LLC.

Pinkwater, Daniel M. The Worms of Kukumlima. 1981. (J). (gr. 4-7). 9.95 o.p. (*0-525-43380-5*, Dutton) Dutton/Plume.

Raban, Jonathan. Foreign Land. 352p. 1986. pap. 6.95 o.p. (*0-14-008266-2*, Penguin Bks.); 1985. 16.95 o.p. (*0-670-80767-2*) Viking Penguin.

—Foreign Land: A Novel. 2001. 352p. pap. 14.00 (*0-375-72594-6*, Vintage) Knopf Publishing Group.

Resnick, Mike. Ivory. 1989. mass mkt. 4.95 o.p. (*0-8125-0042-3*, Tor Bks.) Doherty, Tom Assocs., LLC.

—Ivory. E-Book 7.49 (*1-930936-27-3*) Fictionwise, Inc.

Rettino, Ernie & Kerner, Debby. Psalty on Safari. 1991. 6.99 o.p. (*0-8499-0896-5*) W Publishing Group.

Robinson, Sandra C. The Rainstick: A Fable. 1994. (Illus.). 40p. (gr. 2 up). pap. 9.95 (*1-56044-284-0*, Falcon) Globe Pequot Pr., The.

Roman, Kathy Blankley, illus. Dume's Roar. unabr. ed. 1998. 32p. (J). (ps-3). 14.95 (*0-7737-3003-6*) Stoddart Kids CAN. *Dist:* Fitzhenry & Whiteside, Ltd.

Roy, Lucinda. The Hotel Alleluia: A Novel. 1999. 368p. 25.00 (*0-06-019395-6*) HarperCollins Pubs.

—Lady Moses: A Novel. 1998. 400p. 24.00 o.s.i (*0-06-018244-X*) HarperCollins Pubs.

—Lady Moses: A Novel. 1998. 400p. pap. 13.00 (*0-06-093084-5*, Perennial) HarperTrade.

Ruheni, Mwangi. The Future Leaders. 1973. (African Writers Ser.). pap. text 7.00 o.p. (*0-435-90139-7*) Heinemann.

—The Minister's Daughter. 1975. (African Writers Ser.). pap. 7.95 o.p. (*0-435-90156-7*) Heinemann.

Sabatini, Rafael. Sea Hawk. 1980. reprint ed. 17.00 o.p. (*0-89783-012-1*) Larlin Corp.

—Sea Hawk. 2002. 373p. pap. 13.95 (*0-393-32331-5*) Norton, W. W. & Co., Inc.

Salkey, Andrew. The Late Emancipation of Jerry Stover. Date not set. pap. text 9.95 (*0-582-78559-6*) Addison-Wesley Longman, Ltd. GBR. *Dist:* Trans-Atlantic Pubns., Inc.

Salvatore, R. A. Tarzan: The Epic Adventures. 1997. 280p. mass mkt. 5.99 o.s.i (*0-345-41295-8*, Del Rey) Ballantine Bks.

Samkange, Stanlake. The Mourned One. 1975. (African Writers Ser.). 150p. (C). pap. 9.95 (*0-435-90169-9*, 90169) Heinemann.

—The Year of the Uprising. 1978. (African Writers Ser.). pap. text 7.00 o.p. (*0-435-90190-7*) Heinemann.

Sassine, Williams. Wirriyamu. Reed, John & Wake, Clive, trs. 1980. (African Writers Ser.). 148p. pap. 7.00 o.p. (*0-435-90199-0*) Heinemann.

Savarin, Julian J. Wolf Run. 1992. 464p. mass mkt. 4.50 o.p. (*0-06-100474-X*, HarperTorch) Morrow/Avon.

—Wolf Run. 1994. 2.99 o.p. (*0-517-12527-7*) Random Hse. Value Publishing.

—Wolf Run. 1991. 288p. 19.95 (*0-8027-1148-0*) Walker & Co.

Scanlon, Paul, ed. Stories from Central & Southern Africa. 1983. (African Writers Ser.). 207p. (Orig.). (C). pap. 9.95 (*0-435-90254-7*, 90254) Heinemann.

Schreiner, Olive. Story of an African Farm. 1989. o.s.i (*0-86068-195-5*) Random Hse., Inc.

Settings

—The Story of an African Farm. 1993. 368p. mass mkt. 4.95 o.s.i (*0-553-21412-8*) Bantam Bks.
—The Story of an African Farm. 2003. (Twelve-Point Ser.). lib. bdg. 25.00 (*1-58287-241-4*) North Bks.
—The Story of an African Farm. Bristow, Joseph, ed. & intro. by. 1999. (Oxford World's Classics Ser.). 336p. pap. 11.95 (*0-19-283664-1*) Oxford Univ. Pr., Inc.
—The Story of an African Farm. Bristow, Joseph, ed. 1993. (Oxford World's Classics Ser.). 322p. pap. 7.95 o.p. (*0-19-282885-1*) Oxford Univ. Pr., Inc.
—The Story of an African Farm. 1979. pap. 3.95 o.p. (*0-14-000197-2*) Penguin Group (USA) Inc.
—The Story of an African Farm. 1983. (Classics Ser.). 304p. pap. 11.95 (*0-14-043184-5*, Penguin Classics) Viking Penguin.
—Story of an African Farm. 1977. 258p. reprint ed. 17.00 o.p. (*0-915864-24-X*); pap. 5.00 o.p. (*0-915864-23-1*) Academy Chicago Pubs., Ltd.
—Story of an African Farm. l.t. ed. 1985. (Mainstream Ser.). 395p. 14.95 o.p. (*1-85089-043-9*) ISIS Large Print Bks. GBR. *Dist:* Transaction Pubs.
—The Story of an African Farm. unabr. ed. 1998. 256p. pap. 2.00 (*0-486-40165-0*) Dover Pubns., Inc.
—The Story of an African Farm. Wolff, Robert L., ed. 1975. (Victorian Fiction Ser.). reprint ed. lib. bdg. 73.00 o.p. (*0-8240-1602-5*) Garland Publishing, Inc.
—Trooper Peter: Halket of a Mashonaland. E-Book 2.49 (*1-58627-429-5*) Electric Umbrella Publishing.
Schreiner, Olive & Jacobson, Dan. The Story of an African Farm. 1990. 18.75 (*0-8446-0247-7*) Smith, Peter Pub., Inc.
Schreiner, Oliver. Dream Life & Real Life. E-Book 2.49 (*1-58627-424-4*) Electric Umbrella Publishing.
Sedlack, Robert. The African Safari Papers. 2003. 309p. pap. 13.95 (*1-58567-300-5*) Overlook Pr., The.
Semyonov, Julian. Tass Is Authorized to Announce... 1988. Tr. of Tass Upolnomochen Zayavit. 384p. mass mkt. 4.50 (*0-380-70569-9*, Avon Bks.) Morrow/Avon.
—Tass Is Authorized to Announce... 1995. Tr. of Tass Upolnomochen Zayavit. 350p. 22.95 (*0-88962-359-7*) Mosaic Pr.
—Tass Is Authorized to Announce. . . Buxton, Charles, tr. from RUS. 1987. Tr. of Tass Upolnomochen Zayavit. 352p. 17.95 (*0-7145-4120-6*) Riverrun Pr., Inc.
Shand, Rosa. The Gravity of Sunlight. 2001. 256p. 24.00 (*1-56947-192-4*); reprint ed. pap. 13.00 (*1-56947-240-8*) Soho Pr., Inc.
Sienkiewicz, Henryk. In Deset & Wilderness. Lipinski, Miroslaw, ed. & tr. by. from POL. 1994. 278p. 19.95 (*0-7818-0235-0*) Hippocrene Bks., Inc.
Simenon, Georges. African Trio: Talatala, Tropic Moon, Aboard the Aquitaine. 1979. 9.95 o.p. (*0-15-103955-0*) Harcourt Trade Pubs.
Smith, Wilbur. The Angels Weep. unabr. ed. 1999. audio 124.95 (*0-7540-0400-7*, CAB1823) BBC Audiobooks America.
—The Angels Weep. 1984. mass mkt. 6.99 o.s.i (*0-449-20497-9*, Fawcett) Ballantine Bks.
—The Angels Weep, Pt. 1. unabr. collector's ed. 1988. (Ballantyne Novels Ser.). audio 64.00 (*0-7366-1344-7*, 2246-A ) Books on Tape, Inc.
—The Angels Weep. 1983. 480p. 17.95 o.p. (*0-385-18736-X*) Doubleday Publishing.
—Blue Horizon. 2004. mass mkt. 7.99 (*0-312-99142-8*, St. Martin's Paperbacks) St. Martin's Pr.
—Elephant Song. 1995. 480p. mass mkt. 6.99 (*0-449-22103-2*, Fawcett) Ballantine Bks.
—Elephant Song. unabr. ed. 1993. (Ballantyne Novels Ser.). audio 120.00 (*0-7366-2470-8*, 3233) Books on Tape, Inc.
—Elephant Song. abr. ed. 1993. audio 15.95 o.p. Durkin Hayes Publishing Ltd.
—Elephant Song. 1994. 5.99 o.p. (*0-517-11608-1*) Random Hse. Value Publishing.
—Elephant Song. l.t. ed. 1992. (Adventure Suspense Ser.). 784p. 29.99 o.p. (*0-7089-8663-3*, Ulverscroft) Thorpe, F. A. Pubs. GBR. *Dist:* Ulverscroft Large Print Bks., Ltd., Ulverscroft Large Print Canada, Ltd.
—A Falcon Flies, Pt. 1. unabr. collector's ed. 1988. (Ballantyne Novels Ser.). audio 64.00 (*0-7366-1416-8*, 2303-A) Books on Tape, Inc.
—A Falcon Flies. unabr. ed. 1999. (Ballantyne Novel Ser.). audio 99.95 (*0-7540-0247-0*, CAB1670) Chivers Audio Bks. GBR. *Dist:* BBC Audiobooks America.
—A Falcon Flies. abr. ed. 2001. audio (*0-333-78237-2*) Macmillan U.K. GBR. *Dist:* Macmillan Publishing Co., Inc.
—The Leopard Hunts in Darkness. 1986. 448p. mass mkt. 5.99 o.s.i (*0-449-20725-0*, Fawcett) Ballantine Bks.
—The Leopard Hunts in Darkness. 1984. 432p. 16.95 o.p. (*0-385-18737-8*) Doubleday Publishing.
—The Leopard Hunts in Darkness. abr. ed. audio 15.95 o.p. (*0-88646-135-9*, 7136) Durkin Hayes Publishing Ltd.
—Monsoon, Pt. 1. unabr. collector's ed. 1999. (Courtney Novels). audio 88.00 (*0-7366-4566-7*, 4973-A) Books on Tape, Inc.
—Monsoon. abr. ed. 1999. audio 25.00 (*0-7871-1975-X*, Dove Audio) NewStar Media, Inc.
—Monsoon. 2000. 864p. mass mkt. 7.99 (*0-312-97154-0*, St. Martin's Paperbacks); 1999. 544p. 26.95 (*0-312-20339-X*) St. Martin's Pr.
—The Sunbird. 1992. 480p. mass mkt. 6.99 o.s.i (*0-449-14825-4*, Fawcett) Ballantine Bks.
—The Sunbird, Pt. 1. unabr. collector's ed. 1989. (Ballantyne Novels Ser.). audio 64.00 (*0-7366-1553-9*, 2422-A) Books on Tape, Inc.
—The Sunbird. unabr. ed. 2000. (Ballantyne Novel Ser.). audio 99.95 (*0-7451-8785-4*, CAB 1420) Chivers Audio Bks. GBR. *Dist:* BBC Audiobooks America.
—The Sunbird. 1973. 480p. 17.95 o.p. (*0-385-00710-8*) Doubleday Publishing.
—The Sunbird. abr. ed. 2002. audio (*0-333-90670-5*) Macmillan U.K. GBR. *Dist:* Trafalgar Square.
—The Sunbird. 1978. mass mkt. 2.50 o.p. (*0-451-08256-7*, E8256, Signet Bks.) NAL.
—The Sunbird. l.t. ed. 1977. (Ulverscroft Large Print Ser.). 29.99 o.p. (*0-85456-556-6*, Ulverscroft) Thorpe, F. A. Pubs. GBR. *Dist:* Ulverscroft Large Print Bks., Ltd., Ulverscroft Large Print Canada, Ltd.
—The Sunbird. 1999. lib. bdg. 32.95 (*1-56723-132-2*) Yestermorrow, Inc.
Soyinka, Wole. The Interpreters. 1984. (African Writers Ser.). 260p. (C). pap. 7.95 (*0-435-90076-5*, 90076) Heinemann.
—The Interpreters. 1972. 251p. 29.50 o.s.i (*0-8419-0121-X*, Africana Pub.) Holmes & Meier Pubs., Inc.
St. Pierre, Stephanie. Adventures with Barbie: Wildlife Rescue. 1991. (Adventures with Barbie Ser.: No. 3). (Illus.). 64p. (Orig.). (J). (gr. 1-2). 2.99 o.p. (*0-8431-2918-2*, Price Stern Sloan) Penguin Putnam Bks. for Young Readers.
Stevens, Marcus. The Curve of the World. 2002. 320p. tchr. ed. 24.95 (*1-56512-336-0*) Algonquin Bks. of Chapel Hill.
—The Curve of the World. 2003. 320p. pap. 14.00 (*0-7434-7082-6*, Washington Square Pr.) Simon & Schuster.
Stirling, Emma. A Dangerous Gift. 1998. 160p. 22.00 (*0-7278-5138-1*) Severn Hse. Pubs., Ltd.
—A Dangerous Gift. l.t. ed. 1998. (General Ser.). 208p. pap. 22.95 (*0-7862-1631-X*) Thorndike Pr.
Stirling, Emma, contrib. by. A Dangerous Gift. 1999. 198 p. (*0-7540-3470-4*) BBC Audiobooks America.
Sutherland, Grant. The Consignment. 2004. 416p. mass mkt. 7.50 (*0-553-58331-X*); 2003. 368p. 23.95 (*0-553-80187-2*) Bantam Bks.
Svoboda, Terese. Cannibal. 1994. 138p. (C). 20.00 (*0-8147-8012-1*) New York Univ. Pr.
—Cannibal. 1994. E-Book 19.95 (*0-585-31629-5*) netLibrary, Inc.
Tansi, Sony L. The Antipeople. Underwood, J. A., tr. from FRE. 1987. Tr. of Anti-Peuple. 192p. 18.95 o.p. (*0-7145-2845-5*) Boyars, Marion Pubs., Inc.
Theroux, Paul. My Other Life. 1996. 448p. 24.95 o.p. (*0-395-82527-X*) Houghton Mifflin Co.
—My Other Life. 1997. 464p. pap. 15.00 (*0-395-87752-0*, Mariner Bks.) Houghton Mifflin Co. Trade & Reference Div.
—My Other Life. 1996. 488p. 33.99 (*0-7710-8575-3*) McClelland & Stewart/Tundra Bks.
—My Other Life. abr. ed. 1996. 24.95 o.p. (*0-7871-1126-0*); 12p. pap. 49.95 o.p. (*0-7871-1127-9*, 134321) NewStar Media, Inc.
—My Other Life. 1999. text 22.95 (*0-670-86583-4*) Viking Penguin.
Thomas, Lucien. Blood Diamonds. 2003. (Illus.). 245p. per. (*0-9740164-1-1*) West Pr.
Thomas, Maria. African Visas. 242p. 1992. pap. 10.95 (*0-939149-76-1*); 1991. 19.95 o.s.i (*0-939149-54-0*) Soho Pr., Inc.
—Come to Africa & Save Your Marriage & Other Stories. 1988. pap. text 6.95 o.p. (*0-939149-21-4*); 1987. 235p. 14.95 o.p. (*0-939149-06-0*); 1995. 235p. reprint ed. pap. 10.00 (*1-56947-039-1*) Soho Pr., Inc.
Thomas, Ross. The Seersucker Whipsaw. reprint ed. 1987. 304p. pap. 3.50 o.p. (*0-06-080849-7*, P 849); 1985. 256p. pap. 2.95 o.p. (*0-06-080728-8*, P728) HarperTrade. (Perennial).
—The Seersucker Whipsaw. 1992. 288p. mass mkt. 5.99 o.p. (*0-446-40169-2*, Mysterious Pr. Paperback Bks.) Warner Bks., Inc.
Trevor, Elleston. The Flight of the Phoenix. 1989. mass mkt. 3.95 o.s.i (*0-515-10089-7*, Jove) Berkley Publishing Group.
—The Flight of the Phoenix. unabr. collector's ed. 1979. audio 42.00 (*0-7366-0157-0*, 1157) Books on Tape, Inc.
—The Flight of the Phoenix. l.t. ed. 1984. (Ulverscroft Large Print Ser.). 368p. 29.99 o.p. (*0-7089-1147-1*, Ulverscroft) Thorpe, F. A. Pubs. GBR. *Dist:* Ulverscroft Large Print Bks., Ltd., Ulverscroft Large Print Canada, Ltd.
Trout, Richard E. Elephant Tears Vol. 2: Mask of the Elephant: MacGregor Family Series. 2000. (Harbor Lights Ser.: Vol. 2). (Illus.). 241p. (J). (gr. 7-12). pap. 9.95 (*1-880292-72-6*) LangMarc Publishing.
Uno, Koji. Love of Mountains: Two Stories by Uno Koji. Gerbert, Elaine T., tr. 1997. 240p. pap. text 23.00 (*0-8248-1756-7*) Univ. of Hawaii Pr.
Updike, John. The Coup. 1978. 320p. 32.50 (*0-394-50268-X*) Knopf, Alfred A. Inc.
Valentine, Jane. Sevenoaks. 2001. pap. 17.95 (*0-595-18094-9*) iUniverse, Inc.
Vanderwerff, Corrine. The Mists of Mbinda: Kate's Busy Life Concealed the Soul of a Woman Lonely for Love. 1997. 6.97 o.p. (*0-8163-1404-7*) Pacific Pr. Publishing Assn.
Vassanji, M. G. Amriika. 424p. 2001. text 25.00 (*0-7710-8723-3*); 2000. pap. 16.95 (*0-7710-8725-X*) McClelland & Stewart/Tundra Bks.
—The Book of Secrets. 1994. 352p. pap. 19.99 (*0-7710-8719-5*) McClelland & Stewart/Tundra Bks.
—The Book of Secrets. 1996. 337p. pap. 14.00 (*0-312-15068-7*); 24.00 o.p. (*0-312-14083-5*) Picador.
Vera, Yvonne. Without a Name & under the Tongue. 2002. (Illus.). 224p. pap. 13.00 (*0-374-52816-0*) Farrar, Straus & Giroux.
Vieira, J. L. Luuanda. Bender, Tamara L., tr. 1980. (African Writers Ser.). 118p. (Orig.). (C). pap. 8.95 (*0-435-90222-9*, 90222) Heinemann.
Vieira, Luandino. The Real Life of Domingos Xavier. 1978. (African Writers Ser.). pap. text 6.50 o.p. (*0-435-90202-4*) Heinemann.
Voien, Steven. Black Leopard. 1997. 287p. 23.00 o.s.i (*0-679-44702-4*) Random Hse., Inc.
Wager, Walter. The Spirit Team. 1998. 317p. mass mkt. 6.99 (*0-8125-5087-0*); 1996. 320p. 22.95 o.p. (*0-312-85826-4*) Doherty, Tom Assocs., LLC. (Forge Bks.).
Walker, Alice. Possessing the Secret of Joy. l.t. ed. 1996. 252p. 24.95 o.p. (*1-56895-351-8*, Wheeler Publishing, Inc.) Gale Group.
—Possessing the Secret of Joy. 1992. 304p. 25.00 (*0-15-173152-7*) Harcourt Trade Pubs.
—Possessing the Secret of Joy. 1997. (Illus.). 304p. pap. 14.00 (*0-671-78945-7*, Washington Square Pr.) Simon & Schuster.
—Possessing the Secret of Joy. Grose, Bill, ed. 1993. 304p. reprint ed. mass mkt. 7.99 (*0-671-78942-2*, Pocket) Simon & Schuster.
—Possessing the Secret of Joy. unabr. ed. 1992. pap. 25.00 incl. audio (*0-671-79306-3*, 592128, Simon & Schuster Audioworks) Simon & Schuster Audio.
Walters, Joseph J. Guanya Pau: A Story of an African Princess. 1994. 114p. pap. 10.00 (*0-8032-9755-6*, Bison Bks.); text 40.00 (*0-8032-4764-8*) Univ. of Nebraska Pr.
Waugh, Evelyn. Scoop. unabr. ed. audio 54.95 o.p. (*1-85549-951-7*, CTC 023) BBC Audiobooks America.
—Scoop. unabr. collector's ed. 1991. audio 48.00 (*0-7366-2080-X*, 2885) Books on Tape, Inc.
—Scoop. audio 44.95 Cover to Cover Cassettes, Ltd.
—Scoop. 1977. 15.95 o.s.i (*0-316-92617-5*); 336p. pap. 14.95 (*0-316-92610-8*, Back Bay) Little Brown & Co.
Weiss, Ellen. Simba's Moon. Date not set. (Illus.). 32p. (J). (ps-2). 12.99 (*0-7868-3267-3*) Disney Pr.
Weissmuller, Johnny, Jr., contrib. by. Tarzan. unabr. ed. 1993. audio 19.95 (*1-55935-118-7*) Soundelux Audio Publishing.
West, Owen, pseud. Sharkman Six. 2001. 320p. 24.00 (*0-7432-0542-1*, Simon & Schuster) Simon & Schuster.
—Sharkman Six: A Novel. 2001. 320p. E-Book 24.00 (*0-7432-1747-0*, Simon & Schuster) Simon & Schuster.
West, Paul. Terrestrials. 1999. 380p. 14.95 (*0-87951-891-X*) Overlook Pr., The.
—Terrestrials. 1997. 384p. 24.00 (*0-684-80032-2*, Scribner) Simon & Schuster.
Westlake, Donald E. Kahawa. 1982. (Illus.). 280p. 15.95 o.p. (*0-670-41132-9*) Viking Penguin.
Whitney, Ruth Linnea. Slim: A Novel. 2003. 320p. 24.95 (*0-87074-478-X*) Southern Methodist Univ. Pr.
Wolf, Sarah. The Harbinger Effect. 1989. 18.95 o.p. (*0-671-68324-1*, Simon & Schuster) Simon & Schuster.
Wolff, Warren. White Lies - Black Ice. 2002. (Illus.). 191p. pap. 16.95 (*1-882897-69-2*) Lost Coast Pr.
Wren, Percival C. Beau Geste. 24.95 (*0-8488-1515-7*) Amereon, Ltd.
—Beau Geste. 1996. 414p. pap. 16.95 (*1-873631-07-3*) B & W Publishing GBR. *Dist:* Interlink Publishing Group, Inc.
—Beau Geste. unabr. ed. 1998. audio 69.95 (*0-7861-1290-5*, 2191) Blackstone Audio Bks., Inc.
—Beau Geste. unabr. collector's ed. 1993. audio 88.00 (*0-7366-2508-9*, 3264) Books on Tape, Inc.
—Beau Geste. 1976. lib. bdg. 28.95 (*0-89968-135-2*, Lightyear Pr.) Buccaneer Bks., Inc.
—Beau Geste. 1998. (Gateway Movie Classics Ser.). 431 p. pap. 12.95 o.s.i (*0-89526-380-7*, Gateway Editions) Regnery Publishing, Inc., An Eagle Publishing Co.
—Beau Geste. 1998. (Classics Library). 368p. pap. 3.95 (*1-85326-211-0*, 2110WW) Wordsworth Editions, Ltd. GBR. *Dist:* Casemate Pubs. & Bk. Distributors, LLC.
Wren, Percival C. & Hoppenstand, Gary. Beau Geste. 1999. (Penguin Twentieth-Century Classics Ser.). 368p. pap. 12.95 (*0-14-118151-6*) Viking Penguin.
Zabor, Rafi. I, Wabenzi. 2005. 26.00 (*0-86547-583-0*, North Point Pr.) Farrar, Straus & Giroux.
Zameenzad, Adam. My Friend Matt & Hena the Whore. 1993. 224p. (Orig.). pap. 11.00 o.p. (*0-14-013163-9*, Penguin Bks.) Penguin Group (USA) Inc.
Zwelonke, D. M. Robben Island. 1973. (African Writers Ser.). 151p. (C). pap. 8.95 (*0-435-90128-1*, 90128) Heinemann.

## ALABAMA—FICTION

Atherton, Charles. The First Stone: A Novel. 2001. 15.95 (*1-58838-037-8*, Court Street Pr.) NewSouth, Inc.
Atherton, Charles R. Death on the Hook: A Will Abbott Mystery. 2002. 15.95 (*1-58838-106-4*, Court Street Pr.) NewSouth, Inc.
Bailey, Douglas F. Devil Make a Third. 1989. (Library of Alabama Classics). 400p. reprint ed. pap. 14.95 o.s.i (*0-8173-0420-7*) Univ. of Alabama Pr.
Barr, John G. Rowdy Tales from Early Alabama. 1982. 15.95 o.p. (*0-8173-0057-0*) Univ. of Alabama Pr.
Barton, Beverly. After Dark. 2000. 384p. mass mkt. 5.99 (*0-8217-6693-7*, Zebra Bks.) Kensington Publishing Corp.
—Every Move She Makes. 2001. 384p. mass mkt. 6.50 (*0-8217-6838-7*) Kensington Publishing Corp.
Barton, Marlin. The Dry Well. 2001. 277p. 24.95 (*1-929490-07-0*) Beil, Frederic C. Pub., Inc.
Beidler, Philip D. The Art of Fiction in the Heart of Dixie: An Anthology of Alabama Writers. 1986. 352p. (C). pap. 22.95 o.s.i (*0-8173-0314-6*) Univ. of Alabama Pr.
Bell, Robert E. The Butterfly Tree. 1991. (Library of Alabama Classics). 264p. text 19.95 (*0-8173-0560-2*) Univ. of Alabama Pr.
Blackshear, Helen F. The Creek Captives. 2001. 216p. pap. 9.95 (*1-58838-057-2*) NewSouth, Inc.
Bonnie, Fred. Thanh Ho Delivers. 2000. 448p. 24.95 (*1-880216-51-5*, Black Belt Pr.) River City Publishing.
Braselton, Jeanne. A False Sense of Well Being. 2001. 352p. 23.95 (*0-345-44311-X*, Ballantine Bks.) Ballantine Bks.
—A False Sense of Well Being. 2002. 400p. pap. 13.95 (*0-345-44312-8*) Random Hse., Inc.
Brasher, Nell. The Weaning: And Other Stories. 1993. 192p. 9.95 (*1-881548-01-5*) Crane Hill Pubs.
Brown, Jerry E., ed. Clearings in the Thicket: An Alabama Humanities Reader. 1985. xix, 188p. text 16.50 o.s.i (*0-86554-144-2*, MUP/H134) Mercer Univ. Pr.
Brown, Mary W. Tongues of Flame. 1986. 15.95 o.p. (*0-525-24431-X*, Seymour Lawrence) NAL.
—Tongues of Flame. 1987. mass mkt. (*0-671-64157-3*, Washington Square Pr.) Simon & Schuster.
—Tongues of Flame. 2001. (Library of Alabama Classics). xvii, 162p. (C). pap. 17.95 (*0-8173-0722-2*) Univ. of Alabama Pr.
Brown, Mary Ward. It Wasn't All Dancing: And Other Stories. 2003. (Deep South Books). 160p. reprint ed. pap. 16.95 (*0-8173-5007-1*) Univ. of Alabama Pr.
Carter, Lee. Carry Me Home. 1995. 12.99 o.p. (*0-7852-7858-3*) Nelson, Thomas Inc.
Childers, James S. In the Deep South: A Novel about a White Man & a Black Man. 1988. (Library of Alabama Classics). (Illus.). 304p. reprint ed. pap. 16.50 o.p. (*0-8173-0387-1*) Univ. of Alabama Pr.
Childress, Mark. Crazy in Alabama. 1999. 448p. mass mkt. 6.99 (*0-345-43247-9*); 1994. 384p. reprint ed. pap. 12.00 (*0-345-38924-7*) Ballantine Bks.
—Crazy in Alabama, Set. abr. ed. 1999. audio 18.00 Highsmith Inc.
—Crazy in Alabama. 1993. 384p. 22.95 o.p. (*0-399-13855-2*) Penguin Group (USA) Inc.
Clark, Stephen J. Southern Latitudes. 2002. 272p. mass mkt. 6.50 o.s.i (*0-425-18637-7*, Prime Crime) Berkley Publishing Group.
Cobb, William. Spring of Souls: A Novel. 1999. 304p. 25.95 (*1-57587-137-8*); pap. 15.95 (*1-57587-138-6*) Crane Hill Pubs.
—A Walk Through Fire: A Novel. 1992. 544p. 22.00 o.p. (*0-688-11366-4*, Morrow, William & Co.) Morrow/Avon.

Settings

Colquitt, James E., ed. Alabama Bound: Contemporary Stories of a State. 1994. 224p. pap. 13.95 (*0-942979-26-5*); text 24.95 (*0-942979-25-7*) Livingston Pr.

Cook, Thomas H. Breakheart Hill. 1996. 320p. mass mkt. 6.50 (*0-553-57192-3*) Bantam Bks.

—Breakheart Hill. l.t. ed. 1995. (Large Print Bks.). pap. 22.95 o.p. (*1-56895-251-1*, Wheeler Publishing, Inc.) Gale Group.

Covington, Vicki. Bird of Paradise. 1991. 256p. mass mkt. 4.95 o.s.i (*0-8041-0798-X*, Ivy Bks.) Ballantine Bks.

—Bird of Paradise. l.t. ed. 1991. (General Ser.). 322p. lib. bdg. 19.95 o.p. (*0-8161-5118-0*, Macmillan Reference USA) Gale Group.

—Bird of Paradise. 1999. (Voices of the South Ser.). 208p. pap. 14.95 (*0-8071-2386-2*) Louisiana State Univ. Pr.

—Bird of Paradise. 1990. 18.95 o.p. (*0-671-68634-8*, Simon & Schuster) Simon & Schuster.

—Gathering Home. 1988. 240p. 17.95 o.p. (*0-671-66055-1*, Simon & Schuster) Simon & Schuster.

—Gathering Home. 1999. (Deep South Bks.). 240p. pap. 14.95 (*0-8173-1002-9*) Univ. of Alabama Pr.

—Gathering Home. 1990. 240p. pap. 7.95 o.p. (*0-14-012709-7*, Penguin Bks.) Viking Penguin.

—The Last Hotel for Women. 1996. 304p. 23.00 (*0-684-81111-1*, Simon & Schuster) Simon & Schuster.

—The Last Hotel for Women. 1999. (Deep South Book Ser.). 304p. pap. 16.95 (*0-8173-1003-7*) Univ. of Alabama Pr.

—Night Ride Home. 1992. 20.00 (*0-671-74345-7*, Simon & Schuster) Simon & Schuster.

—Night Ride Home: A Novel. 2001. (Literature & the Religious Spirit Ser.: Vol. 2). ix, 242p. pap. 11.95 (*0-918954-78-9*) Baylor Univ. Pr.

Daugherty, Franklin. Isle of Joy. 1996. 320p. 23.00 (*1-881320-78-2*, Black Belt Pr.) River City Publishing.

Deal, Babs H. It's Always Three O'Clock. 1990. E-Book 17.50 (*0-585-20786-0*) netLibrary, Inc.

—It's Always Three O'clock. 1990. (Library of Alabama Classics). 344p. reprint ed. pap. text 17.50 (*0-8173-0494-0*) Univ. of Alabama Pr.

Deal, Borden. The Least One. 1992. (Library of Alabama Classics). 368p. (YA). (ps up). pap. text 17.95 (*0-8173-0673-0*) Univ. of Alabama Pr.

Devoto, Pat Cunningham. My Last Days as Roy Rogers. 1999. (Illus.). 358p. 20.00 o.p. (*0-446-52388-7*) Warner Bks., Inc.

—My Last Days As Roy Rogers. 2000. 384p. reprint ed. pap. 13.95 (*0-446-67564-4*) Warner Bks., Inc.

—Out of the Night That Covers Me. l.t. ed. 2001. 434p. 28.95 (*1-58724-095-5*, Wheeler Publishing, Inc.) Gale Group.

—Out of the Night That Covers Me. 2001. 448p. pap. 13.95 (*0-446-67802-3*); 432p. 23.95 o.p. (*0-446-52751-3*) Warner Bks., Inc.

Duff, Gerald. Indian Giver. 1983. 244p. reprint ed. pap. 69.60 o.p. (*0-7837-9648-X*, 2059281) Bks. on Demand.

—Indian Giver. 1983. 256p. 12.95 o.p. (*0-253-13999-6*) Indiana Univ. Pr.

—Indian Giver. E-Book 7.00 (*1-930486-12-X*) Salvo Pr.

Ebersole, Lucinda. Death in Equality. 1997. 160p. 19.95 (*0-312-15106-3*) St. Martin's Pr.

Ellis, Helen. Eating the Cheshire Cat. 2001. 288p. pap. 13.00 (*0-684-86441-X*, Scribner) Simon & Schuster.

—Eating the Cheshire Cat: A Novel. 2000. 288p. 23.00 o.s.i (*0-684-86440-1*, Scribner) Simon & Schuster.

Erickson, Ben. A Parting Gift. l.t. ed. 2000. (Wheeler Large Print Book Ser.). 282p. 28.95 (*1-56895-932-X*, Wheeler Publishing, Inc.) Gale Group.

—A Parting Gift. 2000. E-Book 14.95 (*0-446-91482-7*); 2001. 288p. reprint ed. pap. 13.95 (*0-446-67722-1*) Warner Bks., Inc.

Evans, Augusta J. St. Elmo. Date not set. lib. bdg. 30.95 (*0-8488-1973-X*); 1976. 29.95 (*0-8488-1307-3*) Amereon, Ltd.

—St. Elmo. reprint ed. 1984. 415p. lib. bdg. 32.95 (*0-89966-487-3*); 1980. 440p. lib. bdg. 37.95 (*0-89968-210-3*, Lightyear Pr.) Buccaneer Bks., Inc.

—St. Elmo. (Early Best Sellers Ser.). reprint ed. lib. bdg. 48.00 (*0-7426-1023-3*) Classic Bks.

—St. Elmo. 1992. (Library of Alabama Classics). 392p. (C). reprint ed. pap. 14.95 o.s.i (*0-8173-0577-7*) Univ. of Alabama Pr.

—St. Elmo: A Novel. 1975. (Popular Culture in America Ser.). 576p. reprint ed. 41.95 (*0-405-06371-7*) Ayer Co. Pubs., Inc.

Flagg, Fannie. Fried Green Tomatoes at the Whistle Stop Cafe. 1988. pap. 11.00 (*0-449-45860-1*); 1997. 432p. pap. 14.95 (*0-449-91135-7*) Ballantine Bks. (Fawcett).

—Fried Green Tomatoes at the Whistle Stop Cafe. 1989. 420p. 7.95 o.p. (*0-07-021257-0*) McGraw-Hill Cos., The.

—Fried Green Tomatoes at the Whistle Stop Cafe. l.t. ed. 1993. 528p. pap. 18.00 (*0-679-74495-9*) Random Hse. Large Print.

—Fried Green Tomatoes at the Whistle Stop Cafe. 1987. 416p. 25.00 o.s.i (*0-394-56152-X*) Random Hse., Inc.

—Fried Green Tomatoes at the Whistle Stop Cafe. 1999. (*0-7621-0253-5*) Reader's Digest Assn., Inc., The.

—Fried Green Tomatoes at the Whistle Stop Cafe. 2000. (Illus.). (J). 13.55 (*0-606-17986-0*); 1997. 16.10 o.p. (*0-606-12298-2*) Turtleback Bks.

—Fried Green Tomatoes at the Whistle Stop Cafe: A Novel. 2002. 416p. 23.00 (*0-375-50841-4*) Random Hse., Inc.

—Fried Green Tomatoes at the Whistlestop Cafe. 2000. 416p. mass mkt. 7.99 (*0-8041-1561-3*, Ballantine Bks.) Ballantine Bks.

Funderburk, Robert. Rainbow's End. 1997. (Innocent Years Ser.: Vol. 6). 256p. pap. 8.99 o.p. (*1-55661-465-9*) Bethany Hse. Pubs.

George, Anne. Murder Boogies with Elvis. (Southern Sisters Mysteries Ser.). 2002. 288p. mass mkt. 6.99 (*0-06-103102-X*, Avon Bks.); 2001. 256p. 23.00 (*0-06-019870-2*, Morrow, William & Co.) Morrow/Avon.

—Murder Boogies with Elvis: A Southern Sisters Mystery. l.t. ed. 2001. (Mystery Ser.). 27.95 (*1-57490-380-2*, Beeler Large Print Bks.) Beeler, Thomas T. Publisher.

—Murder Carries a Torch. 2000. (Southern Sisters Mysteries Ser.). 272p. 23.00 (*0-380-97810-5*, Morrow, William & Co.) Morrow/Avon.

—Murder Carries a Torch: A Southern Sisters Mystery. l.t. ed. 2001. (Large Print Bks.). 274p. pap. 23.95 (*1-58724-127-7*, Wheeler Publishing, Inc.) Gale Group.

—Murder Carries a Torch: A Southern Sisters Mystery. 2001. 288p. mass mkt. 6.99 (*0-380-80938-9*, Avon Bks.) Morrow/Avon.

—Murder Gets a Life. l.t. ed. 2000. (Beeler Large Print Mystery Ser.). 234p. 26.95 (*1-57490-290-3*, Beeler Large Print Bks.) Beeler, Thomas T. Publisher.

—Murder Gets a Life: A Southern Sisters Mystery. (Southern Sisters Mysteries Ser.). 1999. 272p. mass mkt. 6.99 (*0-380-79366-0*); 1998. 256p. 20.00 o.p. (*0-380-97558-0*) Morrow/Avon. (Avon Bks.).

—Murder Makes Waves. l.t. ed. 2000. (Beeler Large Print Mystery Ser.). 246p. 26.95 (*1-57490-274-1*, Beeler Large Print Bks.) Beeler, Thomas T. Publisher.

—Murder Makes Waves. (Southern Sisters Mysteries Ser.). 1998. 272p. mass mkt. 6.99 (*0-380-78450-5*); 1997. 256p. 20.00 o.p. (*0-380-97527-0*) Morrow/Avon. (Avon Bks.).

—Murder on a Bad Hair Day. l.t. ed. 1999. (Beeler Large Print Mystery Ser.). 277p. 26.95 (*1-57490-238-5*, Beeler Large Print Bks.) Beeler, Thomas T. Publisher.

—Murder on a Bad Hair Day. 1996. (Southern Sisters Mysteries Ser.). 256p. mass mkt. 6.99 (*0-380-78087-9*, Avon Bks.) Morrow/Avon.

—Murder on a Girl's Night Out. 1996. (Southern Sisters Mysteries Ser.). 256p. mass mkt. 6.99 (*0-380-78086-0*, Avon Bks.) Morrow/Avon.

—Murder on a Girls' Night Out. l.t. ed. 1999. (Beeler Large Print Mystery Ser.). 26.95 (*1-57490-212-1*, Beeler Large Print Bks.) Beeler, Thomas T. Publisher.

—Murder Runs in the Family. l.t. ed. 2000. (Beeler Large Print Mystery Ser.). 243p. 26.95 (*1-57490-258-X*, Beeler Large Print Bks.) Beeler, Thomas T. Publisher.

—Murder Runs in the Family. 1997. (Southern Sisters Mysteries Ser.). 288p. mass mkt. 6.99 (*0-380-78449-1*, Avon Bks.) Morrow/Avon.

—Murder Shoots the Bull. 2000. (Southern Sisters Mysteries Ser.). 272p. mass mkt. 6.99 (*0-380-80149-3*, Avon Bks.) Morrow/Avon.

—Murder Shoots the Bull: A Southern Sisters Mystery. l.t. ed. 1999. (*0-07-862222-0*) McGraw-Hill Cos., The.

—Murder Shoots the Bull: A Southern Sisters Mystery. 1999. (Southern Sisters Mysteries Ser.). 247p. 22.00 (*0-380-97688-9*, Avon Bks.) Morrow/Avon.

—Murder Shoots the Bull: A Southern Sisters Mystery. l.t. ed. 1999. (Americana Ser.). 358p. 26.95 (*0-7862-2222-0*) Thorndike Pr.

Gibbons, Faye. King Shoes & Clown Pockets. 1989. 240p. (J). (gr. 4 up). 12.95 o.p. (*0-688-06592-9*, Morrow, William & Co.) Morrow/Avon.

Greenhaw, Wayne. The Spider's Web: A Novella & Other Stories. 2003. 200p. 23.95 (*1-57966-044-4*) River City Publishing.

Hager, Betty. Miss Tilly & the Haunted Mansion. 1994. (Tales from the Bayou Ser.: Bk. 2). 112p. (J). (gr. 3-7). 5.99 o.p. (*0-310-38411-7*) Zondervan.

—Old Jake & the Pirate's Treasure. 1994. (Tales from the Bayou Ser.: Bk. 1). (Illus.). 112p. (J). (gr. 3-7). 5.99 o.p. (*0-310-38401-X*) Zondervan.

Hale, S. Dennis. The Prayer Amendment: A Novel. 2003. pap. 17.95 (*1-58838-118-8*) NewSouth, Inc.

Hannah, Barry. Ray. 1987. 12p. pap. 5.95 o.p. (*0-14-010515-8*, Penguin Bks.) Viking Penguin.

Harrison, Henry F. Jimbo on Board the Nettie Quill: An Alabama Riverboat Adventure. 1995. (Illus.). 40p. (Orig.). (J). (ps-3). pap. 16.00 (*1-881320-19-7*, Black Belt Pr.) River City Publishing.

Harvatich, Mary L. Perfect Love. 2000. 200p. pap. 12.95 (*1-888725-29-X*, BeachHouse Bks.) Science & Humanities Pr.

—Perfect Love: A Novel. l.t. ed. 2000. 206p. per. 18.95 (*1-888725-15-X*, MacroPrintBooks) Science & Humanities Pr.

Hassell, Harriet. Rachel's Children. 1990. (Library of Alabama Classics). 336p. reprint ed. pap. text 16.50 (*0-8173-0499-1*) Univ. of Alabama Pr.

Hegwood, Martin. Massacre Island. 2001. (Illus.). 288p. 23.95 (*0-312-28095-5*, Saint Martin's Minotaur) St. Martin's Pr.

Henderson, George W. Jule. 1989. (Library of Alabama Classics). 256p. (C). reprint ed. pap. text 29.95 (*0-8173-0438-X*) Univ. of Alabama Pr.

—Ollie Miss. 1973. 276p. reprint ed. 15.95 (*0-911860-41-X*) Chatham Bookseller.

—Ollie Miss. 1988. (Library of Alabama Classics). (Illus.). 304p. reprint ed. pap. text 14.50 o.s.i (*0-8173-0388-X*) Univ. of Alabama Pr.

Higginbotham, Jay. Mauvila. 2000. 307p. 25.00 (*1-887650-31-8*, A&B Bahr & Co.) Factor Pr.

Hobson, Anne. In Old Alabama: Being the Chronicles of Miss Mouse, the Little Black Merchant. 1977. (Short Story Index Reprint Ser.). reprint ed. 25.95 (*0-8369-4246-9*) Ayer Co. Pubs., Inc.

Hodges, Sam. B-Four. 2000. (Deep South Bks.). 278p. pap. 17.95 (*0-8173-1049-5*) Univ. of Alabama Pr.

—B-Four: A Novel. 1992. 288p. 18.95 o.p. (*0-312-07647-9*) St. Martin's Pr.

Hoff, B. J. Masquerade. 1996. (Portraits Ser.: No. 1). 224p. pap. 8.99 o.p. (*1-55661-860-3*) Bethany Hse. Pubs.

—Masquerade. l.t. ed. 2000. (Christian Mystery Ser.). 279p. 24.95 (*0-7862-2376-6*) Thorndike Pr.

Hooper, Johnson J. Adventures of Captain Simon Suggs, Late of the Tallapoosa Volunteers: Together with Taking the Census & Other Alabama Sketches. 1993. (Library of Alabama Classics). 272p. pap. 15.95 (*0-8173-0706-0*) Univ. of Alabama Pr.

—Some Adventures of Captain Simon Suggs. (Illus.). reprint ed. lib. bdg. 19.50 (*0-8398-0789-9*) Irvington Pubs.

Howard, Linda. Shades of Twilight. l.t. ed. 1996. (Large Print Bks.). 23.95 o.p. (*1-56895-378-X*, Wheeler Publishing, Inc.) Gale Group.

—Shades of Twilight. 1996. (Illus.). 400p. mass mkt. 6.50 (*0-671-79937-1*, Pocket) Simon & Schuster.

—Tears of the Renegade. 2001. 256p. mass mkt. (*1-55166-786-X*, 1-66786-4, Mira Bks.); 1985. mass mkt. (*0-373-07092-6*, Harlequin Bks.) Harlequin Enterprises, Ltd.

Hubbs, G. Ward, ed. Rowdy Tales from Early Alabama: The Humor of John Gorman Barr. 1989. (Illus.). 232p. pap. text 17.95 (*0-8173-0477-0*) Univ. of Alabama Pr.

Hudson, Helen. Criminal Trespass. 1985. 256p. 17.95 o.p. (*0-399-13055-1*, G. P. Putnam's Sons) Penguin Putnam Bks. for Young Readers.

—Criminal Trespass. 1986. (Contemporary American Fiction Ser.). pap. 6.95 o.p. (*0-14-008494-0*, Penguin Bks.) Viking Penguin.

Huff Fisk, Sarah. Found among the Fragments: A Story of Love & Courage. 1997. (Illus.). 320p. (Orig.). pap. 15.95 (*0-9655917-2-7*) Pinhook Publishing Co.

Ivey, Caroline. The Family. 1991. (Library of Alabama Classics). 400p. pap. 14.95 (*0-8173-0524-6*) Univ. of Alabama Pr.

Jenkins, Jerry B. Hometown Legend. 2001. audio 24.98. audio 24.98 (*1-58621-187-0*) Time Warner AudioBooks.

—Hometown Legend. 2001. 320p. 24.95 o.p. (*0-446-52902-8*); 416p. 24.95 o.p. (*0-446-52998-2*) Warner Bks., Inc.

Johnson, Allen, Jr. Picker McClikker. 1993. (Illus.). (J). (gr. k-3). 16.95 o.s.i (*1-878561-20-0*) Seacoast Publishing, Inc.

Jones, Annie. The Snowbirds. 2003. 336p. pap. 11.99 (*1-57673-623-7*) Multnomah Pubs., Inc.

—The Snowbirds. l.t. ed. 2003. 25.95 (*0-7862-5490-4*) Thorndike Pr.

Kiernan, Caitlín R. Low Red Moon. 2003. 352p. pap. 14.00 (*0-451-45948-2*, ROC) NAL.

—Low Red Moon. 2003. 370p. 40.00 (*1-931081-84-0*) Subterranean Pr.

King, Cassandra. Making Waves. 2003. 304p. 13.95 (*0-7868-8793-1*) Hyperion Pr.

Knight, Michael. Divining Rod: A Novel. 1998. 256p. 23.95 o.p. (*0-525-94379-X*) Dutton/Plume.

Lacy, Al. A Heart Divided: Mobile Bay, 8 vols. 2003. (Battles of Destiny Ser.: Vol. 2). 353p. pap. 9.99 (*0-88070-591-4*, Multnomah Bks.) Multnomah Pubs., Inc.

March, William. Company K. 1989. (Library of Alabama Classics). 288p. pap. 15.95 (*0-8173-0480-0*) Univ. of Alabama Pr.

—Trial Balance: The Collected Short Stories of William March. 1987. (Library of Alabama Classics). 536p. reprint ed. pap. 14.95 (*0-8173-0372-3*) Univ. of Alabama Pr.

Meador, D. J. His Father's House. 1994. 384p. (YA). (gr. 10-12). 25.00 (*1-56554-032-8*) Pelican Publishing Co., Inc.

Meador, Daniel J. Unforgotten. 1999. 400p. 25.00 (*1-56554-349-1*) Pelican Publishing Co., Inc.

Miller, Brenda Rhodes. The Laying on of Hands. 2004. 256p. pap. 12.95 (*0-7679-1556-9*) Broadway Bks.

Miller, Charlotte. Through a Glass, Darkly. 2001. 340p. (*1-58838-054-8*) NewSouth, Inc.

Murray, Albert. Train Whistle Guitar. 1989. (Library of Black Literature). 183p. reprint ed. pap. text 12.95 o.p. (*1-55553-051-6*) Northeastern Univ. Pr.

—Train Whistle Guitar: A Novel. 1998. 192p. pap. 13.00 (*0-375-70336-5*, Vintage) Knopf Publishing Group.

Naslund, Sena Jeter. Four Spirits. 2003. 544p. 26.95 (*0-06-621238-3*); 242.55 (*0-06-057537-9*); pap. (*0-06-093669-X*) Morrow/Avon. (Morrow, William & Co.).

Nicholson, Charles. The Skinner's Tale. 1991. 208p. 19.95 o.s.i (*0-8117-1939-1*) Stackpole Bks.

Oliver, Julia. Goodbye to the Buttermilk Sky. 1995. 192p. pap. 10.95 o.p. (*0-452-27425-7*, Plume) Dutton/Plume.

—Goodbye to the Buttermilk Sky. 1994. 192p. 18.00 o.p. (*1-881320-18-9*, Black Belt Pr.) River City Publishing.

—Goodbye to the Buttermilk Sky. 2001. (Deep South Bks.). pap. text 16.95 (*0-8173-1145-9*) Univ. of Alabama Pr.

Perdue, Tito. Opportunities in Alabama Agriculture. 1994. 222p. 18.00 (*1-880909-24-3*) Baskerville Pubs., Inc.

—The Sweet-Scented Manuscript. Date not set. 21.00 (*1-880909-68-5*) Baskerville Pubs., Inc.

Phillips, W. Glasgow. Tuscaloosa. 1995. 192p. pap. 10.95 o.s.i (*0-452-27439-7*, Plume) Dutton/Plume.

Pruett, Lynn. Ruby River. 2004. 288p. pap. 13.00 (*0-8021-4039-4*, Grove Pr.); 2002. 336p. 24.00 (*0-87113-855-7*, Atlantic Monthly Pr.) Grove/Atlantic, Inc.

—Ruby River. 2003. (Americana Ser.). 28.95 (*0-7862-5144-1*) Thorndike Pr.

Raines, Howell. Whiskey Man. 1980. mass mkt. 2.50 o.p. (*0-449-24335-4*, Fawcett) Ballantine Bks.

—Whiskey Man. 2000. (Deep South Book Ser.). 264p. pap. 17.95 (*0-8173-1067-3*) Univ. of Alabama Pr.

—Whiskey Man. 1977. 8.95 o.p. (*0-670-76190-7*) Viking Penguin.

Rayford, Julian L. Cottonmouth. 1991. (Library of Alabama Classics). 424p. pap. text 18.95 (*0-8173-0529-7*) Univ. of Alabama Pr.

Richmond, Michelle. The Girl in the Fall-Away Dress: Stories. 2001. (Associated Writing Programs Award for Short Fiction Ser.). 176p. 24.95 (*1-55849-315-8*) Univ. of Massachusetts Pr.

Rogers-Pruitt, Ruth. Wind along the Waste. 1991. o.p. (*0-87152-448-1*) Reprint Co.

Sanguinetti, Elise. The Last of the Whitfields. 1986. (Library of Alabama Classics). 288p. pap. 14.95 o.s.i (*0-8173-0309-X*) Univ. of Alabama Pr.

Saums, Mary. The Valley of Jewels. 2001. v, 184p. pap. 15.00 (*1-57072-189-0*); 24.50 (*1-57072-188-2*) Overmountain Pr. (Silver Dagger Mysteries).

Shulman, Neil. Backyard Tribe. 1994. 192p. 16.95 o.p. (*0-312-10513-4*) St. Martin's Pr.

Siddons, Anne Rivers. Heartbreak Hotel. 1984. 336p. mass mkt. 5.99 o.s.i (*0-345-31953-2*) Ballantine Bks.

—Heartbreak Hotel. l.t. ed. 1996. lib. bdg. 24.95 (*1-57490-075-7*, Beeler Large Print Bks.) Beeler, Thomas T. Publisher.

—Heartbreak Hotel. 1993. 416p. mass mkt. 7.99 (*0-06-104278-1*, HarperTorch) Morrow/Avon.

—Heartbreak Hotel. unabr. ed. 1999. audio 70.00 (*0-7887-0295-5*, 94488E7) Recorded Bks., LLC.

Simms, William Gilmore. Richard Hurdis: A Tale of Alabama. Guilds, John C., ed. 1995. (Selected Fiction of William Gilmore Simms Ser.). text 40.00 (*1-55728-334-6*) Univ. of Arkansas Pr.

—Richard Hurdis: A Tale of Alabama. rev. ed. reprint ed. 29.50 (*0-404-06035-8*) AMS Pr., Inc.

—Richard Hurdis: A Tale of Alabama. 1995. (Simms Ser.: Vol. 8). 395p. pap. text 29.95 (*1-55728-347-8*) Univ. of Arkansas Pr.

Sport, Kathryn M. & Hitchcock, Bert, eds. De Remnant Truth: The Tales of Jake Mitchell & Robert Wilton Burton. 1991. 256p. pap. text 19.95 (*0-8173-0515-7*) Univ. of Alabama Pr.

Sprinkle, Patricia. When Did We Lose Harriet? l.t. ed. 1998. (Christian Mystery Ser.). 440p. 22.95 o.p. (*0-7862-1472-4*) Thorndike Pr.

—When Did We Lose Harriet? 1997. (MacLaren Yarbrough Mysteries Ser.). 304p. pap. 19.99 (*0-310-21294-4*) Zondervan.

Stanley, Marie. Gulf Stream. 1993. (Library of Alabama Classics). 352p. pap. text 17.95 (*0-8173-0695-1*) Univ. of Alabama Pr.
—Gulf Stream. 1993. E-Book 17.95 (*0-585-14782-5*) netLibrary, Inc.
Stribling, T. S. The Store. 1991. lib. bdg. 21.95 (*1-56849-056-9*) Buccaneer Bks., Inc.
—The Store. 1985. (Library of Alabama Classics). reprint ed. 27.50 o.p. (*0-8173-0250-6*); 592p. pap. text 39.95 (*0-8173-0251-4*) Univ. of Alabama Pr.
Taylor, Joe. Oldcat & Ms. Puss: A Book of Days for You & Me. 1997. 176p. 23.00 (*1-881320-72-3*, Black Belt Pr.) River City Publishing.
Wallace, Daniel. The Watermelon King: A Novel. 2003. 240p. tchr. ed. 23.00 (*0-618-22138-7*) Houghton Mifflin Co.
—The Watermelon King: A Novel. 2003. 240p. pap. 13.00 (*0-618-40081-8*, Mariner Bks.) Houghton Mifflin Co. Trade & Reference Div.
Wallace, Rangeley. No Defense. 1997. 272p. mass mkt. 5.99 (*0-312-96169-3*, St. Martin's Paperbacks); 1995. 256p. 21.95 o.p. (*0-312-13571-8*) St. Martin's Pr.
Walter, Eugene. The Untidy Pilgrim. 1988. 250p. (C). pap. 9.95 (*0-413-55340-X*, A0304, Methuen Drama) Heinemann.
—The Untidy Pilgrim. (Library of Alabama Classics). 264p. 1987. reprint ed. pap. 14.95 o.s.i (*0-8173-0370-7*); 2nd ed. 2002. pap. 18.95 (*0-8173-1143-2*) Univ. of Alabama Pr.
Warren, Lella. Family Fiction: Unpublished Narratives by Lella Warren. 1989. (Southern Literary Ser.: Vol. II). (Illus.). 102p. (Orig.). pap. 14.95 (*0-917786-73-4*) Summa Pubns.
—Foundation Stone. 1986. (Library of Alabama Classics). 672p. pap. text 17.95 (*0-8173-0288-3*) Univ. of Alabama Pr.
—Foundation Stone. 1986. E-Book 18.95 (*0-585-26146-6*) netLibrary, Inc.
Warren, Lella & Anderson, Nancy G. Foundation Stone. 1986. 32.50 o.p. (*0-8173-0287-5*) Univ. of Alabama Pr.
Woodward, Margaret. Still Waters. 1995. 256p. 22.95 o.p. (*0-399-13990-7*, G. P. Putnam's Sons) Penguin Group (USA) Inc.
Young, Bard. The Snake of God: A Story of Memory & Imagination. 1996. (Illus.). 176p. 25.00 o.p. (*1-881320-86-3*, Black Belt Pr.) River City Publishing.

## ALASKA—FICTION

Alberts, Laurie. Tempting Fate. 1987. 17.95 o.p. (*0-395-43041-0*) Houghton Mifflin Co.
Anderson, Jean. In Extremis & Other Alaskan Stories. 1989. 120p. 14.95 (*0-917635-06-X*); pap. 9.95 (*0-917635-07-8*) Plover Pr.
Arnout, Susan. The Frozen Lady. 1984. mass mkt. 3.95 o.p. (*0-8217-1338-8*, Zebra Bks.) Kensington Publishing Corp.
—Frozen Lady. 1983. 581p. 15.95 o.p. (*0-87795-368-6*, Morrow, William & Co.) Morrow/Avon.
Arthur, Elizabeth. Bad Guys. 1986. 288p. 16.95 o.s.i (*0-394-55442-6*) Knopf, Alfred A. Inc.
Barer, Burl. Murder in the Family. 2000. (Illus.). 320p. mass mkt. 6.50 (*0-7860-1135-1*) Kensington Publishing Corp.
Barlow, Arthur. Sourdoughs & Scallawags. 2002. 118p. pap. (*1-55369-312-4*) Trafford Publishing.
Bergren, Lisa Tawn. Midnight Sun. 2000. (Northern Lights Ser.: Vol. 3). 384p. pap. 10.95 (*1-57856-113-2*) WaterBrook Pr.
Biggar, Joan R. Danger at Half-Moon Lake. 1991. (Adventure Quest Ser.). (Illus.). 143p. (J). (gr. 5-8). pap. 4.99 o.s.i (*0-570-04194-5*, 56-1653) Concordia Publishing Hse.
Blair, Cynthia. Once More with Feeling. 1996. mass mkt. 5.99 o.s.i (*0-345-38638-8*) Ballantine Bks.
Bodett, Tom. The Big Garage on Clear Shot: Growing up, Growing Old, & Going Fishing at the End of the Road. 1990. 320p. 18.95 o.p. (*0-688-09525-9*, Morrow, William & Co.) Morrow/Avon.
—The Free Fall of Webster Cummings, abr. ed. 1995. (Tom Bodett's American Odyssey Ser.: Vol.1). audio 16.95 o.p. (*1-56100-855-9*, 470, Nova Audio Bks.) Brilliance Audio.
—The Free Fall of Webster Cummings. 1996. 384p. (J). 22.95 (*0-7868-6209-2*) Hyperion Pr.
Boyd, Donna. The Promise. 2000. 336p. mass mkt. 6.99 (*0-380-79096-3*) HarperCollins Pubs.
Boyer, G. G. Morgette & the Alaskan Bandits. 1987. 192p. 16.95 o.s.i (*0-8027-0971-0*) Walker & Co.
—Morgette in the Yukon. 1983. 11.95 o.s.i (*0-8027-4020-0*) Walker & Co.
—Morgette on the Barbary Coast. 1984. 192p. 12.95 o.s.i (*0-8027-4033-2*) Walker & Co.
Boyle, T. Coraghessan. Drop City. 2004. 512p. pap. 14.00 (*0-14-200380-8*) Penguin Group (USA) Inc.
—Drop City. 2003. 464p. 25.95 (*0-670-03172-0*, Viking) Viking Penguin.
Brand, Max. The Bells of San Carlos & Other Stories. 1998. 320p. reprint ed. mass mkt. 4.99 (*0-8439-4355-6*, Leisure Bks.) Dorchester Publishing Co., Inc.
—Chinook. l.t. ed. 1999. (Western Ser.). 397p. 22.95 (*0-7862-1167-9*) Thorndike Pr.
—The Lightning Warrior. 1998. 272p. mass mkt. 4.50 (*0-8439-4420-X*, Leisure Bks.) Dorchester Publishing Co., Inc.
—The Lightning Warrior. l.t. ed. Date not set. 20.00 (*0-7838-1667-7*, Macmillan Reference USA) Gale Group.
—The Lightning Warrior. 1998. E-Book 9.95 (*0-585-28870-4*) netLibrary, Inc.
—The Masterman. 2000. (Five Star Western Ser.). 211p. 21.95 (*0-7862-2099-6*, Five Star) Gale Group.
—Sixteen in Nome. unabr. ed. 1996. audio 42.00 (*0-7366-3624-2*, 4284) Books on Tape, Inc.
—Sixteen in Nome. abr. ed. (Five Star Westerns Ser.). 1996. audio 7.99 o.p. (*1-56740-125-2*, 1372, Paperback Nova Audio Bks.); 1995. audio 16.95 o.p. (*1-56100-853-2*, 1371, Nova Audio Bks.); 1995. audio 19.95 o.p. (*1-56100-661-0*, 1551, Bookcassette); 1995. audio 57.25 o.p. (*1-56100-286-0*, 1046, Unabridged Library Editions) Brilliance Audio.
—Sixteen in Nome. 1999. 240p. mass mkt. 4.50 (*0-8439-4486-2*, Leisure Bks.) Dorchester Publishing Co., Inc.
—Sixteen in Nome. 1995. 214p. 18.95 (*0-7862-0509-1*, Five Star) Gale Group.
—Sixteen in Nome. l.t. ed. 1996. (Western Ser.). 299p. lib. bdg. 22.95 (*0-7862-0718-3*) Thorndike Pr.
—Sixteen in Nome. 1999. E-Book 9.95 (*0-585-30569-2*) netLibrary, Inc.
Brown, Tricia. Groucho's Eyebrows. Lavallee, Barbara, tr. & illus. by. 2003. 32p. (J). 15.95 (*0-88240-556-X*, Alaska Northwest Bks.) Graphic Arts Ctr. Publishing Co.
Buchanan, James David. Horde of Fools: A North-Western Story. l.t. ed. 2001. (Five Star First Edition Western Ser.). 237p. 23.95 (*0-7862-3667-1*, Five Star) Gale Group.
Butler, Robert Olen. Sun Dogs. 1985. 240p. mass mkt. 2.95 o.s.i (*0-345-32125-1*) Ballantine Bks.
—Sun Dogs. 1994. 25.00 o.p. (*0-8050-3201-0*); 218p. pap. 11.00 o.s.i (*0-8050-3143-X*, Owl Bks.) Holt, Henry & Co.
—Sun Dogs. 1982. 250p. 12.95 o.p. (*0-8180-0636-6*) Horizon Pr.
Caldwell, Francis E. The Search for the Amigo. 2000. (Illus.). 276p. pap. (*1-55212-469-X*) Trafford Publishing.
Calhoun, Richard S. Cheechako: An Alaskan Adventure. 2001. 160p. pap. 20.99 (*0-7388-4612-0*) Xlibris Corp.
Callanan, Liam. The Cloud Atlas: A Novel. 2004. 368p. 22.95 (*0-385-33694-2*, Delacorte Pr.) Dell Publishing.
Cates, David. Hunger in America: A Novel. 1992. 208p. 19.00 o.p. (*0-671-73817-8*) Summit Bks.
Champlin, Tim. By Flare of Northern Lights. l.t. ed. 2001. (Five Star First Edition Western Ser.). (Illus.). 226p. 23.95 (*0-7862-2730-3*, Five Star) Gale Group.
Charbonneau, Louis. White Harvest. 1994. 288p. 21.00 o.p. (*1-55611-362-5*) Fine, Donald I. Bks.
—White Harvest. l.t. ed. 1997. (Ulverscroft Large Print Ser.). 576p. 31.50 (*0-7089-3681-4*, Ulverscroft) Thorpe, F. A. Pubs. GBR. *Dist:* Ulverscroft Large Print Bks., Ltd., Ulverscroft Large Print Canada, Ltd.
Cherry, Bob. Spirit of the Raven: An Alaskan Novel. 2002. 275p. pap. 18.50 (*0-9665430-6-8*); 1999. (Illus.). 279p. 19.95 (*0-9665430-0-9*) One Eyed Pr.
Clarkson, Ewan. Ice Trek. 1987. 192p. 13.95 o.p. (*0-312-01046-X*) St. Martin's Pr.
Coyle, Daniel. Waking Samuel. 2003. 304p. 23.95 (*1-58234-281-4*) Bloomsbury Publishing.
Crane, Elizabeth. Time Remembered. 1993. E-Book 9.95 (*0-585-31413-6*) netLibrary, Inc.
Crawford, Kenneth C. Yuki. 1998. 96p. (J). (ps up). pap. 7.99 o.p. (*0-8280-1051-X*) Review & Herald Publishing Assn.
Croman, Dorothy Y. Trouble on the Blue Fox Island. 1985. (Outlands Adventure Ser.). 176p. (J). (gr. 4-7). 3.50 o.p. (*0-8423-7345-4*) Tyndale Hse. Pubs.
Cushman, Dan. In Alaska with Shipwreck Kelly. abr. ed. 1997. (Five Star Westerns Ser.). audio 7.99 o.p. (*1-56740-157-0*, 722, Paperback Nova Audio Bks.) Brilliance Audio.
—In Alaska with Shipwreck Kelly. l.t. ed. 1997. 20.00 (*0-7838-1474-7*, Macmillan Reference USA) Gale Group.
—In Alaska with Shipwreck Kelly: A North-Western Story. 1996. (Western Ser.). 226p. 17.95 (*0-7862-0534-2*, Five Star) Gale Group.
Dailey, Janet. The Great Alone. l.t. ed. 1987. Vol. I. 18.95 o.p. (*1-55504-188-4*); Vol. I. pap. 16.95 o.p. (*1-55504-212-0*); Vol. II. pap. 18.95 o.p. (*1-55504-189-2*); Vol. II. pap. 16.95 o.p. (*1-55504-213-9*) BBC Audiobooks America.
—The Great Alone. 1986. 768p. 18.45 o.p. (*0-671-61276-X*, Simon & Schuster) Simon & Schuster.
Davis, Val. The Return of the Spanish Lady. 2001. 307p. 22.95 (*0-312-26224-8*, Saint Martin's Minotaur) St. Martin's Pr.
Delis, Leftare P. The Inside Passage. 1994. 493p. pap. 12.95 o.p. (*0-89716-556-X*) Peanut Butter Publishing.
Doig, Ivan. The Sea Runners. unabr. collector's ed. 1987. audio 48.00 (*0-7366-1227-0*, 2145) Books on Tape, Inc.
—The Sea Runners. 1983. 288p. pap. 14.00 (*0-14-006780-9*, Penguin Bks.) Penguin Group (USA) Inc.
—The Sea Runners. 1982. (Illus.). 288p. 13.95 o.s.i (*0-689-11302-1*, Scribner) Simon & Schuster.
—The Sea Runners. 1992. 24.25 (*0-8446-6538-X*) Smith, Peter Pub., Inc.
Douglass, Keith. Arctic Fire, No. 9. 1997. (Carrier Ser.). 336p. mass mkt. 5.99 o.s.i (*0-515-12084-7*, Jove) Berkley Publishing Group.
Du Brul, Jack. Charon's Landing. abr. ed. 1999. audio 17.95 o.p. (*1-56740-823-0*, 1569, Nova Audio Bks.); audio 30.95 (*1-56740-402-2*, 1567, Bookcassette); audio 105.25 (*1-56740-631-9*, 1571, Unabridged Library Editions) Brilliance Audio.
—Charon's Landing. 2000. 512p. mass mkt. 7.99 o.s.i (*0-8125-7550-4*, Tor Bks.); 1999. 384p. 24.95 (*0-312-86816-2*, Forge Bks.) Doherty, Tom Assocs., LLC.
—Charon's Landing. unabr. ed. 1999. audio 17.95 Highsmith Inc.
Elkins, Aaron. Icy Clutches. l.t. ed. 1992. (Mystery Ser.). 388p. 29.99 (*0-7505-0353-X*) Magna Large Print Bks. GBR. *Dist:* Ulverscroft Large Print Bks., Ltd.
—Icy Clutches. 1990. 304p. 16.95 o.p. (*0-89296-377-8*) Mysterious Pr.
—Icy Clutches. 1991. 304p. mass mkt. 5.99 o.p. (*0-446-40040-8*, Mysterious Pr. Paperback Bks.) Warner Bks., Inc.
Eto, Motokuni, et al, trs. An Alaskan Tale by Jiro Nitta. 1989. 368p. 54.00 (*0-8191-7389-4*) Univ. Pr. of America.
Fenady, Andrew J. The Summer of Jack London. l.t. ed. 2002. pap. 24.95 (*0-7862-4079-2*) Gale Group.
Froetschel, Susan. Alaska Gray. 1996. per. (*0-373-26206-X*, 1-26206-2, Worldwide Library) Harlequin Enterprises, Ltd.
—Alaska Gray. 1994. 256p. 20.95 o.p. (*0-312-11233-5*, Saint Martin's Minotaur) St. Martin's Pr.
Grace, Carol. Under Alaskan Skies. 2003. (Harlequin American Romance Ser.: No. 956). 256p. mass mkt. o.s.i (*0-373-16956-6*, Harlequin Bks.) Harlequin Enterprises, Ltd.
Haldeman, Joe W. Guardian. 2002. 240p. 22.95 (*0-441-00977-8*) Ace Bks.
Hannah, Kristin. A Handful of Heaven. 1995. mass mkt. 2.99 o.s.i (*0-449-14972-2*, Fawcett) Ballantine Bks.
Harner, Michael. The Way of the Shaman. 1990. (Illus.). 208p. reprint ed. 17.95 o.p. (*0-06-250382-0*) HarperSanFrancisco.
Harrison, Kathryn. The Seal Wife: A Novel. unabr. ed. 2002. audio 24.95 (*1-59086-145-0*, 3692, Brilliance Audio Unabridged); audio 62.25 (*1-59086-146-9*, 3693, Unabridged Library Editions) Brilliance Audio.
—The Seal Wife: A Novel. 2003. 248p. pap. 12.95 (*0-8129-6845-X*) Random House Adult Trade Publishing Group.
—The Seal Wife: A Novel. 2002. 224p. 23.95 (*0-375-50629-2*) Random Hse., Inc.
Harrison, Sue. Brother Wind: A Novel. 1994. 494p. 22.00 o.p. (*0-688-12888-2*, Morrow, William & Co.) Morrow/Avon.
—Call down the Stars. 2002. 544p. mass mkt. 7.99 (*0-380-72605-X*, Avon Bks.); 2001. (Illus.). 464p. 26.00 (*0-380-97372-3*, Morrow, William & Co.) Morrow/Avon.
—Cry of the Wind. 2000. (Storyteller Trilogy Ser.: Vol. 2). 512p. mass mkt. 6.99 (*0-380-72604-1*, Avon Bks.) Morrow/Avon.
—Cry of the Wind: Book Two of the Storyteller Trilogy. 1998. (Storyteller Trilogy Ser.: Bk. 2). 464p. 24.00 (*0-380-97371-5*, Avon Bks.) Morrow/Avon.
—Song of the River. 1998. 608p. mass mkt. 6.99 (*0-380-72603-3*); 1997. (Bright & Early Bks.: Vol. 1). 496p. mass mkt. 24.00 (*0-380-97370-7*) Morrow/Avon. (Avon Bks.).
Hawkes, John. Adventures in the Alaskan Skin Trade. 1986. (Contemporary American Fiction Ser.). 400p. pap. 10.95 o.p. (*0-14-009283-8*, Penguin Bks.) Viking Penguin.
Henry, Sue. Beneath the Ashes. 2001. 336p. mass mkt. 6.99 (*0-380-79892-1*, Avon Bks.); 2000. 288p. 23.00 (*0-380-97662-5*, Morrow, William & Co.) Morrow/Avon.
—Cold Company. l.t. ed. 2002. (Large Print Ser.). 27.95 (*1-57490-457-4*) Beeler, Thomas T. Publisher.
—Cold Company. 2002. (Alaska Mystery Ser.). (Illus.). 304p. 23.95 (*0-380-97882-2*, Morrow, William & Co.) Morrow/Avon.
—Dead North. 2002. 384p. mass mkt. 6.99 (*0-380-81684-9*); 2001. (Illus.). 288p. 24.00 (*0-380-97881-4*, Morrow, William & Co.) Morrow/Avon.
—Deadfall: An Alaska Mystery. unabr. ed. 2000. (Alaska Mystery Ser.). audio 29.95 (*0-7366-4428-8*) Books on Tape, Inc.
—Deadfall: An Alaska Mystery. (Alaska Mysteries Ser.). 1999. 320p. mass mkt. 6.99 (*0-380-79891-3*); 1998. 304p. 22.00 (*0-380-97661-7*) Morrow/Avon. (Avon Bks.).
—Death Takes Passage: An Alex Jensen Mystery. (Alaska Mysteries Ser.). 1998. (Illus.). 352p. mass mkt. 6.99 (*0-380-78863-2*); 1997. 272p. (YA). mass mkt. 22.00 o.p. (*0-380-97469-X*) Morrow/Avon. (Avon Bks.).
—Death Trap: An Alaska Mystery. 2003. 288p. 23.95 (*0-380-97883-0*, Morrow, William & Co.) Morrow/Avon.
—Murder on the Iditarod Trail. unabr. collector's ed. 1999. audio 48.00 (*0-7366-4413-X*, 4874) Books on Tape, Inc.
—Murder on the Iditarod Trail. 1991. 18.95 o.p. (*0-87113-440-3*) Grove/Atlantic, Inc.
—Murder on the Iditarod Trail. 1993. (Alaska Mysteries Ser.). 320p. reprint ed. mass mkt. 6.99 (*0-380-71758-1*, Avon Bks.) Morrow/Avon.
—Murder on the Yukon Quest. Grader, T. L., ed. 2000. (Alaska Mysteries Ser.). 320p. mass mkt. 6.99 (*0-380-78864-0*, Avon Bks.) Morrow/Avon.
—Murder on the Yukon Quest. 1999. (Illus.). 304p. 22.00 (*0-380-97764-8*, Avon Bks.) Morrow/Avon.
—Sleeping Lady. unabr. ed. 1999. audio 48.00 (*0-7366-4458-X*, 4903) Books on Tape, Inc.
—Sleeping Lady. 320p. 1996. 22.00 o.p. (*0-688-13747-4*, Morrow, William & Co.); 1997. reprint ed. mass mkt. 6.99 (*0-380-72407-3*, Avon Bks.) Morrow/Avon.
—Termination Dust. (Alex Jensen Ser.). 1996. 320p. mass mkt. 6.99 (*0-380-72406-5*, Avon Bks.); 1995. 305p. 23.00 o.p. (*0-688-13746-6*, Morrow, William & Co.) Morrow/Avon.
Hobbs, William. Wild Man Island. 2002. (Illus.). 192p. (J). (gr. 5 up). 15.95 (*0-688-17473-6*) HarperCollins Children's Bk. Group.
Howard, Jean G. Tuk, the Timid: The Story of a Sea Otter. 1984. (Illus.). 80p. (Orig.). (J). (gr. 3 up). pap. 10.95 o.p. (*0-930954-20-3*) Tidal Pr.
Johnson, Linda O. The Ballad of Jack O'Dair. 2000. (Timeswept Ser.). 368p. mass mkt. 5.50 (*0-505-52404-X*, Love Spell) Dorchester Publishing Co., Inc.
Jones, Stan. Shaman Pass: A Nathan Active Mystery. 2003. 288p. 23.00 (*1-56947-332-3*) Soho Pr., Inc.
—White Sky, Black Ice. 2003. 284p. pap. 13.00 (*1-56947-333-1*) Soho Pr., Inc.
—White Sky, Black Ice: An Alaskan Mystery. 1999. 264p. 22.00 (*1-56947-152-5*) Soho Pr., Inc.
Kafka, Kimberly. True North: A Novel. 288p. 2001. pap. 13.00 o.s.i (*0-452-28223-3*, Plume); 2000. 23.95 o.s.i (*0-525-94530-X*, Dutton) Dutton/Plume.
Kemp, Jewel: Pieces of a Dream. 1998. (Illus.). 144p. (J). (gr. 4-6). pap. 4.99 (*0-671-02455-8*, Simon Pulse) Simon & Schuster Children's Publishing.
Kesey, Ken. Sailor Song. 1993. 544p. pap. 13.95 (*0-14-013997-4*, Penguin Bks.) Penguin Group (USA) Inc.
—Sailor Song. 1992. 528p. 23.50 o.p. (*0-670-83521-8*, Viking) Viking Penguin.
Kittredge, Frances. Neeluk: An Eskimo Boy in the Days of the Whaling Ships. 2001. (Illus.). 88p. (J). (gr. 3-7). pap. 11.95 (*0-88240-546-2*, Alaska Northwest Bks.) Graphic Arts Ctr. Publishing Co.
Kohler, Vincent. Raven's Widows. 1997. 256p. text 22.95 o.p. (*0-312-14714-7*, Saint Martin's Minotaur) St. Martin's Pr.
Koho, Sharon Lewis. The Painting on the Pond. 2003. 198p. pap. 13.95 (*1-55517-703-4*, 77034, Bonneville Bks.) Cedar Fort, Inc./CFI Distribution.
L'Amour, Louis. Sitka. 1996. 256p. mass mkt. 4.99 o.s.i (*0-553-13965-7*); 1984. mass mkt. 2.95 o.s.i (*0-553-24289-X*); 1984. mass mkt. 3.50 o.s.i (*0-553-26119-3*); 1984. 245p. mass mkt. 4.99 o.s.i (*0-553-27881-9*) Bantam Bks.
—Sitka. 352p. 2001. mass mkt. 5.99 (*0-451-20308-9*); 1997. (Signet Historical Fiction Ser.: Vol. 9401). mass mkt. 5.99 o.s.i (*0-451-19401-2*, Signet Bks.) NAL.
—Sitka. l.t. ed. 2000. (Famous Authors Ser.). 431p. 27.95 (*0-7862-2435-5*) Thorndike Pr.
Landers, Gunnard. Eskimo Money. 1999. (Wilderness Badge Ser.: Vol. 1). 206p. pap. 14.95 (*1-57223-149-1*, 1491) Willow Creek Pr., Inc.
Lane, Christopher. The Elements of a Kill. 1998. 416p. mass mkt. 5.99 (*0-380-79870-0*, Avon Bks.) Morrow/Avon.
—The Season of Death: An Inupiat Eskimo Mystery. 1999. 352p. mass mkt. 5.99 (*0-380-79872-7*, Avon Bks.) Morrow/Avon.
—A Shroud of Midnight Sun. 2000. (Inupiat Eskimo Mysteries Ser.). 352p. mass mkt. 5.99 (*0-380-79873-5*, Avon Bks.) Morrow/Avon.

—Silent as the Hunter. 2001. (Inupiat Eskimo Mysteries Ser.). 352p. mass mkt. 6.50 (*0-380-81625-3*, Avon Bks.) Morrow/Avon.

Leon, Bonnie. The Journey of Eleven Moons: A Novel. 1994. pap. 10.99 o.p. (*0-7852-7974-1*) Nelson, Thomas Inc.

—Return to the Misty Shore: A Novel, Vol. 3. 1997. (Northern Lights Ser.). pap. text 10.99 o.p. (*0-7852-7413-8*) Nelson, Thomas Inc.

—A Sacred Place: A Novel. 2000. 310p. pap. 12.99 (*0-8054-2152-1*) Broadman & Holman Pubs.

—Valley of Promises. 2001. (Matanuska Ser.: Bk. 1). vi, 314p. pap. 12.99 (*0-8054-2153-X*) Broadman & Holman Pubs.

—Worthy of Riches, 3 vols., Vol. 2. 2002. (Matanuska Ser.: No. 2). 320p. pap. 12.99 (*0-8054-2154-8*) Broadman & Holman Pubs.

Lesley, Craig. Storm Riders. 2000. 352p. 24.00 o.s.i (*0-312-24554-8*) Picador.

London, Jack. The Call of the Wild. 2000. 252p. E-Book 9.95 (*0-594-05540-7*) 1873 Pr.

—The Call of the Wild. 1997. (Classics Illustrated Study Guides). (Illus.). mass mkt. 4.99 (*1-57840-042-2*) Acclaim Bks.

—The Call of the Wild. 16.95 (*0-8488-0106-7*) Amereon, Ltd.

—The Call of the Wild. 1994. (Illus.). pap. 2.95 o.p. (*0-681-00695-1*) Borders Pr.

—The Call of the Wild. 1983. 271p. reprint ed. lib. bdg. 19.95 (*0-89966-473-3*) Buccaneer Bks., Inc.

—The Call of the Wild. (Collected Works of Jack London). 231p. reprint ed. 2001. pap. 28.00 (*0-7426-5705-1*); 1998. lib. bdg. 88.00 (*1-58201-705-0*) Classic Bks.

—The Call of the Wild. 1999. 96p. pap. 9.95 o.p. (*1-930128-03-7*, JNMedia Bks.) JNMedia, Inc.

—The Call of the Wild. 1990. (Vintage-Library of America ). 112p. pap. 8.50 o.s.i (*0-679-72535-0*, Vintage) Knopf Publishing Group.

—The Call of the Wild. 1997. pap. 3.95 (*0-89375-344-0*) NAL.

—The Call of the Wild. 1989. (Enriched Classics Ser.). (Illus.). 208p. reprint ed. mass mkt. 4.50 (*0-671-70494-X*, 42070, Pocket) Simon & Schuster.

—The Call of the Wild. Dyer, Daniel, ed. & notes by. 1995. (Illus.). 320p. 37.95 (*0-8061-2757-0*) Univ. of Oklahoma Pr.

—The Call of the Wild & Selected Stories. 1960. mass mkt. 2.25 o.p. (*0-451-52316-4*); 1960. 176p. mass mkt. 3.95 o.s.i (*0-451-52390-3*, Signet Classics); 1998. 192p. mass mkt. 3.95 (*0-451-52703-8*, Signet Bks.) NAL.

—The Call of the Wild & Selected Stories. 1960. 10.00 (*0-606-01829-8*) Turtleback Bks.

—The Call of the Wild & White Fang. 1998. (Twelve-Point Ser.). 310p. reprint ed. lib. bdg. 25.00 (*1-58287-020-9*) North Bks.

—The Call of the Wild & White Fang. 1985. (Illus.). 304p. 12.95 o.p. (*0-89577-211-6*) Reader's Digest Assn., Inc., The.

—The Call of the Wild & White Fang. 1984. (Bantam Classics Ser.). 10.00 (*0-606-00168-9*) Turtleback Bks.

—The Call of the Wild & White Fang. unabr. ed. 1997. reprint ed. pap. 14.95 o.p. (*1-57002-040-X*) University Publishing Hse., Inc.

—The Call of the Wild & White Fang. 1997. 240p. pap. 3.95 (*1-85326-571-3*); pap. 3.95 (*1-85326-026-6*, 0266WW) Wordsworth Editions, Ltd. GBR. *Dist:* Combined Publishing.

—The Call of the Wild Readalong. 1994. (Illustrated Classics Collection). 64p. pap. 13.50 o.p. incl. audio (*1-56103-419-3*); pap. 14.95 incl. audio (*0-7854-0704-9*, 40336) American Guidance Service, Inc.

—The Call of the Wild, White Fang, & Other Stories. Labor, Earle & Leitz, Robert C., III, eds. 1998. (Oxford World's Classics Ser.). (Illus.). 400p. (Orig.). pap. 7.95 (*0-19-283514-9*) Oxford Univ. Pr., Inc.

—The Call of the Wild, White Fang, & Other Stories. Leitz, Robert C., III, ed. 1990. (Oxford World's Classics Ser.). (Illus.). 392p. (Orig.). pap. 6.95 o.p. (*0-19-282709-X*) Oxford Univ. Pr., Inc.

—The Call of the Wild, White Fang, & Other Stories. Sinclair, Andrew, ed. (Penguin Twentieth-Century Classics Ser.). 416p. (Orig.). 1993. pap. 7.95 (*0-14-018651-4*); 1981. pap. 5.95 o.p. (*0-14-039001-4*) Viking Penguin. (Penguin Classics).

—Call of the Wild, White Fang, & Other Stories. 1993. (Penguin Twentieth-Century Classics Ser.). 14.00 (*0-606-00170-0*) Turtleback Bks.

—The Call of the Wild, White Fang & to Build a Fire. 2000. E-Book 4.95 (*0-679-64168-8*); 98th ed. 2002. 288p. pap. 7.95 (*0-375-75251-X*) Random House Adult Trade Publishing Group. (Modern Library).

—The Tales of the Klondyke. E-Book 2.49 (*1-58627-871-1*) Electric Umbrella Publishing.

London, Jack & Dyer, Daniel. The Call of the Wild. 1995. E-Book 37.95 (*0-8061-7113-8*) Univ. of Oklahoma Pr.

London, Jack, et al. The Call of the Wild, White Fang, & Other Stories. 1990. (Orig.). E-Book 8.35 (*0-585-35764-1*) netLibrary, Inc.

Lord, Nancy. Survival. 1991. 176p. pap. 10.95 (*0-918273-84-6*) Coffee Hse. Pr.

Loring, Emilie Baker. Behind the Cloud. l.t. ed. 1999. 30.00 o.p. (*0-7862-1754-5*, Macmillan Reference USA) Gale Group.

—Lighted Windows. reprint ed. lib. bdg. 24.95 (*0-88411-378-7*) Amereon, Ltd.

—Lighted Windows. l.t. ed. 1999. (Paperback Ser.). 339p. pap. 23.95 (*0-7838-0342-7*) Thorndike Pr.

Macomber, Debbie. Because of the Baby. 1996. (Harlequin Romance Ser.). 185p. per. (*0-373-03395-8*, 1-03395-0, Harlequin Bks.) Harlequin Enterprises, Ltd.

—Because of the Baby. l.t. ed. 1997. (Harlequin Romance Ser.). 20.95 (*0-263-15007-0*) Harlequin Mills & Boon, Ltd. GBR. *Dist:* Ulverscroft Large Print Bks., Ltd.

—Brides for Brothers. 1995. 187p. per. (*0-373-03379-6*, 1-03379-4, Harlequin Bks.) Harlequin Enterprises, Ltd.

—Brides for Brothers. l.t. ed. 1997. 20.95 o.s.i (*0-263-14919-6*) Harlequin Mills & Boon, Ltd. GBR. *Dist:* Ulverscroft Large Print Bks., Ltd.

—Daddy's Little Helper. 1995. 185p. per. (*0-373-03387-7*, 1-03387-7, Harlequin Bks.) Harlequin Enterprises, Ltd.

—Ending in Marriage. 1996. (Harlequin Romance Ser.). 186p. per. (*0-373-03403-2*, 1-03403-2, Harlequin Bks.) Harlequin Enterprises, Ltd.

—Falling for Him (Midnight Sons) 1996. (Harlequin Romance Ser.). 184p. per. (*0-373-03399-0*, 1-03399-2, Harlequin Bks.) Harlequin Enterprises, Ltd.

—Falling for Him (Midnight Sons) l.t. ed. 1997. (Harlequin Romance Ser.). 20.95 o.s.i (*0-263-15044-5*) Harlequin Mills & Boon, Ltd. GBR. *Dist:* Ulverscroft Large Print Bks., Ltd.

—Family Men: Daddy's Little Helper & Because of the Baby, 2 bks. in 1. 2000. (Harlequin Midnight Sons Ser.). 384p. mass mkt. (*0-373-83435-7*, 1-83435-7, Harlequin Bks.) Harlequin Enterprises, Ltd.

—Mail-Order Marriages. 2000. (Harlequin Midnight Sons Ser.: Vol. 1). 384p. mass mkt. (*0-373-83434-9*, Harlequin Bks.) Harlequin Enterprises, Ltd.

—The Marriage Risk. 1995. (Harlequin Romance Ser.: Vol. 3383). 189p. per. (*0-373-03383-4*, Harlequin Bks.) Harlequin Enterprises, Ltd.

Macomber, Debbie & Wisdom, Linda Randall. The Last Two Bachelors. 2000. (Harlequin Midnight Sons Ser.: Vol. 3). 384p. mass mkt. (*0-373-83436-5*, 1-83436-5, Harlequin Bks.) Harlequin Enterprises, Ltd.

Marquis, Christopher. A Hole in the Heart: A Novel. 2003. 320p. 24.95 (*0-312-30630-X*) St. Martin's Pr.

Martin, Guenn. Forty Miles from Nowhere. 1986. (Illus.). 152p. (Orig.). (J). (gr. 3-8). pap. 4.95 o.p. (*0-8361-3417-6*) Herald Pr.

—Remember the Eagle Day. 1983. (Illus.). 128p. (J). (gr. 7-9). pap. 4.95 o.p. (*0-8361-3351-X*) Herald Pr.

Masiel, David. 2182 kHz. l.t. ed. 2002. 28.95 (*0-7862-4475-5*) Thorndike Pr.

—2182 kHz: A Novel. 2002. 304p. 22.95 (*0-375-50606-3*) Random Hse., Inc.

McCloskey, William B., Jr. Breakers: A Novel. 2000. (Illus.). 368p. 24.95 (*1-58574-084-5*, Lyons Pr.) Globe Pequot Pr., The.

—Highliners: The Classic Novel of Alaska & Its Fishermen. 1995. 416p. pap. 16.95 o.p. (*1-55821-375-9*, Lyons Pr.) Globe Pequot Pr., The.

Mergler, Wayne, ed. The Last New Land: Stories of Alaska, Past & Present. 1996. (Illus.). 816p. 34.95 o.p. (*0-88240-481-4*); pap. 26.95 (*0-88240-483-0*) Graphic Arts Ctr. Publishing Co. (Alaska Northwest Bks.).

Meyerhoff, Paul, 2nd. Sabotage Flight. 1995. (Illus.). 200p. (Orig.). (J). (gr. 5-9). pap. 9.95 (*0-931625-24-6*) DIMI Pr.

Michener, James A. Alaska. 1994. mass mkt. 6.99 o.s.i (*0-449-45313-8*, Fawcett); 1989. 1088p. mass mkt. 7.99 (*0-449-21726-4*, Fawcett); 1989. mass mkt. 5.95 o.s.i (*0-449-21716-7*) Ballantine Bks.

—Alaska. 1994. 96.00 (*0-7366-2711-1*, 3441-C) Books on Tape, Inc.

—Alaska. 2002. 896p. pap. 14.95 (*0-375-76142-X*) Random House Adult Trade Publishing Group.

—Alaska. Set. abr. ed. 1988. audio 16.00 o.s.i (*0-394-57078-2*, RH Audio) Random Hse. Audio Publishing Group.

—Alaska. 1990. 7.99 o.p. (*0-517-05062-5*) Random Hse. Value Publishing.

—James Michener: Two Complete Novels. 1994. 14.99 o.s.i (*0-517-14683-5*) Random Hse. Value Publishing.

Mitchell, John. Alaska Stories. 1984. 75p. 11.50 (*0-917635-00-0*); pap. 6.95 (*0-917635-01-9*) Plover Pr.

—Exile in Alaska. 1987. 113p. 13.95 (*0-917635-02-7*); pap. 7.95 (*0-917635-03-5*) Plover Pr.

Morey, Walt. Deep Trouble. 1989. (Walt Morey Adventure Library). 168p. (YA). (ps-3). reprint ed. pap. 7.95 o.p. (*0-936085-15-0*) Blue Heron Publishing.

Murie, Margaret E. Island Between. 1977. (Illus.). 228p. 9.95 (*0-912006-04-8*) Univ. of Alaska Pr.

—Island Between. 1977. E-Book 9.95 (*0-585-18622-7*) netLibrary, Inc.

North, E. Lee. Mark of the White Wolf. 1999. 3.5 hd 13.95 (*1-892775-06-9*) Blue Knight Enterprises.

Osborne, Maggie. I Do, I Do, I Do. l.t. ed. 2001. 369p. 27.95 (*1-57490-400-0*, Beeler Large Print Bks.) Beeler, Thomas T. Publisher.

Pade, Victoria. The Baby Surprise. 2003. (Silhouette Special Edition Ser.: No. 1544). 256p. mass mkt. (*0-373-24544-0*, Silhouette) Harlequin Enterprises, Ltd.

Parry, Richard. The Winter Wolf: Wyatt Earp in Alaska. 1998. 308p. mass mkt. 6.99 o.p. (*0-8125-4946-5*); 1996. 384p. 24.95 (*0-312-86017-X*) Doherty, Tom Assocs., LLC. (Forge Bks.).

—The Wolf's Cub. 1999. (Illus.). 380p. mass mkt. 6.99 (*0-8125-4947-3*); 1997. 384p. 23.95 (*0-312-86018-8*) Doherty, Tom Assocs., LLC. (Forge Bks.).

Perry, Richard. Winter Wolf. unabr. ed. 1996. audio 78.00 (*0-7887-2000-7*, 95387E7) Recorded Bks., LLC.

Peterson, Tracie. Ashes & Ice. 2001. (Yukon Quest Ser.). 384p. pap. 12.99 (*0-7642-2379-8*) Bethany Hse. Pubs.

—Treasures of the North: Dreams of Gold & the Promise of a New Tomorow Lured Them to the Land of the Midnight Sun. 2000. (Yukon Quest Ser.). (Illus.). 384p. pap. 12.99 (*0-7642-2378-X*) Bethany Hse. Pubs.

Plemmons, Fred M. Had She Not Been a Wolf He Would Have Married Her. 1997. 160p. pap. 7.95 (*1-57502-642-2*, PO 1821) Morris Publishing.

Plunkett, Susan. Bethany's Song. 2001. 368p. mass mkt. 5.50 (*0-505-52463-5*, Love Spell) Dorchester Publishing Co., Inc.

Quackenbush, Robert. Dogsled to Dread. 1988. (Miss Mallard Mystery Ser.). (Illus.). 48p. (J). (gr. 2-6). 12.95 o.s.i (*0-671-66518-9*, Simon & Schuster Children's Publishing) Simon & Schuster Children's Publishing.

Quick, Barbara. Northern Edge. 1990. 18.95 o.p. (*1-55611-173-8*) Fine, Donald I. Bks.

—Northern Edge. 1994. 224p. pap. 10.00 o.p. (*0-06-258521-5*, Perennial) HarperTrade.

Quinn, Elizabeth. Murder Most Grizzly. Marrow, Linda, ed. 1993. 224p. (Orig.). mass mkt. 4.99 (*0-671-74990-0*, Pocket) Simon & Schuster.

—A Wolf in Death's Clothing. 1995. 224p. mass mkt. 5.50 (*0-671-74991-9*, Pocket) Simon & Schuster.

Randles, Slim. Raven's Prey. 1999. 24.95 (*0-9632596-9-5*); pap. 16.95 (*0-9632596-8-7*) McRoy & Blackburn, Pubs.

Rettino, Ernie & Kerner, Debby. Psalty in Alaska. 1991. 6.99 o.p. (*0-8499-0893-0*) W Publishing Group.

Rizzo, Kay D. When Love Returns. 1988. (Destiny Ser.: Vol. II). 96p. pap. 6.95 o.p. (*0-8163-0771-7*) Pacific Pr. Publishing Assn.

Rodahl, Kaare. Akiviak. 1979. 9.95 o.p. (*0-393-01181-X*) Norton, W. W. & Co., Inc.

Roddy, Lee. Stranded on Terror Island, No. 14. 1996. (Ladd Family Adventure Ser.). (J). (gr. 3-7). pap. 6.00 o.p. (*1-56179-482-1*) Focus on the Family Publishing.

Roesch, E. P. Ashana. 1991. mass mkt. 5.99 o.s.i (*0-345-37298-0*) Ballantine Bks.

Rowan, Ronald R. Attua the Aleut. 1999. 508p. pap. 26.99 (*0-7388-0747-8*); text 36.99 (*0-7388-0746-X*) Xlibris Corp.

Rust, Megan Mallory. Dead Stick. 1998. (New Alaskan Murder Mysteries Ser.). 208p. mass mkt. 5.99 o.s.i (*0-425-16296-6*, Prime Crime) Berkley Publishing Group.

—Red Line, 1 vol. 1999. 224p. mass mkt. 5.99 o.s.i (*0-425-16897-2*) Berkley Publishing Group.

Sarff, Extry. Light Reading from Alaska. 1998. 63p. (*0-9662515-0-4*) Sarff, Extry R.

Savage, Les, Jr. In the Land of Little Sticks. 2000. (Five Star Western Ser.). 303p. 21.95 (*0-7862-2111-9*, Five Star) Gale Group.

—In the Land of Little Sticks. l.t. ed. 2001. (Western Ser.). 452p. 24.95 o.p. (*0-7862-2132-1*) Thorndike Pr.

Shahan, Sherry. Frozen Stiff. 1998. 160p. (gr. 4-7). text 14.95 o.s.i (*0-385-32303-4*, Delacorte Pr.) Dell Publishing.

Shaine, Benjamin A. Alaska Dragon. 1991. 365p. pap. 10.95 (*0-914221-11-6*); lib. bdg. 21.95 (*0-914221-12-4*) Fireweed Pr.

Shankle, Sam Boone. The Radioactive Satellite: An Alaskan Adventure. 2000. (Alaskan Adventures Ser.). 148p. pap. 9.95 (*0-595-09739-1*, Writers Club Pr.) iUniverse, Inc.

Simpson, Marcia. Crow in Stolen Colors. 2000. (Alaska Panhandle Mysteries Ser.). 320p. mass mkt. 6.99 o.s.i (*0-425-17463-8*, Prime Crime) Berkley Publishing Group.

—Crow in Stolen Colors. 2000. 264p. 24.95 (*1-890208-36-1*) Poisoned Pen Pr.

—Rogue's Yarn. 2003. 320p. pap. 14.00 (*0-425-19198-2*) Berkley Publishing Group.

—Sound Tracks. 2001. (Illus.). 244p. 24.95 o.s.i (*1-890208-72-8*) Poisoned Pen Pr.

—Sound Tracks: An Alaska Panhandle Mystery. 2001. (Illus.). 320p. mass mkt. 6.50 o.s.i (*0-425-17944-3*, Prime Crime) Berkley Publishing Group.

Smith, Mitchell. Due North: A Novel. 1992. 333p. 21.00 o.p. (*0-671-73877-1*, Simon & Schuster) Simon & Schuster.

Spitzer, Mark. Chum: Novel. 2001. 227p. 21.00 o.p. (*1-58195-031-4*, Zoland Bks., Inc.) Steerforth Pr.

Spring, Joel. Alaskan Visions. 2000. 249p. pap. 21.99 (*0-7388-0921-7*); text 31.99 (*0-7388-0920-9*); E-Book 8.00 (*0-7388-8330-1*) Xlibris Corp.

Stabenow, Dana. Better to Rest. 2002. 29.95 (*1-58724-352-0*, Wheeler Publishing, Inc.) Gale Group.

—Better to Rest. 2003. 304p. mass mkt. 6.99 (*0-451-20960-5*, Signet Bks.); 2002. 272p. 23.95 (*0-451-20702-5*) NAL.

—Blood Will Tell: A Kate Shugak Mystery. 1997. (Kate Shugak Mystery Ser.). 256p. mass mkt. 6.99 (*0-425-15798-9*) Berkley Publishing Group.

—Blood Will Tell: A Kate Shugak Mystery. 1996. (Kate Shugak Mystery Ser.). 256p. 21.95 o.p. (*0-399-14124-3*, G. P. Putnam's Sons) Penguin Group (USA) Inc.

—Breakup: A Kate Shugak Mystery. 1998. (Kate Shugak Mysteries Ser.). 256p. mass mkt. 6.99 (*0-425-16261-3*) Berkley Publishing Group.

—Breakup: A Kate Shugak Mystery. 1997. (Kate Shugak Mystery Ser.). 256p. 21.95 o.s.i (*0-399-14250-9*, G. P. Putnam's Sons) Penguin Group (USA) Inc.

—A Cold-Blooded Business: A Kate Shugak Mystery. 1995. (Kate Shugak Mystery Ser.). 240p. (Orig.). mass mkt. 6.99 (*0-425-15849-7*, Prime Crime) Berkley Publishing Group.

—Cold-Blooded Business: A Kate Shugak Mystery. 1994. (Kate Shugak Mysteries Ser.). 231p. (Orig.). 17.95 o.s.i (*0-425-14173-X*) Berkley Publishing Group.

—A Cold Day for Murder. unabr. ed. 1999. audio 24.95 (*0-7366-4423-7*, 4830) Books on Tape, Inc.

—A Cold Day for Murder: A Kate Shugak Mystery. l.t. ed. 2001. 189p. 26.95 (*1-57490-355-1*, Beeler Large Print Bks.) Beeler, Thomas T. Publisher.

—A Cold Day for Murder: A Kate Shugak Mystery. 1992. (Kate Shugak Mystery Ser.). 208p. mass mkt. 6.99 (*0-425-13301-X*) Berkley Publishing Group.

—Dead in the Water: A Kate Shugak Mystery. 1993. (Kate Shugak Mysteries Ser.). 224p. mass mkt. 6.99 (*0-425-13749-X*) Berkley Publishing Group.

—A Fatal Thaw. unabr. collector's ed. 1999. (Kate Shugak Mystery Ser.). audio 40.00 (*0-7366-4459-8*, 4904) Books on Tape, Inc.

—A Fatal Thaw: A Kate Shugak Mystery. 1993. (Kate Shugak Mystery Ser.). 208p. mass mkt. 6.99 (*0-425-13577-2*) Berkley Publishing Group.

—A Fine & Bitter Snow: A Kate Shugak Novel. 2002. 304p. 24.95 (*0-312-20548-1*, Saint Martin's Minotaur) St. Martin's Pr.

—Fire & Ice: A Liam Campbell Mystery. unabr. collector's ed. 1999. audio 56.00 (*0-7366-4860-7*, 5187) Books on Tape, Inc.

—Fire & Ice: A Liam Campbell Mystery. 1998. 272p. 23.95 o.p. (*0-525-94438-9*) Dutton/Plume.

—Fire & Ice: A Liam Campbell Mystery. 1999. (Liam Campbell Mysteries Ser.). 304p. mass mkt. 6.99 (*0-451-19770-4*, Signet Bks.) NAL.

—Fire & Ice: A Liam Campbell Mystery. l.t. ed. 1999. (Mystery Ser.). 463p. 29.95 (*0-7862-1903-3*) Thorndike Pr.

—A Grave Denied: A Kate Shugak Novel. 2003. 304p. 24.95 (*0-312-30681-4*, Saint Martin's Minotaur) St. Martin's Pr.

—Hunter's Moon. unabr. collector's ed. 1999. audio 40.00 (*0-7366-4635-3*, 5007) Books on Tape, Inc.

—Hunter's Moon: A Kate Shugak Mystery. 1999. (Prime Crime Mysteries Ser.). 256p. reprint ed. mass mkt. 6.99 (*0-425-17259-7*, Prime Crime) Berkley Publishing Group.

—Hunter's Moon: A Kate Shugak Mystery. 1999. (Kate Shugak Mystery Ser.). 260p. 23.95 o.s.i (*0-399-14468-4*) Penguin Group (USA) Inc.

—Killing Grounds. 1999. (Kate Shugak Mysteries Ser.). 256p. reprint ed. mass mkt. 6.99 (*0-425-16773-9*, Prime Crime) Berkley Publishing Group.

—Killing Grounds. 1999. 12.04 (*0-606-16389-1*) Turtleback Bks.

—The Killing Grounds: A Kate Shugak Mystery. 1998. (Kate Shugak Mystery Ser.). 273p. 22.95 o.p. (*0-399-14356-4*, G. P. Putnam's Sons) Penguin Group (USA) Inc.

Settings

—Midnight Come Again. l.t. ed. 2001. (Large Print Book Ser.). 351p. pap. 23.95 o.p. (*1-58724-031-9*, Wheeler Publishing, Inc.) Gale Group.

—Midnight Come Again. E-Book 23.95 (*0-312-27415-7*); 2001. 320p. reprint ed. mass mkt. 6.99 (*0-312-97876-6*, St. Martin's Paperbacks) St. Martin's Pr.

—Midnight Come Again: A Kate Shugak Novel. 2000. (Kate Shugak Mysteries Ser.). 291p. 23.95 o.p. (*0-312-20596-1*, Saint Martin's Minotaur) St. Martin's Pr.

—Nothing Gold Can Stay: A Liam Campbell Mystery. 2000. (Liam Campbell Mysteries Ser.). 288p. 23.95 o.s.i (*0-525-94559-8*, Dutton) Dutton/Plume.

—Play with Fire: A Kate Shugak Mystery. (Kate Shugak Mystery Ser.). 1996. 320p. mass mkt. 6.99 (*0-425-15254-5*); 1995. 288p. 19.95 o.p. (*0-425-14717-7*, Prime Crime) Berkley Publishing Group.

—The Singing of the Dead. 2001. E-Book 23.95 (*1-58945-791-9*) Adobe Systems, Inc.

—The Singing of the Dead. l.t. ed. 2001. (Illus.). 392p. 30.95 o.p. (*0-7838-9516-X*, Macmillan Reference USA) Gale Group.

—The Singing of the Dead. 2001. (Kate Shugak Mysteries Ser.: No. 11). (Illus.). 254p. 23.95 (*0-312-20957-6*, Saint Martin's Minotaur) St. Martin's Pr.

—So Sure of Death. 2000. (Liam Campbell Mysteries Ser.). 304p. mass mkt. 6.99 (*0-451-19944-8*, Signet Bks.) NAL.

—So Sure of Death: A Liam Campbell Mystery. 1999. (Liam Campbell Mysteries Ser.). 288p. 23.95 o.s.i (*0-525-94519-9*) Dutton/Plume.

—So Sure of Death: A Liam Campbell Mystery. l.t. ed. 2000. (Mystery Ser.). 477p. 29.95 (*0-7862-2478-9*) Thorndike Pr.

Stein, Garth. Raven Stole the Moon: A Novel. 1998. (*0-16-710045-9*) Pocket Bks.

Straley, John. The Angels Will Not Care. 2000. 256p. mass mkt. 5.99 (*0-553-58064-7*); 1998. 240p. 22.95 o.s.i (*0-553-10642-2*) Bantam Bks.

—Cold Water Burning. 2001. 224p. mass mkt. 6.50 (*0-553-58076-0*); 208p. 23.95 o.s.i (*0-553-10643-0*) Bantam Bks.

—Curious Eat Themselves: An Alaskan Mystery. 1993. 264p. 19.95 (*0-939149-94-X*) Soho Pr., Inc.

—The Curious Eat Themselves: An Alaskan Mystery. 1995. 240p. mass mkt. 5.99 (*0-553-56805-1*, Crimeline) Bantam Bks.

—The Music of What Happens. 1997. 272p. mass mkt. 5.99 (*0-553-57205-9*, Crimeline) Bantam Bks.

—The Woman Who Married a Bear: An Alaskan Mystery. 1994. 240p. mass mkt. 5.99 o.s.i (*0-451-40421-1*, Signet Bks.) NAL.

—The Woman Who Married a Bear: An Alaskan Mystery. 1992. 240p. 19.95 o.p. (*0-939149-64-8*) Soho Pr., Inc.

Sutherland, William L. News from Fort God. 1993. (First Novel Ser.). 224p. pap. 12.00 o.p. (*0-922811-17-2*) Mid-List Pr.

Tuska, Jon, ed. Odyssey to the North: North-Western Stories. 2003. 245p. 25.95 (*0-7862-3805-4*, Five Star) Gale Group.

—Stories of the Far North. 1998. (Bison Book Ser.). 146p. pap. 15.00 (*0-8032-9434-4*) Univ. of Nebraska Pr.

Vidal, Gore. Williwaw. 2003. 222p. pap. 15.00 (*0-226-85585-6*) Univ. of Chicago Pr.

Von der Heydt, James A. Mother Sawtooth's Nome: A Novel of Alaskan History. 1990. (Illus.). 136p. (Orig.). pap. 7.95 (*0-88196-003-9*) Oak Woods Media.

Weiner, Ellis. Letters from Cicely. 1992. 224p. pap. 10.00 (*0-671-77735-1*, Pocket) Simon & Schuster.

Westbrook, Robert. Insomnia. movie tie-in ed. 2002. (Illus.). 256p. mass mkt. 6.50 (*0-451-41049-1*) NAL.

White, Alan L. Standing Ground: Alaska Stories, Police Tales & Things I'd Rather not Talk About. 2001. 224p. 21.95 (*0-9663201-2-3*); pap. 14.95 (*0-9663201-3-1*) Dark River Publishing.

Wilde, Lori. A Thrill to Remember. 2002. (Harlequin Blaze Ser.: No. 66). 256p. mass mkt. o.s.i (*0-373-79070-8*, Harlequin Bks.) Harlequin Enterprises, Ltd.

—A Thrill to Remember: The Bachelors of Bear Creek. 2002. (Harlequin Blaze Ser.). 256p. mass mkt. (*0-373-79061-9*, Harlequin Bks.) Harlequin Enterprises, Ltd.

Wisdom, Linda R. The Last Two Bachelors: Delaney's Grooms. 1999. (Harlequin American Romance Ser.: No. 774). per. (*0-373-16774-1*, 1-16774-1, Harlequin Bks.) Harlequin Enterprises, Ltd.

Young, Laura D. Love on the Line. 1997. 224p. (Orig.). pap. 11.95 o.p. (*1-56280-162-7*) Naiad Pr., Inc.

### ALBANY (N.Y.)—FICTION

Davies, June W. Storm Before Sunrise. 1993. 574p. 24.95 o.p. (*0-312-10552-5*) St. Martin's Pr.

Herrick, Robert. The Master of the Inn. 2000. 252p. E-Book 3.95 (*0-594-06245-4*) 1873 Pr.

—The Master of the Inn. 1980. 274p. reprint ed. lib. bdg. 12.95 o.s.i (*0-89968-188-3*, Lightyear Pr.) Buccaneer Bks., Inc.

—The Master of the Inn. reprint ed. pap. text 8.50 (*0-8290-1683-X*); lib. bdg. 19.50 (*0-8398-0779-1*) Irvington Pubs.

—The Master of the Inn. 1988. (Collected Works of Robert Herrick). reprint ed. lib. bdg. 59.00 (*0-7812-1269-3*) Reprint Services Corp.

—The Master of the Inn. 1971. reprint ed. 10.00 (*0-403-03055-2*) Somerset Pubs., Inc.

Kennedy, William. Billy Phelan's Greatest Game. 1983. 288p. 14.00 (*0-14-006340-4*); 1978. 9.95 o.p. (*0-670-16667-7*) Viking Penguin.

—The Flaming Corsage. unabr. collector's ed. 1996. audio 48.00 (*0-7366-3405-3*, 4051) Books on Tape, Inc.

—The Flaming Corsage. l.t. ed. 1997. (Large Print Bks.). 24.95 (*1-56895-397-6*, Wheeler Publishing, Inc.) Gale Group.

—The Flaming Corsage. 1997. 224p. pap. 11.95 (*0-14-024270-8*) Penguin Group (USA) Inc.

—The Flaming Corsage. 1996. 224p. 23.95 o.s.i (*0-670-85872-2*, Viking) Viking Penguin.

—The Flaming Corsage: Selections from the Novel. abr. ed. 1996. audio 18.95 o.p. (*0-14-086342-7*, Penguin AudioBooks) Viking Penguin.

—Ironweed. 1984. 19.00 (*0-606-14236-3*) Turtleback Bks.

—Legs. abr. ed. audio 14.95 (*0-945353-30-8*, M20330, Audio Editions Bks. on Cassette) Audio Partners Publishing Corp.

—Legs. unabr. collector's ed. 1986. (Albany Trilogy: Vol. 1). audio 64.00 (*0-7366-1100-2*, 2026) Books on Tape, Inc.

—Legs. abr. ed. 2000. audio 7.95 (*1-57815-188-0*, 1128, Media Bks. Audio Publishing) Media Bks., L. L. C.

—Legs. 1975. 322p. 8.95 o.p. (*0-698-10672-5*) Putnam Publishing Group, The.

—Legs. l.t. ed. 2000. (Perennial Bestsellers Ser.). 427p. 29.95 (*0-7838-8860-0*) Thorndike Pr.

—Legs. 1983. 320p. 14.00 (*0-14-006484-2*) Viking Penguin.

—Legs. 1976. pap. 1.75 o.s.i (*0-446-84140-4*) Warner Bks., Inc.

—Quinn's Book. l.t. ed. 1991. pap. 8.95 o.p. (*1-55504-805-6*, 524) BBC Audiobooks America.

—Quinn's Book. 1989. 304p. pap. 13.95 (*0-14-007737-5*, Penguin Bks.) Penguin Group (USA) Inc.

—Quinn's Book. 1988. 304p. 75.00 o.p. (*0-670-82213-2*); 18.95 o.p. (*0-670-80437-1*) Viking Penguin.

—Roscoe. l.t. ed. 2002. 563p. 30.95 (*0-7862-4038-5*) Gale Group.

—Roscoe. 2002. 306p. pap. 14.00 (*0-14-200173-2*) Penguin Group (USA) Inc.

—Roscoe. 2002. 304p. 24.95 o.s.i (*0-670-03029-5*, Viking) Viking Penguin.

—Very Old Bones. 1992. 304p. 22.00 o.p. (*0-670-83457-2*, Viking) Viking Penguin.

Listfield, Emily. Acts of Love. 1995. 384p. pap. 10.95 o.p. (*0-14-023281-8*, Penguin Bks.) Penguin Group (USA) Inc.

—Acts of Love. 370p. pap. 3.98 o.p. (*0-7651-0409-1*) Smithmark Pubs., Inc.

—Acts of Love. 1994. 384p. 21.95 o.p. (*0-670-85278-3*, Viking) Viking Penguin.

Michaels, Joanne. Nun in the Closet. 1994. 200p. (Orig.). pap. 9.95 (*0-934678-43-X*) New Victoria Pubs., Inc.

O'Kane, Leslie. The Cold, Hard Fax: A Molly Masters Mystery. 1998. (Molly Masters Mysteries Ser.). 288p. mass mkt. 5.99 o.s.i (*0-449-00158-X*, Fawcett) Ballantine Bks.

—The Cold, Hard Fax: A Molly Masters Mystery. l.t. ed. 2000. (Mystery Ser.). 381p. 26.95 (*0-7862-2833-4*) Thorndike Pr.

—Death & Faxes. 1997. per. (*0-373-26248-5*, 1-26248-4, Worldwide Library) Harlequin Enterprises, Ltd.

—Death & Faxes. 1996. 240p. 19.95 o.p. (*0-312-13960-8*, Saint Martin's Minotaur) St. Martin's Pr.

—Just the Fax, Ma'am. 1997. per. (*0-373-26254-X*, 1-26254-2, Worldwide Library) Harlequin Enterprises, Ltd.

—Just the Fax, Ma'am. 1996. 256p. 21.95 o.p. (*0-312-14637-X*, Saint Martin's Minotaur) St. Martin's Pr.

—The School Board Murder. 2000. (Molly Masters Mysteries Ser.). 240p. mass mkt. 6.50 o.s.i (*0-449-00567-4*, Fawcett) Ballantine Bks.

—When the Fax Lady Sings: A Molly Masters Mystery. 2001. (Molly Masters Mysteries Ser.). 256p. mass mkt. 6.50 (*0-449-00568-2*, Fawcett) Ballantine Bks.

—When the Fax Lady Sings: A Molly Masters Mystery. l.t. ed. 2001. 351p. 27.95 (*0-7862-3483-0*) Thorndike Pr.

Sinclair, Alison. Legacies. 1996. 448p. mass mkt. 5.50 o.s.i (*0-06-105699-5*, Eos) Morrow/Avon.

Stevenson, Richard. Chain of Fools. 1996. 208p. 20.95 o.p. (*0-312-14563-2*, Saint Martin's Minotaur) St. Martin's Pr.

—Chain of Fools: A Donald Strachey Mystery. 1997. (Donald Strachey Mystery Ser.). 192p. pap. 11.95 (*0-312-16796-2*, Saint Martin's Griffin) St. Martin's Pr.

—Death Trick. 190p. reprint ed. 1983. pap. 6.95 o.p. (*0-932870-27-9*); 2nd ed. 1996. pap. 9.95 o.p. (*1-55583-387-X*) Alyson Pubns.

—Death Trick. 1981. 224p. 10.95 o.p. (*0-312-18876-5*) St. Martin's Pr.

—Death Trick: A Murder Mystery. 2003. 199p. pap. 15.95 (*1-56023-470-9*, Southern Tier Editions) Haworth Pr., Inc., The.

—Ice Blues. 1987. 224p. mass mkt. 3.95 o.p. (*0-14-009403-2*, Penguin Bks.) Viking Penguin.

—Ice Blues: A Donald Strachey Mystery. 1995. 224p. pap. 8.95 (*0-312-13517-3*, Saint Martin's Griffin); 1986. 256p. 15.95 o.p. (*0-312-40379-8*) St. Martin's Pr.

—On the Other Hand, Death. 1995. 216p. 8.95 (*0-312-11871-6*, Saint Martin's Griffin) St. Martin's Pr.

—On the Other Hand, Death. 1985. (Crime Monthly Ser.). 224p. pap. 3.95 o.p. (*0-14-008319-7*, Penguin Bks.) Viking Penguin.

—On the Other Hand, Death: A Donald Strachey Mystery. 1984. 224p. 12.95 o.p. (*0-312-58458-X*) St. Martin's Pr.

—A Shock to the System: A Donald Strachey Mystery. 192p. 1996. pap. 9.95 (*0-312-14732-5*, Saint Martin's Griffin); 1995. 19.95 o.p. (*0-312-13610-2*, Saint Martin's Minotaur) St. Martin's Pr.

—Strachey's Folly. (Donald Strachey Mystery Ser.). 1999. 224p. pap. 11.95 (*0-312-24328-6*, Saint Martin's Griffin); 1998. 216p. 22.95 o.p. (*0-312-18669-X*, Saint Martin's Minotaur) St. Martin's Pr.

—Third Man Out: A Donald Strachey Mystery. pap. 15.95 (*0-312-30214-2*, Saint Martin's Griffin); 1993. pap. 8.95 (*0-312-08906-6*, Saint Martin's Griffin); 1992. 224p. 17.95 o.p. (*0-312-07110-8*, Saint Martin's Minotaur) St. Martin's Pr.

—Tongue Tied: A Donald Strachey Mystery. 2003. 224p. 22.95 (*0-312-30974-0*, Saint Martin's Minotaur) St. Martin's Pr.

### ALBERTA—FICTION

Badami, Anita Rau. Tamarind Woman. 2002. 272p. 23.95 (*1-56512-335-2*) Algonquin Bks. of Chapel Hill.

—Tamarind Woman. 2004. 304p. pap. 13.95 (*0-345-46494-X*) Ballantine Bks.

Coughlan, Eileen. Dying by Degrees: An Emily Goodstriker Mystery. 2000. (Illus.). 320p. pap. 12.95 (*0-88801-247-0*) Turnstone Pr. CAN. *Dist:* General Distribution Services, Inc.

Dedman, Stephen. The Art of Arrow Cutting. 2001. 304p. mass mkt. 6.99 (*0-8125-4534-6*); 1999. 284p. pap. 13.95 (*0-312-86832-4*); 1997. 320p. 22.95 (*0-312-86320-9*) Doherty, Tom Assocs., LLC. (Tor Bks.).

Flanagan, Jackie. Grass Castles. 1998. 144p. pap. (*1-896209-23-8*) Bayeux Arts, Inc.

King, Thomas. Truth & Bright Water. 2001. 272p. pap. 13.00 (*0-8021-3840-3*, Grove Pr.); 2000. 266p. 24.00 o.p. (*0-87113-818-2*, Atlantic Monthly Pr.) Grove/Atlantic, Inc.

Kinsella, W. P. The Fencepost Chronicles. 1987. 192p. 16.95 o.p. (*0-395-44646-5*); pap. 7.95 o.p. (*0-395-45393-3*) Houghton Mifflin Co.

Mitchell, W. O. The Black Bonspiel of Willie MacCrimmon. 1993. (Illus.). 144p. 14.95 (*0-7710-6081-5*) McClelland & Stewart/Tundra Bks.

North, Suzanne. Healthy, Wealthy & Dead: A Phoebe Fairfax Mystery. 1994. pap. 6.95 (*0-920897-55-X*) NeWest Pubs., Ltd. CAN. *Dist:* General Distribution Services, Inc.

—Seeing Is Deceiving. 1997. (Phoebe Fairfax Mystery Ser.). 336p. mass mkt. 6.99 (*0-7710-6806-9*) McClelland & Stewart/Tundra Bks.

—Seeing Is Deceiving: A Phoebe Fairfax Mystery. 1996. 288p. 25.99 o.p. (*0-7710-6805-0*) McClelland & Stewart/Tundra Bks.

Oke, Janette. Beyond the Gathering Storm. 2000. 256p. pap. 11.99 (*0-7642-2400-X*); 256p. text 16.99 o.p. (*0-7642-2401-8*); 368p. pap. 16.99 (*0-7642-2403-4*) Bethany Hse. Pubs.

—Beyond the Gathering Storm. l.t. ed. 2000. (Christian Fiction Ser.). 357p. 26.95 o.p. (*0-7862-2942-X*) Thorndike Pr.

—Drums of Change: The Story of Running Fawn. 1996. (Women of the West Ser.). 240p. text 15.99 o.p. (*1-55661-818-2*); 240p. pap. 10.99 (*1-55661-812-3*); 352p. pap. 12.99 o.p. (*1-55661-817-4*) Bethany Hse. Pubs.

—Drums of Change: The Story of Running Fawn. l.t. ed. 1996. 318p. lib. bdg. 23.95 o.p. (*0-7838-1822-X*, Macmillan Reference USA) Gale Group.

### ALBION (IMAGINARY PLACE)—FICTION

Lawhead, Stephen R. The Endless Knot. 1994. 416p. pap. 11.95 o.p. (*0-7459-2240-6*); 1993. 450p. 19.95 (*0-7459-2231-7*) Lion Publishing.

—The Endless Knot. 1994. (Song of Albion Ser.: Bk. 3). 416p. pap. 5.99 o.p. (*0-380-71648-8*, Avon Bks.) Morrow/Avon.

—The Endless Knot, 3. 1998. (Song of Albion Ser.). 416p. pap. 27.99 (*0-310-21901-9*) Zondervan.

—The Paradise War. (Song of Albion Ser.: Bk. 1). 1992. 420p. pap. 11.95 (*0-7459-2242-2*); 1991. 450p. 19.95 o.p. (*0-7459-1850-6*) Lion Publishing.

—The Paradise War. 1993. (Song of Albion Ser.: Bk. 1). 432p. pap. 5.99 o.p. (*0-380-71646-1*, Avon Bks.) Morrow/Avon.

—The Silver Hand. (Song of Albion Ser.: Bk. 2). 450p. 1993. pap. 11.95 o.p. (*0-7459-2245-7*); 1992. 19.95 o.p. (*0-7459-2230-9*) Lion Publishing.

—The Silver Hand. 1993. (Song of Albion Ser.: Bk. 2). 400p. mass mkt. 5.99 (*0-380-71647-X*, Avon Bks.) Morrow/Avon.

### ALBUQUERQUE (N.M.)—FICTION

Anaya, Rudolfo A. Rio Grande Fall. 1997. 352p. mass mkt. 6.99 (*0-446-60486-0*); 1996. 368p. 23.00 o.p. (*0-446-51844-1*) Warner Bks., Inc.

—Shaman Winter. 2000. 432p. mass mkt. 7.50 (*0-446-60801-7*); 1999. (Illus.). 374p. 30.00 o.p. (*0-446-52374-7*) Warner Bks., Inc.

—Zia Summer. 1996. 13.04 (*0-606-17163-0*) Turtleback Bks.

—Zia Summer. 1996. 368p. mass mkt. 7.50 (*0-446-60316-3*); 1995. 400p. (YA). 21.95 o.p. (*0-446-51843-3*) Warner Bks., Inc.

Brewer, Steve. Baby Face. 2000. (Bubba Mabry Mystery Ser.). 256p. mass mkt. 5.95 (*1-890768-20-0*, Intrigue Pr.) Corvus Publishing.

—Baby Face. 1995. (Illus.). 256p. (J). mass mkt. 5.50 (*0-671-74735-5*, Pocket) Simon & Schuster.

—Cheap Shot: A Drew Gavin Mystery. 2002. (Drew Gavin Mysteries Ser.: No. 2). 321p. 23.95 (*1-890768-45-6*, Intrigue Pr.) Corvus Publishing.

—Crazy Love. 2001. (Bubba Mabry Mystery Ser.: No. 6). 252p. 23.95 (*1-890768-31-6*, Intrigue Pr.) Corvus Publishing.

—Crazy Love. 2003. (WWL Mystery Ser.: No. 477). 256p. mass mkt. (*0-373-26477-1*, Worldwide Library) Harlequin Enterprises, Ltd.

—Dirty Pool. 2003. (WWL Mystery Ser.: No. 462). 272p. mass mkt. (*0-373-26462-3*, Worldwide Library) Harlequin Enterprises, Ltd.

—Dirty Pool. 1999. 272p. 23.95 o.p. (*0-312-20203-2*, Saint Martin's Minotaur) St. Martin's Pr.

—Lonely Street. unabr. ed. 1999. (Bubba Mabry Mystery Ser.). audio 39.95 (*1-55686-867-7*) Books in Motion.

—Lonely Street. 1999. (Bubba Mabry Mystery Ser.: No. 1). 256p. mass mkt. 5.95 (*1-890768-19-7*, Intrigue Pr.) Corvus Publishing.

—Lonely Street. Grad, Doug, ed. 1994. 224p. mass mkt. 4.99 (*0-671-74734-7*, Pocket) Simon & Schuster.

—Shaky Ground. 2003. (WWL Mystery Ser.: No. 454). 256p. mass mkt. (*0-373-26454-2*, Worldwide Library) Harlequin Enterprises, Ltd.

—Shaky Ground. 1997. 233p. 22.95 o.p. (*0-312-15652-9*, Saint Martin's Minotaur) St. Martin's Pr.

—Witchy Woman. 1996. 208p. 21.95 o.p. (*0-312-14076-2*, Saint Martin's Minotaur) St. Martin's Pr.

—Witchy Woman: A Bubba Mabry P. I. Mystery. 1999. (Bubba Mabry Mystery Ser.). 256p. reprint ed. mass mkt. 5.95 (*1-890768-13-8*, Intrigue Pr.) Corvus Publishing.

Evasdaughter, Elizabeth N. Albuquerque Gold. 2002. 199p. pap. 20.99 (*1-4010-1332-5*); text 30.99 (*1-4010-5540-0*) Xlibris Corp.

Shelton, Connie. Deadly Gamble. unabr. ed. 1996. (Charlie Parker Ser.: Bk. 1). audio 39.95 (*1-55686-653-4*) Books in Motion.

—Deadly Gamble: The First Charlie Parker Mystery. Lenz, Leslie, ed. 1995. 216p. 21.95 o.p. (*0-9643161-0-2*, Intrigue Pr.) Corvus Publishing.

—Deadly Gamble: The First Charlie Parker Mystery. 1997. (The Charlie Parker Mystery Ser.: Vol. 1). 288p. reprint ed. mass mkt. 5.50 (*1-890768-00-6*, Intrigue Pr.) Corvus Publishing.

—Memories Can Be Murder. Ellison, Lee, ed. 1999. (The Charlie Parker Mystery Ser.: 5). 224p. 22.95 (*1-890768-18-9*, Intrigue Pr.) Corvus Publishing.

—Partnerships Can Kill. unabr. ed. 1996. (Charlie Parker Ser.: Bk. 3). audio 26.95 (*1-55686-667-4*) Books in Motion.

—Partnerships Can Kill. 1998. (The Charlie Parker Mystery Ser.: No. 3). 240p. mass mkt. 5.50 (*1-890768-02-2*, Intrigue Pr.) Corvus Publishing.

—Partnerships Can Kill. Ellison, Lee, ed. 1997. 208p. 21.95 o.p. (*0-9643161-4-5*, Intrigue Pr.) Corvus Publishing.

—Small Towns Can Be Murder. (The Charlie Parker Mystery Ser.: No. 4). 1999. (Illus.). 256p. mass mkt. 5.95 (*1-890768-16-2*); 1998. 224p. 22.95 (*1-890768-05-7*) Corvus Publishing. (Intrigue Pr.).

—Vacations Can Be Murder. unabr. ed. 1996. (Charlie Parker Ser.: Bk. 2). audio 39.95 (*1-55686-660-7*) Books in Motion.

—Vacations Can Be Murder: The Second Charlie Parker Mystery. Lenz, Leslie, ed. 1995. (Charlie Parker Mysteries Ser.). 216p. 21.95 o.p. (*0-9643161-1-0*, Intrigue Pr.) Corvus Publishing.
—Vacations Can Be Murder: The Second Charlie Parker Mystery. 1997. (The Charlie Parker Mystery Ser.: Vol. 2). 272p. reprint ed. mass mkt. 5.50 (*1-890768-01-4*, Intrigue Pr.) Corvus Publishing.
Van Gieson, Judith. Ditch Rider: A Neil Hamel Mystery. (Neil Hamel Mystery Ser.). 240p. 1999. mass mkt. 5.99 (*0-06-109515-X*); 1998. 23.00 (*0-06-017513-3*) HarperCollins Pubs.
—Hotshots. 1996. (Neil Hamel Mystery Ser.). 256p. 22.00 o.p. (*0-06-017512-5*) HarperCollins Pubs.
—The Lies That Bind: A Neil Hamel Mystery. 1994. 304p. mass mkt. 4.99 o.p. (*0-06-109051-4*) HarperCollins Pubs.
—The Lies That Bind: A Neil Hamel Mystery. 1993. 256p. 20.00 o.p. (*0-06-017705-5*) HarperTrade.
—North of the Border: A Neil Hamel Mystery. 1993. 176p. mass mkt. 4.99 (*0-671-76967-7*, Pocket) Simon & Schuster.
—North of the Border: A Neil Hamel Mystery. 2002. 178p. pap. 13.95 (*0-8263-2886-5*) Univ. of New Mexico Pr.
—North of the Border: A Neil Hamel Mystery. 1988. 16.95 o.p. (*0-8027-5706-5*) Walker & Co.
—The Other Side of Death. 1991. 224p. 18.95 o.p. (*0-06-016581-2*) HarperTrade.
—The Other Side of Death. 2003. 224p. pap. 13.95 (*0-8263-3207-2*) Univ. of New Mexico Pr.
—Parrot Blues. 1995. 256p. 20.00 o.p. (*0-06-017706-3*) HarperTrade.
—Parrot Blues. 1995. 272p. mass mkt. 4.99 o.p. (*0-06-109048-4*, HarperTorch) Morrow/Avon.
—Raptor. 1990. 17.95 o.p. (*0-06-016167-1*) HarperTrade.
—Raptor. Isaacson, Dana, ed. 1991. 256p. reprint ed. mass mkt. 4.99 (*0-671-73243-9*, Pocket) Simon & Schuster.
—Raptor. 2002. 252p. pap. 13.95 (*0-8263-2974-8*) Univ. of New Mexico Pr.
—The Wolf Path: A Neil Hamel Mystery. 1992. 224p. 19.00 o.p. (*0-06-016804-8*) HarperTrade.
—The Wolf Path: A Neil Hamel Mystery. 1993. 256p. mass mkt. 4.50 o.p. (*0-06-109139-1*, HarperTorch) Morrow/Avon.

**ALEFORD (MASS.: IMAGINARY PLACE)—FICTION**

Page, Katherine Hall. The Body in the Belfry. 1991. 320p. reprint ed. mass mkt. 6.99 (*0-380-71328-4*, Avon Bks.) Morrow/Avon.
—The Body in the Belfry. 1990. 272p. 16.95 (*0-312-03798-8*, Saint Martin's Minotaur) St. Martin's Pr.
—The Body in the Bog. l.t. ed. 1997. 299p. lib. bdg. 23.95 (*1-57490-087-0*, Beeler Large Print Bks.) Beeler, Thomas T. Publisher.
—The Body in the Bog. 1997. 384p. mass mkt. 6.99 (*0-380-72712-9*, Avon Bks.); 1996. 256p. 22.00 o.p. (*0-688-14573-6*, Morrow, William & Co.) Morrow/Avon.
—The Body in the Bookcase. (Faith Fairchild Mysteries Ser.). 1999. 384p. mass mkt. 6.99 (*0-380-73237-8*, Avon Bks.); 1998. 272p. 22.00 (*0-688-15747-5*, Morrow, William & Co.) Morrow/Avon.
—The Body in the Cast. l.t. ed. 1999. (Beeler Large Print Mystery Ser.). 24.95 (*1-57490-239-3*, Beeler Large Print Bks.) Beeler, Thomas T. Publisher.
—The Body in the Cast. 1994. 368p. mass mkt. 6.99 (*0-380-72338-7*, Avon Bks.) Morrow/Avon.
—The Body in the Cast. 1993. 224p. 19.95 o.p. (*0-312-09755-7*, Saint Martin's Minotaur) St. Martin's Pr.

**ALFAR (IMAGINARY PLACE)—FICTION**

Boyer, Elizabeth A. The Dragon's Carbuncle. 1990. (Wizard's War: 3). 320p. (Orig.). mass mkt. 4.95 o.s.i (*0-345-35459-1*, Del Rey) Ballantine Bks.
Boyer, Elizabeth H. The Curse of Slagfid. 1989. (Wizard's War: 2). 352p. mass mkt. 3.95 o.s.i (*0-345-33265-2*, Del Rey) Ballantine Bks.
—The Elves & the Otterskin. 1984. (World of the Alfar Ser.: 1). 304p. mass mkt. 4.99 o.s.i (*0-345-32054-9*, Del Rey) Ballantine Bks.
—Lord of Chaos. 1991. (Wizard's War: 4). (Illus.). 320p. mass mkt. 4.99 o.s.i (*0-345-36302-7*, Del Rey) Ballantine Bks.
—The Sword & the Satchel. 1986. (World of the Alfar Ser.: 2). mass mkt. 3.95 o.s.i (*0-345-33601-1*); 1983. mass mkt. 2.95 o.p. (*0-345-30986-3*, Del Rey) Ballantine Bks.
—The Thrall & the Dragon's Heart. 1986. (World of the Alfar Ser.: 4). 304p. mass mkt. 3.50 o.s.i (*0-345-33749-2*); 1983. mass mkt. 2.95 o.p. (*0-345-31445-X*); 1982. mass mkt. 2.75 o.p. (*0-345-30236-2*) Ballantine Bks. (Del Rey).
—The Troll's Grindstone. 1986. (Wizard's War: 1). 352p. mass mkt. 4.95 o.s.i (*0-345-32182-0*, Del Rey) Ballantine Bks.
—The Wizard & the Warlord. 1987. (World of the Alfar Ser.: 3). mass mkt. 3.95 o.s.i (*0-345-34711-0*, Del Rey) Ballantine Bks.

**ALGERIA—FICTION**

Belamri, Rabah. Shattered Vision. Harter, Hugh A., tr. from FRE. 1994. (French Expressions Ser.). 180p. 19.95 (*0-8419-1258-0*) Holmes & Meier Pubs., Inc.
Bensmaia, Reda. Years of Passages. 1995. (Theory Out of Bounds Ser.: Vol. 5). 147p. pap. 21.95 (*0-8166-2393-7*) Univ. of Minnesota Pr.
Boudjedra, Rachid. The Repudiation. Lambrova, Golda, tr. from FRE. 1995. 195p. 28.00 (*0-89410-729-1*); pap. 14.00 (*0-89410-730-5*) Rienner, Lynne Pubs., Inc. (Three Continents).
—Repudiation. 1986. (Folio Ser.: No. 1326). (FRE.). 251p. pap. 8.95 (*2-07-037326-6*) Schoenhof's Foreign Bks., Inc.
Bouraoui, Nina. Forbidden Vision. 1998. 112p. pap. 9.95 (*1-886449-69-4*) Barrytown, Ltd.
—Forbidden Vision. Marcus, Melissa, tr. from FRE. 1995. 106p. pap. 9.95 (*0-88268-177-X*) Station Hill Pr.
Camus, Albert. The First Man. Hapgood, David, tr. from FRE. 1995. 336p. 25.00 o.s.i (*0-679-43937-4*) Knopf, Alfred A. Inc.
—The First Man. 1996. 336p. pap. o.s.i (*0-676-97005-2*, Vintage) Random Hse. of Canada, Ltd. CAN. *Dist:* Random Hse., Inc.
—The First Man. Hapgood, David, tr. 1996. 336p. pap. 12.00 (*0-679-76816-5*) Random Hse., Inc.
—The First Man. Hapgood, David, tr. l.t. ed. 1996. 371p. lib. bdg. 22.95 (*0-7838-1601-4*) Thorndike Pr.
—The Stranger. 20.95 (*0-89190-220-1*) Amereon, Ltd.
—The Stranger. 1988. 156p. reprint ed. lib. bdg. 24.95 (*0-89966-623-X*) Buccaneer Bks., Inc.
—The Stranger. Ward, Matthew, tr. from FRE. l.t. ed. 2001. 125p. pap. 22.95 o.p. (*1-58724-032-7*, Wheeler Publishing, Inc.) Gale Group.
—The Stranger. Ward, Matthew, tr. 1989. (International Ser.). 144p. pap. 9.95 (*0-679-72020-0*, Vintage) Knopf Publishing Group.
—The Stranger. Ward, Matthew, tr. from FRE. 1993. 160p. 15.00 (*0-679-42026-6*) Knopf, Alfred A. Inc.
—The Stranger. Laredo, Joseph, tr. 1988. 144p. 25.00 (*0-394-53305-4*) Knopf, Alfred A. Inc.
—The Stranger. 1946. 12.95 o.p. (*0-394-44748-4*) Knopf, Alfred A. Inc.
—The Stranger. 1954. pap. 2.95 o.p. (*0-394-70002-3*) Random Hse., Inc.
—The Stranger. 1989. (Vintage International Ser.). 15.05 (*0-606-01426-8*) Turtleback Bks.
—The Stranger. Griffith, Kate, tr. 1982. 110p. pap. text 9.00 o.p. (*0-8191-2142-8*) Univ. Pr. of America.
De Wohl, Louis. Restless Flame: Novel St. Augustine. 1997. 303p. pap. text 12.95 (*0-89870-603-3*) Ignatius Pr.
Dib, Mohammed. The Savage Night. Dickson, C., tr. from FRE. 2001. 191p. pap. 20.00 (*0-8032-6620-0*); text 50.00 (*0-8032-1713-7*) Univ. of Nebraska Pr.
—Who Remembers the Sea. Tremaine, Louis, tr. from FRE. 1985. Tr. of Qui Se Souvient de la Mer. 122p. pap. 9.50 o.p. (*0-89410-445-4*); 15.00 o.s.i (*0-89410-444-6*) Rienner, Lynne Pubs., Inc. (Three Continents).
Djebar, Assia. Fantasia. 1993. 288p. 19.95 (*0-7043-2610-8*) Quartet Bks., Ltd. GBR. *Dist:* Interlink Publishing Group, Inc.
—Fantasia: An Algerian Cavalcade. Blair, Dorothy S., tr. 1993. 227p. (C). pap. 12.95 (*0-435-08621-9*, 08621) Heinemann.
—A Sister to Scheherazade. Blair, Dorothy S., tr. 1993. 160p. (C). pap. 13.95 (*0-435-08622-7*, 08622) Heinemann.
—A Sister to Scheherazade. 1991. 170p. 19.95 (*0-7043-2670-1*) Quartet Bks., Ltd. GBR. *Dist:* Interlink Publishing Group, Inc.
—Women of Algiers in Their Apartment. De Jager, Marjoli, tr. 1999. (African & Caribbean Literature Translated from French Ser.). 224p. pap. 15.95 (*0-8139-1880-4*) Univ. Pr. of Virginia.
—Women of Algiers in Their Apartment. de Jager, Marjolijn, tr. from FRE. 1992. (Caraf Bks.). 224p. (C). text 30.00 (*0-8139-1402-7*) Univ. Pr. of Virginia.
Emerson, Gloria. Loving Graham Greene. 2001. 192p. pap. 12.00 (*0-385-72035-1*, Knopf Bks. for Young Readers) Random Hse. Children's Bks.
Givon, Thomas. Running Through the Tall Grass: A Novel. 1997. 288p. 23.00 o.p. (*0-06-039200-2*, ReganBooks) HarperTrade.
Guyotat, Pierre. Eden, Eden, Eden. Fox, Graham, tr. from FRE. 2003. (Modern Classics Ser.: 2). 192p. pap. 13.95 (*1-84068-063-6*) Creation Bks.
—Eden, Eden, Eden. 1996. 192p. pap. 13.95 (*1-871592-47-X*) Creation Bks.
Hostetler, Marian. Fear in Algeria. 1979. (Illus.). 128p. (J). (gr. 5-10). pap. 3.95 o.p. (*0-8361-1905-3*) Herald Pr.
Khadra, Yasmina. In the Name of God. Black, Linda, tr. from FRE. 2000. 224p. pap. 12.95 (*1-902881-11-7*) Toby Pr.
—In the Name of God. 2000. 29.95 (*1-902881-06-0*) Toby Pr.
—Wolf Dreams. 2003. 272p. 19.95 (*1-902881-75-3*) Toby Pr.
Laugel, Marcel G. The Sons of the Clouds. 1987. (Illus.). 224p. 20.00 (*0-8022-2479-2*) Philosophical Library, Inc.
Little, Denise, ed. Vengeance. 2002. 336p. mass mkt. 6.99 (*0-7564-0084-8*) DAW Bks., Inc.
Marouane, Leila. The Abductor. McNab, Felicity, tr. from FRE. 2001. 240p. pap. 12.95 (*0-7043-8142-7*) Quartet Bks., Ltd. GBR. *Dist:* Interlink Publishing Group, Inc.
Messud, Claire. The Last Life. 2000. 400p. pap. 14.00 (*0-15-601165-4*, Harvest Bks.) Harcourt Trade Pubs.
—The Last Life: A Novel. 1999. 368p. 24.00 (*0-15-100471-4*, Harvest Bks.) Harcourt Trade Pubs.
Mokeddem, Malika. Of Dreams & Assassins. Marcus, K. Melissa, tr. from FRE. 2000. (Caraf Bks.). 128p. 45.00 (*0-8139-1933-9*); pap. 16.95 (*0-8139-1994-0*) Univ. Pr. of Virginia.
Moore, Brian. The Magician's Wife. 1998. 358 p. (*0-7540-1142-9*) BBC Audiobooks America.
—The Magician's Wife. 1997. 215p. (*0-7475-3718-6*) Bloomsbury Publishing, Ltd.
—The Magician's Wife. unabr. ed. 2000. audio 49.95 (*0-7540-0191-1*, CAB 1614) Chivers Audio Bks. GBR. *Dist:* BBC Audiobooks America.
—The Magician's Wife. (William Abrahams Book Ser.). 240p. 1999. pap. 12.95 (*0-452-27959-3*, Plume); 1998. 23.95 o.p. (*0-525-94400-1*, Abrahams, William Bks.) Dutton/Plume.
—The Magician's Wife. 1997. 300p. (J). 28.01 o.s.i (*0-676-97090-7*) Random Hse., Inc.
—The Magician's Wife. unabr. ed. 1997. audio 44.00 (*0-7887-1980-7*, 95367E7) Recorded Bks., LLC.
—The Magician's Wife. l.t. ed. 1998. (Basic Ser.). 359p. 28.95 (*0-7862-1388-4*) Thorndike Pr.
Musser, Elizabeth. Two Crosses. 1996. 425p. 11.99 (*1-56476-577-6*, 6-3577) Cook Communications Ministries.
Ouida. Under Two Flags, 3 vols., 2 bks. reprint ed. 84.50 (*0-404-62088-4*);1. o.p. (*0-404-62089-2*);Vol. 2. o.p. (*0-404-62090-6*) AMS Pr., Inc.
Pendleton, Don. Vengeance. 1999. (SuperBolan Ser.: Vol. 69). mass mkt. (*0-373-61469-1*, Worldwide Library) Harlequin Enterprises, Ltd.
Sutherland, John, ed. Under Two Flags: A Story of the Household & the Desert. 1995. (Oxford Popular Fiction Ser.). 550p. pap. 12.95 o.p. (*0-19-282328-0*) Oxford Univ. Pr., Inc.
Tyler, Royall. The Algerine Captive: Or, the Life & Adventures of Doctor Updike Underhill [Pseud] Six Years a Prisoner among the Algerines . . . 2002. (Modern Library Classics). (Illus.). 304p. pap. 13.95 (*0-375-76034-2*) Random Hse., Inc.
—The Algerine Captive: Or, the Life & Adventures of Doctor Updike Underhill [Pseud] Six Years a Prisoner among the Algerines . . . Cook, Donald L., ed. 1970. pap. 19.95 (*0-8084-0049-5*) Rowman & Littlefield Pubs., Inc.
—The Algerine Captive: Or, the Life & Adventures of Doctor Updike Underhill [Pseud] Six Years a Prisoner among the Algerines . . . 1967. reprint ed. 50.00 (*0-8201-1046-9*) Scholars' Facsimiles & Reprints.

**AMBER (IMAGINARY PLACE)—FICTION**

Zelazny, Roger. Blood of Amber. 224p. 1986. 14.95 o.p. (*0-87795-829-7*, Morrow, William & Co.); 1987. (Chronicles of Amber Ser.: Bk. 7). reprint ed. mass mkt. 4.99 (*0-380-89636-2*, Avon Bks.) Morrow/Avon.
—Blood of Amber. l.t. ed. 2000. (Science Fiction Ser.). 303p. 25.95 (*0-7838-9294-2*) Thorndike Pr.
—Blood of Amber. 1986. 215p. 50.00 o.p. (*0-88733-058-4*) Underwood Bks., Inc.
—The Courts of Chaos. 1978. 183p. 9.95 o.p. (*0-385-13685-4*) Doubleday Publishing.
—The Courts of Chaos. 1979. (Chronicles of Amber Ser.: Bk. 5). 144p. (YA). (gr. 9 up). reprint ed. pap. 4.99 (*0-380-47175-2*, Avon Bks.) Morrow/Avon.
—The Courts of Chaos. l.t. ed. 2000. (Science Fiction Ser.). 208p. 25.95 (*0-7838-9064-8*) Thorndike Pr.
—The Great Book of Amber: The Complete Amber Chronicles. 1-10, 10 vols., set. 1999. (Amber Ser.). 1264p. pap. 22.95 (*0-380-80906-0*, Avon Bks.) Morrow/Avon.
—The Guns of Avalon. 1976. 224p. reprint ed. mass mkt. 5.99 (*0-380-00083-0*, Avon Bks.) Morrow/Avon.
—The Guns of Avalon. l.t. ed. 1999. (Science Fiction Ser.). 287p. 24.95 (*0-7838-8504-0*) Thorndike Pr.
—The Hand of Oberon. 1977. 192p. (YA). (gr. 7 up). reprint ed. pap. 5.99 (*0-380-01664-8*, Avon Bks.) Morrow/Avon.
—The Hand of Oberon. l.t. ed. 2000. (Science Fiction Ser.). 261p. 25.95 (*0-7838-8985-2*) Thorndike Pr.
—Knight of Shadows. 2004. audio compact disk 25.00 (*1-58807-261-4*); 2004. audio compact disk (*1-58807-692-X*); 2003. audio (*1-58807-534-6*); 2003. (Amber Ser.: No. 9). audio 18.00 (*1-58807-134-0*) Americana Publishing, Inc.
—Knight of Shadows. 256p. 1990. pap. 5.99 (*0-380-75501-7*, Avon Bks.); 1989. 14.95 o.p. (*0-688-08726-4*, Morrow, William & Co.) Morrow/Avon.
—Knight of Shadows. l.t. ed. 2001. (Chronicles of Amber Ser.: Vol. 9). 302p. 27.95 (*0-7838-9293-4*) Thorndike Pr.
—Nine Princes in Amber. 1977. 176p. (YA). (gr. 9 up). reprint ed. pap. 5.99 (*0-380-01430-0*, Avon Bks.) Morrow/Avon.
—Nine Princes in Amber. l.t. ed. 1998. (Science Fiction Ser.). 255p. 23.95 (*0-7838-8425-7*) Thorndike Pr.
—Prince of Chaos. 2004. audio compact disk 25.00 (*1-58807-262-2*); 2004. audio compact disk (*1-58807-693-8*); 2003. (Amber Ser.: No. 10). audio 18.00 (*1-58807-135-9*); 2003. audio (*1-58807-538-9*) Americana Publishing, Inc.
—Prince of Chaos. 1992. pap. 5.99 (*0-380-75502-5*, Avon Bks.); 1991. 225p. 18.00 o.p. (*0-688-08727-2*, Morrow, William & Co.) Morrow/Avon.
—Prince of Chaos. l.t. ed. 2001. (Chronicles of Amber Ser.: Vol. 10). 143p. 27.95 (*0-7838-9292-6*) Thorndike Pr.
—Sign of Chaos. 2004. audio compact disk 25.00 (*1-58807-260-6*); 2004. audio compact disk (*1-58807-691-1*); 2003. audio (*1-58807-530-3*); 2003. (Amber Ser.: No. 8). audio 18.00 (*1-58807-133-2*) Americana Publishing, Inc.
—Sign of Chaos. (Amber Ser.: Vol. 8). 224p. 1988. mass mkt. 4.99 (*0-380-89637-0*, Avon Bks.); 1987. 15.95 o.p. (*0-87795-926-9*) Morrow/Avon.
—Sign of Chaos. 1989. 2.99 o.p. (*0-517-69430-1*) Random Hse. Value Publishing.
—Sign of Chaos. l.t. ed. 2001. (Chronicles of Amber Ser.). (Illus.). 288p. (J). 27.95 (*0-7838-9291-8*) Thorndike Pr.
—Sign of the Unicorn. 1986. 192p. reprint ed. pap. 5.99 o.p. (*0-380-00831-9*, Avon Bks.) Morrow/Avon.
—Sign of the Unicorn. l.t. ed. 1999. (Science Fiction Ser.). 243p. 24.95 (*0-7838-8505-9*) Thorndike Pr.
—Trumps of Doom. 1985. (Amber Ser.). 157p. 14.95 o.p. (*0-87795-718-5*); 1986. (Chronicles of Amber Ser.: Bk. 6). 192p. reprint ed. mass mkt. 5.99 (*0-380-89635-4*, Avon Bks.) Morrow/Avon.
—Trumps of Doom. l.t. ed. 2000. (Science Fiction Ser.). 255p. 25.95 (*0-7838-9160-1*) Thorndike Pr.

**AMHEARST (PA.: IMAGINARY PLACE)—FICTION**

Roper, Gayle G. Caught in a Bind. 2000. (Amhearst Mystery Ser.). 320p. pap. 10.99 (*0-310-21850-0*) Zondervan.
—Caught in the Act. 2000. (Five Star Christian Fiction Ser.). 311p. 24.95 (*0-7862-2776-1*, Five Star) Gale Group.
—Caught in the Act? 1998. (Amhearst Mystery Ser.: 2). 272p. pap. 10.99 (*0-310-21909-4*) Zondervan.
—Caught in the Middle. 1997. (Amhearst Mystery Ser.: Vol. 1). 240p. pap. 10.99 (*0-310-20995-1*) Zondervan.

**AMSTERDAM (NETHERLANDS)—FICTION**

Bhabra, H. S. Gestures: A Novel. 2003. 318p. 17.95 (*1-56792-235-X*) Godine, David R. Pub.
Field, Carol. Mangoes & Quince. 2001. 288p. 24.95 (*1-58234-114-1*) Bloomsbury Publishing.
Foy, George. Coaster. 1986. mass mkt. 3.95 o.s.i (*0-671-62326-5*, Pocket) Simon & Schuster.
—Coaster. 1986. 320p. 16.95 o.p. (*0-670-80491-6*) Viking Penguin.
Freeling, Nicolas. Arlette. 1982. pap. 2.95 o.p. (*0-394-75260-0*, Pantheon) Knopf Publishing Group.
—Aupres de Ma Blonde. 1979. pap. 2.95 o.p. (*0-394-74550-7*, Vintage) Knopf Publishing Group.
—Because of the Cats. 2000. 190p. pap. (*1-900850-36-2*) Arcadia Bks.
—Because of the Cats. l.t. ed. 1987. pap. 13.95 o.p. (*1-55504-040-3*) BBC Audiobooks America.
—Because of the Cats. 1975. (Crime Ser.). 192p. pap. 3.95 o.p. (*0-14-002282-1*, Penguin Bks.) Viking Penguin.
—Criminal Conversation. 2001. 218p. pap. 9.95 (*1-84232-842-5*) House of Stratus, Inc. GBR. *Dist:* Midpoint Trade Bks., Inc.
—Criminal Conversation. 1981. (Inspector Van der Valk Suspense Novel Ser.). 213p. pap. 2.50 o.p. (*0-394-74692-9*, V-692) Random Hse., Inc.
—Double - Barrel. 1981. (Inspector Van der Valk Suspense Novel Ser.). 224p. pap. 2.50 o.p. (*0-394-74693-7*, V-693) Random Hse., Inc.
—Double - Barrel. 1975. 208p. pap. 1.95 o.p. (*0-14-002585-5*, Penguin Bks.) Viking Penguin.
—Gun Before Butter. 2001. 216p. pap. 9.95 (*1-84232-838-7*) House of Stratus, Inc. GBR. *Dist:* Midpoint Trade Bks., Inc.
—The King of the Rainy Country. 2001. 167p. pap. 9.95 (*1-84232-843-3*) House of Stratus, Inc. GBR. *Dist:* Midpoint Trade Bks., Inc.

—The King of the Rainy Country. 1975. (Crime Ser.). 160p. pap. 3.95 o.p. (*0-14-002853-6*, Penguin Bks.) Viking Penguin.

—Love in Amsterdam. 1990. 190p. pap. 3.95 o.p. (*0-88184-613-9*, Carroll & Graf Pubs.) Avalon Publishing Group.

—Love in Amsterdam. 2001. 196p. pap. 9.95 (*1-84232-839-5*) House of Stratus, Inc. GBR. *Dist:* Midpoint Trade Bks., Inc.

—Love in Amsterdam. 1975. (Crime Ser.). 192p. pap. 3.95 o.p. (*0-14-002281-3*, Penguin Bks.) Viking Penguin.

—The Lovely Ladies. 1981. (Inspector Van der Valk Suspense Novel Ser.). pap. 3.95 o.p. (*0-394-74694-5*, V-694) Random Hse., Inc.

—The Lovely Ladies. 1989. 288p. pap. 3.95 o.p. (*0-14-011367-3*, Penguin Bks.) Viking Penguin.

—Sand Castles. l.t. ed. 1990. 17.95 o.p. (*0-7451-9898-8*, C0626); pap. 15.95 o.p. (*0-7927-0358-8*, C0820) BBC Audiobooks America.

—Sand Castles. 2001. 210p. pap. 9.95 (*1-84232-864-6*) House of Stratus, Inc. GBR. *Dist:* Midpoint Trade Bks., Inc.

—Sand Castles. 1990. 17.95 (*0-89296-372-7*) Mysterious Pr.

—Sand Castles. 1991. mass mkt. 4.95 o.s.i (*0-445-40925-8*) Warner Bks., Inc.

—Strike Out Where Not Applicable. 2001. 206p. pap. 9.95 (*1-84232-845-X*) House of Stratus, Inc. GBR. *Dist:* Midpoint Trade Bks., Inc.

—Strike Out Where Not Applicable. 1985. (Crime Ser.). 176p. pap. 3.95 o.p. (*0-14-003009-3*, Penguin Bks.) Viking Penguin.

—The Widow. 2001. 280p. pap. 9.95 (*1-84232-850-6*) House of Stratus, Inc. GBR. *Dist:* Midpoint Trade Bks., Inc.

—The Widow. 1980. 256p. pap. 3.95 o.p. (*0-394-74467-5*, Vintage); 1979. 8.95 o.p. (*0-394-50336-8*, Pantheon) Knopf Publishing Group.

Gould, Judith. The Best Is yet to Come. 2003. 448p. mass mkt. 7.99 (*0-451-21016-6*, Signet Bks.) NAL.

Grunberg, Arnon. Blue Mondays. Pomerans, Arnold J. & Pomerans, Erica, trs. from DUT. 1997. 278p. 22.00 o.p. (*0-374-11485-4*) Farrar, Straus & Giroux.

—Blue Mondays. 1997. 278p. o.s.i (*0-436-20458-4*) Random Hse. of Canada, Ltd.

Liss, David. The Coffee Trader: A Novel. 2004. 416p. pap. 14.95 (*0-375-76090-3*) Ballantine Bks.

—The Coffee Trader: A Novel. 2003. 400p. 24.95 (*0-375-50854-6*) Random Hse., Inc.

McEwan, Ian. Amsterdam: A Novel. unabr. ed. 1999. audio 24.00 (*0-7366-4451-2*, 4896) Books on Tape, Inc.

—Amsterdam: A Novel. Oeser, Hans-Christian, tr. from ENG. 1999. (GER.). 224p. (*3-257-06220-6*) Diogenes Verlag AG CHE. *Dist:* International Bk. Import Service, Inc.

—Amsterdam: A Novel. 1998. 208p. 21.00 o.s.i (*0-385-49423-8*, Talese, Nan A.) Doubleday Publishing.

—Amsterdam: A Novel. unabr. ed. 1999. audio 24.95 (*1-57511-060-1*) Publishing Mills, Inc., The.

—Amsterdam: A Novel. 1999. 208p. pap. 13.00 (*0-385-49424-6*, Knopf Bks. for Young Readers) Random Hse. Children's Bks.

—Amsterdam: A Novel. l.t. ed. 1999. (Basic Ser.). 232p. 29.95 (*0-7862-1796-0*) Thorndike Pr.

—Amsterdam: A Novel. abr. ed. 1999. audio 18.70 (*0-00-105566-6*) Ulverscroft Audio (U.S.A.).

Moggach, Deborah. Tulip Fever. unabr. ed. 2000. audio 69.95 (*0-7540-0440-6*, CAB 1863) Chivers Audio Bks. GBR. *Dist:* BBC Audiobooks America.

—Tulip Fever. l.t. ed. 2000. (General Ser.). 263p. pap. 22.95 (*0-7862-2300-6*) Thorndike Pr.

Moody, Bill. Looking for Chet Baker: An Evan Horne Mystery. 2003. (WWL Mystery Ser.: No. 450). 272p. mass mkt. (*0-373-26450-X*, Worldwide Library) Harlequin Enterprises, Ltd.

—Looking for Chet Baker: An Evan Horne Mystery. 2002. 253p. 23.95 (*0-8027-3368-9*) Walker & Co.

Morley, John D. The Anatomy Lesson. 1996. 184p. pap. o.s.i (*0-349-10721-1*) Little Brown & Co.

—The Anatomy Lesson: A Novel. 1995. (Illus.). 184p. 21.95 o.p. (*0-312-13426-6*) St. Martin's Pr.

Richardson, V. A. The House of Windjammer. 2003. (Illus.). 300p. (J). 17.95 (*1-58234-811-1*, Bloomsbury Children) Bloomsbury Publishing.

Van de Wetering, Janwillem. The Amsterdam Cops: Collected Stories. 2000. 240p. pap. 12.00 (*1-56947-210-6*); 1999. 254p. 22.00 (*1-56947-171-1*) Soho Pr., Inc.

—The Blond Baboon. 1987. 224p. mass mkt. 2.95 o.s.i (*0-345-34497-9*) Ballantine Bks.

—The Blond Baboon. l.t. ed. 1993. 12.50 o.p. (*0-8161-6646-3*, Macmillan Reference USA) Gale Group.

—The Blond Baboon, 001. 1978. 7.95 o.p. (*0-395-26307-7*) Houghton Mifflin Co.

—The Blond Baboon. 1979. (gr. 12). pap. 1.95 o.s.i (*0-671-82318-3*, Pocket) Simon & Schuster.

—The Blond Baboon. 1996. 218p. pap. 12.00 (*1-56947-063-4*) Soho Pr., Inc.

—The Corpse on the Dike. 1987. 224p. mass mkt. 3.50 o.s.i (*0-345-33130-3*) Ballantine Bks.

—The Corpse on the Dike, 001. 1976. 6.95 o.p. (*0-395-24675-X*) Houghton Mifflin Co.

—The Corpse on the Dike. 1982. mass mkt. 2.95 o.s.i (*0-671-43527-2*, Pocket) Simon & Schuster.

—The Corpse on the Dike. 1995. 232p. pap. 12.00 (*1-56947-049-9*) Soho Pr., Inc.

—Death of a Hawker. 1987. 256p. mass mkt. 3.50 o.s.i (*0-345-33131-1*) Ballantine Bks.

—Death of a Hawker. 1977. 6.95 o.p. (*0-395-25171-0*) Houghton Mifflin Co.

—Death of a Hawker. 1980. (gr. 12). pap. 2.25 o.s.i (*0-671-83557-2*, Pocket) Simon & Schuster.

—Hard Rain. 1987. pap. o.s.i (*0-345-00732-8*); mass mkt. 3.95 o.s.i (*0-345-33964-9*) Ballantine Bks.

—Hard Rain. 1986. 288p. 15.95 o.s.i (*0-394-54924-4*, Pantheon) Knopf Publishing Group.

—Hard Rain. 1997. 313p. pap. 12.00 (*1-56947-104-5*) Soho Pr., Inc.

—The Hollow-Eyed Angel. 282p. 1997. pap. 13.00 (*1-56947-091-X*); 1996. 22.00 (*1-56947-056-1*) Soho Pr., Inc.

—The Japanese Corpse. 1987. mass mkt. 3.50 o.s.i (*0-345-33128-1*) Ballantine Bks.

—The Japanese Corpse, 001. 1977. 7.95 o.p. (*0-395-25777-8*) Houghton Mifflin Co.

—The Japanese Corpse. 1982. mass mkt. 2.95 o.s.i (*0-671-43528-0*, Pocket) Simon & Schuster.

—The Japanese Corpse. 1996. 296p. pap. 12.00 (*1-56947-057-X*) Soho Pr., Inc.

—Just a Corpse at Twilight. unabr. ed. 1998. (Grijpstra & De Gier Mystery Ser.). audio 44.00 (*0-7887-2181-X*, 95477E7) Recorded Bks., LLC.

—Just a Corpse at Twilight. 1995. 266p. pap. 12.00 (*1-56947-075-8*); 1994. 265p. 20.00 (*1-56947-016-2*) Soho Pr., Inc.

—The Maine Massacre. 1988. 240p. reprint ed. mass mkt. 3.95 o.s.i (*0-345-34496-0*) Ballantine Bks.

—The Maine Massacre, 001. 1978. 8.95 o.p. (*0-395-27395-1*) Houghton Mifflin Co.

—The Maine Massacre, unabr. ed. 1998. (Grijpstra & De Gier Mystery Ser.). audio 51.00 (*0-7887-2025-2*, 95400E7) Recorded Bks., LLC.

—The Maine Massacre. 1980. pap. 2.50 o.s.i (*0-671-82865-7*, Pocket) Simon & Schuster.

—The Maine Massacre. 1996. 231p. pap. 12.00 (*1-56947-064-2*) Soho Pr., Inc.

—The Mind-Murders. 1988. 208p. mass mkt. 3.95 o.s.i (*0-345-34495-2*) Ballantine Bks.

—The Mind-Murders, 001. 1981. 9.95 o.p. (*0-395-30544-6*) Houghton Mifflin Co.

—The Mind-Murders. 1984. mass mkt. 3.95 o.s.i (*0-671-54065-3*, Pocket) Simon & Schuster.

—The Mind-Murders. 1997. 224p. pap. 12.00 (*1-56947-092-8*) Soho Pr., Inc.

—Outsider in Amsterdam. 1986. mass mkt. 3.50 o.s.i (*0-345-33126-5*) Ballantine Bks.

—Outsider in Amsterdam. 1976. ix, 245p. (*0-434-85920-6*, Butterworth-Heinemann) Elsevier Science & Technology Bks.

—Outsider in Amsterdam, 001. 1975. 256p. 6.95 o.p. (*0-395-20705-3*) Houghton Mifflin Co.

—Outsider in Amsterdam. 1978. pap. 2.50 o.s.i (*0-671-43471-3*, Pocket) Simon & Schuster.

—Outsider in Amsterdam. 1994. 304p. pap. 12.00 (*1-56947-017-0*) Soho Pr., Inc.

—The Perfidious Parrot. 280p. 1998. (Amsterdam Cops Ser.: No. 14). pap. 12.00 (*1-56947-130-4*); 1997. 22.00 (*1-56947-102-9*) Soho Pr., Inc.

—The Rattle-Rat. 1986. mass mkt. 3.50 o.s.i (*0-345-32872-8*) Ballantine Bks.

—The Rattle-Rat. l.t. ed. 1986. 392p. 17.95 o.p. (*0-8161-4121-5*, Macmillan Reference USA) Gale Group.

—The Rattle-Rat. 1985. 14.95 o.s.i (*0-394-54710-1*, Pantheon) Knopf Publishing Group.

—The Rattle-Rat. 1997. 294p. pap. 12.00 (*1-56947-103-7*) Soho Pr., Inc.

—The Sergeant's Cat. l.t. ed. 1991. 8.95 o.p. (*0-7451-9503-2*, 78) BBC Audiobooks America.

—The Streetbird. 1983. 288p. 13.95 o.p. (*0-399-12808-5*, G. P. Putnam's Sons) Penguin Putnam Bks. for Young Readers.

—The Streetbird. 1985. mass mkt. 3.50 o.s.i (*0-671-47521-5*, Pocket) Simon & Schuster.

—The Streetbird. 1997. 288p. pap. 12.00 (*1-56947-093-6*) Soho Pr., Inc.

—Tumbleweed. 1987. mass mkt. 3.50 o.s.i (*0-345-33127-3*) Ballantine Bks.

—Tumbleweed. l.t. ed. 1978. lib. bdg. 11.50 o.p. (*0-8161-6569-6*, Macmillan Reference USA) Gale Group.

—Tumbleweed, 001. 1976. 6.95 o.p. (*0-395-24352-1*) Houghton Mifflin Co.

—Tumbleweed. 1994. (Crime Ser.). 224p. pap. 12.00 (*1-56947-018-9*) Soho Pr., Inc.

Vernon, Claire. The Doctor Had a Double. l.t. ed. 2002. 183p. pap. 23.95 (*0-7862-3938-7*) Gale Group.

Vreeland, Susan. Girl in Hyacinth Blue. 1999. 242p. 17.50 (*1-878448-90-0*); 150p. 17.50 o.p. MacMurray & Beck, Inc.

—Girl in Hyacinth Blue. 2000. (Illus.). 256p. pap. 13.00 (*0-14-029628-X*) Penguin Group (USA) Inc.

—Girl in Hyacinth Blue. l.t. ed. 2000. (Basic Ser.). 227p. 28.95 (*0-7862-2440-1*) Thorndike Pr.

—Girl in Hyacinth Blue. 2000. 17.05 (*0-606-20671-X*) Turtleback Bks.

Weil, Grete. Last Trolley from Beethovenstraat. Barrett, John, tr. from GER. 1997. (Verba Mundi Ser.). 176p. 22.95 (*1-56792-031-4*) Godine, David R. Pub.

## ANGRIA (IMAGINARY PLACE)—FICTION

Bronte, Charlotte. Charlotte Bronte's High Life in Verdopolis: A Story from the Glass Town Saga. Alexander, Christine, ed. 1996. (Illus.). 320p. (*0-7123-0408-8*) Univ. of Toronto Pr.

—An Edition of the Early Writings of Charlotte Bronte: The Rise of Angria, 1834-1835. Alexander, Christine, ed. Vol. I: 1826-1832. 1986. 408p. text 100.00 o.p. (*0-631-12988-X*); Vol. II, Pts. 1. 1991. (Edition of the Early Writings of Charlotte Bronte: Vol. II). 448p. 241.95 (*0-631-12989-8*); Vol. II, Pts. 1. 1991. 448p. o.p. (*0-631-17942-9*) Blackwell Publishing.

—Mina Laury. 1996. (Classic Ser.). 64p. pap. 0.95 o.p. (*0-14-600192-3*) Penguin Group (USA) Inc.

Collins, Robert G., comment & intro. The Hand of the Arch-Sinner: Two Angrian Chronicles of Branwell Bronte, a Reader's Edition. 1993. (Illus.). 300p. (C). text 49.95 o.p. (*0-19-812258-6*, Clarendon Press) Oxford Univ. Pr., Inc.

## ANTARCTICA—FICTION

Alexander, Caroline. Mrs. Chippy's Last Expedition: The Newly Discovered Journal of Shackleton's Polar-Bound Cat. 1997. (Illus.). 176p. 16.00 (*0-06-017546-X*) HarperCollins Pubs.

—Mrs. Chippy's Last Expedition: The Remarkable Journal of Shackleton's Polar-Bound Cat. l.t. ed. 2000. (Wheeler Large Print Book Ser.). (Illus.). xviii, 169p. (J). pap. 23.95 (*1-56895-847-1*, Wheeler Publishing, Inc.) Gale Group.

—Mrs. Chippy's Last Expedition: The Remarkable Journal of Shackleton's Polar-Bound Cat. 1999. (Illus.). 176p. pap. 11.95 (*0-06-093261-9*, Perennial) HarperTrade.

—Mrs. Chippy's Last Expedition: The Remarkable Journal of Shakleton's Polar-Bound Cat. unabr. ed. 1998. audio 26.00 (*0-7887-2003-1*, 95390E7) Recorded Bks., LLC.

Arthur, Elizabeth. Antarctic Navigation. 1996. 816p. pap. 14.00 o.s.i (*0-345-40207-3*) Ballantine Bks.

Batchelor, John Calvin. The Birth of the People's Republic of Antarctica. 1995. 416p. pap. 14.00 o.p. (*0-8050-3786-1*, Owl Bks.) Holt, Henry & Co.

Billing, Graham. Forbush & the Penguins. 1995. 168p. (Orig.). pap. 24.95 (*0-908812-40-X*) Canterbury Univ. Pr. NZL. *Dist:* Accents Pubns. Service, Inc.

Charbonneau, Louis. The Ice: A Novel of Antarctica. 1991. 19.95 o.p. (*1-55611-177-0*) Fine, Donald I. Bks.

—The Ice: A Novel of Antarctica. 1993. 320p. reprint ed. mass mkt. 5.50 (*0-671-74714-2*, Pocket) Simon & Schuster.

Cobb, James H. Choosers of the Slain. l.t. ed. 1996. lib. bdg. 24.95 (*1-57490-076-5*, Beeler Large Print Bks.) Beeler, Thomas T. Publisher.

—Choosers of the Slain. 1997. 352p. mass mkt. 6.99 o.s.i (*0-425-16053-X*) Berkley Publishing Group.

—Choosers of the Slain. 1996. 352p. 23.95 o.p. (*0-399-14197-9*, G. P. Putnam's Sons) Penguin Group (USA) Inc.

Dietrich, Bill. Ice Reich. 1998. 375p. 25.00 o.p. (*0-446-52339-9*) Warner Bks., Inc.

Dietrich, William. Dark Winter. 2001. (Illus.). 400p. 24.95 o.p. (*0-446-52675-4*) Warner Bks., Inc.

Farren, Mick. Underland. 2002. (Renquist Quartet Ser.). 496p. 27.95 (*0-7653-0321-3*, Tor Bks.) Doherty, Tom Assocs., LLC.

Francis, Dick. Enquiry. unabr. ed. 2000. audio compact disk 49.99 (*0-7861-9933-4*, z1736) Blackstone Audio Bks., Inc.

Harrison, Payne. Thunder of Erebus. 1993. mass mkt. 5.99 o.s.i (*0-8041-0877-3*, Ivy Bks.) Ballantine Bks.

Herbert, Marie. Winter of the White Seal. 1983. 256p. mass mkt. 3.50 o.p. (*0-451-12061-2*, AE2061, Signet Bks.) NAL.

Jenkin-Pearce, Susie. Peppi & Poppy Search for Santa. 1988. (Illus.). 32p. (J). (gr. k-3). 0.90 o.p. (*0-8120-4129-1*) Barron's Educational Series, Inc.

Keegan, Claire. Antarctica. 1999. 224p. pap. (*0-571-19712-4*) Faber & Faber, Inc.

Keneally, Thomas. Victim of the Aurora. 1978. 219p. 7.95 o.p. (*0-15-193631-5*) Harcourt Trade Pubs.

Marshall, James Vance. White-Out. (Illus.). 256p. 2002. pap. 13.00 (*1-56947-277-7*); 2000. 23.00 (*1-56947-224-6*) Soho Pr., Inc.

—White-Out. l.t. ed. 2001. (Adventure Ser.). 384p. 28.95 (*0-7862-3320-6*) Thorndike Pr.

Mayer, Bob. Eternity Base: A Dave Riley Novel. 1996. 320p. 21.95 o.p. (*0-89141-509-2*, Presidio Pr.) Ballantine Bks.

Morris, M. E. The Icemen: A Novel of Antarctica. 1988. 336p. 17.95 o.p. (*0-89141-281-6*, Presidio Pr.) Ballantine Bks.

—The Icemen: A Novel of Antarctica. 1989. mass mkt. 4.95 o.p. (*0-671-67869-8*, Pocket) Simon & Schuster.

Preston, Douglas J. & Child, Lincoln. The Ice Limit: News Reports on Recent Mysterious Events in the Antarctic Sea. l.t. ed. 2000. (G. K. Hall Core Ser.). 608p. 29.95 (*0-7838-9194-6*, Macmillan Reference USA) Gale Group.

—The Ice Limit: News Reports on Recent Mysterious Events in the Antarctic Sea. 2000. (Illus.). 464p. 25.95 (*0-446-52587-1*); 2001. 512p. reprint ed. mass mkt. 7.99 (*0-446-61023-2*) Warner Bks., Inc.

Reeves-Stevens, Garfield & Reeves-Stevens, Judith. Icefire. 1999. (Illus.). 736p. reprint ed. mass mkt. 7.99 (*0-671-01403-X*, Pocket) Simon & Schuster.

Reeves-Stevens, Judith & Reeves-Stevens, Garfield. Icefire. 1998. (Illus.). 384p. 23.00 (*0-671-01402-1*, Atria) Simon & Schuster.

Reilly, Matthew. Ice Station. 2001. audio (*1-74030-109-9*, 500321) Bolinda Publishing Pty, Ltd.

—Ice Station. (Illus.). 2000. 544p. reprint ed. mass mkt. 6.99 (*0-312-97123-0*, St. Martin's Paperbacks); 2nd ed. 1999. 390p. 24.95 (*0-312-20551-1*) St. Martin's Pr.

—Ice Station. 2000. (GER.). 448p. (*3-548-25045-9*) Ullstein-Taschenbuch-Verlag DEU. *Dist:* International Bk. Import Service, Inc.

Reiss, Bob. Purgatory Road. l.t. ed. 1996. pap. 23.95 (*1-56895-384-4*, Wheeler Publishing, Inc.) Gale Group.

—Purgatory Road. 1996. 240p. 22.00 o.p. (*0-684-81119-7*, Simon & Schuster) Simon & Schuster.

Robinson, Kim Stanley. Antarctica. 1999. 672p. reprint ed. mass mkt. 6.99 (*0-553-57402-7*) Bantam Bks.

—Antarctica. 1999. 13.04 (*0-606-19270-0*) Turtleback Bks.

Rucker, Mike. Terry & The South Pole Breakdown. pap. (*0-615-11379-6*) Univ. Editions.

Savile, Frank. Beyond the Great South Wall: The Secret of the Antarctic. Reginald, R. & Melville, Douglas, eds. 1978. (Lost Race & Adult Fantasy Ser.). (Illus.). reprint ed. lib. bdg. 31.95 (*0-405-11006-5*) Ayer Co. Pubs., Inc.

—Beyond the Great South Wall: The Secret of the Antarctic. 1996. reprint ed. spiral bd. 22.05 (*0-7873-0741-6*) Health Research.

Willingham, Bess. The Smuggler's Bride. abr. ed. 2000. (Zebra Regency Romance Ser.). 256p. mass mkt. 4.99 o.s.i (*0-8217-6690-2*, Zebra Bks.) Kensington Publishing Corp.

## APPALACHIAN MOUNTAINS—FICTION

Baldacci, David. Wish You Well. l.t. ed. 2000. 624p. 24.95 (*0-375-43091-1*) Random Hse. Large Print.

—Wish You Well. 2001. 368p. E-Book 14.95 (*0-7595-0012-6*); 2000. 416p. pap. 16.00 (*0-446-67759-0*); 2001. 384p. reprint ed. mass mkt. 7.99 (*0-446-61010-0*) Warner Bks., Inc.

Baldwin, Mart. Kill the Benefactor. 1995. 336p. pap. 7.95 (*1-57087-166-3*) Professional Pr.

—Kill the Benefactor. 2000. 312p. reprint ed. pap. 16.00 (*1-892323-13-3*) Vivisphere Publishing.

Best, Bill. The Great Appalachian Sperm Bank & Other Stories. 1986. (Illus.). 125p. (Orig.). pap. 6.95 (*0-935680-32-2*) Kentucke Imprints.

Breeding, Robert L. Appalachian Haven. 1981. (Tennessee History Ser.). 280p. pap. 10.95 (*1-880258-00-5*) Thriftecon Publications.

Cassell, Robert P. Echoes of Love: An Appalachian Story. 1993. 160p. (Orig.). pap. 12.95 (*1-881692-08-6*) Trillium Pr.

Corderman, Esther B. Out of the Night. 1994. 340p. pap. 12.95 (*0-87012-519-2*) McClain Printing Co.

Ehle, John. The Road. 1998. (Appalachian Echoes Ser.). 416p. reprint ed. pap. 19.95 (*1-57233-016-3*) Univ. of Tennessee Pr.

—The Winter People. 1982. pap. 3.95 o.p. (*0-440-39770-7*) Dell Publishing.

—The Winter People. 4th ed. 1999. 272p. reprint ed. pap. 14.95 (*1-878086-74-X*) Down Home Pr.

—The Winter People. 1982. 256p. 13.95 o.p. (*0-06-014930-2*); 1989. 320p. reprint ed. mass mkt. 4.95 o.p. (*0-06-080939-6*, P 939, Perennial) HarperTrade.

Elliott, Carter. Riding a Blue Horse. 2003. (Otto Penzler Book Ser.). 224p. 24.00 (*0-7867-1181-7*, Carroll & Graf Pubs.) Avalon Publishing Group.

Fisher, Ben C. Mountain Preacher Stories: Laughter among the Trumpets. 1990. 76p. (Orig.). pap. 5.95 (*0-913239-64-X*) Appalachian Consortium Pr.

Francisco, Edward. The Dealmaker. 2002. 280p. 29.95 (*0-9679527-2-7*) WP.

Garrett, Annie. Because I Wanted You. l.t. ed. 1997. lib. bdg. 21.95 (*1-57490-105-2*, Beeler Large Print Bks.) Beeler, Thomas T. Publisher.

—Because I Wanted You. 1998. (Because I Wanted You Ser.: Vol. 1). 240p. pap. 5.99 (*0-312-96659-8*, St. Martin's Paperbacks); 1997. 226p. 18.95 (*0-312-15427-5*); 1997. 18.95 (*0-312-15473-9*) St. Martin's Pr.

Giancola, Anthony. Appalachian Homestead: By Marge Lawsin. 1992. 50p. pap. text 4.95 (*1-881692-02-7*) Trillium Pr.

Grubb, Davis. Fools' Parade. 2001. (Appalachian Echoes Ser.). 336p. reprint ed. pap. 19.95 (*1-57233-114-3*) Univ. of Tennessee Pr.

Hankla, Cathryn. A Blue Moon in Poorwater. 1988. 288p. 17.95 o.p. (*0-89919-534-2*) Houghton Mifflin Co.

—A Blue Moon in Poorwater. 1998. (Virginia Bookshelf Ser.). 288p. reprint ed. pap. 14.95 (*0-8139-1846-4*) Univ. Pr. of Virginia.

Hill, Chip. The Invisible Wilderness. 1993. 140p. (Orig.). pap. 6.99 o.p. (*1-56043-657-3*) Destiny Image Pubs.

Hirsohn, Don. The Appalachian Tale: The Adventures of the Poetry Man. 1986. (Illus.). 128p. (Orig.). pap. 5.00 (*0-942568-14-1*) Canyon Publishing Co.

Kingsolver, Barbara. Prodigal Summer. 2000. 464p. 26.00 (*0-06-019965-2*) HarperCollins Pubs.

—Prodigal Summer. 2001. 464p. pap. 14.00 (*0-06-095903-7*, Perennial) HarperTrade.

Lyon, George Ella. With a Hammer for My Heart. 1997. (Illus.). 224p. (J). pap. 21.95 o.p. (*0-7894-2460-6*) Dorling Kindersley Publishing, Inc.

—With a Hammer for My Heart. 1999. 224p. reprint ed. pap. 12.00 (*0-380-73217-3*, Avon Bks.) Morrow/Avon.

Marshall, Catherine. Christy. abr. ed. 1995. pap. 19.95 o.p. incl. audio (*1-55927-324-0*) Audio Renaissance.

—Christy. 1994. reprint ed. lib. bdg. 35.95 (*1-56849-309-6*) Buccaneer Bks., Inc.

—Christy. 1967. text 14.95 o.p. (*0-07-040605-7*) McGraw-Hill Cos., The.

—Christy. 1976. 512p. mass mkt. 6.99 (*0-380-00141-1*, Avon Bks.) Morrow/Avon.

—Christy. 1968. 348p. mass mkt. 4.50 o.p. (*0-8007-8008-6*); 1995. (Illus.). 160p. (J). (gr. 6-9). 10.99 o.p. (*0-8007-1708-2*) Revell, Fleming H. Co.

—Christy. 1968. 13.04 (*0-606-00470-X*) Turtleback Bks.

—Christy. 2001. 512p. pap. 12.99 (*0-310-24163-4*) Zondervan.

—Christy: The Collectors Edition. 2001. (Illus.). 480p. (gr. 13 up). 24.99 (*0-8007-9290-4*) Chosen Bks.

—Christy: The Collectors Edition. l.t. ed. 1987. 721p. 20.95 o.p. (*0-8161-4186-X*, Macmillan Reference USA) Gale Group.

—Christy: The Young Readers Edition. 2001. (Illus.). 160p. (J). (gr. 6-9). 9.99 (*0-8007-9293-9*) Chosen Bks.

—Christy Books. 1995. pap. 19.99 (*0-8499-3947-X*) W Publishing Group.

—Christy's Choice. 1996. (Christy Fiction Ser.: No. 6). 128p. (Orig.). (J). (gr. 4-8). mass mkt. 4.99 (*0-8499-3919-4*) Nelson, Tommy.

—The Macmillan International Film Encyclopedia. 4th ed. 2001. 1520p. reprint ed. pap. 12.99 (*0-333-90690-X*, HarperResource) HarperInformation.

Morgan, Robert. Gap Creek: The Story of a Marriage. 2000. (Oprah's Book Club Ser.). 324p. tchr. ed. 22.95 (*1-56512-296-8*) Algonquin Bks. of Chapel Hill.

—Gap Creek: The Story of a Marriage. abr. ed. 2000. 24.95 (*1-56511-386-1*) HighBridge Co.

—Gap Creek: The Story of a Marriage. unabr. ed. 2000. audio 76.00 Recorded Bks., LLC.

—Gap Creek: The Story of a Marriage. 2000. 336p. pap. 14.00 (*0-7432-0363-1*); pap. 7.99 (*0-7432-0334-8*) Simon & Schuster. (Touchstone).

—Gap Creek: The Story of a Marriage. l.t. ed. 2000. (Basic Ser.). 488p. 30.95 (*0-7862-2545-9*) Thorndike Pr.

—The Hinterlands. 1994. 378p. tchr. ed. 21.95 o.p. (*1-56512-021-3*) Algonquin Bks. of Chapel Hill.

—The Hinterlands. 1999. 335p. reprint ed. pap. 17.95 (*0-89587-178-5*) Blair, John F. Pub.

—The Hinterlands. audio o.p. National Humanities Ctr.

Nahai, Gina B. Sunday's Silence. 2001. 320p. 24.00 (*0-15-100627-X*) Harcourt Trade Pubs.

—Sunday's Silence. 2003. 320p. pap. 14.00 (*0-7434-5945-8*, Washington Square Pr.) Simon & Schuster.

Noble, Diane. Kingdom Come. l.t. ed. 2001. 257p. 24.95 (*0-7862-3461-X*) Thorndike Pr.

Pyle, Jack R. The Sound of Distant Thunder: An Appalachian Novel. 1998. 228p. 13.95 (*0-9663666-2-X*) AAcorn Bks.

Rash, Ron. One Foot in Eden. 2002. 240p. 21.95 (*0-9708972-5-1*) Novello Festival Pr.

Richardson, Joyce. On Sunday Creek. 2000. 206p. pap. 12.00 (*0-9700935-0-0*) Dirty Creek Pubns. Co. Ltd.

Russell, E. S. Death of a Cloudwalker. 1991. 192p. 18.95 (*0-8027-5784-7*) Walker & Co.

Wilson, John M. To See the Other Side: A Novel of an Appalachian Trail Thru-Hike. 1998. (Illus.). 400p. pap. 14.95 (*0-9649394-5-2*) Paint Rock Publishing, Inc.

Young, Malone. Latchpins of the Lost Cove. 1987. (Appalachian Ser.). (Illus.). 216p. (Orig.). pap. 9.98 (*0-9625490-0-2*) Latchpins Pr.

**ARCTIC REGIONS—FICTION**

Barrett, Andrea. The Voyage of the Narwhal: A Novel. l.t. ed. pap. 30.00 (*0-7862-1752-9*, Macmillan Reference USA) Gale Group.

—The Voyage of the Narwhal: A Novel. 2000. pap. (*0-393-10269-6*); 1999. (Illus.). 400p. pap. 14.00 (*0-393-31950-4*); 1998. (Illus.). 416p. 24.95 o.p. (*0-393-04632-X*) Norton, W. W. & Co., Inc.

—The Voyage of the Narwhal: A Novel. unabr. ed. 1999. audio 80.00 (*0-7887-2921-7*, 95712E7); audio compact disk 99.00 Recorded Bks., LLC.

—The Voyage of the Narwhal: A Novel. l.t. ed. 1999. (Basic Ser.). 624p. 30.95 (*0-7862-1751-0*) Thorndike Pr.

Brown, Dan. Deception Point. 2003. 576p. 17.95 (*0-7434-9030-4*, Atria); 2002. E-Book 9.99 (*0-7434-7543-7*, Atria); 2001. 384p. 25.00 o.s.i (*0-671-02737-9*, Atria); 2002. 576p. reprint ed. mass mkt. 7.99 (*0-671-02738-7*, Pocket) Simon & Schuster.

Debenham, Frank. In the Arctic: Tales Told at Tea-Time. Debenham, Barbara, ed. & intro. by. 1998. pap. 82.50 (*1-85297-049-9*) Erskine Pr., The GBR. *Dist:* State Mutual Bk. & Periodical Service, Ltd.

Dudman, Clare. One Day the Ice Will Reveal All Its Dead. 2004. 416p. 25.95 (*0-670-03276-X*) Viking Penguin.

Edric, Robert. The Broken Lands: A Novel of Arctic Disaster. (Illus.). 2003. 352p. pap. 14.95 (*0-312-31113-3*, Saint Martin's Griffin); 2002. 384p. 24.95 (*0-312-28889-1*) St. Martin's Pr.

Houston, James. The Ice Master: A Novel of the Arctic. (Illus.). 384p. 1999. pap. 17.95 (*0-7710-4209-4*); 1998. 24.95 o.p. (*0-7710-4207-8*) McClelland & Stewart/Tundra Bks.

Jackson, Loretta & Britton, Vickie. Arctic Legacy. 1997. 192p. lib. bdg. 18.95 (*0-8034-9359-2*, Avalon Bks.) Bouregy, Thomas & Co., Inc.

Johnston, Wayne. The Navigator of New York: A Novel. 496p. 2003. pap. 15.95 (*1-4000-3109-5*); 2002. 27.95 (*0-385-50767-4*) Doubleday Publishing.

Koontz, Dean. Icebound. 1997. pap. 12.95 o.p. (*0-345-41947-2*); 1994. 416p. mass mkt. 7.99 o.s.i (*0-345-38435-0*) Ballantine Bks.

—Icebound. 2000. 416p. mass mkt. 7.99 (*0-553-58290-9*) Bantam Bks.

—Icebound. l.t. ed. 1995. pap. 19.00 o.s.i (*0-679-75942-5*) Random Hse., Inc.

Poyer, David. The Circle. 1993. 543p. mass mkt. 6.99 (*0-312-92964-1*, St. Martin's Paperbacks); 1992. 416p. 21.95 o.p. (*0-312-07671-1*) St. Martin's Pr.

Quick, Barbara. Northern Edge. 1990. 18.95 o.p. (*1-55611-173-8*) Fine, Donald I. Bks.

—Northern Edge. 1994. 224p. pap. 10.00 o.p. (*0-06-258521-5*, Perennial) HarperTrade.

Stebel, S. L. Spring Thaw. 1989. 252p. 17.95 (*0-8027-1068-9*) Walker & Co.

Vollmann, William T. The Rifles. 1995. (Seven Dreams Ser.: Vol. 6). 432p. pap. 13.95 (*0-14-017623-3*) Penguin Group (USA) Inc.

—The Rifles. 1994. (Seven Dreams Ser.: Vol. 6). (Illus.). 432p. 22.95 o.s.i (*0-670-84856-5*, Viking) Viking Penguin.

White, Robin. Typhoon. 2004. 448p. mass mkt. 7.99 (*0-515-13683-2*, Jove) Berkley Publishing Group.

—Typhoon. 2003. (Illus.). 400p. 24.95 (*0-399-14935-X*) Penguin Group (USA) Inc.

Wiebe, Rudy. A Discovery of Strangers. 1995. 336p. pap. 13.95 (*0-394-28083-0*) Knopf, Alfred A. Inc.

Wilson, John. North with Franklin: The Lost Journals of James Fitzjames. 2002. (Illus.). 308p. pap. (*1-55041-630-8*) Fitzhenry & Whiteside, Ltd.

—North with Franklin: The Lost Journals of James Fitzjames. 1999. (Illus.). xix, 308p. 19.95 (*1-55041-406-2*) Fitzhenry & Whiteside, Ltd. CAN. *Dist:* General Distribution Services, Inc.

**ARDEL (IMAGINARY PLACE)—FICTION**

Jensen, Kris. FreeMaster. 1990. (People of Ardel Ser.: 1). 288p. mass mkt. 3.95 o.p. (*0-88677-404-7*) DAW Bks., Inc.

—Healer. 1993. (People of Ardel Ser.: 3). 336p. (Orig.). mass mkt. 4.99 o.p. (*0-88677-570-1*) DAW Bks., Inc.

—Mentor. 1991. (People of Ardel Ser.: 2). 336p. (Orig.). mass mkt. 4.50 o.p. (*0-88677-464-0*) DAW Bks., Inc.

**ARGENTINA—FICTION**

Allende, Isabel. The Stories of Eva Luna. 1992. 384p. mass mkt. 7.99 (*0-553-57535-X*) Bantam Bks.

—The Stories of Eva Luna. Peden, Margaret Sayers, tr. l.t. ed. 1991. lib. bdg. 20.95 o.p. (*0-8161-5253-5*, Macmillan Reference USA) Gale Group.

—The Stories of Eva Luna. 1999. (Scribner Classics). 352p. 26.00 (*0-684-87359-1*, Scribner) Simon & Schuster.

Arlt, Roberto. Mad Toy. Aynesworth, Michele McKay, tr. from SPA. & intro. by. 2002. 120p. 54.95 (*0-8223-2911-5*); pap. 16.95 (*0-8223-2940-9*) Duke Univ. Pr.

Barragan, Nina. Losers & Keepers in Argentina. 2001. (Jewish Latin America Ser.). (Illus.). (*0-8263-2221-2*) Univ. of New Mexico Pr.

—Losers & Keepers in Argentina: A Work of Fiction. 2001. (Jewish Latin America Ser.). xv, 254p. pap. 19.95 (*0-8263-2222-0*) Univ. of New Mexico Pr.

Bioy Casares, Adolfo. The Dream of Heroes. 1988. 17.95 o.p. (*0-525-24687-8*, Dutton) Dutton/Plume.

—A Russian Doll & Other Stories. Levine, Suzanne J., tr. from SPA. 1992. 128p. 22.95 (*0-8112-1211-4*); pap. 10.95 (*0-8112-1212-2*, NDP745) New Directions Publishing Corp.

Borinsky, Alicia. Mean Woman (Mina Cruel) Franzen, Cola, tr. & intro. by. 1993. (Latin American Women Writers Ser.: Vol. 2). 179p. (C). pap. 10.95 (*0-8032-6112-8*, Bison Bks.); text 50.00 (*0-8032-1234-8*) Univ. of Nebraska Pr.

Cortázar, Julio. Blow-Up: And Other Stories. Blackburn, Paul, tr. from SPA. 1985. 288p. pap. 13.00 (*0-394-72881-5*, RH8815, Pantheon) Knopf Publishing Group.

—We Love Glenda So Much & Other Tales. 1984. pap. 14.95 o.p. (*0-394-72297-3*, Vintage) Knopf Publishing Group.

Demitropulos, Libertad. River of Sorrows. Berg, Mary G., tr. from SPA. 2000. (Secret Weavers Ser.: Vol. 14). 147p. pap. 14.00 (*1-877727-88-1*) White Pine Pr.

Dunham, Donald Carl. Assignment Bucharest: An American Diplomat's View of the Communist Takeover of Romania. 2000. 200p. 39.95 (*973-9432-06-9*) Ctr. for Romanian Studies, The ROM. *Dist:* International Specialized Bk. Services.

Frank, Waldo D., ed. Tales from the Argentine. Brenner, Anita, tr. from SPA. 1977. (Short Story Index Reprint Ser.). (Illus.). 19.95 (*0-8369-3539-X*) Ayer Co. Pubs., Inc.

Gerchunoff, Alberto. Jewish Gauchos of the Pampas. de Pereda, Prudencio, tr. from SPA. 1998. (Jewish Latin America Ser.). xxx, 149p. pap. 18.95 (*0-8263-1767-7*) Univ. of New Mexico Pr.

Gombrowicz, Witold. Trans-Atlantyk. 1995. pap. 12.95 (*0-300-06503-5*) Yale Univ. Pr.

—Trans-Atlantyk. Karsov, Nina & Carroll, Frances, trs. 1994. 152p. (C). 35.00 (*0-300-05384-3*) Yale Univ. Pr.

Greene, Graham. The Honorary Consul. 2000. (Simon & Schuster Classic Editions). (Illus.). 288p. 25.00 (*0-684-87125-4*, Simon & Schuster) Simon & Schuster.

Griffin, W. E. B. Blood & Honor. 1997. (Honor Bound Ser.: No. 2). 736p. mass mkt. 7.99 (*0-515-12194-0*, Jove) Berkley Publishing Group.

—Blood & Honor, Pt. 1. unabr. ed. 1996. (Honor Bound Ser.: No. 2). audio 80.00 (*0-7366-3594-7*, 4246A ) Books on Tape, Inc.

—Blood & Honor. l.t. ed. 1997. (Honor Bound Ser.: No. 2). 1105p. 28.95 (*0-7838-8125-8*, Macmillan Reference USA) Gale Group.

—Blood & Honor. 2001. 34.95 (*0-399-14481-1*); 1996. (Honor Bound Ser.: No. 2). 480p. 24.95 o.s.i (*0-399-14190-1*, G. P. Putnam's Sons); Set. 1996. (Honor Bound Ser.: No. 2). 4p. 24.95 o.p. (*0-399-14226-6*, 694560, Putnam Berkley Audio) Penguin Group (USA) Inc.

—Honor Bound. 1994. (Honor Bound Ser.: No. 1). 560p. mass mkt. 7.99 (*0-515-11486-3*, Jove) Berkley Publishing Group.

—Honor Bound, Pt. 1. unabr. ed. (Honor Bound Ser.: No. 1). audio 64.00 (*0-7366-2732-4*, 3460-A/B) Books on Tape, Inc.

—Honor Bound. unabr. ed. 1994. (Honor Bound Ser.: No. 1). audio 130.55 (*1-56100-184-8*, 901, Unabridged Library Editions); audio 29.95 (*1-56100-558-4*, 138, Bookcassette) Brilliance Audio.

—Honor Bound. l.t. ed. 1994. (Honor Bound Ser.: No. 1). 25.95 o.p. (*1-56895-100-0*, Wheeler Publishing, Inc.) Gale Group.

—Honor Bound. abr. ed. 2000. (Honor Bound Ser.: No. 1). audio 7.95 (*1-57815-012-4*, 1002, Media Bks. Audio Publishing) Media Bks., L. L. C.

—Honor Bound. 1994. (Honor Bound Ser.: No. 1). 384p. 22.95 o.p. (*0-399-13862-5*, G. P. Putnam's Sons) Penguin Group (USA) Inc.

—Honor Bound. 22.95 o.s.i (*0-399-14117-0*) Putnam Publishing Group, The.

—Secret Honor. 2000. (Honor Bound Ser.: No. 3). 624p. mass mkt. 7.99 (*0-515-13009-5*, Jove) Berkley Publishing Group.

—Secret Honor. unabr. ed. 2000. (Honor Bound Ser.: No. 3). audio 104.00 Books on Tape, Inc.

—Secret Honor. l.t. ed. 2000. (Honor Bound Ser.: No. 3). 28.95 (*1-56895-868-4*, Wheeler Publishing, Inc.) Gale Group.

—Secret Honor. 2000. (Honor Bound Ser.: No. 3). 544p. 25.95 o.s.i (*0-399-14568-0*) Penguin Group (USA) Inc.

—Secret Honor. (Honor Bound Ser.: No. 3). 512p. (*0-7278-5504-2*) Severn Hse. Pubs., Ltd.

Hudson, William Henry. 3 Tales of the Pampas. 1979. (Illus.). 264p. pap. 5.95 o.p. (*0-916870-23-5*) Creative Arts Bk. Co.

Katz, Judith. The Escape Artist: A Novel. 1997. 288p. (C). pap. 12.95 (*1-56341-084-2*); lib. bdg. 26.95 (*1-56341-085-0*) Firebrand Bks.

Kozameh, Alicia. Steps under Water: A Novel. Davis, David E., tr. from SPA. 1996. (Illus.). 161p. (C). pap. 15.95 (*0-520-20388-7*); text 40.00 (*0-520-20387-9*) Univ. of California Pr.

Kozameh, Alicia & Davis, David E. Steps under Water: A Novel. 1996. E-Book 40.00 (*0-585-23251-2*) netLibrary, Inc.

Martinez, Tomas E. The Peron Novel. 1988. 320p. 19.95 o.s.i (*0-394-55838-3*, Pantheon) Knopf Publishing Group.

Medina, Enrique. Las Tumbas: The Tombs. 1992. (Library of World Literature in Translation: Vol. 4). 334p. text 20.00 (*0-8240-7436-X*) Garland Publishing, Inc.

Osorio, Elsa. My Name Is Light: A Novel. 2003. 388p. pap. 15.95 (*1-58234-182-6*) Bloomsbury Publishing.

Piglia, Ricardo. The Absent City. Waisman, Sergio, tr. from SPA. 2000. 136p. lib. bdg. 54.95 (*0-8223-2557-8*) Duke Univ. Pr.

—The Absent City. Waisman, Sergio, tr. from SPA. & intro. by. 2000. 136p. pap. 17.95 (*0-8223-2586-1*) Duke Univ. Pr.

—Artificial Respiration. Balderston, Daniel, tr. 1994. (Latin America in Translation Ser.). 240p. text 39.95 (*0-8223-1426-6*); pap. text 15.95 (*0-8223-1414-2*) Duke Univ. Pr.

Porter, Jane. In Dante's Debt. 2003. (Harlequin Presents Ser.: No. 2298). 192p. mass mkt. (*0-373-12298-5*, Harlequin Bks.) Harlequin Enterprises, Ltd.

Puig, Manuel. Heartbreak Tango: A Serial. 1987. pap. 7.95 o.p. (*0-525-48288-1*, Plume) Dutton/Plume.

—Heartbreak Tango: A Serial. Levine, Suzanne J., tr. 1975. pap. 2.45 o.p. (*0-525-47397-1*, Dutton) Dutton/Plume.

—Heartbreak Tango: A Serial. Levine, Suzanne J., tr. 1991. 22p. pap. 8.95 o.p. (*0-14-015346-2*, 0772-230, Penguin Bks.) Penguin Group (USA) Inc.

—Heartbreak Tango: A Serial. 1996. (Penguin Twentieth-Century Classics Ser.). 224p. pap. 11.95 o.s.i (*0-14-018997-1*, Viking) Viking Penguin.

Raspail, Jean. Who Will Remember the People . . . Leggatt, Jeremy, tr. from FRE. 1988. 213p. 18.95 o.p. (*0-916515-42-7*) Mercury Hse.

Renskoff, Eugenia. Different Flags. 2000. disk 6.95 (*0-87714-564-4*) Denlingers Pubs., Ltd.

Renskoff, Eugenia M. Different Flags. 2002. 264p. 15.95 (*0-87714-257-2*) Denlingers Pubs., Ltd.

Rios, Lara. Conquest. 2000. 28p. mass mkt. 3.99 o.s.i (*0-7860-1157-2*, Pinnacle Bks.) Kensington Publishing Corp.

Rivabella, Omar. Requiem for a Woman's Soul. 1986. 128p. 14.95 o.s.i (*0-394-54917-1*) Random Hse., Inc.

Saer, Juan J. The Investigation. 1999. (Illus.). 224p. pap. 14.99 (*1-85242-297-1*) Serpent's Tail Ltd. GBR. *Dist:* Consortium Bk. Sales & Distribution.

—Nobody Nothing Never. 1994. (Masks Ser.). 224p. pap. (*1-85242-273-4*) Serpent's Tail Ltd.

Singer, Isaac Bashevis. Scum. Schwartz, Rosaline Dukalsky, tr. 1992. 224p. reprint ed. pap. 9.95 o.p. (*0-452-26786-2*, Plume) Dutton/Plume.

—Scum. 2003. pap. 19.00 (*0-374-52907-8*) Farrar, Straus & Giroux.

—Scum. Schwartz, Rosaline Dukalsky, tr. 1991. 224p. 19.95 o.p. (*0-374-25511-3*) Farrar, Straus & Giroux.

—Scum. 1993. 5.99 o.p. (*0-517-10827-5*) Random Hse. Value Publishing.

—Scum. Schwartz, Rosaline Dukalsky, tr. 1996. (Penguin Twentieth-Century Classics Ser.). 224p. pap. 11.95 o.s.i (*0-14-018842-8*, Viking) Viking Penguin.

Sorrentino, Fernando. Sanitary Centennial & Selected Short Stories. Meehan, Thomas C., tr. from SPA. 1988. (Texas Pan American Ser.). 216p. 19.95 (*0-292-77608-X*) Univ. of Texas Pr.

Thornton, Lawrence. Imagining Argentina. 1991. 240p. pap. 14.95 (*0-553-34579-6*) Bantam Bks.

Toibin, Colm. The Story of the Night. 1998. 304p. pap. 13.00 (*0-8050-5825-7*, Owl Bks.); 1997. 312p. 23.00 o.s.i (*0-8050-5211-9*) Holt, Henry & Co.

—The Story of the Night. 1997. 320p. pap. 19.99 (*0-7710-8556-7*) McClelland & Stewart/Tundra Bks.

Unger, Douglas. Voices from Silence. 1995. 304p. text 21.95 o.p. (*0-312-13204-2*) St. Martin's Pr.

Valenzuela, Luisa. Clara. Labinger, Andrea G., tr. from SPA. 2000. (Series Discoveries Ser.). 159p. pap. 15.95 (*1-891270-09-5*) Latin American Literary Review Pr.

—Strange Things Happen Here: Twenty-Six Short Stories & a Novel. 1979. 264p. 9.95 o.p. (*0-15-185782-2*) Harcourt Trade Pubs.

Zech, Paul. The Birds in Langfoot's Belfry. Odio, Elena B., tr. 1994. (GERM Ser.). 180p. 55.00 (*1-57113-007-1*) Camden Hse.

**ARGYLLE (IMAGINARY PLACE)—FICTION**

Willey, Elizabeth. The Price of Blood & Honor. 1997. 445p. pap. text 5.99 o.p. (*0-8125-5049-8*); 1996. 480p. 25.95 o.p. (*0-312-85784-5*) Doherty, Tom Assocs., LLC. (Tor Bks.).

—A Sorcerer & a Gentleman. 1995. 416p. 23.95 o.p. (*0-312-85783-7*); Vol. 1. 1996. (Sorcerer & a Gentleman Ser.: Vol. 1). mass mkt. 5.99 (*0-8125-5047-1*) Doherty, Tom Assocs., LLC. (Tor Bks.).

—The Well-Favored Man: The Tale of the Sorcerer's Nephew. 448p. 1994. mass mkt. 4.99 (*0-8125-1988-4*); 1993. 23.95 o.p. (*0-312-85590-7*) Doherty, Tom Assocs., LLC. (Tor Bks.).

**ARIZONA—FICTION**

Adler, C. S. More Than a Horse. 1997. 192p. (J). (gr. 4-6). tchr. ed. 15.00 (*0-395-79769-1*, Clarion Bks.) Houghton Mifflin Co. Trade & Reference Div.

Allen, Garrison. Baseball Cat. (Big Mike Mystery Ser.: Vol. 4). 1998. 336p. mass mkt. 5.99 (*1-57566-309-0*); 1997. 304p. 18.95 o.s.i (*1-57566-183-7*) Kensington Publishing Corp.

—Desert Cat. 1994. 304p. mass mkt. 3.99 o.s.i (*0-8217-4503-4*, Zebra Bks.) Kensington Publishing Corp.

—Dinosaur Cat. (Big Mike Mystery Ser.). 336p. 1999. mass mkt. 5.99 o.s.i (*1-57566-426-7*); 1998. (J). 20.00 o.s.i (*1-57566-304-X*, Kensington Bks.) Kensington Publishing Corp.

—Movie Cat. 1999. (Big Mike Mystery Ser.). 304p. 20.00 o.s.i (*1-57566-413-5*) Kensington Publishing Corp.

—Royal Cat: A Big Mike Mystery. 1996. (Big Mike Mystery Ser.: Vol. 2). 304p. mass mkt. 4.99 o.s.i (*1-57566-045-8*); 1995. mass mkt. 16.95 o.s.i (*0-8217-4957-9*, Zebra Bks.) Kensington Publishing Corp.

—Stable Cat. 304p. 1997. mass mkt. 5.50 o.s.i (*1-57566-188-8*); 1996. pap. 18.95 o.p. (*1-57566-042-3*) Kensington Publishing Corp.

Amidon, Stephen. Thirst. 1993. 240p. o.p. (*0-88001-296-X*, Ecco) HarperTrade.

Axinn, Donald E. Spin. 1994. 328p. reprint ed. pap. 11.95 (*1-55970-250-8*) Arcade Publishing, Inc.

—Spin. 1991. 256p. 19.95 (*0-88268-125-7*) Station Hill Pr.

Baldwin, Faith. Arizona Star. 1976. reprint ed. lib. bdg. 24.95 (*0-88411-601-8*) Amereon, Ltd.

Bass, Milton. The Broken-Hearted Detective. Isaacson, Dana, ed. 1994. 256p. (Orig.). mass mkt. 4.99 (*0-671-74243-4*, Pocket) Simon & Schuster.

Berger, Edward F. Spirit of the Sycamore. 2001. 503p. pap. 24.95 (*1-58500-351-4*) 1stBooks Library.

Berrington, Patricia. The Famous Rose Callahan. 1997. 485p. lthr. 27.95 (*0-9658379-0-4*) Silver Rose Productions.

Bjorkquist, Elena D. Suffer Smoke. 1996. 202p. pap. 11.95 o.p. (*1-55885-168-2*) Arte Publico Pr.

Blair, Kerry. Closing In: A Novel. 2002. (Illus.). 280p. 14.95 (*1-59156-012-8*) Covenant Communications.

Bly, Stephen A. Son of an Arizona Legend. 1994. (Stuart Brannon Western Ser.: Vol. 6). 192p. pap. 8.99 (*0-89107-770-7*) Crossway Bks.

—Son of an Arizona Legend. l.t. ed. 1996. (Western Ser.). 242p. 19.95 o.p. (*0-7838-1783-5*, Macmillan Reference USA) Gale Group.

Borthwick, J. S. Dude on Arrival: A Christmas Mystery. 1992. 306p. mass mkt. 6.50 (*0-312-92955-2*, St. Martin's Paperbacks); 1991. 320p. 19.95 o.p. (*0-312-06341-5*, Saint Martin's Minotaur) St. Martin's Pr.

Boswell, Robert. Crooked Hearts. 1994. 208p. reprint ed. pap. 13.00 o.p. (*0-06-097586-5*, Perennial) HarperTrade.

—Crooked Hearts. 1987. 17.95 o.s.i (*0-394-55706-9*) Knopf, Alfred A. Inc.

Boxleitner, Bruce. Frontier Earth. 2001. (Babylon 5 Ser.). 336p. reprint ed. mass mkt. 6.99 o.s.i (*0-441-00794-5*) Ace Bks.

—Frontier Earth: A Novel. 1999. 336p. 21.95 o.s.i (*0-441-00589-6*) Ace Bks.

—Frontier Earth: Searcher. 2001. 336p. 23.95 o.s.i (*0-441-00799-6*) Ace Bks.

Brooksby, L. J. Queen of the Strip. 2000. 240p. pap. 14.95 (*0-88739-234-2*) Creative Arts Bk. Co.

Browning, Sinclair. The Last Song Dogs. 1999. (Trade Ellis Mysteries Ser.). 288p. mass mkt. 5.50 (*0-553-57940-1*) Bantam Bks.

Callahan, John. Kincaid. 2001. 187p. (*0-7838-9417-1*, Macmillan Reference USA) Gale Group.

Carroll, Jenny. Shadowland. E-Book 4.99 (*1-58945-553-3*) Adobe Systems, Inc.

Champlin, Tim. Colt Lightning. 2002. 176p. 19.00 (*0-7540-8194-X*, Gunsmoke) BBC Audiobooks America.

—Colt Lightning. l.t. ed. 1995. (Western Ser.). 242p. 18.95 (*0-7862-0029-4*) Thorndike Pr.

—Shadow Catcher. l.t. ed. 2001. 273p. 24.95 (*0-7838-9494-5*, Macmillan Reference USA) Gale Group.

—The White Lights Roar: A Western Story. 2003. 246p. 25.95 (*0-7862-3807-0*, Five Star) Gale Group.

Clarke, Jaime. We're So Famous. 2001. 185p. pap. 14.95 (*1-58234-113-3*) Bloomsbury Publishing.

Cole, David. The Killing Maze. 2001. 336p. mass mkt. 6.50 (*0-06-101395-1*, Avon Bks.) Morrow/Avon.

—Stalking Moon. 2002. 304p. mass mkt. 6.50 (*0-380-81970-8*, Avon Bks.) Morrow/Avon.

Cook, Will. Temporary Duty. l.t. ed. 2002. lib. bdg. 26.95 (*1-58547-102-X*, Western) Ctr. Point Large Print.

—The Wranglers. 1999. 241 p. (*0-7540-3540-9*); (*0-7540-3539-5*) BBC Audiobooks America.

—The Wranglers. l.t. ed. 1999. (Nightingale Ser.). 248p. pap. 21.95 (*0-7838-0356-7*) Thorndike Pr.

Cramer, Rebecca. Mission to Sonora. 1998. 298p. pap. 10.95 (*1-881542-50-5*) Book World, Inc.

—View from Frog Mountain. Date not set. 10.95 (*1-881542-63-7*) Book World, Inc.

Cummings, Jack. The Last Lawmen. 1994. 177p. 19.95 (*0-8027-4143-6*) Walker & Co.

—Once a Legend. 1992. 224p. reprint ed. mass mkt. 3.50 o.p. (*1-55817-650-0*, Pinnacle Bks.) Kensington Publishing Corp.

—Once a Legend. 1988. 16.95 o.p. (*0-8027-4075-8*) Walker & Co.

Cunningham, Chet. Bloody Gold: Jim Steel. l.t. ed. 1995. (Large Print Western Ser.). 216p. pap. 17.95 o.p. (*0-7838-1239-6*, Macmillan Reference USA) Gale Group.

Dailey, J. R. The Yellow Ribbon Snake. 2000. 144p. pap. 12.00 (*1-880284-37-5*) Daniel, John & Co., Pubs.

Dawson, Peter. The Outlaw of Longbow. 1981. 160p. pap. 1.95 o.p. (*0-553-14997-0*) Bantam Bks.

De la Garza, Phyllis. Bounty Hunter's Daughter. 2000. 256p. mass mkt. 4.50 (*0-8439-4741-1*, Leisure Bks.) Dorchester Publishing Co., Inc.

—Bounty Hunter's Daughter. 1998. (Five Star Western Ser.). 248p. 19.95 (*0-7862-0996-8*, Five Star) Gale Group.

De la Garza, Phyllis, et al. Bounty Hunter's Daughter. l.t. ed. 1999. (Western Ser.). 368p. 21.95 o.p. (*0-7862-1035-4*) Thorndike Pr.

Dengler, Sandy. Fatal Fishes. 1942. (Mirage Mysteries Ser.: No. 5). (Illus.). o.p. (*1-56476-324-2*) Cook Communications Ministries.

—Gila Monster. 1994. (Mirage Mysteries Ser.: No. 4). 276p. (Orig.). pap. 9.99 (*1-56476-238-6*, 6-3238) Cook Communications Ministries.

—The Last Dinosaur. 1994. (Mirage Mysteries Ser.). 276p. (Orig.). pap. 9.99 (*1-56476-235-1*, 6-3235) Cook Communications Ministries.

Edson, J. T. Arizona Range War. 1996. 192p. mass mkt. 4.99 o.s.i (*0-440-22217-6*) Dell Publishing.

—Arizona Range War. l.t. ed. 1997. (Large Print Bks.). pap. 23.95 (*1-56895-412-3*, Wheeler Publishing, Inc.) Gale Group.

Ellis, Scott. The Borzoi Control. 1988. 320p. pap. 3.95 o.p. (*0-8125-0239-6*, Tor Bks.) Doherty, Tom Assocs., LLC.

—The Borzoi Control. 1986. 320p. 16.95 o.p. (*0-312-09309-8*) St. Martin's Pr.

Estleman, Loren D. Bloody Season, Set. unabr. ed. 1999. audio 54.95 (*0-7927-2304-X*, CSL193, Chivers Sound Library) BBC Audiobooks America.

—Bloody Season. 1989. mass mkt. 3.95 o.s.i (*0-553-27494-5*) Bantam Bks.

—Bloody Season. 1999. 256p. mass mkt. 5.99 o.s.i (*0-515-12531-8*, Jove) Berkley Publishing Group.

Feldman, Ron & McPherson, M. Zigzag Canyon: The Legend of Gold Gulch. 1994. 288p. pap. 14.95 (*0-86534-212-1*) Sunstone Pr.

Finney, Charles G. The Circus of Dr. Lao. 1993. reprint ed. lib. bdg. 18.95 (*0-89968-402-5*, Lightyear Pr.) Buccaneer Bks., Inc.

—The Circus of Dr. Lao. 1976. pap. 3.95 o.p. (*0-380-00750-9*, 36368, Avon Bks.) Morrow/Avon.

—The Circus of Dr. Lao. 1961. pap. 1.25 o.p. (*0-670-00082-5*) Penguin Group (USA) Inc.

—The Circus of Dr. Lao. 2002. (Bison Frontiers of Imagination Ser.). (Illus.). 157p. pap. 12.95 (*0-8032-6907-2*, Bison Bks.) Univ. of Nebraska Pr.

Finney, Charles G. & Hoagland, Edward. The Circus of Dr. Lao. 1983. 128p. pap. 3.95 o.p. (*0-394-71617-5*, Vintage) Knopf Publishing Group.

Fodor's Travel Publications, Inc. Staff. Fodor's Arizona 2002: The Guide for All Budgets, Updated Every Year, with a Pullout Map & Color Photos. 2001. (Illus.). 352p. pap. 17.95 o.s.i (*0-676-90146-8*) Fodor's Travel Pubns.

Foster, Nicole. Hallie's Hero. 2003. (Harlequin Historicals Ser.: No. 642). 304p. mass mkt. (*0-373-29242-2*, Harlequin Bks.) Harlequin Enterprises, Ltd.

Gerard, Philip. Desert Kill. 1994. 270p. 23.00 o.p. (*0-688-12641-3*, Morrow, William & Co.) Morrow/Avon.

Gottlieb, Samuel H. Overbooked in Arizona. (Illus.). 112p. 1995. 20.00 (*0-9639966-1-4*); 1994. pap. 9.95 (*0-9639966-0-6*) Camelback Gallery.

Greene, Jennifer. Arizona Heat. 1995. 187p. per. (*0-373-05966-3*, 1-05966-6, Silhouette) Harlequin Enterprises, Ltd.

Greenwood, T. Nearer Than the Sky. 2000. 306p. 23.95 (*0-312-26503-4*) St. Martin's Pr.

Grey, Zane. The Desert Crucible: A Western Story. 2003. 344p. 25.95 (*0-7862-3784-8*, Five Star) Gale Group.

—The Desert Crucible: A Western Story. l.t. ed. 2004. 465p. 26.95 (*0-7862-3767-8*) Thorndike Pr.

—Tonto Basin: A Western Story. 2004. (*1-59414-050-2*, Five Star) Gale Group.

—Wanderer of the Wasteland. 28.95 (*0-88411-660-3*) Amereon, Ltd.

—Wanderer of the Wasteland. 1982. mass mkt. 2.95 (*0-671-45645-8*, Pocket) Simon & Schuster.

—Woman of the Frontier. 1998. (Western Ser.). 320p. 19.95 (*0-7862-1156-3*, Five Star) Gale Group.

—The Young Forester. Date not set. lib. bdg. 21.95 (*0-8488-1031-7*) Amereon, Ltd.

—The Young Forester. l.t. ed. 1998. 210p. (*0-7540-3491-7*) BBC Audiobooks America.

—The Young Forester. E-Book 2.49 (*1-58744-200-0*) Electric Umbrella Publishing.

—The Young Forester. l.t. ed. 1998. (Paperback Ser.). 211p. pap. 23.95 (*0-7838-0295-1*) Thorndike Pr.

Grove, Fred. Into the Far Mountains. l.t. ed. 2000. (Western Ser.). 408p. 21.95 (*0-7862-1339-6*) Thorndike Pr.

Gutcheon, Beth Richardson. Five Fortunes: A Novel. 416p. 1999. pap. 13.95 (*0-06-092995-2*, Perennial); 1998. 24.00 o.s.i (*0-06-017679-2*, HarperCollins) HarperTrade.

Hannon, Steven M. Glen Canyon. 1997. (Illus.). x, 635p. 28.95 (*0-9655125-0-9*) Kokopelli Bks.

Harper, Brian. Blind Pursuit. 1997. 384p. mass mkt. 5.99 o.s.i (*0-451-18199-9*, Signet Bks.) NAL.

Harper, Richard. Death Raid. 1986. pap. 3.50 o.p. (*0-440-11685-6*) Dell Publishing.

Harris, Marian. Tuesday in Arizona. 1998. (Illus.). 32p. (J). (ps-3). 15.95 (*1-56554-233-9*) Pelican Publishing Co., Inc.

Hayes, J. M. The Grey Pilgrim, Vol. 27. 2000. (Missing Mysteries Ser.: Vol. 27). 246p. pap. 14.95 (*1-890208-50-7*) Poisoned Pen Pr.

Haywood, Gar Anthony. Going Nowhere Fast. 1995. 224p. mass mkt. 5.99 o.s.i (*0-425-15051-8*, Prime Crime) Berkley Publishing Group.

—Going Nowhere Fast. abr. ed. 1994. audio 16.95 o.p. (*1-56100-378-6*, 1312, Nova Audio Bks.); audio 57.25 o.p. (*1-56100-204-6*, 1222, Unabridged Library Editions); audio 23.95 o.p. (*1-56100-578-9*, 124, Bookcassette) Brilliance Audio.

—Going Nowhere Fast. abr. ed. 2000. audio 7.95 (*1-57815-010-8*, 1063, Media Bks. Audio Publishing) Media Bks., L. L. C.

—Going Nowhere Fast. 1994. 240p. 19.95 o.p. (*0-399-13917-6*, G. P. Putnam's Sons) Penguin Group (USA) Inc.

Heller, Jane. Crystal Clear. 1999. 384p. mass mkt. 5.99 (*1-57566-388-0*); 1998. 288p. 23.00 o.s.i (*1-57566-257-4*) Kensington Publishing Corp.

Henry, L. D. Terror at Hellhole. 1994. 168p. 18.95 o.p. (*0-87131-745-1*) Evans, M. & Co., Inc.

Hillerman, Tony. The Blessing Way. unabr. ed. 1993. audio 36.00 (*0-7366-2510-0*, 3266) Books on Tape, Inc.

—The Blessing Way. l.t. ed. 1992. (General Ser.). 304p. pap. 17.95 o.p. (*0-8161-5431-7*); lib. bdg. 20.95 o.p. (*0-8161-5430-9*) Gale Group. (Macmillan Reference USA).

—The Blessing Way. (Harper Novel of Suspense Ser.). 1970. 10.00 o.p. (*0-06-011896-2*); 1990. 304p. reprint ed. mass mkt. 6.99 (*0-06-100001-9*) HarperCollins Pubs.

—The Blessing Way. abr. ed. 1995. (Joe Leaphorn Mystery Ser.). 3p. audio 18.00 (*1-55994-160-X*, 394151, HarperAudio) HarperTrade.

—The Blessing Way. 1993. audio 39.80 (*1-56544-006-4*, 250020); audio Literate Ear, Inc.

—The Blessing Way. 1978. (gr. 7 up). pap. 2.95 o.p. (*0-380-39941-5*, Avon Bks.) Morrow/Avon.

—The Blessing Way. unabr. ed. 1990. (Joe Leaphorn Mystery Ser.: Vol. 1). audio 44.00 (*1-55690-058-9*, 90080E7) Recorded Bks., LLC.

—The Blessing Way. 1990. 12.55 (*0-606-16174-0*) Turtleback Bks.

—Coyote Waits. unabr. ed. 1990. audio 42.00 (*0-7366-1788-4*, 2625) Books on Tape, Inc.

—Coyote Waits. 1990. 292p. 75.00 o.p. (*0-06-016422-0*); 1990. 292p. 19.95 o.p. (*0-06-016370-4*); 1995. 3p. audio 18.00 o.s.i (*1-55994-198-7*, 390569, HarperAudio); 1990. pap. 19.95 o.p. (*0-06-016423-9*) HarperTrade.

—Coyote Waits. 1992. 368p. mass mkt. 6.99 (*0-06-109932-5*, HarperTorch) Morrow/Avon.

—Coyote Waits. 1990. audio 10.00 New Letters on Air.

—Coyote Waits. 1990. (J). 13.04 (*0-606-01125-0*) Turtleback Bks.

—Dance Hall of the Dead. abr. ed. 1986. audio 15.95 (*0-88690-127-8*, N20024, Audio Editions Bks. on Cassette) Audio Partners Publishing Corp.

—Dance Hall of the Dead. unabr. ed. 1994. audio 36.00 (*0-7366-2610-7*, 3352) Books on Tape, Inc.

—Dance Hall of the Dead. 1997. lib. bdg. 37.95 (*1-56849-695-8*) Buccaneer Bks., Inc.

—Dance Hall of the Dead. 2004. 224p. pap. 11.95 (*0-06-056374-5*); 1990. 272p. reprint ed. mass mkt. 6.99 (*0-06-100002-7*) HarperTrade. (Perennial).

—Dance Hall of the Dead. 1993. audio 37.20 (*1-56544-025-0*, 250021); audio Literate Ear, Inc.

—Dance Hall of the Dead. 1982. (YA). (gr. 9 up). mass mkt. 2.95 o.p. (*0-380-00217-5*, 60093-5, Avon Bks.) Morrow/Avon.

—Dance Hall of the Dead. unabr. ed. 1991. (Joe Leaphorn Mystery Ser.: Vol. 2). (YA). (gr. 10). audio 44.00 (*1-55690-134-8*, 91122E7) Recorded Bks., LLC.

—Dance Hall of the Dead. l.t. ed. (Paperback Bestsellers Ser.). 239p. 1994. pap. 20.95 (*0-8161-5433-3*); 1993. lib. bdg. 25.95 (*0-8161-5432-5*) Thorndike Pr.

—Dance Hall of the Dead. 1990. 12.55 (*0-606-16124-4*) Turtleback Bks.

—The Dark Wind. unabr. ed. 1994. audio 42.00 (*0-7366-2689-1*, 3424) Books on Tape, Inc.

—The Dark Wind. 1982. 224p. o.p. (*0-06-014936-1*) HarperCollins Pubs.

—The Dark Wind. 1990. 320p. reprint ed. mass mkt. 6.99 (*0-06-100003-5*, Perennial); Set. 1993. audio 18.00 (*1-55994-774-8*, CPN 4032, HarperAudio) HarperTrade.

—The Dark Wind. 1993. audio 39.80. audio Literate Ear, Inc.

—The Dark Wind. 1992. 79p. mass mkt. 5.99 o.p. (*0-06-100491-X*, HarperTorch); 1983. 224p. pap. 3.50 o.p. (*0-380-63321-3*, Avon Bks.) Morrow/Avon.

—The Dark Wind. unabr. ed. 1990. (Jim Chee Mystery Ser.: Vol. 2). (YA). (gr. 10 up). audio 51.00 (*1-55690-136-4*, 91101E7) Recorded Bks., LLC.

—The Fallen Man, unabr. ed. 1997. audio 42.00 (*0-913369-37-3*, 4211) Books on Tape, Inc.

—The Fallen Man. 1996. 304p. 24.00 o.p. (*0-06-017773-X*) HarperCollins Pubs.

—The Fallen Man, Set. abr. ed. 1996. (Joe Leaphorn Mystery Ser.). audio 25.00 (*1-55994-978-3*, 694496, HarperAudio) HarperTrade.

—The Fallen Man. 1997. 320p. mass mkt. 6.99 (*0-06-109288-6*, HarperTorch) Morrow/Avon.

—The Fallen Man. unabr. ed. 1997. (Jim Chee Mystery Ser.: Vol. 9). audio 51.00 (*0-7887-0907-0*, 94961E7) Recorded Bks., LLC.

—The Fallen Man. 1998. 5.98 o.p. (*0-7651-0823-2*) Smithmark Pubs., Inc.

—The First Eagle. 1998. 224p. 25.00 (*0-00-224569-8*); 288p. 25.00 o.s.i (*0-06-017581-8*); 25.00 o.s.i (*0-06-099536-X*) HarperCollins Pubs.

—The First Eagle. unabr. ed. 1998. audio 34.95 (*0-694-52051-9*, 896038);Set. audio 25.00 (*0-694-52011-X*, 696034) HarperTrade. (HarperAudio).

—The First Eagle. 1999. 336p. mass mkt. 6.99 (*0-06-109785-3*, HarperTorch) Morrow/Avon.

—The First Eagle. unabr. ed. (Joe Leaphorn Mystery Ser.). 1999. audio compact disk 58.00 (*0-7887-3445-8*, C1051E7); 1998. audio 56.00 (*0-7887-2160-7*, 95456E7) Recorded Bks., LLC.

—The First Eagle. l.t. ed. (Paperback Bestsellers Ser.). 360p. 1999. pap. 28.95 o.p. (*0-7862-1625-5*); 1998. 30.95 (*0-7862-1624-7*) Thorndike Pr.

—The First Eagle. 1999. 13.04 (*0-606-16536-3*) Turtleback Bks.

—The Ghostway. unabr. ed. 1994. audio 42.00 (*0-7366-2748-0*, 3473) Books on Tape, Inc.

—The Ghostway. 1985. 224p. 13.95 o.p. (*0-06-015396-2*); 1992. 3p. audio 18.00 (*1-55994-606-7*, CPN 2301, HarperAudio) HarperTrade.

—The Ghostway. 1993. audio. audio 47.20 (*1-56544-040-4*, 250033) Literate Ear, Inc.

—The Ghostway. 1992. 320p. mass mkt. 6.99 (*0-06-100345-X*, HarperTorch); 1986. 208p. mass mkt. 4.95 (*0-380-70024-7*, Avon Bks.) Morrow/Avon.

—The Ghostway. unabr. ed. 1990. (Jim Chee Mystery Ser.: Vol. 3). audio 44.00 (*1-55690-194-1*, 90098E7) Recorded Bks., LLC.

—The Ghostway. 1984. (J). 12.55 (*0-606-01124-2*) Turtleback Bks.

—Hunting Badger. 1999. 288p. 26.00 (*0-00-224550-7*); 26.00 (*0-06-019289-5*) HarperCollins Pubs.

—Hunting Badger. l.t. ed. 1999. 256p. pap. 26.00 (*0-06-095564-3*, HarperLargePrint); 2000. audio compact disk 29.95 (*0-694-52287-2*, HarperAudio); Set. 2000. 30p. audio 25.00 (*0-694-52057-8*, HarperAudio) HarperTrade.
—Hunting Badger. 2001. 352p. mass mkt. 7.50 (*0-06-109786-1*, HarperTorch) Morrow/Avon.
—Hunting Badger. unabr. ed. 1999. (Joe Leaphorn Mystery Ser.). audio 29.95 (*0-7887-3894-1*, 96076) Recorded Bks., LLC.
—The Jim Chee Mysteries: Three Classic Hillerman Mysteries Featuring Officer Jim Chee: The Dark Wind, People of Darkness & The Ghostway. 1990. 576p. 26.00 (*0-06-016478-6*) HarperTrade.
—The Jim Chee Mysteries: Three Classic Hillerman Mysteries Featuring Officer Jim Chee: The Dark Wind, People of Darkness & The Ghostway. 1993. 576p. 13.99 o.s.i (*0-517-09281-6*) Random Hse. Value Publishing.
—The Joe Leaphorn Mysteries: Three Classic Hillerman Mysteries Featuring Lt. Joe Leaphorn: The Blessing Way, Dance Hall of the Dead, Listening Woman. 1989. 448p. 19.00 o.p. (*0-06-016174-4*) HarperTrade.
—Leaphorn & Chee: Three Classic Mysteries Featuring Lt. Joe Leaphorn & Officer Jim Chee. 1992. 512p. 19.00 o.p. (*0-06-016909-5*) HarperTrade.
—Listening Woman. unabr. ed. 1994. audio 36.00 (*0-7366-2671-9*, 3408) Books on Tape, Inc.
—Listening Woman. l.t. ed. (General Ser.). 303p. 1994. pap. 18.95 o.p. (*0-8161-5435-X*); 1993. lib. bdg. 22.95 (*0-8161-5434-1*) Gale Group. (Macmillan Reference USA).
—Listening Woman. 1978. (Harper Novel of Suspense Ser.). o.p. (*0-06-011901-2*) HarperCollins Pubs.
—Listening Woman. 1993. audio. audio 44.20 (*1-56544-036-6*, 250022) Literate Ear, Inc.
—Listening Woman. 1990. 336p. mass mkt. 6.99 (*0-06-100029-9*, HarperTorch); 1979. pap. 3.95 (*0-380-43554-3*, Avon Bks.) Morrow/Avon.
—Listening Woman. unabr. ed. 1990. (Joe Leaphorn Mystery Ser.: Vol. 3). audio 44.00 (*1-55690-310-3*, 90073E7) Recorded Bks., LLC.
—People of Darkness. unabr. ed. 1994. audio 36.00 (*0-7366-2725-1*, 3455) Books on Tape, Inc.
—People of Darkness. 1988. 196p. reprint ed. mass mkt. 4.95 o.p. (*0-06-080950-7*, P 950, Perennial) HarperTrade.
—People of Darkness. 1993. audio 44.20 (*1-56544-037-4*, 250034); audio Literate Ear, Inc.
—People of Darkness. 1991. 304p. mass mkt. 6.99 (*0-06-109915-5*, HarperTorch); 1983. 192p. pap. 2.95 o.p. (*0-380-57778-X*, Avon Bks.) Morrow/Avon.
—People of Darkness. unabr. ed. 1990. (Jim Chee Mystery Ser.: Vol. 1). audio 44.00 (*1-55690-405-3*, 90087E7) Recorded Bks., LLC.
—Sacred Clowns. unabr. ed. 1994. audio 48.00 (*0-7366-2645-X*, 3382) Books on Tape, Inc.
—Sacred Clowns. 1994. 368p. mass mkt. 6.99 (*0-06-109260-6*) HarperCollins Pubs.
—Sacred Clowns. 1993. 304p. 100.00 o.p. (*0-06-016830-7*); 304p. 23.00 o.p. (*0-06-016767-X*); audio 17.00 (*1-55994-549-4*, 391505, HarperAudio) HarperTrade.
—Sacred Clowns. unabr. ed. 1993. (Jim Chee Mystery Ser.: Vol. 8). audio 51.00 (*1-55690-910-1*, 93406E7) Recorded Bks., LLC.
—Sacred Clowns. 1994. 13.04 (*0-606-16175-9*) Turtleback Bks.
—Sacred Clowns: A Novel. 2003. 320p. pap. 11.95 (*0-06-053805-8*, Perennial) HarperTrade.
—Skinwalkers. unabr. ed. 1994. audio 36.00 (*0-7366-2795-2*, 3510) Books on Tape, Inc.
—Skinwalkers. 1990. 320p. mass mkt. 6.99 (*0-06-100017-5*); 1987. mass mkt. 4.95 o.p. (*0-06-080893-4*, P/893) HarperCollins Pubs.
—Skinwalkers. 1990. audio 15.95; 1987. 224p. 19.95 o.p. (*0-06-015695-3*); 1991. audio 18.00 (*1-55994-166-9*, CPN 2152, HarperAudio) HarperTrade.
—Skinwalkers. 1993. audio 39.80 (*1-56544-007-2*, 250032); audio Literate Ear, Inc.
—Skinwalkers. unabr. ed. 1990. (Jim Chee Mystery Ser.: Vol. 4). audio 44.00 (*1-55690-480-0*, 90074E7) Recorded Bks., LLC.
—Skinwalkers. 1987. 13.04 (*0-606-03655-5*) Turtleback Bks.
—Talking God. unabr. ed. 1989. audio 42.00 (*0-7366-1656-X*, 2507) Books on Tape, Inc.
—Talking God. 2003. E-Book 6.99 (*0-06-054725-1*) HarperCollins Pubs.
—Talking God. 1991. 368p. mass mkt. 6.99 (*0-06-109918-X*, Perennial); 1989. 17.95 o.p. (*0-06-016118-3*) HarperTrade.
—Talking God. 1989. 13.04 (*0-606-04823-5*) Turtleback Bks.
—A Thief of Time. unabr. ed. 1994. audio 36.00 (*0-7366-2841-X*, 3549) Books on Tape, Inc.
—A Thief of Time. l.t. ed. 1990. 14.95 o.p. (*0-8161-5061-3*); 1989. 344p. 18.95 o.p. (*0-8161-4699-3*) Gale Group. (Macmillan Reference USA).
—A Thief of Time. 2002. E-Book 6.99 (*0-06-054713-8*); E-Book (*0-06-054720-0*) HarperCollins Pubs.
—A Thief of Time. 1988. 224p. 15.45 o.p. (*0-06-015938-3*); 2002. 176p. audio 9.99 (*0-06-008296-8*, HarperAudio); Set. 1995. audio 18.00 (*0-89845-794-7*, 391761, HarperAudio) HarperTrade.
—A Thief of Time. 1990. 352p. reprint ed. mass mkt. 6.99 (*0-06-100004-3*, HarperTorch) Morrow/Avon.
—A Thief of Time. 1989. 13.04 (*0-606-04346-2*) Turtleback Bks.
Hillerman, Tony, reader. Talking God, , abr. ed. 1995. audio 18.00 (*0-89845-956-7*, CPN 2122, HarperAudio) HarperTrade.
Hirt, Douglas. A Good Town. 2001. 320p. mass mkt. 4.99 (*0-8439-4861-2*, Leisure Bks.) Dorchester Publishing Co., Inc.
—A Good Town. l.t. ed. 2002. (Thorndike Western Ser.). 295p. 25.95 (*0-7862-3812-7*) Gale Group.
Hogan, Ray. The Outlawed. l.t. ed. 1996. (G. K. Hall Western Ser.). 205p. 21.95 (*0-7838-1908-0*, Macmillan Reference USA) Gale Group.
Horowitz, Renee B. Deadly Rx. 2001. 172p. per. 13.75 (*0-7433-0363-6*) Clocktower Bks.
—Deadly Rx. 1997. mass mkt. 5.50 (*0-380-78620-6*, Avon Bks.) Morrow/Avon.
—Rx for Murder. 2001. 160p. per. 13.50 (*0-7433-0116-1*) Clocktower Bks.
—Rx for Murder. 1997. mass mkt. 5.50 (*0-380-78619-2*, Avon Bks.) Morrow/Avon.
Howard, Linda. Come Lie with Me. 1999. 248p. mass mkt. (*1-55166-549-2*, Mira Bks.); 1993. mass mkt. (*0-373-48271-X*, Silhouette); 1984. mass mkt. (*0-373-53677-1*, Harlequin Bks.) Harlequin Enterprises, Ltd.
—The Touch of Fire. 1997. 336p. mass mkt. 7.99 (*0-671-01972-4*, Pocket) Simon & Schuster.
—The Touch of Fire. Zion, Claire, ed. 1992. 336p. mass mkt. 5.99 (*0-671-72858-X*, Pocket) Simon & Schuster.
—The Touch of Fire. l.t. ed. 2001. (Famous Authors Ser.). 479p. 28.95 (*0-7862-2846-6*) Thorndike Pr.
Hutchison, Wick. The Adventures of Inquisitive Englebert. 1991. (Illus.). 64p. (J). (gr. k-3). pap. 7.95 (*0-929690-11-7*) Heritage Pubs., Inc.
Jance, J. A. Dead to Rights. unabr. ed. 1999. (Joanna Brady Mystery Ser.: Bk. 4). audio 49.95 (*1-55686-831-6*) Books in Motion.
—Dead to Rights. abr. ed. (Joanna Brady Mystery Ser.). 1997. audio 7.99 o.p. (*1-56740-189-9*, 641, Paperback Nova Audio Bks.); 1996. audio 16.95 o.p. (*1-56100-958-X*, 1174, Nova Audio Bks.); 1996. 9p. audio 23.95 o.p. (*1-56100-719-6*, 85, Bookcassette); 1996. 9p. audio 57.25 o.p. (*1-56100-344-1*, 857, Unabridged Library Editions) Brilliance Audio.
—Dead to Rights. (Joanna Brady Mystery Ser.). 2003. 384p. mass mkt. 7.50 (*0-380-72432-4*); 1996. 373p. mass mkt. 22.00 o.p. (*0-380-97394-4*) Morrow/Avon. (Avon Bks.).
—Desert Heat. l.t. ed. 2001. 269p. 26.95 (*1-57490-371-3*, Beeler Large Print Bks.) Beeler, Thomas T. Publisher.
—Desert Heat. 1993. (Joanna Brady Mystery Ser.). 384p. mass mkt. 7.50 (*0-380-76545-4*, Avon Bks.) Morrow/Avon.
—Devil's Claw. l.t. ed. 2000. (Wheeler Softcover Ser.). 449p. 25.95 (*1-56895-140-X*, Wheeler Publishing, Inc.) Gale Group.
—Devil's Claw. 2001. (Joanna Brady Mystery Ser.). 416p. mass mkt. 7.50 (*0-380-79249-4*) HarperCollins Pubs.
—Devil's Claw. 2000. (Joanna Brady Mystery Ser.). 384p. 24.00 (*0-380-97501-7*, Morrow, William & Co.) Morrow/Avon.
—Exit Wounds: A Novel of Suspense. l.t. ed. 2003. 480p. pap. 24.95 (*0-06-054549-6*, HarperLarge-Print) HarperTrade.
—Exit Wounds: A Novel of Suspense. 2003. 384p. 24.95 (*0-380-97731-1*, Morrow, William & Co.) Morrow/Avon.
—Outlaw Mountain. Set. abr. ed. 1999. audio 25.00. audio 36.00 Highsmith Inc.
—Outlaw Mountain. (Joanna Brady Mystery Ser.). 384p. 2000. mass mkt. 6.99 (*0-380-79248-6*); 1999. 24.00 (*0-380-97500-9*) Morrow/Avon. (Avon Bks.).
—Outlaw Mountain. abr. ed. 1999. (Joanna Brady Mystery Ser.). audio 25.00 (*0-7871-1970-9*); audio 36.00 (*0-7871-1973-3*) NewStar Media, Inc. (Dove Audio).
—Paradise Lost. 2001. E-Book 7.99 (*0-06-001044-4*) HarperCollins Pubs.
—Paradise Lost. abr. ed. 2001. audio 25.95 (*0-694-52573-1*, HarperAudio); 448p. pap. 25.00 (*0-06-621403-3*) HarperTrade.
—Paradise Lost. (Joanna Brady Mystery Ser.). 2002. 432p. mass mkt. 7.99 (*0-380-80469-7*, Avon Bks.); 2001. 384p. 25.00 (*0-380-97729-X*, Morrow, William & Co.) Morrow/Avon.
—Partner in Crime. 2002. E-Book 19.95 (*0-06-009828-7*); E-Book 19.95 (*0-06-009827-9*); E-Book 19.95 (*0-06-009825-2*); E-Book 19.95 (*0-06-009826-0*) HarperCollins General Bks. Group. (Perfect-Bound).
—Partner in Crime. l.t. ed. 2002. 512p. pap. 24.95 (*0-06-009393-5*, HarperLargePrint) HarperTrade.
—Partner in Crime. 2003. 400p. mass mkt. 7.99 (*0-380-80470-0*); 2002. 384p. 24.95 (*0-380-97730-3*) Morrow/Avon. (Morrow, William & Co.).
—Rattlesnake Crossing. l.t. ed. 2000. (Large Print Book Ser.). 408p. pap. 25.95 (*1-56895-938-9*, Wheeler Publishing, Inc.) Gale Group.
—Rattlesnake Crossing. (Joanna Brady Mystery Ser.). 2003. 384p. mass mkt. 6.99 (*0-380-79247-8*); 1998. 371p. 23.00 o.p. (*0-380-97499-1*) Morrow/Avon. (Avon Bks.).
—Sequel to the Hour of the Hunter. 1924. o.s.i (*0-688-10922-5*, Morrow, William & Co.) Morrow/Avon.
—Sheriff Brady, Vol. 5. 1924. o.s.i (*0-688-13822-5*, Morrow, William & Co.) Morrow/Avon.
—Shoot, Don't Shoot. unabr. ed. 1996. (Joanna Brady Mystery Ser.: Bk. 3). audio 49.95 (*1-55686-656-9*) Books in Motion.
—Shoot, Don't Shoot. l.t. ed. 1998. (Large Print Book Ser.). 25.95 (*1-56895-517-0*, Wheeler Publishing, Inc.) Gale Group.
—Shoot, Don't Shoot. (Joanna Brady Mystery Ser.). 1996. 384p. mass mkt. 7.99 (*0-380-76548-9*, Avon Bks.); 1995. 320p. (YA). 21.00 o.p. (*0-688-13821-7*, Morrow, William & Co.) Morrow/Avon.
—Shoot, Don't Shoot. unabr. ed. 1996. audio 70.00 (*0-7887-0477-X*, 94670E7) Recorded Bks., LLC.
—Skeleton Canyon. unabr. ed. 1999. (Joanna Brady Mystery Ser.: Bk. 5). audio 49.95 (*1-55686-883-9*) Books in Motion.
—Skeleton Canyon. abr. ed. (Joanna Brady Mystery Ser.). 1998. audio 7.99 o.p. (*1-56740-206-2*, 1370, Paperback Nova Audio Bks.); 1997. 9p. audio 57.25 o.p. (*1-56100-836-2*, 1047, Unabridged Library Editions); 1997. audio 23.95 (*1-56100-761-7*, 266, Bookcassette) Brilliance Audio.
—Skeleton Canyon. (Joanna Brady Mystery Ser.). 1998. 400p. mass mkt. 7.50 (*0-380-72433-2*); 1997. 384p. mass mkt. 23.00 o.p. (*0-380-97395-2*) Morrow/Avon. (Avon Bks.).
—Skeleton Canyon. l.t. ed. 1998. (Mystery Ser.). 437p. 28.95 (*0-7838-8356-0*) Thorndike Pr.
—Tombstone Courage. unabr. ed. 1998. (Joanna Brady Mystery Ser.: Bk. 2). audio 49.95 (*1-55686-817-0*) Books in Motion.
—Tombstone Courage. (Joanna Brady Mystery Ser.). 1995. 416p. mass mkt. 7.99 (*0-380-76546-2*, Avon Bks.); 1994. 300p. 20.00 o.p. (*0-688-13247-2*, Morrow, William & Co.) Morrow/Avon.
—Tombstone Courage. l.t. ed. 2001. (Joanna Brady Mystery Ser.). 496p. 28.95 (*0-7862-3115-7*) Thorndike Pr.
Johansen, Iris. The Search. l.t. ed. 2001. 12.95 (*1-56895-190-6*); 349p. 30.95 (*1-58724-052-1*) Gale Group. (Wheeler Publishing, Inc.).
Jones, Rennie. Behind the Scenes. 1997. 255p. 22.50 (*0-684-80751-3*, Simon & Schuster) Simon & Schuster.
Judd, Bob. Burn. 1993. 290p. mass mkt. 4.99 o.p. (*0-425-13946-8*) Berkley Publishing Group.
Kalam, Murad. Night Journey. 2003. (Illus.). 320p. 23.00 (*0-7432-4418-4*, Simon & Schuster) Simon & Schuster.
Kaminsky, Howard & Kaminsky, Susan. The Twelve. 2000. 306p. mass mkt. 6.99 (*0-312-97140-0*, St. Martin's Paperbacks); 1999. 304p. 23.95 o.p. (*0-312-20601-1*) St. Martin's Pr.
Kimmel, Mark. Trillion: Once You Know, You Can Never Go Back to Merely Believing. 2002. 363p. per. 26.95 (*0-9720151-0-8*) Paradigm Bks.
King, Laurie R. A Darker Place. 1999. (Illus.). 512p. mass mkt. 6.99 (*0-553-57824-3*); mass mkt. (*0-553-84027-4*); (Illus.). 400p. 23.95 o.s.i (*0-553-10711-9*) Bantam Bks.
—A Darker Place. l.t. ed. 1999. (Large Print Book Ser.). (Illus.). 27.95 (*1-56895-738-6*, Wheeler Publishing, Inc.) Gale Group.
—A Darker Place. unabr. ed. 1999. audio 87.00 (*0-7887-3121-1*, 95648 E7) Recorded Bks., LLC.
Kittinger, J. Iverson. The Winding Road. 2000. 176p. pap. 15.00 (*0-8059-4885-6*) Dorrance Publishing Co., Inc.
Knight, Alanna. Angel Eyes. (*0-7540-3371-6*) BBC Audiobooks America.
Kraus, Krandall. Love's Last Chance. 2000. (Nigel & Nicky Mysteries Ser.). (Illus.). xiv, 312p. pap. 11.95 (*1-55583-505-8*, Alyson Bks.) Alyson Pubns.
Krentz, Jayne Ann. Between the Lines. 2000. 256p. mass mkt. (*1-55166-595-6*, 1-66595-8, Mira Bks.); 1993. mass mkt. (*0-373-83270-2*, 1-83270-8, Harlequin Bks.); 1986. mass mkt. (*0-373-25225-0*, Harlequin Bks.) Harlequin Enterprises, Ltd.
—Between the Lines. l.t. ed. 2002. (Thorndike Romance Ser.). 288p. 30.95 (*0-7862-4002-4*) Thorndike Pr.
—The Cowboy. abr. ed. 1999. audio 7.99 (*1-55204-169-7*, MIR-1169) Durkin Hayes Publishing Ltd.
—The Cowboy. 1999. 251p. mass mkt. (*1-55166-494-1*, 1-66494-5, Mira Bks.); 1990. (Harlequin Temptation Ser.: No. 302). pap. (*0-373-25402-4*, Harlequin Bks.) Harlequin Enterprises, Ltd.
—The Cowboy. l.t. ed. 2001. (G. K. Hall Romance Ser.). 244p. 29.95 (*0-7838-9050-8*) Thorndike Pr.
—Eye of the Beholder. l.t. ed. 1999. 28.95 (*1-56895-760-2*, Wheeler Publishing, Inc.) Gale Group.
—Eye of the Beholder. abr. ed. 1999. audio 24.00 Highsmith Inc.
—Eye of the Beholder. 1999. 400p. mass mkt. 7.99 (*0-671-52307-4*, Pocket); 352p. 24.00 o.s.i (*0-671-52306-6*, Atria) Simon & Schuster.
—Eye of the Beholder. abr. ed. 1999. audio 24.00 o.s.i (*0-671-57615-1*, 498547, Simon & Schuster Audioworks) Simon & Schuster Audio.
Lacy, Al & Lacy, JoAnna. Until the Daybreak. 2003. (Mail Order Bride Ser.: No. 6). 322p. pap. 10.99 (*1-57673-624-5*) Multnomah Pubs., Inc.
—Until the Daybreak. l.t. ed. 2001. (Christian Fiction Ser.). 501p. 27.95 (*0-7862-3607-8*) Thorndike Pr.
Laird, Brian A. Bowman's Line. 1995. 224p. 20.95 o.p. (*0-312-13033-3*, Saint Martin's Minotaur) St. Martin's Pr.
Lawless, Jim. Shootout at Casa Grande. l.t. ed. 2001. (Dales Large Print Ser.). 192p. pap. 21.99 (*1-84262-126-2*) Dales Large Print Bks. GBR. *Dist:* Ulverscroft Large Print Bks., Ltd., Ulverscroft Large Print Canada, Ltd.
Lewis, Alfred H. Faro Nell & Her Friends: Wolfville Stories. 1977. (Short Story Index Reprint Ser.). (Illus.). reprint ed. 26.95 (*0-8369-3956-5*) Ayer Co. Pubs., Inc.
—Sandburrs. 1977. (Short Story Index Reprint Ser.). (Illus.). 23.95 (*0-8369-3068-1*) Ayer Co. Pubs., Inc.
—Sandburrs. 318p. reprint ed. (Illus.). lib. bdg. 21.00 (*0-8398-1158-6*); 1986. (C). pap. text 7.95 (*0-8290-2029-2*) Irvington Pubs.
Little, Bentley. The Revelation. 1999. 336p. mass mkt. 6.99 (*0-451-19225-7*, Signet Bks.) NAL.
—The Revelation. 1991. 2.99 o.p. (*0-517-06899-0*) Random Hse. Value Publishing.
—The Summoning. 544p. 2001. mass mkt. 6.99 (*0-7860-1480-6*); 2000. mass mkt. 5.99 o.s.i (*0-7860-1312-5*) Kensington Publishing Corp.
Lowell, Elizabeth. Too Hot to Handle. 2002. 256p. mass mkt. (*1-55166-895-5*, Mira Bks.) Harlequin Enterprises, Ltd.
—Too Hot to Handle. 2003. (Famous Authors Ser.). 29.95 (*0-7862-4555-7*) Thorndike Pr.
Martin, Patricia P. El Milagro & Other Stories. 1996. (Camino del Sol). 92p. 22.95 o.p. (*0-8165-1547-6*); pap. 9.95 (*0-8165-1548-4*) Univ. of Arizona Pr.
Mason, Connie. To Tempt a Rogue. l.t. ed. 2002. 488p. 27.95 (*0-7862-3951-4*) Gale Group.
—To Tempt a Rogue. 1999. (Avon Romantic Treasure Ser.). 384p. mass mkt. 5.99 (*0-380-79342-3*, Avon Bks.) Morrow/Avon.
Matthews, Patricia. Rendezvous at Midnight. 2002. 25.95 (*0-7862-3698-1*, Five Star) Gale Group.
Matthews, Patricia & Matthews, Clayton. The Scent of Fear. 1992. 320p. 18.95 o.p. (*0-7278-4350-8*) Severn Hse. Pubs., Ltd.
—The Sound of Murder. 1994. 20.00 o.p. (*0-7278-4594-2*) Severn Hse. Pubs., Ltd.
—Taste of Evil. 1993. 256p. lib. bdg. 20.00 o.p. (*0-7278-4505-5*) Severn Hse. Pubs., Ltd.
—Touch of Terror. 1995. 256p. 20.00 (*0-7278-4746-5*) Severn Hse. Pubs., Ltd.
—Vision of Death. 1993. 256p. lib. bdg. 19.00 (*0-7278-4397-4*) Severn Hse. Pubs., Ltd.
Maxim, John R. Bannerman's Promise. 2001. 608p. mass mkt. 7.50 (*0-380-73011-1*, Avon Bks.) Morrow/Avon.
McMillan, Terry. Waiting to Exhale. unabr. ed. 1992. audio 80.00 (*0-7366-2320-5*, 3100) Books on Tape, Inc.
—Waiting to Exhale. l.t. ed. 1993. (General Ser.). 600p. pap. 17.95 (*0-8161-5618-2*); lib. bdg. 23.95 o.p. (*0-8161-5617-4*) Gale Group. (Macmillan Reference USA).
—Waiting to Exhale. abr. ed. 1995. pap. 16.95 incl. audio (*0-453-00960-3*, 391864); 1992. 15.95 o.p. incl. audio (*0-453-00777-5*, 51855-01595) Penguin/HighBridge.
—Waiting to Exhale. 1996. 155p. per. 20.97 (*0-671-85153-5*); 1993. 416p. mass mkt. 6.50 (*0-671-86417-3*); 1992. 264.00 o.p. (*0-670-77972-5*); 1995. 416p. reprint ed. mass mkt. 7.99 (*0-671-53745-8*) Simon & Schuster. (Pocket).
—Waiting to Exhale. Rosenman, Jane, ed. 1994. 416p. reprint ed. pap. 14.00 (*0-671-50148-8*, Washington Square Pr.) Simon & Schuster.
—Waiting to Exhale. 1992. 416p. 22.95 (*0-670-83980-9*, Viking) Viking Penguin.
McNally, T. M. Almost Home. 1998. 240p. 22.00 (*0-684-84469-9*, Scribner) Simon & Schuster.
—Almost Home: A Novel. 1999. 240p. pap. 12.00 (*0-684-85445-7*, Scribner Paper Fiction) Simon & Schuster.
McWilliams, A. L. Penny Town Justice. 2000. (First Edition Romance Ser.). 270p. 25.95 (*0-7862-2812-1*, Five Star) Gale Group.
Mendez, Miguel. From Labor to Letters: A Novel Autobiography. Foster, David W., tr. from SPA. 1997. 128p. 20.00 (*0-927534-70-3*); pap. 11.00 (*0-927534-66-5*) Bilingual Pr./Editorial Bilingue.

Meyers, Harold B. Reservations. 1999. 287p. 24.95 (*0-87081-524-5*) Univ. Pr. of Colorado.

Michaels, Fern. Golden Lasso. l.t. ed. 1985. (Nightingale Ser.). 318p. 9.95 o.p. (*0-8161-3742-0*, Macmillan Reference USA) Gale Group.

—Golden Lasso. 2002. 256p. mass mkt. (*1-55166-912-9*, 1-66912-6, Mira Bks.); 1994. per. (*0-373-48297-3*, 5-48297-1, Silhouette) Harlequin Enterprises, Ltd.

Michaels, Lisa. Grand Ambition: A Novel. l.t. ed. 2001. 275p. 26.95 (*1-57490-374-8*, Beeler Large Print Bks.) Beeler, Thomas T. Publisher.

—Grand Ambition: A Novel. 288p. 2002. pap. 13.95 (*0-393-32295-5*); 2001. (Illus.). 23.95 (*0-393-05047-5*) Norton, W. W. & Co., Inc.

Mills, Kyle. Storming Heaven. 1998. audio compact disk 80.00 (*0-7366-8286-4*); 1999. audio 64.00 (*0-7366-4278-1*, 4776) Books on Tape, Inc.

—Storming Heaven. 2000. 528p. mass mkt. 6.99 (*0-06-101251-3*); 1998. 400p. 25.00 o.s.i (*0-06-101250-5*) HarperCollins Pubs.

—Storming Heaven, Set. abr. ed. 1998. audio 18.00 o.s.i (*0-694-51971-5*, HarperAudio) HarperTrade.

Mitchell, James C. Lovers Crossing. Date not set. pap. (*0-312-31531-7*, St. Martin's Paperbacks); 2003. 304p. 23.95 (*0-312-31530-9*, Saint Martin's Minotaur) St. Martin's Pr.

Mitchell, Kirk. Cry Dance. 2000. (Illus.). 368p. mass mkt. 6.50 (*0-553-57914-2*) Bantam Bks.

—Cry Dance. l.t. ed. 2003. 560p. 25.95 (*0-375-43265-5*) Random Hse. Large Print.

—The Cry Dance: A Novel of Suspense. 1999. 368p. 23.95 o.s.i (*0-553-10810-7*) Bantam Bks.

Monroe, Debra. Newfangled: A Novel. 304p. 2000. pap. 12.00 (*0-684-85197-0*, Touchstone); 1998. 22.00 (*0-684-81905-8*, Simon & Schuster) Simon & Schuster.

Moore, Alison. Synonym for Love. 1996. 256p. pap. 10.95 o.p. (*0-452-27622-5*, Plume) Dutton/Plume.

—Synonym for Love. 1995. 256p. text 19.95 (*1-56279-074-9*) Mercury Hse.

Muehl, Chips. Buckskins, Bedbugs & Bacon: Daily Adventures in the Old West. 2001. (Wild West Ser.: Vol. 9). (Illus.). 141p. pap. 7.95 (*1-893860-22-1*) Arizona Highways.

Murkoff, Bruce. Waterborne. 2004. 416p. 25.00 (*1-4000-4038-8*) Knopf Publishing Group.

Niswander, Adam. The Serpent Slayers: A Southwestern Supernatural Thriller. 1994. (Shaman Cycle Ser.: Bk. 2). 320p. lib. bdg. 21.95 (*0-9626148-2-3*) Integra Pr.

Nobel, Sylvia. Deadly Sanctuary. Lebowitz, Max, ed. 1998. (Kendall O'Dell Mysteries Ser.). (Illus.). iii, 360p. pap. 15.95 (*0-9661105-7-9*) Nite Owl Bks.

—The Devil's Cradle. Williams, Jerry R., ed. l.t. ed. 1999. (Kendall O'Dell Mystery Ser.). (Illus.). 445p. pap. 17.95 (*0-9661105-8-7*) Nite Owl Bks.

Novak, Brenda. Taking the Heat. 2003. (Illus.). 384p. mass mkt. (*0-373-83570-1*, Silhouette) Harlequin Enterprises, Ltd.

Nye, Nelson C. Gunfight at the O. K. Corral. 1982. 244p. pap. 1.95 o.p. (*0-8439-1093-3*) Dorchester Publishing Co., Inc.

—The Seven Six-Gunners. 1987. 144p. 2.50 o.s.i (*0-441-75972-6*, Diamond Bks.) Berkley Publishing Group.

—The Seven Six-Gunners. l.t. ed. 2000. (Paperback Ser.). 199p. 23.95 (*0-7838-9179-2*) Thorndike Pr.

O'Callaghan, Maxine. Only in the Ashes. 1997. 320p. mass mkt. 5.99 o.s.i (*0-515-12077-4*, Jove) Berkley Publishing Group.

—Shadow of the Child. 1996. 336p. mass mkt. 5.99 o.s.i (*0-515-11822-2*, Jove) Berkley Publishing Group.

Olsen, Theodore V. The Vanishing Herd. 2000. 30.00 (*0-7862-2113-5*, Macmillan Reference USA) Gale Group.

Olson, Toby. The Blond Box. 2003. 220p. pap. 14.95 (*1-57366-110-4*) Fiction Collective Two, Inc.

Owens, Louis. Dark River: A Novel. 1999. (American Indian Literature & Critical Studies Ser.: Vol. 30). 296p. 23.95 (*0-8061-3115-2*); E-Book 23.95 (*0-8061-7202-9*) Univ. of Oklahoma Pr.

Paine, Lauran. Apache Trail. l.t. ed. 2000. (G. K. Hall Paperback Ser.). 228p. pap. 23.95 (*0-7838-8928-3*, Macmillan Reference USA) Gale Group.

Parks, Joey Robert. Die Reading: An Espionage Fable. 2002. 256p. 26.75 (*0-9716502-0-9*) Liquid Gravity Publishing.

Parrish, Richard. Abandoned Heart. 1996. 368p. 23.95 o.p. (*0-525-94161-4*, Dutton) Dutton/Plume.

—Abandoned Heart. 1997. 432p. mass mkt. 5.99 o.s.i (*0-451-40693-1*, Onyx) NAL.

—The Dividing Line. 1993. 368p. 20.00 o.p. (*0-525-93561-4*) Dutton/Plume.

—The Dividing Line. 1994. 432p. mass mkt. 5.99 o.s.i (*0-451-40430-0*, Onyx) NAL.

—Nothing but the Truth. 1995. (Joshua Rabb Ser.). 304p. 20.95 o.p. (*0-525-93852-4*, Dutton) Dutton/Plume.

—Nothing but the Truth. 1996. (Joshua Rabb Ser.). 352p. mass mkt. 5.99 o.s.i (*0-451-40538-2*, Onyx) NAL.

Peters, Elizabeth, pseud. Summer of the Dragon. 1980. 256p. mass mkt. 2.25 o.s.i (*0-449-24291-9*, Fawcett) Ballantine Bks.

—Summer of the Dragon. unabr. ed. 1998. audio 44.95 (*0-7861-1354-5*, 2257) Blackstone Audio Bks., Inc.

—Summer of the Dragon. 1989. 256p. mass mkt. 4.99 (*0-8125-0754-1*, Tor Bks.) Doherty, Tom Assocs., LLC.

—Summer of the Dragon, Set. unabr. ed. 1999. audio 44.95 Highsmith Inc.

—Summer of the Dragon. 2001. 352p. mass mkt. 6.99 (*0-380-73122-3*, Avon Bks.) Morrow/Avon.

—Summer of the Dragon. l.t. ed. 1981. (Ulverscroft Large Print Ser.). 389p. 29.99 o.p. (*0-7089-0624-9*, Ulverscroft) Thorpe, F. A. Pubs. GBR. *Dist:* Ulverscroft Large Print Bks., Ltd., Ulverscroft Large Print Canada, Ltd.

Peterson, Tracie. Across the Years. 2002. (Desert Roses Ser.: Bk. 2). 384p. pap. 12.99 (*0-7642-2518-9*) Bethany Hse. Pubs.

—Across the Years. abr. ed. (Desert Roses Ser.: Vol. 2). 2003. audio 17.95 (*1-59086-818-8*, 4412, Bookcassette); 2003. audio 44.25 (*1-59086-819-6*, 4413, CD Library Edition); 2003. audio compact disk 24.95 (*1-59086-820-X*, 4414, CD); 2003. audio compact disk 62.25 (*1-59086-821-8*, 4415, CD Library Edition); 1900. audio 7.99 (*1-59086-822-6*, 4416, Brilliance Audio Paperback Audiobooks) Brilliance Audio.

—Across the Years. l.t. ed. 2004. (Desert Roses Ser.: No. 2). 458p. 27.95 (*0-7862-5780-6*) Thorndike Pr.

—Shadows of the Canyon. 2002. (Desert Roses Ser.: Bk. 1). 368p. pap. 12.99 (*0-7642-2517-0*) Bethany Hse. Pubs.

—Shadows of the Canyon. l.t. ed. 2003. 482p. 26.95 (*0-7862-5784-9*) Gale Group.

—Veiled Reflection. 2000. (Westward Chronicles Ser.: No. 3). 288p. pap. 11.99 (*0-7642-2114-0*) Bethany Hse. Pubs.

—A Veiled Reflection. 2002. 317p. 24.95 (*0-7862-3679-5*, Five Star) Gale Group.

Phelan, Twist. Heir Apparent: A Pinnacle Peak Mystery. 2002. pap. 14.99 (*1-59025-017-6*, 1 59025 017 6) SANDS Publishing, LLC.

Pickard, Nancy. The Twenty-Seven Ingredient Chili con Carne Murders. 1994. (Eugenia Potter Mysteries Ser.). 288p. mass mkt. 5.99 (*0-440-21641-9*) Dell Publishing.

Plumlee, Harry J. Shadow of the Wolf: An Apache Tale. 1997. 216p. 21.95 (*0-8061-2905-0*) Univ. of Oklahoma Pr.

Plumley, Lisa. Reconsidering Riley. 2002. 320p. mass mkt. 5.99 (*0-8217-7340-2*) Kensington Publishing Corp.

Poirier, Mark Jude. Naked Pueble: Stories. 2001. 208p. pap. 12.95 (*0-7868-8593-9*) Talk Miramax Bks.

—Naked Pueblo: Stories. 1999. (Illus.). 224p. 21.00 o.s.i (*0-609-60447-3*, Crown) Crown Publishing Group.

Prescott, Michael. Stealing Faces. 1999. 432p. mass mkt. 6.99 (*0-451-19851-4*); E-Book 6.99 (*0-451-19928-6*) NAL. (Signet Bks.).

—Stealing Faces. l.t. ed. 2001. (Ulverscroft Large Print Ser.). 544p. 31.99 (*0-7089-4350-0*, Ulverscroft) Thorpe, F. A. Pubs. GBR. *Dist:* Ulverscroft Large Print Bks., Ltd., Ulverscroft Large Print Canada, Ltd.

Quinn, Tara Taylor. Sheltered in His Arms. 2001. 304p. mass mkt. (*0-373-83466-7*, Harlequin Bks.) Harlequin Enterprises, Ltd.

Rainey, Yvonne. Dear Lover. Taylor, Chandra Sparks, ed. 2001. 306p. pap. 19.99 (*0-9706847-2-X*) Beginning II End Publishing, Inc.

Rawley, Donald. The Night Bird Cantata. 256p. 1998. 23.00 (*0-380-97609-9*, Avon Bks.); 1999. reprint ed. pap. 12.00 (*0-380-79584-1*) Morrow/Avon.

Reece, Colleen L. Arizona Angel. l.t. ed. 2002. 199p. 23.95 (*0-7862-4081-4*) Gale Group.

—Honor Bound. 1983. 176p. 3.95 o.p. (*0-8024-0153-8*) Moody Pr.

—Honor Bound. l.t. ed. 2001. 101p. 24.95 (*0-7862-3443-1*) Thorndike Pr.

Richards, Dusty. The Lawless Land. 2000. 272p. mass mkt. 5.99 (*0-312-97410-8*, St. Martin's Paperbacks) St. Martin's Pr.

Ring, Ray. Arizona Kiss. 1991. 17.95 o.p. (*0-316-74656-8*) Little Brown & Co.

Ritchie, James A. The Wagon Wars: A Sequel to "The Last Free Range" 1997. 190p. 20.95 (*0-8027-4157-6*) Walker & Co.

Ross, JoAnn. Confessions. l.t. ed. 2003. 477p. 29.95 (*1-58724-504-3*, Wheeler Publishing, Inc.) Gale Group.

—Confessions. 2003. 400p. mass mkt. (*1-55166-752-5*, Mira Bks.) Harlequin Enterprises, Ltd.

Ross, Val Gene. Secret Treasures of the Superstition Mountains. 2001. ix, 409p. (*1-55517-538-4*, Bonneville Bks.) Cedar Fort, Inc./CFI Distribution.

Sala, Sharon. Legend. 1998. 352p. mass mkt. 6.99 (*0-06-108701-7*, HarperTorch) Morrow/Avon.

Sarrantonio, Al. Kitt Peak. 1993. (Novel of the West Ser.). 154p. 16.95 o.p. (*0-87131-656-0*) Evans, M. & Co., Inc.

Savage, Les, Jr. Fire Dance at Spider Rock. unabr. ed. 1997. audio 42.00 (*0-7366-3812-1*, 4480) Books on Tape, Inc.

—Fire Dance at Spider Rock. abr. ed. (Five Star Westerns Ser.). 1996. audio 7.99 o.p. (*1-56740-143-0*, 837, Paperback Nova Audio Bks.); 1995. audio 14.95 o.p. (*1-56100-863-X*, 540, Nova Audio Bks.) Brilliance Audio.

—Fire Dance at Spider Rock. 2000. 240p. mass mkt. 4.50 (*0-8439-4696-2*, Leisure Bks.) Dorchester Publishing Co., Inc.

—Fire Dance at Spider Rock. 2000. E-Book 9.95 (*0-585-32712-2*) netLibrary, Inc.

—Last of the Breed. l.t. ed. 2001. (Paperback Ser.). 269p. 23.95 (*0-7838-9342-6*) Thorndike Pr.

Scott, Barbara & Younce, Carrie. Sedona Storm. 1993. 10.99 o.p. (*0-7852-8266-1*) Nelson, Thomas Inc.

Seltzer, Charles A. West of Apache Pass. 1975. 309p. reprint ed. lib. bdg. 24.95 (*0-88411-108-3*) Amereon, Ltd.

—West of Apache Pass. l.t. ed. 1993. 20.95 o.p. (*0-7927-1494-6*) BBC Audiobooks America.

Sharpe, Jon. Arizona Silver Strike. 2000. (Trailsman Ser.: Vol. 219). 176p. mass mkt. 4.99 o.s.i (*0-451-19932-4*) NAL.

Sinclair, John L. The Day the Bear Came off the Mountain. 1994. 120p. 22.95 o.p. (*0-940666-48-0*); pap. 12.95 o.p. (*0-940666-49-9*) Clear Light Pubs.

Sipherd, Ray. The Devil's Hawk: A Mystery. 2002. 272p. 23.95 (*0-312-24428-2*, Saint Martin's Minotaur) St. Martin's Pr.

Sonnichsen, Charles L. Arizona Humoresque: A Century of Arizona Humor. 1992. (Illus.). 306p. pap. 9.95 (*0-88289-900-7*) Pelican Publishing Co., Inc.

Sonnichsen, Charles L., ed. Arizona Humoresque: A Century of Arizona Humor. 1992. (Illus.). 306p. 17.95 (*0-88289-869-8*) Pelican Publishing Co., Inc.

Straub, Peter. Shadowland. 2003. 480p. mass mkt. 7.99 (*0-425-18822-1*); 1985. mass mkt. 4.50 o.s.i (*0-425-08207-5*); 1984. mass mkt. 3.95 o.s.i (*0-425-07321-1*); 1981. mass mkt. 3.50 o.s.i (*0-425-05056-4*); 1981. mass mkt. 3.50 o.s.i (*0-425-05152-8*) Berkley Publishing Group.

—Shadowland. ltd. ed. 1995. (Classics Revisited Ser.). 60.00 (*1-887368-00-0*) Gauntlet, Inc.

—Shadowland. 1980. 400p. 12.95 o.p. (*0-698-11045-5*) Putnam Publishing Group, The.

Talton, Jon. Concrete Desert: David Mapstone Mystery. 2001. 212p. 22.95 (*0-312-26953-6*, Saint Martin's Minotaur) St. Martin's Pr.

Taylor, Janelle. Chase the Wind. 1994. mass mkt. 14.95 o.s.i (*0-8217-4553-0*) Kensington Publishing Corp.

Thoene, Jake & Thoene, Luke. Legend of the Desert Bigfoot. 1996. (Last Chance Detectives Ser.: No. 2). 131p. (J). (gr. 7 up). pap. 3.99 o.p. (*0-8423-2084-9*, Tyndale Kids) Tyndale Hse. Pubs.

—Mystery Lights of Navajo Mesa. 1994. (Last Chance Detectives Ser.: No. 1). 126p. (J). (gr. 3-7). pap. 3.99 o.p. (*0-8423-2082-2*, Tyndale Kids) Tyndale Hse. Pubs.

Thompson, Vicki Lewis, et al. Escapade: Shattered Vows; Loverboy; The Keeper; The Veranchetti Marriage, 4 bks. in 1. 1998. (Promo Ser.). 971p. per. (*0-373-83408-X*, 1-83408-4, Harlequin Bks.) Harlequin Enterprises, Ltd.

Thornton, Betsy. The Cowboy Rides Away. 1997. 288p. mass mkt. 5.50 o.s.i (*0-440-22327-X*) Dell Publishing.

—The Cowboy Rides Away. 1996. 256p. 21.95 o.p. (*0-312-14301-X*, Saint Martin's Minotaur) St. Martin's Pr.

—Ghost Towns. 2003. 256p. reprint ed. mass mkt. 5.99 (*0-425-18889-2*, Prime Crime) Berkley Publishing Group.

—Ghost Towns. 2002. 272p. 23.95 (*0-312-28041-6*, Saint Martin's Minotaur) St. Martin's Pr.

—High Lonesome Road. E-Book 23.95 (*1-58945-672-6*) Adobe Systems, Inc.

—High Lonesome Road. 2001. 233p. 23.95 (*0-312-26861-0*, Saint Martin's Minotaur) St. Martin's Pr.

—The High Lonesome Road. 2002. 256p. mass mkt. 5.99 o.s.i (*0-425-18455-2*) Berkley Publishing Group.

Tomlinson, Dar. Unbreak My Heart. 2003. 320p. pap. 8.95 (*1-58571-101-2*, 909-645, Love Spectrum) Genesis Pr., Inc.

Udall, Brady. The Miracle Life of Edgar Mint: A Novel. 2002. 432p. pap. 14.00 (*0-375-71918-0*, Vintage) Knopf Publishing Group.

—The Miracle Life of Edgar Mint: A Novel. 2001. 384p. 24.95 (*0-393-02036-3*) Norton, W. W. & Co., Inc.

Urrea, Luis A. In Search of Snow: A Novel. 1994. 272p. 20.00 o.p. (*0-06-017089-1*) HarperTrade.

Vea, Alfredo, Jr. La Maravilla. 320p. 1994. pap. 13.95 (*0-452-27160-6*, Plume); 1993. 21.00 o.p. (*0-525-93588-6*) Dutton/Plume.

Vernon, John. The Last Canyon. 2001. 352p. 24.00 (*0-618-17454-0*) Houghton Mifflin Co.

Webb, Betty. Desert Noir: A Lena Jones Mystery. 2001. 240p. 23.95 o.s.i (*1-890208-63-9*); 251p. pap. 14.95 (*1-890208-70-1*) Poisoned Pen Pr.

West, Carter. Lockwood's Law. l.t. ed. 2001. (Dales Large Print Ser.). 208p. pap. 21.99 (*1-84262-127-0*) Dales Large Print Bks. GBR. *Dist:* Ulverscroft Large Print Bks., Ltd., Ulverscroft Large Print Canada, Ltd.

West, Paul. O. K. The Corral, the Earps & Doc Holliday. 2000. 304p. 24.00 (*0-684-84865-1*, Scribner) Simon & Schuster.

Whatley, Tom V. He Ain't Dead: A Novel of the Wicked West. 2002. 160p. pap. 16.95 (*0-86534-344-6*) Sunstone Pr.

Wheeler, Richard S. Flint's Gift. unabr. ed. 1999. audio 56.95 (*0-7861-1355-3*, 106028) Blackstone Audio Bks., Inc.

—Flint's Gift. 1999. 351p. mass mkt. 5.99 (*0-8125-5019-6*); 1997. 384p. 23.95 o.p. (*0-312-86366-7*) Doherty, Tom Assocs., LLC. (Forge Bks.).

—Flint's Gift. unabr. ed. 1998. audio 70.00 (*0-7887-2280-8*, 95449E7 ) Recorded Bks., LLC.

—Flint's Gift. l.t. ed. 1998. (Western Ser.). 479p. 25.95 (*0-7838-0270-6*) Thorndike Pr.

—Flint's Honor. 2001. 384p. mass mkt. 6.99 (*0-8125-5022-6*); 2nd ed. 1999. 320p. 23.95 (*0-312-86368-3*) Doherty, Tom Assocs., LLC. (Forge Bks.).

—Flint's Honor. l.t. ed. 2001. (G. K. Hall Western Ser.). 462p. 25.95 (*0-7838-9503-8*, Macmillan Reference USA) Gale Group.

White, Stewart Edward. Arizona Nights. 2000. 252p. E-Book 3.95 (*0-594-06443-0*) 1873 Pr.

—Arizona Nights. 1972. pap. 1.50 o.p. (*0-345-23000-0*) Ballantine Bks.

—Arizona Nights. 1976. lib. bdg. 15.75 o.s.i (*0-89968-124-7*, Lightyear Pr.) Buccaneer Bks., Inc.

—Arizona Nights. 1999. E-Book 2.49 (*1-58627-471-6*) Electric Umbrella Publishing.

—Arizona Nights. 2001. 212p. 24.99 (*1-58827-592-2*); per. 19.99 (*1-58827-593-0*) IndyPublish.com.

—Arizona Nights. E-Book 5.00 (*0-7410-0827-0*) SoftBook Pr.

—Arizona Nights: Cowboy Campfire Tales of the Territory. 1985. (Illus.). 356p. reprint ed. pap. 12.00 o.p. (*0-87380-155-5*) Popular E Commerce, Inc.

Wilhelmsen, Romain. Buckskin & Satin: A Novel of the American West. 2000. 213p. pap. 18.95 (*0-86534-307-1*); 1999. 216p. 28.95 (*0-86534-279-2*) Sunstone Pr.

Wilkerson, Carolyn. Hasta Maanana. 2003. 245p. 25.95 (*0-7862-5439-4*, Five Star) Gale Group.

Williams, Joy. The Quick & the Dead. 2002. (Vintage Contemporaries Ser.). 320p. pap. 13.00 (*0-375-72764-7*, Vintage) Knopf Publishing Group.

Willman, Marianne. Pieces of Sky. 2000. 408p. mass mkt. (*1-55166-564-6*); 1993. per. (*0-373-28795-X*, 1-28795-2); 1986. 400p. per. (*0-373-97022-6*) Harlequin Enterprises, Ltd. (Harlequin Bks.).

Windling, Terri. The Wood Wife. 2003. 320p. pap. 14.95 (*0-7653-0293-4*, Orb Bks.); 1997. 294p. pap. text 6.99 (*0-8125-4929-5*, Tor Bks.); 1996. 320p. 22.95 o.p. (*0-312-85988-0*, Tor Bks.) Doherty, Tom Assocs., LLC.

—The Wood Wife. l.t. ed. 1998. (Science Fiction Ser.). 421p. 24.95 (*0-7838-0301-X*) Thorndike Pr.

Wright, Herbert. Bombing at Greenstaff. Magner Publishing Staff, ed. 1999. 138p. pap. 10.95 (*1-929416-13-X*) Magner Publishing & American Binding & Publishing.

Yorke, Christy. The Wishing Garden. l.t. ed. 2000. (G. K. Hall Core Ser.). 439p. 27.95 (*0-7838-9302-7*, Macmillan Reference USA) Gale Group.

The Young Forester. 2000. mass mkt. 4.99 (*1-55902-582-4*, Aerie) Doherty, Tom Assocs., LLC.

Zelle, Steve. Wizard. 1993. 368p. 22.95 o.p. (*0-312-10577-0*) St. Martin's Pr.

## ARKANSAS—FICTION

Adcock, Patrick. Muggsbottom & Me: A Study in Anglo-Arkansas Relations. 1993. 268p. 18.00 (*1-880909-10-3*) Baskerville Pubs., Inc.

Askew, Rilla. The Mercy Seat. 1998. 448p. pap. 13.95 (*0-14-026515-5*) Penguin Group (USA) Inc.

—The Mercy Seat. 1997. 448p. 23.95 o.p. (*0-670-87467-1*) Viking Penguin.

Baker, William M. & Simpson, Ethel C., eds. Arkansas in Short Fiction: Stories from 1841 to 1984. 1986. 220p. (Orig.). 19.95 o.p. (*0-87483-007-9*); pap. 9.95 o.p. (*0-87483-006-0*) August Hse. Pubs., Inc.

Barry, Louise M. A Price Beyond Rubies: A Novel of the Civil War. 1996. (Illus.). 492p. pap. 25.95 (*0-89745-201-1*) Sunflower Univ. Pr.

Bayer, John F. Satan's Ring: A Novel. 2002. 320p. pap. 12.99 (*0-8054-2431-8*) Broadman & Holman Pubs.

Butler, Jack. Living in Little Rock with Miss Little Rock. 1994. (Contemporary American Fiction Ser.). 672p. pap. 11.95 o.p. (*0-14-023713-5*, Penguin Bks.) Penguin Group (USA) Inc.

Campbell, Bethany. Flirtation River. l.t. ed. 1997. (Romance-Hall Ser.). 248p. 23.95 o.p. (*0-7838-8129-0*, Macmillan Reference USA) Gale Group.

—Flirtation River. 1988. pap. (*0-373-02911-X*, Harlequin Bks.) Harlequin Enterprises, Ltd.

Campbell, Bethany, contrib. by. The Roses of Constant. 2000. 26.95 (0-7862-2352-9, Five Star) Gale Group.
Charles, D. L. Object Eve. 2000. 280p. pap. (1-55212-501-7) Trafford Publishing.
Coulter, Hope N. Dry Bones: A Novel. 1990. 264p. 17.95 o.p. (0-87483-152-0) August Hse. Pubs., Inc.
Dane, Dan. Bloodlines of Tyranny. 2001. pap. 15.54 (0-7596-2897-1) 1stBooks Library.
Edwards, Cassie. Savage Pride. 2000. 448p. mass mkt. 5.99 (0-505-52406-6, Love Spell) Dorchester Publishing Co., Inc.
Evanick, Marcia. Family First. 1996. 240p. mass mkt. 3.50 o.s.i (0-553-44468-9) Bantam Bks.
Fleming, Julie Elaine. Moving Lila. E-Book 22.95 (0-312-27533-1); 2000. 212p. 22.95 (0-312-24409-6) St. Martin's Pr.
Fowler, Earlene. Arkansas Traveler. 2001. 304p. 21.95 o.s.i (0-425-17808-0, Prime Crime) Berkley Publishing Group.
Garlock, Dorothy. Dream River. l.t. ed. 1999. (Romance Ser.). 517p. 27.95 (0-7838-8636-5, Macmillan Reference USA) Gale Group.
—Dream River. 1990. 19.00 o.p. (0-7278-4058-4) Severn Hse. Pubs., Ltd.
—Dream River. 384p. 1989. mass mkt. 5.99 (0-445-20676-4); 1988. mass mkt. 3.95 o.s.i (0-445-20364-1) Warner Bks., Inc.
Giles, Janice Holt. The Plum Thicket. 1978. mass mkt. 1.95 o.s.i (0-449-23767-2, Fawcett) Ballantine Bks.
—The Plum Thicket. 1984. (General Ser.). lib. bdg. 17.95 o.p. (0-8161-3647-5, Macmillan Reference USA) Gale Group.
Giles, Janice Holt, ed. The Plum Thicket. 1996. 284p. 30.00 (0-8131-1947-2); pap. 17.00 (0-8131-0859-4) Univ. Pr. of Kentucky.
Glancy, Diane H. Monkey Secret. 1995. 116p. 24.00 (0-8101-5016-6) Northwestern Univ. Pr.
Gossett, Parthy. Jody, Quack, & Me. 2003. pap. 9.95 (0-595-30046-4) iUniverse, Inc.
Grisham, John. A Painted House. 2004. 384p. pap. 13.00 (0-385-33793-0, Delta); 2001. 480p. mass mkt. 7.99 (0-440-23722-X) Dell Publishing.
—A Painted House. 2001. 400p. 27.95 (0-385-50120-X, Image); 250.00 o.s.i (0-385-50121-8, Talese, Nan A.) Doubleday Publishing.
—A Painted House. l.t. ed. 576p. 2004. pap. 13.95 (0-375-72812-0); 2001. 27.95 (0-375-43101-2) Random Hse. Large Print.
Hale, Keith. Cody. (Orig.). 1987. 190p. pap. 6.95 o.p. (1-55583-105-2); 1994. 191p. reprint ed. pap. 5.95 o.p. (1-55583-601-1) Alyson Pubns.
Harington, Donald. The Architecture of the Arkansas Ozarks. 1987. (Illus.). 384p. pap. 20.00 o.p. (0-15-607880-5, Harvest Bks.) Harcourt Trade Pubs.
—The Architecture of the Arkansas Ozarks. 2004. pap. 14.95 (1-59264-073-7) Toby Pr.
—Butterfly Weed. 1996. 384p. 24.00 o.s.i (0-15-100164-2); pap. 19.00 (0-15-600219-1, Harvest Bks.) Harcourt Trade Pubs.
—Thirteen Albatrosses: Or, Falling off the Mountain. 2002. 432p. 26.00 o.s.i (0-8050-6855-4) Holt, Henry & Co.
Harris, Charlaine. Shakespeare's Champion. 1998. 274p. pap. 19.00 o.s.i (0-440-61352-3, Delta); 272p. mass mkt. 5.99 (0-440-22421-7) Dell Publishing.
—Shakespeare's Champion. 1997. (Lily Bard Mysteries Ser.). 224p. 20.95 o.p. (0-312-17005-X, Saint Martin's Minotaur) St. Martin's Pr.
—Shakespeare's Champion. l.t. ed. 1998. (Cloak & Dagger Ser.). 327p. 26.95 (0-7862-1454-6) Thorndike Pr.
—Shakespeare's Christmas: A Lily Bard Mystery. 1999. (Lily Bard Mysteries Ser.). 256p. mass mkt. 5.99 (0-440-23499-9) Dell Publishing.
—Shakespeare's Christmas: A Lily Bard Mystery. 1998. 224p. 20.95 (0-312-19330-0, Saint Martin's Minotaur) St. Martin's Pr.
—Shakespeare's Counselor: A Lily Bard Mystery. 2001. 240p. 22.95 (0-312-27762-8, Saint Martin's Minotaur) St. Martin's Pr.
—Shakespeare's Landlord. 1997. 256p. pap. 19.00 (0-440-61406-6, Dell Bks.); mass mkt. 5.99 (0-440-22418-7) Dell Publishing.
—Shakespeare's Landlord. 1996. 224p. 20.95 o.p. (0-312-14415-6, Saint Martin's Minotaur) St. Martin's Pr.
—Shakespeare's Trollop. 2004. 208p. mass mkt. 5.99 (0-425-19699-2) Berkley Publishing Group.
—Shakespeare's Trollop. 2000. 227p. 23.95 (0-312-26228-0, Saint Martin's Minotaur) St. Martin's Pr.
—Shakespeare's Trollop. l.t. ed. 2000. (Mystery Ser.). (Illus.). 296p. 28.95 (0-7862-3030-4) Thorndike Pr.
Hays, Donald. The Dixie Association. 1997. (Voices of the South Ser.). 392p. pap. 14.95 (0-8071-2226-2) Louisiana State Univ. Pr.
—The Dixie Association. 1984. 352p. 16.45 o.p. (0-671-47564-9, Simon & Schuster) Simon & Schuster.
—The Dixie Association. 1985. 416p. mass mkt. 3.95 o.s.i (0-446-32815-4) Warner Bks., Inc.
Hefley, Howard J. Way Back in the Ozarks. 1992. 280p. pap. 5.95 (0-929292-26-X) Hannibal Bks.
—Way Back in the Ozarks: The Tale of Danny Boy, Bk. 2. 1993. 260p. pap. 5.95 (0-929292-38-3) Hannibal Bks.
Hess, Joan. Busy Bodies. 1995. (Claire Malloy Mystery Ser.). 256p. 19.95 o.p. (0-525-93910-5) Dutton/Plume.
—Closely Akin to Murder. 1996. (Claire Malloy Mystery Ser.). 240p. 21.95 o.s.i (0-525-93911-3, Dutton) Dutton/Plume.
—Closely Akin to Murder. 1997. (Claire Malloy Mysteries Ser.). 272p. mass mkt. 5.99 o.s.i (0-451-40561-7, Onyx) NAL.
—A Conventional Corpse. l.t. ed. 2000. (Wheeler Softcover Ser.). 293p. pap. 24.95 (1-56895-995-8, Wheeler Publishing, Inc.) Gale Group.
—A Conventional Corpse. 2001. 304p. mass mkt. 6.50 o.s.i (0-312-97726-3, St. Martin's Paperbacks); 2000. 275p. 23.95 (0-312-24662-5, Saint Martin's Minotaur) St. Martin's Pr.
—Dear Miss Demeanor. 1990. (Claire Malloy Ser.: No. 3). 195p. mass mkt. 4.99 o.s.i (0-345-34911-3) Ballantine Bks.
—Dear Miss Demeanor. (Claire Malloy Mysteries Ser.). 2000. 208p. mass mkt. 5.99 (0-312-97313-6, St. Martin's Paperbacks); 1987. 192p. 13.95 o.p. (0-312-00702-7, Saint Martin's Minotaur) St. Martin's Pr.
—Death by the Light of the Moon. 208p. 1995. pap. 15.00 (0-345-47171-7); 1994. mass mkt. 6.50 (0-345-37838-5) Ballantine Bks.
—Death by the Light of the Moon. (Claire Malloy Mystery Ser.). 240p. 2003. mass mkt. 6.99 (0-312-99101-0, St. Martin's Paperbacks); 1992. 18.95 o.p. (0-312-06949-9, Saint Martin's Minotaur) St. Martin's Pr.
—A Diet to Die For. 1992. (Claire Mallory Mystery Ser.). reprint ed. mass mkt. 5.50 o.s.i (0-345-36654-9) Ballantine Bks.
—A Diet to Die For. 1989. 192p. 14.95 o.p. (0-312-03326-5, Saint Martin's Minotaur) St. Martin's Pr.
—A Holly, Jolly Murder. l.t. ed. 2003. (Mystery Ser.). 27.95 (1-57490-531-7) Beeler, Thomas T. Publisher.
—A Holly, Jolly Murder. 1997. (Claire Malloy Mystery Ser.). 272p. 22.95 o.s.i (0-525-94240-8) Dutton/Plume.
—A Holly, Jolly Murder. 1998. (Claire Malloy Mystery Ser.). 288p. mass mkt. 5.99 o.s.i (0-451-40728-8, Onyx) NAL.
—Madness in Maggody. 1992. (Arly Hanks Mystery Ser.). 240p. mass mkt. 5.99 o.s.i (0-451-40299-5, Onyx) NAL.
—Madness in Maggody. 1990. 16.95 o.p. (0-312-05465-3, Saint Martin's Minotaur) St. Martin's Pr.
—Maggody & the Moonbeams. 2001. 256p. 23.00 (0-7432-0229-5, Simon & Schuster) Simon & Schuster.
—Maggody in Manhattan. 1992. (Arly Hanks Mystery Ser.). 272p. 18.00 o.p. (0-525-93519-3, Dutton) Dutton/Plume.
—Maggody in Manhattan. 1993. (Arly Hanks Mystery Ser.). 256p. reprint ed. mass mkt. 5.50 o.s.i (0-451-40376-2, Onyx) NAL.
—The Maggody Militia. 1997. (Arly Hanks Mystery Ser.). 320p. 21.95 o.s.i (0-525-94236-X) Dutton/Plume.
—The Maggody Militia. 1998. (Arly Hanks Mystery Ser.). 224p. mass mkt. 5.99 o.s.i (0-451-40726-1, Onyx) NAL.
—Malice in Maggody. 1991. (Arly Hanks Mystery Ser.). 240p. mass mkt. 5.99 o.s.i (0-451-40236-7, Onyx) NAL.
—Martians in Maggody. 1994. (Arly Hanks Mystery Ser.). 256p. 18.95 o.s.i (0-525-93840-0) Dutton/Plume.
—Martians in Maggody. 1995. (Arly Hanks Mystery Ser.). 304p. mass mkt. 5.50 o.s.i (0-451-40592-7, Onyx) NAL.
—Miracles in Maggody, unabr. ed. 1999. audio 39.95 Blackstone Audio Bks., Inc.
—Miracles in Maggody. 1995. (Arly Hanks Mystery Ser.). 288p. 20.95 o.p. (0-525-94051-0, Dutton) Dutton/Plume.
—Miracles in Maggody. 1996. (Arly Hanks Mystery Ser.). 288p. mass mkt. 5.99 o.s.i (0-451-40656-7) NAL.
—Mischief in Maggody. 1991. (Arly Hanks Mystery Ser.). 256p. mass mkt. 5.99 o.s.i (0-451-40253-7, Onyx) NAL.
—Mischief in Maggody. 1988. 176p. 14.95 o.p. (0-312-01792-8, Saint Martin's Minotaur) St. Martin's Pr.
—Misery Loves Maggody. 1999. 288p. 22.00 (0-684-84562-8, Simon & Schuster); 1999. 288p. 22.00 (0-684-86212-3, Simon & Schuster); 2000. (Illus.). 304p. reprint ed. pap. 6.99 (0-671-01684-9, Pocket) Simon & Schuster.
—Mortal Remains in Maggody. 1991. (Arly Hanks Mystery Ser.). 304p. 18.95 o.p. (0-525-93368-9, Dutton) Dutton/Plume.
—Mortal Remains in Maggody. 1992. (Arly Hanks Mystery Ser.). 272p. mass mkt. 4.50 o.s.i (0-451-40326-6, Onyx) NAL.
—Much Ado in Maggody. 1991. (Arly Hanks Mystery Ser.). 256p. mass mkt. 5.99 o.s.i (0-451-40268-5, Onyx) NAL.
—Much Ado in Maggody. 1989. 15.95 o.p. (0-312-02952-7, Saint Martin's Minotaur) St. Martin's Pr.
—Muletrain to Maggody. 2004. 288p. 23.00 (0-7432-2638-0, Simon & Schuster) Simon & Schuster.
—The Murder at the Murder at the Mimosa Inn. 1987. mass mkt. 4.99 o.s.i (0-345-34324-7) Ballantine Bks.
—The Murder at the Murder at the Mimosa Inn. 1999. 192p. mass mkt. 5.99 (0-312-97178-8, St. Martin's Paperbacks); 1986. 208p. 13.95 o.p. (0-312-55293-9) St. Martin's Pr.
—Murder@Maggody.com. l.t. ed. 2000. (Wheeler Large Print Book Ser.). 312p. pap. 24.95 (1-56895-886-2, Wheeler Publishing, Inc.) Gale Group.
—Murder@Maggody.com. 2000. 256p. 22.00 o.s.i (0-684-84563-6, Simon & Schuster) Simon & Schuster.
—O Little Town of Maggody. 1993. (Arly Hanks Mystery Ser.). 256p. 19.00 o.p. (0-525-93654-8, Dutton) Dutton/Plume.
—O Little Town of Maggody. abr. ed. 1994. (Arly Hanks Mystery Ser.). audio 16.00 o.p. (0-453-00871-2, Penguin AudioBooks) HighBridge Co.
—O Little Town of Maggody. 1994. (Arly Hanks Mystery Ser.). 256p. mass mkt. 4.50 o.s.i (0-451-40457-2, Onyx) NAL.
—Out on a Limb. E-Book 17.95 (0-312-70895-5); 2003. mass mkt. o.p. (0-312-98967-9, St. Martin's Paperbacks); 2003. 336p. mass mkt. 6.99 (0-312-98632-7, St. Martin's Paperbacks); 2002. 304p. 23.95 (0-312-26680-4, Saint Martin's Minotaur) St. Martin's Pr.
—Out on a Limb. 2003. (Americana Ser.). 28.95 (0-7862-5102-6) Thorndike Pr.
—Poisoned Pins. 1993. (Claire Malloy Mystery Ser.). 256p. 18.00 o.p. (0-525-93591-6) Dutton/Plume.
—Poisoned Pins. 1994. (Claire Malloy Mystery Ser.). 256p. mass mkt. 5.99 o.s.i (0-451-40390-8, Onyx) NAL.
—A Really Cute Corpse. 1988. 192p. 14.95 o.p. (0-312-02271-9, Saint Martin's Minotaur) St. Martin's Pr.
—Roll over & Play Dead. 1992. reprint ed. mass mkt. 5.50 o.s.i (0-345-37586-6) Ballantine Bks.
—Roll over & Play Dead. (Claire Mallory Mystery Ser.). 2003. 208p. mass mkt. 5.99 (0-312-98828-1, St. Martin's Paperbacks); 1991. 17.95 o.p. (0-312-05956-6, Saint Martin's Minotaur) St. Martin's Pr.
—Strangled Prose. 1987. mass mkt. 5.99 o.s.i (0-345-34059-0) Ballantine Bks.
—Strangled Prose. 192p. 1998. mass mkt. 5.99 (0-312-96864-7, St. Martin's Paperbacks); 1985. 12.95 o.p. (0-312-76428-6) St. Martin's Pr.
—Tickled to Death. 1994. (Claire Malloy Mystery Ser.). 224p. 18.95 o.p. (0-525-93810-9) Dutton/Plume.
—Tickled to Death. l.t. ed. 1994. pap. 19.95 o.p. (1-56895-079-9, Wheeler Publishing, Inc.) Gale Group.
—Tickled to Death. 1995. (Claire Malloy Mystery Ser.). 304p. mass mkt. 5.99 o.s.i (0-451-40550-1, Onyx) NAL.
Hickman, Patricia. Fallen Angels. l.t. ed. 2004. 417p. pap. 16.95 (1-59415-001-X, Walker Large Print) Gale Group.
—Fallen Angels. l.t. ed. 2003. (Millwood Hollow Ser.). 417p. 27.95 (0-7862-5608-7) Thorndike Pr.
—Fallen Angels. 2003. (Millwood Hollow Ser.). 320p. pap. 12.95 (0-446-69101-1, Warner Faith) Warner Bks., Inc.
Hill, Mars. The Moaner's Bench. 1998. 384p. o.s.i (0-06-019102-3, HarperFlamingo) HarperCollins Pubs. Canada, Ltd.
—The Moaner's Bench: A Novel. 1999. 384p. pap. 14.00 (0-06-093058-6, Perennial) HarperTrade.
Hunter, Stephen. Black Light. 1997. 528p. mass mkt. 7.99 (0-440-22313-X) Dell Publishing.
—Black Light. unabr. ed. 1996. audio 23.95 o.s.i (0-553-47748-X, RH Audio) Random Hse. Audio Publishing Group.
—Hot Springs. 2003. (Illus.). 560p. reprint ed. pap. 7.99 (0-671-03545-2, Pocket) Simon & Schuster.
—The Point of Impact. 1993. 592p. mass mkt. 7.99 (0-553-56351-3) Bantam Bks.
—The Point of Impact. 1993. audio 12.79 o.s.i (0-553-70063-4, RH Audio) Random Hse. Audio Publishing Group.
—Point of Impact. abr. ed. 1999. audio 9.99 o.s.i (0-553-70193-2, RH Audio) Random Hse. Audio Publishing Group.
Joe, Yolanda. The Hatwearer's Lesson. l.t. ed. 2003. lib. bdg. 28.95 (1-58547-339-1, Platinum) Ctr. Point Large Print.
—The Hatwearer's Lesson. 2003. 288p. 23.95 (0-525-94716-7) Dutton/Plume.
Jones, Douglas C. Come Winter. 1989. 19.95 o.p. (0-8050-0944-2) Holt, Henry & Co.
—Come Winter. 1992. (Reprint Ser.). 432p. pap. 24.95 (1-55728-259-5) Univ. of Arkansas Pr.
—Hickory Cured. 1987. 16.95 o.p. (0-8050-0383-5) Holt, Henry & Co.
—This Savage Race, Set. l.t. ed. 1994. (Studio Ser.). 109.95 o.p. incl. audio (0-7862-9992-4, Macmillan Reference USA) Gale Group.
—This Savage Race. 1994. 512p. mass mkt. 4.50 o.p. (0-06-100770-6) HarperCollins Pubs.
—This Savage Race. 1993. 320p. 23.00 o.p. (0-8050-2243-0) Holt, Henry & Co.
—Weedy Rough. 1989. mass mkt. 4.95 o.p. (0-8125-8463-5, Tor Bks.) Doherty, Tom Assocs., LLC.
—Weedy Rough. 1981. 352p. o.p. (0-03-050931-9) Holt, Henry & Co.
Judd, Cameron. Confederate Gold. 1993. 208p. mass mkt. 3.99 o.s.i (0-553-56051-4) Bantam Bks.
—Confederate Gold. 2000. 212p. mass mkt. 5.99 (0-312-97498-1, St. Martin's Paperbacks) St. Martin's Pr.
Lewis, Preston. The Redemption of Jesse James. Lewis, Preston, ed. 1995. 368p. mass mkt. 5.50 o.s.i (0-553-56542-7) Bantam Bks.
—The Redemption of Jesse James. l.t. ed. 1995. 496p. 20.95 o.p. (0-7838-1500-X, Macmillan Reference USA) Gale Group.
Macomber, Debbie. Country Brides: A Little Bit Country; Country Bride. 1998. mass mkt. (1-55166-475-5, 1-66475-4, Mira Bks.) Harlequin Enterprises, Ltd.
Mailer, Norris Church. Windchill Summer. 2001. (Reader's Circle Ser.). 432p. pap. 14.00 (0-345-43533-8, Ballantine Bks.) Ballantine Bks.
—Windchill Summer: A Novel. E-Book 19.95 (1-58945-599-1) Adobe Systems, Inc.
—Windchill Summer: A Novel. 2000. E-Book 19.95 (0-375-50572-5) Random Hse., Inc.
—Windchill Summer: A Novel. l.t. ed. 2000. (Basic Ser.). 767p. 27.95 (0-7862-2819-9) Thorndike Pr.
Marlow, Herb. The Guns of Devil's Den. 2000. (Guns of the Civil War Ser.: No. 2). (Illus.). 150p. 21.95 (1-893595-12-9, Guns-2) Four Seasons Bks., Inc.
—The Guns of Prairie Grove. 1999. (Illus.). vi, 153p. pap. 10.95 (1-893595-03-X); (Guns of the Civil War Ser.: No. 1). lib. bdg. 21.95 (1-893595-02-1) Four Seasons Bks., Inc.
McFadden, Bernice L. Sugar. 240p. 2000. 22.95 (0-525-94531-8, Dutton); 2001. reprint ed. pap. 13.00 (0-452-28220-9, Plume) Dutton/Plume.
—Sugar. l.t. ed. 2002. (African American Ser.). 386p. 28.95 (0-7862-3871-2) Thorndike Pr.
—Sugar. 2001. 19.05 (0-606-20932-8) Turtleback Bks.
—This Bitter Earth. 2002. 288p. pap. 13.00 (0-452-28381-7, Plume); 23.95 o.s.i (0-525-94636-5, Dutton) Dutton/Plume.
—This Bitter Earth. l.t. ed. 2002. (African American Ser.). 420p. 29.95 (0-7862-3882-8) Thorndike Pr.
McLarey, Myra. Water from the Well. 1995. 256p. 21.00 o.p. (0-87113-610-4, Atlantic Monthly Pr.) Grove/Atlantic, Inc.
—Water from the Well. 1996. 256p. pap. 11.00 (0-684-83097-3, Touchstone) Simon & Schuster.
Reynolds, April. Knee-Deep in Wonder: A Novel. 2003. 320p. 23.00 (0-8050-7346-9, Metropolitan Bks.) Holt, Henry & Co.
Rudy, Vicky. Call Me Jillian. 2000. 316p. pap. 22.99 (0-7388-1247-1); text 32.99 (0-7388-1246-3) Xlibris Corp.
Shankman, Sarah. He Was Her Man. Chelius, Jane, ed. 288p. 1993. 20.00 (0-671-77553-7, Atria); 1994. reprint ed. mass mkt. 5.50 (0-671-77563-4, Pocket) Simon & Schuster.
Simon, Charlie M. The Arkansas Stories of Charlie May Simon. Hagen, Lyman B., ed. 1981. (Illus.). 83p. (J). (gr. 1-7). 7.95 o.s.i (0-935304-22-3) August Hse. Pubs., Inc.
Simpson, Ethel C. Simpkinsville & Vicinity: Arkansas Stories of Ruth McEnery Stuart. 1999. (Classics Ser.). (Illus.). 214p. pap. text 18.95 (1-55728-575-6) Univ. of Arkansas Pr.
Simpson, Ethel C., ed. Simpkinsville & Vicinity: Arkansas Stories of Ruth McEnery Stuart. 1983. 224p. 19.00 o.p. (0-938626-12-4); pap. 8.95 o.p. (0-938626-16-7) Univ. of Arkansas Pr.
Stockley, Grif. Blind Judgment. 1999. (Gideon Page Mystery Ser.). 384p. mass mkt. 6.50 o.s.i (0-06-101317-X) HarperCollins Pubs.
—Blind Judgment. 1997. 21.50 (0-684-81564-8, Simon & Schuster) Simon & Schuster.
—Expert Testimony. 1994. pap. 5.99 o.p. (0-8041-9832-2); 1993. pap. 5.99 o.p. (0-8041-9810-1); 1992. mass mkt. 5.99 o.s.i (0-8041-1094-8) Ballantine Bks. (Ivy Bks.).
—Expert Testimony. 1991. 19.95 o.p. (0-671-70920-8) Summit Bks.
—Illegal Motion: A Gideon Page Mystery. 1997. 408p. mass mkt. 6.99 o.s.i (0-449-18332-7, Fawcett); 1996. mass mkt. 6.99 o.p. (0-449-22557-7, Fawcett); 1995. mass mkt. 5.99 o.s.i (0-8041-1401-3, Ivy Bks.) Ballantine Bks.
—Illegal Motion: A Gideon Page Mystery. 1995. 301p. 21.00 (0-684-80355-0, Simon & Schuster) Simon & Schuster.

—Probable Cause. 1993. (Southern Mysteries Ser.). mass mkt. 5.99 o.s.i (*0-8041-1133-2*, Ivy Bks.) Ballantine Bks.

—Probable Cause. 1992. 287p. 19.00 o.p. (*0-671-74601-4*, Simon & Schuster) Simon & Schuster.

—Religious Conviction. 1995. reprint ed. mass mkt. 5.99 o.s.i (*0-8041-1255-X*, Ivy Bks.) Ballantine Bks.

—Religious Conviction. 1994. 286p. 21.00 (*0-671-79869-3*, Simon & Schuster) Simon & Schuster.

Stone, Gerald Eugene Nathan. Rockhand Lizzie. 1999. 177p. pap. 12.95 (*0-9640513-6-2*) Tattersall Publishing.

Stuart, Ruth M. In Simpkinsville. 1977. (Short Story Index Reprint Ser.). 19.95 (*0-8369-3174-2*) Ayer Co. Pubs., Inc.

Thoene, Bodie. In My Father's House. l.t. ed. 1993. (Inspirational Ser.). 626p. pap. 21.95 o.p. (*0-8161-5669-7*, Macmillan Reference USA) Gale Group.

—Say to This Mountain. 1993. (Shiloh Legacy Ser.: Vol. 3). 448p. (J). pap. 12.99 (*1-55661-191-9*) Bethany Hse. Pubs.

—Shiloh Autumn. 1999. (Galway Chronicles Ser.). 324p. pap. text 9.97 (*0-7852-6922-3*) Nelson, Thomas Pubs.

—The Shiloh Legacy, Vols. 1-3. 1993. (Shiloh Legacy Ser.). pap. 38.99 (*1-55661-774-7*, 252774) Bethany Hse. Pubs.

—A Thousand Shall Fall. 1992. (Shiloh Legacy Ser.: Vol. 2). 432p. pap. 12.99 (*1-55661-190-0*) Bethany Hse. Pubs.

—A Thousand Shall Fall. l.t. ed. 1993. (General Ser.). 606p. lib. bdg. 22.95 (*0-8161-5718-9*, Macmillan Reference USA) Gale Group.

Thoene, Bodie & Thoene, Brock. Shiloh Autumn. 1996. 480p. 21.99 o.p. (*0-7852-8066-9*); 24.99 o.p. incl. audio (*0-7852-7273-9*) Nelson, Thomas Inc.

—Shiloh Autumn. 1997. 480p. pap. 14.99 (*0-7852-7134-1*) Nelson, Thomas Pubs.

Walsh, Michael. And All the Saints. 2004. 592p. mass mkt. 7.99 (*0-446-61369-X*); 2003. (Illus.). 432p. 24.95 (*0-446-51815-8*) Warner Bks., Inc.

Williams, Miller. The Lives of Kelvin Fletcher: Stories Mostly Short. 2002. 224p. 24.95 (*0-8203-2439-6*) Univ. of Georgia Pr.

Wood, Jane Roberts. A Place Called Sweet Shrub. 1991. 320p. pap. 10.00 o.s.i (*0-440-50305-1*, Dell Bks.) Dell Publishing.

—A Place Called Sweet Shrub, Set. unabr. ed. 1996. audio 67.00 Recorded Bks., LLC.

—A Place Called Sweet Shrub. 3rd ed. 2000. (Lucinda Richards Trilogy Ser.: Vol. 2). 286p. reprint ed. pap. 15.95 (*1-57441-079-2*) Univ. of North Texas Pr.

### ASPEN (COLO.)—FICTION

Clark, Carol Higgins. Iced. 1996. o.s.i (*0-316-87854-5*) Little Brown & Co.

—Iced. unabr. ed. 1995. 29.95 o.p. (*0-7871-0575-9*);Set. audio 17.95 o.p. (*0-7871-0220-2*, 392963) NewStar Media, Inc.

—Iced. 1999. 320p. mass mkt. 4.50 (*0-446-60778-9*); 1996. 320p. mass mkt. 7.99 (*0-446-60198-5*); 1995. 272p. 28.00 (*0-446-51764-X*) Warner Bks., Inc.

Temple, Lou Jane. Stiff Risotto. 1997. 224p. mass mkt. 6.50 (*0-312-96321-1*, St. Martin's Paperbacks) St. Martin's Pr.

Zigal, Thomas. Hardrock Stiff: A Kurt Muller Mystery. 1997. (Kurt Muller Mysteries Ser.). 384p. mass mkt. 5.99 o.s.i (*0-440-22452-7*) Dell Publishing.

—Into Thin Air: A Novel. 1996. (Kurt Muller Mysteries Ser.). 368p. mass mkt. 5.50 o.s.i (*0-440-22251-6*) Dell Publishing.

—Pariah. 2000. (Kurt Muller Mysteries Ser.). 336p. mass mkt. 5.99 o.s.i (*0-440-22443-8*) Dell Publishing.

### ATLANTA (GA.)—FICTION

Abrahams, Peter. The Last of the Dixie Heroes. 2002. 352p. mass mkt. 6.99 (*0-345-43940-6*) Ballantine Bks.

Bambara, Toni Cade. Those Bones Are Not My Child. 2000. (Illus.). 688p. pap. 16.00 (*0-679-77408-4*, Vintage) Knopf Publishing Group.

Barclay, Max. Red Mercury. 1997. pap. 5.99 o.p. (*0-7871-1416-2*, NewStar Pr.); 1996. 17.95 o.p. (*0-7871-0972-X*, 394019) NewStar Media, Inc.

—Red Mercury. 1996. 416p. 22.95 o.p. (*0-7871-0920-7*, Signet Bks.) Penguin Group (USA) Inc.

Bernhardt, William. Final Round. 2003. 336p. mass mkt. 7.50 (*0-345-44963-0*); 2002. 256p. 23.95 (*0-345-44962-2*) Ballantine Bks. (Ballantine Bks.).

—Final Round. l.t. ed. 2003. 307p. 25.95 (*0-375-43276-0*, Random House Large Print) Random Hse. Large Print.

Berry, Linda. Death & the Hubcap. 2000. 240p. 23.95 (*1-885173-75-X*) Write Way Publishing.

Bird, Beverly. When Winter Comes. 2003. E-Book 12.95 incl. cd-rom (*1-58444-031-7*); 1999. 376p. pap. 19.95 (*1-58444-067-8*) Disc-Us Bks., Inc.

Birmingham, Ruth. Atlanta Graves. 1998. (Sunny Childs Mysteries Ser.). 288p. mass mkt. 5.99 o.s.i (*0-425-16267-2*) Berkley Publishing Group.

—Fulton County Blues. 1999. (Fulton County Blues Ser.: Vol. 2). 288p. mass mkt. 5.99 o.s.i (*0-425-16697-X*, Prime Crime) Berkley Publishing Group.

—Fulton County Blues. 2000. 12.04 (*0-606-19296-4*) Turtleback Bks.

—Sweet Georgia. 2000. (Sunny Childs Mysteries Ser.). 320p. mass mkt. 5.99 o.s.i (*0-425-17671-1*, Prime Crime) Berkley Publishing Group.

Bishop, Michael. Ancient of Days. 1995. 354p. pap. 13.95 (*0-312-89027-3*); 1986. 416p. reprint ed. mass mkt. 3.95 (*0-8125-3197-3*) Doherty, Tom Assocs., LLC. (Tor Bks.).

—Ancient of Days. 1985. 310p. 16.95 o.p. (*0-87795-724-X*, Morrow, William & Co.) Morrow/Avon.

Byrd, Adrianne. All I've Ever Wanted. 2001. (Arabesque Ser.). 256p. mass mkt. 5.99 (*1-58314-137-5*) BET Bks.

Coleman, Evelyn. What a Woman's Gotta Do. 1999. 400p. mass mkt. 6.99 (*0-440-23500-6*) Dell Publishing.

—What a Woman's Gotta Do. 1998. 320p. 23.00 (*0-684-83175-9*, Simon & Schuster) Simon & Schuster.

Coram, Robert. Atlanta Heat. 1997. 368p. mass mkt. 5.99 o.s.i (*0-451-19391-1*, Signet Bks.) NAL.

—Dead South. 1999. 336p. mass mkt. 5.99 o.s.i (*0-451-19688-0*, Signet Bks.) NAL.

—Kill the Angels. 1996. 352p. mass mkt. 5.99 o.s.i (*0-451-40340-1*, Onyx) NAL.

DePoy, Phillip. Dancing Made Easy. 1999. (Flap Tucker Mysteries Ser.). 304p. mass mkt. 5.99 o.s.i (*0-440-22618-X*) Dell Publishing.

—Dead Easy. 2000. (Flap Tucker Mysteries Ser.). 288p. mass mkt. 5.99 o.s.i (*0-440-23643-6*) Dell Publishing.

—Easy. 1997. (Flap Tucker Mysteries Ser.). 288p. mass mkt. 5.99 o.s.i (*0-440-22494-2*) Dell Publishing.

—Easy: A Flap Tucker Mystery. 1999. E-Book 5.99 (*0-440-33375-X*) Random Hse., Inc.

—Easy as One, Two, Three: A Flap Tucker Mystery. 1999. (Flap Tucker Mysteries Ser.: Bk. 3). 288p. mass mkt. 5.99 o.s.i (*0-440-22617-1*) Dell Publishing.

—Too Easy. 1998. (Flap Tucker Mysteries Ser.). 288p. mass mkt. 5.99 o.s.i (*0-440-22495-0*) Dell Publishing.

Ellis, Jamellah. That Faith, That Trust, That Love: A Novel. 2003. (Strivers Row Ser.). 352p. pap. 12.95 (*0-8129-6656-2*, Villard Bks.) Random House Adult Trade Publishing Group.

Evans, Eric C. The Key. 2000. 198p. 18.95 (*0-8034-9398-3*, Avalon Bks.) Bouregy, Thomas & Co., Inc.

Fitzwater, Judy. Dying to Get Even. 1999. (Jennifer Marsh Mysteries Ser.). 240p. mass mkt. 6.50 (*0-449-00386-8*, Fawcett) Ballantine Bks.

Ford-Williamson, Estelle. Abbeville Farewell: A Novel of Early Atlanta & North Georgia. 2001. 264p. pap. 18.00 (*0-9708320-0-1*); 2nd ed. per. 18.00 (*0-9708320-1-X*) Other Voices.

Francis, Suzette. Rules for a Pretty Woman. 2003. 320p. pap. 13.95 (*0-06-053542-3*, Avon Bks.) Morrow/Avon.

Gallant, James. The Big Bust at Tyrone's Rooming House: A Novel of Atlanta. 2003. 227p. pap. 18.00 (*1-930180-09-8*) Glad Day Bks.

Griffith, Nicola. The Blue Place: A Novel of Suspense. 1999. 320p. pap. 13.00 (*0-380-79088-2*, Perennial) HarperTrade.

—The Blue Place: A Novel of Suspense. 1998. 320p. pap. 23.00 (*0-380-97446-0*, Avon Bks.) Morrow/Avon.

Hooper, Kay. After Caroline. l.t. ed. 1997. 368p. mass mkt. 6.99 (*0-553-57184-2*) Bantam Bks.

Johansen, Roy. Answer Man. unabr. ed. 1999. audio 66.00 (*0-7887-3134-3*, 95826E7) Recorded Bks., LLC.

—Beyond Belief. 2002. 400p. mass mkt. 5.99 (*0-553-58228-3*) Bantam Bks.

Jones, Tayari. Leaving Atlanta. 272p. 2003. pap. 13.95 (*0-446-69089-9*); 2002. 23.95 (*0-446-52830-7*) Warner Bks., Inc.

Kay, Terry. The Kidnapping of Aaron Greene. 1999. 288p. 25.00 (*0-688-15034-9*, Morrow, William & Co.) Morrow/Avon.

Kelly, Lelia. False Witness. 2000. 416p. mass mkt. 6.99 o.s.i (*0-7860-1193-9*); 312p. 23.00 o.s.i (*1-57566-490-9*, Kensington Bks.) Kensington Publishing Corp.

—Presumption of Guilt. 1998. 352p. mass mkt. 5.99 (*0-7860-0584-X*, Pinnacle Bks.); 224p. 22.95 o.s.i (*1-57566-249-3*) Kensington Publishing Corp.

Kingsbury, Suzanne. The Gospel According to Gracey. 2004. 288p. pap. 12.00 (*0-7432-2306-3*); 2003. 240p. 23.00 (*0-7432-2305-5*) Simon & Schuster. (Scribner).

Minnick, Wayne. The Crossbow Murder. 2000. 208p. pap. 13.95 (*0-88739-301-2*) Creative Arts Bk. Co.

Olshaker, Mark. Unnatural Causes. 1986. 480p. 18.95 o.p. (*0-688-05896-5*, Morrow, William & Co.) Morrow/Avon.

—Unnatural Causes. 1989. mass mkt. 4.50 o.s.i (*0-671-64435-1*, Pocket) Simon & Schuster.

O'Neal, Charles. Three Wishes for Jamie. 1976. 22.95 (*0-8488-0184-9*) Amereon, Ltd.

—Three Wishes for Jamie. 1991. 256p. reprint ed. pap. 5.95 (*1-56129-066-1*) Knightsbridge Publishing.

—Three Wishes for Jamie. 1980. 256p. reprint ed. 26.00 (*0-933256-08-6*); pap. text 16.00 (*0-933256-09-4*) Second Chance Pr.

Owens, Michael T. Pick-Up Lines: A Novel. Cadet, Guichard, ed. 2003. (YA). (gr. 11 up). pap. 15.00 (*0-9718191-5-7*, 212-591-6465) La Caille Nous Publishing Co.

Price, Eugenia. Beauty from Ashes. l.t. ed. 1995. 1008p. 28.50 o.s.i (*0-385-42314-4*);Vol. 3. (Beauty from Ashes Ser.: Vol. 3). 640p. 23.50 o.s.i (*0-385-26703-7*) Doubleday Publishing.

—Beauty from Ashes. 1996. 631p. mass mkt. 7.50 (*0-312-95917-6*, St. Martin's Paperbacks) St. Martin's Pr.

Randall, Alice. The Wind Done Gone. 2001. (Illus.). 224p. 22.00 (*0-618-10450-X*); 210p. 23.00 (*0-618-13309-7*) Houghton Mifflin Co.

—The Wind Done Gone: A Novel. 2002. (Illus.). 224p. pap. 12.00 (*0-618-21906-4*, Mariner Bks.) Houghton Mifflin Co. Trade & Reference Div.

Ray, Jeanne. Step-Ball-Change: A Novel. unabr. ed. 2002. audio 62.25 (*1-59086-083-7*, 3632, Unabridged Library Editions) Brilliance Audio.

—Step-Ball-Change: A Novel. 2002. 240p. 22.95 (*0-609-61003-1*, Shaye Areheart Bks.) Crown Publishing Group.

—Step-Ball-Change: A Novel. l.t. ed. 2002. (Core Collection). 284p. 31.95 (*0-7862-4371-6*) Thorndike Pr.

Rutland, Eva. No Crystal Stair. 2003. 368p. pap. (*1-55166-662-6*); 2000. 480p. per. (*1-55166-519-0*, 1-66519-9) Harlequin Enterprises, Ltd. (Mira Bks.).

Shankman, Sarah. First Kill All the Lawyers. 1991. mass mkt. 5.99 (*0-671-74893-9*); 1988. 224p. mass mkt. 3.50 (*0-671-64529-3*) Simon & Schuster. (Pocket).

Shriner, Larry. Epilogue for Murder. 1994. 264p. 21.95 (*0-8027-3182-1*) Walker & Co.

Siddons, Anne Rivers. Downtown. 1994. 352p. 288.00 o.p. (*0-06-017602-4*) HarperCollins Pubs.

—Downtown. 1994. 352p. 24.00 o.p. (*0-06-017934-1*); Set. 1999. audio (*1-55994-732-2*, 692189, Harper-Audio) HarperTrade.

—Downtown. 1995. 512p. mass mkt. 7.99 (*0-06-109968-6*, HarperTorch) Morrow/Avon.

—Downtown. unabr. ed. 1994. audio 97.00 (*0-7887-0062-6*, 94318E7) Recorded Bks., LLC.

—Downtown. 374p. 6.98 o.p. (*0-7651-0027-4*) Smithmark Pubs., Inc.

—Downtown. l.t. ed. (Paperback Bestsellers Ser.). 647p. 1995. 22.95 (*0-8161-7411-3*); 1994. lib. bdg. 27.95 (*0-8161-7410-5*) Thorndike Pr.

—Peachtree Road. 1989. 608p. mass mkt. 6.99 o.s.i (*0-345-36272-1*) Ballantine Bks.

—Peachtree Road. l.t. ed. 1995. 969p. lib. bdg. 19.95 o.p. (*0-8161-7413-X*, Macmillan Reference USA) Gale Group.

—Peachtree Road. 1988. 18.95 o.p. (*0-06-015799-2*) HarperTrade.

—Peachtree Road. 10th anniv. ed. 1998. 832p. mass mkt. 7.99 (*0-06-109723-3*, HarperTorch) Morrow/Avon.

—Peachtree Road. 1996. 576p. reprint ed. 27.50 (*0-937036-05-6*) Old New York Bk. Shop Pr.

—Peachtree Road. abr. ed. 1989. audio 16.00 o.s.i (*0-394-58044-3*, RH Audio) Random Hse. Audio Publishing Group.

—Peachtree Road. l.t. ed. 1994. (Core Collection). 969p. lib. bdg. 28.95 (*0-8161-7412-1*) Thorndike Pr.

Simms, William Gilmore. Joscelyn: A Tale of the Revolution. Butterworth, Keen, ed. 1975. (Centennial Edition of the Writings of William Gilmore Simms). xxx, 338p. 34.95 o.s.i (*0-87249-322-9*) Univ. of South Carolina Pr.

Skoryna, Stanley C. Atlanta on My Mind, Vol. 1. Mullen, Joseph A., ed. 1996. (Illus.). 335p. 38.95 (*0-943100-01-1*, 100-03) Home Museum Pr.

Smith, Faye M. Flight of the Blackbird. 1996. 348p. 22.50 (*0-684-82971-1*, Scribner) Simon & Schuster.

—The Flight of the Blackbird. 1997. 464p. reprint ed. mass mkt. 6.50 (*0-446-60561-1*) Warner Bks., Inc.

Sorrells, Walter. Will to Murder. 1996. 304p. (Orig.). mass mkt. 5.50 (*0-380-78020-8*, Avon Bks.) Morrow/Avon.

Sprinkle, Patricia H. Murder on Peachtree Street. 1991. 17.95 o.p. (*0-312-05476-9*, Saint Martin's Minotaur) St. Martin's Pr.

—Somebody's Dead in Snellville. 1992. 256p. 18.95 o.p. (*0-312-07809-9*, Saint Martin's Minotaur) St. Martin's Pr.

Staats, Marilyn D. Looking for Atlanta. 1999. 232p. pap. 12.95 (*0-8203-2120-6*); 1992. 240p. 19.95 (*0-8203-1470-6*) Univ. of Georgia Pr.

—Looking for Atlanta. 1993. 240p. mass mkt. 5.99 (*0-446-36574-2*) Warner Bks., Inc.

Sutton, Remar. Long Lines. 1988. 304p. 16.95 o.p. (*1-55584-140-6*) Grove/Atlantic, Inc.

—Long Lines. 1989. 272p. mass mkt. 3.95 o.s.i (*0-445-40794-8*, Mysterious Pr. Paperback Bks.) Warner Bks., Inc.

Trocheck, Kathy Hogan. Every Crooked Nanny. 1992. 208p. 19.00 o.p. (*0-06-017923-6*) HarperTrade.

—Every Crooked Nanny. 1993. (Callahan Garrity Mystery Ser.). 336p. mass mkt. 6.50 (*0-06-109170-7*, HarperTorch) Morrow/Avon.

—Every Crooked Nanny. l.t. ed. 1997. (Ulverscroft Large Print Ser.). 544p. 29.99 o.p. (*0-7089-3748-9*, Ulverscroft) Thorpe, F. A. Pubs. GBR. *Dist:* Ulverscroft Large Print Bks., Ltd., Ulverscroft Large Print Canada, Ltd.

—Happy Never After. 1995. 306p. 22.00 o.p. (*0-06-017637-7*) HarperCollins Pubs.

—Happy Never After. 1996. (Callahan Garrity Mystery Ser.). 320p. mass mkt. 5.99 (*0-06-109360-2*, HarperTorch) Morrow/Avon.

—Heart Trouble. 1996. (Callahan Garrity Mystery Ser.). 304p. 22.00 o.p. (*0-06-017638-5*) HarperCollins Pubs.

—Heart Trouble. 1997. 304p. mass mkt. 5.99 (*0-06-109585-0*, HarperTorch) Morrow/Avon.

—Heart Trouble. l.t. ed. 1998. (Ulverscroft Large Print Ser.). 448p. 29.99 (*0-7089-3947-3*, Ulverscroft) Thorpe, F. A. Pubs. GBR. *Dist:* Ulverscroft Large Print Bks., Ltd., Ulverscroft Large Print Canada, Ltd.

—Homemade Sin. l.t. ed. 1994. 379p. pap. 19.95 (*0-7838-1163-2*, Macmillan Reference USA) Gale Group.

—Homemade Sin. 1994. 256p. 20.00 o.p. (*0-06-017765-9*) HarperTrade.

—Homemade Sin. 1995. (Callahan Garrity Mystery Ser.). 304p. mass mkt. 5.99 (*0-06-109256-8*, HarperTorch) Morrow/Avon.

—Irish Eyes. 2000. (Callahan Garrity Mystery Ser.). 304p. 24.00 (*0-06-019421-9*) HarperCollins Pubs.

—Irish Eyes. 2001. (Callahan Garrity Mystery Ser.). 320p. mass mkt. 5.99 (*0-06-109869-8*, Avon Bks.) Morrow/Avon.

—Irish Eyes. l.t. ed. 2000. (Mystery Ser.). 473p. 28.95 (*0-7862-2837-7*) Thorndike Pr.

—Midnight Clear. l.t. ed. 2000. 360p. 26.95 (*1-57490-323-3*, Beeler Large Print Bks.) Beeler, Thomas T. Publisher.

—Midnight Clear. 1998. (Callahan Garrity Mystery Ser.). 288p. 23.00 o.s.i (*0-06-017543-5*) HarperCollins Pubs.

—Midnight Clear. 1999. (Callahan Garrity Mystery Ser.). 416p. mass mkt. 5.99 (*0-06-109800-0*, HarperTorch) Morrow/Avon.

—Strange Brew. l.t. ed. 1999. 24.95 (*1-57490-219-9*, Beeler Large Print Bks.) Beeler, Thomas T. Publisher.

—Strange Brew. 1997. (Callahan Garrity Mystery Ser.). 288p. 23.00 o.s.i (*0-06-017542-7*) HarperCollins Pubs.

—Strange Brew. 1998. (Callahan Garrity Mystery Ser.). 336p. reprint ed. mass mkt. 5.99 (*0-06-109173-1*, HarperTorch) Morrow/Avon.

—To Live & Die in Dixie. 1993. 288p. 20.00 o.p. (*0-06-017924-4*) HarperTrade.

—To Live & Die in Dixie. 1994. (Callahan Garrity Mystery Ser.). 320p. mass mkt. 5.99 (*0-06-109171-5*, HarperTorch) Morrow/Avon.

—To Live & Die in Dixie. l.t. ed. 1997. (Ulverscroft Large Print Ser.). 496p. 29.99 o.p. (*0-7089-3837-X*, Ulverscroft) Thorpe, F. A. Pubs. GBR. *Dist:* Ulverscroft Large Print Bks., Ltd., Ulverscroft Large Print Canada, Ltd.

Walker, Alice. Meridian. Bernard, Andre, ed. 2003. 264p. pap. 13.00 (*0-15-602834-4*, Harvest Bks.) Harcourt Trade Pubs.

—Meridian. 1981. mass mkt. 2.75 o.p. (*0-671-43750-X*, Washington Square Pr.) Simon & Schuster.

Wieland, Liza. The Names of the Lost: A Novel. 1992. 312p. 19.95 (*0-87074-337-6*) Southern Methodist Univ. Pr.

Willard, Fred. Down on Ponce. 1997. 288p. (Orig.). pap. 12.00 (*1-56352-431-7*) Longstreet Pr., Inc.

Windham, Donald. The Dog Star: A Novel. 1999. (Hill Street Classics Ser.). 224p. reprint ed. pap. 14.95 (*1-892514-09-5*, Hill Street Classics) Hill Street Pr., LLC.

Wolfe, Tom. A Man in Full. 2001. 704p. pap. 14.95 (*0-553-38133-4*); 1999. 800p. mass mkt. 8.50 (*0-553-58093-0*) Bantam Bks.

—A Man in Full, Pt. 1. unabr. ed. 1999. audio 104.00 (*0-7366-4373-7*, 4814-A) Books on Tape, Inc.

—A Man in Full. 1998. 742p. 28.95 (*0-374-27032-5*); 528p. 200.00 o.p. (*0-374-27030-9*) Farrar, Straus & Giroux.

—A Man in Full. l.t. ed. 1998. 33.95 o.p. (*1-56895-694-0*, Wheeler Publishing, Inc.) Gale Group.

—A Man in Full. abr. ed. 1999. audio 27.50 Highsmith Inc.

—A Man in Full. abr. ed. 1998. audio 27.50 (*0-553-47890-7*, 756001); audio compact disk 39.95 (*0-553-45619-9*) Random Hse. Audio Publishing Group. (RH Audio).

Woods, Sherryl. Bank on It. 2000. 235p. 26.95 (*0-7351-0306-2*); pap. 16.95 (*0-7351-0307-0*) Replica Bks.
—Bank on It. 1993. 240p. mass mkt. 4.99 o.s.i (*0-446-36404-5*) Warner Bks., Inc.
—Body & Soul. 2000. 254p. 26.95 (*0-7351-0310-0*); pap. 16.95 (*0-7351-0311-9*) Replica Bks.
—Body & Soul. 1990. 19.00 o.p. (*0-7278-4111-4*) Severn Hse. Pubs., Ltd.
—Body & Soul. 1994. 256p. mass mkt. 5.50 o.s.i (*0-446-60155-1*, Mysterious Pr. Paperback Bks.); 1989. 3.95 (*0-445-20900-3*) Warner Bks., Inc.
—Deadly Obsession. 2000. 236p. 26.95 (*0-7351-0314-3*); pap. 16.95 (*0-7351-0315-1*) Replica Bks.
—Deadly Obsession. 1995. 256p. mass mkt. 5.50 (*0-446-60091-1*) Warner Bks., Inc.
—Hide & Seek. unabr. collector's ed. 1994. audio 36.00 (*0-7366-2778-2*, 3497) Books on Tape, Inc.
—Hide & Seek. 2000. 339p. 28.95 (*0-7351-0304-6*); pap. 18.95 (*0-7351-0305-4*) Replica Bks.
—Hide & Seek. 1993. 240p. mass mkt. 4.99 o.s.i (*0-446-36405-3*) Warner Bks., Inc.
—Reckless. 2000. 240p. 26.95 (*0-7351-0312-7*); 235p. pap. 16.95 (*0-7351-0313-5*) Replica Bks.
—Reckless. 1990. reprint ed. 18.00 o.p. (*0-7278-4048-7*) Severn Hse. Pubs., Ltd.
—Reckless. 1993. 240p. mass mkt. 4.99 o.s.i (*0-446-36549-1*); 1989. pap. 3.95 (*0-445-20819-8*) Warner Bks., Inc.
—Stolen Moments. 2000. 253p. 26.95 (*0-7351-0300-3*); pap. 16.95 (*0-7351-0301-1*) Replica Bks.
—Stolen Moments. 1991. reprint ed. 18.95 o.p. (*0-7278-4174-2*) Severn Hse. Pubs., Ltd.
—Stolen Moments. 1995. 256p. mass mkt. 5.99 o.s.i (*0-446-60163-2*); 1990. mass mkt. 4.95 (*0-445-21010-9*, Mysterious Pr. Paperback Bks.) Warner Bks., Inc.
—Ties That Bind. 2000. 255p. 26.95 (*0-7351-0308-9*); 16.95 (*0-7351-0309-7*) Replica Bks.
—Ties That Bind. 1991. 256p. reprint ed. 19.00 o.p. (*0-7278-4245-5*) Severn Hse. Pubs., Ltd.
—Ties That Bind. 1991. 256p. mass mkt. 4.99 (*0-446-36117-8*) Warner Bks., Inc.
—White Lightning. 2000. 316p. 28.95 (*0-7351-0302-X*); pap. 18.95 (*0-7351-0303-8*) Replica Bks.
—White Lightning. 1995. 320p. mass mkt. 5.99 o.p. (*0-446-60090-3*) Warner Bks., Inc.
Woolner, Ann. Washed Gold. 1994. 391p. 25.00 o.s.i (*0-671-74194-2*, Simon & Schuster) Simon & Schuster.
Wyrick, E. L. A Strange & Bitter Crop. 1994. 304p. 20.95 o.p. (*0-312-11075-8*, Saint Martin's Minotaur) St. Martin's Pr.

## ATLANTIC CITY (N.J.)—FICTION

Blauner, Peter. Casino Moon. 1996. 320p. mass mkt. 5.99 o.p. (*0-380-72589-4*, Avon Bks.) Morrow/Avon.
—Casino Moon. 1994. 288p. 21.00 o.p. (*0-671-88177-9*, Simon & Schuster) Simon & Schuster.
Bretton, Barbara. The Day We Met. 1999. 320p. mass mkt. 6.99 (*0-425-17190-6*) Berkley Publishing Group.
Dezenhall, Eric. Jackie Disaster: A Novel. 2003. 416p. 24.95 (*0-312-30769-1*) St. Martin's Pr.
—Money Wanders. E-Book 13.95 (*0-312-70428-3*); 2002. 338p. 24.95 (*0-312-28275-3*) St. Martin's Pr.
Elwood, Roger. Where Angels Dare: A Novel. 1999. 240p. pap. 9.99 (*0-8054-1877-6*) Broadman & Holman Pubs.
Engelhard, Jack. Deadly Deception. 1997. 288p. 24.00 (*0-914839-43-8*) Gollehon Pr.
Erdman, Paul E. The Palace. 1988. 320p. mass mkt. 4.95 o.s.i (*0-553-27538-0*) Bantam Bks.
Heggan, Christiane. Blind Faith. 2001. 408p. mass mkt. (*1-55166-783-5*, 1-66783-1, Mira Bks.) Harlequin Enterprises, Ltd.
Jacobs, David. Snake Eyes. 1998. 208p. mass mkt. 6.50 o.s.i (*0-425-16637-6*) Berkley Publishing Group.
Kent, Bill. Down by the Sea. 1993. 320p. 19.95 o.p. (*0-312-09277-6*, Saint Martin's Minotaur) St. Martin's Pr.
—On a Blanket with My Baby. 1995. ix, 275p. 21.00 o.p. (*0-312-11870-8*, Saint Martin's Minotaur) St. Martin's Pr.
—Under the Boardwalk. 1990. mass mkt. 4.50 o.s.i (*1-55817-347-1*, Pinnacle Bks.) Kensington Publishing Corp.
—Under the Boardwalk. 1988. 320p. 18.95 o.p. (*1-55710-019-5*, Morrow, William & Co.) Morrow/Avon.
Leonard, Elmore. Glitz. l.t. ed. 1985. (General Ser.). 407p. 15.95 o.p. (*0-8161-3834-6*); 9.95 o.p. (*0-8161-3835-4*) Gale Group. (Macmillan Reference USA).
—Glitz. 1998. 432p. pap. 12.00 (*0-688-16095-6*, Quill) HarperTrade.
—Glitz. 2002. 432p. mass mkt. 7.50 (*0-06-008953-9*); 1983. 14.95 o.p. (*0-87795-632-4*, Morrow, William & Co.) Morrow/Avon.
—Glitz. 1987. 368p. mass mkt. 6.99 (*0-446-34343-9*); 1986. mass mkt. 3.95 (*0-446-32920-7*) Warner Bks., Inc.
Litwin, Bob, et al. The Last Bookmaker. 2000. 288p. 24.95 (*1-880325-18-7*) Borderlands Pr.
May, Jesse. Shut up & Deal. 1998. 224p. pap. 15.00 (*0-385-48940-4*) Doubleday Publishing.
Ratner, Rochelle. Bobby's Girl. 1986. 128p. (Orig.). pap. 9.95 (*0-918273-22-6*) Coffee Hse. Pr.
Reuss, Frederick. Henry of Atlantic City. 1999. 249p. 22.00 (*1-878448-89-7*) MacMurray & Beck, Inc.
—Henry of Atlantic City: A Novel. 2001. (Vintage Contemporaries Ser.). 256p. reprint ed. pap. 12.00 (*0-375-72623-3*, Vintage) Knopf Publishing Group.
Roberts, Gillian. How I Spent My Summer Vacation. 1995. 256p. mass mkt. 5.99 (*0-345-38594-2*); pap. 19.00 o.s.i (*0-345-46533-4*) Ballantine Bks.
Rubino, Jane, et al. Homicide for the Holidays: Fruitcake; Milwaukee Winters Can Be Murder; A Perfect Time for Murder. 2000. (WWL Mystery Ser.: Vol. 362). 512p. mass mkt. (*0-373-26362-7*, 1-26362-3, Worldwide Library) Harlequin Enterprises, Ltd.
Shankman, Sarah. She Walks in Beauty. l.t. ed. 1993. (General Ser.). 484p. 20.95 o.p. (*0-8161-5478-3*, Macmillan Reference USA) Gale Group.
—She Walks in Beauty. 1991. 320p. 20.00 (*0-671-73657-4*, Atria) Simon & Schuster.
—She Walks in Beauty. Chelius, Jane, ed. 1992. 352p. reprint ed. mass mkt. 5.99 (*0-671-73658-2*, Pocket) Simon & Schuster.
Swain, James. Funny Money: A Tony Valentine Novel. 2003. 336p. mass mkt. 6.99 (*0-345-46344-7*, Ballantine Bks.) Ballantine Bks.
—Funny Money: A Tony Valentine Novel. 2003. 352p. mass mkt. 6.99 (*0-7434-3687-3*, Pocket); 2002. 304p. 24.00 (*0-7434-3686-5*, Atria); 2002. 304p. E-Book 23.95 (*0-7434-3988-0*, Atria) Simon & Schuster.
Wells, John. Death in a Dry Season. 1997. 352p. 24.95 o.p. (*0-312-15509-3*, Saint Martin's Minotaur) St. Martin's Pr.
Wilson, F. Paul & Lyon, Steve. Nightkill. 1999. 288p. mass mkt. 6.99 (*0-8125-6536-3*, Tor Bks.); 1997. 304p. 23.95 (*0-312-85910-4*, Forge Bks.) Doherty, Tom Assocs., LLC.

## AUSTIN (TEX.)—FICTION

Bauld, Jane S. Hector's Escapades: The First Night Out. 1997. (Illus.). 39p. (J). 14.95 (*1-57168-185-X*) Eakin Pr.
Blackwood, Scott. In the Shadow of Our House. 2001. 128p. 19.95 (*0-87074-464-X*) Southern Methodist Univ. Pr.
Braun, Matt. Deathwalk. 2000. 280p. mass mkt. 5.99 (*0-312-97516-3*, St. Martin's Paperbacks) St. Martin's Pr.
Crider, Bill. The Texas Capitol Murders. 1992. 336p. 21.95 o.p. (*0-312-07093-4*, Saint Martin's Minotaur) St. Martin's Pr.
Denton, Bradley. Lunatics. unabr. ed. 1998. audio 64.00 (*0-7366-4036-3*, 4535) Books on Tape, Inc.
—Lunatics. 1996. 336p. 23.95 (*0-312-14363-X*) St. Martin's Pr.
—Lunatics: A Novel. 1997. 352p. pap. 19.00 (*0-553-37891-0*) Bantam Bks.
Grape, Jan. Austin City Blues. l.t. ed. 2001. (Five Star First Edition Mystery Ser.). 224p. 23.95 (*0-7862-3014-2*) Thorndike Pr.
—Found Dead in Texas. 2002. (Five Star First Edition Mystery Ser.). 233p. 25.95 (*0-7862-4841-6*, Five Star) Gale Group.
Meyer, Charles. Beside the Still Waters. 1997. (Reverend Lucas Holt Mystery Ser.). 232p. pap. 6.50 (*0-9631149-4-8*) Stone Angel Bks.
—Blessed Are the Merciless. 1996. 272p. mass mkt. 5.50 o.s.i (*0-425-15140-9*) Berkley Publishing Group.
—Blessed Are the Merciless. 2nd ed. 1997. (Reverend Lucas Holt Mystery Ser.). 266p. reprint ed. pap. 6.50 (*0-9631149-5-6*) Stone Angel Bks.
—The Saints of God Murders. 1995. 256p. (Orig.). mass mkt. 5.99 o.s.i (*0-425-14869-6*, Prime Crime) Berkley Publishing Group.
Michaels, Fern. Texas Rich. 1995. pap. 8.95 o.p. (*0-345-40114-X*); 1987. 576p. mass mkt. 6.99 (*0-345-33540-6*, Ivy Bks.); 1985. mass mkt. 3.95 o.p. (*0-345-31374-7*) Ballantine Bks.
—Texas Rich. 1989. reprint ed. 19.95 o.p. (*0-7278-1758-2*) Severn Hse. Pubs., Ltd.
Mooney, Chris. World Without End. 2001. 400p. 25.00 (*0-671-04063-4*, Atria); 2002. 528p. reprint ed. mass mkt. 7.99 (*0-671-04064-2*, Pocket) Simon & Schuster.
Palfrey, Evelyn. The Price of Passion. 1997. 350p. pap. 14.95 o.p. (*0-9654190-1-0*) Moon Child Bks.
—The Price of Passion. 2002. 384p. E-Book 9.99 (*0-7434-2716-5*, Atria); 2000. (Illus.). 384p. pap. 12.95 (*0-671-04220-3*, Atria); 1999. mass mkt. (*0-671-04221-1*, Pocket) Simon & Schuster.
Pendergrass, Tess. Austin City Blues. 2003. (WWL Mystery Ser.: No. 460). 256p. mass mkt. (*0-373-26460-7*, Worldwide Library) Harlequin Enterprises, Ltd.
Pendergrass, Tess, ed. Austin City Blues. 2002. 250p. pap. 18.95 (*1-4104-0067-0*, Five Star Trade) Gale Group.
Riordan, Rick. The Devil Went down to Austin. 2002. 368p. reprint ed. mass mkt. 6.50 (*0-553-57994-0*) Bantam Bks.
Smith, Mark. Riddle. 1992. (Illus.). vi, 78p. (Orig.). pap. 6.95 (*0-9634181-0-6*) Argo Pr.
Spencer, William B. Resume with Monsters. 1995. 212p. 22.00 o.p. (*1-877946-53-2*) Permanent Pr., The.
—Resume with Monsters. 1996. (Illus.). pap. text 5.99 (*1-56504-913-6*, 13351) White Wolf Publishing, Inc.
Spencer, William Browning. Resume with Monsters. 2000. 212p. reprint ed. pap. 16.00 (*1-57962-026-4*) Permanent Pr., The.
Sublett, Jesse. Rock Critic Murders. 1990. 240p. mass mkt. 3.50 o.s.i (*0-440-20703-7*) Dell Publishing.
—Rock Critic Murders. 1989. pap. 3.95 o.p. (*0-14-011208-1*) Penguin Group (USA) Inc.
—Rock Critic Murders. 1989. 240p. 16.95 o.p. (*0-670-82302-3*) Viking Penguin.
—Tough Baby. 1999. pap. 4.95 (*0-14-012397-0*); 1990. 256p. 16.95 o.p. (*0-670-83325-8*) Viking Penguin. (Viking).
Taylor, Chuck. The Lights of the City. 1984. 125p. (Orig.). lib. bdg. 12.95 (*0-941720-15-2*) Slough Pr.
Walker, Mary Willis. All the Dead Lie Down. unabr. ed. 1998. audio 64.00 (*0-7366-4220-X*, 4718) Books on Tape, Inc.
—All the Dead Lie Down. l.t. ed. 1998. (Large Print Bks.). 26.95 (*1-56895-669-X*, Wheeler Publishing, Inc.) Gale Group.
—All the Dead Lie Down. unabr. ed. 1998. audio 78.00 (*0-7887-2166-6*, 95462E7) Recorded Bks., LLC.
—The Red Scream. 1995. 416p. mass mkt. 6.99 (*0-553-57172-9*, Crimeline) Bantam Bks.
—The Red Scream. unabr. ed. 1996. audio 64.00 (*0-7366-3381-2*, 4031) Books on Tape, Inc.
—The Red Scream. 1994. 19.95 o.s.i (*0-385-46858-X*) Doubleday Publishing.
—The Red Scream. unabr. ed. 1996. audio 85.00 (*0-7887-0468-0*, 94661E7) Recorded Bks., LLC.
—The Red Scream. l.t. ed. 1997. (Niagara Large Print Ser.). 524p. 29.50 o.p. (*0-7089-5814-1*, Ulverscroft) Thorpe, F. A. Pubs. GBR. *Dist:* Ulverscroft Large Print Bks., Ltd., Ulverscroft Large Print Canada, Ltd.
—Under the Beetle's Cellar. 1996. 368p. reprint ed. mass mkt. 6.50 (*0-553-57173-7*, Crimeline) Bantam Bks.
—Under the Beetle's Cellar. unabr. ed. 1996. audio 64.00 (*0-7366-3382-0*, 4032) Books on Tape, Inc.
—Under the Beetle's Cellar. l.t. ed. 1996. pap. 22.95 o.p. (*1-56895-313-5*, Wheeler Publishing, Inc.) Gale Group.
—Under the Beetle's Cellar. unabr. ed. audio 75.00 (*0-7887-0515-6*, 94709E7); 1999. audio compact disk 99.00 (*0-7887-3410-5*, C1016E7) Recorded Bks., LLC.
—Zero at the Bone. 1997. 336p. mass mkt. 6.50 (*0-553-57505-8*) Bantam Bks.
—Zero at the Bone. unabr. ed. 1998. audio 56.00 (*0-7366-4131-9*, 4634) Books on Tape, Inc.
—Zero at the Bone. 1993. (Mystery Ser.). mass mkt. (*0-373-26122-5*, 1-26122-1, Harlequin Bks.) Harlequin Enterprises, Ltd.
—Zero at the Bone. 1991. 336p. 18.95 (*0-312-06495-0*, Saint Martin's Minotaur) St. Martin's Pr.
—Zero at the Bone. l.t. ed. 1998. (Niagara Large Print Ser.). 392p. 29.50 o.p. (*0-7089-5830-3*, Ulverscroft) Thorpe, F. A. Pubs. GBR. *Dist:* Ulverscroft Large Print Bks., Ltd., Ulverscroft Large Print Canada, Ltd.

## AUSTRALIA—FICTION

Aalborg, Gordon. Cat Tracks. 2002. 192p. 14.95 (*0-9663397-6-2*) Delphi Bks.
Adams, Jessica. Tom, Dick & Debbie Harry. 2002. 304p. 23.95 (*0-312-29062-4*) St. Martin's Pr.
Aldridge, James. The True Story of Spit Macphee. 1988. 208p. (Orig.). (J). (gr. 7 up). pap. 3.95 o.p. (*0-14-032073-3*, Puffin Bks.) Penguin Putnam Bks. for Young Readers.
Andersen, Honey & Reinholdt, Bill. Don't Cut down This Tree. 1993. (Voyages Ser.). (Illus.). (J). 3.75 (*0-383-03621-6*) SRA/McGraw-Hill.
Anderson, Jessica. The Only Daughter. (Fiction Ser.). 256p. 1986. pap. 6.95 o.p. (*0-14-006333-1*, Penguin Bks.); 1985. 15.95 o.p. (*0-670-80431-2*) Viking Penguin.
—Tirra Lirra by the River. 1984. 16p. pap. 8.95 o.p. (*0-14-006945-3*, Penguin Bks.) Viking Penguin.
Armanno, Venero. The Volcano. 2001. (Illus.). 677p. (*1-74051-053-4*) Knopf, Alfred A. Inc.
Armanno, Vince. Gabriella's Book of Fire: A Novel. 2001. 352p. 14.95 (*0-7868-8510-6*); (Illus.). ix, 337p. 23.95 (*0-7868-6597-0*) Hyperion Pr.
Armstrong, Lindsay. Playboy Lover. 1998. (Harlequin Presents Ser.: Vol. 5). per. (*0-373-82575-7*, Harlequin Bks.) Harlequin Enterprises, Ltd.
—A Question of Marriage. 2001. (Harlequin Presents Ser.: No. 2208). 192p. mass mkt. (*0-373-12208-X*, Harlequin Bks.) Harlequin Enterprises, Ltd.
—Wildcat Wife. 1999. (Harlequin Presents Ser.: Vol. 10). per. (*0-373-82582-X*, 1-82582-7, Harlequin Bks.) Harlequin Enterprises, Ltd.
—Wildcat Wife. l.t. ed. 1998. (Mills & Boon Large Print Ser.). 288p. 25.99 o.p. (*0-263-15559-5*) Harlequin Mills & Boon, Ltd. GBR. *Dist:* Ulverscroft Large Print Bks., Ltd., Ulverscroft Large Print Canada, Ltd.
Astley, Thea. Drylands. 1999. 293p. (*0-670-88619-X*) Viking.
—Hunting the Wild Pineapple. 1992. 184p. pap. 10.00 o.p. (*0-14-005843-5*, Penguin Bks.); 1991. 192p. 19.95 o.p. (*0-399-13561-8*, G. P. Putnam's Sons) Penguin Group (USA) Inc.
—It's Raining in Mango. 1987. 208p. 17.95 o.p. (*0-399-13302-X*, G. P. Putnam's Sons) Penguin Putnam Bks. for Young Readers.
—It's Raining in Mango. 1988. (King Penguin Ser.). 208p. pap. 6.95 o.p. (*0-14-011403-3*, Penguin Bks.) Viking Penguin.
—Reaching Tin River. 1990. 224p. 19.95 o.p. (*0-399-13532-4*, G. P. Putnam's Sons) Penguin Putnam Bks. for Young Readers.
—The Slow Natives. 1967. 4.95 o.p. (*0-87131-015-5*) Evans, M. & Co., Inc.
—The Slow Natives. 1993. 224p. 21.95 o.p. (*0-399-13875-7*) Penguin Group (USA) Inc.
Bail, Murray. Camouflage: Stories. 2002. 160p. 20.00 o.p. (*0-374-11827-2*) Farrar, Straus & Giroux.
—Camouflage: Stories. 2003. (Illus.). 208p. pap. 14.00 (*0-312-42087-0*) Picador.
—The Drover's Wife. 1986. 192p. pap. o.p. (*0-571-13860-8*) Faber & Faber Ltd.
—Eucalyptus: A Novel. 1998. 272p. 23.00 o.p. (*0-374-14857-0*) Farrar, Straus & Giroux.
—Eucalyptus: A Novel. 1999. (Harvest Book Ser.). 264p. pap. 13.00 (*0-15-600781-9*, Harvest Bks.) Harcourt Trade Pubs.
—Holden's Performance. 1989. 368p. o.p. (*0-571-14826-3*) Faber & Faber Ltd.
—Holden's Performance. 1990. 368p. pap. 8.95 o.p. (*0-571-15200-7*) Faber & Faber, Inc.
—Holden's Performance. 2002. 384p. pap. 14.00 (*0-312-42080-3*) Picador.
Baker, Candida. Women & Horses: Infidelity & Treachery in Both a Modern & an Ancient Tale of Foolish Lovers. 1992. 192p. 16.95 o.p. (*0-312-07127-2*) St. Martin's Pr.
Baker, Jeannie. Where the Forest Meets the Sea. 1988. (Illus.). 32p. (J). (ps-3). 16.99 (*0-688-06363-2*); 16.89 (*0-688-06364-0*) HarperCollins Children's Bk. Group. (Greenwillow Bks.).
Balint, Christine. The Salt Letters: A Novel. 2001. (Illus.). 192p. pap. 12.00 (*0-393-32160-6*) Norton, W. W. & Co., Inc.
Bannister, Bronwyn. Haunt. 2000. 152p. pap. 24.95 (*1-877133-84-1*) Univ. of Otago Pr. NZL. *Dist:* International Specialized Bk. Services.
Barnes, Helen. Killing Aurora. 1999. 230p. (*0-14-028774-4*) Penguin Group (USA) Inc.
Barnes, John, ed. & intro. The Penguin Henry Lawson. 1987. 240p. pap. 6.95 o.p. (*0-14-009215-3*, Penguin Bks.) Viking Penguin.
Barr, Emily. Baggage. 2002. 336p. pap. 13.00 (*0-452-28382-5*, Plume) Dutton/Plume.
Barrett, Robert G. Leaving Bondi. 2000. 239p. (*0-7322-6871-0*) HarperCollins Pubs.
Battle, Lois. The Past Is Another Country. 1990. 352p. 19.95 o.p. (*0-670-82576-X*, Viking) Viking Penguin.
Bell, Helen. Idjhil... & the Land Cried for Its Lost Soul. 1996. (Illus.). 40p. (J). 19.95 o.s.i (*1-875560-61-0*) International Specialized Bk. Services.
Bennett, Bruce & Miller, Susan. Daughters of the Sun: Short Stories from Western Australia. 1994. pap. 16.95 (*1-875560-26-2*) Univ. of Western Australia Pr. AUS. *Dist:* International Specialized Bk. Services.
Bianchin, Helen. Dark Tyrant. l.t. ed. 1994. 18.95 o.p. (*0-7927-2152-7*); pap. 17.95 o.p. (*0-7927-2151-9*) BBC Audiobooks America.
—Dark Tyrant. 1984. mass mkt. (*0-373-10751-X*, Harlequin Bks.) Harlequin Enterprises, Ltd.
Bickmore, Barbara. The Back of Beyond. l.t. ed. 1999. 578p. 27.95 (*1-57490-194-X*, Beeler Large Print Bks.) Beeler, Thomas T. Publisher.
—The Back of Beyond. 1995. 576p. mass mkt. 5.99 o.s.i (*0-8217-4893-9*); 1994. mass mkt. 18.95 o.p. (*0-8217-4517-4*) Kensington Publishing Corp. (Zebra Bks.).
Bird, Carmel. Woodpecker Point & Other Stories. 1988. 160p. 19.95 (*0-8112-1072-3*); pap. 9.95 (*0-8112-1073-1*, NDP662) New Directions Publishing Corp.

Bird, Carmel, ed. Australian Short Stories. 1991. 272p. 22.95 o.p. (*0-395-58839-1*) Houghton Mifflin Co.
—The Penguin Century of Australian Stories. 2000. xxxiii, 733p. (*0-670-89233-5*, Viking) Viking Penguin.
Birtles, Dora. Overlanders: A Classic Story of the Australian Outback. 1990. 224p. pap. 7.95 o.p. (*0-14-016209-7*, Penguin Bks.) Viking Penguin.
Blacklock, Dianne. Call Waiting: A Novel. 2003. 384p. 24.95 (*0-312-30348-3*) St. Martin's Pr.
Blee, Jill. Liberator's Birthday. 2002. 248p. pap. 17.95 o.s.i (*0-9578735-3-0*) Indra Publishing AUS. *Dist:* International Specialized Bk. Services.
Bobis, Merlinda. The Kissing: A Collection of Short Stories. 2001. (Illus.). 183p. pap. 11.95 (*1-879960-60-5*) Aunt Lute Bks.
Boldrewood, Rolf. Robbery under Arms. 1999. E-Book 2.49 (*1-58627-214-4*) Electric Umbrella Publishing.
Bradley, James. The Deep Field: A Novel. 2000. 358p. 26.00 o.s.i (*0-8050-6111-8*) Holt, Henry & Co.
—Wrack. 340p. 2000. pap. 13.00 (*0-8050-6447-8*, Owl Bks.); 1999. 25.00 o.s.i (*0-8050-6108-8*) Holt, Henry & Co.
—Wrack. 1997. (Illus.). (*0-09-183494-5*) Trafalgar Square.
—Wrack: Roman. (GER.). 318p. (*3-612-65019-X*) Econ-Verlag GmbH DEU. *Dist:* International Bk. Import Service, Inc.
Brandewyne, Rebecca. The Jacaranda Tree. 1996. (Illus.). 384p. reprint ed. 24.00 (*0-7278-4857-7*) Severn Hse. Pubs., Ltd.
Brent, Madeleine. Golden Urchin. 1987. 336p. 16.95 o.s.i (*0-385-23015-X*) Doubleday Publishing.
—Golden Urchin. l.t. ed. 1988. (General Ser.). 518p. 18.95 o.p. (*0-8161-4399-4*, Macmillan Reference USA) Gale Group.
—Golden Urchin. l.t. ed. 1987. 560p. 17.95 o.p. (*0-7089-8415-0*, Charnwood) Thorpe, F. A. Pubs. GBR. *Dist:* Ulverscroft Large Print Bks., Ltd.
Brett, Lily. What God Wants. 2000. (Illus.). 264p. 18.95 (*1-55972-193-6*, Birch Lane Pr.) Kensington Publishing Corp.
Burke, John. Bridge of Triangles. 2000. 140p. pap. 18.50 o.s.i (*0-7022-2639-4*) Univ. of Queensland Pr. AUS. *Dist:* International Specialized Bk. Services.
Burke, Ross D. When the Music's Over: My Journey into Schizophrenia. Gates, Richard & Hammond, Robin, eds. 1994. 272p. text 20.00 o.p. (*0-465-09141-5*) Basic Bks.
—When the Music's Over: My Journey into Schizophrenia. Gates, Richard & Hammond, Robin, eds. 1996. 272p. reprint ed. pap. 10.95 o.p. (*0-452-27584-9*, Plume) Dutton/Plume.
Campbell, David. Evening under Lamplight. 1987. 193p. pap. 14.95 (*0-7022-2106-6*) Univ. of Queensland Pr. AUS. *Dist:* International Specialized Bk. Services.
Campion, Anna & Campion, Jane. Holy Smoke: A Novel. 1999. (Illus.). 272p. pap. 14.00 (*0-7868-8563-7*); 259p. 22.95 (*0-7868-6349-8*) Hyperion Pr.
Carey, Peter. Bliss. 1986. 304p. reprint ed. pap. 10.00 o.p. (*0-06-091355-X*, PL-1355, Perennial) HarperTrade.
—Bliss. 1996. 304p. pap. 13.00 (*0-679-76719-3*) Random Hse., Inc.
—Bliss. 304p. pap. 14.95 (*0-7022-2759-5*) Univ. of Queensland Pr. AUS. *Dist:* International Specialized Bk. Services.
—The Fat Man in History. anniv. ed. 1998. reprint ed. pap. 19.95 (*0-7022-3020-0*) Univ. of Queensland Pr. AUS. *Dist:* International Specialized Bk. Services.
—Illywhacker. 1985. 512p. 18.95 o.p. (*0-06-015425-X*); 1986. 608p. reprint ed. pap. 10.00 o.p. (*0-06-091331-2*, Perennial) HarperTrade.
—Illywhacker. 1996. 608p. pap. 16.00 (*0-679-76790-8*, Vintage) Knopf Publishing Group.
—Illywhacker. 608p. pap. 18.95 (*0-7022-2762-5*) Univ. of Queensland Pr. AUS. *Dist:* International Specialized Bk. Services.
—My Life As a Fake. 2003. (Illus.). 288p. 24.00 (*0-375-41498-3*) Knopf, Alfred A. Inc.
—Oscar & Lucinda. 448p. 1988. 18.95 o.p. (*0-06-015908-1*); 1992. reprint ed. pap. 13.00 o.p. (*0-06-091592-7*, PL 1592, Perennial) HarperTrade.
—Oscar & Lucinda. l.t. ed. 1989. 818p. reprint ed. 20.95 (*1-85089-318-7*) ISIS Large Print Bks. GBR. *Dist:* Transaction Pubs.
—Oscar & Lucinda. 1997. 448p. pap. 14.95 (*0-679-77750-4*) Knopf Publishing Group.
—Oscar & Lucinda. pap. 18.95 (*0-7022-2760-9*) Univ. of Queensland Pr. AUS. *Dist:* International Specialized Bk. Services.
—True History of the Kelly Gang. 2001. (Illus.). 368p. 25.00 (*0-375-41084-8*) Knopf, Alfred A. Inc.
—True History of the Kelly Gang, 8 cass. 2002. audio 34.99 (*1-4025-1177-9*, 01224) Recorded Bks., LLC.
—True History of the Kelly Gang. 2000. (Illus.). 400p. 50.00 (*0-7022-3167-3*); pap. 30.00 (*0-7022-3188-6*) Univ. of Queensland Pr. AUS. *Dist:* International Specialized Bk. Services.
—True History of the Kelly Gang: A Novel. 2001. (Illus.). 384p. reprint ed. pap. 14.00 (*0-375-72467-2*, Vintage) Knopf Publishing Group.
Carlon, Patricia. Crime of Silence. 1999. 208p. pap. 12.00 (*1-56947-172-X*); 1998. 196p. 21.00 (*1-56947-131-2*) Soho Pr., Inc.
—Crime of Silence. l.t. ed. 1999. (Mystery Ser.). 287p. 26.95 (*0-7862-1905-X*) Thorndike Pr.
—Death by Demonstration. 192p. 2002. pap. 12.00 (*1-56947-257-2*); 2001. 22.00 (*1-56947-246-7*) Soho Pr., Inc.
—Hush, It's a Game. 2001. 188p. 22.00 (*1-56947-214-9*) Soho Pr., Inc.
—Hush, It's a Game: Death by Demonstration. 2001. 189p. pap. 13.00 (*1-56947-245-9*) Soho Pr., Inc.
—The Price of an Orphan. 1999. 190p. 22.00 (*1-56947-173-8*) Soho Pr., Inc.
—The Running Woman. 1998. 189p. pap. 12.00 (*1-56947-132-0*); 196p. 21.00 (*1-56947-110-X*) Soho Pr., Inc.
—The Running Woman. l.t. ed. 1998. (Mystery Ser.). 320p. 26.95 (*0-7862-1671-9*) Thorndike Pr.
—The Souvenir. 1996. 183p. pap. 12.00 (*1-56947-065-0*); 20.00 (*1-56947-048-0*) Soho Pr., Inc.
—The Souvenir. 2000. E-Book 12.95 (*1-86254-541-3*) Wakefield Pr. Pty, Ltd. AUS. *Dist:* BHB International, Inc.
—The Unquiet Night. 2001. 192p. pap. 12.00 (*1-56947-213-0*); 2000. 196p. 22.00 (*1-56947-194-0*) Soho Pr., Inc.
—The Whispering Wall. 1998. 208p. pap. 12.00 (*1-56947-111-8*); 1996. 212p. 20.00 (*1-56947-066-9*) Soho Pr., Inc.
—Who Are You, Linda Condrick? 2002. 190p. 22.00 (*1-56947-258-0*) Soho Pr., Inc.
Carr, Roger. The Clinker. 1989. 144p. (J). (gr. 5-9). 14.95 o.p. (*0-395-51737-0*) Houghton Mifflin Co.
Carver, Caroline. Blood Junction. 2002. 336p. 24.95 (*0-89296-770-6*) Mysterious Pr.
—Blood Junction. 2003. (Basic Ser.). 28.95 (*0-7862-5058-5*) Thorndike Pr.
—Blood Junction. 2003. 400p. mass mkt. 6.99 (*0-446-61319-3*) Warner Bks., Inc.
Caswell, Brian. Dreamslip. 1994. (Illus.). 197p. (J). pap. 12.95 (*0-7022-2641-6*) Univ. of Queensland Pr. AUS. *Dist:* International Specialized Bk. Services.
Cato, Nancy. All the Rivers Run. 1984. 640p. mass mkt. 3.95 o.p. (*0-451-12535-5*, AE2535); 1982. mass mkt. 3.50 o.p. (*0-451-11345-4*); 1979. mass mkt. 2.95 o.p. (*0-451-08693-7*) NAL. (Signet Bks.).
—All the Rivers Run. 1978. 10.95 o.p. (*0-312-02021-X*) St. Martin's Pr.
—All the Rivers Run. l.t. ed. 1987. Vol. 2, Pt. 1. 752p. 15.95 o.p. (*0-7089-8432-0*); Vol. 2, Pt. 2. 416p. 15.95 o.p. (*0-7089-8433-9*) Thorpe, F. A. Pubs. GBR. (Charnwood). *Dist:* Ulverscroft Large Print Bks., Ltd.
—Forefathers. 1984. mass mkt. 4.50 o.p. (*0-451-14087-7*); mass mkt. 3.95 o.p. (*0-451-12798-6*) NAL. (Signet Bks.).
—Forefathers. 1983. 704p. 15.95 o.p. (*0-312-29831-5*) St. Martin's Pr.
Charlton, Ann. Baby down Under. 1999. (Harlequin Presents Ser.: Vol. 8). per. (*0-373-82580-3*, Harlequin Bks.) Harlequin Enterprises, Ltd.
Clark, Manning. Manning Clark: Collected Short Stories. 1987. 176p. pap. 4.95 o.p. (*0-14-009294-3*, Penguin Bks.) Viking Penguin.
Clarke, Arthur C. Dolphin Island. 1987. 192p. mass mkt. 2.95 o.s.i (*0-441-15220-1*) Ace Bks.
—Dolphin Island. 1983. 2.50 o.s.i (*0-425-07143-X*); 1981. 2.25 o.s.i (*0-425-05144-7*); 1978. 1.75 o.s.i (*0-425-03431-3*); 1978. 1.75 o.s.i (*0-425-04302-9*); 1976. 1.25 o.s.i (*0-425-03131-4*); 1975. 0.95 o.s.i (*0-425-02936-0*); 1971. 0.75 o.p. (*0-425-01914-4*) Berkley Publishing Group.
Clarke, Judith. Friend of My Heart. 1994. 148p. pap. 12.95 (*0-7022-2699-8*) Univ. of Queensland Pr. AUS. *Dist:* International Specialized Bk. Services.
—Wolf on the Fold. 2002. 176p. (J). (gr. 7 up). 16.95 (*1-886910-79-0*) Front Street, Inc.
Clarke, Marcus. His Natural Life. Tulloch, Graham, ed. 1997. (Oxford World's Classics Ser.). (Illus.). 524p. pap. 14.95 o.p. (*0-19-282418-X*) Oxford Univ. Pr., Inc.
—His Natural Life. Stuart, Lurline, ed. 2001. (Academy Editions of Australian Literature Ser.). (Illus.). 686p. 175.00 (*0-7022-3176-2*); pap. 80.00 (*0-7022-3177-0*) Univ. of Queensland Pr. AUS. *Dist:* International Specialized Bk. Services.
—His Natural Life. Murray-Smith, Stephen, ed. 1985. (English Library). 928p. pap. 7.95 o.p. (*0-14-043051-2*, Penguin Classics) Viking Penguin.
Cleary, Jon. Autumn Maze: A Scobie Malone Mystery. 1995. 320p. 22.00 o.p. (*0-688-13697-4*, Morrow, William & Co.) Morrow/Avon.
—Babylon South. 1990. 352p. 19.95 o.p. (*0-688-08976-3*, Morrow, William & Co.) Morrow/Avon.
—Bleak Spring. l.t. ed. 1994. 416p. lib. bdg. 22.95 (*0-8161-7437-7*, Macmillan Reference USA) Gale Group.
—Bleak Spring. 1994. 22.00 o.p. (*0-688-12332-5*, Morrow, William & Co.) Morrow/Avon.
—Dark Summer. 1993. 269p. 20.00 o.p. (*0-688-11414-8*, Morrow, William & Co.) Morrow/Avon.
—A Different Turf. unabr. ed. 2001. audio (*1-86340-796-0*, 580336) Bolinda Publishing Pty, Ltd.
—Dilemma. l.t. ed. 2000. (G. K. Hall Core Ser.). 393p. 28.95 (*0-7838-9069-9*, Macmillan Reference USA) Gale Group.
—Dilemma. 2000. 272p. 23.00 (*0-688-17192-3*, Morrow, William & Co.) Morrow/Avon.
—Dragons at the Party. 1988. 320p. 17.95 o.p. (*0-688-07487-1*, Morrow, William & Co.) Morrow/Avon.
—Dragons at the Party. unabr. ed. 1999. audio 79.95 Soundings, Ltd. GBR. *Dist:* Ulverscroft Large Print Bks., Ltd.
—Dragons at the Party. l.t. ed. 1988. (Charnwood Large Print Ser.). 464p. 29.99 o.p. (*0-7089-8474-6*, Ulverscroft) Thorpe, F. A. Pubs. GBR. *Dist:* Ulverscroft Large Print Bks., Ltd., Ulverscroft Large Print Canada, Ltd.
—Endpeace: A Scobie Malone Mystery. 1997. 272p. 23.00 (*0-688-14710-0*, Morrow, William & Co.) Morrow/Avon.
—Endpeace: A Scobie Malone Mystery. l.t. ed. 1998. (Core Ser.). 421p. 28.95 (*0-7838-8369-2*) Thorndike Pr.
—Five Ring Circus. unabr. ed. 2001. audio (*1-86442-364-1*, 590270) Bolinda Publishing Pty, Ltd.
—Five-Ring Circus: Suspense Down Under. 1999. 256p. 23.00 (*0-688-16468-4*, Morrow, William & Co.) Morrow/Avon.
—Five-Ring Circus: Suspense down Under. l.t. ed. 1999. (Core Ser.). 399p. 28.95 (*0-7838-8617-9*) Thorndike Pr.
—The High Commissioner. audio 33.95 o.p. Ulverscroft Audio (U.S.A.).
—Murder Song. l.t. ed. 1992. pap. 21.95 o.p. (*0-7927-1183-1*); 23.95 o.p. (*0-7927-1182-3*, CH0243) BBC Audiobooks America.
—Murder Song. 1990. 288p. 18.95 o.p. (*0-688-09458-9*, Morrow, William & Co.) Morrow/Avon.
—Now & Then, Amen. 1989. 320p. 18.95 o.p. (*0-688-08390-0*, Morrow, William & Co.) Morrow/Avon.
—Now & Then, Amen. l.t. ed. 1989. (Charnwood Large Print Ser.). 29.99 o.p. (*0-7089-8528-9*, Charnwood) Thorpe, F. A. Pubs. GBR. *Dist:* Ulverscroft Large Print Bks., Ltd., Ulverscroft Large Print Canada, Ltd.
—Pride's Harvest. 1991. (Scobie Malone Mystery Ser.). 336p. 20.00 o.p. (*0-688-10408-8*, Morrow, William & Co.) Morrow/Avon.
—Pride's Harvest. unabr. ed. 2001. audio 69.95 (*1-85496-811-4*, 68114) Soundings, Ltd. GBR. *Dist:* Ulverscroft Large Print Bks., Ltd.
—Pride's Harvest. l.t. ed. 1993. (Charnwood Large Print Ser.). 432p. 29.99 o.p. (*0-7089-8690-0*, Charnwood) Thorpe, F. A. Pubs. GBR. *Dist:* Ulverscroft Large Print Bks., Ltd., Ulverscroft Large Print Canada, Ltd.
—Winter Chill. l.t. ed. 1996. 24.95 o.p. (*1-56895-331-3*, Wheeler Publishing, Inc.) Gale Group.
—Winter Chill: A Scobie Malone Mystery. 1996. 269p. 23.00 o.p. (*0-688-14311-3*, Morrow, William & Co.) Morrow/Avon.
Climo, Shirley. Monkey Business. 2001. 16.95 (*0-8050-6392-7*, Holt, Henry & Co. Bks. For Young Readers) Holt, Henry & Co.
Cockington, James. When the Man in the Gold Mustang Met the Girl from the Pink Pussycat. 1997. (*0-09-183389-2*) Trafalgar Square.
Coetzee, J. M. Elizabeth Costello. 2003. 240p. 21.95 (*0-670-03130-5*) Viking Penguin.
Cohen, Bernard, contrib. by. Snowdome. 1998. 144p. (*1-86448-690-2*) Allen & Unwin Pty., Ltd.
Collins, Alan. Jacob's Ladder. 1989. 160p. (YA). (gr. 7 up). 13.95 o.p. (*0-525-67272-9*, Dutton Children's Bks.) Penguin Putnam Bks. for Young Readers.
Cooke, Kaz. Crocodile Club. 1997. vii, 230p. pap. (*1-86448-315-6*) Allen & Unwin Pty., Ltd. AUS. *Dist:* Independent Pubs. Group.
Coote, Cathy. Innocents. 2002. 256p. pap. 12.00 (*0-8021-3927-2*, Grove Pr.) Grove/Atlantic, Inc.
Cornelius, Patricia. My Sister Jill: A Novel. 2003. 224p. 23.95 (*0-312-31228-8*) St. Martin's Pr.
Corris, Peter. Beware of the Dog. 1994. 288p. mass mkt. 4.99 o.s.i (*0-440-21753-9*) Dell Publishing.
—The Big Drop & Other Cliff Hardy Stories. 1988. 208p. mass mkt. 3.50 o.s.i (*0-449-13228-5*, Fawcett) Ballantine Bks.
—Deal Me Out. l.t. ed. 1991. 11.95 o.p. (*0-947072-56-X*, C0376); pap. 17.95 o.p. (*1-86340-123-7*, AUS058) BBC Audiobooks America.
—Deal Me Out. 1987. mass mkt. 2.95 o.s.i (*0-449-13229-3*, Fawcett) Ballantine Bks.
—The Dying Trade. 1986. 256p. mass mkt. 2.95 o.s.i (*0-449-13030-4*, Fawcett) Ballantine Bks.
—The Empty Beach. l.t. ed. 1988. pap. 9.95 o.p. (*1-86340-081-8*) BBC Audiobooks America.
—The Empty Beach. 1986. mass mkt. 2.95 o.s.i (*0-449-13029-0*, Fawcett) Ballantine Bks.
—The Greenwich Apartments. 1986. 173p. pap. (*0-04-820030-1*) Allen & Unwin Pty., Ltd. AUS. *Dist:* Paul & Co. Pubs. Consortium, Inc.
—The Greenwich Apartments. 1988. mass mkt. 3.50 o.s.i (*0-449-14514-X*, Fawcett) Ballantine Bks.
—Heroin Annie. l.t. ed. 1990. pap. 9.95 o.p. (*1-86340-071-0*); 1988. lib. bdg. 15.95 o.p. (*0-947072-17-9*) BBC Audiobooks America.
—Heroine Annie & Other Cliff Hardy Stories. 1987. 256p. mass mkt. 2.95 o.s.i (*0-449-13031-2*, Fawcett) Ballantine Bks.
—The January Zone. l.t. ed. 1991. 21.95 o.p. (*1-86340-200-4*, AUH082); 12.95 o.p. (*0-7451-9609-8*, AUS150) BBC Audiobooks America.
—The January Zone. 1988. mass mkt. 3.50 o.s.i (*0-449-14513-1*, Fawcett) Ballantine Bks.
—Make Me Rich. 1987. 192p. mass mkt. 2.95 o.s.i (*0-449-13021-5*, Fawcett) Ballantine Bks.
—Man in the Shadows, Vol. 5. 1991. (Spanish Bit Saga). 176p. mass mkt. 3.99 o.s.i (*0-553-29087-8*) Bantam Bks.
—The Marvellous Boy. 1986. mass mkt. 2.95 o.s.i (*0-449-13028-2*, Fawcett) Ballantine Bks.
—Matrimonial Causes: A Cliff Hardy Mystery. 1994. 288p. mass mkt. 4.99 o.s.i (*0-440-21747-4*) Dell Publishing.
—O'Fear. 1991. 208p. 15.00 o.s.i (*0-385-42119-2*) Doubleday Publishing.
—Wet Graves. unabr. ed. 2001. audio (*1-86442-312-9*, 590376) Bolinda Publishing Pty, Ltd.
—Wet Graves. 1995. 288p. mass mkt. 4.99 o.s.i (*0-440-21750-4*) Dell Publishing.
—White Meat. 1986. mass mkt. 2.95 o.s.i (*0-449-13027-4*, Fawcett) Ballantine Bks.
Corseri, Gary. A Fine Excess: An Australian Odyssey. 2000. 233p. E-Book 8.00 (*0-7388-7798-0*) Xlibris Corp.
Courtenay, Bryce. Jessica. 1998. 600p. (*0-670-88351-4*) Viking Penguin.
—The Potato Factory. 1996. 739p. mass mkt. o.s.i (*0-7493-2263-2*) Random Hse. of Canada, Ltd.
—Solomon's Song. 2000. 682p. 29.95 (*1-55278-156-9*) McArthur & Co. CAN. *Dist:* HarperCollins Pubs. Canada, Ltd.
—Solomon's Song. 1999. (Illus.). ix, 658p. (*0-670-87878-2*, Viking) Viking Penguin.
—Tommo & Hawk. 1998. (Illus.). 672p. (*0-14-027156-2*) Penguin Bks. Canada, Ltd.
Crew, Gary. Angel's Gate. 1995. 256p. (YA). (gr. 4-7). pap. 16.00 (*0-689-80166-1*, Simon & Schuster Children's Publishing) Simon & Schuster Children's Publishing.
Culton, Wilma. Down at the Billabong. 1993. (Voyages Ser.). (Illus.). (J). 3.75 (*0-383-03565-1*) SRA/McGraw-Hill.
D'Alpuget, Blanche. White Eye. 1994. 254p. pap. 22.00 (*0-671-62005-3*, Simon & Schuster) Simon & Schuster.
Darcy, Emma. Dark Heritage. l.t. ed. 1995. 194p. 21.95 o.p. (*0-7838-1236-1*, Macmillan Reference USA) Gale Group.
—An Impossible Dream. 1993. (Harlequin Presents Ser.). per. (*0-373-11536-9*, 1-11536-9, Harlequin Bks.) Harlequin Enterprises, Ltd.
—The Marriage Risk. 2001. (Harlequin Presents Ser.: No. 2157). 187p. mass mkt. (*0-373-12157-1*, 1-12157-3, Harlequin Bks.) Harlequin Enterprises, Ltd.
—The Wedding. l.t. ed. 1996. (G. K. Hall Romance Ser.). 210p. 22.95 o.p. (*0-7838-1241-8*); 217 p. (*0-7451-4883-2*) Gale Group. (Macmillan Reference USA).
—The Wedding. 1992. (Harlequin Presents Ser.: No. 463). per. (*0-373-11463-X*, 1-11463-6, Harlequin Bks.) Harlequin Enterprises, Ltd.
David, Trisha. Borrowed-One Bride. 1998. (Harlequin Presents Ser.: Vol. 5). 192p. per. (*0-373-82577-3*, 1-82577-7, Harlequin Bks.) Harlequin Enterprises, Ltd.
Davidson, Robyn. Ancestors. l.t. unabr. ed. 1998. 451p. 27.95 (*1-85089-408-6*, 894086) ISIS Large Print Bks. GBR. *Dist:* Transaction Pubs.
—Ancestors. 1991. 304p. pap. 8.95 o.p. (*0-14-014529-X*) Penguin Group (USA) Inc.
—Ancestors. 1989. 19.95 o.p. (*0-671-68062-5*, Simon & Schuster) Simon & Schuster.
Davies, Luke. Isabelle the Navigator. 2002. 272p. pap. 12.95 (*0-425-18604-0*) Berkley Publishing Group.
Day, Marele. The Case of the Chinese Boxes. 1993. 192p. pap. 9.95 o.p. (*0-04-442277-6*) Allen & Unwin Pty., Ltd. AUS. *Dist:* Independent Pubs. Group.
—The Disappearances of Madalena Grimaldi: A Claudia Valentine Mystery. abr. ed. 1996. 224p. 19.95 (*0-8027-3277-1*) Walker & Co.
De Bernieres, Louis. Red Dog. 2001. (Illus.). 128p. 21.00 (*0-375-42155-6*, Pantheon) Knopf Publishing Group.

Dengler, Sandra. Code of Honor. 1988. (Australian Destiny Ser.: Vol. 1). 256p. (Orig.). pap. 8.99 o.p. (*0-87123-994-9*) Bethany Hse. Pubs.

Dengler, Sandy. Code of Honor. 2000. (Five Star Christian Fiction Ser.). 277p. 24.95 (*0-7862-2710-9*, Five Star) Gale Group.

—East of Outback. 1990. (Australian Destiny Ser.: Vol. 4). 336p. pap. 8.99 o.p. (*1-55661-117-X*) Bethany Hse. Pubs.

—Power of Pinjarra. 1989. (Australian Destiny Ser.: No. 2). 272p. pap. 8.99 o.p. (*1-55661-057-2*) Bethany Hse. Pubs.

—Taste of Victory. 1989. (Australian Destiny Ser.: Vol. 3). 272p. (Orig.). pap. 8.99 o.p. (*1-55661-085-8*) Bethany Hse. Pubs.

Denison, Lyn. Dream Lover. 2004. 224p. reprint ed. pap. 12.95 (*1-931513-96-1*) Bella Bks., Inc.

—Dream Lover. 1997. 240p. pap. 11.95 o.p. (*1-56280-173-2*) Naiad Pr., Inc.

—Gold Fever. 1998. 224p. (Orig.). pap. 11.95 (*1-56280-201-1*) Naiad Pr., Inc.

Dennis, C. J. A Sentimental Bloke. 1999. (Illus.). 130p. pap. 14.95 (*1-875892-35-4*) Editions Tom Thompson AUS. *Dist:* International Specialized Bk. Services.

Dickins, Barry. The House of the Lord. 1999. 209p. (*1-86330-562-9*, Vintage) Knopf Publishing Group.

Dietrich, William. Getting Back. 2000. 384p. 24.95 (*0-446-52457-3*) Warner Bks., Inc.

Disher, Garry. Crosskill. 1995. 216p. pap. 5.95 o.p. (*1-86373-634-4*) Independent Pubs. Group.

—Port Vila Blues: A Wyatt Novel. 1996. 232p. (Orig.). pap. 6.95 (*1-86448-025-4*) Allen & Unwin Pty., Ltd. AUS. *Dist:* Independent Pubs. Group.

Drewe, Robert. The Drowner. 1997. 336p. 23.95 (*0-312-16821-7*) St. Martin's Pr.

—Ned Kelly. movie tie-in ed. 2004. 224p. pap. 13.00 (*0-14-200315-8*) Penguin Group (USA) Inc.

Drinnan, Neal. Glove Puppet. 1999. 256p. pap. 12.95 (*0-312-24444-4*, Saint Martin's Griffin); 1998. 236p. 22.95 (*0-312-19271-1*) St. Martin's Pr.

—Quill. 2001. 240p. 23.95 (*0-312-26989-7*) St. Martin's Pr.

Earls, Nick. After January. 1996. 194p. pap. 14.95 (*0-7022-2823-0*) Univ. of Queensland Pr. AUS. *Dist:* International Specialized Bk. Services.

—Bachelor Kisses. 1998. 408p. (*0-14-026963-0*) Penguin Group (USA) Inc.

—Headgames. 1999. 290p. pap. (*0-670-88634-3*) Viking.

—Perfect Skin. 2001. 368p. 24.95 (*0-312-28056-4*) St. Martin's Pr.

—Perfect Skin. 2000. 353p. (*0-670-89104-5*) Viking.

—Perfect Skin: A Novel. 2002. 368p. pap. 13.95 (*0-312-30303-3*, Saint Martin's Griffin) St. Martin's Pr.

Eden, Dorothy. Bridge of Fear. 1981. mass mkt. 2.25 o.s.i (*0-441-07979-2*); 1978. 1.95 o.s.i (*0-441-07978-4*) Ace Bks.

—Bridge of Fear. 1993. 192p. reprint ed. lib. bdg. 18.00 o.p. (*0-7278-4394-X*) Severn Hse. Pubs., Ltd.

—Bridge of Fear. l.t. ed. 2001. 261p. pap. 23.95 (*0-7838-9500-3*) Thorndike Pr.

Edge, Arabella. The Company. 2002. 384p. E-Book 9.99 (*0-7432-1840-X*, Simon & Schuster) Simon & Schuster.

—The Company: Story of a Murderer. 2001. (Illus.). 384p. 23.00 (*0-7432-1342-4*, Simon & Schuster) Simon & Schuster.

—The Company: The Story of a Murderer. 2000. 371p. (*0-330-36220-8*) Picador.

—The Company: The Story of a Murderer. 2003. 384p. pap. 12.00 (*0-7434-1918-9*, Simon & Schuster) Simon & Schuster.

Edwards, Jane. A Whisper of Suspicion. 2002. (Five Star First Edition Romance Ser.). 249p. 26.95 (*0-7862-3747-3*, Five Star) Gale Group.

Elderkin, Susan. The Voices. 2003. 336p. 24.00 (*0-8021-1757-0*, Grove Pr.) Grove/Atlantic, Inc.

Eldridge, Marian. Walking the Dog & Other Stories. 1985. 220p. pap. 14.95 (*0-7022-1785-9*) International Specialized Bk. Services.

—Walking the Dog & Other Stories. 1985. 220p. 10.00 o.p. (*0-7022-1784-0*) Univ. of Queensland Pr. AUS. *Dist:* International Specialized Bk. Services.

Elliott, Summer L. Waiting for Childhood. 1987. 256p. 16.95 o.p. (*0-06-015797-6*) HarperTrade.

English, Robert. More Deaths Than One. 1995. 408p. pap. 5.95 o.p. (*1-86373-651-4*) Independent Pubs. Group.

Eversole, Robyn H. The Gift Stone. 1998. (Illus.). 32p. (J). (gr. k-3). 17.00 o.s.i (*0-679-88684-2*) Knopf, Alfred A. Inc.

—The Gift Stone. 1998. (Illus.). 32p. (J). (gr. k-3). 18.99 o.s.i (*0-679-98684-7*, Knopf Bks. for Young Readers) Random Hse. Children's Bks.

Fairbairn, John. Bindi. 1996. 96p. (J). pap. 10.95 (*0-7022-2805-2*) Univ. of Queensland Pr. AUS. *Dist:* International Specialized Bk. Services.

—More about the Mob. 1995. (Storybridge Ser.). 96p. (J). (gr. 4-7). pap. 11.95 (*0-7022-2790-0*) Univ. of Queensland Pr. AUS. *Dist:* International Specialized Bk. Services.

Favenc, Ernest. Tales of the Austral Tropics. Taylor, Cheryl, ed. 1997. 197p. pap. (*0-86840-381-4*) UNSW Pr.

Flanagan, Richard. Gould's Book of Fish: A Novel in Twelve Fish. 2003. 404p. pap. 14.00 (*0-8021-3959-0*); 2002. 416p. 27.50 (*0-8021-1711-2*) Grove/Atlantic, Inc. (Grove Pr.).

—The Sound of One Hand Clapping. 432p. 2001. pap. 12.00 (*0-8021-3784-9*); 2000. 24.00 o.p. (*0-87113-802-6*, Atlantic Monthly Pr.) Grove/Atlantic, Inc.

—The Sound of One Hand Clapping. 1997. 422p. (*0-7329-0896-5*) Macmillan Education Australia.

Fletcher, Aaron. Wallaby Track. mass mkt. 5.99 (*0-8439-4784-5*); 2000. 480p. mass mkt. 5.99 (*0-8439-3615-0*, Leisure Bks.) Dorchester Publishing Co., Inc.

Fletcher, Beryl. The Bloodwood Clan. 1999. (Illus.). 214p. pap. 14.95 (*1-875559-80-9*) Spinifex Pr. AUS. *Dist:* Stackpole Bks.

Ford, Peter Shann. The Keeper of Dreams: A Novel. 2000. 304p. 24.00 (*0-684-87219-6*, Simon & Schuster) Simon & Schuster.

Fox, Mem. Because of the Bloomers. 2000. (Illus.). (J). 15.00 (*0-15-200250-2*) Harcourt Trade Pubs.

Fox, Stuart. The Back of Beyond. 1995. 320p. mass mkt. 4.99 (*0-8125-2081-5*, Forge Bks.); 1994. 352p. 21.95 o.p. (*0-312-85366-1*, Tor Bks.) Doherty, Tom Assocs., LLC.

Franklin, Miles. My Brilliant Career. 2002. 288p. pap. 13.95 (*0-207-19724-5*) Angus & Robertson, Ltd. GBR. *Dist:* Consortium Bk. Sales & Distribution.

—My Brilliant Career. l.t. ed. 1987. (General Ser.). 17.95 o.p. (*0-8161-4158-4*, Macmillan Reference USA) Gale Group.

—My Brilliant Career. 1992. 81p. pap. 14.00 o.p. (*0-207-18695-2*) HarperTrade.

—My Brilliant Career. 1982. 272p. mass mkt. 3.95 o.s.i (*0-671-45915-5*, Pocket) Simon & Schuster.

—My Brilliant Career. 1980. 252p. 9.95 o.p. (*0-312-55599-7*) St. Martin's Pr.

Gare, Nene. Kent Town. 1997. (*1-86254-355-0*) Wakefield Pr. Pty, Ltd.

Garper, Helen. Postcards from Surfers. 1986. 112p. pap. 4.95 o.p. (*0-14-008462-2*, Penguin Bks.) Viking Penguin.

Geason, Susan. Dogfish. 1993. 208p. (Orig.). pap. 9.95 o.p. (*1-86373-088-5*) Allen & Unwin Pty., Ltd. AUS. *Dist:* Independent Pubs. Group.

—Sharkbait. 1994. 176p. pap. 9.95 o.p. (*1-86373-632-8*) Independent Pubs. Group.

—Shaved Fish. 1993. 168p. (Orig.). pap. 9.95 o.p. (*0-04-442274-1*) Allen & Unwin Pty., Ltd. AUS. *Dist:* Independent Pubs. Group.

Gemmell, Nikki. Alice Springs. 2000. 272p. pap. 12.95 o.s.i (*0-14-028642-X*, Penguin Bks.) Penguin Group (USA) Inc.

—Alice Springs. 1999. 256p. 23.95 o.p. (*0-670-88347-6*) Viking Penguin.

Gilling, Tom. The Adventures of Miles & Isabel. 2002. 208p. 23.00 (*0-87113-861-1*, Atlantic Monthly Pr.) Grove/Atlantic, Inc.

—The Sooterkin. 2001. 224p. reprint ed. pap. 13.00 o.s.i (*0-14-100201-8*) Penguin Group (USA) Inc.

—The Sooterkin. 2000. 224p. 23.95 o.s.i (*0-670-89152-5*, Viking) Viking Penguin.

Golding, William. Close Quarters. 1987. 281p. (*0-571-14779-8*) Faber & Faber Ltd.

—Close Quarters. 1999. 281p. pap. 24.00 (*0-374-52636-2*); 1987. 224p. 16.95 o.s.i (*0-374-12510-4*) Farrar, Straus & Giroux.

—Close Quarters, Bk. 2. unabr. ed. 2001. audio 69.95 (*1-85089-790-5*, 90061) ISIS Audio Bks. GBR. *Dist:* Ulverscroft Large Print Bks., Ltd.

—Fire down Below. 1989. 17.95 o.s.i (*0-374-25381-1*) Farrar, Straus & Giroux.

—Rites of Passage. 1980. 278p. 14.95 o.p. (*0-374-25086-3*) Farrar, Straus & Giroux.

Goldsmith, Andrea. The Prosperous Thief. 2002. 291p. (*1-86508-756-4*) Allen & Unwin Pty., Ltd.

Gordon, Victoria. Beguiled & Bedazzled. 1998. (Harlequin Presents Ser.: Vol. 4). per. (*0-373-82576-5*, 1-82576-9, Harlequin Bks.) Harlequin Enterprises, Ltd.

Gough, Sue, contrib. by. Here Comes the Night. 182p. (*0-7022-2979-2*) Univ. of Queensland Pr. AUS. *Dist:* International Specialized Bk. Services.

Green, Evan. Adam's Empire. 1987. 768p. 19.95 o.p. (*0-312-00557-1*) St. Martin's Pr.

—Alice to Nowhere. l.t. ed. 1990. lib. bdg. 15.95 o.p. (*0-947072-01-2*) BBC Audiobooks America.

—Alice to Nowhere. 1988. 288p. 16.95 o.p. (*0-312-01384-1*) St. Martin's Pr.

Greenwood, Kerry. Murder on the Ballarat Train. 1993. (Orig.). mass mkt. 4.50 o.s.i (*0-449-14832-7*, Fawcett) Ballantine Bks.

Grenville, Kate. Albion's Story. 384p. 1994. 21.95 (*0-15-100122-7*); 1996. reprint ed. pap. 13.00 (*0-15-600241-8*, Harvest Bks.) Harcourt Trade Pubs.

—The Idea of Perfection. 2003. 416p. pap. 14.00 (*0-14-200285-2*) Penguin Group (USA) Inc.

—The Idea of Perfection. 2002. 416p. 24.95 (*0-670-03080-5*, Viking) Viking Penguin.

—Lilian's Story. l.t. ed. 15.95 o.p. (*0-947072-06-3*) BBC Audiobooks America.

—Lilian's Story. 1994. (Harvest Book Ser.). 240p. pap. 10.95 (*0-15-600123-3*, Harvest Bks.) Harcourt Trade Pubs.

—Lilian's Story. 1987. 240p. pap. 6.95 o.p. (*0-14-008547-5*, Penguin Bks.); 1986. 288p. 16.95 o.p. (*0-670-80929-2*) Viking Penguin.

Gross, Gwendolen. Field Guide. 2002. (Illus.). 288p. reprint ed. pap. 14.00 (*0-15-600766-5*, Harvest Bks.) Harcourt Trade Pubs.

Hall, Rodney. Captivity Captive. 1988. 192p. 15.95 o.s.i (*0-374-11889-2*) Farrar, Straus & Giroux.

—Captivity Captive. 1989. pap. 7.95 o.p. (*0-671-67441-2*, Fireside) Simon & Schuster.

—The Grisly Wife. 1993. 261p. 20.00 o.p. (*0-374-16704-4*) Farrar, Straus & Giroux.

—Just Relations. 1989. pap. 9.95 o.p. (*0-671-67575-3*, Fireside) Simon & Schuster.

—The Second Bridegroom. 1991. 214p. 19.95 o.s.i (*0-374-25668-3*) Farrar, Straus & Giroux.

—The Second Bridegroom. 1993. 3.99 o.p. (*0-517-10828-3*) Random Hse. Value Publishing.

Hannay, Barbara. Outback Baby. 2002. (Harlequin Romance Ser.: No. 3690). 192p. mass mkt. (*0-373-03690-6*, 1-03690-4, Harlequin Bks.) Harlequin Enterprises, Ltd.

—A Wedding at Windaroo. 2004. (Harlequin Romance Ser.: No. 3794). 192p. mass mkt. (*0-373-03794-5*); (Harlequin Large Print Ser.: No. 640). 256p. mass mkt. (*0-373-18140-X*) Harlequin Enterprises, Ltd. (Harlequin Bks.).

Hartnett, Sonya. Forest. 2001. 216p. (*0-670-89920-8*, Viking) Viking Penguin.

Hasluck, Nicholas P. Our Man K. 1999. 359p. (*0-14-028249-1*) Penguin Group (USA) Inc.

Hawkins, Mary. Australian Outback: Four Journeys to a New Country Ride on the Wings of Faith & Love. 2003. (Historical Collections). 464p. pap. 6.97 (*1-58660-968-8*) Barbour Publishing, Inc.

Hazzard, Shirley. The Transit of Venus. 1981. 368p. 3.95 o.p. (*0-425-07511-7*) Berkley Publishing Group.

—The Transit of Venus. 1990. 352p. pap. 13.95 (*0-14-010747-9*, Penguin Bks.) Penguin Group (USA) Inc.

—The Transit of Venus. 1980. 11.95 o.p. (*0-670-72426-2*) Viking Penguin.

Henty, G. A. A Final Reckoning: A Tale of Bush Life in Australia. E-Book 3.95 (*0-594-02383-1*) 1873 Pr.

—A Final Reckoning: A Tale of Bush Life in Australia. 2002. 368p. 29.95 (*1-59087-003-4*, GAH003); per. 19.95 (*1-59087-002-6*, GAH002) Althouse Pr.

—A Final Reckoning: A Tale of Bush Life in Australia. collector's ed. 2002. (Illus.). im. lthr. 38.85 (*1-4115-1283-9*); pap. 19.95 (*1-4115-0586-7*); 25.95 (*1-4115-0932-3*); pap. 17.95 (*1-4115-0162-4*) Polyglot Pr., Inc.

Hergenhan, Laurie, ed. The Australian Short Story: An Anthology from the 1890's to the 1980's. 1986. (UQP Australian Authors Ser.). 352p. pap. 18.95 (*0-7022-1787-5*) International Specialized Bk. Services.

Heseltine, Harry, ed. The Penguin Book of Australian Short Stories. 1984. (Illus.). 304p. pap. 6.95 o.p. (*0-14-004303-9*, Penguin Bks.) Viking Penguin.

Hewett, Dorothy. Neap Tide. 1999. 278p. pap. (*0-14-028843-0*) Penguin Group (USA) Inc.

Hickman, Patricia, Jr. Angel of the Outback. 1995. (Land of the Far Horizons Ser.: Bk. 2). 320p. pap. 9.99 o.p. (*1-55661-542-6*) Bethany Hse. Pubs.

Hickman, Patricia. Beyond the Wild Shores. 1997. (Land of the Far Horizons Ser.: Vol. 4). 288p. pap. 9.99 o.p. (*1-55661-544-2*) Bethany Hse. Pubs.

—The Emerald Flame. 1996. (Land of the Far Horizons Ser.: Bk. 3). 288p. pap. 9.99 o.p. (*1-55661-543-4*) Bethany Hse. Pubs.

—Voyage of the Exiles. 1995. (Land of the Far Horizons Ser.: Bk. 1). 320p. pap. 9.99 o.p. (*1-55661-541-8*) Bethany Hse. Pubs.

—Voyage of the Exiles, Angel of the Outback & the Emerald Frame, Vols. 1-3. 1997. (Land of the Far Horizons Ser.). 29.99 o.p. (*0-7642-8151-8*) Bethany Hse. Pubs.

Holt, R. F., ed. Neighbours: Multicultural Writing of the 1980s. 1991. 256p. (Orig.). pap. 16.95 (*0-7022-2318-2*) Univ. of Queensland Pr. AUS. *Dist:* International Specialized Bk. Services.

Hooker, John, contrib. by. Beyond the Pale. 1998. 261p. (*1-86448-640-6*) Allen & Unwin Pty., Ltd.

Hooper, Chloe. A Child's Book of True Crime. (Illus.). 240p. 2003. pap. 13.00 (*0-7432-2513-9*); 2002. 24.00 (*0-7432-2512-0*) Simon & Schuster. (Scribner).

Hornadge, Bill. The Search for an Australian Paradise. 1999. 292p. pap. 16.95 (*1-875892-70-2*) Editions Tom Thompson AUS. *Dist:* International Specialized Bk. Services.

Jacobs, Pat. Going Inland. Padayachee, Vishnu, ed. 2002. 216p. pap. 17.95 o.s.i (*1-86368-374-7*) Fremantle Arts Centre Pr. AUS. *Dist:* International Specialized Bk. Services.

—Going Inland. l.t. ed. 2000. (Ulverscroft Large Print Ser.). 320p. 31.99 (*0-7089-4282-2*, Ulverscroft) Thorpe, F. A. Pubs. GBR. *Dist:* Ulverscroft Large Print Bks., Ltd., Ulverscroft Large Print Canada, Ltd.

Jaivin, Linda. Miles Walker, You're Dead. 2001. 272p. pap. 13.95 (*0-312-28274-5*, Saint Martin's Griffin) St. Martin's Pr.

Jameson, Bronwyn. Zane: The Wild One. 2002. (Silhouette Desire Ser.). mass mkt. (*0-373-76452-9*, Silhouette) Harlequin Enterprises, Ltd.

Jennings, Kate. Snake. 1997. 157p. o.p. (*0-88001-538-1*, Ecco) HarperTrade.

—Snake. 1999. 176p. pap. 12.00 (*0-316-91258-1*); pap. 12.00 (*0-316-19098-5*) Little Brown & Co.

Johnson, Susan. A Big Life. 1993. 320p. 22.95 o.p. (*0-571-16957-0*) Faber & Faber, Inc.

Johnston, Dorothy, contrib. by. One for the Master. 1997. 270p. (*1-86254-408-5*) Wakefield Pr. Pty, Ltd. AUS. *Dist:* BHB International, Inc.

Jolley, Elizabeth. Miss Peabody's Inheritance. (Fiction Ser.). 1985. 176p. pap. 6.95 o.p. (*0-14-007743-X*, Penguin Bks.); 1984. 168p. 13.95 o.p. (*0-670-47952-7*) Viking Penguin.

—The Newspaper of Claremont Street. 132p. pap. 12.95 (*0-949206-59-8*) Fremantle Arts Centre Pr. AUS. *Dist:* International Specialized Bk. Services.

—The Newspaper of Claremont Street. 128p. 1988. pap. 6.95 o.p. (*0-14-008582-3*, Penguin Bks.); 1987. 14.95 o.p. (*0-670-80946-2*) Viking Penguin.

—Palomino. 260p. 1988. 15.95 o.p. (*0-89255-116-X*); 1987. pap. 8.95 (*0-89255-136-4*) Persea Bks., Inc.

—Palomino. 1998. 264p. reprint ed. pap. 19.95 (*0-7022-1948-7*) Univ. of Queensland Pr. AUS. *Dist:* International Specialized Bk. Services.

—Stories. 1989. 320p. pap. 7.95 o.p. (*0-14-008581-5*, Penguin Bks.); 1988. 308p. 17.95 o.p. (*0-670-82113-6*) Viking Penguin.

—The Sugar Mother. 1988. 192p. 16.95 o.p. (*0-06-015940-5*) HarperTrade.

—The Well. 192p. 1987. pap. 6.95 o.p. (*0-14-008901-2*, Penguin Bks.); 1986. 14.95 o.p. (*0-670-81103-3*) Viking Penguin.

—Woman in a Lampshade. 1986. 232p. pap. 6.95 o.p. (*0-14-008418-5*, Penguin Bks.) Viking Penguin.

Jolley, Elizabeth & Milech, Barbara H. Fellow Passengers: Collected Stories. 1997. 396p. (*0-14-027080-9*) Penguin Bks. Canada, Ltd.

Jones, Brian. Billabong Dreaming: An Australian Adventure Tale. 1996. 108p. mass mkt. 4.99 (*0-942444-05-1*, Pelican Pond) Blue Dolphin Publishing, Inc.

Jose, Nicholas. The Custodians. 1997. 512p. 26.95 (*0-312-18073-X*) St. Martin's Pr.

Keegan, Mel. Storm Tide. 1996. 208p. pap. 12.95 (*0-85449-227-5*) Millivres Prowler Group GBR. *Dist:* LPC Group.

Kelly, Alison. Boots in the Bedroom! 1999. (Harlequin Presents Ser.: No. 9). mass mkt. (*0-373-82581-1*, 1-82581-9, Harlequin Bks.) Harlequin Enterprises, Ltd.

Kelly, Carolyn. Sisters of One Heart. 2002. 234p. pap. 14.99 (*1-57646-629-9*); 2000. 302p. pap. 14.99 o.p. (*1-57646-200-5*); 2000. 302p. lib. bdg. 24.99 o.p. (*1-57646-250-1*); 1999. 569p. E-Book 3.99 o.p. incl. cd-rom (*1-57646-168-8*); 2000. 488p. pap. 29.99 (*1-57646-325-7*); 2000. 488p. lib. bdg. 52.99 o.p. (*1-57646-326-5*) Quiet Vision Publishing.

Keneally, Thomas. Bettany's Book. 2000. 598p. (*1-86471-000-4*) Doubleday Publishing.

—Bring Larks & Heroes. 1989. 264p. pap. 11.95 o.p. (*0-14-010929-3*, Penguin Bks.); 1968. 4.95 o.p. (*0-670-19186-8*) Viking Penguin.

—The Chant of Jimmie Blacksmith. 2001. 184p. pap. 13.95 (*0-207-19716-4*) Angus & Robertson, Ltd. GBR. *Dist:* Consortium Bk. Sales & Distribution.

—The Chant of Jimmie Blacksmith. unabr. ed. 1998. audio (*1-86340-648-4*, 561218) Bolinda Publishing Pty, Ltd.

—The Chant of Jimmie Blacksmith. 1989. 192p. pap. 11.95 o.p. (*0-14-003620-2*); 1983. 178p. pap. 6.95 o.p. (*0-14-006973-9*, Penguin Bks.); 1972. 178p. 6.50 o.p. (*0-670-21165-6*) Viking Penguin.

—Ned Kelly & the City of the Bees. 2nd ed. 1981. (Illus.). 128p. (J). (gr. 4-7). pap. 11.95 (*1-56792-022-5*) Godine, David R. Pub.

—The Office of Innocence. 2003. 336p. 25.00 (*0-385-50763-1*, Talese, Nan A.) Doubleday Publishing.

—A River Town. 1996. 336p. pap. 14.00 o.s.i (*0-452-27655-1*, Plume) Dutton/Plume.

—A River Town. l.t. ed. 1995. (Large Print Bks.). 463p. 24.95 o.p. (*1-56895-264-3*, Wheeler Publishing, Inc.) Gale Group.

—Woman of the Inner Sea. 1994. 288p. pap. 13.00 (*0-452-27177-0*, Plume) Dutton/Plume.

Khan, Adib. Seasonal Adjustments. 1995. 240p. pap. 11.95 (*1-86373-652-2*) Allen & Unwin Pty., Ltd. AUS. *Dist:* Paul & Co. Pubs. Consortium, Inc.

Klein, Robin. The Sky in Silver Lace. 1996. 184p. (J). (gr. 5-7). text 13.99 (*0-670-86266-5*, Viking Children's Bks.) Penguin Putnam Bks. for Young Readers.

Knight, Stephen, ed. Dead Witness: Best Australian Mystery Stories. 1990. 288p. pap. 7.95 o.p. (*0-14-011502-1*, Penguin Bks.) Viking Penguin.

—More Crimes for a Summer Christmas. 1993. (Crimes for a Summer Christmas Ser.). (Illus.). 248p. (Orig.). pap. 14.95 o.p. (*1-86373-106-7*) Allen & Unwin Pty., Ltd. AUS. *Dist:* Independent Pubs. Group.

Knox, Malcolm. Summerland. 2002. 272p. pap. 13.00 (*0-312-29166-3*); 2001. 272p. 23.00 (*0-312-28094-7*); 2001. 256p. (*0-330-48678-0*) Picador.

Koch, Christopher J. Highways to a War. 1995. 496p. 23.95 o.p. (*0-670-86155-3*, Viking) Viking Penguin.

Krauth, Nigel & Sheahan, Robyn, eds. From Paradise to Paranoia: New Queensland Writing. 1995. 272p. pap. 18.95 (*0-7022-2785-4*) Univ. of Queensland Pr. AUS. *Dist:* International Specialized Bk. Services.

Lawrence, Anthony. In the Half Light. 384p. 2003. pap. 14.00 (*0-7867-1230-9*); 2002. 26.00 (*0-7867-0999-5*, Carroll & Graf Pubs.) Avalon Publishing Group.

—In the Half Light. 2000. 384p. (*0-330-36235-6*) Picador.

Lawrence, D. H. The Boy in the Bush. 1972. pap. 2.95 o.p. (*0-670-00331-X*) Penguin Group (USA) Inc.

—The Boy in the Bush. 400p. 1992. pap. 9.95 o.p. (*0-14-018446-5*, Penguin Classics); 1981. pap. 6.95 o.p. (*0-14-001935-9*, Penguin Bks.) Viking Penguin.

Lawrence, D. H. & Skinner, M. L. The Boy in the Bush. Eggert, Paul, ed. 1990. (Cambridge Edition of the Works of D. H. Lawrence). (Illus.). 561p. 130.00 (*0-521-30704-X*) Cambridge Univ. Pr.

—The Boy in the Bush. Eggert, Paul, ed. 1996. (Penguin Twentieth-Century Classics Ser.). 432p. pap. 12.95 o.s.i (*0-14-018817-7*) Viking Penguin.

Le Nay, Louise. The Hero: A Story of Family & Belonging. 1997. 252p. (Orig.). pap. 12.95 (*1-86448-157-9*) Allen & Unwin Pty., Ltd. AUS. *Dist:* Independent Pubs. Group.

Lee, Miranda. Marriage at a Price. 2001. (Harlequin Presents Ser.: No. 2181). 185p. mass mkt. (*0-373-12181-4*, 1-12181-3, Harlequin Bks.) Harlequin Enterprises, Ltd.

—Marriage at a Price. l.t. ed. 2001. (Mills & Boon Large Print Ser.). 288p. 27.99 (*0-263-17222-8*) Harlequin Mills & Boon, Ltd. GBR. *Dist:* Thorndike Pr., Ulverscroft Large Print Bks., Ltd., Ulverscroft Large Print Canada, Ltd.

—Simply Irresistible. 1999. (Harlequin Presents Ser.: No. 12). per. (*0-373-82584-6*, 1-82584-3, Harlequin Bks.) Harlequin Enterprises, Ltd.

Lee, Miranda & Way, Margaret. Australian Nights: Simply Irresistible/Her Outback Man, 2 bks. in 1. 2003. 384p. mass mkt. (*0-373-23009-5*, Harlequin Bks.) Harlequin Enterprises, Ltd.

Livingston, Nancy. Two Sisters. 1994. 592p. 25.95 o.p. (*0-312-11346-3*) St. Martin's Pr.

Lofts, Pamela, illus. & retold by. Dunbi the Owl. 2nd ed. 1985. (Dreamtime Ser.). 32p. (J). (gr. 1-6). reprint ed. pap. 3.95 o.s.i (*0-915391-07-4*) Slawson Communications, Inc.

—The Echidna & the Shade Tree. 1985. (Dreamtime Ser.). 32p. (J). (gr. 1-6). reprint ed. pap. 3.95 o.p. (*0-915391-05-8*) Slawson Communications, Inc.

—How the Birds Got Their Colors. 2nd ed. 1985. (Dreamtime Ser.). 32p. (J). (gr. 1-6). reprint ed. pap. 3.95 o.p. (*0-915391-08-2*) Slawson Communications, Inc.

—When the Snake Bites the Sun. 2nd ed. 1985. (Dreamtime Ser.). 32p. (J). (gr. 1-6). reprint ed. pap. 3.95 o.s.i (*0-915391-06-6*) Slawson Communications, Inc.

London, Joan. Gilgamesh. 272p. 2004. pap. 13.00 (*0-8021-4121-8*); 2003. 23.00 (*0-8021-1741-4*) Grove/Atlantic, Inc. (Grove Pr.).

—Sister Ships: And Other Stories. 1988. pap. 5.95 o.p. (*0-14-010571-9*, Penguin Bks.) Viking Penguin.

Long, William S. The Colonists. 1984. (Australians Ser.: No. 6). 496p. (Orig.). mass mkt. 4.50 o.s.i (*0-440-11342-3*) Dell Publishing.

—The Exiles. 1981. (Australians Ser.: No. 1). 688p. mass mkt. 4.95 o.s.i (*0-440-12374-7*) Dell Publishing.

—The Explorers. 1982. (Australians Ser.: No. 4). 512p. (Orig.). mass mkt. 4.50 o.s.i (*0-440-12391-7*) Dell Publishing.

—The Gallant. 1986. (Australians Ser.: No. 8). 448p. (Orig.). mass mkt. 4.95 o.s.i (*0-440-12785-8*) Dell Publishing.

—The Gold Seekers. 1985. (Australians Ser.: No. 7). 400p. mass mkt. 4.95 o.s.i (*0-440-13169-3*) Dell Publishing.

—The Nationalists No. 11: The Australians. 1989. 464p. mass mkt. 4.95 o.s.i (*0-440-20354-6*) Dell Publishing.

Lowell, Elizabeth. Chain Lightning. unabr. ed. 1999. audio 7.99 (*1-55204-189-1*, MIR-1189) Durkin Hayes Publishing Ltd.

—Chain Lightning. 1999. 256p. mass mkt. (*1-55166-538-7*, Mira Bks.); 1997. per. (*1-55166-312-0*, 1-66312-9, Mira Bks.); 1993. per. (*0-373-48278-7*, Harlequin Bks.); 1988. mass mkt. (*0-373-07256-2*, Harlequin Bks.) Harlequin Enterprises, Ltd.

—Pearl Cove. abr. ed. 2000. audio 7.99 o.s.i (*1-56740-348-4*, 2109, Paperback Nova Audio Bks.); 1999. audio 17.95 o.p. (*1-56740-835-4*, 1670, Nova Audio Bks.); 1999. audio 39.95 (*1-56740-422-7*, 1668, Brilliance Audio Unabridged); 1999. audio 73.25 (*1-56740-648-3*, 1669, Unabridged Library Editions) Brilliance Audio.

—Pearl Cove. l.t. ed. 1999. (Wheeler Press Paperback Ser.). pap. 11.95 (*1-56895-964-8*); 28.95 o.p. (*1-56895-746-7*) Gale Group. (Wheeler Publishing, Inc.).

—Pearl Cove. 2002. E-Book 7.50 (*0-06-050383-1*); E-Book 7.50 (*0-06-050384-X*); E-Book 7.50 (*0-06-050385-8*); E-Book 7.50 (*0-06-050382-3*) HarperCollins General Bks. Group. (PerfectBound).

—Pearl Cove. 2000. 432p. mass mkt. 7.50 (*0-380-78988-4*); 1999. 376p. 24.00 (*0-380-97404-5*) Morrow/Avon. (Avon Bks.).

Lumley, Brian. Invaders. 2nd ed. 1999. (Necroscope Ser.: 10). 384p. 25.95 (*0-312-86814-6*, Tor Bks.) Doherty, Tom Assocs., LLC.

Lurie, Morris. The Night We Ate the Sparrow. 1986. 160p. pap. 4.95 o.p. (*0-14-008864-4*, Penguin Bks.) Viking Penguin.

—Outrageous Behavior: Best Stories of Morris Lurie. 1985. 304p. pap. 6.95 o.p. (*0-14-007097-4*, Penguin Bks.) Viking Penguin.

MacColl, Mary-Rose. Angels in the Architecture. 1999. v, 300p. (*1-86508-061-6*) Allen & Unwin Pty., Ltd.

—No Safe Place: A Novel about Sex & Power. 1997. 180p. pap. 12.95 o.p. (*1-86448-174-9*) Allen & Unwin Pty., Ltd. AUS. *Dist:* Independent Pubs. Group.

Mackay, James Alexander Kenneth. The Yellow Wave: A Romance of the Asiatic Invasion of Australia. Enstice, Andrew & Webb, Janeen, eds. 2003. (Wesleyan Early Classics of Science Fiction Ser.). (Illus.). 352p. pap. 19.95 (*0-8195-6632-2*); text 60.00 (*0-8195-6631-4*) Wesleyan Univ. Pr.

Mackintosh, Patricia. The Devil's Madness. 2003. 246p. pap. 19.95 (*1-59286-471-6*) PublishAmerica, Inc.

MacPherson, H. M. And Those Who Trespass Against Us. 2001. 316p. pap. 18.99 (*1-930928-21-1*, 0032) Renaissance Alliance Publishing, Inc.

Maloney, Shane. The Brush-Off: An Arcade Mystery. 1998. 320p. 23.95 (*1-55970-440-3*) Arcade Publishing, Inc.

—Nice Try: A Murray Whelan Mystery. 2000. (Murray Whelan Mystery Ser.). 259p. 24.95 (*1-55970-513-2*) Arcade Publishing, Inc.

—Stiff. 1999. (Murray Whelan Thrillers Ser.). 227p. 23.95 (*1-55970-481-0*) Arcade Publishing, Inc.

Malouf, David. Conversations at Curlow Creek. l.t. ed. 1997. (Thorndike Basic Ser.). 314p. lib. bdg. 23.95 o.p. (*0-7862-1149-0*, Macmillan Reference USA) Gale Group.

—Conversations at Curlow Creek. l.t. ed. 1998. 240p. pap. 15.00 (*0-679-77905-1*, Vintage); 1997. 233p. 23.00 o.s.i (*0-679-44266-9*, Pantheon) Knopf Publishing Group.

—Dream Stuff. 2000. 192p. 22.00 o.s.i (*0-375-42053-3*, Pantheon) Knopf Publishing Group.

—Dream Stuff: Stories. 2001. 208p. pap. 12.00 (*0-375-72449-4*, Knopf Bks. for Young Readers) Random Hse. Children's Bks.

—Remembering Babylon. 1994. 200p. pap. (*0-394-28043-1*) Knopf, Alfred A. Inc.

—Remembering Babylon: A Novel. 1994. 224p. pap. 12.00 (*0-679-74951-9*, Vintage) Knopf Publishing Group.

Marranca, Bonnie, ed. American Dreams: The Imagination of Sam Shepard. 1981. 223p. 22.95 o.p. (*0-933826-12-5*) PAJ Pubns.

Martin, Catherine. The Silent Sea. Foxton, Rosemary, ed. 1996. 569p. pap. (*0-86840-373-3*) UNSW Pr.

Masson, Sophie. The Sun Is Rising. 1996. 114p. (YA). pap. 12.95 (*0-7022-2789-7*) Univ. of Queensland Pr. AUS. *Dist:* International Specialized Bk. Services.

Masters, Olga. Home Girls. l.t. ed. 1991. 11.95 o.p. (*0-947072-85-3*, C0368); pap. 9.95 o.p. (*1-86340-114-8*, AUS017) BBC Audiobooks America.

—Home Girls. 1990. 18.95 o.p. (*0-393-02853-4*) Norton, W. W. & Co., Inc.

—Loving Daughters. l.t. ed. 1991. pap. 17.95 o.p. (*1-86340-061-3*, AUS055); 1989. 11.95 o.p. (*0-947072-57-8*, 25) BBC Audiobooks America.

—Loving Daughters. unabr. ed. 1998. audio (*1-86340-591-7*, 551004) Bolinda Publishing Pty, Ltd.

—Loving Daughters. 1993. 320p. 21.95 o.p. (*0-393-03498-4*) Norton, W. W. & Co., Inc.

—The Rose Fancier: Stories. 1991. 144p. 18.95 o.p. (*0-393-03031-8*) Norton, W. W. & Co., Inc.

Matthews, Greg. The Wisdom of Stones: A Novel. 1994. 480p. 23.00 o.p. (*0-06-017738-1*, HarperCollins) HarperTrade.

Maxwell, Ann. The Diamond Tiger. l.t. ed. 1999. (Core Ser.). 543p. 29.95 (*0-7838-8789-2*, Macmillan Reference USA) Gale Group.

—The Diamond Tiger. 1994. 480p. mass mkt. 2.99 o.p. (*0-06-108260-0*) HarperCollins Children's Bk. Group.

—The Diamond Tiger. 480p. 1997. mass mkt. 5.99 (*0-06-104079-7*); 1992. mass mkt. 4.99 (*0-06-104181-5*) Morrow/Avon. (HarperTorch).

McCarthy, Steven. Black Angels, Red Blood. 1998. 141p. pap. 18.95 (*0-7022-2963-6*) Univ. of Queensland Pr. AUS. *Dist:* International Specialized Bk. Services.

McConnochie, Mardi. Coldwater. 2002. 320p. pap. 14.95 (*0-345-44812-X*, Ballantine Bks.) Ballantine Bks.

McCullough, Colleen. The Ladies of Missalonghi. l.t. ed. 1987. (General Ser.). 268p. 17.95 o.p. (*0-8161-4366-8*, Macmillan Reference USA) Gale Group.

—The Ladies of Missalonghi. 1987. (Illus.). 192p. 12.95 o.p. (*0-06-015739-9*) HarperTrade.

—The Ladies of Missalonghi. 1988. 192p. mass mkt. 5.99 (*0-380-70458-7*, Avon Bks.) Morrow/Avon.

—Morgan's Run. E-Book 28.00 (*1-930161-95-6*) Adobe Systems, Inc.

—Morgan's Run. 2000. E-Book 28.00 (*0-7432-1467-6*, Simon & Schuster); 2000. (Illus.). 608p. 28.00 (*0-684-85329-9*, Simon & Schuster); 2001. 848p. reprint ed. mass mkt. 7.99 (*0-7434-1719-4*, Pocket) Simon & Schuster.

—Morgan's Run. l.t. ed. 2001. 918p. 30.95 (*0-7862-3083-5*); 31.95 (*0-7862-3082-7*) Thorndike Pr.

—The Thorn Birds. abr. ed. audio 12.95 (*0-89926-151-5*, 839); 1985. audio 95.20 Audio Bk. Co.

—The Thorn Birds. unabr. ed. 1993. audio 99.95 (*0-7861-0388-4*, 1340) Blackstone Audio Bks., Inc.

—The Thorn Birds. unabr. ed. Pt. A. audio 40.00; Pt. B. audio 40.00; Pts. A & B. audio 80.00 Books on Tape, Inc.

—The Thorn Birds. 1998. lib. bdg. 11.95 (*1-56849-697-4*) Buccaneer Bks., Inc.

—The Thorn Birds. 1977. 19.95 o.p. (*0-06-012956-5*) HarperTrade.

—The Thorn Birds. 1978. 540p. mass mkt. 6.95 o.p. (*0-380-56390-8*, 56390-8); 704p. mass mkt. 7.99 (*0-380-01817-9*) Morrow/Avon. (Avon Bks.).

—The Thorn Birds. 1998. (Modern Classics Ser.). 704p. 9.99 o.s.i (*0-517-20165-8*) Random Hse. Value Publishing.

—The Thorn Birds. unabr. ed. 1991. audio 144.00 (*1-55690-512-2*, 91308E7) Recorded Bks., LLC.

—The Thorn Birds. 1978. 13.04 (*0-606-01301-6*) Turtleback Bks.

—Tim. 1974. 256p. 15.95 o.p. (*0-06-012891-7*) HarperTrade.

McGahan, Andrew. 1988. 1998. 320p. pap. 12.95 (*0-312-18032-2*, 837237, Saint Martin's Griffin); 1996. 314p. 22.95 o.p. (*0-312-15043-1*) St. Martin's Pr.

McKinley, Tamara. Jacaranda Vines. l.t. ed. 2002. (Magna Large Print Ser.). 512p. 32.50 (*0-7505-1781-6*) Magna Large Print Bks. GBR. *Dist:* Ulverscroft Large Print Bks., Ltd., Ulverscroft Large Print Canada, Ltd.

—Jacaranda Vines: A Novel of Australia. 2001. 416p. 25.95 (*0-312-28434-9*) St. Martin's Pr.

McLaren, Philip. Scream Black Murder: A WorldKrime Mystery. 2002. 288p. 21.95 (*1-890768-42-1*, Intrigue Pr.) Corvus Publishing.

McLeod, Keith A. The Shore & the Shelter. 2000. 232p. pap. 17.95 (*1-86368-272-4*) Fremantle Arts Centre Pr. AUS. *Dist:* International Specialized Bk. Services.

McMullen, Sean. Eyes for the Calculor. 2001. 592p. 27.95 (*0-312-87736-6*, Tor Bks.) Doherty, Tom Assocs., LLC.

McNab, Claire. Body Guard. 1994. (Detective Inspector Carol Ashton Mysteries Ser.: Vol. 6). 224p. pap. 11.95 (*1-56280-073-6*) Naiad Pr., Inc.

—Chain Letter: A Carol Ashton Mystery. 1997. (Detective Inspector Carol Ashton Mysteries Ser.: Vol. 9). 224p. (Orig.). pap. 11.95 (*1-56280-181-3*) Naiad Pr., Inc.

—Cop Out. 1991. (Detective Inspector Carol Ashton Mysteries Ser.: Vol. 4). 224p. (Orig.). pap. 10.95 (*0-941483-84-3*) Naiad Pr., Inc.

—Dead Certain. 1992. (Detective Inspector Carol Ashton Mysteries Ser.: No. 5). 224p. pap. 11.95 (*1-56280-027-2*) Naiad Pr., Inc.

—Death down Under. 1990. (Detective Inspector Carol Ashton Mysteries Ser.: Vol. 3). 240p. pap. 11.95 (*0-941483-39-8*) Naiad Pr., Inc.

—Death Understood: A Denise Cleever Thriller. 2000. 222p. pap. 11.95 (*1-56280-264-X*) Naiad Pr., Inc.

—Double Bluff. 1995. (Detective Inspector Carol Ashton Mysteries Ser.: Vol. 7). 192p. pap. 12.95 (*1-56280-096-5*) Naiad Pr., Inc.

—Fatal Reunion. 1989. (Detective Inspector Carol Ashton Mysteries Ser.: Vol. 2). 224p. pap. 11.95 (*0-941483-40-1*) Naiad Pr., Inc.

—Inner Circle: A Carol Ashton Mystery. 1996. (Detective Inspector Carol Ashton Mysteries Ser.: Vol. 8). 256p. pap. 11.95 (*1-56280-135-X*) Naiad Pr., Inc.

—Lessons in Murder. 1988. (Detective Inspector Carol Ashton Mysteries Ser.: Vol. 1). 216p. pap. 11.95 (*0-941483-14-2*) Naiad Pr., Inc.

—Murder Undercover: A Denise Cleever Thriller. 1999. (Denise Cleever Thrillers Ser.). 240p. pap. 12.95 (*1-56280-259-3*) Naiad Pr., Inc.

—Out of Sight: A Denise Cleever Thriller. 2002. (Denise Cleever Thrillers Ser.: No. 3). 240p. pap. 12.95 (*1-56280-268-2*) Naiad Pr., Inc.

—Past Due: A Detective Inspector Carol Ashton Mystery. 1998. (Detective Inspector Carol Ashton Mysteries Ser.: No. 10). 224p. pap. 11.95 (*1-56280-217-8*) Naiad Pr., Inc.

—Set Up. 1999. (Detective Inspector Carol Ashton Mysteries Ser.: Vol. 11). 202p. pap. 11.95 (*1-56280-255-0*) Naiad Pr., Inc.

—Under Suspicion. 2000. (Detective Inspector Carol Ashton Mysteries Ser.). 204p. pap. 11.95 (*1-56280-261-5*) Naiad Pr., Inc.

—Under the Southern Cross. 1992. 224p. pap. 11.95 (*1-56280-011-6*) Naiad Pr., Inc.

Mears, Gillian. Collected Stories. 1997. 400p. 17.95 (*0-7022-2950-4*) Univ. of Queensland Pr. AUS. *Dist:* International Specialized Bk. Services.

Measday, Stephen. The News They Didn't Use. 1995. 171p. (YA). pap. 12.95 (*0-7022-2711-0*) Univ. of Queensland Pr. AUS. *Dist:* International Specialized Bk. Services.

Meehan, Michael. The Salt of Broken Tears: A Novel. 2001. 304p. 24.95 (*1-55970-567-1*) Arcade Publishing, Inc.

Miles, Franklin. The End of My Career: Purporting to Be the Autobiography of Sybylla Penelope Melvyn. 1981. 234p. 10.95 o.p. (*0-312-25075-4*) St. Martin's Pr.

Miller, Alex. Conditions of Faith. 2002. 400p. reprint ed. pap. 13.95 (*0-425-18177-4*) Berkley Publishing Group.

—Conditions of Faith. 2000. (Illus.). 352p. 25.00 o.s.i (*0-684-86935-7*, Scribner) Simon & Schuster.

Miller, Linda Lael. Just Kate. l.t. ed. 1992. (Romance Ser.). pap. 14.95 o.p. (*0-373-58228-5*) BBC Audiobooks America.

—Just Kate. 2000. 256p. mass mkt. (*1-55166-631-6*, 1-66631-2, Mira Bks.); 1995. per. (*1-55166-055-5*, Mira Bks.); 1989. (Silhouette Desire Ser.: No. 516). pap. (*0-373-05516-1*, Silhouette) Harlequin Enterprises, Ltd.

—Wild about Harry. abr. ed. 1999. (Silhouette Romance Ser.). audio 7.99 o.p. (*1-56740-528-2*, 1704, Silhouette Romance Audio) Brilliance Audio.

—Wild about Harry. 2000. 256p. mass mkt. (*1-55166-575-1*, Harlequin Bks.); 1996. mass mkt. (*0-373-48340-6*, 1-48340-3, Harlequin Bks.); 1995. 187p. mass mkt. (*0-373-15310-4*, 1-15310-5, Harlequin Bks.); 1991. (Silhouette Desire Ser.: No. 667). pap. (*0-373-05667-2*, Silhouette) Harlequin Enterprises, Ltd.

Moloney, James. Swashbuckler. 1995. (Storybridge Ser.). 96p. (J). (gr. 4-7). pap. 11.95 (*0-7022-2825-7*) Univ. of Queensland Pr. AUS. *Dist:* International Specialized Bk. Services.

Montero, Gloria. The Villa Marini. 1998. 320p. pap. 15.00 o.p. (*0-88001-609-4*, Ecco) HarperTrade.

—The Villa Marini. l.t. ed. 1998. (Ulverscroft Large Print Ser.). 432p. 29.99 (*0-7089-3929-5*, Ulverscroft) Thorpe, F. A. Pubs. GBR. *Dist:* Ulverscroft Large Print Bks., Ltd., Ulverscroft Large Print Canada, Ltd.

—The Villa Marini: A Family Saga. 1997. 309p. o.p. (*0-88001-577-2*, Ecco) HarperTrade.

Moorhead, Finola. Still Murder. 1997. 293p. pap. 15.95 (*0-7043-4397-5*) Women's Pr., Ltd., The GBR. *Dist:* Trafalgar Square.

Moorhouse, Frank. Dark Palace. 2000. 678p. (*0-09-183676-X*) Hutchinson Children's Bks, Ltd.

Moran, Thomas. What Harry Saw. 2003. 368p. pap. 14.00 (*1-57322-341-7*, Riverhead Trade (Paperbacks)) Berkley Publishing Group.

—What Harry Saw. 2002. 320p. 25.95 o.s.i (*1-57322-224-0*, Riverhead Bks. (Hardcovers)) Putnam Publishing Group, The.

Morgan, Marlo. Message from Forever. abr. ed. 1998. audio 18.00 (*0-694-51961-8*, HarperAudio) HarperTrade.

—Message from Forever: A Novel of Aboriginal Wisdom. 1998. 336p. 24.00 o.s.i (*0-06-019107-4*, HarperCollins) HarperTrade.

—Mutant Message down Under. 1995. 240p. pap. 80.00 o.p. (*0-06-092668-6*); 1994. 208p. 216.00 o.p. (*0-06-017193-6*); 1994. 240p. 18.00 o.p. (*0-06-017192-8*) HarperCollins Pubs.

—Mutant Message down Under. mass mkt. o.s.i (*0-06-109374-2*, HarperTorch) Morrow/Avon.

—Mutant Message Down Under. 2004. 224p. pap. 12.95 (*0-06-072351-3*); 1995. 208p. pap. 13.00 (*0-06-092631-7*) HarperTrade. (Perennial).

—Mutant Message down Under. abr. ed. 1994. audio 18.00 (*0-694-51515-9*, CPN 2461, HarperAudio) HarperTrade.

—Mutant Message down Under. unabr. ed. 1995. audio 40.00 (*0-7887-0193-2*, 94417E7) Recorded Bks., LLC.

—Mutant Message from Forever: A Novel of Aboriginal Wisdom. 1999. 336p. pap. 13.00 (*0-06-093026-8*, Perennial) HarperTrade.

—Mutant Message from Forever: A Novel of Aboriginal Wisdom. unabr. ed. 1999. audio 60.00 (*0-7887-2923-3*, 95713E7) Recorded Bks., LLC.

Moriarty, Jaclyn. Feeling Sorry for Celia: Novel. 2001. 288p. (YA). (gr. 7 up). 16.95 (*0-312-26923-4*) St. Martin's Pr.

Moriarty, Liane. Three Wishes. 2004. 352p. (Orig.). 24.95 (*0-06-058612-5*) HarperCollins Pubs.

Morrison, John. This Freedom. 1986. 208p. pap. 5.95 o.p. (*0-14-008633-1*, Penguin Bks.) Viking Penguin.

Mudrooroo. Wild Cat Falling. 2001. 152p. pap. 13.95 (*0-207-19732-6*) Angus & Robertson, Ltd. GBR. *Dist:* Consortium Bk. Sales & Distribution.

Mudrooroo, Narogin. Master of the Ghost Dreaming. 1993. 81p. (Orig.). pap. 10.00 o.p. (*0-207-16952-7*) HarperCollins Pubs.

Murray, Les. Fredy Neptune. 2000. 272p. pap. 14.00 (*0-374-52676-1*) Farrar, Straus & Giroux.

—Fredy Neptune: A Novel in Verse. 1999. 208p. 27.50 (*0-374-15854-1*) Farrar, Straus & Giroux.

Ng, Lillian. Swallowing Clouds. 1999. 306p. o.p. (*0-88001-644-2*, Ecco) HarperTrade.

Noonan, Michael. Magwitch. 1982. 224p. 11.95 o.p. (*0-312-50426-8*) St. Martin's Pr.

Nowra, Louis, contrib. by. Red Nights. 1997. 19.95 (*0-330-35986-X*) Picador GBR. *Dist:* Trans-Atlantic Pubns., Inc.

Nyoongah, Mudrooroo. The Kwinkan. 1994. 130p. (Orig.). pap. 10.00 o.p. (*0-207-17944-1*) HarperCollins General Bks. Group.

Oliver, Maria-Antonia. Antipodes. McNerney, Kathleen, tr. from SPA. 1989. (International Women's Crime Ser.). 224p. (Orig.). reprint ed. pap. 8.95 o.p. (*0-931188-82-2*, Seal Pr.) Avalon Publishing Group.

Ottley, Reginald. Bates Family. 1969. (J). (gr. 4-6). 4.50 o.p. (*0-15-205726-9*) Harcourt Children's Bks.

Papaellinas, George. Ikons: A Collection of Stories. 1986. 208p. pap. 4.95 o.p. (*0-14-008852-0*, Penguin Bks.) Viking Penguin.

Park, Ruth. Missus. 1986. 256p. 15.95 o.p. (*0-312-00154-1*) St. Martin's Pr.

Pascoe, Bruce. Shark. 1999. 205p. pap. 16.95 (*1-875641-48-3*) Magabala Bks. AUS. *Dist:* International Specialized Bk. Services.

Perlman, Elliot. Three Dollars. 1999. 358p. 22.00 (*1-878448-88-9*) MacMurray & Beck, Inc.

Pettigrew, Cinda Wombes & Warner, Robyn D. Seeking the White Root: An Australian Story. 1998. pap. text 14.95 (*0-9666739-0-5*) Bald Eagle Pr.

Phipson, Joan. Six & Silver. 1971. (Illus.). 190p. (J). (gr. 4-6). 5.95 o.p. (*0-15-275330-3*) Harcourt Children's Bks.

Pierce, Todd. The Australia Stories. 2003. 223p. 20.00 (*1-931561-28-1*) MacAdam/Cage Publishing, Inc.

Pinney, Estelle R. A Net Full of Honey. 1996. 181p. (YA). pap. 13.95 (*0-7022-2744-7*) Univ. of Queensland Pr. AUS. *Dist:* International Specialized Bk. Services.

Plaidy, Jean. Beyond the Blue Mountains. 1981. 480p. mass mkt. 2.95 o.s.i (*0-449-24451-2*, Fawcett) Ballantine Bks.

Platt, Pamela. Pig with a View. 1995. (Illus.). 80p. (J). (gr. 2-6). pap. 11.95 (*0-7022-2589-4*) Univ. of Queensland Pr. AUS. *Dist:* International Specialized Bk. Services.

Porter, Dorothy. The Witch Number. 1993. 124p. (YA). pap. 11.95 (*0-7022-2460-X*) Univ. of Queensland Pr. AUS. *Dist:* International Specialized Bk. Services.

Power, Karen E. Kajo. 1998. 123p. pap. 9.95 o.p. (*0-533-12359-3*) Vantage Pr., Inc.

Prichard, Katharine S. Tribute: Selected Stories of Katharine Susannah Prichard. Throssell, Ric, ed. 1989. 288p. (Orig.). pap. 16.95 (*0-7022-2166-X*) Univ. of Queensland Pr. AUS. *Dist:* International Specialized Bk. Services.

Prior, Natalie Jane. West End Shuffle. 1996. 212p. (YA). pap. 13.95 (*0-7022-2882-6*) Univ. of Queensland Pr. AUS. *Dist:* International Specialized Bk. Services.

—Yesterday's Heroes. 1995. (YA). pap. 13.95 (*0-7022-2808-7*) Univ. of Queensland Pr. AUS. *Dist:* International Specialized Bk. Services.

Proctor, Candice. September Moon. 1999. 368p. mass mkt. 6.99 (*0-449-00127-X*, Fawcett) Ballantine Bks.

—Whispers of Heaven. 2001. 416p. mass mkt. 6.99 (*0-8041-1931-7*, Ivy Bks.) Ballantine Bks.

Proctor, Candice E. September Moon. l.t. ed. 2000. (Large Print Book Ser.). 467p. 27.95 (*1-56895-917-6*, Wheeler Publishing, Inc.) Gale Group.

—Whispers of Heaven. l.t. ed. 2001. (Large Print Bks.). 512p. pap. 23.95 (*1-58724-098-X*, Wheeler Publishing, Inc.) Gale Group.

Rettino, Ernie & Kerner, Debby. Psalty in Australia. 1991. 6.99 o.p. (*0-8499-0897-3*) W Publishing Group.

Rice, Ben. Pobby & Dingan. E-Book 14.50 (*1-58945-535-5*) Adobe Systems, Inc.

—Pobby & Dingan. 2003. 112p. reprint ed. pap. 10.00 (*1-4000-3188-5*, Vintage) Knopf Publishing Group.

—Pobby & Dingan. 2000. (Illus.). 112p. 18.00 (*0-375-41127-5*) Knopf, Alfred A. Inc.

—Pobby & Dingan. 2001. E-Book 14.50 (*0-375-41261-1*) Random Hse., Inc.

—Pobby y Dingan. (SPA.). 128p. 20.00 (*84-08-03629-7*) GeoPlaneta, Editorial, S. A. ESP. *Dist:* Lectorum Pubns., Inc.

Richards, Tim, contrib. by. Duckness. 1998. 162p. (*1-86448-761-5*) Allen & Unwin Pty., Ltd. AUS. *Dist:* Independent Pubs. Group.

—The Prince. 1997. 168p. (*1-86448-285-0*) Allen & Unwin Pty., Ltd. AUS. *Dist:* Independent Pubs. Group.

Roads, Michael J. Getting There. 1998. 376p. pap. 12.95 (*1-57174-104-6*) SilverRoads Publishing.

Rogers, Jane. Promised Lands. 1998. 376p. pap. 14.95 (*0-87951-866-9*); 1997. 388p. 24.95 (*0-87951-753-0*) Overlook Pr., The.

Ross, Robert. Australia. 1998. (Travelers' Literary Companions Ser.: Vol. 6). 228p. pap. 13.95 (*1-883513-05-7*) Whereabouts.

Rossiter, Richard. The Model: Selected Writings of Kenneth Seaforth McKenzie. 2000. (Illus.). 236p. pap. 19.95 (*1-876268-34-4*) Univ. of Western Australia Pr. AUS. *Dist:* International Specialized Bk. Services.

Rowe, Jennifer. Death in Store. 1994. 208p. mass mkt. 4.99 o.s.i (*0-553-56875-2*) Bantam Bks.

—Death in Store. 1992. 192p. 17.00 o.s.i (*0-385-42598-8*) Doubleday Publishing.

—Grim Pickings. l.t. ed. 1991. 11.95 o.p. (*0-947072-39-X*, 152); pap. 9.95 o.p. (*1-86340-083-4*, C1135) BBC Audiobooks America.

—Grim Pickings. 1991. 416p. mass mkt. 4.99 o.s.i (*0-553-29122-X*) Bantam Bks.

—Grim Pickings. unabr. ed. 1998. audio (*1-86340-605-0*, 551105) Bolinda Publishing Pty, Ltd.

—Lamb to the Slaughter. 1996. 288p. mass mkt. 4.99 o.s.i (*0-553-56820-5*, Crimeline) Bantam Bks.

—The Makeover Murders. 1994. 304p. mass mkt. 4.99 o.s.i (*0-553-29740-6*) Bantam Bks.

—The Makeover Murders. unabr. ed. 1998. audio (*1-86340-569-0*, 571230) Bolinda Publishing Pty, Ltd.

—The Makeover Murders: Moonrider. 1994. 352p. mass mkt. 5.50 o.s.i (*0-553-29693-0*) Bantam Bks.

—Murder by the Book. 1991. 304p. mass mkt. 4.50 o.s.i (*0-553-29373-7*) Bantam Bks.

—Murder by the Book. unabr. ed. 1998. audio (*1-86340-604-2*, 560309) Bolinda Publishing Pty, Ltd.

—Stranglehold. 1995. 256p. mass mkt. 4.99 o.s.i (*0-553-56819-1*) Bantam Bks.

—Stranglehold. l.t. ed. 1995. 338p. lib. bdg. 19.95 (*0-7838-1247-7*, Macmillan Reference USA) Gale Group.

Roy, James. Almost Wednesday. 1996. 140p. (YA). pap. 12.95 (*0-7022-2826-5*) Univ. of Queensland Pr. AUS. *Dist:* International Specialized Bk. Services.

Rudd, Steele. A Steele Rudd Selection: The Best Dad & Dave Stories with Other Rudd Classics. Moorhouse, Frank, ed. 1987. (Illus.). 240p. (Orig.). pap. 15.95 (*0-7022-1978-9*) Univ. of Queensland Pr. AUS. *Dist:* International Specialized Bk. Services.

Ryan, Richard. Funnelweb. 1997. 339p. (*0-7329-0888-4*) Macmillan Education Australia.

Saint-Clair, North & Left from Here. 2001. 252p. pap. 19.95 (*0-7596-3279-0*) 1stBooks Library.

Savage, Georgia. The Estuary. 1993. 224p. (Orig.). 20.00 o.p. (*1-55597-172-5*) Graywolf Pr.

—The Estuary. 1989. 216p. (Orig.). pap. 14.95 o.p. (*0-7022-2115-5*) Univ. of Queensland Pr. AUS. *Dist:* International Specialized Bk. Services.

—House Tibet. 1991. 352p. 18.95 o.p. (*1-55597-144-X*) Graywolf Pr.

Saxton, Judith. Still Waters. 1998. 504p. 26.95 o.p. (*0-312-18185-X*) St. Martin's Pr.

Scott, Bill. The Banshee & the Bullocky: Tales of My Uncle Arch. 1996. (Illus.). 127p. pap. 19.95 (*0-7022-2775-7*) Univ. of Queensland Pr. AUS. *Dist:* International Specialized Bk. Services.

Scott, Kim. Benang. 1999. 440p. pap. 19.95 (*1-86368-240-6*) Fremantle Arts Centre Pr. AUS. *Dist:* International Specialized Bk. Services.

Scott, Phillip. Gay Resort Murder Shock. 2003. 320p. pap. 13.95 (*1-55583-757-3*) Alyson Pubns.

Shapiro, Laurie G. The Unexpected Salami. 308p. 1999. pap. 10.95 (*1-56512-232-1*, 72232); 1998. tchr. ed. 18.95 (*1-56512-194-5*, 72194) Algonquin Bks. of Chapel Hill.

Sharp, Damian. When a Monkey Speaks: And Other Stories from Australia. 1994. 224p. 15.00 o.p. (*0-06-258500-2*) HarperSanFrancisco.

Shaw, Patricia. Cry of the Rain Bird. 1995. 352p. 23.95 o.p. (*0-312-13457-6*) St. Martin's Pr.

—The Feather & the Stone. 1993. 320p. 21.95 o.p. (*0-312-10462-6*) St. Martin's Pr.

—River of the Sun. 1992. 384p. 21.95 o.p. (*0-312-08284-3*) St. Martin's Pr.

—Where the Willows Weep. 1994. 22.95 o.p. (*0-312-11914-3*) St. Martin's Pr.

Shute, Nevil. A Town Like Alice. 23.95 (*0-8488-0848-7*) Amereon, Ltd.

—A Town Like Alice. 1987. 288p. mass mkt. 6.99 (*0-345-35374-9*); 1985. mass mkt. 2.95 o.p. (*0-345-33029-3*); 1981. mass mkt. 2.75 o.p. (*0-345-30565-5*) Ballantine Bks.

—A Town Like Alice. l.t. ed. 2001. (Dales Large Print Ser.). pap. (*1-84262-100-9*) Dales Large Print Bks. GBR. *Dist:* Ulverscroft Large Print Canada, Ltd.

—A Town Like Alice. l.t. ed. 1976. (Ulverscroft Large Print Ser.). 12.00 o.p. (*0-85456-410-1*, Ulverscroft) Thorpe, F. A. Pubs. GBR. *Dist:* Ulverscroft Large Print Bks., Ltd., Ulverscroft Large Print Canada, Ltd.

Skrzynecki, Peter. The Wild Dogs. l.t. ed. 1991. 11.95 o.p. (*0-947072-53-5*, 5030) BBC Audiobooks America.

—The Wild Dogs. 1988. 202p. 14.95 (*0-7022-2014-0*) Univ. of Queensland Pr. AUS. *Dist:* International Specialized Bk. Services.

Snoe, Eboni. Followin' a Dream. 2001. 384p. mass mkt. 5.99 (*0-380-81396-3*, Avon Bks.) Morrow/Avon.

Southall, Ivan. Josh. 1988. 192p. (YA). (gr. 7 up). 13.95 o.s.i (*0-02-786280-1*, Simon & Schuster Children's Publishing) Simon & Schuster Children's Publishing.

—Rachel, RS. 1986. 147p. (J). (gr. 5 up). 14.00 o.p. (*0-374-36163-0*, Farrar, Straus & Giroux (BYR)) Farrar, Straus & Giroux.

Stead, Christina. For Love Alone. 1999. pap. 16.95 (*1-875892-71-0*); 256p. pap. 16.95 (*1-875892-59-1*) Editions Tom Thompson AUS. *Dist:* International Specialized Bk. Services.

—For Love Alone. 1979. 491p. pap. 5.95 o.p. (*0-15-632535-7*, Harvest Bks.) Harcourt Trade Pubs.

—Seven Poor Men of Sydney. 1999. pap. 16.95 (*1-875892-60-5*) Editions Tom Thompson AUS. *Dist:* International Specialized Bk. Services.

Stewart, Maureen. Dear Emily. 1988. 112p. (Orig.). (J). (gr. 3-7). pap. 3.95 o.p. (*0-14-032059-8*, Puffin Bks.) Penguin Putnam Bks. for Young Readers.

Stiller, Eric. Keep Australia on Your Left: A True Story of an Attempt to Circumnavigate Australia by Kayak. 2000. (Illus.). 416p. 25.95 (*0-312-87458-8*, Forge Bks.) Doherty, Tom Assocs., LLC.

Sussex, Lucy. The Scarlet Rider. 2001. pap. 15.95 (*0-312-87294-1*, Forge Bks.); 1999. 352p. mass mkt. 5.99 (*0-8125-4923-6*, Tor Bks.); 1996. 352p. 23.95 o.p. (*0-312-85293-2*, Forge Bks.) Doherty, Tom Assocs., LLC.

Tanner, Janet. Daughter of Riches. 1993. 524p. 24.95 o.p. (*0-312-09266-0*) St. Martin's Pr.

—Shadows of the Past. 2003. 288p. 26.99 (*0-7278-5926-9*) Severn Hse. Pubs., Ltd.

Throssell, Ric, contrib. by. Tomorrow - 1997. 289p. (*0-646-28766-4*) Welles, Dorian Proprietary, Ltd.

Thubron, C. Turning Back the Sun. 1994. pap. 12.00 o.p. (*0-06-092508-6*) HarperCollins Pubs.

Thubron, Colin. Turning Back the Sun: A Novel. 1992. 208p. 20.00 o.p. (*0-06-018227-X*) HarperTrade.

Townsend, Helen. Love Tangle. 1998. 410p. (*0-7322-5866-9*) HarperCollins Pubs.

Trollope, Anthony. The Fixed Period, 2 vols. Hall, N. John, ed. 1981. (Selected Works of Anthony Trollope). reprint ed. lib. bdg. 49.95 (*0-405-14195-5*) Ayer Co. Pubs., Inc.

—The Fixed Period, vols. of 2. reprint ed. lib. bdg. 196.00 (*0-7426-2490-0*); 2001. pap. text 56.00 (*0-7426-7490-8*) Classic Bks.

—The Fixed Period. 1993. (Oxford World's Classics Ser.). 214p. pap. 8.95 o.p. (*0-19-282842-8*) Oxford Univ. Pr., Inc.

—The Fixed Period. Super, R. H., ed. 1990. (Illus.). 207p. (C). reprint ed. text 50.00 (*0-472-09448-3*, 09448) Univ. of Michigan Pr.

—The Fixed Period. Super, Robert H., ed. 1990. (Illus.). 207p. reprint ed. pap. 19.95 (*0-472-06448-7*, 06448) Univ. of Michigan Pr.

—Harry Heathcote of Gangoil: A Tale of Australian Bush Life. Hall, N. John, ed. 1981. (Selected Works of Anthony Trollope). reprint ed. lib. bdg. 38.95 (*0-405-14163-7*) Ayer Co. Pubs., Inc.

—Harry Heathcote of Gangoil: A Tale of Australian Bush Life. 2001. (Collected Works of Anthony Trollope). 313p. reprint ed. pap. text 28.00 (*0-7426-7472-X*) Classic Bks.

—Harry Heathcote of Gangoil: A Tale of Australian Bush Life. 1987. 159p. reprint ed. pap. 4.95 o.p. (*0-486-25317-1*) Dover Pubns., Inc.

—Harry Heathcote of Gangoil: A Tale of Australian Bush Life. 1992. (Oxford World's Classics Ser.). 158p. pap. 6.95 o.p. (*0-19-282846-0*) Oxford Univ. Pr., Inc.

—Harry Heathcote of Gangoil: A Tale of Australian Bush Life. 1994. (Penguin Trollope Ser.: Vol. 35). 320p. pap. 6.95 o.p. (*0-14-043835-1*, Penguin Classics) Viking Penguin.

Turner, George. Down There in Darkness. 352p. 2000. pap. 15.95 (*0-312-87258-5*); 1999. 24.95 (*0-312-86829-4*) Doherty, Tom Assocs., LLC. (Tor Bks.).

Upfield, Arthur W. An Author Bites the Dust. (Napoleon Bonaparte Mysteries Ser.). 21.95 (*0-89190-566-9*) Amereon, Ltd.

—The Bachelors of Broken Hill. 1998. (Inspector Napoleon Bonaparte Mystery Ser.). 256p. pap. 11.00 (*0-684-85058-3*, Touchstone) Simon & Schuster.

—The Bachelors of Broken Hill. l.t. ed. 1974. (Ulverscroft Large Print Ser.). 29.99 o.p. (*0-85456-296-6*, Ulverscroft) Thorpe, F. A. Pubs. GBR. *Dist:* Ulverscroft Large Print Bks., Ltd., Ulverscroft Large Print Canada, Ltd.

—The Bachelors of Broken Hill: An Inspector Napoleon Bonaparte Mystery. 1984. 256p. pap. 6.00 (*0-684-18246-7*, Macmillan Reference USA) Gale Group.

—The Battling Prophet. (Napoleon Bonaparte Mysteries Ser.). reprint ed. lib. bdg. 21.95 (*0-89190-551-0*, Rivercity Pr.) Amereon, Ltd.

—The Battling Prophet. 1994. reprint ed. lib. bdg. 29.95 (*1-56849-352-5*) Buccaneer Bks., Inc.

—The Body at Madmen's Bend. (Napoleon Bonaparte Mysteries Ser.). reprint ed. lib. bdg. 23.95 (*0-89190-552-9*) Amereon, Ltd.

—The Bone Is Pointed. (Napoleon Bonaparte Mysteries Ser.). 23.95 (*0-89190-568-5*) Amereon, Ltd.

—The Bone Is Pointed. 1976. (Crime Fiction Ser.). reprint ed. lib. bdg. 21.00 o.p. (*0-8240-2395-1*) Garland Publishing, Inc.

—The Bone Is Pointed. 2nd l.t. ed. 1993. 385p. 21.95 (*1-85695-335-1*) ISIS Large Print Bks. GBR. *Dist:* Transaction Pubs.

—The Bone Is Pointed. 1998. (Inspector Napoleon Bonaparte Mystery Ser.). 304p. pap. 11.00 (*0-684-85057-5*, Touchstone) Simon & Schuster.

—The Bone Is Pointed: An Inspector Napoleon Bonaparte Mystery. 1984. 288p. pap. 6.00 o.p. (*0-684-18247-5*, Macmillan Reference USA) Gale Group.

—The Bone Is Pointed: An Inspector Napoleon Bonaparte Mystery. unabr. ed. 1994. audio 58.00 (*0-7887-0030-8*, 94229) Recorded Bks., LLC.

—Bony & the Black Virgin. (Napoleon Bonaparte Mysteries Ser.). reprint ed. lib. bdg. 20.95 (*0-89190-553-7*, Rivercity Pr.) Amereon, Ltd.

—Bony & the Kelly Gang. (Napoleon Bonaparte Mysteries Ser.). 21.95 (*0-89190-554-5*) Amereon, Ltd.

—Bony & the Mouse. (Napoleon Bonaparte Mysteries Ser.). 22.95 (*0-89190-561-8*) Amereon, Ltd.

—Bony & the Mouse. l.t. ed. 1973. 12.00 o.p. (*0-85456-186-2*, Ulverscroft) Thorpe, F. A. Pubs. GBR. *Dist:* Ulverscroft Large Print Bks., Ltd.

—Bony & the White Savage. l.t. ed. 1976. (Ulverscroft Large Print Ser.). 29.99 o.p. (*0-85456-407-1*, Ulverscroft) Thorpe, F. A. Pubs. GBR. *Dist:* Ulverscroft Large Print Bks., Ltd., Ulverscroft Large Print Canada, Ltd.

—Bony Buys a Woman. 1984. 21.95 (*0-89190-555-3*) Amereon, Ltd.

—Breakaway House. l.t. ed. 1991. 11.95 o.p. (*0-947072-72-1*, 1033); pap. 9.95 o.p. (*1-86340-102-4*, AUS027) BBC Audiobooks America.

—Bushranger of the Skies. unabr. ed. 1999. audio (*1-86442-387-0*, 590378) Bolinda Publishing Pty, Ltd.

—Bushranger of the Skies. l.t. ed. 1978. (Ulverscroft Large Print Ser.). 29.99 o.p. (*0-7089-0132-8*, Ulverscroft) Thorpe, F. A. Pubs. GBR. *Dist:* Ulverscroft Large Print Bks., Ltd., Ulverscroft Large Print Canada, Ltd.

—Cake in the Hat Box. (Napoleon Bonaparte Mysteries Ser.). 20.95 (*0-89190-567-7*) Amereon, Ltd.

—Cake in the Hat Box. l.t. ed. 1979. 12.00 o.p. (*0-7089-0335-5*, Ulverscroft) Thorpe, F. A. Pubs. GBR. *Dist:* Ulverscroft Large Print Bks., Ltd.

—The Clue of the New Shoe. l.t. ed. 1974. (Ulverscroft Large Print Ser.). 29.99 o.p. (*0-85456-258-3*, Ulverscroft) Thorpe, F. A. Pubs. GBR. *Dist:* Ulverscroft Large Print Bks., Ltd., Ulverscroft Large Print Canada, Ltd.

—Death of a Lake. 1983. 192p. pap. 6.00 o.s.i (*0-684-17886-9*, Macmillan Reference USA) Gale Group.

—Death of a Swagman. unabr. ed. 1999. audio (*1-86442-385-4*, 590372) Bolinda Publishing Pty, Ltd.

—Death of a Swagman. 1982. 224p. pap. 6.00 o.s.i (*0-684-17482-0*, Macmillan Reference USA) Gale Group.

—Death of a Swagman. l.t. ed. 1975. 12.00 o.p. (*0-85456-374-1*, Ulverscroft) Thorpe, F. A. Pubs. GBR. *Dist:* Ulverscroft Large Print Bks., Ltd.

—The Devil's Steps. (Napoleon Bonaparte Mysteries Ser.). reprint ed. lib. bdg. 22.95 (*0-89190-556-1*) Amereon, Ltd.

—The Devil's Steps. unabr. ed. 1999. audio (*1-876584-28-9*, 590788) Bolinda Publishing Pty, Ltd.

—The Devil's Steps: An Inspector Napoleon Bonaparte Mystery. 1982. 288p. pap. 6.00 o.s.i (*0-684-17668-8*, Macmillan Reference USA) Gale Group.

—Gripped by Drought. 1990. 288p. reprint ed. 30.00 o.p. (*0-939767-19-8*) McMillan, Dennis Pubns.

—The House of Cain. 1983. (Illus.). 296p. reprint ed. 20.00 o.p. (*0-9609986-0-8*) McMillan, Dennis Pubns.

—The Lake Frome Monster. (Napoleon Bonaparte Mysteries Ser.). reprint ed. lib. bdg. 18.95 (*0-89190-557-X*) Amereon, Ltd.

—The Lake Frome Monster. 2nd l.t. ed. 1993. 273p. 21.95 (*1-85695-340-8*) ISIS Large Print Bks. GBR. *Dist:* Transaction Pubs.

—The Lake Frome Monster: An Inspector Napoleon Bonaparte Mystery, Set. unabr. ed. 1994. audio 34.00 (*1-85695-505-2*, 94370) Recorded Bks., LLC.

—The Lure of the Bush. (Napoleon Bonaparte Mysteries Ser.). 21.95 (*0-89190-569-3*) Amereon, Ltd.

—Madman's Bend. l.t. ed. 1977. (Ulverscroft Large Print Ser.). 29.99 o.p. (*0-7089-0032-1*, Ulverscroft) Thorpe, F. A. Pubs. GBR. *Dist:* Ulverscroft Large Print Bks., Ltd., Ulverscroft Large Print Canada, Ltd.

—Man of Two Tribes. Date not set. (Napoleon Bonaparte Mysteries Ser.). lib. bdg. 20.95 (*0-8488-2170-X*) Amereon, Ltd.

—The Mountains Have a Secret. 20.95 (*0-8488-0653-0*) Amereon, Ltd.

—The Mountains Have a Secret. 1985. 192p. pap. 4.95 o.s.i (*0-684-18501-6*, Macmillan Reference USA) Gale Group.

—The Mountains Have a Secret. l.t. ed. 1975. (Ulverscroft Large Print Ser.). 29.99 o.p. (*0-85456-341-5*, Ulverscroft) Thorpe, F. A. Pubs. GBR. *Dist:* Ulverscroft Large Print Bks., Ltd., Ulverscroft Large Print Canada, Ltd.

—Mr. Jelly's Business: Murder down Under. (Napoleon Bonaparte Mysteries Ser.). reprint ed. lib. bdg. 24.95 (*0-89190-558-8*, Rivercity Pr.) Amereon, Ltd.

—The Murchison Murders. ltd. ed. 1987. 96p. reprint ed. 15.00 o.p. (*0-9609986-9-1*) McMillan, Dennis Pubns.

—Murder down Under. 1983. 304p. pap. 6.00 (*0-684-17887-7*, Macmillan Reference USA) Gale Group.

—Murder down Under. 1998. (Inspector Napoleon Bonaparte Mystery Ser.). 304p. pap. 12.00 (*0-684-85059-1*, Touchstone) Simon & Schuster.

—Murder Must Wait. (Napoleon Bonaparte Mysteries Ser.). reprint ed. lib. bdg. 21.95 (*0-89190-559-6*, Rivercity Pr.) Amereon, Ltd.

—The Mystery of Swordfish Reef. (Napoleon Bonaparte Mysteries Ser.). 20.95 (*0-89190-562-6*) Amereon, Ltd.

—The Mystery of Swordfish Reef. 1994. reprint ed. lib. bdg. 32.95 (*1-56849-351-7*) Buccaneer Bks., Inc.

—The Mystery of Swordfish Reef. 1998. (Inspector Napoleon Bonaparte Mystery Ser.). 272p. pap. 12.00 (*0-684-85060-5*, Touchstone) Simon & Schuster.

—The Mystery of Swordfish Reef: An Inspector Napoleon Bonaparte Mystery. 1985. 272p. pap. 5.95 o.s.i (*0-684-18412-5*, Macmillan Reference USA) Gale Group.

—The New Shoe. 1983. 192p. pap. 4.95 (*0-684-18020-0*, Macmillan Reference USA) Gale Group.

—No Footprints in the Bush. 20.95 (*0-89190-560-X*) Amereon, Ltd.

—The Sands of Windee. (Napoleon Bonaparte Mysteries Ser.). 21.95 (*0-89190-570-7*) Amereon, Ltd.

—The Sands of Windee. 2nd l.t. ed. 1993. 282p. 22.95 (*1-85695-345-9*) ISIS Large Print Bks. GBR. *Dist:* Transaction Pubs.

—The Sands of Windee. 1985. 224p. pap. 4.95 o.s.i (*0-684-18502-4*, Scribner Paper Fiction) Simon & Schuster.

—The Sands of Windee: A Napoleon Bonaparte Mystery. unabr. ed. 1994. audio 58.00 (*1-55690-983-7*, 94122) Recorded Bks., LLC.

—Sinister Stones. (Napoleon Bonaparte Mysteries Ser.). 19.95 (*0-8488-1211-5*) Amereon, Ltd.

—Sinister Stones. 1983. 192p. pap. 6.00 o.s.i (*0-684-18021-9*, Scribner Paper Fiction) Simon & Schuster.

—The Torn Branch. Date not set. (Napoleon Bonaparte Mysteries Ser.). lib. bdg. 18.95 (*0-8488-2171-8*) Amereon, Ltd.

—The Torn Branch. 1986. 160p. pap. 5.95 o.s.i (*0-02-025930-1*, Scribner Paper Fiction) Simon & Schuster.

—Venom House. (Napoleon Bonaparte Mysteries Ser.). 22.95 (*0-8488-1212-3*) Amereon, Ltd.

—Venom House. unabr. ed. 1998. audio (*1-86442-318-8*, 581157) Bolinda Publishing Pty, Ltd.

—Venom House. 1989. 268p. pap. 6.00 o.s.i (*0-02-025901-8*, Scribner Paper Fiction) Simon & Schuster.

—The Widows of Broome. l.t. ed. 1980. (Ulverscroft Large Print Ser.). 354p. 29.99 o.p. (*0-7089-0490-4*, Ulverscroft) Thorpe, F. A. Pubs. GBR. *Dist:* Ulverscroft Large Print Bks., Ltd., Ulverscroft Large Print Canada, Ltd.

—The Widows of Broome: An Inspector Napoleon Bonaparte Mystery. 1985. 256p. pap. 5.95 (*0-684-18389-7*, Scribner Paper Fiction) Simon & Schuster.

—The Will of the Tribe. (Napoleon Bonaparte Mysteries Ser.). 20.95 (*0-8488-1213-1*) Amereon, Ltd.

—The Will of the Tribe. 1984. 216p. pap. 5.95 o.s.i (*0-684-18141-X*, Scribner Paper Fiction) Simon & Schuster.

—Winds of Evil. (Napoleon Bonaparte Mysteries Ser.). 20.95 (*0-89190-563-4*) Amereon, Ltd.

—Winds of Evil. 1987. 256p. pap. 4.95 o.s.i (*0-02-025910-7*, Scribner Paper Fiction) Simon & Schuster.

—Winds of Evil. l.t. ed. 1977. (Ulverscroft Large Print Ser.). 29.99 o.p. (*0-7089-0054-2*, Ulverscroft) Thorpe, F. A. Pubs. GBR. *Dist:* Ulverscroft Large Print Bks., Ltd., Ulverscroft Large Print Canada, Ltd.

—Wings above the Diamantina. Date not set. (Napoleon Bonaparte Mysteries Ser.). lib. bdg. 23.95 (*0-8488-2172-6*) Amereon, Ltd.

—Wings above the Diamantina. l.t. ed. 1977. (Ulverscroft Large Print Ser.). 29.99 o.p. (*0-7089-0009-7*, Ulverscroft) Thorpe, F. A. Pubs. GBR. *Dist:* Ulverscroft Large Print Bks., Ltd., Ulverscroft Large Print Canada, Ltd.

Vajda, Tibor Timothy. Inspector Bourke in Sydney, Bangkok & Moscow: Crime, Politics, Sex. 2001. 214p. pap. 21.99 (*0-7388-6460-9*) Xlibris Corp.

Wagner, Jenny. Message from Avalon. 1994. 182p. pap. 12.95 (*0-7022-2741-2*) Univ. of Queensland Pr. AUS. *Dist:* International Specialized Bk. Services.

Watt, Peter. Flight of the Eagle. 2003. (Illus.). 672p. mass mkt. 11.95 (*0-552-14796-6*) Transworld Publishers Ltd. GBR. *Dist:* Trafalgar Square.

Way. Outback Fire: The Australians. 2001. mass mkt. (*0-373-03679-5*, Harlequin Bks.) Harlequin Enterprises, Ltd.

Way, Margaret. Claiming His Child. 1999. (Harlequin Romance Ser.: No. 3571). per. (*0-373-03571-3*, 1-03571-6); (Harlequin Large Print Ser.: No. 417). per. (*0-373-15817-3*, 1-15817-9) Harlequin Enterprises, Ltd. (Harlequin Bks.).

—Claiming His Child. l.t. ed. 2000. (Harlequin I Romance Ser.). 22.95 (*0-263-16412-8*) Harlequin Mills & Boon, Ltd. GBR. *Dist:* Thorndike Pr.

—The English Bride. 2000. (Harlequin Romance Ser.: Vol. 3619). 184p. mass mkt. (*0-373-03619-1*, 1-03619-3, Harlequin Bks.) Harlequin Enterprises, Ltd.

—The English Bride: Legends of the Outback. l.t. ed. 2000. (Harlequin Romance Ser.: Vol. 465). 250p. mass mkt. (*0-373-15865-3*, Harlequin Bks.) Harlequin Enterprises, Ltd.

—Fuego Austral. 2002. (Harlequin Jazmin Ser.). (SPA.). 160p. pap. (*0-373-68131-3*, Harlequin Bks.) Harlequin Enterprises, Ltd.

—L' Heritiere Australienne. 1999. (Harlequin Amours d'Aujourd'Hui Ser.: No. 333). (FRE.). mass mkt. (*0-373-38333-9*, 1-38333-0, Harlequin Bks.) Harlequin Enterprises, Ltd.

—Master of Maramba. 2001. (Harlequin Romance Ser.: No. 3671). mass mkt. (*0-373-03671-X*); (Harlequin Presents Ser.). mass mkt. (*0-373-15917-X*) Harlequin Enterprises, Ltd. (Harlequin Bks.).

—Master of Maramba. l.t. ed. 2002. (Mills & Boon Large Print Ser.). 288p. 27.99 (*0-263-17272-4*) Harlequin Mills & Boon, Ltd. GBR. *Dist:* Thorndike Pr., Ulverscroft Large Print Bks., Ltd., Ulverscroft Large Print Canada, Ltd.

—Outback Fire. l.t. ed. 2001. (Harlequin Presents Ser.). mass mkt. (*0-373-15925-0*, Harlequin Bks.) Harlequin Enterprises, Ltd.

—Outback Fire. l.t. ed. 2002. (Mills & Boon Large Print Ser.). 288p. 27.99 (*0-263-17289-9*) Harlequin Mills & Boon, Ltd. GBR. *Dist:* Thorndike Pr., Ulverscroft Large Print Bks., Ltd., Ulverscroft Large Print Canada, Ltd.

—Secrets of the Outback. 2002. (Harlequin Superromance Ser.: No. 1039). 296p. mass mkt. (*0-373-71039-9*, 1-71039-1, Harlequin Bks.) Harlequin Enterprises, Ltd.

Webber, Meredith. Christmas Knight. l.t. ed. 2003. 25.95 (*0-263-17979-6*) Harlequin Mills & Boon, Ltd. GBR. *Dist:* Thorndike Pr.

Webster, Susan. Small Tales of a Town. 1988. 192p. 14.95 o.p. (*0-312-02641-2*) St. Martin's Pr.

Weller, Archie. Land of the Golden Clouds. 1999. xii, 378p. pap. o.p. (*1-86448-338-5*) Allen & Unwin Pty., Ltd.

Wels, Barbara. The Lifestyles of Previous Tenants. 1995. 162p. pap. 19.95 (*0-7022-2781-1*) Univ. of Queensland Pr. AUS. *Dist:* International Specialized Bk. Services.

White, Patrick. The Cockatoos: New Stories. 1975. 312p. 12.95 o.p. (*0-670-22648-3*) Viking Penguin.

—Memoirs of Many in One. 1988. 192p. 15.95 o.p. (*0-670-81320-6*) Viking Penguin.

—Riders in the Chariot. 2002. (New York Review Books Classics Ser.). 624p. pap. 16.95 (*1-59017-002-4*) New York Review of Bks., Inc., The.

Wilde, Hilary. Red As a Rose. l.t. ed. 2003. 220p. pap. 24.45 (*0-7862-5410-6*) Thorndike Pr.

Williams, Darren. Angel Rock: A Novel. 2003. 320p. pap. 13.00 (*0-375-71924-5*) Knopf, Alfred A. Inc.

Williamson, Kristin. Treading on Dreams. 1998. (*0-14-027932-6*) Penguin Group (USA) Inc.

Winton, Tim. Blueback. 1998. 96p. 14.00 (*0-684-84565-2*, Scribner) Simon & Schuster.

—Cloudstreet. 432p. 1993. pap. 12.50 o.p. (*1-55597-183-0*); 1992. 20.00 o.p. (*1-55597-158-X*) Graywolf Pr.

—Dirt Music: A Novel. 2001. 465p. (*0-330-36323-9*) Picador.

—Dirt Music: A Novel. 416p. 2003. pap. 14.00 (*0-7432-2848-0*); 2002. 26.00 (*0-7432-2802-2*) Simon & Schuster. (Scribner).

—Shallows. 1993. 260p. reprint ed. pap. 12.50 (*1-55597-193-8*) Graywolf Pr.

—Shallows. 1986. 235p. 14.95 o.p. (*0-689-11806-6*, Scribner) Simon & Schuster.

Witting, Amy. Isobel on the Way to the Corner Shop. 1999. 352p. (*0-14-028634-9*) Penguin Group (USA) Inc.

—Marias War. 1998. 254p. text (*0-670-88312-3*) Viking.

Wood, Barbara. The Dreaming. 1992. 528p. mass mkt. 5.99 (*0-380-71593-7*, Avon Bks.) Morrow/Avon.

—The Dreaming: A Novel of Australia. 1993. 4.99 o.p. (*0-517-10604-3*) Random Hse. Value Publishing.

Woolfe, Sue. Leaning Towards Infinity: A Novel. 420p. 1998. pap. 14.95 (*0-571-19939-9*); 1997. 24.95 o.p. (*0-571-19905-4*) Faber & Faber, Inc.

Wrightson, Patricia. The Nargun & the Stars. 1988. 168p. (YA). (gr. 7 up). pap. 3.95 o.s.i (*0-14-030780-X*, Puffin Bks.) Penguin Putnam Bks. for Young Readers.

Yedidya & the Esrog Tree. 1982. pap. 2.95 (*0-87306-235-3*) Feldheim, Philipp Inc.

Zelman, Anita. Dead down Under: A Rebecca Lewis Mystery. 2002. 188p. 12.95 (*1-56474-398-5*) Fithian Pr.

### AUSTRIA—FICTION

Alexander, Nina. Rose's Magic Touch. 1997. (Magic Attic Club Ser.). (Illus.). 80p. (J). (gr. 2-6). 18.90 (*1-57513-184-6*, Magic Attic Pr.) Millbrook Pr., Inc.

—Rose's Magic Touch. 1997. (Magic Attic Club Ser.). (J). (gr. 2-6). 12.10 (*0-606-18797-9*) Turtleback Bks.

Alexander, Nina & Williams, Laura E. Rose's Magic Touch. Korman, Susan, ed. 1997. (Magic Attic Club Ser.). (Illus.). 80p. (J). (gr. 2-6). pap. 5.95 (*1-57513-105-6*, Magic Attic Pr.) Millbrook Pr., Inc.

Bernhard, Thomas. Old Masters: A Comedy. Osers, Ewald, tr. 1992. (Phoenix Fiction Ser.). iv, 160p. pap. 15.00 (*0-226-04391-6*) Univ. of Chicago Pr.

Biggins, John. The Emperor's Coloured Coat. 1995. 23.95 o.p. (*0-312-13485-1*) St. Martin's Pr.

—A Sailor of Austria. 1994. 384p. 22.95 o.p. (*0-312-10534-7*) St. Martin's Pr.

Brandstetter, Alois, et al. The Abbey: A Novel. Firchow, Peter E. & Firchow, Evelyn S., trs. from GER. 1998. (Studies in Austrian Literature, Culture & Thought). 232p. pap. 19.95 (*1-57241-045-0*) Ariadne Pr.

Breznik, Melitta. Night Duty. Theobold, Roslyn, tr. from GER. 1999. 131p. pap. 12.00 o.p. (*1-883642-85-X*) Steerforth Pr.

Burgess, Anthony. The End of the World News: An Entertainment. 1983. 388p. text 15.95 o.p. (*0-07-008965-5*) McGraw-Hill Cos., The.

—The End of the World News: An Entertainment. 1984. 400p. pap. 6.95 o.p. (*0-14-006746-9*, Penguin Bks.) Viking Penguin.

Canetti, Veza. The Tortoises. Mitchell, Ian, tr. from GER. 2001. 224p. 24.95 (*0-8112-1468-0*) New Directions Publishing Corp.

—Yellow Street. Mitchell, Ian, tr. from GER. 1991. 144p. 18.95 (*0-8112-1159-2*); pap. 10.95 (*0-8112-1160-6*, NDP709) New Directions Publishing Corp.

Carroll, Jonathan. Sleeping in Flame. 1990. 288p. pap. 13.00 (*0-679-72777-9*, Vintage) Knopf Publishing Group.

—Sleeping in Flames. 1989. 288p. 17.95 o.s.i (*0-385-24957-8*) Doubleday Publishing.

Carter, Peter. Children of the Book. 1987. 272p. (J). (gr. 3-6). 13.95 o.p. (*0-19-271456-2*) Oxford Univ. Pr., Inc.

Chotzinoff, Samuel. Eroica: A Novel Based on the Life of Ludwig Von Beethoven. reprint ed. 45.00 (*0-404-01529-8*) AMS Pr., Inc.

Disch, Irene & Enzenberger, Hans Magnus. Esterhazy: Rabbit Prince. 2000. (Illus.). 36p. (YA). (gr. 3 up). reprint ed. pap. 19.95 (*0-9702768-3-4*) Image Connection America, Inc.

Dukthas, Ann. Time of Murder at Mayerling. 1996. 224p. text 20.95 o.p. (*0-312-14676-0*, Saint Martin's Minotaur) St. Martin's Pr.

Ebner, Jeannie. The Bengal Tiger. Bangerter, Lowell A., tr. & afterword by by. 1992. (Studies in Austrian Literature, Culture & Thought). (GER.). 101p. pap. 12.50 (*0-929497-54-6*) Ariadne Pr.

—Three Flute Notes. Bangerter, Lowell A., tr. & afterword by by. 1993. (Studies in Austrian Literature, Culture & Thought). pap. 21.50 (*0-929497-62-7*) Ariadne Pr.

Fagan, Cary. Animals Waltz. 1996. 288p. 21.95 (*0-312-13921-7*) St. Martin's Pr.

Fell, Doris Elaine. Blue Mist on the Danube. 1999. (Sagas of a Kindred Heart Ser.). 448p. (gr. 13 up). pap. 11.99 o.p. (*0-8007-5677-0*) Revell, Fleming H. Co.

—The Twelfth Rose of Spring. 1995. (Seasons of Intrigue Ser.: Vol. 4). 352p. pap. 9.99 o.p. (*0-89107-861-4*) Crossway Bks.

—The Twelfth Rose of Spring. l.t. ed. 1998. (Christian Mystery Ser.). 544p. 23.95 (*0-7862-1488-0*) Thorndike Pr.

Findley, Timothy. Famous Last Words. 1983. mass mkt. 3.95 o.s.i (*0-440-32543-9*, Laurel); 1982. 13.95 o.s.i (*0-385-28271-0*, Delacorte Pr.) Dell Publishing.

—Famous Last Words. l.t. ed. 1988. (Mainstream Ser.). 576p. reprint ed. lib. bdg. 18.95 o.p. (*1-85089-229-6*) ISIS Large Print Bks. GBR. *Dist:* Transaction Pubs.

Frischmuth, Barbara. The Convent School. Chapple, Gerald & Lawson, James B., trs. from GER. 1993. (Studies in Austrian Literature, Culture & Thought).Tr. of Klosterschule. xii, 93p. 15.95 (*0-929497-75-9*) Ariadne Pr.

Gale, Adela. Angel among Witches. l.t. ed. 1994. 18.95 o.p. (*0-7927-2070-9*); pap. 17.95 o.p. (*0-7927-2069-5*) BBC Audiobooks America.

Goyer, Tricia. From Dust & Ashes: A Story of Liberation. 2003. 448p. pap. 12.99 (*0-8024-1554-7*) Moody Pr.

Gruber, Marianne. The Death of the Plover & Trace of the Buckskin: Two Stories. 1994. (Studies in Austrian Literature, Culture & Thought). 119p. pap. 12.95 (*0-929497-91-0*) Ariadne Pr.

Handke, Peter. On a Dark Night I Left My Silent House. Winston, Krishna, tr. from GER. 2000. Tr. of In Einer Nacht Ging Ich Aus Meinem Stillen Haus. 186p. 23.00 (*0-374-17547-0*) Farrar, Straus & Giroux.

Harris, Rosemary. Summers of the Wild Rose. 1988. 188p. (YA). 11.95 o.p. (*0-571-14702-X*) Faber & Faber, Inc.

Hartling, Peter. Schubert. Smith, Rosemary, tr. from GER. 1995. 260p. 27.95 (*0-8419-1347-1*) Holmes & Meier Pubs., Inc.

Heaven, Constance. Castle of Eagles. l.t. ed. 1993. 21.95 o.p. (*0-7927-1480-6*); pap. 19.95 o.p. (*0-7927-1479-2*) BBC Audiobooks America.

Ibbotson, Eva. Madensky Square. 1988. 256p. 16.95 o.p. (*0-312-02246-8*) St. Martin's Pr.

—The Morning Gift. 1993. 336p. 19.95 o.p. (*0-312-09338-1*) St. Martin's Pr.

—A Song for Summer. unabr. ed. 1998. audio 69.95 (*0-7540-0229-2*, CAB 1652) BBC Audiobooks America.

—A Song for Summer. 1999. mass mkt. (*0-312-96987-2*, St. Martin's Paperbacks); 1998. 288p. 22.95 (*0-312-18181-7*) St. Martin's Pr.

—A Song for Summer. l.t. ed. 1998. (Charnwood Large Print Ser.). 432p. 29.99 o.p. (*0-7089-9041-X*, Charnwood) Thorpe, F. A. Pubs. GBR. *Dist:* Ulverscroft Large Print Bks., Ltd., Ulverscroft Large Print Canada, Ltd.

Jones, J. Sydney. Time of the Wolf. 1990. mass mkt. 4.95 o.p. (*0-451-16734-1*, Signet Bks.) NAL.

Katkov, Norman. Judas Kiss. 1991. 432p. 21.95 o.p. (*0-525-93366-2*) Dutton/Plume.

Kerschbaumer, Marie-Therese & Bangerter, Lowell A. Woman's Face of Resistance. Bangerter, Lowell A., tr. from GER. 1996. (Studies in Austrian Literature, Culture & Thought). Orig. Title: Der Weibliche Name des Widerstands. 260p. pap. 19.95 (*1-57241-027-2*) Ariadne Pr.

Korber, Lili. Night over Vienna. Hertling, Viktoria & Stone, Kay M., trs. from GER. 1989. (Studies in Austrian Literature, Culture & Thought). 147p. pap. 14.95 (*0-929497-12-0*) Ariadne Pr.

Lauterstein, Ingeborg. Vienna Girl. 1986. 16.95 o.p. (*0-393-02264-1*) Norton, W. W. & Co., Inc.

Lippi, Rosina. Homestead: A Novel. 2000. 224p. 21.00 (*1-883285-14-3*) Delphinium Bks., Inc.

—Homestead: A Novel. 1999. 208p. pap. 12.00 (*0-395-97771-1*) Houghton Mifflin Co.

Martinusen, Cindy McCormick. Blue Night: A Novel. 2001. 416p. pap. 10.99 (*0-8423-5236-8*) Tyndale Hse. Pubs.

Maurensig, Paolo. Canone Inverso: A Novel. 1999. 208p. pap. 12.00 (*0-8050-6302-1*, Owl Bks.) Holt, Henry & Co.

—Canone Inverso: A Novel. McPhee, Jenny, tr. 1998. 160p. 21.00 o.s.i (*0-8050-5538-X*) Holt, Henry & Co.

Montano, Mary. Loving Mozart: A Past Life Memory of the Composer's Final Years. 1995. 239p. pap. 21.00 (*0-9642577-0-X*) Cantus Verus Bks.

Musil, Robert. The Man Without Qualities. 1965. pap. 12.00 o.p. (*0-399-50152-5*, Perigee Bks.) Berkley Publishing Group.

—The Man Without Qualities. Wilkins, Sophie & Pike, Burton, trs. 1996. (Man Without Qualities Ser.: Vol. 1). Vol. 1. 752p. pap. 20.00 (*0-679-76787-8*); Vol. 2. 1072p. pap. 24.00 (*0-679-76802-5*) Knopf Publishing Group. (Vintage).

Neider, Charles. Mozart & the Archbooby. 1991. (Contemporary American Fiction Ser.). 96p. (Orig.). pap. 8.95 o.p. (*0-14-015402-7*, Penguin Bks.) Penguin Group (USA) Inc.

Peretz, David. The Mosel Legacy. 2000. E-Book 16.95 incl. cd-rom (*1-58444-027-9*); 1999. 272p. pap. 15.95 (*1-58444-098-8*) Disc-Us Bks., Inc.

Phillips, Max. The Artist's Wife: A Novel. 2001. 272p. 23.00 o.s.i (*0-8050-6670-5*) Holt, Henry & Co.

—The Artist's Wife: A Novel. 2003. 256p. pap. 15.00 (*1-56649-273-4*) Welcome Rain Pubs.

Powers, Tim. The Drawing of the Dark. (Del Rey Impact Ser.). 1999. 336p. pap. 11.95 (*0-345-43081-6*); 1987. mass mkt. 3.99 o.s.i (*0-345-35008-1*, Del Rey) Ballantine Bks.

Reichart, Elisabeth. La Valse & Foreign. Demeritt, Linda C., tr. from GER. 2000. (SUNY Series, Women Writers in Translation). 147p. (C). text 17.50 (*0-7914-4773-1*); pap. text 16.95 (*0-7914-4774-X*) State Univ. of New York Pr.

Rosei, Peter. Try Your Luck. Thorpe, Kathleen E., tr. from GER. & afterword by by. 1994. (Studies in Austrian Literature, Culture & Thought).Tr. of Schnelle Gluck. pap. 10.50 (*0-929497-76-7*) Ariadne Pr.

Rosenfield, Israel. Freud's Megalomania: A Novel. 2000. 160p. 21.95 o.p. (*0-393-04898-5*) Norton, W. W. & Co., Inc.

Roth, Gerhard. The Calm Ocean. Schreckenberger, Helga & Vansant, Jacqueline, trs. 1993. (Studies in Austrian Literature, Culture & Thought). 238p. pap. 20.50 (*0-929497-64-3*) Ariadne Pr.

Roth, Joseph. The Tale of the 1002nd Night. 1999. 272p. pap. 14.00 (*0-312-24494-0*) Picador.

—The Tale of the 1002nd Night: A Novel. Hofmann, Michael, tr. 1998. 272p. 23.95 o.p. (*0-312-19341-6*) Picador.

—The Tale of the 1002nd Night: A Novel. Hofmann, Michael, tr. 1999. E-Book 23.95 (*0-312-24618-8*) St. Martin's Pr.

Roth, Joseph & Hofmann, Michael. The String of Pearls. 1999. 272p. (*1-86207-254-X*) Granta Bks.

Schnitzler, Arthur. The Road into the Open. Byers, Roger, tr. 1992. 314p. (C). pap. 18.95 (*0-520-07774-1*); text 55.00 (*0-520-07575-7*) Univ. of California Pr.

—The Road to the Open. Samuel, Horace, tr. from GER. 1991. 416p. reprint ed. 35.00 o.p. (*0-8101-0921-2*) Northwestern Univ. Pr.

—Vienna, 1900: Games with Love & Death. 1974. 365p. pap. 3.95 o.p. (*0-14-003759-4*, Penguin Bks.) Viking Penguin.

—Viennese Idylls. Eisemann, Frederick, tr. 1977. (Short Story Index Reprint Ser.). reprint ed. 19.95 (*0-8369-4226-4*) Ayer Co. Pubs., Inc.

Schonberg, Leonard. Legacy: A Novel of Three Generations. 2002. 336p. pap. 22.95 (*0-86534-357-8*) Sunstone Pr.

Scott, Joanna. Arrogance. 1991. 288p. pap. 13.00 (*0-393-30792-1*) Norton, W. W. & Co., Inc.

—Arrogance. 1990. 288p. bds. 18.95 o.p. (*0-671-69547-9*, Simon & Schuster) Simon & Schuster.

Sebestyen, Gyorgy. Works of Solitude. Mitchell, Michael, tr. & comment by. 1991. (Studies in Austrian Literature, Culture & Thought). 28.50 (*0-929497-21-X*); pap. 22.50 (*0-929497-26-0*) Ariadne Pr.

Seth, Vikram. An Equal Music. abr. ed. 1999. audio 25.00 o.s.i (*0-553-52636-7*, RH Audio) Random Hse. Audio Publishing Group.

—An Equal Music. unabr. ed. 2000. audio 102.00 (*0-7887-4493-3*, H1080E7, Clipper Audio) Recorded Bks., LLC.

—An Equal Music: A Novel. 2000. (International Ser.). 400p. pap. 14.00 (*0-375-70924-X*, Vintage) Knopf Publishing Group.

Shields, Jody. The Fig Eater: A Novel. l.t. ed. 2000. (Wheeler Hardcover Ser.). (Illus.). 432p. 25.95 (*1-56895-961-3*, Wheeler Publishing, Inc.) Gale Group.

—The Fig Eater: A Novel. 2001. 320p. E-Book 9.95 (*0-7595-9238-1*); 2001. 320p. E-Book 9.95 (*0-7595-4212-0*); 2001. 320p. E-Book 9.95 (*0-7595-0209-9*); 2001. 320p. E-Book 9.95 (*0-7595-6209-1*); 2001. (Illus.). 368p. pap. 13.95 (*0-316-78526-1*, Back Bay); 2000. 240p. 23.95 o.p. (*0-316-78564-4*) Little Brown & Co.

—The Fig Eater: A Novel. 2001. 320p. E-Book 9.95 (*0-7595-8215-7*) Mysterious Pr.

Singerman, Philip. Proof Positive. 2001. 352p. 24.95 (*0-312-87686-6*, Forge Bks.) Doherty, Tom Assocs., LLC.

Sorell, Walter. Choreography of the Heart: Stories about Love & Fulfillment. 1997. (Studies in Austrian Literature, Culture & Thought). 224p. (Orig.). pap. 21.50 (*1-57241-049-3*) Ariadne Pr.

Szyszkowitz, Gerald. On the Other Side. Hanlin, Todd C., tr. 1991. (Studies in Austrian Literature, Culture & Thought). 156p. pap. 12.50 (*0-929497-42-2*) Ariadne Pr.

—Puntigam or the Art of Forgetting. Del Caro, Adrian, tr. 1990. (Studies in Austrian Literature, Culture & Thought). 280p. 24.50 (*0-929497-20-1*); pap. 18.50 (*0-929497-24-4*) Ariadne Pr.

Thoene, Bodie. Vienna Prelude. (Zion Covenant Ser.: No. 1). 2000. 464p. pap. 7.99 (*0-7642-2427-1*); 1989. 416p. pap. 12.99 (*1-55661-066-1*) Bethany Hse. Pubs.

Vogel, Alois. Refractions. Kreeger, Walter L., tr. 1995. (Studies in Austrian Literature, Culture & Thought). 235p. pap. 21.95 (*0-929497-97-X*) Ariadne Pr.

Von Ebner-Eschenbach, Marie. Beyond Atonement. Van Ornam, Vanessa, tr. & intro. by. 1997. (GERM Ser.). 152p. 60.00 (*1-57113-113-2*) Camden Hse.

West, Paul. The Dry Danube: A Hitler Forgery. 2000. 152p. 21.95 (*0-8112-1432-X*) New Directions Publishing Corp.

Winkler, Josef. The Serf. Mitchell, Michael, tr. from GER. & afterword by by. 1997. (Studies in Austrian Literature, Culture & Thought). 306p. pap. 22.50 (*1-57241-024-8*) Ariadne Pr.

Wray, John. The Right Hand of Sleep: A Novel. 2002. 336p. pap. 14.00 (*0-375-70640-2*) Knopf, Alfred A. Inc.

Yorke, Margaret. Silent Witness. l.t. unabr. ed. 1999. 208p. 32.50 o.p. (*0-7531-6028-5*, 160285) ISIS Large Print Bks. GBR. *Dist:* Ulverscroft Large Print Bks., Ltd., Ulverscroft Large Print Canada, Ltd.

—Silent Witness. l.t. ed. 1976. o.p. (*0-85456-455-1*, Ulverscroft) Thorpe, F. A. Pubs.

—Silent Witness. 1975. 5.95 (*0-8027-5318-3*) Walker & Co.

### AVERIDAN (IMAGINARY PLACE)—FICTION

Clough, Brenda W. The Crystal Crown. 1984. 208p. mass mkt. 3.50 o.p. (*0-87997-922-4*);Bk. 1. mass mkt. 3.50 o.p. (*0-88677-283-4*) DAW Bks., Inc.

—The Dragon of Mishbil. 1985. mass mkt. 2.95 o.p. (*0-88677-078-5*) DAW Bks., Inc.

—The Name of the Sun, Bk. 3. 1988. mass mkt. 3.95 o.p. (*0-88677-282-6*) DAW Bks., Inc.

—The Realm Beneath. 1986. mass mkt. 2.95 o.p. (*0-88677-137-4*) DAW Bks., Inc.

## B

### BADGER'S END (ENGLAND: IMAGINARY PLACE)—FICTION

Kingsbury, Kate. Check-Out Time. 1995. 224p. (Orig.). mass mkt. 5.50 o.s.i (*0-425-14640-5*, Prime Crime) Berkley Publishing Group.

—Chivalry Is Dead. 1996. mass mkt. 5.50 o.s.i (*0-425-15515-3*) Berkley Publishing Group.

—Death with Reservations: A Pennyfoot Hotel Mystery. 1998. (Pennyfoot Hotel Mystery Ser.). 224p. mass mkt. 5.99 o.s.i (*0-425-16144-7*, Prime Crime) Berkley Publishing Group.

—Do Not Disturb. 1994. (Orig.). mass mkt. 4.99 o.s.i (*0-425-14914-5*); 208p. mass mkt. 4.50 o.s.i (*0-515-11282-8*) Berkley Publishing Group. (Jove).

—Dying Room Only. 1998. (Pennyfoot Hotel Mystery Ser.). 224p. mass mkt. 5.99 o.s.i (*0-425-16568-X*, Prime Crime) Berkley Publishing Group.

—Eat, Drink, & Be Buried. 1994. 208p. mass mkt. 4.50 o.p. (*0-425-14352-X*, Prime Crime) Berkley Publishing Group.

—Grounds for Murder. 1995. (Pennyfoot Hotel Mystery Ser.). 240p. (Orig.). mass mkt. 5.50 o.s.i (*0-425-14901-3*) Berkley Publishing Group.

—Maid to Murder, 1 vol. 1999. (Pennyfoot Hotel Mystery Ser.: Vol.12). 224p. mass mkt. 5.99 o.s.i (*0-425-16967-7*) Berkley Publishing Group.

—Pay the Piper. 1996. 224p. (Orig.). mass mkt. 5.50 o.s.i (*0-425-15231-6*) Berkley Publishing Group.

—Ring for Tomb Service: In Edwardian England Murder Rings a Bell. 1997. 240p. mass mkt. 5.99 o.s.i (*0-425-15857-8*, Prime Crime) Berkley Publishing Group.

—Room with a Clue. 1993. 208p. (Orig.). mass mkt. 3.99 o.s.i (*0-515-11188-0*, Jove) Berkley Publishing Group.

—A Room with a Clue. 1993. 208p. (Orig.). mass mkt. 5.50 o.s.i (*0-425-14326-0*) Berkley Publishing Group.

—Service for Two. 1994. 208p. (Orig.). mass mkt. 4.99 o.s.i (*0-425-14223-X*, Prime Crime) Berkley Publishing Group.

### BAHAMAS—FICTION

Antoni, Brian. Paradise Overdose. 1997. 256p. reprint ed. pap. 12.00 (*0-8021-3487-4*, Grove Pr.) Grove/Atlantic, Inc.

—Paradise Overdose. 1994. 320p. 21.00 (*0-671-88426-3*, Simon & Schuster) Simon & Schuster.

Berry, Carole. Island Girl. 1991. 256p. 18.95 o.p. (*0-312-06381-4*, Saint Martin's Minotaur) St. Martin's Pr.

Bland, Eleanor Taylor. Whispers in the Dark. l.t. ed. 2002. 28.95 o.p. (*1-58724-187-0*, Wheeler Publishing, Inc.) Gale Group.

—Whispers in the Dark. mass mkt. (*0-312-97990-8*, St. Martin's Paperbacks); 2001. 244p. 23.95 (*0-312-20379-9*, Saint Martin's Minotaur) St. Martin's Pr.

Butler, Tajuana. The Night Before Thirty: A Novel. 2003. 240p. 19.95 (*1-4000-6020-6*, Villard Bks.) Random House Adult Trade Publishing Group.

Collins, Max Allan. Carnal Hours. abr. ed. 1999. audio 16.95 (*1-882071-71-9*) B&B Audio, Inc.

—Carnal Hours. 1994. (Nathan Heller Ser.). 336p. 20.95 o.p. (*0-525-93758-7*) Dutton/Plume.

—Carnal Hours. 1995. (Nathan Heller Ser.). 400p. mass mkt. 5.99 o.s.i (*0-451-17975-7*, Signet Bks.) NAL.

Ducker, Bruce. Mooney in Flight. 2003. 22.00 (*1-931561-52-4*) MacAdam/Cage Publishing, Inc.

Gandolfi, Simon. White Sands. 1997. 272p. 23.00 o.p. (*0-06-018720-4*) HarperCollins Pubs.

—White Sands. mass mkt. o.s.i (*0-06-109576-1*, HarperTorch) Morrow/Avon.

Giusto, Layle. Wind Across Kylarni. 1993. 416p. pap. 5.95 (*0-9633851-2-7*) Iami Bks.

Hall, Russ. Wildcat Did Growl: Adventure in the Bahamas. 2000. 216p. pap. 14.95 (*0-9666173-3-9*) Tropical Pr., Inc.

Hemingway, Ernest. Islands in the Stream. 1984. mass mkt. 4.50 o.s.i (*0-553-25007-8*) Bantam Bks.

—Islands in the Stream. unabr. collector's ed. 1992. audio 72.00 (*0-7366-2179-2*, 2976) Books on Tape, Inc.

—Islands in the Stream. (Hudson River Editions Ser.). 466p. 1980. 50.00 (*0-684-16499-X*); 1976. pap. 16.00 (*0-684-14642-8*) Gale Group. (Macmillan Reference USA).

—Islands in the Stream. 2003. E-Book 9.99 (*0-7432-3726-9*); 2003. 448p. 27.50 (*0-7432-5342-6*); 1997. 448p. pap. 14.00 (*0-684-83787-0*) Simon & Schuster. (Scribner).

Kincheloe, Steve. The Song & the Stream. 2000. 272p. 24.00 (*1-883911-38-9*) Brandylane Pubs., Inc.

Mansell, Patrick J. Abaco Gold: A Bimini Twist Adventure. 2002. 168p. 21.79 (*0-7596-1730-9*); pap. 13.98 (*0-7596-1729-5*) 1stBooks Library.

—Abaco Gold: A Bimini Twist Adventure. 312p. 2001. 23.50 (*0-9676853-5-4*); 2000. per. 11.50 (*0-9676853-7-0*) Bimini Twist Adventures, Inc.

—Bimini Twist. 234p. 2002. 24.91 (*0-7596-1191-2*); 2001. pap. 17.10 (*0-7596-1190-4*) 1stBooks Library.

—Bimini Twist. 1999. 288p. per. 11.00 (*0-9676853-6-2*); 22.50 (*0-9676853-4-6*) Bimini Twist Adventures, Inc.

—Exuma Tide: A Bimini Twist Adventure. Mansell, Lisa, ed. 2002. 232p. 23.50 (*0-9676853-1-1*); per. 11.00 (*0-9676853-9-7*) Bimini Twist Adventures, Inc.

Poyer, David. Bahamas Blue: A Tiller Galloway Thriller. 1992. mass mkt. 5.99 (*0-312-92846-7*, St. Martin's Paperbacks); 1991. 17.95 o.p. (*0-312-04858-0*) St. Martin's Pr.

Pozzessere, Heather G. A Matter of Circumstance. 2000. mass mkt. (*1-55166-642-1*, Harlequin Bks.); 1994. mass mkt. (*0-373-48281-7*, 5-48281-5, Silhouette); 1994. 256p. per. (*1-55166-005-9*, 1-66005-9, Mira Bks.); 1986. pap. (*0-373-07174-4*, Harlequin Bks.) Harlequin Enterprises, Ltd.

Pozzessere, Heather Graham. A Matter of Circumstance. l.t. ed. 2001. (Thorndike Press Large Print Romance Ser.). 339p. 28.95 (*0-7862-2623-4*) Thorndike Pr.

Robinson, Gregor. Hotel Paradiso. 2001. (Illus.). 207p. pap. (*1-55192-358-0*) Raincoast Bk. Distribution.

Ruzic, Neil. The Shallow Sea. 1995. 544p. 19.95 (*0-9632357-0-2*) St. Clair Pr.

Simpson, Thomas W. The Fingerprints of Armless Mike. 1996. 390p. 19.95 o.p. (*0-446-51809-3*) Warner Bks., Inc.

White, Randy Wayne. Shark River. l.t. ed. 2002. 332p. lib. bdg. 28.95 (*1-58547-160-7*) Ctr. Point Large Print.

—Shark River. 2001. 320p. 24.95 o.p. (*0-399-14729-2*, Putnam & Grosset) Penguin Group (USA) Inc.

### BAKERHAVEN (CONN.: IMAGINARY PLACE)—FICTION

Hall, Parnell. A Clue for the Puzzle Lady. 2000. 336p. mass mkt. 6.50 (*0-553-58140-6*); 1999. 304p. 23.95 o.s.i (*0-553-80096-5*) Bantam Bks.

—A Clue for the Puzzle Lady. l.t. ed. 2000. (Thorndike Senior Lifestyle Ser.). 456p. 28.95 o.p. (*0-7862-2542-4*) Thorndike Pr.

—The Last Puzzle & Testament. 2001. (Illus.). 400p. mass mkt. 6.50 (*0-553-58143-0*, Spectra) Bantam Bks.

—Last Puzzle & Testament. l.t. ed. 2001. (Senior Lifestyles Ser.). 511p. 28.95 (*0-7862-2944-6*) Thorndike Pr.

### BALACLAVA JUNCTION (MASS.: IMAGINARY PLACE)—FICTION

MacLeod, Charlotte. The Corpse in Oozak's Pond. 1987. 224p. 15.45 o.p. (*0-89296-188-0*) Mysterious Pr.

—The Corpse in Oozak's Pond. 1989. 2.99 o.p. (*0-517-00184-5*) Random Hse. Value Publishing.

—The Corpse in Oozak's Pond. 1988. 203p. mass mkt. 5.99 o.p. (*0-445-40683-6*, Mysterious Pr. Paperback Bks.) Warner Bks., Inc.

—Curse of the Giant Hogweed. 1986. (Peter Shandy Ser.). 176p. pap. 3.50 (*0-380-70051-4*, Avon Bks.) Morrow/Avon.

—Exit the Milkman. l.t. ed. 1996. 22.95 o.p. (*1-56895-388-7*, Wheeler Publishing, Inc.) Gale Group.

—Exit the Milkman. 1996. 364p. 21.95 o.s.i (*0-89296-572-X*) Mysterious Pr.

—Exit the Milkman. 1997. 256p. mass mkt. 5.99 o.p. (*0-446-40398-9*) Warner Bks., Inc.

—Exit the Milkman. 2003. 320p. pap. 6.99 (*0-7434-4537-6*) ibooks, Inc.

—The Luck Runs Out. 1981. 192p. pap. 3.50 (*0-380-54171-8*, Avon Bks.) Morrow/Avon.

—An Owl Too Many. l.t. ed. 1991. (General Ser.). 355p. lib. bdg. 20.95 (*0-8161-5235-7*, Macmillan Reference USA) Gale Group.

—An Owl Too Many. 1991. 17.95 o.p. (*0-89296-431-6*) Mysterious Pr.

—An Owl Too Many. 1992. 240p. mass mkt. 4.99 o.p. (*0-446-40101-3*, Mysterious Pr. Paperback Bks.) Warner Bks., Inc.

—Rest You Merry. 1979. (General Ser.). lib. bdg. 13.50 o.p. (*0-8161-3000-0*, Macmillan Reference USA) Gale Group.

—Rest You Merry. 1980. 224p. reprint ed. mass mkt. 4.99 o.p. (*0-380-47530-8*, Avon Bks.) Morrow/Avon.

—Something in the Water. 1994. 272p. 18.95 o.s.i (*0-89296-430-8*) Mysterious Pr.

—Something in the Water. 1995. 240p. mass mkt. 5.50 o.p. (*0-446-40446-2*, Mysterious Pr. Paperback Bks.) Warner Bks., Inc.

—Something the Cat Dragged In. l.t. ed. 1984. (Nightingale Ser.). 10.95 o.p. (*0-8161-3710-2*, Macmillan Reference USA) Gale Group.

—Something the Cat Dragged In. 1984. 208p. mass mkt. 3.99 (*0-380-69096-9*, Avon Bks.) Morrow/Avon.

—Vane Pursuit: A Peter Shandy Mystery. l.t. ed. 1990. 368p. lib. bdg. 19.95 o.p. (*0-8161-4850-3*, Macmillan Reference USA) Gale Group.

—Vane Pursuit: A Peter Shandy Mystery. 1989. 15.95 o.p. (*0-89296-369-7*) Mysterious Pr.

—Vane Pursuit: A Peter Shandy Mystery. 1990. 224p. mass mkt. 5.50 o.p. (*0-445-40780-8*, Mysterious Pr. Paperback Bks.) Warner Bks., Inc.

—Wrack & Rune. 1983. 208p. mass mkt. 3.99 (*0-380-61911-3*, Avon Bks.) Morrow/Avon.

—Wrack & Rune. l.t. ed. 1982. 322p. reprint ed. 11.95 o.p. (*0-89621-372-2*) Thorndike Pr.

### BALKAN PENINSULA—FICTION

Ambler, Eric. Background to Danger. 1990. 280p. mass mkt. 3.95 o.p. (*0-88184-611-2*, Carroll & Graf Pubs.) Avalon Publishing Group.

—Background to Danger. 1978. mass mkt. 1.75 o.s.i (*0-345-25908-4*) Ballantine Bks.

—Background to Danger. 1984. 256p. mass mkt. 2.95 o.p. (*0-425-06420-4*) Berkley Publishing Group.

—Background to Danger. 2001. 288p. pap. 12.00 (*0-375-72673-X*, Vintage) Knopf Publishing Group.

Ignatieff, Michael. Charlie Johnson in the Flames. 2003. 224p. 24.00 (*0-8021-1755-4*, Grove Pr.) Grove/Atlantic, Inc.

Kadare, Ismail. The File on H. A Novel. 2002. 192p. pap. 12.95 (*1-55970-627-9*) Arcade Publishing, Inc.

—The Palace of Dreams. Vrioni, Jusuf & Bray, Barbara, trs. 1998. 208p. pap. 12.95 (*1-55970-416-0*) Arcade Publishing, Inc.

—The Palace of Dreams: A Novel. 1993. 205p. 19.00 o.p. (*0-688-11183-1*, Morrow, William & Co.) Morrow/Avon.

### BALTIMORE (MD.)—FICTION

Alvarez, Rafael. The Fountain of Highlandtown: Stories. 1997. 192p. pap. 14.95 o.p. (*0-9656342-8-0*) Woodholme Hse. Pubs.

Auster, Paul. Timbuktu. 1999. 192p. 22.00 o.s.i (*0-8050-5407-3*) Holt, Henry & Co.
—Timbuktu. 2000. 192p. pap. 11.00 (*0-312-26399-6*); mass mkt. 7.99 o.s.i (*0-312-97528-7*) Picador.
Bell, Madison Smartt. Ten Indians. 1996. 264p. 23.00 o.s.i (*0-679-44246-4*) McKay, David Co., Inc.
—Ten Indians. 1997. 272p. pap. 12.95 o.s.i (*0-14-026846-4*) Penguin Group (USA) Inc.
Boland, John. Rich Man's Blood. 1993. 240p. 17.95 o.p. (*0-312-09371-3*, Saint Martin's Minotaur) St. Martin's Pr.
Brown, Parry. Sittin' in the Front Pew: A Novel. 2002. 256p. pap. 13.95 (*0-375-75705-8*, Villard Bks.) Random House Adult Trade Publishing Group.
Cockey, Tim. Backstabber. 2004. 368p. 23.95 (*0-7868-6713-2*) Hyperion Pr.
—The Hearse Case Scenario. 2003. 448p. mass mkt. 7.99 (*0-7868-8995-0*); 2002. (Illus.). 338p. 23.95 (*0-7868-6711-6*) Hyperion Pr.
—Hearse of a Different Color. 2003. (*1-57490-536-8*, Beeler Large Print Bks.) Beeler, Thomas T. Publisher.
—Hearse of a Different Color. 2002. E-Book 5.95 (*0-7868-6955-0*); 2001. 318p. 23.95 (*0-7868-6571-7*); 2003. 416p. reprint ed. mass mkt. 7.99 (*0-7868-8963-2*) Hyperion Pr.
—The Hearse You Came in On. l.t. ed. 28.95 (*1-58724-216-8*, Wheeler Publishing, Inc.) Gale Group.
—The Hearse You Came in On. 2002. E-Book 5.95 (*0-7868-6961-5*); 2000. viii, 308p. 22.95 (*0-7868-6570-9*); 2003. 416p. reprint ed. mass mkt. 6.99 (*0-7868-8962-4*) Hyperion Pr.
—Murder in the Hearse Degree. 2003. 440p. 30.95 (*1-58724-428-4*) Gale Group.
—Murder in the Hearse Degree. 2004. mass mkt. 6.99 (*0-7868-8997-7*); 2003. 336p. 22.95 (*0-7868-6712-4*) Hyperion Pr.
Coulter, Catherine. The Valentine Legacy. 1996. 432p. mass mkt. 7.99 (*0-515-11836-2*, Jove) Berkley Publishing Group.
—The Valentine Legacy. unabr. ed. 1995. (Legacy Ser.). 12p. audio 73.25 (*1-56100-284-4*, 1114, Unabridged Library Editions); audio 23.95 o.p. (*1-56100-659-9*, 305, Bookcassette) Brilliance Audio.
—The Valentine Legacy. l.t. ed. 1995. 573p. 25.95 o.p. (*0-7838-1497-6*, Macmillan Reference USA) Gale Group.
—The Valentine Legacy. 1995. 400p. 19.95 o.p. (*0-399-14094-8*, G. P. Putnam's Sons) Penguin Group (USA) Inc.
Criswell, Millie. The Trouble with Mary. l.t. ed. 2001. 325p. 26.95 (*1-57490-342-X*) Beeler, Thomas T. Publisher.
—What to Do about Annie. 2001. 336p. mass mkt. 6.99 (*0-8041-1951-1*) Ballantine Bks.
Crone, Moira. A Period of Confinement. 1987. 304p. reprint ed. pap. 6.95 o.p. (*0-06-097108-8*, PL 7108, Perennial) HarperTrade.
—A Period of Confinement. 1986. 336p. 19.95 o.p. (*0-399-13136-1*, G. P. Putnam's Sons) Penguin Putnam Bks. for Young Readers.
Crow, Michael. The Bite: A Luther Ewing Thriller. 2003. 304p. text 24.95 (*0-670-03222-0*, Viking) Viking Penguin.
—Red Rain. 2003. 304p. reprint ed. mass mkt. 6.99 (*0-451-41086-6*, Onyx) NAL.
—Red Rain. 2002. 368p. 25.95 o.s.i (*0-670-03090-2*, Viking) Viking Penguin.
Dawson, David L. Double Blind. 1991. 240p. 17.95 o.p. (*0-312-07085-3*, Saint Martin's Minotaur) St. Martin's Pr.
DeFord, Frank. An American Summer: A Novel. 2002. 256p. 24.00 (*1-57071-992-6*, Sourcebooks Landmark) Sourcebooks, Inc.
Fuqua, Jonathon Scott. The Re-Appearance of Sam Webber. 1999. 240p. 23.95 (*1-890862-02-9*) Bancroft Pr.
Grimes, Martha. The Horse You Came in On. 1994. 384p. mass mkt. 7.99 (*0-345-38755-4*) Ballantine Bks.
—The Horse You Came in On. l.t. ed. 1993. 19.00 o.s.i (*0-679-74770-2*) Random Hse. Large Print.
—The Horse You Came in On. unabr. ed. 1994. audio 70.00 (*0-7887-0003-0*, 94142E7) Recorded Bks., LLC.
—The Horse You Came in On. abr. ed. 1993. (Inspector Richard Jury Ser.). audio 17.00 (*0-671-87223-0*, 390934, Simon & Schuster Audioworks) Simon & Schuster Audio.
Jaffe, John. Thief of Words. 2005. mass mkt. (*0-446-61391-6*); 2003. 256p. 19.95 (*0-446-53080-8*) Warner Bks., Inc.
Jones, Patricia. Red on a Rose: A Novel. 2001. 352p. (Orig.). pap. 14.00 (*0-380-81730-6*, Avon Bks.) Morrow/Avon.
Keech, Thomas. The Crawlspace Conspiracy. 1995. 328p. 22.00 (*1-880909-34-0*) Baskerville Pubs., Inc.
Kotlowitz, Robert. His Master's Voice. 1992. 21.00 o.s.i (*0-679-40868-1*) Knopf, Alfred A. Inc.
Lancelotta, Victoria. Far: A Novel. 2003. 224p. text 24.00 (*1-58243-114-0*, Counterpoint Pr.) Basic Bks.
Levinson, Barry. Sixty-Six. 2003. 288p. 24.00 (*0-7679-1533-X*) Broadway Bks.
Lippman, Laura. Baltimore Blues. 1997. 304p. mass mkt. 6.99 (*0-380-78875-6*, Avon Bks.) Morrow/Avon.
—Butcher's Hill. 1998. (Tess Monaghan Mysteries Ser.: Vol. 3). 288p. mass mkt. 5.99 (*0-380-79846-8*, Avon Bks.) Morrow/Avon.
—Charm City. l.t. ed. 2002. (Wheeler Large Print Book Ser.). 27.95 (*1-58724-214-1*, Wheeler Publishing, Inc.) Gale Group.
—Charm City. 1997. (Tess Monaghan Mysteries Ser.: Vol. 2). 304p. mass mkt. 6.99 (*0-380-78876-4*, Avon Bks.) Morrow/Avon.
—Every Secret Thing: 10c Signed Carton. 2003. 249.50 (*0-06-057536-0*, Morrow, William & Co.) Morrow/Avon.
—In a Strange City. 16th l.t. ed. 2002. 368p. lib. bdg. 27.95 (*1-58547-171-2*) Ctr. Point Large Print.
—In a Strange City. 2002. 400p. mass mkt. 6.99 (*0-380-81023-9*); 2001. 320p. 24.00 (*0-380-97818-0*, Morrow, William & Co.) Morrow/Avon.
—In Big Trouble. 1999. (Tess Monaghan Mysteries Ser.). 352p. mass mkt. 6.99 (*0-380-79847-6*, Avon Bks.) Morrow/Avon.
—The Last Place. 2003. 432p. mass mkt. 7.50 (*0-380-81024-7*, Avon Bks.); 2002. 352p. 23.95 (*0-380-97819-9*, Morrow, William & Co.) Morrow/Avon.
—The Sugar House. 2000. (Tess Monaghan Mysteries Ser.). 320p. 24.00 (*0-380-97817-2*, Morrow, William & Co.) Morrow/Avon.
—The Sugar House: A Tess Monaghan Mystery. 2001. 384p. mass mkt. 6.99 (*0-380-81022-0*, Avon Bks.) Morrow/Avon.
—The Sugar House: A Tess Monaghan Mystery. l.t. ed. 2001. (Thorndike Americana Ser.). 483p. 28.95 (*0-7862-3288-9*) Thorndike Pr.
Miller, Dinah. Monday at the Charm. 2001. 214p. pap. 19.95 (*1-58851-558-3*) PublishAmerica, Inc.
Neihart, Ben. Burning Girl. 2000. 256p. pap. 13.00 (*0-688-17689-5*); 1999. 245p. 24.00 (*0-688-15691-6*) Morrow/Avon. (Morrow, William & Co.).
Oke, Janette & Bunn, T. Davis. Another Homecoming. 1997. 256p. pap. 11.99 (*1-55661-934-0*); 256p. text 15.99 o.p. (*1-55661-978-2*); 1p. audio 15.99 o.p. (*1-55661-980-4*); 384p. pap. 14.99 o.p. (*1-55661-979-0*) Bethany Hse. Pubs.
—Another Homecoming. l.t. ed. 1997. 25.95 (*0-7838-8332-3*, Macmillan Reference USA) Gale Group.
Pairo, Preston. Breach of Trust. 1995. 342p. 22.95 o.p. (*0-312-13034-1*, Saint Martin's Minotaur) St. Martin's Pr.
—Bright Eyes. 1996. 320p. mass mkt. 5.99 o.s.i (*0-451-40706-7*, Onyx) NAL.
Price, Hugh B. & Walker, Blair S. Up Jumped the Devil. 1997. 292p. 22.00 o.s.i (*0-380-97420-7*, Avon Bks.) Morrow/Avon.
Putney, Mary Jo. The Burning Point. Date not set. (*0-449-00035-4*, Fawcett) Ballantine Bks.
—The Burning Point. 2000. 352p. mass mkt. 6.99 o.s.i (*0-425-17428-X*) Berkley Publishing Group.
—The Burning Point. l.t. ed. 2000. (Wheeler Large Print Book Ser.). 442p. 26.95 (*1-56895-997-4*, Wheeler Publishing, Inc.) Gale Group.
Roberts, Nora. Inner Harbor. 1999. (Chesapeake Bay Ser.: Bk. 3). 352p. mass mkt. 7.99 (*0-515-12421-4*, Jove) Berkley Publishing Group.
—Inner Harbor. abr. ed. (Chesapeake Bay Ser.: Bk. 3). 1999. audio 7.99 o.s.i (*1-56740-323-9*, 1883, Paperback Nova Audio Bks.); 1998. audio 17.95 o.p. (*1-56740-758-7*, 1276, Nova Audio Bks.); 1998. audio 24.95 (*1-56100-780-3*, 1275, Bookcassette); 1998. 9p. audio 57.25 (*1-56740-559-2*, 1277, Unabridged Library Editions) Brilliance Audio.
—Inner Harbor. abr. ed. 1999. (Chesapeake Bay Ser.: Bk. 3). audio 17.95. audio 73.25 Highsmith Inc.
—Inner Harbor. l.t. ed. 1999. (Chesapeake Bay Ser.: Bk. 3). 488p. 29.95 (*0-7862-1442-2*) Thorndike Pr.
Schechter, Harold. Nevermore. 2000. 480p. reprint ed. pap. 6.99 (*0-671-79856-1*, Pocket) Simon & Schuster.
—Nevermore. l.t. ed. 1999. (Basic Ser.). 599p. 28.95 (*0-7862-1939-4*) Thorndike Pr.
—Nevermore: A Novel. 1999. 352p. 23.00 (*0-671-79855-3*, Atria) Simon & Schuster.
Tanner, Ron. A Bed of Nails: Stories. 2003. (*1-886157-42-1*) BkMk Pr. of the Univ. of Missouri-Kansas City.
Taube, Herman. My Baltimore Landsmen: A Documentary Novel. 1995. (Orig.). pap. 12.95 o.p. (*0-931848-90-3*) Dryad Pr.
Thoene, Jake. Hands of Deliverance. 2000. (Portraits of Destiny Ser.: Vol. 3). 320p. pap. 12.99 (*0-7852-7147-3*) Nelson, Thomas Pubs.
Thoene, Jake & Thoene, Luke, contrib. by. Hands of Deliverance: A Novel. 2003. pap. 9.99 (*0-7852-6385-3*) Nelson, Thomas Inc.
Tucker, Augusta. Miss Susie Slagle's. 1968. (Maryland Paperback Bookshelf Ser.). 352p. reprint ed. pap. 17.95 (*0-8018-3419-8*) Johns Hopkins Univ. Pr.
Tyler, Anne. The Amateur Marriage. 2004. 320p. 24.95 (*1-4000-4207-0*) Knopf Publishing Group.
—The Amateur Marriage. l.t. ed. 2004. 512p. 26.95 (*0-375-43336-8*) Random Hse. Large Print.
—Back When We Were Grownups. 2001. 288p. 25.00 (*0-375-41253-0*) Knopf, Alfred A. Inc.
—Back When We Were Grownups. l.t. ed. 2001. 416p. 25.00 (*0-375-43118-7*) Random Hse. Large Print.
—Celestial Navigation. l.t. ed. 1994. 366p. 24.95 o.p. (*0-7927-1977-8*); pap. 22.95 o.p. (*0-7927-1976-X*) BBC Audiobooks America.
—Celestial Navigation. 1996. 288p. pap. 13.95 (*0-449-91180-2*, Fawcett); 1992. 256p. mass mkt. 5.99 o.s.i (*0-8041-0888-9*, Ivy Bks.) Ballantine Bks.
—Celestial Navigation. mass mkt. 3.95 o.s.i (*0-425-08638-0*); 1986. 256p. mass mkt. 5.95 o.p. (*0-425-09840-0*); 1985. mass mkt. 3.95 o.s.i (*0-425-09142-2*); 1984. mass mkt. 3.50 o.s.i (*0-425-07013-1*) Berkley Publishing Group.
—Celestial Navigation. 1974. 7.95 o.p. (*0-394-49038-X*, Knopf Bks. for Young Readers) Random Hse. Children's Bks.
—Celestial Navigation. 1983. 256p. pap. 3.50 o.p. (*0-446-31169-3*) Warner Bks., Inc.
—A Patchwork Planet. 1999. 304p. pap. 13.95 (*0-449-00398-1*, Fawcett) Ballantine Bks.
—A Patchwork Planet. unabr. ed. 1998. audio 64.00 (*0-7366-4250-1*, 4749) Books on Tape, Inc.
—A Patchwork Planet. abr. ed. 1998. audio 24.00 (*0-375-40308-6*, 595762, RH Audio) Random Hse. Audio Publishing Group.
—A Patchwork Planet. aut. ed. 1998. 24.00 o.p. (*0-676-54925-X*) Random Hse., Inc.
—A Patchwork Planet. unabr. ed. 1999. audio 60.00 (*0-7887-2020-1*, 95397E7) Recorded Bks., LLC.
—A Patchwork Planet. l.t. ed. 1999. (Charnwood Large Print Ser.). 352p. 31.99 o.p. (*0-7089-9085-1*, Ulverscroft) Thorpe, F. A. Pubs. GBR. *Dist:* Ulverscroft Large Print Bks., Ltd., Ulverscroft Large Print Canada, Ltd.
—A Patchwork Planet, Set. abr. ed. 1999. audio 24.35 (*1-85686-711-0*) Ulverscroft Audio (U.S.A.).
Tyler, Anne, ed. The Accidental Tourist. 1999. 360p. (*0-7621-0250-0*) Reader's Digest Assn., Inc., The.
Verne, Jules. From the Earth to the Moon. 1967. (Airmont Classics Ser.). (YA). (gr. 8 up). mass mkt. 1.75 (*0-8049-0142-2*, CL-142) Airmont Publishing Co., Inc.
—From the Earth to the Moon. (Illus.). reprint ed. lib. bdg. 21.95 (*0-88411-901-7*) Amereon, Ltd.
—From the Earth to the Moon. 1993. 208p. mass mkt. 5.95 (*0-553-21420-9*, Bantam Classics) Bantam Bks.
—From the Earth to the Moon. 1975. (Dent's Illustrated Children's Classics Ser.). (Illus.). 192p. (YA). reprint ed. 9.00 o.p. (*0-460-05088-5*) Biblio Distribution.
—From the Earth to the Moon. l.t. ed. 2000. (LRS Large Print Heritage Ser.). 223p. (YA). (gr. 7-12). lib. bdg. 27.95 (*1-58118-070-5*) LRS.
—From the Earth to the Moon. E-Book 2.95 (*1-57799-848-0*) Logos Research Systems, Inc.
—From the Earth to the Moon. E-Book 1.95 (*1-58515-183-1*) MesaView, Inc.
—From the Earth to the Moon. 1999. (Twelve-Point Ser.). 245p. lib. bdg. 25.00 (*1-58287-103-5*); 400p. lib. bdg. 26.00 (*0-939495-96-1*) North Bks.
—From the Earth to the Moon. l.t. ed. 2000. (Science Fiction Ser.). 245p. 25.95 (*0-7838-9075-3*) Thorndike Pr.
—From the Earth to the Moon & a Trip Round It! E-Book 2.49 (*1-58627-446-5*) Electric Umbrella Publishing.
—From the Earth to the Moon & a Trip Round It! 1998. (Pocket Classics). xi, 208p. pap. 10.95 (*0-7509-0824-6*) Sutton Publishing, Ltd. GBR. *Dist:* International Publishers Marketing.
Wade, Brent. Company Man. 1993. 240p. pap. 10.95 o.s.i (*0-385-42563-5*) Doubleday Publishing.
—Company Man: A Novel. 1992. 240p. 18.95 o.p. (*0-945575-73-4*) Algonquin Bks. of Chapel Hill.
Walker, Blair S. Hidden in Plain View. abr. ed. 2001. audio 12.99 (*1-57815-207-0*, Media Bks. Audio Publishing) Media Bks., L. L. C.
—Hidden in Plain View. 1999. (Easy Rawlins Mystery Ser.). 240p. 22.00 o.s.i (*0-380-97421-5*, Avon Bks.) Morrow/Avon.
—Hidden in Plain View. abr. ed. 1999. audio 24.95 (*1-57511-061-X*) Publishing Mills, Inc., The.
—Hidden in Plain View: A Darryl Billups Mystery. 2000. (Darryl Billups Ser.). 240p. mass mkt. 5.99 o.s.i (*0-380-79026-2*, Avon Bks.) Morrow/Avon.
—Up Jumped the Devil. abr. ed. 2001. audio 12.99 (*1-57815-210-0*, Media Bks. Audio Publishing) Media Bks., L. L. C.
—Up Jumped the Devil. 1999. 272p. mass mkt. 5.99 o.s.i (*0-380-79025-4*, Avon Bks.) Morrow/Avon.
—Up Jumped the Devil, Set. abr. ed. 1997. audio 24.95 (*1-57511-027-X*) Publishing Mills, Inc., The.
Ward, Robert. Grace: A Fictional Memoir. 2000. (Illus.). 240p. pap. 12.95 (*0-312-25390-7*, Golden Guides from Saint Martin's Pr.); 1998. 224p. 20.00 (*0-307-44007-9*, Golden Bks. Adult Publishing Group) St. Martin's Pr.
—Grace: A Fictional Memoir. l.t. ed. 1999. (Core Ser.). 352p. 28.95 (*0-7838-0427-X*) Thorndike Pr.
—The King of Cards. Rosenman, Jane, ed. 1993. 336p. 20.00 (*0-671-79568-6*, Atria) Simon & Schuster.

## BANGLADESH—FICTION

Ali, Monica. Seven Seas, Thirteen Rivers. 2004. 288p. pap. 13.00 (*0-7432-4331-5*, Scribner) Simon & Schuster.
Gardner, Katy. Songs at the River's Edge: Stories from a Bangladeshi Village. 1997. pap. 22.50 (*0-7453-1094-X*); 39.95 (*0-7453-1095-8*) Pluto Pr. GBR. *Dist:* Stylus Publishing, LLC.
—Songs at the River's Edge: Stories from a Bangladeshi Village. 1997. E-Book 60.00 (*0-585-33023-9*) netLibrary, Inc.
Khan, Adib. Seasonal Adjustments. 1995. 240p. pap. 11.95 (*1-86373-652-2*) Allen & Unwin Pty., Ltd. AUS. *Dist:* Paul & Co. Pubs. Consortium, Inc.
Nasrin, Taslima. Shame: A Novel. Datta, Kankabati, tr. 1997. 302p. 33.00 (*1-57392-165-3*) Prometheus Bks., Pubs.
Warner, Rachel. Going Fishing. (J). 10.95 o.p. (*0-7136-3211-9*, 92010) A & C Black GBR. *Dist:* Lubrecht & Cramer, Ltd., Talman Co.

## BARCELONA (SPAIN)—FICTION

Caminals-Heath, Roser. Once Remembered, Twice Lived. 1993. (Catalan Studies: Vol. 4). 258p. (Orig.). (C). pap. text 32.95 (*0-8204-1969-9*) Lang, Peter Publishing, Inc.
Hall, David A. Return Trip Ticket. 1992. 176p. 16.95 o.p. (*0-312-08283-5*, Saint Martin's Minotaur) St. Martin's Pr.
Laforet, Carmen. Nada. 25th ed. (Classicos Contemporaneos Comentados Ser.). (SPA., Illus.). 276p. pap. 19.95 (*84-233-0989-4*, DE2057) Ediciones Destino ESP. *Dist:* Continental Bk. Co., Inc.
—Nada. Ennis, Glafyra, tr. from SPA. 1993. (Catalan Studies: Vol. 8). 250p. (C). pap. text 29.95 (*0-8204-2064-6*) Lang, Peter Publishing, Inc.
—Nada. 1958. 286p. (gr. 11-12). pap. text 22.95 (*0-19-500942-8*) Oxford Univ. Pr., Inc.
Prado, Benjamin. Never Shake Hands with a Left-Handed Gunman. Cordero, Kristina, tr. from SPA. 1998. 176p. 19.95 (*0-312-20084-6*) St. Martin's Pr.
Rann, Sheila. Anything for Love. 1995. 288p. 21.95 o.p. (*0-446-51830-1*) Warner Bks., Inc.
Rodoreda, Mercé. Camellia Street: A Novel. Rosenthal, David H., tr. from SPA. & intro. by. 1993. 256p. 20.00 o.p. (*1-55597-192-X*) Graywolf Pr.
—The Time of the Doves. Rosenthal, David H., tr. from CAT. 1986. 208p. reprint ed. pap. 14.00 (*0-915308-75-4*) Graywolf Pr.
—The Time of the Doves. Rosenthall, David, tr. 1980. 8.95 o.s.i (*0-8008-7731-4*) Taplinger Publishing Co., Inc.
Wilson, Barbara. Gaudi Afternoon: A Cassandra Reilly Mystery. 2001. 172p. pap. 12.95 (*1-58005-056-5*, Seal Pr.) Avalon Publishing Group.

## BARNARD'S CROSSING (MASS.: IMAGINARY PLACE)—FICTION

Kemelman, Harry. The Day the Rabbi Resigned. l.t. ed. 1993. (Large Print Mystery Ser.). 345p. 24.95 o.p. (*0-7927-1414-8*); pap. 19.95 o.p. (*0-7927-1413-X*) BBC Audiobooks America.
—The Day the Rabbi Resigned. 1992. mass mkt. 5.99 o.s.i (*0-449-21908-9*); 273p. 20.00 o.s.i (*0-449-90681-7*) Ballantine Bks. (Fawcett).
—The Day the Rabbi Resigned. 2004. 288p. mass mkt. 6.99 (*0-7434-7979-3*) ibooks, Inc.
—Friday the Rabbi Slept Late. 1993. pap. o.p. (*0-449-45127-5*); 1986. mass mkt. 5.99 o.s.i (*0-449-21180-0*) Ballantine Bks. (Fawcett).
—Friday the Rabbi Slept Late. l.t. ed. 1983. (General Ser.). 339p. lib. bdg. 13.95 o.p. (*0-8161-3537-1*, Macmillan Reference USA) Gale Group.
—Monday the Rabbi Took Off. 1988. mass mkt. o.s.i (*0-449-20785-4*); 1986. 288p. mass mkt. 5.99 o.s.i (*0-449-21001-4*, Fawcett); 1981. mass mkt. 2.50 o.s.i (*0-449-23872-5*, Fawcett) Ballantine Bks.
—Monday the Rabbi Took Off. 1972. 316p. 5.95 o.p. (*0-399-10550-6*) Putnam Publishing Group, The.
—Monday the Rabbi Took Off. 2002. 368p. pap. 6.99 (*0-7434-5271-2*) ibooks, Inc.
—Rabbi Small, Bk. 2. 1924. o.s.i (*0-688-05617-2*, Morrow, William & Co.) Morrow/Avon.
—Saturday the Rabbi Went Hungry. 1987. 224p. mass mkt. 5.99 o.s.i (*0-449-21392-7*, Fawcett) Ballantine Bks.
—Saturday the Rabbi Went Hungry. 1988. 4.95 o.s.i (*0-517-01307-X*) Crown Publishing Group.
—Saturday the Rabbi Went Hungry. l.t. ed. 1983. 14.95 o.p. (*0-8161-3531-2*, Macmillan Reference USA) Gale Group.

—Someday the Rabbi Will Leave. 1986. 288p. mass mkt. 5.99 o.s.i (0-449-20945-8, Fawcett) Ballantine Bks.
—Someday the Rabbi Will Leave. 1985. 264p. 15.95 o.p. (0-688-04174-4, Morrow, William & Co.) Morrow/Avon.
—Someday the Rabbi Will Leave. 2003. 288p. pap. 6.99 (0-7434-5911-3) ibooks, Inc.
—Sunday the Rabbi Stayed Home. Date not set. mass mkt. (0-449-20784-6); 1985. 224p. mass mkt. 5.99 o.s.i (0-449-21000-6) Ballantine Bks. (Fawcett).
—Sunday the Rabbi Stayed Home. l.t. ed. 1977. (General Ser.). 420p. lib. bdg. 11.95 o.p. (0-8161-6499-1, Macmillan Reference USA) Gale Group.
—Sunday the Rabbi Stayed Home. 2002. (Rabbi Small Mystery Ser.). (Illus.). 304p. pap. 6.99 (0-7434-5238-0) ibooks, Inc.
—That Day the Rabbi Left Town. (Rabbi Small Mystery Ser.). 1997. 263p. mass mkt. 5.99 o.s.i (0-449-22570-4); 1996. 256p. 22.00 o.s.i (0-449-91002-4); 1996. 233p. lib. bdg. 22.95 (1-57490-040-4) Ballantine Bks. (Fawcett).
—Thursday the Rabbi Walked Out. 1986. mass mkt. 5.99 o.s.i (0-449-21157-6, Fawcett) Ballantine Bks.
—Thursday the Rabbi Walked Out. 2003. 256p. mass mkt. 6.99 (0-7434-5860-5) ibooks, Inc.
—Tuesday the Rabbi Saw Red. 1986. (Rabbi Ser.). mass mkt. 5.99 o.s.i (0-449-21321-8, Fawcett) Ballantine Bks.
—Tuesday the Rabbi Saw Red. 1974. (Adult Ser.). 508p. reprint ed. lib. bdg. 11.95 o.p. (0-8161-6230-1, Macmillan Reference USA) Gale Group.
—Tuesday the Rabbi Saw Red. 2003. 352p. pap. 6.99 (0-7434-4534-1) ibooks, Inc.
—Wednesday the Rabbi Got Wet. (Rabbi Ser.). 1986. mass mkt. 5.99 o.s.i (0-449-21328-5); 1983. mass mkt. 2.50 o.s.i (0-449-20344-1); 1981. mass mkt. 2.50 o.s.i (0-449-23291-3) Ballantine Bks. (Fawcett).
—Wednesday the Rabbi Got Wet. l.t. ed. 1977. (Winter Adult Ser.). 497p. reprint ed. lib. bdg. 13.50 o.p. (0-8161-6413-4, Macmillan Reference USA) Gale Group.
—Wednesday the Rabbi Got Wet. 2003. 336p. pap. 6.99 (0-7434-5830-3) ibooks, Inc.

**BARSETSHIRE (ENGLAND: IMAGINARY PLACE)—FICTION**

Thirkell, Angela. Cheerfulness Breaks In. 2002. 188p. pap. 12.95 (1-55921-312-4) Moyer Bell.
—High Rising. l.t. ed. 2000. 304p. pap. 21.99 (0-7531-6194-X); 32.50 (0-7531-6086-2, 160862) ISIS Large Print Bks. GBR. Dist: Ulverscroft Large Print Bks., Ltd., Ulverscroft Large Print Canada, Ltd.
—High Rising. 2002. 256p. pap. 12.95 (1-55921-330-2); 2004. 264p. reprint ed. pap. 12.95 (1-55921-305-1) Moyer Bell.
—Summer Half. l.t. ed. 2001. 296p. pap. 21.99 o.p. (0-7531-6413-2) ISIS Large Print Bks. GBR. Dist: Ulverscroft Large Print Bks., Ltd., Ulverscroft Large Print Canada, Ltd.
—Summer Half. 2003. (Angela Thirkell Barsetshire Ser.). 288p. pap. 12.95 (1-55921-311-6) Moyer Bell.
—Summer Half. 16th l.t. ed. 2001. 296p. 32.50 (0-7531-6412-4) Thorpe, F. A. Pubs. GBR. Dist: Ulverscroft Large Print Bks., Ltd., Ulverscroft Large Print Canada, Ltd.
Thirkell, Angela M. Ankle Deep. lib. bdg. 20.95 (0-8488-1879-2) Amereon, Ltd.
—August Folly. 1995. 272p. pap. 11.95 (0-7867-0272-9); 1988. 297p. pap. 4.95 o.p. (0-88184-421-7) Avalon Publishing Group. (Carroll & Graf Pubs.).
—August Folly. 1980. 312p. reprint ed. pap. o.p. (0-06-080525-0, P 525) HarperCollins Pubs.
—August Folly. l.t. ed. 1993. (Magna Large Print Ser.). 406p. o.p. (0-7505-0500-1) Magna Large Print Bks. GBR. Dist: Ulverscroft Large Print Canada, Ltd.
—Before Lunch. 1988. (Barsetshire Novels Ser.). 336p. mass mkt. 5.95 o.p. (0-88184-397-0, Carroll & Graf Pubs.) Avalon Publishing Group.
—Before Lunch. 1979. pap. o.p. (0-06-080498-X, P 498) HarperCollins Pubs.
—Before Lunch. l.t. ed. 1994. (Magna Large Print Ser.). 414p. o.p. (0-7505-0703-9) Magna Large Print Bks. GBR. Dist: Ulverscroft Large Print Canada, Ltd.
—The Brandons. 1997. 368p. pap. 12.95 o.p. (0-7867-0362-8); 1987. 358p. reprint ed. pap. 4.95 o.p. (0-88184-361-X) Avalon Publishing Group. (Carroll & Graf Pubs.).
—The Brandons. 1979. pap. o.p. (0-06-080497-1, P 497) HarperCollins Pubs.
—Cheerfulness Breaks In: A Barsetshire Novel. 1996. 320p. pap. 11.95 o.p. (0-7867-0318-0, Carroll & Graf Pubs.) Avalon Publishing Group.
—Cheerfulness Breaks In: A Barsetshire Novel. l.t. ed. 1999. (Magna Large Print Ser.). 448p. 31.99 o.p. (0-7505-1339-X) Magna Large Print Bks. GBR. Dist: Ulverscroft Large Print Bks., Ltd., Ulverscroft Large Print Canada, Ltd.
—County Chronicle. 1998. 352p. pap. 12.95 (1-55921-213-6) Moyer Bell.
—The Demon in the House: A Novel. 1996. 254p. pap. 12.95 (1-55921-159-8) Moyer Bell.
—A Double Affair. 2000. 290p. pap. 12.95 (1-55921-249-7) Moyer Bell.
—The Duke's Daughter. 1998. 355p. pap. 12.95 (1-55921-214-4) Moyer Bell.
—Enter Sir Robert. 2000. (Angela Thirkell Barsetshire Ser.). (Illus.). 265p. pap. 12.95 (1-55921-236-5) Moyer Bell.
—Growing Up. 1995. 272p. pap. 12.95 (1-55921-149-0) Moyer Bell.
—Happy Returns. 1998. (Angela Thirkell Barsetshire Ser.). 324p. pap. 12.95 (1-55921-255-1) Moyer Bell.
—The Headmistress. 1996. 296p. reprint ed. pap. 12.95 (1-55921-150-4) Moyer Bell.
—High Rising. (Barsetshire Novels Ser.). 1989. 282p. mass mkt. 5.95 o.p. (0-88184-463-2); 2nd ed. 1997. 288p. pap. 11.95 o.p. (0-7867-0422-5) Avalon Publishing Group. (Carroll & Graf Pubs.).
—High Rising. 1980. (Barsetshire Ser.). 296p. reprint ed. pap. o.p. (0-06-080524-2, P 524) HarperCollins Pubs.
—Jutland Cottage. 1999. (Angela Thirkell Barsetshire Ser.). 298p. pap. 12.95 (1-55921-273-X) Moyer Bell.
—Love among the Ruins. 1997. 464p. pap. 13.95 (1-55921-204-7) Moyer Bell.
—Marling Hall. 1995. 400p. pap. 11.95 (0-7867-0273-7); 1990. 319p. pap. 4.95 o.p. (0-88184-676-7) Avalon Publishing Group. (Carroll & Graf Pubs.).
—Miss Bunting: A Novel. l.t. ed. 1999. (Magna Large Print Ser.). 432p. 31.99 o.p. (0-7505-1341-1) Magna Large Print Bks. GBR. Dist: Ulverscroft Large Print Bks., Ltd., Ulverscroft Large Print Canada, Ltd.
—Miss Bunting: A Novel. 1996. (Illus.). 336p. reprint ed. pap. 12.95 (1-55921-174-1) Moyer Bell.
—Never Too Late. 2000. 285p. pap. 12.95 (1-55921-235-7) Moyer Bell.
—Northbridge Rectory. (Barsetshire Ser.). 320p. 1991. pap. 5.95 o.p. (0-88184-718-6); 2nd ed. 1997. pap. 12.95 o.p. (0-7867-0380-6) Avalon Publishing Group. (Carroll & Graf Pubs.).
—Northbridge Rectory. l.t. ed. 1999. (Magna Large Print Ser.). 480p. 31.99 (0-7505-1340-3) Magna Large Print Bks. GBR. Dist: Ulverscroft Large Print Bks., Ltd., Ulverscroft Large Print Canada, Ltd.
—The Old Bank House. 1997. 400p. pap. 12.95 (1-55921-205-5) Moyer Bell.
—Peace Breaks Out. 1997. (Angela Thirkell Barsetshire Ser.). 328p. pap. 12.95 (1-55921-188-1) Moyer Bell.
—Pomfret Towers. 1986. 272p. mass mkt. 4.95 o.p. (0-88184-276-1, Carroll & Graf Pubs.) Avalon Publishing Group.
—Pomfret Towers. 1979. pap. o.p. (0-06-080496-3, P 496) HarperCollins Pubs.
—Pomfret Towers. l.t. ed. 1992. (Magna Large Print Ser.). 425p. o.p. (0-7505-0458-7) Magna Large Print Bks. GBR. Dist: Ulverscroft Large Print Canada, Ltd.
—Private Enterprise. 1997. 381p. pap. 13.95 (1-55921-189-X) Moyer Bell.
—Summer Half, Set. unabr. ed. 1998. audio 76.95 o.p. (1-85903-012-2) Magna Story Sound GBR. Dist: Ulverscroft Large Print Bks., Ltd.
—Summer Half: A Barsetshire Novel. 1996. 256p. pap. 10.95 (0-7867-0331-8, Carroll & Graf Pubs.) Avalon Publishing Group.
—What Did It Mean? 1999. 318p. pap. 12.95 (1-55921-274-8) Moyer Bell.
—Wild Strawberries. 1989. 265p. pap. 4.95 o.p. (0-88184-555-8); 2nd ed. 1996. 272p. pap. 11.95 (0-7867-0438-1) Avalon Publishing Group. (Carroll & Graf Pubs.).
—Wild Strawberries. 1980. (Barsetshire Ser.). 280p. reprint ed. pap. o.p. (0-06-080526-9, P526) HarperCollins Pubs.
—Wild Strawberries. l.t. ed. 1992. 288p. 18.95 o.p. (1-85089-294-6) ISIS Large Print Bks. GBR. Dist: Transaction Pubs.

**BARSOOM (IMAGINARY PLACE)—FICTION**

Burroughs, Edgar Rice. The Chessmen of Mars. E-Book 3.95 (0-594-03498-1) 1873 Pr.
—The Chessmen of Mars. rev. ed. 2001. 250p. per. 9.90 (1-58396-014-7) Blue Unicorn Editions.
—The Chessmen of Mars. E-Book 3.49 (1-929120-16-8) Electric Umbrella Publishing.
—The Chessmen of Mars. E-Book 1.95 (1-58515-085-1) MesaView, Inc.
—The Chessmen of Mars. (John Carter of Mars Ser.: Vol. 5). 2000. 172p. pap. 9.99 (1-57646-234-X); 2000. 172p. lib. bdg. 16.99 (1-57646-459-8); 1999. 437p. E-Book 3.99 o.p. incl. cd-rom (1-891595-52-0); 2000. 358p. pap. 17.99 (1-57646-460-1); 2000. 358p. lib. bdg. 34.99 (1-57646-461-X) Quiet Vision Publishing.
—A Fighting Man of Mars. 1986. 192p. mass mkt. 4.99 o.s.i (0-345-34511-8); 1984. mass mkt. 2.25 o.p. (0-345-32052-2, Del Rey); 1979. mass mkt. 1.95 o.s.i (0-345-27840-2); 1973. mass mkt. 1.25 o.p. (0-345-23584-3) Ballantine Bks.
—A Fighting Man of Mars. 1975. (Illus.). reprint ed. 30.00 o.p. (0-940724-02-2) Hunt, Paul.
—The Gods of Mars. 2000. 252p. pap. 9.95 (0-594-04715-3); E-Book 3.95 (0-594-04718-8) 1873 Pr.
—The Gods of Mars. Date not set. 190p. 20.95 (0-8488-2222-6) Amereon, Ltd.
—The Gods of Mars. abr. ed. 1999. (Mars Ser.). audio 16.95 (1-882071-77-8, 394313) B&B Audio, Inc.
—The Gods of Mars. rev. ed. 2001. 250p. per. 9.90 (1-58396-015-5) Blue Unicorn Editions.
—The Gods of Mars. E-Book 3.49 (1-929120-17-6) Electric Umbrella Publishing.
—The Gods of Mars. 1975. (Illus.). reprint ed. 35.00 o.p. (0-940724-03-0) Hunt, Paul.
—The Gods of Mars. E-Book 1.95 (1-58515-078-9) MesaView, Inc.
—The Gods of Mars. (John Carter of Mars Ser.: Vol. 2). 2000. 164p. pap. 9.99 (1-57646-227-7); 2000. 164p. lib. bdg. 16.99 (1-57646-447-4); 1999. 418p. E-Book 3.99 o.p. incl. cd-rom (1-891595-34-2); 2000. 338p. pap. 17.99 (1-57646-448-2); 2000. 338p. lib. bdg. 33.99 (1-57646-449-0) Quiet Vision Publishing.
—John Carter of Mars. 1985. 158p. mass mkt. 4.99 o.s.i (0-345-32955-4, Del Rey); 1979. mass mkt. 1.95 o.p. (0-345-27844-5, Del Rey); 1973. mass mkt. 1.25 o.p. (0-345-23588-6) Ballantine Bks.
—John Carter of Mars. 1982. (Illus.). 12.50 o.p. (0-940724-04-9) Hunt, Paul.
—The John Carter of Mars Collection. 1999. E-Book 8.99 incl. cd-rom (1-57646-062-2) Quiet Vision Publishing.
—Llana of Gathol. 1985. 192p. mass mkt. 4.99 o.s.i (0-345-32443-9, Del Rey); 1979. mass mkt. 1.95 o.p. (0-345-27843-7, Del Rey); 1977. mass mkt. 1.50 o.p. (0-345-25829-0, Del Rey); 1973. mass mkt. 1.25 o.p. (0-345-23587-8) Ballantine Bks.
—The Martian Tales, 4 vols. 1982. pap. 7.80 o.s.i (0-345-26213-1, Del Rey) Ballantine Bks.
—A Princess of Mars. 2000. 252p. pap. 9.95 (0-594-04525-8); E-Book 3.95 (0-594-04528-2) 1873 Pr.
—A Princess of Mars. Date not set. 159p. 18.95 (0-8488-2221-8) Amereon, Ltd.
—A Princess of Mars. unabr. ed. 2000. audio 35.95 Audio Bk. Contractors, Inc.
—A Princess of Mars. abr. ed. 1999. (Mars Ser.). (YA). (gr. 8-12). audio 16.95 (1-882071-51-4, 393368) B&B Audio, Inc.
—A Princess of Mars. 1985. (Mars Ser.: Vol. 1). 160p. mass mkt. 6.50 (0-345-33138-9, Del Rey) Ballantine Bks.
—A Princess of Mars. 2001. per. 12.50 (1-891355-72-4); per. 15.50 (1-58396-238-7) Blue Unicorn Editions.
—A Princess of Mars, Bk. 1. unabr. ed. 1993. (Mars Ser.: Bk. 1). audio 39.95 (1-55686-482-5, 482) Books in Motion.
—A Princess of Mars. unabr. collector's ed. 1988. audio 48.00 (0-7366-3945-4, 9191) Books on Tape, Inc.
—A Princess of Mars. E-Book 3.50 (1-929120-14-1) Electric Umbrella Publishing.
—A Princess of Mars. unabr. ed. 1989. audio 36.00 Jimcin Recordings.
—A Princess of Mars. E-Book 1.95 (1-58515-076-2) MesaView, Inc.
—A Princess of Mars. (John Carter of Mars Ser.). 2000. 156p. lib. bdg. 16.99 (1-57646-444-X); 2000. 156p. pap. 9.99 (1-57646-226-9); 1999. 301p. E-Book 3.99 o.p. incl. cd-rom (1-891595-33-4); 2000. 272p. pap. 17.99 (1-57646-445-8); 2000. 272p. lib. bdg. 29.99 (1-57646-446-6) Quiet Vision Publishing.
—A Princess of Mars. E-Book 5.00 (0-7410-0764-9) SoftBook Pr.
—A Princess of Mars. l.t. ed. 2001. (Science Fiction Ser.). 288p. 26.95 (0-7838-9347-7) Thorndike Pr.
—Swords of Mars. 1985. 190p. mass mkt. 4.99 o.s.i (0-345-32956-2, Del Rey); 1979. mass mkt. 1.95 o.p. (0-345-27841-0, Del Rey); 1977. mass mkt. 1.50 o.p. (0-345-27546-2) Ballantine Bks.
—Thuvia, Maid of Mars. 2000. 252p. pap. 9.95 (0-594-04545-2); E-Book 3.95 (0-594-04548-7) 1873 Pr.
—Thuvia, Maid of Mars. abr. ed. 2000. (Martian Tales of Edgar Rice Burroughs: No. 4). audio 16.95 (1-882071-96-4) B&B Audio, Inc.
—Thuvia, Maid of Mars, No. 4. 1986. 160p. mass mkt. 4.99 o.s.i (0-345-33993-2, Del Rey) Ballantine Bks.
—Thuvia, Maid of Mars. unabr. ed. 2002. audio 39.95 (0-7861-2124-6); audio compact disk 19.95 (0-7861-9151-1); audio compact disk 40.00 (0-7861-9632-7) Blackstone Audio Bks., Inc.
—Thuvia, Maid of Mars. E-Book 1.49 (1-929120-38-9) Electric Umbrella Publishing.
—Thuvia, Maid of Mars. E-Book 1.95 (1-58515-088-6) MesaView, Inc.
—Thuvia, Maid of Mars. (John Carter of Mars Ser.: Vol. 4). 2000. 122p. pap. 9.99 (1-57646-229-3); 2000. 122p. lib. bdg. 16.99 (1-57646-453-9); 1999. 268p. E-Book 3.99 o.p. incl. cd-rom (1-891595-51-2); 2000. 210p. pap. 17.99 (1-57646-454-7); 2000. 210p. lib. bdg. 26.99 (1-57646-455-5) Quiet Vision Publishing.
—Thuvia, Maid of Mars. unabr. ed. 2001. (Mars Ser.: Vol. 4). audio compact disk 33.00 (1-4001-0019-4); audio compact disk 20.00 (1-4001-5019-1) Tantor Media, Inc.
—The Warlord of Mars. 2000. 252p. pap. 9.95 (0-594-04540-1); (Martian Tales Ser.: No. 3). E-Book 3.95 (0-594-04543-6) 1873 Pr.
—The Warlord of Mars. Date not set. 158p. 18.95 (0-8488-2224-2) Amereon, Ltd.
—The Warlord of Mars. abr. ed. 2000. (Martian Tales of Edgar Rice Burroughs). audio 16.95 (1-882071-91-3) B&B Audio, Inc.
—The Warlord of Mars. 1985. (Mars Ser.: Vol. 3). 160p. mass mkt. 5.99 (0-345-32453-6, Del Rey) Ballantine Bks.
—The Warlord of Mars. 1976. reprint ed. lib. bdg. 21.95 (0-89966-045-2) Buccaneer Bks., Inc.
—The Warlord of Mars. (John Carter of Mars Ser.: Vol. 3). 2000. 138p. pap. 9.99 (1-57646-228-5); 2000. 138p. lib. bdg. 16.99 (1-57646-450-4); 1999. 291p. E-Book 3.99 o.p. incl. cd-rom (1-891595-50-4); 2000. 240p. pap. 17.99 (1-57646-451-2); 2000. 240p. lib. bdg. 28.99 (1-57646-452-0) Quiet Vision Publishing.

**BATON ROUGE (LA.)—FICTION**

Parrish, Timothy A. Red Stick Men: Stories. 2000. 227p. 22.00 o.p. (1-57806-263-2) Univ. Pr. of Mississippi.
Shuman, Malcolm. Burial Ground. 1998. 224p. mass mkt. 5.50 (0-380-79423-3, Avon Bks.) Morrow/Avon.

**BATTLE SCHOOL (IMAGINARY PLACE)—FICTION**

Card, Orson Scott. Ender's Game. abr. ed. 1991. audio 15.95 o.p. (1-55927-162-0) Audio Renaissance.
—Ender's Game. Date not set. mass mkt. (0-7655-5070-9, Tor Bks.); 2000. (Ender Ser.: Bk. 1). 349p. mass mkt. 3.99 o.p. (0-8125-8904-1, Tor Bks.); 1994. (Ender Ser.: Bk. 1). 384p. mass mkt. 6.99 (0-8125-2358-X, Tor Bks.); 1992. (Ender Ser.: Bk. 1). 256p. pap. 13.95 (0-312-85323-8, Tor Bks.); 1991. (Ender Ser.: Bk. 1). mass mkt. 4.95 o.s.i (0-8125-1349-5, Tor Bks.); 1987. (Ender Ser.: Bk. 1). pap. 3.95 o.s.i (0-8125-3355-0, Tor Bks.); ltd. ed. 1992. (Ender Ser.: Bk. 1). 256p. 200.00 (0-312-85402-1, Tor Bks.); 2002. 324p. (J). reprint ed. mass mkt. 5.99 (0-7653-4229-4, Starscape); 1991. (Ender Ser.: Bk. 1). 368p. reprint ed. mass mkt. 4.99 o.s.i (0-8125-1911-6, Tor Bks.); rev. ed. 1994. (Ender Ser.: Bk. 1). 384p. pap. 6.99 (0-8125-5070-6, Tor Bks.); 4th rev. ed. 1985. (Ender Ser.: Bk. 1). 226p. 24.95 (0-312-93208-1, Tor Bks.) Doherty, Tom Assocs., LLC.
—Ender's Game. 1993. audio. audio 55.00 (1-56544-043-9, 550001) Literate Ear, Inc.
—Ender's Game. 1985. (Ender Ser.: Bk. 1). 13.04 (0-606-04043-9) Turtleback Bks.
—Ender's Shadow. Date not set. E-Book (0-312-70367-8, Tor Bks.); (Ender Ser.: Bk. 5). mass mkt., tchr. ed. (0-7653-4061-5, Tor Bks.); (Ender Ser.: Bk. 5). E-Book 47.80 (0-312-27772-5, Tor Bks.); 2002. (YA). (gr. 5 up). mass mkt. 5.99 (0-7653-4240-5, Starscape); 2000. (Ender Ser.: Bk. 5). 469p. mass mkt. 7.99 (0-8125-7571-7, Tor Bks.); 2000. (Ender Ser.: Bk. 5). 24.95 (0-312-85758-6, Tor Bks.); deluxe ed. 2000. (Ender Ser.: Bk. 5). 384p. lib. bdg. 200.00 (0-312-87297-6, Tor Bks.); 5th ed. 1999. (Ender Ser.: Bk. 5). 379p. 24.95 (0-312-86860-X, Tor Bks.) Doherty, Tom Assocs., LLC.
—Ender's Shadow. abr. ed. 1999. audio 25.00 (0-7871-1997-0) NewStar Media, Inc.
—Ender's Shadow. (Ender Ser.: Bk. 5). E-Book 24.95 (0-312-87922-9) St. Martin's Pr.
—Ender's Shadow. 2000. 13.04 (0-606-20510-1) Turtleback Bks.

**BEARN (IMAGINARY PLACE)—FICTION**

Reichert, Mickey Zucker. Beyond Ragnarok. (Renshai Chronicles Ser.: Vol. 1). 1996. 744p. mass mkt. 7.99 (0-88677-701-1); 1995. 688p. 21.95 o.s.i (0-88677-658-9) DAW Bks., Inc.
—Child of Thunder. 1993. (Daw Book Collectors Ser.: Bk. 3). 592p. (Orig.). mass mkt. 7.99 (0-88677-549-3) DAW Bks., Inc.
—The Children of Wrath. (Renshai Chronicles Ser.: Vol. VOL). 1999. 640p. mass mkt. 7.99 (0-88677-860-3, D A W Fiction); 1998. 688p. 24.95 o.s.i (0-88677-785-2) DAW Bks., Inc.
—The Last of the Renshai. 1992. (Renshai Trilogy Ser.). 640p. (Orig.). mass mkt. 7.99 (0-88677-503-5) DAW Bks., Inc.
—Prince of Demons Vol. 2: The Renshai Chronicles. (Renshai Chronicles Ser.: Vol. 2). 1996. 640p. 22.95 o.s.i (0-88677-715-1); Vol. 2. 1997. 704p. mass mkt. 7.99 (0-88677-759-3) DAW Bks., Inc.

—The Western Wizard. 1992. (Renshai Chronicles Ser.: Bk. 2). (Illus.). 640p. (Orig.). mass mkt. 7.99 (*0-88677-520-5*) DAW Bks., Inc.

**BEIJING (CHINA)—FICTION**

Gambone, Philip. Beijing. 2003. viii, 312p. 26.95 (*0-299-18490-0*) Univ. of Wisconsin Pr.

Mones, Nicole. A Cup of Light. 304p. 2003. pap. 13.95 (*0-385-31945-2*, Delta); 2002. 24.95 (*0-385-31937-1*, Delacorte Pr.) Dell Publishing.

West, Christopher. The Third Messiah. 2000. 260p. 23.95 (*0-312-26665-0*, Saint Martin's Minotaur) St. Martin's Pr.

**BEKLAN EMPIRE (IMAGINARY PLACE)—FICTION**

Adams, Richard. Maia, Vol. 1. unabr. collector's ed. 1987. audio 96.00 (*0-7366-1165-7*, 2090A ) Books on Tape, Inc.

—Maia. 1986. mass mkt. 6.95 o.p. (*0-451-16811-9*); mass mkt. 4.95 o.p. (*0-451-14035-4*) NAL. (Signet Bks.).

—Shardik. 1976. (YA). (gr. 7 up). mass mkt. 4.95 o.p. (*0-380-00516-6*, 62554-7, Avon Bks.) Morrow/Avon.

**BELGIUM—FICTION**

Bailey, Michele. The Cuckoo Case. l.t. ed. 1997. (Ulverscroft Large Print Ser.). 304p. 31.50 o.p. (*0-7089-3695-4*, Ulverscroft) Thorpe, F. A. Pubs. GBR. *Dist:* Ulverscroft Large Print Bks., Ltd., Ulverscroft Large Print Canada, Ltd.

—Dreadful Lies. 1996. 192p. 19.95 o.p. (*0-312-14323-0*, Saint Martin's Minotaur) St. Martin's Pr.

Bogner, Norman. The Deadliest Art. 2001. 384p. 25.95 (*0-312-86856-1*, Forge Bks.) Doherty, Tom Assocs., LLC.

Bourdouxhe, Madeleine. La Femme de Gilles. Evans, Faith, tr. from FRE. 1994. (European Classics Ser.). 122p. reprint ed. pap. 11.95 (*0-8101-1197-7*) Northwestern Univ. Pr.

Bronte, Charlotte. The Professor. (Modern Library Ser.). E-Book 4.95 (*1-931208-19-0*) Adobe Systems, Inc.

—The Professor. unabr. ed. audio 41.95 (*1-55685-026-3*, 1985) Audio Bk. Contractors, Inc.

—The Professor. Set. unabr. ed. 2000. audio 69.95 (*0-7540-0420-1*, CAB 1843, Sterling Audio Bks.) BBC Audiobooks America.

—The Professor. unabr. ed. 2000. audio 49.95 (*0-7861-1752-4*, 2556); audio compact disk 64.00 (*0-7861-9899-0*, z2556) Blackstone Audio Bks., Inc.

—The Professor. 2. reprint ed. lib. bdg. 196.00 (*0-7426-2191-X*); 2001. 283p. pap. text 56.00 (*0-7426-7191-7*) Classic Bks.

—The Professor. 1972. 5.95 o.p. (*0-460-01417-X*); 1954. 10.50 o.p. (*0-460-00417-4*) Dutton/Plume. (Dutton).

—The Professor. E-Book 2.49 (*0-7574-0384-0*) Electric Umbrella Publishing.

—The Professor. 1999. (Twelve-Point Ser.). 250p. lib. bdg. 25.00 (*1-58287-095-0*) North Bks.

—The Professor. Smith, Margaret & Rosengarten, Herbert, eds. (Oxford World's Classics Ser.). 1999. 336p. pap. 7.95 (*0-19-283511-4*); 1991. 336p. pap. 5.95 o.p. (*0-19-282741-3*); 1987. (Illus.). 390p. 110.00 o.p. (*0-19-812694-8*) Oxford Univ. Pr., Inc.

—The Professor. 2000. E-Book 4.95 (*0-679-63999-3*, Modern Library) Random House Adult Trade Publishing Group.

—The Professor. E-Book 5.00 (*0-7410-0451-8*) SoftBook Pr.

—The Professor. Glen, Heather, ed. & intro. by. 1989. (Classics Ser.). 320p. pap. 8.95 (*0-14-043311-2*, Penguin Classics) Viking Penguin.

—The Professor. abr. ed. 1997. audio 16.95 o.s.i (*0-14-086392-3*, Penguin AudioBooks) Viking Penguin.

—The Professor. 1998. (Classics Library). 215p. pap. 3.95 (*1-85326-208-0*, 2080WW) Wordsworth Editions, Ltd. GBR. *Dist:* Casemate Pubs. & Bk. Distributors, LLC.

—The Professor: 1997 Edition. 1997. 288p. 14.50 o.s.i (*0-679-60273-9*) Random Hse., Inc.

—The Professor & Emma: A Fragment. 1910. 272p. pap. 5.95 o.p. (*0-460-02508-2*, Everyman's Classic Library in Paperback) Tuttle Publishing.

—Villette. Set. 1990. audio 83.95 (*1-55685-171-5*) Audio Bk. Contractors, Inc.

—Villette. 1986. (Bantam Classics Ser.). 512p. mass mkt. 5.95 (*0-553-21243-5*) Bantam Bks.

—Villette. 1974. reprint ed. 9.95 o.p. (*0-460-00351-8*) Biblio Distribution.

—Villette. unabr. ed. 1997. audio 89.95 (*0-7861-1104-6*, 1871) Blackstone Audio Bks., Inc.

—Villette. 1992. reprint ed. lib. bdg. 24.95 (*0-89966-998-0*) Buccaneer Bks., Inc.

—Villette. audio HarperTrade.

—Villette. l.t. unabr. ed. 1991. (Isis Large Print Bks.). 601p. 29.99 o.p. (*1-85089-449-3*, 894493) ISIS Large Print Bks. GBR. *Dist:* Ulverscroft Large Print Bks., Ltd., Ulverscroft Large Print Canada, Ltd.

—Villette. 1992. 256p. 20.00 (*0-679-40988-2*) McKay, David Co., Inc.

—Villette. 496p. 2004. mass mkt. 5.95 (*0-451-52922-7*); 1987. mass mkt. 5.95 o.s.i (*0-451-52083-1*) NAL. (Signet Classics).

—Villette. 1999. (Twelve-Point Ser.). lib. bdg. 25.00 (*1-58287-114-0*) North Bks.

—Villette. Smith, Margaret & Rosengarten, Herbert, eds. (Oxford World's Classics Ser.). 698p. 1998. pap. 9.95 o.p. (*0-19-283433-9*); 1990. pap. 6.95 o.p. (*0-19-281836-8*) Oxford Univ. Pr., Inc.

—Villette. Rosengarten, Herbert & Smith, Margaret, eds. 1985. (Illus.). 824p. 160.00 o.p. (*0-19-812597-6*) Oxford Univ. Pr., Inc.

—Villette. 1968. (Oxford World's Classics Ser.). 16.95 o.p. (*0-19-250047-3*) Oxford Univ. Pr., Inc.

—Villette. Smith, Margaret & Rosengarten, Herbert, eds. 2nd ed. 2001. (Oxford World's Classics Ser.). 592p. pap. 10.95 (*0-19-283964-0*) Oxford Univ. Pr., Inc.

—Villette. Nestor, Pauline, ed. 1992. (New Casebooks Ser.). 184p. 45.00 o.p. (*0-312-07909-5*) Palgrave Macmillan.

—Villette. 2000. E-Book 4.95 (*0-679-64008-8*); 1997. 608p. 18.50 o.s.i (*0-679-60274-7*) Random House Adult Trade Publishing Group. (Modern Library).

—Villette. 1994. o.s.i (*1-85381-136-X*) Random Hse., Inc.

—Villette. Kemp, Sandra, ed. 1993. 576p. pap. 5.95 o.p. (*0-460-87247-8*, Everyman's Classic Library in Paperback) Tuttle Publishing.

—Villette. 1909. 529p. pap. 5.95 o.p. (*0-460-11351-8*, Everyman's Classic Library in Paperback) Tuttle Publishing.

—Villette. Tillotson, Geoffrey & Hawes, Donald, eds. 1978. (Riverside Editions). reprint ed. 26.25 o.p. (*0-8357-0347-9*, ST-00024) University Microfilms, Inc.

—Villette. Lilly, Mark, ed. 1980. (Classics Ser.). 624p. pap. 10.95 (*0-14-043118-7*, Penguin Classics) Viking Penguin.

—Villette. abr. ed. 1995. (Classics on Audio Ser.). pap. 16.95 o.s.i incl. audio (*0-14-086076-2*) Viking Penguin.

Chevalier, Tracy. The Lady & the Unicorn. 2003. 256p. 23.95 (*0-525-94767-1*, Dutton) Dutton/Plume.

Claus, Hugo. Desire. 1998. 288p. pap. 12.95 o.s.i (*0-14-025538-9*) Penguin Group (USA) Inc.

—Desire. Knecht, Stacey, tr. 1997. 224p. 24.95 o.p. (*0-670-86746-2*) Viking Penguin.

—The Sorrow of Belgium. 1990. 24.95 o.s.i (*0-394-56263-1*, Pantheon) Knopf Publishing Group.

—The Sorrow of Belgium. 2003. (Tusk Ivories Ser.). 608p. pap. 17.95 (*1-58567-238-6*) Overlook Pr., The.

—The Sorrow of Belgium. Pomerans, Arnold J., tr. 1994. (Penguin Twentieth-Century Classics Ser.). 624p. pap. 11.95 o.p. (*0-14-018801-0*, Penguin Classics) Viking Penguin.

Dunnett, Dorothy. The Spring of the Ram: Second Book of the House of Niccolo. 1992. reprint ed. lib. bdg. 33.95 (*0-89966-964-6*) Buccaneer Bks., Inc.

—The Spring of the Ram: Second Book of the House of Niccolo. 1989. mass mkt. 4.95 o.s.i (*0-440-20355-4*) Dell Publishing.

—The Spring of the Ram: Second Book of the House of Niccolo. 1999. (House of Niccolo Ser.: Vol. II). (Illus.). 496p. pap. 15.00 (*0-375-70478-7*, Vintage) Knopf Publishing Group.

Feather, Jane. Virtue. 1993. 448p. mass mkt. 6.50 (*0-553-56054-9*) Bantam Bks.

—Virtue. l.t. ed. 1993. 549p. lib. bdg. 21.95 (*0-8161-5871-1*, Macmillan Reference USA) Gale Group.

Fitch, Stona. Senseless. 160p. 2002. pap. 12.00 (*1-56947-306-4*); 2001. 22.00 o.p. (*1-56947-268-8*) Soho Pr., Inc.

Freeling, Nicolas. The Back of the North Wind. (Crime Monthly Ser.). 1984. 224p. pap. 3.95 o.p. (*0-14-006953-4*, Penguin Bks.); 1983. 192p. 13.95 o.p. (*0-670-14398-7*) Viking Penguin.

—The Bugles Blowing. 1980. (Henri Castang Mystery Ser.). pap. 1.95 o.p. (*0-394-74551-5*) Random Hse., Inc.

—Castang's City. 2001. 284p. pap. 9.95 (*1-84232-855-7*) House of Stratus, Inc. GBR. *Dist:* Midpoint Trade Bks., Inc.

—Castang's City. 1980. 9.95 o.p. (*0-394-50895-5*, Pantheon) Knopf Publishing Group.

—Castang's City. 1981. (Henri Castang Mystery Ser.). 304p. pap. 3.95 o.p. (*0-394-74747-X*) Random Hse., Inc.

—Cold Iron. 2001. 260p. pap. (*1-84232-861-1*) House of Stratus, Inc.

—Cold Iron. 1990. 24p. pap. 4.50 o.p. (*0-14-009984-0*); 1988. 240p. pap. 3.95 o.p. (*0-14-009252-8*, Penguin Bks.); 1986. 15.95 o.p. (*0-670-81180-7*) Viking Penguin.

—A Dressing of Diamond. 1974. (Harper Novel of Suspense Ser.). 256p. 7.95 o.p. (*0-06-011352-9*) HarperCollins Pubs.

—A Dressing of Diamond. 1976. (Crime Ser.). 232p. pap. 3.95 o.p. (*0-14-004131-1*, Penguin Bks.) Viking Penguin.

—A Dwarf Kingdom. l.t. ed. 1996. 325p. pap. 20.95 o.p. (*0-7838-1867-X*, Macmillan Reference USA) Gale Group.

—A Dwarf Kingdom. 2001. 210p. pap. 9.95 (*1-84232-869-7*) House of Stratus, Inc. GBR. *Dist:* Midpoint Trade Bks., Inc.

—A Dwarf Kingdom. 214p. 1997. mass mkt. o.s.i (*0-7515-1867-0*); 1996. o.s.i (*0-316-87892-8*) Little Brown & Co.

—A Dwarf Kingdom. 1996. 256p. 21.95 o.s.i (*0-89296-615-7*) Mysterious Pr.

—A Dwarf Kingdom. 1997. 208p. mass mkt. 5.99 (*0-446-40518-3*) Warner Bks., Inc.

—Flanders Sky. 1992. 224p. 25.00 (*0-89296-492-8*) Mysterious Pr.

—Flanders Sky. 1993. 224p. mass mkt. 5.50 o.s.i (*0-446-40352-0*) Warner Bks., Inc.

—Lady Macbeth. 2001. 276p. pap. (*1-84232-862-X*) House of Stratus, Inc.

—The Night Lords. 2001. 290p. pap. 9.95 (*1-84232-854-9*) House of Stratus, Inc. GBR. *Dist:* Midpoint Trade Bks., Inc.

—The Night Lords. 1978. 7.95 o.p. (*0-394-50281-7*, Pantheon) Knopf Publishing Group.

—The Night Lords. 1980. (Henri Castang Mystery Ser.). pap. 1.95 o.s.i (*0-394-74552-3*) Random Hse., Inc.

—No Part in Your Death. 2001. 254p. pap. 9.95 (*1-84232-859-X*) House of Stratus, Inc. GBR. *Dist:* Midpoint Trade Bks., Inc.

—No Part in Your Death. (Crime Monthly Ser.). 240p. 1986. pap. 3.95 o.p. (*0-14-007450-3*, Penguin Bks.); 1984. 13.95 o.p. (*0-670-51441-1*) Viking Penguin.

—Not As Far As Velma. 2001. 246p. pap. 9.95 (*1-84232-863-8*) House of Stratus, Inc. GBR. *Dist:* Midpoint Trade Bks., Inc.

—Not as Far as Velma. 1989. 17.95 o.s.i (*0-89296-380-8*) Mysterious Pr.

—Not as Far as Velma. 1990. 240p. mass mkt. 4.95 o.s.i (*0-445-40811-1*, Mysterious Pr. Paperback Bks.) Warner Bks., Inc.

—Sabine. 1978. (Harper Novel of Suspense Ser.). 7.95 o.p. (*0-06-011356-1*) HarperCollins Pubs.

—Sabine. 1980. (Henri Castang Mystery Ser.). pap. 1.95 o.p. (*0-394-74553-1*) Random Hse., Inc.

—The Seacoast of Bohemia: A Henri Castang Mystery. l.t. ed. 1995. 312p. pap. 20.95 o.p. (*0-7838-1567-0*, Macmillan Reference USA) Gale Group.

—The Seacoast of Bohemia: A Henri Castang Mystery. 1996. 213p. mass mkt. o.s.i (*0-7515-1494-2*) Little Brown & Co.

—The Seacoast of Bohemia: A Henri Castang Mystery. 1995. 213p. 18.95 o.s.i (*0-89296-555-X*) Mysterious Pr.

—The Seacoast of Bohemia: A Henri Castang Mystery. 1996. 208p. mass mkt. 5.99 o.s.i (*0-446-40371-7*) Warner Bks., Inc.

—Those in Peril. l.t. ed. 1991. 17.95 o.p. (*0-7451-8172-4*, AH0226); pap. 15.95 o.p. (*0-7927-0707-9*, AS0262) BBC Audiobooks America.

—Those in Peril. 2001. 218p. pap. 9.95 (*1-84232-865-4*) House of Stratus, Inc. GBR. *Dist:* Midpoint Trade Bks., Inc.

—Those in Peril. 1991. 18.95 o.p. (*0-89296-412-X*) Mysterious Pr.

—Those in Peril. 1992. mass mkt. 4.99 o.s.i (*0-446-40089-0*) Warner Bks., Inc.

—Wolfnight. 2001. 242p. pap. 9.95 (*1-84232-857-3*) House of Stratus, Inc. GBR. *Dist:* Midpoint Trade Bks., Inc.

—Wolfnight. (Henri Castang Mystery Ser.). 1983. 288p. pap. 2.95 o.p. (*0-394-71381-8*, Vintage); 1982. 12.00 o.p. (*0-394-52266-4*, Pantheon) Knopf Publishing Group.

—You Know Who. l.t. ed. 1995. 279p. 21.95 (*0-7838-1182-9*, Macmillan Reference USA) Gale Group.

—You Know Who. 1995. 250p. mass mkt. o.s.i (*0-7515-1028-9*) Little Brown & Co.

—You Know Who. 1994. 192p. 18.95 o.s.i (*0-89296-554-1*) Mysterious Pr.

—You Know Who. 1995. 208p. mass mkt. 5.50 o.s.i (*0-446-40370-9*) Warner Bks., Inc.

Friedman, Carl. The Shovel & the Loom. Ringold, Jeannette K., tr. from DUT. 1996. 176p. 20.00 o.p. (*0-89255-216-6*) Persea Bks., Inc.

—The Shovel & the Loom. 1996. 176p. (C). pap. 12.00 (*0-89255-231-X*) Persea Bks., Inc.

Grant, Jan. Shed the Rain & Dance into the Wind. 2001. pap. 23.35 (*0-7596-2509-3*) 1stBooks Library.

Hollinghurst, Alan. Folding Star. 1995. pap. 14.00 o.s.i (*0-679-76231-0*) Random Hse., Inc.

Keene, Carolyn. The Secret in the Old Lace. (Nancy Drew Mystery Stories Ser.: No. 59). (J). (gr. 3-6). 1989. pap. 3.99 (*0-671-69067-1*); 1987. pap. 3.50 (*0-671-63822-X*) Simon & Schuster Children's Publishing. (Aladdin).

Kelby, N. M. In the Company of Angels: A Novel. 2002. (Illus.). 192p. pap. 12.00 (*0-7868-8583-1*) Hyperion Pr.

Magdalen, I. I. Emma H. 2003. 192p. pap. 12.95 (*1-902881-67-2*) Toby Pr.

Mairesse, Michelle & Mairesse, Jean. The Season Is Over. 1999. (Illus.). 300p. (C). E-Book (*1-929485-04-2*) Hermes Pr.

Norman, Hilary. The Pact. 1997. 432p. (YA). 24.95 o.p. (*0-525-94256-4*) Dutton/Plume.

Rucker, Rudolf V. B. As above, So Below: A Novel of Peter Bruegel. 2002. (Illus.). 320p. 23.95 (*0-7653-0403-1*, Forge Bks.) Doherty, Tom Assocs., LLC.

Sellar, Maurice. The Allies. l.t. ed. 1999. (General Ser.). 384p. pap. 23.95 o.p. (*0-7862-1983-1*) Thorndike Pr.

Shreve, Anita. Resistance. unabr. collector's ed. 1995. audio 48.00 (*0-7366-3121-6*, 3797) Books on Tape, Inc.

—Resistance. 1999. 222p. reprint ed. text 22.00 (*0-7881-6622-0*) DIANE Publishing Co.

—Resistance. 1998. pap. 13.00 (*0-316-19062-4*, Back Bay); 1995. 222p. 21.95 (*0-316-78999-2*); 1997. 256p. reprint ed. pap. 13.95 (*0-316-78984-4*, Back Bay) Little Brown & Co.

Simenon, Georges. Maigret at the Gai-Moulin. Sainsbury, Geoffrey, tr. 2nd ed. 1991. Tr. of Danseuse du Gai-Moulin. 166p. 17.95 o.s.i (*0-15-155568-0*) Harcourt Trade Pubs.

**BELIZE—FICTION**

Edgell, Zee. Beka Lamb. 1986. (Caribbean Writers Ser.). 172p. (Orig.). (C). pap. 10.95 (*0-435-98844-1*, 98844) Heinemann.

McKay, Claudia. Twist of Lime: A Lynn Evans Mystery. 1997. (Lynn Evans Mystery Ser.). 166p. pap. 10.95 (*0-934678-88-X*) New Victoria Pubs., Inc.

Miller, Carlos. Belize: A Novel. 2000. 402p. E-Book 8.00 (*0-7388-8251-8*) Xlibris Corp.

Miller, Carlos Ledson. Belize: A Novel. 2000. 402p. pap. 24.99 (*0-7388-0717-6*); text 34.99 (*0-7388-0716-8*) Xlibris Corp.

Schurch, Maylan. Danger Signals in Belize. 2002. (Justin Case Adventures Ser.: 3). 121p. (YA). pap. 7.99 (*0-8280-1613-5*) Review & Herald Publishing Assn.

Stevens, Katie S. The Church of the Day of Reckoning P. O. Belize. 1998. 246p. (*0-7541-0140-1*) Communications Plus USA.

Weber, Janice. Hot Ticket. 2000. 384p. mass mkt. 6.50 (*0-446-60788-6*); 1998. 337p. 24.00 o.p. (*0-446-51773-9*) Warner Bks., Inc.

**BELLEHAVEN (WASH.: IMAGINARY PLACE)—FICTION**

Dereske, Jo. Final Notice, Bk. 3. 1998. (Miss Zukas Mystery Ser.). 240p. mass mkt. 5.99 (*0-380-78245-6*, Avon Bks.) Morrow/Avon.

—Miss Zukas & Stroke of Death. 1995. (Miss Zukas Mystery Ser.: No. 3). 224p. mass mkt. 6.50 (*0-380-77033-4*, Avon Bks.) Morrow/Avon.

—Miss Zukas & the Island Murders. 1995. (Miss Zukas Mystery Ser.). 224p. (Orig.). mass mkt. 5.99 (*0-380-77031-8*, Avon Bks.) Morrow/Avon.

—Miss Zukas & the Library Murders. l.t. ed. 2003. (Mystery Ser.). (Orig.). 27.95 (*1-57490-511-2*) Beeler, Thomas T. Publisher.

—Miss Zukas & the Library Murders. 1994. (Miss Zukas Mystery Ser.). 224p. (Orig.). mass mkt. 5.99 (*0-380-77030-X*, Avon Bks.) Morrow/Avon.

—Miss Zukas & the Raven's Dance. 1996. (Miss Zukas Mystery Ser.). 256p. mass mkt. 5.99 (*0-380-78243-X*, Avon Bks.) Morrow/Avon.

—Miss Zukas in Death's Shadow. 1999. 224p. mass mkt. 5.99 (*0-380-80472-7*, Avon Bks.) Morrow/Avon.

—Miss Zukas Shelves the Evidence. l.t. ed. 2002. (Paperback Ser.). 310p. pap. 25.95 (*0-7838-9734-0*) Gale Group.

—Miss Zukas Shelves the Evidence. 2001. (Miss Zukas Mystery Ser.). 256p. mass mkt. 5.99 (*0-380-80474-3*, Avon Bks.) Morrow/Avon.

—Out of Circulation. 1997. (Miss Zukas Mystery Ser.). mass mkt. 5.99 (*0-380-78244-8*, Avon Bks.) Morrow/Avon.

**BENTROCK (MONT.: IMAGINARY PLACE)—FICTION**

Watson, Larry. White Crosses. 384p. 1998. pap. 14.00 (*0-671-56773-X*, Washington Square Pr.); 1997. 23.00 o.s.i (*0-671-56771-3*, Atria) Simon & Schuster.

**BERKELEY (CALIF.)—FICTION**

Dunlap, Susan. As a Favor. 1991. 208p. mass mkt. 5.99 o.s.i (*0-440-20999-4*) Dell Publishing.

—As a Favor. 1984. 192p. 12.95 o.p. (*0-312-05594-3*) St. Martin's Pr.

—Cop Out. unabr. ed. 1997. audio 44.95 (*0-7861-1192-5*, 1949) Blackstone Audio Bks., Inc.

—Cop Out. 1998. (Jill Smith Mystery Ser.). 352p. mass mkt. 5.99 o.s.i (*0-440-22479-9*) Dell Publishing.

—Cop Out: A Jill Smith Mystery. 1997. 304p. 20.95 o.s.i (*0-385-31600-3*, Delacorte Pr.) Dell Publishing.

—Death & Taxes. 1993. 288p. mass mkt. 5.50 o.s.i (*0-440-21406-8*) Dell Publishing.

—Diamond in the Buff. 1991. 192p. mass mkt. 5.50 o.s.i (*0-440-20788-6*) Dell Publishing.

—Diamond in the Buff. 1990. 176p. 14.95 o.p. (*0-312-03814-3*, Saint Martin's Minotaur) St. Martin's Pr.

—A Dinner to Die For. 1989. 240p. mass mkt. 5.99 o.s.i (*0-440-20495-X*) Dell Publishing.

—A Dinner to Die For. 1987. 224p. 15.95 o.p. (*0-312-01019-2*, Saint Martin's Minotaur) St. Martin's Pr.

—Karma. 1991. 240p. pap. 15.00 o.s.i (*0-440-61365-5*); mass mkt. 5.99 o.s.i (*0-440-20982-X*) Dell Publishing.

—Karma. 1991. reprint ed. 18.95 o.p. (*0-7278-4229-3*) Severn Hse. Pubs., Ltd.

—Not Exactly a Brahmin. 1991. 240p. mass mkt. 4.99 o.s.i (*0-440-20998-6*) Dell Publishing.

—Not Exactly a Brahmin. 1985. (Jill Smith Mystery Ser.). 192p. 12.95 o.p. (*0-312-57947-0*) St. Martin's Pr.

—Sudden Exposure. unabr. ed. 1998. audio 44.95 Blackstone Audio Bks., Inc.

—Sudden Exposure. 1997. 320p. pap. 19.00 o.s.i (*0-440-61350-7*); mass mkt. 5.50 o.s.i (*0-440-21563-3*) Dell Publishing.

—Sudden Exposure. abr. ed. 1996. (Jill Smith Mystery Ser.). audio 16.99 (*0-88646-408-0*, 7408) Durkin Hayes Publishing Ltd.

—Time Expired. l.t. ed. 1994. 24.95 o.p. (*0-7927-1779-1*); pap. 22.95 o.p. (*0-7927-1778-3*) BBC Audiobooks America.

—Time Expired. 1994. (Jill Smith Mystery Ser.). 304p. mass mkt. 5.99 o.s.i (*0-440-21683-4*) Dell Publishing.

—Too Close to the Edge. 1989. 224p. reprint ed. mass mkt. 5.50 o.s.i (*0-440-20356-2*) Dell Publishing.

—Too Close to the Edge. 1987. 240p. 14.95 o.p. (*0-312-00198-3*) St. Martin's Pr.

Fuchs, Jake. Death of a Dad: The Nursery School Murders. 1998. 180p. pap. 13.95 (*0-88739-159-1*) Creative Arts Bk. Co.

—Death of a Prof: Nursery School Murders II. 2001. 255p. pap. 13.95 (*0-88739-335-7*) Creative Arts Bk. Co.

Gores, Joe. Menaced Assassin. 1995. 384p. mass mkt. 5.50 (*0-446-40390-3*) Warner Bks., Inc.

Nasaw, Jonathan. Shakedown Street. 1995. 208p. (J). mass mkt. 3.99 o.s.i (*0-440-21930-2*) Dell Publishing.

—Shakedown Street. 1993. (J). o.s.i (*0-385-30951-1*, Dell Books for Young Readers) Random Hse. Children's Bks.

VanDenburgh, Jane. The Physics of Sunset. 1999. 304p. 24.00 o.s.i (*0-679-42483-0*, Pantheon) Knopf Publishing Group.

—Physics of Sunset. 2001. 304p. pap. text 15.00 (*1-58243-100-0*, Counterpoint Pr.) Basic Bks.

—The Physics of Sunset. l.t. ed. 1999. (Americana Ser.). 461p. 27.95 (*0-7862-2298-0*) Thorndike Pr.

Vizenor, Gerald Robert. Chancers: A Novel. 2001. pap. (*0-8061-3388-0*); 2000. (American Indian Literature & Critical Studies: Vol. 36). 159p. 19.95 (*0-8061-3266-3*); 2000. E-Book 19.95 (*0-8061-7185-5*) Univ. of Oklahoma Pr.

Wong, Geoffrey. A Golden State of Mind. 2001. 317p. pap. (*1-55212-635-8*) Trafford Publishing.

**BERLIN (GERMANY)—FICTION**

Abbott, Margot. The Last Innocent Hour. 1993. 553p. mass mkt. 5.99 (*0-312-92942-0*, St. Martin's Paperbacks); 1991. 512p. 21.95 o.p. (*0-312-06377-6*) St. Martin's Pr.

Allbeury, Ted. Mission Berlin. 1988. 224p. pap. 3.95 o.p. (*0-380-70444-7*, Avon Bks.) Morrow/Avon.

—Mission Berlin. 1986. 15.95 (*0-8027-0892-7*) Walker & Co.

Bailey, Eleanor. Marlene Dietrich Lived Here. 439p. pap. 11.95 (*0-552-99863-X*) Corgi Bks. Ltd. GBR. *Dist:* Trafalgar Square.

—Marlene Dietrich Lived Here. 2002. 359p. (*0-385-60120-4*) Doubleday Publishing.

Bedford, Sybille. Legacy. 2001. 384p. pap. text 15.00 (*1-58243-142-6*, Counterpoint Pr.) Basic Bks.

Berliner, Janet. Children of the Dusk, Bk. 3. 1997. (Madagascar Manifesto Ser.). 447p. mass mkt. 5.99 (*1-56504-932-2*, Borealis) White Wolf Publishing, Inc.

Berliner, Janet & Guthridge, George. Child of the Light. 1996. (Madagascar Manifesto Ser.: Bk. 1). (Illus.). 440p. (Orig.). pap. 5.99 (*1-56504-931-4*, 12100, Borealis) White Wolf Publishing, Inc.

Bernau, George. Black Phoenix. 304p. 1995. mass mkt. 5.99 o.s.i (*0-446-60182-9*); 1994. (Illus.). 22.95 o.s.i (*0-446-51610-4*) Warner Bks., Inc.

Bunn, T. Davis. Berlin Encounter. 1995. (Rendezvous with Destiny Ser.: Bk. 4). 192p. pap. 8.99 o.p. (*1-55661-382-2*) Bethany Hse. Pubs.

—Berlin Encounter. l.t. ed. 1997. (Christian Mystery Ser.). 227p. 22.95 o.p. (*0-7862-1234-9*) Thorndike Pr.

Carroll, James. Secret Father. l.t. ed. 2003. 626p. 29.95 (*0-7862-6051-3*) Gale Group.

—Secret Father. 2003. 352p. tchr. ed. 25.00 (*0-618-15284-9*) Houghton Mifflin Co.

Cartland, Barbara. Bewildered in Berlin, No. 47. 1987. mass mkt. 2.75 o.s.i (*0-515-09054-9*, Jove) Berkley Publishing Group.

—Bewildered in Berlin. l.t. ed. 2000. (G. K. Hall Paperback Ser.). 205p. pap. 23.95 (*0-7838-9103-2*, Macmillan Reference USA) Gale Group.

Cerda, Carlos. To Die in Berlin. Labinger, Andrea G., tr. from SPA. 1999. (Series Discoveries Ser.).Tr. of Morir en Berlin. 176p. pap. 15.95 (*1-891270-02-8*) Latin American Literary Review Pr.

Deaver, Jeffery. Garden of Beasts. 2004. 416p. 25.00 (*0-7432-2201-6*, Simon & Schuster) Simon & Schuster.

Deighton, Len. Charity. l.t. ed. 1997. (Large Print Book Ser.). 27.95 (*1-56895-436-0*, Wheeler Publishing, Inc.) Gale Group.

—Charity. 1996. 288p. 25.00 o.p. (*0-06-018728-X*) HarperCollins Pubs.

Dold, Gaylord. The Last Man in Berlin. 2003. 368p. 25.00 (*1-4022-0124-9*, Sourcebooks Landmark) Sourcebooks, Inc.

Fedin, Konstantin. Cities & Years. Scammell, Michael, tr. from RUS. 1993. (European Classics Ser.). 350p. reprint ed. pap. 21.00 (*0-8101-1066-0*) Northwestern Univ. Pr.

—Cities & Years: A Novel. Scammell, Michael, tr. 1975. (ENG & RUS.). 415p. reprint ed. lib. bdg. 45.00 o.p. (*0-8371-8029-5*, FECY) Greenwood Publishing Group, Inc.

Fleming, Ian. Octopussy & the Living Daylights. 2004. 128p. pap. 13.00 (*0-14-200329-8*) Penguin Group (USA) Inc.

Fontane, Theodor. Effi Briest. Rorrison, Hugh & Chambers, Helen, trs. from GER. 1996. 246p. pap. 16.95 (*0-946162-44-1*) Angel Bks. GBR. *Dist:* Dufour Editions, Inc.

—Effi Briest. unabr. ed. 1999. (World Classic Literature Ser.). (GER.). pap. 6.95 (*3-89507-004-1*) Bookking International FRA. *Dist:* Distribooks, Inc.

—Effi Briest. (GER.). audio 69.95 o.p. Olivia & Hill Pr., The.

—Effi Briest. Cooper, W. A., tr. abr. ed. 1966. pap. 7.50 o.p. (*0-8044-6156-2*) Ungar, Frederick A Bk.

—Effi Briest. Parmee, Douglas, tr. 1976. (Penguin Classics Ser.). 272p. pap. 11.95 o.s.i (*0-14-044190-5*, Penguin Classics) Viking Penguin.

Gerson, Jack. Death's Head Berlin. 1988. 224p. 15.95 o.p. (*0-312-02569-6*, Saint Martin's Minotaur) St. Martin's Pr.

Grass, Gunter. Too Far Afield. Winston, Krishna, tr. 672p. 2001. pap. 15.00 (*0-15-601416-5*, Harvest Bks.); 2000. 30.00 o.s.i (*0-15-100230-4*) Harcourt Trade Pubs.

Harrington, William. Endgame in Berlin. 1991. 320p. 19.95 o.p. (*1-55611-313-7*) Fine, Donald I. Bks.

Harris, Robert. Fatherland. unabr. ed. 2000. audio 59.95 (*0-7451-4115-3*, CAB 798) Chivers Audio Bks. GBR. *Dist:* BBC Audiobooks America.

—Fatherland. 400p. 1994. mass mkt. 6.50 o.p. (*0-06-100881-8*); 1993. mass mkt. 7.99 (*0-06-100662-9*) Morrow/Avon. (HarperTorch).

—Fatherland. abr. ed. 2002. audio 9.99 (*0-553-70229-7*); 1993. audio 8.99 o.s.i (*0-679-42955-7*); 1992. audio 16.00 o.p. (*0-679-41413-4*) Random Hse. Audio Publishing Group. (RH Audio).

Hein, Christoph. Willenbrock. Boehm, Philip, tr. from GER. 2003. 336p. 24.00 (*0-8050-6731-0*, Metropolitan Bks.) Holt, Henry & Co.

Hoffmann, Yoel. Katschen & The Book of Joseph. Kriss, David et al, trs. from HEB. 1998. 160p. 17.95 (*0-8112-1373-0*); 1999. 161p. reprint ed. pap. 11.95 (*0-8112-1405-2*, NDP875) New Directions Publishing Corp.

Isherwood, Christopher. The Berlin of Sally Bowles. 1975. 583 p. (*0-7012-0407-9*) Hogarth Pr., The.

—The Berlin Stories. 1963. pap. 11.95 (*0-8112-0070-1*, NDP134) New Directions Publishing Corp.

—Mr. Norris Changes Trains. l.t. ed. 1985. (Mainstream Ser.). 271p. 14.95 o.p. (*1-85089-018-8*) ISIS Large Print Bks. GBR. *Dist:* Transaction Pubs.

Isherwood, Christopher, intro. The Berlin Stories. 1979. reprint ed. lib. bdg. 18.00 (*0-8376-0449-4*) Bentley Pubs.

Just, Ward. The Weather in Berlin: A Novel. l.t. ed. 2003. lib. bdg. 29.95 (*1-58547-262-X*, Platinum) Ctr. Point Large Print.

—The Weather in Berlin: A Novel. 2002. 306p. tchr. ed. 24.00 (*0-618-03668-7*) Houghton Mifflin Co.

—The Weather in Berlin: A Novel. 2003. 320p. pap. 13.00 (*0-618-34079-3*, Mariner Bks.) Houghton Mifflin Co. Trade & Reference Div.

Kanon, Joseph. The Good German: A Novel. l.t. ed. 2002. (Basic Ser.). 809p. 31.95 (*0-7862-3655-8*) Gale Group.

—The Good German: A Novel. 2001. (Illus.). 496p. 26.00 o.s.i (*0-8050-6422-2*) Holt, Henry & Co.

—The Good German: A Novel. 2002. mass mkt. 7.99 o.s.i (*0-312-98253-4*); 496p. pap. 14.00 (*0-312-42126-5*); pap. (*0-312-42139-7*) Picador.

—The Good German: A Novel. l.t. ed. 2002. 805p. 28.95 (*0-7862-3656-6*); (*0-7540-1734-6*) Thorndike Pr.

Kaye, M. M. Death in Berlin. unabr. ed. 2000. audio 49.95 (*0-7451-6080-8*, CAB 237) Chivers Audio Bks. GBR. *Dist:* BBC Audiobooks America.

—Death in Berlin. 2000. 272p. pap. 12.95 (*0-312-26308-2*, Saint Martin's Griffin); 1986. 320p. mass mkt. 3.95 (*0-312-90103-8*, St. Martin's Paperbacks); 1985. 288p. 14.95 o.p. (*0-312-18621-5*) St. Martin's Pr.

Kerr, Philip. Berlin Noir: March Violets - The Pale Criminal - A German Requiem. 1994. (Penguin Crime/Mystery Ser.). 848p. 15.95 (*0-14-023170-6*) Viking Penguin.

—A German Requiem. 1993. (Crime Ser.). 320p. pap. 4.95 o.p. (*0-14-017561-X*, Penguin Bks.) Penguin Group (USA) Inc.

—A German Requiem. 1991. 320p. 19.95 o.p. (*0-670-83516-1*, Viking) Viking Penguin.

—March Violets. (Crime Ser.). 256p. 1990. pap. 4.95 o.p. (*0-14-011466-1*, Penguin Bks.); 1989. 17.95 o.p. (*0-670-82431-3*) Viking Penguin.

—The Pale Criminal. 1991. (Crime Monthly Ser.). 288p. reprint ed. pap. 4.95 o.p. (*0-14-015393-4*, Penguin Bks.) Penguin Group (USA) Inc.

—The Pale Criminal. 1990. 288p. 18.95 o.p. (*0-670-82433-X*) Viking Penguin.

Klein, Olaf G. Aftertime. Dembo, Margot B., tr. from GER. 1999. 124p. 28.00 (*0-8101-1504-2*, Hydra Bks.) Northwestern Univ. Pr.

Kolmar, Gertrud. A Jewish Mother from Berlin & Susanna. Goldstein, Brigitte, tr. from GER. 1997. (Modern German Voices Ser.).Tr. of Judische Mutter, Susanna. 225p. 24.00 (*0-8419-1345-5*) Holmes & Meier Pubs., Inc.

La Plante, Lynda. Entwined. 1993. 22.00 o.p. (*0-688-09243-8*, Morrow, William & Co.) Morrow/Avon.

Lindquist, Donald. Berlin Tunnel, Twenty-One. 1978. pap. 2.95 o.p. (*0-380-01843-8*, 78394-0, Avon Bks.) Morrow/Avon.

Maristed, Kai. Broken Ground: A Novel. 2003. 320p. (*1-59376-005-1*) Shoemaker & Hoard.

Marks, John. The Wall. 1999. 448p. reprint ed. 14.00 (*1-57322-757-9*, Riverhead Trade (Paperbacks)) Berkley Publishing Group.

—The Wall. unabr. ed. 2000. audio 79.95 (*0-7927-2277-9*, CSL 166) Chivers Audio Bks. GBR. *Dist:* BBC Audiobooks America.

—The Wall. 1998. 384p. 24.95 o.p. (*1-57322-122-8*, Riverhead Bks. (Hardcovers)) Putnam Publishing Group, The.

Nebenzal, Harold. Cafe Berlin. 1992. 290p. 22.95 o.p. (*0-87951-458-2*) Overlook Pr., The.

Nelson, Penelope. Beyond Berlin. 1996. 256p. (Orig.). pap. 11.95 o.p. (*1-86373-847-9*) Allen & Unwin Pty., Ltd. AUS. *Dist:* Independent Pubs. Group.

Nooteboom, Cees. All Souls Day. Massotty, Susan, tr. from DUT. 2001. 352p. 25.00 (*0-15-100566-4*) Harcourt Trade Pubs.

Ohanna, Karin. Star Crossed: A Novel. 1999. pap. 12.95 o.p. (*0-533-12976-1*) Vantage Pr., Inc.

Oren, Aras. Please, No Police: A Novella. Sipahigil, Teoman, tr. from TUR. 1992. (Modern Middle Eastern Literature in Translation Ser.). 174p. pap. 8.95 (*0-292-76038-8*) Ctr. for Middle Eastern Studies.

Parrinder, Patrick & Rolfe, Christopher, eds. H. G. Wells under Revision: Proceedings of the International H. G. Wells Symposium, London, July 1986. 1990. 264p. 40.00 (*0-945636-05-9*) Susquehanna Univ. Pr.

Phillips, Michael. Escape to Freedom. (Secret of the Rose Ser.: No. 3). 1995. 16.99 o.p. (*0-8423-5951-6*); 1994. 487p. pap. 11.99 (*0-8423-5942-7*) Tyndale Hse. Pubs.

—A Rose Remembered. (Secret of the Rose Ser.: Vol. 2). 2001. 528p. mass mkt. 7.99 (*0-8423-4291-5*, Living Bks.); 1994. 576p. pap. 11.99 o.p. (*0-8423-5929-X*) Tyndale Hse. Pubs.

Pye, Michael. The Pieces from Berlin. 2004. 352p. pap. 14.00 (*0-375-71416-2*, Vintage) Knopf Publishing Group.

—The Pieces from Berlin. 2003. 352p. 24.00 (*0-375-41436-3*) Knopf, Alfred A. Inc.

Rahlens, Holly-Jane. Becky Bernstein Goes Berlin. 1997. 256p. 22.95 (*1-55970-381-4*) Arcade Publishing, Inc.

Robbe-Grillet, Alain. Repetition. 2004. 208p. pap. 13.00 (*0-8021-4057-2*, Grove Pr.) Grove/Atlantic, Inc.

—Repetition. Howard, Richard, tr. from FRE. 2003. 168p. 23.00 (*0-8021-1736-8*, Grove Pr.) Grove/Atlantic, Inc.

Roth, Joseph. Right & Left: The Legend of the Holy Drinker. Hoffman, Michael, tr. 1993. 304p. pap. 15.95 (*0-87951-456-6*) Overlook Pr., The.

—Right & Left & The Legend of the Holy Drinker. Hofmann, Michael, tr. 1992. 320p. 23.95 (*0-87951-448-5*) Overlook Pr., The.

Rothmann, Ralf. Knife Edge. Mitchell, Breon, tr. from GER. 1992. 128p. 19.95 (*0-8112-1204-1*); pap. 9.95 (*0-8112-1210-6*, NDP744) New Directions Publishing Corp.

Schneider, Peter. The Wall Jumper: A Berlin Story. Hafrey, Leigh, tr. 1985. pap. 9.95 o.s.i (*0-394-72882-3*, Pantheon) Knopf Publishing Group.

Sebastian, Tim. The Memory Church: A Novel. 1993. 288p. 20.00 o.p. (*0-688-11447-4*, Morrow, William & Co.) Morrow/Avon.

Shea, Michael. The Iron Veil. 192p. 25.00 (*0-7278-5465-8*) Severn Hse. Pubs., Ltd.

—The Iron Veil. l.t. ed. 2000. (General Ser.). viii, 220p. 22.95 (*0-7862-2806-7*); (*0-7540-4249-9*); (*0-7540-4250-2*) Thorndike Pr.

Strauss, Botho. Living, Glimmering, Lying. Theobald, Roslyn, tr. from GER. 1999. 176p. 26.95 (*0-8101-1283-3*, Hydra Bks.) Northwestern Univ. Pr.

Taylor, Frederick. The Kinder Garden. 1991. 432p. 21.95 o.p. (*0-88184-697-X*, Carroll & Graf Pubs.) Avalon Publishing Group.

Turtledove, Harry. In the Presence of Mine Enemies. 2003. 464p. pap. 24.95 (*0-451-52902-2*) NAL.

Ugresic, Dubravka. The Museum of Unconditional Surrender. Hawkesworth, Celia, tr. from CRO. 1999. 256p. 24.95 o.s.i (*0-8112-1421-4*) New Directions Publishing Corp.

Welt, Elly. Berlin Wild. 1988. 400p. mass mkt. 4.50 o.p. (*0-451-40028-3*, Onyx) NAL.

—Berlin Wild. 1986. 384p. 17.95 o.p. (*0-670-80925-X*) Viking Penguin.

Wilson, Robert. The Company of Strangers. 2002. 496p. pap. 14.00 (*0-15-602710-0*, Harvest Bks.); 2001. 480p. 25.00 o.s.i (*0-15-100846-9*); 2001. 480p. 25.00 (*0-15-100745-4*) Harcourt Trade Pubs.

Zimmerman, R. D. Deadfall in Berlin. 1990. 18.95 o.p. (*1-55611-222-X*) Fine, Donald I. Bks.

**BERMUDA ISLANDS—FICTION**

Fubler, Anson. Genuine Love - The Conspiracy: Bermuda - New York Connection. 1996. 264p. 18.95 o.p. (*0-944957-56-0*) Rivercross Publishing, Inc.

Hart, Carolyn G. Resort to Murder. 2001. 304p. 24.00 (*0-380-97773-7*, Morrow, William & Co.) Morrow/Avon.

—Resort to Murder. l.t. ed. 2001. 456p. 29.95 (*0-7862-3490-3*) Thorndike Pr.

Manuel, David. A Matter of Time. 2003. (Faith Abbey Mystery Ser.). 304p. mass mkt. 6.99 (*0-446-61255-3*) Warner Bks., Inc.

—A Matter of Time: A Faith Abbey Mystery. 2002. 288p. 23.00 (*1-55725-305-6*) Paraclete Pr., Inc.

Walther, Anne Newton. A Time for Treason: A Novel of the American Revolution. 2000. 451p. 24.95 (*0-9676703-0-6*) Tapestries.

**BEVERLY HILLS (CALIF.)—FICTION**

Cunningham, E. V., pseud. The Case of the Angry Actress. 1984. 192p. pap. 2.95 o.p. (*0-440-11093-9*) Dell Publishing.

—The Case of the Kidnapped Angel. 192p. 1983. (Masao Masuto Mystery Ser.: No. 5). pap. 2.95 o.p. (*0-440-11224-9*); 1982. 12.95 o.s.i (*0-385-28118-8*, Delacorte Pr.) Dell Publishing.

—The Case of the Kidnapped Angel. l.t. ed. 1983. 216p. pap. 7.95 o.p. (*0-8161-3471-5*, Macmillan Reference USA) Gale Group.

—The Case of the Murdered MacKenzie. 1984. (Masao Masuto Mystery Ser.). 192p. 11.95 o.s.i (*0-385-29337-2*, Delacorte Pr.) Dell Publishing.

—The Case of the Murdered MacKenzie. l.t. ed. 1985. (Nightingale Ser.). 386p. 9.95 o.p. (*0-8161-3771-4*, Macmillan Reference USA) Gale Group.

—The Case of the One-Penny Orange. l.t. ed. 1982. (Nightingale Ser.). lib. bdg. 11.95 o.p. (*0-8161-3334-4*, Macmillan Reference USA) Gale Group.

—The Case of the One-Penny Orange. 1982. (Masao Masuto Mystery Ser.). 176p. pap. o.p. (*0-03-059858-3*, Owl Bks.) Holt, Henry & Co.

—The Case of the Poisoned Eclairs. 1980. pap. 2.25 o.p. (*0-440-11256-7*) Dell Publishing.

—The Case of the Poisoned Eclairs. 1982. (Nightingale Ser.). pap. 9.95 o.p. (*0-8161-3333-6*, Macmillan Reference USA) Gale Group.

—The Case of the Poisoned Eclairs. 1979. o.p. (*0-03-044721-6*) Holt, Henry & Co.

—The Case of the Russian Diplomat. 1979. 1.75 o.s.i (*0-515-04881-X*, 04881-X, Jove) Berkley Publishing Group.

—The Case of the Russian Diplomat. (Masao Masuto Mystery Ser.). 1982. 176p. pap. o.p. (*0-03-059857-5*, Owl Bks.); 1978. o.p. (*0-03-022456-X*) Holt, Henry & Co.

—The Case of the Sliding Pool. 1983. pap. 2.95 o.p. (*0-440-12092-6*); 1981. 10.95 o.s.i (*0-440-01114-0*, Delacorte Pr.) Dell Publishing.

—The Case of the Sliding Pool. 1982. (Nightingale Ser.). pap. 9.95 o.p. (*0-8161-3348-4*, Macmillan Reference USA) Gale Group.

Dexter, Pete. Train. 2003. 288p. 26.00 (*0-385-50591-4*) Doubleday Publishing.

Settings

Fenady, Andrew J. A Night in Beverly Hills. 2003. 257p. 25.95 (*1-59414-068-5*, Five Star) Gale Group.

Harmon, Renee. Beverly Hills Murder Game. 2001. 280p. (Orig.). pap. 21.99 (*1-4010-1200-0*) Xlibris Corp.

Heller, Jane. The Secret Ingredient. l.t. ed. 2002. 523p. 30.95 (*0-7862-3916-6*) Gale Group.

—The Secret Ingredient. 2002. 336p. 24.95 (*0-312-26172-1*); 2003. 352p. reprint ed. mass mkt. 6.99 (*0-312-98673-4*, St. Martin's Paperbacks) St. Martin's Pr.

Leslie, Diane. Fleur de Leigh's Life of Crime: A Novel. 304p. 2000. pap. 12.00 (*0-684-86741-9*); 1999. (Illus.). 23.00 o.s.i (*0-684-85695-6*) Simon & Schuster. (Simon & Schuster).

Martin, Steve. Shopgirl: A Novella. l.t. ed. 2001. (Wheeler Large Print Book Ser.). 151p. 28.95 (*1-58724-012-2*, Wheeler Publishing, Inc.) Gale Group.

—Shopgirl: A Novella. 2001. 112p. pap. 10.95 (*0-7868-8568-8*); 2001. 144p. E-Book 12.95 (*0-7868-7165-2*); 2001. 144p. E-Book 12.95 (*0-7868-7163-6*); 2001. 144p. E-Book 12.95 (*0-7868-7161-X*); 2001. 144p. E-Book 12.95 (*0-7868-7162-8*); 2001. 144p. E-Book 12.95 (*0-7868-7160-1*); 2000. (Illus.). 130p. 17.95 (*0-7868-6658-6*) Hyperion Pr.

Saroyan, Aram. Artists in Trouble: New Stories. 2001. 200p. 30.00 (*1-57423-172-3*); 35.00 (*1-57423-173-1*) Godine, David R. Pub. (Black Sparrow Pr.).

—Artists in Trouble: New Stories. 2001. 200p. pap. 16.50 (*1-57423-171-5*) HarperCollins Pubs.

### BILOXI (MISS.)—FICTION

Barthelme, Frederick. The Brothers: A Novel. 2001. 272p. pap. text 14.00 (*1-58243-130-2*, Counterpoint Pr.) Basic Bks.

Dunbar, Sophie. Redneck Riviera: An Eclaire Mystery. 1998. (Eclaire Mysteries Ser.: Vol. 2). 290p. mass mkt. 5.50 (*1-890768-06-5*, Intrigue Pr.) Corvus Publishing.

Grisham, John. The Partner. 1998. 480p. pap. 7.99 (*0-440-22604-X*); 1998. 480p. mass mkt. 7.99 (*0-440-22476-4*); 1997. mass mkt. 7.99 (*0-440-29555-6*) Dell Publishing.

—The Partner. 1997. 368p. 27.95 (*0-385-47295-1*); 528p. 31.95 o.s.i (*0-385-48578-6*); 368p. 250.00 o.s.i (*0-385-48592-1*) Doubleday Publishing.

—The Partner, Level 5. 2001. pap. 7.66 (*0-582-43406-8*) Longman Publishing Group.

—The Partner. abr. ed. 1997. audio 26.95 (*0-553-47283-6*, 694963); audio compact disk 29.95 (*0-553-45553-2*) Random Hse. Audio Publishing Group. (RH Audio).

—The Partner. 1998. 14.04 (*0-606-15672-0*) Turtleback Bks.

—The Runaway Jury. 1997. 560p. mass mkt. 7.99 (*0-440-22147-1*) Bantam Dell Publishing Group.

—The Runaway Jury. unabr. ed. 1997. audio 80.00 (*0-913369-34-9*, 4198) Books on Tape, Inc.

—The Runaway Jury. 1997. mass mkt. 10.99 (*0-440-22441-1*); 1997. 215.73 o.s.i (*0-440-78693-2*); 1997. 383.52 o.s.i (*0-440-78694-0*); 1996. mass mkt. 7.99 (*0-440-29552-1*) Dell Publishing.

—The Runaway Jury. 1996. 416p. 30.00 (*0-385-47294-3*); 656p. 30.95 o.s.i (*0-385-48015-6*); 416p. 250.00 o.s.i (*0-385-48016-4*) Doubleday Publishing.

—The Runaway Jury, Level 6. 2001. pap. 7.93 (*0-582-43405-X*) Longman Publishing Group.

—The Runaway Jury. abr. ed. 2003. audio 27.95 (*0-553-47282-8*, 693510); 1996. audio compact disk 29.95 (*0-553-45548-6*, ) Random Hse. Audio Publishing Group. (RH Audio).

—The Runaway Jury. l.t. ed. 2003. 704p. pap. 15.95 (*0-375-43344-9*) Random Hse. Large Print.

—The Runaway Jury, unabr. ed. 1997. audio 97.00 (*0-7887-0724-8*, 94901E7) Recorded Bks., LLC.

—The Runaway Jury. 1997. 14.04 (*0-606-18108-3*) Turtleback Bks.

### BLACK CAT RIDGE (TEX.: IMAGINARY PLACE)—FICTION

Cooper, Susan Rogers. A Crooked Little House. 1999. (E. J. Pugh Mysteries Ser.: No. 6). 352p. mass mkt. 5.99 o.s.i (*0-380-79469-1*, Avon Bks.) Morrow/Avon.

—Hickory Dickory Stalk. 1996. (E. J. Pugh Mysteries Ser.). (Orig.). mass mkt. 5.50 o.s.i (*0-380-78155-7*, Avon Bks.) Morrow/Avon.

—Home Again, Home Again. 1997. (E. J. Pugh Mysteries Ser.). mass mkt. 5.99 o.s.i (*0-380-78156-5*, Avon Bks.) Morrow/Avon.

—Not in My Backyard. 1999. (E. J. Pugh Mysteries Ser.). 256p. mass mkt. 5.99 o.s.i (*0-380-80532-4*, Avon Bks.) Morrow/Avon.

—One, Two, What Did Daddy Do? 1996. (E. J. Pugh Mysteries Ser.). mass mkt. 5.50 o.s.i (*0-380-78417-3*, Avon Bks.) Morrow/Avon.

—One, Two, What Did Daddy Do? 1992. 224p. 17.95 o.p. (*0-312-08209-6*, Saint Martin's Minotaur) St. Martin's Pr.

—There Was a Little Girl. 1998. (E. J. Pugh Mysteries Ser.). 224p. mass mkt. 5.50 o.s.i (*0-380-79468-3*, Avon Bks.) Morrow/Avon.

### BLACKSTONE (NEW ENGLAND: IMAGINARY PLACE)—FICTION

Saul, John. Ashes to Ashes: The Dragon's Flame. 1997. (Blackstone Chronicles Ser.: Pt. 3). 86p. mass mkt. 2.99 o.s.i (*0-449-22786-3*, Fawcett) Ballantine Bks.

—Asylum. 1997. (Blackstone Chronicles Ser.: Pt. 6). 128p. mass mkt. 3.99 (*0-449-22794-4*, Fawcett) Ballantine Bks.

—The Blackstone Chronicles. (Blackstone Chronicles Ser.). 1998. (Illus.). 544p. pap. 14.95 (*0-449-00192-X*); 1997. 18.94 o.s.i (*0-449-00197-0*) Ballantine Bks. (Fawcett).

—Day of Reckoning: The Stereoscope. 1997. (Blackstone Chronicles Ser.: Pt. 5). 84p. mass mkt. 2.99 o.s.i (*0-449-22789-8*, Fawcett) Ballantine Bks.

—An Eye for an Eye: The Doll. 1996. (Blackstone Chronicles Ser.: Pt. 1). 82p. mass mkt. 2.99 (*0-449-22781-2*, Fawcett) Ballantine Bks.

—In the Shadow of Evil: The Handkerchief. 1997. (Blackstone Chronicles Ser.: Pt. 4). 96p. mass mkt. 2.99 (*0-449-22788-X*, Fawcett) Ballantine Bks.

—Twist of Fate: The Locket. 1997. (Blackstone Chronicles Ser.: Pt. 2). 86p. mass mkt. 2.99 o.s.i (*0-449-22784-7*, Fawcett) Ballantine Bks.

### BLISS (SASKATCHEWAN: IMAGINARY PLACE)—FICTION

Glover, Ruth. A Place Called Bliss. 2001. (Saskatchewan Saga Ser.: Vol. 1). 240p. (gr. 13 up). pap. 10.99 (*0-8007-5743-2*) Revell, Fleming H. Co.

—With Love from Bliss. 2001. (Saskatchewan Saga Ser.: Vol. 2). 240p. (gr. 13 up). pap. 10.99 (*0-8007-5744-0*) Revell, Fleming H. Co.

### BLOSSOM (OREGON: IMAGINARY PLACE)—FICTION

Freeman, Mary. Bleeding Heart. 2000. (Gardening Mysteries Ser.). 288p. mass mkt. 5.99 o.s.i (*0-425-17669-X*) Berkley Publishing Group.

—Devil's Trumpet. 1999. (Gardening Mysteries Ser.). 272p. (Orig.). mass mkt. 5.99 o.s.i (*0-425-16821-2*, Prime Crime) Berkley Publishing Group.

Freeman, Mary E. Wilkins. Deadly Nightshade. 1999. (Gardening Mysteries Ser.). 224p. mass mkt. 5.99 o.s.i (*0-425-17196-5*, Prime Crime) Berkley Publishing Group.

### BLUE DEER (MONT.: IMAGINARY PLACE)—FICTION

Harrison, Jamie. Blue Deer Thaw: A Mystery. l.t. ed. 2001. (Softcover Ser.). 376p. pap. 23.95 (*1-58724-082-3*, Wheeler Publishing, Inc.) Gale Group.

—Blue Deer Thaw: A Mystery. 2000. 271p. 22.95 (*0-7868-6422-2*) Hyperion Pr.

—Blue Deer Thaw: A Mystery. 2001. 288p. mass mkt. 6.50 (*0-312-97885-5*, St. Martin's Paperbacks) St. Martin's Pr.

—The Edge of the Crazies. 1995. 384p. 20.95 (*0-7868-6085-5*) Hyperion Pr.

—The Edge of the Crazies. 1996. 324p. mass mkt. 6.99 (*0-312-95942-7*, St. Martin's Paperbacks) St. Martin's Pr.

—Going Local. 1996. (Sheriff Jules Clement Ser.: Bk. 2). 323p. 21.95 o.p. (*0-7868-6108-8*) Hyperion Pr.

—Going Local. (Dead Letter Mysteries Ser.). 1998. 336p. mass mkt. 5.99 (*0-312-96484-6*, St. Martin's Paperbacks); Vol. 1. 1997. mass mkt. (*0-312-96271-1*) St. Martin's Pr.

—An Unfortunate Prairie Occurrence. 1998. 304p. 22.95 o.p. (*0-7868-6260-2*) Hyperion Pr.

—An Unfortunate Prairie Occurrence. 1999. (Dead Letter Mysteries Ser.). 400p. mass mkt. 5.99 (*0-312-96829-9*, St. Martin's Paperbacks) St. Martin's Pr.

—An Unfortunate Prairie Occurrence. l.t. ed. 1998. (Americana Ser.). 624p. 28.95 (*0-7862-1459-7*) Thorndike Pr.

### BLUE ISLE (IMAGINARY PLACE)—FICTION

Rusch, Kristine K. The Changeling. 1996. (Fey Ser.: Vol. 2). 640p. mass mkt. 5.99 o.s.i (*0-553-56895-7*, Spectra) Bantam Bks.

—The Resistance. 1998. (Fey Ser.: Vol. 4). 544p. mass mkt. 6.50 o.s.i (*0-553-57713-1*) Bantam Bks.

—The Rival. 1997. (Fey Ser.: No. 3). 592p. mass mkt. 6.50 o.s.i (*0-553-56896-5*, Spectra) Bantam Bks.

—The Sacrifice: The First Book of the Fey. 1995. (Fey Ser.: Vol. 1). 688p. mass mkt. 6.99 o.s.i (*0-553-56894-9*, Spectra) Bantam Bks.

—The Victory. 1998. (Fey Ser.: Vol. 5). 512p. mass mkt. 6.50 o.s.i (*0-553-57714-X*, Spectra) Bantam Bks.

### BLUE RIDGE MOUNTAINS—FICTION

Barr, Nevada & Perry, Anne. Naked Came the Phoenix: A Serial Novel. Talley, Marcia, ed. l.t. ed. 2002. 375p. 30.95 (*0-7862-3639-6*) Gale Group.

—Naked Came the Phoenix: A Serial Novel. Talley, Marcia, ed. 2001. 320p. 24.95 (*0-312-25194-7*, Saint Martin's Minotaur) St. Martin's Pr.

Barr, Nevada, et al. Naked Came the Phoenix: A Serial Novel. Talley, Marcia, ed. 2002. (Illus.). 352p. mass mkt. 6.99 (*0-312-98019-1*, St. Martin's Paperbacks) St. Martin's Pr.

Coe, Marian. Eve's Mountain: A Novel of Passion & Mystery in the Blue Ridge. (Illus.). 1998. 384p. pap. 14.98 o.p. (*0-9633341-5-8*); 4th ed. 2002. 363p. 18.95 (*0-9633341-7-4*) SouthLore Pr.

Feagans, Carolyn T. In the Shadow of the Blue Ridge, Vol. 1. 1998. 389p. pap. 9.95 (*1-890306-10-X*) Warwick Hse. Publishing.

Gwinne, Jean Q. Mollie O'neill. 1997. (Illus.). 224p. 22.95 (*1-879384-31-0*) Cypress Hse.

Hammonds, Michael. Edge of Fear. 1992. 320p. mass mkt. 4.50 o.s.i (*0-8217-3996-4*, Zebra Bks.) Kensington Publishing Corp.

—Edge of Terror. 1993. 320p. mass mkt. 4.50 o.s.i (*0-8217-4224-8*, Zebra Bks.) Kensington Publishing Corp.

Harper, Jon. Blue Ridge. 1995. (Illus.). 160p. (J). pap. 8.95 (*0-9611872-7-1*) Our Child Pr.

Morgan, Robert. The Blue Valley: A Collection of Stories. 2000. 176p. pap. 11.00 (*0-7432-0422-0*, Touchstone) Simon & Schuster.

—The Blue Valleys: A Collection of Stories. 1989. 176p. 15.95 (*0-934601-71-2*) Peachtree Pubs., Ltd.

—The Mountains Won't Remember Us: And Other Stories. 2000. 256p. pap. 12.00 (*0-7432-0421-2*, Touchstone) Simon & Schuster.

—The Mountains Won't Remember Us & Other Stories. 1992. 256p. 15.95 (*1-56145-049-9*) Peachtree Pubs., Ltd.

Parker, Gary E. Highland Grace. 2003. (Blue Ridge Legacy Ser.). 400p. pap. 12.99 (*0-7642-2454-9*) Bethany Hse. Pubs.

—Highland Mercies. 2002. (Blue Ridge Legacy Ser.). 400p. pap. 12.99 (*0-7642-2453-0*) Bethany Hse. Pubs.

### BOLIVIA—FICTION

Aguirre, Nataniel. Juan de la Rosa: Memoirs of the Last Soldier of the Independence Movement. 1999. (Illus.). 368p. pap. 22.50 (*0-19-511328-4*) Oxford Univ. Pr., Inc.

—Juan de la Rosa: Memoirs of the Last Soldier of the Independence Movement. Soldan, Alba M., ed. Waisman, Sergio G., tr. from SPA. 1998. (Library of Latin America). (Illus.). 368p. 30.00 o.p. (*0-19-511327-6*) Oxford Univ. Pr., Inc.

Grace, Alexander M. Coup! A Novel. 1992. (Lyford Bks.). 256p. 19.95 o.p. (*0-89141-418-5*, Presidio Pr.) Ballantine Bks.

Jacobs, Mark. The Liberation of Little Heaven: And Other Stories. 1999. 254p. 23.00 (*1-56947-135-5*) Soho Pr., Inc.

—Stone Cowboy. 1997. 304p. 24.00 (*1-56947-098-7*) Soho Pr., Inc.

—Stone Cowboy: A Novel. 1999. 304p. 13.00 (*1-56947-136-3*) Soho Pr., Inc.

Moore, Marvin. Conquering High Mountains. 1979. (Destiny Ser). pap. 4.95 o.p. (*0-8163-0327-4*, 03514-7) Pacific Pr. Publishing Assn.

Posey, Carl. Bushmaster Fall. 1992. 19.95 o.p. (*1-55611-245-9*) Fine, Donald I. Bks.

Rabinovich, Dalia. Flora's Suitcase. 1998. 256p. o.s.i (*0-06-019137-6*, HarperFlamingo) HarperCollins Pubs. Canada, Ltd.

—Flora's Suitcase: A Novel. 1999. 256p. pap. 13.00 (*0-06-093249-X*) HarperCollins Pubs.

Scalia, Joseph E. Pearl: A New Chapter in an Old Story. 2001. 95p. pap. 16.99 (*1-4010-0045-2*) Xlibris Corp.

### BORDERLANDS (IMAGINARY PLACE)—FICTION

Bull, Emma. Finder. 2003. 320p. (YA). mass mkt. 6.99 (*0-7653-4777-6*, Tor Teen); 1996. 320p. pap. 14.95 (*0-312-86291-1*, Tor Bks.); 1995. 320p. mass mkt. 4.99 (*0-8125-2296-6*, Tor Bks.); 1994. 317p. 21.95 o.p. (*0-312-85418-8*, Tor Bks.) Doherty, Tom Assocs., LLC.

Shetterly, Will. Elsewhere. 1992. (Novel of the Borderlands Ser.). 272p. (YA). reprint ed. pap. text 3.99 (*0-8125-2003-3*, Tor Bks.) Doherty, Tom Assocs., LLC.

—Elsewhere. 1991. 272p. (YA). (gr. 9 up). 16.95 (*0-15-200731-8*) Harcourt Children's Bks.

—Nevernever. 1995. 214p. (YA). (gr. 9-12). reprint ed. pap. text 4.99 (*0-8125-5151-6*, Tor Bks.) Doherty, Tom Assocs., LLC.

—Nevernever. 1993. 256p. (YA). (gr. 9 up). 16.95 o.s.i (*0-15-257022-5*) Harcourt Children's Bks.

Windling, Terri, et al, eds. The Essential Bordertown. 1999. 383p. pap. 14.95 (*0-312-86703-4*, Tor Bks.) Doherty, Tom Assocs., LLC.

### BORDERVILLE (VA.: IMAGINARY PLACE)—FICTION

Landrum, Graham Gordon. The Famous DAR Murder Mystery. 1995. 198p. mass mkt. 4.50 (*0-312-95568-5*, St. Martin's Paperbacks); 1992. 208p. 18.95 o.p. (*0-312-06968-5*, Saint Martin's Minotaur) St. Martin's Pr.

—The Historical Society Murder Mystery. 1996. 224p. text 21.95 o.p. (*0-312-14355-9*, Saint Martin's Minotaur) St. Martin's Pr.

—The Rotary Club Murder Mystery. 1996. 217p. pap. text 4.99 (*0-312-95796-3*, St. Martin's Paperbacks); 1993. 224p. 17.95 o.p. (*0-312-09375-6*, Saint Martin's Minotaur) St. Martin's Pr.

—The Sensational Music Club Mystery. l.t. ed. 1995. 250p. lib. bdg. 21.95 (*0-7838-1278-7*, Macmillan Reference USA) Gale Group.

—The Sensational Music Club Mystery. 208p. 1994. 18.95 o.p. (*0-312-11331-5*, Saint Martin's Minotaur); Vol. 1. 1997. (Sensational Music Club Murder Ser.: Vol. 1). mass mkt. 5.99 (*0-312-96261-4*, St. Martin's Paperbacks) St. Martin's Pr.

### BOSNIA AND HERCEGOVINA—FICTION

Andric, Ivo. The Bridge on the Drina. mass mkt. 0.95 o.p. (*0-451-02143-6*, Signet Bks.); 1967. mass mkt. 0.95 o.p. (*0-451-50347-3*, Signet Classics); 1967. mass mkt. 0.75 o.p. (*0-451-01798-6*, Signet Bks.) NAL.

—The Bridge on the Drina. Edwards, Lovett, tr. 1959. 13.50 o.p. (*0-04-823017-0*) Routledge.

—The Bridge on the Drina. Edwards, Lovett F., tr. from SER. 1977. (Phoenix Book, P746 Ser.). iv, 314p. reprint ed. pap. 12.00 (*0-226-02045-2*, P746) Univ. of Chicago Pr.

—The Days of the Consuls. Hawkesworth, Celia & Rakic, Bogdan, trs. from CRO. 1993. 416p. pap. 27.00 (*1-85610-024-3*) Forest Bks. GBR. *Dist:* Dufour Editions, Inc.

Drakulic, Slavenka. S. A Novel about the Balkans. Ivic, Marko, tr. 2001. 224p. pap. 13.00 (*0-14-029844-4*) Penguin Group (USA) Inc.

—S. A Novel about the Balkans. 2000. 208p. 22.95 o.s.i (*0-670-89097-9*, Viking) Viking Penguin.

Fesperman, Dan. Lie in the Dark. 2000. (Crime - Black Lizard Ser.). 304p. pap. 12.00 (*0-375-70767-0*, Vintage) Knopf Publishing Group.

—Lie in the Dark. pap. o.p. (*1-56947-167-3*); 1999. 288p. 24.00 (*1-56947-153-3*) Soho Pr., Inc.

—The Small Boat of Great Sorrows: A Novel. 2003. 307p. (*1-4000-3047-1*) Knopf, Alfred A. Inc.

Foley, Tom. This Way to Heaven. (Illus.). 2001. 432p. mass mkt. 7.99 (*0-8125-9008-2*); 2000. 352p. 24.95 o.s.i (*0-312-87402-2*) Doherty, Tom Assocs., LLC. (Forge Bks.).

Fullerton, John. The Monkey House. abr. ed. 1997. audio 7.99 o.p. (*1-56740-180-5*, 676, Paperback Nova Audio Bks.); 1996. audio 16.95 o.p. (*1-56100-922-9*, 1297); 1996. audio 23.95 o.p. (*1-56100-712-9*, 178, Bookcassette); 1996. audio 57.25 o.p. (*1-56100-337-9*, 944, Unabridged Library Editions) Brilliance Audio.

—The Monkey House. 1996. o.s.i (*0-517-70695-4*) Crown Publishing Group.

—The Monkey House. 1996. 384p. 23.00 o.s.i (*0-517-70660-1*) Random Hse. Value Publishing.

—The Monkey House. 2000. 286p. 27.50 (*0-593-04052-X*); 347p. pap. 10.95 (*0-553-50475-4*) Transworld Publishers Ltd. GBR. *Dist:* Trafalgar Square.

Hemon, Aleksandar. Nowhere Man. 2002. 256p. 23.95 (*0-385-49924-8*, Talese, Nan A.) Doubleday Publishing.

—Nowhere Man. 2004. 256p. pap. 13.00 (*0-375-72702-7*, Vintage) Knopf Publishing Group.

—The Question of Bruno. 2000. E-Book 18.50 (*1-58945-546-0*) Adobe Systems, Inc.

Jergovic, Miljenko. Sarajevo Marlboro. Tomasevic, Stela, tr. from MIS. 2004. Orig. Title: Sarajevski Marlboro. 180p. pap. 14.00 (*0-9728692-2-0*) Archipelago Bks.

—Sarajevo Marlboro. 1997. Orig. Title: Sarajevski Marlboro. 192p. pap. 13.95 (*0-14-026071-4*) Penguin Bks., Ltd. GBR. *Dist:* Trafalgar Square.

Kent-Payne, Vaughan. Dark Tide. 2003. 242p. 29.95 (*0-7090-7143-4*) Hale, Robert Ltd. GBR. *Dist:* Trafalgar Square.

Morrell, David. Double Image. audio 12.99 (*1-57815-292-5*, 4438); 2002. audio compact disk 14.99 (*1-57815-549-5*, 4438CD5) Media Bks., L. L. C. (Media Bks. Audio Publishing).

—Double Image, Set. abr. ed. 1998. audio 25.00 (*0-7871-1701-3*, Dove Audio) NewStar Media, Inc.

—Double Image. l.t. ed. 1998. (Core Ser.). 599p. 28.95 (*0-7838-0144-0*) Thorndike Pr.

—Double Image. 1998. 448p. 25.00 o.p. (*0-446-51963-4*) Warner Bks., Inc.

—Double Image. Warner, ed. 1999. 528p. reprint ed. mass mkt. 7.50 (*0-446-60696-0*) Warner Bks., Inc.

O'Donnelly, Kristina. Terra Dolorosa. 2000. pap. 15.95 (*1-930574-08-8*) Rose International Publishing Hse., Inc.

Pendleton, Don. Triple Strike. 1998. (StonyMan Ser.: Vol. 37). 352p. per. (*0-373-61921-9*, 1-61921-2, Worldwide Library) Harlequin Enterprises, Ltd.

Radojcic-Kane, Natasha. Homecoming: A Novel. 2002. 192p. 19.95 (*1-56858-239-0*) Four Walls Eight Windows.

Salazar, Michael. Drop Zone. 2001. 336p. mass mkt. 6.50 (*0-553-58133-3*) Bantam Bks.

—Drop Zone. l.t. ed. 2001. (Softcover Ser.). 338p. pap. 23.95 (*1-58724-053-X*, Wheeler Publishing, Inc.) Gale Group.

Samokovlija, Isak, et al. Tales of Old Sarajevo. Lenic, Zdenko, ed. Hawkesworth, Celia & Pribicevic-Zoric, Christina, trs. from CRO. 1997. (Illus.). 192p. 29.50 (*0-85303-332-3*); pap. 17.50 (*0-85303-331-5*) Vallentine Mitchell Pubs. GBR. *Dist:* International Specialized Bk. Services.

Selimovic, Mesa. Death & the Dervish. Rakic, Bogdan, tr. 1996. (Writings from an Unbound Europe). 480p. 64.00 (*0-8101-1296-5*); pap. 24.00 (*0-8101-1297-3*) Northwestern Univ. Pr.

**BOSTON (MASS.)—FICTION**

Abel, Kenneth. Bait. 1995. 384p. mass mkt. 4.99 o.s.i (*0-440-21720-2*) Dell Publishing.

—Bait. l.t. ed. 1994. 411p. lib. bdg. 23.95 (*0-8161-7436-9*, Macmillan Reference USA) Gale Group.

Abrahams, Peter. A Perfect Crime. l.t. ed. 1999. (Core Ser.). 447p. 29.95 o.p. (*0-7838-8476-1*) Thorndike Pr.

Adler, Elizabeth A. Now or Never. l.t. ed. 1997. 448p. mass mkt. 6.99 (*0-440-22464-0*) Dell Publishing.

Allen, Nancy Campbell. Faith of Our Fathers. 2001. (Illus.). 458p. 22.95 (*1-57734-897-4*) Covenant Communications.

Angoff, Charles. When I Was a Boy in Boston. 1977. (Short Story Index Reprint Ser.). (Illus.). 19.95 (*0-8369-3668-X*) Ayer Co. Pubs., Inc.

Arellano, Robert. Fast Eddie, King of the Bees. 2001. (Illus.). 256p. pap. 14.95 (*1-888451-22-X*) Akashic Bks.

Arnold, Margot, pseud. Death of a Voodoo Doll. 1989. 220p. reprint ed. pap. 7.95 (*0-88150-132-8*, Foul Play) Norton, W. W. & Co., Inc.

Barlow, Linda. Leaves of Fortune. 1990. 560p. reprint ed. mass mkt. 4.95 o.s.i (*0-440-20471-2*) Dell Publishing.

Barnes, Linda. The Big Dig. l.t. ed. 2003. lib. bdg. 29.95 (*1-58547-264-6*, Platinum) Ctr. Point Large Print.

—The Big Dig. 2003. 352p. mass mkt. 6.99 (*0-312-98969-5*, St. Martin's Paperbacks); 2002. 288p. 23.95 (*0-312-28270-2*, Saint Martin's Minotaur) St. Martin's Pr.

—Bitter Finish. 1985. 208p. mass mkt. 4.95 o.s.i (*0-449-20690-4*, Fawcett) Ballantine Bks.

—Bitter Finish. l.t. ed. 2000. 263p. lib. bdg. 28.95 (*1-58547-031-7*) Ctr. Point Large Print.

—Bitter Finish. 1994. 272p. mass mkt. 5.99 o.s.i (*0-440-21606-0*) Dell Publishing.

—Bitter Finish. 1983. 192p. 11.95 o.p. (*0-312-08236-3*) St. Martin's Pr.

—Blood Will Have Blood. 1986. 192p. mass mkt. 5.99 o.s.i (*0-449-20901-6*, Fawcett) Ballantine Bks.

—Blood Will Have Blood. 1985. 192p. pap. 2.25 o.p. (*0-380-79368-7*, 79368, Avon Bks.) Morrow/Avon.

—Cities of the Dead. l.t. ed. 1991. 8.95 o.p. (*0-7451-9581-4*, 5059); pap. 10.95 o.p. (*0-7927-0009-0*, 4616) BBC Audiobooks America.

—Cities of the Dead. 1987. mass mkt. 4.99 o.s.i (*0-449-21188-6*, Fawcett) Ballantine Bks.

—Cities of the Dead. 1996. 272p. mass mkt. 5.99 o.s.i (*0-440-22095-5*) Dell Publishing.

—Cities of the Dead. 1985. 224p. 14.95 o.p. (*0-312-13940-3*) St. Martin's Pr.

—Cold Case. 1998. 496p. mass mkt. 5.99 o.s.i (*0-440-21226-X*, Dell Bks.) Dell Publishing.

—Cold Case. l.t. ed. 1997. (Large Print Book Ser.). 27.95 (*1-56895-427-1*, Wheeler Publishing, Inc.) Gale Group.

—Coyote. 1991. 304p. mass mkt. 5.99 o.s.i (*0-440-21089-5*) Dell Publishing.

—Coyote. l.t. ed. 1991. (General Ser.). 332p. lib. bdg. 20.95 (*0-8161-5197-0*, Macmillan Reference USA) Gale Group.

—Coyote. unabr. ed. 1994. audio. (Carlotta Carlyle Mysteries Ser. : No. 3). audio 44.00 (*0-7887-0036-7*, 94235E7) Recorded Bks., LLC.

—Dead Heat. 1985. 256p. mass mkt. 4.99 o.s.i (*0-449-20689-0*, Fawcett) Ballantine Bks.

—Dead Heat. l.t. ed. 2001. 280p. lib. bdg. 26.95 (*1-58547-114-3*) Ctr. Point Large Print.

—Dead Heat. 1995. 288p. mass mkt. 5.99 o.s.i (*0-440-21862-4*) Dell Publishing.

—Dead Heat. 1984. 224p. 11.95 o.p. (*0-312-18498-0*) St. Martin's Pr.

—Flashpoint. l.t. ed. 2000. (Wheeler Large Print Book Ser.). 354p. 26.95 (*1-56895-856-0*, Wheeler Publishing, Inc.) Gale Group.

—Flashpoint. 2001. 432p. mass mkt. 6.99 (*0-7868-8948-9*); 1999. 288p. 22.95 (*0-7868-6317-X*) Hyperion Pr.

—Hardware. 1996. 400p. mass mkt. 5.99 o.s.i (*0-440-21223-5*) Dell Publishing.

—Hardware. unabr. ed. 2000. (Carlotta Carlyle Mysteries Ser. : No. 6). audio 70.00 (*0-7887-0262-9*, 94471E7) Recorded Bks., LLC.

—The Snake Tattoo. 1990. 208p. mass mkt. 5.99 o.s.i (*0-449-21759-0*, Fawcett) Ballantine Bks.

—The Snake Tattoo. l.t. ed. 1990. (General Ser.). 350p. lib. bdg. 19.95 o.p. (*0-8161-4866-X*, Macmillan Reference USA) Gale Group.

—The Snake Tattoo. unabr. ed. 1993. (Carlotta Carlyle Mysteries Ser. : No. 2). audio 44.00 (*1-55690-923-3*, 93419E7) Recorded Bks., LLC.

—The Snake Tattoo. 2004. 320p. mass mkt. 6.99 (*0-312-99355-2*, St. Martin's Paperbacks); 1989. 288p. 17.95 o.p. (*0-312-02643-9*) St. Martin's Pr.

—Snapshot. 1994. 400p. mass mkt. 5.99 o.s.i (*0-440-21220-0*) Dell Publishing.

—Snapshot. l.t. ed. 1994. (Magna Large Print Ser.). 530p. (*0-7505-0706-3*) Magna Large Print Bks. GBR. *Dist:* Ulverscroft Large Print Canada, Ltd.

—Snapshot. unabr. ed. 1994. (Carlotta Carlyle Mysteries Ser. : No. 5). audio 70.00 (*1-55690-969-1*, 94112E7) Recorded Bks., LLC.

—Steel Guitar. 1992. 272p. pap. 19.00 o.s.i (*0-440-61399-X*); mass mkt. 5.99 o.s.i (*0-440-21268-5*) Dell Publishing.

—Steel Guitar. unabr. ed. 1993. (Carlotta Carlyle Mysteries Ser. : No. 4). audio 44.00 (*1-55690-787-7*, 93102E7) Recorded Bks., LLC.

—A Trouble of Fools. 1988. mass mkt. 5.99 o.s.i (*0-449-21640-3*, Fawcett) Ballantine Bks.

—A Trouble of Fools. l.t. ed. 1989. (General Ser.). 370p. lib. bdg. 19.95 o.p. (*0-8161-4714-0*, Macmillan Reference USA) Gale Group.

—A Trouble of Fools. 2001. 224p. mass mkt. 4.50 (*0-7868-8953-5*) Hyperion Pr.

—A Trouble of Fools. unabr. ed. 2000. (Carlotta Carlyle Mysteries Ser. : No. 1). audio 51.00 (*1-55690-834-2*, 93202E7) Recorded Bks., LLC.

—A Trouble of Fools. 1987. 228p. 15.95 o.p. (*0-312-01100-8*) St. Martin's Pr.

Barrett, Andrea. The Forms of Water. 1994. 304p. pap. 12.95 (*0-671-79522-8*, Washington Square Pr.) Simon & Schuster.

—The Forms of Water. Rosenman, Jane, ed. 1993. 304p. 20.00 o.p. (*0-671-79521-X*, Atria) Simon & Schuster.

Bennett, James W. & Raycraft, Donald R. Old Hoss: A Fictional Baseball Biography of Charles Radbourn. 2002. (Illus.). 201p. per. 24.95 (*0-7864-1321-2*) McFarland & Co., Inc. Pubs.

Blake, Cindy. Second Wives. 2000. 432p. mass mkt. 6.99 (*0-312-97121-4*, St. Martin's Paperbacks); 2000. mass mkt. (*0-312-97568-6*); 1999. 336p. 24.95 o.p. (*0-312-19328-9*) St. Martin's Pr.

Blake, Michelle. The Book of Light: A Lily Connor Mystery. 2003. 224p. 24.95 (*0-399-15046-3*) Putnam Publishing Group, The.

—Earth Has No Sorrow. 2001. 272p. 23.95 o.p. (*0-399-14747-0*, Putnam & Grosset) Penguin Group (USA) Inc.

—The Tentmaker: A Lily Connor Mystery. 1999. (Lily Connor Mysteries Ser.). 273p. 23.95 o.p. (*0-399-14577-X*, G. P. Putnam's Sons) Penguin Group (USA) Inc.

Blanchard, Al. The Disappearance of Jenna Drago. 2002. 306p. pap. 19.95 (*0-9718758-8-X*) Koenisha Pubns.

—The Iscariot Conspiracy. 2001. (Leiutenant James Callahan Mystery: Vol. 1). 278p. pap. 19.95 (*0-9700458-6-7*) Koenisha Pubns.

Bradley, Don. Angels in a Harsh World. 1997. pap. text 17.95 (*1-888298-02-2*) Native Planet Publishing.

—Angels in a Harsh World. 1998. 19.95 o.p. (*0-399-14359-9*, G. P. Putnam's Sons) Penguin Group (USA) Inc.

Bradley, Don & Olsten, Haley. Angels in a Harsh World: A Novel. 1999. 320p. reprint ed. pap. 13.00 o.s.i (*0-425-16690-2*) Berkley Publishing Group.

Braver, Gary. Elixir. 2000. 352p. 25.95 (*0-312-87308-5*, Forge Bks.); 2001. 448p. reprint ed. mass mkt. 7.99 (*0-8125-7591-1*, Tor Bks.) Doherty, Tom Assocs., LLC.

Breton, Laurie. Final Exit. 2003. 384p. mass mkt. (*1-55166-660-X*, Mira Bks.) Harlequin Enterprises, Ltd.

Brogan, Jan. Final Copy. 2001. 320p. 25.00 (*0-9678199-4-6*) Larcom Pr.

Bromell, Henry. Little America. 2001. E-Book 19.00 (*1-59061-173-X*) Adobe Systems, Inc.

—Little America. 2002. 416p. pap. 14.00 (*0-375-71891-5*, Vintage) Knopf Publishing Group.

Butler, Pierce. A Riddle of Stars. 1999. 287p. pap. o.p. (*1-58195-007-1*, Zoland Bks., Inc.) Steerforth Pr.

Carroll, James. The City Below. 1996. 432p. pap. 14.00 (*0-395-82522-9*); 1994. 422p. 22.95 o.s.i (*0-395-59070-1*) Houghton Mifflin Co.

Cassara, Ernest. Murder on Beacon Hill. 1995. 201p. (Orig.). pap. 10.00 (*0-9625794-6-7*) Miniver, Anne Pr.

—Murder on Boston Common: A Father Ballou & His Dog Spot Mystery. 1998. 174p. pap. 9.95 (*0-9662870-0-2*) Cambridge Cornerstone Pr.

Cather, Willa. Alexander's Bridge. 1977. reprint ed. lib. bdg. 19.95 (*0-89190-520-0*, Queens Hse., Inc.) Amereon, Ltd.

—Alexander's Bridge, Set. unabr. ed. 1993. audio 20.95 (*1-55685-287-8*) Audio Bk. Contractors, Inc.

—Alexander's Bridge. 2001. per. 12.50 (*1-58396-412-6*); per. 15.50 (*1-58396-413-4*) Blue Unicorn Editions.

—Alexander's Bridge. 1990. reprint ed. lib. bdg. 16.95 (*0-89968-491-2*) Buccaneer Bks., Inc.

—Alexander's Bridge. (Collected Works of Willa Cather). 174p. reprint ed. 2001. pap. 28.00 (*0-7426-5566-0*); 1998. lib. bdg. 88.00 (*1-58201-566-X*) Classic Bks.

—Alexander's Bridge. 2002. (Thrift Editions Ser.). 160p. pap. 2.00 (*0-486-42450-2*) Dover Pubns., Inc.

—Alexander's Bridge. 1999. E-Book 2.49 (*1-58627-088-5*) Electric Umbrella Publishing.

—Alexander's Bridge. l.t. ed. 79p. pap. 13.58 (*0-7583-0120-0*); 336p. pap. 35.67 (*0-7583-0126-X*); 390p. pap. 40.00 (*0-7583-0127-8*); 222p. pap. 26.47 (*0-7583-0124-3*); 99p. pap. 14.60 (*0-7583-0121-9*); 136p. pap. 18.72 (*0-7583-0122-7*); 174p. pap. 22.55 (*0-7583-0123-5*); 273p. pap. 30.60 (*0-7583-0125-1*); 99p. lib. bdg. 20.60 (*0-7583-0113-8*); 136p. lib. bdg. 24.72 (*0-7583-0114-6*); 174p. lib. bdg. 29.66 (*0-7583-0115-4*); 222p. lib. bdg. 34.47 (*0-7583-0116-2*); 273p. lib. bdg. 38.09 (*0-7583-0117-0*); 336p. lib. bdg. 42.54 (*0-7583-0118-9*); 390p. lib. bdg. 46.34 (*0-7583-0119-7*); 79p. lib. bdg. 19.58 (*0-7583-0112-X*) Huge Print Pr.

—Alexander's Bridge. 2001. 128p. 22.99 (*1-58827-482-9*); per. 18.99 (*1-58827-483-7*) IndyPublish.com.

—Alexander's Bridge, l.t. ed. 2001. 135p. lib. bdg. 24.95 net. (*1-58118-080-2*) LRS.

—Alexander's Bridge. 2001. (Twelve-Point Ser.). 205p. lib. bdg. 25.00 (*1-58287-168-X*); 309p. lib. bdg. 26.00 (*1-58287-651-7*) North Bks.

—Alexander's Bridge. Lindemann, Marilee, ed. & intro. by. 1997. (Oxford World's Classics Ser.). 152p. pap. 8.95 o.p. (*0-19-283214-X*) Oxford Univ. Pr., Inc.

—Alexander's Bridge. 1998. 112p. 22.00 (*0-684-81907-4*, Simon & Schuster) Simon & Schuster.

—Alexander's Bridge. (Ebook Classic Ser.). E-Book 5.00 (*0-7410-1301-0*) SoftBook Pr.

—Alexander's Bridge. 1977. 140p. reprint ed. pap. 9.95 (*0-8032-5863-1*, Bison Bks.) Univ. of Nebraska Pr.

—Alexander's Bridge. 1990. xxiii, 176p. pap. 12.00 o.s.i (*1-85381-163-7*) Virago Pr., Ltd. GBR. *Dist:* Trafalgar Square.

—Alexander's Bridge. l.t. ed. 2000. 201p. 16.99 (*1-930142-29-3*); pap. 9.99 (*1-930142-28-5*) Write Together Publishing.

Cather, Willa & O'Brien, Sharon. Alexander's Bridge. 1988. 216p. pap. 6.00 o.p. (*0-452-00875-1*, Meridian Bks.) NAL.

Cavanaugh, Jack. The Colonists. (American Family Portrait Ser.). 500p. (Orig.). pap. 13.99 (*1-56476-346-3*, 6-3346) Cook Communications Ministries.

Ceremony. 1982. 12.95 o.s.i (*0-385-28127-7*) Doubleday Publishing.

Chamberlin, Holly. Living Single. 2004. 352p. mass mkt. 6.99 (*0-7582-0144-3*, Kensington Bks.) Kensington Publishing Corp.

Charyn, Jerome. The Seventh Babe. 1984. 352p. pap. 2.95 o.p. (*0-380-51540-7*, 51540, Avon Bks.); 1979. 9.95 o.p. (*0-87795-220-5*, Morrow, William & Co.) Morrow/Avon.

—The Seventh Babe. 1996. 352p. (C). 46.00 (*0-87805-898-2*); pap. 16.95 (*0-87805-882-6*) Univ. Pr. of Mississippi.

Chute, Carolyn. Snow Man. 256p. 2001. (Illus.). pap. 14.00 (*0-15-601140-9*, Harvest Bks.); 1999. 23.00 o.s.i (*0-15-100390-4*) Harcourt Trade Pubs.

Cluster, Dick. Obligations of the Bone. 1992. 18.95 o.p. (*0-312-08274-6*, Saint Martin's Minotaur) St. Martin's Pr.

Cook, Robin. Harmful Intent. 1991. 368p. mass mkt. 7.99 (*0-425-12546-7*) Berkley Publishing Group.

—Harmful Intent. 1990. 368p. 18.95 o.p. (*0-399-13481-6*, G. P. Putnam's Sons) Penguin Putnam Bks. for Young Readers.

—Harmful Intent. 18.95 o.s.i (*0-399-13700-9*) Putnam Publishing Group, The.

—Harmful Intent. abr. ed. 1999. audio 9.98 (*0-671-77506-5*, Simon & Schuster Audioworks) Simon & Schuster Audio.

—Harmful Intent. l.t. ed. 2000. (Famous Authors Ser.). 663p. 28.95 (*0-7862-2504-1*) Thorndike Pr.

—Harmful Intent. 1991. 14.04 (*0-606-00927-2*) Turtleback Bks.

—Mortal Fear. 1989. 368p. mass mkt. 7.99 (*0-425-11388-4*) Berkley Publishing Group.

—Mortal Fear. 17.95 o.s.i (*0-399-13690-8*) Penguin Group (USA) Inc.

—Mortal Fear. 1988. 368p. 17.95 o.p. (*0-399-13318-6*, G. P. Putnam's Sons) Penguin Putnam Bks. for Young Readers.

—Mortal Fear. 1989. 14.04 (*0-606-00930-2*) Turtleback Bks.

Cooper, James Fenimore. Lionel Lincoln: Or, The Leaguer of Boston. 1985. (Writings of James Fenimore Cooper Ser.). 437p. (C). text 25.50 (*0-87395-416-5*); pap. text 24.95 (*0-87395-671-0*) State Univ. of New York Pr.

Costello, Mark. Bag Men. 2003. 276p. pap. 14.00 (*0-15-602821-2*, Harvest Bks.) Harcourt Trade Pubs.

Craig, Philip R. & Tapply, William G. First Light. l.t. ed. 2002. 443p. 29.95 (*0-7862-4185-3*) Gale Group.

Dailey, Janet. That Boston Man: Massachusetts. l.t. ed. 2000. (G. K. Hall Core Ser.). 216p. 29.95 (*0-7838-9122-9*, Macmillan Reference USA) Gale Group.

—That Boston Man: Massachusetts. 1991. (Americana Ser.: No. 871). mass mkt. (*0-373-89871-1*); 1987. pap. (*0-373-89821-5*) Harlequin Enterprises, Ltd. (Harlequin Bks.).

—That Boston Man: Massachusetts. 2002. 128p. pap. 6.99 (*0-7592-3831-6*); E-Book 6.99 (*0-7592-0172-2*); E-Book 6.99 (*1-58586-392-0*); E-Book 6.99 (*0-7592-0916-2*) ereads.com.

Day, Dianne. Beacon Street Mourning: A Fremont Jones Mystery. 2001. 304p. mass mkt. 5.99 (*0-553-58061-2*) Bantam Bks.

—Beacon Street Mourning: A Fremont Jones Mystery. 2000. (Fremont Jones Mystery Ser.). 288p. 22.95 o.s.i (*0-385-48610-3*) Doubleday Publishing.

Devane, Terry. Juror Number Eleven: A Novel. 2003. 336p. mass mkt. 6.99 (*0-425-19066-8*) Berkley Publishing Group.

—Juror Number Eleven: A Novel. 2002. 320p. 24.95 o.s.i (*0-399-14886-8*) Penguin Group (USA) Inc.

—A Stain upon the Robe. 2004. 352p. mass mkt. 6.99 (*0-425-19742-5*) Berkley Publishing Group.

—A Stain upon the Robe. 2003. 304p. 24.95 (*0-399-15108-7*) Putnam Publishing Group, The.

—Uncommon Justice. 2002. 352p. reprint ed. mass mkt. 6.99 (*0-425-18424-2*) Berkley Publishing Group.

—Uncommon Justice. 2001. 240p. 24.95 o.p. (*0-399-14717-9*) Penguin Group (USA) Inc.

Doolittle, Jerome. Half Nelson. Grose, Bill, ed. 1994. 288p. 20.00 o.p. (*0-671-50289-1*, Atria) Simon & Schuster.

—Half Nelson: A Tom Bethany Mystery. 1995. 288p. mass mkt. 5.50 (*0-671-79979-7*, Pocket) Simon & Schuster.

—Kill Story. 304p. 1996. mass mkt. 5.99 (*0-671-79981-9*, Pocket); 1995. 22.00 o.p. (*0-671-79980-0*, Atria) Simon & Schuster.

—Strangle Hold. Grose, Bill, ed. 1992. 304p. reprint ed. mass mkt. 4.99 (*0-671-74571-9*, Pocket) Simon & Schuster.

—Stranglehold: A Tom Bethany Mystery. 1991. 304p. 20.00 (*0-671-70754-X*, Atria) Simon & Schuster.

Downing, Michael. Perfect Agreement. 1997. 224p. 22.00 (*1-887178-45-7*, Counterpoint Pr.) Basic Bks.

—Perfect Agreement. 1998. 288p. reprint ed. pap. 12.95 o.s.i (*0-425-16628-7*) Berkley Publishing Group.

Drogin, Karen. Solitary Man. 2000. (Romance Ser.: Vol. 74). 256p. mass mkt. 4.99 o.p. (*0-8217-6734-8*) Kensington Publishing Corp.

Dwyer, Kelly. The Tracks of Angels. 1994. 22.95 o.p. (*0-399-13882-X*, G. P. Putnam's Sons) Penguin Group (USA) Inc.

—The Tracks of Angels. 1995. 272p. pap. 17.99 (*0-446-67052-9*) Warner Bks., Inc.

Eastlake, William. The Long Naked Descent into Boston. 1977. (Richard Seaver Bks.). 10.00 o.p. (*0-670-43852-9*) Viking Penguin.

Eidson, Bill. Dangerous Waters. 1991. 304p. 19.95 o.p. (*0-8050-1767-4*) Holt, Henry & Co.

—The Guardian. 1996. 288p. 22.95 o.p. (*0-312-86115-X*, Forge Bks.) Doherty, Tom Assocs., LLC.

—Guardian. 1998. 288p. mass mkt. 5.99 (*0-8125-4444-7*, Tor Bks.) Doherty, Tom Assocs., LLC.

—The Little Brother. 1990. 272p. 18.95 o.p. (*0-8050-1236-2*) Holt, Henry & Co.

—The Little Brother. 1991. 288p. mass mkt. 4.50 o.s.i (*0-8217-3397-4*, Zebra Bks.) Kensington Publishing Corp.

Emmet, Alan. The Mr. & Mrs. Club: A Novel. 224p. 2002. pap. 18.00 (*1-57962-087-6*); 2001. 24.00 (*1-57962-032-9*) Permanent Pr., The.

Engel, Monroe. Fish. 1981. 12.95 o.p. (*0-689-11219-X*, Scribner) Simon & Schuster.

—Fish. 1985. (Phoenix Fiction Ser.). vi, 218p. pap. 6.95 o.s.i (*0-226-20835-4*) Univ. of Chicago Pr.

Ephron, G. H. Amnesia. 2000. 295p. 23.95 (*0-312-26867-X*, Saint Martin's Minotaur) St. Martin's Pr.

—Delusion. E-Book 24.95 (*0-312-70838-6*) St. Martin's Pr.

—Delusion: A Mystery. 2003. 320p. mass mkt. 6.99 (*0-312-99352-8*, St. Martin's Paperbacks); 2002. 336p. 24.95 (*0-312-30500-1*, Saint Martin's Minotaur) St. Martin's Pr.

Faherty, Terence. Orion Rising: An Owen Keane Mystery. 1999. (Owen Keane Mysteries Ser.). 256p. 22.95 (*0-312-20351-9*, Saint Martin's Minotaur) St. Martin's Pr.

Farber, Thomas. Learning to Love It: Seven Stories & a Novella. 1993. 134p. (Orig.). lib. bdg. 31.00 o.p. (*0-8095-4121-1*) Millefleurs.

Fast, Howard. Bunker Hill: The Prequel to the Crossing. 2001. (Illus.). 208p. pap. 14.00 (*0-7434-2384-4*) ibooks, Inc.

—The Crossing. E-Book 11.95 (*1-58824-009-6*) ibooks, Inc.

Fielding, Joy. Don't Cry Now. 1996. 480p. mass mkt. 7.99 (*0-7704-2721-9*) Bantam Bks.

—Don't Cry Now. abr. ed. 1996. audio 7.99 o.p. (*1-56740-111-2*, 1578, Paperback Nova Audio Bks.); 1995. audio 17.95 o.p. (*1-56100-422-7*, 1576, Nova Audio Bks.); 1995. audio 73.25 o.p. (*1-56100-254-2*, 868); 1995. audio 23.95 o.p. (*1-56100-629-7*, 93, Bookcassette) Brilliance Audio.

—Don't Cry Now. l.t. ed. 1995. pap. 21.95 o.p. (*1-56895-259-7*, Wheeler Publishing, Inc.) Gale Group.

—Don't Cry Now. 1996. 400p. mass mkt. 7.99 (*0-380-71153-2*, Avon Bks.); 1995. 356p. (YA). 23.00 o.p. (*0-688-12673-1*, Morrow, William & Co.) Morrow/Avon.

—See Jane Run. unabr. ed. 1991. audio 23.95 o.p. (*0-930435-82-6*, 419, Bookcassette); audio 73.25 o.p. (*1-56100-076-0*, 601, Unabridged Library Editions) Brilliance Audio.

—See Jane Run. l.t. ed. 1992. (Magna Large Print Ser.). 624p. o.p. (*0-7505-0333-5*) Magna Large Print Bks. GBR. *Dist:* Ulverscroft Large Print Canada, Ltd.

—See Jane Run. 1991. 420p. 20.00 o.p. (*0-688-08867-8*, Morrow, William & Co.); 1992. 416p. reprint ed. mass mkt. 7.99 (*0-380-71152-4*, Avon Bks.) Morrow/Avon.

—See Jane Run. abr. ed. 1993. 15.95 o.p. (*1-55800-408-4*) NewStar Media, Inc.

Finder, Joseph. Extraordinary Powers. 1995. 448p. mass mkt. 6.99 o.s.i (*0-345-39436-4*); 1994. 464p. 22.00 o.s.i (*0-345-38621-3*) Ballantine Bks.

—Extraordinary Powers. abr. ed. 1995. audio 8.99 o.s.i (*0-679-44352-5*) Knopf, Alfred A. Inc.

—Extraordinary Powers. 1994. audio 17.00 o.p. (*0-679-43051-2*, RH Audio) Random Hse. Audio Publishing Group.

—High Crimes. abr. ed. 1998. audio 7.99 o.s.i (*1-56740-274-7*, 1682, Paperback Nova Audio Bks.); audio 24.95 o.p. (*1-56100-789-7*, 134, Bookcassette); audio 57.25 (*1-56740-568-1*, 896, Unabridged Library Editions) Brilliance Audio.

—High Crimes. 1999. 400p. mass mkt. 7.99 (*0-380-72880-X*, Avon Bks.); 1998. 352p. 24.95 (*0-688-14962-6*, Morrow, William & Co.) Morrow/Avon.

—High Crimes. l.t. ed. 2000. (Charnwood Large Print Ser.). 440p. (*0-7089-9128-9*, Ulverscroft) Thorpe, F. A. Pubs. GBR. *Dist:* Ulverscroft Large Print Bks., Ltd., Ulverscroft Large Print Canada, Ltd.

—High Crimes. 1999. 13.04 (*0-606-19265-4*) Turtleback Bks.

Flood, John. Bag Men. 1997. 256p. pap. 9.95 o.s.i (*0-385-32000-0*) Doubleday Publishing.

—Bag Men: A Novel. 1997. 240p. 24.00 o.p. (*0-393-03998-6*) Norton, W. W. & Co., Inc.

Flora, Kate. Chosen for Death. 2003. 256p. pap. 13.00 (*1-932325-00-X*) Crum Creek Pr.

—Chosen for Death. 288p. 1995. mass mkt. 4.99 (*0-8125-3429-8*); 1994. 20.95 o.p. (*0-312-85598-2*) Doherty, Tom Assocs., LLC. (Forge Bks.).

—Death at the Wheel. (Thea Kozak Mystery Ser.). 320p. 1998. mass mkt. 5.99 (*0-8125-6484-7*); 1996. 22.95 o.p. (*0-312-85599-0*) Doherty, Tom Assocs., LLC. (Forge Bks.).

—Death in a Funhouse Mirror. 1995. 352p. 23.95 o.p. (*0-312-85600-8*); Vol. 1. 1996. mass mkt. 5.99 o.p. (*0-8125-3432-8*) Doherty, Tom Assocs., LLC. (Forge Bks.).

—An Educated Death. 384p. 1999. mass mkt. 6.99 (*0-8125-7156-8*); 1997. 23.95 (*0-312-86079-X*) Doherty, Tom Assocs., LLC. (Forge Bks.).

Flynn, Jack. Buddy Reardon in Pursuit of the Lone Ranger. 2002. 29.45 (*1-4033-1909-X*); 2001. 276p. pap. 18.67 (*0-7596-2252-3*) 1stBooks Library.

Ford, Elaine. Life Designs. 1997. 192p. 22.95 o.p. (*0-944072-80-1*, Zoland Bks., Inc.) Steerforth Pr.

Franzen, Jonathan. Strong Motion: A Novel. 1992. 508p. 22.95 o.p. (*0-374-27105-4*) Farrar, Straus & Giroux.

—Strong Motion: A Novel. 1993. 512p. pap. 10.95 (*0-393-30996-7*) Norton, W. W. & Co., Inc.

—Strong Motion: A Novel. 2001. 512p. pap. 14.00 (*0-312-42051-X*) Picador.

Frede, Richard. The Nurses, 001. 1985. 480p. 17.95 o.p. (*0-395-38169-X*) Houghton Mifflin Co.

Fredrickson, Michael. A Cinderella Affidavit. 2000. 450p. mass mkt. 6.99 (*0-8125-8013-3*, Tor Bks.); 1999. 384p. 25.95 (*0-312-86723-9*, Forge Bks.) Doherty, Tom Assocs., LLC.

—A Cinderella Affidavit. unabr. ed. 2000. audio compact disk 119.00 (*0-7887-4210-8*, C1139E7); 1999. audio 96.00 (*0-7887-3764-3*, 95981E7) Recorded Bks., LLC.

—Witness for the Dead. 2001. 384p. 25.95 (*0-312-87447-2*, Forge Bks.); 2002. reprint ed. mass mkt. 7.99 (*0-8125-6528-2*, Tor Bks.) Doherty, Tom Assocs., LLC.

French, Allen. The Colonials. E-Book 3.95 (*0-594-02223-1*) 1873 Pr.

Gaines, Charles. Survival Games. 1997. 240p. 23.00 o.p. (*0-87113-684-8*, Atlantic Monthly Pr.) Grove/Atlantic, Inc.

Gardner, Barbara. The Sai Prophecy: A Novel. 1999. (Illus.). 260p. pap. 14.95 (*1-55874-679-X*) Health Communications, Inc.

—The Sai Prophecy: A Novel. 1998. 260p. 21.95 (*0-935699-12-0*) Illumination Arts Publishing Co., Inc.

—The Sai Prophecy: A Novel. 1997. E-Book 14.95 (*0-585-10258-9*) netLibrary, Inc.

Gardner, Lisa. The Other Daughter. 10p. 2003. pap. 94.95 incl. audio compact disk (*0-7927-2901-3*); 2000. audio 84.95 (*0-7927-2356-2*, CSL 245, Chivers Sound Library) BBC Audiobooks America.

—The Other Daughter. 1999. 416p. mass mkt. 7.50 (*0-553-57679-8*) Bantam Bks.

—The Other Daughter. l.t. ed. (Thorndike/G. K. Hall Paperback Bestsellers Ser.). 2000. 523p. 28.95 (*0-7862-2291-3*); 1999. 619p. 31.95 (*0-7862-2290-5*) Thorndike Pr.

Gerritsen, Tess. The Surgeon. 2001. E-Book 19.95 (*1-59061-359-7*) Adobe Systems, Inc.

—The Surgeon. 368p. 2002. mass mkt. 7.99 (*0-345-44784-0*); 2001. 24.95 (*0-345-44783-2*) Ballantine Bks. (Ballantine Bks.).

—The Surgeon. abr. ed. 2001. audio 25.00 (*0-553-52876-9*, RH Audio) Random Hse. Audio Publishing Group.

—The Surgeon. l.t. ed. 2001. 550p. 30.95 (*0-7862-3574-8*); 528p. (*0-7540-1720-6*) Thorndike Pr.

Goldberg, Myra. Rosalind: A Family Romance. 1998. 128p. pap. 13.00 o.p. (*0-944072-60-7*); 1996. 304p. 22.95 o.p. (*0-944072-59-3*) Steerforth Pr. (Zoland Bks., Inc.).

Goodman, Jo. My Reckless Heart. l.t. ed. 2001. (Thorne Brothers Trilogy Ser.). (Illus.). 456p. 26.95 (*0-7862-2947-0*, Five Star) Gale Group.

Gotti, Victoria. The Senator's Daughter. 1998. 320p. mass mkt. 6.99 o.p. (*0-8125-7176-2*); 1997. 304p. 23.95 o.p. (*0-312-86323-3*) Doherty, Tom Assocs., LLC. (Forge Bks.).

—The Senator's Daughter. l.t. ed. 1997. (Core Ser.). 464p. 26.95 (*0-7838-8196-7*, Macmillan Reference USA) Gale Group.

—The Senator's Daughter. abr. ed. 1997. audio 23.00 (*1-56876-065-5*) Soundlines Entertainment, Inc.

—The Senator's Daughter. 1999. 6.99 (*0-312-87111-2*) St. Martin's Pr.

Graham, Brendan. Element of Fire. 2001. 356p. (*0-00-225977-X*) HarperCollins Pubs.

Graham, Heather. Night of the Blackbird. 2001. 384p. mass mkt. (*1-55166-812-2*, Mira Bks.) Harlequin Enterprises, Ltd.

—Night of the Blackbird. l.t. ed. 2002. (Americana Ser.). 566p. 31.95 (*0-7862-3976-X*) Thorndike Pr.

Habegger, Alfred, ed. The Bostonians. 1985. 496p. pap. text 17.33 o.p. (*0-02-348560-4*, Macmillan College) Prentice Hall PTR.

Hawthorne, Nathaniel. The Scarlet Letter. 2002. pap. 3.95 (*1-59109-017-2*) Booksurge, LLC.

—The Scarlet Letter. l.t. ed. 1997. 352p. pap. 19.95 (*1-58855-005-2*) Cyber Classics, Inc.

—The Scarlet Letter. 1972. 3.95 o.p. (*0-460-01122-7*); 1957. 11.50 o.p. (*0-460-00122-1*) Dutton/Plume. (Dutton).

—The Scarlet Letter. 2002. (Illus.). 410p. (*0-9710756-1-1*) Everbind/Marco Bk. Co.

—The Scarlet Letter. 2003. (Barnes & Noble Classics Ser.). 320p. pap. 3.95 (*1-59308-012-3*) Fine Communications.

—The Scarlet Letter. 1977. mass mkt. 1.25 o.p. (*0-451-07499-8*, Signet Bks.); 1973. mass mkt. 0.95 o.p. (*0-451-05362-1*, Signet Bks.); 1959. mass mkt. 0.60 o.p. (*0-451-50650-2*, Signet Classics); 1959. mass mkt. 0.95 o.p. (*0-451-50910-2*, Signet Classics); 1959. mass mkt. 1.25 o.p. (*0-451-51067-4*, Signet Classics); 1959. mass mkt. 1.50 o.p. (*0-451-51188-3*, Signet Classics); 1959. mass mkt. 0.50 o.p. (*0-451-50008-3*, Signet Classics); 1959. mass mkt. 1.75 o.p. (*0-451-51431-9*, Signet Classics); 1959. mass mkt. 1.50 o.p. (*0-451-51232-4*, Signet Classics) NAL.

—The Scarlet Letter. abr. ed. 1995. 29.95 o.p. (*0-7871-0119-2*) NewStar Media, Inc.

—The Scarlet Letter. 2001. E-Book 2.95 (*1-58882-567-1*) PublishingOnline.

—The Scarlet Letter. 2004. 352p. mass mkt. 3.95 (*0-7434-8756-7*, Pocket) Simon & Schuster.

—The Scarlet Letter. (Ebook Classic Ser.). E-Book 5.00 (*0-7410-0475-5*) SoftBook Pr.

—The Scarlet Letter. l.t. ed. 2002. (Perennial Bestsellers Ser.). 435p. 28.95 (*0-7862-4628-6*) Thorndike Pr.

—The Scarlet Letter. 2000. (Signature Classics Ser.). xiv, 298p. 24.95 (*1-58279-071-X*); (*1-58279-077-9*) Trident Pr. International.

—The Scarlet Letter. 2001. 185p. pap. 9.95 (*1-57002-158-9*) University Publishing Hse., Inc.

—The Scarlet Letter. 2002. 272p. pap. 6.00 (*0-14-243726-3*, Penguin Classics) Viking Penguin.

—The Scarlet Letter: Complete Text with Introduction, Historical Contexts, Critical Essays. 2002. (New Riverside Editions Ser.). (Illus.). ix, 418p. pap. 11.56 (*0-618-10734-7*) Houghton Mifflin Co.

Hawthorne, Nathaniel & Martin, John Stephen. The Scarlet Letter. 1998. E-Book 9.95 (*0-585-25257-2*) netLibrary, Inc.

Hayes, Joseph George, ed. This Thing Called Courage: South Boston Stories. 2002. 246p. (C). 27.95 (*1-56023-380-X*, Southern Tier Editions); pap. 17.95 (*1-56023-381-8*, Harrington Park Pr.) Haworth Pr., Inc., The.

Healy, Jeremiah. Act of God. Chelius, Jane, ed. 1995. 336p. mass mkt. 5.50 (*0-671-79559-7*, Pocket); 1994. 352p. 20.00 (*0-671-79558-9*, Atria) Simon & Schuster.

—Blunt Darts. l.t. ed. 1985. lib. bdg. 16.95 o.p. (*0-89340-918-9*, 482) BBC Audiobooks America.

—Blunt Darts. Chelius, Jane, ed. 1991. 192p. reprint ed. mass mkt. 5.50 (*0-671-73742-2*, Pocket) Simon & Schuster.

—Blunt Darts. 1984. 192p. 12.95 o.s.i (*0-8027-5570-4*) Walker & Co.

—Blunt Darts. 1986. 192p. mass mkt. 3.50 o.s.i (*0-445-20210-6*) Warner Bks., Inc.

—The Concise Cuddy: A Collection of John Francis Cuddy Stories. 1998. 293p. pap. 17.00 (*1-885941-27-7*); 42.00 o.p. (*1-885941-26-9*) Crippen & Landru, Pubs.

—Foursome. 1993. 352p. 20.00 (*0-671-79556-2*, Atria) Simon & Schuster.

—Foursome. Chelius, Jane, ed. 1994. 352p. reprint ed. mass mkt. 5.99 (*0-671-79557-0*, Pocket) Simon & Schuster.

—Invasion of Privacy. l.t. ed. 1997. (Large Print Book Ser.). pap. 23.95 (*1-56895-484-0*, Wheeler Publishing, Inc.) Gale Group.

—Invasion of Privacy. (John Francis Cuddy Mystery Ser.). 1997. 320p. pap. 5.99 (*0-671-89874-4*, Pocket); 1996. 352p. 21.00 o.p. (*0-671-89876-0*, Atria) Simon & Schuster.

—The Only Good Lawyer. (John Francis Cuddy Mystery Ser.). 1998. 304p. 23.00 o.s.i (*0-671-00953-2*, Atria); 1999. (Illus.). 400p. reprint ed. pap. 6.99 (*0-671-00954-0*, Pocket) Simon & Schuster.

—Rescue. 1996. 384p. pap. 5.99 (*0-671-89875-2*, Pocket) Simon & Schuster.

—Rescue. Chelius, Jane, ed. 1995. 368p. 20.00 o.p. (*0-671-89877-9*, Atria) Simon & Schuster.

—Right to Die. Chelius, Jane, ed. 1991. 256p. 18.95 o.p. (*0-671-70809-0*, Atria); 1992. 288p. reprint ed. mass mkt. 5.99 (*0-671-70810-4*, Pocket) Simon & Schuster.

—Shallow Graves. Chelius, Jane, ed. 1992. 288p. 19.00 (*0-671-70811-2*, Atria) Simon & Schuster.

—Shallow Graves. 1993. 288p. reprint ed. mass mkt. 5.99 (*0-671-70812-0*, Pocket) Simon & Schuster.

—So Like Sleep. 1987. 256p. 15.95 o.p. (*0-06-015693-7*) HarperTrade.

—So Like Sleep. 1991. mass mkt. 4.50 (*0-671-74328-7*, Pocket) Simon & Schuster.

—Spiral: A John Frances Cuddy Mystery. (John Francis Cuddy Mystery Ser.). 1999. 368p. 23.00 o.s.i (*0-671-00955-9*, Atria); 2000. 400p. reprint ed. pap. 6.99 (*0-671-00956-7*, Pocket) Simon & Schuster.

—The Staked Goat. 1986. 224p. 14.95 o.p. (*0-06-015515-9*) HarperTrade.

—Swan Dive. 1991. mass mkt. 5.99 (*0-671-74329-5*); 1989. mass mkt. 3.95 (*0-671-67185-5*) Simon & Schuster. (Pocket).

—Swan Dive: A Novel of Suspense. 1988. 224p. 16.95 o.p. (*0-06-015921-9*) HarperTrade.

—Yesterday's News: A Novel of Suspense. l.t. ed. 1990. 19.95 o.p. (*0-7927-0586-6*, C0581); pap. 17.95 o.p. (*0-7927-0587-4*) BBC Audiobooks America.

—Yesterday's News: A Novel of Suspense. 1989. 16.95 o.p. (*0-06-015922-7*) HarperTrade.

—Yesterday's News: A Novel of Suspense. Chelius, Jane, ed. 1990. 256p. reprint ed. mass mkt. 5.50 (*0-671-69584-3*, Pocket) Simon & Schuster.

Higgins, George V. The Agent. 1999. 352p. 24.00 o.s.i (*0-15-100357-2*) Harcourt Trade Pubs.

—At End of Day: A Novel of Suspense. 2000. 392p. 24.00 (*0-15-100358-0*); (*0-15-100532-X*) Harcourt Trade Pubs.

—Bomber's Law. unabr. ed. 1994. audio 72.00 (*0-7366-2805-3*, 3519) Books on Tape, Inc.

—Bomber's Law. unabr. ed. 1997. audio 85.00 (*0-7887-0668-3*, 94845E7) Recorded Bks., LLC.

—Bomber's Law: A Novel. 304p. 1994. pap. 11.00 o.s.i (*0-8050-3566-4*, Owl Bks.); 1993. 22.50 o.p. (*0-8050-2329-1*) Holt, Henry & Co.

—A Change of Gravity. unabr. ed. 1998. audio 85.95 (*0-7861-1300-6*, 2212) Blackstone Audio Bks., Inc.

—The Friends of Eddie Coyle. 1980. 176p. mass mkt. 2.50 o.s.i (*0-345-28635-9*) Ballantine Bks.

—The Friends of Eddie Coyle. unabr. collector's ed. 1990. audio 36.00 (*0-7366-1859-7*, 2690) Books on Tape, Inc.

—The Friends of Eddie Coyle. (John MacRae Bks.). 192p. 2000. pap. 13.00 (*0-8050-6598-9*); 1995. pap. 13.00 o.s.i (*0-8050-4152-4*) Holt, Henry & Co. (Owl Bks.).

—The Friends of Eddie Coyle. 1972. 15.95 o.s.i (*0-394-47327-2*) Knopf, Alfred A. Inc.

—The Friends of Eddie Coyle. unabr. ed. 1996. audio. audio 35.00 (*0-7887-0643-8*, 94820E7) Recorded Bks., LLC.

—The Friends of Eddie Coyle. 1987. 192p. mass mkt. 3.95 o.p. (*0-14-010232-9*, Penguin Bks.) Viking Penguin.

Hobbie, Douglas. Boomfell. 1993. 448p. pap. 10.95 o.p. (*0-8050-2663-0*, Owl Bks.); 1991. 288p. 19.95 o.p. (*0-8050-1534-5*) Holt, Henry & Co.

—Boomfell. 1994. 3.99 o.p. (*0-517-11417-8*) Random Hse. Value Publishing.

Howells, William Dean. The Landlord at Lion's Head. 2000. 252p. E-Book 3.95 (*0-594-05125-8*) 1873 Pr.

—The Landlord at Lion's Head. (Illus.). reprint ed. 45.00 (*0-404-14778-X*) AMS Pr., Inc.

—The Landlord at Lion's Head. 1897. (YA). reprint ed. 461p. pap. text 28.00 (*1-4047-6925-0*); 318p. pap. text 28.00 (*1-4047-3250-0*) Classic Textbooks.

—The Landlord at Lion's Head. 1983. (Illus.). 512p. reprint ed. pap. 8.95 o.p. (*0-486-24455-5*) Dover Pubns., Inc.

—The Landlord at Lion's Head. 2002. Vol. 1. 152p. 93.99 (*1-4043-1242-0*); Vol. 1. 152p. per. 88.99 (*1-4043-1243-9*); Vol. 2. 196p. 94.99 (*1-4043-1244-7*); Vol. 2. 196p. per. 89.99 (*1-4043-1245-5*) IndyPublish.com.

—The Landlord at Lion's Head. 1992. (Notable American Authors Ser.). reprint ed. lib. bdg. 75.00 (*0-7812-3250-3*) Reprint Services Corp.

—A Modern Instance. unabr. ed. 1997. (J). (gr. 10 up). audio 65.95 (*1-55685-461-7*, 461-7) Audio Bk. Contractors, Inc.

—A Modern Instance. 1882. 255p. (YA). reprint ed. pap. text 28.00 (*1-4047-3235-7*) Classic Textbooks.

—A Modern Instance, 001. Gibson, W., ed. 1957. (YA). (gr. 9 up). pap. 13.16 o.p. (*0-395-05119-3*, Riverside Editions) Houghton Mifflin Co.

—A Modern Instance. 1977. (Selected Edition of W. D. Howells Ser.: Vol. 10). 608p. 20.00 o.p. (*0-253-33864-6*) Indiana Univ. Pr.

—A Modern Instance. mass mkt. 0.75 o.p. (*0-451-50249-3*, Signet Classics) NAL.

—A Modern Instance. 2003. (Twelve-Point Ser.). lib. bdg. 25.00 (*1-58287-220-1*); lib. bdg. 26.00 (*1-58287-704-1*) North Bks.

—A Modern Instance. 1992. (Notable American Authors Ser.). reprint ed. lib. bdg. 75.00 (*0-7812-3235-X*) Reprint Services Corp.

—A Modern Instance. l.t. ed. 1999. 524p. text 27.95 (*1-56000-487-8*) Transaction Pubs.

—A Modern Instance. 1984. (Classics Ser.). 480p. (C). 14.00 (*0-14-039027-8*, Penguin Classics) Viking Penguin.

—The Rise of Silas Lapham. reprint ed. lib. bdg. 25.95 (*0-89190-456-5*, Rivercity Pr.) Amereon, Ltd.

—The Rise of Silas Lapham. 1990. audio 53.95 (*1-55685-168-5*) Audio Bk. Contractors, Inc.

—The Rise of Silas Lapham. reprint ed. 1992. lib. bdg. 21.95 (*0-89968-261-8*, Lightyear Pr.); 1990. lib. bdg. 21.95 (*0-89968-528-5*) Buccaneer Bks., Inc.

—The Rise of Silas Lapham. 1971. (Selected Edition of W. D. Howells Ser.: Vol. 12). 434p. 29.95 o.p. (*0-253-35016-6*) Indiana Univ. Pr.

—The Rise of Silas Lapham. unabr. ed. 1993. audio 49.00 Jimcin Recordings.

—The Rise of Silas Lapham. 1991. 368p. pap. 10.50 o.s.i (*0-679-72517-2*, Vintage) Knopf Publishing Group.

—The Rise of Silas Lapham. 1998. (Cloth Bound Pocket Ser.). 7.95 (*3-8290-0874-0*, 520657) Konemann.

—The Rise of Silas Lapham. Cook, Don L., ed. 1982. (Critical Editions Ser.). (C). 24.95 o.p. (*0-393-04433-5*); 519p. pap. text 12.00 (*0-393-09165-1*) Norton, W. W. & Co., Inc.

—The Rise of Silas Lapham. Dixson, Robert James, ed. rev. ed. 1988. (American Classics: No. 8). pap. text 5.75 o.p. (*0-13-024589-5*, 18127) Prentice Hall, ESL Dept.

—The Rise of Silas Lapham. 1977. reprint ed. lib. bdg. 21.95 o.s.i (*0-89244-043-0*) Queens Hse./Focus Service.

—The Rise of Silas Lapham. 1992. (Notable American Authors Ser.). reprint ed. lib. bdg. 75.00 (*0-7812-3237-6*) Reprint Services Corp.

—The Rise of Silas Lapham. 1983. (American Library). 400p. pap. 12.00 (*0-14-039030-8*, Penguin Classics) Viking Penguin.

Hughes, Dean. Lucky Fights Back. 1991. (Lucky Ladd Ser.: Bk. 4). 150p. (Orig.). (J). (gr. 3-6). pap. text 4.95 (*0-87579-559-5*, Cinnamon Tree) Deseret Bk. Co.

Hughes, Richard. Bound for Boston. Wheeler, Jill, ed. 1989. (Great Cities Adventures Ser.). (Illus.). 48p. (J). (gr. 4). lib. bdg. 10.95 o.p. (*0-939179-44-X*) ABDO Publishing Co.

James, Henry. The Bostonians. 2000. 252p. E-Book 3.95 (*0-594-06195-4*) 1873 Pr.

—The Bostonians. 1976. 27.95 (*0-8488-0542-9*) Amereon, Ltd.

—The Bostonians. 1984. 416p. mass mkt. 2.95 o.s.i (*0-553-21153-6*, Bantam Classics) Bantam Bks.

—The Bostonians. 1999. 462p. pap. 9.95 o.p. (*1-930128-02-9*, JNMedia Bks.) JNMedia, Inc.

—The Bostonians. 1992. 17.00 (*0-679-41150-2*, Everyman's Library); 1991. 448p. pap. 10.50 o.s.i (*0-679-73381-7*, Vintage) Knopf Publishing Group.

—The Bostonians. 1992. (Everyman's Library: Vol. 82). 442p. 20.00 (*0-679-41750-8*) Knopf, Alfred A. Inc.

—The Bostonians. 1964. (Modern Library College Editions Ser.). 464p. (C). pap. 10.63 o.p. (*0-07-553642-0*, T59, McGraw-Hill Humanities, Social Sciences & World Languages) McGraw-Hill Higher Education.

—The Bostonians. 1984. 384p. mass mkt. 3.50 o.p. (*0-451-52550-7*, CE1285); 1980. mass mkt. 2.95 o.p. (*0-451-51285-5*) NAL. (Signet Classics).

—The Bostonians. Gooder, R. D., ed. & intro. by. 1998. (Oxford World's Classics Ser.). (Illus.). 504p. pap. 7.95 (*0-19-283442-8*) Oxford Univ. Pr., Inc.

—The Bostonians. 2003. 496p. pap. 8.95 (*0-8129-6996-0*, Modern Library) Random House Adult Trade Publishing Group.

—The Bostonians. 1994. 464p. pap. 4.95 (*0-460-87493-4*, Everyman's Classic Library in Paperback) Tuttle Publishing.

—The Bostonians. 2001. (Classics Ser.). 480p. pap. 9.00 (*0-14-043766-5*, Penguin Classics) Viking Penguin.

—The Bostonians. Anderson, Charles, ed. & intro. by. 1984. (Penguin Classics Ser.). 448p. pap. 8.95 o.s.i (*0-14-043225-6*, Penguin Classics) Viking Penguin.

—The Bostonians. 1974. 400p. pap. 2.95 o.p. (*0-14-002450-6*, Penguin Bks.) Viking Penguin.

—The Bostonians. Gooder, R. D., ed. & intro. by. 1985. 498p. (C). pap. 5.95 o.p. (*0-19-281639-X*) Oxford Univ. Pr., Inc.

—The Bostonians, Set. unabr. ed. 1989. audio 71.95 (*1-55685-150-2*) Audio Bk. Contractors, Inc.

—The Bostonians. 1986. 384p. reprint ed. lib. bdg. 25.95 (*0-89966-522-5*) Buccaneer Bks., Inc.

—The Bostonians. l.t. ed. 2000. (Large Print Ser.). 606p. lib. bdg. 28.00 (*1-58287-608-8*); 250p. reprint ed. lib. bdg. 25.00 (*1-58287-131-0*) North Bks.

—The Bostonians. 1992. (Notable American Authors Ser.). reprint ed. lib. bdg. 75.00 (*0-7812-3387-9*) Reprint Services Corp.

—The Europeans. l.t. ed. 2001. per. 15.50 (*1-58396-136-4*); 200p. per. 9.90 (*1-58396-039-2*) Blue Unicorn Editions.

—The Europeans. 1987. 166p. reprint ed. lib. bdg. 25.95 (*0-89966-608-6*) Buccaneer Bks., Inc.

—The Europeans. 1999. E-Book 2.49 (*1-58627-944-0*) Electric Umbrella Publishing.

—The Europeans. l.t. ed. 723p. pap. 57.18 (*0-7583-0862-0*); 478p. pap. 40.76 (*0-7583-0860-4*); 374p. pap. 32.97 (*0-7583-0859-0*); 839p. pap. 66.86 (*0-7583-0863-9*); 292p. pap. 26.47 (*0-7583-0858-2*); 213p. pap. 21.06 (*0-7583-0857-4*); 170p. pap. 18.64 (*0-7583-0856-6*); 588p. pap. 48.94 (*0-7583-0861-2*); 213p. lib. bdg. 27.06 (*0-7583-0849-3*); 170p. lib. bdg. 24.64 (*0-7583-0848-5*); 374p. lib. bdg. 38.97 (*0-7583-0851-5*); 478p. lib. bdg. 46.76 (*0-7583-0852-3*); 588p. lib. bdg. 54.94 (*0-7583-0853-1*); 839p. lib. bdg. 85.08 (*0-7583-0855-8*); 292p. lib. bdg. 32.47 (*0-7583-0850-7*); 723p. lib. bdg. 63.18 (*0-7583-0854-X*) Huge Print Pr.

—The Europeans. 1964. pap. 4.95 o.p. (*0-452-01021-7*, Meridian Bks.); mass mkt. 1.75 o.p. (*0-451-51351-7*, CE 1351, Signet Classics); mass mkt. 0.60 o.p. (*0-451-50232-9*, Signet Classics) NAL.

—The Europeans. Ross, Ain C., ed. 2nd ed. 1985. (Oxford World's Classics Ser.). 208p. (C). reprint ed. pap. 5.95 o.p. (*0-19-281683-7*) Oxford Univ. Pr., Inc.

—The Europeans. 1979. pap. 2.50 o.p. (*0-14-005398-0*); 1975. pap. 2.50 o.p. (*0-14-002070-5*) Penguin Group (USA) Inc.

—The Europeans. 1976. 176p. reprint ed. lib. bdg. 18.95 (*0-89244-018-X*) Queens Hse./Focus Service.

—The Europeans. 1992. (Notable American Authors Ser.). reprint ed. lib. bdg. 75.00 (*0-7812-3372-0*) Reprint Services Corp.

—The Europeans. 1980. 8.00 o.p. (*0-8446-5205-9*) Smith, Peter Pub., Inc.

—The Europeans. (Ebook Classic Ser.). E-Book 5.00 (*0-7410-0438-0*) SoftBook Pr.

—The Europeans. l.t. ed. 2000. (Perennial Bestsellers Ser.). 255p. 26.95 (*0-7838-9060-5*) Thorndike Pr.

—The Europeans. Tanner, Tony, ed. & intro. by. 1985. (Classics Ser.). 576p. 7.95 (*0-14-043232-9*, Penguin Classics) Viking Penguin.

—The Europeans. 1998. (Classics Library). 160p. pap. 3.95 (*1-85326-262-5*, 2625WW) Wordsworth Editions, Ltd. GBR. *Dist:* Combined Publishing.

—The Europeans: A Sketch. Ross, Ian C., ed. & intro. by. 2000. (Oxford World's Classics Ser.). 208p. pap. 7.95 (*0-19-283500-9*) Oxford Univ. Pr., Inc.

Johnson, Darlene. As We Lay: A Novel. 2003. 368p. pap. 13.95 (*0-375-75842-9*, Villard Bks.) Random House Adult Trade Publishing Group.

Johnstone, William W. Rage of the Mountain Man. 1996. mass mkt. 4.99 o.s.i (*0-8217-5361-4*); 1994. 288p. mass mkt. 3.99 o.s.i (*0-8217-4567-0*) Kensington Publishing Corp. (Zebra Bks.).

—Rage of the Mountain Man. 2003. (Western Ser.). 25.95 (*0-7862-4633-2*) Thorndike Pr.

Joyce, Joe. Trigger Man: A Novel. 1991. 18.95 o.p. (*0-393-02980-8*) Norton, W. W. & Co., Inc.

Juniper, Alex. A Very Proper Death. l.t. ed. 1992. 18.95 o.p. (*0-7451-8384-0*); pap. 16.95 o.p. (*0-7927-1124-6*) BBC Audiobooks America.

—A Very Proper Death. 1991. 256p. 18.95 o.s.i (*0-684-19301-9*, Scribner) Simon & Schuster.

Kennedy, Raud A. Sex on the Beach. 2000. 156p. pap. 20.99 (*0-7388-2386-4*) Xlibris Corp.

Kenney, Charles. Code of Vengeance. 1997. mass mkt. 5.99 o.s.i (*0-449-28779-3*, Fawcett) Ballantine Bks.

—Code of Vengeance. 1995. 303p. 22.00 (*0-671-89697-0*, Simon & Schuster) Simon & Schuster.

—The Last Man. 2002. 352p. mass mkt. 6.99 (*0-345-44180-X*) Ballantine Bks.

Kilmer, Nicholas. Dirty Linen. 1999. (Fred Taylor Mystery Ser.). 256p. 25.00 o.s.i (*0-8050-5034-5*) Holt, Henry & Co.

—Dirty Linen. 2001. 218p. pap. 14.95 o.s.i (*1-890208-53-1*) Poisoned Pen Pr.

—Harmony in Flesh & Black. 1995. 261p. 21.00 o.p. (*0-8050-3663-6*) Holt, Henry & Co.

—Harmony in Flesh & Black. 1996. 272p. mass mkt. 4.99 o.p. (*0-06-104425-3*, HarperTorch) Morrow/Avon.

—Man with a Squirrel. unabr. ed. 1997. audio 44.95 (*0-7861-1226-3*, 1969) Blackstone Audio Bks., Inc.

—Man with a Squirrel. 1996. 88p. 22.50 o.p. (*0-8050-3666-0*) Holt, Henry & Co.

—O Sacred Head. 1997. 288p. 23.00 o.p. (*0-8050-5033-7*) Holt, Henry & Co.

Kinsman, Lawrence. Birds of Prey: A Detective Novel. 2nd ed. 2002. 330p. 25.00 (*0-9648817-4-8*); 350p. pap. 15.00 (*0-9648817-5-6*) Abelard Pr., The.

Klass, Perri. The Mystery of Breathing: A Novel. 2004. 288p. tchr. ed. 24.00 (*0-618-10961-7*) Houghton Mifflin Co.

Knight, Kathryn L. Dark Swan. 1996. (WWL Mystery Ser.). per. (*0-373-26203-5*, 1-26203-9, Worldwide Library) Harlequin Enterprises, Ltd.

—Dark Swan. 1994. 224p. 19.95 o.p. (*0-312-10961-X*, Saint Martin's Minotaur) St. Martin's Pr.

—Mortal Words. 1990. 17.95 o.p. (*0-671-68446-9*, Simon & Schuster) Simon & Schuster.

—Mortal Words. Chelius, Jane, ed. 1991. 352p. reprint ed. mass mkt. 4.50 (*0-671-68449-3*, Pocket) Simon & Schuster.

—Mumbo Jumbo. 1991. 17.95 o.p. (*0-671-68448-5*, Simon & Schuster) Simon & Schuster.

—Mumbo Jumbo. Chelius, Jane, ed. 1992. 224p. reprint ed. mass mkt. 4.99 (*0-671-68447-7*, Pocket) Simon & Schuster.

—Trace Elements. 1986. 15.95 o.p. (*0-393-02333-8*) Norton, W. W. & Co., Inc.

—Trace Elements. 1987. mass mkt. 3.50 (*0-671-64089-5*, Pocket) Simon & Schuster.

Kraft, Eric. Reservations Recommended. 1995. 288p. pap. 12.00 (*0-312-13597-1*) Picador.

—Reservations Recommended. 1992. 2.99 o.p. (*0-517-08814-2*); 1991. 2.99 o.p. (*0-517-07617-9*) Random Hse. Value Publishing.

Lamb, J. Dayne. A Question of Preference: A Teal Stewart Mystery. 1995. mass mkt. 4.99 o.s.i (*0-8217-5099-2*); 1994. 304p. mass mkt. 16.95 o.s.i (*0-8217-4631-6*) Kensington Publishing Corp.

—Questionable Behavior. 1993. 288p. mass mkt. 3.99 o.s.i (*0-8217-4333-3*, Zebra Bks.) Kensington Publishing Corp.

—Unquestioned Loyalty: A Teal Stewart Mystery. 1996. 352p. mass mkt. 4.99 o.s.i (*1-57566-054-7*); 1995. mass mkt. 16.95 o.s.i (*0-8217-5090-9*) Kensington Publishing Corp.

Landay, William. Mission Flats. 2003. 384p. 23.95 (*0-385-33614-4*, Delacorte Pr.); E-Book (*0-440-33455-1*) Dell Publishing.

LeClaire, Anne D. Sideshow. 1995. 400p. mass mkt. 5.99 o.s.i (*0-451-40610-9*, Onyx) NAL.

—Sideshow. 308p. 3.98 o.p. (*0-8317-4551-7*) Smithmark Pubs., Inc.

—Sideshow. 1994. 320p. 20.95 o.p. (*0-670-84328-8*, Viking) Viking Penguin.

Lee, Linda Francis. Nightingale's Gate. 2001. 352p. mass mkt. 6.99 (*0-449-00207-1*, Ivy Bks.) Ballantine Bks.

Lee, Michael. Paradise Dance. 2002. 211p. pap. 14.95 (*0-9679520-6-9*) Leapfrog Pr.

Lee, Wendi. Crazy Like a Fox: An Angela Matelli Mystery. 2002. 240p. 22.95 (*0-312-26139-X*, Saint Martin's Minotaur) St. Martin's Pr.

—Deadbeat. 2000. 256p. mass mkt. (*0-373-26339-2*, Harlequin Bks.) Harlequin Enterprises, Ltd.

—Deadbeat. 1999. (Angela Matelli Mysteries Ser.). 256p. 22.95 o.p. (*0-312-16812-8*, Saint Martin's Minotaur) St. Martin's Pr.

—The Good Daughter. 1996. pap. 4.99 (*0-312-95696-7*, St. Martin's Paperbacks); 1994. 224p. 19.95 o.p. (*0-312-11259-9*, Saint Martin's Minotaur) St. Martin's Pr.

—He Who Dies. 2001. (WWL Mystery Ser.: No. 386). 252p. mass mkt. (*0-373-26386-4*, Worldwide Library) Harlequin Enterprises, Ltd.

—He Who Dies. E-Book 5.99 (*0-312-27437-8*) St. Martin's Pr.

—He Who Dies: An Angela Matelli Mystery. 2000. (Angela Matelli Mysteries Ser.). 247p. 23.95 (*0-312-20894-4*, Saint Martin's Minotaur) St. Martin's Pr.

—Missing Eden. 1999. per. (*0-373-26301-5*, Harlequin Bks.) Harlequin Enterprises, Ltd.

—Missing Eden. 1996. 240p. 21.95 o.p. (*0-312-14370-2*, Saint Martin's Minotaur) St. Martin's Pr.

Lehane, Dennis. Darkness, Take My Hand. 1996. 320p. 24.00 (*0-688-14380-6*, Morrow, William & Co.) Morrow/Avon.

—A Drink Before the War. 2003. 300p. pap. 14.00 (*0-15-602902-2*, Harvest Bks.); 1994. 288p. 22.95 (*0-15-100093-X*) Harcourt Trade Pubs.

—A Drink Before the War. 1996. 320p. mass mkt. 7.99 (*0-380-72623-8*, Avon Bks.) Morrow/Avon.

—A Drink Before the War. 336p. (*0-7278-5537-9*) Severn Hse. Pubs., Ltd.

—Gone, Baby, Gone. abr. ed. 1999. audio 7.99 o.s.i (*1-56740-305-0*, 1869, Paperback Nova Audio Bks.); 1998. audio 17.95 o.p. (*1-56740-783-8*, 450, Nova Audio Bks.); 1998. audio 26.95 (*1-56740-058-2*, 18, Bookcassette); 1998. audio 73.25 (*1-56740-587-8*, 881, Unabridged Library Editions) Brilliance Audio.

—Gone, Baby, Gone. 1999. 448p. mass mkt. 7.99 (*0-380-73035-9*, Avon Bks.); 1998. 256p. 24.00 (*0-688-15332-1*, Morrow, William & Co.) Morrow/Avon.

—Mystic River. 2002. 496p. mass mkt. 7.99 (*0-06-009310-2*) HarperCollins Pubs.

—Mystic River. 2003. 416p. pap. 13.95 (*0-06-058475-0*) HarperTrade.

—Mystic River. 2002. 496p. mass mkt. 7.99 (*0-380-73185-1*); 2001. 416p. 25.00 (*0-688-16316-5*, Morrow, William & Co.); 2001. 640p. pap. 25.00 (*0-06-018563-5*, Morrow, William & Co.) Morrow/Avon.

—Prayers for Rain. abr. ed. 1999. audio 17.95 o.p. (*1-56740-840-0*, 1698, Nova Audio Bks.); audio 35.95 (*1-56740-428-6*, 1696, Brilliance Audio Unabridged); audio 57.25 (*1-56740-654-8*, 1697, Unabridged Library Editions) Brilliance Audio.

—Prayers for Rain, Set. abr. ed. 1999. audio 17.95. audio 35.95 Highsmith Inc.

—Prayers for Rain. 2000. 416p. mass mkt. 7.99 (*0-380-73036-7*); 1999. 352p. 25.00 (*0-688-15333-X*, Morrow, William & Co.) Morrow/Avon.

—Prayers for Rain. l.t. ed. 1999. (Core Ser.). 570p. 29.95 (*0-7838-8786-8*) Thorndike Pr.

—Sacred. abr. ed. 1998. audio 7.99 o.p. (*1-56740-238-0*, 1650, Nova Audio Bks.); 1997. audio 16.95 o.p. (*1-56100-979-2*, 505, Nova Audio Bks.); 1997. audio 73.25 o.p. (*1-56100-829-X*, 1022, Unabridged Library Editions); 1997. audio 23.95 (*1-56100-754-4*, 244, Bookcassette) Brilliance Audio.

—Sacred. 1998. 400p. mass mkt. 7.99 (*0-380-72629-7*, Avon Bks.); 1997. 256p. 23.00 (*0-688-14381-4*, Morrow, William & Co.) Morrow/Avon.

Lesourd, Leonard. The Rookie. 1996. 18.99 (*0-345-40504-8*) Ballantine Bks.

Let's Go, Inc. Staff. Boston. rev. ed. 2000. (Let's Go City Guides). (Illus.). 336p. pap. 16.99 (*0-312-24692-7*, Let's Go Pubns.) St. Martin's Pr.

Lipman, Elinor. The Ladies' Man. l.t. ed. 2000. 26.95 (*1-56895-837-4*, Wheeler Publishing, Inc.) Gale Group.

—The Ladies' Man. 2000. (Contemporaries Ser.). 272p. pap. 13.00 (*0-375-70731-X*, Vintage) Knopf Publishing Group.

—The Pursuit of Alice Thrift. 2004. 288p. pap. 12.95 (*0-375-72459-1*, Vintage) Knopf Publishing Group.

—The Pursuit of Alice Thrift: A Novel. 2003. 288p. 23.95 (*0-679-46313-5*) Random Hse., Inc.

Little, Eddie. Steel Toes. 2001. 320p. 23.95 (*0-312-28291-5*, L. A. Weekly Bks.) St. Martin's Pr.

—Steel Toes: A Novel. 2002. 320p. pap. 13.95 (*0-312-30320-3*, L. A. Weekly Bks.) St. Martin's Pr.

Logan, Margaret. The End of an Altruist. 1993. 288p. 21.95 o.p. (*0-312-10459-6*, Saint Martin's Minotaur) St. Martin's Pr.

—Never Let a Stranger in Your House. 1995. 256p. 21.95 o.p. (*0-312-13130-5*, Saint Martin's Minotaur) St. Martin's Pr.

Lowry, Lois. Taking Care of Terrific, 001. 1983. 176p. (J). (gr. 4-6). 16.00 (*0-395-34070-5*) Houghton Mifflin Co.

—Taking Care of Terrific. l.t. ed. 1989. 208p. (YA). reprint ed. lib. bdg. 16.95 o.s.i (*1-55736-119-3*, Cornerstone Bks.) Pages, Inc.

MacLeod, Charlotte. The Balloon Man. 1998. (Sarah Kelling & Max Bittersohn Mysteries Ser.). 240p. 23.00 o.s.i (*0-89296-657-2*) Mysterious Pr.

—The Balloon Man. 2000. 288p. mass mkt. 6.50 (*0-446-60835-1*) Warner Bks., Inc.

—The Bilbao Looking Glass. 1983. (Crime Club Ser.). 192p. 11.95 o.p. (*0-385-18336-4*) Doubleday Publishing.

—The Bilbao Looking Glass. 1984. 208p. pap. 3.50 (*0-380-67454-8*, Avon Bks.) Morrow/Avon.

—The Bilbao Looking Glass. 2003. 192p. pap. 6.99 (*0-7434-7492-9*) ibooks, Inc.

—The Convivial Codfish. 1984. (Crime Club Ser.). 192p. 11.95 o.p. (*0-385-19333-5*) Doubleday Publishing.

—The Convivial Codfish. 1985. 224p. pap. 3.50 (*0-380-69865-X*, Avon Bks.) Morrow/Avon.

—The Family Vault. 1979. 10.95 o.p. (*0-385-14871-2*) Doubleday Publishing.

—The Family Vault. 1980. 240p. mass mkt. 4.50 (*0-380-49080-3*, Avon Bks.) Morrow/Avon.

—The Gladstone Bag: A Sarah Kelling Mystery. 1990. 16.95 o.p. (*0-89296-370-0*) Mysterious Pr.

—The Gladstone Bag: A Sarah Kelling Mystery. 1992. 3.99 o.p. (*0-517-08076-1*) Random Hse. Value Publishing.

—The Gladstone Bag: A Sarah Kelling Mystery. 1991. mass mkt. 5.99 o.p. (*0-446-40002-5*, Mysterious Pr. Paperback Bks.) Warner Bks., Inc.

—The Odd Job. l.t. ed. 1995. 352p. reprint ed. 21.95 o.p. (*0-7838-1374-0*, Macmillan Reference USA) Gale Group.

—The Odd Job. 1995. 288p. 18.95 o.s.i (*0-89296-571-1*) Mysterious Pr.

—The Odd Job. 1996. 272p. mass mkt. 5.99 o.p. (*0-446-40397-0*) Warner Bks., Inc.

—The Palace Guard. 1981. 192p. 10.95 o.p. (*0-385-17533-7*) Doubleday Publishing.

—The Palace Guard. 1982. 176p. mass mkt. 3.99 (*0-380-59857-4*, Avon Bks.) Morrow/Avon.

—The Palace Guard. l.t. ed. 1982. 325p. reprint ed. 11.95 o.p. (*0-89621-345-5*) Thorndike Pr.

—The Palace Guard. 2003. 192p. mass mkt. 6.99 (*0-7434-5912-1*) ibooks, Inc.

—The Plain Old Man. 1985. (Crime Club Ser.). 192p. 12.95 o.p. (*0-385-23003-6*) Doubleday Publishing.

—The Plain Old Man. l.t. ed. 1986. (Nightingale Ser.). 336p. 10.95 o.p. (*0-8161-4025-1*, Macmillan Reference USA) Gale Group.

—The Plain Old Man. 1986. 224p. mass mkt. 3.99 (*0-380-70148-0*, Avon Bks.) Morrow/Avon.

—The Plain Old Man. 2003. 224p. mass mkt. 6.99 (*0-7434-7479-1*) ibooks, Inc.

—The Recycled Citizen. l.t. ed. 1989. (General Ser.). 352p. lib. bdg. 19.95 o.p. (*0-8161-4777-9*, Macmillan Reference USA) Gale Group.

—The Recycled Citizen. 1988. 208p. 15.45 o.p. (*0-89296-187-2*) Mysterious Pr.

—The Recycled Citizen. 1992. 4.50 (*0-446-77518-5*); 1989. 272p. mass mkt. 4.99 o.p. (*0-445-40689-5*, Mysterious Pr. Paperback Bks.) Warner Bks., Inc.

—The Resurrection Man: A Sarah Kelling & Max Bittersohn Mystery. l.t. ed. 1993. (Magna Large Print Ser.). 381p. o.p. (*0-7505-0496-X*) Magna Large Print Bks. GBR. *Dist:* Ulverscroft Large Print Canada, Ltd.

—The Resurrection Man: A Sarah Kelling & Max Bittersohn Mystery. 1992. 256p. 17.95 o.p. (*0-89296-443-X*) Mysterious Pr.

—The Resurrection Man: A Sarah Kelling & Max Bittersohn Mystery. 1993. 256p. mass mkt. 5.99 o.p. (*0-446-40332-6*, Mysterious Pr. Paperback Bks.) Warner Bks., Inc.

—The Resurrection Man: A Sarah Kelling & Max Bittersohn Mystery. 2001. 256p. mass mkt. 6.99 (*0-7434-2377-1*) ibooks, Inc.

—The Silver Ghost: A Sarah Kelling Mystery. l.t. ed. 1990. (Magna Large Print Ser.). 339p. 29.99 o.p. (*1-85057-592-4*) Magna Large Print Bks. GBR. *Dist:* Ulverscroft Large Print Bks., Ltd., Ulverscroft Large Print Canada, Ltd.

—The Silver Ghost: A Sarah Kelling Mystery. 1988. (Sarah Kelling Mystery Ser.). 224p. 15.95 (*0-89296-189-9*) Mysterious Pr.

—The Silver Ghost: A Sarah Kelling Mystery. 1989. 224p. reprint ed. mass mkt. 4.99 o.p. (*0-445-40828-6*, Mysterious Pr. Paperback Bks.) Warner Bks., Inc.

—The Withdrawing Room. 1980. (Crime Club Ser.). 192p. 8.95 o.p. (*0-385-17181-1*) Doubleday Publishing.

—The Withdrawing Room. 1982. 192p. mass mkt. 3.99 (*0-380-56473-4*, Avon Bks.) Morrow/Avon.

—The Withdrawing Room. 2002. 192p. pap. 6.99 (*0-7434-5258-5*) ibooks, Inc.

Maddison, Lauren. Epitaph for an Angel: A Connor Hawthorne Mystery. 2003. (Connor Hawthorne Mystery Ser.). 400p. pap. 14.95 (*1-55583-812-X*, Alyson Bks.) Alyson Pubns.

Maness, Larry. Nantucket Revenge: A Jake Eaton Mystery. 1995. 208p. 19.95 o.s.i (*0-89141-566-1*, Presidio Pr.) Ballantine Bks.

—A Once Perfect Place: A Jake Eaton Mystery. 1996. 208p. 19.95 o.s.i (*0-89141-567-X*, Presidio Pr.) Ballantine Bks.

—Strangler: A Jake Eaton Mystery. 1998. 192p. 19.95 o.p. (*0-89141-568-8*, Presidio Pr.) Ballantine Bks.

Marquand, John P. The Late George Apley. 1937. 18.95 o.s.i (*0-316-54652-6*) Aspen Pubs., Inc.

—The Late George Apley. 1994. lib. bdg. 24.95 (*1-56849-446-7*) Buccaneer Bks., Inc.

—The Late George Apley. 2004. 368p. pap. 14.95 (*0-316-73567-1*, Back Bay) Little Brown & Co.

—The Late George Apley. 1982. mass mkt. 3.95 o.s.i (*0-671-45929-5*, Pocket) Simon & Schuster.

Mars, Peter. A Taste for Money: A Novel Based on the True Story of a Dirty Boston Cop. 1999. (Illus.). 320p. pap. 14.95 (*0-9664475-1-4*) Commonwealth Publishing.

Maso, Carole. Defiance. 272p. 1999. pap. 12.95 o.s.i (*0-452-27829-5*, Plume); 1998. 23.95 o.p. (*0-525-94307-2*) Dutton/Plume.

Matson, Suzanne. The Hunger Moon: A Novel. 1999. 272p. pap. 12.00 (*0-345-42553-7*) Ballantine Bks.

—The Hunger Moon: A Novel. 1997. 252p. 23.00 (*0-393-04099-2*) Norton, W. W. & Co., Inc.

McAleer, Andrew. Appearance of Counsel: A Suspense Mystery of Boston. 2001. 235p. pap. 16.95 (*1-883707-72-2*); (Illus.). 28.95 (*1-883707-26-9*) Protea Publishing Co.

McCauley, Stephen. True Enough: A Novel. 320p. 2002. pap. 14.00 (*0-7434-4403-5*, Washington Square Pr.); 2001. 24.00 (*0-684-81054-9*, Simon & Schuster) Simon & Schuster.

Mcdonald, Gregory. The Buck Passes Flynn. 1986. 224p. mass mkt. 4.95 o.s.i (*0-345-33690-9*); 1983. mass mkt. 2.50 o.s.i (*0-345-31610-X*); 1981. mass mkt. 2.25 o.s.i (*0-345-30029-7*) Ballantine Bks.

—The Buck Passes Flynn. 2000. E-Book (*1-930351-03-8*) FairHillBooks.com.

—The Buck Passes Flynn. l.t. ed. 1993. 12.95 o.p. (*0-8161-3394-8*, Macmillan Reference USA) Gale Group.

—The Buck Passes Flynn. 2004. 224p. pap. 12.00 (*0-375-71360-3*, Vintage) Knopf Publishing Group.

—Flynn. 2000. E-Book (*1-930351-04-6*) FairHillBooks.com.

—Flynn. 2003. (Vintage Crime/Black Lizard Ser.). 256p. pap. 12.00 (*0-375-71357-3*, Vintage) Knopf Publishing Group.

—Flynn. 1977. 1977p. pap. 3.95 (*0-380-01764-4*, Avon Bks.) Morrow/Avon.

—Flynn's In. 2000. E-Book (*1-930351-02-X*) FairHillBooks.com.

—Flynn's In. 2004. 208p. pap. 12.00 (*0-375-71361-1*, Vintage) Knopf Publishing Group.

—Flynn's In. ("Flynn" Ser.). 1999. 15.45 o.s.i (*0-89296-085-X*); 1987. 45.00 o.p. (*0-89296-086-8*) Mysterious Pr.

—Flynn's In. 1988. mass mkt. 4.95 o.s.i (*0-445-20864-3*) Warner Bks., Inc.

—Flynn's World. E-Book 23.50 (*1-930351-05-4*) FairHillBooks.com.

—Flynn's World. 224p. 2004. pap. 12.00 (*0-375-71358-1*, Vintage); 2003. 23.00 (*0-375-42236-6*, Pantheon) Knopf Publishing Group.

—Skylar in Yankeeland. 1997. 275p. 23.00 o.p. (*0-688-14164-1*, Morrow, William & Co.) Morrow/Avon.

McFarland, Dennis. Singing Boy: A Novel. 2001. 320p. 25.00 o.s.i (*0-8050-6608-X*) Holt, Henry & Co.

—Singing Boy: A Novel. l.t. ed. 2001. 560p. 28.95 (*0-7862-3517-9*) Thorndike Pr.

McGoldrick, May. Captured Dreams. 2003. 384p. mass mkt. 6.99 (*0-451-21077-8*, Signet Bks.) NAL.

Merullo, Roland. Revere Beach Boulevard: A Novel. 336p. 1999. (Revere Beach Trilogy Ser.: Vol. 1). pap. 13.00 o.s.i (*0-8050-6006-5*, Owl Bks.); 1998. (Book One of the Revere Beach Trilogy Ser.). 23.00 o.s.i (*0-8050-6005-7*) Holt, Henry & Co.

Michaels, Grant. Body to Dye For. 1991. (Stonewall Inn Editions Ser.: Vol. 1). 241p. pap. 11.95 (*0-312-05825-X*, Saint Martin's Griffin); 1990. 17.95 o.p. (*0-312-04273-6*, Saint Martin's Minotaur) St. Martin's Pr.

—Dead As a Doornail. (Stan Kraychik Mystery Ser.). 256p. 1999. pap. 12.95 (*0-312-20644-5*, Saint Martin's Griffin); 1998. 22.95 o.p. (*0-312-18077-2*, Saint Martin's Minotaur) St. Martin's Pr.

—Dead on Your Feet. 256p. 1993. 12.99 o.p. (*0-312-09781-6*, Saint Martin's Minotaur); 4th ed. 1994. (Stonewall Inn Editions Ser.: Vol. 1). pap. 11.95 (*0-312-11457-5*, Saint Martin's Griffin) St. Martin's Pr.

—Love You to Death. (Stonewall Inn Editions Ser.). 1993. 10.95 (*0-312-08841-8*, Saint Martin's Griffin); 1992. 256p. 18.95 (*0-312-07027-6*, Saint Martin's Minotaur) St. Martin's Pr.

—Mask for a Diva. 1996. 304p. pap. 10.95 (*0-312-14120-3*, Saint Martin's Griffin); 1994. 272p. 20.95 o.p. (*0-312-11462-1*, Saint Martin's Minotaur) St. Martin's Pr.

—Time to Check Out: A Stan Kraychik Mystery. 1996. 272p. 21.95 o.p. (*0-312-14434-2*, Saint Martin's Minotaur); 1997. 256p. reprint ed. pap. 12.95 (*0-312-15673-1*, NPB 0273, Saint Martin's Griffin) St. Martin's Pr.

Minichino, Camille. The Beryllium Murder. 2000. 272p. 24.00 (*0-688-17207-5*, Morrow, William & Co.) Morrow/Avon.

—The Helium Murder. 1998. (Periodic Table Mystery Ser.: Bk. 2). 192p. 18.95 (*0-8034-9298-7*, Avalon Bks.) Bouregy, Thomas & Co., Inc.

—The Hydrogen Murder. 1997. (Periodic Table Mystery Ser.: Bk. 1). 228p. 18.95 (*0-8034-9268-5*, Avalon Bks.) Bouregy, Thomas & Co., Inc.

—The Hydrogen Murder. 2003. (WWL Mystery Ser.: No. 467). 256p. mass mkt. (*0-373-26467-4*, Worldwide Library) Harlequin Enterprises, Ltd.

—The Lithium Murder: A Gloria Lamerino Mystery. 1999. 231p. 24.00 (*0-688-16784-5*, Morrow, William & Co.) Morrow/Avon.

Minot, Susan. Folly. l.t. ed. 1993. 21.95 o.p. (*0-7927-1566-7*); pap. o.p. (*0-7927-1565-9*) BBC Audiobooks America.

—Folly. 1992. 256p. 19.95 o.p. (*0-395-60339-0*) Houghton Mifflin Co. Trade & Reference Div.

—Folly. Rosenman, Jane, ed. 1994. 288p. reprint ed. pap. 12.00 (*0-671-74951-X*, Pocket) Simon & Schuster.

Mlynowski, Sarah. Milkrun. 2003. 352p. mass mkt. (*0-373-25035-5*); 2001. 288p. pap. (*0-373-25012-6*) Harlequin Enterprises, Ltd. (Red Dress Ink).

Mooney, Chris. World Without End. 2001. 400p. 25.00 (*0-671-04063-4*, Atria); 2002. 528p. reprint ed. mass mkt. 7.99 (*0-671-04064-2*, Pocket) Simon & Schuster.

Moore, Christine P. The Virgin Knows. 1995. 320p. 22.95 o.p. (*0-312-13203-4*) St. Martin's Pr.

Munson, Ronald. Night Vision. 1995. 336p. 21.95 o.p. (*0-525-93781-1*, Dutton) Dutton/Plume.

—Night Vision. 1996. pap. 5.99 o.s.i (*0-451-40659-1*, Onyx); 416p. mass mkt. 5.99 o.s.i (*0-451-18013-5*, Signet Bks.) NAL.

Murphy, Gloria. Down Will Come Baby. 1991. 18.95 o.p. (*1-55611-196-7*) Fine, Donald I. Bks.

Murray, Victoria. Friendly Enemies: The Lambert Series-Book Three. 2003. 200p. pap. 19.95 (*1-59129-873-3*) PublishAmerica, Inc.

Myles, Eileen. Cool for You. 2000. 196p. pap. 14.00 (*1-887128-59-X*) Soft Skull Pr., Inc.

Neely, Barbara. Blanche Cleans Up. 1999. 352p. mass mkt. 6.99 (*0-14-027747-1*) Penguin Group (USA) Inc.

—Blanche Cleans Up. 1998. 288p. 19.95 o.p. (*0-670-87626-7*) Viking Penguin.

Neggers, Carla. On Fire. unabr. ed. 1999. audio 7.99 (*1-55204-192-1*, MIR-1192) Durkin Hayes Publishing Ltd.

—On Fire. 384p. 2003. mass mkt. (*1-55166-970-6*); 1999. per. (*1-55166-541-7*, 1-66541-3) Harlequin Enterprises, Ltd. (Mira Bks.).

Nelson, D. L. Vegetable Lover, Not a Cookbook. 2003. (Five Star First Edition Women's Fiction Ser.). 256p. 26.95 (*0-7862-4706-1*, Five Star) Gale Group.

Nevins, Linda M. Commonwealth Avenue. 1996. 432p. 24.95 o.p. (*0-312-13949-7*) St. Martin's Pr.

Norman, Diana. A Catch of Consequence. 2003. 400p. pap. 14.00 (*0-425-19015-3*) Berkley Publishing Group.

O'Connor, Edward. The Last Hurrah. Date not set. 437p. 28.95 (*0-8488-2373-7*) Amereon, Ltd.

O'Connor, Edwin. The Last Hurrah. 1970. pap. 2.95 o.p. (*0-553-14088-4*, G14088-4) Bantam Bks.

—The Last Hurrah. 1998. pap. 14.00 (*0-316-19092-6*, Back Bay); 1985. 427p. reprint ed. pap. 14.95 o.p. (*0-316-62659-7*) Little Brown & Co.

Packer, George. Central Square. 1998. 304p. 24.95 (*1-55597-277-2*) Graywolf Pr.

Page, David A. Surviving Frank. l.t. ed. 2003. (Five Star First Edition Speculative Fiction Ser.). 272p. 25.95 (*0-7862-5634-6*, Five Star) Gale Group.

Palmer, Michael. Michael Palmer: Three Complete Novels. 1996. 784p. 13.99 (*0-517-14959-1*) Random Hse. Value Publishing.

—Miracle Cure. 1998. 416p. 23.95 o.s.i (*0-553-10523-X*); 1999. 448p. reprint ed. mass mkt. 7.50 (*0-553-57662-3*) Bantam Bks.

—Miracle Cure. unabr. ed. 1998. audio 64.00 (*0-7366-4158-0*, 4661) Books on Tape, Inc.

—Miracle Cure. l.t. ed. 1998. 27.95 o.p. (*1-56895-612-6*, Wheeler Publishing, Inc.) Gale Group.

—Miracle Cure. abr. ed. 1998. audio 23.95 (*0-553-47816-8*); audio compact disk 29.95 (*0-553-45591-5*, ) Random Hse. Audio Publishing Group. (RH Audio).

—Miracle Cure. unabr. ed. 1998. audio 78.00 (*0-7887-1897-5*, 95319E7) Recorded Bks., LLC.

—Natural Causes. 1994. 496p. mass mkt. 7.50 (*0-553-56876-0*) Bantam Bks.

—Natural Causes. abr. ed. 2000. audio 9.99 (*0-553-52727-4*, RH Audio) Random Hse. Audio Publishing Group.

—Natural Causes. unabr. ed. 1994. audio audio 91.00 (*0-7887-0085-5*, 94325E7) Recorded Bks., LLC.

Parker, Robert B. All Our Yesterdays. 1995. 480p. mass mkt. 7.50 (*0-440-22146-3*); 1994. 528p. 27.95 o.s.i (*0-385-31374-8*, Delacorte Pr.) Dell Publishing.

—A Catskill Eagle. unabr. collector's ed. 1990. (Spenser Ser.). audio 40.00 (*0-7366-1676-4*, 2524) Books on Tape, Inc.

—A Catskill Eagle. 1986. (Spencer Mystery Ser.). 384p. mass mkt. 7.50 (*0-440-11132-3*) Dell Publishing.

—A Catskill Eagle. l.t. ed. 1985. (Spencer Mystery Ser.). 16.95 o.p. (*0-8161-3892-3*, Macmillan Reference USA) Gale Group.

—Ceremony. unabr. collector's ed. 1989. (Spenser Ser.). audio 30.00 (*0-7366-1628-4*, 2486) Books on Tape, Inc.

—Ceremony. 1992. (Spencer Mystery Ser.). 224p. mass mkt. 7.50 (*0-440-10993-0*) Dell Publishing.

—Ceremony. l.t. ed. 1985. (Nightingale-Lythway Ser.). 9.95 o.p. (*0-8161-3833-8*, Macmillan Reference USA) Gale Group.

—Chance. 1997. (Spenser Mystery Ser.). 336p. reprint ed. mass mkt. 7.99 (*0-425-15747-4*) Berkley Publishing Group.

—Chance. l.t. ed. 1996. (Spenser Mystery Ser.). 26.95 o.p. (*1-56895-335-6*, Wheeler Publishing, Inc.) Gale Group.

—Chance. unabr. ed. 1996. (Spenser Mystery Ser.). 24.95 o.p. (*0-7871-0712-3*, 693925) NewStar Media, Inc.

—Chance. 1996. 21.95 (*0-399-14688-1*); 1996. 320p. 21.95 o.p. (*0-399-14134-0*, G. P. Putnam's Sons); 2015. 100.00 (*0-399-14167-7*) Penguin Group (USA) Inc.

—Crimson Joy. unabr. collector's ed. 1990. (Spenser Ser.). audio 30.00 (*0-7366-1758-2*, 2597) Books on Tape, Inc.

—Crimson Joy. (Spencer Mystery Ser.). 1989. 304p. mass mkt. 7.99 (*0-440-20343-0*); 1988. 75.00 o.s.i (*0-385-29668-1*, Delacorte Pr.) Dell Publishing.

—Crimson Joy. abr. ed. 1988. (Spencer Mystery Ser.). audio 14.95 (*0-671-66617-7*, Simon & Schuster Audioworks) Simon & Schuster Audio.

—Double Deuce. 1993. (Spenser Mystery Ser.). 256p. mass mkt. 7.99 (*0-425-13793-7*) Berkley Publishing Group.

—Double Deuce. unabr. ed. 2000. (Spenser Mystery Ser.). audio (*1-56054-857-6*, SAB 053) Chivers Audio Bks. GBR. *Dist:* BBC Audiobooks America.

—Double Deuce. l.t. ed. 1993. (Spencer Mystery Ser.). 233p. pap. 17.95 o.p. (*0-8161-5597-6*); 20.95 o.p. (*0-8161-5596-8*) Gale Group. (Macmillan Reference USA).

—Double Deuce. unabr. ed. 1993. (Spenser Mystery Ser.). 24.95 o.p. (*1-55800-473-4*, 492065) NewStar Media, Inc.

—Double Deuce. 1992. (Spenser Mystery Ser.). 224p. 100.00 o.p. (*0-399-13754-8*); 19.95 o.s.i (*0-399-13721-1*) Penguin Group (USA) Inc. (G. P. Putnam's Sons).

—Early Autumn. unabr. collector's ed. 1989. (Spenser Ser.). audio 30.00 (*0-7366-1589-X*, 2452) Books on Tape, Inc.

—Early Autumn. (Spencer Mystery Ser.). 1992. 224p. mass mkt. 2.99 o.s.i (*0-440-21387-8*); 1992. 224p. mass mkt. 7.99 (*0-440-12214-7*); 1981. 10.95 o.s.i (*0-440-02248-7*, Delacorte Pr.) Dell Publishing.

—The Early Spenser - Three Complete Novels: The Godwulf Manuscript, God Save the Child, Mortal Stakes. 1989. 504p. 13.95 o.s.i (*0-385-29728-9*, Delacorte Pr.) Dell Publishing.

—Family Honor. 2000. (Sunny Randall Ser.). 338p. mass mkt. 7.50 (*0-425-17706-8*) Berkley Publishing Group.

—Family Honor. l.t. ed. (Wheeler Press Paperback Ser.). 2000. 10.95 (*1-56895-977-X*); 1999. 27.95 (*1-56895-788-2*) Gale Group. (Wheeler Publishing, Inc.).

—Family Honor, Set. abr. ed. 1999. audio 18.00 Highsmith Inc.

—Family Honor. 1999. audio 30.00 (*0-7871-2354-4*); audio compact disk 36.00 (*0-7871-2369-2*); audio 18.00 (*0-7871-2355-2*, Dove Audio); audio 30.00 NewStar Media, Inc.

—Family Honor. l.t. ed. 1999. (Sunny Randall Ser.). 322p. 22.95 o.p. (*0-399-14566-4*, G. P. Putnam's Sons) Penguin Group (USA) Inc.

—God Save the Child. unabr. collector's ed. 1988. (Spenser Ser.). audio 36.00 (*0-7366-1381-1*, 2274) Books on Tape, Inc.

—God Save the Child. 1987. (Spencer Mystery Ser.). 208p. mass mkt. 7.99 (*0-440-12899-4*) Dell Publishing.

—God Save the Child. 1974. (Spenser Mystery Ser.). 192p. 5.95 o.p. (*0-395-19955-7*) Houghton Mifflin Co.

—God Save the Child. 1995. (Spenser Mystery Ser.). Random Hse., Inc.

—The Godwulf Manuscript. l.t. ed. 1994. (Spenser Mystery Ser.). pap. 18.95 o.p. (*0-7927-1883-6*); 19.95 o.p. (*0-7927-1884-4*) BBC Audiobooks America.

—The Godwulf Manuscript. 1978. (Spenser Mystery Ser.). 1.50 o.s.i (*0-425-03967-6*) Berkley Publishing Group.

—The Godwulf Manuscript. unabr. collector's ed. 1988. (Spenser Ser.). audio 36.00 (*0-7366-1353-6*, 2254) Books on Tape, Inc.

—The Godwulf Manuscript. 1994. (Spenser Mystery Ser.). 192p. reprint ed. lib. bdg. 29.95 (*1-56849-317-7*) Buccaneer Bks., Inc.

—The Godwulf Manuscript. 1992. (Spencer Mystery Ser.). 208p. mass mkt. 7.99 (*0-440-12961-3*) Dell Publishing.

—The Godwulf Manuscript. 1974. (Spenser Mystery Ser.). 5.95 o.p. (*0-395-18011-2*) Houghton Mifflin Co.

—The Godwulf Manuscript. 1995. (Spenser Mystery Ser.). Random Hse., Inc.

—Hugger Mugger. 2001. (Spenser Mystery Ser.: Bk. 27). 336p. reprint ed. mass mkt. 7.99 (*0-425-17955-9*) Berkley Publishing Group.

—Hugger Mugger. unabr. ed. 2000. audio 34.95 (*0-7366-4915-8*, 5222) Books on Tape, Inc.

—Hugger Mugger. l.t. ed. 2000. (Spenser Mystery Ser.). 309p. 27.95 (*1-56895-865-X*, Wheeler Publishing, Inc.) Gale Group.

—Hugger Mugger. unabr. ed. 2000. (Spenser Mystery Ser.). audio 29.95 (*0-553-50246-8*); audio compact disk 34.99 (*0-553-45673-3*) Random Hse. Audio Publishing Group. (RH Audio).

—Hush Money. 2000. (Spenser Mystery Ser.). 336p. pap. 7.99 (*0-425-17401-8*) Berkley Publishing Group.

—Hush Money. l.t. ed. 1999. (Spenser Mystery Ser.). 27.95 (*1-56895-739-4*, Wheeler Publishing, Inc.) Gale Group.

—Hush Money. abr. ed. 1999. (Spenser Mystery Ser.). audio 18.00 (*0-7871-1898-2*, 394162); audio 30.00 (*0-7871-1870-2*, 890100) NewStar Media, Inc.

—Hush Money. 1999. (Spenser Mystery Ser.). 336p. 22.95 o.p. (*0-399-14458-7*) Penguin Group (USA) Inc.

—Hush Money. 2000. 13.55 (*0-606-20394-X*); 13.55 (*0-606-20098-3*) Turtleback Bks.

—The Judas Goat. (Spenser Mystery Ser.). 20.95 (*0-89190-371-2*) Amereon, Ltd.

—The Judas Goat. 1979. (Spenser Mystery Ser.). 1.95 o.p. (*0-425-04204-9*) Berkley Publishing Group.

—The Judas Goat. unabr. collector's ed. 1989. (Spenser Ser.). audio 36.00 (*0-7366-1571-7*, 2438) Books on Tape, Inc.

—The Judas Goat. 1992. (Spencer Mystery Ser.). 208p. mass mkt. 7.99 (*0-440-14196-6*) Dell Publishing.

—The Judas Goat, 001. 1978. (Spenser Mystery Ser.). 7.95 o.p. (*0-395-26682-3*) Houghton Mifflin Co.

—Looking for Rachel Wallace. unabr. collector's ed. 1989. (Spenser Ser.). audio 36.00 (*0-7366-1597-0*, 2458) Books on Tape, Inc.

—Looking for Rachel Wallace. (Spencer Mystery Ser.). 1987. 224p. mass mkt. 7.50 (*0-440-15316-6*); 1980. 10.95 o.s.i (*0-440-04764-1*, Delacorte Pr.) Dell Publishing.

—Mortal Stakes. unabr. collector's ed. 1989. (Spenser Ser.). audio 36.00 (*0-7366-1530-X*, 2400) Books on Tape, Inc.

—Mortal Stakes. 1994. (Spenser Mystery Ser.). reprint ed. lib. bdg. 32.95 (*1-56849-316-9*) Buccaneer Bks., Inc.

—Mortal Stakes. 1987. (Spencer Mystery Ser.). 336p. mass mkt. 7.50 (*0-440-15758-7*) Dell Publishing.

—Mortal Stakes, 001. 1975. (Spenser Mystery Ser.). 192p. 6.95 o.p. (*0-395-21969-8*) Houghton Mifflin Co.

—Mortal Stakes. 2002. (Best Mysteries of All Time Ser.). 288p. (*0-7621-8875-8*, Impress) Scriptorium Pr., The.

—Pale Kings & Princes. unabr. collector's ed. 1990. (Spenser Ser.). audio 30.00 (*0-7366-1772-8*, 2611) Books on Tape, Inc.

—Pale Kings & Princes. (Spencer Mystery Ser.). 1993. 320p. mass mkt. 3.99 o.s.i (*0-440-21584-6*); 1987. 288p. 75.00 o.s.i (*0-385-29568-5*, Delacorte Pr.); 1988. 320p. reprint ed. mass mkt. 7.99 (*0-440-20004-0*) Dell Publishing.

—Pale Kings & Princes. abr. ed. 1988. (Spencer Mystery Ser.). 14.95 incl. audio (*0-671-66073-X*, Simon & Schuster Audioworks) Simon & Schuster Audio.

—Paper Doll. 1994. (Spenser Mystery Ser.). 288p. mass mkt. 7.99 (*0-425-14155-1*) Berkley Publishing Group.

—Paper Doll. unabr. ed. 1993. (Spenser Ser.). audio 36.00 (*0-7366-2636-0*, 3375) Books on Tape, Inc.

—Paper Doll. unabr. ed. 2000. (Spenser Mystery Ser.). audio (*0-7862-9942-8*, SAB 072) Chivers Audio Bks. GBR. *Dist:* BBC Audiobooks America.

—Paper Doll. unabr. ed. 1993. (Spenser Mystery Ser.). 24.95 o.p. (*1-55800-707-5*, 592092) NewStar Media, Inc.

—Paper Doll. 1993. (Spenser Mystery Ser.). 224p. 19.95 o.p. (*0-399-13818-8*, G. P. Putnam's Sons) Penguin Group (USA) Inc.

—Paper Doll. (Spencer Mystery Ser.). 5.98 o.p. (*0-8317-5332-3*) Smithmark Pubs., Inc.

—Pastime. 1992. (Spenser Mystery Ser.). 352p. reprint ed. mass mkt. 7.99 (*0-425-13293-5*) Berkley Publishing Group.

—Pastime. unabr. ed. 2000. (Spenser Mystery Ser.). audio 49.95 (*1-56054-910-6*, SAB 035) Chivers Audio Bks. GBR. *Dist:* BBC Audiobooks America.

—Pastime. l.t. ed. 1992. (Spencer Mystery Ser.). 269p. lib. bdg. 20.95 o.p. (*0-8161-5347-7*, Macmillan Reference USA) Gale Group.

—Pastime. abr. ed. 1993. (Spencer Mystery Ser.). 15.95 o.p. (*1-55800-272-3*, 41180); audio 8.99 o.p. (*1-55800-902-7*, Dove Audio); 24.95 o.p. (*1-55800-433-5*, 692282) NewStar Media, Inc.

—Pastime. (Select Sound, Dove Ser.). 1995. pap. 4.99 o.p. (*0-7871-0305-5*); 1991. 224p. 19.95 o.s.i (*0-399-13628-2*, G. P. Putnam's Sons); 1991. 100.00 o.p. (*0-399-13630-4*) Penguin Group (USA) Inc.

—Pastime. 1992. (Spencer Mystery Ser.). 5.99 o.p. (*0-517-09584-X*) Random Hse. Value Publishing.

—Perish Twice. 2001. 352p. reprint ed. mass mkt. 7.99 (*0-425-18215-0*) Berkley Publishing Group.

—Perish Twice. l.t. ed. (Wheeler Press Paperback Ser.). 2001. 12.95 (*1-56895-180-9*); 2000. 279p. 28.95 (*1-56895-992-3*) Gale Group. (Wheeler Publishing, Inc.).

—Perish Twice. 2000. 320p. 23.95 o.s.i (*0-399-14668-7*) Penguin Group (USA) Inc.

—Playmates. 1990. (Spenser Mystery Ser.). 288p. mass mkt. 7.99 (*0-425-12001-5*) Berkley Publishing Group.

—Playmates. unabr. collector's ed. 1990. (Spenser Ser.). audio 30.00 (*0-7366-1774-4*, 2613) Books on Tape, Inc.

—Playmates. 1989. (Spencer Mystery Ser.). 17.95 o.p. (*0-399-13425-5*, G. P. Putnam's Sons) Penguin Putnam Bks. for Young Readers.

—Playmates. abr. ed. 1989. (Spencer Mystery Ser.). audio 14.95 (*0-671-67832-9*, Simon & Schuster Audioworks) Simon & Schuster Audio.

—Potshot. l.t. ed. 2001. 359p. (*0-7540-1661-7*); (*0-7540-9075-2*) BBC Audiobooks America.

—Potshot. 2002. 352p. reprint ed. mass mkt. 7.99 (*0-425-18288-6*) Berkley Publishing Group.

—Potshot. 2001. (Spenser Ser.). 294p. 23.95 o.p. (*0-399-14710-1*) Penguin Group (USA) Inc.

—Potshot. l.t. ed. (Paperback Bestsellers Ser.). 2002. 359p. pap. 29.95 (*0-7862-3237-4*); 2001. 407p. 32.95 (*0-7862-3232-3*) Thorndike Pr.

—Promised Land. 1978. (Spenser Mystery Ser.). 1.75 o.p. (*0-425-03614-6*) Berkley Publishing Group.

—Promised Land. unabr. collector's ed. 1989. (Spenser Ser.). audio 36.00 (*0-7366-1551-2*, 2420) Books on Tape, Inc.

—Promised Land. 1992. (Spencer Mystery Ser.). 224p. mass mkt. 7.50 (*0-440-17197-0*) Dell Publishing.

—Promised Land. 2002. E-Book 6.99 (*0-7953-0732-2*) RosettaBooks.

—A Savage Place. unabr. collector's ed. 1989. (Spenser Ser.). audio 30.00 (*0-7366-1621-7*, 2481) Books on Tape, Inc.

—A Savage Place. (Spencer Mystery Ser.). 1982. 192p. mass mkt. 6.99 (*0-440-18095-3*); 1981. 6.99 (*0-440-08094-0*); 1981. 14.95 o.s.i (*0-385-28951-0*, Delacorte Pr.) Dell Publishing.

—A Savage Place. l.t. ed. 1982. (Spenser Mystery Ser.). 264p. reprint ed. 12.95 o.p. (*0-89621-343-9*) Thorndike Pr.

—Shrink Rap. 2003. 352p. mass mkt. 7.99 (*0-515-13620-4*, Jove) Berkley Publishing Group.

—Shrink Rap. 2002. 320p. 24.95 o.s.i (*0-399-14930-9*, Putnam & Grosset) Putnam Publishing Group, The.

—Small Vices. 1998. (Spenser Mystery Ser.). 352p. mass mkt. 7.99 (*0-425-16248-6*) Berkley Publishing Group.

—Small Vices. l.t. ed. 1997. (Spenser Mystery Ser.). 25.95 o.p. (*1-56895-466-2*, Wheeler Publishing, Inc.) Gale Group.

—Small Vices. unabr. ed. 1997. (Spenser Mysteries Ser.). 29.95 o.p. (*0-7871-1133-3*, 754969) NewStar Media, Inc.

—Small Vices. 1997. (Spenser Mystery Ser.). 320p. (J). 21.95 o.p. (*0-399-14244-4*, G. P. Putnam's Sons) Penguin Group (USA) Inc.

—Stardust, Set. unabr. ed. 1995. (Spenser Mystery Ser.). audio 54.95 (*1-56054-968-8*, SAB 012, Sterling Audio Bks.) BBC Audiobooks America.

—Stardust. 1991. (Spenser Mystery Ser.). 304p. mass mkt. 7.99 (*0-425-12723-0*) Berkley Publishing Group.

—Stardust. unabr. collector's ed. 1990. (Spenser Ser.). audio 36.00 (*0-7366-1840-6*, 2673) Books on Tape, Inc.

—Stardust. 1990. (Spencer Mystery Ser.). 224p. 18.95 o.s.i (*0-399-13537-5*); 75.00 o.p. (*0-399-13514-6*) Penguin Putnam Bks. for Young Readers. (G. P. Putnam's Sons).

—Stardust. 1992. (Spencer Mystery Ser.). 4.99 o.p. (*0-517-08606-9*) Random Hse. Value Publishing.

—Stardust. abr. ed. 1990. (Spencer Mystery Ser.). audio 14.95 (*0-671-70481-8*, Simon & Schuster Audioworks) Simon & Schuster Audio.

—Sudden Mischief. l.t. ed. 1998. (Spenser Mystery Ser.). 27.95 (*1-56895-569-3*, Wheeler Publishing, Inc.) Gale Group.

—Sudden Mischief. 1998. 22.95 o.s.i (*0-399-14696-2*); 304p. 22.95 o.p. incl. audio (*0-399-14370-X*, G. P. Putnam's Sons) Penguin Group (USA) Inc.

—Taming a Seahorse. unabr. collector's ed. 1990. (Spenser Ser.). audio 30.00 (*0-7366-1750-7*, 2589) Books on Tape, Inc.

—Taming a Seahorse. 1987. (Spencer Mystery Ser.). 320p. mass mkt. 7.99 (*0-440-18841-5*) Dell Publishing.

—Taming a Seahorse. l.t. ed. 1987. (Spencer Mystery Ser.). 362p. 18.95 o.p. (*0-8161-4166-5*, Macmillan Reference USA) Gale Group.

—Thin Air. 1996. (Spenser Mystery Ser.). 304p. reprint ed. mass mkt. 7.99 (*0-425-15290-1*) Berkley Publishing Group.

—Thin Air. l.t. ed. 1995. (Spencer Mystery Ser.). 26.95 o.p. (*1-56895-212-0*, Wheeler Publishing, Inc.) Gale Group.

—Thin Air. unabr. ed. 1995. (Spenser Mystery Ser.). 24.95 o.p. (*0-7871-0277-6*, 692871) NewStar Media, Inc.

—Thin Air. (*0-399-19276-X*); 1995. 293p. 21.95 o.p. (*0-399-14020-4*, G. P. Putnam's Sons); 1995. 125.00 o.p. (*0-399-14063-8*, G. P. Putnam's Sons) Penguin Group (USA) Inc.

—Three Complete Novels, 3 vols. Incl. God Save the Child. 1995. Godwulf Manuscript. 1995. Mortal Stakes. 192p. 1975. 6.95 o.p. (*0-395-21969-8*); 560p. 1995. 13.99 o.s.i (*0-517-14802-1*) Random Hse., Inc.

—Valediction. unabr. collector's ed. 1989. (Spenser Ser.). audio 30.00 (*0-7366-1670-5*, 2519) Books on Tape, Inc.

—Valediction. (Spencer Mystery Ser.). 1992. 288p. mass mkt. 7.50 (*0-440-19246-3*); 1984. 240p. 12.95 o.s.i (*0-385-29330-5*, Delacorte Pr.) Dell Publishing.

—Valediction. 1985. (Spencer Mystery Ser.). mass mkt. 3.50 o.s.i (*0-440-19247-1*) Doubleday Publishing.

—Valediction. l.t. ed. 1984. (Spencer Mystery Ser.). 14.95 o.p. (*0-8161-3702-1*, Macmillan Reference USA) Gale Group.

—Walking Shadow. 1995. (Spenser Mystery Ser.). 304p. mass mkt. 7.99 (*0-425-14774-6*) Berkley Publishing Group.

—Walking Shadow. unabr. ed. 1995. (Spenser Ser.). audio 48.00 (*0-7366-2924-6*, 3622) Books on Tape, Inc.

—Walking Shadow. l.t. ed. 1994. (Spencer Mystery Ser.). 25.95 o.p. (*1-56895-106-X*, Wheeler Publishing, Inc.) Gale Group.

—Walking Shadow. abr. ed. 1993. (Spencer Mystery Ser.). audio 24.95 o.p. (*1-55800-999-X*, Dove Audio) NewStar Media, Inc.

—Walking Shadow. 1994. (Spenser Mystery Ser.). 224p. 19.95 o.p. (*0-399-13920-6*); 100.00 o.p. (*0-399-13961-3*) Penguin Group (USA) Inc. (G. P. Putnam's Sons).

—The Widening Gyre. unabr. collector's ed. 1989. (Spenser Ser.). audio 30.00 (*0-7366-1655-1*, 2506) Books on Tape, Inc.

—The Widening Gyre. (Spencer Mystery Ser.). 192p. 1992. mass mkt. 7.99 (*0-440-19535-7*); 1983. 13.95 o.p. (*0-385-29220-1*, Delacorte Pr.) Dell Publishing.

—Widow's Walk. 2003. 336p. mass mkt. 7.99 (*0-425-18904-X*) Berkley Publishing Group.

—Widow's Walk. 2002. 320p. 24.95 o.s.i (*0-399-14845-0*) Putnam Publishing Group, The.

—Widow's Walk. l.t. ed. 2003. 343p. pap. 13.95 (*1-4104-0099-9*, Large Print Pr.) Thorndike Pr.

—Widow's Walk: A Spenser Novel. 2003. (Paperback Bestsellers Ser.). pap. 13.95 (*0-7862-4216-7*) Thorndike Pr.

Parker, Robert B. & Cohen, Stan. Sudden Mischief. 1999. (Spenser Mystery Ser.). 306p. reprint ed. pap. 7.99 (*0-425-16828-X*) Berkley Publishing Group.

Patterson, James. Cradle & All. l.t. ed. 2000. (Large Print Book Ser.). 305p. 31.95 (*1-56895-879-X*, Wheeler Publishing, Inc.) Gale Group.

—Cradle & All. 2000. 368p. 25.95 o.p. (*0-316-69061-9*) Little Brown & Co.

—Cradle & All. 2001. 384p. reprint ed. mass mkt. 7.99 (*0-446-60940-4*) Warner Bks., Inc.

Peale, Cynthia. The Death of Colonel Mann. 2001. (Beacon Hill Mysteries Ser.). 352p. mass mkt. 6.50 (*0-440-23565-0*) Dell Publishing.

—The Death of Colonel Mann. l.t. ed. 2002. (Ulverscroft Large Print Ser.). 488p. 32.50 (*0-7089-4655-0*, Ulverscroft) Thorpe, F. A. Pubs. GBR. *Dist:* Ulverscroft Large Print Bks., Ltd., Ulverscroft Large Print Canada, Ltd.

—The White Crow. 2003. 336p. mass mkt. 6.50 (*0-440-23566-9*) Dell Publishing.

—The White Crow. 2002. 336p. 24.95 (*0-385-49638-9*) Doubleday Publishing.

Pearl, Matthew. The Dante Club. l.t. ed. 2003. 615p. 32.95 (*1-58724-465-9*, Wheeler Publishing, Inc.) Gale Group.

—The Dante Club: A Novel. 2004. 400p. pap. 13.95 (*0-8129-7104-3*, Random Hse. Trade Paperbacks) Random House Adult Trade Publishing Group.

—The Dante Club: A Novel. 2003. (Illus.). 384p. 24.95 (*0-375-50529-6*); E-Book 17.50 (*1-58836-310-4*) Random Hse., Inc.

—The Dante Club: A Novel. 2003. audio compact disk 30.00 (*0-7435-1792-X*, Simon & Schuster Audioworks) Simon & Schuster Audio.

Pease, R. Runaway: P. I. Jeeter in Boston. 1996. 174p. per. 12.95 (*1-889455-00-8*) Flagg Mountain Pr.

Philpin, John. The Murder Channel. 2001. 336p. mass mkt. 6.50 (*0-553-58009-4*) Bantam Bks.

Piercy, Marge. The Longings of Women. 1995. 448p. mass mkt. 6.99 o.s.i (*0-449-22349-3*, Fawcett) Ballantine Bks.

—The Longings of Women. l.t. ed. 1994. (G. K. Hall Core Ser.). 752p. lib. bdg. 25.95 (*0-8161-7457-1*, Macmillan Reference USA) Gale Group.

—The Longings of Women. abr. ed. 1994. audio 17.00 o.s.i (*1-57042-044-0*, 4-520440) Time Warner AudioBooks.

Preston, Douglas J. Jennie. 1994. 336p. text 21.95 o.p. (*0-312-11294-7*) St. Martin's Pr.

Ray, Jeanne. Julie & Romeo. abr. ed. 2000. audio 17.95 (*1-56740-900-8*, Nova Audio Bks.); audio 44.25 (*1-56740-722-6*, 2076, Unabridged Library Editions); audio 24.95 (*1-56740-355-7*, 2075, Brilliance Audio Unabridged) Brilliance Audio.

—Julie & Romeo. 2000. (Illus.). 240p. 21.00 (*0-609-60672-7*, Harmony) Crown Publishing Group.

—Juliet & Romeo: A Novel. l.t. ed. 2000. (Basic Ser.). 303p. 29.95 (*0-7862-2660-9*) Thorndike Pr.

Reed, Barry. The Deception. l.t. ed. 1997. (Niagara Large Print Ser.). 592p. 29.50 o.p. (*0-7089-5884-2*, Ulverscroft) Thorpe, F. A. Pubs. GBR. *Dist:* Ulverscroft Large Print Bks., Ltd.

—The Deception: Courtroom Drama. 1998. 432p. mass mkt. 6.99 (*0-312-96494-3*, St. Martin's Paperbacks) St. Martin's Pr.

—The Indictment. 1995. 436p. mass mkt. 6.99 (*0-312-95416-6*, St. Martin's Paperbacks) St. Martin's Pr.

Reed, Kelvin L. Rookie Year: Journey of a First-Year Teacher. 1999. 336p. 21.95 (*0-9667631-2-2*) Peralta Publishing Co.

Reynolds, John L. And Leave Her Lay Dying. 1992. (Crime Ser.). 272p. pap. 4.95 o.p. (*0-14-012298-2*, Penguin Bks.) Penguin Group (USA) Inc.

—And Leave Her Lay Dying. 1990. 304p. 16.95 o.p. (*0-670-82875-0*) Viking Penguin.

—The Man Who Murdered God. 272p. 1989. 16.95 o.p. (*0-670-82736-3*); 1990. reprint ed. pap. 4.50 o.p. (*0-14-012037-8*, Penguin Bks.) Viking Penguin.

—Whisper Death. 1992. 256p. 18.95 o.p. (*0-670-83669-9*, Viking) Viking Penguin.

Rosen, Dorothy & Rosen, Sidney. Death & Blintzes. 1998. 180p. reprint ed. pap. 10.95 (*0-89733-450-7*) Academy Chicago Pubs., Ltd.

—Death & Blintzes. 1985. 192p. 14.95 o.p. (*0-8027-5625-5*) Walker & Co.

—Death & Strudel. 1999. 272p. 23.00 (*0-89733-478-7*) Academy Chicago Pubs., Ltd.

Rosen, Richard D. Dead Ball: A Harvey Blissberg Mystery. 2001. 252p. 23.95 (*0-8027-3366-2*) Walker & Co.

—Fadeaway. 1986. 256p. 15.95 o.p. (*0-06-015599-X*) HarperTrade.

—Fadeaway. 1987. mass mkt. 3.95 o.p. (*0-451-40046-1*); 288p. mass mkt. 3.95 o.p. (*0-451-40148-4*) NAL. (Onyx).

—Saturday Night Dead. 1989. mass mkt. 3.95 o.p. (*0-451-40134-4*, Onyx) NAL.

—Saturday Night Dead. 1988. 28p. 16.95 o.p. (*0-670-81977-8*) Viking Penguin.

—Strike Three, You're Dead. l.t. ed. 1986. 19.95 o.p. (*1-55504-143-4*) BBC Audiobooks America.

—Strike Three, You're Dead. 1986. mass mkt. 2.95 o.p. (*0-451-14233-0*, Signet Bks.); 256p. mass mkt. 3.95 o.p. (*0-451-40142-5*, Onyx) NAL.

—Strike Three, You're Dead. 1984. 192p. 12.95 o.s.i (*0-8027-5587-9*) Walker & Co.

—World of Hurt. 1994. 264p. 20.95 (*0-8027-3251-8*) Walker & Co.

Russell, E. S. Death of a Cloudwalker. 1991. 192p. 18.95 (*0-8027-5784-7*) Walker & Co.

Ryan, Conall. The House of Cards. 2002. 298p. reprint ed. pap. 14.95 (*1-902881-61-3*) Toby Pr.

Sarton, May. The Education of Harriet Hatfield. 1989. 18.95 o.p. (*0-393-02695-7*) Norton, W. W. & Co., Inc.

Scott, Holden. Skeptic. E-Book 6.99 (*0-312-26468-2*); 2000. 400p. mass mkt. 6.99 (*0-312-96928-7*, St. Martin's Paperbacks); 1999. 322p. 24.95 o.p. (*0-312-19334-3*) St. Martin's Pr.

Sedgwick, John. The Dark House: A Novel. 2000. 432p. 25.00 (*0-06-019560-6*, HarperCollins) HarperTrade.

—The Education of Mrs. Bemis. 2002. 400p. 24.95 (*0-06-019565-7*) HarperCollins Pubs.

—The Education of Mrs. Bemis: A Novel. 2003. 400p. pap. 13.95 (*0-06-051259-8*, Perennial) HarperTrade.

Senna, Danzy. Caucasia. 1998. 353p. 24.95 o.s.i (*1-57322-091-4*); 1999. 432p. reprint ed. pap. 14.00 (*1-57322-716-1*) Berkley Publishing Group. (Riverhead Trade (Paperbacks)).

—Caucasia. pap. (*1-57322-772-2*, Riverhead Bks. (Hardcovers)) Putnam Publishing Group, The.

—Caucasia. 1999. 19.00 (*0-606-18969-6*) Turtleback Bks.

Shafak, Elif. The Saint of Incipient Insanities. 2004. (*0-374-25357-9*) Farrar, Straus & Giroux.

Shattuck, Jessica. The Hazards of Good Breeding. 2003. 288p. 23.95 (*0-393-05132-3*) Norton, W. W. & Co., Inc.

Sinclair, Upton. Boston: A Documentary Novel of the Sacco-Vanzetti Case. 1978. reprint ed. 32.00 (*0-8376-0420-6*) Bentley Pubs.

—Boston: A Documentary Novel of the Sacco-Vanzetti Case. 1999. (Works of Upton Sinclair). 148.00 (*1-58201-826-X*) Classic Bks.

—Boston: A Documentary Novel of the Sacco-Vanzetti Case, 2 vols. 1928. reprint ed. 59.00 (*0-403-00295-8*) Scholarly Pr., Inc.

Smith, David A. In the Cube: A Novel of Future Boston. 1993. 288p. (YA). 18.95 o.p. (*0-312-85448-X*, Tor Bks.) Doherty, Tom Assocs., LLC.

Smith, David A., ed. Future Boston. 384p. 1995. pap. 13.95 (*0-312-89028-1*, Orb Bks.); 1993. 22.95 o.p. (*0-312-85589-3*, Tor Bks.) Doherty, Tom Assocs., LLC.

Smith, J. P. Breathless. unabr. ed. 1995. audio 64.00 (*0-7366-3128-3*, 3803); audio compact disk 12.95 Books on Tape, Inc.

—Breathless. 1999. pap. 9.95 (*0-14-024524-3*); 1995. 336p. 23.95 o.p. (*0-670-86046-8*) Viking Penguin. (Viking).

Smith, Mary-Ann Tirone. She Smiled Sweetly: A Poppy Rice Mystery. 2004. 25.00 (*0-8050-7224-1*) Holt, Henry & Co.

Soos, Troy. Murder at Fenway Park. 1995. 256p. mass mkt. 4.99 o.s.i (*0-8217-4909-9*, Zebra Bks.); 1994. mass mkt. 14.95 o.s.i (*0-8217-4518-2*) Kensington Publishing Corp.

—Murder at Fenway Park. unabr. ed. (Mickey Rawlings Baseball Ser.: Vol. 1). 1999. audio compact disk 58.00 (*0-7887-3418-0*, C1024E7); 1997. audio 51.00 (*0-7887-0874-0*, 95009E7) Recorded Bks., LLC.

—Murder at Fenway Park. l.t. ed. 1995. (Niagara Large Print Ser.). 277p. 29.50 o.p. (*0-7089-5813-3*, Ulverscroft) Thorpe, F. A. Pubs. GBR. *Dist:* Ulverscroft Large Print Bks., Ltd.

Sparks, Nicholas. Message in a Bottle. l.t. ed. (Paperback Bestsellers Ser.). 464p. 1999. pap. 27.95 (*0-7862-1423-6*); 1998. 30.95 (*0-7862-1422-8*) Thorndike Pr.

—Message in a Bottle. 2000. 288p. E-Book 4.95 (*0-446-92352-4*) Time Warner Bk. Group.

—Message in a Bottle. 2000. 288p. E-Book 5.95 (*0-446-96104-3*); 2000. 214p. E-Book 5.95 (*0-446-96076-4*); 2000. 214p. E-Book 5.95 (*0-446-92009-6*); 2000. E-Book 5.95 (*0-446-93041-5*); 2000. 288p. E-Book 5.95 (*0-446-96021-7*); 2000. 288p. E-Book 4.95 (*0-446-91460-6*); 1998. 336p. 20.00 (*0-446-52356-9*); 1999. 352p. reprint ed. pap. 12.95 (*0-446-67607-1*); 1999. 384p. reprint ed. mass mkt. 7.50 (*0-446-60681-2*) Warner Bks., Inc.

Sparks, Nicholas & South, Nigel. Message in a Bottle. 1983. 192p. text 49.95 o.p. (*0-566-00621-9*) Ashgate Publishing Co.

St. John, Nicole. The Medici Ring. 1975. 6.95 o.p. (*0-394-49342-7*) Random Hse., Inc.

—The Medici Ring. 1976. pap. 1.95 o.s.i (*0-671-80444-8*, Pocket) Simon & Schuster.

—The Medici Ring. l.t. ed. 1978. (Ulverscroft Large Print Ser.). 29.99 o.p. (*0-7089-0160-3*, Ulverscroft) Thorpe, F. A. Pubs. GBR. *Dist:* Ulverscroft Large Print Bks., Ltd., Ulverscroft Large Print Canada, Ltd.

—The Medici Ring. 1999. 286p. reprint ed. pap. 16.00 (*1-892323-25-7*) Vivisphere Publishing.

Steel, Danielle. The Ghost. abr. ed. 1997. audio 25.95 (*0-553-47882-6*, 695424); audio compact disk 29.95 (*0-553-45563-X*) Random Hse. Audio Publishing Group. (RH Audio).

Stephenson, Neal. Zodiac: The Eco-Thriller. 1995. 320p. mass mkt. 7.50 (*0-553-57386-1*, Spectra) Bantam Bks.

—Zodiac: The Eco-Thriller. 1988. 300p. pap. 7.95 o.p. (*0-87113-181-1*, Atlantic Monthly Pr.) Grove/ Atlantic, Inc.

Stuart, Sarah P. The Year Roger Wasn't Well: A Novel. 1994. 256p. 20.00 o.p. (*0-06-017079-4*) Harper-Trade.

Sullivan, Winona. A Sudden Death at the Norfolk Cafe: A Sister Cecile Mystery. 1995. (Sister Cecile Mystery Ser.). mass mkt. 5.99 o.s.i (*0-8041-1213-4*, Ivy Bks.) Ballantine Bks.

—A Sudden Death at the Norfolk Cafe: A Sister Cecile Mystery. 1993. 214p. 17.95 o.p. (*0-312-08899-X*, Saint Martin's Minotaur) St. Martin's Pr.

Tanger, Woody. The Dead Cure. Caso, Adolph, ed. 1996. 180p. pap. 13.95 (*0-8283-2021-7*) Branden Bks.

Tapply, William G. Client Privilege. l.t. ed. 1991. 23.95 o.p. (*0-7927-0888-1*, CH099); pap. 21.95 o.p. (*0-7927-0889-X*, CS0199) BBC Audiobooks America.

—Client Privilege. 1991. 288p. mass mkt. 4.50 o.s.i (*0-440-20866-1*) Dell Publishing.

—Close to the Bone. 1996. 224p. 20.95 o.p. (*0-312-14567-5*, Saint Martin's Minotaur) St. Martin's Pr.

—Close to the Bone: A Brady Coyne Mystery. unabr. ed. 2000. audio 49.95 (*0-7927-2212-4*, CSL 101) Chivers Audio Bks. GBR. *Dist:* BBC Audiobooks America.

—Cutter's Run. l.t. ed. 1999. pap. 24.95 (*1-56895-706-8*, Wheeler Publishing, Inc.) Gale Group.

—Cutter's Run. 1998. (Brady Coyne Mysteries Ser.). 274p. 23.95 (*0-312-18561-8*, Saint Martin's Minotaur) St. Martin's Pr.

—Dead Meat. l.t. ed. 1991. pap. 8.95 o.p. (*1-55504-857-9*, 162); 1989. 15.95 o.p. (*0-7451-9473-7*, 546) BBC Audiobooks America.

—Dead Meat. 1988. 240p. mass mkt. 3.50 o.s.i (*0-345-34730-7*) Ballantine Bks.

—Dead Meat: A Brady Coyne Mystery. 1987. 14.95 o.p. (*0-684-18682-9*, Macmillan Reference USA) Gale Group.

—Dead Winter. 1990. 240p. mass mkt. 3.95 o.s.i (*0-440-20566-2*); 1989. 16.95 o.s.i (*0-440-50171-7*, Delacorte Pr.) Dell Publishing.

—Dead Winter. l.t. ed. 1991. (General Ser.). 350p. lib. bdg. 18.95 o.p. (*0-8161-5003-6*, Macmillan Reference USA) Gale Group.

—Dead Winter. l.t. ed. 1991. (Magna Large Print Ser.). 318p. o.p. (*0-7505-0126-X*) Magna Large Print Bks. GBR. *Dist:* Ulverscroft Large Print Canada, Ltd.

—Death at Charity's Point. l.t. ed. 1991. pap. 10.95 o.p. (*0-7927-0109-7*, C0136) BBC Audiobooks America.

—Death at Charity's Point. 1985. 240p. mass mkt. 2.95 o.s.i (*0-345-32014-X*) Ballantine Bks.

—Death at Charity's Point. 1984. 224p. 12.95 o.p. (*0-684-18056-1*, Macmillan Reference USA) Gale Group.

—Death at Charity's Point. 1997. (Missing Mysteries Ser.: Vol. 2). 244p. reprint ed. pap. 7.95 (*1-890208-02-7*) Poisoned Pen Pr.

—The Dutch Blue Error. 1985. 224p. mass mkt. 2.95 o.s.i (*0-345-32341-6*) Ballantine Bks.

—The Dutch Blue Error. 1984. 240p. 12.95 o.s.i (*0-684-18213-0*, Macmillan Reference USA) Gale Group.

—Dutch Blue Error. l.t. ed. 1986. 321p. 16.95 o.p. (*0-89340-937-5*) BBC Audiobooks America.

—A Fine Line. 2004. mass mkt. (*0-312-98978-4*, St. Martin's Paperbacks) St. Martin's Pr.

—A Fine Line: A Brady Coyne Novel. 2002. 320p. 24.95 (*0-312-30352-1*, Saint Martin's Minotaur) St. Martin's Pr.

—A Fine Line: A Brady Coyne Novel. l.t. ed. 2003. (Mystery Ser.). 30.95 (*0-7862-5208-1*) Thorndike Pr.

—Follow the Sharks. 1985. (Brady Coyne Mystery Ser.). 224p. 13.95 o.p. (*0-684-18446-X*, Macmillan Reference USA) Gale Group.

—Follow the Sharks! 1986. mass mkt. 4.99 o.s.i (*0-345-32906-6*) Ballantine Bks.

—Follow the Sharks. l.t. ed. 1988. pap. 8.95 o.p. (*1-55504-346-1*) BBC Audiobooks America.

—The Marine Corpse. 1987. 240p. mass mkt. 3.95 o.s.i (*0-345-34057-4*) Ballantine Bks.

—The Marine Corpse: A Brady Coyne Mystery. 1986. 240p. 13.95 o.s.i (*0-684-18681-0*, Macmillan Reference USA) Gale Group.

—Past Tense. 2004. mass mkt. 6.99 (*0-312-99551-2*, St. Martin's Paperbacks) St. Martin's Pr.

—Past Tense. l.t. ed. 2002. (Core Collection). 382p. 28.95 (*0-7862-4678-2*) Thorndike Pr.

—Rodent of Doubt. l.t. ed. 1988. pap. 13.95 o.p. (*1-55504-548-0*) BBC Audiobooks America.

—Scar Tissue. 2000. 276p. 24.95 (*0-312-26679-0*, Saint Martin's Minotaur) St. Martin's Pr.

—Seventh Enemy: A Brady Coyne Mystery. 1995. 234p. 21.00 (*1-883402-99-9*, Scribner) Simon & Schuster.

—Shadow of Death: A Brady Coyne Novel. 2003. 320p. 24.95 (*0-312-30377-7*, Saint Martin's Minotaur) St. Martin's Pr.

—The Snake Eater. 1993. 273p. 20.00 o.p. (*1-883402-04-2*, Scribner) Simon & Schuster.

—The Spotted Cats: A Brady Coyne Mystery. 1992. 256p. mass mkt. 4.50 o.s.i (*0-440-21191-3*) Dell Publishing.

—Tight Lines. l.t. ed. 1995. (Magna Large Print Ser.). 421p. (*0-7505-0796-9*) Magna Large Print Bks. GBR. *Dist:* Ulverscroft Large Print Canada, Ltd.

—Tight Lines: A Brady Coyne Mystery. 1993. 288p. mass mkt. 4.99 o.s.i (*0-440-21410-6*) Dell Publishing.

—A Void in Hearts. 1990. 192p. mass mkt. 3.95 o.s.i (*0-345-35868-6*) Ballantine Bks.

—A Void in Hearts. l.t. ed. 1990. (General Ser.). 427p. lib. bdg. 18.95 o.p. (*0-8161-4822-8*, Macmillan Reference USA) Gale Group.

—A Void in Hearts. 1988. (Brady Coyne Mystery Ser.: No. 7). 224p. 16.95 o.s.i (*0-684-18793-0*, Scribner) Simon & Schuster.

—The Vulgar Boatman. l.t. ed. 1991. 8.95 o.p. (*0-7451-9583-0*, 5054); pap. 10.95 o.p. (*0-7927-0011-2*, 618) BBC Audiobooks America.

—The Vulgar Boatman. 1989. 256p. mass mkt. 3.95 o.s.i (*0-345-35577-6*) Ballantine Bks.

—The Vulgar Boatman. l.t. ed. 1989. viii, 315 p. pap. (*0-7451-9595-4*) Chivers Pr.

—The Vulgar Boatman. 1988. (Brady Coyne Mystery Ser.). 240p. 14.95 o.s.i (*0-684-18792-2*, Scribner) Simon & Schuster.

Taylor, Phoebe Atwood. The Iron Clew. 1992. (Leonidas Witherall Mystery Ser.). 216p. pap. 6.00 (*0-88150-241-3*, Foul Play) Norton, W. W. & Co., Inc.

Thomson, Maynard F. Breaking Faith. 1997. 352p. per. 6.50 (*0-671-86789-X*, Pocket) Simon & Schuster.

—Breaking Faith. Wolverton, Pete R., ed. 1996. 384p. 22.00 (*0-671-74900-5*, Atria) Simon & Schuster.

—Dreams of Gold. 2001. 464p. E-Book 4.95 (*0-7595-0628-0*); 2001. 464p. E-Book 4.95 (*0-7595-6629-1*); 2001. 464p. E-Book 4.95 (*0-7595-8638-1*); 2001. 464p. E-Book 4.95 (*0-7595-9699-9*); 2001. 464p. E-Book 4.95 (*0-7595-4631-2*); 2000. 464p. mass mkt. 6.99 (*0-446-60775-4*); 1999. 452p. 22.00 o.p. (*0-446-52445-X*) Warner Bks., Inc.

—Trade Secrets. Chelius, Jane, ed. 256p. 1994. mass mkt. 4.99 (*0-671-86788-1*, Pocket); 1993. 20.00 (*0-671-74899-8*, Atria) Simon & Schuster.

—Trade Secrets. 244p. 3.98 o.p. (*0-8317-2322-X*) Smithmark Pubs., Inc.

Tucker, Kerry. Drift Away: A Libby Kincaid Mystery. 1995. 240p. mass mkt. 4.99 o.p. (*0-06-109176-6*); 1994. 224p. 20.00 o.p. (*0-06-017999-6*) Harper-Collins Pubs.

Waugh, Carol-Lynn R., et al, eds. Murder & Mystery in Boston. 1987. (Murder & Mystery in Ser.). 304p. 15.95 o.p. (*0-934878-95-1*, Dembner Bks.) Barricade Bks., Inc.

Weber, Janice. Devil's Food. 1996. 480p. 22.95 o.p. (*0-446-51772-0*) Warner Bks., Inc.

Weller, Marilyn. Fatal Flaws. 2003. 253p. pap. 15.00 (*0-9722925-0-0*) Aihole Publishing.

Wensberg, Peter C. The Last Bastion. 1995. 224p. 22.00 o.p. (*1-877946-58-3*); pap. 16.00 (*1-57962-001-9*) Permanent Pr., The.

West, Dorothy. Living Is Easy. 1970. (American Negro). reprint ed. 45.95 (*0-405-01942-4*) Ayer Co. Pubs., Inc.

—Living Is Easy. 1982. 376p. (C). reprint ed. pap. 14.95 o.p. (*0-912670-97-5*) Feminist Pr. at The City Univ. of New York.

Wiggs, Susan. The Charm School. abr. ed. 2001. audio 7.99 (*1-55204-174-3*, MIR-1174) Durkin Hayes Publishing Ltd.

—The Charm School. 1999. (Mira Bks.). 408p. per. (*1-55166-491-7*, 1-66491-1, Mira Bks.) Harlequin Enterprises, Ltd.

Willett, Sabin. The Deal. 1997. 496p. mass mkt. 6.99 o.s.i (*0-515-12182-7*, Jove) Berkley Publishing Group.

—Present Value: A Novel. 2003. 416p. 24.95 (*1-4000-6086-9*, Villard Bks.) Random House Adult Trade Publishing Group.

Woods, Sherryl. Ryan's Place. 2002. (Silhouette Special Edition Ser.). mass mkt. (*0-373-24489-4*, Silhouette) Harlequin Enterprises, Ltd.

Ziporyn, Terra. Time's Fool. 2001. 231p. text 31.99 (*1-4010-0486-5*) Xlibris Corp.

### BOTANY (IMAGINARY PLACE)—FICTION

McCaffrey, Anne. Freedom's Challenge. 1999. 320p. reprint ed. mass mkt. 6.99 (*0-441-00625-6*) Ace Bks.

—Freedom's Challenge. 1998. 288p. 23.95 o.p. (*0-399-14397-1*) Penguin Group (USA) Inc.

—Freedom's Challenge. 1999. 12.04 (*0-606-20078-9*); 13.00 (*0-606-20392-3*) Turtleback Bks.

—Freedom's Choice. 1998. 336p. mass mkt. 6.99 (*0-441-00531-4*) Ace Bks.

—Freedom's Choice. 1997. 293p. 23.95 o.s.i (*0-399-14270-3*, Ace/Putnam) Penguin Group (USA) Inc.

—Freedom's Landing. 1996. 336p. mass mkt. 6.99 (*0-441-00338-9*) Ace Bks.

—Freedom's Landing. 1995. 22.95 o.p. (*0-399-14062-X*, G. P. Putnam's Sons) Penguin Group (USA) Inc.

—Freedom's Landing. 1999. 13.04 (*0-606-15538-4*) Turtleback Bks.

—Freedom's Ransom. 2003. 304p. reprint ed. mass mkt. 6.99 (*0-441-01020-2*) Ace Bks.

—Freedom's Ransom. 2002. 304p. 23.95 (*0-399-14889-2*, Putnam & Grosset) Penguin Group (USA) Inc.

### BOTSWANA—FICTION

Bosman, Herman Charles & MacKenzie, Craig. Mafeking Road & Other Stories. 1998. (Illus.). (*0-7981-3902-1*) Human & Rousseau.

Rush, Norman. Mortals. 2004. (Illus.). 736p. pap. 15.95 (*0-679-73711-1*, Vintage) Knopf Publishing Group.

—Mortals. 2003. (Illus.). 736p. 26.95 (*0-679-40622-0*) Knopf, Alfred A. Inc.

Smith, Alexander McCall. The Full Cupboard of Life. 2004. 208p. 19.95 (*0-375-42218-8*, Pantheon) Knopf Publishing Group.

—The Full Cupboard of Life. l.t. ed. 2004. 352p. 21.95 (*0-375-43335-X*) Random Hse. Large Print.

—The Kalahari Typing School for Men. l.t. ed. 2003. lib. bdg. 29.95 (*1-58547-331-6*, Platinum) Ctr. Point Large Print.

—The Kalahari Typing School for Men. 192p. 2004. pap. 11.95 (*1-4000-3180-X*, Anchor); 2003. 19.95 (*0-375-42217-X*, Pantheon) Knopf Publishing Group.

—The Kalahari Typing School for Men. 2003. 192p. 32.95 (*0-676-97568-2*) Knopf, Alfred A. Inc.

—The Kalahari Typing School for Men. audio 24.99 (*1-4025-4178-3*); audio compact disk 29.99 (*1-4025-4706-4*) Recorded Bks., LLC.

—Morality for Beautiful Girls. l.t. ed. 2003. lib. bdg. 29.95 (*1-58547-330-8*, Premier) Ctr. Point Large Print.

—Morality for Beautiful Girls. 2001. 236p. pap. 12.95 (*0-7486-6297-9*) Polygon GBR. *Dist:* Interlink Publishing Group, Inc.

—Morality for Beautiful Girls. 2002. 240p. pap. 11.95 (*1-4000-3136-2*) Random Hse., Inc.

—Morality for Beautiful Girls. audio compact disk 29.99 (*1-4025-4368-9*) Recorded Bks., LLC.

—The No. 1 Ladies' Detective Agency. l.t. ed. 2003. lib. bdg. 29.95 (*1-58547-328-6*, Platinum) Ctr. Point Large Print.

—The No. 1 Ladies' Detective Agency. 2003. 240p. pap. 11.95 (*1-4000-3477-9*, Anchor) Knopf Publishing Group.

—The No. 1 Ladies' Detective Agency. 2001. 202p. pap. 12.95 o.p. (*0-7486-6252-9*) Polygon GBR. *Dist:* AK Pr. Distribution.

—The No. 1 Ladies' Detective Agency. 2002. 240p. pap. 11.95 o.s.i (*1-4000-3134-6*, Knopf Bks. for Young Readers) Random Hse. Children's Bks.

—The No. 1 Ladies' Detective Agency. audio compact disk 29.99 (*1-4025-4535-5*) Recorded Bks., LLC.

—Tears of the Giraffe. 2001. 208p. 12.95 (*0-7486-6273-1*) Edinburgh Univ. Pr. GBR. *Dist:* Columbia Univ. Pr.

—Tears of the Giraffe. 2002. 240p. pap. 11.95 (*1-4000-3135-4*, Knopf Bks. for Young Readers) Random Hse. Children's Bks.

—Tears of the Giraffe. audio 24.99 (*1-4025-4177-5*); audio compact disk 29.99 (*1-4025-4705-6*) Recorded Bks., LLC.

### BOULDER (COLO.)—FICTION

Blume, Judy. Wifey & Smart Women. 2001. 544p. pap. 13.95 (*0-7434-3757-8*, Pocket) Simon & Schuster.

Cail, Carol. Unsafe Keeping. 1996. 304p. mass mkt. 5.50 o.s.i (*0-440-22298-2*) Dell Publishing.

—Unsafe Keeping. pap. 15.95 (*0-312-29194-9*, Saint Martin's Griffin); pap. (*0-312-30031-X*, Saint Martin's Griffin); 1995. 218p. 15.95 (*0-312-13198-4*, Saint Martin's Minotaur) St. Martin's Pr.

—Who Was Sylvia? 1999. (Maxey Burnell Mystery Ser.). 180p. pap. text 16.99 (*1-886199-04-3*, Madison Publishing Co.) Deadly Alibi Pr., Ltd.

Kerr, Baine. Harmful Intent. 2000. 384p. reprint ed. mass mkt. 6.99 (*0-515-12924-0*, Jove) Berkley Publishing Group.

—Harmful Intent. 1999. 368p. 25.00 (*0-684-85413-9*, Scribner) Simon & Schuster.

Millhiser, Marlys. It's Murder Going Home. 1997. (Charlie Greene Mystery Ser.). 288p. mass mkt. 6.95 o.s.i (*0-14-026586-4*) Penguin Group (USA) Inc.

—It's Murder Going Home. 1996. 304p. 22.95 (*0-312-14628-0*, Saint Martin's Minotaur) St. Martin's Pr.

O'Kane, Leslie. Play Dead. 1998. (Allie Babcock Mysteries Ser.). 261p. mass mkt. 5.99 o.s.i (*0-449-00159-8*, Fawcett) Ballantine Bks.

—Play Dead. l.t. ed. 2000. (Mystery Ser.). 391p. o.p. (*0-7862-2329-4*) Thorndike Pr.

—Ruff Way to Go. 2000. (Allie Babcock Mysteries Ser.). 240p. mass mkt. 6.50 o.s.i (*0-449-00161-X*, Fawcett) Ballantine Bks.

—Ruff Way to Go. l.t. ed. 2001. (Thorndike Mystery Ser.). 383p. 28.95 (*0-7862-3193-9*) Thorndike Pr.

Wesson, Marianne. Render up the Body: A Novel of Suspense. l.t. ed. 1998. 432p. mass mkt. 6.99 (*0-06-109392-0*, HarperTorch) Morrow/Avon.

White, Stephen. Blinded. 2004. 400p. 24.95 (*0-385-33620-9*, Delacorte Pr.) Dell Publishing.

—Cold Case. 2000. (Illus.). 368p. 24.95 (*0-525-94526-1*, Dutton) Dutton/Plume.

—Cold Case. 2001. 432p. mass mkt. 7.99 (*0-451-20155-8*, Signet Bks.) NAL.

—Cold Case. l.t. ed. 2000. (Mystery Ser.). 623p. 29.95 (*0-7862-2530-0*) Thorndike Pr.

—Critical Conditions. l.t. ed. 2000. 27.95 (*1-57490-280-6*, Beeler Large Print Bks.) Beeler, Thomas T. Publisher.

—Critical Conditions. unabr. ed. 1998. (Alan Gregory Ser.). audio 64.00 (*0-7366-4184-X*, 4682) Books on Tape, Inc.

—Critical Conditions. 1998. (Alan Gregory Ser.). 320p. 24.95 o.p. (*0-525-94270-X*) Dutton/Plume.

—Critical Conditions. 1999. (Alan Gregory Ser.). 416p. mass mkt. 7.99 (*0-451-19170-6*, Signet Bks.) NAL.

—Harm's Way. l.t. ed. 1996. lib. bdg. 24.95 (*1-57490-066-8*, Beeler Large Print Bks.) Beeler, Thomas T. Publisher.

—Harm's Way. unabr. collector's ed. 1997. (Alan Gregory Ser.). audio 56.00 (*0-913369-39-X*, 4215) Books on Tape, Inc.

—Harm's Way. 1997. 432p. mass mkt. 7.99 (*0-451-18368-1*, Signet Bks.) NAL.

—Harm's Way. 1996. 352p. 22.95 o.p. (*0-670-85861-7*, Viking) Viking Penguin.

—Higher Authority. unabr. collector's ed. 1995. (Alan Gregory Ser.). audio 80.00 (*0-7366-3042-2*, 3724) Books on Tape, Inc.

—Higher Authority. 1996. 432p. mass mkt. 7.99 (*0-451-18511-0*, Signet Bks.) NAL.

—Higher Authority. 1994. 464p. 22.95 o.p. (*0-670-85040-3*) Viking Penguin.

—Manner of Death. l.t. ed. 1999. 450p. 26.95 (*1-57490-177-X*) Beeler, Thomas T. Publisher.

—Manner of Death. unabr. ed. 1999. (Alan Gregory Ser.). audio 72.00 (*0-7366-4403-2*, 4864) Books on Tape, Inc.

—Manner of Death. 1999. (Alan Gregory Ser.). 416p. 23.95 o.p. (*0-525-94440-0*) Dutton/Plume.

—Manner of Death. 2000. 416p. reprint ed. mass mkt. 7.50 (*0-451-19703-8*, Signet Bks.) NAL.

—Private Practices. unabr. collector's ed. 1993. (Alan Gregory Ser.). audio 80.00 (*0-7366-2592-5*, 3337) Books on Tape, Inc.

—Private Practices. 1994. 432p. mass mkt. 7.99 (*0-451-40431-9*, Signet Bks.) NAL.

—Private Practices. 1999. pap. (*0-14-017328-5*); 1993. 432p. 20.00 o.p. (*0-670-84673-2*) Viking Penguin. (Viking).

—Privileged Information. unabr. collector's ed. 1992. (Alan Gregory Ser.). audio 72.00 (*0-7366-2262-4*, 3050) Books on Tape, Inc.

—Privileged Information. 2001. 384p. mass mkt. 6.99 (*0-7860-1356-7*, Pinnacle Bks.); 1999. 383p. mass mkt. 5.99 o.s.i (*0-7860-0624-2*); 1992. 384p. reprint ed. mass mkt. 5.99 o.s.i (*0-8217-3951-4*, Zebra Bks.) Kensington Publishing Corp.

—Privileged Information. 1991. 368p. 19.95 o.p. (*0-670-83765-2*) Viking Penguin.

—The Program. abr. ed. 2001. audio 24.95 o.s.i (*1-58788-359-7*, 2545, Nova Audio Bks.); audio 34.95 (*1-58788-357-0*, 2543, Brilliance Audio Unabridged); audio 87.25 (*1-58788-358-9*, 2544) Brilliance Audio.

—The Program. l.t. ed. 2002. pap. 28.95 (*0-7862-3412-1*); 2001. 480p. 31.95 (*0-7862-3411-3*) Thorndike Pr.

—Remote Control. unabr. ed. 1997. (Alan Gregory Ser.). audio 64.00 (*0-7366-3769-9*, 4442) Books on Tape, Inc.

—Remote Control. 1997. (Alan Gregory Ser.). 320p. 22.95 o.s.i (*0-525-94269-6*) Dutton/Plume.

—Remote Control. 1998. (Alan Gregory Ser.). 432p. mass mkt. 6.99 (*0-451-19169-2*, Signet Bks.) NAL.

—Remote Control. abr. ed. 1997. (Alan Gregory Ser.). audio 16.95 o.s.i (*0-14-086549-7*, Penguin Audio-Books) Viking Penguin.

—Warning Signs. abr. ed. 2003. (Dr. Alan Gregory Series: Vol. 10). audio 12.99 (*1-59086-573-1*, 4163, Brilliance Audio Paperback Audiobooks); 2002. audio 24.95 o.p. (*1-58788-362-7*, 2548, Nova Audio Bks.); 2002. audio 34.95 (*1-58788-360-0*, 2546, Brilliance Audio Unabridged); 2002. audio 73.25 (*1-58788-361-9*, 2547, Unabridged Library Editions) Brilliance Audio.

—Warning Signs. 2002. lib. bdg. 29.95 (*1-58547-186-0*, Platinum) Ctr. Point Large Print.

—Warning Signs. 2003. 512p. mass mkt. 7.99 (*0-440-23741-6*); 2003. E-Book 7.99 (*0-440-33406-3*, Dell Bks.); 2002. 432p. 24.95 (*0-385-33618-7*, Delacorte Pr.) Dell Publishing.

—Warning Signs. unabr. ed. 2003. audio 19.99 (*1-59335-120-8*, 30216) Soulmate Audio Bks., Inc.

**BRANSON (MO.)—FICTION**

Westlake, Donald E. Baby, Would I Lie? unabr. ed. 2000. audio 29.95 (*1-57270-139-0*, N61139u, Audio Editions Mystery Masters) Audio Partners Publishing Corp.

—Baby, Would I Lie? abr. ed. 1994. audio 17.00 o.p. (*1-56100-374-3*, 799, Nova Audio Bks.); audio 57.25 o.p. (*1-56100-197-X*, 1127, Unabridged Library Editions); audio 21.95 o.p. (*1-56100-571-1*, 35, Bookcassette) Brilliance Audio.

—Baby, Would I Lie? unabr. ed. 2000. audio 59.95 (*0-7927-2275-2*, CSL 164) Chivers Audio Bks. GBR. *Dist:* BBC Audiobooks America.

—Baby, Would I Lie? 1994. 304p. 19.95 o.s.i (*0-89296-532-0*) Mysterious Pr.

—Baby, Would I Lie? 1995. 320p. mass mkt. 5.99 (*0-446-40342-3*) Warner Bks., Inc.

**BRATTLEBORO (VT.)—FICTION**

Mayor, Archer. Bellows Falls. 1997. 224p. 22.00 o.p. (*0-89296-637-8*) Mysterious Pr.

—Bellows Falls. l.t. ed. 1998. (Mystery Ser.). 392p. 27.95 (*0-7838-8405-2*) Thorndike Pr.

—Bellows Falls. 1998. 352p. reprint ed. mass mkt. 6.99 (*0-446-60630-8*) Warner Bks., Inc.

—Borderlines. 1991. 320p. mass mkt. 4.50 (*0-380-71600-3*, Avon Bks.) Morrow/Avon.

—Borderlines. 1990. 256p. 19.95 o.s.i (*0-399-13553-7*, G. P. Putnam's Sons) Penguin Putnam Bks. for Young Readers.

—Borderlines. 1994. 336p. reprint ed. mass mkt. 6.99 (*0-446-40443-8*) Warner Bks., Inc.

—The Dark Root. 1995. 82p. 19.95 o.p. (*0-89296-558-4*) Mysterious Pr.

—The Dark Root. 1996. 400p. reprint ed. mass mkt. 6.99 (*0-446-40376-8*) Warner Bks., Inc.

—The Disposable Man. 1998. (Joe Gunther Mysteries Ser.). 294p. 22.00 o.p. (*0-89296-685-8*) Mysterious Pr.

—The Disposable Man. 1999. 336p. reprint ed. mass mkt. 6.99 (*0-446-60768-1*) Warner Bks., Inc.

—Fruits of the Poisonous Tree. 1994. 224p. 19.95 o.s.i (*0-89296-557-6*) Mysterious Pr.

—Fruits of the Poisonous Tree. 1995. (Joe Gunther Mysteries Ser.). 304p. reprint ed. mass mkt. 6.99 (*0-446-40374-1*) Warner Bks., Inc.

—Occam's Razor. l.t. ed. 2000. (Core Ser.). 544p. 30.00 o.p. (*0-7838-8814-7*, Macmillan Reference USA) Gale Group.

—Occam's Razor. 1999. 304p. 23.95 (*0-89296-682-3*) Mysterious Pr.

—Occam's Razor. 2000. 480p. reprint ed. mass mkt. 6.99 (*0-446-60887-4*) Warner Bks., Inc.

—Open Season. 1989. 320p. pap. 3.95 (*0-380-70756-X*, Avon Bks.) Morrow/Avon.

—Open Season. 1988. 304p. 18.95 o.p. (*0-399-13398-4*, G. P. Putnam's Sons) Penguin Putnam Bks. for Young Readers.

—Open Season. 1994. (Joe Gunther Mysteries Ser.). 320p. reprint ed. mass mkt. 6.99 (*0-446-40414-4*) Warner Bks., Inc.

—The Ragman's Memory. l.t. ed. 1997. (G. K. Hall Mystery Ser.). 483p. lib. bdg. 25.95 o.p. (*0-7838-8208-4*, Macmillan Reference USA) Gale Group.

—The Ragman's Memory. 1997. 368p. 6.50 (*0-446-40524-8*) Mysterious Pr.

—The Ragman's Memory. 1996. 336p. 22.00 o.p. (*0-89296-636-X*); 1997. 368p. reprint ed. mass mkt. 6.99 (*0-446-60590-5*) Warner Bks., Inc.

—Scent of Evil. 1992. 368p. 18.95 o.p. (*0-89296-471-5*) Mysterious Pr.

—Scent of Evil. 1993. (Joe Gunther Mysteries Ser.). 416p. reprint ed. mass mkt. 6.99 (*0-446-40335-0*) Warner Bks., Inc.

—The Skeleton's Knee. 1993. 320p. 18.95 (*0-89296-470-7*) Mysterious Pr.

—The Skeleton's Knee. 1994. (Joe Gunther Mysteries Ser.). 320p. reprint ed. mass mkt. 6.99 (*0-446-40099-8*) Warner Bks., Inc.

**BRAZIL—FICTION**

Abreu, Ciao Fernando. Whatever Happened to Dulce Veiga? A B-Novel. Frizzi, Adia, tr. from POR. & afterword by by. 2001. (Texas Pan American Ser.). 206p. 35.00 o.p. (*0-292-70500-X*) Univ. of Texas Pr.

Abreu, Ciao Fernando & Frizzi, Adria. Whatever Happened to Dulce Veiga? A B-Novel. 2001. (Texas Pan American Ser.). 206p. pap. 15.95 (*0-292-70501-8*) Univ. of Texas Pr.

Agualusa, Jose Eduardo. Creole Nation. 2002. 288p. pap. 16.00 (*1-900850-61-3*) Arcadia Bks. GBR. *Dist:* Consortium Bk. Sales & Distribution.

Alencar, Jose de. Senhora: Profile of a Woman. Edinger, Catarina F., tr. from POR. 1994. (Texas Pan American Ser.). 219p. (C). 30.00 o.p. (*0-292-70449-6*); pap. 12.95 (*0-292-70450-X*) Univ. of Texas Pr.

Amado, Jorge. The Golden Harvest. Landers, Clifford E., tr. from POR. 1992. Orig. Title: Sao jorge dos ilheus. 368p. (Orig.). pap. 12.50 (*0-380-76100-9*, Avon Bks.) Morrow/Avon.

Andrade, Mario de. Macunaima. Goodland, E. A., tr. from POR. 1985. 176p. 14.95 o.p. (*0-394-53412-3*) Random Hse., Inc.

Anthony, Patricia. Cradle of Splendor. (Orig.). 1996. 320p. 22.95 o.p. (*0-441-00301-X*); 1997. 304p. reprint ed. mass mkt. 5.99 o.s.i (*0-441-00426-1*) Ace Bks.

Azevedo, Aluisio. Mulatto. MacNicoll, Murray G., ed. & tr. by. from POR. 1990. 304p. 39.50 (*0-8386-3380-3*) Fairleigh Dickinson Univ. Pr.

—Mulatto. Patai, Daphne, ed. MacNicoll, Murray G., tr. from POR. 1993. (Texas Pan American Ser.). 298p. (C). reprint ed. pap. 16.95 o.p. (*0-292-70438-0*) Univ. of Texas Pr.

Bingley, David. Rendezvous in Rio. l.t. ed. 2001. (Linford Mystery Large Print Ser.). 320p. pap. 19.99 (*0-7089-5995-4*, Ulverscroft) Thorpe, F. A. Pubs. GBR. *Dist:* Ulverscroft Large Print Bks., Ltd., Ulverscroft Large Print Canada, Ltd.

Blasi, Vera. Woman on Top: A Sexy Delicious Fairytale. 2000. (Illus.). 112p. 20.00 (*0-06-039396-3*, ReganBooks) HarperTrade.

Bowman, Elizabeth Atkins. Twilight. 2003. 448p. mass mkt. 6.99 (*0-7653-4507-2*, Forge Bks.) Doherty, Tom Assocs., LLC.

Bullen, Fiona. The Deep Blue Sea. 1992. 464p. 22.95 o.p. (*0-312-07706-8*) St. Martin's Pr.

Caminha, Adolfo. Bom-Crioulo: The Black Man & the Cabin Boy. Lacey, E. A., tr. from POR. 1982. 144p. 25.00 (*0-917342-89-5*); pap. 14.95 (*0-917342-88-7*) Gay Sunshine Pr., Inc.

Coelho, Paulo. El Demonio y la Senorita Prym. 2002. Tr. of Devil & Miss Prym. (SPA.). 220p. 15.48 (*970-05-1297-5*) Grijalbo, Editorial MEX. *Dist:* AIMS International Bks., Inc., Forsa Editores.

—Eleven Minutes. 2004. 288p. 24.95 (*0-06-058927-2*, HarperCollins) HarperTrade.

Courter, Gay. River of Dreams. l.t. ed. 1984. (General Ser.). 18.95 o.p. (*0-8161-3768-4*, Macmillan Reference USA) Gale Group.

—River of Dreams, 001. 1984. (Illus.). 544p. 16.95 o.p. (*0-395-35301-7*) Houghton Mifflin Co.

Dee, Jonathan. The Liberty Campaign. l.t. ed. 1994. 22.95 o.p. (*0-7927-1946-8*); 1994. pap. 21.95 o.p. (*0-7927-1945-X*); 1995. audio 69.95 (*0-7862-9978-9*, CSL 082) BBC Audiobooks America.

—The Liberty Campaign. 1995. 288p. pap. 17.95 (*0-671-89085-9*, Pocket) Simon & Schuster.

Dourado, Autran. Pattern for a Tapestry. Parker, John M., tr. from POR. 1984. 170p. 30.00 (*0-7206-0608-X*) Owen, Peter Ltd. GBR. *Dist:* Dufour Editions, Inc.

—Voices of the Dead: A Novel. Parker, John M., tr. from POR. 1981. Orig. Title: Opera Dos Mortos. 248p. 10.95 o.s.i (*0-8008-8030-7*) Taplinger Publishing Co., Inc.

Feldmanis, Erik. The Jungle. 125p. mass mkt. (*1-55197-366-9*);Pt. I. 1999. 120p. pap. (*1-55279-017-7*);Pt. II. 1999. 144p. pap. (*1-55279-015-0*);Pt. III. 1999. 112p. pap. (*1-55279-016-9*) Picasso Pubns., Inc.

Fonesca, Rubem. High Art. Watson, Ellen, tr. 1986. 256p. 17.95 o.p. (*0-06-015572-8*) HarperTrade.

Fonseca, Rubem. Vast Emotions & Imperfect Thoughts. Landers, Clifford E., tr. from POR. 1998. 312p. 24.00 o.p. (*0-88001-583-7*) HarperCollins Pubs.

Garner, Sharon K. River of Dreams. 2000. (First Edition Romance Ser.). 192p. 25.95 (*0-7862-2317-0*, Five Star) Gale Group.

Ghose, Zulfikar. A Different World. 318p. 1986. pap. 9.95 o.s.i (*0-87951-207-5*); 1985. 22.50 (*0-87951-982-7*) Overlook Pr., The.

Grisham, John. The Partner. 1998. 480p. pap. 7.99 (*0-440-22604-X*); 1998. 480p. mass mkt. 7.99 (*0-440-22476-4*); 1997. mass mkt. 7.99 (*0-440-29555-6*) Dell Publishing.

—The Partner. 1997. 368p. 27.95 (*0-385-47295-1*); 528p. 31.95 o.s.i (*0-385-48578-6*); 368p. 250.00 o.s.i (*0-385-48592-1*) Doubleday Publishing.

—The Partner, Level 5. 2001. pap. 7.66 (*0-582-43406-8*) Longman Publishing Group.

—The Partner. abr. ed. 1997. audio 26.95 (*0-553-47283-6*, 694963); audio compact disk 29.95 (*0-553-45553-2*) Random Hse. Audio Publishing Group. (RH Audio).

—The Partner. 1998. 14.04 (*0-606-15672-0*) Turtleback Bks.

—The Testament. 1999. mass mkt. 7.99 (*0-440-29573-4*) Bantam Dell Publishing Group.

—The Testament. 1999. audio compact disk 88.00 (*0-7366-8905-2*); audio 54.95 (*0-7366-4527-6*, 4884) Books on Tape, Inc.

—The Testament. 1999. 544p. mass mkt. 7.99 (*0-440-23474-3*) Dell Publishing.

—The Testament. 1999. 448p. 27.95 (*0-385-49380-0*); 432p. 250.00 o.s.i (*0-385-49382-7*); 576p. 32.95 o.s.i (*0-385-49381-9*) Doubleday Publishing.

—The Testament. abr. ed. 1999. audio 27.95 Highsmith Inc.

—The Testament. abr. ed. 1999. audio compact disk 29.95 (*0-553-45635-0*); audio 49.95 (*0-553-50227-1*, 134242) Random Hse. Audio Publishing Group. (RH Audio).

—The Testament. 2000. 14.04 (*0-606-18110-5*) Turtleback Bks.

—The Testament. abr. ed. 1999. audio 24.35 (*1-85686-601-7*) Ulverscroft Audio (U.S.A.).

Hatoum, Milton. The Brothers. Gledson, John, tr. from POR. 2002. 240p. 23.00 (*0-374-14118-5*) Farrar, Straus & Giroux.

Helprin, Mark. Memoir from Antproof Case. l.t. ed. 1995. 26.95 (*1-56895-256-2*, Wheeler Publishing, Inc.) Gale Group.

—Memoir from Antproof Case. 1995. 514p. 24.00 o.s.i (*0-15-100097-2*) Harcourt Trade Pubs.

—Memoir from Antproof Case. 1996. 528p. pap. 15.95 (*0-380-72733-1*, Avon Bks.) Morrow/Avon.

Higgins, Jack. Three Complete Novels: The Last Place God Made, the Savage Day, a Prayer for the Dying. unabr. ed. 1994. 608p. 11.98 o.p. (*0-399-13992-3*, G. P. Putnam's Sons) Penguin Group (USA) Inc.

Hill, Lloyd E. The Village of Bom Jesus. 1993. 238p. 16.95 o.p. (*0-945575-88-2*, 71588) Algonquin Bks. of Chapel Hill.

House, Richard. Bruiser. 1997. (High Risk Ser.). 254p. pap. o.p. (*1-85242-437-0*) Serpent's Tail Ltd.

Howard, Linda. Heart of Fire. 1997. 320p. mass mkt. 7.99 (*0-671-01974-0*, Pocket) Simon & Schuster.

—Heart of Fire. Zion, Claire, ed. 1993. 320p. mass mkt. 6.99 (*0-671-72859-8*, Pocket) Simon & Schuster.

—Heart of Fire. l.t. ed. 2001. (Famous Authors Ser.). 531p. 28.95 o.p. (*0-7862-2850-4*) Thorndike Pr.

Hyde, Anthony. Double Helix. 1999. 320p. text (*0-670-87825-1*) Viking.

Kaiser, Gloria. Dona Leopoldina: The Habsburg Empress of Brazil. Bangerter, Lowell A., tr. from GER. 1998. (Studies in Austrian Literature, Culture & Thought). 379p. pap. 21.50 (*1-57241-022-1*) Ariadne Pr.

L'Abbe, Pierre. Ten Days in Rio: A Novella in Verse. 1998. 194p. pap. (*1-894205-07-3*) Watershed Bks.

Lins, Osman. Avalovara. Rabassa, Gregory, tr. from POR. & intro. by. 2002. (Illus.). 332p. pap. 15.95 (*1-56478-320-0*) Dalkey Archive Pr.

—Avalovara. Rabassa, Gregory, tr. from POR. 1980. 12.95 o.p. (*0-394-49851-8*) Knopf, Alfred A. Inc.

—Avalovara. Rabassa, Gregory, tr. from SPA. 1990. (Texas Pan American Ser.). 336p. reprint ed. pap. 14.95 o.p. (*0-292-70416-X*) Univ. of Texas Pr.

—The Queen of the Prisons of Greece. Frizzi, Adria, tr. from POR. 1995. 192p. (Orig.). pap. 12.95 (*1-56478-056-2*) Dalkey Archive Pr.

Lispector, Clarice. Family Ties. Pontiero, Giovanni, tr. from POR. (Texas Pan American Ser.). 156p. 1984. pap. 14.95 (*0-292-72448-9*); 1972. 7.95 o.p. (*0-292-72404-7*) Univ. of Texas Pr.

—Soulstorm: Stories. Levitin, Alexis, tr. from POR. 1989. 160p. pap. 11.95 (*0-8112-1091-X*, NDP671); 19.95 (*0-8112-1090-1*) New Directions Publishing Corp.

Machado de Assis, Joaquim Maria. Counselor Ayres' Memorial. Caldwell, Helen, tr. from POR. 1973. 32.50 o.p. (*0-520-02227-0*) Univ. of California Pr.

—Iaia Garcia. Bagby, Albert I., Jr., tr. 1977. (Studies in Romance Languages: No. 17). 192p. 18.00 o.p. (*0-8131-1353-9*) Univ. Pr. of Kentucky.

Mason, Anita. The Racket. 1991. 224p. 19.95 o.p. (*0-525-93351-4*, Abrahams, William Bks.) Dutton/Plume.

Melo, Patricia. The Killer: A Psychological Thriller. Landers, Clifford E., tr. 1997. 192p. o.p. (*0-88001-574-8*); 1999. 217p. reprint ed. pap. o.p. (*0-88001-608-6*) HarperTrade. (Ecco).

Miranda, Ana. Bay of All Saints & Every Conceivable Sin. Pontiero, Giovanni, tr. 1992. 320p. 21.00 o.p. (*0-670-83455-6*, Viking) Viking Penguin.

Mustian, Mark. The Return. 2000. 303p. 18.95 (*1-56164-190-1*) Pineapple Pr., Inc.

Pritchett, V. S. Dead Man Leading. 1984. (Twentieth Century Classics Ser.). 224p. pap. 6.95 o.p. (*0-19-281469-9*) Oxford Univ. Pr., Inc.

Ramos, Graciliano. Barren Lives. Dimmick, Ralph E., tr. from SPA. (Texas Pan American Ser.). (Illus.). 165p. 1971. pap. 12.95 (*0-292-70133-0*); 1965. 12.95 o.p. (*0-292-73172-8*) Univ. of Texas Pr.

Ribeiro, Darcy. Maira. 1984. (Library of Contemporary World Literature). 304p. pap. 7.95 o.p. (*0-394-72214-0*, Vintage) Knopf Publishing Group.

Ribeiro, Joaao Ubaldo. The Lizard's Smile. Landers, Clifford E., tr. 1994. 320p. text 21.00 (*0-689-12125-3*, Scribner) Simon & Schuster.

Ribeiro, Joao Ubaldo. An Invincible Memory. 1989. 25.00 o.p. (*0-06-015622-8*) HarperTrade.

Ripley, J. R. The Body from Ipanema: A Tony Kozol Mystery. 2002. (Tony Kozol Mystery Ser.: Vol. 4). 244p. (YA). kivar 22.95 (*1-892695-08-1*) Long Wind Publishing.

Rollins, James. Amazonia: A Novel. 2003. 528p. mass mkt. 7.99 (*0-06-000249-2*, HarperTorch); 2003. mass mkt. 142.35 (*0-06-057173-X*, Avon Bks.); 2002. 432p. 24.95 (*0-06-008906-7*, Morrow, William & Co.); 2002. (Illus.). 432p. 24.95 (*0-06-000248-4*, Morrow, William & Co.) Morrow/Avon.

Rubiao, Murilo. The Ex-Magician & Other Stories. Colchie, Thomas, tr. from POR. 1979. 13.95 o.p. (*0-06-013708-8*) HarperTrade.

Scott, Evelyn. Escapade. 1971. reprint ed. 39.00 o.p. (*0-403-01199-X*) Scholarly Pr., Inc.

—Escapade. exp. ed. 1995. 286p. (C). pap. 16.95 (*0-8139-1641-0*) Univ. Pr. of Virginia.

Sguiglia, Eduardo. Fordlandia. Duncan, Patricia J., tr. E-Book 22.95 (*0-312-27165-4*); 2000. 245p. 22.95 (*0-312-26592-1*) St. Martin's Pr.

Stangerup, Henrik. The Road to Lagoa Santa. Bluestone, Barbara, tr. from DAN. 288p. 1984. 24.95 o.p. (*0-7145-2797-1*); 1996. reprint ed. pap. 14.95 o.p. (*0-7145-3016-6*) Boyars, Marion Pubs., Inc.

Telles, Lygia Fagundes. Tigrela: And Other Stories. 1986. (Latin American Ser.). 160p. pap. 3.95 (*0-380-89627-3*, Avon Bks.) Morrow/Avon.

Uys, Errol. Brazil: A Novel. 2000. (Illus.). xiii, 776p. pap. 19.95 (*0-916562-51-4*, Silver Spring Bks.) Truck Pr.

Uys, Errol L. Brazil. 1986. 18.45 o.p. (*0-671-46028-5*, Simon & Schuster) Simon & Schuster.

Van Steen, Edla. A Bag of Stories. George, David, tr. from POR. & intro. by. 1991. (Discoveries Ser.). 174p. pap. 14.95 (*0-935480-54-4*) Latin American Literary Review Pr.

—Early Mourning. George, David, tr. from POR. 1997. 150p. (Orig.). (C). pap. 13.95 (*0-935480-84-6*) Latin American Literary Review Pr.

Vargas Llosa, Mario. The War of the End of the World. unabr. ed. 1993. (ENG & SPA.). audio 13.95 (*1-55644-394-3*, 13051) American Audio Prose Library, Inc.

—The War of the End of the World. Lane, Helen, tr. from SPA. 1984. 568p. 18.95 o.s.i (*0-374-28651-5*); 624p. 75.00 o.p. (*0-374-28652-3*) Farrar, Straus & Giroux.

—The War of the End of the World. Lane, Helen R., tr. 1985. pap. 11.95 (*0-380-69987-7*, Avon Bks.) Morrow/Avon.

—The War of the End of the World. 1997. 576p. pap. 17.00 (*0-14-026260-1*, Penguin Bks.) Penguin Group (USA) Inc.

Verissimo, Erico. Consider the Lillies of the Field. Karnoff, Jean N., tr. 1969. 371p. reprint ed. 65.00 o.s.i (*0-8371-2320-8*, VELF, Greenwood Pr.) Greenwood Publishing Group, Inc.

—Time & the Wind. Barrett, L. L., tr. 1970. 624p. reprint ed. 75.00 o.s.i (*0-8371-2111-6*, VETW, Greenwood Pr.) Greenwood Publishing Group, Inc.

Waugh, Evelyn. A Handful of Dust. 2002. 256p. 18.00 (*0-375-41420-7*) Knopf, Alfred A. Inc.

Williams, Anita. The Treasure Keeper. 1995. (Pennant Ser.). (Illus.). 90p. (J). (gr. 1-5). pap. 7.95 (*0-89084-835-1*, 091710) Jones, Bob Univ. Pr.

Yamashita, Karen T. Brazil-Maru. 1992. 248p. 19.95 (*1-56689-000-4*) Coffee Hse. Pr.

—Through the Arc of the Rain Forest. (gr. 11). 1993. 248p. (J). pap. 12.95 o.p. (*1-56689-016-0*); 1990. 192p. (YA). pap. 12.95 (*0-918273-82-X*) Coffee Hse. Pr.

**BRITISH COLUMBIA—FICTION**

Anderson-Dargatz, Gail. The Cure for Death by Lightning. 1996. 297p. 21.95 o.p. (*0-395-77184-6*) Houghton Mifflin Co.

—The Cure for Death by Lightning: A Novel. 2002. 304p. pap. 13.00 (*0-385-72047-5*, Knopf Bks. for Young Readers) Random Hse. Children's Bks.

Bain, Donald. Murder, She Wrote: Destination Murder. 2003. 288p. 19.95 (*0-451-21048-4*) NAL.

Blackbridge, Persimmon. Prozac Highway. 2000. 373p. pap. 14.95 (*0-7145-3059-X*) Boyars, Marion Pubs., Inc.

—Prozac Highway: A Novel. 1997. 256p. pap. (*0-88974-078-X*, Press Gang Pubs.) Raincoast Bk. Distribution.

Bowers, Elisabeth. Ladies' Night. 1988. (International Women's Crime Ser.). 238p. pap. 8.95 o.p. (*0-931188-65-2*, Seal Pr.) Avalon Publishing Group.

—No Forwarding Address. 288p. 1991. 18.95 o.p. (*1-878067-13-3*); 1994. reprint ed. pap. 10.95 o.p. (*1-878067-46-X*) Avalon Publishing Group. (Seal Pr.).

Braithwaite, Lawrence Ytzhak. Ratz Are Nice (PSP) A Novel. 2000. 192p. pap. 11.95 (*1-55583-554-6*, Alyson Bks.) Alyson Pubns.

Cameron, Anne. Sarah's Children. 2001. 288p. pap. (*1-55017-274-3*) Harbour Publishing Co., Ltd.

Choy, Wayson. The Jade Peony. 240p. 1998. pap. 12.00 o.s.i (*0-312-18692-4*); 1997. 22.00 o.p. (*0-312-15556-5*) Picador.

Clarke, Denise. Featherland: The Magical True Tale of an Extraordinary Love Triangle. 2003. 96p. pap. 15.95 (*0-88995-244-2*) Red Deer Pr. CAN. *Dist:* Fitzhenry & Whiteside, Ltd.

Darty, Peggy. Sundance. 1996. (Palisades Pure Romance Ser.). 252p. pap. 9.99 o.s.i (*0-88070-952-9*, Palisades) Multnomah Pubs., Inc.

Deverell, William. Trial of Passion. 2002. 400p. pap. 15.95 (*1-55022-542-1*) ECW Pr. CAN. *Dist:* Independent Pubs. Group.
—Trial of Passion. 1997. 400p. (*0-7710-2673-0*) McClelland & Stewart/Tundra Bks.
—A Trial of Passion. 1999. 448p. mass mkt. 29.99 (*0-7704-2781-2*) McClelland & Stewart/Tundra Bks.
Douglas, Lauren W. The Always Anonymous Beast. 1987. (Caitlin Reece Mysteries Ser.). 224p. pap. 8.95 o.p. (*0-941483-04-5*) Naiad Pr., Inc.
—The Daughters of Artemis. 1991. (Caitlin Reece Mystery Ser.). 240p. (Orig.). pap. 9.95 (*0-941483-95-9*) Naiad Pr., Inc.
—Goblin Market. 1993. (Caitlin Reece Mysteries Ser.: No. 5). 224p. pap. 10.95 (*1-56280-047-7*) Naiad Pr., Inc.
—Ninth Life. 1990. (Caitlin Reece Mysteries Ser.). 256p. pap. 9.95 (*0-941483-50-9*) Naiad Pr., Inc.
—A Rage of Maidens: Sixth Caitlin Reece Mystery. 1994. (Caitlin Reece Mysteries Ser.). 224p. pap. 10.95 (*1-56280-068-X*) Naiad Pr., Inc.
—A Tiger's Heart. 1992. (Caitlin Reece Mysteries Ser.: No. 4). 240p. pap. 9.95 (*1-56280-018-3*) Naiad Pr., Inc.
Ferone, Joseph. Boomboom. 1998. 317p. pap. (*0-9684336-0-X*) Bitterroot Pr.
—Boomboom. 2000. 204p. pap. 13.95 (*0-936085-64-9*, West Coast Crime) Blue Heron Publishing.
French, Roy. The Raven Re-Born. 2000. 300p. pap. o.p. (*1-55212-511-4*) Trafford Publishing.
Furlong, Nicola. Teed Off! 399p. mass mkt. o.p. (*1-55197-091-0*) Picasso Pubns., Inc.
Gill, Judy. A Harvest of Jewels. l.t. ed. 2003. (Candlelight Romance Ser.). 231p. 24.95 (*0-7862-5081-X*) Thorndike Pr.
Giroux, E. X. A Death for a Dancing Doll. 1992. mass mkt. 3.99 o.s.i (*0-345-37609-9*) Ballantine Bks.
—A Death for a Dancing Doll. 1991. 17.95 o.p. (*0-312-05848-9*, Saint Martin's Minotaur) St. Martin's Pr.
Godfrey, Rebecca. The Torn Skirt. 2002. 208p. pap. 11.95 (*0-06-009485-0*, Perennial) HarperTrade.
Grant, Vanessa. Think about Love. 2001. (Romance Ser.). 256p. mass mkt. 4.99 o.s.i (*0-8217-6835-2*) Kensington Publishing Corp.
Haig-Brown, Roderick L. On the Highest Hill. 1994. (Northwest Reprints Ser.). 336p. reprint ed. 27.95 (*0-87071-518-6*); pap. 15.95 (*0-87071-519-4*) Oregon State Univ. Pr.
Hale, Amanda. Sounding the Blood. 2002. 326p. pap. (*1-55192-484-6*) Raincoast Bk. Distribution.
Kelly, Nora. Bad Chemistry, Vol. 21. 2000. (Missing Mysteries Ser.: Vol. 21). 240p. pap. 14.95 (*1-890208-34-5*) Poisoned Pen Pr.
—Bad Chemistry. 1994. 256p. 20.95 o.p. (*0-312-10934-2*, Saint Martin's Minotaur) St. Martin's Pr.
—In the Shadow of Kings. 2000. (Missing Mysteries Ser.: Vol. 12). 189p. pap. 14.95 (*1-890208-22-1*) Poisoned Pen Pr.
—In the Shadow of Kings. 1984. 12.95 o.p. (*0-312-41171-5*) St. Martin's Pr.
—In the Shadow of Kings. l.t. ed. 1995. (Linford Mystery Library). 400p. pap. 17.99 o.p. (*0-7089-7733-2*, Linford) Thorpe, F. A. Pubs. GBR. *Dist:* Ulverscroft Large Print Bks., Ltd., Ulverscroft Large Print Canada, Ltd.
—My Sister's Keeper. 1992. 224p. 17.95 o.p. (*0-312-08268-1*, Saint Martin's Minotaur) St. Martin's Pr.
—Old Wounds. l.t. ed. 1999. (Magna Large Print Ser.). 464p. (*0-7505-1410-8*) Magna Large Print Bks. GBR. *Dist:* Ulverscroft Large Print Canada, Ltd.
—Old Wounds. 2000. 300p. pap. 12.95 (*1-890208-25-6*) Poisoned Pen Pr.
McCormack, Pete. Shelby. 1994. 267p. 28.00 (*1-877946-47-8*) Permanent Pr., The.
Mildon, Marsha. Stalking the Goddess Ship. 1999. 210p. pap. 10.95 (*1-892281-02-3*) New Victoria Pubs., Inc.
O'Brien, Michael. Strangers & Sojourners: A Novel. 573p. 2002. pap. 16.95 (*0-89870-923-7*); 1997. 24.95 (*0-89870-609-2*) Ignatius Pr.
Odhiambo, David N. Diss/Ed Banded Nation. 1999. 160p. pap. (*1-896095-26-7*, Polestar Book Pubs.) Raincoast Bk. Distribution.
O'Hagan, Howard. Trees Are Lonely Company. 1993. 320p. pap. 19.95 (*0-88922-327-0*) Talonbooks, Ltd. CAN. *Dist:* General Distribution Services, Inc.
Perrin, Kayla. Again, My Love. 1999. 286p. mass mkt. 5.99 (*0-345-43255-X*) Ballantine Bks.
—Again, My Love. 1998. (Indigo Love Stories Ser.). 212p. pap. 10.95 (*1-885478-23-2*) Genesis Pr., Inc.
Power, Margo. Image of Conspiracy: A Mystery Adventure. abr. ed. 1999. audio 10.95 (*1-894188-03-9*) APG Sales and Fulfillment.
—Image of Conspiracy: A Mystery Adventure. 1997. pap. text 5.99 (*1-886199-02-7*) Deadly Alibi Pr., Ltd.
Richardson, Bill. Bachelor Brothers' Bed & Breakfast. l.t. ed. 1997. 21.95 (*1-57490-131-1*, Beeler Large Print Bks.) Beeler, Thomas T. Publisher.
—Bachelor Brothers' Bed & Breakfast Pillow Book. 1998. 208p. pap. 10.95 (*0-312-19440-4*, Saint Martin's Griffin); 1997. 18.95 (*0-312-16779-2*); 1997. 384p. pap. 11.95 (*0-312-17183-8*, Saint Martin's Griffin); 1996. 160p. 18.95 (*0-312-14546-2*) St. Martin's Pr.
Robinson, Eden. Monkey Beach. 2000. 384p. 24.00 (*0-618-10168-3*) Houghton Mifflin Co.
—Monkey Beach. 2000. 384p. (*0-676-97075-3*) Knopf, Alfred A. Inc.
—Monkey Beach: A Novel. 2002. (Illus.). 384p. pap. 13.00 (*0-618-21905-6*, Mariner Bks.) Houghton Mifflin Co. Trade & Reference Div.
Slade, Michael. Cutthroat. 1992. 400p. (Orig.). mass mkt. 5.99 o.s.i (*0-451-17452-6*, Signet Bks.) NAL.
—Evil Eye. 1997. 432p. mass mkt. 6.99 o.s.i (*0-451-40695-8*, Onyx) NAL.
—Ghoul. 1988. 416p. 18.95 o.p. (*0-688-07550-9*, Morrow, William & Co.) Morrow/Avon.
—Ghoul. 1989. 400p. mass mkt. 6.99 o.s.i (*0-451-15959-4*, Signet Bks.) NAL.
—Headhunter. 1985. (Illus.). 480p. 17.95 o.p. (*0-688-04710-6*, Morrow, William & Co.) Morrow/Avon.
—Headhunter. 1986. mass mkt. 3.95 o.p. (*0-451-40005-4*); mass mkt. 4.50 o.p. (*0-451-40137-9*); 424p. mass mkt. 6.99 o.s.i (*0-451-40172-7*, Onyx) NAL.
—Primal Scream: Scream If You Want, Live If You Can. 1998. 432p. mass mkt. 6.99 o.s.i (*0-451-19566-3*, Signet Bks.) NAL.
—Ripper. 1994. 416p. (Orig.). mass mkt. 4.99 o.s.i (*0-451-17702-9*, Signet Bks.) NAL.
Smith, Lyndsay. Proximate Causes. 1999. 302p. pap. (*1-55017-214-X*) Harbour Publishing Co., Ltd.
Snaden, Andrew & Dow, Rosey. Vancouver Mystery: A Novel of Suspense. 2002. 272p. pap. 11.99 (*1-58660-589-5*, Promise Pr.) Barbour Publishing, Inc.
Sullivan, Mark T. The Purification Ceremony. 1998. mass mkt. 6.99 o.s.i (*0-380-79042-4*); 1997. 335p. 24.00 o.s.i (*0-380-97428-2*) Morrow/Avon. (Avon Bks.).
Toombs, Jane. The Restless Obsession. 2000. (Five Star Romance Ser.). 227p. pap. 26.95 (*0-7862-2632-3*, Five Star) Gale Group.
Vreeland, Susan. The Forest Lover. 2004. 352p. 24.95 (*0-670-03267-0*) Viking Penguin.
Wright, Laurali R. Acts of Murder. 1998. 288p. 22.00 (*0-684-81381-5*, Scribner) Simon & Schuster.
—Acts of Murder. l.t. ed. 1998. (Mystery Ser.). 381p. 27.95 (*0-7862-1678-6*) Thorndike Pr.
—A Chill Rain in January. 1991. 336p. mass mkt. 7.99 (*0-7704-2417-1*) Bantam Bks.
—A Chill Rain in January. 1991. (Crime Monthly Ser.). 288p. pap. 4.50 o.p. (*0-14-012982-0*, Penguin Bks.) Penguin Group (USA) Inc.
—A Chill Rain in January. 1990. 288p. 17.95 o.p. (*0-670-83129-8*, Viking) Viking Penguin.
—Fall from Grace. l.t. ed. 1992. pap. 17.95 o.p. (*0-7927-1270-6*); 19.95 o.p. (*0-7927-1271-4*) BBC Audiobooks America.
—Fall from Grace. 1999. pap. (*0-14-099717-2*) NAL.
—Fall from Grace. 1992. (Crime Ser.). 256p. reprint ed. pap. 5.95 o.p. (*0-14-012981-2*, Penguin Bks.) Penguin Group (USA) Inc.
—Fall from Grace. 1991. 256p. 18.95 o.p. (*0-670-83130-1*, Viking) Viking Penguin.
—Love in the Temperate Zone. 1988. 17.95 o.p. (*0-670-81173-4*) Viking Penguin.
—Mother Love: A Karl Alberg Mystery with Cassandra Mitchell. 1996. 264p. mass mkt. 7.99 o.s.i (*0-7704-2716-2*) Bantam Bks.
—Mother Love: A Karl Alberg Mystery with Cassandra Mitchell. 1995. 288p. 26.95 o.p. (*0-385-25477-6*) Doubleday Publishing.
—Mother Love: A Karl Alberg Mystery with Cassandra Mitchell. 1995. (Illus.). 304p. 21.00 o.p. (*0-684-19673-5*, Scribner) Simon & Schuster.
—Prized Possessions, No. 5. 1997. 336p. mass mkt. 7.50 (*0-7704-2543-7*) Bantam Bks.
—Prized Possessions. 1994. (Crime Ser.). 272p. pap. 5.95 o.p. (*0-14-017146-0*, Penguin Bks.) Penguin Group (USA) Inc.
—Prized Possessions. 1993. 272p. 19.00 o.p. (*0-670-84565-5*, Viking) Viking Penguin.
—Sleep While I Sing. l.t. ed. 1991. 17.95 o.p. (*0-7451-8072-8*, AH0107); pap. 15.95 o.p. (*0-7927-0555-6*, AS0143) BBC Audiobooks America.
—Sleep While I Sing. 1988. 240p. mass mkt. 6.99 (*0-7704-2300-0*) Bantam Bks.
—Sleep While I Sing. 1988. o.s.i (*0-385-25042-8*) Doubleday Publishing.
—Sleep While I Sing. 1987. 224p. pap. 3.95 o.p. (*0-14-008880-6*, Penguin Bks.); 1987. 39.50 o.p. (*0-14-778226-0*); 1986. 224p. 15.95 o.p. (*0-670-81089-4*) Viking Penguin.
—Strangers among Us. 1997. 256p. mass mkt. 8.99 (*0-7704-2758-8*) Bantam Bks.
—Strangers among Us. 1996. 256p. 20.50 o.p. (*0-684-81382-3*, Scribner) Simon & Schuster.
—Strangers among Us. l.t. ed. 2000. (Mystery Ser.). 360p. 27.95 (*0-7862-2557-2*) Thorndike Pr.
—The Suspect. (Crime Ser.). 224p. 1987. pap. 5.95 o.p. (*0-14-010477-1*, Penguin Bks.); 1985. 15.95 o.p. (*0-670-80596-3*) Viking Penguin.
—A Touch of Panic: A Karl Alberg Mystery. 1995. 288p. mass mkt. 7.99 o.s.i (*0-7704-2620-4*) Bantam Bks.
—A Touch of Panic: A Karl Alberg Mystery. 1995. (Crime Ser.). 288p. pap. 5.95 o.s.i (*0-14-023300-8*, Penguin Bks.) Penguin Group (USA) Inc.
—A Touch of Panic: A Karl Alberg Mystery. 1994. 288p. 20.00 o.s.i (*0-684-19672-7*, Scribner) Simon & Schuster.
Zaremba, Eve. Beyond Hope. 1990. 184p. pap. 11.95 (*0-921299-02-8*) Second Story Pr. CAN. *Dist:* SCB Distributors.
—Uneasy Lies: A Helen Keremos Mystery. 1994. 255p. pap. 11.95 (*0-929005-17-1*) Second Story Pr. CAN. *Dist:* LPC/InBook.
—White Noise: A Helen Keremos Mystery Novel. 1997. 248p. pap. 9.95 (*0-929005-97-X*) Second Story Pr. CAN. *Dist:* SCB Distributors.
—Work for a Million. (NFS Canada Ser.). 200p. pap. 11.95 o.p. (*0-921299-00-1*) Second Story Pr. CAN. *Dist:* SCB Distributors.

**BROWARD'S ROCK (S.C.: IMAGINARY PLACE)—FICTION**

Hart, Carolyn G. The Christie Caper. 1992. (Annie Darling Ser.). 400p. mass mkt. 6.99 (*0-553-29569-1*) Bantam Bks.
—The Christie Caper. unabr. ed. 1996. (Annie Laurance Darling Ser.). audio 64.00 (*0-7366-3457-6*, 4101) Books on Tape, Inc.
—Deadly Valentine. 1991. (Death on Demand Ser.). 272p. mass mkt. 6.99 incl. audio (*0-553-28847-4*) Bantam Bks.
—Deadly Valentine. unabr. ed. 1996. (Annie Laurance Darling Ser.). audio 48.00 (*0-7366-3407-X*, 4053) Books on Tape, Inc.
—Death on Demand. 1989. 208p. mass mkt. 1.95 o.s.i (*0-553-18502-0*); 1987. 224p. mass mkt. 6.99 (*0-553-26351-X*) Bantam Bks.
—Death on Demand. l.t. ed. 2000. (Mystery Ser.). (Illus.). 227p. 26.95 (*1-57490-276-8*, Beeler Large Print Bks.) Beeler, Thomas T. Publisher.
—Death on Demand. 2000. audio 40.00 (*0-7366-4838-0*); audio compact disk 48.00 (*0-7366-7500-0*); (Books on Demand Ser.: 1). audio 30.00 Books on Tape, Inc.
—Death on Demand. l.t. ed. 2000. (Wheeler Softcover Ser.). 280p. pap. 24.95 (*1-56895-914-1*, Wheeler Publishing, Inc.) Gale Group.
—Honeymoon with Murder. 1988. 256p. mass mkt. 6.99 (*0-553-27608-5*) Bantam Bks.
—A Little Class on Murder. l.t. ed. 1992. pap. 21.95 o.p. (*0-7927-1140-8*, CS0306); 1991. 23.95 o.p. (*0-7927-1139-4*, CH0234) BBC Audiobooks America.
—A Little Class on Murder. 1989. 272p. mass mkt. 6.99 (*0-553-28208-5*) Bantam Bks.
—A Little Class on Murder. unabr. collector's ed. 1996. (Annie Laurance Darling Ser.). audio 48.00 (*0-7366-3419-3*, 894409) Books on Tape, Inc.
—A Little Class on Murder. 1989. 12.95 o.s.i (*0-385-26452-6*) Doubleday Publishing.
—Mint Julep Murder. 1996. 256p. mass mkt. 6.99 (*0-553-57202-4*); 1995. 288p. 19.95 o.s.i (*0-553-09463-7*) Bantam Bks.
—Mint Julep Murder. unabr. ed. 1996. (Annie Laurance Darling Ser.). audio 48.00 (*0-7366-3498-3*, 4138) Books on Tape, Inc.
—Mint Julep Murder. l.t. ed. 1996. 362p. 23.95 o.p. (*0-7838-1496-8*, Macmillan Reference USA) Gale Group.
—Southern Ghost. 1993. (Annie Darling Ser.). 320p. mass mkt. 6.99 (*0-553-56275-4*) Bantam Bks.
—Southern Ghost. unabr. ed. 1996. (Annie Laurance Darling Ser.). audio 56.00 (*0-7366-3501-7*, 4141) Books on Tape, Inc.
—White Elephant Dead. (Death on Demand Mysteries Ser.). 2000. 304p. mass mkt. 6.99 (*0-380-79325-3*); 1999. 277p. 23.00 (*0-380-97530-0*) Morrow/Avon. (Avon Bks.).
—White Elephant Dead. l.t. ed. 2000. (Mystery Ser.). 431p. 29.95 o.p. (*0-7862-2341-3*) Thorndike Pr.
—Yankee Doodle Dead. l.t. ed. 1999. pap. 24.95 (*1-56895-718-1*, Wheeler Publishing, Inc.) Gale Group.
—Yankee Doodle Dead. 1999. 304p. mass mkt. 6.99 (*0-380-79326-1*); 1998. 288p. 21.00 (*0-380-97529-7*) Morrow/Avon. (Avon Bks.).

**BUCKSKIN (OKLA.: IMAGINARY PLACE)—FICTION**

Hager, Jean. The Fire Carrier. 1996. 82p. 21.95 o.s.i (*0-89296-566-5*) Mysterious Pr.
—The Fire Carrier. 1997. 224p. reprint ed. mass mkt. 5.99 o.s.i (*0-446-40387-3*) Warner Bks., Inc.
—Ghostland. 1993. mass mkt. (*0-373-26117-9*, 1-26117-1, Harlequin Bks.) Harlequin Enterprises, Ltd.
—Ghostland. 1991. 272p. 18.95 o.p. (*0-312-06982-0*, Saint Martin's Minotaur) St. Martin's Pr.
—The Grandfather Medicine. 1993. per. (*0-373-83303-2*, 1-83303-7); 1990. 224p. mass mkt. (*0-373-26059-8*) Harlequin Enterprises, Ltd. (Harlequin Bks.).
—The Grandfather Medicine. 1998. 248p. pap. 11.95 (*0-9662145-2-8*) Southmont Publishing.
—The Grandfather Medicine. 1989. 16.95 o.p. (*0-312-02923-3*, Saint Martin's Minotaur) St. Martin's Pr.
—Masked Dancers. 1998. 288p. 23.00 o.p. (*0-89296-641-6*) Mysterious Pr.
—Masked Dancers. l.t. ed. 1998. (Cloak & Dagger Ser.). 376p. 25.95 (*0-7862-1485-6*) Thorndike Pr.
—Night Walker. 1991. reprint ed. mass mkt. (*0-373-26085-7*, Harlequin Bks.) Harlequin Enterprises, Ltd.
—Night Walker. 1990. 15.95 o.p. (*0-312-05138-7*, Saint Martin's Minotaur) St. Martin's Pr.

**BUDAPEST (HUNGARY)—FICTION**

Eversz, Robert M. Gypsy Hearts. 1997. 272p. 23.00 o.p. (*0-8021-1609-4*, Grove Pr.) Grove/Atlantic, Inc.
Kertesz, Imre. Fateless. 1996. pap. 14.95 o.p. (*0-8101-1465-8*) Northwestern Univ. Pr.
—Fateless. Wilson, Christopher & Wilson, Katharina, trs. from HUN. 1996. 191p. pap. 19.95 (*0-8101-1049-0*, Hydra Bks.); 1992. 200p. 68.00 (*0-8101-1024-5*) Northwestern Univ. Pr.
Kosztolanyi, Dezso. Anna Edes. Szirtes, George, tr. from HUN. & intro. by. 1993. (Revived Modern Classic Ser.). 240p. pap. 10.95 (*0-8112-1255-6*, NDP772) New Directions Publishing Corp.
Nyiri, Janos. Battlefields & Playgrounds. Nyiri, Janos & Brandon, William, trs. from HUN. 1995. 536p. 25.00 o.p. (*0-374-10918-4*) Farrar, Straus & Giroux.
—Battlefields & Playgrounds. Brandon, William, tr. from HUN. 1997. (Tauber Institute Ser.: No. 23). 544p. reprint ed. per. 19.95 (*0-87451-801-6*) Univ. Pr. of New England.
Pressburger, Giorgio & Pressburger, Nicola. Homage to the Eighth District: Tales from Budapest. Moore, Gerald, tr. from ITA. 1990. 200p. (Orig.). pap. 17.95 (*0-930523-75-X*); pap. 9.95 (*0-930523-76-8*) Readers International.
Rosner, Elizabeth. The Speed of Light. 2003. 272p. pap. 12.95 (*0-345-44225-3*); 2001. 256p. 23.95 (*0-345-44224-5*) Ballantine Bks. (Ballantine Bks.).
—The Speed of Light. l.t. ed. 2002. 398p. 28.95 (*0-7862-4041-5*) Gale Group.
Truman, Margaret. Murder in the CIA. 1999. 6.99 (*0-449-45925-X*); 1988. 320p. reprint ed. mass mkt. 6.99 (*0-449-21275-0*) Ballantine Bks. (Fawcett).
—Murder in the CIA. l.t. ed. 1988. (General Ser.). 412p. 19.95 o.p. (*0-8161-4406-0*); 11.95 o.p. (*0-8161-4407-9*) Gale Group. (Macmillan Reference USA).
—Murder in the CIA. 1993. audio. audio 49.00 (*1-56544-013-7*, 250030) Literate Ear, Inc.
—Murder in the CIA. abr. ed. 1988. audio 16.00 o.s.i (*0-394-57184-3*); Set. 1996. audio 8.99 o.s.i (*0-679-45597-3*, 391229) Random Hse. Audio Publishing Group. (RH Audio).
—Murder in the CIA. unabr. ed. 1991. audio 70.00 (*1-55690-364-2*, 91219E7) Recorded Bks., LLC.

**BUENOS AIRES (ARGENTINA)—FICTION**

Bemau, George. Black Phoenix. 304p. 1995. mass mkt. 5.99 o.s.i (*0-446-60182-9*); 1994. (Illus.). 22.95 o.s.i (*0-446-51610-4*) Warner Bks., Inc.
Bioy Casares, Adolfo. The Dream of Heroes. 1988. 17.95 o.p. (*0-525-24687-8*, Dutton) Dutton/Plume.
Cambaceres, Eugenio. Pot Pourri: Whistlings of an Idler. Ludmer, Josefina, ed. Dillman, Lisa, tr. from SPA. 2003. (Library of Latin America). 192p. 35.00 (*0-19-514463-5*); pap. 16.95 (*0-19-514464-3*) Oxford Univ. Pr., Inc.
Griffin, W. E. B. Blood & Honor. 1997. (Honor Bound Ser.: No. 2). 736p. mass mkt. 7.99 (*0-515-12194-0*, Jove) Berkley Publishing Group.
—Blood & Honor, Pt. 1. unabr. ed. 1996. (Honor Bound Ser.: No. 2). audio 80.00 (*0-7366-3594-7*, 4246A ) Books on Tape, Inc.
—Blood & Honor. l.t. ed. 1997. (Honor Bound Ser.: No. 2). 1105p. 28.95 (*0-7838-8125-8*, Macmillan Reference USA) Gale Group.
—Blood & Honor. 2001. 34.95 (*0-399-14481-1*); 1996. (Honor Bound Ser.: No. 2). 480p. 24.95 o.s.i (*0-399-14190-1*, G. P. Putnam's Sons); Set. 1996. (Honor Bound Ser.: No. 2). 4p. 24.95 o.p. (*0-399-14226-6*, 694560, Putnam Berkley Audio) Penguin Group (USA) Inc.
—Honor Bound. 1994. (Honor Bound Ser.: No. 1). 560p. mass mkt. 7.99 (*0-515-11486-3*, Jove) Berkley Publishing Group.
—Honor Bound, Pt. 1. unabr. ed. (Honor Bound Ser.: No. 1). audio 64.00 (*0-7366-2732-4*, 3460-A/B) Books on Tape, Inc.
—Honor Bound. unabr. ed. 1994. (Honor Bound Ser.: No. 1). audio 130.55 (*1-56100-184-8*, 901, Unabridged Library Editions); audio 29.95 (*1-56100-558-4*, 138, Bookcassette) Brilliance Audio.

—Honor Bound. l.t. ed. 1994. (Honor Bound Ser.: No. 1). 25.95 o.p. (*1-56895-100-0*, Wheeler Publishing, Inc.) Gale Group.

—Honor Bound. abr. ed. 2000. (Honor Bound Ser.: No. 1). audio 7.95 (*1-57815-012-4*, 1002, Media Bks. Audio Publishing) Media Bks., L. L. C.

—Honor Bound. 1994. (Honor Bound Ser.: No. 1). 384p. 22.95 o.p. (*0-399-13862-5*, G. P. Putnam's Sons) Penguin Group (USA) Inc.

—Honor Bound. 22.95 o.s.i (*0-399-14117-0*) Putnam Publishing Group, The.

—Secret Honor. 2000. (Honor Bound Ser.: No. 3). 624p. mass mkt. 7.99 (*0-515-13009-5*, Jove) Berkley Publishing Group.

—Secret Honor. unabr. ed. 2000. (Honor Bound Ser.: No. 3). audio 104.00 Books on Tape, Inc.

—Secret Honor. l.t. ed. 2000. (Honor Bound Ser.: No. 3). 28.95 (*1-56895-868-4*, Wheeler Publishing, Inc.) Gale Group.

—Secret Honor. 2000. (Honor Bound Ser.: No. 3). 544p. 25.95 o.s.i (*0-399-14568-0*) Penguin Group (USA) Inc.

—Secret Honor. (Honor Bound Ser.: No. 3). 512p. (*0-7278-5504-2*) Severn Hse. Pubs., Ltd.

Katz, Judith. The Escape Artist: A Novel. 1997. 288p. (C). pap. 12.95 (*1-56341-084-2*); lib. bdg. 26.95 (*1-56341-085-0*) Firebrand Bks.

Ludlum, Robert. The Rhinemann Exchange. 1989. 448p. mass mkt. 7.99 (*0-553-28063-5*); 464p. mass mkt. 3.99 o.s.i (*0-553-19952-8*) Bantam Bks.

—The Rhinemann Exchange. 1991. 464p. reprint ed. lib. bdg. 31.95 (*0-89966-778-3*) Buccaneer Bks., Inc.

—The Rhinemann Exchange. 1975. 448p. mass mkt. 3.50 o.s.i (*0-440-15079-5*) Dell Publishing.

—The Rhinemann Exchange. 1974. 8.95 o.p. (*0-385-27476-9*) Doubleday Publishing.

—The Rhinemann Exchange. l.t. ed. 1983. (Charnwood Large Print Ser.). 672p. 29.99 o.p. (*0-7089-8100-3*, Ulverscroft) Thorpe, F. A. Pubs. GBR. *Dist:* Ulverscroft Large Print Bks., Ltd., Ulverscroft Large Print Canada, Ltd.

Montalban, Manuel Vazquez. The Buenos Aires Quintet. 2003. 252p. pap. 15.00 (*1-85242-640-3*) Serpent's Tail Ltd. GBR. *Dist:* Consortium Bk. Sales & Distribution.

Piglia, Ricardo. The Absent City. Waisman, Sergio, tr. from SPA. 2000. 136p. lib. bdg. 54.95 (*0-8223-2557-8*) Duke Univ. Pr.

—The Absent City. Waisman, Sergio, tr. from SPA. & intro. by. 2000. 136p. pap. 17.95 (*0-8223-2586-1*) Duke Univ. Pr.

Puig, Manuel. Heartbreak Tango: A Serial. 1987. pap. 7.95 o.p. (*0-525-48288-1*, Plume) Dutton/Plume.

—Heartbreak Tango: A Serial. Levine, Suzanne J., tr. 1975. pap. 2.45 o.p. (*0-525-47397-1*, Dutton) Dutton/Plume.

—Heartbreak Tango: A Serial. Levine, Suzanne J., tr. 1991. 22p. pap. 8.95 o.p. (*0-14-015346-2*, 0772-230, Penguin Bks.) Penguin Group (USA) Inc.

—Heartbreak Tango: A Serial. 1996. (Penguin Twentieth-Century Classics Ser.). 224p. pap. 11.95 o.s.i (*0-14-018997-1*, Viking) Viking Penguin.

Visbal-Arroyo, Luz. Rain. 2000. 72p. pap. 9.00 (*0-8059-4914-3*) Dorrance Publishing Co., Inc.

**BUFFALO (N.Y.)—FICTION**

Belfer, Lauren. City of Light. 2003. 512p. pap. 12.95 (*0-385-33764-7*, Delta); 2000. 704p. mass mkt. 6.99 (*0-440-23512-X*); 1999. 518p. pap. 24.95 (*0-385-22401-X*, Delacorte Pr.) Dell Publishing.

—The City of Light. abr. ed. 1999. audio 25.00 (*0-553-52625-1*, RH Audio) Random Hse. Audio Publishing Group.

—City of Light. l.t. ed. 1999. (Basic Ser.). 851p. 29.95 (*0-7862-1991-2*) Thorndike Pr.

Clement, Peter. Death Rounds. 1999. 345p. mass mkt. 6.99 (*0-449-00450-3*, Fawcett) Ballantine Bks.

—Lethal Practice. 1998. mass mkt. 6.99 (*0-8041-1781-0*, Ivy Bks.); 1998. 352p. mass mkt. 7.99 (*0-449-00281-0*, Fawcett); 1997. mass mkt. 6.99 (*0-345-40776-8*) Ballantine Bks.

Oates, Joyce Carol. Broke Heart Blues. 384p. 2000. pap. 13.95 (*0-452-28034-6*, Plume); 1999. 24.95 o.p. (*0-525-94451-6*) Dutton/Plume.

Perry, Thomas. Dance for the Dead. 1997. (Jane Whitefield Novels Ser.). 416p. mass mkt. 6.99 (*0-8041-1425-0*, Ivy Bks.) Ballantine Bks.

—Dance for the Dead. l.t. ed. 1996. 416p. lib. bdg. 24.95 (*1-57490-065-X*, Beeler Large Print Bks.) Beeler, Thomas T. Publisher.

—Dance for the Dead, Set. abr. ed. 1998. (Jane Whitefield Mystery Ser.). audio 8.99 o.s.i (*0-375-40298-5*, 393900, RH Audio) Random Hse. Audio Publishing Group.

—Dance for the Dead. l.t. ed. 1997. (Charnwood Large Print Ser.). 464p. 34.50 o.p. (*0-7089-8938-1*, Ulverscroft) Thorpe, F. A. Pubs. GBR. *Dist:* Ulverscroft Large Print Bks., Ltd., Ulverscroft Large Print Canada, Ltd.

—Dance for the Dead: A Jane Whitefield Novel. abr. ed. 1996. audio 18.00 o.s.i (*0-679-45169-2*, 393900, RH Audio) Random Hse. Audio Publishing Group.

—The Face-Changers. 1999. (Jane Whitefield Novels Ser.). 432p. mass mkt. 7.50 (*0-8041-1540-0*, Ivy Bks.) Ballantine Bks.

—The Face-Changers. l.t. ed. 1998. (Americana Ser.). 640p. 28.95 (*0-7862-1611-5*) Thorndike Pr.

—The Face-Changers: A Novel. aut. ed. 1998. 372p. 24.00 o.s.i (*0-676-57765-2*) Random Hse., Inc.

—Shadow Woman. 1998. (Jane Whitefield Novels Ser.). 432p. mass mkt. 6.99 (*0-8041-1539-7*, Ivy Bks.) Ballantine Bks.

—Shadow Woman. l.t. ed. 1997. (Large Print Book Ser.). pap. 24.95 (*1-56895-513-8*, Wheeler Publishing, Inc.) Gale Group.

—Shadow Woman. l.t. ed. 1999. (Charnwood Large Print Ser.). 480p. 31.99 (*0-7089-9098-3*, Ulverscroft) Thorpe, F. A. Pubs. GBR. *Dist:* Ulverscroft Large Print Bks., Ltd., Ulverscroft Large Print Canada, Ltd.

—Vanishing Act. 1997. mass mkt. 2.99 o.s.i (*0-8041-1648-2*); 1996. 368p. mass mkt. 6.99 (*0-8041-1387-4*) Ballantine Bks. (Ivy Bks.).

—Vanishing Act. l.t. ed. 1995. (Large Print Bks.). pap. 22.95 (*1-56895-234-1*, Wheeler Publishing, Inc.) Gale Group.

Porter, Connie Rose. Imani All Mine. 2000. (Illus.). 208p. pap. 12.00 (*0-618-05678-5*); 1999. 212p. tchr. ed. 23.00 o.p. (*0-395-83808-8*) Houghton Mifflin Co.

—Imani All Mine. 2000. 18.05 (*0-606-19008-2*) Turtleback Bks.

Simmons, Dan. Hard as Nails. Date not set. mass mkt. (*0-312-99468-0*, St. Martin's Paperbacks); 2003. 288p. pap. 24.95 (*0-312-30528-1*, Saint Martin's Minotaur) St. Martin's Pr.

—Hard Freeze: A Joe Kurtz Novel. 2002. 304p. 24.95 (*0-312-27854-3*, Saint Martin's Minotaur) St. Martin's Pr.

**BULGARIA—FICTION**

Gilman, Dorothy. The Elusive Mrs. Pollifax. 1987. 208p. mass mkt. 6.99 (*0-449-21523-7*); 1985. mass mkt. 2.95 o.s.i (*0-449-20855-9*) Ballantine Bks. (Fawcett).

—The Elusive Mrs. Pollifax. 1971. 8.95 o.p. (*0-385-09463-9*) Doubleday Publishing.

—The Elusive Mrs. Pollifax. (Nightingale Ser.). 1983. pap. 8.95 o.p. (*0-8161-3370-0*); 1993. 275p. 17.95 o.p. (*0-8161-5354-X*) Gale Group. (Macmillan Reference USA).

—The Elusive Mrs. Pollifax. unabr. ed. 1990. (Mrs. Pollifax Mystery Ser.: Vol. 3). audio 44.00 (*1-55690-162-3*, 90005E7) Recorded Bks., LLC.

Haitov, Nikolai. Wild Tales. Holman, M., tr. from BUL. 1979. 239p. 30.00 (*0-7206-0543-1*) Owen, Peter Ltd. GBR. *Dist:* Dufour Editions, Inc.

Kirilov, Nikolai & Kirk, Frank, eds. Introduction to Modern Bulgarian Literature: An Anthology of Short Stories. Alexieva, Marguerite, tr. 1969. text 32.50 (*0-8057-3106-7*); pap. text 16.50 (*0-8290-2128-0*) Irvington Pubs.

McGonigle, Thomas. The Corpse Dream of N. Petkov. 1987. 134p. 20.00 (*0-916583-19-8*) Dalkey Archive Pr.

—The Corpse Dream of N. Petkov. 2000. 133p. pap. 14.95 (*0-8101-1797-5*) Northwestern Univ. Pr.

Ward, Annie. The Making of June. abr. ed. 2002. audio 24.95 o.p. (*1-59086-055-1*, 3598, Nova Audio Bks.); audio 87.25 (*1-59086-054-3*, 3597, CD Unabridged Library Edition); audio 34.95 (*1-59086-053-5*, 3596, Brilliance Audio Unabridged) Brilliance Audio.

—The Making of June. 2002. 320p. 24.95 o.s.i (*0-399-14890-6*, Putnam & Grosset) Penguin Group (USA) Inc.

**BURLINGTON (VT.)—FICTION**

Baruth, Philip E. The Dream of the White Village: A Novel in Stories. 333p. 1999. pap. 14.00 (*0-9657144-2-X*); 1998. 24.00 (*0-9657144-1-1*) Onion River Pr.

## C

**CABOT COVE (ME.: IMAGINARY PLACE)—FICTION**

Bain, Donald. Brandy & Bullets: Murder, She Wrote. l.t. ed. 1999. (G. K. Hall Nightingale Ser.). 288p. pap. 20.95 (*0-7838-8596-2*) Thorndike Pr.

Bain, Donald & Fletcher, Jessica. A Little Yuletide Murder. 1998. (Murder She Wrote Ser.: Vol. 10). 304p. mass mkt. 6.50 (*0-451-19475-6*, Signet Bks.) NAL.

—A Little Yuletide Murder: A Murder, She Wrote, Mystery. l.t. ed. 2000. (Nightingale Ser.). 279p. pap. 21.95 (*0-7838-9101-6*) Thorndike Pr.

Fletcher, Jessica. Gin & Daggers: Jessica Fletcher & Donald Bain Mystery. 2000. (Murder She Wrote Ser.). 272p. mass mkt. 6.50 (*0-451-19998-7*, Signet Bks.) NAL.

—Murder She Wrote: Knock 'em Dead, Vol. 12. 1999. (Murder She Wrote Ser.). 288p. mass mkt. 6.50 (*0-451-19477-2*, Signet Bks.) NAL.

—Murder She Wrote: Trick or Treachery. 2000. (Murder She Wrote Ser.). 272p. mass mkt. 6.50 (*0-451-20152-3*, Signet Bks.) NAL.

Fletcher, Jessica & Bain, Donald. Brandy & Bullets. 1995. (Murder She Wrote Ser.: Vol. 3). 288p. (Orig.). mass mkt. 6.50 (*0-451-18491-2*, Signet Bks.) NAL.

—Deadly Judgement. 1996. (Murder She Wrote Ser.). 304p. mass mkt. 6.50 (*0-451-18771-7*) NAL.

—Gin & Daggers. 1990. reprint ed. pap. 3.50 (*0-380-71166-4*, Avon Bks.) Morrow/Avon.

—Gin & Daggers: A Murder, She Wrote Mystery. 1989. 272p. text 17.95 o.p. (*0-07-003239-4*) McGraw-Hill Cos., The.

**CADWAL (IMAGINARY PLACE)—FICTION**

Vance, Jack. Araminta Station. (Cadwal Chronicles Ser.: 1). 1989. 560p. mass mkt. 4.95 (*0-8125-5709-3*); 1988. 540p. 19.95 o.p. (*0-312-93044-5*) Doherty, Tom Assocs., LLC. (Tor Bks.).

—Ecce & Old Earth. 1992. 448p. mass mkt. 5.99 (*0-8125-5701-8*); 1991. (Cadwal Chronicles Ser.: 2). 21.95 o.p. (*0-312-85132-4*) Doherty, Tom Assocs., LLC. (Tor Bks.).

—Ecce & Old Earth. 1991. (Cadwal Chronicles Ser.: Bk. 2). 313p. 75.00 o.p. (*0-88733-127-0*) Underwood Bks., Inc.

—Throy. 1993. 256p. 18.95 o.p. (*0-312-85133-2*, Tor Bks.) Doherty, Tom Assocs., LLC.

—Throy. deluxe ltd. ed. 1992. (Cadwal Chronicles Ser.: Bk. 3). 256p. 75.00 o.p. (*0-88733-135-1*) Underwood Bks., Inc.

**CAIRO (EGYPT)—FICTION**

Coonts, Stephen. Liberty. l.t. ed. 2003. 688p. 32.95 (*1-58724-442-X*, Wheeler Publishing, Inc.) Gale Group.

—Liberty. 2004. 544p. mass mkt. 7.99 (*0-312-98970-9*); 2003. mass mkt. 7.99 (*0-312-99062-6*) St. Martin's Pr. (St. Martin's Paperbacks).

—Liberty: A Jake Grafton Novel. 2003. (Jake Grafton Novels Ser.). 352p. 25.95 (*0-312-28361-X*) St. Martin's Pr.

Deighton, Len. City of Gold. 1992. 368p. 240.00 o.p. (*0-06-017702-0*) HarperCollins Pubs.

—City of Gold. 1992. 368p. 20.00 o.p. (*0-06-017937-6*) HarperTrade.

—City of Gold. 1993. 416p. mass mkt. 5.99 o.p. (*0-06-109041-7*, HarperTorch) Morrow/Avon.

Ducornet, Rikki. Gazelle: A Novel. 2003. 208p. 21.00 (*0-375-41124-0*) Knopf, Alfred A. Inc.

Kiteley, Brian. I Know Many Songs, But I Cannot Sing. 1996. 192p. 20.00 o.p. (*0-684-80905-2*, Simon & Schuster) Simon & Schuster.

Mahfouz, Naguib. Midaq Alley. 1992. 21.50 o.s.i (*0-385-26475-5*); 1992. 304p. pap. 7.99 (*0-385-26940-4*); 1991. 304p. pap. 12.95 (*0-385-26476-3*) Doubleday Publishing.

—Midaq Alley. 1991. reprint ed. 18.00 o.p. (*0-89410-657-0*); pap. 11.00 o.p. (*0-89410-658-9*) Rienner, Lynne Pubs., Inc. (Three Continents).

—Midaq Alley. Le Gassick, Trevor, tr. from ARA. 1981. ix, 246p. reprint ed. 15.00 o.p. (*0-89410-282-6*, Three Continents) Rienner, Lynne Pubs., Inc.

—Midaq Alley. 2002. 27.00 (*0-8446-7225-4*) Smith, Peter Pub., Inc.

—Palace of Desire. 432p. 1992. pap. 8.95 (*0-385-40208-2*); 1990. 22.95 o.s.i (*0-385-26467-4*); 1990. 13.99 o.s.i (*0-385-26936-6*) Doubleday Publishing.

—Palace of Desire. 1991. (Cairo Trilogy: Vol. II). 432p. pap. 14.95 (*0-385-26468-2*, Knopf Bks. for Young Readers) Random Hse. Children's Bks.

Nasir, Jamil. Tower of Dreams. 1999. 240p. pap. 15.00 (*0-553-76316-4*); mass mkt. 5.99 (*0-553-58089-2*) Bantam Bks. (Spectra).

Pearce, Michael. The Mamur Zapt & the Girl in the Nile. 1994. 224p. 19.95 o.s.i (*0-89296-509-6*) Mysterious Pr.

—The Mamur Zapt & the Men Behind. 1993. 256p. 17.95 (*0-89296-487-1*) Mysterious Pr.

—Mamur Zapt & the Night of the Dog. 1991. 192p. 15.00 o.s.i (*0-385-41521-4*) Doubleday Publishing.

—Mamur Zapt & the Return of the Carpet. 1990. 14.95 o.s.i (*0-385-41520-6*) Doubleday Publishing.

—The Mamur Zapt & the Return of the Carpet. 2001. 200p. pap. 13.95 (*1-890208-77-9*) Poisoned Pen Pr.

—The Mamur Zapt & the Spoils of Egypt. 1995. 240p. 19.95 o.s.i (*0-89296-560-6*) Mysterious Pr.

—The Snake-Catcher's Daughter. 1998. 192p. mass mkt. 9.95 (*0-00-649036-0*) HarperCollins Pubs. Ltd. GBR. *Dist:* Trafalgar Square.

—The Snake-Catcher's Daughter. l.t. ed. 1998. (Linford Mystery Library). 352p. pap. 17.99 o.p. (*0-7089-5217-8*, Linford) Thorpe, F. A. Pubs. GBR. *Dist:* Ulverscroft Large Print Bks., Ltd., Ulverscroft Large Print Canada, Ltd.

—The Snake Catcher's Daughter: A Mamur Zapt Mystery. 2003. (Mamur Zapt Mystery Ser.). 250p. 24.95 o.s.i (*1-59058-051-6*) Poisoned Pen Pr.

Talley, Linda. Bastet. (Key Concepts in Personal Development Ser.). (Illus.). 2001. 32p. pap., tchr. ed. 79.95 incl. VHS (*1-55942-176-2*, 9390K3); 2000. 30p. (J). 79.95 incl. VHS (*1-55942-161-4*) Marsh Media.

Warmington, Mary Jane. Pyramid of Love. l.t. ed. 1997. (Nightingale Ser.). 245p. lib. bdg. 17.95 o.p. (*0-7838-8110-X*, Macmillan Reference USA) Gale Group.

**CAITHE (IMAGINARY PLACE)—FICTION**

Smith, Julie D. The Wizard King. 1993. mass mkt. 5.50 o.s.i (*0-345-37153-4*, Del Rey) Ballantine Bks.

Smith, Julie Dean. Call of Madness. 1990. (Caithan Crusade: 1). 320p. mass mkt. 4.95 o.s.i (*0-345-36327-2*, Del Rey) Ballantine Bks.

—Mission of Magic. 1991. (Caithan Crusade: 2). (Orig.). mass mkt. 4.95 o.s.i (*0-345-36627-1*, Del Rey) Ballantine Bks.

—Sage of Sare. 1992. (Caithan Crusade: 3). mass mkt. 4.99 o.s.i (*0-345-37154-2*, Del Rey) Ballantine Bks.

**CALEDON (IMAGINARY PLACE)—FICTION**

Harris, Deborah T. Caledon of the Mists. 1994. (Orig.). mass mkt. 5.50 o.s.i (*0-441-00029-0*) Ace Bks.

—The City of Exile. 1997. 384p. mass mkt. 6.50 o.s.i (*0-441-00463-6*) Ace Bks.

—The Queen of Ashes. 1995. 464p. (Orig.). mass mkt. 5.99 o.s.i (*0-441-00118-1*) Ace Bks.

**CALIFORNIA—FICTION**

Abbott, Keith. Gush: A Comic Novel about Unemployment in California. 1975. 140p. 29.95 (*0-912652-16-0*); pap. 12.95 (*0-912652-17-9*); 49.95 (*0-912652-18-7*) Blue Wind Pr.

Abella, Alex. Dead of Night. 1998. 304p. 23.00 (*0-684-81426-9*, Simon & Schuster) Simon & Schuster.

—The Killing of the Saints. 1993. (Crime Ser.). 320p. pap. 5.95 o.p. (*0-14-017419-2*, Penguin Bks.) Penguin Group (USA) Inc.

Abramo, J. L. Catching Water in a Net. l.t. ed. 2002. 367p. 28.95 (*0-7862-3996-4*) Gale Group.

Adair, Cherry. Kiss & Tell. 2000. 320p. mass mkt. 6.99 (*0-449-00683-2*, Ivy Bks.) Ballantine Bks.

Adams, Alice. Caroline's Daughters. l.t. ed. 1991. 432p. lib. bdg. 23.95 o.p. (*0-8161-5302-7*, Macmillan Reference USA) Gale Group.

Adler, Bill, Jr., et al. Murder in Los Angeles. 1987. 320p. 16.95 o.p. (*0-688-06684-4*, Morrow, William & Co.) Morrow/Avon.

Adler, Dick. The Mozart Code. 1999. 168p. E-Book 6.00 (*1-58200-107-3*); E-Book 6.00 (*1-58200-227-4*) Hard Shell Word Factory.

Adler, Elizabeth A. All or Nothing. 2000. 368p. mass mkt. 6.99 (*0-440-23496-4*, Dell Bks.) Dell Publishing.

—All or Nothing. l.t. ed. 1999. 27.95 (*1-56895-825-0*, Wheeler Publishing, Inc.) Gale Group.

—Sooner or Later. 1998. 432p. mass mkt. 6.99 (*0-440-22465-9*) Dell Publishing.

—Sooner or Later. l.t. ed. 1998. (Romance Ser.). 27.95 (*1-56895-575-8*, Wheeler Publishing, Inc.) Gale Group.

Ala Maududi, S. Abul. Evidence of Truth. 1985. 36p. (Orig.). pap. 3.00 (*1-56744-267-6*) Kazi Pubns., Inc.

Alcala, Kathleen. The Flower in the Skull: A Novel. 1998. 182p. 22.95 o.p. (*0-8118-1916-7*) Chronicle Bks. LLC.

—The Flower in the Skull: A Novel. 1999. 192p. pap. 13.00 (*0-15-600634-0*, Harvest Bks.) Harcourt Trade Pubs.

Alder, Elizabeth A. All or Nothing. E-Book 6.99 (*1-930161-75-1*) Adobe Systems, Inc.

Allen, Steve. Die Laughing. 1998. 304p. 21.00 o.s.i (*1-57566-241-8*) Kensington Publishing Corp.

Allende, Isabel. The Infinite Plan: A Novel. Peden, Margaret Sayers, tr. from ENG. 1993. 384p. 23.00 o.p. (*0-06-017016-6*) HarperTrade.

Allman, Kevin. Hot Shot. 1998. 256p. 22.95 (*0-312-16866-7*, Saint Martin's Minotaur) St. Martin's Pr.

—Tight Shot. 1995. 262p. 21.00 o.p. (*0-312-11904-6*, Saint Martin's Minotaur) St. Martin's Pr.

Alvarado, Steven. The Angel of Venice Beach. 2001. 104p. pap. 20.99 (*0-7388-5366-6*) Xlibris Corp.

Alwyn, Cynthia G. Scent of Murder. 2001. E-Book 23.95 (*1-59061-037-7*) Adobe Systems, Inc.

—Scent of Murder. 2001. 294p. 23.95 (*0-312-26559-X*, Saint Martin's Minotaur) St. Martin's Pr.

Ambrose, David. Mother of God, abr. ed. 1999. audio 23.00 (*1-56876-062-0*, 595071) Soundlines Entertainment, Inc.

Settings

—Mother of God. l.t. ed. 1997. (Charnwood Large Print Ser.). 464p. 34.50 o.p. (*0-7089-8936-5*, Ulverscroft) Thorpe, F. A. Pubs. GBR. *Dist:* Ulverscroft Large Print Bks., Ltd., Ulverscroft Large Print Canada, Ltd.

Ambrose, David P. Mother of God. l.t. ed. 1997. (G. K. Hall Mystery Ser.). 537p. lib. bdg. 25.95 o.p. (*0-7838-1974-9*, Macmillan Reference USA) Gale Group.

—Mother of God. 1996. 352p. 22.50 o.p. (*0-684-82418-3*, Simon & Schuster) Simon & Schuster.

Andersdatter, Karla. The Doorway. 3rd ed. 2004. per. (*0-935430-25-3*) In Between Bks.

—The Doorway. 1990. 275p. 17.95 (*0-911051-50-3*) Plain View Pr.

Andersen, Susan. Baby, Don't Go. 2000. 384p. mass mkt. 6.50 (*0-380-80712-2*, Avon Bks.) Morrow/Avon.

Anderson, Robert Mailer. Boonville: A Novel. 2003. 272p. pap. 12.95 (*0-06-051621-6*, Perennial) HarperTrade.

Andresen, Julie T. The Blue Hour. 1998. 16.95 (*0-9654499-4-7*); (Illus.). 400p. 23.50 (*0-9654499-1-2*) Windows on History Pr., Inc.

Andrews, Brian. Knife under Fire. 1993. (*1-881529-01-0*) Custom & Limited Editions.

Andrews, Sarah. Mother Nature. 1997. 352p. 23.95 (*0-312-15591-3*, Saint Martin's Minotaur) St. Martin's Pr.

Andrews, V. C. Unfinished Symphony. 1997. (Logan Ser.). 352p. 24.00 o.s.i (*0-671-53469-6*, Atria); 384p. mass mkt. 7.99 (*0-671-53473-4*, Pocket) Simon & Schuster.

—Unfinished Symphony. l.t. ed. 1998. (Core Ser.). 479p. 30.95 (*0-7838-8407-9*) Thorndike Pr.

—Unfinished Symphony. 1997. 14.04 (*0-606-13883-8*) Turtleback Bks.

Andrus, Jeff. The Neighborhood Watch: A Tracer Family Mystery. 1996. 288p. 20.50 (*0-684-19706-5*, Scribner) Simon & Schuster.

—Tracer, Inc. 1994. 256p. 20.00 (*0-684-19705-7*, Scribner) Simon & Schuster.

Anobile, Richard J., ed. The Maltese Falcon. 1974. (Film Classics Library). (Illus.). 256p. mass mkt. 5.50 o.p. (*0-380-01485-8*, 19109-1, Avon Bks.) Morrow/Avon.

Apodaca, Jennifer. Dating Can Be Murder: A Samantha Shaw Mystery. 2003. 256p. mass mkt. 5.99 (*0-7582-0075-7*); 2002. 34p. 22.00 (*0-7582-0073-0*) Kensington Publishing Corp.

Apollo. Concrete Candy: Stories. 1996. 144p. pap. 15.00 (*0-385-47780-5*) Doubleday Publishing.

Appelman, William. Claim to Fame. 1993. 256p. 19.95 o.p. (*0-88184-935-9*, Carroll & Graf Pubs.) Avalon Publishing Group.

Arkham, Candice. Forbidden Yearnings. l.t. ed. 1994. 19.95 o.p. (*0-7927-1901-8*); pap. 17.95 o.p. (*0-7927-1900-X*) BBC Audiobooks America.

Armstrong, Campbell. A Concert of Ghosts: A Novel. 1993. 256p. 20.00 o.p. (*0-06-017946-5*) HarperTrade.

Arnoldi, Katie. Chemical Pink. 2002. 272p. reprint ed. pap. 13.95 (*0-312-87891-5*, Forge Bks.) Doherty, Tom Assocs., LLC.

Ashley, Mary Anne. Fragments I Saved from the Fire. 1989. 120p. (Orig.). pap. 9.00 (*0-918949-06-8*, Papier-Mache Pr.) Moyer Bell.

Ashour, Linda Phillips. A Comforting Lie. 1999. 336p. 24.00 (*0-684-81834-5*, Simon & Schuster) Simon & Schuster.

Atherton, Gertrude Franklin Horn. The Californians. 2000. 252p. E-Book 3.95 (*0-594-03823-5*) 1873 Pr.

—Rezanov. 2000. 252p. pap. 9.95 (*0-594-03580-5*); E-Book 3.95 (*0-594-03583-X*) 1873 Pr.

—Rezanov. (Illus.). 320p. reprint ed. lib. bdg. 32.00 (*0-8398-0067-3*); 1986. pap. text 6.95 (*0-8290-1924-3*) Irvington Pubs.

Atkins, Peter. Morningstar. 1992. 304p. mass mkt. 4.50 o.p. (*0-06-100512-6*, HarperTorch) Morrow/Avon.

Austin, Mary H. The Basket Woman. 1969. reprint ed. 37.50 (*0-404-00429-6*) AMS Pr., Inc.

—The Basket Woman. 1998. (Collected Works of Mary Hunter Austin). 222p. reprint ed. lib. bdg. 88.00 (*1-58201-512-0*) Classic Bks.

—The Basket Woman: A Book of Indian Tales. 1999. (Western Literature Ser.). 136p. (gr. 3-7). reprint ed. pap. 17.00 (*0-87417-336-1*) Univ. of Nevada Pr.

—The Ford. (Collected Works of Mary Hunter Austin). 440p. reprint ed. 2001. (Illus.). pap. text 28.00 (*0-7426-5517-2*); 1998. lib. bdg. 108.00 (*1-58201-517-1*) Classic Bks.

—The Ford. 1997. (California Fiction Ser.). 440p. pap. 16.95 (*0-520-20757-2*) Univ. of California Pr.

—Stories from the Country of Lost Borders. Pryse, Marjorie, ed. 1987. (American Women Writers Ser.). 267p. text 40.00 (*0-8135-1217-4*); pap. text 16.00 (*0-8135-1218-2*) Rutgers Univ. Pr.

Austin, Mary Hunter. The Ford. 1997. E-Book 29.95 (*0-585-32065-9*) netLibrary, Inc.

Ayres, Noreen. Carcass Trade. unabr. ed. 1995. audio 56.00 (*0-7366-2934-3*, 3630) Books on Tape, Inc.

—Carcass Trade. 1994. 285p. 20.00 o.p. (*0-688-10875-X*, Morrow, William & Co.); 1995. 352p. reprint ed. mass mkt. 4.99 o.p. (*0-380-71572-4*, Avon Bks.) Morrow/Avon.

—The Juan Doe Murders: A Smokey Brandon Mystery. 2000. (Five Star Mystery Ser.). 204p. 20.95 (*0-7862-2897-0*, Five Star) Gale Group.

—A World the Color of Salt. unabr. ed. 1992. audio 32.00 (*0-7366-2321-3*, 3101) Books on Tape, Inc.

—A World the Color of Salt. 1993. 304p. mass mkt. 4.99 (*0-380-71571-6*, Avon Bks.); 1992. 352p. 19.00 o.p. (*0-688-10824-5*, Morrow, William & Co.) Morrow/Avon.

Babb, Sanora. Whose Names Are Unknown: A Novel. 2004. (*0-8061-3579-4*) Univ. of Oklahoma Pr.

Babula, William. According to St. John. 2000. (Jeremiah St. John Detective Ser.: Vol. 2). 240p. pap. 12.95 (*1-58345-501-9*) Domhan Bks.

—St. John & the Seven Veils. 2000. (Jeremiah St. John Detective Ser.: Vol. 3). 208p. pap. 12.95 (*1-58345-506-X*) Domhan Bks.

—St. John's Baptism. 2000. (Jeremiah St. John Detective Ser.: Vol. 1). 260p. pap. 12.95 (*1-58345-496-9*) Domhan Bks.

—St. John's Bestiary. 2000. (Jeremiah St. John Detective Ser.: Vol. 4). 264p. pap. 12.95 (*1-58345-511-6*) Domhan Bks.

—St. John's Bestiary. 1994. 264p. 19.95 o.p. (*1-885173-01-6*) Write Way Publishing.

Bain, Donald & Fletcher, Jessica. Murder, She Wrote: Martinis & Mayhem. l.t. ed. 1999. (Nightingale Ser.). 280p. pap. 21.95 (*0-7838-8665-9*) Thorndike Pr.

Bakeer, Donald. Crips: The Story of a South Central L.A. Street Gang. 1992. 195p. reprint ed. 19.95 (*0-9634969-0-5*) Precocious Publishing Co.

Baker, James Robert. Testosterone: A Novel. 2000. viii, 200p. 22.95 o.p. (*1-55583-567-8*, Alyson Bks.) Alyson Pubns.

—Tim & Pete: A Novel. 2001. 256p. pap. 12.95 (*1-55583-566-X*, Alyson Bks.) Alyson Pubns.

Baker, Madeline. Unforgettable. 2000. 400p. mass mkt. 5.99 (*0-8439-4762-4*, Leisure Bks.) Dorchester Publishing Co., Inc.

Ball, John. The Cool Cottontail. 1985. 176p. (Orig.). mass mkt. 3.50 o.p. (*0-06-080734-2*, P734, Perennial) HarperTrade.

—The Eyes of Buddha: A Virgil Tibbs Mystery. 1985. 256p. reprint ed. mass mkt. 3.50 o.p. (*0-06-080751-2*, P751, Perennial) HarperTrade.

—Five Pieces of Jade. l.t. ed. 1983. (Ulverscroft Large Print Ser.). 352p. 29.99 o.p. (*0-7089-0997-3*, Ulverscroft) Thorpe, F. A. Pubs. GBR. *Dist:* Ulverscroft Large Print Bks., Ltd., Ulverscroft Large Print Canada, Ltd.

—Then Came Violence. 1980. (Crime Club Ser.). 8.95 o.p. (*0-385-15726-6*) Doubleday Publishing.

—Then Came Violence. l.t. ed. 1982. (Ulverscroft Large Print Ser.). 352p. 29.99 o.p. (*0-7089-0870-5*, Ulverscroft) Thorpe, F. A. Pubs. GBR. *Dist:* Ulverscroft Large Print Bks., Ltd., Ulverscroft Large Print Canada, Ltd.

—Then Came Violence: A Virgil Tibbs Mystery. 1988. 208p. reprint ed. mass mkt. 3.95 o.p. (*0-06-080883-7*, P-883, Perennial) HarperTrade.

Banbury, Jen. Like a Hole in the Head: A Novel. 1998. 304p. (YA). (gr. 8 up). 21.95 o.p. (*0-316-17110-7*) Little Brown & Co.

—Like a Hole in the Head: A Novel. 1999. 304p. pap. 12.00 o.s.i (*0-446-67517-2*) Warner Bks., Inc.

Barbara, Wood. Sacred Ground. 2002. mass mkt. (*0-312-98298-4*, St. Martin's Paperbacks) St. Martin's Pr.

Barger, Ralph, et al. Dead in 5 Heartbeats: A Novel. 2003. (*0-06-053253-X*, Morrow, William & Co.) Morrow/Avon.

Barger, Ralph "Sonny". Dead in 5 Heartbeats: A Novel. 2003. 320p. 24.95 (*0-06-053251-3*, 53789205, Morrow, William & Co.) Morrow/Avon.

Barich, Bill. Carson Valley. 1998. 352p. pap. 19.00 (*0-679-75857-7*, Vintage) Knopf Publishing Group.

—Carson Valley. l.t. ed. 1997. (Niagara Large Print Ser.). 528p. 29.50 o.p. (*0-7089-5885-0*, Ulverscroft) Thorpe, F. A. Pubs. GBR. *Dist:* Ulverscroft Large Print Bks., Ltd.

Barkhordar-Nahai, Gina. Moonlight on the Avenue of Faith. 2000. 400p. reprint ed. pap. 13.95 (*0-671-04283-1*, Washington Square Pr.) Simon & Schuster.

Barnes, Joanna. The Deceivers. 1970. 6.95 o.p. (*0-87795-007-5*, Morrow, William & Co.) Morrow/Avon.

Barnes, Steven. Firedance. 1993. 416p. 21.95 o.p. (*0-312-85094-8*, Tor Bks.) Doherty, Tom Assocs., LLC.

—Iron Shadows. 2000. 320p. mass mkt. 6.99 (*0-8125-4808-6*); 1998. 416p. 24.95 o.p. (*0-312-85708-X*) Doherty, Tom Assocs., LLC. (Tor Bks.).

Barr, Nevada. Firestorm. l.t. ed. 1997. (Large Print Bks.). 24.95 o.p. (*1-56895-399-2*, Wheeler Publishing, Inc.) Gale Group.

—Firestorm. 1997. (Anna Pigeon Mysteries Ser.). 336p. reprint ed. mass mkt. 7.99 (*0-380-72582-7*, Avon Bks.) Morrow/Avon.

—Firestorm. 1996. 320p. 22.95 o.p. (*0-399-14126-X*, G. P. Putnam's Sons) Penguin Group (USA) Inc.

—High Country. 2004. 336p. 24.95 (*0-399-15144-3*) Putnam Publishing Group, The.

Barre, Richard. Bearing Secrets: A Wil Hardesty Mystery. 1998. (Wil Hardesty Ser.: Vol. 2). 288p. reprint ed. mass mkt. 5.99 o.s.i (*0-425-16641-4*) Berkley Publishing Group.

—Bearing Secrets: A Wil Hardesty Mystery. 1996. (Wil Hardesty Ser.). 312p. 22.95 (*0-8027-3280-1*) Walker & Co.

—Blackheart Highway. (Wil Hardesty Ser.: Vol. 4). 2000. 326p. mass mkt. 6.99 o.s.i (*0-425-17467-0*); 1999. 336p. 21.95 o.s.i (*0-425-16903-0*, Prime Crime) Berkley Publishing Group.

—Burning Moon: A Wil Hardesty Novel. 2003. (Illus.). 330p. 25.95 (*1-59266-011-8*) Capra Pr.

—The Ghosts of Morning: A Will Hardesty Mystery. 1998. 336p. 21.95 o.s.i (*0-425-16300-8*); 1999. 320p. reprint ed. mass mkt. 6.50 o.s.i (*0-425-16931-6*, Prime Crime) Berkley Publishing Group.

—The Innocents. 1997. (Wil Hardesty Ser.: Vol. 1). 288p. mass mkt. 6.50 o.s.i (*0-425-16109-9*, Prime Crime) Berkley Publishing Group.

—The Innocents. 1995. 332p. 19.95 (*0-8027-3261-5*) Walker & Co.

Barrett, Suzanne. Hearts at Risk. 2000. (Romance Ser.: Vol. 75). 256p. mass mkt. 4.99 o.p. (*0-8217-6735-6*) Kensington Publishing Corp.

Barry, Max. Syrup. 2000. 304p. pap. 11.95 (*0-14-029187-3*) Penguin Group (USA) Inc.

—Syrup. 1999. 320p. 23.95 o.p. (*0-670-88640-8*) Viking Penguin.

Barton, Wayne. Lockhart's Nightmare. 2000. 350p. mass mkt. 6.99 (*0-8125-7196-7*, Forge Bks.) Doherty, Tom Assocs., LLC.

Barton, Wayne & Williams, Stan. Lockharts Nightmare. 1998. 384p. 24.95 o.p. (*0-312-86142-7*, Forge Bks.) Doherty, Tom Assocs., LLC.

Bass, Milton. The Half-Hearted Detective. Isaacson, Dana, ed. 1993. 256p. (Orig.). mass mkt. 4.99 (*0-671-74242-6*, Pocket) Simon & Schuster.

Baxt, George. The Greta Garbo Murder Case. 1992. 208p. 17.95 o.p. (*0-312-06988-X*, Saint Martin's Minotaur) St. Martin's Pr.

—The Humphrey Bogart Murder Case. 1995. 200p. 18.95 o.p. (*0-312-11828-7*, Saint Martin's Minotaur) St. Martin's Pr.

—The Mae West Murder Case. 1993. 208p. 17.95 o.p. (*0-312-09864-2*, Saint Martin's Minotaur) St. Martin's Pr.

—The Marlene Dietrich Murder Case. 1993. 224p. 17.95 o.p. (*0-312-09334-9*, Saint Martin's Minotaur) St. Martin's Pr.

—The Talking Pictures Murder Case. 1990. 208p. 15.95 o.p. (*0-312-05043-7*, Saint Martin's Minotaur) St. Martin's Pr.

—The Tallulah Bankhead Murder Case. 1987. 240p. 15.95 o.p. (*0-312-01098-2*, Saint Martin's Minotaur) St. Martin's Pr.

—The William Powell & Myrna Loy Murder Case. 1996. 208p. 20.95 o.p. (*0-312-14071-1*, Saint Martin's Minotaur) St. Martin's Pr.

Beale, Elaine. Murder in the Castro. 1997. 192p. pap. 10.95 (*0-934678-87-1*) New Victoria Pubs., Inc.

Bear, Greg. Infinity Concerto. 1987. mass mkt. 3.95 o.s.i (*0-441-37059-4*) Ace Bks.

—Infinity Concerto. 1986. 352p. 3.50 o.s.i (*0-425-09536-3*); 1984. 2.95 o.s.i (*0-425-07308-4*) Berkley Publishing Group.

—The Serpent Mage. (Orig.). 1987. mass mkt. 3.95 o.s.i (*0-441-75910-6*); 1986. mass mkt. 2.75 o.s.i (*0-441-79066-6*) Ace Bks.

—The Serpent Mage. 1986. 352p. (Orig.). 3.50 o.s.i (*0-425-09337-9*) Berkley Publishing Group.

—Songs of Earth & Power. 1996. 695p. pap. text 6.99 (*0-8125-3603-7*); 1994. 560p. 24.95 o.p. (*0-312-85669-5*) Doherty, Tom Assocs., LLC. (Tor Bks.).

—Songs of Earth & Power. 1992. (*0-7126-5494-1*) Random Hse. UK, Ltd. GBR. *Dist:* Random Hse. of Canada, Ltd.

Beardwood, Roger. The Winner's Share. 1980. 10.00 o.p. (*0-385-14426-1*) Doubleday Publishing.

Beath, Warren N. Bloodletter. 352p. 1994. 21.95 o.p. (*0-312-85731-4*); Vol. 1. 1996. mass mkt. 5.99 o.p. (*0-8125-3393-3*) Doherty, Tom Assocs., LLC. (Tor Bks.).

Beatty, Paul. The White Boy Shuffle. 2001. 240p. pap. 13.00 (*0-312-28019-X*) Picador.

Beck, K. K. Murder in a Mummy Case. l.t. ed. 1989. 8.95 o.p. (*0-7451-9460-5*, 352) BBC Audiobooks America.

—Murder in a Mummy Case. 1987. 176p. mass mkt. 3.95 o.s.i (*0-8041-0117-5*, Ivy Bks.) Ballantine Bks.

—Murder in a Mummy Case. 1986. 176p. 15.95 o.s.i (*0-8027-5655-7*) Walker & Co.

Beers, Terry, ed. Unfolding Beauty: Celebrating California's Landscapes. 2000. (California Legacy Ser.). (Illus.). 416p. pap. 17.95 (*1-890771-34-1*, Roundhouse Pr., The) Heyday Bks.

Belanger, Sean Pierre. Savage Mountain: A Novel. 2002. 194p. pap. 13.00 (*1-59209-002-8*) USA Bks.

Bell, James S. Circumstantial Evidence. 1997. 480p. pap. 13.99 o.p. (*0-8054-6359-3*) Broadman & Holman Pubs.

Bender, Karen E. Like Normal People. l.t. ed. 2000. (G. K. Hall Core Ser.). 384p. 27.95 (*0-7838-9301-9*, Macmillan Reference USA) Gale Group.

—Like Normal People. 2000. 288p. tchr. ed. 23.00 (*0-395-94515-1*) Houghton Mifflin Co.

—Like Normal People. 2001. 288p. pap. 13.00 (*0-618-12692-9*, Mariner Bks.) Houghton Mifflin Co. Trade & Reference Div.

Benke, Patricia D. False Witness. 1996. mass mkt. 5.99 (*0-380-78184-0*, Avon Bks.) Morrow/Avon.

Berg, Patti. Born to Be Wild. 2001. 384p. mass mkt. 5.99 (*0-380-81682-2*, Avon Bks.) Morrow/Avon.

Berlinski, David. The Body Shop: An Aaron Asherfeld Mystery. 1996. 208p. text 20.95 o.p. (*0-312-13935-7*, Saint Martin's Minotaur) St. Martin's Pr.

—A Clean Sweep. 1992. 240p. 17.95 o.p. (*0-312-08744-6*, Saint Martin's Minotaur) St. Martin's Pr.

—Less than Meets the Eye: An Aaron Asherfield Mystery. 1994. (Aaron Asherfield Mystery Ser.). 208p. 18.95 o.p. (*0-312-11298-X*, Saint Martin's Minotaur) St. Martin's Pr.

—Less Than Meets the Eye: An Aaron Asherfield Mystery. 1994. 240p. 19.95 (*0-312-10611-4*, Saint Martin's Minotaur) St. Martin's Pr.

Berrenson, Marc. Bodily Harm. 1992. 224p. (Orig.). mass mkt. 4.50 (*0-380-76613-2*, Avon Bks.) Morrow/Avon.

—L. A. Snitch. 1991. 256p. (Orig.). pap. 3.95 (*0-380-76324-9*, Avon Bks.) Morrow/Avon.

Berriault, Gina. The Lights of Earth. 2nd ed. 1997. 156p. pap. text 12.50 (*1-887178-53-8*, Counterpoint Pr.) Basic Bks.

—The Lights of Earth: A Novel. 1982. 176p. (Orig.). 12.50 o.p. (*0-86547-141-X*, North Point Pr.) Farrar, Straus & Giroux.

Bevarly, Elizabeth. Taming the Prince. 2002. (Silhouette Desire Ser.). 192p. mass mkt. (*0-373-76474-X*, Silhouette) Harlequin Enterprises, Ltd.

Bills, Greg. Fearful Symmetry. 336p. 1997. pap. 12.95 o.p. (*0-452-27574-1*, Plume); 1996. 23.95 o.s.i (*0-525-94081-2*, Dutton) Dutton/Plume.

Bishop, Paul. Chalk Whispers. 2000. 368p. 25.00 (*0-684-87157-2*, Scribner) Simon & Schuster.

—Chalk Whispers: A Fey Croaker LAPD Crime Novel. 2000. (Fey Croaker Novels Ser.). 368p. 25.00 o.s.i (*0-684-83010-8*, Scribner) Simon & Schuster.

—Chapel of the Ravens, Bk. 3. unabr. ed. 1998. audio 64.95 (*1-55686-781-6*) Books in Motion.

—Chapel of the Ravens. 1992. 352p. mass mkt. 4.99 o.p. (*0-8125-0583-2*); 1991. 18.95 o.p. (*0-312-93155-7*) Doherty, Tom Assocs., LLC. (Tor Bks.).

—Kill Me Again. unabr. ed. 1996. (Fey Croaker Mystery Ser.: Bk. 1). audio 49.95 (*1-55686-614-3*) Books in Motion.

—Kill Me Again. 1994. 288p. mass mkt. 4.99 (*0-380-76890-9*, Avon Bks.) Morrow/Avon.

—Sand Against the Tide. 1992. 307p. mass mkt. 4.99 o.p. (*0-8125-0918-8*); 1990. 12.99 o.p. (*0-312-93158-1*) Doherty, Tom Assocs., LLC. (Tor Bks.).

—Tequila Mockingbird. 1998. (Fey Croaker Novels Ser.). 400p. pap. 6.99 (*0-671-02531-7*, Pocket) Simon & Schuster.

—Tequila Mockingbird: A Fey Croaker Novel. 1997. (Fey Croaker Novels Ser.). 400p. 23.00 o.s.i (*0-684-83009-4*, Scribner) Simon & Schuster.

—Twice Dead. unabr. ed. 1996. (Fey Croaker Mystery Ser.: Bk. 2). audio 64.95 (*1-55686-710-7*) Books in Motion.

—Twice Dead. 1996. 336p. mass mkt. 5.50 (*0-380-77862-9*, Avon Bks.) Morrow/Avon.

Blankenship, William D. Brotherly Love. 1981. 12.95 o.p. (*0-87795-301-5*, Morrow, William & Co.) Morrow/Avon.

—Brotherly Love. 1983. mass mkt. 3.50 o.s.i (*0-671-44765-3*, Pocket) Simon & Schuster.

Blatty, William P. Demons Five, Exorcists Nothing: A Fable. 1996. 188p. 18.95 o.p. (*1-55611-501-6*) Fine, Donald I. Bks.

Blaylock, James P. All the Bells on Earth. 1995. 384p. 21.95 o.p. (*0-441-00247-1*) Ace Bks.

—The Rainy Season. 2000. 368p. mass mkt. 6.99 o.s.i (*0-441-00756-2*); 1999. 356p. 21.95 o.s.i (*0-441-00618-3*) Ace Bks.

—Winter Tides. 352p. 1997. 21.95 o.s.i (*0-441-00444-X*); 1998. reprint ed. mass mkt. 6.50 o.s.i (*0-441-00575-6*) Ace Bks.

Blitz, Renee. In Berkeley's Green & Pleasant Land: Songs of Innocence, Songs of Experience. 2001. 268p. pap. 12.95 (*1-58790-011-4*) Regent Pr.

Blum, Bill. The Face of Justice. 1999. pap. 19.95 (*0-525-93906-7*); 1998. 400p. mass mkt. 6.99 o.s.i (*0-451-40803-9*, Onyx) NAL.

—The Last Appeal. 1997. 416p. mass mkt. 6.99 o.s.i (*0-451-18311-8*, Signet Bks.) NAL.

—Prejudicial Error. 1995. 304p. 21.95 o.p. (*0-525-93905-9*, Dutton) Dutton/Plume.

—Prejudicial Error. 1996. 368p. mass mkt. 5.99 o.s.i (*0-451-18309-6*, Signet Bks.) NAL.

Bly, Stephen A. The Last Swan in Sacramento. 1999. (Old California Ser.: Vol. 2). 224p. pap. 10.99 o.p. (*1-58134-109-1*) Crossway Bks.

—The Last Swan in Sacramento. l.t. ed. 2000. (G. K. Hall Western Ser.). 326p. 25.95 (*0-7838-9127-X*) Thorndike Pr.

—Proud Quail of the San Joaquin. 2000. (Old California Ser.: Vol. 3). 232p. pap. 10.99 (*1-58134-152-0*) Crossway Bks.

—Proud Quail of the San Joaquin. l.t. ed. 2000. (G. K. Hall Western Ser.). (Illus.). 345p. (J). 25.95 (*0-7838-9277-2*, Macmillan Reference USA) Gale Group.

—The Red Dove of Monterey. 1998. (Old California Ser.: Vol. 1). 224p. pap. 10.99 (*1-58134-004-4*) Crossway Bks.

Board, Sherri L. Angels of Anguish. 1999. (Katlin Lamar Mystery Ser.). 304p. pap. 11.95 (*0-9634767-5-0*) Crime-Zone Bks.

Bockoven, Georgia. Far from Home. l.t. ed. 1999. 26.95 (*1-57490-246-6*, Beeler Large Print Bks.) Beeler, Thomas T. Publisher.

Bogart, Humphrey, et al. The Maltese Falcon. 1946. audio 7.95 National Recording Co.

Bogner, Norman. Honor Thy Wife. 2000. 536p. mass mkt. 6.99 (*0-8125-7556-3*); 1999. 448p. 25.95 (*0-312-86808-1*) Doherty, Tom Assocs., LLC. (Forge Bks.).

Boorstin, Jon. Pay or Play. 1997. 256p. 22.00 o.p. (*0-7867-0359-8*, Carroll & Graf Pubs.) Avalon Publishing Group.

—Pay or Play. 2000. 278p. pap. 12.95 (*1-890085-04-9*) Siles Pr.

Booth, Pat. Malibu. 1991. 384p. mass mkt. 5.99 o.s.i (*0-345-35218-1*) Ballantine Bks.

—Malibu. 1990. (Illus.). 19.95 o.s.i (*0-517-57506-X*, Crown) Crown Publishing Group.

—Malibu. 1993. 4.99 o.p. (*0-517-10680-9*); 1992. 4.99 o.p. (*0-517-08894-0*) Random Hse. Value Publishing.

Borg, Todd. Tahoe Blowup: An Owen McKenna Mystery Thriller. 2001. (Illus.). 320p. per. 16.95 (*1-931296-12-X*) Thriller Pr.

Boswell, Robert. Mystery Ride. 1994. 352p. pap. 72.00 o.p. (*0-06-097600-4*); reprint ed. pap. 13.00 (*0-06-097585-7*) HarperTrade. (Perennial).

—Mystery Ride: A Novel. 1993. 22.00 o.s.i (*0-679-41292-1*) Knopf, Alfred A. Inc.

Boucher, Anthony. Nine Times Nine. 1986. 254p. pap. 4.95 o.p. (*0-930330-37-4*) International Polygonics, Ltd.

—Rocket to the Morgue. 1988. 176p. pap. 4.95 (*0-930330-82-X*) International Polygonics, Ltd.

Bowman, Robert J. The Screaming Buddha. 1994. 256p. 20.95 o.p. (*0-312-11056-1*, Saint Martin's Minotaur) St. Martin's Pr.

Boyd, William. The New Confessions. 1989. 480p. pap. 8.95 o.p. (*0-14-010699-5*, Penguin Bks.) Viking Penguin.

Boyle, Alistair. Bluebeard's Last Stand: A Gil Yates Private Investigator Novel. 1998. (Gil Yates Private Investigator Ser.). 155p. 20.00 (*1-888310-45-6*) Knoll, Allen A. Pubs.

—The Con: A Gil Yates Private Investigator Novel. 1996. 222p. 19.95 (*0-9627297-9-5*) Knoll, Allen A. Pubs.

—The Missing Link: A Gil Yates Private Investigator Novel. 1995. 224p. 19.95 (*0-9627297-3-6*) Knoll, Allen A. Pubs.

—Ship Shapely: A Gil Yates Private Investigator Novel. 1999. 228p. 20.00 (*1-888310-99-5*) Knoll, Allen A. Pubs.

—The Unholy Ghost: A Gil Yates Private Investigator Novel. 2003. (Gil Yates Private Investigator Ser.: 7). 271p. 23.00 (*1-888310-67-7*) Knoll, Allen A. Pubs.

—The Unlucky Seven: A Gil Yates Private Investigator Novel. 1997. 176p. 20.00 (*1-888310-77-4*) Knoll, Allen A. Pubs.

Boyle, T. Coraghessan. Budding Prospects. 1984. 320p. 16.95 o.p. (*0-670-19439-5*) Viking Penguin.

—Drop City. 2004. 512p. pap. 14.00 (*0-14-200380-8*) Penguin Group (USA) Inc.

—Drop City. 2003. 464p. 25.95 (*0-670-03172-0*, Viking) Viking Penguin.

—A Friend of the Earth. 2000. 256p. 24.95 o.s.i (*0-670-89177-0*, Viking) Viking Penguin.

—The Tortilla Curtain. Set. abr. ed. 1995. audio 16.95 (*1-55927-353-4*, 393174) Audio Renaissance.

—The Tortilla Curtain. unabr. ed. 1996. audio 80.00 (*0-7366-3300-6*, 3955) Books on Tape, Inc.

—The Tortilla Curtain. l.t. ed. 1996. 25.95 (*1-56895-287-2*, Wheeler Publishing, Inc.) Gale Group.

—The Tortilla Curtain. 1996. 368p. pap. 14.00 (*0-14-023828-X*) Penguin Group (USA) Inc.

—The Tortilla Curtain. unabr. ed. audio 85.00 (*0-7887-0457-5*, 94650E7) Recorded Bks., LLC.

—The Tortilla Curtain. 1995. 368p. 23.95 o.s.i (*0-670-85604-5*, Viking) Viking Penguin.

Bradbury, Ray. A Graveyard for Lunatics. 1991. 304p. mass mkt. 5.99 o.s.i (*0-553-18046-0*) Bantam Bks.

—A Graveyard for Lunatics. 2001. 320p. pap. 13.00 (*0-380-81200-2*, Perennial) HarperTrade.

—A Graveyard for Lunatics. 1994. 3.99 o.p. (*0-517-11536-0*); 1992. 4.99 o.p. (*0-517-08571-2*) Random Hse. Value Publishing.

—Let's All Kill Constance. 2003. pap. 13.95 (*0-06-051585-6*); 224p. 23.95 (*0-06-051584-8*) HarperCollins Pubs.

—Let's All Kill Constance. 2004. 256p. mass mkt. 7.50 (*0-06-056178-5*, Avon Bks.) Morrow/Avon.

—Let's All Kill Constance. l.t. ed. 2003. (Core Ser.). 28.95 (*0-7862-5523-4*) Thorndike Pr.

Bradfield, Scott. History of Luminous Motion. 1996. 288p. pap. 13.00 o.p. (*0-312-14089-4*) Picador.

—The History of Luminous Motion. 1990. (Vintage Contemporaries Ser.). 288p. pap. 11.00 o.s.i (*0-679-72943-7*, Vintage) Knopf Publishing Group.

—What's Wrong with America. 1995. pap. 10.00 o.p. (*0-312-13619-6*) Picador.

—What's Wrong with America. 1994. 196p. 18.95 o.p. (*0-312-11349-8*) St. Martin's Pr.

Brady, Catherine. Curled in the Bed of Love: Stories. 2003. (Flannery O'Connor Award for Short Fiction Ser.). xii, 193p. 24.95 (*0-8203-2545-7*) Univ. of Georgia Pr.

Brady, Taylor. Westward Winds Bk. 4: The Kincaids. 1993. (Orig.). pap. 4.99 (*0-380-77134-9*, Avon Bks.) Morrow/Avon.

Braithwaite, Kent. The Wonderland Murders. 2000. 324p. pap. 14.95 (*1-891929-33-X*) Four Seasons Pubs.

Bram, Christopher. The Father of Frankenstein. 288p. 1996. pap. 12.95 (*0-452-27337-4*, Plume); 1995. 19.95 o.s.i (*0-525-93913-X*) Dutton/Plume.

Braudy, Susan. Who Killed Sal Mineo? 1982. 14.50 o.s.i (*0-671-61009-0*, Simon & Schuster) Simon & Schuster.

Brauner, Asher. Love Songs of the Tone-Deaf. 1999. 300p. pap. 12.95 (*0-9670861-0-8*) Brown Bear Books.

Braverman, Kate. Lithium for Medea. 1989. 256p. pap. 8.95 o.p. (*0-14-012641-4*, Penguin Bks.) Viking Penguin.

—Small Craft Warnings: Stories. 1998. (Western Literature Ser.). 192p. pap. 17.00 (*0-87417-321-3*) Univ. of Nevada Pr.

Bray, Marian F. Stars over East L. A. 1993. (Young Adult Fiction Ser.). 216p. (Orig.). (YA). (gr. 8-12). pap. 6.99 o.p. (*0-87788-798-5*, Shaw) WaterBrook Pr.

Breen, Jon. The Gathering Place. 1984. (Mysteries Ser.). 192p. 12.95 o.p. (*0-8027-5575-5*) Walker & Co.

Breen, Jon L. Hot Air: A Jerry Brogan Mystery. 1991. 208p. 19.00 o.p. (*0-671-68105-2*, Simon & Schuster) Simon & Schuster.

—Listen for the Click. 1983. 192p. 12.95 o.p. (*0-8027-5492-9*) Walker & Co.

—Loose Lips. 1992. 2.99 o.p. (*0-517-08070-2*) Random Hse. Value Publishing.

—Loose Lips. 1990. 17.95 o.p. (*0-671-68104-4*, Simon & Schuster) Simon & Schuster.

—Touch of the Past. l.t. ed. 1990. 16.95 o.p. (*0-7451-9711-6*, C0053); pap. 14.95 o.p. (*0-7927-0123-2*, C0201) BBC Audiobooks America.

—Touch of the Past. 1988. 192p. 16.95 o.p. (*0-8027-5704-9*) Walker & Co.

—Triple Crown. 1986. 192p. 13.95 o.p. (*0-8027-5627-1*) Walker & Co.

Breen, Jon L. & Ball, John, eds. Murder California Style: The Southern California Chapter of the Mystery Writers of America. 1987. 304p. 17.95 o.p. (*0-312-00620-9*) St. Martin's Pr.

Brenna, Duff. The Holy Book of the Beard. 1996. 368p. 24.95 o.s.i (*0-385-47962-X*, Talese, Nan A.) Doubleday Publishing.

Brennan, Carol. In the Dark. l.t. ed. 1995. 288p. lib. bdg. 23.95 (*1-57490-029-3*, Beeler Large Print Bks.) Beeler, Thomas T. Publisher.

—In the Dark. 1995. 256p. mass mkt. 4.99 o.p. (*0-425-14579-4*, Prime Crime) Berkley Publishing Group.

—In the Dark. 1994. 288p. 21.95 o.p. (*0-399-13940-0*, G. P. Putnam's Sons) Penguin Group (USA) Inc.

Brennan, Kevin. Parts Unknown: A Novel. 2004. 320p. pap. 13.95 (*0-06-001277-3*, Perennial) HarperTrade.

—Parts Unknown: A Novel. 2003. 320p. 24.95 (*0-06-001276-5*, Morrow, William & Co.) Morrow/Avon.

Brenner, Leslie. Greetings from the Golden State. 2002. 288p. pap. 14.00 (*0-312-42057-9*) Picador.

—Greetings from the Golden State: A Novel. 2001. 288p. 23.00 o.s.i (*0-8050-6564-4*) Holt, Henry & Co.

Brewer, Steve. Fool's Paradise. 2003. 182p. 22.95 (*0-8263-3124-6*) Univ. of New Mexico Pr.

Briskin, Jacqueline. California Generation. l.t. ed. 1995. 812p. lib. bdg. 24.95 o.p. (*0-7838-1216-7*, Macmillan Reference USA) Gale Group.

—Paloverde. l.t. ed. 1995. 828p. 25.95 o.p. (*0-7838-1217-5*, Macmillan Reference USA) Gale Group.

—Paloverde. (SPA.). 9.95 (*84-01-37080-9*) Plaza & Janés Editories, S.A. ESP. *Dist:* AIMS International Bks., Inc.

—Rich Friends. 1993. 464p. mass mkt. 3.99 o.s.i (*0-440-21521-8*, Dell Bks.); 1977. 464p. mass mkt. 4.50 o.s.i (*0-440-17380-9*); 1976. 468p. 8.95 o.s.i (*0-440-07367-7*, Delacorte Pr.) Dell Publishing.

—Rich Friends. l.t. ed. 1994. 704p. lib. bdg. 25.95 o.p. (*0-7838-1132-2*, Macmillan Reference USA) Gale Group.

—Too Much, Too Soon. 1986. 496p. mass mkt. 5.95 o.p. (*0-425-08783-2*); 1985. mass mkt. 3.95 o.s.i (*0-425-09156-2*) Berkley Publishing Group.

—Too Much, Too Soon. l.t. ed. 1986. (Special Editions Ser.). 760p. 19.95 o.p. (*0-8161-3984-9*); 11.95 o.p. (*0-8161-3987-3*) Gale Group. (Macmillan Reference USA).

—Too Much, Too Soon. 1985. 480p. 17.95 o.p. (*0-399-13071-3*, G. P. Putnam's Sons) Penguin Putnam Bks. for Young Readers.

Britto, Anthony. Tattoo. pap. 15.95 (*0-312-30230-4*, Saint Martin's Griffin); 1997. 400p. 24.95 o.p. (*0-312-15220-5*, Saint Martin's Minotaur) St. Martin's Pr.

Brockmann, Suzanne. Frisco's Kid. 2003. 256p. mass mkt. (*1-55166-759-2*, Mira Bks.) Harlequin Enterprises, Ltd.

Bronson, Po. The First $20 Million Is Always the Hardest: A Silicon Valley Novel. unabr. ed. 1997. audio 73.25 o.p. (*1-56100-811-7*, 838, Unabridged Library Editions) Brilliance Audio.

—The First $20 Million Is Always the Hardest: A Silicon Valley Novel. 2000. 304p. pap. 13.00 (*0-380-81624-5*, Perennial) HarperTrade.

—The First $20 Million Is Always the Hardest: A Silicon Valley Novel. 1998. 352p. pap. 6.99 (*0-380-73155-X*, Avon Bks.) Morrow/Avon.

Brown, Dale. The Tin Man. 1999. 464p. reprint ed. mass mkt. 7.99 (*0-553-58000-0*, Bantam Classics) Bantam Bks.

—The Tin Man. l.t. ed. 1998. (Large Print Book Ser.). 26.95 (*1-56895-684-3*, Wheeler Publishing, Inc.) Gale Group.

Brown, James. Final Performance. 1988. 320p. 18.95 o.p. (*0-688-06842-1*, Morrow, William & Co.) Morrow/Avon.

Brown, Sandra. Breakfast in Bed. 1991. 192p. mass mkt. 2.75 o.s.i (*0-553-21623-6*); 1996. 240p. mass mkt. 7.50 (*0-553-57158-3*) Bantam Bks.

—Breakfast in Bed. l.t. ed. 1996. (Large Print Bks.). 25.95 o.p. (*1-56895-307-0*, Wheeler Publishing, Inc.) Gale Group.

—Breakfast in Bed. abr. ed. 1995. audio 16.99 o.s.i (*0-553-47432-4*, RH Audio) Random Hse. Audio Publishing Group.

—Breakfast in Bed. unabr. ed. 1997. audio 35.00 (*0-7887-0845-7*, 94991E7) Recorded Bks., LLC.

—Send No Flowers. 2000. 256p. mass mkt. 6.99 (*0-553-57601-1*); 1984. 192p. mass mkt. 2.25 o.s.i (*0-553-21659-7*) Bantam Bks.

—Send No Flowers. l.t. ed. (Wheeler Press Paperback Ser.). 2000. pap. 10.95 (*1-56895-974-5*); 1999. 27.95 (*1-56895-720-3*) Gale Group. (Wheeler Publishing, Inc.).

—Send No Flowers, abr. ed. 1999. audio 18.00 Highsmith Inc.

—A Treasure Worth Seeking. 288p. reprint ed. 1997. mass mkt. 3.99 (*0-446-60567-0*); 1992. mass mkt. 6.99 (*0-446-36073-2*) Warner Bks., Inc.

Browne, Juanita K. Thomasina & the Tommyknocker. 1993. (Illus.). viii, 85p. (Orig.). (J). (gr. 4-7). pap. 8.75 (*0-9636621-0-4*) Browne Bks. in The Hollow.

Brownlow, Leroy. A Father's World. 1965. 7.95 o.p. (*0-915720-46-9*) Brownlow Publishing Co., Inc.

Brownrigg, Sylvia. The Metaphysical Touch. 24.00 o.p. (*0-374-20873-5*); 1999. 390p. 24.00 o.s.i (*0-374-19965-5*) Farrar, Straus & Giroux.

—The Metaphysical Touch. 2000. 400p. pap. 15.00 (*0-312-26357-0*) Picador.

Bryan, Kate. Murder at Bent Elbow. 1998. (Maggie Maguire Mysteries Ser.: Vol. 1). 224p. mass mkt. 5.99 o.s.i (*0-425-16194-3*, Prime Crime) Berkley Publishing Group.

—A Record of Death. 1998. (Maggie Maguire Mysteries Ser.: Vol. 2). 224p. mass mkt. 5.99 o.s.i (*0-425-16537-X*) Berkley Publishing Group.

Bryant, Dorothy. Ella Price's Journal. reprint ed. 1998. 265p. pap. 14.95 (*1-55861-175-4*); 1997. 256p. lib. bdg. 35.00 (*1-55861-181-9*); 1982. 225p. pap. text 14.95 (*0-931688-08-6*) Feminist Pr. at The City Univ. of New York.

—Ella Price's Journal. 1976. 192p. mass mkt. 1.50 o.p. (*0-451-07040-2*, W7040, Signet Bks.) NAL.

—Miss Giardino. 1978. 160p. pap. 11.95 (*0-931688-01-9*); 1997. 192p. reprint ed. pap. 11.95 (*1-55861-174-6*); 1997. 192p. reprint ed. lib. bdg. 32.00 (*1-55861-180-0*) Feminist Pr. at The City Univ. of New York.

Bryant, Joy L. & Day, A. Steven. Whiskey Row. Diaz, Arthur S., ed. 2001. IX,520p. 27.95 (*0-9705259-5-8*) St. Aztec Publishing.

Buettner, Stewart. The Confessions of Ines: A Novel. 2002. 176p. pap. 12.95 (*1-56474-367-5*) Fithian Pr.

Bugliosi, Vincent T. & Hurwitz, Ken. Shadow of Cain. 1982. 304p. 3.95 o.p. (*0-553-20922-1*) Bantam Bks.

—Shadow of Cain. 1981. 12.95 o.p. (*0-393-01466-5*) Norton, W. W. & Co., Inc.

Bukowski, Charles. Hollywood. 1989. 35.00 o.p. (*0-87685-765-9*, Black Sparrow Pr.) Godine, David R. Pub.

—Hollywood. 1998. reprint ed. 244p. 25.00 (*0-87685-764-0*); 248p. pap. 16.00 (*0-87685-763-2*) HarperCollins Pubs.

—Pulp. deluxe ed. 1994. 200p. 40.00 o.p. (*0-87685-928-7*, Black Sparrow Pr.) Godine, David R. Pub.

—Pulp. 1998. reprint ed. 202p. 25.00 (*0-87685-927-9*); 208p. pap. 15.00 (*0-87685-926-0*) HarperCollins Pubs.

Bunker, Edward. The Animal Factory. 1979. pap. 1.95 o.p. (*0-440-10642-7*) Dell Publishing.

—The Animal Factory. 2000. 208p. reprint ed. pap. 11.95 (*0-312-26711-8*, NPB 0329, Saint Martin's Griffin) St. Martin's Pr.

—The Animal Factory. 1977. 8.95 o.p. (*0-670-12709-4*) Viking Penguin.

—Dog Eat Dog. 240p. 1997. pap. 13.95 (*0-312-16818-7*, Saint Martin's Griffin); 1996. 22.95 o.p. (*0-312-14314-1*) St. Martin's Pr.

—No Beast So Fierce: A Novel. 1993. (Vintage Crime/Black Lizard Ser.). pap. 10.00 o.s.i (*0-679-74155-0*, Vintage) Knopf Publishing Group.

Bunting, Eve. Will You Be My POSSLQ. 1987. 160p. (YA). (gr. 7 up). 12.95 (*0-15-297399-0*) Harcourt Children's Bks.

Burke, Jan. Bones: An Irene Kelly Novel. l.t. ed. 2000. (Wheeler Large Print Book Ser.). 561p. pap. 25.95 (*1-56895-940-0*, Wheeler Publishing, Inc.) Gale Group.

—Bones: An Irene Kelly Novel. 2001. 448p. mass mkt. 6.99 (*0-451-20247-3*, Signet Bks.) NAL.

—Bones: An Irene Kelly Novel. 1999. (Irene Kelly Mystery Ser.: No. 7). 384p. 23.00 o.s.i (*0-684-85551-8*, Simon & Schuster) Simon & Schuster.

—Dear Irene, An Irene Kelly Novel. 1996. pap. 5.50 (*0-380-72556-8*, Avon Bks.) Morrow/Avon.

—Dear Irene, An Irene Kelly Novel. 1995. 288p. 20.00 o.s.i (*0-671-78216-9*, Simon & Schuster) Simon & Schuster.

—Flight: A Novel of Suspense. l.t. ed. 2001. 601p. 28.95 o.p. (*1-58724-051-3*, Wheeler Publishing, Inc.) Gale Group.

—Flight: A Novel of Suspense. 2001. 400p. 24.00 (*0-684-85552-6*); 24.00 (*0-7432-0170-1*) Simon & Schuster. (Simon & Schuster).

—Goodnight, Irene: An Irene Kelly Novel. 1994. (Irene Kelly Mystery Ser.). 256p. pap. 5.99 (*0-380-72279-8*, Avon Bks.) Morrow/Avon.

—Goodnight, Irene: An Irene Kelly Novel. 1993. 18.00 o.p. (*0-671-78200-2*, Simon & Schuster) Simon & Schuster.

—Goodnight, Irene: An Irene Kelly Novel. l.t. ed. 1995. (Ulverscroft Large Print Ser.). 528p. 29.99 o.p. (*0-7089-3287-8*, Ulverscroft) Thorpe, F. A. Pubs. GBR. *Dist:* Ulverscroft Large Print Bks., Ltd., Ulverscroft Large Print Canada, Ltd.

—Hocus: An Irene Kelly Novel. l.t. ed. 1997. lib. bdg. 24.95 (*1-57490-106-0*, Beeler Large Print Bks.) Beeler, Thomas T. Publisher.

—Hocus: An Irene Kelly Novel. 1998. (Irene Kelly Mystery Ser.). 480p. mass mkt. 6.99 o.p. (*0-06-104439-3*) HarperCollins Pubs.

—Hocus: An Irene Kelly Novel. 1997. 22.00 (*0-684-00492-5*); 336p. 22.00 (*0-684-80344-5*) Simon & Schuster. (Simon & Schuster).

—Liar: An Irene Kelly Mystery. 1999. (Irene Kelly Mystery Ser.). 400p. mass mkt. 7.50 (*0-06-104440-7*) HarperCollins Pubs.

—Liar: An Irene Kelly Mystery. 1998. (Irene Kelly Mystery Ser.). 352p. 23.00 (*0-684-80345-3*, Simon & Schuster) Simon & Schuster.

—Remember Me, Irene: An Irene Kelly Novel. 1997. 352p. mass mkt. 5.50 o.s.i (*0-06-104438-5*, HarperTorch) Morrow/Avon.

—Remember Me, Irene: An Irene Kelly Novel. 1996. 304p. 21.00 o.p. (*0-684-80343-7*, Simon & Schuster) Simon & Schuster.

—Sweet Dreams, Irene: An Irene Kelly Novel. 1995. pap. 4.99 (*0-380-72350-6*, Avon Bks.) Morrow/Avon.

—Sweet Dreams, Irene: An Irene Kelly Novel. 1994. 287p. 18.00 (*0-671-78210-X*, Simon & Schuster) Simon & Schuster.

Burrill, Richard. River of Sorrows: Life History of the Maidu-Nisenan Indians. 1988. (Illus.). 219p. pap. 8.95 (*0-87961-187-1*); (YA). (gr. 8-12). 14.95 o.p. (*0-87961-186-3*) Naturegraph Pubs., Inc.

Burrows, Geraldine. Chinatown Mission. 2002. (Five Star First Edition Women's Fiction Ser.). 381p. 25.95 (*0-7862-3613-2*, Five Star) Gale Group.

Bush, Beverly. Evidence of Things Unseen. 1997. (Zoe Journals Ser.: Vol. 2). 350p. pap. 12.99 o.s.i (*0-8499-4040-0*) W Publishing Group.

Butler, Octavia E. Parable of the Sower. 1993. 299p. 19.95 o.p. (*0-941423-99-9*) Four Walls Eight Windows.
—Parable of the Sower. unabr. ed. 2000. audio 80.00 (*0-7887-3782-1*, 95999E7) Recorded Bks., LLC.
—Parable of the Sower. 1993. 352p. 19.95 (*1-888363-25-8*) Seven Stories Pr.
—Parable of the Sower. 2000. 20.00 (*0-606-19220-4*) Turtleback Bks.
—Parable of the Sower. 2000. 352p. reprint ed. pap. 13.95 (*0-446-67550-4*) Warner Bks., Inc.
—Parable of the Talents. 1998. 365p. 24.95 (*1-888363-81-9*) Seven Stories Pr.
—Parable of the Talents. 2000. 20.00 (*0-606-21854-8*) Turtleback Bks.
—Parable of the Talents. 2000. 464p. pap. 13.95 (*0-446-67578-4*) Warner Bks., Inc.
Butler, Octavia E., contrib. by. Parable of the Talents. 1998. Seven Stories Pr.
Butler, Octavia E. & Butler, Cctavia E. Parable of the Sower. 1995. 304p. reprint ed. mass mkt. 6.99 (*0-446-60197-7*) Warner Bks., Inc.
Byrne, Robert. Thrill. 1995. 224p. 19.95 o.p. (*0-7867-0199-4*, Carroll & Graf Pubs.) Avalon Publishing Group.
Byrnes, W. P. The Marvelous Crucifixion on Twin Peaks. 2000. 232p. pap. 21.99 (*0-7388-1207-2*); text 31.99 (*0-7388-1206-4*) Xlibris Corp.
Cadnum, Michael. The Horses of the Night. 1993. 320p. 19.95 o.p. (*0-88184-930-8*, Carroll & Graf Pubs.) Avalon Publishing Group.
—Skyscape. 1994. 368p. 21.95 o.p. (*0-7867-0135-8*, Carroll & Graf Pubs.) Avalon Publishing Group.
Cadre, Adam. Ready, Okay! A Novel. 2000. 389p. 25.00 (*0-06-019558-4*, HarperCollins) HarperTrade.
Cain, James M. Double Indemnity. Date not set. lib. bdg. 14.95 (*0-8488-1754-0*) Amereon, Ltd.
—Double Indemnity. l.t. ed. 1985. (Nightingale Ser.). 184p. 9.95 o.p. (*0-8161-3830-3*, Macmillan Reference USA) Gale Group.
—Double Indemnity, Set. abr. ed. 1996. audio 17.00 (*0-89845-777-7*, 390675, HarperAudio) HarperTrade.
—Double Indemnity. 1992. pap. 8.00 (*0-394-23901-6*); 1989. 128p. pap. 10.00 (*0-679-72322-6*); 1978. pap. 2.95 o.p. (*0-394-72581-6*) Knopf Publishing Group. (Vintage).
—Double Indemnity. mass mkt. 0.25 o.p. (*0-451-01427-8*); 1950. mass mkt. 0.25 o.p. (*0-451-00784-0*) NAL. (Signet Bks.).
—Double Indemnity. 1992. pap. 8.00 (*0-679-74096-1*) Random Hse., Inc.
—The Postman Always Rings Twice. 20.95 (*0-89190-815-3*) Amereon, Ltd.
—The Postman Always Rings Twice. 1981. 457p. reprint ed. lib. bdg. 27.95 (*0-89968-234-0*, Lightyear Pr.) Buccaneer Bks., Inc.
—The Postman Always Rings Twice. 1992. pap. 8.00 (*0-394-23899-0*); 1989. 128p. pap. 10.00 (*0-679-72325-0*) Knopf Publishing Group. (Vintage).
—The Postman Always Rings Twice. 1993. 4.99 o.p. (*0-517-10682-5*) Random Hse. Value Publishing.
—The Postman Always Rings Twice. 1992. pap. 8.00 (*0-679-74097-X*) Random Hse., Inc.
—The Postman Always Rings Twice. 1995. 200p. reprint ed. 35.00 (*1-883402-18-2*, Scribner) Simon & Schuster.
Calder, James. About Face. 2003. (Silicon Valley Ser.). 224p. pap. 11.95 (*0-8118-3680-0*) Chronicle Bks. LLC.
—Knockout Mouse: A Silicon Valley Mystery. 2002. 224p. pap. 11.95 (*0-8118-3499-9*) Chronicle Bks. LLC.
Cameron, Carey. Daddy Boy. 1989. 377p. 15.95 o.p. (*0-912697-84-9*) Algonquin Bks. of Chapel Hill.
Cameron, Julia. Popcorn: Hollywood Stories. 2000. 233p. pap. 14.95 (*1-893329-12-7*) Really Great Bks.
Cameron, Sue. Honey Dust. 1993. 368p. 18.95 o.s.i (*0-446-51513-2*) Warner Bks., Inc.
—Love, Sex & Murder. 1996. 368p. 23.95 o.s.i (*0-446-51852-2*) Warner Bks., Inc.
Campbell, Bebe Moore. Brothers & Sisters. abr. ed. 1994. audio 19.95 (*1-55927-303-8*, 492032) Audio Renaissance.
—Brothers & Sisters. 2000. 480p. pap. 13.95 (*0-425-17267-8*); 1995. 560p. mass mkt. 7.99 (*0-425-14940-4*) Berkley Publishing Group.
—Brothers & Sisters. unabr. ed. 1996. audio 112.00 (*0-7366-3202-6*, 3866) Books on Tape, Inc.
—Brothers & Sisters. l.t. ed. 1995. (Large Print Bks.). 26.95 o.p. (*1-56895-211-2*, Wheeler Publishing, Inc.) Gale Group.
—Brothers & Sisters. 1994. 480p. 22.95 o.p. (*0-399-13929-X*, G. P. Putnam's Sons) Penguin Group (USA) Inc.
—Brothers & Sisters. 476p. pap. 22.95 o.p. (*0-7651-0630-2*) Smithmark Pubs., Inc.
—Brothers & Sisters. 1995. 14.04 (*0-606-19295-6*) Turtleback Bks.
—Brothers & Sisters. 1997. 4.98 (*0-681-56088-6*) Waldenbooks, Inc.
—Singing in the Comeback Choir. 1999. 400p. reprint ed. mass mkt. 7.99 (*0-425-16662-7*) Berkley Publishing Group.
—Singing in the Comeback Choir. l.t. ed. 1998. (Large Print Book Ser.). 27.95 (*1-56895-613-4*, Wheeler Publishing, Inc.) Gale Group.
—Singing in the Comeback Choir. 1998. 320p. 24.95 o.p. (*0-399-14298-3*, G. P. Putnam's Sons) Penguin Group (USA) Inc.
—Singing in the Comeback Choir. 1999. 13.55 (*0-606-19302-2*) Turtleback Bks.
Campbell, Federico. Tijuana: Stories on the Border. Castillo, Debra A., tr. 1995. 167p. (ENG & SPA.). text 45.00 o.p. (*0-520-08946-4*); pap. text 17.95 (*0-520-08603-1*) Univ. of California Pr.
Campbell, Federico & Castillo, Debra A. Tijuana: Stories on the Border. 1995. E-Book 45.00 (*0-585-22963-5*) netLibrary, Inc.
Campbell, Robert. Alice in La-La Land. 1999. 232p. pap. 17.95 (*1-58444-024-4*) Disc-Us Bks., Inc.
—Alice in La-La Land. Chelius, Jane, ed. 1990. mass mkt. 4.95 (*0-671-73343-5*, Pocket) Simon & Schuster.
—Alice in La-La Land. 1987. 256p. 16.45 o.p. (*0-671-64483-1*, Simon & Schuster) Simon & Schuster.
—In La-La Land We Trust. 2000. E-Book 19.95 incl. cd-rom (*1-58444-076-7*); 1999. 230p. pap. 17.95 (*1-58444-051-1*) Disc-Us Bks., Inc.
—In La-La Land We Trust. 1986. 15.45 o.p. (*0-89296-170-8*) Mysterious Pr.
—In La-La Land We Trust. 1987. mass mkt. 4.95 o.p. (*0-445-40596-1*, Mysterious Pr. Paperback Bks.) Warner Bks., Inc.
—Juice. Chelius, Jane, ed. 1990. 320p. mass mkt. 4.95 (*0-671-67454-4*, Pocket) Simon & Schuster.
—Juice. 1989. pap. 18.95 o.p. (*0-671-66624-X*, Simon & Schuster) Simon & Schuster.
—The La-La Land Quartet: Contains 4 Titles- Alice in La-La Land, in La-La Land We Trust, Sweet La-La Land, & Wizard of La-La Land. 2000. E-Book 24.95 incl. cd-rom (*1-58444-083-X*) Disc-Us Bks., Inc.
—Sweet La-La Land. 2000. E-Book 16.95 incl. cd-rom (*1-58444-075-9*); 1999. 232p. pap. 17.95 (*1-58444-050-3*) Disc-Us Bks., Inc.
—Sweet La-La Land. 1990. 18.95 o.p. (*0-671-64484-X*, Simon & Schuster) Simon & Schuster.
—Sweet La-La Land. Chelius, Jane, ed. 1991. 320p. reprint ed. mass mkt. 4.99 (*0-671-73236-6*, Pocket) Simon & Schuster.
—The Wizard of La-La Land. 1999. 244p. pap. 17.95 (*1-58444-052-X*) Disc-Us Bks., Inc.
—The Wizard of La-La Land. Chelius, Jane, ed. 1995. 288p. 20.00 o.p. (*0-671-70321-8*, Atria) Simon & Schuster.
Cannell, Stephen J. The Tin Collectors. l.t. ed. 2001. (Wheeler Large Print Book Ser.). viii, 467p. 29.95 o.p. (*1-58724-080-7*, Wheeler Publishing, Inc.) Gale Group.
—The Tin Collectors. E-Book 24.95 (*0-312-70062-8*); 2001. E-Book 24.95 (*0-312-27411-4*); 2001. viii, 389p. 24.95 o.p. (*0-312-26959-5*); 2002. 384p. reprint ed. mass mkt. 6.99 (*0-312-97951-7*, St. Martin's Paperbacks) St. Martin's Pr.
Cannery Row. 2000. 11.95 (*1-56137-507-1*) Novel Units, Inc.
Cannon, Taffy. Class Reunions Are Murder. 9999. mass mkt. o.p. (*0-449-14951-X*); 1996. mass mkt. 5.50 o.s.i (*0-449-22389-2*) Ballantine Bks. (Fawcett).
—A Pocketful of Karma. 1993. 256p. 19.95 o.p. (*0-88184-906-5*, Carroll & Graf Pubs.) Avalon Publishing Group.
—A Pocketful of Karma. 1995. mass mkt. 5.50 o.s.i (*0-449-22388-4*, Fawcett) Ballantine Bks.
—Tangled Roots. 1995. 320p. 19.95 o.p. (*0-7867-0137-4*, Carroll & Graf Pubs.) Avalon Publishing Group.
—Tangled Roots. Date not set. mass mkt. (*0-449-14950-1*); 1995. mass mkt. 5.99 o.s.i (*0-449-22390-6*) Ballantine Bks. (Fawcett).
Caputo, Philip. Equation for Evil. 1996. 416p. 25.00 o.p. (*0-06-018360-8*) HarperCollins Pubs.
—Equation for Evil. 1997. 496p. pap. 13.50 o.p. (*0-06-098411-2*, Perennial) HarperTrade.
—Equation for Evil. 488p. pap. 4.98 o.p. (*0-7651-0610-8*) Smithmark Pubs., Inc.
Carabine, Sue. The Night Before Christmas in California. gif. ed. 2001. (Illus.). 60p. 5.95 (*1-58685-123-3*) Smith, Gibbs Pub.
Caraganis, Lynn. Cousin It. 1991. 224p. 19.95 o.p. (*0-89919-945-3*) Houghton Mifflin Co.
Carr, Robyn. Deep in the Valley. 2000. 384p. mass mkt. (*1-55166-609-X*, 1-66609-8, Mira Bks.) Harlequin Enterprises, Ltd.
—Down By The River. 2003. 384p. mass mkt. (*1-55166-704-5*, Mira Bks.) Harlequin Enterprises, Ltd.
—The House on Olive Street. 1999. 408p. mass mkt. (*1-55166-545-X*, Mira Bks.) Harlequin Enterprises, Ltd.
—Just Over the Mountain. 2002. 384p. mass mkt. (*1-55166-940-4*, Mira Bks.) Harlequin Enterprises, Ltd.
Carroll, Jonathan. Sleeping in Flame. 1990. 288p. pap. 13.00 (*0-679-72777-9*, Vintage) Knopf Publishing Group.
—Sleeping in Flames. 1989. 288p. 17.95 o.s.i (*0-385-24957-8*) Doubleday Publishing.
Cebulash, Mel. Dirty Money. 1993. 3.95 (*1-56420-002-7*) New Readers Pr.
—Dirty Money: A Sully Gomez Mystery. 1993. (J). audio 10.95 (*1-56420-003-5*) New Readers Pr.
—Knockout Punch: A Sully Gomez Mystery. 1993. audio 9.95 o.p. (*1-56420-009-4*); 3.95 o.p. (*1-56420-008-6*) New Readers Pr.
—Set to Explode: A Sully Gomez Mystery. 1993. 3.95 o.p. (*1-56420-004-3*) New Readers Pr.
—Set to Explode: A/Sully Gomez Mystery. 1993. (J). audio 10.00 o.p. (*1-56420-005-1*) New Readers Pr.
—A Sucker for Redheads: A Sully Gomez Mystery. 1993. audio 9.95 o.p. (*1-56420-007-8*); 3.95 o.p. (*1-56420-006-X*) New Readers Pr.
Cech, John. Rush of Dreamers: The Remarkabe Story of Norton I, Emperor of the United States & Protector of Mexico. 1997. (Illus.). 192p. 20.00 (*1-56924-775-7*, Marlowe & Co.) Avalon Publishing Group.
Cendrars, Blaise. Gold: Being the Marvelous History of General John Augustus Sutter. 1996. 128p. pap. 10.95 o.p. (*1-56924-807-9*, Marlowe & Co.) Avalon Publishing Group.
—Gold: Being the Marvelous History of General John Augustus Sutter. Rootes, Nina, tr. from FRE. 1984. reprint ed. 16.95 o.p. (*0-935576-08-8*); pap. 8.95 o.p. (*0-935576-09-6*) Kesend, Michael Publishing, Ltd.
Chamberlain, Diane. Fire & Rain. 1993. 448p. 20.00 o.p. (*0-06-017712-8*) HarperTrade.
Chambers, Peter. Dames Can Be Deadly. l.t. ed. 1993. (Dales Large Print Ser.). 291p. pap. 19.99 (*1-85389-427-3*) Dales Large Print Bks. GBR. *Dist:* Ulverscroft Large Print Bks., Ltd.
—The Lady Who Never Was. l.t. ed. 1995. (Linford Mystery Large Print Ser.). 272p. pap. 17.99 o.p. (*0-7089-7809-6*, Linford) Thorpe, F. A. Pubs. GBR. *Dist:* Ulverscroft Large Print Bks., Ltd., Ulverscroft Large Print Canada, Ltd.
—Lady, You're Killing Me. l.t. ed. 1994. (Linford Mystery Library). 304p. pap. 17.99 o.p. (*0-7089-7568-2*, Ulverscroft) Thorpe, F. A. Pubs. GBR. *Dist:* Ulverscroft Large Print Bks., Ltd., Ulverscroft Large Print Canada, Ltd.
—Somebody Has to Lose. l.t. ed. 1992. (Dales Mystery Ser.). 211p. pap. 19.99 o.p. (*1-85389-307-2*) Dales Large Print Bks. GBR. *Dist:* Ulverscroft Large Print Bks., Ltd.
—Speak Ill of the Dead. l.t. ed. 1993. (Linford Mystery Library). 368p. pap. 17.99 o.p. (*0-7089-7385-X*, Linford) Thorpe, F. A. Pubs. GBR. *Dist:* Ulverscroft Large Print Bks., Ltd., Ulverscroft Large Print Canada, Ltd.
Chambers, Rick. Anything but Free. 1993. (Open Door Bks.). pap. 4.75 (*1-56212-033-6*, 350700, Faith Alive Christian Resources) CRC Pubns.
Champion, David. Celebrity Trouble: A Bomber Hanson Mystery. 1997. 200p. 20.00 (*1-888310-97-9*) Knoll, Allen A. Pubs.
—The Mountain Massacres: A Bomber Hanson Mystery. 1995. 161p. 14.95 (*0-9627297-4-4*) Knoll, Allen A. Pubs.
—Nobody Roots for Goliath: A Bomber Hanson Mystery. 1996. 319p. 22.95 (*1-888310-44-8*) Knoll, Allen A. Pubs.
—Phantom Virus: A Bomber Hanson Mystery. 1999. 275p. 23.00 (*1-888310-93-6*) Knoll, Allen A. Pubs.
—The Snatch. 1994. 266p. 19.95 (*0-9627297-2-8*) Knoll, Allen A. Pubs.
Champlin, Tim. Deadly Season. 2003. 256p. mass mkt. 4.99 (*0-8439-5131-1*) Dorchester Publishing Co., Inc.
—Deadly Season. 1997. (Western Ser.). 256p. lib. bdg. 18.95 o.p. (*0-7862-0783-3*, Five Star) Gale Group.
—King of the Highbinders. 1989. 192p. mass mkt. 2.95 o.s.i (*0-345-36320-5*) Ballantine Bks.
—King of the Highbinders. l.t. ed. 1997. (Western Ser.). 284p. 20.95 (*0-7862-0898-8*) Thorndike Pr.
—Wayfaring Strangers. 2003. (Spur Ser.). 320p. mass mkt. 5.50 (*0-8439-5210-5*, Leisure Bks.) Dorchester Publishing Co., Inc.
—Wayfaring Strangers. 2000. (Five Star Western Ser.). 312p. 21.95 (*0-7862-2104-6*, Five Star) Gale Group.
Chandler, Raymond. Adieu, Ma Jolie. 1988. Orig. Title: Farewell, My Lovely. (FRE.). 301p. pap. 11.95 (*0-7859-2102-8*, 2070380793) French & European Pubns., Inc.
—The Adventures of Philip Marlowe, Vol. 1. collector's ed. 1999. 34.98 incl. audio Radio Spirits, Inc.
—The Big Sleep. deluxe ltd. ed. 1986. (Illus.). 250p. 425.00 o.p. (*0-910457-09-3*) Arion Pr.
—The Big Sleep. 1975. 224p. mass mkt. 1.50 o.s.i (*0-345-24565-2*); 1973. mass mkt. 0.95 o.s.i (*0-345-22201-6*) Ballantine Bks.
—The Big Sleep. 1986. (Mystery Ser.). mass mkt. 9.95 o.p. (*0-553-06513-0*) Bantam Bks.
—The Big Sleep. 1994. reprint ed. lib. bdg. 29.95 o.p. (*1-56849-261-8*) Buccaneer Bks., Inc.
—The Big Sleep. l.t. ed. 2002. 232p. lib. bdg. 27.95 (*1-58547-164-X*) Ctr. Point Large Print.
—The Big Sleep. abr. ed. audio 15.95 o.p. (*0-88646-007-7*, 7009) Durkin Hayes Publishing Ltd.
—The Big Sleep. 1989. (Illus.). 256p. reprint ed. 22.95 o.p. (*0-86547-402-8*, North Point Pr.) Farrar, Straus & Giroux.
—The Big Sleep. Garrett, George P. et al, eds. 1989. (Film Scripts Ser.). reprint ed. pap. 19.95 (*0-89197-677-9*) Irvington Pubs.
—The Big Sleep. 1992. pap. 9.00 (*0-394-23906-7*); 1988. 240p. reprint ed. pap. 12.00 (*0-394-75828-5*) Knopf Publishing Group. (Vintage).
—The Big Sleep. abr. ed. 1993. 16.95 o.p. (*1-55800-690-7*); audio 29.95 o.p. (*1-55800-848-9*, 752391) NewStar Media, Inc.
—The Big Sleep. 1992. pap. 9.00 o.p. (*0-679-74091-0*); 1978. pap. 3.95 o.p. (*0-394-72631-6*) Random Hse., Inc.
—The Big Sleep. 2002. (Best Mysteries of All Time Ser.). 261p. (*0-7621-8880-4*, Impress) Scriptorium Pr., The.
—The Big Sleep. 1995. 288p. reprint ed. 35.00 (*1-883402-16-6*, Scribner) Simon & Schuster.
—The Big Sleep & Farewell, My Lovely. 1995. (Modern Library Ser.). 544p. 18.95 (*0-679-60140-6*) Random Hse., Inc.
—The Big Sleep & The High Window. abr. ed. 1999. audio 16.85 (*0-563-55892-X*) BBC Bk. Publishing GBR. *Dist:* Ulverscroft Large Print Bks., Ltd.
—La Dame du Lac. 1988. Orig. Title: Lady of the Lake. (FRE.). 258p. pap. 10.95 (*0-7859-2088-9*, 2070379434) French & European Pubns., Inc.
—Farewell, My Lovely. 1983. 256p. mass mkt. 2.25 o.s.i (*0-345-31528-6*, Ballantine Bks.); 1973. mass mkt. 0.95 o.s.i (*0-345-22202-4*) Ballantine Bks.
—Farewell, My Lovely. 1992. pap. 10.00 (*0-394-23907-5*); 1988. 304p. reprint ed. pap. 12.00 (*0-394-75827-7*) Knopf Publishing Group. (Vintage).
—Farewell, My Lovely. abr. ed. 1993. 16.95 o.p. (*1-55800-672-9*); audio 29.95 o.p. (*1-55800-769-5*) NewStar Media, Inc.
—Farewell, My Lovely. 1986. audio 14.95 o.p. (*0-394-55466-3*); 1985. audio 16.00 o.p. (*0-394-55048-X*) Random Hse. Audio Publishing Group. (RH Audio).
—Farewell, My Lovely. 1992. pap. 10.00 (*0-679-74090-2*); 1976. pap. 3.95 o.p. (*0-394-72138-1*) Random Hse., Inc.
—Farewell, My Lovely & The Lady in the Lake. abr. ed. 1999. audio 16.85 (*0-563-55897-0*) BBC Bk. Publishing GBR. *Dist:* Ulverscroft Large Print Bks., Ltd.
—La Grande Fenetre. 1989. Orig. Title: High Window. (FRE.). 276p. pap. 10.95 (*0-7859-2236-9*, 207038103X) French & European Pubns., Inc.
—Le Grande Sommeil. 1987. Orig. Title: Big Sleep. (FRE.). 252p. pap. 10.95 (*0-7859-2071-4*, 2070378659) French & European Pubns., Inc.
—The High Window. 1971. mass mkt. 0.95 o.s.i (*0-345-22203-2*) Ballantine Bks.
—The High Window. l.t. ed. 23.95 (*1-85695-367-X*) ISIS Large Print Bks. GBR. *Dist:* Transaction Pubs.
—The High Window. 1992. pap. 10.00 (*0-394-23908-3*); 1976. pap. 3.95 o.p. (*0-394-72141-1*); 1988. 272p. reprint ed. pap. 12.00 (*0-394-75826-9*) Knopf Publishing Group. (Vintage).
—The High Window. abr. ed. 1993. audio 15.95 o.p. (*1-55800-091-7*, 40290, Dove Audio) NewStar Media, Inc.
—Killer in the Rain. 1987. mass mkt. 3.95 o.s.i (*0-345-35185-1*); 1986. mass mkt. 2.95 o.s.i (*0-345-34195-3*); 1984. mass mkt. 2.50 o.s.i (*0-345-32020-4*); 1980. mass mkt. 2.25 o.s.i (*0-345-28858-0*); 1977. mass mkt. 1.95 o.s.i (*0-345-25728-6*) Ballantine Bks.
—Killer in the Rain & Other Stories. abr. ed. 1996. 24.95 o.p. (*0-7871-0555-4*, 693446) NewStar Media, Inc.
—The Lady in the Lake. Date not set. lib. bdg. 20.95 (*0-8488-2136-X*) Amereon, Ltd.
—The Lady in the Lake. 1976. (Crime Fiction Ser). reprint ed. lib. bdg. 21.00 o.p. (*0-8240-2358-7*) Garland Publishing, Inc.
—The Lady in the Lake. l.t. ed. 23.95 (*1-85695-362-9*) ISIS Large Print Bks. GBR. *Dist:* Transaction Pubs.
—The Lady in the Lake. 1992. pap. 10.00 (*0-394-23909-1*); 1988. 272p. pap. 12.00 (*0-394-75825-0*); 1976. pap. 3.95 o.p. (*0-394-72145-4*) Knopf Publishing Group. (Vintage).
—The Lady in the Lake. abr. ed. 2002. audio 18.00 (*1-59007-093-3*, New Millennium Audio) New Millennium Entertainment.
—The Lady in the Lake. abr. ed. 1993. audio 8.99 o.p. (*1-55800-916-7*); audio 15.95 o.p. (*1-55800-069-0*, 40240) NewStar Media, Inc. (Dove Audio).

—The Lady in the Lake. 1992. pap. 10.00 (*0-679-74088-0*) Random Hse., Inc.
—The Lady in the Lake. 1994. 288p. 35.00 (*1-883402-94-8*, Scribner) Simon & Schuster.
—Later Novels & Other Writings: The Lady in the Lake; The Little Sister; The Long Goodbye; Playback; Double Indemnity; Essays & Letters. MacShane, Frank, ed. 1995. 1088p. 35.00 (*1-883011-08-6*) Library of America, The.
—The Little Sister. l.t. ed. 1993. 21.95 o.p. (*0-7927-1654-X*); pap. 19.95 o.p. (*0-7927-1653-1*); audio 54.95 (*0-7451-5823-4*, CAB 057) BBC Audiobooks America.
—The Little Sister. 1985. mass mkt. 2.95 o.s.i (*0-345-32217-7*); 1983. mass mkt. 2.25 o.s.i (*0-345-31643-6*); 1977. mass mkt. 1.95 o.s.i (*0-345-25727-8*) Ballantine Bks.
—The Little Sister. 1988. (Vintage Crime Ser.). 256p. pap. 12.00 (*0-394-75767-X*, Vintage) Knopf Publishing Group.
—The Little Sister. abr. ed. 1993. pap. 15.95 o.p. incl. audio (*1-55800-082-8*, 40270) NewStar Media, Inc.
—The Little Sister. 1994. 256p. 35.00 (*1-883402-79-4*, Scribner) Simon & Schuster.
—The Little Sister. unabr. ed. 1983. (J). audio 49.95 o.p. (*0-8161-9777-6*) Thorndike Pr.
—The Long Goodbye. 1987. mass mkt. 3.95 o.s.i (*0-345-34938-5*); 1985. mass mkt. 2.95 o.s.i (*0-345-32132-4*); 1982. mass mkt. 2.50 o.s.i (*0-345-30582-5*); 1980. mass mkt. 2.25 o.s.i (*0-345-28859-9*); 1977. mass mkt. 1.95 o.s.i (*0-345-25734-0*) Ballantine Bks.
—The Long Goodbye. 1992. pap. 10.00 (*0-394-23910-5*); 1988. 384p. pap. 13.00 (*0-394-75768-8*) Knopf Publishing Group. (Vintage).
—The Long Goodbye. abr. ed. 1993. audio 15.95 o.p. (*1-55800-002-X*, 40010, Dove Audio) NewStar Media, Inc.
—The Long Goodbye. 1992. pap. 10.00 (*0-679-74087-2*) Random Hse., Inc.
—The Long Goodbye & The Little Sister. abr. ed. 1999. audio 16.85 (*0-563-55803-2*) BBC Bk. Publishing GBR. *Dist:* Ulverscroft Large Print Bks., Ltd.
—Midnight Raymond Chandler, 001. 1971. 10.25 o.p. (*0-395-13152-9*) Houghton Mifflin Co.
—Philip Marlowe. 1999. (Illus.). 416p. pap. 16.00 (*0-671-03890-7*) ibooks, Inc.
—Playback. 1987. mass mkt. 2.95 o.s.i (*0-345-32226-6*); 1987. mass mkt. 3.95 o.s.i (*0-345-34933-4*); 1984. mass mkt. 2.50 o.s.i (*0-345-31961-3*); 1980. mass mkt. 2.25 o.s.i (*0-345-28857-2*); 1976. mass mkt. 1.50 o.s.i (*0-345-25169-5*) Ballantine Bks.
—Playback. l.t. ed. 2001. (Dales Large Print Ser.). 240p. pap. 20.99 (*1-84262-094-0*) Dales Large Print Bks. GBR. *Dist:* Ulverscroft Large Print Bks., Ltd., Ulverscroft Large Print Canada, Ltd.
—Playback. 1988. (Vintage Crime Ser.). 176p. pap. 11.00 (*0-394-75766-1*, Vintage) Knopf Publishing Group.
—Playback. unabr. ed. 1993. pap. 24.95 o.p. (*1-55800-270-7*) NewStar Media, Inc.
—Raymond Chandler: Four Complete Philip Marlowe Novels. 1986. 8.99 o.s.i (*0-517-61811-7*) Random Hse. Value Publishing.
—Stories & Early Novels: Pulp Stories; The Big Sleep; Farewell, My Lovely; The High Window. MacShane, Frank, ed. 1995. 1216p. 35.00 (*1-883011-07-8*) Library of America, The.
—Trouble Is My Business. 1987. mass mkt. 3.95 o.s.i (*0-345-35494-X*); 1984. mass mkt. 2.50 o.s.i (*0-345-32021-2*); 1980. mass mkt. 2.25 o.s.i (*0-345-28862-9*) Ballantine Bks.
—Trouble Is My Business. 1992. pap. 9.00 (*0-394-23911-3*); 1988. 224p. pap. 12.00 (*0-394-75764-5*) Knopf Publishing Group. (Vintage).
—Trouble Is My Business. unabr. ed. 1993. audio 15.95 o.p. (*1-55800-090-9*, 40320, Dove Audio) NewStar Media, Inc.
—Trouble Is My Business. 1992. pap. 9.00 (*0-679-74086-4*) Random Hse., Inc.
—Un Tueur sous la Pluie. 1988. Orig. Title: Killer in the Rain. (FRE.). 245p. pap. 10.95 (*0-7859-2082-X*, 2070379108) French & European Pubns., Inc.
Chandler, Raymond & Parker, Robert B. Farewell, My Lovely & Poodle Springs. abr. ed. 1993. audio 17.95 (*1-55800-778-4*, Dove Audio) NewStar Media, Inc.
—Poodle Springs. 1990. (J). mass mkt. 7.50 o.s.i (*0-425-12343-X*) Berkley Publishing Group.
—Poodle Springs. abr. ed. 1993. audio 14.95 o.p. (*1-55800-168-9*, Dove Audio) NewStar Media, Inc.
—Poodle Springs. 1989. 18.95 o.p. (*0-399-13482-4*, G. P. Putnam's Sons) Penguin Putnam Bks. for Young Readers.
Chang, Leonard. Over the Shoulder. 2001. 400p. 26.00 (*0-06-019839-7*, Ecco) HarperTrade.
Chapman, Sally. Cyberkiss. 1997. (WWL Mystery Ser.: No. 242). 252p. per. (*0-373-26242-6*, 1-26242-7, Worldwide Library) Harlequin Enterprises, Ltd.
—Cyberkiss. 1996. 272p. 21.95 o.p. (*0-312-13952-7*, Saint Martin's Minotaur) St. Martin's Pr.
—Hardwired. 1998. (WWL Mystery Ser.: Vol. 288). per. (*0-373-26288-4*, 1-26288-0, Worldwide Library) Harlequin Enterprises, Ltd.
—Hardwired. 1997. 272p. 22.95 (*0-312-15542-5*, Saint Martin's Minotaur) St. Martin's Pr.
—Love Bytes. 1996. (WWL Mystery Ser.). per. (*0-373-26197-7*, 1-26197-3, Worldwide Library) Harlequin Enterprises, Ltd.
—Love Bytes. 1994. 256p. 20.95 o.p. (*0-312-11023-5*, Saint Martin's Minotaur) St. Martin's Pr.
—Raw Data. 1991. 17.95 o.p. (*0-312-05953-1*, Saint Martin's Minotaur) St. Martin's Pr.
Charbonneau, Eileen. Waltzing in Ragtime. 1997. 399p. mass mkt. 6.99 (*0-8125-4468-4*); 1996. 480p. 26.95 o.p. (*0-312-86180-X*) Doherty, Tom Assocs., LLC. (Forge Bks.).
Charbonneau, Louis. The Devil's Menagerie. 1996. 288p. 23.95 o.p. (*1-55611-494-X*, Dutton) Fine, Donald I. Bks.
Cheever, John. Falconer. 1982. mass mkt. 2.95 o.s.i (*0-345-30792-5*); 1980. mass mkt. 2.75 o.s.i (*0-345-28589-1*); 1978. mass mkt. 2.25 o.s.i (*0-345-27300-1*) Ballantine Bks.
—Falconer. 1977. (Adult Ser.). lib. bdg. 10.95 o.p. (*0-8161-6506-8*, Macmillan Reference USA) Gale Group.
Child, Maureen. Last Virgin in California. 2001. (Silhouette Desire Ser.: No. 1398). mass mkt. (*0-373-76398-0*, Silhouette) Harlequin Enterprises, Ltd.
Chin, Frank. Gunga Din Highway. 400p. 1995. pap. 14.95 (*1-56689-037-3*); 1994. 24.95 (*1-56689-024-1*) Coffee Hse. Pr.
Chittenden, Margaret. Dead Beat & Deadly, 1. (Charlie Plato Mysteries Ser.). 1999. 320p. mass mkt. 5.99 o.s.i (*1-57566-436-4*); 1998. 304p. 20.00 o.s.i (*1-57566-314-7*, Kensington Bks.) Kensington Publishing Corp.
—Dead Men Don't Dance. 1998. (Charlie Plato Mysteries Ser.: Vol. 2). 304p. mass mkt. 5.99 o.s.i (*1-57566-318-X*); 1997. 320p. pap. 18.95 o.p. (*1-57566-184-5*, Kensington Bks.) Kensington Publishing Corp.
—Don't Forget to Die. 2000. 320p. mass mkt. 5.99 o.s.i (*1-57566-566-2*); 1999. 293p. 20.00 o.s.i (*1-57566-435-6*) Kensington Publishing Corp.
—Dying to See You: A Charlie Plato Mystery. 2000. (Charlie Plato Mysteries Ser.). 311p. 20.00 o.s.i (*1-57566-561-1*) Kensington Publishing Corp.
—Dying to Sing. 288p. 1997. (Charlie Plato Mysteries Ser.: Vol. 1). mass mkt. 5.50 o.s.i (*1-57566-189-6*); 1996. 18.95 o.s.i (*1-57566-052-0*) Kensington Publishing Corp.
Choi, Susan. American Woman: A Novel. 2003. 384p. 24.95 (*0-06-054221-7*) HarperCollins Pubs.
Clark, Leigh. Shock Radio. 1998. 352p. mass mkt. 6.99 (*0-8125-2372-5*, Tor Bks.); 1996. 381p. 24.95 o.p. (*0-312-85724-1*, Forge Bks.) Doherty, Tom Assocs., LLC.
Clark, Mary Higgins. Weep No More, My Lady. E-Book 9.95 (*1-930161-66-2*) Adobe Systems, Inc.
—Weep No More, My Lady. 1993. reprint ed. lib. bdg. 37.95 (*0-89968-446-7*, Lightyear Pr.) Buccaneer Bks., Inc.
—Weep No More, My Lady. 1993. 384p. mass mkt. 3.99 o.s.i (*0-440-21473-4*); reprint ed. mass mkt. 6.99 o.s.i (*0-440-20098-9*) Dell Publishing.
—Weep No More, My Lady. 1997. 384p. pap. 11.95 o.s.i (*0-385-31921-5*) Doubleday Publishing.
—Weep No More, My Lady. l.t. ed. 1988. (General Ser.). 441p. 19.95 o.p. (*0-8161-4367-6*, Macmillan Reference USA) Gale Group.
—Weep No More, My Lady. 2000. E-Book 9.95 (*0-7432-0616-9*, Simon & Schuster); 1998. (Illus.). 336p. mass mkt. 7.99 (*0-671-02558-9*, Pocket); 1987. (Illus.). 320p. bds. 17.45 o.p. (*0-671-55664-9*, Simon & Schuster) Simon & Schuster.
—Weep No More, My Lady. 1987. 12.09 o.p. (*0-606-04108-7*) Turtleback Bks.
Clarke, Arthur C. & McQuay, Mike. Richter 10. 1997. 416p. mass mkt. 6.99 o.s.i (*0-553-57333-0*) Bantam Bks.
Clarke, Marion. The Jade Pagoda. 1992. 272p. mass mkt. 4.99 o.s.i (*0-440-21182-4*) Dell Publishing.
Cliffs Notes Staff. The Grapes of Wrath. 2000. (Cliffs-Notes Ser.). (Illus.). 112p. pap. 5.99 (*0-7645-8596-7*, Cliff Notes) Wiley, John & Sons, Inc.
Coburn, Laura. Uncertain Death. 1996. 368p. mass mkt. 5.99 o.s.i (*0-451-40640-0*, Onyx) NAL.
Coffman, Virginia. Golden Gate People. 224p. 26.00 (*0-7278-5624-3*) Severn Hse. Pubs., Ltd.
—The Lombard Cavalcade. l.t. ed. 2001. 597p. 28.95 (*0-7838-9400-7*, Macmillan Reference USA) Gale Group.
—The Lombard Cavalcade. 1982. 464p. 15.50 o.p. (*0-87795-355-4*, Morrow, William & Co.) Morrow/Avon.
—Pacific Cavalcade. 1982. 560p. mass mkt. 3.50 o.s.i (*0-449-20002-7*, Fawcett) Ballantine Bks.
—Pacific Cavalcade. l.t. ed. 2001. 728p. (*0-7540-1584-X*, Macmillan Reference USA) Gale Group.
—Pacific Cavalcade. 1981. 12.95 o.p. (*0-87795-277-9*, Morrow, William & Co.) Morrow/Avon.
—Pacific Cavalcade. l.t. ed. 2001. (G. K. Hall Core Ser.). 728p. 29.95 (*0-7838-9397-3*) Thorndike Pr.
Cohen, Joe. The Minefield. 2002. 152p. pap. 12.00 (*1-58790-029-7*) Regent Pr.
Coker, Carolyn. Appearance of Evil. 1995. 250p. per. (*0-373-26185-3*, 1-26185-8, Worldwide Library) Harlequin Enterprises, Ltd.
—Appearance of Evil. 1993. 240p. 17.95 o.p. (*0-312-09243-1*, Saint Martin's Minotaur) St. Martin's Pr.
Coleman, Wanda. Mambo Hips & Make Believe. ltd. ed. 1999. 250p. 35.00 o.p. (*1-57423-096-4*, Black Sparrow Pr.) Godine, David R. Pub.
—Mambo Hips & Make Believe: A Novel. 1999. 403p. 25.00 o.p. (*1-57423-095-6*, Black Sparrow Pr.) Godine, David R. Pub.
—Mambo Hips & Make Believe: A Novel. 1999. 403p. pap. 16.00 (*1-57423-094-8*) HarperCollins Pubs.
Coll, Susan. Karlmarx.com: A Love Story. 2000. (*0-316-15060-6*) Little Brown & Co.
—Karlmarx.com: A Love Story. 2001. 256p. 23.00 o.s.i (*0-7432-0003-9*, Simon & Schuster) Simon & Schuster.
Collins, Brandilyn. Dread Champion. 2002. 416p. pap. 12.99 (*0-310-23827-7*) Zondervan.
Collins, Cassandra. Dark Angel. 2000. 368p. mass mkt. 5.50 (*0-505-52414-7*, Love Spell) Dorchester Publishing Co., Inc.
Collins, Jackie. Chances. abr. ed. 1991. audio 15.95 (*0-671-73807-0*); Pt. 2. 1995. audio 15.95 (*0-671-75510-2*) Simon & Schuster Audio. (Simon & Schuster Audioworks).
—Chances. 816p. 1981. 14.95 o.s.i (*0-446-51237-0*); 1991. reprint ed. mass mkt. 7.99 (*0-446-35717-0*) Warner Bks., Inc.
—Dangerous Kiss: A Lucky Santangelo Novel. l.t. ed. 2000. (Thorndike/G. K. Hall Paperback Bestsellers Ser.). 620p. pap. 28.95 (*0-7838-8748-5*, Macmillan Reference USA) Gale Group.
—Dangerous Kiss: A Lucky Santangelo Novel, Set. abr. ed. 1999. audio 25.00 Highsmith Inc.
—Dangerous Kiss: A Lucky Santangelo Novel. abr. ed. 2001. audio (*0-333-78160-0*) Macmillan U.K. GBR. *Dist:* Macmillan Publishing Co., Inc.
—Dangerous Kiss: A Lucky Santangelo Novel. unabr. ed. 2001. audio 94.00 (*0-7887-4979-X*, 96486L8) Recorded Bks., LLC.
—Dangerous Kiss: A Lucky Santangelo Novel. 2000. E-Book 25.00 (*0-684-87371-0*, Simon & Schuster); 1999. 528p. 25.00 (*0-684-85030-3*, Simon & Schuster); 2000. (Illus.). 592p. reprint ed. pap. 7.99 (*0-671-02095-1*, Pocket) Simon & Schuster.
—Dangerous Kiss: A Lucky Santangelo Novel. abr. ed. 1999. audio 25.00 (*0-671-58199-6*, Simon & Schuster Audioworks) Simon & Schuster Audio.
—Dangerous Kiss: A Lucky Santangelo Novel. l.t. ed. 1999. (Core Ser.). 620p. 31.95 (*0-7838-8747-7*) Thorndike Pr.
—Hollywood Husbands. 1986. 512p. 18.45 o.p. (*0-671-52500-X*, Simon & Schuster) Simon & Schuster.
—Hollywood Kids. l.t. ed. 1995. (G. K. Hall Core Ser.). 850p. 25.95 (*0-7838-1211-6*); 733p. 20.95 o.p. (*0-7838-1212-4*) Gale Group. (Macmillan Reference USA).
—Hollywood Kids. 1999. per. 7.99 (*0-671-02356-X*, Pocket); 1995. pap. 6.50 (*0-671-89856-6*, Pocket); 1994. 624p. 23.50 (*0-671-66627-4*, Simon & Schuster); 1995. 624p. reprint ed. mass mkt. 7.99 (*0-671-89849-3*, Pocket) Simon & Schuster.
—Hollywood Kids. abr. ed. 1999. 5p. audio 23.00 (*0-671-88859-5*, 492040, Simon & Schuster Audioworks) Simon & Schuster Audio.
—Hollywood Wives: The New Generation. 2001. 528p. 26.00 (*0-7432-1634-2*, Simon & Schuster); 1999. per. 7.99 (*0-671-02355-1*, Pocket); 1986. 560p. mass mkt. 4.95 o.s.i (*0-671-62425-3*, Pocket); 1985. mass mkt. 4.50 o.s.i (*0-671-54764-X*, Pocket); 1984. mass mkt. 4.50 o.s.i (*0-671-49227-6*, Pocket); 1983. 512p. 16.50 o.p. (*0-671-47406-5*, Simon & Schuster); 1987. 560p. reprint ed. mass mkt. 7.99 (*0-671-70459-1*, Pocket) Simon & Schuster.
—Lady Boss. l.t. ed. 1991. (General Ser.). 760p. 16.95 o.p. (*0-8161-5189-X*); lib. bdg. 22.95 o.p. (*0-8161-5193-8*) Gale Group. (Macmillan Reference USA).
—Lady Boss. Peters, Sally, ed. 1992. mass mkt. 5.99 (*0-671-79571-6*, Pocket) Simon & Schuster.
—Lady Boss. 1990. 21.95 o.p. (*0-671-61937-3*); 21.95 (*0-671-94826-1*) Simon & Schuster. (Simon & Schuster).
—Lady Boss. Grose, Bill, ed. 1991. 640p. reprint ed. mass mkt. 7.99 (*0-671-74418-6*, Pocket) Simon & Schuster.
—Lady Boss. rev. ed. 1998. 640p. mass mkt. 7.99 (*0-671-02347-0*, Pocket) Simon & Schuster.
—Lady Boss. abr. ed. 1990. audio 15.95 (*0-671-73710-4*, Simon & Schuster Audioworks) Simon & Schuster Audio.
—Lucky. 1990. 608p. mass mkt. 5.95 o.s.i (*0-671-63845-9*); 1987. mass mkt. 6.99 (*0-671-70419-2*); 1986. 608p. mass mkt. 4.95 o.s.i (*0-671-52496-8*); 1998. 624p. mass mkt. 7.99 (*0-671-02348-9*) Simon & Schuster. (Pocket).
—Lucky. abr. ed. 1991. audio 15.95 (*0-671-73808-9*, Simon & Schuster Audioworks) Simon & Schuster Audio.
—Vendetta: Lucky's Revenge. l.t. ed. 1997. (Large Print Book Ser.). 28.95 (*1-56895-435-2*, Wheeler Publishing, Inc.) Gale Group.
—Vendetta: Lucky's Revenge. 1997. 544p. 25.00 o.p. (*0-06-039209-6*, ReganBooks); audio 25.00 o.p. (*0-694-51809-3*, CPN 4048, HarperAudio) HarperTrade.
—Vendetta: Lucky's Revenge. 1998. 5.98 o.p. (*0-7651-0824-0*) Smithmark Pubs., Inc.
Collins, Joan. Infamous. 1996. 320p. 23.95 o.p. (*0-525-94129-0*, Dutton) Dutton/Plume.
Collins, Michael. The Cadillac Cowboy. 1995. 288p. 20.95 o.p. (*1-55611-461-3*) Fine, Donald I. Bks.
—Cassandra in Red. 1992. 256p. 19.95 o.p. (*1-55611-316-1*) Fine, Donald I. Bks.
Comfort, Bonnie. Denial. 1996. pap. 5.99 (*0-380-72716-1*, Avon Bks.) Morrow/Avon.
—Denial. 1995. 302p. 22.00 o.p. (*0-671-89696-2*, Simon & Schuster) Simon & Schuster.
Compo, Susan. Life after Death & Other Stories. (New American Fiction Ser.). 1991. 214p. pap. 9.95 o.p. (*0-571-12914-5*); 1990. 224p. 18.95 o.p. (*0-571-12902-1*) Faber & Faber, Inc.
—Malingering: Short Stories. 1993. 220p. (Orig.). pap. 13.95 o.p. (*0-571-19818-X*) Faber & Faber, Inc.
Conley, Martha. Growing Light. 1993. 224p. 18.95 o.p. (*0-312-09823-5*, Saint Martin's Minotaur) St. Martin's Pr.
—The Growing Light. 1995. 240p. mass mkt. 4.99 o.s.i (*0-425-14792-4*) Berkley Publishing Group.
Connelly, Michael. Angels Flight. unabr. ed. 1999. (Harry Bosch Novel Ser.). audio 39.95 (*1-56740-410-3*, 1512, Brilliance Audio Unabridged) Brilliance Audio.
—Angels Flight. unabr. ed. 1999. audio 73.25 Highsmith Inc.
—Angels Flight. 1999. (Detective Harry Bosch Mysteries Ser.). 400p. (YA). (gr. 8 up). 25.00 o.p. (*0-316-15219-6*) Little Brown & Co.
—Angels Flight. l.t. ed. (Thorndike/G. K. Hall Paperback Bestsellers Ser.). 595p. 2000. pap. 27.95 (*0-7862-1865-7*); 1999. 30.95 (*0-7862-1864-9*) Thorndike Pr.
—Angels Flight. abr. ed. 1999. (Detective Harry Bosch Mysteries Ser.). (gr. 8 up). audio 24.00 (*1-57042-645-7*) Time Warner AudioBooks.
—Angels Flight. 2000. 480p. reprint ed. mass mkt. 7.99 (*0-446-60727-4*) Warner Bks., Inc.
—The Black Echo. 1992. 19.95 o.p. (*0-316-15361-3*) Little Brown & Co.
—The Black Echo. 10th ed. 1993. 418p. mass mkt. 7.99 (*0-312-95048-9*, St. Martin's Paperbacks) St. Martin's Pr.
—The Black Echo. l.t. ed. 2001. 647p. 30.95 (*0-7862-3309-5*); 584p. (*0-7540-1659-5*); 584p. (*0-7540-9073-6*) Thorndike Pr.
—The Black Echo. 2002. 496p. reprint ed. mass mkt. 7.99 (*0-446-61273-1*) Warner Bks., Inc.
—The Black Ice. unabr. ed. 1998. (Harry Bosch Ser.). audio 26.95 (*1-56740-095-7*, 1479, Bookcassette); 11p. audio 73.25 (*1-56740-624-6*, 1480, Unabridged Library Editions) Brilliance Audio.
—The Black Ice. l.t. ed. 1994. 90.95 o.p. (*0-7862-9985-1*, Macmillan Reference USA) Gale Group.
—The Black Ice. 1993. 322p. 19.95 o.p. (*0-316-15382-6*) Little Brown & Co.
—The Black Ice. 1994. 374p. mass mkt. 7.99 o.s.i (*0-312-95281-3*, St. Martin's Paperbacks) St. Martin's Pr.
—The Black Ice. 2003. 448p. mass mkt. 7.99 (*0-446-61344-4*, Warner Vision) Warner Bks., Inc.
—Blood Work. abr. ed. 1998. audio 7.99 (*1-56740-279-8*, 1679, Paperback Nova Audio Bks.); audio 25.95 o.p. (*1-56100-763-3*, 50, Bookcassette); 15p. audio 89.25 (*1-56100-838-9*, 813, Unabridged Library Editions);Set. audio 17.95 o.p. (*1-56100-988-1*, 461, Nova Audio Bks.) Brilliance Audio.
—Blood Work. l.t. ed. 1998. (Large Print Book Ser.). 26.95 o.p. (*1-56895-622-3*, Wheeler Publishing, Inc.) Gale Group.
—Blood Work, Set. unabr. ed. 1999. audio 89.25 Highsmith Inc.
—Blood Work, Vol. 1. 1998. (Blood Work Ser.: Vol. 1). 400p. (gr. 8). 23.95 (*0-316-15399-0*) Little Brown & Co.
—Blood Work. 2003. E-Book 5.95 (*0-7595-4786-6*) Time Warner Bk. Group.
—Blood Work. reprint ed. 2002. 480p. pap. 14.95 (*0-446-69044-9*); 1998. 528p. mass mkt. 7.99 (*0-446-60262-0*) Warner Bks., Inc.
—Chasing the Dime. 2002. 384p. 25.95 (*0-316-15391-5*); E-Book 14.95 (*0-7595-4710-6*); (Illus.). 544p. 25.95 (*0-316-16046-6*) Little Brown & Co.
—Chasing the Dime. 2003. 448p. mass mkt. 7.99 (*0-446-61162-X*, Warner Vision) Warner Bks., Inc.

Settings

—The Concrete Blonde. abr. ed. 1994. (Harry Bosch Ser.). audio 16.95 o.p. (*1-56100-375-1*, 1642, Nova Audio Bks.); 13p. audio 89.25 (*1-56100-198-8*, 1160, Unabridged Library Editions); 13p. audio 25.95 (*1-56100-572-X*, 67, Bookcassette) Brilliance Audio.

—The Concrete Blonde. 1994. 382p. 21.95 o.p. (*0-316-15383-4*) Little Brown & Co.

—The Concrete Blonde. abr. ed. 2000. audio 7.95 (*1-57815-004-3*, 1031, Media Bks. Audio Publishing) Media Bks., L. L. C.

—The Concrete Blonde. 1995. 397p. mass mkt. 7.99 (*0-312-95500-6*, St. Martin's Paperbacks) St. Martin's Pr.

—A Darkness More Than Night. 2001. 432p. 25.95 o.p. (*0-316-15407-5*); 400p. E-Book 14.95 (*0-7595-4069-1*) Little Brown & Co.

—A Darkness More Than Night. l.t. ed. 608p. 2002. 30.95 (*0-7862-2821-0*); 2001. 31.95 (*0-7862-2820-2*) Thorndike Pr.

—A Darkness More Than Night. deluxe ltd. ed. 2000. 150.00 (*1-890885-10-X*) Trice, B.E. Publishing.

—A Darkness More Than Night. 2002. 488p. reprint ed. mass mkt. 7.99 (*0-446-66790-0*) Warner Bks., Inc.

—The Last Coyote. abr. ed. (Harry Bosch Novel Ser.). 1996. audio 7.99 o.s.i (*1-56740-118-X*, 671, Paperback Nova Audio Bks.); 1995. audio 16.95 o.p. (*1-56100-409-X*, 1270, Nova Audio Bks.); 1995. 13p. audio 89.25 (*1-56100-241-0*, 922, Unabridged Library Editions); 1995. audio 25.95 (*1-56100-616-5*, 157, Bookcassette) Brilliance Audio.

—The Last Coyote. l.t. ed. 1995. (Large Print Bks.). pap. 24.95 (*1-56895-272-4*, Wheeler Publishing, Inc.) Gale Group.

—The Last Coyote. l.t. ed. 1995. 383p. 22.95 o.p. (*0-316-15390-7*) Little Brown & Co.

—The Last Coyote. 5th ed. 1996. 416p. reprint ed. mass mkt. 7.99 (*0-312-95845-5*, St. Martin's Paperbacks) St. Martin's Pr.

—Lost Light. 2004. mass mkt. 7.99 (*0-446-61163-8*, Warner Vision) Warner Bks., Inc.

—Trunk Music. abr. ed. 1997. (Harry Bosch Novel Ser.). audio 7.99 o.s.i (*1-56740-201-1*, 713, Paperback Nova Audio Bks.); audio 25.95 o.s.i (*1-56100-724-2*, 301, Bookcassette); 15p. audio 89.25 (*1-56100-801-X*, 1110, Unabridged Library Editions) Brilliance Audio.

—Trunk Music. l.t. ed. 1997. 27.95 (*1-56895-440-9*, Wheeler Publishing, Inc.) Gale Group.

—Trunk Music. 1997. 400p. 23.45 o.p. (*0-316-15244-7*) Little Brown & Co.

—Trunk Music. 1998. 438p. mass mkt. 7.99 (*0-312-96329-7*, St. Martin's Paperbacks) St. Martin's Pr.

Conner, K. Patrick. Kingdom Road. 1991. 192p. 18.95 o.p. (*1-55611-302-1*) Fine, Donald I. Bks.

Cook, Bruce. Death As a Career Move. 1992. 272p. 18.95 o.p. (*0-312-06946-4*, Saint Martin's Minotaur) St. Martin's Pr.

—Mexican Standoff. 1988. 256p. 16.95 o.p. (*0-531-15089-5*, Watts, Franklin) Scholastic Library Publishing.

—Mexican Standoff. 1990. mass mkt. 3.95 (*0-312-92114-4*, St. Martin's Paperbacks) St. Martin's Pr.

—Rough Cut. 1992. 2.99 o.p. (*0-517-09052-X*) Random Hse. Value Publishing.

—Rough Cut. 1990. 240p. 16.95 o.p. (*0-312-05149-2*, Saint Martin's Minotaur) St. Martin's Pr.

—The Sidewalk Hilton. 1994. 320p. 21.95 o.p. (*0-312-11062-6*, Saint Martin's Minotaur) St. Martin's Pr.

Cooley, Leland F. California. 1984. 612p. 17.95 o.s.i (*0-8128-2987-5*); pap. 4.95 o.p. (*0-8128-8172-9*) Madison Bks., Inc. (Scarborough Hse.).

Cooper, Bernard. A Year of Rhymes. 1994. (Contemporary American Fiction Ser.). 240p. pap. 9.95 o.p. (*0-14-017403-6*, Penguin Bks.) Penguin Group (USA) Inc.

—A Year of Rhymes. 1993. 240p. 20.00 o.p. (*0-670-84732-1*, Viking) Viking Penguin.

Copper, Basil. Bad Scene. l.t. ed. 2000. (G. K. Hall Nightingale Ser.). 217p. pap. 20.95 (*0-7838-8997-6*, Macmillan Reference USA) Gale Group.

—Bad Scene. l.t. ed. 1991. (Linford Mystery Large Print Ser.). pap. 17.99 o.p. (*0-7089-7021-4*, Ulverscroft) Thorpe, F. A. Pubs. GBR. *Dist:* Ulverscroft Large Print Bks., Ltd., Ulverscroft Large Print Canada, Ltd.

—The Breaking Point. l.t. ed. 1995. (Linford Mystery Large Print Ser.). 320p. pap. 17.99 o.p. (*0-7089-7805-3*, Linford) Thorpe, F. A. Pubs. GBR. *Dist:* Ulverscroft Large Print Bks., Ltd., Ulverscroft Large Print Canada, Ltd.

—The Caligari Complex. l.t. ed. 1999. (Linford Mystery Large Print Ser.). 304p. pap. 18.99 (*0-7089-5504-5*, Linford) Thorpe, F. A. Pubs. GBR. *Dist:* Ulverscroft Large Print Bks., Ltd., Ulverscroft Large Print Canada, Ltd.

—Crack in the Sidewalk. l.t. ed. 1997. (Linford Mystery Library). 320p. pap. 17.99 o.p. (*0-7089-5065-5*, Linford) Thorpe, F. A. Pubs. GBR. *Dist:* Ulverscroft Large Print Bks., Ltd., Ulverscroft Large Print Canada, Ltd.

—The Dark Mirror. (Black Dagger Crime Ser.). 16.50 o.p. (*0-86220-796-7*, BD001, Black Dagger) BBC Audiobooks America.

—The Dark Mirror. l.t. ed. 1997. (Linford Mystery Library). 416p. pap. 17.99 o.p. (*0-7089-5101-5*, Linford) Thorpe, F. A. Pubs. GBR. *Dist:* Ulverscroft Large Print Bks., Ltd., Ulverscroft Large Print Canada, Ltd.

—Dead File. l.t. ed. 1991. (Linford Mystery Large Print Ser.). pap. 17.99 o.p. (*0-7089-7001-X*, Ulverscroft) Thorpe, F. A. Pubs. GBR. *Dist:* Ulverscroft Large Print Bks., Ltd., Ulverscroft Large Print Canada, Ltd.

—Death Squad. l.t. ed. 1999. (Linford Mystery Large Print Ser.). 304p. pap. 18.99 (*0-7089-5460-X*, Linford) Thorpe, F. A. Pubs. GBR. *Dist:* Ulverscroft Large Print Bks., Ltd., Ulverscroft Large Print Canada, Ltd.

—Die Now, Live Later. l.t. ed. 1993. (Linford Mystery Library). 336p. pap. 17.99 o.p. (*0-7089-7341-8*, Ulverscroft) Thorpe, F. A. Pubs. GBR. *Dist:* Ulverscroft Large Print Bks., Ltd., Ulverscroft Large Print Canada, Ltd.

—Don't Bleed on Me. l.t. ed. 1991. (Linford Mystery Library). pap. 17.99 o.p. (*0-7089-7081-8*, Ulverscroft) Thorpe, F. A. Pubs. GBR. *Dist:* Ulverscroft Large Print Bks., Ltd., Ulverscroft Large Print Canada, Ltd.

—The Far Horizon. 2001. 219p. (*0-7540-4399-1*); (*0-7540-4400-9*) Gale Group. (Macmillan Reference USA).

—The Far Horizon. l.t. ed. 2001. (G. K. Hall Nightingale Ser.). 219p. pap. 23.95 (*0-7838-9327-2*) Thorndike Pr.

—The Far Horizon. l.t. ed. 1993. (Linford Mystery Library). 336p. pap. 17.99 o.p. (*0-7089-7378-7*, Ulverscroft) Thorpe, F. A. Pubs. GBR. *Dist:* Ulverscroft Large Print Bks., Ltd., Ulverscroft Large Print Canada, Ltd.

—Feedback. l.t. ed. 2001. 225p. pap. 23.95 (*0-7838-9592-5*) Thorndike Pr.

—Feedback. l.t. ed. 1991. (Linford Mystery Library). pap. 17.99 o.p. (*0-7089-7129-6*, Ulverscroft) Thorpe, F. A. Pubs. GBR. *Dist:* Ulverscroft Large Print Bks., Ltd., Ulverscroft Large Print Canada, Ltd.

—A Good Place to Die. l.t. ed. 1989. (Linford Mystery Library). pap. 17.99 o.p. (*0-7089-6742-6*, Ulverscroft) Thorpe, F. A. Pubs. GBR. *Dist:* Ulverscroft Large Print Bks., Ltd., Ulverscroft Large Print Canada, Ltd.

—A Great Year for Dying. l.t. ed. 1993. (Linford Mystery Library). 352p. pap. 17.99 o.p. (*0-7089-7349-3*, Ulverscroft) Thorpe, F. A. Pubs. GBR. *Dist:* Ulverscroft Large Print Bks., Ltd., Ulverscroft Large Print Canada, Ltd.

—The High Wall. l.t. ed. 1987. (Linford Mystery Library). 304p. pap. 17.99 o.p. (*0-7089-6455-9*, Linford) Thorpe, F. A. Pubs. GBR. *Dist:* Ulverscroft Large Print Bks., Ltd., Ulverscroft Large Print Canada, Ltd.

—Impact. l.t. ed. 1997. (Linford Mystery Library). 320p. pap. 17.99 o.p. (*0-7089-5070-1*, Linford) Thorpe, F. A. Pubs. GBR. *Dist:* Ulverscroft Large Print Bks., Ltd., Ulverscroft Large Print Canada, Ltd.

—The Lonely Place. l.t. ed. 1997. (Linford Mystery Library). 304p. pap. 17.99 o.p. (*0-7089-5060-4*, Ulverscroft) Thorpe, F. A. Pubs. GBR. *Dist:* Ulverscroft Large Print Bks., Ltd., Ulverscroft Large Print Canada, Ltd.

—The Long Rest. l.t. ed. 1994. 221p. lib. bdg. 16.95 (*0-8161-7421-0*, Macmillan Reference USA) Gale Group.

—The Marble Orchard. l.t. ed. 1998. (Linford Mystery Large Print Ser.). 256p. pap. 17.99 (*0-7089-5265-8*, Linford) Thorpe, F. A. Pubs. GBR. *Dist:* Ulverscroft Large Print Bks., Ltd., Ulverscroft Large Print Canada, Ltd.

—No Letters from the Grave. l.t. ed. 1998. (Linford Mystery Library). 240p. pap. 17.99 (*0-7089-5223-2*, Linford) Thorpe, F. A. Pubs. GBR. *Dist:* Ulverscroft Large Print Bks., Ltd., Ulverscroft Large Print Canada, Ltd.

—Print-Out. l.t. ed. 1993. (Dales Mystery Ser.). 246p. pap. 19.99 o.p. (*1-85389-380-3*) Dales Large Print Bks. GBR. *Dist:* Ulverscroft Large Print Bks., Ltd., Ulverscroft Large Print Canada, Ltd.

—Print-Out. l.t. ed. 1996. (Linford Mystery Library). 304p. pap. 17.99 o.p. (*0-7089-7861-4*, Linford) Thorpe, F. A. Pubs. GBR. *Dist:* Ulverscroft Large Print Bks., Ltd., Ulverscroft Large Print Canada, Ltd.

—A Quiet Room in Hell. l.t. ed. 1998. (Linford Mystery Large Print Ser.). 288p. pap. 17.99 (*0-7089-5294-1*, Linford) Thorpe, F. A. Pubs. GBR. *Dist:* Ulverscroft Large Print Bks., Ltd., Ulverscroft Large Print Canada, Ltd.

—Ricochet. l.t. ed. 1993. (Linford Mystery Library). 304p. pap. 17.99 o.p. (*0-7089-7382-5*, Linford) Thorpe, F. A. Pubs. GBR. *Dist:* Ulverscroft Large Print Bks., Ltd., Ulverscroft Large Print Canada, Ltd.

—Scratch on the Dark. 2002. 192p. 21.95 (*0-7540-8610-0*, Black Dagger) BBC Audiobooks America.

—Scratch on the Dark. l.t. ed. 2000. (Linford Mystery Large Print Ser.). 264p. pap. 18.99 (*0-7089-5767-6*, Ulverscroft) Thorpe, F. A. Pubs. GBR. *Dist:* Ulverscroft Large Print Bks., Ltd., Ulverscroft Large Print Canada, Ltd.

—Shock-Wave. l.t. ed. 1994. (Linford Mystery Library). 320p. pap. 17.99 o.p. (*0-7089-7629-8*, Linford) Thorpe, F. A. Pubs. GBR. *Dist:* Ulverscroft Large Print Bks., Ltd., Ulverscroft Large Print Canada, Ltd.

—Strong-Arm. l.t. ed. 1989. (Linford Mystery Library). 319p. pap. 17.99 o.p. (*0-7089-6629-2*, Linford) Thorpe, F. A. Pubs. GBR. *Dist:* Ulverscroft Large Print Bks., Ltd., Ulverscroft Large Print Canada, Ltd.

—Tight Corner. l.t. ed. 1994. (Linford Mystery Library). 304p. pap. 17.99 o.p. (*0-7089-7564-X*, Linford) Thorpe, F. A. Pubs. GBR. *Dist:* Ulverscroft Large Print Bks., Ltd., Ulverscroft Large Print Canada, Ltd.

—Trigger-Man. l.t. ed. 1994. (Linford Mystery Library). 320p. pap. 17.99 o.p. (*0-7089-7561-5*, Linford) Thorpe, F. A. Pubs. GBR. *Dist:* Ulverscroft Large Print Bks., Ltd., Ulverscroft Large Print Canada, Ltd.

—A Voice from the Dead. l.t. ed. 1998. (Linford Mystery Large Print Ser.). 304p. pap. 17.99 (*0-7089-5287-9*, Linford) Thorpe, F. A. Pubs. GBR. *Dist:* Ulverscroft Large Print Bks., Ltd., Ulverscroft Large Print Canada, Ltd.

—The Year of the Dragon. l.t. ed. 1991. (Linford Mystery Library). pap. 17.99 o.p. (*0-7089-7077-X*, Linford) Thorpe, F. A. Pubs. GBR. *Dist:* Ulverscroft Large Print Bks., Ltd., Ulverscroft Large Print Canada, Ltd.

Corbett, David. Done for a Dime. 368p. 2004. pap. 12.95 (*0-449-00715-4*); 2003. 24.95 (*0-345-44753-0*, Ballantine Bks.) Ballantine Bks.

Corpi, Lucha. Black Widow's Wardrobe. 1999. (Gloria Damasco Detective Ser.). 193p. pap. 12.95 o.p. (*1-55885-288-3*) Arte Publico Pr.

—Cactus Blood: A Mystery Novel. 1995. 249p. 9.50 o.p. (*1-55885-134-8*) Arte Publico Pr.

—Eulogy for a Brown Angel: A Mystery Novel. 2002. 208p. pap. 12.95 (*1-55885-356-1*); 1992. 200p. 9.00 (*1-55885-050-3*) Arte Publico Pr.

Coscarelli, Kate. Heir Apparent. abr. ed. 1993. audio 16.99 (*0-88646-366-1*, LFP 7366) Durkin Hayes Publishing Ltd.

—Heir Apparent. 1994. 392p. mass mkt. 5.99 o.p. (*0-312-95200-7*, St. Martin's Paperbacks); 1993. 320p. 21.95 o.p. (*0-312-09305-5*) St. Martin's Pr.

—Leading Lady. 1991. 19.95 o.p. (*0-312-05889-6*) St. Martin's Pr.

Cosin, Elizabeth M. Zen & the Art of Murder. (St. Martin's Minotaur Mysteries Ser.). 1999. 304p. mass mkt. 5.99 (*0-312-96948-1*, St. Martin's Paperbacks); 1998. 288p. 22.95 o.p. (*0-312-19376-9*, Saint Martin's Minotaur) St. Martin's Pr.

Coulter, Catherine. Beyond Eden. 1992. 368p. 20.00 o.p. (*0-525-93397-2*, Dutton) Dutton/Plume.

—Beyond Eden. l.t. ed. 1998. 25.95 o.p. (*1-56895-658-4*, Wheeler Publishing, Inc.) Gale Group.

—Beyond Eden. 448p. 1993. mass mkt. 7.50 o.s.i (*0-451-40339-8*, Onyx); 2000. reprint ed. mass mkt. 7.99 (*0-451-20231-7*, Signet Bks.) NAL.

—Midnight Star. l.t. ed. 2000. (Wheeler Large Print Book Ser.). 465p. 26.95 o.p. (*1-56895-862-5*, Wheeler Publishing, Inc.) Gale Group.

—Midnight Star. 1986. 464p. mass mkt. 5.99 o.p. (*0-451-16254-4*, Onyx); 464p. mass mkt. 7.99 (*0-451-40446-7*, Onyx); mass mkt. 3.95 o.p. (*0-451-14297-7*, Signet Bks.); mass mkt. 4.50 o.p. (*0-451-15379-0*, Signet Bks.) NAL.

—Midnight Star. 2001. 464p. 26.00 (*0-7278-5625-1*) Severn Hse. Pubs., Ltd.

—Wild Star. l.t. ed. 2000. (Wheeler Large Print Book Ser.). 508p. 28.95 o.p. (*1-56895-915-X*, Wheeler Publishing, Inc.) Gale Group.

—Wild Star. 2002. 400p. mass mkt. 7.99 (*0-451-20639-8*, Signet Bks.); 1986. 464p. mass mkt. 7.99 o.s.i (*0-451-40447-5*, Onyx) NAL.

—Wild Star. 1994. reprint ed. lib. bdg. 22.00 (*0-7278-4687-6*) Severn Hse. Pubs., Ltd.

Coulter, Kathryn A. Does Cupid Do Takeout? l.t. ed. 1995. 211p. per. 20.95 (*0-7838-1518-2*, Macmillan Reference USA) Gale Group.

Covino, Michael. The Negative. 1993. 368p. 21.00 o.p. (*0-670-85078-0*, Viking) Viking Penguin.

Coyle, Neva. Inside the Private Hedge. 1996. (Summerwind Ser.: Vol. 2). 256p. (Orig.). pap. 8.99 o.p. (*1-55661-547-7*) Bethany Hse. Pubs.

—Inside the Privet Hedge: A Novel. 2001. 290p. 23.95 (*0-7862-2938-1*, Five Star) Gale Group.

Crais, Robert. Demolition Angel. 2001. 400p. mass mkt. 6.99 (*0-345-43448-X*, Ballantine Bks.) Ballantine Bks.

—Demolition Angel. l.t. ed. 2000. (Wheeler Large Print Book Ser.). 474p. 29.95 (*1-56895-921-4*, Wheeler Publishing, Inc.) Gale Group.

—The Devil's Cantina. 1999. 288p. 22.95 (*0-7868-6355-2*) Hyperion Pr.

—Free Fall. 1994. (Elvis Cole Mystery Ser.). mass mkt. 4.99 o.s.i (*0-553-56831-0*, Crimeline); 304p. mass mkt. 6.99 (*0-553-56509-5*) Bantam Bks.

—Indigo Slam. 2003. (Elvis Cole Mystery Ser.). 320p. mass mkt. 7.99 (*0-345-43564-8*, Ballantine Bks.) Ballantine Bks.

—Indigo Slam. unabr. ed. 1997. (Elvis Cole Mystery Ser.). audio 48.00 (*0-7366-3833-4*, 4553) Books on Tape, Inc.

—Indigo Slam. abr. ed. (Elvis Cole Mystery Ser.). 2000. audio 7.99 o.s.i (*1-58788-097-0*, 2352, Paperback Nova Audio Bks.); 1998. audio 7.99 o.s.i (*1-56740-252-6*, 2379, Nova Audio Bks.); 1997. audio 16.95 o.p. (*1-56100-977-6*, 1236, Nova Audio Bks.); 1997. audio 16.95 o.p.; 1997. audio 23.95 (*1-56100-752-8*, 144, Bookcassette); 1997. audio 57.25 (*1-56100-827-3*, 907, Unabridged Library Editions) Brilliance Audio.

—Indigo Slam. (Elvis Cole Mystery Ser.). 1999. 384p. mass mkt. 5.99 (*0-7868-8929-2*); 1997. 304p. 22.95 (*0-7868-6261-0*) Hyperion Pr.

—L. A. Requiem. 2000. (Elvis Cole Mystery Ser.). 416p. mass mkt. 6.99 (*0-345-43447-1*, Ballantine Bks.) Ballantine Bks.

—L. A. Requiem. l.t. ed. 2000. (Elvis Cole Mystery Ser.). 538p. 27.95 (*1-56895-881-1*, Wheeler Publishing, Inc.) Gale Group.

—L. A. Requiem. Set. abr. ed. 1999. (Elvis Cole Mystery Ser.). audio 25.00 Highsmith Inc.

—L. A. Requiem. abr. ed. 1999. (Elvis Cole Mystery Ser.). audio 25.00 (*0-553-52648-0*, RH Audio) Random Hse. Audio Publishing Group.

—Lullaby Town. (Elvis Cole Mystery Ser.). 1993. 352p. mass mkt. 6.99 (*0-553-29951-4*); 1992. 304p. 20.00 o.s.i (*0-553-08197-7*) Bantam Bks.

—The Monkey's Raincoat. (Elvis Cole Mystery Ser.). 1987. 208p. mass mkt. 2.95 o.s.i (*0-553-26336-6*); 1992. 224p. reprint ed. mass mkt. 7.50 (*0-553-27585-2*) Bantam Bks.

—Stalking the Angel. 1992. (Elvis Cole Mystery Ser.). 288p. mass mkt. 7.50 (*0-553-28644-7*) Bantam Bks.

—Sunset Express. unabr. ed. 1997. (Elvis Cole Mystery Ser.). audio 56.00 (*0-913369-89-6*, 4389) Books on Tape, Inc.

—Sunset Express. abr. ed. (Elvis Cole Mystery Ser.). 1997. audio 7.99 o.p. (*1-56740-166-X*, 707, Nova Audio Bks.); 1996. audio 16.95 o.p. (*1-56100-905-9*, 1066, Nova Audio Bks.); 1996. audio 57.25 o.p. (*1-56100-320-4*, 1065, Unabridged Library Editions); 1996. audio 23.95 o.p. (*1-56100-695-5*, 284, Bookcassette) Brilliance Audio.

—Sunset Express. (Elvis Cole Mystery Ser.). 1996. 288p. 21.95 o.p. (*0-7868-6096-0*); 2002. 416p. reprint ed. mass mkt. 6.99 (*0-7868-8915-2*) Hyperion Pr.

—Sunset Express. l.t. ed. 2001. 485p. (*0-7540-1644-7*); (*0-7540-2496-2*) Thorndike Pr.

—Voodoo River. l.t. ed. 2002. (Elvis Cole Mystery Ser.). 499p. 29.95 (*0-7862-3404-0*) Gale Group.

—Voodoo River. (Elvis Cole Mystery Ser.). 1995. 304p. 21.95 (*0-7868-6076-6*); 2003. 416p. reprint ed. mass mkt. 7.99 (*0-7868-8905-5*) Hyperion Pr.

Cramer, Cahroul. Twisted. 1998. 196p. pap. 9.95 (*1-881164-82-9*) Intercontinental Publishing, Inc.

Cresse, Gina. A Deadly Bargain: Plan C. 2000. 207p. 19.95 (*0-8034-9409-2*, Avalon Bks.) Bouregy, Thomas & Co., Inc.

Crichton, Michael. Rising Sun. 1997. pap. 12.00 o.s.i (*0-345-41896-4*); 1992. mass mkt. 6.99 o.p. (*0-345-90226-2*); 1992. 416p. mass mkt. 7.99 (*0-345-38037-1*) Ballantine Bks.

—Rising Sun. 1992. 355p. 26.00 (*0-394-58942-4*) Knopf, Alfred A. Inc.

—Rising Sun. abr. ed. 1999. audio 8.99 o.s.i (*0-375-40575-5*); 1992. audio 16.00 o.s.i (*0-679-41099-6*, 391477) Random Hse. Audio Publishing Group. (RH Audio).

—Rising Sun. l.t. ed. 1992. 24.00 o.s.i (*0-679-41017-1*) Random Hse. Large Print.

Crocker, H. W., III. The Old Limey. 2001. 250p. 19.95 (*0-89526-232-0*) Regnery Publishing, Inc., An Eagle Publishing Co.

Crosby, Harry W. Portrait of Paloma: A Novel. 2001. (Illus.). 320p. pap. 14.95 (*0-916251-56-X*) Sunbelt Pubns., Inc.

Crum, Laura. Breakaway. 2001. (Gail McCarthy Mysteries Ser.). 224p. 22.95 (*0-312-27181-6*, Saint Martin's Minotaur) St. Martin's Pr.

—Cutter. (Gail McCarthy Mysteries Ser.). 1995. 196p. mass mkt. 4.99 (*0-312-95674-6*, St. Martin's Paperbacks); 1994. 208p. 18.95 o.p. (*0-312-10960-1*, Saint Martin's Minotaur) St. Martin's Pr.

—Hayburner: A Gail McCarthy Mystery. 2003. 208p. 22.95 (*0-312-29047-0*, Saint Martin's Minotaur) St. Martin's Pr.

—Hoofprints. 1995. 208p. 21.95 o.p. (*0-312-13983-7*, Saint Martin's Minotaur); Vol. 1. 1996. mass mkt. 5.99 (*0-312-96040-9*, St. Martin's Paperbacks) St. Martin's Pr.

—Roped. 1998. (Gail McCarthy Mysteries Ser.). 256p. 22.95 o.p. (*0-312-19325-4*, Saint Martin's Minotaur) St. Martin's Pr.

—Roughstock. 1997. 224p. text 20.95 o.p. (*0-312-15643-X*, Saint Martin's Minotaur) St. Martin's Pr.

—Slickrock. 1999. (Gail McCarthy Mysteries Ser.). 256p. 22.95 (*0-312-20910-X*, Saint Martin's Minotaur) St. Martin's Pr.

Culea, John. Light the Night. 1997. 389p. pap. 11.99 o.p. (*0-7814-0296-4*) Cook Communications Ministries.

Cunningham, E. V., pseud. The Case of the Angry Actress. 1984. 192p. pap. 2.95 o.p. (*0-440-11093-9*) Dell Publishing.

—The Case of the Kidnapped Angel. 192p. 1983. (Masao Masuto Mystery Ser.: No. 5). pap. 2.95 o.p. (*0-440-11224-9*); 1982. 12.95 o.s.i (*0-385-28118-8*, Delacorte Pr.) Dell Publishing.

—The Case of the Kidnapped Angel. l.t. ed. 1983. 216p. pap. 7.95 o.p. (*0-8161-3471-5*, Macmillan Reference USA) Gale Group.

—The Case of the Murdered MacKenzie. 1984. (Masao Masuto Mystery Ser.). 192p. 11.95 o.s.i (*0-385-29337-2*, Delacorte Pr.) Dell Publishing.

—The Case of the Murdered MacKenzie. l.t. ed. 1985. (Nightingale Ser.). 386p. 9.95 o.p. (*0-8161-3771-4*, Macmillan Reference USA) Gale Group.

—The Case of the One-Penny Orange. l.t. ed. 1982. (Nightingale Ser.). lib. bdg. 11.95 o.p. (*0-8161-3334-4*, Macmillan Reference USA) Gale Group.

—The Case of the One-Penny Orange. 1982. (Masao Masuto Mystery Ser.). 176p. pap. o.p. (*0-03-059858-3*, Owl Bks.) Holt, Henry & Co.

—The Case of the Poisoned Eclairs. 1980. pap. 2.25 o.p. (*0-440-11256-7*) Dell Publishing.

—The Case of the Poisoned Eclairs. 1982. (Nightingale Ser.). pap. 9.95 o.p. (*0-8161-3333-6*, Macmillan Reference USA) Gale Group.

—The Case of the Poisoned Eclairs. 1979. o.p. (*0-03-044721-6*) Holt, Henry & Co.

—The Case of the Russian Diplomat. 1979. 1.75 o.s.i (*0-515-04881-X*, 04881-X, Jove) Berkley Publishing Group.

—The Case of the Russian Diplomat. (Masao Masuto Mystery Ser.). 1982. 176p. pap. o.p. (*0-03-059857-5*, Owl Bks.); 1978. o.p. (*0-03-022456-X*) Holt, Henry & Co.

—The Case of the Sliding Pool. 1983. pap. 2.95 o.p. (*0-440-12092-6*); 1981. 10.95 o.s.i (*0-440-01114-0*, Delacorte Pr.) Dell Publishing.

—The Case of the Sliding Pool. 1982. (Nightingale Ser.). pap. 9.95 o.p. (*0-8161-3348-4*, Macmillan Reference USA) Gale Group.

Cuthbert, Margaret. The Silent Cradle. 1999. 496p. mass mkt. 6.99 (*0-671-01514-1*, Pocket); 1998. 368p. 23.00 o.s.i (*0-671-01513-3*, Atria) Simon & Schuster.

—The Silent Cradle. abr. ed. 1998. audio 18.00 (*0-671-58064-7*, 393598, Simon & Schuster Audioworks) Simon & Schuster Audio.

—The Silent Cradle. abr. ed. 1999. audio 16.85 (*0-671-01116-2*) Ulverscroft Audio (U.S.A.).

Cutler, Stan. Best Performance by a Patsy. 1991. (Goodman-Bradley Mystery Ser.). 352p. 18.95 o.p. (*0-525-93317-4*) Dutton/Plume.

—Best Performance by a Patsy. 1993. (Goodman-Bradley Mystery Ser.). 336p. mass mkt. 4.50 o.p. (*0-451-40359-2*, Onyx) NAL.

—The Face on the Cutting Room Floor. 1991. 320p. 18.95 o.p. (*0-525-93381-6*, Dutton) Dutton/Plume.

—The Face on the Cutting Room Floor. 1993. (Goodman-Bradley Mystery Ser.). 272p. mass mkt. 4.50 o.s.i (*0-451-40394-0*, Signet Bks.) NAL.

—Rough Cut. 1994. 336p. (Orig.). mass mkt. 4.99 o.s.i (*0-451-18253-7*) NAL.

—Shot on Location. 1993. (Goodman-Bradley Mystery Ser.). 352p. 19.00 o.p. (*0-525-93576-2*) Dutton/Plume.

—Shot on Location. 1994. (Goodman-Bradley Mystery Ser.). 336p. mass mkt. 4.99 o.p. (*0-451-40391-6*, Signet Bks.) NAL.

Dain, Catherine. Death of the Party: A Faith Cassidy Mystery. 2000. (Five Star Mystery Ser.). 238p. 21.95 (*0-7862-2538-6*, Five Star) Gale Group.

—Follow the Murder: A Faith Cassidy Mystery. 2002. (Five Star First Edition Mystery Ser.). 222p. 25.95 (*0-7862-4316-3*, Five Star) Gale Group.

Dalessandro, James. Bohemian Heart. 1993. 256p. 19.95 o.p. (*0-312-09756-5*, Saint Martin's Minotaur) St. Martin's Pr.

Dallas, Joe. Unforgiven Sins. 1995. pap. 10.99 o.p. (*1-56507-167-0*) Harvest Hse. Pubs.

Dana, Richard & Paine, Lauran. Death Was the Echo. l.t. ed. 2000. (G. K. Hall Nightingale Ser.). 184p. pap. 20.95 (*0-7838-8846-5*, Macmillan Reference USA) Gale Group.

Daniel, John. Generous Helpings: Stories. 2001. 157p. pap. (*1-885375-08-5*) Shoreline Pr.

Dann, Joshua. Timeshare: ATime for War. 1999. (Timeshare Trilogy Ser.). 288p. mass mkt. 5.99 o.s.i (*0-441-00638-8*) Ace Bks.

—Timeshare: Do You Believe in Yesterday? 1997. 256p. mass mkt. 5.99 o.s.i (*0-441-00457-1*) Ace Bks.

—Timeshare: Second Time Around. 1998. (Timeshare Trilogy Ser.). 256p. mass mkt. 5.99 o.s.i (*0-441-00567-5*) Ace Bks.

Darby, Ann. The Orphan Game. l.t. ed. 1999. (Core Ser.). 521p. 28.95 (*0-7838-8749-3*) Thorndike Pr.

—The Orphan Game: A Novel. 2000. 336p. pap. 13.00 (*0-688-17782-4*, Perennial) HarperTrade.

—The Orphan Game: A Novel. 1999. 326p. 24.00 (*0-688-16778-0*, Morrow, William & Co.) Morrow/Avon.

Dart, Iris Rainer. I'll Be There. l.t. ed. 1994. 22.95 o.p. (*0-7927-2087-3*); pap. 21.95 o.p. (*0-7927-2086-5*) BBC Audiobooks America.

—I'll Be There. 1991. 19.95 o.p. (*0-316-17328-2*) Little Brown & Co.

—I'll Be There. 1993. 15.95 o.p. (*1-55800-414-9*) NewStar Media, Inc.

—Show Business Kills. 1995. 310p. 21.95 o.p. (*0-316-17334-7*) Little Brown & Co.

—Show Business Kills. 1996. 400p. mass mkt. 6.50 o.p. (*0-446-36511-4*) Warner Bks., Inc.

—The Stork Club. l.t. ed. 1993. 22.95 o.p. (*0-7927-1670-1*); pap. 20.95 o.p. (*0-7927-1669-8*) BBC Audiobooks America.

—The Stork Club. 1992. 400p. 21.95 o.p. (*0-316-17332-0*) Little Brown & Co.

—When I Fall in Love. abr. ed. 1999. audio 7.99 o.s.i (*1-56740-336-0*, 1951, Paperback Nova Audio Bks.); audio 17.95 o.p. (*1-56100-833-8*, 1667, Nova Audio Bks.); audio 35.95 (*1-56740-420-0*, 1664, Brilliance Audio Unabridged); 7p. audio 57.25 (*1-56740-646-7*, 1665, Unabridged Library Editions) Brilliance Audio.

—When I Fall in Love. l.t. ed. 1999. 27.95 (*1-56895-734-3*, Wheeler Publishing, Inc.) Gale Group.

—When I Fall in Love. abr. ed. 1999. audio 17.95 Highsmith Inc.

—When I Fall in Love. 1999. 352p. mass mkt. 6.99 (*0-380-73198-3*, Avon Bks.); 258p. 25.00 (*0-688-16034-4*, Morrow, William & Co.) Morrow/Avon.

Davidson, Sara. Cowboy: A Love Story. l.t. ed. 1999. 26.95 (*1-56895-758-0*, Wheeler Publishing, Inc.) Gale Group.

—Cowboy: A Love Story. 288p. 2000. pap. 13.00 (*0-06-093135-3*, Perennial); 1999. 24.00 (*0-06-099582-3*, HarperCollins); 1999. 24.00 o.p. (*0-06-019326-3*, HarperCollins) HarperTrade.

Davies, June W. Golden Destiny. 1993. 22.95 o.p. (*0-312-08800-0*) St. Martin's Pr.

Davis, Kenn. Acts of Homicide. 1989. 224p. mass mkt. 3.50 o.s.i (*0-449-13351-6*, Fawcett) Ballantine Bks.

—As October Dies. 1987. 240p. mass mkt. 2.95 o.s.i (*0-449-13097-5*, Fawcett) Ballantine Bks.

—Blood of Poets. 1990. 208p. (Orig.). mass mkt. 3.95 o.s.i (*0-449-13352-4*, Fawcett) Ballantine Bks.

—Melting Point. 1986. 256p. (Orig.). mass mkt. 2.95 o.s.i (*0-449-12901-2*, Fawcett) Ballantine Bks.

—Nijinsky Is Dead. 1987. 240p. mass mkt. 2.95 o.s.i (*0-449-13096-7*, Fawcett) Ballantine Bks.

—Words Can Kill. 1984. (Orig.). mass mkt. 2.50 o.s.i (*0-449-12667-6*, Fawcett) Ballantine Bks.

Davis, Thomas D. Consuming Fire. 1996. 240p. 21.95 o.p. (*0-312-14575-6*, Saint Martin's Minotaur) St. Martin's Pr.

—Murdered Sleep: A Dave Strickland Mystery. 1994. 264p. 21.95 o.p. (*0-8027-3177-5*) Walker & Co.

Davis, W. E. Black Dragon. l.t. ed. 1995. (Gil Beckman Mystery Ser.: Bk. 3). 192p. pap. 8.99 o.p. (*0-89107-870-3*) Crossway Bks.

—Drastic Park: A Gil Beckman Mystery. 1997. (Gil Beckman Mystery Ser.). 208p. pap. 8.99 (*0-89107-962-9*) Crossway Bks.

—Drastic Park: A Gil Beckman Mystery. l.t. ed. 1998. (Christian Fiction Ser.). 315p. 24.95 (*0-7862-1403-1*) Thorndike Pr.

—The Gathering Storm. 1996. (Valley of the Peacemaker Ser.: Vol. 1). 384p. pap. 10.99 o.p. (*0-89107-887-8*) Crossway Bks.

—The Proving Ground. 1996. (Valley of the Peacemaker Ser.: Vol. 2). 368p. pap. 10.99 o.p. (*0-89107-884-3*) Crossway Bks.

—Suspended Animation, No. 1. 1994. (Gil Beckman Mystery Ser.: Bk. 1). 192p. pap. 8.99 o.p. (*0-89107-802-9*) Crossway Bks.

—Victim of Circumstance. 1995. (Gil Beckman Mystery Ser.: Vol. 2). 208p. pap. 8.99 o.p. (*0-89107-843-6*) Crossway Bks.

—Victim of Circumstance, No. 2. l.t. ed. 1996. 320p. 21.95 o.p. (*0-7838-1701-0*, Macmillan Reference USA) Gale Group.

Dawson, Janet. A Credible Threat. (Jeri Howard Mystery Ser.). 1997. mass mkt. 5.99 o.s.i (*0-449-22357-4*); 1996. 256p. 21.00 o.p. (*0-449-90977-8*) Ballantine Bks. (Fawcett).

—Don't Turn Your Back on the Ocean. 1994. 336p. 20.00 o.p. (*0-449-90766-X*, Fawcett) Ballantine Bks.

—Kindred Crimes. 1992. mass mkt. 4.99 o.s.i (*0-449-22014-1*, Fawcett) Ballantine Bks.

—Kindred Crimes. 1990. 17.95 o.p. (*0-312-04464-X*, Saint Martin's Minotaur) St. Martin's Pr.

—Kindred Crimes. l.t. ed. 1993. (Ulverscroft Large Print Ser.). 480p. 29.99 o.p. (*0-7089-2929-X*, Ulverscroft) Thorpe, F. A. Pubs. GBR. *Dist:* Ulverscroft Large Print Bks., Ltd., Ulverscroft Large Print Canada, Ltd.

—Nobody's Child. 1995. 352p. 21.00 o.s.i (*0-449-90976-X*, Fawcett) Ballantine Bks.

—Nobody's Child: A Jeri Howard Mystery. 1996. 320p. mass mkt. 6.99 o.s.i (*0-449-22356-6*, Fawcett) Ballantine Bks.

—Take a Number. (Northern California Mysteries Ser.). 1994. mass mkt. 4.99 o.s.i (*0-449-22183-0*); 1993. 352p. 20.00 o.s.i (*0-449-90765-1*) Ballantine Bks. (Fawcett).

—Till the Old Men Die. 1993. 275p. mass mkt. 4.50 o.s.i (*0-449-22133-4*, Fawcett) Ballantine Bks.

—Where the Bodies Are Buried. (Jeri Howard Mystery Ser.). 1999. 304p. mass mkt. 6.50 o.s.i (*0-449-00322-1*); 1998. 288p. 23.50 o.s.i (*0-449-00198-9*) Ballantine Bks. (Fawcett).

—Witness to Evil. 1998. 21.95 (*0-449-91060-1*); 1998. 304p. mass mkt. 6.50 (*0-449-22471-6*); 1997. 304p. 21.95 o.s.i (*0-449-00042-7*) Ballantine Bks. (Fawcett).

Day, A. Grove. Great California Stories. 1991. 268p. pap. text 13.95 (*0-8032-6583-2*, Bison Bks.) Univ. of Nebraska Pr.

Day, A. Grove, ed. Great California Stories. 1991. viii, 268p. 35.00 o.p. (*0-8032-1688-2*) Univ. of Nebraska Pr.

Day, A. Steven. Generations. Diaz, Arthur S., ed. 2001. pap. 8.99 (*0-9705259-2-3*); (Illus.). ix, 545p. 27.95 (*0-9705259-4-X*) St. Aztec Publishing.

Day, Dianne. The Bohemian Murders. 1998. (Fremont Jones Mystery Ser.). 288p. reprint ed. mass mkt. 6.50 (*0-553-57412-4*, Crimeline) Bantam Bks.

—The Bohemian Murders: A Fremont Jones Mystery. l.t. ed. 1999. 25.95 (*1-57490-217-2*) Beeler, Thomas T. Publisher.

—The Bohemian Murders: A Fremont Jones Mystery. 1997. 256p. 21.95 o.s.i (*0-385-47923-9*) Doubleday Publishing.

—Emperor Norton's Ghost. 1999. (Fremont Jones Mystery Ser.). 336p. mass mkt. 6.50 (*0-553-58078-7*) Bantam Bks.

—Emperor Norton's Ghost, , unabr. ed. 1999. (Fremont Jones Mystery Ser.). audio 56.00 (*0-7366-4505-5*, 4920) Books on Tape, Inc.

—Fire & Fog. 1997. 288p. mass mkt. 6.50 (*0-553-56922-8*, Crimeline) Bantam Bks.

—Fire & Fog. 2000. audio 48.00 (*0-7366-4839-9*); (Fremont Jones Mystery Ser.: 2). audio 36.00 Books on Tape, Inc.

—Fire & Fog. 1996. 320p. 21.00 o.s.i (*0-385-47550-0*) Doubleday Publishing.

—The Strange Files of Fremont Jones. 1996. (Fremont Jones Mystery Ser.: Vol. 1). 272p. mass mkt. 5.99 (*0-553-56921-X*, Crimeline) Bantam Bks.

—The Strange Files of Fremont Jones. 1999. audio 48.00 (*0-7366-4788-0*); Set. 2000. audio 48.00 Books on Tape, Inc.

—The Strange Files of Fremont Jones. 1995. 240p. 19.95 o.s.i (*0-385-47549-7*) Doubleday Publishing.

—The Strange Files of Fremont Jones. l.t. ed. 1996. (Niagara Large Print Ser.). 336p. 29.50 o.p. (*0-7089-5824-9*, Ulverscroft) Thorpe, F. A. Pubs. GBR. *Dist:* Ulverscroft Large Print Bks., Ltd.

De Csipkay, Nicolette & De Csipkay, Francesca. Black Umbrella Stories. 2003. (*0-9703165-7-7*) Starcherone Bks.

De la Pena, Terri. Latin Satins. 1994. (Djuna Bks.). 220p. (Orig.). pap. 10.95 (*1-878067-52-4*, Seal Pr.) Avalon Publishing Group.

Dean, Donna. Deep Six: A Novel of Life, Death, Deception & Betrayal. 2001. 224p. pap. 14.95 (*1-889901-19-9*, Palo Alto Bks.) Glencannon Pr.

Deaver, Jeffery. The Blue Nowhere: A Novel. 2001. E-Book 9.99 (*1-58945-684-X*) Adobe Systems, Inc.

—The Blue Nowhere: A Novel. 2001. 544p. E-Book 7.99 (*0-7434-3517-6*, Pocket); 432p. pap. 16.00 (*0-7432-1514-1*, Simon & Schuster); (Illus.). 432p. 26.00 (*0-684-87127-0*, Simon & Schuster); E-Book 9.99 (*0-7432-1166-9*, Simon & Schuster); 608p. pap. 26.00 (*0-7432-3048-5*, Simon & Schuster); 608p. 26.00 (*0-7432-1336-X*, Simon & Schuster) Simon & Schuster.

—The Blue Nowhere: A Novel. 2001. E-Book 9.99 (*0-7410-0379-1*) SoftBook Pr.

Debin, David. The Big O: An Albie Marx Caper. 1994. 256p. 19.95 o.p. (*0-7867-0005-X*, Carroll & Graf Pubs.) Avalon Publishing Group.

—Murder Live at Five. 1995. 304p. 21.00 o.p. (*0-7867-0190-0*, Carroll & Graf Pubs.) Avalon Publishing Group.

DeCure, John. Bluebird Rising: A Mystery. 2003. 384p. 25.95 (*0-312-27308-8*, Saint Martin's Minotaur) St. Martin's Pr.

Decure, John. Reef Dance. 2001. 384p. 24.95 (*0-312-27297-9*, Saint Martin's Minotaur) St. Martin's Pr.

Dedman, Stephen. The Art of Arrow Cutting. 2001. 304p. mass mkt. 6.99 (*0-8125-4534-6*); 1999. 284p. pap. 13.95 (*0-312-86832-4*); 1997. 320p. 22.95 (*0-312-86320-9*) Doherty, Tom Assocs., LLC. (Tor Bks.).

—Foreign Bodies. 286p. 2000. pap. 14.95 (*0-312-87259-3*); 1999. 23.95 (*0-312-86864-2*) Doherty, Tom Assocs., LLC. (Tor Bks.).

Deighton, Len. Violent Ward. l.t. ed. 1995. pap. 18.95 o.p. (*0-7927-2022-9*); 1994. 19.95 o.p. (*0-7927-2023-7*) BBC Audiobooks America.

—Violent Ward. 1993. 416p. 23.00 o.p. (*0-06-017938-4*) HarperTrade.

Delacorte, Peter. Time on My Hands. 2000. E-Book 23.00 (*0-684-86459-2*); 1998. (Illus.). 400p. pap. 14.00 o.s.i (*0-671-02324-1*) Simon & Schuster. (Scribner).

—Time on My Hands: A Novel with Photographs. 1997. 397p. 23.00 (*0-684-82651-8*, Scribner) Simon & Schuster.

Delinsky, Barbara. Coast Road. unabr. ed. 2000. 8p. audio 69.95 (*0-7927-2362-7*, CSL 251, Chivers Sound Library) BBC Audiobooks America.

—Coast Road. l.t. ed. 1998. (Large Print Book Ser.). 26.95 o.p. (*1-56895-666-5*, Wheeler Publishing, Inc.) Gale Group.

—Coast Road. 2003. 480p. mass mkt. 5.99 (*0-7434-6717-5*, Pocket); 1999. E-Book 24.00 (*0-684-86788-5*, Simon & Schuster); 1998. 480p. pap. 7.99 (*0-671-02604-6*, Pocket); 1998. 368p. (gr. 10 up). 24.00 o.s.i (*0-684-84576-8*, Simon & Schuster); 1998. 365p. (*0-684-85575-5*, Simon & Schuster); 1999. 480p. reprint ed. mass mkt. 7.99 (*0-671-02766-2*, Pocket) Simon & Schuster.

—Coast Road. abr. ed. 1998. audio 18.00 (*0-671-58220-8*, 396067, Simon & Schuster Audioworks) Simon & Schuster Audio.

DeMarinis, Rick. The Mortician's Apprentice. 1994. 303p. 21.00 o.p. (*0-393-03662-6*) Norton, W. W. & Co., Inc.

—The Year of the Zinc Penny. l.t. ed. 1990. (General Ser.). 288p. lib. bdg. 19.95 o.p. (*0-8161-5056-7*, Macmillan Reference USA) Gale Group.

—The Year of the Zinc Penny. 1990. 176p. reprint ed. pap. 9.00 o.p. (*0-06-097339-0*, Perennial) HarperTrade.

—The Year of the Zinc Penny. 1989. 17.95 o.p. (*0-393-02758-9*) Norton, W. W. & Co., Inc.

—The Year of the Zinc Penny. 1999. pap. 18.95 (*0-670-82575-1*) Viking Penguin.

Dentinger, Jane. Dead Pan: A Jocelyn O'Roarke Mystery. 1992. (Jocelyn O'Roarke Mystery Ser.). 256p. 19.00 o.p. (*0-670-84108-0*, Viking) Viking Penguin.

Devon, Gary. Wedding Night. 1997. pap. 5.99 (*0-380-72812-5*, Avon Bks.) Morrow/Avon.

—Wedding Night. 1995. 252p. 21.00 (*0-684-80183-3*, Simon & Schuster) Simon & Schuster.

Dick, Philip K. The Broken Bubble. 1988. 288p. 16.95 o.p. (*1-55710-012-8*, Morrow, William & Co.) Morrow/Avon.

—Mary & the Giant. 1987. 224p. 16.95 o.p. (*0-87795-850-5*, Morrow, William & Co.) Morrow/Avon.

—Mary & the Giant. 1989. 240p. pap. 8.95 o.p. (*0-312-03398-2*, Saint Martin's Griffin) St. Martin's Pr.

—A Scanner Darkly. 1979. (Del Rey Bk.). mass mkt. 1.95 o.s.i (*0-345-26064-3*) Ballantine Bks.

—A Scanner Darkly. 1984. 224p. mass mkt. 2.50 o.p. (*0-87997-923-2*) DAW Bks., Inc.

—A Scanner Darkly. 1991. 288p. pap. 12.00 (*0-679-73665-4*, Vintage) Knopf Publishing Group.

Dickey, Eric Jerome. Between Lovers. 2002. 400p. mass mkt. 7.50 (*0-451-20467-0*, Signet Bks.) NAL.

—Between Lovers: A Novel. 2001. 320p. 23.95 o.p. (*0-525-94603-9*, Dutton) Dutton/Plume.

—Between Lovers: A Novel. l.t. ed. 2002. 28.95 (*1-58724-172-2*, Wheeler Publishing, Inc.) Gale Group.

—Cheaters. 1999. 224p. 24.95 o.s.i (*0-525-94386-2*) Dutton/Plume.

—Cheaters. 2000. 448p. mass mkt. 7.50 (*0-451-19407-1*, Signet Bks.) NAL.

—Cheaters. abr. ed. 1999. audio 18.95 (*0-14-180024-0*, Penguin AudioBooks) Viking Penguin.

—Liar's Game. 2000. 336p. 23.95 o.s.i (*0-525-94483-4*) Dutton/Plume.

—Liar's Game. l.t. ed. 2000. (Wheeler Large Print Book Ser.). 28.95 (*1-56895-986-9*, Wheeler Publishing, Inc.) Gale Group.

—Liar's Game. 2001. 400p. reprint ed. mass mkt. 7.50 (*0-451-20134-5*, Signet Bks.) NAL.

—Sister, Sister. 1996. 256p. 23.95 (*0-525-94126-6*) Dutton/Plume.

—Sister, Sister. 1997. 368p. mass mkt. 7.50 (*0-451-18802-0*, Signet Bks.) NAL.

—Sister, Sister. 1997. 13.04 (*0-606-15705-0*) Turtleback Bks.

—Sister Sister. 2000. 256p. pap. 13.95 (*0-451-20101-9*, Signet Bks.) NAL.

—Thieves' Paradise: A Novel. 2002. 320p. 19.95 (*0-525-94663-2*, Dutton) Dutton/Plume.

Didion, Joan. Play It As It Lays. 1983. 266p. mass mkt. 3.95 o.s.i (*0-671-49590-9*, Pocket) Simon & Schuster.

—Run River. 1961. 18.95 (*0-8392-1094-9*) Astor-Honor, Inc.

Diehl, William. Eureka. 2003. 480p. mass mkt. 7.99 (*0-345-41147-1*, Fawcett); 2002. 448p. 25.00 (*0-345-41146-3*, Ballantine Bks.) Ballantine Bks.

—Eureka. l.t. ed. 2002. (Mystery Ser.). 737p. 30.95 (*0-7862-4416-X*) Thorndike Pr.

DiGirolamo, Vincent. Whispers under the Wharf. 1990. 144p. (J). pap. 8.95 o.p. (*0-931832-52-7*) Fithian Pr.

Dillon, Millicent. A Version of Love: A Novel. 2003. 288p. 23.95 (*0-393-05216-8*) Norton, W. W. & Co., Inc.

Divakaruni, Chitra Banerjee. The Mistress of Spices. 1997. 352p. 22.95 o.s.i (*0-385-48237-X*) Doubleday Publishing.

—The Mistress of Spices: A Novel. 1998. 352p. pap. 12.95 (*0-385-48238-8*, Knopf Bks. for Young Readers) Random Hse. Children's Bks.

Doherty, Patricia. The Face of Evil. 2001. 220p. pap. 13.95 (*0-87714-239-4*); 2000. E-Book 6.95 (*0-87714-618-7*) Denlingers Pubs., Ltd.

Dold, Gaylord. Schedule 2, Vol. 1. 1996. 256p. text 21.95 o.p. (*0-312-14730-9*, Saint Martin's Minotaur) St. Martin's Pr.

Donahue, Marilyn. Reach with All Your Heart. 1988. (Quick Fox Line Ser.). Orig. Title: To Catch a Golden Ring. 224p. (YA). pap. 4.49 o.p. (*1-55513-755-5*) Cook Communications Ministries.

—To Catch a Golden Ring. 1980. (J). (gr. 4-9). pap. 2.95 o.p. (*0-89191-330-0*) Cook Communications Ministries.

Donnelly, Nisa. The Love Songs of Phoenix Bay. (Stonewall Inn Editions Ser.). 1995. 320p. pap. 12.95 o.p. (*0-312-13561-0*, Saint Martin's Griffin); 1994. 304p. 13.99 o.p. (*0-312-11391-9*) St. Martin's Pr.

Douglas, John E. Man Down: A Broken Wings Thriller. 2002. 336p. 24.00 (*0-671-02392-6*, Atria) Simon & Schuster.

Douglas, John E. & Olshaker, Mark. Broken Wings. l.t. ed. 2000. (G. K. Hall Core Ser.). 570p. 29.95 (*0-7838-9027-3*, Macmillan Reference USA) Gale Group.

—Broken Wings. 1999. 336p. 24.00 o.s.i (*0-671-02391-8*, Atria); 2001. 384p. reprint ed. pap. 7.99 (*0-671-00395-X*, Pocket) Simon & Schuster.

Douglas, Kirk. Dance with the Devil. l.t. ed. 1994. 554p. lib. bdg. 23.95 o.p. (*0-8161-7464-4*, Macmillan Reference USA) Gale Group.

—Dance with the Devil. abr. ed. 1993. 15.95 o.p. (*1-55800-406-8*) NewStar Media, Inc.

—Dance with the Devil. 1992. 3.99 o.p. (*0-517-08346-9*) Random Hse. Value Publishing.

—Dance with the Devil. 1991. 384p. mass mkt. 5.99 o.s.i (*0-446-36191-7*) Warner Bks., Inc.

Doumani, Carol. Indiscretions. unabr. ed. 1999. audio 29.95 (*0-7366-4480-6*) Books on Tape, Inc.

—Indiscretions. 1999. 336p. 25.00 (*0-9642359-9-4*) Wave Publishing.

Downing, Warwick. A Lingering Doubt. Isaacson, Dana, ed. 1993. 320p. (Orig.). mass mkt. 4.99 (*0-671-76034-3*, Pocket) Simon & Schuster.

Drinkard, Michael. Disobedience. 1993. 324p. 21.95 (*0-393-03478-X*) Norton, W. W. & Co., Inc.

—Disobedience. 1996. (California Fiction Ser.). 349p. pap. 14.95 (*0-520-20683-5*) Univ. of California Pr.

Drury, Joan M. The Other Side of Silence. 1993. 256p. pap. 9.95 (*0-933216-92-0*) Spinsters Ink Bks.

Dubus, Andre, III. House of Sand & Fog: A Novel. 2000. (Vintage Contemporaries Ser.). 368p. pap. 14.00 o.s.i (*0-375-70841-3*); pap. 14.00 (*0-375-72734-5*) Knopf Publishing Group. (Vintage).

—House of Sand & Fog: A Novel. E-Book 14.00 (*0-393-10407-9*); 1999. (Illus.). 368p. 24.95 (*0-393-04697-4*); 1999. E-Book 14.00 (*0-393-10410-9*) Norton, W. W. & Co., Inc.

—House of Sand & Fog: A Novel. l.t. ed. (Paperback Bestsellers Ser.). 2002. 613p. pap. 28.95 (*0-7862-3236-6*); 2001. 664p. 31.95 (*0-7862-3235-8*) Thorndike Pr.

—House of Sand & Fog: A Novel. 2000. 20.05 (*0-606-20293-5*) Turtleback Bks.

Due, Linnea. Life Savings. 1992. 250p. (Orig.). pap. 10.95 o.p. (*0-933216-89-0*) Spinsters Ink Bks.

Dukore, Margaret M. Bloom: A Novel. 1985. 304p. 17.95 o.p. (*0-531-09708-0*, Watts, Franklin) Scholastic Library Publishing.

Dunaway, Laramie. Earth Angel. 1995. 384p. 21.95 o.p. (*0-446-51835-2*) Warner Bks., Inc.

—Lessons in Survival. 1994. (Fresh Voices Ser.). 424p. 30.00 (*0-446-51700-3*) Warner Bks., Inc.

Duncan, Lois. Summer of Fear. 2002. (Illus.). (J). 13.38 (*0-7587-8962-9*) Book Wholesalers, Inc.

—Summer of Fear. 1976. 252p. (J). (gr. 7-12). 15.95 o.p. (*0-316-19548-0*) Little Brown & Co.

—Summer of Fear. (YA). (gr. 7 up). 224p. pap. 4.99 (*0-8072-1372-1*); 1987. audio 15.98 (*0-8072-1852-9*, JRH118SP) Random Hse. Audio Publishing Group. (Listening Library).

—Summer of Fear. 1977. 208p. (YA). (gr. 7-12). mass mkt. 5.50 (*0-440-98324-X*, Laurel Leaf) Random Hse. Children's Bks.

—Summer of Fear. unabr. ed. 1998. (YA). (gr. 8). audio 44.00 (*0-7887-1817-7*, 95283E7); Set (gr. 5). audio 56.75 (*0-7887-1844-4*, 40624); Set (gr. 5). audio 109.80 (*0-7887-2790-7*, 46478) Recorded Bks., LLC.

—Summer of Fear. 1976. (Laurel-Leaf Suspense Ser.). (J). 11.04 (*0-606-02179-5*) Turtleback Bks.

Dunlap, Susan. As a Favor. 1991. 208p. mass mkt. 5.99 o.s.i (*0-440-20999-4*) Dell Publishing.

—As a Favor. 1984. 192p. 12.95 o.p. (*0-312-05594-3*) St. Martin's Pr.

—The Bohemian Connection. 1994. 240p. pap. 15.00 o.s.i (*0-440-61356-6*); mass mkt. 5.50 o.s.i (*0-440-21569-2*) Dell Publishing.

—The Bohemian Connection. 1985. 192p. 12.95 o.p. (*0-312-08745-4*, 087454) St. Martin's Pr.

—Cop Out. unabr. ed. 1997. audio 44.95 (*0-7861-1192-5*, 1949) Blackstone Audio Bks., Inc.

—Cop Out. 1998. (Jill Smith Mystery Ser.). 352p. mass mkt. 5.99 o.s.i (*0-440-22479-9*) Dell Publishing.

—Cop Out: A Jill Smith Mystery. 1997. 304p. 20.95 o.s.i (*0-385-31600-3*, Delacorte Pr.) Dell Publishing.

—Death & Taxes. l.t. ed. 1992. 24.95 o.p. (*0-7927-1329-X*); pap. 20.95 o.p. (*0-7927-1328-1*) BBC Audiobooks America.

—Diamond in the Buff. 1991. 192p. mass mkt. 5.50 o.s.i (*0-440-20788-6*) Dell Publishing.

—Diamond in the Buff. 1990. 176p. 14.95 o.p. (*0-312-03814-3*, Saint Martin's Minotaur) St. Martin's Pr.

—A Dinner to Die For. 1989. 240p. mass mkt. 5.99 o.s.i (*0-440-20495-X*) Dell Publishing.

—A Dinner to Die For. 1987. 224p. 15.95 o.p. (*0-312-01019-2*, Saint Martin's Minotaur) St. Martin's Pr.

—An Equal Opportunity Death. 1994. 240p. mass mkt. 5.50 o.s.i (*0-440-21566-8*) Dell Publishing.

—An Equal Opportunity Death: A Mystery. 1984. 192p. 12.95 o.p. (*0-312-25775-9*) St. Martin's Pr.

—High Fall. 1995. (Kiernan O'Shaugnessy Mystery Ser.). 320p. mass mkt. 5.99 o.s.i (*0-440-21560-9*) Dell Publishing.

—High Fall. l.t. ed. 1995. (Large Print Bks.). pap. 20.95 (*1-56895-093-4*, Wheeler Publishing, Inc.) Gale Group.

—Karma. 1991. 240p. pap. 15.00 o.s.i (*0-440-61365-5*); mass mkt. 5.99 o.s.i (*0-440-20982-X*) Dell Publishing.

—Karma. 1991. reprint ed. 18.95 o.p. (*0-7278-4229-3*) Severn Hse. Pubs., Ltd.

—The Last Annual Slugfest. 1994. 256p. mass mkt. 4.99 o.s.i (*0-440-21558-7*) Dell Publishing.

—The Last Annual Slugfest. 1986. 224p. 14.95 o.p. (*0-312-46969-1*) St. Martin's Pr.

—No Immunity: A Kiernan O'Shaughnessy Mystery. 1999. (Kiernan O'Shaugnessy Mystery Ser.). 352p. mass mkt. 5.99 o.s.i (*0-440-22480-2*) Dell Publishing.

—No Immunity: A Kiernan O'Shaughnessy Mystery. l.t. ed. 1999. pap. 23.95 (*1-56895-782-3*, Wheeler Publishing, Inc.) Gale Group.

—Not Exactly a Brahmin. 1991. 240p. mass mkt. 4.99 o.s.i (*0-440-20998-6*) Dell Publishing.

—Not Exactly a Brahmin. 1985. (Jill Smith Mystery Ser.). 192p. 12.95 o.p. (*0-312-57947-0*) St. Martin's Pr.

—Pious Deception. 1990. 256p. mass mkt. 5.99 o.s.i (*0-440-20746-0*) Dell Publishing.

—Rogue Wave. 1992. 272p. mass mkt. 5.99 o.s.i (*0-440-21197-2*) Dell Publishing.

—Rogue Wave. 1994. 3.99 o.p. (*0-517-13047-5*) Random Hse. Value Publishing.

—Sudden Exposure. unabr. ed. 1998. audio 44.95 Blackstone Audio Bks., Inc.

—Sudden Exposure. 1997. 320p. pap. 19.00 o.s.i (*0-440-61350-7*); mass mkt. 5.50 o.s.i (*0-440-21563-3*) Dell Publishing.

—Sudden Exposure. abr. ed. 1996. (Jill Smith Mystery Ser.). audio 16.99 (*0-88646-408-0*, 7408) Durkin Hayes Publishing Ltd.

—Time Expired. l.t. ed. 1994. 24.95 o.p. (*0-7927-1779-1*); pap. 22.95 o.p. (*0-7927-1778-3*) BBC Audiobooks America.

—Time Expired. 1994. (Jill Smith Mystery Ser.). 304p. mass mkt. 5.99 o.s.i (*0-440-21683-4*) Dell Publishing.

—Too Close to the Edge. 1989. 224p. reprint ed. mass mkt. 5.50 o.s.i (*0-440-20356-2*) Dell Publishing.

—Too Close to the Edge. 1987. 240p. 14.95 o.p. (*0-312-00198-3*) St. Martin's Pr.

Dunne, Dominick. Another City, Not My Own: A Novel in the Form of a Memoir. 1999. mass mkt. 7.99 (*0-449-00419-8*, Fawcett); 1998. 406p. mass mkt. 7.99 (*0-345-43051-4*); 1998. mass mkt. o.p. (*0-345-42703-3*) Ballantine Bks.

—Another City, Not My Own: A Novel in the Form of a Memoir. 1998. mass mkt. o.s.i (*0-553-57986-X*) Bantam Bks.

—Another City, Not My Own: A Novel in the Form of a Memoir. l.t. ed. 1997. pap. 25.00 o.p. (*0-7838-8248-3*, Macmillan Reference USA) Gale Group.

—Another City, Not My Own: A Novel in the Form of a Memoir. abr. ed. 1997. 25.00 o.p. (*0-7871-1612-2*) NewStar Media, Inc.

Dunne, John Gregory. Playland. 1995. 512p. pap. 13.95 o.s.i (*0-452-27495-8*, Plume) Dutton/Plume.

Duran, Miguel. Don't Spit on My Corner. 1992. 187p. (gr. 8-12). pap. 9.50 o.p. (*1-55885-042-2*) Arte Publico Pr.

Dwiggins, Toni. Interrupt. 1998. 317p. text 20.00 (*0-7881-5679-9*) DIANE Publishing Co.

—Interrupt. 1995. 319p. pap. text 4.99 o.p. (*0-8125-2037-8*); 1993. 320p. 19.95 o.p. (*0-312-85345-9*) Doherty, Tom Assocs., LLC. (Tor Bks.).

Dwyer, Kelly. Self-Portrait with Ghosts. 2000. 272p. mass mkt. 6.99 o.s.i (*0-425-17696-7*) Berkley Publishing Group.

—Self-Portrait with Ghosts. 1999. 320p. 23.95 o.p. (*0-399-14440-4*, G. P. Putnam's Sons) Penguin Group (USA) Inc.

Easton, Robert. The Saga of California: Power & Glory. 1996. 400p. reprint ed. mass mkt. 4.99 (*0-8439-4074-3*, Leisure Bks.) Dorchester Publishing Co., Inc.

—This Promised Land. 1988. (Saga of California Ser.: Vol. 1). 328p. (Orig.). (C). reprint ed. lib. bdg. 35.00 o.p. (*0-8095-4050-9*) Millefleurs.

Easton, Robert Olney. Blood & Money. l.t. ed. 1999. (Western Ser.). 477p. 24.95 o.p. (*0-7862-1166-0*) Thorndike Pr.

Eberhardt, Michael C. Body of a Crime. 1994. 368p. 19.95 o.p. (*0-525-93623-8*, Dutton) Dutton/Plume.

—Body of a Crime. unabr. ed. 1998. audio 103.95 (*1-85903-136-6*) Magna Story Sound GBR. *Dist:* Ulverscroft Large Print Bks., Ltd.

—Body of a Crime. 1995. 448p. mass mkt. 5.99 o.s.i (*0-451-40569-2*, Onyx) NAL.

—Body of a Crime. l.t. ed. 1997. (Niagara Large Print Ser.). 546p. 29.50 o.p. (*0-7089-5803-6*, Ulverscroft) Thorpe, F. A. Pubs. GBR. *Dist:* Ulverscroft Large Print Bks., Ltd., Ulverscroft Large Print Canada, Ltd.

Ebershoff, David. Pasadena: A Novel. 2003. 520p. pap. 13.95 (*0-8129-6848-4*, Modern Library) Random House Adult Trade Publishing Group.

—Pasadena: A Novel. 2002. (Illus.). 512p. 24.95 (*0-375-50456-7*) Random Hse., Inc.

Edwards, Jane. Tangled Heritage. 1992. 192p. 13.95 o.p. (*0-8034-8942-0*) Bouregy, Thomas & Co., Inc.

—Tangled Heritage. l.t. ed. 1999. (Thorndike Candlelight Romance Ser.). 213p. 30.00 o.p. (*0-7862-1739-1*, Macmillan Reference USA) Gale Group.

—A Whisper of Suspicion. 2002. (Five Star First Edition Romance Ser.). 249p. 26.95 (*0-7862-3747-3*, Five Star) Gale Group.

Egan, Lesley. Chain of Violence. 1985. (Crime Club Ser.). 192p. 12.95 o.p. (*0-385-19807-8*) Doubleday Publishing.

—Little Boy Lost. 1983. (Crime Club Ser.). (Illus.). 192p. 11.95 o.p. (*0-385-18840-4*) Doubleday Publishing.

—Little Boy Lost. l.t. ed. 1986. (Ulverscroft Large Print Ser.). 384p. 29.99 o.p. (*0-7089-1417-9*, Ulverscroft) Thorpe, F. A. Pubs. GBR. *Dist:* Ulverscroft Large Print Bks., Ltd., Ulverscroft Large Print Canada, Ltd.

—Look Back on Death. 1978. 7.95 o.p. (*0-385-14303-6*) Doubleday Publishing.

—Look Back on Death. l.t. ed. 1981. reprint ed. 9.95 o.p. (*0-89621-267-X*) Thorndike Pr.

—The Miser. 1981. (Crime Club Ser.). 192p. 9.95 o.p. (*0-385-17626-0*) Doubleday Publishing.

—The Miser. l.t. ed. 1984. 368p. o.p. (*0-7089-1069-6*, Ulverscroft) Thorpe, F. A. Pubs.

—Motive in Shadow. 1980. (Crime Club Ser.). 10.95 o.p. (*0-385-15605-7*) Doubleday Publishing.

—Motive in Shadow. l.t. ed. 1986. (Ulverscroft Large Print Ser.). 384p. 29.99 o.p. (*0-7089-1471-3*, Ulverscroft) Thorpe, F. A. Pubs. GBR. *Dist:* Ulverscroft Large Print Bks., Ltd., Ulverscroft Large Print Canada, Ltd.

Elkjer, Thom. Hook, Line & Murder. 1997. 240p. 21.95 o.p. (*1-885173-38-5*) Write Way Publishing.

—Hook, Line & Murder: A Rigel Lynx Mystery. 1999. (WWL Mystery Ser.: Vol. 323). 256p. pap. (*0-373-26323-6*, Worldwide Library) Harlequin Enterprises, Ltd.

Ellis, Bret Easton. The Informers. 1994. 240p. 22.00 o.s.i (*0-679-43587-5*) Knopf, Alfred A. Inc.

—The Informers. 1995. 240p. pap. 12.00 (*0-679-74324-3*); pap. 7.00 o.p. (*0-679-76085-7*) Random Hse., Inc.

—Less Than Zero. 1998. 208p. pap. 12.00 (*0-679-78149-8*, Vintage) Knopf Publishing Group.

—Less Than Zero. 1985. 15.45 o.p. (*0-671-54329-6*, Simon & Schuster) Simon & Schuster.

—Less Than Zero. 1986. 14.95 o.p. (*0-671-62140-8*, Simon & Schuster Audioworks) Simon & Schuster Audio.

—Less Than Zero. 208p. 1987. mass mkt. 3.95 o.p. (*0-14-010927-7*, Penguin Bks.); 1986. pap. 11.95 o.s.i (*0-14-008894-6*) Viking Penguin.

Ellroy, James. Because the Night. 1987. pap. 5.99 (*0-380-70063-8*, Avon Bks.) Morrow/Avon.

—Because the Night. 1986. 15.95 (*0-89296-071-X*) Mysterious Pr.

—The Black Dahlia. unabr. collector's ed. 1990. (L. A. Quartet). audio 88.00 (*0-7366-1816-3*, 2652) Books on Tape, Inc.

—The Black Dahlia. 1987. 336p. 16.95 (*0-89296-206-2*) Mysterious Pr.

—The Black Dahlia. 1998. 336p. pap. 13.99 (*0-446-67436-2*); 1988. 384p. mass mkt. 5.99 (*0-445-40525-2*) Warner Bks., Inc.

—Blood on the Moon. 1986. 14.45 o.p. (*0-89296-069-8*) Mysterious Pr.

—Brown's Requiem. 1998. 256p. pap. 13.00 (*0-380-73177-0*); 1981. pap. 4.99 (*0-380-78741-5*) Morrow/Avon. (Avon Bks.).

—Clandestine. 1999. 336p. pap. 12.95 (*0-380-80529-4*); 1982. 352p. mass mkt. 5.99 (*0-380-81141-3*) Morrow/Avon. (Avon Bks.).

—Hollywood Nocturnes. unabr. collector's ed. 1996. audio 48.00 (*0-7366-3255-7*, 3912) Books on Tape, Inc.

—Hollywood Nocturnes. 1995. 368p. mass mkt. 5.99 o.s.i (*0-440-22098-X*) Dell Publishing.

—Hollywood Nocturnes. 1994. (Illus.). 272p. bds. 20.00 o.s.i (*1-883402-54-9*, Scribner) Simon & Schuster.

—Killer on the Road. 1999. 272p. pap. 13.00 (*0-380-80896-X*, Perennial) HarperTrade.

—Killer on the Road. 1986. 288p. mass mkt. 5.99 (*0-380-89934-5*, Avon Bks.) Morrow/Avon.

—L. A. Confidential. unabr. collector's ed. 1991. (L. A. Quartet). audio 80.00 (*0-7366-2012-5*, 116014) Books on Tape, Inc.

—L. A. Confidential. 1990. 75.00 o.p. (*0-89296-424-3*); 19.95 (*0-89296-293-3*) Mysterious Pr.

—L. A. Confidential. abr. ed. 2001. audio 9.99 (*0-553-70244-0*); Set. 1997. audio 18.00 o.s.i (*0-375-40213-6*, 390277) Random Hse. Audio Publishing Group. (RH Audio).

—L. A. Confidential. 1997. 480p. pap. text 9.23 (*0-09-925508-1*) Random Hse. Value Publishing.

—L. A. Confidential. 1997. (*0-446-60605-7*); 1997. 512p. pap. 14.95 (*0-446-67424-9*); 1991. mass mkt. 5.99 (*0-446-40010-6*) Warner Bks., Inc.

—L. A. Noir. 2000. 648p. 25.00 (*0-89296-686-6*); E-Book 14.95 (*0-7595-6040-4*); 600p. E-Book 14.95 (*0-7595-8042-1*); 600p. E-Book 14.95 (*0-7595-9046-X*); 600p. E-Book 14.95 (*0-7595-4041-1*); 600p. E-Book 14.95 (*0-7595-0040-1*) Mysterious Pr.

—Suicide Hill. 1986. 288p. 15.95 (*0-89296-235-6*) Mysterious Pr.

—Suicide Hill. 1989. mass mkt. 5.99 o.s.i (*0-445-40852-9*); 1987. mass mkt. 3.95 (*0-445-40585-6*, Mysterious Pr. Paperback Bks.) Warner Bks., Inc.

—White Jazz. 1997. 368p. pap. 13.00 o.s.i (*0-449-00088-5*, Fawcett) Ballantine Bks.

—White Jazz. unabr. collector's ed. 1992. (L. A. Quartet). audio 64.00 (*0-7366-2323-X*, 3103) Books on Tape, Inc.

—White Jazz. 2001. 368p. pap. 13.00 (*0-375-72736-1*, Vintage) Knopf Publishing Group.

—White Jazz: A Novel. 1993. (Los Angeles Mysteries Ser.). 368p. mass mkt. 5.99 o.s.i (*0-449-14841-6*, Fawcett) Ballantine Bks.

Ellroy, James, et al. Hollywood Nocturnes. 1998. 304p. pap. 13.95 (*0-385-33328-5*) Dell Publishing.

Elton, Ben. Popcorn. 2003. 320p. mass mkt. (*0-552-15101-7*, Corgi) Bantam Bks.

—Popcorn. 1998. 304p. pap. 13.95 (*0-312-19472-2*, Saint Martin's Griffin); 1997. 298p. 22.95 (*0-312-16965-5*) St. Martin's Pr.

Ely, Ron. East Beach. 1997. (Jake Sands Mystery Ser.). 304p. per. (*0-373-26227-2*, 1-26227-8, Worldwide Library) Harlequin Enterprises, Ltd.

—East Beach. 1995. 331p. 21.00 (*0-671-87281-8*, Simon & Schuster) Simon & Schuster.

—The East Beach, Set. abr. ed. 1995. 17.95 o.p. (*0-7871-0135-4*, 390701) NewStar Media, Inc.

—Night Shadows. 1996. per. (*0-373-26218-3*, 1-26218-7, Worldwide Library) Harlequin Enterprises, Ltd.

—Night Shadows. abr. ed. 1993. 16.95 o.p. (*0-7871-0003-X*) NewStar Media, Inc.

—Night Shadows. 1994. 20.00 (*0-671-87280-X*, Simon & Schuster) Simon & Schuster.

Ephron, Amy. Biodegradable Soap. 1991. 176p. 19.95 o.p. (*0-395-57227-4*) Houghton Mifflin Co.

Epstein, Leslie. Pandaemonium. 1998. 416p. pap. 14.95 (*0-312-18752-1*, Saint Martin's Griffin); 1997. 384p. 24.95 o.p. (*0-312-15622-7*) St. Martin's Pr.

—Pinto & Sons. 1990. 380p. 19.95 o.p. (*0-395-54704-0*) Houghton Mifflin Co.

—Pinto & Sons. 1992. 420p. pap. 9.95 o.p. (*0-393-30846-4*) Norton, W. W. & Co., Inc.

Erickson, Steve. Amnesiascope. 1997. 240p. pap. 12.00 o.p. (*0-8050-5361-1*, Owl Bks.) Holt, Henry & Co.

—Amnesiascope: A Novel. 1996. 88p. 23.00 o.p. (0-8050-3503-6) Holt, Henry & Co.
Escandon, Maria Amparo. Santitos: Sexo, Humor y Realismo en una Novela Magica. 1999. (SPA.). 288p. pap. 14.95 o.s.i (0-553-06098-8) Bantam Bks.
Estela, Linda. Reflections of a Healing Heart. 1994. pap. 4.95 (0-9624626-8-3) Astarte Shell Pr.
Estleman, Loren D. Black Powder, White Smoke. 2003. 288p. mass mkt. 6.99 (0-7653-4110-7); 2002. 320p. 24.95 (0-7653-0189-X) Doherty, Tom Assocs., LLC. (Forge Bks.).
—Black Powder, White Smoke. 2002. (Western Ser.). 26.95 (0-7862-4851-3) Thorndike Pr.
Eulo, Ken & Mauck, Joe. Claw. 1994. 22.00 o.s.i (0-671-79963-0, Simon & Schuster) Simon & Schuster.
—Claw. 320p. 3.98 o.p. (0-7651-0133-5) Smithmark Pubs., Inc.
—Claw. 1995. 319p. pap. text 5.50 (0-312-95595-2, St. Martin's Paperbacks) St. Martin's Pr.
Evans, Sheila. Stanley, California. 2003. (1-57962-094-9) Permanent Pr., The.
Eversz, Robert M. Shooting Elvis. 224p. 1996. pap. 21.00 o.p. (0-8021-1582-9); 1997. reprint ed. pap. 12.00 (0-8021-3501-3) Grove/Atlantic, Inc. (Grove Pr.).
Faber, Gail & Lasagna, Michele. Pasquala: The Story of a California Indian Girl. 1990. (Whispers Ser.). (Illus.). 95p. (J). (gr. 4-8). 12.95 (0-936480-07-6) Magpie Pubns.
Faherty, Terence. Come Back Dead. 1997. 336p. 22.00 o.p. (0-684-83084-1, Simon & Schuster) Simon & Schuster.
—Kill Me Again: A Scott Elliott Mystery. 1996. 304p. 22.00 o.p. (0-684-82688-7, Simon & Schuster) Simon & Schuster.
Fairbanks, Nancy. Chocolate Quake. 2003. 304p. mass mkt. 5.99 (0-425-18946-5, Prime Crime) Berkley Publishing Group.
—Chocolate Quake. l.t. ed. 2004. (Culinary Mystery with Recipes Ser.). 390p. pap. 24.95 (1-58724-617-1, Wheeler Publishing, Inc.) Gale Group.
Fairweather, Lori. Blood & Water: A Pacific Northwest Mystery. 1999. 321p. 24.00 (0-688-16118-9, Morrow, William & Co.) Morrow/Avon.
Farmer, Jerrilyn. Immaculate Reception. l.t. ed. 2002. (Mystery Ser.). 396p. 28.95 (0-7862-4755-X) Gale Group.
—Immaculate Reception. 1999. (Madeline Bean Catering Mysteries Ser.). 256p. mass mkt. 6.50 (0-380-79597-3, Avon Bks.) Morrow/Avon.
—Killer Wedding. 2000. (Madeline Bean Catering Mysteries Ser.). 256p. mass mkt. 6.50 (0-380-79598-1, Avon Bks.) Morrow/Avon.
—Sympathy for the Devil. 1998. (Madeline Bean Mystery Ser.). 256p. mass mkt. 5.99 (0-380-79596-5, Avon Bks.) Morrow/Avon.
—Sympathy for the Devil. l.t. ed. 2002. (Mystery Ser.). 404p. 28.95 (0-7862-4743-6) Thorndike Pr.
Farren, Mick. Darklost. 2000. 412p. 24.95 (0-312-86979-7, Tor Bks.) Doherty, Tom Assocs., LLC.
Farrington, Tim. The California Book of the Dead. 1998. (Illus.). 352p. pap. 21.95 (0-671-51959-X, Pocket) Simon & Schuster.
—The California Book of the Dead: A Novel. 1997. 352p. 23.00 o.p. (0-671-51960-3, Atria) Simon & Schuster.
Fast, Howard. The Establishment, 001. 1979. 11.95 o.p. (0-395-28160-1) Houghton Mifflin Co.
—The Immigrants, 001. 1977. 12.95 o.p. (0-395-25699-2) Houghton Mifflin Co.
—An Independent Woman. 1997. 340p. 25.00 (0-15-100271-1) Harcourt Trade Pubs.
—The Second Generation, 001. 1978. 10.95 o.p. (0-395-26683-1) Houghton Mifflin Co.
Febick, Walter. Different Voices: A Different Voice & Other Stories. 1999. (Illus.). 176p. pap. 12.95 (1-879194-26-0) GLB Pubs.
Feehan, Christine. Dark Challenge. 2000. 400p. mass mkt. 6.99 (0-505-52409-0, Love Spell) Dorchester Publishing Co., Inc.
—Dark Challenge. l.t. ed. 2003. 474p. 29.95 (1-58724-531-0, Wheeler Publishing, Inc.) Gale Group.
Feinsod, Ethan. The Habits of a Lifetime. 1992. 240p. 17.95 o.p. (0-312-08205-3, Saint Martin's Minotaur) St. Martin's Pr.
Fell, Doris Elaine. The Wedding Jewel. 1999. (Steeple Hill Love Inspired Ser.: Vol. 74). mass mkt. (0-373-87074-4, 1-87074-0, Harlequin Bks.) Harlequin Enterprises, Ltd.
Femling, Jean. Getting Mine. 1991. pap. text 18.95 o.p. (0-312-05437-8, Saint Martin's Minotaur) St. Martin's Pr.
—Hush, Money. 1989. 16.95 o.p. (0-312-02931-4, Saint Martin's Minotaur) St. Martin's Pr.
Ferrarella, Marie. Baby Talk. 1999. per. (0-373-48384-8, 1-48384-1, Harlequin Bks.) Harlequin Enterprises, Ltd.
Ferri, Richard S. Blossom River Drive: A Novel. 2000. 203p. pap. 13.95 (0-9676723-0-9) Panhelenic Pr.
Ferrigno, Robert. Dead Man's Dance. 1996. 336p. reprint ed. mass mkt. 6.99 o.s.i (0-425-15410-6) Berkley Publishing Group.
—Dead Man's Dance. 1995. 384p. 23.95 o.p. (0-399-14025-5, G. P. Putnam's Sons) Penguin Group (USA) Inc.
—Dead Silent. l.t. ed. 1998. 320p. mass mkt. 6.99 o.s.i (0-425-16149-8) Berkley Publishing Group.
—Dead Silent. 1996. 320p. 24.95 o.p. (0-399-14148-0, G. P. Putnam's Sons) Penguin Group (USA) Inc.
Files, Lolita. Blind Ambitions. 288p. 2000. 23.00 o.s.i (0-684-87144-0); 2001. reprint ed. pap. 13.00 (0-684-87145-9) Simon & Schuster. (Simon & Schuster).
Fillerup, Michael. Beyond the River: A Novel. 1995. 256p. (Orig.). pap. 14.95 o.p. (1-56085-068-X) Signature Bks., Inc.
Finch, Phillip. F2F. 1997. 320p. mass mkt. 6.50 o.s.i (0-553-57216-4) Bantam Bks.
—F2F: The Ultimate Thriller of High Tech Terror. abr. ed. 1996. audio 17.00 (0-671-52282-5, 393930, Simon & Schuster Audioworks) Simon & Schuster Audio.
—Paradise Junction. abr. ed. 1993. audio 16.99 (0-88646-362-9, LFP 7362) Durkin Hayes Publishing Ltd.
—Paradise Junction. 1994. mass mkt. 5.99 o.p. (0-312-95304-6, St. Martin's Paperbacks); 1993. 19.95 o.p. (0-312-08869-8) St. Martin's Pr.
Finney, Ernest J. The Lady with the Alligator Purse. 1992. 288p. 19.00 (0-944439-46-2) Clark City Pr.
—Winterchill. 1991. 240p. pap. 8.95 (0-380-71101-X, Avon Bks.); 1989. 256p. 16.95 o.p. (0-688-08305-6, Morrow, William & Co.) Morrow/Avon.
—Winterchill: A Novel. 1995. (Western Literature Ser.). 240p. pap. 18.00 (0-87417-258-6) Univ. of Nevada Pr.
—Words of My Roaring. 1998. (California Fiction Ser.). 380p. pap. text 16.95 (0-520-21638-5) Univ. of California Pr.
Fischer-Dixon, Eva. The Third Cloud: A Novel. 1900. 552p. pap. 26.99 (0-7388-0751-6); text 36.99 (0-7388-0750-8) Xlibris Corp.
Fisher, David E. Hostage One. 1990. mass mkt. 4.95 o.p. (0-312-92144-6, St. Martin's Paperbacks) St. Martin's Pr.
Fitch, Janet. White Oleander, Set. abr. ed. 1999. audio 24.98 Highsmith Inc.
—White Oleander. (Oprah's Book Club Selection Ser. ). 1999. pap. 7.99 (0-316-28508-0, Back Bay); 1999. 390p. (gr. 8). 24.95 (0-316-56932-1); 1999. 400p. 24.00 o.p. (0-316-28526-9); 2000. 464p. pap. 13.95 (0-316-28495-5, Back Bay) Little Brown & Co.
—White Oleander. unabr. ed. 1999. audio 96.00 (0-7887-3471-7, 95890E7); audio compact disk 112.00 (0-7887-3970-0, C1089E7) Recorded Bks., LLC.
—White Oleander. l.t. ed. 2002. 14.00 (1-4104-0081-6, Large Print Pr.); 2000. 613p. pap. 27.95 (0-7862-2166-6); 1999. 613p. 30.95 (0-7862-2095-3) Thorndike Pr.
—White Oleander. abr. ed. 1999. audio 24.98 (1-57042-821-2) Time Warner AudioBooks.
—White Oleander. 2000. 19.75 (0-606-19031-7) Turtleback Bks.
Fitch, Marian. The Seventh Heart. 1997. 320p. mass mkt. 5.99 o.s.i (0-441-00451-2) Ace Bks.
Fitzgerald, F. Scott. F. Scott Fitzgerald: The Love of The Last Tycoon. Bruccoli, Matthew J., ed. 1993. (Works of F. Scott Fitzgerald). (Illus.). 448p. 45.00 (0-521-40231-X) Cambridge Univ. Pr.
—The Love of the Last Tycoon. 1995. 17.05 (0-606-20777-5) Turtleback Bks.
Fletcher, Jessica & Bain, Donald. Blood on the Vine. 2001. (Murder She Wrote Ser.). 272p. mass mkt. 6.50 (0-451-20275-9, Signet Bks.) NAL.
—Murder, She Wrote: Martinis & Mayhem. 1995. (Murder She Wrote Ser.: Vol. 4). 304p. mass mkt. 6.50 (0-451-18512-9, Signet Bks.) NAL.
Fluke, Joanne. Deadly Memories. 1995. 352p. mass mkt. 4.50 o.s.i (0-8217-4841-6, Zebra Bks.) Kensington Publishing Corp.
Follett, Ken. The Hammer of Eden. 1999. 448p. mass mkt. (0-449-00677-8); 448p. mass mkt. 7.99 (0-449-22754-5, Fawcett); mass mkt. (0-449-00458-9, Ballantine Bks.) Ballantine Bks.
—The Hammer of Eden. l.t. ed. 1998. 672p. 25.95 o.p. (0-7838-0265-X, Macmillan Reference USA) Gale Group.
—The Hammer of Eden: A Novel. l.t. ed. 1998. 672p. pap. 25.95 o.s.i (0-375-70419-1) Random Hse., Inc.
Foreman, Walter C., Jr. Fairy Tale. 2003. 350p. 22.95 (1-880909-63-4) Baskerville Pubs., Inc.
Forrest, Katherine V. Amateur City. 1984. (Kate Delafield Mystery Ser.: Vol. 1). 224p. pap. 11.95 (0-930044-55-X) Naiad Pr., Inc.
—Apparition Alley. (Kate Delafield Mystery Ser.). 256p. 1997. 21.95 o.s.i (0-425-15966-3); 1998. reprint ed. mass mkt. 5.99 o.s.i (0-425-16632-5) Berkley Publishing Group. (Prime Crime).
—The Beverly Malibu. (Kate Delafield Mystery Ser.). 1989. 16.95 o.p. (0-941483-47-9); 1991. 288p. reprint ed. pap. 11.95 (0-941483-48-7) Naiad Pr., Inc.
—Flashpoint. 256p. 1995. pap. 10.95 o.p. (1-56280-079-5); 1994. 22.95 (1-56280-043-4) Naiad Pr., Inc.
—Liberty Square: A Kate Delafield Mystery. (Kate Delafield Mystery Ser.). 256p. 2000. pap. 13.00 o.s.i (0-425-17675-4); 1997. mass mkt. 5.99 o.s.i (0-425-15899-3); 1996. 21.95 o.s.i (0-425-15467-X) Berkley Publishing Group. (Prime Crime).
—Murder by Tradition. 288p. 1991. text 18.95 o.p. (0-941483-89-4); 1993. (Kate Delafield Mystery Ser.: Vol. 4). reprint ed. pap. 11.95 (1-56280-002-7) Naiad Pr., Inc.
Forster, R. A. Character Witness. 1997. 304p. mass mkt. 5.99 o.s.i (0-7860-0378-2, Pinnacle Bks.) Kensington Publishing Corp.
Forster, Suzanne. Come Midnight. (Orig.). mass mkt. 6.99 o.s.i (0-515-12946-1, Jove); 1995. 304p. mass mkt. 5.99 o.s.i (0-425-14565-4) Berkley Publishing Group.
—Shameless. l.t. ed. 2001. (Wheeler Large Print Book Ser.). 497p. 26.95 o.p. (1-58724-023-8, Wheeler Publishing, Inc.) Gale Group.
Foster, Alan Dean. The Mocking Program. 2003. 336p. mass mkt. 6.99 (0-446-61307-X); 2002. 288p. 24.95 (0-446-52774-2) Warner Bks., Inc. (Aspect).
Fowler, Earlene. Dove in the Window. l.t. ed. 2001. (Beeler Large Print Mystery Ser.). 310p. 25.95 (1-57490-368-3, Beeler Large Print Bks.) Beeler, Thomas T. Publisher.
—Dove in the Window. 1999. (Benni Harper Mystery Ser.). 320p. reprint ed. mass mkt. 6.99 (0-425-16894-8, Prime Crime) Berkley Publishing Group.
—Dove in the Window. 1999. 12.55 (0-606-22164-6) Turtleback Bks.
—Dove in the Window: A Benni Harper Mystery, No. 5. 1998. (Benni Harper Mystery Ser.). 304p. 21.95 o.s.i (0-425-16299-0) Berkley Publishing Group.
—Fool's Puzzle. l.t. ed. 1999. (Beeler Large Print Mystery Ser.). 25.95 (1-57490-211-3, Beeler Large Print Bks.) Beeler, Thomas T. Publisher.
—Fool's Puzzle. (Benni Harper Mystery Ser.). 1995. 256p. mass mkt. 6.99 (0-425-14545-X); 1994. 17.95 o.p. (0-425-14041-5) Berkley Publishing Group. (Prime Crime).
—Fool's Puzzle. 1995. 12.55 (0-606-22783-0) Turtleback Bks.
—Goose in the Pond. l.t. ed. 2001. (Beeler Large Print Mystery Ser.). 320p. 26.95 (1-57490-335-7, Beeler Large Print Bks.) Beeler, Thomas T. Publisher.
—Goose in the Pond. (Benni Harper Mystery Ser.: Vol. 4). 320p. 1998. mass mkt. 6.99 (0-425-16239-7); 1997. 21.95 o.s.i (0-425-15782-2) Berkley Publishing Group. (Prime Crime).
—Irish Chain. 320p. 1996. mass mkt. 6.99 (0-425-15137-9); 1995. 18.95 o.p. (0-425-14619-7, Prime Crime) Berkley Publishing Group.
—Mariner's Compass: A Benni Harper Mystery. l.t. ed. 2001. (Beeler Large Print Mystery Ser.). 338p. 26.95 (1-57490-401-9, Beeler Large Print Bks.) Beeler, Thomas T. Publisher.
—Mariner's Compass: A Benni Harper Mystery. (Benni Harper Mystery Ser.: Vol. 6). 336p. 2000. mass mkt. 6.99 (0-425-17408-5); 1999. 21.95 o.s.i (0-425-16891-3, Prime Crime) Berkley Publishing Group.
—Seven Sisters. (Benni Harper Mystery Ser.). 2000. 308p. 21.95 o.s.i (0-425-17296-1); 2001. 320p. reprint ed. mass mkt. 6.99 (0-425-17917-6) Berkley Publishing Group. (Prime Crime).
—Steps to the Altar. 2003. 320p. mass mkt. 6.99 (0-425-18944-9, Prime Crime) Berkley Publishing Group.
—Steps to the Altar. l.t. ed. 2002. (Wheeler Hardcover Ser.). 423p. 28.95 (1-58724-280-X, Wheeler Publishing, Inc.) Gale Group.
—Steps to the Altar: A Benni Harper Mystery. 2002. 320p. 22.95 (0-425-18349-1) Berkley Publishing Group.
Fowler, Karen Joy. The Jane Austen Book Club. 2004. 256p. 23.95 (0-399-15161-3) Putnam Publishing Group, The.
—Sister Noon. 2002. 336p. pap. 14.00 (0-452-28328-0, Plume) Dutton/Plume.
—Sister Noon. 2001. 288p. 24.95 o.p. (0-399-14750-0, Wood, Marian Bks.) Penguin Group (USA) Inc.
—Sister Noon. l.t. ed. 2001. (Women's Fiction Ser.). 423p. 28.95 (0-7862-3549-7) Thorndike Pr.
Fowles, John. Daniel Martin. 1997. 640p. pap. 12.95 (0-316-29039-4); 1977. 19.95 o.p. (0-316-28959-0) Little Brown & Co.
—Daniel Martin. 1978. mass mkt. 2.95 o.p. (0-451-08249-4); mass mkt. 4.50 o.p. (0-451-12210-0, AE2210); mass mkt. 3.50 o.p. (0-451-11484-1); 688p. mass mkt. 5.95 o.p. (0-451-16761-9) NAL. (Signet Bks.).
Fox, Paula. The Western Coast. 2001. 19p. pap. 13.00 (0-393-32286-6) Norton, W. W. & Co., Inc.
Fox, Zachary Alan. All Fall Down. 1997. 480p. mass mkt. 5.99 o.s.i (0-7860-0450-9, Pinnacle Bks.); 384p. 22.00 o.p. (1-57566-139-X, Kensington Bks.) Kensington Publishing Corp.
Frame, Janet. Living in the Maniototo. 1979. 8.95 o.p. (0-8076-0926-9); 2nd ed. 1980. pap. 12.50 (0-8076-0958-7) Braziller, George Inc.
Francisco, Ruth. Confessions of a Deathmaiden: A Novel. 2003. 352p. 23.95 (0-89296-773-0) Mysterious Pr.
Freadhoff, Chuck. Blue Rain. 2000. 368p. mass mkt. 6.99 (0-06-109727-6); 1999. 336p. 24.00 o.p. (0-06-019217-8) HarperCollins Pubs.
—Blue Rain. l.t. ed. 1999. (Americana Ser.). 493p. 26.95 (0-7862-2068-6) Thorndike Pr.
—A Permanent Twilight. 2000. 352p. 25.00 (0-06-019216-X) HarperCollins Pubs.
Freedman, J. F. House of Smoke. 1996. 448p. 23.95 o.p. (0-670-85347-X, Viking) Viking Penguin.
Freeman, David. A Hollywood Education: Tales of Movie Dreams & Easy Money. 1992. 288p. pap. 10.95 (0-88184-870-0, Carroll & Graf Pubs.) Avalon Publishing Group.
—A Hollywood Education: Tales of Movie Dreams & Easy Money. 1987. pap. 6.95 o.s.i (0-440-53738-X, Laurel) Dell Publishing.
—A Hollywood Education: Tales of Movie Dreams & Easy Money. 1986. 256p. 17.95 o.p. (0-399-13044-6) Putnam Publishing Group, The.
—A Hollywood Life. 1991. 19.95 o.p. (0-671-72738-9, Simon & Schuster) Simon & Schuster.
Freeman, Judith. The Chinchilla Farm. 1990. (Vintage Contemporaries Ser.). 320p. pap. 14.00 o.s.i (0-679-73052-4, Vintage) Knopf Publishing Group.
—Chinchilla Farm. 1989. 19.95 o.p. (0-393-02722-8) Norton, W. W. & Co., Inc.
—The Chinchilla Farm: A Novel. 2003. 320p. pap. 13.95 (0-393-32426-5) Norton, W. W. & Co., Inc.
Frey, James. Came a Dead Cat. 1991. 256p. 18.95 o.p. (0-312-06314-8, Saint Martin's Minotaur) St. Martin's Pr.
Friedman. A-Hunting We Will Go. 1998. 448p. mass mkt. 6.99 o.s.i (0-06-109590-7) HarperCollins Pubs.
Friedman, Hal. A Hunting We Will Go. 1998. 368p. 23.00 o.p. (0-06-018264-4) HarperCollins Pubs.
—Over the Edge. 1999. 416p. mass mkt. 6.99 o.s.i (0-06-109367-X); 1998. 320p. 24.00 (0-06-018265-2) HarperCollins Pubs.
Friedman, Steven. Station Break. 1993. 312p. 19.95 o.p. (0-312-08895-7) St. Martin's Pr.
Fritz, Taylor. Take a Byte Out of Crime. 2000. (ByteLady Mysteries Ser.: Vol. 1). 336p. pap. 8.50 (0-9704891-0-2) ByteLady Publishing.
Fuchs, Jake. Death of a Dad: The Nursery School Murders. 1998. 180p. pap. 13.95 (0-88739-159-1) Creative Arts Bk. Co.
Fuguet, Alberto. The Movies of My Life. Fitz, Ezra E., tr. from SPA. 2003. 304p. 24.95 (0-06-053462-1, Rayo) HarperTrade.
—Las Peliculas de Mi Vida. 2003. (SPA.). 304p. 24.95 (0-06-055940-3, Rayo) HarperTrade.
Fulbeck, Kip. Paper Bullets: A Fictional Autobiography. 2001. (Scott & Laurie Oki Series in Asian American Studies). xi, 273p. 35.00 (0-295-98078-8); (Illus.). pap. 18.95 (0-295-98079-6) Univ. of Washington Pr.
Furutani, Dale. Death in Little Tokyo. unabr. collector's ed. 1999. (Ken Tanaka Ser. ). audio 32.00 (0-7366-4414-8, 4875) Books on Tape, Inc.
—Death in Little Tokyo. 1996. 256p. 21.95 o.p. (0-312-14580-2, Saint Martin's Minotaur); Vol. 1. 1997. (Death in Little Tokyo Ser.: Vol. 1). 224p. mass mkt. 5.99 o.p. (0-312-96323-8, St. Martin's Paperbacks) St. Martin's Pr.
—The Toyotomi Blades, Vol. 1. 1998. (Toyotomi Blades Ser.: Vol. 1). 240p. mass mkt. 5.99 (0-312-96667-9, St. Martin's Paperbacks) St. Martin's Pr.
—The Toyotomi Blades: A Ken Tanaka Mystery. 1997. (Ken Tanaka Mystery Ser.). 224p. 21.95 (0-312-17050-5, Saint Martin's Minotaur) St. Martin's Pr.
Futcher, Jane. Dream Lover. 1997. 260p. (Orig.). pap. 9.95 o.p. (1-55583-375-6) Alyson Pubns.
Gadol, Peter. Closer to the Sun. 256p. 1997. pap. 12.00 o.s.i (0-312-15495-X); 1995. 22.00 o.p. (0-312-14084-3) Picador.
—The Long Rain. 2000. 304p. pap. 13.00 (0-312-26354-6); 1998. (Long Rain Ser.: Vol. 1). 295p. mass mkt. 6.99 o.p. (0-312-96638-5); 1997. 320p. 23.00 o.p. (0-312-15571-9) Picador.
—The Long Rain. unabr. ed. 1997. audio 75.00 (0-7887-1314-0, 95172E7) Recorded Bks., LLC.
Gage, Elizabeth. Taboo. l.t. ed. 1994. pap. 23.95 o.p. (0-7927-1731-7); 1993. 25.95 o.p. (0-7927-1732-5) BBC Audiobooks America.
—Taboo. abr. ed. 1993. 16.95 o.p. (1-55800-698-2); audio 8.99 o.p. (1-55800-905-1, Dove Audio) NewStar Media, Inc.
—Taboo. Zion, Claire, ed. 1993. 480p. 22.00 (0-671-78641-5, Atria); 576p. reprint ed. mass mkt. 5.99 (0-671-78644-X, Pocket) Simon & Schuster.
Galbraith, Liam Patrick. Honda Dream. 2000. 256p. pap. 24.50 (0-88739-222-9) Creative Arts Bk. Co.

Galde, Dorothy A. Avalanche! 1901. (Making Choices Ser.). 144p. (J). (gr. 4-7). pap. 3.95 o.p. (*0-89191-253-3*) Cook Communications Ministries.

Gale, Patrick. Tree Surgery for Beginners. 1999. (Illus.). 275p. 25.00 (*0-571-19958-5*) Faber & Faber, Inc.

Garcia, Guy. Skin Deep. 1989. 176p. 16.95 o.s.i (*0-374-26573-9*) Farrar, Straus & Giroux.

—Skin Deep. 1997. 186p. pap. 15.95 (*0-520-20836-6*) Univ. of California Pr.

Gardner, Erle Stanley. The Case of the Amorous Aunt. 1994. mass mkt. 4.50 o.s.i (*0-345-37878-4*) Ballantine Bks.

—The Case of the Amorous Aunt. l.t. ed. 1985. (Nightingale Ser.). 11.95 o.p. (*0-8161-3752-8*, Macmillan Reference USA) Gale Group.

—The Case of the Angry Mourner. 1989. (*1-55504-971-0*); 1991. 12.95 o.p. (*1-55504-970-2*, 215) BBC Audiobooks America.

—The Case of the Angry Mourner. 1993. mass mkt. 4.50 o.s.i (*0-345-37870-9*) Ballantine Bks.

—The Case of the Baited Hook. (Perry Mason Bks.). 288p. reprint ed. lib. bdg. 23.95 (*0-88411-416-3*) Amereon, Ltd.

—The Case of the Baited Hook. (Perry Mason Mysteries Ser.). 1999. mass mkt. 4.99 (*0-345-91478-3*); 1995. 224p. pap. 15.00 (*0-345-46896-1*); 1986. 224p. mass mkt. 5.99 (*0-345-32942-2*) Ballantine Bks.

—The Case of the Beautiful Beggar. 1976. 21.95 (*0-8488-0498-8*) Amereon, Ltd.

—The Case of the Beautiful Beggar. 1986. mass mkt. 3.50 o.s.i (*0-345-34318-2*) Ballantine Bks.

—The Case of the Beautiful Beggar. l.t. ed. 1998. (G. K. Hall Paperback Ser.). 272p. 22.95 o.p. (*0-7838-0269-2*, Macmillan Reference USA) Gale Group.

—The Case of the Beautiful Beggar. abr. ed. 1988. audio 14.95 (*1-55800-118-2*, 40450, Dove Audio) NewStar Media, Inc.

—The Case of the Bigamous Spouse. l.t. ed. 1988. pap. 18.95 o.p. (*1-55504-668-1*); lib. bdg. 20.95 o.p. (*1-55504-687-8*) BBC Audiobooks America.

—The Case of the Bigamous Spouse. 1987. mass mkt. 2.95 o.s.i (*0-345-34378-6*) Ballantine Bks.

—The Case of the Bigamous Spouse. 1972. pap. 0.95 o.p. (*0-671-77865-X*, Pocket) Simon & Schuster.

—The Case of the Black-Eyed Blonde. 1976. 21.95 (*0-8488-0271-3*) Amereon, Ltd.

—The Case of the Black-Eyed Blonde. 1985. 208p. mass mkt. 3.50 o.s.i (*0-345-32311-4*) Ballantine Bks.

—The Case of the Black-Eyed Blonde. 1975. pap. 1.50 o.p. (*0-671-78782-9*, Pocket) Simon & Schuster.

—The Case of the Blonde Bonanza. 1994. mass mkt. 4.50 o.s.i (*0-345-37877-6*) Ballantine Bks.

—The Case of the Blonde Bonanza. l.t. ed. 1987. (Nightingale Ser.). 291p. pap. 11.95 o.p. (*0-8161-4283-1*, Macmillan Reference USA) Gale Group.

—The Case of the Borrowed Brunette. 1987. 224p. mass mkt. 4.99 o.s.i (*0-345-34374-3*) Ballantine Bks.

—The Case of the Borrowed Brunette. 1976. pap. 1.95 o.p. (*0-671-80470-7*, Pocket) Simon & Schuster.

—The Case of the Buried Clock. 1976. 22.95 (*0-8488-0273-X*) Amereon, Ltd.

—The Case of the Buried Clock. 1997. mass mkt. 4.99 (*0-345-90799-X*); 1986. mass mkt. 3.95 o.s.i (*0-345-33691-7*); 1983. mass mkt. 4.99 o.s.i (*0-345-31013-6*, Ballantine Bks.) Ballantine Bks.

—The Case of the Buried Clock. l.t. ed. 1998. (Paperback Ser.). 312p. pap. 24.95 (*0-7838-0366-4*) Thorndike Pr.

—The Case of the Calendar Girl. 1976. 21.95 (*0-8488-0499-6*) Amereon, Ltd.

—The Case of the Calendar Girl. 1987. 224p. mass mkt. 4.99 o.s.i (*0-345-34375-1*) Ballantine Bks.

—The Case of the Careless Cupid. 1995. mass mkt. 4.99 o.s.i (*0-345-39226-4*) Ballantine Bks.

—The Case of the Careless Cupid. l.t. ed. 2003. (Dales Large Print Ser.). 304p. pap. 21.99 (*1-84262-216-1*) Dales Large Print Bks. GBR. *Dist:* Ulverscroft Large Print Bks., Ltd., Ulverscroft Large Print Canada, Ltd.

—The Case of the Careless Cupid. 1977. lib. bdg. 9.95 o.p. (*0-8161-6447-9*, Macmillan Reference USA) Gale Group.

—The Case of the Careless Kitten. 1976. 23.95 (*0-8488-0272-1*) Amereon, Ltd.

—The Case of the Careless Kitten. 1989. (Perry Mason Mysteries Ser.). 224p. mass mkt. 4.99 o.s.i (*0-345-36223-3*) Ballantine Bks.

—The Case of the Caretaker's Cat. 1976. (Perry Mason Bks.). reprint ed. lib. bdg. 24.95 (*0-88411-407-4*) Amereon, Ltd.

—The Case of the Caretaker's Cat. 1985. (Perry Mason Mysteries Ser.). reprint ed. mass mkt. 4.99 o.s.i (*0-345-32156-1*) Ballantine Bks.

—The Case of the Caretaker's Cat. l.t. ed. 1998. (Perry Mason Mysteries Ser.). 283p. 21.95 o.p. (*0-7838-8439-7*, Macmillan Reference USA) Gale Group.

—The Case of the Cautious Coquette. 1997. 18.95 (*0-88411-440-6*); 1976. 21.95 (*0-8488-0500-3*) Amereon, Ltd.

—The Case of the Cautious Coquette. l.t. ed. 1991. 19.95 o.p. (*0-7927-0847-4*, CS0189); pap. 17.95 o.p. (*0-7927-0848-2*) BBC Audiobooks America.

—The Case of the Cautious Coquette. 1988. 240p. reprint ed. mass mkt. 4.99 o.s.i (*0-345-35202-5*) Ballantine Bks.

—The Case of the Counterfeit Eye. 1976. (Perry Mason Books Ser.). reprint ed. lib. bdg. 24.95 (*0-88411-406-6*) Amereon, Ltd.

—The Case of the Counterfeit Eye. (*0-7540-3701-0*); 1999. 296 p. (*0-7540-3702-9*) BBC Audiobooks America.

—The Case of the Counterfeit Eye. (Perry Mason Mysteries Ser.). 1998. mass mkt. 4.99 (*0-345-91229-2*); 1986. 256p. mass mkt. 4.99 o.s.i (*0-345-33195-8*) Ballantine Bks.

—The Case of the Counterfeit Eye. 1974. pap. 0.95 o.p. (*0-671-77895-1*, Pocket) Simon & Schuster.

—The Case of the Crimson Kiss. 1972. pap. 0.95 o.p. (*0-671-77881-1*, Simon Pulse) Simon & Schuster Children's Publishing.

—The Case of the Crooked Candle. 1976. 21.95 (*0-8488-0275-6*) Amereon, Ltd.

—The Case of the Crooked Candle. l.t. ed. 1989. vi, 339 p. (*1-55504-787-4*) BBC Audiobooks America.

—The Case of the Crooked Candle. 1989. mass mkt. 3.99 o.p. (*0-345-01834-6*); 1987. mass mkt. 3.99 o.s.i (*0-345-34164-3*) Ballantine Bks.

—The Case of the Crooked Candle. 1976. (Crime Fiction Ser.). reprint ed. lib. bdg. 21.00 o.p. (*0-8240-2368-4*) Garland Publishing, Inc.

—The Case of the Crying Swallow: A Perry Mason Novelette & Other Stories. l.t. ed. 1987. (Nightingale Ser.). 295p. 11.95 o.p. (*0-8161-4284-X*, Macmillan Reference USA) Gale Group.

—The Case of the Curious Bride. 1976. (Perry Mason Bks.). reprint ed. lib. bdg. 23.95 (*0-88411-405-8*) Amereon, Ltd.

—The Case of the Curious Bride. (Perry Mason Mysteries Ser.). 2000. 192p. mass mkt. 5.99 o.s.i (*0-345-43783-7*, Fawcett); 1989. 224p. mass mkt. 4.99 o.s.i (*0-345-36222-5*) Ballantine Bks.

—The Case of the Curious Bride. l.t. ed. 2001. (G. K. Hall Paperback Ser.). 319p. pap. 24.95 (*0-7838-9432-5*); (*0-7540-4535-8*); (*0-7540-4536-6*) Gale Group. (Macmillan Reference USA).

—The Case of the Curious Bride. 1992. pap. 46.00 o.p. (*0-671-82708-1*, Pocket) Simon & Schuster.

—The Case of the Dangerous Dowager. 1976. (Perry Mason Bks.). reprint ed. lib. bdg. 19.95 (*0-88411-410-4*) Amereon, Ltd.

—The Case of the Dangerous Dowager. (Perry Mason Mysteries Ser.). 1998. mass mkt. 4.99 (*0-345-91231-4*); 1986. 224p. mass mkt. 4.99 o.s.i (*0-345-33192-3*) Ballantine Bks.

—The Case of the Dangerous Dowager. l.t. ed. 2000. (G. K. Hall Paperback Ser.). 299p. pap. 23.95 (*0-7838-9225-X*, Macmillan Reference USA) Gale Group.

—The Case of the Daring Decoy. 1989. (Perry Mason Mysteries Ser.). 224p. mass mkt. 4.99 o.s.i (*0-345-36220-9*) Ballantine Bks.

—The Case of the Daring Divorcee. 1984. 192p. mass mkt. 3.95 o.s.i (*0-345-32003-4*) Ballantine Bks.

—The Case of the Deadly Toy. (Perry Mason Mysteries Ser.). 224p. 2000. mass mkt. 6.99 (*0-345-43784-5*, Fawcett); 1985. mass mkt. 3.50 o.s.i (*0-345-33494-9*) Ballantine Bks.

—The Case of the Deadly Toy. 1981. 288p. reprint ed. lib. bdg. 18.00 (*0-8376-0397-8*) Bentley Pubs.

—The Case of the Deadly Toy. l.t. ed. 1993. (Nightingale Ser.). 378p. lib. bdg. 15.95 o.p. (*0-8161-5632-8*, Macmillan Reference USA) Gale Group.

—The Case of the Demure Defendant. 1991. 192p. mass mkt. 3.95 o.s.i (*0-345-37148-8*, Ballantine Bks.) Ballantine Bks.

—The Case of the Demure Defendant. l.t. ed. 1988. 336p. 15.95 o.p. (*0-7089-1785-2*, Ulverscroft) Thorpe, F. A. Pubs. GBR. *Dist:* Ulverscroft Large Print Bks., Ltd.

—The Case of the Drowning Duck. (Perry Mason Bks.). 284p. reprint ed. lib. bdg. 23.95 (*0-88411-420-1*) Amereon, Ltd.

—The Case of the Drowning Duck. l.t. ed. 1990. (Perry Mason Mystery Ser.). 21.95 o.p. (*0-7927-0635-8*, C0595); pap. 19.95 o.p. (*0-7927-0636-6*) BBC Audiobooks America.

—The Case of the Drowning Duck. 1993. reprint ed. mass mkt. 4.50 o.s.i (*0-345-37868-7*) Ballantine Bks.

—The Case of the Drowning Duck. 1976. pap. 1.95 o.p. (*0-671-80281-X*, Pocket) Simon & Schuster.

—The Case of the Drowsy Mosquito. 1976. 22.95 (*0-8488-0274-8*) Amereon, Ltd.

—The Case of the Drowsy Mosquito. 1994. reprint ed. mass mkt. 4.99 o.s.i (*0-345-37869-5*) Ballantine Bks.

—The Case of the Drowsy Mosquito. 1976. (Two-in-One Ser.). pap. 1.95 o.p. (*0-671-80390-5*, Pocket) Simon & Schuster.

—The Case of the Drowsy Mosquito. l.t. ed. 1978. 12.00 o.p. (*0-7089-0235-9*, Ulverscroft) Thorpe, F. A. Pubs. GBR. *Dist:* Ulverscroft Large Print Bks., Ltd.

—The Case of the Dubious Bridegroom. l.t. ed. 1994. 22.95 o.p. (*0-7927-2103-9*); pap. 21.95 o.p. (*0-7927-2102-0*) BBC Audiobooks America.

—The Case of the Dubious Bridegroom. 1986. 224p. mass mkt. 3.50 o.s.i (*0-345-34186-4*); 1984. mass mkt. 2.50 o.p. (*0-345-31811-0*); 1983. mass mkt. 4.99 o.s.i (*0-345-30881-6*) Ballantine Bks.

—The Case of the Duplicate Daughter. 1988. mass mkt. 3.50 o.s.i (*0-345-35681-0*) Ballantine Bks.

—The Case of the Duplicate Daughter. 1975. pap. 1.50 o.p. (*0-671-78779-9*, Pocket) Simon & Schuster.

—The Case of the Empty Tin. (Perry Mason Bks.). 282p. reprint ed. lib. bdg. 23.95 (*0-88411-419-8*) Amereon, Ltd.

—The Case of the Empty Tin. 1985. 240p. mass mkt. 4.99 o.s.i (*0-345-33198-2*); 1996. reprint ed. mass mkt. 4.99 (*0-345-90798-1*) Ballantine Bks.

—The Case of the Empty Tin. l.t. ed. 1979. (Ulverscroft Large Print Ser.). 12.00 o.p. (*0-7089-0244-8*, Ulverscroft) Thorpe, F. A. Pubs. GBR. *Dist:* Ulverscroft Large Print Bks., Ltd., Ulverscroft Large Print Canada, Ltd.

—The Case of the Fabulous Fake. l.t. ed. 1990. (Perry Mason Mystery Ser.). pap. 10.95 o.p. (*0-89340-024-6*, C0148) BBC Audiobooks America.

—The Case of the Fabulous Fake. 1986. mass mkt. 3.95 o.s.i (*0-345-33548-1*) Ballantine Bks.

—The Case of the Fabulous Fake. 1969. 7.95 o.p. (*0-688-01276-0*, Morrow, William & Co.) Morrow/Avon.

—The Case of the Fan-Dancer's Horse. 1992. reprint ed. mass mkt. 4.99 o.s.i (*0-345-37144-5*) Ballantine Bks.

—The Case of the Fan-Dancer's Horse & the Case of the Hesitant Hostess. 1977. pap. 1.95 o.p. (*0-671-81386-2*, Pocket) Simon & Schuster.

—The Case of the Fenced-In Woman. 1994. (Perry Mason Mysteries Ser.). 224p. mass mkt. 5.99 o.s.i (*0-345-39223-X*) Ballantine Bks.

—The Case of the Fiery Fingers. 1987. mass mkt. 3.50 o.s.i (*0-345-35161-4*) Ballantine Bks.

—The Case of the Fiery Fingers. 1975. pap. 1.50 o.p. (*0-671-78783-7*, Pocket) Simon & Schuster.

—The Case of the Foot-Loose Doll. 1975. pap. 24.95 o.p. (*0-671-78787-X*, Atria) Simon & Schuster.

—The Case of the Fugitive Nurse. 1993. mass mkt. 4.99 o.s.i (*0-345-37873-3*) Ballantine Bks.

—The Case of the Gilded Lily. l.t. ed. 1991. 8.95 o.p. (*1-55504-899-4*, 16) BBC Audiobooks America.

—The Case of the Gilded Lily. 1999. mass mkt. 4.99 (*0-345-91480-5*); 1985. 199p. mass mkt. 5.99 o.s.i (*0-345-32318-1*) Ballantine Bks.

—The Case of the Gilded Lily. 1981. (Perry Mason Mysteries Ser.). 256p. reprint ed. lib. bdg. 18.00 (*0-8376-0396-X*) Bentley Pubs.

—The Case of the Glamorous Ghost. l.t. ed. 1992. pap. 20.95 o.p. (*0-7927-1044-4*, CS0279); 1991. 22.95 o.p. (*0-7927-1043-6*, CH0211) BBC Audiobooks America.

—The Case of the Glamorous Ghost. 240p. 2000. mass mkt. 5.99 (*0-345-43786-1*, Fawcett); 1986. mass mkt. 3.95 o.s.i (*0-345-34440-5*) Ballantine Bks.

—The Case of the Glamorous Ghost. 1977. pap. 1.95 o.p. (*0-671-81691-8*, Pocket) Simon & Schuster.

—The Case of the Golddigger's Purse. 1997. mass mkt. 4.99 (*0-345-90800-7*); 1984. 224p. mass mkt. 4.99 o.s.i (*0-345-31680-0*, Ballantine Bks.) Ballantine Bks.

—The Case of the Green-Eyed Sister. 1978. xii, 426p. (*0-89340-140-4*) BBC Audiobooks America.

—The Case of the Green-Eyed Sister. 1993. mass mkt. 4.50 o.s.i (*0-345-37872-5*) Ballantine Bks.

—The Case of the Green-Eyed Sister. 1975. pap. 1.50 o.p. (*0-671-80074-4*, Pocket) Simon & Schuster.

—The Case of the Grinning Gorilla. 1986. mass mkt. 2.95 o.s.i (*0-345-34187-2*) Ballantine Bks.

—The Case of the Grinning Gorilla. 1973. pap. 0.95 o.p. (*0-671-77889-7*, Star Trek) Simon & Schuster.

—The Case of the Half-Wakened Wife. 1991. 256p. mass mkt. 4.99 o.s.i (*0-345-37147-X*, Ballantine Bks.) Ballantine Bks.

—The Case of the Haunted Husband. 281p. reprint ed. lib. bdg. 23.95 (*0-88411-418-X*) Amereon, Ltd.

—The Case of the Haunted Husband. 1986. vii, 374 p. (*1-55504-067-5*) BBC Audiobooks America.

—The Case of the Haunted Husband. 1985. 208p. mass mkt. 4.99 o.s.i (*0-345-33495-7*) Ballantine Bks.

—The Case of the Haunted Husband. abr. ed. 1991. 2p. audio 16.99 (*0-88646-299-1*) Durkin Hayes Publishing Ltd.

—The Case of the Hesitant Hostess. 1993. mass mkt. 4.50 o.s.i (*0-345-37871-7*) Ballantine Bks.

—The Case of the Hesitant Hostess. l.t. ed. 1991. 377p. pap. 15.95 o.p. (*0-8161-5064-8*, Macmillan Reference USA) Gale Group.

—The Case of the Horrified Heirs. 1995. 192p. mass mkt. 5.99 (*0-345-39227-2*); pap. 15.00 (*0-345-47043-5*) Ballantine Bks.

—The Case of the Howling Dog. 1976. (Perry Mason Bks.). reprint ed. lib. bdg. 24.95 (*0-88411-404-X*) Amereon, Ltd.

—The Case of the Howling Dog. 1987. mass mkt. 4.99 o.s.i (*0-345-34783-8*); 1984. mass mkt. 2.50 o.p. (*0-345-31679-7*) Ballantine Bks.

—The Case of the Howling Dog. l.t. ed. 1999. (Paperback Ser.). 279p. pap. 23.95 (*0-7838-8775-2*, Macmillan Reference USA) Gale Group.

—The Case of the Ice-Cold Hands. 1989. mass mkt. 3.95 o.s.i (*0-345-35939-9*) Ballantine Bks.

—The Case of the Ice-Cold Hands. 1980. (General Ser.). lib. bdg. 11.95 o.p. (*0-8161-3174-0*, Macmillan Reference USA) Gale Group.

—The Case of the Irate Witness. 1973. pap. 0.95 o.p. (*0-671-77883-8*, Pocket) Simon & Schuster.

—The Case of the Lame Canary. (Perry Mason Bks.). 281p. reprint ed. lib. bdg. 23.95 (*0-88411-411-2*) Amereon, Ltd.

—The Case of the Lame Canary. 1996. mass mkt. 4.99 (*0-345-90796-5*); 1987. 256p. mass mkt. 4.99 o.s.i (*0-345-35162-2*); 1984. mass mkt. 2.50 o.s.i (*0-345-31547-2*) Ballantine Bks.

—The Case of the Lazy Lover. l.t. ed. 1982. vii, 438 p. (*0-89340-362-8*) BBC Audiobooks America.

—The Case of the Lazy Lover. 1997. mass mkt. 4.99 (*0-345-90801-5*); 1987. mass mkt. 2.95 o.s.i (*0-345-35007-3*); 1981. mass mkt. 4.99 o.s.i (*0-345-29496-3*) Ballantine Bks.

—The Case of the Lazy Lover. l.t. ed. 1997. 21.95 (*0-7838-8348-X*, Macmillan Reference USA) Gale Group.

—The Case of the Lazy Lover. abr. ed. 1989. audio 14.95 (*1-55800-119-0*, 40460, Dove Audio) NewStar Media, Inc.

—The Case of the Lonely Heiress. (Perry Mason Mysteries Ser.). 1997. mass mkt. 4.99 (*0-345-90802-3*); 1986. 224p. mass mkt. 3.95 o.s.i (*0-345-34012-4*); 1984. mass mkt. 2.50 o.p. (*0-345-31797-1*); 1983. 224p. mass mkt. 5.99 o.s.i (*0-345-31012-8*, Ballantine Bks.) Ballantine Bks.

—The Case of the Lonely Heiress. l.t. ed. 2001. 216p. pap. 24.95 (*0-7838-9506-2*, Macmillan Reference USA) Gale Group.

—The Case of the Lonely Heiress. 1973. pap. 0.95 o.p. (*0-671-77886-2*, Atria) Simon & Schuster.

—The Case of the Long-Legged Models. 1994. mass mkt. 4.99 o.s.i (*0-345-37876-8*) Ballantine Bks.

—The Case of the Long-Legged Models. 1971. pap. 0.75 o.p. (*0-671-75556-0*, Pimsleur) Simon & Schuster Audio.

—The Case of the Lucky Legs. 1976. (Perry Mason Bks.). reprint ed. lib. bdg. 23.95 (*0-88411-403-1*) Amereon, Ltd.

—The Case of the Lucky Legs. 1999. (*0-7540-3826-2*); (*0-7540-3827-0*) BBC Audiobooks America.

—The Case of the Lucky Legs. 1973. pap. 0.95 o.p. (*0-671-77891-9*, Simon & Schuster Audioworks) Simon & Schuster Audio.

—The Case of the Lucky Legs. l.t. ed. 1999. (G. K. Hall Paperback Ser.). 320p. pap. 23.95 (*0-7838-8612-8*) Thorndike Pr.

—The Case of the Lucky Loser. l.t. ed. 1991. 12.95 o.p. (*0-7927-0227-1*, 4764); 1990. pap. 17.95 o.p. (*0-7927-0228-X*, C0247) BBC Audiobooks America.

—The Case of the Lucky Loser. 1990. 192p. mass mkt. 4.99 o.s.i (*0-345-36497-X*) Ballantine Bks.

—The Case of the Mischievous Doll. 1989. mass mkt. 4.99 o.s.i (*0-345-35940-2*) Ballantine Bks.

—The Case of the Mischievous Doll. 1981. (General Ser.). lib. bdg. 11.95 o.p. (*0-8161-3215-1*, Macmillan Reference USA) Gale Group.

—The Case of the Moth-Eaten Mink. 1990. (Perry Mason Mysteries Ser.: No. 57). 240p. mass mkt. 3.95 o.p. (*0-345-36928-9*) Ballantine Bks.

—The Case of the Moth-Eaten Mink. l.t. ed. 1992. (General Ser.). 365p. lib. bdg. 19.95 o.p. (*0-8161-5063-X*, Macmillan Reference USA) Gale Group.

—The Case of the Moth-Eaten Mink. 1971. pap. 0.75 o.p. (*0-671-75539-0*, Star Trek) Simon & Schuster.

—The Case of the Mythical Monkeys. 1984. mass mkt. 3.95 o.s.i (*0-345-31404-2*) Ballantine Bks.

—The Case of the Mythical Monkeys. 1981. 288p. reprint ed. lib. bdg. 18.00 (*0-8376-0398-6*) Bentley Pubs.

—The Case of the Mythical Monkeys. l.t. ed. 1993. 13.95 o.p. (*0-8161-3384-0*, Macmillan Reference USA) Gale Group.

—The Case of the Negligent Nymph. 1986. 176p. mass mkt. 3.95 o.s.i (*0-345-34013-2*) Ballantine Bks.

—The Case of the Negligent Nymph. 1973. pap. 0.95 o.p. (*0-671-77892-7*, Pocket) Simon & Schuster.

—The Case of the Nervous Accomplice. 1992. mass mkt. 3.99 o.s.i (*0-345-37874-1*) Ballantine Bks.

—The Case of the Nervous Accomplice. 1974. pap. 0.95 o.p. (*0-671-77926-5*, Pocket) Simon & Schuster.

—The Case of the One-Eyed Witness. 1995. 240p. mass mkt. 5.99 (*0-345-39225-6*) Ballantine Bks.

—The Case of the One-Eyed Witness. l.t. ed. 1990. pap. 15.95 o.p. (*0-8161-5062-1*, Macmillan Reference USA) Gale Group.

—The Case of the One-Eyed Witness. 1971. pap. 0.75 o.p. (0-671-75536-6, Star Trek) Simon & Schuster.

—The Case of the Perjured Parrot. (Perry Mason Bks.). 288p. reprint ed. lib. bdg. 23.95 (0-88411-414-7) Amereon, Ltd.

—The Case of the Perjured Parrot. (Perry Mason Mysteries Ser.). 1987. mass mkt. 4.99 o.s.i (0-345-34685-8); 1982. mass mkt. 2.25 o.p. (0-345-30396-2) Ballantine Bks.

—The Case of the Perjured Parrot. l.t. ed. 2001. 253p. (0-7540-4401-7); (0-7540-4402-5) Gale Group. (Macmillan Reference USA).

—The Case of the Perjured Parrot. 1975. pap. 1.50 o.p. (0-671-78944-9, Pocket) Simon & Schuster.

—The Case of the Perjured Parrot. l.t. ed. 2001. (G. K. Hall Nightingale Ser.). 253p. pap. 23.95 (0-7838-9322-1) Thorndike Pr.

—The Case of the Phantom Fortune. 1986. mass mkt. 3.50 o.s.i (0-345-33191-5) Ballantine Bks.

—The Case of the Phantom Fortune. l.t. ed. 1984. (Nightingale Ser.). 9.95 o.p. (0-8161-3754-4, Macmillan Reference USA) Gale Group.

—The Case of the Phantom Fortune. 1974. pap. 0.95 o.p. (0-671-77896-X, Pocket) Simon & Schuster.

—The Case of the Postponed Murder. 1995. mass mkt. 4.99 o.s.i (0-345-39229-9) Ballantine Bks.

—The Case of the Postponed Murder. 1973. (General Ser.). reprint ed. lib. bdg. 8.95 o.p. (0-8161-6090-2, Macmillan Reference USA) Gale Group.

—The Case of the Postponed Murder. 1973. 7.95 o.p. (0-688-00033-9, Morrow, William & Co.) Morrow/Avon.

—The Case of the Postponed Murder. 1974. pap. 0.95 o.p. (0-671-77894-3, Pocket) Simon & Schuster.

—The Case of the Queenly Contestant. l.t. ed. 1990. (Perry Mason Mystery Ser.). pap. 18.95 o.p. (0-89340-025-4, C0160) BBC Audiobooks America.

—The Case of the Queenly Contestant. 1993. reprint ed. mass mkt. 4.50 o.s.i (0-345-37879-2) Ballantine Bks.

—The Case of the Reluctant Model. 1990. 208p. mass mkt. 3.95 o.s.i (0-345-36689-1) Ballantine Bks.

—The Case of the Reluctant Model, abr. ed. audio 16.99 (0-88646-301-7, DHA7301) Durkin Hayes Publishing Ltd.

—The Case of the Restless Redhead. 1980. xiv, 435 p. (0-89340-261-3) BBC Audiobooks America.

—The Case of the Restless Redhead. 1985. mass mkt. 3.95 o.s.i (0-345-33199-0) Ballantine Bks.

—The Case of the Rolling Bones. (Perry Mason Bks.). 288p. reprint ed. lib. bdg. 23.95 (0-88411-415-5) Amereon, Ltd.

—The Case of the Rolling Bones. 1999. 4.99 (0-345-91481-3); 1985. 208p. reprint ed. mass mkt. 4.99 o.s.i (0-345-32979-1) Ballantine Bks.

—The Case of the Rolling Bones. l.t. ed. 1986. (Nightingale Ser.). 350p. 11.95 o.p. (0-8161-4080-4, Macmillan Reference USA) Gale Group.

—The Case of the Rolling Bones. 1976. (Two-in-One Ser.). pap. 1.95 o.p. (0-671-80583-5, Pocket) Simon & Schuster.

—The Case of the Runaway Corpse. 1990. 224p. mass mkt. 4.99 o.s.i (0-345-36498-8) Ballantine Bks.

—The Case of the Runaway Corpse. l.t. ed. 1988. lib. bdg. 14.95 o.p. (1-85057-453-7, Macmillan Reference USA) Gale Group.

—The Case of the Screaming Woman. l.t. ed. 1992. pap. 18.95 o.p. (0-7927-0969-1) BBC Audiobooks America.

—The Case of the Screaming Woman. 1994. mass mkt. 4.99 o.s.i (0-345-37875-X); 1992. 20.95 o.p. (0-7927-1228-5, CH0260) Ballantine Bks.

—The Case of the Shapely Shadow. 1986. mass mkt. 3.50 o.s.i (0-345-33496-5) Ballantine Bks.

—The Case of the Shoplifter's Shoe. (Perry Mason Bks.). 312p. reprint ed. lib. bdg. 24.95 (0-88411-413-9) Amereon, Ltd.

—The Case of the Shoplifter's Shoe. 1998. mass mkt. 4.99 (0-345-91233-0); 1986. 224p. mass mkt. 5.99 o.s.i (0-345-32943-0) Ballantine Bks.

—The Case of the Shoplifter's Shoe. 1973. pap. 0.95 o.p. (0-671-77888-9, Pocket) Simon & Schuster.

—The Case of the Silent Partner. (Perry Mason Bks.). reprint ed. lib. bdg. 23.95 (0-88411-417-1) Amereon, Ltd.

—The Case of the Silent Partner. 1999. 4.99 (0-345-91482-1); 1986. 224p. mass mkt. 4.99 o.s.i (0-345-33684-4) Ballantine Bks.

—The Case of the Silent Partner. 2003. (Paperback Ser.). pap. 25.95 (0-7862-5047-X) Thorndike Pr.

—The Case of the Singing Skirt. 1992. mass mkt. 3.99 o.s.i (0-345-37149-6) Ballantine Bks.

—The Case of the Singing Skirt. 1981. 256p. reprint ed. 18.00 (0-8376-0399-4) Bentley Pubs.

—The Case of the Singing Skirt. l.t. ed. 1988. (Nightingale Ser.). 183p. 12.95 o.p. (0-8161-4515-6, Macmillan Reference USA) Gale Group.

—The Case of the Sleepwalker's Niece. 1976. (Perry Mason Bks.). reprint ed. lib. bdg. 21.95 (0-88411-408-2) Amereon, Ltd.

—The Case of the Sleepwalker's Niece. 1991. (Perry Mason Mysteries Ser.). mass mkt. 3.99 o.s.i (0-345-37146-1, Ballantine Bks.) Ballantine Bks.

—The Case of the Sleepwalker's Niece. l.t. ed. 1993. (Nightingale Ser.). 344p. 14.95 o.p. (0-8161-5633-6, Macmillan Reference USA) Gale Group.

—The Case of the Sleepwalker's Niece. 1973. pap. 0.95 o.p. (0-671-77893-5, Pocket) Simon & Schuster.

—The Case of the Spurious Spinster. 1988. mass mkt. 3.50 o.s.i (0-345-35203-3) Ballantine Bks.

—The Case of the Stepdaughter's Secret. 1989. (Perry Mason Mysteries Ser.). 192p. mass mkt. 3.95 o.s.i (0-345-36221-7) Ballantine Bks.

—The Case of the Stepdaughter's Secret. l.t. ed. 1985. (Nightingale Ser.). 288p. 9.95 o.p. (0-8161-3753-6, Macmillan Reference USA) Gale Group.

—The Case of the Stepdaughter's Secret. 1977. pap. 1.95 o.p. (0-671-80968-7, Pocket) Simon & Schuster.

—The Case of the Stuttering Bishop. 1976. (Perry Mason Bks.). reprint ed. lib. bdg. 23.95 (0-88411-409-0) Amereon, Ltd.

—The Case of the Stuttering Bishop. l.t. ed. 1994. 21.95 o.p. (0-7927-1907-7); pap. 19.95 o.p. (0-7927-1906-9) BBC Audiobooks America.

—The Case of the Stuttering Bishop. 1998. mass mkt. 4.99 (0-345-91230-6); 1988. 192p. mass mkt. 6.99 (0-345-35680-2) Ballantine Bks.

—The Case of the Substitute Face. (Perry Mason Bks.). 310p. reprint ed. lib. bdg. 24.95 (0-88411-412-0) Amereon, Ltd.

—The Case of the Substitute Face. l.t. ed. 1993. 22.95 o.p. (0-7927-1562-4); pap. 20.95 o.p. (0-7927-1561-6) BBC Audiobooks America.

—The Case of the Substitute Face. (Perry Mason Mysteries Ser.). 1998. mass mkt. 4.99 (0-345-91232-2); 1987. pap. o.s.i (0-345-01849-4); 1987. 256p. mass mkt. 4.99 o.s.i (0-345-34377-8) Ballantine Bks.

—The Case of the Substitute Face. 1974. pap. 1.25 o.p. (0-671-78448-X, Pocket) Simon & Schuster.

—The Case of the Sulky Girl. 1976. (Perry Mason Books Ser.). reprint ed. lib. bdg. 24.95 (0-88411-402-3) Amereon, Ltd.

—The Case of the Sulky Girl. 1992. mass mkt. 4.99 o.s.i (0-345-37145-3) Ballantine Bks.

—The Case of the Sulky Girl, unabr. ed. 1991. (Listen for Pleasure Ser.). audio 16.99 (0-88646-298-3, LFP 7298) Durkin Hayes Publishing Ltd.

—The Case of the Sun Bather's Diary. 1995. 244p. pap. 15.00 (0-345-47042-7, Fawcett); 1985. 208p. mass mkt. 2.95 o.s.i (0-345-33503-1) Ballantine Bks.

—The Case of the Sun Bather's Diary. 1971. pap. 1.25 o.p. (0-671-82704-9, Pocket) Simon & Schuster.

—The Case of the Sun Bather's Diary. l.t. ed. 2001. (Paperback Ser.). 328p. 24.95 (0-7838-9338-8) Thorndike Pr.

—The Case of the Sun Bather's Diary: A Perry Mason Mystery. 2000. (Perry Mason Mysteries Ser.). 240p. mass mkt. 5.99 (0-345-43788-8, Fawcett) Ballantine Bks.

—The Case of the Terrified Typist. 1999. 4.99 (0-345-91483-X); 1987. 192p. mass mkt. 5.99 o.s.i (0-345-34165-1) Ballantine Bks.

—The Case of the Terrified Typist. l.t. ed. 1989. 296p. 14.95 o.p. (0-8161-4514-8, Macmillan Reference USA) Gale Group.

—The Case of the Terrified Typist. 1975. pap. 1.50 o.p. (0-671-78780-2, Simon Pulse) Simon & Schuster Children's Publishing.

—The Case of the Troubled Trustee. 1995. mass mkt. 4.99 o.s.i (0-345-39224-8) Ballantine Bks.

—The Case of the Vagabond Virgin. l.t. ed. 1990. pap. 17.95 o.p. (0-7927-0534-3, C0794); 19.95 o.p. (0-7927-0533-5, C0286) BBC Audiobooks America.

—The Case of the Vagabond Virgin. 1997. pap. 4.99 (0-345-90803-1); 1986. mass mkt. 3.50 o.s.i (0-345-34319-0); 1982. mass mkt. 4.99 o.s.i (0-345-30393-8) Ballantine Bks.

—The Case of the Vagabond Virgin. 1973. pap. 0.95 o.p. (0-671-77885-4, Simon Pulse) Simon & Schuster Children's Publishing.

—The Case of the Velvet Claws. 1976. (Perry Mason Books Ser.). reprint ed. lib. bdg. 24.95 (0-88411-401-5) Amereon, Ltd.

—The Case of the Velvet Claws. 1996. mass mkt. 4.99 (0-345-90793-0); 1985. 224p. mass mkt. 5.99 o.s.i (0-345-32317-3) Ballantine Bks.

—The Case of the Velvet Claws. 2002. (Best Mysteries of All Time Ser.). 261p. (0-7621-8878-2, IM Pr.) Reader's Digest Assn., Inc., The.

—The Case of the Waylaid Wolf. 1990. (Perry Mason Mysteries Ser.). 208p. mass mkt. 3.95 o.s.i (0-345-36690-5) Ballantine Bks.

—The Case of the Waylaid Wolf. 1976. pap. 1.95 o.p. (0-671-80860-5, Pocket) Simon & Schuster.

—The Case of the Worried Waitress. 1986. 160p. mass mkt. 2.95 o.s.i (0-345-33193-1) Ballantine Bks.

—Perry Mason: Seven Complete Novels. 19th ed. 1994. 832p. 13.99 o.s.i (0-517-29363-3) Random Hse. Value Publishing.

Gardner, Leonard. Fat City. 1986. (Vintage Contemporaries Ser.). 208p. pap. 6.95 o.s.i (0-394-74316-4, Vintage) Knopf Publishing Group.

—Fat City. 1996. (California Fiction Ser.). 183p. pap. text 15.95 (0-520-20657-6) Univ. of California Pr.

Gardner, Theodore R., 2nd. Flip Side: A Novel of Suspense. 1997. 269p. 22.00 (1-888310-96-0) Knoll, Allen A. Pubs.

Garey, Berton D. Death Dance: A Novel. 1999. 354 p. reprint ed. pap. 11.95 (0-943389-29-1) Snow Lion Graphics/SLG Bks.

Garfield, Henry. Room 13. 2001. 320p. (YA). (gr. 7 up). pap. 5.99 (0-689-84153-1, Simon Pulse) Simon & Schuster Children's Publishing.

—Room 13. 1997. 320p. 23.95 o.p. (0-312-15203-5, Saint Martin's Minotaur) St. Martin's Pr.

Garnett, Gale Z. Visible Amazement. 2001. (Illus.). 288p. 23.00 (0-684-87306-0, Simon & Schuster) Simon & Schuster.

Garrison, Zoe. Golden Triple Time. 1986. mass mkt. 2.95 o.p. (0-451-15163-1, Signet Bks.); 1986. mass mkt. 3.95 o.p. (0-451-14150-4, Signet Bks.); 1985. 448p. 15.95 o.p. (0-453-00478-4) NAL.

Garton, Ray. Shackled. 1997. 560p. mass mkt. 5.99 o.s.i (0-553-29891-7) Bantam Bks.

Garwood, Julie. Make Friends with Murder. 1991. 224p. 17.95 o.p. (0-312-07030-6); 1958. o.p. (0-312-06408-X) St. Martin's Pr. (Saint Martin's Minotaur).

Gaslin, Glenn. Beemer: A Novel. 2003. 288p. 23.00 (1-56947-329-3) Soho Pr., Inc.

Gault, William C. Cat & Mouse. 1988. 176p. 12.95 o.p. (0-312-01398-1, Saint Martin's Minotaur) St. Martin's Pr.

—The Chicano War. 1986. 192p. 14.95 o.p. (0-8027-5640-9) Walker & Co.

—Come Die with Me. 1987. 188p. 2.95 o.s.i (0-441-11539-X, Diamond Bks.) Berkley Publishing Group.

—County Kill. 1988. 2.95 (1-55773-017-2, Diamond Bks.) Berkley Publishing Group.

—Day of the Ram. 1988. 2.95 (1-55773-091-1, Diamond Bks.) Berkley Publishing Group.

—Dead Hero. 1988. 2.95 (1-55773-037-7, Diamond Bks.) Berkley Publishing Group.

—Dead Pigeon. 1992. (Mystery Scene Bk.). 160p. pap. 3.95 o.p. (0-88184-839-5, Carroll & Graf Pubs.) Avalon Publishing Group.

—Dead Seed. l.t. ed. 1987. pap. 13.95 o.p. (1-55504-039-X) BBC Audiobooks America.

—Dead Seed. 1985. 12.95 o.p. (0-8027-5604-2) Walker & Co.

—Death in Donegal Bay. 1984. 192p. 12.95 o.p. (0-8027-5591-7) Walker & Co.

—Murder in the Raw. 1988. 2.95 (1-55773-061-X, Diamond Bks.) Berkley Publishing Group.

Gautreaux, Tim. Next Step in the Dance. 352p. 1999. pap. 14.00 (0-312-19936-8); 1998. 23.00 o.p. (0-312-18143-4) Picador.

Geller, Shari P. Fatal Convictions. 1996. 416p. 24.00 o.p. (0-06-039181-2) HarperCollins Pubs.

—Fatal Convictions. 1998. 544p. mass mkt. 6.50 o.s.i (0-06-101223-8, HarperTorch) Morrow/Avon.

Gentry, Anita. Night Summons. 1998. (WWL Mystery Ser.). per. (0-373-26276-0, 1-26276-5, Worldwide Library) Harlequin Enterprises, Ltd.

—Night Summons. 1996. 256p. 22.95 o.p. (0-312-14691-4, Saint Martin's Minotaur) St. Martin's Pr.

Gerber, Merrill J. Anna in Chains. 1997. (Library of Modern Jewish Literature). 136p. 19.95 (0-8156-0484-X) Syracuse Univ. Pr.

Gibbs, Tony. Fade to Black. 1997. 256p. 22.50 o.p. (0-89296-602-5); 1996. 328p. 21.95 o.p. (0-89296-603-3) Mysterious Pr.

—Shot in the Dark. 1997. 320p. mass mkt. 5.99 (0-446-40519-1) Warner Bks., Inc.

Gibson, William. Virtual Light. 1994. 368p. mass mkt. 7.50 (0-553-56606-7) Bantam Bks.

—Virtual Light. abr. ed. 1994. audio 16.98 o.s.i (0-553-74542-5, RH Audio) Random Hse. Audio Publishing Group.

—Virtual Light, unabr. ed. 1994. audio 51.00 (1-55690-967-5, 94110E7) Recorded Bks., LLC.

Gilb, Dagoberto. The Magic of Blood. 1994. 304p. pap. 12.00 (0-8021-3399-1, Grove Pr.) Grove/Atlantic, Inc.

—The Magic of Blood. 1993. 289p. reprint ed. 10.95 o.p. (0-8263-1436-8) Univ. of New Mexico Pr.

—The Magic of Blood. 1993. E-Book 10.95 (0-585-18787-8) netLibrary, Inc.

Gilbar, Steven, ed. California Shorts. 1999. 352p. pap. 15.95 (1-890771-18-X) Heyday Bks.

—Santa Barbara Stories: An Anthology of the Best Short Fiction Set in the California Riviera. 1998. 208p. pap. 14.95 (1-880284-31-6) Daniel, John & Co., Pubs.

Giles, Molly. Iron Shoes: A Novel. 240p. 2000. 22.00 (0-7432-0246-5); 2000. (Illus.). 22.00 o.s.i (0-684-85993-9); 2001. reprint ed. pap. 13.00 (0-684-85992-0) Simon & Schuster. (Simon & Schuster).

—Iron Shoes: A Novel. l.t. ed. 2001. (Thorndike Basic Ser.). 377p. 28.95 (0-7862-3078-9) Thorndike Pr.

Gilligan, Roy. Chinese Restaurants Never Serve Breakfast. 1988. 163p. (Orig.). reprint ed. 29.00 o.p. (0-8095-4203-X, 19624135) Millefleurs.

—Chinese Restaurants Never Serve Breakfast: Murder in Carmel. 1986. (Pat Riordan Mystery Ser.). 180p. reprint ed. pap. 8.95 (0-9626136-2-2) Brendan Bks.

—Happiness Is Often Deadly. 1992. (Pat Riordan Mystery Ser.). pap. 8.95 (0-9626136-3-0) Brendan Bks.

—Happiness Is Often Deadly. 1992. (Pat Riordan Mystery Ser.). 180p. reprint ed. lib. bdg. 24.00 o.p. (0-8095-4211-0) Millefleurs.

—Live Oaks Also Die. 1990. (Pat Riordan Mystery Ser.). 184p. (Orig.). pap. 8.95 (0-9626136-0-6) Brendan Bks.

—Live Oaks Also Die. 1991. (Pat Riordan Mystery Ser.). 188p. (Orig.). (C). reprint ed. pap. text 26.00 o.p. (0-8095-4209-9) Millefleurs.

—Playing God . . . & Other Games. 1993. (Pat Riordan Mystery Ser.). 180p. (Orig.). pap. 8.95 (0-9626136-4-9) Brendan Bks.

Gilmore, Monique. Soul Deep. 1997. 256p. mass mkt. 4.99 o.s.i (0-7860-0395-2, Pinnacle Bks.) Kensington Publishing Corp.

Gilmour, H. B. Billy Moon. 1993. 17.95 (0-932279-44-9) World Citizens.

Girdner, Jaqueline. Adjusted to Death. 1991. 3.99 (1-55773-453-4) Ace Bks.

—Adjusted to Death. 1994. mass mkt. 4.99 o.s.i (0-425-14706-1) Berkley Publishing Group.

—A Cry for Self-Help. (Kate Jasper Mysteries Ser.). 288p. 1998. mass mkt. 5.99 o.s.i (0-425-16265-6); 1997. 21.95 o.s.i (0-425-15630-3, Prime Crime) Berkley Publishing Group.

—Death Hits the Fan. 1999. (Kate Jasper Mystery Ser.). 288p. reprint ed. mass mkt. 5.99 o.s.i (0-425-16808-5, Prime Crime) Berkley Publishing Group.

—Death Hits the Fan: A Kate Jasper Mystery. 1998. (Kate Jasper Mysteries Ser.). 288p. 21.95 o.s.i (0-425-16148-X) Berkley Publishing Group.

—Fat-Free & Fatal. 1993. (Orig.). 3.99 o.s.i (1-55773-917-X) Ace Bks.

—Fat-Free & Fatal. 1993. 224p. (Orig.). mass mkt. 5.99 o.s.i (0-425-15811-X, Prime Crime) Berkley Publishing Group.

—The Last Resort. 1991. 3.95 (1-55773-525-5) Ace Bks.

—The Last Resort. 1991. mass mkt. 5.50 o.s.i (0-425-14431-3, Prime Crime) Berkley Publishing Group.

—Most Likely to Die. (Mistery Ser.). 288p. 1996. 21.95 o.s.i (0-425-15145-X, Prime Crime); 1996. pap. 10.00 o.p. (0-425-15146-8); 1997. reprint ed. mass mkt. 5.99 o.s.i (0-425-15721-0, Prime Crime) Berkley Publishing Group.

—Murder Most Mellow. 1992. 3.99 o.s.i (1-55773-721-5, Diamond Bks.) Ace Bks.

—Murder Most Mellow. 1992. mass mkt. 5.50 o.s.i (0-425-14707-X, Prime Crime) Berkley Publishing Group.

—Murder, My Deer. 2001. (Kate Jasper Mysteries Ser.). 288p. mass mkt. 5.99 o.s.i (0-425-17885-4, Prime Crime) Berkley Publishing Group.

—Murder, My Deer: A Kate Jasper Mystery. 2000. (Kate Jasper Mysteries Ser.). (Illus.). 275p. 21.95 o.s.i (0-425-17328-3) Berkley Publishing Group.

—Murder on the Astral Plane. 2000. (Kate Jasper Mysteries Ser.: Vol. 10). 309p. mass mkt. 5.99 o.s.i (0-425-17359-3, Prime Crime) Berkley Publishing Group.

—Murder on the Astral Plane: A Kate Jasper Mystery. 1999. (Kate Jasper Ser.). 320p. 21.95 o.s.i (0-425-16701-1, Prime Crime) Berkley Publishing Group.

—A Stiff Critique. 1995. 272p. (Orig.). mass mkt. 4.99 o.s.i (0-425-14719-3, Prime Crime) Berkley Publishing Group.

—Tea-Totally Dead. 1994. mass mkt. 4.99 o.s.i (0-425-14210-8) Berkley Publishing Group.

Godbout, Jacques. An American Story. Saint-Pierre, Yves, tr. from FRE. 1988. (Emergent Literatures Ser.).Tr. of Histoire Americaine. 161p. (Orig.). pap. 12.95 (0-8166-1710-4); pap. text 19.95 o.p. (0-8166-1709-0) Univ. of Minnesota Pr.

Goddard, Kenneth M. Balefire. 1996. 401p. mass mkt. 6.99 (0-8125-3383-6, Forge Bks.) Doherty, Tom Assocs., LLC.

Goddard, Kenneth W. Balefire. 1983. 352p. text 14.95 o.p. (0-553-05034-6) Bantam Bks.

Godwin, Gail. Glass People. 1996. 224p. pap. 15.00 (0-345-38990-5) Ballantine Bks.

—Glass People. 1986. (Contemporary American Fiction Ser.). 224p. pap. 6.95 o.p. (0-14-008222-0, Penguin Bks.) Viking Penguin.

Gold, Herbert. Daughter Mine. E-Book 23.95 (0-312-27576-5) St. Martin's Pr.

—Dreaming. 1988. 288p. 17.95 o.s.i (*1-55611-071-5*) Fine, Donald I. Bks.
—A Girl of Forty. 1986. 254p. 16.95 o.s.i (*0-917657-63-2*) Fine, Donald I. Bks.
—She Took My Arm As If She Loved Me. 256p. 1998. pap. 12.95 (*0-312-19525-7*, Saint Martin's Griffin); 1997. 21.95 (*0-312-15653-7*) St. Martin's Pr.
—Travels in San Francisco. 1991. pap. 8.95 o.p. (*1-55970-086-6*) Arcade Publishing, Inc.
Goldberg, Lee. Beyond the Beyond. 1997. 320p. 23.95 o.p. (*0-312-15064-4*) St. Martin's Pr.
—My Gun Has Bullets. 1995. 262p. 21.00 o.p. (*0-312-11862-7*, Saint Martin's Minotaur) St. Martin's Pr.
Goldberg, Leonard S. Deadly Harvest. 1997. 320p. 23.95 o.s.i (*0-525-94093-6*) Dutton/Plume.
—Deadly Harvest. 1998. 416p. mass mkt. 6.99 o.s.i (*0-451-18743-1*, Signet Bks.) NAL.
—Deadly Medicine. 1992. 352p. (Orig.). mass mkt. 6.99 (*0-451-17439-9*, Signet Bks.) NAL.
—Deadly Practice. 1994. 320p. (Orig.). mass mkt. 6.99 (*0-451-17945-5*) NAL.
Goldberg, Tod B. Fake Liar Cheat. 2000. 176p. pap. 12.95 (*0-7434-0056-9*, MTV) Simon & Schuster.
Goldemberg, Rose Leiman. Adios, Hollywood: My Story by Dick, Dog of Oaxaca As Told to Rose Leiman Goldemberg. 2000. 180p. pap. 16.95 (*0-595-08907-0*) iUniverse, Inc.
Goldemberg, Rose Leiman, told to. Adios, Hollywood: My Story by Dick, Dog of Oaxaca As Told to Rose Leiman Goldemberg. 1994. 176p. 18.95 o.p. (*0-312-10455-3*) St. Martin's Pr.
Goldman, William. Tinsel. 1980. mass mkt. 2.75 o.s.i (*0-440-18735-4*); 1979. pap. 10.95 o.s.i (*0-385-29031-4*, Delacorte Pr.) Dell Publishing.
Goldsmith, Olivia. Flavor of the Month. 1993. 704p. 23.00 o.p. (*0-671-79449-3*, Simon & Schuster) Simon & Schuster.
Gomez, Jeff. Geniuses of Crack. 1997. 432p. pap. 12.00 o.s.i (*0-684-83194-5*, Touchstone) Simon & Schuster.
Gonzalez, Rigoberto. Crossing Vines: A Novel. 2003. (Chicana & Chicano Visions of the Americas Ser.: Vol. 2). 216p. 24.95 (*0-8061-3528-X*) Univ. of Oklahoma Pr.
Goodbye, Saigon. audio Thorsons.
Gordon, Nadia. Death by the Glass. 224p. pap. 11.95 (*0-8118-3678-9*) Chronicle Bks. LLC.
—Sharpshooter: A Napa Valley Mystery. 2002. 224p. pap. 11.95 (*0-8118-3462-X*) Chronicle Bks. LLC.
Gores, Joe. Cases. 1999. 354p. 23.00 (*0-89296-593-2*) Mysterious Pr.
—Cases. l.t. ed. 1999. (Mystery Ser.). 555p. 27.95 (*0-7862-1882-7*) Thorndike Pr.
—Cases. 1999. mass mkt. (*0-446-60703-7*) Warner Bks., Inc.
—Contract Null & Void. 1996. 82p. 21.95 o.s.i (*0-89296-592-4*) Mysterious Pr.
—Contract Null & Void. 1997. (Dka File Novel Ser.). 336p. mass mkt. 6.50 o.s.i (*0-446-40447-0*) Warner Bks., Inc.
—Dead Skip. 1981. mass mkt. 2.25 o.s.i (*0-345-29206-5*); 1974. mass mkt. 1.25 o.p. (*0-345-24129-0*) Ballantine Bks.
—Dead Skip. 1992. 208p. reprint ed. mass mkt. 4.99 o.s.i (*0-446-40312-1*, Mysterious Pr. Paperback Bks.) Warner Bks., Inc.
—Final Notice. 1992. 208p. reprint ed. mass mkt. 4.99 (*0-446-40314-8*, Mysterious Pr. Paperback Bks.) Warner Bks., Inc.
—Gone, No Forwarding. 1981. mass mkt. 2.25 o.s.i (*0-345-29208-1*) Ballantine Bks.
—Gone, No Forwarding. 1993. 224p. mass mkt. 5.50 o.s.i (*0-446-40315-6*) Warner Bks., Inc.
—Menaced Assassin. 1994. 336p. 19.95 o.s.i (*0-89296-542-8*) Mysterious Pr.
—Menaced Assassin. 1995. 384p. mass mkt. 5.50 (*0-446-40390-3*) Warner Bks., Inc.
—32 Cadillacs. 1992. 352p. 18.95 (*0-89296-298-4*) Mysterious Pr.
—32 Cadillacs. 1993. 352p. mass mkt. 5.99 o.s.i (*0-446-40360-1*) Warner Bks., Inc.
Gorman, S. S. Daredevil Bladers. Clancy, Lisa, ed. 1993. (High-Fives Ser.). 144p. (Orig.). (J). pap. 2.99 (*0-671-78901-5*, Aladdin) Simon & Schuster Children's Publishing.
Goudge, Eileen. One Last Dance. abr. ed. 1999. audio 17.95 o.p. (*1-56740-842-7*, 1724, Nova Audio Bks.); audio 28.95 (*1-56740-431-6*, 1722, Bookcassette); 14p. audio 89.25 (*1-56740-657-2*, 1723, Unabridged Library Editions) Brilliance Audio.
—One Last Dance. l.t. ed. 1999. 29.95 (*0-7862-2005-8*, Macmillan Reference USA) Gale Group.
—One Last Dance. abr. ed. 1999. audio 17.95 Highsmith Inc.
—One Last Dance. l.t. ed. 2001. (Magna Large Print Ser.). 576p. (*0-7505-1750-6*) Magna Large Print Bks. GBR. *Dist:* Ulverscroft Large Print Canada, Ltd.
—One Last Dance. 2000. 448p. mass mkt. 7.99 (*0-451-19948-0*, Signet Bks.) NAL.
—One Last Dance. 1999. 398p. 24.95 o.p. (*0-670-88575-4*) Viking Penguin.
—Stranger in Paradise. 2002. 432p. reprint ed. mass mkt. 7.99 (*0-451-20577-4*, Signet Bks.) NAL.
—Stranger in Paradise. l.t. ed. 2002. (Carson Spring Ser.: Bk. 1). 573p. pap. 13.95 (*0-7862-3447-4*); 2001. 586p. 31.95 (*0-7862-3446-6*) Thorndike Pr.
—Stranger in Paradise. 2001. (Carson Spring Ser.: Bk. 1). 384p. 24.95 o.s.i (*0-670-89987-9*, Viking) Viking Penguin.
—Taste of Honey. 2003. 432p. reprint ed. mass mkt. 7.99 (*0-451-20734-3*, Signet Bks.) NAL.
—Taste of Honey. l.t. ed. 2002. (Basic Ser.). 699p. 32.95 (*0-7862-4562-X*) Thorndike Pr.
—Taste of Honey. 2002. 336p. 24.95 o.s.i (*0-670-03098-8*, Viking) Viking Penguin.
—Wish Come True. 2004. 416p. mass mkt. 7.99 (*0-451-21061-1*, Signet Bks.) NAL.
—Wish Come True. l.t. ed. 2004. 640p. pap. 13.95 (*1-59413-030-2*, Large Print Pr.); 2003. 737p. 31.95 (*0-7862-5921-3*) Thorndike Pr.
—Wish Come True: A Carson Springs Novel. 2003. 384p. 24.95 (*0-670-03216-6*, Viking) Viking Penguin.
Goulart, Ron. Groucho Marx, Private Eye. 1999. 263p. 23.95 (*0-312-19895-7*, Saint Martin's Minotaur) St. Martin's Pr.
Gould, Judith. My Second Love. 1997. 464p. 25.95 o.p. (*0-525-93930-X*) Dutton/Plume.
Grafton, Sue. A Is for Alibi. 1987. (Kinsey Millhone Mystery Ser.). 224p. mass mkt. 7.99 (*0-553-27991-2*); mass mkt. 3.50 o.s.i (*0-553-26563-6*) Bantam Bks.
— A Is for Alibi. unabr. collector's ed. 1993. (Kinsey Millhone Mystery Ser.). audio 48.00 (*0-7366-2455-4*, 3219) Books on Tape, Inc.
— A Is for Alibi. 1994. (Kinsey Millhone Mystery Ser.). reprint ed. lib. bdg. 29.95 o.p. (*1-56849-284-7*) Buccaneer Bks., Inc.
— A Is for Alibi. l.t. ed. 1991. (Kinsey Millhone Mystery Ser.). 354p. 20.95 o.p. (*0-8161-5144-X*, Macmillan Reference USA) Gale Group.
— A Is for Alibi. 1982. (Kinsey Millhone Mystery Ser.). 256p. o.p. (*0-03-059048-5*); 288p. 27.00 (*0-8050-1334-2*) Holt, Henry & Co.
— A Is for Alibi. 1984. (Kinsey Millhone Mystery Ser.). 192p. mass mkt. 2.75 o.p. (*0-451-12862-1*) NAL.
— A Is for Alibi, Set. abr. ed. 1990. (Kinsey Millhone Mystery Ser.). audio 18.00 o.s.i (*0-394-57977-1*, 390310, RH Audio) Random Hse. Audio Publishing Group.
— A Is for Alibi. 2001. (Kinsey Millhone Mystery Ser.). 285p. (*0-7621-8860-X*) Reader's Digest Assn., Inc., The.
— A Is for Alibi. l.t. ed. 1988. (Kinsey Millhone Mystery Ser.). 432p. 15.95 o.p. (*0-7089-1744-5*, Ulverscroft) Thorpe, F. A. Pubs. GBR. *Dist:* Ulverscroft Large Print Bks., Ltd.
—B Is for Burglar. 1986. (Kinsey Millhone Mystery Ser.). 224p. mass mkt. 7.99 (*0-553-28034-1*); mass mkt. 3.50 o.s.i (*0-553-26061-8*) Bantam Bks.
—B Is for Burglar. 1994. (Kinsey Millhone Mystery Ser.). reprint ed. lib. bdg. 29.95 (*1-56849-283-9*) Buccaneer Bks., Inc.
—B Is for Burglar. l.t. ed. 1991. (Kinsey Millhone Mystery Ser.). 20.95 o.p. (*0-8161-5145-8*, Macmillan Reference USA) Gale Group.
—B Is for Burglar. 1985. (Kinsey Millhone Mystery Ser.). 240p. 27.00 (*0-8050-1632-5*) Holt, Henry & Co.
—B Is for Burglar. l.t. ed. 1988. (Kinsey Millhone Mystery Ser.). 448p. 17.95 o.p. (*0-7089-1786-0*, Ulverscroft) Thorpe, F. A. Pubs. GBR. *Dist:* Ulverscroft Large Print Bks., Ltd.
—C Is for Corpse. 1987. mass mkt. 3.50 o.s.i (*0-553-26468-0*) Bantam Bks.
—C Is for Corpse. 1986. (Kinsey Millhone Mystery Ser.). 256p. 19.95 o.p. (*0-03-001888-9*); 258p. 27.00 (*0-8050-2818-8*) Holt, Henry & Co.
—C Is for Corpse. l.t. ed. 1991. (Kinsey Millhone Mystery Ser.). 371p. pap. 22.95 (*0-8161-5146-6*) Thorndike Pr.
—C Is for Corpse. l.t. ed. 1988. (Kinsey Millhone Mystery Ser.). 432p. 15.95 o.p. (*0-7089-1898-0*, Ulverscroft) Thorpe, F. A. Pubs. GBR. *Dist:* Ulverscroft Large Print Bks., Ltd.
—D Is for Deadbeat. 1988. (Kinsey Millhone Mystery Ser.). 256p. reprint ed. mass mkt. 7.99 (*0-553-27163-6*) Bantam Bks.
—D Is for Deadbeat. unabr. collector's ed. 1993. (Kinsey Millhone Mystery Ser.). audio 42.00 (*0-7366-2568-2*, 3317) Books on Tape, Inc.
—D Is for Deadbeat. l.t. ed. 1992. (Kinsey Millhone Mystery Ser.). 345p. 16.95 o.p. (*0-8161-5147-4*, Macmillan Reference USA) Gale Group.
—D Is for Deadbeat, Set. abr. ed. 1993. (Kinsey Millhone Mystery Ser.). audio 18.00 (*0-679-40354-X*, 390596, RH Audio) Random Hse. Audio Publishing Group.
—D Is for Deadbeat. l.t. ed. 1990. (Kinsey Millhone Mystery Ser.). 18.95 o.p. (*0-7089-2118-3*, Ulverscroft) Thorpe, F. A. Pubs. GBR. *Dist:* Ulverscroft Large Print Bks., Ltd.
—E Is for Evidence. 1989. (Kinsey Millhone Mystery Ser.). 208p. mass mkt. 7.99 (*0-553-27955-6*) Bantam Bks.
—E Is for Evidence. unabr. collector's ed. 1994. (Kinsey Millhone Mystery Ser.). audio 42.00 (*0-7366-2615-8*, 3357) Books on Tape, Inc.
—E Is for Evidence. l.t. ed. 1989. (Kinsey Millhone Mystery Ser.). 319p. 20.95 o.p. (*0-8161-4715-9*, Macmillan Reference USA) Gale Group.
—E Is for Evidence. 1988. (Kinsey Millhone Mystery Ser.). 240p. 27.00 (*0-8050-0459-9*) Holt, Henry & Co.
—E Is for Evidence. abr. ed. 1989. (Kinsey Millhone Mystery Ser.). audio 18.00 (*0-394-57982-8*, 390695, RH Audio) Random Hse. Audio Publishing Group.
—F Is for Fugitive. 1990. (Kinsey Millhone Mystery Ser.). 352p. mass mkt. 7.99 (*0-553-28478-9*) Bantam Bks.
—F Is for Fugitive. unabr. collector's ed. 1994. (Kinsey Millhone Mystery Ser.). audio 48.00 (*0-7366-2620-4*, 3360) Books on Tape, Inc.
—F Is for Fugitive. l.t. ed. 1990. (Kinsey Millhone Mystery Ser.). 368p. 21.95 (*0-8161-4901-1*, Macmillan Reference USA) Gale Group.
—F Is for Fugitive. 1989. (Kinsey Millhone Mystery Ser.). 272p. 25.00 (*0-8050-0460-2*) Holt, Henry & Co.
—F Is for Fugitive. abr. ed. 1989. (Kinsey Millhone Mystery Ser.). audio 18.00 (*0-394-57983-6*, 390742); audio 17.00 (*0-394-58173-3*) Random Hse. Audio Publishing Group. (RH Audio).
—G Is for Gumshoe. (Kinsey Millhone Mystery Ser.). 1997. pap. 12.95 o.s.i (*0-449-00062-1*); 1995. mass mkt. 6.99 o.p. (*0-449-45491-6*); 1993. mass mkt. 5.99 o.p. (*0-449-45161-5*); 1991. pap. 6.99 (*0-449-45764-8*); 1991. 352p. mass mkt. 7.99 (*0-449-21936-4*) Ballantine Bks. (Fawcett).
—G Is for Gumshoe. unabr. collector's ed. 1994. (Kinsey Millhone Mystery Ser.). audio 48.00 (*0-7366-2679-4*, 3415) Books on Tape, Inc.
—G Is for Gumshoe. l.t. ed. 1991. (Kinsey Millhone Mystery Ser.). 355p. 20.95 o.p. (*0-8161-5090-7*, Macmillan Reference USA) Gale Group.
—G Is for Gumshoe. 1990. (Kinsey Millhone Mystery Ser.). 272p. 27.00 (*0-8050-0461-0*) Holt, Henry & Co.
—G Is for Gumshoe. abr. ed. 1990. (Kinsey Millhone Mystery Ser.). audio 16.00 o.p. (*0-394-58632-8*);Set. audio 18.00 (*0-394-58563-1*, 390833) Random Hse. Audio Publishing Group. (RH Audio).
—G Is for Gumshoe. l.t. ed. 1991. (Kinsey Millhone Mystery Ser.). 355p. pap. 22.95 o.p. (*0-8161-5091-5*) Thorndike Pr.
—H Is for Homicide. (Kinsey Millhone Mystery Ser.). 1997. pap. 11.00 o.s.i (*0-449-00063-X*); 1995. mass mkt. 6.99 o.p. (*0-449-45492-4*); 1993. mass mkt. 5.99 o.p. (*0-449-45162-3*); 1992. pap. 6.99 (*0-449-45765-6*); 1992. 304p. mass mkt. 7.99 (*0-449-21946-1*) Ballantine Bks. (Fawcett).
—H Is for Homicide. unabr. collector's ed. 1994. (Kinsey Millhone Mystery Ser.). audio 48.00 (*0-7366-2728-6*, 3458) Books on Tape, Inc.
—H Is for Homicide. l.t. ed. 1992. (Kinsey Millhone Mystery Ser.). 390p. 16.95 o.p. (*0-8161-5281-0*, Macmillan Reference USA) Gale Group.
—H Is for Homicide. (Kinsey Millhone Mystery Ser.). 1991. 272p. 25.00 (*0-8050-1084-X*); 1992. 390p. lib. bdg. 20.95 (*0-8161-5280-2*) Holt, Henry & Co.
—H Is for Homicide, Set. abr. ed. 1991. (Kinsey Millhone Mystery Ser.). 18.00 incl. audio (*0-394-58698-0*, 390890, RH Audio) Random Hse. Audio Publishing Group.
—I Is for Innocent. (Kinsey Millhone Mystery Ser.). 1997. 304p. pap. 12.95 (*0-449-00064-8*); 1995. mass mkt. 6.99 o.p. (*0-449-45493-2*); 1994. mass mkt. 5.99 o.p. (*0-449-45335-9*); 1993. pap. 6.99 (*0-449-45766-4*); 1993. 352p. mass mkt. 7.99 (*0-449-22151-2*) Ballantine Bks. (Fawcett).
—I Is for Innocent. unabr. ed. 1993. (Kinsey Millhone Mystery Ser.). audio 56.00 (*0-7366-2433-3*, 3198) Books on Tape, Inc.
—I Is for Innocent. l.t. ed. 1994. (Kinsey Millhone Mystery Ser.). 373p. 16.95 o.p. (*0-8161-5538-0*, Macmillan Reference USA) Gale Group.
—I Is for Innocent. 1992. (Kinsey Millhone Mystery Ser.). 272p. 27.00 (*0-8050-1085-8*) Holt, Henry & Co.
—I Is for Innocent. abr. ed. 1992. (Kinsey Millhone Mystery Ser.). audio 18.00 (*0-679-41115-1*, 390946, RH Audio) Random Hse. Audio Publishing Group.
—I Is for Innocent. l.t. ed. 1993. (Kinsey Millhone Mystery Ser.). 373p. 24.95 (*0-8161-5537-2*) Thorndike Pr.
—J Is for Judgment. (Kinsey Millhone Mystery Ser.). 1997. pap. 11.00 o.s.i (*0-449-00065-6*); 1995. mass mkt. 6.99 o.p. (*0-449-45495-9*); 1994. pap. 6.99 (*0-449-45767-2*); 1994. 384p. mass mkt. 7.99 (*0-449-22148-2*) Ballantine Bks. (Fawcett).
—J Is for Judgment. unabr. ed. 1994. (Kinsey Millhone Mystery Ser.). audio 56.00 (*0-7366-2736-7*, 3463) Books on Tape, Inc.
—J Is for Judgment. l.t. ed. 1993. (Kinsey Millhone Mystery Ser.). lib. bdg. 23.95 o.p. (*0-8161-5750-2*, Macmillan Reference USA) Gale Group.
—J Is for Judgment. 1993. (Kinsey Millhone Mystery Ser.). 304p. 27.00 (*0-8050-1935-9*) Holt, Henry & Co.
—J Is for Judgment, Set. abr. ed. 1993. (Kinsey Millhone Mystery Ser.). audio 18.00 (*0-679-41368-5*, 390993, RH Audio) Random Hse. Audio Publishing Group.
—J Is for Judgment. l.t. ed. 1994. (Kinsey Millhone Mystery Ser.). 410p. pap. 20.95 (*0-8161-5751-0*) Thorndike Pr.
—K Is for Killer. (Kinsey Millhone Mystery Ser.). 1997. pap. 11.00 o.s.i (*0-449-00066-4*); 1995. pap. 6.99 (*0-449-45768-0*); 1995. 320p. mass mkt. 7.99 (*0-449-22150-4*) Ballantine Bks. (Fawcett).
—K Is for Killer. unabr. ed. 1995. (Kinsey Millhone Mystery Ser.). audio 56.00 (*0-7366-3043-0*, 3725) Books on Tape, Inc.
—K Is for Killer. l.t. ed. 1994. (Kinsey Millhone Mystery Ser.). 26.95 o.p. (*1-56895-101-9*, Wheeler Publishing, Inc.) Gale Group.
—K Is for Killer. 1994. (Kinsey Millhone Mystery Ser.). 304p. 27.00 (*0-8050-1936-7*) Holt, Henry & Co.
—Kinsey Millhone Mystery Series Boxed Set: G Is for Gumshoe; H Is for Homicide; I Is for Innocent, 3 vols. 1993. (Kinsey Millhone Mystery Ser.). 23.97 o.s.i (*0-449-22262-4*, Fawcett) Ballantine Bks.
—L Is for Lawless. (Kinsey Millhone Mystery Ser.). 1997. pap. 11.00 o.s.i (*0-449-00067-2*); 1996. pap. 6.99 (*0-449-45769-9*); 1996. 336p. mass mkt. 7.99 (*0-449-22149-0*) Ballantine Bks. (Fawcett).
—L Is for Lawless. unabr. ed. 1996. (Kinsey Millhone Mystery Ser.). audio 56.00 (*0-7366-3305-7*, 3959) Books on Tape, Inc.
—L Is for Lawless. 1995. (Kinsey Millhone Mystery Ser.). 304p. 24.00 (*0-8050-1937-5*) Holt, Henry & Co.
—L Is for Lawless, Set. abr. ed. 1995. (Kinsey Millhone Mystery Ser.). audio 18.00 (*0-679-42462-8*, 393143, RH Audio) Random Hse. Audio Publishing Group.
—L Is for Lawless. 1997. (Kinsey Millhone Mystery Ser.). 5.98 o.p. (*0-7651-0722-8*) Smithmark Pubs., Inc.
—L Is for Lawless. l.t. ed. (Kinsey Millhone Mystery Ser.). 384p. 1996. pap. 26.95 (*0-7838-1383-X*); 1995. 29.95 (*0-7838-1382-1*) Thorndike Pr.
—M Is for Malice. 1997. (Kinsey Millhone Mystery Ser.). 352p. mass mkt. 7.99 (*0-449-22360-4*, Fawcett) Ballantine Bks.
—M Is for Malice. unabr. collector's ed. 1997. (Kinsey Millhone Mystery Ser.). audio 56.00 (*0-913369-70-5*, 4322) Books on Tape, Inc.
—M Is for Malice. 1996. (Kinsey Millhone Mystery Ser.). (Illus.). 304p. 27.00 (*0-8050-3637-7*) Holt, Henry & Co.
—M Is for Malice. l.t. ed. 1997. (Kinsey Millhone Mystery Ser.). 458p. pap. 27.95 (*0-7838-1834-3*); lib. bdg. 29.95 (*0-7838-1833-5*) Thorndike Pr.
—N Is for Noose. 1999. (Kinsey Millhone Mystery Ser.). mass mkt. (*0-449-00457-0*); 336p. mass mkt. 7.99 (*0-449-22361-2*) Ballantine Bks. (Fawcett).
—N Is for Noose. unabr. ed. 1998. (Kinsey Millhone Mystery Ser.). audio 56.00 (*0-7366-4141-6*, 4645) Books on Tape, Inc.
—N Is for Noose, unabr. ed. 1999. (Kinsey Millhone Mystery Ser.). audio 39.95 Highsmith Inc.
—N Is for Noose. 1998. (Kinsey Millhone Mystery Ser.). 320p. 25.00 (*0-8050-3650-4*) Holt, Henry & Co.
—N Is for Noose. abr. ed. 2002. audio compact disk 25.95 (*0-553-71339-6*); 1998. audio 24.00 (*0-375-40289-6*, 495734); 1998. audio 34.95 (*0-375-40326-4*, AD37D) Random Hse. Audio Publishing Group. (RH Audio).
—N Is for Noose. l.t. ed. (Kinsey Millhone Mystery Ser.). 455p. 1999. pap. 27.95 (*0-7862-1297-7*); 1998. 30.95 (*0-7862-1296-9*) Thorndike Pr.
—O Is for Outlaw. 2001. (Kinsey Millhone Mystery Ser.). 368p. mass mkt. 7.99 (*0-449-00378-7*, Ballantine Bks.) Ballantine Bks.
—O Is for Outlaw. 2000. (Kinsey Millhone Mystery Ser.). audio 39.95 Blackstone Audio Bks., Inc.
—O Is for Outlaw. 1999. (Kinsey Millhone Mystery Ser.). audio 44.95 Books on Tape, Inc.
—O Is for Outlaw. abr. ed. 1999. (Kinsey Millhone Mystery Ser.). audio 25.95. audio 39.95 Highsmith Inc.
—O Is for Outlaw. 1999. (Kinsey Millhone Mystery Ser.). 336p. 26.00 (*0-8050-5955-5*) Holt, Henry & Co.

—O Is for Outlaw. abr. ed. 2004. audio 17.99 (*0-7393-1219-7*, RH Audio Price-Less); 1999. audio compact disk 29.95 (*0-375-40661-1*, RH Audio); 1999. audio 25.95 (*0-375-40415-5*, RH Audio); 1999. audio 39.95 (*0-375-40662-X*, N160, RH Audio) Random Hse. Audio Publishing Group.
—O Is for Outlaw. l.t. ed. 1999. (Kinsey Millhone Mystery Ser.). 534p. 31.95 (*0-7862-2044-9*) Thorndike Pr.
—P Is for Peril. 2001. (Kinsey Millhone Mystery Ser.). 304p. 26.95 (*0-399-14719-5*, Wood, Marian Bks.) Penguin Group (USA) Inc.
—P Is for Peril. l.t. ed. 2003. (Paperback Bestsellers Ser.). 557p. pap. 14.95 (*0-7862-2948-9*) Thorndike Pr.
—Q Is for Quarry. 2002. 400p. 26.95 (*0-399-14915-5*) Putnam Publishing Group, The.
—Q Is for Quarry. pap. o.p. (*0-7862-4369-4*); 2002. 640p. 33.95 (*0-7862-4370-8*) Thorndike Pr.
—Sue Grafton: D is for Deadbeat; E is for Evidence; F is for Fugitive, 3 vols. 2001. (Kinsey Millhone Mystery Ser.). 736p. 13.99 (*0-517-16271-7*) Random Hse. Value Publishing.
Graham, Heather. Long, Lean & Lethal. l.t. ed. 2000. (Large Print Book Ser.). 410p. 28.95 (*1-56895-928-1*, Wheeler Publishing, Inc.) Gale Group.
—Long, Lean & Lethal. 2000. 400p. mass mkt. 6.99 o.s.i (*0-451-40915-9*, Onyx) NAL.
Grant, Jean. The Promise of the Harvest: A Novel, No. 4. 1996. (Salinas Valley Saga Ser.: Bk. 4). 228p. pap. 10.99 (*0-7852-8105-3*) Nelson, Thomas Inc.
—The Promise of Victory: A Novel, No. 3. 1995. (Salinas Valley Saga Ser.: Vol. 3). 9.99 o.p. (*0-7852-8103-7*) Nelson, Thomas Inc.
Grant, Linda. Blind Trust. 1991. (Catherine Sayler Mystery Ser.). mass mkt. 5.99 o.s.i (*0-8041-0791-2*, Ivy Bks.) Ballantine Bks.
—Blind Trust. 1990. 224p. 18.95 o.s.i (*0-684-19165-2*, Macmillan Reference USA) Gale Group.
—Lethal Genes. 1997. mass mkt. 5.99 o.s.i (*0-8041-1558-3*, Ivy Bks.) Ballantine Bks.
—Lethal Genes. 1996. 256p. 21.00 (*0-684-82653-4*, Scribner) Simon & Schuster.
—Love nor Money: An Inspector Catherine Sayler. 1992. (Northern California Mysteries Ser.). mass mkt. 4.50 o.s.i (*0-8041-0947-8*, Ivy Bks.) Ballantine Bks.
—Love nor Money: An Inspector Catherine Sayler. 1991. 288p. 19.95 o.s.i (*0-684-19379-5*, Macmillan Reference USA) Gale Group.
—Random Access Murder: The First Catherine Sayler Mystery. 1998. (Catherine Sayler Mystery Ser.: No. 1). 192p. reprint ed. mass mkt. 5.50 o.p. (*1-890768-09-X*, Intrigue Pr.) Corvus Publishing.
—Random Access Murder: The First Catherine Sayler Mystery. 1988. 192p. pap. 2.95 (*0-380-75534-3*, Avon Bks.) Morrow/Avon.
—Vampire Bytes: A Crime Novel with Catherine Sayler. 1999. mass mkt. 5.99 o.s.i (*0-8041-1862-0*, Ivy Bks.) Ballantine Bks.
—Vampire Bytes: A Crime Novel with Catherine Sayler. 1998. (Crime Novels Ser.). 288p. 22.00 (*0-684-82675-5*, Scribner) Simon & Schuster.
—A Woman's Place. 1995. (Catherine Sayler Mystery Ser.). mass mkt. 5.50 o.s.i (*0-8041-1327-0*, Ivy Bks.) Ballantine Bks.
—A Woman's Place. 1994. 288p. 20.00 o.p. (*0-684-19631-X*, Scribner) Simon & Schuster.
Gray, Genevieve. Fair Laughs the Morn: A Novel. 1994. 288p. pap. 14.95 (*0-86534-213-X*) Sunstone Pr.
Gray, Leonard. Scudding: A Novel. 2000. 228p. pap. 21.99 (*0-7388-2196-9*); text 31.99 (*0-7388-2195-0*); E-Book 8.00 (*0-7388-8810-9*) Xlibris Corp.
Graysmith, Robert. Zodiac. 1987. 384p. mass mkt. 7.99 (*0-425-09808-7*) Berkley Publishing Group.
—Zodiac. 1985. (Illus.). 384p. 16.95 o.p. (*0-312-89895-9*) St. Martin's Pr.
Green, Jane. Jemima J. A Novel about Ugly Ducklings & Swans. 2001. 384p. reprint ed. pap. 11.95 (*0-7679-0518-0*) Broadway Bks.
Green, Kate. Black Dreams: A Theresa Fortunato Mystery. 1993. 288p. 20.00 o.p. (*0-06-017984-8*) HarperTrade.
—Black Dreams: A Theresa Fortunato Mystery. 1994. 464p. mass mkt. 5.99 o.p. (*0-06-109103-0*, HarperTorch) Morrow/Avon.
Greenberg, Martin H. & Waugh, Charles, eds. Hollywood Unreel: Fantasies About Hollywood & the Movies. 1982. 304p. 14.95 o.s.i (*0-8008-3197-7*) Taplinger Publishing Co., Inc.
Greenleaf, Stephen. Beyond Blame. 1986. pap. o.s.i (*0-345-00733-6*); mass mkt. 4.99 o.s.i (*0-345-33670-4*) Ballantine Bks.
—Blood Type: The New John Marshall Tanner Mystery. 1993. 304p. mass mkt. 4.99 o.s.i (*0-553-56106-5*) Bantam Bks.
—Blood Type: The New John Marshall Tanner Mystery. 1992. 304p. 20.00 o.p. (*0-688-11268-4*, Morrow, William & Co.) Morrow/Avon.
—Book Case: A John Marshall Tanner Mystery. 1991. 352p. mass mkt. 4.99 o.s.i (*0-553-29061-4*) Bantam Bks.
—Book Case: A John Marshall Tanner Mystery. 1991. 19.95 o.p. (*0-688-07669-6*, Morrow, William & Co.) Morrow/Avon.
—Death Bed. 1982. mass mkt. 2.50 o.s.i (*0-345-30189-7*) Ballantine Bks.
—Death Bed. 1991. 304p. mass mkt. 4.99 o.s.i (*0-553-29348-6*) Bantam Bks.
—Death Bed. 1980. 320p. 10.95 o.p. (*0-385-27139-5*) Doubleday Publishing.
—Death Bed. 1980. 306p. (J). o.p. (*0-8037-1701-6*, Dial Bks. for Young Readers) Penguin Putnam Bks. for Young Readers.
—The Death Bed. 1985. mass mkt. 2.95 o.s.i (*0-345-32742-X*) Ballantine Bks.
—False Conception: A John Marshall Tanner Novel. (John Marshall Tanner Mysteries Ser.). 1997. 336p. pap. 5.99 (*0-671-00794-7*, Pocket); 1994. 320p. 22.00 (*1-883402-87-5*, Scribner) Simon & Schuster.
—Fatal Obsession. 1985. mass mkt. 2.95 o.s.i (*0-345-33287-3*); 1984. mass mkt. 2.50 o.s.i (*0-345-31485-9*) Ballantine Bks.
—Fatal Obsession. 1991. 256p. mass mkt. 4.99 o.s.i (*0-553-29350-8*) Bantam Bks.
—Fatal Obsession. 1983. 264p. 14.95 o.p. (*0-385-27886-1*) Doubleday Publishing.
—Flesh Wounds: A John Marshall Tanner Mystery. (John Marshall Tanner Mysteries Ser.). 1997. 288p. per. 5.99 (*0-671-00795-5*, Pocket); 1996. 318p. 22.00 (*0-684-81583-4*, Scribner) Simon & Schuster.
—Grave Error. 1982. 240p. mass mkt. 2.50 o.s.i (*0-345-30188-9*) Ballantine Bks.
—Grave Error. 1991. 272p. mass mkt. 4.99 o.s.i (*0-553-29347-8*) Bantam Bks.
—Grave Error. 1985. 8.95 o.p. (*0-385-27058-5*) Doubleday Publishing.
—Past Tense. 1997. (John Marshall Tanner Mysteries Ser.). 352p. 22.00 (*0-684-83249-6*, Scribner) Simon & Schuster.
—Southern Cross: A John Marshall Tanner Novel. 1995. 320p. mass mkt. 4.99 o.s.i (*0-553-56817-5*) Bantam Bks.
—Southern Cross: A John Marshall Tanner Novel. 1993. 320p. 20.00 o.p. (*0-688-12772-X*, Morrow, William & Co.) Morrow/Avon.
—State's Evidence. 1985. 288p. mass mkt. 2.95 o.s.i (*0-345-32534-6*); 1983. mass mkt. 2.50 o.s.i (*0-345-30869-7*) Ballantine Bks.
—State's Evidence. 1991. 320p. mass mkt. 4.99 o.s.i (*0-553-29349-4*) Bantam Bks.
—State's Evidence. 1982. 320p. 15.95 o.p. (*0-385-27236-7*) Doubleday Publishing.
—Strawberry Sunday: A John Marshall Tanner Novel, 2000. audio 44.95 (*0-7861-1574-2*, P2403) Blackstone Audio Bks., Inc.
—Strawberry Sunday: A John Marshall Tanner Novel. 1999. 288p. 23.00 o.p. (*0-684-84954-2*, Scribner) Simon & Schuster.
—Strawberry Sunday: A John Marshall Tanner Novel. l.t. ed. 1999. (Americana Ser.). 439p. 27.95 (*0-7862-1951-3*) Thorndike Pr.
—Toll Call. 1988. mass mkt. 4.99 o.s.i (*0-345-35349-8*) Ballantine Bks.
Grenville, Hilary. Past Imperfect. l.t. ed. 2001. (Nightingale Ser.). 332p. pap. 23.95 (*0-7838-9325-6*) Thorndike Pr.
Grey, Zane. Forlorn River. (Gunsmoke Western Ser.). 12.95 o.p. (*0-86220-961-7*, C0502, Gunsmoke) BBC Audiobooks America.
—Forlorn River. 1977. lib. bdg. 11.95 o.p. (*0-8161-6526-2*, Macmillan Reference USA) Gale Group.
—Forlorn River. 1994. 288p. mass mkt. 3.99 o.p. (*0-06-100391-3*, HarperTorch) Morrow/Avon.
—Forlorn River. 1986. mass mkt. 2.50 (*0-671-83535-1*, Pocket) Simon & Schuster.
—Forlorn River: The Authorized Edition. 1995. 340p. (C). pap. 12.00 (*0-8032-7055-0*, Bison Bks.) Univ. of Nebraska Pr.
Griffin, Annie. Date with the Perfect Dead Man. 1999. (Hannah & Kiki Mysteries Ser.: Vol. 2). 288p. mass mkt. 5.99 o.s.i (*0-425-16985-5*) Berkley Publishing Group.
—Love & the Single Corpse. 2000. (Hannah & Kiki Mysteries Ser.). 288p. mass mkt. 5.99 o.s.i (*0-425-17612-6*, Prime Crime) Berkley Publishing Group.
—Tall, Dead & Handsome. 2001. 304p. mass mkt. 6.50 o.s.i (*0-425-18223-1*, Prime Crime) Berkley Publishing Group.
—A Very Eligible Corpse. 1998. (Hannah & Kiki Mysteries Ser.). 272p. mass mkt. 5.99 o.s.i (*0-425-16535-3*) Berkley Publishing Group.
Grimes, Terris M. Blood Will Tell. 1997. 272p. mass mkt. 5.50 o.s.i (*0-451-40696-6*, Onyx) NAL.
—Somebody Else's Child. 1996. 272p. mass mkt. 5.99 o.s.i (*0-451-18672-9*, Signet Bks.) NAL.
Grimson, Todd. Brand New Cherry Flavor. 1996. 368p. mass mkt. 20.00 o.p. (*0-06-105233-7*) HarperCollins Pubs.
—Brand New Cherry Flavor. 1997. mass mkt. 13.00 o.s.i (*0-06-105320-1*, Eos) Morrow/Avon.
Grimwood, Ken. Into the Deep. 1995. 368p. 20.00 o.p. (*0-688-08799-X*, Morrow, William & Co.) Morrow/Avon.
—Into the Deep. 1996. 384p. mass mkt. 5.99 o.s.i (*0-451-40645-1*, Onyx) NAL.
Grobeson, Mitchell. Outside the Badge. 2000. pap. 14.95 o.p. (*0-533-11559-0*) Vantage Pr., Inc.
Groom, Winston. Such a Pretty, Pretty Girl. l.t. ed. 1999. 30.00 o.p. (*0-7838-8485-0*, Macmillan Reference USA) Gale Group.
—Such a Pretty, Pretty Girl. abr. ed. 1999. audio 24.00 o.s.i (*0-375-40588-7*, 494172, RH Audio) Random Hse. Audio Publishing Group.
Gross, Shelly. Stardust. 1985. 448p. 18.95 o.p. (*0-312-75588-0*) St. Martin's Pr.
Gruenfeld, Lee. The Halls of Justice. unabr. ed. 1996. audio 83.95 (*0-7861-0997-1*, 1774) Blackstone Audio Bks., Inc.
—The Halls of Justice. 1996. 448p. 24.95 o.p. (*0-525-94130-4*, Dutton) Dutton/Plume.
—The Halls of Justice. 1997. 480p. mass mkt. 6.99 o.s.i (*0-451-18806-3*, Onyx) NAL.
—The Halls of Justice. 1996. 6p. audio 24.95 (*1-57511-021-0*) Publishing Mills, Inc., The.
Guerrero, Vicente. Street Kazaultiez: Welcome to the Streets. 2000. 192p. text 30.99 (*0-7388-2485-2*) Xlibris Corp.
—Street Kazaultiez: Welcome to the Streets. 2000. 192p. pap. 20.99 (*0-7388-2486-0*) Xlibris Corp.
Guiver, Patricia. Delilah Doolittle & the Canine Chorus. 2001. (Delilah Doolittle, Pet Detective Ser.: No. 5). 192p. 5.99 o.s.i (*0-425-17801-3*, Prime Crime) Berkley Publishing Group.
—Delilah Doolittle & the Careless Coyote. 1998. (Pet Detective Mystery Ser.: Bk. 3). 208p. mass mkt. 5.99 o.s.i (*0-425-16612-0*, Prime Crime) Berkley Publishing Group.
—Delilah Doolittle & the Missing Macaw. 2000. (Pet Detective Mystery Ser.). 192p. mass mkt. 5.99 o.s.i (*0-425-17342-9*, Prime Crime) Berkley Publishing Group.
—Delilah Doolittle & the Motley Mutts. 1998. (Pet Detective Mystery Ser.: Vol. 2). 208p. mass mkt. 5.99 o.s.i (*0-425-16266-4*, Prime Crime) Berkley Publishing Group.
—Delilah Doolittle & the Purloined Pooch. 1997. (Pet Detective Mystery Ser.: Vol. 1). 208p. mass mkt. 5.99 o.s.i (*0-425-15963-9*, Prime Crime) Berkley Publishing Group.
Gullick, Charlotte. By Way of Water. 2002. 256p. 24.95 o.s.i (*0-399-14898-1*, BlueHen Bks.) Putnam Publishing Group, The.
Gummerman, Jay. Chez Chance. 1996. pap. o.p. (*0-679-75845-3*) Knopf, Alfred A. Inc.
—Chez Chance: A Novel. 1997. (California Fiction Ser.). 211p. pap. 15.95 (*0-520-21080-8*) Univ. of California Pr.
Gunn, Gay G. Nowhere to Run. 1997. 261p. pap. 10.95 (*1-885478-13-5*) Genesis Pr., Inc.
Gutcheon, Beth Richardson. Saying Grace: A Novel. 1995. 312p. 23.00 o.p. (*0-06-017678-4*) HarperTrade.
Guthrie, Feliz. The Last Californian. 1987. (Illus.). 400p. text 15.95 o.p. (*0-918466-13-X*) Quintessence Pubns.
Haake, Katharine. That Water, Those Rocks. 2003. (Western Literature Ser.). 192p. pap. 18.00 (*0-87417-530-5*) Univ. of Nevada Pr.
Haas, Barbara. When California Was an Island. 1987. 160p. (Orig.). 15.00 (*0-934257-11-6*); pap. 8.00 (*0-934257-10-8*) Story Line Pr.
Hagan, Patricia. Orchids in Moonlight. l.t. ed. 1994. 22.95 o.p. (*1-56895-059-4*, Wheeler Publishing, Inc.) Gale Group.
—Orchids in Moonlight. 1993. 384p. mass mkt. 5.50 o.p. (*0-06-108038-1*, HarperTorch) Morrow/Avon.
Hagberg, David. Critical Mass. unabr. ed. 1992. audio 23.95 o.p. (*1-56100-466-9*, 73, Bookcassette); audio 73.25 o.p. (*1-56100-100-7*, 1158, Unabridged Library Editions) Brilliance Audio.
—Critical Mass. 1999. 472p. mass mkt. 6.99 (*0-8125-2497-7*); 1992. 384p. 4.99 o.p. (*0-312-85255-X*) Doherty, Tom Assocs., LLC. (Tor Bks.).
Hailes, Steve. The Quicksilver Kid: A Gold Rush Adventure. 2000. 193p. pap. 20.99 (*0-7388-0811-3*); text 30.99 (*0-7388-0810-5*) Xlibris Corp.
Hall, Jennifer. Star Quality: A Novel. 1993. 21.00 o.p. (*1-55611-346-3*) Fine, Donald I. Bks.
Hall, Mary B. Emma Chizzit & the Mother Lode Marauder. 1995. per. (*0-373-26178-0*, Harlequin Bks.) Harlequin Enterprises, Ltd.
—Emma Chizzit & the Mother Lode Marauder. 1993. 19.95 (*0-8027-3225-9*) Walker & Co.
—Emma Chizzit & the Napa Nemesis. 1992. 202p. 19.95 (*0-8027-3211-9*) Walker & Co.
—Emma Chizzit & the Queen Anne Killer. 1989. 224p. 17.95 o.s.i (*0-8027-5751-0*) Walker & Co.
—Emma Chizzit & the Sacramento Stalker. 1995. (WWL Mystery Ser.). pap. (*0-373-28023-8*, 1-28023-9, Harlequin Bks.) Harlequin Enterprises, Ltd.
—Emma Chizzit & the Sacramento Stalker. 1991. 192p. 17.95 o.s.i (*0-8027-5777-4*) Walker & Co.
Hall, Oakley M. Ambrose Bierce & the Queen of Spades: A Novel. 2000. 288p. pap. 5.99 (*0-14-028860-0*, Penguin Bks.) Penguin Group (USA) Inc.
—Ambrose Bierce & the Queen of Spades: A Novel. 1998. 321p. text 22.95 (*0-520-21555-9*) Univ. of California Pr.
—Separations. 1997. (Western Literature Ser.). 288p. pap. 17.00 (*0-87417-292-6*) Univ. of Nevada Pr.
Hallinan, Timothy. The Bone Polisher. 1996. (Simeon Grist Mystery Ser.). 304p. mass mkt. 5.99 o.p. (*0-380-71372-1*, Avon Bks.) Morrow/Avon.
—Bone Polisher. 1995. 305p. 22.00 o.p. (*0-688-10345-6*, Morrow, William & Co.) Morrow/Avon.
—Everything but the Squeal: A Simeon Grist Suspense Novel. 1990. (Simeon Grist Mystery Ser.). 352p. 17.95 o.p. (*0-453-00694-9*) NAL.
—The Four Last Things. 1989. (Simeon Grist Mystery Ser.). 336p. 16.95 o.p. (*0-453-00650-7*) NAL.
—Incinerator. 1993. 304p. mass mkt. 4.99 (*0-380-71370-5*, Avon Bks.) Morrow/Avon.
—Incinerator: A Simeon Grist Mystery. 1992. 288p. 19.00 o.p. (*0-688-10343-X*, Morrow, William & Co.) Morrow/Avon.
—The Man with No Time: A Simeon Grist Mystery. 1993. 22.00 o.p. (*0-688-10344-8*, Morrow, William & Co.) Morrow/Avon.
—Skin Deep: A Simeon Grist Suspense Novel. 1991. (Simeon Grist Mystery Ser.). 336p. 18.95 o.p. (*0-525-24978-8*, Dutton) Dutton/Plume.
Hamilton, Laurell K. A Caress of Twilight. 2003. 368p. mass mkt. 7.50 (*0-345-42342-9*, Fawcett); 2002. 336p. 23.95 o.s.i (*0-345-43527-3*) Ballantine Bks.
—A Caress of Twilight. abr. ed. (Meredith Gentry Ser.: Vol. 2). 2003. audio 12.99 (*1-59086-037-3*, 3580, Brilliance Audio Paperback Audiobooks); 2002. audio 24.95 o.p. (*1-59086-036-5*, 3579, Nova Audio Bks.); 2002. audio 87.25 (*1-59086-035-7*, 3578, Unabridged Library Editions); 2002. audio 32.95 (*1-59086-034-9*, 3577, Brilliance Audio Unabridged) Brilliance Audio.
—A Caress of Twilight. unabr. ed. 2003. (Meredith Gentry Ser.). audio 19.99 (*1-59335-055-4*, 30140) Soulmate Audio Bks., Inc.
Hammett, Dashiell. The Maltese Falcon. Date not set. 148p. 18.95 (*0-8488-2436-9*) Amereon, Ltd.
—The Maltese Falcon. 1983. (Illus.). 300p. 325.00 o.p. (*0-910457-01-8*) Arion Pr.
—The Maltese Falcon. 1985. (Mystery Ser.). mass mkt. 9.95 o.p. (*0-553-06509-2*) Bantam Bks.
—The Maltese Falcon. (Illus.). 352p. reprint ed. 1987. pap. 9.95 o.p. (*0-86547-157-6*); 1982. 20.00 o.p. (*0-86547-156-8*) Farrar, Straus & Giroux. (North Point Pr.).
—The Maltese Falcon. l.t. ed. 2001. 217p. 28.95 (*0-7838-9459-7*, Macmillan Reference USA) Gale Group.
—The Maltese Falcon. 1992. pap. 9.00 (*0-394-23903-2*); 1989. 224p. pap. 11.00 (*0-679-72264-5*) Knopf Publishing Group. (Vintage).
—The Maltese Falcon, Set. l.t. ed. (YA). (gr. 10 up). reprint ed. 10.00 (*0-89064-044-0*) National Assn. for Visually Handicapped.
—The Maltese Falcon. 1992. pap. 9.00 (*0-679-74094-5*); 1972. pap. 4.95 o.p. (*0-394-71772-4*) Random Hse., Inc.
—The Maltese Falcon. 2001. (Best Mysteries of All Time Ser.). 271p. (*0-7621-8867-7*, IM Pr.) Reader's Digest Assn., Inc., The.
—The Maltese Falcon. 1993. 284p. reprint ed. 35.00 o.p. (*1-883402-15-8*, Scribner) Simon & Schuster.
—The Maltese Falcon. 1989. (Vintage Crime Ser.). 16.05 (*0-606-12411-X*) Turtleback Bks.
Hammond, Emily. Milk. 256p. 2002. pap. 20.00 (*1-57962-086-8*); 2001. 26.00 o.s.i (*1-57962-034-5*) Permanent Pr., The.
Hanadel, Kraig, et al. Catch Me If You Can: A California Saga of Murder, Greed & Two Heroic Detectives. 2000. (Reith Lectures). (Illus.). 416p. mass mkt. 7.50 (*0-380-80287-2*, Avon Bks.) Morrow/Avon.
Handler, David. The Boy Who Never Grew Up. 1993. 384p. mass mkt. 4.99 o.s.i (*0-553-29739-2*) Bantam Bks.
—The Boy Who Never Grew Up. unabr. ed. 1998. (Stewart Hoag Mystery Ser.: Vol. 5). audio 85.00 (*0-7887-2283-2*, 95534E7) Recorded Bks., LLC.
Hanford, Martin. Wheres Waldo in Hollywood. 2003. (Big Bks.). (Illus.). 32p. 19.99 (*0-7636-2238-9*) Candlewick Pr.
Hansen, Joseph. The Boy Who Was Buried This Morning. 1991. 192p. reprint ed. pap. 5.95 o.p. (*0-452-26617-3*, Plume) Dutton/Plume.
—The Boy Who Was Buried This Morning. 1990. 176p. 16.95 o.p. (*0-670-83324-X*) Viking Penguin.
—Brandstetter & Others. 1984. 235p. 12.95 o.s.i (*0-88150-031-3*) Countryman Pr.
—Brandstetter & Others. 1986. 256p. pap. 3.95 o.p. (*0-14-007738-3*, Penguin Bks.) Viking Penguin.
—Country of Old Men: The Last Dave Brandstetter Mystery. 1992. 192p. pap. 7.00 o.p. (*0-452-26805-2*, Plume) Dutton/Plume.

—Country of Old Men: The Last Dave Brandstetter Mystery. 1991. 192p. 17.95 o.p. (*0-670-83826-8*) Viking Penguin.

—Death Claims. 1980. 88p. pap. 5.95 o.p. (*0-8050-0622-2*); pap. 3.95 o.p. (*0-03-057484-6*) Holt, Henry & Co. (Owl Bks.).

—Death Claims. 192p. pap. 9.95 o.p. (*1-874061-62-9*) Oldcastle Bks., Ltd. GBR. *Dist:* Trafalgar Square.

—Early Graves. 1987. 208p. 15.95 o.p. (*0-89296-249-6*) Mysterious Pr.

—Early Graves. 1988. 208p. mass mkt. 3.95 o.s.i (*0-445-40735-2*, Mysterious Pr. Paperback Bks.) Warner Bks., Inc.

—Fadeout. 2000. (Dave Brandstetter Mysteries Ser.). 256p. reprint ed. pap. 11.95 o.p. (*1-55583-552-X*, Alyson Bks.) Alyson Pubns.

—Fadeout. unabr. ed. 1995. (Dave Brandstetter Mystery Ser.: No. 1). audio 24.95 (*1-888348-01-1*, HCB201) Hall Closet Bk. Co.

—Fadeout. 1980. 88p. pap. 5.95 o.p. (*0-8050-1054-8*);Vol. 1. pap. 3.95 o.p. (*0-03-057486-2*) Holt, Henry & Co. (Owl Bks.).

—Gravedigger. (Dave Brandsetter Mystery Ser.). 1985. 192p. pap. 5.95 o.p. (*0-8050-0196-4*, Owl Bks.); 1985. pap. o.p. (*0-03-003682-8*, Owl Bks.); 1982. o.p. (*0-03-056063-2*) Holt, Henry & Co.

—Jack of Hearts. 1995. 224p. 19.95 o.p. (*0-525-93924-5*, Dutton) Dutton/Plume.

—The Little Dog Laughed: A Dave Brandstetter Mystery. 1987. 192p. pap. 5.95 o.p. (*0-8050-0627-3*, Owl Bks.); 1986. 15.95 o.p. (*0-8050-0083-6*) Holt, Henry & Co.

—Living Upstairs. 1993. 224p. (J). (gr. 5 up). 20.00 o.p. (*0-525-93682-3*, Dutton) Dutton/Plume.

—The Man Everybody Was Afraid Of. 1981. pap. o.p. (*0-03-059894-X*, Owl Bks.); 1981. 192p. pap. 5.95 o.p. (*0-8050-0723-7*, Owl Bks.); 1978. 192p. o.p. (*0-03-042376-7*) Holt, Henry & Co.

—The Man Everybody Was Afraid Of. 192p. pap. 9.95 o.p. (*1-874061-66-1*) Oldcastle Bks., Ltd. GBR. *Dist:* Trafalgar Square.

—Nightwork. 1985. (Dave Brandsetter Mystery Ser.). 88p. pap. 5.95 o.p. (*0-8050-1055-6*); pap. 3.95 o.p. (*0-03-003679-8*) Holt, Henry & Co. (Owl Bks.).

—Obedience. 1988. 208p. 16.95 (*0-89296-296-8*) Mysterious Pr.

—Obedience. 1989. mass mkt. 4.95 (*0-445-40844-8*, Mysterious Pr. Paperback Bks.) Warner Bks., Inc.

—Skinflick. 1980. 192p. pap. o.p. (*0-03-057641-5*, Owl Bks.); 1980. 89p. pap. 5.95 o.p. (*0-8050-0197-2*, Owl Bks.); 1979. 192p. o.p. (*0-03-048931-8*) Holt, Henry & Co.

—Troublemaker: A Dave Brandstetter Mystery. 2002. 176p. pap. 12.95 (*1-55583-710-7*) Alyson Pubns.

—Troublemaker: A Dave Brandstetter Mystery. 1981. pap. 3.95 o.p. (*0-03-057487-0*); 1988. 89p. reprint ed. pap. 5.95 o.p. (*0-8050-0812-8*) Holt, Henry & Co. (Owl Bks.).

Hanson, Jacquelyn. Susan's Quest. 1998. (Illus.). 280p. pap. 5.95 (*0-9637265-2-8*, 9802); 268p. (*0-9637265-7-9*) Glenhaven Pr.

Harmetz, Aljean. Off the Face of the Earth. 1998. 320p. per. 6.99 (*0-671-00465-4*, Pocket); 1997. 288p. 22.00 (*0-684-83617-3*, Scribner) Simon & Schuster.

Harmon, Renee. Beverly Hills Murder Game. 2001. 280p. (Orig.). pap. 21.99 (*1-4010-1200-0*) Xlibris Corp.

—Evil Covenant. 2001. 166p. pap. 20.99 (*0-7388-6020-4*); E-Book 8.00 (*1-4010-0746-5*) Xlibris Corp.

Harper, Andrew. Bad Karma. 1998. 304p. mass mkt. 5.99 o.s.i (*0-7860-0480-0*, Pinnacle Bks.); 1997. 240p. 22.00 o.s.i (*1-57566-160-8*) Kensington Publishing Corp.

Harper, Brian. Mortal Pursuit. 1997. 432p. mass mkt. 5.99 o.s.i (*0-451-18200-6*, Signet Bks.) NAL.

—Shatter. 1995. 384p. mass mkt. 4.99 o.s.i (*0-451-17338-4*, Signet Bks.) NAL.

—Shudder. 1994. 416p. mass mkt. 4.99 o.s.i (*0-451-17693-6*, Signet Bks.) NAL.

Harrington, William. Columbo: The Game Show Killer. 1996. 224p. 21.95 o.p. (*0-312-86178-8*, Forge Bks.) Doherty, Tom Assocs., LLC.

—Columbo: The Glitter Murder. (Columbo Ser.). 1997. 240p. 21.95 o.p. (*0-312-86161-3*); Vol. 5. 1998. 192p. mass mkt. 5.99 (*0-8125-6273-9*) Doherty, Tom Assocs., LLC. (Forge Bks.).

—Columbo: The Glitter Murder. l.t. ed. 1998. (Nightingale Ser.). 256p. pap. 21.95 (*0-7838-0134-3*) Thorndike Pr.

—Columbo: The Grassy Knoll. l.t. ed. 1994. 22.95 o.p. (*0-7927-2032-6*); pap. 21.95 o.p. (*0-7927-2031-8*) BBC Audiobooks America.

—Columbo: The Grassy Knoll. 1994. 320p. mass mkt. 4.99 (*0-8125-3024-1*, Tor Bks.); 1993. 288p. 18.95 o.p. (*0-312-85536-2*, Forge Bks.) Doherty, Tom Assocs., LLC.

—Columbo: The Helter Skelter Murders. (Columbo Ser.). 1995. 303p. mass mkt. 5.99 (*0-8125-3026-8*); 1994. 288p. 19.95 o.p. (*0-312-85537-0*) Doherty, Tom Assocs., LLC. (Forge Bks.).

—Columbo: The Hoffa Connection. 1995. 288p. 21.95 o.p. (*0-312-85816-7*, Forge Bks.) Doherty, Tom Assocs., LLC.

—Columbo: The Hoover Files. (Columbo Ser.). 224p. 1999. mass mkt. 5.99 (*0-8125-6274-7*); 1997. 21.95 o.p. (*0-312-86027-7*) Doherty, Tom Assocs., LLC. (Forge Bks.).

—Columbo: The Hoover Files. l.t. ed. 2000. (G. K. Hall Nightingale Ser.). 272p. pap. 21.95 (*0-7838-8925-9*, Macmillan Reference USA) Gale Group.

—The Game Show Killer. 1997. (Columbo Ser.: Vol. 4). 211p. pap. 5.99 (*0-8125-5080-3*, Forge Bks.) Doherty, Tom Assocs., LLC.

—Hoffa Connection. 1996. (Columbo Ser.). 245p. mass mkt. 5.99 (*0-8125-5078-1*, Forge Bks.) Doherty, Tom Assocs., LLC.

Harriss, Will. Noble Rot. 1993. 197p. 17.95 o.p. (*0-312-08865-5*, Saint Martin's Minotaur) St. Martin's Pr.

Hart, Carolyn G. The Rich Die Young. 2000. (Five Star Mystery Ser.). 179p. 22.95 (*0-7862-2898-9*, Five Star) Gale Group.

Hart, William. Never Fade Away: A Novel. 2002. 202p. pap. 12.95 (*1-56474-386-1*) Fithian Pr.

Harte, Bret. Maruja & Other Tales. 1977. (Short Story Index Reprint Ser.: Vol. 1). 32.95 (*0-8369-3400-8*) Ayer Co. Pubs., Inc.

—Three Partners. 1896. (YA). reprint ed. pap. text 28.00 (*1-4047-7847-0*) Classic Textbooks.

—Three Partners. 1999. (Works of Bret Harte: Vol. 15). 346p. reprint ed. lib. bdg. 90.00 (*0-7812-7847-3*) Reprint Services Corp.

—Under the Redwoods. 2000. 252p. E-Book 3.95 (*0-594-05574-1*) 1873 Pr.

—Under the Redwoods. 1977. (Short Story Index Reprint Ser.). 23.95 (*0-8369-3403-2*) Ayer Co. Pubs., Inc.

—Under the Redwoods. 1896. (YA). reprint ed. pap. text 38.00 (*1-4047-7842-X*) Classic Textbooks.

—Under the Redwoods. 1999. (Works of Bret Harte: Vol. 10). 340p. reprint ed. lib. bdg. 90.00 (*0-7812-7842-2*) Reprint Services Corp.

Hartman, Melissa. The Sure Thing. 1994. 208p. pap. 9.95 o.p. (*1-56280-078-7*) Naiad Pr., Inc.

Hartog, Diana. The Photographer's Sweethearts. 228p. 1997. pap. 13.95 (*0-87951-796-4*); 1996. 22.95 o.s.i (*0-87951-646-1*) Overlook Pr., The.

Haslam, Gerald. Okies: Selected Short Stories. 1975. (Illus.). 110p. reprint ed. pap. 4.95 o.p. (*0-87905-042-X*) Smith, Gibbs Pub.

—Snapshots: Glimpses of the Other California. 1985. 130p. (Orig.). pap. 8.95 o.p. (*0-915685-03-5*) Devil Mountain Bks.

Haslam, Gerald W. Condor Dreams & Other Fictions. 1994. (Western Literature Ser.). 216p. pap. 17.00 (*0-87417-232-2*); 25.00 (*0-87417-227-6*) Univ. of Nevada Pr.

—The Great Tejon Club Jubilee: Stories. 1996. (Illus.). 154p. (C). pap. 11.95 (*0-915685-09-4*) Devil Mountain Bks.

—That Constant Coyote: California Stories. 1990. 192p. 22.00 (*0-87417-160-1*); 224p. pap. 17.00 (*0-87417-161-X*) Univ. of Nevada Pr.

Hauck, Charlie. Artistic Differences. 1993. 238p. 21.00 o.p. (*0-688-12152-7*, Morrow, William & Co.) Morrow/Avon.

Hayes, Helen & Chastain, Thomas. Where the Truth Lies. 1988. 288p. 16.95 o.p. (*0-688-06933-9*, Morrow, William & Co.) Morrow/Avon.

Haywood, Gar Anthony. All the Lucky Ones Are Dead: An Aaron Gunner Mystery. 2000. 240p. 23.95 o.s.i (*0-399-14540-0*, G. P. Putnam's Sons) Penguin Group (USA) Inc.

—Fear of the Dark. 1988. 192p. 13.95 o.p. (*0-312-01796-0*, Saint Martin's Minotaur) St. Martin's Pr.

—Fear of the Dark. 1990. 192p. pap. 3.95 o.p. (*0-14-013153-1*, Penguin Bks.) Viking Penguin.

—It's Not a Pretty Sight: An Aaron Gunner Mystery. 1998. 256p. mass mkt. 5.99 o.s.i (*0-425-16196-X*, Prime Crime) Berkley Publishing Group.

—It's Not a Pretty Sight: An Aaron Gunner Mystery. 1996. 240p. 22.95 o.p. (*0-399-14132-4*, G. P. Putnam's Sons) Penguin Group (USA) Inc.

—Not Long for This World. 1991. (Crime Monthly Ser.). 272p. pap. 4.95 o.p. (*0-14-015265-2*, Penguin Bks.) Penguin Group (USA) Inc.

—Not Long for This World. 1990. 17.95 o.p. (*0-312-04398-8*, Saint Martin's Minotaur) St. Martin's Pr.

—When Last Seen Alive. 1999. 256p. mass mkt. 5.99 o.s.i (*0-425-17027-6*) Berkley Publishing Group.

—When Last Seen Alive. 1997. 240p. 22.95 o.p. (*0-399-14303-3*, G. P. Putnam's Sons) Penguin Group (USA) Inc.

—You Can Die Trying. 1993. 224p. 17.95 o.p. (*0-312-09425-6*, Saint Martin's Minotaur) St. Martin's Pr.

—You Can Die Trying: An Aaron Gunner Mystery. 1994. (Crime Ser.). 224p. reprint ed. pap. 5.95 o.p. (*0-14-023946-4*, Penguin Bks.) Penguin Group (USA) Inc.

Heath, Monica. Falconlough. l.t. ed. 1997. (Romance-Hall Ser.). 216p. 23.95 o.p. (*0-7838-8128-2*, Macmillan Reference USA) Gale Group.

—Falconlough. 1977. mass mkt. 1.50 o.p. (*0-451-07627-3*, W7627); 1971. mass mkt. 0.50 o.p. (*0-451-02875-9*); 1971. mass mkt. 0.75 o.p. (*0-451-04525-4*) NAL. (Signet Bks.).

Heggan, Christiane. Enemy Within. 2000. 408p. mass mkt. (*1-55166-577-8*, Harlequin Bks.) Harlequin Enterprises, Ltd.

—Trust No One. 1999. 408p. mass mkt. (*1-55166-536-0*, 1-66536-3, Mira Bks.) Harlequin Enterprises, Ltd.

Hegland, Jean. Into the Forest. 1998. 256p. pap. 13.95 (*0-553-37961-5*) Bantam Bks.

—Into the Forest. 1996. 208p. 25.95 o.p. (*0-934971-50-1*); pap. 13.95 o.p. (*0-934971-49-8*) Calyx Bks.

—Into the Forest, unabr. ed. 1998. audio 60.00 (*0-7887-1989-0*, 95376E7) Recorded Bks., LLC.

Heitzmann, Kristen. The Tender Vine. 2002. (Diamond of the Rockies Ser.). 384p. pap. 12.99 (*0-7642-2417-4*) Bethany Hse. Pubs.

Heller, Zoe. Everything You Know. 2000. 224p. 22.00 o.s.i (*0-375-40724-3*) Knopf, Alfred A. Inc.

—Everything You Know. 2001. (Illus.). 224p. reprint ed. pap. 12.95 (*0-7434-1195-1*, Washington Square Pr.) Simon & Schuster.

Henderson, M. R. Victim. 2002. (Five Star First Edition Mystery Ser.). 250p. 24.95 (*0-7862-3930-1*, Five Star) Gale Group.

Hensley, Dennis. Misadventures in the (213) 1999. 304p. pap. 15.00 (*0-688-17128-1*, Perennial) HarperTrade.

—Misadventures in the (213) 1998. 304p. 24.00 (*0-688-15452-2*, Morrow, William & Co.) Morrow/Avon.

—Misadventures in the (213), abr. ed. 1999. audio 18.00 (*1-57511-063-6*) Publishing Mills, Inc., The.

Hertzog, Francis. Closer to My Home: A Novel. 2003. 192p. pap. 14.95 (*1-56474-416-7*) Fithian Pr.

Hill, Morgan. Ghost of Sonora. 2003. (Ghosts of Sonora (ABA ONLY) Ser.). 256p. pap. 5.99 o.s.i (*1-59052-134-X*) Multnomah Pubs., Inc.

Hill, Russell. Lucy Boomer. 1992. mass mkt. 4.99 o.s.i (*0-345-38163-7*) Ballantine Bks.

Hiller, Catherine. California Time. 1993. 256p. 19.95 o.p. (*0-312-09760-3*) St. Martin's Pr.

Hillmer, Timothy. The Hookmen. 1996. 256p. pap. 11.00 (*0-684-81386-6*, Touchstone) Simon & Schuster.

—The Hookmen. 1994. 280p. 22.50 o.p. (*0-87081-348-X*) Univ. Pr. of Colorado.

Hilton, Joni. Scrambled Home Evenings: A Novel. 1994. 9.95 o.p. (*1-55503-651-1*) Covenant Communications, Inc.

Himes, Chester B. The Lonely Crusade. 1986. (Classic Reprint Ser.). 408p. (C). reprint ed. pap. 14.95 o.p. (*0-938410-37-7*, Thunder's Mouth Pr.) Avalon Publishing Group.

—Lonely Crusade. 1973. reprint ed. 9.50 o.p. (*0-911860-35-5*) Chatham Bookseller.

—The Lonely Crusade: A Novel. 2nd ed. 1997. 398p. reprint ed. pap. 14.95 (*1-56025-142-5*, Thunder's Mouth Pr.) Avalon Publishing Group.

Hinze, Vicki. Shades of Gray. 1999. (Romance Ser.). 312p. 24.95 (*0-7862-1689-1*, Five Star) Gale Group.

—Shades of Grey. 1998. (Shades of Gray Ser.: Vol. 1). 326p. pap. 5.99 (*0-312-96610-5*, St. Martin's Paperbacks) St. Martin's Pr.

Hoffman, Alice. Fortune's Daughter. 1986. 272p. mass mkt. 5.99 o.s.i (*0-449-20976-8*, Fawcett) Ballantine Bks.

—Fortune's Daughter. 1999. 320p. pap. 13.00 (*0-425-16870-0*) Berkley Publishing Group.

—Fortune's Daughter. l.t. ed. 2000. (G. K. Hall Core Ser.). 338p. 30.95 (*0-7838-9026-5*, Macmillan Reference USA) Gale Group.

—Fortune's Daughter. 1985. 272p. 15.95 o.p. (*0-399-13056-X*, G. P. Putnam's Sons) Penguin Putnam Bks. for Young Readers.

—White Horses. 1999. 320p. pap. 12.95 (*0-425-17050-0*); 1993. 304p. mass mkt. 7.99 (*0-425-13980-8*); 1983. mass mkt. 3.50 o.s.i (*0-425-06325-9*) Berkley Publishing Group.

—White Horses. 1982. 256p. 12.95 o.p. (*0-399-12709-7*) Putnam Publishing Group, The.

—White Horses. l.t. ed. 2000. (Basic Ser.). 469p. 29.95 (*0-7862-2313-8*) Thorndike Pr.

Hoffman, Blair. Murder for the Prosecution. 1993. 208p. 18.95 o.p. (*0-88184-995-2*, Carroll & Graf Pubs.) Avalon Publishing Group.

Hoffman, Lauran. Bar Girls. 1995. pap. text 10.95 o.p. (*1-56280-115-5*) Naiad Pr., Inc.

Hohl, Joan. California Copper. 1986. per. (*0-373-05312-6*, Harlequin Bks.) Harlequin Enterprises, Ltd.

Holland, Cecelia. The Bear Flag. 1990. 448p. 19.95 o.p. (*0-395-48886-9*) Houghton Mifflin Co.

—The Bear Flag. 1996. 320p. 15.00 o.s.i (*1-57566-086-5*, Kensington Bks.); 1992. 480p. mass mkt. 5.99 o.s.i (*1-55817-635-7*, Pinnacle Bks.) Kensington Publishing Corp.

—An Ordinary Woman: The Remarkable Story of the First American Woman in California. 224p. 1999. 21.95 (*0-312-86528-7*); 2001. reprint ed. pap. 13.95 (*0-312-87417-0*) Doherty, Tom Assocs., LLC. (Forge Bks.).

—Pacific Street. 1991. 21.95 o.p. (*0-395-56144-2*) Houghton Mifflin Co.

—Railroad Schemes. 1999. 276p. mass mkt. 5.99 (*0-8125-7900-3*); 1999. mass mkt. (*0-8125-5398-5*); 1997. 304p. 23.95 (*0-312-86405-1*) Doherty, Tom Assocs., LLC. (Forge Bks.).

—Railroad Schemes. l.t. ed. 1998. (Basic Ser.). 429p. 27.95 o.p. (*0-7862-1321-3*) Thorndike Pr.

Hollis, Tom. Honky Tonk Logic: A Novel. 1996. 352p. 23.95 o.p. (*0-312-13981-0*) St. Martin's Pr.

Holt, Tim & Hood, Sandra, eds. On Higher Ground: A Postmodern Romance. 2000. (Illus.). 288p. pap. 12.95 (*0-914485-19-9*) Trill Pr.

Holtzer, Susan. Better Than Sex. 240p. 2002. mass mkt. 6.50 (*0-312-98005-1*, St. Martin's Paperbacks); 2001. 22.95 (*0-312-25345-1*, Saint Martin's Minotaur) St. Martin's Pr.

Hopkins, Bradd. The Fourth Corner of the Ninth Room. 1998. 265p. 23.95 (*1-891954-21-0*, Four Ravens) Russell Dean & Co.

—The Fourth Corner of the 9th Room. 1999. 352p. pap. 15.95 (*1-891954-22-9*) Russell Dean & Co.

Hornsby, Wendy. Bad Intent: A Maggie MacGowen Mystery. 1994. (Maggie MacGowen Mystery Ser.). 304p. 18.95 o.p. (*0-525-93817-6*, Dutton) Dutton/Plume.

—Bad Intent: A Maggie MacGowen Mystery. 1995. (Maggie MacGowen Mystery Ser.). 384p. mass mkt. 5.50 o.s.i (*0-451-18501-3*, Onyx) NAL.

—Half a Mind. 304p. 1991. mass mkt. 3.99 o.p. (*0-451-40245-6*, Onyx); 1990. 16.95 o.p. (*0-453-00710-4*) NAL.

—A Hard Light: A Maggie MacGowen Mystery. 1997. (Maggie MacGowen Mystery Ser.). 272p. 22.95 o.p. (*0-525-94067-7*) Dutton/Plume.

—A Hard Light: A Maggie MacGowen Mystery. 1998. (Maggie Macgowen Mystery Ser.). 272p. mass mkt. 5.99 o.s.i (*0-451-18690-7*, Signet Bks.) NAL.

—Midnight Baby: A Maggie MacGowen Mystery. 1993. (Maggie MacGowen Mystery Ser.). 272p. 19.00 o.p. (*0-525-93615-7*, Dutton) Dutton/Plume.

—Midnight Baby: A Maggie MacGowen Mystery. 1994. (Maggie MacGowen Mystery Ser.). 304p. mass mkt. 5.99 o.s.i (*0-451-18136-0*, Signet Bks.) NAL.

—No Harm. 1989. (WWL Mystery Ser.: No. 30). mass mkt. (*0-373-26030-X*, Harlequin Bks.) Harlequin Enterprises, Ltd.

—Telling Lies: A Maggie MacGowen Mystery. 1992. 256p. 18.00 o.p. (*0-525-93472-3*, Dutton) Dutton/Plume.

—Telling Lies: A Maggie MacGowen Mystery. 1993. (Maggie MacGowen Mystery Ser.). 288p. mass mkt. 5.99 o.s.i (*0-451-40380-0*, Onyx) NAL.

—77th Street Requiem: A Maggie MacGowan Mystery. 1996. (Maggie MacGowen Mystery Ser.). 384p. mass mkt. 5.99 o.s.i (*0-451-40675-3*, Signet Bks.) NAL.

—77th Street Requiem: A Maggie MacGowen Mystery. 1995. (Maggie MacGowen Mystery Ser.). 288p. 21.95 o.p. (*0-525-93998-9*, Dutton) Dutton/Plume.

—77th Street Requiem: A Maggie MacGowen Mystery. l.t. ed. 1996. (Large Print Bks.). pap. 21.95 (*1-56895-334-8*, Wheeler Publishing, Inc.) Gale Group.

Houston-Davila, Daniel. Malinche's Children. 2003. 362p. 27.00 (*1-57806-521-6*) Univ. Pr. of Mississippi.

Houston, James D. Continental Drift. 1987. 336p. pap. text 4.95 o.p. (*0-07-030488-2*) McGraw-Hill Cos., The.

—Continental Drift. 1978. 8.95 o.p. (*0-394-50124-1*, Knopf Bks. for Young Readers) Random Hse. Children's Bks.

—Continental Drift. 1996. (California Fiction Ser.). 337p. (C). pap. 15.95 (*0-520-20713-0*) Univ. of California Pr.

—Snow Mountain Passage: A Novel of the Donner Party. 2002. (Harvest Book Ser.). (Illus.). 336p. reprint ed. pap. 14.00 (*0-15-601143-3*, Harvest Bks.) Harcourt Trade Pubs.

—Snow Mountain Passage: A Novel of the Donner Party. 2001. (Illus.). 336p. 24.00 (*0-375-41103-8*) Knopf, Alfred A. Inc.

Houston, Jeanne Wakatsuki. The Legend of Fire Horse Woman. 2003. 336p. 23.00 (*0-7582-0455-8*) Kensington Publishing Corp.

Howe, Melodie J. Beauty Dies. 1996. (Crime Ser.). 272p. pap. 5.95 o.s.i (*0-14-023565-5*) Penguin Group (USA) Inc.

—Beauty Dies: A Claire Conrad - Maggie Hill Mystery. 1994. 272p. 19.95 o.p. (*0-670-85449-2*, Viking) Viking Penguin.

—The Mother Shadow. (Crime Ser.). 272p. 1990. pap. 5.95 o.p. (*0-14-011778-4*, Penguin Bks.); 1989. 16.95 o.p. (*0-670-82602-2*) Viking Penguin.

Howell, Daedalus. The Late Projectionist: Or, from Angst to Zilch: The Portable Buntel Eriksson Filmography. 1999. 156p. pap. 12.95 (*0-9671001-0-0*) Daedalus Howell Co.

Hudson, Wayne. The Beams of Our House. 2003. per. 13.95 (*1-888237-46-5*) Baxter Pr.

—The Beams of Our House. 2002. 165p. pap. 12.99 (*0-9705259-8-2*) St. Aztec Publishing.

Hunt, Joy. 1994. o.s.i (*1-85381-297-8*) Random Hse., Inc.

Hunt, David, pseud. The Magician's Tale. 1998. 416p. reprint ed. mass mkt. 7.50 o.s.i (*0-425-16482-9*) Berkley Publishing Group.

—The Magician's Tale. 1997. 416p. 24.95 o.s.i (*0-399-14260-6*, G. P. Putnam's Sons) Penguin Group (USA) Inc.

—Trick of Light. 1999. 416p. reprint ed. mass mkt. 7.50 o.s.i (*0-425-17035-7*) Berkley Publishing Group.

—Trick of Light. 1998. 400p. 24.95 o.p. (*0-399-14393-9*, G. P. Putnam's Sons) Penguin Group (USA) Inc.

Hunt, Marsha. Joy. 1991. 352p. 19.95 o.p. (*0-525-24942-7*, Dutton); 1992. 384p. reprint ed. pap. 12.95 o.p. (*0-452-26753-6*, Plume) Dutton/Plume.

Huo, T. C. Land of Smiles: A Novel. 224p. 2000. 12.95 o.s.i (*0-452-28185-7*, Plume); 1999. 23.95 (*0-525-94281-5*, Dutton) Dutton/Plume.

Hurst, Jim. Fatal Image. 1998. 200p. (Orig.). pap. 14.50 (*0-88739-120-6*) Creative Arts Bk. Co.

Huston, Bo. The Listener: A Novella & Four Stories. 1993. 176p. 17.95 o.p. (*0-312-09931-2*) St. Martin's Pr.

—The Listener: A Novella & Other Stories. 1994. 176p. pap. 5.99 o.p. (*0-312-11313-7*, Saint Martin's Griffin) St. Martin's Pr.

Huxley, Aldous. After Many a Summer Dies the Swan. 1977. reprint ed. lib. bdg. 25.95 (*0-89190-395-X*, Queens Hse., Inc.) Amereon, Ltd.

—After Many a Summer Dies the Swan. 1993. 95p. reprint ed. pap. 14.95 (*1-56663-018-5*, Elephant Paperbacks) Dee, Ivan R. Pub.

—After Many a Summer Dies the Swan. 1965. pap. 2.25 o.p. (*0-06-083046-8*, P3046) HarperCollins Pubs.

—After Many a Summer Dies the Swan. 1983. 256p. mass mkt. 5.95 o.p. (*0-06-091063-1*, CN1063, Perennial) HarperTrade.

Hyde, Bill. Bodie Gone: A Novel of Suspense. 2001. (First Fiction Ser.). 256p. 26.95 (*0-86534-317-9*) Sunstone Pr.

Hyde, Catherine R. Funerals for Horses. 1997. (Emerging Writers Ser.). 256p. 19.95 (*0-9653524-3-9*) Russian Hill Pr.

Hyde, Catherine Ryan. Electric God. 2002. 320p. pap. 13.00 (*0-7434-3756-X*, Pocket) Simon & Schuster.

Hynd, Noel. Cemetery of Angels. 2002. 416p. mass mkt. 6.99 o.s.i (*0-7860-1487-3*); 1996. 416p. mass mkt. 5.99 o.s.i (*0-7860-0261-1*, Pinnacle Bks.); 1995. 368p. mass mkt. 19.95 o.p. (*0-8217-5029-1*, Zebra Bks.) Kensington Publishing Corp.

Hynes, Angela. California Natural. 2000. 300p. pap. 14.95 (*0-595-00459-8*, Writers Club Pr.) iUniverse, Inc.

Inclan, Jessica Barksdale. The Matter of Grace. 2004. 320p. mass mkt. 6.99 (*0-451-21185-5*, Signet Bks.) NAL.

—The Matter of Grace. 2002. 272p. pap. 12.95 (*0-451-20575-8*) Penguin Group (USA) Inc.

Indiana, Gary. Resentment: A Comedy. 320p. 1998. pap. 12.95 o.s.i (*0-385-49336-3*); 1997. 22.95 o.s.i (*0-385-48429-1*) Doubleday Publishing.

Isberg, Art. The Search for the Golden Bucket Mine. 2000. E-Book 6.95 (*0-87714-457-5*) Denlingers Pubs., Ltd.

Islas, Arturo. La Mollie & the King of Tears. 1996. 200p. (C). pap. 14.95 (*0-8263-1732-4*) Univ. of New Mexico Pr.

Ison, Tara. A Child Out of Alcatraz: A Novel. 1997. 264p. 22.95 o.p. (*0-571-19910-0*) Faber & Faber, Inc.

Iyer, Pico. Abandon: A Romance. 2003. 368p. 24.00 (*0-375-41505-X*) Knopf, Alfred A. Inc.

Jackson, Helen Hunt. Ramona. E-Book 3.95 (*0-594-02290-8*) 1873 Pr.

Jackson, Lisa. Mystic. l.t. ed. 2003. (Romance Ser.). 28.95 (*1-58724-403-9*, Wheeler Publishing, Inc.) Gale Group.

—Mystic. 2002. (Illus.). 256p. mass mkt. (*1-55166-957-9*, Mira Bks.); 1986. pap. (*0-373-07158-2*, Harlequin Bks.) Harlequin Enterprises, Ltd.

Jackson, Sheneska. Blessings. 2003. mass mkt. 6.99 (*0-7434-8246-8*); 1999. 400p. pap. 13.00 (*0-684-85312-4*); 1998. 400p. 23.00 (*0-684-85035-4*) Simon & Schuster. (Simon & Schuster).

—Caught up in the Rapture. 1996. 272p. 20.50 (*0-684-81487-0*, Simon & Schuster) Simon & Schuster.

—Caught up in the Rapture: A Novel. 1997. 272p. pap. 13.00 (*0-684-83153-8*, Simon & Schuster) Simon & Schuster.

Jacobs, Jonnie. Evidence of Guilt. (Kali O'Brien Mystery Ser.). 1998. 384p. mass mkt. 5.99 (*1-57566-279-5*); 1997. 368p. 18.95 o.p. (*1-57566-141-1*) Kensington Publishing Corp. (Kensington Bks.).

—Motion to Dismiss. (Kali O'Brien Mystery Ser.). 2000. 400p. mass mkt. 5.99 (*1-57566-543-3*); 1999. 304p. 22.00 (*1-57566-395-3*) Kensington Publishing Corp.

—Motion to Dismiss. 2002. 284p. per. 17.95 (*0-7592-1227-9*) ereads.com.

—Murder among Friends. 2001. 352p. mass mkt. 5.99 (*0-7582-0098-6*); 1996. 352p. mass mkt. 5.99 o.s.i (*1-57566-089-X*, Kensington Bks.); 1995. 304p. mass mkt. 16.95 o.s.i (*0-8217-5030-5*) Kensington Publishing Corp.

—Murder among Neighbors. 304p. 1995. mass mkt. 5.99 (*1-57566-275-2*); 1995. mass mkt. 4.99 o.s.i (*0-8217-5039-9*); 1994. mass mkt. 16.95 o.p. (*0-8217-4680-4*, Zebra Bks.) Kensington Publishing Corp.

—Murder among Strangers. 2000. (Kate Austen Mystery Ser.). 378p. 20.00 o.s.i (*1-57566-540-9*) Kensington Publishing Corp.

—Murder among Us: A Kate Austen Mystery. 1999. 304p. mass mkt. 5.99 (*1-57566-398-8*); 1998. 336p. 20.00 (*1-57566-276-0*) Kensington Publishing Corp.

—Shadow of Doubt. (Kali O'Brien Mystery Ser.). 1997. 308p. mass mkt. 5.50 o.s.i (*1-57566-146-2*, Kensington Bks.); 1996. 304p. pap. 18.95 o.p. (*1-57566-017-2*); 1996. mass mkt. 18.95 o.s.i (*0-8217-5254-5*) Kensington Publishing Corp.

Jacobsen, Clay. The Lasko Interview. 1998. 412p. pap. 12.99 (*0-8054-1660-9*) Broadman & Holman Pubs.

Jacoby, Kathleen. Vision of the Grail: A Spiritual Adventure at the Dawn of the 21st Century. 2001. 304p. (Orig.). 14.95 (*1-930126-07-7*) Lightlines Publishing Co.

Jakes, John. California Gold. 1990. 768p. mass mkt. 7.99 o.s.i (*0-345-36943-2*) Ballantine Bks.

—California Gold. abr. ed. 1989. audio 16.00 o.s.i (*0-394-57732-9*, RH Audio) Random Hse. Audio Publishing Group.

—California Gold. unabr. ed. Pt. 1. 1990. audio 90.00 (*1-55690-080-5*, 90072E7); Pt. 2. audio 72.00 (*1-55690-081-3*, 90078E7) Recorded Bks., LLC.

Jan, Calamity. Goodbye God, I'm Going to Bodie. Jan, Calamity, ed. 2002. (Ghosttowners Ser.: Vol. 1). 112p. (J). (gr. 4-8). pap. 10.00 (*0-9721800-0-1*) WildWest Publishing.

Jaramillo, Stephan. Going Postal: A Novel. 1997. 256p. pap. 12.00 o.s.i (*0-425-15768-7*) Berkley Publishing Group.

—The Scoundrel. 1999. 256p. (Orig.). pap. 12.00 o.s.i (*0-425-16859-X*) Berkley Publishing Group.

Jenkins, Victoria. Cruise Control. 2002. 144p. pap. 16.00 (*1-57962-045-0*) Permanent Pr., The.

Jennings, Patrick. Faith & the Rocket Cat. 1998. (Illus.). 224p. (J). (gr. 3-6). pap. 15.95 (*0-590-11004-7*) Scholastic, Inc.

Jiménez, Francisco. The Circuit: Stories from the Life of a Migrant Child. 1997. Tr. of Cajas de Carton. 134p. pap. 10.95 (*0-8263-1797-9*) Univ. of New Mexico Pr.

—The Circuit: Stories from the Life of a Migrant Child. 1997. Tr. of Cajas de Carton. E-Book 10.95 (*0-585-18784-3*) netLibrary, Inc.

John, Sally D. To Dream Again. 2000. 256p. pap. 10.99 o.p. (*1-58134-186-5*) Crossway Bks.

Johnson, Allison. The Way Home. 2001. (Five Star First Edition Romance Ser.). 315p. 26.95 (*0-7862-3033-9*, Five Star) Gale Group.

Johnson, Denis. Already Dead: A California Gothic. 1997. 448p. 25.00 o.p. (*0-06-018737-9*) HarperCollins Pubs.

—Already Dead: A California Gothic. 1998. 448p. pap. 13.95 (*0-06-092909-X*, Perennial) HarperTrade.

Johnson, Diane. Health & Happiness. 1991. mass mkt. 5.99 o.s.i (*0-449-21841-4*, Fawcett) Ballantine Bks.

—Health & Happiness. 1998. 272p. pap. 14.00 (*0-452-28000-1*, Plume) Dutton/Plume.

—The Shadow Knows. 1988. 288p. mass mkt. 3.95 o.s.i (*0-449-21560-1*, Fawcett) Ballantine Bks.

—The Shadow Knows. 1998. (William Abrahams Book Ser.). 288p. pap. 12.95 (*0-452-27736-1*) Dutton/Plume.

—The Shadow Knows. 1974. 7.95 o.p. (*0-394-48035-X*, Knopf Bks. for Young Readers) Random Hse. Children's Bks.

—The Shadow Knows, Vol. 193. 1982. 256p. pap. 3.50 o.p. (*0-394-71193-9*) Random Hse., Inc.

—The Shadow Knows. 1976. pap. 2.75 o.p. (*0-671-83370-7*, 80249, Pocket) Simon & Schuster.

Johnson, Margaret. Riches of the Heart. 1995. 192p. 18.95 o.s.i (*0-8034-9144-1*, Avalon Bks.) Bouregy, Thomas & Co., Inc.

Johnston, Joan. The Cowboy. 2000. 400p. mass mkt. 7.50 (*0-440-22380-6*) Dell Publishing.

—The Cowboy. l.t. ed. 2000. (Wheeler Large Print Book Ser.). 425p. 28.95 (*1-56895-903-6*, Wheeler Publishing, Inc.) Gale Group.

Johnstone, William W. Power of the Mountain Man. 1995. (Zebra Bks.). mass mkt. 4.99 o.s.i (*0-8217-5363-0*, Zebra Bks.); 256p. mass mkt. 3.99 o.s.i (*0-8217-4871-8*) Kensington Publishing Corp.

Jones, Idwal. The Vineyard. 1973. mass mkt. 1.25 o.p. (*0-345-23371-9*) Ballantine Bks.

—The Vineyard. 1997. (California Fiction Ser.). 285p. pap. text 15.95 (*0-520-21090-5*) Univ. of California Pr.

Jones, Louis B. California's Over. 1998. 336p. pap. 19.00 (*0-679-74600-5*, Vintage) Knopf Publishing Group.

—Particles & Luck. 1994. (Vintage Contemporaries Ser.). 305p. pap. 19.00 (*0-679-74599-8*, Vintage) Knopf Publishing Group.

Jong, Erica. How to Save Your Own Life. 1995. 320p. pap. 11.95 o.p. (*0-452-27454-0*, Plume) Dutton/Plume.

—How to Save Your Own Life. 1977. 8.95 o.p. (*0-03-017726-X*) Holt, Henry & Co.

Kadohata, Cynthia. In the Heart of the Valley of Love. 1993. 240p. pap. 10.00 o.p. (*0-14-013449-2*, Penguin Bks.) Penguin Group (USA) Inc.

—In the Heart of the Valley of Love. 1997. (California Fiction Ser.). 224p. pap. text 15.95 (*0-520-20728-9*) Univ. of California Pr.

—In the Heart of the Valley of Love. 1992. 240p. 20.00 o.p. (*0-670-83415-7*, Viking) Viking Penguin.

Kaiser, R. J. Fruitcake. 2000. 448p. mass mkt. (*1-55166-625-1*, Harlequin Bks.) Harlequin Enterprises, Ltd.

—Jane Doe. abr. ed. 1999. audio 7.99 (*1-55204-177-8*, MIR-1177) Durkin Hayes Publishing Ltd.

—Jane Doe. 1999. (Mira Bks.). 442p. per. (*1-55166-510-7*, 1-66510-8, Mira Bks.) Harlequin Enterprises, Ltd.

Kalpakian, Laura. Graced Land. 1992. 18.95 o.p. (*0-8021-1474-1*) Grove/Atlantic, Inc.

Kaminsky, Stuart M. Bullet for a Star. unabr. ed. 1994. audio 23.95 (*0-7861-0731-6*, 1482) Blackstone Audio Bks., Inc.

—Bullet for a Star. 1985. (Toby Peters Mystery Ser.). pap. 3.95 o.p. (*0-89296-147-3*) Mysterious Pr.

—Bullet for a Star. 1977. (Toby Peters Mystery Ser.). 188p. 7.95 o.p. (*0-312-10797-8*) St. Martin's Pr.

—Bullet for a Star. 1991. (Toby Peters Mystery Ser.). 192p. mass mkt. 4.99 (*0-446-40061-0*, Mysterious Pr. Paperback Bks.) Warner Bks., Inc.

—Buried Caesars. l.t. ed. 1991. (Toby Peters Mystery Ser.). 281p. 18.95 o.p. (*0-7927-0490-8*); pap. 16.95 o.p. (*0-7927-0491-6*, C0783) BBC Audiobooks America.

—Buried Caesars. 1989. (Toby Peters Mystery Ser.). 192p. 15.45 o.p. (*0-89296-374-3*) Mysterious Pr.

—Buried Caesars. unabr. ed. 1997. (Toby Peters Mystery Ser.: Vol. 14). audio 44.00 (*0-7887-0401-X*, 94593E7) Recorded Bks., LLC.

—Buried Caesars. 1990. (Toby Peters Mystery Ser.). 192p. mass mkt. 4.50 (*0-445-40878-2*, Mysterious Pr. Paperback Bks.) Warner Bks., Inc.

—Catch a Falling Clown. 1981. (Toby Peters Mystery Ser.). 182p. 10.95 o.p. (*0-312-12377-9*) St. Martin's Pr.

—Catch a Falling Clown. 1984. (Toby Peters Mystery Ser.). 182p. reprint ed. pap. 3.95 o.p. (*0-14-007022-2*, Penguin Bks.) Viking Penguin.

—Dancing in the Dark. unabr. ed. 1996. (Toby Peters Mystery Ser.). 30p. audio 39.95 (*0-7861-0961-0*, 754074) Blackstone Audio Bks., Inc.

—Dancing in the Dark. 1996. (Toby Peters Mystery Ser.). 228p. 19.95 o.s.i (*0-89296-528-2*) Mysterious Pr.

—Dancing in the Dark. unabr. ed. audio. 1996. (Toby Peters Mystery Ser.: Vol. 19). audio 44.00 (*0-7887-0621-7*, 94795E7) Recorded Bks., LLC.

—Dancing in the Dark. 1997. (Toby Peters Mystery Ser.). 224p. mass mkt. 5.99 o.p. (*0-446-40337-7*) Warner Bks., Inc.

—The Devil Met a Lady. unabr. ed. 1995. audio 39.95 (*0-7861-0881-9*, 1536) Blackstone Audio Bks., Inc.

—The Devil Met a Lady. 1993. (Toby Peters Mystery Ser.). 208p. 18.95 (*0-89296-436-7*) Mysterious Pr.

—The Devil Met a Lady. 1995. (Toby Peters Mystery Ser.). 208p. mass mkt. 5.50 (*0-446-40423-3*, Mysterious Pr. Paperback Bks.) Warner Bks., Inc.

—The Devil Met a Lady. 2000. (Toby Peters Mysteries Ser.). 240p. pap. 12.00 (*0-7434-0004-6*) ibooks, Inc.

—Devil on My Doorstep. 1998. (Rockford Files: Vol. 2). 304p. 22.95 (*0-312-86444-2*, Forge Bks.) Doherty, Tom Assocs., LLC.

—Down for the Count. l.t. ed. 1986. (Toby Peters Mystery Ser.). 307p. 11.95 o.p. (*0-8161-4000-6*, Macmillan Reference USA) Gale Group.

—Down for the Count. 1985. (Toby Peters Mystery Ser.). 192p. 12.95 o.p. (*0-312-21862-1*) St. Martin's Pr.

—Down for the Count. 1990. (Toby Peters Mystery Ser.). mass mkt. 4.50 o.s.i (*0-445-40908-8*, Mysterious Pr. Paperback Bks.) Warner Bks., Inc.

—The Fala Factor. 1985. (Toby Peters Mystery Ser.). pap. 3.95 o.p. (*0-89296-148-1*) Mysterious Pr.

—The Fala Factor. 1984. (Toby Peters Mystery Ser.). 174p. 11.95 o.p. (*0-312-27967-1*) St. Martin's Pr.

—The Fala Factor. 1993. (Toby Peters Mystery Ser.). 224p. mass mkt. 4.99 (*0-446-40065-3*, Mysterious Pr. Paperback Bks.) Warner Bks., Inc.

—A Fatal Glass of Beer. unabr. ed. 1998. (Toby Peters Mystery Ser.). audio 29.95 (*0-7861-1465-7*); audio 44.95 (*0-7861-1346-4*, 1766) Blackstone Audio Bks., Inc.

—A Fatal Glass of Beer, Set. unabr. ed. 1999. audio 44.95 Highsmith Inc.

—A Fatal Glass of Beer. 1997. (Toby Peters Mystery Ser.). (ACE.). 256p. 21.50 o.p. (*0-89296-630-0*) Mysterious Pr.

—A Fatal Glass of Beer. unabr. ed. 1997. (Toby Peters Mystery Ser.: Vol. 20). audio 51.00 (*0-7887-0650-0*, 94827E7) Recorded Bks., LLC.

—The Green Bottle. unabr. ed. 1999. audio 69.95 (*0-7927-2300-7*, CSL189, Chivers Sound Library) BBC Audiobooks America.

—The Green Bottle. (Rockford Files: Vol. 1). 320p. 1996. 22.95 (*0-312-86229-6*); 1999. mass mkt. 5.99 (*0-8125-7105-3*) Doherty, Tom Assocs., LLC. (Forge Bks.).

—The Green Bottle. l.t. ed. 1998. (Americana Ser.). 437p. 28.95 (*0-7862-1521-6*) Thorndike Pr.

—He Done Her Wrong. unabr. ed. 1998. audio 39.95 (*0-7861-1280-8*, 2175) Blackstone Audio Bks., Inc.

—He Done Her Wrong. 1984. (Toby Peters Mystery Ser.). reprint ed. pap. 3.95 o.p. (*0-89296-095-7*) Mysterious Pr.

—He Done Her Wrong. 1983. (Toby Peters Mystery Ser.). 168p. 10.95 o.p. (*0-312-36491-1*) St. Martin's Pr.

—He Done Her Wrong. 1995. (Toby Peters Mystery Ser.). 208p. mass mkt. 5.50 (*0-446-40191-9*, Mysterious Pr. Paperback Bks.) Warner Bks., Inc.

—High Midnight. unabr. ed. 1995. audio 32.95 (*0-7861-0765-0*, 1614) Blackstone Audio Bks., Inc.

—High Midnight. 1984. (Toby Peters Mystery Ser.). reprint ed. pap. 3.95 o.p. (*0-89296-091-4*) Mysterious Pr.

—High Midnight. 1981. (Toby Peters Mystery Ser.). 188p. 9.95 o.p. (*0-312-37234-5*) St. Martin's Pr.

—The Howard Hughes Affair. 1980. (Toby Peters Mystery Ser.). 192p. 2.25 o.s.i (*0-441-34462-3*) Ace Bks.

—The Howard Hughes Affair. unabr. ed. 1999. audio 32.95 (*0-7861-1397-9*, 1570); 1995. audio 32.95 (*0-7861-0668-9*, 1570) Blackstone Audio Bks., Inc.

—The Howard Hughes Affair. 1979. (Toby Peters Mystery Ser.). 207p. 8.95 o.p. (*0-312-39617-1*) St. Martin's Pr.

—The Howard Hughes Affair. 1990. (Toby Peters Mystery Ser.). 224p. mass mkt. 4.95 o.s.i (*0-445-40905-3*, Mysterious Pr. Paperback Bks.) Warner Bks., Inc.

—The Man Who Shot Lewis Vance. unabr. ed. 1998. audio 5.99 (*0-88646-963-5*, PAC-7963) Durkin Hayes Publishing Ltd.

—The Man Who Shot Lewis Vance. 1986. (Toby Peters Mystery Ser.). 224p. 14.95 o.p. (*0-312-51394-1*) St. Martin's Pr.

—The Man Who Shot Lewis Vance. 1990. (Toby Peters Mystery Ser.). 208p. mass mkt. 4.50 o.s.i (*0-445-40909-6*, Mysterious Pr. Paperback Bks.) Warner Bks., Inc.

—The Melting Clock. l.t. ed. 1992. (Toby Peters Mystery Ser.). 260p. 19.95 o.p. (*0-7927-1280-3*); pap. 17.95 o.p. (*0-7927-1281-1*) BBC Audiobooks America.

—The Melting Clock. unabr. ed. 1998. (Toby Peters Mystery Ser.). audio 32.95 (*0-7861-1468-1*, 2227) Blackstone Audio Bks., Inc.

—The Melting Clock. 1991. (Toby Peters Mystery Ser.). 192p. 17.45 o.p. (*0-89296-435-9*) Mysterious Pr.

—The Melting Clock. 1993. (Toby Peters Mystery Ser.). 208p. mass mkt. 4.99 (*0-446-40304-0*, Mysterious Pr. Paperback Bks.) Warner Bks., Inc.

—Murder on the Yellow Brick Road. unabr. ed. 1994. audio 23.95 (*0-7861-0785-5*, 1511) Blackstone Audio Bks., Inc.

—Murder on the Yellow Brick Road. 1978. (Toby Peters Mystery Ser.). 197p. 7.95 o.p. (*0-312-55318-8*) St. Martin's Pr.

—Murder on the Yellow Brick Road. 1979. (Toby Peters Mystery Ser.). 208p. pap. 3.95 o.p. (*0-14-005124-4*, Penguin Bks.) Viking Penguin.

—Murder on the Yellow Brick Road. 2000. (Toby Peters Mysteries Ser.). 192p. pap. 12.00 (*0-7434-0000-3*) ibooks, Inc.

—Never Cross a Vampire. unabr. ed. 2000. audio compact disk 48.00 (*0-7861-9943-1*, z2256); 1999. audio compact disk 24.95 (*0-7861-1461-4*); 1998. audio 32.95 (*0-7861-1353-7*, 2256) Blackstone Audio Bks., Inc.

—Never Cross a Vampire, unabr. ed. 1999. audio 32.95 Highsmith Inc.

—Never Cross a Vampire. 1984. (Toby Peters Mystery Ser.). reprint ed. pap. 3.95 o.s.i (*0-89296-087-6*) Mysterious Pr.



For book reviews, descriptive annotations, tables of contents, cover images, author biographies & additional information, updated daily, subscribe to **www.booksinprint.com** 637

—Never Cross a Vampire. 1980. (Toby Peters Mystery Ser.). 182p. 8.95 o.p. (*0-312-56471-6*) St. Martin's Pr.

—Never Cross a Vampire. 1995. (Toby Peters Mystery Ser.). 192p. mass mkt. 5.50 (*0-446-40190-0*, Mysterious Pr. Paperback Bks.) Warner Bks., Inc.

—Never Cross a Vampire. 2000. 224p. pap. 12.00 (*0-7434-0713-X*) ibooks, Inc.

—Poor Butterfly. unabr. ed. 1996. audio 32.95 (*0-7861-1018-X*, 1796) Blackstone Audio Bks., Inc.

—Poor Butterfly. 1990. (Toby Peters Mystery Ser.). 179p. 17.95 o.p. (*0-89296-411-1*) Mysterious Pr.

—Poor Butterfly. unabr. ed. 1997. (Toby Peters Mystery Ser.: Vol. 15). audio 35.00 (*0-7887-0833-3*, 94978E7) Recorded Bks., LLC.

—Poor Butterfly. 1991. (Toby Peters Mystery Ser.). mass mkt. 4.95 o.s.i (*0-446-40011-4*) Warner Bks., Inc.

—The Rockford Files: Devil on My Doorstep. unabr. ed. 2000. audio 49.95 (*0-7927-2313-9*, CSL 202) Chivers Audio Bks. GBR. *Dist:* BBC Audiobooks America.

—Smart Moves. unabr. ed. 1997. audio 39.95 (*0-7861-1167-4*, 1934) Blackstone Audio Bks., Inc.

—Smart Moves. 1987. (Toby Peters Mystery Ser.). 272p. 15.95 o.p. (*0-312-00190-8*) St. Martin's Pr.

—Smart Moves. 1996. (Toby Peters Mystery Ser.). 224p. reprint ed. mass mkt. 5.99 o.p. (*0-446-40438-1*, Mysterious Pr. Paperback Bks.) Warner Bks., Inc.

—Think Fast, Mr. Peters. 1996. (Toby Peters Mystery Ser.). 224p. mass mkt. 5.99 (*0-446-40440-3*, Mysterious Pr. Paperback Bks.) Warner Bks., Inc.

—Tomorrow Is Another Day. 1995. (Toby Peters Mystery Ser.). 208p. 18.95 o.s.i (*0-89296-527-4*) Mysterious Pr.

—Tomorrow Is Another Day. unabr. ed. 1995. (Toby Peters Mystery Ser.: Vol. 18). audio 51.00 (*0-7887-0354-4*, 94546E7) Recorded Bks., LLC.

—Tomorrow Is Another Day. 1996. (Toby Peters Mystery Ser.). 224p. mass mkt. 5.99 (*0-446-40336-9*, Mysterious Pr. Paperback Bks.) Warner Bks., Inc.

—You Bet Your Life. 1979. (Toby Peters Mystery Ser.). 215p. 8.95 o.p. (*0-312-89662-X*) St. Martin's Pr.

—You Bet Your Life. 1990. (Toby Peters Mystery Ser.). 224p. mass mkt. 4.95 o.s.i (*0-445-40906-1*, Mysterious Pr. Paperback Bks.) Warner Bks., Inc.

Kandel, Susan. I Dreamed I Married Perry Mason: A Cece Caruso Mystery. 2004. 288p. (*0-06-058105-0*, Morrow, William & Co.) Morrow/Avon.

Kanin, Garson. Moviola. 1979. 12.95 o.s.i (*0-671-24822-7*, Simon & Schuster) Simon & Schuster.

Karabo, Karen. Trespassers Welcome Here. 1990. pap. 8.95 o.p. (*0-671-70024-3*, Fireside) Simon & Schuster.

Karbo, Karen. The Diamond Lane. 1991. 320p. 21.95 o.p. (*0-399-13597-9*, G. P. Putnam's Sons) Penguin Group (USA) Inc.

—Trespassers Welcome Here. 1989. 192p. 19.95 o.p. (*0-399-13437-9*, G. P. Putnam's Sons) Penguin Putnam Bks. for Young Readers.

Kaye, John. Stars Screaming. 336p. 1997. 25.00 o.p. (*0-87113-691-0*, Atlantic Monthly Pr.); 1999. reprint ed. pap. 13.00 (*0-87113-742-9*) Grove/Atlantic, Inc.

Keannealy, Jerry. Vintage Polo. 1993. 256p. 19.95 o.p. (*0-312-09932-0*, Saint Martin's Minotaur) St. Martin's Pr.

Keller, Janet. Necessary Risks. 1994. 192p. mass mkt. 5.99 o.s.i (*0-553-56784-5*) Bantam Bks.

Kellerman, Faye. Day of Atonement: A Peter Decker & Rina Lazarus Novel. 1998. 368p. mass mkt. 6.99 o.s.i (*0-449-00323-X*); 1992. mass mkt. 6.99 o.s.i (*0-449-14824-6*) Ballantine Bks. (Fawcett).

—Day of Atonement: A Peter Decker & Rina Lazarus Novel. l.t. ed. 1992. (Large Print Bks.). 401p. lib. bdg. 21.95 (*0-8161-5351-5*, Macmillan Reference USA) Gale Group.

—Day of Atonement: A Peter Decker & Rina Lazarus Novel. 2004. 400p. mass mkt. 7.99 (*0-06-055489-4*, HarperTorch); 1991. 359p. 20.00 o.p. (*0-688-08604-7*, Morrow, William & Co.) Morrow/Avon.

—False Prophet: A Peter Decker & Rina Lazarus Novel. 1998. 416p. mass mkt. 7.99 (*0-449-00329-9*); 1994. mass mkt. 5.99 o.p. (*0-449-45337-5*); 1993. mass mkt. 5.99 o.s.i (*0-449-14840-8*); 1993. mass mkt. 5.99 o.s.i (*0-449-14898-X*) Ballantine Bks. (Fawcett).

—False Prophet: A Peter Decker & Rina Lazarus Novel. l.t. ed. 1994. (Large Print Bks.). 554p. lib. bdg. 23.95 (*0-8161-7458-X*, Macmillan Reference USA) Gale Group.

—False Prophet: A Peter Decker & Rina Lazarus Novel. 1992. 367p. 20.00 o.p. (*0-688-10553-X*, Morrow, William & Co.) Morrow/Avon.

—The Forgotten: A Peter Decker & Rina Lazarus Novel. l.t. ed. 2001. 592p. pap. 25.00 (*0-06-620958-7*) HarperCollins Pubs.

—The Forgotten: A Peter Decker & Rina Lazarus Novel. 2001. 384p. 26.00 (*0-688-15614-2*, Morrow, William & Co.) Morrow/Avon.

—The Forgotten: A Peter Decker & Rina Lazarus Novel. abr. ed. 2001. audio 25.00 (*0-671-58271-2*); audio compact disk 30.00 o.s.i (*0-7435-0761-4*) Simon & Schuster Audio. (Simon & Schuster Audioworks).

—Grievous Sin: A Peter Decker & Rina Lazarus Novel. 1998. 400p. mass mkt. 7.99 (*0-449-00330-2*); 1994. mass mkt. 6.99 o.s.i (*0-449-14839-4*) Ballantine Bks. (Fawcett).

—Grievous Sin: A Peter Decker & Rina Lazarus Novel. unabr. ed. 1996. audio 72.00 (*0-7366-3321-9*, 3973) Books on Tape, Inc.

—Grievous Sin: A Peter Decker & Rina Lazarus Novel. unabr. ed. 1993. audio 23.95 o.p. (*1-56100-518-5*, 129, Bookcassette); audio 73.25 (*1-56100-150-3*, 885, Unabridged Library Editions) Brilliance Audio.

—Grievous Sin: A Peter Decker & Rina Lazarus Novel. l.t. ed. 1994. (Large Print Bks.). 552p. lib. bdg. 24.95 (*0-8161-7460-1*, Macmillan Reference USA) Gale Group.

—Grievous Sin: A Peter Decker & Rina Lazarus Novel. 1993. 368p. 20.00 o.p. (*0-688-10554-8*, Morrow, William & Co.) Morrow/Avon.

—Jupiter's Bones: A Peter Decker & Rina Lazarus Novel. l.t. ed. 552p. 2000. pap. 28.95 (*0-7838-8783-3*); 1999. 31.95 (*0-7838-8782-5*) Gale Group. (Macmillan Reference USA).

—Jupiter's Bones: A Peter Decker & Rina Lazarus Novel. Feron, C. F., ed. 2000. 448p. mass mkt. 7.50 (*0-380-73082-0*, Avon Bks.) Morrow/Avon.

—Jupiter's Bones: A Peter Decker & Rina Lazarus Novel. 1999. 375p. 25.00 o.p. (*0-688-15612-6*, Morrow, William & Co.) Morrow/Avon.

—Jupiter's Bones: A Peter Decker & Rina Lazarus Novel. abr. ed. 1999. audio 25.00 (*0-671-57759-X*, Simon & Schuster Audioworks) Simon & Schuster Audio.

—Justice: A Peter Decker & Rina Lazarus Novel. unabr. ed. 1996. audio 80.00 (*0-7366-3275-1*, 3931) Books on Tape, Inc.

—Justice: A Peter Decker & Rina Lazarus Novel. abr. ed. 1996. audio 7.99 o.p. (*1-56740-129-5*, 665, Paperback Nova Audio Bks.); 1995. audio 16.95 o.p. (*1-56100-850-8*, 1258, Nova Audio Bks.); 1995. audio 89.25 o.p. (*1-56100-283-6*, 914, Unabridged Library Editions); 1995. audio 25.95 o.p. (*1-56100-658-0*, 150, Bookcassette) Brilliance Audio.

—Justice: A Peter Decker & Rina Lazarus Novel. l.t. ed. 1995. 563p. 26.95 (*0-7838-1494-1*, Macmillan Reference USA) Gale Group.

—Justice: A Peter Decker & Rina Lazarus Novel. abr. ed. 2000. audio 7.95 (*1-57815-172-4*, 1115, Media Bks. Audio Publishing) Media Bks., L. L. C.

—Justice: A Peter Decker & Rina Lazarus Novel. 1996. 465p. mass mkt. 7.99 (*0-380-72498-7*); 1995. 388p. 23.00 o.p. (*0-688-04613-4*, Morrow, William & Co.) Morrow/Avon.

—Milk & Honey: A Peter Decker & Rina Lazarus Novel. 384p. 1998. mass mkt. 6.99 o.s.i (*0-449-00313-2*); 1991. mass mkt. 5.99 o.s.i (*0-449-14728-2*) Ballantine Bks. (Fawcett).

—Milk & Honey: A Peter Decker & Rina Lazarus Novel. 1990. 384p. 18.95 o.p. (*0-688-08603-9*, Morrow, William & Co.) Morrow/Avon.

—Prayers for the Dead: A Peter Decker & Rina Lazarus Novel. unabr. ed. 1997. audio 80.00 Books on Tape, Inc.

—Prayers for the Dead: A Peter Decker & Rina Lazarus Novel. abr. ed. 1997. audio 7.99 o.p. (*1-56740-181-3*, 689, Nova Audio Bks.); 1996. audio 16.95 o.p. (*1-56100-919-9*, 1349, Nova Audio Bks.); 1996. audio 25.95 o.p. (*1-56100-709-9*, 218, Bookcassette); 1996. audio 89.25 o.p. (*1-56100-334-4*, 991, Unabridged Library Editions) Brilliance Audio.

—Prayers for the Dead: A Peter Decker & Rina Lazarus Novel. l.t. ed. 1996. (Large Print Bks.). 586p. 26.95 (*0-7838-1910-2*, Macmillan Reference USA) Gale Group.

—Prayers for the Dead: A Peter Decker & Rina Lazarus Novel. 1997. 424p. mass mkt. 7.99 (*0-380-72624-6*); 1996. 406p. 24.00 o.p. (*0-688-14367-9*, Morrow, William & Co.) Morrow/Avon.

—The Ritual Bath: A Peter Decker & Rina Lazarus Novel. 1998. mass mkt. 6.99 (*0-449-45814-8*); 1987. 288p. mass mkt. 6.99 o.s.i (*0-449-21373-0*) Ballantine Bks. (Fawcett).

—The Ritual Bath: A Peter Decker & Rina Lazarus Novel. l.t. ed. 2000. (G. K. Hall Core Ser.). 368p. 30.95 (*0-7838-9046-X*, Macmillan Reference USA) Gale Group.

—The Ritual Bath: A Peter Decker & Rina Lazarus Novel. 1999. 384p. mass mkt. 6.99 (*0-380-73266-1*) Morrow/Avon.

—Sacred & Profane: A Peter Decker & Rina Lazarus Novel. 1998. mass mkt. 6.99 (*0-449-45815-6*); 1988. mass mkt. 6.99 o.s.i (*0-449-21502-4*, Fawcett) Ballantine Bks.

—Sacred & Profane: A Peter Decker & Rina Lazarus Novel. l.t. ed. 2001. (Magna Large Print Ser.). 400p. (*0-7505-1667-4*) Magna Large Print Bks. GBR. *Dist:* Ulverscroft Large Print Canada, Ltd.

—Sacred & Profane: A Peter Decker & Rina Lazarus Novel. 1999. 384p. mass mkt. 6.99 (*0-380-73267-X*, Avon Bks.); 1987. 311p. 16.95 o.p. (*0-87795-887-4*, Morrow, William & Co.) Morrow/Avon.

—Sacred & Profane: A Peter Decker & Rina Lazarus Novel. 1990. 3.99 o.p. (*0-517-05799-9*) Random Hse. Value Publishing.

—Sanctuary: A Peter Decker & Rina Lazarus Novel. unabr. ed. 1996. audio 72.00 (*0-7366-3355-3*, 4006) Books on Tape, Inc.

—Sanctuary: A Peter Decker & Rina Lazarus Novel. abr. ed. 1994. audio 16.95 o.p. (*1-56100-386-7*, 1359, Nova Audio Bks.); audio 89.25 o.p. (*1-56100-221-6*, 1023, Unabridged Library Editions); audio 25.95 o.p. (*1-56100-596-7*, 246, Bookcassette) Brilliance Audio.

—Sanctuary: A Peter Decker & Rina Lazarus Novel. l.t. ed. 1995. 509p. pap. 23.95 o.p. (*1-56895-090-X*, Wheeler Publishing, Inc.) Gale Group.

—Sanctuary: A Peter Decker & Rina Lazarus Novel. abr. ed. 2000. audio 7.95 (*1-57815-022-1*, 1006, Media Bks. Audio Publishing) Media Bks., L. L. C.

—Sanctuary: A Peter Decker & Rina Lazarus Novel. 1994. 396p. 22.00 o.p. (*0-688-04612-6*, Morrow, William & Co.); 1995. 428p. reprint ed. pap. 6.99 (*0-380-72497-9*, Avon Bks.) Morrow/Avon.

—Serpent's Tooth: A Peter Decker & Rina Lazarus Novel. unabr. ed. 1997. audio 72.00 (*0-7366-4049-5*, 4548) Books on Tape, Inc.

—Serpent's Tooth: A Peter Decker & Rina Lazarus Novel. l.t. ed. 539p. 2001. pap. 30.00 (*0-7838-8323-4*); 1997. lib. bdg. 28.95 o.p. (*0-7838-8322-6*) Gale Group. (Macmillan Reference USA).

—Serpent's Tooth: A Peter Decker & Rina Lazarus Novel. 1998. 432p. mass mkt. 6.99 (*0-380-72625-4*, Avon Bks.); 1997. 416p. 24.50 (*0-688-14368-7*, Morrow, William & Co.); 1997. 416p. 294.00 (*0-688-15649-5*, Morrow, William & Co.) Morrow/Avon.

—Serpent's Tooth: A Peter Decker & Rina Lazarus Novel. abr. ed. 1997. audio 24.00 (*0-671-57757-3*, 495448, Simon & Schuster Audioworks) Simon & Schuster Audio.

—Stalker: A Peter Decker & Rina Lazarus Novel. l.t. ed. 2000. 624p. pap. 25.00 (*0-06-019729-3*, HarperLargePrint) HarperTrade.

—Stalker: A Peter Decker & Rina Lazarus Novel. 2000. 416p. 25.00 (*0-688-15613-4*, Morrow, William & Co.) Morrow/Avon.

—Stone Kiss. 2003. 528p. mass mkt. 7.99 (*0-446-61147-6*, Warner Vision); 2002. 400p. 25.95 (*0-446-53038-7*); 2002. 668p. 25.95 (*0-446-53078-6*) Warner Bks., Inc.

Kellerman, Jonathan. Bad Love. 2003. 512p. mass mkt. 7.99 (*0-345-46072-3*, Ballantine Bks.) Ballantine Bks.

—Bad Love. 1994. 496p. mass mkt. 6.99 o.s.i (*0-553-18118-1*); 512p. mass mkt. 7.99 o.s.i (*0-553-56870-1*); 27.50 o.s.i (*0-553-09636-2*) Bantam Bks.

—Bad Love. l.t. ed. 2001. 386p. 31.95 (*0-7838-9456-2*, Macmillan Reference USA) Gale Group.

—Bad Love. 1994. audio 13.59 o.s.i (*0-553-70076-6*, RH Audio) Random Hse. Audio Publishing Group.

—Blood Test. 2003. 320p. mass mkt. 7.99 (*0-345-46661-6*, Ballantine Bks.) Ballantine Bks.

—Blood Test. 1995. (Alex Delaware Novel Ser.). 320p. mass mkt. 7.99 o.s.i (*0-553-56963-5*) Bantam Bks.

—Blood Test. l.t. ed. 2002. (Famous Authors Ser.). 405p. 29.95 (*0-7862-3753-8*) Gale Group.

—Blood Test. 1987. mass mkt. 4.50 o.p. (*0-451-15434-7*, Signet Bks.); mass mkt. 4.50 o.p. (*0-451-14737-5*, Signet Bks.); 352p. mass mkt. 5.99 o.p. (*0-451-15929-2*, Signet Bks.); mass mkt. 5.99 o.s.i (*0-451-17802-5*) NAL.

—Blood Test. 1986. 258p. bds. 14.95 o.s.i (*0-689-11634-9*, Scribner) Simon & Schuster.

—The Clinic. 2003. 496p. mass mkt. 7.99 (*0-345-46074-X*, Ballantine Bks.) Ballantine Bks.

—The Clinic. 1997. (Alex Delaware Novel Ser.). 496p. mass mkt. 7.99 o.s.i (*0-553-57230-X*); mass mkt. 6.99 (*0-553-84009-6*) Bantam Bks.

—The Clinic. unabr. ed. 1997. (Alex Delaware Mystery Ser.). audio 64.00 (*0-913369-47-0*, 4251) Books on Tape, Inc.

—The Clinic. abr. ed. 1997. (Alex Delaware Mystery Ser.). audio compact disk 29.95 (*0-553-45552-4*, RH Audio) Random Hse. Audio Publishing Group.

—The Clinic. l.t. ed. 1998. (Thorndike/G. K. Hall Paperback Bestsellers Ser.). 600p. pap. 28.95 (*0-7862-0983-6*) Thorndike Pr.

—Devil's Waltz. 2003. 528p. mass mkt. 7.99 (*0-345-46071-5*, Ballantine Bks.) Ballantine Bks.

—Devil's Waltz. 1993. (Alex Delaware Novel Ser.). 528p. mass mkt. 7.99 (*0-553-56352-1*); 512p. mass mkt. 6.50 o.s.i (*0-553-18101-7*) Bantam Bks.

—Devil's Waltz. unabr. ed. 1993. audio 72.00 (*0-7366-2424-4*, 3189) Books on Tape, Inc.

—Devil's Waltz. 1993. audio 15.95 o.s.i (*0-553-74528-X*); 1993. audio 12.79 o.s.i (*0-553-70060-X*); 1999. audio 9.99 o.s.i (*0-553-70211-4*) Random Hse. Audio Publishing Group. (RH Audio).

—Devil's Waltz. 6.98 o.p. (*0-8317-4339-5*) Smithmark Pubs., Inc.

—Flesh & Blood. 2001. E-Book 21.95 (*1-58836-141-1*) Random Hse., Inc.

—Over the Edge. 1988. 448p. mass mkt. 5.99 o.p. (*0-451-15219-0*); mass mkt. 7.99 o.s.i (*0-451-17801-7*) NAL. (Signet Bks.).

—Over the Edge. 1987. 384p. bds. 17.95 o.s.i (*0-689-11635-7*, Scribner) Simon & Schuster.

—Private Eyes. 2003. 560p. mass mkt. 7.99 (*0-345-46070-7*, Ballantine Bks.) Ballantine Bks.

—Private Eyes. audio 15.99. 1992. 560p. mass mkt. 7.99 o.s.i (*0-553-29950-6*); 1992. pap. 5.50 (*0-553-18085-1*) Bantam Bks.

—Private Eyes. l.t. ed. 1992. 720p. 25.00 o.s.i (*0-385-42283-0*, Bantam Large Type) Bantam Doubleday Dell Large Print Group, Inc.

—Private Eyes. unabr. ed. 1993. audio 88.00 (*0-7366-2351-5*, 3128) Books on Tape, Inc.

—Private Eyes. 1992. audio 12.79 o.s.i (*0-553-70022-7*, RH Audio); 2004. audio compact disk 14.99 (*0-7393-1223-5*, RH Audio Price-Less); 1999. audio 9.99 o.s.i (*0-553-70201-7*, RH Audio) Random Hse. Audio Publishing Group.

—Self-Defense. 1995. 528p. mass mkt. 6.99 o.s.i (*0-553-84002-9*); (Illus.). reprint ed. mass mkt. 7.99 o.s.i (*0-553-57220-2*) Bantam Bks.

—Self-Defense. unabr. ed. 1995. audio 64.00 (*0-7366-2958-0*, 3651) Books on Tape, Inc.

—Self-Defense. l.t. ed. 1995. (Large Print Bks.). 556p. 26.95 o.p. (*1-56895-206-6*, Wheeler Publishing, Inc.) Gale Group.

—Self-Defense. abr. ed. 1995. audio 16.98 o.s.i (*0-553-74598-0*, RH Audio) Random Hse. Audio Publishing Group.

—Self-Defense. 2002. (Illus.). 528p. mass mkt. 7.99 (*0-345-45883-4*) Random Hse., Inc.

—Silent Partner. 2003. 512p. mass mkt. 7.99 (*0-345-46068-5*, Ballantine Bks.) Ballantine Bks.

—Silent Partner. 1990. 512p. mass mkt. 5.50 o.s.i (*0-553-17339-1*); mass mkt. 7.99 o.s.i (*0-553-28592-0*) Bantam Bks.

—Silent Partner. unabr. ed. 1992. (Alex Delaware Mystery Ser.). audio 88.00 (*0-7366-2266-7*, 3054) Books on Tape, Inc.

—Silent Partner. l.t. ed. 1996. (Large Print Bks.). 585p. pap. 23.95 o.p. (*1-56895-362-3*, Wheeler Publishing, Inc.) Gale Group.

—Silent Partner. 1989. audio 15.95 o.s.i (*0-553-74579-4*, RH Audio); 2003. audio compact disk 14.99 (*0-7393-0376-7*, RH Audio Price-Less); 1999. audio 9.99 o.s.i (*0-553-70196-7*, RH Audio); 1989. audio 16.99 o.s.i (*0-553-45191-X*, RH Audio) Random Hse. Audio Publishing Group.

—Survival of the Fittest. l.t. ed. 1998. 621p. (*0-7540-2083-5*) BBC Audiobooks America.

—Survival of the Fittest. 1998. (Alex Delaware Novel Ser.). 544p. mass mkt. 7.99 o.s.i (*0-553-57232-6*) Bantam Bks.

—Survival of the Fittest. unabr. ed. 1998. audio 72.00 (*0-7366-3995-0*, 4461) Books on Tape, Inc.

—Survival of the Fittest. abr. ed. 1997. (Alex Delaware Mystery Ser.). audio compact disk 29.95 o.s.i (*0-553-45569-9*, , RH Audio) Random Hse. Audio Publishing Group.

—Survival of the Fittest. 2002. (Illus.). 544p. mass mkt. 7.99 (*0-345-45884-2*) Random Hse., Inc.

—Survival of the Fittest. l.t. ed. (Paperback Bestsellers Ser.). 667p. 1999. 27.95 o.p. (*0-7862-1283-7*); 1998. 30.95 (*0-7862-1282-9*) Thorndike Pr.

—Time Bomb. 2003. 496p. mass mkt. 7.99 (*0-345-46069-3*, Ballantine Bks.) Ballantine Bks.

—Time Bomb. 1991. (Alex Delaware Novel Ser.). 496p. mass mkt. 7.99 o.s.i (*0-553-29170-X*); 480p. mass mkt. 5.95 o.s.i (*0-553-18041-X*) Bantam Bks.

—Time Bomb. unabr. ed. 1992. audio 88.00 (*0-7366-2267-5*, 3055) Books on Tape, Inc.

—Time Bomb. abr. ed. 1990. audio 16.99 o.s.i (*0-553-45237-1*, RH Audio) Random Hse. Audio Publishing Group.

—The Web. 2003. 448p. mass mkt. 7.99 (*0-345-46073-1*, Ballantine Bks.) Ballantine Bks.

—The Web. 1996. 448p. mass mkt. 7.99 o.s.i (*0-553-57227-X*) Bantam Bks.

—The Web. unabr. ed. 1996. (Alex Delaware Mystery Ser.). audio 64.00 (*0-7366-3277-8*, 3933) Books on Tape, Inc.

—The Web. l.t. ed. 1996. (Alex Delaware Ser.). 454p. 26.95 o.p. (*1-56895-311-9*, Wheeler Publishing, Inc.) Gale Group.

—The Web. abr. ed. 1996. (Alex Delaware Mystery Ser.). audio 23.95 o.s.i (*0-553-47430-8*, 693452, RH Audio) Random Hse. Audio Publishing Group.

—When the Bough Breaks. 2003. 448p. mass mkt. 7.99 (*0-345-46660-8*, Ballantine Bks.) Ballantine Bks.

—When the Bough Breaks. 1994. (Alex Delaware Novel Ser.). 448p. mass mkt. 7.99 o.s.i (0-553-56961-9) Bantam Bks.
—When the Bough Breaks. 1986. mass mkt. 4.95 o.p. (0-451-15874-1); mass mkt. 4.50 o.p. (0-451-14870-3); mass mkt. 3.95 o.p. (0-451-14249-7); 352p. mass mkt. 5.99 o.p. (0-451-16862-3); mass mkt. 5.99 o.s.i (0-451-17803-3) NAL. (Signet Bks.).
—When the Bough Breaks. 1985. 304p. bds. 15.95 o.s.i (0-689-11519-9, Scribner) Simon & Schuster.
—When the Bough Breaks. l.t. ed. 2001. 608p. 28.95 o.p. (0-7862-3752-X); (0-7540-1721-4); (0-7540-9118-X) Thorndike Pr.
Kennealy, Jerry. All That Glitters: A Nick Polo Mystery. 1996. 240p. 21.95 o.p. (0-312-15049-0, Saint Martin's Minotaur) St. Martin's Pr.
—Beggar's Choice. 1994. 256p. 20.95 o.p. (0-312-11478-8, Saint Martin's Minotaur) St. Martin's Pr.
—Green with Envy: A Nick Polo Mystery. 1991. 240p. 17.95 o.p. (0-312-06572-8, Saint Martin's Minotaur) St. Martin's Pr.
—Polo, Anyone? 1988. 224p. 15.95 o.p. (0-312-01491-0, Saint Martin's Minotaur) St. Martin's Pr.
—Polo in the Rough. 1989. 14.95 o.p. (0-312-02964-0, Saint Martin's Minotaur) St. Martin's Pr.
—Polo Solo. 1988. pap. 2.95 o.p. (0-312-91074-6, St. Martin's Paperbacks); 1987. 192p. 13.95 o.p. (0-312-00671-3) St. Martin's Pr.
—Polo's Ponies. 1988. 176p. 14.95 o.p. (0-312-02267-0, Saint Martin's Minotaur) St. Martin's Pr.
—Polo's Wild Card. 1992. 1.99 o.p. (0-517-08490-2) Random Hse. Value Publishing.
—Polo's Wild Card. 1990. 15.95 o.p. (0-312-04437-2, Saint Martin's Minotaur) St. Martin's Pr.
—Special Delivery: A Case for Nick Polo. 1992. 224p. 17.95 o.p. (0-312-08304-1, Saint Martin's Minotaur) St. Martin's Pr.
Kenner, Julie. Aphrodite's Kiss. 2001. (Time of Your Life Ser.). 400p. mass mkt. 5.99 (0-505-52438-4, Love Spell) Dorchester Publishing Co., Inc.
—The Cat's Fancy. 2000. (Time of Your Life Ser.). 400p. mass mkt. 5.99 (0-505-52397-3, Love Spell) Dorchester Publishing Co., Inc.
Kensington Ladies' Erotica Society Staff. Look Homeward Erotica. 1987. 240p. pap. 8.95 o.p. (0-89815-195-3) Ten Speed Pr.
Kerr, Larry L. The Neon Nightmare. l.t. ed. 1999. E-Book 14.99 incl. cd-rom (1-929077-71-8, Books OnScreen) PageFree Publishing, Inc.
—The Neon Nightmare. deluxe unabr. ed. 2002. lib. bdg. 35.00 incl. audio (0-932079-26-1, 79261) TimeFare Audio Bk. Productions.
Kerr, Philip. The Grid. l.t. ed. 1996. 578p. 25.95 o.p. (0-7838-1654-5, Macmillan Reference USA) Gale Group.
—The Grid. abr. ed. 1996. audio 12.98 (1-57042-406-3, 394054) Time Warner AudioBooks.
—The Grid. 1997. 464p. mass mkt. 6.99 (0-446-60340-6); 1996. 82p. 21.95 o.s.i (0-446-52053-5) Warner Bks., Inc.
Kerr, Phillip. The Grid. unabr. ed. 1996. audio 72.00 (0-7366-3468-1, 4112) Books on Tape, Inc.
Keys, Elizabeth. Irish Blessing: Reilly's Gold. 2000. (Irish Blessings Ser.). 32p. mass mkt. 5.50 o.s.i (0-8217-6730-5) Kensington Publishing Corp.
Kihn, Greg. The Horror Show. 1997. 274p. pap. text 5.99 (0-8125-5108-7, Tor Bks.) Doherty, Tom Assocs., LLC.
Kijewski, Karen. Alley Kat Blues. 1996. (Kat Colorado Mysteries Ser.). 384p. mass mkt. 6.99 (0-553-57315-2, Crimeline) Bantam Bks.
—Alley Kat Blues. 1995. 22.95 o.s.i (0-385-46852-0) Doubleday Publishing.
—Kat Scratch Fever. 1998. (Kat Colorado Mysteries Ser.). 368p. mass mkt. 6.99 o.s.i (0-425-16339-3) Berkley Publishing Group.
—Kat Scratch Fever. 1997. 323p. 22.95 o.p. (0-399-14245-2) Penguin Group (USA) Inc.
—Katapult. 1992. (Kat Colorado Mysteries Ser.). 288p. reprint ed. mass mkt. 6.99 (0-380-71486-8, Avon Bks.) Morrow/Avon.
—Katapult. 1990. 244p. 16.95 o.p. (0-312-04679-0, Saint Martin's Minotaur) St. Martin's Pr.
—Kat's Cradle. 1997. (Kat Colorado Mysteries Ser.). 320p. mass mkt. 6.99 (0-553-29391-5) Bantam Bks.
—Katwalk. 1990. (Kat Colorado Mysteries Ser.). 240p. reprint ed. mass mkt. 6.99 (0-380-71187-7, Avon Bks.) Morrow/Avon.
—Katwalk. 1989. 232p. 16.95 o.p. (0-312-02969-1, Saint Martin's Minotaur) St. Martin's Pr.
—Stray Kat Waltz. 1999. (Kat Colorado Mysteries Ser.). 352p. reprint ed. pap. 6.99 o.s.i (0-425-16988-X) Berkley Publishing Group.
—Stray Kat Waltz. 1998. (Kat Colorado Mysteries Ser. ). 311p. 22.95 o.s.i (0-399-14368-8, G. P. Putnam's Sons) Penguin Group (USA) Inc.
—Wild Kat. 1994. (Kat Colorado Mysteries Ser.). 400p. mass mkt. 6.99 (0-553-56877-9) Bantam Bks.
Kilworth, Garry D. Angel. 1996. 320p. 22.95 o.p. (0-312-86107-9, Forge Bks.) Doherty, Tom Assocs., LLC.
Kim, Nancy. Chinhominey's Secret: A Novel. 1999. 240p. 22.95 (1-882593-28-6) Bridge Works Publishing Co., Inc.
Kim, Willyce. Dancer Dawkins & the California Kid. 1985. 133p. (Orig.). pap. 5.95 o.p. (0-932870-59-7) Alyson Pubns.
Kincaid, Tim. Today, Tomorrow & Always. 1997. 480p. mass mkt. 5.99 o.s.i (1-57566-187-X); 1996. 432p. 22.00 o.p. (1-57566-077-6, Kensington Bks.) Kensington Publishing Corp.
King, Laurie R. A Grave Talent. 1995. 368p. mass mkt. 6.99 (0-553-57399-3, Crimeline) Bantam Bks.
—A Grave Talent. unabr. ed. 1996. (Kate Martinelli Mystery Ser.: Vol. 1). audio 85.00 (0-7887-0395-1, 94587E7) Recorded Bks., LLC.
—A Grave Talent. 1993. 310p. 19.95 (0-312-08804-3, Saint Martin's Minotaur) St. Martin's Pr.
—Night Work. 2000. (Kate Martinelli Mysteries Ser.). 416p. mass mkt. 6.99 (0-553-57825-1) Bantam Bks.
—To Play the Fool. 1996. 320p. mass mkt. 6.99 (0-553-57455-8, Crimeline) Bantam Bks.
—To Play the Fool. unabr. ed. 1996. (Kate Martinelli Mystery Ser.: Vol. 2). audio 60.00 (0-7887-0406-0, 94598E7); audio Recorded Bks., LLC.
—To Play the Fool. 1995. 260p. 21.00 o.p. (0-312-11907-0, Saint Martin's Minotaur) St. Martin's Pr.
—With Child. 1997. 320p. mass mkt. 6.99 (0-553-57458-2) Bantam Bks.
—With Child. unabr. ed. 1996. (Kate Martinelli Mystery Ser.: Vol. 3). audio 70.00 (0-7887-0579-2, 94757E7) Recorded Bks., LLC.
—With Child. 1996. 275p. 21.95 o.p. (0-312-14077-0, Saint Martin's Minotaur) St. Martin's Pr.
—With Child. l.t. ed. 1998. (Ulverscroft Large Print Ser.). 528p. 29.99 (0-7089-3904-X, Ulverscroft) Thorpe, F. A. Pubs. GBR. Dist: Ulverscroft Large Print Bks., Ltd., Ulverscroft Large Print Canada, Ltd.
Kiraly, Sherwood. California Rush: A Novel. 1997. 256p. reprint ed. pap. 12.00 o.s.i (0-425-15979-5) Berkley Publishing Group.
Klavan, Andrew. Dynamite Road. Date not set. mass mkt. (0-7653-4694-X); 2003. 320p. 25.95 (0-7653-0785-5) Doherty, Tom Assocs., LLC. (Forge Bks.).
Klein, Michael. The Voice of Free Earth. Hughes, Kyra B., ed. 1996. 285p. pap. 11.95 (0-9637981-0-3) One Horse Rhino Pr.
Kliewer, Dorothy. Murder in the Swamp. 2004. (WWL Mystery Ser.: No. 490). 256p. mass mkt. (0-373-26490-9, Worldwide Library) Harlequin Enterprises, Ltd.
Knox, Elizabeth. Black Oxen. 2001. 448p. 25.00 o.p. (0-374-11405-6) Farrar, Straus & Giroux.
—Black Oxen. 2002. 448p. pap. 14.00 (0-312-42049-8) Picador.
Koontz, Dean. Dragon Tears. unabr. ed. audio 69.95 o.p. BBC Audiobooks America.
—Dragon Tears. 1994. pap. 6.98 (0-8317-4384-0); 1993. 416p. mass mkt. 7.99 (0-425-14003-2) Berkley Publishing Group.
—Dragon Tears. 1993. 384p. 22.95 o.p. (0-399-13773-4, G. P. Putnam's Sons) Penguin Group (USA) Inc.
—Dragon Tears. ltd. ed. 1993. 150.00 o.s.i (0-399-13789-0) Putnam Publishing Group, The.
—Dragon Tears. unabr. ed. 2003. audio 39.95 (0-671-86585-4, Simon & Schuster Audioworks) Simon & Schuster Audio.
—Dragon Tears. 1993. (J). 14.04 (0-606-05243-7) Turtleback Bks.
—Fear Nothing. 1998. mass mkt. 7.99 (0-553-84021-5); 448p. mass mkt. 7.99 (0-553-57975-4); 400p. 26.95 o.s.i (0-553-10664-3) Bantam Bks.
—Fear Nothing. l.t. ed. 1998. (Core Ser.). 577p. 29.95 o.p. (0-7838-8358-7, Macmillan Reference USA) Gale Group.
—Fear Nothing. unabr. ed. 1998. (Christopher Snow Stories Ser.). 12p. audio 39.95 (0-553-47900-8, 105583, RH Audio) Random Hse. Audio Publishing Group.
—Fear Nothing. 1998. 14.04 (0-606-16374-3) Turtleback Bks.
—Intensity. 1997. pap. text 7.99 (0-345-91189-X); 1997. pap. 12.95 o.p. (0-345-41948-0); 1996. 448p. mass mkt. 7.99 o.s.i (0-345-38436-9); 1996. mass mkt. 6.99 (0-345-40514-5) Ballantine Bks.
—Intensity. l.t. ed. 1996. 752p. 25.00 o.p. (0-7838-1678-2, Macmillan Reference USA) Gale Group.
—Intensity. deluxe ed. 1996. 25.00 o.s.i (0-676-51387-5) Random Hse., Inc.
—Mr. Murder. 1994. 496p. mass mkt. 7.99 (0-425-14442-9) Berkley Publishing Group.
—Mr. Murder. 1993. 416p. 23.95 o.p. (0-399-13874-9, G. P. Putnam's Sons); (Illus.). (J). 150.00 o.p. (0-399-13899-4, Puffin Bks.) Penguin Group (USA) Inc.
—Phantoms. 432p. 1997. mass mkt. 7.50 o.s.i (0-425-16202-8); 1986. mass mkt. 7.99 o.s.i (0-425-10145-2) Berkley Publishing Group.
—Phantoms. 1983. 352p. 15.95 o.p. (0-399-12655-4, G. P. Putnam's Sons) Penguin Putnam Bks. for Young Readers.
—Phantoms. 1983. 14.04 (0-606-03685-7) Turtleback Bks.
—Seize the Night. 1999. 480p. mass mkt. 7.99 (0-553-58019-1); 480p. mass mkt. 7.99 o.s.i (0-553-58229-1); mass mkt. 7.99 (0-553-84020-7) Bantam Bks.
—Seize the Night, unabr. ed. 1999. audio 39.95 Highsmith Inc.
—Seize the Night. unabr. ed. 1998. (Christopher Snow Stories Ser.). audio 39.95 (0-553-47901-6, 116030, RH Audio) Random Hse. Audio Publishing Group.
—Seize the Night. l.t. ed. (Paperback Bestsellers Ser.). 2000. 617p. pap. 27.95 (0-7838-8529-6); 1999. 605p. 30.95 (0-7838-8528-8) Thorndike Pr.
—Seize the Night. l.t. ed. 2000. (Charnwood Large Print Ser.). 616p. (0-7089-9144-0, Ulverscroft) Thorpe, F. A. Pubs. GBR. Dist: Ulverscroft Large Print Bks., Ltd., Ulverscroft Large Print Canada, Ltd.
—Seize the Night. 1999. 14.04 (0-606-18001-X) Turtleback Bks.
—The Servants of Twilight. 1990. 432p. mass mkt. 7.99 (0-425-12125-9); 1988. 18.95 o.p. (0-913165-24-7) Berkley Publishing Group.
—The Servants of Twilight. l.t. ed. 1994. (Magna Large Print Ser.). 721p. o.p. (0-7505-0637-7) Magna Large Print Bks. GBR. Dist: Ulverscroft Large Print Canada, Ltd.
—The Servants of Twilight. 1996. (SPA.). 496p. (84-01-49545-8) Plaza & Janés Editories, S.A.
—The Servants of Twilight. l.t. ed. 2001. (Famous Authors Ser.). 765p. 29.95 (0-7862-2866-0) Thorndike Pr.
—The Servants of Twilight. 1984. 14.04 (0-606-04537-6) Turtleback Bks.
—Ticktock. 1997. 352p. mass mkt. 7.99 o.s.i (0-345-38430-X) Ballantine Bks.
—Ticktock. l.t. ed. 1997. pap. 20.00 o.p. (0-7838-8136-3, Macmillan Reference USA) Gale Group.
—Winter Moon. 1997. pap. 12.95 o.p. (0-345-41949-9); 1993. 480p. mass mkt. 7.99 o.s.i (0-345-38610-8) Ballantine Bks.
Koretsky, Judy Lea. The Eternity Look. 2003. 231p. pap. 14.95 (1-58790-052-1) Regent Pr.
Kotzwinkle, William. The Exile. 1998. 277p. pap. 12.95 (1-56924-728-5, Marlowe & Co.) Avalon Publishing Group.
—The Exile. 1988. 288p. pap. 7.95 o.p. (0-525-48378-0, Obelisk); 1987. 17.95 o.p. (0-525-24526-X, Seymour Lawrence) NAL.
—The Exile. 1990. 4.99 o.p. (0-517-02758-5) Random Hse. Value Publishing.
Krantz, Judith. Lovers. 1995. 544p. mass mkt. 7.99 (0-553-56135-9) Bantam Bks.
—Lovers. unabr. ed. 1997. audio 99.95 (1-85695-924-4, 950304) ISIS Audio Bks. GBR. Dist: Ulverscroft Large Print Bks., Ltd.
—Lovers. abr. ed. 1995. audio 8.99 o.s.i (0-679-44348-7, 391115, RH Audio) Random Hse. Audio Publishing Group.
—Lovers. l.t. ed. Date not set. pap. 4.99 (0-517-19680-8) Random Hse. Large Print.
Kraus, Jim & Kraus, Terri. The Price: A Novel. 2000. (Circle of Destiny Ser.). 368p. pap. 8.99 o.p. (0-8423-1835-6) Tyndale Hse. Pubs.
Krentz, Jayne Ann. Ghost of a Chance. l.t. ed. 2003. 280p. 31.95 (1-58724-498-5, Wheeler Publishing, Inc.) Gale Group.
—Ghost of a Chance. 1999. 250p. mass mkt. (1-55166-524-7, 1-66524-9, Mira Bks.) Harlequin Enterprises, Ltd.
—Gift of Fire. l.t. ed. 1994. 22.95 o.p. (0-7927-1954-9); pap. o.p. (0-7927-1953-0) BBC Audiobooks America.
—Gift of Fire. 1992. 352p. reprint ed. 20.00 o.p. (0-7278-4354-0) Severn Hse. Pubs., Ltd.
—The Ties That Bind. 2002. 256p. mass mkt. (1-55166-903-X, Mira Bks.); 1993. per. (0-373-83269-9, 1-83269-0, Harlequin Bks.) Harlequin Enterprises, Ltd.
—The Ties That Bind. 2003. (Famous Authors Ser.). 288p. 29.95 (0-7862-5060-7) Thorndike Pr.
—True Colors. l.t. ed. 2002. (Wheeler Large Print Book Ser.). 28.95 (1-58724-193-5, Wheeler Publishing, Inc.) Gale Group.
—True Colors. 2001. 256p. mass mkt. (1-55166-798-3, Mira Bks.); 1985. mass mkt. (0-373-25191-2, Harlequin Bks.) Harlequin Enterprises, Ltd.
—Witchcraft. 1996. per. (1-55166-158-6, 1-66158-6, Mira Bks.); 1985. mass mkt. (0-373-25174-2, Harlequin Bks.) Harlequin Enterprises, Ltd.
—Witchcraft. l.t. ed. 2000. (Romance Ser.). (Illus.). 315p. 28.95 (0-7862-2600-5) Thorndike Pr.
Krich, Rochelle Majer. Angel of Death. 1994. 384p. 27.00 (0-89296-508-8) Mysterious Pr.
—Angel of Death. 372p. pap. 4.98 o.p. (0-7651-0305-2) Smithmark Pubs., Inc.
—Angel of Death. 1996. 368p. mass mkt. 5.99 o.s.i (0-446-40311-3) Warner Bks., Inc.
—Blood Money: A Mystery. 2000. 352p. mass mkt. 6.99 (0-380-78954-X); 1999. 341p. 23.00 (0-380-97379-0) Morrow/Avon. (Avon Bks.).
—Fair Game. 1994. 320p. mass mkt. 5.50 o.s.i (0-446-40310-5) Warner Bks., Inc.
—Fertile Ground: A Mystery. 1999. mass mkt. 6.99 (0-380-78953-1); 1998. 352p. mass mkt. 22.00 (0-380-97378-2) Morrow/Avon. (Avon Bks.).
—Speak No Evil. 1996. 82p. 21.95 o.p. (0-89296-584-3) Mysterious Pr.
—Speak No Evil. 1997. 384p. mass mkt. 6.50 o.p. (0-446-40505-1) Warner Bks., Inc.
Krich, Rochelle Majer, et al, eds. Murder on Sunset Boulevard. 2002. 221p. pap. 12.95 (1-929976-19-4) Top Pubns., Ltd.
Kuhlken, Ken. The Angel Gang. 1994. 288p. 20.95 o.p. (0-312-10930-X, Saint Martin's Minotaur) St. Martin's Pr.
Kyne, Jon. Henrietta. 2002. 156p. per. 19.95 (1-930859-07-4) Elderberry Pr., LLC.
La Plante, Lynda. Cold Blood. 1999. 480p. mass mkt. 6.99 o.s.i (0-515-12479-6, Jove) Berkley Publishing Group.
—Cold Blood. unabr. ed. 2000. (Lorraine Page Mystery Ser.). audio 89.95 (0-7451-8782-X, CAB 1417) Chivers Audio Bks. GBR. Dist: BBC Audiobooks America.
—Cold Heart. unabr. ed. 1998. audio 84.95 (0-7540-0213-6, CAB 1636) BBC Audiobooks America.
—Cold Shoulder. 1997. 464p. mass mkt. 6.99 o.s.i (0-515-12128-2, Jove) Berkley Publishing Group.
—Cold Shoulder. unabr. ed. 2000. (Lorraine Page Mystery Ser.). audio 79.95 (0-7451-6511-7, CAB 1127) Chivers Audio Bks. GBR. Dist: BBC Audiobooks America.
Lachtman, Ofelia D. A Shell for Angela. 1995. 214p. (Orig.). pap. 9.95 (1-55885-123-2) Arte Publico Pr.
Lackey, Mercedes. The Fire Rose. 1996. 448p. pap. 6.99 (0-671-87750-X); 1995. 22.00 (0-671-87687-2); 2001. 448p. reprint ed. 6.99 (0-671-31967-1) Baen Bks.
Lacy, Al. A Dream Fulfilled, 10 vols. 2003. (Angel of Mercy Ser.: Vol. 4). 270p. pap. 10.99 (0-88070-940-5, Multnomah Bks.) Multnomah Pubs., Inc.
—Faithful Heart, 10 vols. 2003. (Angel of Mercy Ser.: Vol. 2). 308p. pap. 10.99 (0-88070-835-2, Multnomah Bks.) Multnomah Pubs., Inc.
Lacy, Al & Lacy, JoAnna. So Little Time. l.t. ed. 2003. (Mail Order Bride Ser.). 517p. 27.95 (0-7862-5360-6) Thorndike Pr.
—So Little Time Bk #9. 2003. (Mail Order Bride Ser.). 304p. pap. 10.99 (1-57673-898-1) Multnomah Pubs., Inc.
Lafferty, Perry. Jablonski & the Erotomaniac: A Jack Jablonski Thriller. 1992. 19.95 o.p. (1-55611-323-4) Fine, Donald I. Bks.
—Jablonski of L. A. 1991. 18.95 o.p. (1-55611-262-9) Fine, Donald I. Bks.
Laidlaw, Marc. Kalifornia: A Novel. 1993. 245p. 18.95 o.p. (0-312-08830-2) St. Martin's Pr.
—The Orchid Eater. 1994. 240p. 19.95 o.p. (0-312-10515-0) St. Martin's Pr.
Lamb, Bette Golden & J. J. Lamb. Bone Dry. 2003. 256p. pap. 13.95 (1-4104-0130-8, Five Star Trade) Gale Group.
Lamb, Bette Golden & Lamb, J. J. Bone Dry. 2003. (Five Star First Edition Mystery Ser.). 256p. 25.95 (0-7862-4912-9, Five Star) Gale Group.
Lambert, Mercedes. Dogtown: A Whitney Logan Mystery. 1991. (Whitney Logan Mystery Ser.). 272p. 18.95 o.p. (0-670-83479-3) Viking Penguin.
—Soultown. 1997. (Whitney Logan Mystery Ser.). 256p. pap. 5.95 o.s.i (0-14-025492-7) Penguin Group (USA) Inc.
—Soultown: A Whitney Logan Mystery. 1996. (Whitney Logan Mystery Ser.). 256p. 21.95 o.s.i (0-670-86684-9, Viking) Viking Penguin.
Landers, Gunnard. The Violators. 1991. 250p. 19.95 o.p. (0-8027-1179-0) Walker & Co.
Landreth, Marsha. The Holiday Murders. 1992. 243p. 19.95 o.s.i (0-8027-1246-0) Walker & Co.
Lanigan, Catherine. California Moon. 2000. 376p. per. (1-55166-578-6, Harlequin Bks.) Harlequin Enterprises, Ltd.
Lankford, Terrill. Angry Moon. unabr. ed. 1998. audio 49.95 (0-7861-1347-2, 2250) Blackstone Audio Bks., Inc.
—Angry Moon. 317p. 1999. mass mkt. 5.99 (0-8125-4834-5, Tor Bks.); 1997. 22.95 (0-312-85726-8, Forge Bks.) Doherty, Tom Assocs., LLC.
—Shooters. 224p. 1998. mass mkt. 5.99 (0-8125-5538-4); 1996. 20.95 o.p. (0-312-86272-5) Doherty, Tom Assocs., LLC. (Forge Bks.).
—Shooters. abr. ed. 1997. audio 17.00 (1-56876-068-X) Soundlines Entertainment, Inc.
Lapierre, Janet. Baby Mine: A Port Silva Mystery. 1999. (Port Silva Mysteries Ser.). (Illus.). 255p. pap. 12.95 (1-880284-32-4) Daniel, John & Co., Pubs.
—Children's Games. 1989. 16.95 o.s.i (0-684-19064-8, Macmillan Reference USA) Gale Group.
—Children's Games. 1990. mass mkt. (0-373-26052-0, Harlequin Bks.) Harlequin Enterprises, Ltd.



For book reviews, descriptive annotations, tables of contents, cover images, author biographies & additional information, updated daily, subscribe to **www.booksinprint.com** 639

—Children's Games. 1990. pap. o.s.i (*1-85381-112-2*) Virago Pr., Ltd. GBR. *Dist:* Little Brown & Co.
—The Cruel Mother. 1991. reprint ed. per. (*0-373-26078-4*, Harlequin Bks.) Harlequin Enterprises, Ltd.
—The Cruel Mother: A Meg Halloran Mystery. 1990. 224p. 18.95 o.s.i (*0-684-19170-9*, Macmillan Reference USA) Gale Group.
—Grandmother's House. 1991. 288p. 19.95 o.s.i (*0-684-19382-5*, Macmillan Reference USA) Gale Group.
—Grandmother's House. 1993. (Mystery Ser.). per. (*0-373-26120-9*, 1-26120-5, Harlequin Bks.) Harlequin Enterprises, Ltd.
—Keepers. 2001. (Port Silva Mystery Ser.). (Illus.). 240p. pap. 12.95 (*1-880284-44-8*) Daniel, John & Co., Pubs.
—Old Enemies. 1993. 256p. text 20.00 (*0-684-19614-X*, Macmillan Reference USA) Gale Group.
—The Unquiet Grave. 1987. 240p. 15.95 o.p. (*0-312-01102-4*, Saint Martin's Minotaur) St. Martin's Pr.
Lark, Michael. Graphic Comic Book: Raymond Chandler's 'The Little Sister' 1997. (Illus.). 136p. pap. 15.00 o.s.i (*0-684-82933-9*, Fireside) Simon & Schuster.
Larsen, Michael. Uncertainty. 1998. Tr. of Uden Sikker Viden. 272p. pap. 12.00 o.s.i (*0-449-91236-1*, Fawcett) Ballantine Bks.
—Uncertainty. Blecher, Lone T. & Blecher, George, trs. from DAN. 1996. Tr. of Uden Sikker Viden. 272p. 22.00 o.s.i (*0-15-100202-9*) Harcourt Trade Pubs.
Larsgaard, Chris. The Heir Hunter. 2001. 448p. mass mkt. 6.99 (*0-440-23462-X*) Dell Publishing.
Latiolais, Michelle. Even Now. 1990. 18.95 o.s.i (*0-374-14993-3*) Farrar, Straus & Giroux.
—Even Now. 1992. 2.99 o.p. (*0-517-08587-9*) Random Hse. Value Publishing.
Latt, Mimi. Powers of Attorney. 1993. 512p. 23.00 o.p. (*0-671-78708-X*, Simon & Schuster) Simon & Schuster.
—Powers of Attorney. Rubenstein, Julie, ed. 1994. 544p. reprint ed. mass mkt. 6.99 (*0-671-86916-7*, Pocket) Simon & Schuster.
—Pursuit of Justice. l.t. ed. 1998. (Large Print Bks.). pap. 24.95 (*1-56895-589-8*, Wheeler Publishing, Inc.) Gale Group.
—Pursuit of Justice. 1999. (Illus.). 480p. mass mkt. 6.99 o.s.i (*0-671-03411-1*, Pocket); 1998. 384p. 23.00 (*0-684-81184-7*, Simon & Schuster) Simon & Schuster.
Lawrence, Cynthia. Take-Out City. 1993. 208p. 18.95 o.p. (*0-88184-942-1*, Carroll & Graf Pubs.) Avalon Publishing Group.
Lawrence, Cynthia P. Chill Before Serving: A Mystery for Food Lovers. 2002. 262p. pap. 14.95 (*0-595-21791-5*, Mystery & Suspense Pr.) iUniverse, Inc.
Lawrence, Martha C. Aquarius Descending. (Elizabeth Chase Mysteries Ser.). 2000. 320p. mass mkt. 5.99 (*0-312-97284-9*, St. Martin's Paperbacks); 1998. 304p. 23.95 o.p. (*0-312-19829-9*, Saint Martin's Minotaur) St. Martin's Pr.
—Aquarius Descending Newsletter Kit. Date not set. pap. (*0-312-20695-X*, Saint Martin's Griffin) St. Martin's Pr.
—The Cold Heart of Capricorn. 240p. 1996. text 21.95 o.p. (*0-312-14569-1*, Saint Martin's Minotaur); Vol. 1. 1998. mass mkt. 5.99 o.s.i (*0-312-96294-0*, St. Martin's Paperbacks) St. Martin's Pr.
—Murder in Scorpio. 1996. 227p. mass mkt. 5.50 (*0-312-95984-2*, St. Martin's Paperbacks); 1995. 256p. 21.95 (*0-312-13567-X*, Saint Martin's Minotaur) St. Martin's Pr.
—Pisces Rising. 2000. 254p. 23.95 o.p. (*0-312-20298-9*, Saint Martin's Minotaur) St. Martin's Pr.
Laws, Jay B. The Unfinished. 1993. 283p. pap. 9.95 o.p. (*1-55583-217-2*) Alyson Pubns.
Laymon, Richard. Among the Missing. 2000. 320p. mass mkt. 5.99 (*0-7472-6072-9*) Headline Bk. Publishing, Ltd. GBR. *Dist:* Trafalgar Square.
—Darkness, Tell Us. 2003. 400p. mass mkt. 6.99 (*0-8439-5047-1*) Dorchester Publishing Co., Inc.
—The Quake. 1995. 400p. 22.95 o.p. (*0-312-13150-X*) St. Martin's Pr.
Le Guin, Ursula K. Always Coming Home. 1985. 25.00 o.p. (*0-06-015456-X*) HarperCollins Pubs.
—Always Coming Home. 1985. (Illus.). 576p. 33.75 o.p. (*0-06-015562-0*); 50.00 o.p. incl. audio (*0-06-015545-0*) HarperTrade.
—Always Coming Home. 2001. (California Fiction Ser.). (Illus.). 525p. reprint ed. pap. text 16.95 (*0-520-22735-2*) Univ. of California Pr.
Leason, Barney. Grand Cru. 2001. 22.95 (*0-312-87198-8*, Forge Bks.) Doherty, Tom Assocs., LLC.
—Rodeo Drive. 2001. 464p. mass mkt. 6.99 (*0-8125-7169-X*, Forge Bks.) Doherty, Tom Assocs., LLC.
Lee, Don. Yellow: Stories. 2002. 256p. pap. 13.95 (*0-393-32308-0*); 2001. 192p. 22.95 (*0-393-02562-4*) Norton, W. W. & Co., Inc.
Lee, Gus. China Boy. 336p. 1994. pap. 14.00 (*0-452-27158-4*, Plume); 1991. 19.95 o.p. (*0-525-24994-X*) Dutton/Plume.
—China Boy. 1992. 400p. mass mkt. 5.99 o.p. (*0-451-17434-8*, Signet Bks.) NAL.
—China Boy. 1994. 19.00 (*0-606-16250-X*) Turtleback Bks.
—No Physical Evidence. 1998. 400p. 24.95 o.s.i (*0-449-91139-X*, Fawcett) Ballantine Bks.
—No Physical Evidence. abr. ed. 1998. audio 17.95 o.p. (*1-56740-785-4*, 1462, Nova Audio Bks.); audio 28.95 (*1-56740-060-4*, 1460, Bookcassette); audio 89.25 (*1-56740-589-4*, 1461, Unabridged Library Editions) Brilliance Audio.
—No Physical Evidence: A Courtroom Novel. 2000. 384p. mass mkt. 6.99 o.s.i (*0-8041-1779-9*, Ivy Bks.) Ballantine Bks.
Lee, Hector. The Bodega War, & Other Tales from Western Lore. 1988. 200p. (C). reprint ed. lib. bdg. 23.00 o.p. (*0-8095-4003-7*) Millefleurs.
Lee, Rebecca L. Concha: My Dancing Saint. 1997. (Illus.). 240p. (YA). (gr. 7-12). pap. 12.95 (*1-56474-215-6*) Fithian Pr.
—Kori & the Island of Enchantment. 1990. 80p. (Orig.). (YA). (gr. 8 up). pap. 6.95 o.p. (*0-931832-46-2*) Fithian Pr.
Leebron, Fred G. Out West. 1997. (Harvest Book Ser.). 256p. pap. 12.00 o.s.i (*0-15-600546-8*, Harvest Bks.) Harcourt Trade Pubs.
—Out West: A Novel. 1996. 256p. 21.95 o.s.i (*0-385-48420-8*) Doubleday Publishing.
Leiber, Fritz. The Dealings of Daniel Kesserich. 1997. 125p. 18.95 (*0-312-85408-0*, Tor Bks.) Doherty, Tom Assocs., LLC.
Leigh, Janet. House of Destiny. 1996. 507p. mass mkt. (*1-55166-159-4*, 1-66159-4); 1995. 512p. (*1-55166-125-X*) Harlequin Enterprises, Ltd. (Mira Bks.).
Lemann, Nancy. Malaise. l.t. ed. 2002. 28.95 (*1-58724-338-5*, Wheeler Publishing, Inc.) Gale Group.
—Malaise. 256p. 2003. pap. 13.00 (*0-7432-1549-4*); 2002. 24.00 (*0-7432-1548-6*) Simon & Schuster. (Scribner).
LeMone, Charles S. A Dance in the Street. 1993. 256p. (Orig.). mass mkt. 3.99 (*0-380-76713-9*, Avon Bks.) Morrow/Avon.
Leonard, Elmore. Be Cool. 1999. (*0-7540-1295-6*) BBC Audiobooks America.
—Be Cool. unabr. ed. 1999. audio 40.00 (*0-7366-4449-0*, 4894) Books on Tape, Inc.
—Be Cool. 2000. 368p. mass mkt. 7.50 o.s.i (*0-440-23505-7*); 1999. mass mkt. 7.99 (*0-440-29577-7*) Dell Publishing.
—Be Cool. abr. ed. 1999. audio 25.00 o.s.i (*0-553-52604-9*, RH Audio) Random Hse. Audio Publishing Group.
—Be Cool. 2000. E-Book 7.50 (*0-440-33423-3*) Random Hse., Inc.
—Be Cool, unabr. ed. 1999. audio 51.00 (*0-7887-2916-0*, 95708E7) Recorded Bks., LLC.
—Be Cool. l.t. ed. (Thorndike/G. K. Hall Paperback Bestsellers Ser.). 383p. 2000. pap. 27.95 (*0-7862-1839-8*); 1999. lib. bdg. 30.95 (*0-7862-1838-X*) Thorndike Pr.
—Get Shorty. unabr. ed. 1992. audio 48.00 (*0-7366-2222-5*, 3012) Books on Tape, Inc.
—Get Shorty. 2000. 368p. mass mkt. 4.99 o.s.i (*0-440-23614-2*); 1998. 304p. pap. 9.95 o.s.i (*0-385-32398-0*); 1995. 304p. pap. 8.95 o.s.i (*0-385-31567-8*, Delacorte Pr.); 1991. 384p. mass mkt. 6.99 o.s.i (*0-440-20980-3*); 1991. 368p. mass mkt. 5.50 o.s.i (*0-440-29515-7*) Dell Publishing.
—Get Shorty. l.t. ed. 1993. pap. 18.95 (*0-8161-5809-6*, Macmillan Reference USA) Gale Group.
—Get Shorty. 1990. audio 14.98 o.s.i (*0-553-74582-4*); audio 12.79 o.s.i (*0-553-19964-1*) Random Hse. Audio Publishing Group. (RH Audio).
Leonard, Elmore, contrib. by. Be Cool. 1999. (*0-7540-2221-8*) BBC Audiobooks America.
Leonard, John. Crybaby of the Western World: A Novel of Petit Guignol in Long Beach, California. 1968. 308p. (J). (*0-356-02457-1*) Little Brown U.K.
Leonardi, Susan J. And Then They Were Nuns. 2003. pap. 14.95 (*1-56341-126-1*) Firebrand Bks.
Lescroart, John. A Certain Justice. 1996. pap. 6.99 (*0-440-29547-5*) Bantam Bks.
—A Certain Justice. 1996. 544p. mass mkt. 7.99 (*0-440-22104-8*) Dell Publishing.
—A Certain Justice. 1995. 448p. 22.95 o.p. (*1-55611-445-1*) Fine, Donald I. Bks.
—A Certain Justice. l.t. ed. 1996. 756p. 25.95 (*0-7838-1565-4*, Macmillan Reference USA) Gale Group.
—Dead Irish. 1996. 416p. mass mkt. 7.99 (*0-440-20783-5*) Dell Publishing.
—Dead Irish. 1990. 18.95 o.p. (*1-55611-159-2*) Fine, Donald I. Bks.
—Guilt. 1998. 656p. mass mkt. 7.99 (*0-440-22281-8*) Doubleday Publishing.
—Guilt. l.t. ed. 1997. (Large Print Book Ser.). 26.95 (*1-56895-477-8*, Wheeler Publishing, Inc.) Gale Group.
—Hard Evidence. 1994. (Northern California Mysteries Ser.). 512p. mass mkt. 6.99 o.s.i (*0-8041-1275-4*, Ivy Bks.) Ballantine Bks.
—Hard Evidence. 1993. 478p. 21.95 o.p. (*1-55611-344-7*) Fine, Donald I. Bks.
—The Hearing. 2001. (Illus.). 464p. 25.95 o.s.i (*0-525-94575-X*, Dutton) Dutton/Plume.
—The Hearing. l.t. ed. 2002. 655p. pap. 29.95 (*0-7838-9394-9*, Macmillan Reference USA); 2001. 480p. 32.95 (*0-7838-9393-0*, Hall, G. K. & Co.) Gale Group.
—The Hearing. 2001. 544p. pap. 7.99 (*0-451-20450-6*); 2002. 560p. reprint ed. mass mkt. 7.99 (*0-451-20489-1*) NAL. (Signet Bks.).
—The Mercy Rule. 1999. 640p. mass mkt. 7.99 (*0-440-22282-6*) Dell Publishing.
—The Mercy Rule. l.t. ed. (Paperback Bestsellers Ser.). 684p. 1999. pap. 27.95 (*0-7838-0394-X*); 1998. 30.95 (*0-7838-0344-3*) Thorndike Pr.
—Nothing but the Truth. 1999. mass mkt. 7.99 (*0-440-29574-2*) Bantam Dell Publishing Group.
—Nothing but the Truth. 2000. mass mkt. 7.99 (*0-440-22664-3*); 448p. 24.95 o.s.i (*0-385-33353-6*, Delacorte Pr.) Dell Publishing.
—Nothing but the Truth. l.t. ed. 2000. 27.95 (*1-56895-813-7*, Wheeler Publishing, Inc.) Gale Group.
—Nothing but the Truth. 2001. 464p. mass mkt. 7.99 (*0-451-20285-6*) NAL.
—Nothing but the Truth. abr. ed. 2000. audio 25.95 (*0-553-52662-6*, RH Audio) Random Hse. Audio Publishing Group.
—The Vig. 1998. 384p. mass mkt. 7.99 (*0-440-20986-2*) Dell Publishing.
—The Vig. 1991. 18.95 o.p. (*1-55611-221-1*) Fine, Donald I. Bks.
—The Vig. abr. ed. 1998. audio 16.99 o.p. Random Hse. Audio Publishing Group.
—The 13th Juror. 1995. 560p. mass mkt. 7.99 (*0-440-22079-3*) Dell Publishing.
—The 13th Juror. 1994. 480p. 22.95 o.s.i (*1-55611-402-8*) Fine, Donald I. Bks.
—The 13th Juror. l.t. ed. 1994. 803p. lib. bdg. 24.95 o.p. (*0-8161-7448-2*, Macmillan Reference USA) Gale Group.
Leslie, Diane. Fleur de Leigh's Life of Crime: A Novel. 304p. 2000. pap. 12.00 (*0-684-86741-9*); 1999. (Illus.). 23.00 o.s.i (*0-684-85695-6*) Simon & Schuster. (Simon & Schuster).
Lethem, Jonathan. As She Climbed Across the Table. 1998. 224p. pap. 13.00 (*0-375-70012-9*, Vintage) Knopf Publishing Group.
—Gun, with Occasional Music. 5th ed. 1995. 262p. pap. 12.95 (*0-312-85878-7*, CPB1189, Tor Bks.) Doherty, Tom Assocs., LLC.
—Gun, with Occasional Music. 1994. 262p. 19.95 o.s.i (*0-15-136458-3*) Harcourt Trade Pubs.
Levin, Bob. Fully Armed: The Story of Jimmy Don Polk. 1995. 245p. 21.00 (*1-880909-38-3*) Baskerville Pubs., Inc.
Levin, Donna. California Street. 1992. 336p. mass mkt. 4.50 o.s.i (*0-451-40303-7*, Onyx) NAL.
—California Street. 1990. 18.95 o.p. (*0-671-69300-X*, Simon & Schuster) Simon & Schuster.
Levy, JoAnn. Daughter of Joy. 1997. (Women of the West Novels Ser.). 320p. 23.95 (*0-312-86502-3*, Tor Bks.) Doherty, Tom Assocs., LLC.
—The Daughter of Joy. 1999. (Women of the West Novels Ser.). 320p. pap. 6.99 (*0-8125-4029-8*, Forge Bks.) Doherty, Tom Assocs., LLC.
—For California's Gold. 2000. x, 268p. 24.95 (*0-87081-566-0*) Univ. Pr. of Colorado.
Lewis, Fiona. Between Men: A Novel. 1995. 304p. 21.00 o.p. (*0-87113-586-8*, Atlantic Monthly Pr.) Grove/Atlantic, Inc.
Lewis, Sara. The Answer Is Yes. 1998. 288p. (C). 23.00 o.s.i (*0-15-100326-2*) Harcourt Trade Pubs.
—The Answer Is Yes. l.t. ed. 1998. (Inspirational Ser.). 407p. 26.95 o.p. (*0-7838-0392-3*) Thorndike Pr.
—The Answer Is Yes: A Novel. 1999. (Harvest Book Ser.). 272p. pap. 13.00 (*0-15-600564-6*, Harvest Bks.) Harcourt Trade Pubs.
L'Heureux, John. The Handmaid of Desire. 256p. 1998. pap. 12.00 (*1-56947-123-1*); 1996. 23.00 o.p. (*1-56947-073-1*) Soho Pr., Inc.
Litherland, Donna. The Great Flood of California. 2000. 122p. 24.95 (*0-9607888-5-9*) Barney Pr.
Little, Eddie. Steel Toes. 2001. 320p. 23.95 (*0-312-28291-5*, L. A. Weekly Bks.) St. Martin's Pr.
—Steel Toes: A Novel. 2002. 320p. pap. 13.95 (*0-312-30320-3*, L. A. Weekly Bks.) St. Martin's Pr.
Liu, Aimee. Cloud Mountain. abr. ed. 1997. audio 17.98 (*1-57042-480-2*) Time Warner AudioBooks.
Liu, Aimee E. Cloud Mountain. abr. ed. 1997. audio 19.00 o.p. Beeler, Thomas T. Publisher.
—Cloud Mountain. 1998. mass mkt. (*0-446-60544-1*); 1997. 368p. 24.00 o.p. (*0-446-51987-1*); 1998. 672p. reprint ed. pap. 14.99 (*0-446-67434-6*) Warner Bks., Inc.
Lochte, Dick. Laughing Dog. 1988. (Leo Bloodworth-Serendipity Dahlquist Mystery Ser.: Bk. 2). 272p. 17.95 o.p. (*0-87795-941-2*, Morrow, William & Co.) Morrow/Avon.
—Laughing Dog. 1989. 400p. reprint ed. mass mkt. 3.95 o.s.i (*0-446-35724-3*) Warner Bks., Inc.
—Lucky Dog & Other Tales of Murder. 2000. (Five Star Mystery Ser.). 207p. 20.95 (*0-7862-2688-9*, Five Star) Gale Group.
—Sleeping Dog. 1985. 288p. 15.95 o.p. (*0-87795-738-X*, Morrow, William & Co.) Morrow/Avon.
—Sleeping Dog. 2001. (Missing Mystery Ser.: Vol. 29). 292p. pap. 14.95 (*1-890208-51-5*) Poisoned Pen Pr.
—Sleeping Dog. 1986. 288p. mass mkt. 3.95 o.s.i (*0-446-32661-5*) Warner Bks., Inc.
Logue, John. A Rain of Death. 1998. (Morris & Sullivan Mystery Ser.). 304p. mass mkt. 5.99 o.s.i (*0-440-22397-0*) Dell Publishing.
Loh, Sandra Tsing. If You Lived Here, You'd Be Home by Now: A Novel. 1998. 240p. 13.00 o.s.i (*1-57322-695-5*, Riverhead Trade (Paperbacks)) Berkley Publishing Group.
—If You Lived Here, You'd Be Home by Now: A Novel. 1997. 224p. 23.95 o.p. (*1-57322-068-X*, Riverhead Bks. (Hardcovers)) Putnam Publishing Group, The.
London, Jack. Jack London's Golden State: Selected California Writings. Haslam, Gerald, ed. 1999. 304p. pap. 15.95 (*1-890771-02-3*) Heyday Bks.
—The Valley of the Moon. unabr. ed. 1992. audio 64.95 (*1-55686-434-5*, 434) Books in Motion.
—The Valley of the Moon. 1998. (Collected Works of Jack London). 530p. reprint ed. lib. bdg. 118.00 (*1-58201-748-4*) Classic Bks.
—The Valley of the Moon. E-Book 1.95 (*1-58515-165-3*) MesaView, Inc.
—The Valley of the Moon. 1999. (California Fiction Ser.). 436p. pap. text 16.95 (*0-520-21820-5*) Univ. of California Pr.
—White Fang. 1994. (Illus.). 2.95 o.p. (*0-681-00649-8*) Borders Pr.
London, Mary. Look Fatter in Jeans: An Adventure in Growing Older & Wiser. 1997. (Illus.). vi, 306p. (Orig.). pap. 12.95 (*0-9656648-0-5*) Boomer Pubns.
Lowe, Tom. Spin. 1998. 327p. 23.00 (*0-671-01923-6*, Atria) Simon & Schuster.
—Spin: A Novel. 1999. 304p. pap. 18.95 (*0-671-01924-4*, Pocket) Simon & Schuster.
Lowell, Elizabeth. Moving Target. 2002. E-Book 19.95 (*0-06-001063-0*); 2001. E-Book 19.95 (*0-06-001065-7*); 2001. 592p. pap. 24.00 (*0-06-620962-5*) HarperCollins Pubs.
—Moving Target. abr. ed. 2001. audio 25.95 (*0-694-52562-6*, HarperAudio) HarperTrade.
—Moving Target. 464p. 2002. mass mkt. 7.99 (*0-06-103107-0*, Avon Bks.); 2001. 24.00 (*0-06-019875-3*, Morrow, William & Co.) Morrow/Avon.
Lucas, Frances. If Looks Could Kill. 1995. 190p. (Orig.). pap. 9.95 (*0-934678-63-4*) New Victoria Pubs., Inc.
Lucke, Margaret. A Relative Stranger. 1991. 320p. 19.95 o.p. (*0-312-06307-5*, Saint Martin's Minotaur) St. Martin's Pr.
Luna, Louisa. Brave New Girl. 2001. E-Book 11.95 (*0-7434-2144-2*); (Illus.). 208p. pap. 11.95 (*0-7434-0786-5*) Simon & Schuster. (MTV).
Lupoff, Richard A. The Bessie Blue Killer: A Hobart Lindsey - Marvia Plum Mystery. 1994. 304p. 20.95 o.p. (*0-312-10425-1*, Saint Martin's Minotaur) St. Martin's Pr.
—The Classic Car Killer. 1992. 288p. (Orig.). mass mkt. 4.99 o.s.i (*0-553-29607-8*) Bantam Bks.
—The Comic Book Killer. 1989. mass mkt. 3.95 o.s.i (*0-553-27781-2*) Bantam Bks.
—The Cover Girl Killer: A Hobart Lindsey - Marvia Plum Mystery. 1995. 224p. 21.95 o.p. (*0-312-13455-X*, Saint Martin's Minotaur) St. Martin's Pr.
—The Radio Red Killer. 1997. (Marvia Plum Mystery Ser.). 268p. text 22.95 o.p. (*0-312-17181-1*, Saint Martin's Minotaur) St. Martin's Pr.
—The Sepia Siren Killer. 1994. (Hobart Lidsey-Mariva Plum Mystery Ser.). 304p. 20.95 o.p. (*0-312-11332-3*, Saint Martin's Minotaur) St. Martin's Pr.
Luzkow, Jack Lawerence. The Birthday Present. 2001. 260p. pap. 14.00 (*0-9701723-1-1*) Parma Hse., Ltd.
Lynch, Patrick. Figure of Eight. 2000. (Illus.). 320p. 24.95 o.s.i (*0-525-94510-5*, Dutton) Dutton/Plume.
—Omega. 1997. 384p. 23.95 o.s.i (*0-525-94327-7*) Dutton/Plume.
—Omega. 1998. 432p. mass mkt. 6.99 o.s.i (*0-451-19323-7*, Signet Bks.) NAL.
Lyon, Bentley. Summer Stalk. 1992. 288p. 18.95 o.p. (*0-312-08312-2*, Saint Martin's Minotaur) St. Martin's Pr.
Lyons. Castles Burning. 1981. mass mkt. 2.50 (*0-671-41864-5*, Pocket) Simon & Schuster.
Lyons, Arthur. All God's Children. 1976. mass mkt. 1.50 o.s.i (*0-345-25020-6*) Ballantine Bks.
—All God's Children. 1982. 224p. pap. o.p. (*0-03-060394-3*, Owl Bks.) Holt, Henry & Co.
—At the Hands of Another. 240p. 1986. pap. o.p. (*0-03-008533-0*, Owl Bks.); 1983. o.p. (*0-03-059616-5*) Holt, Henry & Co.
—Castles Burning. 1982. (Rinehart Suspense Novel Ser.). 224p. pap. o.p. (*0-03-062417-7*, Owl Bks.) Holt, Henry & Co.
—The Dead Are Discreet. 1983. 224p. pap. o.p. (*0-03-060393-5*, Owl Bks.) Holt, Henry & Co.

—Dead Ringer. 1983. 240p. pap. o.p. (*0-03-060396-X*, Owl Bks.) Holt, Henry & Co.
—False Pretenses. 1994. 240p. 18.95 o.s.i (*0-89296-220-8*) Mysterious Pr.
—False Pretenses. 1995. 224p. mass mkt. 5.50 o.s.i (*0-446-40422-5*) Warner Bks., Inc.
—Fast Fade: A Jacob Asch Mystery. 1987. 224p. 15.45 (*0-89296-216-X*) Mysterious Pr.
—Fast Fade: A Jacob Asch Mystery. 1988. 208p. mass mkt. 3.95 o.s.i (*0-445-40703-4*, Mysterious Pr. Paperback Bks.) Warner Bks., Inc.
—Hard Trade. 264p. 1983. pap. o.p. (*0-03-063333-8*, Owl Bks.); 1981. o.p. (*0-03-053621-9*) Holt, Henry & Co.
—The Killing Floor. 1982. pap. o.p. (*0-03-060397-8*, Owl Bks.) Holt, Henry & Co.
—Other People's Money. 1989. 213p. 17.95 o.s.i (*0-89296-218-6*) Mysterious Pr.
—Other People's Money. 1990. 224p. mass mkt. 4.95 o.s.i (*0-445-40903-7*, Mysterious Pr. Paperback Bks.) Warner Bks., Inc.
—Three with a Bullet. 240p. 1986. pap. 3.95 o.p. (*0-03-008539-X*, Owl Bks.); 1985. o.p. (*0-03-059617-3*) Holt, Henry & Co.
MacDonald, Ross, pseud. Archer in Jeopardy, 3 bks., Set. Incl. Zebra-Striped Hearse. 1979. (Lew Archer Mystery Ser.). 1979. 24.95 o.s.i (*0-394-50804-1*) Knopf, Alfred A. Inc.
—The Barbarous Coast. 1975. (Lew Archer Mystery Ser.). 192p. pap. 2.95 o.s.i (*0-553-12249-5*) Bantam Bks.
—The Barbarous Coast. unabr. ed. (Lew Archer Mystery Ser.). 2000. audio compact disk 48.00 (*0-7861-9916-4*, z1819); 1996. audio 39.95 (*0-7861-1047-3*, 1819) Blackstone Audio Bks., Inc.
—The Barbarous Coast. 1990. (Lew Archer Mystery Ser.). 240p. mass mkt. 3.95 o.s.i (*0-446-35882-7*) Warner Bks., Inc.
—Blue City. 1988. 2.99 o.p. (*0-517-68432-2*) Random Hse. Value Publishing.
—Blue City. 1992. (Lew Archer Mystery Ser.). 224p. mass mkt. 4.50 o.s.i (*0-446-35884-3*) Warner Bks., Inc.
—The Blue Hammer. Date not set. (Lew Archer Mystery Ser.). pap. 16.95 (*0-8488-1722-2*); 23.95 (*0-89190-095-0*) Amereon, Ltd.
—The Blue Hammer. 1988. (Lew Archer Mystery Ser.). pap. 3.95 o.s.i (*0-553-27548-8*) Bantam Bks.
—The Blue Hammer, unabr. ed. 1999. (Lew Archer Mystery Ser.). audio 44.95 (*0-7861-1031-7*, 894402) Blackstone Audio Bks., Inc.
—The Blue Hammer. 1976. (Lew Archer Mystery Ser.). reprint ed. lib. bdg. 13.50 o.p. (*0-8161-6431-2*, Macmillan Reference USA) Gale Group.
—The Blue Hammer. 1990. (Lew Archer Mystery Ser.). mass mkt. 3.95 o.s.i (*0-446-35885-1*) Warner Bks., Inc.
—The Chill. 1983. (Lew Archer Mystery Ser.). mass mkt. 2.75 o.s.i (*0-553-24282-2*) Bantam Bks.
—The Chill, unabr. ed. 1996. (Lew Archer Mystery Ser.). audio 44.95 (*0-7861-1066-X*, 894596) Blackstone Audio Bks., Inc.
—The Chill. 2001. 288p. pap. 8.42 (*1-84195-118-8*) Canongate Bks. GBR. *Dist:* Grove/Atlantic, Inc.
—The Chill. 1996. (Lew Archer Mystery Ser.). 288p. pap. 12.00 (*0-679-76807-6*) Random Hse., Inc.
—The Chill. 1990. (Lew Archer Mystery Ser.). mass mkt. 3.95 o.s.i (*0-446-35887-8*) Warner Bks., Inc.
—The Doomsters. 1990. (Lew Archer Mystery Ser.). mass mkt. 3.95 o.s.i (*0-446-35888-6*) Warner Bks., Inc.
—The Drowning Pool. 1975. (Lew Archer Mystery Ser.). 224p. pap. 2.75 o.p. (*0-553-24135-4*) Bantam Bks.
—The Drowning Pool. l.t. ed. 2002. pap. 25.95 (*0-7838-9783-9*) Gale Group.
—The Drowning Pool. Barzun, Jacques & Taylor, Wendell H., eds. 1976. (Lew Archer Mystery Ser.). reprint ed. lib. bdg. 21.00 o.p. (*0-8240-2382-X*) Garland Publishing, Inc.
—The Drowning Pool. 1996. (Lew Archer Mystery Ser.). 256p. pap. 12.00 (*0-679-76806-8*) Random Hse., Inc.
—The Drowning Pool. 1993. (Lew Archer Mystery Ser.). 224p. mass mkt. 4.99 o.s.i (*0-446-35889-4*) Warner Bks., Inc.
—The Far Side of the Dollar. (Lew Archer Mystery Ser.). 2000. audio compact disk 56.00 (*0-7861-9889-3*, ZP1769); 1996. audio 44.95 (*0-7861-0990-4*, 1767) Blackstone Audio Bks., Inc.
—The Far Side of the Dollar. 1990. (Lew Archer Mystery Ser.). mass mkt. 4.99 o.s.i (*0-446-35890-8*) Warner Bks., Inc.
—Find a Victim, unabr. ed. 1999. (Lew Archer Mystery Ser.). audio 39.95 (*0-7861-1493-2*, 758945) Blackstone Audio Bks., Inc.
—Find a Victim, Set. unabr. ed. 1999. (Lew Archer Mystery Ser.). audio 39.95 Highsmith Inc.
—Find a Victim. 2001. (Lew Archer Mystery Ser.). 224p. pap. 12.00 (*0-375-70867-7*, Vintage) Knopf Publishing Group.
—Find a Victim. 1991. (Lew Archer Mystery Ser.). mass mkt. 4.50 o.s.i (*0-446-35892-4*) Warner Bks., Inc.
—The Galton Case. 1980. (Lew Archer Mystery Ser.). pap. 2.75 o.p. (*0-553-22621-5*) Bantam Bks.
—The Galton Case. 1990. (Lew Archer Mystery Ser.). mass mkt. 3.95 o.s.i (*0-446-35893-2*) Warner Bks., Inc.
—The Galton Case: A Lew Archer Novel. 1996. (Lew Archer Mystery Ser.). 256p. pap. 12.00 (*0-679-76864-5*) McKay, David Co., Inc.
—The Goodbye Look. 2000. (Lew Archer Mystery Ser.). 256p. pap. 12.00 (*0-375-70865-0*, Vintage) Knopf Publishing Group.
—The Goodbye Look. 1992. (Lew Archer Mystery Ser.). 224p. mass mkt. 4.50 o.s.i (*0-446-35894-0*) Warner Bks., Inc.
—The Instant Enemy. 1991. (Lew Archer Mystery Ser.). 224p. mass mkt. 4.50 o.s.i (*0-446-35895-9*) Warner Bks., Inc.
—The Ivory Grin. 1998. (Lew Archer Mystery Ser.). 192p. 19.50 (*0-7540-8519-8*, Black Dagger) BBC Audiobooks America.
—The Ivory Grin. 1992. (Lew Archer Mystery Ser.). 224p. reprint ed. mass mkt. 4.50 o.s.i (*0-446-35896-7*) Warner Bks., Inc.
—Lew Archer Private Investigator. l.t. ed. 1988. (Lew Archer Mystery Ser.). 20.95 o.p. (*1-55504-639-8*); pap. 18.95 o.p. (*1-55504-640-1*) BBC Audiobooks America.
—Lew Archer Private Investigator. 1986. (Lew Archer Mystery Ser.). 10.00 o.p. (*0-89296-033-7*) Mysterious Pr.
—Lew Archer Private Investigator II. l.t. ed. 1988. (Lew Archer Mystery Ser.). pap. 17.95 o.p. (*1-55504-703-3*) BBC Audiobooks America.
—The Moving Target. l.t. ed. 1991. (Lew Archer Mystery Ser.). pap. 10.95 o.p. (*0-89340-171-4*, C0096) BBC Audiobooks America.
—The Moving Target. 1979. (Lew Archer Mystery Ser.). lib. bdg. 9.95 o.p. (*0-8398-2538-2*, Macmillan Reference USA) Gale Group.
—The Moving Target. 1998. (Lew Archer Mystery Ser.). 256p. pap. 11.00 (*0-375-70146-X*, Vintage) Knopf Publishing Group.
—The Moving Target. 1990. (Lew Archer Mystery Ser.). mass mkt. 4.99 o.s.i (*0-446-35898-3*) Warner Bks., Inc.
—Sleeping Beauty. (Lew Archer Mystery Ser.). 23.95 (*0-89190-096-9*) Amereon, Ltd.
—Sleeping Beauty, unabr. ed. 1997. (Lew Archer Mystery Ser.). audio 29.95 (*1-57270-049-1*, N61049u) Audio Partners Publishing Corp.
—Sleeping Beauty. 1984. mass mkt. 3.50 o.s.i (*0-553-27101-6*) Bantam Bks.
—Sleeping Beauty. unabr. ed. 1998. (Lew Archer Mystery Ser.). audio 44.95 (*0-7861-1320-0*, 2245) Blackstone Audio Bks., Inc.
—Sleeping Beauty. 2000. (Lew Archer Mystery Ser.). 288p. pap. 12.00 (*0-375-70866-9*, Vintage) Knopf Publishing Group.
—Sleeping Beauty. 1973. (Lew Archer Mystery Ser). 5.95 o.p. (*0-394-48474-6*, Knopf Bks. for Young Readers) Random Hse. Children's Bks.
—Sleeping Beauty. 1991. (Lew Archer Mystery Ser.). mass mkt. 4.50 o.s.i (*0-446-35899-1*) Warner Bks., Inc.
—The Underground Man. 1984. (Lew Archer Mystery Ser.). mass mkt. 3.95 o.s.i (*0-553-27183-0*) Bantam Bks.
—The Underground Man. 1992. (Lew Archer Mystery Ser.). mass mkt. 4.50 o.s.i (*0-446-35901-7*) Warner Bks., Inc.
—The Underground Man: A Lew Archer Novel. 1996. (Lew Archer Mystery Ser.). (SPA.). 288p. pap. 12.00 (*0-679-76808-4*, Vintage) Knopf Publishing Group.
—The Way Some People Die. 1990. (Lew Archer Mystery Ser.). mass mkt. 3.95 o.s.i (*0-446-35902-5*) Warner Bks., Inc.
—The Wycherly Woman. 1984. (Lew Archer Mystery Ser.). mass mkt. 2.95 o.s.i (*0-553-23855-8*) Bantam Bks.
—The Wycherly Woman. 1998. (Lew Archer Mystery Ser.). 288p. pap. 12.00 (*0-375-70144-3*, Vintage) Knopf Publishing Group.
—The Wycherly Woman. 1990. (Lew Archer Mystery Ser.). mass mkt. 3.95 o.s.i (*0-446-35903-3*) Warner Bks., Inc.
—The Zebra-Striped Hearse. 1998. (Lew Archer Mystery Ser.). 19.50 o.p. (*0-7540-8511-2*, Black Dagger) BBC Audiobooks America.
—The Zebra-Striped Hearse. 1984. (Lew Archer Mystery Ser.). 224p. mass mkt. 3.95 o.s.i (*0-553-27362-0*); pap. text 2.95 o.p. (*0-553-23996-1*) Bantam Bks.
—The Zebra-Striped Hearse. 1998. (Lew Archer Mystery Ser.). 288p. pap. 12.00 (*0-375-70145-1*, Vintage) Knopf Publishing Group.
—The Zebra-Striped Hearse. 1979. (Lew Archer Mystery Ser.). Knopf, Alfred A. Inc.
—The Zebra-Striped Hearse. 1993. (Lew Archer Mystery Ser.). 272p. mass mkt. 4.99 o.s.i (*0-446-35904-1*) Warner Bks., Inc.
MacDonald, Ross, pseud, ed. The Ivory Grin. 1988. (Lew Archer Mystery Ser.). 256p. mass mkt. 3.95 o.s.i (*0-553-27352-3*) Bantam Bks.
MacLean, Amanda. Everlasting. 1996. (Palisades Pure Romance Ser.). 316p. pap. 9.99 o.p. (*0-88070-929-4*, Palisades) Multnomah Pubs., Inc.
Macomber, Debbie. Shirley, Goodness & Mercy. unabr. ed. 1999. 3p. audio 7.99 (*1-55204-194-8*, MIR-1194) Durkin Hayes Publishing Ltd.
—Shirley, Goodness & Mercy. 1999. 136p. (*1-55166-529-8*, 1-66529-8); mass mkt. (*1-55166-562-X*, 1-66562-9) Harlequin Enterprises, Ltd. (Mira Bks.).
—Someday Soon. l.t. ed. 2000. (Wheeler Large Print Book Ser.). 353p. pap. 24.95 (*1-56895-900-1*, Wheeler Publishing, Inc.) Gale Group.
—Someday Soon. 1998. 352p. mass mkt. 3.99 o.p. (*0-06-104478-4*, HarperBusiness) HarperInformation.
—Someday Soon. 1995. 352p. mass mkt. 6.99 (*0-06-108309-7*, HarperTorch) Morrow/Avon.
MacPherson, Malcolm C. Deadlock. 1998. 320p. 23.00 (*0-684-83157-0*, Simon & Schuster) Simon & Schuster.
Maddison, Lauren. Death by Prophecy: A Connor Hawthorne Mystery. 2002. (Connor Hawthorne Mystery Ser.). 408p. pap. 14.95 (*1-55583-764-6*) Alyson Pubns.
Maiman, Jaye. I Left My Heart. 1991. (Robin Miller Mysteries Ser.: Vol. 1). 320p. pap. 11.95 o.p. (*0-941483-72-X*) Naiad Pr., Inc.
Maino, Jeannette G. Left Hand Turn: A Story of the Donner Party Women. 1987. (Illus.). 19.50 o.p. (*0-941885-02-X*); (Illus.). pap. 16.50 o.p. (*0-941885-03-8*); 2nd ed. 15.00 o.p. (*0-941885-04-6*) Dry Creek Bks.
Majer Krich, Rochelle. Fair Game. 1993. 384p. 29.00 (*0-89296-507-X*) Mysterious Pr.
Mallory, Carole. Flash. 1991. 2.99 o.p. (*0-517-07575-X*) Random Hse. Value Publishing.
—Flash. 1989. mass mkt. 4.50 o.s.i (*0-671-64465-3*, Pocket); 1988. 16.95 o.p. (*0-671-64464-5*, Simon & Schuster) Simon & Schuster.
Manaster, Benjamin. Skyla. Caso, Adolph, ed. 1995. 246p. 21.95 (*0-8283-2002-0*) Branden Bks.
Mandeville, Joyce. Careful Mistakes. 1996. 184p. o.s.i (*0-316-87899-5*) Little Brown & Co.
—Careful Mistakes: A Novel. 1997. 432p. 21.95 (*0-316-87999-1*) Little Brown & Co.
Manning, Jason. Frontier Road. 2002. 256p. mass mkt. 5.99 o.s.i (*0-312-98202-X*, St. Martin's Paperbacks) St. Martin's Pr.
Manning, Kate. Whitegirl. 416p. 2003. pap. 13.95 (*0-385-33721-3*); 2002. 23.95 (*0-385-33287-4*, Delacorte Pr.) Dell Publishing.
Manson, Cynthia & Stern, Adam, eds. Silver Screams: Murder Goes Hollywood. 1994. 8.95 o.p. (*0-681-00753-2*) Borders Pr.
Mapson, Jo-Ann. Along Came Mary. 2003. 368p. 24.00 (*0-7432-2461-2*); E-Book 24.00 (*0-7432-3878-8*) Simon & Schuster. (Simon & Schuster).
—Along Came Mary. l.t. ed. 2003. 30.95 (*1-58724-414-4*, Wheeler Publishing, Inc.) Gale Group.
—Along Came Mary: A Bad Girl Creek Novel. 2004. 384p. pap. 13.00 (*0-7432-2462-0*, Simon & Schuster) Simon & Schuster.
—Bad Girl Creek. 2002. 384p. pap. 13.00 (*0-7432-1771-3*, Simon & Schuster) Simon & Schuster.
—Bad Girl Creek: A Novel. l.t. ed. 2001. 529p. 29.95 o.p. (*1-58724-126-9*, Wheeler Publishing, Inc.) Gale Group.
—Bad Girl Creek: A Novel. 2001. 384p. 24.00 (*0-7432-0256-2*, Simon & Schuster) Simon & Schuster.
—Hank & Chloe: A Novel. l.t. ed. 1993. 24.95 o.p. (*0-7927-1718-X*); pap. 22.95 o.p. (*0-7927-1699-X*) BBC Audiobooks America.
—Hank & Chloe: A Novel. 1993. 320p. 20.00 o.p. (*0-06-016943-5*) HarperTrade.
—Shadow Ranch: A Novel. l.t. ed. 1999. 25.95 (*1-57490-176-1*, Beeler Large Print Bks.) Beeler, Thomas T. Publisher.
—Shadow Ranch: A Novel. 1996. 384p. 24.00 o.p. (*0-06-017216-9*) HarperCollins Pubs.
—Shadow Ranch: A Novel. 1997. 384p. pap. 13.00 (*0-06-092843-3*, Perennial) HarperTrade.
—Shadow Ranch: A Novel. 376p. pap. 4.98 o.p. (*0-7651-0612-4*) Smithmark Pubs., Inc.
Maracotta, Lindsay. The Dead Celeb. 1998. mass mkt. 5.99 (*0-380-72689-0*, Avon Bks.); 1997. 288p. 24.00 o.p. (*0-688-14499-3*, Morrow, William & Co.) Morrow/Avon.
—The Dead Hollywood Moms Society. 320p. 1997. mass mkt. 5.99 (*0-380-72688-2*, Avon Bks.); 1996. 24.00 o.p. (*0-688-14498-5*, Morrow, William & Co.) Morrow/Avon.
—Playing Dead: A Hollywood Mystery. 1999. 288p. 24.00 (*0-688-15867-6*, Morrow, William & Co.) Morrow/Avon.
Marino, Anne N. The Collapsible World. 2000. 171p. 22.95 (*0-393-04909-4*) Norton, W. W. & Co., Inc.
Martel, John. Conflicts of Interest. 2002. 480p. mass mkt. 6.99 (*0-451-41040-8*, Onyx) NAL.
—Conflicts of Interest. 1996. 480p. mass mkt. 6.99 (*0-671-89095-6*, Pocket); 1995. 448p. 23.00 (*0-671-89094-8*, Atria) Simon & Schuster.
Martin, Ann M. Dawn on the Coast. 1997. (Baby-Sitters Club Ser.: No. 23). 160p. (J). (gr. 3-7). mass mkt. 3.99 (*0-590-67391-2*) Scholastic, Inc.
—Maggie. 1997. (California Diaries). (YA). (gr. 6-8). 10.04 (*0-606-11181-6*) Turtleback Bks.
—Sunny. 1997. (California Diaries). (YA). (gr. 6-8). 10.04 (*0-606-11180-8*) Turtleback Bks.
—Sunny: Diary Two. 1998. (California Diaries). (YA). (gr. 6-8). pap. 71.82 (*0-590-65607-4*) Scholastic, Inc.
—Sunny: Diary Two. 1998. (California Diaries). (YA). (gr. 6-8). 10.04 (*0-606-13237-6*) Turtleback Bks.
Martin, Dannie. In the Hat. 1997. 320p. 23.00 (*0-684-83335-2*, Simon & Schuster); 2000. 304p. reprint ed. pap. 6.99 (*0-671-02404-3*, Pocket) Simon & Schuster.
Martin, Dannie M. The Dishwasher. 1995. 192p. 20.00 o.p. (*0-393-03790-8*) Norton, W. W. & Co., Inc.
Martin, L. J. Candor Canyon. 2000. 256p. mass mkt. 5.99 (*0-7860-1131-9*, Pinnacle Bks.) Kensington Publishing Corp.
Martin, Larry J. The Benicia Belle. l.t. ed. 1993. (General Ser.). 316p. lib. bdg. 19.95 o.p. (*0-8161-5609-3*, Macmillan Reference USA) Gale Group.
Martinez, Nina Marie. Caramba! A Tale Told in Turns of the Card. 2004. (Illus.). 384p. 24.95 (*0-375-41375-8*) Knopf, Alfred A. Inc.
Martini, Steve. The Arraignment. 2003. 416p. 25.95 (*0-399-14878-7*) Putnam Publishing Group, The.
—The Attorney. unabr. ed. 2001. audio compact disk 110.95 (*0-7927-9952-6*, SLD 003); 2000. audio 84.95 (*0-7927-2408-9*, CSL 297) BBC Audiobooks America. (Chivers Sound Library).
—The Attorney. 2001. 448p. mass mkt. 7.99 (*0-515-13004-4*, Jove) Berkley Publishing Group.
—The Attorney. 2000. 448p. 25.95 o.s.i (*0-399-14536-2*) Penguin Group (USA) Inc.
—The Attorney. abr. ed. 2000. (Paul Madriani Novels Ser.). 5p. audio 25.00 (*0-671-04696-9*); audio compact disk 32.00 (*0-7435-0006-7*) Simon & Schuster Audio. (Simon & Schuster Audioworks).
—The Attorney. l.t. ed. 2000. (Basic Ser.). 613p. 31.95 (*0-7862-2433-9*) Thorndike Pr.
—Compelling Evidence. 1993. 448p. mass mkt. 7.99 (*0-515-11039-6*, Jove) Berkley Publishing Group.
—Compelling Evidence. l.t. ed. 1992. (General Ser.). 608p. lib. bdg. 23.95 o.p. (*0-8161-5548-8*, Macmillan Reference USA) Gale Group.
—Compelling Evidence. abr. ed. 1993. (Super Sound Buy, Dove Ser.). audio 8.99 o.p. (*1-55800-802-0*); 15.95 o.p. (*1-55800-613-3*) NewStar Media, Inc.
—Compelling Evidence. 1992. 384p. 21.95 o.p. (*0-399-13712-2*, G. P. Putnam's Sons) Penguin Group (USA) Inc.
—Compelling Evidence. l.t. ed. 1993. (G. K. Hall Large Print Book Ser.). 657p. pap. 19.95 (*0-8161-5549-6*) Thorndike Pr.
—Compelling Evidence & Prime Witness. abr. ed. 1998. (Steve Martini Collections). audio 25.00 (*0-7871-1759-5*, Dove Audio) NewStar Media, Inc.
—The Judge. 1996. 512p. mass mkt. 6.99 o.s.i (*0-515-11915-6*, Jove); reprint ed. pap. 7.99 (*0-515-11964-4*) Berkley Publishing Group.
—The Judge. 1996. 400p. 23.95 o.p. (*0-399-14043-3*, G. P. Putnam's Sons) Penguin Group (USA) Inc.
—The Judge, unabr. ed. audio 85.00 (*0-7887-0466-4*, 94659E7) Recorded Bks., LLC.
—The Judge. abr. ed. 1996. audio 24.00 (*0-671-53453-X*); Set. 1998. audio 12.98 (*0-671-58209-7*, 493061) Simon & Schuster Audio. (Simon & Schuster Audioworks).
—The Judge. l.t. ed. 1996. (Thorndike/G. K. Hall Paperback Bestsellers Ser.). 567p. pap. 27.95 (*0-7838-1611-1*); lib. bdg. 28.95 (*0-7838-1610-3*) Thorndike Pr.
—Prime Witness. 1994. 416p. mass mkt. 7.99 (*0-515-11264-X*, Jove) Berkley Publishing Group.
—Prime Witness. l.t. ed. 590p. 1994. 19.95 o.p. (*0-8161-5870-3*); 1993. 23.95 o.p. (*0-8161-5869-X*) Gale Group. (Macmillan Reference USA).
—Prime Witness. abr. ed. 1993. audio 16.95 o.p. (*1-55800-813-6*, 391400) NewStar Media, Inc.
—Prime Witness. 1993. 384p. 21.95 o.p. (*0-399-13802-1*, G. P. Putnam's Sons) Penguin Group (USA) Inc.
—Undue Influence. 480p. 1995. mass mkt. 7.99 (*0-515-11605-X*); 1996. pap. 6.99 o.s.i (*0-515-12072-3*) Berkley Publishing Group. (Jove).
—Undue Influence. l.t. ed. 1996. 567p. 19.95 o.p. (*0-7838-1129-2*); 1994. 714p. lib. bdg. 25.95 o.p. (*0-7838-1128-4*) Gale Group. (Macmillan Reference USA).
—Undue Influence. 1994. 400p. 22.95 o.p. (*0-399-13932-X*) Penguin Group (USA) Inc.
—Undue Influence, unabr. ed. 1995. audio 85.00 (*0-7887-0190-8*, 94425E7) Recorded Bks., LLC.

—Undue Influence. abr. ed. 1994. audio 17.00 (*0-671-89520-6*); Set. 1998. audio 9.98 (*0-671-58129-5*, 391836) Simon & Schuster Audio. (Simon & Schuster Audioworks).
—Undue Influence, Compelling Evidence, Prime Witness. 1995. 20.97 o.s.i (*0-515-11795-1*, Jove) Berkley Publishing Group.
Marx, Arthur. Set to Kill. 1993. 361p. 17.95 (*0-942637-80-1*) Barricade Bks., Inc.
Marx, Pat. Blockbuster. 1988. 224p. pap. 15.00 (*0-553-34498-6*) Bantam Bks.
Mason. Cyberweb. 2000. 20.00 (*0-380-97248-4*) Morrow/Avon.
Mason, Lisa. Cyberweb. 1998. 272p. pap. 12.00 (*0-380-79917-0*, Eos); 1996. 272p. mass mkt. 4.99 (*0-380-77486-0*, Avon Bks.); 1995. 256p. 20.00 (*0-688-13987-6*, Avon Bks.) Morrow/Avon.
—Summer of Love. 1994. (Illus.). 400p. pap. 12.95 o.s.i (*0-553-37330-7*) Bantam Bks.
Masters, Alexis. The Giuliana Legacy: A Novel. 2000. ix, 462p. pap. 14.95 (*1-55874-785-0*) Health Communications, Inc.
Masters, J. G. Sarah Elizabeth: A Tale of Old Colorado. 1985. 208p. 13.95 (*0-940672-29-4*) Shearer Publishing.
Masterton, Graham. Master of Lies. 1995. 336p. mass mkt. 4.99 (*0-8125-1166-2*); 1991. 320p. 19.95 o.p. (*0-312-85102-2*) Doherty, Tom Assocs., LLC. (Tor Bks.).
Matera, Lia. Designer Crimes: A Laura Di Palma Mystery. (Laura Di Palma Mystery Ser.). 1996. 288p. pap. 6.50 (*0-671-00196-5*, Pocket); 1995. 240p. 21.00 o.s.i (*0-684-80312-7*, Simon & Schuster) Simon & Schuster.
—Face Value: A Laura Di Palma Mystery. (Laura Di Palma Ser.). 1995. o.s.i (*0-684-88840-8*, Pocket); 1995. (Illus.). 272p. mass mkt. 5.99 (*0-671-88840-4*, Pocket); 1994. 221p. 20.00 (*0-671-74197-7*, Simon & Schuster) Simon & Schuster.
—The Good Fight. 1991. (Laura Di Palma Ser.). mass mkt. 5.99 o.s.i (*0-345-37107-0*, Ballantine Bks.) Ballantine Bks.
—The Good Fight. 1990. 17.95 o.p. (*0-671-68561-9*, Simon & Schuster) Simon & Schuster.
—A Hard Bargain. 1993. (Laura Di Palma Ser.). mass mkt. 5.99 o.s.i (*0-345-38059-2*) Ballantine Bks.
—A Hard Bargain. 1992. 224p. 19.00 o.p. (*0-671-74196-9*, Simon & Schuster) Simon & Schuster.
—Havana Twist: A Willa Jansson Mystery. abr. ed. 1998. (Willa Jansson Mystery Ser.). 3p. audio 18.00 (*0-7871-1735-8*, Dove Audio) NewStar Media, Inc.
—Havana Twist: A Willa Jansson Mystery. (Willa Jansson Mystery Ser.). 1999. 352p. pap. 6.99 o.s.i (*0-671-00421-2*, Pocket); 1998. 256p. 22.00 (*0-684-83470-7*, Simon & Schuster) Simon & Schuster.
—Hidden Agenda. 1992. (Willa Jansson Ser.). mass mkt. 5.99 o.s.i (*0-345-37128-3*, Ballantine Bks.) Ballantine Bks.
—Hidden Agenda. 1988. mass mkt. 3.50 o.s.i (*0-553-27721-9*) Bantam Bks.
—Last Chants. (Willa Jansson Mystery Ser.). 1997. 320p. pap. 5.99 (*0-671-88096-9*, Pocket); 1996. 240p. 21.00 (*0-684-81085-9*, Simon & Schuster) Simon & Schuster.
—Prior Convictions. 1992. (Northern California Mysteries Ser.). mass mkt. 5.99 o.s.i (*0-345-37445-2*) Ballantine Bks.
—Prior Convictions. 1991. 224p. 17.95 o.p. (*0-671-68560-0*, Simon & Schuster) Simon & Schuster.
—Radical Departure. 1991. (Laura Di Palma Ser.). 224p. (Orig.). mass mkt. 5.99 o.s.i (*0-345-37126-7*) Ballantine Bks.
—A Radical Departure. 1988. mass mkt. 3.50 o.s.i (*0-553-27072-9*) Bantam Bks.
—The Smart Money. 1991. 192p. (Orig.). mass mkt. 5.99 o.s.i (*0-345-37127-5*) Ballantine Bks.
—The Smart Money. 1988. 208p. (Orig.). mass mkt. 3.50 o.s.i (*0-553-27268-3*) Bantam Bks.
—Star Witness. (Willa Jansson Mystery Ser.). 1998. 336p. pap. 6.50 (*0-671-00420-4*, Pocket); 1997. 240p. 21.50 (*0-684-83469-3*, Simon & Schuster) Simon & Schuster.
—Where Lawyers Fear to Tread. 1991. (Willa Jansson Ser.). mass mkt. 5.99 o.s.i (*0-345-37125-9*) Ballantine Bks.
—Where Lawyers Fear to Tread. 1987. mass mkt. 3.50 o.s.i (*0-553-27588-7*) Bantam Bks.
—Where Lawyers Fear to Tread. 1999. (Mystery Ser.). 209p. 20.95 o.p. (*0-7862-1814-2*, Five Star) Gale Group.
Mathes, Charles. The Girl Who Remembered the Snow. 1996. 304p. 23.95 (*0-312-13977-2*, Saint Martin's Minotaur) St. Martin's Pr.
Matheson, Richard. Hunted Past Reason. E-Book 24.95 (*0-312-70739-8*); 2002. 304p. 24.95 (*0-7653-0271-3*) Doherty, Tom Assocs., LLC. (Tor Bks.).
Matlin, David. How the Night Is Divided: A Novel. 1993. 201p. 20.00 (*0-929701-33-X*) McPherson & Co.
Matthews, Greg. The Further Adventures of Huckleberry Finn. 1983. o.s.i (*0-517-55141-1*) Crown Publishing Group.
—The Further Adventures of Huckleberry Finn. 1984. 480p. mass mkt. 3.95 o.p. (*0-451-13188-6*, Signet Bks.) NAL.
Matthews, Patricia. Tame the Restless Heart. 1985. 352p. pap. 6.95 o.s.i (*0-553-34220-7*) Bantam Bks.
—Tame the Restless Heart. l.t. ed. 2001. 446p. lib. bdg. 27.95 (*1-58547-056-2*) Ctr. Point Large Print.
Maupin, Armistead. Babycakes. 1994. (Tales of the City Ser.: Vol. 4). 336p. pap. 14.00 (*0-06-092483-7*, Perennial); 1984. 254p. 15.95 o.p. (*0-06-015262-1*); 1984. 254p. pap. 9.95 o.p. (*0-06-091099-2*, CN 1099, Perennial); 1990. audio 17.00 o.s.i (*1-55994-276-2*, CPN 2179, HarperAudio) HarperTrade.
—Babycakes Reiss. 1989. 336p. reprint ed. pap. 12.00 o.p. (*0-06-096407-3*, Perennial) HarperTrade.
—Back to Barbary Lane: The Final Tales of the City Omnibus. 1991. 720p. 34.95 (*0-06-016649-5*) HarperTrade.
—Further Tales of the City. 1982. 176p. o.p. (*0-06-014991-4*); pap. 9.95 o.p. (*0-06-090916-1*) HarperCollins Pubs.
—Further Tales of the City. 1994. (Tales of the City Ser.: Vol. 3). 384p. pap. 14.00 (*0-06-092492-6*, Perennial); 1989. 368p. reprint ed. pap. 12.00 o.p. (*0-06-096406-5*, Perennial); Set. 1990. audio 16.00 o.s.i (*1-55994-301-7*, CPN 2186, HarperAudio) HarperTrade.
—Further Tales of the City. unabr. ed. 1995. (Tales of the City Ser.: Vol. 3). audio 70.00 (*0-7887-0254-8*, 94463E7) Recorded Bks., LLC.
—Maybe the Moon: A Novel. ltd. ed. 1992. 320p. 100.00 o.p. (*0-06-016947-8*) HarperTrade.
—More Tales of the City. 1994. 352p. pap. 13.00 o.p. (*0-06-092479-9*, Perennial) HarperTrade.
—The Night Listener: A Novel. 2000. (Illus.). 352p. 26.00 (*0-06-017143-X*, HarperCollins); audio 34.95 (*0-694-52144-2*, HarperAudio) HarperTrade.
—The Night Listener: A Novel. l.t. ed. 2001. (Thorndike Americana Ser.). 451p. 31.95 (*0-7862-3180-7*); pap. 28.95 (*0-7862-3181-5*) Thorndike Pr.
—Significant Others. 1987. pap. 9.95 o.p. (*0-06-096126-0*) HarperCollins Pubs.
—Significant Others. 1994. (Tales of the City Ser.: Vol. 5). 336p. pap. 14.00 (*0-06-092481-0*, Perennial); 1987. 19.95 o.p. (*0-06-055086-4*, Perennial); 1999. audio 18.00 o.s.i (*1-55994-300-9*, CPN 2185, HarperAudio); 1989. 384p. reprint ed. pap. 12.00 o.p. (*0-06-096408-1*, Perennial) HarperTrade.
—Sure of You. 1990. pap. 65.70 o.p. (*0-06-092034-3*) HarperCollins Pubs.
—Sure of You. 1994. (Tales of the City Ser.: Vol. 6). 272p. pap. 14.00 (*0-06-092484-5*, Perennial); 1989. 288p. 18.95 o.p. (*0-06-016164-7*, Perennial); 1990. (Tales of the City Ser.). 272p. reprint ed. 11.00 o.p. (*0-06-092033-5*, Perennial); Set. 1991. audio 15.95 o.s.i (*1-55994-299-1*, CPN 2184, HarperAudio) HarperTrade.
—Tales of the City. 1987. mass mkt. 3.50 o.s.i (*0-345-35190-8*); 1984. mass mkt. 2.95 o.s.i (*0-345-32037-9*); 1983. mass mkt. 2.75 o.s.i (*0-345-31170-1*); 1979. mass mkt. 2.50 o.s.i (*0-345-28422-4*) Ballantine Bks.
—Tales of the City. 1994. 384p. pap. 72.00 o.p. (*0-06-092493-4*); 1978. pap. 10.95 o.p. (*0-06-090654-5*); 1996. 384p. 18.00 o.p. (*0-06-018669-0*) HarperCollins Pubs.
—Tales of the City. annuals 384p. 1989. (Tales of the City Ser.: Vol. 1). pap. 14.00 (*0-06-096404-9*); 1994. reprint ed. pap. 12.00 o.p. (*0-06-092480-2*) HarperTrade. (Perennial).
—Tales of the City. 1994. 371p. lib. bdg. 33.00 o.p. (*0-8095-9139-1*) Millefleurs.
—28 Barbary Lane: A "Tales of the City" Omnibus. 1990. 768p. 34.95 (*0-06-016466-2*) HarperTrade.
Maxwell, A. E. Art of Survival. 1993. 336p. mass mkt. 4.99 o.p. (*0-06-104115-7*, HarperTorch) Morrow/Avon.
—The Art of Survival. 1990. mass mkt. 4.50 o.s.i (*0-553-28479-7*) Bantam Bks.
—Frog & the Scorpion. 1986. 264p. 16.95 o.p. (*0-385-19260-6*) Doubleday Publishing.
—The Frog & the Scorpion. 1987. 224p. mass mkt. 3.50 o.s.i (*0-553-26876-7*) Bantam Bks.
—The Frog & the Scorpion. 1993. 320p. mass mkt. 4.99 o.p. (*0-06-104113-0*, HarperTorch) Morrow/Avon.
—Gatsby's Vineyard. 1988. 240p. mass mkt. 3.50 o.s.i (*0-553-27409-0*) Bantam Bks.
—Gatsby's Vineyard. 1987. 240p. 15.95 o.s.i (*0-385-23712-X*) Doubleday Publishing.
—Gatsby's Vineyard. 1993. 320p. mass mkt. 4.99 o.p. (*0-06-104112-2*, HarperTorch) Morrow/Avon.
—The Golden Empire. 1979. (Orig.). mass mkt. 2.50 o.s.i (*0-449-14267-1*, Fawcett) Ballantine Bks.
—Just Another Day in Paradise. 1986. mass mkt. 2.95 o.s.i (*0-553-25789-7*) Bantam Bks.
—Just Another Day in Paradise. 1985. 240p. 14.95 o.p. (*0-385-19259-2*) Doubleday Publishing.
—Just Another Day in Paradise. 1993. 304p. mass mkt. 4.99 o.p. (*0-06-104114-9*, HarperTorch) Morrow/Avon.
—Just Enough Light to Kill. 1989. mass mkt. 3.95 o.s.i (*0-553-28213-1*) Bantam Bks.
—Just Enough Light to Kill. 1993. 336p. mass mkt. 4.99 o.s.i (*0-06-104111-4*, HarperTorch) Morrow/Avon.
—The King of Nothing. 1994. 320p. mass mkt. 5.50 o.p. (*0-06-104230-7*, HarperTorch) Morrow/Avon.
—Money Burns. 1993. 368p. mass mkt. 5.50 o.p. (*0-06-104123-8*, HarperTorch) Morrow/Avon.
—Money Burns. 1993. 3.99 o.p. (*0-517-10621-3*) Random Hse. Value Publishing.
—Murder Hurts. 1995. 352p. mass mkt. 4.99 o.p. (*0-06-104318-4*, HarperTorch) Morrow/Avon.
—Redwood Empire. (Harlequin Historicals Ser.). 1995. 440p. per. (*0-373-28867-0*, 1-28867-9); 1987. 416p. mass mkt. (*0-373-97049-8*) Harlequin Enterprises, Ltd. (Harlequin Bks.).
Mayersberg, Paul. Homme Fatale. 1992. 352p. 19.95 o.p. (*0-312-06996-0*) St. Martin's Pr.
Maynard, Joyce. The Usual Rules. E-Book 24.95 (*0-312-70971-4*) St. Martin's Pr.
—The Usual Rules. l.t. ed. 2003. 542p. 29.95 (*0-7862-5548-X*) Thorndike Pr.
—The Usual Rules: A Novel. 2004. 400p. pap. 13.95 (*0-312-28369-5*); 2003. 320p. 24.95 (*0-312-24261-1*) St. Martin's Pr.
Mazza, Cris. Dog People. 1997. 200p. (Orig.). pap. 13.95 (*1-56689-055-1*) Coffee Hse. Pr.
—Your Name Here. 1995. 280p. (Orig.). pap. 12.95 (*1-56689-031-4*) Coffee Hse. Pr.
McAllester, Melanie. The Lessons. 1994. 240p. pap. 9.95 (*0-933216-99-8*) Spinsters Ink Bks.
McCabe, Peter. Wasteland: A Novel. 1994. 258p. 20.00 (*0-684-19681-6*, Scribner) Simon & Schuster.
McCarthy, Gary. The Gringo Amigo. 1997. 192p. reprint ed. pap. 4.50 (*0-8439-4256-8*, Leisure Bks.) Dorchester Publishing Co., Inc.
McConnell, Frank. The Frog King: A Harry Garnish/Bridget O'Toole Mystery. l.t. ed. 1992. pap. 19.95 o.p. (*0-7927-1175-0*); 21.95 o.p. (*0-7927-1149-1*, CH0241) BBC Audiobooks America.
—The Frog King: A Harry Garnish/Bridget O'Toole Mystery. 1990. 192p. 18.95 o.p. (*0-8027-5748-0*) Walker & Co.
McCoy, Horace. I Should Have Stayed Home. Kupelnick, Bruce S., ed. 1978. (Classics of Film Literature Ser.). lib. bdg. 21.00 o.p. (*0-8240-2883-X*) Garland Publishing, Inc.
Mcdonald, Gregory. Carioca Fletch. unabr. ed. 1989. audio 42.00 (*0-7366-1538-5*, 2408) Books on Tape, Inc.
—Carioca Fletch. 2002. (Illus.). 192p. pap. 12.00 (*0-375-71347-6*) Random Hse., Inc.
—Carioca Fletch. 1988. 288p. mass mkt. 4.99 o.s.i (*0-446-34899-6*) Warner Bks., Inc.
—Confess, Fletch. unabr. ed. 1988. audio 42.00 (*0-7366-1323-4*, 2227) Books on Tape, Inc.
—Confess, Fletch. 1976. 272p. mass mkt. 4.99 (*0-380-00814-9*, Avon Bks.) Morrow/Avon.
—Fletch. unabr. ed. 1988. audio 36.00 (*0-7366-1352-8*, 2253) Books on Tape, Inc.
—Fletch. 1976. 256p. mass mkt. 4.99 (*0-380-00645-6*, Avon Bks.) Morrow/Avon.
—Fletch & the Man Who. unabr. ed. 1988. audio 42.00 (*0-7366-1380-3*, 2273) Books on Tape, Inc.
—Fletch & the Man Who. l.t. ed. 1988. (General Ser.). 352p. pap. 17.95 o.p. (*0-8161-4654-3*, Macmillan Reference USA) Gale Group.
—Fletch & the Man Who. 1988. 288p. mass mkt. 4.99 o.s.i (*0-446-35560-7*) Warner Bks., Inc.
—Fletch & the Widow Bradley. unabr. ed. 1988. audio 36.00 (*0-7366-1418-4*, 2304) Books on Tape, Inc.
—Fletch & the Widow Bradley. 2000. E-Book (*1-930351-09-7*) FairHillBooks.com.
—Fletch & the Widow Bradley. 1982. (General Ser.). 11.95 o.p. (*0-8161-3377-8*, Macmillan Reference USA) Gale Group.
—Fletch & the Widow Bradley. 1989. mass mkt. 4.99 o.s.i (*0-446-35997-1*) Warner Bks., Inc.
—The Fletch Chronicle Vol. 1: Fletch Won; Fletch, Too; Fletch & the Widow Bradley. 1989. 8.99 o.p. (*0-517-00308-2*) Random Hse. Value Publishing.
—The Fletch Chronicle Vol. 2: Fletch; Carioca Fletch; Confess, Fletch. 1989. 8.99 o.p. (*0-517-00307-4*) Random Hse. Value Publishing.
—The Fletch Chronicle Vol. 3: Fletch's Fortune; Fletch's Moxie; Fletch & the Man Who. 1989. 8.99 o.p. (*0-517-00309-0*) Random Hse. Value Publishing.
—Fletch Reflected. 1995. 288p. mass mkt. 6.50 o.s.i (*0-515-11676-9*, Jove) Berkley Publishing Group.
—Fletch Reflected. unabr. ed. 1996. audio 36.00 (*0-7366-3287-5*, 3942) Books on Tape, Inc.
—Fletch Reflected. 1994. 240p. 21.95 o.p. (*0-399-13983-4*, G. P. Putnam's Sons) Penguin Group (USA) Inc.
—Fletch Reflected. 224p. 4.98 o.p. (*0-7651-0180-7*) Smithmark Pubs., Inc.
—Fletch, Too. 2000. E-Book (*1-930351-06-2*) FairHillBooks.com.
—Fletch, Too. 2002. 256p. pap. 12.00 (*0-375-71353-0*, Vintage) Knopf Publishing Group.
—Fletch, Too. 1987. o.s.i (*0-446-51326-1*); mass mkt. 4.99 o.s.i (*0-446-34614-4*) Warner Bks., Inc.
—Fletch, Too. unabr. ed. 1989. audio 36.00 (*0-7366-1492-3*, 2368) Books on Tape, Inc.
—Fletch Won. unabr. ed. 1988. audio 42.00 (*0-7366-1452-4*, 2334) Books on Tape, Inc.
—Fletch's Fortune. unabr. ed. 1988. audio 36.00 (*0-7366-1398-6*, 2287) Books on Tape, Inc.
—Fletch's Fortune. 1988. pap. 4.99 (*0-380-37978-3*, Avon Bks.) Morrow/Avon.
—Fletch's Moxie. unabr. ed. 1988. audio 42.00 (*0-7366-1442-7*, 2325) Books on Tape, Inc.
—Fletch's Moxie. 2000. E-Book (*1-930351-08-9*) FairHillBooks.com.
—Fletch's Moxie. 1989. 288p. mass mkt. 4.99 o.s.i (*0-446-35976-9*) Warner Bks., Inc.
—Son of Fletch. 1994. 272p. mass mkt. 5.99 o.s.i (*0-515-11470-7*, Jove) Berkley Publishing Group.
—Son of Fletch. 1993. 240p. 19.95 o.p. (*0-399-13831-5*, G. P. Putnam's Sons) Penguin Group (USA) Inc.
—Son of Fletch. 4.98 o.s.i (*0-8317-6523-2*) Smithmark Pubs., Inc.
McDonald, Ian. Terminal Cafe. 1994. 277p. pap. 19.00 (*0-553-37416-8*) Bantam Bks.
McDonald, Ross, photos by. Black Money. 1988. (Lew Archer Mystery Ser.). 208p. pap. 3.95 o.s.i (*0-553-27219-5*) Bantam Bks.
—Black Money. 1996. (Lew Archer Mystery Ser.). 256p. pap. 11.95 (*0-679-76810-6*) Random Hse., Inc.
McDougall, Ruth B. Tell Me a Story. 1985. (Illus.). 152p. (Orig.). pap. 7.95 (*0-89407-070-3*) Strawberry Hill Pr.
McDowell, Josh. Vote of Intolerance. 1998. 416p. pap. 12.99 o.p. (*0-8423-7816-2*) Tyndale Hse. Pubs.
McDowell, Josh & Stewart, Ed. Vote of Intolerance. 1997. 416p. 12.99 o.p. (*0-8423-3905-1*); audio compact disk 14.99 o.p. (*0-8423-3902-7*) Tyndale Hse. Pubs.
McGoogan, Ken. Kerouac's Ghost. rev. ed. 1996. 192p. pap. text 12.99 (*1-895854-54-7*) Davies, Robert Publishing CAN. *Dist:* General Distribution Services, Inc.
McGrady, Sean. Dead Letter. Chelius, Jane, ed. 1992. 240p. (Orig.). mass mkt. 4.99 (*0-671-74267-1*, Pocket) Simon & Schuster.
McGuire, Christine. Until Death Do Us Part. 1996. 352p. pap. 6.50 (*0-671-53618-4*, Pocket) Simon & Schuster.
—Until Judgment Day. 2003. 368p. mass mkt. 6.99 (*0-7434-2230-9*, Pocket) Simon & Schuster.
McKay, Gardner. Toyer. unabr. ed. 1999. audio 39.95 (*1-56740-424-3*, 1677, Brilliance Audio Unabridged); audio 73.25 (*1-56740-650-5*, 1678, Unabridged Library Editions) Brilliance Audio.
—Toyer. abr. ed. 1999. audio 17.98 (*1-57042-626-0*) Time Warner AudioBooks.
—Toyer. 1999. 496p. mass mkt. 7.50 (*0-446-60773-8*) Warner Bks., Inc.
—Toyer: A Novel. 1999. 464p. (YA). (gr. 8 up). 24.00 o.p. (*0-316-56118-5*) Little Brown & Co.
McKenna, Bridget. Caught Dead. 1995. 240p. (Orig.). mass mkt. 4.99 o.s.i (*0-425-14493-3*, Prime Crime) Berkley Publishing Group.
—Dead Ahead. 1994. 208p. (Orig.). mass mkt. 4.50 o.s.i (*0-425-14300-7*, Prime Crime) Berkley Publishing Group.
—Murder Beach. 1993. 208p. (Orig.). 4.50 o.p. (*1-55773-967-6*, Diamond Bks.) Ace Bks.
McKenna, K. C. Survival: A Novel of the Donner Party. 1994. 320p. (Orig.). mass mkt. 4.99 o.s.i (*0-515-11405-7*, Jove) Berkley Publishing Group.
McKenna, Lindsay. Protecting His Own. 2002. (Silhouette Intimate Moments Ser.). 256p. mass mkt. (*0-373-27255-3*, Silhouette) Harlequin Enterprises, Ltd.
McKevett, G. A. Bitter Sweets. 304p. 1997. mass mkt. 5.50 o.s.i (*1-57566-169-1*); 1996. 18.95 o.p. (*1-57566-032-6*) Kensington Publishing Corp.
—Cooked Goose. 1999. 320p. mass mkt. 6.50 (*0-7582-0205-9*); 1999. 32p. mass mkt. 5.99 (*1-57566-479-8*); 1998. (Illus.). 304p. 20.00 o.s.i (*1-57566-359-7*) Kensington Publishing Corp.
—Death by Chocolate: A Savannah Reid Mystery. 2003. 256p. 22.00 (*1-57566-712-6*) Kensington Publishing Corp.
—Death by Chocolate: A Savannah Reid Mystery. l.t. ed. 2003. (Paperback Ser.). 25.95 (*0-7862-5324-X*) Thorndike Pr.
—Just Desserts. (Savannah Reid Mystery Ser.). 1996. 320p. mass mkt. 4.99 o.s.i (*1-57566-037-7*); 1995. mass mkt. 5.99 (*0-7582-0061-7*); 1995. mass mkt. 16.95 o.s.i (*0-8217-4924-2*) Kensington Publishing Corp.
—Just Desserts. l.t. ed. 2003. (Savannah Reid Mystery Ser.). 439p. pap. 24.95 (*0-7862-6000-9*) Thorndike Pr.

—Killer Calories. (Savannah Reid Mystery Ser.). 2000. 320p. mass mkt. 5.99 (*1-57566-521-2*, Kensington Bks.); 1998. 320p. mass mkt. 5.99 o.s.i (*1-57566-298-1*); 1997. 304p. 18.95 o.s.i (*1-57566-163-2*) Kensington Publishing Corp.

—Sugar & Spite. (Savannah Reid Mystery Ser.). 2001. 34p. mass mkt. 5.99 (*1-57566-637-5*); 2000. 288p. 20.00 o.s.i (*1-57566-493-3*) Kensington Publishing Corp.

—Sugar & Spite. l.t. ed. 2003. (Savannah Reid Mystery Ser.). 397p. pap. 24.95 (*0-7862-5890-X*) Thorndike Pr.

McLaughlin, Christian. Glamourpuss. 1994. 256p. 19.95 o.p. (*0-525-93866-4*) Dutton/Plume.

McMurtry, Larry. Somebody's Darling. unabr. collector's ed. 1986. audio 64.00 (*0-7366-0791-9*, 1743) Books on Tape, Inc.

—Somebody's Darling. 2002. 352p. pap. 14.00 (*0-684-85389-2*, Simon & Schuster) Simon & Schuster.

—Somebody's Darling. Grose, Bill, ed. 1991. 352p. mass mkt. 5.99 o.s.i (*0-671-74585-9*, Pocket) Simon & Schuster.

—Somebody's Darling. 1990. 416p. mass mkt. 5.50 (*0-671-72777-X*, Pocket); 1987. 352p. pap. 10.00 (*0-671-63319-8*, Simon & Schuster); 1978. 10.00 o.s.i (*0-671-24394-2*, Simon & Schuster) Simon & Schuster.

McNamara, Joseph D. The Blue Mirage. 1991. 320p. mass mkt. 5.99 o.s.i (*0-449-14755-X*, Fawcett) Ballantine Bks.

—The Blue Mirage. 1990. 324p. 19.95 o.p. (*0-688-09518-6*, Morrow, William & Co.) Morrow/Avon.

—Code 211 Blue. 1996. mass mkt. 5.99 o.s.i (*0-449-14894-7*, Fawcett) Ballantine Bks.

—Fatal Command. 1988. 288p. mass mkt. 5.99 o.s.i (*0-449-13393-1*, Fawcett) Ballantine Bks.

—Fatal Command. 1987. 17.95 o.p. (*0-87795-874-2*, Morrow, William & Co.) Morrow/Avon.

—The First Directive. 1985. 320p. mass mkt. 5.99 o.s.i (*0-449-12863-6*, Fawcett) Ballantine Bks.

—The First Directive. 1988. 320p. 2.99 o.p. (*0-517-55454-2*) Random Hse. Value Publishing.

Meallet, Sandro. Edgewater Angels: A Novel. 2002. 336p. pap. 13.00 (*0-375-72561-X*, Vintage) Knopf Publishing Group.

Mercer, Judy. Blind Spot. 2000. 480p. 23.95 (*0-671-03424-3*, Atria) Simon & Schuster.

—Fast Forward. l.t. ed. 1996. (G. K. Hall Mystery Ser.). 593p. 22.95 o.p. (*0-7838-1495-X*, Macmillan Reference USA) Gale Group.

—Fast Forward. Date not set. pap. 3.99 (*0-671-02431-0*); 1997. (Illus.). 400p. pap. 6.99 (*0-671-89961-9*) Simon & Schuster. (Pocket).

—Fast Forward. Chernoff, Dona, ed. 1995. 352p. 22.00 o.p. (*0-671-89960-0*, Atria) Simon & Schuster.

Merek, Jack. Target Stealth. 1990. 352p. 18.45 o.s.i (*0-446-51470-5*); mass mkt. 4.95 (*0-446-34843-0*) Warner Bks., Inc.

Meschery, Joanne. Home & Away. 1994. 284p. 21.00 (*0-671-88419-0*, Simon & Schuster) Simon & Schuster.

—Home & Away: A Novel. 1998. (California Fiction Ser.). 284p. pap. 15.95 (*0-520-21342-4*) Univ. of California Pr.

Michaels, Fern. Wish List. 1996. (Romances Ser.). lib. bdg. 24.95 (*0-7862-0851-1*, Five Star); 26.95 (*1-56895-336-4*, Wheeler Publishing, Inc.) Gale Group.

—Wish List. 352p. 2002. mass mkt. 7.50 (*0-8217-7363-1*); 1996. mass mkt. 6.99 o.s.i (*0-8217-5228-6*, Zebra Bks.) Kensington Publishing Corp.

—Wish List. abr. ed. 1996. audio 6.99 (*1-57096-040-2*, RAZ 941) Romance Alive Audio.

Michaels, Kasey, et al. The Coltons: Sapphire Bride; Colton's Bride; Destiny's Bride, 3 bks. in 1. 2001. 384p. mass mkt. (*0-373-48444-5*, 1-48444-3, Harlequin Bks.) Harlequin Enterprises, Ltd.

Michaels, Leonard. The Men's Club. 1981. 181p. 10.95 o.p. (*0-374-20782-8*) Farrar, Straus & Giroux.

—The Men's Club. exp. ed. 1993. 200p. pap. 10.00 o.p. (*1-56279-039-0*) Mercury Hse.

—The Men's Club. 1982. 128p. pap. 2.95 o.p. (*0-380-58131-0*, 58131-0, Avon Bks.) Morrow/Avon.

Michaels, Melisa C. Through the Eyes of the Dead. 2000. (WWL Mystery Ser.: Vol. 370). 256p. mass mkt. (*0-373-26370-8*, 1-26370-6, Worldwide Library) Harlequin Enterprises, Ltd.

—Through the Eyes of the Dead. 1989. 192p. 17.95 o.p. (*0-8027-5718-9*) Walker & Co.

Mickelbury, Penny. Where to Choose. 2001. 240p. reprint ed. mass mkt. 6.50 (*0-312-97708-5*, 20-3261, St. Martin's Paperbacks) St. Martin's Pr.

Millar, Margaret. The Cannibal Heart. 1985. 207p. pap. 4.95 o.p. (*0-930330-32-3*) International Polygonics, Ltd.

—The Cannibal Heart. l.t. ed. 2000. 283p. (*0-7540-4053-4*); (*0-7540-4054-2*); 26.95 (*0-7862-2335-9*) Thorndike Pr.

Miller, John & Smith, Tim, eds. San Francisco Thrillers: True Crimes & Dark Mysteries from the City by the Bay. 1995. (Illus.). 272p. pap. 14.95 o.p. (*0-8118-1043-7*) Chronicle Bks. LLC.

Miller, Joshua. The Mao Game. 1997. 224p. 21.00 o.s.i (*0-06-039185-5*, ReganBooks) HarperTrade.

—The Mao Game. 1998. pap. 12.00 (*0-380-73182-7*, Avon Bks.) Morrow/Avon.

Miller, Mary. Tales of Topanga. 1994. 144p. (Orig.). pap. 9.95 (*1-56474-068-4*) Fithian Pr.

Millhiser, Marlys. Death of the Office Witch. 1995. (Charlie Green Mystery Ser.). 304p. pap. 5.95 o.p. (*0-14-024340-2*, Penguin Bks.) Penguin Group (USA) Inc.

—Death of the Office Witch. 1993. 289p. 20.00 (*1-883402-02-6*, Scribner) Simon & Schuster.

—Killer Commute: A Charlie Greene Mystery. 2000. (Charlie Greene Mysteries Ser.). 275p. 23.95 (*0-312-26610-3*, Saint Martin's Minotaur) St. Martin's Pr.

—Nobody Dies in a Casino. 1999. 288p. 22.95 (*0-312-20344-6*, Saint Martin's Minotaur) St. Martin's Pr.

Miner, Valerie. Murder in the English Department. 1983. 176p. 9.95 o.p. (*0-312-55310-2*) St. Martin's Pr.

—Winter's Edge. 1997. 216p. (gr. 11-12). reprint ed. pap. 10.95 (*1-55861-150-9*) Feminist Pr. at The City Univ. of New York.

—Winter's Edge: A Novel. 1985. (Feminist Ser.). 184p. (Orig.). (C). 20.95 o.p. (*0-89594-176-7*) Crossing Pr., Inc., The.

Minger, Elda. Coup de Foudre a Malibu. 1998. (FRE.). mass mkt. (*0-373-37479-8*, 1-37479-2, Harlequin Bks.) Harlequin Enterprises, Ltd.

Miss Giardino. 1987. pap. 7.95 o.p. (*0-931688-26-4*) Ata Bks.

Mitchell, John. On the Window Licks the Night: A Nivola. 1994. (Plover Nivola Ser.). 104p. pap. 8.95 (*0-917635-18-3*) Plover Pr.

Mitchell, Kirk. Black Dragon. 1989. mass mkt. 4.95 o.s.i (*0-440-20469-0*) Dell Publishing.

—Black Dragon. 1988. 448p. 18.95 o.p. (*0-312-01774-X*) St. Martin's Pr.

Moeri, Louise. Downwind. 1987. (J). (gr. k-12). mass mkt. 2.75 o.s.i (*0-440-92132-5*, Laurel Leaf) Random Hse. Children's Bks.

Montecino, Marcel. The Crosskiller. 1988. 352p. 18.95 o.p. (*0-87795-908-0*, Morrow, William & Co.) Morrow/Avon.

—Crosskiller. 1990. 3.99 o.p. (*0-517-03359-3*) Random Hse. Value Publishing.

—Crosskiller. 1989. 592p. mass mkt. 6.99 (*0-671-67894-9*, Pocket) Simon & Schuster.

Montgomery, Lee. Absolute Disaster: New Fiction from Los Angeles. 1996. 352p. pap. 15.95 o.p. (*0-7871-1052-3*) NewStar Media, Inc.

Moody, Bill. Bird Lives! An Evan Horne Mystery. 2000. (Evan Horne Mysteries Ser.: Bk. 350). per. (*0-373-26350-3*, 1-26350-8, Worldwide Library) Harlequin Enterprises, Ltd.

—Bird Lives! An Evan Horne Mystery. 1999. (Evan Horne Mysteries Ser.). 256p. 22.95 (*0-8027-3327-1*) Walker & Co.

—Solo Hand. 1996. 304p. mass mkt. 5.50 o.s.i (*0-440-22322-9*) Dell Publishing.

—Solo Hand. 2003. 193p. pap. 13.95 (*0-9644138-3-3*, Dark City Bks.) OffByOne Pr.

—Solo Hand. 1994. 19.95 (*0-8027-3248-8*) Walker & Co.

Moore, Brian. Cold Heaven. 1997. 272p. reprint ed. pap. 12.95 o.s.i (*0-452-27867-8*, Plume) Dutton/Plume.

—Cold Heaven. 1983. o.p. (*0-03-063257-9*) Holt, Henry & Co.

Moore, Christopher. Bloodsucking Friends: A Love Story. 1995. 300p. 23.00 o.p. (*0-684-81097-2*, Simon & Schuster) Simon & Schuster.

—The Lust Lizard of Melancholy Cove. 320p. 2000. pap. 13.00 (*0-380-79274-5*); 1999. 23.00 (*0-380-97506-8*) Morrow/Avon. (Avon Bks.).

Moore, Michael Scott. Too Much of Nothing. 2003. 13.00 (*0-7867-1196-5*, Carroll & Graf Pubs.) Avalon Publishing Group.

Moore, Rod V. Igloo among Palms. 1997. 216p. pap. 11.00 (*0-9660829-0-7*) Hinterlands Pr.

—Igloo among Palms. 1994. (Iowa Short Fiction Award Ser.). 145p. 11.50 (*0-87745-475-2*) Univ. of Iowa Pr.

Morales, Alejandro. The Brick People. 2nd ed. 1992. 320p. pap. 11.95 (*0-934770-91-3*) Arte Publico Pr.

Mori, Toshio. Unfinished Message: Selected Works of Toshio Mori. 2000. (California Legacy Ser.). (Illus.). 256p. pap. 15.95 (*1-890771-35-X*, Roundhouse Pr., The) Heyday Bks.

Morris, Gilbert. The Silver Star, Vol. 20. 1997. (House of Winslow Ser.: Vol. 20). 336p. pap. 11.99 (*1-55661-688-0*) Bethany Hse. Pubs.

Morris, Lynn & Morris, Gilbert. In the Twilight, in the Evening, 6. 1997. (Cheney Duvall, M. D. Ser.: Vol. 6). 320p. pap. 11.99 (*1-55661-427-6*) Bethany Hse. Pubs.

—In the Twilight, in the Evening. 1998. 23.95 (*0-7862-1365-5*, Five Star) Gale Group.

Morris, Wright. Love among the Cannibals. 1977. 253p. reprint ed. pap. 8.95 o.p. (*0-8032-5842-9*, Bison Bks.) Univ. of Nebraska Pr.

Morrison, Faye & Cusick, Kathryn. Golden Poppies: California History & Contemporary Life in Books & Other Media for Young Readers - An Annotated Bibliography. 1987. viii, 280p. pap. 25.00 o.p. (*0-208-02099-3*, Library Professional Pubns.) Shoe String Pr., Inc.

Mosley, Walter. Always Outnumbered, Always Outgunned. abr. ed. 1997. (Easy Rawlins Mystery Ser.). 25.00 o.p. (*0-7871-1646-7*, 695538) NewStar Media, Inc.

—Always Outnumbered, Always Outgunned. 1997. 224p. 23.00 (*0-393-04539-0*) Norton, W. W. & Co., Inc.

—Always Outnumbered, Always Outgunned. 1998. 208p. pap. 14.00 (*0-671-01499-4*, Washington Square Pr.) Simon & Schuster.

—Always Outnumbered, Always Outgunned. l.t. ed. 1998. (Basic Ser.). 360p. 30.95 (*0-7862-1268-3*) Thorndike Pr.

—Black Betty. abr. ed. 1994. (Easy Rawlins Mystery Ser.: No. 4). 3p. audio 16.95 (*1-55927-290-2*, 390399) Audio Renaissance.

—Black Betty. unabr. ed. 1994. (Easy Rawlins Mystery Ser.). audio 56.00 (*0-7366-2853-3*, 3561) Books on Tape, Inc.

—Black Betty. 1994. (Easy Rawlins Mystery Ser.). 255p. 19.95 (*0-393-03644-8*) Norton, W. W. & Co., Inc.

—Black Betty. 368p. 1997. pap. 14.00 (*0-671-01983-X*, Pocket); 1995. (Illus.). mass mkt. 6.99 (*0-671-88427-1*, Pocket); 2002. reprint ed. pap. 14.00 (*0-7434-5178-3*, Washington Square Pr.) Simon & Schuster.

—Black Betty: Library Edition, Set. unabr. ed. 1994. audio 59.95 o.p. (*1-55927-302-X*) Audio Renaissance.

—Blue Light. l.t. ed. 1999. 27.95 (*1-56895-639-8*, Wheeler Publishing, Inc.) Gale Group.

—Blue Light. 1998. 304p. (YA). (gr. 8 up). 24.00 o.p. (*0-316-57098-2*) Little Brown & Co.

—Blue Light. 1999. 400p. reprint ed. mass mkt. 6.99 (*0-446-60692-8*, Aspect) Warner Bks., Inc.

—Devil in a Blue Dress. abr. ed. 1993. (Easy Rawlins Mystery Ser.). audio 16.95 (*1-55927-238-4*, 390653) Audio Renaissance.

—Devil in a Blue Dress. unabr. ed. 1994. (Easy Rawlins Mystery Ser.). audio 36.00 (*0-7366-2810-X*, 3524) Books on Tape, Inc.

—Devil in a Blue Dress. 1990. (Easy Rawlins Mystery Ser.). 219p. 19.95 (*0-393-02854-2*) Norton, W. W. & Co., Inc.

—Devil in a Blue Dress. (Easy Rawlins Mystery Ser.). 1997. 240p. pap. 14.00 (*0-671-01982-1*); 2002. 272p. reprint ed. pap. 14.00 (*0-7434-5179-1*) Simon & Schuster. (Washington Square Pr.).

—Devil in a Blue Dress. Ryan, Kevin, ed. 1995. (Easy Rawlins Mystery Ser.). 240p. reprint ed. mass mkt. 6.99 (*0-671-51142-4*, Pocket) Simon & Schuster.

—Devil in a Blue Dress. Chelius, Jane, ed. 1991. 224p. reprint ed. mass mkt. 5.99 (*0-671-74050-4*, Pocket) Simon & Schuster.

—Devil in a Blue Dress: Library Edition, Set. unabr. ed. 1994. audio 39.95 o.p. (*1-55927-269-4*) Audio Renaissance.

—Fearless Jones. l.t. ed. 2001. (Hardcover Ser.). 322p. 31.95 (*1-58724-050-5*, Wheeler Publishing, Inc.) Gale Group.

—Gone Fishin' 1997. 208p. 22.00 o.p. (*1-57478-025-5*) Black Classic Pr.

—Gone Fishin', Set. abr. ed. 1997. (Easy Rawlins Mystery Ser.). 17.95 o.p. (*0-7871-1402-2*, 394867) NewStar Media, Inc.

—Gone Fishin' (Easy Rawlins Mystery Ser.). 1998. 272p. mass mkt. 6.50 (*0-671-01011-5*, Pocket); 1999. 256p. reprint ed. pap. 14.00 (*0-671-02746-8*, Washington Square Pr.) Simon & Schuster.

—Gone Fishin' l.t. ed. 1997. (Americana Ser.). 203p. 29.95 (*0-7862-1060-5*) Thorndike Pr.

—A Little Yellow Dog. unabr. ed. 1997. (Easy Rawlins Mystery Ser.). audio 48.00 (*0-7366-3732-X*, 4410) Books on Tape, Inc.

—A Little Yellow Dog. (Easy Rawlins Mystery Ser.). 1997. 336p. pap. 14.00 (*0-671-01986-4*, Washington Square Pr.); 1997. 336p. mass mkt. 6.50 (*0-671-88429-8*, Pocket); 2002. 384p. reprint ed. pap. 14.00 (*0-7434-5180-5*, Washington Square Pr.) Simon & Schuster.

—A Little Yellow Dog: An Easy Rawlins Mystery. abr. ed. 1996. (Easy Rawlins Mystery Ser.). audio 16.95 (*1-55927-374-7*, 394056) Audio Renaissance.

—A Little Yellow Dog: An Easy Rawlins Mystery. (Easy Rawlins Mystery Ser.). 1996. 300p. 23.00 (*0-393-03924-2*); 100.00 (*0-393-03978-1*) Norton, W. W. & Co., Inc.

—A Little Yellow Dog: An Easy Rawlins Mystery. l.t. ed. 1996. (Basic Ser.). 447p. 28.95 (*0-7862-0810-4*) Thorndike Pr.

—A Red Death. abr. ed. (Easy Rawlins Mystery Ser.). 1993. audio 16.95 (*1-55927-234-1*, 391455); Set. 1994. audio 59.95 o.p. (*1-55927-270-8*) Audio Renaissance.

—A Red Death. unabr. ed. 1994. audio 48.00 (*0-7366-2833-9*, 3541) Books on Tape, Inc.

—A Red Death. 1991. (Easy Rawlins Mystery Ser.). 284p. 19.95 (*0-393-02998-0*) Norton, W. W. & Co., Inc.

—A Red Death. 1997. (Easy Rawlins Mystery Ser.). 272p. pap. 14.00 (*0-671-01984-8*, Washington Square Pr.); pap. 3.99 (*0-671-01006-9*, Pocket) Simon & Schuster.

—A Red Death. Chelius, Jane, ed. 1992. (Easy Rawlins Mystery Ser.). 256p. reprint ed. mass mkt. 6.99 (*0-671-74989-7*, Pocket) Simon & Schuster.

—White Butterfly. abr. ed. 1993. (Easy Rawlins Mystery Ser.). audio 16.95 (*1-55927-224-4*, 391901) Audio Renaissance.

—White Butterfly. unabr. ed. 1994. (Easy Rawlins Mystery Ser.). audio 48.00 (*0-7366-2798-7*, 3513) Books on Tape, Inc.

—White Butterfly. 1992. (Easy Rawlins Mystery Ser.). 256p. 19.95 (*0-393-03366-X*) Norton, W. W. & Co., Inc.

—White Butterfly. (Easy Rawlins Mystery Ser.). 2002. 320p. pap. 14.00 (*0-7434-5177-5*); 1997. pap. 14.00 (*0-671-01985-6*) Simon & Schuster. (Washington Square Pr.).

—White Butterfly. Chelius, Jane, ed. 1993. (Easy Rawlins Mystery Ser.). 304p. reprint ed. mass mkt. 6.50 (*0-671-86787-3*, Pocket) Simon & Schuster.

—White Butterfly: Library Edition. unabr. ed. 1994. (Easy Rawlins Mystery Ser.). audio 59.95 o.p. (*1-55927-271-6*) Audio Renaissance.

Mowry, Jess. Six Out of Seven. 1993. 501p. 22.00 o.p. (*0-374-22083-2*) Farrar, Straus & Giroux.

—Six out Seven. 1994. 512p. pap. 13.95 (*0-385-47534-9*) Doubleday Publishing.

—Way Past Cool. 1992. 288p. 17.00 o.p. (*0-374-28669-8*) Farrar, Straus & Giroux.

—Way Past Cool: A Novel. 1993. 320p. pap. 60.00 o.p. (*0-06-097547-4*); pap. 13.95 o.s.i (*0-06-097545-8*) HarperTrade. (Perennial).

Mukherjee, Bharati. Leave It to Me. 1998. 240p. pap. 12.95 (*0-449-00396-5*, Fawcett) Ballantine Bks.

—Leave It to Me. 1997. 288p. 23.00 o.s.i (*0-679-43427-5*) Knopf, Alfred A. Inc.

Mullen, Jack. Behind the Shield. 1996. 352p. (Orig.). mass mkt. 5.99 (*0-380-78236-7*, Avon Bks.) Morrow/Avon.

—In the Line of Duty. 1995. 320p. (Orig.). mass mkt. 5.50 o.p. (*0-380-77614-6*, Avon Bks.) Morrow/Avon.

Muller, Eddie. The Distance: A Crime Novel Introducing Billy Nichols. 2002. 304p. 25.00 (*0-7432-1762-4*); (Illus.). 25.00 (*0-7432-1443-9*) Simon & Schuster. (Scribner).

Muller, Marcia. Ask the Cards a Question. unabr. ed. 1996. (Sharon McCone Ser.). audio 36.00 (*0-7366-3454-1*, 4098) Books on Tape, Inc.

—Ask the Cards a Question: A Sharon McCone Mystery. l.t. ed. 1996. 239p. pap. 19.95 o.p. (*0-7838-1480-1*, Macmillan Reference USA) Gale Group.

—Ask the Cards a Question: A Sharon McCone Mystery. 1982. 168p. 10.95 o.p. (*0-312-05653-2*) St. Martin's Pr.

—Ask the Cards a Question: A Sharon McCone Mystery. 1990. 224p. reprint ed. mass mkt. 6.99 (*0-445-40849-9*) Warner Bks., Inc.

—Both Ends of the Night. unabr. ed. 1997. (Sharon McCone Ser.). audio 48.00 (*0-7366-3802-4*, 4473) Books on Tape, Inc.

—Both Ends of the Night. abr. ed. (Sharon Mccone Ser.). 1998. audio 7.99 o.p. (*1-56740-250-X*, 629, Paperback Nova Audio Bks.); 1997. audio 16.95 o.p. (*1-56100-985-7*, 1137); 1997. audio 73.25 o.p. (*1-56100-834-6*, 814, Unabridged Library Editions); 1997. audio 23.95 (*1-56100-759-5*, 51, Bookcassette) Brilliance Audio.

—Both Ends of the Night. l.t. ed. 1997. (Wheeler Large Print Book Ser.). pap. 24.95 (*1-56895-463-8*, Wheeler Publishing, Inc.) Gale Group.

—Both Ends of the Night. 1997. 368p. 22.50 o.p. (*0-89296-622-X*) Mysterious Pr.

—Both Ends of the Night. 1998. (Sharon McCone Mysteries Ser.). 384p. reprint ed. mass mkt. 6.99 (*0-446-60550-6*) Warner Bks., Inc.

—The Broken Promise Land. unabr. ed. 1996. (Sharon McCone Ser.). audio 64.00 (*0-7366-3383-9*, 4033) Books on Tape, Inc.

—The Broken Promise Land. abr. ed. (Sharon Mccone Ser.). 1997. audio 7.99 o.p. (*1-56740-177-5*, 630, Paperback Nova Audio Bks.); 1996. audio 16.95 o.p. (*1-56100-956-3*, 817, Nova Audio Bks.); 1996. audio 23.95 o.p. (*1-56100-718-8*, 53, Bookcassette); 1996. audio 73.25 o.p. (*1-56100-343-3*, 816, Unabridged Library Editions) Brilliance Audio.

—The Broken Promise Land. 1996. 82p. 22.95 o.s.i (*0-89296-621-1*) Mysterious Pr.

—The Broken Promise Land. 1997. (Sharon McCone Mysteries Ser.). 400p. reprint ed. mass mkt. 6.50 (*0-446-60410-0*) Warner Bks., Inc.

—The Cavalier in White. l.t. ed. 1990. 19.95 o.p. (*0-7927-0633-1*, C0594); pap. 17.95 o.p. (*0-7927-0634-X*) BBC Audiobooks America.

—The Cavalier in White. 1993. per. (*0-373-83304-0*, 1-83304-5); 1988. 224p. reprint ed. pap. (*0-373-26008-3*) Harlequin Enterprises, Ltd. (Harlequin Bks.).

—The Cavalier in White. 1986. 256p. 15.95 o.p. (*0-312-12539-9*) St. Martin's Pr.

—The Cheshire Cat's Eye: A Sharon McCone Mystery. unabr. ed. 1996. (Sharon McCone Ser.). audio 36.00 (*0-7366-3490-8*, 4130) Books on Tape, Inc.

—The Cheshire Cat's Eye: A Sharon McCone Mystery. l.t. ed. 1988. (Nightingale Ser.). 278p. pap. 12.95 o.p. (*0-8161-4396-X*, Macmillan Reference USA) Gale Group.

—The Cheshire Cat's Eye: A Sharon McCone Mystery. 1983. 160p. 10.95 o.p. (*0-312-13175-5*) St. Martin's Pr.

—The Cheshire Cat's Eye: A Sharon McCone Mystery. 1990. 224p. reprint ed. mass mkt. 6.99 (*0-445-40850-2*) Warner Bks., Inc.

—Cyanide Wells. 2003. (Illus.). 304p. 24.95 (*0-89296-781-1*) Mysterious Pr.

—Cyanide Wells. l.t. ed. 2003. 432p. 30.95 (*0-7862-5837-3*) Thorndike Pr.

—Cyanide Wells. 2004. mass mkt. (*0-446-61421-1*) Warner Bks., Inc.

—Dark Star. l.t. ed. 2000. 218p. 27.95 (*1-57490-327-6*, Beeler Large Print Bks.) Beeler, Thomas T. Publisher.

—Dark Star. 1993. per. (*0-373-83308-3*, 1-83308-6); 1990. 224p. mass mkt. (*0-373-26058-X*) Harlequin Enterprises, Ltd. (Harlequin Bks.).

—Dark Star. 1989. 15.95 o.p. (*0-312-02897-0*, Saint Martin's Minotaur) St. Martin's Pr.

—Edwin of the Iron Shoes. 1993. (Black Dagger Crime Ser.). 184p. 16.50 o.p. (*0-7451-8617-3*, Black Dagger) BBC Audiobooks America.

—Edwin of the Iron Shoes. unabr. ed. 1996. (Sharon McCone Ser.). audio 36.00 (*0-7366-3408-8*, 4054) Books on Tape, Inc.

—Edwin of the Iron Shoes. 1977. (McKay-Washburn Mystery Ser.). 7.95 o.p. (*0-679-50782-5*) McKay, David Co., Inc.

—Edwin of the Iron Shoes. 1978. (Crime Ser.). pap. 1.95 o.p. (*0-14-004915-0*, Penguin Bks.) Viking Penguin.

—Edwin of the Iron Shoes. 1990. 224p. reprint ed. mass mkt. 6.99 (*0-445-40902-9*) Warner Bks., Inc.

—Eye of the Storm. unabr. ed. 1998. (Sharon McCone Ser.). audio 56.00 (*0-7366-4135-1*, 4640) Books on Tape, Inc.

—Eye of the Storm. 1988. 15.95 o.p. (*0-89296-269-0*) Mysterious Pr.

—Eye of the Storm. 1989. 256p. reprint ed. mass mkt. 6.99 o.s.i (*0-445-40625-9*) Warner Bks., Inc.

—Games to Keep the Dark Away: A Sharon McCone Mystery. unabr. ed. 1997. (Sharon McCone Ser.). audio 36.00 (*0-7366-3566-1*, 4212) Books on Tape, Inc.

—Games to Keep the Dark Away: A Sharon McCone Mystery. l.t. ed. 1986. (Nightingale Ser.). 278p. 11.95 o.p. (*0-8161-3903-2*, Macmillan Reference USA) Gale Group.

—Games to Keep the Dark Away: A Sharon McCone Mystery. 2003. 320p. pap. 14.95 (*0-312-31620-8*, L. A. Weekly Bks.) St. Martin's Pr.

—Games to Keep the Dark Away: A Sharon McCone Mystery. 1990. reprint ed. mass mkt. 6.99 (*0-445-40851-0*) Warner Bks., Inc.

—Leave a Message for Willie: A Sharon McCone Mystery. unabr. ed. 1997. (Sharon McCone Ser.). audio 42.00 (*0-7366-3779-6*, 4452) Books on Tape, Inc.

—Leave a Message for Willie: A Sharon McCone Mystery. l.t. ed. 1995. 266p. pap. 20.95 o.p. (*0-7838-1481-X*, Macmillan Reference USA) Gale Group.

—Leave a Message for Willie: A Sharon McCone Mystery. 1984. 192p. 11.95 o.p. (*0-312-47728-7*) St. Martin's Pr.

—Leave a Message for Willie: A Sharon McCone Mystery. 1990. 224p. reprint ed. mass mkt. 6.99 (*0-445-40900-2*) Warner Bks., Inc.

—The Legend of the Slain Soldiers: An Elena Oliverez Mystery. 1987. 224p. mass mkt. 3.50 o.p. (*0-451-15050-3*, Signet Bks.) NAL.

—The Legend of the Slain Soldiers: An Elena Oliverez Mystery. 1985. 181p. 13.95 o.p. (*0-8027-5617-4*) Walker & Co.

—The Legend of the Slain Soldiers: An Elena Oliverez Mystery. 1996. 192p. mass mkt. 5.99 (*0-446-40421-7*) Warner Bks., Inc.

—Listen to the Silence. 2000. 304p. 23.95 (*0-89296-689-0*) Mysterious Pr.

—McCone & Friends. 2000. 202p. (Illus.). (J). pap. 16.00 (*1-885941-38-2*); 40.00 o.p. (*1-885941-37-4*) Crippen & Landru, Pubs.

—Pennies on a Dead Woman's Eyes. 1992. 304p. 18.95 (*0-89296-454-5*) Mysterious Pr.

—Pennies on a Dead Woman's Eyes. 1993. 366p. reprint ed. mass mkt. 6.99 (*0-446-40033-5*) Warner Bks., Inc.

—Point Deception. 2001. (Illus.). 320p. 23.95 o.p. (*0-89296-690-4*) Mysterious Pr.

—Point Deception. l.t. ed. 2001. 484p. 30.95 (*0-7862-3367-2*) Thorndike Pr.

—The Shape of Dread. unabr. ed. 1999. audio 48.00 (*0-7366-4455-5*, 4900) Books on Tape, Inc.

—The Shape of Dread. 1989. 16.95 o.p. (*0-89296-271-2*) Mysterious Pr.

—The Shape of Dread. 1990. 288p. reprint ed. mass mkt. 6.99 (*0-445-40916-9*) Warner Bks., Inc.

—There Hangs the Knife. 1993. per. (*0-373-83307-5*, 1-83307-8); 1989. mass mkt. (*0-373-26034-2*) Harlequin Enterprises, Ltd. (Harlequin Bks.).

—There Hangs the Knife. 1990. 2.99 o.p. (*0-517-05927-4*) Random Hse. Value Publishing.

—There Hangs the Knife. 1988. 240p. 15.95 o.p. (*0-312-01833-9*, Saint Martin's Minotaur) St. Martin's Pr.

—There's Nothing to Be Afraid Of. unabr. ed. 1997. (Sharon McCone Ser.). audio 48.00 (*0-7366-3780-X*, 4453) Books on Tape, Inc.

—There's Nothing to Be Afraid Of. 1985. 256p. 14.95 o.p. (*0-312-79955-1*) St. Martin's Pr.

—There's Nothing to Be Afraid Of. 1990. 224p. reprint ed. mass mkt. 6.99 o.s.i (*0-445-40901-0*) Warner Bks., Inc.

—There's Something in a Sunday: A Sharon McCone Mystery. unabr. ed. 1998. (Sharon McCone Ser.). audio 48.00 (*0-7366-4136-X*, 4641) Books on Tape, Inc.

—There's Something in a Sunday: A Sharon McCone Mystery. 1989. 15.95 o.p. (*0-89296-270-4*) Mysterious Pr.

—There's Something in a Sunday: A Sharon McCone Mystery. 1990. 224p. reprint ed. mass mkt. 6.99 (*0-445-40865-0*) Warner Bks., Inc.

—Till the Butchers Cut Him Down: A Sharon McCone Mystery. 1994. 352p. 18.95 o.s.i (*0-89296-455-3*) Mysterious Pr.

—Till the Butchers Cut Him Down: A Sharon McCone Mystery. 1995. pap. (*0-446-40034-3*, Mysterious Pr. Paperback Bks.); 336p. reprint ed. mass mkt. 5.99 (*0-446-60302-3*) Warner Bks., Inc.

—The Tree of Death. 1987. mass mkt. 3.50 o.p. (*0-451-14749-9*, Signet Bks.) NAL.

—The Tree of Death. 1983. (Mysteries Ser.). 192p. 12.95 o.s.i (*0-8027-5576-3*) Walker & Co.

—The Tree of Death. 1996. 208p. mass mkt. 5.99 o.s.i (*0-446-40420-9*) Warner Bks., Inc.

—Trophies & Dead Things: A Sharon McCowe Mystery. unabr. ed. 1999. audio 48.00 Books on Tape, Inc.

—Trophies & Dead Things: A Sharon McCowe Mystery. l.t. ed. 1991. (General Ser.). 379p. lib. bdg. 19.95 o.p. (*0-8161-5134-2*, Macmillan Reference USA) Gale Group.

—Trophies & Dead Things: A Sharon McCowe Mystery. 1990. 272p. 16.95 o.p. (*0-89296-417-0*) Mysterious Pr.

—Trophies & Dead Things: A Sharon McCowe Mystery. 1991. 272p. reprint ed. mass mkt. 5.99 o.s.i (*0-446-40039-4*) Warner Bks., Inc.

—A Walk Through the Fire. 1999. 362p. 23.00 o.s.i (*0-89296-688-2*) Mysterious Pr.

—Where Echoes Live. 1991. 17.95 o.p. (*0-89296-418-9*) Mysterious Pr.

—Where Echoes Live. 1992. 368p. reprint ed. mass mkt. 6.99 (*0-446-40161-7*) Warner Bks., Inc.

—While Other People Sleep. unabr. ed. 1999. (Sharon McCone Ser.). audio 48.00 (*0-7366-4318-4*, 4790) Books on Tape, Inc.

—While Other People Sleep. unabr. ed. 1998. (Sharon McCone Ser.). audio 25.95 (*1-56740-061-2*, 1, Bookcassette); audio 57.25 (*1-56740-590-8*, 1095, Unabridged Library Editions);Set. audio 17.95 o.p. (*1-56740-786-2*, 448, Nova Audio Bks.) Brilliance Audio.

—While Other People Sleep. 1998. (Sharon McCone Mysteries Ser.). 344p. 23.00 o.p. (*0-89296-650-5*) Mysterious Pr.

—While Other People Sleep. l.t. ed. 1998. (Mystery Ser.). 432p. 28.95 o.p. (*0-7862-1615-8*) Thorndike Pr.

—While Other People Sleep. 1999. 304p. reprint ed. mass mkt. 6.99 (*0-446-60721-5*) Warner Bks., Inc.

—A Wild & Lonely Place: A Sharon McCone Mystery. unabr. ed. 2000. (Sharon McCone Ser.: 16). audio 48.00 Books on Tape, Inc.

—A Wild & Lonely Place: A Sharon McCone Mystery. 1995. 300p. 19.95 o.s.i (*0-89296-526-6*) Mysterious Pr.

—A Wild & Lonely Place: A Sharon McCone Mystery. 1996. 336p. reprint ed. mass mkt. 6.99 (*0-446-60328-7*) Warner Bks., Inc.

—Wolf in the Shadows. 1993. 368p. 18.95 (*0-89296-525-8*) Mysterious Pr.

—Wolf in the Shadows. 1994. 384p. reprint ed. mass mkt. 5.50 (*0-446-40383-0*) Warner Bks., Inc.

Muller, Marcia & Pronzini, Bill. Beyond the Grave. 240p. 1999. mass mkt. 5.95 (*0-7867-0650-3*); 1991. mass mkt. 3.95 o.p. (*0-88184-731-3*) Avalon Publishing Group. (Carroll & Graf Pubs.).

—Beyond the Grave. l.t. ed. 2001. 388p. pap. 24.95 (*0-7838-9537-2*, Macmillan Reference USA) Gale Group.

—Beyond the Grave. 1986. 224p. 15.95 o.p. (*0-8027-5651-4*) Walker & Co.

—Double. unabr. ed. 1997. audio 64.00 (*0-7366-3710-9*, 4394) Books on Tape, Inc.

—Double. 1984. 288p. 13.95 o.p. (*0-312-21807-9*) St. Martin's Pr.

—Double. 1995. 288p. reprint ed. mass mkt. 5.50 o.s.i (*0-446-40413-6*) Warner Bks., Inc.

Mulligan, John. Shopping Cart Soldiers. 1997. 239p. 22.95 (*1-880684-48-9*) Curbstone Pr.

—Shopping Cart Soldiers. 1999. 256p. pap. 12.00 (*0-684-85605-0*, Touchstone) Simon & Schuster.

Mulvihill, William. Night of the Axe. 1999. 168p. (*0-395-13650-4*) Houghton Mifflin Co.

Munn, Vella. Spirit of the Eagle. 1996. 352p. 23.95 o.p. (*0-312-86096-X*, Forge Bks.) Doherty, Tom Assocs., LLC.

—The Wind Warrior. 350p. 1999. pap. 6.99 (*0-8125-3876-5*); 1998. 23.95 o.p. (*0-312-86446-9*) Doherty, Tom Assocs., LLC. (Forge Bks.).

Munoz, Elias M. Brand New Memory. 1998. 224p. pap. 12.95 (*1-55885-227-1*) Arte Publico Pr.

Murphy, Garth. The Indian Lover. 2002. (Illus.). 448p. 26.00 (*0-7432-1943-0*, Simon & Schuster) Simon & Schuster.

Murphy, Shirley Rousseau. Cat in the Dark. 1999. 272p. 22.00 o.s.i (*0-06-105096-2*) HarperCollins Pubs.

—Cat in the Dark. 1999. (Joe Grey Mysteries Ser.). 320p. mass mkt. 6.99 (*0-06-105947-1*, Eos) Morrow/Avon.

—Cat Laughing Last: A Joe Grey Mystery. 2002. 288p. 23.95 (*0-06-620951-X*) HarperCollins Pubs.

—Cat on the Edge. 1996. 288p. mass mkt. 6.99 (*0-06-105600-6*, Eos) Morrow/Avon.

—Cat Raise the Dead. 1997. 304p. mass mkt. 6.99 (*0-06-105602-2*, Eos) Morrow/Avon.

—Cat Spitting Mad. l.t. ed. 2002. (Wheeler Large Print Book Ser.). 281p. pap. 23.95 o.p. (*1-58724-158-7*, Wheeler Publishing, Inc.) Gale Group.

—Cat Spitting Mad. 2000. (Joe Grey Mysteries Ser.). 240p. 23.00 (*0-06-105098-9*) HarperCollins Pubs.

—Cat Spitting Mad. 2001. 304p. mass mkt. 6.99 (*0-06-105989-7*, Avon Bks.) Morrow/Avon.

—Cat to the Dogs: A Joe Grey Mystery. l.t. ed. 2000. 243p. 24.95 (*1-57490-264-4*, Beeler Large Print Bks.) Beeler, Thomas T. Publisher.

—Cat to the Dogs: A Joe Grey Mystery. 1999. (Joe Grey Mysteries Ser.). 256p. 23.00 (*0-06-105097-0*) HarperCollins Pubs.

—Cat to the Dogs: A Joe Grey Mystery. 2000. (Joe Grey Mysteries Ser.). 304p. mass mkt. 6.99 (*0-06-105988-9*, Avon Bks.) Morrow/Avon.

—Cat under Fire. 1997. 256p. mass mkt. 6.99 (*0-06-105601-4*, Eos) Morrow/Avon.

Murray, Lynne. At Large. 2002. 288p. mass mkt. 6.50 (*0-312-98004-3*, St. Martin's Paperbacks); 2001. 260p. 23.95 (*0-312-28029-7*, Saint Martin's Minotaur); 2001. 287.40 (*0-312-28026-2*, Saint Martin's Minotaur) St. Martin's Pr.

—Large Target: A Josephine Fuller Mystery. E-Book 6.50 (*0-312-27388-6*); 2001. 304p. mass mkt. 6.50 (*0-312-97537-6*, St. Martin's Paperbacks); 2000. viii, 258p. 23.95 (*0-312-25456-3*, Saint Martin's Minotaur) St. Martin's Pr.

—Larger Than Death: A Josephine Fuller Mystery. 1997. 300p. 23.00 (*0-9642949-0-7*) Orloff Pr.

—Larger Than Death: A Josephine Fuller Mystery. 2000. (Josephine Fuller Mystery Ser.). 304p. mass mkt. 5.99 (*0-312-97277-6*, St. Martin's Paperbacks) St. Martin's Pr.

—A Ton of Trouble. mass mkt. (*0-312-98467-7*, St. Martin's Paperbacks); E-Book 21.95 (*0-312-70744-4*); 2002. 160p. 22.95 (*0-312-30077-8*, Saint Martin's Minotaur) St. Martin's Pr.

Murray, Victoria Christopher. Joy. l.t. ed. 2002. (African American Ser.). 643p. 29.95 (*0-7862-3864-X*) Thorndike Pr.

—Joy. 2002. 400p. pap. 13.95 (*0-446-67944-5*); 2001. 384p. 23.95 o.p. (*0-446-52875-7*) Warner Bks., Inc. (Walk Worthy Pr.).

Murray, William. The Getaway Blues. 1991. 288p. mass mkt. 4.99 o.s.i (*0-553-29103-3*) Bantam Bks.

—The Hard Knocker's Luck. 1985. 276p. 14.95 o.p. (*0-670-80621-8*) Viking Penguin.

—I'm Getting Killed Right Here. 1992. 304p. mass mkt. 4.99 o.s.i (*0-553-29638-8*) Bantam Bks.

—The King of the Nightcap. 1990. 336p. mass mkt. 4.50 o.s.i (*0-553-28426-6*) Bantam Bks.

—Now You See Her, Now You Don't. 1994. 244p. 22.00 o.p. (*0-8050-2971-0*) Holt, Henry & Co.

—Tip on a Dead Crab. (Crime Monthly Ser.). 1985. 230p. pap. 3.95 o.p. (*0-14-007662-X*, Penguin Bks.); 1984. 13.95 o.p. (*0-670-71620-0*) Viking Penguin.

—We're off to See the Killer. 1993. 18.50 o.s.i (*0-385-47035-5*) Doubleday Publishing.

—When the Fat Man Sings. 1990. 56p. mass mkt. 2.25 o.s.i (*0-553-18511-X*); 1988. mass mkt. 3.95 o.s.i (*0-553-27305-1*) Bantam Bks.

Murray, Yxta M. Locas. 1997. 256p. 22.00 o.p. (*0-8021-1605-1*, Grove Pr.) Grove/Atlantic, Inc.

Mystery Scene Magazine Editors. Hollywood Kills. 1993. 416p. 21.00 o.p. (*0-88184-879-4*, Carroll & Graf Pubs.) Avalon Publishing Group.

Nagy, Gloria. Marriage: A Novel. 1995. 448p. 22.95 o.p. (*0-316-59675-2*) Little Brown & Co.

Nahai, Gina B. Moonlight on the Avenue of Faith. 1999. 384p. 24.00 o.s.i (*0-15-100388-2*) Harcourt Trade Pubs.

Narayan, Kirin. Love, Stars & All That. 1994. 320p. 20.00 (*0-671-79395-0*, Atria) Simon & Schuster.

Nasaw, Jonathan. Shakedown Street. 1995. 208p. (J). mass mkt. 3.99 o.s.i (*0-440-21930-2*) Dell Publishing.

—Shakedown Street. 1993. (J). o.s.i (*0-385-30951-1*, Dell Books for Young Readers) Random Hse. Children's Bks.

—The World on Blood. 1996. 352p. 22.95 o.s.i (*0-525-94066-9*, Dutton) Dutton/Plume.

—The World on Blood. 1997. 448p. mass mkt. 6.99 o.s.i (*0-451-18658-3*, Signet Bks.) NAL.

Nathanson, E. M. Lovers & Schemers. 2002. (Illus.). 587p. 28.00 (*0-9704662-1-8*) Regenesis Pr.

Nava, Michael. The Burning Plain. 1999. 432p. mass mkt. 5.99 o.s.i (*0-553-58085-X*) Bantam Bks.

—The Burning Plain. 1998. 240p. 23.95 o.p. (*0-399-14310-6*, G. P. Putnam's Sons) Penguin Group (USA) Inc.

—Death of Friends. 1996. 288p. 22.95 o.p. (*0-399-13977-X*, G. P. Putnam's Sons) Penguin Group (USA) Inc.

—The Death of Friends. 1998. 256p. reprint ed. mass mkt. 5.99 o.s.i (*0-553-57763-8*) Bantam Bks.

—Goldenboy. 1988. 216p. 5.95 o.p. (*1-55583-141-9*); 1996. 224p. reprint ed. pap. 10.00 o.p. (*1-55583-366-7*); 1991. 215p. reprint ed. pap. 8.95 o.p. (*1-55583-130-3*) Alyson Pubns.

—The Hidden Law. 1994. (Los Angeles Mysteries Ser.). 192p. mass mkt. 4.99 o.s.i (*0-345-38406-7*) Ballantine Bks.

—The Hidden Law. 1992. 288p. 19.00 o.p. (*0-06-016783-1*) HarperTrade.

—How Town. 1991. (Los Angeles Mysteries Ser.). 240p. mass mkt. 4.99 o.s.i (*0-345-36987-4*) Ballantine Bks.

—How Town. 1990. 224p. 16.95 o.p. (*0-06-016207-4*) HarperTrade.

—The Little Death. 165p. 1986. pap. 7.95 o.p. (*0-932870-96-1*); 1997. reprint ed. pap. 9.95 o.p. (*1-55583-388-8*) Alyson Pubns.

—Rag & Bone: A Henry Rios Novel. 2001. 304p. 24.95 o.s.i (*0-399-14708-X*) Penguin Group (USA) Inc.

Nelson, Curt. Darkstar. 2001. 390p. pap. 22.99 (*0-7388-1825-9*); text 32.99 (*0-7388-1824-0*) Xlibris Corp.

Nelson-Weyh, Christie. Woodacre: A Novel. 1998. 258p. (*0-9654951-2-4*) Thumbprint Pr.

Nesbit, Jeff. Mountaintop Rescue. 1994. (High Sierra Adventure Ser.: Vol. 4). (J). (gr. 4 up). pap. 5.99 o.p. (*0-8407-9257-3*) Nelson, Thomas Inc.

—Setting the Trap. 1994. (High Sierra Adventure Ser.: Vol. 3). 162p. (J). (gr. 7 up). pap. 5.99 o.p. (*0-8407-9256-5*) Nelson, Thomas Inc.

Nesheim, Gisela. High Tech Murder: A Silicon Valley Murder Mystery. McGuire, Beverly, ed. 1998. 316p. 17.95 (*0-9663167-0-3*) Strategic Enterprise Consulting.

Newman, Sandra. The Only Good Thing Anyone Has Ever Done. 2003. 400p. 24.95 (*0-06-051498-1*) HarperCollins Pubs.

Ng, Fae M. Bone: A Novel. 1993. 208p. (J). 19.95 o.p. (*1-56282-944-0*) Hyperion Pr.

—Bone: Novel, A. 1994. 208p. reprint ed. pap. 12.95 (*0-06-097592-X*, Perennial) HarperTrade.

Nichols, Linda. Handyman. 2000. 272p. mass mkt. 6.99 (*0-440-23542-1*) Dell Publishing.

—Handyman. abr. ed. 2000. audio 25.00 (*0-694-52266-X*, HarperAudio) HarperTrade.

—Handyman. l.t. ed. 2000. (Americana Ser.). 431p. 28.95 (*0-7862-2503-3*) Thorndike Pr.

Nicholson, Geoff. The Food Chain. 1993. 192p. 21.95 (*0-87951-508-2*) Overlook Pr., The.

Nicholson, Joy. Road to Esmeralda. Date not set. (*0-312-26863-7*) St. Martin's Pr.

—The Tribes of Palos Verdes. 224p. 1997. 19.95 o.p. (*0-312-15677-4*); 3rd ed. 1998. pap. 11.95 (*0-312-19532-X*, CPB1114, Saint Martin's Griffin) St. Martin's Pr.

Nietzke, Ann. Windowlight. 1996. 200p. 12.00 o.p. (*1-56947-060-X*) Soho Pr., Inc.

—Windowlight: A Woman's Journal from the Edge of America. 1988. 224p. (Orig.). (C). reprint ed. pap. text 22.95 o.p. (*0-8095-4052-5*) Millefleurs.

Nightingale Staff. Lost Coast. 1997. 272p. pap. 11.95 o.p. (*0-312-15572-7*, Saint Martin's Griffin) St. Martin's Pr.

Nightingale, Steven. Lost Coast. 1996. 208p. 21.95 o.p. (*0-312-14007-X*) St. Martin's Pr.

—The Thirteenth Daughter of the Moon. 1997. 256p. 23.95 o.p. (*0-312-16911-6*) St. Martin's Pr.

—Thirteenth Daughter of the Moon. 1998. 256p. pap. 12.95 (*0-312-19528-1*, Saint Martin's Griffin) St. Martin's Pr.

Nisbet, Jim. Prelude to a Scream. 1997. 400p. 4.50 (*0-7867-0408-X*, Carroll & Graf Pubs.) Avalon Publishing Group.

Noble, Diane. At Play in the Promised Land. 2001. (California Chronicles Ser.: Vol. 3). 384p. pap. 11.95 (*1-57856-091-8*) WaterBrook Pr.

—The Blossom & the Nettle. 2000. (California Chronicles Ser.: Vol. 2). 400p. pap. 11.95 (*1-57856-090-X*) WaterBrook Pr.

—When the Far Hills Bloom. 1999. (California Chronicles Ser.: Vol. 1). 384p. pap. 11.99 (*1-57856-140-X*) WaterBrook Pr.

Noguchi, Thomas T. & Lyons, Arthur. Unnatural Causes. 1989. 4.95 (*1-55773-264-7*, Diamond Bks.) Berkley Publishing Group.

—Unnatural Causes. 1988. 320p. 17.95 o.p. (*0-399-13354-2*) Putnam Publishing Group, The.

Nolan, William F. Sharks Never Sleep, unabr. ed. 1999. audio 44.95 (*0-7861-1629-3*, 2457) Blackstone Audio Bks., Inc.

—Sharks Never Sleep. 1998. 288p. 22.95 o.p. (*0-312-19331-9*, Saint Martin's Minotaur) St. Martin's Pr.

Nordhoff, Walter. The Journey of the Flame. 2002. (California Legacy Ser.). (Illus.). 240p. reprint ed. pap. 14.95 (*1-890771-58-9*) Heyday Bks.

Norman, Barry. Birddog Tape. 1995. 236 p. 19.95 o.p. (*0-312-11753-1*, Saint Martin's Minotaur) St. Martin's Pr.

Norris, Frank. McTeague. unabr. ed. 1998. (Classic Books on Cassettes Collection). audio 53.95 (*1-55685-273-8*) Audio Bk. Contractors, Inc.

—McTeague. unabr. ed. 1993. audio 69.95 (*0-7861-0462-7*, 1414) Blackstone Audio Bks., Inc.

—McTeague. 1976. lib. bdg. 18.95 o.s.i (*0-89968-071-2*, Lightyear Pr.) Buccaneer Bks., Inc.

—McTeague. E-Book 2.49 (*1-58627-817-7*) Electric Umbrella Publishing.

—McTeague. Collins, Carvel, ed. 1950. 343p. (C). pap. text 25.00 (*0-03-009250-7*) Harcourt College Pubs.

—McTeague. 2002. 312p. 96.99 (*1-4043-1838-0*); per. 91.99 (*1-4043-1839-9*) IndyPublish.com.

—McTeague. unabr. ed. 1990. audio 79.95 (*1-58081-104-3*, RDP9) L. A. Theatre Works.

—McTeague. 201p. 1999. 14.95 (*1-57002-135-X*); 1997. reprint ed. pap. 14.95 o.p. (*1-57002-056-6*) University Publishing Hse., Inc.

—McTeague: A Story of California. 1971. 340p. lib. bdg. 20.00 (*0-8376-0406-0*) Bentley Pubs.

—McTeague: A Story of San Francisco. 1980. mass mkt. 2.25 o.s.i (*0-449-30810-3*, Fawcett) Ballantine Bks.

—McTeague: A Story of San Francisco. 1990. (Vintage-Library of America ). 324p. pap. 10.50 o.p. (*0-679-73273-X*, Vintage) Knopf Publishing Group.

—McTeague: A Story of San Francisco. 1964. mass mkt. 3.95 o.p. (*0-451-52281-8*); 352p. mass mkt. 6.95 o.s.i (*0-451-52421-7*, Signet Classics) NAL.

—McTeague: A Story of San Francisco. Pizer, Donald, ed. 1978. (C). pap. text o.p. (*0-393-09136-8*); 1977. 12.95 o.p. (*0-393-04460-2*) Norton, W. W. & Co., Inc.

—McTeague: A Story of San Francisco. Loving, Jerome, ed. 2001. (Oxford World's Classics Ser.). 384p. pap. 10.95 (*0-19-284059-2*) Oxford Univ. Pr., Inc.

—McTeague: A Story of San Francisco. Loving, Jerome, ed. & intro. by. 1996. 372p. pap. 9.95 o.p. (*0-19-282356-6*) Oxford Univ. Pr., Inc.

—McTeague: A Story of San Francisco. 2002. (Modern Library Classics). 544p. pap. 10.95 (*0-375-76129-2*) Random Hse., Inc.

—McTeague: A Story of San Francisco. 1992. (BCL1-PS American Literature Ser.). 442p. reprint ed. lib. bdg. 99.00 (*0-7812-6809-5*) Reprint Services Corp.

—McTeague: A Story of San Francisco. 1988. 18.75 o.p. (*0-8446-2663-5*) Smith, Peter Pub., Inc.

—McTeague: A Story of San Francisco. E-Book 5.00 (*0-7410-0477-1*) SoftBook Pr.

—McTeague: A Story of San Francisco. 1981. 12.05 o.p. (*0-606-03855-8*) Turtleback Bks.

—McTeague: A Story of San Francisco. Starr, Kevin, ed. & intro. by. 1994. (Penguin Twentieth-Century Classics Ser.). 496p. 10.95 (*0-14-018769-3*, Penguin Classics) Viking Penguin.

—McTeague: A Story of San Francisco. Starr, Kevin, ed. 1982. (American Library). 496p. pap. 9.95 o.p. (*0-14-039017-0*, Penguin Classics) Viking Penguin.

—McTeague: A Story of San Francisco: an Authoritative Text, Contexts, Criticism. Pizer, Donald, ed. 2nd ed. 1996. (Critical Editions Ser.). (C). pap. text 9.00 (*0-393-97013-2*) Norton, W. W. & Co., Inc.

—Moran of the Lady Letty, a Story of Adventure off the California Coast. 1971. 293p. reprint ed. 29.50 (*0-404-04790-4*) AMS Pr., Inc.

—Octopus. 1968. (Airmont Classics Ser.). (J). (gr. 11 up). mass mkt. 1.95 o.p. (*0-8049-0179-1*, CL-179) Airmont Publishing Co., Inc.

—Octopus. 446p. 29.95 o.s.i (*0-8488-2443-1*) Amereon, Ltd.

—Octopus. 1986. (gr. 8 up). pap. 1.75 o.p. (*0-553-10686-4*) Bantam Bks.

—Octopus. 1964. mass mkt. 3.50 o.p. (*0-451-51711-3*, CE1711, Signet Classics) NAL.

—The Octopus: A Story of California. 1997. audio 83.95 (*1-55685-474-9*) Audio Bk. Contractors, Inc.

—The Octopus: A Story of California. 1994. (Twentieth Century Classics Ser.). 688p. pap. 14.95 (*0-14-018770-7*, Penguin Classics) Viking Penguin.

—The Octopus: A Story of California. 2003. 400p. pap. 8.95 (*0-486-43212-2*) Dover Pubns., Inc.

—The Octopus: A Story of California. 1992. (BCL1-PS American Literature Ser.). 361p. reprint ed. lib. bdg. 89.00 (*0-7812-6812-5*) Reprint Services Corp.

North, Darian. Violation. 1998. 304p. 23.95 o.p. (*0-525-93736-6*) Dutton/Plume.

—Violation. 1999. 448p. reprint ed. mass mkt. 6.99 o.s.i (*0-451-17915-3*, Signet Bks.) NAL.

—Violation. l.t. ed. 1999. (Americana Ser.). 496p. 26.95 (*0-7862-1719-7*) Thorndike Pr.

Nova, Craig. The Book of Dreams. 1994. 336p. 22.95 o.p. (*0-395-63650-7*) Houghton Mifflin Co.

—The Universal Donor. 1997. 288p. tchr. ed. 23.00 o.p. (*0-395-70938-5*) Houghton Mifflin Co.

—The Universal Donor. 1998. (Norton Paperback Fiction Ser.). 256p. pap. 13.00 (*0-393-31845-1*, Norton Paperbacks) Norton, W. W. & Co., Inc.

Novak, Karen. Ordinary Monsters. 2003. 288p. pap. 13.95 (*1-58234-291-1*) Bloomsbury Publishing.

—Ordinary Monsters: A Novel. 2002. 288p. 24.95 (*1-58234-241-5*) Bloomsbury Publishing.

Nunn, Kem. The Dogs of Winter. 1998. 368p. pap. 14.00 o.s.i (*0-671-79334-9*); 1997. 400p. 23.50 (*0-684-82647-X*) Simon & Schuster. (Scribner).

—Pomona Queen. 2000. 224p. pap. 12.95 (*1-56858-176-9*, No Exit Pr.) Four Walls Eight Windows.

—Pomona Queen. Rosenman, Jane, ed. 1992. 240p. 19.00 o.p. (*0-671-73528-4*, Atria) Simon & Schuster.

—Pomona Queen. Sacco, Maryanne, ed. 1993. 240p. reprint ed. pap. (*0-671-79877-4*, Scribner) Simon & Schuster.

—Tapping the Source. 1988. mass mkt. 7.95 o.s.i (*0-440-20078-4*); 1988. 304p. pap. 7.95 o.s.i (*0-440-50031-1*, Laurel); 1984. 310p. 14.95 o.s.i (*0-385-29272-4*, Delacorte Pr.) Dell Publishing.

—Tapping the Source. 2000. 288p. reprint ed. pap. 13.95 (*1-56858-162-9*) Four Walls Eight Windows.

—Unassigned Territory. 1988. 320p. pap. 7.95 o.s.i (*0-440-50009-5*) Dell Publishing.

Obenzinger, Hilton. Cannibal Eliot & the Lost Histories of San Francisco. 1993. 256p. (Orig.). pap. 12.95 (*1-56279-047-1*) Mercury Hse.

O'Brien, Darcy. Margaret in Hollywood. 1991. 320p. 20.95 o.p. (*0-688-09169-5*, Morrow, William & Co.) Morrow/Avon.

O'Brien, Keith. Between Friends. 2000. 208p. pap. 13.95 (*0-9679394-4-5*) Global Learning Systems, LLC.

O'Brien, Meg. The Keeper. 1992. 18.50 o.s.i (*0-385-42482-5*) Doubleday Publishing.

—Sacred Trust. abr. ed. 2000. (Mira Ser.). audio 9.99 (*1-55204-216-2*, MIR-1216) Durkin Hayes Publishing Ltd.

—Sacred Trust. 2000. 403p. per. (*1-55166-586-7*, Mira Bks.) Harlequin Enterprises, Ltd.

O'Callaghan, Maxine. Death Is Forever. l.t. ed. 1999. (Five Star Mystery Ser.). 205p. 19.95 o.p. (*0-7862-1729-4*, Five Star) Gale Group.

—Down for the Count: A Delilah West Novel. 1998. (WWL Mystery Ser.: No. 294). per. (*0-373-26294-9*, 0-26294-9, Worldwide Library) Harlequin Enterprises, Ltd.

—Down for the Count: A Delilah West Novel. 1997. (Delilah West Mystery Ser.: Vol. 60). 240p. 20.95 (*0-312-16820-9*, Saint Martin's Minotaur) St. Martin's Pr.

—Down for the Count: A Delilah West Novel. l.t. ed. 1998. (Mystery Ser.). 307p. 26.95 (*0-7838-8404-4*) Thorndike Pr.

—Hit & Run. 1991. pap. 3.95 o.p. (*0-312-92440-2*, St. Martin's Paperbacks); 1989. 192p. 14.95 o.p. (*0-312-02584-X*, Saint Martin's Minotaur) St. Martin's Pr.

—Set-Up: A Delilah West Mystery. 1994. mass mkt. (*0-373-26144-6*, Harlequin Bks.) Harlequin Enterprises, Ltd.

—Set-Up: A Delilah West Mystery. 1991. 208p. 18.95 o.p. (*0-312-06462-4*, Saint Martin's Minotaur) St. Martin's Pr.

—Trade-Off. 1996. (Mystery Ser.). per. (*0-373-26191-8*, 1-26191-6, Worldwide Library) Harlequin Enterprises, Ltd.

—Trade-Off. 1994. 224p. 19.95 o.p. (*0-312-11081-2*, Saint Martin's Minotaur) St. Martin's Pr.

O'Connor, Joey. In His Steps: The Promise. 1998. 192p. (YA). (gr. 11 up). pap. 8.99 o.p. (*0-8007-5678-9*) Revell, Fleming H. Co.

O'Donnelly, Kristina. The Scorpion Child. 2000. pap. 15.95 (*1-930574-01-0*); (Illus.). 320p. 27.95 (*1-930574-11-8*) Rose International Publishing Hse., Inc.

Offit, Avodah K. Virtual Love. 1994. 317p. 22.00 (*0-671-87436-5*, Simon & Schuster) Simon & Schuster.

Olafsson, Olaf. Walking into the Night: A Novel. 2003. 272p. 23.00 (*0-375-42254-4*, Pantheon) Knopf Publishing Group.

Olivas, Daniel A. Assumption & Other Stories. 2003. 136p. pap. text 11.00 (*1-931010-19-6*) Bilingual Pr./Editorial Bilingue.

Olsen, Theodore V. The Burning Sky. 1991. 144p. (Orig.). mass mkt. 3.95 o.s.i (*0-449-14691-X*, Fawcett) Ballantine Bks.

—The Burning Sky. l.t. ed. 1997. (G. K. Hall Nightingale Ser.). 215p. (Orig.). pap. 17.95 o.p. (*0-7838-1978-1*, Macmillan Reference USA) Gale Group.

O'Marie, Carol Anne. Advent of Dying: A Sister Mary Helen Mystery. 1987. 256p. mass mkt. 4.99 o.s.i (*0-440-10052-6*); 1986. 288p. 14.95 o.p. (*0-385-29506-5*, Delacorte Pr.) Dell Publishing.

—Death Goes on Retreat. unabr. ed. 2001. (Sister Mary Helen Mystery Ser.). audio 29.95 (*1-57270-187-0*, N61187u, Audio Editions Mystery Masters) Audio Partners Publishing Corp.

—Death Goes on Retreat. unabr. ed. 2000. (Sister Mary Helen Mystery Ser.). audio 49.95 (*0-7927-2213-2*, CSL 102) Chivers Audio Bks. GBR. *Dist:* BBC Audiobooks America.

—Death Goes on Retreat: A Sister Mary Helen Mystery. 1996. 272p. mass mkt. 5.50 o.s.i (*0-440-21610-9*) Dell Publishing.

—Death of an Angel: A Sister Mary Helen Mystery. unabr. ed. 1998. audio 39.95 (*0-7861-1452-5*, 2314) Blackstone Audio Bks., Inc.

—Death of an Angel: A Sister Mary Helen Mystery. l.t. ed. 1997. pap. 23.95 (*1-56895-442-5*, Wheeler Publishing, Inc.) Gale Group.

—Death of an Angel: A Sister Mary Helen Mystery. 1996. 256p. 21.95 (*0-312-15107-1*, Saint Martin's Minotaur); 3rd ed. 1997. 304p. mass mkt. 6.50 (*0-312-96396-3*, St. Martin's Paperbacks) St. Martin's Pr.

—Death Takes up a Collection: A Sister Mary Helen Mystery. (Sister Mary Helen Mystery Ser.: Vol. 8). 1998. 224p. 21.95 o.p. (*0-312-19256-8*, Saint Martin's Minotaur); 1999. 256p. reprint ed. mass mkt. 6.50 (*0-312-97193-1*, St. Martin's Paperbacks) St. Martin's Pr.

—Death Takes up a Collection: A Sister Mary Helen Mystery. l.t. ed. 1999. (Mystery Ser.). 347p. 27.95 (*0-7862-1663-8*) Thorndike Pr.

—The Missing Madonna: A Sister Mary Helen Mystery. 1989. 272p. reprint ed. mass mkt. 4.99 o.s.i (*0-440-20473-9*) Dell Publishing.

—The Missing Madonna: A Sister Mary Helen Mystery. l.t. ed. 1990. (General Ser.). 371p. lib. bdg. 20.95 o.p. (*0-8161-4814-7*, Macmillan Reference USA) Gale Group.

—Murder in Ordinary Time: A Sister Mary Helen Mystery. 256p. 1992. mass mkt. 4.99 o.s.i (*0-440-21353-3*); 1991. 18.00 o.s.i (*0-385-30226-6*, Delacorte Pr.) Dell Publishing.

—Murder in Ordinary Time: A Sister Mary Helen Mystery. l.t. ed. 1992. (General Ser.). 352p. lib. bdg. 20.95 o.p. (*0-8161-5425-2*); lib. bdg. 16.95 o.p. (*0-8161-5426-0*) Gale Group. (Macmillan Reference USA).

—Murder Makes a Pilgrimage: A Sister Mary Helen Mystery, unabr. ed. 2000. audio 69.95 (*0-7927-2325-2*, CSL 214, Chivers Sound Library) BBC Audiobooks America.

—A Novena for Murder: A Sister Mary Helen Mystery. 1986. 192p. mass mkt. 4.99 o.s.i (*0-440-16469-9*) Dell Publishing.

—A Novena for Murder: A Sister Mary Helen Mystery. 1984. 224p. 12.95 o.s.i (*0-684-18087-1*, Macmillan Reference USA) Gale Group.

—Requiem at the Refuge: A Sister Mary Helen Mystery. 2000. (Sister Mary Helen Mystery Ser.). 276p. 23.95 (*0-312-20906-1*, Saint Martin's Minotaur) St. Martin's Pr.

—Requiem at the Refuge: A Sister Mary Helen Mystery. l.t. ed. 2000. (Mystery Ser.). 421p. 29.95 (*0-7862-2844-X*) Thorndike Pr.

O'Neal, David. What Goes Around. 1998. 240p. per. 5.99 (*0-9660851-0-8*) Pacific Coast Pr.

O'Rourke, F. M. The Poison Tree: A Novel. 1996. 368p. 23.00 o.p. (*0-684-80214-7*, Simon & Schuster) Simon & Schuster.

Ortiz Taylor, Sheila. Coachella. 1998. x, 187p. pap. 14.95 (*0-8263-1843-6*) Univ. of New Mexico Pr.

Osborn, David. Murder in the Napa Valley. unabr. ed. 1993. audio 30.00 (*0-7366-2534-8*, 3286) Books on Tape, Inc.

—Murder in the Napa Valley. 1995. 224p. mass mkt. 4.99 o.s.i (*0-8217-4844-0*, Zebra Bks.) Kensington Publishing Corp.

—Murder in the Napa Valley. 2000. 176p. pap. 12.95 (*0-7432-1294-0*, Simon & Schuster) Simon & Schuster.

—Murder in the Napa Valley: A Margaret Barlow Mystery. 1993. 224p. 19.00 (*0-671-70487-7*, Simon & Schuster) Simon & Schuster.

Osborne, Denise. Murder Offscreen. 1994. 310p. 19.95 o.p. (*0-8050-3113-8*) Holt, Henry & Co.

O'Shaughnessy, Perri. Acts of Malice. abr. ed. 1999. audio 17.95 o.p. (*1-56740-852-4*, 1759, Nova Audio Bks.); audio 73.25 (*1-56740-668-8*, 1758, Unabridged Library Editions); audio 26.95 (*1-56740-442-1*, 1757, Bookcassette) Brilliance Audio.

—Acts of Malice. 2000. 480p. mass mkt. 7.99 (*0-440-22581-7*) Dell Publishing.

—Acts of Malice. l.t. ed. 1999. 503p. 27.95 (*1-56895-766-1*, Wheeler Publishing, Inc.) Gale Group.

—Acts of Malice, Set. abr. ed. 1999. audio 17.95. audio 73.25 Highsmith Inc.

—Breach of Promise. 1999. 560p. mass mkt. 7.99 (*0-440-22473-X*) Broadway Bks.

—Breach of Promise. l.t. ed. 1999. pap. 23.95 (*1-56895-808-0*, Wheeler Publishing, Inc.) Gale Group.

—Invasion of Privacy. 1997. 544p. mass mkt. 7.99 (*0-440-22069-6*) Dell Publishing.

—Move to Strike. 2001. 512p. reprint ed. mass mkt. 7.99 (*0-440-22582-5*) Dell Publishing.

—Move to Strike. l.t. ed. 2000. (Wheeler Large Print Book Ser.). 540p. 27.95 (*1-56895-988-5*, Wheeler Publishing, Inc.) Gale Group.

—Obstruction of Justice. abr. ed. 1998. audio 7.99 o.s.i (*1-56740-240-2*, 1333, Paperback Nova Audio Bks.); 1997. audio 16.95 o.p. (*1-56740-753-6*, 498, Nova Audio Bks.); 1997. audio 89.25 (*1-56740-553-3*, 969, Unabridged Library Editions); 1997. audio 25.95 (*1-56100-774-9*, 201, Bookcassette) Brilliance Audio.

—Obstruction of Justice. 1998. 512p. reprint ed. mass mkt. 7.99 (*0-440-22472-1*) Dell Publishing.

—Obstruction of Justice. 1997. 400p. 23.95 o.s.i (*0-385-31870-7*) Doubleday Publishing.

—Obstruction of Justice. l.t. ed. 2000. 27.95 (*1-56895-845-5*, Wheeler Publishing, Inc.) Gale Group.

—Obstruction of Justice. unabr. ed. 1999. audio 89.25 Highsmith Inc.

Oster, Jerry. Rancho Maria. 1986. 232p. 14.95 o.p. (*0-06-015519-1*) HarperTrade.

Otsuka, Julie. When the Emperor Was Divine: A Novel. 2003. 160p. pap. 9.95 (*0-385-72181-1*) Doubleday Publishing.

—When the Emperor Was Divine: A Novel. 2002. 160p. 18.00 (*0-375-41429-0*) Knopf, Alfred A. Inc.

—When the Emperor Was Divine: A Novel. l.t. ed. 2003. 256p. 20.00 (*0-375-43278-7*) Random Hse. Large Print.

Otto, Whitney. A Collection of Beauties at the Height of Their Popularity. 2002. E-Book 19.00 (*1-58836-154-3*) Random Hse., Inc.

—A Collection of Beauties at the Height of Their Popularity: A Novel. 2003. (Illus.). 320p. pap. 12.95 (*0-8129-6681-3*) Random House Adult Trade Publishing Group.

—How to Make an American Quilt. 1994. 240p. pap. 12.95 (*0-345-38896-8*); 1992. 272p. reprint ed. mass mkt. 6.99 (*0-345-37080-5*, Ballantine Bks.) Ballantine Bks.

—How to Make an American Quilt. l.t. ed. 1992. 294p. pap. 17.95 o.p. (*0-8161-5365-5*); lib. bdg. 19.95 o.p. (*0-8161-5338-8*) Gale Group. (Macmillan Reference USA).

—How to Make an American Quilt. 1993. (Illus.). 3.99 o.p. (*0-517-09819-9*) Random Hse. Value Publishing.

—How to Make an American Quilt. 1991. pap. o.s.i (*0-679-73533-X*) Random Hse., Inc.

Outland, Orland. Death Wore a Fabulous New Fragrance. 1998. (Doan & Binky Mysteries Ser.). 208p. mass mkt. 5.99 o.s.i (*0-425-16197-8*, Prime Crime) Berkley Publishing Group.

—Death Wore a Smart Little Outfit. 1997. 224p. mass mkt. 5.50 o.s.i (*0-425-15855-1*, Prime Crime) Berkley Publishing Group.

Owens, Durrell. The Song of a Manchild. 2004. 293p. pap. 19.95 (*1-56023-480-6*, Harrington Park Pr.) Haworth Pr., Inc., The.

Padgett, Abigail. Blue. 1998. 288p. 22.00 (*0-89296-671-8*) Mysterious Pr.

—Blue. 1999. mass mkt. (*0-446-60763-0*) Warner Bks., Inc.

—Child of Silence. 1993. 208p. 17.95 (*0-89296-488-X*) Mysterious Pr.

—Child of Silence. 1994. 208p. mass mkt. 5.99 o.p. (*0-446-40184-6*, Mysterious Pr. Paperback Bks.) Warner Bks., Inc.

—The Dollmaker's Daughters. (Bo Bradley Mystery Ser.). 1998. 320p. mass mkt. 6.50 (0-446-40536-1); 1997. 288p. 22.00 o.p. (0-89296-614-9) Warner Bks., Inc.

—Moonbird Boy. 1996. 82p. 21.95 o.s.i (0-89296-613-0) Mysterious Pr.

—Moonbird Boy. 1997. 256p. mass mkt. 5.99 o.p. (0-446-40513-2, Mysterious Pr. Paperback Bks.) Warner Bks., Inc.

—Strawgirl. 1994. 256p. 18.95 o.s.i (0-89296-489-8) Mysterious Pr.

—Strawgirl. 1995. 240p. mass mkt. 5.50 o.p. (0-446-40199-4, Mysterious Pr. Paperback Bks.) Warner Bks., Inc.

—Turtle Baby. 1995. 288p. 19.95 o.s.i (0-89296-580-0) Mysterious Pr.

—Turtle Baby. l.t. ed. 1996. (Large Print Ser.). 496p. 29.99 o.p. (0-7089-3560-5, Ulverscroft) Thorpe, F. A. Pubs. GBR. *Dist:* Ulverscroft Large Print Bks., Ltd., Ulverscroft Large Print Canada, Ltd.

—Turtle Baby. 1996. 256p. mass mkt. 5.99 o.p. (0-446-40478-0, Mysterious Pr. Paperback Bks.) Warner Bks., Inc.

Padilla, Mike. Hard Language. 2000. 164p. pap. 12.95 (1-55885-298-0) Arte Publico Pr.

Paine, Lauran. The Triangle Murder. l.t. ed. 1996. 202p. pap. 20.95 o.p. (0-7838-1898-X, Macmillan Reference USA) Gale Group.

Palmer, Karen. Border Dogs: A Novel. 2002. 305p. 24.00 (1-56947-315-3) Soho Pr., Inc.

Palmer, Michael. Critical Judgment. 1997. 464p. mass mkt. 6.99 o.s.i (0-553-84015-0); 1998. 480p. reprint ed. mass mkt. 7.50 (0-553-57408-6) Bantam Bks.

—Critical Judgment. unabr. ed. 1997. audio 80.00 (0-913369-35-7, 4206) Books on Tape, Inc.

—Critical Judgment. l.t. ed. 1996. (Core Collection). 605p. 27.95 (0-7838-1940-4) Thorndike Pr.

Palmer, Shirley. The Trade. 2003. 304p. (1-55166-735-5, Mira Bks.) Harlequin Enterprises, Ltd.

Parker, Robert B. Perchance to Dream. 1993. 288p. mass mkt. 6.99 o.s.i (0-425-13131-9) Berkley Publishing Group.

—Perchance to Dream. unabr. ed. 1994. (Spenser Ser.). audio 30.00 (0-7366-2694-8, 3428) Books on Tape, Inc.

—Perchance to Dream. abr. ed. 1993. 15.95 o.p. (1-55800-291-X, 41250) NewStar Media, Inc.

—Perchance to Dream. 1991. (Spenser Thriller Ser.). 272p. 19.95 o.p. (0-399-13580-4, G. P. Putnam's Sons) Penguin Group (USA) Inc.

Parker, Robert B. & Chandler, Raymond. Poodle Springs & Pastime. abr. ed. 1999. audio 25.00 (0-7871-1894-X, Dove Audio) NewStar Media, Inc.

Parker, T. Jefferson. Black Water. 2002. lib. bdg. 29.95 (1-58547-255-7, Platinum) Ctr. Point Large Print.

—Black Water. 2002. 352p. 23.95 (0-7868-6804-X) Hyperion Pr.

—The Blue Hour. unabr. ed. 1999. audio 64.00 (0-7366-4563-2, 4970) Books on Tape, Inc.

—The Blue Hour. aut. ltd. ed. 1999. 384p. 23.95 (0-7868-6559-8) Disney Pr.

—The Blue Hour, Set. abr. ed. 1999. audio 25.00 Highsmith Inc.

—The Blue Hour. 1999. 359p. 23.95 (0-7868-6288-2); 2003. 480p. reprint ed. mass mkt. 7.99 (0-7868-8969-1) Hyperion Pr.

—The Blue Hour. abr. ed. 1999. audio 26.95 (0-7871-1935-0); audio 39.95 (0-7871-1938-5) NewStar Media, Inc. (Dove Audio).

—The Blue Hour. l.t. ed. 1999. (Americana Ser.). 597p. 29.95 (0-7862-2164-X) Thorndike Pr.

—Laguna Heat. 1985. 288p. 15.95 o.p. (0-312-46434-7) St. Martin's Pr.

—Pacific Beat. abr. ed. 1991. audio 15.95 o.p. (1-55927-157-4) Audio Renaissance.

—Pacific Beat. 1992. 421p. pap. text 5.99 o.p. (0-312-92792-4, St. Martin's Paperbacks); 1991. 18.95 o.p. (0-312-05943-4) St. Martin's Pr.

—Silent Joe. l.t. ed. 2001. 501p. lib. bdg. 28.95 (1-58547-125-9) Ctr. Point Large Print.

—Silent Joe. 2001. vii, 341p. 23.95 (0-7868-6728-0); 2003. 400p. reprint ed. mass mkt. 7.99 (0-7868-9003-7) Hyperion Pr.

—Summer of Fear. l.t. ed. 1995. pap. 22.95 o.p. (0-7927-2059-8); 1994. 23.95 o.p. (0-7927-2060-1) BBC Audiobooks America.

—Summer of Fear. 4.98 o.p. (0-8317-4640-8) Smithmark Pubs., Inc.

—Summer of Fear. 1993. 384p. 19.95 o.p. (0-312-09396-9) St. Martin's Pr.

—The Triggerman's Dance. 1996. 352p. 21.95 (0-7868-6142-8); 2003. 576p. reprint ed. mass mkt. 6.99 (0-7868-8917-9) Hyperion Pr.

—Where Serpents Lie. 1999. mass mkt. 6.99 (0-7868-8949-7); 2003. 576p. reprint ed. mass mkt. 7.50 (0-7868-8944-6) Hyperion Pr.

—Where Serpents Lie. l.t. ed. 1998. (Cloak & Dagger Ser.). 655p. 28.95 (0-7862-1526-7) Thorndike Pr.

Parvin, Roy. The Loneliest Road in America: Stories. 1996. 192p. pap. 11.95 o.p. (0-8118-1435-1) Chronicle Bks. LLC.

Passman, Don. The Visionary. 2000. 432p. mass mkt. 7.99 o.s.i (0-446-60831-9) Warner Bks., Inc.

Passman, Donald S. The Visionary. 1999. 448p. 25.00 o.p. (0-446-52159-0) Warner Bks., Inc.

Patchett, Ann. The Magician's Assistant. 368p. 1998. pap. 14.00 (0-15-600621-9, Harvest Bks.); 1997. 23.00 (0-15-100263-0) Harcourt Trade Pubs.

Patterson, James. 1st to Die. 2001. 432p. 26.95 o.p. (0-316-66600-9) Little Brown & Co.

—1st to Die. l.t. ed. 2001. 464p. 32.95 (0-7862-3291-9); pap. 29.95 (0-7862-3292-7); (0-7540-1631-5); (0-7540-2486-5) Thorndike Pr.

—1st to Die. 2001. E-Book 4.95 (0-7595-8434-6) Time Warner Bk. Group.

—1st to Die. 2001. 432p. pap. 16.00 (0-446-67842-2); 2002. 488p. reprint ed. mass mkt. 7.99 (0-446-61003-8) Warner Bks., Inc.

—1st to Die. 2001. E-Book 4.95 (0-7595-6427-2) ereads.com.

Patterson, James & de Jonge, Peter. Miracle on the 17th Green. l.t. ed. 2001. (Thorndike Famous Authors Ser.). 176p. 28.95 (0-7862-3315-X) Thorndike Pr.

Patterson, Richard North. Degree of Guilt. 1998. pap. 7.99 (0-345-91454-6); 1997. pap. 12.00 o.s.i (0-345-41811-5); 1992. mass mkt. o.s.i (0-345-38408-3); 1993. 544p. reprint ed. mass mkt. 7.99 (0-345-38184-X) Ballantine Bks.

—Degree of Guilt. unabr. ed. 1993. audio 16.00 o.s.i (0-679-42131-9, RH Audio) Random Hse. Audio Publishing Group.

—Degree of Guilt. l.t. ed. 1993. 25.00 o.s.i (0-679-42211-0) Random Hse., Inc.

—Eyes of a Child. 1998. pap. 7.99 (0-345-91463-5); 1997. pap. 12.00 o.s.i (0-345-41813-1); 1995. 576p. mass mkt. 7.99 (0-345-38613-2); 1995. mass mkt. 6.99 o.s.i (0-345-40007-0); 1994. mass mkt. o.p. (0-345-39526-3) Ballantine Bks.

—Eyes of a Child. abr. ed. 2003. audio compact disk 14.99 (0-7393-0377-5, RH Audio Price-Less); 1995. audio 17.00 o.s.i (0-679-43952-8, RH Audio); Set. 1997. audio 8.99 o.s.i (0-679-46021-7, RH Audio) Random Hse. Audio Publishing Group.

—Eyes of a Child. l.t. ed. 1995. pap. 23.00 o.s.i (0-679-76031-8) Random Hse., Inc.

—No Safe Place. 2001. E-Book 7.99 (1-58945-583-5) Adobe Systems, Inc.

—No Safe Place. 1999. mass mkt. 7.99 (0-345-38612-4);Vol. 2. 544p. mass mkt. 7.99 (0-345-40477-7) Ballantine Bks.

—No Safe Place. l.t. ed. 1998. pap. 25.95 o.p. (0-7838-0161-0, Macmillan Reference USA) Gale Group.

—No Safe Place. 1999. E-Book 7.99 (0-375-41075-9); 1998. 25.95 o.s.i (0-676-54935-7) Random Hse., Inc.

—No Safe Place: A Novel. l.t. ed. 1998. 512p. pap. 25.95 o.s.i (0-375-70296-2) Random Hse., Inc.

Paul, Jim. Medieval in L. A. A Delightful Romp Through Los Angeles as Seen Through the Mind of a Medieval Man. 1997. (Harvest Book Ser.). 240p. pap. 12.00 (0-15-600537-9, Harvest Bks.) Harcourt Trade Pubs.

—Medieval in L. A. A Fiction. 1988. 240p. text 21.00 o.p. (1-887178-15-5, Counterpoint Pr.) Basic Bks.

Pavese, Cesare. The Moon & the Bonfire. Sinclair, Louis, tr. 1974. 15.95 o.p. (0-7206-0383-8) Dufour Editions, Inc.

—The Moon & the Bonfires. Flint, R. W., tr. from ITA. 2002. (New York Review Books Classics Ser.). 176p. pap. 12.95 (1-59017-021-0) New York Review of Bks., Inc., The.

—The Moon & the Bonfires. Sinclair, Louise, tr. from ITA. 2002. (Peter Owen Modern Classics Ser.). 189p. reprint ed. pap. 18.95 (0-7206-1119-9) Owen, Peter Ltd. GBR. *Dist:* Dufour Editions, Inc.

Peak, John. Mortal Judgments. E-Book 23.95 (0-312-26461-5); 1999. 352p. 23.95 o.p. (0-312-19837-X) St. Martin's Pr.

Peak, John A. Spare Change. 1994. 512p. 24.95 o.p. (0-312-11071-5, Saint Martin's Minotaur) St. Martin's Pr.

Pearce, Jonathan. Buds: A Story about Friendship. 2003. 154p. per. 12.95 (1-59411-006-9) Writers' Collective, The.

Pearson, Carol Lynn. A Stranger for Christmas: A Novel. 2003. 14.95 (0-8294-1762-1) Loyola Pr.

Pearson, Ridley. Hard Fall. unabr. ed. 1993. audio 80.00 (0-7366-2528-3, 3280) Books on Tape, Inc.

—Hard Fall. 1992. 416p. mass mkt. 6.99 o.s.i (0-440-21262-6) Dell Publishing.

—Probable Cause. 1991. 401p. mass mkt. 6.99 (0-312-92385-6, St. Martin's Paperbacks); 1990. 320p. 18.95 o.p. (0-312-03914-X) St. Martin's Pr.

—Probable Cause. l.t. ed. 2000. (Basic Ser.). (Illus.). 501p. 29.95 (0-7862-2849-0) Thorndike Pr.

Pearson, Ryne Douglas. Capitol Punishment. 1996. 352p. mass mkt. 5.99 (0-380-72228-3, Avon Bks.); 1995. 320p. 22.00 o.p. (0-688-12983-8, Morrow, William & Co.) Morrow/Avon.

Peart, Jane. Circle of Love. l.t. ed. 2002. (Christian Romance Ser.). 263p. 26.95 (0-7862-4110-1) Gale Group.

—Circle of Love. 1999. (Steeple Hill Love Inspired Ser.). 238p. per. (0-373-87093-0, 1-87093-0, Harlequin Bks.) Harlequin Enterprises, Ltd.

—Promise of the Valley. l.t. ed. 2001. (Westward Dreams Ser.). 416p. 24.95 (0-7862-3129-7) Thorndike Pr.

—Promise of the Valley. 1995. (Westward Dreams Ser.: Vol. 2). 288p. pap. 18.99 (0-310-41281-1) Zondervan.

Peeples, Samuel. The Man Who Died Twice. 1984. 252p. pap. 8.00 (0-89733-121-4) Academy Chicago Pubs., Ltd.

—The Man Who Died Twice. 1976. 7.95 o.p. (0-399-11777-6) Putnam Publishing Group, The.

Peiffer, Lila. Rosehaven. 1994. 10.99 o.p. (0-7852-8227-0) Nelson, Thomas Inc.

—The Secrets of the Roses. 1992. (Orig.). pap. 9.99 o.p. (0-89840-358-8); pap. 10.99 o.p. (0-8407-4860-4) Nelson, Thomas Inc.

—The Secrets of the Roses: A Novel. 1994. pap. 10.99 o.p. (0-7852-8192-4) Nelson, Thomas Inc.

Pella, Judith. Beloved Stranger. l.t. ed. 1999. (Romance Ser.). 392p. 27.95 (0-7838-8495-8, Macmillan Reference USA) Gale Group.

—Blind Faith. 1996. (Portraits Ser.). 304p. pap. 8.99 o.p. (1-55661-880-8) Bethany Hse. Pubs.

—Blind Faith. l.t. ed. 2002. 581p. 26.95 o.p. (0-7862-4011-3) Gale Group.

—Toward the Sunrise. 2003. (Daughters of Fortune Ser.). 720p. pap. 16.99 (0-7642-2845-5); 464p. 16.99 (0-7642-2846-3); 464p. pap. 12.99 (0-7642-2423-9) Bethany Hse. Pubs.

Pence, Joanne. Cook in Time. 1999. (Angie Amalfi Mysteries Ser.). 352p. mass mkt. 6.99 (0-06-104454-7) HarperCollins Pubs.

—Cooking Most Deadly. 1996. (Angie Amalfi Mysteries Ser.). 256p. mass mkt. 6.50 (0-06-104395-8, HarperTorch) Morrow/Avon.

—Cooking up Trouble. 1995. (Angie Amalfi Mysteries Ser.). 320p. mass mkt. 6.99 (0-06-108200-7, HarperTorch) Morrow/Avon.

—Cook's Night Out. 1998. (Angie Amalfi Mysteries Ser.). 304p. mass mkt. 5.99 (0-06-104396-6) HarperCollins Pubs.

—Cooks Overboard. 1998. (Angie Amalfi Mysteries Ser.: Vol. 6). 304p. mass mkt. 5.99 (0-06-104453-9, HarperTorch) Morrow/Avon.

—Something's Cooking. 650th ed. 1993. (Angie Amalfi Mysteries Ser.). 336p. mass mkt. 6.50 (0-06-108096-9, HarperTorch) Morrow/Avon.

—Too Many Cooks. 1994. (Angie Amalfi Mysteries Ser.). 352p. mass mkt. 6.50 (0-06-108199-X, HarperTorch) Morrow/Avon.

Pendleton, Don. Copp for Hire. 1987. 272p. 16.95 o.p. (1-55611-064-2) Fine, Donald I. Bks.

—Copp in Deep. 1989. 252p. 17.95 o.p. (1-55611-141-X) Fine, Donald I. Bks.

—Copp in Deep. 1991. 256p. mass mkt. 4.50 o.p. (0-06-100248-8, HarperTorch) Morrow/Avon.

—Copp in Shock. 1992. 256p. 19.95 o.p. (1-55611-287-4) Fine, Donald I. Bks.

—Copp in Shock. 1993. 256p. mass mkt. 4.99 o.p. (0-06-100459-6, HarperTorch) Morrow/Avon.

—Copp in the Dark. l.t. ed. 1991. 19.95 o.p. (0-7927-0982-9, CH0157); pap. 17.95 o.p. (0-7927-0983-7, CS0256) BBC Audiobooks America.

—Copp in the Dark. 1990. (Joe Copp Ser.: No. 4). 18.95 o.p. (1-55611-210-6) Fine, Donald I. Bks.

—Copp in the Dark. 1992. 256p. mass mkt. 4.99 o.p. (0-06-100347-6, HarperTorch) Morrow/Avon.

—Copp on Fire. 1988. 16.95 o.p. (1-55611-088-X) Fine, Donald I. Bks.

—Copp on Fire. 1990. 256p. mass mkt. 4.50 o.p. (0-06-100036-1, HarperTorch) Morrow/Avon.

—Copp on Ice. 1991. 18.95 o.p. (1-55611-235-1) Fine, Donald I. Bks.

—Copp on Ice. 1992. 240p. mass mkt. 4.99 o.p. (0-06-100458-8, HarperTorch) Morrow/Avon.

Penn, W. S. The Absence of Angels: A Novel. 1995. (American Indian Literature & Critical Studies Ser.: Vol. 14). 272p. pap. 19.95 (0-8061-2714-7) Univ. of Oklahoma Pr.

Penn, William. The Absence of Angels. 1994. 274p. 28.00 (1-877946-42-7) Permanent Pr., The.

The People Is Grass! The Novel. 2001. E-Book 19.95 (0-9713623-4-3) EBOOKSITES.ORG.

Perison, Eben Paul. The Seventh Sin. 2000. 304p. mass mkt. 6.99 o.s.i (0-451-40912-4, Onyx) NAL.

Pete, Eric E. Real for Me. 2000. 214p. pap. 14.95 (0-9704995-2-3) E-fect Publishing.

Peterson, Tracie & Bell, James Scott. City of Angels #1: Shannon Saga. 2000. (Shannon Saga Ser.: Vol. 1). 384p. pap. 12.99 (0-7642-2418-2) Bethany Hse. Pubs.

Petracca, Michael. Doctor Syntax. 1989. 240p. pap. 9.95 o.p. (0-88739-138-9, Black Mask) Creative Arts Bk. Co.

—Doctor Syntax. 1991. 272p. (C). reprint ed. 29.00 o.p. (0-8095-4083-5) Millefleurs.

Petree, Sheree. Number, Please. 2002. 288p. pap. 9.95 (1-892343-25-8, Oak Tree Pr.) Oak Tree Publishing.

Phillips, Clyde. Blindsided. 2001. 384p. mass mkt. 7.50 (0-380-81763-2) Morrow/Avon.

—Blindsided: A Mystery. 2000. 320p. 24.00 (0-688-17154-0, Morrow, William & Co.) Morrow/Avon.

—Fall from Grace: A Noir Thriller. 1998. 320p. 24.00 o.p. (0-688-15744-0, Morrow, William & Co.) Morrow/Avon.

—Fall from Grace: A Noir Thriller. 1999. 448p. reprint ed. pap. 6.50 (0-671-03428-6, Pocket) Simon & Schuster.

Phillips, Gary. Bad Night Is Falling. 1998. (Ivan Monk Mysteries Ser.). 320p. 21.95 o.s.i (0-425-16302-4) Berkley Publishing Group.

—Perdition, U. S. A. 1997. 272p. mass mkt. 5.99 o.s.i (0-425-15900-0, Prime Crime) Berkley Publishing Group.

—Perdition, U. S. A. 1994. 260p. pap. 13.00 o.p. (0-9639050-6-6, West Coast Crime) Blue Heron Publishing.

—Violent Spring. 1997. 27p. reprint ed. mass mkt. 5.99 o.s.i (0-425-15625-7, Prime Crime) Berkley Publishing Group.

—Violent Spring. 1994. 275p. pap. 9.00 o.p. (1-883303-13-3, West Coast Crime) Blue Heron Publishing.

Phillips, Michael. Daughter of Grace. 1996. (Journals of Corrie Belle Hollister). 304p. text 14.99 o.p. (1-55661-906-5) Bethany Hse. Pubs.

—Home for My Heart. 1994. (Journals of Corrie Belle Hollister: Vol. 8). 320p. pap. 10.99 o.p. (1-55661-440-3) Bethany Hse. Pubs.

—My Father's World. 1996. (Journals of Corrie Belle Hollister: No. 1). 288p. text 14.99 o.p. (1-55661-905-7) Bethany Hse. Pubs.

—On the Trail of the Truth. l.t. ed. 1995. 450p. 21.95 (0-7838-1490-9, Macmillan Reference USA) Gale Group.

—On the Trail of Truth No. 3: The Journal of Corrie Belle Hollister. 1991. (Journals of Corrie Belle Hollister: Vol. 3). 320p. (Orig.). pap. 10.99 o.p. (1-55661-106-4) Bethany Hse. Pubs.

—A Place in the Sun: The Journals of Corrie Belle Hollister, Bk. 4. l.t. ed. 1996. 448p. 23.95 (0-7838-1702-9, Macmillan Reference USA) Gale Group.

Phillips, Michael & Pella, Judith. Daughter of Grace. 1990. (Journals of Corrie Belle Hollister: Bk. 2). 304p. pap. 10.99 o.p. (1-55661-105-6) Bethany Hse. Pubs.

—Daughter of Grace. l.t. ed. 1995. 376p. 21.95 (0-7838-1179-9, Macmillan Reference USA) Gale Group.

—My Father's World. 1990. (Journals of Corrie Belle Hollister: No. 1). 288p. pap. 10.99 o.p. (1-55661-104-8) Bethany Hse. Pubs.

—My Father's World. l.t. ed. 1994. 366p. lib. bdg. 20.95 (0-8161-5994-7, Macmillan Reference USA) Gale Group.

—A Place in the Sun. 1991. (Journals of Corrie Belle Hollister: Bk. 4). 304p. (Orig.). pap. 10.99 o.p. (1-55661-222-2) Bethany Hse. Pubs.

—Sea to Shining Sea. 1992. (Journals of Corrie Belle Hollister: Vol. 5). 320p. (J). pap. 10.99 o.p. (1-55661-227-3) Bethany Hse. Pubs.

Phillips, Michael R. A New Beginning. 1997. (Journals of Corrie & Christopher: No. 2). 240p. text 14.99 o.p. (1-55661-945-6); pap. 10.99 o.p. (1-55661-933-2) Bethany Hse. Pubs.

Phillips, Michael R. & Pella, Judith. My Father's World. 2000. 300p. 24.95 o.p. (0-7862-2871-7, Five Star) Gale Group.

Pieper, Bill. So Trust Me. 2000. 166p. pap. 13.95 (0-88739-267-9) Creative Arts Bk. Co.

Pierce, David M. Angels in Heaven. 1992. 240p. 17.95 o.p. (0-89296-483-9) Mysterious Pr.

—Angels in Heaven. 1993. 208p. mass mkt. 4.99 (0-446-40163-3, Mysterious Pr. Paperback Bks.) Warner Bks., Inc.

—As She Rides By. 1996. 224p. 20.95 o.p. (0-312-13924-1, Saint Martin's Minotaur) St. Martin's Pr.

—Down in the Valley. 1990. 224p. pap. 4.95 o.p. (0-14-011411-4, Penguin Bks.) Viking Penguin.

—Hear the Wind Blow, Dear. 1990. 192p. pap. 4.95 o.p. (0-14-011413-0, Penguin Bks.) Viking Penguin.

—Roses Love Sunshine. 1990. 240p. pap. 4.95 o.p. (0-14-011414-9, Penguin Bks.) Viking Penguin.

—Write Me a Letter. 1993. 272p. 18.95 (0-89296-484-7) Mysterious Pr.

Pillsbury, Samuel H. Conviction: A Novel. 1992. 213p. 21.95 o.p. (0-8027-1225-8) Walker & Co.

Pimentel, Ricardo. House with Two Doors. 1997. 176p. pap. 14.00 (0-927534-67-3) Bilingual Pr./Editorial Bilingue.

—Voices from the River. 2001. 144p. pap. 12.00 (1-931010-00-5) Bilingual Pr./Editorial Bilingue.

Pincus, Elizabeth. The Hangdog Hustle. 1995. (Neil Fury Ser.). 205p. (Orig.). pap. 9.95 (1-883523-05-2) Spinsters Ink Bks.

—The Solitary Twist. 1993. (Neil Fury Ser.). 225p. (Orig.). pap. 9.95 (*0-933216-93-9*) Spinsters Ink Bks.
—The Two Bit Tango. 1992. (Neil Fury Ser.). (Illus.). 193p. (Orig.). pap. 9.95 (*0-933216-88-2*) Spinsters Ink Bks.
Pineiro, R. J. Breakthrough. unabr. ed. 1999. audio 56.95 (*0-7861-1283-2*, 2178) Blackstone Audio Bks., Inc.
—Breakthrough. 1999. 381p. mass mkt. 6.99 (*0-8125-4390-4*, Tor Bks.); 1997. 384p. 23.95 o.p. (*0-312-85983-X*, Forge Bks.) Doherty, Tom Assocs., LLC.
Plate, Peter. The Angels of Catastrophe. 2001. 256p. 22.95 (*1-58322-050-X*); pap. 13.00 (*1-58322-063-1*) Seven Stories Pr.
Platt, Randall Beth. The Royalscope Fe-As-Ko. 1997. 288p. 21.95 (*0-945774-35-4*, PS3566.L293R68) Catbird Pr.
Plesko, Les. The Last Bongo Sunset: A Novel. 1995. 269p. 21.00 o.s.i (*0-671-88049-7*, Simon & Schuster) Simon & Schuster.
Pohlmann, Lillian. The Unsuitable Behavior of America Martin. 1976. (J). 6.95 o.p. (*0-664-32603-X*) Westminster John Knox Pr.
Poverman, C. E. On the Edge. 1997. 311p. 22.95 (*0-86538-087-2*) Ontario Review Pr.
—On the Edge. 1999. 368p. mass mkt. 6.99 (*0-312-97089-7*, St. Martin's Paperbacks) St. Martin's Pr.
Powell, Lawrence C. Eucalyptus Fair. 1992. 271p. 20.00 (*0-9632966-0-4*); 100.00 (*0-9632966-1-2*) Books West Southwest.
Powers, Richard. Operation Wandering Soul. 2002. 352p. reprint ed. pap. 13.95 (*0-06-097611-X*, Perennial) HarperTrade.
—Operation Wandering Soul: A Novel. 1993. 352p. 23.00 o.p. (*0-688-11548-9*, Morrow, William & Co.) Morrow/Avon.
Powers, Tim. Expiration Date. 1995. 384p. 23.95 o.p. (*0-312-86086-2*); 1996. 534p. pap. text 6.99 (*0-8125-5517-1*) Doherty, Tom Assocs., LLC. (Tor Bks.).
—Expiration Date. 1924. o.s.i (*0-688-10733-8*, Morrow, William & Co.) Morrow/Avon.
Prather, Richard S. Shellshock. 1987. 352p. 16.95 o.p. (*0-312-93034-8*, Tor Bks.) Doherty, Tom Assocs., LLC.
Pratt, James Michael. Paradise Bay. E-Book 23.95 (*0-312-70638-3*); 2003. 352p. mass mkt. 6.99 (*0-312-98674-2*, St. Martin's Paperbacks); 2002. 304p. 23.95 (*0-312-26634-0*) St. Martin's Pr.
Preiss, Byron. Raymond Chandler's Philip Marlowe. 1990. 6.99 o.p. (*0-517-05641-0*) Random Hse. Value Publishing.
Preiss, Byron, ed. Raymond Chandler's Philip Marlowe. 1990. 384p. reprint ed. pap. 12.95 o.p. (*0-399-51616-6*) Putnam Publishing Group, The.
—Raymond Chandler's Philip Marlowe: A Centennial Celebration. unabr. ed. 1993. 24.95 o.p. (*1-55800-485-8*) NewStar Media, Inc.
Pronzini, Bill. Bindlestiff. 1983. 208p. 11.95 o.p. (*0-312-07864-1*) St. Martin's Pr.
—Blowback. 1983. 149p. reprint ed. pap. 4.95 o.p. (*0-88150-034-8*) Countryman Pr.
—Blowback. 1977. 6.95 o.p. (*0-394-40793-8*) Random Hse., Inc.
—Bones. l.t. ed. 1991. 21.95 o.p. (*0-7927-0937-3*, CH0147); pap. 19.95 o.p. (*0-7927-0938-1*, CS0244) BBC Audiobooks America.
—Bones. 1985. (Nameless Detective Ser.). 224p. 12.95 o.p. (*0-312-08769-1*, 087691) St. Martin's Pr.
—Boobytrap: A "Nameless Detective" Mystery. 1998. (Nameless Detective Mystery Ser.). 256p. 23.00 (*0-7867-0505-1*, Carroll & Graf Pubs.) Avalon Publishing Group.
—Boobytrap: A "Nameless Detective" Mystery. unabr. ed. 1999. ("Nameless Detective" Mystery Ser.). audio 54.95 (*0-7927-2269-8*, CSL158, Chivers Sound Library) BBC Audiobooks America.
—Boobytrap: A "Nameless Detective" Mystery. l.t. ed. 1999. (Mystery Ser.). 317p. 28.95 (*0-7862-1718-9*) Thorndike Pr.
—Breakdown. l.t. ed. 1992. 19.95 o.p. (*0-7927-1050-9*); pap. 17.95 o.p. (*0-7927-1051-7*) BBC Audiobooks America.
—Breakdown. 1991. 256p. mass mkt. 4.50 o.s.i (*0-440-21157-3*) Dell Publishing.
—Crazybone: A "Nameless Detective" Mystery. 2000. 208p. 23.00 (*0-7867-0730-5*, Carroll & Graf Pubs.) Avalon Publishing Group.
—Crazybone: A "Nameless Detective" Mystery. l.t. ed. 2000. (Mystery Ser.). 317p. 29.95 (*0-7862-2694-3*) Thorndike Pr.
—Deadfall. 1986. 272p. 15.95 o.p. (*0-312-18525-1*) St. Martin's Pr.
—Demons: A "Nameless Detective" Mystery. 1994. 288p. mass mkt. 4.99 o.s.i (*0-440-21118-2*) Dell Publishing.
—Demons: A "Nameless Detective" Mystery. l.t. ed. 1994. 65.95 o.p. (*0-7862-9982-7*, Macmillan Reference USA) Gale Group.
—Dragonfire: A "Nameless Detective" Mystery. 1982. 208p. 10.95 o.p. (*0-312-21893-1*) St. Martin's Pr.
—Dragonfire & Casefile. 1990. (Nameless Detective Ser.). 576p. reprint ed. pap. 5.95 (*1-877961-95-7*) Knightsbridge Publishing.
—Epitaphs: A "Nameless Detective" Mystery. 1993. 304p. mass mkt. 4.99 o.s.i (*0-440-21117-4*); 1992. 240p. 19.00 o.s.i (*0-385-30504-4*, Delacorte Pr.) Dell Publishing.
—Hardcase. unabr. ed. 2000. (Nameless Detective Mystery Ser.). audio 49.95 (*0-7927-2215-9*, CSL 104) Chivers Audio Bks. GBR. *Dist:* BBC Audiobooks America.
—Hardcase. 1996. 288p. mass mkt. 5.50 o.s.i (*0-440-22149-8*) Dell Publishing.
—Hoodwink: A "Nameless Detective" Mystery. l.t. ed. 1990. pap. 17.95 o.p. (*0-7927-0193-3*, C0242) BBC Audiobooks America.
—Hoodwink: A "Nameless Detective" Mystery. 1981. 238p. 10.95 o.p. (*0-312-38969-8*) St. Martin's Pr.
—Illusions: A "Nameless Detective" Mystery. 1997. 256p. 23.00 o.p. (*0-7867-0403-9*, Carroll & Graf Pubs.) Avalon Publishing Group.
—Illusions: A "Nameless Detective" Mystery. unabr. ed. 2000. (Nameless Detective Mystery Ser.). audio 49.95 (*0-7927-2234-5*, CSL 123) Chivers Audio Bks. GBR. *Dist:* BBC Audiobooks America.
—Illusions: A "Nameless Detective" Mystery. 1999. 254p. lib. bdg. 26.95 (*0-7351-0222-8*) Replica Bks.
—Jackpot. 1990. 240p. reprint ed. mass mkt. 3.95 o.s.i (*0-440-20821-1*) Dell Publishing.
—Jackpot. l.t. ed. 1991. (General Ser.). 342p. lib. bdg. 20.95 (*0-8161-5037-0*, Macmillan Reference USA) Gale Group.
—Labyrinth. 2001. 186p. pap. 12.95 (*1-931755-01-9*) Mystery Vault, Inc.
—Labyrinth. 1980. 8.95 o.p. (*0-312-46352-9*) St. Martin's Pr.
—The Nameless Detective: Dragonfire-Bindlestiff. 1990. pap. 5.95 (*1-877961-15-9*) Knightsbridge Publishing.
—The Nameless Detective: Hoodwink & Scattershot. 1990. 560p. reprint ed. pap. 5.95 (*1-877961-94-9*) Knightsbridge Publishing.
—The Nameless Detective: Labyrinth & Bones. 1990. 560p. pap. 5.95 (*1-877961-92-2*) Knightsbridge Publishing.
—Nightshades: A "Nameless Detective" Mystery. 1984. 208p. 11.95 o.p. (*0-312-57338-3*) St. Martin's Pr.
—Nothing but the Night. unabr. ed. 2000. (Chivers Sound Library American Collections). audio 54.95 (*0-7927-2312-0*, CSL 201, Chivers Sound Library) BBC Audiobooks America.
—Nothing but the Night. l.t. ed. 2000. 24.95 (*1-57490-266-0*, Beeler Large Print Bks.) Beeler, Thomas T. Publisher.
—Nothing but the Night. 272p. 1999. 23.95 (*0-8027-3330-1*); 2000. reprint ed. pap. 8.95 (*0-8027-7582-9*) Walker & Co.
—Quarry: A "Nameless Detective" Mystery. l.t. ed. 1992. 22.95 o.p. (*0-7927-1392-3*); pap. 20.95 o.p. (*0-7927-1391-5*) BBC Audiobooks America.
—Quarry: A "Nameless Detective" Mystery. 1992. 224p. mass mkt. 4.99 o.s.i (*0-440-21116-6*) Dell Publishing.
—Quicksilver: A "Nameless Detective" Mystery. 1984. 192p. 11.95 o.p. (*0-312-66081-2*) St. Martin's Pr.
—Scattershot: A "Nameless Detective" Mystery. l.t. ed. 1989. 18.95 o.p. (*1-55504-833-1*, 296) BBC Audiobooks America.
—Scattershot: A "Nameless Detective" Mystery. 1983. 176p. pap. 5.95 o.p. (*0-312-70047-4*, Saint Martin's Griffin); 1982. 182p. 10.95 o.p. (*0-312-70046-6*) St. Martin's Pr.
—Sentinels: A "Nameless Detective" Mystery. 1996. 288p. 20.00 (*0-7867-0311-3*); 2002. 224p. reprint ed. pap. 11.00 (*0-7867-1014-4*) Avalon Publishing Group. (Carroll & Graf Pubs.).
—Sentinels: A "Nameless Detective" Mystery. l.t. ed. 1996. lib. bdg. 23.95 (*1-57490-074-9*, Beeler Large Print Bks.) Beeler, Thomas T. Publisher.
—Sentinels: A "Nameless Detective" Mystery. unabr. ed. 2000. (Nameless Detective Mystery Ser.). audio 49.95 (*0-7927-2207-8*, CSL 096) Chivers Audio Bks. GBR. *Dist:* BBC Audiobooks America.
—Shackles: A "Nameless Detective" Mystery. 1988. 272p. 16.95 o.p. (*0-312-01818-5*, Saint Martin's Minotaur) St. Martin's Pr.
—The Snatch. 1984. (Nameless Detective Mystery Ser.). reprint ed. pap. 4.95 o.p. (*0-88150-021-6*) Countryman Pr.
—Spadework: A Collection of "Nameless Detective" Stories. 1996. 192p. pap. 16.00 (*1-885941-07-2*); 30.00 o.p. (*1-885941-06-4*) Crippen & Landru, Pubs.
—Step to the Graveyard Easy. l.t. ed. 2002. (Mystery Ser.). 319p. 30.45 (*0-7862-4512-3*) Thorndike Pr.
—Step to the Graveyard Easy. 2002. 180p. 23.95 (*0-8027-3375-1*) Walker & Co.
—Undercurrent. 1984. 213p. pap. 4.95 o.p. (*0-88150-033-X*) Countryman Pr.
—The Vanished. 1984. (Nameless Detective Mystery Ser.). reprint ed. pap. 4.95 o.p. (*0-88150-022-4*) Countryman Pr.
—The Vanished. 1974. pap. 0.95 o.p. (*0-671-77714-9*, Pocket) Simon & Schuster.
—The Vanished. l.t. ed. 1999. (G. K. Hall Nightingale Ser.). 236p. pap. 20.95 (*0-7838-8766-3*) Thorndike Pr.
—A Wasteland of Strangers. l.t. ed. 2001. 339p. 26.95 (*1-57490-370-5*, Beeler Large Print Bks.) Beeler, Thomas T. Publisher.
—A Wasteland of Strangers. 1997. 256p. 21.95 (*0-8027-3301-8*); 1999. 264p. reprint ed. pap. 8.95 (*0-8027-7560-8*) Walker & Co.
—With an Extreme Burning. 1994. 304p. 19.95 (*0-7867-0139-0*, Carroll & Graf Pubs.) Avalon Publishing Group.
Pronzini, Bill & Greenberg, Martin H., eds. The Californians: The Best of the West. 1989. mass mkt. 2.95 o.s.i (*0-449-13471-7*, Fawcett) Ballantine Bks.
—The Californians: The Best of the West. l.t. ed. 1990. lib. bdg. 19.50 o.p. (*0-8161-4975-5*, Macmillan Reference USA) Gale Group.
Pronzini, Bill & Wilcox, Collin. Two-Spot. 1993. 272p. mass mkt. 12.95 (*0-7867-0042-4*, Carroll & Graf Pubs.) Avalon Publishing Group.
—Two-Spot. 1978. 8.95 o.p. (*0-399-12129-3*) Putnam Publishing Group, The.
Pugh, Dianne G. Cold Call. Isaacson, Dana, ed. 1993. 288p. 20.00 (*0-671-77841-2*, Atria) Simon & Schuster.
—Fast Friends. 1997. 320p. 22.00 (*0-671-51912-3*, Atria) Simon & Schuster.
—Foolproof. 1998. (Iris Thorne Mystery Ser.). 344p. 23.00 (*0-671-01424-2*, Atria) Simon & Schuster.
—Slow Squeeze. Isaacson, Dana, ed. 1994. 320p. 20.00 o.p. (*0-671-77843-9*, Atria) Simon & Schuster.
—Slow Squeeze: An Iris Thorne Mystery. 1995. 288p. mass mkt. 5.99 (*0-671-77844-7*, Pocket) Simon & Schuster.
Purl, Mara. Closer Than You Think. 1998. (Milford-Haven: Bk. 2). 190p. (Orig.). pap. 11.95 (*0-9659480-2-1*) Haven Bks.
Puzo, Mario. The Last Don. 1997. mass mkt. 7.99 (*0-345-91220-9*); 512p. mass mkt. 7.99 (*0-345-41221-4*) Ballantine Bks.
—The Last Don, Set. abr. ed. 1996. audio 24.00 o.s.i (*0-679-45270-2*, RH Audio) Random Hse. Audio Publishing Group.
—The Last Don. l.t. ed. 1996. 720p. 25.95 o.p. (*0-7838-1916-1*) Random Hse. Large Print.
Queen, Ellery. And on the Eighth Day. 1979. mass mkt. 1.75 o.s.i (*0-345-28291-4*); 1975. mass mkt. 1.25 o.s.i (*0-345-24552-0*) Ballantine Bks.
—And on the Eighth Day. l.t. ed. 1998. (G. K. Hall Paperback Ser.). 248p. 21.95 o.p. (*0-7838-8428-1*, Macmillan Reference USA) Gale Group.
—And on the Eighth Day. 1994. (Ellery Queen Mystery Ser.). 192p. pap. 8.00 o.p. (*0-06-097603-9*, Perennial) HarperTrade.
—The Four of Hearts: An Ellery Queen Mystery. 1994. 224p. reprint ed. pap. 8.00 o.p. (*0-06-097604-7*, Perennial) HarperTrade.
—The Hollywood Murders. 2000. 468p. pap. 17.00 (*1-56858-173-4*) Four Walls Eight Windows.
Racina, Thom. Snow Angel. 1996. 304p. 23.95 o.s.i (*0-525-94030-8*) Dutton/Plume.
—Snow Angel. 1997. 416p. mass mkt. 6.99 (*0-451-18599-4*, Signet Bks.) NAL.
Raphael, Neil & Raphael, Ray. Comic Cops. 1992. 182p. (Orig.). (J). (gr. 4-8). pap. 6.95 (*1-881102-10-0*) Real Bks.
Rawles, Nancy. Love Like Gumbo. 1997. (Discoveries Ser.: No. 2). 272p. pap. 14.00 (*0-940242-75-3*) Fjord Pr.
Rayner, Richard. Los Angeles Without a Map: A Love Story. 1990. 208p. pap. 7.95 o.p. (*0-452-26370-0*, Plume) Dutton/Plume.
— Los Angeles Without a Map: A Love Story. 1988. 16.95 o.p. (*1-55584-268-2*) Grove/Atlantic, Inc.
— Los Angeles Without a Map: A Love Story. 1997. (Illus.). 192p. pap. 12.00 o.p. (*0-395-83809-6*, Mariner Bks.) Houghton Mifflin Co. Trade & Reference Div.
—Murder Book. 1999. 432p. mass mkt. 5.99 o.s.i (*0-06-109737-3*) HarperCollins Pubs.
—Murder Book. 2001. 384p. pap. 14.00 (*0-06-093828-5*, Perennial) HarperTrade.
—Murder Book. 1997. 384p. tchr. ed. 25.00 o.p. (*0-395-83625-5*) Houghton Mifflin Co.
Reagan, Jim. The Scene: And Other Stories. 1994. 176p. pap. 9.95 (*1-56474-103-6*) Fithian Pr.
Reaves, Michael. Night Hunter. 1997. 276p. mass mkt. 5.99 (*0-8125-1994-9*); 1995. 256p. 21.95 o.p. (*0-312-85318-1*) Doherty, Tom Assocs., LLC. (Tor Bks.).
Rechy, John. Bodies & Souls: A Novel. 2001. 448p. pap. 14.00 (*0-8021-3846-2*, Grove Pr.) Grove/Atlantic, Inc.
—The Coming of the Night. 256p. 1999. 23.00 o.p. (*0-8021-1650-7*); 2000. reprint ed. pap. 12.00 (*0-8021-3742-3*) Grove/Atlantic, Inc. (Grove Pr.).
—The Miraculous Day of Amalia Gomez: A Novel. 2001. 224p. pap. 13.00 (*0-8021-3847-0*, Grove Pr.) Grove/Atlantic, Inc.
Reed, Ishmael. The Last Days of Louisiana Red. 1989. 192p. pap. 8.95 o.p. (*0-689-70731-2*, Scribner) Simon & Schuster.
Reed, Philip. Bird Dog. (Car Noir Thrillers Ser.). 1998. 336p. pap. 6.50 (*0-671-00165-5*, Pocket Star); 1997. 304p. 22.00 (*0-671-00163-9*, Atria) Simon & Schuster.
—Low Rider. 1999. 320p. pap. 6.50 (*0-671-00167-1*, Pocket); 1998. 336p. 23.00 (*0-671-00166-3*, Atria) Simon & Schuster.
—Low Rider. l.t. ed. 1999. (Americana Ser.). 456p. 27.95 (*0-7862-1758-8*) Thorndike Pr.
Reese, Laura. Topping from Below. abr. ed. 1997. audio 16.95 (*1-882071-58-1*) B&B Audio, Inc.
—Topping from Below. 1995. 368p. 22.95 o.p. (*0-312-12000-1*); 4th ed. 1996. 384p. pap. 13.95 (*0-312-14435-0*, CPB1157, Saint Martin's Griffin) St. Martin's Pr.
Reese, Robert. Flying with One Wing. 1992. 176p. (Orig.). pap. 8.95 (*0-9633351-2-X*) Blue Pacific Pr.
Reidinger, Paul. Good Boys. 272p. 1994. pap. 10.95 o.p. (*0-452-27220-3*, Plume); 1993. 20.00 o.p. (*0-525-93616-5*, Dutton) Dutton/Plume.
Reinstedt, Randall A. Otters, Octopuses & Odd Creatures of the Deep: A Tale of History, Science & Mystery. Bergez, John, ed. 1987. (History & Happenings of California Ser.). (Illus.). 64p. (J). (gr. 3-7). 13.95 (*0-933818-21-1*) Ghost Town Pubns.
—Stagecoach Santa. Bergez, John, ed. 1986. (History & Happenings of California Ser.). (Illus.). 46p. (J). (gr. 3-7). 13.95 (*0-933818-20-3*) Ghost Town Pubns.
Relling, William, Jr. The Criminalist. 2003. 368p. mass mkt. 6.99 (*0-8439-5278-4*, Leisure Bks.) Dorchester Publishing Co., Inc.
—Deadly Vintage. 1999. (WWL Mystery Ser.: Vol. 330). mass mkt. (*0-373-26330-9*, Worldwide Library) Harlequin Enterprises, Ltd.
—Deadly Vintage: A Jack Donne Mystery. 1995. 200p. 19.95 o.s.i (*0-8027-3262-3*) Walker & Co.
Resnick, Rachel. Go West Young F*cked-Up Chick: A Novel of Separation. 256p. 2000. pap. 12.95 (*0-312-26329-5*, Saint Martin's Griffin); 1999. 22.95 o.p. (*0-312-19889-2*) St. Martin's Pr.
Revoyr, Nina. The Necessary Hunger. 1998. 368p. pap. 14.95 (*0-312-18142-6*, Saint Martin's Griffin) St. Martin's Pr.
Richer, Lois. Baby on the Way. 1999. (Steeple Hill Love Inspired Ser.: Vol. 73). mass mkt. (*0-373-87073-6*, 1-87073-2, Harlequin Bks.) Harlequin Enterprises, Ltd.
Riefe, Barbara. Against All Odds: The Lucy Scott Mitchum Story. 2000. 288p. mass mkt. 5.99 (*0-8125-5522-8*); 1996. 304p. 22.95 (*0-312-86075-7*) Doherty, Tom Assocs., LLC. (Forge Bks.).
Rigbey, Liz. Summertime. 2003. 384p. 24.95 (*0-399-15094-3*, Putnam & Grosset) Putnam Publishing Group, The.
Rimmer, Christine. Marriage - Jones Style! Wagered Woman; Man of the Mountain; A Home for the Hunter, 3 bks. in 1. 2001. 736p. mass mkt. o.s.i (*0-373-20184-2*, Harlequin Bks.) Harlequin Enterprises, Ltd.
Rivers, Francine. The Atonement Child. l.t. ed. 2003. 565p. pap. 17.95 (*1-4104-0049-2*, Walker Large Print) Gale Group.
—The Atonement Child. 2003. (Christian Fiction Ser.). 27.95 (*0-7862-4850-5*) Thorndike Pr.
—The Atonement Child. 1999. 384p. pap. 12.99 (*0-8423-0052-X*); 1997. audio 14.99 (*0-8423-0283-2*); 1997. 256p. 12.99 o.p. (*0-8423-0041-4*) Tyndale Hse. Pubs.
—Redeeming Love. 1991. 432p. mass mkt. 3.99 o.s.i (*0-553-29368-0*) Bantam Bks.
—Redeeming Love. l.t. ed. 1993. 670p. lib. bdg. 23.95 o.p. (*0-8161-5823-1*, Macmillan Reference USA) Gale Group.
—Redeeming Love. 2000. 464p. pap. 13.99 o.p. (*1-57673-186-3*, Multnomah Bks.); 2003. 486p. reprint ed. pap. 14.99 (*1-57673-816-7*) Multnomah Pubs., Inc.
—The Scarlet Thread. l.t. ed. 2002. 651p. 26.95 (*0-7862-4363-5*) Gale Group.
—The Scarlet Thread. 2000. 416p. mass mkt. 6.99 (*0-8423-4271-0*, Living Bks.); 1997. (Illus.). 352p. pap. 12.99 (*0-8423-3568-4*) Tyndale Hse. Pubs.
Robbins, Harold. The Storyteller. l.t. ed. 1987. 8.95 o.p. (*1-55504-244-9*); pap. 18.95 o.p. (*1-55504-359-3*) BBC Audiobooks America.
—The Storyteller. 1985. 17.45 o.p. (*0-671-55749-1*, Simon & Schuster) Simon & Schuster.
Roberts, Gillian. Time & Trouble. 1999. 336p. mass mkt. 5.99 (*0-312-96996-1*, St. Martin's Paperbacks); 1998. 384p. 24.95 (*0-312-18673-8*, Saint Martin's Minotaur) St. Martin's Pr.
—Whatever Doesn't Kill You: An Emma Howe & Billie August Mystery. 2001. 312p. 23.95 (*0-312-26269-8*, Saint Martin's Minotaur) St. Martin's Pr.

Roberts, Les. A Carrot for the Donkey: A Saxon Mystery. 1989. 256p. 16.95 o.p. (0-312-02554-8, Saint Martin's Minotaur) St. Martin's Pr.

—An Infinite Number of Monkeys. 1988. mass mkt. 2.95 (0-312-91095-9, St. Martin's Paperbacks); 1987. 176p. 12.95 o.p. (0-312-00610-1) St. Martin's Pr.

—The Lemon Chicken Jones. 1993. 288p. 20.95 o.p. (0-312-10490-1, Saint Martin's Minotaur) St. Martin's Pr.

—Not Enough Horses. 1988. 224p. mass mkt. 3.50 o.p. (0-312-91225-0, St. Martin's Paperbacks); 256p. 15.95 o.p. (0-312-01485-6, Saint Martin's Minotaur) St. Martin's Pr.

—Seeing the Elephant. 1992. 352p. 18.95 o.p. (0-312-07081-0, Saint Martin's Minotaur) St. Martin's Pr.

—Snake Oil. 1990. 17.95 o.p. (0-312-04424-0, Saint Martin's Minotaur) St. Martin's Pr.

Roberts, Lillian. Almost Human. 1998. mass mkt. 5.99 o.s.i (0-449-00228-4, Fawcett) Ballantine Bks.

—The Hand That Feeds You. 1997. mass mkt. 5.50 o.s.i (0-449-14986-2, Fawcett) Ballantine Bks.

—Riding for a Fall. 1996. (Veterinarian Mystery Ser.). mass mkt. 5.50 o.s.i (0-449-14985-4, Fawcett) Ballantine Bks.

Roberts, Lora. Murder Bone by Bone. 1997. (Liz Sullivan Mysteries Ser.). mass mkt. 5.50 o.s.i (0-449-14946-3, Fawcett) Ballantine Bks.

—Murder Crops Up. 1998. (Liz Sullivan Mysteries Ser.). 240p. mass mkt. 5.99 o.s.i (0-449-15048-8, Fawcett) Ballantine Bks.

—Murder Follows Money. 2000. (Liz Sullivan Mysteries Ser.). 240p. mass mkt. 6.50 o.s.i (0-449-00539-9, Fawcett) Ballantine Bks.

—Murder Follows Money. l.t. ed. 2001. 262p. pap. 24.95 (0-7838-9591-7, Macmillan Reference USA) Gale Group.

—Murder in a Nice Neighborhood. 1994. (Liz Sullivan Mysteries Ser.). (Orig.). mass mkt. 4.99 o.s.i (0-449-14891-2, Fawcett) Ballantine Bks.

—Murder in the Marketplace. 1995. mass mkt. 5.50 o.s.i (0-449-14890-4, Fawcett) Ballantine Bks.

Roberts, Nora. Daring to Dream. 1996. 384p. mass mkt. 7.99 (0-515-11920-2, Jove) Berkley Publishing Group.

—Daring to Dream. abr. ed. (Dream Ser.). 1997. audio 7.99 o.p. (1-56740-204-6, 637, Paperback Nova Audio Bks.); 1996. audio 73.25 o.p. (1-56100-813-3, 852, Unabridged Library Editions); 1996. audio 23.95 o.p. (1-56100-738-2, 81, Bookcassette) Brilliance Audio.

—Daring to Dream. 1998. 384p. 25.00 (0-7278-5310-4) Severn Hse. Pubs., Ltd.

—Daring to Dream. l.t. ed. 1997. (Romance Ser.). 528p. lib. bdg. 27.95 (0-7862-0894-5) Thorndike Pr.

—Finding the Dream. 1997. 352p. mass mkt. 7.99 (0-515-12087-1, Jove) Berkley Publishing Group.

—Finding the Dream. abr. ed. (Dream Ser.). 1998. audio 7.99 o.p. (1-56740-205-4, 1303, Paperback Nova Audio Bks.); 1997. audio 16.95 o.p. (1-56100-929-6, 469, Nova Audio Bks.); 1997. audio 73.25 o.p. (1-56100-815-X, 835, Unabridged Library Editions); 1997. audio 23.95 o.p. (1-56100-740-4, 108, Bookcassette) Brilliance Audio.

—Finding the Dream. 1999. 368p. 26.00 (0-7278-2295-0) Severn Hse. Pubs., Ltd.

—Finding the Dream. l.t. ed. 1998. (Romance Ser.). 525p. 28.95 (0-7862-1130-X) Thorndike Pr.

—Genuine Lies. 1991. 528p. reprint ed. mass mkt. 7.99 (0-553-29078-9) Bantam Bks.

—Genuine Lies. l.t. ed. 1998. (Large Print Book Ser.). 27.95 (1-56895-678-9, Wheeler Publishing, Inc.) Gale Group.

—Holding the Dream. l.t. ed. 1997. 368p. mass mkt. 7.99 (0-515-12000-6, Jove) Berkley Publishing Group.

—Holding the Dream. abr. ed. 1997. (Dream Ser.). audio 7.99 o.p. (1-56740-203-8, 658, Paperback Nova Audio Bks.); audio 16.95 o.p. (1-56100-928-8, 1230, Nova Audio Bks.); audio 73.25 o.p. (1-56100-814-1, 898, Unabridged Library Editions); audio 23.95 o.p. (1-56100-739-0, 135, Bookcassette) Brilliance Audio.

—Holding the Dream. 1999. 352p. 26.00 (0-7278-2215-2) Severn Hse. Pubs., Ltd.

—Holding the Dream. l.t. ed. 1997. (Romance Ser.). 552p. 26.95 o.p. (0-7862-1053-2) Thorndike Pr.

—The Villa. 2001. 421p. 25.95 o.s.i (0-399-14712-8) Penguin Group (USA) Inc.

—The Villa. 2001. E-Book 25.95 (0-7865-0269-X) Penguin Putnam, Inc E-Books.

—The Villa. l.t. ed. 2001. 704p. 25.95 (0-375-43103-9) Random Hse. Large Print.

Roberts, Paul W. Palace of Fears. 1997. 23.00 o.s.i (0-679-43077-6) Random Hse., Inc.

Robinson, Jill. Star Country. 9999. mass mkt. o.p. (0-449-22257-8, Fawcett); 1997. mass mkt. 6.50 o.s.i (0-8041-1551-6, Ivy Bks.) Ballantine Bks.

Robinson, Kim Stanley. The Gold Coast. (Three Californias Ser.). 1995. 400p. pap. 14.95 (0-312-89037-0, Orb Bks.); 1988. 416p. pap. 3.95 o.p. (0-8125-5239-3, Tor Bks.); 1988. 18.95 o.p. (0-312-93050-X, Tor Bks.) Doherty, Tom Assocs., LLC.

—Pacific Edge. (Three Californias Ser.). 1995. 336p. pap. 14.95 (0-312-89038-9, Orb Bks.); 1991. mass mkt. 4.99 (0-8125-0056-3, Tor Bks.); 1990. 18.95 o.p. (0-312-85097-2, Tor Bks.) Doherty, Tom Assocs., LLC.

—The Wild Shore. Carr, Terry, ed. 1985. (New Ace Science Fiction Specials Ser.). mass mkt. 3.50 o.s.i (0-441-88874-7) Ace Bks.

—The Wild Shore. 1984. mass mkt. 2.95 o.s.i (0-441-88871-2); mass mkt. 2.95 o.s.i (0-441-88870-4) Ace Bks.

—The Wild Shore. 1995. 384p. pap. 14.95 (0-312-89036-2, Orb Bks.) Doherty, Tom Assocs., LLC.

Robinson, Patrick. Barracuda 945. 2004. 512p. mass mkt. 7.99 (0-06-008663-7, HarperTorch) Morrow/Avon.

Robitaille, Julie. Iced. 1994. (Kit Powell Mystery Ser.). 224p. 19.95 o.p. (0-312-11434-6, Saint Martin's Minotaur) St. Martin's Pr.

—Jinx. (Brown Bag Mystery Line Ser.). 1995. 358p. 3.00 o.p. (0-933031-58-0); 1992. 14.95 o.p. (0-933031-44-0) Council Oak Bks.

Roddy, Lee. Shiloh's Choice. 1996. (Giants on the Hill Ser.: No. 3). 288p. pap. 10.99 o.s.i (0-8499-3833-3) W Publishing Group.

—Yesterday's Shadows. (Pinkerton Lady Chronicles Ser.: 2). 335p. pap. 10.99 (1-56476-687-X) Cook Communications Ministries.

—Yesterday's Shadows. l.t. ed. 2002. (Pinkerton Lady Chronicles: No. 2). 470p. pap. 16.95 (1-4104-0037-9, Walker Large Print) Gale Group.

—Yesterday's Shadows. l.t. ed. 2001. (Pinkerton Lady Chronicles Ser.). 467p. 23.95 (0-7862-3208-0) Thorndike Pr.

Roderus, Frank. J. A. Whitford & the Great California Gold Hunt. 1990. 14.95 o.s.i (0-385-26690-1) Doubleday Publishing.

—J. A. Whitford & the Great California Gold Hunt. l.t. ed. 1991. (Nightingale Series Large Print Bks.). 276p. pap. 14.95 o.p. (0-8161-5173-3, Macmillan Reference USA) Gale Group.

Rodriguez, Luis. The Republic of East L. A. Stories. 2002. 256p. 23.95 (0-06-621263-4) HarperCollins Pubs.

—The Republic of East L. A. Stories. 2003. 256p. pap. 12.95 (0-06-093686-X, Rayo) HarperTrade.

Roessner, Michaela. Vanishing Point. 1993. 384p. (YA). 21.95 o.p. (0-312-85213-4, Tor Bks.) Doherty, Tom Assocs., LLC.

Roley, Brian Ascalon. The American Son: A Novel. 2001. 256p. pap. 13.00 (0-393-32154-1, Norton Paperbacks) Norton, W. W. & Co., Inc.

Romano, Mike. Murder in Palm Springs. 2002. 201p. pap. 14.95 (0-88100-129-5); 2000. 190p. pap. 14.95 (0-88100-116-3) National Writers Pr., The.

Romero, Leo. Rita & Los Angeles. 1994. 144p. (Orig.). pap. 13.00 (0-927534-44-4) Bilingual Pr./Editorial Bilingue.

Rooney, Mickey. The Search for Sonny Skies: A Novel. l.t. ed. 1995. 314p. lib. bdg. 22.95 (0-7838-1254-X, Macmillan Reference USA) Gale Group.

Roper, Robert. Cuervo Tales. 1993. 256p. 19.95 o.p. (0-89919-988-7) Houghton Mifflin Co.

—The Trespassers. 1992. 288p. 19.95 o.p. (0-89919-987-9) Houghton Mifflin Co.

Rosen, Marion. Death by Education. 1993. 224p. 17.95 o.p. (0-312-09268-7, Saint Martin's Minotaur) St. Martin's Pr.

Rosenberg, Nancy. Sullivan's Law. 2004. 400p. 24.00 (0-7582-0618-6, Kensington Bks.) Kensington Publishing Corp.

Rosenberg, Nancy Taylor. Abuse of Power. unabr. ed. 1997. audio 72.00 (0-913369-73-X, 4326) Books on Tape, Inc.

—Abuse of Power. 1997. 336p. 23.95 o.p. (0-525-93768-4) Dutton/Plume.

—Abuse of Power. l.t. ed. 1997. 448p. mass mkt. 7.99 (0-451-18006-2, Signet Bks.) NAL.

—Abuse of Power. unabr. ed. 1997. audio 78.00 (0-7887-0916-X, 94957E7) Recorded Bks., LLC.

—Abuse of Power. abr. ed. 1997. 3p. audio 16.95 o.s.i (0-14-086507-1, Penguin AudioBooks) Viking Penguin.

—Buried Evidence. 2000. 359p. 24.95 (0-7868-6619-5) Disney Pr.

—Buried Evidence. 2002. E-Book 5.95 (0-7868-6986-0); 2003. 368p. reprint ed. mass mkt. 7.99 (0-7868-8983-7) Hyperion Pr.

—Buried Evidence. l.t. ed. 2000. (Americana Ser.). 575p. 30.95 (0-7862-2924-1) Thorndike Pr.

—California Angel. 1995. 272p. (J). 17.95 o.p. (0-525-93945-8, Dutton Children's Bks.) Dutton/Plume.

—California Angel. l.t. ed. 1995. 25.95 o.p. (1-56895-214-7, Wheeler Publishing, Inc.) Gale Group.

—California Angel. abr. ed. 1995. 16.95 o.p. incl. audio (0-453-00925-5) HighBridge Co.

—California Angel. 1995. pap. 6.50 o.s.i (0-451-18757-1); 1995. 400p. mass mkt. 6.50 o.p. (0-451-18628-1); 1996. 400p. mass mkt. 6.99 o.s.i (0-451-19177-3) NAL. (Signet Bks.).

—Conflict of Interest. 2002. 320p. 24.95 (0-7868-6620-9) Hyperion Pr.

—Conflict of Interest. l.t. ed. 2002. (Americana Ser.). 475p. 31.95 (0-7862-4226-4); 28.95 (0-7862-4227-2) Thorndike Pr.

—Interest of Justice. unabr. ed. 1996. audio 80.00 (0-913369-20-9, 4169) Books on Tape, Inc.

—Interest of Justice. l.t. ed. 1993. 384p. 21.00 o.p. (0-525-93680-7, Dutton) Dutton/Plume.

—Interest of Justice. l.t. ed. 1993. 26.95 (1-56895-047-0, Wheeler Publishing, Inc.) Gale Group.

—Interest of Justice. 1994. 448p. mass mkt. 7.99 o.s.i (0-451-18021-6, Signet Bks.) NAL.

—Interest of Justice. abr. ed. 1993. (Classics on Cassette). 2p. audio 16.00 o.p. (0-453-00855-0) Penguin/HighBridge.

—Interest of Justice. 5.98 o.s.i (0-8317-2670-9) Smithmark Pubs., Inc.

—Mitigating Circumstances. l.t. ed. 1994. 21.95 o.p. (0-7927-1753-8); pap. 21.95 o.p. (0-7927-1752-X) BBC Audiobooks America.

—Mitigating Circumstances. unabr. ed. 1996. audio 72.00 (0-7366-3476-2, 4119) Books on Tape, Inc.

—Mitigating Circumstances. 1993. 368p. 21.00 o.p. (0-525-93587-8) Dutton/Plume.

—Mitigating Circumstances. 1993. 448p. mass mkt. 7.99 o.s.i (0-451-17672-3, Signet Bks.) NAL.

—Mitigating Circumstances. abr. ed. 1993. audio 16.00 o.p. (0-453-00817-8) Penguin/HighBridge.

—Mitigating Circumstances. unabr. ed. 1997. audio 78.00 (0-7887-0822-8, 94972E7) Recorded Bks., LLC.

Rosenberg, Robert. House of Guilt, Vol. 25. 2000. (Missing Mysteries Ser.: Vol. 25). 277p. pap. 14.95 o.s.i (1-890208-41-8) Poisoned Pen Pr.

Ross, Dana Fuller, pseud. California! 1984. mass mkt. 3.99 o.s.i (0-553-80006-X); mass mkt. 3.95 o.s.i (0-553-24655-0); 384p. mass mkt. 4.99 o.s.i (0-553-26377-3) Bantam Bks.

—California! l.t. ed. 1982. (Reader's Request Ser.). lib. bdg. 17.95 o.p. (0-8161-3319-0, Macmillan Reference USA) Gale Group.

—California Glory. 1991. (Holts: An American Dynasty Ser.: No. 4). 336p. mass mkt. 5.99 o.s.i (0-553-28970-5) Bantam Bks.

—California Glory. l.t. ed. 1992. (General Ser.). 476p. lib. bdg. 21.95 o.p. (0-8161-5310-8, Macmillan Reference USA) Gale Group.

—Sierra Triumph. l.t. ed. 1992. (General Ser.). 400p. 21.95 o.p. (0-8161-5450-3); 16.95 o.p. (0-8161-5451-1) Gale Group. (Macmillan Reference USA).

Ross, Lillian B. The Stranger in Big Sur. 1988. 282p. (C). reprint ed. lib. bdg. 24.95 o.p. (0-8095-4049-5) Millefleurs.

Rossner, Judith. His Little Women. 1990. 19.95 o.p. (0-671-64858-6, Simon & Schuster) Simon & Schuster.

—His Little Women. Rubenstein, Julie, ed. 1991. 448p. reprint ed. mass mkt. 5.95 (0-671-70124-X, Pocket) Simon & Schuster.

Rothenberg, Rebecca. The Bulrush Murders: A Botanical Mystery. 1991. 240p. 18.95 o.p. (0-88184-749-6, Carroll & Graf Pubs.) Avalon Publishing Group.

—The Bulrush Murders: A Botanical Mystery. 1994. 256p. mass mkt. 5.99 o.s.i (0-446-40404-7) Warner Bks., Inc.

—The Dandelion Murders. 1994. 304p. 18.95 o.s.i (0-89296-561-4) Mysterious Pr.

—The Dandelion Murders. 1995. 272p. mass mkt. 5.50 (0-446-40378-4, Mysterious Pr. Paperback Bks.) Warner Bks., Inc.

—The Shy Tulip Murders. 1996. 336p. 21.95 o.s.i (0-89296-607-6) Mysterious Pr.

—The Shy Tulip Murders. 1997. 304p. mass mkt. 5.99 (0-446-40462-4, Mysterious Pr. Paperback Bks.) Warner Bks., Inc.

Rothenberg, Rebecca & Cannon, Taffy. The Tumbleweed Murders: A Claire Sharples Botanical Mystery. 2001. (Claire Sharples Botanical Mystery Ser.). (Illus.). 240p. pap. 12.95 (1-880284-43-X) Daniel, John & Co., Pubs.

Rovin, Jeff. Fatalis. 2000. 355p. 25.95 (0-312-24103-8); 2001. 368p. reprint ed. mass mkt. 6.99 (0-312-98120-1, St. Martin's Paperbacks) St. Martin's Pr.

Royce, Josiah. The Feud of Oakfield Creek: A Novel of California Life. reprint ed. lib. bdg. 32.50 (0-8398-1770-3) Irvington Pubs.

Rubin, Charles. 4-F Blues: A Novel of WWII Hollywood. 2002. 308p. pap. 14.00 (0-9679790-0-5) NewCentury Pubs.

Rucker, Lance. Intimate Falls: A Brandon Drake Novel. 2001. (Brandon Drake Mysteries). 405p. pap. (0-9688274-0-3) Lochenlode Publishing.

Ruiz, Ronald L. Happy Birthday Jesus. 1994. 320p. 9.95 (1-55885-108-9); 2nd ed. 2003. 216p. pap. 11.95 (1-55885-398-7) Arte Publico Pr.

Russell, Alan. The Fat Innkeeper. 1995. 352p. 19.95 (0-89296-539-8) Mysterious Pr.

—The Fat Innkeeper. 1996. 304p. mass mkt. 5.99 (0-446-40349-0, Mysterious Pr. Paperback Bks.) Warner Bks., Inc.

—The Forest Prime Evil. 1992. 192p. 18.95 o.s.i (0-8027-3204-6) Walker & Co.

—The Hotel Detective. 1994. 352p. 18.95 o.s.i (0-89296-538-X) Mysterious Pr.

—The Hotel Detective. 1995. 304p. mass mkt. 5.50 (0-446-40348-2) Warner Bks., Inc.

—Multiple Wounds. 1996. 288p. 21.50 o.p. (0-684-81526-5, Simon & Schuster) Simon & Schuster.

Russell, Jay. Greed & Stuff. 2001. 264p. 23.95 (0-312-26168-3, Saint Martin's Minotaur) St. Martin's Pr.

Russell, Jay S. Burning Bright. 1998. 288p. 23.95 o.p. (0-312-18545-6) St. Martin's Pr.

—Celestial Dogs. 1997. 272p. 22.95 o.p. (0-312-15076-8, Saint Martin's Minotaur) St. Martin's Pr.

Russell, Kirk. Shell Games: A John Marquez Crime Novel. pap. 12.95 o.s.i (0-8118-4111-1); 2003. 352p. 23.95 (0-8118-4186-3) Chronicle Bks. LLC.

Rust, Megan Mallory. Coffin Corner. 2000. (Alaskan Mystery Ser.). 224p. mass mkt. 5.99 o.s.i (0-425-17508-1) Berkley Publishing Group.

Ryan, Pam Muñoz. Riding Freedom. 1998. (Illus.). 144p. (J). (gr. 3-7). pap. 15.95 (0-590-95766-X) Scholastic, Inc.

Ryman, Geoff. Was. 1993. 384p. pap. 13.95 (0-14-017872-4, Penguin Bks.) Penguin Group (USA) Inc.

—Was. 1994. 4.99 o.p. (0-517-11656-1) Random Hse. Value Publishing.

Saban, Cheryl. The Sins of the Mother. 1997. 256p. 19.95 o.p. (0-7871-1268-2) NewStar Media, Inc.

—Sins of the Mother. abr. ed. 1997. 18.00 o.p. (0-7871-1398-0) NewStar Media, Inc.

Sadownick, Douglas. Sacred Lips of the Bronx. 1995. pap. 9.95 o.p. (0-312-13165-8, Saint Martin's Griffin); 1994. 240p. 21.95 o.p. (0-312-11052-9) St. Martin's Pr.

Sahgal, Ajay. Pool: A Novel. 224p. 1995. pap. 10.00 (0-8021-3343-6, Grove Pr.); 1994. 20.00 o.p. (0-87113-559-0, Atlantic Monthly Pr.) Grove/Atlantic, Inc.

Sala, Sharon. Gentle Persuasion. 2000. 256p. mass mkt. (0-373-48418-6, 1-48418-7, Harlequin Bks.) Harlequin Enterprises, Ltd.

Salzman, Mark. Lying Awake: A Novel. 2000. (Illus.). 192p. 22.00 (0-375-40632-8) Knopf, Alfred A. Inc.

—Lying Awake: A Novel. l.t. ed. 2001. (G. K. Hall Inspirational Ser.). 183p. 27.95 (0-7838-9395-7) Thorndike Pr.

Sanders, Evelin. A Rainbow High. 1997. (YA). (gr. 9 up). pap. 9.99 (0-88092-345-8) Royal Fireworks Publishing Co.

Sanders, Lawrence. The Dream Lover. 1987. 320p. mass mkt. 7.50 (0-425-09473-1) Berkley Publishing Group.

Sandford, John, pseud. The Night Crew. 1998. 368p. mass mkt. 7.99 (0-425-16338-5) Berkley Publishing Group.

—The Night Crew. l.t. ed. 1997. 25.95 o.p. (1-56895-497-2, Wheeler Publishing, Inc.) Gale Group.

—The Night Crew. 1997. 368p. 23.95 o.s.i (0-399-14237-1, G. P. Putnam's Sons) Penguin Group (USA) Inc.

—The Night Crew. 23.95 o.s.i (0-399-14552-4) Putnam Publishing Group, The.

Sandifer, Linda. The Daughters of Luke McCall. 2000. (First Edition Romance Ser.). 228p. 25.95 (0-7862-2583-1, Five Star) Gale Group.

Santora, The Good Daughter. 2002. 320p. per. 14.95 (0-9712357-0-8) Xipactli Publishing.

Saul, John. The Homing. 1995. 448p. mass mkt. 7.99 (0-449-22379-5, Fawcett) Ballantine Bks.

Sawyer, Corinne Holt. The Geezer Factory Murders. 1997. 263p. mass mkt. 5.99 o.s.i (0-449-22532-1, Fawcett) Ballantine Bks.

—The Geezer Factory Murders. 1996. (Benbow/Wingate Mystery Ser.). 240p. 21.95 o.s.i (1-55611-497-4, Dutton) Fine, Donald I. Bks.

—Ho-Ho Homicide. 1996. mass mkt. 5.99 o.s.i (0-449-22409-0, Fawcett) Ballantine Bks.

—Ho-Ho Homicide. 1995. (Benbow/Wingate Mystery Ser.). 256p. 20.95 o.s.i (1-55611-459-1) Fine, Donald I. Bks.

—The J. Alfred Prufrock Murders. 1989. 256p. mass mkt. 4.99 o.s.i (0-449-21743-4, Fawcett) Ballantine Bks.

—The J. Alfred Prufrock Murders. 1988. (Benbow/Wingate Mystery Ser.). 17.95 o.s.i (1-55611-081-2) Fine, Donald I. Bks.

—Murder by Owl Light. 1994. mass mkt. 4.99 o.s.i (0-449-22171-7) Ballantine Bks.

—Murder by Owl Light. 1992. (Benbow/Wingate Mystery Ser.). 240p. 19.00 o.p. (1-55611-332-3) Fine, Donald I. Bks.

—Murder Has No Calories. 1995. mass mkt. 5.99 o.s.i (0-449-22338-8, Fawcett) Ballantine Bks.

—Murder Has No Calories. 1994. (Benbow/Wingate Mystery Ser.). 224p. 19.95 o.p. (1-55611-412-5) Fine, Donald I. Bks.

—Murder in Gray & White. 1989. (Benbow/Wingate Mystery Ser.). 17.95 o.p. (*1-55611-153-3*) Fine, Donald I. Bks.
—Murder Ole! 1998. 260p. mass mkt. 5.99 o.s.i (*0-449-00034-6*, Fawcett) Ballantine Bks.
—Murder Ole! 1997. (Benbow/Wingate Mystery Ser.). 272p. 22.95 (*1-55611-514-8*) Fine, Donald I. Bks.
—The Peanut Butter Murders. 1994. mass mkt. 4.99 o.s.i (*0-449-22172-5*) Ballantine Bks.
—The Peanut Butter Murders. 1993. (Benbow/Wingate Mystery Ser.). 233p. 18.95 o.p. (*1-55611-350-1*) Fine, Donald I. Bks.
Sawyer, Meryl. A Kiss in the Dark. l.t. ed. 1995. 605p. 23.95 o.p. (*0-7838-1371-6*, Macmillan Reference USA) Gale Group.
—Trust No One. 2000. 416p. mass mkt. 6.99 (*0-8217-6676-7*, Zebra Bks.) Kensington Publishing Corp.
Sawyer, Robert J. Illegal Alien. 1997. 304p. 21.95 o.s.i (*0-441-00476-8*); 1999. 320p. reprint ed. mass mkt. 5.99 o.s.i (*0-441-00592-6*) Ace Bks.
Saxton, Alexander. Bright Web in the Darkness. 1997. (California Fiction Ser.). 312p. pap. text 15.95 (*0-520-20931-1*) Univ. of California Pr.
Schalesky, Marlo M. Only the Wind Remembers. 2003. 12.99 (*0-8024-3324-3*) Moody Pr.
Schermerhorn, James. Night of the Cat. 1993. 224p. 18.95 o.p. (*0-312-09887-1*, Saint Martin's Minotaur) St. Martin's Pr.
Schiller, Gerald A. Death Underground. unabr. ed. 1999. 220p. pap. 9.95 (*1-881164-84-5*) Intercontinental Publishing, Inc.
Schlossstein, Steven. Yakuza: The Japanese Godfather. 1990. 320p. 19.95 (*0-9627060-1-9*) Stratford Bks.
Schmidt, Carol. Cabin Fever. 1995. (Laney Samms Mysteries Ser.). 224p. pap. 10.95 (*1-56280-098-1*) Naiad Pr., Inc.
—Silverlake Heat. 1993. 224p. pap. 9.95 o.p. (*1-56280-031-0*) Naiad Pr., Inc.
—Sweet Cherry Wine. 1994. (Laney Samms Mysteries Ser.). 272p. pap. 9.95 (*1-56280-063-9*) Naiad Pr., Inc.
Schopen, Bernard. The Iris Deception. 1996. (Western Literature Ser.). 296p. pap. 18.00 (*0-87417-286-1*) Univ. of Nevada Pr.
Schow, David J., ed. Bullets of Rain: A Novel of Suspense. 2003. 304p. pap. 13.95 (*0-06-053667-5*, Dark Alley) HarperTrade.
Schulberg, Budd. The Disenchanted. 1975. 416p. pap. 3.95 o.p. (*0-670-00584-3*, Penguin Bks.) Viking Penguin.
—What Makes Sammy Run? 1979. reprint ed. lib. bdg. 16.00 (*0-8376-0435-4*) Bentley Pubs.
—What Makes Sammy Run? 1994. reprint ed. lib. bdg. 32.95 (*1-56849-333-9*) Buccaneer Bks., Inc.
—What Makes Sammy Run? 1993. 352p. pap. 14.00 (*0-679-73422-8*, Vintage) Knopf Publishing Group.
—What Makes Sammy Run? 1990. 19.95 o.s.i (*0-394-57618-7*) Random Hse., Inc.
—What Makes Sammy Run? 1978. pap. 3.95 o.p. (*0-14-004795-6*, Penguin Bks.) Viking Penguin.
Schulte, Elaine L. Eternal Passage. 1989. (California Pioneer Ser.). 288p. (J). pap. 7.99 (*1-55513-988-4*, 39883) Cook Communications Ministries.
—Mercies So Tender. 1995. 312p. pap. 8.99 o.p. (*0-7814-0158-5*) Cook Communications Ministries.
—Peace Like a River. 1993. (California Pioneer Ser.). 288p. pap. 8.99 o.p. (*0-7814-0358-8*) Cook Communications Ministries.
—With Wings As Eagles. 1990. (California Pioneer Ser.). 275p. (J). pap. 8.99 o.p. (*1-55513-989-2*, 39891) Cook Communications Ministries.
Schulze, Dallas. Loving Jessie. 2002. 384p. mass mkt. (*1-55166-791-6*, 1-66791-4, Mira Bks.) Harlequin Enterprises, Ltd.
—Substitute Wife. 2003. 384p. mass mkt. (*1-55166-677-4*, Mira Bks.) Harlequin Enterprises, Ltd.
Scott, Robin. Death by Degrees. 1995. 224p. 20.95 o.p. (*0-312-13462-2*, Saint Martin's Minotaur) St. Martin's Pr.
Scoville, Shelagh. Ulu's Dog: And Other Stories. 2003. 320p. pap. 14.95 (*1-56474-415-9*) Fithian Pr.
Scoville, Thomas. Silicon Follies: A Dot.Comedy. 2002. 336p. pap. 13.00 (*0-7434-1121-8*, Washington Square Pr.); 2001. 336p. 23.95 o.s.i (*0-7434-1120-X*, Atria); 2001. reprint ed. E-Book 22.95 (*0-7434-1945-6*, Atria) Simon & Schuster.
See, Carolyn. Golden Days. 1987. mass mkt. 3.95 o.s.i (*0-449-21437-0*, Fawcett) Ballantine Bks.
—Golden Days. 1987. 208p. text 15.95 o.p. (*0-07-056120-6*) McGraw-Hill Cos., The.
—Golden Days. 1996. (California Fiction Ser.). 196p. (C). pap. 15.95 (*0-520-20673-8*) Univ. of California Pr.
—Golden Days. 1996. E-Book 29.95 (*0-585-28774-0*) netLibrary, Inc.
—The Handyman. 2000. 272p. pap. 13.95 (*0-345-42660-6*, Ballantine Bks.) Ballantine Bks.
—The Handyman. unabr. ed. 1999. audio 24.95 (*1-57511-059-8*) Publishing Mills, Inc., The.
—The Handyman. l.t. ed. 1999. (Basic Ser.). 345p. 27.95 (*0-7862-2078-3*) Thorndike Pr.
—The Handyman: A Novel. 1999. 240p. 22.95 o.s.i (*0-375-50155-X*) Random Hse., Inc.
Seelig, Tina L. Games for Your Brain: Bug Cards. 2003. (Illus.). 224p. (J). 9.95 (*0-8118-3474-3*) Chronicle Bks. LLC.
—Games for Your Brain: Dinosaur Cards. 2003. (Illus.). 61p. (YA). 9.95 (*0-8118-3498-0*) Chronicle Bks. LLC.
Seranella, Barbara. No Human Involved. 1998. 304p. mass mkt. 6.99 o.s.i (*0-06-101361-7*, HarperTorch) Morrow/Avon.
—No Human Involved. 1997. 256p. 22.95 o.p. (*0-312-15614-6*, Saint Martin's Minotaur) St. Martin's Pr.
—No Man Standing. 2002. (Wheeler Hardcover Ser.). 28.95 (*1-58724-304-0*, Wheeler Publishing, Inc.) Gale Group.
—No Man Standing. 2003. (Illus.). 368p. pap. 6.99 (*0-7434-2033-0*, Pocket) Simon & Schuster.
—No Offense Intended. 1998. 272p. 24.00 o.p. (*0-06-019212-7*) HarperCollins Pubs.
—No Offense Intended. 1999. 336p. mass mkt. 6.99 o.s.i (*0-06-109724-1*, HarperTorch) Morrow/Avon.
—Unfinished Business: A Munch Mancini Crime Novel. 2001. 272p. 24.00 (*0-7432-1266-5*, Scribner) Simon & Schuster.
—Unwanted Company. 2000. 304p. 24.00 o.s.i (*0-06-019213-5*) HarperCollins Pubs.
Serros, Michele M. How to Be a Chicana Role Model: A Novel. 2000. 240p. pap. 12.95 (*1-57322-824-9*, Riverhead Trade (Paperbacks)) Berkley Publishing Group.
Sethi, Robbie Clipper. Fifty-Fifty: A Novel in Many Voices. 2003. (Illus.). 217p. 24.95 (*0-929306-24-4*) Silicon Pr.
Shafquat, Sofia. The Shadow Man. 1993. 269p. 28.00 (*1-877946-25-7*) Permanent Pr., The.
Shagan, Steve. A Cast of Thousands. l.t. ed. 1993. 22.95 o.p. (*1-56895-021-7*, Wheeler Publishing, Inc.) Gale Group.
—A Cast of Thousands. Grose, Bill, ed. 1993. 368p. 22.00 (*0-671-74132-2*, Atria); 1994. 384p. reprint ed. mass mkt. 5.99 (*0-671-74133-0*, Pocket) Simon & Schuster.
Shah, Diane K. Dying Cheek to Cheek. 1992. 464p. 18.50 o.s.i (*0-385-42250-4*) Doubleday Publishing.
—High Heel Blue. 1997. 318p. 22.50 (*0-684-81431-5*, Simon & Schuster) Simon & Schuster.
Shalet, Diane. Grief in a Sunny Climate. 1994. 288p. 20.95 o.p. (*0-312-11054-5*) St. Martin's Pr.
Shallit, Barney. Song of Anger: Tales of Tule Lake. 2001. (Michi Nishiura & Walter Weglyn Multicultural Publication Ser.). (Illus.). xvii, 121p. pap. (*0-930046-15-3*) California State Univ. Fullerton, Ctr. for Oral & Public History.
Shannon, Dell. The Ace of Spades. l.t. ed. 1992. 18.95 o.p. (*0-7451-8385-9*); pap. 16.95 o.p. (*0-7927-1151-3*) BBC Audiobooks America.
—The Ace of Spades. 1984. reprint ed. pap. 3.95 o.p. (*0-89296-078-7*) Mysterious Pr.
—Appearances of Death. 1980. 208p. pap. 1.95 o.p. (*0-553-13953-3*) Bantam Bks.
—Appearances of Death. l.t. ed. 1981. 319p. reprint ed. 12.95 o.p. (*0-89621-319-6*) Thorndike Pr.
—Blood Count. 1988. 224p. mass mkt. (*0-373-26006-7*, Harlequin Bks.) Harlequin Enterprises, Ltd.
—Blood Count. 1989. 2.99 o.p. (*0-517-69441-7*) Random Hse. Value Publishing.
—Blood Count: The 37th Volume of a Detective Series. 1986. 224p. 15.95 o.p. (*0-688-06394-2*, Morrow, William & Co.) Morrow/Avon.
—Case Pending. l.t. ed. 1991. pap. 14.95 o.p. (*0-7927-0173-9*, C0214); 1990. 16.95 o.p. (*0-7451-9742-6*, C0066) BBC Audiobooks America.
—Case Pending. 1984. reprint ed. pap. 3.95 o.p. (*0-89296-076-0*) Mysterious Pr.
—Chaos of Crime. l.t. ed. 1988. lib. bdg. 14.95 o.p. (*1-85057-443-X*, Macmillan Reference USA) Gale Group.
—Chaos of Crime. 1988. 224p. reprint ed. pap. (*0-373-26015-6*, Harlequin Bks.) Harlequin Enterprises, Ltd.
—Chaos of Crime. 1985. 256p. 14.95 o.p. (*0-688-02297-9*, Morrow, William & Co.) Morrow/Avon.
—Cold Trail. 1989. 224p. reprint ed. mass mkt. (*0-373-26027-X*, Harlequin Bks.) Harlequin Enterprises, Ltd.
—The Death Bringers. l.t. ed. 1993. 21.95 o.p. (*0-7927-1513-6*) BBC Audiobooks America.
—The Death-Bringers. l.t. ed. 1993. pap. 19.95 o.p. (*0-7927-1512-8*); 1996. audio 54.95 (*0-7927-2205-1*, CSL094, Chivers Sound Library) BBC Audiobooks America.
—Death by Inches. l.t. ed. 1992. 18.95 o.p. (*0-7451-8425-1*); pap. 16.95 o.p. (*0-7927-1343-5*) BBC Audiobooks America.
—Death of a Busybody. l.t. ed. 1991. 17.95 o.p. (*0-7451-8024-8*, AH083); pap. 15.95 o.p. (*0-7927-0500-9*, AS0119) BBC Audiobooks America.
—Death of a Busybody. 1985. (Lt. Luis Mendoza Mystery Ser.). pap. 3.95 o.s.i (*0-89296-149-X*) Mysterious Pr.
—Destiny of Death. 1984. 227p. 14.95 o.p. (*0-688-03109-9*, Morrow, William & Co.) Morrow/Avon.
—Destiny of Death: A Luis Mendoza Mystery. 1991. 224p. reprint ed. mass mkt. (*0-373-26073-3*, Harlequin Bks.) Harlequin Enterprises, Ltd.
—The Dispossessed. 1988. 352p. 18.95 o.p. (*0-688-07998-9*, Morrow, William & Co.) Morrow/Avon.
—Double Bluff. l.t. ed. 1991. 17.95 o.p. (*0-7451-8173-2*, AH0227); pap. 15.95 o.p. (*0-7927-0708-7*, AS0263) BBC Audiobooks America.
—Double Bluff. 1985. (Lt. Luis Mendoza Mystery Ser.). pap. 3.95 o.p. (*0-89296-150-3*) Mysterious Pr.
—Exploit of Death. 1990. mass mkt. (*0-373-26061-X*, Harlequin Bks.) Harlequin Enterprises, Ltd.
—Exploit of Death. l.t. ed. 1983. (Luis Mendoza Mystery Ser.). 349p. reprint ed. 12.95 o.p. (*0-89621-493-1*) Thorndike Pr.
—Extra Kill. 1984. 256p. reprint ed. pap. 3.95 o.p. (*0-89296-080-9*) Mysterious Pr.
—Felony at Random. 1980. 224p. pap. 1.95 o.p. (*0-553-13954-1*) Bantam Bks.
—Felony at Random. l.t. ed. 1981. (Ulverscroft Large Print Ser.). 355p. 29.99 o.p. (*0-7089-0660-5*, Ulverscroft) Thorpe, F. A. Pubs. GBR. *Dist:* Ulverscroft Large Print Bks., Ltd., Ulverscroft Large Print Canada, Ltd.
—Felony File. l.t. ed. 1981. 374p. reprint ed. 10.95 o.p. (*0-89621-281-5*) Thorndike Pr.
—Knave of Hearts. 1984. reprint ed. pap. 3.95 o.p. (*0-89296-082-5*) Mysterious Pr.
—The Manson Curse. l.t. ed. 1992. 18.95 o.p. (*0-7451-8253-4*, AH0264); pap. 16.95 o.p. (*0-7927-0814-8*, AS0300) BBC Audiobooks America.
—The Manson Curse. 1990. 288p. 17.95 o.p. (*0-688-10119-4*, Morrow, William & Co.) Morrow/Avon.
—Mark of Murder. 1994. 256p. mass mkt. 4.50 o.p. (*0-7867-0043-2*, Carroll & Graf Pubs.) Avalon Publishing Group.
—Mark of Murder. l.t. ed. 1991. 12.95 o.p. (*0-7927-0147-X*, 4662); pap. 17.95 o.p. (*0-7927-0148-8*, C0079) BBC Audiobooks America.
—Mark of Murder: A Lieutenant Luis Mendoza Mystery. 1986. 240p. mass mkt. 3.95 (*0-445-40262-8*, Mysterious Pr. Paperback Bks.) Warner Bks., Inc.
—Motive on Record. 1990. mass mkt. (*0-373-26049-0*, Harlequin Bks.) Harlequin Enterprises, Ltd.
—The Motive on Record. l.t. ed. 1982. 364p. reprint ed. 12.95 o.p. (*0-89621-394-3*) Thorndike Pr.
—Murder by the Tale. 1987. 224p. 16.95 o.p. (*0-688-07538-X*, Morrow, William & Co.) Morrow/Avon.
—Murder by the Tale. 1989. 2.99 o.p. (*0-517-69454-9*) Random Hse. Value Publishing.
—Murder Most Strange. 1989. mass mkt. (*0-373-26037-7*, Harlequin Bks.) Harlequin Enterprises, Ltd.
—Murder Most Strange. l.t. ed. 1982. 354p. 12.95 o.p. (*0-89621-377-3*) Thorndike Pr.
—Root of All Evil. 1993. 208p. mass mkt. 3.95 o.p. (*0-88184-978-2*, Carroll & Graf Pubs.) Avalon Publishing Group.
—Root of All Evil. l.t. ed. 1993. 21.95 o.p. (*0-7927-1771-6*); pap. 19.95 o.p. (*0-7927-1770-8*) BBC Audiobooks America.
—Root of All Evil. 1986. 288p. reprint ed. mass mkt. 3.95 (*0-445-40259-8*, Mysterious Pr. Paperback Bks.) Warner Bks., Inc.
—The Scalpel & the Sword. 1987. 416p. 18.95 o.p. (*0-688-07216-X*, Morrow, William & Co.) Morrow/Avon.
—Sorrow to the Grave. 1992. 18.00 o.p. (*0-688-11577-2*, Morrow, William & Co.) Morrow/Avon.
—Streets of Death. 1980. 192p. pap. 1.95 o.p. (*0-553-13952-5*) Bantam Bks.
—Streets of Death. l.t. ed. 1980. 315p. reprint ed. 9.95 o.p. (*0-89621-250-5*) Thorndike Pr.
Shannon, John. The Concrete River. 1998. (Jack Liffey Mystery Ser.). 240p. reprint ed. mass mkt. 5.99 o.s.i (*0-425-16193-5*, Prime Crime) Berkley Publishing Group.
—The Concrete River. 1996. 192p. pap. 12.00 o.p. (*0-9639050-5-8*, West Coast Crime) Blue Heron Publishing.
—The Cracked Earth. 1999. (Jack Liffey Mystery Ser.). 288p. mass mkt. 5.99 o.s.i (*0-425-16732-1*) Berkley Publishing Group.
—The Poison Sky. 2000. (Jack Liffey Mystery Ser.). 241p. mass mkt. 5.99 o.s.i (*0-425-17424-7*, Prime Crime) Berkley Publishing Group.
Sharpe, Jon. California Quarry. 1994. (Trailsman Ser.: No. 148). 176p. (Orig.). mass mkt. 3.50 o.s.i (*0-451-17883-1*, Signet Bks.) NAL.
Sheen, Anitra. Things Unspoken. 2001. 288p. reprint ed. pap. 12.95 (*0-8118-3157-4*) Chronicle Bks. LLC.
Sheldon, Sidney. Nothing Lasts Forever. 1994. 398p. 23.00 o.p. (*0-688-08491-5*, Morrow, William & Co.) Morrow/Avon.
—A Stranger in the Mirror. 1976. 21.50 o.p. (*0-688-03002-5*, Morrow, William & Co.) Morrow/Avon.
—A Stranger in the Mirror. l.t. ed. 1983. (Charnwood Large Print Ser.). 400p. o.p. (*0-7089-8111-9*, Charnwood) Thorpe, F. A. Pubs. GBR. *Dist:* Ulverscroft Large Print Canada, Ltd.
—A Stranger in the Mirror. 1988. 320p. reprint ed. mass mkt. 7.99 (*0-446-35657-3*) Warner Bks., Inc.
Shepard, Fern. An Old-Fashioned Love. l.t. ed. 1994. 18.95 o.p. (*0-7927-2121-7*); pap. 17.95 o.p. (*0-7927-2120-9*) BBC Audiobooks America.
Sherwood, Frances. Green. 1995. 419p. 23.00 o.p. (*0-374-16673-0*) Farrar, Straus & Giroux.
Shigekuni, Julie. A Bridge Between Us. 1995. 253p. 18.95 o.s.i (*0-385-47678-7*) Doubleday Publishing.
Shirley, John. Wetbones. 1999. 352p. mass mkt. 5.50 (*0-8439-4525-7*, Leisure Bks.) Dorchester Publishing Co., Inc.
—Wetbones. 1992. 25.00 o.p. (*0-929480-63-5*); 65.00 o.p. (*0-929480-64-3*) Ziesing, Mark V.
—Wetbones. 1999. E-Book 9.95 (*0-585-29892-0*) netLibrary, Inc.
Shoemaker, Bill. Fire Horse. 1996. mass mkt. 5.99 o.s.i (*0-449-14974-9*, Fawcett) Ballantine Bks.
—Fire Horse. l.t. ed. 1995. (Niagara Large Print Ser.). 415p. 29.50 o.p. (*0-7089-5802-8*, Ulverscroft) Thorpe, F. A. Pubs. GBR. *Dist:* Ulverscroft Large Print Bks., Ltd.
Shuken, Julia. In the House of My Pilgrimage. 1995. 256p. pap. 10.99 (*0-89107-839-8*) Crossway Bks.
Siegel, Barry. Actual Innocence. 2001. 320p. mass mkt. 6.99 (*0-345-41310-5*, Ballantine Bks.) Ballantine Bks.
—The Perfect Witness. 1999. 339p. mass mkt. 6.99 (*0-345-43084-0*) Ballantine Bks.
—The Perfect Witness. abr. ed. 1998. audio 25.00 (*0-7871-1693-9*, Dove Audio) NewStar Media, Inc.
—The Perfect Witness, unabr. ed. 1998. audio 78.00 (*0-7887-1976-9*, 95363E7) Recorded Bks., LLC.
Siegel, Lee. Love & Other Games of Chance. 2004. 432p. pap. 14.00 (*0-14-200391-3*) Penguin Group (USA) Inc.
Simon, Roger L. The Big Fix. 1924. o.s.i (*1-55710-050-0*, Morrow, William & Co.) Morrow/Avon.
—The Big Fix. 1978. pap. 1.95 o.p. (*0-671-82010-9*, Pocket) Simon & Schuster.
—The Big Fix. 1986. 208p. mass mkt. 3.50 o.s.i (*0-446-30043-8*) Warner Bks., Inc.
—The Big Fix. 2000. (Moses Wine Mystery Ser.). (Illus.). 192p. reprint ed. pap. 14.00 (*0-671-03906-7*) ibooks, Inc.
—California Roll. 1986. 208p. mass mkt. 3.50 o.s.i (*0-446-32965-7*) Warner Bks., Inc.
—The Lost Coast. 1997. 79p. 22.50 o.p. (*0-06-017707-1*) HarperTrade.
—The Lost Coast. 272p. 2003. mass mkt. 6.99 (*0-7434-5913-X*); 2000. reprint ed. pap. 14.00 (*0-671-03904-0*) ibooks, Inc.
—The Straight Man. 1987. 240p. mass mkt. 3.95 (*0-446-34389-7*) Warner Bks., Inc.
—Wild Turkey: A Moses Wine Mystery. 1986. 240p. mass mkt. 3.50 o.s.i (*0-446-30044-6*) Warner Bks., Inc.
—Wild Turkey: A Moses Wine Mystery. 2000. (Moses Wine Mysteries Ser.). 208p. pap. 14.00 (*0-7434-0012-7*) ibooks, Inc.
Simpson, Lawrence R. Brother Sam: A Novel of Early California. 1988. 277p. (Orig.). pap. 10.95 o.p. (*0-936784-50-4*) Daniel, John & Co., Pubs.
Simpson, Mona. Anywhere but Here. 1987. audio 13.95 (*1-55644-195-9*, 7071) American Audio Prose Library, Inc.
—Anywhere but Here. l.t. ed. 1999. 660p. 25.95 (*1-57490-214-8*, Beeler Large Print Bks.) Beeler, Thomas T. Publisher.
—Anywhere but Here. 1999. pap. 14.00 (*0-676-58970-7*); 1992. 544p. pap. 14.00 (*0-679-73738-3*); 1987. 416p. pap. 9.95 o.p. (*0-394-75559-6*) Knopf Publishing Group. (Vintage).
—Anywhere but Here. 1986. 18.95 o.s.i (*0-394-55283-0*) Knopf, Alfred A. Inc.
—A Regular Guy. 1997. pap. 13.00 (*0-679-77271-5*); 1996. 372p. 25.00 o.s.i (*0-679-45091-2*) McKay, David Co., Inc.
Sinclair, April. Ain't Gonna Be the Same Fool Twice: A Novel. 1996. 336p. (J). 19.95 (*0-7868-6069-3*) Hyperion Pr.
Sinclair, Upton. Oil! 1981. reprint ed. lib. bdg. 32.00 (*0-8376-0444-3*) Bentley Pubs.
—Oil! 1997. 528p. pap. 18.95 (*0-520-20727-0*) Univ. of California Pr.
Singer, Rochelle. Samson's Deal. 1983. 192p. 11.95 o.p. (*0-312-69849-6*) St. Martin's Pr.
Singer, Shelley. Free Draw: A Jake Samson Mystery. 1984. 192p. 12.95 o.p. (*0-312-30366-1*) St. Martin's Pr.
—Full House. 1988. (Jake Samson/Rosie Vicente Series). 224p. reprint ed. mass mkt. (*0-373-26007-5*, Harlequin Bks.) Harlequin Enterprises, Ltd.
—Full House: A Jake Samson Mystery. 1986. 208p. 13.95 o.p. (*0-312-30973-2*, 39-1127) St. Martin's Pr.

—Royal Flush: A Jake Samson & Rosie Vicente Mystery. 1999. 237p. pap. 12.95 (*1-880284-33-2*) Daniel, John & Co., Pubs.

—Spit in the Ocean. 1989. (Jake Samson/Rosie Vicente Series). 224p. reprint ed. mass mkt. (*0-373-26026-1*, Harlequin Bks.) Harlequin Enterprises, Ltd.

—Spit in the Ocean: A Jake Samson Mystery. 1987. 208p. 14.95 o.p. (*0-312-00685-3*, Saint Martin's Minotaur) St. Martin's Pr.

—Suicide King. 1989. per. (*0-373-26040-7*, Harlequin Bks.) Harlequin Enterprises, Ltd.

—Suicide King. 1988. 224p. 15.95 o.p. (*0-312-02293-X*, Saint Martin's Minotaur) St. Martin's Pr.

Sisters in Crime, Los Angeles Chapter Staff. Murder by Thirteen. English, Priscilla et al, eds. 1997. 176p. pap. 10.95 (*0-9647945-3-5*, Intrigue Pr.) Corvus Publishing.

Skye, Christina. Hot Pursuit. 2003. 448p. mass mkt. 6.99 (*0-440-23759-9*) Dell Publishing.

Slim, Iceberg. Doom Fox. 1998. 256p. pap. 12.00 (*0-8021-3588-9*, Grove Pr.) Grove/Atlantic, Inc.

—Doom Fox. viii, 260p. pap. 11.95 (*0-86241-762-7*) Payback Pr. GBR. *Dist:* AK Pr. Distribution.

Smart, Ariel. The Green Lantern: And Other Stories. 1999. 112p. (Orig.). pap. 10.00 (*1-56474-271-7*) Fithian Pr.

—Stolen Moments: And Other Stories. 2003. 160p. pap. 12.95 (*1-56474-422-1*) Fithian Pr.

Smith, April. Good Morning, Killer. 2003. 368p. 24.00 (*0-375-41240-9*) Knopf, Alfred A. Inc.

—North of Montana. 1995. 368p. mass mkt. 6.99 (*0-449-22502-X*, Fawcett) Ballantine Bks.

—North of Montana. l.t. ed. 1995. (Large Print Ser.). 352p. lib. bdg. 23.95 (*1-57490-035-8*, Beeler Large Print Bks.) Beeler, Thomas T. Publisher.

—North of Montana. abr. ed. 1994. audio 17.00 o.s.i (*0-679-43652-9*, RH Audio) Random Hse. Audio Publishing Group.

Smith, Charlie. Chimney Rock: A Novel. 1997. 352p. pap. 14.00 o.p. (*0-8050-5592-4*, Owl Bks.); 1993. 400p. 22.50 o.p. (*0-8050-2244-9*) Holt, Henry & Co.

Smith, Jerry. Deadman's Throttle. 1998. (Jason Street Mysteries Ser.). 191p. pap. 12.95 (*1-884313-13-2*, DT) Whitehorse Pr.

Smith, Julie. Dead in the Water. (Orig.). 1993. pap. 4.99 o.p. (*0-8041-9804-7*); 1991. mass mkt. 4.99 o.s.i (*0-8041-0855-2*) Ballantine Bks. (Ivy Bks.).

—Death Turns a Trick. 1993. pap. 3.99 o.p. (*0-8041-9805-5*); 1992. reprint ed. mass mkt. 5.99 o.s.i (*0-8041-0856-0*) Ballantine Bks. (Ivy Bks.).

—Huckleberry Fiend. 1987. (Paul McDonald Mystery Ser.). 224p. 15.95 (*0-89296-237-2*) Mysterious Pr.

—Huckleberry Fiend. 1988. 224p. mass mkt. 5.50 (*0-445-40696-8*, Mysterious Pr. Paperback Bks.) Warner Bks., Inc.

—Other People's Skeletons. 1995. 240p. pap. 15.00 (*0-345-47164-4*); 1994. pap. 4.99 o.p. (*0-8041-9820-9*, Ivy Bks.); 1993. mass mkt. 5.99 o.s.i (*0-8041-1086-7*, Ivy Bks.) Ballantine Bks.

—Other People's Skeletons. 1999. (Mystery Ser.). 232p. 20.95 (*0-7862-1953-X*, Five Star) Gale Group.

—The Sourdough Wars. 1993. pap. 4.99 o.p. (*0-8041-9807-1*); 1992. mass mkt. 5.99 o.s.i (*0-8041-0929-X*) Ballantine Bks. (Ivy Bks.).

—Tourist Trap. 1993. pap. 4.99 o.p. (*0-8041-9806-3*); 1992. mass mkt. 5.99 o.s.i (*0-8041-0930-3*) Ballantine Bks. (Ivy Bks.).

—Tourist Trap. 1986. 240p. 15.45 o.p. (*0-89296-162-7*) Mysterious Pr.

—Tourist Trap. 1987. 240p. mass mkt. 3.95 o.s.i (*0-445-40640-2*, Mysterious Pr. Paperback Bks.) Warner Bks., Inc.

—True-Life Adventure. 1986. 15.45 o.p. (*0-89296-120-1*) Mysterious Pr.

—True-Life Adventure. 1986. 256p. reprint ed. mass mkt. 4.99 o.s.i (*0-445-40505-8*, Mysterious Pr. Paperback Bks.) Warner Bks., Inc.

Smith, Lawrence R. Annie's Soup Kitchen: A Novel. 2003. (Literature of the American West Ser.: Vol. 13). 236p. 24.95 (*0-8061-3529-8*) Univ. of Oklahoma Pr.

Smith, Lisa. The Hunter. MacDonald, Patricia, ed. 1994. (Forbidden Game Ser.: Vol. 1). 240p. (Orig.). (YA). (gr. 7 up). mass mkt. 3.99 (*0-671-87451-9*, Simon Pulse) Simon & Schuster Children's Publishing.

Smith, Taylor. Random Acts. abr. ed. 1998. audio 7.99 (*1-55204-154-9*) Durkin Hayes Publishing Ltd.

—Random Acts. 1998. (Mira Bks.). 441p. mass mkt. (*1-55166-431-3*, 1-66431-7, Mira Bks.) Harlequin Enterprises, Ltd.

Snow, Marina. The Walking Wounded. 2001. 255p. 19.95 (*1-882897-57-9*) Lost Coast Pr.

Snyder, Keith. Coffin's Got the Dead Guy on the Inside. 1999. mass mkt. 5.99 (*0-440-23536-7*); 320p. mass mkt. 5.99 o.s.i (*0-440-23541-3*) Dell Publishing.

—Coffin's Got the Dead Guy on the Inside. l.t. ed. 1998. (Jason Keltner Mysteries Ser.). 300p. 22.95 (*0-8027-3320-4*) Walker & Co.

—Show Control. 1996. 267p. 20.95 o.p. (*1-885173-11-3*) Write Way Publishing.

—Trouble Comes Back. 1999. (Jason Keltner Mysteries Ser.). 318p. 22.95 (*0-8027-3338-7*) Walker & Co.

Sobel, Steven. Collecting Sins. 1999. (Illus.). 282p. pap. 13.00 (*1-891661-04-3*, 1043, Offbeat Pr.) Santa Monica Pr.

Songer, C. J. Bait. 1999. 384p. mass mkt. 6.99 (*0-06-101424-9*, HarperTorch) Morrow/Avon.

—Bait. 1998. 320p. 23.00 (*0-684-85042-7*, Scribner) Simon & Schuster.

—Hook. 1999. 304p. 24.00 o.s.i (*0-684-85043-5*, Scribner) Simon & Schuster.

Sonnett, Sherry. Restraint. 1996. 320p. mass mkt. 5.99 o.s.i (*0-451-18642-7*, Signet Bks.) NAL.

Sonnett, Sherry. Restraint. 1995. 319p. 21.00 (*0-671-87958-8*, Simon & Schuster) Simon & Schuster.

Sontag, Susan. In America. 2001. E-Book 9.00 o.p. (*0-374-97519-1*); 2001. E-Book 9.00 o.p. (*0-374-97517-5*); 2000. E-Book 9.00 (*0-374-70020-6*); 2000. E-Book 9.00 (*0-374-97515-9*); 2000. (Illus.). 387p. 26.00 o.p. (*0-374-17540-3*); 1998. (*0-374-94114-9*) Farrar, Straus & Giroux.

—In America. l.t. ed. 2000. 540p. 28.95 (*1-56895-898-6*, Wheeler Publishing, Inc.) Gale Group.

—In America. 2001. 400p. pap. 14.00 (*0-312-27320-7*) Picador.

Soto, Gary. Amnesia in a Republican County: A Novel. 2003. 208p. 23.95 (*0-8263-2931-4*) Univ. of New Mexico Pr.

—Chato y Su Cena. Ada, Alma Flor, tr. unabr. ed. 1998. (SPA., Illus.). (J). (gr. k-3). pap. 15.95 incl. audio (*0-87499-437-3*) Live Oak Media.

—Nickel & Dime. 2000. 189p. 29.95 (*0-8263-2185-2*); pap. 16.95 (*0-8263-2186-0*) Univ. of New Mexico Pr.

Southern, Terry. Blue Movie. 6.95 o.p. (*0-453-00331-1*, Dutton); 1985. pap. 7.95 o.p. (*0-452-25723-9*, Plume) Dutton/Plume.

—Blue Movie. 2001. 256p. reprint ed. pap. 12.00 (*0-8021-3466-1*) Grove/Atlantic, Inc.

—Blue Movie. 1971. mass mkt. 1.50 o.p. (*0-451-06173-X*, W6173); mass mkt. 1.25 o.p. (*0-451-04608-0*) NAL. (Signet Bks.).

Spencer, John B. Quake City. 1997. 158p. pap. 12.95 (*1-899344-02-0*) Dufour Editions, Inc.

Spicer, Jack. The Tower of Babel. 1994. vi, 170p. (Orig.). lib. bdg. 33.95 (*1-883689-05-8*); pap. 12.95 (*1-883689-04-X*) Talisman Hse., Pubs.

Spizer, Joyce. The Cop Was White As Snow. 1998. (Harbour Pointe Mysteries Ser.). 298p. pap. 10.95 (*1-881164-83-7*) Intercontinental Publishing, Inc.

Stadler, Matthew. Landscape: Memory. 1991. (Contemporary Fiction Ser.). (Illus.). 320p. pap. 9.95 o.p. (*0-452-26647-5*, Plume) Dutton/Plume.

—Landscape: Memory. 1990. (Illus.). 416p. 19.95 o.s.i (*0-684-19185-7*, Macmillan Reference USA) Gale Group.

Stansberry, Domenic. Exit Paradise. 1992. 146p. (Orig.). pap. 10.00 (*0-89924-081-X*) Lynx Hse. Pr.

Starhawk. The Fifth Sacred Thing. 1994. 496p. pap. 16.00 (*0-553-37380-3*); 1993. 496p. 21.95 o.s.i (*0-553-09522-6*); 1993. 486p. 22.50 o.s.i (*0-553-08916-1*) Bantam Bks.

Stebel, S. L. The Boss's Wife. 1992. 252p. 19.95 o.p. (*0-8027-1198-7*) Walker & Co.

Steel, Danielle. Accident. 1995. 448p. mass mkt. 7.99 (*0-440-21754-7*); 1994. 312p. 23.95 (*0-385-30602-4*, Delacorte Pr.); 1994. 312p. 200.00 (*0-385-31215-6*, Delacorte Pr.) Dell Publishing.

—Accident. l.t. ed. 2004. 480p. 24.95 (*0-375-43320-1*) Random Hse. Large Print.

—Accident. 1995. 12.09 o.p. (*0-606-07173-3*) Turtleback Bks.

—Heartbeat. l.t. ed. 1991. 608p. 24.95 o.s.i (*0-385-30320-3*, Delacorte Large Type) Bantam Doubleday Dell Large Print Group, Inc.

—Heartbeat. 1992. 416p. mass mkt. 7.50 (*0-440-21189-1*); 1991. 368p. 23.95 o.s.i (*0-385-29908-7*, Delacorte Pr.) Dell Publishing.

—Heartbeat. l.t. ed. 1994. 428p. pap. 20.95 o.p. (*0-8161-5789-8*, Macmillan Reference USA) Gale Group.

—Heartbeat. l.t. ed. 2004. 592p. 24.95 (*0-375-43324-4*) Random Hse. Large Print.

—Heartbeat. 1991. 13.04 (*0-606-05346-8*) Turtleback Bks.

—The House on Hope Street. 2000. 240p. 19.95 (*0-385-33306-4*, Delacorte Pr.) Dell Publishing.

—Irresistible Forces. 2000. 384p. mass mkt. 7.99 (*0-440-22486-1*); 2000. 18.87 (*0-385-33461-3*, Delacorte Pr.); 1999. 384p. 26.95 (*0-385-31960-6*, Delacorte Pr.); 1999. 384p. 200.00 (*0-385-33476-1*, Delacorte Pr.) Dell Publishing.

—Irresistible Forces, Set. abr. ed. 1999. audio 26.95 Highsmith Inc.

—Irresistible Forces. abr. ed. 1999. audio 26.95 (*0-553-47935-0*); audio compact disk 29.95 (*0-553-45574-5*); audio 39.95 (*0-553-50215-8*) Random Hse. Audio Publishing Group. (RH Audio).

—Irresistible Forces. l.t. ed. 528p. 2000. pap. 13.95 (*0-375-70787-5*); 1999. 26.95 (*0-375-40863-0*) Random Hse. Large Print.

—Mixed Blessings. 1993. 432p. mass mkt. 7.50 (*0-440-21411-4*); 1992. 384p. 23.50 (*0-385-29910-9*, Delacorte Pr.) Dell Publishing.

—Mixed Blessings. l.t. ed. 1994. 493p. pap. 20.95 o.p. (*0-8161-5792-8*, Macmillan Reference USA) Gale Group.

—Secrets. 1985. 336p. 19.95 o.s.i (*0-385-29418-2*, Delacorte Pr.) Dell Publishing.

—Secrets. l.t. ed. 1986. (Special Editions Ser.). 18.95 o.p. (*0-8161-4013-8*, Macmillan Reference USA) Gale Group.

—Silent Honor. 1997. 416p. mass mkt. 7.50 (*0-440-22405-5*); 1996. 360p. 24.95 (*0-385-31301-2*, Delacorte Pr.); 1996. 360p. 200.00 (*0-385-31810-3*, Delacorte Pr.) Dell Publishing.

—Silent Honor. l.t. ed. 1996. 360p. 29.95 (*0-385-31712-3*) Doubleday Publishing.

—Silent Honor. abr. ed. 1996. audio 24.95 (*0-553-47761-7*, 694379); audio compact disk 29.95 (*0-553-45550-8*) Random Hse. Audio Publishing Group. (RH Audio).

Stegner, Lynn. Undertow. 367p. 1996. pap. 12.00 (*1-880909-42-1*, Basset Bks.); 1993. 21.00 (*1-880909-02-2*) Baskerville Pubs., Inc.

Stegner, Wallace. All the Little Live Things. 1979. vi, 345p. reprint ed. 25.95 o.p. (*0-8032-4110-0*) Univ. of Nebraska Pr.

—Angle of Repose. 1981. mass mkt. 2.95 o.p. (*0-449-23796-6*); 1985. 512p. reprint ed. mass mkt. 5.95 o.s.i (*0-449-20988-1*) Ballantine Bks. (Fawcett).

—Angle of Repose. unabr. collector's ed. 1996. Pt. 1. audio 72.00 (*0-7366-3281-6*, 3937 A ); Pt. 2. audio 80.00 (*0-7366-3282-4*, 3937-B) Books on Tape, Inc.

—Angle of Repose. 1971. 12.95 o.p. (*0-385-07882-X*) Doubleday Publishing.

—Angle of Repose. 1998. (*0-14-771245-9*); 1997. (*0-14-771219-X*); 1992. 512p. pap. 13.95 (*0-14-016930-X*, Penguin Bks.) Penguin Group (USA) Inc.

—Angle of Repose. 1996. 9.99 o.p. (*0-517-18489-3*) Random Hse. Value Publishing.

—Angle of Repose. 2000. (Modern Library Ser.). 656p. 23.95 o.s.i (*0-679-60338-7*) Random Hse., Inc.

—Angle of Repose. 2000. 21.05 (*0-606-21897-1*) Turtleback Bks.

—Angle of Repose. 2000. (Classics Ser.). 512p. 15.00 (*0-14-118547-3*, Penguin Classics) Viking Penguin.

—A Shooting Star. 1996. 448p. pap. 15.00 (*0-14-025241-X*, Viking) Penguin Group (USA) Inc.

—A Shooting Star. 1991. 24.75 (*0-8446-6919-9*) Smith, Peter Pub., Inc.

—A Shooting Star. 1961. 5.00 o.p. (*0-670-64071-9*) Viking Penguin.

—The Spectator Bird. 1976. 240p. 6.95 o.p. (*0-385-07890-0*) Doubleday Publishing.

—The Spectator Bird. 1977. (Spring Adult Ser.). lib. bdg. 11.50 o.p. (*0-8161-6443-6*, Macmillan Reference USA) Gale Group.

—The Spectator Bird. 1992. 24.25 (*0-8446-6607-6*) Smith, Peter Pub., Inc.

—The Spectator Bird. 1979. 214p. reprint ed. pap. 6.95 o.p. (*0-8032-9107-8*, Bison Bks.) Univ. of Nebraska Pr.

—The Spectator Bird. 1990. (Contemporary American Fiction Ser.). 224p. reprint ed. 14.00 (*0-14-013940-0*) Viking Penguin.

Steinbeck, John. Cannery Row. 1982. mass mkt. 2.50 o.s.i (*0-553-23416-1*); 128p. mass mkt. 2.75 o.s.i (*0-553-26603-9*); 128p. mass mkt. 2.95 o.s.i (*0-553-27823-1*, Bantam Classics) Bantam Bks.

—Cannery Row. l.t. ed. 2001. 196p. 28.95 (*0-7838-9520-8*, Macmillan Reference USA) Gale Group.

—Cannery Row. l.t. ed. 1989. (Mainstream Ser.). 319p. lib. bdg. 15.95 o.p. (*1-85089-109-5*) ISIS Large Print Bks. GBR. *Dist:* Transaction Pubs.

—Cannery Row. (Steinbeck's Centennial Ser.). 2002. 192p. pap. 12.00 (*0-14-200068-X*); 1963. pap. 1.95 o.p. (*0-670-00131-7*) Penguin Group (USA) Inc.

—Cannery Row. 1992. 12.00 (*0-606-08948-9*) Turtleback Bks.

—Cannery Row. (Great Books of the 20th Century Ser.). 1994. 224p. 11.00 (*0-14-018737-5*, Penguin Classics); 1993. 208p. 8.00 (*0-14-017738-8*); 1945. 20p. 18.95 o.p. (*0-670-20281-9*, Penguin Classics); 1999. 16.95 incl. audio (*0-14-086199-8*, Penguin AudioBooks) Viking Penguin.

—East of Eden. 1976. 704p. pap. 2.75 o.p. (*0-553-12909-0*) Bantam Bks.

—East of Eden. 2004. (*1-58724-562-0*, Wheeler Publishing, Inc.) Gale Group.

—East of Eden. (Steinbeck's Centennial Ser.). 2002. 608p. pap. 16.00 (*0-14-200065-5*); 1981. pap. 4.95 o.p. (*0-14-005829-X*); 1970. pap. 3.95 o.p. (*0-670-00278-X*) Penguin Group (USA) Inc.

—East of Eden. abr. l.t. ed. 1976. 12.00 o.p. (*0-85456-562-0*, Ulverscroft) Thorpe, F. A. Pubs. GBR. *Dist:* Ulverscroft Large Print Bks., Ltd.

—East of Eden. 1992. 19.00 (*0-606-00591-9*) Turtleback Bks.

—East of Eden. 2003. 608p. pap. 16.00 (*0-14-200423-5*, Penguin Bks.); 1992. 624p. 14.00 (*0-14-018639-5*, Penguin Classics); 1979. 782p. (C). pap. 7.95 o.s.i (*0-14-004997-5*, Penguin Bks.); 1952. 784p. 27.95 o.p. (*0-670-28738-5*) Viking Penguin.

—The Grapes of Wrath. Ehrenhaft, George & Krailing, Tessa, eds. 1984. (Barron's Book Notes Ser.). 120p. (YA). (gr. 10-12). pap. 3.95 (*0-8120-3413-9*) Barron's Educational Series, Inc.

—The Grapes of Wrath. 1998. (Bloom's Notes Ser.). pap. text 19.95 (*0-7910-4122-0*) Chelsea Hse. Pubs.

—The Grapes of Wrath. 2002. 517p. reprint ed. 25.00 (*0-7567-5706-1*) DIANE Publishing Co.

—The Grapes of Wrath. adapted ed. 1991. per. 6.50 (*0-8222-0475-4*) Dramatists Play Service, Inc.

—The Grapes of Wrath. 1993. (Everyman's Library: Vol. 154). 608p. 20.00 o.s.i (*0-679-42040-1*) Knopf, Alfred A. Inc.

—The Grapes of Wrath. o.p. (*0-582-78130-2*) Moonbeam Pubns., Inc.

—The Grapes of Wrath. (YA). 1999. 9.95 (*1-56137-299-4*); 1998. 32p. 11.95 (*1-56137-300-1*, NU3001SP) Novel Units, Inc.

—The Grapes of Wrath. (Steinbeck's Centennial Ser.). 2002. 464p. pap. 15.00 (*0-14-200066-3*); 1999. 464p. (C). pap. 15.00 (*0-14-028162-2*); 1991. 592p. pap. 8.95 o.p. (*0-14-015724-7*); 1972. pap. 4.95 o.p. (*0-670-01808-2*); 1958. pap. 3.50 o.p. (*0-670-00033-7*) Penguin Group (USA) Inc.

—The Grapes of Wrath. 1990. 5.99 o.p. (*0-517-03017-9*) Random Hse. Value Publishing.

—The Grapes of Wrath. 1991. (World's Best Reading Ser.). 445p. (*0-89577-387-2*) Reader's Digest Assn., Inc., The.

—The Grapes of Wrath. 1992. 19.05 (*0-606-00174-3*) Turtleback Bks.

—The Grapes of Wrath. (Twentieth Century Classics Ser.). 1992. 672p. pap. 14.00 (*0-14-018640-9*, Penguin Classics); 1989. 640p. 25.00 o.p. (*0-670-82638-3*) Viking Penguin.

—The Grapes of Wrath. Lisca, Peter, ed. 1977. (Critical Studies). 896p. pap. 15.95 o.p. (*0-14-015508-2*, Viking) Viking Penguin.

—The Grapes of Wrath. (Fiction Ser.). 1976. 586p. pap. 7.95 o.p. (*0-14-004239-3*, Penguin Bks.); 1972. xiii, 881 p. pap. 11.95 o.p. (*0-670-34792-2*); 1939. 22.95 o.p. (*0-670-34791-4*); 1998th abr. unabr. ed. 1998. 640p. audio 49.95 (*0-14-086844-5*, Penguin AudioBooks) Viking Penguin.

—The Grapes of Wrath. 2000. text 6.00 (*0-8220-7081-2*, Cliff Notes) Wiley, John & Sons, Inc.

—The Grapes of Wrath: Text & Criticism. Lisca, Peter, ed. 2nd ed. 1997. (Viking Critical Library). 736p. pap. 19.95 (*0-14-024775-0*, Penguin Bks.) Penguin Group (USA) Inc.

—The Grapes of Wrath & Other Writings, 1936-1941: The Long Valley; The Grapes of Wrath; The Log from the Sea of Cortez; The Harvest Gypsies. DeMott, Robert & Steinbeck, Elaine A., eds. 1996. (Library of America). 1088p. 35.00 (*1-883011-15-9*) Library of America, The.

—In Dubious Battle. unabr. collector's ed. 1994. audio 56.00 (*0-7366-2878-9*, 3581) Books on Tape, Inc.

—In Dubious Battle. 1963. pap. 2.95 o.p. (*0-670-00132-5*) Penguin Group (USA) Inc.

—In Dubious Battle. l.t. ed. 2000. (Perennial Bestsellers Ser.). 405p. 28.95 (*0-7838-9162-8*) Thorndike Pr.

—In Dubious Battle. 1964. 17.05 o.p. (*0-606-03036-0*) Turtleback Bks.

—In Dubious Battle. (Great Books of the 20th Century Ser.). 1992. 384p. pap. 14.00 (*0-14-018641-7*, Penguin Classics); 1979. 368p. pap. 6.00 o.p. (*0-14-004888-X*, Penguin Bks.); 1936. 5.95 o.p. (*0-670-39523-4*) Viking Penguin.

—The Long Valley. 1970. (gr. 7-12). pap. 1.95 o.p. (*0-553-12824-8*) Bantam Bks.

—The Long Valley. 1956. pap. 2.75 o.p. (*0-670-00001-9*) Penguin Group (USA) Inc.

—The Long Valley. l.t. ed. 2000. (Perennial Bestsellers Ser.). 311p. 28.95 (*0-7838-9164-4*) Thorndike Pr.

—The Long Valley. (Twentieth Century Classics Ser.). 1995. 304p. 14.00 (*0-14-018745-6*, Penguin Classics); 1986. 320p. pap. 6.95 o.p. (*0-14-008038-4*, Penguin Bks.); 1938. 320p. 19.95 o.p. (*0-670-43888-X*); 1999. pap. 39.95 (*0-14-180009-7*, Penguin AudioBooks) Viking Penguin.

—Of Mice & Men. 1950. per. 6.50 (*0-8222-0838-5*) Dramatists Play Service, Inc.

—Of Mice & Men. audio 7.95 National Recording Co.

—Of Mice & Men. 1979. 13.00 o.p. (*0-394-60472-5*) Random Hse., Inc.

—Of Mice & Men. unabr. ed. 1999. audio compact disk 31.00 (*0-7887-3724-4*, C1081E7) Recorded Bks., LLC.

—Of Mice & Men. 1980. (Radio Ser.). audio 5.95 o.p. (*0-88142-407-2*, 410) Soundelux Audio Publishing.

—Of Mice & Men. l.t. ed. 1995. 126p. lib. bdg. 20.95 (*0-7838-1358-9*) Thorndike Pr.

—Of Mice & Men. abr. ed. 1998. audio 8.00 Time Warner AudioBooks.

—Of Mice & Men. 1992. 13.00 (*0-606-00200-6*) Turtleback Bks.

—Of Mice & Men. Austin, Sarat, ed. 1997. pap. 19.95 (*0-14-018829-0*) Viking Penguin.

—Of Mice & Men. (Great Books of the 20th Century Ser.). 1994. 160p. 11.00 (*0-14-018642-5*, Penguin Classics); 1993. 112p. 8.00 (*0-14-017739-6*); 1978. 320p. pap. 7.95 o.p. (*0-14-004891-X*, Penguin Bks.); 1992. 18.95 (*0-453-00790-2*, 391299) Viking Penguin.

—Of Mice & Men: The Play. 1983. 128p. mass mkt. 3.50 o.s.i (*0-553-27824-X*, Bantam Classics) Bantam Bks.

—Of Mice & Men: The Play. 1989. 124p. (C). pap. 14.95 (*0-09-175758-4*) Dufour Editions, Inc.

—Of Mice & Men: The Play. 1992. (Illus.). 112p. pap. 4.50 o.p. (*0-14-017320-X*, Penguin Bks.) Penguin Group (USA) Inc.

—Of Mice & Men: The Play. 1937. 19.95 o.s.i (*0-670-52071-3*) Viking Penguin.

—The Pastures of Heaven. reprint ed. 21.50 (*0-404-20244-6*, PS3537) AMS Pr., Inc.

—The Pastures of Heaven. mass mkt. 0.25 o.p. (*0-451-00509-0*, Signet Bks.) NAL.

—The Pastures of Heaven. 1963. pap. 1.45 o.p. (*0-670-00133-3*) Penguin Group (USA) Inc.

—The Pastures of Heaven. (Great Books of the 20th Century Ser.). 1995. 256p. 13.00 (*0-14-018748-0*, Penguin Classics); 1982. 240p. pap. 6.95 o.p. (*0-14-004998-3*, Penguin Bks.); 1932. 4.50 o.p. (*0-670-54245-8*) Viking Penguin.

—The Short Novels of John Steinbeck. 1963. 544p. 16.95 o.p. (*0-670-64138-3*) Viking Penguin.

—Sweet Thursday. l.t. ed. 2001. (G. K. Hall Perennial Bestsellers Ser. ). 312p. 28.95 (*0-7838-9163-6*) Thorndike Pr.

—Sweet Thursday. (Great Books of the 20th Century Ser.). 1996. 288p. 13.00 (*0-14-018750-2*, Penguin Classics); 1979. 288p. pap. 7.00 o.p. (*0-14-004889-8*, Penguin Bks.); 1954. 3.75 o.p. (*0-670-68686-7*) Viking Penguin.

—To a God Unknown. unabr. collector's ed. 1992. audio 48.00 (*0-7366-2124-5*, 2926) Books on Tape, Inc.

—To a God Unknown. l.t. ed. 1974. (Ulverscroft Large Print Ser.). 29.99 o.p. (*0-85456-304-0*, Ulverscroft) Thorpe, F. A. Pubs. GBR. *Dist:* Ulverscroft Large Print Bks., Ltd., Ulverscroft Large Print Canada, Ltd.

—To a God Unknown. (Great Books of the 20th Century Ser.). 1995. 288p. 12.95 (*0-14-018751-0*, Penguin Classics); 1976. 272p. pap. 6.95 o.p. (*0-14-004233-4*, Penguin Bks.) Viking Penguin.

—Tortilla Flat. mass mkt. 0.25 o.p. (*0-451-00599-6*); mass mkt. 0.25 o.p. (*0-451-00816-2*); mass mkt. 0.25 o.p. (*0-451-01380-8*); mass mkt. 0.35 o.p. (*0-451-01737-4*); mass mkt. 0.60 o.p. (*0-451-02189-4*) NAL. (Signet Bks.).

—Tortilla Flat. (Fiction Ser.). 1977. 224p. pap. 8.00 (*0-14-004240-7*, Penguin Bks.); 1963. pap. 2.25 o.p. (*0-670-00134-1*) Penguin Group (USA) Inc.

—Tortilla Flat, unabr. ed. 1999. audio 44.00 (*0-7887-2928-4*, 95715E7) Recorded Bks., LLC.

—Tortilla Flat. 1986. 13.00 (*0-606-00987-6*) Turtleback Bks.

—Tortilla Flat. 1999. audio; 1997. 192p. 10.00 (*0-14-018740-5*, Penguin Classics); 1935. 16.95 o.s.i (*0-670-72109-3*); 1999. 6p. audio 29.95 (*0-14-086894-1*) Viking Penguin.

—The Wayward Bus. 2004. (*0-14-243787-5*) Penguin Group (USA) Inc.

—The Wayward Bus. l.t. ed. 1998. (G. K. Hall Perennial Bestsellers Ser. ). 352 p. 26.95 (*0-7838-0138-6*) Thorndike Pr.

—The Wayward Bus. (Great Books of the 20th Century Ser.). 1995. 304p. 13.00 (*0-14-018752-9*, Penguin Classics); 1979. 320p. pap. 7.95 o.p. (*0-14-005001-9*, Penguin Bks.); 1947. 2.75 o.p. (*0-670-75277-0*) Viking Penguin.

Steinbeck, Thomas. Down to a Soundless Sea. 2003. 320p. pap. 13.95 (*0-345-45577-0*, Ballantine Bks.) Ballantine Bks.

—Down to a Soundless Sea. 2002. (Core Ser.). 31.95 (*0-7862-4729-0*) Thorndike Pr.

Steinberg, Janice. The Dead Man & the Sea. 1997. 256p. mass mkt. 5.99 o.s.i (*0-425-16037-8*, Prime Crime) Berkley Publishing Group.

—Death Crosses the Border. 1995. 240p. mass mkt. 4.99 o.s.i (*0-425-15052-6*) Berkley Publishing Group.

—Death-Fires Dance. 1996. 272p. (Orig.). mass mkt. 5.99 o.s.i (*0-425-15551-X*, Prime Crime) Berkley Publishing Group.

—Death of a Postmodernist. 1995. 256p. (Orig.). mass mkt. 5.99 o.s.i (*0-425-14546-8*, Prime Crime) Berkley Publishing Group.

Steinke, Darcey. Suicide Blonde. 2000. 200p. pap. 12.00 (*0-8021-3664-8*, Grove Pr.); 1992. 191p. 19.00 o.p. (*0-87113-479-9*, Atlantic Monthly Pr.) Grove/Atlantic, Inc.

—Suicide Blonde. Rosenman, Jane, ed. 1994. 204p. reprint ed. pap. (*0-671-87315-6*, Washington Square Pr.) Simon & Schuster.

Stewart, Ed. Doomsday Flight. 1995. 475p. pap. 11.99 (*1-56476-482-6*, 6-3482) Cook Communications Ministries.

—Millennium's Dawn. 1994. 480p. pap. 11.99 o.p. (*1-56476-345-5*, 6-3345) Cook Communications Ministries.

—Millennium's Eve. 1993. 448p. pap. 12.99 (*1-56476-133-9*, 6-3133) Cook Communications Ministries.

Stewart, Fred M. The Glitter & the Gold. 1989. 480p. 19.95 o.p. (*0-453-00676-0*) NAL.

Stinson, Jim. Double Exposure. 1988. (Illus.). 160p. mass mkt. 3.50 o.s.i (*0-553-26665-9*) Bantam Bks.

—Double Exposure. 1986. (Stoney Winston Mystery Ser.). 224p. 13.95 o.s.i (*0-684-18458-3*, Macmillan Reference USA) Gale Group.

—Low Angles: A Stoney Winston Mystery. 1986. 240p. 13.95 o.s.i (*0-684-18626-8*, Macmillan Reference USA) Gale Group.

—Truck Shot: A Stoney Winston Mystery. 1989. 256p. 17.95 o.p. (*0-684-18876-7*, Scribner) Simon & Schuster.

—TV Safe. 1991. 256p. 19.95 o.p. (*0-684-19225-X*, Scribner) Simon & Schuster.

Stone, Katherine. Thief of Hearts. 1999. 416p. 23.00 o.p. (*0-446-52181-7*) Warner Bks., Inc.

Stone, Katherine. Bel Air. l.t. ed. 1996. pap. 22.95 o.p. (*1-56895-383-6*, Wheeler Publishing, Inc.) Gale Group.

—Bel Air. (Zebra Bks.). 1996. 448p. mass mkt. 6.99 (*0-8217-5201-4*, Zebra Bks.); 1993. mass mkt. 4.95 o.s.i (*0-8217-4418-6*); 1990. mass mkt. 4.95 o.s.i (*0-8217-2979-9*, Zebra Bks.) Kensington Publishing Corp.

—The Carlton Club. (Zebra Book Ser.). 544p. 1996. mass mkt. 6.99 o.s.i (*0-8217-5204-9*); 1988. mass mkt. 4.50 o.p. (*0-8217-2296-4*) Kensington Publishing Corp. (Zebra Bks.).

—Carlton Club. 1988. mass mkt. 4.95 o.s.i (*0-8217-3614-0*, Zebra Bks.) Kensington Publishing Corp.

—The Carlton Club. l.t. ed. 1997. pap. 24.95 (*1-56895-414-X*, Wheeler Publishing, Inc.) Gale Group.

—Happy Endings. l.t. ed. 1995. 23.95 o.p. (*1-56895-216-3*, Wheeler Publishing, Inc.) Gale Group.

—Happy Endings. 1996. 384p. mass mkt. 6.99 (*0-8217-5250-2*); 1995. 384p. mass mkt. 5.99 o.s.i (*0-8217-4856-4*); 1994. 368p. mass mkt. 15.95 o.p. (*0-8217-4646-4*) Kensington Publishing Corp. (Zebra Bks.).

—Illusions. l.t. ed. 1994. 512p. reprint ed. lib. bdg. 20.95 o.p. (*0-8161-5946-7*, Macmillan Reference USA) Gale Group.

—Illusions. 1996. 418p. mass mkt. 6.99 (*0-8217-5247-2*, Zebra Bks.); 1994. 448p. mass mkt. 5.99 o.s.i (*0-8217-4617-0*); 1994. mass mkt. 18.95 o.s.i (*0-8217-4453-4*, Zebra Bks.) Kensington Publishing Corp.

—Promises. l.t. ed. 1995. 23.95 o.p. (*0-7927-2018-0*); 1994. pap. 25.95 o.p. (*0-7927-2019-9*) BBC Audiobooks America.

—Roommates. l.t. ed. 1996. (Large Print Bks.). 24.95 o.p. (*1-56895-356-9*, Wheeler Publishing, Inc.) Gale Group.

—Roommates. 1996. mass mkt. 6.99 o.s.i (*0-8217-5206-5*, Zebra Bks.); 1995. mass mkt. 5.99 o.s.i (*0-8217-5243-X*); 1987. mass mkt. 4.95 o.s.i (*0-8217-3355-9*, Zebra Bks.) Kensington Publishing Corp.

—Thief of Hearts. 2000. 448p. E-Book 4.95 (*0-446-92329-X*) Time Warner Bk. Group.

—Thief of Hearts. 2000. E-Book 4.95 (*0-446-91275-1*) Warner Bks., Inc.

—A Thief of Hearts. 2000. 448p. mass mkt. 7.50 (*0-446-60829-7*) Warner Bks., Inc.

Straight, Susan. Aquaboogie: A Novel in Stories. 1990. (Illus.). 196p. pap. 12.95 (*0-915943-59-X*) Milkweed Editions.

—Blacker Than a Thousand Midnights. 1994. 400p. (J). 21.95 o.p. (*0-7868-6003-0*) Hyperion Pr.

—Blacker Than a Thousand Midnights. 1995. 400p. pap. 12.95 (*0-385-47434-2*, Knopf Bks. for Young Readers) Random Hse. Children's Bks.

—Highwire Moon: A Novel. 2001. (Illus.). 320p. tchr. ed. 24.00 (*0-618-05614-9*) Houghton Mifflin Co.

—Highwire Moon: A Novel. 2002. (Illus.). 320p. pap. 14.00 (*0-385-72261-3*, Anchor) Knopf Publishing Group.

Strom, Dao. Grass Roof, Tin Roof: A Novel. 2003. 240p. pap. 12.00 (*0-618-14559-1*) Houghton Mifflin Co.

Strupp, Joe. The City & County: A Novel of San Francisco's Newsmakers. 2001. 425p. per. 19.95 (*1-931333-01-7*) Dry Bones Pr.

Stubbs, Jean. The Golden Crucible. 1995. 280p. 18.50 o.p. (*0-7451-8664-5*, Black Dagger) BBC Audiobooks America.

—The Golden Crucible. 1977. (General Ser.). reprint ed. lib. bdg. 12.50 o.p. (*0-8161-6488-6*, Macmillan Reference USA) Gale Group.

—The Golden Crucible. 1976. 8.95 o.p. (*0-8128-1903-9*, Scarborough Hse.) Madison Bks., Inc.

Sublett, Jesse. Boiled in Concrete. 1999. pap. 3.95 (*0-14-015230-X*); 1992. 320p. 20.00 o.p. (*0-670-83888-8*) Viking Penguin. (Viking).

Sussman, Ellen. On a Night Like This. 2004. 304p. 23.95 (*0-446-53141-3*) Warner Bks., Inc.

Swick, Marly. Evening News. 2000. 352p. E-Book 4.95 (*0-7595-4015-2*); E-Book 4.95 (*0-7595-0015-0*) Little Brown & Co.

—Evening News. unabr. ed. 1999. audio 83.00 (*0-7887-3132-7*, 95687E7) Recorded Bks., LLC.

—Evening News. abr. ed. 1999. audio 17.98 (*1-57042-653-8*) Time Warner AudioBooks.

—Evening News. 2000. 352p. E-Book 4.95 (*0-7595-9023-0*); E-Book 4.95 (*0-7595-8016-2*) Warner Bks., Inc.

—Evening News: A Novel. 368p. 2000. pap. 13.95 (*0-316-82564-6*, Back Bay); 1999. (YA). (gr. 8 up). 23.00 o.p. (*0-316-82533-6*) Little Brown & Co.

Swick, Marly & Williams, JoBeth. The Evening News. abr. ed. 1999. audio 17.98 Highsmith Inc.

Tan, Amy. The Kitchen God's Wife. 1996. mass mkt. 6.99 (*0-8041-9897-7*); 1992. 544p. mass mkt. 7.99 (*0-8041-0753-X*) Ballantine Bks. (Ivy Bks.).

—The Kitchen God's Wife. 1993. 432p. pap. 13.00 (*0-679-74808-3*, Vintage) Knopf Publishing Group.

—The Kitchen God's Wife. unabr. ed. 1993. audio 39.95 o.p. (*0-7871-0018-8*, Dove Audio); 39.95 o.p. (*1-55800-434-3*, 133134);Set. 15.95 o.p. (*1-55800-266-9*, 391032) NewStar Media, Inc.

—The Kitchen God's Wife. 1991. 320p. 22.95 o.p. (*0-399-13578-2*) Putnam Publishing Group, The.

—The Kitchen God's Wife. 1992. 14.04 (*0-606-01177-3*) Turtleback Bks.

Tatlock, Ann. All the Way Home: A Friendship That Once Bridged Two Cultural Will It Survive The Span of Time. 2002. 448p. pap. 12.99 (*0-7642-2663-0*) Bethany Hse. Pubs.

Taylor, Elizabeth Atwood. The Cable Car Murder. 1988. 240p. reprint ed. mass mkt. 4.99 o.s.i (*0-8041-0281-3*, Ivy Bks.) Ballantine Bks.

—The Cable Car Murder. (Fingerprint Mysteries Ser.). 224p. 1983. pap. 5.95 o.p. (*0-312-11312-9*, Saint Martin's Griffin); 1981. 11.95 o.p. (*0-312-11311-0*) St. Martin's Pr.

—The Cable Car Murders. l.t. ed. 1982. 412p. reprint ed. 12.95 o.p. (*0-89621-360-9*) Thorndike Pr.

—Murder at Vassar. 1988. mass mkt. 4.95 o.s.i (*0-8041-0212-0*, Ivy Bks.) Ballantine Bks.

—Murder at Vassar. 1987. 256p. 15.95 o.p. (*0-312-00160-6*) St. Martin's Pr.

—The Northwest Murders. 1992. 288p. 18.95 o.p. (*0-312-07753-X*, Saint Martin's Minotaur) St. Martin's Pr.

Taylor, Erika. The Sun Maiden. 1991. 288p. 19.95 o.p. (*0-689-12130-X*, Scribner) Simon & Schuster.

Taylor, Jean. The Last of Her Lies: A Maggie Garrett Mystery. 1996. 238p. (Orig.). pap. 10.95 (*1-878067-75-3*, Seal Pr.) Avalon Publishing Group.

—We Know Where You Live. 1995. 240p. pap. 9.95 (*1-878067-62-1*, Seal Pr.) Avalon Publishing Group.

Taylor, Robert L. The Travels of Jaimie McPheeters. 1981. 544p. mass mkt. 3.50 o.s.i (*0-441-82269-X*) Ace Bks.

—The Travels of Jaimie McPheeters. 1958. 13.95 o.p. (*0-385-04930-7*) Doubleday Publishing.

Taylor, Robert Lewis. The Travels of Jaimie McPheeters. 37.95 (*0-8488-1483-5*) Amereon, Ltd.

—The Travels of Jaimie McPheeters. 1991. 550p. reprint ed. lib. bdg. 36.95 o.p. (*0-89966-835-6*) Buccaneer Bks., Inc.

—The Travels of Jaimie McPheeters: Arbor House Library of Contemporary Americana. 1992. 548p. pap. 25.00 (*0-385-42222-9*) Broadway Bks.

Tea, Michelle. Valencia. 2000. 202p. pap. 13.00 (*1-58005-035-2*, Seal Pr.) Avalon Publishing Group.

Telushkin, Joseph. An Eye for an Eye. 1992. 288p. mass mkt. 4.99 o.s.i (*0-553-29620-5*) Bantam Bks.

—An Eye for an Eye. 1991. 272p. 15.00 o.s.i (*0-385-42116-8*) Doubleday Publishing.

Teran, Boston. God Is a Bullet. aut. ed. 1999. 24.00 o.s.i (*0-676-54976-4*) Knopf, Alfred A. Inc.

—The Prince of Deadly Weapons: A Novel. 2002. 368p. 24.95 (*0-312-27118-2*, Saint Martin's Minotaur) St. Martin's Pr.

Tervalon, Jervey. Understand This. 1999. pap. 15.00 (*0-385-50021-1*) Doubleday Publishing.

—Understand This. 1995. 272p. pap. 19.00 o.s.i (*0-385-47824-0*) Knopf, Alfred A. Inc.

—Understand This. 1994. 271p. 20.00 o.p. (*0-688-04560-X*, Morrow, William & Co.) Morrow/Avon.

—Understand This. 2000. (California Fiction Ser.). 271p. pap. text 15.95 (*0-520-22355-1*) Univ. of California Pr.

Thackrey, Ted, Jr. King of Diamonds. 1989. mass mkt. 4.50 o.s.i (*0-515-10169-9*, Jove) Berkley Publishing Group.

Thoene, Brock. The Legend of Storey County. 1995. 288p. 16.99 o.p. (*0-7852-8070-7*) Nelson, Thomas Inc.

Thoene, Brock & Thoene, Bodie. Cannons of the Comstock. 1992. (Saga of the Sierras Ser.: Vol. 5). 208p. (J). (ps up). pap. 8.99 o.p. (*1-55661-166-8*) Bethany Hse. Pubs.

—Cannons of the Comstock. l.t. ed. 2002. lib. bdg. 27.95 (*1-58547-182-8*, Western) Ctr. Point Large Print.

—Gold Rush Prodigal. 1991. (Saga of the Sierras Ser.: Bk. 3). 224p. (J). (ps up). pap. 8.99 o.p. (*1-55661-162-5*) Bethany Hse. Pubs.

—The Man from Shadow Ridge. 1990. (Saga of the Sierras Ser.: No. 1). 240p. pap. 8.99 o.p. (*1-55661-098-X*) Bethany Hse. Pubs.

—The Man from Shadow Ridge. l.t. ed. 2002. lib. bdg. 27.95 (*1-58547-181-X*, Western) Ctr. Point Large Print.

—Riders of the Silver Rim. 1990. (Saga of the Sierras Ser.: Vol. 2). 208p. pap. 8.99 o.p. (*1-55661-099-8*) Bethany Hse. Pubs.

—Sequoia Scout. 1991. (Saga of the Sierras Ser.: Bk. 4). 240p. pap. 8.99 o.p. (*1-55661-165-X*) Bethany Hse. Pubs.

—Shooting Star. 1993. (Saga of the Sierras Ser.: Vol. 7). 208p. pap. 8.99 o.p. (*1-55661-320-2*) Bethany Hse. Pubs.

—Shooting Star. l.t. ed. 1994. 214p. lib. bdg. 21.95 (*0-8161-5908-4*, Macmillan Reference USA) Gale Group.

—Year of the Grizzly. 1992. (Saga of the Sierras Ser.: Vol. 6). 192p. pap. 8.99 o.p. (*1-55661-167-6*) Bethany Hse. Pubs.

Thomas, Michael M. Black Money. abr. ed. 1994. audio 16.95 o.p. (*1-55927-285-6*) Audio Renaissance.

—Black Money. 1994. 309p. 22.00 o.s.i (*0-517-59523-0*) Crown Publishing Group.

—Black Money. 1995. 343p. pap. text 6.50 o.p. (*0-312-95680-0*, St. Martin's Paperbacks) St. Martin's Pr.

Thomas, Ross. Ah, Treachery! 1994. 288p. 21.95 o.s.i (*0-89296-452-9*) Mysterious Pr.

—Ah, Treachery!, unabr. ed. audio 51.00 (*0-7887-0260-2*, 94469E7) Recorded Bks., LLC.

—Ah, Treachery! 2004. 288p. pap. 13.95 (*0-312-32704-8*, Saint Martin's Griffin) St. Martin's Pr.

—Ah, Treachery! 1995. 272p. mass mkt. 5.99 o.s.i (*0-446-40031-9*) Warner Bks., Inc.

—The Fourth Durango. 1989. 320p. 18.95 o.p. (*0-89296-213-5*) Mysterious Pr.

—No Questions Asked. 1993. 192p. mass mkt. 4.99 o.p. (*0-446-40180-3*, Mysterious Pr. Paperback Bks.) Warner Bks., Inc.

Thompson, Jim. The Grifters. 1985. 196p. reprint ed. pap. 3.95 o.p. (*0-916870-90-1*, Black Mask) Creative Arts Bk. Co.

—The Grifters. 1990. (Vintage Crime/Black Lizard Ser.). 208p. pap. 11.00 (*0-679-73248-9*, Vintage) Knopf Publishing Group.

—Now & on Earth. 1994. 320p. pap. 12.00 (*0-679-74013-9*) Random Hse., Inc.

Thomson, Rupert. Air & Fire. 1995. 320p. pap. 14.00 (*0-679-74730-3*, Vintage) Knopf Publishing Group.

—Air & Fire. 1994. 309p. 23.00 o.s.i (*0-679-42506-3*) Knopf, Alfred A. Inc.

Thoreau, David. City at Bay. 1979. 9.95 o.p. (*0-87795-231-0*, Morrow, William & Co.) Morrow/Avon.

Thornburg, Newton. Eve's Men. 1999. 277p. mass mkt. 6.99 (*0-8125-8419-8*); 1998. 288p. 22.95 (*0-312-86399-3*) Doherty, Tom Assocs., LLC. (Forge Bks.).

—To Die in California. 1982. mass mkt. 1.50 o.p. (*0-380-00001-6*, 18622, Avon Bks.) Morrow/Avon.

—To Die in California. 2002. 288p. pap. 14.00 (*1-85242-806-6*) Serpent's Tail Ltd. GBR. *Dist:* Consortium Bk. Sales & Distribution.

Thorne, Tamara. Eternity. 2001. 4p. mass mkt. 5.99 (*0-7860-1310-9*, Pinnacle Bks.) Kensington Publishing Corp.

—Moonfall. 2000. 432p. mass mkt. 5.99 o.s.i (*0-7860-1132-7*, Pinnacle Bks.); 1996. 384p. mass mkt. 4.99 o.s.i (*0-8217-5315-0*) Kensington Publishing Corp.

Thornton, Lawrence. Ghost Woman. 1992. 288p. 19.95 o.p. (*0-395-61592-5*) Houghton Mifflin Co.

—Ghost Woman. 1999. (California Fiction Ser.). (Illus.). 302p. pap. 15.95 (*0-520-22068-4*) Univ. of California Pr.

Thrasher, L. L. Charlie's Bones. l.t. ed. 2000. (Dales Large Print Ser.). 304p. pap. (*1-84137-000-2*) Magna Large Print Bks. GBR. *Dist:* Ulverscroft Large Print Bks., Ltd., Ulverscroft Large Print Canada, Ltd.

—Charlie's Bones. 1998. 224p. 21.95 (*1-885173-47-4*) Write Way Publishing.

—Charlie's Web. 2000. 225p. 23.95 (*1-885173-66-0*) Write Way Publishing.

Thrush, Robin A., ed. The Gray Whales Are Missing. 1987. (Illus.). 144p. (YA). (gr. 4-7). 14.95 o.s.i (*0-15-200455-6*, Gulliver Bks.) Harcourt Children's Bks.

Tierney, Ronald. Eclipse of the Heart. 1995. pap. 8.95 o.p. (*0-312-11780-9*, Saint Martin's Griffin); 1993. 224p. 12.99 o.p. (*0-312-09792-1*, Saint Martin's Minotaur) St. Martin's Pr.

Tiller, Denise. Calculated Risk. 2000. 250p. pap. 14.95 (*1-58752-015-X*); 2000. E-Book 14.95 (*1-58752-031-1*); 1999. E-Book 14.95 (*1-58752-035-4*) Timberwolf Pr., Inc.

—Calculated Risk. unabr. ed. 2000. lib. bdg. 29.95 incl. audio (*1-58752-016-8*); lib. bdg. 34.95 incl. audio compact disk (*1-58752-017-6*) Timberwolf Pr., Inc.

Tobar, Hector. Tattooed Soldier: A Novel. 2000. 320p. 23.00 (*1-883285-15-1*) Delphinium Bks., Inc.

—Tattooed Soldier: A Novel. 2000. 320p. 12.95 (*0-14-028861-9*) Viking Penguin.

Tolkin, Michael. The Player. 1997. 208p. pap. 12.00 (*0-8021-3513-7*, Grove Pr.); 1988. 204p. 17.95 o.p. (*0-87113-228-1*) Grove/Atlantic, Inc.

—The Player. 1992. pap. 10.00 (*0-394-23924-5*); 1989. pap. 10.00 o.s.i (*0-679-72254-8*) Knopf Publishing Group. (Vintage).

—The Player. 1992. audio 16.00 o.p. (*0-679-41849-0*, RH Audio) Random Hse. Audio Publishing Group.

—The Player. 1993. 3.99 o.p. (*0-517-10912-3*) Random Hse. Value Publishing.

Toll, Emily. Murder Pans Out. 2003. 288p. (Orig.). mass mkt. 6.50 (*0-425-18995-3*, Prime Crime) Berkley Publishing Group.

Tolnay, Tom. The Big House. 1992. 188p. 19.95 o.p. (*0-8027-3218-6*) Walker & Co.

Townsend, Larry. The Case of the Severed Head. 1994. 239p. (Orig.). pap. 8.95 (*1-881684-04-0*) L.T. Pubns.

—One for the Master, Two for the Fool: A Bruce MacLeod Mystery. 1992. 214p. pap. 9.95 (*1-55583-209-1*) Alyson Pubns.

Trachtenberg, Paul. Ben's Exit. 1993. 128p. (Orig.). pap. 7.00 (*0-916156-91-5*) Cherry Valley Editions.

Trackler, Richard. The Roll-Call Vote. 2001. 300p. pap. 17.95 (*1-57197-277-3*) Pentland Pr., Inc.

Traylor, James L., ed. Hollywood Troubleshooter: W. T. Ballards Bill Lennox Stories. 1985. 156p. 19.95 (*0-87972-316-5*, Popular Pr.) Univ. of Wisconsin Pr.

Trevino, Jesus. The Fabulous Sinkhole & Other Stories. 1995. 164p. pap. 9.95 o.p. (*1-55885-129-1*) Arte Publico Pr.

Trolley, Jack. Balboa Firefly. 1994. 272p. 3.95 (*0-7867-0117-X*, Carroll & Graf Pubs.) Avalon Publishing Group.

—Juarez Justice. 1996. 272p. 22.00 o.p. (*0-7867-0356-3*, Carroll & Graf Pubs.) Avalon Publishing Group.

—Manila Time: A Novel. 1995. 304p. 21.00 o.p. (*0-7867-0255-9*, Carroll & Graf Pubs.) Avalon Publishing Group.

Trott, Susan. The Housewife & the Assassin. 1987. 270p. mass mkt. 6.95 o.p. (*0-06-097118-5*, PL/7118, Perennial) HarperTrade.

—The Housewife & the Assassin. 1979. 8.95 o.p. (*0-312-39346-6*) St. Martin's Pr.

Trujillo, Carla Mari. What Night Brings. 2003. 242p. pap. 15.95 (*1-880684-94-2*) Curbstone Pr.

Tsukiyama, Gail. Dreaming Water. E-Book 23.95 (*0-312-70692-8*); 2002. 224p. 23.95 (*0-312-20607-0*); 2003. 240p. reprint ed. pap. 12.95 (*0-312-31608-9*, Saint Martin's Griffin) St. Martin's Pr.

—Dreaming Water. 2002. (Women's Fiction Ser.). 29.95 (*0-7862-4797-5*) Thorndike Pr.

—Night of Many Dreams. unabr. ed. 1999. audio 29.95 (*0-7861-1546-7*); pap. 44.95 incl. audio (*0-7861-1335-9*, 2229) Blackstone Audio Bks., Inc.

—Night of Many Dreams. 1999. E-Book 12.95 o.s.i (*0-312-20733-6*); 1998. 288p. 22.95 o.p. (*0-312-17194-3*); 1998. 288p. reprint ed. pap. 12.95 (*0-312-19940-6*, NPB 0230, Saint Martin's Griffin) St. Martin's Pr.

Tubach, Sally Patterson. Memoirs of a Terrorist. 1996. (SUNY Series, The Margins of Literature). 174p. (C). pap. text 19.95 (*0-7914-3006-5*); text 20.50 (*0-7914-3005-7*) State Univ. of New York Pr.

Tufts, Kingsley. Pico Street Stories. 1998. 208p. pap. 12.00 (*1-880284-27-8*) Daniel, John & Co., Pubs.

Turtledove, Harry. Gunpowder Empire. Date not set. mass mkt. (*0-7653-4609-5*); 2003. 288p. 24.95 (*0-7653-0693-X*) Doherty, Tom Assocs., LLC. (Tor Bks.).

Twain, Mark. Gold Miners & Guttersnipes: Tales of California. 1991. 224p. pap. 10.95 o.p. (*0-87701-881-2*) Chronicle Bks. LLC.

—The Jumping Frog. 14.95 (*0-89190-256-2*) Amereon, Ltd.

—The Jumping Frog. 1994. reprint ed. lib. bdg. 18.95 (*1-56849-349-5*) Buccaneer Bks., Inc.

—The Jumping Frog. rev. ed. 1971. (Illus.). 66p. (J). pap. 3.95 (*0-486-22686-7*) Dover Pubns., Inc.

—The Jumping Frog: In English, Then in French, Then Clawed Back into a Civilized Language Once More by Patient, Unremunerated Toil. 1987. (Illus.). 80p. 12.95 o.p. (*0-87701-442-6*) Chronicle Bks. LLC.

—The Jumping Frog: In English, Then in French, Then Clawed Back into a Civilized Language Once More by Patient, Unremunerated Toil. 1993. (ENG & FRE., Illus.). 48p. reprint ed. pap. 7.95 (*1-55921-097-4*) Moyer Bell.

—The Jumping Frog & Other Stories. 1985. (Gift Editions Ser.). (Illus.). 64p. (C). 6.95 o.p. (*0-88088-544-0*, 885440) Peter Pauper Pr. Inc.

—The Jumping Frog & 18 Other Stories. 2000. (Illus.). 128p. per. 12.95 (*1-58509-200-2*, BT-002) Book Tree, The.

—Jumping Frogs to Cannibalism, Set. unabr. ed. 1994. (Mark Twain Ser.). 16.95 incl. audio (*1-883049-17-2*, 390212, Commuters Library) Sound Room Pubs., Inc.

—Jumping Frogs to Cannibalism: Library Edition. unabr. ed. 1994. lib. bdg. 18.95 incl. audio (*1-883049-31-8*) Sound Room Pubs., Inc.

Twyman, James F. The Proposing Tree: A Love Story. 2003. 112p. 16.95 (*1-57174-394-4*) Hampton Roads Publishing Co., Inc.

Tyler, Lee. The Case of the Missing Links. 1999. 190p. pap. 10.95 (*1-56474-302-0*) Fithian Pr.

Uchida, Yoshiko. Picture Bride. 1987. 200p. 14.95 o.p. (*0-87358-429-5*) Northland Publishing.

—Picture Bride. 1988. 224p. 20.85 o.p. (*0-671-92720-5*); pap. 6.95 o.p. (*0-671-66874-9*) Simon & Schuster. (Fireside).

—Picture Bride. E-Book 12.95 (*0-295-97998-4*); 2003. 222p. reprint ed. pap. 14.95 (*0-295-97616-0*) Univ. of Washington Pr.

Ullman, Ellen. The Bug. 2003. 368p. 23.95 (*0-385-50860-3*, Talese, Nan A.) Doubleday Publishing.

—The Bug. 2004. 368p. pap. 13.95 (*1-4000-3235-0*, Anchor) Knopf Publishing Group.

Upton, Robert. Dead on the Stick. 256p. 1987. pap. 3.50 o.p. (*0-14-007601-8*, Penguin Bks.); 1986. 15.95 o.p. (*0-670-80331-6*) Viking Penguin.

—The Faberge Egg. 1988. 208p. 16.95 o.p. (*0-525-24692-4*, Dutton) Dutton/Plume.

—Fade Out. 1984. (Amos McGuffin Mystery Ser.). 13.95 o.p. (*0-670-30469-7*) Viking Penguin.

—Fade Out: An Amos McGuffin Mystery. 1986. 192p. pap. 3.95 o.p. (*0-14-008312-X*, Penguin Bks.) Viking Penguin.

—A Golden Fleecing. 1979. 10.95 o.p. (*0-312-33730-2*) St. Martin's Pr.

—A Killing in Real Estate: An Amos McGuffin Mystery. 1990. 192p. 17.95 o.p. (*0-525-24927-3*, Dutton) Dutton/Plume.

—Who'd Want to Kill Old George? 1982. 224p. pap. 2.50 o.p. (*0-523-41537-0*, Pinnacle Bks.) Kensington Publishing Corp.

—Who'd Want to Kill Old George? 1976. 7.95 o.p. (*0-399-11867-5*) Putnam Publishing Group, The.

Van der Veer, Judy. Higher Than the Arrow. 1975. (J). (gr. 4-6). pap. 1.50 o.p. (*0-380-00194-2*, 44859-9, Avon Bks.) Morrow/Avon.

Van Loan, Derek. Sausalito Waterfront Stories. 1992. (Illus.). 144p. (Orig.). pap. 9.95 (*0-9614068-2-8*) Epoch Pr.

VanDenburgh, Jane. The Physics of Sunset. 1999. 304p. 24.00 o.s.i (*0-679-42483-0*, Pantheon) Knopf Publishing Group.

—Physics of Sunset. 2001. 304p. pap. text 15.00 (*1-58243-100-0*, Counterpoint Pr.) Basic Bks.

—The Physics of Sunset. l.t. ed. 1999. (Americana Ser.). 461p. 27.95 (*0-7862-2298-0*) Thorndike Pr.

Vanderhaeghe, Guy. The Englishman's Boy. 1998. 352p. pap. 14.00 (*0-312-19544-3*); 1997. 336p. 24.00 o.p. (*0-312-16823-3*) Picador.

Vardeman, Robert E. The Resonance of Blood. 1992. 224p. (Orig.). mass mkt. 4.50 (*0-380-75857-1*, Avon Bks.) Morrow/Avon.

Varni, Steven. The Inland Sea. 2000. 269p. 22.00 (*0-688-16906-6*, Morrow, William & Co.) Morrow/Avon.

Vaz, Katherine. Saudade. 1994. o.p. (*0-345-37992-6*) Ballantine Bks.

—Saudade. 1996. 304p. pap. 12.95 (*0-312-14408-3*, Saint Martin's Griffin); 1994. 297p. 20.95 o.p. (*0-312-11055-3*) St. Martin's Pr.

Vea, Alfredo, Jr. Reckoning of Angels. 1996. 352p. 24.95 o.s.i (*0-525-94077-4*, Dutton) Dutton/Plume.

Velasquez, Gloria. Rina's Family Secret. 1998. 112p. (J). 16.95 o.p. (*1-55885-236-0*); (Roosevelt High School Series Bks.: Vol. 4). (gr. 4-7). pap. 9.95 (*1-55885-233-6*) Arte Publico Pr. (Piñata Books).

—Rina's Family Secret. 1998. (Roosevelt High School Series). 16.00 (*0-606-16036-1*) Turtleback Bks.

Ventura, Michael. The Zoo Where You're Fed to God: A Novel. 1994. 256p. 21.00 o.s.i (*0-671-89222-3*, Simon & Schuster) Simon & Schuster.

Victor, Frances F. Women of the Gold Rush: "The New Penelope" & Other Stories. Egli, Ida R., ed. 1998. 192p. reprint ed. pap. 12.95 (*1-890771-03-1*) Heyday Bks.

Vida. Goodbye, Saigon. Date not set. mass mkt. (*0-449-22404-X*, Fawcett) Ballantine Bks.

Vida, Nina. Goodbye, Saigon. 1995. mass mkt. 5.99 o.s.i (*0-449-22422-8*, Fawcett) Ballantine Bks.

—Goodbye, Saigon, Set. abr. ed. 1994. 17.95 o.p. (*0-7871-0218-0*) NewStar Media, Inc.

Vidal, Gore. Hollywood: A Novel of America in the 1920's. 1991. (American Chronicle Ser.). 432p. mass mkt. 7.99 o.s.i (*0-345-37013-9*, Ballantine Bks.) Ballantine Bks.

—Hollywood: A Novel of America in the 1920's. unabr. ed. 1993. (American Chronicles Ser.). audio 104.00 (*0-7366-2529-1*, 3281) Books on Tape, Inc.

—Hollywood: A Novel of America in the 1920's. 2000. (International Ser.). 448p. pap. 15.00 (*0-375-70875-8*, Vintage) Knopf Publishing Group.

—Hollywood: A Novel of America in the 1920's. aut. ed. 1999. 24.95 (*0-676-58932-4*, Modern Library) Random House Adult Trade Publishing Group.

—Hollywood: A Novel of America in the 1920's. 1993. 4.99 o.p. (*0-517-10710-4*); 1992. 5.99 o.p. (*0-517-08085-0*) Random Hse. Value Publishing.

—Hollywood: A Novel of America in the 1920's. 1999. (Modern Library Ser.). 640p. 24.95 o.s.i (*0-679-60292-5*) Random Hse., Inc.

—Myron. 1975. mass mkt. 1.75 o.s.i (*0-345-24625-X*, Ballantine Bks.) Ballantine Bks.

Villanueva, Alma Luz. Luna's California Poppies. 2001. 176p. 24.00 (*0-927534-98-3*); pap. 14.00 (*0-927534-99-1*) Bilingual Pr./Editorial Bilingue.

Villarreal, Jose A. Pocho. 1970. 192p. reprint ed. pap. 10.95 (*0-385-06118-8*) Doubleday Publishing.

—Pocho. 1994. (SPA.). 272p. pap. 19.00 (*0-385-47407-5*) Knopf, Alfred A. Inc.

Villarreal, Rosa Martha. Chronicles of Air & Dreams. 1999. (Illus.). 235p. 22.00 (*0-9662299-2-4*) Archer Bks.

Villasenor, Victor. Trece Sentidos. 2002. (SPA.). 528p. pap. 14.95 (*0-06-050511-7*, Rayo) HarperTrade.

Villegas, Anna T. All We Know of Heaven. 1997. 208p. 19.95 o.p. (*0-312-14613-2*) St. Martin's Pr.

Vollmann, William T. The Rainbow Stories. 1992. (Contemporary American Fiction Ser.). 560p. pap. 17.95 (*0-14-017154-1*) Penguin Group (USA) Inc.

—The Rainbow Stories. 1989. 541p. 19.95 o.s.i (*0-689-11961-5*, Scribner) Simon & Schuster.

—The Royal Family: A Novel. 2000. (Illus.). 566p. 40.00 o.s.i (*0-670-89167-3*) Viking Penguin.

Von Herzen, Lane. The Unfastened Heart. 256p. 1995. pap. 12.95 o.s.i (*0-452-27290-4*, Plume); 1994. 19.95 o.p. (*0-525-93890-7*, Dutton) Dutton/Plume.

—The Unfastened Heart. l.t. ed. 1995. 341p. lib. bdg. 19.95 (*0-7838-1288-4*, Macmillan Reference USA) Gale Group.

Vreeland, Susan. What Love Sees. unabr. ed. 1996. audio 85.00 (*0-7887-0645-4*, 94822E7) Recorded Bks., LLC.

Wagner, Bruce. I'm Losing You. 1997. 336p. pap. 12.95 (*0-452-27868-6*, Signet Bks.) Dutton/Plume.

Wakefield, Hannah. The Price You Pay. 1990. 16.95 o.p. (*0-312-04989-7*, Saint Martin's Minotaur) St. Martin's Pr.

Waldorf, Mary. Thousand Camps, 001. 1982. (J). (gr. 5-9). 8.95 o.p. (*0-395-31866-1*) Houghton Mifflin Co.

Walker, Dale L. Bear Flag Rising: The Conquest of California, 1846. 320p. 1999. 24.95 (*0-312-86685-2*); 2000. reprint ed. pap. 14.95 o.s.i (*0-312-87512-6*, NPB 0239) Doherty, Tom Assocs., LLC. (Forge Bks.).

Walker, Jim. The Nightriders. l.t. ed. 1994. (Wells Fargo Trail Ser.: Bk. 2). 272p. pap. 8.99 o.p. (*1-55661-429-2*) Bethany Hse. Pubs.

—The Nightriders. l.t. ed. 1997. (Christian Fiction Ser.). 439p. 23.95 o.p. (*0-7862-1066-4*) Thorndike Pr.

Walker, Walter. The Appearance of Impropriety. Rosenman, Jane, ed. 1993. 336p. 20.00 (*0-671-74042-3*, Atria) Simon & Schuster.

Wallace, Connie. Any Way the Wind Blows. 1999. 351p. mass mkt. 6.99 (*0-9668039-0-6*) Wallace, Connie.

Wallace, Marilyn. A Single Stone. 1991. 292p. 15.00 o.s.i (*0-385-42118-4*) Doubleday Publishing.

Walpow, Nathan. The Cactus Club Killings. 1999. 288p. pap. 19.00 (*0-440-61382-5*, Dell Bks.); mass mkt. 5.99 o.s.i (*0-440-23491-3*) Dell Publishing.

—Death of an Orchid Lover. 2000. (Joe Portugal Mysteries Ser.). 320p. mass mkt. 5.99 o.s.i (*0-440-23492-1*) Bantam Dell Publishing Group.

—Death of an Orchid Lover. 2000. 320p. pap. 19.00 (*0-440-61385-X*, Dell Bks.) Dell Publishing.

Wambaugh, Joseph. The Choirboys. unabr. ed. 1976. audio 64.00 (*0-7366-0014-0*, 1024) Books on Tape, Inc.

—The Choirboys. 1987. 384p. mass mkt. 7.50 (*0-440-11188-9*); 1975. 8.95 o.p. (*0-440-05363-3*, Delacorte Pr.) Dell Publishing.

—Finnegan's Week. 1994. 352p. mass mkt. 7.50 (*0-553-56440-4*) Bantam Bks.

—Finnegan's Week. abr. ed. 1993. audio 16.95 o.p. (*1-56100-350-6*, 1305); audio 73.25 o.p. (*1-56100-155-4*, 836); audio 23.95 o.p. (*1-56100-527-4*, 343, Bookcassette) Brilliance Audio.

—Finnegan's Week. abr. ed. 2000. audio 7.95 (*1-57815-008-6*, 1009, Media Bks. Audio Publishing) Media Bks., L. L. C.

—Finnegan's Week. 1993. 348p. 22.00 o.p. (*0-688-12801-7*, Morrow, William & Co.) Morrow/Avon.

—Floaters. 1997. 304p. mass mkt. 6.99 (*0-553-57595-3*) Bantam Bks.

—Floaters. l.t. ed. 1996. 375p. 26.95 o.p. (*1-56895-365-8*, Wheeler Publishing, Inc.) Gale Group.

—Fugitive Nights. 1992. 384p. mass mkt. 7.50 (*0-553-29578-0*) Bantam Bks.

—Fugitive Nights. unabr. ed. 1992. audio 22.95 o.p. (*1-56100-455-3*, 431, Bookcassette); audio 57.25 o.p. (*1-56100-088-4*, 613, Unabridged Library Editions) Brilliance Audio.

—Fugitive Nights. 1992. 336p. 22.00 o.p. (*0-688-11128-9*, Morrow, William & Co.) Morrow/Avon.

—The Glitter Dome. 1984. mass mkt. 4.50 o.s.i (*0-553-26302-1*); 1982. 352p. mass mkt. 6.99 (*0-553-27259-4*) Bantam Bks.

—The Golden Orange. l.t. ed. 1992. 16.95 o.p. (*0-7927-0621-8*); 1991. 363p. 20.95 o.p. (*0-7927-0620-X*, E0005) BBC Audiobooks America.

—The Golden Orange. 1991. 416p. mass mkt. 7.50 (*0-553-29026-6*) Bantam Bks.

—The Golden Orange. unabr. ed. 1991. audio 73.25 o.p. (*1-56100-070-1*, 596); audio 23.95 o.p. (*0-930435-75-3*, 414, Bookcassette) Brilliance Audio.

—The Golden Orange. 1990. 317p. 19.95 o.p. (*0-688-09408-2*, Morrow, William & Co.) Morrow/Avon.

—Lines & Shadows. 1984. 384p. mass mkt. 4.50 o.s.i (*0-553-24607-0*); 416p. mass mkt. 6.99 (*0-553-27148-2*) Bantam Bks.

—Lines & Shadows. unabr. ed. 1985. lib. bdg. 73.25 o.p. incl. audio (*1-56100-002-7*, 926, Unabridged Library Editions); audio 19.95 o.p. (*0-930435-03-6*, 350, Bookcassette) Brilliance Audio.

—Lines & Shadows. 1984. 383p. 15.95 o.p. (*0-688-02619-2*, Morrow, William & Co.) Morrow/Avon.

—The New Centurions. unabr. ed. audio 59.50 Audio Bk. Co.

—The New Centurions. 1987. 368p. mass mkt. 7.50 (*0-440-16417-6*) Dell Publishing.

—The New Centurions. 1971. 30.00 o.p. (*0-316-92145-9*) Little Brown & Co.

—The Secrets of Harry Bright. 1986. 352p. pap. 19.00 (*0-553-76287-7*); 320p. mass mkt. 4.50 o.s.i (*0-553-26021-9*); 352p. mass mkt. 6.99 (*0-553-27430-9*) Bantam Bks.

—The Secrets of Harry Bright. l.t. ed. 1986. 444p. 18.95 o.p. (*0-8161-4066-9*); pap. 10.95 o.p. (*0-8161-4069-3*) Gale Group. (Macmillan Reference USA).

—The Secrets of Harry Bright. 1985. 345p. 17.95 o.p. (*0-688-05958-9*, Morrow, William & Co.) Morrow/Avon.

Ward, Robert. The Cactus Garden. 1996. 320p. mass mkt. 6.99 (*0-671-88266-X*, Pocket) Simon & Schuster.

—The Cactus Garden. Grose, William, ed. 1995. 304p. 22.00 o.p. (*0-671-88265-1*, Atria) Simon & Schuster.

Warner, Penny. Dead Body Language. 1997. (Connor Westphal Mystery Ser.). 288p. mass mkt. 5.50 o.s.i (*0-553-57586-4*, Crimeline) Bantam Bks.

—A Quiet Undertaking. 2000. 272p. mass mkt. 5.50 o.s.i (*0-553-57965-7*) Bantam Bks.

—Right to Remain Silent. 1998. 288p. mass mkt. 5.50 o.s.i (*0-553-57962-2*, Crimeline) Bantam Bks.

—Sign of Foul Play: A Connor Westphal Mystery. 1997. (Connor Westphal Mystery Ser.). 288p. mass mkt. 5.50 o.s.i (*0-553-57587-2*, Crimeline) Bantam Bks.

Warren, Bill. Nukin' Denham. 2000. 152p. pap. 20.99 (*0-7388-3020-8*) Xlibris Corp.

Washburn, L. J. Dead-Stick. l.t. ed. 1992. pap. 20.95 o.p. (*0-7927-1177-7*); 22.95 o.p. (*0-7927-1176-9*, CH0242) BBC Audiobooks America.

—Dead-Stick, Vol. 1. 1989. 16.95 o.p. (*0-312-93133-6*, Tor Bks.) Doherty, Tom Assocs., LLC.

—Dog Heavies: A Lucas Hallam Mystery. 1990. 288p. 17.95 o.p. (*0-312-93160-3*, Tor Bks.) Doherty, Tom Assocs., LLC.

—Wild Night. l.t. ed. 1991. 12.95 o.p. (*0-7927-0188-7*, 4718); pap. 10.95 o.p. (*0-7927-0189-5*, C0086) BBC Audiobooks America.

—Wild Night. 1987. 320p. pap. 3.95 o.p. (*0-8125-1041-0*, Tor Bks.) Doherty, Tom Assocs., LLC.

—Wild Night. 1998. (Mystery Ser.). 253p. 20.95 (*0-7862-1658-1*, Five Star) Gale Group.

Washburn, Stan. Intent to Harm. Chelius, Jane, ed. 1995. 384p. mass mkt. 5.99 (*0-671-88458-1*, Pocket); 1994. 352p. 22.00 o.p. (*0-671-88457-3*, Atria) Simon & Schuster.

—Into Thin Air. 1996. 336p. mass mkt. 6.99 (*0-671-56246-0*, Pocket) Simon & Schuster.

Waters, Frank. The Lizard Woman. 1995. Orig. Title: Fever Pitch. 146p. pap. 14.95 (*0-8040-0987-2*) Swallow Pr.

—The Lizard Woman. 1985. Orig. Title: Fever Pitch. 18.00 (*0-914476-99-8*) Thorp Springs Pr.

Waugh, Evelyn. The Loved One. unabr. collector's ed. 1992. audio 24.00 (*0-7366-2108-3*, 2912) Books on Tape, Inc.

—The Loved One. 1994. reprint ed. lib. bdg. 27.95 (*1-56849-358-4*) Buccaneer Bks., Inc.

—The Loved One. rev. ed. 1977. 13.95 o.s.i (*0-316-92618-3*) Little Brown & Co.
—The Loved One. l.t. ed. 1999. (Perennial Bestsellers Ser.). 131p. 27.95 (*0-7838-8787-6*) Thorndike Pr.
—The Loved One. lib. bdg. 20.95 (*1-56723-177-2*) Yestermorrow, Inc.
—The Loved One: A Novel. rev. ed. 1977. (Illus.). 176p. pap. 13.95 (*0-316-92608-6*, Back Bay) Little Brown & Co.
Weaver, Mary Cesario. A Mendocino Mystery. 2003. 184p. pap. 14.95 (*1-882897-74-9*) Lost Coast Pr.
Webster, Brenda. Sins of the Mothers. 1993. 364p. 21.00 (*1-880909-05-7*) Baskerville Pubs., Inc.
Weinberg, Robert & Gresh, Lois. The Termination Node. 1999. 320p. mass mkt. 6.99 o.s.i (*0-345-41246-X*, Del Rey) Ballantine Bks.
—The Termination Node. 1999. 13.04 (*0-606-18957-2*) Turtleback Bks.
Weiss, Mike. A Dry & Thirsty Ground. 1992. 240p. 17.95 o.p. (*0-312-06956-1*, Saint Martin's Minotaur) St. Martin's Pr.
Wellington, Janet. Forever Rose. 2000. (Time Passages Romance Ser.). 272p. mass mkt. 5.99 o.s.i (*0-515-12782-5*, Jove) Berkley Publishing Group.
Wells, Jess. AfterShocks: A Novel. 1992. 240p. (Orig.). pap. 9.95 o.p. (*1-879427-08-7*) 3rd Side Pr., Inc.
Wesner, Maralene & Wesner, Miles E. The God Unknown: What God Do You Worship? 1989. (What God Do You Worship? Ser.). 195p. pap. 11.95 (*0-936715-15-4*) Diversity Pr.
West, Charles G. The Sacred Disc. 2000. (San Joaquin Mysteries Ser.). 192p. pap. 12.95 (*0-9664520-4-6*); E-Book 7.00 (*1-930486-04-9*) Salvo Pr.
West, Jessamyn. The State of Stony Lonesome. 1984. 256p. 12.95 o.s.i (*0-15-184903-X*) Harcourt Trade Pubs.
Westmiller, Robin C. Red Wine for Breakfast. 1999. 220p. E-Book 8.95 incl. disk (*1-58519-015-2*); 220p. E-Book 4.95 (*1-58519-016-0*); 220p. E-Book 4.95 incl. cd-rom (*1-58519-017-9*); (Illus.). E-Book 12.95 incl. cd-rom (*1-58519-018-7*) Book-On-Disc.Com.
—Red Wine for Breakfast. 1999. 310p. pap. 14.95 o.p. (*1-893652-36-X*, Writers Club Pr.) iUniverse, Inc.
Wheeler, Richard. Sierra. l.t. ed. 1998. 448p. mass mkt. 5.99 (*0-8125-4288-6*, Forge Bks.) Doherty, Tom Assocs., LLC.
Wheeler, Richard S. Sierra: A Novel of the California Gold Rush. 1996. 380p. 24.95 o.p. (*0-312-86185-0*, Forge Bks.) Doherty, Tom Assocs., LLC.
White, Curtis. The Idea of Home. 1992. (New American Fiction Ser.: No. 27). 208p. (Orig.). pap. 12.95 (*1-55713-144-9*) Sun & Moon Pr.
White, Gloria. Charged with Guilt. 1995. 336p. mass mkt. 5.50 o.s.i (*0-440-22049-1*) Dell Publishing.
—Money to Burn. 1993. 320p. mass mkt. 4.99 o.s.i (*0-440-21612-5*, Dell Bks.) Dell Publishing.
—Money to Burn. unabr. ed. 1993. (Ronnie Ventana Mystery Ser.). audio 36.00 (*0-9624010-6-4*, 752466) Reader's Chair, Inc., The.
—Murder on the Run. 1991. 288p. mass mkt. 5.50 o.s.i (*0-440-20983-8*) Dell Publishing.
—Murder on the Run. unabr. ed. 1993. (Ronnie Ventana Mystery Ser.). audio 30.00 (*0-9624010-4-8*) Reader's Chair, Inc., The.
—Murder on the Run. 1992. 304p. 20.00 o.p. (*0-7278-4317-6*) Severn Hse. Pubs., Ltd.
—Sunset & Santiago. 1997. 320p. mass mkt. 5.50 o.s.i (*0-440-22326-1*) Dell Publishing.
White, Stewart Edward. The Story of California: Gold, the Gray Dawn, the Rose Dawn. reprint ed. 64.50 (*0-404-06936-3*) AMS Pr., Inc.
White, Teri. Fault Lines. 1988. 16.95 o.s.i (*0-89296-254-2*) Mysterious Pr.
—Fault Lines. 1989. mass mkt. 4.50 o.s.i (*0-445-40820-0*, Mysterious Pr. Paperback Bks.) Warner Bks., Inc.
—Tightrope. 228p. 1987. mass mkt. 3.95 o.s.i (*0-445-40579-1*); 1986. 15.95 o.p. (*0-89296-234-8*) Mysterious Pr.
White, Vicki Mason. Deadly Demise. 1997. mass mkt. 5.99 o.s.i (*0-449-14999-4*, Fawcett) Ballantine Bks.
Wicinas, David. Sagebrush & Cappuccino: Confessions of an L. A. Naturalist. 2000. 228p. pap. 14.95 (*0-595-00198-X*) iUniverse, Inc.
—Sagebrush & Cappuccino: Confessions of an LA Naturalist. 1995. 160p. (Orig.). pap. 13.00 o.p. (*0-87156-435-1*) Sierra Club Bks.
Wick, Lori. As Time Goes By. (Californians Ser.: Vol. 2). 279p. 2000. pap. 9.99 (*0-7369-0256-2*); 1992. pap. 9.99 o.s.i (*1-56507-005-4*) Harvest Hse. Pubs.
—As Time Goes By, Vol. 1. l.t. ed. 1999. (Christian Fiction Ser.). 376p. 25.95 (*0-7862-1832-0*) Thorndike Pr.
—Donovan's Daughter. (Californians Ser.: Vol. 4). 2000. 312p. pap. 9.99 (*0-7369-0257-0*); 1994. pap. 9.99 o.p. (*1-56507-129-8*) Harvest Hse. Pubs.
—Donovan's Daughter. l.t. ed. 1999. (Christian Fiction Ser.). 411p. 25.95 (*0-7862-2147-X*) Thorndike Pr.
—Sean Donovan. (Californians Ser.: Vol. 3). 2000. 276p. pap. 9.99 (*0-7369-0258-9*); 1993. 269p. pap. 9.99 o.p. (*1-56507-046-1*) Harvest Hse. Pubs.
—Sean Donovan. l.t. ed. 1999. (Christian Fiction Ser.). 355p. 25.95 (*0-7862-2053-8*) Thorndike Pr.
—Whatever Tomorrow Brings. 2000. (Californians Ser.: Vol. 1). 323p. pap. 9.99 (*0-7369-0259-7*); 1992. 250p. pap. 9.99 o.s.i (*0-89081-969-6*) Harvest Hse. Pubs.
—Whatever Tomorrow Brings. l.t. ed. 1999. (Christian Fiction Ser.). 480p. 25.95 (*0-7862-1802-9*) Thorndike Pr.
Wilcox, Collin. Aftershock. unabr. ed. 1997. (Frank Hastings Ser.). audio 48.00 (*0-7366-3554-8*, 4199) Books on Tape, Inc.
—Bernhardt's Edge. 1991. pap. 3.95 o.p. (*0-8125-1148-4*); 1988. 320p. 17.95 o.p. (*0-312-93076-3*) Doherty, Tom Assocs., LLC. (Tor Bks.).
—Calculated Risk. unabr. ed. 1996. (Frank Hastings Ser.). audio 48.00 (*0-7366-3203-4*, 3867) Books on Tape, Inc.
—Calculated Risk. 1995. 256p. 22.50 o.p. (*0-8050-3003-4*) Holt, Henry & Co.
—Dead Aim. unabr. ed. 1996. (Frank Hastings Ser.). audio 48.00 (*0-7366-3373-1*, 4023) Books on Tape, Inc.
—Dead Center. unabr. ed. 1993. (Frank Hastings Ser.). audio 48.00 (*0-7366-2519-4*, 3274) Books on Tape, Inc.
—Dead Center. 1995. pap. 5.95 o.p. (*0-8050-4232-6*, Owl Bks.); 1992. 256p. 18.95 o.p. (*0-8050-1615-5*) Holt, Henry & Co.
—A Death Before Dying. unabr. ed. 1992. (Frank Hastings Ser.). audio 56.00 (*0-7366-2212-8*, 3005) Books on Tape, Inc.
—A Death Before Dying. 1994. 231p. pap. 5.95 o.p. (*0-8050-3122-7*, Owl Bks.) Holt, Henry & Co.
—A Death Before Dying: A Lt. Hastings Mystery. 1990. 240p. 18.95 o.p. (*0-8050-0979-5*) Holt, Henry & Co.
—The Disappearance. 19.95 (*0-89190-580-4*) Amereon, Ltd.
—The Disappearance. unabr. ed. 1996. (Frank Hastings Ser.). audio 48.00 (*0-7366-3346-4*, 3996) Books on Tape, Inc.
—Doctor, Lawyer ... 1981. (Mystery Ser.). 192p. 1.95 o.s.i (*0-515-05194-2*, Jove) Berkley Publishing Group.
—Doctor, Lawyer ... 1977. 6.95 o.p. (*0-394-40061-5*) Random Hse., Inc.
—Doctor, Lawyer... unabr. ed. 1997. (Frank Hastings Ser.). audio 48.00 (*0-7366-3530-0*, 4168) Books on Tape, Inc.
—Except for the Bones. 1991. 288p. 18.95 o.p. (*0-312-93162-X*, Tor Bks.) Doherty, Tom Assocs., LLC.
—Find Her a Grave. 1993. 288p. 19.95 o.p. (*0-312-85244-4*, Forge Bks.) Doherty, Tom Assocs., LLC.
—Full Circle. 1994. 352p. 21.95 o.p. (*0-312-85521-4*, Forge Bks.) Doherty, Tom Assocs., LLC.
—Hiding Place. 20.95 (*0-89190-581-2*) Amereon, Ltd.
—Hiding Place. unabr. ed. 1996. (Frank Hastings Ser.). audio 48.00 (*0-7366-3404-5*, 4050) Books on Tape, Inc.
—Hire a Hangman. 1994. 248p. pap. 5.95 o.p. (*0-8050-3121-9*, Owl Bks.) Holt, Henry & Co.
—Hire a Hangman: A Lt. Hastings Mystery. Haun, Joann, ed. 1991. 256p. 18.95 o.p. (*0-8050-0980-9*) Holt, Henry & Co.
—The Lonely Hunter. unabr. ed. 1996. (Frank Hastings Ser.). audio 48.00 (*0-7366-3325-1*, 3977) Books on Tape, Inc.
—Long Way Down. unabr. ed. 1996. (Frank Hastings Ser.). audio 48.00 (*0-7366-3474-6*, 4117) Books on Tape, Inc.
—Mankiller. unabr. ed. 1997. (Frank Hastings Ser.). audio 48.00 (*0-7366-3788-5*, 4462) Books on Tape, Inc.
—Mankiller. 1980. 224p. 8.95 o.p. (*0-394-50550-6*) Random Hse., Inc.
—Night Games. 1986. 240p. 15.45 o.p. (*0-89296-160-0*) Mysterious Pr.
—Night Games. 1987. 240p. mass mkt. 3.95 o.s.i (*0-445-40590-2*, Mysterious Pr. Paperback Bks.) Warner Bks., Inc.
—The Pariah. 1988. 15.45 o.p. (*0-89296-280-1*) Mysterious Pr.
—The Pariah. 1989. mass mkt. 4.95 (*0-445-40790-5*, Mysterious Pr. Paperback Bks.) Warner Bks., Inc.
—Power Plays. 21.95 (*0-89190-582-0*) Amereon, Ltd.
—Power Plays. unabr. ed. 1997. (Frank Hastings Ser.). audio 48.00 (*0-7366-3737-0*, 4414) Books on Tape, Inc.
—Power Plays. 1979. 7.95 o.p. (*0-394-50172-1*) Random Hse., Inc.
—Silent Witness. 1992. mass mkt. 3.99 (*0-8125-1149-2*); 1990. 17.95 o.p. (*0-312-93161-1*) Doherty, Tom Assocs., LLC. (Tor Bks.).
—Stalking Horse: A Mystery. 1982. 10.50 o.p. (*0-394-51173-5*) Random Hse., Inc.
—Switchback. unabr. ed. 1994. (Frank Hastings Ser.). audio 56.00 (*0-7366-2701-4*, 3435) Books on Tape, Inc.
—Switchback. 1995. 89p. pap. 5.95 o.p. (*0-8050-4233-4*, Owl Bks.) Holt, Henry & Co.
—Switchback: A Lt. Hastings Mystery. 1993. 256p. 19.95 o.p. (*0-8050-2104-3*) Holt, Henry & Co.
—Victims. 1986. 14.95 o.p. (*0-89296-066-3*); pap. 3.95 o.p. (*0-445-40252-0*) Mysterious Pr.
Wilhelm, Kate. Justice for Some. 1994. (Northwest Mysteries Ser.). mass mkt. 5.99 o.s.i (*0-449-22247-0*, Fawcett) Ballantine Bks.
—Justice for Some. 1993. 272p. 18.95 o.p. (*0-312-09319-5*, Saint Martin's Minotaur) St. Martin's Pr.
Wilkerson, Ken. Blue Ride. 1998. 25.00 o.p. (*1-879378-34-5*); pap. 15.00 (*1-879378-33-7*) Xenos Bks.
Wilkins, Barbara. In Name Only: A Novel. 1992. 432p. 20.00 o.p. (*0-06-017957-0*) HarperTrade.
Williams, Susan D. Sunset Coast. 1995. 320p. pap. 11.99 o.p. (*0-89107-854-1*) Crossway Bks.
Willis, Connie. Remake. 1996. 176p. mass mkt. 5.99 (*0-553-57441-8*) Bantam Bks.
—Remake. ltd. ed. 1994. 45.00 (*0-929480-48-1*) Ziesing, Mark V.
Wilson, John Morgan. Justice at Risk: A Benjamin Justice Mystery. 2000. (Benjamin Justice Mystery Ser.). 368p. mass mkt. 6.50 (*0-553-57860-X*) Bantam Bks.
—Justice at Risk: A Benjamin Justice Mystery. 1999. (Benjamin Justice Mystery Ser.). 304p. 22.95 o.s.i (*0-385-49116-6*) Doubleday Publishing.
—Revision of Justice: A Benjamin Justice Mystery. 1999. (Benjamin Justice Mystery Ser.). 416p. mass mkt. 5.99 (*0-553-57533-3*) Bantam Bks.
—Simple Justice: A Benjamin Justice Mystery. 1997. (Benjamin Justice Mystery Ser.). 304p. mass mkt. 6.50 o.s.i (*0-553-57532-5*) Bantam Bks.
—Simple Justice: A Benjamin Justice Mystery. 1996. 256p. 21.00 o.s.i (*0-385-48234-5*) Doubleday Publishing.
Wilson, Staci Layne. The Dance: An Inspirational Romance. 2000. 212p. pap. 21.99 (*0-7388-2656-1*) Xlibris Corp.
Wings, Mary. She Came in a Flash. 1990. 24p. pap. 10.00 o.p. (*0-452-26384-0*, Plume) Dutton/Plume.
—She Came in a Flash. 1989. 208p. 17.95 o.p. (*0-453-00648-5*) NAL.
—She Came in Drag. 1999. (Emma Victor Mysteries Ser.). 352p. mass mkt. 6.50 o.s.i (*0-425-16935-9*) Berkley Publishing Group.
—She Came to the Castro. (Emma Victor Mysteries Ser.). 272p. 1998. mass mkt. 5.99 o.s.i (*0-425-16222-2*); 1997. 21.95 o.s.i (*0-425-15629-X*) Berkley Publishing Group. (Prime Crime).
Winslow, Don. California Fire & Life. 2001. 416p. mass mkt. 6.99 (*0-8041-1611-3*) Ballantine Bks.
—California Fire & Life. unabr. ed. 1999. audio 80.00 (*0-7887-3770-8*, 95987E7, Clipper Audio) Recorded Bks., LLC.
—While Drowning in the Desert. 1998. (Neal Carey Mysteries Ser.). 224p. mass mkt. 5.99 (*0-312-96118-9*, St. Martin's Paperbacks) St. Martin's Pr.
Winters, Angela. Know by Heart. 2001. (Arabesque Ser.). 256p. mass mkt. 5.99 (*1-58314-215-0*) BET Bks.
Wojciechowska, Maia. The Hollywood Kid. 1966. (YA). (gr. 7 up). lib. bdg. 11.89 o.p. (*0-06-026573-6*) HarperCollins Children's Bk. Group.
Wolfe, Susan. The Last Billable Hour. 1989. 240p. 15.95 o.p. (*0-312-02566-1*, Saint Martin's Minotaur) St. Martin's Pr.
Wolford, Shirley K. Design for Love. l.t. ed. 1999. 291p. pap. 12.95 (*1-58345-688-0*) Domhan Bks.
Wolitzer, Hilma. Tunnel of Love. 384p. 1995. pap. 12.00 o.p. (*0-06-118010-6*, Perennial); 1994. 20.00 o.p. (*0-06-118007-6*) HarperTrade.
Wolper, Carol. The Cigarette Girl. 1999. 208p. 22.95 o.p. (*1-57322-137-6*, Riverhead Bks. (Hardcovers)) Putnam Publishing Group, The.
—The Cigarette Girl: A Novel. 2000. 288p. pap. 12.95 (*1-57322-818-4*, Riverhead Trade (Paperbacks)) Berkley Publishing Group.
Wong, Geoffrey. A Golden State of Mind. 2001. 317p. pap. (*1-55212-635-8*) Trafford Publishing.
Wood, Barbara. Sacred Ground. E-Book 24.95 (*1-59061-241-8*) Adobe Systems, Inc.
—Sacred Ground. 2001. 340p. 24.95 (*0-312-27537-4*) St. Martin's Pr.
Wood, William P. Gangland. 1989. mass mkt. 4.95 o.p. (*0-312-91575-6*, St. Martin's Paperbacks); 1988. 384p. 18.95 o.p. (*0-312-01764-2*) St. Martin's Pr.
—Stay of Execution. Zion, Claire, ed. 1994. 416p. mass mkt. 5.99 (*0-671-73179-3*, Pocket) Simon & Schuster.
—Stay of Execution. 1993. o.s.i (*0-671-73178-5*, Atria) Simon & Schuster.
Woodman, Nancy. Sea-Fari Deep. 1998. (Illus.). 48p. (J). (gr. 3-7). 17.95 (*0-7922-7340-0*) National Geographic Society.
Woodruff, Charles. A Farm Where People Grow. 2000. 152p. pap. 20.99 (*0-7388-3149-2*) Xlibris Corp.
Woods, Paula L. Inner City Blues: A Charlotte Justice Novel. 1999. 316p. 23.95 (*0-393-04680-X*) Norton, W. W. & Co., Inc.
Woods, Stuart. Dead Eyes. 1994. 320p. 22.00 o.p. (*0-06-017715-2*) HarperTrade.
—Dead Eyes. 368p. 1995. mass mkt. 3.99 o.p. (*0-06-109480-3*); 1994. mass mkt. 7.99 (*0-06-109157-X*) Morrow/Avon. (HarperTorch).
—Dead Eyes. unabr. ed. 1995. audio 60.00 (*0-7887-0161-4*, 94386E7) Recorded Bks., LLC.
—L. A. Times. 1994. 400p. mass mkt. 7.99 (*0-06-109156-1*) HarperCollins Pubs.
—L. A. Times. 1993. 320p. 21.00 o.p. (*0-06-017714-4*) HarperTrade.
—L. A. Times. l.t. ed. 1995. 79p. mass mkt. 3.99 o.p. (*0-06-109479-X*, HarperTorch) Morrow/Avon.
—L. A. Times. unabr. ed. 1993. audio 60.00 (*1-55690-905-5*, 93401E7) Recorded Bks., LLC.
—L. A. Times. pap. 5.98 o.p. (*0-8317-0036-X*) Smithmark Pubs., Inc.
—Swimming to Catalina. unabr. ed. 1998. audio 64.00 (*0-7366-4188-2*, 4686) Books on Tape, Inc.
—Swimming to Catalina. l.t. ed. 1998. (Wheeler Large Print Book Ser.). 27.95 (*1-56895-620-7*, Wheeler Publishing, Inc.) Gale Group.
—Swimming to Catalina. 1998. 320p. 25.00 o.s.i (*0-06-018369-1*) HarperCollins Pubs.
—Swimming to Catalina. abr. ed. 2004. audio 14.95 (*0-06-072533-8*); Set. 1998. audio 25.00 (*0-694-51938-3*, 693583) HarperTrade. (HarperAudio).
—Swimming to Catalina. 1998. 416p. mass mkt. 7.99 (*0-06-109980-5*, HarperTorch) Morrow/Avon.
—Swimming to Catalina, unabr. ed. 1998. audio 60.00 (*0-7887-1973-4*, 95360E7) Recorded Bks., LLC.
Wooley, Marilyn. Jackpot Justice. E-Book 24.95 (*0-312-27384-3*); 2000. 352p. 24.95 (*0-312-25455-5*, Saint Martin's Minotaur) St. Martin's Pr.
Wrede, Barbara. Death in the Redwoods. deluxe unabr. ed. 2001. lib. bdg. 35.00 incl. audio (*0-932079-13-X*, 7913X) TimeFare Audio Bk. Productions.
Wright, Harold Bell. The Winning of Barbara Worth. Date not set. 516p. 31.95 (*0-8488-2510-1*) Amereon, Ltd.
—The Winning of Barbara Worth. unabr. ed. 1994. audio 59.95 (*1-55686-520-1*) Books in Motion.
—The Winning of Barbara Worth. 1975. lib. bdg. 20.60 (*0-89966-208-0*) Buccaneer Bks., Inc.
—The Winning of Barbara Worth. 1999. (Collected Works of Harold Bell Wright). 511p. reprint ed. lib. bdg. 118.00 (*1-58201-898-7*) Classic Bks.
—The Winning of Barbara Worth. 1999. 512p. pap. 5.95 (*1-56554-472-2*) Pelican Publishing Co., Inc.
—The Winning of Barbara Worth. Burke, Quentin, ed. enl. ed. 1998. (Illus.). 392p. reprint ed. 29.95 (*0-9618473-6-0*, 98-96669); 49.95 (*0-9618473-5-2*, 98-88051) Quellen Co., The.
—The Winning of Barbara Worth. 1987. (Illus.). 512p. reprint ed. 24.95 o.p. (*0-9618473-0-1*) Quellen Co., The.
Wuamett, Victor. Artichoke Hearts: A Chase Randel Mystery. 1991. 224p. 17.95 o.p. (*0-312-06294-X*, Saint Martin's Minotaur) St. Martin's Pr.
Wurlitzer, Rudolph. Quake. 2nd ed. 1995. (Midnight Classics Ser.). 158p. pap. (*1-85242-409-5*) Serpent's Tail Ltd.
—Slow Fade. 1984. 209p. (Orig.). 13.95 o.p. (*0-394-53610-X*) Knopf, Alfred A. Inc.
Wurlitzer, Rudy. Quake. 2000. 158p. pap. 39.95 o.p. (*1-56649-116-9*) Welcome Rain Pubs.
Wyman, Margaret. Mission: The Birth of California, the Death of a Nation. Orton, Jerry, ed. 2002. 316p. per. 16.95 (*1-931857-00-8*) Idyllwild Publishing Co.
Yalom, Irvin D. Lying on the Couch. 1996. 384p. text 25.00 o.p. (*0-465-04295-3*) Basic Bks.
—Lying on the Couch: A Novel. 1997. 384p. pap. 14.00 (*0-06-092851-4*, Perennial) HarperTrade.
Yamaguchi, Yoji. Face of a Stranger. 1995. 208p. 18.00 o.p. (*0-06-017235-5*) HarperTrade.
Yamashita, Karen T. Tropic of Orange. 1997. 280p. (Orig.). pap. 14.95 (*1-56689-064-0*) Coffee Hse. Pr.
Ybarra, Ricardo M. Brotherhood of Dolphins. 1997. 160p. pap. 12.95 (*1-55885-215-8*) Arte Publico Pr.
Yelverton, Therese. Zanita: A Tale of the Yo-Semite. 1991. 209p. reprint ed. pap. 9.95 o.s.i (*0-89815-410-3*) Ten Speed Pr.
Yorke, Christy. Song of the Seals. 2003. 320p. pap. 14.00 (*0-425-18824-8*) Berkley Publishing Group.
Young, Al. Seduction by Light. 1988. 352p. pap. 8.95 o.s.i (*0-385-29943-5*, Delta) Dell Publishing.
—Who Is Angelina? 1996. (California Fiction Ser.). 280p. (C). pap. text 15.95 (*0-520-20712-2*) Univ. of California Pr.
Young & Dead. 2001. mass mkt. (*1-931297-55-X*); E-Book 7.99 net. (*1-931297-47-9*) Bookbooters Pr.
Yukic, Eleanor. The Devil's Punchbowl. 1997. 152p. 14.00 o.p. (*0-8059-4109-6*) Dorrance Publishing Co., Inc.
Zackel, Fred. Cinderella After Midnight. 1980. 11.95 o.p. (*0-698-10990-2*) Putnam Publishing Group, The.
—Cocaine & Blue Eyes. 1983. 320p. mass mkt. 2.95 o.p. (*0-425-06241-4*) Berkley Publishing Group.
—Cocaine & Blue Eyes. 1978. 8.95 o.p. (*0-698-10934-1*) Putnam Publishing Group, The.

Settings

Zappa, Moon Unit. America the Beautiful: A Novel. 2001. 304p. pap. 14.00 (0-7432-1383-1); E-Book 9.99 (0-7432-1913-9) Simon & Schuster. (Touchstone).

Zavala, Ann. The San Francisco Gold. 1995. 288p. 21.95 o.p. (0-312-85441-2, Forge Bks.) Doherty, Tom Assocs., LLC.

—San Francisco Gold. 1996. 286p. pap. text 5.99 (0-8125-2360-1, Forge Bks.) Doherty, Tom Assocs., LLC.

Zelman, Anita. Dead down Under: A Rebecca Lewis Mystery. 2002. 188p. 12.95 (1-56474-398-5) Fithian Pr.

Zimmerman, Bruce. Blood under the Bridge. 1989. 16.95 o.p. (0-06-016087-X) HarperTrade.

—Blood under the Bridge. 1990. mass mkt. 3.95 o.p. (0-312-92244-2, St. Martin's Paperbacks) St. Martin's Pr.

—Crimson Green: A Quinn Parker Novel of Suspense. 1994. 320p. 20.00 o.p. (0-06-017069-7) HarperCollins Pubs.

—Crimson Green: A Quinn Parker Suspense Novel. 1995. 368p. mass mkt. 4.50 o.p. (0-06-109359-9) HarperCollins Pubs.

—Full-Bodied Red. 1994. 400p. mass mkt. 4.50 o.p. (0-06-109175-8, HarperTorch) Morrow/Avon.

—Full-Bodied Red: A Quinn Parker Novel of Suspense. 1993. 288p. 20.00 o.p. (0-06-017931-7) HarperTrade.

—Thicker Than Water: A Novel of Suspense. 1991. 288p. 19.95 o.p. (0-06-016387-9) HarperTrade.

—Thicker Than Water: A Quinn Parker Mystery. 1993. 368p. mass mkt. 4.50 o.p. (0-06-109026-3, HarperTorch) Morrow/Avon.

### CALLOWAY CORNERS (IMAGINARY PLACE)—FICTION

Burton, Katherine. Tess. 1993. (Calloway Corners Ser.). per. (0-373-83280-X, 1-83280-7, Harlequin Bks.) Harlequin Enterprises, Ltd.

Canfield, Sandra. Mariah. 1993. (Calloway Corners Ser.). per. (0-373-83278-8, 1-83278-1); 1988. (Harlequin Superromance Ser.: No. 338). pap. (0-373-70338-4) Harlequin Enterprises, Ltd. (Harlequin Bks.).

Hughes, Tracy. Jo. 1993. (Calloway Corners Ser.). per. (0-373-83279-6, 1-83279-9, Harlequin Bks.) Harlequin Enterprises, Ltd.

Richards, Penny. Eden. 1993. (Calloway Corners Ser.). per. (0-373-83281-8, 1-83281-5, Harlequin Bks.) Harlequin Enterprises, Ltd.

### CALUSA (FLA.: IMAGINARY PLACE)—FICTION

McBain, Ed, pseud. Beauty & the Beast. unabr. ed. 1985. (Matthew Hope Ser.). audio 42.00 (0-7366-1034-0, 1964) Books on Tape, Inc.

—Beauty & the Beast. 1983. 228p. o.p. (0-03-062198-4) Holt, Henry & Co.

—Beauty & the Beast. 1988. 256p. mass mkt. 3.99 o.s.i (1-55817-662-4); mass mkt. 3.95 o.p. (1-55817-134-7) Kensington Publishing Corp. (Pinnacle Bks.).

—Beauty & the Beast. 1994. 224p. mass mkt. 5.99 o.s.i (0-446-60131-4) Warner Bks., Inc.

—Cinderella. unabr. ed. 1992. (Matthew Hope Ser.). audio 48.00 (0-7366-2245-4, 3035) Books on Tape, Inc.

—Cinderella. 1986. (Matthew Hope Ser.). 256p. (J). o.p. (0-03-004959-8) Holt, Henry & Co.

—Cinderella. 1993. 15.95 o.p. (1-55800-396-7); audio 8.95 o.p. (1-55800-494-7, Dove Audio) NewStar Media, Inc.

—Cinderella. 272p. 1994. mass mkt. 5.99 o.s.i (0-446-60134-9); 1989. mass mkt. 4.99 (0-445-40898-7, Mysterious Pr. Paperback Bks.); 1987. mass mkt. 3.95 o.s.i (0-445-40618-6) Warner Bks., Inc.

—Gladly the Cross-Eyed Bear. unabr. ed. 1997. (Matthew Hope Ser.). audio 48.00 (0-913369-38-1, 4214) Books on Tape, Inc.

—Gladly the Cross-Eyed Bear, Set. abr. ed. 1996. (Matthew Hope Mystery Ser.). 3p. audio 16.99 (0-88646-423-4, 394439) Durkin Hayes Publishing Ltd.

—Gladly the Cross-Eyed Bear. l.t. ed. 1996. (G. K. Hall Core Ser.). 424p. 25.95 (0-7838-1899-8, Macmillan Reference USA) Gale Group.

—Gladly the Cross-Eyed Bear. l.t. ed. 1998. (Paperback Bestsellers Ser.). 424p. pap. 25.95 (0-7838-1900-5) Thorndike Pr.

—Gladly the Cross-Eyed Bear. (Matthew Hope Novels Ser.). 336p. 1998. mass mkt. 6.50 o.s.i (0-446-60494-1); 1996. 22.50 o.p. (0-446-51989-8) Warner Bks., Inc.

—Goldilocks. 1979. pap. 2.25 o.p. (0-553-12158-8, 13158-3) Bantam Bks.

—Goldilocks. unabr. ed. 1985. (Matthew Hope Ser.). audio 36.00 (0-7366-1032-4, 1962) Books on Tape, Inc.

—Goldilocks. 224p. 1988. mass mkt. 3.95 o.s.i (1-55817-108-8); 1985. pap. 3.50 o.p. (0-523-42452-3) Kensington Publishing Corp. (Pinnacle Bks.).

—Goldilocks. 1978. 8.95 o.p. (0-87795-177-2, Morrow, William & Co.) Morrow/Avon.

—Goldilocks. 1996. 224p. mass mkt. 5.99 o.s.i (0-446-60305-8) Warner Bks., Inc.

—The House That Jack Built. unabr. ed. 1992. (Matthew Hope Ser.). audio 48.00 (0-7366-2177-6, 2974) Books on Tape, Inc.

—The House That Jack Built. l.t. ed. 1989. (General Ser.). 320p. 13.95 o.p. (0-8161-4934-8); lib. bdg. 20.95 (0-8161-4758-2) Gale Group. (Macmillan Reference USA).

—The House That Jack Built. 1988. 16.95 o.p. (0-8050-0787-3) Holt, Henry & Co.

—The House That Jack Built. 256p. 1994. mass mkt. 5.99 o.s.i (0-446-60136-5); 1989. mass mkt. 4.99 (0-445-40623-2, Mysterious Pr. Paperback Bks.) Warner Bks., Inc.

—Jack & the Beanstalk. unabr. ed. 1985. (Matthew Hope Ser.). audio 48.00 Books on Tape, Inc.

—Jack & the Beanstalk. 1984. o.p. (0-03-062197-6) Holt, Henry & Co.

—Jack & the Beanstalk. 288p. 1992. mass mkt. 3.99 o.s.i (1-55817-663-2); 1985. pap. 3.50 o.p. (0-523-42559-7) Kensington Publishing Corp. (Pinnacle Bks.).

—Jack & the Beanstalk. 1994. 256p. mass mkt. 5.99 (0-446-60132-2) Warner Bks., Inc.

—The Last Best Hope. unabr. ed. 1998. (Matthew Hope Ser.). audio 40.00 (0-7366-4215-3, 4713) Books on Tape, Inc.

—The Last Best Hope. l.t. ed. 1998. (Basic Ser.). 397p. pap. 29.95 (0-7862-1605-0) Thorndike Pr.

—The Last Best Hope. (Matthew Hope Novels Ser.). 1999. 304p. mass mkt. 7.50 o.s.i (0-446-60673-1); 1998. 320p. 24.00 o.p. (0-446-51990-1) Warner Bks., Inc.

—Mary, Mary. l.t. ed. 1993. 24.95 o.p. (0-7927-1662-0); pap. 22.95 o.p. (0-7927-1661-2) BBC Audiobooks America.

—Mary, Mary. unabr. ed. 1993. (Matthew Hope Ser.). audio 72.00 (0-7366-2480-5, 3242) Books on Tape, Inc.

—Mary, Mary. unabr. ed. 1993. 73.25 o.p. incl. audio (1-56100-137-6, 1280, Unabridged Library Editions); audio 23.95 o.p. (1-56100-508-8, 173, Bookcassette) Brilliance Audio.

—Mary, Mary. 384p. 1994. mass mkt. 5.99 o.s.i (0-446-60054-7); 1993. 19.95 o.s.i (0-446-51738-0) Warner Bks., Inc.

—Puss in Boots. unabr. ed. 1992. (Matthew Hope Ser.). audio 48.00 (0-7366-2193-8, 2988) Books on Tape, Inc.

—Puss in Boots. 1987. 15.95 o.p. (0-8050-0371-1) Holt, Henry & Co.

—Puss in Boots. 1993. audio 15.95 o.p. (1-55800-259-6) NewStar Media, Inc.

—Puss in Boots. 1994. 224p. mass mkt. 5.99 o.s.i (0-446-60135-7); 1988. mass mkt. 4.95 o.s.i (0-445-40621-6) Warner Bks., Inc.

—Rumpelstiltskin. 1985. 240p. mass mkt. 4.95 o.s.i (0-345-33149-4); 1982. mass mkt. 2.50 o.p. (0-345-30436-5) Ballantine Bks.

—Rumpelstiltskin. 1981. (Matthew Hope Mystery Ser.). 12.95 o.p. (0-670-61059-3) Viking Penguin.

—Rumpelstiltskin. 1994. 240p. mass mkt. 5.99 o.s.i (0-446-60130-6) Warner Bks., Inc.

—Snow White & Rose Red. unabr. ed. 1995. audio 54.95 (0-7451-6155-3, CAB 162) BBC Audiobooks America.

—Snow White & Rose Red. unabr. ed. 1986. (Matthew Hope Ser.). audio 48.00 (0-7366-1036-7, 1966) Books on Tape, Inc.

—Snow White & Rose Red. 1985. o.p. (0-03-002603-2) Holt, Henry & Co.

—Snow White & Rose Red. abr. ed. 1993. audio 15.95 o.p. (1-55800-256-1, Dove Audio) NewStar Media, Inc.

—Snow White & Rose Red. 256p. 1994. mass mkt. 5.99 o.p. (0-446-60133-0); 1986. reprint ed. mass mkt. 4.99 o.s.i (0-445-40513-9) Warner Bks., Inc.

—There Was a Little Girl. unabr. ed. 1995. (Matthew Hope Ser.). audio 56.00 (0-7366-2972-6, 3663) Books on Tape, Inc.

—There Was a Little Girl. l.t. ed. 1995. 424p. pap. 19.95 o.p. (0-7838-1181-0); 480p. 24.95 o.p. (0-7838-1180-2) Gale Group. (Macmillan Reference USA).

—There Was a Little Girl. 1999. audio (1-57042-777-1) Time Warner AudioBooks.

—There Was a Little Girl. 1995. 352p. mass mkt. 6.50 (0-446-60214-0); 1994. 336p. 21.95 o.s.i (0-446-51739-9) Warner Bks., Inc.

—Three Blind Mice. unabr. ed. 1991. (Matthew Hope Ser.). audio 56.00 (0-7366-1963-1, 2784) Books on Tape, Inc.

—Three Blind Mice. l.t. ed. 1991. (General Ser.). 396p. lib. bdg. 21.95 (0-8161-5169-5, Macmillan Reference USA) Gale Group.

—Three Blind Mice. abr. ed. (Super Sound Buy, Dove Ser.). 1994. audio 8.99 o.p. (0-7871-0233-4); 1993. 15.95 o.p. (1-55800-392-4, 41460) NewStar Media, Inc.

—Three Blind Mice. 1994. 304p. mass mkt. 5.99 o.s.i (0-446-60137-3); 1991. mass mkt. 4.99 o.s.i (0-446-40035-1) Warner Bks., Inc.

### CAMBODIA—FICTION

Beld, Gordon. A Gentle Breeze from Gossamer Wings: A Fictional Depiction of Refugees from the Pol Pot Era. 1999. (Judeo-Christian Ethics Ser.). (Illus.). ix, 304p. pap. 18.00 (1-885288-07-7) PREP Publishing.

Bergin, Bob. Stone Gods, Wooden Elephants. 2001. 318p. pap. 14.95 (1-57023-177-X) Impact Pubns.

Bingham, Robert. Lightning on the Sun: A Novel. 2001. 304p. reprint ed. pap. 13.00 (0-385-48868-8, Knopf Bks. for Young Readers) Random Hse. Children's Bks.

Bosco, Rosco Lo. Buddha Wept: A Novel of Terror & Transcendence. 2003. 144p. 21.95 (0-9671851-8-1) GreyCore Pr.

Fowler, William. Speedin' A Strange & Savage Trip Thru the Thai & Cambodian Badlands. 2000. 168p. E-Book 8.00 (0-7388-8972-5) Xlibris Corp.

Keeley, Edmund. A Wilderness Called Peace. 1985. 16.45 o.p. (0-671-47416-2, Simon & Schuster) Simon & Schuster.

Keeley, Edmund. A Wilderness Called Peace. 1987. 368p. reprint ed. mass mkt. 4.95 o.s.i (0-440-39376-0, Laurel) Dell Publishing.

May, Peter. The Noble Path. 1993. 19.95 o.p. (0-312-08864-7, Saint Martin's Minotaur) St. Martin's Pr.

Ryan, Paul R. Khmer Rouge End Game. 1998. x, 236p. pap. 16.95 (0-9662707-4-6); xvi, 192 p. (0-9662707-3-8) Munewata Pr.

Sam, Sien. In the Land of the Red Prince. 1994. 14.95 o.p. (0-533-10698-2) Vantage Pr., Inc.

Schow, Vione I. Phay Vanneth: Dead or Alive? 2002. 180p. pap. 12.95 (1-55517-605-4, Bonneville Bks.) Cedar Fort, Inc./CFI Distribution.

Webber, Elsie. The Saving Rain. 1989. (Illus.). 220p. 17.95 (0-8283-1911-1) Branden Bks.

### CAMBRIDGE (MASS.)—FICTION

Allen, Irene. Quaker Silence: An Elizabeth Elliot Mystery. 1992. 210p. 17.00 o.s.i (0-679-41414-2, Villard Bks.) Random House Adult Trade Publishing Group.

—Quaker Testimony. 272p. 1996. text 21.95 o.p. (0-312-14709-0, Saint Martin's Minotaur); Vol. 1. 1998. (Quaker Testimony Ser.: Vol. 1). (Illus.). mass mkt. 5.99 (0-312-96424-2, St. Martin's Paperbacks) St. Martin's Pr.

—Quaker Witness. 1993. 254p. 18.00 o.s.i (0-679-41415-0, Villard Bks.) Random House Adult Trade Publishing Group.

—Quaker Witness. 2001. 272p. mass mkt. 5.99 (0-312-97285-7, St. Martin's Paperbacks) St. Martin's Pr.

Conant, Susan. Animal Appetite: A Dog Lover's Mystery. 1998. (Dog Lover's Mysteries Ser.). 304p. reprint ed. mass mkt. 5.99 o.s.i (0-553-57186-9, Crimeline) Bantam Bks.

—The Barker Street Regulars: A Dog Lover's Mystery. 1999. (Dog Lover's Mysteries Ser.). 288p. mass mkt. 6.99 (0-553-57655-0) Bantam Bks.

—The Barker Street Regulars: A Dog Lover's Mystery. l.t. ed. 1998. (Large Print Book Ser.). pap. 23.95 (1-56895-609-6, Wheeler Publishing, Inc.) Gale Group.

—Bite of Death. 1991. 4.50 (1-55773-490-9) Ace Bks.

—Bite of Death. 1994. mass mkt. 5.99 o.s.i (0-425-14542-5) Berkley Publishing Group.

—Black Ribbon: A Dog Lover's Mystery. 1995. (Dog Lover's Mysteries Ser.). 288p. reprint ed. mass mkt. 5.99 o.s.i (0-553-29875-5, Crimeline) Bantam Bks.

—Bloodlines. 1993. (Dog Lover's Mysteries Ser.). 272p. mass mkt. 5.99 (0-553-29886-0) Bantam Bks.

—Bride & Groom. 2004. 272p. 22.95 (0-425-19412-4) Berkley Publishing Group.

—Creature Discomforts. 2001. (Dog Lover's Mysteries Ser.). 224p. mass mkt. 6.99 (0-553-58059-0, Spectra) Bantam Bks.

—Creature Discomforts: A Dog Lover's Mystery. l.t. ed. 2001. (Beeler Large Print Mystery Ser.). 228p. 25.95 (1-57490-360-8, Beeler Large Print Bks.) Beeler, Thomas T. Publisher.

—Creature Discomforts: A Dog Lover's Mystery. 2000. 256p. 22.95 o.s.i (0-385-49446-7) Doubleday Publishing.

—Dead & Doggone. 2003. (Mystery Ser.). 27.95 (1-57490-466-3) Beeler, Thomas T. Publisher.

—Dead & Doggone. 1990. mass mkt. 5.99 o.s.i (0-425-14429-1, Prime Crime) Berkley Publishing Group.

—Evil Breeding. 2000. (Dog Lover's Mysteries Ser.). 224p. reprint ed. mass mkt. 6.99 (0-553-58052-3) Bantam Bks.

—Gone to the Dogs: A Dog Lover's Mystery. 1992. (Dog Lover's Mysteries Ser.). 272p. mass mkt. 5.99 (0-553-29734-1) Bantam Bks.

—Gone to the Dogs: A Dog Lover's Mystery. l.t. ed. 2003. (Mystery Ser.). 27.95 (1-57490-488-4, Beeler Large Print Bks.) Beeler, Thomas T. Publisher.

—Gone to the Dogs: A Dog Lover's Mystery. 1992. 224p. 16.50 o.s.i (0-385-42378-0) Doubleday Publishing.

—New Leash on Death. 1990. 4.50 (1-55773-385-6) Berkley Publishing Group.

—A New Leash on Death. 1994. 192p. mass mkt. 5.99 (0-425-14622-7) Berkley Publishing Group.

—Paws Before Dying. 1991. 4.50 (1-55773-550-6) Ace Bks.

—Paws Before Dying. 1991. mass mkt. 5.99 o.s.i (0-425-14430-5) Berkley Publishing Group.

—Ruffly Speaking: A Dog Lover's Mystery. 1994. (Dog Lover's Mysteries Ser.). 304p. mass mkt. 6.99 (0-553-29484-9) Bantam Bks.

—Stud Rites: A Dog Lover's Mystery. 1997. (Dog Lover's Mysteries Ser.). 272p. mass mkt. 5.99 o.s.i (0-553-57300-4, Crimeline) Bantam Bks.

Dershowitz, Alan M. The Advocate's Devil. abr. ed. 1994. audio 17.95 o.p. (0-7871-0408-6, Dove Audio) NewStar Media, Inc.

—The Advocate's Devil. 1999. 352p. reprint ed. lib. bdg. 35.95 (0-7351-0066-7) Replica Bks.

—The Advocate's Devil. 384p. 2001. pap. 4.95 (0-446-51759-3); 1995. mass mkt. 6.50 (0-446-60291-4) Warner Bks., Inc.

Desmond, Sean. Adams Fall. 2000. 245p. 22.95 (0-312-26254-X) St. Martin's Pr.

Greeley, Andrew M. Star Bright! A Christmas Story. l.t. ed. 1998. 19.95 (1-57490-166-4) Beeler, Thomas T. Publisher.

—Star Bright! A Christmas Story. 1997. 127p. 13.95 (0-312-86387-X); 128p. 111.60 o.s.i (0-312-86500-7) Doherty, Tom Assocs., LLC. (Forge Bks.).

—Star Bright! A Christmas Story, Set. abr. ed. 1997. audio 16.99 Durkin Hayes Publishing Ltd.

—Star Bright! A Christmas Story. 1999. 13.95 (0-312-87116-3) St. Martin's Pr.

Gregory, Susanna. A Killer in Winter. 2003. (Illus.). 496p. (0-316-86011-5) Time Warner Bks. UK GBR. *Dist:* Trafalgar Square.

Kelly, Susan. The Gemini Man. 1986. 304p. mass mkt. 2.95 o.s.i (0-345-33113-3) Ballantine Bks.

—The Gemini Man. 1985. 221p. 14.95 o.s.i (0-8027-5613-1) Walker & Co.

—Out of the Darkness. unabr. ed. 1992. audio 21.95 o.p. (1-56100-478-2, 204, Bookcassette); audio 57.25 o.p. (1-56100-112-0, 974, Unabridged Library Editions) Brilliance Audio.

—Out of the Darkness. 1994. 352p. mass mkt. 4.50 o.s.i (0-8217-4620-0) Kensington Publishing Corp.

—Out of the Darkness. 1992. 278p. 18.00 o.s.i (0-679-41131-3, Villard Bks.) Random House Adult Trade Publishing Group.

—The Summertime Soldiers. 1986. 192p. 14.95 o.p. (0-8027-5646-8) Walker & Co.

—Trail of the Dragon. 1990. 256p. mass mkt. 3.95 o.s.i (0-345-35749-3) Ballantine Bks.

—Trail of the Dragon. 1988. 282p. 17.95 (0-8027-5696-4) Walker & Co.

—Until Proven Innocent. unabr. ed. 1991. audio 57.25 o.p. (1-56100-067-1, 593); audio 21.95 o.p. (0-930435-73-7, 411) Brilliance Audio.

—Until Proven Innocent. 1990. 288p. 16.95 o.s.i (0-394-58414-7, Villard Bks.) Random House Adult Trade Publishing Group.

Kraus, Jim & Kraus, Terri. The Quest: A Novel. 2002. (Circle of Destiny Ser.). 384p. pap. 10.99 o.p. (0-8423-1838-0) Tyndale Hse. Pubs.

Langton, Jane. Dark Nantucket Noon. 1993. (Black Dagger Crime Ser.). (Illus.). 304p. 16.50 o.p. (0-7451-8604-1, Black Dagger) BBC Audiobooks America.

—Dark Nantucket Noon. unabr. ed. 1982. audio 48.00 (0-7366-0630-0, 1591) Books on Tape, Inc.

—Dark Nantucket Noon. 1981. (Fiction Ser.). 304p. pap. 5.99 (0-14-005836-2, Penguin Bks.) Penguin Group (USA) Inc.

—Divine Inspiration: A Homer Kelly Mystery. unabr. collector's ed. 1994. audio 56.00 (0-7366-2722-7, 3452) Books on Tape, Inc.

—Divine Inspiration: A Homer Kelly Mystery. abr. ed. 1994. (Homer Kelly Mystery Ser.). audio 16.00 o.p. (0-453-00888-7, Penguin AudioBooks) HighBridge Co.

—Divine Inspiration: A Homer Kelly Mystery. 1994. (Homer Kelly Mystery Ser.). (Illus.). 416p. reprint ed. pap. 5.99 o.s.i (0-14-017376-5, Penguin Bks.) Penguin Group (USA) Inc.

—Divine Inspiration: A Homer Kelly Mystery. 1993. (Homer Kelly Mystery Ser.). (Illus.). 416p. 20.00 o.p. (0-670-84709-7, Viking) Viking Penguin.

—Emily Dickinson Is Dead. unabr. collector's ed. 1987. audio 48.00 (0-7366-1077-4, 2004) Books on Tape, Inc.

—Emily Dickinson Is Dead. 1984. 256p. 13.95 o.p. (0-312-24434-7) St. Martin's Pr.

—Emily Dickinson Is Dead. l.t. ed. 1992. (Linford Mystery Large Print Ser.). 448p. pap. 17.99 o.p. (0-7089-7162-8, Ulverscroft) Thorpe, F. A. Pubs. GBR. *Dist:* Ulverscroft Large Print Bks., Ltd., Ulverscroft Large Print Canada, Ltd.

—Emily Dickinson Is Dead. 1985. (Crime Ser.). 256p. pap. 5.95 o.p. (*0-14-007771-5*, Penguin Bks.) Viking Penguin.

—The Escher Twist: A Homer Kelly Mystery. 2002. (Homer Kelly Mystery Ser.). (Illus.). 256p. 22.95 o.s.i (*0-670-03067-8*, Viking) Viking Penguin.

—The Face on the Wall: A Homer Kelly Mystery. l.t. ed. 1999. (Large Print Mystery Ser.). 25.95 (*1-57490-205-9*, Beeler Large Print Bks.) Beeler, Thomas T. Publisher.

—The Face on the Wall: A Homer Kelly Mystery, , unabr. ed. 1999. audio 48.00 (*0-7366-4369-9*, 4827) Books on Tape, Inc.

—The Face on the Wall: A Homer Kelly Mystery. 1999. (Homer Kelly Mystery Ser.). (Illus.). 304p. pap. 5.99 o.s.i (*0-14-028157-6*) Penguin Group (USA) Inc.

—The Face on the Wall: A Homer Kelly Mystery. 1998. (Homer Kelly Mystery Ser.). (Illus.). 288p. 21.95 o.p. (*0-670-87674-7*) Viking Penguin.

—Good & Dead. unabr. collector's ed. 1992. audio 48.00 (*0-7366-2223-3*, 3013) Books on Tape, Inc.

—Good & Dead. 1986. 320p. 15.95 o.p. (*0-312-33865-1*) St. Martin's Pr.

—Good & Dead. (Homer Kelly Mystery Ser.). 256p. 1989. pap. 5.95 o.s.i (*0-14-012687-2*); 1987. pap. 3.95 o.p. (*0-14-010088-1*) Viking Penguin. (Penguin Bks.).

—The Memorial Hall Murder. unabr. ed. 1982. audio 48.00 (*0-7366-0631-9*, 1592) Books on Tape, Inc.

—The Memorial Hall Murder. 1996. pap. (*0-14-771166-5*) Penguin Group (USA) Inc.

—The Memorial Hall Murder. 1981. (Fiction Ser.). 272p. pap. 5.95 o.p. (*0-14-005704-8*, Penguin Bks.) Viking Penguin.

—Murder at the Gardner. unabr. collector's ed. 1990. audio 56.00 (*0-7366-1741-8*, 2581) Books on Tape, Inc.

—Murder at the Gardner. 1989. (Penguin Crime Fiction Ser.). 368p. pap. 6.99 (*0-14-011382-7*, Penguin Bks.) Penguin Group (USA) Inc.

—Murder at the Gardner. 1988. (Illus.). 288p. 17.95 o.p. (*0-312-01479-1*, Saint Martin's Minotaur) St. Martin's Pr.

—Natural Enemy. unabr. collector's ed. 1992. audio 48.00 (*0-7366-2231-4*, 3021) Books on Tape, Inc.

—Natural Enemy. 1982. (Joan Kahn Bk.). (Illus.). 288p. 11.95 o.p. (*0-89919-081-2*) Houghton Mifflin Co.

—Natural Enemy. (Homer Kelly Mystery Ser.). 1990. 28p. pap. 5.95 o.p. (*0-14-013393-3*); 1987. (Illus.). 228p. pap. 3.95 o.p. (*0-14-009345-1*) Viking Penguin. (Penguin Bks.).

—The Shortest Day: Murder at the Revels. 1996. (Homer Kelly Mystery Ser.). (Illus.). 272p. pap. 5.95 o.s.i (*0-14-017377-3*, Viking) Penguin Group (USA) Inc.

—The Shortest Day: Murder at the Revels. 1995. (Homer Kelly Mystery Ser.). (Illus.). 272p. 19.95 o.p. (*0-670-84710-0*) Viking Penguin.

—The Transcendental Murder. unabr. collector's ed. 1982. audio 48.00 (*0-7366-0499-5*, 1473) Books on Tape, Inc.

—The Transcendental Murder. (Homer Kelly Mystery Ser.). 1990. 36p. pap. 6.95 o.p. (*0-14-014852-3*); 1989. 288p. pap. 3.95 o.p. (*0-14-011384-3*) Viking Penguin. (Penguin Bks.).

Medwed, Mameve. The End of an Error. 320p. 2003. (Illus.). 24.95 (*0-446-53079-4*); 2000. 23.95 (*0-446-52166-3*) Warner Bks., Inc.

—The Host Family. 2001. 320p. pap. 13.95 o.s.i (*0-446-67661-6*) Warner Bks., Inc.

Swann, E. L. Night Gardening. unabr. ed. 1999. audio 24.95 (*1-56740-825-7*, 1592, Brilliance Audio Unabridged) Brilliance Audio.

—Night Gardening. l.t. ed. 2000. (G. K. Hall Core Ser.). 256p. 28.95 (*0-7838-9036-2*, Macmillan Reference USA) Gale Group.

—Night Gardening. 2000. (Illus.). 208p. mass mkt. 6.50 o.s.i (*0-7868-8952-7*) Hyperion Pr.

—Night Gardening: A Novel. 1999. 215p. 16.95 (*0-7868-6498-2*) Hyperion Pr.

Thomas-Graham, Pamela. A Darker Shade of Crimson: An Ivy League Mystery. (Ivy League Mysteries Ser.). 1999. (Illus.). 416p. pap. 6.99 (*0-671-01670-9*, Pocket); 1998. 288p. 23.00 (*0-684-84526-1*, Simon & Schuster) Simon & Schuster.

Traxler, Patricia. Blood. 2001. 352p. 24.95 (*0-312-27484-X*, Saint Martin's Minotaur) St. Martin's Pr.

—Blood: A Novel. 2002. 368p. pap. 13.95 (*0-312-30401-3*, Saint Martin's Griffin) St. Martin's Pr.

**CAMELOT (LEGENDARY PLACE)—FICTION**

Ashley, Mike, ed. The Camelot Chronicles: Heroic Adventures from the Time of King Arthur. 1994. 432p. pap. 12.95 (*0-7867-0085-8*); 1992. 400p. 21.00 o.s.i (*0-88184-912-X*) Avalon Publishing Group. (Carroll & Graf Pubs.).

—The Camelot Chronicles: Heroic Adventures from the Time of King Arthur. 1995. 432p. 11.99 o.s.i (*0-517-12450-5*) Random Hse. Value Publishing.

Brown, Thomas Airlie. Celtic Roots. 2001. 276p. pap. (*1-55212-585-8*) Trafford Publishing.

Evans, Quinn Taylor. Daughter of Camelot. 1999. (Merlin's Legacy Ser.: Vol. 6). 416p. mass mkt. 5.99 o.s.i (*0-8217-6255-9*) Kensington Publishing Corp.

—Daughter of Fire. (Merlin's Legacy Ser.). 1999. mass mkt. 5.99 (*0-8217-6632-5*); 1998. 432p. mass mkt. 5.50 o.s.i (*0-8217-6052-1*, Zebra Bks.); 1996. 448p. mass mkt. 5.50 o.s.i (*0-8217-5187-5*, Zebra Bks.) Kensington Publishing Corp.

—Daughter of Fire Bk. 1: Merlin's Legacy. 1998. (Romance Ser.: Vol. 1). 496p. 25.95 o.p. (*0-7862-1714-6*, Five Star) Gale Group.

—Merlin's Legacy: Daughter of Fire. 1998. (Merlin's Legacy Ser.: Vol. 1). 448p. pap. 12.00 o.s.i (*1-57566-306-6*, Kensington Bks.) Kensington Publishing Corp.

—Merlin's Legacy: Daughter of the Mist. (Merlin's Legacy Ser.: Vol. 2). 1999. 384p. pap. 12.00 o.s.i (*1-57566-406-2*); 1996. 480p. mass mkt. 5.50 o.s.i (*0-8217-5347-9*, Zebra Bks.) Kensington Publishing Corp.

—Merlin's Legacy: Dawn of Camelot. 1998. (Merlin's Legacy Ser.: Vol. 5). 320p. mass mkt. 5.50 o.s.i (*0-8217-6028-9*) Kensington Publishing Corp.

—Merlin's Legacy No. 3: Daughter of Light. (Merlin's Legacy Ser.). 1998. 320p. mass mkt. 5.50 o.s.i (*0-8217-6051-3*); 1997. 480p. mass mkt. 5.50 o.s.i (*0-8217-5549-8*) Kensington Publishing Corp. (Zebra Bks.).

—Merlin's Legacy No. 4: Shadows of Camelot. 1997. (Merlin's Legacy Ser.: Vol. 4). 320p. mass mkt. 5.50 o.s.i (*0-8217-5760-1*) Kensington Publishing Corp.

—Shadows of Camelot. 1999. (Romances Ser.). pap. 25.95 (*0-7862-2083-X*, Five Star) Gale Group.

Foss, Michael. The World of Camelot: King Arthur & the Knights of the Round Table. (Illus.). 240p. 1998. pap. 17.95 (*0-8069-4230-4*); 1995. 19.95 o.p. (*0-8069-1314-2*) Sterling Publishing Co., Inc.

Matthews, John. Secret Camelot. 1997. (Illus.). 176 p. 29.95 (*0-7137-2646-6*) Blandford Pr. GBR. *Dist:* Sterling Publishing Co., Inc.

Miles, Rosalind. The Knight of the Sacred Lake. 2001. (Guenevere Ser.: Bk. 2). 448p. pap. 11.95 (*0-609-80802-8*, Three Rivers Pr.) Crown Publishing Group.

Twain, Mark. A Connecticut Yankee in King Arthur's Court. 1994. (Illustrated Classics Collection: No. 3). 64p. pap. 3.60 o.p. (*1-56103-525-4*); pap. 4.95 (*0-7854-0695-6*, 40447) American Guidance Service, Inc.

—A Connecticut Yankee in King Arthur's Court. 1983. 288p. mass mkt. 4.95 (*0-553-21143-9*, Bantam Classics) Bantam Bks.

—A Connecticut Yankee in King Arthur's Court. 2000. (Stratford Festival Ser.). audio 12.92 (*0-660-18178-9*) Canadian Broadcasting Corp./Societe Radio-Canada CAN. *Dist:* Georgetown Terminal Warehouse.

—A Connecticut Yankee in King Arthur's Court. E-Book 2.95 (*1-57799-844-8*) Logos Research Systems, Inc.

—A Connecticut Yankee in King Arthur's Court. E-Book 1.95 (*1-58515-199-8*) MesaView, Inc.

—A Connecticut Yankee in King Arthur's Court. 1963. 334p. mass mkt. 2.25 o.p. (*0-451-52353-9*, Signet Classics); mass mkt. 1.95 o.p. (*0-451-51874-8*) NAL.

—A Connecticut Yankee in King Arthur's Court. Ensor, Allison E., ed. 1982. (Critical Editions Ser.). (Illus.). (C). 455p. 24.95 o.p. (*0-393-01378-2*); 450p. pap. text 16.35 (*0-393-95137-5*) Norton, W. W. & Co., Inc.

—A Connecticut Yankee in King Arthur's Court. Inge, M. Thomas, ed. (Oxford World's Classics Ser.). (Illus.). 1999. 400p. pap. 7.95 (*0-19-283902-0*); 1997. 386p. pap. 5.95 o.p. (*0-19-282721-9*) Oxford Univ. Pr., Inc.

—A Connecticut Yankee in King Arthur's Court. 1987. (Regents Illustrated Classics Ser.). 62p. pap. text 4.65 net. o.p. (*0-13-167701-2*, 20468) Prentice Hall, ESL Dept.

—A Connecticut Yankee in King Arthur's Court. 2000. (Illus.). 260p. pap. 19.99 (*1-57646-258-7*) Quiet Vision Publishing.

—A Connecticut Yankee in King Arthur's Court. 1984. (Illus.). 334p. 12.95 o.p. (*0-89577-185-3*) Reader's Digest Assn., Inc., The.

—A Connecticut Yankee in King Arthur's Court. 1979. 368p. pap. 2.50 (*0-671-41017-2*, Simon Pulse) Simon & Schuster Children's Publishing.

—A Connecticut Yankee in King Arthur's Court. 1960. (Signet Classics Ser.). 11.00 (*0-606-01831-X*) Turtleback Bks.

—A Connecticut Yankee in King Arthur's Court. 1983. (Mark Twain Library: No. 4). (Illus.). 482p. (C). 30.00 o.p. (*0-520-05089-4*); pap. 14.95 (*0-520-05109-2*) Univ. of California Pr.

—A Connecticut Yankee in King Arthur's Court. Stein, Bernard L., ed. 1979. (Iowa-California Edition of the Works of Mark Twain: No. 9). (Illus.). 847p. text 75.00 (*0-520-03621-2*) Univ. of California Pr.

—A Connecticut Yankee in King Arthur's Court. Kaplan, Justin, ed. & intro. by. 1972. (Classics Ser.). 416p. 7.95 (*0-14-043064-4*, Penguin Classics) Viking Penguin.

—A Connecticut Yankee in King Arthur's Court. Fishkin, Shelley Fisher, ed. 1996. (Oxford Mark Twain Ser.). (Illus.). 656p. 22.00 o.p. (*0-19-510141-3*) Oxford Univ. Pr., Inc.

—A Connecticut Yankee in King Arthur's Court. unabr. ed. 1991. audio 34.95 o.p. (*1-55656-089-3*, DAB015) BBC Audiobooks America.

—A Connecticut Yankee in King Arthur's Court, unabr. ed. 2000. audio 56.95 (*0-7861-1721-4*, 2525) Blackstone Audio Bks., Inc.

—A Connecticut Yankee in King Arthur's Court. 1982. reprint ed. lib. bdg. 19.95 (*0-89966-381-8*) Buccaneer Bks., Inc.

—A Connecticut Yankee in King Arthur's Court. unabr. ed. audio 29.95 o.s.i (*1-55656-034-6*); 1997. pap. 29.95 incl. audio (*1-55656-200-4*) Dercum Audio.

—A Connecticut Yankee in King Arthur's Court. abr. ed. 1992. audio 16.99 (*0-88646-324-6*, 7324) Durkin Hayes Publishing Ltd.

—A Connecticut Yankee in King Arthur's Court. 1980. (Holiday Editions). (Illus.). reprint ed. 7.95 o.p. (*0-06-014445-9*) HarperCollins Pubs.

—A Connecticut Yankee in King Arthur's Court. abr. ed. 1989. audio 21.00 Jimcin Recordings.

—A Connecticut Yankee in King Arthur's Court. abr. ed. (Ultimate Classics Ser.). 1994. 29.95 o.p. incl. audio compact disk (*0-7871-0059-5*); 1993. 16.95 o.p. incl. audio (*1-55800-739-3*) NewStar Media, Inc.

—A Connecticut Yankee in King Arthur's Court. 2000. (Twelve-Point Ser.). 245p. reprint ed. lib. bdg. 25.00 (*1-58287-118-3*) North Bks.

—A Connecticut Yankee in King Arthur's Court. 1988. (Works of Mark Twain). reprint ed. lib. bdg. 79.00 (*0-7812-1121-2*) Reprint Services Corp.

—A Connecticut Yankee in King Arthur's Court: 1889. 1988. mass mkt. 4.95 (*0-938819-79-8*, Aerie) Doherty, Tom Assocs., LLC.

—A Connecticut Yankee in King Arthur's Court: 1889. Fishkin, Shelley Fisher, ed. 1997. (Oxford Mark Twain Ser.). (Illus.). 656p. text 28.00 (*0-19-511410-8*) Oxford Univ. Pr., Inc.

—A Connecticut Yankee in King Arthur's Court Readalong. 1994. (Illustrated Classics Collection: No. 3). 64p. pap. 14.95 incl. audio (*0-7854-0736-7*, 40449) American Guidance Service, Inc.

Whyte, Jack. The Skystone. (Illus.). 2002. 352p. pap. 14.95 (*0-7653-0372-8*, Forge Bks.); 1996. (Camulod Chronicles: Bk. 1). 498p. mass mkt. 6.99 (*0-8125-5138-9*, Tor Bks.); 1996. (Camulod Chronicles: Bk. 1). 352p. 22.95 o.p. (*0-312-86091-9*, Forge Bks.) Doherty, Tom Assocs., LLC.

**CAMULOD (IMAGINARY PLACE)—FICTION**

Whyte, Jack. The Eagles' Brood. 1998. (Camulod Chronicles: Bk. 3). (Illus.). 623p. mass mkt. 6.99 (*0-8125-5140-0*, Tor Bks.) Doherty, Tom Assocs., LLC.

—The Saxon Shore. 2003. (Arthurian Novel Ser.). 736p. pap. 17.95 (*0-7653-0650-6*, Forge Bks.); 1999. (Camulod Chronicles: Bk. 4). (Illus.). 719p. mass mkt. 7.99 (*0-8125-4416-1*, Tor Bks.) Doherty, Tom Assocs., LLC.

—The Singing Sword. 1997. (Camulod Chronicles: Bk. 2). (Illus.). 547p. mass mkt. 6.99 (*0-8125-5139-7*, Tor Bks.); 1996. (Camulod Chronicles: Bk. 2). 352p. 23.95 o.p. (*0-312-85292-4*, Forge Bks.); 2nd ed. 2002. (Illus.). 384p. reprint ed. pap. 14.95 (*0-7653-0458-9*, NPB0851, Forge Bks.) Doherty, Tom Assocs., LLC.

—The Sorcerer: Metamorphosis. 1999. (Camulod Chronicles: Bk. 6). (Illus.). 352p. 23.95 (*0-312-86598-8*, Forge Bks.) Doherty, Tom Assocs., LLC.

**CANADA—FICTION**

Adderson, Caroline. Bad Imaginings. 1993. 160p. pap. 12.95 (*0-88984-172-1*) Porcupine's Quill, Inc. CAN. *Dist:* General Distribution Services, Inc.

Alguire, Judith. Iced. 1995. 202p. pap. 10.95 (*0-934678-60-X*) New Victoria Pubs., Inc.

—Iced: A Novel By... 1995. 192p. (*0-88961-214-5*) Women's Pr. CAN. *Dist:* Univ. of Toronto Pr.

Ali, Ansara. The Sacred Adventures of a Taxi Driver. rev. ed. 1993. (Illus.). 544p. reprint ed. 27.95 o.s.i (*0-9636170-1-X*); pap. 16.95 (*0-9636170-0-1*) Royal Rags Publishing.

Allinson, Sidney. Jeremy Kane: A Canadian Historical Adventure Novel of the 1837 Mackenzie Rebellion & Its Brutal Aftermath in the Australian Penal Colonies. 1998. 366p. E-Book 8.00 (*0-7388-7966-5*) Xlibris Corp.

Anderson-Dargatz, Gail. A Recipe for Bees. l.t. ed. 2000. (Thorndike Senior Lifestyle Ser.). (Illus.). 422p. 27.95 (*0-7862-2666-8*) Thorndike Pr.

—A Rhinestone Button. 2002. 336p. 25.99 (*0-676-97549-6*) Knopf, Alfred A. Inc.

Arengo, Sue. A Taste of Murder. 4th ed. 1998. (Illus.). 32p. pap. text 4.95 (*0-19-421970-4*) Oxford Univ. Pr., Inc.

Armstrong, Luanne. Bordering. 1995. 176p. pap. 10.95 o.p. (*0-921881-35-5*) Ragweed Pr. CAN. *Dist:* Univ. of Toronto Pr.

Arnason, David. The Happiest Man in the World: And Other Stories. 1989. 236p. pap. 13.95 (*0-88922-269-X*) Talonbooks, Ltd. CAN. *Dist:* General Distribution Services, Inc.

Atkinson, Diana. Highways & Dancehalls. 1996. pap. 12.95 (*0-394-28162-4*); 1995. 226p. (*0-394-28062-8*) Knopf, Alfred A. Inc.

—Highways & Dancehalls. 1997. (Illus.). 235p. 21.95 o.p. (*0-312-15139-X*) St. Martin's Pr.

Atwood, Margaret. Alias Grace. 1997. 576p. mass mkt. 7.99 o.s.i (*0-7704-2759-6*) Bantam Bks.

—Alias Grace. 1996. 464p. 24.95 o.s.i (*0-385-47571-3*, Talese, Nan A.); mass mkt. o.s.i (*0-385-48624-3*) Doubleday Publishing.

—Alias Grace. l.t. ed. 1997. (G. K. Hall Core Ser.). 718p. lib. bdg. 27.95 o.p. (*0-7838-8040-5*, Macmillan Reference USA) Gale Group.

—Alias Grace. abr. ed. 1996. audio 24.95 (*0-553-47772-2*, 694514, RH Audio) Random Hse. Audio Publishing Group.

—Alias Grace. 1997. 480p. pap. 15.00 (*0-385-49044-5*, Knopf Bks. for Young Readers) Random Hse. Children's Bks.

—Bluebeard's Egg. 1996. 304p. pap. 10.95 o.s.i (*0-553-37860-0*); 1984. 272p. mass mkt. 7.99 o.s.i (*0-7704-2134-2*) Bantam Bks.

—Bluebeard's Egg. 1998. 256p. pap. 12.00 (*0-385-49104-2*, Knopf Bks. for Young Readers) Random Hse. Children's Bks.

—Bluebeard's Egg. l.t. ed. 1997. (Basic Ser.). 421p. lib. bdg. 26.95 (*0-7862-1252-7*) Thorndike Pr.

—Bluebeard's Egg & Other Stories. 1987. 336p. mass mkt. 5.95 o.s.i (*0-449-21417-6*, Fawcett) Ballantine Bks.

—Bluebeard's Egg & Other Stories, 001. 1986. 15.95 o.p. (*0-395-40424-X*) Houghton Mifflin Co.

—Bodily Harm. 1995. 304p. pap. 10.95 o.s.i (*0-553-37789-2*); 1983. mass mkt. 4.50 o.p. (*0-553-23289-4*); 1983. mass mkt. 4.50 o.s.i (*0-553-26969-0*); 1983. 304p. mass mkt. 6.50 o.s.i (*0-553-27455-4*) Bantam Bks.

—Bodily Harm. 2002. lib. bdg. 27.95 (*1-58547-236-0*, Premier) Ctr. Point Large Print.

—Bodily Harm. 1998. 304p. pap. 12.95 (*0-385-49107-7*) Doubleday Publishing.

—Bodily Harm. 1982. 45.00 (*0-671-44153-1*) Ultramarine Publishing Co., Inc.

—Dancing Girls: And Other Stories. 1995. 256p. pap. 10.95 o.s.i (*0-553-37791-4*); 1993. 256p. mass mkt. 5.99 o.s.i (*0-553-56169-3*); 1985. pap. 6.95 o.s.i (*0-553-34115-4*); 1985. 240p. pap. 9.50 o.s.i (*0-553-34501-X*); 1982. 256p. mass mkt. 6.99 o.s.i (*0-7704-2332-9*) Bantam Bks.

—Dancing Girls: And Other Stories. 1998. 256p. pap. 12.00 (*0-385-49109-3*) Doubleday Publishing.

—Dancing Girls: And Other Stories. 1982. 14.50 o.p. (*0-671-24249-0*, Simon & Schuster) Simon & Schuster.

—Murder in the Dark: Short Fictions & Prose Poems. 1984. pap. 10.95 o.p. (*0-88910-258-9*) Consortium Bk. Sales & Distribution.

—The Robber Bride. 544p. 1995. mass mkt. 6.50 o.s.i (*0-553-56905-8*); 1994. mass mkt. 6.99 o.s.i (*0-7704-2616-6*) Bantam Bks.

—The Robber Bride. l.t. ed. 1993. 880p. 27.00 o.s.i (*0-385-47216-1*, Bantam Large Type) Bantam Doubleday Dell Large Print Group, Inc.

—The Robber Bride. 1998. 528p. pap. 15.00 (*0-385-49103-4*); 1993. 480p. 23.50 o.s.i (*0-385-26008-3*, Talese, Nan A.) Doubleday Publishing.

—The Robber Bride. 1998. 20.05 (*0-606-20887-9*) Turtleback Bks.

Atwood, Margaret & Weaver, Robert, eds. The New Oxford Book of Canadian Short Stories. 2nd ed. 1995. 480p. 30.00 o.p. (*0-19-541025-4*) Oxford Univ. Pr., Inc.

—The Oxford Book of Canadian Short Stories in English. 1987. 456p. 27.95 o.p. (*0-19-540565-X*) Oxford Univ. Pr., Inc.

Aubert, Rosemary. The Feast of Stephen. 2001. 272p. mass mkt. 6.99 o.s.i (*0-425-17799-8*, Prime Crime) Berkley Publishing Group.

—The Feast of Stephen: An Ellis Portal Mystery. 1999. (Ellis Portal Mystery Ser.). 224p. 22.95 (*1-882593-27-8*) Bridge Works Publishing Co., Inc.

—Free Reign. 1998. 304p. mass mkt. 6.99 o.s.i (*0-425-16427-6*) Berkley Publishing Group.

—Free Reign: A Suspense Novel. 1997. (Ellis Portal Mystery Ser.). 240p. 21.95 o.s.i (*1-882593-18-9*) Bridge Works Publishing Co., Inc.

Bacon, Charlotte. Lost Geography. 2002. 288p. pap. 13.00 (*0-312-42052-8*) Picador.

Badami, Anita Rau. The Hero's Walk. 2001. 359p. 23.95 (*1-56512-312-3*) Algonquin Bks. of Chapel Hill.

Baker, Nancy. The Night Inside. 1994. 320p. 20.00 o.p. (*0-449-90904-2*, Fawcett) Ballantine Bks.

Bell, Mary S. Sonata for Mind & Heart. 1992. 224p. (YA). (gr. 7 up). lib. bdg. 14.95 o.s.i (*0-689-31734-4*, Atheneum) Simon & Schuster Children's Publishing.

Beresford-Howe, Constance. A Serious Widow. 1993. pap. (*0-7710-1103-2*) McClelland & Stewart/ Tundra Bks.

Bernhard, Thomas. The Loser. Dawson, Jack, tr. from GER. 1993. pap. 10.00 o.p. (*0-679-74179-8*, Vintage) Knopf Publishing Group.

—The Loser. Dawson, Jack, tr. 1996. (Phoenix Fiction Ser.). 200p. pap. 14.00 (*0-226-04388-6*) Univ. of Chicago Pr.

—The Loser: A Novel. Dawson, Jack, tr. from GER. 1991. 190p. 19.00 o.p. (*0-394-57239-4*) Knopf, Alfred A. Inc.

Berry, Michelle. How to Get There from Here. 1997. 190p. pap. 16.95 (*0-88801-212-8*) Turnstone Pr. CAN. *Dist:* General Distribution Services, Inc.

Birdsell, Sandra. The Two-Headed Calf. 1997. 280p. pap. 19.99 (*0-7710-1454-6*) McClelland & Stewart/Tundra Bks.

Blais, Marie-Claire. St. Lawrence Blues. Manheim, Ralph, tr. from FRE. 1974. 229p. 7.95 o.p. (*0-374-25350-1*) Farrar, Straus & Giroux.

—St. Lawrence Blues. 1985. mass mkt. o.p. (*0-7710-9337-3*) McClelland & Stewart CAN. *Dist:* Random Hse. of Canada, Ltd.

Blaise, Clark. Resident Alien. 1986. 208p. pap. 5.95 o.p. (*0-14-008234-4*, Penguin Bks.) Viking Penguin.

Block, Kevin James. Without Shedding of Blood. 1994. 185p. pap. (*1-895308-17-8*) Hyperion Pr., Ltd.

Bock, Dennis. Olympia. 1999. 272p. 22.95 (*1-58234-023-4*) Bloomsbury Publishing.

—Olympia. 1998. 256p. pap. o.s.i (*0-385-25698-1*) Doubleday Publishing.

Bock, Dennis, contrib. by. Olympia. 1998. 252p. (*0-7475-3680-5*) Bloomsbury Publishing, Ltd. GBR. *Dist:* Trafalgar Square.

Boraks-Nemetz, Lillian. The Old Brown Suitcase: A Teenager's Story of War & Peace. 1994. 210p. (Orig.). (YA). (gr. 8-12). pap. 9.50 (*0-914539-10-8*) Ben-Simon Pubns.

Boswell, Hazel. Town House, Country House: Recollections of a Quebec Childhood. 1990. (Illus.). 152p. (C). 29.95 (*0-7735-0721-3*) McGill-Queen's Univ. Pr. CAN. *Dist:* CUP Services.

Bowen, Gail. A Killing Spring. 1997. (Joanne Kilbourn Mystery Ser.). 272p. mass mkt. 5.95 (*0-7710-1486-4*) McClelland & Stewart/Tundra Bks.

—A Killing Spring: A Joanne Kilburn Mystery. 1997. 264p. 22.95 o.p. (*0-7710-1484-8*) McClelland & Stewart/Tundra Bks.

—Striking Out. 1996. 256p. mass mkt. 5.99 (*0-7710-3415-6*) McClelland & Stewart/Tundra Bks.

—The Wandering Soul Murders: A Joanne Kilbourn Mystery. 1994. 207p. 19.95 o.p. (*0-312-10574-6*, Saint Martin's Minotaur) St. Martin's Pr.

Bowering, Marilyn. Visible Worlds. 1999. 304p. pap. 13.00 o.s.i (*0-06-092926-X*) HarperCollins Pubs.

—Visible Worlds. 1998. 304p. o.s.i (*0-06-019148-1*, HarperFlamingo) HarperCollins Pubs. Canada, Ltd.

Boyer, Elizabeth. Marguerite De la Roque: A Story of Survival. 1975. 20.00 (*0-915964-01-5*) Veritie Pr.

Brand, Max. The Tyrant: A North-Western Story. l.t. ed. 2001. (Five Star First Edition Western Ser.). 248p. 23.95 (*0-7862-2760-5*) Thorndike Pr.

Brandis, Marianne. The Tinder-Box. 1982. Orig. Title: Fyrtojet. 160p. pap. (*0-88984-064-4*) Porcupine's Quill, Inc.

Braun, Lois. Stone Watermelon. 1997. pap. 10.95 (*0-88801-107-5*) Turnstone Pr. CAN. *Dist:* General Distribution Services, Inc.

Brill, Ethel C. Madeleine Takes Command. 1996. (Living History Library). (Illus.). 208p. (J). (gr. 4-7). reprint ed. pap. 12.95 (*1-883937-17-5*, 17-5) Bethlehem Bks.

Brooke, Frances. The History of Emily Montague. Shugrue, Michael F., ed. 1975. (Flowering of the Novel Ser.: Vol. 85). lib. bdg. 110.00 o.s.i (*0-8240-1184-8*) Garland Publishing, Inc.

—The History of Emily Montague. 1995. (New Canadian Library). 416p. mass mkt. 8.95 (*0-7710-3457-1*) McClelland & Stewart/Tundra Bks.

—The History of Emily Montague. Edwards, Mary Jane, ed. 459p. (*0-88629-025-2*); pap. (*0-88629-027-9*) McGill-Queen's Univ. Pr.

Burke, Betsy. Lucy's Launderette. 2003. 320p. pap. (*0-373-25034-7*, Red Dress Ink) Harlequin Enterprises, Ltd.

Burnard, Bonnie. A Good House: A Novel. 2000. 309p. 25.00 o.s.i (*0-8050-6495-8*) Holt, Henry & Co.

—A Good House: A Novel. 2001. 320p. pap. 14.00 (*0-312-42032-3*) Picador.

Burnford, Sheila. The Incredible Journey. 1989. (Illus.). 212p. (J). (gr. 6-8). 13.95 o.p. (*0-8161-4724-8*, Macmillan Reference USA) Gale Group.

Burns, Mary. Suburbs of the Arctic Circle. 1988. 158p. 12.95 (*0-920806-79-1*) Penumbra Pr. CAN. *Dist:* Univ. of Toronto Pr.

—Vengeance is Mine. 2001. 231p. pap. 21.99 (*0-7388-9911-9*) Xlibris Corp.

Bush, Catherine. Minus Time. 2nd ed. 1995. (High Risk Ser.). 320p. pap. (*1-85242-408-7*) Serpent's Tail Ltd.

—Minus Time: A Novel. 1993. 352p. 19.95 o.p. (*1-56282-881-9*) Hyperion Pr.

Calce, Fiorella D. Vinnie & Me, No. 31. 1996. (Prose Ser.: No. 31). 90p. (C). pap. 10.00 (*1-55071-017-6*) Guernica Editions, Inc.

Callaghan, Morley. Native Argosy. 1977. (Short Story Index Reprint Ser.). 22.95 (*0-8369-3292-7*) Ayer Co. Pubs., Inc.

Carrier, Roch. The Boxing Champion. ed. 1995. Tr. of Champion. (J). (gr. 2). spiral bd. (*0-616-01612-3*) Canadian National Institute for the Blind/Institut National Canadien pour les Aveugles.

—The Boxing Champion.Tr. of Champion. (Illus.). 24p. (J). (gr. 3-7). 1993. pap. 7.95 (*0-88776-257-3*); 1991. 15.95 (*0-88776-249-2*) Tundra Bks. of Northern New York.

—The Hockey Sweater. ed. 1988. Orig. Title: Le Chandail de Hockey. (J). (gr. 2). spiral bd. (*0-616-01613-1*) Canadian National Institute for the Blind/ Institut National Canadien pour les Aveugles.

—The Hockey Sweater. 1984. Orig. Title: Le Chandail de Hockey. (Illus.). 24p. (J). (gr. 3-7). 17.95 (*0-88776-169-0*) Tundra Bks. of Northern New York.

Catherwood, Mary Hartwell. Romance of Dollard. 1977. (American Fiction Reprint Ser.). 22.95 (*0-8369-7024-1*) Ayer Co. Pubs., Inc.

Cave, Hugh B. The Dawning. 2000. 368p. mass mkt. 5.50 (*0-8439-4739-X*, Leisure Bks.) Dorchester Publishing Co., Inc.

Choy, Wayson. The Jade Peony. 240p. 1998. pap. 12.00 o.s.i (*0-312-18692-4*); 1997. 22.00 o.p. (*0-312-15556-5*) Picador.

Clark, Joan. Wild Man of the Woods. 1986. (Viking Kestrel Novels Ser.). 172p. (J). (gr. 5-9). 11.95 o.p. (*0-670-80015-5*, Viking Children's Bks.) Penguin Putnam Bks. for Young Readers.

Clarke, Austin. Nine Men Who Laughed. 1987. 240p. pap. 6.95 o.p. (*0-14-008560-2*, Penguin Bks.) Viking Penguin.

Clarke, George Elliott. Beatrice Chancy. 1999. (Illus.). 160p. pap. 14.95 (*1-896095-94-1*, Polestar Book Pubs.) Raincoast Bk. Distribution CAN. *Dist:* Orca Bk. Pubs.

Coady, Lynn. Strange Heaven. 2002. 256p. pap. (*0-385-65914-8*, Anchor Canada) Doubleday Canada, Ltd. CAN. *Dist:* Random Hse., Inc.

—Strange Heaven. (GLE Library). 198p. 2000. pap. (*0-86492-320-1*); 1998. pap. (*0-86492-230-2*) Goose Lane Editions.

Cohen, Leonard. Beautiful Losers. 1993. 256p. pap. 13.00 (*0-679-74825-3*, Vintage) Knopf Publishing Group.

—Beautiful Losers. 1969. pap. 1.75 o.p. (*0-670-00261-5*) Penguin Group (USA) Inc.

—Beautiful Losers. 1966. 5.75 o.p. (*0-670-15291-9*) Viking Penguin.

Collins, Angela. Learning by Heart: A Poignant Account of Teaching in Rural Newfoundland in the 1950s. 2001. 150p. pap. (*1-894294-39-4*) Creative Bk. Publishing CAN. *Dist:* General Distribution Services, Inc.

Compton, Wayde. 49th Parallel Psalm. 1999. 175p. pap. 15.95 (*1-55152-065-6*) Arsenal Pulp Pr., Ltd. CAN. *Dist:* LPC Group.

Cook, Hugh. Cracked Wheat & Other Stories. 1984. 127p. (YA). (gr. 7 up). 12.95 (*0-931940-09-5*) Middleburg Pr., The.

—Cracked Wheat & Other Stories. 1994. 122p. pap. 9.95 (*0-88962-265-5*) Mosaic Pr.

Cooper, Barbara. The Choosing. l.t. ed. 1999. (General Ser.). 232p. pap. 22.95 (*0-7862-2177-1*) Thorndike Pr.

Courtney, Dayle. The Trail of Bigfoot. 1983. (Thorne Twins Adventure Bks.). (Illus.). 192p. (Orig.). (J). (gr. 7-12). pap. 2.98 o.p. (*0-87239-681-9*, 2901) Standard Publishing.

Craig, Alisa, pseud. A Dismal Thing to Do. 1986. (Crime Club Ser.). 192p. 12.95 o.p. (*0-385-23263-2*) Doubleday Publishing.

—Trouble in the Brasses. 1989. 224p. mass mkt. 4.50 (*0-380-75539-4*, Avon Bks.) Morrow/Avon.

—The Wrong Rite. 1992. (Madoc & Janet Rhys Mystery Ser.: No. 5). 224p. 19.00 o.p. (*0-688-08643-8*, Morrow, William & Co.) Morrow/Avon.

Cumyn, Alan. Burridge Unbound. 2000. 352p. pap. (*0-7710-2486-X*) McClelland & Stewart.

Curtis, Herb. The Americans Are Coming. 263p. 1989. pap. (*0-86492-108-X*); 1999. reprint ed. pap. (*0-86492-275-2*) Goose Lane Editions.

Curwood, James Oliver. Kazan. 1976. reprint ed. lib. bdg. 25.95 (*0-88411-855-X*) Amereon, Ltd.

—Kazan. 1990. reprint ed. lib. bdg. 21.95 (*0-89968-501-3*) Buccaneer Bks., Inc.

—Kazan: Father of Baree. 2004. 240p. (YA). (gr. 4-7). pap. 4.95 (*1-55704-225-X*) Newmarket Pr.

Cussler, Clive. Inca Gold. 2001. (Dirk Pitt Adventure Ser.). (Illus.). 592p. reprint ed. pap. 16.00 (*0-7434-2680-0*, Pocket) Simon & Schuster.

—Shock Wave. 2002. (Dirk Pitt Adventure Ser.). 576p. pap. 16.00 (*0-7434-2679-7*, Pocket) Simon & Schuster.

D'Alfonso, Antonio. Fabrizio's Passion. No. 12. 2nd ed. 2000. (Picas Ser.: No. 12). 213p. pap. 10.00 (*1-55071-082-6*); Vol. 1. 1995. (Prose Ser.: No. 34). 214p. pap. 15.00 o.p. (*1-55071-023-0*) Guernica Editions, Inc.

Dalton, Margot. Under Prairie Skies. 2000. 352p. mass mkt. (*1-55166-594-8*, 1-66594-2, Mira Bks.); 1990. (Harlequin Superromance Ser.: No. 401). per. (*0-373-70401-1*, Harlequin Bks.) Harlequin Enterprises, Ltd.

Dandurand, Anne. The Cracks. 1992. pap. 11.95 (*0-920544-93-2*) Mercury Bks. CAN. *Dist:* LPC/InBook.

Davies, Robertson. The Cornish Trilogy: The Rebel Angels; What's Bred in the Bone; The Lyre of Orpheus. 1992. 1200p. 22.95 (*0-14-015850-2*) Viking Penguin.

—The Cunning Man. unabr. ed. 1996. audio 76.95 (*0-7861-1060-0*, 1831) Blackstone Audio Bks., Inc.

—The Cunning Man. l.t. ed. 1995. pap. 23.95 o.p. (*1-56895-230-9*, Wheeler Publishing, Inc.) Gale Group.

—The Cunning Man. 1994. 472p. (*0-7710-2581-5*) McClelland & Stewart/Tundra Bks.

—The Cunning Man. 1996. (*0-14-771176-2*); 478p. pap. 13.95 (*0-14-024830-7*, Viking) Penguin Group (USA) Inc.

—The Cunning Man. unabr. ed. 1996. audio 97.00 (*0-7887-0294-7*, 94487E7) Recorded Bks., LLC.

—The Cunning Man. 1995. 480p. 23.95 o.p. (*0-670-85911-7*, Viking) Viking Penguin.

—The Lyre of Orpheus. l.t. ed. 1990. (General Ser.). 586p. 21.95 o.p. (*0-8161-4839-2*, Macmillan Reference USA) Gale Group.

—The Lyre of Orpheus. 1990. (Cornish Trilogy Ser.). 480p. pap. 15.00 (*0-14-011433-5*, Penguin Bks.) Penguin Group (USA) Inc.

—The Lyre of Orpheus. 1989. (Cornish Trilogy Ser.). 480p. 19.95 o.p. (*0-670-82416-X*) Viking Penguin.

—Murther & Walking Spirits. l.t. ed. 1992. (General Ser.). 480p. 22.95 o.p. (*0-8161-5466-X*); pap. 16.95 o.p. (*0-8161-5467-8*) Gale Group. (Macmillan Reference USA).

—Murther & Walking Spirits. 1992. 352p. reprint ed. pap. 13.95 (*0-14-016884-2*, Penguin Bks.) Penguin Group (USA) Inc.

—Murther & Walking Spirits. unabr. ed. 1991. audio 85.00 (*1-55690-632-3*, 91422E7) Recorded Bks., LLC.

—Murther & Walking Spirits. 1991. 368p. 21.95 o.p. (*0-670-84189-7*, Viking) Viking Penguin.

—The Rebel Angels. 1983. (Cornish Trilogy Ser.). 336p. pap. 13.95 (*0-14-006271-8*, Penguin Bks.) Penguin Group (USA) Inc.

—What's Bred in the Bone. l.t. ed. 1987. 641p. 20.95 o.p. (*0-8161-4133-9*, Macmillan Reference USA) Gale Group.

—What's Bred in the Bone. 1986. (Cornish Trilogy Ser.). 448p. pap. 15.00 (*0-14-009711-2*, Penguin Bks.) Penguin Group (USA) Inc.

—What's Bred in the Bone. 1985. (Cornish Trilogy Ser.). 17.95 o.p. (*0-670-80916-0*, Viking) Viking Penguin.

Davis, Kathleen Legeia. Serpentina: A Novel. 2003. (Illus.). 323p. 18.50 (*0-9715402-1-7*, 410-707-6686) Barnhardt & Ashe Publishing, Inc.

De La Roche, Mazo. The Building of Jalna. unabr. ed. 1993. 69.95 incl. audio (*0-7451-6246-0*); 1990. audio 64.95 o.s.i (*0-8161-9513-7*) BBC Audiobooks America.

—The Building of Jalna. 1976. 288p. mass mkt. 1.50 o.s.i (*0-449-23071-6*, Fawcett) Ballantine Bks.

—The Building of Jalna. 1944. (Jalna Ser.). 8.95 o.p. (*0-316-17996-5*) Little Brown & Co.

—The Building of Jalna. l.t. ed. 1972. (Whiteoak Chronicles Ser.). 16.95 o.p. (*0-85456-673-2*, Ulverscroft) Thorpe, F. A. Pubs. GBR. *Dist:* Ulverscroft Large Print Bks., Ltd.

—Centenary at Jalna. l.t. ed. 1973. (Whiteoak Chronicles Ser.). 12.00 o.p. (*0-85456-688-0*, Ulverscroft) Thorpe, F. A. Pubs. GBR. *Dist:* Ulverscroft Large Print Bks., Ltd.

—Finch's Fortune. 1976. mass mkt. 1.50 o.s.i (*0-449-23053-8*, Fawcett) Ballantine Bks.

—Finch's Fortune. l.t. ed. 1973. (Whiteoak Chronicles Ser.). 12.00 o.p. (*0-85456-681-3*, Ulverscroft) Thorpe, F. A. Pubs. GBR. *Dist:* Ulverscroft Large Print Bks., Ltd.

—Jalna. 1979. mass mkt. 1.95 o.s.i (*0-449-24118-1*, Fawcett); 1976. mass mkt. 1.50 o.s.i (*0-449-23138-0*) Ballantine Bks.

—Jalna. l.t. ed. 2002. 400p. pap. 21.99 (*0-7531-6462-0*) ISIS Large Print Bks. GBR. *Dist:* Ulverscroft Large Print Bks., Ltd., Ulverscroft Large Print Canada, Ltd.

—Jalna. l.t. ed. 2001. 400p. 32.50 (*0-7531-6461-2*); 1973. 29.99 o.p. (*0-85456-679-1*, Ulverscroft) Thorpe, F. A. Pubs. GBR. *Dist:* Ulverscroft Large Print Bks., Ltd., Ulverscroft Large Print Canada, Ltd.

—Mary Wakefield. unabr. ed. 1991. (Audio Bks.). audio 69.95 (*0-7451-6244-4*) BBC Audiobooks America.

—Mary Wakefield. 1976. mass mkt. 1.50 o.s.i (*0-449-23057-0*, Fawcett) Ballantine Bks.

—Mary Wakefield. l.t. ed. 1973. (Whiteoak Chronicles Ser.). 12.00 o.p. (*0-85456-675-9*, Ulverscroft) Thorpe, F. A. Pubs. GBR. *Dist:* Ulverscroft Large Print Bks., Ltd., Ulverscroft Large Print Canada, Ltd.

—The Master of Jalna. (Jalna Ser.). 1979. mass mkt. 1.95 o.s.i (*0-449-23932-2*, Fawcett); 1975. mass mkt. 1.50 o.s.i (*0-449-22797-9*) Ballantine Bks.

—The Master of Jalna. l.t. ed. 1973. (Whiteoak Chronicles Ser.). 29.99 o.p. (*0-85456-682-1*, Ulverscroft) Thorpe, F. A. Pubs. GBR. *Dist:* Ulverscroft Large Print Bks., Ltd., Ulverscroft Large Print Canada, Ltd.

—Morning at Jalna. unabr. ed. 1991. (Audio Bks.). audio 69.95 (*0-7451-6245-2*) BBC Audiobooks America.

—Morning at Jalna. (Jalna Ser.). 1978. mass mkt. 1.75 o.s.i (*0-449-23712-5*, Fawcett); 1975. mass mkt. 1.25 o.s.i (*0-449-22411-2*) Ballantine Bks.

—Morning at Jalna. 1960. (Jalna Ser.). 8.95 o.p. (*0-316-18003-3*) Little Brown & Co.

—Morning at Jalna. l.t. ed. 1972. (Whiteoak Chronicles Ser.). 29.99 o.p. (*0-85456-674-0*, Ulverscroft) Thorpe, F. A. Pubs. GBR. *Dist:* Ulverscroft Large Print Bks., Ltd., Ulverscroft Large Print Canada, Ltd.

—Renny's Daughter. 1975. 304p. mass mkt. 1.50 o.s.i (*0-449-22550-X*, Q2550, Fawcett) Ballantine Bks.

—Renny's Daughter. l.t. ed. 1973. (Whiteoak Chronicles Ser.). 29.99 o.p. (*0-85456-686-4*, Ulverscroft) Thorpe, F. A. Pubs. GBR. *Dist:* Ulverscroft Large Print Bks., Ltd., Ulverscroft Large Print Canada, Ltd.

—Return to Jalna. 1977. (Jalna Ser.). mass mkt. 1.75 o.s.i (*0-449-23386-3*, Fawcett) Ballantine Bks.

—Return to Jalna. l.t. ed. 1973. (Whiteoak Chronicles Ser.). 12.00 o.p. (*0-85456-685-6*, Ulverscroft) Thorpe, F. A. Pubs. GBR. *Dist:* Ulverscroft Large Print Bks., Ltd.

—Variable Winds at Jalna. l.t. ed. 1973. (Whiteoak Chronicles Ser.). 12.00 o.p. (*0-85456-687-2*, Ulverscroft) Thorpe, F. A. Pubs. GBR. *Dist:* Ulverscroft Large Print Bks., Ltd.

—Wakefield's Course. 1977. (Jalna Ser.). mass mkt. 1.95 o.s.i (*0-449-23431-2*, Fawcett) Ballantine Bks.

—Wakefield's Course. l.t. ed. 1973. (Whiteoak Chronicles Ser.). o.p. (*0-85456-684-8*, Ulverscroft) Thorpe, F. A. Pubs.

—Whiteoak Brothers. 1978. (Jalna Ser.). mass mkt. 1.75 o.s.i (*0-449-23643-9*, Fawcett) Ballantine Bks.

—The Whiteoak Brothers. l.t. ed. 1973. (Whiteoak Chronicles Ser.). 29.99 o.p. (*0-85456-678-3*, Ulverscroft) Thorpe, F. A. Pubs. GBR. *Dist:* Ulverscroft Large Print Bks., Ltd., Ulverscroft Large Print Canada, Ltd.

—Whiteoak Harvest. 1978. (Jalna Ser.). mass mkt. 1.75 o.s.i (*0-449-23521-1*, Fawcett) Ballantine Bks.

—Whiteoak Harvest. 1936. (Jalna Ser.). 7.95 o.p. (*0-316-18013-0*) Little Brown & Co.

—Whiteoak Harvest. l.t. ed. 1973. (Whiteoak Chronicles Ser.). 12.00 o.p. (*0-85456-683-X*, Ulverscroft) Thorpe, F. A. Pubs. GBR. *Dist:* Ulverscroft Large Print Bks., Ltd.

—Whiteoak Heritage. 1979. mass mkt. 1.95 o.s.i (*0-449-22214-4*, Fawcett) Ballantine Bks.

—Whiteoak Heritage. 1940. (Jalna Ser.). 8.95 o.p. (*0-316-18012-2*) Little Brown & Co.

—Whiteoak Heritage. l.t. ed. 1973. (Whiteoak Chronicles Ser.). o.p. (*0-85456-677-5*, Ulverscroft) Thorpe, F. A. Pubs.

—Whiteoaks of Jalna. (Jalna Ser.). 1980. mass mkt. 2.25 o.s.i (*0-449-23510-6*, Fawcett); 1975. mass mkt. 1.50 o.s.i (*0-449-22764-2*) Ballantine Bks.

De Lint, Charles. Moonheart. 1985. mass mkt. 3.50 o.s.i (*0-441-53720-0*); 1984. mass mkt. 2.95 o.s.i (*0-441-53719-7*) Ace Bks.

—Moonheart. 1985. 496p. mass mkt. 3.95 o.s.i (*0-441-53721-9*, Diamond Bks.) Berkley Publishing Group.

—Moonheart. 1994. 439p. pap. 14.95 (*0-312-89004-4*, Orb Bks.); 1992. mass mkt. (*0-8125-1622-2*, Tor Bks.) Doherty, Tom Assocs., LLC.

—The Road to Lisdoonvarna. 2001. 190p. 40.00 (*1-892284-91-X*) Subterranean Pr.

Decter, Ann. Paper, Scissors, Rock. 1992. 290p. pap. (*0-88974-040-2*, Press Gang Pubs.) Raincoast Bk. Distribution.

Deverell, William. Mindfield. 1989. 17.95 o.s.i (*0-945167-22-9*) British American Publishing, Ltd.

—Mindfield. 1989. o.p. (*0-7710-2659-5*) McClelland & Stewart/Tundra Bks.

—Street Legal: The Betrayal. 1996. 344p. 22.95 o.p. (*0-7710-2669-2*) McClelland & Stewart/Tundra Bks.

Dey, Claudia. Beaver. 2000. 75p. pap. (*0-921368-97-6*) Blizzard Publishing, Inc.

Dohaney, M. T. A Fit Month for Dying. 2000. 264p. pap. (*0-86492-312-0*) Goose Lane Editions.

Dorsey, Candas Jane. A Paradigm of Earth. 2001. E-Book 24.95 (*1-59061-421-6*) Adobe Systems, Inc.
—A Paradigm of Earth. 2001. 368p. 26.95 (*0-312-87796-X*, Tor Bks.) Doherty, Tom Assocs., LLC.
—Vanilla & Other Stories. 2000. 161p. pap. 12.95 (*1-896300-21-9*) NeWest Pubs., Ltd. CAN. *Dist:* General Distribution Services, Inc.
Douglas, Lauren W. The Always Anonymous Beast. 1987. (Caitlin Reece Mysteries Ser.). 224p. pap. 8.95 o.p. (*0-941483-04-5*) Naiad Pr., Inc.
—The Daughters of Artemis. 1991. (Caitlin Reece Mystery Ser.). 240p. (Orig.). pap. 9.95 (*0-941483-95-9*) Naiad Pr., Inc.
—Goblin Market. 1993. (Caitlin Reece Mysteries Ser.: No. 5). 224p. pap. 10.95 (*1-56280-047-7*) Naiad Pr., Inc.
—Ninth Life. 1990. (Caitlin Reece Mysteries Ser.). 256p. pap. 9.95 (*0-941483-50-9*) Naiad Pr., Inc.
—A Rage of Maidens: Sixth Caitlin Reece Mystery. 1994. (Caitlin Reece Mysteries Ser.). 224p. pap. 10.95 (*1-56280-068-X*) Naiad Pr., Inc.
—A Tiger's Heart. 1992. (Caitlin Reece Mysteries Ser.: No. 4). 240p. pap. 9.95 (*1-56280-018-3*) Naiad Pr., Inc.
Douglas, Marion. Bending at the Bow. 1995. 80p. pap. (*0-88974-051-8*, Press Gang Pubs.) Raincoast Bk. Distribution.
—The Doubtful Guests. 1993. 192p. pap. 7.99 o.p. (*0-920501-92-3*) Orca Bk. Pubs.
Duncan, Sara Jeannette. The Pool in the Desert. 1985. (Fiction Ser.). 224p. pap. 6.95 o.p. (*0-14-007457-0*, Penguin Bks.) Viking Penguin.
Dunford, Warren. Making a Killing. 2001. 325p. pap. 13.95 (*1-55583-657-7*) Alyson Pubns.
—Soon to Be a Major Motion Picture: A Novel. 2000. 255p. pap. 12.95 (*1-55583-582-1*, Alyson Bks.) Alyson Pubns.
Durham, Charles. The Last Exile. 1992. mass mkt. 5.99 o.s.i (*0-345-37382-0*); 1989. 448p. pap. 23.00 (*0-345-35495-8*) Ballantine Bks.
Dyer, Bernadette. Villa Fair. 2000. (Illus.). ix, 174p. pap. 14.95 (*0-88878-410-4*) Beach Holme Pubs., Ltd. CAN. *Dist:* Stackpole Bks.
Dyment, Margaret. Drawing the Spaces. 1994. 240p. pap. 7.99 o.p. (*1-55143-015-0*) Orca Bk. Pubs.
Earth Magic. 2001. E-Book 6.95 (*0-9710473-5-9*) Dragonfly Publishing, Inc.
Easson, Roger R., et al. Grandpa Beaver: His Amazing Tales. 1987. (Illus.). 98p. (Orig.). (J). (gr. 5-12). pap. 6.95 (*0-942179-01-3*) Shelby Hse.
Eddenden, A. E. A Good Year for Murder. 1988. (Academy Book Ser.). 184p. 18.95 o.p. (*0-89733-284-9*) Academy Chicago Pubs., Ltd.
—Murder at the Movies. 1996. 159p. 20.00 (*0-89733-428-0*) Academy Chicago Pubs., Ltd.
—Murder on the Thirteenth. 1992. 168p. 20.00 (*0-89733-380-2*) Academy Chicago Pubs., Ltd.
Eddie, David. Chump Change: A Novel. 1999. 230p. 13.00 (*1-57322-736-6*, Riverhead Trade (Paperbacks)) Berkley Publishing Group.
Ellis, Deb. Haley & Scotia. 1995. 132p. (Orig.). pap. 7.95 (*0-9603628-8-6*) Frog in the Well.
Ellis, Peter B. The Rising of the Moon. 1987. 640p. 19.95 o.p. (*0-312-00676-4*) St. Martin's Pr.
Epp, Margaret. The Earth Is Round. 1974. 228p. (Orig.). pap. 4.50 o.p. (*0-919797-00-8*) Kindred Productions.
Epp, Margaret A. The Earth Is Round. 1998. 228 p. (Orig.). mass mkt. 4.95 (*0-87813-575-8*) Christian Light Pubns., Inc.
Estleman, Loren D. White Desert. 240p. 2001. mass mkt. 5.99 (*0-8125-8436-8*); 2000. reprint ed. 22.95 o.p. (*0-312-86969-X*, NHC 0145) Doherty, Tom Assocs., LLC. (Forge Bks.).
—White Desert. l.t. ed. 2002. (Western Ser.). 324p. 26.95 (*0-7862-3854-2*) Thorndike Pr.
Findley, Timothy. Dinner along the Amazon. 1985. (Fiction Ser.). 272p. pap. 6.95 o.p. (*0-14-007304-3*, Penguin Bks.) Viking Penguin.
—Headhunter. 1994. 23.00 o.s.i (*0-517-59827-2*) Crown Publishing Group.
—The Wars. 1983. mass mkt. 3.95 o.s.i (*0-440-39239-X*); 1977. 8.95 o.s.i (*0-440-09397-X*, Delacorte Pr.) Dell Publishing.
Foster, Marion. Legal Tender. 1992. 240p. (Orig.). pap. 9.95 (*1-56341-010-9*); pap. text 20.95 (*1-56341-011-7*) Firebrand Bks.
Fournier, Claude. Rene LeVesque: Portrait of a Man Alone. Fournier, Jean-Pierre, tr. 1995. 272p. pap. o.p. (*0-7710-3216-1*) McClelland & Stewart/Tundra Bks.
Fox, Kathryn. The Second Vow: The Mounties. 2001. 384p. mass mkt. 5.99 o.s.i (*0-8217-6821-2*) Kensington Publishing Corp.
Frith, Ellen. Man-S-Laughter. 1995. 268p. pap. (*0-88982-147-X*) Oolichan Bks.
Gabriele, Lisa. Tempting Faith DiNapoli. 2002. (Illus.). 304p. 24.00 (*0-7432-2522-8*, Simon & Schuster) Simon & Schuster.
Gage, S. R. A Few Rustic Huts: Ranger Cabins & Logging Camps of Algonquin Park. 1994. (Illus.). 96p. pap. 12.95 (*0-88962-291-4*) Mosaic Pr.
Gallant, Mavis. The Pegnitz Junction. 1988. (Short Fiction Ser.). 180p. (C). pap. 6.00 o.p. (*0-915308-60-6*) Graywolf Pr.
Galloway, Steven. Finnie Walsh. 2000. (Illus.). 165p. pap. (*1-55192-372-6*) Raincoast Bk. Distribution.
Galt, George. Scribes & Scoundrels. 1997. 220p. pap. (*1-55022-333-X*) ECW Pr.
Gardiner, Scott. The Dominion of Wyley McFadden. 2001. 352p. pap. 12.95 (*0-679-31105-X*, Random Hse. Bks. for Young Readers) Random Hse. Children's Bks.
Gasco, Elyse. Can You Wave Bye Bye, Baby? 2000. 256p. pap. 12.00 (*0-312-26300-7*) Picador.
—Can You Wave Bye, Bye Baby? 1999. 256p. pap. 17.00 (*0-312-20631-3*) Picador.
Gaston, Bill. Sex is Red. 1998. 230p. pap. (*1-896951-09-0*) Cormorant Bks.
Gerber, Joanne. In the Misleading Absence of Light. 1997. 280p. pap. 12.95 (*1-55050-115-1*) Coteau Bks. CAN. *Dist:* General Distribution Services, Inc.
Gerson, Carole. A Purer Taste: The Reading & Writing of Fiction in English in Nineteenth-Century Canada. 1989. (Illus.). 224p. text (*0-8020-5820-5*); pap. text (*0-8020-6733-6*) Univ. of Toronto Pr.
Gibson, Graeme. Gentleman Death. 1995. 256p. pap. 12.95 (*0-7710-3312-5*) McClelland & Stewart/Tundra Bks.
—Perpetual Motion. 1998. (New Canadian Library). 272p. mass mkt. 8.95 (*0-7710-3462-8*) McClelland & Stewart/Tundra Bks.
—Perpetual Motion. 1983. 283p. 12.95 o.p. (*0-312-60132-8*) St. Martin's Pr.
—Perpetual Motion. 1988. 288p. pap. 6.95 o.p. (*0-14-010382-1*, Penguin Bks.) Viking Penguin.
Gilmour, David. Lost Between Houses. 2000. 240p. pap. 14.95 (*0-679-31029-0*) Random Hse., Inc.
—Sparrow Nights. 2002. 224p. text 24.00 (*1-58243-203-1*, Counterpoint Pr.) Basic Bks.
Giroux, E. X. A Death for a Dancing Doll. 1992. mass mkt. 3.99 o.s.i (*0-345-37609-9*) Ballantine Bks.
—A Death for a Dancing Doll. 1991. 17.95 o.p. (*0-312-05848-9*, Saint Martin's Minotaur) St. Martin's Pr.
Glover, Ruth. Bittersweet Bliss: A Novel. 2003. (Saskatchewan Saga Ser.). 272p. pap. 11.99 (*0-8007-5828-5*) Revell, Fleming H. Co.
Godbout, Jacques. Knife on the Table. 1976. mass mkt. o.p. (*0-7710-9230-X*) McClelland & Stewart CAN. *Dist:* Random Hse. of Canada, Ltd.
Godfrey, Ellen. Murder Behind Locked Doors. 1988. 336p. 17.95 o.p. (*0-312-02258-1*, Saint Martin's Minotaur) St. Martin's Pr.
Goodman, Joan Elizabeth. Paradise: A Tale of Survival. 2002. 224p. (J). (gr. 7 up). tchr. ed. 16.00 (*0-618-11450-5*) Houghton Mifflin Co.
Gordon, Alison. The Dead Pull Hitter. 1991. 256p. mass mkt. 3.99 o.p. (*0-451-40240-5*, Onyx) NAL.
—The Dead Pull Hitter. 1989. 224p. 15.95 o.p. (*0-312-03319-2*, Saint Martin's Minotaur) St. Martin's Pr.
—The Dead Pull Hitter: A Kate Henry Mystery. 1996. 224p. mass mkt. 6.99 (*0-7710-3420-2*) McClelland & Stewart/Tundra Bks.
—Prairie Hardball. 1998. (Kate Henry Mysteries Ser.: Bk. 5). 288p. mass mkt. 6.95 (*0-7710-3413-X*) McClelland & Stewart/Tundra Bks.
—Prairie Hardball: A Kate Henry Mystery. 1998. (Kate Henry Mystery Ser.). 288p. 20.95 o.p. (*0-7710-3412-1*) McClelland & Stewart/Tundra Bks.
—Safe at Home. 1991. 17.95 o.p. (*0-312-05959-0*, Saint Martin's Minotaur) St. Martin's Pr.
—Safe at Home: A Kate Henry Mystery. 1996. 248p. mass mkt. 5.95 (*0-7710-3417-2*) McClelland & Stewart/Tundra Bks.
—Striking Out: A Kate Henry Mystery. 1995. 240p. 19.95 o.p. (*0-7710-3423-7*) McClelland & Stewart/Tundra Bks.
Gorgas, Paula Blais. Earth Magic. 2001. pap. 13.95 (*0-9710473-4-0*) Dragonfly Publishing, Inc.
Gosselin, Henry. Eustache Lambert: Donne Extraordinaire. 2001. pap. 13.98 (*0-7596-1852-6*) 1stBooks Library.
Gostick, Adrian R. Eddy & the Habs. 1994. vii, 157p. (J). (gr. 3-7). pap. o.p. (*0-87579-832-2*) Deseret Bk. Co.
Gough, Laurence. Death on a No. 8 Hook. 2001. (Willows & Parker Mystery Ser.). 232p. mass mkt. 7.95 (*0-7710-3533-0*) McClelland & Stewart/Tundra Bks.
—The Goldfish Bowl. 1988. 192p. 13.95 o.p. (*0-312-01434-1*, Saint Martin's Minotaur) St. Martin's Pr.
—Hot Shots. 2002. 224p. mass mkt. 6.95 (*0-7710-3545-4*) McClelland & Stewart/Tundra Bks.
—Hot Shots. 1991. (Crime Monthly Ser.). 192p. pap. 4.95 o.p. (*0-14-015488-4*, Penguin Bks.) Penguin Group (USA) Inc.
—Hot Shots. 1990. 192p. 16.95 o.p. (*0-670-83014-3*) Viking Penguin.
—Karaoke Rap. 1998. (Willows & Parker Mystery Ser.). 368p. 20.95 o.p. (*0-7710-3403-2*) McClelland & Stewart/Tundra Bks.
—Killers. 1995. 256p. pap. 8.95 o.p. (*0-575-05782-3*) Gollancz, Victor GBR. *Dist:* Trafalgar Square.
—Killers. 1993. o.p. (*0-7710-3439-3*) McClelland & Stewart/Tundra Bks.
—Memory Lane. 1997. (Willows & Parker Mystery Ser.). 304p. mass mkt. 5.95 (*0-7710-3404-0*) McClelland & Stewart/Tundra Bks.
—Memory Lane: A Willows & Parker Mystery. 1997. 296p. 24.95 o.p. (*0-7710-3437-7*) McClelland & Stewart/Tundra Bks.
—Serious Crimes. 2002. 256p. mass mkt. 6.95 (*0-7710-3546-2*) McClelland & Stewart/Tundra Bks.
—Serious Crimes. 1999. pap. (*0-670-83675-3*) Viking Penguin.
—Shutterbug. 1999. (Willows & Parker Mystery Ser.). 288p. mass mkt. 7.95 (*0-7710-3429-6*) McClelland & Stewart/Tundra Bks.
—Shutterbug: A Willows & Parker Mystery. 1998. (Willows & Parker Mystery Ser.: Bk. 11). 288p. 20.95 o.p. (*0-7710-3531-4*) McClelland & Stewart/Tundra Bks.
—Silent Knives. 1988. 192p. 13.95 o.p. (*0-312-01747-2*, Saint Martin's Minotaur) St. Martin's Pr.
—Silent Knives. 1990. 192p. pap. 3.95 o.p. (*0-14-012189-7*, Penguin Bks.) Viking Penguin.
Gray, Ed. Lake of the Beginning: A Fable of Salmon & Northern Lights. 1998. (Illus.). 126p. tchr. ed. 22.50 (*1-57223-085-1*, 0851) Willow Creek Pr., Inc.
Green, Terence M. Blue Limbo. 1998. (Blue Limbo Ser.: Vol. 1). 288p. mass mkt. 5.99 (*0-8125-7134-7*); 1996. 253p. 22.95 o.p. (*0-312-86282-2*) Doherty, Tom Assocs., LLC. (Tor Bks.).
—Blue Limbo. 1999. 5.99 (*0-312-87119-8*) St. Martin's Pr.
—A Witness to Life. (Illus.). 240p. 2000. pap. 12.95 (*0-312-87300-X*); 1999. 20.95 (*0-312-86672-0*) Doherty, Tom Assocs., LLC. (Forge Bks.).
Guilford, Irene. The Embrace, Vol. 1. 1999. (Prose Ser.: Vol. 55). 150p. pap. 13.00 (*1-55071-086-9*) Guernica Editions, Inc.
Haig-Brown, Roderick L. On the Highest Hill. 1994. (Northwest Reprints Ser.). 336p. reprint ed. 27.95 (*0-87071-518-6*); pap. 15.95 (*0-87071-519-4*) Oregon State Univ. Pr.
Haley, Susan. Getting Married in Buffalo Jump. 1987. 256p. 17.95 o.p. (*0-525-24528-6*, 01646-490, Dutton) Dutton/Plume.
Hall, Linda. August Gamble. 1995. (Royal Canadian Mounted Police Ser.: Vol. 1). 256p. pap. 9.99 (*0-934998-62-0*) Evangel Publishing Hse.
Hampson, Cy, contrib. by. All Sorts—all Shorts: Short Stories. 1997. (Illus.). (*0-9680850-1-6*) Ardmore Pr.
Harlow, Joan Hiatt. Star in the Storm. 2000. (Illus.). 160p. (J). (gr. 3-7). 16.00 (*0-689-82905-1*, McElderry, Margaret K.) Simon & Schuster Children's Publishing.
Hart, Bill. Don't Blink ... or You'll Miss It! 2001. (Illus.). 200p. (*1-55212-790-7*) Trafford Publishing.
Hay, Elizabeth. A Student of Weather. 2001. 384p. pap. text 15.00 (*1-58243-181-7*, Counterpoint Pr.) Basic Bks.
Hedley, Leslie B. Twelve Sisters. 1993. vi, 201p. pap. o.p. (*0-87579-779-2*) Deseret Bk. Co.
Hemon, Louis. Maria Chapdelaine. reprint ed. lib. bdg. 48.00 (*0-7426-1383-6*); 2001. pap. text 28.00 (*0-7426-6383-3*) Classic Bks.
—Maria Chapdelaine. 1989. (FRE.). pap. 8.95 (*0-7859-3068-X*, 2253005665) French & European Pubns., Inc.
—Maria Chapdelaine. 2002. 128p. 22.99 (*1-4043-1638-8*); per. 18.99 (*1-4043-1639-6*) IndyPublish.com.
—My Fair Lady. Bradley, William A., tr. 1977. (Short Story Index Reprint Ser.). reprint ed. 23.95 (*0-8369-4219-1*) Ayer Co. Pubs., Inc.
Hessayon, Joan. Thorsby. 1989. 208p. 22.95 o.p. (*0-7126-1828-7*) Century GBR. *Dist:* Trafalgar Square.
—Thorsby. l.t. ed. 1989. (Ulverscroft Large Print Ser.). 352p. 29.99 o.p. (*0-7089-2037-3*, Ulverscroft) Thorpe, F. A. Pubs. GBR. *Dist:* Ulverscroft Large Print Bks., Ltd., Ulverscroft Large Print Canada, Ltd.
Heurtelou, Maude. The Bonplezi Family: The Adventures of a Haitian Family in North America. Vilsaint, Fequiere, ed. Nickrosz, John D., tr. 1998. 242p. pap. (*1-881839-69-9*) Educa Vision.
Highway, Tomson. The Kiss of the Fur Queen. 1999. 320p. pap. (*0-385-25880-1*) Doubleday Canada, Ltd. CAN. *Dist:* Random Hse., Inc.
—The Kiss of the Fur Queen. 2000. (American Indian Literature & Critical Studies Ser.: Vol. 34). 320p. 24.95 (*0-8061-3236-1*) Univ. of Oklahoma Pr.
Hillis, Rick. Limbo River. 1991. 144p. pap. 9.95 o.p. (*0-88001-315-X*) HarperCollins Pubs.
—Limbo River. 1991. pap. (*0-7710-4098-9*) McClelland & Stewart/Tundra Bks.
—Limbo River. 1990. (Drue Heinz Literature Prize Ser.). 142p. 22.50 (*0-8229-3653-4*) Univ. of Pittsburgh Pr.
Hoagland, Edward. Seven Rivers West. 1986. 320p. 18.45 o.p. (*0-671-60753-7*) Summit Bks.
—Seven Rivers West. 1987. 320p. pap. 6.95 o.p. (*0-14-010276-0*, Penguin Bks.) Viking Penguin.
Hollingshead, Greg. The Healer: A Novel. 1999. 336p. 24.00 o.s.i (*0-06-019227-5*) HarperCollins Pubs.
—The Healer: A Novel. 2000. 336p. pap. 14.00 (*0-06-092967-7*, Perennial) HarperTrade.
—The Roaring Girl. 1998. (Harvest Book Ser.). 208p. pap. 12.00 o.s.i (*0-15-600584-0*, Harvest Bks.) Harcourt Trade Pubs.
—The Roaring Girl. 1997. 208p. 21.95 o.s.i (*0-399-14222-3*, G. P. Putnam's Sons) Penguin Group (USA) Inc.
Hood, Hugh. Around the Mountain. 1994. 160p. pap. (*0-88984-141-1*) Porcupine's Quill, Inc.
Houston, James. River Runners: A Tale of Hardship & Bravery. 1979. (Illus.). 160p. (J). (gr. 7 up). 11.95 o.s.i (*0-689-50151-X*, McElderry, Margaret K.) Simon & Schuster Children's Publishing.
—Running West. 1996. pap. 14.00 o.p. (*1-57566-044-X*); 1992. (Illus.). 380p. mass mkt. 4.99 o.s.i (*0-8217-3505-5*, Zebra Bks.) Kensington Publishing Corp.
—Running West. 1990. mass mkt. 5.95 (*0-7710-4268-X*); 1989. o.p. (*0-7710-4262-0*) McClelland & Stewart/Tundra Bks.
Howarth, Jean. Treasure Island. 1985. (Fiction Ser.). 208p. pap. 5.95 o.p. (*0-14-007066-4*, Penguin Bks.) Viking Penguin.
Hubert, Cam. Dreamspeaker. 1981. pap. 3.50 (*0-380-56622-2*, Avon Bks.) Morrow/Avon.
Humphreys, Helen. Leaving Earth. 1998. 224p. 22.00 o.s.i (*0-8050-5957-1*, Metropolitan Bks.) Holt, Henry & Co.
—Leaving Earth. 2000. 256p. pap. 13.00 (*0-312-25500-4*) Picador.
Huston, Nancy. Plainsong. 1995. 224p. pap. o.p. (*0-00-647937-5*) HarperCollins Pubs. Canada, Ltd.
Innes, Hammond. High Stand. 1988. 336p. pap. text 4.95 o.p. (*0-07-031738-0*) McGraw-Hill Cos., The.
—High Stand. 1986. 336p. 17.95 o.p. (*0-689-11850-3*, Scribner) Simon & Schuster.
Itani, Frances. Leaning, Leaning Over Water: A Novel In Ten Stories. 1998. 206p. (*0-00-225501-4*) HarperCollins Pubs.
—Leaning, Leaning Over Water: A Novel in Ten Stories. 1998. pap. (*0-00-638582-6*) HarperCollins Pubs.
Jackson, Lorna. Dressing for Hope. 1996. 148p. (J). pap. (*0-86492-167-5*) Goose Lane Editions.
Johnson, E. Pauline. The Moccasin Maker. 1987. 272p. reprint ed. pap. 84.40 (*0-608-00729-3*, 206150500009) Bks. on Demand.
—The Moccasin Maker. 1987. 267p. reprint ed. pap. 12.95 o.p. (*0-8165-0910-7*) Univ. of Arizona Pr.
Johnson, E. Pauline, et al. The Moccasin Maker. 1998. (Illus.). 272p. pap. 12.95 (*0-8061-3079-2*) Univ. of Oklahoma Pr.
Johnston, Basil. Ojibway Heritage. 1990. (Illus.). 171p. reprint ed. pap. 11.95 (*0-8032-7572-2*, Bison Bks.) Univ. of Nebraska Pr.
—Ojibway Tales. 1993. Orig. Title: Moose Meat & Wild Rice. 188p. reprint ed. pap. 13.95 (*0-8032-7578-1*, Bison Bks.) Univ. of Nebraska Pr.
Johnston, Basil H. Ojibway Ceremonies. 1987. 192p. pap. 16.99 (*0-7710-4445-3*) McClelland & Stewart/Tundra Bks.
—Ojibway Ceremonies. 1990. (Illus.). 188p. reprint ed. pap. 13.95 (*0-8032-7573-0*, Bison Bks.) Univ. of Nebraska Pr.
—Ojibway Heritage. 1976. (Illus.). 171p. 20.50 o.p. (*0-231-04168-3*) Columbia Univ. Pr.
Josefchak-Pugh, Patricia. Angel on Her Knees. 1999. 126p. pap. 12.45 (*1-58500-617-3*) 1stBooks Library.
Keegan, Gerald. Famine Diary: Journey to a New World. 1997. 144p. reprint ed. pap. 10.95 (*0-86327-300-9*) Wolfhound Pr. IRL. *Dist:* Irish American Bk. Co.
Kelly, Nora. Bad Chemistry, Vol. 21. 2000. (Missing Mysteries Ser.: Vol. 21). 240p. pap. 14.95 (*1-890208-34-5*) Poisoned Pen Pr.
—Bad Chemistry. 1994. 256p. 20.95 o.p. (*0-312-10934-2*, Saint Martin's Minotaur) St. Martin's Pr.
—In the Shadow of Kings. 2000. (Missing Mysteries Ser.: Vol. 12). 189p. pap. 14.95 (*1-890208-22-1*) Poisoned Pen Pr.
—In the Shadow of Kings. 1984. 12.95 o.p. (*0-312-41171-5*) St. Martin's Pr.
—In the Shadow of Kings. l.t. ed. 1995. (Linford Mystery Library). 400p. pap. 17.99 o.p. (*0-7089-7733-2*, Linford) Thorpe, F. A. Pubs. GBR. *Dist:* Ulverscroft Large Print Bks., Ltd., Ulverscroft Large Print Canada, Ltd.
—My Sister's Keeper. 2000. (Missing Mysteries Ser.: Vol. 15). 221p. pap. 14.95 (*1-890208-28-0*) Poisoned Pen Pr.
—My Sister's Keeper. 1992. 224p. 17.95 o.p. (*0-312-08268-1*, Saint Martin's Minotaur) St. Martin's Pr.
—Old Wounds. l.t. ed. 1999. (Magna Large Print Ser.). 464p. (*0-7505-1410-8*) Magna Large Print Bks. GBR. *Dist:* Ulverscroft Large Print Canada, Ltd.

—Old Wounds. 2000. 300p. pap. 12.95 (*1-890208-25-6*) Poisoned Pen Pr.

Kelso, Irene Landry. A Passion in Winter. 2002. (Illus.). 302p. pap. (*1-55212-414-2*) Trafford Publishing.

Kidd, Monica. Beatrice: A Novel. 2001. 224p. pap. 16.95 (*0-88801-265-9*) Turnstone Pr. CAN. *Dist:* General Distribution Services, Inc.

Kilbourne, Christina. Day of the Dog-Tooth Violets. 2001. (Illus.). 200p. pap. 13.50 (*1-896647-44-8*) Broken Jaw Pr. CAN. *Dist:* General Distribution Services, Inc.

Kilpatrick, Nancy. Eternal City. 2003. 304p. pap. 13.95 (*1-4104-0153-7*, Five Star Trade) Gale Group.

Kilpatrick, Nancy & Kilpatrick, Michael. Eternal City. 2003. (Five Star First Edition Speculative Fiction Ser.). 290p. 25.95 (*0-7862-4960-9*, Five Star) Gale Group.

King, Thomas, ed. All My Relations: An Anthology of Contemporary Canadian Native Fiction. 1992. (American Indian Literature & Critical Studies Ser.: Vol. 4). 236p. reprint ed. pap. 15.95 (*0-8061-2429-6*) Univ. of Oklahoma Pr.

—All My Relations: An Anthology of Contemporary Canadian Native Prose. 1990. 240p. pap. 18.99 (*0-7710-6706-2*) McClelland & Stewart/Tundra Bks.

Kirby, William. The Golden Dog. 2000. 252p. E-Book 3.95 (*0-594-02549-4*) 1873 Pr.

—The Golden Dog. 2002. 592p. 24.99 (*1-4043-0426-6*); per. 19.99 (*1-4043-0427-4*) IndyPublish.com.

Knister, Raymond, ed. Canadian Short Stories. 1977. (Short Story Index Reprint Ser.). xix, 340p. reprint ed. 22.95 (*0-8369-3917-4*) Ayer Co. Pubs., Inc.

Kogawa, Joy. Itsuka. 1993. 352p. pap. 19.00 (*0-385-46885-7*) Knopf, Alfred A. Inc.

—Obasan. unabr. collector's ed. 1986. audio 56.00 (*0-7366-1009-X*, 1942) Books on Tape, Inc.

—Obasan. 1993. 320p. pap. 12.95 (*0-385-46886-5*) Doubleday Publishing.

—Obasan. 1982. 256p. reprint ed. 14.95 o.p. (*0-87923-429-6*); pap. 11.95 o.p. (*0-87923-491-1*) Godine, David R. Pub.

Kroetsch, Robert. The Man from the Creeks. 1998. 320p. o.s.i (*0-679-30917-9*) Random Hse. of Canada, Ltd. CAN. *Dist:* Random Hse., Inc.

Laurence, Margaret. A Bird in the House. 1993. (Phoenix Fiction Ser.). 192p. (C). reprint ed. pap. text 14.00 (*0-226-46934-4*) Univ. of Chicago Pr.

—The Diviners. 1984. 480p. mass mkt. 4.95 o.s.i (*0-7704-2176-8*) Bantam Bks.

—The Diviners. 1984. mass mkt. o.s.i (*0-7704-2045-1*) Seal Bks.

—The Diviners. 1993. (Phoenix Fiction Ser.). 392p. (C). pap. 14.00 (*0-226-46935-2*) Univ. of Chicago Pr.

—The Fire-Dwellers. 1984. mass mkt. o.s.i (*0-7704-2039-7*) Seal Bks.

—The Fire-Dwellers. 1993. (Phoenix Fiction Ser.). viii, 288p. pap. 13.00 (*0-226-46951-4*) Univ. of Chicago Pr.

—A Jest of God. 1988. 224p. mass mkt. 7.95 (*0-7710-9988-6*) McClelland & Stewart/Tundra Bks.

—A Jest of God. 1993. (Phoenix Fiction Ser.). 224p. pap. 13.50 (*0-226-46952-2*) Univ. of Chicago Pr.

—The Stone Angel. 1984. mass mkt. 4.50 o.s.i (*0-7704-2140-7*); 304p. mass mkt. 4.50 o.s.i (*0-7704-2177-6*) Bantam Bks.

—The Stone Angel. 1988. 328p. mass mkt. 7.95 (*0-7710-9989-4*) McClelland & Stewart/Tundra Bks.

—The Stone Angel. 1993. (Phoenix Fiction Ser.). 320p. (C). pap. 14.00 (*0-226-46936-0*) Univ. of Chicago Pr.

Lavery, John. Very Good Butter. 2000. 150p. pap. 14.95 (*1-55022-411-5*) ECW Pr. CAN. *Dist:* Independent Pubs. Group.

Leacock, Stephen. Sunshine Sketches of a Little Town. 1980. (Short Story Index Reprint Ser.). 26.95 (*0-8369-3595-0*) Ayer Co. Pubs., Inc.

—Sunshine Sketches of a Little Town. Spadoni, Carl, ed. 2002. (Broadview Literary Texts Ser.). (Illus.). lxxxv, 321p. (*1-55111-178-0*) Broadview Pr.

—Sunshine Sketches of a Little Town. 1999. (Illus.). 184p. 26.95 o.s.i (*0-7710-5001-1*); 1996. 200p. mass mkt. 6.95 (*0-7710-9984-3*) McClelland & Stewart/Tundra Bks.

—Sunshine Sketches of a Little Town. 2000. (Humour Classics Ser.). 224p. 15.95 (*1-85375-367-X*) Prion GBR. *Dist:* Trafalgar Square.

Leddy, Elfie. On Silver Wings: A Mystic Tale from Celtic Lore. 2001. 520p. 21.95 (*1-57733-080-3*, Pelican Pond) Blue Dolphin Publishing, Inc.

Lee, Sky. Disappearing Moon Cafe. 1991. 237p. 18.95 o.p. (*1-878067-11-7*, Seal Pr.) Avalon Publishing Group.

Levine, Norman. Champagne Barn. 1985. (Fiction Ser.). 272p. pap. 6.95 o.p. (*0-14-007255-1*, Penguin Bks.) Viking Penguin.

London, Jack. White Fang. 1989. (Illus.). 206p. (J). mass mkt. 2.99 (*0-8125-0512-3*, Tor Classics) Doherty, Tom Assocs., LLC.

Luke, Pearl. Burning Ground. 2001. 256p. pap. 13.00 (*0-452-28267-5*, Plume) Dutton/Plume.

—Burning Ground. 2000. 249p. (*0-00-225504-9*) HarperCollins Pubs.

Lundin, Steve. A Ruin of Feathers. 1992. pap. text (*0-920661-23-8*) TSAR Pubns.

MacDonald, D. R. Eyestone. 1988. (Editor's Book Award Ser.). 15.95 (*0-916366-48-0*) Pushcart Pr., The.

—Eyestone. 1989. 224p. pap. 6.95 o.p. (*0-14-012020-3*, Penguin Bks.) Viking Penguin.

MacLennan, Hugh. Each Man's Son. 2003. pap. (*0-7735-2488-6*); 222p. mass mkt. (*0-7735-2489-4*) McGill-Queen's Univ. Pr.

MacLeod, Alistair. Island: The Collected Stories. 2002. 448p. pap. 14.00 (*0-375-71304-2*, Vintage) Knopf Publishing Group.

—Island: The Collected Stories. 2001. v, 434p. 25.95 (*0-393-05035-1*) Norton, W. W. & Co., Inc.

MacMillan, Gail. The Hermit of Hart's Hollow. 2000. 186p. 18.95 (*0-8034-9397-5*, Avalon Bks.) Bouregy, Thomas & Co., Inc.

Malton, H. Mel. Dead Cow in Aisle Three: A Polly Deacon Mystery. 2001. (Rendezvous Crime Ser.). 304p. pap. 10.95 (*0-929141-82-2*, Rendezvous Press) Napoleon Publishing/Rendezvous Pr. CAN. *Dist:* Words Distributing Co.

Maracle, Lee. Sojourner's Truth: First Nations Fiction. 1995. pap. o.p. (*0-88974-023-2*, Press Gang Pubs.) Raincoast Bk. Distribution.

—Sojourners, Truth & Sundogs: First Nations Fiction. 1999. 342p. pap. (*0-88974-061-5*, Press Gang Pubs.) Raincoast Bk. Distribution.

—Sundogs. 1992. 224p. pap. 10.95 o.p. (*0-919441-41-6*) Theytus Bks., Ltd. CAN. *Dist:* Orca Bk. Pubs.

Marchand, Clement. Vanishing Villages. 1993. (Prose Ser.: No. 19). 270p. pap. 13.00 (*0-920717-73-X*) Guernica Editions, Inc.

Marshall, Tom. The Adventures of John Montgomery. 1997. (Illus.). 398p. pap. 12.95 (*1-55082-135-0*) Quarry Pr. CAN. *Dist:* LPC/InBook.

Martel, Suzanne. King's Daughter. 1998. 232p. (gr. 5-9). 14.95 (*0-88899-323-4*) Publishers Group West.

—The King's Daughter. rev. ed. 1998. 192p. (YA). (gr. 5-9). pap. 6.95 (*0-88899-218-1*) Groundwood Bks. CAN. *Dist:* Publishers Group West.

Matheson, Shirlee Smith. Keeper of the Mountains. 2002. (Illus.). 152p. pap. (*1-894345-13-4*) Thistledown Pr., Ltd.

McKinnon, K. C. Dancing at the Harvest Moon. 1999. (Illus.). 248p. mass mkt. 6.50 o.s.i (*0-449-00527-5*, Fawcett) Ballantine Bks.

—Dancing at the Harvest Moon. l.t. ed. 1998. 25.95 o.p. (*1-56895-551-0*, Wheeler Publishing, Inc.) Gale Group.

McNamee, Stephen. Ten Thousand Days Has Our Youth, Vol. 1. 1987. 328p. 17.75 (*0-930950-03-8*) Nopoly Pr., Inc.

Metcalf, Jill. Marriage by Design. 1999. 320p. pap. 4.99 (*0-8439-4553-2*) Dorchester Publishing Co., Inc.

Metcalf, John, ed. Making It New. 1983. (Contemporary Canadian Stories Ser.). 272p. pap. 13.95 o.p. (*0-458-95470-5*, NO. 3891) Routledge.

Miller, K. D. A Litany in Time of Plague. 1994. 160p. pap. (*0-88984-145-4*) Porcupine's Quill, Inc.

Mitchell, W. O. How I Spent My Summer Holidays. 2000. (Douglas Gibson Bks.). 264p. pap. 18.95 (*0-7710-6110-2*) McClelland & Stewart/Tundra Bks.

—Roses Are Difficult Here. 2000. (Douglas Gibson Bks.). 328p. pap. 18.95 (*0-7710-6109-9*) McClelland & Stewart/Tundra Bks.

Monroe, Alice. Open Secrets. unabr. ed. 1995. audio 24.99 (*0-88646-383-1*, 7383) Durkin Hayes Publishing Ltd.

Moore, Brian. Black Robe. 1991. mass mkt. 4.99 o.p. (*0-449-45066-X*, Fawcett); 1986. mass mkt. 5.99 o.s.i (*0-449-20947-4*) Ballantine Bks.

—Black Robe. 1997. 256p. pap. 14.00 (*0-452-27865-1*, Plume); 1985. 15.95 o.p. (*0-525-24311-9*, Dutton) Dutton/Plume.

—Black Robe. 1995. 80p. pap. 10.00 o.p. (*0-586-08615-3*) HarperCollins Pubs. Ltd. GBR. *Dist:* HarperCollins Pubs.

Morris, Alan. Bright Sword of Justice. 1997. (Guardians of the North Ser.: Vol. 3). 256p. pap. 9.99 o.p. (*1-55661-694-5*) Bethany Hse. Pubs.

—Bright Sword of Justice. l.t. ed. 1998. (Guardians of the North Ser.: Vol. 3). 376p. 24.95 (*0-7862-1470-8*) Thorndike Pr.

—By Honor Bound. 1996. (Guardians of the North Ser.: Bk. 1). 288p. pap. 9.99 (*1-55661-692-9*) Bethany Hse. Pubs.

—By Honor Bound. l.t. ed. 1998. (Guardians of the North Ser.: Vol. 1). 549p. 24.95 (*0-7862-1300-0*) Thorndike Pr.

—Heart of Valor. 1996. (Guardians of the North Ser.: Bk. 2). 256p. pap. 9.99 o.p. (*1-55661-693-7*) Bethany Hse. Pubs.

—Heart of Valor. l.t. ed. 1998. (Christian Fiction Ser.). 445p. 24.95 (*0-7862-1406-6*) Thorndike Pr.

—Wings of Healing. 1999. (Guardians of the North Ser.: Vol. 5). 272p. pap. 9.99 (*1-55661-696-1*) Bethany Hse. Pubs.

—Wings of Healing. l.t. ed. 2000. (Christian Fiction Ser.). 408p. 24.95 (*0-7862-2378-2*) Thorndike Pr.

Mowat, Farley. The Farfarers: Before the Norse. 2002. (Illus.). 528p. pap. (*0-385-65926-1*, Anchor Canada) Doubleday Canada, Ltd. CAN. *Dist:* Random Hse., Inc.

—The Farfarers: Before the Norse. 2000. (Illus.). 377p. pap. 16.00 (*1-883642-56-6*) Steerforth Pr.

—Mowat Adventure Stories, 3 vols. 1987. mass mkt. 20.99 (*0-7710-6682-1*) McClelland & Stewart/Tundra Bks.

Munro, Alice. Hateship, Friendship, Courtship, Loveship, Marriage: Stories. l.t. ed. 2002. 501p. 29.95 (*0-7862-4231-0*) Gale Group.

—Hateship, Friendship, Courtship, Loveship, Marriage: Stories. 336p. 2002. pap. 14.00 (*0-375-72743-4*); 2001. 24.00 (*0-375-41300-6*) Knopf, Alfred A. Inc.

—Lives of Girls & Women. 1983. pap. 6.95 o.p. (*0-452-25433-7*, Plume) Dutton/Plume.

—Lives of Girls & Women. 2001. 288p. pap. 13.00 (*0-375-70749-2*, Vintage) Knopf Publishing Group.

—Lives of Girls & Women. 1974. mass mkt. 4.95 o.p. (*0-451-16754-6*); mass mkt. 4.50 o.p. (*0-451-14733-2*); mass mkt. 1.25 o.p. (*0-451-05740-6*); mass mkt. 1.75 o.p. (*0-451-07961-2*); mass mkt. 2.50 o.p. (*0-451-11298-9*); mass mkt. 3.50 o.p. (*0-451-12294-1*); mass mkt. 3.95 o.p. (*0-451-13643-8*) NAL. (Signet Bks.).

—The Love of a Good Woman: Stories. unabr. ed. 1999. audio 69.95 (*0-7927-2316-3*, CSL205, Chivers Sound Library) BBC Audiobooks America.

—The Love of a Good Woman: Stories. 1999. 352p. pap. 13.00 (*0-375-70363-2*); 1998. 320p. 24.00 (*0-375-40395-7*) Knopf, Alfred A. Inc.

—Open Secrets: Stories. 1995. 304p. pap. 13.00 (*0-679-75562-4*, Vintage) Knopf Publishing Group.

—Open Secrets: Stories. 1994. 293p. 23.00 o.s.i (*0-679-43575-1*) Knopf, Alfred A. Inc.

Namjoshi, Suniti. Goja: An Autobiographical Myth. 2001. 160p. pap. 13.95 (*1-875559-97-3*) Spinifex Pr. AUS. *Dist:* Stackpole Bks.

Neilan, Sarah. Paradise. 1982. 368p. 13.95 o.p. (*0-312-59596-4*) St. Martin's Pr.

—Paradise. l.t. ed. 1984. (Ulverscroft Large Print Ser.). 560p. 29.99 o.p. (*0-7089-1188-9*, Ulverscroft) Thorpe, F. A. Pubs. GBR. *Dist:* Ulverscroft Large Print Bks., Ltd., Ulverscroft Large Print Canada, Ltd.

Norman, Howard. Kiss in the Hotel, Joseph Conrad & Other Stories. 1989. 18.95 o.p. (*0-671-64419-X*) Summit Bks.

—The Northern Lights. 2001. 240p. pap. 13.00 (*0-312-28337-7*) Picador.

—The Northern Lights. 1988. 240p. pap. (*0-671-65877-8*, Washington Square Pr.) Simon & Schuster.

—The Northern Lights. 1987. 224p. 17.45 o.p. (*0-671-53231-6*) Summit Bks.

North, Suzanne. Healthy, Wealthy & Dead: A Phoebe Fairfax Mystery. 1994. pap. 6.95 (*0-920897-55-X*) NeWest Pubs., Ltd. CAN. *Dist:* General Distribution Services, Inc.

—Seeing Is Deceiving. 1997. (Phoebe Fairfax Mystery Ser.). 336p. mass mkt. 6.99 (*0-7710-6806-9*) McClelland & Stewart/Tundra Bks.

—Seeing Is Deceiving: A Phoebe Fairfax Mystery. 1996. 288p. 25.99 o.p. (*0-7710-6805-0*) McClelland & Stewart/Tundra Bks.

Oke, Janette. Beyond the Gathering Storm. 2000. 256p. pap. 11.99 (*0-7642-2400-X*); 256p. text 16.99 o.p. (*0-7642-2401-8*); 368p. pap. 16.99 (*0-7642-2403-4*) Bethany Hse. Pubs.

—Beyond the Gathering Storm. l.t. ed. 2000. (Christian Fiction Ser.). 357p. 26.95 o.p. (*0-7862-2942-X*) Thorndike Pr.

—The Birthright. ltd. ed. 2001. (Song of Acadia Ser.). 288p. pap. 10.99 o.p. (*0-7642-8801-6*) Bethany Hse. Pubs.

—A Bride for Donnigan. 1993. (Women of the West Ser.). 224p. pap. 11.99 (*1-55661-327-X*) Bethany Hse. Pubs.

—A Bride for Donnigan. l.t. ed. 1994. 316p. 20.95 o.p. (*0-8161-5958-0*, Macmillan Reference USA) Gale Group.

—The Calling of Emily Evans. 2003. (Classics for Girls Ser.). (Illus.). 176p. (J). 9.99 (*0-7642-2713-0*); 1998. (Women of the West Ser.: Bk. 1). 288p. mass mkt. 5.99 o.p. (*0-7642-2098-5*, 202098); 1990. (Women of the West Ser.). 224p. pap. 11.99 (*1-55661-118-8*); 1990. (Women of the West Ser.). 224p. pap. 12.99 o.p. (*1-55661-121-8*) Bethany Hse. Pubs.

—The Calling of Emily Evans. l.t. ed. 2000. (Christian Fiction Ser.). 345p. 26.95 (*0-7862-2701-X*) Thorndike Pr.

—Canadian West Saga: Four Bestselling Novels Complete in One Volume. 1995. 656p. 12.99 (*0-88486-112-0*, Arrowood Pr.) BBS Publishing Corp.

—The Matchmakers. 1997. 144p. text 12.99 o.p. (*0-7642-2002-0*); pap. 12.99 o.p. (*0-7642-2020-9*) Bethany Hse. Pubs.

—The Matchmakers. l.t. ed. 2001. (Illus.). 197p. 25.95 (*0-7862-3256-0*); (*0-7540-4523-4*); (*0-7540-4524-2*) Thorndike Pr.

—The Measure of a Heart. (Women of the West Ser.: Bk. 6). 1998. 288p. mass mkt. 5.99 o.p. (*0-7642-2100-0*, 202100); 1992. 224p. pap. 11.99 (*1-55661-296-6*); 1992. 224p. pap. 12.99 o.p. (*1-55661-297-4*) Bethany Hse. Pubs.

—The Measure of a Heart. l.t. ed. 1994. 293p. 19.95 (*0-8161-5850-9*, Macmillan Reference USA) Gale Group.

—Roses for Mama. (Classics for Girls Ser.). 2002. 176p. (J). 9.99 (*0-7642-2709-2*); 1999. 288p. pap. 5.99 (*0-7642-2243-0*); 1991. 224p. pap. 11.99 (*1-55661-185-4*); 1991. 224p. pap. 10.99 o.p. (*1-55661-199-4*) Bethany Hse. Pubs.

—Roses for Mama. l.t. ed. 2002. 27.95 (*1-58547-211-5*, Premier) Ctr. Point Large Print.

—When Breaks the Dawn. 1986. (Canadian West Ser.: Vol. 3). 224p. pap. 10.99 (*0-87123-882-9*); pap. 10.99 o.p. (*0-87123-895-0*) Bethany Hse. Pubs.

—When Breaks the Dawn. l.t. ed. 2001. (Christian Fiction Ser.). 317p. 26.95 o.p. (*0-7862-3053-3*) Thorndike Pr.

—When Calls the Heart. (Canadian West Ser.: Vol. 1). 1983. (Illus.). 224p. pap. 10.99 (*0-87123-611-7*); 1985. 226p. pap. 10.99 o.p. (*0-87123-885-3*) Bethany Hse. Pubs.

—When Calls the Heart. l.t. ed. 1992. (General Ser.). 322p. 17.95 o.p. (*0-8161-5366-3*, Macmillan Reference USA) Gale Group.

—When Comes the Spring. 1985. (Canadian West Ser.: Vol. 2). 256p. pap. 10.99 (*0-87123-795-4*); pap. 10.99 o.p. (*0-87123-884-5*) Bethany Hse. Pubs.

—When Comes the Spring. l.t. ed. 1993. (General Ser.). 375p. 19.95 o.p. (*0-8161-5395-7*, Macmillan Reference USA) Gale Group.

—When Hope Springs New. (Canadian West Ser.: Vol. 4). 2001. 288p. pap. 6.99 (*0-7642-2535-9*); 1986. 224p. pap. 10.99 (*0-87123-657-5*); 1986. 224p. pap. 10.99 o.p. (*0-87123-675-3*) Bethany Hse. Pubs.

—When Hope Springs New. l.t. ed. 2001. (Canadian West Ser.). 309p. 28.95 (*0-7862-3054-1*) Thorndike Pr.

—When Tomorrow Comes. 2001. 256p. pap. 11.99 (*0-7642-2555-3*); pap. 15.99 (*0-7642-2557-X*); 368p. pap. 16.99 (*0-7642-2558-8*) Bethany Hse. Pubs.

—When Tomorrow Comes. l.t. ed. 2002. 351p. 28.95 (*0-7862-4031-8*) Gale Group.

Oke, Janette & Bunn, T. Davis. The Birthright. 2001. (Song of Acadia Ser.). 288p. pap. 11.99 (*0-7642-2229-5*); 1p. pap. 15.99 o.p. (*0-7642-2231-7*); 288p. text 16.99 o.p. (*0-7642-2230-9*) Bethany Hse. Pubs.

—The Meeting Place. 1999. (Song of Acadia Ser.). 288p. pap. 11.99 (*0-7642-2176-0*); 288p. text 15.99 o.p. (*0-7642-2177-9*); 1p. pap. 15.99 o.p. incl. audio (*0-7642-2179-5*); 432p. pap. 16.99 o.p. (*0-7642-2178-7*) Bethany Hse. Pubs.

—The Meeting Place. l.t. ed. 1999. (Inspirational Ser.). 384p. 27.95 (*0-7838-8658-6*) Thorndike Pr.

—The Sacred Shore. 2000. (Song of Acadia Ser.). 272p. pap. 11.99 (*0-7642-2247-3*); 272p. text 16.99 o.p. (*0-7642-2249-X*); 384p. pap. 16.99 o.p. (*0-7642-2248-1*) Bethany Hse. Pubs.

—The Sacred Shore. l.t. ed. 2000. (G. K. Hall Inspirational Ser.). 344p. 27.95 (*0-7838-9090-7*, Macmillan Reference USA) Gale Group.

Ondaatje, Michael. In the Skin of a Lion: A Novel. 1987. 16.95 o.s.i (*0-394-56363-8*) Knopf, Alfred A. Inc.

—In the Skin of a Lion: A Novel. 1997. 256p. pap. 12.00 (*0-679-77266-9*) McKay, David Co., Inc.

—In the Skin of a Lion: A Novel. abr. ed. 1998. audio 15.00 (*0-333-72603-0*) Ulverscroft Audio (U.S.A.).

—In the Skin of a Lion: A Novel. 1988. 256p. pap. 10.95 o.p. (*0-14-011309-6*, Penguin Bks.) Viking Penguin.

—In the Skin of a Lion & Running in the Family. unabr. ed. 1993. audio 13.95 (*1-55644-385-4*, 13021) American Audio Prose Library, Inc.

Ondaatje, Michael, selected by. From Ink Lake: Canadian Stories. 1992. 736p. reprint ed. pap. 15.95 o.p. (*0-14-011832-2*, Penguin Bks.) Penguin Group (USA) Inc.

Oxley, Dorothy. Summer Dreams. 1984. Orig. Title: Wheelchair Summer. 144p. (J). (gr. 6-10). reprint ed. pap. 3.95 o.p. (*0-89107-319-1*) Crossway Bks.

Packer, Miriam. Take Me to Coney Island, No. 25. 1993. (Prose Ser.: No. 25). 180p. pap. 15.00 (*0-920717-92-6*) Guernica Editions, Inc.

Parameswaran, Uma. The Sweet Smell of Mother's Milk-Wet Bodice. 2001. 80p. pap. 10.00 (*1-896647-72-3*) Broken Jaw Pr. CAN. *Dist:* General Distribution Services, Inc.

Parker, Gilbert. The Seats of the Mighty. 2000. 252p. E-Book 9.95 (*0-594-02709-8*) 1873 Pr.

—The Seats of the Mighty, 23 vols. 2001. (Works of Gilbert Parker ). reprint ed. pap. text 28.00 (*0-7426-8822-4*) Classic Bks.

Peck, Robert Newton. Eagle Fur. 1986. (J). pap. 1.95 o.p. (*0-380-45039-9*, 45039, Avon Bks.) Morrow/ Avon.

Pilling, Marilyn Gear. The Roseate Spoonbill of Happiness. 2002. 160p. pap. 14.95 (*1-894498-10-0*) Boheme Pr. CAN. *Dist:* Independent Pubs. Group, Univ. of Toronto Pr.

Porczeny-Dalrymple, Edna. Rather a Ruby. 2000. 232p. pap. 21.99 (*0-7388-3066-6*) Xlibris Corp.

Porter, Anna. Hidden Agenda. 1986. 280p. 14.95 o.p. (*0-525-24427-1*, Dutton) Dutton/Plume.

—Mortal Sins. 1988. 288p. 17.95 o.p. (*0-453-00616-7*) NAL.

Potrebenko, Helen. A Flight of Average Persons: Stories & Other Writings. 1979. 228p. pap. 9.95 o.p. (*0-919888-95-X*) New Star Bks., Ltd. CAN. *Dist:* General Distribution Services, Inc.

Power, Margo. Image of Conspiracy: A Mystery Adventure. abr. ed. 1999. audio 10.95 (*1-894188-03-9*) APG Sales and Fulfillment.

—Image of Conspiracy: A Mystery Adventure. 1997. pap. text 5.99 (*1-886199-02-7*) Deadly Alibi Pr., Ltd.

Pronzini, Bill & Greenberg, Martin H., eds. The Northerners. 1990. 256p. (Orig.). mass mkt. 3.50 o.s.i (*0-449-14641-3*, Fawcett) Ballantine Bks.

Pyper, Andrew. Lost Girls. 2001. 464p. reprint ed. mass mkt. 6.50 (*0-440-23546-4*) Dell Publishing.

Quarrington, Paul. King Leary. 1994. 256p. pap. 12.95 o.s.i (*0-385-25484-9*); 1988. 288p. 16.95 o.s.i (*0-385-25138-6*) Doubleday Publishing.

Reddick, Don. Dawson City Seven. 1994. 272p. pap. (*0-86492-158-6*) Goose Lane Editions.

Reece, Colleen L. Angel of the North. l.t. ed. 2001. (Thorndike Press Large Print Christian Romance Ser.). 236p. 24.95 (*0-7862-3663-9*) Thorndike Pr.

Reed, Ishmael. Flight to Canada. 1989. 180p. pap. 11.00 (*0-689-70733-9*) Central Bureau voor Schimmelcultures NLD. *Dist:* Lubrecht & Cramer, Ltd.

—Flight to Canada. 1977. pap. 2.75 o.p. (*0-380-01798-9*, 52019, Avon Bks.) Morrow/Avon.

—Flight to Canada. 1998. 192p. pap. 11.00 (*0-684-84750-7*, Scribner) Simon & Schuster.

Reed, Nat. Thunderbird Gold. 1997. 154p. (J). (gr. 4-7). pap. 6.49 (*0-89084-919-6*, 103325) Jones, Bob Univ. Pr.

Ricci, Nino. Where She Has Gone. 336p. 1999. pap. 13.00 o.s.i (*0-312-20681-X*); 1998. 25.00 o.p. (*0-312-18700-9*) Picador.

Richards, David Adams. The Bay of Love & Sorrows. 2003. (Illus.). 320p. 24.95 (*1-55970-650-3*) Arcade Publishing, Inc.

—The Bay of Love & Sorrows. 2002. 320p. pap. (*0-385-66005-7*, Anchor Canada) Doubleday Canada, Ltd. CAN. *Dist:* Random Hse., Inc.

—Mercy among the Children. 2001. 384p. 24.95 (*1-55970-586-8*) Arcade Publishing, Inc.

—Mercy among the Children. 2001. 432p. pap. (*0-385-25995-6*, Anchor Canada) Doubleday Canada, Ltd. CAN. *Dist:* Random Hse., Inc.

Richardson, Bill. Bachelor Brothers' Bed & Breakfast. l.t. ed. 1997. 21.95 (*1-57490-131-1*, Beeler Large Print Bks.) Beeler, Thomas T. Publisher.

—Bachelor Brothers' Bed & Breakfast. 1998. (Between the Covers Collection). audio (*0-86492-207-8*) Goose Lane Editions.

—Bachelor Brothers' Bed & Breakfast Pillow Book. 1998. 208p. pap. 10.95 (*0-312-19440-4*, Saint Martin's Griffin); 1997. 18.95 (*0-312-16779-2*); 1997. 384p. pap. 11.95 (*0-312-17183-8*, Saint Martin's Griffin); 1996. 160p. 18.95 (*0-312-14546-2*) St. Martin's Pr.

Richardson, Tracey. Northern Blue. 1996. 224p. pap. 10.95 o.p. (*1-56280-118-X*) Naiad Pr., Inc.

Riche, Edward. Rare Birds. 2001. 304p. pap. (*0-385-65862-1*, Anchor Canada) Doubleday Canada, Ltd. CAN. *Dist:* Random Hse., Inc.

—Rare Birds. 1997. 272p. pap. o.s.i (*0-385-25635-3*) Doubleday Publishing.

Richler, Mordecai. The Apprenticeship of Duddy Kravitz. 2000. 320p. 24.95 (*0-8488-2769-4*) Amereon, Ltd.

—The Apprenticeship of Duddy Kravitz. Young, George, ed. 1974. (Illus.). 288p. mass mkt. 1.50 o.p. (*0-345-24154-1*) Ballantine Bks.

—The Apprenticeship of Duddy Kravitz. 1981. 304p. pap. 2.95 o.p. (*0-553-14584-3*) Bantam Bks.

—The Apprenticeship of Duddy Kravitz. 1989. (New Canadian Library). 328p. mass mkt. 6.95 (*0-7710-9972-X*) McClelland & Stewart/Tundra Bks.

—The Apprenticeship of Duddy Kravitz. 1991. 384p. pap. 9.95 o.p. (*0-14-015296-2*, Penguin Bks.) Penguin Group (USA) Inc.

—The Apprenticeship of Duddy Kravitz. 1999. 384p. pap. 14.00 (*0-671-02847-2*, Pocket) Simon & Schuster.

—Barney's Version. 1999. 368p. pap. 14.00 (*0-671-02846-4*, Washington Square Pr.) Simon & Schuster.

—Joshua Then & Now. 1997. 384p. mass mkt. 7.95 (*0-7710-9864-2*) McClelland & Stewart/Tundra Bks.

—Joshua Then & Now. 1991. 448p. pap. 9.95 o.p. (*0-14-015280-6*, Penguin Bks.) Penguin Group (USA) Inc.

Rivard, Ken. Skin Tests. 2000. 120p. 18.95 (*0-88753-337-X*) Black Moss Pr. CAN. *Dist:* Firefly Bks., Ltd.

Robinson, Grant. Great Expectations. 2000. (Illus.). 272p. pap. (*0-88984-206-X*) Porcupine's Quill, Inc.

Robinson, Margaret A. A Woman of Her Tribe. 1991. 160p. (YA). (gr. 7-12). mass mkt. 4.50 o.s.i (*0-449-70405-X*, Fawcett) Ballantine Bks.

—A Woman of Her Tribe. 1990. 144p. (YA). (gr. 7 up). mass mkt. 13.95 (*0-684-19223-3*, Atheneum) Simon & Schuster Children's Publishing.

Rodriguez, Nice. Throw It to the River. 1993. 156p. pap. 12.95 (*0-88961-187-4*) Women's Pr. CAN. *Dist:* Univ. of Toronto Pr.

Roy, Gabrielle. Windflower. 1991. (New Canadian Library). 176p. mass mkt. 5.95 (*0-7710-9879-0*) McClelland & Stewart/Tundra Bks.

Rubinsky, Holley. At First I Hope for Rescue. 256p. 1999. pap. 12.00 (*0-312-19967-8*); 1998. 22.00 o.p. (*0-312-18043-8*) Picador.

Sakamoto, Kerri. The Electrical Field. 2000. 320p. pap. text 13.00 (*0-393-32048-0*, Norton Paperbacks); 1999. 305p. 23.95 o.p. (*0-393-04692-3*) Norton, W. W. & Co., Inc.

Sale, Medora. Murder in a Good Cause. 1990. 224p. 18.95 o.s.i (*0-684-19216-0*) Macmillan Information.

—Murder in Focus. 1989. 288p. 17.95 o.s.i (*0-684-19082-6*, Macmillan Reference USA) Gale Group.

—Murder on the Run. unabr. ed. 1998. (Inspector John Sanders Mystery Ser.). audio 39.95 (*1-55686-825-1*) Books in Motion.

—Pursued by Shadows. 1992. (Inspector John Sanders Mystery Ser.). 256p. text 20.00 (*0-684-19505-4*, Scribner) Simon & Schuster.

—Shortcut to Santa Fe. 1994. 256p. 20.00 (*0-684-19680-8*, Scribner) Simon & Schuster.

—Sleep of the Innocent. unabr. ed. 1999. (Inspector John Sanders Mystery Ser.). audio 49.95 (*1-55686-906-1*) Books in Motion.

—Sleep of the Innocent. 1991. 256p. 18.95 o.s.i (*0-684-19305-1*, Scribner) Simon & Schuster.

Savage, Les, Jr. In the Land of Little Sticks. 2000. (Five Star Western Ser.). 303p. 21.95 (*0-7862-2111-9*, Five Star) Gale Group.

—In the Land of Little Sticks. l.t. ed. 2001. (Western Ser.). 452p. 24.95 o.p. (*0-7862-2132-1*) Thorndike Pr.

Sawyer, Robert J. Factoring Humanity. 352p. 1999. pap. 6.99 (*0-8125-7129-0*); 1998. 23.95 o.p. (*0-312-86458-2*) Doherty, Tom Assocs., LLC. (Tor Bks.).

—Factoring Humanity. 1999. (Illus.). (J). 12.04 (*0-606-18640-9*) Turtleback Bks.

Schermbrucker, Bill. Chameleon & Other Stories. 1993. 160p. pap. 12.95 (*0-88922-208-8*) Talonbooks, Ltd. CAN. *Dist:* General Distribution Services, Inc.

Schoemperlen, Diane. Red Plaid Shirt: Stories. 2003. 320p. pap. 14.00 (*0-14-200320-4*) Penguin Group (USA) Inc.

Shields, Carol. Dressing up for the Carnival. unabr. ed. 2000. audio 25.00 (*1-57453-352-5*) Audio Literature.

—Dressing up for the Carnival. 2001. 224p. pap. 13.00 (*0-14-100191-7*) Penguin Group (USA) Inc.

—Dressing up for the Carnival. l.t. ed. 2000. (Basic Ser.). 285p. 27.95 (*0-7862-2792-3*); (*0-7540-4271-5*); (*0-7540-4272-3*) Thorndike Pr.

—Dressing up for the Carnival. 2000. (Illus.). 208p. 23.95 o.s.i (*0-670-88921-0*, Viking) Viking Penguin.

—Larry's Party. unabr. ed. 1998. audio 64.00 (*0-7366-4112-2*, 4617) Books on Tape, Inc.

—Larry's Party. l.t. ed. 1998. 25.95 o.p. (*1-56895-537-5*, Wheeler Publishing, Inc.) Gale Group.

—Larry's Party. 1998. (Between the Covers Collection). audio (*0-86492-191-8*) Goose Lane Editions.

—Larry's Party. 1998. 352p. pap. 12.95 (*0-14-026677-1*) Penguin Group (USA) Inc.

—Larry's Party. unabr. ed. 1998. audio 78.00 (*0-7887-1873-8*, 95295E7) Recorded Bks., LLC.

—Larry's Party. 1997. 320p. 23.95 o.s.i (*0-670-87392-6*); audio 24.95 o.s.i (*0-14-086621-3*, Penguin AudioBooks); audio 24.95 Viking Penguin.

—Swann. 1990. (King Penguin Ser.). 320p. pap. 12.95 (*0-14-013429-8*, Penguin Bks.) Penguin Group (USA) Inc.

—Swann. 1989. 320p. 17.95 o.p. (*0-670-82822-X*) Viking Penguin.

—Various Miracles. l.t. ed. 1996. pap. 22.95 o.p. (*1-56895-364-X*, Wheeler Publishing, Inc.) Gale Group.

—Various Miracles. 1989. (King Penguin Ser.). 192p. pap. 12.00 (*0-14-011837-3*, Penguin Bks.) Penguin Group (USA) Inc.

Silver, Alfred. Lord of the Plains. 1992. mass mkt. 5.99 o.s.i (*0-345-37700-1*) Ballantine Bks.

—Where the Ghost Horse Runs. 1994. 468p. mass mkt. 5.99 o.s.i (*0-345-38670-1*); 1991. pap. 10.00 o.s.i (*0-345-36734-0*) Ballantine Bks.

Silvera, Makeda. The Heart Does Not Bend. 2003. 272p. pap. 12.95 (*0-679-31187-4*) Knopf, Alfred A. Inc.

Skvorecky, Josef. The Engineer of Human Souls. Wilson, Paul, tr. from CZE. 1999. 571p. reprint ed. pap. 14.95 (*1-56478-199-2*) Dalkey Archive Pr.

—The Engineer of Human Souls. 1985. reprint ed. pap. 9.95 o.s.i (*0-671-55682-7*, Pocket) Simon & Schuster.

—Two Murders in My Double Life. 2001. 175p. 22.00 o.p. (*0-374-28025-8*) Farrar, Straus & Giroux.

—Two Murders in My Double Life. 1999. 183p. pap. (*1-55263-021-8*) Key Porter Bks. CAN. *Dist:* BookWorld Services, Inc.

—Two Murders in My Double Life. 2002. 192p. pap. 12.00 (*0-312-42026-9*) Picador.

Slade, Michael. Cutthroat. 1992. 400p. (Orig.). mass mkt. 5.99 o.s.i (*0-451-17452-6*, Signet Bks.) NAL.

—Evil Eye. 1997. 432p. mass mkt. 6.99 o.s.i (*0-451-40695-8*, Onyx) NAL.

—Ghoul. 1988. 416p. 18.95 o.p. (*0-688-07550-9*, Morrow, William & Co.) Morrow/Avon.

—Ghoul. 1989. 400p. mass mkt. 6.99 o.s.i (*0-451-15959-4*, Signet Bks.) NAL.

—Headhunter. 1985. (Illus.). 480p. 17.95 o.p. (*0-688-04710-6*, Morrow, William & Co.) Morrow/Avon.

—Headhunter. 1986. mass mkt. 3.95 o.p. (*0-451-40005-4*); mass mkt. 4.50 o.p. (*0-451-40137-9*); 424p. mass mkt. 6.99 o.s.i (*0-451-40172-7*, Onyx) NAL.

—Primal Scream: Scream If You Want, Live If You Can. 1998. 432p. mass mkt. 6.99 o.s.i (*0-451-19566-3*, Signet Bks.) NAL.

—Ripper. 1994. 416p. (Orig.). mass mkt. 4.99 o.s.i (*0-451-17702-9*, Signet Bks.) NAL.

Slater, Sandra. A Song for Ben. 1998. (Illus.). 24p. pap. text 5.50 (*0-19-421953-4*) Oxford Univ. Pr., Inc.

Smith, Brad. All Hat: A Novel. 2003. 320p. 24.00 (*0-8050-7217-9*) Holt, Henry & Co.

—All Hat: A Novel. 2004. 320p. pap. 14.00 (*0-312-42317-9*) Picador.

Smucker, Barbara. Amish Adventure. 1983. (Illus.). 144p. (Orig.). (J). (gr. 6-9). pap. 6.95 o.p. (*0-8361-3339-0*) Herald Pr.

—Underground to Canada. 1993. pap. (*0-14-031122-X*) Prentice Hall PTR.

Southwell, Tim G. Fractured Spirits. 2001. pap. 14.95 (*0-595-19595-4*) iUniverse, Inc.

Speare, Elizabeth George. Calico Captive. 1973. 288p. (gr. 4-7). pap. text 4.99 o.s.i (*0-440-41156-4*, Yearling) Random Hse. Children's Bks.

Spinka, Penina Keen. Dream Weaver. 2003. (Illus.). 464p. 26.95 (*0-525-94684-5*, Dutton) Dutton/ Plume.

—Dream Weaver. 2004. 512p. mass mkt. 7.99 (*0-451-41111-0*, Onyx) NAL.

Steinfeld, J. J. Dancing at the Club Holocaust: Stories New & Selected. 1993. 224p. pap. 14.95 o.p. (*0-921556-30-6*) Ragweed Pr. CAN. *Dist:* LPC/InBook.

Stenson, Fred. Teeth. 1994. 152p. pap. 12.95 (*1-55050-060-0*) Coteau Bks. CAN. *Dist:* General Distribution Services, Inc.

—The Trade. 2000. (Illus.). 344p. pap. (*1-55054-816-6*) Douglas & McIntyre, Ltd.

Stonich, Sarah. The Ice Chorus. 2004. 288p. (*0-316-81555-1*) Little Brown & Co.

Svendsen, Linda. Marine Life. 1992. 180p. 17.00 o.p. (*0-374-10088-8*) Farrar, Straus & Giroux.

—Marine Life. 1993. (Contemporary American Fiction Ser.). 176p. pap. 9.00 o.p. (*0-14-023048-3*, Penguin Bks.) Penguin Group (USA) Inc.

Sweatman, Margaret. When Alice Lay Down with Peter. 2002. 472p. pap. (*0-676-97316-7*, Vintage) Random Hse. of Canada, Ltd. CAN. *Dist:* Random Hse., Inc.

Taylor, Timothy L. Silent Cruise: A Novella & Stories. 2002. 416p. pap. text 15.00 (*1-58243-216-3*, Counterpoint Pr.) Basic Bks.

Tefs, Wayne. Home Free. 1997. (Willow Island Trilogy Ser.). 224p. pap. 14.95 (*0-88801-217-9*) Turnstone Pr. CAN. *Dist:* General Distribution Services, Inc.

Tefs, Wayne, et al, eds. Due West. 1996. 400p. mass mkt. 8.99 (*1-55050-096-1*) Coteau Bks. CAN. *Dist:* General Distribution Services, Inc.

Thomson, Colin A. Klanty's Daughters. 1993. 181p. pap. 14.95 (*1-55059-065-0*) Temeron Bks., Inc.

Thomson, Edward W. Old Man Savarin Stories: Tales of Canada & Canadians. 1977. (Short Story Index Reprint Ser.). reprint ed. 25.95 (*0-8369-4126-8*) Ayer Co. Pubs., Inc.

Tregebov, Rhea, ed. Frictions II: Stories by Women. 1993. 410p. pap. text 12.95 (*0-929005-47-3*) Second Story Pr. CAN. *Dist:* LPC/InBook.

Tucker, Ernest. Underworld Dwellers. 1994. 160p. 15.95 o.p. (*0-944957-22-6*) Rivercross Publishing, Inc.

Urquhart, Jane. Away. 1998. (BTC Audiobooks). audio (*0-86492-211-6*); incl. audio compact disk (*0-86492-209-4*) Goose Lane Editions.

—Away. 1995. 368p. pap. 14.00 (*0-14-024926-5*, Penguin Bks.) Penguin Group (USA) Inc.

—Away. 1994. 304p. 21.95 o.s.i (*0-670-85504-9*, Viking) Viking Penguin.

Van Shelton, Ricky. Quacker Meets Canadian Goose: Tales from a Duck Named Quacker. 1994. (Illus.). 40p. (Orig.). (J). pap. 7.00 (*0-9634257-2-2*) RVS Bks., Inc.

Van Stockum, Hilda. Canadian Summer. 1996. (Mitchells Ser.: Vol. 2). (Illus.). 208p. (J). (ps up). reprint ed. pap. 11.95 o.p. (*1-883937-14-0*, 14-0) Bethlehem Bks.

—Friendly Gables. 1996. (Mitchells Ser.: Vol. 3). (Illus.). 192p. (J). (gr. 4-7). pap. 11.95 o.p. (*1-883937-19-1*, 19-1) Bethlehem Bks.

Vanderhaeghe, Guy. The Englishman's Boy. 1998. 352p. pap. 14.00 (*0-312-19544-3*); 1997. 336p. 24.00 o.p. (*0-312-16823-3*) Picador.

—Man Descending: Selected Stories. 1985. 230p. pap. 7.95 o.p. (*0-89919-385-4*) Houghton Mifflin Co.

Vollmann, William T. Second Dream, Fathers & Crows. 1992. (Seven Dreams Ser.). (Illus.). 1008p. 30.00 o.p. (*0-670-84333-4*, Viking) Viking Penguin.

Ward, Gregory. The Internet Bride. 2000. 392p. pap. 21.95 (*1-55278-163-1*) McArthur & Co. CAN. *Dist:* HarperCollins Pubs. Canada, Ltd.

Watmough, David. Hunting with Diana. 1996. 172p. (Orig.). pap. 14.95 (*1-55152-032-X*) Arsenal Pulp Pr., Ltd. CAN. *Dist:* LPC Group.

Wiebe, Rudy. The Temptations of Big Bear. 1996. 408p. (J). mass mkt. 7.95 (*0-7710-3454-7*) McClelland & Stewart/Tundra Bks.

—The Temptations of Big Bear. 2000. (Illus.). 423p. pap. 16.95 (*0-8040-1029-3*) Swallow Pr.

Wilson, Doug. Labour of Love. 1994. 208p. pap. 8.95 o.p. (*0-312-11408-7*, Saint Martin's Griffin); 1993. 224p. 18.95 o.p. (*0-312-09839-1*) St. Martin's Pr.

Woo, Terry. Banana Boys. 2000. (Illus.). 381p. pap. (*1-896332-15-3*) Riverbank, Pr., The CAN. *Dist:* General Distribution Services, Inc.

Wright, Eric. A Body Surrounded by Water. (Inspector Charlie Salter Mystery Ser.). 1987. 208p. 14.95 o.s.i (*0-684-18873-2*); 1992. 264p. pap. 14.95 o.p. (*0-8161-5319-1*) Gale Group. (Macmillan Reference USA).

—A Body Surrounded by Water. 1989. mass mkt. 3.95 o.p. (*0-451-16385-0*, Signet Bks.) NAL.

—Death by Degrees. 1995. 192p. reprint ed. mass mkt. 6.99 o.s.i (*0-7704-2601-8*) Bantam Bks.

—Death by Degrees. 1993. 192p. o.s.i (*0-385-25436-9*) Doubleday Canada, Ltd. CAN. *Dist:* Random Hse., Inc.

—Death by Degrees. 1993. (Inspector Charlie Salter Mystery Ser.). 224p. 20.00 (*0-684-19648-4*, Macmillan Reference USA) Gale Group.

—Death by Degrees. 1995. (WWL Mystery Ser.). 251p. mass mkt. (*0-373-26169-1*, 1-26169-2, Harlequin Bks.) Harlequin Enterprises, Ltd.

—Death of a Sunday Writer. 1996. 224p. text 21.00 (*0-88150-377-0*) Norton, W. W. & Co., Inc.

—Death on the Rocks: A Lucy Trimble Mystery. 1999. 240p. 15.95 (*0-312-20525-2*, Saint Martin's Minotaur) St. Martin's Pr.

—Final Cut: An Inspector Charlie Salter Novel. 1991. 256p. 22.50 o.s.i (*0-385-25289-7*) Doubleday Publishing.

—Final Cut: An Inspector Charlie Salter Novel. 1991. 256p. 18.95 o.s.i (*0-684-19300-0*, Macmillan Reference USA) Gale Group.

—Final Cut: An Inspector Charlie Salter Novel. 1992. (Inspector Charlie Salter Mystery Ser.). reprint ed. per. (*0-373-26107-1*, Harlequin Bks.) Harlequin Enterprises, Ltd.

—A Fine Italian Hand. l.t. ed. 1993. 21.95 o.p. (*0-7927-1564-0*); pap. 19.95 o.p. (*0-7927-1563-2*) BBC Audiobooks America.

—A Fine Italian Hand. 1993. 240p. mass mkt. 6.99 o.s.i (*0-7704-2569-0*) Bantam Bks.

—A Fine Italian Hand. 1992. 192p. 23.50 o.s.i (*0-385-25371-0*) Doubleday Publishing.

—A Fine Italian Hand. 1992. (Inspector Charlie Salter Mystery Ser.). 192p. text 20.00 (*0-684-19504-6*, Macmillan Reference USA) Gale Group.

—A Fine Italian Hand. 1994. mass mkt. (*0-373-26143-8*, Harlequin Bks.) Harlequin Enterprises, Ltd.

—The Hemingway Caper: A Joe Barley Mystery. 2003. 260p. pap. 14.99 (*1-55002-451-5*) Dundurn Pr. CAN. *Dist:* Univ. of Toronto Pr.

—The Kidnapping of Rosie Dawn: A Joe Barley Mystery. 2000. 213p. pap. 12.95 (*1-880284-40-5*, Perseverance Pr.) Daniel, John & Co., Pubs.

Settings

—The Kidnapping of Rosie Dawn: A Joe Barley Mystery. l.t. ed. 2001. 306p. 27.95 (*0-7862-3478-4*); 296p. (*0-7540-4673-7*); 296p. (*0-7540-4674-5*) Thorndike Pr.

—The Man Who Changed His Name. l.t. ed. 1987. (Nightingale Ser.). 288p. 11.95 o.p. (*0-8161-4285-8*, Macmillan Reference USA) Gale Group.

—The Man Who Changed His Name. 1987. 224p. mass mkt. 3.50 o.p. (*0-451-14930-0*, Signet Bks.) NAL.

—The Night the Gods Smiled. 1983. 192p. 12.95 o.s.i (*0-684-18009-X*, Macmillan Reference USA) Gale Group.

—The Night the Gods Smiled. 1985. mass mkt. 2.95 o.p. (*0-451-13409-5*, Signet Bks.) NAL.

—A Question of Murder. l.t. ed. 1992. 330p. pap. 14.95 o.p. (*0-8161-5372-8*, Macmillan Reference USA) Gale Group.

—A Question of Murder. 1989. mass mkt. (*0-373-26039-3*, Harlequin Bks.) Harlequin Enterprises, Ltd.

—A Question of Murder. 1988. 208p. 15.95 o.s.i (*0-684-19000-1*, Scribner) Simon & Schuster.

—A Sensitive Case. 1990. 224p. 22.95 o.s.i (*0-385-25250-1*) Doubleday Publishing.

—A Sensitive Case. 1991. (Inspector Charlie Salter Mystery Ser.). 224p. mass mkt. (*0-373-26083-0*, Harlequin Bks.) Harlequin Enterprises, Ltd.

—A Sensitive Case: A Charlie Salter Novel. l.t. ed. 1991. (Magna Large Print Ser.). 284p. (*0-7505-0119-7*) Magna Large Print Bks. GBR. *Dist:* Ulverscroft Large Print Canada, Ltd.

—A Sensitive Case: A Charlie Salter Novel. 1990. 224p. 17.95 o.s.i (*0-684-19132-6*, Scribner) Simon & Schuster.

—Smoke Detector. l.t. ed. 1985. (Nightingale Ser.). 286p. 10.95 o.p. (*0-8161-3900-8*, Macmillan Reference USA) Gale Group.

—Smoke Detector. 1986. mass mkt. 2.95 o.p. (*0-451-14123-7*, Signet Bks.) NAL.

Yashinsky, Dan, ed. The Next Teller: A Book of Canadian Storytelling. 1994. (Illus.). 262p. (YA). (gr. 7 up). pap. 12.95 (*0-921556-46-2*) Ragweed Pr. CAN. *Dist:* Univ. of Toronto Pr.

Young, Scott. Murder in a Cold Climate. 1989. mass mkt. o.s.i (*0-449-21746-9*) Ballantine Bks.

—Murder in a Cold Climate. (Crime Ser.). 1990. 240p. pap. 4.50 o.p. (*0-14-012336-9*, Penguin Bks.); 1989. 256p. 16.95 o.p. (*0-670-82889-0*) Viking Penguin.

—The Shaman's Knife. 1994. (Crime Ser.). 288p. pap. 5.95 o.p. (*0-14-014353-X*, Penguin Bks.) Penguin Group (USA) Inc.

—The Shaman's Knife. 1993. 288p. 20.00 o.p. (*0-670-83555-2*, Viking) Viking Penguin.

Zaremba, Eve. The Butterfly Effect: A Helen Keremos Detective Novel. 1994. 332p. pap. 9.95 (*0-929005-56-2*) Second Story Pr. CAN. *Dist:* SCB Distributors.

—Uneasy Lies: A Helen Keremos Mystery. 1994. 255p. pap. 11.95 (*0-929005-17-1*) Second Story Pr. CAN. *Dist:* LPC/InBook.

—Work for a Million. (NFS Canada Ser.). 200p. pap. 11.95 o.p. (*0-921299-00-1*) Second Story Pr. CAN. *Dist:* SCB Distributors.

## CAPE BRETON ISLAND (N.S.)—FICTION

MacDonald, D. R. Cape Breton Road. 2002. 304p. reprint ed. pap. 14.00 (*0-15-601324-X*, Harvest Bks.) Harcourt Trade Pubs.

—Cape Breton Road: A Novel. 2001. 336p. (gr. 9). pap. (*0-385-25911-5*, Anchor Canada) Doubleday Canada, Ltd. CAN. *Dist:* Random Hse., Inc.

—Cape Breton Road: A Novel. 2001. 320p. 23.00 (*0-15-100523-0*) Harcourt Trade Pubs.

MacLeod, Alistair. The Lost Salt Gift of Blood. 1996. 168p. mass mkt. 6.95 (*0-7710-9969-X*) McClelland & Stewart/Tundra Bks.

—The Lost Salt Gift of Blood. 1988. 227p. pap. 11.95 o.p. (*0-86538-063-5*) Ontario Review Pr.

—No Great Mischief. 2001. (Vintage International Ser.). 304p. pap. 13.00 (*0-375-72665-9*, Vintage) Knopf Publishing Group.

—No Great Mischief. 2000. (Illus.). 283p. 23.95 o.p. (*0-393-04970-1*) Norton, W. W. & Co., Inc.

Magruder, Owen. The Strange Case of Mr. Nobody. 2000. 212p. pap. 7.95 (*1-892059-01-0*) Edmonston Publishing, Inc.

## CAPE COD (MASS.)—FICTION

Abrahams, Peter. Revolution, No. 9. 2002. 320p. mass mkt. 6.99 (*0-345-44580-5*, Fawcett) Ballantine Bks.

—Revolution, No. 9. 1993. 320p. mass mkt. 5.50 o.p. (*0-446-40156-0*, Mysterious Pr. Paperback Bks.) Warner Bks., Inc.

Andrews, V. C. Heart Song. 1997. 384p. 23.00 (*0-671-53468-8*, Atria); pap. 7.99 (*0-671-53472-6*, Pocket) Simon & Schuster.

—Heart Song. l.t. ed. 1998. (Core Ser.). 477p. 29.95 (*0-7838-8346-3*) Thorndike Pr.

—Heart Song. 1997. 14.04 (*0-606-13471-9*) Turtleback Bks.

—Melody. 1999. 15.70 (*0-613-01437-5*) CRC Pr. LLC.

—Melody. l.t. ed. 1996. (G. K. Hall Core Ser.). 451p. 25.95 (*0-7838-1906-4*, Macmillan Reference USA) Gale Group.

—Melody. 1996. 384p. 23.00 o.p. (*0-671-53470-X*, Atria); pap. 7.99 (*0-671-53471-8*, Pocket) Simon & Schuster.

—Melody. 1996. 14.04 (*0-606-13603-7*) Turtleback Bks.

—Music in the Night. 1998. (Logan Ser.). 320p. 24.00 o.s.i (*0-671-53467-X*, Atria); (Illus.). 336p. pap. 7.99 (*0-671-53474-2*, Pocket) Simon & Schuster.

—Music in the Night. l.t. ed. 1999. (Core Ser.). 436p. 29.95 (*0-7838-8533-4*) Thorndike Pr.

—Music in the Night. 1998. 14.04 (*0-606-13627-4*) Turtleback Bks.

—Olivia. 1999. (Logan Ser.). 384p. 24.00 (*0-671-00760-2*, Atria); pap. 7.99 (*0-671-00761-0*, Pocket) Simon & Schuster.

—Olivia. l.t. ed. 1999. (Core Ser.). 456p. 28.95 (*0-7838-8592-X*) Thorndike Pr.

—Olivia. 1999. 14.04 (*0-606-17529-6*) Turtleback Bks.

—Unfinished Symphony. 1997. (Logan Ser.). 352p. 24.00 o.s.i (*0-671-53469-6*, Atria); 384p. mass mkt. 7.99 (*0-671-53473-4*, Pocket) Simon & Schuster.

—Unfinished Symphony. l.t. ed. 1998. (Core Ser.). 479p. 30.95 (*0-7838-8407-9*) Thorndike Pr.

—Unfinished Symphony. 1997. 14.04 (*0-606-13883-8*) Turtleback Bks.

Arnold, Margot, pseud. The Cape Cod Caper. 1982. (Murder Mystery Ser.). 192p. 2.50 (*0-86721-206-3*, Jove) Berkley Publishing Group.

—The Cape Cod Caper. 1988. (Penny Spring & Sir Toby Glendower Mystery Ser.). 192p. pap. 7.95 (*0-88150-116-6*, Foul Play) Norton, W. W. & Co., Inc.

—The Cape Cod Conundrum. 1994. (Penny Spring & Sir Toby Glendower Mystery Ser.). 224p. reprint ed. pap. 7.95 (*0-88150-293-6*, Foul Play) Norton, W. W. & Co., Inc.

Clark, Mary Higgins. The Lottery Winner. E-Book 9.95 (*1-930161-64-6*) Adobe Systems, Inc.

—The Lottery Winner. 1997. reprint ed. lib. bdg. 32.95 (*1-56849-588-9*) Buccaneer Bks., Inc.

—The Lottery Winner. 2000. E-Book 9.95 (*0-7432-0626-6*, Simon & Schuster); 1995. 304p. mass mkt. 7.99 (*0-671-86717-2*, Pocket); 1994. 26.00 o.s.i (*0-684-80222-8*, Simon & Schuster); 1994. (Illus.). 256p. 22.00 (*0-671-86716-4*, Simon & Schuster) Simon & Schuster.

—The Lottery Winner. abr. ed. 1994. (Willy & Alvirah Mystery Ser.). audio 22.00 (*0-671-50136-4*, 592256, Simon & Schuster Audioworks) Simon & Schuster Audio.

—The Lottery Winner. 265p. pap. 5.98 o.p. (*0-7651-0558-6*) Smithmark Pubs., Inc.

—Where Are the Children? E-Book 9.95 (*1-930161-68-9*) Adobe Systems, Inc.

—Where Are the Children? 2000. E-Book 9.95 (*0-7432-0611-8*); 1999. (Illus.). 272p. 25.00 (*0-684-86356-1*); 1975. 7.95 o.s.i (*0-671-21942-1*) Simon & Schuster. (Simon & Schuster).

Connors, Rose. Absolute Certainty. 2003. 304p. E-Book 24.00 (*0-7432-3366-2*, Scribner); 2003. (Illus.). 320p. mass mkt. 6.99 (*0-7434-4881-2*, Pocket Star); 2002. 304p. 24.00 (*0-7432-2906-1*, Scribner) Simon & Schuster.

—Absolute Certainty. 2002. (Basic Ser.). 27.95 (*0-7862-4791-6*) Thorndike Pr.

Diamond, Diana. The Babysitter. 2002. 368p. mass mkt. 6.99 (*0-312-98364-6*, St. Martin's Paperbacks); 2001. 313p. 23.95 (*0-312-28047-5*) St. Martin's Pr.

—The Babysitter. l.t. ed. 2001. 592p. 28.95 (*0-7862-3637-X*) Thorndike Pr.

Flynn, Raymond & Moore, Robin. The Accidental Pope. 2000. 394p. 24.95 (*0-312-26801-7*) St. Martin's Pr.

Jarrett, Miranda. Wishing. 1999. 368p. pap. 6.50 (*0-671-00341-0*, Pocket) Simon & Schuster.

Kemprecos, Paul. Bluefin Blues: An Aristotle "Soc" Socarides Mystery. 1997. 224p. 20.95 o.p. (*0-312-16787-3*, Saint Martin's Minotaur) St. Martin's Pr.

—Cool Blue Tomb. 1991. 288p. mass mkt. 4.50 o.s.i (*0-553-28881-4*) Bantam Bks.

—Death in Deep Water. 1993. 336p. mass mkt. 4.99 o.s.i (*0-553-29735-X*) Bantam Bks.

—Death in Deep Water: An Aristotle "Soc" Socraides Mystery. 1992. 368p. 16.50 o.s.i (*0-385-42379-9*) Doubleday Publishing.

—A Feeding Frenzy. 1994. 336p. mass mkt. 4.99 o.s.i (*0-553-56774-8*) Bantam Bks.

—Mayflower Murder. 1996. 22.95 (*0-312-14852-6*, Saint Martin's Minotaur) St. Martin's Pr.

—Neptune's Eye. 1991. 320p. mass mkt. 4.50 o.s.i (*0-553-29353-2*) Bantam Bks.

Lippincott, Robin. Our Arcadia: An American Watercolor. 2001. (Illus.). 224p. 23.95 o.p. (*0-670-89273-4*, Viking) Viking Penguin.

Manuel, David. A Matter of Diamonds. 2000. (Faith Abbey Mystery Ser.: Vol. 2). xiv, 314p. 23.00 (*1-55725-258-0*, 930-059) Paraclete Pr., Inc.

—A Matter of Diamonds. 2002. 408p. mass mkt. 6.99 (*0-446-60989-7*) Warner Bks., Inc.

—A Matter of Roses. 1999. (Faith Abbey Mystery Ser.). 330p. 23.00 (*1-55725-234-3*, 930-006) Paraclete Pr., Inc.

—A Matter of Roses. 2001. 480p. mass mkt. 6.99 (*0-446-60988-9*) Warner Bks., Inc.

—A Matter of Time. 2003. (Faith Abbey Mystery Ser.). 304p. mass mkt. 6.99 (*0-446-61255-3*) Warner Bks., Inc.

—A Matter of Time: A Faith Abbey Mystery. 2002. 288p. 23.00 (*1-55725-305-6*) Paraclete Pr., Inc.

Martin, William. Cape Cod. abr. ed. 1993. 15.95 o.p. (*1-55800-399-1*, 41500) NewStar Media, Inc.

—Cape Cod. 2003. 864p. pap. 14.00 (*0-446-69260-3*); 1991. 672p. 21.95 o.p. (*0-446-51510-8*); 1992. 736p. reprint ed. mass mkt. 7.99 (*0-446-36317-0*) Warner Bks., Inc.

Mitchard, Jacquelyn. Twelve Times Blessed. 2003. 14p. pap. 110.95 (*0-7927-2882-3*); 17p. pap. 124.95 (*0-7927-2883-1*) BBC Audiobooks America.

—Twelve Times Blessed. 2003. (Illus.). 544p. 25.95 (*0-06-621475-0*, HarperCollins); 912p. pap. 25.95 (*0-06-053419-2*, HarperLargePrint); 640p. audio compact disk 29.95 (*0-06-053469-9*, HarperAudio) HarperTrade.

—Twelve Times Blessed. 2004. 624p. mass mkt. 7.99 (*0-06-103247-6*, HarperTorch) Morrow/Avon.

Moodie, Craig. A Sailor's Valentine. 1994. 208p. 17.95 o.p. (*0-312-11053-7*) St. Martin's Pr.

—A Sailor's Valentine: Stories. 1999. pap. text 14.95 (*0-940160-80-3*) Parnassus Imprints.

Nagy, Gloria. The Beauty. 2001. 290p. 26.95 (*1-58567-149-5*) Overlook Pr., The.

Pease, R. Book & Page: A Cape Cod Novel. 1997. 185p. per. 12.95 (*1-889455-02-4*) Flagg Mountain Pr.

—Dead Ahead: A Cape Cod Novel. 1994. 183p. per. 12.95 (*0-9637154-1-0*) Flagg Mountain Pr.

—Head in the Sand: Murder on Sandy Neck. 1999. 131p. pap. 12.95 (*1-889455-07-5*) Flagg Mountain Pr.

—Never Let Go: P. I. Jeeter on Cape Cod. 1996. 162p. per. 12.95 (*0-9637154-8-8*) Flagg Mountain Pr.

Rouillard, Wendy W. Barnaby's Cape Cod Coloring Book. 1996. 16p. (J). (ps-4). pap. 2.50 (*0-9642836-4-6*) Barnaby & Co.

Taylor, Phoebe Atwood. The Annulet of Gilt. 1986. (Asey Mayo Cape Cod Mystery Ser.). 288p. reprint ed. pap. 6.95 (*0-88150-078-X*, Foul Play) Norton, W. W. & Co., Inc.

—The Asey Mayo Trio. 1990. 256p. reprint ed. pap. 7.95 (*0-88150-171-9*, Foul Play) Norton, W. W. & Co., Inc.

—Banbury Bog. 1978. reprint ed. lib. bdg. 16.95 o.p. (*0-89966-247-1*) Buccaneer Bks., Inc.

—Banbury Bog. 1987. (Asey Mayo Cape Cod Mystery Ser.). 176p. reprint ed. pap. 5.95 (*0-88150-090-9*, Foul Play) Norton, W. W. & Co., Inc.

—The Cape Cod Mystery. 1985. (Asey Mayo Cape Cod Mystery Ser.). 192p. pap. 7.95 (*0-88150-046-1*, Foul Play) Norton, W. W. & Co., Inc.

—The Deadly Sunshade. l.t. ed. 1992. 19.95 o.p. (*0-7927-1318-4*); pap. 17.95 o.p. (*0-7927-1317-6*) BBC Audiobooks America.

—The Deadly Sunshade. 1989. (Asey Mayo Cape Cod Mystery Ser.). 300p. reprint ed. pap. 6.00 o.p. (*0-88150-136-0*) Countryman Pr.

—Death Lights a Candle. 1989. (Asey Mayo Cape Cod Mystery Ser.). 304p. reprint ed. pap. 7.95 (*0-88150-145-X*, Foul Play) Norton, W. W. & Co., Inc.

—Deathblow Hill. 1993. (Asey Mayo Cape Cod Mystery Ser.). 286p. pap. 6.50 (*0-88150-262-6*, Foul Play) Norton, W. W. & Co., Inc.

—Diplomatic Corpse. 1989. (Asey Mayo Cape Cod Mystery Ser.). 244p. reprint ed. pap. 5.95 o.p. (*0-88150-146-8*) Countryman Pr.

—Figure Away. 1979. (Foul Play Press Bks.). reprint ed. pap. 4.50 o.p. (*0-914378-48-1*) Countryman Pr.

—Figure Away. 1991. (Asey Mayo Cape Cod Mystery Ser.). 286p. reprint ed. pap. 5.95 o.p. (*0-88150-206-5*, Foul Play) Norton, W. W. & Co., Inc.

—Going, Going, Gone. 21.95 (*0-8488-1201-8*) Amereon, Ltd.

—The Mystery of the Cape Cod Players. 1987. (Asey Mayo Cape Cod Mystyery Ser.). 272p. reprint ed. pap. 6.00 o.p. (*0-88150-091-7*) Countryman Pr.

—The Mystery of the Cape Cod Tavern. 1985. (Asey Mayo Cape Cod Mystery Ser.). 288p. pap. 7.95 (*0-88150-047-X*, Foul Play) Norton, W. W. & Co., Inc.

—Octagon House. 1983. pap. 4.50 o.p. (*0-914378-47-3*) Countryman Pr.

—Octagon House. 1991. (Asey Mayo Cape Cod Mystery Ser.). 296p. pap. 6.95 (*0-88150-194-8*, Foul Play) Norton, W. W. & Co., Inc.

—Octagon House. 1999. lib. bdg. 22.95 (*1-56723-139-X*, 148) Yestermorrow, Inc.

—Proof of the Pudding. 1979. (Foul Play Press Bks.). reprint ed. pap. 4.95 o.p. (*0-914378-55-4*) Countryman Pr.

—Proof of the Pudding. 1991. 192p. pap. 6.00 (*0-88150-193-X*, Foul Play) Norton, W. W. & Co., Inc.

—Punch with Care. 21.95 (*0-8488-1202-6*) Amereon, Ltd.

—Punch with Care. 1992. (Asey Mayo Cape Cod Mystery Ser.). 224p. pap. 7.95 (*0-88150-229-4*, Foul Play) Norton, W. W. & Co., Inc.

—The Six Iron Spiders. 1979. (Foul Play Press Bks.). reprint ed. pap. 4.95 o.p. (*0-914378-53-8*) Countryman Pr.

—The Six Iron Spiders. 1992. (Asey Mayo Cape Cod Mystery Ser.). 288p. pap. 6.95 (*0-88150-230-8*, Foul Play) Norton, W. W. & Co., Inc.

—Three Plots for Asey Mayo. 1969. 5.95 o.p. (*0-393-08534-1*); 1991. 320p. reprint ed. pap. 6.95 o.p. (*0-88150-205-7*, Foul Play) Norton, W. W. & Co., Inc.

—The Tinkling Symbol. 1993. (Asey Mayo Cape Cod Mystery Ser.). 288p. pap. 7.95 (*0-88150-263-4*, Foul Play) Norton, W. W. & Co., Inc.

Theroux, Marcel. The Confessions of Mycroft Holmes: A Paper Chase. 2001. (Illus.). 224p. 23.00 o.s.i (*0-15-100647-4*); 2002. 228p. reprint ed. pap. 14.00 (*0-15-600743-6*, Harvest Bks.) Harcourt Trade Pubs.

## CARIBBEAN AREA—FICTION

Abrahams, Peter. This Island Now. 1985. 256p. pap. o.p. (*0-571-13439-4*) Faber & Faber Ltd.

—The View from Coyaba. 1985. 440p. o.p. (*0-571-13288-X*) Faber & Faber Ltd.

—The View from Coyaba. 1985. 440p. pap. 8.95 o.p. (*0-571-13289-8*) Faber & Faber, Inc.

Ada, Alma Flor, et al. Choices & Other Stories from the Caribbean. 1993. (J). (gr. 3-5). pap. 6.95 (*0-377-00257-7*) Friendship Pr.

Alvarez, Julia. In the Name of Salome. 2001. 368p. pap. 14.00 (*0-452-28243-8*, Plume) Dutton/Plume.

—In the Name of Salome. 2001. 19.05 (*0-606-21792-4*) Turtleback Bks.

Anthony, Michael. The Year in San Fernando. 1997. (Caribbean Writers Ser.). 156p. pap. 10.95 (*0-435-98943-X*) Heinemann.

Anthony, Michael & Griffiths, Gareth. Green Days by the River. (Caribbean Writers Ser.). 2000. xxi, 198p. pap. 12.95 (*0-435-98955-3*); 1985. 192p. (C). pap. 7.95 (*0-435-98030-0*, 98030) Heinemann.

Antoni, Robert & Morrow, Bradford, eds. Conjunctions Vol. 27: The Archipelago, New Writing from & about the Caribbean. 1996. 360p. pap. text 12.00 (*0-941964-43-4*) Conjunctions.

Arthur, Kevyn A. The View from Belmont. 1997. 230p. pap. 14.95 (*1-900715-02-3*) Peepal Tree Pr., Ltd. GBR. *Dist:* Independent Pubs. Group, Paul & Co. Pubs. Consortium, Inc.

Atwood, Margaret. Bodily Harm. 1995. 304p. pap. 10.95 o.s.i (*0-553-37789-2*); 1983. mass mkt. 4.50 o.p. (*0-553-23289-4*); 1983. mass mkt. 4.50 o.s.i (*0-553-26969-0*); 1983. 304p. mass mkt. 6.50 o.s.i (*0-553-27455-4*) Bantam Bks.

—Bodily Harm. 2002. lib. bdg. 27.95 (*1-58547-236-0*, Premier) Ctr. Point Large Print.

—Bodily Harm. 1998. 304p. pap. 12.95 (*0-385-49107-7*) Doubleday Publishing.

—Bodily Harm. 1982. 45.00 (*0-671-44153-1*) Ultramarine Publishing Co., Inc.

Baldeosingh, Kevin. Virgin's Triangle. 1997. (Caribbean Writers Ser.). 180p. pap. 13.95 (*0-435-98947-2*) Heinemann.

Barthold, Bonnie J. Black Time: Fiction of Africa, the Caribbean, & the United States. 1981. (Illus.). 224p. 25.00 o.p. (*0-300-02573-4*) Yale Univ. Pr.

Behn, Aphra. Oroonoko: The Royal Slave. 1997. (Critical Editions Ser.). (Illus.). v, 90p. pap. 8.95 (*0-393-31205-4*) Norton, W. W. & Co., Inc.

Benjamin, Clinton L. Belinda. 2001. 144p. pap. 13.00 (*1-57197-243-9*) Pentland Pr., Inc.

Benitez Rojo, Antonio. A View from the Mangrove. Maraniss, James, tr. 256p. 2000. pap. 19.95 (*1-55849-261-5*); 1998. text 27.50 o.p. (*1-55849-136-8*) Univ. of Massachusetts Pr.

Bingham, Linda S. FlashPoint. 2000. (John & Mary Bolt Mystery Ser.). 248p. 11.95 (*0-945199-16-3*) Double SS Pr.

Boodhoo, I. J. Between Two Seasons Caribbean Writrs Series. 1995. (Longman Caribbean Writers Ser.). 314p. (C). pap. 16.80 (*0-582-22869-7*) Addison-Wesley Longman, Inc.

Boullosa, Carmen. They're Cows, We're Pigs. Chambers, Leland H., tr. 192p. 2001. pap. 12.00 (*0-8021-3786-5*); 1997. 23.00 o.p. (*0-8021-1610-8*, Grove Pr.) Grove/Atlantic, Inc.

Brand, Dionne. At the Full & Change of the Moon. 1999. 302p. 24.00 o.p. (*0-8021-1649-3*); 2000. 320p. reprint ed. pap. 13.50 (*0-8021-3723-7*) Grove/Atlantic, Inc. (Grove Pr.).

—In Another Place, Not Here. 2000. 256p. pap. 13.00 (*0-8021-3633-8*, Grove Pr.) Grove/Atlantic, Inc.

Breton, Marcela, ed. Rhythm & Revolt: Tales of the Antilles. 1995. 304p. pap. 12.95 o.p. (*0-452-27178-9*, Plume) Dutton/Plume.

Brown, Stewart, ed. Caribbean New Wave: Contemporary Short Stories. 1990. (Caribbean Writers Ser.). 192p. (Orig.). (C). pap. 10.95 (0-435-98814-X, 98814) Heinemann.

Buffett, Jimmy. Where Is Joe Merchant? l.t. ed. 1993. 22.95 o.p. (1-56895-011-X, Wheeler Publishing, Inc.) Gale Group.

—Where Is Joe Merchant? 1992. 19.95 o.p. (0-15-196299-5) Harcourt Trade Pubs.

—Where Is Joe Merchant? 2002. 416p. mass mkt. 7.99 (0-380-72118-X, Avon Bks.) Morrow/Avon.

—Where Is Joe Merchant? A Novel Tale. 1992. 416p. 25.00 (0-15-196296-0); 1992. 75.00 (0-15-196297-9); 2003. 496p. reprint ed. pap. 14.00 (0-15-602699-6, Harvest Bks.) Harcourt Trade Pubs.

Buslik, Gary. The Missionary's Position. 1999. 312p. pap. 12.95 (0-9665513-0-3) Sunny Bks.

Cambeira, Alan. Azucar! The Story of Sugar. 2001. 290p. pap. 14.50 (0-9720821-1-5) Belecam & Assocs.

Carpentier, Alejo. Explosion in a Cathedral. Sturrock, John, tr. 1989. 351p. pap. 14.00 o.p. (0-374-52198-0) Farrar, Straus & Giroux.

—Explosion in a Cathedral. 2001. 360p. reprint ed. pap. 15.95 (0-8166-3808-X) Univ. of Minnesota Pr.

Carrington, Roslyn. Candy Don't Come in Gray. 2002. 32p. pap. 14.00 (1-57566-852-1) Kensington Publishing Corp.

—Every Bitter Thing Sweet. 2001. 32p. pap. 14.00 (1-57566-851-3) Kensington Publishing Corp.

—A Thirst for Rain. 2000. 28p. pap. 12.00 (1-57566-575-1, Kensington Bks.); 1999. 208p. 22.00 o.s.i (1-57566-446-1) Kensington Publishing Corp.

Chaikin, Linda L. The Pirate & His Lady. 1997. (Buccaneers Ser.: No. 2). 384p. pap. 11.99 (0-8024-1072-3, 251) Moody Pr.

—Port Royal. 1995. (Buccaneers Ser.: No. 1). pap. 11.99 (0-8024-1071-5, 252) Moody Pr.

—Silver Dreams. 1998. (Trade Winds Ser.: Vol. 2). 215p. pap. 8.99 o.p. (1-56507-756-3) Harvest Hse. Pubs.

—Silver Dreams. l.t. ed. 2000. (Trade Winds Ser.). 360p. 23.95 (0-7862-2748-6) Thorndike Pr.

Chamoiseau, Patrick. Chronicle of the Seven Sorrows. Coverdale, Linda, tr. from FRE. & afterword by. 1999. (Illus.). 226p. text 30.00 (0-8032-1495-2); pap. 15.00 (0-8032-6426-7, Bison Bks.) Univ. of Nebraska Pr.

—Texaco: A Novel. 1998. 416p. pap. 15.00 (0-679-75175-0, Vintage) Knopf Publishing Group.

Chieftains Carnival & Other Stories. 1995. (C). pap. text o.p. (0-582-21805-5, TG7668) Longman Publishing Group.

Christmas, Joyce. A Perfect Day for Dying. 1993. (Orig.). mass mkt. 4.99 o.s.i (0-449-14703-7, Fawcett) Ballantine Bks.

Clarke, Austin. The Polished Hoe: A Novel. 2002. 480p. tchr. ed. (0-88762-110-4) Allen, Thomas & Son, Ltd.

—The Polished Hoe: A Novel. 2003. 480p. 24.95 (0-06-055565-3, Amistad Pr.) HarperTrade.

Collymore, Frank. The Man Who Loved Attending Funerals. 1993. (Caribbean Writers Ser.). 192p. pap. 9.95 (0-435-98931-6, 98931) Heinemann.

Conde, Maryse. Land of Many Colors & Nanna-Ya: Pays Mele Suivi de Nanna-Ya. Ball, Nicole, tr. from FRE. 1999. 113p. pap. 12.00 (0-8032-6395-3) Univ. of Nebraska Pr.

—Land of Many Colors & Nanna-Ya (Pays Mele Suivi de Nanna-Ya) Pays Mele Suivi de Nanna-Ya. Ball, Nicole, tr. from FRE. 1999. 113p. text 30.00 o.p. (0-8032-1488-X) Univ. of Nebraska Pr.

—The Last of the African Kings. Philcox, Richard, tr. 1997. 216p. pap. 12.00 (0-8032-6384-8, Bison Bks.); text 45.00 (0-8032-1489-8) Univ. of Nebraska Pr.

—Windward Heights. Philcox, Richard, tr. from FRE. 2000. 352p. pap. 13.00 (1-56947-216-5); 1999. 364p. 24.00 (1-56947-161-4) Soho Pr., Inc.

Coulter, Catherine. Impulse. l.t. ed. 1998. 25.95 o.p. (1-56895-611-8, Wheeler Publishing, Inc.) Gale Group.

—Impulse. 1991. 400p. mass mkt. 7.50 o.s.i (0-451-40250-2, Onyx); 1990. 40p. 18.95 o.p. (0-453-00726-0) NAL.

Courlander, Harold. The Bordeaux Narrative. 1990. 192p. 21.95 o.p. (0-8263-0915-1) Univ. of New Mexico Pr.

D'Aguiar, Fred. Dear Future. 1996. 224p. 22.00 o.s.i (0-679-44248-0) McKay, David Co., Inc.

—Dear Future. 1998. pap. 12.00 (0-380-72967-9, Avon Bks.) Morrow/Avon.

Danticat, Edwidge. The Farming of Bones. 1999. 320p. pap. 14.00 (0-14-028049-9, Penguin Bks.) Penguin Group (USA) Inc.

—The Farming of Bones. 1998. 312p. 23.00 (1-56947-126-6); pap. o.p. (1-56947-141-X) Soho Pr., Inc.

—The Farming of Bones. l.t. ed. 1999. (Basic Ser.). 416p. 29.95 (0-7862-1732-4) Thorndike Pr.

DeBrosse, Jim. Southern Cross. 1994. 240p. 19.95 o.p. (0-312-11070-7, Saint Martin's Minotaur) St. Martin's Pr.

Delinsky, Barbara. A Single Rose. 1994. 249p. mass mkt. (0-373-83293-1, 1-83293-0); 1987. mass mkt. (0-373-25250-1) Harlequin Enterprises, Ltd. (Harlequin Bks.).

—A Single Rose. l.t. ed. 2001. (Thorndike Famous Authors Ser.). 320p. 29.95 (0-7862-3055-X) Thorndike Pr.

Diamond, Diana. The Trophy Wife. l.t. ed. 2000. 26.95 (1-57490-305-5, Beeler Large Print Bks.) Beeler, Thomas T. Publisher.

—The Trophy Wife. 2000. 261p. 23.95 (0-312-20600-3) St. Martin's Pr.

Didion, Joan. The Last Thing He Wanted. 1997. 240p. pap. 12.00 (0-679-75285-4, Vintage) Knopf Publishing Group.

—The Last Thing He Wanted. 1996. 227p. 23.00 o.s.i (0-679-43331-7) Knopf, Alfred A. Inc.

Donovan, Rosalind. Come to My Island. Taylor, Maxwell, ed. 1996. (Illus.). 32p. (J). (ps-2). pap. 7.95 (1-881316-47-5) A & B Distributors & Pubs. Group.

Drayton, Geoffrey. Christopher. 1972. (Caribbean Writers Ser.). 192p. (C). pap. 7.95 (0-435-98235-4, 98235) Heinemann.

Eakins, Patricia. The Marvelous Adventures of Pierre Baptiste. 1999. 264p. 20.00 (0-8147-2209-1) New York Univ. Pr.

Edwards, Jane. Island Interlude. unabr. ed. 1994. audio 26.95 (1-55686-554-6) Books in Motion.

—Island Interlude. l.t. ed. 2000. (Paperback Ser.). 222p. pap. 23.95 (0-7838-9131-8) Thorndike Pr.

Edwards, Jonathan. Tales in the Key of Sea. 2001. 185p. pap. 13.95 (0-595-16841-8) iUniverse, Inc.

Flanagan, Brenda. You Alone Are Dancing. 1996. (Ann Arbor Paperback Ser.). (Illus.). 208p. (Orig.). (C). text 37.50 o.s.i (0-472-09627-3, 09627); pap. text 16.95 (0-472-06627-7, 06627) Univ. of Michigan Pr.

Fox, Paula. A Servant's Tale. 1982. 336p. 16.50 o.p. (0-86547-164-9, North Point Pr.) Farrar, Straus & Giroux.

—A Servant's Tale. 2001. (Norton Paperback Fiction Ser.). 336p. pap. 13.00 (0-393-32285-8) Norton, W. W. & Co., Inc.

—A Servant's Tale. 1986. (Contemporary American Fiction Ser.). 336p. pap. 6.95 o.p. (0-14-008386-3, Penguin Bks.) Viking Penguin.

Francis, Dick. Second Wind. 2000. 272p. mass mkt. 6.99 (0-515-12923-2, Jove) Berkley Publishing Group.

—Second Wind. l.t. ed. 1999. 24.95 o.p. (0-7838-8691-8, Macmillan Reference USA) Gale Group.

—Second Wind. 1999. 293p. 24.95 o.s.i (0-399-14562-1) Penguin Group (USA) Inc.

—Second Wind. l.t. ed. 2000. 416p. pap. 11.95 (0-375-70772-7) Random Hse. Large Print.

—Second Wind. 2000. 13.04 (0-606-19301-4) Turtleback Bks.

Freydont, Shelley. High Seas Murder: A Lindy Haggerty Mystery. 2000. (Linda Haggerty Mysteries Ser. ). 336p. 20.00 o.s.i (1-57566-627-8) Kensington Publishing Corp.

Furst, Peter. Don Quixote in Exile. 1996. (Jewish Lives Ser.). 210p. (C). 64.00 (0-8101-1447-X); pap. 21.00 (0-8101-1448-8) Northwestern Univ. Pr.

Furthman, Jules & Faulkner, William. To Have & Have Not. Kawin, Bruce F., ed. 1980. (Warner Bros. Screenplay Ser.). (Illus.). 232p. 14.95 o.p. (0-299-08090-0) Univ. of Wisconsin Pr.

Garne, S. T. By a Blazing Blue Sea. 1999. (Illus.). 32p. (J). (ps-3). 16.00 (0-15-201780-1, Gulliver Bks.) Harcourt Children's Bks.

Garrison, Paul. Sea Hunter: A Novel of Suspense. 2003. 352p. 25.95 (0-06-008167-8) HarperCollins Pubs.

—Sea Hunter: A Novel of Suspense. 2003. 384p. mass mkt. 7.99 (0-06-008168-6, HarperTorch) Morrow/Avon.

Gerber, Alain. The Slave Trail. Leggatt, Jeremy, tr. from FRE. 1989. 160p. 18.95 o.p. (0-916515-51-6) Mercury Hse.

Gibbs, Tony. Dead Run. 1989. mass mkt. 3.50 o.s.i (0-8041-0420-4, Ivy Bks.) Ballantine Bks.

—Landfall: A Novel. 1992. 256p. 20.00 o.p. (0-688-11102-5, Morrow, William & Co.) Morrow/Avon.

—Running Fix. 1990. 18.95 o.s.i (0-394-57580-6) Random Hse., Inc.

Gilroy, Beryl. Frangipani House. 1986. (Caribbean Writers Ser.). 111p. (Orig.). (C). pap. 8.95 (0-435-98852-2, 98852) Heinemann.

Gittens-Jones, Cheryl. The Cleansing. 2003. 242p. pap. 19.95 (1-59286-467-8) PublishAmerica, Inc.

Grant-Adamson, Lesley, ed. Dangerous Games. 1995. 234p. 19.95 o.p. (0-312-11766-3, Saint Martin's Minotaur) St. Martin's Pr.

Green, Chloe. Fashion Victim. 2003. mass mkt. 5.99 (1-57566-716-9); 2002. 288p. 22.00 (1-57566-715-0) Kensington Publishing Corp. (Kensington Bks.).

Gulland, Sandra. The Many Lives & Secret Sorrows of Josephine B. A Novel. 1999. 448p. pap. 14.00 (0-684-85606-9, Touchstone) Simon & Schuster.

Guy, Rosa. My Love, My Friend: Or the Pleasant Girl. 1985. 128p. 12.95 o.p. (0-03-000507-8) Holt, Henry & Co.

—My Love, My Friend or the Peasant Girl. 1990. 128p. pap. 9.95 o.p. (0-8050-1659-7, Owl Bks.) Holt, Henry & Co.

—My Love, My Love or the Peasant Girl. 2002. 168p. pap. 11.95 (1-56689-131-0) Coffee Hse. Pr.

Hall, Russ. Island: A Novel. 2001. 262p. pap. 16.95 (0-9666173-6-3) Tropical Pr., Inc.

Handley, George B. Postslavery Literatures in the Americas: Family Portraits in Black & White. 2000. (New World Studies). x, 231p. 57.50 (0-8139-1976-2); pap. 18.50 (0-8139-1977-0) Univ. Pr. of Virginia.

Harris, Wilson. The Angel at the Gate. 1983. 128p. o.p. (0-571-11929-8) Faber & Faber Ltd.

—Carnival. 1985. 176p. (C). 19.95 o.s.i (0-571-13449-1) Faber & Faber, Inc.

—The Carnival Trilogy: Carnival, The Infinite Rehersal, & The Four Banks of the River of Space. 1993. 464p. pap. 16.95 o.p. (0-571-15435-2) Faber & Faber, Inc.

—Da Silva Cultivated Wilderness & Genesis of the Clowns. 1978. 160p. 9.95 o.p. (0-571-10819-9) Faber & Faber, Inc.

—Resurrection at Sorrow Hill. 1993. 256p. text 22.95 o.p. (0-571-16978-3) Faber & Faber, Inc.

Heller, Jane. Princess Charming. l.t. ed. 1997. lib. bdg. 24.95 (1-57490-102-8, Beeler Large Print Bks.) Beeler, Thomas T. Publisher.

—Princess Charming. 1998. 352p. mass mkt. 5.99 (1-57566-261-2); 1997. 304p. 22.00 o.s.i (1-57566-148-9) Kensington Publishing Corp.

—Princess Charming. unabr. ed. 1998. audio 78.00 (0-7887-1927-0, 95348E7) Recorded Bks., LLC.

Hemingway, Ernest. To Have & Have Not. (Scribner Classics). 1999. 176p. 25.00 (0-684-85923-8, Scribner); 1996. 272p. pap. 12.00 (0-684-81898-1, Scribner); 1983. 272p. pap. 4.95 o.s.i (0-684-17952-0, Scribner Paper Fiction); 1977. 272p. 40.00 (0-684-15328-9, Scribner); 1937. 272p. pap. 10.95 o.s.i (0-684-71809-X, Scribner Paper Fiction) Simon & Schuster.

Hodge, Merle. Crick Crack Monkey. 1981. (Caribbean Writers Ser.). 112p. (C). reprint ed. pap. 7.95 (0-435-98401-2, 98401) Heinemann.

Hoover, Thomas. Caribbee. 1985. (Illus.). 408p. 17.95 o.p. (0-385-19366-1) Doubleday Publishing.

—Caribbee. 1987. 512p. mass mkt. 4.50 o.p. (0-8217-2400-2, Zebra Bks.) Kensington Publishing Corp.

Hopkinson, Nalo. The Salt Roads. 2003. 400p. 22.95 (0-446-53302-5) Warner Bks., Inc.

Jacobson, Jeffrey P. Mystery of the Compass Rose. 2000. 191p. pap. 14.95 (0-9677814-0-X) Bluewater Publishing.

James, Dana. Love's Ransom. l.t. ed. 2001. 227p. pap. 22.95 (0-7838-9476-7, Macmillan Reference USA) Gale Group.

—Love's Ransom. 1990. (Harlequin Romance Ser.: No. 3068). pap. (0-373-03068-1, Harlequin Bks.) Harlequin Enterprises, Ltd.

Jarrett, Miranda. Wishing. 1999. 368p. pap. 6.50 (0-671-00341-0, Pocket) Simon & Schuster.

Kaiser, R. J. Hoodwinked. 2001. 440p. mass mkt. (1-55166-820-3, Mira Bks.) Harlequin Enterprises, Ltd.

—Payback. 1998. 448p. mass mkt. (1-55166-460-7, 1-66460-6, Mira Bks.) Harlequin Enterprises, Ltd.

Kamau, Kwadwo A. Flickering Shadows. 1996. 304p. 21.95 (1-56689-049-7) Coffee Hse. Pr.

—Flickering Shadows. 1997. 320p. pap. 13.00 o.p. (0-8050-5472-3, Owl Bks.) Holt, Henry & Co.

Kennedy, William P. Dark Tide: A Novel of Suspense. l.t. ed. 1995. 535p. lib. bdg. 25.95 o.p. (0-7838-1286-8, Macmillan Reference USA) Gale Group.

—Dark Tide: A Novel of Suspense. 1996. 374p. pap. text 5.99 (0-312-95776-9, St. Martin's Paperbacks); 1995. 359p. 22.95 o.p. (0-312-11768-X) St. Martin's Pr.

Kilian, Michael. Looker. 1990. 19.95 o.p. (0-312-05123-9) St. Martin's Pr.

Kincaid, Jamaica. At the Bottom of the River. 1992. 96p. reprint ed. pap. 9.95 o.s.i (0-452-26754-4, Plume) Dutton/Plume.

—At the Bottom of the River. 2000. 96p. pap. 11.00 (0-374-52734-2); 1983. 82p. 15.00 o.s.i (0-374-10660-6) Farrar, Straus & Giroux.

—At the Bottom of the River. 1985. 82p. pap. 8.00 o.s.i (0-394-73683-4, Vintage) Knopf Publishing Group.

—Mr. Potter. (0-374-99619-9); 2003. 208p. pap. 11.00 (0-374-52874-8); 2002. E-Book 15.00 (0-374-70343-4); 2002. E-Book (0-374-70344-2); 2002. E-Book 15.00 o.p. (0-374-70345-0); 2002. E-Book 15.00 (0-374-70346-9); 2002. E-Book (0-374-70347-7); 2002. 144p. 20.00 (0-374-21494-8) Farrar, Straus & Giroux.

Kingsolver, Barbara. Homeland & Other Stories. 1999. reprint ed. 26.95 (1-56849-724-5) Buccaneer Bks., Inc.

—Homeland & Other Stories. l.t. ed. 2001. (Wheeler Large Print Book Ser.). 316p. 29.95 (1-58724-091-2, Wheeler Publishing, Inc.) Gale Group.

—Homeland & Other Stories. 1989. 244p. 16.95 o.p. (0-06-016112-4) HarperTrade.

Kirkland, Martha. The Seductive Spy. 2000. (Five Star Romance Ser.). 200p. 25.95 (0-7862-2725-7, Five Star) Gale Group.

Kraus, Jim & Kraus, Terri. Passages of Gold. 1997. (Treasures of the Caribbean Ser.: No. 2). 510p. pap. 8.99 o.p. (0-8423-0382-0) Tyndale Hse. Pubs.

—Pirates of the Heart. 1996. (Pirates of the Heart Ser.: No. 1). 600p. pap. 8.99 o.p. (0-8423-0381-2) Tyndale Hse. Pubs.

Kraus, Jim & Kraus, Terry. Journey to the Crimson Sea. 1997. (Treasures of the Caribbean Ser.: No. 3). 384p. pap. 9.99 o.p. (0-8423-0383-9) Tyndale Hse. Pubs.

Kurlansky, Mark. The White Man in the Tree: And Other Stories. 2000. (Illus.). 320p. 23.95 o.s.i (0-671-03605-X); 2001. 336p. reprint ed. pap. 13.00 (0-671-03606-8) Simon & Schuster. (Washington Square Pr.).

Ladd, Garland. A Cruise to Remember. 2001. 242p. pap. 21.99 (1-4010-0329-X) Xlibris Corp.

Lambdin, Dewey. The Gun Ketch: An Alan Lewrie Naval Adventure. 1996. (Alan Lewrie Navel Adventures Ser.). 336p. mass mkt. 6.99 (0-449-22450-3, Fawcett) Ballantine Bks.

—The Gun Ketch: An Alan Lewrie Naval Adventure. 1993. 21.95 o.s.i (1-55611-356-0) Fine, Donald I. Bks.

—Havoc's Sword: An Alan Lewrie Naval Adventure. 2003. (Illus.). 384p. 25.95 (0-312-28688-0) St. Martin's Pr.

Lamming, George. In the Castle of My Skin. 1987. 352p. pap. 13.00 o.s.i (0-8052-0750-3, Schocken) Knopf Publishing Group.

—In the Castle of My Skin. 1992. 21.50 o.p. (0-8446-6634-3) Smith, Peter Pub., Inc.

—In the Castle of My Skin. 1991. (Ann Arbor Paperback Ser.). (Illus.). 344p. (C). reprint ed. text 52.50 (0-472-09468-8, 09468); pap. text 17.95 (0-472-06468-1, 06468) Univ. of Michigan Pr.

Lindsey, Johanna. A Pirate's Love. 1997. (Five Star Romance Ser.). 373p. 23.95 o.p. (0-7862-0953-4, Five Star) Gale Group.

—A Pirate's Love. 1978. 384p. mass mkt. 7.99 (0-380-40048-0, Avon Bks.) Morrow/Avon.

—A Pirate's Love. 1991. 384p. reprint ed. 17.95 o.p. (0-7278-1592-X) Severn Hse. Pubs., Ltd.

—A Pirate's Love. l.t. ed. 1996. (Americana Ser.). 482p. 27.95 (0-7862-0724-8) Thorndike Pr.

Lopez, Barry. Light Action in the Caribbean: Stories. 2001. 176p. pap. 12.00 (0-679-75448-2, Vintage) Knopf Publishing Group.

Lovelace, Earl. A Brief Conversion & Other Stories. 1988. (Caribbean Writers Ser.). 141p. (Orig.). (C). pap. 7.50 (0-435-98882-4, 98882) Heinemann.

—A Brief Conversion & Other Stories. 2002. 160p. (Orig.). pap. 14.00 (0-89255-271-9) Persea Bks., Inc.

—The Dragon Can't Dance. 1998. 240p. 24.00 (0-89255-234-4); 2002. 242p. reprint ed. pap. 15.00 (0-89255-272-7) Persea Bks., Inc.

Lovell, Glenville. Fire in the Canes. 1997. 272p. mass mkt. 6.99 o.s.i (0-425-16040-8) Berkley Publishing Group.

—Fire in the Canes. 1995. 272p. 22.00 (1-56947-044-8) Soho Pr., Inc.

—Song of Night. 1998. 256p. 23.00 (1-56947-122-3) Soho Pr., Inc.

Mais, Roger. Black Lightning. 1983. (Caribbean Writers Ser.). 159p. (Orig.). (C). reprint ed. pap. 8.95 o.p. (0-435-98584-1, 98584) Heinemann.

—Brother Man. 1974. (Caribbean Writers Ser.). 191p. (C). pap. 8.95 (0-435-98585-X) Heinemann.

—The Hills Were Joyful Together. 1981. (Caribbean Writers Ser.). 304p. (C). pap. 9.95 (0-435-98586-8, 98586) Heinemann.

The Many Lives & Secret Sorrows of Josephine B: A Novel. 2000. E-Book 14.00 (0-7432-1357-2, Scribner Paper Fiction) Simon & Schuster.

Maran, Rene. Batouala. 1989. reprint ed. lib. bdg. 25.95 (0-89966-640-X) Buccaneer Bks., Inc.

—Batouala. 1988. (African Writers Ser.). 150p. (C). pap. 11.95 (0-435-90135-4, 90135, African Writers Series) Heinemann.

Markham, E. A. Caribbean Short Stories. 1997. 464p. 15.00 (0-14-024503-0) Viking Penguin.

Marshall, Paule. The Chosen Place, the Timeless People. 1992. pap. 13.00 (0-394-23987-3); 1984. 480p. pap. 15.00 (0-394-72633-2) Knopf Publishing Group. (Vintage).

McCafferty, Kate. Testimony of an Irish Slave Girl. 2003. 240p. pap. 13.00 (0-14-200183-X) Penguin Group (USA) Inc.

—Testimony of an Irish Slave Girl: A Novel. 2002. 224p. 24.95 o.s.i (0-670-03065-1, Viking) Viking Penguin.


Settings

McGarrity, Mark. White Rush - Green Fire. 1992. 464p. mass mkt. 4.99 (*0-380-71097-8*, Avon Bks.); 1991. 504p. 20.00 o.p. (*0-688-08658-6*, Morrow, William & Co.) Morrow/Avon.
McKee, Lynn Armistead. Daughter of the Fifth Moon. 2001. 384p. mass mkt. 6.99 o.s.i (*0-451-20356-9*, Signet Bks.) NAL.
McKernan, Victoria. Point Deception. 1992. 288p. 19.95 o.p. (*0-88184-798-4*, Carroll & Graf Pubs.) Avalon Publishing Group.
Michener, James A. Caribbean. 1990. 832p. mass mkt. 7.99 (*0-449-21749-3*, Fawcett) Ballantine Bks.
—Caribbean. 1993. audio 96.00 (*0-7366-2375-2*) Books on Tape, Inc.
—Caribbean. 1989. o.s.i (*5-550-28705-6*) Nairi.
—Caribbean. abr. ed. 1989. audio 16.00 o.s.i (*0-394-58046-X*, RH Audio) Random Hse. Audio Publishing Group.
—Caribbean. 1991. 6.99 o.p. (*0-517-07226-2*) Random Hse. Value Publishing.
Mickelbury, Penny. Paradise Interrupted. 2001. 288p. 23.00 (*0-684-85991-2*, Simon & Schuster) Simon & Schuster.
Miller, Linda Lael. Pirates. l.t. ed. 1995. (Large Print Bks.). 24.95 o.p. (*1-56895-249-X*, Wheeler Publishing, Inc.) Gale Group.
—Pirates. 1996. (Illus.). 336p. mass mkt. 6.99 (*0-671-87316-4*, Pocket) Simon & Schuster.
—Pirates. Marrow, Linda, ed. 1995. 304p. 20.00 o.p. (*0-671-52732-0*, Atria) Simon & Schuster.
Milstein, Linda B. Coconut Mon. 1995. (Illus.). 32p. (J). (ps up). 16.00 o.p. (*0-688-12862-9*); lib. bdg. 15.93 o.p. (*0-688-12863-7*) Morrow/Avon. (Morrow, William & Co.).
Mittleholzer, Edgar. Corentyne Thunder. 1970. (Caribbean Writers Ser.). 229p. (C). pap. 8.95 o.p. (*0-435-98593-0*, 98593) Heinemann.
Montero, Mayra. The Red of His Shadow. Grossman, Edith, tr. from SPA. 176p. 2002. pap. 12.95 (*0-06-095291-1*); 2001. (Illus.). 22.00 (*0-06-621059-3*) HarperTrade. (Ecco).
Moore, Brian. No Other Life. 1997. (William Abrahams Book Ser.). 224p. pap. 11.95 o.s.i (*0-452-27878-3*, Plume) Dutton/Plume.
—No Other Life. l.t. ed. 1993. 277p. lib. bdg. 22.95 (*0-8161-5897-5*, Macmillan Reference USA) Gale Group.
Mootoo, Shani. Cereus Blooms at Night. 1998. 272p. 23.00 o.p. (*0-8021-1633-7*, Grove Pr.) Grove/Atlantic, Inc.
—Cereus Blooms at Night. 1999. 272p. pap. 13.00 (*0-380-73199-1*, Perennial) HarperTrade.
—Cereus Blooms at Night. 1996. 216p. pap. (*0-88974-064-X*, Press Gang Pubs.) Raincoast Bk. Distribution.
—Cereus Blooms at Night, unabr. ed. 2000. audio 63.00 (*1-84197-102-2*, H1091E7, Clipper Audio) Recorded Bks., LLC.
—Cereus Blooms at Night. l.t. ed. 1999. (Basic Ser.). 423p. 28.95 (*0-7862-1734-0*) Thorndike Pr.
Morgan, Trudy J. Whatcha Doin Alex? 1994. (J). mass mkt. 5.99 o.p. (*0-8280-0849-3*) Review & Herald Publishing Assn.
Morris, Lynn & Morris, Gilbert. Where Two Seas Met. l.t. ed. 2001. (Cheney Duvall, M. D. Ser.). 480p. pap. 17.99 (*0-7642-2610-X*) Bethany Hse. Pubs.
—Where Two Seas Met Bk #1. 2001. (Cheney Duvall, M. D. Ser.). 320p. pap. 12.99 (*1-55661-437-3*) Bethany Hse. Pubs.
Morris, Mary. House Arrest. 1997. 272p. pap. 12.00 (*0-312-15547-6*) Picador.
Morris, Mervyn, ed. The Faber Book of Contemporary Caribbean Short Stories. 1991. 250p. pap. 10.95 o.p. (*0-571-15299-6*) Faber & Faber, Inc.
Morrison, Toni. Tar Baby. 1987. pap. 8.95 o.p. (*0-452-25258-X*); 1987. 352p. pap. 7.95 o.p. (*0-452-26012-4*, Z5326); 1987. 320p. pap. 12.95 (*0-452-26479-0*); 1982. pap. 6.95 o.p. (*0-452-25326-8*) Dutton/Plume. (Plume).
—Tar Baby. 2004. 320p. pap. 13.00 (*1-4000-3344-6*, Vintage) Knopf Publishing Group.
—Tar Baby. 1981. 320p. 26.95 (*0-394-42329-1*) Knopf, Alfred A. Inc.
—Tar Baby. 1993. pap. 5.99 o.s.i (*0-451-18238-3*); 1983. mass mkt. 3.95 o.p. (*0-451-12224-0*); 1983. 272p. mass mkt. 5.99 o.p. (*0-451-16639-6*); 1983. 320p. mass mkt. 4.50 o.p. (*0-451-15260-3*) NAL. (Signet Bks.).
—Tar Baby. 1983. 19.00 (*0-606-01962-6*) Turtleback Bks.
Munroe, Andrew A. The Obeah Woman May: A Caribbean Novel of Mystery & Magic. 1998. 181p. pap. 12.95 (*0-9643010-1-6*) Golden Grove Publishing.
Naipaul, V. S. Miguel Street. 1974. (Caribbean Writers Ser.). 172p. (C). pap. 7.95 (*0-435-98645-7*, 98645) Heinemann.
—Miguel Street. 1984. 176p. pap. 6.95 o.s.i (*0-394-72065-2*, Vintage) Knopf Publishing Group.
—Miguel Street. 1977. 176p. pap. 11.95 o.s.i (*0-14-003302-5*, Penguin Bks.) Viking Penguin.
—Vintage Naipaul. 2004. 208p. pap. 9.95 (*1-4000-3400-0*, Vintage) Knopf Publishing Group.
Neff, Heather. Wisdom. 336p. 2003. pap. 13.95 (*0-345-44744-1*, One World/Ballantine); 2002. 24.00 (*0-345-44743-3*) Ballantine Bks.
Newcomb, Kerry. Mad Morgan. E-Book 24.95 (*0-312-27596-X*); 2001. 320p. mass mkt. 6.50 (*0-312-97741-7*, St. Martin's Paperbacks); 2000. 276p. 24.95 (*0-312-26197-7*) St. Martin's Pr.
Nunez, Elizabeth. Bruised Hibiscus: A Novel. 2001. 295p. reprint ed. pap. 13.95 (*1-58005-061-1*, Seal Pr.) Avalon Publishing Group.
—Bruised Hibiscus: A Novel. 2003. 304p. pap. 13.95 (*0-345-45109-0*) Ballantine Bks.
O'Connor, Dan. Spice: An Island Intrigue. 2002. 348p. 14.95 (*0-9667235-5-4*) Waterton Pr.
O'Donnell, Lillian. The Goddess Affair. 1997. mass mkt. 5.99 o.s.i (*0-449-28805-6*, Fawcett) Ballantine Bks.
—The Goddess Affair. l.t. ed. 1997. (Large Print Book Ser.). 25.95 o.p. (*1-56895-461-1*, Wheeler Publishing, Inc.) Gale Group.
—The Goddess Affair. 1996. 240p. 21.95 o.p. (*0-399-14183-9*, G. P. Putnam's Sons) Penguin Group (USA) Inc.
Owen, Richard. White Slave. 1987. 320p. 16.95 o.p. (*0-688-06939-8*, Morrow, William & Co.) Morrow/Avon.
—White Slave. 1988. 352p. mass mkt. 4.50 o.p. (*0-451-15395-2*, Signet Bks.) NAL.
Pemberton-Strong, Sarah. Burning the Sea. 2002. (Illus.). 344p. pap. 13.95 (*1-55583-644-5*) Alyson Pubns.
Phillips, Caryl. A State of Independence. 1986. 158p. 13.95 o.s.i (*0-374-26976-9*) Farrar, Straus & Giroux.
—A State of Independence. 1995. 160p. pap. 15.00 (*0-679-75930-1*, Vintage) Knopf Publishing Group.
Poyer, David. The Passage. 1997. 560p. mass mkt. 6.99 (*0-312-95450-6*, St. Martin's Paperbacks); 1994. (*0-312-11381-1*); 1994. 516p. 22.95 o.p. (*0-312-11874-0*) St. Martin's Pr.
Rice, Patricia. Volcano. 1999. mass mkt. 5.99 (*0-449-15064-X*); 352p. mass mkt. 5.99 (*0-449-00609-3*) Ballantine Bks. (Fawcett).
Ripley, J. R. Murder in St. Barts. 2003. 243p. 25.00 (*1-892339-55-2*) Beachfront Publishing.
Roberts, Nora. The Reef. 1999. 448p. mass mkt. 7.99 (*0-515-12608-X*, Jove) Berkley Publishing Group.
—The Reef. 1998. 448p. 23.95 o.p. (*0-399-14441-2*, G. P. Putnam's Sons) Penguin Group (USA) Inc.
—The Reef. 2002. E-Book 7.50 (*0-7865-2663-7*) Penguin Putnam, Inc E-Books.
—The Reef. l.t. ed. (Thorndike/G. K. Hall Paperback Bestsellers Ser.). 629p. 2000. pap. 27.95 (*0-7862-1699-9*); 1999. 30.95 (*0-7862-1698-0*) Thorndike Pr.
Rosshandler, Felicia. Passing Through Havana: A Novel of a Wartime Girlhood in the Caribbean. 1983. 240p. 13.95 o.p. (*0-312-59779-7*) St. Martin's Pr.
Santos-Febres, Mayra. Sirena Selena. Lytle, Stephen, tr. E-Book 21.00 (*0-312-27601-X*) Picador.
Santos, Mayra. Sirena Selena. Lytle, Stephen, tr. from SPA. 2000. 224p. 21.00 (*0-312-25227-7*) Picador.
Schwarz-Bart, Simone. The Bridge of Beyond. Bray, Barbara, tr. from FRE. 1982. (Caribbean Writers Ser.). 192p. (C). reprint ed. pap. 10.95 (*0-435-98770-4*, 98770) Heinemann.
Scott, C. H. Tales from the Tropics: Seven Sea Stories. 1992. 208p. (Orig.). pap. 9.95 o.p. (*1-56474-025-0*) Fithian Pr.
Scott, Lawrence. Ballad for the New World & Other Stories. 1994. (Caribbean Writers Ser.). 114p. pap. 9.95 (*0-435-98939-1*, 98939) Heinemann.
Shacochis, Bob. Easy in the Islands. 1985. 224p. 13.95 o.s.i (*0-517-55549-2*, Crown) Crown Publishing Group.
—Easy in the Islands. 2004. 224p. pap. 13.00 (*0-8021-4059-9*, Grove Pr.) Grove/Atlantic, Inc.
—Easy in the Islands. 284th ed. 1986. (Contemporary American Fiction Ser.). 224p. pap. 14.00 o.s.i (*0-14-008301-4*, Penguin Bks.) Viking Penguin.
—Swimming in the Volcano. 1994. (Contemporay American Fiction Ser.). 528p. pap. 14.95 o.s.i (*0-14-023658-9*, Penguin Bks.) Penguin Group (USA) Inc.
—Swimming in the Volcano. 2002. 480p. pap. 24.95 (*0-7432-3758-7*, Scribner) Simon & Schuster.
—Swimming in the Volcano. Grossman, B., ed. 1993. 480p. 22.00 o.p. (*0-684-19260-8*, Scribner) Simon & Schuster.
—Swimming in the Volcano. 520p. 3.98 o.p. (*0-7651-0135-1*) Smithmark Pubs., Inc.
Skye, Christina. Going Overboard. 2001. 352p. mass mkt. 6.99 (*0-440-23575-8*) Dell Publishing.
—Going Overboard. l.t. ed. 2001. (Americana Ser.). 517p. 28.95 (*0-7862-3591-8*) Thorndike Pr.
Slade, Esther. Ayla's Paradise. 2001. 150p. pap. 11.95 (*1-885003-87-0*) Reed, Robert D. Pubs.
Smith, Carol. Charmed Circle. 1998. 355p. 24.00 o.p. (*0-446-52238-4*) Warner Bks., Inc.
—The Charmed Circle. 1999. 352p. mass mkt. 6.99 (*0-446-60704-5*) Warner Bks., Inc.
Snoe, Eboni. Tell Me I'm Dreamin' 1998. 384p. mass mkt. 5.99 o.s.i (*0-380-79562-0*, Avon Bks.) Morrow/Avon.
Spark, Debra. The Ghost of Bridgetown. 2001. 300p. 24.95 (*1-55597-352-3*) Graywolf Pr.
Sprechman, J. R. Caribe. 1986. 17.95 o.p. (*0-525-24320-8*, Dutton) Dutton/Plume.
—Caribe. 1988. 288p. pap. text 4.95 o.p. (*0-07-060345-6*) McGraw-Hill Cos., The.
Stone, Robert. Bay of Souls: A Novel. 2003. 256p. tchr. ed. 25.00 (*0-395-96349-4*) Houghton Mifflin Co.
—Bay of Souls: A Novel. 2004. 272p. pap. 13.00 (*0-618-44674-5*, Mariner Bks.) Houghton Mifflin Co. Trade & Reference Div.
Styron, Alexandra. All the Finest Girls. Pietsch, Michael, ed. 2001. 272p. 23.95 o.p. (*0-316-89080-4*) Little Brown & Co.
—All the Finest Girls. 2002. 288p. reprint ed. pap. 13.95 (*0-316-12086-3*, Back Bay) Little Brown & Co.
Szeps-Fralin, C. & Fralin, A. G., eds. Schwartz-Bart: Pluie et Vent sur Telumee Miracle. 1997. (French Texts). (ENG & FRE., Illus.). 128p. (C). pap. text 20.95 (*1-85399-483-9*) Bristol Classical Pr. GBR. *Dist:* Focus Publishing/R. Pullins Co., Inc.
Thomas, William H. Learning from Hannah: Secrets for a Life Worth Living. 1999. (Illus.). x, 227p. 21.95 (*1-889242-09-8*) VanderWyk & Burnham.
Vargas Llosa, Mario. La Fiesta del Chivo. 2000. (SPA., Illus.). 518p. (*968-19-0699-3*) Alfaguara, Ediciones, S.A.- Grupo Santillana.
—La Fiesta del Chivo. 2nd ed. 2000. (SPA., Illus.). 520p. 22.95 (*84-204-4169-4*) Alfaguara, Ediciones, S.A.- Grupo Santillana ESP. *Dist:* Santillana USA Publishing Co., Inc.
—La Fiesta del Chivo. 2001. (SPA.). 570p. 11.00 (*84-663-0331-6*, SN13360) Suma de Letras, S.L. ESP. *Dist:* Lectorum Pubns., Inc., Santillana USA Publishing Co., Inc.
Warner, Marina. Indigo, or, Mapping the Waters. 1992. 380p. 22.00 o.p. (*0-671-70156-8*, Simon & Schuster) Simon & Schuster.
Wilks, Eileen. Proposition: Marriage. 1999. (Silhouette Desire Ser.: No. 1239). 185p. per. (*0-373-76239-9*, 1-76239-2, Silhouette) Harlequin Enterprises, Ltd.
Williams, John A. The Berhama Account. 1985. 264p. 16.95 o.p. (*0-88282-009-5*) New Horizon Pr. Pubs., Inc.
Woods, Stuart. Dead in the Water. l.t. ed. 1997. 26.95 o.p. (*1-56895-508-1*, Wheeler Publishing, Inc.) Gale Group.
—Dead in the Water. 1998. 432p. mass mkt. 7.99 (*0-06-109349-1*) HarperCollins Pubs.
—Dead in the Water. 1997. 336p. 25.00 o.p. (*0-06-018368-3*, HarperCollins) HarperTrade.
Wouk, Herman. Don't Stop the Carnival. 1973. 416p. 25.00 o.s.i (*0-385-02003-1*) Doubleday Publishing.
—Don't Stop the Carnival. 1999. mass mkt. 7.99 (*0-316-95534-5*); 1998. mass mkt. 15.00 (*0-316-19223-6*); 1992. 416p. reprint ed. pap. 14.95 (*0-316-95512-4*) Little Brown & Co. (Back Bay).
—Don't Stop the Carnival. 1987. mass mkt. 4.95 o.s.i (*0-671-65678-3*); 1985. mass mkt. 4.50 o.s.i (*0-671-60544-5*) Simon & Schuster. (Pocket).
—Don't Stop the Carnival. 1999. lib. bdg. 28.95 (*1-56723-174-8*) Yestermorrow, Inc.
Zschokke, Magdalena. Salt Rock Mysteries. 2000. 208p. pap. 11.95 (*1-892281-07-4*) New Victoria Pubs., Inc.

## CARLSBAD CAVERNS (N.M.)—FICTION

Barr, Nevada. Blind Descent. l.t. ed. 1998. 25.95 o.p. (*1-56895-547-2*, Wheeler Publishing, Inc.) Gale Group.
—Blind Descent. 1999. (Anna Pigeon Mysteries Ser.). (Illus.). 384p. mass mkt. 7.99 (*0-380-72826-5*, Avon Bks.) Morrow/Avon.
—Blind Descent. 1998. 352p. (gr. 5 up). 22.95 o.p. (*0-399-14371-8*, G. P. Putnam's Sons) Penguin Group (USA) Inc.
—Blind Descent. 1999. audio compact disk 99.00; 1998. audio 83.00 (*0-7887-2038-4*, 95402E7) Recorded Bks., LLC.

## CARMEL (CALIF.)—FICTION

Day, Dianne. The Bohemian Murders. 1998. (Fremont Jones Mystery Ser.). 288p. reprint ed. mass mkt. 6.50 (*0-553-57412-4*, Crimeline) Bantam Bks.
—The Bohemian Murders: A Fremont Jones Mystery. l.t. ed. 1999. 25.95 (*1-57490-217-2*) Beeler, Thomas T. Publisher.
—The Bohemian Murders: A Fremont Jones Mystery. 1997. 256p. 21.95 o.s.i (*0-385-47923-9*) Doubleday Publishing.
—Emperor Norton's Ghost. 1999. (Fremont Jones Mystery Ser.). 336p. mass mkt. 6.50 (*0-553-58078-7*) Bantam Bks.
—Emperor Norton's Ghost, , unabr. ed. 1999. (Fremont Jones Mystery Ser.). audio 56.00 (*0-7366-4505-5*, 4920) Books on Tape, Inc.
—Fire & Fog. 1997. 288p. mass mkt. 6.50 (*0-553-56922-8*, Crimeline) Bantam Bks.
—Fire & Fog. 2000. audio 48.00 (*0-7366-4839-9*); (Fremont Jones Mystery Ser.: 2). audio 36.00 Books on Tape, Inc.
—Fire & Fog. 1996. 320p. 21.00 o.s.i (*0-385-47550-0*) Doubleday Publishing.
—The Strange Files of Fremont Jones. 1996. (Fremont Jones Mystery Ser.; Vol. 1). 272p. mass mkt. 5.99 (*0-553-56921-X*, Crimeline) Bantam Bks.
—The Strange Files of Fremont Jones. 1999. audio 48.00 (*0-7366-4788-0*); Set. 2000. audio 48.00 Books on Tape, Inc.
—The Strange Files of Fremont Jones. 1995. 240p. 19.95 o.s.i (*0-385-47549-7*) Doubleday Publishing.
—The Strange Files of Fremont Jones. l.t. ed. 1996. (Niagara Large Print Ser.). 336p. 29.50 o.p. (*0-7089-5824-9*, Ulverscroft) Thorpe, F. A. Pubs. GBR. *Dist:* Ulverscroft Large Print Bks., Ltd.
Stone, Katherine. The Other Twin. 2003. 368p. mass mkt. (*1-55166-747-9*); 304p. (*1-55166-655-3*) Harlequin Enterprises, Ltd. (Mira Bks.).
—The Other Twin. 2003. (Basic Ser.). 433p. 29.95 (*0-7862-5393-2*) Thorndike Pr.

## CARROLL (TEX.: IMAGINARY PLACE)—FICTION

Meredith, Doris R. The Sheriff & the Branding Iron Murders. 1992. mass mkt. 3.99 o.s.i (*0-345-36950-5*) Ballantine Bks.
—The Sheriff & the Branding Iron Murders. l.t. ed. 1997. (Nightingale Ser.). pap. 18.95 o.p. (*0-7838-2044-5*, Macmillan Reference USA) Gale Group.
—The Sheriff & the Branding Iron Murders. 1986. 160p. pap. 2.95 (*0-380-70050-6*, Avon Bks.) Morrow/Avon.
—The Sheriff & the Branding Iron Murders. Holland, Stephen, ed. abr. ed. 1994. audio 24.95 (*1-883268-12-5*) Spellbinders, Inc.
—The Sheriff & the Branding Iron Murders. 1985. 159p. 14.95 (*0-8027-4050-2*) Walker & Co.
—The Sheriff & the Folsom Man Murders. 1992. mass mkt. 3.99 o.s.i (*0-345-36949-1*) Ballantine Bks.
—The Sheriff & the Folsom Man Murders. 1987. 208p. pap. 2.95 (*0-380-70364-5*, Avon Bks.) Morrow/Avon.
—The Sheriff & the Folsom Man Murders. 1989. 2.99 o.p. (*0-517-00603-0*) Random Hse. Value Publishing.
—The Sheriff & the Folsom Man Murders. l.t. ed. 1999. 261p. pap. 24.95 (*0-7838-8582-2*) Thorndike Pr.
—The Sheriff & the Folsom Man Murders. 1987. 192p. 16.95 (*0-8027-5663-8*) Walker & Co.
—The Sheriff & the Panhandle Murders. l.t. ed. 1986. 13.95 o.p. (*1-55504-028-4*, 317) BBC Audiobooks America.
—The Sheriff & the Panhandle Murders. 1991. mass mkt. 4.99 o.s.i (*0-345-36951-3*) Ballantine Bks.
—The Sheriff & the Panhandle Murders. 1985. 224p. pap. 2.95 o.p. (*0-380-69929-X*, Avon Bks.) Morrow/Avon.
—The Sheriff & the Panhandle Murders. Holland, Stephen, ed. abr. ed. 1994. audio 24.95 (*1-883268-08-7*) Spellbinders, Inc.
—The Sheriff & the Panhandle Murders. 1984. 192p. 12.95 o.s.i (*0-8027-4036-7*) Walker & Co.
—The Sheriff & the Pheasant Hunt Murders. 1993. mass mkt. 4.50 o.s.i (*0-345-36948-3*) Ballantine Bks.
—The Sheriff & the Pheasant Hunt Murders. Holland, Stephen, ed. abr. ed. 1994. audio 24.95 (*1-883268-07-9*) Spellbinders, Inc.

## CARTHAGE (EXTINCT CITY)—FICTION

Craft, Elisabeth R. A Spy for Hannibal: A Novel of Carthage. 1996. 290p. 21.95 (*0-910155-33-X*) Bartleby Pr.
Hamilton, Lyn. The African Quest: An Archaeological Mystery. 2001. (Archaeological Mystery Ser.). (Illus.). 304p. 21.95 o.s.i (*0-425-17806-4*) Berkley Publishing Group.
Huby, Peter. Carthage. 2003. (Illus.). 192p. pap. 13.95 (*1-899235-29-9*) Lewis, Dewi Publishing GBR. *Dist:* Consortium Bk. Sales & Distribution.
Leckie, Ross. Carthage. 2001. (Illus.). 240p. 24.00 (*0-86241-944-1*) Canongate Bks. GBR. *Dist:* Grove/Atlantic, Inc.
—Hannibal. 1996. ix, 245p. pap. o.s.i (*0-349-10826-9*) Little Brown & Co.
—Hannibal. 1996. (Illus.). 245p. 19.95 o.p. (*0-89526-443-9*) Regnery Publishing, Inc., An Eagle Publishing Co.
Roberts, John Maddox. Hannibal's Children. 2002. 368p. 22.95 o.s.i (*0-441-00933-6*) Ace Bks.
—Hannibal's Children: A Novel of Alternate History. 2003. 368p. mass mkt. 6.99 (*0-441-01038-5*) Ace Bks.
Taleb, Mirza. Hannibal, Man of Destiny. 1974. 300p. 25.95 o.p. (*0-8283-1501-9*) Branden Bks.

## CASTLE AMBER (IMAGINARY PLACE)—FICTION

*see Amber (Imaginary Place)—Fiction*

**CASTLE PERILOUS (IMAGINARY PLACE)—FICTION**

DeChancie, John. Bride of the Castle. 1994. 192p. (Orig.). mass mkt. 4.99 o.s.i (*0-441-00120-3*) Ace Bks.

—Bride of the Castle. 2002. 176p. (Orig.). per. 14.95 (*0-7592-3240-7*) ereads.com.

—Castle Dreams. 1992. mass mkt. 4.99 o.s.i (*0-441-09414-7*) Ace Bks.

—Castle for Rent. 1989. mass mkt. 4.99 o.s.i (*0-441-09406-6*) Ace Bks.

—Castle for Rent. 2002. 200p. per. 14.95 (*0-7592-3204-0*) ereads.com.

—Castle Kidnapped. 1989. mass mkt. 4.99 o.s.i (*0-441-09408-2*) Ace Bks.

—Castle Kidnapped. 2002. 220p. per. 15.95 (*0-7592-3216-4*) ereads.com.

—Castle Murders. 1991. mass mkt. 4.99 o.s.i (*0-441-09273-X*) Ace Bks.

—Castle Perilous. 1988. mass mkt. 4.99 o.s.i (*0-441-09418-X*) Ace Bks.

—Castle Perilous. 1999. 212p. per. 15.95 (*0-7592-3198-2*) ereads.com.

—Castle Spellbound. 1992. 240p. (Orig.). mass mkt. 4.99 o.s.i (*0-441-09407-4*) Ace Bks.

—Castle War. 1990. mass mkt. 4.99 o.s.i (*0-441-09270-5*) Ace Bks.

—Castle War. 2002. 240p. per. 15.95 (*0-7592-3222-9*) ereads.com.

**CASTLE ROCK (ME.: IMAGINARY PLACE)—FICTION**

King, Stephen. Needful Things. l.t. ed. 1992. (General Ser.). 1044p. pap. 19.95 o.p. (*0-8161-5477-5*); lib. bdg. 25.95 o.p. (*0-8161-5476-7*) Gale Group. (Macmillan Reference USA).

—Needful Things. abr. unabr. ed. Pt. 1. 1991. 704p. 29.95 o.p. incl. audio (*0-453-00759-7*, Penguin Bks.); Pt. 2. 1991. 704p. 29.95 o.p. incl. audio (*0-453-00760-0*, Penguin Bks.); Pt. 2. audio 29.95 o.p.; Pt. 3. 1991. audio 29.95 o.p. (*0-453-00761-9*); Pt. 3. audio 29.95 o.p. HighBridge Co.

—Needful Things. 752p. 1993. mass mkt. 6.99 o.p. (*0-451-17859-9*); 1992. mass mkt. 7.99 (*0-451-17281-7*) NAL. (Signet Bks.).

—Needful Things. abr. unabr. ed. 1993. 49.95 incl. audio (*0-453-00859-3*) Penguin/HighBridge.

—Needful Things. 1992. 14.04 (*0-606-01485-3*) Turtleback Bks.

—Needful Things. 1991. 704p. text 35.00 (*0-670-83953-1*, Penguin Bks.) Viking Penguin.

**CATSKILL MOUNTAINS REGION (N.Y.)—FICTION**

Goodman, Carol. The Seduction of Water. 2003. 368p. 23.95 (*0-345-45090-6*, Ballantine Bks.) Ballantine Bks.

—The Seduction of Water. l.t. ed. 2003. 28.95 (*1-58724-421-7*, Wheeler Publishing, Inc.) Gale Group.

Hanyen, Jim. All the Way Home. 1995. 230p. 10.75 o.p. (*1-880664-06-2*) E. M. Productions.

Hayes, John R. Catskill. 2001. (Illus.). 272p. 23.95 (*0-312-28153-6*, Saint Martin's Minotaur) St. Martin's Pr.

Irving, Washington. The Sketch Book of Geoffrey Crayon, Vol. 19. 1973. (Works of Washington Irving Ser.). 532 p. (*0-404-03529-9*) AMS Pr., Inc.

—The Sketch Book of Geoffrey Crayon. reprint ed. lib. bdg. 48.00 (*0-7426-1034-9*); 2001. (Illus.). pap. text 28.00 (*0-7426-6034-6*) Classic Bks.

—The Sketch Book of Geoffrey Crayon. 1961. (Signet Classics). 384p. mass mkt. 5.95 (*0-451-52495-0*); mass mkt. 0.60 o.p. (*0-451-50101-2*); mass mkt. 0.75 o.p. (*0-451-50282-5*); mass mkt. 0.95 o.p. (*0-451-50599-9*); mass mkt. 1.50 o.p. (*0-451-51094-1*); mass mkt. 1.75 o.p. (*0-451-51263-4*); mass mkt. 2.95 o.p. (*0-451-51614-1*) NAL. (Signet Classics).

—The Sketch Book of Geoffrey Crayon. 1992. (BCL1-PS American Literature Ser.). 487p. reprint ed. lib. bdg. 99.00 (*0-7812-6755-2*) Reprint Services Corp.

—The Sketch Book of Geoffrey Crayon. 1981. (Illus.). 512p. reprint ed. 23.95 (*0-912882-47-6*) Sleepy Hollow Pr.

—The Sketch Book of Geoffrey Crayon. Bradbury, Malcolm & Bigsby, Christopher, eds. 1993. 400p. pap. 6.95 (*0-460-87151-X*, Everyman's Classic Library in Paperback) Tuttle Publishing.

—The Sketch Book of Geoffrey Crayon. 1988. 368p. pap. 7.95 o.p. (*0-14-039032-4*, Penguin Classics) Viking Penguin.

—The Sketch Book of Geoffrey Crayon. 24.95 o.p. (*0-8488-0539-9*); 1998. lib. bdg. 26.95 (*1-56723-063-6*) Yestermorrow, Inc.

Irving, Washington, et al. The Sketch Book of Geoffrey Crayon. 1981. xii, 465p. (*0-912882-51-4*) Sleepy Hollow Pr.

Pollack, Eileen. Paradise, New York: A Novel. 2000. 288p. 49.50 (*1-56639-657-3*); pap. 17.95 (*1-56639-789-8*) Temple Univ. Pr.

Van Valkenburgh, Norman J. & Blessing, Airilee Ellyn. Murder in the Shawangunks & the Class of '68: A Ward Eastman Mystery. 1999. 166p. pap. 12.50 (*1-930098-01-4*) Purple Mountain Pr., Ltd.

**CEDAR RAPIDS (IOWA)—FICTION**

Gorman, Ed. Harlot's Moon. 256p. 1999. mass mkt. 5.99 (*0-312-96771-3*, St. Martin's Paperbacks); 1998. 21.95 o.p. (*0-312-18108-6*, Saint Martin's Minotaur) St. Martin's Pr.

**CELYDONN (IMAGINARY PLACE)—FICTION**

Edgerton, Teresa. The Castle of the Silver Wheel. 1993. 288p. (Orig.). mass mkt. 4.99 o.s.i (*0-441-09275-6*) Ace Bks.

—Child of Saturn. 1990. mass mkt. 3.95 o.s.i (*0-441-10401-0*); 1989. mass mkt. 3.50 o.s.i (*0-441-10400-2*) Ace Bks.

—The Grail & the Ring. 1994. 320p. (Orig.). mass mkt. 4.99 o.s.i (*0-441-30157-6*) Ace Bks.

—The Moon & The Thorn. 1995. 336p. (Orig.). mass mkt. 5.99 o.s.i (*0-441-00188-2*) Ace Bks.

—The Moon in Hiding. 1989. mass mkt. 3.50 o.s.i (*0-441-54215-8*) Ace Bks.

—The Work of the Sun. 1990. mass mkt. 3.95 o.s.i (*0-441-90911-6*) Ace Bks.

**CENOTAPH ROAD (IMAGINARY PLACE)—FICTION**

Vardeman, Robert E. Cenotaph Road. 1984. mass mkt. 2.75 o.s.i (*0-441-09846-0*); 1983. mass mkt. 2.75 o.s.i (*0-441-09845-2*) Ace Bks.

—Fire & Fog. 1984. (Cenotaph Road Ser.: No. 5). 224p. mass mkt. 2.75 o.s.i (*0-441-23824-6*) Ace Bks.

—Pillar of Night. 1984. (Cenotaph Road Ser.: No. 6). mass mkt. 2.75 o.s.i (*0-441-66397-4*) Ace Bks.

—Sorcerers Skull. 1984. 224p. mass mkt. 2.75 o.s.i (*0-441-77542-X*) Ace Bks.

—World of Mazes. 1984. (Cenotaph Road Ser.: No. 3). 224p. mass mkt. 2.75 o.s.i (*0-441-91031-9*) Ace Bks.

**CENTRAL AMERICA—FICTION**

Ambler, Eric. Doctor Frigo. 1982. pap. 7.95 o.p. (*0-689-70617-0*, 276, Scribner Paper Fiction) Simon & Schuster.

Barbas-Rhoden, Laura. Writing Women in Central America: Gender & the Fictionalization of History. 2003. (Research in International Studies : Vol. 41). (C). pap. text 23.00 (*0-89680-233-7*, Ohio Univ. Ctr. for International Studies) Ohio Univ. Pr.

Belli, Gioconda. The Inhabited Woman. 1995. 416p. pap. 19.99 o.p. (*0-446-67206-8*) Warner Bks., Inc.

—The Inhabited Woman: A Novel. March, Kathleen N., tr. from SPA. 1994. 430p. 22.95 (*1-880684-17-9*) Curbstone Pr.

Benitez, Sandra. Bitter Grounds. 1998. pap. (*0-312-20863-4*); 464p. pap. 15.00 (*0-312-19541-9*) Picador.

—The Weight of All Things. 2002. (Illus.). 256p. pap. 13.95 (*0-7868-8703-6*); 2001. 241p. 22.95 (*0-7868-6399-4*) Hyperion Pr.

Boswell, Robert. Geography of Desire. 1990. 2.99 o.p. (*0-517-05994-0*) Random Hse. Value Publishing.

—The Geography of Desire. 1994. 320p. reprint ed. pap. 12.00 o.p. (*0-06-097587-3*, Perennial) HarperTrade.

Castañeda, Omar S. Cunuman. 1987. 228p. 14.95 o.p. (*0-910923-43-4*) Pineapple Pr., Inc.

Coulter, Catherine. The Edge. 2000. 352p. mass mkt. 7.99 (*0-515-12860-0*, Jove) Berkley Publishing Group.

—The Edge. unabr. ed. 1999. audio 39.95 (*1-56740-430-8*, 1708, Brilliance Audio Unabridged); audio 73.25 (*1-56740-653-X*, 1709, Unabridged Library Editions) Brilliance Audio.

—The Edge, Set. unabr. ed. 1999. audio 39.95 Highsmith Inc.

—The Edge. 1999. 388p. 22.95 o.p. (*0-399-14506-0*); 24.95 o.p. (*0-399-14519-2*, Putnam Berkley Audio) Penguin Group (USA) Inc.

—The Edge. l.t. ed. 1999. (Basic Ser.). 493p. 31.95 o.p. (*0-7862-2240-9*) Thorndike Pr.

Cowley, Joseph G. Dust Be My Destiny. 2001. 220p. pap. 13.95 (*0-87714-219-X*) Denlingers Pubs., Ltd.

Davis, Patti. Deadfall. 1991. 4.99 o.p. (*0-517-07155-X*) Random Hse. Value Publishing.

Didion, Joan. A Book of Common Prayer. 1995. 272p. pap. 13.00 (*0-679-75486-5*, Vintage) Knopf Publishing Group.

—A Book of Common Prayer. 1986. mass mkt. 4.50 o.s.i (*0-671-63808-4*, Pocket); 1983. mass mkt. 3.50 o.s.i (*0-671-47098-1*, Pocket); 1983. 288p. mass mkt. 3.95 o.s.i (*0-671-49589-5*, Pocket); 1977. 8.95 o.p. (*0-671-22491-3*, Simon & Schuster) Simon & Schuster.

Faust, Ron. In the Forest of the Night. 1993. 288p. 18.95 o.p. (*0-312-85165-0*, Tor Bks.) Doherty, Tom Assocs., LLC.

A Flag for Sunrise. audio American Audio Prose Library, Inc.

Freedman, J. F. Fallen Idols. 2003. 432p. 19.95 (*0-446-53189-8*) Warner Bks., Inc.

Hall, James W. Off the Chart. 2003. (Illus.). audio compact disk 30.00 (*1-55927-825-0*); pap. 25.95 incl. audio (*1-55927-883-8*) Audio Renaissance.

—Off the Chart. 2003. 8p. 69.95 (*0-7927-2890-4*); 10p. pap. 94.95 (*0-7927-2891-2*) BBC Audiobooks America.

—Off the Chart. E-Book 20.95 (*0-312-71013-5*); 2003. 352p. 24.95 (*0-312-27178-6*, Saint Martin's Minotaur) St. Martin's Pr.

—Off the Chart. l.t. ed. 2003. 586p. 30.95 (*0-7862-5796-2*, Large Print Pr.) Thorndike Pr.

Hoover, Thomas. Life Blood. 2000. 352p. mass mkt. 6.99 o.s.i (*0-7860-1313-3*, Pinnacle Bks.) Kensington Publishing Corp.

Hornig, Doug. Stinger. 1990. 400p. mass mkt. 4.95 o.p. (*0-451-16691-4*, Signet Bks.) NAL.

Jacobs, Mark. Cast of Spaniards. 1994. 208p. pap. 12.95 (*1-883689-18-X*); lib. bdg. 33.95 (*1-883689-19-8*) Talisman Hse., Pubs.

Lundin, Steve. A Ruin of Feathers. 1992. pap. text (*0-920661-23-8*) TSAR Pubns.

Macomber, Debbie. Sooner or Later. l.t. ed. 2000. (Wheeler Softcover Ser.). 346p. pap. 25.95 (*1-56895-141-8*, Wheeler Publishing, Inc.) Gale Group.

—Sooner or Later. 1998. 368p. mass mkt. 3.99 o.p. (*0-06-104475-X*) HarperCollins Pubs.

—Sooner or Later. 1996. 368p. mass mkt. 6.99 (*0-06-108345-3*, HarperTorch) Morrow/Avon.

McClelland, Michael. Oyster Blues. E-Book 8.95 (*1-58929-165-4*) PocketPCpr.

—Oyster Blues. 2002. 288p. 19.95 (*0-7434-5259-3*) ibooks, Inc.

Moeri, Louise. The Forty-Third War. 1989. 208p. (J). (gr. 5-9). 13.95 o.p. (*0-395-50215-2*) Houghton Mifflin Co.

Newton, C. J. Costa Azul. 1998. (Illus.). 190p. pap. 14.50 (*0-88739-170-2*) Creative Arts Bk. Co.

—Costa Azul. E-Book 9.95 (*0-942871-26-X*) Serendipity Systems.

O'Donnell, Peter. Last Day in Limbo. 2003. (Modesty Blaise Series Ser.). 256p. pap. 14.95 (*0-285-63675-8*) Souvenir Pr. Ltd. GBR. *Dist:* Independent Pubs. Group.

Omang, Joanne. Incident at Akabal. 1992. 19.95 o.p. (*0-395-58840-5*) Houghton Mifflin Co.

Paschke, Barbara & Volpendesta, David, eds. Clamor of Innocence: Central American Short Stories. 1988. 224p. (Orig.). pap. 9.95 o.p. (*0-87286-227-5*) City Lights Bks.

Peters, Daniel. Tikal: A Novel about the Maya. 1983. 422p. 16.95 o.s.i (*0-394-53278-3*) Random Hse., Inc.

Portis, Charles. The Dog of the South. 1999. 246p. 15.95 (*0-87951-931-2*) Overlook Pr., The.

Poulson, Clair. Samuel: Gadianton's Foe. 1994. pap. 9.95 o.p. (*1-55503-658-9*, 01111574) Covenant Communications, Inc.

—Samuel, Gadianton's Foe. audio 11.98 (*1-55503-662-7*, 0700967) Covenant Communications, Inc.

Smith, Michael. Sanctuary Stories. 1996. 242p. (Orig.). pap. 16.00 (*0-927534-50-9*) Bilingual Pr./Editorial Bilingue.

Stone, Robert. A Flag for Sunrise. 1987. mass mkt. 4.95 o.s.i (*0-345-34249-6*); 1982. mass mkt. 3.95 o.p. (*0-345-30650-3*) Ballantine Bks.

—A Flag for Sunrise. 1992. 448p. pap. 15.95 (*0-679-73762-6*, Vintage) Knopf Publishing Group.

Weinman, Irving. Stealing Home: A Novel. 2003. 224p. pap. 14.95 (*1-880284-72-3*) Daniel, John & Co., Pubs.

Zietlow, E. R. Matada: Seeds of Terror. (*1-894694-11-2*) Granville Island Publishing.

**CHAMBERLAIN (ME.: IMAGINARY PLACE)—FICTION**

King, Stephen. Carrie. 1990. 192p. 32.50 (*0-385-08695-4*) Doubleday Publishing.

—Carrie. 1991. (Stephen King Collectors Editions Ser.). 176p. pap. 12.95 o.p. (*0-452-26719-6*, Plume) Dutton/Plume.

—Carrie. 1992. (SPA.). 288p. pap. 3.95 (*1-56780-057-2*) La Costa Pr., Inc.

—Carrie. 1975. mass mkt. 3.95 o.p. (*0-451-15071-6*); 256p. reprint ed. mass mkt. 7.99 o.s.i (*0-451-15744-3*) NAL. (Signet Bks.).

—Carrie. 1999. (SPA., Illus.). 288p. (*84-01-49966-6*) Plaza & Janés Editories, S.A.

—Carrie. (SPA.). 288p. 12.95 (*84-01-49888-0*) Plaza & Janés Editories, S.A. ESP. *Dist:* Distribooks, Inc.

—Carrie. 2002. 272p. pap. 7.99 (*0-671-03972-5*); 2000. 208p. pap. 12.95 (*0-671-03973-3*) Simon & Schuster. (Pocket).

—Carrie. 1975. 14.04 (*0-606-00823-3*) Turtleback Bks.

**CHARLESTON (S.C.)—FICTION**

Brouwer, Sigmund. Crown of Thorns. 2002. (Moving Fiction Ser.). 384p. 17.97 (*0-8423-3038-0*); xii, 365p. pap. 12.99 (*0-8423-6581-8*) Tyndale Hse. Pubs.

Chesnut, Mary Boykin Miller. Two Novels by Mary Chesnut. Muhlenfeld, Elisabeth, ed. & intro. by. 2002. (Publications of the Southern Texts Society). xx, 216p. 29.95 (*0-8139-2058-2*) Univ. Pr. of Virginia.

Durban, Pam. So Far Back. 272p. 2001. pap. 13.00 (*0-312-28347-4*); 2000. 23.00 o.s.i (*0-312-26869-6*) Picador.

—So Far Back. E-Book 23.00 (*0-312-27168-9*) St. Martin's Pr.

Farrow, David A. The Root of All Evil. 2002. E-Book 20.00 o.p. (*0-941711-54-4*); 1997. 350p. 23.95 (*0-941711-36-6*) Wyrick & Co.

Frank, Dorothea Benton. Sullivan's Island. 2004. 464p. pap. 13.95 (*0-425-19394-2*); 2000. 416p. mass mkt. 7.99 (*0-515-12722-1*, Jove) Berkley Publishing Group.

—Sullivan's Island. l.t. ed. 2000. (Core Ser.). 567p. 31.95 (*0-7838-9078-8*, Macmillan Reference USA) Gale Group.

—Sullivan's Island. l.t. ed. 2001. 567p. pap. 29.95 (*0-7838-9079-6*) Thorndike Pr.

Heins, Henry C., Jr. Dr. Thomas Chalmers' Secret Diary. 1998. 213p. 20.00 (*1-887301-03-8*) Palmetto Bookworks.

Humphreys, Josephine. The Fireman's Fair. 1992. 272p. pap. 13.00 (*0-14-016838-9*, Penguin Bks.) Penguin Group (USA) Inc.

—The Fireman's Fair. 1991. 272p. 19.95 o.p. (*0-670-83907-8*) Viking Penguin.

Lacy, Al & Lacy, JoAnna. Ransom of Love. 2003. (Mail Order Bride Ser.: Vol. 5). 336p. pap. 10.99 (*1-57673-609-1*, Multnomah Bks.) Multnomah Pubs., Inc.

Michaels, Fern. Finders Keepers. l.t. ed. 1998. 27.95 (*1-56895-693-2*, Wheeler Publishing, Inc.) Gale Group.

—Finders Keepers. 2002. 432p. mass mkt. 7.50 (*0-8217-7364-X*); 1999. 432p. mass mkt. 6.99 o.s.i (*0-8217-6307-5*, Zebra Bks.); 1998. 352p. 24.00 o.s.i (*1-57566-323-6*, Kensington Bks.) Kensington Publishing Corp.

Morris, Lynn & Morris, Gilbert. Toward the Sunrising. 1996. (Cheney Duvall, M. D. Ser.: Vol. 4). 368p. pap. 11.99 (*1-55661-425-X*) Bethany Hse. Pubs.

—Toward the Sunrising. 1998. (Cheney Duvall, M. D. Ser.: Vol. 4). 362p. 23.95 (*0-7862-1436-8*, Five Star) Gale Group.

Pinckney, Josephine. Three O'Clock Dinner. 2001. (Southern Classics Ser.). 320p. pap. text 21.95 (*1-57003-423-0*) Univ. of South Carolina Pr.

—Three O'Clock Dinner. 1945. 2.50 o.p. (*0-670-70879-8*) Viking Penguin.

Robards, Karen. To Trust a Stranger. 2003. (Illus.). 448p. mass mkt. 7.99 (*0-671-78660-1*, Pocket Star); 2001. 352p. 25.00 (*0-671-78653-9*, Atria); 2001. E-Book 25.00 (*0-7434-2456-5*, Atria); 2002. 512p. pap. 25.00 (*0-7434-6628-4*, Pocket) Simon & Schuster.

Sprinkle, Patricia H. Murder in the Charleston Manner. 1993. (Mystery Ser.). per. (*0-373-26119-5*, 1-26119-7, Harlequin Bks.) Harlequin Enterprises, Ltd.

Trollope, Joanna. Girl from the South. 2003. 352p. pap. 14.00 (*0-425-19350-0*) Berkley Publishing Group.

—Girl from the South. 2002. 304p. 24.95 (*0-670-03097-X*, Viking) Viking Penguin.

Williams, Philip Lee. The True & Authentic History of Jenny Dorset. 1997. 512p. 24.95 (*1-56352-365-5*) Longstreet Pr., Inc.

Williamson, Denise. The Dark Sun Rises: A Novel. 1999. (Roots of Faith Ser.: Bk. 1). 448p. pap. 12.99 (*1-55661-882-4*) Bethany Hse. Pubs.

Woodiwiss, Kathleen E. The Elusive Flame. abr. ed. 1999. audio 7.99 o.s.i (*1-56740-316-6*, 1866, Paperback Nova Audio Bks.); 1998. audio 39.95 (*1-56740-407-3*, 1492, Brilliance Audio Unabridged); 1998. 16p. audio 89.25 (*1-56740-605-X*, 1632, Unabridged Library Editions) Brilliance Audio.

—The Elusive Flame. l.t. ed. 1998. (Large Print Book Ser.). 27.95 o.p. (*1-56895-692-4*, Wheeler Publishing, Inc.) Gale Group.

—The Elusive Flame. 1999. 496p. mass mkt. 7.50 (*0-380-80786-6*); 1998. 432p. pap. 14.00 o.p. (*0-380-76655-8*) Morrow/Avon. (Avon Bks.).

**CHARLOTTE (N.C.)—FICTION**

Jaffe, Jody. Chestnut Mare, Beware. 1997. mass mkt. 5.99 o.s.i (*0-8041-1552-4*, Ivy Bks.); 1996. 288p. 21.00 o.s.i (*0-449-90998-0*, Fawcett) Ballantine Bks.

—Chestnut Mare, Beware. unabr. collector's ed. 1997. audio 64.00 (*0-7366-3599-8*, 4250) Books on Tape, Inc.

—Horse of a Different Killer. 1996. mass mkt. 5.99 o.s.i (*0-8041-1472-2*, Ivy Bks.); 1995. 288p. 21.00 o.s.i (*0-449-90997-2*) Ballantine Bks.

—Horse of a Different Killer. unabr. collector's ed. 1997. audio 48.00 (*0-913369-53-5*, 4265) Books on Tape, Inc.

—In Colt Blood. 1999. mass mkt. 5.99 o.s.i (*0-8041-1711-X*, Ivy Bks.) Ballantine Bks.

—In Colt Blood. collector's ed. 1999. audio 56.00 (*0-7366-4787-2*, 5134) Books on Tape, Inc.

Kee, John P. Not Guilty: The Script. 2002. (Illus.). 139p. pap. 11.99 (*0-8024-1517-2*) Moody Pr.

Leebron, Fred. Six Figures. 2001. (Harvest Book Ser.). 240p. reprint ed. pap. 13.00 (*0-15-601064-X*, Harvest Bks.) Harcourt Trade Pubs.

Myers, Tamar. Baroque & Desperate. 1999. (Den of Antiquity Ser.). 256p. mass mkt. 6.99 (*0-380-80225-2*, Avon Bks.) Morrow/Avon.

—Estate of Mind. 1999. 320p. mass mkt. 6.50 (*0-380-80227-9*, Avon Bks.) Morrow/Avon.

—Guilt by Association. 1996. (Den of Antiquity Ser.). 256p. mass mkt. 6.50 (*0-380-78237-5*, Avon Bks.) Morrow/Avon.

—Larceny & Old Lace. 1996. (Den of Antiquity Ser.). 224p. (Orig.). mass mkt. 6.99 (*0-380-78239-1*, Avon Bks.) Morrow/Avon.

—Ming & I. 1997. (Den of Antiquity Ser.). 256p. mass mkt. 6.99 (*0-380-79255-9*, Avon Bks.) Morrow/Avon.

—So Faux, So Good. 1998. (Den of Antiquity Ser.). 256p. mass mkt. 6.50 (*0-380-79254-0*, Avon Bks.) Morrow/Avon.

## CHARLOTTESVILLE (VA.)—FICTION

Even, Aaron Roy. Bloodroot. 2000. 261p. 22.95 (*0-312-26561-1*) St. Martin's Pr.

Hornig, Doug. Deep Dive. l.t. ed. 1989. (General Ser.). 373p. lib. bdg. 18.95 o.p. (*0-8161-4690-X*, Macmillan Reference USA) Gale Group.

—Deep Dive. 1988. 15.45 o.p. (*0-89296-257-7*) Mysterious Pr.

—Deep Dive. 1989. mass mkt. 4.50 (*0-445-40788-3*, Mysterious Pr. Paperback Bks.) Warner Bks., Inc.

Leebron, Fred G. Six Figures. 2000. 240p. 22.00 o.s.i (*0-375-40640-9*) Knopf, Alfred A. Inc.

## CHICAGO (ILL.)—FICTION

Ade, George. Stories of Chicago. Meine, Franklin J., ed. & intro. by. 2003. (Illus.). 312p. pap. 15.95 (*0-252-07143-3*); text 29.95 (*0-252-02870-8*) Univ. of Illinois Pr.

Algren, Nelson. The Neon Wilderness: 24 Short Stories. 1988. 23.95 (*0-8488-0415-5*) Amereon, Ltd.

—The Neon Wilderness: 24 Short Stories. Simon, Dan, ed. 1997. 304p. reprint ed. pap. 10.95 (*1-888363-21-5*) Seven Stories Pr.

—Never Come Morning. 1995. 5.60 (*0-87129-597-0*, N40) Dramatic Publishing Co.

—Never Come Morning. 1987. 336p. pap. text 8.95 o.p. (*0-941423-00-X*) Four Walls Eight Windows.

—Never Come Morning. 2001. 320p. pap. 10.95 (*1-58322-279-0*) Seven Stories Pr.

Allbeury, Ted. The Stalking Angel. 208p. 1989. mass mkt. 3.95 o.s.i (*0-445-40834-0*); 1988. 17.95 (*0-89296-184-8*) Mysterious Pr.

Allen, Shirley S. Roxanna Britton. 2001. 388p. per. 16.00 (*1-884162-08-8*) Criterion Hse.

Amberg, Jay. Blackbird Singing. 2000. mass mkt. 6.99 (*0-8125-9006-6*); 1998. 302p. 23.95 (*0-312-86554-6*) Doherty, Tom Assocs., LLC. (Forge Bks.).

Anshaw, Carol. Seven Moves. 1996. 220p. tchr. ed. 21.95 o.p. (*0-395-69131-1*) Houghton Mifflin Co.

—Seven Moves. 1997. 240p. pap. 11.00 (*0-395-87756-3*, Mariner Bks.) Houghton Mifflin Co. Trade & Reference Div.

—Seven Moves. 1998. 242p. pap. o.s.i (*1-86049-436-6*) Virago Pr., Ltd. GBR. *Dist:* Little Brown & Co.

Ashby, Gil, illus. Summer Sands. 1997. (*0-7802-8035-0*) Wright Group, The.

Axelrod, Larry. The Advocate. 2000. 254p. 22.95 (*1-58182-137-9*) Cumberland Hse. Publishing.

Axelrood, Larry. Plea Bargain: A Novel. 2002. (Darcy Cole Mystery Ser.). 352p. 22.95 (*1-58182-273-1*) Cumberland Hse. Publishing.

Ayala, E. L. Will You Be Made Whole. 2000. 195p. 15.00 (*1-55630-954-6*) Brentwood Communications Group.

Baisden, Michael. God's Gift to Women: A Novel. 2003. 304p. pap. 13.00 (*0-7432-4997-6*, Touchstone) Simon & Schuster.

—God's Gift to Women: A Novel. 2003. (African American Ser.). 29.95 (*0-7862-5147-6*) Thorndike Pr.

Baker, Nikki. In the Game. 1991. (Virginia Kelly Mystery Ser.). 224p. (Orig.). pap. 9.95 (*1-56280-004-3*) Naiad Pr., Inc.

—The Lavender House Murder. 1992. (Virginia Kelly Mystery Ser.). 224p. pap. 9.95 o.p. (*1-56280-012-4*) Naiad Pr., Inc.

—The Long Goodbyes. 1993. (Virginia Kelly Mystery Ser.: No. 3). 208p. pap. 9.95 o.p. (*1-56280-042-6*) Naiad Pr., Inc.

—The Ultimate Exit Strategy: A Virginia Kelly Mystery. 2001. 240p. pap. 11.95 (*1-931513-03-1*) Bella Bks., Inc.

Barrett, Neal, Jr. Pink Vodka Blues. 1997. 304p. mass mkt. 5.99 o.s.i (*1-57566-237-X*) Kensington Publishing Corp.

—Pink Vodka Blues. 1992. 320p. 18.95 (*0-312-07766-1*, Saint Martin's Minotaur) St. Martin's Pr.

Barrow, Adam. Blind Spot. 1997. 304p. 22.95 o.p. (*0-525-94186-X*) Dutton/Plume.

—Blind Spot. 1998. 416p. mass mkt. 5.99 o.s.i (*0-451-19187-0*, Signet Bks.) NAL.

Bassingthwaite, Don. If Whispers Call. 2000. (Dark Matter Ser.). 288p. mass mkt. 6.99 o.s.i (*0-7869-1679-6*) Wizards of the Coast.

Bell, James Scott. The Nephilim Seed: A Novel. 2001. 375p. pap. 12.99 (*0-8054-2438-5*) Broadman & Holman Pubs.

Bellow, Saul. The Dean's December. 1982. (General Ser.). lib. bdg. 16.95 o.p. (*0-8161-3404-9*, Macmillan Reference USA) Gale Group.

—The Dean's December. 1982. 320p. 14.95 o.p. (*0-06-014849-7*) HarperTrade.

—The Dean's December. 1985. 346p. mass mkt. 4.50 (*0-671-60254-3*); 1983. mass mkt. 3.95 o.s.i (*0-671-46476-0*) Simon & Schuster. (Pocket).

—The Dean's December. 1998. (Great Books of the 20th Century Ser.). 320p. 13.95 (*0-14-018913-0*, Penguin Classics) Viking Penguin.

Beverly, Elizabeth. How to Trap a Tycoon. 2000. 384p. mass mkt. 5.99 (*0-380-81048-4*, Avon Bks.) Morrow/Avon.

Black, Michael A. A Killing Frost. 2003. 270p. pap. 13.95 (*1-4104-0131-6*, Five Star Trade); 2002. 287p. 24.95 (*0-7862-4309-0*, Five Star) Gale Group.

Bland, Eleanor Taylor. Fatal Remains. 2003. 288p. 23.95 (*0-312-30097-2*, Saint Martin's Minotaur) St. Martin's Pr.

—Whispers in the Dark. l.t. ed. 2002. 28.95 o.p. (*1-58724-187-0*, Wheeler Publishing, Inc.) Gale Group.

—Whispers in the Dark. mass mkt. (*0-312-97990-8*, St. Martin's Paperbacks); 2001. 244p. 23.95 (*0-312-20379-9*, Saint Martin's Minotaur) St. Martin's Pr.

—Windy City Dying: A Marti MacAlister Mystery. 320p. 2003. pap. 13.95 (*0-312-32048-5*, Saint Martin's Griffin); 2002. 24.95 (*0-312-30098-0*, Saint Martin's Minotaur) St. Martin's Pr.

Bonansinga, Jay. The Killer's Game. Set. abr. ed. 1997. 24.95 o.p. (*0-7871-1428-6*, 694908) NewStar Media, Inc.

Bonansinga, Jay R. The Killer's Game. 1997. 300p. 22.50 o.p. (*0-684-82513-9*, Simon & Schuster) Simon & Schuster.

Brand, Max. Seven Faces. l.t. ed. 1999. 271p. (*0-7540-3552-2*) BBC Audiobooks America.

—Seven Faces. l.t. ed. 1999. (Nightingale Ser.). 280p. pap. 21.95 (*0-7838-0360-5*) Thorndike Pr.

—Seven Faces. 1998. 180p. text 40.00 (*0-8032-1281-X*) Univ. of Nebraska Pr.

Branton, Matthew. The House of Whacks. 1999. 256p. pap. 13.95 (*1-58234-024-2*) Bloomsbury Publishing.

Brod, D. C. Masquerade in Blue. 1991. 208p. 19.95 (*0-8027-5792-8*) Walker & Co.

—Paid in Full. 2000. (Five Star Mystery Ser.). 280p. 21.95 (*0-7862-2673-0*, Five Star) Gale Group.

Brown, Carrie. The Hatbox Baby. 2000. 333p. tchr. ed. 22.95 (*1-56512-299-2*) Algonquin Bks. of Chapel Hill.

—The Hatbox Baby. unabr. ed. 2003. audio compact disk 79.95 (*0-7927-2844-0*, SLD 319); 2001. audio 69.95 (*0-7927-2430-5*, CSL 319) BBC Audiobooks America. (Chivers Sound Library).

—The Hatbox Baby. 2002. 352p. pap. 14.00 (*0-425-18465-X*) Berkley Publishing Group.

—The Hatbox Baby. l.t. ed. 2000. (Compass Press Large Print Book Ser.). 410p. 26.95 (*1-56895-962-1*, Wheeler Publishing, Inc.) Gale Group.

Brown, Fredric. Fabulous Clipjoint. 1986. 192p. pap. 8.95 o.p. (*0-87923-597-7*) Godine, David R. Pub.

—Hunter & Hunted Pt. One: The Ed & Am Hunter Novels. 2002. 640p. 29.99 (*0-9718185-0-9*) Stewart Masters Publishing, Ltd.

Browne, Howard. Pork City. 1988. 272p. 16.95 o.p. (*0-312-01493-7*) St. Martin's Pr.

Buckman, Daniel. Water in Darkness. 2001. 193p. pap. 21.00 (*1-888451-19-X*) Akashic Bks.

Cameron, Julia. The Dark Room. 1998. 448p. 25.00 o.p. (*0-7867-0564-7*, Carroll & Graf Pubs.) Avalon Publishing Group.

Campbell, Robert. Boneyards. Chelius, Jane, ed. 304p. 1992. 21.00 o.p. (*0-671-70319-6*, Atria); 1993. reprint ed. mass mkt. 5.50 (*0-671-70320-X*, Pocket) Simon & Schuster.

—The Cat's Meow. (Jimmy Flannery Mystery Ser.). 1990. 208p. mass mkt. 4.50 o.p. (*0-451-16431-8*, Signet Bks.); 1988. 240p. 16.95 o.p. (*0-453-00615-9*) NAL.

—A Flannery Trilogy: Featuring The Junkyard Dog, 600-Pound Gorilla & Hip-Deep in Alligators. rev. ed. 1999. (Flannery Trilogies Ser.: Vol. 1). 384p. pap. 24.95 (*1-58444-073-2*) Disc-Us Bks., Inc.

—A Flannery Trilogy: Featuring the Junkyard Dog, 600-Pound Gorilla & Hip-Deep in Alligators, I. 2003. (Jimmy Flannery Mystery Ser.). E-Book 16.95 incl. cd-rom (*1-58444-084-8*) Disc-Us Bks., Inc.

—The Gift Horse's Mouth. Chelius, Jane, ed. 208p. 1990. 17.95 o.p. (*0-671-67586-9*, Atria); 1991. reprint ed. mass mkt. 4.99 (*0-671-74340-6*, Pocket) Simon & Schuster.

—Hip Deep in Alligators. 1988. 208p. mass mkt. 3.95 o.p. (*0-451-40096-8*, Onyx); 1987. 16.95 o.p. (*0-453-00577-2*) NAL.

—In a Pig's Eye. Chelius, Jane, ed. 224p. 1991. 19.00 (*0-671-70327-7*, Atria); 1992. reprint ed. mass mkt. 4.99 (*0-671-70328-5*, Pocket) Simon & Schuster.

—The Junkyard Dog. 2000. E-Book 14.50 o.p. incl. cd-rom (*1-58444-047-3*) Disc-Us Bks., Inc.

—The Junkyard Dog. 1986. mass mkt. 2.95 o.p. (*0-451-14396-5*); 192p. mass mkt. 3.99 o.s.i (*0-451-15899-7*) NAL. (Signet Bks.).

—The Junkyard Dog. unabr. ed. 1991. (Jimmy Flannery Mystery Ser.: Vol. 1). audio 35.00 (*1-55690-277-8*, 91231E7) Recorded Bks., LLC.

—The Lion's Share. 1996. 82p. 21.95 o.s.i (*0-89296-609-2*) Mysterious Pr.

—The Lion's Share. 1997. 224p. mass mkt. 5.99 o.s.i (*0-446-40464-0*) Warner Bks., Inc.

—Nibbled to Death by Ducks. unabr. ed. 1992. (Jimmy Flannery Mystery Ser.: Vol. 6). audio 44.00 (*1-55690-703-6*, 92105E7) Recorded Bks., LLC.

—Nibbled to Death by Ducks. 1989. 208p. 17.95 o.p. (*0-671-67585-0*, Atria) Simon & Schuster.

—Nibbled to Death by Ducks. Chelius, Jane, ed. 1990. 288p. reprint ed. mass mkt. 4.99 (*0-671-67583-4*, Pocket) Simon & Schuster.

—Pigeon Pie. 1998. (Jimmy Flannery Mystery Ser.: Vol. 27). 240p. 22.00 o.s.i (*0-89296-665-3*) Mysterious Pr.

—Pigeon Pie. l.t. ed. 1999. (Cloak & Dagger Ser.). 301p. 29.95 (*0-7862-1528-3*) Thorndike Pr.

—Sauce for the Goose. 1995. 240p. 18.95 o.s.i (*0-89296-608-4*) Mysterious Pr.

—Sauce for the Goose. 1996. 208p. mass mkt. 5.99 o.p. (*0-446-40463-2*) Warner Bks., Inc.

—Thinning the Turkey Herd. 1989. mass mkt. 3.50 o.p. (*0-451-15920-9*, Signet Bks.); 1988. 16.95 o.p. (*0-453-00583-7*) NAL.

—600-Pound Gorilla. 1987. 240p. mass mkt. 3.95 o.p. (*0-451-15390-1*, Signet Bks.) NAL.

—The 600-Pound Gorilla. unabr. ed. 1991. (Jimmy Flannery Mystery Ser.: Vol. 2). audio 35.00 (*1-55690-582-3*, 91307E7) Recorded Bks., LLC.

Cappetta, Gary Michael. Fall for the Dream: A Script of Wrestling Fiction. 2000. 168p. (Orig.). pap. 14.95 (*0-9703991-5-4*) Little Bro' Ltd.

Castillo, Ana. Peel My Love Like an Onion. 1999. 240p. 23.95 o.s.i (*0-385-49676-1*) Doubleday Publishing.

—Peel My Love Like an Onion: A Novel. 2000. 240p. reprint ed. pap. 12.00 (*0-385-49677-X*) Doubleday Publishing.

Castillo, Linda. The Shadow Side. 2003. 384p. mass mkt. 5.99 (*0-425-19102-8*) Berkley Publishing Group.

Chernoff, Maxine. A Boy in Winter. 1999. 256p. 22.00 o.s.i (*0-609-60522-4*) Crown Publishing Group.

—Signs of Devotion: Stories. 1993. 192p. 19.00 o.s.i (*0-671-79812-X*, Simon & Schuster) Simon & Schuster.

Child, Lee. Die Trying. 1999. 448p. reprint ed. mass mkt. 7.99 (*0-515-12502-4*, Jove) Berkley Publishing Group.

—Die Trying. abr. ed. 1999. audio 7.99 (*1-56740-296-8*, 1855, Paperback Nova Audio Bks.); 1998. audio 28.95 (*1-56100-791-9*, 14, Bookcassette); 1998. audio 89.25 (*1-56740-570-3*, 864, Unabridged Library Editions); Set. 1998. audio 17.95 o.p. (*1-56740-766-8*, 445, Nova Audio Bks.) Brilliance Audio.

—Die Trying. 1998. 384p. 23.95 o.s.i (*0-399-14379-3*, G. P. Putnam's Sons) Penguin Group (USA) Inc.

Churchill, Jill. Class Menagerie. 1999. (Jane Jeffry Mystery Ser.). 224p. mass mkt. 6.99 (*0-380-77380-5*, Avon Bks.) Morrow/Avon.

—Farewell to Yarns. 1991. (Jane Jeffry Mystery Ser.). 256p. mass mkt. 6.99 (*0-380-76399-0*, Avon Bks.) Morrow/Avon.

—Fear of Frying. (Jane Jeffry Mystery Ser.). 1998. 256p. mass mkt. 6.99 (*0-380-78707-5*); 1997. 224p. pap. 22.00 (*0-380-97324-3*) Morrow/Avon. (Avon Bks.).

—From Here to Paternity. 1995. (Jane Jeffry Mystery Ser.). 256p. (Orig.). mass mkt. 6.99 (*0-380-77715-0*, Avon Bks.) Morrow/Avon.

—Grime & Punishment. 1989. 208p. (Orig.). mass mkt. 3.50 o.s.i (*0-553-27646-8*) Bantam Bks.

—Grime & Punishment. 1992. (Jane Jeffry Mystery Ser.). 256p. (Orig.). mass mkt. 6.99 (*0-380-76400-8*, Avon Bks.) Morrow/Avon.

—A Groom with a View: A Jane Jeffry Mystery. (Jane Jeffry Mystery Ser.). 2000. 288p. mass mkt. 6.50 (*0-380-79450-0*); Bk. C. 1999. 224p. 22.00 (*0-380-97570-X*) Morrow/Avon. (Avon Bks.).

—A Groom with a View: A Jane Jeffry Mystery. l.t. ed. 2000. (Americana Ser.). 293p. 27.95 (*0-7862-2454-1*) Thorndike Pr.

—The House of Seven Mabels: A Jane Jeffry Mystery. 2002. 240p. 23.95 (*0-380-97736-2*, Morrow, William & Co.) Morrow/Avon.

—A Knife to Remember. 1999. (Jane Jeffry Mystery Ser.). 224p. mass mkt. 6.99 (*0-380-77381-3*, Avon Bks.) Morrow/Avon.

—The Merchant of Menace: A Jane Jeffry Mystery. 1999. 256p. mass mkt. 6.99 (*0-380-79449-7*); 1998. 224p. 21.00 (*0-380-97569-6*) Morrow/Avon. (Avon Bks.).

—Mulch Ado about Nothing: A Jane Jeffry Mystery. 2001. 272p. mass mkt. 6.50 (*0-380-80491-3*); 2000. 216p. 23.00 (*0-380-97735-4*, Morrow, William & Co.) Morrow/Avon.

—Quiche Before Dying. 1993. (Jane Jeffry Mystery Ser.). 192p. mass mkt. 6.99 (*0-380-76932-8*, Avon Bks.) Morrow/Avon.

—Silence of the Hams. 1996. (Jane Jeffry Mystery Ser.). 288p. mass mkt. 6.99 (*0-380-77716-9*, Avon Bks.) Morrow/Avon.

—War & Peas. (Jane Jeffry Mystery Ser.). 1997. 288p. mass mkt. 6.99 (*0-380-78706-7*); 1996. 224p. mass mkt. 20.00 (*0-380-97323-5*) Morrow/Avon. (Avon Bks.).

Cisneros, Sandra. Caramelo. unabr. ed. 2002. 112p. audio 39.95 (*0-06-051591-0*, HarperAudio) HarperTrade.

—Caramelo. 2003. (SPA.). 496p. pap. 13.95 (*1-4000-3099-4*, Vintage); 464p. pap. 13.95 (*0-679-74258-1*, Vintage); 464p. 24.00 (*1-4000-4150-3*) Knopf Publishing Group.

—Caramelo. 2002. 464p. 24.00 (*0-679-43554-9*) Knopf, Alfred A. Inc.

—Caramelo. 2002. (SPA.). 496p. 24.00 (*0-375-41509-2*) Random Hse., Inc.

—Caramelo. 2003. (Spanish Language Ser.). (SPA.). 28.95 (*0-7862-5124-7*); 30.95 (*0-7862-5138-7*) Thorndike Pr.

—La Casa en Mango Street. 2002. (SPA.). 150p. 27.95 (*0-7862-4298-1*) Thorndike Pr.

—La Casa en Mango Street. 1994. 16.00 (*0-606-19185-2*) Turtleback Bks.

—The House on Mango Street. 1989. 80p. 7.50 o.p. (*0-934770-20-4*) Arte Publico Pr.

—The House on Mango Street. 1991. (Contemporaries Ser.). 128p. pap. 9.95 (*0-679-73477-5*, RH4775, Vintage) Knopf Publishing Group.

—The House on Mango Street. 1996. (ESOL Companion Guide Ser.). 128p. pap. 13.13 (*0-07-009429-2*) McGraw-Hill Higher Education.

—The House on Mango Street. 1999. 11.95 (*1-58130-559-1*) Novel Units, Inc.

—The House on Mango Street. 1994. 160p. 24.00 (*0-679-43335-X*) Random Hse., Inc.

—The House on Mango Street. 1991. (Vintage Contemporaries Ser.). 16.00 (*0-606-05352-2*) Turtleback Bks.

Clark, Jack. Westerfield's Chain: A Mystery. 2002. 304p. 24.95 (*0-312-28960-X*, Saint Martin's Minotaur) St. Martin's Pr.

Clark, Mary Higgins, et al. Great Mysteries, Great Writers. abr. ed. 1994. audio 24.95 o.p. (*0-7871-0047-1*, 692220, Dove Audio) NewStar Media, Inc.

Clason, Clyde B. The Man from Tibet. 1998. 224p. pap. 14.00 (*0-915230-17-8*) Rue Morgue Pr.

Collins, Max Allan. Chicago Confidential. 2002. 304p. 22.95 (*0-451-20650-9*) NAL.

—Damned in Paradise. 1996. (Nathan Heller Ser.). 320p. 23.95 o.p. (*0-525-94225-4*) Dutton/Plume.

—Damned in Paradise. 1998. (Nathan Heller Ser.: Vol. 8). 320p. mass mkt. 5.99 o.s.i (*0-451-19104-8*, Signet Bks.) NAL.

—Damned in Paradise. unabr. ed. 1997. audio 70.00 (*0-7887-0855-4*, 95001E7) Recorded Bks., LLC.

—The Million Dollar Wound. 1987. 320p. reprint ed. pap. 3.95 o.p. (*0-8125-0159-4*, Tor Bks.) Doherty, Tom Assocs., LLC.

—The Million Dollar Wound. 1986. (Illus.). 400p. 16.95 o.p. (*0-312-53252-0*) St. Martin's Pr.

—The Million Dollar Wound. 2003. (Illus.). 352p. mass mkt. 6.99 (*0-7434-7463-5*) ibooks, Inc.

—Neon Mirage. 1991. 288p. mass mkt. 4.99 o.s.i (*0-553-28548-3*) Bantam Bks.

—Neon Mirage. 1988. (Illus.). 384p. 18.95 o.p. (*0-312-01484-8*, Saint Martin's Minotaur) St. Martin's Pr.

—Road to Perdition. Heifer, Andrew, ed. 1998. (Illus.). 304p. pap. 13.95 (*1-56389-449-1*) DC Comics.

—Road to Perdition. 2002. 256p. mass mkt. 6.99 (*0-451-41029-7*) Penguin Group (USA) Inc.

—Road to Perdition. (Illus.). 304p. 2002. pap. 14.00 (*0-7434-4224-5*); 1998. per. 14.00 (*0-671-00921-4*) Simon & Schuster. (Pocket).

—True Crime. 1986. 384p. reprint ed. pap. 3.95 o.p. (*0-8125-0152-7*, Tor Bks.) Doherty, Tom Assocs., LLC.

—True Crime. 1984. 15.95 o.p. (*0-312-82045-3*) St. Martin's Pr.

—True Crime. 2003. (Illus.). 368p. mass mkt. 6.99 (*0-7434-5900-8*) ibooks, Inc.

—True Detective. 1986. 384p. reprint ed. pap. 3.95 o.p. (*0-8125-0150-0*, Tor Bks.) Doherty, Tom Assocs., LLC.
—True Detective. 1983. (Illus.). 368p. 14.95 o.p. (*0-312-82051-8*) St. Martin's Pr.
Conrad, James. Making Love to the Minor Poets of Chicago. E-Book 14.95 (*0-312-27372-X*); 2001. 432p. pap. 14.95 (*0-312-27073-9*, Saint Martin's Griffin); 2000. 436p. 25.95 (*0-312-20472-8*) St. Martin's Pr.
Converse, Jane. Alias Miss Saunders, R. N. l.t. ed. 2002. 247p. 23.95 (*0-7862-4151-9*) Thorndike Pr.
—Alias Miss Saunders, R.N. l.t. ed. 1981. 266p. reprint ed. 10.95 o.p. (*0-89621-315-3*) Thorndike Pr.
Cooper, Susan Rogers. Funny As a Dead Comic. 1993. 224p. 18.95 o.p. (*0-312-09815-4*, Saint Martin's Minotaur) St. Martin's Pr.
Cormany, Michael. Lost Daughter. 1991. 224p. reprint ed. pap. 3.50 (*0-8439-3063-2*) Dorchester Publishing Co., Inc.
—Polaroid Man. 1993. 240p. reprint ed. pap. 3.99 (*0-8439-3542-1*) Dorchester Publishing Co., Inc.
—Red Winter. 1991. 224p. (Orig.). reprint ed. pap. 3.50 (*0-8439-3142-6*) Dorchester Publishing Co., Inc.
—Red Winter. 1991. (Orig.). 2.99 o.p. (*0-517-06332-8*) Random Hse. Value Publishing.
—Rich or Dead. 1991. 208p. reprint ed. pap. 3.50 (*0-8439-3186-8*) Dorchester Publishing Co., Inc.
Craft, Michael. Eye Contact. (Mark Manning Mystery Ser.). 1999. 342p. pap. 12.00 (*1-57566-425-9*); 1998. 352p. 21.95 o.s.i (*1-57566-292-2*) Kensington Publishing Corp. (Kensington Bks.).
—Flight Dreams. 1998. 256p. pap. 10.95 o.s.i (*1-57566-294-9*); 1997. (Mark Manning Mystery Ser.: Vol. 1). 224p. 19.95 o.s.i (*1-57566-174-8*) Kensington Publishing Corp. (Kensington Bks.).
Cresswell, Jasmine. The Inheritance. 2000. 408p. mass mkt. (*1-55166-511-5*, 1-66511-6, Mira Bks.) Harlequin Enterprises, Ltd.
Croft, Barbara. Moon's Crossing. 2003. 208p. pap. 12.00 (*0-618-34153-6*, Mariner Bks.) Houghton Mifflin Co. Trade & Reference Div.
—Moon's Crossing. l.t. ed. 2003. 336p. 28.95 (*0-7862-5958-2*) Thorndike Pr.
D'Amato, Barbara. Authorized Personnel Only. 2000. 352p. 24.95 (*0-312-86564-3*, Forge Bks.) Doherty, Tom Assocs., LLC.
—Good Cop, Bad Cop. 1999. 304p. mass mkt. 6.99 (*0-8125-9014-7*); 1998. 320p. 22.95 o.p. (*0-312-86562-7*) Doherty, Tom Assocs., LLC. (Forge Bks.).
—Hard Bargain: A Cat Marsala Mystery. 1999. (Cat Marsala Ser.). 288p. mass mkt. 5.99 o.s.i (*0-425-16898-0*) Berkley Publishing Group.
—Hard Bargain: A Cat Marsala Mystery. 1997. (Illus.). 288p. 21.00 o.s.i (*0-684-83353-0*, Scribner) Simon & Schuster.
—Hard Case: A Cat Marsala Mystery. 1995. 240p. mass mkt. 4.99 o.s.i (*0-425-15009-7*, Prime Crime) Berkley Publishing Group.
—Hard Case: A Cat Marsala Mystery. 1994. 288p. 20.00 o.p. (*0-684-19686-7*, Macmillan Reference USA) Gale Group.
—Hard Christmas: A Cat Marsala Mystery. 1996. 288p. mass mkt. 5.99 o.s.i (*0-425-15465-3*, Prime Crime) Berkley Publishing Group.
—Hard Christmas: A Cat Marsala Mystery. 1995. 288p. 20.00 (*0-684-19687-5*, Scribner) Simon & Schuster.
—Hard Evidence: A Cat Marsala Mystery. 2000. (Cat Marsala Mysteries Ser.). (Illus.). 255p. mass mkt. 6.50 o.s.i (*0-425-17412-3*, Prime Crime) Berkley Publishing Group.
—Hard Evidence: A Cat Marsala Mystery. l.t. ed. 2000. (Wheeler Large Print Bks.). (Illus.). 247p. pap. 23.95 (*1-56895-861-7*, Wheeler Publishing, Inc.) Gale Group.
—Hard Evidence: A Cat Marsala Mystery. 1999. (Cat Marsala Mysteries Ser.). 256p. 22.00 (*0-684-83354-9*, Scribner) Simon & Schuster.
—Hard Luck: A Cat Marsala Mystery. 1992. 224p. text 20.00 (*0-684-19408-2*, Macmillan Reference USA) Gale Group.
—Hard Luck: A Cat Marsala Mystery. 1993. (Mystery Ser.). per. (*0-373-26124-1*, 1-26124-7, Harlequin Bks.) Harlequin Enterprises, Ltd.
—Hard Tack: A Cat Marsala Mystery. 1991. 224p. 18.95 o.s.i (*0-684-19299-3*, Macmillan Reference USA) Gale Group.
—Hard Tack: A Cat Marsala Mystery. 1992. (WWL Mystery Ser.: No. 97). per. (*0-373-26097-0*, 1-26097-5, Harlequin Bks.) Harlequin Enterprises, Ltd.
—Hard Women: A Cat Marsala Mystery. 1993. 256p. 20.00 o.p. (*0-684-19564-X*, Macmillan Reference USA) Gale Group.
—Hard Women: A Cat Marsala Mystery. 1994. per. (*0-373-26150-0*, 1-26150-2, Harlequin Bks.) Harlequin Enterprises, Ltd.
—Hardball. 2003. 224p. pap. 13.00 (*1-932325-01-8*) Crum Creek Pr.
—Hardball. 1990. 224p. 17.95 o.s.i (*0-684-19140-7*, Macmillan Reference USA) Gale Group.
—Hardball. 1993. (Illus.). per. (*0-373-83302-4*, 1-83302-9); 1991. mass mkt. (*0-373-26066-0*) Harlequin Enterprises, Ltd. (Harlequin Bks.).
—Help Me, Please! 2nd ed. 1999. 336p. 23.95 (*0-312-86563-5*, Forge Bks.) Doherty, Tom Assocs., LLC.
—Killer.app. 350p. 1997. mass mkt. 5.99 (*0-8125-5391-8*); 1996. 22.95 o.p. (*0-312-85991-0*) Doherty, Tom Assocs., LLC. (Forge Bks.).
Davis-Gardner, Angela. Forms of Shelter. l.t. ed. 1993. (General Ser.). 346p. 16.95 o.p. (*0-8161-5423-6*, Macmillan Reference USA) Gale Group.
—Forms of Shelter. 1991. 256p. 19.95 o.p. (*0-395-59312-3*) Houghton Mifflin Co.
De Rosa, Tina. Paper Fish. 2003. (Contemporary Classics by Women Ser.). 176p. pap. 15.95 (*1-55861-439-7*) Feminist Pr. at The City Univ. of New York.
Deep End of the Ocean. 1996. (*0-670-78102-9*) Penguin Group (USA) Inc.
Dickson, Gordon R. Necromancer. 1981. 189p. 2.25 o.s.i (*0-441-56851-3*) Ace Bks.
—Necromancer. 1999. 5.99 (*0-312-87091-4*) St. Martin's Pr.
Diehl, William. Primal Fear. 1998. pap. 6.99 (*0-345-91452-X*); 1995. mass mkt. 6.99 o.p. (*0-345-90885-6*); 1995. mass mkt. 6.99 o.p. (*0-345-90644-6*); 1994. 432p. mass mkt. 7.99 (*0-345-38877-1*, Ballantine Bks.); 1993. mass mkt. 6.99 (*0-345-38391-5*) Ballantine Bks.
—Primal Fear. unabr. ed. 1993. audio 25.95 o.p. (*1-56100-490-1*, 220, Bookcassette);Set. audio 89.25 o.p. (*1-56100-124-4*, 993) Brilliance Audio.
—Primal Fear. 1994. audio 8.99 o.s.i (*0-679-43414-3*); 1993. audio 18.00 o.s.i (*0-679-42014-2*, 391398); Set. 1999. audio 8.99 o.s.i (*0-375-40574-7*) Random Hse. Audio Publishing Group. (RH Audio).
—Reign in Hell. 1998. 480p. mass mkt. 7.99 (*0-345-39506-9*, Ballantine Bks.) Ballantine Bks.
—Show of Evil. 1998. pap. 6.99 (*0-345-91453-8*); 1996. 416p. mass mkt. 7.99 (*0-345-37536-X*, Ballantine Bks.); 1995. mass mkt. 6.99 (*0-345-40133-6*) Ballantine Bks.
—Show of Evil. abr. ed. 1995. audio 17.00 o.s.i (*0-679-44304-5*, RH Audio) Random Hse. Audio Publishing Group.
Donovan, Susan. Knock Me off My Feet. 2002. 320p. mass mkt. 6.50 (*0-312-98374-3*, St. Martin's Paperbacks) St. Martin's Pr.
Dopp, Peggy H. & Vroman, Barbara F. Tomorrow Is a River. 1977. 390p. 15.95 (*0-931762-00-6*) Phunn Pubs.
Dreiser, Theodore. Sister Carrie. (Modern Library Ser.). E-Book 4.95 (*1-931208-42-5*) Adobe Systems, Inc.
—Sister Carrie. 1967. (Airmont Classics Ser.). mass mkt. 2.95 o.p. (*0-8049-0147-3*, CL-147) Airmont Publishing Co., Inc.
—Sister Carrie. 1976. 27.95 (*0-8488-0993-9*) Amereon, Ltd.
—Sister Carrie. 1982. 432p. mass mkt. 2.95 o.s.i (*0-553-21264-8*); mass mkt. 5.99 (*0-553-21374-1*) Bantam Bks. (Bantam Classics).
—Sister Carrie. 1971. 472p. reprint ed. lib. bdg. 20.00 (*0-8376-0401-X*) Bentley Pubs.
—Sister Carrie. 1980. 557p. reprint ed. lib. bdg. 37.95 (*0-89968-207-3*, Lightyear Pr.) Buccaneer Bks., Inc.
—Sister Carrie. (Collected Works of Theodore Drieser). 382p. reprint ed. 2001. (Illus.). pap. text 28.00 (*0-7426-5625-X*); 1998. lib. bdg. 98.00 (*1-58201-625-9*) Classic Bks.
—Sister Carrie. E-Book 2.49 (*0-7574-0316-6*); E-Book 2.49 (*0-7574-0213-5*) Electric Umbrella Publishing.
—Sister Carrie. 1957. 474p. (C). pap. text 24.00 (*0-03-009075-X*) Harcourt College Pubs.
—Sister Carrie. Simpson, Claude, ed. 1972. pap. 12.36 o.p. (*0-395-05134-7*, Riverside Editions) Houghton Mifflin Co.
—Sister Carrie. l.t. ed. 808p. pap. 60.08 (*0-7583-2330-1*); 1035p. pap. 71.70 (*0-7583-2331-X*); 1324p. pap. 85.64 (*0-7583-2332-8*); 590p. pap. 42.40 (*0-7583-2329-8*); 1629p. pap. 108.27 (*0-7583-2333-6*); 2004p. pap. 123.01 (*0-7583-2334-4*); 2324p. pap. 145.14 (*0-7583-2335-2*); 1035p. lib. bdg. 83.70 (*0-7583-2323-9*); 2324p. lib. bdg. 174.31 (*0-7583-2327-1*); 2004p. lib. bdg. 144.15 (*0-7583-2326-3*); 1629p. lib. bdg. 126.27 (*0-7583-2325-5*); 808p. lib. bdg. 72.08 (*0-7583-2322-0*); 1324p. lib. bdg. 97.64 (*0-7583-2324-7*); 472p. lib. bdg. 41.72 (*0-7583-2320-4*); 590p. lib. bdg. 48.40 (*0-7583-2321-2*) Huge Print Pr.
—Sister Carrie. 1962. mass mkt. 1.75 o.p. (*0-451-51206-5*); 1962. mass mkt. 2.25 o.p. (*0-451-51319-3*); 1962. mass mkt. 2.50 o.p. (*0-451-51462-9*); 1962. mass mkt. 2.25 o.p. (*0-451-51725-3*); 1962. mass mkt. 1.50 o.p. (*0-451-50904-8*); 1962. mass mkt. 0.75 o.p. (*0-451-50086-5*); 1962. mass mkt. 0.95 o.p. (*0-451-50758-4*); 1962. mass mkt. 2.95 o.p. (*0-451-51969-8*); 1962. 480p. mass mkt. 5.95 o.s.i (*0-451-52273-7*); 2000. 512p. mass mkt. 5.95 (*0-451-52760-7*) NAL. (Signet Classics).
—Sister Carrie. l.t. ed. (Large Print Ser.). reprint ed. 1997. 632p. lib. bdg. 28.00 (*0-939495-16-3*); 1998. 453p. lib. bdg. 25.00 (*1-58287-071-3*) North Bks.
—Sister Carrie. 1970. (C). pap. o.p. (*0-393-09949-0*) Norton, W. W. & Co., Inc.
—Sister Carrie. Pizer, Donald, ed. 2nd ed. 1991. (Critical Editions Ser.). 600p. (C). pap. text 12.00 (*0-393-96042-0*, 9949) Norton, W. W. & Co., Inc.
—Sister Carrie. Mitchell, Lee Clark, ed. 1999. (Oxford World's Classics Ser.). 512p. pap. 12.95 (*0-19-283574-2*) Oxford Univ. Pr., Inc.
—Sister Carrie. 1991. (Oxford World's Classics Ser.). 508p. pap. 9.95 o.p. (*0-19-282742-1*, 9673) Oxford Univ. Pr., Inc.
—Sister Carrie. 2000. E-Book 4.95 (*0-679-64138-6*); 1999. 752p. pap. 12.95 (*0-375-75321-4*) Random House Adult Trade Publishing Group. (Modern Library).
—Sister Carrie. 1997. (Modern Library Ser.). 658p. 19.50 o.s.i (*0-679-60250-X*) Random Hse., Inc.
—Sister Carrie. E-Book 5.00 (*0-7410-0562-X*) SoftBook Pr.
—Sister Carrie. 1994. (Penguin Twentieth-Century Classics Ser.). 19.00 (*0-606-04903-7*) Turtleback Bks.
—Sister Carrie. Berkey, John C. et al, eds. 1997. (University of Pennsylvania Dreiser Edition Ser.). 544p. pap. 22.50 (*0-8122-1638-5*) Univ. of Pennsylvania Pr.
—Sister Carrie. West, James L. W., III et al, eds. 1981. (Dreiser Edition Ser.). (Illus.). 704p. 49.95 o.p. (*0-8122-7784-8*); pap. 24.95 o.p. (*0-8122-1110-3*) Univ. of Pennsylvania Pr.
—Sister Carrie. unabr. ed. 1997. 297p. reprint ed. pap. 14.95 o.p. (*1-57002-041-8*) University Publishing Hse., Inc.
—Sister Carrie. 1994. (Twentieth Century Classics Ser.). 496p. 12.95 (*0-14-018828-2*, Penguin Classics) Viking Penguin.
—Sister Carrie. Berkey, John C. et al, eds. 1981. (American Library). 528p. pap. 8.95 o.p. (*0-14-039002-2*, Penguin Classics) Viking Penguin.
—Sister Carrie: An Authoritative Text, Backgrounds & Sources Criticism. 1970. (Critical Editions Ser.). (Illus.). x, 591p. (*0-393-04325-8*) Norton, W. W. & Co., Inc.
—Sister Carrie, Jennie Gerhardt, Twelve Men. Lehan, Richard, ed. 1987. (Library of America). 1168p. 40.00 (*0-940450-41-0*) Library of America, The.
Duberman, Martin B. Haymarket: A Novel. 2004. 24.95 (*1-58322-618-4*) Seven Stories Pr.
Duncan, Alice. Just North of Bliss. 2002. (Zebra Ballad Romance Ser.). 352p. mass mkt. 5.99 o.s.i (*0-8217-7277-5*, Zebra Bks.) Kensington Publishing Corp.
Dunlop, Susan, et al. Crime's Leading Ladies. unabr. ed. 1995. 3p. audio 16.99 (*0-88646-376-9*, 390575) Durkin Hayes Publishing Ltd.
Dybek, Stuart. Childhood & Other Neighborhoods: Stories. 2003. 212p. pap. 16.00 (*0-226-17658-4*) Univ. of Chicago Pr.
—The Coast of Chicago. 2003. 192p. pap. 13.00 (*0-312-42282-2*) Picador.
—I Sailed with Magellan. 2003. 320p. 24.00 (*0-374-17407-5*) Farrar, Straus & Giroux.
Dymmoch, Michael A. Incendiary Designs. 1998. 304p. 15.95 (*0-312-19245-2*, Saint Martin's Minotaur) St. Martin's Pr.
Dymmoch, Michael Allen. The Feline Friendship: Thinnes & Caleb Together Again. 2003. 304p. 24.95 o.s.i (*0-312-31016-1*, Saint Martin's Minotaur) St. Martin's Pr.
Eberhart, Mignon G. The House on the Roof. 1976. reprint ed. lib. bdg. 23.95 (*0-88411-762-6*) Amereon, Ltd.
—The House on the Roof. 1996. 304p. pap. 13.00 (*0-8032-6734-7*, Bison Bks.) Univ. of Nebraska Pr.
—Postmark Murder. 1983. 208p. mass mkt. 5.50 (*0-446-31181-2*) Warner Bks., Inc.
Elliott, Stephen. A Life Without Consequences. 2002. pap. 12.50 (*1-931561-19-2*); 2001. 186p. 25.00 (*0-9673701-7-5*) MacAdam/Cage Publishing, Inc.
—What It Means to Love You. 2002. (Illus.). 195p. 19.50 (*1-931561-18-4*) MacAdam/Cage Publishing, Inc.
Elrod, P. N. A Chill in the Blood. (Vampire Files Ser.: Vol. 7). 336p. 1998. 20.95 o.s.i (*0-441-00501-2*); 1999. reprint ed. mass mkt. 6.50 o.s.i (*0-441-00627-2*) Ace Bks.
—Dark Sleep. (Vampire Files Ser.: Vol. 8). 368p. 2000. mass mkt. 6.99 (*0-441-00723-6*); 1999. 21.95 o.s.i (*0-441-00591-8*) Ace Bks.
—Lady Crymsyn: A Novel of the Vampire Files. 2000. (Vampire Files Ser.: Vol. 9). (Illus.). 416p. 22.95 o.s.i (*0-441-00724-4*) Ace Bks.
—Vampire Files: Blood Art. 1991. (Vampire Files Ser.: Vol. 4). 208p. mass mkt. 5.99 o.s.i (*0-441-85945-3*) Ace Bks.
—Vampire Files: Blood on the Water. 1992. (Vampire Files Ser.: Vol. 6). 208p. mass mkt. 5.99 o.s.i (*0-441-85947-X*) Ace Bks.
—Vampire Files: Fire in the Blood. 1991. (Vampire Files Ser.: Vol. 5). mass mkt. 5.99 o.s.i (*0-441-85946-1*) Ace Bks.
—Vampire Files: The Bloodlist, No. 1. 2003. 464p. pap. 14.00 (*0-441-01090-3*) Ace Bks.
—Vampire Files No. 01: Bloodlist. 1990. (Vampire Files Ser.). 208p. mass mkt. 6.50 o.s.i (*0-441-06795-6*) Ace Bks.
—Vampire Files No. 2: Lifeblood. 1990. (Vampire Files Ser.: Vol. 2). 208p. mass mkt. 5.99 o.s.i (*0-441-84776-5*) Ace Bks.
—Vampire Files No. 3: Bloodcircle. 1990. (Vampire Files Ser.: Vol. 3). mass mkt. 5.99 o.s.i (*0-441-06717-4*) Ace Bks.
Engleman, Paul. The Man with My Cat. 2000. 228p. 23.95 o.p. (*0-312-24651-X*, Saint Martin's Minotaur) St. Martin's Pr.
Enright, Michael. Daisies in the Junkyard. 2002. 240p. 23.95 (*0-7653-0144-X*, Forge Bks.) Doherty, Tom Assocs., LLC.
Farrell, James T. Studs Lonigan: A Trilogy. 2004. (Library of America: Vol. 148). 1024p. 35.00 (*1-931082-55-3*) Library of America, The.
—Young Lonigan. 2003. 224p. mass mkt. 7.95 (*0-451-52913-8*, Signet Classics) NAL.
—Young Lonigan. 2003. 224p. pap. 13.00 (*0-14-218007-6*, Penguin Classics) Viking Penguin.
Faust, Ron. Split Image. 2000. 224p. pap. 12.95 (*0-312-87719-6*, Forge Bks.); 1999. mass mkt. (*0-8125-4924-4*, Tor Bks.); 1997. 224p. 20.95 o.p. (*0-312-86011-0*, Forge Bks.) Doherty, Tom Assocs., LLC.
Fielding, Joy. The First Time. l.t. ed. 2001. (Wheeler Large Print Book Ser.). 510p. 29.95 o.p. (*1-58724-057-2*, Wheeler Publishing, Inc.) Gale Group.
—The First Time. 2003. (Illus.). 512p. mass mkt. 5.99 (*0-7434-6714-0*, Pocket Star); 2000. (Illus.). 400p. 24.95 (*0-7434-0705-9*, Atria); 1999. (*0-7434-2268-6*, Atria); 1999. 512p. mass mkt. 7.99 (*0-7434-4636-4*, Pocket); 2001. (Illus.). 512p. reprint ed. mass mkt. 7.99 (*0-7434-0706-7*, Pocket Star); 2001. 400p. reprint ed. mass mkt. 7.99 (*0-7434-1724-0*, Pocket) Simon & Schuster.
Fiffer, Sharon. The Wrong Stuff. Date not set. pap. (*0-312-31415-9*, St. Martin's Paperbacks); 2003. 320p. 24.95 (*0-312-31414-0*, Saint Martin's Minotaur) St. Martin's Pr.
Fink, John. Painted Leaves. 1995. 266p. 22.95 o.p. (*0-312-13137-2*, Saint Martin's Minotaur) St. Martin's Pr.
Fleming, Kathleen Anne. The Jazz Age Murders. 1999. 180p. pap. 14.50 (*0-88739-203-2*) Creative Arts Bk. Co.
Flint, Eric & Freer, Dave. Pyramid Scheme. 2001. 432p. 21.00 (*0-671-31839-X*) Baen Bks.
Ford, John M. The Last Hot Time. 2000. 224p. 22.95 (*0-312-85545-1*); 2001. reprint ed. pap. 12.95 (*0-312-87578-9*) Doherty, Tom Assocs., LLC. (Tor Bks.).
Forrest, Leon. The Bloodworth Orphans. 2001. 383p. pap. 18.00 (*0-226-25722-3*) Univ. of Chicago Pr.
—There Is a Tree More Ancient Than Eden. 2001. 213p. pap. 13.00 (*0-226-25721-5*) Univ. of Chicago Pr.
Foster, Sharon Ewell. Passing by Samaria. 2003. 566p. pap. 16.95 (*1-4104-0157-X*, Walker Large Print) Gale Group.
—Passing by Samaria. 2003. 384p. pap. 12.99 (*1-57673-615-6*, Alabaster) Multnomah Pubs., Inc.
—Passing by Samaria. l.t. ed. 2003. 566p. 26.95 (*0-7862-5572-2*) Thorndike Pr.
Frasier, Anne. Hush. 2002. (Illus.). 384p. mass mkt. 6.99 (*0-451-41031-9*, Onyx) NAL.
Fuller, Jack. The Best of Jackson Payne: Novel. 2001. (Phoenix Fiction Ser.). 321p. pap. 15.00 (*0-226-26868-3*) Univ. of Chicago Pr.
Gagliano, Peter. The Rosary Roulette. 1999. 139p. 15.95 o.p. (*1-58141-008-5*) Rivercross Publishing, Inc.
Garland, Ardella. Details at Ten. E-Book 21.00 (*1-58945-169-4*) Adobe Systems, Inc.
—Details at Ten: A Georgia Barnett Mystery. 2000. 208p. 21.00 o.s.i (*0-684-87375-3*, Simon & Schuster) Simon & Schuster.
Garland, Ardella & Joe, Yolanda. Details at Ten. 2002. (Illus.). 272p. reprint ed. mass mkt. 6.99 (*0-7434-1480-2*, Pocket) Simon & Schuster.
Glass, Joseph. Blood: A Susan Shader Novel. 2000. (Susan Shader Novels Ser.). 400p. 24.00 (*0-684-85963-7*, Simon & Schuster) Simon & Schuster.
—Eyes. 1999. mass mkt. 6.99 o.s.i (*0-449-00512-7*, Fawcett) Ballantine Bks.
Gleiter, Jan. Lie down with Dogs. (Dead Letter Mysteries Ser.). 240p. 1997. mass mkt. 5.99 o.p. (*0-312-96175-8*, St. Martin's Paperbacks); 1996. 21.95 o.p. (*0-312-14003-7*, Saint Martin's Minotaur) St. Martin's Pr.

Granger, Bill. Drover & the Zebras. 1993. 240p. mass mkt. 4.99 (*0-380-71211-3*, Avon Bks.); 1992. 20.00 o.p. (*0-688-09857-6*, Morrow, William & Co.) Morrow/Avon.

Greeley, Andrew M. The Bishop & the Missing L Train: A Blackie Ryan Mystery. 2002. lib. bdg. 27.95 (*1-58547-254-9*, Premier) Ctr. Point Large Print.

—The Bishop & the Missing L Train: A Blackie Ryan Mystery. E-Book 6.99 (*0-312-70218-3*, Tor Bks.); 2001. 304p. reprint ed. mass mkt. 6.99 (*0-8125-7596-2*, Forge Bks.); 2000. 288p. reprint ed. 24.95 o.p. (*0-312-86875-8*, NHC 0141, Forge Bks.) Doherty, Tom Assocs., LLC.

—The Bishop at Sea: A Blackie Ryan Mystery. 1997. (Blackie Ryan Novels Ser.). 304p. mass mkt. 6.99 (*0-425-16080-7*) Berkley Publishing Group.

—The Bishop at Sea: A Blackie Ryan Mystery. l.t. ed. 2000. (Americana Ser.). 407p. 27.95 (*0-7862-2322-7*) Thorndike Pr.

—A Christmas Wedding. l.t. ed. 2001. lib. bdg. 27.95 (*1-58547-158-5*) Ctr. Point Large Print.

—A Christmas Wedding. 2000. 349p. 24.95 (*0-312-87224-0*); 2001. 512p. reprint ed. mass mkt. 7.99 (*0-8125-6667-X*) Doherty, Tom Assocs., LLC. (Forge Bks.).

—Contract with an Angel: A Novel of Angelic Intervention. abr. ed. 1999. audio 7.99 o.s.i (*1-56740-300-X*, 1862, Paperback Nova Audio Bks.); 1998. audio 26.95 (*1-56740-068-X*, 13, Bookcassette); 1998. 10p. audio 73.25 (*1-56740-597-5*, 830, Unabridged Library Editions); Set. 1998. audio 17.95 o.p. (*1-56740-793-5*, 444, Nova Audio Bks.) Brilliance Audio.

—Contract with an Angel: A Novel of Angelic Intervention. 1999. 384p. mass mkt. 6.99 (*0-8125-4443-9*); 1998. 304p. 23.95 o.p. (*0-312-86081-1*) Doherty, Tom Assocs., LLC. (Tor Bks.).

—Happy Are the Clean of Heart: A Blackie Ryan Novel. l.t. ed. 1987. 412p. 18.95 o.p. (*0-8161-4278-5*, Macmillan Reference USA) Gale Group.

—Happy Are the Clean of Heart: A Blackie Ryan Novel. 1988. mass mkt. 4.95 (*0-446-35722-7*) Warner Bks., Inc.

—Happy Are the Meek: A Blackie Ryan Novel. l.t. ed. 1986. (General Ser.). 373p. 16.95 o.p. (*0-8161-4029-4*, Macmillan Reference USA) Gale Group.

—Happy Are the Meek: A Blackie Ryan Novel. 1985. 288p. mass mkt. 3.95 (*0-446-32706-9*) Warner Bks., Inc.

—Happy Are the Merciful: A Blackie Ryan Novel. 1992. 336p. mass mkt. 6.99 o.s.i (*0-515-10726-3*, Jove) Berkley Publishing Group.

—Happy Are the Oppressed: A Blackie Ryan Novel. l.t. ed. 1997. lib. bdg. 24.95 (*1-57490-083-8*, Beeler Large Print Bks.) Beeler, Thomas T. Publisher.

—Happy Are the Oppressed: A Blackie Ryan Novel. 1996. (Illus.). 320p. mass mkt. 7.50 (*0-515-11921-0*, Jove) Berkley Publishing Group.

—Happy Are the Peace Makers: A Blackie Ryan Novel. l.t. ed. 1993. 24.95 o.p. (*0-7927-1680-9*); 22.95 o.p. (*0-7927-1679-5*) BBC Audiobooks America.

—Happy Are the Peace Makers: A Blackie Ryan Novel. 1993. 320p. mass mkt. 6.99 o.s.i (*0-515-11075-2*, Jove) Berkley Publishing Group.

—Happy Are the Poor in Spirit: A Blackie Ryan Novel. 1994. (Blackie Ryan Novels Ser.). (Illus.). 304p. mass mkt. 6.99 o.s.i (*0-515-11502-9*, Jove) Berkley Publishing Group.

—Happy Are the Poor in Spirit: A Blackie Ryan Novel. l.t. ed. 2000. (Americana Ser.). 392p. 28.95 (*0-7862-2323-5*) Thorndike Pr.

—Happy Are Those Who Mourn: A Blackie Ryan Novel. l.t. ed. 1996. (Large Print Ser.). 352p. lib. bdg. 23.95 (*1-57490-038-2*, Beeler Large Print Bks.) Beeler, Thomas T. Publisher.

—Happy Are Those Who Mourn: A Blackie Ryan Novel. 1995. (Illus.). 304p. mass mkt. 6.99 o.s.i (*0-515-11761-7*, Jove) Berkley Publishing Group.

—Happy Are Those Who Thirst for Justice: A Blackie Ryan Novel. l.t. ed. 1988. (General Ser.). 440p. 18.95 o.p. (*0-8161-4488-5*, Macmillan Reference USA) Gale Group.

—Happy Are Those Who Thirst for Justice: A Blackie Ryan Novel. 1987. 320p. 16.95 (*0-89296-180-5*) Mysterious Pr.

—Happy Are Those Who Thirst for Justice: A Blackie Ryan Novel. 1988. mass mkt. 4.50 (*0-446-34946-1*) Warner Bks., Inc.

—Irish Eyes: A Nuala Anne McGrail Novel. 2000. 320p. 24.95 (*0-312-86570-8*); 2001. 352p. reprint ed. mass mkt. 6.99 (*0-8125-9024-4*) Doherty, Tom Assocs., LLC. (Forge Bks.).

—Irish Eyes: A Nuala Anne McGrail Novel. l.t. ed. 2001. 525p. 29.95 (*0-7862-3091-6*); (*0-7540-1621-8*) Thorndike Pr.

—Irish Lace: A Nuala Anne McGrail Novel. (Nuala Anne McGrail Novel Ser.). 1997. 345p. pap. 6.99 (*0-8125-5077-3*, Tor Bks.); 1996. 304p. 23.95 o.p. (*0-312-86234-2*, Forge Bks.) Doherty, Tom Assocs., LLC.

—Irish Lace: A Nuala Anne McGrail Novel. abr. ed. 1996. 17.95 o.p. (*0-7871-1022-1*, 394462) NewStar Media, Inc.

—Irish Lace: A Nuala Anne McGrail Novel. 1998. 4.98 o.p. (*0-7651-1156-X*) Smithmark Pubs., Inc.

—Irish Stew: A Nuala Anne McGrail Novel. 2002. 304p. 25.95 (*0-312-87188-0*, Forge Bks.) Doherty, Tom Assocs., LLC.

—Irish Stew: A Nuala Anne McGrail Novel. l.t. ed. 2003. 25.95 (*1-58724-413-6*, Wheeler Publishing, Inc.) Gale Group.

—Irish Whiskey: A Nuala Anne McGrail Novel. 1998. (Nuala Anne McGrail Novel Ser.). 309p. pap. 6.99 (*0-8125-7770-1*, Tor Bks.); 304p. 23.95 o.p. (*0-312-85596-6*, Forge Bks.) Doherty, Tom Assocs., LLC.

—Irish Whiskey: A Nuala Anne McGrail Novel. l.t. ed. 2000. (Basic Ser.). 549p. 28.95 (*0-7862-2930-6*) Thorndike Pr.

—A Midwinter's Tale. 1999. 448p. mass mkt. 6.99 (*0-8125-9025-2*); No. 1. 1998. (Midwinter's Tale Ser.: Vol. 1). 383p. 24.95 (*0-312-86571-6*) Doherty, Tom Assocs., LLC. (Forge Bks.).

—A Midwinter's Tale. l.t. ed. 2000. 542p. 26.95 (*1-56895-949-4*, Wheeler Publishing, Inc.) Gale Group.

—Rite of Spring. 1988. 416p. mass mkt. 4.95 o.s.i (*0-446-34341-2*) Warner Bks., Inc.

—Star Bright! A Christmas Story. l.t. ed. 1998. 19.95 (*1-57490-166-4*) Beeler, Thomas T. Publisher.

—Star Bright! A Christmas Story. 1997. 127p. 13.95 (*0-312-86387-X*); 128p. 111.60 o.s.i (*0-312-86500-7*) Doherty, Tom Assocs., LLC. (Forge Bks.).

—Star Bright! A Christmas Story, Set. abr. ed. 1997. audio 16.99 Durkin Hayes Publishing Ltd.

—Star Bright! A Christmas Story. 1999. 13.95 (*0-312-87116-3*) St. Martin's Pr.

—Wages of Sin. 1993. mass mkt. 6.99 o.s.i (*0-515-11222-4*, Jove) Berkley Publishing Group.

—Wages of Sin. 1992. 352p. 21.95 o.p. (*0-399-13752-1*, G. P. Putnam's Sons) Penguin Group (USA) Inc.

—Younger Than Springtime, collector's ed. 1999. audio 72.00 (*0-7366-4654-X*, 5036) Books on Tape, Inc.

—Younger Than Springtime. 1999. 348p. 24.95 (*0-312-86572-4*); 2000. 469p. reprint ed. mass mkt. 6.99 (*0-8125-9026-0*) Doherty, Tom Assocs., LLC. (Forge Bks.).

Haddad, C. A. Caught in the Shadows: A Mystery. 1994. (WWL Mystery Ser.). per. (*0-373-26138-1*, 1-26138-7, Harlequin Bks.) Harlequin Enterprises, Ltd.

—Caught in the Shadows: A Mystery. 1992. 272p. 17.95 o.p. (*0-312-07666-5*, Saint Martin's Minotaur) St. Martin's Pr.

Hamilton, Jane. Disobedience: A Novel. 2001. 288p. pap. 13.00 (*0-385-72046-7*, Knopf Bks. for Young Readers) Random Hse. Children's Bks.

—Disobedience: A Novel. l.t. ed. 2001. (Thorndike Basic Ser.). 463p. 31.95 (*0-7862-3159-9*); pap. 29.95 (*0-7862-3158-0*) Thorndike Pr.

Hartzmark, Gini. A Bitter Business. (Kate Millholland Novel Ser.). 1997. 340p. mass mkt. 5.99 o.s.i (*0-8041-1241-X*, Ivy Bks.); 1995. 320p. 4.99 o.s.i (*0-449-90989-1*, Fawcett) Ballantine Bks.

—Dead Certain. 2000. (Kate Millholland Novel Ser.). 320p. mass mkt. 6.50 o.s.i (*0-8041-1900-7*, Ivy Bks.) Ballantine Bks.

—Fatal Reaction. 1998. (Kate Millholland Novel Ser.). 352p. mass mkt. 6.50 o.s.i (*0-8041-1743-8*, Ivy Bks.) Ballantine Bks.

—Final Option. 1994. (Midwest Mysteries Ser.). (Orig.). mass mkt. 5.99 o.s.i (*0-8041-1227-4*, Ivy Bks.) Ballantine Bks.

—Principal Defense. 1992. (Midwest Mysteries Ser.). mass mkt. 5.99 o.s.i (*0-8041-1074-3*, Ivy Bks.) Ballantine Bks.

—Rough Trade. 1999. 293p. mass mkt. 6.50 (*0-8041-1829-9*, Ivy Bks.) Ballantine Bks.

Hecht, Ben. A Thousand & One Afternoons in Chicago. 1992. (Illus.). 290p. pap. text 27.00 (*0-226-32279-3*) Univ. of Chicago Pr.

Hellman, Libby Fischer. Image of Death. 2004. 320p. mass mkt. 6.50 (*0-425-19504-X*) Berkley Publishing Group.

Hemon, Aleksandar. Nowhere Man. 2002. 256p. 23.95 (*0-385-49924-8*, Talese, Nan A.) Doubleday Publishing.

—Nowhere Man. 2004. 256p. pap. 13.00 (*0-375-72702-7*, Vintage) Knopf Publishing Group.

—The Question of Bruno. 2000. E-Book 18.50 (*1-58945-546-0*) Adobe Systems, Inc.

—The Question of Bruno. 2000. E-Book 2.99 (*0-385-50223-0*, Talese, Nan A.) Doubleday Publishing.

—The Question of Bruno. 2001. (Illus.). 240p. reprint ed. pap. 12.00 (*0-375-72700-0*, Vintage) Knopf Publishing Group.

Holton, Hugh. Chicago Blues. 1997. 373p. mass mkt. 5.99 (*0-8125-4464-1*); 1996. 384p. 23.95 o.p. (*0-312-85984-8*) Doherty, Tom Assocs., LLC. (Forge Bks.).

—The Devil's Shadow. 2001. 382p. 25.95 (*0-312-87784-6*, Forge Bks.) Doherty, Tom Assocs., LLC.

—The Left Hand of God. 2000. 416p. mass mkt. 6.99 (*0-8125-7084-7*); 1998. (Illus.). 384p. 24.95 (*0-312-86763-8*) Doherty, Tom Assocs., LLC. (Forge Bks.).

—Presumed Dead. 1995. 351p. pap. 5.99 (*0-8125-4813-2*); 1994. 320p. 21.95 o.p. (*0-312-85710-1*) Doherty, Tom Assocs., LLC. (Forge Bks.).

—Presumed Dead. 318p. 3.98 o.p. (*0-8317-5214-9*) Smithmark Pubs., Inc.

—Red Lightning. 320p. 1999. mass mkt. 6.99 (*0-8125-8912-2*); 1998. 23.95 o.p. (*0-312-86687-9*) Doherty, Tom Assocs., LLC. (Forge Bks.).

—Red Lightning. 1998. 6.99 (*0-312-87125-2*) St. Martin's Pr.

—Time of the Assassins. 2000. 383p. 24.95 (*0-312-87333-6*, Forge Bks.) Doherty, Tom Assocs., LLC.

—Violent Crimes. 1998. (Illus.). 512p. mass mkt. 6.99 (*0-8125-7187-8*); 1996. 384p. text 23.95 o.p. (*0-312-86281-4*) Doherty, Tom Assocs., LLC. (Forge Bks.).

—Violent Crimes. 1999. 6.99 (*0-312-87126-0*) St. Martin's Pr.

—Windy City. 1996. 310p. mass mkt. 5.99 (*0-8125-6714-5*, Tor Bks.); 1996. mass mkt. 5.99 (*0-8125-3695-9*, Forge Bks.); 1995. 352p. 22.95 o.p. (*0-312-85711-X*, Forge Bks.) Doherty, Tom Assocs., LLC.

House, Richard. Bruiser. 1997. (High Risk Ser.). 254p. pap. o.p. (*1-85242-437-0*) Serpent's Tail Ltd.

Howard, Clark. City Blood: A Novel of Revenge. 1994. 320p. 23.00 (*1-883402-39-5*, Scribner) Simon & Schuster.

Hunter, Fred. Capital Queers. (Alex Reynolds Mysteries Ser.). 2000. 232p. pap. 12.95 (*0-312-26301-5*, Saint Martin's Griffin); 1999. 224p. 23.95 o.p. (*0-312-20463-9*, Saint Martin's Minotaur) St. Martin's Pr.

—The Chicken Asylum. 2001. 272p. 23.95 (*0-312-27117-4*, Saint Martin's Minotaur) St. Martin's Pr.

—Federal Fag. (Alex Reynolds Mysteries Ser.). 272p. 1999. pap. 11.95 (*0-312-20649-6*, Saint Martin's Griffin); 1998. 22.95 o.p. (*0-312-18580-4*, Saint Martin's Minotaur) St. Martin's Pr.

—Government Gay. (Alex Reynolds Mysteries Ser.). 1998. 224p. pap. 11.95 (*0-312-18721-1*, Saint Martin's Griffin); 1997. 215p. text 21.95 o.p. (*0-312-15536-0*, Saint Martin's Minotaur) St. Martin's Pr.

—The Mummy's Ransom. 2003. (WWL Mystery Ser.: No. 451). 288p. mass mkt. (*0-373-26451-8*, Worldwide Library) Harlequin Enterprises, Ltd.

—The Mummy's Ransom. 2002. 272p. 23.95 (*0-312-27123-9*, Saint Martin's Minotaur) St. Martin's Pr.

—National Nancys. 2000. (Alex Reynolds Mysteries Ser.). 240p. 22.95 (*0-312-25233-1*, Saint Martin's Minotaur) St. Martin's Pr.

—Presence of Mind. 1998. (WWL Mystery Ser.). per. (*0-373-26282-5*, 1-26282-3, Worldwide Library) Harlequin Enterprises, Ltd.

—Presence of Mind. 1994. 19.95 (*0-8027-3245-3*) Walker & Co.

—Ransom at Sea. 2003. 272p. 23.95 (*0-312-30066-2*, Saint Martin's Minotaur) St. Martin's Pr.

—Ransom at the Opera. E-Book 22.95 (*0-312-27643-5*); 2000. 244p. 22.95 (*0-312-26257-4*, Saint Martin's Minotaur) St. Martin's Pr.

—Ransom for a Holiday. 1997. (Jeremy Ransom/Emily Charters Mysteries Ser.). 240p. 20.95 (*0-312-16976-0*, Saint Martin's Minotaur) St. Martin's Pr.

—Ransom for a Killing. 329. 1999. (WWL Mystery Ser.: Vol. 329). mass mkt. (*0-373-26329-5*, Worldwide Library) Harlequin Enterprises, Ltd.

—Ransom for a Killing. 1998. (Jeremy Ransom/Emily Charters Mysteries Ser.). 240p. 21.95 o.p. (*0-312-19323-8*, Saint Martin's Minotaur) St. Martin's Pr.

—Ransom for an Angel. 1996. mass mkt. (*0-373-26224-8*, 1-26224-5, Worldwide Library) Harlequin Enterprises, Ltd.

—Ransom for an Angel. 1995. 246p. 19.95 (*0-8027-3253-4*) Walker & Co.

—Ransom for Our Sins. 1997. per. (*0-373-26249-3*, 1-26249-2, Worldwide Library) Harlequin Enterprises, Ltd.

—Ransom for Our Sins. 1996. 238p. 22.95 (*0-8027-3284-4*) Walker & Co.

—Ransom Unpaid. 2000. (WWL Mystery Ser.: Vol. 365). mass mkt. (*0-373-26365-1*, 1-26365-6, Worldwide Library) Harlequin Enterprises, Ltd.

—Ransom Unpaid. 1999. 216p. 22.95 (*0-312-24233-6*, Saint Martin's Minotaur) St. Martin's Pr.

Izzi, Eugene. A Matter of Honor. 1998. pap. 6.99 (*0-380-78842-X*); 1997. 432p. 24.00 (*0-380-97342-1*) Morrow/Avon. (Avon Bks.).

—The Take. 1988. mass mkt. 3.50 (*0-312-91120-3*, St. Martin's Paperbacks); 1987. 256p. 16.95 o.p. (*0-312-01038-9*) St. Martin's Pr.

Jackson, Edwardo. Ever After: A Novel. 2002. 384p. pap. 13.95 (*0-375-75773-2*, Villard Bks.) Random House Adult Trade Publishing Group.

Jakes, John. American Dreams. unabr. collector's ed. 1999. audio 112.00 (*0-7366-4355-9*, 4812) Books on Tape, Inc.

—American Dreams. 1998. 464p. 24.95 o.p. (*0-525-94437-0*, Dutton) Dutton/Plume.

—American Dreams. l.t. ed. 1998. (G. K. Hall Core Ser.). 802p. 28.95 o.p. (*0-7838-0379-6*, Macmillan Reference USA) Gale Group.

—American Dreams. 1999. 560p. reprint ed. mass mkt. 7.99 (*0-451-19701-1*, Signet Bks.) NAL.

—American Dreams. abr. ed. 1998. audio 30.00 (*0-7871-1733-1*, 896030, Dove Audio) NewStar Media, Inc.

Johnson, Charles. Dreamer: A Novel. 240p. 1999. pap. 12.00 (*0-684-85443-0*); 1998. 23.00 (*0-684-81224-X*) Simon & Schuster. (Scribner).

—Dreamer. A Novel. abr. ed. 1998. audio 25.00 (*0-671-58240-2*, Simon & Schuster Audioworks) Simon & Schuster Audio.

Johnson, R. M. The Harris Men. 336p. 1999. 23.00 o.s.i (*0-684-84470-2*); 2000. reprint ed. pap. 12.95 (*0-7434-0059-3*) Simon & Schuster. (Simon & Schuster).

Jones, D. J. H. Murder at the MLA: A Novel. 2000. 224p. pap. 13.95 (*0-8263-2150-X*) Univ. of New Mexico Pr.

Jones, Dylan. Unnatural Acts. 1996. 320p. text 22.95 o.p. (*0-312-14753-8*, Saint Martin's Minotaur) St. Martin's Pr.

Joyce, Graham. Indigo. 2001. 272p. pap. 14.00 (*0-671-03938-5*, Washington Square Pr.) Simon & Schuster.

Kahn, Michael A. Death Benefits: A Rachel Gold Mystery. 1992. (Rachel Gold Mystery Ser.). 320p. 19.00 o.p. (*0-525-93456-1*, Dutton) Dutton/Plume.

—Death Benefits: A Rachel Gold Mystery. 1994. (Rachel Gold Mystery Ser.). 320p. mass mkt. 4.99 o.s.i (*0-451-17687-1*, Signet Bks.) NAL.

—Grave Designs: A Rachel Gold Mystery. 1992. (Rachel Gold Mystery Ser.). 352p. mass mkt. 5.50 o.s.i (*0-451-40293-6*, Signet Bks.) NAL.

Kaminsky, Stuart M. The Big Silence. 2000. 288p. 23.95 (*0-312-86926-6*, Forge Bks.) Doherty, Tom Assocs., LLC.

—The Big Silence. l.t. ed. 2001. (Thorndike Basic Ser.). 411p. 29.95 (*0-7862-3148-3*) Thorndike Pr.

—Lieberman's Choice. l.t. ed. 1994. 222p. 24.95 o.p. (*0-7927-2109-8*); pap. 23.95 o.p. (*0-7927-2108-X*) BBC Audiobooks America.

—Lieberman's Choice. 1994. (Midwest Mysteries Ser.). mass mkt. 4.99 o.s.i (*0-8041-1176-6*, Ivy Bks.) Ballantine Bks.

—Lieberman's Choice. abr. ed. 1995. (Abe Lieberman Mystery Ser.). audio 16.99 (*0-88646-384-X*, 391066) Durkin Hayes Publishing Ltd.

—Lieberman's Choice. 1993. 216p. 18.95 o.p. (*0-312-08836-1*, Saint Martin's Minotaur) St. Martin's Pr.

—Lieberman's Day. 1994. mass mkt. 4.99 o.s.i (*0-8041-1286-X*, Ivy Bks.) Ballantine Bks.

—Lieberman's Day. abr. ed. 1994. (Abe Lieberman Mystery Ser.). audio 16.99 (*0-88646-346-7*, 391067) Durkin Hayes Publishing Ltd.

—Lieberman's Day. l.t. ed. 1994. 286p. 23.95 o.p. (*1-56895-115-9*, Wheeler Publishing, Inc.) Gale Group.

—Lieberman's Day. 1994. (Henry Holt Mystery Ser.). 260p. 19.95 o.p. (*0-8050-2575-8*) Holt, Henry & Co.

—Lieberman's Day. unabr. ed. 2000. (Abe Lieberman Mystery Ser.). audio 51.00 (*0-7887-0418-4*, 94610E7) Recorded Bks., LLC.

—Lieberman's Folly. l.t. ed. 1994. 290p. 20.95 o.p. (*0-7927-1979-4*); pap. 19.95 o.p. (*0-7927-1978-6*) BBC Audiobooks America.

—Lieberman's Folly. 1992. (Midwest Mysteries Ser.). mass mkt. 4.99 o.s.i (*0-8041-0924-9*, Ivy Bks.) Ballantine Bks.

—Lieberman's Folly. 1991. 216p. 15.95 o.p. (*0-312-05398-3*, Saint Martin's Minotaur) St. Martin's Pr.

—Lieberman's Law. unabr. ed. 1999. audio 49.95 Blackstone Audio Bks., Inc.

—Lieberman's Law. 1996. (Henry Holt Mystery Ser.). 309p. 22.50 o.p. (*0-8050-3749-7*) Holt, Henry & Co.

—Lieberman's Law. unabr. ed. 1996. (Abe Lieberman Mystery Ser.). audio 60.00 (*0-7887-0586-5*, 94705E7) Recorded Bks., LLC.

—Lieberman's Thief. 1996. mass mkt. 5.50 o.s.i (*0-8041-1287-8*, Ivy Bks.) Ballantine Bks.

—Lieberman's Thief. abr. ed. 1996. audio 7.99 o.p. (*1-56740-112-0*, 1321, Paperback Nova Audio Bks.); 1995. (Abe Lieberman Mystery Ser.: Bk. 4). audio 16.95 o.p. (*1-56100-430-8*, 1320, Nova Audio Bks.); 1995. (Abe Lieberman Mystery Ser.: Vol. 4). audio 57.25 o.p. (*1-56100-263-1*, 1266, Unabridged Library Editions); 1995. (Abe Lieberman Mystery Ser.: Vol. Bk. 4). audio 23.95 o.p. (*1-56100-638-6*, 162, Bookcassette) Brilliance Audio.

—Lieberman's Thief. 1995. (Henry Holt Mystery Ser.). 238p. 22.50 o.p. (*0-8050-2576-6*) Holt, Henry & Co.

—Not Quite Kosher. 2002. (Abe Lieberman Ser.). 256p. 23.95 (*0-312-87453-7*, Forge Bks.) Doherty, Tom Assocs., LLC.

Katz, Michael J. The Big Freeze. 1991. 256p. 21.95 o.p. (*0-399-13558-8*, G. P. Putnam's Sons) Penguin Group (USA) Inc.

—Last Dance in Redondo Beach. 1989. 256p. 17.95 o.p. (*0-399-13445-X*, G. P. Putnam's Sons) Penguin Putnam Bks. for Young Readers.

—Last Dance in Redondo Beach. 1990. 288p. bds. 3.95 (*0-671-67913-9*, Pocket) Simon & Schuster.

—Murder off the Glass. 1987. 16.95 o.p. (*0-8027-5667-0*) Walker & Co.

Kelly, Mary P. Special Intentions. 1998. 380p. pap. 13.95 (*1-874597-71-5*) New Island Bks. IRL. *Dist:* Irish Bks. & Media, Inc.

Konrath, J. A. Whiskey Sour: A Jack Daniels Mystery. unabr. ed. 2004. audio 27.95 (*1-59355-486-9*, 5111, Brilliance Audio Unabridged); audio 69.25 (*1-59355-487-7*, 5113, Brilliance Audio Unabridged Lib Ed); audio compact disk 82.25 (*1-59355-489-3*, 5115, Brilliance Audio on CD Unabridged Lib Ed); audio compact disk 29.95 (*1-59355-488-5*, 5114, Brilliance Audio on CD Unabridged) Brilliance Audio.

—Whiskey Sour: A Jack Daniels Mystery. 2004. 23.95 (*1-4013-0087-1*) Hyperion Pr.

Laird, Thomas. Cutter. 2001. 256p. 24.00 (*0-7867-0944-8*, Carroll & Graf Pubs.) Avalon Publishing Group.

—Cutter. l.t. ed. 2002. (General Ser.). 320p. pap. 24.95 (*0-7862-4228-0*) Thorndike Pr.

Laird, Tom. Season of the Assassin. 2003. 288p. 24.00 (*0-7867-1124-8*, Carroll & Graf Pubs.) Avalon Publishing Group.

Langer, Adam. Crossing California. 2004. 24.95 (*1-57322-274-7*, Riverhead Bks. (Hardcovers)) Putnam Publishing Group, The.

Lanigan, Catherine. In Love's Shadow. 1998. 384p. mass mkt. (*1-55166-435-6*, 1-66435-8, Mira Bks.) Harlequin Enterprises, Ltd.

Lindsay, Tony. One Dead Preacher. 2000. (Downlow Mystery Ser.). (Illus.). 208p. pap. 14.95 (*1-888018-20-8*) BlackWords Pr.

Linz, Cathie. Private Account. 1984. (Candlelight Regency Romance Ser.: No. 242). 192p. pap. 1.95 o.p. (*0-440-17072-9*) Dell Publishing.

—Private Account. l.t. ed. 2001. 217p. 28.95 (*0-7838-9599-2*, Macmillan Reference USA) Gale Group.

Mackenzie, Myrna. The Billionaire's Bargain. 2002. (Silhouette Romance Ser.). 192p. mass mkt. (*0-373-19622-9*, Silhouette) Harlequin Enterprises, Ltd.

Maher, Mary. The Devil's Card. 1992. 288p. 18.95 o.p. (*0-312-07715-7*, Saint Martin's Minotaur) St. Martin's Pr.

Mallon, James. Magazine. 2000. 278p. 22.95 o.p. (*1-57197-181-5*) Pentland Pr., Inc.

Mamet, David. The Old Religion. 2002. 194p. 14.95 (*1-58567-190-8*) Overlook Pr., The.

Manderino, John. The Man Who Once Played Catch with Nellie Fox. 1998. 280p. 22.50 (*0-89733-448-5*) Academy Chicago Pubs., Ltd.

Matthews, Alex. Cat's Claw. (Cassidy McCabe Mystery Ser.: No. 5). 2001. 325p. mass mkt. 6.99 (*1-890768-35-9*); 2000. 272p. 22.95 (*1-890768-22-7*) Corvus Publishing. (Intrigue Pr.).

—Death's Domain: Sixth Cassidy McCabe Mystery. 2001. 320p. 23.95 (*1-890768-37-5*, Intrigue Pr.) Corvus Publishing.

—Satan's Silence. 1998. (Cassidy McCabe Mysteries Ser.: No. 2). 368p. mass mkt. 5.50 (*1-890768-04-9*, Intrigue Pr.) Corvus Publishing.

—Satan's Silence. Ellison, Lee, ed. 1997. (Cassidy McCabe Mystery Ser.: No. 2). 304p. 22.50 o.p. (*0-9643161-5-3*, Intrigue Pr.) Corvus Publishing.

—Secret's Shadow. unabr. ed. 1998. (Cassidy McCabe Mystery Ser.). audio 49.95 (*1-55686-745-X*) Books in Motion.

—Secret's Shadow: The First Cassidy McCabe Mystery. 1998. (Cassidy McCabe Mysteries Ser.: Vol. 1). 352p. mass mkt. 5.50 (*1-890768-03-0*, Intrigue Pr.) Corvus Publishing.

—Secret's Shadow: The First Cassidy McCabe Mystery. Ellison, Lee, ed. 1996. 296p. 22.50 o.p. (*0-9643161-3-7*, Intrigue Pr.) Corvus Publishing.

—Vendetta's Victim: The Third Cassidy McCabe Mystery. (Cassidy McCabe Mysteries Ser.). 1999. 256p. mass mkt. 5.95 (*1-890768-14-6*); 1998. 222p. 22.95 o.p. (*0-9643161-9-6*) Corvus Publishing. (Intrigue Pr.).

—Wanton's Web. 2001. (Cassidy McCabe Mystery Ser.: No. 4). 304p. mass mkt. 6.99 (*1-890768-34-0*); 1999. (Cassidy McCabe Mysteries Ser.). 316p. 22.95 (*1-890768-12-X*) Corvus Publishing. (Intrigue Pr.).

Mayer, Bob. Synbat: A Novel. 1993. 286p. 19.95 o.p. (*0-89141-416-9*, Presidio Pr.) Ballantine Bks.

McConnell, Frank. Blood Lake: A Harry Garnish/Bridget O'Toole Mystery. l.t. ed. 1988. 19.95 o.p. (*1-55504-590-1*); pap. 17.95 o.p. (*1-55504-573-1*) BBC Audiobooks America.

—Blood Lake: A Harry Garnish/Bridget O'Toole Mystery. 1988. (Crime Ser.). 256p. pap. 3.95 o.p. (*0-14-010755-X*, Penguin Bks.); 39.50 o.p. (*0-14-778359-3*) Viking Penguin.

—Blood Lake: A Harry Garnish/Bridget O'Toole Mystery. 1987. 256p. 16.95 o.s.i (*0-8027-5673-5*) Walker & Co.

—The Frog King: A Harry Garnish/Bridget O'Toole Mystery. l.t. ed. 1992. pap. 19.95 o.p. (*0-7927-1175-0*); 21.95 o.p. (*0-7927-1149-1*, CH0241) BBC Audiobooks America.

—The Frog King: A Harry Garnish/Bridget O'Toole Mystery. 1990. 192p. 18.95 o.p. (*0-8027-5748-0*) Walker & Co.

—Liar's Poker: A Harry Garnish/Bridget O'Toole Mystery. 1993. 234p. 19.95 (*0-8027-3229-1*) Walker & Co.

—Murder among Friends: A Harry Garnish/Bridget O'Toole Mystery. l.t. ed. 1986. pap. 13.95 o.p. (*0-7451-9149-5*) BBC Audiobooks America.

—Murder among Friends: A Harry Garnish/Bridget O'Toole Mystery. 1988. pap. 39.50 o.p. (*0-14-778313-5*); 192p. mass mkt. 3.95 o.p. (*0-451-82189-0*, Penguin Bks.) Viking Penguin.

—Murder among Friends: A Harry Garnish/Bridget O'Toole Mystery. 1983. 192p. 12.95 o.s.i (*0-8027-5567-4*) Walker & Co.

McMillan, Terry. A Day Late & a Dollar Short. l.t. ed. 661p. 2002. 29.95 (*0-7862-3350-8*); 2001. 32.95 (*0-7862-3349-4*) Thorndike Pr.

—A Day Late & a Dollar Short. Date not set. (*0-670-78287-4*, Viking); 2001. (Illus.). 448p. 25.95 o.s.i (*0-670-89676-4*); 2000. 23.95 (*0-670-86042-5*, Viking) Viking Penguin.

Merkel, Earl. Dirty Fire. 2003. 384p. mass mkt. 6.99 (*0-451-21017-4*, Signet Bks.) NAL.

Miles, Keith. Saint's Rest. 1999. (Merlin Richards Mystery Ser.). 312p. 23.95 (*0-8027-3332-8*) Walker & Co.

Mitchard, Jacquelyn. The Deep End of the Ocean. unabr. ed. 1999. audio 88.00 (*0-7366-3466-5*, 4110) Books on Tape, Inc.

—The Deep End of the Ocean. 1999. 448p. mass mkt. 7.99 (*0-451-19774-7*); 1997. 448p. mass mkt. 7.50 o.s.i (*0-451-18692-3*); 1997. 300.00 o.p. (*0-451-98390-4*) NAL. (Signet Bks.).

—The Deep End of the Ocean. 1999. 448p. pap. 14.00 (*0-14-028627-6*, Penguin Bks.) Penguin Group (USA) Inc.

—The Deep End of the Ocean. l.t. ed. 1997. (Niagara Large Print Ser.). 608p. 29.50 (*0-7089-5848-6*, Ulverscroft) Thorpe, F. A. Pubs. GBR. *Dist:* Ulverscroft Large Print Bks., Ltd., Ulverscroft Large Print Canada, Ltd.

—The Deep End of the Ocean. 1996. 448p. 23.95 o.p. (*0-670-86579-6*, Viking); 1999. 2p. audio 16.95 o.s.i (*0-14-086887-9*); 1996. audio 16.95 o.p. (*0-14-086355-9*, Penguin AudioBooks) Viking Penguin.

Moquist, Richard. Eye of the Agency, Vol. 1. 1997. ix, 207p. text 22.95 o.p. (*0-312-15526-3*, Saint Martin's Minotaur) St. Martin's Pr.

Moriarty, Daniel P. The World's Greatest Surgeon. 2000. 160p. pap. 10.95 (*0-595-15653-3*) iUniverse, Inc.

Nelscott, Kris. Smoke-Filled Rooms: Smokey Dalton Novel. 320p. 2002. mass mkt. 6.99 (*0-312-98290-9*, St. Martin's Paperbacks); 2001. 24.95 (*0-312-26265-5*, Saint Martin's Minotaur) St. Martin's Pr.

—Stone Cribs. E-Book 18.95 (*0-312-71111-5*); 2004. 320p. 24.95 (*0-312-28784-4*, Saint Martin's Minotaur) St. Martin's Pr.

—Thin Walls: A Smokey Dalton Novel. 2004. 400p. pap. 13.95 (*0-312-32044-2*, Saint Martin's Griffin); 2002. 320p. 24.95 (*0-312-28783-6*, Saint Martin's Minotaur) St. Martin's Pr.

Norris, Frank. The Pit: A Story of Chicago. 1976. lib. bdg. 19.95 (*0-89968-069-0*, Lightyear Pr.) Buccaneer Bks., Inc.

—The Pit: A Story of Chicago. reprint ed. lib. bdg. 48.00 (*0-7426-1189-2*) Classic Bks.

—The Pit: A Story of Chicago. 1983. 7.50 o.p. (*0-8446-0825-4*) Smith, Peter Pub., Inc.

Ojikutu, Bayo. 47th Street Black: A Novel. 2003. 432p. pap. 12.95 (*0-609-80847-8*, Crown) Crown Publishing Group.

Paretsky, Sara. At the Old Swimming Hole. abr. ed. 1999. audio 5.99 Durkin Hayes Publishing Ltd.

—Bitter Medicine. 1988. 272p. mass mkt. 6.99 o.s.i (*0-345-34722-6*) Ballantine Bks.

—Bitter Medicine. 1993. audio compact disk 56.00 (*0-7366-7125-0*); audio 48.00 (*0-7366-2417-1*, 3184) Books on Tape, Inc.

—Bitter Medicine. 1999. 352p. mass mkt. 7.50 (*0-440-23476-X*) Dell Publishing.

—Bitter Medicine. l.t. ed. 1989. 352p. 19.95 o.p. (*0-8161-4467-2*, Macmillan Reference USA) Gale Group.

—Bitter Medicine. 1987. 320p. 17.95 o.p. (*0-688-06448-5*, Morrow, William & Co.) Morrow/Avon.

—Bitter Medicine. unabr. ed. 2000. audio 58.00 (*1-55690-695-1*, 92428) Recorded Bks., LLC.

—Blacklist. abr. ed. (V. I. Warshawski Ser.). 2004. audio 12.99 (*1-58788-871-8*, 3384, Brilliance Audio Paperback Audiobooks); 2003. audio 24.95 (*1-58788-868-8*, 3381, Brilliance Audio Unabridged); 2003. audio 34.95 (*1-58788-866-1*, 3379, Brilliance Audio Unabridged); 2003. audio 97.25 (*1-58788-867-X*, 3380, Brilliance Audio Unabridged Lib Ed); 2003. audio compact disk 40.95 (*1-58788-869-6*, 3382, Brilliance Audio on CD Unabridged); 2003. audio compact disk 117.25 (*1-58788-870-X*, 3383, Brilliance Audio on CD Unabridged Lib Ed) Brilliance Audio.

—Blacklist. 2003. (V. I. Warshawski Novel Ser.). 448p. 24.95 (*0-399-15085-4*) Putnam Publishing Group, The.

—Blood Shot. unabr. ed. 1993. (V. I. Warshawski Ser.). audio 56.00 (*0-7366-2328-0*, 3108) Books on Tape, Inc.

—Blood Shot. 1989. (V.I. Warshawski Novels Ser.). 384p. mass mkt. 7.99 (*0-440-20420-8*) Dell Publishing.

—Blood Shot. l.t. ed. 1989. (General Ser.). 20.95 o.p. (*0-8161-4775-2*, Macmillan Reference USA) Gale Group.

—Blood Shot. abr. ed. 1990. audio 14.95 o.s.i (*0-553-45215-0*, RH Audio) Random Hse. Audio Publishing Group.

—Blood Shot. unabr. ed. 1993. (V. I. Warshawski Mystery Ser.: Vol. 1). audio 70.00 (*1-55690-899-7*, 93341E7) Recorded Bks., LLC.

—Burn Marks. unabr. ed. 1992. (V. I. Warshawski Ser.). audio 64.00 (*0-7366-2168-7*, 2967) Books on Tape, Inc.

—Burn Marks. 1991. (V.I. Warshawski Novels Ser.). 416p. mass mkt. 7.99 (*0-440-20845-9*) Dell Publishing.

—Burn Marks. l.t. ed. 1990. (Large Print Bks.). 533p. lib. bdg. 21.95 o.p. (*0-8161-5004-4*, Macmillan Reference USA) Gale Group.

—Burn Marks. abr. ed. 1990. audio 14.95 o.s.i (*0-553-45208-8*, RH Audio) Random Hse. Audio Publishing Group.

—Deadlock. l.t. ed. 1985. lib. bdg. 13.95 o.p. (*0-89340-898-0*, 842) BBC Audiobooks America.

—Deadlock. 1984. 272p. mass mkt. 5.95 o.s.i (*0-345-31954-0*) Ballantine Bks.

—Deadlock. unabr. collector's ed. 1993. (V. I. Warshawski Ser.). audio 48.00 (*0-7366-2382-5*, 3153) Books on Tape, Inc.

—Deadlock. unabr. ed. 1985. audio 14.95 o.p. (*0-930435-02-8*, 364); audio 57.25 o.p. (*1-56100-001-9*, 549, Unabridged Library Editions) Brilliance Audio.

—Deadlock. 1992. (V.I. Warshawski Novels Ser.). 320p. mass mkt. 6.99 (*0-440-21332-0*) Dell Publishing.

—Deadlock. 1984. 264p. 14.95 o.p. (*0-385-27933-7*) Doubleday Publishing.

—Deadlock. l.t. ed. 1993. (General Ser.). 271p. pap. 18.95 o.p. (*0-8161-5562-3*); lib. bdg. 20.95 o.p. (*0-8161-5561-5*) Gale Group. (Macmillan Reference USA).

—Ghost Country. 1999. 416p. pap. 14.95 (*0-385-33336-6*, Delta) Dell Publishing.

—Ghost Country. l.t. ed. 1998. 26.95 o.p. (*1-56895-682-7*, Wheeler Publishing, Inc.) Gale Group.

—Guardian Angel. unabr. ed. 1992. (V. I. Warshawski Ser.). audio 72.00 (*0-7366-2203-9*, 2998) Books on Tape, Inc.

—Guardian Angel. 1993. 432p. mass mkt. 7.99 (*0-440-21399-1*) Dell Publishing.

—Guardian Angel. l.t. ed. 1992. (General Ser.). 544p. 18.95 o.p. (*0-8161-5542-9*); lib. bdg. 21.95 o.p. (*0-8161-5541-0*) Gale Group. (Macmillan Reference USA).

—Guardian Angel. 1992. audio 15.95 o.s.i (*0-553-74558-1*); audio 16.99 o.s.i (*0-553-47035-3*) Random Hse. Audio Publishing Group. (RH Audio).

—Guardian Angel. 1993. 5.99 o.p. (*0-517-10926-3*) Random Hse. Value Publishing.

—Guardian Angel. unabr. ed. 1992. (V. I. Warshawski Mystery Ser.: Vol. 7). audio 85.00 (*1-55690-669-2*, 92233E7) Recorded Bks., LLC.

—Guardian Angel. 1992. (Audio Books Ser.). 69.95 o.p. incl. audio (*0-7838-8000-6*) Thorndike Pr.

—Guardian Angel: International Edition. 1992. 432p. mass mkt. 5.50 o.s.i (*0-440-29522-X*) Dell Publishing.

—Hard Time. (V.I. Warshawski Novels Ser.). 2000. 512p. mass mkt. 7.99 (*0-440-22470-5*, Delta); 1999. 400p. 24.95 (*0-385-31363-2*, Delacorte Pr.) Dell Publishing.

—Hard Time. l.t. ed. 1999. pap. 24.95 o.p. (*0-7838-8696-9*, Macmillan Reference USA) Gale Group.

—Hard Time, Set. abr. ed. 1999. audio 25.00 Highsmith Inc.

—Hard Time. abr. ed. 1999. audio 25.00 (*0-7871-2013-8*); audio compact disk 50.00 (*0-7871-2371-4*); audio 36.00 (*0-7871-2012-X*) NewStar Media, Inc. (Dove Audio).

—Hard Time. l.t. ed. 2000. 656p. pap. 13.95 (*0-375-70780-8*) Random Hse. Large Print.

—Hard Time. 2000. 13.04 (*0-606-18985-8*) Turtleback Bks.

—Indemnity Only. 1985. 224p. mass mkt. 4.95 o.s.i (*0-345-33634-8*); 1983. mass mkt. 2.50 o.s.i (*0-345-30684-8*) Ballantine Bks.

—Indemnity Only. unabr. ed. 1992. (V. I. Warshawski Ser.). audio 48.00 (*0-7366-2282-9*, 3069) Books on Tape, Inc.

—Indemnity Only. 1991. (V.I. Warshawski Novels Ser.). 336p. mass mkt. 6.99 (*0-440-21069-0*) Dell Publishing.

—Indemnity Only. 1982. 14.95 o.p. (*0-385-27213-8*) Doubleday Publishing.

—Indemnity Only. (Nightingale Ser.). 1982. pap. 9.95 o.p. (*0-8161-3439-1*); 1992. 381p. lib. bdg. 20.95 (*0-8161-5455-4*) Gale Group. (Macmillan Reference USA).

—Indemnity Only. abr. ed. 1991. audio 15.99 o.s.i (*0-553-45271-1*, RH Audio) Random Hse. Audio Publishing Group.

—Indemnity Only. l.t. ed. 1992. (Novels Ser.). 381p. pap. 20.95 (*0-8161-5456-2*) Thorndike Pr.

—Killing Orders. l.t. ed. 1986. lib. bdg. 17.95 o.p. (*1-55504-024-1*) BBC Audiobooks America.

—Killing Orders. 1988. pap. o.p. (*0-345-00730-1*); 1986. 288p. mass mkt. 5.95 o.s.i (*0-345-32777-2*) Ballantine Bks.

—Killing Orders. unabr. collector's ed. 1993. (V. I. Warshawski Ser.). audio 48.00 (*0-7366-2391-4*, 3162) Books on Tape, Inc.

—Killing Orders. 1993. 352p. mass mkt. 7.99 (*0-440-21528-5*, Dell Bks.) Dell Publishing.

—Sara Paretsky, 3 vols., Set. 1992. pap. 14.85 o.s.i (*0-440-36046-3*) Dell Publishing.

—Sara Paretsky: Three Complete Novels. 1995. 704p. 13.99 o.s.i (*0-517-14801-3*) Random Hse., Inc.

—The Sara Paretsky Value Collection: Indemnity Only, Blood Shots, & Burn Marks. abr. ed. 2000. audio 29.95 (*0-553-52724-X*, RH Audio) Random Hse. Audio Publishing Group.

—Settled Score. abr. ed. 1998. audio 4.99 (*0-88646-964-3*, 7964) Durkin Hayes Publishing Ltd.

—Skin Deep & Other Stories. unabr. ed. 1994. (V. I. Warshawski Mystery Ser.). audio 16.99 (*0-88646-373-4*, 391592) Durkin Hayes Publishing Ltd.

—Strung Out. unabr. ed. 1997. audio 4.99 (*0-88646-940-6*, 7940) Durkin Hayes Publishing Ltd.

—Three-Dot Po. unabr. ed. 1994. audio 8.95 o.p. (*1-879371-80-4*, 30030) Publishing Mills, Inc., The.

—Total Recall. 2002. 544p. mass mkt. 7.99 (*0-440-22471-3*) Dell Publishing.

—Total Recall. l.t. ed. 2001. 25.95 (*0-375-43136-5*) Random Hse. Large Print.

—Tunnel Vision. unabr. ed. 1994. (V. I. Warshawski Ser.). audio 80.00 (*0-7366-2842-8*, 3550) Books on Tape, Inc.

—Tunnel Vision. (V.I. Warshawski Novels Ser.). 1995. 480p. mass mkt. 7.50 (*0-440-21752-0*); 1995. E-Book 6.99 (*0-440-33393-8*); 1994. 736p. 26.95 o.s.i (*0-385-31307-1*, Delacorte Pr.) Dell Publishing.

—Tunnel Vision. l.t. ed. 1994. (Large Print Bks.). pap. 22.95 o.p. (*1-56895-084-5*, Wheeler Publishing, Inc.) Gale Group.

—Tunnel Vision. abr. ed. 1993. (V.I. Warshawski Novels Ser.). audio 24.95 o.p. (*1-55800-975-2*, 692333) NewStar Media, Inc.

—Windy City Blues. unabr. ed. 1996. (V. I. Warshawski Ser.). audio 48.00 (*0-7366-3243-3*, 3902) Books on Tape, Inc.

—Windy City Blues. 1996. (V.I. Warshawski Novels Ser.). 352p. mass mkt. 7.99 (*0-440-21873-X*) Dell Publishing.

—Windy City Blues. 1996. pap. 6.99 (*0-440-29546-7*) Doubleday Publishing.

—Windy City Blues. unabr. ed. 1995. (V. I. Warshawski Mystery Ser.). 24.95 o.p. (*0-7871-0478-7*, 693248) NewStar Media, Inc.

—Windy City Blues. l.t. ed. 1996. (Paperback Bestsellers Ser.). 336p. pap. 24.95 (*0-7838-1562-X*); 26.95 (*0-7838-1561-1*) Thorndike Pr.

—A Woman's Eye. 1992. 464p. reprint ed. mass mkt. 6.99 (*0-440-21335-5*) Dell Publishing.

—A Woman's Eye. 1993. 5.99 o.p. (*0-517-11187-X*) Random Hse. Value Publishing.

—Women on the Case: 26 Original Stories by the Best Women Crime Writers of Our Times. 1997. 464p. mass mkt. 7.50 (*0-440-22325-3*) Dell Publishing.

Paretsky, Sara, ed. Beastly Tales. 1995. (Select Sound, Dove Ser.). 4.99 o.p. (*0-7871-0326-8*); 4.99 o.p. (*0-7871-0311-X*) Penguin Group (USA) Inc.

—Beastly Tales. 1989. 17.95 o.p. (*0-922066-14-0*) Wynwood.

Paretsky, Sara, intro. A Woman's Eye. l.t. ed. 1992. (General Ser.). 569p. lib. bdg. 21.95 o.p. (*0-8161-5457-0*, Macmillan Reference USA) Gale Group.

Paretsky, Sara & McCrumb, Sharyn. Lily & the Sockeyes & Happiness Is a Dead Poet. unabr. ed. 1994. audio 4.99 (*0-88646-725-X*) Durkin Hayes Publishing Ltd.

Perilli, Sylvia. Make Me Nice. 2001. 283p. per. 16.95 (*0-9700957-9-1*) Irite Publishing.

Perrin, Kayla. If You Want Me. 2001. 384p. mass mkt. 6.50 (*0-380-81378-5*, HarperTorch) Morrow/Avon.

Pickart, Joan Elliott, et al. Body of Evidence: Verdict: Marriage/Behind the Badge/Premeditated Passion, 3 bks. in 1. 2003. 384p. mass mkt. (*0-373-21829-X*, Harlequin Bks.) Harlequin Enterprises, Ltd.

Possley, Maurice & Kogan, Rick. Everybody Pays. 2002. 352p. reprint ed. mass mkt. 7.99 (*0-425-18867-1*) Berkley Publishing Group.

Power, Susan. Roofwalker. 2002. 224p. 20.00 (*1-57131-039-8*) Milkweed Editions.

Powers, John R. The Last Catholic in America. 1981. reprint ed. lib. bdg. 18.00 (*0-8376-0439-7*) Bentley Pubs.

—The Last Catholic in America. 1993. 224p. mass mkt. 4.99 o.p. (*0-451-17614-6*, Signet Bks.) NAL.

—The Last Catholic in America. 1988. 224p. mass mkt. 4.95 (*0-446-31252-5*) Warner Bks., Inc.

Purdy, James. Gertrude of Stony Island Avenue. 1999. 192p. pap. 13.00 o.s.i (*0-688-17226-1*, Quill) HarperTrade.

—Gertrude of Stony Island Avenue. 1998. 144p. 19.95 (*0-688-15901-X*, Morrow, William & Co.) Morrow/Avon.

—Gertrude of Stony Island Avenue. 1996. 256p. 27.95 (*0-7206-1011-7*) Owen, Peter Ltd. GBR. *Dist:* Dufour Editions, Inc.

Quill, Monica. Half Past Nun: A Sister Mary Teresa Mystery. 1997. 198p. 20.95 o.p. (*0-312-15541-7*, Saint Martin's Minotaur) St. Martin's Pr.

—Sister Hood: A Sister Mary Teresa Mystery. 1991. 16.95 o.p. (*0-312-04602-2*, Saint Martin's Minotaur) St. Martin's Pr.

—The Veil of Ignorance: A Sister Mary Teresa Mystery. 1988. 208p. 15.95 o.p. (*0-312-02308-1*, Saint Martin's Minotaur) St. Martin's Pr.

Raleigh, Michael. A Body in Belmont Harbor. 1993. 277p. 17.95 o.p. (*0-312-08707-1*, Saint Martin's Minotaur) St. Martin's Pr.

—A Body in Belmont Harbor. 2000. (Paul Whelan Mystery Ser.). 292p. pap. 15.95 (*0-595-09340-X*) iUniverse, Inc.

—Death in Uptown. 2000. (Paul Whelan Mystery Ser.). 256p. pap. 14.95 (*0-595-09341-8*) iUniverse, Inc.

—Death in Uptown: A Paul Whelan Mystery. 1991. 17.95 o.p. (*0-312-05849-7*, Saint Martin's Minotaur) St. Martin's Pr.

—In the Castle of the Flynns. 2003. 368p. pap. 14.00 (*0-425-19036-6*) Berkley Publishing Group.

—In the Castle of the Flynns. abr. ed. 2003. audio 12.99 o.s.i (*1-59086-060-8*, 3603, Brilliance Audio Paperback Audiobooks); 2002. audio 24.95 o.p. (*1-59086-059-4*, 3602, Nova Audio Bks.); 2002. audio 34.95 (*1-59086-057-8*, 3600, Brilliance Audio Unabridged); 2002. audio 87.25 (*1-59086-058-6*, 3601, Unabridged Library Editions) Brilliance Audio.

—In the Castle of the Flynns. unabr. ed. 2003. audio 19.99 (*1-59335-021-X*, 30103) Soulmate Audio Bks., Inc.

—In the Castle of the Flynns. 2002. 352p. 22.00 (*1-57071-797-4*, Sourcebooks Landmark) Sourcebooks, Inc.

—Killer on Argyle Street. 2000. (Paul Whelan Mystery Ser.). 256p. pap. 14.95 (*0-595-09343-4*) iUniverse, Inc.

—Killer on Argyle Street: A Chicago Mystery Featuring Paul Whelan. 1995. 298p. 21.95 o.p. (*0-312-13532-7*, Saint Martin's Minotaur) St. Martin's Pr.

—The Maxwell Street Blues. 1994. 280p. 20.95 o.p. (*0-312-11394-3*, Saint Martin's Minotaur) St. Martin's Pr.

—The Maxwell Street Blues. 2000. (Paul Whelan Mystery Ser.). 288p. pap. 15.95 (*0-595-09342-6*) iUniverse, Inc.

—The Riverview Murders. 1997. 213p. 21.95 o.p. (*0-312-15641-3*, Saint Martin's Minotaur) St. Martin's Pr.

Reasoner, James. Battle Lines: The Last Good War. 2001. 384p. 24.95 (*0-312-87345-X*, Forge Bks.) Doherty, Tom Assocs., LLC.

Reaves, Sam. Dooley's Back. 2002. 288p. 24.00 (*0-7867-1094-2*, Carroll & Graf Pubs.) Avalon Publishing Group.

—Get What's Coming. 1995. 252p. 23.95 o.p. (*0-399-14018-2*, G. P. Putnam's Sons) Penguin Group (USA) Inc.

—A Long Cold Fall. 1992. 304p. pap. 4.50 (*0-380-71641-0*, Avon Bks.) Morrow/Avon.

Reed, Myrtle. The Shadow of Victory. 2000. 252p. E-Book 9.95 (*0-594-02741-1*) 1873 Pr.

Robinson, Chet Kelly. No More Mr. Nice Guy: A Love Story. 2002. 288p. pap. 13.95 (*0-375-76047-4*, Villard Bks.) Random House Adult Trade Publishing Group.

Roby, Kimberla Lawson. Behind Closed Doors. 1997. 244p. reprint ed. pap. 12.00 (*1-57478-005-0*) Black Classic Pr.

—Behind Closed Doors. 1997. x, 250p. pap. 12.00 (*0-9653470-4-4*) Lenox Pr.

—Casting the First Stone. 2000. x, 300p. 22.00 o.s.i (*1-57566-489-5*, Kensington Bks.); 2001. 32p. reprint ed. pap. 14.00 (*1-57566-633-2*) Kensington Publishing Corp.

—Here & Now. 288p. 2000. pap. 13.00 o.s.i (*1-57566-494-1*, Dafina); 1998. 22.00 o.s.i (*1-57566-336-8*) Kensington Publishing Corp.

Rodi, Robert. Drag Queen. 272p. 1996. pap. 12.95 o.s.i (*0-452-27344-7*, Plume); 1995. 21.95 o.p. (*0-525-93925-3*, Dutton) Dutton/Plume.

—Fag Hag. (Plume Fiction Ser.). 304p. 1993. pap. 14.00 (*0-452-26940-7*, Plume); 1992. 20.00 o.p. (*0-525-93406-5*, Dutton) Dutton/Plume.

Roe, Edward Payson. Barriers Burned Away. reprint ed. 24.50 (*0-404-05378-5*) AMS Pr., Inc.

—Barriers Burned Away. reprint ed. lib. bdg. 48.00 (*0-7426-1039-X*); 2001. (Illus.). pap. text 28.00 (*0-7426-6039-7*) Classic Bks.

—Barriers Burned Away. (YA). reprint ed. 1898. 472p. pap. text 28.00 (*1-4047-6845-9*); 1872. pap. text 28.00 (*1-4047-8809-3*) Classic Textbooks.

—Barriers Burned Away. 1988. (Illus.). 480p. (C). reprint ed. lib. bdg. 11.00 (*0-8398-1762-2*) Irvington Pubs.

—Barriers Burned Away. (Notable American Authors Ser.). reprint ed. 1999. lib. bdg. 125.00 (*0-7812-8809-6*); 1992. 472p. lib. bdg. 99.00 (*0-7812-6845-1*) Reprint Services Corp.

—Barriers Burned Away. 1971. (Illus.). reprint ed. 9.00 (*0-403-01185-X*) Scholarly Pr., Inc.

Rogers, Kenny. The Gift. 1996. (Illus.). 64p. 10.99 o.p. (*0-7852-7174-0*) Nelson, Thomas Inc.

Rose, Karen. Don't Tell. 2003. 512p. reprint ed. mass mkt. 5.99 (*0-446-61280-4*, Warner Romance) Warner Bks., Inc.

Rosemoor, Patricia. Improper Conduct. 2002. (Harlequin Blaze Ser.). 256p. mass mkt. (*0-373-79059-7*, Harlequin Bks.) Harlequin Enterprises, Ltd.

Rubino, Jane, et al. Homicide for the Holidays: Fruitcake; Milwaukee Winters Can Be Murder; A Perfect Time for Murder. 2000. (WWL Mystery Ser.: Vol. 362). 512p. mass mkt. (*0-373-26362-7*, 1-26362-3, Worldwide Library) Harlequin Enterprises, Ltd.

Rutkoff, Peter M. Shadow Ball: A Novel of Baseball & Chicago. 2001. 232p. per. 24.95 (*0-7864-0981-9*) McFarland & Co., Inc. Pubs.

Saberhagen, Fred. A Matter of Taste. 1992. 288p. mass mkt. 3.99 (*0-8125-2575-2*); 1990. 16.95 o.p. (*0-312-85046-8*) Doherty, Tom Assocs., LLC. (Tor Bks.).

Saenz, Benjamin Alire. The House of Forgetting. 1998. mass mkt. 6.99 o.s.i (*0-8041-1831-0*, Ivy Bks.) Ballantine Bks.

Saenz, Benjamin Alire, ed. The House of Forgetting. 1998. pap. (*0-449-00308-6*, Fawcett) Ballantine Bks.

—The House of Forgetting. 1997. 352p. 24.00 o.s.i (*0-06-018738-7*) HarperCollins Pubs.

Sharpe, Jon. Chicago Six-Guns. 1993. (Canyon O'Grady Ser.: No. 24). 176p. (Orig.). mass mkt. 3.50 o.p. (*0-451-17529-8*, Signet Bks.) NAL.

Sherer, Michael W. A Forever Death. l.t. ed. 2001. (Mystery Ser.). 277p. 23.95 (*0-7862-3016-9*, Five Star) Gale Group.

Shields, Carol. Happenstance. 1980. 224p. 12.95 o.p. (*0-07-092377-9*) McGraw-Hill Cos., The.

—Happenstance. 1994. pap. 10.95 (*0-14-771022-7*) NAL.

—Happenstance. 1994. 416p. pap. 14.00 (*0-14-017951-8*, Penguin Bks.) Penguin Group (USA) Inc.

Sinclair, April. Coffee Will Make You Black: A Novel. 1995. 256p. pap. 12.00 (*0-380-72459-6*, Perennial) HarperTrade.

—Coffee Will Make You Black: A Novel. 1994. 256p. 19.95 o.p. (*1-56282-796-0*) Hyperion Pr.

—Coffee Will Make You Black: A Novel. 1995. 18.05 (*0-606-12860-3*) Turtleback Bks.

—I Left My Back Door Open. 1999. 290p. 22.95 (*0-7868-6229-7*) Hyperion Pr.

—I Left My Back Door Open: A Novel. 2000. 304p. pap. 13.00 (*0-380-73280-7*) Morrow/Avon.

Sinclair, Upton. The Jungle. 1997. (C). pap. text (*0-321-02602-0*) Addison-Wesley Educational Pubs., Inc.

—The Jungle. 26.95 (*0-8488-0630-1*) Amereon, Ltd.

—The Jungle, Set. unabr. ed. 1997. audio 59.95 (*1-55685-473-0*, 473-0) Audio Bk. Contractors, Inc.

—The Jungle. 1981. (Bantam Classics Ser.). 400p. reprint ed. mass mkt. 5.95 (*0-553-21245-1*) Bantam Dell Publishing Group.

—The Jungle. 1971. 342p. reprint ed. lib. bdg. 20.00 (*0-8376-0400-1*) Bentley Pubs.

—The Jungle. 1991. 3.95 (*0-425-12527-0*) Berkley Publishing Group.

—The Jungle. unabr. ed. 1994. audio 76.95 (*0-7861-0789-8*, 132758) Blackstone Audio Bks., Inc.

—The Jungle. 2002. pap. 4.50 (*1-59109-049-0*) Booksurge, LLC.

—The Jungle. 1981. reprint ed. lib. bdg. 27.95 (*0-89966-415-6*) Buccaneer Bks., Inc.

—The Jungle. 2002. (Modern Critical Interpretations Ser.). 176p. pap. 19.95 (*0-7910-7169-3*) Chelsea Hse. Pubs.

—The Jungle. (Collected Works of Upton Sinclair). 2001. 413p. pap. text 28.00 (*0-7426-5821-X*); reprint ed. lib. bdg. 48.00 (*0-7426-1156-6*); 2001. reprint ed. pap. text 28.00 (*0-7426-6156-3*); 1999. 413p. reprint ed. lib. bdg. 118.00 (*1-58201-821-9*) Classic Bks.

—The Jungle. l.t. ed. 1998. 555p. pap. 22.95 (*1-58855-013-3*) Cyber Classics, Inc.

—The Jungle. 2001. (Dover Thrift Editions Ser.). 320p. pap. 3.00 (*0-486-41923-1*) Dover Pubns., Inc.

—The Jungle. 2003. (Barnes & Noble Classics Ser.). 448p. pap. 4.95 (*1-59308-008-5*) Fine Communications.

—The Jungle. 2002. 336p. 96.99 (*1-4043-1156-4*); per. 91.99 (*1-4043-1157-2*) IndyPublish.com.

—The Jungle. 1999. 410p. pap. 9.95 o.p. (*1-930128-07-X*, JNMedia Bks.) JNMedia, Inc.

—The Jungle. E-Book 1.95 (*1-57799-892-8*) Logos Research Systems, Inc.

—The Jungle. 2001. 352p. mass mkt. 5.95 (*0-451-52804-2*, Signet Classics); 1970. mass mkt. 0.75 o.p. (*0-451-50522-0*, Signet Classics); 1970. mass mkt. 0.50 o.p. (*0-451-50036-9*, Signet Classics); 1970. mass mkt. 0.60 o.p. (*0-451-50130-6*, Signet Classics); 1960. mass mkt. 1.75 o.p. (*0-451-51318-5*, Signet Classics); 1960. mass mkt. 1.50 o.p. (*0-451-51102-6*, Signet Classics); 1960. mass mkt. 1.25 o.p. (*0-451-50799-1*, Signet Classics); 1960. mass mkt. 2.25 o.p. (*0-451-52210-9*); 1960. mass mkt. 0.95 o.p. (*0-451-50715-0*, Signet Classics); 1960. mass mkt. 1.95 o.p. (*0-451-51504-8*, Signet Classics); 1960. 352p. mass mkt. 5.95 o.s.i (*0-451-52420-9*, Signet Bks.) NAL.

—The Jungle. 1980. pap. 2.25 o.p. (*0-14-000049-6*) Penguin Group (USA) Inc.

—The Jungle. 2002. (Modern Library Classics). 416p. pap. 9.95 (*0-375-75950-6*, Modern Library) Random House Adult Trade Publishing Group.

—The Jungle. unabr. ed. 1994. audio 91.00 (*1-55690-977-2*, 94116E7) Recorded Bks., LLC.

—The Jungle. 1999. 424p. reprint ed. lib. bdg. 29.95 (*0-7351-0120-5*) Replica Bks.

—The Jungle. 2004. 368p. mass mkt. 5.95 (*0-7434-8762-1*, Pocket) Simon & Schuster.

—The Jungle. E-Book 5.00 (*0-7410-0615-4*) SoftBook Pr.

—The Jungle. 2002. (Perennial Bestsellers Ser.). 28.95 (*0-7862-4887-4*) Thorndike Pr.

—The Jungle. 1990. 12.00 (*0-606-00909-4*) Turtleback Bks.

—The Jungle. 1988. (Prairie State Bks.). 388p. pap. text 16.95 (*0-252-01480-4*); 34.95 o.p. (*0-252-01494-4*) Univ. of Illinois Pr.

—The Jungle. 1985. (American Library). 448p. pap. 9.95 (*0-14-039031-6*, Penguin Classics) Viking Penguin.

Skom, Edith. The Charles Dickens Murders: A Beth Austin Mystery. (Beth Austin Mysteries Ser.). 304p. 1999. mass mkt. 5.99 (*0-440-21776-8*); 1998. 21.95 o.s.i (*0-385-31230-X*) Dell Publishing.

—The George Eliot Murders: A Beth Austin Mystery. (Beth Austin Mysteries Ser.). 1996. 288p. mass mkt. 5.99 o.s.i (*0-440-21775-X*); 1995. 243p. 19.95 o.s.i (*0-385-31228-8*, Delacorte Pr.) Dell Publishing.

—The Mark Twain Murders: A Beth Austin Mystery. 1989. (Brown Bag Mystery Line Ser.). 277p. 12.95 o.p. (*0-933031-17-3*) Council Oak Bks.

—The Mark Twain Murders: A Beth Austin Mystery. 1990. (Beth Austin Mysteries Ser.). 304p. mass mkt. 5.99 o.s.i (*0-440-20608-1*) Dell Publishing.

Smith, Barbara B., et al. 'Tis the Season for Murder: Christmas Crimes. 1998. mass mkt. (*0-373-26290-6*, 1-26290-6, Worldwide Library) Harlequin Enterprises, Ltd.

Solwitz, Sharon. Bloody Mary: A Novel. 2003. 224p. pap. 13.95 (*1-889330-93-0*) Sarabande Bks., Inc.

Soos, Troy. Murder at Wrigley Field. (Mickey Rawlings Baseball Mystery Ser.). 304p. 1997. mass mkt. 5.50 o.s.i (*1-57566-155-1*); 1996. pap. 18.95 o.p. (*1-57566-023-7*) Kensington Publishing Corp.

—Murder at Wrigley Field. unabr. ed. 1998. (Mickey Rawlings Baseball Ser.: Vol. 3). audio 53.00 (*0-7887-2282-4*, 95533E7) Recorded Bks., LLC.

Spencer, Ross H. Monastery Nightmare. 240p. reprint ed. 1987. mass mkt. 3.50 o.s.i (*0-445-40567-8*); 1986. 15.95 (*0-89296-233-X*) Mysterious Pr.

Sprinkle, Patricia H. Murder at Markham. 1992. (Sheila Travis Mystery Ser.). reprint ed. per. (*0-373-26108-X*, Harlequin Bks.) Harlequin Enterprises, Ltd.

Stella, Leslie. The Easy Hour: A Novel of Leisure. 2003. 272p. pap. 12.95 (*0-609-80972-5*, Three Rivers Pr.) Crown Publishing Group.

Sussman, Susan. Audition for Murder. 2000. (Morgan Taylor Mysteries Ser.: Bk. 351). per. (*0-373-26351-1*, 1-26351-6, Worldwide Library) Harlequin Enterprises, Ltd.

Sussman, Susan & Avidon, Sarajane. Audition for Murder. 1999. vii, 279p. 23.95 (*0-312-19968-6*, Saint Martin's Minotaur) St. Martin's Pr.

Sutton, Remar. Long Lines. 1988. 304p. 16.95 o.p. (*1-55584-140-6*) Grove/Atlantic, Inc.

—Long Lines. 1989. 272p. mass mkt. 3.95 o.s.i (*0-445-40794-8*, Mysterious Pr. Paperback Bks.) Warner Bks., Inc.

Swartz, Mark. Instant Karma. 2002. (Illus.). 112p. pap. 11.95 (*0-87286-408-1*) City Lights Bks.

Taylor, Valerie. The Girls in 3-B. 2003. (Femmes Fatales Ser.). 208p. pap. 13.95 (*1-55861-456-7*); lib. bdg. 14.95 (*1-55861-462-1*) Feminist Pr. at The City Univ. of New York.

Thompson, Jean. City Boy. 2004. 320p. 24.00 (*0-7432-4282-3*, Simon & Schuster) Simon & Schuster.

Tooley, S. D. Nothing Else Matters. 2000. (Sam Casey Mystery Ser.). 288p. 22.95 (*0-9666021-2-9*) Full Moon Publishing.

—When the Dead Speak. 2000. (Sam Casey Mystery Ser.). 304p. pap. 6.50 (*0-9666021-3-7*) Full Moon Publishing.

—When the Dead Speak. Roerden, Chris, ed. 1999. (Sam Casey Mystery Ser.). 304p. 21.95 (*0-9666021-0-2*) Full Moon Publishing.

Travis, Dempsey J. They Heard a Thousand Thunders. 1999. 166p. 19.75 (*0-941484-28-9*) Urban Research Pr., Inc.

Trice, Dawn T. Only Twice I've Wished for Heaven. l.t. ed. 1997. (Wheeler Large Print Book Ser.). 24.95 (*1-56895-468-9*, Wheeler Publishing, Inc.) Gale Group.

Trice, Dawn Turner. Only Twice I've Wished for Heaven. 1997. 304p. 23.00 o.s.i (*0-517-70428-5*) Random Hse. Value Publishing.

—Only Twice I've Wished for Heaven. 1998. 18.05 (*0-606-19398-7*) Turtleback Bks.

Vachss, Andrew. Shella. 2001. E-Book 11.00 (*1-59061-227-2*) Adobe Systems, Inc.

—Shella. 1994. 240p. pap. 12.00 (*0-679-75681-7*, Vintage) Knopf Publishing Group.

Walker, David J. Applaud the Hollow Ghost. 1997. 288p. 23.95 (*0-312-18041-1*, Saint Martin's Minotaur) St. Martin's Pr.

—A Beer at a Bawdy House. E-Book 23.95 o.p. (*0-312-27340-1*); 2000. 307p. 23.95 (*0-312-25242-0*, Saint Martin's Minotaur) St. Martin's Pr.

—End of Emerald Woods: A Wild Onion. 2000. (Wild Onion Ltd. Mysteries Ser.). 310p. 23.95 (*0-312-25215-3*, Saint Martin's Minotaur) St. Martin's Pr.

—Fixed in His Folly. 1999. (WWL Mystery Ser.: Bk. 315). 256p. per. (*0-373-26315-5*, 1-26315-1, Worldwide Library) Harlequin Enterprises, Ltd.

—Fixed in His Folly: A Malachy Foley Mystery. 1995. 262p. 21.95 o.p. (*0-312-13074-0*, Saint Martin's Minotaur) St. Martin's Pr.

—Half the Truth. 1996. 288p. 22.95 (*0-312-14611-6*, Saint Martin's Minotaur) St. Martin's Pr.

—No Show of Remorse: A Malachy Foley Mystery. E-Book 23.95 (*0-312-70467-4*); 2002. 304p. 23.95 (*0-312-25240-4*, Saint Martin's Minotaur) St. Martin's Pr.

—Ticket to Die For. 1998. (Wild Onion Ltd. Mysteries Ser.). 272p. 22.95 (*0-312-19345-9*, Saint Martin's Minotaur) St. Martin's Pr.

Walsh, Robert J. Back of the Yards. 2000. 564p. pap. 26.99 (*0-7388-3186-7*) Xlibris Corp.

Weis, Margaret & Baldwin, David. Dark Heart. 1998. (Dragon's Disciples Ser.: Vol. 1). 352p. 23.00 o.s.i (*0-06-105298-1*) HarperCollins Pubs.

—Dark Heart. 1999. (Dragon's Disciples Ser.: Vol. 1). 448p. mass mkt. 5.99 (*0-06-105791-6*, Eos) Morrow/Avon.

Wessel, John. Kiss It Goodbye: A Novel. 2002. 336p. E-Book 24.00 (*0-7432-2605-4*, Simon & Schuster) Simon & Schuster.

—Pretty Ballerina. 1998. 240p. 23.50 (*0-684-81464-1*, Simon & Schuster) Simon & Schuster.

—This Far, No Further. 1997. 384p. mass mkt. 6.99 o.s.i (*0-440-22490-X*) Dell Publishing.

—This Far, No Further. l.t. ed. 1997. (Large Print Book Ser.). 25.95 (*1-56895-418-2*, Wheeler Publishing, Inc.) Gale Group.

—This Far, No Further. unabr. ed. 1997. audio 75.00 (*0-7887-0803-1*, 94952E7) Recorded Bks., LLC.

—This Far, No Further. 1996. 336p. 23.00 (*0-684-81463-3*, Simon & Schuster) Simon & Schuster.

—This Far, No Further. 1999. pap. 9.98 (*0-671-04467-2*); Set. 1988. audio 18.00 (*0-671-57433-7*, 394372) Simon & Schuster Audio. (Simon & Schuster Audioworks).

Whack, Rita Coburn. Meant to Be: A Novel. 2002. 320p. pap. 11.95 (*0-375-75809-7*, Villard Bks.) Random House Adult Trade Publishing Group.

Whittingham, Richard. Their Kind of Town. 1994. 384p. 22.50 o.p. (*1-55611-358-7*) Fine, Donald I. Bks.

—Their Kind of Town. 1996. mass mkt. 5.99 (*0-380-72502-9*, Avon Bks.) Morrow/Avon.

Wiggs, Susan. The Firebrand. 2001. 408p. mass mkt. (*1-55166-801-7*, 1-66801-1, Mira Bks.) Harlequin Enterprises, Ltd.

—The Mistress. 2000. 408p. mass mkt. (*1-55166-610-3*, 1-66610-6, Mira Bks.) Harlequin Enterprises, Ltd.

Wilks, Eileen. Expecting... And in Danger. 2002. (Silhouette Desire Ser.). 192p. mass mkt. o.s.i (*0-373-76472-3*, Silhouette) Harlequin Enterprises, Ltd.

Wright, Richard A. Native Son. Date not set. 371p. 26.95 (*0-8488-2577-2*) Amereon, Ltd.

—Native Son. 1997. 594p. 49.95 (*1-56849-694-X*) Buccaneer Bks., Inc.

—Native Son. audio 19.95 Filmic Archives.

—Native Son. abr. ed. 1989. 432p. pap. 7.95 (*0-06-080977-9*) HarperCollins Pubs.

—Native Son. (Perennial Classics Ser.). 2004. 528p. pap. 13.00 (*0-06-092980-4*, Perennial); 1986. 398p. mass mkt. 4.95 o.p. (*0-06-080855-1*, P 855, Perennial); 1942. mass mkt. 3.95 o.p. (*0-06-083055-7*, P 3055, Perennial); 1998. audio 18.00 (*0-89845-916-8*, 393493, HarperAudio); 1993. 624p. reprint ed. pap. 7.00 o.p. (*0-06-081249-4*, P 977, Perennial); 1969. reprint ed. 24.95 o.p. (*0-06-014762-8*) HarperTrade.

—Native Son. unabr. ed. 1998. audio 102.00 audio 102.00 (*0-7887-2112-7*, 95437E7) Recorded Bks., LLC.

—Native Son. l.t. ed. 1993. 619p. lib. bdg. 22.95 (*0-8161-5787-1*) Thorndike Pr.

Wubbels, Lance. In the Shadow of a Secret. 1999. 288p. pap. 10.99 o.p. (*0-7642-2183-3*) Bethany Hse. Pubs.

Zabytko, Irene. When Luba Leaves Home: A Profile in Stories. 2003. 240p. tchr. ed. 22.95 (*1-56512-332-8*, 72332) Algonquin Bks. of Chapel Hill.

Zubro, Mark Richard. Another Dead Teenager. 1995. 194p. 19.95 o.p. (*0-312-13024-4*, Saint Martin's Minotaur) St. Martin's Pr.

—Are You Nuts? (Tom & Scott Mystery Ser.). 256p. 1999. pap. 12.95 (*0-312-20634-8*, Saint Martin's Griffin); 1998. 21.95 (*0-312-18528-6*, Saint Martin's Minotaur) St. Martin's Pr.

—Drop Dead. (Paul Turner Mystery Ser.). 2000. 256p. pap. 12.95 (*0-312-26314-7*, Saint Martin's Griffin); 1999. 245p. 22.95 (*0-312-20532-5*, Saint Martin's Minotaur) St. Martin's Pr.

—An Echo of Death: A Tom & Scott Mystery. (Tom & Scott Mystery Ser.). 1995. 208p. pap. 11.95 (*0-312-13480-0*, Saint Martin's Griffin); 1994. 192p. 18.95 o.p. (*0-312-11268-8*, Saint Martin's Minotaur) St. Martin's Pr.

—Here Comes the Corpse. 2002. (Tom & Scott Mystery Ser.: No. 9). 256p. 23.95 (*0-312-28098-X*, Saint Martin's Minotaur) St. Martin's Pr.

—One Dead Drag Queen. E-Book 22.95 (*0-312-27586-2*); 2001. 256p. pap. 12.95 (*0-312-27702-4*, Saint Martin's Griffin); 2000. 256p. 22.95 o.s.i (*0-312-20937-1*, Saint Martin's Minotaur) St. Martin's Pr.

—The Only Good Priest. (Tom & Scott Mystery Ser.). 1992. 192p. pap. 10.95 (*0-312-07054-3*, Saint Martin's Griffin); 1991. 8.99 o.p. (*0-312-05486-6*, Saint Martin's Minotaur) St. Martin's Pr.

—Political Poison: A Paul Turner Mystery. (Paul Turner Mystery Ser.). 1994. 208p. pap. 11.95 (*0-312-11044-8*, Saint Martin's Griffin); 1993. 192p. 10.99 o.p. (*0-312-09364-0*, Saint Martin's Minotaur) St. Martin's Pr.

—The Principal Cause of Death. (Tom & Scott Mystery Ser.). 1993. 192p. pap. 11.95 (*0-312-09896-0*, Saint Martin's Griffin); 1992. 208p. 11.99 o.p. (*0-312-07767-X*, Saint Martin's Minotaur) St. Martin's Pr.

—Rust on the Razor. (Tom & Scott Mystery Ser.). 224p. 1997. pap. 11.95 (*0-312-15644-8*, Saint Martin's Griffin); 1996. text 20.95 o.p. (*0-312-14404-0*, Saint Martin's Minotaur) St. Martin's Pr.

—Sex & Murder.Com. 2001. (Paul Turner Mystery Ser.). 294p. 23.95 (*0-312-26683-9*, Saint Martin's Minotaur) St. Martin's Pr.

—A Simple Suburban Murder. (Stonewall Inn Editions Ser.). 1990. 6.50 o.p. (*0-312-03887-9*, Saint Martin's Minotaur); 1990. 224p. pap. 8.95 (*0-312-03933-6*, Saint Martin's Griffin); 1989. 224p. 15.95 o.p. (*0-312-02640-4*, Saint Martin's Minotaur) St. Martin's Pr.

—Sorry Now? 1991. 208p. 11.99 o.p. (*0-312-06470-5*, Saint Martin's Minotaur); 3rd ed. 1992. 192p. pap. 10.95 (*0-312-08299-1*, Saint Martin's Griffin) St. Martin's Pr.

—The Truth Can Get You Killed. (Stonewall Inn Editions Ser.). 224p. 1998. pap. 11.95 (*0-312-18765-3*, Saint Martin's Griffin); 1997. 21.95 (*0-312-15679-0*, Saint Martin's Minotaur) St. Martin's Pr.

—Why Isn't Becky Twitchell Dead? 1970. 208p. 15.00 o.p. (*0-312-03955-7*) Palgrave Macmillan.

—Why Isn't Becky Twitchell Dead? 1991. (Stonewall Inn Editions Ser.). 189p. pap. 12.95 (*0-312-05996-5*, Saint Martin's Griffin) St. Martin's Pr.

## CHILE—FICTION

Agosin, Marjorie. Happiness. Horan, Elizabeth, tr. 1993. 238p. pap. 14.00 (*1-877727-34-2*) White Pine Pr.

Alegria, Fernando. Allende: A Novel. 1994. (Illus.). xiv, 303p. pap. 13.95 (*0-8047-2326-5*) Stanford Univ. Pr.

—Allende: A Novel. Janney, Frank, tr. from SPA. 1993. 320p. (C). 45.00 (*0-8047-1998-5*) Stanford Univ. Pr.

—The Maypole Warriors. Miller, Yvette E., ed. Lozano, Carlos, tr. from SPA. 1992. (Discoveries Ser.). 192p. pap. 16.95 (*0-935480-58-7*) Latin American Literary Review Pr.

Allende, Isabel. Daughter of Fortune. 1999. audio 44.95 (*0-7366-4811-9*, 5127) Books on Tape, Inc.

—Daughter of Fortune. 2001. 464p. mass mkt. 7.99 (*0-380-82101-X*) HarperCollins Pubs.

—Daughter of Fortune. Peden, Margaret Sayers, tr. from SPA. 1999. (Oprah's Book Club Ser.). (Illus.). 416p. 26.00 (*0-06-019491-X*) HarperCollins Pubs.

—Daughter of Fortune. Peden, Margaret Sayers, tr. from SPA. 2000. 416p. pap. 14.00 (*0-06-093275-9*, Perennial) HarperTrade.

—Daughter of Fortune. 2000. 20.05 (*0-606-20501-2*) Turtleback Bks.

—Portrait in Sepia. Peden, Margaret Sayers, tr. from SPA. 2001. 320p. 26.00 (*0-06-621161-1*) HarperCollins Pubs.

—Portrait in Sepia. l.t. ed. 2001. 448p. pap. 26.00 (*0-06-621401-7*) HarperCollins Pubs.

—Portrait in Sepia. 2002. 320p. pap. 13.95 (*0-06-093636-3*, Perennial) HarperTrade.

—Portrait in Sepia. l.t. ed. 2002. (SPA.). 512p. 28.95 (*0-7862-4200-0*) Thorndike Pr.

—Portrait in Sepia. l.t. ed. 2002. (French Ser.). 542p. pap. 30.99 o.p. (*2-84011-445-3*) Thorpe, F. A. Pubs. GBR. *Dist:* Ulverscroft Large Print Bks., Ltd., Ulverscroft Large Print Canada, Ltd.

Bolano, Roberto. By Night in Chile. Andrews, Chris, tr. 2003. 144p. pap. 13.95 (*0-8112-1547-4*) New Directions Publishing Corp.

Coloane, Francisco. Cape Horn & Other Stories from the End of the World. Petreman, David A., tr. from SPA. 1991. (Discoveries Ser.). 192p. pap. 14.95 o.p. (*0-935480-50-1*) Latin American Literary Review Pr.

—Cape Horn & Other Stories from the End of the World. Petreman, David A., tr. from SPA. & intro. by. 2nd ed. 2003. 14.95 (*1-891270-17-6*) Latin American Literary Review Pr.

De la Parra, Marco A. Secret Holy War of Santiago de Chile. Thomas, Charles, tr. 1994. (Emerging Voices Ser.). 328p. 29.95 (*1-56656-127-2*); pap. 12.95 (*1-56656-123-X*) Interlink Publishing Group, Inc.

del Rio, Ana Maria. Carmen's Rust. Lazzara, Michael J., tr. from SPA. & intro. by. 2002. 112p. 20.00 (*1-928746-23-3*) Herodias.

Del Rio, Ana Maria. Carmen's Rust. Lazzara, Michael J., tr. 2003. 112p. 19.95 (*1-58567-486-9*) Overlook Pr., The.

Delano, Poli. In This Sacred Place. 2003. 240p. pap. 16.00 (*1-893996-59-X*) White Pine Pr.

Dobyns, Stephen. After Shocks - Near Escapes. 1991. 288p. 19.95 o.p. (*0-670-83914-0*) Viking Penguin.

Donoso, José. Curfew. 1989. 320p. pap. 12.00 (*0-8021-3381-9*, Grove Pr.) Grove/Atlantic, Inc.

—Curfew. Polizzotti, Mark, ed. MacAdam, Alfred, tr. from SPA. 1988. 320p. 18.95 o.p. (*1-55584-166-X*) Grove/Atlantic, Inc.

—Curfew. l.t. ed. 1999. 490p. text 32.95 (*1-56000-450-9*) Transaction Pubs.

Dorfman, Ariel. Hard Rain. Shivers, George, tr. from SPA. 1990. (Readers International Ser.). 220p. (Orig.). (C). pap. 18.95 (*0-930523-77-6*); pap. 10.95 (*0-930523-78-4*) Readers International.

—My House Is on Fire. Shivers, George, tr. 1990. 192p. 17.95 o.p. (*0-670-82021-0*, Viking) Viking Penguin.

—The Nanny & the Iceberg. 1999. 353p. 25.00 o.p. (*0-374-21898-6*) Farrar, Straus & Giroux.

—The Nanny & the Iceberg. 2003. 272p. 14.95 (*1-58322-567-6*) Seven Stories Pr.

Fuguet, Alberto. Bad Vibes. Cordero, Kristina, tr. 1997. 320p. 22.95 o.p. (*0-312-15059-8*) St. Martin's Pr.

Hazuka, Tom. In the City of the Disappeared: A Novel. 2000. 260p. 22.95 (*1-882593-31-6*) Bridge Works Publishing Co., Inc.

O'Brian, Patrick. Blue at the Mizzen. unabr. ed. 1999. (Aubrey-Maturin Ser.). audio 48.00 (*0-7366-4737-6*, 5075) Books on Tape, Inc.

—Blue at the Mizzen. (Aubrey-Maturin Ser.). 1999. (Illus.). 288p. 24.00 (*0-393-04844-6*); 250.00 (*0-393-04874-8*); 2000. (Illus.). 272p. reprint ed. pap. 13.95 (*0-393-32107-X*, Norton Paperbacks) Norton, W. W. & Co., Inc.

—Blue at the Mizzen. abr. ed. 1999. (Aubrey-Maturin Ser.). audio 25.00 (*0-375-40876-2*, RH Audio) Random Hse. Audio Publishing Group.

—Blue at the Mizzen. unabr. ed. (Aubrey-Maturin Ser.). 2000. audio compact disk 81.00 (*0-7887-4204-3*, C1133E7); 1999. audio 60.00 (*0-7887-3769-4*, 95986E7) Recorded Bks., LLC.

—Blue at the Mizzen. l.t. ed. 2000. (Aubrey-Maturin Ser.). 393p. 27.95 (*0-7862-2047-3*); 435p. 30.95 (*0-7862-2046-5*) Thorndike Pr.

Richards, Caroline. Sweet Country. 1979. 9.95 o.p. (*0-15-187332-1*) Harcourt Trade Pubs.

—Sweet Country. 1986. pap. 7.95 o.p. (*0-671-62285-4*, Fireside) Simon & Schuster.

Sepulveda, Luis. The Name of the Bullfighter. Ruta, Suzanne, tr. from SPA. 1996. 224p. 21.00 o.s.i (*0-15-100193-6*) Harcourt Trade Pubs.

Sfeir, Anastassia. Para Olividar tus Besos. 2001. Tr. of In Order to Forget Your Kisses. (SPA., Illus.). 324p. pap. 15.00 (*970-661-130-4*) Edamex, Editores Asociados Mexicanos, S. A. de C. V. MEX. *Dist:* AIMS International Bks., Inc.

Silver, Katherine, ed. Chile Vol. 10: A Traveler's Literary Companion. 2003. (Traveler's Literary Companion Ser.: 10). 256p. pap. 13.95 (*1-883513-13-8*) Whereabouts.

Skármeta, Antonio. Watch Where the Wolf Is Going. 1991. (Orig.). 192p. pap. 18.95 (*0-930523-83-0*); 160p. pap. 10.95 (*0-930523-84-9*) Readers International.

## CHINA—FICTION

Ackerman, A. J. The Buddha's Treasure: A Novel. 1996. (Illus.). ix, 203p. (Orig.). (J). pap. 6.95 o.p. (*0-916147-73-8*) Regent Pr.

Agel, Jerome & Boe, Eugene. Deliverance in Shanghai. 1983. 362p. 14.95 o.p. (*0-934878-32-3*, Dembner Bks.) Barricade Bks., Inc.

Alai. Red Poppies: A Novel of Tibet. Goldblatt, Howard & Li-chun Lin, Sylvia, trs. 2003. 448p. pap. 14.00 (*0-618-34069-6*, Mariner Bks.) Houghton Mifflin Co. Trade & Reference Div.

—Red Poppies: An Epic Saga of Old Tibet. Goldblatt, Howard & Li-Chun Lin, Sylvia, trs. from CHI. 2002. 448p. tchr. ed. 25.00 (*0-618-11964-7*) Houghton Mifflin Co.

Alcorn, Randy. Safely Home: A Novel. 416p. 2003. pap. 13.99 (*0-8423-5991-5*); 2001. 13.99 (*0-8423-3791-1*) Tyndale Hse. Pubs.

Altieri, Daniel & Cooney, Eleanor. The Court of the Lion: A Novel of 8th Century China. 1989. 1117p. 19.95 o.p. (*0-87795-902-1*, Morrow, William & Co.) Morrow/Avon.

Amor, Paul F. The People's Republic. 1990. 224p. 18.95 (*0-8027-1072-7*) Walker & Co.

Anyi, Wang. Baotown. 1989. 17.95 o.p. (*0-393-02711-2*) Norton, W. W. & Co., Inc.

—Brocade Valley. McDougall, Bonnie S. & Maiping, Chen, trs. from CHI. 1992. 128p. 17.95 (*0-8112-1224-6*) New Directions Publishing Corp.

Arnote, Ralph. Hong Kong, China. 1997. 369p. pap. text 6.99 (*0-8125-4289-4*, Tor Bks.); 1996. 304p. 23.95 o.p. (*0-312-86097-8*, Forge Bks.) Doherty, Tom Assocs., LLC.

Bai, Hua. The Remote Country of Women: A Novel by Bai Hua. Wu, Qingyun & Beebee, Thomas O., trs. from CHI. 1994. (Fiction from Modern China Ser.). (Illus.). 384p. 38.00 (*0-8248-1591-2*); pap. 17.00 (*0-8248-1611-0*) Univ. of Hawaii Pr.

Ball, David. China Run: A Novel. 384p. 2003. mass mkt. 7.99 (*0-7434-7113-X*, Pocket); 2002. (Illus.). 24.00 (*0-7432-2743-3*, Simon & Schuster) Simon & Schuster.

Ballard, J. G. Empire of the Sun. unabr. ed. 1996. audio 64.00 (*0-7366-3319-7*, 3971) Books on Tape, Inc.

—Empire of the Sun. 1997. reprint ed. lib. bdg. 39.95 (*1-56849-663-X*) Buccaneer Bks., Inc.

—Empire of the Sun. unabr. ed. 2001. audio 59.95 (*0-7451-5767-X*, CAB 152) Chivers Audio Bks. GBR. *Dist:* BBC Audiobooks America.

—Empire of the Sun. 1987. 384p. mass mkt. 5.99 (*0-671-64877-2*, Pocket); 1984. 320p. 16.45 o.p. (*0-671-53051-8*, Simon & Schuster); 1985. reprint ed. mass mkt. 4.50 (*0-671-53053-4*, Washington Square Pr.) Simon & Schuster.

—Empire of the Sun. l.t. ed. 1985. 480p. 13.95 o.p. (*0-7089-8270-0*, Charnwood) Thorpe, F. A. Pubs. GBR. *Dist:* Ulverscroft Large Print Bks., Ltd.

Barganier, Jeff S. Slash Brokers: And It Shall Come to Pass in the Last Days. 1998. 256p. pap. 14.99 (*1-56384-150-9*) Huntington Hse. Pubs.

Barr, Pat. Jade: A Novel of China. 1982. 640p. 14.95 o.p. (*0-312-43943-1*) St. Martin's Pr.

Bartlett, Robert M. The Obstinate Illusion. 1991. 16.95 o.p. (*0-914339-34-6*) Randall, Peter E. Pub.

Bauer, Wolfgang. The Golden Caskets: Chinese Novellas of Two Millennia. Levenson, Christopher & Franke, Herbert, trs. from GER. 1978. Tr. of Goldeme Truhe. (Illus.). 391p. reprint ed. 35.00 o.s.i (*0-313-20091-2*, BAGO, Greenwood Pr.) Greenwood Publishing Group, Inc.

Bei Dao. Waves. McDougall, Bonnie S. & Cooke, Susette T., trs. from CHI. 1990. (Paperbook Ser.: Vol. 693). 224p. 22.95 (*0-8112-1133-9*) New Directions Publishing Corp.

Benson, Raymond. Zero Minus Ten. 1997. 288p. 22.95 o.p. (*0-399-14257-6*, G. P. Putnam's Sons) Penguin Group (USA) Inc.

Bickmore, Barbara. Distant Star. 1993. (Illus.). 544p. (Orig.). pap. 10.00 o.s.i (*0-345-36109-1*) Ballantine Bks.

Binstock, R. C. Tree of Heaven. 1996. 220p. pap. 12.00 (*1-56947-069-3*); 1995. 212p. 22.00 (*1-56947-038-3*) Soho Pr., Inc.

Blackwood, Grant. The Wall of Night. 2002. 576p. mass mkt. 7.99 o.s.i (*0-515-13278-0*, Jove) Berkley Publishing Group.

Bo, Ma. Blood Red Sunset: A Memoir of the Chinese Cultural Revolution. Goldblatt, Howard, tr. 1995. 384p. 24.95 o.p. (*0-670-84181-1*, Viking) Viking Penguin.

Bosse, Malcolm. The Warlord. Grey, Linda, ed. 1984. 768p. mass mkt. 4.95 o.s.i (*0-553-26523-7*) Bantam Bks.

—The Warlord. 1983. 717p. 17.25 o.p. (*0-671-44332-1*, Simon & Schuster) Simon & Schuster.

Bradby, Tom. The Master of Rain. 2003. (Illus.). 592p. mass mkt. (*0-552-14746-X*, Corgi) Bantam Bks.

—The Master of Rain. 2002. (Illus.). 464p. 24.95 (*0-385-50397-0*) Doubleday Publishing.

Bradby, Tom & Mansbach, Adam. The Master of Rain. 2003. (Illus.). 528p. reprint ed. pap. 14.00 (*0-375-71333-6*, Anchor) Knopf Publishing Group.

Bradley, James. The Deep Field: A Novel. 2000. 358p. 26.00 o.s.i (*0-8050-6111-8*) Holt, Henry & Co.

Brady, James. Warning of War: A Novel of the North China Marines. (Illus.). 352p. 2002. 24.95 (*0-312-28018-1*); 2003. reprint ed. pap. 13.95 (*0-312-30332-7*, Saint Martin's Griffin) St. Martin's Pr.

—Warning of War: A Novel of the North China Marines. l.t. ed. 2002. (Americana Ser.). 31.95 (*0-7862-4440-2*) Thorndike Pr.

Bridges, Shirin Yim. Ruby's Wish. 2002. (Illus.). 36p. (J). (gr. k-3). 15.95 (*0-8118-3490-5*) Chronicle Bks. LLC.

Brightfield, Richard. China: Why Was an Army Made of Clay? 1989. (Earth Inspectors Ser.: Bk. 7). 112p. (J). (gr. 4-6). pap. text 3.95 o.p. (*0-07-047999-2*) McGraw-Hill Cos., The.

Brown, Dale. Fatal Terrain. 1998. 496p. mass mkt. 7.99 (*0-425-16260-5*) Berkley Publishing Group.

—Fatal Terrain. abr. ed. 1997. 25.00 o.p. (*0-7871-1466-9*) NewStar Media, Inc.

—Fatal Terrain. 1997. 448p. 24.95 o.s.i (*0-399-14241-X*, G. P. Putnam's Sons) Penguin Group (USA) Inc.

—Fatal Terrain. 24.95 o.s.i (*0-399-14556-7*) Putnam Publishing Group, The.

Buck, Pearl S. Dragon Seed. expurg. ed. 2004. (Oriental Novels of Peal S. Buck Ser.). 400p. (C). pap. 12.95 (*1-55921-335-3*) Acorn Alliance.

—Dragon Seed. 1993. reprint ed. lib. bdg. 19.95 (*1-56849-133-6*) Buccaneer Bks., Inc.

—Dragon Seed. 1992. (Oriental Novels of Pearl S. Buck Ser.). 378p. reprint ed. pap. 12.95 (*1-55921-033-8*) Moyer Bell.

—Dragon Seed. 1972. pap. 1.25 o.p. (*0-671-78269-X*, Simon Pulse) Simon & Schuster Children's Publishing.

—East Wind - West Wind. 1993. (Oriental Novels of Pearl S. Buck Ser.: Vol. 8). 272p. reprint ed. pap. 11.95 (*1-55921-086-9*) Moyer Bell.

—A Field of Rice. 1993. (J). (gr. 4 up). o.p. (*0-88682-577-6*, Creative Education) Creative Co., The.

—The Good Earth. 17.95 (*0-8488-1251-4*) Amereon, Ltd.

—The Good Earth. 1981. 421p. reprint ed. lib. bdg. 35.95 (*0-89966-299-4*) Buccaneer Bks., Inc.

—The Good Earth. 1999. pap. 14.65 (*0-88103-224-7*) Econo-Clad Bks.

—The Good Earth. Ba'Albaki, Munir, tr. 1978. (ARA.). 200p. pap. 14.95 o.s.i (*0-86685-137-2*) International Bk. Ctr., Inc.

—The Good Earth. 1982. (Oxford Progressive English Readers Ser.). (Illus.). pap. 5.25 o.p. (*0-19-581035-X*) Oxford Univ. Pr., Inc.

—The Good Earth. unabr. ed. 1992. audio 78.00 (*1-55690-671-4*, 92318E7) Recorded Bks., LLC.

—The Good Earth. 1981. (Keith Jennison Large Type Bks.). (gr. 6 up). lib. bdg. 9.95 o.p. (*0-531-00191-1*, Watts, Franklin) Scholastic Library Publishing.

—The Good Earth. 1999. (YA). (gr. 8-12). mass mkt. (*0-671-50086-4*, Pocket); 1990. mass mkt. 5.99 (*0-671-72989-6*, Pocket); 1990. mass mkt. (*0-671-72651-X*, Washington Square Pr.); 1989. mass mkt. 4.50 (*0-671-68954-1*, Washington Square Pr.) Simon & Schuster.

—The Good Earth. Shefter, Harry, ed. 1989. (Enriched Classics Ser.). 320p. mass mkt. 3.95 (*0-671-68813-8*, Pocket) Simon & Schuster.

—The Good Earth. 1983. pap. 3.95 (*0-671-50437-1*, Washington Square Pr.); 1983. pap. 3.50 (*0-671-47226-7*, Washington Square Pr.); 1982. mass mkt. 2.95 (*0-671-45534-6*, Washington Square Pr.); 1999. 368p. reprint ed. pap. 12.00 (*0-671-03577-0*, Washington Square Pr.); 1994. (Illus.). 416p. reprint ed. mass mkt. 6.99 (*0-671-51012-6*, Pocket) Simon & Schuster.

—The Good Earth. 1980. mass mkt. 2.75 (*0-671-42458-0*); 1978. mass mkt. 2.50 (*0-671-49097-4*); 1976. mass mkt. 1.75 (*0-671-48796-5*); 1973. mass mkt. 0.95 (*0-671-47897-4*) Simon & Schuster Children's Publishing. (Simon Pulse).

—The Good Earth. l.t. ed. 1993. (Perennial Bestsellers Ser.). 441p. lib. bdg. 23.95 (*0-8161-5691-3*) Thorndike Pr.

—The Good Earth. 1994. 13.04 (*0-606-12947-2*); 1958. 11.09 o.p. (*0-606-00173-5*) Turtleback Bks.

—A House Divided. 1994. (Oriental Novels of Pearl S. Buck Ser.: Vol. 9). 360p. reprint ed. pap. 11.95 (*1-55921-034-6*) Moyer Bell.

—A House Divided. 1975. pap. 1.95 o.p. (*0-671-81366-8*, Pocket) Simon & Schuster.

—Imperial Woman. expurg. ed. 2004. (Oriental Novels of Peal S. Buck Ser.). 384p. (C). pap. 12.95 (*1-55921-334-5*) Acorn Alliance.

—Imperial Woman. 1992. reprint ed. lib. bdg. 23.95 o.p. (*0-89966-988-3*) Buccaneer Bks., Inc.

—Imperial Woman. 1996. (Oriental Novels of Pearl S. Buck Ser.: Vol. 3). 384p. reprint ed. pap. 11.95 (*1-55921-035-4*) Moyer Bell.

—Imperial Woman. 1980. pap. 1.25 o.p. (*0-671-78270-3*, Simon Pulse) Simon & Schuster Children's Publishing.

—Little Red. 1987. (Collection of Wonder). (YA). (gr. 4 up). lib. bdg. 13.95 o.p. (*0-88682-124-X*, Creative Education) Creative Co., The.

—Peony. 1996. pap. 18.00 (*0-7892-5111-6*) Abbeville Pr., Inc.

—Peony. expurg. ed. 2004. (Oriental Novels of Peal S. Buck Ser.). 336p. (C). pap. 12.95 (*1-55921-338-8*) Acorn Alliance.

—Peony. 1990. (Illus.). 340p. reprint ed. pap. 11.95 o.p. (*0-930395-12-3*) Biblio Pr., the Jewish Women's Pub.

—Peony. 338p. 1990. pap. 11.95 (*0-8197-0593-4*); 1990. lib. bdg. 24.95 o.p. (*0-8197-0592-6*); 1996. (Illus.). reprint ed. lib. bdg. 24.95 o.p. (*0-8197-0617-5*) Bloch Publishing Co.

—Peony. 1996. 320p. reprint ed. pap. 11.95 (*1-55921-168-7*) Moyer Bell.

—The Promise. 1997. (Oriental Novels of Pearl S. Buck Ser.: Vol. 14). 248p. (Orig.). pap. 9.95 (*1-55921-209-8*) Moyer Bell.

—Sons. expurg. ed. 2004. (Oriental Novels of Peal S. Buck Ser.). 336p. (C). pap. 12.95 (*1-55921-339-6*) Acorn Alliance.

—Sons. 1992. (Second Volume in the Good Earth Trilogy Ser.). 314p. pap. 11.95 (*1-55921-039-7*) Moyer Bell.

—The Three Daughters of Madame Liang. 1991. (Oriental Novels of Pearl S. Buck Ser.: Vol. 4). 316p. reprint ed. pap. 11.95 (*1-55921-040-0*) Moyer Bell.

—The Three Daughters of Madame Liang. 1975. pap. 1.50 o.p. (*0-671-80133-3*, Pocket) Simon & Schuster.

—The Three Daughters of Madame Liang. l.t. ed. 1973. (Ulverscroft Large Print Ser.). 457p. 12.00 o.p. (*0-85456-226-5*, Ulverscroft) Thorpe, F. A. Pubs. GBR. *Dist:* Ulverscroft Large Print Bks., Ltd., Ulverscroft Large Print Canada, Ltd.

Bunn, T. Davis. The Great Divide. abr. ed. 2000. audio 24.95 o.p. (*1-56740-928-8*, 2192, Nova Audio Bks.); audio 35.95 (*1-56740-386-7*, 2191, Brilliance Audio Unabridged) Brilliance Audio.

Burdett, John. The Last Six Million Seconds: A Thriller. 1997. 320p. 24.00 o.p. (*0-688-14774-7*, Morrow, William & Co.) Morrow/Avon.

Burgauer, Steven. The Brazen Rule. 1995. 278p. pap. 8.95 (*0-7610-0088-7*) Zero-g Pr.

Caldwell, Bo. The Distant Land of My Father. 2002. (Harvest Book Ser.). (Illus.). 400p. pap. 14.00 (*0-15-602713-5*, Harvest Bks.) Harcourt Trade Pubs.

—The Distant Land of My Father: A Novel of Shanghai. 2001. (Illus.). 384p. 23.95 (*0-8118-3240-6*) Chronicle Bks. LLC.

—The Distant Land of My Father: A Novel of Shanghai. l.t. ed. 2003. (Charnwood Large Print Ser.). 496p. 32.50 (*0-7089-9446-6*) Thorpe, F. A. Pubs. GBR. *Dist:* Ulverscroft Large Print Bks., Ltd., Ulverscroft Large Print Canada, Ltd.

Can Xue. Dialogues in Paradise. Janssen, Ronald & Zhang, Jian, trs. from CHI. 1989. 173p. 24.00 o.p. (*0-8101-0830-5*) Northwestern Univ. Pr.

Cao Xue Qin. A Dream of Red Mansions. 1978. 19.95 (*0-8351-0485-0*); 1978. 46.95 o.p. (*0-8351-0874-0*); Pt. II. 24.95 (*0-8351-0583-0*); Pt. III. 24.95 (*0-8351-0803-1*) China Bks. & Periodicals, Inc.

—A Dream of Red Mansions. Yang, Hsien-yi et al, trs. from CHI. (Illus.). Vol. 1. 1978. 599p. o.s.i (*0-917056-66-3*); Vol. 3. 1980. 586p. (C). o.s.i (*0-917056-68-X*) Foreign Languages Teaching & Research Pr.

—The Dream of the Red Chamber. McHugh, Florence & McHugh, Isabel, trs. from GER. 1975. (Illus.). 604p. reprint ed. 65.95 (*0-8371-8113-5*, TSDR, Greenwood Pr.) Greenwood Publishing Group, Inc.

—The Dream of the Red Chamber. 1996. (Classic Ser.). 96p. pap. 0.95 o.p. (*0-14-600176-1*) Penguin Group (USA) Inc.

—The Dream of the Red Chamber. 1998. lib. bdg. 22.95 (*1-56723-060-1*) Yestermorrow, Inc.

—The Story of the Stone: The Dream of the Red Chamber, 5 vols. (Chinese Literature in Translation Ser.). 120.00 o.p. (*0-253-19266-8*) Indiana Univ. Pr.

—The Story of the Stone Volume 1: The Golden Days. Hawkes, David, tr. from CHI. 1979. (Chinese Literature in Translation Ser.). 544p. 25.00 o.p. (*0-253-19261-7*) Indiana Univ. Pr.

—The Story of the Stone Volume 1: The Golden Days, Vol. 1. Hawkes, David, tr. 1974. (Classics Ser.). 544p. 15.00 (*0-14-044293-6*, Penguin Classics) Viking Penguin.

—The Story of the Stone Volume 2: The Crab-Flower Club. Hawkes, David, tr. 1979. (Chinese Literature in Translation Ser.). 608p. 29.50 o.p. (*0-253-19262-5*) Indiana Univ. Pr.

—The Story of the Stone Volume 2: The Crab-Flower Club, Vol. 2. Hawkes, David, tr. 1977. (Penguin Classics Ser.). 606p. 13.95 (*0-14-044326-6*, Penguin Classics) Viking Penguin.

—The Story of the Stone Volume 3: The Warning Voice. Hawkes, David, tr. 1981. (Chinese Literature in Translation Ser.). 640p. 35.00 (*0-253-19263-3*) Indiana Univ. Pr.

—The Story of the Stone Volume 3: The Warning Voice, Vol. 3. Hawkes, David, tr. 1981. (Classics Ser.). 640p. 13.95 (*0-14-044370-3*, Penguin Classics) Viking Penguin.

—The Story of the Stone Volume 4: The Debt of Tears. Gao, E., ed. Minford, John, tr. 1983. (Chinese Literature in Translation Ser.). 400p. 30.00 o.p. (*0-253-19264-1*) Indiana Univ. Pr.

—The Story of the Stone Volume 4: The Debt of Tears, Vol. 4. Gao, E., ed. Minford, John, tr. 1982. (Penguin Classics Ser.). 400p. 15.00 (*0-14-044371-1*, Penguin Classics) Viking Penguin.

—The Story of the Stone Volume 5: The Dreamer Awakes. Gao E, ed. Minford, John, tr. 1987. (Chinese Literature in Translation Ser.). 384p. 35.00 (*0-253-19265-X*) Indiana Univ. Pr.

—The Story of the Stone Volume 5: The Dreamer Awakes, Vol. 5. Gao, E., ed. Minford, John, tr. from CHI. 1986. (Penguin Classics Ser.). 384p. 13.95 (*0-14-044372-X*, Penguin Classics) Viking Penguin.

Cao Xue Qin & Gao, E. A Dream of Red Mansions. Xianyi, Yang & Yang, Gladys, trs. deluxe ed. 2001. (Library of Chinese Classics). 3577p. 179.95 (*7-119-02411-6*) Beijing Foreign Languages Pr. CHN. *Dist:* China Bks. & Periodicals, Inc.

—A Dream of Red Mansions. Xinqu, Huang, tr. from CHI. abr. ed. 1995. 298p. pap. 14.95 (*0-8351-2529-7*) China Bks. & Periodicals, Inc.

Cao Xue Qin & Kao, Ngo. A Dream of Red Mansions. Yang, Hsien-yi & Yang, Gladys, trs. from CHI. abr. ed. 1996. 503p. (C). pap. 24.95 (*0-88727-178-2*) Cheng & Tsui Co.

Cao Xue Qin, et al. A Dream of Red Mansions, Vol. 2. Yang, Hsien-yi & Yang, Gladys, trs. from CHI. 1978. (Illus.). 701p. o.s.i (*0-917056-67-1*) Foreign Languages Teaching & Research Pr.

Carlisle, Carris. Party in Peking. 1987. 192p. 13.95 o.p. (*0-312-00656-X*) St. Martin's Pr.

Carr, Caleb. El Soldado del Diablo. 2001. Tr. of Devil's Soldier. (SPA.). 416p. 21.43 (*84-406-9307-9*) AIMS International Bks., Inc.

Casserly, Jack. Traitor: The Odyssey of Korean War POWs in Red China-a Novel Based on Actual Events. 2004. 320p. pap. 16.95 (*0-9713318-0-4*) Lucky Pr., LLC.

Cha, Louis. Book & Sword. Minford, John & Earnshw, Graham, trs. from CHI. 2004. (Martial Arts Novels of Louis Cha Ser.). (Illus.). 500p. 35.00 (*0-19-590727-2*) Oxford Univ. Pr., Inc.

Chai, May-Lee. My Lucky Face. 272p. 2000. pap. 13.00 (*1-56947-181-9*); 1997. text 23.00 o.p. (*1-56947-094-4*) Soho Pr., Inc.

Chang, Ai-Ling. The Rice Sprout Song: A Novel of Modern China. 1998. 182p. pap. 16.95 (*0-520-21088-3*) Univ. of California Pr.

—The Rouge of the North. 1998. 185p. pap. 17.95 (*0-520-21087-5*); text 40.00 o.p. (*0-520-21438-2*) Univ. of California Pr.

Chang, Ai-Ling, et al. The Rice Sprout Song: A Novel of Modern China. 1998. 182p. text 40.00 o.p. (*0-520-21437-4*) Univ. of California Pr.

Chen Jo-hsi. Execution of Mayor Yin & Other Stories from the Great Proletarian Cultural Revolution. (Chinese Literature in Translation Series) annuals Ing, Nancy & Goldblatt, Howard, trs. (Chinese Literature in Translation Ser.). 248p. 1979. pap. 12.95 (*0-253-20231-0*, MB-231); 1978. 25.00 o.p. (*0-253-12475-1*) Indiana Univ. Pr.

Chen, Ying. Ingratitude. Volk, Carol, tr. from FRE. 1998. 160p. 20.00 o.p. (*0-374-17554-3*) Farrar, Straus & Giroux.

Chen, Ying & Volk, Carol. Ingratitude. 1999. 154p. pap. text 14.95 (*0-520-22013-7*) Univ. of California Pr.

Ch'en Ying-chen. Exiles at Home: Stories by Ch'en Ying-chen. Miller, Lucien, tr. from CHI. 1986. (Michigan Monographs in Chinese Studies: No. 57). (Illus.). 195p. (Orig.). text 15.00 o.p. (*0-89264-067-7*); pap. text 9.00 o.p. (*0-89264-068-5*) Ctr. for Chinese Studies Pubns.

Chen, Yuan-Tsun. The Dragon's Village. 1981. 304p. pap. 13.95 (*0-14-005811-7*, Penguin Bks.) Penguin Group (USA) Inc.

Chen, Yuan-Tsung. The Dragon's Village. 1980. 10.00 o.s.i (*0-394-50791-6*, Pantheon) Knopf Publishing Group.

Cheng, Francois. Green Mountain, White Cloud: A Novel of Love in the Ming Dynasty. 2004. 224p. 22.95 (*0-312-31574-0*) St. Martin's Pr.

Cheng, Terrance. Sons of Heaven: A Novel. 2002. 320p. 24.95 (*0-06-000243-3*, Morrow, William & Co.) Morrow/Avon.

Cheng, Terrence. Sons of Heaven: A Novel. 2002. E-Book 19.95 (*0-06-009813-9*); E-Book 19.95 (*0-06-009816-3*); E-Book 19.95 (*0-06-009815-5*); E-Book 19.95 (*0-06-009814-7*) HarperCollins General Bks. Group. (PerfectBound).

Chengli, Li, illus. Romance of the Three Kingdoms. 1995. Vol. 1. 9.95 (*981-3029-62-5*); Vol. 2. 9.95 (*981-3029-63-3*); Vol. 3. 9.95 (*981-3029-64-1*); Vol. 4. 9.95 (*981-3029-65-X*); Vol. 5. 9.95 (*981-3029-66-8*); Vol. 6. 9.95 (*981-3029-67-6*); Vol. 7. 9.95 (*981-3029-68-4*); Vol. 8. 9.95 (*981-3029-69-2*); Vol. 9. 9.95 (*981-3029-70-6*); Vol. 10. 9.95 (*981-3029-71-4*) Asiapac SGP. *Dist:* China Bks. & Periodicals, Inc.

Chin, Shunshin. The Taiping Rebellion. Fogel, Joshua, tr. from JPN. 2000. 672p. pap. 35.00 (*0-7656-0100-1*, East Gate Bk.) Sharpe, M.E. Inc.

Christensen, Loren W. Crouching Tiger: Taming the Warrior Within. 2002. 144p. pap. 14.95 (*1-880336-69-3*, CT) Turtle Pr.

Clancy, Tom. The Bear & the Dragon. 2000. 752p. 28.95 (*0-399-14563-X*) Penguin Group (USA) Inc.

—The Bear & the Dragon. l.t. ed. 2000. 1504p. 28.95 (*0-375-43069-5*) Random Hse. Large Print.

Clavell, James. Two Complete Novels. 1995. 13.99 (*0-517-14800-5*) Random Hse., Inc.

Cohen, Stuart. Invisible World. 1998. 352p. 24.00 o.s.i (*0-06-039227-4*, ReganBooks) HarperTrade.

Cooley, Regina F. The Magic Christmas Pony. 1991. (Illus.). 36p. (J). (gr. 1-5). 19.95 (*1-880450-04-6*) Capstone Publishing, Inc.

Cooney, Eleanor & Altieri, Daniel. Court of the Lion. 1990. 1024p. pap. 6.50 (*0-380-70985-6*, Avon Bks.) Morrow/Avon.

—Deception: A Novel of Murder & Madness in T'ang China. 1993. 22.00 o.p. (*0-688-08938-0*, Morrow, William & Co.); 1994. 640p. reprint ed. pap. 5.99 (*0-380-70872-8*, Avon Bks.) Morrow/Avon.

—Shangri-La: The Return to the World of Lost Horizon. 1996. 320p. 25.00 o.p. (*0-688-12872-6*, Morrow, William & Co.) Morrow/Avon.

Coonts, Stephen. Hong Kong: A Jake Grafton Novel. l.t. ed. 2000. (Wheeler Hardcover Ser.). 522p. 27.95 (*1-56895-985-0*, Wheeler Publishing, Inc.) Gale Group.

—Hong Kong: A Jake Grafton Novel. 2001. 416p. mass mkt. 7.99 (*0-312-97837-5*, St. Martin's Paperbacks); 2000. 350p. 25.95 (*0-312-25339-7*) St. Martin's Pr.

Counsilman, J. J. Dragon's Full Glory: A Novel of Love & Prejudice in Modern China. 2002. 236p. pap. 19.95 (*1-58851-198-7*) PublishAmerica, Inc.

Cussler, Clive & Dirgo, Craig. Golden Buddha. 2003. 432p. pap. 15.00 (*0-425-19172-9*) Berkley Publishing Group.

—Golden Buddha. abr. ed. 2003. audio 24.95 (*1-59355-202-5*, 4812); audio 32.95 (*1-59355-200-9*, 4810, Brilliance Audio Unabridged); audio 87.25 (*1-59355-201-7*, 4811, Brilliance Audio Unabridged Lib Ed); audio compact disk 36.95 (*1-59355-203-3*, 4813, Brilliance Audio on CD Unabridged); audio compact disk 102.25 (*1-59355-204-1*, 4814, Brilliance Audio Unabridged Lib Ed) Brilliance Audio.

Dai, Fan. Butterfly Lovers: A Tale of the Chinese Romeo & Juliet. 2003. 251p. pap. 16.95 (*0-9665421-4-2*) Homa & Sekey Bks.

Dao, Bei. Waves. McDougall, Bonnie S. & Cooke, Susette T., trs. from CHI. 1990. (Paperback Ser.). 224p. pap. 13.95 (*0-8112-1134-7*, NDP693) New Directions Publishing Corp.

Darrell, Elizabeth. The Rice Dragon. 2002. 539p. 26.99 (*0-7278-5655-3*) Severn Hse. Pubs., Ltd.

Davis, John F. Chinese Novels. 1976. 296p. reprint ed. 50.00 (*0-8201-1278-X*) Scholars' Facsimiles & Reprints.

de Musset, Alfred. The Confession of a Child of the Century. 1977. reprint ed. 25.00 o.p. (*0-86527-231-X*) Fertig, Howard Inc.

—The Confession of a Child of the Century. 2002. 244p. pap. 94.99 (*1-58827-279-6*); per. 90.99 (*1-58827-280-X*) IndyPublish.com.

Delattre, Pierre. Tales of a Dalai Lama. 1978. (Fiction Ser.). 160p. pap. 5.95 o.p. (*0-916870-10-3*) Creative Arts Bk. Co.

—Tales of a Dalai Lama. 159p. 1999. pap. 14.95 (*0-89924-098-4*); 1998. (Illus.). 24.95 (*0-89924-099-2*) Lost Horse Pr.

DeMarco, Frank. Messenger: A Sequel to Lost Horizon. 1994. 240p. pap. 9.95 (*1-57174-013-9*) Hampton Roads Publishing Co., Inc.

Der Ling. Golden Phoenix. 1977. (Short Story Index Reprint Ser.). (Illus.). 22.95 (*0-8369-3187-4*) Ayer Co. Pubs., Inc.

DiMercurio, Michael. Attack of the Seawolf. 1993. 352p. 21.95 o.s.i (*1-55611-360-9*) Fine, Donald I. Bks.

Dong, He. Ask the Sun: Stories of Childhood in the Cultural Revolution. Hanson, Katherine, tr. from CHI. 1997. Tr. of Spor Solen. 112p. (Orig.). pap. 12.95 (*1-879679-10-8*) Women In Translation.

Douglass, Keith. Alpha Strike. 1997. (Carrier Ser.: No. 8). 336p. mass mkt. 6.99 o.s.i (*0-515-12018-9*, Jove) Berkley Publishing Group.

Drummond, Emma. The Bridge of a Hundred Dragons. 1986. 352p. 16.95 o.p. (*0-312-09549-X*) St. Martin's Pr.

—The Bridge of a Hundred Dragons. l.t. ed. 1987. 608p. 17.95 o.p. (*0-7089-8420-7*, Charnwood) Thorpe, F. A. Pubs. GBR. *Dist:* Ulverscroft Large Print Bks., Ltd.

Eaton, Evelyn. Go Ask the River. 1990. 292p. reprint ed. text 9.95 o.p. (*0-89087-611-8*) Celestial Arts Publishing Co.

Ehrlich, John D. The China Card. 1987. 656p. mass mkt. 4.50 o.s.i (*0-446-34577-6*) Warner Bks., Inc.

Ehrlichman, John D. The China Card. 1986. 523p. 18.45 o.p. (*0-671-50716-8*, Simon & Schuster) Simon & Schuster.

Elegant, Robert S. From a Far Land. 1989. mass mkt. 4.95 o.s.i (*0-449-21685-3*, Fawcett) Ballantine Bks.

—Last Year in Hong Kong: A Love Story. 1997. 256p. 23.00 (*0-688-14890-5*, Morrow, William & Co.) Morrow/Avon.

—Manchu. 1982. 608p. mass mkt. 4.95 o.s.i (*0-449-24445-8*, Fawcett) Ballantine Bks.

—Manchu. 1980. 592p. 12.95 o.p. (*0-07-019163-8*) McGraw-Hill Cos., The.

—Mandarin. 1984. mass mkt. 4.50 o.s.i (*0-671-45175-8*, Pocket); 1983. 544p. 17.25 o.p. (*0-671-45173-1*, Simon & Schuster) Simon & Schuster.

Elegant, Simon. A Floating Life: The Adventures of Li Po, an Historical Novel. 1999. 320p. pap. o.p. (*0-88001-656-6*); 288p. o.p. (*0-88001-559-4*) HarperTrade. (Ecco).

Falla, Jonathan. Blue Poppies. 2003. 240p. pap. 11.95 (*0-385-33680-2*, Delta) Dell Publishing.

—Blue Poppies. 2002. 213p. pap. 15.00 (*1-903238-37-4*) Interlink Publishing Group, Inc.

Fast, Jonathan. The Jade Stalk: An Erotic Novel. 1988. 320p. 18.95 o.p. (*0-525-24650-9*, Dutton) Dutton/Plume.

Feng Ji-cai. Chrysanthemums & Other Stories. Chen, Susan W., tr. from CHI. 1985. 240p. 19.95 o.p. (*0-15-117878-X*) Harcourt Trade Pubs.

—The Three-Inch Golden Lotus. Wakefield, David, tr. from CHI. 1994. (Fiction from Modern China Ser.). 208p. (C). pap. 14.95 (*0-8248-1606-4*); text 28.00 o.p. (*0-8248-1574-2*) Univ. of Hawaii Pr.

Flack, Marjorie. Story about Ping. 1989. (StoryTape Ser.). (J). 6.95 o.p. (*0-14-095038-9*, Puffin Bks.) Penguin Putnam Bks. for Young Readers.

Fleischman, Lisa Huang. Dream of the Walled City. 2000. 432p. 24.95 o.s.i (*0-671-04228-9*, Atria); 2001. 448p. reprint ed. pap. 13.95 (*0-671-04229-7*, Washington Square Pr.) Simon & Schuster.

Flinchbaugh, C. Hope. Daughter of China. 2002. 288p. pap. 11.99 (*0-7642-2731-9*) Bethany Hse. Pubs.

Fraser, George MacDonald. Flashman & the Dragon. unabr. ed. 1995. (Flashman Ser.). audio 72.00 (*0-7366-3053-8*, 3735) Books on Tape, Inc.

—Flashman & the Dragon. 1987. (Flashman Ser.). 336p. pap. 13.95 (*0-452-26191-0*); pap. 7.95 o.p. (*0-452-25930-4*) Dutton/Plume. (Plume).

Frey, Edward. To Please a Chinese Wife: A Romance for Keen Readers - With True Tales of Southeast Asia. 1999. 416p. pap. (*0-9671947-0-9*) Asia Literary Pr., U.S.A.

Frutkin, Mark. The Lion of Venice. 2000. (Porc Epic Book Ser.). 213p. pap. 12.95 (*0-88878-378-7*, Porcepic Bks.) Beach Holme Pubs., Ltd. CAN. *Dist:* Strauss Consultants.

Gaan, Margaret. Blue Mountain. l.t. ed. 1989. (Ulverscroft Large Print Ser.). 464p. 29.99 o.p. (*0-7089-2009-8*, Ulverscroft) Thorpe, F. A. Pubs. GBR. *Dist:* Ulverscroft Large Print Bks., Ltd., Ulverscroft Large Print Canada, Ltd.

—Red Barbarian. l.t. ed. 1989. (Ulverscroft Large Print Ser.). 633p. 29.99 o.p. (*0-7089-1958-8*, Ulverscroft) Thorpe, F. A. Pubs. GBR. *Dist:* Ulverscroft Large Print Bks., Ltd., Ulverscroft Large Print Canada, Ltd.

Garcia, Cristina. Monkey Hunting: A Novel. 2003. (Illus.). 272p. 23.00 (*0-375-41056-2*) Knopf, Alfred A. Inc.

Geddes, Ward, tr. from JPN. & intro. Kara Monogatari: Tales of China. 1984. (Occasional Paper Arizona State Univ., Center for Asian Studies: No.16). 192p. pap. 10.00 (*0-939252-12-0*) Arizona State Univ. Ctr. for Asian Studies.

Gilman, Dorothy. Mrs. Pollifax pursued. 1985. 224p. mass mkt. 6.99 (*0-449-20840-0*, Fawcett) Ballantine Bks.

—Mrs. Pollifax & the China Station. 1983. (Illus.). 192p. 12.95 o.p. (*0-385-14525-X*) Doubleday Publishing.

Gilman, Dorothy. Mrs Pillifax pursued 1995. 240p. mass mkt. 6.99 (*0-449-14956-0*, Fawcett) Ballantine Bks.

Goldblatt, Howard, tr. from CHI. The Garlic Ballads. 1995. Tr. of Tien-Tang Suan Tai Chih Ko. 304p. 23.95 o.p. (*0-670-85401-8*, Viking) Viking Penguin.

Grey, Anthony. Peking. 1988. 560p. 19.95 (*0-316-32823-5*) Little Brown & Co.

Guanzhong, Lou. Romance of the Three Kingdoms, Vol. 2. Brewitt-Taylor, C. H., tr. from CHI. 2nd ed. 1985. 638p. reprint ed. 19.95 (*0-89346-925-4*) Heian International Publishing, Inc.

Hall, Adam. Quiller Bamboo. unabr. collector's ed. 1992. (Quiller Ser.). audio 56.00 (*0-7366-2117-2*, 2920) Books on Tape, Inc.

—Quiller Bamboo. 1992. 320p. mass mkt. 4.99 (*0-380-71161-3*, Avon Bks.); 1991. 288p. 20.00 o.p. (*0-688-09696-4*, Morrow, William & Co.) Morrow/Avon.

Han, Shaogong. A Dictionary of Maqiao. Lovell, Julia, tr. from CHI. 2003. 400p. 27.95 (*0-231-12744-8*) Columbia Univ. Pr.

Haupeur, J. H. Hot Nights in Rangoon. pap. o.p. (*1-56097-232-7*) Fantagraphics Bks.

Hawksley, Humphrey & Holberton, Simon. Dragon Strike. 1999. mass mkt. (*0-312-97125-7*, St. Martin's Paperbacks) St. Martin's Pr.

—Dragon Strike: The Millennium War. 1998. 387p. pap. text 17.00 (*0-7881-5917-8*) DIANE Publishing Co.

—Dragon Strike: The Millennium War. 1997. (Illus.). 350p. mass mkt. 13.95 (*0-330-35036-6*) Macmillan U.K. GBR. *Dist:* Trans-Atlantic Pubns., Inc.

Hawksley, Humphrey, et al. Dragon Strike. 1999. xiv, 387p. 26.95 (*0-312-20531-7*) St. Martin's Pr.

Hearn, Lafcadio. Some Chinese Ghosts. 1887. (YA). reprint ed. 299p. pap. text 28.00 (*1-4047-6736-3*);Vol. 1. pap. text 28.00 (*1-4047-3065-6*) Classic Textbooks.

—Some Chinese Ghosts. 1986. 203p. pap. 7.95 o.p. (*9971-4-9096-X*) Heian International Publishing, Inc.

—Some Chinese Ghosts. 1972. reprint ed. lib. bdg. 32.95 (*0-8422-8074-X*) Irvington Pubs.

—Some Chinese Ghosts. 1992. (Notable American Authors Ser.). reprint ed. lib. bdg. 75.00 (*0-7812-3065-9*) Reprint Services Corp.

—Some Chinese Ghosts. 1887. 11.00 o.p. (*0-403-04286-0*) Somerset Pubs., Inc.

—Some Chinese Ghosts. 1999. 203p. (Illus.). pap. text 15.00 (*1-58715-000-X*); 35.00 (*1-58715-001-8*) Wildside Pr.

Henderson, Jon. Tigers & Dragons. 1993. 392p. pap. 10.99 o.p. (*0-8423-7309-8*) Tyndale Hse. Pubs.

Heng, Liu. Black Snow. Goldblatt, Howard, tr. from CHI. 1993. Tr. of Hei Ti Hsueh. 261p. 20.00 o.p. (*0-87113-530-2*) Grove/Atlantic, Inc.

—Green River Daydreams. Goldblatt, Howard, tr. from CHI. 2001. 384p. 24.00 o.p. (*0-8021-1690-6*); 2002. 336p. reprint ed. pap. 13.00 (*0-8021-3904-3*) Grove/Atlantic, Inc. (Grove Pr.).

Herman, Gail. Little Panda: Picture Book. 1995. (Illus.). 32p. (J). (ps-3). mass mkt. 2.95 (*0-590-55207-4*) Scholastic, Inc.

Herman, Richard, Jr. Dark Wing. 1994. 23.00 (*0-671-87306-7*, Simon & Schuster) Simon & Schuster.

Herman, Richard. The Last Phoenix. 2003. 496p. mass mkt. 7.99 (*0-06-103181-X*, HarperTorch); 2002. 448p. 25.95 (*0-06-620976-5*, Morrow, William & Co.) Morrow/Avon.

Herman, Steven L. Last Assignment. Anderson, Mark, ed. 2001. 192p. pap. 13.95 (*0-9707206-0-2*) Firelight Publishing, Inc.

Herron, Russell R. Empty Rice Bowl. Herron, Susan E., ed. 1995. (Illus.). 313p. (Orig.). pap. 6.95 (*0-9646470-0-1*) Beavercreek Pub. Co.

Hersey, John. The Call. 1986. 704p. pap. 8.95 o.p. (*0-14-008695-1*, Penguin Bks.) Viking Penguin.

Hill, Justin. The Drink & Dream Tea House: A Novel. 2001. 368p. 23.95 o.p. (*0-316-82400-3*) Little Brown & Co.

—The Drink & Dream Teahouse. 2002. 384p. reprint ed. pap. 13.95 (*0-316-82584-0*, Back Bay) Little Brown & Co.

Hill, Porter. China Flyer. 2001. (Illus.). 224p. mass mkt. 5.99 o.s.i (*0-425-17882-X*) Berkley Publishing Group.

Hobart, Alice Tisdale. Oil for the Lamps of China. 2002. 300p. reprint ed. pap. 14.95 (*1-891936-08-5*, D'Asia Vu Reprint Library) EastBridge.

Holt, Victoria. The House of a Thousand Lanterns. 1974. 336p. 9.95 o.s.i (*0-385-00817-1*) Doubleday Publishing.

Hsueh-Chin, Tsao, et al. The Dream of the Red Chamber. 1958. 352p. pap. 13.95 (*0-385-09379-9*) Doubleday Publishing.

Hua, Gu. Pagoda Ridge & Other Stories. Yang, Gladys, tr. from CHI. 1985. 260p. pap. 5.95 o.p. (*0-8351-1335-3*) China Bks. & Periodicals, Inc.

—Pagoda Ridge & Other Stories. 1995. 260p. lib. bdg. 29.00 o.p. (*0-8095-4516-0*) Millefleurs.

Huan Ching & the Golden Fish. 1988. (Publish-a-Book Clippers Ser.). (Illus.). 32p. (J). (gr. 2-4). lib. bdg. 29.28 o.p. incl. audio (*0-8172-2466-1*) Raintree Pubs.

Hughart, Barry. The Bridge of Birds: A Novel of China That Never Was. 1985. 288p. mass mkt. 6.99 (*0-345-32138-3*, Del Rey) Ballantine Bks.

—The Bridge of Birds: A Novel of China That Never Was. 1984. 256p. 13.95 o.p. (*0-312-09551-1*) St. Martin's Pr.

Hunt, E. Howard. Dragon Teeth. 1997. 480p. 26.95 o.s.i (*1-55611-523-7*) Fine, Donald I. Bks.

Hyde-Chambers, Frederick R. Lama: A Novel of Tibet. 1986. 576p. pap. text 4.95 o.p. (*0-07-031601-5*) McGraw-Hill Cos., The.

—Lama: A Story of Tibet. 1985. 480p. text 16.95 o.p. (*0-07-031600-7*) McGraw-Hill Cos., The.

Inoue, Yasushi. Tun Huang. Shaw & Tsuisaki, eds. Moy, Joan O., tr. from JPN. 1993. 216p. 12.95 o.p. (*0-87011-314-3*); pap. 12.00 o.s.i (*0-87011-576-6*) Kodansha America, Inc.

Ishiguro, Kazuo. When We Were Orphans. unabr. ed. 2000. audio 39.95 (*0-694-52384-4*, PH844, Harper-Audio) HarperTrade.

Jenner, William J., ed. & tr. from CHI. Modern Chinese Stories. Yang, Gladys, tr. from CHI. 1974. (Orig.). pap. 8.95 o.p. (*0-19-519788-7*) Oxford Univ. Pr., Inc.

Jin, Ba. Ward Four. Kong, Haili & Goldblatt, Howard, trs. 1999. 224p. pap. 14.95 (*0-8351-2646-3*) China Bks. & Periodicals, Inc.

Jin, Ha. The Bridegroom. E-Book 17.50 (*1-58945-611-4*) Adobe Systems, Inc.

—The Bridegroom. 2001. E-Book 11.00 (*0-375-42120-3*) Random Hse., Inc.

—The Bridegroom: Stories. 2001. 240p. reprint ed. pap. 12.00 (*0-375-72493-1*, Vintage) Knopf Publishing Group.

—The Crazed. 2004. 336p. pap. 13.95 (*0-375-71411-1*, Vintage) Knopf Publishing Group.

—The Crazed: A Novel. 2002. 336p. 24.00 (*0-375-42181-5*, Pantheon) Knopf Publishing Group.

—In the Pond. 1998. 160p. 20.00 (*0-944072-92-5*, Zoland Bks., Inc.) Steerforth Pr.

—In the Pond. 2000. 17.05 (*0-606-21847-5*) Turtleback Bks.

—In the Pond: A Novel. 2000. 192p. pap. 12.00 (*0-375-70911-8*, Vintage) Knopf Publishing Group.

—Ocean of Words: Army Stories. 1996. 204p. (Orig.). pap. 13.95 o.p. (*0-944072-58-5*, Zoland Bks., Inc.) Steerforth Pr.

—Under the Red Flag: Stories by Ha Jin. 1999. (Illus.). 224p. pap. 13.00 (*1-58195-006-3*); pap. (*0-944072-90-9*) Steerforth Pr. (Zoland Bks., Inc.).

—Under the Red Flag: Stories by Ha Jin. 1997. (Flannery O'Connor Award for Short Fiction Ser.). 224p. 22.95 (*0-8203-1939-2*) Univ. of Georgia Pr.

—Waiting. 2001. E-Book 11.50 (*1-58945-644-0*) Adobe Systems, Inc.

—Waiting. l.t. ed. 2000. 374p. 29.95 (*1-56895-885-4*, Wheeler Publishing, Inc.) Gale Group.

—Waiting. 2001. E-Book 11.50 (*0-375-72695-0*) Random Hse., Inc.

—Waiting. 2000. 19.05 (*0-606-21850-5*) Turtleback Bks.

—Waiting: A Novel. (Vintage International Ser.). 320p. 2000. pap. 13.00 (*0-375-70641-0*, Vintage); 1999. 24.00 (*0-375-40653-0*, Pantheon) Knopf Publishing Group.

Jones, Idwal. China Boy. 1977. (Short Story Index Reprint Ser.). reprint ed. 16.95 (*0-8369-3947-6*) Ayer Co. Pubs., Inc.

Jones, Margaret G. The Confucius Enigma. 1982. 224p. 10.95 o.p. (*0-312-16238-3*) St. Martin's Pr.

Jones, Rod. Julia Paradise. 1987. 98p. 12.70 o.p. (*0-671-64663-X*) Summit Bks.

—Julia Paradise. 1989. 128p. pap. 6.95 o.p. (*0-14-010077-6*, Penguin Bks.) Viking Penguin.

Jui, Li. Silver City. Goldblatt, Howard, tr. 1997. 276p. 25.00 o.s.i (*0-8050-4895-2*, Metropolitan Bks.) Holt, Henry & Co.

Kadare, Ismail. The Concert. Vrioni, Jusuf & Ray, Barbara, trs. 1998. 444p. pap. 14.95 (*1-55970-415-2*) Arcade Publishing, Inc.

—The Concert. 1994. 443p. 25.00 o.p. (*0-688-09762-6*, Morrow, William & Co.) Morrow/Avon.

Kenrick, Tony. Shanghai Surprise. 1986. 304p. pap. 3.95 o.p. (*0-14-009405-9*, Penguin Bks.) Viking Penguin.

Kern, Gary. The Last Snow Leopard. 1996. 271p. 35.00 o.p. (*0-8095-6020-8*) Millefleurs.

King, Gail O. Story of Hua Guan Suo. 1989. (Monograph Ser.: No. 23). 279p. pap. 10.00 (*0-939252-20-1*) Arizona State Univ. Ctr. for Asian Studies.

Kok, Marilyn. Stillpoint. 1996. (Portraits Ser.: No. 2). 256p. pap. 8.99 o.p. (*1-55661-821-2*) Bethany Hse. Pubs.

—Stillpoint. l.t. ed. 2000. (Christian Mystery Ser.). 398p. 23.95 (*0-7862-2698-6*) Thorndike Pr.

Kuan-Chung, Lo. Romance of the Three Kingdoms. Brewitt-Taylor, C. H., tr. 2002. reprint ed. Vol. 1. pap. 24.95 (*0-8048-3467-9*); Vol. 2. pap. 24.95 (*0-8048-3468-7*) Tuttle Publishing.

Lachs, Lorraine. Flowers for Mei-Ling. 1997. 416p. 24.00 o.p. (*0-7867-0414-4*, Carroll & Graf Pubs.) Avalon Publishing Group.

Lao She. Rickshaw: The Novel Lo-t'o hsiang Tzu. James, Jean M., tr. from CHI. 1979. Orig. Title: Lo-to Hsiang Tzu. (C). text 12.00 o.p. (*0-8248-0616-6*); xi, 249 p. pap. text 10.00 (*0-8248-0655-7*) Univ. of Hawaii Pr.

Larsen, Jeanne. Bronze Mirror. 1991. 384p. 19.95 o.p. (*0-8050-1110-2*) Holt, Henry & Co.

—Manchu Palaces. abr. ed. 1997. audio 21.95 (*1-57453-133-6*) Audio Literature.

—Manchu Palaces. 1996. (Illus.). 88p. 25.00 o.p. (*0-8050-1111-0*) Holt, Henry & Co.

—Silk Road. 1990. 448p. pap. 9.95 o.s.i (*0-449-90523-3*, Fawcett) Ballantine Bks.

—Silk Road: A Novel of Eighth-Century China. 1989. (Illus.). 400p. 19.95 o.p. (*0-8050-0958-2*) Holt, Henry & Co.

Lattimore, Eleanor F. Little Pear. 1992. (J). (gr. 1-4). 18.00 o.p. (*0-8446-6576-2*) Smith, Peter Pub., Inc.

Lee, C. Y. Gate of Rage: A Novel of One Family Trapped by the Events at Tiananmen Square. 1991. 340p. 20.00 o.p. (*0-688-09764-2*, Morrow, William & Co.) Morrow/Avon.

—The Second Son of Heaven: A Novel. Drew, Lisa, ed. 1990. 384p. 19.95 o.p. (*0-688-05140-5*, Morrow, William & Co.) Morrow/Avon.

Lee, Lilian. Farewell to My Concubine. 1993. Tr. of Pa-wang Pieh Chi. (CHI & ENG.). x, 255p. 18.00 o.p. (*0-688-12020-2*, Morrow, William & Co.) Morrow/Avon.

—Last Princess of Manchuria: A Novel. 1992. 15.00 o.p. (*0-688-10834-2*, Morrow, William & Co.) Morrow/Avon.

Levi, Jean. The Chinese Emperor. Bray, Barbara, tr. 1987. 18.95 (*0-15-117649-3*) Harcourt Trade Pubs.

—The Chinese Emperor. 1989. pap. 8.95 o.s.i (*0-394-75996-6*, Vintage) Knopf Publishing Group.

—The Dream of Confucius. 1992. 22.95 o.s.i (*0-15-126570-4*) Harcourt Trade Pubs.

Li, Leslie. Bittersweet. unabr. ed. 1999. audio 104.00 (*0-7887-0326-9*, 94518E7) Recorded Bks., LLC.

—Bittersweet. 1994. 398p. pap. 12.95 (*0-8048-3036-3*); 1992. x, 388p. 19.95 o.p. (*0-8048-1777-4*) Tuttle Publishing.

Lin Yu-T'ang. Widow, Nun & Courtesan: Three Novelettes from the Chinese. 1971. 266p. reprint ed. 38.50 o.s.i (*0-8371-4716-6*, LIWN, Greenwood Pr.) Greenwood Publishing Group, Inc.

Liu, Aimee. Cloud Mountain. abr. ed. 1997. audio 17.98 (*1-57042-480-2*) Time Warner AudioBooks.

Liu, Aimee E. Cloud Mountain. abr. ed. 1997. audio 19.00 o.p. Beeler, Thomas T. Publisher.

—Cloud Mountain. 1998. mass mkt. (*0-446-60544-1*); 1997. 368p. 24.00 o.p. (*0-446-51987-1*); 1998. 672p. reprint ed. pap. 14.99 (*0-446-67434-6*) Warner Bks., Inc.

—Flash House. 2004. 472p. pap. 13.95 (*0-446-69121-6*); 2003. (Illus.). 464p. 24.95 (*0-446-53097-2*) Warner Bks., Inc.

Lo Kuan-Chung. Romance of the Three Kingdoms. 1985. reprint ed. Set, Vols. 1-2. 1276p. text 39.90 o.p. (*981-218-043-5*); Vol. 1. 623p. text 19.95 o.p. (*9971-947-94-3*) Heian International Publishing, Inc.

—Romance of the Three Kingdoms, Vol. 2. Brewitt-Taylor, C. H., tr. from CHI. 2nd ed. 1985. 638p. reprint ed. text 19.95 o.p. (*981-218-044-3*) Heian International Publishing, Inc.

—Romance of the Three Kingdoms. Brewitt-Taylor, C. H., tr. 1990. 1280p. pap. 39.95 o.p. (*0-8048-1649-2*); 1969. 37.50 o.p. (*0-8048-0726-4*) Tuttle Publishing.

—Three Kingdoms: A Historical Novel. Roberts, Moss, tr. 1977. pap. 15.16 o.s.i (*0-394-73393-2*, Pantheon) Knopf Publishing Group.

—Three Kingdoms: A Historical Novel. Roberts, Moss, ed. 1976. 320p. 10.00 o.s.i (*0-394-40722-9*, Pantheon) Knopf Publishing Group.

—Three Kingdoms: A Historical Novel. 1994. (Illus.). 1096p. pap. text 45.00 o.s.i (*0-520-08930-8*) Univ. of California Pr.

—Three Kingdoms: A Historical Novel. Roberts, Moss, tr. & intro. by. 1992. (Centennial Bk.). 1110p. (C). 100.00 o.p. (*0-520-06821-1*) Univ. of California Pr.

Lo Kuan-Chung, et al. Three Kingdoms: A Historical Novel. abr. ed. 1999. (Illus.). 504p. text 50.00 (*0-520-21584-2*); pap. text 21.95 (*0-520-21585-0*) Univ. of California Pr.

Long, Jeff. Ascent: A Novel. 1992. 20.00 o.p. (*0-688-10888-1*, Morrow, William & Co.) Morrow/Avon.

Lord, Bette Bao. The Middle Heart. 1997. 408p. pap. 12.00 (*0-449-91232-9*); mass mkt. 6.99 o.p. (*0-449-22564-X*); mass mkt. 6.99 o.s.i (*0-449-28808-0*) Ballantine Bks. (Fawcett).

—The Middle Heart. abr. ed. 1996. 24.95 o.p. (*0-7871-0929-0*, 693405) NewStar Media, Inc.

—Spring Moon: A Novel of China. l.t. ed. 1982. 18.95 o.p. (*0-8161-3385-9*, Macmillan Reference USA) Gale Group.

—Spring Moon: A Novel of China. 1981. 400p. 15.45 o.p. (*0-06-014893-4*) HarperCollins Pubs.

—Spring Moon: A Novel of China. 1990. 592p. mass mkt. 7.99 (*0-06-100105-8*, HarperTorch); 1982. mass mkt. 4.95 (*0-380-59923-6*, Avon Bks.) Morrow/Avon.

Louie, Andrea. Moon Cakes. 1995. 341.10 (*0-345-39622-7*); o.s.i (*0-345-39674-X*); 288p. 21.00 o.s.i (*0-345-38554-3*) Ballantine Bks.

Lowe, H. Y. The Adventures of Wu: The Life Cycle of a Peking Man. (Illus.). 274p. reprint ed. Vol. 1. pap. 78.10 o.p. (*0-608-06411-4*, 2066625); Vol. 1-2. 1983. pap. 85.00 (*0-608-06412-2*, 206662500008) Bks. on Demand.

—The Adventures of Wu: The Life Cycle of a Peking Man. 1983. (Illus.). 512p. reprint ed. 55.00 o.p. (*0-691-06552-7*); pap. 17.95 o.p. (*0-691-01400-0*) Princeton Univ. Pr.

Ma, Y. W. & Lau, Joseph S., eds. Traditional Chinese Stories: Themes & Variations. 1991. (C & T Asian Literature Ser.). 619p. (C). reprint ed. pap. text 29.95 (*0-88727-071-9*) Cheng & Tsui Co.

—Traditional Chinese Stories: Themes & Variations. 1978. 603p. 51.50 o.p. (*0-231-04058-X*); pap. 20.00 o.p. (*0-231-04059-8*) Columbia Univ. Pr.

Maas, Peter. China White. l.t. ed. 1995. (Large Print Bks.). pap. 23.95 (*1-56895-096-9*, Wheeler Publishing, Inc.) Gale Group.

—China White. 1994. 272p. 23.00 o.s.i (*0-671-69417-0*, Simon & Schuster) Simon & Schuster.

Malraux, André. The Conquerors. Becker, Stephen, tr. from FRE. 1977. pap. 3.95 o.s.i (*0-394-17023-7*, E701) Grove/Atlantic, Inc.

—The Conquerors. 1976. o.p. (*0-03-007716-8*) Holt, Henry & Co.

—The Conquerors. Becker, Stephen, tr. 1991. (Phoenix Fiction Ser.). 212p. pap. text 16.00 (*0-226-50290-2*) Univ. of Chicago Pr.

—Man's Fate. 1990. 368p. pap. 14.00 (*0-679-72574-1*, Vintage) Knopf Publishing Group.

—Man's Fate. 1965. 360p. (C). 11.25 (*0-07-553654-4*, McGraw-Hill Humanities, Social Sciences & World Languages) McGraw-Hill Higher Education.

—Man's Fate. 1984. 18.95 o.p. (*0-394-54379-3*); Vol. 479. 1969. pap. 5.95 o.p. (*0-394-70479-7*) Random Hse., Inc.

Mao Dun, et al. Rainbow. Zelin, Madeleine, tr. from CHI. 1992. (Fast Forward MBA Ser.: No. 4). 255p. pap. 19.95 (*0-520-07328-2*) Univ. of California Pr.

Martens, Wilfred. River of Glass. 1980. 232p. pap. 6.95 o.p. (*0-8361-1913-4*) Herald Pr.

Maxwell, Ann. Shadow & Silk. l.t. ed. 1997. lib. bdg. 25.95 (*1-57490-085-4*, Beeler Large Print Bks.) Beeler, Thomas T. Publisher.

—Shadow & Silk. 1999. (Romance Ser.). 25.95 (*0-7862-1716-2*, Five Star) Gale Group.

—Shadow & Silk. 432p. 2002. mass mkt. 6.99 (*0-8217-7311-9*); 1997. mass mkt. 6.50 o.s.i (*0-8217-5547-1*, Zebra Bks.) Kensington Publishing Corp.

Mayer, Bob. Dragon SIM-13: A Novel. 1992. 19.95 o.p. (*0-89141-415-0*, Presidio Pr.) Ballantine Bks.

McCune, Evelyn. Empress: A Novel. 1994. 512p. pap. 25.00 (*0-449-90749-X*) Ballantine Bks.

McCunn, Ruthanne Lum. The Moon Pearl. 2000. 316p. 24.00 (*0-8070-8348-8*) Beacon Pr.

McFadden, T. Formosa Straits. E-Book 3.50 (*1-58495-072-2*) DiskUs Publishing.

McKenna, Richard. The Sand Pebbles, Pt. 2. unabr. collector's ed. 1986. audio 56.00 (*0-7366-0553-3*, 1526-B) Books on Tape, Inc.

—The Sand Pebbles. 1991. 608p. reprint ed. lib. bdg. 49.95 (*0-89966-857-7*) Buccaneer Bks., Inc.

—The Sand Pebbles. 1963. 11.95 o.p. (*0-06-012910-7*) HarperCollins Pubs.

—The Sand Pebbles. (Bluejacket Bks.). reprint ed. 2000. xxii, 597p. pap. 21.95 (*1-55750-446-6*); 1984. 597p. 32.95 o.p. (*0-87021-592-2*) Naval Institute Pr.

—The Sand Pebbles. 2002. E-Book 4.99 (*0-7953-0512-5*) RosettaBooks.

McLeay, Alison. After Shanghai. 1996. 432p. 24.95 o.p. (*0-312-14271-4*) St. Martin's Pr.

Meidav, Edie. The Far Field: A Novel of Ceylon. 2002. 592p. pap. 14.00 (*0-618-21916-1*, Mariner Bks.) Houghton Mifflin Co. Trade & Reference Div.

Michael, Judith, pseud. A Certain Smile. 2000. 352p. mass mkt. 7.99 (*0-449-22426-0*); mass mkt. 6.99 (*0-449-00681-6*, Fawcett) Ballantine Bks.

—A Certain Smile. abr. ed. 2000. audio 7.99 o.s.i (*1-56740-984-9*, 2112, Paperback Nova Audio Bks.); 1999. audio 17.95 o.p. (*1-56740-805-2*, 1523, Nova Audio Bks.); 1999. 11p. audio 73.25 (*1-56740-612-2*, 1651, Unabridged Library Editions); 1999. audio 39.95 (*1-56740-083-3*, 1521, Brilliance Audio Unabridged) Brilliance Audio.

—A Certain Smile. l.t. ed. pap. 24.95 o.p. (*0-7838-8544-X*, Macmillan Reference USA) Gale Group.

—A Certain Smile, abr. ed. 1999. audio 17.95 Highsmith Inc.

—A Certain Smile. l.t. ed. 1999. 560p. 24.95 o.s.i (*0-375-70678-X*) Random Hse., Inc.

Min, Anchee. Becoming Madame Mao. 2000. 320p. tchr. ed. 25.00 (*0-618-00407-6*) Houghton Mifflin Co.

—Becoming Madame Mao. 2001. 330p. pap. 13.00 (*0-618-12700-3*, Mariner Bks.) Houghton Mifflin Co. Trade & Reference Div.

—Katherine. 2001. 240p. pap. 13.00 o.s.i (*0-425-18023-9*); 1996. 304p. mass mkt. 6.99 o.s.i (*0-425-15291-X*) Berkley Publishing Group.

—Katherine, Set. abr. ed. 1995. 17.95 o.p. (*0-7871-0252-0*, 392915) NewStar Media, Inc.

—Katherine. 1995. 241p. 22.95 o.p. (*1-57322-005-1*, Riverhead Bks. (Hardcovers)) Putnam Publishing Group, The.

—Wild Ginger: A Novel. 2002. 224p. tchr. ed. 23.00 (*0-618-06886-4*) Houghton Mifflin Co.

—Wild Ginger: A Novel. 2004. 240p. pap. 13.00 (*0-618-38043-4*, Mariner Bks.) Houghton Mifflin Co. Trade & Reference Div.

Mo, Yan. Shifu, You'll Do Anything for a Laugh: A Novel. 2003. (Illus.). 212p. pap. 12.95 (*1-55970-671-6*) Arcade Publishing, Inc.

Mo Yen. Red Sorghum. Goldblatt, Howard, tr. 1993. 368p. 23.50 o.p. (*0-670-84402-0*, Viking) Viking Penguin.

Mones, Nicole. Lost in Translation. 1999. 384p. pap. 13.95 (*0-385-31944-4*, Delta) Dell Publishing.

Monjo, F. N. The Porcelain Pagoda. 1976. (Illus.). 256p. (J). (gr. 7-11). 10.00 o.p. (*0-670-56565-2*) Viking Penguin.

Motley, Annette. Green Dragon, White Tiger. 1988. 592p. mass mkt. 4.95 o.p. (*0-451-40061-5*, Onyx) NAL.

Nai-Shan, Ch'eng. The Piano Tuner. Dean, Britten, tr. from CHI. & intro. by. 1989. 198p. 16.95 o.p. (*0-8351-2142-9*); pap. 8.95 o.p. (*0-8351-2141-0*) China Bks. & Periodicals, Inc.

Namioka, Lensey. The Laziest Boy in the World. 1998. (Illus.). 32p. (J). (ps-3). tchr. ed. 16.95 (*0-8234-1330-6*) Holiday Hse., Inc.

Ng, Lillian. Swallowing Clouds. 1999. 306p. o.p. (*0-88001-644-2*, Ecco) HarperTrade.

Norton, Andre. Imperial Lady. 1990. mass mkt. 3.95 (*0-8125-0722-3*); Vol. 1. 1989. 17.95 o.p. (*0-312-93128-X*) Doherty, Tom Assocs., LLC. (Tor Bks.).

O'Diear, James. Season of the Tigers: A Novel of Pre-Pearl Harbor Espionage & Counterespionage. McDonald, Susie & Ball, Terrie, eds. 1995. (Illus.). 319p. (Orig.). pap. 14.99 (*1-57090-015-9*) aBOOKS Distributing.

Owen, Frank F. The Wind That Tramps the World: Splashes of Chinese Color, Vol. 1. 1977. (Short Story Index Reprint Ser.). reprint ed. 19.95 (*0-8369-4186-1*) Ayer Co. Pubs., Inc.

Oxnam, Robert B. Ming: A Novel of 17th Century China. 1994. xiii, 270p. 21.95 o.p. (*0-312-11315-3*) St. Martin's Pr.

Pacilio, V. J. Ling Cho & His Three Friends, RS. 2000. (Illus.). 32p. (J). (ps-3). 16.00 (*0-374-34545-7*, Farrar, Straus & Giroux (BYR)) Farrar, Straus & Giroux.

Pattison, Eliot. Bone Mountain. Date not set. mass mkt. (*0-312-98949-0*, St. Martin's Paperbacks); E-Book 18.95 (*0-312-70795-9*); 2002. (Illus.). 352p. 24.95 (*0-312-27760-1*, Saint Martin's Minotaur) St. Martin's Pr.

—Water Touching Stone. 2001. E-Book 24.95 (*1-58945-857-5*) Adobe Systems, Inc.

—Water Touching Stone. 2001. 400p. 24.95 o.s.i (*0-312-20612-7*, Saint Martin's Minotaur) St. Martin's Pr.

Peters, Maureen. Night of the Willow. 1981. 210p. 10.95 o.p. (*0-312-57318-9*) St. Martin's Pr.

Pieczenik, Steve. Pax Pacifica. 1995. 352p. mass mkt. 5.99 o.p. (*0-446-60250-7*); 336p. 22.95 o.s.i (*0-446-51557-4*); (*0-446-51818-2*) Warner Bks., Inc.

Pilegard, Virginia Walton. The Warlord's Beads. 2001. (Illus.). 32p. (J). (gr. k-2). 14.95 (*1-56554-863-9*) Pelican Publishing Co., Inc.

Ping, Wang & Wang, Ping. Foreign Devil. 1996. 287p. 21.95 (*1-56689-048-9*) Coffee Hse. Pr.

Pingwa, Jia. Turbulence: Novel. Goldblatt, Howard, tr. from CHI. 1991. 592p. 22.95 (*0-8071-1687-4*) Louisiana State Univ. Pr.

Putney, Mary Jo. The China Bride. 2001. 448p. mass mkt. 6.99 (*0-449-00589-5*, Ballantine Bks.) Ballantine Bks.

—The China Bride. l.t. ed. 2000. (Wheeler Large Print Book Ser.). 451p. 28.95 (*1-56895-916-8*, Wheeler Publishing, Inc.) Gale Group.

Reader's Digest Editors & Buck, Pearl S. A Pearl Buck Reader, 2 vols. 1985. (Illus.). 1008p. 19.95 o.p. (*0-89577-196-9*) Reader's Digest Assn., Inc., The.

Redfield, James. The Secret of Shambhala: In Search of the Eleventh Insight. 256p. 2001. pap. 14.95 (*0-446-67648-9*); 2001. E-Book 9.95 (*0-7595-9320-5*); 2001. E-Book 9.95 (*0-7595-6287-3*); 2001. E-Book 9.95 (*0-7595-8293-9*); 2001. E-Book 9.95 (*0-7595-0287-0*); 2001. E-Book 9.95 (*0-7595-4290-2*); 1999. 23.95 o.p. (*0-446-52308-9*) Warner Bks., Inc.

Reed, John Robert. The Kingfisher's Call. 2002. 304p. 22.00 (*1-57071-796-6*, Sourcebooks Landmark) Sourcebooks, Inc.

Reeman, Douglas. The First to Land. 1985. 293p. 16.95 o.p. (*0-688-04509-X*, Morrow, William & Co.) Morrow/Avon.

—The First to Land. l.t. ed. 1986. 416p. 13.95 o.p. (*0-7089-8368-5*, Charnwood) Thorpe, F. A. Pubs. GBR. *Dist:* Ulverscroft Large Print Bks., Ltd.

Reeser, Michael. Huan Ching & the Golden Fish. 1988. (Publish-a-Book Ser.). (Illus.). 32p. (J). (gr. 1-6). lib. bdg. 22.83 incl. audio (*0-8172-2751-2*) Raintree Pubs.

Robinson, Patrick. The Shark Mutiny. 2002. 512p. mass mkt. 7.99 (*0-06-103066-X*); 2001. (Illus.). 480p. 26.00 (*0-06-019631-9*) HarperCollins Pubs.

—The Shark Mutiny. l.t. ed. 2001. 672p. 25.00 (*0-06-621021-6*, HarperLargePrint) HarperTrade.

—The Shark Mutiny. 2001. 385p. o.s.i (*0-7126-8038-1*) Random Hse. of Canada, Ltd.

Rohmer, Sax, pseud. The Bride of Fu Manchu. 1976. reprint ed. lib. bdg. 21.95 (*0-89190-801-3*, Rivercity Pr.) Amereon, Ltd.

—Daughter of Fu Manchu. lib. bdg. 22.95 (*0-8488-2112-2*) Amereon, Ltd.

—Dream Detective. 1977. reprint ed. pap. 3.95 o.p. (*0-486-23504-1*) Dover Pubns., Inc.

—Drums of Fu Manchu. 20.95 (*0-8488-0619-0*) Amereon, Ltd.

—The Fu Manchu Omnibus. Vol. 1. 1996. 650p. pap. 16.95 (*0-7490-0271-9*); Vol. II. 1997. 656p. pap. 16.95 (*0-7490-0222-0*); Vol. 3. 1998. 650p. pap. 16.95 o.p. (*0-7490-0227-1*); Vol. 4. 1999. pap. 9.95 (*0-7490-0328-6*) Allison & Busby, Ltd. GBR. *Dist:* International Publishers Marketing.

—Fu Manchu Omnibus, Vol. 5. 2001. (Fu Manchu Omnibus Ser.: Vol. 5). 300p. pap. 15.95 (*0-7490-0520-3*) Allison & Busby, Ltd. GBR. *Dist:* International Publishers Marketing.

—The Hand of Fu Manchu. Date not set. reprint ed. lib. bdg. 20.95 (*0-89190-802-1*, American Reprint Co.) Amereon, Ltd.

—The Hand of Fu Manchu. unabr. ed. 1994. audio 44.95 (*0-7861-0794-4*, 2132) Blackstone Audio Bks., Inc.

—The Hand of Fu Manchu, Set. unabr. ed. 1994. audio 29.00 Jimcin Recordings.

—The Hand of Fu Manchu. unabr. ed. 2002. audio compact disk 20.00 (*1-4001-5052-3*) Tantor Media, Inc.

—The Hand of Fu Manchu. 2001. 308p. pap. 14.95 (*1-58715-219-3*) Wildside Pr.

—The Insidious Dr. Fu-Manchu. 1976. lib. bdg. 13.95 o.s.i (*0-89968-143-3*, Lightyear Pr.) Buccaneer Bks., Inc.

—The Insidious Dr. Fu-Manchu. 1997. (Dover Classic Mystery Ser.). (Illus.). 224p. pap. 2.00 (*0-486-29898-1*) Dover Pubns., Inc.

—The Insidious Dr. Fu-Manchu. 2002. 244p. 18.99 (*1-4043-0924-1*); per. 13.99 (*1-4043-0925-X*) IndyPublish.com.

—The Insidious Dr. Fu-Manchu. 1985. mass mkt. 3.50 o.s.i (*0-8217-1668-9*) Kensington Publishing Corp.

—The Insidious Dr. Fu-Manchu. E-Book 1.95 (*1-57799-899-5*) Logos Research Systems, Inc.

—The Insidious Dr. Fu-Manchu. E-Book 5.00 (*0-7410-0442-9*) SoftBook Pr.

—The Island of Fu Manchu. 1986. 320p. mass mkt. 3.50 o.p. (*0-8217-1912-2*, Zebra Bks.) Kensington Publishing Corp.

—The Mask of Fu Manchu. 1976. reprint ed. lib. bdg. 21.95 (*0-89190-803-X*, Rivercity Pr.) Amereon, Ltd.

—The Mask of Fu Manchu. 1985. 362 p. (*0-89621-588-1*) BBC Audiobooks America.

—The Mystery of Dr. Fu Manchu. Date not set. pap. text (*0-17-556692-5*) Addison-Wesley Longman, Inc.

—The Mystery of Dr. Fu Manchu. l.t. ed. 1994. 18.95 o.p. (*0-7451-6454-4*); 1992. 248p. reprint ed. 14.95 o.p. (*0-86220-837-8*, Black Dagger) BBC Audiobooks America.

—The Return of Dr. Fu-Manchu. 20.95 (*0-89190-828-5*) Amereon, Ltd.

—The Return of Dr. Fu-Manchu. 1976. lib. bdg. 13.95 (*0-89968-141-7*, Lightyear Pr.) Buccaneer Bks., Inc.

—The Return of Dr. Fu-Manchu. E-Book 1.95 (*1-57799-900-2*) Logos Research Systems, Inc.

—Shadow of Fu Manchu. 1986. 272p. mass mkt. 3.50 o.p. (*0-8217-1870-3*, Zebra Bks.) Kensington Publishing Corp.

—Trail of Fu Manchu. 25.95 (*0-8488-0317-5*) Amereon, Ltd.

—Trail of Fu Manchu. 1985. mass mkt. 3.50 o.s.i (*0-8217-1619-0*) Kensington Publishing Corp.

Rosenbaum, Ray. Hawks: A Novel. 1994. 314p. 21.95 o.p. (*0-89141-477-0*, Presidio Pr.) Ballantine Bks.

Rosenstock, Patricia Jane. China Nights. 2000. 356p. pap. 16.95 (*0-595-01027-X*) iUniverse, Inc.

Ross, Dana Fuller, pseud. Yankee Rogue. l.t. ed. 1993. 22.95 (*1-56895-044-6*, Wheeler Publishing, Inc.) Gale Group.

Rotenberg, David. The Lake Ching Murders: A Mystery of Fire & Ice. 2002. 208p. 22.95 (*0-312-27671-0*, Saint Martin's Minotaur) St. Martin's Pr.

—The Shanghai Murders. 1998. 320p. o.p. (*0-312-18661-4*); 24.95 o.p. (*0-312-18175-2*, 853565) St. Martin's Pr. (Saint Martin's Minotaur).

Roy, David T., tr. The Plum in the Golden Vase: Chin P'ing Mei The Gathering, Vol. 1. 1993. (Library of Asian Translations). (Illus.). 544p. text 90.00 o.p. (*0-691-06932-8*) Princeton Univ. Pr.

Ruoxi, Chen. The Short Stories of Chen Ruoxi, Translated from the Original Chinese: A Writer at the Crossroads. Kao, Hsin-sheng C., ed. 1992. 420p. 109.95 (*0-7734-9190-2*) Mellen, Edwin Pr., The.

Sa, Shan. The Girl Who Played Go. 2003. 320p. 22.95 (*1-4000-4025-6*, Everyman's Library) Knopf Publishing Group.

Scarborough, Elizabeth Ann. Nothing Sacred. 1991. 352p. pap. 19.00 (*0-385-41530-3*) Broadway Bks.

Schroder, Russell. Mulan Special Collector's Edition. deluxe ed. 1998. (Illus.). 72p. (J). (gr. 4-7). 16.95 (*0-7868-3173-1*) Disney Pr.

See, Lisa. Crooked Shadow. 2000. 512p. reprint ed. mass mkt. 6.99 o.s.i (*0-06-109754-3*, HarperTorch) Morrow/Avon.

—Dragon Bones: A Novel. 2003. 368p. 24.95 (*0-679-46320-8*) Random Hse., Inc.

—Flower Net. 1998. 480p. mass mkt. 6.99 o.s.i (*0-06-109543-5*); 1997. 352p. 24.00 o.p. (*0-06-017527-3*) HarperCollins Pubs.

—The Interior. 1999. 400p. 25.00 o.s.i (*0-06-019261-5*) HarperCollins Pubs.

Segalen, Victor. Rene Leys. 2003. (Classics Ser.). (Illus.). 208p. pap. 14.00 (*1-59017-041-5*) New York Review of Bks., Inc., The.

—Rene Leys. Underwood, J. A., tr. 224p. 1989. pap. 14.95 o.s.i (*0-87951-350-0*); 1988. 24.95 (*0-87951-324-1*) Overlook Pr., The.

Shen, Yen-Ping, pseud. Spring Silkworms & Other Stories. Shapiro, Sidney, tr. reprint ed. 39.50 (*0-404-14486-1*) AMS Pr., Inc.

Sher, William. Peace on Earth & Goodwill among Peoples. 2000. 9p. 11.95 o.p. (*0-533-13403-X*) Vantage Pr., Inc.

Shi Nai'an & Luo, Guanzhong. All Men Are Brothers. Buck, Pearl S., tr. from CHI. 2004. 658p. (C). pap. 16.95 (*1-55921-303-5*) Moyer Bell.

Shuo, Wang. Playing for Thrills: A Mystery. Goldblatt, Howard, tr. from CHI. 1997. 256p. 23.00 (*0-688-13046-1*, Morrow, William & Co.) Morrow/Avon.

—Playing for Thrills: A Mystery. Goldblatt, Howard, tr. 1998. 336p. 12.95 (*0-14-026971-1*) Viking Penguin.

—Please Don't Call Me Human. Goldblatt, Howard, tr. 304p. pap. 19.95 (*0-88727-412-9*) Cheng & Tsui Co.

—Please Don't Call Me Human. Goldblatt, Howard, tr. from CHI. 2000. 304p. 23.95 (*0-7868-6419-2*) Hyperion Pr.

Sijie, Dai. Balzac & the Little Chinese Seamstress: A Novel. 2002. Tr. of Balzac et la Petite Tailleuse Chinoise. 192p. pap. 10.00 (*0-385-72220-6*, Anchor Bible) Doubleday Publishing.

—Balzac & the Little Chinese Seamstress: A Novel. Rilke, Ina, tr. from FRE. 2001. Tr. of Balzac et la Petite Tailleuse Chinoise. 208p. 18.00 (*0-375-41309-X*) Knopf, Alfred A. Inc.

Simon, Roger L. Peking Duck. 1987. 256p. mass mkt. 3.95 (*0-446-34932-1*) Warner Bks., Inc.

—Peking Duck. 2002. E-Book 9.99 (*1-58824-340-0*); 2000. 304p. pap. 14.00 (*0-7434-0716-4*) ibooks, Inc.

Sledge, Linda C. Empire of Heaven. 1991. 640p. mass mkt. 5.95 o.s.i (*0-553-28693-5*) Bantam Bks.

Smith, Sid. Something Like a House. 2004. 224p. 25.00 (*1-56649-271-8*) Welcome Rain Pubs.

Sola, Liu. Chaos & All That: An Irreverent Novel. King, Richard, tr. from CHI. 1994. (Fiction from Modern China Ser.). (C). reprint ed. 142p. 22.00 (*0-8248-1617-X*); 134p. pap. 11.95 (*0-8248-1651-X*) Univ. of Hawaii Pr.

Soulie de Morant, George. Pei Yu: Boy Actress. Fabian, Gerald & Wernham, Guy, trs. from FRE. 1991. (Illus.). 160p. 19.95 (*0-9624751-3-0*); pap. 12.95 (*0-9624751-4-9*) Alamo Square Pr.

Sue, Chun. Beijing Doll. 2004. pap. 14.00 (*1-59448-020-6*, Riverhead Trade (Paperbacks)) Berkley Publishing Group.

Szymanski, Jean Artley & Bushman, Jennifer Scheel. Hard Sleeper: A Novel of Old & New China. 2003. xvii, 253p. 24.95 (*1-882897-73-0*) Lost Coast Pr.

Tan, Amy. The Bonesetter's Daughter. 2003. 400p. pap. 14.95 (*0-345-45737-4*, Ballantine Bks.); 2002. 416p. mass mkt. o.s.i (*0-345-45571-1*); 2002. 416p. reprint ed. mass mkt. 7.99 (*0-8041-1498-6*, Ballantine Bks.) Ballantine Bks.

—The Bonesetter's Daughter. 2001. 400p. 25.95 o.s.i (*0-399-14643-1*); 150.00 (*0-399-14685-7*) Penguin Group (USA) Inc.

—The Bonesetter's Daughter. l.t. ed. 567p. 2002. pap. 29.95 (*0-7862-2951-9*); 2001. 32.95 (*0-7862-2952-7*); 2001. (*0-7540-1594-7*); 2001. (*0-7540-2453-9*) Thorndike Pr.

Tarrant, John. China Gold. 1991. 252p. 19.95 (*0-8128-4020-8*, Scarborough Hse.) Madison Bks., Inc.

Taylor, Barry. The Deadfall Trap. 1990. 250p. 18.95 o.p. (*0-8027-1111-1*) Walker & Co.

Thayer, James Stewart. The Gold Swan. 2002. 352p. 25.00 (*0-684-86286-7*, Simon & Schuster) Simon & Schuster.

Theroux, Paul. Kowloon Tong: A Novel. l.t. ed. 1997. (G. K. Hall Core Ser.). 281p. lib. bdg. 25.95 (*0-7838-8275-0*, Macmillan Reference USA) Gale Group.

—Kowloon Tong: A Novel. 1997. 256p. 23.00 o.p. (*0-395-86029-6*) Houghton Mifflin Co.

—Kowloon Tong: A Novel. 1998. 248p. pap. 12.00 (*0-395-90141-3*, Mariner Bks.) Houghton Mifflin Co. Trade & Reference Div.

—Kowloon Tong: A Novel. 1997. 256p. 29.99 (*0-7710-8576-1*) McClelland & Stewart/Tundra Bks.

—Kowloon Tong: A Novel. unabr. ed. 1997. 25.00 o.p. (*0-7871-1465-0*) NewStar Media, Inc.

Tian-Cheng, Lu. The Embroidered Couch: An Erotic Novel of China. Hu, Lenny, tr. from CHI. 2001. (Illus.). 140p. pap. 12.95 (*1-55152-101-6*) Arsenal Pulp Pr., Ltd. CAN. *Dist:* Consortium Bk. Sales & Distribution.

Tien-Wen, Chu. Notes of a Desolate Man. 1999. (Modern Chinese Literature from Taiwan Ser.). viii, 169p. text 22.00 (*0-231-11608-X*) Columbia Univ. Pr.

—Notes of a Desolate Man. Goldblatt, Howard & Lin, Sylvia Li-Chun, trs. 2000. 184p. reprint ed. pap. 15.95 (*0-231-11609-8*) Columbia Univ. Pr.

Tong, Su. Raise the Red Lantern. 2004. 288p. pap. 12.95 (*0-06-059633-3*, Perennial) HarperTrade.

—Rice. 2004. 288p. pap. 12.95 (*0-06-059632-5*, Perennial) HarperTrade.

—Rice. Goldblatt, Howard, tr. from CHI. 1995. 288p. 23.00 o.p. (*0-688-13245-6*, Morrow, William & Co.) Morrow/Avon.

—Rice. 1996. 270p. pap. 14.00 (*0-14-025644-X*, Penguin Bks.) Penguin Group (USA) Inc.

Topping, Seymour. The Peking Letter: A Novel of the Chinese Civil War. 1999. 320p. text 25.00 (*1-891620-35-5*) PublicAffairs.

Tseng, Grace. White Tiger, Blue Serpent. 1999. (Illus.). 32p. (J). (gr. 1 up). lib. bdg. 16.89 (*0-688-12516-6*) HarperCollins Children's Bk. Group.

—White Tiger, Blue Serpent. 1999. (Illus.). 32p. (J). (ps-3). 16.00 (*0-688-12515-8*, Morrow, William & Co.) Morrow/Avon.

Tsubakiyama, Margaret. Mei-Mei Loves the Morning. 1999. (Illus.). 32p. (J). (ps-3). lib. bdg. 15.95 (*0-8075-5039-6*) Whitman, Albert & Co.

Tsukiyama, Gail. The Language of Threads. 1999. 276p. 23.95 o.p. (*0-312-20376-4*); 2000. (Illus.). 288p. reprint ed. pap. 12.95 (*0-312-26756-8*, Saint Martin's Griffin) St. Martin's Pr.

—Night of Many Dreams. unabr. ed. 1999. audio 29.95 (*0-7861-1546-7*); pap. 44.95 incl. audio (*0-7861-1335-9*, 2229) Blackstone Audio Bks., Inc.

—Night of Many Dreams. 1999. E-Book 12.95 o.s.i (*0-312-20733-6*); 1998. 288p. 22.95 o.p. (*0-312-17194-3*); 1998. 288p. reprint ed. pap. 12.95 (*0-312-19940-6*, NPB 0230, Saint Martin's Griffin) St. Martin's Pr.

—Women of the Silk. 288p. 1991. 18.95 (*0-312-06465-9*); 1993. reprint ed. pap. 12.95 (*0-312-09943-6*, NPB 0229, Saint Martin's Griffin) St. Martin's Pr.

Tuten, Frederic. The Adventures of Mao on the Long March. rev. ed. 1997. 144p. pap. 13.95 o.p. (*0-7145-3021-2*) Boyars, Marion Pubs., Inc.

Twigger, Robert. The Extinction Club: A Mostly True Story about Two Men, a Deer & a Writer. 2002. (Illus.). 240p. 23.95 (*0-688-17539-2*, Morrow, William & Co.) Morrow/Avon.

—The Extinction Club: A Mostly True Story about Two Men, a Deer & a Writer. 2001. 179p. (*0-241-14067-6*, Hamilton, Hamish) Viking Penguin.

Van Gulik, Robert H. Celebrated Cases of Judge Dee: An Authentic Eighteenth Century Chinese Detective Novel. 1976. (Illus.). 237p. reprint ed. pap. 6.95 (*0-486-23337-5*) Dover Pubns., Inc.

—The Chinese Bell Murders. 288p. 2004. pap. 12.95 (*0-06-072888-4*, Perennial); 1983. (Illus.). 10.95 o.p. (*0-06-015205-2*) HarperTrade.

—The Chinese Bell Murders. 1977. (Illus.). x, 298p. pap. 10.00 (*0-226-84862-0*) Univ. of Chicago Pr.

—The Chinese Gold Murders. 224p. 2004. pap. 12.95 (*0-06-072867-1*, Perennial); 1983. (Illus.). 10.95 o.p. (*0-06-015206-0*) HarperTrade.

—The Chinese Gold Murders. 1979. (Illus.). x, 214p. pap. 8.50 (*0-226-84864-7*) Univ. of Chicago Pr.

—The Chinese Lake Murders. 1979. (Illus.). viii, 215p. pap. 10.00 (*0-226-84865-5*) Univ. of Chicago Pr.

—Chinese Maze Murders. 1997. (Judge Dee Mysteries Ser.). (Illus.). 321p. pap. 11.00 (*0-226-84878-7*) Univ. of Chicago Pr.

—The Chinese Nail Murders. 1977. 220p. pap. 9.00 (*0-226-84863-9*) Univ. of Chicago Pr.

—Dee Goong An: Three Murder Cases Solved by Judge Dee. Van Gulik, Robert H., tr. 1980. (Literature of Mystery & Detection Ser.). (Illus.). 237p. reprint ed. 29.95 (*0-405-07875-7*) Ayer Co. Pubs., Inc.

—The Emperor's Pearl: A Judge Dee Mystery. 1982. o.p. (*0-434-82559-X*) David & Charles Pubs.

—The Emperor's Pearl: A Judge Dee Mystery. 1994. (Judge Dee Mysteries Ser.). (Illus.). vi, 186p. pap. 8.50 (*0-226-84872-8*) Univ. of Chicago Pr.

—The Haunted Monastery: A Judge Dee Mystery. 1983. 168p. pap. 2.95 o.p. (*0-684-17975-X*, Macmillan Reference USA) Gale Group.

—The Haunted Monastery: A Judge Dee Mystery, unabr. ed. 1986. (Judge Dee Mysteries Ser.). audio 26.00 (*1-55690-218-2*, 86530E7) Recorded Bks., LLC.

—The Haunted Monastery: A Judge Dee Mystery. 1997. (Judge Dee Mysteries Ser.). (Illus.). 198p. pap. 9.00 (*0-226-84879-5*) Univ. of Chicago Pr.

—The Haunted Monastery & the Chinese Maze Murders: A Judge Dee Mystery. 1978. (Illus.). 328p. 8.95 (*0-486-23502-5*) Dover Pubns., Inc.

—Judge Dee at Work, unabr. ed. 1986. (Judge Dee Mysteries Ser.). audio 26.00 (*1-55690-274-3*, 86560E7) Recorded Bks., LLC.

—Judge Dee at Work: Eight Chinese Detective Stories. 1979. (Judge Dee Mysteries Ser.). pap. 4.95 o.p. (*0-684-16179-6*, SL858, Macmillan Reference USA) Gale Group.

—Judge Dee at Work: Eight Chinese Detective Stories. 1992. (Judge Dee Mysteries Ser.). (Illus.). vi, 174p. pap. 8.00 (*0-226-84866-3*) Univ. of Chicago Pr.

—The Lacquer Screen: A Chinese Detective Story. 1982. o.p. (*0-434-82560-3*) David & Charles Pubs.

—The Lacquer Screen: A Chinese Detective Story. 1982. 192p. pap. 4.95 o.s.i (*0-684-17633-5*, Macmillan Reference USA) Gale Group.

—The Lacquer Screen: A Chinese Detective Story. Barzun, Jacques & Taylor, W. H., eds. 1983. (Crime Fiction 1950-1975 Ser.). (Illus.). 182p. lib. bdg. 5.00 o.p. (*0-8240-4951-9*) Garland Publishing, Inc.

—The Lacquer Screen: A Chinese Detective Story, unabr. ed. 1988. (Judge Dee Mysteries Ser.). audio 35.00 (*1-55690-290-5*, 88080E7) Recorded Bks., LLC.

—The Lacquer Screen: A Chinese Detective Story. 1992. (Judge Dee Mysteries Ser.). (Illus.). x, 180p. pap. 12.00 (*0-226-84867-1*) Univ. of Chicago Pr.

—Monkey & the Tiger. 1980. (J). pap. 2.95 (*0-684-16737-9*, Macmillan Reference USA) Gale Group.

—The Monkey & the Tiger: Two Chinese Detective Stories. 1992. (Judge Dee Mysteries Ser.). (Illus.). vii, 143p. pap. 8.00 (*0-226-84869-8*) Univ. of Chicago Pr.

—Murder in Canton: A Judge Dee Mystery. 1993. (Judge Dee Mysteries Ser.). (Illus.). viii, 207p. pap. 7.95 (*0-226-84874-4*) Univ. of Chicago Pr.

—Necklace & Calabash: A Chinese Detective Story. 1979. (Judge Dee Mysteries Ser.). pap. 3.95 o.p. (*0-684-16329-2*, Macmillan Reference USA) Gale Group.

—Necklace & Calabash: A Chinese Detective Story. 1992. (Illus.). viii, 143p. pap. 8.00 (*0-226-84870-1*) Univ. of Chicago Pr.

—The Phantom of the Temple, unabr. ed. 1986. (Judge Dee Mysteries Ser.). audio 35.00 (*1-55690-411-8*, 86880E7) Recorded Bks., LLC.

—The Phantom of the Temple. 1979. (Judge Dee Mysteries Ser.). pap. 4.95 o.p. (*0-684-16178-8*, Scribner Paper Fiction) Simon & Schuster.

—The Phantom of the Temple. 1995. (Judge Dee Mysteries Ser.). (Illus.). 205p. pap. 9.00 (*0-226-84877-9*) Univ. of Chicago Pr.

—Poets & Murder: A Judge Dee Mystery. 1979. (Judge Dee Mysteries Ser.). 192p. pap. 4.95 o.s.i (*0-684-16180-X*, Scribner Paper Fiction) Simon & Schuster.

—Poets & Murder: A Judge Dee Mystery. 1996. (Judge Dee Mysteries Ser.). (Illus.). vi, 176p. pap. 8.00 (*0-226-84876-0*) Univ. of Chicago Pr.

—The Red Pavilion, unabr. ed. 1986. (Judge Dee Mysteries Ser.). audio 35.00 (*1-55690-438-X*, 86550E7) Recorded Bks., LLC.

—The Red Pavilion. 1984. (Illus.). 184p. pap. 3.50 o.p. (*0-684-18142-8*, Scribner Paper Fiction) Simon & Schuster.

—The Red Pavilion. 1994. (Judge Dee Mysteries Ser.). (Illus.). 173p. (C). pap. 8.00 (*0-226-84873-6*) Univ. of Chicago Pr.

—The Red Tape Murder & Other Stories, unabr. ed. 1986. (Judge Dee Mysteries Ser.). audio 18.00 (*1-55690-440-1*, 86160E7) Recorded Bks., LLC.

—The Willow Pattern: A Judge Dee Mystery, unabr. ed. 1987. (Judge Dee Mysteries Ser.). audio 26.00 (*1-55690-565-3*, 87840E7) Recorded Bks., LLC.

—The Willow Pattern: A Judge Dee Mystery. 1993. (Judge Dee Mysteries Ser.). (Illus.). viii, 183p. pap. 10.00 (*0-226-84875-2*) Univ. of Chicago Pr.

Wainwright, J. A. A Deathful Ridge: A Novel of Everest. 1997. 138p. 19.95 (*0-88962-633-2*, 734028); pap. 14.95 (*0-88962-650-2*) Mosaic Pr.

Wang, Annie R. Lili: A Novel. 2002. 320p. pap. 13.00 (*0-385-72050-5*, Knopf Bks. for Young Readers) Random Hse. Children's Bks.

—Lili: A Novel of Tiananmen. 2001. 320p. 24.00 (*0-375-42085-1*, Pantheon) Knopf Publishing Group.

Wang Chi-Chen, ed. Stories of China at War. 1975. 158p. reprint ed. lib. bdg. 18.75 o.p. (*0-8371-8369-3*, WASC, Greenwood Pr.) Greenwood Publishing Group, Inc.

Wang Chi-Chen, tr. Contemporary Chinese Stories. 1969. 242p. reprint ed. 62.95 (*0-8371-0738-5*, WAC) Greenwood Publishing Group, Inc.

Wang, Dulu. Crouching Tiger, Hidden Dragon. 2004. 448p. pap. 14.00 (*0-7432-2751-4*, Touchstone) Simon & Schuster.

Wang, Meng. Bolshevik Salute: A Modernist Chinese Novel. Larson, Wendy, tr. 1990. 168p. 19.95 (*0-295-96856-7*) Univ. of Washington Pr.

—The Butterfly & Other Stories. Rui An et al, trs. from CHI. 1983. 239p. (Orig.). pap. 4.95 o.p. (*0-8351-1021-4*) China Bks. & Periodicals, Inc.

Waters, Mary Yukari. The Laws of Evening: Stories. 192p. 2004. pap. 12.00 (*0-7432-4333-1*); 2003. 21.00 (*0-7432-4332-3*) Simon & Schuster. (Scribner).

Watts, Mabel. Yin Sun & the Lucky Dragon. 1969. (J). 3.75 o.p. (*0-664-32434-7*) Westminster John Knox Pr.

Weber, Joe. Dancing with the Dragon: A Novel. 2002. 320p. 25.95 (*0-89141-764-8*, Presidio Pr.) Ballantine Bks.

Weighing an Elephant. 1981. pap. 3.95 o.p. (*0-8351-0893-7*) China Bks. & Periodicals, Inc.

Wenfu, Lu. The Gourmet & Other Stories. Burrows, Judith, tr. from CHI. 1988. 243p. (Orig.). 16.95 (*0-930523-38-5*); pap. 8.95 (*0-930523-39-3*) Readers International.

West, Paul. The Tent of Orange Mist. l.t. ed. 1996. 23.95 (*1-56895-279-1*, Wheeler Publishing, Inc.) Gale Group.

—The Tent of Orange Mist. 1997. 272p. 13.95 (*0-87951-792-1*) Overlook Pr., The.

—The Tent of Orange Mist. 1995. 263p. 22.00 (*0-684-80031-4*, Scribner) Simon & Schuster.

Winslow, Don. The Trail to Buddha's Mirror. 384p. 1992. 21.95 o.p. (*0-312-07099-3*, Saint Martin's Minotaur); Vol. 1. 1997. mass mkt. 5.99 (*0-312-96309-2*, St. Martin's Paperbacks) St. Martin's Pr.

Woodman, Richard. A Private Revenge. 1996. (Illus.). 247p. mass mkt. o.s.i (*0-7515-0724-5*) Little Brown & Co.

—A Private Revenge. l.t. ed. 2002. (Magna Large Print Ser.). 384p. (*0-7505-1737-9*) Magna Large Print Bks. GBR. *Dist:* Ulverscroft Large Print Canada, Ltd.

—A Private Revenge. 1990. 16.95 o.p. (*0-312-04405-4*) St. Martin's Pr.

—A Private Revenge: A Nathaniel Drinkwater Novel. 1999. (Mariner's Library). 256p. pap. 14.95 (*1-57409-078-X*) Sheridan Hse., Inc.

Xianliang, Zhang. Half of Man Is Woman. Avery, Martha, tr. from CHI. 1988. 17.95 o.p. (*0-393-02586-1*) Norton, W. W. & Co., Inc.

Xiao Ming & Katie Visit the Zoo. 1981. (J). 1.95 o.p. (*0-8351-0775-2*) China Bks. & Periodicals, Inc.

Xiaolong, Qiu. A Loyal Character Dancer. 360p. 2003. pap. 13.00 (*1-56947-341-2*); 2002. 25.00 (*1-56947-301-3*) Soho Pr., Inc.

Xingjian, Gao. One Man's Bible. Lee, Mabel, tr. from CHI. 2002. Tr. of Yi ge ren de sheng jing. 464p. 26.95 (*0-06-621132-8*) HarperCollins Pubs.

—One Man's Bible: A Novel. 2003. 464p. pap. 13.95 (*0-06-093626-6*, Perennial) HarperTrade.

—Soul Mountain. Date not set. 506p. pap. 15.00 (*0-7322-6651-3*) HarperCollins Pubs.

—Soul Mountain. Lee, Mabel, tr. from CHI. 2000. (Illus.). 528p. 27.00 (*0-06-621082-8*) HarperCollins Pubs.

—Soul Mountain. 2001. 528p. pap. 15.00 (*0-06-093623-1*, Perennial) HarperTrade.

Xiugui, Zhang. CliffsNotes TM Dream of the Red Chamber. 1999. E-Book 3.95 (*0-8220-7060-X*, Cliff Notes) Wiley, John & Sons, Inc.

Yan Li, Mordecai. Daughters of the Red Land. 1996. 532p. pap. (*0-920813-17-8*) Sister Vision Pr.

Yan, Mo. The Republic of Wine. Goldblatt, Howard, tr. from CHI. 2000. v, 355p. 26.95 (*1-55970-531-0*) Arcade Publishing, Inc.

—The Republic of Wine. 2015. 336p. 24.95 (*0-670-86965-1*) Viking Penguin.

—The Republic of Wine: A Novel. Goldblatt, Howard, tr. from CHI. 2001. 384p. reprint ed. pap. 13.95 (*1-55970-576-0*) Arcade Publishing, Inc.

—Shifu, You'll Do Anything for a Laugh. Goldslalt, Howard, tr. from CHI. 2001. 224p. 23.95 (*1-55970-565-5*) Arcade Publishing, Inc.

Yang, Belle. Baba: A Return to China upon My Father's Shoulders. 1996. (Illus.). 240p. pap. 18.00 o.p. (*0-15-600239-6*, Harvest Bks.) Harcourt Trade Pubs.

—The Odyssey of a Manchurian. 1996. (Illus.). 336p. 35.00 o.s.i (*0-15-100175-8*) Harcourt Trade Pubs.

—A Return to China upon the Shoulders of My Father. 1994. (Illus.). 224p. 27.95 o.s.i (*0-15-100063-8*) Harcourt Trade Pubs.

Year of Chance. 1989. 18.95 (*0-9624136-0-7*) Songs of Sottongs.

Ying, Hong. Summer of Betrayal: A Novel. Avery, Martha, tr. from CHI. 1997. 208p. 22.00 o.p. (*0-374-27175-5*) Farrar, Straus & Giroux.

—Summer of Betrayal: A Novel. Avery, Martha, tr. from CHI. 1999. 192p. pap. 12.00 (*0-8021-3594-3*) Grove/Atlantic, Inc.

Yu-T'Ang Lin. Famous Chinese Short Stories. 1979. reprint ed. lib. bdg. 41.50 o.p. (*0-8371-9062-2*, YUFC, Greenwood Pr.) Greenwood Publishing Group, Inc.

Yu Zhu Zher, Carlos. The Pagoda Builders. 1998. 317p. (Orig.). pap. 15.95 o.p. (*0-533-12290-2*) Vantage Pr., Inc.

Zelin, Madeleine, tr. from CHI. Rainbow. 1992. (Voices from Asia Ser.: No. 4). 255p. text 48.00 (*0-520-07327-4*) Univ. of California Pr.

Zhaoyan, Ye. Nanjing 1937: A Love Story. Berry, Michael, tr. from CHI. 2003. (Weatherhead Books on Asia). 234p. 24.95 (*0-231-12754-5*) Columbia Univ. Pr.

—Nanjing 1937: A Love Story. 2004. 368p. pap. 14.00 (*1-4000-3427-2*, Anchor) Knopf Publishing Group.

Zhong, Lou Guan. Romance of the Three Kingdoms. 623p. 19.95 (*0-89346-924-6*); 2000. 39.90 (*0-89346-926-2*) Heian International Publishing, Inc.

Zhu, Lin. Snake's Pillow & Other Stories. King, Richard, tr. from CHI. 1998. (Fiction from Modern China Ser.). 232p. 38.00 (*0-8248-1549-1*); pap. 13.50 (*0-8248-1716-8*) Univ. of Hawaii Pr.

Zongren, Liu. 6 Tianyin Alley. 1989. 17.95 o.p. (*0-8351-2146-1*) China Bks. & Periodicals, Inc.

### CHUNG KUO (IMAGINARY PLACE)—FICTION

Wingrove, David. The Broken Wheel: A Hung Kuo Novel, Bk. 2. 1991. (Chung Kuo Ser.: Vol. 2). 624p. mass mkt. 6.99 o.s.i (*0-440-20928-5*) Dell Publishing.

—The Marriage of the Living Dark. 1999. 480p. pap. 14.95 (*0-385-25736-8*) Bantam Bks.

—The Middle Kingdom, Vol. I. 1991. (Chung Kuo Ser.: Vol. 1). 704p. mass mkt. 6.99 (*0-440-20761-4*) Dell Publishing.

—The Stone Within. 1993. pap. 15.95 o.s.i (*0-385-29876-5*, Delacorte Pr.);Vol. IV. 592p. pap. 14.95 o.s.i (*0-440-50569-0*, Dell Bks.) Dell Publishing.

—The Stone Within: A Chung Kuo Novel, Vol. IV. 1994. (Chung Kuo Ser.: Vol. 4). 608p. mass mkt. 6.99 o.s.i (*0-440-21755-5*) Dell Publishing.

—White Moon, Red Dragon. 1997. (Chung Kuo Ser.: Vol. 6). 720p. mass mkt. 6.99 o.s.i (*0-440-22308-3*) Dell Publishing.

—The White Mountain. 1992. (Chung Kuo Ser.: Bk. 3). 624p. mass mkt. 6.99 o.s.i (*0-440-21356-8*) Dell Publishing.

### CIMMERIA (IMAGINARY PLACE)—FICTION

Anderson, Poul. Conan the Rebel. 1988. mass mkt. 3.95 o.s.i (*0-441-11642-6*) Ace Bks.

—Conan the Rebel. 1980. 224p. pap. 2.50 o.p. (*0-553-22731-9*) Bantam Bks.

Buscema, John & Thomas, Roy. Conan the Rogue. 1991. 64p. 9.95 o.p. (*0-87135-842-5*) Marvel Enterprises.

Carpenter, Leonard. Conan Lord of the Black River. 1996. 274p. mass mkt. 5.99 o.s.i (*0-8125-5266-0*, Tor Bks.) Doherty, Tom Assocs., LLC.

—Conan of the Red Brotherhood. 1993. (Conan the Barbarian Ser.). 288p. (Orig.). mass mkt. 5.99 o.s.i (*0-8125-1413-0*, Tor Bks.) Doherty, Tom Assocs., LLC.

—Conan, Scourge of the Bloody Coast. 1994. 256p. (Orig.). mass mkt. 4.99 (*0-8125-2488-8*, Tor Bks.) Doherty, Tom Assocs., LLC.

—Conan the Gladiator. 1995. (Tor Fantasy Ser.). 288p. mass mkt. 5.99 (*0-8125-2492-6*, Tor Bks.) Doherty, Tom Assocs., LLC.

—Conan the Great. 1990. 277p. mass mkt. 5.99 (*0-8125-0714-2*, Tor Bks.) Doherty, Tom Assocs., LLC.

—Conan the Hero. 1989. mass mkt. 3.50 (*0-8125-3318-6*); 1991. 278p. reprint ed. mass mkt. 5.99 o.s.i (*0-8125-1907-8*) Doherty, Tom Assocs., LLC. (Tor Bks.).

—Conan the Outcast. 1991. mass mkt. 5.99 (*0-8125-0928-5*, Tor Bks.) Doherty, Tom Assocs., LLC.

—Conan the Raider. 288p. 1986. pap. 6.95 o.s.i (*0-8125-4256-8*); 1987. reprint ed. mass mkt. 3.50 (*0-8125-4262-2*) Doherty, Tom Assocs., LLC. (Tor Bks.).

—Conan the Renegade. 1986. 288p. (Orig.). mass mkt. 2.95 (*0-8125-4250-9*, Tor Bks.) Doherty, Tom Assocs., LLC.

—Conan the Savage. 1993. 320p. mass mkt. 5.99 (*0-8125-1412-2*); 1992. 288p. pap. 7.99 o.p. (*0-8125-2238-9*) Doherty, Tom Assocs., LLC. (Tor Bks.).

—Conan the Warlord. 1988. 273p. reprint ed. mass mkt. 5.99 (*0-8125-4268-1*, Tor Bks.) Doherty, Tom Assocs., LLC.

Conan. 2nd ed. 1985. 11.80 (*0-8125-9707-9*, Tor Bks.) Doherty, Tom Assocs., LLC.

de Camp, L. Sprague. Conan & the Spider God. 1989. (Conan the Barbarian Ser.: No. 18). mass mkt. 3.95 o.s.i (*0-441-11609-4*) Ace Bks.

—Conan & the Spider God. 1982. 192p. mass mkt. 2.50 o.s.i (*0-553-22730-0*) Bantam Bks.

de Camp, L. Sprague & Carter, Lin. The Buccaneer. 1986. (Conan the Barbarian Ser.: No. 6). 192p. mass mkt. 4.50 o.s.i (*0-441-11585-3*) Ace Bks.

—Conan of Aquilonia. 1987. 192p. mass mkt. 4.50 o.s.i (*0-441-11484-9*) Ace Bks.

—Conan the Barbarian. 1982. pap. 2.50 o.p. (*0-553-22544-8*) Bantam Bks.

—Conan the Swordsman, No. 1. 1978. pap. 1.95 o.p. (*0-553-12018-2*) Bantam Bks.

de Camp, L. Sprague, et al. The Swordsman. 1987. (Conan the Barbarian Ser.: No. 13). 224p. mass mkt. 3.95 o.s.i (*0-441-11479-2*) Ace Bks.

Green, Roland. Conan & the Gods of the Mountain. 1993. 276p. mass mkt. 5.99 o.s.i (*0-8125-1414-9*, Tor Bks.) Doherty, Tom Assocs., LLC.

—Conan & the Mists of Doom. 1995. mass mkt. 4.99 (*0-8125-2494-2*, Tor Bks.) Doherty, Tom Assocs., LLC.

—Conan at the Demon's Gate. 1996. mass mkt. 5.99 (*0-8125-6355-7*); 1994. 278p. pap. text 7.99 (*0-8125-2491-8*) Doherty, Tom Assocs., LLC. (Tor Bks.).

—Conan the Valiant. 1989. 280p. mass mkt. 5.99 o.s.i (*0-8125-0082-2*); 1988. 288p. pap. 6.95 o.p. (*0-8125-4270-3*) Doherty, Tom Assocs., LLC. (Tor Bks.).

Green, Roland J. Conan & the Death Lord of Thanza. 1997. 272p. mass mkt. 5.99 (*0-8125-5268-7*, Tor Bks.) Doherty, Tom Assocs., LLC.

—Conan the Guardian. 1991. 280p. mass mkt. 5.99 (*0-8125-0961-7*, Tor Bks.) Doherty, Tom Assocs., LLC.

—Conan the Relentless. 1992. mass mkt. 5.99 (*0-8125-0962-5*, Tor Bks.) Doherty, Tom Assocs., LLC.

Hocking, John C. Conan & the Emerald Lotus. (Conan Ser.). 1999. 288p. mass mkt. 5.99 (*0-8125-9061-9*); 1995. pap. 9.99 o.p. (*0-8125-4499-4*) Doherty, Tom Assocs., LLC. (Tor Bks.).

Howard, Robert E. Conan, Nos. 10, 11, 12, 13, 14. 1988. 14.75 o.s.i (*0-441-11606-X*) Ace Bks.

—Conan: The Devil in Iron. 1978. 6.95 o.p. (*0-448-14580-4*) Putnam Publishing Group, The.

—Conan: The Treasure of Tranicos. 1985. 192p. mass mkt. 2.95 o.s.i (*0-441-82246-0*) Ace Bks.

—Conan of Cimmeria, No. 2. 1984. 2.75 o.s.i (*0-441-11455-5*) Ace Bks.

—Conan of the Isles. 1986. (Conan Ser.: No. 12). 192p. reprint ed. mass mkt. 4.50 o.s.i (*0-441-11623-X*) Ace Bks.

—Conan the Warrior. 1986. (Conan Ser.: No. 7). (Illus.). 224p. mass mkt. 4.50 o.s.i (*0-441-11586-1*) Ace Bks.

—Conan the Warrior. de Camp, L. Sprague, ed. 1985. (Conan Ser.: No. 7). 192p. mass mkt. 2.95 o.s.i (*0-441-11704-X*) Ace Bks.

—The Usurper. (Conan Ser.: No. 8). (Orig.). 1986. mass mkt. 3.50 o.s.i (*0-441-11589-6*); 1983. mass mkt. 2.50 o.s.i (*0-441-11602-7*) Ace Bks.

Howard, Robert E. & de Camp, L. Sprague. The Adventurer. 1986. (Conan the Barbarian Ser.: No. 5). 224p. mass mkt. 4.50 o.s.i (*0-441-11858-5*) Ace Bks.

—Conan! The Flame Knife. 1986. (Conan Ser.). 160p. mass mkt. 2.95 o.s.i (*0-441-11716-3*) Ace Bks.

—Conan the Conqueror. 1986. 224p. mass mkt. 4.50 o.s.i (*0-441-11590-X*) Ace Bks.

—Conan, the Freebooter. 1986. (Conan Ser.: No. 3). 224p. mass mkt. 4.50 o.s.i (*0-441-11863-1*) Ace Bks.

—The Usurper. 1990. (Conan the Barbarian Ser.: No. 8). 256p. (Orig.). mass mkt. 4.50 o.s.i (*0-441-11591-8*) Ace Bks.

Howard, Robert E., et al. Conan, No. 1. 1987. 224p. mass mkt. 4.50 o.s.i (*0-441-11481-4*) Ace Bks.

—Conan of Cimmeria. 1990. 192p. mass mkt. 4.50 o.s.i (*0-441-11453-9*) Ace Bks.

—Conan the Avenger, No. 10. 1987. 192p. mass mkt. 4.50 o.s.i (0-441-11483-0) Ace Bks.

—Conan the Wanderer. 1985. 224p. mass mkt. 4.50 o.s.i (0-441-11597-7) Ace Bks.

Jones Staff. Conan Doyle & the Spirits. 1983. 14.95 (0-85030-837-2) Aquarian Pr. GBR. Dist: Harper-SanFrancisco.

Jordan, Robert. Conan, Set. 1984. mass mkt. 11.80 (0-8125-9608-0, Tor Bks.) Doherty, Tom Assocs., LLC.

—The Conan Chronicles. 1995. 510p. 19.95 (0-312-85929-5, Tor Bks.) Doherty, Tom Assocs., LLC.

—Conan the Defender. 1991. mass mkt. 3.95 (0-8125-1394-0); 1983. 298p. mass mkt. 2.95 (0-8125-4228-2); 1982. 298p. mass mkt. 5.95 (0-523-48063-6) Doherty, Tom Assocs., LLC. (Tor Bks.).

—Conan the Destroyer. 2004. (0-7653-0290-X); 2004. pap. (0-7653-0291-8); 1993. 271p. pap. text 4.50 (0-8125-3136-1); 1991. 288p. mass mkt. 3.99 o.s.i (0-8125-1401-7); 1984. mass mkt. 2.95 (0-8125-4238-X) Doherty, Tom Assocs., LLC. (Tor Bks.).

—Conan the Magnificent. (Orig.). 1991. 288p. mass mkt. 3.99 o.s.i (0-8125-1593-5); 1989. mass mkt. 3.95 (0-8125-0099-7); Vol. 5. 1984. mass mkt. 2.95 o.s.i (0-8125-4236-3) Doherty, Tom Assocs., LLC. (Tor Bks.).

—Conan the Triumphant. 1991. mass mkt. 3.95 (0-8125-1398-3); 1988. mass mkt. 3.50 (0-8125-4279-7); 1983. (Illus.). 280p. pap. 6.95 o.s.i (0-8125-4234-7) Doherty, Tom Assocs., LLC. (Tor Bks.).

—Conan the Unconquered. 1991. 286p. mass mkt. 3.99 (0-8125-1400-9); 1988. 3.50 o.s.i (0-8125-4277-0); 1983. (Tor Conan Ser.: Bk. 3). 288p. mass mkt. 2.95 (0-523-48053-9) Doherty, Tom Assocs., LLC. (Tor Bks.).

—Conan the Victorious. 1991. 280p. mass mkt. 3.95 (0-8125-1399-1); 1984. (Illus.). pap. 6.95 o.s.i (0-8125-4240-1) Doherty, Tom Assocs., LLC. (Tor Bks.).

Kraar, et al. Conan: Witch Queen of Acheron. 1985. 64p. 6.50 o.p. (0-87135-085-8) Marvel Enterprises.

Kraar, Don & Severin. Conan the Reaver. 1987. 64p. 9.95 o.p. (0-87135-289-3) Marvel Enterprises.

Moench, et al. Conan: Skull of Set. 1989. 64p. 8.95 o.p. (0-87135-579-5) Marvel Enterprises.

Moore, Roger E. Conan & the Prophecy. Charette, Beverly, ed. 1985. (Endless Quest Bks.). (Illus.). 160p. (J). (gr. 4 up). pap. text 2.25 o.p. (0-88038-121-3) TSR, Inc.

—Conan the Outlaw. 1985. (Endless Quest Bks.). (Illus.). 160p. (J). (gr. 4-7). pap. 2.25 o.p. (0-394-73974-4, Random Hse. Bks. for Young Readers) Random Hse. Children's Bks.

—Conan the Outlaw. Larson, William, ed. 1985. (Endless Quest Bks.). (Illus.). 160p. (J). (gr. 4 up). pap. text 2.25 o.p. (0-88038-222-8) TSR, Inc.

Moore, Sean A. Conan & the Grim Grey God. (Conan Ser.). 1996. 224p. pap. 9.99 o.s.i (0-8125-5267-9); Vol. 1. 1997. 204p. pap. text 5.99 (0-8125-9062-7) Doherty, Tom Assocs., LLC. (Tor Bks.).

—Conan & the Shaman's Curse. 1996. mass mkt. 4.99 (0-8125-5265-2, Tor Bks.) Doherty, Tom Assocs., LLC.

—Conan the Hunter. 1994. 245p. mass mkt. 4.99 (0-8125-3531-6, Tor Bks.) Doherty, Tom Assocs., LLC.

Offutt, Andrew J. Conan, the Mercenary. 1987. (Conan Ser.). 192p. (Orig.). mass mkt. 2.95 o.s.i (0-441-11482-2) Ace Bks.

—The Sword of Skelos. 1987. (Conan the Barbarian Ser.: No. 15). mass mkt. 3.95 o.s.i (0-441-11480-6) Ace Bks.

—The Sword of Skelos. 1979. (Conan Ser.: No. 3). pap. 2.50 o.p. (0-553-22729-7) Bantam Bks.

Perry, Steve. Conan the Defiant. 1988. mass mkt. 3.50 (0-8125-4273-8); 1987. 256p. pap. 6.95 o.p. (0-8125-4264-9) Doherty, Tom Assocs., LLC. (Tor Bks.).

—Conan the Fearless. (Orig.). 1989. mass mkt. 3.95 (0-8125-0096-2); 1987. 288p. pap. 2.95 o.s.i (0-8125-4258-4); 1986. mass mkt. 6.95 (0-8125-4248-7) Doherty, Tom Assocs., LLC. (Tor Bks.).

—Conan the Formidable. 1991. 288p. mass mkt. 5.99 (0-8125-1377-0); 1990. pap. text 7.95 o.p. (0-8125-0998-6) Doherty, Tom Assocs., LLC. (Tor Bks.).

—Conan the Freelance. 1990. 279p. mass mkt. 5.99 (0-8125-0690-1, Tor Bks.) Doherty, Tom Assocs., LLC.

—Conan the Indomitable. 1990. mass mkt. 3.95 (0-8125-0860-2, Tor Bks.) Doherty, Tom Assocs., LLC.

Roberts, John M. Conan & the Amazon. 1995. 288p. mass mkt. 5.99 (0-8125-2493-4, Tor Bks.) Doherty, Tom Assocs., LLC.

—Conan & the Manhunters. 1994. (Conan Ser.). 320p. mass mkt. 5.99 (0-8125-2489-6, Tor Bks.) Doherty, Tom Assocs., LLC.

—Conan & the Treasure of Python. (Orig.). 1994. 288p. mass mkt. 4.99 (0-8125-5000-5); 1993. mass mkt. 7.99 (0-8125-1415-7) Doherty, Tom Assocs., LLC. (Tor Bks.).

—Conan the Bold. 1989. 282p. mass mkt. 5.99 o.s.i (0-8125-5210-5, Tor Bks.) Doherty, Tom Assocs., LLC.

—Conan the Champion. 1989. mass mkt. 3.95 (0-8125-0094-6); 1987. pap. 3.50 o.s.i (0-8125-4260-6) Doherty, Tom Assocs., LLC. (Tor Bks.).

—Conan the Marauder. 1992. 277p. mass mkt. 4.50 (0-8125-3149-3); 1988. pap. 3.50 o.s.i (0-8125-4266-5) Doherty, Tom Assocs., LLC. (Tor Bks.).

—Conan the Rogue. (Orig.). 1992. 304p. mass mkt. 5.99 o.s.i (0-8125-2141-2); 1991. mass mkt. 7.99 (0-8125-1411-4) Doherty, Tom Assocs., LLC. (Tor Bks.).

—Conan the Valorous. (Orig.). 1992. mass mkt. 3.99 (0-8125-1809-8); 1986. 288p. pap. 2.95 o.s.i (0-8125-4252-5); 1985. 320p. mass mkt. 6.95 (0-8125-4244-4) Doherty, Tom Assocs., LLC. (Tor Bks.).

Thomas, Roy, et al. Conan: Ravagers of Time. 1992. 64p. 9.95 o.p. (0-87135-911-1) Marvel Enterprises.

—Conan: The Horn of Azoth. 1990. 64p. 8.95 o.p. (0-87135-639-2) Marvel Enterprises.

—Conan of the Isles. 1988. (Illus.). 96p. 8.95 o.p. (0-87135-483-7) Marvel Enterprises.

Wagner, Karl Edward. Road of Kings. 1987. (Conan the Barbarian Ser.: No. 16). 224p. mass mkt. 3.95 o.s.i (0-441-11618-3) Ace Bks.

## CINCINNATI (OHIO)—FICTION

Borton, D. B. Five Alarm Fire. 1996. 240p. mass mkt. 5.99 o.s.i (0-425-15338-X, Prime Crime) Berkley Publishing Group.

—Four Elements of Murder. 1995. 256p. (Orig.). mass mkt. 5.99 o.s.i (0-425-14722-3, Prime Crime) Berkley Publishing Group.

—One for the Money. 1993. 208p. 4.50 o.s.i (1-55773-869-6) Ace Bks.

—One for the Money. 1993. 208p. mass mkt. 4.99 o.s.i (0-425-15328-2) Berkley Publishing Group.

—Six Feet Under. 1997. 240p. mass mkt. 5.99 o.s.i (0-425-15700-8, Prime Crime) Berkley Publishing Group.

—Three Is a Crowd. 1994. 240p. (Orig.). mass mkt. 4.99 o.s.i (0-425-14327-9, Prime Crime) Berkley Publishing Group.

—Two Points for Murder. 1993. mass mkt. 4.99 o.s.i (0-425-13947-6) Berkley Publishing Group.

Boyle, Kay. Process: A Novel. Spanier, Sandra Whipple, ed. & intro. by. 2002. (Illus.). 168p. 24.95 (0-252-02668-3) Univ. of Illinois Pr.

DeBrosse, Jim. Hidden City: A Rick Decker Mystery. 1991. 304p. 18.95 o.p. (0-312-06368-7, Saint Martin's Minotaur) St. Martin's Pr.

—The Serpentine Wall. 1988. 336p. 17.95 o.p. (0-312-02278-6, Saint Martin's Minotaur) St. Martin's Pr.

—Southern Cross. 1994. 240p. 19.95 o.p. (0-312-11070-7, Saint Martin's Minotaur) St. Martin's Pr.

Fielding, Joy. Grand Avenue. 2001. 400p. 25.00 (0-7434-0707-5, Atria); 2001. 400p. 25.00 (0-7434-4845-6, Atria); 2001. 400p. 25.00 (0-7434-4836-7, Atria); 2002. 528p. pap. 25.00 (0-7434-6667-5, Pocket); 2001. 528p. 25.00 (0-7434-2269-4, Atria); 2002. (Illus.). 560p. reprint ed. mass mkt. 7.99 (0-7434-0708-3, Pocket Star) Simon & Schuster.

Goonan, Kathleen Ann. Queen City Jazz. 2003. 400p. pap. 14.95 (0-7653-0751-0, Orb Bks.) Doherty, Tom Assocs., LLC.

Hightower, Lynn S. Eyeshot. 1996. 368p. 23.00 o.p. (0-06-017649-0) HarperCollins Pubs.

—Eyeshot. 1997. 368p. mass mkt. 6.50 o.p. (0-06-109609-1, HarperTorch) Morrow/Avon.

—Flashpoint. 1995. 352p. 22.00 o.p. (0-06-017648-2) HarperTrade.

—Flashpoint. 1996. 448p. mass mkt. 6.50 o.s.i (0-06-109456-0, HarperTorch) Morrow/Avon.

—No Good Deed. unabr. ed. 1998. audio 44.95 (0-7861-1438-X, 2324) Blackstone Audio Bks., Inc.

—No Good Deed. 1998. (Sonora Blair Mysteries Ser.). 400p. mass mkt. 6.50 (0-440-22531-0); 336p. 22.95 o.s.i (0-385-32359-X, Delacorte Pr.) Dell Publishing.

Holden, Craig. The Jazz Bird: A Novel. l.t. ed. 2002. 408p. lib. bdg. 29.95 (1-58547-165-8, Platinum) Ctr. Point Large Print.

—The Jazz Bird: A Novel. 2003. 400p. mass mkt. 6.99 (0-7434-1881-6, Pocket); 2002. 320p. 25.00 (0-7432-1296-7, Simon & Schuster); 2002. E-Book 5.99 (0-7432-1757-8, Simon & Schuster) Simon & Schuster.

John, Cathie, et al. Add One Dead Critic: Journals of Kate Cavanaugh. 1997. 249p. pap. 12.95 (0-9634183-4-3, Journey Bk. Pr.) C C Publishing.

—Beat a Rotten Egg to the Punch: Journals of Kate Cavanaugh. 1998. (Journals of Kate Cavanaugh Ser.). 287p. pap. 12.95 (0-9634183-5-1) C C Publishing.

—Carve a Witness to Shreds: A Kate Cavanaugh Mystery. 1999. (Journals of Kate Cavanaugh Ser.). 260p. (Orig.). pap. 12.95 (0-9634183-6-X, Journey Bk. Pr.) C C Publishing.

Jones, Annie. Irish Eyes. 1997. (Palisades Pure Romance Ser.). 238p. pap. 9.99 o.s.i (1-57673-108-1, Palisades) Multnomah Pubs., Inc.

Karshner, Roger. Getting Sentimental over You. 2002. (Illus.). 184p. 20.00 (0-9634147-4-7) Noble Porter Pr.

Lutz, Norma Jean. Trouble on the Ohio River: Drought Shuts Down a City. 15th ed. 1998. (American Adventure Ser.: No. 15). (Illus.). (J). (gr. 3-7). pap. 3.97 (1-57748-232-8) Barbour Publishing, Inc.

—Trouble on the Ohio River: Drought Shuts Down a City, 1999. (American Adventure Ser.: No. 15). 144p. (J). (gr. 3-7). lib. bdg. 15.95 (0-7910-5588-4) Chelsea Hse. Pubs.

Meibers, Richard. Steal Away Home. 2000. 362p. pap. 17.95 (0-595-12965-X) iUniverse, Inc.

Pyle, A. M. Murder Moves In. 1987. 256p. mass mkt. 3.50 o.p. (0-451-14889-4, Signet Bks.) NAL.

—Murder Moves In. 1986. 216p. 14.95 o.s.i (0-8027-5635-2) Walker & Co.

—Pure Murder. 1990. 256p. 16.95 o.p. (0-312-03917-4, Saint Martin's Minotaur) St. Martin's Pr.

—Trouble Making Toys. 1986. 256p. mass mkt. 2.95 o.p. (0-451-14570-4, Signet Bks.) NAL.

—Trouble Making Toys. 1985. 192p. 13.95 (0-8027-5610-7) Walker & Co.

Short, Sharon G. The Death We Share. 1995. mass mkt. 5.99 o.s.i (0-449-14916-1, Fawcett) Ballantine Bks.

—Past Pretense. 1994. (Orig.). mass mkt. 4.99 o.s.i (0-449-14915-3, Fawcett) Ballantine Bks.

Short, Sharon Gwyn. Angel's Bidding. 1993. (Midwest Mysteries Ser.). mass mkt. 4.99 o.s.i (0-449-14873-4, Fawcett) Ballantine Bks.

Soos, Troy. Cincinnati Red Stalkings. 1999. 336p. mass mkt. 5.99 o.s.i (1-57566-408-9) Kensington Publishing Corp.

—Cincinnati Red Stalkings, unabr. ed. 1998. (Mickey Rawlings Baseball Ser.: Vol. 5). audio 52.00 (0-7887-2478-9, 95553E7) Recorded Bks., LLC.

—The Cincinnati Red Stalkings: A Mickey Rawlings Baseball Mystery. 1998. (Mickey Rawlings Baseball Mystery Ser.). 352p. 20.00 o.s.i (1-57566-286-8, Kensington Bks.) Kensington Publishing Corp.

Valin, Jonathan. Day of Wrath. 1994. 320p. mass mkt. 4.99 o.s.i (0-440-21041-0) Dell Publishing.

—Day of Wrath. 1983. (Harry Stoner Mystery Ser.). 256p. pap. 3.50 (0-380-63917-3, Avon Bks.) Morrow/Avon.

—Dead Letter. 1994. 320p. mass mkt. 4.99 o.s.i (0-440-21038-0) Dell Publishing.

—Dead Letter. 1983. (Harry Stoner Mystery Ser.). 224p. pap. 3.50 (0-380-61366-2, Avon Bks.) Morrow/Avon.

—Extenuating Circumstances. 1989. 15.95 o.s.i (0-440-50110-5, Delacorte Pr.); 1989. 240p. 15.95 o.s.i (0-385-29683-5, Delacorte Pr.); 1990. 256p. reprint ed. mass mkt. 3.95 o.s.i (0-440-20630-8) Dell Publishing.

—Final Notice. 1994. 320p. mass mkt. 4.99 o.s.i (0-440-21032-1) Dell Publishing.

—Final Notice. 1982. (Harry Stoner Mystery Ser.). 192p. pap. 3.50 (0-380-57893-X, Avon Bks.) Morrow/Avon.

—Fire Lake. 1989. 272p. (YA). reprint ed. mass mkt. 4.99 o.s.i (0-440-20145-4) Dell Publishing.

—Fire Lake: A Harry Stoner Novel. 1987. 264p. 14.95 o.s.i (0-385-29589-8, Delacorte Pr.) Dell Publishing.

—Life's Work. 1987. 256p. reprint ed. mass mkt. 4.99 o.s.i (0-440-14790-5) Dell Publishing.

—Life's Work: A Harry Stoner Novel. 1986. 240p. 14.95 o.s.i (0-385-29503-0, Delacorte Pr.) Dell Publishing.

—The Lime Pit. 1994. 320p. mass mkt. 4.99 o.s.i (0-440-21029-1) Dell Publishing.

—The Lime Pit. 1983. (Harry Stoner Mystery Ser.). 208p. pap. 3.50 (0-380-55442-9, Avon Bks.) Morrow/Avon.

—The Music Lovers: A Harry Stoner Mystery. 1994. 304p. mass mkt. 4.99 o.s.i (0-440-21686-9) Dell Publishing.

—Natural Causes. 1994. 384p. mass mkt. 4.99 o.s.i (0-440-21035-6) Dell Publishing.

—Natural Causes. 1984. (Harry Stoner Mystery Ser.). 304p. pap. 2.95 o.p. (0-380-68247-8, 68247, Avon Bks.) Morrow/Avon.

—Second Chance: A Harry Stoner Mystery. 288p. 1992. mass mkt. 4.99 o.s.i (0-440-21222-7); 1991. 18.00 o.s.i (0-385-29912-5, Delacorte Pr.) Dell Publishing.

## CLEVELAND (OHIO)—FICTION

Bendis, Brian Michael & Andreyko, Marc. Torso: The Definitive Collection. 2001. (Illus.). 280p. pap. 24.95 (1-58240-174-8) Image Comics.

Cielec, Greg. My Cleveland Story. 1998. 288p. 22.00 (0-9665724-0-8) Pink Flamingo Pr.

Collins, Max Allan. Bullet Proof, Vol. 3. 1989. mass mkt. 3.50 o.s.i (0-553-27982-3) Bantam Bks.

—Butcher's Dozen. 1988. 224p. mass mkt. 3.50 o.s.i (0-553-26151-7) Bantam Bks.

—Butcher's Dozen. 1998. (Mystery Ser.). 263p. 20.95 o.p. (0-7862-1662-X, Five Star) Gale Group.

—The Dark City. 1987. mass mkt. 3.50 o.p. (0-553-26539-3) Bantam Bks.

—Murder by the Numbers. 1993. 17.95 o.p. (0-312-08856-6, Saint Martin's Minotaur) St. Martin's Pr.

Cooke, John Peyton. Torsos. 1994. 368p. 19.95 o.s.i (0-89296-522-3) Mysterious Pr.

—Torsos. 1995. 352p. mass mkt. 5.99 o.s.i (0-446-40454-3) Warner Bks., Inc.

Haien, Jeannette. Matters of Chance: A Novel. 1998. 448p. pap. 13.95 (0-06-092952-9, Perennial) HarperTrade.

Lacey, Rick. Cat Fever. 1994. 24.95 (0-9642466-0-0) Karson Publishing.

Martin, James E. And Then You Die: A Novel. 1993. 224p. mass mkt. 4.99 (0-380-71696-8, Avon Bks.); 1992. 18.00 o.p. (0-688-11198-X, Morrow, William & Co.) Morrow/Avon.

—A Fine & Private Place. 1995. 256p. mass mkt. 4.99 (0-380-71697-6, Avon Bks.) Morrow/Avon.

—A Fine & Private Place: A Gil Disbro Mystery. 1994. 23.00 o.p. (0-688-11211-0, Morrow, William & Co.) Morrow/Avon.

—The Flip Side of Life. 1991. 256p. mass mkt. 3.99 (0-380-71407-8, Avon Bks.) Morrow/Avon.

—The Mercy Trap. 1990. 256p. pap. 3.95 (0-380-71041-2, Avon Bks.) Morrow/Avon.

—The Mercy Trap. 1989. 256p. 18.95 o.p. (0-399-13441-7, G. P. Putnam's Sons) Penguin Putnam Bks. for Young Readers.

Mitchell, Sharon. Sheer Necessity. 1999. 304p. 23.95 o.p. (0-525-94523-7) Dutton/Plume.

—Sheer Necessity. 2000. 352p. reprint ed. mass mkt. 6.99 o.s.i (0-451-19947-2, Signet Bks.) NAL.

—Sheer Necessity. 2000. 13.04 (0-606-19634-X) Turtleback Bks.

Montanari, Richard. Deviant Way. 1997. 336p. mass mkt. 6.50 (0-671-51109-2, Pocket); 1995. 288p. 22.00 o.p. (0-684-80357-7, Simon & Schuster) Simon & Schuster.

—Kiss of Evil: A Novel of Suspense. 2002. 368p. mass mkt. 6.99 (0-380-79534-5); 2001. 304p. 25.00 (0-380-97593-9, Morrow, William & Co.) Morrow/Avon.

Pomidor, Bill. Anatomy of a Murder. 1996. (Cal & Plato Marley Mystery Ser.). 272p. mass mkt. 5.50 o.s.i (0-451-18417-3, Signet Bks.) NAL.

—Mind over Murder. 1998. (Cal & Plato Marley Mystery Ser.). 288p. mass mkt. 5.99 o.s.i (0-451-19216-8, Signet Bks.) NAL.

—Murder by Prescription. 1995. (Cal & Plato Marley Ser.). 288p. mass mkt. 4.99 o.s.i (0-451-18416-5, Signet Bks.) NAL.

—Skeletons in the Closet. 1997. (Cal & Plato Marley Mystery Ser.). 288p. mass mkt. 5.50 o.s.i (0-451-18418-1, Signet Bks.) NAL.

—Ten Little Medicine Men. 1998. (Cal & Plato Marley Mystery Ser.). 288p. mass mkt. 5.99 o.s.i (0-451-19214-1, Signet Bks.) NAL.

Richards, Emilie. The Parting Glass. 2003. 464p. (1-55166-709-6, Mira Bks.) Harlequin Enterprises, Ltd.

Roberts, Les. The Best-Kept Secret. (Milan Jacovich Mysteries Ser.). 2000. 311p. mass mkt. 5.99 (0-312-97126-5, St. Martin's Paperbacks); 1999. 308p. 23.95 (0-312-20499-X, Saint Martin's Minotaur) St. Martin's Pr.

—The Cleveland Connection. (Milan Jacovich Mysteries Ser.). 1997. 336p. mass mkt. 5.99 o.s.i (0-312-96218-5, St. Martin's Paperbacks); 1993. 294p. 19.95 (0-312-08746-2, Saint Martin's Minotaur) St. Martin's Pr.

—Cleveland Local. 1998. (Milan Jacovich Mysteries Ser.). 288p. mass mkt. 5.99 (0-312-96678-4, St. Martin's Paperbacks) St. Martin's Pr.

—The Cleveland Local. 1997. (Milan Jacovich Mysteries Ser.). 288p. 22.95 o.p. (0-312-16801-2, Saint Martin's Minotaur) St. Martin's Pr.

—Collision Bend. (Milan Jacovich Mysteries Ser.). 1997. 288p. mass mkt. 5.99 (0-312-96399-8, St. Martin's Paperbacks); 1996. 320p. 22.95 o.p. (0-312-14570-5, Saint Martin's Minotaur) St. Martin's Pr.

—Deep Shaker. 1992. mass mkt. 3.99 (0-312-92795-9, St. Martin's Paperbacks); 1991. 17.95 o.p. (0-312-05855-1, Saint Martin's Minotaur) St. Martin's Pr.

—The Duke of Cleveland: A Milan Jacovich Mystery. 1995. 272p. 21.95 o.p. (0-312-13473-8, Saint Martin's Minotaur) St. Martin's Pr.

—The Dutch. l.t. ed. 2002. 28.95 (0-7862-4096-2) Gale Group.

—The Dutch. mass mkt. (0-312-98028-0, St. Martin's Paperbacks); 2001. 293p. 23.95 (0-312-26579-4, Saint Martin's Minotaur) St. Martin's Pr.

—Full Cleveland. 1990. mass mkt. 3.95 (0-312-92345-7, St. Martin's Paperbacks); 1989. 224p. 15.95 o.p. (0-312-03349-4, Saint Martin's Minotaur) St. Martin's Pr.

—Full Cleveland: A Milan Jacovich Mystery. 1991. 2.99 o.p. (0-517-07803-1) Random Hse. Value Publishing.

—The Indian Sign. E-Book 23.95 (*0-312-27594-3*); 2001. 304p. mass mkt. 6.50 (*0-312-97646-1*, St. Martin's Paperbacks); 2000. 274p. 23.95 (*0-312-25217-X*, Saint Martin's Minotaur) St. Martin's Pr.

—Irish Sports Pages. mass mkt. (*0-312-98380-8*, St. Martin's Paperbacks); 2002. 304p. 23.95 (*0-312-28661-9*, Saint Martin's Minotaur) St. Martin's Pr.

—The Lake Effect: A Milan Jacovich Mystery. 1994. 352p. 21.95 (*0-312-11537-7*, Saint Martin's Minotaur) St. Martin's Pr.

—Pepper Pike. (Milan Jacovich Mysteries Ser.). 1988. 240p. 15.95 o.p. (*0-312-02266-2*, Saint Martin's Minotaur); Vol. 1. 1990. 232p. mass mkt. 5.99 o.s.i (*0-312-92213-2*, St. Martin's Paperbacks) St. Martin's Pr.

—A Shoot in Cleveland. (Milan Jacovich Mysteries Ser.). 1999. 336p. mass mkt. 5.99 (*0-312-96694-6*, St. Martin's Paperbacks); 1999. E-Book 5.99 o.s.i (*0-312-20742-5*); 1998. 368p. 23.95 o.p. (*0-312-18663-0*, Saint Martin's Minotaur) St. Martin's Pr.

Salisbury, Luke. The Cleveland Indian: The Legend of King Saturday. 1992. 288p. (Orig.). pap. 24.95 (*0-912292-95-4*) Smith, The.

—Cleveland Indian: The Legend of King Saturday. 1995. 288p. (Orig.). pap. 14.95 (*1-882986-14-8*) Smith, The.

Wallace, David Foster. The Broom of the System. 1997. pap. 6.99 (*0-380-73030-8*); 1993. 480p. pap. 14.00 (*0-380-71991-6*) Morrow/Avon. (Avon Bks.)

—The Broom of the System. 1987. (Contemporary American Fiction Ser.). 467p. 18.95 o.p. (*0-670-81230-7*); 480p. pap. 7.95 o.p. (*0-14-009868-2*, Penguin Bks.) Viking Penguin.

Whisnant, Luke. Watching TV with the Red Chinese. 1994. 320p. pap. 10.99 o.s.i (*0-446-67007-3*) Warner Bks., Inc.

—Watching TV with the Red Chinese: A Novel. 1992. 320p. 17.95 o.p. (*0-945575-83-1*) Algonquin Bks. of Chapel Hill.

Winegardner, Mark. Crooked River Burning. 2001. 592p. pap. 14.00 (*0-15-601422-X*, Harvest Bks.); 572p. 27.00 (*0-15-100294-0*) Harcourt Trade Pubs.

**COLOMBIA—FICTION**

Atherton, Marc. Where the Rocks Started. 2001. 275p. pap. 15.95 (*0-942996-43-7*) Post-Apollo Pr., The.

García Márquez, Gabriel. El Amor en los Tiempos del Colera. 1997. (SPA.). pap. text (*968-13-1547-2*) Editorial Diana, S.A.

—El Amor en los Tiempos del Colera. 9th ed. 1989. (SPA.). 360p. 24.95 o.p. (*0-8288-2519-X*, S17019); pap. 24.95 (*0-7859-4987-9*) French & European Pubns., Inc.

—El Amor en los Tiempos del Colera. (SPA.). 494p. 18.95 (*84-01-24230-4*, PJ2304) Plaza & Janés Editories, S.A. ESP. *Dist:* Continental Bk. Co., Inc., Distribooks, Inc., Libros Sin Fronteras.

—El Amor en los Tiempos del Colera. (SPA.). 451p. 23.95 (*950-07-0320-3*) Sudamericana (Sudamericana - Planeta) ARG. *Dist:* AIMS International Bks., Inc.

—El Amor en los Tiempos del Colera. 1996. 20.00 (*0-606-20205-6*) Turtleback Bks.

—El Amor en los Tiempos del Colera. 1996. (Penguin Great Books of the 20th Century Ser.). (SPA.). 368p. 15.00 (*0-14-025578-8*) Viking Penguin.

Indiana, Gary. Gone Tomorrow. 1995. 175p. reprint ed. pap. (*1-85242-336-6*) Serpent's Tail Ltd.

Johansen, Iris. No One to Trust. 2003. 336p. mass mkt. 7.50 (*0-553-58437-5*); 2002. 304p. 25.95 (*0-553-80245-3*); 2002. E-Book 19.95 (*0-553-89708-X*) Bantam Bks.

—No One to Trust. l.t. ed. 2002. 384p. 27.95 (*0-375-43157-8*) Random Hse., Inc.

McTeer, Alan. Red Zone. 2003. 300p. 24.00 (*0-9671851-9-X*) GreyCore Pr.

Restrepo, Laura. The Angel of Galilea: A Novel. 1999. 208p. pap. 15.00 (*0-375-70649-6*, Vintage) Knopf Publishing Group.

—La Novia Oscura. 2002. (SPA.). 464p. pap. 14.95 (*0-06-051431-0*, Rayo) HarperTrade.

—La Novia Oscura. 2nd ed. (SPA., Illus.). 465p. pap. 20.95 (*958-04-5588-0*, NR11680) Norma S.A. COL. *Dist:* Lectorum Pubns., Inc.

Windle, Jeanette. The DMZ: A Novel. 2002. 512p. 15.99 (*0-8254-4118-8*) Kregel Pubns.

**COLORADO—FICTION**

Allegretto, Michael. Blood Relative: A Jacob Lomax Mystery. 1992. 224p. text 20.00 (*0-684-19409-0*, Macmillan Reference USA) Gale Group.

—Blood Stone. 1988. 224p. 16.95 o.p. (*0-684-18966-6*, Macmillan Reference USA) Gale Group.

—The Dead of Winter. 1989. 256p. 16.95 o.p. (*0-684-19138-5*, Macmillan Reference USA) Gale Group.

—Death on the Rocks: A Jacob Lomax Mystery. 1987. 15.95 o.p. (*0-684-18758-2*, Macmillan Reference USA) Gale Group.

—Grave Doubt. 1995. 224p. 19.95 o.p. (*0-7867-0186-2*, Carroll & Graf Pubs.) Avalon Publishing Group.

—The Night of Reunion. 1990. 256p. 17.95 o.s.i (*0-684-19133-4*, Macmillan Reference USA) Gale Group.

—The Night of Reunion. 1991. 288p. mass mkt. 4.99 (*0-380-71442-6*, Avon Bks.) Morrow/Avon.

—Shadow House. 1994. 304p. 19.95 o.p. (*0-7867-0070-X*, Carroll & Graf Pubs.) Avalon Publishing Group.

Allen, Kate. Give My Secrets Back: An Alison Kaine Mystery. 1995. 200p. (Orig.). pap. 9.95 (*0-934678-64-2*) New Victoria Pubs., Inc.

—I Knew You Would Call. 1995. 202p. (Orig.). pap. 10.95 (*0-934678-70-7*) New Victoria Pubs., Inc.

—Takes One to Know One: An Alison Kaine Mystery. 1996. 200p. (Orig.). pap. 10.95 (*0-934678-74-X*) New Victoria Pubs., Inc.

Anderson, Catherine. Simply Love. l.t. ed. 1999. pap. 24.95 (*1-56895-641-X*, Wheeler Publishing, Inc.) Gale Group.

—Simply Love. 1997. 400p. mass mkt. 5.99 (*0-380-79102-1*, Avon Bks.) Morrow/Avon.

Andrews, Sarah. A Fall in Denver: An Em Hansen Mystery. 1996. (Em Hansen Mystery Ser.). 272p. mass mkt. 5.50 o.s.i (*0-451-18793-8*) NAL.

—A Fall in Denver: An Em Hansen Mystery. 1995. 288p. 20.00 o.p. (*0-684-81523-0*); 20.00 (*1-883402-34-4*) Simon & Schuster. (Scribner).

—Only Flesh & Bones. 1999. (Dead Letter Mysteries Ser.: Vol. 1). 368p. mass mkt. 6.50 (*0-312-96702-0*, St. Martin's Paperbacks); 1998. 336p. 23.95 (*0-312-18642-8*, Saint Martin's Minotaur) St. Martin's Pr.

Bain, Donald & Fletcher, Jessica. Murder at the Powderhorn Ranch: A Murder, She Wrote Mystery. l.t. ed. 2000. (G. K. Hall Nightingale Ser.). 256p. pap. 21.95 (*0-7838-8926-7*, Macmillan Reference USA) Gale Group.

Barr, Nevada. Ill Wind. 2004. 320p. mass mkt. 6.99 (*0-425-19725-5*) Berkley Publishing Group.

—Ill Wind. l.t. ed. 1995. (Large Print Bks.). pap. 21.95 o.p. (*1-56895-252-X*, Wheeler Publishing, Inc.) Gale Group.

—Ill Wind. 1996. (Anna Pigeon Mysteries Ser.: No. 3). 320p. mass mkt. 7.99 (*0-380-72363-8*, Avon Bks.) Morrow/Avon.

—Ill Wind. abr. ed. 1995. 17.95 o.p. (*0-7871-0370-5*) NewStar Media, Inc.

—Ill Wind. 1995. 309p. 19.95 o.p. (*0-399-14015-8*, G. P. Putnam's Sons) Penguin Group (USA) Inc.

—Ill Wind. unabr. ed. 1999. (Anna Pigeon Mystery Ser. : No. 3). audio 62.00 (*0-7887-2932-2*, 95717E7) Recorded Bks., LLC.

Baxter, Mary L. Lightning Strikes. 1997. (Thirty-Six Hours Ser.: No. 1). per. (*0-373-65006-X*, 1-65006-8, Harlequin Bks.) Harlequin Enterprises, Ltd.

Bixler, Inez French & Artex Publishing. Winds of Caribou. 1997. (Illus.). (*1-57745-024-8*) Artex Publishing, Inc.

Black, Michelle. Never Come Down. 1999. E-Book 6.00 (*1-58200-206-1*) Hard Shell Word Factory.

—Never Come Down. 1996. 270p. pap. 9.95 (*1-57502-210-9*, P0849) Morris Publishing.

—Never Come Down. rev. ed. 1997. 268p. pap. 14.95 (*0-9658014-0-3*) WinterSun Pr.

Bly, Stephen A. Hard Winter at Broken Arrow Crossing. 1991. (Stuart Brannon Western Ser.: No. 1). 192p. pap. 8.99 o.p. (*0-89107-620-4*) Crossway Bks.

—Hard Winter at Broken Arrow Crossing. l.t. ed. 1993. 234p. lib. bdg. 18.95 (*0-8161-5822-3*, Macmillan Reference USA) Gale Group.

Brenna, Duff. Too Cool. 1998. 272p. 22.95 o.s.i (*0-385-48971-4*, Talese, Nan A.) Doubleday Publishing.

—Too Cool. 1999. 272p. pap. 12.95 o.s.i (*0-452-28116-4*, Plume) Dutton/Plume.

Brockett, Deborah A. Stained Glass Rose. 2002. 143p. pap. 14.95 (*1-890437-61-1*) Western Reflections Publishing Co.

Brockway, Connie. Anything for Love. 1994. 384p. mass mkt. 4.50 (*0-380-77754-1*, Avon Bks.) Morrow/Avon.

Brown, Corinne Joy. MacGregor's Lantern. 2001. (Five Star First Edition Western Ser.). 392p. 26.95 (*0-7862-3227-7*, Five Star) Gale Group.

Brown, Dave. Bristlecone Peak. 1998. (Legend of the Golden Feather Ser.: Vol. 1). 320p. pap. 14.95 (*1-878406-13-2*) Parker Distributing.

Brown, David E. The Protectors. 1998. (Legend of the Golden Feather Ser.: Vol. 2). 270p. pap. 14.95 (*1-878406-20-5*) Parker Distributing.

Brown, Harry C. Sundays in August: A Novel. 1997. 196p. 26.95 (*0-86534-261-X*) Sunstone Pr.

Burns, Rex. Angle of Attack. 1979. (Harper Novel of Suspense Ser.). o.p. (*0-06-010523-2*) HarperCollins Pubs.

—The Avenging Angel: A Gabe Wager Mystery. (Crime Monthly Ser.). 1984. 24p. pap. 3.95 o.p. (*0-14-007104-0*, Penguin Bks.); 1983. 240p. 12.50 o.p. (*0-670-14317-0*) Viking Penguin.

—Blood Line. 1995. 204p. 19.95 (*0-8027-3256-9*) Walker & Co.

—Endangered Species. 1993. 288p. 19.00 o.p. (*0-670-84601-5*, Viking) Viking Penguin.

—The Farnsworth Score. 1978. 1.75 o.p. (*0-425-03749-5*) Berkley Publishing Group.

—The Farnsworth Score. 1977. (Harper Novel of Suspense Ser.). o.p. (*0-06-010573-9*) HarperCollins Pubs.

—The Farnsworth Score. 1993. (Crime Ser.). 208p. pap. 5.95 o.p. (*0-14-016949-0*, Penguin Bks.) Penguin Group (USA) Inc.

—Ground Money. 1987. 256p. mass mkt. 3.95 o.p. (*0-14-008515-7*, Penguin Bks.); 1986. 187p. 15.95 o.p. (*0-670-80904-7*) Viking Penguin.

—The Killing Zone. 1989. 272p. pap. 3.95 o.p. (*0-14-010532-8*, Penguin Bks.); 1988. 261p. 17.95 o.p. (*0-670-81955-7*) Viking Penguin.

—The Leaning Land: A Gabe Wager Mystery. 1997. (Gabe Wagner Mystery Ser.). 246p. 22.95 o.p. (*0-8027-3306-9*) Walker & Co.

—Speak for the Dead. 1978. (Harper Novel of Suspense Ser.). 8.95 o.p. (*0-06-010526-7*) Harper-Collins Pubs.

—Strip Search. (Crime Monthly Ser.). 1985. 272p. pap. 3.95 o.p. (*0-14-007747-2*, Penguin Bks.); 1984. 300p. 13.95 o.p. (*0-670-67905-4*) Viking Penguin.

Butler, Luther. County Dublin & Blood on the Moon. 1999. (La Plata County Ser.: 1). 368p. pap. 18.95 (*1-58348-365-9*) iUniverse, Inc.

Cacek, P. D. Canyons. 2000. 304p. 23.95 (*0-312-87383-2*, Tor Bks.) Doherty, Tom Assocs., LLC.

Cail, Carol. If Two of Them Are Dead. 1996. 224p. 15.95 (*0-312-14361-3*, Saint Martin's Minotaur) St. Martin's Pr.

—Unsafe Keeping. 1996. 304p. mass mkt. 5.50 o.s.i (*0-440-22298-2*) Dell Publishing.

—Unsafe Keeping. pap. 15.95 (*0-312-29194-9*, Saint Martin's Griffin); pap. (*0-312-30031-X*, Saint Martin's Griffin); 1995. 218p. 15.95 (*0-312-13198-4*, Saint Martin's Minotaur) St. Martin's Pr.

—Who Was Sylvia? 1999. (Maxey Burnell Mystery Ser.). 180p. pap. text 16.99 (*1-886199-04-3*, Madison Publishing Co.) Deadly Alibi Pr., Ltd.

Carr, Robyn. Mind Tryst. 1992. 304p. 19.95 o.p. (*0-312-07034-9*) St. Martin's Pr.

Cather, Willa. The Song of the Lark. 34.95 (*0-88411-288-8*) Amereon, Ltd.

—The Song of the Lark. unabr. ed. 1991. audio 59.95 (*1-55685-190-1*) Audio Bk. Contractors, Inc.

—The Song of the Lark. 1991. 400p. mass mkt. 4.95 o.s.i (*0-553-21391-1*, Bantam Classics) Bantam Bks.

—The Song of the Lark. 1990. reprint ed. lib. bdg. 31.95 (*0-89968-493-9*) Buccaneer Bks., Inc.

—The Song of the Lark. 1998. (Collected Works of Willa Cather). 489p. reprint ed. lib. bdg. 108.00 (*1-58201-575-9*) Classic Bks.

—The Song of the Lark. 1983. 424p. pap. 5.95 (*0-395-34530-8*) Houghton Mifflin Co.

—The Song of the Lark. 1999. (Vintage Bks.). 448p. pap. 12.00 (*0-375-70645-3*) Knopf, Alfred A. Inc.

—The Song of the Lark. Sharistanian, Janet, ed. 2000. (Oxford World's Classics Ser.). 480p. pap. 10.95 (*0-19-283201-8*) Oxford Univ. Pr., Inc.

—The Song of the Lark, unabr. ed. 2001. audio 91.00 (*0-7887-0657-8*, 94834E7) Recorded Bks., LLC.

—The Song of the Lark. 1915th ed. 1978. xvi, 490p. pap. 6.95 o.p. (*0-8032-6300-7*, BB 670) Univ. of Nebraska Pr.

—The Song of the Lark. 1999. audio 49.95 (*0-14-180014-3*, Penguin AudioBooks) Viking Penguin.

—The Song of the Lark: The Sleeper-McCann House. 1991. 432p. mass mkt. 5.95 (*0-451-52533-7*, Signet Classics) NAL.

Cather, Willa & Harbison, Sherrill. The Song of the Lark. 1999. (Twentieth Century Classics Ser.). 448p. 11.00 (*0-14-118104-4*, Penguin Classics) Viking Penguin.

Champlin, Tim. Iron Trail. l.t. ed. 2001. 252p. 24.95 (*0-7838-9492-9*, Macmillan Reference USA) Gale Group.

Chandler, Jon. The Spanish Peaks: A Novel of Frontier Colorado. 1999. pap. 15.95 (*0-9662696-0-8*) Loveland Pr.

Chastain, Sandra. The Mail Order Groom. 2002. 304p. mass mkt. 5.99 (*0-553-58050-7*) Bantam Bks.

Choate, Jane M. Sweet Lies & Rainbow Skies. 1993. 18.95 o.s.i (*0-8034-9015-1*, Avalon Bks.) Bouregy, Thomas & Co., Inc.

—Sweet Lies & Rainbow Skies. l.t. ed. 1995. (Nightingale Ser.). 192p. reprint ed. pap. 17.95 o.p. (*0-7838-1290-6*, Macmillan Reference USA) Gale Group.

Clark, Carol Higgins. Iced. 1996. o.s.i (*0-316-87854-5*) Little Brown & Co.

—Iced. unabr. ed. 1995. 29.95 o.p. (*0-7871-0575-9*);Set. audio 17.95 o.p. (*0-7871-0220-2*, 392963) NewStar Media, Inc.

—Iced. 1999. 320p. mass mkt. 4.50 (*0-446-60778-9*); 1996. 320p. mass mkt. 7.99 (*0-446-60198-5*); 1995. 272p. 28.00 (*0-446-51764-X*) Warner Bks., Inc.

Coleman, Jane Candia. Matchless: A Western Story. 2003. 244p. 25.95 (*0-7862-3803-8*, Five Star) Gale Group.

Collins, Laurel. Jordan's Heart. 2000. 320p. mass mkt. 5.99 o.s.i (*0-8217-6711-9*, Zebra Bks.) Kensington Publishing Corp.

Connelly, Michael. The Poet. l.t. ed. 2000. pap. 25.95 o.p. (*1-56895-330-5*, Wheeler Publishing, Inc.) Gale Group.

—The Poet. 1996. 440p. 22.95 o.p. (*0-316-15398-2*) Little Brown & Co.

—The Poet. 1997. 528p. reprint ed. mass mkt. 7.99 (*0-446-60261-2*) Warner Bks., Inc.

Copeland, Lori. Roses Will Bloom Again. 2003. 424p. pap. 15.95 (*1-4104-0155-3*, Walker Large Print) Gale Group.

—Roses Will Bloom Again. l.t. ed. 2003. 424p. 26.95 (*0-7862-5562-5*) Thorndike Pr.

—Roses Will Bloom Again. 2002. (HeartQuest Ser.). 304p. pap. 9.99 (*0-8423-1936-0*) Tyndale Hse. Pubs.

—Stranded in Paradise. 2002. (Women of Faith Fiction Ser.). 300p. pap. 13.99 (*0-8499-4378-7*) W Publishing Group.

Creel, Ann Howard. The Magic of Ordinary Days. l.t. ed. 2001. 27.95 o.p. (*0-7862-3741-4*) Thorndike Pr.

—The Magic of Ordinary Days. 288p. 2002. 13.00 (*0-14-200090-6*); 2001. 24.95 o.p. (*0-670-91027-9*, Viking) Viking Penguin.

Cresswell, Jasmine. The Refuge. 2000. 408p. mass mkt. (*1-55166-608-1*, 1-66608-0, Mira Bks.) Harlequin Enterprises, Ltd.

Cunningham, Chet. Devil's Gold. l.t. ed. 1995. (Nightingale Ser.). 242p. pap. 17.95 o.p. (*0-7838-1238-8*, Macmillan Reference USA) Gale Group.

Curtis, Jack. Paradise Valley. l.t. ed. 2001. (Sagebrush Large Print Westerns Ser.). 180p. 20.95 (*1-57490-346-2*, Sagebrush Large Print Westerns) Beeler, Thomas T. Publisher.

Cutler, Bruce. The Massacre at Sand Creek: Narrative Voices. (American Indian Literature & Critical Studies: Vol. 16). 1997. xi, 252p. pap. 14.95 (*0-8061-2990-5*); 1995. 264p. 19.95 o.p. (*0-8061-2730-9*) Univ. of Oklahoma Pr.

—The Massacre at Sand Creek: Narrative Voices. 1995. E-Book 11.95 (*0-585-16865-2*) netLibrary, Inc.

Dailey, Janet. Aspen Gold. 1992. 416p. mass mkt. 5.99 (*0-316-17153-0*); 1991. 22.95 o.s.i (*0-316-17148-4*); 1991. 19.95 o.p. (*0-316-17146-8*) Little Brown & Co.

—Aspen Gold. 1993. 4.99 o.p. (*0-517-10684-1*) Random Hse. Value Publishing.

—Riding High. 1994. (Janet Dailey's Love Scenes Ser.). pap. 4.75 (*1-56420-098-1*) New Readers Pr.

Dale, Ruth Jean. Cupid's Revenge: Camerons of Colorado. 1998. (Harlequin Superromance Ser.: No. 788). per. (*0-373-70788-6*, 0-70788-5, Harlequin Bks.) Harlequin Enterprises, Ltd.

Dallas, Sandra. The Diary of Mattie Spenser. l.t. ed. 1998. (Large Print Book Ser.). pap. 24.95 (*1-56895-523-5*, Wheeler Publishing, Inc.) Gale Group.

—The Diary of Mattie Spenser. 1999. E-Book 11.95 o.s.i (*0-312-20714-X*); 1998. 240p. pap. 12.95 (*0-312-18710-6*, Saint Martin's Griffin); 1997. 229p. 21.95 o.p. (*0-312-15515-8*) St. Martin's Pr.

Dare, Justine. Dangerous Games, 1 vol. 1999. 336p. mass mkt. 5.99 o.s.i (*0-451-40773-3*, Signet Bks.) NAL.

Davidson, Carolyn. The Tender Stranger. 1999. 304p. per. (*0-373-29056-X*, 1-29056-8, Harlequin Bks.) Harlequin Enterprises, Ltd.

Davidson, Diane Mott. Catering to Nobody. 1998. pap. 5.99 (*0-449-45882-2*); 1998. pap. 5.99 (*0-449-45833-4*); 1992. 320p. reprint ed. mass mkt. 5.99 o.s.i (*0-449-22046-X*) Ballantine Bks. (Fawcett).

—Catering to Nobody. l.t. ed. 1999. (Beeler Large Print Mystery Ser.). 25.95 (*1-57490-204-0*, Beeler Large Print Bks.) Beeler, Thomas T. Publisher.

—Catering to Nobody. 1990. 17.95 (*0-312-04277-9*, Saint Martin's Minotaur) St. Martin's Pr.

—The Cereal Murders. 1994. 368p. mass mkt. 6.99 (*0-553-56773-X*) Bantam Bks.

—The Cereal Murders. l.t. ed. 1999. pap. 23.95 o.p. (*1-56895-743-2*, Wheeler Publishing, Inc.) Gale Group.

—Chopping Spree. 2003. 368p. mass mkt. 6.99 (*0-553-57835-9*); 2002. 320p. 23.95 (*0-553-10730-5*) Bantam Bks.

—Chopping Spree. l.t. ed. pap. o.p. (*0-7862-4677-4*); 2003. 484p. 13.95 (*1-4104-0085-9*); 2002. 484p. 32.95 (*0-7862-4676-6*) Thorndike Pr.

—Dying for Chocolate. 1993. (Culinary Mysteries Ser.). (Illus.). 352p. mass mkt. 6.99 (*0-553-56024-7*) Bantam Bks.

—Dying for Chocolate. l.t. ed. 2000. pap. 22.95 o.p. (*1-56895-821-8*, Wheeler Publishing, Inc.) Gale Group.

—The Grilling Season. 1998. 432p. reprint ed. mass mkt. 6.99 (*0-553-57466-3*) Bantam Bks.

—Killer Pancake. 1996. 368p. mass mkt. 6.99 (*0-553-57204-0*) Bantam Bks.

—The Last Suppers. 1995. 304p. mass mkt. 6.99 (*0-553-57258-X*, Crimeline) Bantam Bks.

—The Last Suppers. l.t. ed. 1999. pap. 24.95 o.p. (*1-56895-640-1*, Wheeler Publishing, Inc.) Gale Group.

—The Main Corpse. l.t. ed. 1997. (Large Print Bks.). 25.95 o.p. (*1-56895-409-3*, Wheeler Publishing, Inc.) Gale Group.

—Prime Cut. 2000. (Illus.). 384p. reprint ed. mass mkt. 6.99 (*0-553-57467-1*) Bantam Bks.

—Prime Cut. l.t. ed. 1999. 27.95 o.p. (*1-56895-588-X*, Wheeler Publishing, Inc.) Gale Group.

—Prime Cut. unabr. ed. 1999. (Catering Mystery Ser.). audio 72.00 (*0-7887-2922-5*, 95647E7); audio compact disk 83.00 (*0-7887-3432-6*, C1038E7) Recorded Bks., LLC.

—Sticks & Scones. l.t. ed. 2001. (Large Print Book Ser.). 410p. 29.95 (*1-58724-027-0*, Wheeler Publishing, Inc.) Gale Group.

—Tough Cookie. 2001. 336p. reprint ed. mass mkt. 6.99 (*0-553-57830-8*, Fanfare) Bantam Bks.

—Tough Cookie. l.t. ed. 2001. pap. 12.95 o.p. (*1-56895-149-3*); 2000. 31.95 (*1-56895-892-7*) Gale Group. (Wheeler Publishing, Inc.).

Davidson, Jim. Mine Work: A Novel. 1999. 312p. pap. 10.00 (*0-87421-275-8*) Utah State Univ. Pr.

—Mine Work: A Novel. 1999. E-Book 17.95 (*0-585-06991-3*) netLibrary, Inc.

Davis, Nageeba. A Dying Art: A Maggie Kean Mystery. 2001. 272p. 22.95 o.s.i (*0-425-17951-6*, Prime Crime) Berkley Publishing Group.

Deveraux, Jude. Legend. 2002. E-Book 9.99 (*1-59061-635-9*) Adobe Systems, Inc.

—Legend. l.t. ed. 1997. (Large Print Bks.). 26.95 o.p. (*1-56895-395-X*, Wheeler Publishing, Inc.) Gale Group.

—Legend. unabr. ed. 1997. audio 90.00 (*0-7887-0840-6*, 94986E7) Recorded Bks., LLC.

—Legend. 1998. E-Book 23.00 (*0-671-03694-7*, Atria); 1997. 416p. pap. 7.99 (*0-671-00170-1*, Pocket); 1996. 384p. 23.00 (*0-671-74461-5*, Atria) Simon & Schuster.

—Legend. abr. ed. 1999. audio 9.98 (*0-671-04600-4*); 1995. audio 17.00 (*0-671-53605-2*, 394318) Simon & Schuster Audio. (Simon & Schuster Audioworks).

Dietz, Denise. Beat up a Cookie: An Ellie Bernstein Mystery. 2000. per. (*0-373-26340-6*, Harlequin Bks.) Harlequin Enterprises, Ltd.

—Beat up a Cookie: An Ellie Bernstein Mystery. 1994. 216p. 19.95 o.p. (*0-8027-3186-4*) Walker & Co.

—Footprints in the Butter: An Ingrid Beaumont Mystery Co-Starring Hitchcock the Dog. 1999. 224p. 21.95 (*0-9663397-2-X*, 16579330) Delphi Bks.

—Throw Darts at a Cheesecake. 1999. per. (*0-373-26334-1*, Harlequin Bks.) Harlequin Enterprises, Ltd.

—Throw Darts at a Cheesecake. 1992. 211p. 19.95 o.p. (*0-8027-1237-1*) Walker & Co.

Doss, James D. Dead Soul. Date not set. pap. (*0-312-31746-8*, St. Martin's Paperbacks); Date not set. mass mkt. (*0-312-99462-1*, St. Martin's Paperbacks); mass mkt. (*0-312-99109-6*, St. Martin's Paperbacks); 2003. 352p. 24.95 (*0-312-31744-1*, Saint Martin's Minotaur) St. Martin's Pr.

—The Shaman Laughs. 1995. 272p. 21.95 o.p. (*0-312-13601-3*, Saint Martin's Minotaur) St. Martin's Pr.

—Shaman Laughs. 1997. (Shaman Mysteries Ser.). 352p. mass mkt. 6.99 (*0-380-72690-4*, Avon Bks.) Morrow/Avon.

—The Shaman Sings. 1994. 272p. 3000.00 o.p. (*0-312-10547-9*, Saint Martin's Minotaur) St. Martin's Pr.

—Shaman Sings. 1995. (Shaman Mysteries Ser.). 256p. mass mkt. 6.99 (*0-380-72496-0*, Avon Bks.) Morrow/Avon.

—The Shaman's Bones. 1997. 288p. 22.00 (*0-380-97424-X*, Avon Bks.) Morrow/Avon.

—The Shaman's Game. (Shaman Mysteries Ser.). 1999. 352p. mass mkt. 6.50 (*0-380-79030-0*); 1998. 384p. 22.00 (*0-380-97425-8*) Morrow/Avon. (Avon Bks.).

—The Shaman's Mistake. 1998. (Shaman Mysteries Ser.). 352p. mass mkt. 6.99 (*0-380-79029-7*, Avon Bks.) Morrow/Avon.

—White Shell Woman: A Charlie Moon Mystery. 2002. 304p. 23.95 (*0-06-019932-6*, Morrow, William & Co.) Morrow/Avon.

Downing, Sybil. The Binding Oath. 2001. 200p. 24.95 (*0-87081-607-1*) Univ. Pr. of Colorado.

—Fire in the Hole. (Women's West Ser.). 1998. 239p. pap. 16.95 (*0-87081-515-6*); 1996. 248p. 22.50 o.p. (*0-87081-380-3*) Univ. Pr. of Colorado.

—Fire in the Hole. 1996. E-Book 12.95 (*0-585-02261-5*) netLibrary, Inc.

Dunning, John. Booked to Die. 1993. 384p. reprint ed. pap. 5.99 o.p. (*0-380-71883-9*, Avon Bks.) Morrow/Avon.

—Booked to Die. unabr. ed. 1995. audio 70.00 (*0-7887-0411-7*, 94603E7) Recorded Bks., LLC.

—Booked to Die. 2001. (Illus.). 432p. reprint ed. mass mkt. 6.99 (*0-7434-1065-3*, Pocket Star) Simon & Schuster.

—Booked to Die. l.t. ed. 1998. (Niagara Large Print Ser.). 552p. 29.50 o.p. (*0-7089-5836-2*, Ulverscroft) Thorpe, F. A. Pubs. GBR. *Dist:* Ulverscroft Large Print Bks., Ltd., Ulverscroft Large Print Canada, Ltd.

—The Bookman's Wake. 1996. 448p. mass mkt. 7.99 (*0-671-56782-9*, Pocket Star); 1995. (Illus.). 352p. 21.00 (*0-684-80003-9*, Scribner) Simon & Schuster.

Dunning, John H. Booked to Die: A Mystery Introducing Cliff Janeway. 1992. 288p. 23.00 (*0-684-19383-3*, Scribner) Simon & Schuster.

Edgerton, Clyde. Redeye. 1995. 252p. 17.95 (*1-56512-060-4*) Algonquin Bks. of Chapel Hill.

—Redeye. audio o.p. National Humanities Ctr.

—Redeye. 1996. 256p. pap. 15.00 o.p. (*0-14-025491-9*, Penguin Bks.) Penguin Group (USA) Inc.

Evans, Tabor. Longarm & the Hangman's Daughter, Vol. 20. 2001. (Longarm Ser.: Vol. 20). 320p. mass mkt. 5.99 o.s.i (*0-515-12999-2*, Jove) Berkley Publishing Group.

Everett, Percival. Watershed. 2nd ed. 2003. 224p. pap. 14.00 (*0-8070-8361-5*) Beacon Pr.

—Watershed. 1996. 202p. 22.95 (*1-55597-237-3*) Graywolf Pr.

Fletcher, Jessica & Bain, Donald. Murder at the Powderhorn Ranch. 1999. (Murder She Wrote Ser.: Vol. 11). 272p. mass mkt. 6.50 (*0-451-19476-4*) NAL.

Garlock, Dorothy. Restless Wind. l.t. ed. 2002. 408p. lib. bdg. 29.95 (*1-58547-152-6*) Ctr. Point Large Print.

—Restless Wind. 1997. (Romance Ser.). 353p. 26.95 (*0-7862-1261-6*, Five Star) Gale Group.

—Restless Wind. 1988. 384p. reprint ed. mass mkt. 6.99 (*0-445-20932-1*) Warner Bks., Inc.

—Wayward Wind. l.t. ed. 2002. lib. bdg. 29.95 (*1-58547-155-0*, Premier) Ctr. Point Large Print.

—Wind of Promise. l.t. ed. 2002. lib. bdg. 29.95 (*1-58547-156-9*, Premier) Ctr. Point Large Print.

Gear, Kathleen O'Neal. Thin Moon & Cold Mist. (Women of the West Novels Ser.). 1996. 465p. mass mkt. 6.99 (*0-8125-3657-6*); 1995. 384p. 22.95 o.p. (*0-312-85701-2*) Doherty, Tom Assocs., LLC. (Forge Bks.).

—Thin Moon & Cold Mist. l.t. ed. 1996. 23.95 (*0-7838-1636-7*, Macmillan Reference USA) Gale Group.

Gilman, Charlotte Perkins. The Crux. 2003. 168p. 49.95 (*0-8223-3179-9*); pap. 16.95 (*0-8223-3167-5*) Duke Univ. Pr.

—The Crux. Tuttle, Jennifer S., ed. & intro. by. 2002. (Illus.). 248p. 42.50 (*0-87413-771-3*) Univ. of Delaware Pr.

Glenn, Anne Fitten. Storm Mountain. 2001. 288p. pap. 22.95 (*0-7596-4965-0*) 1stBooks Library.

Goff, Christine. A Nest in the Ashes. 2002. 224p. mass mkt. 5.99 (*0-425-18404-8*, Prime Crime) Berkley Publishing Group.

Goodman, Jo. More Than a Touch. l.t. ed. 1996. lib. bdg. 21.95 o.p. (*0-7838-1574-3*, Macmillan Reference USA) Gale Group.

Goonan, Kathleen Ann. Light Music. 2002. 416p. 25.95 (*0-380-97712-5*, Eos) Morrow/Avon.

Greenberg, Joanne. No Reck'ning Made. l.t. ed. 1994. 25.95 o.p. (*0-7927-1974-3*); pap. 24.95 o.p. (*0-7927-1973-5*) BBC Audiobooks America.

—No Reck'ning Made. 1995. 88p. pap. 12.95 o.p. (*0-8050-3849-3*, Owl Bks.); 1993. 384p. (YA). 23.00 o.p. (*0-8050-2579-0*) Holt, Henry & Co.

—Simple Gifts. 1986. 208p. 15.95 o.p. (*0-8050-0034-8*) Holt, Henry & Co.

Greer, Robert. The Devil's Backbone. 1998. 368p. 22.00 o.p. (*0-89296-653-X*) Mysterious Pr.

—The Devil's Backbone. 1999. (C J Floyd Mystery Ser.). 320p. mass mkt. 6.99 (*0-446-60711-8*) Warner Bks., Inc.

—The Devil's Hatband. 1996. 82p. 21.95 o.p. (*0-89296-634-3*) Mysterious Pr.

—The Devil's Hatband. 1997. 304p. reprint ed. mass mkt. 5.99 (*0-446-40485-3*) Warner Bks., Inc.

—The Devil's Red Nickel. 1997. 368p. 22.00 o.p. (*0-89296-652-1*) Mysterious Pr.

—The Devil's Red Nickel. 1998. (C J Floyd Mystery Ser.). 352p. mass mkt. 5.99 (*0-446-60592-1*); mass mkt. 5.99 (*0-446-40529-9*, Mysterious Pr. Paperback Bks.) Warner Bks., Inc.

—Heat Shock: A Novel. 2003. 320p. 24.95 (*0-89296-753-6*) Mysterious Pr.

Grippando, James M. Found Money. l.t. ed. 2001. (Softcover Ser.). 466p. pap. 23.95 o.p. (*1-58724-069-6*, Wheeler Publishing, Inc.) Gale Group.

—Found Money. 1998. 352p. 25.00 (*0-06-018263-6*) HarperCollins Pubs.

—Found Money, Set. abr. ed. 1999. audio 18.00 (*0-694-52106-X*, 396054, HarperAudio) HarperTrade.

—Found Money, Set. abr. ed. 1999. audio 18.00 Highsmith Inc.

—Found Money. 2000. 480p. mass mkt. 7.50 (*0-06-109762-4*, Avon Bks.) Morrow/Avon.

—Found Money. unabr. ed. 1999. audio 75.00 (*0-7887-3055-X*, 95749E7) Recorded Bks., LLC.

—Found Money: Australian Edition. 1999. 320p. pap. 16.00 (*0-06-107231-1*) HarperCollins Pubs.

Hale, Gena. Dream Mountain. 2001. 256p. mass mkt. 6.99 o.s.i (*0-451-41003-3*, Onyx) NAL.

Hansen, Ron. Atticus. 256p. 1997. pap. 13.00 (*0-06-092786-0*, Perennial); 1996. 22.00 o.p. (*0-06-018217-2*) HarperTrade.

—Atticus. unabr. ed. 1997. audio 44.00 (*0-7887-0943-7*, 95076E7) Recorded Bks., LLC.

Hardin, Clement. Stage Line to Rincon. 1979. mass mkt. 1.75 o.s.i (*0-441-77911-5*) Ace Bks.

—Stage Line to Rincon. l.t. ed. 2002. (Nightingale Ser.). 22.95 (*0-7862-4188-8*) Thorndike Pr.

Harmon, Susan. Colorado Ransom. 1991. 192p. 19.95 o.s.i (*0-8027-4125-8*) Walker & Co.

—Spirit of a Bear. l.t. ed. 1995. 233p. lib. bdg. 20.95 (*0-7838-1155-1*, Macmillan Reference USA) Gale Group.

—Spirit of a Bear. 1994. 155p. 19.95 (*0-8027-4140-1*) Walker & Co.

Harris, Jeane. Black Iris. 1991. 256p. pap. 8.95 o.p. (*0-941483-68-1*) Naiad Pr., Inc.

Haruf, Kent. Eventide. 2004. 320p. 24.95 (*0-375-41158-5*) Knopf, Alfred A. Inc.

—Plainsong. 2001. E-Book 11.50 (*1-58945-682-3*) Adobe Systems, Inc.

—Plainsong. l.t. ed. 2001. 12.95 (*1-56895-147-7*); 2000. 370p. 27.95 (*1-56895-839-0*) Gale Group. (Wheeler Publishing, Inc.).

—Plainsong. 2000. (Contemporaries Ser.). 320p. pap. 13.00 (*0-375-70585-6*, Vintage) Knopf Publishing Group.

—Plainsong. 1999. 320p. 24.00 (*0-375-40618-2*) Knopf, Alfred A. Inc.

—Plainsong. 2000. E-Book 11.50 (*0-375-72693-4*) Random Hse., Inc.

—Plainsong. 2000. 19.05 (*0-606-20073-8*) Turtleback Bks.

—The Tie That Binds: A Vivid Saga of Pioneer Life. 1986. (Contemporary American Fiction Ser.). 256p. pap. 6.95 o.p. (*0-14-008466-5*, Penguin Bks.) Viking Penguin.

Heitzmann, Kristen. Honor's Disguise, 4. 1999. (Rocky Mountain Legacy Ser.: Vol. 4). 288p. pap. 11.99 (*0-7642-2203-1*) Bethany Hse. Pubs.

—Honor's Disguise. 2002. 275p. 24.95 (*0-7862-3568-3*, Five Star) Gale Group.

—Honor's Price. 1998. (Rocky Mountain Legacy Ser.: Vol. 2). 304p. pap. 11.99 (*0-7642-2032-2*) Bethany Hse. Pubs.

—Honor's Price. 2001. 333p. 23.95 (*0-7862-3569-1*, Five Star) Gale Group.

—Honor's Quest. 1999. (Rocky Mountain Legacy Ser.: Bk. 3). 288p. pap. 11.99 (*0-7642-2033-0*) Bethany Hse. Pubs.

—Honor's Quest. 2002. 307p. 23.95 (*0-7862-3570-5*, Five Star) Gale Group.

—Honor's Reward. 2000. (Rocky Mountain Legacy Ser.: Vol. 5). 320p. pap. 11.99 (*0-7642-2204-X*) Bethany Hse. Pubs.

—Honor's Reward. 2002. (Five Star Christian Fiction Ser.). 380p. 24.95 (*0-7862-3571-3*, Five Star) Gale Group.

—The Rose Legacy. 2000. (Diamond of the Rockies Ser.: Vol. 1). 400p. pap. 12.99 (*0-7642-2381-X*) Bethany Hse. Pubs.

—Sweet Boundless. 2001. (Diamond of the Rockies Ser.: Vol. 2). 352p. pap. 12.99 (*0-7642-2382-8*) Bethany Hse. Pubs.

Hendrie, Laura. Stygo. 1994. 225p. 16.95 o.p. (*1-878448-59-5*) MacMurray & Beck, Inc.

Henry, Sue. The Serpent's Trail. 2004. 288p. 23.95 (*0-451-21122-7*) NAL.

Hofer, Andrew. Ahab's Vineyard. 2000. vi, 228p. (*1-890437-43-3*) Western Reflections Publishing Co.

Hooper, Kay. On Her Doorstep. 1994. 192p. mass mkt. 4.50 o.s.i (*0-515-11423-5*, Jove) Berkley Publishing Group.

—On Her Doorstep. 192p. 25.00 (*0-7278-5526-3*); 2001. 288p. 27.00 (*0-7278-7051-3*) Severn Hse. Pubs., Ltd.

—On Her Doorstep. l.t. ed. 2001. (Thorndike Romance Ser.). 237p. 28.95 (*0-7862-3192-0*) Thorndike Pr.

Howard, Linda. Angel Creek. 352p. 1998. pap. 7.99 (*0-671-01976-7*); 1991. mass mkt. 6.99 (*0-671-66081-0*) Simon & Schuster. (Pocket).

—Angel Creek. l.t. ed. 2000. (Famous Authors Ser.). 435p. 27.95 (*0-7862-2851-2*) Thorndike Pr.

Hyde, Elizabeth. Crazy as Chocolate. 2003. 272p. pap. 14.00 (*0-425-19246-6*) Berkley Publishing Group.

Irving, Clifford. The Spring. 1996. 288p. 23.00 (*0-684-81076-X*, Simon & Schuster) Simon & Schuster.

Irving, Mark. Sakura's Stratagem. 1999. 245p. 24.00 (*0-9669050-0-8*) Starmount Pr.

Johansen, Iris. Dead Aim. 2004. 368p. mass mkt. 7.99 (*0-553-58438-3*); 2003. 352p. 24.95 (*0-553-80246-1*) Bantam Bks.

—Dead Aim. abr. ed. 2003. E-Book 19.95 (*0-553-89727-6*, RH Audio) Random Hse. Audio Publishing Group.

Johnson, Bett Reece. The Woman Who Rode to the Moon: A Cordelia Morgan Mystery. 1999. (Cordelia Morgan Mysteries Ser.). 321p. pap. 12.95 (*1-57344-086-8*) Cleis Pr.

Johnson, Dolores. A Dress to Die For: A Mandy Dyer Mystery. 1998. (Mandy Dyer Mystery Ser.: Vol. 3). 272p. mass mkt. 5.99 (*0-440-22355-5*) Dell Publishing.

—Homicide & Old Lace. 2000. (Mandy Dyer Mystery Ser.). 288p. mass mkt. 5.99 o.s.i (*0-440-23524-3*, Dell Bks.) Dell Publishing.

—Hung up to Die. 1997. (Mandy Dyer Mystery Ser.: Vol. 2). 256p. mass mkt. 5.99 o.s.i (*0-440-22353-9*) Dell Publishing.

—Taken to the Cleaners. 1997. (Mandy Dyer Mystery Ser.: Vol. 1). 272p. mass mkt. 5.50 o.s.i (*0-440-22370-9*) Dell Publishing.

—Wash, Fold & Die: A Mandy Dyer Mystery. 1999. (Mandy Dyer Mystery Ser.). 288p. mass mkt. 5.99 o.s.i (*0-440-23523-5*) Dell Publishing.

Johnstone, William W. Battle of the Mountain Man. 1998. 256p. mass mkt. 4.99 o.s.i (*0-8217-5925-6*, Zebra Bks.) Kensington Publishing Corp.

—The Last Mountain Man. 208p. 2000. mass mkt. 5.99 (*0-8217-6856-5*); 1996. mass mkt. 4.99 o.s.i (*0-8217-5274-X*); 1984. mass mkt. 3.50 o.s.i (*0-8217-4084-9*, Zebra Bks.) Kensington Publishing Corp.

—The Last Mountain Man. l.t. ed. 1998. (Western Ser.). 228p. 24.95 (*0-7838-8391-9*) Thorndike Pr.

—Trail of the Mountain Man. 2000. 272p. mass mkt. 5.99 (*0-7860-1297-8*); 1996. 272p. mass mkt. 4.99 o.s.i (*0-8217-5609-5*); 1995. mass mkt. 4.50 o.s.i (*0-8217-5151-4*); 1987. mass mkt. 3.50 o.s.i (*0-8217-3676-0*, Zebra Bks.) Kensington Publishing Corp.

—Trail of the Mountain Man. l.t. ed. 1999. (Western Ser.). 356p. 24.95 (*0-7838-8541-5*) Thorndike Pr.

Jorgensen, Christine T. Curl up & Die. 1998. (WWL Mystery Ser.). per. (*0-373-26266-3*, 1-26266-6, Worldwide Library) Harlequin Enterprises, Ltd.

—Curl up & Die: A Stella the Stargazer Mystery. 1997. (Stella the Stargazer Mystery Ser.). 224p. 21.95 (*0-8027-3288-7*) Walker & Co.

—Dead on Her Feet. 2000. (Stella the Stargazer Mystery Ser.). 253p. per. (*0-373-26344-9*, Harlequin Bks.) Harlequin Enterprises, Ltd.

—Dead on Her Feet. 1999. (Stella the Stargazer Mystery Ser.). 256p. 23.95 (*0-8027-3334-4*) Walker & Co.

—Death of a Dustbunny. 1999. (WWL Mystery Ser.: Bk. 308). per. (*0-373-26308-2*, 1-26308-6, Harlequin Bks.) Harlequin Enterprises, Ltd.

—Death of a Dustbunny. l.t. ed. 1998. (Stella the Stargazer Mystery Ser.). 246p. 22.95 (*0-8027-3315-8*) Walker & Co.

—A Love to Die For. 1997. (Mystery Ser.). 256p. per. (*0-373-26231-0*, 1-262310, Worldwide Library) Harlequin Enterprises, Ltd.

—A Love to Die For. 1994. 214p. 19.95 (*0-8027-3188-0*) Walker & Co.

—You Bet Your Life. 1997. 48p. per. (*0-373-26245-0*, 1-26245-0, Worldwide Library) Harlequin Enterprises, Ltd.

—You Bet Your Life: A Stella the Stargazer Mystery. 1995. 224p. 19.95 (*0-8027-3265-8*) Walker & Co.

Judd, Cameron. The Hanging at Leadville. l.t. ed. 1992. (General Ser.). 306p. lib. bdg. 19.95 o.p. (*0-8161-5427-9*, Macmillan Reference USA) Gale Group.

Julavits, Heidi. The Mineral Palace. 2001. 368p. reprint ed. pap. 14.00 (*0-425-17982-6*) Berkley Publishing Group.

—The Mineral Palace. abr. ed. 2000. audio 24.95 o.p. (*1-56740-931-8*, 2202, Nova Audio Bks.); audio 32.95 (*1-56740-389-1*, 2200, Brilliance Audio Unabridged); audio 73.25 (*1-56740-991-1*, 2201, Unabridged Library Editions) Brilliance Audio.

—The Mineral Palace. 2000. 325p. 23.95 o.s.i (*0-399-14622-9*) Penguin Group (USA) Inc.

Kalla, Alec & Sullivan, M. J. Velvet: A Novel of Suspense. 1993. 224p. 19.00 o.p. (*0-88150-264-2*) Countryman Pr.

Kane, Kathleen. Small Treasures. 1993. (Homespun Ser.). 336p. 4.99 o.p. (*1-55773-866-1*, Diamond Bks.) Ace Bks.

Karr, Leona. Murder in Bandora: An Addie Devore Mystery. 1993. 205p. 19.95 o.s.i (*0-8027-3240-2*) Walker & Co.

Keck, E. Frances. The JJ Ranch on the Purgatory River: The Jones Family & the Prairie Cattle Company. 2001. (Illus.). 144p. pap. 15.00 (*0-9663156-4-2*) Otero Pr.

Kerr, Baine. Harmful Intent. 2000. 384p. reprint ed. mass mkt. 6.99 (*0-515-12924-0*, Jove) Berkley Publishing Group.

—Harmful Intent. 1999. 368p. 25.00 (*0-684-85413-9*, Scribner) Simon & Schuster.

King, Stephen. The Shining. 1990. 464p. 35.00 (*0-385-12167-9*) Doubleday Publishing.

—The Shining. 1991. (Stephen King Collectors Editions Ser.). (Illus.). 432p. pap. 14.95 o.p. (*0-452-26722-6*, Plume) Dutton/Plume.
—The Shining. 1997. 464p. mass mkt. 7.50 o.s.i (*0-451-19388-1*); 1978. mass mkt. 4.50 o.p. (*0-451-15032-5*); 1978. 464p. reprint ed. mass mkt. 7.99 o.s.i (*0-451-16091-6*) NAL. (Signet Bks.).
—The Shining. reprint ed. 2002. 528p. pap. 14.00 (*0-7434-3749-7*); 2001. 704p. pap. 7.99 (*0-7434-2442-5*) Simon & Schuster. (Pocket).
—The Shining. l.t. ed. 1993. 656p. lib. bdg. 23.95 (*0-8161-5685-9*) Thorndike Pr.
—The Shining. 1977. 14.04 (*0-606-01215-X*) Turtleback Bks.
Krentz, Jayne Ann. Ghost of a Chance. l.t. ed. 2003. 280p. 31.95 (*1-58724-498-5*, Wheeler Publishing, Inc.) Gale Group.
—Ghost of a Chance. 1999. 250p. mass mkt. (*1-55166-524-7*, 1-66524-9, Mira Bks.) Harlequin Enterprises, Ltd.
—Gift of Gold. l.t. ed. 1994. pap. 22.95 o.p. (*0-7927-1885-2*); 23.95 o.p. (*0-7927-1886-0*) BBC Audiobooks America.
—Gift of Gold. unabr. collector's ed. 1996. audio 72.00 (*0-7366-3445-2*, 4089) Books on Tape, Inc.
—Gift of Gold. 1997. (Romance Ser.). 407p. lib. bdg. 24.95 (*0-7862-0910-0*, Five Star) Gale Group.
—Gift of Gold. 384p. 1993. mass mkt. 7.99 (*0-446-36381-2*); 1988. mass mkt. 4.95 (*0-445-20658-6*) Warner Bks., Inc.
Krinard, Susan. To Catch a Wolf. 2003. 368p. mass mkt. 6.99 (*0-425-19208-3*) Berkley Publishing Group.
Lacy, Al. A Dream Fulfilled, 10 vols. 2003. (Angel of Mercy Ser.: Vol. 4). 270p. pap. 10.99 (*0-88070-940-5*, Multnomah Bks.) Multnomah Pubs., Inc.
—Not by Might, 10 vols. 2003. (Angel of Mercy Ser.: Vol. 8). 349p. pap. 10.99 (*1-57673-242-8*, Multnomah Fiction) Multnomah Pubs., Inc.
L'Amour, Louis. The Cherokee Trail. 1996. 208p. mass mkt. 4.50 (*0-553-27047-8*); 1982. mass mkt. 2.95 o.s.i (*0-553-20846-2*) Bantam Bks.
—The Cherokee Trail. 1983. (General Ser.). lib. bdg. 12.95 o.p. (*0-8161-3464-2*, Macmillan Reference USA) Gale Group.
—The Cherokee Trail. 1982. (J). 10.55 (*0-606-01540-X*) Turtleback Bks.
Lazar, Zachary. Aaron, Approximately. 1998. 352p. 22.00 o.p. (*0-06-039211-8*, ReganBooks) HarperTrade.
—Aaron, Approximately. 1999. 352p. pap. 13.50 (*0-380-73213-0*, Avon Bks.) Morrow/Avon.
Lee, Rachel. A January Chill. 2001. 384p. mass mkt. (*1-55166-802-5*, 1-66802-9, Mira Bks.) Harlequin Enterprises, Ltd.
Lee, Wendi. Cannon's Revenge. l.t. ed. 1996. 20.00 (*0-7838-1628-6*); pap. 17.95 o.p. (*0-7838-1619-7*) Gale Group. (Macmillan Reference USA).
—Cannon's Revenge. 1995. 171p. 19.95 o.s.i (*0-8027-4147-9*) Walker & Co.
Legg, John P. Blood in the Snow. 1993. 304p. mass mkt. 3.50 o.s.i (*0-8217-4136-5*, Zebra Bks.) Kensington Publishing Corp.
Leiber, Vivian. Three Wishes. 2000. (Zebra Bouquet Ser.: Vol. 58). 256p. mass mkt. 3.99 o.s.i (*0-8217-6668-6*) Kensington Publishing Corp.
Lewis, Sherry. No Place for Death. 1996. 256p. mass mkt. 5.99 o.s.i (*0-425-15383-5*, Prime Crime) Berkley Publishing Group.
—No Place for Secrets. 1995. 256p. (Orig.). mass mkt. 4.99 o.s.i (*0-425-14835-1*, Prime Crime) Berkley Publishing Group.
—No Place for Sin. 1997. (Fred Vickery Novel Ser.). 256p. mass mkt. 5.99 o.s.i (*0-425-16113-7*, Prime Crime) Berkley Publishing Group.
—No Place for Tears. 1997. (Senior Sleuth Fred Vickery Ser.). 256p. (Orig.). mass mkt. 5.99 o.s.i (*0-425-15626-5*, Prime Crime) Berkley Publishing Group.
—No Place Like Home. 1996. 256p. (Orig.). mass mkt. 5.50 o.s.i (*0-425-15185-9*) Berkley Publishing Group.
Lowell, Elizabeth. Granite Man. 2001. 256p. mass mkt. (*1-55166-810-6*, 1-66810-2, Mira Bks.) Harlequin Enterprises, Ltd.
—Only You. l.t. ed. 1996. pap. 22.95 o.p. (*1-56895-363-1*, Wheeler Publishing, Inc.) Gale Group.
—Only You. 1992. 384p. mass mkt. 7.99 (*0-380-76340-0*) Morrow/Avon.
Madl, Linda. Brighter Than Gold. 2000. 368p. mass mkt. 5.99 o.s.i (*0-8217-6755-0*, Zebra Bks.) Kensington Publishing Corp.
Malone, Michael. The Delectable Mountains: Or, Entertaining Strangers. 1977. 8.95 o.p. (*0-394-49729-5*) Random Hse., Inc.
—The Delectable Mountains: Or, Entertaining Strangers. 2002. (Illus.). 352p. pap. 15.00 (*1-4022-0006-4*) Sourcebooks, Inc.
Masters, J. G. Sarah Elizabeth: A Tale of Old Colorado. 1985. 208p. 13.95 (*0-940672-29-4*) Shearer Publishing.
McNary, H. A. The Horse's Lawyer. 2003. 212p. pap. (*1-4120-0035-1*) Trafford Publishing.
—The Horse's Lawyer. 2003. 251p. pap. 21.99 o.p. (*1-4010-7798-6*); text 31.99 o.p. (*1-4010-7799-4*); E-Book 8.00 o.p. (*1-4010-7800-1*) Xlibris Corp.
McNaught, Judith. Perfect. Marrow, Linda, ed. 1993. 528p. 22.00 (*0-671-79552-X*, Atria); 1994. 704p. reprint ed. mass mkt. 7.99 (*0-671-79553-8*, Pocket) Simon & Schuster.
—Perfect. abr. ed. 1993. audio 17.00 (*0-671-86556-0*, 391361, Simon & Schuster Audioworks) Simon & Schuster Audio.
—Perfect. l.t. ed. 1993. (Romance Ser.). 1008p. lib. bdg. 26.95 (*1-56054-731-6*) Thorndike Pr.
Meixsell, Tara. Silverheels. 2002. (Illus.). 128p. pap. 10.95 (*1-890437-58-1*) Western Reflections Publishing Co.
Michael, Judith, pseud. Sleeping Beauty. l.t. ed. 1992. (General Ser.). 832p. lib. bdg. 23.95 o.p. (*0-8161-5490-2*); 16.95 o.p. (*0-8161-5491-0*) Gale Group. (Macmillan Reference USA).
—Sleeping Beauty. 1994. 640p. mass mkt. 7.99 o.s.i (*0-671-89959-7*, Pocket); 1991. 560p. 22.00 o.p. (*0-671-64893-4*, Simon & Schuster) Simon & Schuster.
—Sleeping Beauty. Grose, Bill, ed. 1992. 640p. reprint ed. mass mkt. 5.99 (*0-671-78252-5*, Pocket) Simon & Schuster.
Miles, John. Tenoclock Scholar: A Johnnie Baker Mystery. 1996. 252p. 22.95 (*0-8027-3273-9*) Walker & Co.
Millhiser, Marlys. It's Murder Going Home. 1997. (Charlie Greene Mystery Ser.). 288p. mass mkt. 6.95 o.s.i (*0-14-026586-4*) Penguin Group (USA) Inc.
—It's Murder Going Home. 1996. 304p. 22.95 (*0-312-14628-0*, Saint Martin's Minotaur) St. Martin's Pr.
Minger, Elda. Night Rythms. 2000. 224p. mass mkt. (*0-373-51119-1*, 1-51119-5, Harlequin Bks.) Harlequin Enterprises, Ltd.
Montgomery, Yvonne. Scavengers. 1990. 256p. pap. 3.50 (*0-380-71002-1*, Avon Bks.); 1987. 240p. 16.95 o.p. (*0-87795-897-1*, Morrow, William & Co.) Morrow/Avon.
Moody, Greg. Deadroll: A Cycling Murder Mystery. 2001. xviii, 272p. pap. 14.95 (*1-884737-92-7*) VeloPress.
Morgan, Kathleen. Child of Promise. 2002. (Brides of Culdee Creek Ser.: Bk. 4). 304p. (gr. 13 up). pap. 11.99 (*0-8007-5761-0*) Revell, Fleming H. Co.
—Daughter of Joy. 1999. (Brides of Culdee Creek Ser.: Vol. 1). 336p. (gr. 9 up). pap. 10.99 (*0-8007-5718-1*) Revell, Fleming H. Co.
—Daughter of Joy/Woman of Grace. 2000. pap. 11.99 (*0-8007-6458-7*) Revell, Fleming H. Co.
Morris, Gilbert & Ferguson, J. Landon. Unseen Riches. 1999. (Chronicles of the Golden Frontier Ser.: Bk. 2). 368p. pap. 11.99 (*1-58134-022-2*) Crossway Bks.
Most, Bruce W. Bonded for Murder: A Ruby Dark Mystery. 1996. (Dead Letter Mysteries Ser.). 279p. mass mkt. 5.99 (*0-312-96051-4*, St. Martin's Paperbacks) St. Martin's Pr.
—Missing Bonds, Vol. 1. 1997. (Ruby Dark Ser.). 288p. mass mkt. 5.99 (*0-312-96273-8*, St. Martin's Paperbacks) St. Martin's Pr.
Murray, Earl. In the Arms of the Sky. 2000. 304p. mass mkt. 6.99 (*0-8125-5143-5*); 1998. 301p. 22.95 (*0-312-86123-0*) Doherty, Tom Assocs., LLC. (Forge Bks.).
—South of Eden. 2001. mass mkt. 5.99 (*0-8125-7515-6*); 2001. 304p. mass mkt. 5.99 (*0-8125-7172-X*); 2000. 320p. 23.95 (*0-312-86923-1*) Doherty, Tom Assocs., LLC. (Forge Bks.).
Nelson, Kent. Discoveries: Short Stories of the San Juan Mountains. 1998. 152p. 18.95 (*1-890437-16-6*); pap. 12.95 (*1-890437-15-8*) Western Reflections Publishing Co.
Nicholson, Peggy. Don't Mess with Texans: By the Year 2000: Revenge, No. 834. 1999. (Harlequin Superromance Ser.: Vol. 834). per. (*0-373-70834-3*, Harlequin Bks.) Harlequin Enterprises, Ltd.
Nofziger, Lyn. Tackett & the Teacher. 1998. (Ground Source Chronicles Ser.). pap. 19.95 (*0-915463-81-4*) Jameson Bks., Inc.
—Tackett & the Teacher. 1994. 192p. 16.95 (*0-89526-488-9*) Regnery Publishing, Inc., An Eagle Publishing Co.
OakGrove, Artemis. Led Astray. 1994. 280p. (Orig.). pap. 9.95 (*1-885084-00-5*) Tickerwick Pubns.
O'Brien, Christopher. Mysterious Valley. 1996. 300p. mass mkt. 6.99 (*0-312-95883-8*, St. Martin's Paperbacks) St. Martin's Pr.
O'Kane, Leslie. The Fax of Life, 1. 1999. 256p. mass mkt. 5.99 o.s.i (*0-449-00160-1*, Fawcett) Ballantine Bks.
—The Fax of Life. l.t. ed. 2000. (Mystery Ser.). 381p. 26.95 (*0-7862-2328-6*) Thorndike Pr.
—Play Dead. 1998. (Allie Babcock Mysteries Ser.). 261p. mass mkt. 5.99 o.s.i (*0-449-00159-8*, Fawcett) Ballantine Bks.
—Play Dead. l.t. ed. 2000. (Mystery Ser.). 391p. o.p. (*0-7862-2329-4*) Thorndike Pr.
—Ruff Way to Go. 2000. (Allie Babcock Mysteries Ser.). 240p. mass mkt. 6.50 o.s.i (*0-449-00161-X*, Fawcett) Ballantine Bks.
—Ruff Way to Go. l.t. ed. 2001. (Thorndike Mystery Ser.). 383p. 28.95 (*0-7862-3193-9*) Thorndike Pr.
Oliphant, B. J., pseud. A Ceremonial Death. 1995. mass mkt. 5.99 o.s.i (*0-449-14897-1*, Fawcett) Ballantine Bks.
—Dead in the Scrub. 1990. 240p. mass mkt. 4.95 o.s.i (*0-449-14653-7*, Fawcett) Ballantine Bks.
—Death & the Delinquent. 1992. (Southwest Mysteries Ser.). (Orig.). mass mkt. 4.50 o.s.i (*0-449-14718-5*, Fawcett) Ballantine Bks.
—Death Served up Cold. 1994. (Orig.). mass mkt. 4.99 o.s.i (*0-449-14896-3*, Fawcett) Ballantine Bks.
—Deservedly Dead, No. 1. 1992. (Deservedly Dead Ser.: Vol. 1). mass mkt. 4.99 o.s.i (*0-449-14717-7*, Fawcett) Ballantine Bks.
—The Haunting at Lost Lake. l.t. ed. 1991. (Orig.). pap. 19.95 o.p. (*0-7927-0745-1*, CH023); pap. 17.95 o.p. (*0-7927-0746-X*, CS0129) BBC Audiobooks America.
—The Unexpected Corpse. 1990. 224p. (Orig.). mass mkt. 4.99 o.s.i (*0-449-14674-X*, Fawcett) Ballantine Bks.
Orde, A. J., pseud. Death & the Dogwalker. 1993. mass mkt. 4.50 o.s.i (*0-449-22027-3*, Fawcett) Ballantine Bks.
—Death for Old Times' Sake. 1993. mass mkt. 4.50 o.s.i (*0-449-22193-8*, Fawcett) Ballantine Bks.
—Death for Old Times' Sake. 1992. 240p. 16.50 o.s.i (*0-385-41941-4*) Doubleday Publishing.
—A Little Neighborhood Murder. 1992. mass mkt. 4.50 o.s.i (*0-449-22026-5*, Fawcett) Ballantine Bks.
—A Little Neighborhood Murder. l.t. ed. 1992. (Linford Mystery Library). 448p. pap. 17.99 o.p. (*0-7089-7163-6*, Linford) Thorpe, F. A. Pubs. GBR. *Dist:* Ulverscroft Large Print Bks., Ltd., Ulverscroft Large Print Canada, Ltd.
—A Long Time Dead. 1995. mass mkt. 5.50 o.s.i (*0-449-22359-0*, Fawcett) Ballantine Bks.
Orde, A. J., pseud & Tepper, Sheri S. Death of Innocents. 1997. (Jason Lynx Mystery Ser.). mass mkt. 5.99 o.s.i (*0-449-22519-4*, Fawcett) Ballantine Bks.
Overholser, Stephen. Fire in the Rainbow: A Western Story. 2003. mass mkt. 4.99 (*0-8439-5294-6*) Dorchester Publishing Co., Inc.
—Fire in the Rainbow: A Western Story. 2003. 287p. 25.95 (*0-7862-3795-3*, Five Star) Gale Group.
—Molly & the Gambler. 1984. (Molly Ser.). 160p. pap. 2.50 o.p. (*0-553-24055-2*) Bantam Bks.
—Molly & the Gambler. l.t. ed. 2001. 256p. 24.95 (*0-7862-3611-6*) Gale Group.
—Molly & the Gambler. l.t. ed. 2001. 269p. (*0-7540-4716-4*); (*0-7540-4717-2*) Thorndike Pr.
—Shadow Valley Rising: A Western Story. l.t. ed. 2002. (Five Star First Edition Western Ser.). 235p. 24.95 (*0-7862-3266-8*) Gale Group.
Paine, Lauran. Cache Canon. 2000. 208p. mass mkt. 3.99 (*0-8439-4733-0*, Leisure Bks.) Dorchester Publishing Co., Inc.
—Cache Canon. 1998. (Western Ser.). 207p. 20.95 (*0-7862-0989-5*, Five Star) Gale Group.
—Cache Canon: A Western Story. l.t. ed. 1999. (Western Ser.). 304p. 23.95 o.p. (*0-7862-1028-1*) Thorndike Pr.
Paine, Lauran, contrib. by. Cache Canon. 1999. (*0-7540-3665-0*) BBC Audiobooks America.
Parker, Ann. Silver Lies. 2003. 420p. 24.95 o.s.i (*1-59058-072-9*); 650p. pap. 22.95 o.s.i (*1-59058-084-2*) Poisoned Pen Pr.
Patten, Lewis B. Massacre at White River. l.t. ed. 1994. 18.95 o.p. (*0-7927-2068-7*); pap. 17.95 o.p. (*0-7927-2067-9*) BBC Audiobooks America.
—The Woman at Ox-Yoke: A Western Duo. 2001. 208p. reprint ed. pap. 3.99 (*0-8439-4914-7*, Leisure Bks.) Dorchester Publishing Co., Inc.
—The Woman at Ox-Yoke: A Western Duo. l.t. ed. 2000. (Five Star Western Ser.). 208p. pap. 21.95 (*0-7862-2475-4*, Five Star) Gale Group.
—The Woman at Ox-Yoke: A Western Duo. l.t. ed. 2001. 307p. 23.95 o.p. (*0-7862-2476-2*); 296p. (*0-7540-4712-1*); 296p. (*0-7540-4713-X*) Thorndike Pr.
Patterson, James. The Lake House. 2003. 384p. (gr. 8). 27.95 (*0-316-60328-7*); 448p. 27.95 (*0-316-71113-6*) Little Brown & Co.
—The Lake House. 2003. E-Book 12.75 (*0-7595-4745-9*) Time Warner Bk. Group.
—The Lake House. 2004. 416p. mass mkt. 7.99 (*0-446-61390-8*) Warner Bks., Inc.
—When the Wind Blows. unabr. ed. 1998. audio 56.00 (*0-7366-4249-8*, 4748) Books on Tape, Inc.
—When the Wind Blows. l.t. ed. 1999. (Core Ser.). 521p. 30.95 (*0-7838-0423-7*, Macmillan Reference USA) Gale Group.
—When the Wind Blows. unabr. ed. 1999. audio 39.98 Highsmith Inc.
—When the Wind Blows. 1998. 432p. (YA). (gr. 8 up). 25.00 o.p. (*0-316-69332-4*) Little Brown & Co.
—When the Wind Blows. l.t. ed. 2000. (Paperback Bestsellers Ser.). 423p. pap. 27.95 (*0-7838-0424-5*) Thorndike Pr.
—When the Wind Blows. abr. ed. 1998. audio 24.98 (*1-57042-639-2*, 693811); audio 39.98 (*1-57042-640-6*, 103816) Time Warner AudioBooks.
—When the Wind Blows. 2003. E-Book 5.95 (*0-7595-4740-8*) Time Warner Bk. Group.
—When the Wind Blows. 2000. 20.00 (*0-606-19686-2*) Turtleback Bks.
—When the Wind Blows. reprint ed. 2000. 416p. pap. 13.95 (*0-446-67643-8*); 1999. 448p. mass mkt. 7.99 (*0-446-60765-7*) Warner Bks., Inc.
Peart, Jane. Undaunted Spirit. l.t. ed. 2002. (Westward Dreams Ser.). 350p. 25.95 (*0-7862-3127-0*) Gale Group.
—Undaunted Spirit. 1999. (Westward Dreams Ser.: Vol. 5). 240p. pap. 9.99 (*0-310-22012-2*) Zondervan.
Pendergrass, Tess. Colorado Shadows Bk. 1: Colorado Series. 2000. (First Edition Romance Ser.). 387p. 25.95 (*0-7862-2372-3*, Five Star) Gale Group.
—Colorado Sunrise. 2002. (Five Star First Edition Romance Ser.). 384p. 26.95 (*0-7862-4515-8*, Five Star) Gale Group.
—Colorado Twilight. 2001. (Five Star First Edition Romance Ser.). 355p. 25.95 (*0-7862-3301-X*, Five Star) Gale Group.
Pickard, Nancy. The Blue Corn Murders. 1999. (Eugenia Potter Mysteries Ser.). 356p. pap. (*0-7540-3688-X*) BBC Audiobooks America.
—The Blue Corn Murders. 1998. (Eugenia Potter Mysteries Ser.). 272p. 21.95 o.s.i (*0-385-31224-5*) Dell Publishing.
—The Blue Corn Murders. l.t. ed. 1999. (Eugenia Potter Mysteries Ser.). 353p. 28.95 (*0-7838-8479-6*, Macmillan Reference USA) Gale Group.
Pickard, Nancy, contrib. by. The Blue Corn Murders. 1999. (Eugenia Potter Mysteries Ser.). (*0-7540-3687-1*) BBC Audiobooks America.
Pickard, Nancy & Pickard, Virginia. The Blue Corn Murders. 1999. (Eugenia Potter Mysteries Ser.). 304p. mass mkt. 5.99 (*0-440-21765-2*) Dell Publishing.
Pritchett, Laura. Hell's Bottom, Colorado. 2001. 144p. pap. 14.95 (*1-57131-036-3*) Milkweed Editions.
Quezada, M. Louise. Love's Destiny. 1999. 168p. pap. 8.95 (*1-885478-68-2*) Genesis Pr., Inc.
Raine, William M. Colorado. 1976. reprint ed. lib. bdg. 24.95 (*0-88411-557-7*) Amereon, Ltd.
Ramos. The Last Client of Luis Montez, Vol. 1. 1997. mass mkt. o.p. (*0-312-96105-7*, St. Martin's Paperbacks) St. Martin's Pr.
Ramos, Manuel. The Ballad of Gato Guerrero. 1994. 192p. 18.95 o.p. (*0-312-10935-0*, Saint Martin's Minotaur) St. Martin's Pr.
—Blues for the Buffalo: A Luis Montez Mystery. 1997. 240p. 21.95 o.p. (*0-312-15480-1*, Saint Martin's Minotaur) St. Martin's Pr.
—Death of a Martyr: The Ballad of Rocky Ruiz. 1993. 208p. 17.95 o.p. (*0-312-09271-7*, Saint Martin's Minotaur) St. Martin's Pr.
—The Last Client of Luis Montez. 1996. 208p. 20.95 o.p. (*0-312-13997-7*, Saint Martin's Minotaur) St. Martin's Pr.
Ramthun, Bonnie. Earthquake Games. 2001. 352p. mass mkt. 6.99 o.s.i (*0-515-13177-6*, Jove) Berkley Publishing Group.
—Earthquake Games. 2000. 304p. 24.95 o.s.i (*0-399-14666-0*) Penguin Group (USA) Inc.
—The Thirteenth Skull. Teel, Barbara, ed. 2003. pap. 14.95 (*0-9662696-7-5*, 0966269675) Loveland Pr.
Rice, Pam. Coming to My Senses. 2002. (Five Star First Edition Romance Ser.). 265p. 25.95 (*0-7862-3034-7*, Five Star) Gale Group.
—Coming to My Senses. l.t. ed. 2003. 392p. 28.95 (*0-7862-6028-9*, Large Print Pr.) Thorndike Pr.
Roberts, Lora. Murder Mile High. 1996. (Liz Sullivan Mysteries Ser.). mass mkt. 5.50 o.s.i (*0-449-14947-1*, Fawcett) Ballantine Bks.
Rose, Joanna. Little Miss Strange. 1998. 384p. pap. 12.00 (*0-684-84741-8*, Touchstone) Simon & Schuster.
—Little Miss Strange: A Novel. 1997. 384p. tchr. ed. 20.95 (*1-56512-154-6*, 72154) Algonquin Bks. of Chapel Hill.
Ross, Dana Fuller, pseud. Colorado! 1984. mass mkt. 3.95 o.s.i (*0-553-24694-1*); 368p. mass mkt. 4.95 o.s.i (*0-553-26546-6*) Bantam Bks.
—Colorado! 1982. (Reader's Request Ser.). lib. bdg. 16.95 o.p. (*0-8161-3320-4*, Macmillan Reference USA) Gale Group.
Ryan, Gordon. Threads of Honor. 1996. xv, 80p. pap. o.p. (*1-57345-169-X*, Shadow Mountain) Deseret Bk. Co.
Ryan, Mary. Hope. mass mkt. (*0-312-98744-7*, St. Martin's Paperbacks) St. Martin's Pr.
—Hope: A Novel. 2003. 480p. 27.95 (*0-312-30970-8*) St. Martin's Pr.
Ryan, Nan. Naughty Marietta. 2003. 384p. mass mkt. (*1-55166-676-6*, Mira Bks.) Harlequin Enterprises, Ltd.

—Naughty Marietta. l.t. ed. 2003. 429p. 27.95 (0-7862-5844-6) Thorndike Pr.

Sala, Sharon. Remember Me. unabr. ed. 1999. audio 7.99 (1-55204-196-4, MIR-1196) Durkin Hayes Publishing Ltd.

—Remember Me. 384p. 2003. mass mkt. (1-55166-967-6); 1999. mass mkt. (1-55166-535-2) Harlequin Enterprises, Ltd. (Mira Bks.).

Schaff, Donna. Priceless. 1998. 384p. mass mkt. 5.99 o.s.i (0-440-22586-8) Doubleday Publishing.

Schaller, Bob. Colorado. 1998. (Arlingtons Ser.). (Illus.). 128p. (J). (gr. 3-7). pap. text 7.95 o.p. (1-887002-77-4) Cross Training Publishing.

Schofield, Susan C. Telluride: A Novel. 1993. 344p. 18.95 o.p. (0-945575-96-3) Algonquin Bks. of Chapel Hill.

Schwartz, Steven. Therapy: A Novel. 1995. 352p. pap. 12.95 o.p. (0-452-27431-1, Plume) Dutton/Plume.

—Therapy: A Novel. 1994. 352p. 22.95 o.s.i (0-15-100062-X) Harcourt Trade Pubs.

Sharpe, Jon. Colorado Carnage. 1995. (Trailsman Ser.: No. 166). 176p. mass mkt. 4.50 o.s.i (0-451-18223-5, Signet Bks.) NAL.

—Colorado Diamond Dupe. 2000. (Trailsman Ser.: Vol. 222). 176p. mass mkt. 4.99 o.s.i (0-451-20007-1, Signet Bks.) NAL.

—Colorado Quarry. 1992. (Trailsman Ser.: No. 124). 176p. (Orig.). mass mkt. 3.50 o.s.i (0-451-17213-2, Signet Bks.) NAL.

—Colorado Wolfpack. 1996. (Trailsman Ser.: No. 177). 176p. mass mkt. 4.99 o.s.i (0-451-18759-8, Signet Bks.) NAL.

—Curse of the Grizzly. 1996. (Trailsman Ser.: No. 176). 176p. mass mkt. 4.99 o.s.i (0-451-18689-3, Signet Bks.) NAL.

—The Trailsman: Colorado Diamond Dupe. l.t. ed. 2000. (Wheeler Large Print Book Ser.). 201p. pap. 24.95 o.p. (1-56895-888-9, Wheeler Publishing, Inc.) Gale Group.

—The Trailsman No. 75: Colorado Robber. 1988. (Trailsman Ser.). 176p. mass mkt. 2.75 o.p. (0-451-15226-3, Signet Bks.) NAL.

Simmons, Hal. Deadly Gold: A Novel. 2002. 272p. pap. 14.95 (1-57416-060-5) Clear Light Pubs.

Sinclair, Upton. The Coal War. Graham, John, ed. & intro. by. 1976. 335p. text 25.00 o.p. (0-87081-067-7) Univ. Pr. of Colorado.

—King Coal. 1980. (Labor Movement in Fiction & Non-Fiction Ser.). 408p. reprint ed. 37.50 (0-404-58469-1) AMS Pr., Inc.

—King Coal. lib. bdg. 28.95 (0-8488-1899-7) Amereon, Ltd.

—King Coal. 1994. 448p. mass mkt. 4.95 o.s.i (0-553-21433-0) Bantam Bks.

—King Coal. (Collected Works of Upton Sinclair). 396p. 2001. pap. text 28.00 (0-7426-5822-8); 1999. reprint ed. lib. bdg. 108.00 (1-58201-822-7) Classic Bks.

Smith, Bobbi. Jenny. 2000. (Brides of Durango Ser.). 400p. mass mkt. 5.99 (0-8439-4776-4, Leisure Bks.) Dorchester Publishing Co., Inc.

Spencer, LaVyrle. Hummingbird. 2003. 416p. pap. 10.00 (0-425-19580-5); 1987. 416p. mass mkt. 7.50 (0-515-09160-X, Jove); 1985. mass mkt. 3.95 o.s.i (0-515-08588-X, Jove); 1984. mass mkt. 3.95 o.s.i (0-515-08373-9, Jove); 1983. mass mkt. 3.50 o.s.i (0-515-07108-0, Jove); 1983. mass mkt. 3.95 o.s.i (0-515-07261-3, Jove) Berkley Publishing Group.

—Hummingbird. l.t. ed. 1993. 501p. 18.95 o.p. (0-8161-5296-9); lib. bdg. 22.95 o.p. (0-8161-5295-0) Gale Group. (Macmillan Reference USA).

Stafford, Jean. The Mountain Lion. 1972. 231p. 6.95 o.p. (0-374-21402-6) Farrar, Straus & Giroux.

—The Mountain Lion. 1983. 244p. reprint ed. pap. 5.95 o.p. (0-525-48031-5, Obelisk) NAL.

—The Mountain Lion. 1977. (Zia Bks.). 231p. reprint ed. pap. 3.45 o.p. (0-8263-0432-X) Univ. of New Mexico Pr.

—The Mountain Lion. 1992. 232p. reprint ed. pap. 11.95 (0-292-75136-2) Univ. of Texas Pr.

Stone, Katherine. The Island of Dreams. 2001. 336p. mass mkt. 6.99 (0-446-60954-4); 2000. 272p. 23.95 (0-446-52182-5) Warner Bks., Inc.

—Island of Dreams. l.t. ed. 2000. (Large Print Bks.). 263p. 28.95 (1-56895-955-9, Wheeler Publishing, Inc.) Gale Group.

Stone, Michael. A Long Reach. 1998. (Streeter Mystery Ser.). 240p. pap. 5.99 o.s.i (0-14-024703-3) Penguin Group (USA) Inc.

—A Long Reach. l.t. ed. 1997. (Niagara Large Print Ser.). 320p. 29.50 o.p. (0-7089-5875-3, Ulverscroft) Thorpe, F. A. Pubs. GBR. *Dist:* Ulverscroft Large Print Bks., Ltd.

—A Long Reach. 1997. (Streeter Mystery Ser.). 240p. 20.95 o.s.i (0-670-86166-9) Viking Penguin.

—The Low End of Nowhere: A Streeter Mystery. 1997. (Viking Mystery Suspense Ser.). 240p. pap. 5.95 o.s.i (0-14-024694-0) Penguin Group (USA) Inc.

—The Low End of Nowhere: A Streeter Mystery. l.t. ed. 1997. (Niagara Large Print Ser.). 290p. 29.50 o.p. (0-7089-5863-X, Linford) Thorpe, F. A. Pubs. GBR. *Dist:* Ulverscroft Large Print Bks., Ltd.

—The Low End of Nowhere: A Streeter Mystery. 1996. (Streeter Mystery Ser.). 240p. 20.95 o.p. (0-670-86154-5) Viking Penguin.

—Token of Remorse. 1998. (Streeter Mystery Ser.). 256p. 22.95 o.p. (0-670-87774-3) Viking Penguin.

—Token of Remorse: A Streeter Mystery. 1999. (Streeter Mystery Ser.). 256p. pap. 5.99 (0-14-027546-0, Puffin Bks.) Penguin Group (USA) Inc.

—Totally Dead. 2000. (Streeter Mystery Ser.). 240p. pap. 5.99 o.s.i (0-14-028598-9, Penguin Bks.) Penguin Group (USA) Inc.

—Totally Dead. 1999. (Streeter Mystery Ser.). 256p. 22.95 o.s.i (0-670-88208-9, Viking) Viking Penguin.

Strand, Keith. Grandfather's Christmas Tree. 1999. (Illus.). 32p. (J). (ps-3). 16.00 (0-15-201821-2, Silver Whistle) Harcourt Children's Bks.

Taylor, Lucy. Dancing with Demons. deluxe ed. 1998. (Illus.). 300p. 45.00 (1-891480-02-2) Obsidian Bks., Etc.

Thacker, Shelly. Into the Sunset. 1999. 384p. mass mkt. 6.50 o.s.i (0-440-22518-3) Dell Publishing.

Thompson, Vicki Lewis, et al. Escapade: Shattered Vows; Loverboy; The Keeper; The Veranchetti Marriage, 4 bks. in 1. 1998. (Promo Ser.). 971p. per. (0-373-83408-X, 1-83408-4, Harlequin Bks.) Harlequin Enterprises, Ltd.

Thornburg, Newton. Eve's Men. 1999. 277p. mass mkt. 6.99 (0-8125-8419-8); 1998. 288p. 22.95 (0-312-86399-3) Doherty, Tom Assocs., LLC. (Forge Bks.).

Thurlow, Kathy. A Brand New Life. 2002. (Five Star Romance Ser.). 311p. 26.95 (0-7862-3852-6, Five Star) Gale Group.

—A Brand New Life. 1994. 512p. mass mkt. 4.99 o.s.i (0-8217-4496-8, Zebra Bks.) Kensington Publishing Corp.

—Mrs. Love. 2001. (Five Star First Edition Romance Ser.). 247p. 25.95 (0-7862-3385-0, Five Star) Gale Group.

—Mrs. Love. 1999. E-Book 5.50 (1-58200-268-1); 248p. E-Book 5.50 (1-58200-148-0) Hard Shell Word Factory.

Tomlinson, Dar. Designer Passion. 1999. (Love Spectrum Romance Ser.). 399p. pap. 8.95 (1-885478-79-8, Love Spectrum) Genesis Pr., Inc.

Trainor, J. F. High Country Murder: An Angela Biwaban Mystery. 1996. 400p. mass mkt. 4.99 o.s.i (1-57566-107-1); 1995. 390p. mass mkt. 18.95 o.p. (0-8217-5124-7, Kensington Bks.) Kensington Publishing Corp.

Trammel, Eddie Dean. Colorado Bound. 2002. 224p. pap. 12.95 (1-885373-45-7) Emerald Ink Publishing.

Tremblay, William. The June Rise: The Apocryphal Letters of Joseph Antoine Janis. 2001. 256p. 22.95 (1-55591-452-7) Fulcrum Publishing.

—The June Rise: The Apocryphal Letters of Joseph Antoine Janis. 1994. 225p. pap. 19.95 o.p. (0-87421-176-X) Utah State Univ. Pr.

Tremblay, William & Janis, Joseph Antoine. The June Rise: The Apocryphal Letters of Joseph Antoine Janis. 1994. E-Book 5.00 (0-585-03266-1) netLibrary, Inc.

Underwood, Phillip. Green Valley Justice. 1992. 192p. 18.95 o.s.i (0-8027-4127-4) Walker & Co.

Vernon, John. All for Love: Baby Doe & Silver Dollar. 1995. 288p. 23.00 (0-684-80371-2, Simon & Schuster) Simon & Schuster.

—The Last Canyon. 2001. 352p. 24.00 (0-618-17454-0) Houghton Mifflin Co.

Wall, Judith Henry. Blood Sisters. 1994. 336p. mass mkt. 4.99 o.p. (0-451-40414-9, Onyx) NAL.

—Blood Sisters. 1992. 320p. 22.00 o.p. (0-670-84114-5, Viking) Viking Penguin.

Waters, Frank. Pike's Peak: A Mining Saga. 1987. 743p. 39.95 (0-8040-0503-6) Swallow Pr.

Watt, Laura. Carry Me Back. pap. 15.95 (0-312-30225-8, Saint Martin's Griffin); 1996. 256p. 21.95 (0-312-15075-X) St. Martin's Pr.

Wells, Marian. Colorado Gold. 1988. (Treasure Quest Bks.: Vol. 2). 336p. (Orig.). pap. 8.99 o.p. (0-87123-966-3) Bethany Hse. Pubs.

Wesson, Marianne. Render Up the Body. l.t. ed. 1998. 336p. 24.00 o.s.i (0-06-018292-X) HarperCollins Pubs.

—Render up the Body: A Novel of Suspense. l.t. ed. 1998. 432p. mass mkt. 6.99 (0-06-109392-0, HarperTorch) Morrow/Avon.

—A Suggestion of Death. 2001. 464p. reprint ed. mass mkt. 6.99 (0-671-03560-6, Pocket Star) Simon & Schuster.

—A Suggestion of Death: A Novel. 2000. 352p. 23.95 (0-671-03559-2, Atria) Simon & Schuster.

Wheeler, Richard S. Second Lives. 1999. 436p. mass mkt. 5.99 (0-8125-4517-6, Forge Bks.) Doherty, Tom Assocs., LLC.

—Second Lives: A Novel of the Gilded Age. 1997. 384p. 24.95 o.p. (0-312-86333-0, Forge Bks.) Doherty, Tom Assocs., LLC.

White, Stephen. Cold Case. 2000. (Illus.). 368p. 24.95 (0-525-94526-1, Dutton) Dutton/Plume.

—Cold Case. 2001. 432p. mass mkt. 7.99 (0-451-20155-8, Signet Bks.) NAL.

—Cold Case. l.t. ed. 2000. (Mystery Ser.). 623p. 29.95 (0-7862-2530-0) Thorndike Pr.

—Critical Conditions. l.t. ed. 2000. 27.95 (1-57490-280-6, Beeler Large Print Bks.) Beeler, Thomas T. Publisher.

—Critical Conditions. unabr. ed. 1998. (Alan Gregory Ser.). audio 64.00 (0-7366-4184-X, 4682) Books on Tape, Inc.

—Critical Conditions. 1998. (Alan Gregory Ser.). 320p. 24.95 o.p. (0-525-94270-X) Dutton/Plume.

—Critical Conditions. 1999. (Alan Gregory Ser.). 416p. mass mkt. 7.99 (0-451-19170-6, Signet Bks.) NAL.

—Harm's Way. l.t. ed. 1996. lib. bdg. 24.95 (1-57490-066-8, Beeler Large Print Bks.) Beeler, Thomas T. Publisher.

—Harm's Way. unabr. collector's ed. 1997. (Alan Gregory Ser.). audio 56.00 (0-913369-39-X, 4215) Books on Tape, Inc.

—Harm's Way. 1997. 432p. mass mkt. 7.99 (0-451-18368-1, Signet Bks.) NAL.

—Harm's Way. 1996. 352p. 22.95 o.p. (0-670-85861-7, Viking) Viking Penguin.

—Higher Authority. unabr. collector's ed. 1995. (Alan Gregory Ser.). audio 80.00 (0-7366-3042-2, 3724) Books on Tape, Inc.

—Higher Authority. 1996. 432p. mass mkt. 7.99 (0-451-18511-0, Signet Bks.) NAL.

—Higher Authority. 1994. 464p. 22.95 o.p. (0-670-85040-3) Viking Penguin.

—Manner of Death. l.t. ed. 1999. 450p. 26.95 (1-57490-177-X) Beeler, Thomas T. Publisher.

—Manner of Death. unabr. ed. 1999. (Alan Gregory Ser.). audio 72.00 (0-7366-4403-2, 4864) Books on Tape, Inc.

—Manner of Death. 1999. (Alan Gregory Ser.). 416p. 23.95 o.p. (0-525-94440-0) Dutton/Plume.

—Manner of Death. 2000. 416p. reprint ed. mass mkt. 7.50 (0-451-19703-8, Signet Bks.) NAL.

—Private Practices. unabr. collector's ed. 1993. (Alan Gregory Ser.). audio 80.00 (0-7366-2592-5, 3337) Books on Tape, Inc.

—Private Practices. 1994. 432p. mass mkt. 7.99 (0-451-40431-9, Signet Bks.) NAL.

—Private Practices. 1999. pap. (0-14-017328-5); 1993. 432p. 20.00 o.p. (0-670-84673-2) Viking Penguin. (Viking).

—Privileged Information. unabr. collector's ed. 1992. (Alan Gregory Ser.). audio 72.00 (0-7366-2262-4, 3050) Books on Tape, Inc.

—Privileged Information. 2001. 384p. mass mkt. 6.99 (0-7860-1356-7, Pinnacle Bks.); 1999. 383p. mass mkt. 5.99 o.s.i (0-7860-0624-2); 1992. 384p. reprint ed. mass mkt. 5.99 o.s.i (0-8217-3951-4, Zebra Bks.) Kensington Publishing Corp.

—Privileged Information. 1991. 368p. 19.95 o.p. (0-670-83765-2) Viking Penguin.

—The Program. abr. ed. 2001. audio 24.95 o.s.i (1-58788-359-7, 2545, Nova Audio Bks.); audio 34.95 (1-58788-357-0, 2543, Brilliance Audio Unabridged); audio 87.25 (1-58788-358-9, 2544) Brilliance Audio.

—The Program. 2002. 480p. mass mkt. 7.99 (0-440-23726-2) Dell Publishing.

—The Program. l.t. ed. 2002. pap. 28.95 (0-7862-3412-1); 2001. 480p. 31.95 (0-7862-3411-3) Thorndike Pr.

—Remote Control. unabr. ed. 1997. (Alan Gregory Ser.). audio 64.00 (0-7366-3769-9, 4442) Books on Tape, Inc.

—Remote Control. 1997. (Alan Gregory Ser.). 320p. 22.95 o.s.i (0-525-94269-6) Dutton/Plume.

—Remote Control. 1998. (Alan Gregory Ser.). 432p. mass mkt. 6.99 (0-451-19169-2, Signet Bks.) NAL.

—Remote Control. abr. ed. 1997. (Alan Gregory Ser.). audio 16.95 o.s.i (0-14-086549-7, Penguin AudioBooks) Viking Penguin.

Whitesmith, D. Innocent Prey: A Novel. 1993. 192p. pap. 6.99 o.p. (0-7814-0946-2) Cook Communications Ministries.

Whitney, Phyllis A. Domino. l.t. ed. 1993. 22.95 o.p. (0-7927-1668-X); pap. 21.95 o.p. (0-7927-1667-1) BBC Audiobooks America.

Williams, Arthur. Missing at Tenoclock. 1994. 216p. 19.95 (0-8027-3185-6) Walker & Co.

Wise, Joe. Cannibal Plateau: A Novel. 2002. pap. 12.95 (0-86534-360-8); 1997. 160p. 14.95 (0-86534-262-8) Sunstone Pr.

Work, James C. The Tobermory Manuscript. 2000. (Five Star Western Ser.). 299p. 21.95 (0-7862-2103-8, Five Star) Gale Group.

Wright, Barbara. Easy Money: A Novel. 1995. 402p. 18.95 o.p. (0-945575-63-7) Algonquin Bks. of Chapel Hill.

Wright, Michelle Curry. Miranda Blue Calling. 2004. 320p. pap. 13.95 (0-06-056143-2, Avon Bks.) Morrow/Avon.

—Wait & See, Annie Lee. l.t. ed. 2001. 297p. 26.95 (1-57490-377-2, Beeler Large Print Bks.) Beeler, Thomas T. Publisher.

—Wait & See, Annie Lee. 288p. 2002. pap. 13.95 (0-446-67855-4); 2001. (Illus.). 23.95 (0-446-52690-8) Warner Bks., Inc.

Yaffe, James. Mom among the Liars. 1994. (WWL Mystery Ser.). mass mkt. (0-373-26142-X, 1-26142-9, Harlequin Bks.) Harlequin Enterprises, Ltd.

—Mom among the Liars. 1992. 224p. 17.95 o.p. (0-312-08264-9, Saint Martin's Minotaur) St. Martin's Pr.

—Mom Doth Murder Sleep. 1992. (WWL Mystery Ser.: No. 98). mass mkt. (0-373-26098-9, 1-26098-3, Harlequin Bks.) Harlequin Enterprises, Ltd.

—Mom Doth Murder Sleep. 1991. 16.95 o.p. (0-312-05898-5, Saint Martin's Minotaur) St. Martin's Pr.

—Mom Meets Her Maker. 1991. 224p. mass mkt. (0-373-26067-9, Harlequin Bks.) Harlequin Enterprises, Ltd.

—Mom Meets Her Maker. 1990. 256p. 16.95 o.p. (0-312-03893-3, Saint Martin's Minotaur) St. Martin's Pr.

—A Nice Murder for Mom. 1990. mass mkt. (0-373-26044-X, Harlequin Bks.) Harlequin Enterprises, Ltd.

—A Nice Murder for Mom. 1988. 208p. 15.95 o.p. (0-312-02260-3, Saint Martin's Minotaur) St. Martin's Pr.

Yancey, Wes. Kill that Deputy. l.t. ed. 1994. 19.95 o.p. (0-7927-1903-4); pap. 17.95 o.p. (0-7927-1902-6) BBC Audiobooks America.

Yarbro, Chelsea Quinn. Charity Colorado. 1993. 234p. 18.95 o.p. (0-87131-746-X) Evans, M. & Co., Inc.

York, Kieran. Crystal Mountain Veils: A Royce Madison Mystery. 1995. 240p. (Orig.). pap. 10.95 o.p. (1-879427-19-2) 3rd Side Pr., Inc.

—Timber City Masks: A Royce Madison Mystery. 1993. 230p. (Orig.). pap. 9.95 o.p. (1-879427-13-3) 3rd Side Pr., Inc.

Zapel, Arthur L. Sweet Uncertainty: Action & Suspense, Fantasy & Reality Intersect in a Novel of Discovery. 2002. 448p. pap. 14.00 (1-56608-077-0) Meriwether Publishing, Ltd.

Zigal, Thomas. Hardrock Stiff: A Kurt Muller Mystery. 1997. (Kurt Muller Mysteries Ser.). 384p. mass mkt. 5.99 o.s.i (0-440-22452-7) Dell Publishing.

—Into Thin Air: A Novel. 1996. (Kurt Muller Mysteries Ser.). 368p. mass mkt. 5.50 o.s.i (0-440-22251-6) Dell Publishing.

—Pariah. 2000. (Kurt Muller Mysteries Ser.). 336p. mass mkt. 5.99 o.s.i (0-440-22443-8) Dell Publishing.

## CONCORD (MASS.)—FICTION

Langton, Jane. The Deserter: Murder at Gettysburg. 2003. (Illus.). 256p. 23.95 (0-312-30186-3, Saint Martin's Minotaur) St. Martin's Pr.

—God in Concord: A Homer Kelly Mystery. 1993. (Homer Kelly Mystery Ser.). (Illus.). 352p. pap. 6.99 (0-14-016594-0, Penguin Bks.) Penguin Group (USA) Inc.

—God in Concord: A Homer Kelly Mystery. 1992. (Homer Kelly Mystery Ser.). 384p. 19.00 o.p. (0-670-84260-5, Viking) Viking Penguin.

Luber, Philip. Deliver Us from Evil. 1997. 324p. mass mkt. 5.99 (0-449-14940-4, Fawcett) Ballantine Bks.

—Forgive Us Our Sins. 1994. (Boston Mysteries Ser.). mass mkt. 5.99 o.s.i (0-449-14849-1, Fawcett) Ballantine Bks.

—Pray for Us Sinners. 1997. 294p. (Orig.). mass mkt. 5.99 o.s.i (0-449-18329-7, Fawcett) Ballantine Bks.

## CONFLUENCE (IMAGINARY PLACE)—FICTION

McAuley, Paul J. Ancients of Days. 2000. (Confluence Trilogy Ser.: Vol. 2). 416p. mass mkt. 6.99 o.s.i (0-380-79297-4, Eos) Morrow/Avon.

—Ancients of Days: The Second Book of Confluence. 1999. 400p. 16.00 o.p. (0-380-97516-5, Eos) Morrow/Avon.

—Child of the River, No. 1. 1999. 336p. mass mkt. 6.99 (0-380-79296-6, Eos) Morrow/Avon.

—Child of the River: The First Book of Confluence. 1998. 320p. 14.00 (0-380-97515-7, Eos) Morrow/Avon.

—A Shrine of Stars: The Third Book of Confluence. 2000. (Confluence Trilogy Ser.). 384p. 18.00 (0-380-97517-3, Avon Bks.) Morrow/Avon.

## CONNECTICUT—FICTION

Allen, Charlotte Vale. Claudia's Shadow. 1996. 399p. mass mkt. (1-55166-177-2, 1-66177-6); 304p. per. (1-55166-245-0, 1-66245-1) Harlequin Enterprises, Ltd. (Mira Bks.).

—Dreaming in Color. l.t. ed. 1993. 23.95 o.p. (*1-56895-040-3*, Wheeler Publishing, Inc.); Set. 1994. 104.95 o.p. incl. audio (*0-7862-9980-0*, Macmillan Reference USA) Gale Group.
—Dreaming in Color. 2001. 416p. pap. (*1-55166-856-4*, 1-66856-5, Mira Bks.) Harlequin Enterprises, Ltd.
—Dreaming in Color. l.t. ed. 1994. (Magna Large Print Ser.). 636p. o.p. (*0-7505-0689-X*) Magna Large Print Bks. GBR. *Dist:* Ulverscroft Large Print Canada, Ltd.
—Fresh Air. 2004. 384p. mass mkt. (*0-7783-2023-5*); 2003. 288p. (*1-55166-682-0*) Harlequin Enterprises, Ltd. (Mira Bks.).
—Fresh Air. l.t. ed. 2003. 396p. 29.95 (*0-7862-5543-9*) Thorndike Pr.
—Nightfall. 1999. 234p. reprint ed. pap. 20.00 (*1-892738-28-7*) Island Nation Pr., LLC.
Ambrose, David P. The Man Who Turned into Himself. 1994. text 17.00 o.p. (*0-312-10497-9*) St. Martin's Pr.
—The Man Who Turned into Himself: A Novel. 1995. (Picador Fiction Ser.). 208p. pap. 10.00 (*0-312-13119-4*) Picador.
Archer, Jeffrey. Sons of Fortune. 2003. 544p. mass mkt. 7.99 o.s.i (*0-312-99353-6*, St. Martin's Paperbacks); mass mkt. 7.99 (*0-312-99380-3*, St. Martin's Paperbacks); 400p. 27.95 (*0-312-31319-5*) St. Martin's Pr.
—Sons of Fortune. l.t. ed. 2003. 32.95 (*0-7862-5462-9*) Thorndike Pr.
Argiri, Laura. The God in Flight. 1996. 496p. pap. 22.00 o.s.i (*0-14-025413-7*, Penguin Bks.) Penguin Group (USA) Inc.
Basch, Rachel. The Passion of Reverend Nash: A Novel. 2003. 288p. 23.95 (*0-393-05768-2*) Norton, W. W. & Co., Inc.
Benchley, Peter. Peter Benchley's Creature. 1998. 352p. mass mkt. 6.99 (*0-312-96573-7*, St. Martin's Paperbacks) St. Martin's Pr.
—White Shark. l.t. ed. 1995. (Magna Large Print Ser.). (Illus.). 497p. o.p. (*0-7505-0860-4*) Magna Large Print Bks. GBR. *Dist:* Ulverscroft Large Print Canada, Ltd.
—White Shark. 1995. 340p. mass mkt. 6.50 (*0-312-95573-1*, St. Martin's Paperbacks) St. Martin's Pr.
Berenson, Laurien. Dog Eat Dog: A Melanie Travis Mystery. (Melanie Travis Mystery Ser.). 1997. 336p. mass mkt. 5.99 (*1-57566-227-2*); 1996. 352p. 18.95 o.s.i (*1-57566-103-9*) Kensington Publishing Corp.
—Hair of the Dog: A Melanie Travis Mystery. (Melanie Travis Mystery Ser.). 1998. 336p. mass mkt. 5.99 (*1-57566-356-2*); 1997. 320p. 18.95 o.s.i (*1-57566-222-1*) Kensington Publishing Corp.
—Hush Puppy. (Melanie Travis Mystery Ser.). 2000. 32p. mass mkt. 5.99 (*1-57566-600-6*); 1999. 304p. 20.00 o.s.i (*1-57566-469-0*, Kensington Bks.) Kensington Publishing Corp.
—A Pedigree to Die For: A Melanie Travis Mystery. l.t. ed. 1995. 347p. pap. 20.95 o.p. (*0-7838-1446-1*, Macmillan Reference USA) Gale Group.
—A Pedigree to Die For: A Melanie Travis Mystery, 1. 1998. mass mkt. 5.99 (*1-57566-374-0*); 1997. 288p. pap. 9.95 o.s.i (*1-57566-125-X*); 1996. 288p. mass mkt. 4.99 o.s.i (*1-57566-003-2*); 1996. mass mkt. 4.99 o.p. (*0-8217-5227-8*); 1995. 304p. mass mkt. 16.95 o.p. (*0-8217-4827-0*, Zebra Bks.) Kensington Publishing Corp.
—Underdog: A Melanie Travis Mystery. 1996. 336p. mass mkt. 4.99 o.s.i (*1-57566-108-X*); 320p. 18.95 o.s.i (*1-57566-011-3*); mass mkt. 16.95 o.s.i (*0-8217-5224-3*) Kensington Publishing Corp.
—Watchdog. (Melanie Travis Mystery Ser.). 1999. 320p. mass mkt. 5.99 (*1-57566-472-0*, Kensington Bks.); 1998. 314p. (J). (gr. 10 up). 20.00 o.s.i (*1-57566-350-3*) Kensington Publishing Corp.
Bradford, Barbara Taylor. Love in Another Town. unabr. ed. 1996. audio 30.00 (*0-7366-3257-3*, 3914) Books on Tape, Inc.
—Love in Another Town. 1995. 224p. 225.00 o.p. (*0-06-017684-9*) HarperCollins Pubs.
—Love in Another Town. abr. ed. 1995. audio 17.00 o.s.i (*0-694-51598-1*, 393244, HarperAudio) HarperTrade.
—Love in Another Town. 1996. 240p. mass mkt. 5.99 (*0-06-109209-6*, HarperTorch) Morrow/Avon.
—Love in Another Town. 182p. pap. 3.98 o.p. (*0-7651-0528-4*) Smithmark Pubs., Inc.
—Love in Another Town. l.t. ed. 1996. (Paperback Bestsellers Ser.). 208p. pap. 24.95 (*0-7838-1560-3*); 26.95 (*0-7838-1559-X*) Thorndike Pr.
—The Triumph of Katie Byrne. l.t. ed. 2001. 496p. 24.95 (*0-375-43097-0*) Random Hse. Large Print.
Christmas, Joyce. A Better Class of Murder: A Lady Margaret Priam/Betty Trenka Mystery. 2000. (Lady Margaret Priam Mysteries Ser.). 272p. mass mkt. 6.50 (*0-449-15013-5*, Fawcett) Ballantine Bks.
—A Better Class of Murder: A Lady Margaret Priam/Betty Trenka Mystery. l.t. ed. 2001. 264p. pap. 24.95 (*0-7838-9472-4*, Macmillan Reference USA) Gale Group.
—Death at Face Value. 1995. (Betty Trenka Mystery Ser.). (Orig.). mass mkt. 4.99 o.s.i (*0-449-14801-7*, Fawcett) Ballantine Bks.
—Down-Sized to Death. 1997. (Betty Trenka Mystery Ser.). 199p. mass mkt. 5.99 o.s.i (*0-449-14802-5*, Fawcett) Ballantine Bks.
—Mood to Murder. 1999. (Betty Trenka Mystery Ser.). mass mkt. 5.99 o.s.i (*0-449-15012-7*) Ballantine Bks.
—This Business Is Murder. 1993. (Betty Trenka Mystery Ser.). mass mkt. 4.50 o.s.i (*0-449-14800-9*, Fawcett) Ballantine Bks.
Ciresi, Rita. Pink Slip. 1999. 416p. pap. 12.95 (*0-385-32363-8*, Delta) Dell Publishing.
—Sometimes I Dream in Italian. 2001. 224p. pap. 12.95 (*0-385-33494-X*, Delta) Dell Publishing.
—Sometimes I Dream in Italian. l.t. ed. 2001. (Basic Ser.). 320p. 28.95 (*0-7862-3080-0*) Thorndike Pr.
Clark, Catherine. Gilmore Girls. 2002. (Illus.). 160p. mass mkt. 5.99 (*0-06-051023-4*, HarperEntertainment) Morrow/Avon.
Clark, Mary Higgins. We'll Meet Again. 2000. E-Book 9.95 (*1-930161-67-0*) Adobe Systems, Inc.
—We'll Meet Again. 1999. E-Book 9.95 (*0-684-85767-7*, Simon & Schuster); 1999. 320p. 25.00 (*0-684-83597-5*, Simon & Schuster); 2005. 320p. pap. 12.00 (*0-7432-6133-X*, Simon & Schuster); 1999. 480p. 25.00 (*0-684-86211-5*, Simon & Schuster); 2000. (Illus.). 384p. reprint ed. mass mkt. 7.99 (*0-671-00456-5*, Pocket) Simon & Schuster.
—We'll Meet Again. 2000. 14.04 (*0-606-17764-7*) Turtleback Bks.
Crespi, Camilla T. The Trouble with Thin Ice. 1994. 288p. 18.00 o.p. (*0-06-017726-8*) HarperTrade.
—The Trouble with Thin Ice. 1994. 304p. mass mkt. 4.50 o.p. (*0-06-109154-5*, HarperTorch) Morrow/Avon.
Dank, Gloria. Friends till the End. 1989. 192p. mass mkt. 3.50 o.s.i (*0-553-28152-6*) Bantam Bks.
—Going out in Style. 1989. (Illus.). mass mkt. 3.95 o.s.i (*0-553-28346-4*) Bantam Bks.
Delinsky, Barbara. The Woman Next Door: A Novel. 2001. 368p. 25.00 (*0-7432-0469-7*, Simon & Schuster) Simon & Schuster.
—The Woman Next Door: A Novel. l.t. ed. 2002. 504p. 14.95 (*0-7862-3512-8*); 2001. 541p. 32.95 (*0-7862-3510-1*) Thorndike Pr.
Driscoll, Jack. Lucky Man, Lucky Woman: A Love Story. 2000. (Norton Paperback Fiction Ser.). 272p. pap. 13.00 (*0-393-31945-8*) Norton, W. W. & Co., Inc.
—Lucky Man, Lucky Woman: A Love Story. 1999. (Editor's Book Award Ser.). 264p. 24.50 (*1-888889-08-X*) Pushcart Pr., The.
Dyja, Tom. Meet John Trow. 2002. (Illus.). 336p. 24.95 (*0-670-03099-6*, Viking) Viking Penguin.
Fast, Howard. The Outsider. 1985. 320p. mass mkt. 3.95 o.s.i (*0-440-16778-7*) Dell Publishing.
—The Outsider. l.t. ed. 1984. (Special Editions Ser.). 17.95 o.p. (*0-8161-3760-9*, Macmillan Reference USA) Gale Group.
—The Outsider, 001. 1984. 311p. 15.95 o.p. (*0-395-36101-X*) Houghton Mifflin Co.
Ferber, Edna. American Beauty. 20.95 (*0-88411-596-8*) Amereon, Ltd.
—American Beauty. 1980. mass mkt. 1.95 o.s.i (*0-449-22817-7*, Fawcett) Ballantine Bks.
—American Beauty. 1994. lib. bdg. 24.95 o.p. (*1-56849-494-7*) Buccaneer Bks., Inc.
—American Beauty. 1987. 3.95 o.p. (*0-385-04014-8*) Doubleday Publishing.
—American Beauty. 1947. mass mkt. 0.25 o.p. (*0-451-00650-X*, Signet Bks.) NAL.
—American Beauty. l.t. ed. 1997. (Perennial Ser.). 323p. 23.95 (*0-7838-8142-8*) Thorndike Pr.
Fisher, Nancy. Side Effects. 1994. 384p. mass mkt. 4.99 o.s.i (*0-451-18130-1*, Signet Bks.) NAL.
—Side Effects. 2000. 384p. pap. 22.95 (*0-595-09230-6*, Backinprint.com) iUniverse, Inc.
Forrest, Richard. A Child's Garden of Death. 1982. (Scene of the Crime Ser.: No. 44). pap. 2.25 o.p. (*0-440-11325-3*) Dell Publishing.
—A Child's Garden of Death. 1977. pap. 1.50 o.p. (*0-671-80924-5*, Pocket) Simon & Schuster.
—The Death at Yew Corner. 1984. 176p. pap. 2.95 o.p. (*0-440-11782-8*) Dell Publishing.
—The Death at Yew Corner. 1981. (Rinehart Suspense Novel Ser.). 228p. o.p. (*0-03-053386-4*) Holt, Henry & Co.
—The Death in the Willows. 1979. (Rinehart Suspense Novel Ser.). 228p. o.p. (*0-03-049296-3*) Holt, Henry & Co.
—Death on the Mississippi. 1989. 224p. 15.95 o.p. (*0-312-03323-0*, Saint Martin's Minotaur) St. Martin's Pr.
—Death Through the Looking Glass. 1979. pap. 1.75 o.s.i (*0-671-82157-1*, Pocket) Simon & Schuster.
—Death under the Lilacs. 1985. 208p. 13.95 o.p. (*0-312-18878-1*) St. Martin's Pr.
—Pied Piper of Death: A Lyon & Bea Wentworth Mystery. 1997. 240p. 21.95 o.p. (*0-312-15292-2*, Saint Martin's Minotaur) St. Martin's Pr.
Freydont, Shelley. Backstage Murder: A Lindy Haggerty Mystery. (Lindy Haggerty Mystery Ser.). 2000. 336p. mass mkt. 5.99 o.s.i (*1-57566-590-5*); 1999. 316p. 20.00 o.s.i (*1-57566-458-5*) Kensington Publishing Corp.
Fusco, John. Paradise Salvage. 384p. 2004. pap. 15.95 (*1-58567-382-X*); 2002. 26.95 (*1-58567-209-2*) Overlook Pr., The.
Gertler, Stephanie. Drifting. 2003. 288p. 23.95 (*0-525-94735-3*, Dutton) Dutton/Plume.
—Drifting. 2004. 352p. mass mkt. 6.99 (*0-451-21263-0*, Signet Bks.) NAL.
—Jimmy's Girl. l.t. ed. 2001. (Large Print Book Ser.). 323p. 26.95 o.p. (*1-58724-022-X*, Wheeler Publishing, Inc.) Gale Group.
—Jimmy's Girl: A Novel. 2001. 288p. 22.95 o.s.i (*0-525-94565-2*) Dutton/Plume.
Gordon, Jacquie. Flanders Point. 1997. 336p. 24.95 (*0-312-15531-X*) St. Martin's Pr.
Graham, Heather. A Season of Miracles. 2002. 384p. mass mkt. (*1-55166-892-0*, Mira Bks.) Harlequin Enterprises, Ltd.
Green, Jane. Spellbound. 2004. 432p. 21.95 (*0-7679-1226-8*) Broadway Bks.
Haddam, Jane. Skeleton Key. (Gregor Demarkian Mystery Ser.). 2001. 352p. mass mkt. 6.50 (*0-312-97865-0*, St. Martin's Paperbacks); 2000. 276p. 23.95 o.p. (*0-312-20909-6*, Saint Martin's Minotaur) St. Martin's Pr.
Hall, Parnell. A Clue for the Puzzle Lady. 2000. 336p. mass mkt. 6.50 (*0-553-58140-6*); 1999. 304p. 23.95 o.s.i (*0-553-80096-5*) Bantam Bks.
—A Clue for the Puzzle Lady. l.t. ed. 2000. (Thorndike Senior Lifestyle Ser.). 456p. 28.95 o.p. (*0-7862-2542-4*) Thorndike Pr.
—The Last Puzzle & Testament. 2001. (Illus.). 400p. mass mkt. 6.50 (*0-553-58143-0*, Spectra) Bantam Bks.
—Last Puzzle & Testament. l.t. ed. 2001. (Senior Lifestyles Ser.). 511p. 28.95 (*0-7862-2944-6*) Thorndike Pr.
—Puzzled to Death. 2002. 416p. mass mkt. 6.50 (*0-553-58146-5*) Bantam Bks.
—Puzzled to Death. l.t. ed. 2002. 568p. 27.95 (*0-7862-4281-7*) Gale Group.
—With This Puzzle, I Thee Kill. 2003. 336p. 23.95 (*0-553-80241-0*) Bantam Bks.
Handler, David. The Bright Silver Star. Date not set. pap. (*0-312-30715-2*, Saint Martin's Griffin); Date not set. mass mkt. (*0-312-99620-9*, St. Martin's Paperbacks); Date not set. mass mkt. (*0-312-99461-3*, St. Martin's Paperbacks); mass mkt. (*0-312-98578-9*, St. Martin's Paperbacks); E-Book (*0-312-70566-2*); 2003. 320p. 24.95 (*0-312-30714-4*, Saint Martin's Minotaur) St. Martin's Pr.
—The Cold Blue Blood. 2002. 320p. mass mkt. 6.50 (*0-312-98610-6*, St. Martin's Paperbacks); 2001. 304p. 23.95 (*0-312-28003-3*, Saint Martin's Minotaur) St. Martin's Pr.
—The Girl Who Ran off with Daddy. 1996. 304p. mass mkt. 4.99 o.s.i (*0-553-56902-3*) Bantam Bks.
—The Hot Pink Farmhouse. Date not set. mass mkt. (*0-312-98579-7*, St. Martin's Paperbacks); E-Book 17.95 (*0-312-70893-9*); 2002. 336p. 23.95 (*0-312-28015-7*, Saint Martin's Minotaur) St. Martin's Pr.
Heller, Jane. Cha Cha Cha. 1994. mass mkt. 18.95 o.s.i (*0-8217-4615-4*) Kensington Publishing Corp.
—The Club. 1996. mass mkt. 6.99 (*0-7582-0149-4*); 1996. 352p. mass mkt. 4.99 o.p. (*0-8217-5284-7*); 1996. (Illus.). 352p. mass mkt. 4.99 o.s.i (*1-57566-038-5*); 1995. mass mkt. 18.95 (*0-8217-4887-4*); 1995. 272p. mass mkt. 19.95 o.s.i (*0-8217-4988-9*, Zebra Bks.) Kensington Publishing Corp.
Herzig, Alison C. & Mali, Jane L. The Ten Speed Babysitter. 1987. 144p. (J). (gr. 4-7). 11.95 o.p. (*0-525-44340-1*, 01160-350, Dutton Children's Bks.) Penguin Putnam Bks. for Young Readers.
Hiscox, Edward T. The Hiscox Standard Baptist Manual. 1965. pap. 10.00 (*0-8170-0340-1*) Judson Pr.
Howard, Maureen. Natural History. 1999. (Illus.). 393p. pap. 12.95 (*0-7867-0632-5*, Carroll & Graf Pubs.) Avalon Publishing Group.
—Natural History. 1993. (Illus.). 416p. reprint ed. 12.00 o.p. (*0-06-097569-5*, Perennial) HarperTrade.
—Natural History. 1992. (Illus.). 512p. 22.95 o.p. (*0-393-03405-4*) Norton, W. W. & Co., Inc.
Hrbek, Greg. The Hindenburg Crashes Nightly. 2000. 368p. pap. 13.00 (*0-380-80543-X*, Perennial) HarperTrade.
—The Hindenburg Crashes Nightly. 1999. 368p. 23.00 (*0-380-97741-9*, Avon Bks.) Morrow/Avon.
Huidekoper, Peter. Shelter: A Cold War Memory. 1998. 150p. pap. 7.95 (*0-9660861-0-4*) Shippen Pr.
Hunt, Angela Elwell. Hartford. 1996. (Keepers of the Ring Ser.: No. 3). (Illus.). 350p. pap. 11.99 o.p. (*0-8423-2014-8*) Tyndale Hse. Pubs.
Hynd, Noel. Cemetery of Angels. 2002. 416p. mass mkt. 6.99 o.s.i (*0-7860-1487-3*); 1996. 416p. mass mkt. 5.99 o.s.i (*0-7860-0261-1*, Pinnacle Bks.); 1995. 368p. mass mkt. 19.95 o.p. (*0-8217-5029-1*, Zebra Bks.) Kensington Publishing Corp.
Jackson, Sheneska. Caught up in the Rapture. 1996. 272p. 20.50 (*0-684-81487-0*, Simon & Schuster) Simon & Schuster.
—Caught up in the Rapture: A Novel. 1997. 272p. pap. 13.00 (*0-684-83153-8*, Simon & Schuster) Simon & Schuster.
Kallen, Lucille. C. B. Greenfield: No Lady in the House. 1982. 12.95 o.p. (*0-671-43240-0*, Simon & Schuster) Simon & Schuster.
—C. B. Greenfield: The Piano Bird. 1984. 175p. 13.95 o.p. (*0-394-53081-0*) Random Hse., Inc.
Kauffman, Donna. The Royal Hunter. 2001. 384p. mass mkt. 5.99 (*0-553-58242-9*) Bantam Bks.
Kava, Alex. At the Stroke of Madness. 2003. 336p. (*1-55166-717-7*, Mira Bks.) Harlequin Enterprises, Ltd.
—At the Stroke of Madness. l.t. ed. 2003. (Maggie O'Dell Novel Ser.). 423p. 28.95 (*0-7862-5977-9*) Thorndike Pr.
Kittredge, Mary. Cadaver. 1993. 250p. mass mkt. 3.99 o.p. (*0-312-95002-0*, St. Martin's Paperbacks) St. Martin's Pr.
—Cadaver: An Edwina Crusoe Medical Mystery. 1992. 208p. 17.95 o.p. (*0-312-06920-0*, Saint Martin's Minotaur) St. Martin's Pr.
—Desperate Remedy. 1997. (Crime Line Ser.). 224p. mass mkt. 5.99 o.s.i (*0-553-57591-0*, Crimeline) Bantam Bks.
—Desperate Remedy, Vol. 1. 1994. (Desperate Remedy Ser.: Vol. 1). mass mkt. 4.50 o.p. (*0-312-95330-5*, St. Martin's Paperbacks) St. Martin's Pr.
—Desperate Remedy: An Edwina Crusoe Medical Mystery. 1993. 208p. 18.95 o.p. (*0-312-09784-0*, Saint Martin's Minotaur) St. Martin's Pr.
—Fatal Diagnosis. 1997. 208p. mass mkt. 5.50 o.s.i (*0-553-57590-2*, Crimeline) Bantam Bks.
—Fatal Diagnosis. 1990. pap. 15.95 o.p. (*0-312-04315-5*, Saint Martin's Minotaur) St. Martin's Pr.
—Kill or Cure. 1996. 288p. mass mkt. 5.50 o.s.i (*0-553-57585-6*, Crimeline) Bantam Bks.
—Kill or Cure: An Edwina Crusoe Medical Mystery. 1995. 216p. 19.95 o.p. (*0-312-13103-8*, Saint Martin's Minotaur) St. Martin's Pr.
—Rigor Mortis. 1991. 14.95 o.p. (*0-312-05504-8*, Saint Martin's Minotaur); 1992. 201p. reprint ed. mass mkt. 3.99 o.p. (*0-312-92865-3*, St. Martin's Paperbacks) St. Martin's Pr.
—Walking Dead Man. 1993. mass mkt. 3.99 o.p. (*0-312-95157-4*, St. Martin's Paperbacks); 1992. 208p. 17.95 o.p. (*0-312-08333-5*, Saint Martin's Minotaur) St. Martin's Pr.
Law, Janice. The Big Payoff. 1976. 6.95 o.p. (*0-395-21900-0*) Houghton Mifflin Co.
—The Big Payoff. 1999. 192p. pap. 9.95 (*1-58348-697-6*) iUniverse, Inc.
—Death Under Par, 001. 1981. 9.95 o.p. (*0-395-30227-7*) Houghton Mifflin Co.
—Death Under Par. 2000. 248p. pap. 12.95 (*0-595-00040-1*) iUniverse, Inc.
—Gemini Trip. 1977. 7.95 o.p. (*0-395-25703-4*) Houghton Mifflin Co.
—Gemini Trip. 2000. (Anna Peters Mystery Ser.). 188p. pap. 9.95 (*0-595-08851-1*) iUniverse, Inc.
—Infected Be the Air. 1991. 208p. 18.95 o.p. (*0-8027-5799-5*) Walker & Co.
—The Night Bus. 352p. 2000. 24.95 o.s.i (*0-312-84882-X*); 2001. reprint ed. pap. 15.95 (*0-312-87599-1*) Doherty, Tom Assocs., LLC. (Forge Bks.).
—A Safe Place to Die. 1995. per. (*0-373-26179-9*, 1-26179-1, Harlequin Bks.) Harlequin Enterprises, Ltd.
—A Safe Place to Die. 1993. 208p. 17.95 o.p. (*0-312-09300-4*, Saint Martin's Minotaur) St. Martin's Pr.
—The Shadow of the Palms, 001. 1980. 8.95 o.p. (*0-395-28591-7*) Houghton Mifflin Co.
—The Shadow of the Palms. 2000. (Anna Peters Mystery Ser.). 228p. pap. 13.95 (*0-595-08938-0*) iUniverse, Inc.
—Time Lapse: An Anna Peters Mystery. 1998. (WWL Mystery Ser.). per. (*0-373-26267-1*, 1-26267-4, Worldwide Library) Harlequin Enterprises, Ltd.
—Time Lapse: An Anna Peters Mystery. 1992. 199p. 19.95 o.p. (*0-8027-3221-6*) Walker & Co.
—Under Orion, 001. 1978. 14.95 o.p. (*0-395-26484-7*) Houghton Mifflin Co.
—Under Orion. 2000. 192p. pap. 11.95 (*0-595-08852-X*) iUniverse, Inc.
Loring, Emilie Baker. A Candle in Her Heart. 1976. reprint ed. lib. bdg. 22.95 (*0-88411-353-1*) Amereon, Ltd.
—A Candle in Her Heart. 1980. 224p. pap. 1.75 o.p. (*0-553-13484-1*) Bantam Bks.
Luntta, Karl. Know It by Heart. 2003. 256p. pap. 15.95 (*1-880684-95-0*) Curbstone Pr.
Malone, Michael. Dingley Falls. 1980. 540p. 12.95 o.p. (*0-15-125673-X*) Harcourt Trade Pubs.

—Dingley Falls. 1994. 672p. pap. o.p. (*0-671-87529-9*, Washington Square Pr.); 1989. bds. 4.95 o.p. (*0-671-67180-4*, Pocket) Simon & Schuster.

—Dingley Falls. 2002. 640p. pap. 15.00 (*1-4022-0007-2*) Sourcebooks, Inc.

Marlowe, Katharine, pseud. Nightfall. 1994. 349p. pap. text 4.99 (*0-8125-2415-2*); 1993. 352p. 21.95 o.p. (*0-312-85482-X*) Doherty, Tom Assocs., LLC. (Tor Bks.).

Martin, Kat. The Silent Rose. 1999. 512p. mass mkt. 6.99 (*0-8217-6281-8*) Kensington Publishing Corp.

—The Silent Rose. l.t. ed. 2001. (Thorndike Press Large Print Romance Ser.). 714p. 27.95 o.p. (*0-7862-3479-2*) Thorndike Pr.

McGaughey, Neil. And Then There Were Ten. 1995. 255p. 21.00 (*0-684-19760-X*, Scribner) Simon & Schuster.

—Best Money Murder Can Buy: A Stokes Moran Mystery. 1996. 256p. 21.00 (*0-684-19761-8*, Scribner) Simon & Schuster.

—A Corpse by Any Other Name: A Stokes Moran Mystery. 1998. (Stokes Moran Mystery Ser.). 240p. 22.00 (*0-684-19762-6*, Scribner) Simon & Schuster.

McShea, Susanna H. Hometown Heroes. 1992. (Hometown Heroes Ser.). 320p. mass mkt. 4.99 (*0-380-71675-5*, Avon Bks.) Morrow/Avon.

—Hometown Heroes. 1990. (Hometown Heroes Ser.). 18.95 o.p. (*0-312-04681-2*, Saint Martin's Minotaur) St. Martin's Pr.

—Ladybug, Ladybug. 1995. (Hometown Heroes Ser.). 352p. reprint ed. mass mkt. 5.50 (*0-380-71981-9*, Avon Bks.) Morrow/Avon.

—Ladybug, Ladybug. 1994. (Hometown Heroes Ser.). 3352p. (J). (ps-k). 21.95 o.p. (*0-312-11017-0*, Saint Martin's Minotaur) St. Martin's Pr.

—The Pumpkin-Shell Wife. 1993. (Hometown Heroes Ser.). 352p. mass mkt. 4.99 (*0-380-71980-0*, Avon Bks.) Morrow/Avon.

—The Pumpkin-Shell Wife. 1992. (Hometown Heroes Ser.). 352p. 19.95 o.p. (*0-312-07768-8*, Saint Martin's Minotaur) St. Martin's Pr.

Miano, Mark. Dead of Summer. 224p. 2002. mass mkt. 5.99 o.s.i (*1-57566-717-7*, Kensington Bks.); 1999. 20.00 o.s.i (*1-57566-404-6*) Kensington Publishing Corp.

Millhauser, Steven. Enchanted Night. abr. ed. 1999. audio 18.00 (*0-7871-2274-2*, Dove Audio) NewStar Media, Inc.

—Enchanted Night. unabr. ed. 1999. audio 23.00 (*0-7887-4042-3*, 96152E7) Recorded Bks., LLC.

—Enchanted Night: A Novella. 1999. 112p. 17.00 o.s.i (*0-609-60516-X*) Crown Publishing Group.

—Enchanted Night: A Novella. 2000. (Vintage Contemporaries Ser.). 144p. pap. 11.00 (*0-375-70696-8*, Vintage) Knopf Publishing Group.

Millman, M. C. Juggling Act. 2003. 224p. (J). 17.95 (*0-910818-28-2*) Judaica Pr., Inc., The.

Moody, Rick. The Ice Storm. 1994. 279p. 19.95 o.p. (*0-316-57921-1*); 2002. 288p. reprint ed. pap. 13.95 (*0-316-70600-0*, Back Bay) Little Brown & Co.

—The Ice Storm. 1995. 288p. reprint ed. pap. 11.95 o.s.i (*0-446-67148-7*) Warner Bks., Inc.

Neggers, Carla. Stonebrook Cottage. l.t. ed. 2003. (Wheeler Romance Ser.). 381p. 29.95 (*1-58724-365-2*, Wheeler Publishing, Inc.) Gale Group.

—Stonebrook Cottage. 2002. 384p. mass mkt. (*1-55166-923-4*, Mira Bks.) Harlequin Enterprises, Ltd.

O'Grady, Leslie. The Grateful Undead. 2002. 200p. pap. 22.00 (*0-9678199-8-9*) Larcom Pr.

Osborn, Karen. The River Road. 2002. 288p. 23.95 (*0-688-15899-4*, Morrow, William & Co.) Morrow/Avon.

Pearson, Ridley. Chain of Evidence. 1997. audio 15.99 o.p. (*1-57375-356-4*) Audioscope.

—Chain of Evidence. unabr. ed. 1996. audio 72.00 (*0-7366-3377-4*, 4027) Books on Tape, Inc.

—Chain of Evidence. l.t. ed. 1995. 25.95 o.p. (*1-56895-268-6*, Wheeler Publishing, Inc.) Gale Group.

—Chain of Evidence. 1995. 368p. 22.95 (*0-7868-6172-X*); 2003. 512p. reprint ed. mass mkt. 7.99 (*0-7868-8908-X*) Hyperion Pr.

Petry, Ann. The Narrows. 1988. (Black Women Writers Ser.). 464p. (C). reprint ed. pap. 16.00 o.p. (*0-8070-8303-8*) Beacon Pr.

Pope, Dan. In the Cherry Tree: A Novel. 2003. 288p. pap. 14.00 (*0-312-42236-9*) Picador.

Rice, Luanne. Crazy in Love. 1989. 256p. mass mkt. 4.99 o.s.i (*0-449-21754-X*, Fawcett) Ballantine Bks.

—Crazy in Love. l.t. ed. 2001. 445p. 31.95 o.p. (*0-7838-9441-4*, Macmillan Reference USA) Gale Group.

—Crazy in Love. 1988. (Illus.). 320p. 18.95 o.p. (*0-670-82131-4*) Viking Penguin.

—Follow the Stars Home. abr. ed. 2000. audio 24.95 o.p. (*1-56740-877-X*, 1963, Nova Audio Bks.); audio 35.95 (*1-56740-481-2*, 1961, Brilliance Audio Unabridged); audio 73.25 (*1-56740-699-8*, 1962, Unabridged Library Editions) Brilliance Audio.

—Follow the Stars Home. l.t. ed. 2000. (Large Print Book Ser.). 26.95 o.p. (*1-56895-864-1*, Wheeler Publishing, Inc.) Gale Group.

Ripley, Ann. The Garden Tour Affair: A Gardening Mystery. 1999. (Gardening Mysteries Ser.). 320p. mass mkt. 5.99 o.s.i (*0-553-57736-0*); 22.95 o.s.i (*0-553-10693-7*) Bantam Bks.

Roberts, Nora. Dance of Dreams. l.t. ed. 2000. (G. K. Hall Romance Ser.). 235p. 29.95 (*0-7838-9043-5*, Macmillan Reference USA) Gale Group.

—Dance of Dreams. 1992. (NR Flowers Ser.: No. 8). mass mkt. (*0-373-51008-X*, 5-51008-6, Harlequin Bks.) Harlequin Enterprises, Ltd.

Rogers, Joel T. The Red Right Hand. 1983. 198p. reprint ed. pap. 3.50 o.p. (*0-88184-008-4*, Carroll & Graf Pubs.) Avalon Publishing Group.

Rogers, Joel Townsley. The Red Right Hand. 1997. 192p. mass mkt. 4.95 (*0-7867-0446-2*, Carroll & Graf Pubs.) Avalon Publishing Group.

Schwartz, John Burnham. Reservation Road. 1999. 304p. pap. 13.00 (*0-375-70273-3*) Knopf, Alfred A. Inc.

—Reservation Road. l.t. ed. 1999. (Americana Ser.). 456p. 28.95 (*0-7862-1740-5*) Thorndike Pr.

Scott, Justin. FrostLine. 2003. 300p. 24.95 o.s.i (*1-59058-062-1*) Poisoned Pen Pr.

—HardScape. 1995. (Ben Abbott Mystery Ser.). 288p. pap. 5.95 o.s.i (*0-14-023450-0*, Penguin Bks.) Penguin Group (USA) Inc.

—HardScape. 2003. 250p. pap. 14.95 o.s.i (*1-59058-060-5*) Poisoned Pen Pr.

—HardScape. 218p. 3.98 o.p. (*0-8317-4999-7*) Smithmark Pubs., Inc.

—HardScape. 1994. (Ben Abbott Mystery Ser.). 288p. 19.95 o.p. (*0-670-85212-0*, Viking) Viking Penguin.

—StoneDust. 1996. (Ben Abbott Mystery Ser.). 304p. pap. 5.95 o.s.i (*0-14-023456-X*, Viking) Penguin Group (USA) Inc.

—StoneDust. 2003. 250p. pap. 14.95 o.s.i (*1-59058-061-3*) Poisoned Pen Pr.

—WeakEnd: A Ben Abbott Novel. 1995. (Ben Abbott Mystery Ser.). 304p. 19.95 o.p. (*0-670-85213-9*, Viking) Viking Penguin.

Sipherd, Ray. The Audubon Quartet. 1999. (WWL Mystery Ser.: No. 311). per. (*0-373-26311-2*, 1-26311-0, Worldwide Library) Harlequin Enterprises, Ltd.

—Audubon Quartet, Vol. 1. 1998. (Jonathan Wilder Mysteries Ser.). 272p. 22.95 o.p. (*0-312-18536-7*, Saint Martin's Minotaur) St. Martin's Pr.

—Dance of the Scarecrows. 1998. (WWL Mystery Ser.: Vol. 287). per. (*0-373-26287-6*, 1-26287-2, Worldwide Library) Harlequin Enterprises, Ltd.

—Dance of the Scarecrows. 1996. 256p. 21.95 o.p. (*0-312-14306-0*, Saint Martin's Minotaur) St. Martin's Pr.

Smith, Rosamond, pseud. Nemesis. 1990. 288p. 18.95 o.p. (*0-525-24881-1*, Dutton) Dutton/Plume.

—Nemesis. 1991. 304p. mass mkt. 5.50 o.p. (*0-451-40295-2*, Onyx) NAL.

Steel, Danielle. Bittersweet. 2000. 448p. mass mkt. 7.99 (*0-440-22484-5*); 1999. 384p. 26.95 (*0-385-31957-6*, Delacorte Pr.); 1999. 384p. 200.00 (*0-385-33388-9*, Delacorte Pr.) Dell Publishing.

—Bittersweet. unabr. ed. 1999. audio 39.95 Highsmith Inc.

—Bittersweet. unabr. ed. 1999. audio 39.95 (*0-553-50214-X*, 106254, RH Audio) Random Hse. Audio Publishing Group.

—Bittersweet. l.t. ed. 2004. 576p. 24.95 (*0-375-43321-X*) Random Hse. Large Print.

Sternberg, Alan. Camaro City. 1994. 219p. 19.95 (*0-15-115373-6*) Harcourt Trade Pubs.

Straub, Peter. Circulo Diabolico. 1998. (SPA.). 466p. (*84-08-02053-6*) GeoPlaneta, Editorial, S. A.

—The Hellfire Club. 1997. (ACE.). 544p. mass mkt. 7.99 (*0-345-41500-0*); mass mkt. 6.99 o.s.i (*0-345-41505-1*) Ballantine Bks.

—The Hellfire Club. l.t. ed. 1996. (Large Print Bks.). 25.95 o.p. (*1-56895-337-2*, Wheeler Publishing, Inc.) Gale Group.

—The Hellfire Club. abr. ed. 1996. 6p. audio 25.00 (*0-671-73860-7*, Simon & Schuster Audioworks) Simon & Schuster Audio.

The Tanglewood Murder. 1980. 11.95 o.s.i (*0-671-61018-X*, Simon & Schuster) Simon & Schuster.

Tessier, Thomas. Fog Heart. 320p. 2000. pap. 13.95 (*0-312-25387-7*, Saint Martin's Griffin); 1997. 23.95 o.p. (*0-312-18098-5*) St. Martin's Pr.

Thomas-Graham, Pamela. Blue Blood. (Ivy League Mysteries Ser.). 1999. 288p. 23.00 (*0-684-84527-X*, Simon & Schuster); 2000. 320p. reprint ed. pap. 6.99 (*0-671-01671-7*, Pocket) Simon & Schuster.

Thomas, Roseanne D. Awaiting Grace. 256p. 2000. pap. 12.00 (*0-312-25269-2*); 1999. 22.00 o.s.i (*0-312-20275-X*) Picador.

Travis, Elizabeth. Under the Influence. 1992. (WWL Mystery Ser.: No. 92). per. (*0-373-26092-X*, 1-26092-6, Harlequin Bks.) Harlequin Enterprises, Ltd.

—Under the Influence. 1989. 16.95 o.p. (*0-312-02994-2*, Saint Martin's Minotaur) St. Martin's Pr.

Valentine, Katherine. A Gathering of Angels: A Novel. 2003. (Dorsetville Ser.). 288p. text 23.95 (*0-670-03229-8*, Viking) Viking Penguin.

—A Miracle for St. Cecilia's: A Novel. 2002. (Americana Ser.). 28.95 (*0-7862-4739-8*) Thorndike Pr.

—A Miracle for St. Cecilia's: A Novel. 2002. 288p. 23.95 o.s.i (*0-670-03113-5*, Viking) Viking Penguin.

Van Wormer, Laura. Expose. 2000. 480p. mass mkt. (*1-55166-581-6*, 1-66581-9); 1999. 384p. (*1-55166-526-3*) Harlequin Enterprises, Ltd. (Mira Bks.).

Victor, Cynthia. What Matters Most. 1996. 336p. 23.95 o.s.i (*0-525-94033-2*, Dutton) Dutton/Plume.

—What Matters Most. l.t. ed. 1996. pap. 24.95 (*1-56895-352-6*, Wheeler Publishing, Inc.) Gale Group.

—What Matters Most. 1997. 448p. mass mkt. 6.99 o.s.i (*0-451-18603-6*, Signet Bks.) NAL.

Wallace, Carol M. The Wrong House. 1994. 320p. 21.95 o.p. (*0-312-10579-7*) St. Martin's Pr.

Wallant, Edward Lewis. The Human Season. 1973. 192p. reprint ed. pap. 1.65 o.p. (*0-15-642330-8*, Harvest Bks.) Harcourt Trade Pubs.

—The Human Season. 1998. (Library of Modern Jewish Literature). 181p. pap. text 16.95 (*0-8156-0560-9*) Syracuse Univ. Pr.

Wenner, Kate. Setting Fires. 2001. 352p. reprint ed. pap. 13.00 (*0-425-18210-X*) Berkley Publishing Group.

—Setting Fires. 2000. 304p. 24.00 o.s.i (*0-684-83748-X*, Scribner) Simon & Schuster.

White, Richard W. Jordan Freeman Was My Friend. 1994. 300p. 18.95 o.p. (*0-941423-73-5*) Four Walls Eight Windows.

Wiltse, David. Bone Deep. 1996. 400p. reprint ed. mass mkt. 6.99 o.s.i (*0-425-15340-1*) Berkley Publishing Group.

—Bone Deep. 1995. 320p. 23.95 o.p. (*0-399-14093-X*, G. P. Putnam's Sons) Penguin Group (USA) Inc.

—Bone Deep. abr. ed. 1996. audio 17.00 (*1-56876-052-3*) Soundlines Entertainment, Inc.

—Prayer for the Dead. 1992. 352p. mass mkt. 6.50 o.s.i (*0-425-13398-2*) Berkley Publishing Group.

—Prayer for the Dead. 1991. 320p. 19.95 o.p. (*0-399-13607-X*, G. P. Putnam's Sons) Penguin Group (USA) Inc.

Wolzien, Valerie. All Hallows' Evil. 1992. 256p. (Orig.). mass mkt. 6.99 (*0-449-14745-2*, Fawcett) Ballantine Bks.

—Deck the Halls with Murder. (Josie Pigeon Mystery Ser.). 256p. 1998. mass mkt. 5.99 (*0-449-15036-4*); 1995. pap. 19.00 (*0-345-46621-7*) Ballantine Bks. (Fawcett).

—Elected for Death. 1996. mass mkt. 5.99 o.s.i (*0-449-14959-5*, Fawcett) Ballantine Bks.

—The Fortieth Birthday Body: A Suburban Mystery. 1990. 240p. mass mkt. 6.50 (*0-449-14685-5*, Fawcett) Ballantine Bks.

—The Fortieth Birthday Body: A Suburban Mystery. 1992. 1.99 o.p. (*0-517-08392-2*) Random Hse. Value Publishing.

—The Fortieth Birthday Body: A Suburban Mystery. 1989. 266p. 16.95 o.p. (*0-312-02917-9*, Saint Martin's Minotaur) St. Martin's Pr.

—A Good Year for a Corpse. 1994. mass mkt. 5.99 o.s.i (*0-449-14833-5*, Fawcett) Ballantine Bks.

—Murder at the PTA Luncheon. 1990. 240p. mass mkt. 6.99 (*0-449-14639-1*, Fawcett) Ballantine Bks.

—Murder at the PTA Luncheon. 1988. 256p. 16.95 o.p. (*0-312-01480-5*, Saint Martin's Minotaur) St. Martin's Pr.

—An Old Faithful Murder. 1995. 256p. pap. 19.00 (*0-449-00743-X*); 1992. mass mkt. 5.99 (*0-449-14744-4*) Ballantine Bks. (Fawcett).

—Permit for Murder. 1997. (Josie Pigeon Mystery Ser.). 240p. mass mkt. 7.99 (*0-449-14960-9*, Fawcett) Ballantine Bks.

—Remodeled to Death. 1995. mass mkt. 5.99 o.s.i (*0-449-14921-8*, Fawcett) Ballantine Bks.

—Shore to Die. 1995. mass mkt. 5.50 o.s.i (*0-449-14958-7*, Fawcett) Ballantine Bks.

—A Star-Spangled Murder. 1993. 224p. mass mkt. 6.99 (*0-449-14834-3*, Fawcett) Ballantine Bks.

—The Student Body. 1999. (Susan Henshaw Mysteries Ser.). 240p. mass mkt. 6.99 (*0-449-15037-2*, Fawcett) Ballantine Bks.

—This Old Murder. 2000. (Josie Pigeon Mystery Ser.). 288p. mass mkt. 6.50 (*0-449-00629-8*, Fawcett) Ballantine Bks.

—'Tis the Season to Be Murdered. 240p. (Orig.). 1995. pap. 15.00 (*0-449-00741-3*); 1994. mass mkt. 6.50 (*0-449-14920-X*) Ballantine Bks. (Fawcett).

—We Wish You a Merry Murder. 1993. mass mkt. 4.50 o.p. (*0-449-45259-X*); 1991. 288p. mass mkt. 6.99 (*0-449-14723-1*) Ballantine Bks. (Fawcett).

—Weddings Are Murder. 1998. (Susan Henshaw Mysteries Ser.). 240p. mass mkt. 6.99 (*0-449-15035-6*, Fawcett) Ballantine Bks.

Wood, Bari. The Basement: A Novel. 1995. 352p. 17.95 o.p. (*0-688-13351-7*, Morrow, William & Co.) Morrow/Avon.

Wright, Bill. Sunday You Learn How to Box. 2000. 224p. pap. 12.00 (*0-684-85795-2*, Touchstone) Simon & Schuster.

Yates, Richard. Revolutionary Road. 1983. pap. 7.95 o.s.i (*0-385-29203-1*, Delta); 1983. pap. 7.95 o.s.i (*0-440-57428-5*, Delta); 1971. pap. 1.75 o.p. (*0-440-37412-X*) Dell Publishing.

—Revolutionary Road. 1971. 337p. reprint ed. 74.95 (*0-8371-6221-1*, YARR, Greenwood Pr.) Greenwood Publishing Group, Inc.

—Revolutionary Road. (Contemporaries Ser.). 1989. pap. 15.00 o.p. (*0-679-72191-6*); 2nd ed. 2000. 368p. pap. 14.00 (*0-375-70844-8*) Knopf Publishing Group. (Vintage).

### CONTRARY (KY.: IMAGINARY PLACE)—FICTION

Collins, Tess. The Law of Revenge. 9999. mass mkt. o.p. (*0-345-41484-5*); 1997. (*0-449-91075-X*, Fawcett); 1997. mass mkt. 6.99 (*0-449-22534-8*, Fawcett); 1997. mass mkt. 5.99 o.s.i (*0-8041-1684-9*, Ivy Bks.) Ballantine Bks.

—The Law of Revenge. l.t. ed. 1997. (Niagara Large Print Ser.). 416p. 29.50 o.p. (*0-7089-5888-5*, Ulverscroft) Thorpe, F. A. Pubs. GBR. *Dist:* Ulverscroft Large Print Bks., Ltd.

—The Law of the Dead. 1999. mass mkt. 6.99 o.s.i (*0-8041-1795-0*, Ivy Bks.) Ballantine Bks.

### COPENHAGEN (DENMARK)—FICTION

Cornwell, Bernard. Sharpe's Prey: Richard Sharpe & the Expedition to Copenhagen, 1807. l.t. ed. 2002. 506p. 29.95 (*0-7862-4121-7*) Gale Group.

—Sharpe's Prey: Richard Sharpe & the Expedition to Copenhagen, 1807. 2002. (Illus.). 272p. 24.95 (*0-06-000252-2*) HarperCollins Pubs.

Davis, Philip J. Thomas Gray in Copenhagen: In Which the Philosopher Cat Meets the Ghost of Hans Christian Andersen. 1995. (Illus.). 192p. text 16.00 (*0-387-94493-1*) Springer-Verlag New York, Inc.

Forrest, Anthony. A Balance of Dangers: A Captain Justice Story. 1984. 240p. 14.95 o.p. (*0-8090-2800-X*, Hill & Wang) Farrar, Straus & Giroux.

Hoeg, Peter. Borderliners. 1995. 288p. mass mkt. 6.99 o.s.i (*0-7704-2709-X*) Bantam Bks.

—Borderliners. 1995. 288p. reprint ed. pap. 14.95 (*0-385-31508-2*, Delta) Dell Publishing.

—Borderliners. Haveland, Barbara, tr. 1994. 277p. 22.00 o.p. (*0-374-11554-0*) Farrar, Straus & Giroux.

—Borderliners. Haveland, Barbara, tr. from DAN. l.t. ed. 1995. (Large Print Bks.). 22.95 (*1-56895-202-3*, Wheeler Publishing, Inc.) Gale Group.

—Smilla's Sense of Snow. Haveland, Barbara, tr. from DAN. l.t. ed. 1995. pap. 23.95 o.p. (*0-7927-2024-5*); 1994. 25.95 o.p. (*0-7927-2050-4*) BBC Audiobooks America.

—Smilla's Sense of Snow. 1994. 512p. mass mkt. 6.99 o.s.i (*0-7704-2618-2*) Bantam Bks.

—Smilla's Sense of Snow. 1994. 512p. mass mkt. 6.99 o.s.i (*0-440-21853-5*); 1995. 480p. reprint ed. pap. 12.95 (*0-385-31514-7*, Delta) Dell Publishing.

—Smilla's Sense of Snow. 2001. 480p. pap. (*0-385-65818-4*) Doubleday Canada, Ltd. CAN. *Dist:* Random Hse., Inc.

—Smilla's Sense of Snow. 1993. 456p. 24.95 o.p. (*0-385-25442-3*) Doubleday Publishing.

—Smilla's Sense of Snow. Nunnally, Tiina, tr. from DAN. 1993. 453p. 21.00 o.p. (*0-374-26644-1*) Farrar, Straus & Giroux.

—Smilla's Sense of Snow, Set. abr. ed. 1993. audio 18.00 o.s.i (*1-55994-866-3*, 391604, HarperAudio) HarperTrade.

—Smilla's Sense of Snow, Nannally, Tiina, tr. unabr. ed. 1994. audio 97.00 (*0-7887-0023-5*, 94222E7) Recorded Bks., LLC.

Larsen, Michael. Uncertainty. 1998. Tr. of Uden Sikker Viden. 272p. pap. 12.00 o.s.i (*0-449-91236-1*, Fawcett) Ballantine Bks.

—Uncertainty. Blecher, Lone T. & Blecher, George, trs. from DAN. 1996. Tr. of Uden Sikker Viden. 272p. 22.00 o.s.i (*0-15-100202-9*) Harcourt Trade Pubs.

### CORAMONDE (IMAGINARY PLACE)—FICTION

Daley, Brian. The Doomfarers of Coramonde. 1986. 352p. (Orig.). mass mkt. 3.50 o.s.i (*0-345-33953-3*, Del Rey) Ballantine Bks.

—The Starfollowers of Coramonde. 1986. mass mkt. 3.50 o.s.i (*0-345-33954-1*, Del Rey) Ballantine Bks.

### CORDEN (S.D.: IMAGINARY PLACE)—FICTION

Adams, Harold. The Barbed Wire Noose. l.t. ed. 1991. pap. 10.95 o.p. (*0-7927-0073-2*, C0125) BBC Audiobooks America.

—The Barbed Wire Noose. 192p. 1988. pap. 3.95 o.p. (*0-445-40727-1*); 1987. 15.45 (*0-89296-250-X*) Mysterious Pr.

—Lead, So I Can Follow. (Carl Wilcox Mystery Ser.). 2000. 224p. pap. 8.95 (*0-8027-7596-9*); 1999. 219p. 22.95 (*0-8027-3336-0*) Walker & Co.

—The Man Who Met the Train. (Carl Wilcox Mystery Ser.: No. 7). 240p. 1989. pap. 3.95 o.p. (*0-445-40810-3*); 1988. 15.95 (*0-89296-251-8*) Mysterious Pr.

—The Man Who Missed the Party. l.t. ed. 1992. 18.95 o.p. (*0-7451-8330-1*); pap. 16.95 o.p. (*0-7927-1017-7*) BBC Audiobooks America.

—The Man Who Missed the Party. 1990. 192p. mass mkt. 4.95 o.s.i (*0-445-40885-5*, Mysterious Pr. Paperback Bks.) Warner Bks., Inc.

—The Man Who Missed the Party: A Carol Wilcox Mystery. 1989. 192p. 16.95 (*0-89296-252-6*) Mysterious Pr.

—The Man Who Was Taller Than God. 1998. (Carl Wilcox Mystery Ser.). 156p. (gr. 8). pap. 7.95 (*0-8027-7554-3*) Walker & Co.

—The Man Who Was Taller Than God: A Carl Wilcox Mystery. 1992. (Carl Wilcox Mystery Ser.). 156p. 18.95 (*0-8027-1239-8*) Walker & Co.

—Murder. 1981. 256p. 2.50 o.s.i (*0-441-54706-0*) Ace Bks.

—Murder. l.t. ed. 1991. pap. 8.95 o.p. (*1-55504-839-0*, 102); 1989. 16.95 o.p. (*0-7451-9459-1*, 340) BBC Audiobooks America.

—Murder. 1988. 224p. mass mkt. 3.95 o.s.i (*0-445-40627-5*, Mysterious Pr. Paperback Bks.) Warner Bks., Inc.

—The Naked Liar. 1986. 15.95 o.p. (*0-89296-126-0*) Mysterious Pr.

—The Naked Liar. 1986. mass mkt. 3.95 o.s.i (*0-445-40126-5*, Mysterious Pr. Paperback Bks.) Warner Bks., Inc.

—When Rich Men Die. 1987. 240p. 16.95 o.s.i (*0-385-24005-8*) Doubleday Publishing.

—When Rich Men Die. l.t. ed. 1988. (Mainstream Ser.). 377p. reprint ed. lib. bdg. 19.95 o.p. (*1-55736-085-5*) ISIS Large Print Bks. GBR. *Dist:* Transaction Pubs.

—When Rich Men Die. 1988. 256p. pap. 3.50 (*0-380-70539-7*, Avon Bks.) Morrow/Avon.

**CORNWALL (ENGLAND: COUNTY)—FICTION**

Aitken, Rosemary. Stormy Waters. 2001. 224p. 25.99 (*0-7278-5728-2*); 28.99 (*0-7278-7152-8*) Severn Hse. Pubs., Ltd.

Atherton, Nancy. Aunt Dimity & the Duke. 1995. (Crime Fiction Ser.). 304p. pap. 6.99 (*0-14-017841-4*, Penguin Bks.) Penguin Group (USA) Inc.

—Aunt Dimity & the Duke. 1994. (Aunt Dimity Mystery Ser.). 304p. 19.95 o.p. (*0-670-84964-2*, Viking) Viking Penguin.

—Aunt Dimity Beats the Devil. l.t. ed. 2001. (Thorndike Mystery Ser.). 309p. 29.95 (*0-7862-2935-7*) Thorndike Pr.

—Aunt Dimity Beats the Devil. 2000. (Illus.). 224p. (J). 22.95 o.s.i (*0-670-89179-7*, Viking) Viking Penguin.

—Aunt Dimity Digs In. 1999. 288p. pap. 6.99 (*0-14-027569-X*) Penguin Group (USA) Inc.

—Aunt Dimity Digs In. 1998. (Aunt Dimity Mystery Ser.). 288p. 21.95 o.p. (*0-670-87061-7*) Viking Penguin.

—Aunt Dimity's Christmas. l.t. ed. 2000. (Beeler Large Print Mystery Ser.). 25.95 (*1-57490-260-1*, Beeler Large Print Bks.) Beeler, Thomas T. Publisher.

—Aunt Dimity's Christmas. 2000. (Illus.). 224p. pap. 6.99 (*0-14-029630-1*) Penguin Group (USA) Inc.

—Aunt Dimity's Christmas. 1999. 224p. text 22.95 (*0-670-88453-7*, Viking) Viking Penguin.

—Aunt Dimity's Death. 1993. (Special Study of the Kennan Institute for Advanced Russian S Ser.). 256p. reprint ed. pap. 6.99 (*0-14-017840-6*) Penguin Group (USA) Inc.

—Aunt Dimity's Death. 1992. (Aunt Dimity Mystery Ser.). 256p. 19.00 o.p. (*0-670-84449-7*, Viking) Viking Penguin.

—Aunt Dimity's Good Deed. 1998. (Aunt Dimity Mystery Ser.). 288p. pap. 6.99 (*0-14-025881-7*) Penguin Group (USA) Inc.

—Aunt Dimity's Good Deed. 1996. (Aunt Dimity Mystery Ser.). 288p. 20.95 o.s.i (*0-670-86715-2*, Viking) Viking Penguin.

Beauman, Sally. Rebecca's Tale. l.t. ed. 2002. 29.95 (*1-58724-201-X*, Wheeler Publishing, Inc.) Gale Group.

—Rebecca's Tale. 2002. 528p. mass mkt. 7.99 (*0-06-103204-2*); 512p. mass mkt. 7.99 (*0-00-639189-3*) HarperCollins Pubs.

—Rebecca's Tale. abr. ed. 2001. audio 25.95 (*0-694-52646-0*, HarperAudio) HarperTrade.

Beauman, Sally & Du Maurier, Daphne. Rebecca's Tale. 2001. 438p. (*0-00-200500-X*) HarperCollins Pubs.

—Rebecca's Tale. 2001. 448p. 25.00 (*0-06-621108-5*, Morrow, William & Co.) Morrow/Avon.

Bennett, Rebecca. Vision of Love. l.t. ed. 1994. 173p. lib. bdg. 16.95 (*0-8161-5953-X*, Macmillan Reference USA) Gale Group.

—Vision of Love. 1994. (Rainbow Romances Ser.: No. 898). 160p. 14.95 (*0-7090-4970-6*) Parkwest Pubns., Inc.

Black, Veronica. Fair Kilmeny. l.t. ed. 1997. (Nightingale Ser.). pap. 17.95 o.p. (*0-7838-1972-2*, Macmillan Reference USA) Gale Group.

—A Vow of Adoration: A Sister Joan Mystery. 1997. (Sister Joan Mystery Ser.: Vol. 9). 190p. 20.95 (*0-312-18205-8*, Saint Martin's Minotaur) St. Martin's Pr.

—A Vow of Chastity: A Sister Joan Mystery. 1993. mass mkt. 4.50 o.s.i (*0-8041-1055-7*, Ivy Bks.) Ballantine Bks.

—A Vow of Chastity: A Sister Joan Mystery. 1992. 192p. 16.95 o.p. (*0-312-07112-4*, Saint Martin's Minotaur) St. Martin's Pr.

—A Vow of Chastity: A Sister Joan Mystery. l.t. ed. 1992. (Linford Mystery Library). 400p. pap. 17.99 o.p. (*0-7089-7262-4*, Linford) Thorpe, F. A. Pubs. GBR. *Dist:* Ulverscroft Large Print Bks., Ltd., Ulverscroft Large Print Canada, Ltd.

—A Vow of Compassion: A Sister Joan Mystery. 1998. (Sister Joan Mystery Ser.: Vol. 10). 208p. 20.95 (*0-312-19354-8*, Saint Martin's Minotaur) St. Martin's Pr.

—A Vow of Compassion: A Sister Joan Mystery. l.t. ed. 1998. (Ulverscroft Large Print Ser.). 336p. 29.99 (*0-7089-3972-4*, Ulverscroft) Thorpe, F. A. Pubs. GBR. *Dist:* Ulverscroft Large Print Bks., Ltd., Ulverscroft Large Print Canada, Ltd.

—A Vow of Devotion: A Sister Joan Mystery. (Sister Joan Mystery Ser.). 1997. mass mkt. 5.50 o.s.i (*0-312-96005-0*, St. Martin's Paperbacks); 1995. 186p. 20.95 o.p. (*0-312-13206-9*, Saint Martin's Minotaur) St. Martin's Pr.

—A Vow of Devotion: A Sister Joan Mystery. l.t. ed. 1998. (Nightingale Ser.). 276p. pap. 20.95 (*0-7838-8388-9*) Thorndike Pr.

—A Vow of Fidelity: A Sister Joan Mystery. 1996. 208p. text 19.95 o.p. (*0-312-14064-9*, Saint Martin's Minotaur); Vol. 1. 1997. (Vow of Fidelity Ser.: Vol. 1). 192p. mass mkt. 5.50 (*0-312-96259-2*, St. Martin's Paperbacks) St. Martin's Pr.

—A Vow of Fidelity: A Sister Joan Mystery. l.t. ed. 1997. (Ulverscroft Large Print Ser.). 352p. 29.99 (*0-7089-3697-0*, Ulverscroft) Thorpe, F. A. Pubs. GBR. *Dist:* Ulverscroft Large Print Bks., Ltd., Ulverscroft Large Print Canada, Ltd.

—A Vow of Obedience: A Sister Joan Mystery. 1995. (Sister Joan Mystery Ser.). mass mkt. 5.50 o.s.i (*0-8041-1245-2*, Ivy Bks.) Ballantine Bks.

—A Vow of Obedience: A Sister Joan Mystery. l.t. ed. 1994. 298p. pap. 19.95 (*0-8161-7472-5*, Macmillan Reference USA) Gale Group.

—A Vow of Obedience: A Sister Joan Mystery. 1996. mass mkt. 143.76 (*0-312-95718-1*); 1994. 192p. 18.95 o.p. (*0-312-10573-8*, Saint Martin's Minotaur) St. Martin's Pr.

—A Vow of Penance: A Sister Joan Mystery. 1996. mass mkt. 5.50 (*0-312-95850-1*, St. Martin's Paperbacks); 1994. 270p. 19.95 o.p. (*0-312-11092-8*, Saint Martin's Minotaur) St. Martin's Pr.

—A Vow of Penance: A Sister Joan Mystery. l.t. ed. 1995. (Ulverscroft Large Print Ser.). 352p. 29.99 (*0-7089-3326-2*, Ulverscroft) Thorpe, F. A. Pubs. GBR. *Dist:* Ulverscroft Large Print Bks., Ltd., Ulverscroft Large Print Canada, Ltd.

—A Vow of Poverty: A Sister Joan Mystery. 1996. 208p. 20.95 o.p. (*0-312-14756-2*, Saint Martin's Minotaur) St. Martin's Pr.

—A Vow of Poverty: A Sister Joan Mystery. l.t. ed. 1997. (Ulverscroft Large Print Ser.). 388p. 29.99 (*0-7089-3733-0*, Ulverscroft) Thorpe, F. A. Pubs. GBR. *Dist:* Ulverscroft Large Print Bks., Ltd., Ulverscroft Large Print Canada, Ltd.

—A Vow of Silence: A Sister Joan Mystery. 1991. mass mkt. 4.99 o.s.i (*0-8041-0814-5*, Ivy Bks.) Ballantine Bks.

—A Vow of Silence: A Sister Joan Mystery. 1990. 15.95 o.p. (*0-312-04441-0*, Saint Martin's Minotaur) St. Martin's Pr.

—A Vow of Silence: A Sister Joan Mystery. l.t. ed. 1991. (Ulverscroft Large Print Ser.). 29.99 (*0-7089-2529-4*, Ulverscroft) Thorpe, F. A. Pubs. GBR. *Dist:* Ulverscroft Large Print Bks., Ltd., Ulverscroft Large Print Canada, Ltd.

Bolitho, Janie. Framed in Cornwall. 2001. 192p. pap. 10.95 (*0-7490-0590-4*) Allison & Busby, Ltd. GBR. *Dist:* International Publishers Marketing.

—Framed in Cornwall. l.t. ed. 1999. (Dales Large Print Ser.). 368p. pap. 0.p. (*1-85389-932-1*) Dales Large Print Bks. GBR. *Dist:* Ulverscroft Large Print Canada, Ltd.

—Killed in Cornwall: A Rose Trevelyan Mystery. 2002. 206p. 24.95 (*0-7490-0508-4*) Allison & Busby, Ltd. GBR. *Dist:* International Publishers Marketing.

—Snapped in Cornwall. 2000. 208p. mass mkt. 9.95 (*0-7490-0469-X*, London Hse.) Allison & Busby, Ltd. GBR. *Dist:* International Publishers Marketing.

Brandewyne, Rebecca. Upon a Moon-Dark Moor. l.t. ed. 1989. (General Ser.). 552p. 20.95 o.p. (*0-8161-4731-0*, Macmillan Reference USA) Gale Group.

Cameron, Stella. Finding Ian. l.t. ed. 2001. 400p. 30.95 (*0-7838-9457-0*, Macmillan Reference USA) Gale Group.

—Finding Ian. 2002. 336p. mass mkt. 6.99 (*0-8217-7082-9*); 2001. 34p. 22.00 o.s.i (*1-57566-713-4*) Kensington Publishing Corp.

Carr, Philippa. The Gossamer Cord. l.t. ed. 1993. (General Ser.). 490p. pap. 17.95 o.p. (*0-8161-5614-X*); lib. bdg. 23.95 o.p. (*0-8161-5613-1*) Gale Group. (Macmillan Reference USA).

—The Gossamer Cord. 1992. (Cornwall Saga Ser.). 368p. 21.95 o.p. (*0-399-13725-4*, G. P. Putnam's Sons) Penguin Group (USA) Inc.

Carroll, Susan. The Bride Finder. 1999. 416p. mass mkt. 6.99 (*0-449-00388-4*, Fawcett) Ballantine Bks.

—The Bride Finder. l.t. ed. 1998. (Large Print Book Ser.). 26.95 o.p. (*1-56895-585-5*, Wheeler Publishing, Inc.) Gale Group.

Casley, Dennis. Death Undertow: A Chief Inspector Odhiambo Mystery. 1995. 208p. 19.95 o.p. (*0-312-13643-9*, Saint Martin's Minotaur) St. Martin's Pr.

Clarke, Lindsay. Alice's Masque. 1994. 246p. o.p. (*0-224-03287-9*) Random Hse. UK, Ltd.

Clayton, Mary. Pearls Before Swine. l.t. ed. 1995. (Magna Large Print Ser.). 337p. o.p. (*0-7505-0916-3*) Magna Large Print Bks. GBR. *Dist:* Ulverscroft Large Print Canada, Ltd.

—Pearls Before Swine. 1996. 256p. 21.95 o.p. (*0-312-14026-6*, Saint Martin's Minotaur) St. Martin's Pr.

Coffin, Julie. Shadows of Regret. l.t. ed. 2000. (G. K. Hall Nightingale Ser.). 130p. (*0-7540-4201-4*, Macmillan Reference USA) Gale Group.

—Shadows of Regret. l.t. ed. 2000. (Nightingale Ser.). 130p. pap. 20.95 (*0-7838-9095-8*) Thorndike Pr.

Cook, Gloria. Touch the Silence. 2003. 288p. 26.99 (*0-7278-5894-7*) Severn Hse. Pubs., Ltd.

Coulter, Catherine. The Nightingale Legacy. 1995. 464p. mass mkt. 7.99 (*0-515-11624-6*, Jove) Berkley Publishing Group.

—The Nightingale Legacy. unabr. ed. 1995. (Legacy Ser.). 13p. audio 89.25 (*1-56100-203-8*, 332, Unabridged Library Editions); audio 25.95 o.p. (*1-56100-579-7*, 1301, Bookcassette) Brilliance Audio.

—The Nightingale Legacy. 1994. 384p. 16.95 o.p. (*0-399-13970-2*, G. P. Putnam's Sons) Penguin Group (USA) Inc.

—The Nightingale Legacy. 484p. pap. 5.98 o.p. (*0-7651-0429-6*) Smithmark Pubs., Inc.

Dolan, Charlotte L. The Counterfeit Gentleman. l.t. ed. 1994. 328p. (Orig.). pap. 18.95 (*0-7838-1140-3*, Macmillan Reference USA) Gale Group.

—The Counterfeit Gentleman. 1994. (Signet Regency Romance Ser.). 224p. (Orig.). mass mkt. 3.99 o.s.i (*0-451-17742-8*, Signet Bks.) NAL.

Du Maurier, Daphne. Rebecca. adapted ed. 1999. audio 24.95 (*1-56938-316-2*, AMP-3162) Acorn Media Publishing, Inc.

—Rebecca. unabr. ed. 1999. audio 39.95 (*1-57270-113-7*, F91113u, Cover to Cover Classics) Audio Partners Publishing Corp.

—Rebecca. abr. ed. 1993. audio 24.95 (*1-55927-261-9*, 692908) Audio Renaissance.

—Rebecca. unabr. ed. audio 89.95 o.p. (*1-85549-948-7*, CTC 058) BBC Audiobooks America.

—Rebecca. unabr. ed. audio 80.00 (*0-7366-3650-1*, 1296) Books on Tape, Inc.

—Rebecca. 1946. per. 6.50 (*0-8222-0933-0*); 1989. 599p. 13.00 o.p. (*0-7089-8006-6*) Dramatists Play Service, Inc.

—Rebecca. abr. ed. audio 15.95 o.p. (*0-88646-071-9*, 7092) Durkin Hayes Publishing Ltd.

—Rebecca. 2000. pap. 12.00 (*0-06-093354-2*) HarperCollins Pubs.

—Rebecca. 1997. 416p. pap. 14.00 (*0-380-73040-5*); 1994. 384p. mass mkt. 7.50 (*0-380-77855-6*); 1988. 384p. reprint ed. mass mkt. 5.99 (*0-380-00917-X*) Morrow/Avon. (Avon Bks.).

—Rebecca. audio 89.95 o.p. Olivia & Hill Pr., The.

—Rebecca. 1992. (SPA.). 512p. 12.50 (*84-01-49291-2*, PJ9054) Plaza & Janés Editories, S.A. ESP. *Dist:* Lectorum Pubns., Inc.

—Rebecca. unabr. ed. 1988. audio 91.00 (*1-55690-435-5*, 88340E7) Recorded Bks., LLC.

—Rebecca. abr. ed. 1982. (Radio Ser.). audio 7.95 o.p. (*0-88142-411-0*) Soundelux Audio Publishing.

—Rebecca. 1971. 13.04 (*0-606-04492-2*) Turtleback Bks.

—Rebecca. abr. ed. 1997. (Classic Ser.). 4p. pap. 23.95 o.s.i incl. audio (*0-14-086391-5*, Penguin Audiobooks) Viking Penguin.

—Rebecca: Acting Edition. l.t. ed. 1993. 688p. 25.00 o.s.i (*0-385-47197-1*) Doubleday Publishing.

Du Maurier, Daphne, et al. Rebecca. 1948. 384p. 29.95 (*0-385-04380-5*) Doubleday Publishing.

Gabriel, Hayden. Where the Light Remains: A Novel. 2003. 432p. pap. 14.00 (*0-7432-4314-5*); E-Book (*0-7432-5363-9*) Simon & Schuster. (Touchstone).

—Where the Light Remains: A Novel. l.t. ed. 2003. 603p. 29.95 (*0-7862-5988-4*, Large Print Pr.) Thorndike Pr.

Goddard, Robert. Beyond Recall. unabr. ed. 1998. audio 84.95 (*0-7540-0088-5*, CAB1511) BBC Audiobooks America.

—Beyond Recall. 1998. 368p. mass mkt. (*0-552-14225-5*, Corgi) Bantam Bks.

—Beyond Recall. (Henry Holt Mystery Ser.). 1999. 320p. pap. 14.00 o.s.i (*0-8050-6197-5*, Owl Bks.); 1998. 310p. 25.00 o.s.i (*0-8050-5110-4*) Holt, Henry & Co.

—Beyond Recall. l.t. ed. 1998. (Charnwood Large Print Ser.). 480p. 29.99 o.p. (*0-7089-8991-8*, Ulverscroft) Thorpe, F. A. Pubs. GBR. *Dist:* Ulverscroft Large Print Bks., Ltd., Ulverscroft Large Print Canada, Ltd.

Graham, Winston. The Angry Tide. unabr. ed. 1999. (Poldark Ser. ). Set audio 110.95; Vol. 7. audio 110.95 (*0-7540-0294-2*, CAB 1717) BBC Audiobooks America.

—The Angry Tide. 1979. mass mkt. 2.50 o.s.i (*0-345-28046-6*) Ballantine Bks.

—The Angry Tide. unabr. ed. 2000. (Poldark Ser.: Bk. 7). audio 89.95 Chivers Audio Bks. GBR. *Dist:* BBC Audiobooks America.

—The Angry Tide. 1978. 10.00 o.p. (*0-385-13682-X*) Doubleday Publishing.

—The Angry Tide. 1979. (Reader's Request Ser.). lib. bdg. 19.95 o.p. (*0-8161-6682-X*, Macmillan Reference USA) Gale Group.

—The Angry Tide: Cornwall - As the 18th Century Ebbs. 2002. (Poldark Saga Ser.: Vol. 7). (Illus.). 308p. mass mkt. 8.95 (*0-330-34500-1*) Pan Bks. Ltd. GBR. *Dist:* Trafalgar Square.

—Bella Poldark: A Novel of Cornwall, 1818-1820. 2002. (Poldark Saga). 530p. 24.95 (*0-333-98923-6*) Macmillan U.K. GBR. *Dist:* Trafalgar Square.

—Bella Poldark: A Novel of Cornwall, 1818-1820. 2003. xiii, 688p. pap. 8.95 (*0-330-49149-0*) Pan Bks. Ltd. GBR. *Dist:* Trafalgar Square.

—The Black Moon. 1978. (Poldark Ser.: No.5). mass mkt. 2.25 o.s.i (*0-345-27735-X*); 1977. mass mkt. 1.95 o.s.i (*0-345-26004-X*) Ballantine Bks.

—Black Moon, 2 vols. l.t. ed. 1979. (YA). (gr. 7-12). lib. bdg. 18.95 o.p. (*0-8161-6680-3*, Macmillan Reference USA) Gale Group.

—The Black Moon. unabr. ed. 1997. (Poldark Ser. : Vol. 5). audio 96.95 (*0-7451-6753-5*, CAB 1369) BBC Audiobooks America.

—The Black Moon. unabr. ed. 2000. (Poldark Ser.: Bk. 5). audio 79.95 Chivers Audio Bks. GBR. *Dist:* BBC Audiobooks America.

—The Black Moon: Cornwall 1794. 2002. (Poldark Saga Ser.: Vol. 5). (Illus.). 324p. mass mkt. 8.95 (*0-330-34498-6*) Pan Bks. Ltd. GBR. *Dist:* Trafalgar Square.

—Demelza. unabr. ed. 1995. (Poldark Ser. : Vol. 2). audio 96.95 (*0-7451-6469-2*, CAB 1086) BBC Audiobooks America.

—Demelza. 1977. mass mkt. 1.95 o.s.i (*0-345-26001-5*) Ballantine Bks.

—Demelza. unabr. ed. 2000. (Poldark Ser.: Bk. 2). audio 79.95 Chivers Audio Bks. GBR. *Dist:* BBC Audiobooks America.

—Demelza. 1979. (Reader's Request Ser.). lib. bdg. 17.95 o.p. (*0-8161-6677-3*, Macmillan Reference USA) Gale Group.

—Four Swans. 2002. (Poldark Saga Ser.: Vol. 6). (Illus.). 581p. mass mkt. 8.95 (*0-330-34499-4*) Pan Bks. Ltd. GBR. *Dist:* Trafalgar Square.

—The Four Swans. unabr. ed. 1998. (Poldark Ser. : Vol. 6). audio 110.95 (*0-7540-0124-5*, CAB1547) BBC Audiobooks America.

—The Four Swans. 1978. mass mkt. 2.25 o.s.i (*0-345-26005-8*) Ballantine Bks.

—The Four Swans. unabr. ed. 2000. (Poldark Ser.: Bk. 6). audio 89.95 Chivers Audio Bks. GBR. *Dist:* BBC Audiobooks America.

—The Four Swans. 1977. 8.95 o.p. (*0-385-12338-8*) Doubleday Publishing.

—The Four Swans. 1979. (Reader's Request Ser.). lib. bdg. 19.95 o.p. (*0-8161-6681-1*, Macmillan Reference USA) Gale Group.

—Jeremy Poldark. unabr. ed. 1996. (Poldark Ser. : Vol. 3). audio 69.95 (*0-7451-6612-1*, CAB1228) BBC Audiobooks America.

—Jeremy Poldark. 1977. mass mkt. 1.95 o.s.i (*0-345-26002-3*); No. 3. 1978. mass mkt. 2.25 o.s.i (*0-345-27733-3*) Ballantine Bks.

—Jeremy Poldark. unabr. ed. 2000. (Poldark Ser.: Bk. 3). audio 59.95 Chivers Audio Bks. GBR. *Dist:* BBC Audiobooks America.

—Jeremy Poldark. l.t. ed. 1979. (YA). (gr. 7-12). lib. bdg. 14.95 o.p. (*0-8161-6678-1*, Macmillan Reference USA) Gale Group.

—Loving Cup. 2002. (Poldark Saga Ser.: Vol. 10). (Illus.). 580p. mass mkt. 8.95 (*0-330-34503-6*) Pan Bks. Ltd. GBR. *Dist:* Trafalgar Square.

Settings

—Loving Cup: The Tenth Poldark Novel. 1985. 456p. 17.95 o.p. (*0-385-19834-5*) Doubleday Publishing.
—Miller's Dance. Date not set. lib. bdg. 22.95 (*0-8488-1016-3*) Amereon, Ltd.
—The Miller's Dance. 1983. (Poldark Ser.: No. 9). 384p. 15.95 o.p. (*0-385-18405-0*) Doubleday Publishing.
—The Miller's Dance. 2002. (Poldark Saga Ser.: Vol. 9). (Illus.). 496p. mass mkt. 8.95 (*0-330-34502-8*) Pan Bks. Ltd. GBR. *Dist:* Trafalgar Square.
—Ross Poldark. unabr. ed. 1992. (Poldark Ser. : Vol. 1). audio 84.95 (*0-7451-4035-1*, CAB 732) BBC Audiobooks America.
—Ross Poldark. (Poldark Ser.). 1978. mass mkt. 2.25 o.s.i (*0-345-27731-7*); 1977. mass mkt. 1.95 o.s.i (*0-345-25654-9*) Ballantine Bks.
—Ross Poldark. unabr. ed. 2000. (Poldark Ser.: Bk. 1). audio 69.95 Chivers Audio Bks. GBR. *Dist:* BBC Audiobooks America.
—Ross Poldark, 2 vols. l.t. ed. 1979. (Reader's Request Ser.). lib. bdg. 16.95 o.p. (*0-8161-6676-5*, Macmillan Reference USA) Gale Group.
—Stranger from the Sea. 22.95 (*0-8488-1017-1*) Amereon, Ltd.
—The Stranger from the Sea. unabr. ed. 2000. (Poldark Ser.: Vol. 8). audio 96.95 (*0-7540-0437-6*, CAB 1860) Chivers Audio Bks. GBR. *Dist:* BBC Audiobooks America.
—The Stranger from the Sea. 1982. 432p. 17.95 o.p. (*0-385-17967-7*) Doubleday Publishing.
—The Stranger from the Sea, Bk. 8. 2002. (Poldark Saga Ser.: Vol. 8). (Illus.). 304p. pap. 8.95 (*0-330-34501-X*) Pan Bks. Ltd. GBR. *Dist:* Trafalgar Square.
—The Twisted Sword: Cornwall - January 1815. 1991. (Poldark Novel Ser.). 512p. 21.95 o.p. (*0-88184-693-7*, Carroll & Graf Pubs.) Avalon Publishing Group.
—The Twisted Sword: Cornwall - January 1815, Bk. 11. 2002. (Poldark Saga Ser.: Vol. 11). (Illus.). 544p. pap. 8.95 (*0-330-31749-0*) Pan Bks. Ltd. GBR. *Dist:* Trafalgar Square.
—The Twisted Sword Pt. 1: Cornwall - January 1815. l.t. ed. 1995. (Charnwood Large Print Ser.). 496p. 29.99 o.p. (*0-7089-8822-9*, Charnwood) Thorpe, F. A. Pubs. GBR. *Dist:* Ulverscroft Large Print Bks., Ltd., Ulverscroft Large Print Canada, Ltd.
—The Twisted Sword Pt. 2: Cornwall - January 1815. l.t. ed. 1995. (Charnwood Large Print Ser.). 288p. 29.99 o.p. (*0-7089-8828-8*, Charnwood) Thorpe, F. A. Pubs. GBR. *Dist:* Ulverscroft Large Print Bks., Ltd., Ulverscroft Large Print Canada, Ltd.
—Warleggan. unabr. ed. 1996. (Poldark Ser. : Vol. 4). audio 96.95 (*0-7451-6691-1*, CAB1307) BBC Audiobooks America.
—Warleggan. 1978. (Poldark Ser.: No. 4). mass mkt. 2.25 o.s.i (*0-345-27734-1*); 1977. mass mkt. 1.95 o.s.i (*0-345-26003-1*) Ballantine Bks.
—Warleggan. unabr. ed. 2000. (Poldark Ser.: Bk. 4). audio 79.95 Chivers Audio Bks. GBR. *Dist:* BBC Audiobooks America.
—Warleggan, 2 vols. l.t. ed. 1979. (Reader's Request Ser.). lib. bdg. 17.95 o.p. (*0-8161-6679-X*, Macmillan Reference USA) Gale Group.
—Warleggan, Bk. 4. 2002. (Poldark Saga Ser.: Vol. 4). 471p. pap. 8.95 (*0-330-34496-X*) Pan Bks. Ltd. GBR. *Dist:* Trafalgar Square.
Gregson, Rebecca. Eggshell Days. pap. (*0-312-31042-0*, St. Martin's Paperbacks); mass mkt. (*0-312-98769-2*, St. Martin's Paperbacks); 2003. 320p. 24.95 (*0-312-31041-2*) St. Martin's Pr.
Hill, Susan. Mrs. De Winter. abr. ed. 1993. audio 24.95 (*1-55927-250-3*, 102649) Audio Renaissance.
—Mrs. De Winter. unabr. ed. audio 64.00 (*0-7366-2884-3*, 3586) Books on Tape, Inc.
—Mrs. De Winter. 1993. 349p. 20.00 o.p. (*0-688-12707-X*, Morrow, William & Co.) Morrow/Avon.
—Mrs. de Winter: Library Edition. unabr. ed. 1994. audio 79.95 (*1-55927-273-2*, 102802) Audio Renaissance.
Holt, Victoria. The Legend of the Seventh Virgin. 1993. mass mkt. 5.99 o.s.i (*0-449-45251-4*); 1986. 288p. mass mkt. 5.99 o.s.i (*0-449-21123-1*) Ballantine Bks. (Fawcett).
—The Legend of the Seventh Virgin. 1965. 13.95 o.p. (*0-385-00609-8*) Doubleday Publishing.
—The Legend of the Seventh Virgin. l.t. ed. 2001. (Thorndike Press Large Print Famous Authors Ser.). 519p. 28.95 (*0-7862-3460-1*) Thorndike Pr.
—Menfreya in the Morning. 1966. 5.95 o.p. (*0-385-06098-X*) Doubleday Publishing.
—Menfreya in the Morning. l.t. ed. 2001. (Candlelight Ser.). 255p. 26.95 o.p. (*0-7862-3458-X*) Thorndike Pr.
—Mistress of Mellyn. 1992. mass mkt. 5.99 o.p. (*0-449-45002-3*, Fawcett); 1988. mass mkt. o.s.i (*0-449-20227-5*); 1981. 240p. mass mkt. 3.50 o.s.i (*0-449-23924-1*, Fawcett); 1978. mass mkt. 1.75 o.s.i (*0-449-23124-0*) Ballantine Bks.
—Mistress of Mellyn. 1988. 12.95 o.p. (*0-385-00912-7*) Doubleday Publishing.
—Mistress of Mellyn. l.t. ed. 1969. (Ulverscroft Large Print Ser.). o.p. (*0-85456-705-4*, Ulverscroft) Thorpe, F. A. Pubs. GBR. *Dist:* Ulverscroft Large Print Canada, Ltd.
—Mistress of Mellyn, unabr. ed. 1999. audio 54.95 BBC Audiobooks America.
Jackson, Melanie. Amarantha. 2001. 400p. mass mkt. 5.99 (*0-8439-4900-7*, Leisure Bks.) Dorchester Publishing Co., Inc.
James, Dana. Heart of Glass. l.t. ed. 2001. (Romance Ser.). 239p. pap. 23.95 o.p. (*0-7838-9446-5*) Thorndike Pr.
—Pool of Dreaming. l.t. ed. 2002. 262p. pap. 22.95 (*0-7862-3725-2*) Gale Group.
James, Samantha. The Truest Heart. 2001. 384p. mass mkt. 6.99 (*0-380-80588-X*, Avon Bks.) Morrow/Avon.
—The Truest Heart. l.t. ed. 2001. 466p. 28.95 (*0-7862-3700-7*) Thorndike Pr.
Jones, Jill. The Island. 1999. 320p. mass mkt. 5.99 (*0-312-97073-0*, St. Martin's Paperbacks) St. Martin's Pr.
Lide, Mary. Polmena Cove. l.t. ed. 1995. 323p. pap. 19.95 o.p. (*0-7838-1203-5*, Macmillan Reference USA) Gale Group.
—Polmena Cove. 1994. 230p. 19.95 o.p. (*0-312-11877-5*) St. Martin's Pr.
—The Sea Scape. 1992. 256p. 17.95 o.p. (*0-312-07799-8*) St. Martin's Pr.
Lillington, Kenneth. Selkie. 1985. 145p. (YA). (gr. 7-10). o.p. (*0-571-13421-1*) Faber & Faber Ltd.
Llewellyn, Caroline. False Light. l.t. ed. 1997. (Large Print Bks.). pap. 23.95 (*1-56895-403-4*, Wheeler Publishing, Inc.) Gale Group.
—False Light. 1996. 315p. 21.50 o.p. (*0-684-82460-4*, Scribner) Simon & Schuster.
Llewellyn, Sam. The Sea Garden. 2000. 378p. pap. 17.95 o.p. (*0-7472-7373-1*) Headline Bk. Publishing, Ltd. GBR. *Dist:* Trafalgar Square.
—The Sea Garden. l.t. ed. 2001. (Charnwood Large Print Ser.). 544p. 32.50 o.p. (*0-7089-9244-7*, Ulverscroft) Thorpe, F. A. Pubs. GBR. *Dist:* Ulverscroft Large Print Bks., Ltd., Ulverscroft Large Print Canada, Ltd.
MacDonald, Malcolm. Kernow & Daughter. 1996. 400p. 23.95 o.p. (*0-312-13995-0*) St. Martin's Pr.
—Tamsin Harte. 2000. 384p. 24.95 o.p. (*0-312-20628-3*) St. Martin's Pr.
Macdonald, Malcolm. To the End of Her Days. 1994. 384p. 23.95 o.p. (*0-312-11080-4*) St. Martin's Pr.
—The Trevarton Inheritance. 1996. 400p. 24.95 o.p. (*0-312-14748-1*) St. Martin's Pr.
MacDonald, Malcolm. Woman Alone. 1991. 18.95 o.p. (*0-312-06000-9*) St. Martin's Pr.
Macdonald, Malcolm. A Woman Possessed. 1993. 384p. 21.95 o.p. (*0-312-09416-7*) St. Martin's Pr.
MacDonald, Malcom. Tomorrows Tide. 1997. 336p. 23.95 (*0-312-15676-6*) St. Martin's Pr.
Mann, Jessica. Under a Dark Sun. l.t. ed. 2001. (Thorndike General Ser.). 271p. pap. 22.95 o.p. (*0-7862-3221-8*); (*0-7540-4422-X*); (*0-7540-4423-8*) Thorndike Pr.
McCloud, Susan Evans. Murder by the Sea. 1997. 192p. pap. 9.95 (*1-57008-314-2*, Bookcraft, Inc.) Deseret Bk. Co.
Miles, Rosalind. Isolde: Queen of the Western Isle. 2003. (Tristan & Isolde Trilogy: Bk. 1). (Illus.). 368p. pap. 12.95 (*1-4000-4786-2*) Crown Publishing Group.
Oldfield, Pamela. A Woman Alone. l.t. ed. 2001. 428p. (*0-7540-1569-6*); (*0-7540-2431-8*) Gale Group. (Macmillan Reference USA).
—A Woman Alone. l.t. ed. 2001. (G. K. Hall Romance Ser.). 428p. 26.95 (*0-7838-9364-7*) Thorndike Pr.
Paton Walsh, Jill. The Serpentine Cave. 1997. 224p. 20.95 (*0-312-16999-X*) St. Martin's Pr.
—The Serpentine Cave. l.t. ed. 1998. (Charnwood Large Print Ser.). 272p. 29.99 o.p. (*0-7089-9001-0*, Charnwood) Thorpe, F. A. Pubs. GBR. *Dist:* Ulverscroft Large Print Bks., Ltd., Ulverscroft Large Print Canada, Ltd.
Peake, Lilian. Love in Moonlight. l.t. ed. 1994. 18.95 o.p. (*0-7927-2130-6*); pap. 17.95 o.p. (*0-7927-2129-2*) BBC Audiobooks America.
Peart, Jane. Web of Deception. l.t. ed. 2000. (G. K. Hall Inspirational Ser.). 261p. 26.95 o.p. (*0-7838-8942-9*, Macmillan Reference USA) Gale Group.
—Web of Deception. 1996. (Edgecliffe Manor Mystery Ser.: No. 2). 208p. (gr. 10). pap. 9.99 o.p. (*0-8007-5598-7*) Revell, Fleming H. Co.
Pykare, Nina Coombs. The Haunting of Grey Cliffs. 1992. 192p. 4.50 o.p. (*1-55773-830-0*, Diamond Bks.) Ace Bks.
—The Haunting of Grey Cliffs. l.t. ed. 2000. (Romance Ser.). 234p. 24.95 (*0-7862-2350-2*) Thorndike Pr.
Roe, Jill. A New Leaf. 1997. 224p. 20.95 o.p. (*0-312-15603-0*) St. Martin's Pr.
—A New Leaf. l.t. ed. 1997. (Romance Ser.). 310p. 24.95 (*0-7862-1070-2*) Thorndike Pr.
—A New Leaf. l.t. ed. 1997. (Ulverscroft Large Print Ser.). 368p. 29.99 o.p. (*0-7089-3817-5*, Ulverscroft) Thorpe, F. A. Pubs. GBR. *Dist:* Ulverscroft Large Print Bks., Ltd., Ulverscroft Large Print Canada, Ltd.
Sabatini, Rafael. Sea Hawk. 1980. reprint ed. 17.00 o.p. (*0-89783-012-1*) Larlin Corp.
—Sea Hawk. 2002. 373p. pap. 13.95 (*0-393-32331-5*) Norton, W. W. & Co., Inc.
Seton, Anya. Avalon. 1977. mass mkt. 1.95 o.s.i (*0-449-23308-1*, Fawcett) Ballantine Bks.
—Avalon. 1965. 10.00 o.p. (*0-395-08170-X*) Houghton Mifflin Co.
—Avalon. l.t. ed. 1982. (Ulverscroft Large Print Ser.). 587p. 12.50 o.p. (*0-7089-0750-4*, Ulverscroft) Thorpe, F. A. Pubs. GBR. *Dist:* Ulverscroft Large Print Bks., Ltd., Ulverscroft Large Print Canada, Ltd.
Stubbs, Jean. Family Games. 1995. mass mkt. 4.99 o.p. (*0-312-95479-4*, St. Martin's Paperbacks); 1994. 320p. 21.95 o.p. (*0-312-10437-5*) St. Martin's Pr.
—Kelly Park: A Novel. 1992. 320p. 19.95 o.p. (*0-312-07850-1*) St. Martin's Pr.
—Light in Summer. 1991. 18.95 o.p. (*0-312-05462-9*) St. Martin's Pr.
Summers, Rowena. Primmy's Daughter. l.t. ed. 1999. (Magna Large Print Ser.). 448p. 31.99 (*0-7505-1374-8*) Magna Large Print Bks. GBR. *Dist:* Ulverscroft Large Print Bks., Ltd., Ulverscroft Large Print Canada, Ltd.
—Primmy's Daughter. 1998. 256p. 24.00 o.p. (*0-7278-5326-0*) Severn Hse. Pubs., Ltd.
Thomas, Graham. Malice in Cornwall. 1998. (Erskine Powell Mysteries Ser.: Vol. 2). 240p. mass mkt. 6.50 (*0-8041-1656-3*, Ivy Bks.) Ballantine Bks.
—Malice in Cornwall. l.t. ed. 2000. (Ulverscroft Large Print Ser.). 312p. 31.99 (*0-7089-4324-1*, Ulverscroft) Thorpe, F. A. Pubs. GBR. *Dist:* Ulverscroft Large Print Bks., Ltd., Ulverscroft Large Print Canada, Ltd.
Todd, Charles. Wings of Fire. 1999. (Wings of Fire Ser.: Vol. 1). 320p. mass mkt. 6.99 (*0-312-96568-0*, St. Martin's Paperbacks); 1998. (Inspector Ian Rutledge Mysteries Ser.). 294p. (gr. 5 up). 23.95 (*0-312-17064-5*, Saint Martin's Minotaur) St. Martin's Pr.
Wesley, Mary. Harnessing Peacocks. 1987. 380p. pap. 10.95 o.p. (*0-552-99210-0*) Bantam Bks.
—Harnessing Peacocks. 1986. 288p. 16.95 o.p. (*0-684-18637-3*); 1994. 391p. pap. 18.95 (*0-8161-7490-3*) Gale Group. (Macmillan Reference USA).
—Harnessing Peacocks. unabr. ed. 1994. audio 61.95 (*1-85089-660-7*, 91041) ISIS Audio Bks. GBR. *Dist:* Ulverscroft Large Print Bks., Ltd.
—Harnessing Peacocks. 1990. 288p. pap. 14.00 (*0-14-012393-8*, Penguin Bks.) Penguin Group (USA) Inc.
White, Gill. Veil of Darkness. 2003. 411p. pap. 8.95 (*0-552-15040-1*) Transworld Publishers Ltd. GBR. *Dist:* Trafalgar Square.
Whitnell, Barbara. A Clear Blue Sky. 1995. 320p. 23.95 o.p. (*0-312-13945-4*) St. Martin's Pr.
—The View from the Summer House. 1995. 316p. 21.95 o.p. (*0-312-11913-5*) St. Martin's Pr.
Williams, Mary. Trenhawk. l.t. ed. 1993. (Magna Large Print Ser.). 558p. 29.99 o.p. (*0-7505-0528-1*) Magna Large Print Bks. GBR. *Dist:* Ulverscroft Large Print Bks., Ltd., Ulverscroft Large Print Canada, Ltd.
—Trenhawk. 1982. 322p. 13.95 o.p. (*0-312-81766-5*) St. Martin's Pr.

## CORONNAN (IMAGINARY PLACE)—FICTION

Radford, Irene. Dragon's Touchstone. 1997. (Dragon Nimbus History Ser.: Vol. 1). 384p. mass mkt. 6.99 (*0-88677-744-5*) DAW Bks., Inc.
—The Glass Dragon, Vol. 1. 1994. (Dragon Nimbus Ser.: Vol. 1). 352p. (Orig.). mass mkt. 6.99 (*0-88677-634-1*) DAW Bks., Inc.
—The Last Battlemage. 1998. (Dragon Nimbus History Ser.: No. 2). 352p. mass mkt. 6.99 (*0-88677-774-7*) DAW Bks., Inc.
—The Loneliest Magician. 1996. (Dragon Nimbus Ser.: Vol. 3). 352p. mass mkt. 6.99 (*0-88677-709-7*) DAW Bks., Inc.
—The Perfect Princess, Vol. 2. 1995. (Dragon Nimbus Ser.: No. 2). 352p. mass mkt. 6.99 (*0-88677-678-3*) DAW Bks., Inc.
—Wizard's Treasure. 2000. (Dragon Nimbus Ser.: Vol. 4). 400p. mass mkt. 6.99 o.s.i (*0-88677-913-8*) DAW Bks., Inc.

## COSTA RICA—FICTION

Benavides, Miguel. The Children of Mariplata: Stories from Costa Rica. 1993. 55p. pap. 17.95 (*1-85610-019-7*) Dufour Editions, Inc.
De Vallbona, Rima. Flowering Inferno: Tales of Sinking Hearts. De Tagle, Lillian L., tr. from SPA. 1994. (Discoveries Ser.). 92p. pap. 12.95 (*0-935480-64-1*) Latin American Literary Review Pr.
Gagini, Carlos. Redemptions: A Costa Rican Novel. 1985. Tr. of Arbol Enfermo. (Illus.). 130p. 20.00 (*0-916304-66-3*); pap. 12.50 o.p. (*0-916304-67-1*) San Diego State Univ. Pr.
Levi, Enrique J., ed. When New Flowers Bloomed: Short Stories by Women Writers from Costa Rica & Panama. 1988. (Discoveries Ser.). 208p. pap. 14.95 (*0-935480-47-1*) Latin American Literary Review Pr.

## COTSWOLD HILLS (ENGLAND)—FICTION

Atherton, Nancy. Aunt Dimity: Detective. l.t. ed. 2002. (Mystery Ser.). 274p. 30.45 (*0-7862-3843-7*) Gale Group.
—Aunt Dimity, Detective. 2003. 240p. mass mkt. 6.99 (*0-14-200154-6*) Penguin Group (USA) Inc.
—Aunt Dimity, Detective. 2001. 256p. 22.95 o.s.i (*0-670-03021-X*, Viking) Viking Penguin.
Beaton, M. C., pseud. Agatha Raisin & the Day the Floods Came. l.t. ed. 2002. (Mystery Ser.). 341p. 30.95 (*0-7862-4679-0*) Gale Group.
—Agatha Raisin & the Day the Floods Came. E-Book 22.95 (*0-312-70710-X*); 2003. 240p. mass mkt. 6.50 (*0-312-98586-X*, St. Martin's Paperbacks); 2002. 224p. 22.95 (*0-312-20767-0*, Saint Martin's Minotaur) St. Martin's Pr.
—Agatha Raisin & the Fairies of Fryfam. 2001. 224p. mass mkt. 6.50 (*0-312-97626-7*, St. Martin's Paperbacks); 2000. 197p. 19.95 (*0-312-20496-5*, Saint Martin's Minotaur) St. Martin's Pr.
—Agatha Raisin & the Fairies of Fryfam. l.t. ed. 2000. (Mystery Ser.). (Illus.). 283p. (J). 29.95 (*0-7862-2858-X*) Thorndike Pr.
—Agatha Raisin & the Love from Hell. l.t. ed. 2002. 366p. 30.95 (*0-7862-3862-3*) Gale Group.
—Agatha Raisin & the Love from Hell. 2003. 256p. mass mkt. 6.50 (*0-312-98318-2*, St. Martin's Paperbacks); 2001. 224p. 22.95 (*0-312-20766-2*, Saint Martin's Minotaur) St. Martin's Pr.
—Agatha Raisin & the Murderous Marriage. l.t. ed. 1997. (Large Print Book Ser.). pap. 22.95 (*1-56895-443-3*, Wheeler Publishing, Inc.) Gale Group.
—Agatha Raisin & the Murderous Marriage. (Agatha Raisin Mysteries Ser.). 1997. 224p. mass mkt. 6.50 (*0-312-96186-3*, St. Martin's Paperbacks); 1996. 208p. 20.95 (*0-312-14538-1*, Saint Martin's Minotaur) St. Martin's Pr.
—Agatha Raisin & the Potted Gardener. 1995. 192p. mass mkt. 6.50 (*0-8041-1359-9*, Ivy Bks.) Ballantine Bks.
—Agatha Raisin & the Potted Gardener. l.t. ed. 1998. 204p. 21.95 o.p. (*0-7838-8392-7*, Macmillan Reference USA) Gale Group.
—Agatha Raisin & the Potted Gardener. 1994. 240p. 18.95 (*0-312-10927-X*, Saint Martin's Minotaur) St. Martin's Pr.
—Agatha Raisin & the Quiche of Death. 1993. 192p. mass mkt. 6.50 (*0-8041-1163-4*, Ivy Bks.) Ballantine Bks.
—Agatha Raisin & the Quiche of Death. 1992. 208p. 17.95 o.p. (*0-312-08153-7*, Saint Martin's Minotaur) St. Martin's Pr.
—Agatha Raisin & the Terrible Tourist. l.t. ed. 1998. pap. 22.95 o.p. (*1-56895-574-X*, Wheeler Publishing, Inc.) Gale Group.
—Agatha Raisin & the Terrible Tourist. (Agatha Raisin Mysteries Ser.). 1997. 160p. 20.95 o.p. (*0-312-16761-X*, Saint Martin's Minotaur); 1958. E-Book 5.99 o.s.i (*0-312-20707-7*); 1998. 208p. reprint ed. mass mkt. 6.50 (*0-312-96566-4*, St. Martin's Paperbacks) St. Martin's Pr.
—Agatha Raisin & the Vicious Vet. 1994. 192p. mass mkt. 6.99 (*0-8041-1162-6*, Ivy Bks.) Ballantine Bks.
—Agatha Raisin & the Vicious Vet. 1993. 208p. 17.95 o.p. (*0-312-09242-3*, Saint Martin's Minotaur) St. Martin's Pr.
—Agatha Raisin & the Vicious Vet. l.t. ed. 1998. (Paperback Ser.). 227p. pap. 24.95 (*0-7838-0368-0*) Thorndike Pr.
—Agatha Raisin & the Walkers of Dembley. 1996. (Agatha Raisin Ser.). 176p. mass mkt. 6.50 (*0-8041-1358-0*, Ivy Bks.) Ballantine Bks.
—Agatha Raisin & the Walkers of Dembley. 1995. 170p. 19.95 o.p. (*0-312-11738-8*, Saint Martin's Minotaur) St. Martin's Pr.
—Agatha Raisin & the Wellspring of Death. l.t. ed. 1999. (Large Print Book Ser.). pap. 23.95 (*1-56895-730-0*, Wheeler Publishing, Inc.) Gale Group.
—Agatha Raisin & the Wellspring of Death. (Dead Letter Mysteries Ser.). 1999. 256p. mass mkt. 6.50 (*0-312-96695-4*, St. Martin's Paperbacks); 1998. 272p. 21.95 o.p. (*0-312-18523-5*, Saint Martin's Minotaur) St. Martin's Pr.
—Agatha Raisin & the Witch of Wyckhadden. 2000. 214p. mass mkt. 5.99 (*0-312-97369-1*, St. Martin's Paperbacks); 1999. 208p. 21.95 (*0-312-20494-9*, Saint Martin's Minotaur) St. Martin's Pr.
—Agatha Raisin & the Witch of Wyckhadden. l.t. ed. 2000. (Mystery Ser.). 288p. 28.95 (*0-7862-2418-5*) Thorndike Pr.

—Agatha Raisin & the Wizard of Evesham. pap. text (*0-312-20693-3*, Tor Bks.) Doherty, Tom Assocs., LLC.

—Agatha Raisin & the Wizard of Evesham. 1999. 256p. mass mkt. 5.99 (*0-312-97062-5*, St. Martin's Paperbacks); (Agatha Raisin Mysteries Ser.: Vol. 8). 208p. 20.95 o.p. (*0-312-19822-1*, Saint Martin's Minotaur) St. Martin's Pr.

—Agatha Raisin & the Wizard of Evesham. l.t. ed. 2000. (Mystery Ser.). (Illus.). 272p. 28.95 (*0-7862-2417-7*) Thorndike Pr.

Granger, Ann. Beneath These Stones. 2000. (Meredith & Markby Mysteries Ser.). 250p. 22.95 (*0-312-24178-X*, Saint Martin's Minotaur) St. Martin's Pr.

—Call the Dead Again. l.t. ed. 1999. 30.00 o.p. (*0-7862-1817-7*, Macmillan Reference USA) Gale Group.

—Call the Dead Again. 1999. (Meredith & Markby Mysteries Ser.). 256p. 22.95 (*0-312-20505-8*, Saint Martin's Minotaur) St. Martin's Pr.

—Candle for a Corpse. 1997. (Meredith & Markby Mysteries Ser.: Vol. 8). 288p. mass mkt. 5.99 (*0-380-73012-X*, Avon Bks.) Morrow/Avon.

—Candle for a Corpse. 1996. 256p. text 21.95 o.p. (*0-312-14292-7*, Saint Martin's Minotaur) St. Martin's Pr.

—Cold in the Earth. 1994. 256p. mass mkt. 5.50 (*0-380-72213-5*, Avon Bks.) Morrow/Avon.

—Cold in the Earth. 1993. 218p. 17.95 o.p. (*0-312-08747-0*, Saint Martin's Minotaur) St. Martin's Pr.

—Cold in the Earth. l.t. ed. 1994. (Ulverscroft Large Print Ser.). 576p. 29.99 o.p. (*0-7089-3111-1*, Ulverscroft) Thorpe, F. A. Pubs. GBR. *Dist:* Ulverscroft Large Print Bks., Ltd., Ulverscroft Large Print Canada, Ltd.

—A Fine Place for Death. 1996. (New Meredith & Markby Mystery Ser.: No. 6). 288p. mass mkt. 5.50 (*0-380-72573-8*, Avon Bks.) Morrow/Avon.

—A Fine Place for Death. 1994. 249p. 21.00 o.p. (*0-312-11787-6*, Saint Martin's Minotaur) St. Martin's Pr.

—A Fine Place for Death. l.t. ed. 1995. (Ulverscroft Large Print Ser.). 528p. 29.99 o.p. (*0-7089-3346-7*, Ulverscroft) Thorpe, F. A. Pubs. GBR. *Dist:* Ulverscroft Large Print Bks., Ltd., Ulverscroft Large Print Canada, Ltd.

—Flowers for His Funeral. 1997. mass mkt. 5.50 (*0-380-72887-7*, Avon Bks.) Morrow/Avon.

—Flowers for His Funeral. 1995. 250p. 21.95 o.p. (*0-312-13495-9*, Saint Martin's Minotaur) St. Martin's Pr.

—Murder among Us. 1995. (Meredith & Markby Mysteries Ser.: No. 4). 304p. mass mkt. 5.99 (*0-380-72476-6*, Avon Bks.) Morrow/Avon.

—Murder among Us. 1993. 224p. 18.95 o.p. (*0-312-09875-8*); (*0-312-09343-8*) St. Martin's Pr. (Saint Martin's Minotaur).

—Murder among Us. l.t. ed. 1994. (Ulverscroft Large Print Ser.). 544p. 29.99 o.p. (*0-7089-3146-4*, Ulverscroft) Thorpe, F. A. Pubs. GBR. *Dist:* Ulverscroft Large Print Bks., Ltd., Ulverscroft Large Print Canada, Ltd.

—Say It with Poison. 1993. 224p. mass mkt. 5.50 (*0-380-71823-5*, Avon Bks.) Morrow/Avon.

—Say It with Poison. 1991. 16.95 o.p. (*0-312-05506-4*, Saint Martin's Minotaur) St. Martin's Pr.

—A Season for Murder. 1993. (Meredith & Markby Mysteries Ser.: Vol. 2). 256p. mass mkt. 5.99 o.s.i (*0-380-71997-5*, Avon Bks.) Morrow/Avon.

—A Season for Murder. 1992. 256p. 18.95 o.p. (*0-312-07079-9*, Saint Martin's Minotaur) St. Martin's Pr.

—A Season for Murder. l.t. ed. 1992. (Magna Large Print Ser.). 361p. 29.99 o.p. (*0-7505-0483-8*, Ulverscroft) Thorpe, F. A. Pubs. GBR. *Dist:* Ulverscroft Large Print Bks., Ltd., Ulverscroft Large Print Canada, Ltd.

—A Touch of Mortality. 1998. 288p. mass mkt. 5.99 (*0-380-73087-1*, Avon Bks.) Morrow/Avon.

—A Touch of Mortality. 1997. 256p. 21.95 (*0-312-15231-0*, Saint Martin's Minotaur) St. Martin's Pr.

—Where Old Bones Lie. 1995. (New Meredith & Markby Mystery Ser.: No. 5). 288p. mass mkt. 5.99 (*0-380-72477-4*, Avon Bks.) Morrow/Avon.

—Where Old Bones Lie. 1994. 224p. 19.95 o.p. (*0-312-11097-9*, Saint Martin's Minotaur) St. Martin's Pr.

—Where Old Bones Lie. l.t. ed. 1995. (Ulverscroft Large Print Ser.). 528p. 29.99 o.p. (*0-7089-3391-2*, Ulverscroft) Thorpe, F. A. Pubs. GBR. *Dist:* Ulverscroft Large Print Bks., Ltd., Ulverscroft Large Print Canada, Ltd.

—A Word After Dying. 1998. (Meredith & Markby Mysteries Ser.). 256p. 21.95 (*0-312-17067-X*, Saint Martin's Minotaur) St. Martin's Pr.

—A Word after Dying. 1999. (Meredith & Markby Mysteries Ser.). 304p. mass mkt. 5.99 (*0-380-73227-0*, Avon Bks.) Morrow/Avon.

—A Word after Dying. pap. 14.95 (*0-312-30475-7*, Saint Martin's Griffin) St. Martin's Pr.

—A Word after Dying. l.t. ed. 1997. (Ulverscroft Large Print Ser.). 560p. 29.99 o.p. (*0-7089-3809-4*, Ulverscroft) Thorpe, F. A. Pubs. GBR. *Dist:* Ulverscroft Large Print Bks., Ltd., Ulverscroft Large Print Canada, Ltd.

Grant-Adamson, Lesley. The Girl in the Case. unabr. ed. 1998. pap. text 54.95 incl. audio (*0-7531-0264-1*, 971206) ISIS Audio Bks. GBR. *Dist:* Ulverscroft Large Print Bks., Ltd.

—The Girl in the Case. l.t. ed. 1997. (Paperback Ser.). 370p. pap. 23.95 (*0-7838-8279-3*) Thorndike Pr.

Lively, Penelope. Passing On. 224p. 1990. 17.95 o.p. (*0-8021-1155-6*); 1999. reprint ed. pap. 12.00 (*0-8021-3626-5*, Grove Pr.) Grove/Atlantic, Inc.

—Passing On. 1991. 224p. reprint ed. pap. 12.00 o.s.i (*0-06-097370-6*, Perennial) HarperTrade.

—Passing On. unabr. ed. 2001. audio 61.95 (*1-85089-786-7*, 9007X); 2000. audio compact disk 59.95 (*0-7531-0701-5*, 107015) ISIS Audio Bks. GBR. *Dist:* Ulverscroft Large Print Bks., Ltd.

—Passing On. l.t. ed. 1990. 342p. 19.95 (*1-85089-329-2*) ISIS Large Print Bks. GBR. *Dist:* Transaction Pubs.

Llewellyn, Caroline. Life Blood. 1994. mass mkt. 5.99 o.s.i (*0-8041-1263-0*, Ivy Bks.) Ballantine Bks.

—Life Blood. 1993. 352p. 20.00 o.p. (*0-684-19402-3*); 1994. 571p. lib. bdg. 21.95 (*0-8161-5940-8*) Gale Group. (Macmillan Reference USA).

Tettmar, Elizabeth. Trial Love. 1998. 255p. pap. (*0-7540-3421-6*) BBC Audiobooks America.

—Trial Love. 192p. 22.00 (*0-7278-5234-5*) Severn Hse. Pubs., Ltd.

—Trial Love. l.t. ed. 1998. (Nightingale Ser.). 264p. pap. 20.95 (*0-7838-0249-8*) Thorndike Pr.

### CRAWFORD COUNTY (TEX.: IMAGINARY PLACE)—FICTION

Meredith, Doris R. The Homefront Murders. 1994. (Southwest Mysteries Ser.). mass mkt. 4.99 o.s.i (*0-345-38050-9*) Ballantine Bks.

—The Sheriff & the Branding Iron Murders. 1992. mass mkt. 3.99 o.s.i (*0-345-36950-5*) Ballantine Bks.

—The Sheriff & the Branding Iron Murders. l.t. ed. 1997. (Nightingale Ser.). pap. 18.95 o.p. (*0-7838-2044-5*, Macmillan Reference USA) Gale Group.

—The Sheriff & the Branding Iron Murders. 1986. 160p. pap. 2.95 (*0-380-70050-6*, Avon Bks.) Morrow/Avon.

—The Sheriff & the Branding Iron Murders. Holland, Stephen, ed. abr. ed. 1994. audio 24.95 (*1-883268-12-5*) Spellbinders, Inc.

—The Sheriff & the Branding Iron Murders. 1985. 159p. 14.95 (*0-8027-4050-2*) Walker & Co.

—The Sheriff & the Folsom Man Murders. 1992. mass mkt. 3.99 o.s.i (*0-345-36949-1*) Ballantine Bks.

—The Sheriff & the Folsom Man Murders. 1987. 208p. pap. 2.95 (*0-380-70364-5*, Avon Bks.) Morrow/Avon.

—The Sheriff & the Folsom Man Murders. 1989. 2.99 o.p. (*0-517-00603-0*) Random Hse. Value Publishing.

—The Sheriff & the Folsom Man Murders. l.t. ed. 1999. 261p. pap. 24.95 (*0-7838-8582-2*) Thorndike Pr.

—The Sheriff & the Folsom Man Murders. 1987. 192p. 16.95 (*0-8027-5663-8*) Walker & Co.

—The Sheriff & the Panhandle Murders. l.t. ed. 1986. 13.95 o.p. (*1-55504-028-4*, 317) BBC Audiobooks America.

—The Sheriff & the Panhandle Murders. 1991. mass mkt. 4.99 o.s.i (*0-345-36951-3*) Ballantine Bks.

—The Sheriff & the Panhandle Murders. 1985. 224p. pap. 2.95 o.p. (*0-380-69929-X*, Avon Bks.) Morrow/Avon.

—The Sheriff & the Panhandle Murders. Holland, Stephen, ed. abr. ed. 1994. audio 24.95 (*1-883268-08-7*) Spellbinders, Inc.

—The Sheriff & the Panhandle Murders. 1984. 192p. 12.95 o.s.i (*0-8027-4036-7*) Walker & Co.

—The Sheriff & the Pheasant Hunt Murders. 1993. mass mkt. 4.50 o.s.i (*0-345-36948-3*) Ballantine Bks.

—The Sheriff & the Pheasant Hunt Murders. Holland, Stephen, ed. abr. ed. 1994. audio 24.95 (*1-883268-07-9*) Spellbinders, Inc.

### CROSSROADS (IMAGINARY PLACE)—FICTION

O'Donohoe, Nick. The Healing of Crossroads. 1996. 336p. mass mkt. 5.99 o.s.i (*0-441-00391-5*) Ace Bks.

—The Magic & the Healing. 1994. 352p. (Orig.). mass mkt. 4.99 o.s.i (*0-441-00053-3*) Ace Bks.

—Under the Healing Sun. 1995. 352p. (Orig.). mass mkt. 4.99 o.s.i (*0-441-00180-7*) Ace Bks.

### CRYSTAL COVE (CALIF.: IMAGINARY PLACE)—FICTION

Maxwell, A. E. Art of Survival. 1993. 336p. mass mkt. 4.99 o.p. (*0-06-104115-7*, HarperTorch) Morrow/Avon.

—The Art of Survival. 1990. mass mkt. 4.50 o.s.i (*0-553-28479-7*) Bantam Bks.

—Frog & the Scorpion. 1986. 264p. 16.95 o.p. (*0-385-19260-6*) Doubleday Publishing.

—The Frog & the Scorpion. 1987. 224p. mass mkt. 3.50 o.s.i (*0-553-26876-7*) Bantam Bks.

—The Frog & the Scorpion. 1993. 320p. mass mkt. 4.99 o.p. (*0-06-104113-0*, HarperTorch) Morrow/Avon.

—Gatsby's Vineyard. 1988. 240p. mass mkt. 3.50 o.s.i (*0-553-27409-0*) Bantam Bks.

—Gatsby's Vineyard. 1987. 240p. 15.95 o.s.i (*0-385-23712-X*) Doubleday Publishing.

—Gatsby's Vineyard. 1993. 320p. mass mkt. 4.99 o.p. (*0-06-104112-2*, HarperTorch) Morrow/Avon.

—The Golden Empire. 1979. (Orig.). mass mkt. 2.50 o.s.i (*0-449-14267-1*, Fawcett) Ballantine Bks.

—Just Another Day in Paradise. 1986. mass mkt. 2.95 o.s.i (*0-553-25789-7*) Bantam Bks.

—Just Another Day in Paradise. 1985. 240p. 14.95 o.p. (*0-385-19259-2*) Doubleday Publishing.

—Just Another Day in Paradise. 1993. 304p. mass mkt. 4.99 o.p. (*0-06-104114-9*, HarperTorch) Morrow/Avon.

—Just Enough Light to Kill. 1989. mass mkt. 3.95 o.s.i (*0-553-28213-1*) Bantam Bks.

—Just Enough Light to Kill. 1993. 336p. mass mkt. 4.99 o.s.i (*0-06-104111-4*, HarperTorch) Morrow/Avon.

—The King of Nothing. 1994. 320p. mass mkt. 5.50 o.p. (*0-06-104230-7*, HarperTorch) Morrow/Avon.

—Money Burns. 1993. 368p. mass mkt. 5.50 o.p. (*0-06-104123-8*, HarperTorch) Morrow/Avon.

—Money Burns. 1993. 3.99 o.p. (*0-517-10621-3*) Random Hse. Value Publishing.

—Murder Hurts. 1995. 352p. mass mkt. 4.99 o.p. (*0-06-104318-4*, HarperTorch) Morrow/Avon.

—Redwood Empire. (Harlequin Historicals Ser.). 1995. 440p. per. (*0-373-28867-0*, 1-28867-9); 1987. 416p. mass mkt. (*0-373-97049-8*) Harlequin Enterprises, Ltd. (Harlequin Bks.).

### CUBA—FICTION

Abreu, Juan. Garbageland. 2001. (SPA., Illus.). 224p. pap. (*84-397-0690-1*) Grijalbo Mondadori, S.A.-Junior.

Arenas, Reinaldo. The Color of Summer: Or the New Garden of Earthly Delight. Hurley, Andrew, tr. from SPA. 2000. 544p. 28.95 o.s.i (*0-670-84065-3*) Viking Penguin.

—The Palace of the White Skunks. Hurley, Andrew, tr. 1993. 384p. pap. 13.95 (*0-14-009792-9*, Penguin Bks.) Penguin Group (USA) Inc.

—The Palace of the White Skunks. Hurley, Andrew, tr. 1991. 384p. 21.95 o.p. (*0-670-81510-1*) Viking Penguin.

—Singing from the Well. 1988. (King Penguin Ser.). 240p. pap. 12.95 (*0-14-009444-X*, Penguin Bks.) Penguin Group (USA) Inc.

—Singing from the Well. 1987. 16.95 o.p. (*0-670-80805-9*) Viking Penguin.

Armstrong, Campbell. Mambo. 1990. 18.95 o.p. (*0-06-016285-6*) HarperTrade.

—Mambo. 1991. 560p. mass mkt. 5.95 o.p. (*0-06-109902-3*, HarperTorch) Morrow/Avon.

—Mambo. 1991. 4.99 o.p. (*0-517-07410-9*) Random Hse. Value Publishing.

Badeau, Adam. Conspiracy. 2000. 252p. E-Book 9.95 (*0-594-05608-X*) 1873 Pr.

Barr, Emily. Cuba. 2004. 13.00 (*0-452-28503-8*, Plume) Dutton/Plume.

Bernardo, Jose Raul. Las Sabias Mujeres de la Habana. 2002. (SPA.). 384p. pap. 13.95 (*0-06-093616-9*, Rayo) HarperTrade.

—The Secret of the Bulls: A Novel. 1996. 336p. 22.00 o.p. (*0-684-81817-5*, Simon & Schuster) Simon & Schuster.

—Silent Wing. unabr. ed. 1999. audio 44.95 (*0-7861-1554-8*, 2384) Blackstone Audio Bks., Inc.

—Silent Wing. 1998. 240p. (YA). 23.00 (*0-684-84389-7*, Simon & Schuster) Simon & Schuster.

—Silent Wing. l.t. ed. 1999. (Basic Ser.). 391p. 27.95 (*0-7862-1757-X*) Thorndike Pr.

—The Wise Women of Havana. 2002. 336p. 24.95 (*0-06-621123-9*, Rayo) HarperTrade.

Blackthorn, John, pseud. I, Che Guevara: A Novel. 2000. 352p. 24.00 (*0-688-16760-8*, Morrow, William & Co.) Morrow/Avon.

Brock, Darryl. Havana Heat. 2000. 260p. 24.95 (*1-892129-23-X*) Total Sports Publishing.

Burton, Orville Vernon & Burton, Georganne B., eds. The Free Flag of Cuba: The Lost Novel of Lucy Halcombe Pickens. 2002. (Library of Southern Civilization). (Illus.). 240p. text 59.95 (*0-8071-2831-7*); pap. text 24.95 (*0-8071-2834-1*) Louisiana State Univ. Pr.

Carpentier, Alejo. The Chase. 2001. 136p. reprint ed. pap. 14.95 (*0-8166-3809-8*) Univ. of Minnesota Pr.

Casemore, Robert F. Splendid Morning. l.t. ed. 1999. (Romance Ser.). 439p. 26.95 (*0-7838-8474-5*) Thorndike Pr.

Chaviano, Daína. El Hombre, la Hembra y el Hambre. 1997. (Autores Espanoles E Iberoamericanos Ser.).Tr. of Man, Woman, Hunger. (SPA., Illus.). 312p. 24.95 (*84-08-02530-9*) GeoPlaneta, Editorial, S. A. ESP. *Dist:* Lectorum Pubns., Inc.

Coltrane, James. Good Day to Die: A Novel. 1999. 155p. text 21.95 (*0-393-04766-0*) Norton, W. W. & Co., Inc.

—A Good Day to Die: A Novel of Cuba after Castro. 2000. 160p. pap. 11.00 (*0-385-49898-5*, Knopf Bks. for Young Readers) Random Hse. Children's Bks.

Coonts, Stephen. Cuba. l.t. ed. 1999. 25.95 (*1-56895-801-3*, Wheeler Publishing, Inc.) Gale Group.

—Cuba. 2000. 480p. mass mkt. 7.99 (*0-312-97139-7*, St. Martin's Paperbacks); 2nd ed. 1999. 384p. 24.95 (*0-312-20521-X*) St. Martin's Pr.

Coplin, Keith. Croftons Fire. 2004. 288p. 21.95 (*0-399-15112-5*, G. P. Putnam's Sons) Penguin Putnam Bks. for Young Readers.

Correa, Arnaldo. Cold Havana Ground. Moore, Marjorie, tr. from SPA. 2003. Orig. Title: Spanish. 320p. 22.95 (*1-888451-52-1*) Akashic Bks.

—Spy's Fate. 2002. 302p. 24.95 (*1-888451-28-9*) Akashic Bks.

Doval, Teresa de la Caridad. A Girl Like Che Guevara: A Novel. 2004. (*1-56947-358-7*) Soho Pr., Inc.

Engle, Margarita M. Singing to Cuba. 1993. (Illus.). 164p. (C). pap. 9.50 o.p. (*1-55885-070-8*) Arte Publico Pr.

Ephron, Amy. White Rose: Una Rosa Blanca. 2000. 288p. pap. 12.00 (*0-345-44110-9*, Ballantine Bks.) Ballantine Bks.

—White Rose: Una Rosa Blanca. 1999. 259p. 23.00 (*0-688-16314-9*, Morrow, William & Co.) Morrow/Avon.

Estevez, Abilio. Distant Palaces: A Novel. 2004. 288p. 25.95 (*1-55970-700-3*) Arcade Publishing, Inc.

—Thine Is the Kingdom. Frye, David, tr. from SPA. 336p. 2000. pap. 13.95 (*1-55970-504-3*); 1999. 25.95 (*1-55970-451-9*) Arcade Publishing, Inc.

Firmat, Gustavo Perez. Anything but Love. 2000. 143p. pap. 12.95 (*1-55885-295-6*) Arte Publico Pr.

French, Roy. The Raven Re-Born. 2000. 300p. pap. o.p. (*1-55212-511-4*) Trafford Publishing.

Garcia-Aguilera, Carolina. Havana Heat: A Lupe Solano Mystery. 2001. 352p. mass mkt. 6.99 (*0-380-80740-8*, Avon Bks.) Morrow/Avon.

Garcia, Cristina. The Aguero Sisters. 1998. 103.60 o.s.i (*0-345-91389-2*); 103.60 o.s.i (*0-345-91390-6*); 336p. pap. 14.00 (*0-345-40651-6*, Ballantine Bks.) Ballantine Bks.

—Dreaming in Cuban. 1999. pap. (*0-345-91367-1*, Ballantine Bks.); 1993. (SPA.). 256p. pap. 14.00 (*0-345-38143-2*, One World/Ballantine) Ballantine Bks.

—Dreaming in Cuban. 1992. 20.00 o.s.i (*0-679-40883-5*) Knopf, Alfred A. Inc.

—Las Hermanas Aguero: Una Novela. 1997. (SPA.). 320p. pap. 13.95 (*0-679-78145-5*, RH9081, Vintage) Knopf Publishing Group.

—Monkey Hunting: A Novel. 2003. (Illus.). 272p. 23.00 (*0-375-41056-2*) Knopf, Alfred A. Inc.

—Sonar en Cubano. 1994. (SPA.). 336p. pap. 12.95 (*0-345-39139-X*, RH9018, Ballantine Bks.) Ballantine Bks.

Gonzalez-Cruz, Luis F. Olorun's Rainbow: Anatomy of a Cuban Dreamer. 2001. 188p. 24.95 (*0-7596-3402-5*) 1stBooks Library.

Gonzalez, Edward. Ernesto's Ghost. 2002. 360p. 29.95 (*0-7658-0135-3*) Transaction Pubs.

Gonzalez, Luis. Spirits of the Revolution, 3 Vols., Vol. 1. 1998. 892p. 26.00 (*0-9663058-0-9*) Colonnade Bks.

Gutierrez, Pedro Juan. Dirty Havana Trilogy. Wimmer, Natasha, tr. from SPA. 2001. 392p. 25.00 o.p. (*0-374-14016-2*) Farrar, Straus & Giroux.

—Dirty Havana Trilogy: A Novel in Stories. Wimmer, Natasha, tr. from SPA. 2002. 400p. pap. 13.95 (*0-06-000689-7*, Ecco) HarperTrade.

Hackman, Gene & Lenihan, Daniel F. Wake of the Perdido Star. abr. ed. 1999. audio 24.95 o.p. (*1-56740-888-5*, 2014, Nova Audio Bks.); audio 73.25 (*1-56740-711-0*, 2015, Unabridged Library Editions); audio 35.95 (*1-56740-493-6*, 2011, Brilliance Audio Unabridged) Brilliance Audio.

—Wake of the Perdido Star. l.t. ed. 1999. (Large Print Book Ser.). 27.95 (*1-56895-806-4*, Wheeler Publishing, Inc.) Gale Group.

—Wake of the Perdido Star. l.t. ed. 2001. (Magna Large Print Ser.). 496p. (*0-7505-1680-1*) Magna Large Print Bks. GBR. *Dist:* Ulverscroft Large Print Canada, Ltd.

—Wake of the Perdido Star: A Novel of Shipwrecks, Pirates & the Sea. 2004. 400p. (J). 24.95 (*1-55704-398-1*) Newmarket Pr.

Hackman, Gene, et al. Wake of the Perdido Star. 2000. 432p. mass mkt. 6.99 o.s.i (*0-451-20211-2*, Signet Bks.) NAL.

Heisler-Samuels, Betty. The Last Minyan in Havana. 2000. (Illus.). 192p. pap. 14.95 (*0-9703078-0-2*) Chutzpah Publishing.

Hemingway, Ernest. Elements of Literature: The Old Man & the Sea. 1989. pap. text, stu. ed. 15.33 (*0-03-023452-2*) Holt, Rinehart & Winston.

—Islands in the Stream. 1984. mass mkt. 4.50 o.s.i (*0-553-25007-8*) Bantam Bks.

—Islands in the Stream. unabr. collector's ed. 1992. audio 72.00 (*0-7366-2179-2*, 2976) Books on Tape, Inc.

—Islands in the Stream. (Hudson River Editions Ser.). 466p. 1980. 50.00 (*0-684-16499-X*); 1976. pap. 16.00 (*0-684-14642-8*) Gale Group. (Macmillan Reference USA).

—Islands in the Stream. 2003. E-Book 9.99 (*0-7432-3726-9*); 2003. 448p. 27.50 (*0-7432-5342-6*); 1997. 448p. pap. 14.00 (*0-684-83787-0*) Simon & Schuster. (Scribner).

—The Old Man & the Sea. unabr. ed. audio 17.95 Blackstone Audio Bks., Inc.

—The Old Man & the Sea. Bloom, Harold, ed. 1999. (Modern Critical Interpretations Ser.). vii, 205p. (YA). 34.95 (*0-7910-4778-4*) Chelsea Hse. Pubs.

—The Old Man & the Sea. 128p. 1984. (Illus.). 18.00 (*0-684-18227-0*); 1979. (Illus.). pap. 3.50 o.s.i (*0-684-16326-8*); 1977. 30.00 (*0-684-15363-7*); 1977. text 6.95 o.s.i (*0-684-51528-8*); 1950. 14.00 (*0-684-10245-5*); 1950. pap. 6.95 o.s.i (*0-684-71805-7*) Gale Group. (Macmillan Reference USA).

—The Old Man & the Sea. 1990. 10.92 (*0-02-635123-4*) Glencoe/McGraw-Hill.

—The Old Man & the Sea. unabr. ed. (Annual Review of the Institute for Information Studies). 1998. audio 18.00 (*0-89845-952-4*, CPN 2084, Caedmon); 1992. audio 17.00 (*1-55994-636-9*, DCN 2084, HarperAudio) HarperTrade.

—The Old Man & the Sea. o.p. (*0-582-78224-4*) Moonbeam Pubns., Inc.

—The Old Man & the Sea. l.t. ed. reprint ed. 10.00 (*0-89064-252-4*) National Assn. for Visually Handicapped.

—The Old Man & the Sea. 1952. text, stu. ed. 25.20 o.p. (*0-02-352990-3*, Macmillan College) Prentice Hall PTR.

—The Old Man & the Sea. unabr. ed. 1999. audio 18.00 (*0-7887-0520-2*, 94715E7); audio compact disk 27.00 (*0-7887-3412-1*, C1018E7) Recorded Bks., LLC.

—The Old Man & the Sea. 2003. E-Book 9.99 (*0-7432-3730-7*); 1996. (Illus.). 96p. 20.00 (*0-684-83049-3*); 1995. 128p. pap. 10.00 (*0-684-80122-1*) Simon & Schuster. (Scribner).

—The Old Man & the Sea. l.t. ed. 1994. 113p. lib. bdg. 21.95 (*0-8161-5970-X*) Thorndike Pr.

—The Old Man & the Sea. 1995. 16.05 (*0-606-00201-4*) Turtleback Bks.

—The Old Man & the Sea & The Snows of Kilimanjaro & Other Stories. unabr. collector's ed. 1999. (J). audio 12.95 (*0-7366-4524-1*, 2585) Books on Tape, Inc.

Hemingway, Ernest & Prentice-Hall Staff. The Old Man & the Sea. 2nd ed. text, stu. ed. (*0-13-717273-7*) Prentice Hall (Schl. Div.).

Herrera, Andrea. The Pearl of the Antilles. 2000. (Illus.). 240p. 26.00 (*0-927534-95-9*) Bilingual Pr./Editorial Bilingue.

Herrera, Andrea O'Reilly. The Pearl of the Antilles. 2001. (Illus.). 354p. pap. 16.00 (*0-927534-96-7*) Bilingual Pr./Editorial Bilingue.

Hijuelos, Oscar. A Simple Habana Melody: From When the World Was Good. l.t. ed. 2003. lib. bdg. 29.95 (*1-58547-298-0*, Platinum) Ctr. Point Large Print.

Hijuelos, Oscar. Una Sencilla Melodia Habanera. 2003. (SPA.). 368p. pap. 13.95 (*0-06-054353-1*, Rayo) HarperTrade.

—A Simple Habana Melody: From When the World Was Good. 2002. 352p. 24.95 (*0-06-017569-9*) HarperCollins Pubs.

—A Simple Habana Melody: From When the World Was Good. 2003. 368p. pap. 13.95 (*0-06-092869-7*, Perennial) HarperTrade.

Lamar, Mario. Escape from Castro. 1999. 237p. pap. 14.00 (*1-883911-20-6*) Brandylane Pubs., Inc.

Lamazares, Ivonne. The Sugar Island. 2000. 224p. tchr. ed. 23.00 (*0-395-86040-7*); 2001. 206p. reprint ed. pap. 12.00 (*0-618-15454-X*) Houghton Mifflin Co. Trade & Reference Div. (Mariner Bks.).

Latour, Jose. The Havana World Series. 2004. 272p. 23.00 (*0-8021-1754-6*, Grove Pr.) Grove/Atlantic, Inc.

—Outcast. 1999. 217p. pap. 13.95 o.p. (*1-888451-07-6*, AKB04) Akashic Bks.

—Outcast. 2001. 304p. 24.00 (*0-06-018488-4*, Morrow, William & Co.) Morrow/Avon.

Lemon, Brendan. Last Night. 2002. 288p. 24.95 o.p. (*1-55583-645-3*) Alyson Pubns.

—Last Night: A Novel. 2003. 248p. pap. 13.95 (*1-55583-801-4*, Alyson Bks.) Alyson Pubns.

Lynch, Daniel. Yellow: A Novel. 1992. 211p. 19.95 o.s.i (*0-8027-1226-6*) Walker & Co.

Mann, Mary Peabody. Juanita: A Romance of Real Life in Cuba Fifty Years Ago. Ard, Patricia M., ed. & intro. by. 2000. (New World Studies). (Illus.). xlvii, 222p. 55.00 (*0-8139-1955-X*); pap. 18.50 (*0-8139-1956-8*) Univ. Pr. of Virginia.

Marias, Javier. Dark Back of Time: Novel. Allen, Esther, tr. from SPA. 2001. (Illus.). 336p. 27.95 (*0-8112-1466-4*) New Directions Publishing Corp.

Matera, Lia. Havana Twist. 2002. 272p. pap. 17.95 (*0-7432-4252-1*, Simon & Schuster) Simon & Schuster.

—Havana Twist: A Willa Jansson Mystery. (Willa Jansson Mystery Ser.). 1999. 352p. pap. 6.99 o.s.i (*0-671-00421-2*, Pocket); 1998. 256p. 22.00 (*0-684-83470-7*, Simon & Schuster) Simon & Schuster.

McKinney, Mel. Where There's Smoke. 1999. 224p. 22.95 (*0-312-20623-2*) St. Martin's Pr.

Medina, Pablo. The Return of Felix Nogara. 2002. 272p. pap. 15.00 (*0-89255-279-4*); 2000. 278p. reprint ed. 25.95 (*0-89255-251-4*) Persea Bks., Inc.

Menendez, Ana. In Cuba I Was a German Shepherd. 2001. 229p. 23.00 o.p. (*0-8021-1688-4*); 2002. 240p. reprint ed. pap. 12.00 (*0-8021-3887-X*) Grove/Atlantic, Inc. (Grove Pr.).

—Loving Che. 2003. 240p. 22.00 (*0-87113-908-1*) Grove/Atlantic, Inc.

Mestre, Ernesto. The Lazarus Rumba. 512p. 2000. pap. 15.00 (*0-312-26352-X*); 1999. (Illus.). 27.50 o.p. (*0-312-19907-4*) Picador.

Montero, Mayra. The Messenger: A Novel. Grossman, Edith, tr. from SPA. 1999. 224p. o.p. (*0-06-019223-2*, HarperFlamingo) HarperCollins Pubs. Canada, Ltd.

—The Messenger: A Novel. Grossman, Edith, tr. 2000. 228p. pap. 13.00 (*0-06-092961-8*, Perennial) HarperTrade.

Morell, Luis Grave de Peralta. La Mafia de la Habana: Nuestra Cosa Nostra. 2001. 128p. pap. 14.95 (*0-7596-6199-5*) 1stBooks Library.

Morris, Robert G. Diplomatic Relations. 2002. 256p. 15.95 (*0-87714-259-9*); 2000. E-Book 6.95 (*0-87714-572-5*) Denlingers Pubs., Ltd.

Morse, C. Scott. Ancient Joe: El Bizarron. 2002. (Illus.). 120p. pap. 12.95 (*1-56971-795-8*) Dark Horse Comics.

Munoz, Elias M. Brand New Memory. 1998. 224p. pap. 12.95 (*1-55885-227-1*) Arte Publico Pr.

Nieto, Benigno S. Reina de la Vida. 2001. (Coleccion Caniqui Ser.). 334p. pap. 19.95 (*0-89729-940-X*, 940-X) Ediciones Universal.

Novas, Himilce. Mangos, Bananas & Coconuts: A Cuban Love Story. 1996. 168p. 9.95 (*1-55885-092-9*) Arte Publico Pr.

Ortiz, Oscar F. El Primer - Detective Del Exilio Cubano. 2001. (SPA.). 112p. pap. 12.95 (*1-928612-06-7*, OSOR Productions) Ortiz, Oscar F.

Pearson, Ryne Douglas. Capitol Punishment. 1996. 352p. mass mkt. 5.99 (*0-380-72228-3*, Avon Bks.); 1995. 320p. 22.00 o.p. (*0-688-12983-8*, Morrow, William & Co.) Morrow/Avon.

Ponte, Antonio Jose. In the Cold of the Malecon: And Other Stories. Fravizen, Cola & Cluster, Dick, trs. from SPA. 2000. 127p. pap. 10.95 (*0-87286-374-3*) City Lights Bks.

—Tales from the Cuban Empire. Franzen, Cola, tr. from SPA. 2002. 112p. (Orig.). pap. 11.95 (*0-87286-407-3*) City Lights Bks.

Quinnell, A. J. Siege of Silence. 1986. 16.95 o.p. (*0-525-24429-8*, Dutton) Dutton/Plume.

Raymond, Beverly Mays. Kennedy's Daughter - Castro's Bastard. 2001. 131p. pap. 20.99 (*0-7388-6693-8*) Xlibris Corp.

Sarduy, Severo. From Cuba with a Song. Levine, Suzanne J., tr. from SPA. 1994. (Sun & Moon Classics Ser.: No. 52). 104p. (Orig.). pap. 10.95 o.p. (*1-55713-158-9*) Sun & Moon Pr.

—Maitreya. 1987. 100p. pap. 9.50 (*0-910061-31-9*, 1205) Ediciones del Norte.

Shawver, Brian. Cuban Prospect: A Novel. 2003. 286p. 24.95 (*1-58567-344-7*) Overlook Pr., The.

Simmons, Dan. The Crook Factory. 2000. 592p. mass mkt. 6.99 (*0-380-78917-5*) HarperCollins Pubs.

—The Crook Factory. 1999. 448p. 24.00 (*0-380-97368-5*, Avon Bks.) Morrow/Avon.

Smith, Martin Cruz. Havana Bay. 2001. (Illus.). 352p. mass mkt. 7.99 (*0-345-39045-8*, Ballantine Bks.) Ballantine Bks.

—Havana Bay. l.t. ed. pap. 25.95 o.p. (*0-7838-8547-4*, Macmillan Reference USA) Gale Group.

—Havana Bay. 1999. 416p. 24.95 o.s.i (*0-679-42662-0*) Random Hse., Inc.

Suarez, Virgil. Latin Jazz. 2002. (Voices of the South Ser.). 304p. pap. 16.95 (*0-8071-2790-6*) Louisiana State Univ. Pr.

—Latin Jazz. 1989. 290p. 18.95 o.p. (*0-688-08475-3*, Morrow, William & Co.) Morrow/Avon.

—Latin Jazz. 1990. pap. 9.95 o.p. (*0-671-70535-0*, Fireside) Simon & Schuster.

Thane, Elswyth. Ever After. 1976. reprint ed. lib. bdg. 26.95 (*0-88411-958-0*) Amereon, Ltd.

—Ever After. 1983. mass mkt. 3.50 o.s.i (*0-553-22933-8*) Bantam Bks.

—Ever After. 1993. reprint ed. lib. bdg. 31.95 (*1-56849-230-8*) Buccaneer Bks., Inc.

—Ever After. 1981. (Reader's Request Ser.). lib. bdg. 17.95 o.p. (*0-8161-3165-1*, Macmillan Reference USA) Gale Group.

Valdés, Zoé. I Gave You All I Had. 2000. 256p. pap. 13.95 (*1-55970-541-8*) Arcade Publishing, Inc.

—I Gave You All I Had. Benabid, Nadia, tr. from SPA. 1999. 238p. 24.95 (*1-55970-477-2*) Arcade Publishing, Inc.

Varela, Maria Elena Cruz. Dios En Las Carceles De Cuba: Novela Testimonio. 2001. (Coleccion Caniqui Ser.). (SPA., Illus.). 240p. 19.95 (*0-89729-936-1*, 936-1) Ediciones Universal.

Weber, Joe. Shadow Flight. 1990. 368p. 19.95 o.p. (*0-89141-342-1*, Presidio Pr.) Ballantine Bks.

—Shadow Flight. 1991. mass mkt. 5.99 o.s.i (*0-515-10660-7*, Jove) Berkley Publishing Group.

Wendel, Tim. Castro's Curveball. 2000. 304p. pap. 12.95 (*0-345-43474-9*) Ballantine Bks.

—Castro's Curveball. 1999. audio 27.95 (*0-7861-1700-1*); 2000. audio compact disk 56.00 (*0-7861-9938-5*, z2383); 1999. audio 44.95 (*0-7861-1553-X*, 2383) Blackstone Audio Bks., Inc.

White, Randy Wayne. North of Havana. 1998. 272p. mass mkt. 6.99 (*0-425-16294-X*, Prime Crime) Berkley Publishing Group.

—North of Havana. 1997. 256p. 22.95 o.p. (*0-399-14242-8*, G. P. Putnam's Sons) Penguin Group (USA) Inc.

### CUTLER'S COVE (IMAGINARY PLACE)—FICTION

Andrews, V. C. Darkest Hour. l.t. ed. 471p. 1994. lib. bdg. 18.95 (*0-8161-5876-2*); 1993. lib. bdg. 23.95 (*0-8161-5875-4*) Gale Group. (Macmillan Reference USA).

—Darkest Hour, Vol. 4. Marrow, Linda, ed. 1993. 400p. 22.00 (*0-671-75933-7*, Atria); mass mkt. 7.99 (*0-671-75932-9*, Pocket) Simon & Schuster.

—Darkest Hour. 1993. 14.04 (*0-606-05225-9*) Turtleback Bks.

—Dawn. unabr. ed. 1991. (Cutler Ser.). audio 64.00 (*0-7366-1944-5*, 2765) Books on Tape, Inc.

—Dawn. l.t. ed. 1991. (General Ser.). 472p. pap. 17.95 (*0-8161-5186-5*); lib. bdg. 20.95 (*0-8161-5184-9*) Gale Group. (Macmillan Reference USA).

—Dawn. 2003. audio 76.95 (*0-7531-1772-X*); audio compact disk 89.95 (*0-7531-2231-6*) ISIS Audio Bks. GBR. *Dist:* Ulverscroft Large Print Bks., Ltd.

—Dawn. 1990. 19.95 (*0-671-67067-0*, Atria) Simon & Schuster.

—Dawn. Marrow, Linda, ed. 1990. (Cutler Ser.). 416p. mass mkt. 7.99 (*0-671-67068-9*, Pocket) Simon & Schuster.

—Dawn. 1990. 14.04 (*0-606-04649-6*) Turtleback Bks.

—Midnight Whispers. unabr. ed. 1993. audio 72.00 (*0-7366-2532-1*, 3284) Books on Tape, Inc.

—Midnight Whispers. l.t. ed. 1993. (G. K. Hall Large Print Book Ser.). 515p. 19.95 o.p. (*0-8161-5656-5*); lib. bdg. 23.95 (*0-8161-5655-7*) Gale Group. (Macmillan Reference USA).

—Midnight Whispers. Marrow, Linda, ed. 1992. 448p. (Midnight Whispers Ser.: Vol. 5). mass mkt. 7.99 (*0-671-69516-9*, Pocket);Vol. 5. 22.00 (*0-671-69517-7*, Atria) Simon & Schuster.

—Midnight Whispers. 1992. 14.04 (*0-606-02201-5*) Turtleback Bks.

—Secrets of the Morning. unabr. ed. 1993. (Cutler Ser.). audio 64.00 (*0-7366-2356-6*, 3131) Books on Tape, Inc.

—Secrets of the Morning. l.t. ed. 1992. (General Ser.). 487p. pap. 17.95 (*0-8161-5386-8*); lib. bdg. 20.95 (*0-8161-5385-X*) Gale Group. (Macmillan Reference USA).

—Secrets of the Morning. unabr. ed. 2003. audio 84.95 (*0-7531-1773-8*) ISIS Audio Bks. GBR. *Dist:* Ulverscroft Large Print Bks., Ltd.

—Secrets of the Morning. Marrow, Linda, ed. 1991. (Cutler Ser.). 416p. mass mkt. 7.99 (*0-671-69512-6*, Pocket);Vol. 2. 384p. 21.95 (*0-671-69513-4*, Atria) Simon & Schuster.

—Secrets of the Morning. 1991. 14.04 (*0-606-05012-4*) Turtleback Bks.

—Twilight's Child. unabr. ed. 1993. (Dawn Ser.: Vol. 3). audio 72.00 (*0-7366-2406-6*, 3175) Books on Tape, Inc.

—Twilight's Child. l.t. ed. 1993. (General Ser.). 555p. pap. 17.95 (*0-8161-5525-9*); lib. bdg. 20.95 (*0-8161-5524-0*) Gale Group. (Macmillan Reference USA).

—Twilight's Child. Marrow, Linda, ed. 1992. 416p. (Twilight's Child Ser.: Vol. 3). mass mkt. 7.99 (*0-671-69514-2*, Pocket);Vol. 3. 22.00 o.p. (*0-671-69515-0*, Atria) Simon & Schuster.

—Twilight's Child. 1992. 14.04 (*0-606-00810-1*) Turtleback Bks.

### CYPRUS—FICTION

Beaton, M. C., pseud. Agatha Raisin & the Terrible Tourist. l.t. ed. 1998. pap. 22.95 o.p. (*1-56895-574-X*, Wheeler Publishing, Inc.) Gale Group.

—Agatha Raisin & the Terrible Tourist. (Agatha Raisin Mysteries Ser.). 1997. 160p. 20.95 o.p. (*0-312-16761-X*, Saint Martin's Minotaur); 1958. E-Book 5.99 o.s.i (*0-312-20707-7*); 1998. 208p. reprint ed. mass mkt. 6.50 (*0-312-96566-4*, St. Martin's Paperbacks) St. Martin's Pr.

Cory, Desmond. The Mask of Zeus. 1993. 256p. 19.95 o.p. (*0-312-09873-1*, Saint Martin's Minotaur) St. Martin's Pr.

MacLeod, Robert. A Property in Cyprus. l.t. ed. 1978. (Ulverscroft Large Print Ser.). 29.99 o.p. (*0-7089-0092-5*, Ulverscroft) Thorpe, F. A. Pubs. GBR. *Dist:* Ulverscroft Large Print Bks., Ltd., Ulverscroft Large Print Canada, Ltd.

Masters, Alexis. The Giuliana Legacy: A Novel. 2000. ix, 462p. pap. 14.95 (*1-55874-785-0*) Health Communications, Inc.

### CYTEEN (IMAGINARY PLACE)—FICTION

Cherryh, C. J. Cyteen. 1988. 18.45 o.s.i (*0-446-51428-4*); 1995. 696p. reprint ed. pap. 14.99 (*0-446-67127-4*) Warner Bks., Inc.

—Cyteen Pt. 1: The Betrayal. 1989. 368p. mass mkt. 5.50 (*0-445-20452-4*, Aspect) Warner Bks., Inc.

—Cyteen Pt. 2: The Rebirth. 1989. 256p. mass mkt. 4.99 o.s.i (*0-445-20454-0*) Warner Bks., Inc.

—Cyteen Pt. 3: The Vindication. 1989. 320p. mass mkt. 5.50 o.s.i (*0-445-20430-3*) Warner Bks., Inc.

### CZECHOSLOVAKIA—FICTION

Alcock, Deborah. Crushed yet Conquering: A Story of Constance & Bohemia. 2002. (Reformation Trail Ser.). (Illus.). 430p. (*1-894666-01-1*) Inheritance Pubns.

Goldstein, Lisa. The Alchemist's Door. 2003. 288p. pap. 14.95 (*0-7653-0151-2*); 2002. 256p. 23.95 (*0-7653-0150-4*) Doherty, Tom Assocs., LLC. (Tor Bks.).

Hrabal, Bohumil. Dancing Lessons for the Advanced in Age: A Novel. Heim, Michael H., tr. from CZE. 1995. Tr. of Tanecni Hodiny Pro Starsi a Pokrocile. 128p. 14.00 o.p. (*0-15-123810-3*); 117p. pap. o.p. (*0-15-600232-9*) Harcourt Trade Pubs. (Harvest Bks.).

Kaplicky, Vaclav. Witch Hammer. Newton, John, tr. from CZE. 1990. 384p. 17.95 o.p. (*0-943173-59-0*) Rinehart, Roberts Pubs.

Klima, Ivan. My First Loves. Osers, Ewald, tr. from CZE. 1988. Tr. of Moje Prvni Lasky. 176p. 14.95 o.p. (*0-06-015866-2*) HarperTrade.

—My First Loves. Osers, Ewald, tr. from CZE. 1989. Tr. of Moje Prvni Lasky. pap. 9.95 (*0-393-30601-1*) Norton, W. W. & Co., Inc.

—The Ultimate Intimacy. Brain, A. G., tr. from CZE. Tr. of Posledni Stupen Duvernosti. 400p. 1998. 25.00 o.p. (*0-8021-1625-6*); 1999. reprint ed. pap. 14.00 (*0-8021-3601-X*) Grove/Atlantic, Inc. (Grove Pr.).

Kliment, Alexandr. Living Parallel. Wechsler, Robert, tr. from CZE. 2002. 238p. 21.00 (*0-945774-51-6*) Catbird Pr.

Kundera, Milan. The Farewell Party. Kussi, Peter, tr. 1977. pap. 6.95 o.p. (*0-14-004539-2*) Penguin Group (USA) Inc.

—The Farewell Party. Kussi, Peter, tr. 1976. 7.95 o.p. (*0-394-49660-4*, Knopf Bks. for Young Readers) Random Hse. Children's Bks.

—The Farewell Party. rev. ed. 1987. 224p. pap. 11.95 o.p. (*0-14-009694-9*, Penguin Bks.) Viking Penguin.

Paral, Vladimir. Lovers & Murderers. Cravens, Craig, tr. from CZE. 2002. 416p. 27.00 (*0-945774-52-4*) Catbird Pr.

Paton Walsh, Jill. A Desert in Bohemia. 2001. 288p. pap. (*0-385-60121-2*) Doubleday Publishing.

—A Desert in Bohemia. 2001. 336p. pap. 13.00 (*0-452-28268-3*) Dutton/Plume.

—A Desert in Bohemia. l.t. ed. 2001. (G. K. Hall Core Ser.). 407p. 30.95 (*0-7838-9430-9*, Macmillan Reference USA) Gale Group.

—A Desert in Bohemia. 2000. 332p. 23.95 (*0-312-26263-9*) St. Martin's Pr.

—A Desert in Bohemia. 2001. 19.05 (*0-606-22312-6*) Turtleback Bks.

Skvorecky, Josef. The Bass Saxophone. Polackvoa-Henley, Kaca, tr. 1979. 8.95 o.s.i (*0-394-50267-1*, Knopf Bks. for Young Readers) Random Hse. Children's Bks.

—The Bass Saxophone. 1985. mass mkt. 5.95 (*0-671-55681-9*, Washington Square Pr.) Simon & Schuster.

—Bass Saxophone. 1999. 256p. pap. 12.00 (*0-88001-370-2*, Ecco) HarperTrade.

—The Republic of Whores. (Illus.). 1996. pap. 15.00 o.p. (*0-88001-428-8*); 1994. 248p. 21.00 o.p. (*0-88001-371-0*) HarperCollins Pubs.

Stifter, Adalbert. Witiko. Frye, Wendell, tr. from GER. 1999. 596p. (C). pap. text 34.95 (*0-8204-4624-6*) Lang, Peter Publishing, Inc.

Tielsch, Ilse & Scrase, David. The Ancestral Pyramid. 2001. (Studies in Austrian Literature, Culture, & Thought). 303p. pap. 28.50 (*1-57241-090-6*) Ariadne Pr.

# D

## DALLAS (TEX.)—FICTION

Adams, Marcia. Shadow Patterns: A Novel of Dallas & Padre Island. 1997. pap. 18.95 (*1-57860-022-7*) Emmis Bks.

Ames, Jeffrey. Lethal City. 2003. 384p. mass mkt. 6.99 (*0-451-20798-X*, Signet Bks.) NAL.

Baxter, Mary Lynn. His Touch. 2003. 384p. mass mkt. (*1-55166-686-3*, Mira Bks.) Harlequin Enterprises, Ltd.

Ellroy, James. The Cold Six Thousand. 2002. 688p. pap. 15.95 (*0-375-72740-X*) Knopf, Alfred A. Inc.

Englade, Ken. To Hatred Turned. 1994. mass mkt. 4.99 o.p. (*0-312-95132-9*, St. Martin's Paperbacks) St. Martin's Pr.

—To Hatred Turned: A True Story of Love & Death in Texas. 1993. (Illus.). 368p. 21.95 o.p. (*0-312-09924-X*) St. Martin's Pr.

Gray, A. W. Bino. 1988. 208p. 16.95 o.p. (*0-525-24590-1*, Dutton) Dutton/Plume.

—Bino. 1989. mass mkt. 3.95 o.p. (*0-451-40129-8*, Onyx) NAL.

—Bino's Blues. 1995. 256p. 20.00 (*0-671-88186-8*, Simon & Schuster) Simon & Schuster.

—In Defense of Judges. 1990. 18.95 o.p. (*0-525-24875-7*, Dutton) Dutton/Plume.

—In Defense of Judges. 1991. 368p. mass mkt. 5.99 o.s.i (*0-451-40271-5*, Onyx) NAL.

—Killings. 1993. 304p. 20.00 o.p. (*0-525-93625-4*, Dutton) Dutton/Plume.

—Killings. 1994. 384p. mass mkt. 4.99 o.p. (*0-451-40525-0*, Onyx) NAL.

—The Man Offside. 1991. 240p. 18.95 o.p. (*0-525-93310-7*) Dutton/Plume.

—The Man Offside. 1992. 336p. mass mkt. 4.99 o.s.i (*0-451-40318-5*, Onyx) NAL.

Lackey, Mercedes. Burning Water. 1992. 314p. pap. text 6.99 (*0-8125-2485-3*, Tor Bks.) Doherty, Tom Assocs., LLC.

—Children of the Night. 1992. 313p. pap. text 6.99 (*0-8125-2272-9*); 1990. mass mkt. 3.95 o.s.i (*0-8125-2112-9*) Doherty, Tom Assocs., LLC. (Tor Bks.).

—Jinx High. 1991. 314p. (Orig.). pap. text 4.99 o.s.i (*0-8125-2114-5*, Tor Bks.) Doherty, Tom Assocs., LLC.

McBride, Susan. Blue Blood. 2004. 352p. mass mkt. 6.50 (*0-06-056389-3*, Avon Bks.) Morrow/Avon.

McGlothin, Victor. What's a Woman to Do? 2003. 352p. 19.95 (*0-312-28687-2*) St. Martin's Pr.

Miller, Rex. Stone Shadow. 1989. mass mkt. 3.95 o.p. (*0-451-40164-6*, 036, Onyx) NAL.

—Stone Shadow. E-Book 6.99 (*0-7592-0797-6*); 2000. pap. 19.95 (*1-58586-164-2*); 2000. E-Book 6.99 (*1-58586-162-6*); 2000. E-Book 6.99 (*1-58586-163-4*); 2000. E-Book 6.99 (*1-58586-280-0*) ereads.com.

Myers, Helen R. More Than You Know. 1999. (Mira Bks.). 400p. mass mkt. (*1-55166-504-2*, Mira Bks.) Harlequin Enterprises, Ltd.

Peterson, Tracie. Controlling Interests. 1998. 256p. (YA). (gr. 10 up). pap. 8.99 o.p. (*0-7642-2064-0*) Bethany Hse. Pubs.

—Controlling Interests. l.t. ed. 1999. (Christian Mystery Ser.). 456p. 24.95 o.p. (*0-7862-1999-8*) Thorndike Pr.

Ray, Francis. I Know Who Holds Tomorrow. 2nd ed. 2002. 352p. pap. 13.95 (*0-312-30050-6*, CPB1181, Saint Martin's Griffin) St. Martin's Pr.

Reasoner, James. Hell's Half Acre. 1999. (Walker, Texas Ranger Ser.: Vol. 2). 224p. mass mkt. 5.99 o.s.i (*0-425-16972-3*) Berkley Publishing Group.

—Walker, Texas Ranger: The Novel. 1999. (Walker, Texas Ranger Ser.). 256p. (Orig.). mass mkt. 5.99 o.s.i (*0-425-16815-8*) Berkley Publishing Group.

Rose, Carol. Wild Woman. 2000. (Zebra Bouquet Ser.: Vol. 64). 256p. mass mkt. 4.99 o.s.i (*0-8217-6687-2*, Zebra Bks.) Kensington Publishing Corp.

Rosenberg, Nancy Taylor. Trial by Fire. unabr. ed. 1996. audio 64.00 (*0-7366-3433-9*, 4077) Books on Tape, Inc.

—Trial by Fire. 1996. 352p. 22.95 o.p. (*0-525-93767-6*) Dutton/Plume.

—Trial by Fire. l.t. ed. 1996. (Large Print Bks.). 27.95 (*1-56895-305-4*, Wheeler Publishing, Inc.) Gale Group.

—Trial by Fire. 1996. 448p. mass mkt. 7.99 (*0-451-18005-4*, Signet Bks.) NAL.

—Trial by Fire. unabr. ed. audio 78.00 (*0-7887-0521-0*, 94716E7) Recorded Bks., LLC.

—Trial by Fire. abr. ed. 1996. audio 16.95 o.s.i (*0-14-086200-5*, Penguin AudioBooks) Viking Penguin.

Ross, Carol. Wild Woman. 2001. (Five Star Romance Ser.). 212p. 26.95 (*0-7862-3474-1*, Five Star) Gale Group.

Sala, Sharon. Butterfly. l.t. ed. 2002. (Wheeler Softcover Ser.). 398p. pap. 23.95 (*1-58724-317-2*, Wheeler Publishing, Inc.) Gale Group.

—Butterfly. 384p. 2003. mass mkt. (*1-55166-968-4*); 2000. mass mkt. (*1-55166-616-2*, 1-66616-3) Harlequin Enterprises, Ltd. (Mira Bks.).

Swanson, Doug J. Big Town. 1995. 288p. mass mkt. 4.50 o.p. (*0-06-109213-4*, HarperTorch) Morrow/Avon.

—Big Town: A Novel of Suspense. 1994. 224p. 18.00 o.p. (*0-06-017749-7*) HarperTrade.

—Dreamboat. 1996. 256p. mass mkt. 4.99 o.p. (*0-06-109214-2*); 1995. 288p. 20.00 o.p. (*0-06-017748-9*) HarperCollins Pubs.

—Umbrella Man. 1999. (Jack Flippo Mysteries Ser.: Vol. 4). 273p. 23.95 o.p. (*0-399-14503-6*, G. P. Putnam's Sons) Penguin Group (USA) Inc.

—96 Tears. 1996. 208p. 22.50 o.p. (*0-06-017511-7*) HarperCollins Pubs.

Swindle, Howard. Doin' Dirty. 2000. 292p. 22.95 (*0-312-20389-6*, Saint Martin's Minotaur) St. Martin's Pr.

—Jitter Joint. unabr. ed. 2000. audio compact disk 69.00; 1999. audio 56.00 (*0-7887-3481-4*, 95875E7) Recorded Bks., LLC.

—Jitter Joint. E-Book 5.99 (*0-312-26457-7*); 2000. 272p. mass mkt. 5.99 (*0-312-97611-9*, St. Martin's Paperbacks); 1999. 256p. 21.95 (*0-312-20066-8*, Saint Martin's Minotaur) St. Martin's Pr.

Thompson, Vicki Lewis. Truly, Madly, Deeply. 2002. (Harlequin Blaze Ser.). mass mkt. (*0-373-79056-2*, Harlequin Bks.) Harlequin Enterprises, Ltd.

Willeford, Charles. Deliver Me from Dallas! 2001. 214p. 30.00 (*0-939767-38-4*) McMillan, Dennis Pubns.

## DAMAR (IMAGINARY PLACE)—FICTION

McKinley, Robin. The Blue Sword. 1987. 256p. mass mkt. 5.99 (*0-441-06880-4*) Ace Bks.

—The Blue Sword. 1986. 2.95 o.s.i (*0-425-10142-8*); 1985. 2.95 o.s.i (*0-425-08840-5*); 1984. 2.75 o.s.i (*0-425-07505-2*); 1983. 2.75 o.s.i (*0-425-06318-6*) Berkley Publishing Group.

—The Blue Sword. 2002. (Illus.). (J). 14.21 (*0-7587-0243-4*) Book Wholesalers, Inc.

—The Blue Sword. 1982. 288p. (J). (gr. 7 up). 16.99 (*0-688-00938-7*, Greenwillow Bks.) HarperCollins Children's Bk. Group.

—The Blue Sword. 2000. 288p. pap. 6.99 (*0-14-130975-X*, Puffin Bks.) Penguin Putnam Bks. for Young Readers.

—The Blue Sword. unabr. ed. (YA). (gr. 8). audio 69.00 (*1-55690-616-1*, 92309) Recorded Bks., LLC.

—The Blue Sword. 1950. (J). audio 34.66 (*0-676-30662-4*) SRA/McGraw-Hill.

—The Blue Sword. 2000. 12.04 (*0-606-20223-4*); 2000. 12.04 (*0-606-20349-4*); 1983. 11.09 o.p. (*0-606-01012-2*) Turtleback Bks.

—The Hero & the Crown. 240p. (gr. 7-12). 1998. pap. 12.00 (*0-441-00499-7*); 1987. (J). mass mkt. 5.99 (*0-441-32809-1*) Ace Bks.

—The Hero & the Crown. 1986. (J). 34.66 incl. audio (*0-676-31297-7*) Ballantine Bks.

—The Hero & the Crown. 2002. (Illus.). (J). 14.21 (*0-7587-0189-6*) Book Wholesalers, Inc.

—The Hero & the Crown. 1984. (Illus.). 256p. (J). (gr. 7 up). 16.99 (*0-688-02593-5*, Greenwillow Bks.) HarperCollins Children's Bk. Group.

—The Hero & the Crown. l.t. ed. 1988. (J). (gr. 3-7). reprint ed. lib. bdg. 16.95 o.s.i (*1-55736-078-2*, Cornerstone Bks.) Pages, Inc.

—The Hero & the Crown. 2000. (Illus.). 240p. (J). (gr. 5 up). pap. 6.99 (*0-14-130981-4*, Puffin Bks.) Penguin Putnam Bks. for Young Readers.

—The Hero & the Crown. 1986. (J). 11.09 (*0-606-03294-0*) Turtleback Bks.

## DARK TOWERS (IMAGINARY PLACE)—FICTION

King, Stephen. The Drawing of the Three. (Dark Tower Ser.: Bk. II). 1997. 416p. pap. 18.00 o.s.i (*0-452-27961-5*); 1989. (Illus.). 416p. pap. 16.95 o.s.i (*0-452-26214-3*); 2003. (Illus.). 432p. pap. 17.95 (*0-452-28470-8*) Dutton/Plume. (Plume).

—The Drawing of the Three. 1987. (Dark Tower Ser.: Bk. II). (Illus.). 399p. 35.00 o.p. (*0-937986-91-7*); pap. 100.00 o.p. (*0-937986-90-9*) Grant, Donald M. Pub., Inc.

—The Drawing of the Three. (Dark Tower Ser.: Bk. 2). 1990. 464p. mass mkt. 7.99 o.s.i (*0-451-16352-4*); 2003. 480p. mass mkt. 7.99 (*0-451-21085-9*) NAL. (Signet Bks.).

—The Drawing of the Three. rev. unabr. ed. 2003. (Dark Tower Ser.: Bk. II). audio compact disk 37.95 (*0-14-280038-4*) Penguin Group (USA) Inc.

—The Drawing of the Three. 2003. (Dark Tower Ser.: Bk. II). reprint ed. E-Book 7.99 (*0-7865-3750-7*) Penguin Putnam, Inc E-Books.

—The Drawing of the Three. abr. unabr. ed. 1989. (Dark Tower Ser.). audio 30.00 o.p. (*0-453-00643-4*, 25024-18082) Penguin/HighBridge.

—The Drawing of the Three. 1987. (Dark Tower Ser.: Bk. II). 14.04 (*0-606-00785-7*) Turtleback Bks.

—The Drawing of the Three. rev. ed. (Dark Tower Ser.: Bk. 2). 2003. (Illus.). 432p. 35.00 (*0-670-03255-7*); 1998. 8p. audio 35.95 (*0-14-086715-5*, Penguin AudioBooks) Viking Penguin.

—The Gunslinger. 1976. (Dark Tower Ser.: Bk. I). 21.95 (*0-8488-0780-4*) Amereon, Ltd.

—The Gunslinger. (Dark Tower Ser.: Bk. I). 224p. 1988. (Illus.). pap. 10.95 o.s.i (*0-452-26134-1*); Vol. 1. 1997. pap. 15.00 o.s.i (*0-452-27960-7*) Dutton/Plume. (Plume).

—The Gunslinger. 1982. (Dark Tower Ser.: Bk. I). (Illus.). 224p. 60.00 o.p. (*0-937986-51-8*); pap. 20.00 o.p. (*0-937986-50-X*) Grant, Donald M. Pub., Inc.

—The Gunslinger. 1989. (Dark Tower Ser.: Bk. I). (Illus.). 320p. reprint ed. mass mkt. 7.99 o.s.i (*0-451-16052-5*, Signet Bks.) NAL.

—The Gunslinger. exp. rev. unabr. ed. 2003. (Dark Tower Ser.: Bk. I). 4p. audio 25.95 (*0-14-280036-8*) Penguin Group (USA) Inc.

—The Gunslinger. abr. ed. 1988. (Dark Tower Ser.). audio 29.95 o.p. (*0-453-00636-1*, 1987) Penguin/HighBridge.

—The Gunslinger. unabr. ed. 2003. audio 58.00 (*1-4025-5859-7*, 97135); audio compact disk 58.00 (*1-4025-5944-5*, C2306); audio 34.95 (*1-4025-5860-0*, RG118) Recorded Bks., LLC.

—The Gunslinger. 1978. (Dark Tower Ser.: Bk. I). 20.05 (*0-606-04112-5*) Turtleback Bks.

—The Gunslinger. abr. ed. (Dark Tower Ser.: Bk. I). 1998. 4p. pap. 29.95 incl. audio (*0-14-086716-3*, Penguin AudioBooks); 2003. 6p. audio compact disk 29.99 (*0-14-280037-6*, Penguin Bks.) Viking Penguin.

—The Waste Lands. (Dark Tower Ser.: Bk. III). 2003. (Illus.). 448p. pap. 17.95 (*0-452-28471-6*); 1997. 432p. pap. 17.95 o.s.i (*0-452-27962-3*); 1992. (Illus.). 432p. reprint ed. pap. 17.95 o.s.i (*0-452-26740-4*) Dutton/Plume. (Plume).

—The Waste Lands. 1991. (Dark Tower Ser.: Bk. III). (Illus.). 509p. 38.00 o.p. (*0-937986-17-8*); 2001. 30.00 (*1-880418-23-1*) Grant, Donald M. Pub., Inc.

—The Waste Lands. abr. unabr. ed. 1992. (Dark Tower Ser.: Bk. III). 34.95 o.p. incl. audio (*0-453-00770-8*, 51855-03495, NAL Bks.) HighBridge Co.

—The Waste Lands. (Dark Tower Ser.: No. 3). 2003. 608p. mass mkt. 7.99 (*0-451-21086-7*); 1993. (Illus.). 592p. mass mkt. 7.99 o.s.i (*0-451-17331-7*); 1992. pap. 5.99 o.s.i (*0-451-17475-5*) NAL. (Signet Bks.).

—The Waste Lands, Bk. 3. unabr. ed. 2003. (Dark Tower Ser.). 16p. audio compact disk 49.95 (*0-14-280039-2*) Penguin Group (USA) Inc.

—The Waste Lands. 2003. (Dark Tower Ser.: Bk. 3). E-Book 7.99 (*0-7865-3754-X*) Penguin Putnam, Inc E-Books.

—The Waste Lands. 1991. (Dark Tower Ser.: Bk. III). 14.04 (*0-606-02971-0*) Turtleback Bks.

—The Waste Lands. abr. unabr. ed. (Dark Tower Ser.: Vol. 3). 1998. 12p. audio 44.95 (*0-14-086717-1*, Penguin AudioBooks); 2003. (Illus.). 448p. reprint ed. 35.00 (*0-670-03256-5*) Viking Penguin.

—Wizard & Glass. (Dark Tower Ser.: Bk. IV). 2003. 720p. pap. 18.95 (*0-452-28472-4*, Plume); 1997. (Illus.). 688p. pap. 17.95 o.s.i (*0-452-27917-8*, Signet Bks.) Dutton/Plume.

—Wizard & Glass. 1997. (Dark Tower Ser.: Bk. IV). (Illus.). 792p. 45.00 (*1-880418-38-X*); 787 p. pap. o.p. (*1-880418-37-1*) Grant, Donald M. Pub., Inc.

—Wizard & Glass, Set. unabr. ed. 1999. audio 49.95 Highsmith Inc.

—Wizard & Glass. (Dark Tower Ser.: No. 4). 752p. 2003. mass mkt. 7.99 (*0-451-21087-5*); 1998. (Illus.). mass mkt. 7.99 o.s.i (*0-451-19486-1*) NAL. (Signet Bks.).

—Wizard & Glass. unabr. ed. 2003. (Dark Tower Ser.: Vol. 4). 23p. audio compact disk 59.95 (*0-14-280040-6*) Penguin Group (USA) Inc.

—Wizard & Glass. 2003. (Dark Tower Ser.: Bk. 4). E-Book 7.99 (*0-7865-3758-2*) Penguin Putnam, Inc E-Books.

—Wizard & Glass. 1998. (Dark Tower Ser.). 14.04 (*0-606-15772-7*) Turtleback Bks.

—Wizard & Glass. (Dark Tower Ser.). 2003. (Illus.). 704p. 40.00 (*0-670-03257-3*); 1997. 18p. audio 57.95 (*0-14-086688-4*, Penguin AudioBooks) Viking Penguin.

—Wolves of the Calla. 2003. (Dark Tower Ser.: Bk. 5). (Illus.). 736p. 35.00 (*1-880418-56-8*) Grant, Donald M. Pub., Inc.

—Wolves of the Calla. 2003. (Dark Tower Ser.: Bk. 5). E-Book (*0-7432-5510-0*, Scribner) Simon & Schuster.

## DARKOVER (IMAGINARY PLACE)—FICTION

Bradley, Marion Zimmer. Against the Terrans. 1981. (Darkover Ser.). 368p. mass mkt. 6.99 o.s.i (*0-88677-309-1*) DAW Bks., Inc.

—The Against the Terrans Spell Sword. 1974. (Darkover Ser.). 160p. mass mkt. 5.99 o.s.i (*0-88677-237-0*) DAW Bks., Inc.

—The Ages of Chaos: Storm Queen/Hawk Mistress. 2002. (DAW Book Collectors Ser.: No. 1223). (Illus.). 768p. mass mkt. 7.99 (*0-7564-0072-4*) DAW Bks., Inc.

—The Bloody Sun. 1986. 416p. mass mkt. 4.50 o.s.i (*0-441-06863-4*); 1985. mass mkt. 3.95 o.s.i (*0-441-06859-6*); 1985. mass mkt. 3.50 o.s.i (*0-441-06858-8*); 1982. mass mkt. 2.95 o.s.i (*0-441-06857-X*) Ace Bks.

—The Bloody Sun. 1994. (Darkover Ser.). 416p. mass mkt. 6.99 o.s.i (*0-88677-603-1*) DAW Bks., Inc.

—The Bloody Sun. 1993. 22.00 o.p. (*0-7278-4446-6*) Severn Hse. Pubs., Ltd.

—The City of Sorcery. 1984. (Darkover Ser.). mass mkt. 3.95 o.p. (*0-88677-122-6*); mass mkt. 3.50 o.p. (*0-87997-962-3*) DAW Bks., Inc.

—The City of Sorcery: The Renunciates, Free Amazons. 1984. (Darkover: The Renunciates, Free Amazons Ser.: Vol. 3). 424p. mass mkt. 6.99 o.s.i (*0-88677-332-6*) DAW Bks., Inc.

—Darkover Landfall. (Darkover Ser.). 1976. mass mkt. 1.25 o.p. (*0-87997-256-4*); 1972. 256p. mass mkt. 6.99 o.s.i (*0-88677-234-6*, UE2234); 1972. mass mkt. 0.95 o.p. (*0-87997-036-7*); 1972. mass mkt. 1.50 o.p. (*0-87997-447-8*); 1972. mass mkt. 1.75 o.p. (*0-87997-567-9*); 1972. mass mkt. 1.95 o.p. (*0-87997-684-5*); 1972. mass mkt. 2.25 o.p. (*0-87997-806-6*); 1972. mass mkt. 2.50 o.p. (*0-87997-906-2*) DAW Bks., Inc.

—Darkover Landfall. 1987. mass mkt. o.p. (*0-09-915410-2*) Hutchinson GBR. *Dist:* Random Hse. of Canada, Ltd.

—Darkover Landfall. l.t. ed. 1999. (Science Fiction Ser.). 233p. 24.95 (*0-7838-8672-1*) Thorndike Pr.

—Domains of Darkover. 1990. (Darkover Ser.). 256p. (Orig.). mass mkt. 3.99 o.p. (*0-88677-407-1*) DAW Bks., Inc.

—Exile's Song. 1997. (Darkover Ser.). 496p. mass mkt. 7.99 (*0-88677-734-8*); 1996. (Daw Book Collectors Ser.: Vol. 1024). 400p. 21.95 o.s.i (*0-88677-705-4*) DAW Bks., Inc.

—The Forbidden Tower. 1977. (Darkover Ser.). mass mkt. 1.95 o.p. (*0-87997-323-4*); mass mkt. 2.25 o.p. (*0-87997-599-7*); mass mkt. 2.95 o.p. (*0-87997-752-3*); mass mkt. 3.50 o.p. (*0-87997-894-5*); mass mkt. 3.95 o.p. (*0-88677-029-7*); mass mkt. 3.95 o.p. (*0-88677-235-4*); 368p. reprint ed. mass mkt. 6.99 o.s.i (*0-88677-373-3*) DAW Bks., Inc.

—The Forbidden Tower. 1994. (Darkover Ser.). reprint ed. lib. bdg. 22.00 o.p. (*0-7278-4589-6*) Severn Hse. Pubs., Ltd.

—Hawkmistress. 1982. (Darkover Ser.). (Orig.). mass mkt. 3.50 o.p. (*0-87997-958-5*); 336p. mass mkt. 6.99 o.s.i (*0-88677-239-7*); mass mkt. 2.95 o.p. (*0-87997-762-0*); mass mkt. 3.95 o.p. (*0-88677-064-5*) DAW Bks., Inc.

—The Heirs of Hammerfell. (Darkover Ser.). 1990. mass mkt. 6.99 o.s.i (*0-88677-451-9*); 1989. 304p. mass mkt. 18.95 o.p. (*0-88677-395-4*) DAW Bks., Inc.

—The Heritage of Hastur. (Darkover Ser.). 1984. mass mkt. 3.50 o.p. (*0-87997-967-4*); 1984. mass mkt. 3.95 o.p. (*0-88677-079-3*); 1984. 384p. mass mkt. 6.99 o.s.i (*0-88677-413-6*); 1984. mass mkt. 4.99 o.p. (*0-88677-238-9*); 1977. mass mkt. 1.95 o.p. (*0-87997-307-2*); 1975. mass mkt. 2.50 o.p. (*0-87997-630-6*); 1975. mass mkt. 2.95 o.p. (*0-87997-744-2*); 1975. mass mkt. 1.50 o.p. (*0-87997-189-4*) DAW Bks., Inc.

—The Keeper's Price. 1980. (Darkover Ser.). mass mkt. 2.25 o.p. (*0-87997-517-2*); mass mkt. 2.50 o.p. (*0-87997-837-6*); mass mkt. 2.50 o.p. (*0-87997-931-3*); 208p. mass mkt. 3.99 o.s.i (*0-88677-236-2*, UE2236) DAW Bks., Inc.

—Leroni of Darkover. 1991. (Darkover Ser.). 352p. (Orig.). mass mkt. 4.99 o.s.i (*0-88677-494-2*) DAW Bks., Inc.

—The Other Side of the Mirror. 1987. (Darkover Ser.). 304p. mass mkt. 4.50 o.s.i (*0-88677-185-4*) DAW Bks., Inc.

—The Planet Savers. 1985. mass mkt. 3.50 o.s.i (*0-441-67026-1*); 1982. mass mkt. 2.75 o.s.i (*0-441-67022-9*) Ace Bks.

—The Planet Savers: Also Including The Waterfall. l.t. ed. 2001. (G. K. Hall Science Fiction Ser.). (Illus.). 142p. 27.95 (*0-7838-9065-6*) Thorndike Pr.

—The Planet Savers: The Sword of Aldones. 1988. mass mkt. 3.95 o.s.i (*0-441-67027-X*); 1984. mass mkt. 2.75 o.s.i (*0-441-67025-3*) Ace Bks.

—The Planet Savers: Winds of Darkover. 1995. (Darkover Revival Ser.). 320p. mass mkt. 6.99 o.s.i (*0-88677-630-9*) DAW Bks., Inc.

—Red Sun of Darkover. 1987. (Darkover Ser.). 288p. mass mkt. 3.95 o.p. (*0-88677-230-3*) DAW Bks., Inc.

—Renunciates of Darkover. 1991. (Darkover Ser.). 288p. (Orig.). mass mkt. 4.50 o.p. (*0-88677-469-1*) DAW Bks., Inc.

—The Shadow Matrix. (Darkover Ser.). 1999. 560p. mass mkt. 7.99 (*0-88677-812-3*); 1997. 576p. 22.95 o.s.i (*0-88677-743-7*) DAW Bks., Inc.

—Sharra's Exile. 1981. (Darkover Ser.). mass mkt. 2.95 o.p. (*0-87997-659-4*); mass mkt. 3.50 o.p. (*0-87997-836-8*); mass mkt. 3.50 o.p. (*0-87997-913-5*); mass mkt. 3.95 o.p. (*0-87997-988-7*) DAW Bks., Inc.

—Sharra's Exile. 1996. (Darkover Ser.). 368p. reprint ed. 24.00 (*0-7278-4799-6*) Severn Hse. Pubs., Ltd.

—The Shattered Chain. (Darkover Ser.). 1977. mass mkt. 1.95 o.p. (*0-87997-327-7*); 1976. mass mkt. 1.50 o.p. (*0-87997-229-7*); 1976. mass mkt. 2.25 o.p. (*0-87997-566-0*); 1976. mass mkt. 2.50 o.p. (*0-87997-683-7*); 1976. mass mkt. 2.95 o.p. (*0-87997-840-6*); 1976. mass mkt. 3.50 o.p. (*0-87997-961-5*); 1976. 288p. mass mkt. 5.99 o.s.i (*0-88677-308-3*) DAW Bks., Inc.

—The Spell Sword. 1974. (Darkover Ser.). mass mkt. 0.95 o.p. (*0-87997-131-2*); mass mkt. 1.25 o.p. (*0-87997-284-X*); mass mkt. 1.50 o.p. (*0-87997-440-0*); mass mkt. 1.95 o.p. (*0-87997-675-6*); mass mkt. 2.25 o.p. (*0-87997-891-0*); mass mkt. 2.50 o.p. (*0-88677-091-2*) DAW Bks., Inc.

—The Spell Sword. l.t. ed. 2000. (Science Fiction Ser.). 240p. 25.95 (*0-7838-9066-4*) Thorndike Pr.

—Stormqueen! 1978. (Darkover Ser.). mass mkt. 1.95 o.p. (*0-87997-381-1*); mass mkt. 2.50 o.p. (*0-87997-629-2*); mass mkt. 2.95 o.p. (*0-87997-812-0*); mass mkt. 3.50 o.p. (*0-87997-951-8*); mass mkt. 3.95 o.p. (*0-88677-092-0*); 368p. mass mkt. 6.99 o.s.i (*0-88677-310-5*) DAW Bks., Inc.

—Sword of Chaos. 1982. (Darkover Ser.). mass mkt. 3.50 o.s.i (*0-88677-172-2*); mass mkt. 2.95 o.p. (*0-87997-722-1*) DAW Bks., Inc.

—Thendara House. 1983. (Darkover Ser.). mass mkt. 3.50 o.p. (*0-87997-857-0*); Darkover Ser.). mass mkt. 3.95 o.p. (*0-88677-119-6*); (Darkover: The Renunciates, Free Amazons Ser.: Vol. 2). 416p. mass mkt. 6.99 o.s.i (*0-88677-240-0*) DAW Bks., Inc.

—Thendara House. 1995. (Darkover Ser.). 416p. reprint ed. 22.00 (*0-7278-4723-6*) Severn Hse. Pubs., Ltd.

—Traitor's Sun. (Darkover Ser.). 2000. 544p. mass mkt. 7.99 (*0-88677-811-5*, D A W Fiction); 1999. 496p. 24.95 o.p. (*0-88677-810-7*) DAW Bks., Inc.

—Two to Conquer. 1980. (Orig.). mass mkt. 2.25 o.p. (*0-87997-540-7*); mass mkt. 2.50 o.p. (*0-87997-651-9*); mass mkt. 2.95 o.p. (*0-87997-876-7*); 336p. mass mkt. 6.99 o.s.i (*0-88677-174-9*) DAW Bks., Inc.

—The Winds of Darkover. 1986. 192p. mass mkt. 3.50 o.s.i (*0-441-89261-2*) Ace Bks.

—The Winds of Darkover. 1996. (Darkover Ser.). 192p. 22.00 o.p. (*0-7278-5191-8*) Severn Hse. Pubs., Ltd.

—The Winds of Darkover. l.t. ed. 2000. (Science Fiction Ser.). 221p. 25.95 (*0-7838-9067-2*) Thorndike Pr.

—The World Wreckers. 1988. 224p. mass mkt. 2.95 o.s.i (*0-441-91178-1*) Ace Bks.

—The World Wreckers. 1994. (Against the Terrans Ser.). 288p. mass mkt. 6.99 o.s.i (*0-88677-629-5*) DAW Bks., Inc.

Bradley, Marion Zimmer, ed. Free Amazons of Darkover: An Anthology. 1985. (Darkover Ser.). mass mkt. 3.50 o.p. (*0-88677-096-3*) DAW Bks., Inc.

—Snows of Darkover. 1994. (Darkover Ser.). 336p. (Orig.). mass mkt. 4.99 o.s.i (*0-88677-601-5*) DAW Bks., Inc.

—Towers of Darkover. 1993. (Darkover Ser.). 336p. (Orig.). mass mkt. 4.99 o.s.i (*0-88677-553-1*) DAW Bks., Inc.

Bradley, Marion Zimmer, ed. & intro. Free Amazons of Darkover: An Anthology. 1985. (Darkover Ser.). 303p. mass mkt. 3.95 o.s.i (*0-88677-430-6*) DAW Bks., Inc.

Bradley, Marion Zimmer & Lackey, Mercedes. Rediscovery. (Darkover Ser.). 1993. 320p. 18.00 o.p. (*0-88677-561-2*); 1994. 368p. reprint ed. mass mkt. 6.99 o.s.i (*0-88677-529-9*) DAW Bks., Inc.

Bradley, Marion Zimmer & Ross, Deborah. The Fall of Neskaya, Bk. 1. 2001. (Darkover Ser.). 448p. 24.95 (*0-7564-0034-1*) DAW Bks., Inc.

Bradley, Marion Zimmer & Ross, Deborah J. The Fall of Neskaya. 2002. 576p. reprint ed. mass mkt. 6.99 (*0-7564-0053-8*) DAW Bks., Inc.

Bradley, Marion Zimmer, et al. Four Moons of Darkover. 1988. (Darkover Ser.). mass mkt. 4.99 o.s.i (*0-88677-305-9*) DAW Bks., Inc.

### DARWATH (IMAGINARY PLACE)—FICTION

Hambly, Barbara. The Armies of Daylight. (Darwath Trilogy Ser.). 1997. mass mkt. 5.99 (*0-345-91172-5*); 1983. 309p. mass mkt. 5.99 o.s.i (*0-345-29671-0*) Ballantine Bks. (Del Rey).

—Icefalcon's Quest. 1995. 368p. pap. 19.00 (*0-345-47035-4*, Del Rey) Ballantine Bks.

—Mother of Winter. 1997. (Darwath Trilogy Ser.). 384p. mass mkt. 6.99 (*0-345-39723-1*, Del Rey) Ballantine Bks.

—The Time of the Dark. (Darwath Trilogy Ser.). 1997. mass mkt. 5.99 (*0-345-91168-7*); 1984. 272p. mass mkt. 5.99 o.s.i (*0-345-31965-6*) Ballantine Bks. (Del Rey).

—The Walls of Air. (Darwath Trilogy Ser.). (Orig.). 1997. mass mkt. 5.99 (*0-345-91170-9*); 1983. (Illus.). 297p. mass mkt. 5.99 o.s.i (*0-345-29670-2*) Ballantine Bks. (Del Rey).

### DEATH GATE UNIVERSE (IMAGINARY PLACE)—FICTION

Hickman, Tracy & Weis, Margaret. The Seventh Gate. 1995. (Bantam Spectra Book Ser.). 368p. mass mkt. 7.50 (*0-553-57325-X*, Spectra) Bantam Bks.

Weis, Margaret & Hickman, Tracy. Elven Star. 1991. (Death Gate Cycle Ser.: No. 2). 432p. mass mkt. 7.50 (*0-553-29098-3*, Spectra) Bantam Bks.

—The Hand of Chaos: A Death Gate Novel, No. 5. 1993. (Hands of Chaos Ser.). 512p. mass mkt. 7.50 (*0-553-56369-6*, Spectra); 496p. 21.95 o.s.i (*0-553-09377-0*) Bantam Bks.

### DEATHLANDS (IMAGINARY PLACE)—FICTION

Axler, James. Amazon Gate. 2002. (Deathlands Ser.: No. 59). 352p. mass mkt. (*0-373-62569-3*, Worldwide Library) Harlequin Enterprises, Ltd.

—Bitter Fruit. 1996. (Deathlands Ser.: No. 35). per. (*0-373-62535-9*, Harlequin Bks.) Harlequin Enterprises, Ltd.

—Bloodfire. 2003. (Deathlands Ser.: No. 64). 352p. mass mkt. (*0-373-62574-X*, 1-625748, Gold Eagle) Harlequin Enterprises, Ltd.

—Bloodlines. 1995. (Deathlands Ser.: No. 29). 348p. per. (*0-373-62529-4*, Worldwide Library) Harlequin Enterprises, Ltd.

—Breakthrough. 2002. (Deathlands Ser.: No. 57). 349p. mass mkt. (*0-373-62567-7*, 1-62567-2, Worldwide Library) Harlequin Enterprises, Ltd.

—Chill Factor. abr. ed. 1999. (Deathlands Ser.: No. 15). audio (*1-55204-401-7*, GOL-3401) Durkin Hayes Publishing Ltd.

—Chill Factor. (Deathlands Ser.: No. 15). 1999. mass mkt. (*0-373-62553-7*, 1-62553-2, Worldwide Library); 1992. mass mkt. (*0-373-62515-4*, 1-62515-1, Harlequin Bks.) Harlequin Enterprises, Ltd.

—Circle Thrice. 1996. (Deathlands Ser.: No. 32). per. (*0-373-62532-4*, 1-62532-6, Worldwide Library) Harlequin Enterprises, Ltd.

—Cold Asylum. unabr. ed. 1999. (Deathlands Ser.: No. 20). audio 7.99 (*1-55204-416-5*, GOL-3416) Durkin Hayes Publishing Ltd.

—Cold Asylum. (Deathlands Ser.: No. 20). 1999. mass mkt. (*0-373-62558-8*, 1-62558-1, Worldwide Library); 1994. mass mkt. (*0-373-62520-0*, 1-62520-1, Harlequin Bks.) Harlequin Enterprises, Ltd.

—Crater Lake. abr. ed. 1998. (Deathlands Ser.: No. 2). 3p. audio 7.99 (*1-55204-374-6*) Durkin Hayes Publishing Ltd.

—Crater Lake. (Deathlands Ser.: No. 4). 1997. per. (*0-373-48598-0*, 1-48598-6); 1987. 256p. mass mkt. (*0-373-63060-3*); 1987. mass mkt. (*0-373-62504-9*) Harlequin Enterprises, Ltd. (Harlequin Bks.).

—Crossways. (Deathlands Ser.: No. 30). 2000. mass mkt. (*0-373-62576-6*, 1-62576-3); 1996. 349p. mass mkt. (*0-373-62530-8*, 1-62530-0) Harlequin Enterprises, Ltd. (Worldwide Library).

—Crucible of Time. 1998. (Deathlands Ser.: No. 44). per. (*0-373-62544-8*, 1-62544-1, Mira Bks.) Harlequin Enterprises, Ltd.

—Dark Carnival. abr. ed. 1999. (Deathlands Ser.: No. 14). audio (*1-55204-398-3*, GOL-3398) Durkin Hayes Publishing Ltd.

—Dark Carnival. (Deathlands Ser.: No. 14). 1999. mass mkt. (*0-373-62552-9*, 1-62552-4, Worldwide Library); 1991. mass mkt. (*0-373-62514-6*, Harlequin Bks.) Harlequin Enterprises, Ltd.

—Dark Emblem. (Deathlands Ser.: No. 43). Date not set. E-Book (*0-373-86015-3*, Gold Eagle); 1998. per. (*0-373-62543-X*, 1-62543-3, Worldwide Library) Harlequin Enterprises, Ltd.

—Dark Reckoning. 1999. (Deathlands Ser.: No. 48). per. (*0-373-62548-0*, Harlequin Bks.) Harlequin Enterprises, Ltd.

—Dectra Chain. abr. ed. 1998. (Deathlands Ser.: No. 7). audio 7.99 (*1-55204-380-0*) Durkin Hayes Publishing Ltd.

—Dectra Chain. (Deathlands Ser.: No. 7). 1997. per. (*0-373-89005-2*, 1-89005-2); 1988. 352p. pap. (*0-373-62507-3*) Harlequin Enterprises, Ltd. (Harlequin Bks.).

—Deep Empire. unabr. ed. 1999. (Deathlands Ser.: No. 19). audio 7.99 (*1-55204-413-0*, GOL-3413) Durkin Hayes Publishing Ltd.

—Deep Empire. (Deathlands Ser.: No. 19). 1999. mass mkt. (*0-373-62557-X*, 1-62557-3, Worldwide Library); 1993. mass mkt. (*0-373-62519-7*, 1-62519-3, Harlequin Bks.) Harlequin Enterprises, Ltd.

—Demons of Eden. 1997. (Deathlands Ser.: No. 37). per. (*0-373-62537-5*, 1-62537-5, Worldwide Library) Harlequin Enterprises, Ltd.

—Destiny's Truth. 2002. (Deathlands Ser.: No. 60). 352p. mass mkt. o.s.i (*0-373-62570-7*, 1-62570-6, Gold Eagle) Harlequin Enterprises, Ltd.

—Eclipse at Noon. 1996. (Deathlands Ser.: No. 33). per. (*0-373-62533-2*, Worldwide Library) Harlequin Enterprises, Ltd.

—Emerald Fire. abr. ed. 2000. (Deathlands Ser.: No. 28). audio 7.99 (*1-55204-450-5*, GOL-3450) Durkin Hayes Publishing Ltd.

—Emerald Fire. 1995. (Deathlands Ser.: No. 28). 347p. per. (*0-373-62528-6*, 1-62528-4, Harlequin Bks.) Harlequin Enterprises, Ltd.

—Encounter. collector's ed. 1999. (Deathlands Ser.). 384p. per. (*0-373-81197-7*, Gold Eagle) Harlequin Enterprises, Ltd.

—Freedom Lost. 1998. (Deathlands Ser.: No. 41). per. (*0-373-62541-3*, 1-62541-7, Worldwide Library) Harlequin Enterprises, Ltd.

—Fury's Pilgrims. unabr. ed. 1999. (Deathlands Ser.: No. 17). audio 7.99 (*1-55204-407-6*, GOL-3407) Durkin Hayes Publishing Ltd.

—Fury's Pilgrims. (Deathlands Ser.: No. 17). 1999. mass mkt. (*0-373-62555-3*, 1-62555-7, Worldwide Library); 1992. mass mkt. (*0-373-62517-0*, 1-62517-7, Harlequin Bks.) Harlequin Enterprises, Ltd.

—Gaia's Demise. 1999. (Deathlands Ser.: No. 47). 346p. mass mkt. (*0-373-62547-2*, Worldwide Library) Harlequin Enterprises, Ltd.

—Gemini Rising. 1999. (Deathlands Ser.: No. 46). per. (*0-373-62546-4*, 1-62546-6, Worldwide Library) Harlequin Enterprises, Ltd.

—Genesis Echo. 1995. (Deathlands Ser.: No. 25). mass mkt. (*0-373-62525-1*, 1-62525-0, Harlequin Bks.) Harlequin Enterprises, Ltd.

—Ground Zero. 1995. (Deathlands Ser.: No. 27). mass mkt. (*0-373-62527-8*, 1-62527-6, Harlequin Bks.) Harlequin Enterprises, Ltd.

—Hellbenders. 2000. (Deathlands Ser.: No. 65). 352p. mass mkt. (*0-373-62575-8*, 1-62575-5, Gold Eagle) Harlequin Enterprises, Ltd.

—Homeward Bound. (Deathlands Ser.: No. 5). 1997. per. (*0-373-48599-9*, 1-48599-4); 1987. mass mkt. (*0-373-62505-7*); 1987. 320p. mass mkt. (*0-373-63061-1*) Harlequin Enterprises, Ltd. (Harlequin Bks.).

—Ice & Fire, abr. ed. 1998. (Deathlands Ser.: No. 8). audio 7.99 (*1-55204-382-7*) Durkin Hayes Publishing Ltd.

—Ice & Fire. (Deathlands Ser.: No. 8). 1997. per. (*0-373-89006-0*, 1-89006-0); 1988. 352p. mass mkt. (*0-373-62508-1*) Harlequin Enterprises, Ltd. (Harlequin Bks.).

—Keepers of the Sun. 1996. (Deathlands Ser.: No. 31). per. (*0-373-62531-6*, 1-62531-8, Worldwide Library) Harlequin Enterprises, Ltd.

—Latitude Zero. abr. ed. 1999. (Deathlands Ser.: No. 12). audio 7.99 (*1-55204-390-8*, GOL-3390) Durkin Hayes Publishing Ltd.

—Latitude Zero. (Deathlands Ser.: No. 12). 1999. mass mkt. (*0-373-62550-2*, 1-62550-8, Worldwide Library); 1991. mass mkt. (*0-373-62512-X*, Harlequin Bks.) Harlequin Enterprises, Ltd.

—The Mars Arena. 1997. (Deathlands Ser.: No. 38). per. (*0-373-62538-3*, 1-62538-3, Worldwide Library) Harlequin Enterprises, Ltd.

—Moon Fate. abr. ed. 1999. (Deathlands Ser.: No. 16). audio 7.99 (*1-55204-404-1*, GOL-3404) Durkin Hayes Publishing Ltd.

—Moon Fate. (Deathlands Ser.: No. 16). 1999. mass mkt. (*0-373-62554-5*, 1-62554-0, Worldwide Library); 1992. per. (*0-373-62516-2*, 1-62516-9, Harlequin Bks.) Harlequin Enterprises, Ltd.

—Neutron Solstice. (Deathlands Ser.: No. 3). 1997. per. (*0-373-48597-2*, 1-48597-8); 1987. mass mkt. (*0-373-62503-0*); 1987. 256p. mass mkt. (*0-373-63059-X*) Harlequin Enterprises, Ltd. (Harlequin Bks.).

—Nightmare Passage. 1997. (Deathlands Ser.: No. 40). per. (*0-373-62540-5*, 1-62540-9, Worldwide Library) Harlequin Enterprises, Ltd.

—Northstar Rising. (Deathlands Ser.: No. 10). 1997. per. (*0-373-89008-7*, 1-89008-6); 1989. mass mkt. (*0-373-62510-3*) Harlequin Enterprises, Ltd. (Harlequin Bks.).

—Pandora's Redoubt. 2000. (Deathlands Ser.: No. 50). 352p. per. (*0-373-62560-X*, 1-62560-7, Worldwide Library) Harlequin Enterprises, Ltd.

—Pony Soldiers. 1998. (Deathlands Ser.: No. 6). audio 7.99 (*1-55204-378-9*) Durkin Hayes Publishing Ltd.

—Pony Soldiers. (Deathlands Ser.: No. 6). 1997. per. (*0-373-89004-4*, 1-89004-5); 1988. 352p. pap. (*0-373-62506-5*) Harlequin Enterprises, Ltd. (Harlequin Bks.).

—Red Equinox. (Deathlands Ser.: No. 9). 1997. per. (*0-373-89007-9*, 1-89007-8); 1989. 352p. mass mkt. (*0-373-62509-X*) Harlequin Enterprises, Ltd. (Harlequin Bks.).

—Red Holocaust. abr. ed. 1998. (Deathlands Ser.: No. 2). audio 7.99 (*1-55204-369-X*) Durkin Hayes Publishing Ltd.

—Red Holocaust. (Deathlands Ser.: No. 2). 1997. per. (*0-373-48596-4*, 1-48596-0); 1986. 256p. mass mkt. (*0-373-63058-1*); 1986. mass mkt. (*0-373-62502-2*) Harlequin Enterprises, Ltd. (Harlequin Bks.).

—Rider, Reaper. unabr. ed. 1999. (Deathlands Ser.: No. 22). audio 7.99 (*1-55204-422-X*, GOL-3422) Durkin Hayes Publishing Ltd.

—Rider, Reaper. 1994. (Deathlands Ser.: No. 22). mass mkt. (*0-373-62522-7*, 1-62522-7, Harlequin Bks.) Harlequin Enterprises, Ltd.

—Road Wars. 1994. (Deathlands Ser.: No. 23). per. (*0-373-62523-5*, 1-62523-5, Harlequin Bks.) Harlequin Enterprises, Ltd.

—Salvation Road. 2002. (Deathlands Ser.: No. 58). mass mkt. (*0-373-62568-5*, 1-62568-0, Worldwide Library) Harlequin Enterprises, Ltd.

—Seedling. abr. ed. 1999. (Deathlands Ser.: No. 13). audio (*1-55204-395-9*, GOL-3395) Durkin Hayes Publishing Ltd.

—Seedling. (Deathlands Ser.: No. 13). 1999. mass mkt. (*0-373-62551-0*, 1-62551-6, Worldwide Library); 1991. mass mkt. (*0-373-62513-8*, Harlequin Bks.) Harlequin Enterprises, Ltd.

—Shadow World. 2000. (Deathlands Ser.: No. 49). 352p. per. (*0-373-62559-6*, Worldwide Library) Harlequin Enterprises, Ltd.

—Shadowfall. 1995. (Deathlands Ser.: No. 26). mass mkt. (*0-373-62526-X*, 1-62526-8, Harlequin Bks.) Harlequin Enterprises, Ltd.

—Shockscape. unabr. ed. 1999. (Deathlands Ser.: No. 18). audio 7.99 (*1-55204-410-6*, GOL-3410) Durkin Hayes Publishing Ltd.

—Shockscape. (Deathlands Ser.: No. 18). 1999. mass mkt. (*0-373-62556-1*, 1-62556-5, Worldwide Library); 1993. mass mkt. (*0-373-62518-9*, 1-62518-5, Harlequin Bks.) Harlequin Enterprises, Ltd.

—Skydark. 1997. (Deathlands Ser.: No. 36). 352p. per. (*0-373-62536-7*, 1-62536-7, Worldwide Library) Harlequin Enterprises, Ltd.

—Starfall. 1999. (Deathlands Ser.: No. 45). per. (*0-373-62545-6*, 1-62545-8, Worldwide Library) Harlequin Enterprises, Ltd.

—Stoneface. 1996. (Deathlands Ser.: No. 34). mass mkt. (*0-373-62534-0*, 1-62534-2, Worldwide Library) Harlequin Enterprises, Ltd.

—Time Nomads. (Deathlands Ser.: No. 11). 1999. mass mkt. (*0-373-62549-9*, 1-62549-0, Worldwide Library); 1990. mass mkt. (*0-373-62511-1*, Harlequin Bks.) Harlequin Enterprises, Ltd.

—Trader Redux. 1994. (Deathlands Ser.: No. 24). mass mkt. (*0-373-62524-3*, 1-62524-3, Harlequin Bks.) Harlequin Enterprises, Ltd.

—Twilight Children. unabr. ed. 1999. (Deathlands Ser.: No. 21). 3p. audio 7.99 (*1-55204-419-X*, GOL-3419) Durkin Hayes Publishing Ltd.

—Twilight Children. 1994. (Deathlands Ser.: No. 21). mass mkt. (*0-373-62521-9*, 1-62521-9, Harlequin Bks.) Harlequin Enterprises, Ltd.

—Watersleep. 1997. (Deathlands Ser.: No. 39). per. (*0-373-62539-1*, 1-62539-1, Worldwide Library) Harlequin Enterprises, Ltd.

—Way of the Wolf. 1998. (Deathlands Ser.: No. 42). per. (*0-373-62542-1*, 1-62542-5, Worldwide Library) Harlequin Enterprises, Ltd.

Axler, James & Adrian, Jack. Pilgrimage to Hell. (Deathlands Ser.: No. 1). 1997. per. (*0-373-48595-6*, 1-48595-2); 1986. mass mkt. (*0-373-62501-4*) Harlequin Enterprises, Ltd. (Harlequin Bks.).

### DELAWARE—FICTION

Albensi, Bill. Lenape & the Colony of New Sweden. 1987. 183p. 14.75 (*0-930950-17-8*); pap. 8.75 (*0-930950-18-6*) Nopoly Pr., Inc.

Burcham, Carl. White Dolphin Blues. 1999. 308p. 24.50 (*0-88739-213-X*); pap. 13.95 (*0-88739-212-1*) Creative Arts Bk. Co.

Coyne, Tom. A Gentleman's Game. l.t. ed. 2001. 352p. 25.00 (*0-06-620996-X*, HarperLargePrint) HarperTrade.

—A Gentleman's Game: A Novel. 2001. 224p. 24.00 o.p. (*0-87113-791-7*, Atlantic Monthly Pr.); 2002. 272p. reprint ed. pap. 13.00 (*0-8021-3890-X*, Grove Pr.) Grove/Atlantic, Inc.

—A Gentleman's Game: A Novel. unabr. ed. 2001. audio 34.95 (*0-694-52522-7*, H227, HarperAudio) HarperTrade.

Johnson, Barbara. Bad Moon Rising: A Colleen Fitzgerald Mystery. 1998. (Colleen Fitzgerald Mysteries Ser.). 224p. pap. 11.95 (*1-56280-211-9*) Naiad Pr., Inc.

—The Beach Affair. 1995. (Colleen Fitzgerald Mysteries Ser.). 224p. pap. 10.95 (*1-56280-090-6*) Naiad Pr., Inc.

Paulding, James K. Koningsmarke, the Long Finne: A Story of the New World. 1988. 294p. 24.00 (*0-912756-20-9*) Union College Pr.

Spencer, Candace. Between Friends. l.t. ed. 1993. (Desire Ser.). 17.95 o.p. (*0-373-58810-0*); pap. 16.95 o.p. (*0-373-58910-7*) BBC Audiobooks America.

—Between Friends. 1990. (Silhouette Desire Ser.: No. 581). pap. (0-373-05581-1, Silhouette) Harlequin Enterprises, Ltd.

Tanenbaum, Robert K. True Justice. 2000. 384p. 24.95 o.s.i (0-7434-0589-7, Atria); 2001. (Illus.). 464p. reprint ed. mass mkt. 7.99 (0-7434-0590-0, Pocket) Simon & Schuster.

—True Justice. l.t. ed. 2001. (Thorndike Mystery Ser.). 681p. 30.95 (0-7862-3032-0) Thorndike Pr.

Williamson, Kathryn. The Secret in the Rose Room. 1997. 192p. (Orig.). mass mkt. 5.99 o.p. (1-56315-076-X) SterlingHouse Pubs., Inc.

**DEL MORAY (FLA.: IMAGINARY PLACE)—FICTION**

Lutz, John. Blood Fire. 1991. 17.95 o.p. (0-8050-0969-8) Holt, Henry & Co.

—Blood Fire. 1992. (Fred Carver Mystery Ser.). 224p. reprint ed. mass mkt. 3.99 (0-380-71446-9, Avon Bks.) Morrow/Avon.

—Burn: A Fred Carver Mystery. 1995. (Henry Holt Mystery Ser.). 278p. 22.50 o.p. (0-8050-3480-3) Holt, Henry & Co.

—Flame. unabr. ed. 1990. audio 57.25 o.p. (1-56100-050-7, 1197, Unabridged Library Editions); Set. audio 19.95 o.p. (0-930435-56-7, 344, Bookcassette) Brilliance Audio.

—Flame. 1996. 88p. pap. 5.95 o.p. (0-8050-4567-8, Owl Bks.) Holt, Henry & Co.

—Flame. 1991. 272p. pap. 3.95 (0-380-71070-6, Avon Bks.) Morrow/Avon.

—Hot: A Fred Carver Mystery. 1992. 288p. 18.95 o.p. (0-8050-1584-1) Holt, Henry & Co.

—Hot: A Fred Carver Mystery. 1993. 256p. mass mkt. 4.99 (0-380-71447-7, Avon Bks.) Morrow/Avon.

—Kiss. unabr. ed. 1990. audio 57.25 o.p. (1-56100-056-6, 920, Unabridged Library Editions); audio 19.95 o.p. (0-930435-62-1, 2030, Bookcassette) Brilliance Audio.

—Kiss. (Fred Carver Mystery Ser.). 1996. 88p. pap. 5.95 o.p. (0-8050-4566-X, Owl Bks.); 1988. 17.95 o.p. (0-8050-0412-2) Holt, Henry & Co.

—Kiss. 1990. 272p. pap. 3.95 (0-380-70934-1, Avon Bks.) Morrow/Avon.

—Lightning: A Fred Carver Mystery. unabr. ed. 1996. (P. I. Fred Carver Mystery Ser.). audio 48.00 (0-7366-3519-X, 4156) Books on Tape, Inc.

—Lightning: A Fred Carver Mystery. 1996. 88p. 22.50 o.p. (0-8050-4379-9) Holt, Henry & Co.

—Scorcher. unabr. ed. 1990. audio 57.25 o.p. (1-56100-060-4, 1030, Unabridged Library Editions); audio 19.95 o.p. (0-930435-66-4, 252, Bookcassette) Brilliance Audio.

—Scorcher. 272p. 1995. pap. 5.95 o.p. (0-8050-3829-9, Owl Bks.); 1987. 16.95 o.p. (0-8050-0411-4) Holt, Henry & Co.

—Scorcher. 1988. 256p. pap. 3.95 (0-380-70526-5, Avon Bks.) Morrow/Avon.

—Spark: A Fred Carver Mystery. 1993. 288p. 19.95 o.p. (0-8050-1993-6) Holt, Henry & Co.

—Torch. 1994. (Henry Holt Mystery Ser.). 290p. 22.00 o.p. (0-8050-2610-X) Holt, Henry & Co.

—Tropical Heat. l.t. ed. 1991. 21.95 o.p. (1-55504-579-0); pap. 6.95 o.p. (1-55504-550-2, 456) BBC Audiobooks America.

—Tropical Heat. unabr. ed. 1989. (P. I. Fred Carver Mystery Ser.). audio 19.95 o.p. (0-930435-53-2, 359, Bookcassette); audio 57.25 o.p. (1-56100-047-7, 1107, Unabridged Library Editions) Brilliance Audio.

—Tropical Heat. 1995. 252p. pap. 5.95 o.p. (0-8050-3828-0, Owl Bks.); 1986. 224p. o.p. (0-03-006958-0) Holt, Henry & Co.

—Tropical Heat. 1987. 256p. pap. 3.95 (0-380-70309-2, Avon Bks.) Morrow/Avon.

**DENMARK—FICTION**

Andersen, Benny. Selected Stories. 1983. 96p. pap. 8.95 (0-915306-25-5) Curbstone Pr.

Anderson, Poul. War of the Gods. (Tor Fantasy Ser.). 304p. 1999. mass mkt. 5.99 (0-8125-3925-7); 1997. 22.95 o.p. (0-312-86315-2) Doherty, Tom Assocs., LLC. (Tor Bks.).

—War of the Gods. 1999. 5.99 (0-312-87067-1) St. Martin's Pr.

—War of the Gods. l.t. ed. 1998. (Science Fiction Ser.). 400p. 24.95 (0-7838-0300-1) Thorndike Pr.

Aron, Paul. Ben: The Alien Bird. Aron, Paul & Auswaks, Alex, trs. from DAN. 1999. 248p. 19.95 (965-229-183-8) Gefen Publishing Hse., Ltd ISR. *Dist:* Gefen Bks.

Bergantino, David. Hamlet II: Ophelia's Revenge. 2003. (Bard's Blood Ser.). 256p. reprint ed. pap. 6.99 (0-7434-5624-6, Pocket Star) Simon & Schuster.

Branner, Hans Christian. The Story of Borge. Planck, Kristi, tr. from DAN. 1973. (Library of Scandinavian Literature). lib. bdg. 32.50 (0-8057-3359-0) Irvington Pubs.

Bredsdorff, Elias, tr. Contemporary Danish Prose. 1974. 375p. (C). reprint ed. o.p. (0-8371-7358-2, BRDP, Greenwood Pr.) Greenwood Publishing Group, Inc.

Canning, Victor. Raven's Wind. 1983. 192p. 11.95 o.p. (0-688-02133-6, Morrow, William & Co.) Morrow/Avon.

Davis, Philip J. Thomas Gray in Copenhagen: In Which the Philosopher Cat Meets the Ghost of Hans Christian Andersen. 1995. (Illus.). 192p. text 16.00 (0-387-94493-1) Springer-Verlag New York, Inc.

Ditlevsen, Tove. The Faces. Nunnally, Tiina, tr. from DAN. 153p. (Orig.). 1991. pap. 9.95 (0-940242-11-7); 1990. pap. 19.95 (0-940242-12-5) Fjord Pr.

Enquist, Per Olov. The Royal Physician's Visit. Nunnally, Tiina, tr. from SWE. 2001. 314p. 26.95 (1-58567-196-7) Overlook Pr., The.

Follett, Ken. Hornet Flight. 2002. 416p. 26.95 (0-525-94689-6) Dutton/Plume.

Forrest, Anthony. A Balance of Dangers: A Captain Justice Story. 1984. 240p. 14.95 o.p. (0-8090-2800-X, Hill & Wang) Farrar, Straus & Giroux.

Goldschmidt, Meir. A Jew. Ober, Kenneth, tr. from DAN. 1990. (Library of World Literature in Translation: Vol. 7). 350p. text 20.00 (0-8240-2993-3) Garland Publishing, Inc.

Gunnarsson, Gunnar. Black Cliffs. Wood, Cecil, tr. from DAN. 1967. (Nordic Translation Ser.). 260p. 8.00 o.p. (0-299-04471-8) Univ. of Wisconsin Pr.

Hansen, Martin A. Lucky Kristoffer. Egglishaw, John J., tr. from DAN. 1974. (Library of Scandinavian Literature). 377p. lib. bdg. 7.50 (0-8057-3339-6) Irvington Pubs.

Haugaard, Erik Christian. Untold Tale, 001. 1971. (Illus.). (J). (gr. 5 up). 4.95 o.p. (0-395-12366-6) Houghton Mifflin Co.

Heinesen, William. The Kingdom of the Earth. Bronner, Hedin, tr. from DAN. 1974. (Library of Scandinavian Literature). lib. bdg. 29.50 (0-8057-3324-8) Irvington Pubs.

—The Lost Musicians. Friis, Erick J., tr. from DAN. 1972. 364p. pap. 3.95 o.p. (0-88254-002-5) Hippocrene Bks., Inc.

—The Lost Musicians. Friis, Erik J. & Bronner, Hedin, trs. from DAN. 1971. (Library of Scandinavian Literature). lib. bdg. 10.95 (0-8057-3337-X) Irvington Pubs.

Hoeg, Peter. Borderliners. 1995. 288p. mass mkt. 6.99 o.s.i (0-7704-2709-X) Bantam Bks.

—Borderliners. 1995. 288p. reprint ed. pap. 14.95 (0-385-31508-2, Delta) Dell Publishing.

—Borderliners. Haveland, Barbara, tr. 1994. 277p. 22.00 o.p. (0-374-11554-0) Farrar, Straus & Giroux.

—Borderliners. Haveland, Barbara, tr. from DAN. l.t. ed. 1995. (Large Print Bks.). 22.95 (1-56895-202-3, Wheeler Publishing, Inc.) Gale Group.

—The History of Danish Dreams. 1996. mass mkt. 6.99 o.s.i (0-7704-2734-0) Bantam Bks.

—The History of Danish Dreams. 1996. 416p. pap. 12.95 (0-385-31591-0, Delta) Dell Publishing.

—The History of Danish Dreams. 1995. 352p. mass mkt. 18.95 o.s.i (0-385-25549-7) Doubleday Publishing.

—The History of Danish Dreams. Haveland, Barbara, tr. 1995. 356p. 24.00 o.p. (0-374-17138-6) Farrar, Straus & Giroux.

—The History of Danish Dreams. abr. ed. 1995. audio 24.95 (1-57511-006-7, 70020) Publishing Mills, Inc., The.

—Smilla's Sense of Snow. Haveland, Barbara, tr. from DAN. l.t. ed. 1995. pap. 23.95 o.p. (0-7927-2024-5); 1994. 25.95 o.p. (0-7927-2050-4) BBC Audiobooks America.

—Smilla's Sense of Snow. 1994. 512p. mass mkt. 6.99 o.s.i (0-7704-2618-2) Bantam Bks.

—Smilla's Sense of Snow. 1994. 512p. mass mkt. 6.99 o.s.i (0-440-21853-5); 1995. 480p. reprint ed. pap. 12.95 (0-385-31514-7, Delta) Dell Publishing.

—Smilla's Sense of Snow. 2001. 480p. pap. (0-385-65818-4) Doubleday Canada, Ltd. CAN. *Dist:* Random Hse., Inc.

—Smilla's Sense of Snow. 1993. 456p. 24.95 o.p. (0-385-25442-3) Doubleday Publishing.

—Smilla's Sense of Snow. Nunnally, Tiina, tr. from DAN. 1993. 453p. 21.00 o.p. (0-374-26644-1) Farrar, Straus & Giroux.

—Smilla's Sense of Snow, Set. abr. ed. 1993. audio 18.00 o.s.i (1-55994-866-3, 391604, HarperAudio) HarperTrade.

—Smilla's Sense of Snow. Nannally, Tiina, tr. unabr. ed. 1994. audio 97.00 (0-7887-0023-5, 94222E7) Recorded Bks., LLC.

Holdt, Rigmor C. The Glistening Isle. 2nd ed. 1992. (Illus.). 392p. pap. 14.95 (87-984071-0-4, TX 3362966) American Pictures Foundation.

Jacobsen, Jens Peter. Mogens & Other Stories. Nunnally, Tiina, tr. from DAN. (Modern Classics Ser.: No. 5). 160p. pap. 24.00 o.p. (0-940242-58-3); 1994. pap. 12.00 (0-940242-57-5) Fjord Pr.

Jensen, Johannes V. The Fall of the King. Bower, Alan G., tr. from DAN. 1992. Tr. of Kongens Feld. 288p. (Orig.). (C). pap. 16.95 o.p. (1-880755-06-8) Stonehill Publishing Co.

—The Fall of the King. Bower, Alan, tr. from DAN. 2nd rev. ed. 1995. Tr. of Kongens Feld. vi, 281p. (Orig.). pap. 21.35 (0-9643394-2-0) Stonehill Publishing Co.

Jensen, Niels. Days of Courage. Stallybrass, Oliver, tr. 1973. (J). (gr. 4-6). 5.75 o.p. (0-15-222880-2) Harcourt Children's Bks.

Kristensen, Tom. Havoc. Malmberg, Carl, tr. from DAN. 1968. (Nordic Translation Ser.). 445p. reprint ed. pap. 138.00 (0-608-01887-2, 206253900003) Bks. on Demand.

—Havoc. Malmberg, Carl, tr. from DAN. 1968. (Nordic Translation Ser.). 446p. 17.50 o.p. (0-299-04711-3); pap. 6.00 o.p. (0-299-04714-8) Univ. of Wisconsin Pr.

Larsen, Michael. Uncertainty. 1998. Tr. of Uden Sikker Viden. 272p. pap. 12.00 o.s.i (0-449-91236-1, Fawcett) Ballantine Bks.

—Uncertainty. Blecher, Lone T. & Blecher, George, trs. from DAN. 1996. Tr. of Uden Sikker Viden. 272p. 22.00 o.s.i (0-15-100202-9) Harcourt Trade Pubs.

Leffland, Ella. Breath & Shadows. 2000. 336p. pap. 14.00 (0-345-43923-6) Ballantine Bks.

—Breath & Shadows. 2000. pap. (0-688-17588-0, Quill) HarperTrade.

—Breath & Shadows. 1999. (Illus.). 311p. 24.00 (0-688-14271-0, Morrow, William & Co.) Morrow/Avon.

Levin, Jane W. Star of Danger. 1966. (Illus.). (J). (gr. 7 up). 5.50 o.p. (0-15-279380-1) Harcourt Children's Bks.

Lewis, Janet. Trial of Soren Qvist. 1959. 256p. pap. 12.95 (0-8040-0297-5) Swallow Pr.

Madsen, Svend A. Virtue & Vice in the Middle Time. Ogier, James M., tr. 1992. (Library of World Literature in Translation: Vol. 29). (DAN & ENG.). 584p. text 20.00 (0-8153-0606-7) Garland Publishing, Inc.

Mitchell, P. M. & Ober, Kenneth H., trs. from DAN. The Royal Guest & Other Classical Danish Narrative. 1993. lib. bdg. 15.00 o.s.i (0-226-53213-5); pap. 6.95 o.s.i (0-226-53214-3) Univ. of Chicago Pr.

Morch, Dea T. Winter's Child. Tate, Joan, tr. from DAN. 1986. (Modern Scandinavian Literature in Translation Ser.).Tr. of Vinterborn. (Illus.). 271p. reprint ed. 25.00 o.p. (0-8032-3101-6); pap. text 24.95 (0-8032-8133-1, Bison Bks.) Univ. of Nebraska Pr.

Peters, Elizabeth, pseud. The Copenhagen Connection. 1992. mass mkt. 4.99 (0-8125-2227-3); 1990. mass mkt. 4.50 o.s.i (0-8125-0914-5) Doherty, Tom Assocs., LLC. (Tor Bks.).

—The Copenhagen Connection. 1982. (General Ser.). lib. bdg. 13.95 o.p. (0-8161-3467-7, Macmillan Reference USA) Gale Group.

—The Copenhagen Connection. 2001. 384p. mass mkt. 6.99 (0-380-73338-2, Avon Bks.) Morrow/Avon.

—The Copenhagen Connection. 1994. 224p. mass mkt. 5.50 (0-446-36483-5) Warner Bks., Inc.

Scherfig, Hans. Stolen Spring. Hugus, Frank, tr. from DAN. 1986. Tr. of Det Forsomte Forar. 196p. 15.95 (0-940242-20-6); pap. 7.95 (0-940242-00-1) Fjord Pr.

Sorensen, Villy. Harmless Tales. Hostrup-Jessen, Paula, tr. from DAN. & intro. by. 1991. (Norvik Press Series B: No. 9). 137p. (Orig.). pap. 18.95 (1-870041-15-1) Norvik Pr. GBR. *Dist:* Dufour Editions, Inc.

—Tiger in the Kitchen, & Other Strange Stories. Neiiendam, Maureen, tr. 1977. (Short Story Index Reprint Ser.). 19.95 (0-8369-3060-6) Ayer Co. Pubs., Inc.

—Tutelary Tales. Hostrup-Jessen, Paula, tr. 1988. (Modern Scandinavian Literature in Translation Ser.). vi, 246p. 25.00 o.p. (0-8032-4185-2) Univ. of Nebraska Pr.

Tremain, Rose. Music & Silence. 2000. 485p. 25.00 o.s.i (0-374-19989-2) Farrar, Straus & Giroux.

Updike, John. Gertrude & Claudius. 2000. 224p. 23.00 (0-375-40908-4) Knopf, Alfred A. Inc.

Waller, Pamela. The Glass Rose. 2003. 200p. per. 12.95 (1-892343-32-0, Timeless Love) Oak Tree Publishing.

**DENVER (COLO.)—FICTION**

Allegretto, Michael. Blood Relative: A Jacob Lomax Mystery. 1992. 224p. text 20.00 (0-684-19409-0, Macmillan Reference USA) Gale Group.

—Blood Stone. 1988. 224p. 16.95 o.p. (0-684-18966-6, Macmillan Reference USA) Gale Group.

—The Dead of Winter. 1989. 256p. 16.95 o.p. (0-684-19138-5, Macmillan Reference USA) Gale Group.

—Death on the Rocks: A Jacob Lomax Mystery. 1987. 15.95 o.p. (0-684-18758-2, Macmillan Reference USA) Gale Group.

—Grave Doubt. 1995. 224p. 19.95 o.p. (0-7867-0186-2, Carroll & Graf Pubs.) Avalon Publishing Group.

Allen, Kate. Give My Secrets Back: An Alison Kaine Mystery. 1995. 200p. (Orig.). pap. 9.95 (0-934678-64-2) New Victoria Pubs., Inc.

—I Knew You Would Call. 1995. 202p. (Orig.). pap. 10.95 (0-934678-70-7) New Victoria Pubs., Inc.

—Takes One to Know One: An Alison Kaine Mystery. 1996. 200p. (Orig.). pap. 10.95 (0-934678-74-X) New Victoria Pubs., Inc.

Andrews, Sarah. A Fall in Denver: An Em Hansen Mystery. 1996. (Em Hansen Mystery Ser.). 272p. mass mkt. 5.50 o.s.i (0-451-18793-8) NAL.

—A Fall in Denver: An Em Hansen Mystery. 1995. 288p. 20.00 o.p. (0-684-81523-0); 20.00 (1-883402-34-4) Simon & Schuster. (Scribner).

—Only Flesh & Bones. 1999. (Dead Letter Mysteries Ser.: Vol. 1). 368p. mass mkt. 6.50 (0-312-96702-0, St. Martin's Paperbacks); 1998. 336p. 23.95 (0-312-18642-8, Saint Martin's Minotaur) St. Martin's Pr.

Baer, Will Christopher. Penny Dreadful. 2001. 240p. pap. 13.00 o.s.i (0-14-029850-9) Penguin Group (USA) Inc.

Burns, Rex. Angle of Attack. 1979. (Harper Novel of Suspense Ser.). o.p. (0-06-010523-2) HarperCollins Pubs.

—The Avenging Angel: A Gabe Wager Mystery. (Crime Monthly Ser.). 1984. 24p. pap. 3.95 o.p. (0-14-007104-0, Penguin Bks.); 1983. 240p. 12.50 o.p. (0-670-14317-0) Viking Penguin.

—Blood Line. 1995. 204p. 19.95 (0-8027-3256-9) Walker & Co.

—Endangered Species. 1993. 288p. 19.00 o.p. (0-670-84601-5, Viking) Viking Penguin.

—The Farnsworth Score. 1978. 1.75 o.p. (0-425-03749-5) Berkley Publishing Group.

—The Farnsworth Score. 1977. (Harper Novel of Suspense Ser.). o.p. (0-06-010573-9) HarperCollins Pubs.

—The Farnsworth Score. 1993. (Crime Ser.). 208p. pap. 5.95 o.p. (0-14-016949-0, Penguin Bks.) Penguin Group (USA) Inc.

—Ground Money. 1987. 256p. mass mkt. 3.95 o.p. (0-14-008515-7, Penguin Bks.); 1986. 187p. 15.95 o.p. (0-670-80904-7) Viking Penguin.

—The Killing Zone. 1989. 272p. pap. 3.95 o.p. (0-14-010532-8, Penguin Bks.); 1988. 261p. 17.95 o.p. (0-670-81955-7) Viking Penguin.

—The Leaning Land: A Gabe Wager Mystery. 1997. (Gabe Wagner Mystery Ser.). 246p. 22.95 o.p. (0-8027-3306-9) Walker & Co.

—Speak for the Dead. 1978. (Harper Novel of Suspense Ser.). 8.95 o.p. (0-06-010526-7) HarperCollins Pubs.

—Strip Search. (Crime Monthly Ser.). 1985. 272p. pap. 3.95 o.p. (0-14-007747-2, Penguin Bks.); 1984. 300p. 13.95 o.p. (0-670-67905-4) Viking Penguin.

Cacek, P. D. Canyons. 2000. 304p. 23.95 (0-312-87383-2, Tor Bks.) Doherty, Tom Assocs., LLC.

Cail, Carol. If Two of Them Are Dead. 1996. 224p. 15.95 (0-312-14361-3, Saint Martin's Minotaur) St. Martin's Pr.

Collins, Colleen. Tongue-Tied. 2002. (Harlequin Temptation Ser.). 219p. mass mkt. (0-373-69099-1, Harlequin Bks.) Harlequin Enterprises, Ltd.

Connelly, Michael. The Poet. l.t. ed. 2000. pap. 25.95 o.p. (1-56895-330-5, Wheeler Publishing, Inc.) Gale Group.

—The Poet. 1996. 440p. 22.95 o.p. (0-316-15398-2) Little Brown & Co.

—The Poet. 1997. 528p. reprint ed. mass mkt. 7.99 (0-446-60261-2) Warner Bks., Inc.

Cresswell, Jasmine. The Third Wife. 2002. 400p. mass mkt. (1-55166-931-5, Mira Bks.) Harlequin Enterprises, Ltd.

Dunning, John. Booked to Die. 1993. 384p. reprint ed. pap. 5.99 o.p. (0-380-71883-9, Avon Bks.) Morrow/Avon.

—Booked to Die. unabr. ed. 1995. audio 70.00 (0-7887-0411-7, 94603E7) Recorded Bks., LLC.

—Booked to Die. l.t. ed. 1998. (Niagara Large Print Ser.). 552p. 29.50 o.p. (0-7089-5836-2, Ulverscroft) Thorpe, F. A. Pubs. GBR. *Dist:* Ulverscroft Large Print Bks., Ltd., Ulverscroft Large Print Canada, Ltd.

—The Bookman's Promise. 2005. 384p. mass mkt. (0-7434-7629-8, Pocket) Simon & Schuster.

—The Bookman's Promise: A Cliff Janeway Novel. 2004. 384p. 25.00 (0-7432-4992-5, Scribner) Simon & Schuster.

—The Bookman's Wake. 1996. 448p. mass mkt. 7.99 (0-671-56782-9, Pocket Star); 1995. (Illus.). 352p. 21.00 (0-684-80003-9, Scribner) Simon & Schuster.

Dunning, John H. Booked to Die: A Mystery Introducing Cliff Janeway. 1992. 288p. 23.00 (0-684-19383-3, Scribner) Simon & Schuster.

Greer, Robert. The Devil's Backbone. 1998. 368p. 22.00 o.p. (0-89296-653-X) Mysterious Pr.

—The Devil's Backbone. 1999. (C J Floyd Mystery Ser.). 320p. mass mkt. 6.99 (0-446-60711-8) Warner Bks., Inc.

—The Devil's Hatband. 1996. 82p. 21.95 o.p. (0-89296-634-3) Mysterious Pr.

—The Devil's Hatband. 1997. 304p. reprint ed. mass mkt. 5.99 (0-446-40485-3) Warner Bks., Inc.

—The Devil's Red Nickel. 1997. 368p. 22.00 o.p. (0-89296-652-1) Mysterious Pr.

—The Devil's Red Nickel. 1998. (C J Floyd Mystery Ser.). 352p. mass mkt. 5.99 (0-446-60592-1); mass mkt. 5.99 (0-446-40529-9, Mysterious Pr. Paperback Bks.) Warner Bks., Inc.

Harris, Jeane. Black Iris. 1991. 256p. pap. 8.95 o.p. (0-941483-68-1) Naiad Pr., Inc.

Indigo, Susannah. The Angel of Fuck. 2000. E-Book 12.95 incl. cd-rom (0-9704677-1-0) West Emerald Pr.

Johnson, Dolores. Buttons & Foes. 2004. (WWL Mystery Ser.: No. 487). 256p. mass mkt. (0-373-26487-9, Worldwide Library) Harlequin Enterprises, Ltd.

—Buttons & Foes. E-Book 16.95 (0-312-70760-6); 2002. 240p. 22.95 (0-312-28396-2, Saint Martin's Minotaur) St. Martin's Pr.

—A Dress to Die For: A Mandy Dyer Mystery. 1998. (Mandy Dyer Mystery Ser.: Vol. 3). 272p. mass mkt. 5.99 (0-440-22355-5) Dell Publishing.

—Homicide & Old Lace. 2000. (Mandy Dyer Mystery Ser.). 288p. mass mkt. 5.99 o.s.i (0-440-23524-3, Dell Bks.) Dell Publishing.

—Hung up to Die. 1997. (Mandy Dyer Mystery Ser.: Vol. 2). 256p. mass mkt. 5.99 o.s.i (0-440-22353-9) Dell Publishing.

—Taken to the Cleaners. 1997. (Mandy Dyer Mystery Ser.: Vol. 1). 272p. mass mkt. 5.50 o.s.i (0-440-22370-9) Dell Publishing.

—Wash, Fold & Die: A Mandy Dyer Mystery. 1999. (Mandy Dyer Mystery Ser.). 288p. mass mkt. 5.99 o.s.i (0-440-23523-5) Dell Publishing.

Jorgensen, Christine T. Curl up & Die. 1998. (WWL Mystery Ser.). per. (0-373-26266-3, 1-26266-6, Worldwide Library) Harlequin Enterprises, Ltd.

—Curl up & Die: A Stella the Stargazer Mystery. 1997. (Stella the Stargazer Mystery Ser.). 224p. 21.95 (0-8027-3288-7) Walker & Co.

—Dead on Her Feet. 2000. (Stella the Stargazer Mystery Ser.). 253p. per. (0-373-26344-9, Harlequin Bks.) Harlequin Enterprises, Ltd.

—Dead on Her Feet. 1999. (Stella the Stargazer Mystery Ser.). 256p. 23.95 (0-8027-3334-4) Walker & Co.

—Death of a Dustbunny. 1999. (WWL Mystery Ser.: Bk. 308). per. (0-373-26308-2, 1-26308-6, Harlequin Bks.) Harlequin Enterprises, Ltd.

—Death of a Dustbunny. l.t. ed. 1998. (Stella the Stargazer Mystery Ser.). 246p. 22.95 (0-8027-3315-8) Walker & Co.

—A Love to Die For. 1997. (Mystery Ser.). 256p. per. (0-373-26231-0, 1-262310, Worldwide Library) Harlequin Enterprises, Ltd.

—A Love to Die For. 1994. 214p. 19.95 (0-8027-3188-0) Walker & Co.

—You Bet Your Life. 1997. 48p. per. (0-373-26245-0, 1-26245-0, Worldwide Library) Harlequin Enterprises, Ltd.

—You Bet Your Life: A Stella the Stargazer Mystery. 1995. 224p. 19.95 (0-8027-3265-8) Walker & Co.

Kane, Stephanie. Extreme Indifference. 2004. mass mkt. 6.99 (0-7434-6681-0, Pocket); 2003. 304p. 24.00 (0-7432-4556-3, Scribner) Simon & Schuster.

Kenry, Chris. Can't Buy Me Love. 2002. 336p. pap. 14.00 (1-57566-846-7); 2001. 34p. 23.00 (1-57566-845-9) Kensington Publishing Corp.

Lacy, Al. A Dream Fulfilled, 10 vols. 2003. (Angel of Mercy Ser.: Vol. 4). 270p. pap. 10.99 (0-88070-940-5, Multnomah Bks.) Multnomah Pubs., Inc.

—Not by Might, 10 vols. 2003. (Angel of Mercy Ser.: Vol. 8). 349p. pap. 10.99 (1-57673-242-8, Multnomah Fiction) Multnomah Pubs., Inc.

—One More Sunrise. 2004. pap. (1-59052-308-3) Multnomah Pubs., Inc.

Lazar, Zachary. Aaron, Approximately. 1998. 352p. 22.00 o.p. (0-06-039211-8, ReganBooks) HarperTrade.

—Aaron, Approximately. 1999. 352p. pap. 13.50 (0-380-73213-0, Avon Bks.) Morrow/Avon.

Ledbetter, Suzann. A Lady Never Trifles with Thieves. 2003. (Illus.). 224p. mass mkt. 5.99 (0-7434-5747-1, Pocket) Simon & Schuster.

Montgomery, Yvonne. Scavengers. 1990. 256p. pap. 3.50 (0-380-71002-1, Avon Bks.); 1987. 240p. 16.95 o.p. (0-87795-897-1, Morrow, William & Co.) Morrow/Avon.

Most, Bruce W. Bonded for Murder: A Ruby Dark Mystery. 1996. (Dead Letter Mysteries Ser.). 279p. mass mkt. 5.99 (0-312-96051-4, St. Martin's Paperbacks) St. Martin's Pr.

—Missing Bonds, Vol. 1. 1997. (Ruby Dark Ser.). 288p. mass mkt. 5.99 (0-312-96273-8, St. Martin's Paperbacks) St. Martin's Pr.

OakGrove, Artemis. Led Astray. 1994. 280p. (Orig.). pap. 9.95 (1-885084-00-5) Tickerwick Pubns.

Orde, A. J., pseud. Death & the Dogwalker. 1993. mass mkt. 4.50 o.s.i (0-449-22027-3, Fawcett) Ballantine Bks.

—Death for Old Times' Sake. 1993. mass mkt. 4.50 o.s.i (0-449-22193-8, Fawcett) Ballantine Bks.

—Death for Old Times' Sake. 1992. 240p. 16.50 o.s.i (0-385-41941-4) Doubleday Publishing.

—A Little Neighborhood Murder. 1992. mass mkt. 4.50 o.s.i (0-449-22026-5, Fawcett) Ballantine Bks.

—A Little Neighborhood Murder. l.t. ed. 1992. (Linford Mystery Library). 448p. pap. 17.99 o.p. (0-7089-7163-6, Linford) Thorpe, F. A. Pubs. GBR. *Dist:* Ulverscroft Large Print Bks., Ltd., Ulverscroft Large Print Canada, Ltd.

—A Long Time Dead. 1995. mass mkt. 5.50 o.s.i (0-449-22359-0, Fawcett) Ballantine Bks.

Orde, A. J., pseud & Tepper, Sheri S. Death of Innocents. 1997. (Jason Lynx Mystery Ser.). mass mkt. 5.99 o.s.i (0-449-22519-4, Fawcett) Ballantine Bks.

Overholser, Stephen. Shadow Valley Rising: A Western Story. l.t. ed. 2002. (Five Star First Edition Western Ser.). 235p. 24.95 (0-7862-3266-8) Gale Group.

Proulx, E. Annie. That Old Ace in the Hole: A Novel. 2003. 352p. pap. 12.00 (0-7432-4147-9); 2003. mass mkt. 7.99 (0-7432-4148-7); 2002. 384p. 26.00 (0-684-81307-6); 2002. 560p. 26.00 (0-7432-4092-8) Simon & Schuster. (Scribner).

Ramos. The Last Client of Luis Montez, Vol. 1. 1997. mass mkt. o.p. (0-312-96105-7, St. Martin's Paperbacks) St. Martin's Pr.

Ramos, Manuel. The Ballad of Gato Guerrero. 1994. 192p. 18.95 o.p. (0-312-10935-0, Saint Martin's Minotaur) St. Martin's Pr.

—The Ballad of Gato Guerrero. 2004. (Latino Voices Ser.). 192p. pap. 14.00 (0-8101-2091-7) Northwestern Univ. Pr.

—The Ballad of Rocky Ruiz. 2004. (Latino Voices Ser.). 212p. pap. 14.00 (0-8101-2090-9) Northwestern Univ. Pr.

—Blues for the Buffalo: A Luis Montez Mystery. 1997. 240p. 21.95 o.p. (0-312-15480-1, Saint Martin's Minotaur) St. Martin's Pr.

—Brown-on-Brown. 2003. ix, 178p. 21.95 (0-8263-3169-6) Univ. of New Mexico Pr.

—Death of a Martyr: The Ballad of Rocky Ruiz. 1993. 208p. 17.95 o.p. (0-312-09271-7, Saint Martin's Minotaur) St. Martin's Pr.

—The Last Client of Luis Montez. 1996. 208p. 20.95 o.p. (0-312-13997-7, Saint Martin's Minotaur) St. Martin's Pr.

—Moony's Road to Hell. 2002. 208p. 19.95 (0-8263-2949-7) Univ. of New Mexico Pr.

Roberts, Lora. Murder Mile High. 1996. (Liz Sullivan Mysteries Ser.). mass mkt. 5.50 o.s.i (0-449-14947-1, Fawcett) Ballantine Bks.

Sala, Sharon. Remember Me. unabr. ed. 1999. audio 7.99 (1-55204-196-4, MIR-1196) Durkin Hayes Publishing Ltd.

—Remember Me. 384p. 2003. mass mkt. (1-55166-967-6); 1999. mass mkt. (1-55166-535-2) Harlequin Enterprises, Ltd. (Mira Bks.).

Sharpe, Jon. Colorado Cutthroats, Vol. 257. 2003. 176p. mass mkt. 4.99 (0-451-20827-7) NAL.

Shortridge, Jennie. Riding with the Queen. 2003. 352p. pap. 12.95 (0-451-21027-1) NAL.

Smith, L. Neil. The Probability Broach. 1979. mass mkt. 1.95 o.s.i (0-345-28593-X, Del Rey) Ballantine Bks.

—The Probability Broach. 1996. 305p. pap. text 6.99 (0-8125-3875-7, Tor Bks.); 2001. 320p. reprint ed. pap. 15.95 (0-7653-0153-9, Orb Bks.) Doherty, Tom Assocs., LLC.

Stone, Katherine. The Island of Dreams. 2001. 336p. mass mkt. 6.99 (0-446-60954-4); 2000. 272p. 23.95 (0-446-52182-5) Warner Bks., Inc.

—Island of Dreams. l.t. ed. 2000. (Large Print Bks.). 263p. 28.95 (1-56895-955-9, Wheeler Publishing, Inc.) Gale Group.

Stone, Michael. A Long Reach. 1998. (Streeter Mystery Ser.). 240p. pap. 5.99 o.s.i (0-14-024703-3) Penguin Group (USA) Inc.

—A Long Reach. l.t. ed. 1997. (Niagara Large Print Ser.). 320p. 29.50 o.p. (0-7089-5875-3, Ulverscroft) Thorpe, F. A. Pubs. GBR. *Dist:* Ulverscroft Large Print Bks., Ltd.

—A Long Reach. 1997. (Streeter Mystery Ser.). 240p. 20.95 o.s.i (0-670-86166-9) Viking Penguin.

—The Low End of Nowhere: A Streeter Mystery. 1997. (Viking Mystery Suspense Ser.). 240p. pap. 5.95 o.s.i (0-14-024694-0) Penguin Group (USA) Inc.

—The Low End of Nowhere: A Streeter Mystery. l.t. ed. 1997. (Niagara Large Print Ser.). 290p. 29.50 o.p. (0-7089-5863-X, Linford) Thorpe, F. A. Pubs. GBR. *Dist:* Ulverscroft Large Print Bks., Ltd.

—The Low End of Nowhere: A Streeter Mystery. 1996. (Streeter Mystery Ser.). 240p. 20.95 o.p. (0-670-86154-5) Viking Penguin.

—Token of Remorse. 1998. (Streeter Mystery Ser.). 256p. 22.95 o.p. (0-670-87774-3) Viking Penguin.

—Token of Remorse: A Streeter Mystery. 1999. (Streeter Mystery Ser.). 256p. pap. 5.99 (0-14-027546-0, Puffin Bks.) Penguin Group (USA) Inc.

—Totally Dead. 2000. (Streeter Mystery Ser.). 240p. pap. 5.99 o.s.i (0-14-028598-9, Penguin Bks.) Penguin Group (USA) Inc.

—Totally Dead. 1999. (Streeter Mystery Ser.). 256p. 22.95 o.s.i (0-670-88208-9, Viking) Viking Penguin.

Tomlinson, Dar. Designer Passion. 1999. (Love Spectrum Romance Ser.). 399p. pap. 8.95 (1-885478-79-8, Love Spectrum) Genesis Pr., Inc.

Wright, Barbara. Easy Money: A Novel. 1995. 402p. 18.95 o.p. (0-945575-63-7) Algonquin Bks. of Chapel Hill.

Zeltserman, Dave. In His Shadow. 2002. 263p. pap. 16.95 (0-595-21084-8, Mystery & Suspense Pr.) iUniverse, Inc.

## DERRY HILLS (MO.: IMAGINARY PLACE)—FICTION

Hart, Carolyn G. Death in Lovers' Lane. unabr. ed. 1998. (Henrie O Mysteries Ser.). audio 48.00 (0-7366-4168-8, 4670) Books on Tape, Inc.

—Death in Lovers' Lane. l.t. ed. 1997. (Wheeler Large Print Book Ser.). 25.95 (1-56895-467-0, Wheeler Publishing, Inc.) Gale Group.

—Death in Lovers' Lane. 1997. 288p. mass mkt. 20.00 o.p. (0-380-97413-4); 1998. 320p. reprint ed. mass mkt. 6.50 (0-380-79002-5) Morrow/Avon. (Avon Bks.).

—Death in Paradise. unabr. ed. 1998. (Henrie O Mysteries Ser.). audio 48.00 (0-7366-4263-3, 4762) Books on Tape, Inc.

—Death in Paradise. 1999. 304p. mass mkt. 6.50 (0-380-79003-3); 1998. 288p. 20.00 (0-380-97414-2) Morrow/Avon. (Avon Bks.).

—Death in Paradise, Set. abr. ed. 1998. audio 18.00 (0-7871-1704-8, Dove Audio) NewStar Media, Inc.

—Death in Paradise. l.t. ed. 2000. (Mystery Ser.). 415p. 29.95 (0-7862-2679-X) Thorndike Pr.

## DETROIT (MICH.)—FICTION

Alibrandi, Tom. Killshot. 1979. pap. 2.25 o.p. (0-523-40375-5, Pinnacle Bks.) Kensington Publishing Corp.

Allyn, Doug. The Cheerio Killings. 1989. 256p. 22.95 o.p. (0-312-03302-8, Saint Martin's Minotaur) St. Martin's Pr.

—Motown Underground. 1993. 233p. 17.95 o.p. (0-312-08851-5, Saint Martin's Minotaur) St. Martin's Pr.

Allyn, Douglas. Welcome to Wolf Country. 2001. (Five Star First Edition Mystery Ser.). 216p. 23.95 (0-7862-3421-0, Five Star) Gale Group.

Anthony, Sterling. Cookie Cutter. 2000. 336p. pap. 14.00 (0-345-43568-0, One World/Ballantine) Ballantine Bks.

Apple, Max. Zip. 1978. 8.95 o.p. (0-670-79692-1) Viking Penguin.

Arnow, Harriette. The Dollmaker. 2003. 624p. pap. 13.95 (0-06-052934-2, Perennial) HarperTrade.

Arnow, Harriette Louisa Simpson. The Dollmaker. 1999. (SPA.). 608p. mass mkt. 6.99 (0-380-00947-1, Avon Bks.) Morrow/Avon.

—The Dollmaker. 1985. 560p. 24.00 o.p. (0-8131-1544-2) Univ. Pr. of Kentucky.

Beatty, Robert. Sapo. 1996. 285p. 18.95 o.p. (0-9639705-4-2) Ecopress.

Briskin, Jacqueline. The Onyx. 1983. 512p. mass mkt. 5.99 o.s.i (0-440-16667-5); 1982. 448p. 15.95 o.s.i (0-385-28762-3, Delacorte Pr.) Dell Publishing.

—The Onyx. l.t. ed. 1995. (G. K. Hall Core Ser.). 739p. 24.95 (0-7838-1133-0, Macmillan Reference USA) Gale Group.

Burton, Rainelle. The Root Worker. 2001. 208p. 25.95 (1-58567-140-1) Overlook Pr., The.

—The Root Worker. 2002. 208p. reprint ed. pap. 13.00 (0-14-200085-X) Viking Penguin.

Coughlin, William Jeremiah. Death Penalty. l.t. ed. 1993. pap. 22.95 o.p. (0-7927-1541-1); 22.95 o.p. (0-7927-1542-X) BBC Audiobooks America.

—Death Penalty. 1992. 304p. 20.00 o.p. (0-06-017701-2) HarperTrade.

—Death Penalty. 1993. 432p. mass mkt. 5.99 o.s.i (0-06-109053-0, HarperTorch) Morrow/Avon.

—In the Presence of Enemies. l.t. ed. 1993. (General Ser.). 575p. lib. bdg. 22.95 o.p. (0-8161-5695-6, Macmillan Reference USA) Gale Group.

—In the Presence of Enemies. 1994. mass mkt. 6.99 (0-312-95164-7, St. Martin's Paperbacks); 1993. 309p. 21.95 o.p. (0-312-08818-3) St. Martin's Pr.

—The Judgement. abr. l.t. ed. 1995. 352p. lib. bdg. 27.00 incl. audio (1-57490-025-0, Beeler Large Print Bks.) Beeler, Thomas T. Publisher.

—The Judgement. 1999. mass mkt. 223.68 (0-312-96877-9); 1997. 352p. 24.95 o.p. (0-312-15558-1) St. Martin's Pr.

—The Judgment, Set. abr. ed. 1997. 25.00 o.p. (0-7871-1505-3, 695947) NewStar Media, Inc.

—The Judgment. 1999. E-Book 6.99 (0-312-20724-7); (Judgement Ser.: Vol. 1). 424p. mass mkt. 6.99 (0-312-96244-4, St. Martin's Paperbacks) St. Martin's Pr.

—Shadow of a Doubt. l.t. ed. 1992. (General Ser.). 562p. 18.95 (0-8161-5346-9); lib. bdg. 21.95 (0-8161-5345-0) Gale Group. (Macmillan Reference USA).

—Shadow of a Doubt. 1993. 407p. mass mkt. 6.99 (0-312-92745-2, St. Martin's Paperbacks); 1991. 19.95 o.p. (0-312-05961-2) St. Martin's Pr.

Coughlin, William Jeremiah & Sorrells, Walter. Proof of Intent: A Charley Sloan Courtroom Thriller. 2002. 320p. 24.95 (0-312-28066-1) St. Martin's Pr.

Daniels, Jim Ray. Detroit Tales. 2003. 208p. pap. 22.95 (0-87013-662-3) Michigan State Univ. Pr.

Dobyns, Stephen. The House on Alexandrine. 1990. 236p. (C). text 21.95 o.p. (0-8143-2182-8); pap. text 15.95 (0-8143-2183-6) Wayne State Univ. Pr.

Estleman, Loren D. Angel Eyes. abr. ed. 2001. audio (1-58807-602-4); 2000. audio 25.00 (1-58807-045-X) Americana Publishing, Inc.

—Angel Eyes. 1986. mass mkt. 3.95 o.s.i (0-449-21134-7, Fawcett) Ballantine Bks.

—Angel Eyes. unabr. ed. 1986. (Amos Walker Ser.). audio 19.95 o.p. (0-930435-19-2, 369, Bookcassette); audio 57.25 o.p. (1-56100-014-0, 551) Brilliance Audio.

—Angel Eyes. 1981. 11.95 o.p. (0-395-31558-1) Houghton Mifflin Co.

—Angel Eyes. 1984. 256p. pap. 2.75 o.p. (0-523-42185-0, Pinnacle Bks.) Kensington Publishing Corp.

—Angel Eyes. 2000. (Amos Walker Mysteries Ser.). 256p. reprint ed. pap. 14.00 (0-671-03900-8) ibooks, Inc.

—Any Man's Death. l.t. ed. 1990. (Magna Large Print Ser.). 310p. 29.99 o.p. (1-85057-645-9) Magna Large Print Bks. GBR. *Dist:* Ulverscroft Large Print Bks., Ltd., Ulverscroft Large Print Canada, Ltd.

—Any Man's Death. 1987. 224p. mass mkt. 3.95 o.s.i (0-445-40588-0, Mysterious Pr. Paperback Bks.) Warner Bks., Inc.

—Downriver. 1989. mass mkt. 3.95 o.s.i (0-449-21623-3, Fawcett) Ballantine Bks.

—Downriver, 001. 1988. 192p. 15.95 o.p. (0-395-41073-8) Houghton Mifflin Co.

—Edsel: A Novel of Detroit. 1995. 291p. 21.95 o.p. (0-89296-552-5) Mysterious Pr.

—Edsel: A Novel of Detroit. 1999. E-Book 4.95 (0-446-92306-0) Time Warner Bk. Group.

—Edsel: A Novel of Detroit. 1999. E-Book 4.95 (0-446-91298-0); 1996. 256p. reprint ed. mass mkt. 5.99 o.p. (0-446-40366-0) Warner Bks., Inc.

—Every Brilliant Eye. 1987. mass mkt. 4.95 o.s.i (0-449-21137-1, Fawcett) Ballantine Bks.

—Every Brilliant Eye. unabr. ed. 1986. (Amos Walker Ser.). audio 19.95 o.p. (0-930435-26-5, 378, Bookcassette) Brilliance Audio.

—Every Brilliant Eye. Howe, J. C., ed. unabr. ed. 1986. (Amos Walker Ser.). audio 57.25 o.p. (1-56100-021-3, 560) Brilliance Audio.

—Every Brilliant Eye, 001. 1986. 264p. 15.95 o.p. (0-395-39428-7) Houghton Mifflin Co.

—General Murders: Ten Amos Walker Mysteries. 1989. 192p. mass mkt. 3.95 o.s.i (0-449-21696-9, Fawcett) Ballantine Bks.

—General Murders: Ten Amos Walker Mysteries, 001. 1988. 256p. 16.95 o.p. (0-395-41071-1) Houghton Mifflin Co.

—General Murders: Ten Amos Walker Mysteries. l.t. ed. 1992. (Ulverscroft Large Print Ser.). 432p. 29.99 o.p. (0-7089-2622-3, Ulverscroft) Thorpe, F. A. Pubs. GBR. *Dist:* Ulverscroft Large Print Bks., Ltd., Ulverscroft Large Print Canada, Ltd.

—The Glass Highway. 1987. mass mkt. 3.95 o.s.i (0-449-21136-3, Fawcett) Ballantine Bks.

—The Glass Highway. unabr. ed. 1986. (Amos Walker Ser.). audio 57.25 o.p. (1-56100-019-1, 561) Brilliance Audio.

—The Glass Highway, 001. 1983. (Amos Walker Mysteries Ser.). 179p. 13.95 o.p. (0-395-34636-3) Houghton Mifflin Co.

—The Glass Highway. 1984. 224p. pap. 2.95 o.p. (0-523-42263-6, Pinnacle Bks.) Kensington Publishing Corp.

—The Glass Highway. E-Book 9.99 (1-58824-389-3); 2000. 240p. pap. 14.00 (0-7434-0729-6) ibooks, Inc.

—The Hours of the Virgin. abr. ed. 1999. (Amos Walker Ser.). audio 17.95 o.p. (1-56740-847-8, 1743, Nova Audio Bks.); 7p. audio 24.95 (1-56740-437-5, 1741, Bookcassette); audio 57.25 (1-56740-663-7, 1742, Unabridged Library Editions) Brilliance Audio.

—The Hours of the Virgin. 1999. (Amos Walker Mysteries Ser.). 288p. 23.00 (0-89296-683-1) Mysterious Pr.

—The Hours of the Virgin. 2000. 336p. (gr. 8 up). mass mkt. 6.99 (0-446-60868-8) Warner Bks., Inc.

—Jitterbug: A Novel of Detroit. unabr. ed. 1999. audio 69.95 (0-7927-2264-7, CSL153, Chivers Sound Library) BBC Audiobooks America.

—Jitterbug: A Novel of Detroit. 304p. 2000. mass mkt. 5.99 (0-8125-4537-0); 1998. 22.95 (0-312-86360-8) Doherty, Tom Assocs., LLC. (Forge Bks.).

—Jitterbug: A Novel of Detroit. unabr. ed. 1998. audio 60.00 (0-7887-3120-3, 95783E7) Recorded Bks., LLC.

—Kill Zone. l.t. ed. 1991. 23.95 o.p. (*0-7927-1027-4*, CH0167); pap. 21.95 o.p. (*0-7927-1028-2*, CS0268) BBC Audiobooks America.

—Kill Zone. 1986. mass mkt. 2.95 o.s.i (*0-449-12839-3*, Fawcett) Ballantine Bks.

—Kill Zone. 1986. 224p. 14.95 o.p. (*0-89296-065-5*) Mysterious Pr.

—King of the Corner. 1992. (Detroit Trilogy Ser.: No. 3). 304p. 20.00 o.s.i (*0-553-08926-9*) Bantam Bks.

—Lady Yesterday. 1988. 224p. mass mkt. 3.95 o.s.i (*0-449-21467-2*, Fawcett) Ballantine Bks.

—Lady Yesterday, 001. 1987. 15.95 o.p. (*0-395-41072-X*) Houghton Mifflin Co.

—The Midnight Man. 1987. mass mkt. 4.95 o.s.i (*0-449-21135-5*, Fawcett) Ballantine Bks.

—The Midnight Man. unabr. ed. 1986. (Amos Walker Ser.). audio 19.95 o.p. (*0-930435-18-4*, 370); audio 57.25 o.p. (*1-56100-013-2*, 552) Brilliance Audio.

—The Midnight Man, 001. 1982. 230p. 12.95 o.p. (*0-395-32204-9*) Houghton Mifflin Co.

—The Midnight Man. 1984. (Amos Walker Mysteries Ser.). 256p. pap. 2.95 o.p. (*0-523-42186-9*, Pinnacle Bks.) Kensington Publishing Corp.

—The Midnight Man. 2000. (Amos Walker Mysteries Ser.). 288p. pap. 14.00 (*0-7434-0002-X*) ibooks, Inc.

—Motor City Blue. 1986. mass mkt. 4.95 o.s.i (*0-449-21133-9*, Fawcett) Ballantine Bks.

—Motor City Blue, 001. 1980. 9.95 o.p. (*0-395-29447-9*) Houghton Mifflin Co.

—Motown. 1992. 320p. mass mkt. 4.99 o.s.i (*0-553-29728-7*); 1991. 304p. 19.00 o.s.i (*0-553-07421-0*) Bantam Bks.

—Never Street. abr. ed. (Amos Walker Mysteries Ser.). 1998. audio 7.99 o.p. (*1-56740-245-3*, 684, Paperback Nova Audio Bks.); 1997. audio 16.95 o.p. (*1-56100-934-2*, 1311, Nova Audio Bks.); 1997. audio 57.25 o.p. (*1-56100-823-0*, 961, Unabridged Library Editions); 1997. audio 23.95 o.p. (*1-56100-748-X*, 192, Bookcassette) Brilliance Audio.

—Never Street. l.t. ed. 1999. (Magna Large Print Ser.). 432p. (*0-7505-1448-5*) Magna Large Print Bks. GBR. *Dist:* Ulverscroft Large Print Canada, Ltd.

—Never Street. 1998. mass mkt. (*0-446-40483-7*, Mysterious Pr. Paperback Bks.); 1998. 352p. mass mkt. 6.99 (*0-446-60596-4*); 1997. 352p. 23.00 o.p. (*0-89296-633-5*) Warner Bks., Inc.

—Peeper. l.t. ed. 1991. 17.95 o.p. (*0-7451-8203-8*, AH0239); pap. 15.95 o.p. (*0-7927-0751-6*, AS0275) BBC Audiobooks America.

—Peeper. 1990. 224p. reprint ed. mass mkt. 4.99 o.s.i (*0-553-28605-6*) Bantam Bks.

—Roses Are Dead. l.t. ed. 1991. pap. 17.95 o.p. (*0-7927-0589-0*, CS045); 1990. 19.95 o.p. (*0-7927-0588-2*, C0582) BBC Audiobooks America.

—Roses Are Dead. 240p. 1987. pap. 3.95 o.s.i (*0-445-40574-0*); 1986. 15.95 (*0-89296-136-8*) Mysterious Pr.

—Silent Thunder. 1990. 224p. mass mkt. 4.95 o.s.i (*0-449-21854-6*, Fawcett) Ballantine Bks.

—Silent Thunder. l.t. ed. 1990. (Large Print Bks.). 286p. lib. bdg. 18.95 o.p. (*0-8161-4976-3*, Macmillan Reference USA) Gale Group.

—Silent Thunder, 001. 1989. 224p. 16.95 o.p. (*0-395-41074-6*) Houghton Mifflin Co.

—Silent Thunder. 2003. 240p. mass mkt. 6.99 (*0-7434-7480-5*) ibooks, Inc.

—Sinister Heights. 2002. lib. bdg. 29.95 (*1-58547-223-9*, Premier) Ctr. Point Large Print.

—Sinister Heights. 2002. 272p. 24.95 (*0-89296-738-2*) Mysterious Pr.

—A Smile on the Face of the Tiger. l.t. ed. 2001. (Large Print Book Ser.). 311p. 28.95 (*1-58724-024-6*, Wheeler Publishing, Inc.) Gale Group.

—A Smile on the Face of the Tiger. 2000. 304p. E-Book 14.95 (*0-446-92250-1*); E-Book 14.95 (*0-446-93125-X*); 304p. E-Book 14.95 (*0-446-92366-4*); 304p. 24.95 o.p. (*0-89296-706-4*) Mysterious Pr.

—A Smile on the Face of the Tiger. 2000. 304p. E-Book 14.95 (*0-446-92858-5*); E-Book 14.95 (*0-446-96087-X*); E-Book 14.95 (*0-446-91368-5*) Warner Bks., Inc.

—Stress: A Novel of Detroit. 1996. 82p. 21.95 (*0-89296-553-3*) Mysterious Pr.

—Stress: A Novel of Detroit. 1999. E-Book 4.95 (*0-446-92340-0*) Time Warner Bk. Group.

—Stress: A Novel of Detroit. 1999. E-Book 4.95 (*0-446-91299-9*); 1997. 256p. reprint ed. mass mkt. 5.99 o.p. (*0-446-40367-9*) Warner Bks., Inc.

—Sugartown. l.t. ed. 1985. lib. bdg. 16.95 o.p. (*0-89340-931-6*, 159) BBC Audiobooks America.

—Sugartown. l.t. ed. 1985. mass mkt. 4.99 o.s.i (*0-449-20998-9*, Fawcett) Ballantine Bks.

—Sugartown. unabr. ed. 1986. (Amos Walker Ser.). audio 15.95 o.p. (*0-930435-25-7*, 380, Bookcassette); audio 57.25 o.p. (*1-56100-020-5*, 562) Brilliance Audio.

—Sugartown. 1984. 220p. 13.95 o.p. (*0-395-36449-3*) Houghton Mifflin Co.

—Sugartown. 1984. 220p. 25.00 (*0-89366-256-9*) Ultramarine Publishing Co., Inc.

—Sugartown. E-Book 9.99 (*1-58824-394-X*); 2001. 256p. pap. 14.00 (*0-7434-1293-1*) ibooks, Inc.

—Sweet Women Lie. 1991. mass mkt. 4.99 o.s.i (*0-449-21944-5*, Fawcett) Ballantine Bks.

—Sweet Women Lie. 1990. (Amos Walker Mysteries Ser.). 208p. 18.95 o.p. (*0-395-53767-3*) Houghton Mifflin Co.

—Thunder City: A Novel of Detroit. 2001. 245p. mass mkt. 6.99 (*0-8125-4538-9*); 1999. 256p. 22.95 (*0-312-86369-1*) Doherty, Tom Assocs., LLC. (Forge Bks.).

—Thunder City: A Novel of Detroit. l.t. ed. 2000. (G. K. Hall Core Ser.). 327p. 28.95 (*0-7838-9030-3*, Macmillan Reference USA) Gale Group.

—Whiskey River. 1991. (Detroit Trilogy Ser.: No. 1). 336p. mass mkt. 4.99 o.s.i (*0-553-29025-8*) Bantam Bks.

—The Witchfinder. abr. ed. (Amos Walker Mysteries Ser.). 1999. audio 7.99 o.s.i (*1-56740-292-5*, 1753, Paperback Nova Audio Bks.); 1998. audio 24.95 (*1-56740-052-3*, 7, Bookcassette); 1998. audio 57.25 (*1-56740-581-9*, 1101, Unabridged Library Editions); Set. 1998. audio 17.95 o.p. (*1-56740-778-1*, 440, Nova Audio Bks.) Brilliance Audio.

—The Witchfinder. 1998. (Amos Walker Mysteries Ser.). 320p. 23.00 o.p. (*0-89296-663-7*) Mysterious Pr.

—The Witchfinder. l.t. ed. 1998. (Cloak & Dagger Ser.). 408p. 27.95 (*0-7862-1509-7*) Thorndike Pr.

—The Witchfinder. l.t. ed. 2000. (Ulverscroft Large Print Ser.). 416p. 31.99 (*0-7089-4252-0*, Ulverscroft) Thorpe, F. A. Pubs. GBR. *Dist:* Ulverscroft Large Print Bks., Ltd., Ulverscroft Large Print Canada, Ltd.

—The Witchfinder. 1999. E-Book 4.95 (*0-446-92328-1*) Time Warner Bk. Group.

—The Witchfinder. 1999. 320p. mass mkt. 6.50 (*0-446-60760-6*); E-Book 4.95 (*0-446-91300-6*) Warner Bks., Inc.

Eugenides, Jeffrey. Middlesex: A Novel. 2002. E-Book 15.00 (*0-374-70430-9*); E-Book 15.00 (*0-374-70431-7*); E-Book 15.00 o.p. (*0-374-70432-5*); E-Book 15.00 (*0-374-70433-3*); (Illus.). 544p. 27.00 (*0-374-19969-8*); E-Book (*0-374-70434-1*) Farrar, Straus & Giroux.

—Middlesex: A Novel. 2003. 544p. pap. 15.00 (*0-312-42215-6*) Picador.

—Middlesex: A Novel. 2003. mass mkt. 7.99 (*0-312-99173-8*, St. Martin's Paperbacks) St. Martin's Pr.

—Middlesex: A Novel. l.t. ed. 2003. 877p. 28.95 (*0-7862-5700-8*) Thorndike Pr.

Gilmore, Monique. The Grass Ain't Greener. l.t. ed. 1999. (Romance Ser.). 360p. 27.95 (*0-7838-8508-3*) Thorndike Pr.

Grice, Julia. Cutting Hours. 1993. 20.95 (*0-312-09702-6*, Forge Bks.) Doherty, Tom Assocs., LLC.

Hardwick, Gary. Cold Medina. 1996. 352p. 22.95 o.p. (*0-525-93919-9*) Dutton/Plume.

—Double Dead. 1997. 368p. 23.95 o.s.i (*0-525-93920-2*) Dutton/Plume.

—Double Dead. 1998. 400p. mass mkt. 6.99 o.s.i (*0-451-18276-6*, Onyx) NAL.

—Supreme Justice: A Novel of Suspense. 1999. 368p. 24.00 (*0-688-16513-3*, Morrow, William & Co.) Morrow/Avon.

Harris, Anne. The Nature of Smoke. 1997. 288p. pap. 13.95 (*0-312-86351-9*); 1996. 256p. 22.95 o.p. (*0-312-85286-X*) Doherty, Tom Assocs., LLC. (Tor Bks.).

Henning, Barbara. Black Lace. 2001. 90p. pap. 12.00 (*1-881471-62-4*) Spuyten Duyvil.

Hilmon, Darrious. Five Dimes: A Novel. 2003. 256p. pap. 12.95 (*0-451-20869-2*) NAL.

Hirshberg, Glen. The Snowman's Children. 2003. 336p. pap. 13.00 (*0-7867-1253-8*); 2002. 352p. 24.00 (*0-7867-1082-9*, Carroll & Graf Pubs.) Avalon Publishing Group.

Jackson, Jon A. The Blind Pig. 2001. (Detective Sergeant Mullheisen Mysteries Ser.). 228p. pap. 12.00 (*0-8021-3706-7*) Grove/Atlantic, Inc.

—The Blind Pig. 1988. (Modern Hard-Boiled Detective Ser.). 228p. reprint ed. pap. 7.95 o.p. (*0-939767-07-4*) McMillan, Dennis Pubns.

—The Blind Pig. 1979. 7.95 o.p. (*0-394-42613-4*) Random Hse., Inc.

—The Blind Pig. 1988. 228p. pap. 6.95 (*0-89366-275-5*) Ultramarine Publishing Co., Inc.

—The Blind Pig: A Detective Sergeant Mulheisen Novel. 1995. 288p. mass mkt. 4.99 o.s.i (*0-440-21714-8*) Dell Publishing.

—Dead Folks: A Detective Sergeant Mulheisen Mystery. 1996. 272p. 22.00 o.p. (*0-87113-638-4*, Atlantic Monthly Pr.) Grove/Atlantic, Inc.

—Dead Folks: A Detective Sergeant Mullheisen Mystery. 2001. (Detective Sergeant Mullheisen Mysteries Ser.). 264p. reprint ed. pap. 12.00 (*0-8021-3602-8*) Grove/Atlantic, Inc.

—Deadman. 1994. 272p. 20.00 o.p. (*0-87113-562-0*, Atlantic Monthly Pr.) Grove/Atlantic, Inc.

—Deadman: A Detective Sergeant Mulheisen Novel. 1995. 304p. mass mkt. 4.99 o.s.i (*0-440-22047-5*) Dell Publishing.

—The Die Hard. 2001. (Detective Sergeant Mullheisen Mysteries Ser.). 215p. pap. 12.00 (*0-8021-3707-5*) Grove/Atlantic, Inc.

—The Diehard. 1977. 6.95 o.p. (*0-394-41030-0*) Random Hse., Inc.

—The Diehard: A Detective Sergeant Mulheisen Novel. 1995. 272p. mass mkt. 4.99 o.s.i (*0-440-21717-2*) Dell Publishing.

—Grootka. 1990. 352p. 19.95 o.p. (*0-88150-179-4*) Countryman Pr.

—Grootka. 1992. 352p. mass mkt. 4.99 o.s.i (*0-440-21151-4*) Dell Publishing.

—Hit on the House. 1995. 304p. mass mkt. 4.99 o.s.i (*0-440-21711-3*) Dell Publishing.

—Hit on the House. (Detective Sergeant Mullheisen Mysteries Ser.). 2001. 256p. pap. 12.00 (*0-8021-3705-9*); 1993. 237p. 20.00 o.p. (*0-87113-495-0*) Grove/Atlantic, Inc.

Kantner, Rob. Made in Detroit. 1990. mass mkt. 3.95 o.s.i (*0-553-28458-4*) Bantam Bks.

Kienzle, William X. Assault with Intent. 1987. (Father Koesler Mystery Ser.: No. 4). 273p. 9.95 o.p. (*0-8362-6117-8*) Andrews McMeel Publishing.

—Assault with Intent. 1985. (Father Koesler Mystery Ser.: No. 4). 320p. mass mkt. 5.99 o.s.i (*0-345-33283-0*); 1983. mass mkt. 2.95 o.p. (*0-345-30812-3*) Ballantine Bks.

—Assault with Intent. unabr. collector's ed. 1997. (Father Koesler Mystery Ser.). audio 56.00 (*0-7366-3994-2*, 4459) Books on Tape, Inc.

—Bishop As Pawn. 1994. (Father Koesler Mystery Ser.: No. 16). xiii, 266p. 18.95 o.p. (*0-8362-6130-5*) Andrews McMeel Publishing.

—Bishop As Pawn. 1995. (Father Koesler Mystery Ser.: No. 16). mass mkt. 5.99 o.s.i (*0-345-38800-3*) Ballantine Bks.

—Body Count. 1992. (Father Koesler Mystery Ser.: No. 14). viii, 266p. 18.95 o.p. (*0-8362-6128-3*) Andrews McMeel Publishing.

—Body Count. 1993. (Father Koesler Mystery Ser.: No. 14). reprint ed. mass mkt. 5.99 o.s.i (*0-345-37767-2*) Ballantine Bks.

—Call No Man Father. 1995. (Father Koesler Mystery Ser.: No. 17). 272p. 18.95 o.p. (*0-8362-6131-3*) Andrews McMeel Publishing.

—Call No Man Father. 1996. (Father Koesler Mystery Ser.: No. 17). mass mkt. 5.99 o.s.i (*0-345-38801-1*) Ballantine Bks.

—Chameleon. 1991. (Father Koesler Mystery Ser.: No. 13). 289p. pap. 16.95 o.p. (*0-8362-6127-5*) Andrews McMeel Publishing.

—Chameleon. 1992. (Father Koesler Mystery Ser.: No. 13). mass mkt. 5.99 o.s.i (*0-345-36621-2*) Ballantine Bks.

—Dead Wrong. 1993. (Father Koesler Mystery Ser.: No. 15). 269p. 18.95 o.p. (*0-8362-6129-1*) Andrews McMeel Publishing.

—Dead Wrong. 1994. (Father Koesler Mystery Ser.: No. 15). mass mkt. 5.99 o.s.i (*0-345-37766-4*) Ballantine Bks.

—Deadline for a Critic. 1987. (Father Koesler Mystery Ser.: No. 9). 263p. 14.95 o.p. (*0-8362-6123-2*) Andrews McMeel Publishing.

—Deadline for a Critic. 1988. (Father Koesler Mystery Ser.: No. 9). 352p. mass mkt. 5.99 o.s.i (*0-345-33190-7*) Ballantine Bks.

—Deadline for a Critic. 1990. (Father Koesler Mystery Ser.: No. 9). 2.99 o.p. (*0-517-05975-4*) Random Hse. Value Publishing.

—Death Bed. 1987. (Father Koesler Mystery Ser.: No. 8). mass mkt. 5.99 o.s.i (*0-345-33189-3*) Ballantine Bks.

—Death Wears a Red Hat. 1980. (Father Koesler Mystery Ser.: No. 2). 304p. 9.95 o.p. (*0-8362-6111-9*) Andrews McMeel Publishing.

—Death Wears a Red Hat. 1989. (Father Koesler Mystery Ser.: No. 2). mass mkt. 5.99 o.s.i (*0-345-35669-1*) Ballantine Bks.

—Death Wears a Red Hat. 1981. (Father Koesler Mystery Ser.: No. 2). 288p. pap. 3.50 o.p. (*0-553-26524-5*) Bantam Bks.

—Death Wears a Red Hat. unabr. collector's ed. 1997. (Father Koesler Mystery Ser.). audio 56.00 (*0-7366-4063-0*, 4574) Books on Tape, Inc.

—Death Wears a Red Hat. l.t. ed. 1981. (Father Koesler Mystery Ser.: No. 2). 553p. 29.99 o.p. (*0-7089-0647-8*, Ulverscroft) Thorpe, F. A. Pubs. GBR. *Dist:* Ulverscroft Large Print Bks., Ltd., Ulverscroft Large Print Canada, Ltd.

—Deathbed. 1985. (Father Koesler Mystery Ser.: No. 8). 258p. 14.95 o.p. (*0-8362-6122-4*) Andrews McMeel Publishing.

—Eminence. 1989. (Father Koesler Mystery Ser.: No. 11). 312p. 15.95 o.p. (*0-8362-6125-9*) Andrews McMeel Publishing.

—Eminence. 1990. (Father Koesler Mystery Ser.: No. 11). 368p. mass mkt. 5.99 o.s.i (*0-345-35395-1*) Ballantine Bks.

—Eminence. 1990. 3.99 o.p. (*0-517-05976-2*) Random Hse. Value Publishing.

—The Gathering. 2002. 288p. 22.95 (*0-7407-2229-8*) Andrews McMeel Publishing.

—The Gathering. 2003. 304p. mass mkt. 6.99 (*0-345-45794-3*, Fawcett) Ballantine Bks.

—The Greatest Evil. 1998. (Father Koesler Mystery Ser.: No. 20). vii, 278p. 19.95 o.p. (*0-8362-5206-3*) Andrews McMeel Publishing.

—The Greatest Evil. 1999. (Father Koesler Mystery Ser.: No. 20). 294p. mass mkt. 6.99 (*0-345-42638-X*) Ballantine Bks.

—The Greatest Evil. unabr. collector's ed. 1998. (Father Koesler Mystery Ser.). audio 56.00 (*0-7366-4529-2*, 4720) Books on Tape, Inc.

—Kill & Tell. 1984. (Father Koesler Mystery Ser.: No. 6). 250p. 12.95 o.p. (*0-8362-6120-8*) Andrews McMeel Publishing.

—Kill & Tell. 1985. (Father Koesler Mystery Ser.: No. 6). mass mkt. 5.99 o.s.i (*0-345-31856-0*) Ballantine Bks.

—Kill & Tell. l.t. ed. 1984. (Father Koesler Mystery Ser.: No. 6). 378p. 15.95 o.p. (*0-8161-3779-X*, Macmillan Reference USA) Gale Group.

—The Man Who Loved God. 1997. (Father Koesler Mystery Ser.: No. 19). 274p. 19.95 (*0-8362-2754-9*) Andrews McMeel Publishing.

—The Man Who Loved God. 1998. (Father Koesler Mystery Ser.: No. 19). 304p. mass mkt. 6.99 o.s.i (*0-345-40290-1*) Ballantine Bks.

—Marked for Murder. 1988. (Father Koesler Mystery Ser.: No. 10). 281p. 14.95 o.p. (*0-8362-6124-0*) Andrews McMeel Publishing.

—Marked for Murder. 1989. (Father Koesler Mystery Ser.: No. 10). mass mkt. 5.99 o.s.i (*0-345-35397-8*) Ballantine Bks.

—Masquerade. 1990. (Father Koesler Mystery Ser.: No. 12). 267p. 15.95 o.p. (*0-8362-6126-7*) Andrews McMeel Publishing.

—Masquerade. 1991. (Father Koesler Mystery Ser.: No. 12). 384p. mass mkt. 5.99 o.s.i (*0-345-36620-4*) Ballantine Bks.

—Mind over Murder. 1981. (Father Koesler Mystery Ser.: No. 3). v, 296p. 9.95 o.p. (*0-8362-6114-3*) Andrews McMeel Publishing.

—Mind over Murder. 1989. (Father Koesler Mystery Ser.: No. 3). mass mkt. 5.99 o.s.i (*0-345-35667-5*) Ballantine Bks.

—Mind over Murder. 1982. (Father Koesler Mystery Ser.: No. 3). pap. 3.50 o.p. (*0-553-25008-6*) Bantam Bks.

—Mind over Murder. unabr. collector's ed. 1997. (Father Koesler Mystery Ser.). audio 64.00 (*0-7366-4064-9*, 4575) Books on Tape, Inc.

—No Greater Love. 1999. (Father Koesler Mystery Ser.: No. 21). 292p. 19.95 o.p. (*0-8362-7865-8*) Andrews McMeel Publishing.

—No Greater Love. 2000. (Father Koesler Mystery Ser.). 304p. mass mkt. 6.99 (*0-345-42639-8*, Fawcett) Ballantine Bks.

—Requiem for Moses. 1996. (Father Koesler Mystery Ser.: No. 18). 272p. 19.95 o.p. (*0-8362-1042-5*) Andrews McMeel Publishing.

—Requiem for Moses. 1997. (Father Koesler Mystery Ser.: No. 19). 322p. mass mkt. 5.99 o.s.i (*0-345-40291-X*) Ballantine Bks.

—The Rosary Murders. 1979. (Father Koesler Mystery Ser.: No. 1). 257p. 9.95 o.p. (*0-8362-6101-1*) Andrews McMeel Publishing.

—The Rosary Murders. 1989. (Father Koesler Mystery Ser.: No. 1). 304p. mass mkt. 5.99 o.s.i (*0-345-35668-3*) Ballantine Bks.

—The Rosary Murders. 1984. mass mkt. 3.50 o.s.i (*0-553-25084-1*); 1980. (Father Koesler Mystery Ser.: No. 1). 304p. mass mkt. 3.50 o.s.i (*0-553-26406-0*) Bantam Bks.

—The Sacrifice. 1999. 288p. 22.95 (*0-7407-1226-8*) Andrews McMeel Publishing.

—The Sacrifice. 2002. 320p. mass mkt. 6.99 (*0-449-00712-X*, Fawcett) Ballantine Bks.

—The Sacrifice. unabr. ed. 2001. audio 56.00 (*0-7366-6850-0*) Books on Tape, Inc.

—Shadow of Death. 1983. (Father Koesler Mystery Ser.: No. 5). 252p. 10.95 o.p. (*0-8362-6119-4*) Andrews McMeel Publishing.

—Shadow of Death. (Father Koesler Mystery Ser.: No. 5). 1985. mass mkt. 5.99 o.s.i (*0-345-33110-9*); 1984. mass mkt. 2.95 o.p. (*0-345-31251-1*) Ballantine Bks.

—Shadow of Death, unabr. collector's ed. 1999. (Father Koesler Mystery Ser.). audio 56.00 (*0-7366-4330-3*, 4824) Books on Tape, Inc.

—Shadow of Death. l.t. ed. 1983. (Father Koesler Mystery Ser.: No. 5). lib. bdg. 16.95 o.p. (*0-8161-3582-7*, Macmillan Reference USA) Gale Group.

—Sudden Death. 1985. (Father Koesler Mystery Ser.: No. 7). 257p. 12.95 o.p. (*0-8362-6121-6*) Andrews McMeel Publishing.

—Sudden Death. 1986. (Father Koesler Mystery Ser.: No. 7). mass mkt. 5.99 o.s.i (*0-345-32851-5*) Ballantine Bks.

—Sudden Death. l.t. ed. 1986. (Father Koesler Mystery Ser.: No. 7). 416p. 16.95 o.p. (*0-8161-3965-2*, Macmillan Reference USA) Gale Group.

—Till Death. 2000. 279p. 19.95 (*0-7407-0489-3*) Andrews McMeel Publishing.

Kinkopf, Eric. Shooter. 1993. 288p. 21.95 o.p. (*0-399-13772-6*, G. P. Putnam's Sons) Penguin Group (USA) Inc.

Lenzo, Lisa. Within the Lighted City. 1997. (John Simmons Short Fiction Award Ser.). 112p. 19.95 (*0-87745-611-9*); E-Book 19.95 (*1-58729-134-7*) Univ. of Iowa Pr.

Leonard, Elmore. City Primeval: High Noon in Detroit. l.t. ed. 1986. (General Ser.). 350p. 16.95 o.p. (*0-8161-3948-2*, Macmillan Reference USA) Gale Group.

—City Primeval: High Noon in Detroit. 1980. 10.95 o.p. (*0-87795-282-5*, Morrow, William & Co.) Morrow/Avon.

—Freaky Deaky. unabr. collector's ed. 1997. audio 48.00 (*0-7366-3606-4*, 4260) Books on Tape, Inc.

—Freaky Deaky. unabr. ed. 2000. audio 59.95 (*1-56054-962-9*, SAB 016) Chivers Audio Bks. GBR. *Dist:* BBC Audiobooks America.

—Freaky Deaky. abr. ed. 1988. audio 16.99 (*0-88646-232-0*, LFP 7232) Durkin Hayes Publishing Ltd.

—Freaky Deaky. l.t. ed. 1989. 376p. 20.95 o.p. (*0-8161-4708-6*, Macmillan Reference USA) Gale Group.

—Freaky Deaky. 1998. 320p. pap. 12.00 (*0-688-16096-4*, Quill) HarperTrade.

—Freaky Deaky. 2002. 448p. mass mkt. 7.50 (*0-06-008955-5*); 1988. 18.95 o.p. (*0-87795-975-7*, Morrow, William & Co.) Morrow/Avon.

—Freaky Deaky. 1990. 4.99 o.p. (*0-517-03358-5*) Random Hse. Value Publishing.

—Freaky Deaky, unabr. ed. 1995. audio 51.00 (*0-7887-0324-2*, 94516E7) Recorded Bks., LLC.

—Freaky Deaky. 1989. mass mkt. 5.95 (*0-446-35039-7*) Warner Bks., Inc.

—Killshot. l.t. ed. 1990. (General Ser.). 432p. reprint ed. lib. bdg. 20.95 o.p. (*0-8161-4865-1*, Macmillan Reference USA) Gale Group.

—Killshot. 1999. 288p. pap. 12.00 (*0-688-16638-5*, Quill) HarperTrade.

—Killshot. 2003. 416p. mass mkt. 7.50 (*0-06-051224-5*, HarperTorch); 1989. 288p. 18.95 o.p. (*1-55710-041-1*, Morrow, William & Co.) Morrow/Avon.

—Killshot. abr. ed. 1999. audio 7.99 (*0-7871-2047-2*); 1993. audio 14.95 o.p. (*1-55800-156-5*, 40640, Dove Audio); Set. 1998. audio 18.00 (*0-7871-1740-4*, Dove Audio) NewStar Media, Inc.

—Killshot. 1994. (Super Sound Buy, Dove Ser.). 8.99 o.p. (*0-7871-0112-5*) Penguin Group (USA) Inc.

—Killshot. 1991. 4.99 o.p. (*0-517-07549-0*) Random Hse. Value Publishing.

—Killshot. 1990. 352p. reprint ed. mass mkt. 5.95 (*0-446-35041-9*) Warner Bks., Inc.

—Out of Sight. 1998. 304p. pap. 9.95 o.s.i (*0-385-33291-2*, 892924Q, Delta); 1997. 352p. mass mkt. 6.99 o.s.i (*0-440-21442-4*) Dell Publishing.

—Out of Sight. l.t. ed. 1996. 27.95 (*1-56895-385-2*, Wheeler Publishing, Inc.) Gale Group.

—Out of Sight: International Edition. 1997. mass mkt. 6.50 (*0-440-29553-X*) Dell Publishing.

—Pagan Babies. abr. ed. 2000. audio 25.95 o.s.i (*0-553-52751-7*, RH Audio) Random Hse. Audio Publishing Group.

—Pagan Babies. l.t. ed. 2000. 352p. 24.95 o.s.i (*0-375-43086-5*) Random Hse. Large Print.

—Swag. unabr. collector's ed. 1996. audio 42.00 (*0-7366-3234-4*, 3895) Books on Tape, Inc.

—Swag. l.t. ed. 2000. 279p. lib. bdg. 28.95 (*1-58547-041-4*) Ctr. Point Large Print.

—Swag. 240p. 1978. mass mkt. 6.99 o.s.i (*0-440-18424-X*); 1976. pap. 7.95 o.s.i (*0-440-08449-0*, Delacorte Pr.) Dell Publishing.

—Swag, Set. abr. ed. 1987. audio 16.99 (*0-88646-221-5*, 7221) Durkin Hayes Publishing Ltd.

—Swag, unabr. ed. 1997. audio 44.00 (*0-7887-0502-4*, 94698E7) Recorded Bks., LLC.

—Unknown Man, No. 89. 1977. 8.95 o.s.i (*0-440-09216-7*, Delacorte Pr.) Dell Publishing.

—Unknown Man. l.t. ed. 1993. (General Ser.: No. 89). 379p. pap. 17.95 (*0-8161-5696-4*, Macmillan Reference USA) Gale Group.

Lindsay, Paul. Code Name: Gentkill. 1996. mass mkt. 5.99 o.s.i (*0-449-14902-1*, Fawcett) Ballantine Bks.

—Code Name: Gentkill. l.t. ed. 1996. (Niagara Large Print Ser.). 401p. 29.50 o.p. (*0-7089-5839-7*, Ulverscroft) Thorpe, F. A. Pubs. GBR. *Dist:* Ulverscroft Large Print Bks., Ltd.

—Witness to the Truth. unabr. ed. 1993. audio 21.95 o.p. (*1-56100-491-X*, 320, Bookcassette); audio 57.25 o.p. (*1-56100-125-2*, 1102, Unabridged Library Editions) Brilliance Audio.

McMillan, Rosalyn. Blue Collar Blues. Set. abr. ed. 1998. audio 18.00 (*0-7871-1793-5*, 396117, Dove Audio) NewStar Media, Inc.

—Blue Collar Blues. 2001. 416p. E-Book 4.95 (*0-446-92303-6*); 2000. 400p. mass mkt. 7.50 (*0-446-60764-9*); 1999. E-Book 4.95 (*0-446-91291-3*); 1998. 352p. 30.00 o.p. (*0-446-52243-0*) Warner Bks., Inc.

—Knowing. 2001. 416p. E-Book 4.95 (*0-446-92304-4*); 1997. E-Book 4.95 (*0-446-91290-5*); 1996. 416p. 19.95 o.p. (*0-446-51866-2*); 1997. 416p. reprint ed. mass mkt. 7.50 (*0-446-60376-7*) Warner Bks., Inc.

McMillan, Terry. Mama. l.t. ed. 1994. 23.95 o.p. (*0-7927-1777-5*); pap. 21.95 o.p. (*0-7927-1776-7*) BBC Audiobooks America.

—Mama. 1987. 272p. 16.95 o.p. (*0-395-39974-2*) Houghton Mifflin Co.

Meadows, Lee E. Silent Conspiracy. 2002. (Lincoln Keller Mystery Ser.). pap. 16.95 (*1-928623-06-9*) Proctor Pubns.

—Silent Conspiracy: A Lincoln Keller Mystery. 1997. 270p. 24.95 o.p. (*1-882792-38-6*) Proctor Pubns.

—Silent Suspicion: A Lincoln Keller Mystery. 2000. (Lincoln Keller Mystery Ser.). 437p. 24.95 (*1-882792-93-9*) Proctor Pubns.

Osterman, Mark. Happiness Is a Green Light. 2000. 280p. pap. 8.95 (*1-877633-54-2*) Luthers.

Parker, Al. Murder in Detroit. 2000. 185p. pap. 11.95 (*1-56315-260-6*) SterlingHouse Pubs., Inc.

Pietrzyk, Leslie. Pears on a Willow Tree. 1999. 288p. pap. 13.00 (*0-380-79910-3*, Perennial) HarperTrade.

—Pears on a Willow Tree. 1998. 272p. 23.00 o.p. (*0-380-97667-6*, Avon Bks.) Morrow/Avon.

Richards, John. Working Stiff. 1997. 224p. pap. 15.00 (*1-57650-098-5*) Hi Jinx Pr.

Sims, Elizabeth. Holy Hell: A Lillian Byrd Crime Story. 2002. 270p. pap. 13.95 (*1-55583-653-4*) Alyson Pubns.

Slezak, Ellen. Last Year's Jesus: A Novella & Nine Stories. 2002. pap. 13.95 (*0-7868-8638-2*); 224p. 22.95 (*0-7868-6741-8*) Hyperion Pr.

Soos, Troy. Hunting a Detroit Tiger. 352p. 1998. (Mickey Rawlings Baseball Mystery Ser.: Vol. 4). mass mkt. 5.99 o.s.i (*1-57566-291-4*); 1997. 18.95 o.s.i (*1-57566-150-0*) Kensington Publishing Corp.

—Hunting a Detroit Tiger, unabr. ed. 1999. (Mickey Rawlings Baseball Ser.: Vol. 4). audio 60.00 (*0-7887-0926-7*, 95066E7) Recorded Bks., LLC.

Szymanski, Therese. When Good Girls Go Bad: A Motor City Thriller Featuring Brett Higgins. 2003. 274p. pap. 12.95 (*1-931513-11-2*) Bella Bks., Inc.

Verdelle, A. J. The Good Negress. 1999. 312p. tchr. ed. 19.95 (*1-56512-085-X*, 72085) Algonquin Bks. of Chapel Hill.

—The Good Negress. 1996. 320p. pap. 13.00 (*0-06-097683-7*); pap. 60.00 o.p. (*0-06-097693-4*) HarperTrade. (Perennial).

—The Good Negress. audio o.p. National Humanities Ctr.

—Good Negress. 1996. (Illus.). (J). 19.05 (*0-606-18810-X*) Turtleback Bks.

Walker, Mildred. The Brewers' Big Horses. 1996. 441p. pap. 15.00 (*0-8032-9786-6*, Bison Bks.) Univ. of Nebraska Pr.

Wolf, William. Whacking Jimmy: A Novel. 1998. 244p. pap. 15.00 (*0-8129-9239-3*, Villard Bks.) Random House Adult Trade Publishing Group.

### DEVELOPING COUNTRIES—FICTION

Bunn, T. Davis. A Drummer in the Dark. l.t. ed. 2001. (Wheeler Large Print Book Ser.). 613p. 30.95 (*1-58724-138-2*, Wheeler Publishing, Inc.) Gale Group.

—A Drummer in the Dark. 2001. 432p. 21.95 (*1-57856-390-9*) WaterBrook Pr.

Cartwright, Justin. Interior. 1989. 17.95 o.s.i (*0-394-57512-1*) Random Hse., Inc.

Hamilton-Paterson, James. That Time in Malomba. Orig. Title: Bell-Boy. 180p. 1992. 9.95 (*0-939149-68-0*); 1990. 18.95 o.s.i (*0-939149-42-7*) Soho Pr., Inc.

McAllister, V. A. The Mosquito War. 2001. 320p. 25.95 (*0-312-87870-2*, Forge Bks.) Doherty, Tom Assocs., LLC.

### DEVERRY (IMAGINARY PLACE)—FICTION

Kerr, Katharine. The Black Raven. 2000. (Dragon Mage Ser.: Bk. 20). 432p. mass mkt. 6.99 (*0-553-57919-3*) Bantam Bks.

—The Black Raven. 2000. (Dragon Mage Ser.: Bk. 2). 13.04 (*0-606-19271-9*) Turtleback Bks.

—Daggerspell. 1987. (Deverry Ser.: No. 1). 384p. mass mkt. 4.99 o.s.i (*0-345-34430-8*, Del Rey) Ballantine Bks.

—Daggerspell. 1993. (Deverry Ser.: No. 1). 480p. mass mkt. 6.99 (*0-553-56521-4*, Spectra) Bantam Bks.

—Daggerspell. 1986. (Deverry Ser.: No. 1). (Illus.). xi, 414p. 16.95 o.s.i (*0-385-23108-3*) Doubleday Publishing.

—Darkspell. 1988. (Deverry Ser.: No. 2). mass mkt. 4.99 o.s.i (*0-345-34431-6*, Del Rey) Ballantine Bks.

—Darkspell. 1994. (Deverry Ser.: No. 2). 432p. mass mkt. 6.99 (*0-553-56888-4*, Spectra) Bantam Bks.

—Darkspell. 1987. (Deverry Ser.: No. 2). (Illus.). xi, 369p. 17.95 o.s.i (*0-385-23109-1*) Doubleday Publishing.

—Dawnspell: The Bristling Wood. 1990. (Deverry Ser.: No. 3). 384p. mass mkt. 6.99 (*0-553-28581-5*, Spectra) Bantam Bks.

—Days of Air & Darkness. (Deverry Ser.: No. 8). 1995. 432p. mass mkt. 6.99 (*0-553-57262-8*); 1994. (Illus.). xiii, 415p. pap. 12.95 o.s.i (*0-553-37289-0*) Bantam Bks.

—Days of Blood & Fire. (Deverry Ser.: No. 7). 1994. 528p. mass mkt. 6.99 (*0-553-29012-6*); 1993. 416p. pap. 11.95 o.s.i (*0-553-37204-1*) Bantam Bks.

—The Dragon Revenant. 1991. (Deverry Ser.: No. 4). 432p. mass mkt. 6.99 (*0-553-28909-8*, Spectra) Bantam Bks.

—The Dragon Revenant. 1990. (Deverry Ser.: No. 4). 416p. pap. 19.00 (*0-385-41098-0*) Broadway Bks.

—The Dragon Revenant. 1990. (Deverry Ser.: No. 4). xi, 403p. 18.95 o.s.i (*0-385-26140-3*) Doubleday Publishing.

—The Red Wyvern. 1998. (Dragon Mage Ser.: Bk. 1). 416p. mass mkt. 6.99 (*0-553-57264-4*) Bantam Bks.

—A Time of Exile. 1992. (Deverry Ser.: No. 5). 432p. mass mkt. 6.99 (*0-553-29813-5*, Spectra) Bantam Bks.

—A Time of Exile. 1991. (Deverry Ser.: No. 5). 444p. pap. 19.00 (*0-385-41464-1*) Broadway Bks.

—A Time of Exile. 1991. (Deverry Ser.: No. 5). 444p. 22.00 o.s.i (*0-385-41463-3*) Doubleday Publishing.

—A Time of Omens. (Deverry Ser.: No. 6). 1993. 432p. mass mkt. 6.99 (*0-553-29011-8*); 1992. xi, 406p. 22.50 o.s.i (*0-553-08913-7*, Spectra); 1992. xi, 406p. pap. 11.00 o.s.i (*0-553-35235-0*, Spectra) Bantam Bks.

### D'HARAN EMPIRE (IMAGINARY PLACE)—FICTION

Goodkind, Terry. Blood of the Fold. unabr. ed. 1999. (Sword of Truth Ser.: Bk. 3). audio 34.95 o.p. (*1-56740-415-4*, 1626, Bookcassette); audio 137.25 (*1-56740-638-6*, 1627, Unabridged Library Editions) Brilliance Audio.

—Blood of the Fold. (Sword of Truth Ser.: Vol. 3). 1997. 623p. mass mkt. 7.99 (*0-8125-5147-8*); 1996. 464p. 29.95 (*0-312-89052-4*) Doherty, Tom Assocs., LLC. (Tor Bks.).

—Blood of the Fold. abr. ed. 1998. (Sword of Truth Ser.: Bk. 3). audio 16.95 (*1-55935-238-8*) Soundelux Audio Publishing.

—Faith of the Fallen. (Sword of Truth Ser.: Bk. 6). 2000. 512p. 27.95 (*0-312-86786-7*, NHC 0167); 2000. 512p. pap. 200.00 (*0-312-87521-5*); 2001. 800p. reprint ed. mass mkt. 7.99 (*0-8125-7639-X*) Doherty, Tom Assocs., LLC. (Tor Bks.).

—Soul of the Fire. unabr. ed. 1999. (Sword of Truth Ser.: Bk. 5). audio 34.95 o.p. (*1-56740-403-0*, 1584, Bookcassette); 24p. audio 137.25 (*1-56740-632-7*, 1585, Unabridged Library Editions) Brilliance Audio.

—Soul of the Fire. (Sword of Truth Ser.: Bk. 5). 2000. 800p. mass mkt. 7.99 (*0-8125-5149-4*); 1999. 528p. 27.95 (*0-312-89054-0*) Doherty, Tom Assocs., LLC. (Tor Bks.).

—Stone of Tears. (Sword of Truth Ser.). unabr. ed. 2004. audio 39.95 (*1-59355-555-5*, 5180, Brilliance Audio Unabridged); unabr. ed. 2004. audio 217.25 (*1-59355-556-3*, 5181, Brilliance Audio Unabridged Lib Ed); unabr. ed. 1998. audio 217.25 (*1-56740-556-8*, 1060, Unabridged Library Editions); 2nd unabr. ed. 1998. audio 44.95 (*1-56100-777-3*, 279, Bookcassette) Brilliance Audio.

—Stone of Tears. (Sword of Truth Ser.: Bk. 2). 1996. 982p. mass mkt. 7.99 (*0-8125-4809-4*); 4th ed. 1995. (Illus.). 703p. 27.95 (*0-312-85706-3*, CPHC0706) Doherty, Tom Assocs., LLC. (Tor Bks.).

—The Sword of Truth, 3 vols. 1998. (Sword of Truth Ser.). 23.97 o.s.i (*0-8125-7560-1*, Forge Bks.) Doherty, Tom Assocs., LLC.

—Temple of the Winds. unabr. ed. 1997. (Sword of Truth Ser.: Bk. 4). audio 169.25 (*1-56740-555-X*, 1070, Unabridged Library Editions); audio 35.95 o.p. (*1-56100-776-5*, 287, Bookcassette) Brilliance Audio.

—Temple of the Winds. (Sword of Truth Ser.: Bk. 4). 1999. 0.01 o.p. (*0-312-86406-X*); 1998. 832p. mass mkt. 7.99 (*0-8125-5148-6*); 1997. 416p. 29.95 (*0-312-89053-2*) Doherty, Tom Assocs., LLC. (Tor Bks.).

—Wizard's First Rule. unabr. ed. 1994. (Sword of Truth Ser.: Bk. 1). audio 169.25 (*1-56100-223-2*, 1103, Unabridged Library Editions); audio 35.95 (*1-56100-598-3*, 321, Bookcassette);Set. audio 17.00 o.p. (*1-56100-389-1*, 1410, Nova Audio Bks.) Brilliance Audio.

—Wizard's First Rule. (Sword of Truth Ser.: Bk. 1). 2003. 848p. mass mkt. 2.99 o.s.i (*0-7653-4652-4*); 1997. 836p. (J). mass mkt. 7.99 (*0-8125-4805-1*); 1994. (Illus.). 573p. 29.95 (*0-312-85705-5*) Doherty, Tom Assocs., LLC. (Tor Bks.).

—Wizard's First Rule, abr. ed. 2000. (Sword of Truth Ser.: Bk. 1). audio 7.95 (*1-57815-131-7*, 1090, Media Bks. Audio Publishing) Media Bks., L. L. C.

### DINOSAUR PLANET (IMAGINARY PLACE)—FICTION

McCaffrey, Anne. Dinosaur Planet. 1984. 288p. mass mkt. 6.99 (*0-345-31995-8*); 1982. mass mkt. 2.25 o.p. (*0-345-30776-3*); 1980. mass mkt. 2.25 o.p. (*0-345-29593-5*) Ballantine Bks. (Del Rey).

—Dinosaur Planet. l.t. ed. 2000. (Science Fiction Ser.). 280p. 25.95 (*0-7838-8853-8*) Thorndike Pr.

—Dinosaur Planet; Dinosaur Planet Survivors. 1994. mass mkt. o.p. (*0-345-38897-6*, Del Rey) Ballantine Bks.

—Dinosaur Planet Survivors. 1984. 304p. mass mkt. 6.99 (*0-345-27246-3*, Del Rey) Ballantine Bks.

### DISCWORLD (IMAGINARY PLACE)—FICTION

Briggs, Stephen & Pratchett, Terry, contrib. by. Terry Pratchett's Guards! Guards! The Play. 1997. xix, 180p. 12.95 (*0-552-14431-2*) Transworld Publishers Ltd. GBR. *Dist:* Trafalgar Square.

Pratchett, Terry. Carpe Jugulum. 1999. 432p. (YA). (gr. 9). mass mkt. (*0-552-14615-3*, Corgi) Bantam Bks.

—Carpe Jugulum. unabr. ed. 2000. (Discworld Ser.). 8p. audio 69.95 (*0-7531-0838-0*, 000603) ISIS Audio Bks. GBR. *Dist:* Ulverscroft Large Print Bks., Ltd.

—Carpe Jugulum. (Discworld Ser.). 2000. 400p. mass mkt. 6.99 (*0-06-102039-7*, HarperTorch); 1999. 296p. (J). 24.00 (*0-06-105158-6*, Eos) Morrow/Avon.

—The Colour of Magic. 1990. (Discworld Ser.). 284p. mass mkt. 6.99 (*0-552-12475-3*) Bantam Bks.

—The Colour of Magic. 2000. (Discworld Ser.). 240p. mass mkt. 6.99 (*0-06-102071-0*, Perennial) HarperTrade.

—The Colour of Magic. unabr. ed. 1997. (Discworld Ser.). audio 54.95 (*1-85695-800-0*, 950401) ISIS Audio Bks. GBR. *Dist:* Ulverscroft Large Print Bks., Ltd.

—The Colour of Magic. l.t. ed. (Discworld Ser.). 23.95 (*1-85695-364-5*) ISIS Large Print Bks. GBR. *Dist:* Transaction Pubs.

—The Colour of Magic. 1985. (Discworld Ser.). mass mkt. 3.50 o.p. (*0-451-15705-2*); 256p. mass mkt. 4.99 o.p. (*0-451-45112-0*); mass mkt. 2.95 o.p. (*0-451-13577-6*) NAL. (ROC).

—The Colour of Magic. 1990. (Discworld Ser.). 25.00 (*0-86140-324-X*) Smythe, Colin Ltd. GBR. *Dist:* Dufour Editions, Inc.

—The Colour of Magic. 1983. (Discworld Ser.). 160p. 11.95 o.p. (*0-312-15084-9*) St. Martin's Pr.

—The Colour of Magic. 2000. audio 16.95 (*0-552-14017-1*) Trafalgar Square.

—Death's Domain: A Discworld Map. 2003. (Discworld Ser.). (Illus.). pap. 15.95 (*0-552-14672-2*) Transworld Publishers Ltd. GBR. *Dist:* Trafalgar Square.

—Equal Rites. 1987. (Discworld Ser.). 256p. 18.95 o.p. (*0-575-03950-7*) Gollancz, Victor GBR. *Dist:* Trafalgar Square.

—Equal Rites. 2000. (Discworld Ser.). 240p. mass mkt. 6.99 (*0-06-102069-9*, Perennial) HarperTrade.

—Equal Rites, unabr. ed. 1998. (Discworld Ser.). audio 54.95 (*1-85695-828-0*, 951001) ISIS Audio Bks. GBR. *Dist:* Ulverscroft Large Print Bks., Ltd.

—Equal Rites. l.t. ed. (Discworld Ser.). 23.95 (*1-85695-387-4*) ISIS Large Print Bks. GBR. *Dist:* Transaction Pubs.

—Equal Rites. 1988. (Discworld Ser.). mass mkt. 3.50 o.p. (*0-451-15704-4*); 256p. mass mkt. 5.99 o.p. (*0-451-45092-2*) NAL. (ROC).

—Equal Rites. 2000. audio 16.95 (*0-552-14016-3*) Transworld Publishers Ltd. GBR. *Dist:* Trafalgar Square.

—Eric. 2002. 224p. mass mkt. 6.99 (*0-380-82121-4*) Morrow/Avon.

—Eric. 1995. (Discworld Ser.). 192p. mass mkt. 5.99 o.s.i (*0-451-45357-3*, Signet Bks.) NAL.

—Feet of Clay. 1997. (Discworld Ser.). (Illus.). 414p. mass mkt. 7.99 (*0-552-14237-9*) Bantam Bks.

—Feet of Clay. unabr. ed. (Discworld Ser.). 2000. audio 69.95 (*0-7531-0519-5*, 990903); 1999. 8p. audio compact disk 79.95 (*0-7531-0744-9*, 107449) ISIS Audio Bks. GBR. *Dist:* Ulverscroft Large Print Bks., Ltd.

—Feet of Clay. (Discworld Ser.). pap. o.s.i (*0-06-105339-2*, Eos); 1997. 384p. mass mkt. 6.99 (*0-06-105764-9*, HarperTorch); 1996. 256p. 20.00 o.p. (*0-06-105250-7*, Eos) Morrow/Avon.

—The Fifth Elephant. 2001. 464p. mass mkt. (*0-552-14616-1*, Corgi) Bantam Bks.

—The Fifth Elephant. l.t. ed. 2000. (Discworld Ser.: Vol. 24). 494p. 27.95 (*0-7838-9307-8*, Macmillan Reference USA) Gale Group.

—The Fifth Elephant. 2001. (Discworld Ser.: Vol. 24). 400p. mass mkt. 6.99 (*0-06-102040-0*) HarperCollins Pubs.

—The Fifth Elephant. 2001. audio compact disk 89.95 (*0-7531-1132-2*, 111322); 10p. audio 84.95 (*0-7531-0839-9*, 001205) ISIS Audio Bks. GBR. *Dist:* Ulverscroft Large Print Bks., Ltd.

—The Fifth Elephant. 2002. 108p. pap. 12.95 (*0-413-77115-6*) Methuen Publishing Ltd. GBR. *Dist:* Consortium Bk. Sales & Distribution.

—The Fifth Elephant. 2000. (Discworld Ser.: Vol. 24). 336p. 24.00 (*0-06-105157-8*, Eos) Morrow/Avon.
—The Fifth Elephant. 1999. audio 16.95 (*0-552-14720-6*) Trafalgar Square.
—The First Discworld Novels. 1999. v, 352p. 33.95 (*0-86140-421-1*) Smythe, Colin Ltd. GBR. *Dist:* Dufour Editions, Inc.
—Guards! Guards! 1998. 411p. mass mkt. (*0-552-13462-7*, Corgi) Bantam Bks.
—Guards! Guards! unabr. ed. (Discworld Ser.). 2000. audio compact disk 99.95 (*0-7531-0697-3*, 106973); 1998. audio 69.95 (*0-7531-0016-9*, 951202) ISIS Audio Bks. GBR. *Dist:* Ulverscroft Large Print Bks., Ltd.
—Guards! Guards! 1991. (Discworld Ser.). (Illus.). 352p. mass mkt. 4.99 o.p. (*0-451-45089-2*, ROC) NAL.
—Hogfather. 1998. (Discworld Ser.). 352p. mass mkt. 8.99 (*0-552-14542-4*) Bantam Bks.
—Hogfather. unabr. ed. 2000. (Discworld Ser.). audio compact disk 69.95 (*0-7531-0759-7*, 107597); audio 69.95 (*0-7531-0520-9*, 991202) ISIS Audio Bks. GBR. *Dist:* Ulverscroft Large Print Bks., Ltd.
—Hogfather. 1998. (Discworld Ser.). 304p. 24.00 o.s.i (*0-06-105046-6*, Eos) Morrow/Avon.
—Interesting Times. unabr. ed. 2002. audio compact disk 84.95 (*0-7531-0738-4*); 1997. audio 54.95 (*1-85695-814-0*, 950603) ISIS Audio Bks. GBR. *Dist:* Ulverscroft Large Print Bks., Ltd.
—Interesting Times. l.t. ed. (Discworld Ser.). 23.95 (*1-85695-254-1*) ISIS Large Print Bks. GBR. *Dist:* Transaction Pubs.
—Interesting Times. (Discworld Ser.). pap. o.s.i (*0-06-105341-4*, Eos); 1998. 400p. mass mkt. 6.99 (*0-06-105690-1*, HarperTorch); 1997. 288p. 22.00 o.p. (*0-06-105252-3*, Eos) Morrow/Avon.
—Interesting Times. 2000. audio 16.95 (*0-552-14425-8*) Transworld Publishers Ltd. GBR. *Dist:* Trafalgar Square.
—Jingo. 1999. 413p. mass mkt. (*0-552-14598-X*, Corgi) Bantam Bks.
—Jingo. 1998. (Discworld Ser.). 336p. (YA). 24.00 o.s.i (*0-06-105047-4*) HarperCollins Pubs.
—Jingo. 2000. (Discworld Ser.). audio 69.95 (*0-7531-0521-7*, 000203); 10p. audio compact disk 89.95 (*0-7531-0884-4*, 108844) ISIS Audio Bks. GBR. *Dist:* Ulverscroft Large Print Bks., Ltd.
—Jingo. 1999. (Discworld Ser.). 464p. mass mkt. 6.99 (*0-06-105906-4*, HarperTorch) Morrow/Avon.
—Jingo. abr. ed. 1998. (Discworld Ser.). audio 18.70 (*0-552-14684-6*) Ulverscroft Audio (U.S.A.).
—The Last Continent. 1999. (Illus.). 411p. mass mkt. (*0-552-14614-5*); 1998. 329p. o.s.i (*0-385-40989-3*) Bantam Bks. (Corgi).
—The Last Continent. 1999. (Discworld Ser.). 304p. 24.00 o.p. (*0-06-105048-2*) HarperCollins Pubs.
—The Last Continent. unabr. ed. 1999. (Discworld Ser.). audio 69.95 (*0-7531-0522-5*, 990203) ISIS Audio Bks. GBR. *Dist:* Ulverscroft Large Print Bks., Ltd.
—The Last Continent. 2000. (Discworld Ser.). 400p. mass mkt. 6.99 (*0-06-105907-2*, Eos) Morrow/Avon.
—The Last Hero: A Discworld Fable. 2001. (Illus.). 160p. 35.00 (*0-06-104096-7*) HarperCollins Pubs.
—The Last Hero: A Discworld Fable. 2002. (Discworld Fable Ser.). 176p. pap. 19.95 (*0-06-050777-2*, Eos) Morrow/Avon.
—The Light Fantastic. 1997. (Discworld Ser.). 284p. (YA). (gr. 9). mass mkt. 6.99 (*0-552-12848-1*) Bantam Bks.
—The Light Fantastic. 2000. (Discworld Ser.). (Illus.). 272p. mass mkt. 6.99 (*0-06-102070-2*, Perennial) HarperTrade.
—The Light Fantastic. 1988. (Discworld Ser.). 256p. mass mkt. 3.50 o.p. (*0-451-15297-2*, Signet Bks.); mass mkt. 5.99 o.s.i (*0-451-16241-2*, ROC) NAL.
—The Light Fantastic. 1987. (Discworld Ser.). 218p. 27.95 (*0-86140-203-0*) Smythe, Colin Ltd. GBR. *Dist:* Dufour Editions, Inc.
—The Light Fantastic. 1958. (Discworld Ser.). 240p. 14.95 o.p. (*0-312-48603-0*) St. Martin's Pr.
—Light Fantastic. abr. ed. 2002. (The Discworld Ser.: Vol. 2). audio 16.95 (*0-552-14018-X*) Trafalgar Square.
—The Light Fantastic. unabr. ed. 1997. (Discworld Ser.). audio 54.95 (*1-85695-831-0*, 950508) ISIS Audio Bks. GBR. *Dist:* Ulverscroft Large Print Bks., Ltd.
—The Light Fantastic. l.t. ed. (Discworld Ser.). 24.95 (*1-85695-369-6*) ISIS Large Print Bks. GBR. *Dist:* Transaction Pubs.
—Lords & Ladies. 1994. (Discworld Ser.). 384p. (YA). (gr. 9). mass mkt. 6.99 (*0-552-13891-6*) Bantam Bks.
—Lords & Ladies. unabr. ed. 1998. (Discworld Ser.). audio 69.95 (*0-7531-0018-5*, 960703) ISIS Audio Bks. GBR. *Dist:* Ulverscroft Large Print Bks., Ltd.
—Lords & Ladies. (Discworld Ser.). 1996. 400p. mass mkt. 6.99 (*0-06-105692-8*, Eos); 1995. 320p. pap. 12.00 o.p. (*0-06-109216-9*, HarperTorch) Morrow/Avon.
—Lords & Ladies. abr. ed. 2000. audio 16.95 (*0-552-14417-7*) Trafalgar Square.
—Maskerade. 1997. 380p. mass mkt. (*0-552-14236-0*, Corgi) Bantam Bks.
—Maskerade. 2001. 10p. audio compact disk 89.95 (*0-7531-0743-0*); 1999. audio 69.95 (*0-7531-0518-7*, 990504) ISIS Audio Bks. GBR. *Dist:* Ulverscroft Large Print Bks., Ltd.
—Maskerade. l.t. unabr. ed. 1998. 24.95 (*0-7531-5156-1*, 151561) ISIS Large Print Bks. GBR. *Dist:* ISIS Publishing.
—Maskerade. (Discworld Ser.). 1998. 384p. mass mkt. 6.99 (*0-06-105691-X*, HarperTorch); 1997. 278p. 22.00 o.s.i (*0-06-105251-5*, Eos) Morrow/Avon.
—Maskerade. abr. ed. 2000. audio 16.95 (*0-552-14426-6*) Trafalgar Square.
—Men at Arms. 1995. (Discworld Ser.). mass mkt. 6.99 (*0-552-14028-7*) Bantam Bks.
—Men at Arms. 1996. (Discworld Ser.). 384p. 20.00 o.s.i (*0-06-109218-5*) HarperTrade.
—Men at Arms. unabr. ed. 1998. (Discworld Ser.). audio 69.95 (*0-7531-0017-7*, 960403) ISIS Audio Bks. GBR. *Dist:* ISIS Publishing.
—Men at Arms. 1997. (Discworld Ser.). 400p. mass mkt. 6.99 (*0-06-109219-3*, Eos) Morrow/Avon.
—Men at Arms. 2000. (Discworld Ser.). xviii, 182p. pap. 12.95 (*0-552-14432-0*) Transworld Publishers Ltd. GBR. *Dist:* Trafalgar Square.
—Monstrous Regiment. 2003. (Discworld Ser.). 368p. 24.95 (*0-06-001315-X*); 368p. 24.95 (*0-06-057815-7*); audio 39.95 (*0-06-056996-4*) HarperCollins Pubs.
—Mort. 1989. (Discworld Ser.). 272p. mass mkt. 6.99 (*0-552-13106-7*) Bantam Bks.
—Mort. 2001. (Discworld Ser.). 272p. mass mkt. 6.99 (*0-06-102068-0*) HarperCollins Pubs.
—Mort. unabr. ed. 1998. (Discworld Ser.). audio 54.95 (*1-85695-845-0*, 950901) ISIS Audio Bks. GBR. *Dist:* Ulverscroft Large Print Bks., Ltd.
—Mort. 1989. (Discworld Ser.). 240p. mass mkt. 5.99 o.p. (*0-451-45113-9*); mass mkt. 3.95 o.p. (*0-451-15923-3*) NAL. (ROC).
—Mort. 2000. audio 16.95 (*0-552-14015-5*) Trafalgar Square.
—Mort. 2000. (Discworld Ser.). xix, 167p. pap. 8.95 (*0-552-14429-0*) Transworld Publishers Ltd. GBR. *Dist:* Trafalgar Square.
—Moving Pictures. 1998. (Illus.). 332p. mass mkt. (*0-552-13463-5*, Corgi) Bantam Bks.
—Moving Pictures. 2002. 368p. mass mkt. 6.99 (*0-06-102063-X*) HarperCollins Pubs.
—Moving Pictures. unabr. ed. 1998. (Discworld Ser.). audio 54.95 (*0-7531-0139-4*, 970601) ISIS Audio Bks. GBR. *Dist:* Ulverscroft Large Print Bks., Ltd.
—Moving Pictures. 1992. (Discworld Ser.). 352p. mass mkt. 4.99 o.p. (*0-451-45131-7*, ROC) NAL.
—Moving Pictures. unabr. ed. 2002. audio compact disk 89.95 (*0-7531-1477-1*) Soundings, Ltd. GBR. *Dist:* Ulverscroft Large Print Bks., Ltd.
—Moving Pictures. abr. ed. 2000. audio 16.95 (*0-552-14010-4*) Transworld Publishers Ltd. GBR. *Dist:* Trafalgar Square.
—Night Watch. 2002. (Illus.). 352p. 24.95 (*0-06-001311-7*) HarperCollins Pubs.
—Pyramids. 1999. 308p. mass mkt. (*0-552-13461-9*, Corgi) Bantam Bks.
—Pyramids. unabr. ed. 1998. (Discworld Ser.). audio 69.95 (*0-7531-0140-8*, 970903) ISIS Audio Bks. GBR. *Dist:* Ulverscroft Large Print Bks., Ltd.
—Pyramids. 1989. (Discworld Ser.). 304p. mass mkt. 4.99 o.p. (*0-451-45044-2*, ROC) NAL.
—Pyramids. abr. ed. 2000. audio 16.95 (*0-552-14013-9*) Trafalgar Square.
—Reaper Man. 1992. (Discworld Ser.). 352p. mass mkt. 5.99 o.p. (*0-451-45168-6*, ROC) NAL.
—The Reaper Man. 1998. 286p. mass mkt. (*0-552-13464-3*, Corgi) Bantam Bks.
—Reaper Man. unabr. ed. 1998. (Discworld Ser.). audio 54.95 (*0-7531-0019-3*, 951103) ISIS Audio Bks. GBR. *Dist:* Ulverscroft Large Print Bks., Ltd.
—Reaper Man. unabr. ed. 2000. audio 16.95 (*0-552-14009-0*) Trafalgar Square.
—Small Gods. 1993. 384p. mass mkt. (*0-552-13890-8*, Corgi) Bantam Bks.
—Small Gods. 1994. (Discworld Ser.). 272p. 20.00 o.p. (*0-06-017750-0*) HarperTrade.
—Small Gods. unabr. ed. 1998. (Discworld Ser.). audio 69.95 (*0-7531-0141-6*, 970201) ISIS Audio Bks. GBR. *Dist:* Ulverscroft Large Print Bks., Ltd.
—Small Gods. 1994. (Discworld Ser.). 384p. mass mkt. 6.99 (*0-06-109217-7*, HarperTorch) Morrow/Avon.
—Small Gods. abr. ed. 2000. audio 16.95 (*0-552-14416-9*) Transworld Publishers Ltd. GBR. *Dist:* Trafalgar Square.
—Soul Music. 1995. (Discworld Ser.). 377p. mass mkt. 6.99 (*0-552-14029-5*) Bantam Bks.
—Soul Music. 1995. (Discworld Ser.). 400p. mass mkt. 6.99 (*0-06-105489-5*) HarperCollins Pubs.
—Soul Music. unabr. ed. 1998. (Discworld Ser.). audio 69.95 (*0-7531-0120-3*, 961204) ISIS Audio Bks. GBR. *Dist:* Ulverscroft Large Print Bks., Ltd.
—Soul Music. l.t. unabr. ed. 1998. (Discworld Ser.). 24.95 (*0-7531-5157-X*, 15157X) ISIS Large Print Bks. GBR. *Dist:* ISIS Publishing.
—Soul Music. 1994. (Discworld Ser.). 80p. 20.00 o.p. (*0-06-105203-5*) Prentice Hall PTR.
—Soul Music. abr. ed. 2000. audio (*0-552-14424-X*) Transworld Publishers Ltd.
—Sourcery. 1989. (Discworld Ser.). 240p. mass mkt. 6.99 (*0-552-13107-5*) Bantam Bks.
—Sourcery. unabr. ed. 1997. (Discworld Ser.). audio 54.95 (*1-85695-862-0*, 950701) ISIS Audio Bks. GBR. *Dist:* Ulverscroft Large Print Bks., Ltd.
—Sourcery. 2001. (Discworld Ser.). 288p. mass mkt. 6.99 (*0-06-102067-2*) Morrow/Avon.
—Sourcery. 1989. (Discworld Ser.). 256p. mass mkt. 5.99 o.p. (*0-451-16233-1*, ROC) NAL.
—Thief of Time. 2002. 432p. mass mkt. (*0-552-14840-7*, Corgi) Bantam Bks.
—Thief of Time. 2002. 384p. mass mkt. 6.99 (*0-06-103132-1*); 2001. (Discworld Ser.: Vol. 26). 336p. 25.00 (*0-06-019956-3*) HarperCollins Pubs.
—The Truth. 2001. 443p. mass mkt. (*0-552-14768-0*, Corgi) Bantam Bks.
—The Truth. 2001. 8p. audio 69.95 (*0-7531-1116-0*) ISIS Audio Bks. GBR. *Dist:* Ulverscroft Large Print Bks., Ltd.
—The Truth. 2002. (Methuen Drama Ser.). ix, 125p. pap. 12.95 (*0-413-77116-4*) Methuen Publishing Ltd. GBR. *Dist:* Consortium Bk. Sales & Distribution.
—The Truth. 2001. 368p. mass mkt. 6.99 (*0-380-81819-1*); 2000. (Illus.). 324p. 24.00 (*0-380-97895-4*) Morrow/Avon.
—The Truth. unabr. ed. 2002. audio compact disk 89.95 (*0-7531-1469-0*) Soundings, Ltd. GBR. *Dist:* Ulverscroft Large Print Bks., Ltd.
—Witches Abroad. 1998. 285p. mass mkt. (*0-552-13465-1*, Corgi) Bantam Bks.
—Witches Abroad. unabr. ed. 1998. (Discworld Ser.). audio 69.95 (*0-7531-0020-7*, 960908) ISIS Audio Bks. GBR. *Dist:* Ulverscroft Large Print Bks., Ltd.
—Witches Abroad. 1993. (Discworld Ser.). 320p. mass mkt. 6.99 o.p. (*0-451-45225-9*, ROC) NAL.
—Wyrd Sisters. 1998. 331p. mass mkt. (*0-552-13460-0*, Corgi) Bantam Bks.
—Wyrd Sisters. 2001. (Discworld Ser.). 288p. mass mkt. 6.99 (*0-06-102066-4*) HarperCollins Pubs.
—Wyrd Sisters, unabr. ed. 1998. (Discworld Ser.). audio 69.95 (*0-7531-0021-5*, 960108) ISIS Audio Bks. GBR. *Dist:* Ulverscroft Large Print Bks., Ltd.
—Wyrd Sisters. 1990. (Discworld Ser.). 320p. mass mkt. 6.50 o.p. (*0-451-45012-4*, ROC) NAL.
—Wyrd Sisters. abr. ed. 2000. audio (*0-552-14014-7*) Transworld Publishers Ltd.
—Wyrd Sisters. 2000. (Discworld Ser.). xviii, 154p. pap. 9.95 (*0-552-14430-4*) Transworld Publishers Ltd. GBR. *Dist:* Trafalgar Square.

Pratchett, Terry, afr. Hogfather. 1999. (Discworld Ser.). 384p. mass mkt. 6.99 (*0-06-105905-6*, Eos) Morrow/Avon.

**DOONA (IMAGINARY PLACE)—FICTION**

McCaffrey, Anne. Crisis on Doona. 1992. 336p. mass mkt. 6.99 o.s.i (*0-441-23194-2*) Ace Bks.
—Decision at Doona. 1987. 256p. mass mkt. 6.99 (*0-345-35377-3*, Del Rey); 1986. mass mkt. 2.95 o.p. (*0-345-33774-3*, Del Rey); 1981. mass mkt. 2.50 o.p. (*0-345-30175-7*, Del Rey); 1979. mass mkt. 2.25 o.p. (*0-345-28506-9*, Del Rey); 1978. mass mkt. 1.95 o.p. (*0-345-27864-X*, Del Rey); 1977. mass mkt. 1.75 o.p. (*0-345-27477-6*, Del Rey); 1975. mass mkt. 1.50 o.p. (*0-345-24416-8*) Ballantine Bks.
—Treaty at Doona. Nye, Jody L., ed. 1994. 352p. (Orig.). mass mkt. 5.99 o.s.i (*0-441-00089-4*) Ace Bks.

McCaffrey, Anne & Nye, Jody L. Crisis on Doona & Treaty at Doona. abr. ed. 1994. audio 19.95 o.p. (*0-7871-0239-3*) NewStar Media, Inc.

McCaffrey, Anne & Nye, Jody Lynn. Doona. 2004. 576p. pap. 15.00 (*0-441-01131-4*) Ace Bks.

**DORSAI (IMAGINARY PLACE)—FICTION**

Dickson, Gordon R. Dorsai! 1986. mass mkt. 3.95 o.s.i (*0-441-16025-5*) Ace Bks.
—Dorsai! 1977. (Science Fiction Ser.). 236p. mass mkt. 1.75 o.p. (*0-87997-342-0*, UE1342) DAW Bks., Inc.
—Dorsai! 1993. (Childe Cycle Ser.). 280p. mass mkt. 5.99 (*0-8125-0398-8*, Tor Bks.) Doherty, Tom Assocs., LLC.
—The Dorsai Companion. 1986. 256p. 5.95 o.s.i (*0-441-16026-3*) Ace Bks.
—Dorsai Spirit. E-Book 25.95 (*0-312-70663-4*); 2002. 432p. 25.95 (*0-312-87764-1*) Doherty, Tom Assocs., LLC. (Tor Bks.).
—The Final Encyclopedia. 1986. 704p. mass mkt. 5.95 o.s.i (*0-441-23777-0*) Ace Bks.
—The Final Encyclopedia. (Childe Cycle Ser.). 1984. 684p. 18.95 o.p. (*0-312-93241-3*, Tor Bks.); Vol. 1. 1996. 704p. 25.95 (*0-312-86288-1*, Tor Bks.); Vol. 1. 1996. 384p. pap. 16.95 (*0-312-86186-9*, Orb Bks.); Vol. II. 1996. 350p. 25.95 (*0-312-86289-X*, Tor Bks.); Vol. II. 1996. 352p. pap. 16.95 (*0-312-86188-5*, Orb Bks.) Doherty, Tom Assocs., LLC.
—Lost Dorsai. 1985. 288p. mass mkt. 3.95 o.s.i (*0-441-49303-3*); 1985. mass mkt. 2.95 o.s.i (*0-441-49302-5*); 1981. mass mkt. 2.95 o.s.i (*0-441-49300-9*) Ace Bks.
—Lost Dorsai. 1993. (Childe Cycle Ser.). 278p. mass mkt. 4.99 (*0-8125-0404-6*, Tor Bks.) Doherty, Tom Assocs., LLC.
—The Spirit of Dorsai. 1985. mass mkt. 3.95 o.s.i (*0-441-77806-2*) Ace Bks.
—The Spirit of Dorsai. 1993. (Childe Cycle Ser.). 256p. mass mkt. 4.99 (*0-8125-0403-8*, Tor Bks.) Doherty, Tom Assocs., LLC.

**DRAGAERA (IMAGINARY PLACE)—FICTION**

Brust, Steven. Athyra. 1993. 256p. mass mkt. 5.99 o.s.i (*0-441-03342-3*) Ace Bks.
—The Book of Taltos. 2002. 400p. pap. 14.00 (*0-441-00894-1*); 1988. mass mkt. 5.99 o.s.i (*0-441-18200-3*) Ace Bks.
—Brokedown Palace. 1987. 288p. mass mkt. 5.99 o.s.i (*0-441-07182-1*); 1986. mass mkt. 2.95 o.s.i (*0-441-07181-3*) Ace Bks.
—Dragon. 288p. 1999. mass mkt. 6.99 (*0-8125-8916-5*); 1998. 22.95 (*0-312-86692-5*) Doherty, Tom Assocs., LLC. (Tor Bks.).
—Five Hundred Years After. (Tor Fantasy Ser.). 1995. 576p. mass mkt. 6.99 (*0-8125-1522-6*); 1994. 448p. 23.95 o.p. (*0-312-85179-0*) Doherty, Tom Assocs., LLC. (Tor Bks.).
—Jhereg. 1987. 256p. mass mkt. 5.99 o.s.i (*0-441-38554-0*); 1985. mass mkt. 2.95 o.s.i (*0-441-38553-2*); 1984. mass mkt. 2.75 o.s.i (*0-441-38552-4*); 1983. mass mkt. 2.50 o.s.i (*0-441-38551-6*) Ace Bks.
—Orca. 1996. 304p. (Orig.). mass mkt. 6.50 o.s.i (*0-441-00196-3*) Ace Bks.
—The Phoenix Guards. 1990. mass mkt. 4.99 o.s.i (*0-441-66225-0*) Ace Bks.
—The Phoenix Guards. 1992. 491p. mass mkt. 7.99 (*0-8125-0689-8*); 1991. 16.95 o.p. (*0-312-85157-X*) Doherty, Tom Assocs., LLC. (Tor Bks.).
—Teckla. 1987. 224p. mass mkt. 5.99 o.s.i (*0-441-79977-9*) Ace Bks.
—Yendi. 1984. mass mkt. 2.95 o.s.i (*0-441-94457-4*); mass mkt. 2.75 o.s.i (*0-441-94456-6*) Ace Bks.
—Yendi. 1987. 224p. pap. 2.95 o.s.i (*0-441-94459-0*, Diamond Bks.) Berkley Publishing Group.

**DRAGONREALM (IMAGINARY PLACE)—FICTION**

Knaak, Richard A. Children of the Drake. 1991. 284p. mass mkt. 4.99 (*0-446-36153-4*, Aspect) Warner Bks., Inc.
—Children of the Drake. 2000. (Dragonrealm Ser.). 292p. pap. 17.95 (*0-595-09208-X*, Backinprint.com) iUniverse, Inc.
—The Crystal Dragon. 1993. 304p. mass mkt. 4.99 (*0-446-36432-0*, Aspect) Warner Bks., Inc.
—The Crystal Dragon. 2000. (Dragonrealm Ser.: Vol. 70). 308p. pap. 18.95 (*0-595-09205-5*, Backinprint.com) iUniverse, Inc.
—The Dragon Crown. 1994. 336p. (Orig.). mass mkt. 5.50 o.s.i (*0-446-36464-9*, Aspect) Warner Bks., Inc.
—The Dragon Crown. 2000. (Dragonrealm Ser.). 332p. (Orig.). pap. 19.95 (*0-595-09204-7*, Backinprint.com) iUniverse, Inc.
—Dragon Tome. 1992. 288p. (Orig.). mass mkt. 4.99 (*0-446-36252-2*, Aspect) Warner Bks., Inc.
—Dragon Tome. 2000. (Dragonrealm Ser.). 288p. (Orig.). pap. 17.95 (*0-595-09207-1*, Backinprint.com) iUniverse, Inc.
—Firedrake. 1989. 272p. mass mkt. 4.99 (*0-445-20940-2*, Aspect) Warner Bks., Inc.
—Firedrake. 2000. (Dragonrealm Ser.). 276p. pap. 16.95 (*0-595-09214-4*, Backinprint.com) iUniverse, Inc.
—The Horse King. 1997. 352p. mass mkt. 5.99 o.p. (*0-446-60353-8*, Aspect) Warner Bks., Inc.
—The Horse King. 2000. (Dragonrealm Ser.). 356p. pap. 20.95 (*0-595-09202-0*, Backinprint.com) iUniverse, Inc.
—Ice Dragon. 1989. 256p. mass mkt. 5.50 (*0-445-20942-9*) Warner Bks., Inc.
—Ice Dragon. 2000. (Dragonrealm Ser.). 256p. pap. 15.95 (*0-595-09213-6*, Backinprint.com) iUniverse, Inc.
—Shadow Steed. 1990. 272p. mass mkt. 4.99 (*0-445-20967-4*) Warner Bks., Inc.
—Shadow Steed. 2000. 272p. pap. 16.95 (*0-595-09211-X*, Backinprint.com) iUniverse, Inc.
—The Shrouded Realm. 1991. mass mkt. 4.95 (*0-446-36138-0*) Warner Bks., Inc.
—The Shrouded Realm. 2000. (Dragonrealm Ser.). 304p. pap. 18.95 (*0-595-09209-8*, Backinprint.com) iUniverse, Inc.
—Wolfhelm. 1990. 251p. mass mkt. 4.99 (*0-445-20966-6*, Aspect) Warner Bks., Inc.
—Wolfhelm. 2000. (Dragonrealm Ser.). 260p. pap. 16.95 (*0-595-09212-8*, Backinprint.com) iUniverse, Inc.

Settings

**DREAD EMPIRE (IMAGINARY PLACE)—FICTION**

Cook, Glen. All Darkness Met: Dread Empire No. 3. 1984. 336p. 2.50 o.p. (*0-425-06541-3*) Berkley Publishing Group.

—The Fire in His Hands. 1984. (Orig.). mass mkt. 2.95 o.s.i (*0-671-45907-4*, Pocket) Simon & Schuster.

—An Ill Fate Marshalling. 1988. 320p. pap. 3.50 (*0-8125-5379-9*, Forge Bks.) Doherty, Tom Assocs., LLC.

—October's Baby. 1984. (Dread Empire Ser.: No. 2). 256p. 2.50 o.p. (*0-425-06538-3*) Berkley Publishing Group.

—Reap the East Wind. 1987. 224p. (Orig.). pap. 2.95 o.p. (*0-8125-3376-3*, Tor Bks.) Doherty, Tom Assocs., LLC.

—A Shadow of All Night Falling. 1983. 256p. 2.50 o.p. (*0-425-06320-8*) Berkley Publishing Group.

**DREAM PARK (IMAGINARY PLACE)—FICTION**

Niven, Larry. Dream Park. 1983. mass mkt. 3.50 o.s.i (*0-441-16728-4*) Ace Bks.

Niven, Larry & Barnes, Steven. The California Voodoo Game. 1992. 352p. mass mkt. 5.99 o.s.i (*0-345-38148-3*, Del Rey) Ballantine Bks.

—Dream Park. 1986. 448p. mass mkt. 6.99 (*0-441-16730-6*) Ace Bks.

—Dream Park II: The Barsoom Project. 1989. 352p. mass mkt. 6.99 (*0-441-16712-8*) Ace Bks.

**DRYCO (IMAGINARY PLACE)—FICTION**

Womack, Jack. Ambient. 1991. mass mkt. 3.99 o.p. (*0-8125-1605-2*, Tor Bks.) Doherty, Tom Assocs., LLC.

—Ambient. 272p. 1987. 15.95 o.s.i (*1-55584-082-5*); 1997. reprint ed. pap. 13.00 (*0-8021-3494-7*, Grove Pr.) Grove/Atlantic, Inc.

—Elvissey: A Novel of Elvis Past & Elvis Future. 1997. 319p. reprint ed. pap. text 13.00 o.p. (*0-7881-5117-7*) DIANE Publishing Co.

—Elvissey: A Novel of Elvis Past & Elvis Future. 1992. pap. 12.95 o.p. (*0-312-85202-9*, Tor Bks.) Doherty, Tom Assocs., LLC.

—Elvissey: A Novel of Elvis Past & Elvis Future. 1997. 320p. reprint ed. pap. 13.50 (*0-8021-3495-5*, Grove Pr.) Grove/Atlantic, Inc.

—Heathern. 1991. 215p. mass mkt. 3.99 (*0-8125-0872-6*); 1990. 16.95 o.p. (*0-312-85078-6*) Doherty, Tom Assocs., LLC. (Tor Bks.).

—Heathern. 1998. 224p. reprint ed. pap. 12.00 (*0-8021-3563-3*, Grove Pr.) Grove/Atlantic, Inc.

—Random Acts of Senseless Violence. 256p. 1995. pap. 13.50 (*0-8021-3424-6*, Grove Pr.); 1994. 21.00 o.p. (*0-87113-577-9*, Atlantic Monthly Pr.) Grove/Atlantic, Inc.

—Terraplane. 1990. mass mkt. 3.95 (*0-8125-0623-5*, Tor Bks.) Doherty, Tom Assocs., LLC.

—Terraplane. 240p. 1988. 16.95 o.p. (*1-55584-165-1*); 1998. reprint ed. pap. 12.00 (*0-8021-3562-5*, Grove Pr.) Grove/Atlantic, Inc.

**D'SHAI (IMAGINARY PLACE)—FICTION**

Rosenberg, Joel. D'shai. 1991. mass mkt. 4.95 o.s.i (*0-441-15751-3*) Ace Bks.

—Hour of the Octopus. 1994. 272p. (Orig.). mass mkt. 4.99 o.s.i (*0-441-16975-9*) Ace Bks.

**DUBLIN (IRELAND)—FICTION**

Adler, Curtis. January Colours. 2004. 320p. pap. 10.00 (*0-684-02092-0*) Simon & Schuster, Ltd. GBR. *Dist:* Simon & Schuster, Inc.

Banville, Vincent. Cannon Law. 2002. 300p. pap. 14.95 (*1-902602-61-7*) New Island Bks. IRL. *Dist:* Dufour Editions, Inc.

Beckett, Samuel. Dream of Fair to Middling Women. Date not set. (*0-7145-4212-1*); 1996. 252p. pap. 15.95 (*0-7145-4213-X*) Riverrun Pr., Inc.

—Endgame. 1993. 264p. 21.95 (*1-55970-217-6*) Arcade Publishing, Inc.

—Endgame. Beckett, Samuel, tr. from FRE. 1958. pap. 3.95 o.p. (*0-394-17208-6*, E96) Grove/Atlantic, Inc.

—Endgame: Production Notebook. rev. ed. 1993. (Theatrical Notebooks of Samuel Beckett Ser.: Vol. 2). Tr. of Fin de Partie. (ENG & FRE.). 256p. 75.00 (*0-8021-1089-4*, Grove Pr.) Grove/Atlantic, Inc.

Binchy, Maeve. Circle of Friends. 1991. 608p. mass mkt. 5.99 o.s.i (*0-440-20996-X*); 1991. 608p. mass mkt. 7.99 (*0-440-21126-3*, 2766354); 1990. 576p. 19.95 o.s.i (*0-440-29400-2*) Dell Publishing.

—Circle of Friends. l.t. ed. 1991. (General Ser.). 755p. 22.95 o.p. (*0-8161-5207-1*, Macmillan Reference USA) Gale Group.

—Circle of Friends. abr. ed. 2000. audio 9.99 (*0-553-52729-0*); 1991. 180p. audio 16.99 o.s.i (*0-553-45270-3*) Random Hse. Audio Publishing Group. (RH Audio).

—Circle of Friends. 1999. (*0-7621-0252-7*) Reader's Digest Assn., Inc., The.

—Evening Class. 2001. E-Book 7.99 (*1-58945-902-4*) Adobe Systems, Inc.

—Evening Class. unabr. ed. 1998. audio 96.95 o.p. (*0-7540-0000-1*, CAB 1423) BBC Audiobooks America.

—Evening Class. 1998. 544p. mass mkt. 7.99 (*0-440-22320-2*, 25456916, Dell Bks.); 1997. pap. 6.99 (*0-440-29550-5*) Dell Publishing.

—Evening Class. abr. ed. 1997. audio 24.95 (*0-553-47765-X*, 695019); audio compact disk 29.95 o.s.i (*0-553-45554-0*) Random Hse. Audio Publishing Group. (RH Audio).

—Evening Class. 1999. E-Book 7.50 (*0-440-33414-4*) Random Hse., Inc.

—Evening Class. unabr. ed. 2000. audio 95.00 (*0-7887-3999-9*, H1076K8, Clipper Audio) Recorded Bks., LLC.

—Evening Class. l.t. ed. (Paperback Bestsellers Ser.). 661p. 1998. pap. 27.95 (*0-7838-8113-4*); 1997. 29.95 (*0-7838-8112-6*) Thorndike Pr.

—The Lilac Bus. unabr. ed. 1993. audio 54.95 (*0-7451-5789-0*, CAB 198) BBC Audiobooks America.

—The Lilac Bus. 1992. 400p. mass mkt. 7.50 (*0-440-21302-9*) Dell Publishing.

—The Lilac Bus. l.t. ed. 1992. (General Ser.). 480p. 18.95 o.p. (*0-8161-5384-1*); lib. bdg. 21.95 o.p. (*0-8161-5383-3*) Gale Group. (Macmillan Reference USA).

—The Lilac Bus. 1984. 200p. pap. 7.95 o.p. (*0-907085-79-2*) Irish Bks. & Media, Inc.

—Scarlet Feather. 2001. 528p. 25.95 o.s.i (*0-525-94593-8*, Dutton) Dutton/Plume.

—Scarlet Feather. 2001. 560p. mass mkt. 7.99 (*0-451-20446-8*, Signet Bks.) NAL.

—Scarlet Feather. l.t. ed. 2001. 912p. 25.95 (*0-375-43106-3*) Random Hse. Large Print.

—Tara Road. l.t. ed. 1999. 743p. (*0-7540-2212-9*) BBC Audiobooks America.

—Tara Road. 2000. 656p. mass mkt. 7.99 (*0-440-23559-6*); 1999. 512p. 24.95 o.s.i (*0-385-33395-1*, Delacorte Pr.) Dell Publishing.

—Tara Road. l.t. ed. (Paperback Bestsellers Ser.). 743p. 2000. pap. 28.95 (*0-7862-1837-1*); 1999. 31.95 (*0-7862-1836-3*) Thorndike Pr.

—Tara Road. 2000. 14.04 (*0-606-18987-4*) Turtleback Bks.

Binchy, Maeve, contrib. by. Tara Road. (*0-7540-1282-4*) BBC Audiobooks America.

Boylan, Claire. Holy Pictures. 1983. 208p. 13.50 o.p. (*0-671-46750-6*) Summit Bks.

—Holy Pictures. 1984. 224p. pap. 3.95 o.p. (*0-14-006811-2*, Penguin Bks.) Viking Penguin.

Boylan, Clare. Beloved Stranger. 320p. 2001. text 24.00 o.p. (*1-58243-096-9*); 2002. reprint ed. pap. text 15.00 (*1-58243-224-4*) Basic Bks. (Counterpoint Pr.).

Brady, John. All Souls. 1993. 304p. 20.95 o.p. (*0-312-09735-2*, Saint Martin's Minotaur) St. Martin's Pr.

—The Good Life. 1995. 352p. 22.95 o.p. (*0-312-13083-X*, Saint Martin's Minotaur) St. Martin's Pr.

—Kaddish in Dublin. 1992. 288p. 18.95 o.p. (*0-312-08229-0*, Saint Martin's Minotaur) St. Martin's Pr.

—A Stone of the Heart. 1988. 256p. 16.95 o.p. (*0-312-01829-0*, Saint Martin's Minotaur) St. Martin's Pr.

—A Stone of the Heart. 2001. (Matt Minogue Mystery Ser.). (Illus.). xxiii, 247p. pap. 14.95 (*1-58642-029-1*) Steerforth Pr.

—A Stone of the Heart. 1990. 256p. pap. 3.95 o.p. (*0-14-013847-1*, Penguin Bks.) Viking Penguin.

—Unholy Ground. 1991. 288p. 18.95 o.p. (*0-312-07109-4*, Saint Martin's Minotaur) St. Martin's Pr.

—Unholy Ground. 2002. (Matt Minogue Mystery Ser.). 208p. reprint ed. pap. 14.95 (*1-58642-037-2*) Steerforth Pr.

Brennan, Maeve. The Springs of Affection: Stories of Dublin. 1998. 368p. pap. 13.00 (*0-395-93759-0*); 1997. 358p. tchr. ed. 24.00 o.p. (*0-395-87046-1*) Houghton Mifflin Co.

—The Visitor. 2001. 96p. pap. text 10.00 (*1-58243-161-2*, Counterpoint Pr.) Basic Bks.

—Visitor. 2000. 96p. text 16.95 o.p. (*1-58243-083-7*, Counterpoint Pr.) Basic Bks.

Butler, Pierce. A Riddle of Stars. 1999. 287p. pap. o.p. (*1-58195-007-1*, Zoland Bks., Inc.) Steerforth Pr.

Casey, Phillip. The Fabulists. 2001. 240p. pap. 14.95 (*1-897959-18-4*) Serif GBR. *Dist:* Interlink Publishing Group, Inc.

Center for Learning Network Staff. Tara Road/the Return Journey: Curriculum Unit —Novel Series— Grades 9-12. 1999. (Novel Ser.). 65p. (YA). (gr. 9-12). tchr. ed., spiral bd. 18.95 (*1-56077-636-6*) Ctr. for Learning, The.

Conlon, Evelyn. A Glassful of Letters. 1998. 208p. pap. 16.95 (*0-85640-618-X*) Blackstaff Pr., The IRL. *Dist:* Dufour Editions, Inc.

Conlon-McKenna, Marita. The Magdalen. l.t. ed. 2001. (Magna Large Print Ser.). 384p. (*0-7505-1733-6*) Magna Large Print Bks. GBR. *Dist:* Ulverscroft Large Print Canada, Ltd.

Costello, Peter. The Life of Leopold Bloom: A Novel. 1993. 197p. (Orig.). pap. 9.95 (*1-879373-34-3*) Rinehart, Roberts Pubs.

Cremins, Robert. A Sort of Homecoming: A Novel. 2000. 304p. pap. 13.95 (*0-393-32023-5*, Norton Paperbacks) Norton, W. W. & Co., Inc.

Crowley, Elaine. A Family Cursed. 1996. 309p. 27.00 o.p. (*1-85797-767-X*) Orion Publishing Group, Ltd. GBR. *Dist:* Trafalgar Square.

Devlin, Martina. Three Wise Men. 2000. 437p. pap. (*0-00-651458-8*) HarperCollins Pubs.

Donoghue, Emma. Stir-Fry. 256p. 1995. pap. 11.00 o.p. (*0-06-092624-4*, Perennial); 1994. 20.00 o.p. (*0-06-017109-X*) HarperTrade.

—Stir-Fry: A Novel. 2001. 240p. pap. 12.95 o.p. (*1-55583-723-9*, Alyson Bks.) Alyson Pubns.

Doyle, Roddy. The Barrytown Trilogy: The Commitments, the Snapper, the Van. 1995. 640p. 18.00 (*0-14-025262-2*) Viking Penguin.

—The Commitments. 1989. (Vintage Contemporaries Ser.). 176p. pap. 12.00 (*0-679-72174-6*, Vintage) Knopf Publishing Group.

—Paddy Clarke Ha Ha Ha. 288p. 1995. 14.00 (*0-14-023390-3*); 1994. 20.95 o.p. (*0-670-85345-3*, Viking) Viking Penguin.

—Paddy Clarke Ha, Ha, Ha. abr. ed. 1995. (Classics on Cassette). (J). audio 16.95 (*0-453-00953-0*) Penguin/HighBridge.

—Paddy Clarke Ha Ha Ha. l.t. ed. 1994. 23.95 o.p. (*1-56895-070-5*, Wheeler Publishing, Inc.) Gale Group.

—Paddy Clarke Ha, Ha, Ha!. unabr. ed. 1995. (J). audio 59.95 (*0-7451-4384-9*, CAB 1068) Chivers Audio Bks. GBR. *Dist:* BBC Audiobooks America.

—The Snapper. 1992. 224p. 12.00 (*0-14-017167-3*) Viking Penguin.

—The Van. 1997. 320p. pap. 11.95 o.s.i (*0-14-026002-1*) Penguin Group (USA) Inc.

—The Van. 1993. 320p. 13.00 (*0-14-017191-6*); 1992. 320p. 21.00 o.p. (*0-670-84587-6*, Viking); 1997. audio 16.95 o.s.i (*0-14-086426-1*, Penguin Audio-Books) Viking Penguin.

Doyle, Rose. Alva. l.t. ed. 1999. (Magna Large Print Ser.). 432p. (*0-7505-1432-9*) Magna Large Print Bks. GBR. *Dist:* Ulverscroft Large Print Canada, Ltd.

—Alva. 2003. vii, 422p. pap. (*0-330-34845-0*) Pan Macmillan.

—The Shadow Player. l.t. ed. 2000. (Magna Large Print Ser.). 448p. (*0-7505-1564-3*) Magna Large Print Bks. GBR. *Dist:* Ulverscroft Large Print Canada, Ltd.

—The Shadow Player. 1999. (*1-86059-098-5*) Town Hse.

Easterman, Daniel. Brotherhood of the Tomb. 1991. 480p. mass mkt. 5.50 o.p. (*0-06-100206-2*, HarperTorch) Morrow/Avon.

Enright, Anne. The Wig My Father Wore. 2001. 224p. pap. 12.00 (*0-8021-3832-2*, Grove Pr.) Grove/Atlantic, Inc.

Fallon, Ann C. Blood Is Thicker. 1990. 256p. (Orig.). mass mkt. 3.95 (*0-671-70623-3*, Pocket) Simon & Schuster.

—Dead Ends. Isaacson, Dana, ed. 1992. 256p. (Orig.). mass mkt. 4.99 (*0-671-75134-4*, Pocket) Simon & Schuster.

—Hour of Our Death. Chelius, Jane, ed. 1995. 256p. (Orig.). mass mkt. 5.50 (*0-671-88515-4*, Pocket) Simon & Schuster.

—Potter's Field. Isaacson, Dana, ed. 1993. 256p. (Orig.). mass mkt. 4.99 (*0-671-75136-0*, Pocket) Simon & Schuster.

—Where Death Lies. Isaacson, Dana, ed. 1991. 256p. mass mkt. 4.99 (*0-671-70624-1*, Pocket) Simon & Schuster.

Flanagan, Thomas. The End of the Hunt. 1994. 640p. 24.95 o.p. (*0-525-93681-5*, Dutton) Dutton/Plume.

Gibson, Maggie. The First Holy Chameleon. 2002. 317p. pap. (*0-575-40323-3*) Weidenfeld & Nicolson, Ltd. GBR. *Dist:* Trafalgar Square.

Gill, Bartholomew. Death in Dublin. 2003. 368p. mass mkt. 6.99 (*0-06-000850-4*, Avon Bks.); 304p. 24.95 (*0-06-000849-0*, Morrow, William & Co.) Morrow/Avon.

Greeley, Andrew M. Irish Gold: A Nuala Anne McGrail Novel. (Nuala Anne McGrail Novel Ser.). 1995. 493p. pap. 7.99 (*0-8125-5076-5*); 1994. 336p. 14.29 o.p. (*0-312-85813-2*) Doherty, Tom Assocs., LLC. (Forge Bks.).

—Irish Gold: A Nuala Anne McGrail Novel. abr. ed. 1994. 17.95 o.p. (*0-7871-0332-2*, 390987) NewStar Media, Inc.

Hamill, Denis. Fork in the Road. 496p. 2000. 24.95 o.s.i (*0-671-01673-3*, Atria); 2001. (Illus.). reprint ed. pap. 14.95 (*0-671-01674-1*, Washington Square Pr.) Simon & Schuster.

Hamilton, Hugo. Headbanger. 2001. 230p. pap. 13.95 (*1-56858-195-5*) Four Walls Eight Windows.

—Sad Bastard. 2001. 193p. pap. 13.95 (*1-56858-206-4*) Four Walls Eight Windows.

Hing, Robert J. Ulysses: His Story. 1996. (Illus.). 176p. (Orig.). pap. 12.95 o.p. (*0-9631460-1-7*) Anchor Watch Pr.

Jordan, John. Collected Stories. McFadden, Hugh, ed. 1991. 206p. pap. 16.95 (*1-85371-105-5*) Poolbeg Pr. IRL. *Dist:* Dufour Editions, Inc.

Joyce, James. Dubliners. 1993. (Modern Library Ser.). E-Book 4.95 (*1-931208-61-1*) Adobe Systems, Inc.

—Dubliners. 1976. 24.95 (*0-8488-1064-3*) Amereon, Ltd.

—Dubliners. 1990. 208p. mass mkt. 4.95 (*0-553-21380-6*) Bantam Bks.

—Dubliners. 1992. reprint ed. lib. bdg. 27.95 (*0-89968-285-5*, Lightyear Pr.) Buccaneer Bks., Inc.

—Dubliners. Goodwyn, Andrew, ed. 1995. (Literature Ser.). (Illus.). 240p. pap. text 9.50 (*0-521-48544-4*) Cambridge Univ. Pr.

—Dubliners. (Collected Works of James Joyce). reprint ed. lib. bdg. 98.00 (*0-7426-3126-5*); 2001. pap. text 28.00 (*0-7426-8126-2*) Classic Bks.

—Dubliners. l.t. unabr. ed. (Large Print Classics Ser.). 2001. 269p. pap. 9.95 (*0-486-41782-4*); 1991. 160p. reprint ed. pap. 1.50 (*0-486-26870-5*) Dover Pubns., Inc.

—Dubliners. Gabler, Hans W. & Hettche, Wettche, eds. 1993. 462p. 55.00 o.p. (*0-8153-1277-6*) Garland Publishing, Inc.

—Dubliners. 1992. 33.00 o.p. (*0-7171-1901-7*) Gill & MacMillan, Ltd. IRL. *Dist:* Irish Bks. & Media, Inc.

—Dubliners. 1993. 304p. pap. 10.00 (*0-679-73990-4*, Vintage) Knopf Publishing Group.

—Dubliners. pap., tchr. ed. (*0-451-52617-1*); 1991. 256p. mass mkt. 4.95 (*0-451-52543-4*) NAL. (Signet Classics).

—Dubliners. 2001. (Twelve-Point Ser.). 250p. lib. bdg. 25.00 (*1-58287-174-4*); 400p. lib. bdg. 26.00 (*1-58287-657-6*) North Bks.

—Dubliners. Johnson, Jeri, ed. & intro. by. 2001. (Illus.). 352p. pap. 8.95 (*0-19-283999-3*) Oxford Univ. Pr., Inc.

—Dubliners. 1969. pap. 2.95 o.p. (*0-670-01805-8*); 1968. pap. 1.45 o.p. (*0-670-00041-8*) Penguin Group (USA) Inc.

—Dubliners. 8th abr. unabr. ed. 1993. (Classics on Cassette). 16.00 incl. audio (*0-453-00845-3*, 390003) Penguin/HighBridge.

—Dubliners. 2000. E-Book 4.95 (*0-679-64160-2*, Modern Library) Random House Adult Trade Publishing Group.

—Dubliners. 1993. (Modern Library Ser.). 304p. 14.95 (*0-679-60049-3*); 1991. (Everyman's Library: Vol. 49). 352p. 18.00 (*0-679-40574-7*); 1978. 9.95 o.s.i (*0-394-60464-4*); 1926. 3.95 o.s.i (*0-394-60124-6*) Random Hse., Inc.

—Dubliners. 1998. (Enriched Classics Ser.). (Illus.). 256p. reprint ed. mass mkt. 4.99 (*0-671-01537-0*, Pocket) Simon & Schuster.

—Dubliners. annot. ed. 1995. (Illus.). pap. 19.95 (*0-312-11779-5*, Saint Martin's Griffin) St. Martin's Pr.

—Dubliners. 1992. (Illus.). 192p. (C). reprint ed. 30.00 o.p. (*0-7509-0015-6*) Sutton Publishing, Ltd. GBR. *Dist:* International Publishers Marketing.

—Dubliners. l.t. ed. 2001. (G. K. Hall Perennial Bestsellers Ser. ). 293p. 27.95 (*0-7838-9369-8*) Thorndike Pr.

—Dubliners. 1998. (Washington Square Press Enriched Classic Ser.). (Illus.). (J). 11.04 (*0-606-20641-8*) Turtleback Bks.

—Dubliners. (Twentieth Century Classics Ser.). 1993. 368p. pap. 9.95 (*0-14-018647-6*, Penguin Classics); 1982. 17.50 o.p. (*0-670-28586-2*); 1982. pap. 6.95 o.p. (*0-14-006285-8*, Penguin Bks.); 1976. 512p. pap. 14.95 o.p. (*0-14-015505-8*); 1976. 224p. pap. 7.95 o.p. (*0-14-004222-9*, Viking); 1969. pap. 5.95 o.p. (*0-670-28585-4*); 1968. 4.50 o.p. (*0-670-28584-6*); 1916. 3.50 o.p. (*0-670-28583-8*) Viking Penguin.

—Dubliners. 1998. (Classics Library). 176p. pap. 3.95 (*1-85326-048-7*, 0487WW) Wordsworth Editions, Ltd. GBR. *Dist:* Casemate Pubs. & Bk. Distributors, LLC.

—Dubliners & Portrait of the Artist As a Young Man. 1998. E-Book 5.00 (*0-7607-1284-0*) Barnes & Noble, Inc.

—A Portrait of an Artist As a Young Man. 1992. 256p. mass mkt. 4.95 (*0-553-21404-7*, Bantam Classics) Bantam Bks.

—A Portrait of the Artist As a Young Man. 2001. (Illus.). E-Book 4.95 (*1-931208-62-X*) Adobe Systems, Inc.

—A Portrait of the Artist As a Young Man. 22.95 (*0-89190-725-4*) Amereon, Ltd.

—A Portrait of the Artist As a Young Man. abr. ed. 1993. audio 16.99 (*0-88646-343-2*) Durkin Hayes Publishing Ltd.

—A Portrait of the Artist As a Young Man. Gabler, Hans W. & Hettche, Walter, eds. 1993. 366p. text 61.00 (*0-8153-1278-4*) Garland Publishing, Inc.

—A Portrait of the Artist As a Young Man. abr. ed. audio 12.95 o.p. (*0-694-50084-4*, SWC 1110, Caedmon) HarperTrade.

—A Portrait of the Artist As a Young Man. 1993. 288p. pap. 10.00 (*0-679-73989-0*, Vintage) Knopf Publishing Group.

—A Portrait of the Artist As a Young Man. 1991. (Everyman's Library: Vol. 9). 368p. 17.00 (*0-679-40575-5*) Knopf, Alfred A. Inc.
—A Portrait of the Artist As a Young Man. 1991. 256p. mass mkt. 4.95 (*0-451-52544-2*, Signet Classics) NAL.
—A Portrait of the Artist As a Young Man. abr. ed. 1996. (Works of James Joyce). audio 17.98 (*962-634-570-5*, NA307014, Naxos AudioBooks) Naxos of America, Inc.
—A Portrait of the Artist As a Young Man. Johnson, Jeri, ed. & intro. by. 2001. 352p. pap. 7.95 (*0-19-283998-5*) Oxford Univ. Pr., Inc.
—A Portrait of the Artist As a Young Man. Kershner, R. B., ed. 1993. (Case Studies in Contemporary Criticism). 416p. (C). text 35.00 o.p. (*0-312-08987-2*) Palgrave Macmillan.
—A Portrait of the Artist As a Young Man. 2003. 384p. pap. 9.00 (*0-14-243734-4*); 1999. 240p. pap. 10.95 (*0-14-028328-5*); 1977. pap. 1.95 o.p. (*0-14-004579-1*); 1964. pap. 1.65 o.p. (*0-670-00009-4*) Penguin Group (USA) Inc.
—A Portrait of the Artist As a Young Man. 1996. E-Book 4.95 (*0-679-64161-0*, Modern Library) Random House Adult Trade Publishing Group.
—A Portrait of the Artist As a Young Man. 1996. (Modern Library Ser.). 368p. 17.95 (*0-679-60232-1*) Random Hse., Inc.
—A Portrait of the Artist As a Young Man. 1995. pap. 13.95 o.p. (*0-312-13845-8*) St. Martin's Pr.
—A Portrait of the Artist As a Young Man. 1916. 15.00 (*0-606-02826-9*) Turtleback Bks.
—A Portrait of the Artist As a Young Man. 1993. (Penguin Twentieth-Century Classics Ser.). 384p. pap. 8.95 o.s.i (*0-14-018683-2*, Penguin Classics) Viking Penguin.
—A Portrait of the Artist As a Young Man. Ellmann, Richard, ed. 1982. 17.50 o.p. (*0-670-56683-7*) Viking Penguin.
—A Portrait of the Artist As a Young Man. 1964. 256p. pap. 7.00 o.p. (*0-14-004221-0*, Penguin Bks.); 1964. 10.00 o.p. (*0-670-56682-9*); 1916. 3.50 o.p. (*0-670-56681-0*) Viking Penguin.
—A Portrait of the Artist As a Young Man. 1997. (Classics Ser.). 208p. pap. 3.95 (*1-85326-006-1*, 0061WW) Wordsworth Editions, Ltd. GBR. *Dist:* Casemate Pubs. & Bk. Distributors, LLC.
—A Portrait of the Artist As a Young Man. abr. ed. 1995. (Works of James Joyce). audio compact disk 19.98 (*962-634-070-3*, NA307012, Naxos Audio-Books) Naxos of America, Inc.
—A Portrait of the Artist As a Young Man, Set. unabr. ed. 1994. audio 41.95 (*1-55685-317-3*) Audio Bk. Contractors, Inc.
—A Portrait of the Artist As a Young Man. unabr. ed. 1995. audio 49.95 (*0-7861-0655-7*, 1559) Blackstone Audio Bks., Inc.
—A Portrait of the Artist As a Young Man. unabr. collector's ed. 1992. (J). audio 56.00 (*0-7366-2301-9*, 3085) Books on Tape, Inc.
—A Portrait of the Artist As a Young Man. 1992. 350p. reprint ed. lib. bdg. 26.95 (*0-89966-899-2*) Buccaneer Bks., Inc.
—A Portrait of the Artist As a Young Man. reprint ed. lib. bdg. 98.00 (*0-7426-3127-3*); 2001. pap. text 28.00 (*0-7426-8127-0*) Classic Bks.
—A Portrait of the Artist As a Young Man. 1994. (Thrift Editions Ser.). 192p. reprint ed. pap. 2.00 (*0-486-28050-0*) Dover Pubns., Inc.
—A Portrait of the Artist As a Young Man. unabr. ed. 1993. (YA). (gr. 11-12). audio 28.00 Jimcin Recordings.
—A Portrait of the Artist As a Young Man. l.t. ed. 1995. 410p. lib. bdg. 26.00 (*0-939495-86-4*); 1998. 255p. reprint ed. lib. bdg. 25.00 (*1-58287-057-8*) North Bks.
—A Portrait of the Artist As a Young Man, unabr. ed. 1999. audio 70.00 (*1-55690-421-5*, 91106E7) Recorded Bks., LLC.
—A Portrait of the Artist As a Young Man. 1998. (Enriched Classics Ser.). (Illus.). 288p. reprint ed. mass mkt. 5.99 (*0-671-01538-9*, Pocket) Simon & Schuster.
—A Portrait of the Artist As a Young Man: Text & Criticism. Anderson, Chester G., ed. (Critical Studies). 1977. 576p. 15.95 (*0-14-015503-1*); 1964. (J). (gr. 9 up). pap. 8.95 o.p. (*0-670-56648-9*) Viking Penguin.
—Shorter Finnegans Wake. 1967. 6.00 o.p. (*0-670-64270-3*) Viking Penguin.
—Stephen Hero. rev. ed. 1963. (Illus.). pap. 11.95 (*0-8112-0074-4*, NDP133) New Directions Publishing Corp.
—Ulysses. 2001. (Modern Library Ser.). E-Book 9.95 (*1-931208-63-8*) Adobe Systems, Inc.
—Ulysses. 799p. 38.95 (*0-8488-2569-1*) Amereon, Ltd.
—Ulysses. 1992. reprint ed. lib. bdg. 27.95 (*0-89968-284-7*, Lightyear Pr.) Buccaneer Bks., Inc.
—Ulysses, 3 vols. Gabler, Hans W. & Melchior, Claus, eds. 1984. 1954p. text 202.00 o.p. (*0-8240-4375-8*) Garland Publishing, Inc.
—Ulysses. abr. ed. 1972. audio 12.95 o.s.i (*0-694-50050-X*, SWC 1063, Caedmon); Set. 1984. audio 19.95 (*0-694-50866-7*, SWC 328, Caedmon); Set. 1992. audio 18.00 o.s.i (*1-55994-633-4*, DCN 328, HarperAudio) HarperTrade.
—Ulysses. 1990. 816p. pap. 17.00 (*0-679-72276-9*, Vintage) Knopf Publishing Group.
—Ulysses. 1997. 1136p. 25.00 (*0-679-45513-2*) Knopf, Alfred A. Inc.
—Ulysses. 2015. 880p. mass mkt. 7.95 o.s.i (*0-451-52674-0*, Signet Classics) NAL.
—Ulysses. abr. ed. (Works of James Joyce). 1996. audio 22.98 (*962-634-511-X*, NA401114); 1994. audio compact disk 26.98 (*962-634-011-8*, NA401112) Naxos of America, Inc. (Naxos Audio-Books).
—Ulysses. Date not set. 35.00 (*0-393-03390-2*) Norton, W. W. & Co., Inc.
—Ulysses. 1998. 732p. 75.00 (*0-914061-70-4*) Orchises Pr.
—Ulysses. Johnson, Jeri, ed. & intro. by, unexpurg. ed. 1993. (Oxford World's Classics Ser.). (Illus.). 1056p. pap. 15.95 o.p. (*0-19-282866-5*) Oxford Univ. Pr., Inc.
—Ulysses. 2000. E-Book 9.95 (*0-679-64162-9*, Modern Library) Random House Adult Trade Publishing Group.
—Ulysses. 1993. audio 22.00 o.s.i (*0-553-47163-5*, RH Audio) Random Hse. Audio Publishing Group.
—Ulysses. 2002. 800p. 26.00 (*0-375-50794-9*); 1992. 816p. 22.95 (*0-679-60011-6*); 1967. 20.00 o.p. (*0-394-45005-1*); 1967. pap. 10.95 o.p. (*0-394-70380-4*); 1940. 5.95 o.s.i (*0-394-60752-X*) Random Hse., Inc.
—Ulysses. 2004. audio compact disk 79.99 (*1-4025-7203-4*); Pt. 2, set. audio o.s.i; Set. 1999. audio 186.00 (*0-7887-0225-4*, 94502); Vols. 1 & 2. 1996. audio 186.00 (*0-7887-0309-9*, 94502E7) Recorded Bks., LLC.
—Ulysses. 1040p. 1999. pap. 14.95 (*0-14-118086-2*); 1998. pap. 14.95 (*0-14-018558-5*, Penguin Classics) Viking Penguin.
—Ulysses: A Facsimile of the Manuscript, 3 vols. ltd. ed. 1976. (Octagon Bk.). 1066p. 200.00 o.p. (*0-374-28033-9*) Farrar, Straus & Giroux.
—Ulysses: A Facsimile of the Manuscript & the Manuscript & First Printings Compared, 3 vols. 1975. 100.00 o.p. (*0-374-94440-7*) Univ. Pr. of Virginia.
—Ulysses: A Reader's Edition. Rose, Danis, ed. 1998. 826p. pap. 19.95 (*0-330-35230-X*); 1997. 824p. 47.50 o.p. (*0-330-35229-6*) Picador GBR. *Dist:* Trans-Atlantic Pubns., Inc.
—Ulysses: A Reproduction of the 1922 First Edition. 2002. (Illus.). 736p. pap. 29.95 (*0-486-42444-8*) Dover Pubns., Inc.
—Ulysses: The Corrected Text. 1986. 608p. 29.95 o.s.i (*0-394-55373-X*); 680p. pap. 19.00 (*0-394-74312-1*) Knopf Publishing Group. (Vintage).
—Ulysses: The Corrected Text. rev. ed. 1986. 16.95 (*0-07-544944-7*) McGraw-Hill Cos., The.
Joyce, James, contrib. by. Ulysses. 1997. (*1-874675-98-8*); (*1-874675-99-6*) Dufour Editions, Inc.
Joyce, James, et al. Dubliners. Jackson, John W. & MCGinley, Bernard, eds. 1993. 35.00 (*0-312-09790-5*) St. Martin's Pr.
—A Portrait of the Artist As a Young Man. 1999. (Literature Made Easy Ser.). 85p. pap. 4.95 (*0-7641-0825-5*) Barron's Educational Series, Inc.
Keyes, Marian. Rachel's Holiday. 2002. 592p. pap. 13.95 (*0-06-009038-3*, Perennial) HarperTrade.
—Rachel's Holiday. 2001. 528p. mass mkt. 6.99 (*0-380-81768-3*, Avon Bks.); 2000. 576p. 25.00 (*0-688-18071-X*, Morrow, William & Co.) Morrow/Avon.
—Rachel's Holiday. 1998. (*1-85371-896-3*) Poolbeg Pr. IRL. *Dist:* Dufour Editions, Inc.
—Sushi for Beginners. unabr. ed. 2003. audio 39.95 (*0-06-055780-X*, HarperAudio) HarperTrade.
—Sushi for Beginners. 2004. 560p. mass mkt. 7.99 (*0-06-055725-7*, HarperTorch); 2003. 432p. 24.95 (*0-06-052050-7*, Morrow, William & Co.) Morrow/Avon.
—Watermelon. 2002. 432p. pap. 13.95 (*0-06-009036-7*, Perennial) HarperTrade.
—Watermelon. 1999. 448p. mass mkt. 6.99 (*0-380-79609-0*); 1998. 432p. mass mkt. 15.95 (*0-380-97617-X*) Morrow/Avon. (Avon Bks.).
—Watermelon. 1995. 612p. pap. 11.95 (*1-85371-508-5*) Poolbeg Pr. IRL. *Dist:* Dufour Editions, Inc.
Kiely, David M. The Angel Tapes: A Blade Macken Mystery. 1997. (Blade Macken Mystery Ser.). 304p. text 23.95 o.p. (*0-312-16772-5*) St. Martin's Pr.
Kurtz, Katherine. St. Patrick's Gargoyle. 2001. 240p. 21.95 o.s.i (*0-441-00725-2*) Ace Bks.
Leonard, Hugh. A Wild People: A Novel. 2002. 288p. 23.95 (*0-312-29029-2*) St. Martin's Pr.
Llywelyn, Morgan. 1916: A Novel of the Irish Rebellion. unabr. ed. 1998. audio 28.95 (*1-56740-050-7*, 196, Bookcassette); audio 89.25 (*1-56740-579-7*, 784, Unabridged Library Editions) Brilliance Audio.
—1916: A Novel of the Irish Rebellion. (Illus.). 1999. 544p. pap. text 6.99 (*0-8125-7492-3*, Tor Bks.); 1998. 447p. 24.95 o.p. (*0-312-86101-X*, Forge Bks.) Doherty, Tom Assocs., LLC.
—1916: A Novel of the Irish Rebellion. 1999. 6.99 (*0-312-87140-6*) St. Martin's Pr.
Macdonald, Malcolm. Hell Hath No Fury. 1992. 384p. 21.95 o.p. (*0-312-06994-4*) St. Martin's Pr.
May, Ena. Close Shave with the Devil. 1999. 159p. pap. text 15.95 (*1-901866-17-3*, Liplop Pr.) Goodfellow Catalog Pr., Inc.
McGinley, Patrick. Goosefoot: A Novel with Murder. 1982. 280p. 13.95 o.p. (*0-525-24142-6*, 01354-410, Dutton) Dutton/Plume.
McKenna, Marita C. The Magdelen. 2002. 352p. pap. 14.95 (*0-7653-0513-5*, Forge Bks.) Doherty, Tom Assocs., LLC.
Morrissy, Mary. Mother of Pearl: A Novel. 1995. 281p. 22.00 o.p. (*0-684-19667-0*, Scribner) Simon & Schuster.
Murdoch, Iris. Something Special: A Story. 2000. (Illus.). 55p. 15.95 (*0-393-05007-6*) Norton, W. W. & Co., Inc.
—Something Special: A Story. 1999. (Illus.). 48p. o.p. (*0-7011-6918-4*) Random Hse. of Canada, Ltd. CAN. *Dist:* Random Hse., Inc.
O'Brien, Flann. The Hard Life. 2nd ed. 179p. reprint ed. 1996. pap. 11.95 (*1-56478-141-0*); 1994. pap. 9.95 o.p. (*1-56478-042-2*) Dalkey Archive Pr.
—The Hard Life. 1977. pap. 3.50 o.p. (*0-14-004517-1*, Penguin Bks.) Viking Penguin.
O'Carroll, Brendan. The Chisellers. 2000. 192p. pap. 11.95 (*0-452-28122-9*, Plume) Dutton/Plume.
—The Chisellers. l.t. ed. 2000. (G. K. Hall Core Ser.). 230p. 28.95 (*0-7838-9259-4*, Macmillan Reference USA) Gale Group.
—The Young Wan: An Agnes Browne Novel. 2003. 224p. 23.95 (*0-670-03114-3*, Viking) Viking Penguin.
O'Connor, Joseph. The Salesman. 400p. 2000. pap. 14.00 (*0-312-20431-0*); 1999. (Illus.). 24.00 o.p. (*0-312-19998-8*) Picador.
O'Neill, Jamie. At Swim, Two Boys. 2002. E-Book 28.00 (*1-4014-9977-5*) Barnes & Noble Digital.
—At Swim, Two Boys. 2003. 576p. pap. 15.00 (*0-7432-2295-4*); 2002. E-Book 28.00 (*0-7432-4187-8*); 2002. 576p. 28.00 (*0-7432-2294-6*); 2001. 643p. (*0-7432-0712-2*); 2001. 643p. pap. (*0-7432-0713-0*) Simon & Schuster. (Scribner).
Parsons, Julie. The Courtship Gift. 2000. 320p. 24.00 (*0-684-86982-9*, Simon & Schuster); 2001. (Illus.). 400p. reprint ed. mass mkt. 6.99 (*0-7434-2665-7*, Pocket) Simon & Schuster.
—The Courtship Gift. 1999. 390p. (*1-86059-102-7*) Town Hse. IRL. *Dist:* Rinehart, Roberts Pubs.
Redhill, Michael. Martin Sloane. 2001. 288p. pap. (*0-385-25987-5*, Anchor Canada) Doubleday Canada, Ltd. CAN. *Dist:* Random Hse., Inc.
—Martin Sloane. 2002. 288p. pap. 13.95 (*0-316-73936-7*, Back Bay) Little Brown & Co.
Ridgway, Keith. Standard Time. Date not set. (*0-312-32771-4*); pap. (*0-312-32772-2*, St. Martin's Paperbacks); mass mkt. (*0-312-99652-7*, St. Martin's Paperbacks) St. Martin's Pr.
Roberts, Paul A. The Rasherhouse. 1997. 178p. pap. 14.95 (*1-898256-21-7*) Dufour Editions, Inc.
Roper, Martin. Gone: A Novel. 2002. 256p. 23.00 o.s.i (*0-8050-6775-2*) Holt, Henry & Co.
—Gone: A Novel. 2003. 240p. pap. 13.00 (*0-312-42125-7*) Picador.
Scanlan, Patricia. Francesca's Party. 2003. 512p. mass mkt. (*1-55166-746-0*, Mira Bks.) Harlequin Enterprises, Ltd.
—Francesca's Party. Date not set. (*0-312-30187-1*) St. Martin's Pr.
—Francesca's Party: A Novel. 2002. 464p. 24.95 (*0-312-30172-3*) St. Martin's Pr.
Stirling, Jessica. Shamrock Green. 2003. 480p. 26.95 (*0-312-31770-0*) St. Martin's Pr.

**DUDLEY (ARIZ.: IMAGINARY PLACE)—FICTION**

Thornton, Betsy. The Cowboy Rides Away. 1997. 288p. mass mkt. 5.50 o.s.i (*0-440-22327-X*) Dell Publishing.
—The Cowboy Rides Away. 1996. 256p. 21.95 o.p. (*0-312-14301-X*, Saint Martin's Minotaur) St. Martin's Pr.
—High Lonesome Road. E-Book 23.95 (*1-58945-672-6*) Adobe Systems, Inc.
—High Lonesome Road. 2001. 233p. 23.95 (*0-312-26861-0*, Saint Martin's Minotaur) St. Martin's Pr.
—The High Lonesome Road. 2002. 256p. mass mkt. 5.99 o.s.i (*0-425-18455-2*) Berkley Publishing Group.

**DUE EAST (S.C.: IMAGINARY PLACE)—FICTION**

Sayers, Valerie. Due East. 1988. mass mkt. 3.95 o.p. (*0-425-10895-3*) Berkley Publishing Group.

**DUNCTON WOOD (IMAGINARY PLACE)—FICTION**

Horwood, William. Duncton Wood. 1986. 736p. mass mkt. 4.95 o.s.i (*0-345-34189-9*); 1984. mass mkt. 3.95 o.p. (*0-345-31770-X*); 1981. mass mkt. 3.50 o.s.i (*0-345-29113-1*) Ballantine Bks.
—Duncton Wood. 1980. 12.95 o.p. (*0-07-030434-3*) McGraw-Hill Cos., The.

**DUNE (IMAGINARY PLACE)—FICTION**

Herbert, Brian. Dune: House Atreides. 2000. 13.04 (*0-606-19184-4*) Turtleback Bks.
—Dune: House Corrino. 2002. (Dune Chronicles). (Illus.). 688p. mass mkt. 7.50 (*0-553-58033-7*); mass mkt. 6.99 (*0-553-84036-3*) Bantam Bks. (Spectra).
Herbert, Brian & Anderson, Kevin J. Dune: House Atreides. (Dune Chronicles). 2003. E-Book 4.99 (*0-553-89782-9*); 2000. 704p. mass mkt. 7.50 (*0-553-58027-2*); 1999. 624p. 27.50 o.s.i (*0-553-11061-6*, Spectra) Bantam Bks.
—Dune: House Atreides, , Pt. 2 unabr. ed. 2000. (Dune Chronicles: 4). audio 48.00 Books on Tape, Inc.
—Dune: House Atreides. abr. ed. 1999. (Prelude to Dune Ser.: Vol. 1). audio 29.95 (*0-553-52665-0*, RH Audio) Random Hse. Audio Publishing Group.
—Dune: House Corrino. 2002. (Dune Chronicles). E-Book 4.99 (*0-553-89695-4*) Bantam Bks.
—Dune: House Corrino. 2001. audio 128.00 (*0-7366-9260-6*) Books on Tape, Inc.
—Dune: House Corrino. abr. ed. 2001. audio 29.95 (*0-553-52667-7*, RH Audio) Random Hse. Audio Publishing Group.
—Dune: House Harkonnen. (Dune Chronicles). 2003. E-Book 4.99 (*0-553-89783-7*); 2001. (Illus.). 752p. reprint ed. mass mkt. 7.50 (*0-553-58030-2*, Spectra) Bantam Bks.
—Dune: House Harkonnen. abr. ed. 2000. audio 29.95 (*0-553-52666-9*, RH Audio) Random Hse. Audio Publishing Group.
—Dune: The Butlerian Jihad. unabr. ed. 2002. (Illus.). audio compact disk 60.00 (*1-55927-755-6*) Audio Renaissance.
—Dune: The Butlerian Jihad. (Dune Ser.). 2003. 704p. mass mkt. 7.99 (*0-7653-4077-1*); 2002. 624p. 200.00 (*0-7653-0585-2*); 2002. 624p. 27.95 (*0-7653-0157-1*); 2002. E-Book 27.95 (*0-312-70808-4*) Doherty, Tom Assocs., LLC. (Tor Bks.).
—Dune: The Machine Crusade. (Dune Ser.). 2004. mass mkt. 7.99 (*0-7653-4078-X*); 2003. 624p. 27.95 (*0-7653-0158-X*); 2003. 624p. 200.00 (*0-7653-0586-0*) Doherty, Tom Assocs., LLC. (Tor Bks.).
Herbert, Brian, et al. Dune: House Corrino. 2001. (Illus.). 512p. 27.95 (*0-553-11084-5*) Bantam Bks.
Herbert, Frank. The Best of Frank Herbert. Wells, Angus, ed. 1975. 302 p. (J). 22.50 (*0-283-98173-3*) Sidgwick & Jackson, Ltd. GBR. *Dist:* Trans-Atlantic Pubns., Inc.
—Chapterhouse: Dune. 1987. (Dune Chronicles: Vol. 6). 448p. mass mkt. 7.99 (*0-441-10267-0*) Ace Bks.
—Chapterhouse: Dune. 1986. (Dune Chronicles: Bk. 6). pap. 7.95 o.p. (*0-425-09214-3*) Berkley Publishing Group.
—Chapterhouse: Dune. 1985. (Dune Chronicles: Bk. 6). 464p. pap. 17.95 o.p. (*0-399-13027-6*, G. P. Putnam's Sons) Penguin Putnam Bks. for Young Readers.
—Chapterhouse: Dune. 1985. (Dune Chronicles: Bk. 6). 75.00 o.s.i (*0-399-13075-6*) Putnam Publishing Group, The.
—Chapterhouse: Dune. 1987. (Dune Chronicles: Bk. 6). lib. bdg. 13.04 (*0-606-17104-5*) Turtleback Bks.
—Children of Dune. (Dune Chronicles: Vol. 3). 1987. 416p. mass mkt. 7.99 (*0-441-10402-9*); 1977. pap. 1.50 o.p. (*0-441-10412-6*); 1975. pap. 1.25 o.p. (*0-441-10411-8*) Ace Bks.
—Children of Dune. 1984. pap. 7.95 o.p. (*0-425-07902-3*); 1984. 3.95 o.s.i (*0-425-07499-4*); 1984. 3.50 o.s.i (*0-425-07179-0*); 1983. 3.50 o.s.i (*0-425-06435-2*); 1982. 2.95 o.s.i (*0-425-06174-4*); 1982. 384p. pap. 6.95 o.s.i (*0-425-05315-6*); 1981. 2.75 o.s.i (*0-425-05472-1*); 1981. 2.50 o.s.i (*0-425-04383-5*); 1978. 2.25 o.s.i (*0-425-04075-5*); 1978. 2.25 o.s.i (*0-425-03931-5*); 1977. 1.95 o.s.i (*0-425-03310-4*) Berkley Publishing Group.
—Children of Dune. 1999. pap. 14.55 (*0-8085-2094-6*) Econo-Clad Bks.
—Children of Dune. 1976. (Dune Chronicles: Bk. 3). 19.95 o.s.i (*0-399-11697-4*) Putnam Publishing Group, The.
—Children of Dune. 1991. (Dune Chronicles). 13.04 (*0-606-00827-6*) Turtleback Bks.
—Dune. 2002. pap. 9.99 (*0-441-01062-8*); 1987. mass mkt. 4.95 o.s.i (*0-441-17266-0*); 1999. (Ace Science Fiction Ser.). 528p. reprint ed. 25.95 (*0-441-00590-X*); 25th anniv. ed. 1990. (Dune Chronicles: Vol. 1). (Illus.). 544p. mass mkt. 7.99 (*0-441-17271-7*) Ace Bks.

—Dune. 1987. 4.50 o.s.i (*0-425-10381-1*); 1984. 3.95 o.s.i (*0-425-08002-1*); 1984. 544p. 3.95 o.s.i (*0-425-07160-X*); 1983. 3.95 o.s.i (*0-425-06434-4*); 1982. pap. 7.95 o.p. (*0-425-05313-X*); 1982. 2.95 o.s.i (*0-425-05471-3*); 1980. 2.75 o.s.i (*0-425-04687-7*); 1977. 2.50 o.s.i (*0-425-04376-2*); 1977. 2.25 o.s.i (*0-425-03698-7*); 1975. 1.95 o.s.i (*0-425-02706-6*) Berkley Publishing Group.

—Dune. 2002. audio 36.00 (*0-7366-8959-1*); 2002. audio compact disk 160.00 (*0-7366-9240-1*); 1997. audio 104.00 (*0-7366-3763-X*, 4437) Books on Tape, Inc.

—Dune. abr. ed. 1988. audio 14.00 o.s.i (*0-89845-216-3*, SWC 1555, Caedmon) HarperTrade.

—Dune. 1984. 528p. 26.95 (*0-399-12896-4*, G. P. Putnam's Sons) Penguin Putnam Bks. for Young Readers.

—Dune. 4th ed. 1996. (SPA., Illus.). 704p. (*84-01-46931-7*) Plaza & Janés Editories, S.A.

—Dune. 2002. (SPA.). pap. 13.95 (*84-01-46261-4*, PJ9380) Plaza & Janés Editories, S.A. ESP. *Dist:* Lectorum Pubns., Inc.

—Dune. unabr. ed. 1993. audio 128.00 (*1-55690-933-0*, 93429E7) Recorded Bks., LLC.

—Dune. 1977. (Dune Chronicles). 13.04 (*0-606-03111-1*) Turtleback Bks.

—Dune: Dune, Children of Dune, Dune Messiah, God Emperor of Dune & Chapterhouse Dune. 1988. 22.50 o.s.i (*0-441-17267-9*) Ace Bks.

—The Dune Collection. 1984. 14.90 o.s.i (*0-425-07420-X*) Berkley Publishing Group.

—Dune Coloring Book, 12 bks. 1984. (Illus.). 48p. (J). 23.40 o.p. (*0-448-81710-1*, Grosset & Dunlap) Penguin Putnam Bks. for Young Readers.

—Dune Messiah. 1987. (Dune Chronicles: Vol. 2). 336p. mass mkt. 7.99 (*0-441-17269-5*) Ace Bks.

—Dune Messiah. (Dune Chronicles). 1984. 288p. 7.95 o.p. (*0-425-07901-5*); 1984. 3.95 o.s.i (*0-425-07498-6*); 1984. 3.50 o.s.i (*0-425-07180-4*); 1983. 3.50 o.s.i (*0-425-06436-0*); 1982. 2.95 o.s.i (*0-425-06173-6*); 1982. pap. 5.95 o.p. (*0-425-05314-8*); 1981. 2.75 o.s.i (*0-425-05503-5*); 1980. 2.50 o.s.i (*0-425-04379-7*); 1979. 2.25 o.s.i (*0-425-04346-0*); 1978. 1.95 o.s.i (*0-425-03930-7*); 1977. 1.75 o.s.i (*0-425-03585-9*); 1975. 1.50 o.s.i (*0-425-02952-2*); 1974. 1.25 o.s.i (*0-425-02601-9*) Berkley Publishing Group.

—Dune Messiah. unabr. collector's ed. 1998. (Dune Chronicles: Bk. 2). audio 48.00 (*0-7366-4018-5*, 4516) Books on Tape, Inc.

—Dune Messiah. 1976. (Dune Chronicles). 18.95 o.p. (*0-399-10226-4*, G. P. Putnam's Sons) Penguin Putnam Bks. for Young Readers.

—Dune Messiah. 1994. 13.04 (*0-606-03112-X*) Turtleback Bks.

—God Emperor of Dune. 1987. (Dune Chronicles: Vol. 4). 432p. reprint ed. mass mkt. 7.99 (*0-441-29467-7*) Ace Bks.

—God Emperor of Dune. (Dune Chronicles). 1984. 3.95 o.s.i (*0-425-08003-X*); 1982. 432p. pap. 7.95 o.s.i (*0-425-06128-0*) Berkley Publishing Group.

—God Emperor of Dune, , unabr. collector's ed. 1999. (Dune Chronicles). audio 80.00 (*0-7366-4422-9*, 4839) Books on Tape, Inc.

—God Emperor of Dune. 1994. audio 5.99 (*1-55994-910-4*, HarperAudio); 1982. audio 14.00 o.p. (*0-694-50358-4*, SWC 1694, Caedmon) HarperTrade.

—God Emperor of Dune. 1981. (Dune Chronicles). 432p. 22.50 o.s.i (*0-399-12593-0*, G. P. Putnam's Sons) Penguin Putnam Bks. for Young Readers.

—God Emperor of Dune. 1981. (Dune Chronicles). 12.09 o.p. (*0-606-03081-6*) Turtleback Bks.

—Heretics of Dune. 1987. (Dune Chronicles: Vol. 5). 480p. mass mkt. 7.99 (*0-441-32800-8*) Ace Bks.

—Heretics of Dune. 1986. (Dune Chronicles: Vol. 5). (Illus.). 496p. 4.50 o.s.i (*0-425-08732-8*) Berkley Publishing Group.

—Heretics of Dune. abr. ed. 1988. audio 14.00 o.p. (*0-694-51022-X*, SWC 1742, Caedmon) HarperTrade.

—Heretics of Dune. 1984. (Dune Chronicles). 464p. 75.00 o.p. (*0-399-12947-2*); 16.95 o.s.i (*0-399-12898-0*) Penguin Putnam Bks. for Young Readers. (G. P. Putnam's Sons).

—Heretics of Dune. 1996. (Dune Chronicles). 13.04 (*0-606-01600-7*) Turtleback Bks.

Unknown. Core Roleplaying Game. 1900. (Dune Chronicles). 35.00 (*0-671-03505-3*) Simon & Schuster.

—Narrators Guide. 1900. (Dune Chronicles). (Illus.). 64p. pap. 16.00 (*0-671-03506-1*) Simon & Schuster.

## E

### EARTHSEA (IMAGINARY PLACE)—FICTION

Le Guin, Ursula K. The Other Wind. 2003. 224p. mass mkt. 7.99 (*0-441-01125-X*); 288p. reprint ed. pap. 13.95 (*0-441-00993-X*) Ace Bks.

—The Other Wind. 2001. (Illus.). 256p. 25.00 o.s.i (*0-15-100684-9*) Harcourt Trade Pubs.

—Tales from Earthsea. 2002. 336p. (YA). pap. 13.95 (*0-441-00932-8*) Ace Bks.

### EDINBURGH (SCOTLAND)—FICTION

Boxer, Charlie. The Cloud of Dust. 2001. 112p. o.p. (*0-224-06108-9*) Random Hse. UK, Ltd.

Brookmyre, Christopher. Quite Ugly One Morning. 2002. 224p. pap. 12.00 (*0-8021-3861-6*, Grove Pr.) Grove/Atlantic, Inc.

—Quite Ugly One Morning. 1996. 224p. o.s.i (*0-316-87883-9*) Little Brown & Co.

Davis, Margaret Thomson. Light & Dark. 2001. (Illus.). 448p. pap. 14.95 (*1-873631-43-X*) B & W Publishing GBR. *Dist:* Interlink Publishing Group, Inc.

Deveraux, Jude. Temptation. l.t. ed. 2001. (Wheeler Press Paperback Ser.). 12.95 (*1-56895-176-0*, Wheeler Publishing, Inc.) Gale Group.

—Temptation. 2003. (Illus.). 368p. mass mkt. 5.99 (*0-7434-6725-6*, Pocket); 2000. 352p. 24.95 (*0-671-00203-1*, Atria) Simon & Schuster.

Dunnett, Dorothy. The Game of Kings. 1976. 22.95 o.p. (*0-8488-1298-0*) Amereon, Ltd.

—The Game of Kings. 1983. 425p. lib. bdg. 39.95 (*0-89966-318-4*) Buccaneer Bks., Inc.

—The Game of Kings. 1997. (Legendary Lymond Chronicles: Vol. 1). 560p. pap. 15.00 (*0-679-77743-1*, Vintage) Knopf Publishing Group.

Jardine, Quintin. Autographs in the Rain. 2001. 288p. 24.95 (*0-7472-7446-0*) Headline Bk. Publishing, Ltd. GBR. *Dist:* Trafalgar Square.

—Skinner's Festival. 2001. (J). mass mkt. 8.95 (*0-7472-4140-6*) Headline Bk. Publishing, Ltd. GBR. *Dist:* Trafalgar Square.

—Skinner's Festival. 1995. 310p. 21.95 o.p. (*0-312-11892-9*, Saint Martin's Minotaur) St. Martin's Pr.

—Skinner's Ghosts. l.t. ed. 1999. (Ulverscroft Large Print Ser.). 416p. 31.99 o.p. (*0-7089-4159-1*, Ulverscroft) Thorpe, F. A. Pubs. GBR. *Dist:* Ulverscroft Large Print Bks., Ltd., Ulverscroft Large Print Canada, Ltd.

—Skinner's Mission. 2001. 406p. mass mkt. 9.95 (*0-7472-5043-X*) Headline Bk. Publishing, Ltd. GBR. *Dist:* Trafalgar Square.

—Skinner's Mission. unabr. ed. 1999. audio 83.95 (*1-85903-291-5*) Magna Story Sound GBR. *Dist:* Ulverscroft Large Print Bks., Ltd.

—Skinner's Mission. l.t. ed. 1998. (Ulverscroft Large Print Ser.). 512p. 29.99 o.p. (*0-7089-3914-7*, Ulverscroft) Thorpe, F. A. Pubs. GBR. *Dist:* Ulverscroft Large Print Bks., Ltd., Ulverscroft Large Print Canada, Ltd.

—Skinner's Ordeal. 2001. 438p. mass mkt. 8.95 (*0-7472-5042-1*) Headline Bk. Publishing, Ltd. GBR. *Dist:* Trafalgar Square.

—Skinner's Ordeal. l.t. ed. 1997. (Ulverscroft Large Print Ser.). 720p. 29.99 (*0-7089-3826-4*, Ulverscroft) Thorpe, F. A. Pubs. GBR. *Dist:* Ulverscroft Large Print Bks., Ltd., Ulverscroft Large Print Canada, Ltd.

—Skinner's Round. 2001. 436p. mass mkt. 9.95 (*0-7472-5041-3*) Headline Bk. Publishing, Ltd. GBR. *Dist:* Trafalgar Square.

—Skinner's Round. 1996. 304p. 23.95 (*0-312-14737-6*, Saint Martin's Minotaur) St. Martin's Pr.

—Skinner's Rules. 2001. mass mkt. 8.95 (*0-7472-4139-2*) Headline Bk. Publishing, Ltd. GBR. *Dist:* Trafalgar Square.

—Skinner's Rules. 1994. 320p. 21.95 o.p. (*0-312-11066-9*, Saint Martin's Minotaur) St. Martin's Pr.

—Skinner's Trail. 1996. 320p. 22.95 o.p. (*0-312-14417-2*, Saint Martin's Minotaur) St. Martin's Pr.

Johnston, Paul. The House of Dust. 2003. 352p. mass mkt. 8.95 (*0-340-76613-1*) Hodder & Stoughton, Ltd. GBR. *Dist:* Trafalgar Square.

—Water of Death. 2001. 400p. 24.95 (*0-312-27311-8*, Saint Martin's Minotaur) St. Martin's Pr.

Knight, Alanna. Blood Line: An Inspector Faro Mystery. 1989. 224p. 15.95 o.p. (*0-312-03295-1*, Saint Martin's Minotaur) St. Martin's Pr.

—The Bull Slayers: An Inspector Faro Mystery. l.t. ed. 1997. 290p. 21.95 (*0-7838-8045-6*, Macmillan Reference USA) Gale Group.

—The Coffin Lane Murders. 2001. 218p. pap. 11.95 (*1-902927-23-0*) B & W Publishing GBR. *Dist:* Interlink Publishing Group, Inc.

—Deadly Beloved. l.t. ed. 1992. (Mystery Ser.). 336p. 29.99 o.p. (*0-7089-2646-0*, Ulverscroft) Thorpe, F. A. Pubs. GBR. *Dist:* Ulverscroft Large Print Bks., Ltd., Ulverscroft Large Print Canada, Ltd.

—Enter Second Murderer. 1989. 14.95 o.p. (*0-312-03021-5*) St. Martin's Pr.

—Enter Second Murderer. l.t. ed. 1998. (General Ser.). 269p. pap. 23.95 (*0-7862-1308-6*) Thorndike Pr.

—Enter Second Murderer. l.t. ed. 1990. (Ulverscroft Large Print Ser.). 29.99 o.p. (*0-7089-2236-8*, Ulverscroft) Thorpe, F. A. Pubs. GBR. *Dist:* Ulverscroft Large Print Bks., Ltd., Ulverscroft Large Print Canada, Ltd.

—Enter Second Murderer: An Inspector Faro Mystery. Set. unabr. ed. 1999. audio 54.95 (*0-7540-0352-3*, CAB1775) BBC Audiobooks America.

—The Evil That Men Do. l.t. ed. 1996. 281p. pap. 20.95 o.p. (*0-7838-1649-9*, Macmillan Reference USA) Gale Group.

—Killing Cousins: An Inspector Faro Mystery. l.t. ed. 1992. (Lythway Ser.). 248p. lib. bdg. 20.50 o.p. (*0-7451-1419-9*, Macmillan Reference USA) Gale Group.

—Killing Cousins: An Inspector Faro Mystery. 1991. 256p. 17.95 o.p. (*0-312-07008-X*, Saint Martin's Minotaur) St. Martin's Pr.

—The Missing Duchess. l.t. ed. 1996. pap. 20.95 (*0-7838-1650-2*, Macmillan Reference USA) Gale Group.

—Murder by Appointment: An Inspector Faro Mystery. l.t. ed. 1997. pap. 20.95 o.p. (*0-7838-8044-8*, Macmillan Reference USA) Gale Group.

Knight, Alanna & Lawhead, Stephen R. Deadly Beloved. 1990. 192p. 15.95 o.p. (*0-312-05069-0*, Saint Martin's Minotaur) St. Martin's Pr.

O'Neill, Anthony. The Lamplighter: A Novel. 2004. 432p. mass mkt. 7.99 (*0-7434-6427-3*, Pocket Star); 2003. 320p. 25.00 (*0-7432-4349-8*, Scribner) Simon & Schuster.

Paul, William. Sleeping Dogs. 1995. 192p. 19.95 o.p. (*0-312-13603-X*, Saint Martin's Minotaur) St. Martin's Pr.

—Sleeping Partner. 1997. 192p. 19.95 o.p. (*0-312-15208-6*, Saint Martin's Minotaur) St. Martin's Pr.

—Sleeping Pretty. 1996. 192p. 19.95 o.p. (*0-312-14418-0*, Saint Martin's Minotaur) St. Martin's Pr.

Ramsay, Eileen. The Quality of Mercy. 1997. 310p. pap. o.s.i (*0-7515-1849-2*); o.s.i (*0-316-88114-7*) Little Brown & Co.

—The Quality of Mercy. l.t. ed. 1999. (Magna Large Print Ser.). 416p. (*0-7505-1225-3*) Magna Large Print Bks. GBR. *Dist:* Ulverscroft Large Print Bks., Ltd., Ulverscroft Large Print Canada, Ltd.

Rankin, Ian. Black & Blue. unabr. ed. 1998. audio 80.00 (*0-7366-4176-9*, 4675) Books on Tape, Inc.

—Black & Blue. Date not set. E-Book (*0-312-70694-4*); 1999. (Black & Blue Ser.: Vol. 1). 352p. mass mkt. 6.99 (*0-312-96677-6*, St. Martin's Paperbacks); 1997. (Inspector Rebus Novel Ser.). 394p. 24.95 (*0-312-16783-0*, Saint Martin's Minotaur) St. Martin's Pr.

—Black & Blue: An Inspector Rebus Novel. l.t. ed. 1998. (Mystery Ser.). 623p. 28.95 (*0-7838-8443-5*) Thorndike Pr.

—The Black Book. E-Book 6.50 (*0-312-70693-6*); 2000. 352p. mass mkt. 7.50 (*0-312-97675-5*, St. Martin's Paperbacks) St. Martin's Pr.

—The Black Book: An Inspector Rebus Novel. unabr. ed. 1995. audio 59.95 (*0-7451-6514-1*, CAB 1130) Chivers Audio Bks. GBR. *Dist:* BBC Audiobooks America.

—The Black Book: An Inspector Rebus Novel. 1994. 288p. reprint ed. 21.00 (*1-883402-77-8*, Scribner) Simon & Schuster.

—Dead Souls. 2000. 448p. mass mkt. 6.99 (*0-312-97420-5*, St. Martin's Paperbacks); 1999. 320p. 24.95 o.p. (*0-312-20293-8*, Saint Martin's Minotaur) St. Martin's Pr.

—Death Is Not Enough. mass mkt. (*0-312-97628-3*, St. Martin's Paperbacks) St. Martin's Pr.

—Death Is Not the End: An Instpector Rebus Novella. 2000. 73p. 11.95 (*0-312-26142-X*, Saint Martin's Minotaur) St. Martin's Pr.

—The Falls. 2001. 399p. (*0-7528-2130-X*); pap. (*0-7528-3861-X*) Orion Publishing Group, Ltd. GBR. *Dist:* Trafalgar Square.

—The Falls. 2003. 496p. mass mkt. 7.50 (*0-312-98240-2*, St. Martin's Paperbacks); 2001. 400p. 24.95 (*0-312-20610-0*, Saint Martin's Minotaur) St. Martin's Pr.

—The Hanging Garden. unabr. ed. 1999. audio 64.00 Books on Tape, Inc.

—The Hanging Garden. E-Book 5.99 (*0-312-70698-7*); 1998. 352p. 24.95 o.p. (*0-312-19278-9*, Saint Martin's Minotaur); 1999. 384p. reprint ed. mass mkt. 6.99 (*0-312-96913-9*, St. Martin's Paperbacks) St. Martin's Pr.

—The Hanging Garden. l.t. ed. 1999. (Charnwood Large Print Ser.). 432p. 31.99 o.p. (*0-7089-9124-6*, Ulverscroft) Thorpe, F. A. Pubs. GBR. *Dist:* Ulverscroft Large Print Bks., Ltd., Ulverscroft Large Print Canada, Ltd.

—Hide & Seek. E-Book 6.50 (*0-312-70699-5*); 1997. 224p. mass mkt. 6.50 (*0-312-96397-1*, St. Martin's Paperbacks) St. Martin's Pr.

—Hide & Seek. l.t. ed. 1992. (General Ser.). 464p. 29.99 o.p. (*0-7089-2734-3*, Ulverscroft) Thorpe, F. A. Pubs. GBR. *Dist:* Ulverscroft Large Print Bks., Ltd., Ulverscroft Large Print Canada, Ltd.

—Hide & Seek: A John Rebus Mystery. 1994. 288p. reprint ed. 21.00 (*1-883402-74-3*, Scribner) Simon & Schuster.

—Knots & Crosses. 1987. (Crime Club Ser.). 192p. 12.95 o.s.i (*0-385-24307-3*) Doubleday Publishing.

—Knots & Crosses. 2002. E-Book 6.99 (*0-312-70721-5*); 1995. mass mkt. 7.50 o.s.i (*0-312-95673-8*, St. Martin's Paperbacks); 1995. pap. o.s.i (*0-312-95566-9*, St. Martin's Paperbacks) St. Martin's Pr.

—Let It Bleed. 1996. (Detective John Rebus Novels Ser.). 288p. 20.50 (*0-684-83055-8*, Simon & Schuster); 20.00 (*1-883402-76-X*, Scribner) Simon & Schuster.

—Let It Bleed. E-Book 6.50 (*0-312-70701-0*); 1998. 320p. mass mkt. 7.50 (*0-312-96665-2*, St. Martin's Paperbacks) St. Martin's Pr.

—Let It Bleed: An Inspector Rebus Novel. l.t. ed. 2000. (Mystery Ser.). 502p. 26.95 (*0-7862-2677-3*) Thorndike Pr.

—Mortal Causes. 1995. 21.50 (*1-883402-75-1*, Scribner) Simon & Schuster.

—Mortal Causes. E-Book 6.50 (*0-312-70702-9*); 3rd ed. 1997. 277p. mass mkt. 6.99 (*0-312-96094-8*, St. Martin's Paperbacks) St. Martin's Pr.

—Mortal Causes: A John Rebus Mystery. 1995. 288p. 22.00 o.p. (*0-684-81497-8*, Simon & Schuster) Simon & Schuster.

—Mortal Causes: An Inspector Rebus Novel. unabr. ed. 1996. audio 69.95 BBC Audiobooks America.

—The Question of Blood. unabr. ed. 2004. (Inspector Rebus Novel Ser.). audio 87.25 (*1-59086-490-5*, 4082, Brilliance Audio Unabridged Lib Ed) Brilliance Audio.

—The Question of Blood. 2004. (Inspector Rebus Novel Ser.). 416p. 22.95 (*0-316-09564-8*) Little Brown & Co.

—Resurrection Men. (Inspector Rebus Novel Ser.). 2004. 528p. mass mkt. 7.99 (*0-316-60849-1*); 2003. 448p. 19.95 (*0-316-76684-4*) Little Brown & Co.

—Resurrection Men. 2003. 28.95 (*0-7862-5204-9*) Thorndike Pr.

—Set in Darkness. E-Book 6.99 (*0-312-70703-7*, Tor Bks.) Doherty, Tom Assocs., LLC.

—Set in Darkness. l.t. ed. 2001. 583p. 29.95 (*0-7838-9406-6*, Macmillan Reference USA) Gale Group.

—Set in Darkness. 2000. 432p. 24.95 (*0-312-20609-7*, Saint Martin's Minotaur); 2001. reprint ed. mass mkt. 7.50 (*0-312-97789-1*, St. Martin's Paperbacks) St. Martin's Pr.

—Strip Jack. E-Book 6.50 (*0-312-70704-5*);Vol. 1. 1998. 272p. mass mkt. 6.99 (*0-312-96514-1*, St. Martin's Paperbacks) St. Martin's Pr.

—Strip Jack: An Inspector Rebus Novel. 1994. 272p. 20.95 o.p. (*0-312-10553-3*, Saint Martin's Minotaur) St. Martin's Pr.

—Tooth & Nail. E-Book 6.99 (*0-312-70705-3*); 1996. 304p. reprint ed. mass mkt. 7.50 (*0-312-95878-1*, St. Martin's Paperbacks) St. Martin's Pr.

Spencer, John B. Tooth & Nail. 1998. 184p. pap. 15.95 (*1-899344-31-4*) Do-Not Pr., The GBR. *Dist:* Dufour Editions, Inc.

Wallace, Christopher. The Resurrection Club. 2000. (Illus.). 231p. pap. 12.00 (*0-00-655219-6*) HarperCollins Pubs. Ltd. GBR. *Dist:* Trafalgar Square.

Welsh, Irvine. Filth. 1998. 393p. pap. 14.00 (*0-393-31868-0*) Norton, W. W. & Co., Inc.

—Glue. 2001. ix, 469p. pap. 14.95 (*0-393-32215-7*) Norton, W. W. & Co., Inc.

—The Marabou Stork Nightmares. 1997. 284p. pap. 14.00 (*0-393-31563-0*); 1996. 264p. 21.00 (*0-393-03845-9*) Norton, W. W. & Co., Inc.

—Porno. 2002. 320p. pap. (*0-224-06181-X*) Cape, Jonathan Ltd. GBR. *Dist:* Trafalgar Square.

—Porno. 2002. 484p. 24.95 (*0-393-05723-2*) Norton, W. W. & Co., Inc.

—Trainspotting. Date not set. pap. 5.99 (*0-7493-2173-3*) Heinemann.

—Trainspotting. 23.95 (*0-393-05724-0*); 1996. 340p. pap. 13.95 (*0-393-31480-4*, Norton Paperbacks) Norton, W. W. & Co., Inc.

### EGYPT—FICTION

Adelson, Sandra. Wrap Her in Light. 1981. 448p. 12.95 o.p. (*0-688-03753-4*, Morrow, William & Co.) Morrow/Avon.

—Wrap Her in Light. 1983. 432p. mass mkt. 3.95 o.s.i (*0-671-44162-0*, Pocket) Simon & Schuster.

Al-Hakim, Tawfiq & Eban, A. S. Maze of Justice: Diary of a Country Prosecutor. 1989. 160p. pap. 13.95 o.p. (*0-292-75113-3*); 13.95 o.p. (*0-292-75112-5*) Univ. of Texas Pr.

Algosaibi, Ghazi. An Apartment Called Freedom. McLoughlin, Leslie, tr. from ARA. 1996. 280p. 110.00 (*0-7103-0550-8*) Kegan Paul International Ltd. GBR. *Dist:* Columbia Univ. Pr.

Ashley, Mike, ed. The Mammoth Book of Egyptian Whodunnits. 2002. (Illus.). 512p. pap. 11.95 (*0-7867-1065-9*, Carroll & Graf Pubs.) Avalon Publishing Group.

Bantock, Nick. Alexandria: In Which the Extraordinary Correspondence of Griffin & Sabine Unfolds. 19.95 o.s.i (*0-8118-3699-1*) Chronicle Bks. LLC.

Bantock, Nick, illus. Alexandria: In Which the Extraordinary Correspondence of Griffin & Sabine Unfolds. 2002. 56p. 19.95 (*0-8118-3140-X*) Chronicle Bks. LLC.

Bell, Clare. Tomorrow's Sphinx. 1986. 312p. (YA). (gr. 7 up). lib. bdg. 15.95 o.s.i (*0-689-50402-0*, McElderry, Margaret K.) Simon & Schuster Children's Publishing.

Boullosa, Carmen. Cleopatra Dismounts: A Novel. Hargreaves, Geoff, tr. from SPA. 2003. 22.00 (*0-8021-1753-8*, Grove Pr.) Grove/Atlantic, Inc.

Bradshaw, Gillian. Cleopatra's Heir. 2002. 496p. 25.95 (*0-7653-0228-4*, Forge Bks.) Doherty, Tom Assocs., LLC.

—Render unto Caesar. Date not set. pap. (*0-7653-0654-9*, Forge Bks.); E-Book (*0-312-71073-9*, Tor Bks.); 2003. 464p. 27.95 (*0-7653-0653-0*, Forge Bks.) Doherty, Tom Assocs., LLC.

Brockway, Connie. As You Desire. 1997. 400p. mass mkt. 6.50 (*0-440-22199-4*) Dell Publishing.

Brown, William F. Thursday at Noon. 1988. 384p. reprint ed. pap. (*0-373-97080-3*, Harlequin Bks.) Harlequin Enterprises, Ltd.

—Thursday at Noon. 1987. 288p. 16.95 o.p. (*0-312-00020-0*) St. Martin's Pr.

Bull, Bartle. A Cafe on the Nile. (Illus.). 1999. 480p. 13.95 (*0-7867-0675-9*); 1998. 465p. 26.00 (*0-7867-0556-6*) Avalon Publishing Group. (Carroll & Graf Pubs.).

—The Devil's Oasis. 2001. (Illus.). 356p. 25.00 (*0-7867-0844-1*); 2002. 336p. reprint ed. pap. 14.00 (*0-7867-0990-1*) Avalon Publishing Group. (Carroll & Graf Pubs.).

Byrd-Clarke, Mary. Sothis: Star of Egypt. 2000. E-Book 12.95 incl. cd-rom (*1-58444-032-5*) Disc-Us Bks., Inc.

Caldecott, Moyra. Tutankhamun & the Daughter of Ra. 1200. (Egyptian Ser.). E-Book (*1-899142-62-2*); E-Book (*1-899142-88-6*); E-Book (*1-899142-33-9*); E-Book (*1-899142-17-7*) Mushroom Publishing.

—Tutankhamun & the Daughter of Ra. 1200. (Egyptian Ser.: Vol. 3). E-Book (*1-84319-172-5*); E-Book (*1-84319-016-8*); E-Book (*1-84319-046-X*); E-Book (*1-84319-171-7*); E-Book (*1-84319-170-9*) Mushroom e-books.

Campbell, Jeff, et al. Raiders of the Lost Ark. 1998. (Mighty Chronicles Ser.). (Illus.). 320p. (gr. 3-7). 9.95 o.p. (*0-8118-2209-5*) Chronicle Bks. LLC.

Caute, David. Fatima's Scarf. 1998. 560p. (*0-9530407-0-4*) Totterdown Bks.

Chaikin, Linda L. Arabian Winds: Lions of the Desert. 1997. (Palisades Pure Romance Ser.: Vol. 1). 406p. pap. 11.99 o.p. (*1-57673-105-7*, Palisades) Multnomah Pubs., Inc.

—Valiant Hearts. 1998. 378p. pap. 11.99 o.p. (*1-57673-240-1*) Multnomah Pubs., Inc.

Christie, Agatha. Death Comes As the End. 1982. (Agatha Christie Ser.). 9.95 (*0-396-08109-6*, G. P. Putnam's Sons) Penguin Putnam Bks. for Young Readers.

—Death Comes As the End. 1990. mass mkt. 4.99 o.s.i (*0-671-70610-1*); 1982. mass mkt. 2.95 o.s.i (*0-671-46539-2*) Simon & Schuster. (Pocket).

—Death Comes As the End. l.t. ed. 1970. (Ulverscroft Large Print Ser.). 29.99 o.p. (*0-85456-004-1*, Ulverscroft) Thorpe, F. A. Pubs. GBR. *Dist:* Ulverscroft Large Print Bks., Ltd., Ulverscroft Large Print Canada, Ltd.

—Death Comes As the End. 1992. 12.04 (*0-606-12246-X*) Turtleback Bks.

Chute, Carolyn. Merry Men. 1995. 712p. pap. 17.00 (*0-15-600191-8*, Harvest Bks.); 1994. x, 695p. (C). 24.95 o.s.i (*0-15-159270-5*) Harcourt Trade Pubs.

Cohen-Mor, Dalya. Yusuf Idris: The Piper Dies & Other Stories. 1992. (C). pap. 15.95 (*1-880613-03-4*) Sheba Pr., Ltd.

Conway, Anthony. The Colonel's Renegade. 2003. 352p. pap. 11.95 (*0-340-82209-0*) Hodder & Stoughton, Ltd. GBR. *Dist:* Trafalgar Square.

Danielson, Peter. The Shepherd Kings. 1983. (Orig.). 448p. mass mkt. 3.95 o.s.i (*0-553-23749-7*); 608p. mass mkt. 4.99 o.s.i (*0-553-26971-2*) Bantam Bks.

Deighton, Len. City of Gold. 1992. 368p. 240.00 o.p. (*0-06-017702-0*) HarperCollins Pubs.

—City of Gold. 1992. 368p. 20.00 o.p. (*0-06-017937-6*) HarperTrade.

—City of Gold. 1993. 416p. mass mkt. 5.99 o.p. (*0-06-109041-7*, HarperTorch) Morrow/Avon.

Devine, Laurie. Nile. 1984. 544p. pap. 3.95 o.p. (*0-440-16419-2*) Dell Publishing.

—Nile. 1924. o.s.i (*0-688-04734-3*, Morrow, William & Co.) Morrow/Avon.

Doherty, P. C. The Anubis Slayings: An Egyptian Novel of Intrigue & Murder. 2001. (Illus.). 288p. 23.95 (*0-312-27658-3*, Saint Martin's Minotaur) St. Martin's Pr.

—The Mask of Ra: A Novel of Mystery & Murder in Ancient Egypt. 2001. 288p. mass mkt. 6.50 (*0-425-18093-X*) Berkley Publishing Group.

—The Mask of Ra: A Novel of Mystery & Murder in Ancient Egypt. l.t. ed. 2000. (Magna Large Print Ser.). 368p. (*0-7505-1526-0*) Magna Large Print Bks. GBR. *Dist:* Ulverscroft Large Print Canada, Ltd.

—The Mask of Ra: A Novel of Mystery & Murder in Ancient Egypt. 2nd ed. 1999. 240p. 21.95 (*0-312-20560-0*, Saint Martin's Minotaur) St. Martin's Pr.

—The Slayers of Seth: A Story of Intrigue & Murder Set in Ancient Egypt. 2002. (Illus.). 320p. 23.95 (*0-312-28264-8*, Saint Martin's Minotaur) St. Martin's Pr.

Doyle, Peter R. Trapped in Pharaoh's Tomb. 1993. (Daring Adventure Ser.: Vol. 2). (J). (gr. 4). pap. 5.99 o.p. (*1-56179-143-1*) Focus on the Family Publishing.

Drinnan, W. S. The Scorpion of Avaris. 2001. 135p. pap. (*1-55212-855-5*) Trafford Publishing.

Durrell, Lawrence. Balthazar. unabr. ed. 1994. (Alexandria Ser. ). audio 56.00 (*0-7366-2713-8*, 3443) Books on Tape, Inc.

—Balthazar. abr. ed. (Alexandria Quartet Ser.: Vol. II). 1996. audio 17.98 (*962-634-546-2*, NA304614); 1995. audio compact disk 19.98 (*962-634-046-0*, NA304612) Naxos of America, Inc. (Naxos AudioBooks).

—Balthazar. 2002. (SPA.). 280p. mass mkt. 8.95 (*1-4000-0028-9*) Random Hse., Inc.

—Balthazar. 1981. (Alexandria Quartet Ser.: Vol. 2). 256p. mass mkt. 3.95 o.s.i (*0-671-45102-2*, Pocket) Simon & Schuster.

—Balthazar. l.t. ed. 1999. (Perennial Bestsellers Ser.). 325p. pap. 26.95 (*0-7838-8718-3*) Thorndike Pr.

—Balthazar. 1991. (Alexandria Quartet Ser.). 250p. reprint ed. 14.00 (*0-14-015321-7*) Viking Penguin.

—Clea. unabr. ed. 1994. (Alexandria Quartet Ser.: Vol. IV). audio 64.00 (*0-7366-2808-8*, 3522) Books on Tape, Inc.

—Clea. 1961. (Alexandria Quartet Ser.). pap. 6.25 o.p. (*0-525-47083-2*, Plume) Dutton/Plume.

—Clea. abr. ed. (Alexandria Quartet Ser.: Vol. IV). 1996. audio 17.98 (*962-634-566-7*, NA306614); 1995. audio compact disk 19.98 (*962-634-066-5*, NA306612) Naxos of America, Inc. (Naxos AudioBooks).

—Clea. 2002. (SPA.). 344p. mass mkt. 9.95 (*1-4000-0032-7*) Random Hse., Inc.

—Clea, Vol. 4. 1981. 288p. mass mkt. 3.95 o.s.i (*0-671-45103-0*, Pocket) Simon & Schuster.

—Clea. l.t. ed. 2000. (Perennial Bestsellers Ser.). 381p. 25.95 (*0-7838-8975-5*) Thorndike Pr.

—Clea. 1991. (Alexandria Quartet Ser.). 287p. reprint ed. 14.00 (*0-14-015322-5*) Viking Penguin.

—Justine. 1961. (Alexandria Quartet Ser.). pap. 6.95 o.p. (*0-525-48406-X*, Plume) Dutton/Plume.

—Justine. 1981. (Alexandria Quartet Ser.: Vol. 1). 240p. mass mkt. 3.95 o.s.i (*0-671-45104-9*, Pocket) Simon & Schuster.

—Justine. l.t. ed. 1999. (Perennial Bestsellers Ser.). 320p. 25.95 (*0-7838-8644-6*) Thorndike Pr.

—Mountolive. unabr. ed. 1994. (Alexandria Quartet Ser.: Vol. III). audio 72.00 (*0-7366-2807-X*, 3521) Books on Tape, Inc.

—Mountolive. 1961. (Alexandria Quartet Ser.). pap. 6.25 o.p. (*0-525-47082-4*, Plume) Dutton/Plume.

—Mountolive. 2002. (SPA.). 376p. mass mkt. 10.95 (*1-4000-0031-9*) Random Hse., Inc.

—Mountolive. l.t. ed. 2000. (Perennial Bestsellers Ser.). 447p. 25.95 (*0-7838-8820-1*) Thorndike Pr.

—Mountolive. 1991. (Alexandria Quartet Ser.). 320p. reprint ed. 12.95 (*0-14-015320-9*) Viking Penguin.

Easterman, Daniel. The Name of the Beast. 1992. 384p. 20.00 o.p. (*0-06-017996-1*) HarperTrade.

Ebers, George C. The Sisters. E-Book 3.95 (*0-594-02159-6*) 1873 Pr.

Ebers, George Moritz. Uarda. E-Book 3.95 (*0-594-02161-8*) 1873 Pr.

El Saadawi, Nawal. The Circling Song. 1989. 128p. (C). o.p. (*0-86232-816-0*); pap. o.p. (*0-86232-817-9*) Zed Bks., Ltd.

El-Saadawi, Nawal. Searching. 1991. (C). (*1-85649-008-4*); pap. (*1-85649-009-2*) Zed Bks., Ltd.

Elkins, Aaron. Dead Men's Hearts. 1994. 240p. 18.95 o.s.i (*0-89296-466-9*) Mysterious Pr.

—Dead Men's Hearts. 1995. 256p. mass mkt. 6.99 (*0-446-40056-4*) Warner Bks., Inc.

Essex, Karen. Kleopatra. 2001. (Illus.). 400p. 24.95 o.p. (*0-446-52740-8*) Warner Bks., Inc.

Fielding, Sarah. The Lives of Cleopatra & Octavia. Johnson, Christopher D., ed. 1994. 200p. reprint ed. 36.50 (*0-8387-5257-8*) Bucknell Univ. Pr.

—The Lives of Cleopatra & Octavia, 1757. 1975. (Novel in England, 1700-1775 Ser). lib. bdg. 55.00 o.p. (*0-8240-1147-3*) Garland Publishing, Inc.

Fields, Hillary. Marrying Jezebel. 2000. 368p. mass mkt. 5.99 (*0-312-97567-8*, St. Martin's Paperbacks) St. Martin's Pr.

Flaubert, Gustave. The Temptation of St. Anthony. 1978. reprint ed. 17.50 (*0-86527-312-X*) Fertig, Howard Inc.

—The Temptation of St. Anthony. 2002. (Modern Library Classics). 288p. pap. 13.95 (*0-375-75912-3*, Modern Library) Random House Adult Trade Publishing Group.

—The Temptation of St. Anthony. Mrosovsky, Kitty, tr. from FRE. & intro. by. 1983. (Penguin Classics Ser.). 304p. pap. 11.95 o.p. (*0-14-044410-6*, Penguin Classics) Viking Penguin.

Frank, Suzanne J. Reflections in the Nile. 1999. 528p. E-Book 4.95 (*0-446-92325-7*) Time Warner Bk. Group.

Frank, Suzanne J., ed. Reflections in the Nile. 1999. E-Book 4.95 (*0-446-91282-4*); 1998. (Illus.). 544p. mass mkt. 6.99 o.s.i (*0-446-60579-4*); 1997. 418p. 22.00 o.p. (*0-446-52089-6*) Warner Bks., Inc.

Gedge, Pauline. Child of the Morning. 1976. 30.95 (*0-8488-1335-9*) Amereon, Ltd.

—Child of the Morning. unabr. collector's ed. 1985. Pt. 1. audio 64.00 (*0-7366-0874-5*, 1824A); Pt. 2. audio 56.00 (*0-7366-0875-3*, 1824-B) Books on Tape, Inc.

—Child of the Morning. 1986. 300p. reprint ed. lib. bdg. 32.95 o.p. (*0-89966-567-5*) Buccaneer Bks., Inc.

—Child of the Morning. 1993. (Hera Ser.). 403p. pap. 15.00 (*0-939149-85-0*) Soho Pr., Inc.

—The Hippopotamus Marsh. 2000. (Lord of the Two Lands Ser.: Vol. 1). 408p. pap. 14.00 (*1-56947-220-3*); (Illus.). 368p. 25.00 (*1-56947-191-6*) Soho Pr., Inc.

—The Horus Road. 2001. (Lords of the Two Lands Ser.: Vol. 3). (Illus.). xvii, 507p. 26.00 (*1-56947-236-X*) Soho Pr., Inc.

—The Horus Road. 2000. (Illus.). xvii, 507p. pap. o.p. (*0-670-88670-X*) Viking Penguin.

—The Horus Road Vol. 3: Lords of the Two Lands. 2001. 528p. reprint ed. pap. 15.00 (*1-56947-260-2*) Soho Pr., Inc.

—House of Illusions. 1997. 446p. 24.95 (*1-55921-200-4*) Moyer Bell.

—Lady of the Reeds. (Hera Ser.). 513p. 1997. pap. 16.00 (*1-56947-072-3*); 1995. 25.00 (*1-56947-043-X*) Soho Pr., Inc.

—Mirage: A Novel. 1991. 480p. 21.95 o.p. (*0-06-016541-3*) HarperTrade.

—The Oasis. (Lord of the Two Lands Ser.: Vol. 2). 2000. (Illus.). xi, 532p. 26.00 (*1-56947-219-X*); 2001. 544p. reprint ed. pap. 15.00 (*1-56947-238-6*) Soho Pr., Inc.

—The Oasis, Vol. 2. 1999. (Illus.). 532p. pap. o.p. (*0-670-88671-8*, Viking) Viking Penguin.

—The Twelfth Transforming. 1987. mass mkt. 3.95 o.s.i (*0-8041-0130-2*, Ivy Bks.) Ballantine Bks.

—The Twelfth Transforming. 1984. 544p. 16.95 o.p. (*0-06-015338-5*) HarperTrade.

—The Twelfth Transforming. 1998. 407p. pap. 14.95 (*1-55921-259-4*) Moyer Bell.

George, Margaret. The Memoirs of Cleopatra. unabr. collector's ed. 1998. Pt. 1. audio 104.00 (*0-7366-4093-2*, 4600-A); Pt. 2. audio 88.00 (*0-7366-4094-0*, 4600-B); Pt. 3. audio 88.00 (*0-7366-4095-9*, 4600-C) Books on Tape, Inc.

—The Memoirs of Cleopatra. abr. ed. 1997. audio 22.95 o.p. (*1-55935-254-X*) Soundelux Audio Publishing.

—The Memoirs of Cleopatra. 1999. E-Book 15.95 (*0-312-20730-1*) St. Martin's Pr.

—The Memoirs of Cleopatra: A Novel. 1999. pap. 339.00 (*0-312-24601-3*); 1997. 1024p. 27.95 o.s.i (*0-312-15430-5*); 4th ed. 1998. 964p. pap. 16.95 (*0-312-18745-9*, Saint Martin's Griffin) St. Martin's Pr.

Gormley, Beatrice. Miriam. (J). 1999. 180p. (gr. 4-9). pap. 6.00 (*0-8028-5156-8*, Eerdmans Bks For Young Readers); 1998. (*0-8028-5153-3*) Eerdmans, William B. Publishing Co.

Grant, Joan M. Eyes of Horus. 1988. 480p. pap. 15.99 (*0-89804-146-5*) Ariel Pr.

—Eyes of Horus. 1980. 33.95 (*0-405-11782-5*) Ayer Co. Pubs., Inc.

Haney, Lauren. A Curse of Silence: A Mystery of Ancient Egypt. 2000. 304p. mass mkt. 6.50 (*0-380-81285-1*, Avon Bks.) Morrow/Avon.

—A Face Turned Backward. 1999. (Mystery of Ancient Egypt Ser.). 304p. mass mkt. 5.99 (*0-380-79267-2*, Avon Bks.) Morrow/Avon.

—Path of Shadows. 2003. 320p. mass mkt. 6.99 (*0-06-052190-2*, Avon Bks.) Morrow/Avon.

—The Right Hand of Amon. 1997. 320p. mass mkt. 6.99 (*0-380-79266-4*, Avon Bks.) Morrow/Avon.

—A Vile Justice. 1999. 304p. mass mkt. 5.99 (*0-380-79265-6*, Avon Bks.) Morrow/Avon.

Haqqi, Yaha. Blood & Mud: Three Novelettes by Yaha Haqqi. Cachia, Pierre, tr. 1998. 131p. 18.00 o.p. (*1-57889-092-6*) Passeggiata Pr.

—Blood & Mud: Three Stories by Yaha Haqqi. Cachia, Pierre, tr. from ARA. 1999. 131p. pap. 11.00 (*1-57889-093-4*) Passeggiata Pr.

Hauge, J. D. Sanctuary on the Nile: River of Life. 2nd l.t. ed. 2000. 301p. pap. text 19.95 (*0-9703805-0-X*) Alpha Imagery.

Hibsman, Tim. Cartoon Cartouche: A Humorous Look at Ancient Egypt. 2001. 100p. cd-rom (*1-889858-06-4*) True Arts Graphics & Printing.

Higgins, Jack. In the Hour Before Midnight. 1984. mass mkt. 2.95 o.s.i (*0-449-12807-5*); 1980. mass mkt. 2.25 o.s.i (*0-449-13954-9*) Ballantine Bks. (Fawcett).

—In the Hour Before Midnight. 2000. 304p. reprint ed. mass mkt. 7.50 (*0-425-17631-2*) Berkley Publishing Group.

—In the Hour Before Midnight. unabr. collector's ed. 1984. audio 36.00 (*0-7366-0481-2*, 1456) Books on Tape, Inc.

—In the Hour Before Midnight. unabr. ed. 2000. audio 34.95 (*0-7451-6021-2*, CAB 337) Chivers Audio Bks. GBR. *Dist:* BBC Audiobooks America.

—In the Hour Before Midnight. 1982. 192p. mass mkt. 2.95 o.s.i (*0-440-14350-0*) Dell Publishing.

—In the Hour Before Midnight. l.t. ed. 1978. o.p. (*0-7089-0113-1*, Ulverscroft) Thorpe, F. A. Pubs.

High, Monique R. The Eleventh Year. 1984. pap. 3.95 o.p. (*0-440-12267-8*) Dell Publishing.

Holland, Cecelia. Valley of the Kings. 1999. 231p. pap. 12.95 (*0-312-86862-6*); 1997. 240p. 21.95 (*0-312-86334-9*) Doherty, Tom Assocs., LLC. (Forge Bks.).

Hopkins, Harry. The 1001 Nights of Drummer Donald McLeod. 2000. xi, 441p. pap. 16.00 (*0-86241-890-9*) Canongate Bks. GBR. *Dist:* Grove/Atlantic, Inc.

Hopkinson, Nalo. The Salt Roads. 2003. 400p. 22.95 (*0-446-53302-5*) Warner Bks., Inc.

Hull, E. M. The Sheik. 1976. reprint ed. lib. bdg. 23.95 (*0-89190-734-3*, Rivercity Pr.) Amereon, Ltd.

—The Sheik. 1990. reprint ed. lib. bdg. 25.95 (*0-89968-529-3*) Buccaneer Bks., Inc.

—The Sheik. 2001. 304p. pap. 14.95 (*0-8122-1763-2*) Univ. of Pennsylvania Pr.

Hunt, Angela Elwell. Brothers. 1997. (Legacies of the Ancient River Ser.: Vol. 2). 368p. pap. 12.99 (*1-55661-608-2*) Bethany Hse. Pubs.

—Brothers. 2001. 391p. 24.95 (*0-7862-3090-8*, Five Star) Gale Group.

—Dreamers. 1995. (Legacies of the Ancient River Ser.: Vol. 1). 400p. pap. 12.99 (*1-55661-607-4*) Bethany Hse. Pubs.

—Dreamers. 1998. (Legacies of the Ancient River Ser.: Vol. 1). 413p. pap. 23.95 (*0-7862-1419-8*, Five Star) Gale Group.

—Journey. 1997. (Legacies of the Ancient River Ser.: Vol. 3). 384p. pap. 12.99 (*1-55661-609-0*) Bethany Hse. Pubs.

Ibrahim, Sun'Allah. The Committee. St. Germain, Mary & Constable, Charlene, trs. from ARA. 2001. (Middle East Literature in Translation Ser.). 172p. 22.95 (*0-8156-0726-1*) Syracuse Univ. Pr.

Idris, Yusuf. In the Eye of the Beholder: Tales of Egyptian Life from the Writings of Yusuf Idris. 1978. (Studies in Middle Eastern Literatures: No. 10). 30.00 o.p. (*0-88297-019-4*) Bibliotheca Islamica, Inc.

Irwin, Robert. The Arabian Nightmare. 1987. 288p. 16.95 o.p. (*0-670-81661-2*) Viking Penguin.

Jacq, Christian. The Battle of Kadesh. 1998. (Ramses Ser.: Vol. 3). (Illus.). 384p. pap. 14.99 (*0-446-67358-7*) Warner Bks., Inc.

—The Eternal Temple. 1998. (Ramses Ser.: Vol. 2). (Illus.). 368p. pap. 14.99 (*0-446-67357-9*) Warner Bks., Inc.

—The Lady of Abu Simbel. 1998. (Ramses Ser.: Vol. 4). (Illus.). 384p. pap. 14.99 (*0-446-67359-5*) Warner Bks., Inc.

—Nefer the Silent. 2000. (Stone of Light Ser.: Vol. 1). 400p. pap. 16.00 (*0-7434-0346-0*, Atria) Simon & Schuster.

—Nefer the Silent. abr. ed. 2000. (Stone of Light Ser.: Vol. 1). audio 25.00 (*0-7435-0508-5*, Simon & Schuster Audioworks) Simon & Schuster Audio.

—Paneb the Ardent. 2001. (Stone of Light Ser.: Vol. 3). 400p. pap. 16.00 (*0-7434-0348-7*, Atria) Simon & Schuster.

—The Place of Truth. 2001. (Stone of Light Ser.: Vol. 4). 384p. pap. 16.00 (*0-7434-0349-5*, Atria) Simon & Schuster.

—Ramses Vol. 1: The Son of Light. 2001. 336p. E-Book 9.95 (*0-446-91284-0*) Warner Bks., Inc.

—Ramses Vol. 2: The Eternal Temple. 2001. 368p. E-Book 9.95 (*0-446-92309-5*) Time Warner Bk. Group.

—Ramses Vol. 2: The Eternal Temple. 2001. 368p. E-Book 9.95 (*0-446-91285-9*) Warner Bks., Inc.

—Ramses Vol. 3: The Battle of Kadesh. 2001. 384p. E-Book 9.95 (*0-446-92310-9*) Time Warner Bk. Group.

—Ramses Vol. 3: The Battle of Kadesh. 2001. 384p. E-Book 9.95 (*0-446-91286-7*) Warner Bks., Inc.

—Ramses Vol. 4: The Lady of Abu Simbel. 2001. 384p. E-Book 9.95 (*0-446-92311-7*) Time Warner Bk. Group.

—Ramses Vol. 4: The Lady of Abu Simbel. 2001. 384p. E-Book 9.95 (*0-446-91287-5*) Warner Bks., Inc.

—Ramses Vol. 5: Under the Western Acacia. 2001. 384p. E-Book 9.95 (*0-446-92312-5*) Time Warner Bk. Group.

—Ramses Vol. 5: Under the Western Acacia. 2001. 384p. E-Book 9.95 (*0-446-91288-3*) Warner Bks., Inc.

—The Wise Woman. 2000. (Stone of Light Ser.: Vol. 2). (Illus.). 432p. pap. 16.00 (*0-7434-0347-9*, Atria) Simon & Schuster.

Jong, Erica. Sappho's Leap: A Novel. 2003. (Illus.). 320p. 24.95 (*0-393-05761-5*); 256p. 24.95 (*0-393-05762-3*) Norton, W. W. & Co., Inc.

Jonz, St. Juill. Phleideis: A Pharaoh Story. 2000. 216p. E-Book 8.00 (*0-7388-8486-3*) Xlibris Corp.

Kadare, Ismail. The Pyramid. Vrioni, Jusuf & Bellos, David, trs. from FRE. 1996. 176p. 21.95 (*1-55970-314-8*) Arcade Publishing, Inc.

—The Pyramid. Bellos, David, tr. from FRE. 1998. 176p. pap. 11.00 o.s.i (*0-375-70095-1*, Vintage) Knopf Publishing Group.

Kassem, Abdel-Hakim. The Seven Days of Man. Bell, Joseph, tr. 1996. Tr. of Ayyam Al-Insan Al-Sabah. 220p. 31.00 (*0-8101-1415-1*, Hydra Bks.) Northwestern Univ. Pr.

Kingsley, Charles. Hypatia. 2000. 252p. E-Book 3.95 (*0-594-02545-1*) 1873 Pr.

—Hypatia: New Foes with an Old Face. 1987. 416p. reprint ed. pap. 14.50 o.p. (*0-8334-0020-7*, Spiritual Literature Library) Garber Communications, Inc.

Kiteley, Brian. I Know Many Songs, But I Cannot Sing. 1996. 192p. 20.00 o.p. (*0-684-80905-2*, Simon & Schuster) Simon & Schuster.

Lattimore, Deborah Nourse. The Winged Cat a Tale of Ancient Egypt. 1992. (J). 13.10 (*0-606-08434-7*) Turtleback Bks.

Le Coz, Martine. Le Pharaon Qui n'Avait Pas d'Ombre. 1999. (FRE.). 288p. reprint ed. pap. 14.95 (*1-58348-174-5*) iUniverse, Inc.

Levin, Lee. King Tut's Private Eye. 1996. 272p. 21.95 o.p. (*0-312-14274-9*, Saint Martin's Minotaur) St. Martin's Pr.

Lindsey, Johanna. Captive Bride. (Romance Ser.). 1996. lib. bdg. 24.95 (*0-7862-0880-5*, Five Star); 1992. 342p. lib. bdg. 19.95 o.p. (*0-8161-5291-8*, Macmillan Reference USA) Gale Group.

—Captive Bride. 1999. 384p. mass mkt. 6.99 (*0-380-01697-4*, 88799-1, Avon Bks.) Morrow/Avon.

—Captive Bride. abr. ed. 1994. audio 5.99 (*1-57096-008-9*, RAZ 909) Romance Alive Audio.

—Captive Bride. 1996. 18.00 o.p. (*0-7278-1634-9*) Severn Hse. Pubs., Ltd.

—Captive Bride. l.t. ed. 1992. (Large Print Book Ser.). 342p. pap. 19.95 (*0-8161-5292-6*) Thorndike Pr.

Livesay, Ann & Sutton, Myron D. The Isis Command: An Egyptian Mystery. 1998. (Barry Ross International Mystery Ser.: Vol. 1). 225p. pap., wbk. ed. (*0-9662817-0-5*) Silver River Bks.

Mackin, Jeanne. Dreams of Empire. 256p. 1997. mass mkt. 4.99 o.s.i (*1-57566-133-0*); 1996. 21.00 o.s.i (*1-57566-020-2*) Kensington Publishing Corp.

Mahfouz, Naguib. Adrift on the Nile. 176p. 1994. pap. 7.99 (*0-385-40473-5*); 1994. pap. 15.00 (*0-385-42333-0*); 1993. 13.99 (*0-385-40336-4*) Doubleday Publishing.

—Akhenaten: Dweller in Truth. 1999. 19.95 (*977-424-470-2*) American Univ. in Cairo Pr. EGY. *Dist:* Books International, Incorporated.

—Autumn Quail. 1986. pap. 8.50 o.p. (*977-424-107-X*) American Univ. in Cairo Pr. EGY. *Dist:* Books International, Incorporated.

—The Beggar. Henry, Kristin W., tr. 1987. pap. 10.50 o.p. (*977-424-135-5*) American Univ. in Cairo Pr. EGY. *Dist:* Books International, Incorporated.

—The Cairo Trilogy: Palace Walk, Palace of Desire, Sugar Street, 3 vols. 2001. 1360p. 30.00 (*0-375-41331-6*, Knopf Bks. for Young Readers) Random Hse. Children's Bks.

—Children of the Alley. Theroux, Peter, tr. from ENG. 1995. Tr. of Awlad al-Haratina. (ARA.). 464p. 24.95 o.s.i (*0-385-42094-3*) Doubleday Publishing.

—The Day the Leader Was Killed. 1999. 14.95 (*977-424-454-0*) American Univ. in Cairo Pr. EGY. *Dist:* Books International, Incorporated.

—The Day the Leader Was Killed. 2000. 112p. pap. 11.00 (*0-385-49922-1*) Doubleday Publishing.

—Fountain & Tomb. Kenneson, James et al, trs. 1988. Tr. of Hakayat Haretna. (Illus.). 120p. (C). reprint ed. pap. 12.00 (*0-89410-581-7*, Three Continents) Rienner, Lynne Pubs., Inc.

—The Harafish. Cobham, Catherine, tr. from ARA. 1997. Orig. Title: Malhamat al-Harafish. 416p. pap. 15.95 (*0-385-42335-7*) Doubleday Publishing.

—The Harafish. Orig. Title: Malhamat al-Harafish. 416p. 1995. pap. 9.99 (*0-385-40583-9*); 1994. 15.99 (*0-385-40362-3*) Doubleday Publishing.

—Midaq Alley. 1992. 21.50 o.s.i (*0-385-26475-5*); 1992. 304p. pap. 7.99 (*0-385-26940-4*); 1991. 304p. pap. 12.95 (*0-385-26476-3*) Doubleday Publishing.

—Midaq Alley. 1991. reprint ed. 18.00 o.p. (*0-89410-657-0*); pap. 11.00 o.p. (*0-89410-658-9*) Rienner, Lynne Pubs., Inc. (Three Continents).

—Midaq Alley. Le Gassick, Trevor, tr. from ARA. 1981. ix, 246p. reprint ed. 15.00 o.p. (*0-89410-282-6*, Three Continents) Rienner, Lynne Pubs., Inc.

—Midaq Alley. 2002. 27.00 (*0-8446-7225-4*) Smith, Peter Pub., Inc.

—Miramar. 1993. 192p. pap. 7.99 (*0-385-26941-2*) Doubleday Publishing.

—Miramar. Rodenbeck, John, ed. Mahmoud, Fatma M., tr. 1992. 192p. pap. 15.00 (*0-385-26478-X*) Doubleday Publishing.

—Miramar. Moussa-Mahmoud, Fatma, tr. 2nd enl. ed. 1996. (ARA.). 156p. reprint ed. pap. 12.00 (*1-57889-037-3*) Passeggiata Pr.

—Miramar. Moussa-Mahmoud, Fatma, tr. from ARA. reprint ed. 2nd enl. ed. 1996. 173p. pap. 11.00 o.p. (*0-89410-693-7*); 3rd ed. 1988. pap. 10.00 o.p. (*0-89410-462-4*) Rienner, Lynne Pubs., Inc. (Three Continents).

—Palace of Desire. 432p. 1992. pap. 8.95 (*0-385-40208-2*); 1990. 22.95 o.s.i (*0-385-26467-4*); 1990. 13.99 o.s.i (*0-385-26936-6*) Doubleday Publishing.

—Palace of Desire. 1991. (Cairo Trilogy: Vol. II). 432p. pap. 14.95 (*0-385-26468-2*, Knopf Bks. for Young Readers) Random Hse. Children's Bks.

—Sugar Street. 320p. 1993. pap. 8.99 (*0-385-40306-2*); 1991. 14.99 o.s.i (*0-385-26937-4*); Vol. 3. 1991. 22.50 o.s.i (*0-385-26469-0*) Doubleday Publishing.

—Sugar Street. Hutchins, William M., tr. 1992. (Cairo Trilogy: Vol. 3). 320p. pap. 12.95 (*0-385-26470-4*, Knopf Bks. for Young Readers) Random Hse. Children's Bks.

Mahfouz, Naguib, et al. Akhenaten: Dweller in Truth, a Novel. 2000. 178p. pap. 12.00 (*0-385-49909-4*, Anchor Bible) Doubleday Publishing.

Mailer, Norman. Ancient Evenings. 1983. 800p. 19.95 o.s.i (*0-316-54410-8*) Little Brown & Co.

Makepeace, Joanna. The Chosen of the Gods. l.t. ed. 1997. 227p. pap. 22.95 o.p. (*0-7838-2015-1*, Macmillan Reference USA) Gale Group.

—Daughter of Isis. l.t. ed. 1997. 236p. pap. 21.95 (*0-7838-2017-8*, Macmillan Reference USA) Gale Group.

—Divine Son of Ra. l.t. ed. 1997. 266p. pap. 21.95 (*0-7838-2016-X*, Macmillan Reference USA) Gale Group.

Mann, Jessica. Death Beyond the Nile. l.t. ed. 1991. 15.95 o.p. (*0-7927-9582-2*, 5055); pap. 15.95 o.p. (*0-7927-0010-4*, 4617) BBC Audiobooks America.

—Death Beyond the Nile. 1989. 192p. 14.95 o.p. (*0-312-02564-5*, Saint Martin's Minotaur) St. Martin's Pr.

Marsche, Daniel Tegan. The Eunuch Neferu. 2002. 344p. pap. 20.95 (*0-595-24397-5*, Writers Club Pr.) iUniverse, Inc.

McCoy, Gayle A., illus. Nenfretiti, Woman Pharaoh. 2001. 250p. pap. (*1-55212-739-7*) Trafford Publishing.

Meade, Glenn. The Sands of Sakkara. abr. ed. 1999. audio 17.95 o.p. (*1-55927-543-X*) Audio Renaissance.

—The Sands of Sakkara. 2000. 544p. mass mkt. 6.99 (*0-312-97108-7*, St. Martin's Paperbacks); 1999. 436p. 25.95 o.p. (*0-312-20201-6*) St. Martin's Pr.

Morris, Gilbert. The Beloved Enemy. 2003. (House of Winslow Ser.). 320p. pap. 11.99 (*0-7642-2704-1*) Bethany Hse. Pubs.

Nasir, Jamil. Tower of Dreams. 1999. 240p. pap. 15.00 (*0-553-76316-4*); mass mkt. 5.99 (*0-553-58089-2*) Bantam Bks. (Spectra).

Nelson, Ray F. Dogheaded Death. 1989. (Centurion Bks.). 184p. (Orig.). pap. 9.95 (*0-89407-079-7*) Strawberry Hill Pr.

Nuelle, Helen. Surrender to Love. l.t. ed. 1993. 19.95 o.p. (*0-7927-1688-4*); pap. 17.95 o.p. (*0-7927-1687-6*) BBC Audiobooks America.

Out el Kouloub. Ramza. Atiya, Nayra, tr. from FRE. 1994. (Contemporary Issues in the Middle East Ser.). (Illus.). 128p. pap. 16.95 (*0-8156-0280-4*); text 34.95 (*0-8156-2618-5*) Syracuse Univ. Pr.

—Zanouba: A Novel. Atiya, Nayra, tr. & intro. by. 1996. (Middle East Literature in Translation Ser.). 192p. 39.95 (*0-8156-2718-1*, ATZA); pap. 17.95 (*0-8156-0408-4*, ATZAP) Syracuse Univ. Pr.

Pearce, Michael. The Mamur Zapt & the Donkey-Vous: A Suspense Tale of Old Cairo. 1992. 272p. 17.95 (*0-89296-486-3*) Mysterious Pr.

—The Mamur Zapt & the Girl in the Nile. 1994. 224p. 19.95 o.s.i (*0-89296-509-6*) Mysterious Pr.

—The Mamur Zapt & the Men Behind. 1993. 256p. 17.95 (*0-89296-487-1*) Mysterious Pr.

—Mamur Zapt & the Night of the Dog. 1991. 192p. 15.00 o.s.i (*0-385-41521-4*) Doubleday Publishing.

—Mamur Zapt & the Return of the Carpet. 1990. 14.95 o.s.i (*0-385-41520-6*) Doubleday Publishing.

—The Mamur Zapt & the Spoils of Egypt. 1995. 240p. 19.95 o.s.i (*0-89296-560-6*) Mysterious Pr.

Peters, Elizabeth, pseud. The Ape Who Guards the Balance. l.t. ed. 1999. (Amelia Peabody Mystery Ser.: No. 10). 26.95 (*1-56895-597-9*, Wheeler Publishing, Inc.) Gale Group.

—The Ape Who Guards the Balance. 2002. E-Book 7.50 (*0-06-052324-7*); E-Book 7.50 (*0-06-052322-0*); E-Book 7.50 (*0-06-052323-9*); E-Book 7.50 (*0-06-052325-5*) HarperCollins General Bks. Group. (PerfectBound).

—The Ape Who Guards the Balance. (Amelia Peabody Mystery Ser.: No. 10). 1999. 464p. (gr. 8 up). mass mkt. 7.50 (*0-380-79856-5*); 1998. 384p. 24.00 (*0-380-97657-9*) Morrow/Avon. (Avon Bks.).

—Children of the Storm. 2003. (Amelia Peabody Mystery Ser.). 416p. 25.95 (*0-06-621476-9*) HarperCollins Pubs.

—Crocodile on the Sandbank. 1978. (Amelia Peabody Mystery Ser.: No. 1). mass mkt. 1.75 o.s.i (*0-449-23713-3*, Fawcett) Ballantine Bks.

—Crocodile on the Sandbank. 1988. (Amelia Peabody Mystery Ser.: No. 1). reprint ed. pap. 3.95 o.p. (*0-89296-072-8*) Mysterious Pr.

—Crocodile on the Sandbank. unabr. ed. 1990. (Amelia Peabody Mystery Ser.: No. 1). (YA). audio 60.00 (*1-55690-127-5*, 90085E7) Recorded Bks., LLC.

—Crocodile on the Sandbank. 1988. (Amelia Peabody Mystery Ser.). 272p. reprint ed. mass mkt. 7.50 (*0-445-40651-8*) Warner Bks., Inc.

—The Curse of the Pharaohs. l.t. ed. 1993. (Amelia Peabody Mystery Ser.). 14.95 o.p. (*0-8161-3274-7*, Macmillan Reference USA) Gale Group.

—The Curse of the Pharaohs. unabr. ed. 1990. (Amelia Peabody Mystery Ser.: Vol. 2). (YA). (gr. 10). audio 70.00 (*1-55690-130-5*, 90095E7) Recorded Bks., LLC.

—The Curse of the Pharaohs. 1988. (Amelia Peabody Mystery Ser.). 304p. reprint ed. mass mkt. 7.50 (*0-445-40648-8*) Warner Bks., Inc.

—The Deeds of the Disturber. unabr. ed. 1993. (Amelia Peabody Mystery Ser.: No. 5). audio 85.00 (*1-55690-942-X*, 93438E7) Recorded Bks., LLC.

—The Falcon at the Portal. l.t. ed. 1999. (Amelia Peabody Mystery Ser.: No. 11). 27.95 (*1-56895-765-3*, Wheeler Publishing, Inc.) Gale Group.

—The Falcon at the Portal. 2002. (Amelia Peabody Mystery Ser.). E-Book 7.50 (*0-06-621027-5*); E-Book 7.50 (*0-06-018905-3*); E-Book 7.50 (*0-06-050440-4*); E-Book 7.50 (*0-06-621028-3*) HarperCollins General Bks. Group. (PerfectBound).

—The Falcon at the Portal. (Amelia Peabody Mystery Ser.: No. 11). 2000. 464p. mass mkt. 7.50 (*0-380-79857-3*, Avon Bks.); 1999. 384p. (gr. 8). 24.00 (*0-380-97658-7*, Morrow, William & Co.) Morrow/Avon.

—The Falcon at the Portal. abr. ed. 1999. (Amelia Peabody Mystery Ser.: No. 11). audio 26.95 (*0-7871-1924-5*, Dove Audio) NewStar Media, Inc.

—The Falcon at the Portal, unabr. ed. 1999. (Amelia Peabody Mystery Ser.: No. 11). audio 96.00 (*0-7887-3744-9*, 95650E7) Recorded Bks., LLC.

—The Falcon at the Portal. 2000. (Amelia Peabody Mystery Ser.: No. 11). 13.04 (*0-606-18956-4*) Turtleback Bks.

—The Golden One: A Novel of Suspense. 2002. E-Book 19.95 (*0-06-009840-6*); E-Book 19.95 (*0-06-009892-9*) HarperCollins General Bks. Group. (PerfectBound).

—The Golden One: A Novel of Suspense. 2002. E-Book 19.95 (*0-06-009842-2*); E-Book 19.95 (*0-06-009841-4*) HarperCollins Pubs.

—The Golden One: A Novel of Suspense. l.t. ed. 2002. 688p. 25.95 (*0-06-009386-2*, HarperLargePrint) HarperTrade.

—The Golden One: A Novel of Suspense. 2003. 512p. mass mkt. 7.50 (*0-380-81715-2*, Avon Bks.); 2002. 448p. 25.95 (*0-380-97885-7*, Morrow, William & Co.) Morrow/Avon.

—He Shall Thunder in the Sky. 2001. (Amelia Peabody Mystery Ser.: Bk. 12). 512p. mass mkt. 7.50 (*0-380-79858-1*, Avon Bks.); 2000. (Amelia Peabody Mystery Ser.: Bk. 12). (Illus.). 416p. 25.00 (*0-380-97659-5*, Morrow, William & Co.); 2000. (*0-380-29962-3*) Morrow/Avon.

—He Shall Thunder in the Sky. l.t. ed. (Illus.). 728p. 2001. (Amelia Peabody Mystery Ser.: Bk. 12). pap. 29.95 (*0-7862-2828-8*); 2000. (Amelia Peabody Mystery Ser.: Bk. 12). 31.95 (*0-7862-2827-X*); 2000. (*0-7540-1498-3*) Thorndike Pr.

—The Hippopotamus Pool. l.t. ed. 1996. (Amelia Peabody Mystery Ser.: No. 8). 571p. lib. bdg. 24.95 o.p. (*0-7838-1726-6*, Macmillan Reference USA) Gale Group.

—The Hippopotamus Pool. unabr. ed. 2000. (Amelia Peabody Mystery Ser.: No. 8). (J). audio 85.00 (*0-7887-0607-1*, 94617E7) Recorded Bks., LLC.

—The Hippopotamus Pool. abr. ed. 1996. (Amelia Peabody Mystery Ser.: No. 8). audio 21.95 o.p. (*1-55935-207-8*) Soundelux Audio Publishing.

—The Hippopotamus Pool. (Amelia Peabody Mystery Ser.: No. 8). 1996. 82p. 22.95 o.s.i (*0-446-51833-6*); 1997. 448p. reprint ed. mass mkt. 7.50 (*0-446-60398-8*) Warner Bks., Inc.

—The Jackal's Head. l.t. ed. 2000. 264p. lib. bdg. 26.95 (*1-58547-040-6*) Ctr. Point Large Print.

—The Jackal's Head. 1988. 245p. pap. 4.99 (*0-8125-0002-4*); pap. 3.50 o.s.i (*0-8125-0768-1*) Doherty, Tom Assocs., LLC. (Tor Bks.).

—The Jackal's Head. 1991. reprint ed. 18.95 o.p. (*0-7278-4257-9*) Severn Hse. Pubs., Ltd.

—The Last Camel Died at Noon. l.t. ed. 1992. (Amelia Peabody Mystery Ser.: No. 6). 576p. pap. 24.95 (*0-8161-5358-2*); 574p. lib. bdg. 21.95 o.p. (*0-8161-5357-4*) Gale Group. (Macmillan Reference USA).

—The Last Camel Died at Noon. unabr. ed. 1991. (Amelia Peabody Mystery Ser.: No. 6). audio 91.00 (*1-55690-300-6*, 91318E7) Recorded Bks., LLC.

—The Last Camel Died at Noon. 1992. 448p. mass mkt. 7.50 (*0-446-36338-3*); 1991. (Amelia Peabody Mystery Ser.: No. 6). 18.95 o.p. (*0-446-51483-7*) Warner Bks., Inc.

—Lion in the Valley. unabr. ed. 2001. audio 56.95 (*0-7861-2107-6*); audio compact disk 80.00 (*0-7861-9643-2*, ZR2869) Blackstone Audio Bks., Inc.

—Lion in the Valley. 1990. (Amelia Peabody Mystery Ser.: No. 4). 320p. reprint ed. mass mkt. 4.99 o.p. (*0-8125-1242-1*, Tor Bks.) Doherty, Tom Assocs., LLC.

—Lion in the Valley. 1999. (Amelia Peabody Mystery Ser.: No. 4). 384p. mass mkt. 7.50 (*0-380-73119-3*, Avon Bks.) Morrow/Avon.

—Lion in the Valley. unabr. ed. 1992. (Amelia Peabody Mystery Ser.: No. 4). audio 78.00 (*1-55690-690-0*, 92346E7) Recorded Bks., LLC.

—Lion in the Valley. 1986. (Amelia Peabody Mystery Ser.: No. 4). 288p. 14.95 o.p. (*0-689-11619-5*, Scribner) Simon & Schuster.

—Lord of the Silent. l.t. ed. 2001. 704p. pap. 25.00 (*0-06-620961-7*) HarperCollins Pubs.

—Lord of the Silent. 2002. 496p. mass mkt. 7.50 (*0-380-81714-4*); 2001. (Illus.). 416p. 25.00 (*0-380-97884-9*, Morrow, William & Co.) Morrow/Avon.

—The Mummy Case. (Amelia Peabody Mystery Ser.: No. 3). 1994. mass mkt. 4.50 (*0-8125-3214-7*); 1992. mass mkt. 3.99 o.s.i (*0-8125-2031-9*); 1988. pap. 3.95 o.s.i (*0-8125-0793-2*); 1986. pap. 3.50 o.s.i (*0-8125-0760-6*) Doherty, Tom Assocs., LLC. (Tor Bks.).

—The Mummy Case. l.t. ed. 1985. (Amelia Peabody Mystery Ser.: No. 3). 450p. pap. 17.95 o.p. (*0-8161-3934-2*, Macmillan Reference USA) Gale Group.

—The Mummy Case. unabr. ed. 1991. (Amelia Peabody Mystery Ser.: No. 3). audio 78.00 (*1-55690-631-5*, 91420E7) Recorded Bks., LLC.

—The Mummy Case. 1995. (Amelia Peabody Mystery Ser.). 336p. reprint ed. mass mkt. 7.50 (*0-446-60193-4*) Warner Bks., Inc.

—Night Train to Memphis. unabr. ed. 1997. (Vicky Bliss Mysteries Ser.). audio 28.00 (*1-885608-26-8*) Airplay.

—Night Train to Memphis. unabr. ed. 1996. audio 62.95 (*0-7861-1065-1*, 1836) Blackstone Audio Bks., Inc.

—Night Train to Memphis. unabr. ed. 1995. (Vicky Bliss Mystery Ser.: Vol. 5). audio 85.00 (*0-7887-0109-6*, 94372E7) Recorded Bks., LLC.

—Night Train to Memphis. 354p. pap. 5.98 o.p. (*0-7651-0300-1*) Smithmark Pubs., Inc.

—Night Train to Memphis. 368p. 1995. mass mkt. 7.50 (*0-446-60248-5*); 1994. 21.95 o.s.i (*0-446-51586-8*) Warner Bks., Inc.

—Seeing a Large Cat. unabr. ed. 1997. (Amelia Peabody Mystery Ser.: No. 9). audio 90.00 (*0-7887-1297-7*, 95131E7) Recorded Bks., LLC.

—Seeing a Large Cat. (Amelia Peabody Mystery Ser.: No. 9). 1997. 416p. 24.00 o.p. (*0-446-51834-4*); 1998. 432p. reprint ed. mass mkt. 7.50 (*0-446-60557-3*) Warner Bks., Inc.

—The Snake, the Crocodile & the Dog. l.t. ed. (Amelia Peabody Mystery Ser.: No. 7). 555p. 1994. pap. 17.95 (*0-8161-5682-4*); 1993. 24.95 (*0-8161-5681-6*) Gale Group. (Macmillan Reference USA).

—The Snake, the Crocodile & the Dog. unabr. ed. 1992. (Amelia Peabody Mystery Ser.: No. 7). audio 91.00 (*1-55690-783-4*, 92422E7) Recorded Bks., LLC.

—The Snake, the Crocodile & the Dog. (Amelia Peabody Mystery Ser.: No. 7). 1992. 340p. 28.00 (*0-446-51585-X*); 1994. 448p. reprint ed. mass mkt. 7.50 (*0-446-36478-9*) Warner Bks., Inc.

Preston, Peter. Hor. E-Book (*1-84045-022-3*) Online Originals.

Quayd, Muhammad Y. War in the Land of Egypt. Kenny, Olive E. et al, trs. from ARA. 1998. (Emerging Voices Ser.). 192p. pap. 12.95 (*1-56656-227-9*) Interlink Publishing Group, Inc.

Rabley, Stephen. The Fireboy. 2002. (Illus.). 16p. pap. (*0-582-40296-4*) Penguin Putnam Bks. for Young Readers.

Rettino, Ernie & Kerner, Debby. Psalty in Egypt. 1991. 6.99 o.p. (*0-8499-0894-9*) W Publishing Group.

Roberts, John Maddox. The Temple of the Muses. 3rd ed. 1999. (SPQR Ser.: Vol. 4). 240p. (Orig.). pap. 13.95 (*0-312-24698-6*, CPB1103, Saint Martin's Griffin) St. Martin's Pr.

Robinson, Lynda S. Drinker of Blood. 1998. (Lord Meren Mystery Ser.). 290p. 22.00 (*0-89296-673-4*) Mysterious Pr.

—Eater of Souls. 4th ed. 1998. (Easter of Souls Ser.: Vol. 4). 288p. mass mkt. 6.99 (*0-345-39533-6*) Ballantine Bks.

—Eater of Souls: A Lord Meren Mystery. 1997. (Lord Meren Mystery Ser.). 228p. 21.95 (*0-8027-3294-1*) Walker & Co.

—Murder at the Feast of Rejoicing: A Lord Meren Mystery. 3rd ed. 1997. (Lord Meren Mystery Ser.). 256p. mass mkt. 6.50 (*0-345-39532-8*) Ballantine Bks.

—Murder at the Feast of Rejoicing: A Lord Meren Mystery. 1996. (Lord Meren Mystery Ser.). 240p. (YA). 20.95 (*0-8027-3274-7*) Walker & Co.

—Murder at the God's Gate. 1995. (Lord Meren Mystery Ser.). 288p. mass mkt. 6.50 (*0-345-39531-X*) Ballantine Bks.

—Murder at the God's Gate. 1995. 248p. 19.95 (*0-8027-3198-8*) Walker & Co.

—Murder in the Place of Anubis. 1994. (Lord Meren Mystery Ser.). 224p. mass mkt. 6.99 (*0-345-38922-0*) Ballantine Bks.

—Murder in the Place of Anubis. 1994. 203p. 18.95 (*0-8027-3249-6*) Walker & Co.

—Slayer of Gods. 2001. (Lord Meren Mystery Ser.). (Illus.). 256p. 23.45 o.p. (*0-89296-705-6*) Mysterious Pr.

Rubalcaba, Jill. Place in the Sun. 1998. (Puffin Novel Ser.). 96p. (J). (gr. 3-7). pap. 4.99 (*0-14-130123-6*) Penguin Putnam Bks. for Young Readers.

Ryan, Will H. Nile Nightmare: A Novel of Suspense. 1993. 288p. (Orig.). pap. 12.95 (*1-56474-049-8*) Fithian Pr.

Salem, Ibtihal. Children of the Waters. Booth, Marilyn, tr. from ARA. 2003. (Modern Middle East Literatures in Translation Ser.). 140p. pap. 13.95 (*0-292-77773-6*) Univ. of Texas Pr.

Serageldin, Samia. The Cairo House: A Novel. 2000. (Arab American Writings). ix, 233p. pap. 24.95 (*0-8156-0673-7*) Syracuse Univ. Pr.

Sharouni, Yusuf. Blood Feud & Other Stories. Johnson-Davies, Denys, tr. 1992. 137p. pap. 10.00 (*977-424-268-8*) American Univ. in Cairo Pr. EGY. *Dist:* Books International, Incorporated.

Shults, Sylvia. Golden Horus: A Novel of Ancient Egypt. 2000. 288p. pap. 21.99 (*0-7388-3964-7*); E-Book 8.00 (*0-7388-9515-6*) Xlibris Corp.

Siebert, Steven. Cleopatras Needle. 2000. 426p. mass mkt. 6.99 (*0-8125-7071-5*, Tor Bks.) Doherty, Tom Assocs., LLC.

—Cleopatra's Needle. 2nd ed. 1999. 352p. 23.95 (*0-312-86748-4*, Forge Bks.) Doherty, Tom Assocs., LLC.

Smith, Annette. Terror in Cairo. 1979. (Illus.). (J). (gr. 4-7). 2.95 o.p. (*0-15-284812-6*) Harcourt Children's Bks.

Smith, Wilbur. River God. l.t. ed. 1995. pap. 29.95 o.p. (*0-7927-2016-4*); 1994. 32.95 o.p. (*0-7927-2017-2*) BBC Audiobooks America.

—River God, Pt. 1. unabr. ed. 1995. (Courtney Novels). audio 72.00 (*0-7366-3123-2*, 3799A) Books on Tape, Inc.

—River God. abr. ed. 1994. audio 16.95 o.p. (*1-56100-360-3*, 1354, Nova Audio Bks.); audio 146.55 (*1-56100-179-1*, 1012, Unabridged Library Editions); audio 29.95 (*1-56100-553-3*, 234, Bookcassette) Brilliance Audio.

—River God. abr. ed. 2001. audio 19.95 (*0-333-90483-4*) Macmillan U.K. GBR. *Dist:* Trafalgar Square.

—River God. abr. ed. 2000. audio 7.95 (*1-57815-021-3*, 1044, Media Bks. Audio Publishing) Media Bks., L. L. C.

—River God. 2001. pap. 14.95 (*0-312-28755-0*, Saint Martin's Griffin); 1994. mass mkt. 19.95 (*0-330-33197-3*); 1994. 544p. 24.95 o.p. (*0-312-10612-2*); 1995. 672p. reprint ed. mass mkt. 7.99 (*0-312-95446-8*, St. Martin's Paperbacks) St. Martin's Pr.

—The Seventh Scroll. unabr. ed. 1996. audio 124.95 (*0-7451-6640-7*, CAB 1256) BBC Audiobooks America.

—The Seventh Scroll. unabr. ed. 1995. (Courtney Novels). Pt. 1. audio 64.00 (*0-7366-3152-6*, 3826 A); Pt. 2. audio 64.00 Books on Tape, Inc.

—The Seventh Scroll. abr. ed. 2001. audio 16.95 (*0-333-66113-3*) Macmillan U.K. GBR. *Dist:* Trafalgar Square.

—The Seventh Scroll. abr. ed. 1995. 24.95 o.p. (*0-7871-0438-8*, 692304) NewStar Media, Inc.

—The Seventh Scroll. 1996. 614p. mass mkt. 7.99 (*0-312-95757-2*, St. Martin's Paperbacks); 1995. 496p. 24.95 o.p. (*0-312-11999-2*) St. Martin's Pr.

—Warlock: A Novel of Ancient Egypt. 2002. 704p. mass mkt. 7.99 (*0-312-98038-8*, St. Martin's Paperbacks); 2001. (Illus.). 560p. 27.95 (*0-312-27823-3*) St. Martin's Pr.

Soueif, Ahdaf. The Map of Love. (Illus.). 529p. 2000. pap. (*0-7475-4563-4*); 1999. (*0-7475-4367-4*) Bloomsbury Publishing, Ltd.

—The Map of Love. 2000. 544p. pap. 14.95 (*0-385-72011-4*, Knopf Bks. for Young Readers) Random Hse. Children's Bks.

Stewart, Daniel Blair. Akhnaton: The Extraterrestrial King. 2nd ed. 1995. (Illus.). 220p. pap. 19.95 (*1-883319-34-X*) Frog, Ltd.

Sussman, Paul. The Lost Army of Cambyses. 2003. (Illus.). 384p. 24.95 (*0-312-30153-7*) St. Martin's Pr.

Tarr, Judith. King & Goddess. 1996. 384p. 23.95 o.p. (*0-312-86092-7*, Forge Bks.); Vol. 1. 1998. (King & Goddess Ser.: Vol. 1). 407p. mass mkt. 6.99 o.s.i (*0-8125-5084-6*, Tor Bks.) Doherty, Tom Assocs., LLC.

—The Lord of the Two Lands. 1993. 320p. (YA). 3.99 o.p. (*0-312-85362-9*, Tor Bks.) Doherty, Tom Assocs., LLC.

—Pillar of Fire. unabr. ed. 1996. audio 95.95 (*0-7861-1061-9*, 1832) Blackstone Audio Bks., Inc.

—Pillar of Fire. 1997. 661p. pap. text 6.99 (*0-8125-3903-6*, Tor Bks.); 1995. 448p. 23.95 o.p. (*0-312-85542-7*, Forge Bks.) Doherty, Tom Assocs., LLC.

—The Shepherd Kings. 1999. 512p. 27.95 (*0-312-86113-3*, Forge Bks.) Doherty, Tom Assocs., LLC.

—Throne of Isis. 1994. 352p. (YA). 22.95 o.p. (*0-312-85363-7*, Forge Bks.) Doherty, Tom Assocs., LLC.

Thibaux, Jean-Michel. Le Roman de Cleopatre. l.t. ed. 1998. (French Ser.). (FRE.). 545p. pap. 30.99 (*2-84011-257-4*) Feryane, SA, Editions FRA. *Dist:* Ulverscroft Large Print Bks., Ltd., Ulverscroft Large Print Canada, Ltd.

Tyldesley, Joyce A. Judgement of the Pharoah. 2001. pap. 14.95 (*0-7538-1278-9*) Phoenix Hse. GBR. *Dist:* Trafalgar Square.

Warmington, Mary Jane. Pyramid of Love. l.t. ed. 1997. (Nightingale Ser.). 245p. lib. bdg. 17.95 o.p. (*0-7838-8110-X*, Macmillan Reference USA) Gale Group.

Wilder. The City of Refuge. 2001. 448p. pap. 25.50 (*0-7596-2562-X*) 1stBooks Library.

Wood, Barbara. The Prophetess. abr. ed. 1997. audio 7.99 o.p. (*1-56740-167-8*, 690, Paperback Nova Audio Bks.); 1996. audio 16.95 o.p. (*1-56100-904-0*, 1350, Nova Audio Bks.); 1996. audio 89.25 o.p. (*1-56100-319-0*, 995, Unabridged Library Editions); 1996. audio 25.95 o.p. (*1-56100-694-7*, 222, Bookcassette) Brilliance Audio.

—The Prophetess. 1996. 400p. 23.95 o.p. (*0-316-81652-3*) Little Brown & Co.

—The Prophetess. 1997. 496p. reprint ed. mass mkt. 6.99 o.s.i (*0-446-60380-5*) Warner Bks., Inc.

Woodman, Richard. A Brig of War. 1984. 224p. pap. 2.95 o.p. (*0-523-41978-3*, Pinnacle Bks.) Kensington Publishing Corp.

—A Brig of War. 1995. mass mkt. o.s.i (*0-7515-1304-0*) Little Brown & Co.

—A Brig of War. 1998. 320p. mass mkt. 5.99 o.p. (*0-446-60463-1*) Warner Bks., Inc.

—A Brig of War: A Nathaniel Drinkwater Novel. 2001. (Mariner's Library Fiction Classics). (Illus.). 240p. reprint ed. pap. 14.95 (*1-57409-125-5*) Sheridan Hse., Inc.

**EGYPT (ME.: IMAGINARY PLACE)—FICTION**

Chute, Carolyn. The Beans of Egypt, Maine. l.t. ed. 1985. 14.95 o.p. (*0-8161-3956-3*, Macmillan Reference USA) Gale Group.

—The Beans of Egypt, Maine. 228p. 1985. 15.95 o.p. (*0-89919-314-5*); 1984. pap. 7.95 o.p. (*0-89919-362-5*) Houghton Mifflin Co.

—The Beans of Egypt, Maine. 1987. 14.95 o.s.i (*0-671-64104-2*, Simon & Schuster Audioworks) Simon & Schuster Audio.

—The Beans of Egypt, Maine. 1986. 256p. mass mkt. 6.50 o.s.i (*0-446-30010-1*) Warner Bks., Inc.

—The Beans of Egypt, Maine: The Finished Version. 1995. (Harvest American Writing Ser.). 304p. pap. 13.00 (*0-15-600188-8*, Harvest Bks.) Harcourt Trade Pubs.

—Letourneau's Used Auto Parts. 1995. (Harvest American Writing Ser.). 256p. pap. 11.00 (*0-15-600189-6*, Harvest Bks.) Harcourt Trade Pubs.

—Letourneau's Used Auto Parts. 1989. 256p. reprint ed. pap. 7.95 o.p. (*0-06-097225-4*, PL 7225, Perennial) HarperTrade.

—Letourneau's Used Auto Parts. 1988. 224p. 16.45 (*0-89919-500-8*) Houghton Mifflin Co.

—Merry Men. 1995. 712p. pap. 17.00 (*0-15-600191-8*, Harvest Bks.); 1994. x, 695p. (C). 24.95 o.s.i (*0-15-159270-5*) Harcourt Trade Pubs.

Chute, Carolyn, et al. Inside Vacationland: New Fiction from the Real Maine. Melnicove, Mark, ed. 1985. 192p. (Orig.). pap. 8.95 o.p. (*0-937966-18-5*) Tilbury Hse. Pubs.

**EIGHTY-SEVENTH PRECINCT (IMAGINARY PLACE)—FICTION**

McBain, Ed, pseud. And All Through the House. 1994. 48p. 12.45 o.p. (*0-446-51845-X*) Warner Bks., Inc.

—Ax. unabr. ed. 1996. (Eighty-Seventh Precinct Ser.). audio 30.00 (*0-7366-3506-8*, 4145) Books on Tape, Inc.

—Ax. 1977. (87th Precinct Mystery Ser.). mass mkt. 2.95 o.p. (*0-451-14599-2*); mass mkt. 1.25 o.p. (*0-451-07654-0*, Signet Bks.); 160p. mass mkt. 4.50 o.s.i (*0-451-16407-5*, Signet Bks.) NAL.

—Ax. 1964. 3.50 o.p. (*0-671-06283-2*) Simon & Schuster.

—The Big Bad City. abr. ed. 1998. (Eighty Seventh Precinct Ser.). audio 24.95 (*1-55927-536-7*, 696064) Audio Renaissance.

—The Big Bad City. unabr. ed. 1999. (Eighty-Seventh Precinct Ser.). audio 40.00 (*0-7366-4460-1*, 4905) Books on Tape, Inc.

—The Big Bad City. l.t. ed. 1999. 27.95 (*1-56895-714-9*, Wheeler Publishing, Inc.) Gale Group.

—The Big Bad City. 1999. 272p. mass mkt. 7.99 (*0-671-03473-1*, Pocket); 25.00 (*0-684-85512-7*, Simon & Schuster) Simon & Schuster.

—Blood Relatives. 1977. pap. 1.50 o.p. (*0-394-25462-7*) Ballantine Bks.

—Blood Relatives. 1978. (Eighty-Seventh Precinct Ser). pap. 1.75 o.p. (*0-553-11759-9*) Bantam Bks.

—Blood Relatives. unabr. ed. 1987. (Eighty-Seventh Precinct Ser.). audio 36.00 (*0-7366-1147-9*, 2071) Books on Tape, Inc.

—Blood Relatives. 2002. reprint ed. lib. bdg. 27.95 (*1-58547-183-6*, Premier) Ctr. Point Large Print.

—Blood Relatives. 1987. mass mkt. 3.50 o.p. (*0-451-15084-8*); 1982. mass mkt. 2.50 o.p. (*0-451-11854-5*) NAL. (Signet Bks.).

—Bread. unabr. ed. 1987. (Eighty-Seventh Precinct Ser.). audio 42.00 (*0-7366-1198-3*, 2116) Books on Tape, Inc.

—Bread. 1987. 176p. mass mkt. 4.50 (*0-380-70368-8*, Avon Bks.) Morrow/Avon.

—Bread. 1982. mass mkt. 2.25 o.p. (*0-451-11279-2*, AE1279); 1975. mass mkt. 1.25 o.p. (*0-451-06754-1*) NAL. (Signet Bks.).

—Bread. 1974. 213p. (J). o.p. (*0-394-48580-7*) Random Hse., Inc.

—Bread. 1997. (Eighty Seventh Precinct Ser.). 224p. reprint ed. mass mkt. 6.50 (*0-446-60425-9*) Warner Bks., Inc.

—Calypso. 1980. 208p. pap. 1.95 o.s.i (*0-553-13399-3*) Bantam Bks.

—Calypso. unabr. ed. 1998. (Eighty-Seventh Precinct Ser.). audio 42.00 (*0-7366-3775-3*, 4448) Books on Tape, Inc.

—Calypso. 1988. 208p. mass mkt. 4.99 (*0-380-70591-5*, Avon Bks.) Morrow/Avon.

—Calypso. 1979. 10.95 o.p. (*0-670-20030-1*) Viking Penguin.

—The Con Man. unabr. ed. 1993. audio 54.95 (*0-7451-4157-9*, CAB 840) BBC Audiobooks America.

—The Con Man. unabr. ed. 1990. (Eighty-Seventh Precinct Ser.). audio 36.00 (*0-7366-1787-6*, 2624) Books on Tape, Inc.

—The Con Man. l.t. ed. 1986. (Nightingale Ser.). 296p. 10.95 o.p. (*0-8161-3982-2*, Macmillan Reference USA) Gale Group.

—The Con Man. (Eighty-Seventh Precinct Mysteries Ser.). 1987. 160p. mass mkt. 3.99 o.s.i (*0-451-15085-6*); 1980. mass mkt. 1.75 o.p. (*0-451-09351-8*); 1974. mass mkt. 0.95 o.p. (*0-451-05863-1*) NAL. (Signet Bks.).

—Cop Hater. unabr. ed. 1992. (Eighty-Seventh Precinct Novels Ser.). audio 54.95 (*0-7451-6153-7*, CAB 674) BBC Audiobooks America.

—Cop Hater. unabr. ed. 1990. (Eighty-Seventh Precinct Ser.). audio 36.00 (*0-7366-1710-8*, 2552) Books on Tape, Inc.

—Cop Hater. l.t. ed. 1989. (Nightingale Ser.). 316p. 13.95 o.p. (*0-8161-4517-2*, Macmillan Reference USA) Gale Group.

—Cop Hater. (Eighty-Seventh Precinct Mysteries Ser.). 9999. 160p. mass mkt. 3.95 o.p. (*0-451-16441-5*); 1987. 160p. mass mkt. 3.99 o.p. (*0-451-15079-1*); 1980. mass mkt. 1.75 o.p. (*0-451-09170-1*); 1973. mass mkt. 0.95 o.p. (*0-451-05617-5*) NAL. (Signet Bks.).

—Cop Hater. 1999. (Eighty-Seventh Precinct Ser.). (Illus.). 272p. pap. 7.99 (*0-671-77547-2*, Pocket) Simon & Schuster.

—Doll. 1981. mass mkt. 2.25 o.s.i (*0-345-29289-8*) Ballantine Bks.

—Doll. unabr. ed. 1996. (Eighty-Seventh Precinct Ser.). audio 30.00 (*0-7366-3512-2*, 4151) Books on Tape, Inc.

—Doll. 1986. (Eighty-Seventh Precinct Novel Ser.). 160p. mass mkt. 4.50 (*0-380-70082-4*, Avon Bks.) Morrow/Avon.

—Doll. 1997. (Eighty Seventh Precinct Ser.). 208p. reprint ed. mass mkt. 5.99 (*0-446-60146-2*) Warner Bks., Inc.

—Ed McBain: Three Complete Novels: Wings Suspense. 1992. (Illus.). 528p. 13.99 o.s.i (*0-517-06499-5*) Random Hse. Value Publishing.

—Eight Black Horses. l.t. ed. 1986. (General Ser.). 350p. 15.95 o.p. (*0-8161-4022-7*, Macmillan Reference USA) Gale Group.

—Eight Black Horses. (Eighty-Seventh Precinct Novel Ser.). 1986. 256p. mass mkt. 4.99 (*0-380-70029-8*, Avon Bks.); 1985. 15.95 o.p. (*0-87795-681-2*, Morrow, William & Co.) Morrow/Avon.

—Eight Black Horses. 2003. (Illus.). 336p. pap. 7.99 (*0-7434-6308-0*, Pocket) Simon & Schuster.

—Eighty Million Eyes. 1983. 192p. mass mkt. 2.25 o.s.i (*0-345-29292-8*); 1975. mass mkt. 1.25 o.s.i (*0-345-24604-7*) Ballantine Bks.

—Eighty Million Eyes. unabr. ed. 1997. (Eighty-Seventh Precinct Ser.). audio 30.00 (*0-7366-3565-3*, 4209) Books on Tape, Inc.

—Eighty Million Eyes. l.t. ed. 2000. 229p. lib. bdg. 25.95 (*1-58547-011-2*) Ctr. Point Large Print.

—Eighty Million Eyes. 1987. 176p. mass mkt. 4.50 (*0-380-70367-X*, Avon Bks.) Morrow/Avon.

—Eighty Million Eyes. 1997. (Eighty Seventh Precinct Ser.). 208p. reprint ed. mass mkt. 5.99 (*0-446-60386-4*) Warner Bks., Inc.

—The Eighty-Seventh Precinct Companion. 1995. (Orig.). pap. (*0-89296-989-X*, Mysterious Pr. Paperback Bks.) Warner Bks., Inc.

—The Empty Hours. unabr. ed. 1996. (Eighty-Seventh Precinct Ser.). audio 36.00 (*0-7366-3409-6*, 4056) Books on Tape, Inc.

—The Empty Hours. (87th Precinct Mystery Ser.). 1982. mass mkt. 2.25 o.p. (*0-451-11835-9*); 1982. 256p. mass mkt. 4.50 o.p. (*0-451-14601-8*); 1977. mass mkt. 1.25 o.p. (*0-451-07287-1*) NAL. (Signet Bks.).

—Fat Ollie's Book. 2003. 368p. mass mkt. 7.99 (*0-7434-1033-5*, Pocket); (Illus.). 288p. 25.00 (*0-7432-0270-8*, Simon & Schuster) Simon & Schuster.

—Fat Ollie's Book. 2003. 29.95 (*0-7862-5041-0*) Thorndike Pr.

—The Frumious Bandersnatch: A Novel of the 87th Precinct. 2004. 304p. 25.00 (*0-7432-5034-6*, Simon & Schuster) Simon & Schuster.

—Fuzz. unabr. ed. 1995. (87th Precinct Mystery Ser.). audio 54.95 (*0-7451-6157-X*, CAB 133) BBC Audiobooks America.

—Fuzz. unabr. ed. 1997. (Eighty-Seventh Precinct Ser.). audio 42.00 (*0-7366-3637-4*, 4298) Books on Tape, Inc.

—Fuzz. 1978. mass mkt. 1.75 o.p. (*0-451-08399-7*); 1978. 192p. mass mkt. 3.99 o.p. (*0-451-15554-8*, E8399); 1972. mass mkt. 0.75 o.p. (*0-451-05151-3*); 1969. mass mkt. 0.60 o.p. (*0-451-04001-5*) NAL. (Signet Bks.).

—Fuzz. E-Book 6.99 (*0-7953-0320-3*); E-Book 6.99 (*0-7953-0322-X*) RosettaBooks.

—Fuzz. 2000. (Eighty Seventh Precinct Ser.). 288p. mass mkt. 6.50 o.s.i (*0-446-60971-4*) Warner Bks., Inc.

—Ghosts. 1981. 176p. pap. 2.50 o.p. (*0-553-23240-1*) Bantam Bks.

—Ghosts. unabr. ed. 1998. (Eighty-Seventh Precinct Ser.). audio 36.00 (*0-7366-4109-2*, 4614) Books on Tape, Inc.

—Ghosts. 1980. 212p. 9.95 o.p. (*0-670-33806-0*) Viking Penguin.

—Give the Boys a Great Big Hand. unabr. ed. 1992. (Eighty-Seventh Precinct Ser.). audio 36.00 (*0-7366-2251-9*, 3040) Books on Tape, Inc.

—Give the Boys a Great Big Hand. l.t. ed. 1988. (Nightingale Ser.). 307p. 12.95 o.p. (*0-8161-4516-4*, Macmillan Reference USA) Gale Group.

—Give the Boys a Great Big Hand. (87th Precinct Mystery Ser.). 1981. mass mkt. 2.25 o.p. (*0-451-11081-1*); 1981. 240p. mass mkt. 4.50 o.p. (*0-451-15921-7*); 1981. mass mkt. 2.95 o.p. (*0-451-13900-3*); 1975. mass mkt. 1.25 o.p. (*0-451-06683-9*) NAL. (Signet Bks.).

—Hail, Hail, the Gang's All Here. unabr. ed. 1997. (Eighty-Seventh Precinct Ser.). audio 36.00 (*0-7366-3752-4*, 4427) Books on Tape, Inc.

—Hail, Hail, the Gang's All Here. 1972. 307p. (J). (*0-8161-6025-2*, Macmillan Reference USA) Gale Group.

—Hail, Hail, the Gang's All Here. 1972. 160p. mass mkt. 3.99 o.s.i (*0-451-15609-9*, Signet Bks.) NAL.

—Hail to the Chief. unabr. ed. 1995. audio 36.00 o.p. audio o.p. audio 30.00 (*0-7366-3199-2*, 3863) Books on Tape, Inc.

—Hail to the Chief. l.t. ed. 2003. lib. bdg. 28.95 (*1-58547-307-3*, Premier) Ctr. Point Large Print.

—Hail to the Chief. 1987. (Eighty-Seventh Precinct Novel Ser.). 160p. mass mkt. 4.50 o.p. (*0-380-70370-X*, Avon Bks.) Morrow/Avon.

—Hail to the Chief. 1981. mass mkt. 2.25 o.p. (*0-451-11214-8*); 1975. mass mkt. 1.25 o.p. (*0-451-06548-4*) NAL. (Signet Bks.).

—Hail to the Chief. 1973. 182p. o.p. (*0-394-48581-5*) Random Hse., Inc.

—Hail to the Chief. 1997. 192p. reprint ed. mass mkt. 5.99 (*0-446-60405-4*) Warner Bks., Inc.

—He Who Hesitates. 1981. 160p. mass mkt. 2.25 o.s.i (*0-345-29291-X*); 1975. mass mkt. 1.25 o.s.i (*0-345-24757-4*) Ballantine Bks.

—He Who Hesitates. l.t. ed. 1990. (Nightingale Ser.). 248p. 13.95 o.p. (*0-8161-4769-8*, Macmillan Reference USA) Gale Group.

Settings

—He Who Hesitates. 2000. mass mkt. 3.50 (*0-380-64198-4*); 1986. 160p. mass mkt. 4.50 (*0-380-70084-0*, Avon Bks.) Morrow/Avon.

—He Who Hesitates. 1996. 160p. reprint ed. mass mkt. 5.99 (*0-446-60147-0*) Warner Bks., Inc.

—Heat. 1987. 208p. mass mkt. 3.95 o.s.i (*0-345-34597-5*); 1983. mass mkt. 2.95 o.s.i (*0-345-30673-2*) Ballantine Bks.

—Heat. unabr. ed. 1998. (Eighty-Seventh Precinct Ser.). audio 42.00 (*0-7366-4110-6*, 4615) Books on Tape, Inc.

—Heat. 1992. (Eighty-Seventh Precinct Mysteries Ser.). 208p. mass mkt. 4.99 o.s.i (*0-451-17078-4*, Signet Bks.) NAL.

—Heat. 1981. 288p. 12.95 o.p. (*0-670-36479-7*) Viking Penguin.

—The Heckler. unabr. ed. 1996. (Eighty-Seventh Precinct Ser.). audio 36.00 (*0-7366-3254-9*, 3911) Books on Tape, Inc.

—The Heckler. 1982. mass mkt. 2.25 o.p. (*0-451-11421-3*); 1982. 176p. mass mkt. 4.50 o.p. (*0-451-15970-5*); 1982. mass mkt. 2.95 o.p. (*0-451-13901-1*); 1976. mass mkt. 1.25 o.p. (*0-451-06839-4*) NAL. (Signet Bks.).

—The Heckler. 2003. (Illus.). 288p. pap. 7.99 (*0-7434-6307-2*, Pocket) Simon & Schuster.

—Ice. unabr. ed. 1995. (Eighty-Seventh Precinct Ser.). audio 56.00 (*0-7366-3180-1*, 3849) Books on Tape, Inc.

—Ice. l.t. ed. 1983. 510p. lib. bdg. 17.95 o.p. (*0-8161-3568-1*, Macmillan Reference USA) Gale Group.

—Ice. 1984. 320p. pap. 5.99 (*0-380-67108-5*, Avon Bks.); 1983. 305p. 15.50 o.p. (*0-87795-468-2*, Morrow, William & Co.) Morrow/Avon.

—Ice. 2003. (Best Mysteries of All Time Ser.). 360p. (*0-7621-8889-8*, Impress) Scriptorium Pr., The.

—Ice. 1996. 336p. reprint ed. mass mkt. 5.99 o.p. (*0-446-60390-2*) Warner Bks., Inc.

—Jigsaw. unabr. ed. 1997. (Eighty-Seventh Precinct Ser.). audio 30.00 (*0-7366-3641-2*, 4303) Books on Tape, Inc.

—Jigsaw. 1970. (Eighty-Seventh Precinct Mysteries Ser.). 160p. mass mkt. 4.50 o.p. (*0-451-15480-0*, Signet Bks.) NAL.

—Killer's Choice. 1981. mass mkt. 2.25 o.s.i (*0-345-29288-X*) Ballantine Bks.

—Killer's Choice. unabr. ed. 1991. (Eighty-Seventh Precinct Ser.). audio 36.00 (*0-7366-2064-8*, 2872) Books on Tape, Inc.

—Killer's Choice. 1986. (Eighty-Seventh Precinct Novel Ser.). pap. 4.50 (*0-380-70083-2*, Avon Bks.) Morrow/Avon.

—Killer's Choice. 1996. 160p. mass mkt. 5.99 o.s.i (*0-446-60144-6*) Warner Bks., Inc.

—Killer's Payoff. unabr. ed. 1991. (Eighty-Seventh Precinct Ser.). audio 36.00 (*0-7366-2065-6*, 2873) Books on Tape, Inc.

—Killer's Payoff. l.t. ed. 1987. (Nightingale Ser.). 295p. 11.95 o.p. (*0-8161-4257-2*, Macmillan Reference USA) Gale Group.

—Killer's Payoff. (Eighty-Seventh Precinct Mysteries Ser.). 1987. 160p. mass mkt. 3.99 o.p. (*0-451-15081-3*); 1980. mass mkt. 1.75 o.p. (*0-451-09464-6*); 1974. mass mkt. 0.95 o.p. (*0-451-05939-5*) NAL. (Signet Bks.).

—Killer's Payoff. 2003. (Illus.). 272p. pap. 6.99 (*0-7434-6306-4*, Pocket) Simon & Schuster.

—Killer's Wedge. unabr. ed. 1992. (Eighty-Seventh Precinct Ser.). audio 36.00 (*0-7366-2105-9*, 2909) Books on Tape, Inc.

—Killer's Wedge. l.t. ed. 2000. 198p. lib. bdg. 27.95 o.p. (*1-58547-032-5*) Ctr. Point Large Print.

—Killer's Wedge. 1981. mass mkt. 1.75 o.p. (*0-451-09614-2*); 1981. 160p. mass mkt. 3.99 o.p. (*0-451-16336-2*); 1981. mass mkt. 2.95 o.p. (*0-451-14597-6*); 1974. mass mkt. 0.95 o.p. (*0-451-06219-1*) NAL. (Signet Bks.).

—King's Ransom. unabr. ed. 1991. (Eighty-Seventh Precinct Ser.). audio 42.00 (*0-7366-1894-5*, 2721) Books on Tape, Inc.

—King's Ransom. l.t. ed. 1986. (Nightingale Ser.). 327p. 11.95 o.p. (*0-8161-4127-4*, Macmillan Reference USA) Gale Group.

—King's Ransom. (87th Precinct Mystery Ser.). 1981. mass mkt. 2.25 o.p. (*0-451-09815-3*, Signet Bks.); 1981. 176p. mass mkt. 4.50 o.p. (*0-451-15933-0*); 1981. mass mkt. 2.95 o.p. (*0-451-13898-8*, Signet Bks.); 1975. mass mkt. 1.25 o.p. (*0-451-06467-4*, Signet Bks.) NAL.

—Kiss. unabr. ed. 1992. (Eighty-Seventh Precinct Ser.). audio 64.00 (*0-7366-2286-1*, 3072) Books on Tape, Inc.

—Kiss. unabr. ed. 1992. audio 22.95 o.p. (*1-56100-461-8*, 155, Bookcassette); audio 57.25 o.p. (*1-56100-095-7*, 543, Unabridged Library Editions) Brilliance Audio.

—Kiss. l.t. ed. 1993. (General Ser.). 458p. 16.95 o.p. (*0-8161-5589-5*); 21.95 o.p. (*0-8161-5588-7*) Gale Group. (Macmillan Reference USA).

—Kiss. 2002. 400p. audio 9.99 (*0-06-008392-1*); 1992. audio 16.00 o.p. (*1-55994-461-7*) HarperTrade. (HarperAudio).

—Kiss. abr. ed. 2000. (Eighty Seventh Precinct Novels Ser.). audio 7.95 (*1-57815-052-3*, 1013, Media Bks. Audio Publishing) Media Bks., L. L. C.

—Kiss. 1992. 384p. pap. 5.99 (*0-380-71382-9*, Avon Bks.); 330p. 17.00 o.p. (*0-688-10220-4*, Morrow, William & Co.) Morrow/Avon.

—Kiss. 1993. 4.99 o.p. (*0-517-11033-4*) Random Hse. Value Publishing.

—Lady Killer. unabr. ed. 1995. (Eighty-Seventh Precinct Novels Ser.). audio 39.95 BBC Audiobooks America.

—Lady Killer. unabr. ed. 1996. (Eighty-Seventh Precinct Ser.). audio 30.00 (*0-7366-3219-0*, 3882) Books on Tape, Inc.

—Lady Killer. l.t. ed. 1984. (General Ser.). lib. bdg. 12.95 o.p. (*0-8161-3665-3*, Macmillan Reference USA) Gale Group.

—Lady Killer. (Eighty-Seventh Precinct Mysteries Ser.). 1987. 160p. mass mkt. 4.50 o.s.i (*0-451-15082-1*); 1980. mass mkt. 1.75 o.p. (*0-451-09532-4*); 1974. mass mkt. 0.95 o.p. (*0-451-06067-9*) NAL. (Signet Bks.).

—Lady, Lady, I Did It! unabr. ed. 1996. (Eighty-Seventh Precinct Ser.). audio 30.00 (*0-7366-3495-9*, 4135) Books on Tape, Inc.

—Lady, Lady, I Did It! (87th Precinct Mystery Ser.). 1982. mass mkt. 2.25 o.p. (*0-451-11779-4*); 1982. 256p. mass mkt. 4.50 o.p. (*0-451-15841-5*); 1982. mass mkt. 2.95 o.p. (*0-451-13899-6*); 1976. mass mkt. 1.25 o.p. (*0-451-07151-4*) NAL. (Signet Bks.).

—Lady, Lady, I Did It! 1961. 3.50 o.p. (*0-671-40555-1*) Simon & Schuster.

—The Last Dance. l.t. ed. 2000. (Wheeler Large Print Book Ser.). 27.95 (*1-56895-814-5*, Wheeler Publishing, Inc.) Gale Group.

—The Last Dance. 2000. (Illus.). 272p. 25.00 o.s.i (*0-684-85513-5*, Simon & Schuster); 1999. E-Book 25.00 (*0-7432-0047-0*, Simon & Schuster); 2000. (Illus.). 336p. reprint ed. mass mkt. 7.99 (*0-671-02570-8*, Pocket) Simon & Schuster.

—Let's Hear It for the Deaf Man. unabr. ed. 1998. (Eighty-Seventh Precinct Ser.). audio 36.00 (*0-7366-3776-1*, 4449) Books on Tape, Inc.

—Let's Hear It for the Deaf Man. 1973. 231p. (J). o.p. (*0-385-01600-X*) Doubleday Publishing.

—Let's Hear It for the Deaf Man. 1974. (87th Precinct Mystery Ser.). 160p. mass mkt. 3.99 o.p. (*0-451-15403-7*, Signet Bks.) NAL.

—Lightning. 1999. (Eighty-Seventh Precinct Ser.). audio 56.00 (*0-7366-4624-8*, 5009) Books on Tape, Inc.

—Lightning. abr. ed. audio 17.00 o.p. (*0-694-51547-7*, CPN 2489, HarperAudio) HarperTrade.

—Lightning. (Eighty-Seventh Precinct Novel Ser.). 1985. 304p. mass mkt. 4.95 (*0-380-69974-5*, Avon Bks.); 1984. 15.95 o.p. (*0-87795-581-6*, Morrow, William & Co.) Morrow/Avon.

—Like Love. unabr. ed. 1996. (Eighty-Seventh Precinct Ser.). audio 36.00 (*0-7366-3496-7*, 4136) Books on Tape, Inc.

—Like Love. l.t. ed. 1993. (Nightingale Ser.). 304p. lib. bdg. 15.95 o.p. (*0-8161-5705-7*, Macmillan Reference USA) Gale Group.

—Like Love. (87th Precinct Mystery Ser.). 1982. mass mkt. 2.25 o.p. (*0-451-11628-3*); 1982. 176p. mass mkt. 2.95 o.p. (*0-451-13903-8*); 1982. 160p. mass mkt. 4.50 o.s.i (*0-451-16383-4*); 1976. mass mkt. 1.25 o.p. (*0-451-07221-9*) NAL. (Signet Bks.).

—Long Time No See. 1982. pap. 2.50 o.p. (*0-553-23130-8*) Bantam Bks.

—Long Time No See. unabr. ed. 1986. (Eighty-Seventh Precinct Ser.). audio 40.00 (*0-7366-0823-0*, 1773) Books on Tape, Inc.

—Long Time No See. abr. ed. audio 17.00 o.p. (*0-694-51546-9*, CPN 2488, HarperAudio) HarperTrade.

—Long Time No See. 1987. 272p. mass mkt. 4.99 (*0-380-70369-6*, Avon Bks.) Morrow/Avon.

—Long Time No See. 1997. 304p. mass mkt. 5.99 (*0-446-60449-6*) Warner Bks., Inc.

—Lullaby. unabr. ed. 1992. (Audio Bks.). audio 69.95 (*0-7451-6154-5*, CAB 549) BBC Audiobooks America.

—Lullaby. 1999. audio 48.00 (*0-7366-4872-0*); 1989. audio 48.00 Books on Tape, Inc.

—Lullaby. l.t. ed. 1990. (General Ser.). 437p. 20.95 o.p. (*0-8161-4923-2*, Macmillan Reference USA) Gale Group.

—Lullaby. abr. ed. audio 16.00 o.p. (*1-55994-819-1*, CPN 2392, HarperAudio) HarperTrade.

—Lullaby. abr. ed. 2000. (Eighty Seventh Precinct Novels Ser.). audio 7.95 (*1-57815-050-7*, 1014, Media Bks. Audio Publishing) Media Bks., L. L. C.

—Lullaby. 1990. 352p. mass mkt. 5.99 (*0-380-70384-X*, Avon Bks.); 1989. 17.95 o.p. (*0-87795-994-3*, Morrow, William & Co.) Morrow/Avon.

—McBain's Ladies: The Women of the 87th Precinct. 1988. 320p. 16.95 o.s.i (*0-89296-284-4*) Mysterious Pr.

—McBain's Ladies: The Women of the 87th Precinct. 1989. mass mkt. 4.95 (*0-445-40334-9*, Mysterious Pr. Paperback Bks.) Warner Bks., Inc.

—McBain's Ladies Too. 1989. 272p. 17.95 o.p. (*0-89296-285-2*) Mysterious Pr.

—McBain's Ladies Too. 1990. mass mkt. 4.95 o.s.i (*0-445-40893-6*, Mysterious Pr. Paperback Bks.) Warner Bks., Inc.

—Mischief. l.t. ed. 1995. pap. 23.95 o.p. (*0-7927-2014-8*); 1994. 25.95 o.p. (*0-7927-2015-6*) BBC Audiobooks America.

—Mischief. unabr. ed. 1993. (Eighty-Seventh Precinct Ser.). audio 64.00 (*0-7366-2591-7*, 3336) Books on Tape, Inc.

—Mischief. unabr. ed. 1993. 57.25 o.p. incl. audio (*1-56100-147-3*, 942, Unabridged Library Editions); audio 21.95 o.p. (*1-56100-514-2*, 176, Bookcassette) Brilliance Audio.

—Mischief. abr. ed. 2000. audio 9.99 (*0-694-52329-1*, HarperAudio) HarperTrade.

—Mischief. abr. ed. 2000. (Eighty Seventh Precinct Novels Ser.). audio 7.95 (*1-57815-051-5*, 1043, Media Bks. Audio Publishing) Media Bks., L. L. C.

—Mischief. 1994. 352p. pap. 5.99 (*0-380-71384-5*, Avon Bks.); 1993. 346p. 20.00 o.p. (*0-688-10221-2*, Morrow, William & Co.) Morrow/Avon.

—Money, Money, Money. 2001. E-Book 9.99 (*1-59061-377-5*) Adobe Systems, Inc.

—Money, Money, Money. 2002. 352p. mass mkt. 7.99 (*0-7434-4379-9*, Pocket); 2001. 272p. 25.00 (*0-7432-0269-4*, Simon & Schuster); 2001. 272p. E-Book 25.00 (*0-7432-1767-5*, Simon & Schuster); 2003. 384p. pap. 25.00 (*0-7432-5445-7*, Simon & Schuster); 2001. 384p. 25.00 (*0-7432-2406-X*, Simon & Schuster); 2002. 352p. reprint ed. mass mkt. 7.99 (*0-7434-1032-7*, Pocket) Simon & Schuster.

—Money, Money, Money. abr. ed. 2001. audio 26.00 (*0-7435-0992-7*); audio compact disk 30.00 (*0-7435-0993-5*) Simon & Schuster Audio. (Simon & Schuster Audioworks).

—The Mugger. unabr. ed. 1995. (Eighty-Seventh Precinct Novels Ser.). audio 39.95 (*0-7451-6855-8*, CAB 321) BBC Audiobooks America.

—The Mugger. 1981. 160p. mass mkt. 2.25 o.s.i (*0-345-29290-1*) Ballantine Bks.

—The Mugger. unabr. ed. 1990. (Eighty-Seventh Precinct Ser.). audio 36.00 (*0-7366-1721-3*, 2562) Books on Tape, Inc.

—The Mugger. 1986. (Eighty-Seventh Precinct Novel Ser.). 160p. mass mkt. 3.50 (*0-380-70081-6*, Avon Bks.) Morrow/Avon.

—The Mugger. 1996. 192p. mass mkt. 5.99 (*0-446-60143-8*) Warner Bks., Inc.

—Nocturne. abr. ed. 1997. (Eighty Seventh Precinct Ser.). audio 24.95 (*1-55927-439-5*, 695087) Audio Renaissance.

—Nocturne. unabr. ed. 1997. (Eighty-Seventh Precinct Ser.). audio 48.00 (*0-7366-3777-X*, 4450) Books on Tape, Inc.

—Nocturne. (Eighty Seventh Precinct Ser.). 1998. mass mkt. 188.73 (*0-446-16558-1*); 1997. 320p. 23.50 o.p. (*0-446-51805-0*); 1998. 352p. reprint ed. mass mkt. 6.99 (*0-446-60538-7*) Warner Bks., Inc.

—Poison. 2001. audio 64.00 (*0-7366-5935-8*) Books on Tape, Inc.

—Poison. l.t. ed. 1988. 352p. 19.95 o.p. (*0-8161-4299-8*, Macmillan Reference USA) Gale Group.

—Poison. 1988. 256p. mass mkt. 4.99 (*0-380-70030-1*, Avon Bks.); 1987. 242p. 16.95 o.p. (*0-87795-787-8*, Morrow, William & Co.) Morrow/Avon.

—Poison. abr. ed. 1987. audio 14.95 (*0-671-64160-3*, Simon & Schuster Audioworks) Simon & Schuster Audio.

—The Pusher. unabr. ed. 1994. (Eighty-Seventh Precinct Novels Ser.). audio 54.95 (*0-7451-4228-1*, CAB 911) BBC Audiobooks America.

—The Pusher. unabr. ed. 1992. (Eighty-Seventh Precinct Ser.). audio 36.00 (*0-7366-2155-5*, 2954) Books on Tape, Inc.

—The Pusher. l.t. ed. 1987. (Large Print Books, Nightingale Ser.). 266p. 11.95 o.p. (*0-8161-4258-0*, Macmillan Reference USA) Gale Group.

—The Pusher. 9999. pap. 3.95 o.p. (*0-451-16480-6*); 1987. 160p. mass mkt. 3.99 o.p. (*0-451-15080-5*, Signet Bks.); 1980. mass mkt. 1.75 o.p. (*0-451-09256-2*, Signet Bks.); 1973. mass mkt. 0.95 o.p. (*0-451-05705-8*, Signet Bks.) NAL.

—The Pusher. 2002. 256p. pap. 6.99 (*0-7434-6305-6*, Pocket) Simon & Schuster.

—Romance. unabr. ed. 1995. (Eighty-Seventh Precinct Ser.). audio 48.00 (*0-7366-3122-4*, 3798) Books on Tape, Inc.

—Romance. abr. ed. audio 17.00 o.p. (*1-55994-995-3*, CPN 2484, HarperAudio) HarperTrade.

—Romance. 338p. pap. 5.98 o.p. (*0-7651-0365-6*) Smithmark Pubs., Inc.

—Romance. 1995. 336p. 22.95 o.s.i (*0-446-51804-2*); 1996. 352p. reprint ed. mass mkt. 6.50 o.s.i (*0-446-60280-9*) Warner Bks., Inc.

—Sadie When She Died. unabr. ed. 1998. (Eighty-Seventh Precinct Ser.). audio 30.00 (*0-7366-3993-4*, 4356) Books on Tape, Inc.

—Sadie When She Died. 1973. (87th Precinct Mystery Ser.). 160p. mass mkt. 3.99 o.s.i (*0-451-15366-9*, Signet Bks.) NAL.

—See Them Die. unabr. ed. 1996. (Eighty-Seventh Precinct Ser.). audio 36.00 (*0-7366-3359-6*, 4009) Books on Tape, Inc.

—See Them Die. (87th Precinct Mystery Ser.). 1982. mass mkt. 2.25 o.p. (*0-451-11561-9*, Signet Bks.); 1982. mass mkt. 2.95 o.p. (*0-451-14596-8*); 1976. mass mkt. 1.25 o.p. (*0-451-07030-5*, Signet Bks.); 1982. 160p. reprint ed. mass mkt. 4.50 o.p. (*0-451-16426-1*, Signet Bks.) NAL.

—Shotgun. unabr. ed. 1997. (Eighty-Seventh Precinct Ser.). audio 30.00 (*0-7366-3578-5*, 4230) Books on Tape, Inc.

—Shotgun. 1970. (87th Precinct Mystery Ser.). 176p. mass mkt. 4.50 o.p. (*0-451-15674-9*); mass mkt. 2.50 o.p. (*0-451-11971-1*) NAL. (Signet Bks.).

—So Long As You Both Shall Live. unabr. ed. 1998. (Eighty-Seventh Precinct Ser.). audio 30.00 (*0-7366-3778-8*, 4451) Books on Tape, Inc.

—So Long As You Both Shall Live. 1977. mass mkt. 3.50 o.p. (*0-451-15718-4*); mass mkt. 1.50 o.p. (*0-451-07749-0*) NAL. (Signet Bks.).

—Ten Plus One. unabr. ed. 1997. (Eighty-Seventh Precinct Ser.). audio 36.00 (*0-7366-3532-7*, 4171) Books on Tape, Inc.

—Ten Plus One. (87th Precinct Mystery Ser.). 1982. mass mkt. 2.25 o.p. (*0-451-11923-1*, Signet Bks.); 1982. 176p. mass mkt. 4.50 o.s.i (*0-451-16367-2*, Signet Bks.); 1982. mass mkt. 2.95 o.p. (*0-451-14598-4*); 1977. mass mkt. 1.25 o.p. (*0-451-07463-7*, Signet Bks.) NAL.

—'Til Death. unabr. ed. 1992. (Eighty-Seventh Precinct Ser.). audio 36.00 (*0-7366-2123-7*, 2925) Books on Tape, Inc.

—'Til Death. (Eighty-Seventh Precinct Mysteries Ser.). 1989. 176p. mass mkt. 4.50 o.s.i (*0-451-15891-1*); 1981. mass mkt. 2.25 o.p. (*0-451-09734-3*); 1981. mass mkt. 2.95 o.p. (*0-451-13896-1*) NAL. (Signet Bks.).

—Till Death Us Do Part. 1975. mass mkt. 1.25 o.p. (*0-451-06320-1*, Signet Bks.) NAL.

—Tricks. unabr. ed. 1992. (Eighty-Seventh Precinct Novels Ser.). audio 54.95 (*0-7451-6156-1*, CAB 616) BBC Audiobooks America.

—Tricks. 2001. audio 56.00 (*0-7366-6021-6*) Books on Tape, Inc.

—Tricks. 256p. 1987. 16.95 o.p. (*0-87795-927-7*, Morrow, William & Co.); 1989. reprint ed. mass mkt. 5.99 (*0-380-70383-1*, Avon Bks.) Morrow/Avon.

—Tricks. 1989. 3.99 o.p. (*0-517-69431-X*) Random Hse. Value Publishing.

—Tricks. abr. ed. 1988. audio 14.95 Simon & Schuster Audio.

—Vespers. unabr. ed. 1990. (Eighty-Seventh Precinct Ser.). audio 64.00 (*0-7366-1807-4*, 2644) Books on Tape, Inc.

—Vespers. l.t. ed. 1991. 470p. 24.95 o.p. (*1-85089-498-1*) ISIS Large Print Bks. GBR. *Dist:* Transaction Pubs.

—Vespers. 1991. 352p. mass mkt. 5.99 (*0-380-70385-8*, Avon Bks.); 1990. 350p. 18.95 o.p. (*0-87795-987-0*, Morrow, William & Co.) Morrow/Avon.

—Widows. unabr. ed. 1991. (Eighty-Seventh Precinct Ser.). audio 64.00 (*0-7366-1965-8*, 2786) Books on Tape, Inc.

—Widows. l.t. ed. 1992. (General Ser.). 454p. lib. bdg. 21.95 o.p. (*0-8161-5311-6*, Macmillan Reference USA) Gale Group.

—Widows. abr. ed. 2000. (Eighty Seventh Precinct Novels Ser.). audio 7.95 (*1-57815-056-6*, 1054, Media Bks. Audio Publishing) Media Bks., L. L. C.

—Widows. 1991. 330p. 19.00 o.p. (*0-688-10219-0*, Morrow, William & Co.); 1992. 336p. reprint ed. mass mkt. 6.50 (*0-380-71383-7*, Avon Bks.) Morrow/Avon.

**EL PASO (TEX.)—FICTION**

Fackler, Elizabeth. Patricide. 2000. (Five Star Mystery Ser.). 275p. 22.95 (*0-7862-2363-4*, Five Star) Gale Group.

—When Kindness Fails. l.t. ed. 2003. 314p. 25.95 (*0-7862-5443-2*, Five Star) Gale Group.

Schumacher, Aileen. Affirmative Reaction. 2000. (Tory Travers/David Alvarez Mysteries Ser.: Bk. 355). 256p. mass mkt. (*0-373-26355-4*, 1-26355-7, Worldwide Library) Harlequin Enterprises, Ltd.

—Affirmative Reaction. 1999. (Travers/Alvarez Mystery Ser.: No. 4). 310p. 24.95 o.p. (*1-885173-69-5*) Write Way Publishing.

—Engineered for Murder. 1996. 293p. 21.95 o.p. (*1-885173-17-2*); mass mkt. 5.95 o.p. (*1-885173-43-1*) Write Way Publishing.

—Framework for Death. 1998. (Tory Travers/David Alvarez Mysteries Ser.). 360p. 23.95 o.p. (*1-885173-55-5*) Write Way Publishing.

**ELUNDIUM (IMAGINARY PLACE)—FICTION**

Jefferies, Mike. Citadel of Shadows. 1997. (Loremasters of Elundium Ser.: 5). 352p. mass mkt. 5.99 o.p. (*0-06-105434-8*, Eos) Morrow/Avon.

—Palace of Kings. 1990. (Loremasters of Elundium Ser.: 2). 432p. mass mkt. 4.99 o.p. (*0-06-100018-3*, HarperTorch) Morrow/Avon.

—Road to Underfall. 1990. (Loremasters of Elundium Ser.: 1). 384p. mass mkt. 5.99 o.p. (*0-06-100019-1*, HarperTorch) Morrow/Avon.

—Shadowlight. 1990. (Loremasters of Elundium Ser.: 3). 464p. mass mkt. 5.99 o.p. (*0-06-100031-0*, HarperTorch) Morrow/Avon.

Jeffries, Mike. Knights of Cawdor. 1995. (Loremasters of Elundium Ser.: 4). 352p. mass mkt. 5.99 o.p. (*0-06-100668-8*, Eos) Morrow/Avon.

**EMPTY CREEK (ARIZ.: IMAGINARY PLACE)—FICTION**

Allen, Garrison. Baseball Cat. (Big Mike Mystery Ser.: Vol. 4). 1998. 336p. mass mkt. 5.99 (*1-57566-309-0*); 1997. 304p. 18.95 o.s.i (*1-57566-183-7*) Kensington Publishing Corp.

—Desert Cat. 1994. 304p. mass mkt. 3.99 o.s.i (*0-8217-4503-4*, Zebra Bks.) Kensington Publishing Corp.

—Dinosaur Cat. (Big Mike Mystery Ser.). 336p. 1999. mass mkt. 5.99 o.s.i (*1-57566-426-7*); 1998. (J). 20.00 o.s.i (*1-57566-304-X*, Kensington Bks.) Kensington Publishing Corp.

—Movie Cat. 1999. (Big Mike Mystery Ser.). 304p. 20.00 o.s.i (*1-57566-413-5*) Kensington Publishing Corp.

—Royal Cat: A Big Mike Mystery. 1996. (Big Mike Mystery Ser.: Vol. 2). 304p. mass mkt. 4.99 o.s.i (*1-57566-045-8*); 1995. mass mkt. 16.95 o.s.i (*0-8217-4957-9*, Zebra Bks.) Kensington Publishing Corp.

—Stable Cat. 304p. 1997. mass mkt. 5.50 o.s.i (*1-57566-188-8*); 1996. pap. 18.95 o.p. (*1-57566-042-3*) Kensington Publishing Corp.

**ENGLAND—FICTION**

Abe, Shana. A Kiss at Midnight. 2000. (Meet Me at Midnight Ser.). 368p. mass mkt. 5.99 o.s.i (*0-553-58057-4*) Bantam Bks.

—The Secret Swan. 2001. 400p. mass mkt. 5.99 (*0-553-58200-3*) Bantam Bks.

Ackland, Tom. The Disobedient Servant. 1998. (Illus.). 224p. pap. 10.95 o.p. (*0-575-06187-1*) Gollancz, Victor GBR. *Dist:* Trafalgar Square.

Ackroyd, Peter. First Light. 1991. 336p. pap. 8.95 o.p. (*0-345-36887-8*) Ballantine Bks.

—First Light. 336p. 1989. 19.95 o.p. (*0-8021-1161-0*); 1996. reprint ed. pap. 12.00 (*0-8021-3481-5*, Grove Pr.) Grove/Atlantic, Inc.

—Hawksmoor. 1987. 288p. pap. 8.95 o.p. (*0-06-091390-8*, PL1390, Perennial); 1986. 217p. 16.95 o.p. (*0-06-015503-5*) HarperTrade.

—The Trial of Elizabeth Cree: A Novel of the Limehouse Murders. unabr. collector's ed. 1997. audio 48.00 (*0-7366-3627-7*, 4288) Books on Tape, Inc.

—The Trial of Elizabeth Cree: A Novel of the Limehouse Murders. 1995. 272p. 22.00 o.s.i (*0-385-47707-4*, Talese, Nan A.) Doubleday Publishing.

—The Trial of Elizabeth Cree: A Novel of the Limehouse Murders. unabr. ed. 2000. audio 51.00 (*0-7887-0470-2*, 94663E7) Recorded Bks., LLC.

Ackroyd, Peter, intro. Bleak House. 1991. (Complete Novels of Charles Dickens Ser.). (Illus.). 935p. (C). pap. 5.50 o.p. (*0-7493-0765-X*) Heinemann.

Adair, Gilbert. Closed Book. 1999. 258p. pap. (*0-571-20081-8*) Faber & Faber, Inc.

Adamoli, Vida. Sons, Lovers, Etcetera. 1997. 250p. pap. 13.95 o.p. (*0-7472-5501-6*) Headline Bk. Publishing, Ltd. GBR. *Dist:* Trafalgar Square.

Adams, Jane. Like Angels Falling. l.t. ed. 2002. 320p. pap. 24.95 (*0-7862-3691-4*) Gale Group.

Adrian, Jack, selected by. Desirable Residences & Other Stories. 1991. 304p. 25.00 o.p. (*0-19-212304-1*) Oxford Univ. Pr., Inc.

The Adventures of Sherlock Holmes. audio Audio Bk. Co.

The Adventures of Sherlock Holmes. unabr. collector's ed. Incl. Adventure of the Blue Carbuncle. Doyle, Arthur Conan. audio Beryl Coronet. audio Boscombe Valley Mystery. audio Case of Identity. audio Case of the Five Orange Pips. Doyle, Arthur Conan. audio Copper Beeches. Brett, Jeremy. audio Engineer's Thumb. audio Man with the Twisted Lip. Doyle, Arthur Conan. audio Noble Bachelor. audio Red-Headed League. Doyle, Arthur Conan. audio Scandal in Bohemia. Doyle, Arthur Conan. audio Speckled Band. audio 1984. (Sherlock Holmes Ser.). 1978. Set audio 56.00 (*0-7366-0101-5*, 1109) Books on Tape, Inc.

Aiken, Joan. Jane Fairfax: Jane Austen's Emma, Through Another's Eyes. 1997. 256p. reprint ed. pap. 12.95 (*0-312-15707-X*, Saint Martin's Griffin) St. Martin's Pr.

—Lady Catherines Necklace. 2000. 172p. 21.95 (*0-312-24406-1*) St. Martin's Pr.

—Lady Catherine's Necklace. l.t. ed. 2000. (General Ser.). 230p. pap. 24.95 (*0-7862-2629-3*) Thorndike Pr.

—Mansfield Revisited. 1986. 176p. mass mkt. 2.95 o.s.i (*0-446-34000-6*) Warner Bks., Inc.

Aiken, Joan & Austen, Jane. Eliza's Daughter. 1994. 384p. 20.95 o.p. (*0-312-10972-5*) St. Martin's Pr.

—Emma Watson: The Watsons Completed. l.t. ed. 1997. 25.95 (*1-56895-441-7*, Wheeler Publishing, Inc.) Gale Group.

—Emma Watson: The Watsons Completed. 1996. 224p. 20.95 o.p. (*0-312-14593-4*) St. Martin's Pr.

—Jane Fairfax: Jane Austen's Emma, Through Another's Eyes. 1991. 18.95 o.p. (*0-312-05884-5*) St. Martin's Pr.

—Mansfield Revisited. 1985. 192p. 13.95 o.p. (*0-385-19793-4*) Doubleday Publishing.

—The Youngest Miss Ward. l.t. ed. 1999. (General Ser.). 428p. 30.00 (*0-7862-1826-6*, Macmillan Reference USA) Gale Group.

—The Youngest Miss Ward. 1998. 320p. 23.95 o.p. (*0-312-19375-0*) St. Martin's Pr.

Ainsworth, William Harrison. The Constable of the Tower. 1999. (Library of Classical Historical Fiction). 340p. E-Book 9.95 (*0-594-00158-7*); (Illus.). 340p. pap. 16.95 (*0-594-00156-0*); E-Book 9.95 (*0-594-00157-9*) 1873 Pr.

—The Leaguer of Lathom. 1999. (Library of Classical Historical Fiction). 326p. pap. 16.95 (*0-594-00729-1*); 326p. E-Book 9.95 (*0-594-00731-3*); E-Book 9.95 (*0-594-00730-5*) 1873 Pr.

—Ovingdean Grange. 1999. (Library of Classical Historical Fiction). 236p. E-Book 9.95 (*0-594-00155-2*); (Illus.). pap. 13.95 (*0-594-00153-6*) 1873 Pr.

—The Tower of London. 1999. (Library of Classical Historical Fiction). 504p. pap. 22.95 (*0-594-00735-6*); E-Book 9.95 (*0-594-00737-2*); E-Book 9.95 (*0-594-00736-4*) 1873 Pr.

Aird, Catherine. After Effects. l.t. ed. 1997. (G. K. Hall Nightingale Ser.). 206p. pap. 18.95 o.p. (*0-7838-1967-6*, Macmillan Reference USA) Gale Group.

—After Effects. 1996. (Detective Inspector C. D. Sloan Mystery). 208p. 20.95 (*0-312-14270-6*, Saint Martin's Minotaur) St. Martin's Pr.

—Amendment of Life: A Mystery. 2003. 240p. 22.95 (*0-312-29080-2*, Saint Martin's Minotaur) St. Martin's Pr.

—Body Politic. 1991. 192p. 15.00 o.s.i (*0-385-41780-2*) Doubleday Publishing.

—A Dead Liberty. Set. unabr. ed. 2001. (Inspector C. D. Sloan Mystery Ser.). audio 49.95 (*0-7451-5705-X*, CAB 234) Chivers Audio Bks. GBR. *Dist:* BBC Audiobooks America.

—A Dead Liberty. 1987. (Crime Club Ser.). 192p. 12.95 o.s.i (*0-385-23554-2*) Doubleday Publishing.

—A Dead Liberty. 1987. audio 49.95 (*0-8161-7688-4*) Thorndike Pr.

—A Dead Liberty. l.t. ed. 1987. 384p. 16.95 o.p. (*0-7089-1664-3*, Ulverscroft) Thorpe, F. A. Pubs. GBR. *Dist:* Ulverscroft Large Print Bks., Ltd.

—A Going Concern. l.t. ed. 1995. (G. K. Hall Nightingale Ser.). 235p. pap. 17.95 (*0-7838-1134-9*, Macmillan Reference USA) Gale Group.

—A Going Concern. 1994. 167p. 18.95 o.p. (*0-312-11423-0*, Saint Martin's Minotaur) St. Martin's Pr.

—Harm's Way. 1985. 192p. mass mkt. 2.95 o.s.i (*0-553-25191-0*) Bantam Bks.

—Harm's Way. 1984. (Crime Club Ser.). 192p. 11.95 o.p. (*0-385-19542-7*) Doubleday Publishing.

—Harm's Way. l.t. ed. 1985. (Ulverscroft Large Print Ser.). 384p. 12.50 o.p. (*0-7089-1359-8*, Ulverscroft) Thorpe, F. A. Pubs. GBR. *Dist:* Ulverscroft Large Print Bks., Ltd., Ulverscroft Large Print Canada, Ltd.

—Henrietta Who? 1981. mass mkt. 2.95 o.s.i (*0-553-25463-4*) Bantam Bks.

—Henrietta Who? l.t. ed. 2000. (G. K. Hall Nightingale Ser.). 247p. pap. 21.95 (*0-7838-9003-6*, Macmillan Reference USA) Gale Group.

—Henrietta Who? l.t. ed. 1979. (Ulverscroft Large Print Ser.). 299p. 12.00 o.p. (*0-7089-0352-5*, Ulverscroft) Thorpe, F. A. Pubs. GBR. *Dist:* Ulverscroft Large Print Bks., Ltd., Ulverscroft Large Print Canada, Ltd.

—His Burial Too. 1980. 208p. pap. 2.95 o.p. (*0-553-25441-3*) Bantam Bks.

—His Burial Too. l.t. ed. 1980. (Ulverscroft Large Print Ser.). 316p. 12.00 o.p. (*0-7089-0478-5*, Ulverscroft) Thorpe, F. A. Pubs. GBR. *Dist:* Ulverscroft Large Print Bks., Ltd., Ulverscroft Large Print Canada, Ltd.

—Injury Time: Featuring Inspector C. D. Sloan. unabr. ed. 1997. audio 16.99 (*0-88646-432-3*, 7432) Durkin Hayes Publishing Ltd.

—Injury Time: Featuring Inspector C. D. Sloan. l.t. ed. 1995. 289p. 18.95 o.p. (*0-7838-1458-5*, Macmillan Reference USA) Gale Group.

—Injury Time: Featuring Inspector C. D. Sloan. 1995. 168p. 19.95 o.p. (*0-312-13095-3*, Saint Martin's Minotaur) St. Martin's Pr.

—Last Respects. 1984. 176p. mass mkt. 2.95 o.s.i (*0-553-25811-7*) Bantam Bks.

—Last Respects. 1982. (Crime Club Ser.). 192p. 11.95 o.p. (*0-385-18256-2*) Doubleday Publishing.

—Last Respects. l.t. ed. 1984. (Ulverscroft Large Print Ser.). 304p. 12.50 o.p. (*0-7089-1180-3*, Ulverscroft) Thorpe, F. A. Pubs. GBR. *Dist:* Ulverscroft Large Print Bks., Ltd., Ulverscroft Large Print Canada, Ltd.

—A Late Phoenix. l.t. ed. 1994. 18.95 o.p. (*0-7451-6427-7*) BBC Audiobooks America.

—A Late Phoenix. 1988. mass mkt. o.s.i (*0-552-12794-9*, Corgi); 1981. 176p. pap. 2.95 o.p. (*0-553-25442-1*) Bantam Bks.

—A Late Phoenix. 1988. audio 35.95 o.s.i (*0-8161-7797-X*) Thorndike Pr.

—Little Knell. 2001. 240p. 22.95 (*0-312-26983-8*, Saint Martin's Minotaur) St. Martin's Pr.

—A Most Contagious Game. 1994. 200p. 16.95 o.p. (*0-7451-8630-0*, Black Dagger) BBC Audiobooks America.

—Parting Breath. 1989. mass mkt. o.s.i (*0-552-13426-0*, Corgi); 1985. 176p. mass mkt. 2.95 o.s.i (*0-553-25414-6*); 1984. mass mkt. 2.75 o.s.i (*0-553-24601-1*) Bantam Bks.

—Parting Breath. l.t. ed. 2001. (Thorndike Mystery Ser.). 277p. pap. 23.95 (*0-7838-9431-7*) Thorndike Pr.

—Passing Strange. 1981. (Crime Club Ser.). 192p. 9.95 o.p. (*0-385-17271-0*) Doubleday Publishing.

—The Religious Body. unabr. ed. 2001. (Inspector C. D. Sloan Mystery Ser.). audio 34.95 (*0-7451-5709-2*, CSL 074) Chivers Audio Bks. GBR. *Dist:* BBC Audiobooks America.

—The Religious Body: The First C. D. Sloan Mystery. unabr. ed. 2000. (C. D. Sloan Mystery Ser.). audio 24.95 (*1-57270-149-8*, N41149u, Audio Editions Mystery Masters) Audio Partners Publishing Corp.

—The Religious Body: The First C. D. Sloan Mystery. l.t. ed. 1983. 288p. 12.50 o.p. (*0-7089-1038-6*, Ulverscroft) Thorpe, F. A. Pubs. GBR. *Dist:* Ulverscroft Large Print Bks., Ltd.

—The Religious Body: The First C.D. Sloan Mystery. 2000. 21.95 (*0-7540-8561-9*, Black Dagger) BBC Audiobooks America.

—The Religious Body: The First C.D. Sloan Mystery. 1980. 176p. pap. 2.95 o.p. (*0-553-24602-X*) Bantam Bks.

—Slight Mourning. 1989. mass mkt. o.s.i (*0-552-13427-9*, Corgi); 1982. 192p. mass mkt. 2.95 o.s.i (*0-553-25631-9*) Bantam Bks.

—Slight Mourning. l.t. ed. 1979. (Ulverscroft Large Print Ser.). 287p. o.p. (*0-7089-0271-5*, Ulverscroft) Thorpe, F. A. Pubs. GBR. *Dist:* Ulverscroft Large Print Canada, Ltd.

—Some Die Eloquent. 1981. 208p. pap. 2.95 o.p. (*0-553-25110-4*) Bantam Bks.

—Some Die Eloquent. 1980. (Crime Club Ser.). 10.95 o.p. (*0-385-15747-9*) Doubleday Publishing.

—Some Die Eloquent. l.t. ed. 1981. 328p. 12.00 o.p. (*0-7089-0631-1*, Ulverscroft) Thorpe, F. A. Pubs. GBR. *Dist:* Ulverscroft Large Print Bks., Ltd.

—The Stately Home Murder. 1980. 208p. pap. 2.75 o.p. (*0-553-24078-1*) Bantam Bks.

—Stiff News. 2000. audio compact disk 39.95; 1999. 222 p. (*0-7540-3643-X*) BBC Audiobooks America.

—Stiff News. 1998. 240p. 21.95 o.p. (*0-312-20023-4*, Saint Martin's Minotaur) St. Martin's Pr.

—Stiff News. l.t. ed. 1999. (Nightingale Ser.). 232p. pap. 21.95 (*0-7838-8477-X*) Thorndike Pr.

Airth, Rennie. River of Darkness: A Novel of Suspense in the Shadow of World War I. l.t. ed. 2000. (Mystery Ser.). 600p. 28.95 (*0-7862-2334-0*) Thorndike Pr.

—River of Darkness: A Novel of Suspense in the Shadow of World War I. 2000. 400p. 6.99 (*0-14-029196-2*) Viking Penguin.

Alcott, Louisa May. The Inheritance. l.t. ed. 1997. 26.95 o.p. (*1-56895-505-7*, Wheeler Publishing, Inc.) Gale Group.

—The Inheritance. 1998. 192p. mass mkt. 5.99 o.s.i (*0-14-027729-3*) Penguin Group (USA) Inc.

—The Inheritance. Myerson, Joel & Shealy, Daniel, eds. 1997. 160p. (YA). 18.00 o.s.i (*0-525-45756-9*) Penguin Putnam Bks. for Young Readers.

—The Inheritance. 1998. (Illus.). (J). 12.04 (*0-606-18412-0*) Turtleback Bks.

—The Inheritance. Myerson, Joel & Shealy, Daniel, eds. 1998. (Classics Ser.). 192p. 13.00 (*0-14-043666-9*, Penguin Classics) Viking Penguin.

Aldiss, Brian W. Remembrance Day. 1993. 320p. 21.95 o.p. (*0-312-09370-5*) St. Martin's Pr.

Alexander, Bruce. Blind Justice. unabr. ed. 1998. (Sir John Fielding Mystery Ser.: Vol. 1). audio 56.00 (*0-7366-4081-9*, 4590) Books on Tape, Inc.

—Blind Justice: A Sir John Fielding Mystery. 1995. (Sir John Fielding Mystery Ser.). 336p. mass mkt. 6.50 (*0-425-15007-0*) Berkley Publishing Group.

—Blind Justice: A Sir John Fielding Mystery. 1994. (Sir John Fielding Ser.). 224p. 19.95 o.p. (*0-399-13978-8*, G. P. Putnam's Sons) Penguin Group (USA) Inc.

—Blind Justice: A Sir John Fielding Mystery. l.t. ed. 1996. (Large Print Ser.). 576p. 29.99 o.p. (*0-7089-3606-7*, Ulverscroft) Thorpe, F. A. Pubs. GBR. *Dist:* Ulverscroft Large Print Bks., Ltd., Ulverscroft Large Print Canada, Ltd.

—Death of a Colonial: A Sir John Fielding Mystery. 1999. (Sir John Fielding Mystery Ser.). 288p. 23.95 o.p. (*0-399-14564-8*, G. P. Putnam's Sons) Penguin Group (USA) Inc.

—The Death of a Colonial: A Sir John Fielding Mystery. 2000. (Sir John Fielding Ser.). 304p. mass mkt. 6.50 (*0-425-17702-5*) Berkley Publishing Group.

—Jack, Knave & Fool. unabr. ed. 1999. (Sir John Fielding Mystery Ser.). audio 64.00 Books on Tape, Inc.

—Jack, Knave & Fool: A Sir John Fielding Mystery. 1999. (Sir John Fielding Ser.). 416p. reprint ed. mass mkt. 6.99 (*0-425-17120-5*, Prime Crime) Berkley Publishing Group.

—Jack, Knave & Fool: A Sir John Fielding Mystery. l.t. ed. 1999. (Basic Ser.). 631p. 28.95 (*0-7862-1798-7*) Thorndike Pr.

—Jack Knave the Fool. 1998. (Sir John Fielding Mystery Ser.). 288p. 22.95 o.p. (*0-399-14419-6*, G. P. Putnam's Sons) Penguin Group (USA) Inc.

—Murder in Grub Street. unabr. ed. 1998. (Sir John Fielding Mystery Ser.: Vol. 2). audio 56.00 (*0-7366-3998-5*, 4498) Books on Tape, Inc.

—Murder in Grub Street: A Sir John Fielding Mystery. 1996. (Sir John Fielding Mystery Ser.). 320p. reprint ed. mass mkt. 6.99 (*0-425-15550-1*, Prime Crime) Berkley Publishing Group.

—Murder in Grub Street: A Sir John Fielding Mystery. 1995. (Sir John Fielding Ser.). 256p. 21.95 o.p. (*0-399-14085-9*, G. P. Putnam's Sons) Penguin Group (USA) Inc.

—Murder in Grub Street: A Sir John Fielding Mystery. l.t. ed. 1997. (Ulverscroft Large Print Ser.). 608p. 29.99 (*0-7089-3749-7*, Ulverscroft) Thorpe, F. A. Pubs. GBR. *Dist:* Ulverscroft Large Print Bks., Ltd., Ulverscroft Large Print Canada, Ltd.

—Person or Persons Unknown. unabr. ed. 1999. (Sir John Fielding Mystery Ser.). audio 56.00 (*0-7366-4337-0*, 4826) Books on Tape, Inc.

—Person or Persons Unknown: A Sir John Fielding Mystery. 1998. (Sir John Fielding Mystery Ser.: Bk. 4). 336p. reprint ed. mass mkt. 6.99 (*0-425-16566-3*, Prime Crime) Berkley Publishing Group.

—Person or Persons Unknown: A Sir John Fielding Mystery. 1997. (Sir John Fielding Ser.). 256p. 22.95 o.s.i (*0-399-14309-2*, G. P. Putnam's Sons) Penguin Group (USA) Inc.

—Smuggler's Moon. 2002. (Sir John Fielding Mystery Ser.: Vol. 8). 304p. reprint ed. mass mkt. 6.50 (*0-425-18690-3*, Prime Crime) Berkley Publishing Group.

—Smuggler's Moon. 1998. 23.95 o.p. (*0-399-14778-0*, Putnam & Grosset) Penguin Group (USA) Inc.

—Smuggler's Moon. 2002. 491p. 29.95 (*0-7862-4141-1*) Thorndike Pr.

—Smuggler's Moon: A Sir John Fielding Mystery. 2001. 288p. 24.95 o.s.i (*0-399-14774-8*) Penguin Group (USA) Inc.

—Watery Grave. 1997. (Sir John Fielding Mystery Ser.). 320p. mass mkt. 6.99 (*0-425-16036-X*, Prime Crime) Berkley Publishing Group.

—Watery Grave. unabr. ed. 1998. (Sir John Fielding Mystery Ser.: Vol. 3). audio 56.00 (*0-7366-3997-7*, 4497) Books on Tape, Inc.

—Watery Grave. 1996. (Sir John Fielding Mystery Ser.). 272p. 22.95 o.p. (*0-399-14155-3*, G. P. Putnam's Sons) Penguin Group (USA) Inc.

—Watery Grave. l.t. ed. 1998. (Ulverscroft Large Print Ser.). 544p. 29.99 o.p. (*0-7089-3984-8*, Ulverscroft) Thorpe, F. A. Pubs. GBR. *Dist:* Ulverscroft Large Print Bks., Ltd., Ulverscroft Large Print Canada, Ltd.

Alexander, Kate. The House of Hope. 1994. 352p. 21.95 o.p. (*0-312-10997-0*) St. Martin's Pr.

—The House of Hope. l.t. ed. 1994. (Charnwood Ser.). 528p. 29.99 (*0-7089-8752-4*, Charnwood) Thorpe, F. A. Pubs. GBR. *Dist:* Ulverscroft Large Print Bks., Ltd., Ulverscroft Large Print Canada, Ltd.

—Paths of Peace. 1984. 320p. 14.95 o.p. (*0-312-59801-7*) St. Martin's Pr.

—Paths of Peace. l.t. ed. 1985. (Charnwood Large Print Ser.). 448p. 15.45 o.p. (*0-7089-8300-6*, Charnwood) Thorpe, F. A. Pubs. GBR. *Dist:* Ulverscroft Large Print Bks., Ltd., Ulverscroft Large Print Canada, Ltd.

Alexander, Victoria. Her Highness, My Wife. l.t. ed. 2003. (Romance Ser.). 30.95 (*1-58724-373-3*, Wheeler Publishing, Inc.) Gale Group.

—Her Highness, My Wife. 2002. 384p. mass mkt. 6.99 (*0-06-000144-5*, Avon Bks.) Morrow/Avon.

—The Husband List. l.t. ed. 2002. (Wheeler Large Print Book Ser.). pap. 23.95 (*1-58724-173-0*, Wheeler Publishing, Inc.) Gale Group.

—The Husband List. 2000. (Avon Romantic Treasure Ser.). 384p. mass mkt. 5.99 (*0-380-80631-2*, Avon Bks.) Morrow/Avon.

—The Marriage Lesson. 2001. 384p. mass mkt. 5.99 (0-380-81820-5, Avon Bks.) Morrow/Avon.

Allbeury, Ted. All Our Tomorrows. 1989. 272p. 18.95 o.p. (0-89296-183-X) Mysterious Pr.

—All Our Tomorrows. 1990. 304p. mass mkt. 4.95 (0-445-40914-2, Mysterious Pr. Paperback Bks.) Warner Bks., Inc.

Allen, Grant. The Woman Who Did. Wintle, Sarah & Trotter, David, eds. 1995. (Oxford Popular Fiction Ser.). 148p. pap. 8.95 o.p. (0-19-282312-4) Oxford Univ. Pr., Inc.

Allingham, Margery. The Allingham Case-Book. 18.95 o.p. (0-89190-915-X) Amereon, Ltd.

—The Allingham Case-Book. 2nd ed. 1992. 240p. mass mkt. 3.95 (0-88184-889-1, Carroll & Graf Pubs.) Avalon Publishing Group.

—The Allingham Case-Book. 1998. 224p. lib. bdg. 21.95 (1-56723-000-8) Yestermorrow, Inc.

—The Black Dudley Murder. 176p. reprint ed. lib. bdg. 19.95 o.p. (0-89190-188-4, Rivercity Pr.) Amereon, Ltd.

—The Black Dudley Murder. 2000. 224p. mass mkt. 5.95 (0-7867-0754-2, Carroll & Graf Pubs.) Avalon Publishing Group.

—The Black Dudley Murder. 1994. reprint ed. lib. bdg. 27.95 (1-56849-252-9) Buccaneer Bks., Inc.

—The Black Dudley Murder. 1988. 224p. mass mkt. 3.99 (0-380-70575-3, Avon Bks.) Morrow/Avon.

—The Black Dudley Murder. 1998. 227p. lib. bdg. 22.95 (1-56723-001-6) Yestermorrow, Inc.

—Black Plumes. 1993. 276p. reprint ed. 19.95 o.p. (0-89190-191-4) Amereon, Ltd.

—Black Plumes. 1995. 192p. mass mkt. 3.95 (0-7867-0290-7, Carroll & Graf Pubs.) Avalon Publishing Group.

—Black Plumes. 1985. mass mkt. 2.95 o.s.i (0-553-25214-3) Bantam Bks.

—Black Plumes. 1994. lib. bdg. 18.95 (1-56849-458-0) Buccaneer Bks., Inc.

—Black Plumes. 1944. mass mkt. 0.25 o.p. (0-451-00534-1, Signet Bks.) NAL.

—Black Plumes. 1998. lib. bdg. 23.95 (1-56723-002-4) Yestermorrow, Inc.

—Cargo of Eagles. 1989. pap. (0-7012-0612-8) Chatto & Windus GBR. Dist: Random Hse. of Canada, Ltd.

—Cargo of Eagles. 1990. 224p. reprint ed. mass mkt. 3.99 (0-380-70576-1, Avon Bks.) Morrow/Avon.

—Cargo of Eagles. 1998. 206p. lib. bdg. 21.95 (1-56723-003-2) Yestermorrow, Inc.

—The Case of the Late Pig. (0-7540-3642-1); 1999. 165 p. (0-7540-3641-3) BBC Audiobooks America.

—The Case of the Late Pig. abr. ed. 1990. audio 16.99 (0-88646-264-9, 7264) Durkin Hayes Publishing Ltd.

—The Case of the Late Pig. 1989. 160p. mass mkt. 3.50 (0-380-70577-X, Avon Bks.) Morrow/Avon.

—The Case of the Late Pig. l.t. ed. 1999. (G. K. Hall Nightingale Ser.). 176p. pap. 19.95 (0-7838-8507-5) Thorndike Pr.

—The China Governess. 1990. 272p. mass mkt. 4.50 (0-380-70578-8, Avon Bks.) Morrow/Avon.

—The China Governess. l.t. ed. 1979. (Ulverscroft Large Print Ser.). 463p. 12.50 o.p. (0-7089-0353-3, Ulverscroft) Thorpe, F. A. Pubs. GBR. Dist: Ulverscroft Large Print Bks., Ltd., Ulverscroft Large Print Canada, Ltd.

—The China Governess. 1998. 224p. lib. bdg. 21.95 (1-56723-004-0) Yestermorrow, Inc.

—Coroner's Pidgin. 1993. 243p. 19.95 o.p. (0-89190-177-9) Amereon, Ltd.

—Coroner's Pidgin. unabr. ed. 1996. (Albert Campion Mysteries Ser.). audio 54.95 (0-7451-5734-3, CAB182) BBC Audiobooks America.

—Coroner's Pidgin. l.t. ed. 1979. 418p. 12.00 o.p. (0-7089-0269-3, Ulverscroft) Thorpe, F. A. Pubs. GBR. Dist: Ulverscroft Large Print Bks., Ltd.

—Coroner's Pidgin. 1998. lib. bdg. 22.95 (1-56723-005-9) Yestermorrow, Inc.

—The Crime at Black Dudley. l.t. ed. 1978. 388p. 12.00 o.p. (0-7089-0130-1, Ulverscroft) Thorpe, F. A. Pubs. GBR. Dist: Ulverscroft Large Print Bks., Ltd.

—The Crime at Black Dudley. 1983.; 1950. pap. 2.50 o.p. (0-14-000770-9, Penguin Bks.) Viking Penguin.

—Dancers in Mourning. 1993. 240p. reprint ed. lib. bdg. 19.95 o.p. (0-89190-189-2) Amereon, Ltd.

—Dancers in Mourning. 1996. (Albert Campion Mysteries Ser.). 272p. mass mkt. 4.95 (0-7867-0384-9, Carroll & Graf Pubs.) Avalon Publishing Group.

—Dancers in Mourning. 1984. 256p. pap. text 2.95 o.p. (0-553-24852-9); 1983. 272p. mass mkt. 3.95 o.s.i (0-553-23880-9) Bantam Bks.

—Dancers in Mourning. 1976. (Crime Fiction Ser.). reprint ed. lib. bdg. 21.00 o.p. (0-8240-2351-X) Garland Publishing, Inc.

—Dancers in Mourning. l.t. ed. 1978. 548p. 12.00 o.p. (0-7089-0213-8, Ulverscroft) Thorpe, F. A. Pubs. GBR. Dist: Ulverscroft Large Print Bks., Ltd.

—Dancers in Mourning. 1998. lib. bdg. 22.95 (1-56723-006-7) Yestermorrow, Inc.

—Deadly Duo. 1993. 167p. 16.95 o.p. (0-89190-193-0) Amereon, Ltd.

—Deadly Duo. 1985. 208p. mass mkt. 2.95 o.s.i (0-553-25411-1) Bantam Bks.

—Deadly Duo. 1993. reprint ed. lib. bdg. 15.95 (0-89968-452-1) Buccaneer Bks., Inc.

—Deadly Duo. 1998. lib. bdg. 19.95 (1-56723-007-5) Yestermorrow, Inc.

—Death of a Ghost. 1993. 175p. reprint ed. 16.95 (0-89190-195-7) Amereon, Ltd.

—Death of a Ghost. 1997. 192p. mass mkt. 4.95 (0-7867-0441-1, Carroll & Graf Pubs.) Avalon Publishing Group.

—Death of a Ghost. 1985. 224p. mass mkt. 4.50 o.s.i (0-553-24958-4) Bantam Bks.

—Death of a Ghost. 1993. reprint ed. lib. bdg. 15.95 (0-89968-453-X) Buccaneer Bks., Inc.

—Death of a Ghost. unabr. ed. 2001. (Albert Campion Mystery Ser.: Bk. 6). audio 59.95 (0-7451-5724-6, CAB 228) Chivers Audio Bks. GBR. Dist: BBC Audiobooks America.

—Death of a Ghost. 1987. audio 69.95 o.s.i (0-8161-7680-9) Thorndike Pr.

—Death of a Ghost. 1998. 175p. lib. bdg. 19.95 (1-56723-008-3) Yestermorrow, Inc.

—The Estate of the Beckoning Lady. 1990. 256p. mass mkt. 3.99 (0-380-70574-5, Avon Bks.) Morrow/Avon.

—The Estate of the Beckoning Lady. 1998. lib. bdg. 22.95 (1-56723-009-1) Yestermorrow, Inc.

—Fashion in Shrouds. 1993. 255p. reprint ed. 19.95 o.p. (0-89190-194-9) Amereon, Ltd.

—Fashion in Shrouds. 1995. 280p. mass mkt. 4.95 (0-7867-0224-9, Carroll & Graf Pubs.) Avalon Publishing Group.

—Fashion in Shrouds. 1985. 288p. mass mkt. 2.95 o.s.i (0-553-25412-X) Bantam Bks.

—Fashion in Shrouds. 1993. reprint ed. lib. bdg. 18.95 (0-89968-454-8) Buccaneer Bks., Inc.

—Fashion in Shrouds. 2002. 10p. 94.95 (0-7540-5536-1, CCD 227); Set. 2000. (Albert Campion Mystery Ser.: No. 10). audio 84.95 (0-7540-0418-X, CAB 1841) Chivers Audio Bks. GBR. Dist: BBC Audiobooks America.

—Fashion in Shrouds. 1986. o.p. (0-434-01875-9) David & Charles Pubs.

—Fashion in Shrouds. l.t. ed. 432p. 2001. pap. 21.99 o.p. (0-7531-6208-3); 2000. 32.50 (0-7531-6102-8) ISIS Large Print Bks. GBR. Dist: Ulverscroft Large Print Bks., Ltd., Ulverscroft Large Print Canada, Ltd.

—Fashion in Shrouds. l.t. ed. 1978. 579p. 12.00 o.p. (0-7089-0152-2, Ulverscroft) Thorpe, F. A. Pubs. GBR. Dist: Ulverscroft Large Print Bks., Ltd.

—Fashion in Shrouds. 1998. lib. bdg. 22.95 (1-56723-010-5) Yestermorrow, Inc.

—The Fear Sign. 192p. reprint ed. lib. bdg. 17.95 o.p. (0-89190-190-6, Rivercity Pr.) Amereon, Ltd.

—The Fear Sign. 2000. 240p. mass mkt. 5.95 (0-7867-0755-0, Carroll & Graf Pubs.) Avalon Publishing Group.

—The Fear Sign. 1989. 240p. pap. 3.95 (0-380-70571-0, Avon Bks.) Morrow/Avon.

—The Fear Sign. 1998. lib. bdg. 20.95 (1-56723-011-3) Yestermorrow, Inc.

—Flowers for the Judge. 1995. (Illus.). 248p. mass mkt. 4.50 (0-7867-0291-5, Carroll & Graf Pubs.) Avalon Publishing Group.

—Flowers for the Judge. 1984. 256p. mass mkt. 3.95 o.s.i (0-553-24190-7) Bantam Bks.

—The Gyrth Chalice Mystery. 1989. 256p. mass mkt. 3.99 (0-380-70572-9, Avon Bks.) Morrow/Avon.

—Hide My Eyes. unabr. ed. 1995. audio 54.95 (0-7451-5725-4, CAB 111) BBC Audiobooks America.

—Look to the Lady. unabr. ed. 1989. audio 54.95 (0-7451-5726-2, CAB 365) BBC Audiobooks America.

—Look to the Lady. l.t. unabr. ed. 2000. 320p. o.p. (0-7531-6101-X, 16101X) ISIS Large Print Bks. GBR. Dist: Ulverscroft Large Print Canada, Ltd.

—Look to the Lady. l.t. ed. 1979. 414p. 12.00 o.p. (0-7089-0293-6, Ulverscroft) Thorpe, F. A. Pubs. GBR. Dist: Ulverscroft Large Print Bks., Ltd.

—Look to the Lady. 1983. Viking Penguin.

—The Margery Allingham Omnibus. Incl. Crime at Black Dudley, Look to the Lady, Mystery Mile. Matthews, Francis, reader. 29.95 592p. 1983. Set pap. 7.95 o.p. (0-14-006058-8, Penguin Bks.) Viking Penguin.

—The Mind Readers. 20.95 o.p. (0-89190-179-5) Amereon, Ltd.

—The Mind Readers. 1990. 272p. pap. 3.95 (0-380-70570-2, Avon Bks.) Morrow/Avon.

—The Mind Readers. 1998. 286p. lib. bdg. 23.95 (1-56723-012-1) Yestermorrow, Inc.

—More Work for the Undertaker. 19.95 o.p. (0-89190-180-9) Amereon, Ltd.

—More Work for the Undertaker. 1989. 272p. mass mkt. 3.95 (0-380-70573-7, Avon Bks.) Morrow/Avon.

—More Work for the Undertaker. 1952. pap. 3.50 o.p. (0-14-000864-0) Penguin Group (USA) Inc.

—More Work for the Undertaker. 1988. audio 49.95 o.p. (0-8161-9448-3) Thorndike Pr.

—More Work for the Undertaker. l.t. ed. 1978. (Ulverscroft Large Print Ser.). 470p. 29.99 o.p. (0-7089-0233-2, Ulverscroft) Thorpe, F. A. Pubs. GBR. Dist: Ulverscroft Large Print Bks., Ltd., Ulverscroft Large Print Canada, Ltd.

—More Work for the Undertaker. 1998. 253p. lib. bdg. 22.95 (1-56723-013-X) Yestermorrow, Inc.

—Mr. Campion & Others. 1991. 272p. mass mkt. 3.95 (0-380-70579-6, Avon Bks.) Morrow/Avon.

—Mr. Campion & Others. 1950. pap. 1.95 o.p. (0-14-000762-8, Penguin Bks.) Viking Penguin.

—Mr. Campion's Lucky Day & Other Stories. 1992. 240p. mass mkt. 3.95 (0-88184-890-5, Carroll & Graf Pubs.) Avalon Publishing Group.

—Mystery Mile. 22.95 o.p. (0-89190-178-7) Amereon, Ltd.

—Mystery Mile. unabr. ed. 2000. (Albert Campion Mysteries Ser.). audio 29.95 (1-57270-137-4, N61137u, Audio Editions Bks. on Cassette) Audio Partners Publishing Corp.

—Mystery Mile. 1994. 250p. mass mkt. 4.50 (0-7867-0168-4, Carroll & Graf Pubs.) Avalon Publishing Group.

—Mystery Mile. 1990. 256p. mass mkt. 3.95 o.s.i (0-553-29013-4) Bantam Bks.

—Mystery Mile. unabr. ed. (Albert Campion Mystery Ser.). 2000. 8p. audio compact disk 79.95 (0-7540-5336-9, CCD 027); 1992. audio 59.95 (0-7451-5728-9, CAB 651) Chivers Audio Bks. GBR. Dist: BBC Audiobooks America.

—Mystery Mile. l.t. ed. 1975. 388p. 12.00 o.p. (0-85456-358-X, Ulverscroft) Thorpe, F. A. Pubs. GBR. Dist: Ulverscroft Large Print Bks., Ltd.

—Mystery Mile. 1983. 29.95; 1950. pap. 2.50 o.p. (0-14-000761-X, Penguin Bks.) Viking Penguin.

—Mystery Mile. 1998. 264p. lib. bdg. 25.95 (1-56723-014-8) Yestermorrow, Inc.

—Pearls Before Swine. 192p. reprint ed. lib. bdg. 18.95 (0-89190-196-5, Rivercity Pr.) Amereon, Ltd.

—Pearls Before Swine. 1996. 224p. mass mkt. 4.95 (0-7867-0338-5, Carroll & Graf Pubs.) Avalon Publishing Group.

—Pearls Before Swine. 1984. 224p. mass mkt. 2.95 o.s.i (0-553-24548-1) Bantam Bks.

—Pearls Before Swine. 1998. 240p. lib. bdg. 21.95 (1-56723-016-4) Yestermorrow, Inc.

—Police at the Funeral. 1994. 232p. mass mkt. 3.95 (0-7867-0169-2, Carroll & Graf Pubs.) Avalon Publishing Group.

—Police at the Funeral. 1989. 240p. mass mkt. 3.95 o.s.i (0-553-28506-8) Bantam Bks.

—Police at the Funeral. 1949. pap. 3.50 o.p. (0-14-000219-7, Penguin Bks.) Viking Penguin.

—Police at the Funeral. 1998. lib. bdg. 21.95 (1-56723-017-2) Yestermorrow, Inc.

—The Return of Mr. Campion: Uncollected Stories. Morpurgo, J. E., ed. & intro. by. 1991. 192p. pap. 3.95 (0-380-71448-5, Avon Bks.) Morrow/Avon.

—The Return of Mr. Campion: Uncollected Stories. Morpurgo, J. E., ed. & intro. by. 1990. 15.95 o.p. (0-312-04413-5, Saint Martin's Minotaur) St. Martin's Pr.

—Sweet Danger. l.t. ed. 1981. (Ulverscroft Large Print Ser.). o.p. (0-7089-0589-7, Ulverscroft) Thorpe, F. A. Pubs. GBR. Dist: Ulverscroft Large Print Canada, Ltd.

—Sweet Danger. 1988. 256p. mass mkt. 5.95 (0-14-008779-6, Penguin Bks.); 1950. pap. 3.50 o.p. (0-14-000769-5) Viking Penguin.

—Take Two at Bedtime. Date not set. lib. bdg. 20.95 (0-8488-1951-9) Amereon, Ltd.

—Tether's End. 176p. reprint ed. lib. bdg. 16.95 (0-89190-197-3, Rivercity Pr.) Amereon, Ltd.

—Tether's End. 1984. 208p. mass mkt. 3.95 o.s.i (0-553-25102-3); 1983. mass mkt. 3.95 o.s.i (0-553-23605-9) Bantam Bks.

—Tether's End. 1998. 216p. lib. bdg. 20.95 (1-56723-018-0) Yestermorrow, Inc.

—The Tiger in the Smoke. 21.95 (0-89190-198-1) Amereon, Ltd.

—The Tiger in the Smoke. 232p. 2000. mass mkt. 5.95 (0-7867-0719-4); 1995. mass mkt. 4.95 o.p. (0-7867-0225-7) Avalon Publishing Group. (Carroll & Graf Pubs.).

—The Tiger in the Smoke, Set. unabr. ed. 1990. audio 69.95 (0-7451-5737-8, CAB 482) BBC Audiobooks America.

—The Tiger in the Smoke. 1985. 240p. pap. 2.95 o.p. (0-553-24814-6) Bantam Bks.

—The Tiger in the Smoke. 1994. lib. bdg. 17.95 (1-56849-459-9) Buccaneer Bks., Inc.

—Traitor's Purse. 176p. reprint ed. lib. bdg. 16.95 (0-89190-199-X, Rivercity Pr.) Amereon, Ltd.

—Traitor's Purse. unabr. ed. 2002. audio (1-57270-159-5) Audio Partners Publishing Corp.

—Traitor's Purse. 1997. 224p. mass mkt. 4.95 (0-7867-0447-0, Carroll & Graf Pubs.) Avalon Publishing Group.

—Traitor's Purse. unabr. ed. 1998. audio 54.95 (0-7451-5733-5, CAB259) BBC Audiobooks America.

—Traitor's Purse. 1990. 192p. mass mkt. 4.50 o.s.i (0-553-23822-1) Bantam Bks.

—Traitor's Purse. 1994. reprint ed. lib. bdg. 24.95 (1-56849-251-0) Buccaneer Bks., Inc.

—Traitor's Purse. 1998. 176p. lib. bdg. 19.95 (1-56723-019-9) Yestermorrow, Inc.

Allingham, Margery & Carter, Youngman. Mr. Campion's Farthing. 1990. 191p. mass mkt. 3.95 (0-88184-667-8, Carroll & Graf Pubs.) Avalon Publishing Group.

—Mr. Campion's Quarry. 1991. 240p. mass mkt. 3.95 (0-88184-724-0, Carroll & Graf Pubs.) Avalon Publishing Group.

Amis, Kingsley. Difficulties with Girls. 1991. 3.99 o.p. (0-517-06319-0) Random Hse. Value Publishing.

—Difficulties with Girls. 1989. 304p. 18.95 o.p. (0-671-67582-6) Summit Bks.

—The Folks That Live on the Hill. 1990. 18.95 o.p. (0-671-70816-3) Summit Bks.

—Girl, 20. 1989. 248p. 8.95 o.p. (0-671-67120-0) Summit Bks.

—Jake's Thing. 1980. 288p. pap. 7.95 o.p. (0-14-005096-5, Penguin Bks.); 1979. 11.95 o.p. (0-670-40471-3) Viking Penguin.

—Stanley & the Women. 1988. 256p. reprint ed. pap. 6.95 o.p. (0-06-097145-2, PL-7145, Perennial) HarperTrade.

—Stanley & the Women. 1985. 256p. 14.70 o.p. (0-671-60317-5) Summit Bks.

Amis, Martin. London Fields. 1991. (Vintage International Ser.). 480p. pap. 14.00 (0-679-73034-6, Vintage) Knopf Publishing Group.

—Other People: A Mystery Story. 1994. 224p. pap. 13.00 (0-679-73589-5, Vintage) Knopf Publishing Group.

—Other People: A Mystery Story. 1981. 12.95 o.p. (0-670-52948-6) Viking Penguin.

—The Rachel Papers. 1992. 240p. pap. 12.00 (0-679-73458-9, Vintage) Knopf Publishing Group.

Ammerman, Lisa. Hunger Hill. 2003. 234p. pap. 15.95 (0-595-29881-8) iUniverse, Inc.

Ammerman, Mark. The Rain from God. 1997. (Cross & the Tomahawk Ser.: Vol. I). (Illus.). 320p. (J). pap. 11.99 (0-88965-134-5, Horizon Bks.) Christian Pubns., Inc.

Anand, Valerie. The Cherished Wives: Book V of Bridges over Time. 1995. 352p. 23.95 o.p. (0-312-13943-8) St. Martin's Pr.

Anderson, Caroline. Just a Family Doctor. l.t. ed. 2001. (Mills & Boon Large Print Ser.). 288p. 27.99 (0-263-16832-8) Harlequin Mills & Boon, Ltd. GBR. Dist: Ulverscroft Large Print Bks., Ltd., Ulverscroft Large Print Canada, Ltd.

—Sarah's Gift. 1999. (Promo Ser.). mass mkt. o.s.i (0-373-63117-0, 1-63117-5, Harlequin Bks.) Harlequin Enterprises, Ltd.

—Sarah's Gift. l.t. ed. 1999. (Mills & Boon Large Print Ser.). 288p. 25.99 o.p. (0-263-15904-3) Harlequin Mills & Boon, Ltd. GBR. Dist: Ulverscroft Large Print Bks., Ltd., Ulverscroft Large Print Canada, Ltd.

Anderson, Gabriella. Destiny Coin: A Matter of Convenience. 2000. (Ballad Romances Ser.). 32p. mass mkt. 5.50 o.s.i (0-8217-6682-1, Zebra Bks.) Kensington Publishing Corp.

—The Destiny Coin: A Matter of Pride. 2001. (Romances Ser.). 32p. mass mkt. 5.50 o.s.i (0-8217-6765-8) Kensington Publishing Corp.

Andrews, Lyn. Leaving Liverpool. 2000. 381p. pap. 10.95 (0-552-13933-5) Transworld Publishers Ltd. GBR. Dist: Trafalgar Square.

—Liverpool Lamplight. l.t. ed. 1998. (Magna Large Print Ser.). 544p. o.p. (0-7505-1194-X) Magna Large Print Bks. GBR. Dist: Ulverscroft Large Print Canada, Ltd.

—Liverpool Lou. 2000. 382p. (J). pap. 9.95 (0-552-13718-9) Transworld Publishers Ltd. GBR. Dist: Trafalgar Square.

—Liverpool Songbird. l.t. ed. 1997. (Magna Large Print Ser.). 571p. 29.99 o.p. (0-7505-1124-9) Magna Large Print Bks. GBR. Dist: Ulverscroft Large Print Bks., Ltd., Ulverscroft Large Print Canada, Ltd.

—The Sisters O'Donnell. 2000. pap. 11.95 (0-552-13600-X) Transworld Publishers Ltd. GBR. Dist: Trafalgar Square.

Andrews, Mark. The Return of Jack the Ripper. 1977. pap. 1.75 o.p. (0-8439-0476-3) Dorchester Publishing Co., Inc.

Andrews, V. C. Lightning Strikes. 2001. 424p. (0-7540-2432-6); (0-7540-1570-X) Gale Group. (Macmillan Reference USA).

—Lightning Strikes. 2000. (Hudson Family Ser.: Vol. 2). 368p. 24.95 o.s.i (*0-671-00768-8*, Atria); 384p. pap. 7.99 (*0-671-00769-6*, Pocket) Simon & Schuster.

—Lightning Strikes. l.t. ed. 2001. (G. K. Hall Core Ser.). (Illus.). 352p. 31.95 (*0-7838-9316-7*) Thorndike Pr.

—Lightning Strikes. 2000. (Illus.). (J). 14.04 (*0-606-18830-4*) Turtleback Bks.

Andrews, Val. Sherlock Holmes & the Baker Street Dozen: A Collection of Thirteen Short Stories. 1997. 126p. pap. 13.95 (*0-947533-41-9*) Breese Bks., Ltd. GBR. *Dist:* Midpoint Trade Bks., Inc.

—Sherlock Holmes & the Brighton Pavilion Mystery. 1991. 124p. 25.00 (*0-86025-269-8*) Henry, Ian Pubns. GBR. *Dist:* Empire Publishing Service.

—Sherlock Holmes & the Circus of Fear. 1997. 112p. pap. 13.95 o.s.i (*0-947533-17-6*) Breese Bks., Ltd. GBR. *Dist:* Midpoint Trade Bks., Inc.

—Sherlock Holmes & the Egyptian Hall Adventure. 1997. 112p. pap. 9.95 (*0-947533-43-5*) Breese Bks., Ltd. GBR. *Dist:* Midpoint Trade Bks., Inc.

—Sherlock Holmes & the Egyptian Hall Adventure. l.t. ed. 1998. (Linford Mystery Large Print Ser.). 208p. pap. 17.99 (*0-7089-5346-8*, Linford) Thorpe, F. A. Pubs. GBR. *Dist:* Ulverscroft Large Print Bks., Ltd., Ulverscroft Large Print Canada, Ltd.

—Sherlock Holmes & the Eminent Thespian. 1991. 124p. 25.00 (*0-86025-268-X*) Henry, Ian Pubns. GBR. *Dist:* Empire Publishing Service.

—Sherlock Holmes & the Greyfriars School Mystery. 1997. 109p. pap. 10.95 (*0-947533-55-9*) Breese Bks., Ltd. GBR. *Dist:* Midpoint Trade Bks., Inc.

—Sherlock Holmes & the Greyfriars School Mystery. l.t. ed. 1999. (Linford Mystery Large Print Ser.). 192p. pap. 18.99 (*0-7089-5442-1*, Ulverscroft) Thorpe, F. A. Pubs. GBR. *Dist:* Ulverscroft Large Print Bks., Ltd., Ulverscroft Large Print Canada, Ltd.

—Sherlock Holmes & the Houdini Birthright. 1997. (Sherlock Holmes Mysteries Ser.). 160p. pap. 10.95 (*0-947533-91-5*) Breese Bks., Ltd. GBR. *Dist:* Midpoint Trade Bks., Inc.

—Sherlock Holmes & the Long Acre Vampire: A Sherlock Holmes Mystery. 2000. (Sherlock Holmes Mysteries Ser.). 128p. pap. 14.95 (*0-947533-29-X*) Breese Bks., Ltd. GBR. *Dist:* Midpoint Trade Bks., Inc.

—Sherlock Holmes & the Man Who Lost Himself. 1997. 112p. pap. 10.95 (*0-947533-70-2*) Breese Bks., Ltd. GBR. *Dist:* Midpoint Trade Bks., Inc.

—Sherlock Holmes & the Man Who Lost Himself. l.t. ed. 1998. (Linford Mystery Large Print Ser.). 224p. pap. 17.99 (*0-7089-5334-4*, Linford) Thorpe, F. A. Pubs. GBR. *Dist:* Ulverscroft Large Print Bks., Ltd., Ulverscroft Large Print Canada, Ltd.

—Sherlock Holmes & the Sandringham House Mystery. 1999. pap. (*0-947533-53-2*) Breese Bks., Ltd.

—Sherlock Holmes & the Sandringham House Mystery. l.t. ed. 2000. (Linford Mystery Large Print Ser.). 200p. pap. 18.99 o.p. (*0-7089-5772-2*, Linford) Thorpe, F. A. Pubs. GBR. *Dist:* Ulverscroft Large Print Bks., Ltd., Ulverscroft Large Print Canada, Ltd.

—Sherlock Holmes & the Theatre of Death. 1997. 125p. pap. 13.95 (*0-947533-12-5*) Breese Bks., Ltd. GBR. *Dist:* Midpoint Trade Bks., Inc.

—Sherlock Holmes & the Theatre of Death. l.t. ed. 2000. (Linford Mystery Large Print Ser.). 216p. pap. 18.99 o.p. (*0-7089-5900-8*, Linford) Thorpe, F. A. Pubs. GBR. *Dist:* Ulverscroft Large Print Bks., Ltd., Ulverscroft Large Print Canada, Ltd.

—Sherlock Holmes & the Tomb of Terror. 2000. (Sherlock Holmes Ser.). 160p. pap. 14.95 (*0-947533-72-9*) Breese Bks., Ltd. GBR. *Dist:* Midpoint Trade Bks., Inc.

—Sherlock Holmes & the Yule-Tide Mystery. 1996. 112p. pap. 10.95 (*0-947533-11-7*) Breese Bks., Ltd. GBR. *Dist:* Midpoint Trade Bks., Inc.

—Sherlock Holmes & the Yule-Tide Mystery. l.t. ed. 1998. (Linford Mystery Large Print Ser.). 224p. pap. 17.99 (*0-7089-5394-8*, Linford) Thorpe, F. A. Pubs. GBR. *Dist:* Ulverscroft Large Print Bks., Ltd., Ulverscroft Large Print Canada, Ltd.

—Sherlock Holmes at the Varieties. 2000. (Sherlock Holmes Ser.). 196p. pap. 12.95 (*0-947533-82-6*) Breese Bks., Ltd. GBR. *Dist:* Midpoint Trade Bks., Inc.

—Sherlock Holmes on the Western Front. 2000. (Sherlock Holmes Ser.). 128p. pap. 14.95 (*0-947533-87-7*) Breese Bks., Ltd. GBR. *Dist:* Midpoint Trade Bks., Inc.

Anonymous. Girl's Reformatory. 2001. 256p. pap. 7.95 (*1-56201-237-1*, Blue Moon Bks.) Avalon Publishing Group.

—Sir Gawain & the Green Knight. 2001. 144p. mass mkt. 6.95 (*0-451-52818-2*) NAL.

—Sir Gawain & the Green Knight. Raffel, Burton, ed. & tr. by. 1970. mass mkt. 1.25 o.p. (*0-451-61330-9*); mass mkt. 1.50 o.p. (*0-451-61548-4*); mass mkt. 1.75 o.p. (*0-451-61848-3*); mass mkt. 1.95 o.p. (*0-451-62092-5*); mass mkt. 2.25 o.p. (*0-451-62312-6*); mass mkt. 0.95 o.p. (*0-451-61028-8*) NAL. (Signet Bks.).

Anthony, Evelyn. The Doll's House. 1992. 288p. 20.00 o.p. (*0-06-017981-3*) HarperTrade.

—Exposure. l.t. ed. 1994. 486p. lib. bdg. 23.95 (*0-8161-7429-6*, Macmillan Reference USA) Gale Group.

—Exposure. 1994. 288p. 22.00 o.p. (*0-06-017774-8*) HarperTrade.

—The Legacy. l.t. ed. 1998. 361 p. (*0-7540-2118-1*); audio 69.95 (*0-7540-0121-0*, CAB1544) BBC Audiobooks America.

—The Legacy. 1998. 381p. mass mkt. o.s.i (*0-552-14242-5*, Corgi); 1997. 253p. o.s.i (*0-593-03659-X*) Bantam Bks.

—The Legacy. l.t. ed. 1998. (G. K. Hall Mystery Ser.). 367p. 24.95 o.p. (*0-7838-0176-9*, Macmillan Reference USA) Gale Group.

Anthony, Michael D. Becket Factor. 1991. 17.95 o.p. (*0-312-05821-7*, Saint Martin's Minotaur) St. Martin's Pr.

—Dark Provenance. 1995. 256p. 21.00 o.p. (*0-312-11767-1*, Saint Martin's Minotaur) St. Martin's Pr.

—Dark Provenance. l.t. ed. 1995. (Ulverscroft Large Print Ser.). 528p. 29.99 o.p. (*0-7089-3324-6*, Ulverscroft) Thorpe, F. A. Pubs. GBR. *Dist:* Ulverscroft Large Print Bks., Ltd., Ulverscroft Large Print Canada, Ltd.

—Midnight Come. 1999. 302p. 22.95 (*0-312-20058-7*, Saint Martin's Minotaur) St. Martin's Pr.

Archer, Jeffrey. As the Crow Flies. 1991. 608p. 275.40 o.p. (*0-06-017915-5*) HarperCollins Pubs.

—As the Crow Flies. 1991. 22.95 o.p. (*0-06-017914-7*); 608p. pap. 24.95 o.p. (*0-06-017916-3*) HarperTrade.

—As the Crow Flies. 1992. 800p. mass mkt. 7.99 (*0-06-109934-1*, HarperTorch) Morrow/Avon.

—As the Crow Flies. 1992. 5.99 o.p. (*0-517-09222-0*); 5.99 o.p. (*0-517-09221-2*) Random Hse. Value Publishing.

—Twelve Red Herrings. l.t. ed. 1994. 25.95 o.p. (*1-56895-150-7*, Wheeler Publishing, Inc.) Gale Group.

—Twelve Red Herrings. 1994. 320p. 276.00 o.p. (*0-06-017625-3*) HarperCollins Pubs.

—Twelve Red Herrings. 1994. 320p. 23.00 o.p. (*0-06-017944-9*); Set. 1999. audio (*0-694-51473-X*, 692334, HarperAudio) HarperTrade.

—Twelve Red Herrings. 1995. 384p. mass mkt. 7.99 (*0-06-109365-3*, HarperTorch) Morrow/Avon.

Arditti, Michael. Pagan's Father. 2000. 416p. pap. 14.00 (*1-56947-183-5*); 1996. 436p. 24.00 o.p. (*1-56947-062-6*) Soho Pr., Inc.

Argers, Helen. Noblesse Oblige. l.t. ed. 1995. 424p. reprint ed. lib. bdg. 22.95 (*0-7838-1230-2*, Macmillan Reference USA) Gale Group.

—Noblesse Oblige. 1994. 320p. 21.95 o.p. (*0-312-11324-2*) St. Martin's Pr.

Arkell, Reginald. Old Herbaceous: A Novel of the Garden. 2003. (Modern Library Gardening). (Illus.). 176p. pap. 11.95 (*0-8129-6738-0*, Modern Library) Random House Adult Trade Publishing Group.

Armitage, Aileen. The Dark Arches. l.t. ed. 1997. (General Ser.). 497p. pap. 22.95 (*0-7862-1129-6*) Thorndike Pr.

Armstrong, Martin D. Bazaar & Other Stories. 1977. (Short Story Index Reprint Ser.). 22.95 (*0-8369-3278-1*) Ayer Co. Pubs., Inc.

Armstrong, Vivien. Dead in the Water. l.t. ed. 2000. (Dales Large Print Ser.). 352p. pap. 20.99 o.p. (*1-84137-016-9*) Magna Large Print Bks. GBR. *Dist:* Ulverscroft Large Print Bks., Ltd., Ulverscroft Large Print Canada, Ltd.

—Dead in the Water. 1999. 224p. 25.00 (*0-7278-2229-2*) Severn Hse. Pubs., Ltd.

—Rewind. 2001. 224p. 25.99 (*0-7278-5699-5*); 28.99 (*0-7278-7146-3*) Severn Hse. Pubs., Ltd.

Arnold, Margot, pseud. Death on the Dragon's Tongue. 1982. 224p. 2.50 (*0-86721-150-4*, Jove) Berkley Publishing Group.

—Death on the Dragon's Tongue. 1990. (Penny Spring & Sir Toby Glendower Mystery Ser.). 224p. reprint ed. pap. 7.95 (*0-88150-158-1*, Foul Play) Norton, W. W. & Co., Inc.

—Dirge for a Dorset Druid. (Penny Spring & Sir Toby Glendower Mystery Ser.). 240p. 1995. pap. 7.95 (*0-88150-334-7*); 1993. 20.00 (*0-88150-266-9*) Norton, W. W. & Co., Inc. (Foul Play).

—Toby's Folly. 1990. 256p. 18.95 o.p. (*0-88150-177-8*) Countryman Pr.

—Toby's Folly. 1992. (Penny Spring & Sir Toby Glendower Mystery Ser.). 256p. pap. 7.95 (*0-88150-228-6*, Foul Play) Norton, W. W. & Co., Inc.

Ashford, Jeffrey. Judgement Deferred. l.t. ed. 1995. (Nightingale Ser.). 252p. pap. 17.95 (*0-8161-7470-9*, Macmillan Reference USA) Gale Group.

—Judgment Deferred. 1994. 176p. 18.95 o.p. (*0-312-11012-X*, Saint Martin's Minotaur) St. Martin's Pr.

—Loyal Disloyalty. 1998. 192p. 20.95 (*0-312-19918-X*, Saint Martin's Minotaur) St. Martin's Pr.

—Loyal Disloyalty. l.t. ed. 1999. (Mystery Ser.). 295p. 26.95 (*0-7862-2048-1*); (*0-7540-3895-5*); (*0-7540-3896-3*) Thorndike Pr.

—The Price of Failure. 1997. 195p. 20.95 o.p. (*0-312-18156-6*, Saint Martin's Minotaur) St. Martin's Pr.

—The Price of Failure. l.t. ed. 1998. (Nightingale Ser.). 278p. pap. 20.95 (*0-7838-8111-8*) Thorndike Pr.

Ashley, Mike, ed. The Mammoth Book of Arthurian Legends. 1998. (Mammoth Bks.). x, 566p. pap. 10.95 (*0-7867-0532-9*, Carroll & Graf Pubs.) Avalon Publishing Group.

Asimov, Isaac, et al, eds. Sherlock Holmes Through Time & Space. (Illus.). 368p. 1984. 14.95 o.p. (*0-312-94400-4*); 1986. reprint ed. pap. 8.95 o.p. (*0-312-94401-2*) Bluejay Bks.

Astley, Judy. Just for the Summer. 2000. pap. 12.95 (*0-552-20455-2*) Transworld Publishers Ltd. GBR. *Dist:* Trafalgar Square.

Aston, Elizabeth. Mr. Darcy's Daughters: A Novel. 2003. 368p. pap. 14.00 (*0-7432-4397-8*, Touchstone) Simon & Schuster.

Atherton, Nancy. Aunt Dimity & the Duke. 1994. (Aunt Dimity Mystery Ser.). 304p. 19.95 o.p. (*0-670-84964-2*, Viking) Viking Penguin.

—Aunt Dimity Snowbound. 2004. (Aunt Dimity Mystery Ser.). 240p. 22.95 (*0-670-03278-6*) Viking Penguin.

—Aunt Dimity's Death. 1992. (Aunt Dimity Mystery Ser.). 256p. 19.00 o.p. (*0-670-84449-7*, Viking) Viking Penguin.

Atkins, Meg Elizabeth. Death Out of Season. l.t. ed. 2002. (Nightingale Ser.). 24.45 (*0-7862-4143-8*) Thorndike Pr.

Atkinson, Kate. Behind the Scenes at the Museum. unabr. ed. 1997. audio 84.95 (*0-7451-6749-7*, CAB 1365) BBC Audiobooks America.

—Behind the Scenes at the Museum. 1999. 333p. pap. 14.00 (*0-312-15060-1*) Picador.

—Behind the Scenes at the Museum. 1995. 336p. 22.95 (*0-312-13928-4*) St. Martin's Pr.

—Behind the Scenes at the Museum: A Novel. l.t. ed. 1996. pap. 23.95 (*1-56895-373-9*, Wheeler Publishing, Inc.) Gale Group.

—Behind the Scenes at the Museum: A Novel. 2000. pap. 0.01 (*0-312-25174-2*) St. Martin's Pr.

—Human Croquet. 2000. pap. (*0-312-19076-X*); 1999. 352p. pap. 14.00 (*0-312-18688-6*); 1997. 352p. 24.00 o.s.i (*0-312-15550-6*) Picador.

—The Human Croquet. 1998. (Illus.). 352p. pap. 10.95 (*0-552-99619-X*) Transworld Publishers Ltd. GBR. *Dist:* Trafalgar Square.

—Human Croquet, Set. unabr. ed. 1998. audio 69.95 (*0-7540-0097-4*, CAB1520) BBC Audiobooks America.

Attanasio, A. A. The Wolf & the Crown. 1998. 352p. pap. 14.00 o.s.i (*0-06-105370-8*, Eos) Morrow/Avon.

Attoe, David. Lion at the Door: A Novel. 1989. 240p. 17.95 (*0-316-05800-9*) Little Brown & Co.

Aumonier, Stacy & Belcher, George F. Odd Fish. 1977. (Short Story Index Reprint Ser.). 19.95 (*0-8369-3431-8*) Ayer Co. Pubs., Inc.

Austen, Jane. The Complete Novels of Jane Austen. 1994. 1,548p. pap. 18.95 o.p. (*0-19-282284-5*) Oxford Univ. Pr., Inc.

—The Complete Novels of Jane Austen Vol. 1: Sense & Sensibility, Pride & Prejudice, Mansfield Park. 1992. (Modern Library Ser.: Vol. 1). 912p. 21.95 (*0-679-60026-4*, Modern Library) Random House Adult Trade Publishing Group.

—The Complete Novels of Jane Austen Vol. II: Emma, Nothanger Abbey, Persuasion. 1992. (Modern Library Ser.). 736p. 23.95 o.s.i (*0-679-60025-6*, Modern Library) Random House Adult Trade Publishing Group.

—Emma. 2002. (World Digital Library). E-Book 3.95 (*0-594-08158-0*) 1873 Pr.

—Emma. 1997. (Modern Library Ser.). E-Book 4.95 (*1-931208-08-5*) Adobe Systems, Inc.

—Emma. 1966. (Airmont Classics Ser.). mass mkt. 2.95 o.p. (*0-8049-0102-3*, CL-102) Airmont Publishing Co., Inc.

—Emma. Date not set. 232p. 21.95 (*0-8488-2522-5*) Amereon, Ltd.

—Emma. l.t. ed. 1999. 630p. pap. 24.95 (*1-55701-279-2*) BNI Pubns., Inc.

—Emma. 1984. mass mkt. 1.95 o.s.i (*0-553-21159-5*, Bantam Classics); 432p. mass mkt. 4.95 (*0-553-21273-7*) Bantam Bks.

—Emma. 2002. audio compact disk 120.00 (*0-7366-8766-1*) Books on Tape, Inc.

—Emma. 1986. lib. bdg. 19.95 (*0-89966-242-0*) Buccaneer Bks., Inc.

—Emma, 3 Vols. (Collected Works of Jane Austen). reprint ed. lib. bdg. 294.00 (*0-7426-2073-5*); 2001. pap. text 84.00 (*0-7426-7073-2*) Classic Bks.

—Emma. l.t. ed. 1999. 630p. pap. 24.95 (*1-58855-018-4*) Cyber Classics, Inc.

—Emma. unabr. ed. 1999. 384p. pap. text 2.50 (*0-486-40648-2*) Dover Pubns., Inc.

—Emma. 1956. 10.50 o.p. (*0-460-00024-1*, Dutton) Dutton/Plume.

—Emma. E-Book 2.49 (*1-58744-220-5*) Electric Umbrella Publishing.

—Emma. 1998. (SPA.). 416p. (*84-320-3877-6*) GeoPlaneta, Editorial, S. A.

—Emma. l.t. ed. 2000. 624p. pap. 22.00 (*0-06-095693-3*, HarperCollins) HarperTrade.

—Emma. 2003. audio 14.95 (*1-84032-771-5*) Hodder Headline Audiobooks GBR. *Dist:* Trafalgar Square.

—Emma. Trilling, Lionel, ed. 1972. (C). pap. 16.36 (*0-395-05115-0*) Houghton Mifflin Co.

—Emma. l.t. ed. 555p. pap. 41.61 (*0-7583-0811-6*); 436p. pap. 33.67 (*0-7583-0810-8*); 319p. pap. 27.06 (*0-7583-0809-4*); 254p. pap. 23.38 (*0-7583-0808-6*); 708p. pap. 51.13 (*0-7583-0812-4*); 1233p. pap. 88.84 (*0-7583-0815-9*); 1063p. pap. 79.19 (*0-7583-0814-0*); 865p. pap. 68.70 (*0-7583-0813-2*); 254p. lib. bdg. 29.38 (*0-7583-0800-0*); 319p. lib. bdg. 33.06 (*0-7583-0801-9*); 1233p. lib. bdg. 100.84 (*0-7583-0807-8*); 436p. lib. bdg. 39.67 (*0-7583-0802-7*); 1063p. lib. bdg. 91.19 (*0-7583-0806-X*); 865p. lib. bdg. 81.13 (*0-7583-0805-1*); 555p. lib. bdg. 47.61 (*0-7583-0803-5*); 708p. lib. bdg. 57.13 (*0-7583-0804-3*) Huge Print Pr.

—Emma. 1996. (Illus.). 464p. reprint ed. pap. 9.95 (*0-7868-8183-6*) Hyperion Pr.

—Emma. 1991. (Everyman's Library). 484p. (*1-85715-036-8*, Everyman's Library) Knopf Publishing Group.

—Emma. 1999. (Cloth Bound Pocket Ser.). 7.95 (*3-8290-0827-9*, 520519) Konemann.

—Emma. E-Book 2.95 (*1-57799-980-0*); E-Book 2.95 (*1-57799-846-4*) Logos Research Systems, Inc.

—Emma. Cheetham, Paul, ed. 1984. (Study Texts Ser.). pap. text 4.29 (*0-582-33153-6*, 72058) Longman Publishing Group.

—Emma. E-Book 1.95 (*1-58515-171-8*) MesaView, Inc.

—Emma. (Signet Classics). 1996. 416p. mass mkt. 4.95 (*0-451-52627-9*, Signet Classics); 1968. mass mkt. 0.50 o.p. (*0-451-50216-7*, Signet Classics); 1968. mass mkt. 0.75 o.p. (*0-451-50388-0*, Signet Classics); 1964. mass mkt. 2.25 o.p. (*0-451-51941-8*); 1964. 400p. mass mkt. 4.95 o.p. (*0-451-52306-7*, Signet Classics); 1964. mass mkt. 1.95 o.p. (*0-451-51524-2*, Signet Classics); 1964. mass mkt. 1.25 o.p. (*0-451-50798-3*, Signet Classics); 1964. mass mkt. 0.95 o.p. (*0-451-50705-3*, Signet Classics); 1964. mass mkt. 1.75 o.p. (*0-451-51357-6*, Signet Classics); 1943. mass mkt. 1.50 o.p. (*0-451-51010-0*, Signet Classics) NAL.

—Emma. l.t. ed. reprint ed. 1997. 610p. lib. bdg. 26.00 (*0-939495-08-2*); 1998. 478p. lib. bdg. 25.00 (*1-58287-025-X*) North Bks.

—Emma. Parrish, Stephen M., ed. (Critical Editions Ser.). 430p. (C). 1972. pap. o.p. (*0-393-09667-X*); 2nd ed. 1993. pap. text o.p. (*0-393-96014-5*) Norton, W. W. & Co., Inc.

—Emma. 1999. (Oxford World's Classics Ser.). 464p. 13.00 o.p. (*0-19-210030-0*) Oxford Univ. Pr., Inc.

—Emma. Kinsley, James, ed. (Oxford World's Classics Ser.). 1998. 488p. pap. 6.95 o.p. (*0-19-283357-X*); 1990. 482p. pap. 4.50 o.p. (*0-19-282756-1*) Oxford Univ. Pr., Inc.

—Emma. Kinsley, James & Lodge, David, eds. 1980. (Oxford World's Classics Ser.). pap. 2.50 o.p. (*0-19-281504-0*) Oxford Univ. Pr., Inc.

—Emma. Pinch, Adela, ed. 2nd ed. 2003. (Oxford World's Classics Ser.). 672p. pap. 6.95 (*0-19-280237-2*) Oxford Univ. Pr., Inc.

—Emma. Kinsley, James, ed. 2nd ed. 1995. (Oxford World's Classics Ser.). 484p. pap. 4.95 o.p. (*0-19-282432-5*) Oxford Univ. Pr., Inc.

—Emma, Vol. IV. Chapman, R. W., ed. 3rd ed. 1988. (Illus.). 536p. reprint ed. 20.00 (*0-19-254704-6*) Oxford Univ. Pr., Inc.

—Emma. collector's ed. 2002. (Illus.). im. lthr. 38.85 (*1-931927-22-7*); pap. 19.95 (*1-931927-23-5*); 25.95 (*1-931927-21-9*); pap. 17.95 (*1-931927-14-6*) Polyglot Pr., Inc.

—Emma. (Jane Austen Works). 2000. 364p. lib. bdg. 41.99 (*1-57646-332-X*); 2000. 364p. pap. 19.99 o.p. (*1-57646-261-7*); 1999. 200p. E-Book 3.99 incl. audio compact disk (*1-57646-144-0*); 2000. 646p. pap. 39.99 (*1-57646-333-8*); 2000. 646p. lib. bdg. 49.99 (*1-57646-334-6*) Quiet Vision Publishing.

—Emma. (Modern Library Classics). 2001. 384p. pap. 7.95 (*0-375-75742-2*); 2001. E-Book 4.95 (*0-679-64108-4*); 1995. 14.95 o.s.i (*0-679-60193-7*) Random House Adult Trade Publishing Group. (Modern Library).

—Emma. 1988. (Zodiac Press Ser.). 520p. o.p. (*0-7011-1232-8*) Random Hse. of Canada, Ltd. CAN. *Dist:* Random Hse., Inc.

—Emma. 2002. (SPA.). 600p. mass mkt. 9.95 (*1-4000-0083-1*); 1997. 13.00 o.s.i (*0-679-60257-7*); 1991. 560p. 18.00 (*0-679-40581-X*); 1989. o.s.i (*1-85381-096-7*) Random Hse., Inc.

—Emma. 1994. (World's Best Reading Ser.). 391p. (0-89577-582-4) Reader's Digest Assn., Inc., The.

—Emma. 2000. E-Book 2.95 incl. cd-rom (1-58853-011-6) Sensory Publishing, Inc.

—Emma. E-Book 5.00 (0-7410-0560-3) SoftBook Pr.

—Emma. unabr. ed. 2003. audio 19.99 (1-59335-041-4, 30126) Soulmate Audio Bks., Inc.

—Emma. l.t. ed. 1985. (Charnwood Large Print Ser.). 547p. 29.99 (0-7089-8258-1, Charnwood) Thorpe, F. A. Pubs. GBR. *Dist:* Ulverscroft Large Print Bks., Ltd., Ulverscroft Large Print Canada, Ltd.

—Emma. Daleski, H. M., ed. 2003. 9.95 (1-59264-004-4); 510p. pap. 9.95 (1-59264-003-6) Toby Pr.

—Emma. 2000. (Signature Classics Ser.). 459p. 24.95 (1-58279-090-6); lib. bdg. 29.95 (1-58279-081-7) Trident Pr. International.

—Emma. 1997. 19.00 (0-606-17578-4); 1980. 11.00 (0-606-03147-2) Turtleback Bks.

—Emma. 1994. 464p. pap. 3.95 o.p. (0-460-87467-5); 1964. 432p. pap. 5.95 o.p. (0-460-15024-3) Tuttle Publishing. (Everyman's Classic Library in Paperback).

—Emma. 2000. 9.00 (81-85944-76-8) UBS Pubs. Distributions, Ltd. IND. *Dist:* South Asia Bks.

—Emma. (Classics Ser.). 2003. 512p. pap. 8.00 (0-14-143958-0, Penguin Classics); 1997. 448p. 7.95 (0-14-043415-1); 1971. 4.50 o.p. (0-460-01024-7) Viking Penguin.

—Emma. Blythe, Ronald, ed. 1966. (English Library). 480p. pap. 6.95 o.s.i (0-14-043010-5, Penguin Classics) Viking Penguin.

—Emma. 1999. E-Book 5.99 (0-8220-7063-4, Cliff Notes) Wiley, John & Sons, Inc.

—Emma. 1997. (Classics Library). 384p. pap. 3.95 (1-85326-028-2, 0282WW) Wordsworth Editions, Ltd. GBR. *Dist:* Casemate Pubs. & Bk. Distributors, LLC.

—Emma: Critical Edition. Parrish, Stephen M., ed. 3rd ed. 2000. (Critical Editions Ser.). (Illus.). ix, 449p. pap. 11.00 (0-393-97284-4) Norton, W. W. & Co., Inc.

—Emma, Northanger Abbey & Persuasion, Vol. 2. 1976. pap. 8.95 o.p. (0-394-71892-5, V-892) Random Hse., Inc.

—Jane Austen: The Complete Novels. 1994. 1136p. 12.99 (0-517-11829-7) Random Hse. Value Publishing.

—The Jane Austen Collection: Lady Susan, The Watsons, Sanditon. Drabble, Margaret, ed. 1975. (English Library). 224p. pap. 9.00 (0-14-043102-0, Penguin Classics) Viking Penguin.

—Jane Austen's Pride & Prejudice. Johnson, Claudia L. & Wolfson, Susan J., eds. 2002. (Longman Cultural Edition Ser.). 464p. pap. 16.00 (0-321-10507-9) Longman Publishing Group.

—Lady Susan. 2003. text (0-9746806-1-3) Alcazar Audioworks.

—Lady Susan. 2001. (Collected Works of Jane Austen). (Illus.). reprint ed. pap. text 28.00 (0-7426-7078-3) Classic Bks.

—Lady Susan. E-Book 2.49 (1-58744-261-2) Electric Umbrella Publishing.

—Lady Susan. 2000. (Jane Austen Works: Vol. 2). 84p. lib. bdg. 24.99 (1-57646-335-4); 120p. pap. 10.99 (1-57646-336-2); 120p. lib. bdg. 21.99 (1-57646-337-0) Quiet Vision Publishing.

—Lady Susan. (Ebook Classic Ser.). E-Book 5.00 (0-7410-0416-X) SoftBook Pr.

—Northanger Abbey. (Modern Library Ser.). E-Book 4.95 (1-931208-13-1) Adobe Systems, Inc.

—Northanger Abbey. Date not set. lib. bdg. 20.95 (0-8488-1244-1) Amereon, Ltd.

—Northanger Abbey. unabr. ed. 54.95 o.p. incl. audio (1-85549-915-0, CTC 055) BBC Audiobooks America.

—Northanger Abbey. 1999. 320p. pap. 4.95 (0-553-21494-2, Bantam Classics); 240p. mass mkt. 4.95 (0-553-21197-8) Bantam Bks.

—Northanger Abbey. Grogan, Claire, ed. (Illus.). 1996. 276p. (C). pap. text (1-55111-078-4); 2nd ed. 2002. 280p. pap. (1-55111-479-8) Broadview Pr.

—Northanger Abbey. 1986. 220p. reprint ed. lib. bdg. 18.95 (0-89966-534-9); lib. bdg. 18.95 o.p. (0-89966-539-X) Buccaneer Bks., Inc.

—Northanger Abbey. unabr. ed. 2000. (Thrift Editions Ser.). 192p. pap. 2.00 (0-486-41412-4) Dover Pubns., Inc.

—Northanger Abbey. 1977. 3.95 o.p. (0-460-01893-0, Dutton) Dutton/Plume.

—Northanger Abbey. 1999. E-Book 2.49 (1-58627-076-1) Electric Umbrella Publishing.

—Northanger Abbey. l.t. ed. 2001. 315p. 28.95 (0-7838-9633-6, Hall, G. K. & Co.) Gale Group.

—Northanger Abbey. 2000. (Green Integer Bks.: Vol. 99). 290p. pap. 11.95 (1-892295-92-X) Green Integer.

—Northanger Abbey. l.t. ed. 486p. pap. 41.45 (0-7583-1635-6); 622p. pap. 50.95 (0-7583-1636-4); 1091p. pap. 88.55 (0-7583-1639-9); 379p. pap. 33.50 (0-7583-1634-8); 277p. pap. 26.95 (0-7583-1633-X); 764p. pap. 61.50 (0-7583-1637-2); 213p. pap. 22.00 (0-7583-1632-1); 940p. pap. 74.00 (0-7583-1638-0); 764p. lib. bdg. 80.90 (0-7583-1629-1); 1091p. lib. bdg. 100.55 (0-7583-1631-3); 622p. lib. bdg. 56.94 (0-7583-1628-3); 486p. lib. bdg. 47.45 (0-7583-1627-5); 379p. lib. bdg. 39.54 (0-7583-1626-7); 277p. lib. bdg. 32.95 (0-7583-1625-9); 940p. lib. bdg. 90.94 (0-7583-1630-5); 213p. lib. bdg. 28.06 (0-7583-1624-0) Huge Print Pr.

—Northanger Abbey. l.t. ed. 1991. (Isis Large Print Bks.). 234p. 24.95 (1-85089-434-5) ISIS Large Print Bks. GBR. *Dist:* Transaction Pubs.

—Northanger Abbey. 2002. 204p. 24.99 (1-4043-2098-9); per. 19.99 (1-4043-2099-7) IndyPublish.com.

—Northanger Abbey. 1992. (Everyman's Library). 288p. 15.00 (0-679-41715-X) Knopf, Alfred A. Inc.

—Northanger Abbey. 1999. (Cloth Bound Pocket Ser.). 7.95 (3-8290-3001-0, 521272) Konemann.

—Northanger Abbey. l.t. ed. 1998. (Large Print Heritage Ser.). 357p. lib. bdg. 33.95 (1-58118-030-6, 22022) LRS.

—Northanger Abbey. E-Book 1.95 (1-57799-956-8) Logos Research Systems, Inc.

—Northanger Abbey. 1996. 240p. mass mkt. 4.95 (0-451-52636-8); 1965. mass mkt. 2.50 o.p. (0-451-51748-2, Signet Classics); 1965. 224p. mass mkt. 3.95 o.p. (0-451-52372-5, Signet Classics); 1965. 224p. mass mkt. 2.50 o.p. (0-451-51834-9, Signet Classics); 1965. mass mkt. 1.50 o.p. (0-451-51113-1, Signet Classics); 1965. mass mkt. 0.95 o.p. (0-451-50868-8, Signet Classics); 1965. mass mkt. 0.60 o.p. (0-451-50720-7, Signet Classics); 1965. mass mkt. 0.50 o.p. (0-451-50312-0, Signet Classics); 1965. mass mkt. 0.50 o.p. (0-451-50580-8, Signet Classics); 1965. mass mkt. 2.25 o.p. (0-451-51539-0, Signet Classics) NAL.

—Northanger Abbey. l.t. ed. 2000. reprint ed. 370p. lib. bdg. 26.00 (0-939495-48-1); 230p. lib. bdg. 25.00 (1-58287-121-3) North Bks.

—Northanger Abbey, Vol. V. Chapman, R. W., ed. 3rd ed. 1988. (Illus.). 348p. reprint ed. 20.00 (0-19-254705-4) Oxford Univ. Pr., Inc.

—Northanger Abbey. collector's ed. 2002. (Illus.). im. lthr. 38.85 (1-931927-35-9); pap. 19.95 (1-931927-36-7); 25.95 (1-931927-34-0); pap. 17.95 (1-931927-18-9) Polyglot Pr., Inc.

—Northanger Abbey. (Jane Austen Works: Vol. 4). 2000. 180p. lib. bdg. 29.99 (1-57646-341-9); 2000. 180p. pap. 14.99 o.p. (1-57646-264-1); 1999. 200p. E-Book 3.99 incl. audio compact disk (1-57646-147-5); 2000. 318p. pap. 24.99 (1-57646-342-7); 2000. 318p. lib. bdg. 32.99 (1-57646-343-5) Quiet Vision Publishing.

—Northanger Abbey. 2002. 256p. pap. 6.95 (0-375-75917-4); 2000. E-Book 4.95 (0-679-64110-6); 1995. 192p. 13.95 (0-679-60192-9) Random House Adult Trade Publishing Group. (Modern Library).

—Northanger Abbey. 1988. (Zodiac Press Ser.). 240p. o.p. (0-7011-1234-4) Random Hse. of Canada, Ltd. CAN. *Dist:* Random Hse., Inc.

—Northanger Abbey. 1989. o.s.i (1-85381-094-0) Random Hse., Inc.

—Northanger Abbey. E-Book 5.00 (0-7410-0423-2) SoftBook Pr.

—Northanger Abbey. l.t. ed. 1995. (Charnwood Large Print Ser.). 359p. 29.99 (0-7089-8876-8, Charnwood) Thorpe, F. A. Pubs. GBR. *Dist:* Ulverscroft Large Print Bks., Ltd., Ulverscroft Large Print Canada, Ltd.

—Northanger Abbey. 1998. 12.00 (0-606-20826-7) Turtleback Bks.

—Northanger Abbey. 1994. 304p. 3.95 o.p. (0-460-87434-9, Everyman's Classic Library in Paperback) Tuttle Publishing.

—Northanger Abbey. Butler, Marilyn, ed. 1996. (Penguin Classics Ser.). (Illus.). 288p. 6.95 (0-14-043413-5) Viking Penguin.

—Northanger Abbey. Ehrenpreis, Anne H., ed. 1972. (English Library). 256p. pap. 5.95 o.p. (0-14-043074-1, Penguin Classics) Viking Penguin.

—Northanger Abbey. 1998. (Classics Library). 208p. pap. 3.95 (1-85326-043-6, 0436WW) Wordsworth Editions, Ltd. GBR. *Dist:* Casemate Pubs. & Bk. Distributors, LLC.

—Persuasion. Date not set. 122p. 17.95 (0-8488-2542-X) Amereon, Ltd.

—Persuasion. 1984. (Bantam Classics Ser.). 240p. mass mkt. 4.95 (0-553-21137-4, Bantam Classics) Bantam Bks.

—Persuasion. Bree, Linda, ed. 1998. (Literary Texts Ser.). (Illus.). 306p. pap. (1-55111-131-4) Broadview Pr.

—Persuasion. 1986. 240p. reprint ed. lib. bdg. 18.95 (0-89966-538-1) Buccaneer Bks., Inc.

—Persuasion. 1999. 256p. pap. 3.99 (0-8125-6588-6, Tor Classics) Doherty, Tom Assocs., LLC.

—Persuasion. 1997. 224p. reprint ed. pap. text 2.00 (0-486-29555-9) Dover Pubns., Inc.

—Persuasion. E-Book 2.49 (1-929120-78-8) Electric Umbrella Publishing.

—Persuasion. Clay, N. L., ed. 1986. (Guide Novel Ser.). pap. text 4.50 o.p. (0-435-16040-0) Heinemann.

—Persuasion. 1998. (Cloth Bound Pocket Ser.). 350p. 7.95 (3-8290-0901-1, 520664) Konemann.

—Persuasion. l.t. ed. 1998. (Large Print Heritage Ser.). 371p. lib. bdg. 34.95 (1-58118-027-6, 22023) LRS.

—Persuasion. 1992. (Everyman's Library). 304p. 15.00 (0-679-40986-6) McKay, David Co., Inc.

—Persuasion. 1996. pap., tchr. ed. (0-451-52661-9, Signet Classics); 1996. 288p. mass mkt. 4.95 (0-451-52638-4); 1964. 256p. mass mkt. 4.95 o.p. (0-451-52289-3, Signet Classics) NAL.

—Persuasion. l.t. ed. reprint ed. 1996. 405p. lib. bdg. 26.00 (0-939495-04-X); 1998. 243p. lib. bdg. 25.00 (1-58287-055-1) North Bks.

—Persuasion. Spacks, Patricia M., ed. 1994. (Critical Editions Ser.). 316p. (C). pap. text 7.00 (0-393-96018-8) Norton, W. W. & Co., Inc.

—Persuasion. Davie, John, ed. (Oxford World's Classics Ser.). 1998. 304p. pap. 4.95 (0-19-283361-8); 1990. 302p. pap. 4.50 o.p. (0-19-282759-6) Oxford Univ. Pr., Inc.

—Persuasion. Davie, John N., ed. 1981. (Oxford World's Classics Ser.). pap. 2.95 o.p. (0-19-281546-6) Oxford Univ. Pr., Inc.

—Persuasion. (Jane Austen Works). 1999. 200p. E-Book 3.99 incl. audio compact disk (1-57646-148-3); 2000. 336p. lib. bdg. 33.99 (1-57646-346-X); 2000. 336p. pap. 24.99 (1-57646-345-1) Quiet Vision Publishing.

—Persuasion. (Modern Library Classics). 2001. 224p. pap. 5.95 (0-375-75729-5); 1995. 192p. 14.95 o.s.i (0-679-60191-0) Random House Adult Trade Publishing Group. (Modern Library).

—Persuasion. 1988. (Zodiac Press Ser.). 248p. o.p. (0-7011-1235-2) Random Hse. of Canada, Ltd. CAN. *Dist:* Random Hse., Inc.

—Persuasion. 1995. 15.00 o.s.i (0-676-50518-X); 1989. o.s.i (1-85381-099-1) Random Hse., Inc.

—Persuasion. l.t. ed. 1990. (Charnwood Large Print Ser.). 389p. 29.99 (0-7089-8534-3, Charnwood) Thorpe, F. A. Pubs. GBR. *Dist:* Ulverscroft Large Print Bks., Ltd., Ulverscroft Large Print Canada, Ltd.

—Persuasion. 1999. 9.04 (0-606-18650-6); 1984. 11.00 (0-606-02200-7) Turtleback Bks.

—Persuasion. Beer, Gillian, ed. & intro. by. 1999. (Penguin Classics Ser.). 272p. (C). 5.95 (0-14-043467-4) Viking Penguin.

—Persuasion. Harding, D. W., ed. 1967. (Penguin Classics Ser.). 400p. (C). pap. 5.95 o.s.i (0-14-043005-9) Viking Penguin.

—Persuasion. abr. ed. 1996. 4p. pap. 23.95 o.s.i incl. audio (0-14-086058-4, 693419, Penguin Audio-Books) Viking Penguin.

—Persuasion. 1998. (Classics Library). 192p. pap. 3.95 (1-85326-056-8, 0568WW) Wordsworth Editions, Ltd. GBR. *Dist:* Casemate Pubs. & Bk. Distributors, LLC.

—Persuasion: Penguin Reader Level 2. 1998. pap. 7.00 (0-14-081527-9) Longman Publishing Group.

—Pride & Prejudice. 2000. 252p. E-Book 9.95 (0-594-05313-7) 1873 Pr.

—Pride & Prejudice. 1998. pap. 4.99 o.p. (1-57840-200-X) Acclaim Bks.

—Pride & Prejudice. 1997. pap. text o.p. (0-17-556586-4) Addison-Wesley Longman, Inc.

—Pride & Prejudice. unabr. ed. 1962. (Classics Ser.). mass mkt. 4.95 (0-8049-0001-9, CL-1) Airmont Publishing Co., Inc.

—Pride & Prejudice. Date not set. lib. bdg. 25.95 (0-8488-0420-1) Amereon, Ltd.

—Pride & Prejudice. unabr. ed. 1997. audio 34.95 (1-57270-055-6, F81055u, Cover to Cover Classics) Audio Partners Publishing Corp.

—Pride & Prejudice. unabr. ed. audio 84.95 o.p. (1-85549-911-8, CTC 001); 1998. audio 84.95 (0-7540-0149-0, CAB 1572, Sterling Audio Bks.) BBC Audiobooks America.

—Pride & Prejudice. abr. ed. 1999. audio 16.85 (0-563-55816-4) BBC Bk. Publishing GBR. *Dist:* Ulverscroft Large Print Bks., Ltd.

—Pride & Prejudice. 2001. 7.95 (0-8010-1211-2) Baker Bks.

—Pride & Prejudice. 1991. mass mkt. 4.95 (0-553-54088-2); 1983. mass mkt. 1.95 o.s.i (0-553-21215-X); 1983. 352p. reprint ed. mass mkt. 4.95 (0-553-21310-5, Bantam Classics) Bantam Bks.

—Pride & Prejudice. 1999. (Classic Novels ). 392p. pap. 8.95 (0-7641-1147-7) Barron's Educational Series, Inc.

—Pride & Prejudice. Kendrick, Walter, ed. 1980. (Mcdonald Classics Ser.). 410p. 19.95 (0-8464-1071-0) Beekman Pubs., Inc.

—Pride & Prejudice. unabr. ed. 2000. audio compact disk 88.00 (0-7861-9894-X, z1054); 1989. audio 56.95 (0-7861-0057-5, 1054) Blackstone Audio Bks., Inc.

—Pride & Prejudice. unabr. collector's ed. 1996. audio 72.00 (0-7366-3370-7, 4020) Books on Tape, Inc.

—Pride & Prejudice. unabr. ed. 1993. (For Antoinette Ser.). audio 19.95 o.p. (1-56100-484-7, 219, Bookcassette); audio 59.25 (1-56100-118-X, 992, Unabridged Library Editions) Brilliance Audio.

—Pride & Prejudice. 1988. lib. bdg. 19.95 (0-89966-243-9) Buccaneer Bks., Inc.

—Pride & Prejudice. 1997. (Cambridge Literature Ser.). audio 16.95 o.p. (0-521-59792-7); audio compact disk 22.95 o.p. (0-521-59791-9) Cambridge Univ. Pr.

—Pride & Prejudice. Bain, Richard, ed. 1996. (Literature Ser.). (Illus.). 384p. pap. text 11.95 o.p. (0-521-57654-7) Cambridge Univ. Pr.

—Pride & Prejudice. unabr. ed. 2000. 10p. audio compact disk 94.95 (0-7540-5338-5, CCD 029) Chivers Audio Bks. GBR. *Dist:* BBC Audiobooks America.

—Pride & Prejudice, 3 Vols. reprint ed. lib. bdg. 294.00 (0-7426-2071-9); 2001. pap. text 84.00 (0-7426-7071-6) Classic Bks.

—Pride & Prejudice. audio 59.95 Cover to Cover Cassettes, Ltd.

—Pride & Prejudice. 1994. 332p. mass mkt. 3.99 (0-8125-2336-9, Tor Classics) Doherty, Tom Assocs., LLC.

—Pride & Prejudice. l.t. unabr. ed. (Large Print Classics). 2001. 476p. pap. 14.95 (0-486-41775-1); 1995. 272p. pap. 2.50 (0-486-28473-5) Dover Pubns., Inc.

—Pride & Prejudice. 1942. 107p. pap. 5.60 (0-87129-686-1, P36) Dramatic Publishing Co.

—Pride & Prejudice. abr. ed. audio 15.95 o.p. (0-88646-029-8, 7042); 1986. audio 29.95 o.p. (0-88646-795-0, R 7042) Durkin Hayes Publishing Ltd.

—Pride & Prejudice. 1985. (Illus.). 352p. 20.00 o.p. (0-525-18381-7, Dutton) Dutton/Plume.

—Pride & Prejudice. 2003. (Barnes & Noble Classics Ser.). 400p. pap. 4.95 (1-59308-020-4) Fine Communications.

—Pride & Prejudice. 1980. (Reader's Request Ser.). lib. bdg. 13.95 o.p. (0-8161-3076-0, Macmillan Reference USA) Gale Group.

—Pride & Prejudice. abr. ed. 1984. audio 8.98; 1978. audio 12.95 o.p. (0-694-50321-5, SWC 1595, HarperAudio) HarperTrade.

—Pride & Prejudice. Clay, N. L., ed. 1986. (Guide Novel Ser.). pap. text 4.50 o.p. (0-435-16041-9) Heinemann.

—Pride & Prejudice. abr. ed. 1999. audio 16.95 (1-85998-013-9) Hodder Headline Audiobooks GBR. *Dist:* Trafalgar Square.

—Pride & Prejudice. 1997. pap. 8.25 (0-03-051487-8) Holt, Rinehart & Winston.

—Pride & Prejudice. Schorer, Mark, ed. 1956. pap. 16.36 (0-395-05101-0, Riverside Editions) Houghton Mifflin Co.

—Pride & Prejudice. l.t. ed. 276p. pap. 24.62 (0-7583-1936-3); 349p. pap. 29.76 (0-7583-1937-1); 484p. pap. 36.91 (0-7583-1938-X); 623p. pap. 45.49 (0-7583-1939-8); 995p. pap. 74.61 (0-7583-1941-X); 1224p. pap. 85.50 (0-7583-1942-8); 1444p. pap. 95.94 (0-7583-1943-6); 806p. pap. 63.79 (0-7583-1940-1); 484p. lib. bdg. 42.91 (0-7583-1930-4); 1444p. lib. bdg. 107.94 (0-7583-1935-5); 1224p. lib. bdg. 97.50 (0-7583-1934-7); 276p. lib. bdg. 30.62 (0-7583-1928-2); 995p. lib. bdg. 86.61 (0-7583-1933-9); 806p. lib. bdg. 75.79 (0-7583-1932-0); 623p. lib. bdg. 51.49 (0-7583-1931-2); 349p. lib. bdg. 35.76 (0-7583-1929-0) Huge Print Pr.

—Pride & Prejudice. 1991. 327p. (1-85715-001-5, Everyman's Library) Knopf Publishing Group.

—Pride & Prejudice. 1991. 416p. 17.00 (0-679-40542-9) Knopf, Alfred A. Inc.

—Pride & Prejudice. 1998. (Cloth Bound Pocket Ser.). 240p. 7.95 (3-89508-207-4, 521305) Konemann.

—Pride & Prejudice. l.t. ed. 1997. (Large Print Heritage Ser.). 560p. lib. bdg. 36.95 (1-58118-009-8, 21967) LRS.

—Pride & Prejudice. 1993. audio 50.60 (1-56544-019-6, 350003); audio Literate Ear, Inc.

—Pride & Prejudice. (Longman Fiction Ser.). 1997. pap. 9.07 (0-582-27508-3); 1993. pap. text 6.50 o.p. (0-582-09674-X, 79823) Longman Publishing Group.

—Pride & Prejudice. Adams, Richard, ed. 1983. (Study Texts Ser.). pap. text 5.95 (0-582-33086-6, 72039) Longman Publishing Group.

—Pride & Prejudice. abr. ed. 2000. audio 7.95 (1-57815-123-6, 1085, Media Bks. Audio Publishing) Media Bks., L. L. C.

—Pride & Prejudice. 9999. o.p.; 1996. 336p. mass mkt. 4.95 (0-451-52588-4, Signet Classics); 1961. mass mkt. 1.75 o.p. (0-451-51916-7, Signet Classics); 1961. mass mkt. 1.50 o.p. (0-451-51662-1, Signet Classics); 1961. mass mkt. 1.95 o.p. (0-451-51491-2, Signet Classics); 1961. mass mkt. 1.75 o.p. (0-451-51396-7, Signet Classics); 1961. mass mkt. 1.25 o.p. (0-451-51111-5, Signet Classics); 1961. mass mkt. 0.95 o.p. (0-451-50977-3, Signet Classics); 1961. mass mkt. 0.75 o.p. (0-451-50843-2, Signet Classics); 1961. mass mkt. 0.60 o.p. (0-451-50721-5, Signet Classics); 1961. mass mkt. 1.50 o.p. (0-451-51253-7, Signet Classics); 1961. mass mkt. 0.50 o.p. (0-451-50082-2, Signet

Classics); 1950. 336p. mass mkt. 3.95 o.p. (*0-451-52365-2*); 1950. mass mkt. 2.25 o.p. (*0-451-52226-5*, Signet Classics); 1950. mass mkt. 1.95 o.p. (*0-451-52075-0*, Signet Classics) NAL.

—Pride & Prejudice. audio 7.95 National Recording Co.

—Pride & Prejudice. abr. ed. 1996. (Works of Jane Austen). audio 17.98 (*962-634-604-3*, NA310414); audio compact disk 19.98 (*962-634-104-1*, NA310412) Naxos of America, Inc. (Naxos AudioBooks).

—Pride & Prejudice. Worrall, Andrew, ed. 1997. (Thornes Classic Novels Ser.). (Illus.). 376p. pap. 16.95 (*0-7487-2977-1*) Nelson Thornes GBR. *Dist:* Trans-Atlantic Pubns., Inc.

—Pride & Prejudice. abr. ed. 1996. 19.95 o.p. (*0-7871-0306-3*) NewStar Media, Inc.

—Pride & Prejudice. l.t. ed. 1998. 480p. lib. bdg. 26.00 (*0-939495-50-3*); 355p. reprint ed. lib. bdg. 25.00 (*1-58287-058-6*) North Bks.

—Pride & Prejudice. (C). pap. text (*0-393-99771-5*) Norton, W. W. & Co., Inc.

—Pride & Prejudice. Gray, Donald J., ed. 1966. (Critical Editions Ser.). 450p. (C). pap. o.p. (*0-393-09668-8*) Norton, W. W. & Co., Inc.

—Pride & Prejudice. 1999. 9.95 (*1-56137-766-X*) Novel Units, Inc.

—Pride & Prejudice. 1999. (Oxford World's Classics Ser.). 366p. 12.50 o.p. (*0-19-210026-2*) Oxford Univ. Pr., Inc.

—Pride & Prejudice. Kinsley, James, ed. 1998. (Oxford World's Classics Ser.). 410p. pap. 6.95 (*0-19-283355-3*) Oxford Univ. Pr., Inc.

—Pride & Prejudice. Hedge, Tricia, ed. 1995. (Illus.). 112p. pap. text 5.95 o.p. (*0-19-422710-3*) Oxford Univ. Pr., Inc.

—Pride & Prejudice. Kinsley, James, ed. 1990. (Oxford World's Classics Ser.). 390p. pap. 5.95 o.p. (*0-19-282760-X*) Oxford Univ. Pr., Inc.

—Pride & Prejudice. Kinsley, James & Bradbrook, F. W., eds. 1980. (Oxford World's Classics Ser.). pap. 2.25 o.p. (*0-19-281503-2*) Oxford Univ. Pr., Inc.

—Pride & Prejudice. 2nd ed. 1993. (Illus.). 126p. pap. text 5.95 (*0-19-585472-1*) Oxford Univ. Pr., Inc.

—Pride & Prejudice. 2000. 384p. pap. 2.99 o.s.i (*0-14-130930-X*) Penguin Putnam Bks. for Young Readers.

—Pride & Prejudice. 1996. 144p. pap. 20.00 (*81-209-0025-1*) Pitambar Publishing IND. *Dist:* State Mutual Bk. & Periodical Service, Ltd.

—Pride & Prejudice. collector's ed. 2002. (Illus.). im. lthr. 38.85 (*1-931927-42-1*); pap. 19.95 (*1-931927-43-X*); 25.95 (*1-931927-41-3*); pap. 17.95 (*1-931927-01-4*) Polyglot Pr., Inc.

—Pride & Prejudice. text (*0-13-981465-5*) Prentice Hall (Schl. Div.).

—Pride & Prejudice. (Jane Austen Works: Vol. 7). 2000. 280p. lib. bdg. 36.99 (*1-57646-350-8*); 2000. 280p. pap. 19.99 o.p. (*1-57646-267-6*); 1999. 200p. E-Book 3.99 incl. audio compact disk (*1-57646-150-5*); 2000. 518p. lib. bdg. 42.99 (*1-57646-352-4*); 2000. 518p. pap. 34.99 (*1-57646-351-6*) Quiet Vision Publishing.

—Pride & Prejudice. 1987. (Radiobook Ser.). audio 4.98 (*0-929541-27-8*) Radiola Co.

—Pride & Prejudice. (Modern Library Ser.). 2000. E-Book 4.95 (*0-679-64112-2*); 2000. 320p. pap. 7.95 (*0-679-78326-1*); 1995. (Illus.). 304p. 14.95 (*0-679-60168-6*) Random House Adult Trade Publishing Group. (Modern Library).

—Pride & Prejudice. 1987. audio 14.95 o.p. (*0-394-56408-1*); 1995. audio 24.00 o.s.i (*0-553-47396-4*) Random Hse. Audio Publishing Group. (RH Audio).

—Pride & Prejudice. 1988. 3.99 o.s.i (*0-517-38589-9*) Random Hse. Value Publishing.

—Pride & Prejudice. 1988. (Zodiac Press Ser.). 248p. o.p. (*0-7011-1236-0*) Random Hse. of Canada, Ltd. CAN. *Dist:* Random Hse., Inc.

—Pride & Prejudice. 1996. o.s.i (*0-679-60252-6*); 1989. o.s.i (*1-85381-097-5*); 1986. pap. 16.00 o.s.i incl. audio (*0-394-55731-X*) Random Hse., Inc.

—Pride & Prejudice. 1984. (Illus.). 368p. 25.00 o.p. (*0-89577-198-5*) Reader's Digest Assn., Inc., The.

—Pride & Prejudice, unabr. ed. 1980. audio 70.00 (*1-55690-424-X*, 80020E7) Recorded Bks., LLC.

—Pride & Prejudice. (Literary Classics Ser.). 368p. 2002. 9.00 o.p. (*0-7624-0550-3*); 1992. text 5.98 o.p. (*1-56138-171-3*, Courage Bks.) Running Pr. Bk. Pubs.

—Pride & Prejudice. 2000. 416p. mass mkt. 4.99 (*0-439-10135-2*) Scholastic, Inc.

—Pride & Prejudice. 2000. E-Book 2.95 (*1-58853-022-1*) Sensory Publishing, Inc.

—Pride & Prejudice. 400p. 2005. (Illus.). mass mkt. 4.99 (*0-7434-6748-5*); 2004. mass mkt. 4.95 (*0-7434-8759-1*) Simon & Schuster. (Pocket).

—Pride & Prejudice. Shefter, Harry, ed. 1985. (Enriched Classics Ser.). mass mkt. 2.50 o.p. (*0-671-41678-2*, Pocket) Simon & Schuster.

—Pride & Prejudice. 1982. 464p. mass mkt. 2.95 o.s.i (*0-671-44389-5*, Pocket) Simon & Schuster.

—Pride & Prejudice. 1996. (Classic Library). 12.98 o.p. (*0-7651-9980-7*) Smithmark Pubs., Inc.

—Pride & Prejudice. unabr. ed. 2003. audio 19.99 (*1-59335-191-7*, 30287) Soulmate Audio Bks., Inc.

—Pride & Prejudice. abr. ed. audio 14.95 o.p. (*0-88142-378-5*) Soundelux Audio Publishing.

—Pride & Prejudice. 2003. (Perennial Bestsellers Ser.). 28.95 (*0-7862-4964-1*) Thorndike Pr.

—Pride & Prejudice. l.t. ed. 1984. (Charnwood Large Print Ser.). 532p. 29.99 (*0-7089-8228-X*, Charnwood) Thorpe, F. A. Pubs. GBR. *Dist:* Ulverscroft Large Print Bks., Ltd., Ulverscroft Large Print Canada, Ltd.

—Pride & Prejudice. Daleski, H. M., ed. 2003. 456p. 9.95 (*1-59264-001-X*); pap. 7.95 (*1-59264-000-1*) Toby Pr.

—Pride & Prejudice. 1986. (Illus.). 352p. 25.95 o.p. (*0-7126-1011-1*) Trafalgar Square.

—Pride & Prejudice. 1999. (Signature Classics Ser.). (Illus.). 352p. 24.95 (*1-58279-032-9*); 29.95 (*1-58279-044-2*) Trident Pr. International.

—Pride & Prejudice. 1950. 11.00 (*0-606-01933-2*) Turtleback Bks.

—Pride & Prejudice. Norris, Pamela, ed. 1993. 384p. pap. 3.95 (*0-460-87212-5*, Everyman's Classic Library in Paperback) Tuttle Publishing.

—Pride & Prejudice. 1906. 352p. pap. 4.95 o.p. (*0-460-11022-5*, Everyman's Classic Library in Paperback) Tuttle Publishing.

—Pride & Prejudice. (Penguin Classics Ser.). 2002. 480p. pap. 8.00 (*0-14-143951-3*, Penguin Classics); 1997. 384p. pap. 7.95 o.s.i (*0-14-043426-7*, Penguin Classics); 1996. 400p. pap. 9.95 o.p. (*0-14-043596-4*) Viking Penguin.

—Pride & Prejudice. Tanner, Tony, ed. 1980. pap. 1.95 o.p. (*0-14-005774-9*) Viking Penguin.

—Pride & Prejudice. 1976. 2.95 o.p. (*0-460-01022-0*) Viking Penguin.

—Pride & Prejudice. Tanner, Tony, ed. 1972. (English Library). 400p. pap. 7.95 o.s.i (*0-14-043072-5*, Penguin Classics) Viking Penguin.

—Pride & Prejudice. abr. ed. 2003. (Classics on Audio Ser.). 4p. audio 16.95 (*0-14-086060-6*, 693102, Penguin Classics) Viking Penguin.

—Pride & Prejudice. 2000. text 6.00 (*0-8220-7172-X*, Cliff Notes) Wiley, John & Sons, Inc.

—Pride & Prejudice. 1997. (Classics Library). 288p. pap. 3.95 (*1-85326-000-2*, 0002WW) Wordsworth Editions, Ltd. GBR. *Dist:* Casemate Pubs. & Bk. Distributors, LLC.

—Pride & Prejudice. 1992. E-Book 8.98 (*0-585-25816-3*) netLibrary, Inc.

—Pride And Prejudice. Kinsley, James, ed. 2nd ed. 2004. (Oxford World's Classics Ser.). 368p. (Orig.). pap. 6.95 (*0-19-280238-0*) Oxford Univ. Pr., Inc.

—Pride & Prejudice, Set. unabr. ed. 1986. audio 53.95 (*1-55685-025-5*) Audio Bk. Contractors, Inc.

—Pride & Prejudice, Set. abr. ed. 1992. audio 16.99 (*0-88646-278-9*, 7278) Durkin Hayes Publishing Ltd.

—Pride & Prejudice, Set. unabr. ed. 1999. audio 56.95 Highsmith Inc.

—Pride & Prejudice. 3rd ed. 2000. (Critical Editions Ser.). viii, 413p. (C). pap. 7.25 (*0-393-97604-1*, Norton Paperbacks) Norton, W. W. & Co., Inc.

—Pride & Prejudice, Vol. II. Chapman, R. W., ed. 3rd ed. 1988. (Illus.). 432p. reprint ed. 21.50 (*0-19-254702-X*) Oxford Univ. Pr., Inc.

—Pride & Prejudice: An Authoritative Text. Gray, Donald J., ed. 2001. x, 219p. pap. (*0-393-10321-8*) Norton, W. W. & Co., Inc.

—Sense & Sensibility. unabr. ed. 1996. (Thrift Editions Ser.). 272p. reprint ed. pap. text 2.00 (*0-486-29049-2*) Dover Pubns., Inc.

—Sense & Sensibility. 1992. (Everyman's Library). 416p. 15.95 (*0-679-40987-4*) McKay, David Co., Inc.

—Sense & Sensibility. Kinsley, James, ed. 1990. (Oxford World's Classics Ser.). 398p. pap. 4.95 o.p. (*0-19-282761-8*) Oxford Univ. Pr., Inc.

—Sense & Sensibility. 2000. (Jane Austen Works: Vol. 6). 240p. pap. 18.99 o.p. (*1-57646-266-8*); 496p. lib. bdg. 41.99 (*1-57646-349-4*); 496p. pap. 29.99 (*1-57646-348-6*) Quiet Vision Publishing.

—Sense & Sensibility. (Paperback Classics Ser.). 2001. 304p. pap. 6.95 (*0-375-75673-6*); 1995. 288p. 14.95 (*0-679-60195-3*) Random House Adult Trade Publishing Group. (Modern Library).

—Sense & Sensibility. 1996. 352p. text 8.98 o.p. (*1-56138-705-3*, Courage Bks.) Running Pr. Bk. Pubs.

—Sense & Sensibility. Ballaster, Ros, ed. & intro. by. 1996. (Penguin Classics Ser.). 368p. (C). 6.95 (*0-14-043425-9*) Viking Penguin.

—Sense & Sensibility, Pride & Prejudice & Mansfield Park. 1976. pap. 6.95 (*0-394-71891-7*, V-891) Random Hse., Inc.

—The Watsons. Chapman, R. W., ed. 1985. (Jane Austen Library: vol. 4). 164p. (C). reprint ed. text 39.99 (*0-485-10503-9*) Athlone Pr. GBR. *Dist:* Transaction Pubs.

—The Watsons. reprint ed. lib. bdg. 98.00 (*0-7426-2077-8*); 2001. (Illus.). pap. text 28.00 (*0-7426-7077-5*) Classic Bks.

—The Watsons. 1973. 318p. reprint ed. 65.00 o.s.i (*0-8371-6598-9*, AUTW, Greenwood Pr.) Greenwood Publishing Group, Inc.

—The Works of Jane Austen: Pride & Prejudice, Emma, Sense & Sensibility. 1995. (Classic Bonded Leather Ser.). 960p. (YA). 24.95 o.p. (*0-681-10375-2*) Borders Pr.

Austen, Jane & Butler, Marilyn. Northanger Abbey. 2003. (Classics Ser.). (Illus.). 288p. pap. 7.00 (*0-14-143979-3*, Penguin Classics) Viking Penguin.

Austen, Jane & Crogan, Claire. Northanger Abbey. 1996. E-Book 7.95 (*0-585-23088-9*) netLibrary, Inc.

Austen, Jane & Hemmant, Lynette. Pride & Prejudice. 1980. 14.95 o.p. (*0-437-24575-6*) Trafalgar Square.

Austen, Jane & Kinsley, James. Pride & Prejudice. 1990. E-Book 13.13 (*0-585-37761-8*) netLibrary, Inc.

Austen, Jane, et al. Emma. 1998. E-Book 7.30 (*0-585-36169-X*) netLibrary, Inc.

—Sanditon, 001. 1975. 8.95 o.p. (*0-395-20284-1*) Houghton Mifflin Co.

Austen-Leigh, Joan. Later Days at Highbury. 1996. 160p. 19.95 o.p. (*0-312-14642-6*) St. Martin's Pr.

Avery, Gillian. To Tame a Sister. 1973. (Illus.). 256p. (J). (gr. 4-6). 5.95 o.p. (*0-670-71777-0*) Viking Penguin.

Avery, Graham. Sherlock Holmes & the Strange Events at the Bank of England. Landes, William-Alan, ed. unabr. ed. 1997. (Illus.). 160p. pap. 20.00 (*0-88734-927-7*) Players Pr., Inc.

Avery, Graham & Phillips, Maberly. Sherlock Holmes & the Strange Events at the Bank of England; The Bank of England, Its History & Development, 2 vol. set. Wilkes, Ian, ed. unabr. ed. 1997. (Illus.). 144p. pap. 20.00 (*0-86025-288-4*) Players Pr., Inc.

Aycliffe, Jonathan. A Shadow on the Wall. 224p. 26.00 (*0-7278-5505-0*) Severn Hse. Pubs., Ltd.

—A Shadow on the Wall. 2001. 263p. (*0-7540-4416-5*); pap. 24.95 (*0-7862-3183-1*); (*0-7540-4417-3*) Thorndike Pr.

Azzopardi, Trezza. Remember Me. 2004. 192p. 23.00 (*0-8021-1767-8*, Grove Pr.) Grove/Atlantic, Inc.

Babson, Marian. Break a Leg, Darlings. l.t. ed. 1997. (G. K. Hall Nightingale Ser.). 300p. lib. bdg. 18.95 o.p. (*0-7838-8036-7*, Macmillan Reference USA) Gale Group.

—Break a Leg, Darlings. 1997. 183p. 20.95 o.p. (*0-312-15285-X*, Saint Martin's Minotaur) St. Martin's Pr.

—Canapes for the Kitties. unabr. ed. 1999. audio 44.95 (*0-7861-1565-3*, 2396) Blackstone Audio Bks., Inc.

—Canapes for the Kitties. l.t. ed. 1998. (Large Print Book Ser.). pap. 23.95 (*1-56895-522-7*, Wheeler Publishing, Inc.) Gale Group.

—Canapes for the Kitties. 1997. 272p. 21.95 o.p. (*0-312-16929-9*, Saint Martin's Minotaur); 1999. 256p. reprint ed. mass mkt. 5.99 (*0-312-96897-3*, St. Martin's Paperbacks) St. Martin's Pr.

—Cover-up Story. 1991. 208p. mass mkt. 3.99 o.s.i (*0-553-29330-3*) Bantam Bks.

—Cover-up Story. l.t. ed. 1991. (Nightingale Ser.). 264p. pap. 14.95 o.p. (*0-8161-4926-7*, Macmillan Reference USA) Gale Group.

—Cover-up Story. 2003. 224p. mass mkt. 6.50 (*0-312-98822-2*, St. Martin's Paperbacks); 1988. 192p. 14.95 o.p. (*0-312-02180-1*, Saint Martin's Minotaur) St. Martin's Pr.

—The Diamond Cat. l.t. ed. 1995. 256p. pap. 17.95 o.p. (*0-7838-1456-9*, Macmillan Reference USA) Gale Group.

—The Diamond Cat. unabr. ed. 2000. audio 46.00 (*1-84197-067-0*, H1064E7, Clipper Audio) Recorded Bks., LLC.

—The Diamond Cat. 1996. mass mkt. 5.99 (*0-312-95660-6*, St. Martin's Paperbacks); 1995. 224p. 20.95 o.p. (*0-312-13049-X*, Saint Martin's Minotaur) St. Martin's Pr.

—Encore Murder. l.t. ed. 1991. (Nightingale Ser.). 275p. pap. 14.95 o.p. (*0-8161-5139-3*, Macmillan Reference USA) Gale Group.

—Encore Murder. 1990. 15.95 o.p. (*0-312-04964-1*, Saint Martin's Minotaur) St. Martin's Pr.

—Even Yuppies Die. unabr. ed. 2002. audio 54.95 (*0-7540-0878-9*, CAB 2300) Chivers Pr. GBR. *Dist:* BBC Audiobooks America.

—Even Yuppies Die. 1995. 208p. 20.95 o.p. (*0-312-13969-1*, Saint Martin's Minotaur) St. Martin's Pr.

—Guilty Party. 1991. 192p. 16.95 o.p. (*0-312-06365-2*, Saint Martin's Minotaur) St. Martin's Pr.

—In the Teeth of Adversity. 1992. 208p. mass mkt. 4.99 o.s.i (*0-553-29131-9*) Bantam Bks.

—In the Teeth of Adversity. l.t. ed. 1992. (Nightingale Ser.). 250p. 14.95 o.p. (*0-8161-5259-4*, Macmillan Reference USA) Gale Group.

—In the Teeth of Adversity. 2003. 176p. mass mkt. 6.50 (*0-312-99103-7*, St. Martin's Paperbacks); 1990. 14.95 o.p. (*0-312-04332-5*, Saint Martin's Minotaur) St. Martin's Pr.

—Murder at the Cat Show. 1990. 192p. reprint ed. mass mkt. 3.95 o.s.i (*0-553-28590-4*) Bantam Bks.

—Murder at the Cat Show. l.t. ed. 1992. (Nightingale Ser.). 264p. 14.95 o.p. (*0-8161-5258-6*, Macmillan Reference USA) Gale Group.

—Murder at the Cat Show. pap. 15.95 (*0-312-31278-4*, Saint Martin's Griffin); 2003. 192p. mass mkt. 5.99 (*0-312-98974-1*, St. Martin's Paperbacks); 1989. 14.95 o.p. (*0-312-02954-3*, Saint Martin's Minotaur) St. Martin's Pr.

—Nine Lives to Murder. l.t. ed. 1994. 21.95 o.p. (*0-7927-2150-0*); pap. 20.95 o.p. (*0-7927-2124-1*) BBC Audiobooks America.

—Nine Lives to Murder. 1995. mass mkt. 4.99 (*0-312-95580-4*, St. Martin's Paperbacks); 1994. 192p. 18.95 o.p. (*0-312-10511-8*, Saint Martin's Minotaur) St. Martin's Pr.

—Past Regret. 1992. 192p. 16.95 o.p. (*0-312-07763-7*, Saint Martin's Minotaur) St. Martin's Pr.

—Paws for Alarm. 1998. (Dead Letter Mysteries Ser.). 272p. reprint ed. pap. 6.50 (*0-312-96513-3*, St. Martin's Paperbacks) St. Martin's Pr.

—Reel Murder, unabr. ed. 1993. audio 39.95 (*0-7451-5753-X*, CAT 4025) BBC Audiobooks America.

—Reel Murder. 1988. mass mkt. 3.50 o.s.i (*0-553-27361-2*) Bantam Bks.

—Reel Murder. l.t. ed. 1988. (Nightingale Ser.). 307p. 12.95 o.p. (*0-8161-4492-3*, Macmillan Reference USA) Gale Group.

—Reel Murder. 1987. 192p. 12.95 o.p. (*0-312-00227-0*) St. Martin's Pr.

—Reel Murder. 1988. audio 35.95 o.p. (*0-8161-7780-5*) Thorndike Pr.

—Shadows in Their Blood. l.t. ed. 1994. 322p. lib. bdg. 16.95 (*0-8161-5952-1*, Macmillan Reference USA) Gale Group.

—Shadows in Their Blood. 1993. 192p. 16.95 o.p. (*0-312-09383-7*, Saint Martin's Minotaur) St. Martin's Pr.

—Tightrope for Three. l.t. ed. 1993. (Nightingale Ser.). 251p. lib. bdg. 16.95 (*0-8161-5255-1*, Macmillan Reference USA) Gale Group.

—Tightrope for Three. 1990. 192p. 16.95 (*0-8027-5750-2*) Walker & Co.

—To Catch a Cat. l.t. ed. 2001. (Wheeler Softcover Ser.). 254p. pap. 24.95 (*1-56895-128-0*, Wheeler Publishing, Inc.) Gale Group.

—To Catch a Cat. mass mkt. (*0-312-97732-8*, St. Martin's Paperbacks); 2002. 192p. mass mkt. 5.99 (*0-312-97790-5*, St. Martin's Paperbacks); 2000. 192p. 21.95 (*0-312-20918-5*, Saint Martin's Minotaur) St. Martin's Pr.

—Tourists Are for Trapping. 1991. 192p. mass mkt. 3.99 o.s.i (*0-553-29031-2*) Bantam Bks.

—Tourists Are for Trapping. 1992. 2.99 o.p. (*0-517-09060-0*) Random Hse. Value Publishing.

—Tourists Are for Trapping. 2003. 208p. mass mkt. 5.99 (*0-312-99099-5*, St. Martin's Paperbacks); 1989. 192p. 14.95 o.p. (*0-312-03444-X*, Saint Martin's Minotaur) St. Martin's Pr.

—The Twelve Deaths of Christmas. 1981. 192p. mass mkt. 2.25 o.s.i (*0-440-19183-1*) Dell Publishing.

—The Twelve Deaths of Christmas. l.t. ed. 1993. 11.50 o.p. (*0-8161-3183-X*, Macmillan Reference USA) Gale Group.

—The Twelve Deaths of Christmas, Vol. 1. 1996. (Twelve Deaths of Christmas Ser.: Vol. 1). 170p. mass mkt. 4.99 (*0-312-96039-5*, St. Martin's Paperbacks) St. Martin's Pr.

—The Twelve Deaths of Christmas. 1980. 180p. 10.95 o.p. (*0-8027-5426-0*) Walker & Co.

Bacon, Margaret. The Ewe Lamb. l.t. ed. 2000. (Magna Large Print Ser.). 432p. 31.99 (*0-7505-1589-9*) Magna Large Print Bks. GBR. *Dist:* Ulverscroft Large Print Bks., Ltd., Ulverscroft Large Print Canada, Ltd.

—The Ewe Lamb. 2000. 284p. 26.00 (*0-7278-5435-6*) Severn Hse. Pubs., Ltd.

Baddock, James. The Faust Conspiracy. 1989. 192p. 18.95 o.p. (*0-8027-1081-6*) Walker & Co.

Bader, Ted, et al. Desire & Duty: A Sequel to Jane Austen's Pride & Prejudice. 1997. (Illus.). 286p. 19.95 (*0-9654299-0-3*, 97-1) Revive Publishing.

Baer, Ann. Down the Common: A Year in the Life of a Medieval Woman. 1998. (Illus.). 240p. pap. text 14.95 (*0-87131-874-1*) Evans, M. & Co., Inc.

—Down the Common: The Charmed Life of Marion Carpenter. 1997. (Illus.). 240p. 19.95 (*0-87131-818-0*) Evans, M. & Co., Inc.

Bage, Robert. Hermsprong; or, Man as He Is Not. Perkins, Pamela Ann, ed. 2002. (Broadview Literary Texts Ser.). 387p. (*1-55111-279-5*) Broadview Pr.

Bailey, Eleanor. Idioglossia. 2003. 448p. pap. 13.00 (*0-552-99860-5*) Black Swan GBR. *Dist:* Trafalgar Square.

—Idioglossia. 2000. 381p. (*0-385-60114-X*) Doubleday Publishing.

Bailey, Elizabeth. A Trace of Memory. l.t. ed. 2001. (Mills & Boon Large Print Ser.). 320p. 27.99 (*0-263-17195-7*) Harlequin Mills & Boon, Ltd. GBR. *Dist:* Ulverscroft Large Print Bks., Ltd., Ulverscroft Large Print Canada, Ltd.

Bailey, H. C. The God of Clay. 1999. (Library of Classical Historical Fiction). 240p. E-Book 9.95 (0-594-00182-X); (Illus.). 240p. pap. 13.95 (0-594-00180-3); E-Book 9.95 (0-594-00181-1) 1873 Pr.

Bainbridge, Beryl. An Awfully Big Adventure. 224p. 1995. pap. 8.95 (0-7867-0184-6); 1993. pap. 9.95 o.p. (0-88184-961-8) Avalon Publishing Group. (Carroll & Graf Pubs.).

—An Awfully Big Adventure. 1989. 193 p. (0-7156-2204-8) Duckworth, Gerald & Co., Ltd. GBR. Dist: International Publishers Marketing.

—An Awfully Big Adventure. 1991. 240p. 19.95 o.p. (0-06-016544-8) HarperTrade.

—An Awfully Big Adventure. l.t. unabr. ed. 1999. 196p. pap. 19.95 (0-7531-5120-0, 151200) ISIS Large Print Bks. GBR. Dist: ISIS Publishing.

—An Awfully Big Adventure. l.t. ed. 1997. 24.95 (1-85695-264-9) Isis-Oasis GBR. Dist: Eye in the Ear Inc.

—The Dressmaker. 1996. 160p. pap. 8.95 (0-7867-0322-9, Carroll & Graf Pubs.) Avalon Publishing Group.

—A Quiet Life. 1999. 210p. pap. 10.95 (0-7867-0635-X, Carroll & Graf Pubs.) Avalon Publishing Group.

—A Quiet Life. 1977. 208p. 7.95 o.p. (0-8076-0846-7) Braziller, George Inc.

—A Quiet Life. 1978. mass mkt. 1.75 o.p. (0-451-07969-8, E7969, Signet Bks.) NAL.

—Sweet William. 1976. 192p. 7.95 o.s.i (0-8076-0816-5) Braziller, George Inc.

—Watson's Apology. 2001. 224p. pap. 12.00 (0-7867-0935-9, Carroll & Graf Pubs.) Avalon Publishing Group.

—Watson's Apology. 1985. 222p. text 14.95 o.p. (0-07-003254-8) McGraw-Hill Cos., The.

—Young Adolf. 1995. 208p. pap. 9.95 (0-7867-0258-3, Carroll & Graf Pubs.) Avalon Publishing Group.

—Young Adolf. 1984. pap. 2.50 o.p. (0-553-13194-X) Bantam Bks.

—Young Adolf. 1979. 208p. reprint ed. 7.95 o.p. (0-8076-0910-2) Braziller, George Inc.

Baker, Anne. Moonlight on the Mersey. 1997. 512p. mass mkt. 13.95 (0-7472-5319-6) Headline Bk. Publishing, Ltd. GBR. Dist: Trafalgar Square.

—Moonlight on the Mersey. l.t. ed. 2001. (Magna Large Print Ser.). 576p. (0-7505-1863-4) Magna Large Print Bks. GBR. Dist: Ulverscroft Large Print Canada, Ltd.

Baker, Donna. Ride for a Fall. 1998. 192p. 24.00 (0-7278-5305-8) Severn Hse. Pubs., Ltd.

—Ride for a Fall. l.t. ed. 2000. (Romance Ser.). 266p. 25.95 (0-7862-2648-X); (0-7540-4231-6); (0-7540-4232-4) Thorndike Pr.

Baker, John. Poet in the Gutter. 1996. 240p. 21.95 o.p. (0-312-14393-1, Saint Martin's Minotaur) St. Martin's Pr.

Balogh, Mary. More Than a Mistress. 2001. 384p. reprint ed. mass mkt. 5.99 (0-440-22601-5, Dell Bks.) Dell Publishing.

Balogh, Mary, et al. A Regency Christmas: Five Stories, Vol. IV. 1992. (Super Regency Ser.). 352p. mass mkt. 4.99 o.p. (0-451-17341-4, Signet Bks.) NAL.

Bangs, John K. R. Holmes & Co. Being the Remarkable Adventures of Raffles Holmes, Esq., Detective & Amateur Cracksman by Birth. 1994. (Illus.). 272p. reprint ed. pap. 8.00 o.p. (1-883402-63-8, Scribner) Simon & Schuster.

Banks, Sydney. The Enlightened Gardener. 2001. 176p. 12.95 (1-55105-298-9) Lone Pine Publishing.

Bannister, Jo. A Bleeding of Innocents. 1999. 304p. (0-7540-3481-X); pap. (0-7540-3482-8) BBC Audiobooks America.

—A Bleeding of Innocents. 1997. (WWL Mystery Ser.: No. 241). per. (0-373-26241-8, 1-26241-9, Worldwide Library) Harlequin Enterprises, Ltd.

—A Bleeding of Innocents. unabr. ed. 1998. audio 69.95 (1-872672-97-3) Magna Story Sound GBR. Dist: Ulverscroft Large Print Bks., Ltd.

—A Bleeding of Innocents. 1993. 224p. 18.95 o.p. (0-312-09750-6, Saint Martin's Minotaur) St. Martin's Pr.

—A Bleeding of Innocents. l.t. ed. 1998. (General Ser.). 304p. pap. 24.95 (0-7862-1610-7) Thorndike Pr.

—Broken Lines. 2000. (Castlemere Mystery Ser.). 272p. per. (0-373-26338-4, Harlequin Bks.) Harlequin Enterprises, Ltd.

—Broken Lines. 1999. 304p. 22.95 (0-312-19842-6, Saint Martin's Minotaur) St. Martin's Pr.

—Broken Lines. l.t. ed. 1999. (General Ser.). 336p. pap. 23.95 (0-7862-1682-4) Thorndike Pr.

—Changelings. 2002. (WWL Mystery Ser.: No. 410). mass mkt. (0-373-26410-0, 1-26410-0, Worldwide Library) Harlequin Enterprises, Ltd.

—Changelings. 2000. 374p. (0-333-90189-4) Macmillan Pr.

—Changelings. l.t. ed. 2001. (Magna Large Print Ser.). 368p. (0-7505-1761-1) Magna Large Print Bks. GBR. Dist: Ulverscroft Large Print Canada, Ltd.

—Changelings. 2000. 384p. 23.95 (0-312-26567-0, Saint Martin's Minotaur) St. Martin's Pr.

—Charisma. 1997. per. (0-373-26253-1, 1-26253-4, Worldwide Library) Harlequin Enterprises, Ltd.

—Charisma. 1994. 208p. 18.95 o.p. (0-312-11252-1, Saint Martin's Minotaur) St. Martin's Pr.

—Gilgamesh. unabr. ed. 1998. audio 63.95 o.p. (1-85903-013-0) Magna Story Sound GBR. Dist: Ulverscroft Large Print Bks., Ltd.

—The Going down of the Sun. 1989. 12.95 o.s.i (0-385-26451-8) Doubleday Publishing.

—The Hireling's Tale. 1999. 316p. 23.95 (0-312-24400-2, Saint Martin's Minotaur) St. Martin's Pr.

—The Hireling's Tale. l.t. ed. 1999. (General Ser.). 352p. pap. 22.95 (0-7862-2163-1) Thorndike Pr.

—The Lazarus Hotel. 1999. per. (0-373-26307-4, 1-26307-8, Worldwide Library) Harlequin Enterprises, Ltd.

—The Lazarus Hotel. 1997. 288p. 22.95 o.p. (0-312-15565-4, Saint Martin's Minotaur) St. Martin's Pr.

—The Lazarus Hotel. l.t. ed. 1997. (Ulverscroft Large Print Ser.). 432p. 29.99 o.p. (0-7089-3858-2, Ulverscroft) Thorpe, F. A. Pubs. GBR. Dist: Ulverscroft Large Print Bks., Ltd., Ulverscroft Large Print Canada, Ltd.

—No Birds Sing. 1998. (WWL Mystery Ser.). per. (0-373-26283-3, 1-26283-1, Worldwide Library) Harlequin Enterprises, Ltd.

—No Birds Sing. 1996. 240p. 21.95 (0-312-14382-6, Saint Martin's Minotaur) St. Martin's Pr.

—No Birds Sing. l.t. ed. 1997. (Ulverscroft Large Print Ser.). 464p. 29.99 o.p. (0-7089-3732-2, Ulverscroft) Thorpe, F. A. Pubs. GBR. Dist: Ulverscroft Large Print Bks., Ltd., Ulverscroft Large Print Canada, Ltd.

—The Primrose Convention. l.t. ed. 1998. (0-7540-3254-X); 263p. pap. (0-7540-3253-1) BBC Audiobooks America.

—The Primrose Convention. 1998. 272p. 22.95 o.p. (0-312-18157-4, Saint Martin's Minotaur) St. Martin's Pr.

—The Primrose Convention. l.t. ed. 1998. (General Ser.). 272p. pap. 24.95 (0-7862-1383-3) Thorndike Pr.

—Striving with Gods. 1984. (Crime Club Ser.). 192p. 11.95 o.p. (0-385-19482-X) Doubleday Publishing.

—A Taste for Burning. 1997. (Castlemere Mystery Ser.). per. (0-373-26259-0, 1-26259-1, Worldwide Library) Harlequin Enterprises, Ltd.

—A Taste for Burning. 1995. 208p. 19.95 o.p. (0-312-13191-7, Saint Martin's Minotaur) St. Martin's Pr.

Barbour, Anne. Lord Glenraven's Return. 1994. (Signet Science Ser.). 224p. mass mkt. 3.99 o.s.i (0-451-17843-2, Signet Bks.) NAL.

—Step in Time. 1996. 224p. mass mkt. 4.99 o.s.i (0-451-18723-7) NAL.

Baring-Gould, S. Urith. E-Book 3.95 (0-594-02283-5) 1873 Pr.

Barker, A. L. The Haunt. 2001. 192p. 22.95 (0-7867-0784-4, Carroll & Graf Pubs.) Avalon Publishing Group.

Barker, Ann. The Squire's Daughter. l.t. ed. 2002. 265p. pap. 23.95 (0-7862-3954-9) Gale Group.

—The Squire's Daughter. 2002. 222p. 27.50 (0-7090-6874-3) Hale, Robert Ltd. GBR. Dist: Trafalgar Square.

Barker, Clive. Sacrament. 1996. 79p. 25.00 o.p. (0-06-017949-X) HarperCollins Pubs.

—Sacrament. 1997. 624p. mass mkt. 7.99 (0-06-109199-5, HarperTorch) Morrow/Avon.

Barker, Margaret. Reluctant Partners. l.t. ed. 2001. (Mills & Boon Large Print Ser.). 288p. 27.99 (0-263-17147-7) Harlequin Mills & Boon, Ltd. GBR. Dist: Ulverscroft Large Print Bks., Ltd., Ulverscroft Large Print Canada, Ltd.

Barker, Nicola. Behindlings: A Novel. 544p. 2003. pap. 13.95 (0-06-093362-3); 2002. 27.95 (0-06-018569-4) HarperTrade. (Ecco).

—Five Miles from Outer Hope. 2000. 191p. pap. (0-571-20205-5) Faber & Faber, Inc.

Barker, Pat. Another World. 2000. pap. (0-374-90271-2); 1999. 278p. 24.00 o.p. (0-374-10525-1) Farrar, Straus & Giroux.

—Another World. 2000. 288p. pap. 13.00 (0-312-20397-7) Picador.

—Another World. unabr. ed. 2000. audio 51.00 (0-7887-4151-9, 96181E7, Clipper Audio) Recorded Bks., LLC.

—Another World. l.t. ed. 1999. (Core Ser.). 264p. 30.95 (0-7838-8750-7) Thorndike Pr.

—Another World. 1998. 288p. pap. (0-670-87716-6) Viking.

—Another World. 1998. 320p. text (0-670-87058-7, Viking) Viking Penguin.

—Another World Reading Group Guide, Set. 2000. pap. 0.01 o.s.i (0-312-27107-7) Picador.

—Blow Your House Down. 1985. 224p. mass mkt. 3.50 o.s.i (0-345-32361-0) Ballantine Bks.

—Blow Your House Down. 1984. 180p. 13.95 o.p. (0-399-13011-X, G. P. Putnam's Sons) Penguin Putnam Bks. for Young Readers.

—Blow Your House Down. 2000. (Modern Classics). 170p. reprint ed. 13.00 (0-86068-398-2) Virago Pr., Ltd. GBR. Dist: Trafalgar Square.

—Border Crossing. 2001. 215p. 22.00 o.p. (0-374-18115-2); E-Book 9.00 (0-374-70123-7); E-Book 24.00 (0-374-70085-0); E-Book 24.00 o.p. (0-374-70086-9); E-Book 24.00 (0-374-70087-7) Farrar, Straus & Giroux.

—Border Crossing. 2002. 224p. pap. 13.00 (0-312-42019-6) Picador.

—The Century's Daughter. 1986. 256p. 16.95 o.p. (0-399-13174-4, G. P. Putnam's Sons) Penguin Putnam Bks. for Young Readers.

—Liza's England. 2001. 288p. pap. 14.00 (0-312-25304-4) Picador.

Barker, Raffaella. Hens Dancing: A Novel. 2001. E-Book 19.95 (0-375-50685-3) Random Hse., Inc.

—Summertime. 2003. 336p. reprint ed. pap. 14.00 (0-385-72185-4, Anchor) Knopf Publishing Group.

—Summertime: A Novel. 2002. 336p. 24.95 (0-375-50387-0) Random Hse., Inc.

Barlow, Eleanor Poe. The Master's Cat: The Story of Charles Dickens as Told by His Cat. 1998. (Illus.). 132p. (YA). (gr. 7 up). 24.00 (0-9518525-3-1) Dickens Publishing GBR. Dist: Hood, Alan C. & Co., Inc.

—The Master's Cat: The Story of Charles Dickens as Told by His Cat. 1999. 132p. (YA). pap. 16.50 (1-880158-22-1) Townsend, J.N. Publishing.

Barnard, Robert. The Bad Samaritan. unabr. ed. 1997. audio 54.95 (0-7531-0046-0, 961104) ISIS Audio Bks. GBR. Dist: Ulverscroft Large Print Bks., Ltd.

—The Bad Samaritan. 1996. (Crime Ser.). 240p. pap. 5.95 o.p. (0-14-025730-6) Penguin Group (USA) Inc.

—The Bad Samaritan. 1995. 240p. 21.00 (0-684-81334-3, Scribner) Simon & Schuster.

—Bodies. 1988. 224p. mass mkt. 3.50 o.s.i (0-440-20007-5) Dell Publishing.

—Bodies. 1986. 224p. 13.95 o.p. (0-684-18729-9, Macmillan Reference USA) Gale Group.

—Bodies. 1988. audio 35.95 o.s.i (0-8161-7781-3) Thorndike Pr.

—The Bones in the Attic: A Novel of Suspense. l.t. ed. Date not set. 28.95 (1-58724-200-1, Wheeler Publishing, Inc.) Gale Group.

—The Bones in the Attic: A Novel of Suspense. 2002. (Illus.). 272p. 24.00 (0-684-87379-6, Scribner) Simon & Schuster.

—The Case of the Missing Bronte. 1983. 192p. 11.95 o.s.i (0-684-17910-5); 1984. 248p. 8.95 o.p. (0-8161-3590-8) Gale Group. (Macmillan Reference USA).

—The Cherry Blossom Corpse. 1988. 256p. mass mkt. 3.50 o.s.i (0-440-20178-0) Dell Publishing.

—The Cherry Blossom Corpse. 1996. (Crime Ser.). 256p. pap. 5.95 o.p. (0-14-023789-5, Penguin Bks.) Penguin Group (USA) Inc.

—The Cherry Blossom Corpse. 1987. 14.95 o.p. (0-684-18825-2, Scribner) Simon & Schuster.

—The Corpse at the Haworth Tandoori. l.t. ed. 1999. (Wheeler Large Print Book Ser.). (Illus.). 290p. pap. 24.95 (1-56895-744-0, Wheeler Publishing, Inc.) Gale Group.

—The Corpse at the Haworth Tandoori. l.t. ed. 2000. (Magna Large Print Ser.). 352p. o.p. (0-7505-1502-3) Magna Large Print Bks. GBR. Dist: Ulverscroft Large Print Bks., Ltd., Ulverscroft Large Print Canada, Ltd.

—The Corpse at the Haworth Tandoori. 2002. 288p. pap. 18.95 (0-7432-2427-2); 1999. (Illus.). 283p. 22.00 (0-684-85532-1) Simon & Schuster. (Scribner).

—Death & the Princess, Vol. 66. 1983. 192p. mass mkt. 3.25 o.s.i (0-440-12153-1) Dell Publishing.

—Death & the Princess. 1982. 192p. 10.95 o.s.i (0-684-17759-5); 1985. (Nightingale Ser.: No. 2). pap. 9.95 o.p. (0-8161-3520-7) Gale Group. (Macmillan Reference USA).

—Death by Sheer Torture. 1982. 192p. 10.95 o.s.i (0-684-17437-5, Macmillan Reference USA) Gale Group.

—Death by Sheer Torture. 1995. (Crime Ser.). 192p. pap. 5.95 o.p. (0-14-023787-9, Penguin Bks.) Penguin Group (USA) Inc.

—A Fatal Attachment. 1994. mass mkt. 5.99 o.s.i (0-552-13932-7) Bantam Bks.

—A Fatal Attachment. 1992. 288p. 20.00 (0-684-19412-0, Macmillan Reference USA) Gale Group.

—A Fatal Attachment. l.t. ed. 1993. (Magna Large Print Ser.). 348p. o.p. (0-7505-0506-0) Magna Large Print Bks. GBR. Dist: Ulverscroft Large Print Canada, Ltd.

—A Fatal Attachment. 1994. 240p. mass mkt. 4.99 (0-380-71998-3, Avon Bks.) Morrow/Avon.

—A Hovering of Vultures. 1995. 224p. mass mkt. 6.99 o.p. (0-552-14119-4); 1994. 229p. 24.50 o.s.i (0-593-03397-3) Bantam Bks.

—A Hovering of Vultures. 1993. 224p. text 20.00 (0-684-19625-5, Macmillan Reference USA) Gale Group.

—A Hovering of Vultures. 1995. 224p. mass mkt. 4.99 (0-380-77653-7, Avon Bks.) Morrow/Avon.

—A Hovering of Vultures. 1993. 22.00 o.s.i (0-684-19666-2, Scribner) Simon & Schuster.

—A Little Local Murder. 1984. 192p. mass mkt. 2.95 o.s.i (0-440-14882-0) Dell Publishing.

—A Little Local Murder. 1983. 192p. 11.95 o.s.i (0-684-17882-6); 1985. 320p. pap. 9.95 o.p. (0-8161-3798-6) Gale Group. (Macmillan Reference USA).

—A Little Local Murder. 1995. 192p. pap. 7.95 (0-88150-325-8, Foul Play) Norton, W. W. & Co., Inc.

—The Masters of the House: A Novel of Suspense. 1994. 224p. 20.00 (0-684-19728-6, Macmillan Reference USA) Gale Group.

—The Masters of the House: A Novel of Suspense. 1996. 224p. mass mkt. 4.99 (0-380-72511-8, Avon Bks.) Morrow/Avon.

—A Murder in Mayfair. l.t. ed. 2003. 260p. pap. 22.95 o.s.i (1-59058-081-8) Poisoned Pen Pr.

—A Murder in Mayfair. 2000. (Illus.). 272p. (YA). 23.00 o.s.i (0-684-86445-2, Scribner) Simon & Schuster.

—A Murder in Mayfair. l.t. ed. 2000. (Basic Ser.). 379p. 27.95 (0-7862-2656-0); (0-7540-4229-4); (0-7540-4230-8) Thorndike Pr.

—No Place of Safety. 1998. 192p. 21.50 (0-684-84503-2, Scribner) Simon & Schuster.

—No Place of Safety. l.t. ed. 1998. (Basic Ser.). 312p. 28.95 (0-7862-1452-X); (0-7540-3361-9); (0-7540-3362-7) Thorndike Pr.

—A Scandal in Belgravia. l.t. ed. 1992. (Magna Large Print Ser.). 304p. (0-7505-0395-5) Magna Large Print Bks. GBR. Dist: Ulverscroft Large Print Canada, Ltd.

—A Scandal in Belgravia. 2000. (Missing Mysteries Ser.: Vol. 10). 245p. pap. 14.95 (1-890208-16-7); 2003. 354p. pap. 22.95 o.s.i (1-59058-080-X) Poisoned Pen Pr.

—A Scandal in Belgravia. 1994. 3.99 o.p. (0-517-11431-3) Random Hse. Value Publishing.

—A Scandal in Belgravia. 1991. 288p. 17.95 o.s.i (0-684-19322-1, Scribner) Simon & Schuster.

—Sheer Torture. unabr. ed. 1998. audio 69.95 o.p. (1-872672-22-1) Magna Story Sound GBR. Dist: Ulverscroft Large Print Bks., Ltd.

—Unholy Dying. l.t. ed. 2002. (Magna Large Print Ser.). 368p. (0-7505-1822-7) Magna Large Print Bks. GBR. Dist: Ulverscroft Large Print Canada, Ltd.

—Unholy Dying. 2001. 288p. 23.00 o.s.i (0-7432-0149-3, Scribner) Simon & Schuster.

—Unholy Dying. l.t. ed. 2001. 399p. 28.95 (0-7862-3333-8) Thorndike Pr.

Barnes, Julian. England, England. 2000. 288p. pap. 13.00 (0-375-70550-3); 1999. pap. 0.00 (0-375-70591-0) Knopf, Alfred A. Inc.

—England, England, Set. abr. ed. 1999. audio 26.95 (0-7871-1971-7, Dove Audio) NewStar Media, Inc.

—Metroland. 1992. 176p. pap. 11.00 (0-679-73608-5, Vintage) Knopf Publishing Group.

—Metroland. 1987. 176p. pap. text 4.95 o.p. (0-07-003746-9) McGraw-Hill Cos., The.

—Metroland. 1980. 10.95 o.p. (0-312-53169-9) St. Martin's Pr.

—Staring at the Sun. 1988. 208p. reprint ed. pap. 7.95 o.p. (0-06-097148-7, PL-7148, Perennial) HarperTrade.

—Staring at the Sun. 1987. 15.95 o.s.i (0-394-55821-9) Knopf, Alfred A. Inc.

—Talking It Over. 1992. 288p. pap. 13.00 (0-679-73687-5, Vintage) Knopf Publishing Group.

Barnes, Trevor. Midsummer Night's Killing: A Mystery Introducing Scotland Yard's Blanche Hampton. 1992. 18.00 o.p. (0-688-11047-9, Morrow, William & Co.) Morrow/Avon.

—A Pound of Flesh. 1993. 20.00 o.p. (0-688-11048-7, Morrow, William & Co.) Morrow/Avon.

Barnett, Cheryl Kay & Olson, Alger. Sentimental Journey. 1998. 214p. pap. 6.95 o.p. (1-56315-152-9) SterlingHouse Pubs., Inc.

Barnett, Cheryl Kay & Olson, Alger James. Sentimental Journey. 1999. 181p. pap. 11.95 o.p. (1-56315-195-2) SterlingHouse Pubs., Inc.

Barr, Emily. Cuba. 2004. 13.00 (0-452-28503-8, Plume) Dutton/Plume.

Barr, Robert. The Triumphs of Eugene Valmont. 1985. 192p. reprint ed. pap. 5.95 o.p. (0-486-24894-1) Dover Pubns., Inc.

—The Triumphs of Eugene Valmont. 1997. (Oxford Popular Fiction Ser.). 246p. pap. 9.95 o.p. (0-19-283248-4) Oxford Univ. Pr., Inc.

Barraclough, June. Rooks Nest. 1987. 336p. 17.95 o.p. (0-312-01083-4) St. Martin's Pr.

Barrett, Julia, pseud. Presumption. 238p. pap. 11.95 (1-85479-993-2) O'Mara, Michael Bks., Ltd. GBR. Dist: Andrews McMeel Publishing.

—Presumption: An Entertainment Sequel to Jane Austen's Pride & Prejudice. unabr. collector's ed. 1995. audio 48.00 (0-7366-2954-8, 3648) Books on Tape, Inc.

—The Third Sister: A Continuation of Jane Austen's Sense & Sensibility. 1998. (Mira Bks.). mass mkt. (1-55166-446-1, 1-66446-5, Mira Bks.) Harlequin Enterprises, Ltd.

Barrett, Julia, pseud & Austen, Jane. Jane Austen's Charlotte: Her Fragment of a Last Novel. 2000. 240p. 21.95 (*0-87131-908-X*) Evans, M. & Co., Inc.
—Presumption: An Entertainment: A Sequel to Pride & Prejudice. 1993. 240p. 19.95 o.p. (*0-87131-736-2*) Evans, M. & Co., Inc.
—Presumption: An Entertainment: A Sequel to Pride & Prejudice. 1995. 238p. reprint ed. pap. 12.00 (*0-226-03813-0*) Univ. of Chicago Pr.
—The Third Sister: A Continuation of Jane Austen's Sense & Sensibility. 1996. 256p. 22.95 o.s.i (*1-55611-496-6*) Fine, Donald I. Bks.
Barrie, J. M. The Little White Bird, Vol. 7. reprint ed. 57.50 (*0-404-08787-6*) AMS Pr., Inc.
—The Little White Bird. E-Book 2.49 (*1-58627-195-4*) Electric Umbrella Publishing.
—The Little White Bird. l.t. ed. 516p. lib. bdg. 49.00 (*0-7583-3308-0*) Huge Print Pr.
—The Little White Bird. E-Book 5.00 (*0-7410-1312-6*) SoftBook Pr.
Barron, Stephanie. Jane & the Genius of the Place. 2000. (Jane Austen Mystery Ser.: Vol. 4). 384p. mass mkt. 6.50 (*0-553-57839-1*) Bantam Bks.
—Jane & the Genius of the Place. l.t. ed. 1999. (Mystery Ser.). 517p. 29.95 (*0-7862-2017-1*) Thorndike Pr.
—Jane & the Ghosts of Netley. 2004. 336p. mass mkt. 6.99 (*0-553-58406-5*); 7th ed. 2003. 304p. 23.95 (*0-553-80222-4*) Bantam Bks.
—Jane & the Man of the Cloth. 1997. (Jane Austen Mystery Ser.: No. 2). 368p. reprint ed. mass mkt. 6.50 (*0-553-57489-2*) Bantam Bks.
—Jane & the Man of the Cloth. unabr. collector's ed. 1997. (Jane Austen Ser.). audio 64.00 (*0-7366-3683-8*, 4362) Books on Tape, Inc.
—Jane & the Prisoner of Wool House. 2002. (Jane Austen Mystery Ser.: Bk. 6). 384p. mass mkt. 6.50 (*0-553-57840-5*, Crimeline) Bantam Bks.
—Jane & the Prisoner of Wool House. unabr. ed. 2001. (Jane Austen Ser.: Bk. 6). audio 56.00 (*0-7366-8483-2*) Books on Tape, Inc.
—Jane & the Stillroom Maid. 2001. (Jane Austen Mystery Ser.: Vol. 5). 336p. reprint ed. mass mkt. 6.50 (*0-553-57837-5*) Bantam Bks.
—Jane & the Stillroom Maid. l.t. ed. 2000. (Mystery Ser.). 477p. 29.95 (*0-7862-3006-1*) Thorndike Pr.
—Jane & the Unpleasantness at Scargrave Manor. 1996. (Jane Austen Mystery Ser.: No. 1). 352p. mass mkt. 6.50 (*0-553-57593-7*, Crimeline) Bantam Bks.
—Jane & the Unpleasantness at Scargrave Manor. unabr. collector's ed. 1997. (Jane Austen Ser.). audio 64.00 (*0-7366-3569-6*, 4219) Books on Tape, Inc.
—Jane & the Unpleasantness at Scargrave Manor. l.t. ed. 1997. (Jane Austen Mystery Ser.: No. 1). 24.95 o.p. (*1-56895-400-X*, Wheeler Publishing, Inc.) Gale Group.
—Jane & the Wandering Eye. 1998. (Jane Austen Mystery Ser.: No. 3). 272p. (gr. 5 up). 22.95 o.s.i (*0-553-10204-4*); 336p. mass mkt. 6.99 (*0-553-57817-0*) Bantam Bks.
—Jane & the Wandering Eye. unabr. collector's ed. 1998. (Jane Austen Ser.). audio 56.00 (*0-7366-4164-5*, 4667) Books on Tape, Inc.
—Jane & the Wandering Eye. l.t. ed. 1998. (Cloak & Dagger Ser.). 471p. 29.95 (*0-7862-1353-1*) Thorndike Pr.
Basso, Eric. Bartholomew Fair. 1999. 134p. pap. 13.00 (*1-878580-24-8*) Asylum Arts.
—Bartholomew Fair. 1998. pap. 13.00 (*1-57650-099-3*) Hi Jinx Pr.
Bastable, Bernard. Dead Mr. Mozart. 1996. 183p. mass mkt. o.s.i (*0-7515-1092-0*) Little Brown & Co.
—Dead Mr. Mozart. 1995. 19.95 o.p. (*0-312-11771-X*, Saint Martin's Minotaur) St. Martin's Pr.
—To Die Like a Gentleman. 1993. 192p. 16.95 o.p. (*0-312-09402-7*, Saint Martin's Minotaur) St. Martin's Pr.
—Too Many Notes, Mr. Mozart. 1996. 192p. 21.00 o.p. (*0-7867-0315-6*, Carroll & Graf Pubs.) Avalon Publishing Group.
—Too Many Notes, Mr. Mozart. 1998. 250p. mass mkt. o.s.i (*0-7515-1806-9*) Little Brown & Co.
Bates, H. E. The Best of H. E. Bates. 1977. (Short Story Index Reprint Ser.). reprint ed. 39.95 (*0-8369-3967-0*) Ayer Co. Pubs., Inc.
—The Darling Buds of May. Set. unabr. ed. 2001. (Larkin Family Ser.: Bk. 1). audio 34.95 (*0-7451-5780-7*, CAB 178) Chivers Audio Bks. GBR. *Dist:* BBC Audiobooks America.
—The Darling Buds of May. l.t. ed. 1992. (Magna Large Print Ser.). 208p. o.p. (*0-7505-0426-9*) Magna Large Print Bks. GBR. *Dist:* Ulverscroft Large Print Canada, Ltd.
—The Darling Buds of May: A Comedy. 1996. (*0-573-01751-4*) French, Samuel Inc.
—The Darling Buds of May: The Pop Larkin Chronicles, 3 vols. 1993. 352p. reprint ed. pap. 11.00 o.p. (*0-06-097596-2*, Perennial) HarperTrade.
—The Darling Buds of May: The Pop Larkin Chronicles. 1993. 333p. 20.00 o.p. (*0-688-11960-3*, Morrow, William & Co.) Morrow/Avon.
—A Little of What You Fancy. unabr. ed. 1994. audio 54.95 (*0-7451-4221-4*, CAB 904) BBC Audiobooks America.
—Love for Lydia. l.t. ed. 1993. 24.95 o.p. (*0-7927-1783-X*); pap. 22.95 o.p. (*0-7927-1782-1*) BBC Audiobooks America.
—My Uncle Silas. 1988. (Short Fiction Ser.). (Illus.). 190p. pap. 7.00 o.p. (*0-915308-63-0*); 14.00 o.p. (*0-915308-62-2*) Graywolf Pr.
—My Uncle Silas. 1984. (Twentieth Century Classics Ser.). (Illus.). (C). pap. 0.00 o.p. (*0-19-281854-6*) Oxford Univ. Pr., Inc.
—When the Green Woods Laugh. unabr. ed. 1992. 39.95 incl. audio (*0-7451-4044-0*, CAB 741) BBC Audiobooks America.
Battison, Brian. The Christmas Bow Murder. 2000. (DCI Jim Ashworth Mysteries Ser.). 240p. pap. 12.95 (*0-7490-0475-4*, London Hse.) Allison & Busby, Ltd. GBR. *Dist:* International Publishers Marketing.
—The Christmas Bow Murder. 1994. 224p. 19.95 o.p. (*0-312-11463-X*, Saint Martin's Minotaur) St. Martin's Pr.
—The Christmas Bow Murder. l.t. ed. 1995. (Ulverscroft Large Print Ser.). 480p. 29.99 o.p. (*0-7089-3407-2*, Ulverscroft) Thorpe, F. A. Pubs. GBR. *Dist:* Ulverscroft Large Print Bks., Ltd., Ulverscroft Large Print Canada, Ltd.
—Flying Pigs. 1998. 224p. (*0-09-478550-3*, Constable & Co. Ltd.) Constable & Robinson Ltd.
—Jeopardy's Child: A DCI Jim Ashworth Investigation. 1999. (DCI Jim Ashworth Mysteries Ser.). 352p. mass mkt. 9.95 (*0-7490-0304-9*) Allison & Busby, Ltd. GBR. *Dist:* International Publishers Marketing.
—Jeopardy's Child: A DCI Jim Ashworth Investigation. 1998. 224p. (*0-09-477530-3*, Constable & Co. Ltd.) Constable & Robinson Ltd.
—Jeopardy's Child: A DCI Jim Ashworth Investigation. l.t. ed. 2000. (Ulverscroft Large Print Ser.). 416p. 31.99 (*0-7089-4304-7*, Ulverscroft) Thorpe, F. A. Pubs. GBR. *Dist:* Ulverscroft Large Print Bks., Ltd., Ulverscroft Large Print Canada, Ltd.
—Mirror Image. l.t. ed. 1999. (Ulverscroft Large Print Ser.). 408p. 31.99 (*0-7089-4129-X*, Ulverscroft) Thorpe, F. A. Pubs. GBR. *Dist:* Ulverscroft Large Print Bks., Ltd., Ulverscroft Large Print Canada, Ltd.
—Truths Not Told. 279p. mass mkt. 9.95 (*0-7490-0366-9*) Sutton Publishing.
—Truths Not Told. l.t. ed. 1998. (Linford Mystery Large Print Ser.). 512p. pap. 17.99 (*0-7089-5293-3*, Linford) Thorpe, F. A. Pubs. GBR. *Dist:* Ulverscroft Large Print Bks., Ltd., Ulverscroft Large Print Canada, Ltd.
—The Witch's Familiar. l.t. ed. 1998. (Linford Mystery Large Print Ser.). 528p. pap. 17.99 (*0-7089-5335-2*, Linford) Thorpe, F. A. Pubs. GBR. *Dist:* Ulverscroft Large Print Bks., Ltd., Ulverscroft Large Print Canada, Ltd.
Battrick, Elizabeth. Beatrix Potter's Tale. l.t. ed. 1998. (Ulverscroft Large Print Ser.). 432p. 29.99 (*0-7089-3891-4*, Ulverscroft) Thorpe, F. A. Pubs. GBR. *Dist:* Ulverscroft Large Print Bks., Ltd., Ulverscroft Large Print Canada, Ltd.
Baumbach, Jonathan. My Father More or Less. 1982. 152p. 15.95 (*0-914590-66-9*); pap. 10.95 (*0-914590-67-7*) Fiction Collective Two, Inc.
Bawden, Nina. The Birds on the Trees. 1976. 192p. pap. 1.95 o.p. (*0-14-003430-7*, Penguin Bks.) Viking Penguin.
—Family Money. 1991. 240p. 17.95 o.p. (*0-312-06351-2*) St. Martin's Pr.
—The Ice House. 1983. 236p. 11.95 o.p. (*0-312-40386-0*) St. Martin's Pr.
—A Little Love, a Little Learning. 21.95 (*0-88411-122-9*) Amereon, Ltd.
—A Little Love, a Little Learning. l.t. unabr. ed. 1998. 304p. pap. 21.99 (*0-7531-5863-9*, 158639); 32.50 (*0-7531-5584-2*, 155842) ISIS Large Print Bks. GBR. *Dist:* Ulverscroft Large Print Bks., Ltd., Ulverscroft Large Print Canada, Ltd.
—The Runaway Summer. 1976. (Puffin Story Bks.). 176p. (J). (gr. 5 up). pap. 1.50 o.p. (*0-14-030539-4*, Penguin Bks.) Viking Penguin.
Bayer, Valerie T. City of Childhood. 1992. 320p. 19.95 o.p. (*0-312-06926-X*) St. Martin's Pr.
—The Metaphysics of Sex. 1992. 384p. 21.95 o.p. (*0-312-08263-0*) St. Martin's Pr.
Beagle, Peter S. Tamsin. 1999. 288p. mass mkt. 21.95 o.s.i (*0-451-45763-3*, ROC) NAL.
Beard, Julie. My Fair Lord. 2000. 352p. mass mkt. 6.99 o.s.i (*0-425-17481-6*) Berkley Publishing Group.
Beard, Richard. Damascus. 1999. 320p. 23.95 (*1-55970-460-8*) Arcade Publishing, Inc.
Beaton, M. C., pseud. Agatha Raisin & the Day the Floods Came. l.t. ed. 2002. (Mystery Ser.). 341p. 30.95 (*0-7862-4679-0*) Gale Group.
—Agatha Raisin & the Day the Floods Came. E-Book 22.95 (*0-312-70710-X*); 2003. 240p. mass mkt. 6.50 (*0-312-98586-X*, St. Martin's Paperbacks); 2002. 224p. 22.95 (*0-312-20767-0*, Saint Martin's Minotaur) St. Martin's Pr.
—Agatha Raisin & the Fairies of Fryfam. 2001. 224p. mass mkt. 6.50 (*0-312-97626-7*, St. Martin's Paperbacks); 2000. 197p. 19.95 (*0-312-20496-5*, Saint Martin's Minotaur) St. Martin's Pr.
—Agatha Raisin & the Fairies of Fryfam. l.t. ed. 2000. (Mystery Ser.). (Illus.). 283p. (J). 29.95 (*0-7862-2858-X*) Thorndike Pr.
—Agatha Raisin & the Haunted House. l.t. ed. 2003. 340p. 30.95 (*0-7862-6013-0*) Gale Group.
—Agatha Raisin & the Haunted House. Date not set. mass mkt. (*0-312-99482-6*, St. Martin's Paperbacks); E-Book (*0-312-71122-0*); 2003. 256p. 23.95 (*0-312-20769-7*) St. Martin's Pr.
—Agatha Raisin & the Murderous Marriage. l.t. ed. 1997. (Large Print Book Ser.). pap. 22.95 (*1-56895-443-3*, Wheeler Publishing, Inc.) Gale Group.
—Agatha Raisin & the Murderous Marriage. (Agatha Raisin Mysteries Ser.). 1997. 224p. mass mkt. 6.50 (*0-312-96186-3*, St. Martin's Paperbacks); 1996. 208p. 20.95 (*0-312-14538-1*, Saint Martin's Minotaur) St. Martin's Pr.
—Agatha Raisin & the Potted Gardener. 1995. 192p. mass mkt. 6.50 (*0-8041-1359-9*, Ivy Bks.) Ballantine Bks.
—Agatha Raisin & the Potted Gardener. l.t. ed. 1998. 204p. 21.95 o.p. (*0-7838-8392-7*, Macmillan Reference USA) Gale Group.
—Agatha Raisin & the Potted Gardener. 1994. 240p. 18.95 (*0-312-10927-X*, Saint Martin's Minotaur) St. Martin's Pr.
—Agatha Raisin & the Quiche of Death. 1993. 192p. mass mkt. 6.50 (*0-8041-1163-4*, Ivy Bks.) Ballantine Bks.
—Agatha Raisin & the Quiche of Death. 1992. 208p. 17.95 o.p. (*0-312-08153-7*, Saint Martin's Minotaur) St. Martin's Pr.
—Agatha Raisin & the Terrible Tourist. l.t. ed. 1998. pap. 22.95 o.p. (*1-56895-574-X*, Wheeler Publishing, Inc.) Gale Group.
—Agatha Raisin & the Terrible Tourist. (Agatha Raisin Mysteries Ser.). 1997. 160p. 20.95 o.p. (*0-312-16761-X*, Saint Martin's Minotaur); 1958. E-Book 5.99 o.s.i (*0-312-20707-7*); 1998. 208p. reprint ed. mass mkt. 6.50 (*0-312-96566-4*, St. Martin's Paperbacks) St. Martin's Pr.
—Agatha Raisin & the Vicious Vet. 1994. 192p. mass mkt. 6.99 (*0-8041-1162-6*, Ivy Bks.) Ballantine Bks.
—Agatha Raisin & the Vicious Vet. 1993. 208p. 17.95 o.p. (*0-312-09242-3*, Saint Martin's Minotaur) St. Martin's Pr.
—Agatha Raisin & the Vicious Vet. l.t. ed. 1998. (Paperback Ser.). 227p. pap. 24.95 (*0-7838-0368-0*) Thorndike Pr.
—Agatha Raisin & the Walkers of Dembley. 1996. (Agatha Raisin Ser.). 176p. mass mkt. 6.50 (*0-8041-1358-0*, Ivy Bks.) Ballantine Bks.
—Agatha Raisin & the Walkers of Dembley. 1995. 170p. 19.95 o.p. (*0-312-11738-8*, Saint Martin's Minotaur) St. Martin's Pr.
—Agatha Raisin & the Wellspring of Death. l.t. ed. 1999. (Large Print Book Ser.). pap. 23.95 (*1-56895-730-0*, Wheeler Publishing, Inc.) Gale Group.
—Agatha Raisin & the Wellspring of Death. (Dead Letter Mysteries Ser.). 1999. 256p. mass mkt. 6.50 (*0-312-96695-4*, St. Martin's Paperbacks); 1998. 272p. 21.95 o.p. (*0-312-18523-5*, Saint Martin's Minotaur) St. Martin's Pr.
—Agatha Raisin & the Witch of Wyckhadden. 2000. 214p. mass mkt. 5.99 (*0-312-97369-1*, St. Martin's Paperbacks); 1999. 208p. 21.95 (*0-312-20494-9*, Saint Martin's Minotaur) St. Martin's Pr.
—Agatha Raisin & the Witch of Wyckhadden. l.t. ed. 2000. (Mystery Ser.). 288p. 28.95 (*0-7862-2418-5*) Thorndike Pr.
—Agatha Raisin & the Wizard of Evesham. pap. text (*0-312-20693-3*, Tor Bks.) Doherty, Tom Assocs., LLC.
—Agatha Raisin & the Wizard of Evesham. 1999. 256p. mass mkt. 5.99 (*0-312-97062-5*, St. Martin's Paperbacks); (Agatha Raisin Mysteries Ser.: Vol. 8). 208p. 20.95 o.p. (*0-312-19822-1*, Saint Martin's Minotaur) St. Martin's Pr.
—Agatha Raisin & the Wizard of Evesham. l.t. ed. 2000. (Mystery Ser.). (Illus.). 272p. 28.95 (*0-7862-2417-7*) Thorndike Pr.
—The Skeleton in the Closet. 2001. 218p. 21.95 (*0-312-20772-7*, Saint Martin's Minotaur) St. Martin's Pr.
—The Skeleton in the Closet. l.t. ed. 2001. 318p. 29.95 (*0-7862-3496-2*); 293p. (*0-7540-4671-0*); 293p. (*0-7540-4672-9*) Thorndike Pr.
Bebris, Carrie. Pride & Prescience. 2004. 288p. 21.95 (*0-7653-0508-9*, Forge Bks.) Doherty, Tom Assocs., LLC.
Beckett, Simon. Fine Lines: A Novel. 1994. 304p. 22.00 (*0-671-89206-1*, Simon & Schuster) Simon & Schuster.
Bedford, Martyn. Acts of Revision. 1998. 256p. pap. 19.95 o.s.i (*0-552-99674-2*) Bantam Bks.
—The Houdini Girl: A Novel. 2000. (Crime - Black Lizard Ser.). 320p. pap. 13.00 (*0-375-70476-0*, Vintage) Knopf Publishing Group.
Beechey, Alan. An Embarrassment of Corpses. 1997. 265p. 22.95 (*0-312-16936-1*, Saint Martin's Minotaur) St. Martin's Pr.
Beerbohm, Max. Zuleika Dobson. 1999. E-Book 2.49 (*1-58627-221-7*) Electric Umbrella Publishing.
Belben, Rosalind. Hound Music. 2001. 306p. (*0-7011-7277-0*) Random Hse. of Canada, Ltd. CAN. *Dist:* Random Hse., Inc.
Bell, Donna. A Tangled Web. 2001. (Zebra Regency Romance Ser.). 24p. mass mkt. 4.99 o.s.i (*0-8217-6795-X*, Zebra Bks.) Kensington Publishing Corp.
Bell, James Scott. The Darwin Conspiracy: The Confessions of Sir Max Busby. 2002. 288p. pap. 12.99 (*0-8054-2500-4*) Broadman & Holman Pubs.
Bell, Josephine. A Flat Tyre in Fulham. 2001. 21.95 (*0-7540-8579-1*, Black Dagger) BBC Audiobooks America.
—The Hunter & the Trapped. 2000. 21.95 (*0-7540-8562-7*, Black Dagger) BBC Audiobooks America.
—The Hunter & the Trapped. l.t. ed. 1991. (Ulverscroft Large Print Ser.). 29.99 o.p. (*0-7089-2475-1*, Ulverscroft) Thorpe, F. A. Pubs. GBR. *Dist:* Ulverscroft Large Print Bks., Ltd., Ulverscroft Large Print Canada, Ltd.
Bell, Madison Smartt. Doctor Sleep. 1991. 320p. 19.95 (*0-15-126100-8*) Harcourt Trade Pubs.
Bell, Michele Ashman. Flawless: A Novel. 2002. 279p. 14.95 (*1-59156-017-9*) Covenant Communications.
Bell, Pauline. The Dead Do Not Praise. 1993. 192p. 17.95 o.p. (*0-312-09780-8*, Saint Martin's Minotaur) St. Martin's Pr.
Benison, C. C. Death at Buckingham Palace: Her Majesty Investigates. 1996. (Her Majesty Investigates Ser.). 288p. mass mkt. 6.99 (*0-553-57476-0*, Crimeline) Bantam Bks.
—The Death at Sandringham House. 1996. (Her Majesty Investigates Ser.). 384p. mass mkt. 6.50 (*0-553-57477-9*, Crimeline) Bantam Bks.
—Death at Windsor Castle: Her Majesty Investigates. 1998. (Her Majesty Investigates Ser.). 400p. mass mkt. 6.99 (*0-553-57478-7*, Crimeline) Bantam Bks.
Benison, Teresa. The Arrogance of Women. 1998. 378p. o.p. (*0-09-179214-2*) Random Hse. of Canada, Ltd. CAN. *Dist:* Random Hse., Inc.
Bennett, Arnold. Anna of the Five Towns. 1977. (Collected Works of Arnold Bennett: Vol. 1). reprint ed. 24.95 (*0-518-19082-X*) Ayer Co. Pubs., Inc.
—Anna of the Five Towns. Harris, Margaret, ed. & intro. by. 1995. (Oxford World's Classics Ser.). 256p. pap. 8.95 o.p. (*0-19-282965-3*) Oxford Univ. Pr., Inc.
—Anna of the Five Towns. Preston, Peter, ed. 1997. (Paperback Classics). 304p. pap. 7.50 o.p. (*0-460-87653-8*, Everyman's Classic Library in Paperback) Tuttle Publishing.
—Anna of the Five Towns. 1991. (Penguin Twentieth-Century Classics Ser.). 240p. pap. 9.95 o.p. (*0-14-018015-X*, Penguin Classics) Viking Penguin.
—Clayhanger. 1976. (Fiction Ser.). 528p. pap. 5.95 o.p. (*0-14-000997-3*, Penguin Bks.) Viking Penguin.
—The Grim Smile of the Five Towns. 1977. (Collected Works of Arnold Bennett: Vol. 27). reprint ed. 28.95 (*0-518-19108-7*) Ayer Co. Pubs., Inc.
—The Matador of the Five Towns & Other Stories. 1977. (Collected Works of Arnold Bennett: Vol. 53). reprint ed. 36.95 (*0-518-19134-6*) Ayer Co. Pubs., Inc.
—The Matador of the Five Towns & Other Stories. 1971. reprint ed. 25.00 (*0-403-00862-X*) Scholarly Pr., Inc.
—The Regent: A Five Town Story of Adventure. 1977. (Collected Works of Arnold Bennett: Vol. 70). reprint ed. 27.95 (*0-518-19151-6*) Ayer Co. Pubs., Inc.
—Tales of the Five Towns. 1977. (Collected Works of Arnold Bennett: Vol. 77). reprint ed. 25.95 (*0-518-19158-3*) Ayer Co. Pubs., Inc.
—Tales of the Five Towns. (Collected Works of Arnold Bennett). reprint ed. lib. bdg. 98.00 (*0-7426-2540-0*); 2001. 317p. pap. text 28.00 (*0-7426-7540-8*) Classic Bks.
Bennett, John. Master Skylark. 2000. 252p. E-Book 3.95 (*0-594-01871-4*) 1873 Pr.
Bennett, Rebecca. Vision of Love. l.t. ed. 1994. 173p. lib. bdg. 16.95 (*0-8161-5953-X*, Macmillan Reference USA) Gale Group.
—Vision of Love. 1994. (Rainbow Romances Ser.: No. 898). 160p. 14.95 (*0-7090-4970-6*) Parkwest Pubns., Inc.
Benson, Ann. The Plague Tales. 1998. 688p. mass mkt. 6.99 (*0-440-22510-8*) Dell Publishing.
Benson, E. F. Desirable Residences & Other Stories. 1992. 292p. pap. 12.95 o.p. (*0-19-282977-7*) Oxford Univ. Pr., Inc.

—Fine Feathers & Other Stories. 1995. 320p. pap. 10.95 o.p. (0-19-282416-3) Oxford Univ. Pr., Inc.
—Lucia in London. (Make Way for Lucia Ser.: Pt. 2). 1984. 320p. pap. 3.95 o.p. (0-06-080695-8, P695); Pt. II. 1987. 256p. pap. 12.00 o.p. (0-06-091373-8, PL 1373) HarperTrade. (Perennial).
—Lucia in London. 1999. 232p. pap. 11.95 (1-55921-277-2) Moyer Bell.
—Lucia's Progress. 2000. (Lucia Ser.). 230p. pap. 11.95 (1-55921-233-0) Moyer Bell.
—Mapp & Lucia. (Make Way for Lucia Ser.: Pt. 4). 320p. 1984. mass mkt. 3.95 o.p. (0-06-080714-8, P 714); Pt. IV. 1986. reprint ed. pap. 12.00 o.p. (0-06-091328-2, PL 1328) HarperTrade. (Perennial).
—Mapp & Lucia. 2000. (Illus.). 277p. pap. 12.95 (1-55921-232-2) Moyer Bell.
—Miss Mapp. unabr. ed. 1999. audio 41.95 (1-55685-587-7) Audio Bk. Contractors, Inc.
—Miss Mapp. 1986. pap. o.s.i (0-552-99083-3, Corgi) Bantam Bks.
—Miss Mapp, Pt. III. (Make Way for Lucia Ser.). 1987. 272p. pap. 5.95 o.p. (0-06-091374-6); 1984. mass mkt. 3.95 o.p. (0-06-080696-6) HarperTrade. (Perennial).
—Miss Mapp. 1999. 232p. pap. 11.95 (1-55921-275-6) Moyer Bell.
—Queen Lucia. unabr. ed. 1998. (C). audio 41.95 (1-55685-584-2) Audio Bk. Contractors, Inc.
—Queen Lucia. l.t. ed. 1987. 360p. 16.95 o.p. (0-8161-4163-0, Macmillan Reference USA) Gale Group.
—Queen Lucia, abr. ed. 1987. audio 15.95 (0-89845-590-1, CPN 2105, Caedmon); Pt. 1. 288p. pap. 12.00 o.p. (0-06-091372-X, PL 1372, Perennial) HarperTrade.
—Queen Lucia. unabr. ed. 2001. audio 69.95 (1-85089-641-0, 91013) ISIS Audio Bks. GBR. Dist: Ulverscroft Large Print Bks., Ltd.
—Queen Lucia. 1998. (Lucia Ser.). 176p. pap. 10.95 (1-55921-252-7) Moyer Bell.
—Queen Lucia Pt. 1: Make Way for Lucia. unabr. ed. 1998. audio 44.95 (0-7861-1449-5, 2311) Blackstone Audio Bks., Inc.
—Trouble for Lucia. 1992. reprint ed. lib. bdg. 18.95 (0-89966-960-3) Buccaneer Bks., Inc.
—Trouble for Lucia. (Make Way for Lucia Ser.: Pt. 6). 1984. 320p. pap. 3.95 o.p. (0-06-080716-4, P 716); Pt. VI. 1987. 288p. pap. 5.95 o.p. (0-06-091376-2, PL 1376) HarperTrade. (Perennial).
—Trouble for Lucia. 2001. (Lucia Ser.: Vol. 6). 234p. 12.95 (1-55921-298-5); 2000. 232p. pap. 11.95 (1-55921-281-0) Moyer Bell.
—The Worshipful Lucia, Pt. V. 1987. (Make Way for Lucia Ser.). 272p. pap. 5.95 o.p. (0-06-091375-4, PL1375, Perennial) HarperTrade.
Benson, E. F. & Mitford, Nancy. Queen Lucia. 1984. (Make Way for Lucia Ser.: Pt. 1). 320p. pap. 3.95 o.p. (0-06-080694-X, P694, Perennial) HarperTrade.
Benson, Jessica. Much Obliged. 2001. (Zebra Regency Romance Ser.). 288p. mass mkt. 4.99 o.s.i (0-8217-6783-6, Zebra Bks.) Kensington Publishing Corp.
Benson, Robert H. The King's Achievement. rev. ed. 2000. 500p. E-Book 9.95 (0-594-01875-7) 1873 Pr.
Bentley, E. C. Trent's Last Case. 1997. (Mystery Classics Ser.). (Illus.). 192p. reprint ed. pap. text 2.00 (0-486-29687-3) Dover Pubns., Inc.
—Trent's Last Case. 1976. (Crime Fiction Ser.). reprint ed. lib. bdg. 21.00 o.p. (0-8240-2353-6) Garland Publishing, Inc.
Berdoll, Linda. The Bar Sinister: Pride & Prejudice Continues. 1999. 468p. pap. 18.50 (0-9674817-0-8) Well There It Is Pubs.
Bergengren, Ralph W. Perfect Gentleman. 1977. (Essay Index Reprint Ser.). 13.95 (0-8369-0202-5) Ayer Co. Pubs., Inc.
Berger, Arthur Asa. Durkheim Is Dead! A Sherlock Holmes Mystery of Social Theory. 2003. (Illus.). 272p. 19.95 (0-7591-0300-3); 200p. pap. 70.00 o.s.i (0-7591-0299-6) AltaMira Pr.
Berkeley, Anthony. The Piccadilly Murder. 1983. (Detective Stories Ser.). 352p. reprint ed. pap. 6.95 o.p. (0-486-24518-7) Dover Pubns., Inc.
Besant, Walter. All Sorts & Conditions of Men. 1997. (Oxford Popular Fiction Ser.). (Illus.). 464p. pap. 11.95 o.p. (0-19-283258-1) Oxford Univ. Pr., Inc.
—All Sorts & Conditions of Men: An Impossible Story. 1971. reprint ed. 39.00 o.p. (0-403-00519-1) Scholarly Pr., Inc.
Besant, Walter & Rice, James. Twas in Trafalgar Bay. 2000. 252p. E-Book 9.95 (0-594-02944-9) 1873 Pr.
Bettle, Janet. Unnatural Causes. l.t. ed. 2001. (Magna Large Print Ser.). 400p. (0-7505-1656-9) Magna Large Print Bks. GBR. Dist: Ulverscroft Large Print Canada, Ltd.
—Unnatural Causes. 2000. 320p. 23.95 (0-312-26244-2, Saint Martin's Minotaur) St. Martin's Pr.
Beverley, Jo. The Dragon's Bride. l.t. ed. 2001. (Core Ser.). 479p. 28.95 o.p. (0-7838-9657-3) Thorndike Pr.
—Hazard. l.t. ed. 2002. (Wheeler Hardcover Ser.). 564p. 28.95 (1-58724-288-5, Wheeler Publishing, Inc.) Gale Group.
—Hazard. 2002. 384p. mass mkt. 6.99 (0-451-20580-4, Signet Bks.) NAL.
—St. Raven. l.t. ed. 2003. 28.95 (1-58724-425-X, Wheeler Publishing, Inc.) Gale Group.
—St. Raven. 2003. 384p. mass mkt. 6.99 (0-451-20807-2, Signet Bks.) NAL.
—The Stanforth Secrets. 1991. 256p. mass mkt. 3.99 (0-380-71438-8, Avon Bks.) Morrow/Avon.
—The Stanforth Secrets: A Regency Romantic Intrigue. 1989. 224p. 19.95 o.p. (0-8027-1061-1) Walker & Co.
—An Unwilling Bride. 2000. 352p. mass mkt. 6.99 (0-8217-6724-0); 1994. mass mkt. 3.99 o.s.i (0-8217-4475-5); 1992. mass mkt. 3.99 o.s.i (0-8217-3669-8, Zebra Bks.) Kensington Publishing Corp.
—An Unwilling Bride. l.t. ed. 2001. (Thorndike Press Large Print Romance Ser.). 581p. 28.95 (0-7862-3334-6) Thorndike Pr.
Bickham, Jack M. Breakfast at Wimbledon. 1992. (Brad Smith Ser.: No. 4). 375p. mass mkt. 3.99 o.p. (0-8125-1195-6); 1991. 19.95 o.p. (0-312-85144-8) Doherty, Tom Assocs., LLC. (Tor Bks.).
—Breakfast at Wimbledon. 1991. 19.95 (0-312-51195-7) St. Martin's Pr.
Biderman, Bob. Judgement of Death. l.t. ed. 1992. 18.95 o.p. (0-7451-8226-7); pap. 16.95 o.p. (0-7927-0774-5) BBC Audiobooks America.
—Judgement of Death. 1992. 224p. 19.95 (0-8027-3217-8) Walker & Co.
Biggle, Lloyd, Jr. The Glendower Conspiracy: A Memoir of Sherlock Holmes. 1990. (Brown Bag Mystery Line Ser.). 422p. 14.95 o.p. (0-933031-25-4) Council Oak Bks.
—The Quallsford Inheritance: A Memoir of Sherlock Holmes, from the Papers of Edward Porter Jones, His Late Assistant. 1986. 256p. 15.95 o.p. (0-312-65813-3) St. Martin's Pr.
Biggle, Lloyd. The Quallsford Inheritance: A Memoir of Sherlock Holmes from the Papers of Edward Porter Jones, His Late Assistant. 1987. 288p. pap. 3.95 o.p. (0-14-010007-5, Penguin Bks.) Viking Penguin.
Bigsby, Christopher & Hawthorne, Nathaniel. Pearl. 1996. 256p. 26.00 o.p. (0-297-81533-4) Weidenfeld & Nicolson, Ltd. GBR. Dist: Trafalgar Square.
Billingham, Mark. Scaredy Cat: A Novel. 2003. 384p. 23.95 (0-06-621300-2, Morrow, William & Co.) Morrow/Avon.
—Sleepyhead. 2003. 432p. mass mkt. 7.50 (0-06-103221-2, Avon Bks.); 2002. 320p. 24.95 (0-06-621299-5, Morrow, William & Co.) Morrow/Avon.
Billington, Rachel. Occasion of Sin. 1983. 320p. 14.50 o.p. (0-671-45938-4) Summit Bks.
—Theo & Matilda: A Novel. 1991. 352p. 21.95 o.p. (0-06-016483-2) HarperTrade.
Binchy, Maeve. Silver Wedding. 1990. 432p. reprint ed. mass mkt. 7.99 (0-440-20777-0) Dell Publishing.
—Silver Wedding. l.t. ed. 2001. 382p. 29.95 (0-7862-3583-7); 453p. (0-7540-1708-7); 453p. (0-7540-9107-4) Thorndike Pr.
—Silver Wedding. l.t. ed. 1989. o.p. (0-7089-8522-X, Charnwood) Thorpe, F. A. Pubs.
Binchy, Maeve, et al. Ladies' Night at Finbar's Hotel. Bolger, Dermot, ed. 2000. (Harvest Original Ser.). 276p. pap. 14.00 (0-15-600866-1, Harvest Bks.) Harcourt Trade Pubs.
Binding, Paul. My Cousin the Writer. 2003. 224p. pap. 13.95 (1-899235-09-4) Lewis, Dewi Publishing GBR. Dist: Consortium Bk. Sales & Distribution.
Binding, Tim. A Perfect Execution. 1996. 320p. o.p. (0-385-25587-X) Doubleday Publishing.
Bingham. The Nightingale Sings. 2000. 639p. 29.95 (0-385-40610-X) Transworld Publishers Ltd. GBR. Dist: Trafalgar Square.
Bingham, Charlotte. The Blue Note. 2000. 566p. (0-385-60063-1) Doubleday Publishing.
—The Chestnut Tree. Date not set. pap. (0-312-30760-8, Saint Martin's Griffin); mass mkt. (0-312-98593-2, St. Martin's Paperbacks); E-Book (0-312-70580-8) St. Martin's Pr.
—The Chestnut Tree. l.t. ed. 2003. 555p. 28.95 (0-7862-5951-5) Thorndike Pr.
—The Chestnut Tree: A Novel of the Women of World War II. 2003. 336p. 24.95 (0-312-30759-4) St. Martin's Pr.
—Distant Music. 2002. 570p. (0-385-60267-7) Doubleday Publishing.
—Distant Music. l.t. ed. 2002. (Charnwood Large Print Ser.). 560p. 32.50 (0-7089-9375-3, Charnwood) Thorpe, F. A. Pubs. GBR. Dist: Ulverscroft Large Print Bks., Ltd., Ulverscroft Large Print Canada, Ltd.
Biondine, Shannah. Cachet. E-Book 7.95 (1-931071-22-5, Bookmice) McGraw Publishing, Inc.
Birch, Carol. Little Sister. 2001. 278p. pap. 13.00 (1-86049-530-3); 1998. o.s.i (1-86049-434-X); 1998. 278p. o.s.i (1-86049-267-3) Virago Pr., Ltd. GBR. Dist: Trafalgar Square, Little Brown & Co.
Bishop, Laurie. The Best Laid Plains. 2003. 224p. mass mkt. 4.99 (0-451-20995-8, Signet Bks.) NAL.
Black, Veronica. Fair Kilmeny. l.t. ed. 1997. (Nightingale Ser.). pap. 17.95 o.p. (0-7838-1972-2, Macmillan Reference USA) Gale Group.
—Hoodman Blind. 1999. 200 p. pap. (0-7540-3550-6); (0-7540-3549-2) BBC Audiobooks America.
—Hoodman Blind. l.t. ed. 1999. (Nightingale Ser.). 208p. pap. 20.95 (0-7838-0371-0) Thorndike Pr.
—A Vow of Adoration: A Sister Joan Mystery. 1997. (Sister Joan Mystery Ser.: Vol. 9). 190p. 20.95 (0-312-18205-8, Saint Martin's Minotaur) St. Martin's Pr.
—A Vow of Chastity: A Sister Joan Mystery. 1993. mass mkt. 4.50 o.s.i (0-8041-1055-7, Ivy Bks.) Ballantine Bks.
—A Vow of Chastity: A Sister Joan Mystery. 1992. 192p. 16.95 o.p. (0-312-07112-4, Saint Martin's Minotaur) St. Martin's Pr.
—A Vow of Chastity: A Sister Joan Mystery. l.t. ed. 1992. (Linford Mystery Library). 400p. pap. 17.99 o.p. (0-7089-7262-4, Linford) Thorpe, F. A. Pubs. GBR. Dist: Ulverscroft Large Print Bks., Ltd., Ulverscroft Large Print Canada, Ltd.
—A Vow of Compassion: A Sister Joan Mystery. 1998. (Sister Joan Mystery Ser.: Vol. 10). 208p. 20.95 (0-312-19354-8, Saint Martin's Minotaur) St. Martin's Pr.
—A Vow of Compassion: A Sister Joan Mystery. l.t. ed. 1998. (Ulverscroft Large Print Ser.). 336p. 29.99 (0-7089-3972-4, Ulverscroft) Thorpe, F. A. Pubs. GBR. Dist: Ulverscroft Large Print Bks., Ltd., Ulverscroft Large Print Canada, Ltd.
—A Vow of Devotion: A Sister Joan Mystery. (Sister Joan Mystery Ser.). 1997. mass mkt. 5.50 o.s.i (0-312-96005-0, St. Martin's Paperbacks); 1995. 186p. 20.95 o.p. (0-312-13206-9, Saint Martin's Minotaur) St. Martin's Pr.
—A Vow of Devotion: A Sister Joan Mystery. l.t. ed. 1998. (Nightingale Ser.). 276p. pap. 20.95 (0-7838-8388-9) Thorndike Pr.
—A Vow of Fidelity: A Sister Joan Mystery. 1996. 208p. text 19.95 o.p. (0-312-14064-9, Saint Martin's Minotaur); Vol. 1. 1997. (Vow of Fidelity Ser.: Vol. 1). 192p. mass mkt. 5.50 (0-312-96259-2, St. Martin's Paperbacks) St. Martin's Pr.
—A Vow of Fidelity: A Sister Joan Mystery. l.t. ed. 1997. (Ulverscroft Large Print Ser.). 352p. 29.99 (0-7089-3697-0, Ulverscroft) Thorpe, F. A. Pubs. GBR. Dist: Ulverscroft Large Print Bks., Ltd., Ulverscroft Large Print Canada, Ltd.
—A Vow of Obedience: A Sister Joan Mystery. 1995. (Sister Joan Mystery Ser.). mass mkt. 5.50 o.s.i (0-8041-1245-2, Ivy Bks.) Ballantine Bks.
—A Vow of Obedience: A Sister Joan Mystery. l.t. ed. 1994. 298p. pap. 19.95 (0-8161-7472-5, Macmillan Reference USA) Gale Group.
—A Vow of Obedience: A Sister Joan Mystery. 1996. mass mkt. 143.76 (0-312-95718-1); 1994. 192p. 18.95 o.p. (0-312-10573-8, Saint Martin's Minotaur) St. Martin's Pr.
—A Vow of Penance: A Sister Joan Mystery. 1996. mass mkt. 5.50 (0-312-95850-1, St. Martin's Paperbacks); 1994. 270p. 19.95 o.p. (0-312-11092-8, Saint Martin's Minotaur) St. Martin's Pr.
—A Vow of Penance: A Sister Joan Mystery. l.t. ed. 1995. (Ulverscroft Large Print Ser.). 352p. 29.99 (0-7089-3326-2, Ulverscroft) Thorpe, F. A. Pubs. GBR. Dist: Ulverscroft Large Print Bks., Ltd., Ulverscroft Large Print Canada, Ltd.
—A Vow of Poverty: A Sister Joan Mystery. 1996. 208p. 20.95 o.p. (0-312-14756-2, Saint Martin's Minotaur) St. Martin's Pr.
—A Vow of Poverty: A Sister Joan Mystery. l.t. ed. 1997. (Ulverscroft Large Print Ser.). 388p. 29.99 (0-7089-3733-0, Ulverscroft) Thorpe, F. A. Pubs. GBR. Dist: Ulverscroft Large Print Bks., Ltd., Ulverscroft Large Print Canada, Ltd.
—A Vow of Silence: A Sister Joan Mystery. 1991. mass mkt. 4.99 o.s.i (0-8041-0814-5, Ivy Bks.) Ballantine Bks.
—A Vow of Silence: A Sister Joan Mystery. 1990. 15.95 o.p. (0-312-04441-0, Saint Martin's Minotaur) St. Martin's Pr.
—A Vow of Silence: A Sister Joan Mystery. l.t. ed. 1991. (Ulverscroft Large Print Ser.). 29.99 (0-7089-2529-4, Ulverscroft) Thorpe, F. A. Pubs. GBR. Dist: Ulverscroft Large Print Bks., Ltd., Ulverscroft Large Print Canada, Ltd.
Blackaby, M. Look What They Have Done to the Blu. 1997. 319p. 17.95 (0-575-06393-9) Gollancz, Victor GBR. Dist: Trafalgar Square.
Blackburn, Julia. The Book of Color. 1996. 192p. pap. 15.00 (0-679-75837-2) Random Hse., Inc.
Blackmore, Richard D. Slain by the Doones, & Other Stories. 1977. (Short Story Index Reprint Ser.). 19.95 (0-8369-3041-X) Ayer Co. Pubs., Inc.
Blackwell, Lawana. Catherine's Heart. 2002. (Tales of London Ser.). 416p. pap. 12.99 (0-7642-2259-7) Bethany Hse. Pubs.
—Like a River Glorious. 1995. (Victorian Serenade: No. 1). 334p. pap. 8.99 (0-8423-7954-1) Tyndale Hse. Pubs.
Blackwood, Caroline. Great Granny Webster. 2002. (New York Review Books Classics Ser.). 120p. pap. 12.95 (1-59017-007-5) New York Review of Bks., Inc., The.
Blair, Catherine. Athena's Conquest. 2001. (Zebra Regency Romance Ser.). 224p. mass mkt. 4.99 o.s.i (0-8217-6873-5) Kensington Publishing Corp.
Blair, Emma. The Daffodil Sea. 2000. 26.95 (0-593-02828-7); 509p. pap. 9.95 (0-553-40614-0) Transworld Publishers Ltd. GBR. Dist: Trafalgar Square.
Blair, Jessica. Portrait of Charlotte. l.t. ed. 2000. (Magna Large Print Ser.). 464p. 31.99 (0-7505-1531-7) Magna Large Print Bks. GBR. Dist: Ulverscroft Large Print Bks., Ltd., Ulverscroft Large Print Canada, Ltd.
—Time & Tide. l.t. ed. 2003. (Magna Large Print Ser.). 512p. 32.50 (0-7505-2027-2) Magna Large Print Bks. GBR. Dist: Ulverscroft Large Print Bks., Ltd., Ulverscroft Large Print Canada, Ltd.
Blayne, Sara. His Scandalous Duchess. 2000. 352p. mass mkt. 5.99 o.s.i (0-8217-6694-5, Zebra Bks.) Kensington Publishing Corp.
Blundell, Mary W. Pastorals of Dorset. 1977. (Short Story Index Reprint Ser.). (Illus.). reprint ed. 25.95 (0-8369-3910-7) Ayer Co. Pubs., Inc.
Bolen, Cheryl. The Bride Wore Blue. 2002. (Brides of Bath Ser.). 32p. mass mkt. 5.99 o.s.i (0-8217-7247-3) Kensington Publishing Corp.
Bolger, Dermot, ed. Ladies' Night at Finbars Hotel. 2000. (0-15-100608-3) Harcourt Trade Pubs.
Bolitho, Janie. Baptised in Blood. l.t. ed. 2001. 305p. pap. 24.95 (0-7862-3312-5) Thorndike Pr.
—Dangerous Deceit. l.t. ed. 1997. (Dales Large Print Ser.). 288p. pap. 19.99 o.p. (1-85389-731-0) Dales Large Print Bks. GBR. Dist: Ulverscroft Large Print Bks., Ltd., Ulverscroft Large Print Canada, Ltd.
—Kindness Can Kill. 1996. (Mystery Ser.). 252p. per. (0-373-26193-4, 1-26193-2, Worldwide Library) Harlequin Enterprises, Ltd.
—Kindness Can Kill: A Detective Chief Inspector Roper Mystery. 1993. 208p. 18.95 o.p. (0-312-10488-X, Saint Martin's Minotaur) St. Martin's Pr.
—Ripe for Revenge. 1996. per. (0-373-26220-5, 1-26220-3, Worldwide Library) Harlequin Enterprises, Ltd.
—Ripe for Revenge. 1995. 191p. 18.95 o.p. (0-312-11881-3, Saint Martin's Minotaur) St. Martin's Pr.
—Sequence of Shame. l.t. ed. 1998. (Dales Large Print Ser.). 304p. pap. o.p. (1-85389-836-8) Dales Large Print Bks. GBR. Dist: Ulverscroft Large Print Canada, Ltd.
—Snapped in Cornwall. 2000. 208p. mass mkt. 9.95 (0-7490-0469-X, London Hse.) Allison & Busby, Ltd. GBR. Dist: International Publishers Marketing.
Bolton, Melvin. The Softener. 1986. 14.95 o.p. (0-531-15015-1, Watts, Franklin) Scholastic Library Publishing.
Booth, Stephen. Blind to the Bones. 2003. 432p. 25.00 (0-7432-3796-X, Scribner) Simon & Schuster.
—Blood on the Tongue. 2003. (Illus.). 512p. mass mkt. 7.50 (0-7434-5783-8, Pocket); 2002. 400p. 25.00 (0-7432-3618-1, Scribner) Simon & Schuster.
—Dancing with the Virgins: A Constable Ben Cooper Novel. 2002. (Illus.). 528p. reprint ed. mass mkt. 6.99 (0-7434-3100-6, Pocket) Simon & Schuster.
—Dancing with the Virgins: A Crime Novel. 2001. 384p. (Illus.). 24.00 (0-7432-1690-3); E-Book 24.00 (0-7432-2364-0) Simon & Schuster. (Scribner).
Borowitz, Albert. The Jack the Ripper Walking Tour Murder. 1986. 256p. 15.95 o.p. (0-312-43944-X) St. Martin's Pr.
Borrow, George (Henry). Lavengro: The Classic Account of Gypsy Life in 19th-Century England. 1991. (Illus.). 608p. reprint ed. pap. 12.95 (0-486-26915-9) Dover Pubns., Inc.
—Lavengro: The Scholar, the Gypsy, the Priest. 1961. 8.95 o.p. (0-460-00119-1); 2.95 o.p. (0-460-01119-7) Biblio Distribution.
—Lavengro: The Scholar, the Gypsy, the Priest. 2001. (Works of George Borrow). reprint ed. pap. text 28.00 (0-7426-8853-4) Classic Bks.
—The Romany Rye. 1969. (Illus.). reprint ed. 8.95 o.p. (0-460-00120-5); 3.95 o.p. (0-460-01120-0) Biblio Distribution.
—The Romany Rye. 2001. (Works of George Borrow). reprint ed. pap. text 28.00 (0-7426-8854-2) Classic Bks.
—The Romany Rye. 1948. 7.00 o.p. (0-248-98251-6) Dufour Editions, Inc.
—The Romany Rye. E-Book 2.49 (0-7574-0395-6) Electric Umbrella Publishing.

—The Romany Rye. 2001. (Twelve-Point Ser.). 474p. lib. bdg. 25.00 (*1-58287-149-3*); 633p. lib. bdg. 28.00 (*1-58287-632-0*) North Bks.

—The Romany Rye. 1984. pap. 8.95 o.p. (*0-19-281406-0*) Oxford Univ. Pr., Inc.

—The Romany Rye. E-Book 5.00 (*0-7410-1102-6*) SoftBook Pr.

Bosse, Malcolm. A Vast Memory of Love. 1992. (Illus.). 448p. 22.95 o.p. (*0-395-62943-8*) Houghton Mifflin Co.

Boston, Lucy M. An Enemy at Green Knowe. 2002. (Green Knowe Ser.). (Illus.). 192p. (YA). (gr. 3 up). reprint ed. 17.00 (*0-15-202475-1*, Harcourt Young Classics) Harcourt Children's Bks.

Boucher, Anthony. The New Adventures of Sherlock Holmes, Vol. 5. abr. ed. 1994. (New Adventures of Sherlock Holmes Gift Edition Ser.: Vol. 5). 25.00 o.s.i incl. audio (*0-671-50143-7*, Simon & Schuster Audioworks) Simon & Schuster Audio.

—The New Adventures of Sherlock Holmes Vol. 1: The Unfortunate Tobacconist & the Paradol Chamber. abr. ed. 1999. (New Adventures of Sherlock Holmes Ser.: Vol. 1). audio (*0-671-04341-2*, Simon & Schuster Audioworks) Simon & Schuster Audio.

—The New Adventures of Sherlock Holmes Vol. 2: The Viennese Strangler & the Notorious Canary Trainer. abr. ed. 1999. audio (*0-671-04342-0*, Simon & Schuster Audioworks) Simon & Schuster Audio.

—The New Adventures of Sherlock Holmes Vol. 3: The April Fool's Day Adventure & the Strange Adventure of the Uneasy Chair. abr. ed. 1999. audio (*0-671-04343-9*, Simon & Schuster Audioworks) Simon & Schuster Audio.

—The New Adventures of Sherlock Holmes Vol. 4: The Strange Case of the Demon Barber & the Mystery of the Headless Monk. abr. ed. 1999. audio (*0-671-04344-7*, Simon & Schuster Audioworks) Simon & Schuster Audio.

—The New Adventures of Sherlock Holmes Vol. 5: The Amateur Mendicant Society & the Case of the Vanishing White Elephant. abr. ed. 1999. (New Adventures of Sherlock Holmes Ser.: Vol. 5). audio (*0-671-04346-3*, Simon & Schuster Audioworks) Simon & Schuster Audio.

—The New Adventures of Sherlock Holmes Vol. 6: The Case of the Limping Ghost & the Girl with the Gazelle. abr. ed. 1999. audio 5.98 (*0-671-04340-4*, Simon & Schuster Audioworks); 1998. audio 5.98 Simon & Schuster Audio.

—The New Adventures of Sherlock Holmes Vol. 7: The Case of the Out of Date Murder & the Waltz of Death. abr. ed. 1999. (New Adventures of Sherlock Holmes Ser.: Vol. 7). audio (*0-671-04347-1*, Simon & Schuster Audioworks) Simon & Schuster Audio.

—The New Adventures of Sherlock Holmes Vol. 8: Colonel Warburton's Madness. abr. ed. 1999. (New Adventures of Sherlock Holmes Ser.: Vol. 8). audio (*0-671-04348-X*, Simon & Schuster Audioworks) Simon & Schuster Audio.

—The New Adventures of Sherlock Holmes Vol. 9: A Scandal in Bohemia & the Second Generation. 1999. (New Adventures of Sherlock Holmes Ser.: Vol. 9). audio (*0-671-04349-8*, Simon & Schuster Audioworks) Simon & Schuster Audio.

—The New Adventures of Sherlock Holmes Vol. 10: In Flanders Fields & the Eyes of Mr. Leyton. abr. ed. 1999. (New Adventures of Sherlock Holmes Ser.: Vol. 10). audio (*0-671-04350-1*, Simon & Schuster Audioworks) Simon & Schuster Audio.

—The New Adventures of Sherlock Holmes Vol. 11: The Tell Tale Pigeon Feathers & the Indiscretion of Mr. Edwards. abr. ed. 1999. audio (*0-671-04351-X*, Simon & Schuster Audioworks) Simon & Schuster Audio.

—The New Adventures of Sherlock Holmes Vol. 11: The Tell Tale Pigeon Feathers & The Indiscretion of Mr. Edwards. abr. ed. 1991. audio 9.95 (*0-671-69083-3*, Simon & Schuster Audioworks) Simon & Schuster Audio.

—The New Adventures of Sherlock Holmes Vol. 12: The Problem of Thor Bridge & the Double Zero. 1999. audio (*0-671-04352-8*, Simon & Schuster Audioworks) Simon & Schuster Audio.

—The New Adventures of Sherlock Holmes Vol. 13: Murder in the Casbah & the Tankerville Club. abr. ed. 1999. (New Adventures of Sherlock Holmes Ser.: Vol. 13). audio (*0-671-04353-6*, Simon & Schuster Audioworks) Simon & Schuster Audio.

—The New Adventures of Sherlock Holmes Vol. 14: The Strange Case of the Murderer in Wax & the Man with the Twisted Lip. abr. ed. 1999. audio (*0-671-04354-4*, Simon & Schuster Audioworks) Simon & Schuster Audio.

—The New Adventures of Sherlock Holmes Vol. 15: The Guileless Gypsy & the Camberville Poisoners. abr. ed. 1999. (New Adventures of Sherlock Holmes Ser.: Vol. 15). audio (*0-671-04355-2*, Simon & Schuster Audioworks) Simon & Schuster Audio.

—The New Adventures of Sherlock Holmes Vol. 16: The Terrifying Cats & the Submarine Club. abr. ed. 1999. (New Adventures of Sherlock Holmes Ser.: Vol. 16). audio (*0-671-04356-0*, Simon & Schuster Audioworks) Simon & Schuster Audio.

—The New Adventures of Sherlock Holmes Vol. 17: The Living Doll & the Disappearing Scientists. abr. ed. 1999. audio (*0-671-04357-9*, Simon & Schuster Audioworks) Simon & Schuster Audio.

—The New Adventures of Sherlock Holmes Vol. 18: The Adventure of the Speckled Band & the Purloined Ruby. abr. ed. 1999. audio (*0-671-04358-7*, Simon & Schuster Audioworks) Simon & Schuster Audio.

—The New Adventures of Sherlock Holmes Vol. 19: The Book of Tobit & Murder Beyond the Mountains. abr. ed. 1999. audio (*0-671-04359-5*, Simon & Schuster Audioworks) Simon & Schuster Audio.

—The New Adventures of Sherlock Holmes Vol. 20: The Manor House Case & the Adventure of the Stuttering Ghost. abr. ed. 1999. audio (*0-671-04360-9*, Simon & Schuster Audioworks) Simon & Schuster Audio.

—The New Adventures of Sherlock Holmes Vol. 21: The Great Gandolfo & the Adventure of the Original Hamlet. abr. ed. 1999. audio (*0-671-04361-7*, Simon & Schuster Audioworks) Simon & Schuster Audio.

—The New Adventures of Sherlock Holmes Vol. 22: Murder by Moonlight & the Singular Affair of the Coptic Compass. 1999. (New Adventures of Sherlock Holmes Ser.). audio (*0-671-04362-5*, Simon & Schuster Audioworks) Simon & Schuster Audio.

—The New Adventures of Sherlock Holmes Vol. 23: The Gunpowder Plot & the Babbling Butler. abr. ed. 1999. audio (*0-671-04363-3*, Simon & Schuster Audioworks) Simon & Schuster Audio.

—The New Adventures of Sherlock Holmes Vol. 24: The Accidental Murderess & the Adventure of the Blarney Stone. abr. ed. 1999. (New Adventures of Sherlock Holmes Ser.). audio (*0-671-04364-1*, Simon & Schuster Audioworks) Simon & Schuster Audio.

—The New Adventures of Sherlock Holmes Vol. 25: The Night Before Christmas & the Darlington Substitution. abr. ed. 1999. (New Adventures of Sherlock Holmes Ser.). audio (*0-671-04365-X*, Simon & Schuster Audioworks) Simon & Schuster Audio.

—The New Adventures of Sherlock Holmes Vol. 26: The Haunting of Sherlock Holmes & the Baconian Cipher. abr. ed. 1999. audio (*0-671-04366-8*, Simon & Schuster Audioworks) Simon & Schuster Audio.

Boucher, Anthony & Green, Denis. The New Adventures of Sherlock Holmes. abr. ed. 1990. (Sherlock Holmes Ser.). audio 25.00 o.s.i (*0-671-72702-8*); 1993. (Sherlock Holmes Ser.). audio 25.00 o.s.i (*0-671-87587-6*); 2001. audio 49.95 (*0-7435-2045-9*); Set. 1992. (New Adventures of Sherlock Holmes Gift Edition Ser.: Vol. 3). audio 25.00 o.s.i (*0-671-79367-5*); Vol. 5-18. 1991. (New Adventures of Sherlock Holmes Ser.: Vol. 2). audio 25.00 o.s.i (*0-671-74750-9*); Vol. 10. 1990. audio 9.95 (*0-671-69082-5*) Simon & Schuster Audio. (Simon & Schuster Audioworks).

—The New Adventures of Sherlock Holmes Vol. 1: The Unfortunate Tobacconist & The Paradol Chamber. abr. ed. 1988. 9.95 incl. audio (*0-671-66076-4*, Simon & Schuster Audioworks) Simon & Schuster Audio.

—The New Adventures of Sherlock Holmes Vol. 3: The Aprl Fool's Day Adventure & The Strange Adventure of the Uneasy Easy Chair. abr. ed. 1989. 9.95 incl. audio (*0-671-67785-3*, Simon & Schuster Audioworks) Simon & Schuster Audio.

—The New Adventures of Sherlock Holmes Vol. 4: The Strange Case of the Demon Barber & The Mystery of the Headless Monk. abr. ed. 1989. 9.95 incl. audio (*0-671-68088-9*, Simon & Schuster Audioworks) Simon & Schuster Audio.

—The New Adventures of Sherlock Holmes Vol. 5: The Amateur Mendicant Society & The Case of the Vanishing White Elephant. abr. ed. 1990. audio 9.95 (*0-671-68423-X*, Simon & Schuster Audioworks) Simon & Schuster Audio.

—The New Adventures of Sherlock Holmes Vol. 6: Eight Classic Radio Mysteries. gif. ed. 1995. (New Adventures of Sherlock Holmes Gift Edition Ser.: Vol. 6). audio 25.00 o.s.i (*0-671-53703-2*, Simon & Schuster Audioworks) Simon & Schuster Audio.

—The New Adventures of Sherlock Holmes Vol. 6: The Case of the Limping Ghost & The Girl with the Gazelle. abr. ed. 1989. audio 9.95 (*0-671-68772-7*, Simon & Schuster Audioworks) Simon & Schuster Audio.

—The New Adventures of Sherlock Holmes Vol. 7: The Case of the Out of Date Murder & The Waltz of Death. abr. ed. 1990. audio 9.95 (*0-671-68773-5*, Simon & Schuster Audioworks) Simon & Schuster Audio.

—The New Adventures of Sherlock Holmes Vol. 8: Colonel Warburton's Madness & The Iron Box. abr. ed. 1990. (New Adventures of Sherlock Holmes Ser.: Vol. 8). 60p. audio 9.95 (*0-671-68774-3*, Simon & Schuster Audioworks) Simon & Schuster Audio.

—The New Adventures of Sherlock Holmes Vol. 9: A Scandal in Bohemia & The Second Generation. abr. ed. 1990. audio 9.95 (*0-671-69081-7*, Simon & Schuster Audioworks) Simon & Schuster Audio.

—The New Adventures of Sherlock Holmes Vol. 12: The Problem of Thor Bridge & The Double Zero. abr. ed. 1991. audio 9.95 (*0-671-70744-2*, 326340, Simon & Schuster Audioworks) Simon & Schuster Audio.

—The New Adventures of Sherlock Holmes Vol. 14: The Strange Case of the Murderer in Wax & The Man with the Twisted Lip. abr. ed. 1991. audio 9.95 (*0-671-70746-9*, Simon & Schuster Audioworks) Simon & Schuster Audio.

—The New Adventures of Sherlock Holmes Vol. 20: The Manor House Case & The Adventure of the Stuttering Ghost. abr. ed. 1993. audio 11.00 (*0-671-79411-6*, Simon & Schuster Audioworks) Simon & Schuster Audio.

Boucher, Anthony & Greene, Denis. The New Adventures of Sherlock Holmes Slip Case, Vols. 1-13. unabr. ed. audio 129.35 Simon & Schuster Audio.

Boumelha, Penny & Hardy, Thomas. Jude the Obscure: Thomas Hardy. 2000. (New Casebooks Ser.). 224p. 59.95 (*0-312-22701-9*) Palgrave Macmillan.

Bowen, John. The Girls. 1988. 192p. pap. 7.95 o.p. (*0-452-26077-9*, Plume) Dutton/Plume.

—The Girls. 1987. 192p. 16.95 o.p. (*0-87113-137-4*) Grove/Atlantic, Inc.

Bowen, Marjorie. The Governor of England: A Novel on Oliver Cromwell. 2000. 252p. E-Book 3.95 (*0-594-01887-0*) 1873 Pr.

Bowker, David. The Death You Deserve: A Novel. 2003. 256p. pap. 12.95 (*0-312-31178-8*, Saint Martin's Griffin) St. Martin's Pr.

Boylan, Clare. Emma Brown. 2004. 448p. 25.95 (*0-670-03297-2*) Viking Penguin.

Boyle, Elizabeth. Brazen Temptress. 1999. 368p. pap. 19.00 (*0-440-61376-0*, Delta); mass mkt. 5.99 o.s.i (*0-440-22639-2*) Dell Publishing.

—Once Tempted. 2001. 384p. mass mkt. 5.99 (*0-380-81535-4*, Avon Bks.) Morrow/Avon.

Boyle, Josephine. Holy Terror. 1995. 21.95 o.p. (*0-312-11824-4*, Saint Martin's Minotaur) St. Martin's Pr.

—Maiden's End. 1989. 272p. 17.95 o.p. (*0-312-03391-5*) St. Martin's Pr.

Boyle, Kay. The Crazy Hunter. 1993. (Bibelots Ser.). 144p. reprint ed. pap. 6.00 (*0-8112-1233-5*, NDP769) New Directions Publishing Corp.

Boyt, Susie. The Characters of Love. 1997. 192p. 19.95 o.p. (*0-297-81766-3*) Weidenfeld & Nicolson, Ltd. GBR. *Dist:* Trafalgar Square.

Bradberry, James. Ruins of Civility. 1996. 256p. 21.95 o.p. (*0-312-14041-X*, Saint Martin's Minotaur) St. Martin's Pr.

Bradbury, Malcolm. Eating People Is Wrong. 1991. 248p. reprint ed. pap. 12.00 (*0-89733-189-3*) Academy Chicago Pubs., Ltd.

—The History Man. 1985. (Fiction Ser.). 240p. pap. 10.00 o.p. (*0-14-007630-1*, Penguin Bks.) Viking Penguin.

Braddon, M. E. Eleanor's Victory. 1996. (Pocket Classics Ser.). 416p. pap. 12.95 (*0-7509-1118-2*) Sutton Publishing, Ltd. GBR. *Dist:* International Publishers Marketing.

Braddon, Mary Elizabeth. Aurora Floyd. Nemesvari, Richard & Surridge, Lisa, eds. 1998. (Literary Texts Ser.). (Illus.). 635p. pap. (*1-55111-123-3*) Broadview Pr.

—Aurora Floyd. 1999. (Oxford World's Classics Ser.). 498p. pap. 12.95 (*0-19-283727-3*) Oxford Univ. Pr., Inc.

—Aurora Floyd. Edwards, P. D., ed. 1996. (Oxford World's Classics Ser.). 500p. pap. 12.95 o.p. (*0-19-282402-3*) Oxford Univ. Pr., Inc.

—Aurora Floyd. 1987. o.s.i (*0-86068-510-1*) Random Hse., Inc.

—Lady Audley's Secret. 1987. (Oxford World's Classics Ser.). 496p. pap. 8.95 o.p. (*0-19-281741-8*) Oxford Univ. Pr., Inc.

—Vixen. 1993. (Pocket Classics Ser.). pap. 12.95 (*0-7509-0445-3*) Sutton Publishing, Ltd. GBR. *Dist:* International Publishers Marketing.

Bradford, Barbara Taylor. Everything to Gain. l.t. ed. 1994. 26.95 o.p. (*1-56895-152-3*, Wheeler Publishing, Inc.) Gale Group.

Bradley, Marion Zimmer. The Mists of Avalon. 2001. E-Book 15.00 (*1-58945-945-8*) Adobe Systems, Inc.

—The Mists of Avalon. 2001. E-Book 15.00 (*0-345-44816-2*, Ballantine Bks.); 2000. 896p. 30.00 (*0-345-44118-4*, Del Rey); 1985. 396p. pap. 9.95 o.s.i (*0-345-33385-3*, Del Rey); 1987. 912p. reprint ed. pap. 16.95 (*0-345-35049-9*, Del Rey) Ballantine Bks.

—The Mists of Avalon. 1982. 16.95 o.p. (*0-394-52406-3*) Knopf, Alfred A. Inc.

Bradshaw, Anne Christine. Chamomile Winter. 2001. (Joy to the Lands: Vol. 2). 203p. pap. 12.95 (*1-55517-558-9*, Bonneville Bks.) Cedar Fort, Inc./CFI Distribution.

Brady, James. A Hampton's Christmas. (Illus.). 2001. 288p. mass mkt. 6.99 o.s.i (*0-312-98127-9*, St. Martin's Paperbacks); 2000. 211p. 23.95 (*0-312-26604-9*) St. Martin's Pr.

Bragg, Melvyn. The Maid of Buttermere. 1991. 416p. text 24.95 o.p. (*0-340-40173-7*) Hodder & Stoughton, Ltd. GBR. *Dist:* Lubrecht & Cramer, Ltd., Trafalgar Square.

—The Maid of Buttermere. 1987. 384p. 19.95 o.p. (*0-399-13225-2*, G. P. Putnam's Sons) Penguin Putnam Bks. for Young Readers.

—The Soldier's Return. 2002. 384p. 25.95 (*1-55970-639-2*) Arcade Publishing, Inc.

—The Son of War. A Novel. 2003. 432p. 25.95 (*1-55970-686-4*) Arcade Publishing, Inc.

Braine, John. Life at the Top. 1980. reprint ed. pap. 3.95 o.s.i (*0-416-00591-8*, NO. 0185) Routledge.

—Room at the Top. 22.95 (*0-8488-0921-1*) Amereon, Ltd.

—Room at the Top. 1993. reprint ed. lib. bdg. 18.95 (*1-56849-187-5*) Buccaneer Bks., Inc.

—Room at the Top. l.t. unabr. ed. 1998. 288p. 24.95 (*1-85695-357-2*, 953572) ISIS Large Print Bks. GBR. *Dist:* Transaction Pubs.

—Room at the Top. mass mkt. 0.60 o.p. (*0-451-02318-8*); mass mkt. 0.75 o.p. (*0-451-03192-X*); mass mkt. 0.95 o.p. (*0-451-04672-2*); mass mkt. 0.35 o.p. (*0-451-01569-X*) NAL. (Signet Bks.).

—Room at the Top. 1957. reprint ed. 9.95 o.p. (*0-416-00601-9*, NO. 0186); pap. 4.95 o.p. (*0-416-00611-6*, NO. 0187) Routledge.

—Waiting for Sheila. 1977. 9.95 o.p. (*0-416-00571-3*, NO. 0183) Routledge.

Brand, Christianna. Death in High Heels. unabr. ed. 1993. audio 54.95 (*0-7451-5798-X*, CAT 4037) BBC Audiobooks America.

—Death of Jezebel. unabr. ed. 1994. audio 54.95 (*0-7451-5800-5*, CAB 4050) BBC Audiobooks America.

—Fog of Doubt. 272p. 1995. mass mkt. 4.95 (*0-7867-0219-2*); 1984. pap. 3.50 o.p. (*0-88184-065-3*) Avalon Publishing Group. (Carroll & Graf Pubs.).

—Fog of Doubt. 1979. lib. bdg. 9.95 o.p. (*0-8398-2535-8*, Macmillan Reference USA) Gale Group.

—Green for Danger. 1997. 256p. mass mkt. 4.95 (*0-7867-0386-5*); 1990. 254p. pap. 3.95 o.p. (*0-88184-612-0*); 1989. 254p. pap. 7.95 o.p. (*0-88184-483-7*) Avalon Publishing Group. (Carroll & Graf Pubs.).

—Green for Danger. l.t. ed. 1990. pap. 16.95 o.p. (*0-7927-0442-8*, C0400); 1993. audio 54.95 (*0-7451-2418-6*, CDA 019, Chivers Children's Audio Bks.) BBC Audiobooks America.

—Green for Danger. 1986. (Mystery Ser.). mass mkt. 9.95 o.p. (*0-553-06517-3*) Bantam Bks.

—Green for Danger. 1978. (Illus.). 271p. reprint ed. 18.95 o.p. (*0-89163-046-5*) Boulevard Bks.

—Green for Danger. 1981. 256p. pap. 2.50 o.p. (*0-06-080551-X*, P 551) HarperCollins Pubs.

—Suddenly at His Residence. (Black Dagger Crime Ser.). 1990. 18.50 o.p. (*0-86220-791-6*, C1031, Black Dagger); 1992. audio 54.95 (*0-7451-2404-6*, CD 005) BBC Audiobooks America.

—Suddenly at His Residence. 1988. 176p. mass mkt. 3.50 o.s.i (*0-553-25465-0*) Bantam Bks.

—Suddenly at His Residence. l.t. ed. 1997. (Linford Mystery Library). 416p. pap. 17.99 o.p. (*0-7089-5107-4*, Linford) Thorpe, F. A. Pubs. GBR. *Dist:* Ulverscroft Large Print Bks., Ltd., Ulverscroft Large Print Canada, Ltd.

Brand, Christianna & Boyd, Carole. Death in High Heels. unabr. ed. 1989. audio 53.95 o.s.i (*0-8161-9375-4*) BBC Audiobooks America.

Brand, Christianna & Melling, John K. Death of Jezebel. 1990. (Black Dagger Crime Ser.). 208p. reprint ed. text 12.95 o.p. (*0-86220-774-6*) Chivers Pr. GBR. *Dist:* BBC Audiobooks America.

Brandewyne, Rebecca. The Love Knot. l.t. ed. 2003. 418p. 29.95 (*1-58724-493-4*, Wheeler Publishing, Inc.) Gale Group.

—The Love Knot. 2003. 400p. mass mkt. (*1-55166-685-5*, Mira Bks.) Harlequin Enterprises, Ltd.

—Swan Road. 1995. (Illus.). 384p. reprint ed. 22.00 (*0-7278-4758-9*) Severn Hse. Pubs., Ltd.

—Swan Road. 1994. 384p. mass mkt. 5.99 (*0-446-32701-8*) Warner Bks., Inc.

—Upon a Moon-Dark Moor. l.t. ed. 1989. (General Ser.). 552p. 20.95 o.p. (*0-8161-4731-0*, Macmillan Reference USA) Gale Group.

Branfield, John. Brown Cow. 1985. 160p. (J). (gr. 6-8). 15.95 o.p. (*0-575-03223-5*) Gollancz, Victor GBR. *Dist:* Trafalgar Square.

Brayfield, Celia. Heartswap. l.t. ed. 2000. (General Ser.). 330p. 23.95 (*0-7862-2811-3*) Thorndike Pr.

Breeze, Paul. In Harm's Way. 1995. 240p. 20.95 o.p. (*0-312-13094-5*) St. Martin's Pr.

Brendan, Mary. A Kind & Decent Man. 2001. 256p. mass mkt. (*0-373-51152-3*, Harlequin Bks.) Harlequin Enterprises, Ltd.

Brett, Simon. An Amateur Corpse. l.t. ed. 1990. pap. 5.00 (*0-7451-1285-4*) BBC Audiobooks America.
—An Amateur Corpse. 1980. mass mkt. 1.95 o.p. (*0-425-04489-0*) Berkley Publishing Group.
—An Amateur Corpse. unabr. ed. 1994. audio 39.95 (*0-7861-0483-X*, 1435) Blackstone Audio Bks., Inc.
—An Amateur Corpse. 1986. mass mkt. 3.50 o.s.i (*0-440-10185-9*) Dell Publishing.
—An Amateur Corpse. l.t. ed. 1990. (Nightingale Ser.). 300p. pap. 13.95 (*0-8161-5040-0*, Macmillan Reference USA) Gale Group.
—An Amateur Corpse. unabr. ed. 2000. (Charles Paris Mystery Ser. : Vol. 4). audio 44.00 (*0-7887-1286-1*, 95146E7) Recorded Bks., LLC.
—An Amateur Corpse. 1991. mass mkt. 3.95 o.p. (*0-446-35960-2*) Warner Bks., Inc.
—An Amateur Corpse. 2000. 196p. pap. 12.95 (*0-595-00359-1*) iUniverse, Inc.
—The Body on the Beach. 2000. (Fethering Mysteries Ser.). 320p. 21.95 o.s.i (*0-425-17500-6*, Prime Crime) Berkley Publishing Group.
—Cast, in Order of Disappearance. unabr. ed. 1993. audio 39.95 (*0-7451-5803-X*, CSL 052) BBC Audiobooks America.
—Cast, in Order of Disappearance. 1981. mass mkt. 2.25 o.p. (*0-425-04934-5*) Berkley Publishing Group.
—Cast, in Order of Disappearance. l.t. ed. 1990. (Nightingale Ser.). 279p. pap. 13.95 o.p. (*0-8161-4917-8*, Macmillan Reference USA) Gale Group.
—Cast, in Order of Disappearance. unabr. ed. 1997. (Charles Paris Mystery Ser. : Vol. 1). audio 35.00 (*0-7887-0858-9*, 94984E7) Recorded Bks., LLC.
—A Comedian Dies. 1980. mass mkt. 2.25 o.p. (*0-425-04702-4*) Berkley Publishing Group.
—A Comedian Dies. unabr. ed. 1999. audio 39.95 Blackstone Audio Bks., Inc.
—A Comedian Dies. unabr. ed. 1998. (Charles Paris Mystery Ser. : Vol. 5). audio 44.00 (*0-7887-1886-X*, 95308E7) Recorded Bks., LLC.
—A Comedian Dies. 1990. mass mkt. 3.95 o.p. (*0-446-35958-0*) Warner Bks., Inc.
—A Comedian Dies. 2000. 164p. pap. 11.95 (*0-595-00358-3*) iUniverse, Inc.
—Corporate Bodies. l.t. ed. 1993. 22.95 o.p. (*0-7927-1418-0*); pap. 20.95 o.p. (*0-7927-1417-2*) BBC Audiobooks America.
—Corporate Bodies. unabr. ed. 1993. audio 39.95 (*0-7861-0394-9*, 752393) Blackstone Audio Bks., Inc.
—Corporate Bodies. abr. ed. 1992. 2p. audio 16.99 (*0-88646-323-8*, 7323); Set. 1996. audio 9.99 (*1-55204-012-7*, 393577) Durkin Hayes Publishing Ltd.
—Corporate Bodies. 1992. 256p. 19.00 (*0-684-19397-3*, Macmillan Reference USA) Gale Group.
—Corporate Bodies. 1993. (Mystery Ser.). mass mkt. (*0-373-26130-6*, 1-26130-4, Harlequin Bks.) Harlequin Enterprises, Ltd.
—Corporate Bodies. unabr. ed. 2000. (Charles Paris Mystery Ser. : Vol. 15). audio 44.00 (*1-55690-654-4*, 92406E7) Recorded Bks., LLC.
—Dead Giveaway. 1987. 256p. mass mkt. 3.50 o.s.i (*0-440-11914-6*) Dell Publishing.
—Dead Giveaway. (Charles Paris Mystery Ser.). 1986. 169p. 13.95 o.p. (*0-684-18517-2*); 1987. 237p. 10.95 o.p. (*0-8161-4218-1*) Gale Group. (Macmillan Reference USA).
—Dead Giveaway. 2000. 180p. pap. 12.95 (*0-595-00357-5*) iUniverse, Inc.
—Dead Room Farce. unabr. ed. 1998. audio 54.95 (*0-7540-0150-4*, CAB 1573) BBC Audiobooks America.
—Dead Room Farce. unabr. ed. 1999. audio 39.95 (*0-7861-1642-0*, 2470) Blackstone Audio Bks., Inc.
—Dead Room Farce. 1998. 208p. 20.95 (*0-312-19251-7*, Saint Martin's Minotaur) St. Martin's Pr.
—Dead Room Farce. l.t. ed. 1998. (Mystery Ser.). 344p. 27.95 (*0-7862-1564-X*) Thorndike Pr.
—The Dead Side of the Mike. unabr. ed. 1997. audio 54.95 (*0-7451-6738-1*, CAB 1354) BBC Audiobooks America.
—The Dead Side of the Mike. unabr. ed. 1992. audio 39.95 (*0-7861-0340-X*, 1297) Blackstone Audio Bks., Inc.
—The Dead Side of the Mike. 1986. pap. 3.50 o.p. (*0-440-11763-1*) Dell Publishing.
—The Dead Side of the Mike. unabr. ed. 1998. (Charles Paris Mystery Ser. : No. 6). audio 44.00 (*0-7887-2520-3*, 95593E7) Recorded Bks., LLC.
—The Dead Side of the Mike. 1991. mass mkt. 3.95 o.p. (*0-446-35957-2*) Warner Bks., Inc.
—The Dead Side of the Mike. 2000. 180p. per. 11.95 (*0-595-00354-0*) iUniverse, Inc.
—Death on the Downs. 304p. 2001. 21.95 o.s.i (*0-425-17953-2*); 2002. (Fethering Mysteries Ser.: Vol. 2). reprint ed. mass mkt. 6.99 (*0-425-18636-9*) Berkley Publishing Group. (Prime Crime).
—Death on the Downs. l.t. ed. 2002. 441p. 28.95 (*0-7862-3988-3*) Gale Group.
—Mrs. Pargeter's Package. 1991. 288p. 18.95 o.s.i (*0-684-19286-1*, Macmillan Reference USA) Gale Group.
—Mrs. Pargeter's Package. unabr. ed. 2001. audio 54.95 (*1-85089-648-8*, 91061); 1999. audio compact disk 59.95 (*0-7531-0711-2*, 107112) ISIS Audio Bks. GBR. *Dist:* Ulverscroft Large Print Bks., Ltd.
—Mrs. Pargeter's Package. l.t. ed. 1991. (Magna Large Print Ser.). 270p. o.p. (*0-7505-0130-8*) Magna Large Print Bks. GBR. *Dist:* Ulverscroft Large Print Canada, Ltd.
—Mrs. Pargeter's Package. 1992. 224p. mass mkt. 4.99 (*0-446-36204-2*) Warner Bks., Inc.
—Mrs. Pargeter's Plot. 1999. (WWL Mystery Ser.: No. 322). per. (*0-373-26322-8*, 1-26322-7, Worldwide Library) Harlequin Enterprises, Ltd.
—Mrs. Pargeter's Plot. unabr. ed. 2001. audio 49.95 (*0-7531-0103-3*, 961001); 2000. audio compact disk 59.95 (*0-7531-0904-2*, 109042) ISIS Audio Bks. GBR. *Dist:* Ulverscroft Large Print Bks., Ltd.
—Mrs. Pargeter's Plot. l.t. ed. 1998. (Magna Large Print Ser.). 320p. o.p. (*0-7505-1284-9*) Magna Large Print Bks. GBR. *Dist:* Ulverscroft Large Print Canada, Ltd.
—Mrs. Pargeter's Plot. 1998. (Mrs. Pargeter Mysteries Ser.). 256p. 22.00 (*0-684-83714-5*, Scribner) Simon & Schuster.
—Mrs. Pargeter's Plot. l.t. ed. 1998. (Mystery Ser.). 255p. 30.95 (*0-7838-0172-6*) Thorndike Pr.
—Mrs. Pargeter's Point of Honour. 2003. (Mystery Ser.). 28.95 (*1-57490-465-5*) Beeler, Thomas T. Publisher.
—Mrs. Pargeter's Point of Honour. 2000. (Mrs. Pargeter Mysteries Ser.). 256p. mass mkt. (*0-373-26361-9*, 1-26361-5, Worldwide Library) Harlequin Enterprises, Ltd.
—Mrs. Pargeter's Point of Honour. unabr. ed. 1999. audio 54.95 (*0-7531-0466-0*, 981201) ISIS Audio Bks. GBR. *Dist:* Ulverscroft Large Print Bks., Ltd.
—Mrs. Pargeter's Point of Honour. l.t. ed. 1999. (Magna Large Print Ser.). 320p. o.p. (*0-7505-1394-2*) Magna Large Print Bks. GBR. *Dist:* Ulverscroft Large Print Canada, Ltd.
—Mrs. Pargeter's Point of Honour. 272p. 2002. pap. 18.95 (*0-7432-4186-X*); 1999. 23.00 o.s.i (*0-684-86295-6*) Simon & Schuster. (Scribner).
—Mrs. Pargeter's Pound of Flesh. 1993. 224p. 20.00 o.p. (*0-684-19565-8*, Macmillan Reference USA) Gale Group.
—Mrs. Pargeter's Pound of Flesh. unabr. ed. 2001. audio 54.95 (*1-85695-571-0*, 93051) ISIS Audio Bks. GBR. *Dist:* Ulverscroft Large Print Bks., Ltd.
—Mrs. Pargeter's Pound of Flesh. l.t. ed. 1993. (Magna Large Print Ser.). 307p. (*0-7505-0579-6*) Magna Large Print Bks. GBR. *Dist:* Ulverscroft Large Print Canada, Ltd.
—Mrs. Pargeter's Pound of Flesh. 1994. (Crime Ser.). 208p. pap. 5.95 o.p. (*0-14-023485-3*, Penguin Bks.) Penguin Group (USA) Inc.
—Mrs., Presumed Dead. 1990. 256p. mass mkt. 3.95 o.s.i (*0-440-20552-2*) Dell Publishing.
—Mrs., Presumed Dead. 1989. 256p. 17.95 o.s.i (*0-684-18851-1*, Macmillan Reference USA) Gale Group.
—Mrs., Presumed Dead. unabr. ed. 2001. audio 54.95 (*1-85695-429-3*, 89042) ISIS Audio Bks. GBR. *Dist:* Ulverscroft Large Print Bks., Ltd.
—Murder in the Museum. l.t. ed. 2003. (Fethering Mystery Ser.). 456p. 28.95 (*0-7862-5865-9*) Thorndike Pr.
—Murder in the Title. 1986. pap. 3.50 o.p. (*0-440-16016-2*) Dell Publishing.
—Murder in the Title. 1983. 192p. 11.95 o.s.i (*0-684-17898-2*, Macmillan Reference USA) Gale Group.
—Murder in the Title. 1990. mass mkt. 3.95 o.p. (*0-446-35954-8*) Warner Bks., Inc.
—Murder in the Title. 2000. (Charles Paris Mystery Ser.). 196p. pap. 12.95 (*0-595-00353-2*) iUniverse, Inc.
—Murder Unprompted. unabr. ed. 1992. (Audio Bks.). audio 39.95 (*0-7451-5804-8*, CAB 686) BBC Audiobooks America.
—Murder Unprompted. unabr. ed. 1997. audio 32.95 (*0-7861-1081-3*, 1851) Blackstone Audio Bks., Inc.
—Murder Unprompted. 1986. (Murder Ink Mystery Ser.: No. 69). pap. 3.50 o.p. (*0-440-16145-2*) Dell Publishing.
—Murder Unprompted. (Nightingale Ser.). 1983. 290p. pap. 9.95 o.p. (*0-8161-3540-1*); 1982. 160p. 10.95 o.s.i (*0-684-17659-9*) Gale Group. (Macmillan Reference USA).
—Murder Unprompted. unabr. ed. 2001. audio compact disk 49.00 (*0-7887-3982-4*, C1145E7); 1999. audio 38.00 (*0-7887-4081-4*, H1075E7) Recorded Bks., LLC. (Clipper Audio).
—Murder Unprompted. 1990. mass mkt. 3.95 o.p. (*0-446-35955-6*) Warner Bks., Inc.
—A Nice Class of Corpse. 1988. 224p. mass mkt. 3.50 o.s.i (*0-440-20113-6*) Dell Publishing.
—A Nice Class of Corpse. 1987. 196p. 14.95 o.p. (*0-684-18685-3*, Macmillan Reference USA) Gale Group.
—A Nice Class of Corpse. unabr. ed. 2001. audio 54.95 (*1-85089-755-7*, 87122) ISIS Audio Bks. GBR. *Dist:* Ulverscroft Large Print Bks., Ltd.
—A Nice Class of Corpse. l.t. ed. 1987. (Mainstream Ser.). 236p. reprint ed. lib. bdg. 17.95 o.p. (*1-85089-174-5*) ISIS Large Print Bks. GBR. *Dist:* Transaction Pubs.
—Not Dead, Only Resting. l.t. ed. 1985. (Nightingale Ser.). 304p. 10.95 o.p. (*0-8161-3831-1*, Macmillan Reference USA) Gale Group.
—Not Dead, Only Resting. 1990. mass mkt. 3.95 o.p. (*0-446-35952-1*) Warner Bks., Inc.
—Not Dead, Only Resting. 2000. 180p. pap. 12.95 (*0-595-00356-7*) iUniverse, Inc.
—Not Dead, Only Resting: A Charles Paris Mystery. 1984. 176p. 11.95 o.s.i (*0-684-18193-2*, Macmillan Reference USA) Gale Group.
—A Reconstructed Corpse. unabr. ed. 2000. (Charles Paris Mystery Ser.: Bk. 15). audio (*0-7451-4357-1*, CAB 1040) Chivers Audio Bks. GBR. *Dist:* BBC Audiobooks America.
—A Reconstructed Corpse. l.t. ed. 1994. 234p. 24.95 (*1-56895-117-5*, Wheeler Publishing, Inc.) Gale Group.
—A Reconstructed Corpse. 1996. (WWL Mystery Ser.). per. (*0-373-26194-2*, 1-26194-0, Worldwide Library) Harlequin Enterprises, Ltd.
—A Reconstructed Corpse. l.t. ed. 1994. (Magna Large Print Ser.). 302p. o.p. (*0-7505-0717-9*) Magna Large Print Bks. GBR. *Dist:* Ulverscroft Large Print Canada, Ltd.
—A Reconstructed Corpse. unabr. ed. 1994. audio 44.00 (*0-7887-0110-X*, 94351E7) Recorded Bks., LLC.
—A Reconstructed Corpse. 1994. 192p. 20.00 (*0-684-19700-6*, Scribner) Simon & Schuster.
—A Series of Murders. unabr. ed. 1993. audio 39.95 (*0-7451-5801-3*, CAB 427) BBC Audiobooks America.
—A Series of Murders. 1989. 224p. 16.95 o.s.i (*0-684-19096-6*, Scribner) Simon & Schuster.
—A Series of Murders. 1990. mass mkt. 3.95 o.s.i (*0-446-35949-1*) Warner Bks., Inc.
—Sicken & So Die. unabr. ed. 1996. (Charles Paris Mystery Ser.). audio 54.95 (*0-7451-6698-9*, CAB1314) BBC Audiobooks America.
—Sicken & So Die. unabr. ed. (Charles Paris Mystery Ser.). 2000. audio compact disk 40.00 (*0-7861-9896-6*, z1874); 1997. audio 32.95 (*0-7861-1108-9*, 1874) Blackstone Audio Bks., Inc.
—Sicken & So Die. 1997. per. (*0-373-26262-0*, 1-26262-5, Worldwide Library) Harlequin Enterprises, Ltd.
—Sicken & So Die. 1997. 208p. 20.50 (*0-684-82459-0*, Scribner) Simon & Schuster.
—Simon Brett: Four Complete Mysteries. 1993. 736p. 6.99 o.s.i (*0-517-09330-8*) Random Hse. Value Publishing.
—Situation Tragedy. unabr. ed. 1996. audio 32.95 (*0-7861-0965-3*, 1742) Blackstone Audio Bks., Inc.
—Situation Tragedy. 1986. pap. 3.50 o.p. (*0-440-18792-3*) Dell Publishing.
—Situation Tragedy. unabr. ed. 1998. audio 69.95 o.p. (*1-872672-11-6*) Magna Story Sound GBR. *Dist:* Ulverscroft Large Print Bks., Ltd.
—Situation Tragedy. 1981. (Charles Paris Mystery Ser. : Vol. 7). audio 44.00 (*0-7887-3491-1*, 95898E7) Recorded Bks., LLC.
—Situation Tragedy. 1981. 192p. 9.95 o.s.i (*0-684-17268-2*, Scribner) Simon & Schuster.
—Situation Tragedy. 1990. mass mkt. 3.95 o.s.i (*0-446-35956-4*) Warner Bks., Inc.
—So Much Blood. 1981. mass mkt. 2.25 o.s.i (*0-425-04935-3*); 1979. mass mkt. 1.75 o.s.i (*0-425-04159-X*) Berkley Publishing Group.
—So Much Blood. unabr. ed. 2000. (Charles Paris Mystery Ser.: Bk. 2). audio 49.95 (*0-7451-4251-6*, CAB 934) Chivers Audio Bks. GBR. *Dist:* BBC Audiobooks America.
—So Much Blood. 1986. mass mkt. 3.50 o.s.i (*0-440-18069-4*) Dell Publishing.
—So Much Blood. unabr. ed. 1997. (Charles Paris Mystery Ser. : Vol. 2). audio 44.00 (*0-7887-0931-3*, 95071E7) Recorded Bks., LLC.
—So Much Blood. 2000. 196p. pap. 12.95 (*0-595-00360-5*) iUniverse, Inc.
—Star Trap. unabr. ed. 1995. audio 54.95 (*0-7451-6481-1*, CAB 1097) BBC Audiobooks America.
—Star Trap. unabr. ed. 2000. audio 32.95 (*0-7861-1750-8*, 2554); audio compact disk 40.00 (*0-7861-9901-6*, z2554) Blackstone Audio Bks., Inc.
—Star Trap. 1986. mass mkt. 3.50 o.s.i (*0-440-18300-6*) Dell Publishing.
—Star Trap. l.t. ed. 1989. 315p. 13.95 o.p. (*0-8161-4774-4*, Macmillan Reference USA) Gale Group.
—Star Trap. unabr. ed. 1997. (Charles Paris Mystery Ser. : Vol. 3). audio 44.00 (*0-7887-1146-6*, 95084E7) Recorded Bks., LLC.
—Star Trap. 1990. mass mkt. 3.95 o.p. (*0-446-35959-9*) Warner Bks., Inc.
—What Bloody Man Is That? unabr. ed. 1993. 54.95 incl. audio (*0-7451-5805-6*, CAB 632) BBC Audiobooks America.
—What Bloody Man Is That? 1989. mass mkt. 3.50 o.s.i (*0-440-20344-9*) Dell Publishing.
—What Bloody Man Is That? l.t. ed. 1988. (Nightingale Ser.). 297p. 12.95 o.p. (*0-8161-4398-6*, Macmillan Reference USA) Gale Group.
—What Bloody Man Is That? unabr. ed. 2002. audio 40.00 (*1-4025-1944-3*, Clipper Audio) Recorded Bks., LLC.
—What Bloody Man Is That? 1987. 196p. 14.95 o.p. (*0-684-18824-4*, Scribner) Simon & Schuster.
—What Bloody Man Is That? 2000. 188p. pap. 12.95 (*0-595-00349-4*) iUniverse, Inc.
Brightwell, Emily. The Ghost & Mrs. Jeffries. 1993. (Victorian Mystery Ser.). mass mkt. 5.50 o.s.i (*0-425-13949-2*) Berkley Publishing Group.
—The Inspector & Mrs. Jeffries. 1993. (Victorian Mystery Ser.). 192p. mass mkt. 5.99 (*0-425-13622-1*) Berkley Publishing Group.
—The Inspector & Mrs. Jeffries. l.t. ed. 1999. (Paperback Ser.). 256p. pap. 23.95 (*0-7838-0417-2*) Thorndike Pr.
—Mrs. Jeffries & the Missing Alibi. 1996. (Victorian Mystery Ser.). 240p. mass mkt. 5.99 o.s.i (*0-425-15256-1*) Berkley Publishing Group.
—Mrs. Jeffries Dusts for Clues. 1993. (Victorian Mystery Ser.). 192p. mass mkt. 5.50 o.s.i (*0-425-13704-X*) Berkley Publishing Group.
—Mrs. Jeffries Dusts for Clues. 1999. (G. K. Hall Paperback Ser.). 253p. pap. 23.95 (*0-7838-8721-3*, Macmillan Reference USA) Gale Group.
—Mrs. Jeffries on the Ball. l.t. ed. 1995. (Nightingale Ser.). 282p. reprint ed. pap. 18.95 o.p. (*0-7838-1284-1*, Macmillan Reference USA) Gale Group.
—Mrs. Jeffries on the Ball: A Victorian Mystery. 1994. (Victorian Mystery Ser.). 208p. mass mkt. 5.99 o.s.i (*0-425-14491-7*, Prime Crime) Berkley Publishing Group.
—Mrs. Jeffries on the Trail. 1995. (Victorian Mystery Ser.). 240p. mass mkt. 5.50 o.s.i (*0-425-14691-X*, Prime Crime) Berkley Publishing Group.
—Mrs. Jeffries Plays the Cook. 1995. (Victorian Mystery Ser.). 240p. mass mkt. 5.50 o.s.i (*0-425-15053-4*) Berkley Publishing Group.
—Mrs. Jeffries Pleads Her Case. 2003. 208p. (Orig.). mass mkt. 5.99 (*0-425-18947-3*, Prime Crime) Berkley Publishing Group.
—Mrs. Jeffries Questions the Answer. 1997. (Victorian Mystery Ser.). 240p. mass mkt. 5.99 o.s.i (*0-425-16093-9*, Prime Crime) Berkley Publishing Group.
—Mrs. Jeffries Questions the Answer. l.t. ed. 2000. (G. K. Hall Paperback Ser.). 287p. pap. 23.95 (*0-7838-9266-7*, Macmillan Reference USA) Gale Group.
—Mrs. Jeffries Reveals Her Art. 1998. (Victorian Mystery Ser.). 240p. mass mkt. 5.99 o.s.i (*0-425-16243-5*, Prime Crime) Berkley Publishing Group.
—Mrs. Jeffries Reveals Her Art. l.t. ed. 2000. (G. K. Hall Paperback Ser.). 272p. pap. 23.95 (*0-7838-9104-0*, Macmillan Reference USA) Gale Group.
—Mrs. Jeffries Rocks the Boat. 1999. (Victorian Mystery Ser.: Vol. 12). 208p. mass mkt. 5.99 o.s.i (*0-425-16934-0*) Berkley Publishing Group.
—Mrs. Jeffries Rocks the Boat. l.t. ed. 2002. pap. 24.95 (*0-7862-4463-1*) Thorndike Pr.
—Mrs. Jeffries Stands Corrected. 1996. (Victorian Mystery Ser.). 224p. mass mkt. 5.99 o.s.i (*0-425-15580-3*, Prime Crime) Berkley Publishing Group.
—Mrs. Jeffries Sweeps the Chimney. 2004. 224p. mass mkt. 6.50 (*0-425-19391-8*) Berkley Publishing Group.
—Mrs. Jeffries Takes Stock. 1994. (Victorian Mystery Ser.). 208p. mass mkt. 4.99 o.s.i (*0-425-14282-5*, Prime Crime) Berkley Publishing Group.
—Mrs. Jeffries Takes Stock. l.t. ed. 2000. (Paperback Ser.). 261p. pap. 23.95 (*0-7838-9157-1*) Thorndike Pr.
—Mrs. Jeffries Takes the Cake. 1998. (Victorian Mystery Ser.). 240p. mass mkt. 5.99 o.s.i (*0-425-16569-8*, Prime Crime) Berkley Publishing Group.
—Mrs. Jeffries Takes the Cake. l.t. ed. 1999. (Paperback Ser.). 282p. pap. 24.95 (*0-7838-8798-1*, Macmillan Reference USA) Gale Group.
—Mrs. Jeffries Takes the Stage. 1997. (Victorian Mystery Ser.). 240p. mass mkt. 5.99 o.s.i (*0-425-15724-5*, Prime Crime) Berkley Publishing Group.
—Mrs. Jeffries Takes the Stage. l.t. ed. 2000. (G. K. Hall Paperback Ser.). 280p. pap. 23.95 (*0-7838-9035-4*, Macmillan Reference USA) Gale Group.
Brindley, Louise. In the Shadow of the Brontes. 1983. 272p. 11.95 o.p. (*0-312-41167-7*) St. Martin's Pr.
Brisbin, Terri. The Dumont Bride. 2002. (Harlequin Historicals Ser.). 304p. mass mkt. (*0-373-29234-1*, Harlequin Bks.) Harlequin Enterprises, Ltd.
—The Queen's Man. 2000. (Time Passages Ser.). 320p. mass mkt. 5.99 o.s.i (*0-515-12906-2*, Jove) Berkley Publishing Group.
Brockway, Connie. The Bridal Season. 2001. 384p. mass mkt. 6.99 (*0-440-23671-1*) Dell Publishing.
Bronte, Anne. Agnes Grey. unabr. ed. 1987. (YA). (gr. 9-12). audio 35.95 (*1-55685-087-5*) Audio Bk. Contractors, Inc.
—Agnes Grey. unabr. ed. 2003. audio compact disk 64.95 (*0-7540-5537-X*, CCD 228) BBC Audiobooks America.

—Agnes Grey. unabr. ed. 1995. audio 39.95 (*0-7861-0856-8*, 1654) Blackstone Audio Bks., Inc.
—Agnes Grey. unabr. ed. 2000. audio 49.95 (*0-7540-0165-2*, CAB 1588) Chivers Audio Bks. GBR. *Dist:* BBC Audiobooks America.
—Agnes Grey. E-Book 2.49 (*1-58627-209-8*) Electric Umbrella Publishing.
—Agnes Grey. unabr. ed. 2001. audio 54.95 (*1-85089-766-2*, 89064) ISIS Audio Bks. GBR. *Dist:* Ulverscroft Large Print Bks., Ltd.
—Agnes Grey. Inglesfield, Robert & Marsden, Hilda, eds. 1998. (Oxford World's Classics Ser.). 248p. pap. 8.95 (*0-19-283478-9*) Oxford Univ. Pr., Inc.
—Agnes Grey. Marsden, Hilda, ed. 1991. (Oxford World's Classics Ser.). 240p. pap. 5.95 o.p. (*0-19-282711-1*, 12022) Oxford Univ. Pr., Inc.
—Agnes Grey. Marsden, Hilda & Inglesfield, Robert, eds. 1988. (Clarendon Edition of the Novels of the Brontes). (Illus.). 256p. text 85.00 o.p. (*0-19-812693-X*) Oxford Univ. Pr., Inc.
—Agnes Grey. 2001. pap. (*1-57646-270-6*); 1999. 200p. E-Book 3.99 incl. cd-rom (*1-57646-163-7*) Quiet Vision Publishing.
—Agnes Grey. 1994. o.s.i (*1-85381-132-7*) Random Hse., Inc.
—Agnes Grey. Goreau, Angeline, ed. & intro. by. 1989. (Classics Ser.). 272p. pap. 8.95 (*0-14-043210-8*, Penguin Classics) Viking Penguin.
—Agnes Grey. abr. ed. 1996. audio 16.95 o.s.i (*0-14-086170-X*, Penguin AudioBooks) Viking Penguin.
—Agnes Grey. 1998. (Classics Library). 150p. pap. 3.95 (*1-85326-216-1*, 2161WW) Wordsworth Editions, Ltd. GBR. *Dist:* Casemate Pubs. & Bk. Distributors, LLC.
—Agnes Grey & Poems. 1992. 208p. pap. 4.95 (*0-460-87121-8*, Everyman's Classic Library in Paperback) Tuttle Publishing.
—The Tenant of Wildfell Hall. Rosengarten, Herbert, ed. 1998. (Oxford World's Classics Ser.). 520p. reprint ed. pap. 6.95 (*0-19-283462-2*) Oxford Univ. Pr., Inc.
—The Tenant of Wildfell Hall. 1997. (Modern Library Ser.). 548p. 19.95 o.s.i (*0-679-60279-8*, Modern Library) Random House Adult Trade Publishing Group.
—The Tenant of Wildfell Hall. Davies, Steve, ed. & intro. by. 1996. (Penguin Classics Ser.). 576p. pap. 9.00 (*0-14-043474-7*, Penguin Classics) Viking Penguin.
—The Tenant of Wildfell Hall. 1979. (Banquo Bks.). 389p. reprint ed. pap. 4.95 (*0-912800-70-4*) Woodbridge Pr. Publishing Co.
Bronte, Charlotte. Jane Eyre. (World Digital Library). 2002. E-Book 3.95 (*0-594-08278-1*); 2000. 252p. E-Book 9.95 (*0-594-06663-8*) 1873 Pr.
—Jane Eyre. 8.97 (*0-673-58353-8*); 1997. pap. text o.p. (*0-17-556627-5*) Addison-Wesley Longman, Inc.
—Jane Eyre. (Modern Library Ser.). E-Book 4.95 (*1-931208-17-4*) Adobe Systems, Inc.
—Jane Eyre. 1963. mass mkt. 4.95 (*0-8049-0017-5*, CL-17) Airmont Publishing Co., Inc.
—Jane Eyre. Date not set. lib. bdg. 28.95 (*0-8488-1269-7*) Amereon, Ltd.
—Jane Eyre. l.t. ed. 1997. 741p. pap. 24.95 (*1-55701-207-5*) BNI Pubns., Inc.
—Jane Eyre. 1983. (Bantam Classics Ser.). 528p. reprint ed. mass mkt. 4.95 (*0-553-21140-4*) Bantam Dell Publishing Group.
—Jane Eyre. 1996. (Case Studies in Contemporary Criticism). 696p. pap. text 8.50 (*0-312-09545-7*) Bedford/Saint Martin's.
—Jane Eyre. Kendrick, Walter, ed. 1980. (Macdonald Classics Ser.). 508p. (C). 19.95 (*0-8464-1070-2*) Beekman Pubs., Inc.
—Jane Eyre. 2000. 6.98 (*0-681-99485-1*, 50885537) Borders Pr.
—Jane Eyre. Nemesvari, Richard, ed. 1999. (Literary Texts Ser.). 680p. pap. (*1-55111-180-2*) Broadview Pr.
—Jane Eyre. 1984. 599p. reprint ed. lib. bdg. 27.95 (*0-89966-493-8*) Buccaneer Bks., Inc.
—Jane Eyre. 1997. (Cambridge Literature Ser.). audio compact disk 22.95 o.p. (*0-521-59796-X*) Cambridge Univ. Pr.
—Jane Eyre. Cockcroft, Susan, ed. 1996. (Cambridge Literature Ser.). (Illus.). 528p. pap. text 11.95 o.p. (*0-521-56865-X*) Cambridge Univ. Pr.
—Jane Eyre. 3. reprint ed. lib. bdg. 294.00 (*0-7426-2188-X*); 2001. pap. text 84.00 (*0-7426-7188-7*) Classic Bks.
—Jane Eyre. 1998. 480p. pap. 14.95 incl. disk (*1-55701-233-4*); 1997. 741p. pap. 24.95 (*1-58855-021-4*) Cyber Classics, Inc.
—Jane Eyre. 1994. 488p. pap. text 3.99 (*0-8125-2337-7*, Tor Classics) Doherty, Tom Assocs., LLC.
—Jane Eyre. 1997. (New York Public Library Collector's Edition Ser.). 576p. 18.50 o.s.i (*0-385-48717-7*) Doubleday Publishing.
—Jane Eyre. 2002. (Thrift Editions Ser.). (Illus.). 448p. pap. 3.50 (*0-486-42449-9*) Dover Pubns., Inc.
—Jane Eyre. 1972. 2.95 o.p. (*0-460-01287-8*, Dutton) Dutton/Plume.
—Jane Eyre. E-Book 2.49 (*1-58627-105-9*) Electric Umbrella Publishing.
—Jane Eyre. Luaces, Juan G., tr. 7th ed. 1991. (Nueva Austral Ser.: No. 59). (SPA., Illus.). 488p. 19.95 (*84-239-1859-9*) Elliot's Bks.
—Jane Eyre. 2003. (Barnes & Noble Classics Ser.). 608p. pap. 4.95 (*1-59308-007-7*) Fine Communications.
—Jane Eyre. 2002. (Classics for Young Readers Ser.). (SPA.). (*84-392-0935-5*, EV30620) Gaviota Ediciones ESP. *Dist:* Lectorum Pubns., Inc.
—Jane Eyre. 6th ed. 1998. (Clasicos Universales Ser.: Vol. 5). (SPA., Illus.). 375p. pap. (*84-08-01725-X*) GeoPlaneta, Editorial, S. A.
—Jane Eyre. (HRW Library). 2000. 581p. 17.90 (*0-03-095764-8*); 1997. text 8.25 (*0-03-051488-6*) Holt, Rinehart & Winston.
—Jane Eyre. l.t. ed. 2171p. pap. 132.40 (*0-7583-1190-7*); 1868p. pap. 116.43 (*0-7583-1189-3*); 2704p. pap. 155.70 (*0-7583-1191-5*); 1515p. pap. 100.58 (*0-7583-1188-5*); 661p. pap. 46.42 (*0-7583-1185-0*); 525p. pap. 38.72 (*0-7583-1184-2*); 912p. pap. 64.90 (*0-7583-1186-9*); 1172p. pap. 77.48 (*0-7583-1187-7*); 1515p. lib. bdg. 118.98 (*0-7583-1180-X*); 1172p. lib. bdg. 89.48 (*0-7583-1179-6*); 912p. lib. bdg. 76.90 (*0-7583-1178-8*); 661p. lib. bdg. 52.42 (*0-7583-1177-X*); 525p. lib. bdg. 44.72 (*0-7583-1176-1*); 1868p. lib. bdg. 137.16 (*0-7583-1181-8*); 2704p. lib. bdg. 193.87 (*0-7583-1183-4*); 2171p. lib. bdg. 152.77 (*0-7583-1182-6*) Huge Print Pr.
—Jane Eyre. 1996. (Illus.). 466p. pap. 12.95 o.p. (*0-7868-8118-6*) Hyperion Pr.
—Jane Eyre. 2002. 500p. 29.99 (*1-4043-1064-9*); per. 24.99 (*1-4043-1065-7*) IndyPublish.com.
—Jane Eyre. Ba'Albaki, Munir, tr. (ARA.). 200p. pap. 14.95 (*0-86685-755-9*) International Bk. Ctr., Inc.
—Jane Eyre. 1998. (Cloth Bound Pocket Ser.). 240p. 7.95 (*3-89508-259-7*, 520184) Konemann.
—Jane Eyre. E-Book 2.95 (*1-57799-817-0*) Logos Research Systems, Inc.
—Jane Eyre. Ballantine, Cecil, ed. 1986. (Illus.). 32p. pap. text o.p. (*0-582-33152-8*) Longman Publishing Group.
—Jane Eyre. (English As a Second Language Bk.). 1981. pap. text 5.95 o.p. (*0-582-53843-2*, 74218); 2nd rev. ed. 1996. pap. text 5.90 o.s.i (*0-582-27511-3*); Level 3. 2000. (C). pap. 7.66 (*0-582-41780-5*); Level 5. 2000. (C). pap. 7.66 (*0-582-41932-8*) Longman Publishing Group.
—Jane Eyre. E-Book 1.95 (*1-58515-060-6*) MesaView, Inc.
—Jane Eyre. (Signet Classics). 1997. 480p. (C). mass mkt. 4.95 (*0-451-52655-4*); 1968. mass mkt. 0.60 o.p. (*0-451-50449-6*, Signet Classics); 1968. mass mkt. 0.50 o.p. (*0-451-50011-3*, Signet Classics); 1960. mass mkt. 1.95 o.p. (*0-451-51884-5*); 1960. mass mkt. 0.95 o.p. (*0-451-50871-8*, Signet Classics); 1960. mass mkt. 1.50 o.p. (*0-451-51117-4*, Signet Classics); 1960. mass mkt. 1.75 o.p. (*0-451-51347-9*, Signet Classics); 1960. mass mkt. 2.25 o.p. (*0-451-51465-3*, Signet Classics); 1960. mass mkt. 1.75 o.p. (*0-451-51556-0*, Signet Classics); 1960. mass mkt. 1.25 o.p. (*0-451-51013-5*, Signet Classics); 1960. mass mkt. 0.75 o.p. (*0-451-50726-6*, Signet Classics); 1960. 464p. mass mkt. 4.95 o.s.i (*0-451-52332-6*, Signet Classics) NAL.
—Jane Eyre. Schorer, Mark, ed. 1977. (Gotham Library Ser.). 429p. 12.50 o.p. (*0-8147-7780-5*); pap. 5.50 o.p. (*0-8147-7781-3*) New York Univ. Pr.
—Jane Eyre. 1998. 550p. reprint ed. lib. bdg. 25.00 (*1-58287-089-6*) North Bks.
—Jane Eyre. 2nd ed. 1997. (C). pap. text 16.50 o.p. (*0-393-98367-6*) Norton, W. W. & Co., Inc.
—Jane Eyre. Dunn, Richard J., ed. 2nd ed. 1987. 24.95 o.p. (*0-393-02424-5*) Norton, W. W. & Co., Inc.
—Jane Eyre. 3rd ed. 2002. (C). pap. text 11.50 (*0-393-94110-8*); pap. text 16.00 (*0-393-94097-7*) Norton, W. W. & Co., Inc.
—Jane Eyre. 2000. (Oxford World's Classics Ser.). 544p. 15.00 o.p. (*0-19-210042-4*) Oxford Univ. Pr., Inc.
—Jane Eyre. Smith, Margaret, ed. & intro. by. 1998. (Oxford World's Classics Ser.). 532p. pap. 6.95 o.p. (*0-19-283356-1*) Oxford Univ. Pr., Inc.
—Jane Eyre. Smith, Margaret, ed. 1980. 518p. pap. 5.95 o.p. (*0-19-281513-X*) Oxford Univ. Pr., Inc.
—Jane Eyre. Jack, Jane & Smith, Margaret, eds. 1969. (Clarendon Edition of the Novels of the Brontes). 72.00 o.p. (*0-19-811490-7*) Oxford Univ. Pr., Inc.
—Jane Eyre. Smith, Margaret, ed. 2nd ed. 2001. (Oxford World's Classics Ser.). 542p. pap. 6.95 (*0-19-283965-9*) Oxford Univ. Pr., Inc.
—Jane Eyre. Newman, Beth, ed. 1996. (Case Studies in Contemporary Criticism). 592p. 55.00 (*0-312-12795-2*) Palgrave Macmillan.
—Jane Eyre. 2001. (Embellished Manuscripts). 160p. 14.95 (*1-55156-199-9*) Paperblank Bk. Co.
—Jane Eyre. 2000. (Illustrated Junior Library Ser.). 9.99 o.p. (*0-448-42439-8*, Grosset & Dunlap) Penguin Putnam Bks. for Young Readers.
—Jane Eyre. 2001. pap. (*1-57646-269-2*) Quiet Vision Publishing.
—Jane Eyre. 2000. (Modern Library Classics). 752p. pap. 7.95 (*0-679-78332-6*); E-Book 4.95 (*0-679-64118-1*) Random House Adult Trade Publishing Group. (Modern Library).
—Jane Eyre. annuals (Modern Library Classics Ser.). 1993. 704p. 19.95 (*0-679-42472-5*); 1992. o.s.i (*1-85381-137-8*); 1928. 3.95 o.s.i (*0-394-60064-9*) Random Hse., Inc.
—Jane Eyre. 1984. (Illus.). 480p. 12.95 o.p. (*0-89577-200-0*) Reader's Digest Assn., Inc., The.
—Jane Eyre. (Courage Unabridged Classics Ser.). 1997. 336p. pap. 6.00 o.p. (*0-7624-0547-3*, Courage Bks.); 1991. 336p. text 5.98 o.p. (*1-56138-022-9*, Courage Bks.); 1988. pap. 4.95 o.p. (*0-89471-631-X*) Running Pr. Bk. Pubs.
—Jane Eyre. 2000. E-Book 2.95 (*1-58853-014-0*) Sensory Publishing, Inc.
—Jane Eyre. (Enriched Classics Ser.). 1997. 576p. pap. 5.99 (*0-671-01479-X*, Pocket); 1994. 3.95 o.p. (*0-671-00602-9*) Simon & Schuster.
—Jane Eyre. 1996. (Classic Library). 12.98 o.p. (*0-7651-9981-5*) Smithmark Pubs., Inc.
—Jane Eyre. 1996. 592p. pap. text 14.95 o.p. (*0-312-14202-1*) St. Martin's Pr.
—Jane Eyre. l.t. ed. 1994. 689p. lib. bdg. 23.95 (*0-7838-1135-7*) Thorndike Pr.
—Jane Eyre. l.t. ed. 1997. (Charnwood Large Print Ser.). 740p. 29.99 (*0-7089-8015-5*, Ulverscroft) Thorpe, F. A. Pubs. GBR. *Dist:* Ulverscroft Large Print Bks., Ltd., Ulverscroft Large Print Canada, Ltd.
—Jane Eyre. abr. ed. 2000. mass mkt. 11.95 incl. audio (*1-85998-487-8*) Trafalgar Square.
—Jane Eyre. 2000. (Signature Classics Ser.). 436p. 24.95 (*1-58279-068-X*); lib. bdg. 29.95 (*1-58279-074-4*) Trident Pr. International.
—Jane Eyre. 1998. 19.00 (*0-606-16071-X*); 1981. 11.00 (*0-606-13533-2*); 1960. 11.00 (*0-606-00892-6*) Turtleback Bks.
—Jane Eyre. 1998. xlv, 530p. pap. 6.95 (*0-460-87596-5*); 1991. 474p. pap. 6.95 o.p. (*0-460-87085-8*) Tuttle Publishing. (Everyman's Classic Library in Paperback).
—Jane Eyre. 1999. 9.50 (*81-85944-80-6*) UBS Pubs. Distributions, Ltd. IND. *Dist:* South Asia Bks.
—Jane Eyre. Mason, Michael, ed. & intro. by. (Classics Ser.). 2003. 576p. 8.00 (*0-14-243720-4*); 1996. 560p. pap. 7.95 o.s.i (*0-14-043400-3*) Viking Penguin. (Penguin Classics).
—Jane Eyre. Leavis, Q. D., ed. 1966. 496p. pap. 5.95 o.p. (*0-14-043011-3*, Penguin Classics) Viking Penguin.
—Jane Eyre. 1999. E-Book 5.99 (*0-8220-7104-5*, Cliff Notes) Wiley, John & Sons, Inc.
—Jane Eyre. 1997. (Classics Library). 448p. pap. 3.95 (*1-85326-020-7*, 0207WW) Wordsworth Editions, Ltd. GBR. *Dist:* Casemate Pubs. & Bk. Distributors, LLC.
—Jane Eyre: Critical Edition. 2nd ed. (Critical Editions Ser.). (C). pap. text 38.50 (*0-393-99008-7*); 1999. pap. text 28.00 o.p. (*0-393-98061-8*) Norton, W. W. & Co., Inc.
—Jane Eyre: Critical Edition. Dunn, Richard J., ed. 2nd ed. 1987. (Critical Editions Ser.). 497p. (C). pap. text 10.00 o.p. (*0-393-95589-3*, 95589) Norton, W. W. & Co., Inc.
—Jane Eyre: Critical Edition. 3rd ed. (Critical Editions Ser.). 2001. (C). pap. text 29.00 (*0-393-94427-1*); 2000. xiv, 321p. pap. 8.00 (*0-393-97542-8*, Norton Paperbacks) Norton, W. W. & Co., Inc.
—Jane Eyre Authoritive Text. 1971. (C). pap. o.p. (*0-393-09966-0*) Norton, W. W. & Co., Inc.
—Shirley. annuals 1997. (Modern Library Ser.). 688p. 19.50 o.s.i (*0-679-60275-5*, Modern Library) Random House Adult Trade Publishing Group.
—Shirley. Hook, Andrew & Hook, Judith, eds. 1974. (Classics Ser.). 624p. 7.95 (*0-14-043095-4*, Penguin Classics) Viking Penguin.
—Unfinished Novels. 1993. (Pocket Classics Ser.). pap. 6.95 (*0-7509-0481-X*) Sutton Publishing, Ltd. GBR. *Dist:* International Publishers Marketing.
Bronte, Charlotte & Everyman's Library Staff. Jane Eyre. 1991. (Everyman's Library: Vol. 10). 326p. 20.00 (*0-679-40582-8*) Random Hse., Inc.
Bronte, Charlotte & Johnson, Diane. Jane Eyre. 1997. (Modern Library Ser.). 704p. 19.00 o.s.i (*0-679-60269-0*, Modern Library) Random House Adult Trade Publishing Group.
Bronte, Emily. Wuthering Heights. 2000. 252p. E-Book 9.95 (*0-594-04088-4*) 1873 Pr.
—Wuthering Heights. 1991. pap. text (*0-17-556575-9*) Addison-Wesley Longman, Inc.
—Wuthering Heights. 2001. E-Book 4.95 (*1-931208-21-2*) Adobe Systems, Inc.
—Wuthering Heights. unabr. ed. 1963. (Classics Ser.). mass mkt. 4.95 (*0-8049-0011-6*, CL-11) Airmont Publishing Co., Inc.
—Wuthering Heights. Date not set. 320p. 24.95 (*0-8488-2218-8*) Amereon, Ltd.
—Wuthering Heights. 1997. 386p. pap. 14.95 incl. disk (*1-55701-238-5*); 506p. pap. 22.95 (*1-55701-208-3*) BNI Pubns., Inc.
—Wuthering Heights. 1983. mass mkt. o.s.i (*0-553-19633-2*); mass mkt. 1.95 o.s.i (*0-553-21141-2*) Bantam Bks.
—Wuthering Heights. 1983. (Bantam Classics Ser.). 336p. reprint ed. mass mkt. 4.95 (*0-553-21258-3*) Bantam Dell Publishing Group.
—Wuthering Heights. Seely, Elizabeth & Seely, John, eds. 1999. (Classic Novels ). 368p. pap. 8.95 (*0-7641-1148-5*) Barron's Educational Series, Inc.
—Wuthering Heights. Murfin, Ross C. & Peterson, Linda H., eds. 1991. (Case Studies in Contemporary Criticism). 467p. (C). pap. text 8.50 (*0-312-03547-0*) Bedford/Saint Martin's.
—Wuthering Heights. 2nd ed. 2003. pap. text 8.50 (*0-312-25686-8*) Bedford/Saint Martin's.
—Wuthering Heights. Kendrick, Walter, ed. 1990. (Classics Ser.). 400p. (C). 19.95 (*0-8464-1072-9*) Beekman Pubs., Inc.
—Wuthering Heights. 1988. 360p. 40.00 o.p. (*0-913720-31-3*) Beil, Frederic C. Pub., Inc.
—Wuthering Heights. 1990. (Illus.). 3.75 o.s.i (*0-425-12259-X*, Classics Illustrated) Berkley Publishing Group.
—Wuthering Heights. per. 14.50 (*1-58396-669-2*) Blue Unicorn Editions.
—Wuthering Heights. 2002. audio 64.00 (*0-7366-8796-3*); audio compact disk 80.00 (*0-7366-8797-1*) Books on Tape, Inc.
—Wuthering Heights. 2002. pap. 4.95 (*1-59109-024-5*) Booksurge, LLC.
—Wuthering Heights. 2000. 6.98 (*0-681-99570-X*, 50885620) Borders Pr.
—Wuthering Heights. 1986. 320p. reprint ed. lib. bdg. 25.95 (*0-89966-520-9*) Buccaneer Bks., Inc.
—Wuthering Heights. 1997. (Cambridge Literature Ser.). audio 16.95 o.p. (*0-521-59798-6*) Cambridge Univ. Pr.
—Wuthering Heights. Hoyes, Richard, ed. 1997. (Cambridge Literature Ser.). (Illus.). 416p. pap. text 11.95 o.p. (*0-521-58949-5*) Cambridge Univ. Pr.
—Wuthering Heights. reprint ed. lib. bdg. 98.00 (*0-7426-2197-9*); 2001. (Illus.). 385p. pap. text 28.00 (*0-7426-7197-6*) Classic Bks.
—Wuthering Heights. 1986. o.s.i (*0-517-62145-2*); xxxi, 431p. 2.99 o.s.i (*0-517-60612-7*) Crown Publishing Group.
—Wuthering Heights. l.t. ed. 1997. 506p. pap. 22.95 (*1-58855-022-2*) Cyber Classics, Inc.
—Wuthering Heights. 1961. pap. 2.25 o.s.i (*0-440-39728-6*, Laurel) Dell Publishing.
—Wuthering Heights. 1989. 224p. mass mkt. 3.99 (*0-8125-0516-6*, Tor Classics); 1989. mass mkt. 3.25 o.s.i (*0-8125-0517-4*, Tor Classics); 1988. mass mkt. 4.95 (*0-938819-83-6*, Aerie); 1988. mass mkt. 2.25 (*0-938819-52-6*, Aerie) Doherty, Tom Assocs., LLC.
—Wuthering Heights. unabr. ed. 1996. (Thrift Editions Ser.). 256p. reprint ed. pap. 2.50 (*0-486-29256-8*) Dover Pubns., Inc.
—Wuthering Heights. 1972. 2.50 o.p. (*0-460-01243-6*); 1955. 12.95 o.p. (*0-460-00243-0*) Dutton/Plume. (Dutton).
—Wuthering Heights. E-Book 1.95 (*1-58627-104-0*) Electric Umbrella Publishing.
—Wuthering Heights. 2003. (Barnes & Noble Classics Ser.). 368p. mass mkt. 4.95 (*1-59308-044-1*) Fine Communications.
—Wuthering Heights. 2001. 240p. pap. 16.95 o.p. (*1-929925-57-3*) FirstPublish.
—Wuthering Heights. 1990. 10.92 (*0-02-635143-9*) Glencoe/McGraw-Hill.
—Wuthering Heights. l.t. ed. 2000. 464p. pap. 22.00 (*0-06-095570-8*) HarperCollins Pubs.
—Wuthering Heights. Clay, N. L., ed. 1986. (Guide Novel Ser.). pap. text 4.50 o.p. (*0-435-16100-8*) Heinemann.
—Wuthering Heights. 1979. (Blackie Chosen Classics Ser.). 320p. 3.95 o.p. (*0-216-88523-X*) Hippocrene Bks., Inc.
—Wuthering Heights. 1997. text 8.25 (*0-03-051489-4*) Holt, Rinehart & Winston.
—Wuthering Heights. Pritchett, V. S., ed. 1956. (YA). pap. 16.36 (*0-395-05102-9*, Riverside Editions) Houghton Mifflin Co.
—Wuthering Heights. l.t. ed. 407p. pap. 28.95 (*0-7583-2929-6*); 563p. pap. 35.94 (*0-7583-2930-X*); 1680p. pap. 101.81 (*0-7583-2935-0*); 1426p. pap. 84.35 (*0-7583-2934-2*); 1159p. pap. 72.96 (*0-7583-2933-4*); 939p. pap. 62.39 (*0-7583-2932-6*); 322p. pap. 24.22 (*0-7583-2928-8*); 725p. pap. 44.33 (*0-7583-2931-8*); 1426p. lib. bdg. 100.73 (*0-7583-2926-1*); 1159p. lib. bdg. 87.00 (*0-7583-2925-3*); 939p. lib. bdg. 75.66 (*0-7583-2924-5*); 725p. lib. bdg. 50.99 (*0-7583-2923-7*); 563p. lib. bdg. 42.65 (*0-7583-2922-9*); 407p. lib. bdg. 34.95 (*0-7583-2921-0*); 1680p. lib. bdg. 127.48 (*0-7583-2927-X*); 322p. lib. bdg. 30.22 (*0-7583-2920-2*) Huge Print Pr.
—Wuthering Heights. l.t. ed. 1992. (Clear Type Classics Ser.). 418p. 22.95 o.p. (*1-85695-310-6*) ISIS Large Print Bks. GBR. *Dist:* Transaction Pubs.

—Wuthering Heights. 1999. 348p. pap. 9.95 o.p. (*1-930128-12-6*, JNMedia Bks.) JNMedia, Inc.
—Wuthering Heights. 1977. pap. 1.95 o.p. (*0-523-40126-4*, Pinnacle Bks.) Kensington Publishing Corp.
—Wuthering Heights. 1998. (Cloth Bound Pocket Ser.). 240p. 7.95 (*3-89508-208-2*, 520082) Konemann.
—Wuthering Heights. l.t. ed. 1997. (Large Print Heritage Ser.). 536p. lib. bdg. 35.95 (*1-58118-003-9*, 21964) LRS.
—Wuthering Heights. 1996. (Longman Fiction Ser.). pap. text 5.90 o.s.i (*0-582-27495-8*) Longman Publishing Group.
—Wuthering Heights. Blatchford, Roy, ed. 1993. (Literature Ser.). pap. 5.95 (*0-582-07782-6*, TG7655) Longman Publishing Group.
—Wuthering Heights. 1993. (Fiction Ser.). pap. text 6.50 (*0-582-09672-3*, 79835) Longman Publishing Group.
—Wuthering Heights. E-Book 1.95 (*1-58515-093-2*) MesaView, Inc.
—Wuthering Heights. 2004. 336p. mass mkt. 4.95 (*0-451-52925-1*, Signet Classics); 1993. 328p. mass mkt. o.p. (*0-451-52583-3*, Signet Classics); 1979. o.p.; 1959. mass mkt. 1.50 o.p. (*0-451-51179-4*, Signet Classics); 1959. mass mkt. 1.75 o.p. (*0-451-51240-5*, Signet Classics); 1959. mass mkt. 2.25 o.p. (*0-451-52119-6*); 1959. mass mkt. 1.95 o.p. (*0-451-51958-2*, Signet Classics); 1959. mass mkt. 1.25 o.p. (*0-451-51020-8*, Signet Classics); 1959. mass mkt. 0.95 o.p. (*0-451-50874-2*, Signet Classics); 1959. mass mkt. 1.75 o.p. (*0-451-51650-8*, Signet Classics); 1959. mass mkt. 0.75 o.p. (*0-451-50750-9*, Signet Classics); 1959. mass mkt. 1.95 o.p. (*0-451-51388-6*, Signet Classics); 1959. mass mkt. 0.50 o.p. (*0-451-50010-5*, Signet Classics); 1959. mass mkt. 0.60 o.p. (*0-451-50610-3*, Signet Classics); 1959. 336p. reprint ed. mass mkt. 4.95 (*0-451-52338-5*) NAL.
—Wuthering Heights. 1997. (Thornes Classic Novels Ser.). (Illus.). 354p. pap. 16.95 (*0-7487-2978-X*) Nelson Thornes GBR. *Dist:* Trans-Atlantic Pubns., Inc.
—Wuthering Heights. l.t. ed. (Large Print Ser.). 1992. 566p. lib. bdg. 26.00 (*0-939495-28-7*); 1998. 350p. reprint ed. lib. bdg. 25.00 (*1-58287-083-7*) North Bks.
—Wuthering Heights. Sale, William M., Jr., ed. 1972. (C). pap. o.p. (*0-393-09400-6*) Norton, W. W. & Co., Inc.
—Wuthering Heights. 2nd ed. 2002. (Norton Critical Edition Ser.). 416p. pap. 12.10 (*0-393-97889-3*) Norton, W. W. & Co., Inc.
—Wuthering Heights. 1999. (Oxford World's Classics Ser.). 384p. 15.50 (*0-19-210027-0*) Oxford Univ. Pr., Inc.
—Wuthering Heights. Stoneman, Patsy & Jack, Ian, eds. 1998. (Oxford World's Classics Ser.). (Illus.). 432p. pap. 5.95 (*0-19-283354-5*) Oxford Univ. Pr., Inc.
—Wuthering Heights. Jack, Ian, ed. 1981. (Oxford World's Classics Ser.). (C). pap. 4.50 o.p. (*0-19-281543-1*) Oxford Univ. Pr., Inc.
—Wuthering Heights. Marsden, Hilda & Jack, Ian, eds. 1976. (Clarendon Edition of the Novels of the Brontes). 65.00 o.p. (*0-19-812511-9*) Oxford Univ. Pr., Inc.
—Wuthering Heights. Stoneman, Patsy, ed. 1993. (New Casebooks Ser.). 208p. 49.95 o.p. (*0-312-09689-5*) Palgrave Macmillan.
—Wuthering Heights. Peterson, Linda H., ed. 1992. text 39.95 o.p. (*0-312-06523-X*) Palgrave Macmillan.
—Wuthering Heights. 1997. (*0-14-771199-1*) Penguin Group (USA) Inc.
—Wuthering Heights. 1999. pap. 2.99 o.p. (*0-14-130547-9*); 1990. 352p. pap. 3.99 o.p. (*0-14-035113-2*) Penguin Putnam Bks. for Young Readers. (Puffin Bks.).
—Wuthering Heights. abr. ed. 1993. (Classics on Cassette). 16.00 incl. audio (*0-453-00819-4*) Penguin/HighBridge.
—Wuthering Heights. 2000. pap. (*1-57646-268-4*); 1999. 200p. E-Book 3.99 incl. audio compact disk (*1-57646-161-0*) Quiet Vision Publishing.
—Wuthering Heights. (Classics Ser.). 2000. 464p. pap. 6.95 (*0-375-75644-2*); 2000. E-Book 4.95 (*0-679-64000-2*); 1994. 448p. 17.95 o.s.i (*0-679-60135-X*) Random House Adult Trade Publishing Group. (Modern Library).
—Wuthering Heights. 1987. audio 14.95 o.p. (*0-394-56409-X*, RH Audio) Random Hse. Audio Publishing Group.
—Wuthering Heights. 1987. 9.99 o.s.i (*0-517-64301-4*) Random Hse. Value Publishing.
—Wuthering Heights. 1991. (Everyman's Library: Vol. 2). 544p. 17.00 (*0-679-40543-7*); 1990. o.s.i (*1-85381-138-6*); 1978. (Illus.). 400p. 12.95 o.s.i (*0-394-60458-X*); 1950. (Modern Library College Editions Ser.). pap. text 4.00 o.p. (*0-394-30904-9*, T4) Random Hse., Inc.
—Wuthering Heights. 1982. (Illus.). 303p. 12.95 o.p. (*0-89577-159-4*) Reader's Digest Assn., Inc., The.
—Wuthering Heights. Glen, Heather, ed. 1996. (English Texts Ser.). 400p. (C). pap. 20.99 o.p. (*0-415-00667-8*) Routledge.
—Wuthering Heights. (Courage Unabridged Classics Ser.). 1998. 256p. pap. 6.00 o.p. (*0-7624-0559-7*, Courage Bks.); 1991. 248p. text 5.98 o.p. (*1-56138-035-0*, Courage Bks.); 1986. 256p. pap. 4.95 o.p. (*0-89471-480-5*); 1986. 256p. lib. bdg. 12.90 o.p. (*0-89471-481-3*) Running Pr. Bk. Pubs.
—Wuthering Heights. 1992. 416p. mass mkt. 3.50 o.p. (*0-590-46030-7*, Scholastic Paperbacks) Scholastic, Inc.
—Wuthering Heights. 2000. E-Book 2.95 (*1-58853-026-4*) Sensory Publishing, Inc.
—Wuthering Heights. 2004. 400p. mass mkt. 4.95 (*0-7434-8764-8*, Pocket); 2003. 336p. pap. 4.99 (*0-7434-8507-6*, MTV) Simon & Schuster.
—Wuthering Heights. Peters, Sally, ed. 1992. 352p. mass mkt. 4.99 (*0-671-79022-6*, Pocket) Simon & Schuster.
—Wuthering Heights. 1997. (Enriched Classics Ser.). 400p. reprint ed. mass mkt. 5.99 (*0-671-01480-3*, Pocket) Simon & Schuster.
—Wuthering Heights. 1930. 25.00 (*0-689-83079-3*, Atheneum) Simon & Schuster Children's Publishing.
—Wuthering Heights. (Ebook Classic Ser.). E-Book 5.00 (*0-7410-0464-X*) SoftBook Pr.
—Wuthering Heights. unabr. ed. 2003. audio 19.99 (*1-59335-134-8*, 30230) Soulmate Audio Bks., Inc.
—Wuthering Heights. 1996. pap. text 15.95 o.p. (*0-312-13826-1*) St. Martin's Pr.
—Wuthering Heights. l.t. ed. 2000. (Perennial Bestsellers Ser.). 492p. 27.95 (*0-7838-9062-1*) Thorndike Pr.
—Wuthering Heights. l.t. ed. 1997. (Charnwood Large Print Ser.). 551p. 29.99 (*0-7089-8950-0*, Ulverscroft) Thorpe, F. A. Pubs. GBR. *Dist:* Ulverscroft Large Print Bks., Ltd., Ulverscroft Large Print Canada, Ltd.
—Wuthering Heights. l.t. ed. 1998. 440p. text 29.95 (*1-56000-527-0*) Transaction Pubs.
—Wuthering Heights. 1999. (Signature Classics Ser.). (Illus.). 384p. 24.95 (*1-58279-033-7*); 29.95 (*1-58279-045-0*) Trident Pr. International.
—Wuthering Heights. 1989. 9.04 (*0-606-18662-X*); 1981. 11.00 (*0-606-13932-X*); 1959. 11.00 (*0-606-01582-5*) Turtleback Bks.
—Wuthering Heights. unabr. ed. 1997. 230p. reprint ed. pap. 14.95 o.p. (*1-57002-048-5*) University Publishing Hse., Inc.
—Wuthering Heights. 2002. (Penguin Classics Ser.). (Illus.). 416p. pap. 7.00 (*0-14-143955-6*, Penguin Classics) Viking Penguin.
—Wuthering Heights. Nestor, Pauline, ed. 1996. (Penguin Classics Ser.). 400p. (C). pap. 6.95 o.s.i (*0-14-043418-6*) Viking Penguin.
—Wuthering Heights. Daiches, David, ed. 1990. (English Library). 384p. pap. 5.95 o.p. (*0-14-043001-6*, Penguin Classics) Viking Penguin.
—Wuthering Heights. 2000. text 6.00 (*0-8220-7231-9*, Cliff Notes) Wiley, John & Sons, Inc.
—Wuthering Heights. 1997. (Classics Library). 272p. pap. 3.95 (*1-85326-001-0*, 0010WW) Wordsworth Editions, Ltd. GBR. *Dist:* Casemate Pubs. & Bk. Distributors, LLC.
—Wuthering Heights: Complete Text with Introduction, Contexts, Critical Essays. Hoeveler, Diane Long, ed. 2002. (New Riverside Editions Ser.). (Illus.). viii, 456p. pap. 8.76 (*0-618-08486-X*) Houghton Mifflin Co.
—Wuthering Heights: Norton Critical Edition. Sale, William M., Jr. & Dunn, Richard J., eds. 3rd rev. ed. 1990. (Critical Editions Ser.). 396p. pap. text (*0-393-95760-8*) Norton, W. W. & Co., Inc.
—Wuthering Heights: Study Text. Adams, Richard & Cookson, Linda, eds. 1989. (Study Texts Ser.). (Illus.). 338p. pap. text 5.95 o.p. (*0-582-33098-X*, TG7232) Longman Publishing Group.
—Wuthering Heights: 1818 Version. Jack, Ian, ed. 2nd ed. 1995. (Oxford World's Classics Ser.). 428p. pap. 4.95 o.p. (*0-19-282350-7*) Oxford Univ. Pr., Inc.
—Wuthering Heights & Poems. Drabble, Margaret, ed. 1993. 432p. pap. 4.95 o.p. (*0-460-87311-3*, Everyman's Classic Library in Paperback) Tuttle Publishing.
—Wuthering Heights & Poems. 1991. 403p. pap. 5.95 o.p. (*0-460-87036-X*, Everyman's Classic Library in Paperback) Tuttle Publishing.
—Wuthering Heights with Connections. 2000. (HRW Library). 399p. 17.90 (*0-03-095770-2*) Holt, Rinehart & Winston.
Bronte, Emily, et al. Wuthering Heights. 1998. E-Book 6.25 (*0-585-35916-4*) netLibrary, Inc.
Brookfield, Amanda. Cast of Smiles. 1991. 15.95 o.p. (*0-312-05399-1*) St. Martin's Pr.
Brookner, Anita. Altered States. 1998. 240p. pap. 12.00 (*0-679-77325-8*, Vintage) Knopf Publishing Group.
—Brief Lives. l.t. ed. 2000. 312p. lib. bdg. 27.95 (*1-58547-018-X*) Ctr. Point Large Print.
—Brief Lives. 1992. (Vintage Contemporaries Ser.). 272p. pap. 13.00 (*0-679-73733-2*, Vintage) Knopf Publishing Group.
—Brief Lives. 1993. 4.49 o.p. (*0-517-10943-3*) Random Hse. Value Publishing.
—The Debut. 1981. 11.95 o.p. (*0-671-42626-5*, Simon & Schuster) Simon & Schuster.
—Fraud. (Vintage Contemporaries Ser.). 1994. 272p. pap. 13.00 (*0-679-74308-1*); 1994. mass mkt. o.s.i (*0-394-22272-5*); 1993. 262p. 21.00 o.s.i (*0-679-41606-4*) Random Hse., Inc.
—A Friend from England. l.t. ed. 1989. (General Ser.). 293p. lib. bdg. 19.95 o.p. (*0-8161-4656-X*, Macmillan Reference USA) Gale Group.
—A Friend from England. 1989. 208p. reprint ed. pap. 10.00 o.p. (*0-06-097202-5*, PL 7202, Perennial) HarperTrade.
—Latecomers. l.t. ed. 1990. (General Ser.). 259p. lib. bdg. 19.95 o.p. (*0-8161-4892-9*, Macmillan Reference USA) Gale Group.
—Latecomers. 1990. (Vintage Contemporaries Ser.). 248p. pap. 12.00 (*0-679-72668-3*, Vintage) Knopf Publishing Group.
—Latecomers. 1990. 3.99 o.p. (*0-517-05087-0*) Random Hse. Value Publishing.
—Lewis Percy. l.t. ed. 1991. (General Ser.). 357p. pap. 20.95 o.p. (*0-8161-5074-5*, Macmillan Reference USA) Gale Group.
—Lewis Percy. 1991. (Vintage Contemporaries Ser.). 272p. pap. 14.00 (*0-679-72944-5*, Vintage) Knopf Publishing Group.
—Lewis Percy. 1991. 3.99 o.p. (*0-517-07930-5*) Random Hse. Value Publishing.
—Look at Me. l.t. ed. 1991. 259p. 22.95 o.p. (*1-85089-404-3*) ISIS Large Print Bks. GBR. *Dist:* Transaction Pubs.
—Look at Me. 1997. 208p. pap. 12.00 (*0-679-73813-4*, Vintage) Knopf Publishing Group.
—Look at Me. 1985. pap. 7.95 o.p. (*0-525-48156-7*, Obelisk) NAL.
—A Private View. l.t. ed. 1995. 284p. lib. bdg. 24.95 o.p. (*0-7838-1218-3*, Macmillan Reference USA) Gale Group.
—A Private View. unabr. ed. 2001. audio 54.95 (*1-85695-941-4*, 950511) ISIS Audio Bks. GBR. *Dist:* Ulverscroft Large Print Bks., Ltd.
—A Private View. 1996. 256p. pap. 12.00 (*0-679-75443-1*, Vintage) Knopf Publishing Group.
—A Private View. 1994. (*0-224-03684-X*) Random Hse. UK, Ltd. GBR. *Dist:* Trafalgar Square.
—Providence. 1994. (Vintage Contemporaries Ser.). 192p. pap. 13.00 (*0-679-73814-2*) Knopf, Alfred A. Inc.
—The Rules of Engagement. 2003. 288p. 23.95 (*1-4000-6165-2*, Random House) Random House Adult Trade Publishing Group.
—Undue Influence. l.t. ed. 2000. (G. K. Hall Core Ser.). 306p. 29.95 (*0-7838-9001-X*, Macmillan Reference USA) Gale Group.
—Undue Influence. 2001. 240p. pap. 12.00 (*0-375-70734-4*, Vintage) Knopf Publishing Group.
—Visitors. l.t. ed. 1998. 301p. (*0-7540-2099-1*) BBC Audiobooks America.
—Visitors. l.t. ed. 1998. (G. K. Hall Core Ser.). 305p. 27.95 o.p. (*0-7838-8444-3*, Macmillan Reference USA) Gale Group.
—Visitors. 1998. 256p. pap. 13.00 (*0-679-78147-1*, Vintage) Knopf Publishing Group.
—Visitors. 1997. 242p. 23.00 o.s.i (*0-679-45785-2*) Random Hse., Inc.
Broughton, Rhoda. Cometh up As a Flower: An Autobiography. 1993. (Pocket Classics Ser.). x, 285p. 8.00 o.p. (*0-7509-0448-8*) Sutton Publishing, Ltd. GBR. *Dist:* International Publishers Marketing.
—Cometh up as a Flower: An Autobiography, 2 vols., 1 bk. reprint ed. 44.50 (*0-404-61794-8*) AMS Pr., Inc.
Brouwer, Sigmund. Magnus. 1994. (Illus.). 500p. pap. 11.99 (*1-56476-296-3*, 6-3296) Cook Communications Ministries.
—Wings of Dawn. 1999. 445p. (*0-7459-4083-8*) Cook Communications Ministries.
Brown, Alan. Princess. l.t. ed. 1991. 21.95 o.p. (*0-7927-0694-3*, CH010); pap. 19.95 o.p. (*0-7927-0695-1*, CS0112) BBC Audiobooks America.
Brown, Carrie. Lamb in Love. 1999. 348p. tchr. ed. 21.95 (*1-56512-203-8*, 72203) Algonquin Bks. of Chapel Hill.
—Lamb in Love. unabr. ed. 1999. (Chivers Sound Library American Collections). audio 69.95 (*0-7927-2318-X*, CSL207, Chivers Sound Library) BBC Audiobooks America.
—Lamb in Love. 2000. 320p. reprint ed. pap. 12.95 (*0-553-38085-0*) Bantam Bks.
—Lamb in Love. l.t. ed. 1999. (Large Print Book Ser.). 26.95 (*1-56895-732-7*, Wheeler Publishing, Inc.) Gale Group.
Brown, Dan. The Da Vinci Code: A Novel. 2004. 512p. mass mkt. 7.99 (*0-345-45151-1*, Fawcett) Ballantine Bks.
—The Da Vinci Code: A Novel. 2003. 464p. 24.95 (*0-385-50420-9*); E-Book 12.00 (*0-385-50421-7*) Doubleday Publishing.
—The Da Vinci Code: A Novel. l.t. ed. 2003. 752p. 26.95 (*0-375-43230-2*) Random Hse. Large Print.
Brown, Lizbie. Turkey Tracks. 1995. 178p. 20.95 o.p. (*0-312-13193-3*, Saint Martin's Minotaur) St. Martin's Pr.
Brown, Mary. Here There Be Dragonnes. 2003. 832p. pap. 15.00 (*0-7434-3596-6*) Baen Bks.
Brown, Molly. Cracker: To Say I Love You. (Cracker Ser.). 1996. 249p. mass mkt. 5.99 (*0-312-95996-6*, St. Martin's Paperbacks); 1995. 256p. 21.95 o.p. (*0-312-13951-9*) St. Martin's Pr.
—Invitation to a Funeral: A Tale of Restoration Intrigue. 288p. 1999. mass mkt. 5.99 (*0-312-97094-3*, St. Martin's Paperbacks); 1998. (YA). 22.95 o.p. (*0-312-18598-7*, Saint Martin's Minotaur) St. Martin's Pr.
Brown, Stacy. One Wilde Night. 2000. 352p. mass mkt. 5.99 o.s.i (*0-8217-6728-3*, Zebra Bks.) Kensington Publishing Corp.
Browne, Douglas G. Too Many Cousins. 1984. (Detective Stories Ser.). 192p. reprint ed. pap. 3.95 (*0-486-24774-0*) Dover Pubns., Inc.
—What Beckoning Ghost? 1986. 265p. reprint ed. pap. 5.95 o.p. (*0-486-25055-5*) Dover Pubns., Inc.
Browne, Gretta Curran. Ghosts in Sunlight. 1999. 437p. (*0-86327-728-4*) Wolfhound Pr.
Bruce, Colin. Einstein Paradox: And Other Science Mysteries Solved by Sherlock Holmes. 1963. 272p. text 3.00 o.p. (*0-465-09311-6*) Basic Bks.
—Einstein Paradox: And Other Science Mysteries Solved by Sherlock Holmes. 1998. 272p. reprint ed. pap. text 15.95 (*0-7382-0023-9*) Perseus Publishing.
Bruce, Leo. A Bone & a Hank of Hair. 1985. (Carolus Deene Mystery Ser.). 192p. reprint ed. 20.00 o.p. (*0-89733-176-1*); pap. 5.95 o.s.i (*0-89733-175-3*) Academy Chicago Pubs., Ltd.
—Case for Sergeant Beef. 1985. (Sergeant Beef Mystery Ser.). 14.95 o.s.i (*0-89733-037-4*); pap. 4.95 o.s.i (*0-89733-036-6*) Academy Chicago Pubs., Ltd.
—Case for Sergeant Beef. l.t. ed. 1982. (Ulverscroft Large Print Ser.). 320p. 29.99 o.p. (*0-7089-0842-X*, Ulverscroft) Thorpe, F. A. Pubs. GBR. *Dist:* Ulverscroft Large Print Bks., Ltd., Ulverscroft Large Print Canada, Ltd.
—Case for Three Detectives. 1985. (Sgt. Beef Mystery Ser.). 240p. pap. 10.95 (*0-89733-033-1*) Academy Chicago Pubs., Ltd.
—Case for Three Detectives. 1995. 248p. 19.50 (*0-7451-8661-0*, Black Dagger) BBC Audiobooks America.
—Case with No Conclusion. (Sergeant Beef Mystery Ser.). 288p. pap. 5.95 o.s.i (*0-89733-118-4*); 1984. 15.00 o.s.i (*0-89733-117-6*) Academy Chicago Pubs., Ltd.
—Case with Ropes & Rings. 1990. pap. 4.95 o.s.i (*0-89733-329-2*); 192p. reprint ed. 14.95 o.s.i (*0-89733-034-X*); 192p. reprint ed. pap. 4.95 o.s.i (*0-89733-035-8*) Academy Chicago Pubs., Ltd.
—Case Without a Corpse. 1990. (Sergeant Beef Mystery Ser.). 284p. reprint ed. 14.95 o.p. (*0-89733-052-8*); pap. 4.95 o.p. (*0-89733-051-X*) Academy Chicago Pubs., Ltd.
—Dead Man's Shoes. 1987. (Carolus Deene Mystery Ser.). 216p. pap. 7.95 (*0-89733-271-7*) Academy Chicago Pubs., Ltd.
—Death at Hallows End. 2003. 221p. 22.50 (*0-89733-516-3*) Academy Chicago Pubs., Ltd.
—Death at St Asprey's School. 1984. (Carolus Deene Mystery Ser.). 221p. 14.95 o.p. (*0-89733-095-1*); pap. 7.95 (*0-89733-094-3*) Academy Chicago Pubs., Ltd.
—Death in Albert Park. 1983. (Carolus Deene Mystery Ser.). 239p. reprint ed. pap. 7.95 (*0-89733-073-0*) Academy Chicago Pubs., Ltd.
—Death of a Commuter. 1988. (Carolus Deene Mystery Ser.). 192p. pap. 7.95 (*0-89733-326-8*) Academy Chicago Pubs., Ltd.
—Death on All Hallowe'en. 1988. (Carolus Deene Mystery Ser.). 176p. pap. 7.95 (*0-89733-292-X*) Academy Chicago Pubs., Ltd.
—Death with Blue Ribbon. 1994. (Carolus Deene Mystery Ser.). 176p. pap. 7.95 (*0-89733-345-4*) Academy Chicago Pubs., Ltd.
—Die All, Die Merrily. 1987. (Carolus Deene Mystery Ser.). 192p. pap. 7.95 (*0-89733-253-9*) Academy Chicago Pubs., Ltd.
—Furious Old Women. 1983. (Carolus Deene Mystery Ser.). 191p. reprint ed. pap. 7.95 (*0-89733-084-6*) Academy Chicago Pubs., Ltd.
—Furious Old Women. Barzun, Jacques & Taylor, W. H., eds. 1983. (Crime Fiction 1950-1975 Ser.). 191p. lib. bdg. 5.00 o.p. (*0-8240-4976-4*) Garland Publishing, Inc.
—Jack on the Gallows Tree. 1983. (Carolus Deene Mystery Ser.). 189p. 15.00 (*0-89733-071-4*); pap. 7.95 (*0-89733-072-2*) Academy Chicago Pubs., Ltd.

—Neck & Neck. 1980. (Sergeant Beef Mystery Ser.). 224p. reprint ed. 15.00 o.s.i (*0-89733-041-2*); pap. 5.95 o.s.i (*0-89733-040-4*) Academy Chicago Pubs., Ltd.
—Neck & Neck. l.t. ed. 1983. (Ulverscroft Large Print Ser.). 368p. 29.99 o.p. (*0-7089-0898-5*, Ulverscroft) Thorpe, F. A. Pubs. GBR. *Dist:* Ulverscroft Large Print Bks., Ltd., Ulverscroft Large Print Canada, Ltd.
—Nothing Like Blood. 1986. 4.95 o.p. (*0-89733-127-3*); 1985. 192p. 15.00 (*0-89733-128-1*) Academy Chicago Pubs., Ltd.
—Our Jubilee Is Death. 1986. (Carolus Deene Mystery Ser.). 189p. pap. 7.95 (*0-89733-229-6*) Academy Chicago Pubs., Ltd.
—Such Is Death. (Carolus Deene Mystery Ser.). 192p. 1986. 15.00 (*0-89733-159-1*); 1985. pap. 7.95 (*0-89733-160-5*) Academy Chicago Pubs., Ltd.
Bruen, Ken. Rilke on Black. 1997. (Mask Noir Ser.). 144p. (Orig.). pap. text o.p. (*1-85242-511-3*) Serpent's Tail Ltd.
Buchan, Carole, ed. The Catch: Prize-Winning Stories by Women. 1998. 183p. pap. o.p. (*1-85242-573-3*) Serpent's Tail Ltd.
Buchan, Elizabeth. The Good Wife Strikes Back. 2003. 320p. 24.95 (*0-670-03280-8*) Viking Penguin.
—Perfect Love. unabr. ed. 1996. audio 84.95 (*0-7451-6637-7*, CAB 1253) BBC Audiobooks America.
—Perfect Love. 2003. 448p. pap. 13.95 (*0-312-32464-2*, Saint Martin's Griffin); 1999. 256p. 24.95 o.p. (*0-312-20568-6*) St. Martin's Pr.
—Perfect Love: Rosamunde Pilchers Book Shelf. 2000. (Rosamunde Pilcher's Bookshelf Ser.). 448p. mass mkt. 6.99 (*0-312-97426-4*, St. Martin's Paperbacks) St. Martin's Pr.
—Revenge of the Middle-Aged Woman. 2003. 352p. pap. 14.00 (*0-14-200372-7*) Penguin Group (USA) Inc.
—Revenge of the Middle-Aged Woman. l.t. ed. 2003. 414p. 32.95 (*0-7862-5638-9*) Thorndike Pr.
—Revenge of the Middle-Aged Woman. 2003. 352p. 24.95 (*0-670-03206-9*, Viking) Viking Penguin.
Buchan, John. Midwinter. E-Book 3.95 (*0-594-01897-8*); 2000. 300p. E-Book 9.95 (*0-594-02014-X*) 1873 Pr.
—Midwinter. 1988. reprint ed. lib. bdg. 49.00 (*0-7812-0467-4*) Reprint Services Corp.
—Midwinter. 1971. reprint ed. 59.00 (*0-403-00878-6*) Scholarly Pr., Inc.
Buck, Gayle. Belle's Beau. 2000. (Signet Regency Romance Ser.). 224p. mass mkt. 4.99 o.s.i (*0-451-20197-3*) NAL.
Buckley, Fiona. The Doublet Affair. unabr. ed. 2000. audio 49.95 (*0-7861-1725-7*, 2530) Blackstone Audio Bks., Inc.
—The Doublet Affair. 1999. (Illus.). 416p. mass mkt. 6.99 (*0-671-01532-X*, Pocket) Simon & Schuster.
—The Doublet Affair. l.t. ed. 2000. (Ulverscroft Large Print Ser.). 408p. 31.99 o.p. (*0-7089-4180-X*, Ulverscroft) Thorpe, F. A. Pubs. GBR. *Dist:* Ulverscroft Large Print Bks., Ltd., Ulverscroft Large Print Canada, Ltd.
—The Doublet Affair: An Ursula Blanchard Mystery at Queen Elizabeth I's Court. 1998. 304p. 21.00 o.s.i (*0-684-83842-7*, Scribner) Simon & Schuster.
—A Pawn for a Queen: An Ursula Blanchard Mystery at Queen Elizabeth I's Court. 2002. 288p. 24.00 (*0-7432-0265-1*, Scribner) Simon & Schuster.
—Queen's Ransom. 2003. 336p. reprint ed. mass mkt. 6.99 (*0-671-03293-3*, Pocket) Simon & Schuster.
—The Robsart Mystery. l.t. ed. 1998. (Ulverscroft Large Print Ser.). 480p. 29.99 o.p. (*0-7089-4009-9*, Ulverscroft) Thorpe, F. A. Pubs. GBR. *Dist:* Ulverscroft Large Print Bks., Ltd., Ulverscroft Large Print Canada, Ltd.
—To Shield the Queen. unabr. ed. 1999. audio 49.95 (*0-7861-1532-7*, 2382) Blackstone Audio Bks., Inc.
—To Shield the Queen: A Mystery at Queen Elizabeth I's Court. 1997. (Mystery at Queen Elizabeth I's Court Ser.). (Illus.). 288p. 21.00 (*0-684-83841-9*, Scribner) Simon & Schuster.
Buffong, Jean. Snowflakes in the Sun. 1997. 180p. pap. 14.95 (*0-7043-4423-8*) Women's Pr., Ltd., The GBR. *Dist:* Trafalgar Square.
Bugge, Carole. Haunting of Torre Abbey. 2000. 258p. 22.95 (*0-312-24557-2*, Saint Martin's Minotaur) St. Martin's Pr.
—Star of India. 1997. 256p. 21.95 (*0-312-18034-9*) St. Martin's Pr.
Burdekin, Katharine. Proud Man. 1993. 360p. 35.00 (*1-55861-070-7*); pap. 14.95 (*1-55861-067-7*) Feminist Pr. at The City Univ. of New York.
Burden, Pat. Bury Him Kindly. 1992. 192p. 16.50 o.s.i (*0-385-42234-2*) Doubleday Publishing.
—Bury Him Kindly. l.t. ed. 1992. (Magna Large Print Ser.). 296p. 29.99 o.p. (*0-7505-0368-8*) Magna Large Print Bks. GBR. *Dist:* Ulverscroft Large Print Bks., Ltd., Ulverscroft Large Print Canada, Ltd.
—Screaming Bones. 1992. 224p. mass mkt. 4.50 o.s.i (*0-553-29936-0*) Bantam Bks.
—Screaming Bones. 1990. 192p. 14.95 o.s.i (*0-385-41522-2*) Doubleday Publishing.
—Wreath of Honesty. 1991. 192p. 15.00 o.s.i (*0-385-41863-9*) Doubleday Publishing.
—Wreath of Honesty. l.t. ed. 1992. 368p. 29.99 (*0-7089-2583-9*, Ulverscroft) Thorpe, F. A. Pubs. GBR. *Dist:* Ulverscroft Large Print Bks., Ltd.
Burdett, John. A Personal History of Thirst: A Psychological Thriller in the Tradition of Damage. 1996. 320p. 23.00 o.p. (*0-688-14399-7*, Morrow, William & Co.) Morrow/Avon.
Burgess, Anthony. A Dead Man in Deptford. 1996. 288p. pap. 11.95 (*0-7867-0321-0*); 1995. 272p. 21.00 o.p. (*0-7867-0192-7*); 2003. 272p. reprint ed. 14.00 (*0-7867-1152-3*) Avalon Publishing Group. (Carroll & Graf Pubs.).
—A Dead Man in Deptford. 1994. (*0-09-930256-X*) Hutchinson GBR. *Dist:* Random Hse. of Canada, Ltd.
—Earthly Powers. 1994. 608p. pap. 15.95 (*0-7867-0026-2*, Carroll & Graf Pubs.) Avalon Publishing Group.
—Earthly Powers. 1980. 16.95 o.s.i (*0-671-41490-9*, Simon & Schuster) Simon & Schuster.
—The Pianoplayers. 1986. 256p. 16.95 o.p. (*0-87795-832-7*, Morrow, William & Co.) Morrow/Avon.
—The Pianoplayers. 1987. pap. 4.95 (*0-671-63792-4*, Washington Square Pr.) Simon & Schuster.
Burley, W. J. Death in a Salubrious Place. l.t. ed. 1988. (Linford Mystery Library). 320p. pap. 17.99 o.p. (*0-7089-6612-8*, Ulverscroft) Thorpe, F. A. Pubs. GBR. *Dist:* Ulverscroft Large Print Bks., Ltd., Ulverscroft Large Print Canada, Ltd.
—Death in a Salubrious Place. 1984. (British Mystery Ser.). 175p. reprint ed. pap. 2.95 o.p. (*0-8027-3069-8*) Walker & Co.
—Wycliffe & Death in Stanley Street. l.t. ed. 1997. (Magna Large Print Ser.). 295p. 29.99 o.p. (*0-7505-1143-5*) Magna Large Print Bks. GBR. *Dist:* Ulverscroft Large Print Bks., Ltd., Ulverscroft Large Print Canada, Ltd.
—Wycliffe & Death in Stanley Street. 2003. 220p. mass mkt. 7.95 (*0-7528-4969-7*) Orion Publishing Group, Ltd. GBR. *Dist:* Trafalgar Square.
—Wycliffe & the Beales. 1984. (Crime Club Ser.). 192p. 11.95 o.p. (*0-385-19189-8*) Doubleday Publishing.
—Wycliffe & the Beales. 1987. 192p. pap. 2.95 o.p. (*0-380-70329-7*, Avon Bks.) Morrow/Avon.
—Wycliffe & the Cycle of Death. 1991. 192p. 15.00 o.s.i (*0-385-41800-0*) Doubleday Publishing.
—Wycliffe & the Cycle of Death. l.t. ed. 1991. (Magna Large Print Ser.). 309p. o.p. (*0-7505-0038-7*) Magna Large Print Bks. GBR. *Dist:* Ulverscroft Large Print Canada, Ltd.
—Wycliffe & the Cycle of Death. 2000. pap. 8.95 (*0-552-14109-7*) Transworld Publishers Ltd. GBR. *Dist:* Trafalgar Square.
—Wycliffe & the Dead Flautist. l.t. ed. 1992. (Magna Large Print Ser.). 303p. 29.99 o.p. (*0-7505-0196-0*) Magna Large Print Bks. GBR. *Dist:* Ulverscroft Large Print Bks., Ltd., Ulverscroft Large Print Canada, Ltd.
—Wycliffe & the Dead Flautist. unabr. ed. 1999. audio 49.95 Soundings, Ltd. GBR. *Dist:* Ulverscroft Large Print Bks., Ltd.
—Wycliffe & the Dead Flautist. 1992. 192p. 16.95 o.p. (*0-312-07129-9*, Saint Martin's Minotaur) St. Martin's Pr.
—Wycliffe & the Dead Flautist. 2000. pap. 8.95 (*0-552-14264-6*) Transworld Publishers Ltd. GBR. *Dist:* Trafalgar Square.
—Wycliffe & the Dunes Mystery. 1995. mass mkt. o.s.i (*0-552-14221-2*, Corgi) Bantam Bks.
—Wycliffe & the Dunes Mystery. l.t. ed. 1994. (Magna Large Print Ser.). 299p. o.p. (*0-7505-0629-6*) Magna Large Print Bks. GBR. *Dist:* Ulverscroft Large Print Canada, Ltd.
—Wycliffe & the Dunes Mystery. 1994. 192p. 18.95 o.p. (*0-312-11100-2*, Saint Martin's Minotaur) St. Martin's Pr.
—Wycliffe & the Four Jacks. 1994. mass mkt. 5.99 o.s.i (*0-552-14267-0*) Bantam Bks.
—Wycliffe & the Four Jacks. 1986. (Crime Club Ser.). 192p. 12.95 o.p. (*0-385-23262-4*) Doubleday Publishing.
—Wycliffe & the Four Jacks. 1987. 192p. pap. 2.95 o.p. (*0-380-70328-9*, Avon Bks.) Morrow/Avon.
—Wycliffe & the Guilt Edged Alibi. 1994. mass mkt. o.s.i (*0-552-14115-1*, Corgi) Bantam Bks.
—Wycliffe & the House of Death. 1995. 192p. 19.95 o.p. (*0-312-14080-0*, Saint Martin's Minotaur) St. Martin's Pr.
—Wycliffe & the House of Fear. l.t. ed. 1996. (Magna Large Print Ser.). 327p. o.p. (*0-7505-1006-4*) Magna Large Print Bks. GBR. *Dist:* Ulverscroft Large Print Canada, Ltd.
—Wycliffe & the Last Rites. l.t. ed. 1993. (Magna Large Print Ser.). 337p. o.p. (*0-7505-0492-7*) Magna Large Print Bks. GBR. *Dist:* Ulverscroft Large Print Canada, Ltd.
—Wycliffe & the Last Rites. 1993. 192p. 17.95 o.p. (*0-312-09946-0*, Saint Martin's Minotaur) St. Martin's Pr.
—Wycliffe & the Last Rites. 2000. 219p. pap. 8.95 (*0-552-14265-4*) Transworld Publishers Ltd. GBR. *Dist:* Trafalgar Square.
—Wycliffe & the Pea Green Boat. 1998. 208p. mass mkt. 4.99 o.s.i (*0-552-12804-X*) Bantam Bks.
—Wycliffe & the Quiet Virgin. 1986. (Crime Club Ser.). 192p. 12.95 o.p. (*0-385-23549-6*) Doubleday Publishing.
—Wycliffe & the Quiet Virgin. 1988. 176p. mass mkt. 2.95 (*0-380-70510-9*, Avon Bks.) Morrow/Avon.
—Wycliffe & the Quiet Virgin. 1989. 192p. mass mkt. 8.95 o.s.i (*0-552-13435-X*) Transworld Publishers Ltd. GBR. *Dist:* Trafalgar Square.
—Wycliffe & the Redhead. 1999. (Illus.). 255p. mass mkt. (*0-552-14661-7*, Corgi) Bantam Bks.
—Wycliffe & the Redhead. l.t. ed. 1999. (Magna Large Print Ser.). 320p. o.p. (*0-7505-1373-X*) Magna Large Print Bks. GBR. *Dist:* Ulverscroft Large Print Canada, Ltd.
—Wycliffe & the Redhead. 1998. 192p. 20.95 (*0-312-19374-2*, Saint Martin's Minotaur) St. Martin's Pr.
—Wycliffe & the Scapegoat. 1988. mass mkt. o.s.i (*0-552-12806-6*) Corgi Bks. Ltd.
—Wycliffe & the Scapegoat. l.t. ed. 2001. (Dales Large Print Ser.). 256p. pap. (*1-84262-055-X*) Dales Large Print Bks. GBR. *Dist:* Ulverscroft Large Print Canada, Ltd.
—Wycliffe & the Scapegoat. 1979. (Crime Club Ser.). 9.95 o.p. (*0-385-15126-8*) Doubleday Publishing.
—Wycliffe & the Scapegoat. 1987. 160p. pap. 2.95 o.p. (*0-380-70330-0*, Avon Bks.) Morrow/Avon.
—Wycliffe & the Scapegoat. 1998. 208p. mass mkt. 8.95 o.p. (*0-552-14266-2*) Transworld Publishers Ltd. GBR. *Dist:* Trafalgar Square.
—Wycliffe & the Schoolgirls. 1987. mass mkt. 3.95 o.s.i (*0-552-12805-8*) Bantam Bks.
—Wycliffe & the Schoolgirls. l.t. ed. 1989. 277p. lib. bdg. 11.95 o.p. (*1-85057-477-4*, Macmillan Reference USA) Gale Group.
—Wycliffe & the Schoolgirls. 1984. (British Mystery Ser.). 175p. reprint ed. pap. 2.95 o.p. (*0-8027-3064-7*) Walker & Co.
—Wycliffe & the Tangled Web. 2000. pap. 8.95 (*0-552-14268-9*) Transworld Publishers Ltd. GBR. *Dist:* Trafalgar Square.
—Wycliffe & the Three-Toed Pussy. 1997. 18.50 o.p. (*0-7451-8702-1*, Black Dagger) BBC Audiobooks America.
—Wycliffe & the Three-Toed Pussy. l.t. ed. 1996. (Magna Large Print Ser.). 320p. 29.99 o.p. (*0-7505-0963-5*) Magna Large Print Bks. GBR. *Dist:* Ulverscroft Large Print Bks., Ltd., Ulverscroft Large Print Canada, Ltd.
—Wycliffe & Winsor Blue. 1987. (Crime Club Ser.). 192p. 12.95 o.s.i (*0-385-24311-1*) Doubleday Publishing.
—Wycliffe in Paul's Court. 1980. (Crime Club Ser.). 192p. 10.95 o.p. (*0-385-17208-7*) Doubleday Publishing.
—Wycliffe in Paul's Court. 2003. 192p. mass mkt. 7.95 (*0-7528-4932-8*) Orion Publishing Group, Ltd. GBR. *Dist:* Trafalgar Square.
—Wycliffe in Paul's Court. 1981. 192p. pap. 3.95 o.p. (*0-14-005917-2*, Penguin Bks.) Viking Penguin.
—Wycliffe's Wild Goose Chase. 1982. (Crime Club Ser.). 192p. 11.95 o.p. (*0-385-18254-6*) Doubleday Publishing.
—Wycliffe's Wild Goose Chase. 2000. (J). pap. 8.95 (*0-552-14269-7*) Transworld Publishers Ltd. GBR. *Dist:* Trafalgar Square.
Burnett, Frances Hodgson. A Fair Barbarian. unabr. ed. 1992. audio 26.95 (*1-55686-430-2*, 430) Books in Motion.
—A Fair Barbarian. 1995. 285p. reprint ed. pap. 15.95 (*0-89301-187-8*) Univ. of Idaho Pr.
Burney, Fanny. Camilla. Bloom, Edward A. & Bloom, Lillian D., eds. 1983. (Oxford World's Classics Ser.). 992p. pap. 12.95 o.p. (*0-19-281662-4*) Oxford Univ. Pr., Inc.
—Cecilia: Memoirs of an Heiress. 1986. (Virago Modern Classics Ser.). 938p. pap. 7.95 o.p. (*0-14-016136-8*, Penguin Bks.) Viking Penguin.
—Cecilia: Or, Memoirs of an Heiress. Sabor, Peter & Doody, Margaret Anne, eds. 1988. (Oxford World's Classics Ser.). 1,056p. pap. 11.95 o.p. (*0-19-281742-6*) Oxford Univ. Pr., Inc.
—Evelina: Or, the History of a Young Lady's Entrance into the World, Set. unabr. ed. 1989. (YA). (gr. 9 up). audio 71.95 (*1-55685-140-5*) Audio Bk. Contractors, Inc.
—Evelina: Or, the History of a Young Lady's Entrance into the World. 1992. 464p. mass mkt. 5.50 o.s.i (*0-553-21411-X*, Bantam Classics) Bantam Bks.
—Evelina: Or, the History of a Young Lady's Entrance into the World. 1958. 5.00 o.p. (*0-460-00352-6*) Biblio Distribution.
—Evelina: Or, the History of a Young Lady's Entrance into the World. 1992. 480p. mass mkt. 6.95 o.s.i (*0-451-52560-4*, Signet Classics) NAL.
—Evelina: Or, the History of a Young Lady's Entrance into the World. 2000. (Critical Editions Ser.). (C). pap. text 21.50 (*0-393-94708-4*); pap. text 33.25 (*0-393-94850-1*) Norton, W. W. & Co., Inc.
—Evelina: Or, the History of a Young Lady's Entrance into the World. Cooke, Stewart J., ed. 1998. (Critical Editions Ser.). (C). pap. text 9.50 (*0-393-97158-9*) Norton, W. W. & Co., Inc.
—Evelina: Or, the History of a Young Lady's Entrance into the World. 1965. pap. 11.95 (*0-393-00294-2*) Norton, W. W. & Co., Inc.
—Evelina: Or, the History of a Young Lady's Entrance into the World. Bloom, Edward A., ed. & intro. by. (Oxford World's Classics Ser.). (Illus.). 1998. 464p. pap. 10.95 o.p. (*0-19-283396-0*); 1982. 478p. pap. 8.95 o.p. (*0-19-281596-2*) Oxford Univ. Pr., Inc.
—Evelina: Or, the History of a Young Lady's Entrance into the World. Straub, Kristina, ed. 1997. (Bedford Cultural Editions Ser.). 544p. 35.00 o.p. (*0-312-12796-0*) Palgrave Macmillan.
—Evelina: Or, the History of a Young Lady's Entrance into the World. 2001. (Modern Library Classics). 480p. pap. 11.95 (*0-375-75805-4*); E-Book 9.95 (*1-58836-235-3*) Random House Adult Trade Publishing Group. (Modern Library).
—Evelina: Or, the History of a Young Lady's Entrance into the World. Doody, Margaret Anne, ed. & intro. by. 1994. (Classics Ser.). 544p. 13.95 (*0-14-043347-3*, Penguin Classics) Viking Penguin.
—Evelina: The History of a Young Lady's Entrance into the World. Bloom, Edward A., ed. 2nd ed. 2002. (Oxford World's Classics Ser.). (Illus.). 448p. pap. 10.95 (*0-19-284031-2*) Oxford Univ. Pr., Inc.
—Fanny Burney's Evelina. Straub, Kristina, ed. 1997. (Bedford Cultural Editions Ser.). (Illus.). 693p. pap. text 14.50 (*0-312-09729-8*) Bedford/Saint Martin's.
Burney, Fanny & Howard, Susan Kubica. Evelina: Or, the History of a Young Lady's Entrance into the World. 2000. (Literary Texts Ser.). (Illus.). 694p. (C). pap. (*1-55111-237-X*) Broadview Pr.
Burns, Richard. Why Diamond Had to Die. 1991. text 22.95 o.p. (*0-7475-0275-7*) Trafalgar Square.
Burnside, John. The Locust Room. 2001. 224p. pap. o.p. (*0-224-05292-6*) Random Hse. UK, Ltd.
Burt, Sophie. 2000. pap. 10.95 (*0-552-99532-0*) Transworld Publishers Ltd. GBR. *Dist:* Trafalgar Square.
Busbee, Shirlee. At Long Last. 2000. 450p. E-Book 4.95 (*0-7595-8046-4*); 450p. E-Book 4.95 (*0-7595-9051-6*); 450p. E-Book 4.95 (*0-7595-4045-4*); 450p. E-Book 4.95 (*0-7595-0044-4*); 448p. reprint ed. mass mkt. 6.99 (*0-446-60807-6*) Warner Bks., Inc.
—For Love Alone. 2000. 448p. reprint ed. mass mkt. 6.50 (*0-446-60532-8*) Warner Bks., Inc.
—A Heart for the Taking. 1997. 432p. reprint ed. mass mkt. 5.99 (*0-446-60218-3*) Warner Bks., Inc.
Busch, Frederick. The Mutual Friend. 1983. (Nonpareil Bk.). 224p. reprint ed. pap. 8.95 o.p. (*0-87923-482-2*) Godine, David R. Pub.
—The Mutual Friend. 1978. 8.95 o.p. (*0-06-010527-5*) HarperCollins Pubs.
—The Mutual Friend. 1994. (Paperbook Ser.: Vol. 774). 240p. reprint ed. pap. 9.95 (*0-8112-1258-0*, NDP774) New Directions Publishing Corp.
—War Babies. 2001. 122p. reprint ed. pap. 12.95 (*0-8112-1476-1*) New Directions Publishing Corp.
Butler, Gwendoline. Coffin & the Paper Man. 1993. (WWL Mystery Ser.). mass mkt. o.s.i (*0-373-26133-0*, 1-26133-8, Harlequin Bks.) Harlequin Enterprises, Ltd.
—Coffin & the Paper Man. pap. 15.95 (*0-312-29192-2*, Saint Martin's Griffin); 1991. 16.95 (*0-312-05835-7*, Saint Martin's Minotaur) St. Martin's Pr.
—Coffin for Baby. (Black Dagger Crime Ser.). 1993. 192p. 16.50 o.p. (*0-7451-8606-8*, Black Dagger); 1994. 18.95 o.p. (*0-7451-6458-7*) BBC Audiobooks America.
—A Coffin for Charley. 1996. (WWL Mystery Ser.). mass mkt. o.s.i (*0-373-26200-0*, 1-26200-5, Worldwide Library) Harlequin Enterprises, Ltd.
—A Coffin for Charley. l.t. ed. 1994. (Magna Large Print Ser.). 358p. o.p. (*0-7505-0705-5*) Magna Large Print Bks. GBR. *Dist:* Ulverscroft Large Print Canada, Ltd.
—A Coffin for Charley. 1994. 256p. 20.95 o.p. (*0-312-11466-4*, Saint Martin's Minotaur) St. Martin's Pr.
—A Coffin from the Past. l.t. ed. 1993. pap. 16.95 o.p. (*0-7451-6419-6*); 1992. 18.95 o.p. (*0-7451-6413-7*); 1993. audio 39.95 (*0-7451-5814-5*, CSL 075) BBC Audiobooks America.
—A Coffin from the Past. (Black Dagger Crime Ser.). 224p. 12.95 o.p. (*0-86220-706-1*) Chivers Pr. GBR. *Dist:* BBC Audiobooks America.
—Coffin in Fashion. 1992. mass mkt. o.s.i (*0-373-26100-4*, Harlequin Bks.) Harlequin Enterprises, Ltd.
—Coffin in Fashion. pap. 15.95 (*0-312-29177-9*, Saint Martin's Griffin); 1989. 176p. 16.95 (*0-312-03802-X*, Saint Martin's Minotaur) St. Martin's Pr.
—Coffin in Malta. unabr. ed. 1989. audio 39.95 (*0-7451-5815-3*, CAT 4038) BBC Audiobooks America.

Settings

—Coffin in Malta. 1989. (Black Dagger Crime Ser.). 224p. reprint ed. text 12.95 o.p. (0-86220-752-5) Chivers Pr. GBR. *Dist:* BBC Audiobooks America.

—Coffin in Malta. 1985. (Walker's British Paperback Mysteries Ser.). 192p. reprint ed. pap. 2.95 o.s.i (0-8027-3111-2) Walker & Co.

—Coffin in the Black Museum. unabr. ed. 1991. (Audio Ser.). audio 54.95 (0-7451-5816-1, CAT 4068) BBC Audiobooks America.

—Coffin in the Museum of Crime. 1993. (Mystery Ser.). mass mkt. o.s.i (0-373-26121-7, 1-26121-3, Harlequin Bks.) Harlequin Enterprises, Ltd.

—Coffin in the Museum of Crime. 1990. 16.95 (0-312-04282-5, Saint Martin's Minotaur) St. Martin's Pr.

—Coffin on Murder Street. 1994. (Mystery Ser.). mass mkt. o.s.i (0-373-26147-0, 1-26147-8, Harlequin Bks.) Harlequin Enterprises, Ltd.

—Coffin on Murder Street. 1992. 224p. 16.95 (0-312-07673-8, Saint Martin's Minotaur) St. Martin's Pr.

—Coffin on the Water. 1992. (WWL Mystery Ser.: No. 90). mass mkt. o.s.i (0-373-26090-3, 1-26090-0, Harlequin Bks.) Harlequin Enterprises, Ltd.

—Coffin on the Water. 1990. 2.99 o.p. (0-517-05811-1) Random Hse. Value Publishing.

—Coffin on the Water. 1989. 192p. 14.95 (0-312-02561-0, Saint Martin's Minotaur) St. Martin's Pr.

—The Coffin Tree. 1997. mass mkt. o.s.i (0-373-26250-7, 1-26250-0, Worldwide Library) Harlequin Enterprises, Ltd.

—The Coffin Tree. pap. 15.95 (0-312-29189-2, Saint Martin's Griffin); 1995. 240p. 21.95 (0-312-13946-2, Saint Martin's Minotaur) St. Martin's Pr.

—Coffin Underground. l.t. ed. 1989. 336p. lib. bdg. 11.95 o.p. (1-85057-722-6, Macmillan Reference USA) Gale Group.

—Coffin Underground. 1992. per. (0-373-26110-1, 1-26110-6, Harlequin Bks.) Harlequin Enterprises, Ltd.

—Coffin Underground. pap. 14.95 (0-312-31071-4, Saint Martin's Griffin); 1989. 16.95 (0-312-02886-5, Saint Martin's Minotaur) St. Martin's Pr.

—Coffin Waiting. unabr. ed. 1992. (Crimson Dagger Audio Bks.). audio 39.95 (0-7451-2406-2, CDA 007) BBC Audiobooks America.

—Coffin's Game. l.t. ed. 1999. (Thorndike General Ser.). 307p. pap. 22.95 o.p. (0-7862-1946-7, Macmillan Reference USA) Gale Group.

—Coffin's Game. 2000. (Commander John Coffin Mysteries Ser.: Bk. 353). 256p. mass mkt. o.s.i (0-373-26353-8, 1-26353-2, Worldwide Library) Harlequin Enterprises, Ltd.

—Coffin's Game. 1999. (Commander John Coffin Mysteries Ser.). 240p. 21.95 (0-312-20512-0, Saint Martin's Minotaur) St. Martin's Pr.

—Coffin's Ghost. 2001. 224p. 22.95 (0-312-27997-3, Saint Martin's Minotaur) St. Martin's Pr.

—Coffin's Ghost. l.t. ed. 2000. (General Ser.). 318p. 22.95 (0-7862-2803-2) Thorndike Pr.

—Cracking Open a Coffin. 1995. (WWL Mystery Ser.). 250p. mass mkt. o.s.i (0-373-26171-3, 1-29171-8, Harlequin Bks.) Harlequin Enterprises, Ltd.

—Cracking Open a Coffin. 1993. 240p. 16.95 (0-312-09777-8, Saint Martin's Minotaur) St. Martin's Pr.

—A Dark Coffin. 1998. (WWL Mystery Ser.). mass mkt. o.s.i (0-373-26265-5, 1-26265-8, Worldwide Library) Harlequin Enterprises, Ltd.

—A Dark Coffin. unabr. ed. 2001. audio 54.95 ISIS Audio Bks. GBR. *Dist:* Ulverscroft Large Print Bks., Ltd.

—A Dark Coffin. l.t. ed. 1996. (Magna Large Print Ser.). 325p. o.p. (0-7505-1049-8) Magna Large Print Bks. GBR. *Dist:* Ulverscroft Large Print Canada, Ltd.

—A Dark Coffin. 1996. 240p. 21.95 (0-312-14577-2, Saint Martin's Minotaur) St. Martin's Pr.

—Death Lives Next Door. 1992. (John Coffin Ser.). 192p. 16.95 o.p. (0-312-08175-8, Saint Martin's Minotaur) St. Martin's Pr.

—A Double Coffin. 1999. (WWL Mystery Ser.: No. 313). per. (0-373-26313-9, 1-26313-6, Worldwide Library) Harlequin Enterprises, Ltd.

—A Double Coffin. 1998. 240p. 21.95 o.p. (0-312-18569-3, Saint Martin's Minotaur) St. Martin's Pr.

—A Grave Coffin. 2000. 256p. 22.95 (0-312-26167-5, Saint Martin's Minotaur) St. Martin's Pr.

—A Nameless Coffin. l.t. ed. 2000. (General Ser.). 335p. pap. 23.95 (0-7862-2302-2); (0-7540-3993-5); (0-7540-3994-3) Thorndike Pr.

—A Nameless Coffin. 1985. pap. 2.95 o.s.i (0-8027-3081-7) Walker & Co.

Butler, Gwendoline & Melling, John K. Coffin Waiting. 1990. (Black Dagger Crime Ser.). 200p. reprint ed. text 12.95 o.p. (0-86220-767-3) Chivers Pr. GBR. *Dist:* BBC Audiobooks America.

Butler, Nancy. The Prodigal Hero. 2000. (Signet Regency Romance Ser.). 240p. mass mkt. 4.99 o.s.i (0-451-20172-8) NAL.

—The Rake's Retreat. 1999. (Signet Regency Romance Ser.). 224p. mass mkt. 4.99 o.s.i (0-451-19789-5, Signet Bks.) NAL.

Butler, Nancy, et al. Regency Christmas Eve. 2000. (Signet Regency Romance Ser.). 352p. mass mkt. 6.99 o.s.i (0-451-20167-1, Signet Bks.) NAL.

Butler, Samuel. Ainsi Va Toute Chair. 1977. Orig. Title: Way of all Flesh. (FRE.). Vol. 1. 237p. pap. 11.95 (0-7859-1845-0, 2070369145); Vol. 2. pap. 11.95 (0-7859-1846-9, 2070369153) French & European Pubns., Inc.

—The Way of All Flesh. 1976. reprint ed. 11.95 o.p. (0-460-00895-1) Biblio Distribution.

—The Way of All Flesh. 1983. 345p. reprint ed. lib. bdg. 17.95 o.s.i (0-89966-310-9) Buccaneer Bks., Inc.

—The Way of All Flesh. 1999. (Shrewsbury Edition of the Works of Samuel Butler: Vol. 17). 414p. reprint ed. lib. bdg. 88.00 (1-58201-017-X) Classic Bks.

—The Way of All Flesh. Wolff, Robert L., ed. 1975. (Victorian Fiction Ser.). reprint ed. lib. bdg. 73.00 o.p. (0-8240-1611-4) Garland Publishing, Inc.

—The Way of All Flesh. 1993. (Everyman's Library). 416p. 17.00 (0-679-41718-4) Knopf, Alfred A. Inc.

—The Way of All Flesh. 1993. (Oxford World's Classics Ser.). 518p. pap. 9.95 o.p. (0-19-282980-7) Oxford Univ. Pr., Inc.

—The Way of All Flesh. 2000. (Modern Library Ser.). E-Book 4.95 (0-679-64120-3, Modern Library) Random House Adult Trade Publishing Group.

—The Way of All Flesh. 1998. (Modern Library Ser.). 448p. pap. 10.95 (0-375-75249-8) Random Hse., Inc.

—The Way of All Flesh. l.t. ed. 1999. (Perennial Bestsellers Ser.). 583p. pap. 25.95 (0-7838-8641-1) Thorndike Pr.

—The Way of All Flesh. 1993. 416p. pap. 7.95 (0-460-87240-0, Everyman's Classic Library in Paperback) Tuttle Publishing.

—The Way of All Flesh. Hogart, Richard & Cochrane, James, eds. 1966. (Classics Ser.). 446p. 12.00 (0-14-043012-1, Penguin Classics) Viking Penguin.

—The Way of All Flesh. 1995. (Classics Library). 400p. pap. 3.95 (1-85326-228-5, 2285WW) Wordsworth Editions, Ltd. GBR. *Dist:* Casemate Pubs. & Bk. Distributors, LLC.

Byatt, A. S. Babel Tower. l.t. ed. 1996. 870p. 25.95 o.p. (0-7838-1684-7, Macmillan Reference USA) Gale Group.

—Babel Tower. 1997. 640p. pap. 15.00 (0-679-73680-8, Vintage) Knopf Publishing Group.

—The Djinn in the Nightingale's Eye: Five Fairy Stories. 1998. (Illus.). 288p. pap. 12.00 (0-679-76222-1, Vintage) Knopf Publishing Group.

—The Djinn in the Nightingale's Eye: Five Fairy Stories. unabr. ed. 1997. audio 44.00 (0-7887-1317-5, 95175E7) Recorded Bks., LLC.

—The Oxford Book of English Short Stories. 2000. 480p. (Orig.). pap. 18.95 o.p. (0-19-288111-6) Oxford Univ. Pr., Inc.

—Possession: A Romance. 1991. (International Ser.). 576p. reprint ed. pap. 14.00 (0-679-73590-9, Vintage) Knopf Publishing Group.

—Possession: A Romance. 640p. 2002. 17.95 (0-679-64238-2); 2000. 19.95 o.s.i (0-679-64030-4, Modern Library) Random House Adult Trade Publishing Group.

—Possession: A Romance. 1993. 5.99 o.p. (0-517-09792-3) Random Hse. Value Publishing.

—The Shadow of the Sun. 1993. (Harvest Book Ser.). 324p. pap. 14.00 (0-15-681416-1, Harvest Bks.) Harcourt Trade Pubs.

—Still Life. 1985. 376p. 16.95 o.p. (0-684-18577-6); 1997. 400p. reprint ed. pap. 14.00 (0-684-83503-7) Simon & Schuster. (Scribner).

—A Whistling Woman. 2004. 448p. pap. 15.00 (0-679-77690-7, Vintage) Knopf Publishing Group.

—A Whistling Woman. 2002. 448p. 26.00 (0-375-41534-3) Knopf, Alfred A. Inc.

Byatt, A. S., ed. The Oxford Book of English Short Stories. (Oxford Books of Prose). (Orig.). 2003. (Illus.). 480p. pap. 19.95 (0-19-280376-X); 1998. 472p. 40.00 (0-19-214238-0) Oxford Univ. Pr., Inc.

Byrd, Nicole. Robert's Lady. 2000. 336p. mass mkt. 5.99 o.s.i (0-515-12853-8, Jove) Berkley Publishing Group.

Byrne, Julia. An Independent Lady. 2001. 256p. mass mkt. (0-373-51153-1, Harlequin Bks.) Harlequin Enterprises, Ltd.

Cach, Lisa. The Mermaid of Penperro. 2001. (Wink & a Kiss Ser.). 368p. mass mkt. 5.50 (0-505-52437-6, Love Spell) Dorchester Publishing Co., Inc.

—Of Midnight Born. 2000. 368p. mass mkt. 5.50 (0-505-52399-X, Love Spell) Dorchester Publishing Co., Inc.

Cadell, Elizabeth. Parson's House. l.t. ed. 1999. (0-7540-3477-1); 280 p. pap. (0-7540-3478-X) BBC Audiobooks America.

—Parson's House. l.t. ed. 1977. lib. bdg. 11.95 o.p. (0-8161-6528-9, Macmillan Reference USA) Gale Group.

—Parson's House. l.t. ed. 1999. (General Ser.). 288p. pap. 23.95 (0-7862-1608-5) Thorndike Pr.

Callen, Gayle. His Betrothed. 2001. 384p. mass mkt. 5.99 (0-380-81377-7, Avon Bks.) Morrow/Avon.

Callison, Brian R. The Stollenberg Legacy. l.t. ed. 2001. (Thorndike General Ser.). 380p. pap. 22.95 (0-7862-3200-5) Thorndike Pr.

Calvit, Christina. Pride & Prejudice. unabr. ed. 1997. audio 22.95 (1-58081-052-7, CTA55) L. A. Theatre Works.

Cameron, Stella. All Smiles. 2000. 448p. mass mkt. (1-55166-615-4, 1-66615-5, Mira Bks.) Harlequin Enterprises, Ltd.

Camp, Candace. The Hidden Heart. 2002. 416p. mass mkt. (1-55166-922-6, Mira Bks.) Harlequin Enterprises, Ltd.

—Promise Me Tomorrow. 2000. 408p. mass mkt. (1-55166-607-3, 1-66607-2, Mira Bks.) Harlequin Enterprises, Ltd.

—Secrets of the Heart. 2003. 416p. mass mkt. (1-55166-657-X, Mira Bks.) Harlequin Enterprises, Ltd.

—A Stolen Heart. abr. ed. 2000. (Mira Bks.). audio 9.99 (1-55204-209-X, MIR-1209) Durkin Hayes Publishing Ltd.

—A Stolen Heart. 2000. 408p. mass mkt. (1-55166-552-2, Mira Bks.) Harlequin Enterprises, Ltd.

—Swept Away. abr. ed. 1999. audio 7.99 (1-55204-176-X, MIR-1176) Durkin Hayes Publishing Ltd.

—Swept Away. 1999. (Mira Bks.). mass mkt. (1-55166-508-5, 1-66508-2, Mira Bks.) Harlequin Enterprises, Ltd.

Campbell, Glynnis. My Champion. 2000. (Knights of de Ware Ser.). 336p. mass mkt. 5.99 (0-515-13048-6, Jove) Berkley Publishing Group.

—My Warrior. 2001. 320p. mass mkt. 6.50 (0-515-13153-9, Jove) Berkley Publishing Group.

Campbell, R. T. Bodies in a Bookshop. 1984. 192p. reprint ed. pap. 6.95 (0-486-24720-1) Dover Pubns., Inc.

—Unholy Dying. 1985. 128p. reprint ed. pap. 5.95 (0-486-24977-8) Dover Pubns., Inc.

Camus, Albert. The Stranger. 1988. 16.45 (0-07-543227-7) McGraw-Hill Cos., The.

—The Stranger. Griffith, Kate, tr. 1982. 110p. lib. bdg. 21.75 o.p. (0-8191-2141-X) Univ. Pr. of America.

Cannam, Helen. A High & Lonely Road. 1990. 400p. 19.95 o.p. (0-312-04328-7) St. Martin's Pr.

—The Last Ballad. 1991. 352p. 19.95 o.p. (0-312-06388-1) St. Martin's Pr.

Cannell, Dorothy. Bridesmaids Revisited: An Ellie Haskell Mystery. l.t. ed. 2000. (G. K. Hall Core Ser.). 342p. 30.95 (0-7838-9272-1, Macmillan Reference USA) Gale Group.

—Bridesmaids Revisited: An Ellie Haskell Mystery. 2001. (Ellie Haskell Mysteries Ser.). 256p. mass mkt. 5.99 (0-14-100186-0) Penguin Group (USA) Inc.

—Bridesmaids Revisited: An Ellie Haskell Mystery. 2000. (Ellie Haskell Mysteries Ser.). 256p. 22.95 o.s.i (0-670-89205-X, Viking) Viking Penguin.

—Down the Garden Path: A Pastoral Mystery. 1989. 272p. mass mkt. 3.95 o.s.i (0-553-26895-3) Bantam Bks.

—Down the Garden Path: A Pastoral Mystery. l.t. ed. 2002. 28.95 (1-58547-218-2, Premier) Ctr. Point Large Print.

—Down the Garden Path: A Pastoral Mystery. 1998. (Tessa Fields Mystery Ser.). 288p. pap. 5.99 (0-14-026623-2) Penguin Group (USA) Inc.

—Down the Garden Path: A Pastoral Mystery. 1985. 304p. 14.95 o.p. (0-312-21869-9) St. Martin's Pr.

—Femmes Fatal. 1994. 304p. mass mkt. 6.99 (0-553-29684-1) Bantam Bks.

—Femmes Fatal. l.t. ed. 1993. (General Ser.). 385p. 21.95 o.p. (0-8161-5654-9, Macmillan Reference USA) Gale Group.

—God Save the Queen. 1997. 224p. 22.95 o.s.i (0-553-10163-3); 1998. 272p. reprint ed. mass mkt. 6.50 (0-553-57468-X, Crimeline) Bantam Bks.

—God Save the Queen. l.t. ed. 1998. pap. 23.95 o.p. (1-56895-542-1, Wheeler Publishing, Inc.) Gale Group.

—How to Murder the Man of Your Dreams. 1996. 304p. mass mkt. 6.99 (0-553-57360-8) Bantam Bks.

—How to Murder the Man of Your Dreams. l.t. ed. 1996. 428p. 23.95 o.p. (0-7838-1493-3, Macmillan Reference USA) Gale Group.

—How to Murder Your Mother-in-Law. 1995. 288p. mass mkt. 6.50 (0-553-56951-1); 1994. 272p. 19.95 o.s.i (0-553-07493-8) Bantam Bks.

—How to Murder Your Mother-in-Law. unabr. ed. 1994. audio 57.25 o.p. (1-56100-178-3, 904, Unabridged Library Editions); audio 21.95 o.p. (1-56100-552-5, 141, Bookcassette) Brilliance Audio.

—How to Murder Your Mother-in-Law. l.t. ed. 1994. 385p. lib. bdg. 23.95 (0-8161-5930-0, Macmillan Reference USA) Gale Group.

—The Spring Cleaning Murders: An Ellie Haskell Mystery. l.t. ed. 1998. (Beeler Large Print Mystery Ser.). 26.95 (1-57490-162-1, Beeler Large Print Bks.) Beeler, Thomas T. Publisher.

—The Spring Cleaning Murders: An Ellie Haskell Mystery. 1999. (Ellie Haskell Mysteries Ser.). 288p. pap. 6.99 (0-14-027615-7) Penguin Group (USA) Inc.

—The Spring Cleaning Murders: An Ellie Haskell Mystery. 1998. (Ellie Haskell Mysteries Ser.). 256p. 21.95 o.p. (0-670-87571-6, Viking) Viking Penguin.

—The Thin Woman: An Epicurean Mystery. 1992. 304p. mass mkt. 6.99 (0-553-29195-5) Bantam Bks.

—The Thin Woman: An Epicurean Mystery. l.t. ed. 2000. 376p. lib. bdg. 28.95 (1-58547-008-2) Ctr. Point Large Print.

—The Thin Woman: An Epicurean Mystery. 1984. 288p. 13.95 o.p. (0-312-80005-3) St. Martin's Pr.

—The Thin Woman: An Epicurean Mystery. 1985. (Crime Monthly Ser.). 256p. pap. 4.50 o.p. (0-14-007947-5, Penguin Bks.) Viking Penguin.

—The Trouble with Harriet: An Ellie Haskell Mystery. l.t. ed. 2000. pap. 23.95 (1-56895-833-1, Wheeler Publishing, Inc.) Gale Group.

—The Trouble with Harriet: An Ellie Haskell Mystery. 2000. (Ellie Haskell Mysteries Ser.). 288p. pap. 5.99 (0-14-029182-2) Penguin Group (USA) Inc.

—The Trouble with Harriet: An Ellie Haskell Mystery. 1999. (Ellie Haskell Mysteries Ser.). 256p. 21.95 o.s.i (0-670-88629-7, Viking) Viking Penguin.

—The Widows' Club. 1989. 352p. mass mkt. 6.99 (0-553-27794-4) Bantam Bks.

Caplan, Thomas. Grace & Favor. 336p. 1998. pap. 14.95 (0-312-19459-5, Saint Martin's Griffin); 1997. 24.95 (0-312-17106-4) St. Martin's Pr.

Carlyle, Liz. Beauty Like the Night. 2000. E-Book 6.50 (1-58945-127-9) Adobe Systems, Inc.

—Beauty Like the Night. 2000. (Sonnet Bks.). (Illus.). 448p. mass mkt. 6.50 (0-7434-1054-8, Pocket) Simon & Schuster.

—A Woman of Virtue. Date not set. E-Book 6.50 (0-7434-2267-8); 2001. 464p. pap. 6.50 (0-7434-1055-6) Simon & Schuster. (Pocket).

Carnegie, Dale. Tess of the d'Urbervilles. Hardy, Thomas, ed. 1998. (Enriched Classics Ser.). (Illus.). 480p. reprint ed. mass mkt. 5.99 (0-671-01546-X, Pocket) Simon & Schuster.

Carnell, Jennifer. Murder, Mystery & Mayhem. 1989. 160p. 15.95 o.p. (0-06-016205-8) HarperTrade.

Carr, John Dickson. The Arabian Nights Murder: A Dr. Gideon Fell Mystery. 1989. 320p. reprint ed. pap. 4.95 o.p. (0-06-080981-7, P 981, Perennial) HarperTrade.

—Below Suspicion. 1986. (Library of Crime Classics). 186p. pap. 4.95 o.p. (0-930330-50-1) International Polygonics, Ltd.

—The Blind Barber: A Dr. Gideon Fell Mystery. l.t. ed. 1992. pap. 14.95 o.p. (0-7927-1064-9) BBC Audiobooks America.

—The Blind Barber: A Dr. Gideon Fell Mystery. 1990. 256p. reprint ed. mass mkt. 4.95 o.p. (0-06-081038-6, Perennial) HarperTrade.

—The Blind Barber: A Dr. Gideon Fell Mystery. 1990. 256p. (C). reprint ed. lib. bdg. 20.00 o.p. (0-8095-9027-1) Millefleurs.

—The Case of the Constant Suicides. 2002. 168p. 21.95 (0-7540-8615-1, Black Dagger) BBC Audiobooks America.

—The Crooked Hinge: A Dr. Gideon Fell Mystery. 1976. 283p. 18.95 o.p. (0-89163-026-0) Boulevard Bks.

—The Crooked Hinge: A Dr. Gideon Fell Mystery. 1989. 256p. reprint ed. mass mkt. 3.95 o.p. (0-06-080980-9, P 980, Perennial) HarperTrade.

—Dark of the Moon. 1987. pap. 3.50 o.p. (0-88184-304-0); 2nd ed. 1995. 256p. mass mkt. 4.95 (0-7867-0222-2) Avalon Publishing Group. (Carroll & Graf Pubs.).

—Dark of the Moon. l.t. ed. 2001. (Ulverscroft Large Print Ser.). 448p. 32.50 (0-7089-4441-8) Ulverscroft Large Print Bks., Ltd.

—The Dead Man's Knock. 1987. 272p. mass mkt. 3.50 o.p. (0-8217-2099-6, Zebra Bks.) Kensington Publishing Corp.

—Death Turns the Tables. 1985. 200p. pap. 4.95 o.p. (0-930330-22-6) International Polygonics, Ltd.

—Death-Watch: A Dr. Gideon Fell Mystery. 1990. 256p. reprint ed. mass mkt. 4.95 o.p. (0-06-081040-8, Perennial) HarperTrade.

—The Eight of Swords. 1986. 256p. mass mkt. 3.50 o.p. (0-8217-1881-9); mass mkt. 3.99 o.s.i (0-8217-3649-3) Kensington Publishing Corp. (Zebra Bks.).

—Fell & Foul Play. Greene, Douglas G., ed. 1990. 368p. 19.95 o.p. (1-55882-071-X) International Polygonics, Ltd.

—Hag's Nook. 1976. 291p. lib. bdg. 25.95 (0-89966-047-9) Buccaneer Bks., Inc.

—Hag's Nook. 1985. 1985p. pap. 5.95 o.p. (0-930330-28-5) International Polygonics, Ltd.

—He Who Whispers. 1986. (Ipl Library of Crime Classics). 190p. pap. 5.95 o.p. (0-930330-38-2) International Polygonics, Ltd.

—The Hollow Man. 1994. 264p. 16.95 o.p. (0-7451-8637-8, Black Dagger) BBC Audiobooks America.

—The House at Satan's Elbow. 1980. 1.95 o.s.i (0-441-34372-4) Ace Bks.

—The House at Satan's Elbow. 1987. (Library of Crime Classics). 200p. pap. 4.95 o.p. (*0-930330-61-7*) International Polygonics, Ltd.
—In Spite of Thunder. 1987. 224p. 3.50 o.p. (*0-88184-287-7*, Carroll & Graf Pubs.) Avalon Publishing Group.
—John Dickson Carr. 1988. 5.99 o.s.i (*0-517-65956-5*) Random Hse. Value Publishing.
—The Lost Gallows. 1986. 344p. pap. 3.50 o.p. (*0-88184-202-8*, Carroll & Graf Pubs.) Avalon Publishing Group.
—The Mad Hatter Mystery: A Dr. Gideon Fell Mystery. 1989. 288p. reprint ed. mass mkt. 4.95 o.p. (*0-06-080997-3*, Perennial) HarperTrade.
—Man Who Could Not Shudder. 1986. mass mkt. 3.50 o.s.i (*0-8217-1703-0*, Zebra Bks.) Kensington Publishing Corp.
—Merrivale, March & Murder. Greene, Douglas G., ed. 1992. 350p. 22.95 o.p. (*1-55882-101-5*) International Polygonics, Ltd.
—Panic in Box C. 1987. 272p. mass mkt. 3.50 o.p. (*0-88184-288-5*, Carroll & Graf Pubs.) Avalon Publishing Group.
—The Problem of the Green Capsule. 1986. (Library of Crime Classics). 256p. pap. 5.95 o.p. (*0-930330-51-X*) International Polygonics, Ltd.
—The Problem of the Wire Cage. 1986. mass mkt. 3.95 o.s.i (*0-8217-3384-2*, Zebra Bks.) Kensington Publishing Corp.
—The Problem of the Wire Cage. 1982. 224p. 20.00 o.p. (*0-7278-0249-6*) State Mutual Bk. & Periodical Service, Ltd.
—The Sleeping Sphinx. 1985. (Dr. Fell Detective Ser.). 199p. pap. 4.95 (*0-930330-24-2*) International Polygonics, Ltd.
—The Three Coffins. 1989. lib. bdg. 25.95 (*0-89966-048-7*) Buccaneer Bks., Inc.
—The Three Coffins. 1986. 160p. pap. 6.95 o.s.i (*0-930330-39-0*) International Polygonics, Ltd.
—The Three Coffins. 1979. 306p. reprint ed. 25.00 (*0-89366-259-3*) Ultramarine Publishing Co., Inc.
—Till Death Do Us Part. 1985. 200p. pap. 4.95 o.p. (*0-930330-21-8*); 1989. 224p. reprint ed. pap. 5.95 (*1-55882-017-5*, Library of Crime Classics) International Polygonics, Ltd.
—To Wake the Dead: A Dr. Gideon Fell Mystery. 1989. 256p. reprint ed. mass mkt. 4.50 o.p. (*0-06-080998-1*, Perennial) HarperTrade.
Carr, Philippa. Daughters of England. 1997. mass mkt. 5.99 o.s.i (*0-449-14955-2*, Fawcett) Ballantine Bks.
—Daughters of England. l.t. ed. 1995. 482p. lib. bdg. 24.95 o.p. (*0-7838-1352-X*, Macmillan Reference USA) Gale Group.
—Daughters of England. unabr. ed. 2001. audio 84.95 ISIS Audio Bks. GBR. *Dist:* Ulverscroft Large Print Bks., Ltd.
—Daughters of England. 1995. (YA). 22.95 o.p. (*0-399-14023-9*, G. P. Putnam's Sons) Penguin Group (USA) Inc.
—The Gossamer Cord. l.t. ed. 1993. (General Ser.). 490p. pap. 17.95 o.p. (*0-8161-5614-X*); lib. bdg. 23.95 o.p. (*0-8161-5613-1*) Gale Group. (Macmillan Reference USA).
—The Gossamer Cord. 1992. (Cornwall Saga Ser.). 368p. 21.95 o.p. (*0-399-13725-4*, G. P. Putnam's Sons) Penguin Group (USA) Inc.
Carr, Rocky. Brixton Bwoy: A Novel. 1998. 199p. 15.95 (*1-85702-738-8*) Fourth Estate, Ltd. GBR. *Dist:* Trafalgar Square.
Carris, Joan D. Hedgehogs in the Closet. 1988. (Illus.). 160p. (J). (gr. 5 up). 11.95 (*0-397-32233-X*); lib. bdg. 13.89 (*0-397-32234-8*) HarperCollins Children's Bk. Group.
Carroll, Lewis, pseud, ed. The Works of Charles Dickens, 21 vols. reprint ed. lib. bdg. 2058.00 (*0-7426-2349-1*) Classic Bks.
Carroll, Susan. The Bride Finder. 1999. 416p. mass mkt. 6.99 (*0-449-00388-4*, Fawcett) Ballantine Bks.
—The Bride Finder. l.t. ed. 1998. (Large Print Book Ser.). 26.95 o.p. (*1-56895-585-5*, Wheeler Publishing, Inc.) Gale Group.
—The Night Drifter. 2000. 432p. mass mkt. 6.99 (*0-449-00585-2*, Fawcett) Ballantine Bks.
—The Night Drifter. unabr. ed. 2000. audio 97.00 (*0-7887-4419-4*, 95910E7) Recorded Bks., LLC.
Carson, Michael. Brothers in Arms. 1989. 22p. pap. 9.95 o.p. (*0-452-26309-3*, Plume) Dutton/Plume.
Carter, Angela. Wise Children. 1992. 232p. 21.00 o.p. (*0-374-29133-0*) Farrar, Straus & Giroux.
—Wise Children. 1991. (*0-316-13053-2*) Little Brown & Co.
—Wise Children. 1993. 240p. pap. 12.95 (*0-14-017530-X*, Penguin Bks.) Penguin Group (USA) Inc.
Cartland, Barbara. Beyond the Stars. l.t. ed. 1997. (Nightingale Ser.). pap. 18.95 (*0-7838-1894-7*, Macmillan Reference USA) Gale Group.
—Beyond the Stars No. 145: Camfield. 1995. 176p. (Orig.). mass mkt. 4.50 o.s.i (*0-515-11706-4*, Jove) Berkley Publishing Group.
—Lights, Laughter, & a Lady. l.t. ed. 2001. (Candlelight Ser.). 238p. 24.95 o.p. (*0-7862-3624-8*) Thorndike Pr.
—Love Climbs In. 1998. 288p. 7.99 o.s.i (*0-517-18824-4*) Random Hse. Value Publishing.
—Love Climbs in. 1979. 6.95 o.p. (*0-87272-082-9*) Brodart Co.
—Love Climbs In. l.t. ed. 2001. 210p. (*0-7540-4429-7*); (*0-7540-4430-0*) Gale Group. (Macmillan Reference USA).
—Love Climbs In. l.t. ed. 2001. (Paperback Ser.). 210p. 23.95 (*0-7838-9313-2*) Thorndike Pr.
—Love Climbs in, No. 108. 1979. pap. 1.50 o.p. (*0-553-13035-8*) Bantam Bks.
—Lucky Logan Finds Love. l.t. ed. 2000. (Candlelight Romance Ser.). 185p. 21.95 (*0-7862-2787-7*) Thorndike Pr.
—A Night of Gaiety, No. 142. 1981. pap. 1.95 o.p. (*0-553-14791-9*) Bantam Bks.
—A Night of Gaiety. l.t. ed. 2002. 27.95 (*0-7862-4033-4*) Gale Group.
—Secrets of the Heart. l.t. ed. 2001. (Romance Ser.). 235p. 27.95 (*0-7862-3228-5*); (*0-7540-4463-7*); (*0-7540-4464-5*) Thorndike Pr.
—The Taming of a Tigress. l.t. ed. 2001. (G. K. Hall Paperback Ser.). 183p. 23.95 (*0-7838-9401-5*) Thorndike Pr.
Carvic, Heron. Miss Seeton Draws the Line. l.t. ed. 1991. pap. 10.95 o.p. (*0-7927-0097-X*, C0003) BBC Audiobooks America.
—Miss Seeton Draws the Line. 1988. mass mkt. 4.50 o.s.i (*0-425-11097-4*) Berkley Publishing Group.
—Miss Seeton Sings. l.t. ed. 1991. 19.95 o.p. (*0-7927-0690-0*, CH008); pap. 17.95 o.p. (*0-7927-0691-9*, CS0110) BBC Audiobooks America.
—Miss Seeton Sings. Fowler, Kathy, ed. 1988. 208p. reprint ed. mass mkt. 4.50 o.s.i (*0-425-10714-0*) Berkley Publishing Group.
—Odds on Miss Seeton. l.t. ed. 1991. 18.95 o.p. (*0-7927-0933-0*, CH0145); pap. 19.95 o.p. (*0-7927-0934-9*, CS0242) BBC Audiobooks America.
—Odds on Miss Seeton. 1989. mass mkt. 4.50 o.s.i (*0-425-11307-8*) Berkley Publishing Group.
—Odds on Miss Seeton. 1981. 279p. reprint ed. lib. bdg. 16.95 o.p. (*0-89966-307-9*) Buccaneer Bks., Inc.
—Odds on Miss Seeton. 1975. (Harper Novel of Suspense Ser.). 160p. 7.95 o.p. (*0-06-010654-9*) HarperCollins Pubs.
—Picture Miss Seeton. (Black Dagger Crime Ser.). 1993. 176p. 16.50 o.p. (*0-7451-8615-7*, Black Dagger); 1991. 12.95 o.p. (*0-7927-0041-4*, 476) BBC Audiobooks America.
—Picture Miss Seeton. 1988. (Heron Carvic's Miss Seeton Ser.). mass mkt. 4.50 o.s.i (*0-425-10929-1*) Berkley Publishing Group.
—Witch Miss Seeton. l.t. ed. 1990. pap. 16.95 o.p. (*0-7927-0428-2*, C0486); 18.95 o.p. (*0-7927-0427-4*, C0258) BBC Audiobooks America.
—Witch Miss Seeton. 1988. 192p. mass mkt. 4.50 o.s.i (*0-425-10713-2*) Berkley Publishing Group.
Casley, Dennis. Death Undertow: A Chief Inspector Odhiambo Mystery. 1995. 208p. 19.95 o.p. (*0-312-13643-9*, Saint Martin's Minotaur) St. Martin's Pr.
Castle, Linda Lea. Promise the Moon. 2002. 352p. mass mkt. 5.99 o.s.i (*0-8217-7266-X*) Kensington Publishing Corp.
Caudwell, Sarah L. The Shortest Way to Hades. 1995. 320p. mass mkt. 6.50 (*0-440-21233-2*) Dell Publishing.
—The Shortest Way to Hades. (Crime, Penguin Ser.). 2015. 208p. pap. 3.50 o.p. (*0-14-008488-6*); 1986. pap. 3.50 o.p. (*0-14-009401-6*) Penguin Group (USA) Inc.
—The Shortest Way to Hades. 1985. 208p. 12.95 o.s.i (*0-684-18292-0*, Scribner) Simon & Schuster.
—The Shortest Way to Hades. 1989. 208p. pap. 5.95 o.p. (*0-14-012874-3*, Penguin Bks.) Viking Penguin.
—The Sibyl in Her Grave. 2000. (Illus.). 304p. 23.95 o.s.i (*0-385-29934-6*, Delacorte Pr.) Dell Publishing.
—The Sirens Sang of Murder. l.t. ed. 1991. 17.95 o.p. (*0-7451-8046-9*, AH096); pap. 15.95 o.p. (*0-7927-0503-3*, AS0132) BBC Audiobooks America.
—The Sirens Sang of Murder. 1990. 288p. mass mkt. 5.99 (*0-440-20745-2*) Dell Publishing.
—Thus Was Adonis Murdered. 1994. 320p. mass mkt. 5.99 (*0-440-21231-6*) Dell Publishing.
—Thus Was Adonis Murdered. 1982. 256p. pap. 5.95 o.p. (*0-14-006310-2*, Penguin Bks.) Viking Penguin.
Caxton, Tony. Bowker's Bonfire. 1996. 272p. 21.95 o.p. (*0-312-13936-5*, Saint Martin's Minotaur) St. Martin's Pr.
—Murder in a Quiet Place. 1994. 288p. 20.95 o.p. (*0-312-11031-6*, Saint Martin's Minotaur) St. Martin's Pr.
Celine, Louis-Ferdinand. London Bridge. Di Bernardi, Dominic, tr. from FRE. 1995. 449p. 23.95 (*1-56478-071-6*); 1999. 390p. reprint ed. pap. 14.50 (*1-56478-175-5*) Dalkey Archive Pr.
Chadwick, Elizabeth. Marsh King's Daughter. 2000. 416p. 25.95 (*0-312-26491-7*) St. Martin's Pr.
Chaikin, Linda L. Friday's Child. 2001. (Day to Remember Ser.: Bk. 5). (Illus.). 350p. pap. 10.99 (*0-7369-0657-6*) Harvest Hse. Pubs.
—Jamaican Sunset. 1997. (Buccaneers Ser.: No. 3). pap. 10.99 (*0-8024-1073-1*, 6) Moody Pr.
Chalmers, Robert. Who's Who in Hell. 2002. 368p. pap. 13.00 (*0-8021-3924-8*, Grove Pr.) Grove/Atlantic, Inc.
Chambers, Peter. Lady, This Is Murder. 2000. 21.95 (*0-7540-8573-2*, Black Dagger) BBC Audiobooks America.
—The Vanishing Holes Murders. l.t. ed. 2001. 201p. pap. 23.95 (*0-7838-9570-4*) Thorndike Pr.
—The Vanishing Holes Murders. l.t. ed. 1996. (Linford Mystery Library). 304p. pap. 17.99 o.p. (*0-7089-7942-4*, Linford) Thorpe, F. A. Pubs. GBR. *Dist:* Ulverscroft Large Print Bks., Ltd., Ulverscroft Large Print Canada, Ltd.
Chance, John Newton. The Psychic Trap. l.t. ed. 2001. 166p. pap. 23.95 (*0-7838-9445-7*) Thorndike Pr.
Chaplin, Sid. In Blackberry Time. Chaplin, Michael, ed. (Illus.). 240p. 1996. 42.00 (*1-85224-031-8*); 1988. pap. 18.95 (*1-85224-032-6*) Bloodaxe Bks. GBR. *Dist:* Dufour Editions, Inc.
Chapman, Jean. And a Golden Pear. 2002. 384p. 26.99 (*0-7278-5863-7*) Severn Hse. Pubs., Ltd.
Chapman, R. W., ed. The Oxford Illustrated Jane Austen, 6 vols. 3rd ed. Incl. Vol. I. Sense & Sensibility. 3rd ed. Austen, Jane. 446p. 20.00 (*0-19-254701-1*); Vol. III. Joseph Andrews. 3rd ed. Fielding, Henry. 584p. 20.00 (*0-19-254703-8*); Vol. IV. Emma. 3rd ed. Austen, Jane. 536p. 20.00 (*0-19-254704-6*); Vol. V. Northanger Abbey. 3rd ed. Austen, Jane. 348p. 20.00 (*0-19-254705-4*); Vol. VI. Minor Works. Austen, Jane. 486p. 20.00 (*0-19-254706-2*); reprint ed. (Oxford Illustrated Austen Ser.). (Illus.). 3184p. 1988. 95.00 (*0-19-254707-0*) Oxford Univ. Pr., Inc.
Chapman, Vera. The Three Damosels. 1996. (Illus.). 383p. (*0-575-06340-8*) Gollancz, Victor.
Charles, Hampton. Miss Seeton at the Helm. 1990. mass mkt. 3.99 o.s.i (*0-425-12264-6*) Berkley Publishing Group.
—Miss Seeton at the Helm. l.t. ed. 1998. (G. K. Hall Nightingale Ser.). pap. 18.95 o.p. (*0-8161-5926-2*, Macmillan Reference USA) Gale Group.
Charles, Kate. Appointed to Die. 1994. 368p. 19.95 o.s.i (*0-89296-548-7*) Mysterious Pr.
—Appointed to Die. 1995. 352p. mass mkt. 5.99 o.s.i (*0-446-40361-X*) Warner Bks., Inc.
—Cruel Habitations. 2001. 438p. 28.00 o.p. (*0-316-64622-9*) Little Brown & Co.
—Cruel Habitations. 2001. 515p. mass mkt. 8.95 (*0-7515-2533-2*) Warner Futura GBR. *Dist:* Trafalgar Square.
—A Dead Man Out of Mind. l.t. ed. 1996. (G. K. Hall Mystery Ser.). 429p. 22.95 o.p. (*0-7838-1706-1*, Macmillan Reference USA) Gale Group.
—A Dead Man Out of Mind. 1995. 82p. 19.95 o.p. (*0-89296-585-1*) Mysterious Pr.
—A Dead Man Out of Mind. 1996. 288p. mass mkt. 5.99 o.p. (*0-446-40432-2*) Warner Bks., Inc.
—A Drink of Deadly Wine. 1992. 336p. 17.95 (*0-89296-501-0*) Mysterious Pr.
—A Drink of Deadly Wine. 1993. (Book of Psalms Mysteries Ser.). 304p. mass mkt. 5.99 o.s.i (*0-446-40194-3*) Warner Bks., Inc.
—Evil Angels among Them. l.t. ed. 1997. (G. K. Hall Mystery Ser.). 371p. lib. bdg. 25.95 o.p. (*0-7838-2024-0*, Macmillan Reference USA) Gale Group.
—Evil Angels among Them. 352p. 1997. mass mkt. 6.50 (*0-446-40521-3*, Mysterious Pr. Paperback Bks.); 1996. 21.50 o.p. (*0-89296-639-4*) Warner Bks., Inc.
—The Snares of Death. 1993. 368p. 18.95 (*0-89296-498-7*) Mysterious Pr.
—The Snares of Death. 1994. 352p. mass mkt. 5.50 (*0-446-40195-1*) Warner Bks., Inc.
—Unruly Passions. 2001. 440p. pap. 8.95 (*0-7515-2437-9*) Warner Bks. GBR. *Dist:* Trafalgar Square.
Charles, Paul. Fountain of Sorrow. 1999. 230p. 31.00 (*1-899344-38-1*); pap. 14.95 (*1-899344-39-X*) Do-Not Pr., The GBR. *Dist:* Dufour Editions, Inc.
Charnock, Ian. Elementary Cases of Sherlock Holmes. 1999. (Sherlock Holmes Ser.). 160p. pap. text o.s.i (*0-947533-97-4*) Breese Bks., Ltd.
Charriere, Isabelle De. Letters of Mistress Henley Published by Her Friend. Stewart, Philip & Vache, Jean, trs. from FRE. 1993. (MLA Texts & Translations Ser.: No. 1b). xxix, 42p. (Orig.). pap. 3.95 (*0-87352-776-3*, P001P) Modern Language Assn. of America.
Charteris, Leslie. Follow the Saint. 1982. (Saint Ser.). (Illus.). 288p. 2.50 o.s.i (*0-441-24211-1*) Ace Bks.
—Follow the Saint. 1976. 202p. reprint ed. lib. bdg. 21.95 (*0-89190-382-8*, Rivercity Pr.) Amereon, Ltd.
—Follow the Saint. (Black Dagger Crime Ser.). 12.95 o.p. (*0-86220-807-6*, BD008) Chivers Pr. GBR. *Dist:* BBC Audiobooks America.
—Holy Terror. 1977. (Short Story Index Reprint Ser.). 22.95 (*0-8369-3298-6*) Ayer Co. Pubs., Inc.
Chase, Loretta. The Sandalwood Princess. 1991. 240p. pap. 3.99 (*0-380-71455-8*, Avon Bks.) Morrow/Avon.
—The Sandalwood Princess. 1991. 224p. 18.95 (*0-8027-1128-6*) Walker & Co.
—Viscount Vagabond. 1990. pap. 2.95 (*0-380-70836-1*, Avon Bks.) Morrow/Avon.
—Viscount Vagabond. 1988. 192p. 18.95 (*0-8027-1046-8*) Walker & Co.
Chatwin, Bruce. On the Black Hill. 1983. 256p. 14.75 o.p. (*0-670-52492-1*) Viking Penguin.
Cheaney, Janie B. The Playmaker. Siscoe, Nancy, ed. 2000. 320p. (J). (gr. 5-7). lib. bdg. 17.99 (*0-375-90577-4*, Knopf Bks. for Young Readers) Random Hse. Children's Bks.
Cheek, Mavis. Getting Back Brahms. l.t. ed. 2001. 293p. pap. 24.95 (*0-7862-3508-X*) Thorndike Pr.
—Mrs. Fytton's Country Life. 352p. 2002. pap. 14.95 (*0-312-30295-9*, Saint Martin's Griffin); 2001. 24.95 (*0-312-28334-2*) St. Martin's Pr.
—Parlor Games. 1989. 18.95 o.p. (*0-671-68309-8*, Simon & Schuster) Simon & Schuster.
—The Sex Life of My Aunt. Date not set. pap. (*0-312-30784-5*, Saint Martin's Griffin); mass mkt. (*0-312-98601-7*, St. Martin's Paperbacks); E-Book 23.95 (*0-312-70588-3*); 2003. 288p. pap. 14.95 (*0-312-32039-6*, Saint Martin's Griffin); 2002. 288p. 23.95 (*0-312-30782-9*) St. Martin's Pr.
—The Sex Life of My Aunt. l.t. ed. 2003. 320p. pap. 25.95 (*0-7862-5379-7*) Thorndike Pr.
Chekhov, Anton. Swan Song. 1999. E-Book 0.99 (*1-58515-027-4*) MesaView, Inc.
Cheshire, Chloe. A Gypsy at Almack's. 1992. 18.95 o.p. (*0-312-08805-1*) St. Martin's Pr.
Cheska, Anna. Moving to the Country. 2001. 374p. 25.95 (*0-312-28132-3*) St. Martin's Pr.
Chesney, Marion. Animating Maria. l.t. ed. 1991. (School for Manners Ser.: Vol. 5). 232p. pap. 14.95 o.p. (*0-8161-5099-0*, Macmillan Reference USA) Gale Group.
—Animating Maria. 1990. (School for Manners Ser.: Vol. 5). pap. 3.95 o.p. (*0-312-92343-0*, St. Martin's Paperbacks); 160p. 14.95 o.p. (*0-312-03820-8*) St. Martin's Pr.
—Back in Society. l.t. ed. 1995. (G. K. Hall Nightingale Ser.: Vol. 6). pap. 18.95 o.p. (*0-7838-1454-2*, Macmillan Reference USA) Gale Group.
—Back in Society. (Poor Relation Ser.: Vol. 6). 1995. mass mkt. 4.50 (*0-312-95338-0*, St. Martin's Paperbacks); 1994. 160p. 12.99 o.p. (*0-312-10932-6*) St. Martin's Pr.
—The Banishment. 1996. (Daughters of Mannerling Ser.: Vol. 1). mass mkt. 4.50 o.s.i (*0-449-22419-8*, Fawcett) Ballantine Bks.
—The Banishment. l.t. ed. 1996. (Daughters of Mannerling Ser.: Vol. 1). 221p. pap. 17.95 o.p. (*0-7838-1519-0*, Macmillan Reference USA) Gale Group.
—The Banishment. 1995. (Daughters of Mannerling Ser.: Vol. 1). 17.95 o.p. (*0-312-11749-3*) St. Martin's Pr.
—Beatrice Goes to Brighton. l.t. ed. 1993. (Travelling Matchmaker Ser.: Vol. 4). 252p. lib. bdg. 15.95 o.p. (*0-8161-5546-1*, Macmillan Reference USA) Gale Group.
—Beatrice Goes to Brighton. (Travelling Matchmaker Ser.: Vol. 4). 1992. mass mkt. 3.99 o.p. (*0-312-92794-0*, St. Martin's Paperbacks); 1991. 160p. 16.95 o.p. (*0-312-06302-4*) St. Martin's Pr.
—Belinda Goes to Bath. l.t. ed. 1992. (Travelling Matchmaker Ser.: Vol. 2). 232p. pap. 14.95 o.p. (*0-8161-5375-2*, Macmillan Reference USA) Gale Group.
—Belinda Goes to Bath. 1991. (Travelling Matchmaker Ser.: Vol. 2). 160p. mass mkt. 3.99 (*0-312-92642-1*, St. Martin's Paperbacks); 14.95 o.p. (*0-312-05382-7*) St. Martin's Pr.
—Colonel Sandhurst to the Rescue. l.t. ed. 1995. (G. K. Hall Nightingale Ser.: Vol. 5). 208p. pap. 18.95 o.p. (*0-8161-7415-6*, Macmillan Reference USA) Gale Group.
—Colonel Sandhurst to the Rescue. (Poor Relation Ser.: Vol. 5). 1995. 152p. mass mkt. 4.50 (*0-312-95337-2*, St. Martin's Paperbacks); 1994. 160p. 17.95 o.p. (*0-312-10444-8*) St. Martin's Pr.
—The Constant Companion. 1987. mass mkt. 2.50 o.s.i (*0-449-21324-2*); 1980. 224p. mass mkt. 1.75 o.s.i (*0-449-50114-0*) Ballantine Bks. (Fawcett).
—The Constant Companion. l.t. ed. 2001. 248p. 27.95 (*0-7862-3634-5*); (*0-7540-4724-5*); (*0-7540-4725-3*) Thorndike Pr.
—Daphne. 1985. (Six Sisters Ser.: Vol. 4). 176p. mass mkt. 2.50 o.s.i (*0-449-20583-5*, Fawcett) Ballantine Bks.
—Daphne. l.t. ed. 1986. (Six Sisters Ser.: Vol. 4). 280p. 9.95 o.p. (*0-8161-3910-5*, Macmillan Reference USA) Gale Group.
—Daphne. 1984. (Six Sisters Ser.: Vol. 4). 192p. 10.95 o.p. (*0-312-18221-X*) St. Martin's Pr.

—Deborah Goes to Dover. l.t. ed. 1993. (Travelling Matchmaker Ser.: Vol. 5). 254p. lib. bdg. 15.95 (*0-8161-5545-3*, Macmillan Reference USA) Gale Group.
—Deborah Goes to Dover. 1992. (Travelling Matchmaker Ser.: Vol. 5). mass mkt. 3.99 (*0-312-92902-1*, St. Martin's Paperbacks); 160p. 16.95 o.p. (*0-312-06952-9*) St. Martin's Pr.
—The Deception. 1997. (Daughters of Mannerling Ser.: Vol. 3). mass mkt. 4.50 o.s.i (*0-449-22559-3*, Fawcett) Ballantine Bks.
—The Deception. 1996. (Daughters of Mannerling Ser.: Vol. 3). 160p. 18.95 o.p. (*0-312-13465-7*) St. Martin's Pr.
—Deirdre & Desire. 1985. (Six Sisters Ser.: Vol. 3). 208p. mass mkt. 2.50 o.s.i (*0-449-20582-7*, Fawcett) Ballantine Bks.
—Deirdre & Desire. l.t. ed. 1985. (Six Sisters Ser.: Vol. 3). 352p. 10.95 o.p. (*0-8161-3824-9*, Macmillan Reference USA) Gale Group.
—Deirdre & Desire. 1984. (Six Sisters Ser.: Vol. 3). 192p. 10.95 o.p. (*0-312-19136-7*) St. Martin's Pr.
—Diana the Huntress. 1986. (Six Sisters Ser.: Vol. 5). mass mkt. 2.50 o.s.i (*0-449-20584-3*, Fawcett) Ballantine Bks.
—Diana the Huntress. l.t. ed. 1986. (Six Sisters Ser.: Vol. 5). 294p. 10.95 o.p. (*0-8161-3997-0*, Macmillan Reference USA) Gale Group.
—Diana the Huntress. 1985. (Six Sisters Ser.: Vol. 5). 192p. 12.95 o.p. (*0-312-19937-6*) St. Martin's Pr.
—The Dreadful Debutante. l.t. ed. 1999. 199p. (*0-7540-3631-6*) BBC Audiobooks America.
—The Dreadful Debutante. 1994. (Regency Romance Ser.). mass mkt. 3.99 o.s.i (*0-449-22261-6*, Fawcett) Ballantine Bks.
—The Dreadful Debutante. l.t. ed. 1999. (Nightingale Ser.). 199p. pap. 21.95 (*0-7838-8502-4*) Thorndike Pr.
—Emily Goes to Exeter. l.t. ed. 1992. (Travelling Matchmaker Ser.: Vol. 1). 245p. pap. 14.95 o.p. (*0-8161-5157-1*, Macmillan Reference USA) Gale Group.
—Emily Goes to Exeter. (Travelling Matchmaker Ser.: Vol. 1). 1991. 160p. mass mkt. 3.99 (*0-312-92582-4*, St. Martin's Paperbacks); 1990. 15.95 o.p. (*0-312-05078-X*) St. Martin's Pr.
—Enlightening Delilah. l.t. ed. 1991. (School for Manners Ser.: Vol. 3). 248p. 14.95 o.p. (*0-8161-4950-X*, Macmillan Reference USA) Gale Group.
—Enlightening Delilah. 1990. 2.99 o.p. (*0-517-05815-4*) Random Hse. Value Publishing.
—Enlightening Delilah. (School for Manners Ser.: Vol. 3). 1990. mass mkt. 3.50 (*0-312-92157-8*, St. Martin's Paperbacks); 1989. 14.95 o.p. (*0-312-02912-8*) St. Martin's Pr.
—Finessing Clarissa. l.t. ed. 1991. (School for Manners Ser.: Vol. 4). 243p. lib. bdg. 14.95 o.p. (*0-8161-5013-3*, Macmillan Reference USA) Gale Group.
—Finessing Clarissa. (School for Manners Ser.: Vol. 4). 1990. pap. 3.95 o.p. (*0-312-92283-3*, St. Martin's Paperbacks); 1989. 160p. 14.95 o.p. (*0-312-03341-9*) St. Martin's Pr.
—The Folly. 1997. (Daughters of Mannerling Ser.: Vol. 4). mass mkt. 4.50 o.s.i (*0-449-28775-0*, Fawcett) Ballantine Bks.
—The Folly. 1996. (Daughters of Mannerling Ser.: Vol. 4). 192p. 16.00 (*0-312-14338-9*) St. Martin's Pr.
—The Folly. l.t. ed. 1998. (Nightingale Ser.). 255p. pap. 21.95 (*0-7838-8288-2*) Thorndike Pr.
—Frederica in Fashion. 1986. (Six Sisters Ser.: Vol. 6). mass mkt. 2.50 o.s.i (*0-449-20585-1*, Fawcett) Ballantine Bks.
—Frederica in Fashion. l.t. ed. 1986. (Six Sisters Ser.: Vol. 6). 272p. pap. 10.95 o.p. (*0-8161-3996-2*, Macmillan Reference USA) Gale Group.
—Frederica in Fashion. 1985. (Six Sisters Ser.: Vol. 6). 176p. 11.95 o.p. (*0-312-30363-7*) St. Martin's Pr.
—The Homecoming. 1998. (Daughters of Mannerling Ser.: Vol. 6). mass mkt. 4.99 o.s.i (*0-449-28777-7*, Fawcett) Ballantine Bks.
—The Homecoming. l.t. ed. 2000. (G. K. Hall Nightingale Ser.). 226p. pap. 21.95 (*0-7838-8982-8*, Macmillan Reference USA) Gale Group.
—The Homecoming. 1997. (Daughters of Mannerling Ser.: Vol. 6). 144p. 18.95 o.p. (*0-312-16865-9*) St. Martin's Pr.
—The Intrigue. 1996. (Daughters of Mannerling Ser.: Vol. 2). mass mkt. 4.50 o.p. (*0-449-22420-1*, Fawcett) Ballantine Bks.
—The Intrigue. l.t. ed. 1997. (Daughters of Mannerling Ser.: Vol. 2). pap. 18.95 o.p. (*0-7838-8034-0*, Macmillan Reference USA) Gale Group.
—The Intrigue. 1995. (Daughters of Mannerling Ser.: Vol. 2). 160p. 18.95 o.p. (*0-312-13096-1*) St. Martin's Pr.
—Lady Fortescue Steps Out. l.t. ed. 1994. (Poor Relation Ser.: Vol. 1). 196p. lib. bdg. 15.95 o.p. (*0-8161-5836-3*, Macmillan Reference USA) Gale Group.
—Lady Fortescue Steps Out. (Poor Relation Ser.: Vol. 1). 1993. 152p. mass mkt. 3.99 (*0-312-95129-9*, St. Martin's Paperbacks); 1992. 160p. 17.95 o.p. (*0-312-08231-2*) St. Martin's Pr.
—The Loves of Lord Granton. 1996. mass mkt. 4.50 o.s.i (*0-449-22260-8*, Fawcett) Ballantine Bks.
—The Loves of Lord Granton. l.t. ed. 1997. (Romance-Hall Ser.). 206p. lib. bdg. 25.95 (*0-7838-8301-3*, Macmillan Reference USA) Gale Group.
—Marrying Harriet. l.t. ed. 1992. (School for Manners Ser.: Vol. 6). 252p. pap. 15.95 (*0-8161-5158-X*, Macmillan Reference USA) Gale Group.
—Marrying Harriet. (School for Manners Ser.: Vol. 6). 1991. pap. 3.95 o.p. (*0-312-92420-8*, St. Martin's Paperbacks); 1990. 14.95 o.p. (*0-312-04276-0*) St. Martin's Pr.
—Minerva. 1984. (Six Sisters Ser.: Vol. 1). 192p. mass mkt. 2.25 o.s.i (*0-449-20580-0*, Fawcett) Ballantine Bks.
—Minerva. l.t. ed. 1985. (Six Sisters Ser.: Vol. 1). 10.95 o.p. (*0-8161-3745-5*, Macmillan Reference USA) Gale Group.
—Minerva. 1983. (Six Sisters Ser.: Vol. 1). 192p. 10.95 o.p. (*0-312-53360-8*) St. Martin's Pr.
—Miss Tonks Takes a Risk. 1994. (Poor Relation Ser.: Vol. 2). 152p. mass mkt. 3.99 (*0-312-95219-8*, St. Martin's Paperbacks) St. Martin's Pr.
—Miss Tonks Turns to Crime. l.t. ed. 1994. (Poor Relation Ser.: Vol. 2). 251p. lib. bdg. 17.95 (*0-8161-5898-3*, Macmillan Reference USA) Gale Group.
—Miss Tonks Turns to Crime. 1993. (Poor Relation Ser.: Vol. 2). 16.95 o.p. (*0-312-08846-9*) St. Martin's Pr.
—Mrs. Budley Falls from Grace. l.t. ed. 1994. (Poor Relation Ser.: Vol. 3). 274p. lib. bdg. 15.95 o.p. (*0-8161-5980-7*, Macmillan Reference USA) Gale Group.
—Mrs. Budley Falls from Grace. (Poor Relation Ser.: Vol. 3). 160p. 1994. mass mkt. 3.99 (*0-312-95275-9*, St. Martin's Paperbacks); 1993. 16.95 o.p. (*0-312-09342-X*) St. Martin's Pr.
—Penelope Goes to Portsmouth. l.t. ed. 1992. (Travelling Matchmaker Ser.: Vol. ). 247p. pap. 14.95 o.p. (*0-8161-5547-X*, Macmillan Reference USA) Gale Group.
—Penelope Goes to Portsmouth. (Travelling Matchmaker Ser.: Vol. 3). 1992. mass mkt. 3.99 (*0-312-92720-7*, St. Martin's Paperbacks); 1991. 15.95 o.p. (*0-312-05945-0*) St. Martin's Pr.
—Perfecting Fiona. l.t. ed. 1990. (School for Manners Ser.: Vol. 2). 244p. 14.95 o.p. (*0-8161-4869-4*, Macmillan Reference USA) Gale Group.
—Perfecting Fiona. 1990. 2.99 o.p. (*0-517-05822-7*) Random Hse. Value Publishing.
—Perfecting Fiona. (School for Manners Ser.: Vol. 2). 1990. pap. 3.50 o.p. (*0-312-92059-8*, St. Martin's Paperbacks); 1989. 176p. 14.95 o.p. (*0-312-02577-7*) St. Martin's Pr.
—The Rake's Progress. l.t. unabr. ed. 1989. (House for the Season Ser.: Vol. 4). 282p. 12.95 o.p. (*0-8161-4653-5*, Macmillan Reference USA) Gale Group.
—The Rake's Progress. 1987. (House for the Season Ser.: Vol. 4). 176p. 12.95 o.p. (*0-312-00674-8*) St. Martin's Pr.
—Refining Felicity. l.t. ed. 1989. (School for Manners Ser.: Vol. 1). 248p. 13.95 o.p. (*0-8161-4797-3*, Macmillan Reference USA) Gale Group.
—Refining Felicity. (School for Manners Ser.: Vol. 1). 1989. pap. 3.50 o.p. (*0-312-91585-3*, St. Martin's Paperbacks); 1988. 176p. 14.95 o.p. (*0-312-02288-3*) St. Martin's Pr.
—The Romance. 1998. (Daughters of Mannerling Ser.: Vol. 5). mass mkt. 4.99 o.s.i (*0-449-28776-9*, Fawcett) Ballantine Bks.
—The Romance. 1997. (Daughters of Mannerling Ser.: Vol. 5). 192p. 20.95 (*0-312-15202-7*) St. Martin's Pr.
—The Romance. l.t. ed. 1998. (Nightingale Ser.). 238p. pap. 21.95 (*0-7838-8385-4*) Thorndike Pr.
—Sir Philip's Folly. l.t. ed. 1994. (Poor Relation Ser.: Vol. 4). 223p. lib. bdg. 17.95 (*0-8161-7414-8*, Macmillan Reference USA) Gale Group.
—Sir Philip's Folly. 1993. (Poor Relation Ser.: Vol. 4). 160p. 17.95 o.p. (*0-312-09912-6*) St. Martin's Pr.
—Sweet Masquerade. 1984. 176p. mass mkt. 2.25 o.s.i (*0-449-20120-1*, Fawcett) Ballantine Bks.
—The Taming of Annabelle. (Six Sisters Ser.: Vol. 2). 1987. 176p. mass mkt. 2.50 o.s.i (*0-449-21457-5*); 1984. 192p. mass mkt. 2.25 o.p. (*0-449-20581-9*) Ballantine Bks. (Fawcett).
—The Taming of Annabelle. l.t. ed. 1985. (Six Sisters Ser.: Vol. 2). 10.95 o.p. (*0-8161-3823-0*, Macmillan Reference USA) Gale Group.
—The Taming of Annabelle. 1983. (Six Sisters Ser.: Vol. 2). 208p. 10.95 o.p. (*0-312-78489-9*) St. Martin's Pr.
—Yvonne Goes to York. l.t. ed. 1993. (Travelling Matchmaker Ser.: Vol. 6). 264p. lib. bdg. 15.95 (*0-8161-5834-7*, Macmillan Reference USA) Gale Group.
—Yvonne Goes to York. 1992. (Travelling Matchmaker Ser.: Vol. 6). mass mkt. 3.99 (*0-312-92849-1*, St. Martin's Paperbacks); 160p. 16.95 o.p. (*0-312-07892-7*) St. Martin's Pr.
Chesterton, G. K. The Annotated Innocence of Father Brown. 1998. (Illus.). 336p. pap. 12.95 (*0-486-29859-0*) Dover Pubns., Inc.
—The Annotated Innocence of Father Brown. Gardner, Martin, ed. 1988. 288p. pap. 7.95 o.p. (*0-19-282164-4*); 1987. (Illus.). 256p. 18.95 o.p. (*0-19-217748-6*) Oxford Univ. Pr., Inc.
—The Astonishing Father Brown. 1998. (Father Brown Mystery Ser.). audio 21.95 o.s.i (*1-55656-301-9*); audio 16.95 o.p. (*1-55656-300-0*) Dercum Audio.
—The Best of Father Brown. 1991. (Father Brown Mystery Ser.). 282p. pap. 7.95 o.p. (*0-460-87073-4*, Everyman's Classic Library in Paperback) Tuttle Publishing.
—The Best of Father Brown. Keating, H. R. F., ed. abr. ed. 1993. (Father Brown Mystery Ser.). 310p. pap. 9.95 (*0-460-87395-4*, Everyman's Classic Library in Paperback) Tuttle Publishing.
—The Blue Cross - A Father Brown Mystery. abr. ed. 1997. (Father Brown Mysteries Ser.). 3p. audio 16.99 (*0-88646-447-1*, 7447) Durkin Hayes Publishing Ltd.
—The Book of Father Brown. (Father Brown Mystery Ser.). reprint ed. lib. bdg. 19.95 (*0-89190-576-6*, Rivercity Pr.) Amereon, Ltd.
—The Book of Father Brown. 1990. (Father Brown Mystery Ser.). reprint ed. lib. bdg. 16.95 (*0-89968-494-7*) Buccaneer Bks., Inc.
—The Complete Father Brown. 1987. (Father Brown Mystery Ser.). 720p. pap. 16.95 (*0-14-009766-X*, Penguin Bks.) Penguin Group (USA) Inc.
—Father Brown: Selected Stories. 1995. (Father Brown Mystery Ser.). 582p. pap. (*0-19-282309-4*) Oxford Univ. Pr., Inc.
—Father Brown: Selected Stories. 1998. (Father Brown Mystery Ser.). pap. 3.95 (*1-85326-003-7*, 0037WW) Wordsworth Editions, Ltd. GBR. *Dist:* Casemate Pubs. & Bk. Distributors, LLC.
—Father Brown & the Church of Rome. 270p. 2002. pap. 13.95 (*0-89870-953-9*); 1996. 17.95 (*0-89870-590-8*) Ignatius Pr.
—Father Brown Crime Stories. 1990. (Father Brown Mystery Ser.). 12.99 o.s.i (*0-517-00182-9*) Random Hse. Value Publishing.
—The Father Brown Stories, Set. 1992. (Father Brown Mystery Ser.). audio 65.95 (*1-55685-269-X*) Audio Bk. Contractors, Inc.
—Favorite Father Brown Stories. 1993. (Father Brown Mystery Ser.). (Illus.). 96p. reprint ed. pap. 1.00 (*0-486-27545-0*) Dover Pubns., Inc.
—Following Father Brown. unabr. ed. (Father Brown Mystery Ser.). audio 21.95 o.p. (*1-55656-013-3*, DAB 038) BBC Audiobooks America.
—The Incredulity of Father Brown. (Father Brown Mystery Ser.). 20.95 (*0-89190-339-9*) Amereon, Ltd.
—The Incredulity of Father Brown. unabr. ed. 1992. (Father Brown Ser.). audio 44.95 (*0-7861-0126-1*, 1112) Blackstone Audio Bks., Inc.
—The Incredulity of Father Brown. unabr. collector's ed. 1986. (Father Brown Mystery Ser.). audio 48.00 (*0-7366-0893-1*, 1837) Books on Tape, Inc.
—The Incredulity of Father Brown. l.t. ed. 1984. (Father Brown Mystery Ser.). 9.95 o.p. (*0-8161-3680-7*); lib. bdg. 11.95 o.p. (*0-8161-3732-3*) Gale Group. (Macmillan Reference USA).
—The Incredulity of Father Brown. audio 38.95 NorthStar Audio Bks.
—The Incredulity of Father Brown. 1975. (Father Brown Mystery Ser.). pap. 3.95 o.p. (*0-14-001069-6*) Penguin Group (USA) Inc.
—The Incredulity of Father Brown. 1987. (Father Brown Mystery Ser.). 192p. pap. 4.95 o.p. (*0-14-008258-1*, Penguin Bks.) Viking Penguin.
—The Innocence of Father Brown. (Father Brown Mystery Ser.). 22.95 (*0-89190-338-0*) Amereon, Ltd.
—The Innocence of Father Brown. l.t. ed. 1991. (Father Brown Mystery Ser.). pap. 16.95 o.p. (*0-7927-0373-1*, CS042) BBC Audiobooks America.
—The Innocence of Father Brown. unabr. ed. 1992. (Father Brown Ser.). audio 44.95 (*0-7861-0124-5*, 1110) Blackstone Audio Bks., Inc.
—The Innocence of Father Brown. unabr. collector's ed. 1984. (Father Brown Mystery Ser.). audio 48.00 (*0-7366-0812-5*, 1762) Books on Tape, Inc.
—The Innocence of Father Brown. 1976. (Father Brown Mystery Ser.). reprint ed. lib. bdg. 21.00 o.p. (*0-8240-2359-5*) Garland Publishing, Inc.
—The Innocence of Father Brown. audio 42.95 NorthStar Audio Bks.
—The Innocence of Father Brown. 1975. (Father Brown Mystery Ser.). pap. 3.95 o.p. (*0-14-000765-2*) Penguin Group (USA) Inc.
—The Innocence of Father Brown. unabr. ed. 1989. (Father Brown Mystery Ser.). audio 51.00 (*1-55690-255-7*, 89930E7) Recorded Bks., LLC.
—The Innocence of Father Brown. 1987. (Father Brown Mystery Ser.). 256p. pap. 4.95 o.p. (*0-14-008257-3*, Penguin Bks.) Viking Penguin.
—The Invisible Man - A Father Brown Mystery. unabr. ed. 1998. (Father Brown Mysteries Ser.). audio 16.99 (*0-88646-455-2*, 7455) Durkin Hayes Publishing Ltd.
—The Man Who Was Thursday. reprint ed. lib. bdg. 20.95 (*0-89190-577-4*, Rivercity Pr.) Amereon, Ltd.
—The Man Who Was Thursday. 1986. 196p. pap. 3.50 o.p. (*0-88184-225-7*, Carroll & Graf Pubs.) Avalon Publishing Group.
—The Man Who Was Thursday. 1908. E-Book (*1-58734-005-4*) Bartleby.com.
—The Man Who Was Thursday. 1990. reprint ed. lib. bdg. 16.95 (*0-89968-495-5*) Buccaneer Bks., Inc.
—The Man Who Was Thursday. l.t. unabr. ed. (Large Print Classics). 2002. vi, 249p. pap. 10.95 (*0-486-42250-X*); 1986. (Illus.). 128p. reprint ed. pap. 4.95 (*0-486-25121-7*) Dover Pubns., Inc.
—The Man Who Was Thursday. l.t. ed. 1987. (Nightingale Ser.). 296p. 11.95 o.p. (*0-8161-4322-6*, Macmillan Reference USA) Gale Group.
—The Man Who Was Thursday. 1960. pap. 5.95 o.p. (*0-399-50151-7*) Putnam Publishing Group, The.
—The Man Who Was Thursday. 2001. (Modern Library Classics). 224p. pap. 8.95 (*0-375-75791-0*, Modern Library) Random House Adult Trade Publishing Group.
—The Man Who Was Thursday. l.t. ed. 1999. 288p. text 24.95 (*1-56000-492-4*) Transaction Pubs.
—The Man Who Was Thursday. 1990. (Penguin Twentieth-Century Classics Ser.). 192p. 8.95 (*0-14-018388-4*, Penguin Classics) Viking Penguin.
—The Man Who Was Thursday. 1998. (Classics Library). 184p. pap. 3.95 (*1-85326-236-6*, 2366WW) Wordsworth Editions, Ltd. GBR. *Dist:* Casemate Pubs. & Bk. Distributors, LLC.
—The Man Who Was Thursday: And Related Pieces. Metcalf, Stephen, ed. 1996. (Oxford World's Classics Ser.). (Illus.). 238p. pap. 7.95 o.p. (*0-19-282359-0*) Oxford Univ. Pr., Inc.
—The Napoleon of Notting Hill. 1991. (Illus.). 160p. pap. 5.95 (*0-486-26551-X*) Dover Pubns., Inc.
—The Napoleon of Notting Hill. Bergonzi, Bernard, ed. 1994. (Oxford World's Classics Ser.). (Illus.). 202p. pap. 8.95 o.p. (*0-19-283145-3*) Oxford Univ. Pr., Inc.
—The Scandal of Father Brown. unabr. ed. 1993. (Father Brown Mystery Ser.). audio 39.95 (*0-7451-5828-5*, CAT 4027) BBC Audiobooks America.
—The Scandal of Father Brown. unabr. ed. 1988. (Father Brown Ser.). audio 32.95 (*0-7861-0058-3*, 1055) Blackstone Audio Bks., Inc.
—The Scandal of Father Brown. unabr. collector's ed. 1994. (Father Brown Mystery Ser.). audio 36.00 (*0-7366-2756-1*, 3479) Books on Tape, Inc.
—The Scandal of Father Brown. l.t. ed. 1986. (Father Brown Mystery Ser.). 292p. 10.95 o.p. (*0-8161-3930-X*, Macmillan Reference USA) Gale Group.
—The Scandal of Father Brown. 2000. 182p. pap. 9.95 (*0-7551-0026-3*) House of Stratus, Inc. GBR. *Dist:* Midpoint Trade Bks., Inc.
—The Scandal of Father Brown. 1988. (Father Brown Mystery Ser.). audio 35.95 o.s.i (*0-8161-7782-1*) Thorndike Pr.
—The Scandal of Father Brown. (Father Brown Mystery Ser.). 1988. 176p. pap. 4.95 o.p. (*0-14-008256-5*); 1982. pap. 3.50 o.p. (*0-14-004739-5*) Viking Penguin. (Penguin Bks.).
—The Secret of Father Brown. (Father Brown Mystery Ser.). 20.95 (*0-89190-337-2*) Amereon, Ltd.
—The Secret of Father Brown. unabr. ed. 1999. (Father Brown Mystery Ser.). audio 39.95 (*0-7861-0016-8*, 1016) Blackstone Audio Bks., Inc.
—The Secret of Father Brown. unabr. collector's ed. 1994. (Father Brown Mystery Ser.). audio 42.00 (*0-7366-2755-3*, 3478) Books on Tape, Inc.
—The Secret of Father Brown. l.t. ed. 1985. (Father Brown Mystery Ser.). 312p. 9.95 o.p. (*0-8161-3929-6*, Macmillan Reference USA) Gale Group.
—The Secret of Father Brown. 2000. 204p. pap. 9.95 (*0-7551-0027-1*) House of Stratus, Inc. GBR. *Dist:* Midpoint Trade Bks., Inc.
—The Secret of Father Brown. 1975. (Father Brown Mystery Ser.). pap. 3.50 o.p. (*0-14-003807-8*) Penguin Group (USA) Inc.
—The Secret of Father Brown. 1989. (Father Brown Mystery Ser.). audio 53.95 o.s.i (*0-8161-7726-0*) Thorndike Pr.
—The Secret of Father Brown. 1987. (Father Brown Mystery Ser.). 176p. pap. 4.95 o.p. (*0-14-008255-7*, Penguin Bks.) Viking Penguin.
—The Wisdom of Father Brown. (Father Brown Mystery Ser.). 21.95 (*0-89190-336-4*) Amereon, Ltd.
—The Wisdom of Father Brown. unabr. ed. 1992. (Father Brown Mystery Ser.). audio 44.95 (*0-7861-0125-3*, 1111) Blackstone Audio Bks., Inc.
—The Wisdom of Father Brown. unabr. collector's ed. 1986. (Father Brown Mystery Ser.). audio 48.00 (*0-7366-0813-3*, 1763) Books on Tape, Inc.
—The Wisdom of Father Brown. 2001. audio 42.95 NorthStar Audio Bks.

—The Wisdom of Father Brown. 1975. (Father Brown Mystery Ser.). pap. 3.50 o.p. (*0-14-003118-9*) Penguin Group (USA) Inc.
—The Wisdom of Father Brown. l.t. ed. 2000. (Father Brown Mystery Ser.). 280p. pap. 18.95 (*1-888725-27-3*, MacroPrintBooks) Science & Humanities Pr.
—The Wisdom of Father Brown. 1987. (Father Brown Mystery Ser.). 208p. pap. 4.95 o.p. (*0-14-008159-3*, Penguin Bks.) Viking Penguin.
Chevalier, Tracy. Falling Angels: A Novel. 2001. 324p. 24.95 o.s.i (*0-525-94581-4*, Dutton) Dutton/Plume.
Child, Lee. Running Blind. abr. ed. 2000. audio 24.95 o.p. (*1-56740-906-7*, 2100, Nova Audio Bks.); audio 32.95 (*1-56740-362-X*, 2099); audio 73.25 (*1-56740-729-3*, 2101, Unabridged Library Editions) Brilliance Audio.
—Running Blind. 2000. (Jack Reacher Ser.). 360p. 18.95 o.s.i (*0-399-14623-7*) Penguin Group (USA) Inc.
Cholmondeley, Mary. Moth & Rust & Other Stories. 1977. (Short Story Index Reprint Ser.). 22.95 (*0-8369-3182-3*) Ayer Co. Pubs., Inc.
Chopra, Deepak. El Retorno de Merlin. 1998. (SPA.). 416p. (*84-270-2152-6*) Ediciones Martinez Roca.
—El Retorno de Merlin. (SPA.). pap. 25.00 (*958-04-3512-X*, NR9053) Norma S.A. COL. *Dist:* Lectorum Pubns., Inc.
—The Return of Merlin. 1996. 432p. pap. 14.95 (*0-449-91074-1*, Fawcett) Ballantine Bks.
—The Return of Merlin. l.t. ed. 1996. 24.95 (*1-56895-288-0*, Wheeler Publishing, Inc.) Gale Group.
Christie, Agatha. The A. B. C. Murders. 1991. (Hercule Poirot Mystery Ser.). 240p. mass mkt. 5.99 (*0-425-13024-X*); E-Book 5.99 (*0-425-17788-2*) Berkley Publishing Group.
—The A. B. C. Murders. l.t. ed. (Popular Author Ser.). 344p. 1989. 12.95 o.p. (*0-8161-4500-8*); 1988. lib. bdg. 20.95 o.p. (*0-8161-4459-1*) Gale Group. (Macmillan Reference USA).
—The A. B. C. Murders. 1985. (Agatha Christie Ser.). 256p. 12.95 (*0-396-08698-5*, G. P. Putnam's Sons) Penguin Putnam Bks. for Young Readers.
—The A. B. C. Murders. 1985. 240p. mass mkt. 3.50 o.s.i (*0-671-60063-X*); 1982. mass mkt. 2.95 o.s.i (*0-671-46477-9*) Simon & Schuster. (Pocket).
—The A. B. C. Murders. 1991. 12.04 (*0-606-12156-0*) Turtleback Bks.
—Affair of the Pink Pearl. unabr. ed. 1992. audio 5.99 (*0-88646-602-4*, PAC-7602) Durkin Hayes Publishing Ltd.
—After the Funeral. 2000. (Hercule Poirot Mystery Ser.). 256p. mass mkt. 5.99 (*0-425-17390-9*) Berkley Publishing Group.
—After the Funeral. 1985. mass mkt. 3.50 o.s.i (*0-671-55695-9*); 1983. mass mkt. 2.95 o.s.i (*0-671-47287-9*) Simon & Schuster. (Pocket).
—Agatha Christie: Five Complete Hercule Poirot Novels. 1990. 672p. 13.99 o.s.i (*0-517-03583-9*) Random Hse. Value Publishing.
—Agatha Christie: Five Complete Miss Marple Novels. 1990. 13.99 o.s.i (*0-517-03580-4*) Random Hse. Value Publishing.
—At Bertram's Hotel. unabr. ed. 1997. (Miss Marple Mysteries Ser.). audio 54.95 o.p. (*0-7451-6812-4*, CAB 313) BBC Audiobooks America.
—At Bertram's Hotel. 1987. (HC Collection). 9.95 o.p. (*0-553-82243-8*) Bantam Bks.
—At Bertram's Hotel. l.t. ed. (Agatha Christie Ser.). 329p. 1992. 14.95 o.p. (*0-8161-4532-6*); 1991. lib. bdg. 19.95 o.p. (*0-8161-4531-8*) Gale Group. (Macmillan Reference USA).
—At Bertram's Hotel. 2000. (Miss Marple Mysteries Ser.). 224p. mass mkt. 5.99 (*0-451-19993-6*, Signet Bks.) NAL.
—At Bertram's Hotel. 1992. 208p. 22.95 o.s.i (*0-399-13706-8*, G. P. Putnam's Sons) Penguin Group (USA) Inc.
—At Bertram's Hotel. 1982. mass mkt. 2.75 o.s.i (*0-671-45761-6*); 1984. mass mkt. 3.50 o.s.i (*0-671-54385-7*) Simon & Schuster. (Pocket).
—At Bertram's Hotel. 1988. audio 53.95 o.p. (*0-8161-9107-7*) Thorndike Pr.
—At Bertram's Hotel. l.t. ed. 1968. (Ulverscroft Large Print Ser.). 367p. 12.00 o.p. (*0-85456-586-8*, Ulverscroft) Thorpe, F. A. Pubs. GBR. *Dist:* Ulverscroft Large Print Bks., Ltd., Ulverscroft Large Print Canada, Ltd.
—The Big Four. 1986. mass mkt. 9.95 o.p. (*0-553-35041-2*) Bantam Bks.
—The Big Four. 1987. 208p. mass mkt. 5.99 (*0-425-09882-6*); 1986. mass mkt. 2.95 o.s.i (*0-425-09362-X*); 1984. mass mkt. 2.95 o.s.i (*0-425-06776-9*) Berkley Publishing Group.
—The Big Four. 1982. pap. 2.95 o.p. (*0-440-10562-5*) Dell Publishing.
—The Big Four. l.t. ed. (Agatha Christie Ser.). 280p. 1992. pap. 12.95 o.p. (*0-8161-4534-2*); 1991. 19.95 o.p. (*0-8161-4533-4*) Gale Group. (Macmillan Reference USA).
—The Big Four. l.t. ed. 1974. (Ulverscroft Large Print Ser.). 312p. 12.00 o.p. (*0-85456-283-4*, Ulverscroft) Thorpe, F. A. Pubs. GBR. *Dist:* Ulverscroft Large Print Bks., Ltd., Ulverscroft Large Print Canada, Ltd.
—Black Coffee. l.t. ed. 1999. 26.95 o.p. (*1-56895-625-8*, Wheeler Publishing, Inc.) Gale Group.
—Black Coffee. unabr. ed. 1998. (Hercule Poirot Mystery Ser.). 6p. audio 24.95 (*1-55935-281-7*, 696051) Soundelux Audio Publishing.
—Black Coffee. (Hercule Poirot Mystery Ser.). 1998. (Illus.). 221p. 22.95 o.p. (*0-312-19241-X*, Saint Martin's Minotaur); 3rd ed. 1999. 290p. mass mkt. 6.99 (*0-312-97007-2*, St. Martin's Paperbacks) St. Martin's Pr.
—Black Coffee. abr. ed. 1998. audio 24.35 (*0-00-105536-4*) Ulverscroft Audio (U.S.A.).
—The Body in the Library. 1987. (HC Collection). 9.95 o.p. (*0-553-35058-7*) Bantam Bks.
—The Body in the Library. l.t. ed. (Popular Author Ser.). 249p. 1989. 10.95 o.p. (*0-8161-4501-6*); 1988. lib. bdg. 19.95 o.p. (*0-8161-4458-3*) Gale Group. (Macmillan Reference USA).
—The Body in the Library. 2000. (Miss Marple Mysteries Ser.). 224p. mass mkt. 5.99 (*0-451-19987-1*, Signet Bks.) NAL.
—The Body in the Library. 1985. (Agatha Christie Ser.). 240p. 14.95 o.s.i (*0-399-15017-X*, G. P. Putnam's Sons) Penguin Group (USA) Inc.
—The Body in the Library. 1985. 12.95 o.s.i (*0-396-08699-3*) Putnam Publishing Group, The.
—The Body in the Library. 1985. mass mkt. 3.50 o.s.i (*0-671-60255-1*); 1984. 11.80 o.p. (*0-671-90084-6*); 1983. mass mkt. 2.95 o.s.i (*0-671-46496-5*) Simon & Schuster. (Pocket).
—The Body in the Library. 1992. (Miss Marple Mysteries Ser.). 12.04 (*0-606-12195-1*) Turtleback Bks.
—The Boomerang Clue. mass mkt. 3.50 o.s.i (*0-425-12582-3*); 1985. mass mkt. 2.95 o.s.i (*0-425-08802-2*); 1984. mass mkt. 2.95 o.s.i (*0-425-06777-7*) Berkley Publishing Group.
—The Boomerang Clue. (Popular Author Ser.). 1988. lib. bdg. 20.95 o.p. (*0-8161-4535-0*); 1989. 375p. 12.95 o.p. (*0-8161-4536-9*) Gale Group. (Macmillan Reference USA).
—The Boomerang Clue. 1987. 224p. 14.95 o.s.i (*0-396-09155-5*, G. P. Putnam's Sons) Penguin Putnam Bks. for Young Readers.
—By the Pricking of My Thumbs. abr. ed. 2003. (Agatha Christie Audio Mystery Ser.). (Illus.). audio 12.95 (*1-55927-904-4*) Audio Renaissance.
—By the Pricking of My Thumbs. unabr. ed. 1995. audio 69.95 o.p. (*0-7451-4197-8*, CAB 880) BBC Audiobooks America.
—By the Pricking of My Thumbs. 2000. (Tommy & Tuppence Mysteries Ser.). 224p. mass mkt. 5.99 (*0-451-20052-7*, Signet Bks.) NAL.
—By the Pricking of My Thumbs. 1986. (Agatha Christie Ser.). 14.95 o.s.i (*0-396-08863-5*, G. P. Putnam's Sons) Penguin Putnam Bks. for Young Readers.
—By the Pricking of My Thumbs. 1990. mass mkt. 4.99 o.p. (*0-671-70609-8*); 1983. mass mkt. 2.95 o.s.i (*0-671-46807-3*) Simon & Schuster. (Pocket).
—By the Pricking of My Thumbs. l.t. ed. 1987. (Ulverscroft Large Print Ser.). 432p. o.p. (*0-7089-1571-X*, Ulverscroft) Thorpe, F. A. Pubs. GBR. *Dist:* Ulverscroft Large Print Canada, Ltd.
—By the Pricking of My Thumbs. 1992. 12.04 (*0-606-12207-9*) Turtleback Bks.
—Cards on the Table. mass mkt. 3.50 o.s.i (*0-425-12577-7*); 2001. E-Book 5.99 (*0-425-17790-4*); 1998. mass mkt. 3.99 o.s.i (*0-425-16924-3*); 1986. mass mkt. 2.95 o.s.i (*0-425-09317-4*); 1984. mass mkt. 2.95 o.s.i (*0-425-06778-5*) Berkley Publishing Group.
—Cards on the Table. 1980. pap. 2.95 o.p. (*0-440-11052-1*) Dell Publishing.
—Cards on the Table. 1987. (Agatha Christie Ser.). 14.95 (*0-396-09010-9*, G. P. Putnam's Sons) Penguin Putnam Bks. for Young Readers.
—Cards on the Table. 1984. (Hercule Poirot Mystery Ser.). 12.04 (*0-606-12211-7*) Turtleback Bks.
—The Cards on the Table. 1987. (Hercule Poirot Mystery Ser.). 224p. mass mkt. 5.99 (*0-425-10567-9*) Berkley Publishing Group.
—Cards on the Table. l.t. ed. 1983. 352p. 12.50 o.p. (*0-7089-1151-X*, Ulverscroft) Thorpe, F. A. Pubs. GBR. *Dist:* Ulverscroft Large Print Bks., Ltd.
—Cat among the Pigeons. 2000. (Hercule Poirot Mystery Ser.). 256p. mass mkt. 5.99 (*0-425-17547-2*) Berkley Publishing Group.
—Cat among the Pigeons. 1986. (Agatha Christie Ser.). 224p. 12.95 o.s.i (*0-396-08802-3*, G. P. Putnam's Sons) Penguin Putnam Bks. for Young Readers.
—Cat among the Pigeons. 1985. mass mkt. 3.50 o.s.i (*0-671-55700-9*); 1983. mass mkt. 2.95 o.s.i (*0-671-46766-2*) Simon & Schuster. (Pocket).
—Cat among the Pigeons. l.t. ed. 1983. 400p. 12.50 o.p. (*0-85456-771-2*, Ulverscroft) Thorpe, F. A. Pubs. GBR. *Dist:* Ulverscroft Large Print Bks., Ltd.
—Cat among the Pigeons. 1991. (Hercule Poirot Mystery Ser.). 12.04 (*0-606-12214-1*) Turtleback Bks.
—The Christmas Tragedy & Other Stories. unabr. ed. 1994. audio 5.99 (*0-88646-723-3*, PAC-7723) Durkin Hayes Publishing Ltd.
—The Clocks. unabr. ed. 1997. (Hercule Poirot Mystery Ser.). audio 69.95 o.p. (*0-7451-6814-0*, CAB 640) BBC Audiobooks America.
—The Clocks. 1988. (HC Collection). 9.95 o.s.i (*0-553-35071-4*) Bantam Bks.
—The Clocks. 2000. 272p. mass mkt. 5.99 (*0-425-17391-7*) Berkley Publishing Group.
—The Clocks. 1985. mass mkt. 3.50 o.s.i (*0-671-55822-6*); 1983. mass mkt. 2.95 o.s.i (*0-671-47296-8*) Simon & Schuster. (Pocket).
—The Clocks. l.t. ed. 1983. (Ulverscroft Large Print Ser.). 432p. o.p. (*0-85456-666-X*, Ulverscroft) Thorpe, F. A. Pubs. GBR. *Dist:* Ulverscroft Large Print Canada, Ltd.
—The Clocks. 1991. (Hercule Poirot Mystery Ser.). 12.04 (*0-606-12222-2*) Turtleback Bks.
—Crooked House. 1986. (Mystery Ser.). 224p. mass mkt. 9.95 o.p. (*0-553-35054-4*) Bantam Bks.
—Crooked House. l.t. ed. (Popular Author Ser.). 300p. 1989. 12.95 o.p. (*0-8161-4502-4*); 1988. lib. bdg. 19.95 o.p. (*0-8161-4463-X*) Gale Group. (Macmillan Reference USA).
—Crooked House. 1987. (Agatha Christie Ser.). 14.95 o.s.i (*0-396-09157-1*, G. P. Putnam's Sons) Penguin Putnam Bks. for Young Readers.
—Crooked House. 1984. 224p. mass mkt. 3.50 o.s.i (*0-671-54321-0*); 1983. mass mkt. 2.95 o.s.i (*0-671-47161-9*) Simon & Schuster. (Pocket).
—Crooked House. 1991. 12.04 (*0-606-12231-1*) Turtleback Bks.
—Curtain. 1976. 22.95 (*0-88411-386-8*) Amereon, Ltd.
—Curtain. 2000. (Hercule Poirot Mystery Ser.). 224p. mass mkt. 5.99 (*0-425-17374-7*) Berkley Publishing Group.
—Curtain. pap. 14.95 (*0-8161-4540-7*); 1992. 289p. lib. bdg. 19.95 o.p. (*0-8161-4539-3*) Gale Group. (Macmillan Reference USA).
—Curtain. 1995. 24.95 (*0-399-14016-6*, Philomel) Penguin Group (USA) Inc.
—Curtain. 1985. 288p. mass mkt. 4.99 o.p. (*0-671-54717-8*, Pocket) Simon & Schuster.
—Curtain. 1993. 12.04 (*0-606-12235-4*) Turtleback Bks.
—A Daughter's a Daughter. 1988. mass mkt. 3.95 o.s.i (*0-515-09494-3*, Jove) Berkley Publishing Group.
—A Daughter's a Daughter & Other Novels. 2001. 576p. pap. 17.95 (*0-312-27472-6*, Saint Martin's Griffin) St. Martin's Pr.
—Dead Man's Folly. unabr. ed. 1997. audio 54.95 o.p. (*0-7451-6815-9*, CAB 314) BBC Audiobooks America.
—Dead Man's Folly. 2000. (Hercule Poirot Mystery Ser.). 240p. mass mkt. 5.99 (*0-425-17473-5*) Berkley Publishing Group.
—Dead Man's Folly. 1986. (Agatha Christie Ser.). 14.95 o.s.i (*0-396-08864-3*, G. P. Putnam's Sons) Penguin Putnam Bks. for Young Readers.
—Dead Man's Folly. 1990. 224p. mass mkt. 3.95 o.p. (*0-671-69484-7*); 1984. mass mkt. 3.50 o.s.i (*0-671-54318-0*); 1983. mass mkt. 2.95 o.s.i (*0-671-47317-4*) Simon & Schuster. (Pocket).
—Dead Man's Folly. 1988. audio 53.95 o.p. (*0-8161-9109-3*) Thorndike Pr.
—Dead Man's Folly. l.t. ed. 1983. 336p. 12.50 o.p. (*0-85456-772-0*, Ulverscroft) Thorpe, F. A. Pubs. GBR. *Dist:* Ulverscroft Large Print Bks., Ltd.
—Dead Man's Mirror. 1986. mass mkt. 2.95 o.s.i (*0-425-08765-4*); 1984. mass mkt. 2.95 o.s.i (*0-425-06779-3*) Berkley Publishing Group.
—Dead Man's Mirror. 1981. 192p. pap. 2.95 o.p. (*0-440-11699-6*) Dell Publishing.
—Dead Man's Mirror. abr. ed. 1990. 2p. audio 16.99 (*0-88646-203-7*, 7203) Durkin Hayes Publishing Ltd.
—Death in the Clouds. Orig. Title: Death in the Air. 2000. E-Book 5.99 (*0-425-17791-2*); 1998. mass mkt. 3.99 o.s.i (*0-425-16921-9*); 1987. 240p. mass mkt. 5.99 (*0-425-09914-8*) Berkley Publishing Group.
—Death in the Clouds. 1998. (Hercule Poirot Mystery Ser.). Orig. Title: Death in the Air. (Illus.). 256p. 24.95 (*0-399-14432-3*, G. P. Putnam's Sons) Penguin Group (USA) Inc.
—Death in the Clouds. l.t. ed. 1987. Orig. Title: Death in the Air. 16.95 (*0-7089-1738-0*, Ulverscroft) Thorpe, F. A. Pubs. GBR. *Dist:* Ulverscroft Large Print Bks., Ltd.
—Death in the Clouds. 2000. Orig. Title: Death in the Air. 12.04 (*0-606-20623-X*) Turtleback Bks.
—Double Sin & Other Stories. 1987. (HC Collection). 9.95 o.p. (*0-553-35057-9*) Bantam Bks.
—Double Sin & Other Stories. 1984. 224p. mass mkt. 5.99 o.s.i (*0-425-06781-5*) Berkley Publishing Group.
—Double Sin & Other Stories. 1977. pap. 1.95 o.p. (*0-440-12144-2*) Dell Publishing.
—Double Sin & Other Stories. l.t. ed. (Popular Author Ser.). 1991. 12.95 o.p. (*0-8161-4542-3*); 1990. 266p. lib. bdg. 19.95 o.p. (*0-8161-4541-5*) Gale Group. (Macmillan Reference USA).
—Double Sin & Other Stories. 1987. (Agatha Christie Ser.). 224p. 14.95 o.s.i (*0-396-09158-X*, G. P. Putnam's Sons) Penguin Putnam Bks. for Young Readers.
—Dumb Witness. 1986. (Hercule Poirot Mystery Ser.). 272p. mass mkt. 5.99 (*0-425-09854-0*) Berkley Publishing Group.
—Easy to Kill. l.t. ed. (Agatha Christie Ser.). 1991. 336p. 14.95 o.p. (*0-8161-4544-X*); 1990. 312p. lib. bdg. 19.95 o.p. (*0-8161-4543-1*) Gale Group. (Macmillan Reference USA).
—Easy to Kill. 1987. (Agatha Christie Ser.). 224p. 14.95 o.s.i (*0-396-09159-8*, G. P. Putnam's Sons) Penguin Group (USA) Inc.
—Easy to Kill. 1990. mass mkt. 4.99 o.p. (*0-671-70599-7*, Pocket) Simon & Schuster.
—Easy to Kill: HC Collection Ser. 1987. mass mkt. 9.95 o.p. (*0-553-35055-2*) Bantam Bks.
—Elephants Can Remember. 1984. (Agatha Christie Ser.). 224p. mass mkt. 5.99 (*0-425-06782-3*) Berkley Publishing Group.
—Elephants Can Remember. 1976. pap. 1.25 o.p. (*0-440-12329-1*) Dell Publishing.
—Elephants Can Remember. l.t. ed. (Agatha Christie Ser.). 1991. 291p. pap. 12.95 o.p. (*0-8161-4546-6*); 1990. 328p. lib. bdg. 19.95 o.p. (*0-8161-4545-8*); 1984. pap. 9.95 o.p. (*0-8161-3122-8*); 1973. reprint ed. lib. bdg. 9.95 o.p. (*0-8161-6086-4*) Gale Group. (Macmillan Reference USA).
—Elephants Can Remember. 1972. (Agatha Christie Ser.). 8.95 (*0-396-07769-2*, G. P. Putnam's Sons) Penguin Group (USA) Inc.
—Elephants Can Remember. 1992. 12.04 (*0-606-12274-5*) Turtleback Bks.
—Elephants Can Remember. l.t. ed. 2001. (Ulverscroft Large Print Ser.). 368p. 32.50 (*0-7089-2657-6*) Ulverscroft Large Print Bks., Ltd.
—Elephants Can Remember: A Hercule Poirot Mystery. unabr. ed. 1999. audio 49.95 (*0-7540-0334-5*, CAB1757) Chivers Audio Bks. GBR. *Dist:* BBC Audiobooks America.
—Endless Night. 1985. (Mystery Ser.). 208p. 9.95 o.p. (*0-553-35039-0*) Bantam Bks.
—Endless Night. l.t. ed. (Agatha Christie Ser.). 336p. 1990. 13.95 o.p. (*0-8161-4548-2*); 1989. lib. bdg. 20.95 (*0-8161-4547-4*) Gale Group. (Macmillan Reference USA).
—Endless Night. 1985. (Agatha Christie Ser.). 224p. 12.95 o.s.i (*0-396-08700-0*, G. P. Putnam's Sons) Penguin Putnam Bks. for Young Readers.
—Endless Night. 1985. mass mkt. 3.50 o.s.i (*0-671-60427-9*); 1983. mass mkt. 2.95 o.s.i (*0-671-49453-8*) Simon & Schuster. (Pocket).
—Endless Night. l.t. ed. 1972. (Ulverscroft Large Print Ser.). 342p. 12.00 o.p. (*0-85456-115-3*, Ulverscroft) Thorpe, F. A. Pubs. GBR. *Dist:* Ulverscroft Large Print Bks., Ltd., Ulverscroft Large Print Canada, Ltd.
—Endless Night. 1992. 12.04 (*0-606-12279-6*) Turtleback Bks.
—Evil under the Sun. unabr. ed. 1997. (Hercule Poirot Mystery Ser.). audio 54.95 (*0-7451-4014-9*, CAB 711) BBC Audiobooks America.
—Evil under the Sun. 1991. (Hercule Poirot Mystery Ser.). 208p. mass mkt. 5.99 (*0-425-12960-8*) Berkley Publishing Group.
—Evil under the Sun. l.t. ed. 291p. 1989. pap. 12.95 o.p. (*0-8161-4550-4*); 1988. lib. bdg. 20.95 o.p. (*0-8161-4549-0*) Gale Group. (Macmillan Reference USA).
—Evil under the Sun. 1985. 12.95 (*0-396-08701-9*) Putnam Publishing Group, The.
—Evil under the Sun. 1990. mass mkt. 3.95 o.s.i (*0-671-70612-8*); 1985. mass mkt. 3.50 o.p. (*0-671-60174-1*); 1983. mass mkt. 2.95 o.p. (*0-671-47427-8*) Simon & Schuster. (Pocket).
—Evil under the Sun. l.t. ed. 1971. (Ulverscroft Large Print Ser.). 362p. o.p. (*0-85456-042-4*, Ulverscroft) Thorpe, F. A. Pubs. GBR. *Dist:* Ulverscroft Large Print Canada, Ltd.
—Evil under the Sun. 1991. (Hercule Poirot Mystery Ser.). 12.04 (*0-606-12281-8*) Turtleback Bks.
—Five Little Pigs. 2000. E-Book 5.99 (*0-425-17787-4*); 1998. mass mkt. 3.99 o.s.i (*0-425-16923-5*); 1985. 224p. reprint ed. mass mkt. 5.99 (*0-425-09325-5*) Berkley Publishing Group.
—Five Little Pigs. l.t. ed. 1982. (Ulverscroft Large Print Ser.). 316p. (*0-7089-0814-4*, Ulverscroft) Thorpe, F. A. Pubs. GBR. *Dist:* Ulverscroft Large Print Canada, Ltd.
—Funerals Are Fatal. 224p. 21.95 o.s.i (*0-8488-2446-6*) Amereon, Ltd.
—Funerals Are Fatal. l.t. ed. pap. 14.95 (*0-8161-4552-0*); 1992. lib. bdg. 19.95 o.p. (*0-8161-4551-2*) Gale Group. (Macmillan Reference USA).
—Funerals Are Fatal. 1988. 14.95 (*0-396-09295-0*, G. P. Putnam's Sons) Penguin Group (USA) Inc.

—Funerals Are Fatal. 1990. 208p. 22.95 (*0-399-13560-X*, G. P. Putnam's Sons) Penguin Putnam Bks. for Young Readers.
—Funerals Are Fatal. 1992. (Hercule Poirot Mystery Ser.). 12.04 (*0-606-12301-6*) Turtleback Bks.
—The Golden Ball & Other Stories. 1987. (HC Collection). 9.95 o.s.i (*0-553-35065-X*) Bantam Bks.
—The Golden Ball & Other Stories. 1986. 240p. mass mkt. 5.99 o.s.i (*0-425-09922-9*) Berkley Publishing Group.
—The Golden Ball & Other Stories. 1972. pap. 2.25 o.s.i (*0-440-13272-X*) Dell Publishing.
—The Golden Ball & Other Stories. (Agatha Christie Ser.). 1991. 416p. pap. 12.95 o.p. (*0-8161-4554-7*); 1990. 393p. lib. bdg. 19.95 o.p. (*0-8161-4553-9*) Gale Group. (Macmillan Reference USA).
—The Golden Ball & Other Stories. 1988. 14.95 (*0-396-09296-9*, G. P. Putnam's Sons) Penguin Group (USA) Inc.
—Hallowe'en Party, Set. unabr. ed. 1999. audio 54.95 (*0-7540-0377-9*, CAB1800) BBC Audiobooks America.
—Hallowe'en Party. 2000. E-Book 5.99 (*0-425-17789-0*); 1998. mass mkt. 3.99 o.s.i (*0-425-16922-7*); 1991. 240p. mass mkt. 5.99 (*0-425-12963-2*) Berkley Publishing Group.
—Hallowe'en Party. unabr. ed. 2000. (Hercule Poirot Mystery Ser.). audio compact disk 64.95 (*0-7540-5335-0*, CCD 026) Chivers Audio Bks. GBR. *Dist:* BBC Audiobooks America.
—Hallowe'en Party. 2003. (Hercule Poirot Investigates Ser.). E-Book 5.99 (*0-06-072146-4*, PerfectBound) HarperCollins General Bks. Group.
—Hallowe'en Party. 1987. (Agatha Christie Ser.). 14.95 o.s.i (*0-396-09012-5*, G. P. Putnam's Sons) Penguin Putnam Bks. for Young Readers.
—Hallowe'en Party. 1984. mass mkt. 3.50 o.s.i (*0-671-54203-6*); 1982. mass mkt. 2.95 o.s.i (*0-671-45935-X*); 1989. reprint ed. mass mkt. 4.99 o.p. (*0-671-70231-9*) Simon & Schuster. (Pocket).
—Hallowe'en Party. l.t. ed. 1987. (Ulverscroft Large Print Ser.). 400p. o.p. (*0-7089-1666-X*, Ulverscroft) Thorpe, F. A. Pubs. GBR. *Dist:* Ulverscroft Large Print Canada, Ltd.
—Hallowe'en Party. 1992. (Hercule Poirot Mystery Ser.). 12.04 (*0-606-12321-0*) Turtleback Bks.
—The Harlequin Tea Set & Other Stories. 1998. 224p. reprint ed. mass mkt. 5.99 (*0-425-16515-9*) Berkley Publishing Group.
—The Harlequin Tea Set & Other Stories. abr. ed. 2001. audio 24.95 (*1-56511-570-8*) HighBridge Co.
—The Harlequin Tea Set & Other Stories. 1997. 208p. 21.95 o.s.i (*0-399-14287-8*, G. P. Putnam's Sons) Penguin Group (USA) Inc.
—The Harlequin Tea Set & Other Stories. unabr. ed. 1998. audio 21.95 (*1-55935-260-4*) Soundelux Audio Publishing.
—The Herb of Death & Other Stories. unabr. ed. 1989. 7p. audio 16.99 (*0-88646-241-X*) Durkin Hayes Publishing Ltd.
—Hercule Poirot's Casebook: Fifty Stories. 1998. 18.95 (*0-399-15021-8*); 1984. 18.95 (*0-396-08417-6*) Penguin Group (USA) Inc. (G. P. Putnam's Sons).
—Hercule Poirot's Early Cases. 22.95 (*0-88411-388-4*) Amereon, Ltd.
—Hercule Poirot's Early Cases. 1986. mass mkt. 9.95 o.p. (*0-553-35045-5*) Bantam Bks.
—Hercule Poirot's Early Cases. l.t. ed. 1979. (gr. 7-12). lib. bdg. 8.95 o.p. (*0-8161-6734-6*, Macmillan Reference USA) Gale Group.
—Hickory, Dickory, Death. 1987. (Agatha Christie Ser.). 224p. 14.95 o.s.i (*0-396-09160-1*, G. P. Putnam's Sons) Penguin Putnam Bks. for Young Readers.
—Hickory, Dickory, Death. 1989. mass mkt. 4.99 o.p. (*0-671-70263-7*, Pocket) Simon & Schuster.
—Hickory, Dickory, Death. l.t. ed. 1987. 352p. 14.95 o.p. (*0-7089-1637-6*, Ulverscroft) Thorpe, F. A. Pubs. GBR. *Dist:* Ulverscroft Large Print Bks., Ltd.
—Hickory, Dickory, Dock. 2000. (Hercule Poirot Mystery Ser.). 224p. mass mkt. 5.99 (*0-425-17546-4*) Berkley Publishing Group.
—A Holiday for Murder. 1983. mass mkt. 2.95 o.s.i (*0-553-24144-3*); 1962. 176p. mass mkt. 3.50 o.s.i (*0-553-26795-7*) Bantam Bks.
—The Hollow. 1986. 240p. mass mkt. 9.95 o.p. (*0-553-35050-1*) Bantam Bks.
—The Hollow. 1984. (Hercule Poirot Mystery Ser.). 272p. mass mkt. 5.99 (*0-425-06784-X*) Berkley Publishing Group.
—The Hollow. 1992. 304p. 24.95 (*0-399-13727-0*, G. P. Putnam's Sons) Penguin Group (USA) Inc.
—The Hollow. l.t. ed. 1974. (Ulverscroft Large Print Ser.). 431p. (*0-85456-301-6*, Ulverscroft) Thorpe, F. A. Pubs. GBR. *Dist:* Ulverscroft Large Print Canada, Ltd.
—The Hollow: A Hercule Poirot Mystery. l.t. ed. (Agatha Christie Ser.). 1992. 385p. pap. 12.95 o.p. (*0-8161-4556-3*); 1991. 370p. 19.95 o.p. (*0-8161-4555-5*) Gale Group. (Macmillan Reference USA).
—The Incredible Theft. unabr. ed. 1992. audio 4.99 (*0-88646-619-9*) Durkin Hayes Publishing Ltd.
—The Labors of Hercules, unabr. ed. 1995. audio 54.95 o.p. (*0-7451-5835-8*, CAB 134) BBC Audiobooks America.
—The Labors of Hercules. 1984. (Hercule Poirot Mystery Ser.). 272p. reprint ed. mass mkt. 5.99 (*0-425-06785-8*) Berkley Publishing Group.
—The Labors of Hercules. 1982. pap. 2.95 o.p. (*0-440-14620-8*) Dell Publishing.
—The Labors of Hercules, Vol. 111. unabr. ed. (Agatha Christie Mysteries Ser.). audio 16.99 Durkin Hayes Publishing Ltd.
—The Labors of Hercules. l.t. ed. 1993. 448p. 12.95 o.p. (*0-8161-4558-X*); 1992. 434p. lib. bdg. 20.95 o.p. (*0-8161-4557-1*) Gale Group. (Macmillan Reference USA).
—The Labors of Hercules. 1993. (Hercule Poirot Ser.). 224p. 24.95 (*0-399-13777-7*, G. P. Putnam's Sons) Penguin Group (USA) Inc.
—The Labors of Hercules. 1967. (Agatha Christie Ser.). 8.95 (*0-396-05578-8*, G. P. Putnam's Sons) Penguin Putnam Bks. for Young Readers.
—The Labors of Hercules. l.t. ed. 1978. (Ulverscroft Large Print Ser.). 344p. 32.50 o.p. (*0-7089-0119-0*, Ulverscroft) Thorpe, F. A. Pubs. GBR. *Dist:* Ulverscroft Large Print Bks., Ltd., Ulverscroft Large Print Canada, Ltd.
—The Listerdale Mystery. Date not set. lib. bdg. 20.95 (*0-8488-1964-0*) Amereon, Ltd.
—Lord Edgware Dies. 1986. 256p. mass mkt. 5.99 (*0-425-09961-X*) Berkley Publishing Group.
—Lord Edgware Dies. l.t. ed. 1989. 380p. o.p. (*0-85456-479-9*, Ulverscroft) Thorpe, F. A. Pubs.
—The Love Detectives. unabr. ed. 1993. audio 4.99 (*0-88646-648-2*) Durkin Hayes Publishing Ltd.
—The Million Dollar Bond Robbery. unabr. ed. 1999. (Agatha Christie Ser.). audio 5.99 (*1-55204-602-8*, PAC-8602) Durkin Hayes Publishing Ltd.
—The Mirror Crack'd. l.t. ed. 1992. 370p. lib. bdg. 19.95 o.p. (*0-8161-4559-8*, Macmillan Reference USA) Gale Group.
—The Mirror Crack'd. 2000. (Miss Marple Mysteries Ser.). 224p. mass mkt. 5.99 (*0-451-19989-8*, Signet Bks.) NAL.
—The Mirror Crack'd from Side to Side, unabr. ed. 1996. audio 54.95 (*0-7451-4060-2*, CAB 757) BBC Audiobooks America.
—The Mirror Crack'd from Side to Side. l.t. ed. 1966. (Ulverscroft Large Print Ser.). 401p. o.p. (*0-85456-698-8*, Ulverscroft) Thorpe, F. A. Pubs. GBR. *Dist:* Ulverscroft Large Print Canada, Ltd.
—Miss Marple: The Complete Short Stories. l.t. ed. 1988. 12.95 o.p. (*0-8161-4129-0*); 1987. 436p. 20.95 o.p. (*0-8161-4128-2*) Gale Group. (Macmillan Reference USA).
—Miss Marple: The Complete Short Stories. 1985. (Agatha Christie Ser.). 320p. 16.95 (*0-396-08747-7*, G. P. Putnam's Sons) Penguin Group (USA) Inc.
—The Moving Finger. (Miss Marple Mysteries Ser.). 1987. 208p. mass mkt. 5.99 o.s.i (*0-425-10569-5*); 1985. 208p. mass mkt. 2.95 o.s.i (*0-425-08796-4*); 1984. mass mkt. 2.95 o.s.i (*0-425-06787-4*) Berkley Publishing Group.
—The Moving Finger. 1982. 192p. pap. 2.95 o.p. (*0-440-15861-3*) Dell Publishing.
—The Moving Finger. l.t. ed. (Agatha Christie Ser.). 264p. 1990. pap. 12.95 o.p. (*0-8161-4562-8*); 1989. lib. bdg. 19.95 o.p. (*0-8161-4561-X*) Gale Group. (Macmillan Reference USA).
—The Moving Finger. 2000. (Miss Marple Mysteries Ser.). 224p. mass mkt. 5.99 (*0-451-20116-7*) NAL.
—The Moving Finger. 1986. (Agatha Christie Ser.). 12.95 o.s.i (*0-396-08803-1*, G. P. Putnam's Sons) Penguin Putnam Bks. for Young Readers.
—The Moving Finger. 1991. 10.60 (*0-606-12432-2*); 1984. 12.04 (*0-606-19947-0*) Turtleback Bks.
—The Moving Finger: A Miss Marple Murder Mystery. unabr. ed. 2001. audio 24.95 (*1-57270-123-4*, N41123u, Audio Editions Mystery Masters) Audio Partners Publishing Corp.
—The Moving Finger: A Miss Marple Mystery. unabr. ed. 1996. audio 54.95 (*0-7451-4045-9*, CAB742) BBC Audiobooks America.
—Mr. Parker Pyne, Detective. 1985. mass mkt. 2.95 o.s.i (*0-425-07999-6*); 1984. mass mkt. 2.95 o.s.i (*0-425-06788-2*) Berkley Publishing Group.
—Mr. Parker Pyne, Detective. l.t. ed. (Agatha Christie Ser.). 296p. 1990. pap. 13.95 (*0-8161-4564-4*); 1989. lib. bdg. 19.95 o.p. (*0-8161-4563-6*) Gale Group. (Macmillan Reference USA).
—Mr. Parker Pyne, Detective. 1986. (Agatha Christie Ser.). 14.95 o.s.i (*0-396-08865-1*, G. P. Putnam's Sons) Penguin Putnam Bks. for Young Readers.
—Mrs. McGinty's Dead. 1987. (HC Collection). 9.95 o.p. (*0-553-35059-5*) Bantam Bks.
—Mrs. McGinty's Dead. 1993. (Hercule Poirot Ser.). 304p. 24.95 (*0-399-13823-4*, G. P. Putnam's Sons) Penguin Group (USA) Inc.
—Mrs. McGinty's Dead. 1985. 240p. mass mkt. 3.50 o.s.i (*0-671-83440-1*); 1983. mass mkt. 2.95 o.s.i (*0-671-49806-1*) Simon & Schuster. (Pocket).
—Mrs. McGinty's Dead. l.t. ed. 1988. (Ulverscroft Large Print Ser.). 320p. 17.95 o.p. (*0-7089-1771-2*, Ulverscroft) Thorpe, F. A. Pubs. GBR. *Dist:* Ulverscroft Large Print Bks., Ltd., Ulverscroft Large Print Canada, Ltd.
—Mrs. McGinty's Dead. 1992. (Hercule Poirot Mystery Ser.). 12.04 (*0-606-12434-9*) Turtleback Bks.
—Mrs. McGinty's Dead: A Hecule Poirit Novel. 2000. (Hercule Poirot Mystery Ser.). 240p. mass mkt. 5.99 (*0-425-17545-6*) Berkley Publishing Group.
—Murder after Hours. 256p. 22.95 o.s.i (*0-8488-2447-4*) Amereon, Ltd.
—Murder at Hazelmoor. 1986. mass mkt. 2.95 o.s.i (*0-425-09471-5*); 1984. mass mkt. 2.95 o.s.i (*0-425-06789-0*) Berkley Publishing Group.
—Murder at Hazelmoor. 1970. 192p. pap. 2.50 o.s.i (*0-440-15940-7*) Dell Publishing.
—Murder at Hazelmoor. 1987. (Agatha Christie Ser.). 14.95 (*0-396-09013-3*, G. P. Putnam's Sons) Penguin Putnam Bks. for Young Readers.
—Murder at Hazelmoor. l.t. ed. 1973. (Ulverscroft Large Print Ser.). o.p. (*0-85456-203-6*, Ulverscroft) Thorpe, F. A. Pubs. GBR. *Dist:* Ulverscroft Large Print Canada, Ltd.
—Murder at the Vicarage. unabr. ed. audio 69.95 o.p. (*0-7451-6817-5*, CAB 611) BBC Audiobooks America.
—Murder at the Vicarage. (Agatha Christie Ser.). 1986. 240p. mass mkt. 5.99 o.s.i (*0-425-09453-7*); 1984. mass mkt. 2.95 o.s.i (*0-425-06790-4*) Berkley Publishing Group.
—Murder at the Vicarage. 1970. 224p. pap. 2.50 o.s.i (*0-440-15946-6*) Dell Publishing.
—Murder at the Vicarage. l.t. ed. (Agatha Christie Ser.). 408p. 1990. 12.95 o.p. (*0-8161-4566-0*); 1989. 16.95 o.p. (*0-8161-4565-2*) Gale Group. (Macmillan Reference USA).
—Murder at the Vicarage. 2000. (Miss Marple Mysteries Ser.). 256p. mass mkt. 5.99 (*0-451-20115-9*); 70th anniv. ed. (Illus.). pap. 12.00 o.s.i (*0-451-19978-2*) NAL. (Signet Bks.).
—Murder at the Vicarage. 1986. (Agatha Christie Ser.). 12.95 (*0-396-08804-X*, G. P. Putnam's Sons) Penguin Putnam Bks. for Young Readers.
—Murder at the Vicarage. abr. ed. 1997. (BBC Radio Presents Ser.). audio 18.00 o.s.i (*0-553-47767-6*, RH Audio) Random Hse. Audio Publishing Group.
—Murder for Christmas. 1987. (Agatha Christie Ser.). 224p. 14.95 (*0-396-09161-X*, G. P. Putnam's Sons) Penguin Putnam Bks. for Young Readers.
—Murder for Christmas. l.t. ed. 1987. 400p. (*0-7089-1724-0*, Ulverscroft) Thorpe, F. A. Pubs.
—Murder in Retrospect. 1985. mass mkt. 9.95 o.p. (*0-553-35038-2*) Bantam Bks.
—Murder in Retrospect. mass mkt. 3.50 o.s.i (*0-425-12575-0*); 1984. mass mkt. 2.95 o.s.i (*0-425-06792-0*) Berkley Publishing Group.
—Murder in Retrospect. 1970. 192p. pap. 2.50 o.s.i (*0-440-16030-8*) Dell Publishing.
—Murder in the Mews. abr. ed. 1984. audio 16.99 (*0-88646-090-5*, TC-LFP 7020) Durkin Hayes Publishing Ltd.
—Murder in the Mews. l.t. ed. 1986. 416p. o.p. (*0-7089-1443-8*, Ulverscroft) Thorpe, F. A. Pubs.
—Murder in the Mews. 1984. 12.04 (*0-606-00967-1*) Turtleback Bks.
—Murder in the Mews & Other Stories. 1987. (Hercule Poirot Mystery Ser.). 256p. mass mkt. 5.99 (*0-425-10435-4*) Berkley Publishing Group.
—Murder in Three Acts. 1988. (HC Collection). 9.95 o.p. (*0-553-35069-2*) Bantam Bks.
—Murder in Three Acts. 1986. mass mkt. 2.95 o.s.i (*0-425-09041-8*); 1984. mass mkt. 2.95 o.s.i (*0-425-06793-9*) Berkley Publishing Group.
—Murder in Three Acts. l.t. ed. (Agatha Christie Ser.). 360p. 1990. pap. 12.95 o.p. (*0-8161-4570-9*); 1989. lib. bdg. 19.95 o.p. (*0-8161-4569-5*) Gale Group. (Macmillan Reference USA).
—Murder in Three Acts. 1986. (Agatha Christie Ser.). 14.95 o.s.i (*0-396-08866-X*, G. P. Putnam's Sons) Penguin Group (USA) Inc.
—A Murder Is Announced. 1986. mass mkt. 9.95 o.p. (*0-553-35040-4*) Bantam Bks.
—A Murder Is Announced. 1991. (Miss Marple Mysteries Ser.). 240p. mass mkt. 5.99 o.s.i (*0-425-12962-4*) Berkley Publishing Group.
—A Murder Is Announced. l.t. ed. 1988. (Popular Author Ser.). 368p. pap. 9.95 o.p. (*0-8161-4572-5*); lib. bdg. 19.95 o.p. (*0-8161-4571-7*) Gale Group. (Macmillan Reference USA).
—A Murder Is Announced. 2001. (Miss Marple Mysteries Ser.). 240p. mass mkt. 5.99 (*0-451-20119-1*) NAL.
—A Murder Is Announced. 1967. (Agatha Christie Ser.). 12.95 (*0-396-08702-7*, G. P. Putnam's Sons) Penguin Group (USA) Inc.
—A Murder Is Announced. 1985. mass mkt. 3.50 o.s.i (*0-671-55267-8*, Pocket) Simon & Schuster.
—A Murder Is Announced. 1988. (G. K. Hall Audio Bks.). audio 69.95 o.s.i (*0-8161-9108-5*) Thorndike Pr.
—A Murder Is Announced. 1991. (Miss Marple Mysteries Ser.). 12.04 (*0-606-12436-5*) Turtleback Bks.
—A Murder Is Announced: A Miss Marple Mystery. unabr. ed. 1996. audio 69.95 o.p. (*0-7451-6818-3*, CAB297) BBC Audiobooks America.
—Murder Is Easy. 1981. (Agatha Christie Ser.). 8.95 (*0-396-08016-2*, G. P. Putnam's Sons) Penguin Putnam Bks. for Young Readers.
—Murder Is Easy. 1992. 12.04 (*0-606-12437-3*) Turtleback Bks.
—The Murder of Roger Ackroyd. Date not set. 277p. 23.95 (*0-8488-2236-6*) Amereon, Ltd.
—The Murder of Roger Ackroyd, unabr. ed. 2000. (YA). (gr. 10 up). audio 35.95 (*1-55685-638-5*) Audio Bk. Contractors, Inc.
—The Murder of Roger Ackroyd. unabr. ed. 1995. audio 54.95 o.p. (*0-7451-5836-6*, CAB 199) BBC Audiobooks America.
—The Murder of Roger Ackroyd. 2000. (Hercule Poirot Mystery Ser.). 256p. reprint ed. pap. 12.00 (*0-425-17651-7*) Berkley Publishing Group.
—The Murder of Roger Ackroyd. l.t. ed. 1989. 12.95 o.p. (*0-8161-4499-0*); 1988. 376p. lib. bdg. 19.95 o.p. (*0-8161-4460-5*) Gale Group. (Macmillan Reference USA).
—The Murder of Roger Ackroyd. 1976. (Crime Fiction Ser). reprint ed. lib. bdg. 21.00 o.p. (*0-8240-2360-9*) Garland Publishing, Inc.
—The Murder of Roger Ackroyd. 1985. (Agatha Christie Ser.). 276p. 12.95 o.s.i (*0-396-08574-1*, G. P. Putnam's Sons) Penguin Putnam Bks. for Young Readers.
—The Murder of Roger Ackroyd. 1989. (Hercule Poirot Mystery Ser.). 256p. mass mkt. 4.99 o.p. (*0-671-70118-5*, Pocket) Simon & Schuster.
—The Murder of Roger Ackroyd. l.t. ed. 1972. (Ulverscroft Large Print Ser.). 414p. 12.00 o.p. (*0-85456-144-7*, Ulverscroft) Thorpe, F. A. Pubs. GBR. *Dist:* Ulverscroft Large Print Bks., Ltd., Ulverscroft Large Print Canada, Ltd.
—The Murder of Roger Ackroyd. 1991. (Hercule Poirot Mystery Ser.). 12.04 (*0-606-12438-1*) Turtleback Bks.
—The Murder of Roger Ackroyd: A Hercule Poirot Novel. 2000. (Hercule Poirot Mystery Ser.). 256p. mass mkt. 5.99 (*0-425-17389-5*) Berkley Publishing Group.
—Murder on the Links, unabr. ed. 1998. 35.95 incl. audio (*1-55685-504-4*) Audio Bk. Contractors, Inc.
—Murder on the Links. 1984. (Hercule Poirot Mystery Ser.). 240p. mass mkt. 5.99 (*0-425-06794-7*) Berkley Publishing Group.
—Murder on the Links. 1983. pap. 2.95 o.p. (*0-440-16102-9*) Dell Publishing.
—Murder on the Links. l.t. ed. (Popular Author Ser.). 1991. pap. 12.95 o.p. (*0-8161-4574-1*); 1990. 323p. lib. bdg. 19.95 o.p. (*0-8161-4573-3*) Gale Group. (Macmillan Reference USA).
—Murder on the Links. 1987. (Agatha Christie Ser.). 224p. 14.95 o.s.i (*0-396-09162-8*, G. P. Putnam's Sons) Penguin Putnam Bks. for Young Readers.
—Murder on the Links. l.t. ed. 1990. (Ulverscroft Large Print Ser.). 12.00 o.p. (*0-85456-516-7*, Ulverscroft) Thorpe, F. A. Pubs. GBR. *Dist:* Ulverscroft Large Print Bks., Ltd., Ulverscroft Large Print Canada, Ltd.
—Murder on the Links. 1984. 12.04 (*0-606-00970-1*) Turtleback Bks.
—Murder with Mirrors. 1985. 192p. 9.95 o.p. (*0-553-35027-7*) Bantam Bks.
—Murder with Mirrors. 1986. (Agatha Christie Ser.). 14.95 (*0-396-08867-8*, G. P. Putnam's Sons) Penguin Putnam Bks. for Young Readers.
—Murder with Mirrors. 1990. mass mkt. 3.95 o.p. (*0-671-70603-9*, Pocket) Simon & Schuster.
—The Mysterious Affair at Styles. 22.95 (*0-88411-385-X*) Amereon, Ltd.
—The Mysterious Affair at Styles, 1995. audio 29.95 (*1-55685-373-4*) Audio Bk. Contractors, Inc.
—The Mysterious Affair at Styles. unabr. ed. 2004. audio compact disk 29.95 (*1-57270-297-4*); 1996. audio 22.95 (*1-57270-017-3*, N51017u, Audio Editions Mystery Masters) Audio Partners Publishing Corp.
—The Mysterious Affair at Styles. abr. ed. 2003. (Agatha Christie Audio Mystery Ser.). (Illus.). audio 12.95 (*1-55927-906-0*) Audio Renaissance.
—The Mysterious Affair at Styles. 1992. 19.95 incl. audio (*1-882071-21-2*); 1998. audio 19.95 (*1-882071-59-X*, 023) B&B Audio, Inc.
—The Mysterious Affair at Styles. 1983. 192p. mass mkt. 3.50 o.s.i (*0-553-26587-3*) Bantam Bks.
—The Mysterious Affair at Styles. 1920. E-Book (*1-58734-006-2*) Bartleby.com.
—The Mysterious Affair at Styles. 1991. 208p. mass mkt. 5.99 (*0-425-12961-6*) Berkley Publishing Group.
—The Mysterious Affair at Styles. audio 26.95 (*1-885546-07-6*) Big Ben Audio, Inc.

—The Mysterious Affair at Styles. unabr. ed. 2000. audio compact disk 48.00 (*0-7861-9928-8*, z1362); 1996. audio 39.95 (*0-7861-0410-4*, 1362) Blackstone Audio Bks., Inc.
—The Mysterious Affair at Styles. unabr. collector's ed. 1996. audio 48.00 (*0-7366-3226-3*, 3887) Books on Tape, Inc.
—The Mysterious Affair at Styles. 1997. (Dover Mystery Classics Ser.). 160p. reprint ed. pap. text 2.00 (*0-486-29695-4*) Dover Pubns., Inc.
—The Mysterious Affair at Styles. 1980. pap. 8.95 o.p. (*0-8161-3105-8*); 1976. lib. bdg. 10.95 o.p. (*0-8161-6343-X*); 1992. lib. bdg. 19.95 o.p. (*0-8161-4575-X*) Gale Group. (Macmillan Reference USA).
—The Mysterious Affair at Styles, unabr. ed. 1999. audio 39.95 Highsmith Inc.
—The Mysterious Affair at Styles. E-Book 2.95 (*1-57799-806-5*) Logos Research Systems, Inc.
—The Mysterious Affair at Styles. 1985. (Agatha Christie Ser.). 236p. 12.95 o.s.i (*0-396-08703-5*, G. P. Putnam's Sons) Penguin Putnam Bks. for Young Readers.
—The Mysterious Affair at Styles. 1999. E-Book 8.99 incl. cd-rom (*1-891595-60-1*) Quiet Vision Publishing.
—The Mysterious Affair at Styles. l.t. ed. 2001. (Ulverscroft Large Print Ser.). 32.50 o.p. (*0-7089-1955-3*) Ulverscroft Large Print Bks., Ltd.
—The Mysterious Affair at Styles & The Secret Adversary: An Agatha Christie Omnibus. 1998. 464p. pap. 12.95 (*0-7867-0434-9*, Carroll & Graf Pubs.) Avalon Publishing Group.
—The Mysterious Mr. Quin. 1987. (Hercule Poirot Mystery Ser.). 256p. mass mkt. 5.99 o.s.i (*0-425-10353-6*) Berkley Publishing Group.
—The Mysterious Mr. Quin. 1976. pap. 2.50 o.s.i (*0-440-16246-7*) Dell Publishing.
—The Mysterious Mr. Quin. l.t. ed. (Agatha Christie Ser.). 420p. 1992. pap. 13.95 o.p. (*0-8161-4578-4*); 1991. lib. bdg. 19.95 o.p. (*0-8161-4577-6*) Gale Group. (Macmillan Reference USA).
—The Mysterious Mr. Quin. l.t. ed. 1977. (Ulverscroft Large Print Ser.). 457p. o.p. (*0-85456-546-9*, Ulverscroft) Thorpe, F. A. Pubs. GBR. *Dist:* Ulverscroft Large Print Canada, Ltd.
—The Mystery of the Blue Train. Date not set. lib. bdg. 20.95 (*0-8488-2138-6*) Amereon, Ltd.
—The Mystery of the Blue Train. 1987. (Hardcover Collection). 9.95 o.s.i (*0-553-35068-4*) Bantam Bks.
—The Mystery of the Blue Train. 1991. (Hercule Poirot Mystery Ser.). 288p. reprint ed. mass mkt. 5.99 (*0-425-13026-6*) Berkley Publishing Group.
—The Mystery of the Blue Train. l.t. ed. 1992. 391p. 13.95 o.p. (*0-8161-4580-6*); 1991. 350p. 19.95 o.p. (*0-8161-4579-2*) Gale Group. (Macmillan Reference USA).
—The Mystery of the Blue Train. abr. ed. 1993. (BBC Radio Presents Ser.). audio 18.00 o.s.i (*0-553-47181-3*, RH Audio) Random Hse. Audio Publishing Group.
—The Mystery of the Blue Train. 1989. 224p. mass mkt. 4.99 o.p. (*0-671-70264-5*); 1985. mass mkt. 3.50 o.s.i (*0-671-60637-9*) Simon & Schuster. (Pocket).
—The Mystery of the Blue Train. l.t. ed. 1976. 423p. 12.00 o.p. (*0-85456-438-1*, Ulverscroft) Thorpe, F. A. Pubs. GBR. *Dist:* Ulverscroft Large Print Bks., Ltd.
—The Mystery of the Blue Train. 1991. 12.04 (*0-606-12445-4*) Turtleback Bks.
—N or M? unabr. ed. 1997. (Tuppence & Tommy Beresford Mysteries Ser.). audio 54.95 o.p. (*0-7451-5832-3*, CAB 653) BBC Audiobooks America.
—N or M? (Agatha Christie Ser.). 1998. mass mkt. 3.99 o.s.i (*0-425-16929-4*); 1986. 240p. mass mkt. 5.99 o.s.i (*0-425-09845-1*); 1986. mass mkt. 2.95 o.s.i (*0-425-09329-8*); 1984. mass mkt. 2.95 o.s.i (*0-425-06796-3*) Berkley Publishing Group.
—N or M? 1974. 192p. pap. 2.50 o.s.i (*0-440-16254-8*) Dell Publishing.
—N or M? 2000. (Tommy & Tuppence Mysteries Ser.). 224p. mass mkt. 5.99 (*0-451-20113-2*, Signet Bks.) NAL.
—N or M? 1987. (Agatha Christie Ser.). 14.95 o.s.i (*0-396-09163-6*, G. P. Putnam's Sons) Penguin Putnam Bks. for Young Readers.
—N or M? l.t. ed. 1984. (Ulverscroft Large Print Ser.). 336p. 32.50 (*0-7089-1156-0*, Ulverscroft) Thorpe, F. A. Pubs. GBR. *Dist:* Ulverscroft Large Print Bks., Ltd., Ulverscroft Large Print Canada, Ltd.
—Nemesis. abr. ed. 1998. audio 16.85 (*0-563-55728-1*) BBC Bk. Publishing GBR. *Dist:* Ulverscroft Large Print Bks., Ltd.
—Nemesis. (Agatha Christie Ser.). 1991. 400p. 12.95 o.p. (*0-8161-4582-2*); 1990. 368p. lib. bdg. 13.95 o.p. (*0-8161-4581-4*) Gale Group. (Macmillan Reference USA).
—Nemesis. (SPA.). 240p. 7.95 (*84-272-0294-6*) Molino, Editorial ESP. *Dist:* AIMS International Bks., Inc.
—Nemesis. 2000. 224p. mass mkt. 5.99 (*0-451-20018-7*, Signet Bks.) NAL.
—Nemesis. 1989. mass mkt. 4.99 o.p. (*0-671-70416-8*); 1984. mass mkt. 3.50 o.s.i (*0-671-54206-0*) Simon & Schuster. (Pocket).
—Nemesis. 1992. (J). 12.04 (*0-606-12448-9*) Turtleback Bks.
—One, Two, Buckle My Shoe. 2000. E-Book 5.99 (*0-425-17792-0*); 1998. mass mkt. 3.99 o.s.i (*0-425-16925-1*) Berkley Publishing Group.
—One, Two, Buckle My Shoe. Cooper, Roger, ed. 1987. 256p. reprint ed. mass mkt. 5.99 (*0-425-10570-9*) Berkley Publishing Group.
—One, Two, Buckle My Shoe. l.t. ed. 1973. (Ulverscroft Large Print Ser.). 322p. 12.00 o.p. (*0-85456-185-4*, Ulverscroft) Thorpe, F. A. Pubs. GBR. *Dist:* Ulverscroft Large Print Bks., Ltd., Ulverscroft Large Print Canada, Ltd.
—One, Two, Buckle My Shoe. 1984. 12.04 (*0-606-00968-X*) Turtleback Bks.
—Ordeal by Innocence. unabr. ed. 1997. audio 69.95 o.p. (*0-7451-5833-1*, CAB 593) BBC Audiobooks America.
—Ordeal by Innocence. 1987. 9.95 o.s.i (*0-553-35067-6*) Bantam Bks.
—Ordeal by Innocence. l.t. ed. (Agatha Christie Ser.). 1990. 384p. 13.95 o.p. (*0-8161-4584-9*); 1989. 350p. lib. bdg. 19.95 o.p. (*0-8161-4583-0*) Gale Group. (Macmillan Reference USA).
—Ordeal by Innocence. 1985. (Agatha Christie Ser.). 256p. 12.95 o.s.i (*0-396-08704-3*, G. P. Putnam's Sons) Penguin Putnam Bks. for Young Readers.
—Ordeal by Innocence. 1989. 256p. mass mkt. 3.95 o.p. (*0-671-70265-3*); 1985. mass mkt. 3.50 o.s.i (*0-671-54209-5*); 1983. mass mkt. 2.95 o.s.i (*0-671-47424-3*) Simon & Schuster. (Pocket).
—Ordeal by Innocence. 1991. 12.04 (*0-606-12463-2*) Turtleback Bks.
—An Overdose of Death. 1972. mass mkt. 2.95 o.s.i (*0-440-16780-9*) Dell Publishing.
—The Pale Horse. 1986. mass mkt. 9.95 o.p. (*0-553-35046-3*) Bantam Bks.
—The Pale Horse. 1985. (Agatha Christie Ser.). 256p. 12.95 o.s.i (*0-396-08705-1*, G. P. Putnam's Sons) Penguin Putnam Bks. for Young Readers.
—The Pale Horse. 1991. 224p. mass mkt. 3.95 o.p. (*0-671-70600-4*); 1983. mass mkt. 2.95 o.s.i (*0-671-47422-7*) Simon & Schuster. (Pocket).
—The Pale Horse. 2002. 288p. mass mkt. 5.99 (*0-312-98171-6*, St. Martin's Paperbacks) St. Martin's Pr.
—The Pale Horse. l.t. ed. 1987. (Ulverscroft Large Print Ser.). o.p. (*0-7089-1739-9*, Ulverscroft) Thorpe, F. A. Pubs. GBR. *Dist:* Ulverscroft Large Print Canada, Ltd.
—The Pale Horse. 1992. 12.04 (*0-606-12472-1*) Turtleback Bks.
—Partners in Crime. 224p. 21.95 o.s.i (*0-8488-2448-2*) Amereon, Ltd.
—Partners in Crime. 1987. (Agatha Christie Ser.). 240p. mass mkt. 5.99 o.s.i (*0-425-10352-8*) Berkley Publishing Group.
—Partners in Crime. 1971. 224p. pap. 2.50 o.s.i (*0-440-16848-1*) Dell Publishing.
—Partners in Crime. unabr. ed. audio 42.25 o.p. 1989. audio 15.95 o.p. Durkin Hayes Publishing Ltd.
—Partners in Crime. l.t. ed. 1986. 416p. (*0-7089-1540-X*, Ulverscroft) Thorpe, F. A. Pubs.
—The Patriotic Murders. 1986. mass mkt. 9.95 o.p. (*0-553-35042-0*) Bantam Bks.
—The Patriotic Murders. 1985. mass mkt. 2.95 o.s.i (*0-425-08900-2*); 1984. mass mkt. 2.95 o.s.i (*0-425-06797-1*) Berkley Publishing Group.
—The Patriotic Murders. l.t. ed. (Agatha Christie Ser.). 312p. 1990. 12.95 o.p. (*0-8161-4586-5*); 1989. lib. bdg. 20.95 (*0-8161-4585-7*) Gale Group. (Macmillan Reference USA).
—The Patriotic Murders. 1986. (Agatha Christie Ser.). 14.95 (*0-396-08868-6*, G. P. Putnam's Sons) Penguin Putnam Bks. for Young Readers.
—Peril at End House. 1991. (Hercule Poirot Mystery Ser.). 224p. mass mkt. 5.99 (*0-425-13025-8*) Berkley Publishing Group.
—Peril at End House. l.t. ed. (Popular Author Ser.). 281p. 1989. 13.95 o.p. (*0-8161-4588-1*); 1988. lib. bdg. 19.95 o.p. (*0-8161-4587-3*) Gale Group. (Macmillan Reference USA).
—Peril at End House. 1985. (Agatha Christie Ser.). 12.95 o.s.i (*0-396-08706-X*, G. P. Putnam's Sons) Penguin Putnam Bks. for Young Readers.
—Peril at End House. 1985. mass mkt. 3.50 o.s.i (*0-671-61120-8*); 1982. mass mkt. 2.95 o.s.i (*0-671-46538-4*) Simon & Schuster. (Pocket).
—Peril at End House. l.t. ed. 1978. (Ulverscroft Large Print Ser.). 327p. 12.00 (*0-7089-0153-0*, Ulverscroft) Thorpe, F. A. Pubs. GBR. *Dist:* Ulverscroft Large Print Bks., Ltd., Ulverscroft Large Print Canada, Ltd.
—Peril at End House. 1991. (Hercule Poirot Mystery Ser.). 12.04 (*0-606-12477-2*) Turtleback Bks.
—A Pocket Full of Rye. unabr. ed. 1995. audio 54.95 o.p. (*0-7451-5831-5*, CAB 099) BBC Audiobooks America.
—A Pocket Full of Rye. 2000. (Miss Marple Mysteries Ser.). 224p. mass mkt. 5.99 (*0-451-19986-3*, Signet Bks.) NAL.
—A Pocket Full of Rye. 1985. mass mkt. 3.50 o.s.i (*0-671-55796-3*); 1983. mass mkt. 2.95 o.s.i (*0-671-49203-9*); 1982. mass mkt. 2.75 o.s.i (*0-671-44727-0*) Simon & Schuster. (Pocket).
—A Pocket Full of Rye. l.t. ed. 1983. 384p. o.p. (*0-7089-1066-1*, Ulverscroft) Thorpe, F. A. Pubs.
—Poirot Investigates. 1983. mass mkt. 2.95 o.s.i (*0-553-23908-2*); 208p. mass mkt. 3.50 o.s.i (*0-553-27001-X*) Bantam Bks.
—Poirot Investigates. 2000. (Hercule Poirot Mystery Ser.). 256p. mass mkt. 5.99 (*0-425-17472-7*) Berkley Publishing Group.
—Poirot Investigates. unabr. ed. 1990. (Hercule Poirot Mystery Ser.). Set. audio 16.99 (*0-88646-168-5*, 7169); Vol. 2. audio 16.99 (*0-88646-237-1*) Durkin Hayes Publishing Ltd.
—Poirot Investigates. pap. 14.95 (*0-8161-4590-3*); 1992. 330p. lib. bdg. 19.95 o.p. (*0-8161-4589-X*) Gale Group. (Macmillan Reference USA).
—Poirot Investigates. l.t. ed. 2001. (Ulverscroft Large Print Ser.). 32.50 (*0-7089-2282-1*) Ulverscroft Large Print Bks., Ltd.
—Poirot Loses a Client. (Hercule Poirot Ser.). 1986. mass mkt. 2.95 o.s.i (*0-425-09038-8*); 1984. mass mkt. 2.95 o.s.i (*0-425-06799-8*) Berkley Publishing Group.
—Poirot Loses a Client. 1974. 224p. pap. 2.50 o.s.i (*0-440-16984-4*) Dell Publishing.
—Poirot Loses a Client. l.t. ed. (Agatha Christie Ser.). 420p. 1992. 14.95 o.p. (*0-8161-4592-X*); 1991. lib. bdg. 19.95 o.p. (*0-8161-4591-1*) Gale Group. (Macmillan Reference USA).
—Poirot Loses a Client. 1991. (Hercule Poirot Ser.). 336p. 22.95 (*0-399-13604-5*, G. P. Putnam's Sons) Penguin Group (USA) Inc.
—Poirot's Early Cases. l.t. ed. 2001. (Ulverscroft Large Print Ser.). 32.50 (*0-7089-2326-7*) Ulverscroft Large Print Bks., Ltd.
—Postern of Fate. 1974. (HC Collection). 288p. reprint ed. mass mkt. 3.50 o.s.i (*0-553-25493-6*) Bantam Bks.
—Postern of Fate. l.t. ed. (General Ser.). 1992. 376p. lib. bdg. 19.95 o.p. (*0-8161-4593-8*); 1985. 488p. 10.95 o.p. (*0-8161-3123-6*); 1974. 492p. reprint ed. lib. bdg. 11.95 o.p. (*0-8161-6197-6*) Gale Group. (Macmillan Reference USA).
—Postern of Fate. 2000. (Tommy & Tuppence Mysteries Ser.). 240p. mass mkt. 5.99 (*0-451-20053-5*, Signet Bks.) NAL.
—Postern of Fate. 1991. (General Ser.). 12.04 (*0-606-12483-7*) Turtleback Bks.
—Postern of Fate. l.t. ed. 2001. (Ulverscroft Large Print Ser.). 480p. 32.50 (*0-7089-2708-4*) Ulverscroft Large Print Bks., Ltd.
—The Regatta Mystery & Other Stories. 1986. 176p. mass mkt. 5.99 (*0-425-10041-3*) Berkley Publishing Group.
—The Regatta Mystery & Other Stories. 1976. mass mkt. 2.95 o.s.i (*0-440-17336-1*) Dell Publishing.
—The Regatta Mystery & Other Stories. l.t. ed. (Agatha Christie Ser.). 280p. 1990. 12.95 o.p. (*0-8161-4596-2*); 1989. 12.95 o.p. (*0-8161-4595-4*) Gale Group. (Macmillan Reference USA).
—The Regatta Mystery & Other Stories. 1986. (Agatha Christie Ser.). 229p. 12.95 o.s.i (*0-396-08805-8*, G. P. Putnam's Sons) Penguin Putnam Bks. for Young Readers.
—Remembered Death. l.t. ed. 368p. 1993. pap. 12.95 o.p. (*0-8161-4598-9*); 1992. lib. bdg. 19.95 o.p. (*0-8161-4597-0*) Gale Group. (Macmillan Reference USA).
—Remembered Death. 1984. mass mkt. 3.50 o.s.i (*0-671-54320-2*); 1982. mass mkt. 2.95 o.s.i (*0-671-46531-7*) Simon & Schuster. (Pocket).
—Sad Cypress. (Hercule Poirot Ser.). 1986. mass mkt. 2.95 o.s.i (*0-425-09328-X*); 1984. mass mkt. 2.95 o.s.i (*0-425-06801-3*) Berkley Publishing Group.
—Sad Cypress. 1970. 224p. pap. 2.50 o.s.i (*0-440-17552-6*) Dell Publishing.
—Sad Cypress. 1994. (Hercule Poirot Ser.). 320p. 24.95 (*0-399-13924-9*, G. P. Putnam's Sons) Penguin Group (USA) Inc.
—Sad Cypress. 1982. (Agatha Christie Ser.). 9.95 o.p. (*0-425-46801-1*, G. P. Putnam's Sons) Penguin Putnam Bks. for Young Readers.
—Sad Cypress. (Hercule Poirot Ser.). 9.95 o.s.i (*0-396-08112-6*) Putnam Publishing Group, The.
—Sad Cypress. abr. ed. 1993. (BBC Radio Presents Ser.). audio 16.99 o.s.i (*0-553-47132-5*, RH Audio) Random Hse. Audio Publishing Group.
—Sad Cypress. l.t. ed. 1965. (Ulverscroft Large Print Ser.). 384p. o.p. (*0-85456-690-2*, Ulverscroft) Thorpe, F. A. Pubs. GBR. *Dist:* Ulverscroft Large Print Canada, Ltd.
—Sad Cypress. 1984. (Hercule Poirot Mystery Ser.). 12.04 (*0-606-00971-X*) Turtleback Bks.
—Sad Cypress: A Hercule Poirot Mystery. unabr. ed. 1995. audio 54.95 o.p. (*0-7451-4186-2*, CAB 869) BBC Audiobooks America.
—Sad Cypress: A Hercule Poirot Novel. 1986. (Hercule Poirot Mystery Ser.). 240p. mass mkt. 5.99 (*0-425-09853-2*) Berkley Publishing Group.
—The Secret Adversary, unabr. ed. 1996. audio 35.95 (*1-55685-450-1*) Audio Bk. Contractors, Inc.
—The Secret Adversary. unabr. ed. audio 69.95 o.p. BBC Audiobooks America.
—The Secret Adversary. 1983. 224p. mass mkt. 3.50 o.s.i (*0-553-26477-X*) Bantam Bks.
—The Secret Adversary. 1991. (Agatha Christie Ser.). 240p. mass mkt. 5.99 o.s.i (*0-425-13027-4*) Berkley Publishing Group.
—The Secret Adversary, unabr. ed. 1998. audio 44.95 (*0-7861-1336-7*, 2230) Blackstone Audio Bks., Inc.
—The Secret Adversary. unabr. collector's ed. 1998. audio 56.00 (*0-7366-4213-7*, 4711) Books on Tape, Inc.
—The Secret Adversary. 1988. lib. bdg. 19.95 o.p. (*0-8161-4464-8*); 1989. 363p. 13.95 o.p. (*0-8161-4503-2*) Gale Group. (Macmillan Reference USA).
—The Secret Adversary, unabr. ed. 1999. audio 44.95 Highsmith Inc.
—The Secret Adversary. E-Book 1.95 (*1-58515-018-5*) MesaView, Inc.
—The Secret Adversary. 1999. E-Book 8.99 incl. cd-rom (*1-891595-61-X*) Quiet Vision Publishing.
—The Secret Adversary. l.t. ed. 2001. (Ulverscroft Large Print Ser.). 32.50 (*0-7089-2441-7*) Ulverscroft Large Print Bks., Ltd.
—The Seven Dials Mystery. 1983. mass mkt. 2.95 o.s.i (*0-553-23905-8*); 224p. mass mkt. 3.50 o.s.i (*0-553-26896-1*) Bantam Bks.
—The Seven Dials Mystery. 1986. (Agatha Christie Ser.). 14.95 o.s.i (*0-396-08871-6*, G. P. Putnam's Sons) Penguin Putnam Bks. for Young Readers.
—The Seven Dials Mystery. l.t. ed. 1984. (Ulverscroft Large Print Ser.). 400p. o.p. (*0-7089-1097-1*, Ulverscroft) Thorpe, F. A. Pubs. GBR. *Dist:* Ulverscroft Large Print Canada, Ltd.
—The Sittaford Mystery. unabr. ed. 2002. audio 25.95 (*1-57270-316-4*) Audio Partners Publishing Corp.
—The Sittaford Mystery. abr. ed. 1999. audio (*0-563-41062-0*) BBC Bk. Publishing GBR. *Dist:* Ulverscroft Large Print Bks., Ltd.
—The Sittaford Mystery. 1987. 240p. pap. 4.99 (*0-425-01040-6*); reprint ed. mass mkt. 5.99 o.s.i (*0-425-10406-0*) Berkley Publishing Group.
—The Sittaford Mystery. abr. unabr. ed. 1995. (BBC Radio Presents Ser.). audio 18.00 o.s.i (*0-553-47273-9*, RH Audio) Random Hse. Audio Publishing Group.
—Sleeping Murder. 22.95 (*0-88411-387-6*) Amereon, Ltd.
—Sleeping Murder. unabr. ed. 1997. (Miss Marple Mysteries Ser.). audio 54.95 o.p. (*0-7451-5834-X*, CAB 620) BBC Audiobooks America.
—Sleeping Murder. l.t. ed. (Agatha Christie Ser.). 1991. 336p. 13.95 o.p. (*0-8161-4600-4*); 1990. 298p. lib. bdg. 19.95 o.p. (*0-8161-4599-7*) Gale Group. (Macmillan Reference USA).
—Sleeping Murder. 2000. (Miss Marple Mysteries Ser.). 224p. mass mkt. 5.99 (*0-451-20019-5*, Signet Bks.) NAL.
—Sleeping Murder. l.t. ed. 1978. (Ulverscroft Large Print Ser.). 344p. 12.00 o.p. (*0-7089-0109-3*, Ulverscroft) Thorpe, F. A. Pubs. GBR. *Dist:* Ulverscroft Large Print Bks., Ltd., Ulverscroft Large Print Canada, Ltd.
—Sleeping Murder. 1992. 12.04 (*0-606-12521-3*) Turtleback Bks.
—Sparkling Cyanide. unabr. ed. audio 54.95 o.p. (*0-7451-6820-5*, CAB 316) BBC Audiobooks America.
—Sparkling Cyanide. 1988. audio 53.95 o.p. (*0-8161-9106-9*) Thorndike Pr.
—Sparkling Cyanide. l.t. ed. 1978. (Ulverscroft Large Print Ser.). 12.00 o.p. (*0-7089-0223-5*, Ulverscroft) Thorpe, F. A. Pubs. GBR. *Dist:* Ulverscroft Large Print Bks., Ltd., Ulverscroft Large Print Canada, Ltd.
—Sparkling Cyanide. 1992. 12.04 (*0-606-12526-4*) Turtleback Bks.
—Spider's Web. 2001. 304p. mass mkt. 6.99 (*0-312-97950-9*, St. Martin's Paperbacks); 2000. (Illus.). 223p. 23.95 (*0-312-26650-2*, Saint Martin's Minotaur) St. Martin's Pr.
—Taken at the Flood. (Agatha Christie Ser.). 1998. mass mkt. 3.99 o.s.i (*0-425-16927-8*); 1984. 256p. mass mkt. 5.99 (*0-425-06803-X*) Berkley Publishing Group.
—Taken at the Flood. l.t. ed. 1990. 386p. 12.00 o.p. (*0-85456-084-X*, Ulverscroft) Thorpe, F. A. Pubs. GBR. *Dist:* Ulverscroft Large Print Bks., Ltd.
—There Is a Tide. 1987. 9.95 o.s.i (*0-553-35066-8*) Bantam Bks.
—There Is a Tide. 1970. pap. 1.95 o.s.i (*0-440-18692-7*) Dell Publishing.
—There Is a Tide. l.t. ed. (Agatha Christie Ser.). 374p. 1992. pap. 12.95 o.p. (*0-8161-4604-7*); 1991. lib. bdg. 19.95 o.p. (*0-8161-4603-9*) Gale Group. (Macmillan Reference USA).
—There Is a Tide. 1988. 14.95 (*0-396-09299-3*, G. P. Putnam's Sons) Penguin Group (USA) Inc.

—They Do It with Mirrors. unabr. ed. 1995. audio 54.95 o.p. (*0-7451-5837-4*, CAB 086) BBC Audiobooks America.
—They Do It with Mirrors. 2000. (Miss Marple Mysteries Ser.). 224p. mass mkt. 5.99 (*0-451-19990-1*, Signet Bks.) NAL.
—They Do It with Mirrors. 1985. audio 53.95 o.p. (*0-8161-9897-7*) Thorndike Pr.
—They Do It with Mirrors. l.t. ed. 1987. (Ulverscroft Large Print Ser.). 16.95 o.p. (*0-7089-1737-2*, Ulverscroft) Thorpe, F. A. Pubs. GBR. *Dist:* Ulverscroft Large Print Bks., Ltd., Ulverscroft Large Print Canada, Ltd.
—They Do It with Mirrors. 1992. (Miss Marple Mysteries Ser.). 12.04 (*0-606-12440-3*) Turtleback Bks.
—They Do It with Mirrors: A Miss Marple Murder Mystery. unabr. ed. 2000. audio 24.95 (*1-57270-143-9*, N41143u, Audio Editions Mystery Masters) Audio Partners Publishing Corp.
—Third Girl. 1991. (Agatha Christie Ser.). 400p. 12.95 o.p. (*0-8161-4608-X*, Macmillan Reference USA) Gale Group.
—Third Girl. 1990. (Hercule Poirot Ser.). 208p. 21.95 o.s.i (*0-399-13512-X*, G. P. Putnam's Sons) Penguin Putnam Bks. for Young Readers.
—Third Girl. 1984. mass mkt. 3.50 o.s.i (*0-671-54212-5*); 1982. mass mkt. 2.95 o.s.i (*0-671-46719-0*) Simon & Schuster. (Pocket).
—Third Girl. 1992. (Hercule Poirot Mystery Ser.). 12.04 (*0-606-12536-1*) Turtleback Bks.
—The Third Girl. 2000. (Hercule Poirot Mystery Ser.). 272p. mass mkt. 5.99 (*0-425-17471-9*) Berkley Publishing Group.
—Third Girl. l.t. ed. 1990. (Agatha Christie Ser.). 360p. lib. bdg. 13.95 o.p. (*0-8161-4607-1*, Macmillan Reference USA) Gale Group.
—Third Girl. l.t. ed. 1989. 406p. 12.00 o.p. (*0-85456-585-X*, Ulverscroft) Thorpe, F. A. Pubs. GBR. *Dist:* Ulverscroft Large Print Bks., Ltd.
—Third Girl: A Hercule Poirot Mystery. unabr. ed. 1997. audio 54.95 o.p. (*0-7451-5838-2*, CAB 105) BBC Audiobooks America.
—Thirteen at Dinner. 224p. 21.95 o.s.i (*0-8488-2445-8*) Amereon, Ltd.
—Thirteen at Dinner. 1985. mass mkt. 2.95 o.s.i (*0-425-08902-9*); 1984. mass mkt. 2.95 o.s.i (*0-425-06805-6*) Berkley Publishing Group.
—Thirteen at Dinner. 1969. 240p. pap. 2.50 o.s.i (*0-440-18742-7*) Dell Publishing.
—Thirteen at Dinner. l.t. ed. (Agatha Christie Ser.). 1990. 368p. 12.95 o.p. (*0-8161-4610-1*); 1989. 340p. lib. bdg. 19.95 o.p. (*0-8161-4609-8*) Gale Group. (Macmillan Reference USA).
—Thirteen at Dinner. 1986. (Agatha Christie Ser.). 255p. 12.95 (*0-396-08806-6*, G. P. Putnam's Sons) Penguin Putnam Bks. for Young Readers.
—Thirteen at Dinner. 1992. audio 15.95 o.s.i (*0-553-74533-6*); audio 18.00 o.s.i (*0-553-47109-0*) Random Hse. Audio Publishing Group. (RH Audio).
—The Thirteen Problems. (Agatha Christie Ser.). 1998. mass mkt. 3.99 o.s.i (*0-425-16926-X*); 1985. 224p. mass mkt. 5.99 o.s.i (*0-425-08903-7*) Berkley Publishing Group.
—The Thirteen Problems. 2000. (Miss Marple Mysteries Ser.). 224p. mass mkt. 5.99 (*0-451-20020-9*, Signet Bks.) NAL.
—The Thirteen Problems. l.t. ed. 1968. (Ulverscroft Large Print Ser.). 358p. 12.00 o.p. (*0-85456-475-6*, Ulverscroft) Thorpe, F. A. Pubs. GBR. *Dist:* Ulverscroft Large Print Bks., Ltd., Ulverscroft Large Print Canada, Ltd.
—Three Act Tragedy. 1986. (Hercule Poirot Mystery Ser.). 224p. mass mkt. 5.99 (*0-425-09180-5*) Berkley Publishing Group.
—Three Act Tragedy. l.t. ed. 1989. 351p. 12.00 o.p. (*0-85456-326-1*, Ulverscroft) Thorpe, F. A. Pubs. GBR. *Dist:* Ulverscroft Large Print Bks., Ltd.
—Three Act Tragedy. 1984. (Hercule Poirot Mystery Ser.). 12.04 (*0-606-12538-8*) Turtleback Bks.
—Three Blind Mice & Other Stories. 1984. 224p. mass mkt. 5.99 o.s.i (*0-425-06806-4*) Berkley Publishing Group.
—Three Blind Mice & Other Stories. 1980. pap. 2.50 o.s.i (*0-440-15867-2*) Dell Publishing.
—Three Blind Mice & Other Stories. l.t. ed. (Popular Author Ser.). 338p. 1989. 10.95 o.p. (*0-8161-4462-1*); 1988. lib. bdg. 19.95 o.p. (*0-8161-4461-3*) Gale Group. (Macmillan Reference USA).
—Three Blind Mice & Other Stories. 1985. (Agatha Christie Ser.). 240p. 12.95 (*0-396-08707-8*, G. P. Putnam's Sons) Penguin Putnam Bks. for Young Readers.
—Three Blind Mice & Other Stories. 2001. 288p. reprint ed. mass mkt. 5.99 (*0-312-97976-2*, St. Martin's Paperbacks) St. Martin's Pr.
—Three Puzzles for Poirot. 1989. (Hercule Poirot Ser.). 400p. 29.95 o.s.i (*0-399-13496-4*, G. P. Putnam's Sons) Penguin Putnam Bks. for Young Readers.
—Thumbmark of St. Peter. unabr. ed. 1993. (Miss Marple Mysteries Ser.). audio 4.99 (*0-88646-649-0*) Durkin Hayes Publishing Ltd.
—Towards Zero. 1998. (Agatha Christie Ser.). mass mkt. 3.99 o.s.i (*0-425-16928-6*) Berkley Publishing Group.
—Towards Zero. 1985. mass mkt. 3.50 o.s.i (*0-671-60256-X*); 1982. mass mkt. 2.95 o.s.i (*0-671-47049-3*) Simon & Schuster. (Pocket).
—Towards Zero. l.t. ed. 1989. 347p. 12.00 o.p. (*0-85456-126-9*, Ulverscroft) Thorpe, F. A. Pubs. GBR. *Dist:* Ulverscroft Large Print Bks., Ltd.
—Towards Zero: Acting Edition. 1986. (Agatha Christie Ser.). 14.95 o.s.i (*0-396-08872-4*, G. P. Putnam's Sons) Penguin Putnam Bks. for Young Readers.
—The Tuesday Club Murders. unabr. ed. 2004. audio 25.95 (*1-57270-359-8*); audio compact disk 29.95 (*1-57270-360-1*) Audio Partners Publishing Corp.
—The Tuesday Club Murders. 1984. mass mkt. 2.95 o.s.i (*0-425-06807-2*) Berkley Publishing Group.
—The Tuesday Club Murders. 1971. 192p. pap. 2.50 o.s.i (*0-440-19136-X*) Dell Publishing.
—The Tuesday Club Murders. unabr. ed. 1987. audio 16.99 (*0-88646-196-0*, 7197) Durkin Hayes Publishing Ltd.
—The Tuesday Club Murders. l.t. ed. 1992. lib. bdg. 19.95 o.p. (*0-8161-4613-6*); 1989. 328p. 12.95 o.p. (*0-8161-4612-8*) Gale Group. (Macmillan Reference USA).
—The Under Dog & Other Stories. 1988. (HC Collection). mass mkt. 9.95 o.s.i (*0-553-35070-6*) Bantam Bks.
—The Under Dog & Other Stories. 1984. 208p. mass mkt. 5.99 (*0-425-06808-0*) Berkley Publishing Group.
—The Under Dog & Other Stories. 1969. 192p. pap. 2.25 o.s.i (*0-440-19228-5*) Dell Publishing.
—The Under Dog & Other Stories. l.t. ed. 1992. 290p. pap. 12.95 o.p. (*0-8161-4616-0*); 1991. 320p. lib. bdg. 19.95 o.p. (*0-8161-4615-2*) Gale Group. (Macmillan Reference USA).
—The Unexpected Guest: A Novel. unabr. ed. 1999. audio 24.95 (*1-55935-323-6*) Soundelux Audio Publishing.
—The Unexpected Guest: A Novel. 2000. 304p. mass mkt. 6.99 (*0-312-97512-0*, St. Martin's Paperbacks); 1999. (Illus.). 224p. 23.95 (*0-312-24262-X*, Saint Martin's Minotaur) St. Martin's Pr.
—The Unexpected Guest: A Novel. l.t. ed. 1999. (Basic Ser.). 215p. 30.95 (*0-7862-2201-8*) Thorndike Pr.
—What Mrs. McGillicuddy Saw! l.t. ed. (Popular Author Ser.). 1991. 12.95 o.p. (*0-8161-4618-7*); 1990. 342p. lib. bdg. 12.95 o.p. (*0-8161-4617-9*) Gale Group. (Macmillan Reference USA).
—What Mrs. McGillicuddy Saw! 1987. (Agatha Christie Ser.). 14.95 o.s.i (*0-396-09014-1*, G. P. Putnam's Sons) Penguin Putnam Bks. for Young Readers.
—What Mrs. McGillicuddy Saw! 1991. mass mkt. 3.95 o.p. (*0-671-70602-0*); 1983. mass mkt. 2.95 o.s.i (*0-671-49454-6*) Simon & Schuster. (Pocket).
—Why Didn't They Ask Evans? 1986. 240p. mass mkt. 5.99 o.s.i (*0-425-09855-9*) Berkley Publishing Group.
—Why Didn't They Ask Evans? 1971. 224p. pap. 2.25 o.s.i (*0-440-10704-0*) Dell Publishing.
—Why Didn't They Ask Evans? 1984. 12.04 (*0-606-00963-9*) Turtleback Bks.
—Witness for the Prosecution. 1985. mass mkt. 2.95 o.s.i (*0-425-07997-X*) Berkley Publishing Group.
—Witness for the Prosecution. 1972. pap. 2.50 o.s.i (*0-440-19619-1*) Dell Publishing.
—Witness for the Prosecution & Other Stories. 1984. 240p. mass mkt. 5.99 o.s.i (*0-425-06809-9*) Berkley Publishing Group.
—Witness for the Prosecution & Other Stories. abr. ed. 1986. audio 16.99 (*0-88646-169-3*, 7170) Durkin Hayes Publishing Ltd.
—Witness for the Prosecution & Other Stories. l.t. ed. 1989. 392p. 9.95 o.p. (*0-8161-4620-9*); 1988. 375p. 21.95 o.p. (*0-8161-4619-5*) Gale Group. (Macmillan Reference USA).
—Witness for the Prosecution & Other Stories. 1985. (Agatha Christie Ser.). 297p. 12.95 o.s.i (*0-396-08576-8*, G. P. Putnam's Sons) Penguin Putnam Bks. for Young Readers.
—Witness for the Prosecution & Other Stories. 1996. 12.04 (*0-606-00961-2*) Turtleback Bks.
—4:50 from Paddington. 2000. (Miss Marple Mysteries Ser.). 224p. mass mkt. 5.99 (*0-451-20051-9*, Signet Bks.) NAL.
—4:50 from Paddington. 1982. (Agatha Christie Ser.). 9.95 (*0-396-08110-X*, G. P. Putnam's Sons) Penguin Putnam Bks. for Young Readers.
—4:50 from Paddington. l.t. ed. 1965. (Ulverscroft Large Print Ser.). 391p. (*0-85456-474-8*, Ulverscroft) Thorpe, F. A. Pubs. GBR. *Dist:* Ulverscroft Large Print Canada, Ltd.
Christie, Agatha & Verner, Gerald. Towards Zero. 1957. per. 6.50 (*0-8222-1162-9*) Dramatists Play Service, Inc.
Clancy, Tom. Red Rabbit. 2002. 640p. 28.95 (*0-399-14870-1*); (Illus.). 896p. 150.00 (*0-399-14914-7*) Penguin Group (USA) Inc.
—Red Rabbit. l.t. ed. 2002. 33.95 (*0-7862-4064-4*) Thorndike Pr.
Clare, Alys. The Tavern in the Morning. mass mkt. (*0-312-98379-4*, St. Martin's Paperbacks); 2002. (Illus.). 240p. 23.95 (*0-312-26237-X*, Saint Martin's Minotaur) St. Martin's Pr.
Clare, Alys & Johnson-Hodge, Margaret. Fortune Like the Moon. 2000. (Hawkenlye Mysteries Ser.). (Illus.). 256p. 22.95 (*0-312-26162-4*, Saint Martin's Minotaur) St. Martin's Pr.
Clark, Carol Higgins. Decked: A Regan Reilly Mystery. 1993. (Super Sound Buy, Dove Ser.). 8.99 o.p. (*1-55800-804-7*); audio 16.95 o.p. (*1-55800-575-7*, Dove Audio) NewStar Media, Inc.
—Decked: A Regan Reilly Mystery. 1999. 288p. mass mkt. 4.50 o.s.i (*0-446-60777-0*); 1993. 288p. mass mkt. 7.99 (*0-446-36470-3*); 1992. 230p. 17.95 (*0-446-51549-3*) Warner Bks., Inc.
Clark, Catherine C. The Saturday Treat. 1993. 384p. 22.95 o.p. (*0-312-09908-8*) St. Martin's Pr.
Clark, Douglas. The Big Grouse: A Masters & Green Mystery. 1987. 224p. 18.95 o.p. (*0-575-03909-4*) Gollancz, Victor GBR. *Dist:* Trafalgar Square.
—The Big Grouse: A Masters & Green Mystery. 1988. 272p. reprint ed. pap. 3.95 o.p. (*0-06-080918-3*, P-918, Perennial) HarperTrade.
—Bouquet Garni. l.t. ed. 1986. 368p. 12.50 o.p. (*0-7089-1415-2*, Ulverscroft) Thorpe, F. A. Pubs. GBR. *Dist:* Ulverscroft Large Print Bks., Ltd.
—Dead Letter: A Masters & Green Mystery. l.t. ed. 1989. (Ulverscroft Large Print Ser.). 379p. 29.99 o.p. (*0-7089-1972-3*, Ulverscroft) Thorpe, F. A. Pubs. GBR. *Dist:* Ulverscroft Large Print Bks., Ltd., Ulverscroft Large Print Canada, Ltd.
—Doone Walk. l.t. ed. 1987. (Linford Mystery Library). 336p. pap. 17.99 o.p. (*0-7089-6394-3*, Linford) Thorpe, F. A. Pubs. GBR. *Dist:* Ulverscroft Large Print Bks., Ltd., Ulverscroft Large Print Canada, Ltd.
—Dread & Water. l.t. ed. 1991. 17.95 o.p. (*0-7451-9999-2*, AH035); pap. 15.95 o.p. (*0-7927-0463-0*, AS071) BBC Audiobooks America.
—The Gimmel Flask. 1982. (Murder Ink Mystery Ser.: No. 41). pap. 2.25 o.p. (*0-440-13160-X*) Dell Publishing.
—Golden Rain. 1982. (Murder Ink Mystery Ser.: No. 47). 224p. pap. 2.50 o.p. (*0-440-12932-X*) Dell Publishing.
—Heberden's Seat. l.t. ed. 1991. 17.95 o.p. (*0-7451-8118-X*, AH0167); pap. 15.95 o.p. (*0-7927-0618-8*, AS0203) BBC Audiobooks America.
—Heberden's Seat. 1985. 192p. mass mkt. 3.50 o.p. (*0-06-080724-5*, P724, Perennial) HarperTrade.
—Jewelled Eye: A Masters & Green Mystery. l.t. ed. 1987. pap. 13.95 o.p. (*1-55504-251-1*) BBC Audiobooks America.
—Jewelled Eye: A Masters & Green Mystery. 1986. 189p. 17.95 o.p. (*0-575-03728-8*) Gollancz, Victor GBR. *Dist:* Trafalgar Square.
—Jewelled Eye: A Masters & Green Mystery. 1988. 272p. reprint ed. pap. 3.95 o.p. (*0-06-080919-1*, P-919, Perennial) HarperTrade.
—The Longest Pleasure. 1984. 192p. reprint ed. pap. 2.95 o.p. (*0-06-080689-3*, P689) HarperCollins Pubs.
—The Monday Theory. 1985. 208p. mass mkt. 3.50 o.p. (*0-06-080737-7*, P737, Perennial) HarperTrade.
—Nobody's Perfect. l.t. ed. (Atlantic Mystery Ser.). pap. 8.95 o.p. (*1-55504-561-8*, 844) BBC Audiobooks America.
—Nobody's Perfect. 1986. 192p. reprint ed. mass mkt. 3.50 o.p. (*0-06-080796-2*, P 796, Perennial) HarperTrade.
—Performance. 1986. 224p. reprint ed. mass mkt. 3.50 o.p. (*0-06-080810-1*, P 810, Perennial) HarperTrade.
—Plain Sailing: A Masters & Green Mystery. 1988. 272p. reprint ed. pap. 3.95 o.p. (*0-06-080917-5*, P-917, Perennial) HarperTrade.
—Plain Sailing: A Masters & Green Mystery. l.t. ed. 1989. (Ulverscroft Large Print Ser.). 384p. 29.99 o.p. (*0-7089-2008-X*, Ulverscroft) Thorpe, F. A. Pubs. GBR. *Dist:* Ulverscroft Large Print Bks., Ltd., Ulverscroft Large Print Canada, Ltd.
—Poacher's Bag. l.t. ed. 1989. (Atlantic Mystery Ser.). pap. 14.95 o.p. (*1-55504-716-5*, 149) BBC Audiobooks America.
—Poacher's Bag. 1983. 176p. pap. o.p. (*0-06-080643-5*, P 643) HarperCollins Pubs.
—Roast Eggs. 1983. 176p. pap. o.p. (*0-06-080644-3*, P 644) HarperCollins Pubs.
—Shelf Life. l.t. ed. 1992. 18.95 o.p. (*0-7451-8252-6*, AH0262); pap. 16.95 o.p. (*0-7927-0812-1*, AS0298) BBC Audiobooks America.
—Shelf Life. 1983. 176p. pap. o.p. (*0-06-080675-3*, P675) HarperCollins Pubs.
—Sick to Death. l.t. ed. 1990. 17.95 o.p. (*0-7451-9897-X*, C0628); pap. 15.95 o.p. (*0-7927-0360-X*, C0822) BBC Audiobooks America.
—Sick to Death. 1983. 176p. pap. o.p. (*0-06-080676-1*, P676) HarperCollins Pubs.
—Storm Centre. 1986. 18.95 o.p. (*0-575-03833-0*) Gollancz, Victor GBR. *Dist:* Trafalgar Square.
—Storm Centre. 1988. (Master & Green Mystery Ser.). 240p. reprint ed. pap. 3.95 o.p. (*0-06-080920-5*, P-920, Perennial) HarperTrade.
—Storm Centre. l.t. ed. 1987. (Linford Mystery Library). 368p. pap. 17.99 o.p. (*0-7089-6388-9*, Linford) Thorpe, F. A. Pubs. GBR. *Dist:* Ulverscroft Large Print Bks., Ltd., Ulverscroft Large Print Canada, Ltd.
—Table d'Hote. 1985. 208p. mass mkt. 3.50 o.p. (*0-06-080723-7*, P723, Perennial) HarperTrade.
—Table d'Hote. l.t. ed. 1981. (Ulverscroft Large Print Ser.). 315p. 29.99 o.p. (*0-7089-0603-6*, Ulverscroft) Thorpe, F. A. Pubs. GBR. *Dist:* Ulverscroft Large Print Bks., Ltd., Ulverscroft Large Print Canada, Ltd.
—Vicious Circle: A Masters & Green Mystery. l.t. ed. 1988. pap. 14.95 o.p. (*1-55504-629-0*, 313) BBC Audiobooks America.
—Vicious Circle: A Masters & Green Mystery. 1985. 208p. reprint ed. mass mkt. 3.50 o.p. (*0-06-080778-4*, P 778, Perennial) HarperTrade.
Clark, Simon. Blood Crazy. 2001. 460p. 40.00 (*1-58767-028-3*) Cemetery Dance Pubns.
—Blood Crazy. 2001. 400p. mass mkt. 5.99 (*0-8439-4825-6*, Leisure Bks.) Dorchester Publishing Co., Inc.
—Darkness Demands. ltd. ed. 2001. 440p. 40.00 (*1-58767-008-9*) Cemetery Dance Pubns.
—Darkness Demands. 2001. 400p. mass mkt. 5.99 (*0-8439-4898-1*, Leisure Bks.) Dorchester Publishing Co., Inc.
Clarke, Anna. Cabin Three Thousand Thirty-Three. 1989. 3.50 (*1-55773-251-5*, Diamond Bks.) Berkley Publishing Group.
—Cabin Three Thousand Thirty-Three. 1986. (Crime Club Ser.). 192p. 12.95 o.p. (*0-385-23264-0*) Doubleday Publishing.
—Cabin Three Thousand Thirty-Three. l.t. ed. 1988. (Nightingale Ser.). 285p. 12.95 o.p. (*0-8161-4387-0*, Macmillan Reference USA) Gale Group.
—The Case of the Anxious Aunt. 1996. 208p. mass mkt. 5.99 o.p. (*0-425-15311-8*) Berkley Publishing Group.
—The Case of the Ludicrous Letters. 1994. 208p. (Orig.). mass mkt. 4.50 o.p. (*0-425-14048-2*) Berkley Publishing Group.
—The Case of the Paranoid Patient. 1993. 192p. mass mkt. 3.99 o.p. (*0-425-13858-5*) Berkley Publishing Group.
—The Case of the Paranoid Patient. l.t. ed. 1993. (Nightingale Ser.). 300p. lib. bdg. 15.95 (*0-8161-5845-2*, Macmillan Reference USA) Gale Group.
—Last Judgment. 1985. (Crime Club Ser.). 192p. 11.95 o.p. (*0-385-19666-0*) Doubleday Publishing.
—Last Seen in London. 1987. (Crime Club Ser.). 192p. o.s.i (*0-385-23559-3*) Doubleday Publishing.
—Last Seen in London. l.t. ed. 1992. 340p. pap. 14.95 o.p. (*0-8161-5452-X*, Macmillan Reference USA) Gale Group.
—Murder in Writing. 1990. 3.50 (*1-55773-326-0*, Diamond Bks.) Berkley Publishing Group.
—Murder in Writing. 1988. (Crime Club Ser.). 192p. pap. 15.00 (*0-385-24325-1*) Doubleday Publishing.
—Mystery Lady. 1986. (Crime Club Ser.). 192p. 12.95 o.p. (*0-385-23546-1*) Doubleday Publishing.
—The Whitelands Affair. 1992. mass mkt. 3.99 o.p. (*0-425-13268-4*) Berkley Publishing Group.
Clarke, Lindsay. Alice's Masque. 1994. 246p. o.p. (*0-224-03287-9*) Random Hse. UK, Ltd.
—The Chymical Wedding. 1997. 536p. pap. 25.00 (*0-449-00118-0*); 1991. 512p. mass mkt. 5.95 o.s.i (*0-8041-0702-5*, Ivy Bks.) Ballantine Bks.
Clarkson, Ewan. The Flight of the Osprey. 1996. 192p. 19.95 o.p. (*0-312-13973-X*) St. Martin's Pr.
—The Flight of the Osprey. l.t. ed. 1996. (Large Print Ser.). 368p. 29.99 o.p. (*0-7089-3567-2*, Ulverscroft) Thorpe, F. A. Pubs. GBR. *Dist:* Ulverscroft Large Print Bks., Ltd., Ulverscroft Large Print Canada, Ltd.
Claybourne, Casey. Thing of Beauty. 2000. 336p. mass mkt. 6.99 o.s.i (*0-425-17695-9*) Berkley Publishing Group.
Clayton, Mary. Pearls Before Swine. l.t. ed. 1995. (Magna Large Print Ser.). 337p. o.p. (*0-7505-0916-3*) Magna Large Print Bks. GBR. *Dist:* Ulverscroft Large Print Canada, Ltd.
—Pearls Before Swine. 1996. 256p. 21.95 o.p. (*0-312-14026-6*, Saint Martin's Minotaur) St. Martin's Pr.
Clayton, Victoria. Running Wild. 2002. 384p. pap. 16.95 (*0-7528-2517-8*) Orion Publishing Group, Ltd. GBR. *Dist:* Trafalgar Square.
—Running Wild. l.t. ed. 2002. (Charnwood Large Print Ser.). 560p. 32.50 (*0-7089-9312-5*, Charnwood) Thorpe, F. A. Pubs. GBR. *Dist:* Ulverscroft Large Print Bks., Ltd., Ulverscroft Large Print Canada, Ltd.
Cleeves, Ann. Another Man's Poison. 1993. mass mkt. 4.50 o.s.i (*0-449-14850-5*, Fawcett) Ballantine Bks.

—Another Man's Poison. l.t. ed. 1994. (Ulverscroft Large Print Ser.). 400p. 29.99 o.p. (*0-7089-3038-7*, Ulverscroft) Thorpe, F. A. Pubs. GBR. *Dist:* Ulverscroft Large Print Bks., Ltd., Ulverscroft Large Print Canada, Ltd.

—A Bird in the Hand. 1987. mass mkt. 4.99 o.s.i (*0-449-13349-4*, Fawcett) Ballantine Bks.

—A Bird in the Hand. l.t. ed. 1988. 416p. 15.95 o.p. (*0-7089-1830-1*, Ulverscroft) Thorpe, F. A. Pubs. GBR. *Dist:* Ulverscroft Large Print Bks., Ltd.

—Come Death & High Water. 1988. 224p. mass mkt. 4.50 o.s.i (*0-449-13348-6*, Fawcett) Ballantine Bks.

—Come Death & High Water. l.t. ed. 1989. (Ulverscroft Large Print Ser.). 29.99 o.p. (*0-7089-2101-9*, Ulverscroft) Thorpe, F. A. Pubs. GBR. *Dist:* Ulverscroft Large Print Bks., Ltd., Ulverscroft Large Print Canada, Ltd.

—A Day in the Death of Dorothea Cassidy. 1992. mass mkt. 4.99 o.s.i (*0-449-14789-4*, Fawcett) Ballantine Bks.

—A Day in the Death of Dorothea Cassidy. l.t. ed. 1993. (Mystery Ser.). 384p. 29.99 o.p. (*0-7089-2965-6*, Ulverscroft) Thorpe, F. A. Pubs. GBR. *Dist:* Ulverscroft Large Print Bks., Ltd., Ulverscroft Large Print Canada, Ltd.

—The Healers. 1995. (Stephen Ramsay Mysteries Ser.). mass mkt. 5.99 o.s.i (*0-449-14944-7*, Fawcett) Ballantine Bks.

—High Island Blues. 1996. mass mkt. 5.50 o.s.i (*0-449-14979-X*) Ballantine Bks.

—Killjoy. 1995. (Orig.). mass mkt. 4.99 o.s.i (*0-449-14893-9*, Fawcett) Ballantine Bks.

—A Lesson in Dying. 1990. 176p. mass mkt. 4.99 o.s.i (*0-449-14677-4*, Fawcett) Ballantine Bks.

—A Lesson in Dying. l.t. ed. 1992. (Ulverscroft Large Print Ser.). 336p. 29.99 o.p. (*0-7089-2566-9*, Ulverscroft) Thorpe, F. A. Pubs. GBR. *Dist:* Ulverscroft Large Print Bks., Ltd., Ulverscroft Large Print Canada, Ltd.

—The Mill on the Shore. 1994. mass mkt. 4.99 o.s.i (*0-449-14918-8*, Fawcett) Ballantine Bks.

—Murder in My Backyard. 1991. (Stephen Ramsay Mysteries Ser.). 256p. mass mkt. 4.99 o.s.i (*0-449-14720-7*, Fawcett) Ballantine Bks.

—Murder in Paradise. 1988. mass mkt. 4.99 o.s.i (*0-449-14540-9*, Fawcett) Ballantine Bks.

—Murder in Paradise. l.t. ed. 1990. (Ulverscroft Large Print Ser.). 29.99 o.p. (*0-7089-2200-7*, Ulverscroft) Thorpe, F. A. Pubs. GBR. *Dist:* Ulverscroft Large Print Bks., Ltd., Ulverscroft Large Print Canada, Ltd.

—A Prey to Murder. 1989. 192p. mass mkt. 4.99 o.s.i (*0-449-14575-1*, Fawcett) Ballantine Bks.

—A Prey to Murder. l.t. ed. 1991. (Ulverscroft Large Print Ser.). 29.99 o.p. (*0-7089-2386-0*, Ulverscroft) Thorpe, F. A. Pubs. GBR. *Dist:* Ulverscroft Large Print Bks., Ltd., Ulverscroft Large Print Canada, Ltd.

—Sea Fever. 1991. (Illus.). 192p. mass mkt. 3.99 o.s.i (*0-449-14707-X*, Fawcett) Ballantine Bks.

Cleland, John. Fanny Hill: Or Memoirs of a Woman of Pleasure. l.t. unabr. ed. 1991. (Large Print Bks.). 225p. 22.95 (*1-85089-454-X*, 89454X) ISIS Large Print Bks. GBR. *Dist:* Transaction Pubs., Ulverscroft Large Print Canada, Ltd.

—Fanny Hill: Or Memoirs of a Woman of Pleasure. 2001. (Modern Library Classics). 288p. pap. 9.95 (*0-375-75808-9*, Modern Library) Random House Adult Trade Publishing Group.

—Memoirs of a Woman of Pleasure. 1999. (Oxford World's Classics Ser.). 240p. pap. 8.95 (*0-19-283565-3*) Oxford Univ. Pr., Inc.

—Memoirs of a Woman of Pleasure. Sabor, Peter, ed. 1985. (WC-P Ser.). 236p. pap. 8.95 o.p. (*0-19-281634-9*) Oxford Univ. Pr., Inc.

—Memoirs of a Woman of Pleasure (Fannie Hill) (Early Best Sellers Ser.). reprint ed. lib. bdg. 48.00 (*0-7426-1011-X*) Classic Bks.

—Memoirs of a Woman of Pleasure (Fanny Hill) 1998. 270p. pap. text 15.00 (*0-7881-5871-6*) DIANE Publishing Co.

Clements, Bruce. The Treasure of Plunderell Manor, RS. 1987. 192p. (YA). (gr. 7 up). 15.00 o.p. (*0-374-37746-4*, Farrar, Straus & Giroux (BYR)) Farrar, Straus & Giroux.

Cline, Edward. Sparrowhawk: Jack Frake: A Novel. (Sparrowhawk Ser.: Bk. 1). 2002. pap. 13.50 (*1-931561-21-4*); 2001. 360p. 25.00 (*1-931561-00-1*) MacAdam/Cage Publishing, Inc.

Clitheroe, Susan. The Devil's Protection. 1995. 320p. 21.95 o.p. (*0-312-13466-5*) St. Martin's Pr.

Clive, Caroline A. Paul Ferroll. 1997. (Oxford Popular Fiction Ser.). 236p. pap. 9.95 o.p. (*0-19-283247-6*) Oxford Univ. Pr., Inc.

—Paul Ferroll. 2002. 244p. pap. 18.95 (*1-59224-848-9*); lib. bdg. 29.95 (*1-59224-849-7*) Wildside Pr.

—Paul Ferroll: A Tale. reprint ed. 44.50 (*0-404-61821-9*) AMS Pr., Inc.

Clynes, Michael, pseud. A Brood of Vipers: Being the Fourth Journal of Sir Roger Shallot Concerning Certain Wicked Conspiracies & Horrible Murders Perpetrated in the Reign of King Henry VIII. unabr. ed. 1998. audio 76.95 (*1-85903-164-1*) Magna Story Sound GBR. *Dist:* Ulverscroft Large Print Bks., Ltd.

—A Brood of Vipers: Being the Fourth Journal of Sir Roger Shallot Concerning Certain Wicked Conspiracies & Horrible Murders Perpetrated in the Reign of King Henry VIII. 1995. 256p. 21.95 o.p. (*0-312-13938-1*, Saint Martin's Minotaur) St. Martin's Pr.

—The Gallows Murders: Being the Fifth Journal of Sir Roger Shallot Concerning Certain Wicked Conspiracies & Horrible Murders Perpetrated in the Reign of King Henry VIII. 1996. 256p. text 21.95 o.p. (*0-312-14605-1*, Saint Martin's Minotaur) St. Martin's Pr.

—The Gallows Murders: Being the Fifth Journal of Sir Roger Shallot Concerning Certain Wicked Conspiracies & Horrible Murders Perpetrated in the Reign of King Henry VIII. l.t. ed. 1997. (Large Print Ser.). 448p. 29.99 (*0-7089-3789-6*, Ulverscroft) Thorpe, F. A. Pubs. GBR. *Dist:* Ulverscroft Large Print Bks., Ltd., Ulverscroft Large Print Canada, Ltd.

—The Grail Murders: Being the Third Journal of Sir Roger Shallot Concerning Certain Wicked Conspiracies & Horrible Murders Perpetrated in the Reign of King Henry the Eighth. unabr. ed. 1998. audio 76.95 (*1-85903-158-7*) Magna Story Sound GBR. *Dist:* Ulverscroft Large Print Bks., Ltd.

—The Grail Murders: Being the Third Journal of Sir Roger Shallot Concerning Certain Wicked Conspiracies & Horrible Murders Perpetrated in the Reign of King Henry the Eighth. 1994. 256p. reprint ed. 21.00 (*1-883402-49-2*, Scribner) Simon & Schuster.

—The Poisoned Chalice: Being the Second Journal of Sir Roger Shallot Concerning Wicked Conspiracies & Horrible Murders Perpetrated in the Reign of King Henry VIII. unabr. ed. 1998. audio 76.95 (*1-85903-137-4*) Magna Story Sound GBR. *Dist:* Ulverscroft Large Print Bks., Ltd.

—The Poisoned Chalice: Being the Second Journal of Sir Roger Shallot Concerning Wicked Conspiracies & Horrible Murders Perpetrated in the Reign of King Henry VIII. 1994. 288p. reprint ed. 20.00 (*1-883402-48-4*, Scribner) Simon & Schuster.

—The White Rose Murders: Being the First Journal of Sir Roger Shallot Concerning Wicked Conspiracies & Horrible Murders Perpetrated in the Reign of King Henry VIII. unabr. ed. 1998. audio 76.95 (*1-85903-113-7*) Magna Story Sound GBR. *Dist:* Ulverscroft Large Print Bks., Ltd.

—The White Rose Murders: Being the First Journal of Sir Roger Shallot Concerning Wicked Conspiracies & Horrible Murders Perpetrated in the Reign of King Henry VIII. l.t. ed. 1993. viii, 244p. 18.95 o.p. (*0-312-08920-1*, Saint Martin's Minotaur) St. Martin's Pr.

—The White Rose Murders: Being the First Journal of Sir Roger Shallot Concerning Wicked Conspiracies & Horrible Murders Perpetrated in the Reign of King Henry VIII. l.t. ed. 1995. (Ulverscroft Large Print Ser.). 464p. 29.99 o.p. (*0-7089-3218-5*, Ulverscroft) Thorpe, F. A. Pubs. GBR. *Dist:* Ulverscroft Large Print Bks., Ltd., Ulverscroft Large Print Canada, Ltd.

Cobbold, Marika. Guppies for Tea. 1994. 288p. 20.95 o.p. (*0-312-10992-X*) St. Martin's Pr.

—The Purveyor of Enchantment. l.t. ed. 1997. 240p. 22.95 o.p. (*0-312-18160-4*) St. Martin's Pr.

—The Purveyor of Enchantment. l.t. ed. 1998. (Romance Ser.). 293p. 28.95 (*0-7838-0122-X*) Thorndike Pr.

—The Purveyor of Enchantment. 2000. 235p. 27.95 (*0-593-04076-7*); pap. 12.95 (*0-552-99687-4*) Transworld Publishers Ltd. GBR. *Dist:* Trafalgar Square.

Cochran, Molly. The Broken Sword. 1997. 384p. 24.95 o.p. (*0-312-86283-0*, Tor Bks.) Doherty, Tom Assocs., LLC.

Cochran, Molly & Murphy, Warren. The Broken Sword. 1998. 480p. mass mkt. 6.99 (*0-8125-4513-3*, Tor Bks.) Doherty, Tom Assocs., LLC.

Cody, Liza. Backhand. 1992. 288p. mass mkt. 4.99 o.s.i (*0-553-29627-2*); mass mkt. 5.99 o.s.i (*0-7704-2531-3*) Bantam Bks.

—Backhand. unabr. ed. 1993. (Anna Lee Mystery Ser.: Vol. 6). audio 60.00 (*1-55690-808-3*, 93117E7) Recorded Bks., LLC.

—Backhand: An Anna Lee Mystery. 1992. 288p. 18.50 o.s.i (*0-385-42231-8*) Doubleday Publishing.

—Bad Company. 1983. 260p. 11.95 o.p. (*0-684-17760-9*, Macmillan Reference USA) Gale Group.

—Bad Company. 1992. pap. o.p. (*0-09-982120-6*) Hutchinson GBR. *Dist:* Random Hse. of Canada, Ltd.

—Bad Company. unabr. ed. 2000. audio compact disk 64.95 (*0-7531-0906-9*, 109069); 1997. audio 54.95 (*1-85695-740-3*, 940506) ISIS Audio Bks. GBR. *Dist:* Ulverscroft Large Print Bks., Ltd.

—Bad Company. 1984. 288p. mass mkt. 2.95 o.s.i (*0-446-30738-6*) Warner Bks., Inc.

—Bucket Nut. 1993. 240p. 18.50 o.s.i (*0-385-46776-1*) Doubleday Publishing.

—Bucket Nut. l.t. unabr. ed. 1998. 24.95 (*0-7531-5173-1*, 151731) ISIS Large Print Bks. GBR. *Dist:* ISIS Publishing.

—Bucket Nut. 1995. 224p. mass mkt. 5.50 o.p. (*0-446-40459-4*) Warner Bks., Inc.

—Dupe. 1992. mass mkt. 4.99 o.s.i (*0-7704-2439-2*); 256p. mass mkt. 4.99 o.s.i (*0-553-29641-8*) Bantam Bks.

—Dupe. 1981. 252p. 10.95 o.s.i (*0-684-17153-8*, Macmillan Reference USA) Gale Group.

—Dupe. 1992. pap. o.p. (*0-09-982110-9*) Hutchinson GBR. *Dist:* Random Hse. of Canada, Ltd.

—Dupe. 1984. mass mkt. 2.95 o.s.i (*0-446-30527-8*) Warner Bks., Inc.

—Head Case. l.t. ed. 1992. 18.95 o.p. (*0-7451-8282-8*, AH0274); pap. 16.95 o.p. (*0-7927-0951-9*, AS0310) BBC Audiobooks America.

—Head Case. 1989. 192p. reprint ed. mass mkt. 3.95 o.s.i (*0-553-27645-X*) Bantam Bks.

—Head Case. unabr. ed. 1997. audio 54.95 (*1-85695-745-4*, 940201) ISIS Audio Bks. GBR. *Dist:* Ulverscroft Large Print Bks., Ltd.

—Head Case: An Anna Lee Mystery. 1986. 196p. 13.95 o.s.i (*0-684-18586-5*, Macmillan Reference USA) Gale Group.

—Monkey Wrench. 1995. 256p. 18.95 o.s.i (*0-89296-600-9*) Mysterious Pr.

—Monkey Wrench. 1996. 240p. mass mkt. 5.99 o.p. (*0-446-40457-8*) Warner Bks., Inc.

—Muscle Bound. 1997. 288p. 22.00 o.p. (*0-89296-601-7*) Mysterious Pr.

—Stalker. 1986. 208p. mass mkt. 3.50 o.s.i (*0-446-32807-3*) Warner Bks., Inc.

—The Stalker. 1989. mass mkt. 1.95 o.s.i (*0-553-18503-9*) Bantam Bks.

—Stalker: A Mystery. 1985. 168p. 11.95 o.s.i (*0-684-18234-3*, Scribner) Simon & Schuster.

—Under Contract. 1990. 208p. mass mkt. 3.95 o.s.i (*0-553-28345-6*) Bantam Bks.

—Under Contract. unabr. ed. 1993. (Anna Lee Mystery Ser.: Vol. 5). audio 51.00 (*1-55690-929-2*, 93425E7) Recorded Bks., LLC.

—Under Contract: An Anna Lee Mystery. 1987. 16.95 o.p. (*0-684-18780-9*, Scribner) Simon & Schuster.

Cody, Pat. His Wicked Will. 2000. 320p. mass mkt. 4.99 (*0-8439-4791-8*, Leisure Bks.) Dorchester Publishing Co., Inc.

Coe, Jonathan. The House of Sleep. 1999. (Vintage Contemporaries Ser.). 352p. pap. 13.00 (*0-375-70088-9*, Vintage) Knopf Publishing Group.

—The House of Sleep. 1998. 337p. 24.00 o.s.i (*0-375-40093-1*) Knopf, Alfred A. Inc.

—The Rotters' Club. 2003. 432p. pap. 14.00 (*0-375-71312-3*, Vintage) Knopf Publishing Group.

—The Rotters' Club. 2001. 405p. (*0-670-89252-1*, Viking) Viking Penguin.

—The Winshaw Legacy: or What a Carve Up! 1996. 512p. pap. 15.00 (*0-679-75405-9*) Random Hse., Inc.

Coffman, Elaine. The Fifth Daughter. l.t. ed. 2002. (Wheeler Large Print Book Ser.). 28.95 (*1-58724-222-2*, Wheeler Publishing, Inc.) Gale Group.

—The Fifth Daughter. 2001. 448p. mass mkt. (*1-55166-842-4*, Mira Bks.) Harlequin Enterprises, Ltd.

Coffman, Virginia. Emerald Flame. 1996. (Jewels Ser.: Bk. 1). 320p. 24.00 (*0-7278-4890-9*); 416p. 28.00 o.p. (*0-7278-7000-9*) Severn Hse. Pubs., Ltd.

Colegate, Isabel. The Shooting Party. 1981. 192p. 11.95 o.p. (*0-670-64064-6*) Viking Penguin.

—Winter Journey. l.t. ed. 2001. (Senior Lifestyles Ser.). 323p. 28.95 (*0-7862-3374-5*) Thorndike Pr.

—A Winter Journey. 2002. 208p. reprint ed. pap. text 14.00 (*1-58243-250-3*, Counterpoint Pr.) Basic Bks.

Coleridge, Mary E. Gathered Leaves from the Prose of Mary E. Coleridge: With a Memoir by Edith Sichel. 1977. (Short Story Index Reprint Ser.). reprint ed. 29.95 (*0-8369-4006-7*) Ayer Co. Pubs., Inc.

Colgan, Jenny. Amanda's Wedding. 2001. 288p. E-Book 14.95 (*0-7595-6142-7*); E-Book 14.95 (*0-7595-9162-8*); E-Book 14.95 (*0-7595-0142-4*); E-Book 14.95 (*0-7595-4144-2*); E-Book 14.95 (*0-7595-8146-0*) Warner Bks., Inc.

—Talking to Addison. abr. ed. 2003. audio 9.99 (*1-58788-922-6*, 3440, Brilliance Audio Paperback Audiobooks); 2002. audio 19.95 (*1-58788-921-8*, 3439, Nova Audio Bks.); 2002. audio 29.95 (*1-58788-919-6*, 3437, Brilliance Audio Unabridged); 2002. audio 69.25 (*1-58788-920-X*, 3438, Unabridged Library Editions) Brilliance Audio.

—Talking to Addison. unabr. ed. 2003. audio 19.99 (*1-59335-171-2*, 30267) Soulmate Audio Bks., Inc.

—Talking to Addison. 320p. 2003. pap. 13.95 (*0-446-69015-5*); 2002. 23.95 o.p. (*0-446-52661-4*) Warner Bks., Inc.

Collier, G. K. The Gamester. 1994. 21.95 o.p. (*0-312-11277-7*) St. Martin's Pr.

Collier, Iris. Day of Wrath. l.t. ed. 2002. (Magna Large Print Ser.). 448p. 32.50 (*0-7505-1783-2*) Magna Large Print Bks. GBR. *Dist:* Ulverscroft Large Print Bks., Ltd., Ulverscroft Large Print Canada, Ltd.

—Day of Wrath. 2002. 320p. 24.95 (*0-312-29020-9*, Saint Martin's Minotaur) St. Martin's Pr.

Collins, Warwick. The Rationalist. 1994. 251p. 21.00 o.s.i (*0-671-86939-6*, Simon & Schuster) Simon & Schuster.

Collins, Wilkie. Armadale. 1999. (Works of Wilkie Collins: Vol. 8). reprint ed. Pt. 1. 579p. lib. bdg. 98.00 (*1-58201-029-3*); Pt. 2. 575p. lib. bdg. 98.00 (*1-58201-030-7*) Classic Bks.

—Armadale. 1977. (Illus.). 597p. pap. 9.95 o.p. (*0-486-23429-0*) Dover Pubns., Inc.

—Armadale. Peters, Catharine, ed. 1999. (Oxford World's Classics Ser.). 880p. pap. 12.95 (*0-19-283467-3*) Oxford Univ. Pr., Inc.

—Armadale. Peters, Catherine, ed. 1990. (Oxford World's Classics Ser.). (Illus.). 716p. pap. 11.95 o.p. (*0-19-281802-3*) Oxford Univ. Pr., Inc.

—Armadale, 2 vols., Set. 1988. reprint ed. lib. bdg. 150.00 (*0-7812-0752-5*) Reprint Services Corp.

—Armadale, 2 vols., Set. 1972. (Illus.). reprint ed. 69.00 (*0-403-00433-0*) Scholarly Pr., Inc.

—Armadale. Sutherland, John, ed. & intro. by. 1995. (Classics Ser.). 752p. 11.95 (*0-14-043411-9*, Penguin Classics) Viking Penguin.

—Hide & Seek. 1982. (Illus.). 384p. reprint ed. pap. 8.95 (*0-486-24211-0*) Dover Pubns., Inc.

—Hide & Seek. 1993. (Oxford World's Classics Ser.). 472p. pap. 9.95 o.p. (*0-19-283092-9*) Oxford Univ. Pr., Inc.

—The Legacy of Cain. 1993. (Pocket Classics Ser.). pap. 10.95 o.s.i (*0-7509-0453-4*) Sutton Publishing.

—Man & Wife. (Works of Wilkie Collins: Vol. 3). reprint ed. Pt. 1. 2001. 574p. pap. text 28.00 (*0-7426-5024-3*); Pt. 1. 1999. 574p. lib. bdg. 98.00 (*1-58201-024-2*); Pt. 2. 2001. 615p. pap. text 28.00 (*0-7426-5025-1*); Pt. 2. 1999. 615p. lib. bdg. 98.00 (*1-58201-025-0*) Classic Bks.

—Man & Wife. 1983. (Illus.). 239p. reprint ed. pap. 5.95 o.p. (*0-486-24451-2*) Dover Pubns., Inc.

—Man & Wife. 2002. 696p. 32.99 (*1-4043-1608-6*); per. 27.99 (*1-4043-1609-4*) IndyPublish.com.

—Man & Wife. 1999. E-Book 1.95 (*1-58515-264-1*) MesaView, Inc.

—Man & Wife. Page, Norman, ed. & intro. by. 1999. (Oxford World's Classics Ser.). 688p. pap. 14.95 (*0-19-283696-X*) Oxford Univ. Pr., Inc.

—Man & Wife. Page, Norman, ed. 1995. (Oxford World's Classics Ser.). 682p. pap. 13.95 o.p. (*0-19-283146-1*) Oxford Univ. Pr., Inc.

—The Moonstone. (World Digital Library). 2002. E-Book 3.95 (*0-594-08173-4*); 2000. 252p. E-Book 9.95 (*0-594-04118-X*) 1873 Pr.

—The Moonstone. 1965. (Airmont Classics Ser.). (gr. 10 up). mass mkt. 2.95 o.p. (*0-8049-0076-0*, CL-76) Airmont Publishing Co., Inc.

—The Moonstone. 1976. reprint ed. lib. bdg. 29.95 (*0-89190-241-4*, Rivercity Pr.) Amereon, Ltd.

—The Moonstone. unabr. ed. 1998. audio 71.95 (*1-55685-553-2*) Audio Bk. Contractors, Inc.

—The Moonstone. 1982. 464p. mass mkt. 4.50 o.s.i (*0-553-21156-0*, Bantam Classics) Bantam Bks.

—The Moonstone. unabr. ed. 1986. Pt. 1. audio 56.95 (*0-7861-0553-4*, 2047-A); Pt. 2. audio 49.95 (*0-7861-0554-2*, 2047-B) Blackstone Audio Bks., Inc.

—The Moonstone, Pt. 1. unabr. collector's ed. 1984. audio 64.00 (*0-7366-3896-2*, 9127-A) Books on Tape, Inc.

—The Moonstone. Farmer, Steve, ed. 1999. 720p. pap. (*1-55111-243-4*) Broadview Pr.

—The Moonstone. 1990. reprint ed. lib. bdg. 25.95 (*0-89968-498-X*) Buccaneer Bks., Inc.

—The Moonstone. (Works of Wilkie Collins: Vol. 7). reprint ed. 1999. 602p. lib. bdg. 98.00 (*1-58201-028-5*); Pt. 1. 1999. 580p. lib. bdg. 98.00 (*1-58201-027-7*); Pt.1. 2001. 580p. pap. text 28.00 (*0-7426-5027-8*) Classic Bks.

—The Moonstone. 1988. audio 87.95 Cover to Cover Cassettes, Ltd.

—The Moonstone. 2002. (Thrift Editions Ser.). 400p. pap. 3.50 (*0-486-42451-0*) Dover Pubns., Inc.

—The Moonstone. 1972. 5.95 o.p. (*0-460-01979-1*, Dutton) Dutton/Plume.

—The Moonstone. abr. ed. 10.00 o.p. (*0-06-010820-7*) HarperCollins Pubs.

—The Moonstone. l.t. ed. 1992. (Isis Large Print Bks.). 605p. 27.95 (*1-85089-543-0*) ISIS Large Print Bks. GBR. *Dist:* Transaction Pubs., Ulverscroft Large Print Canada, Ltd.

—The Moonstone. 2002. 528p. 23.99 (*1-4043-1934-4*); per. 18.99 (*1-4043-1935-2*) IndyPublish.com.

—The Moonstone. 1989. audio 89.00 Jimcin Recordings.

—The Moonstone. 1992. (Everyman's Library: Vol. 122). 480p. 17.00 (*0-679-41722-2*) Knopf, Alfred A. Inc.

—The Moonstone, Level 6. 2000. pap. 7.66 (*0-582-41822-4*) Longman Publishing Group.

—The Moonstone. 2002. 512p. mass mkt. 6.95 (*0-451-52829-8*); 1984. mass mkt. 2.95 o.p. (*0-451-51837-3*, Signet Classics); 1984. mass mkt. 3.50 o.p. (*0-451-52167-6*); 1984. mass mkt. 3.25 o.p. (*0-451-52031-9*, Signet Classics); 1984. 480p. mass mkt. 6.95 o.s.i (*0-451-52394-6*, Signet Classics) NAL.

—The Moonstone. abr. ed. 1995. audio 17.98 (*962-634-527-6*, NA302714); audio compact disk 19.98 (*962-634-027-4*, NA302712) Naxos of America, Inc. (Naxos AudioBooks).

—The Moonstone. 1998. 570p. reprint ed. lib. bdg. 25.00 (*1-58287-094-2*) North Bks.

—The Moonstone. 1999. (Oxford World's Classics Ser.). 576p. 16.50 o.p. (*0-19-210028-9*) Oxford Univ. Pr., Inc.

—The Moonstone. Trodd, Anthea, ed. & intro. by. 1998. (Oxford World's Classics Ser.). 572p. pap. 6.95 o.p. (*0-19-283471-1*) Oxford Univ. Pr., Inc.

—The Moonstone. Trodd, Anthea, ed. 1982. (Oxford World's Classics Ser.). 572p. pap. 6.95 o.p. (*0-19-281579-2*) Oxford Univ. Pr., Inc.

—The Moonstone. Sutherland, John, ed. 2nd ed. 2000. (Oxford World's Classics Ser.). 560p. pap. 6.95 (*0-19-283338-3*) Oxford Univ. Pr., Inc.

—The Moonstone. 1987. (Regents Illustrated Classics Ser.). 62p. (gr. 7-12). pap. text o.p. (*0-13-600677-9*, 20420) Prentice Hall, ESL Dept.

—The Moonstone. 2001. (Modern Library Classics). 528p. pap. 6.95 (*0-375-75785-6*, Modern Library) Random House Adult Trade Publishing Group.

—The Moonstone. 2002. (Best Mysteries of All Time Ser.). 557p. (*0-7621-8873-1*, IM Pr.) Reader's Digest Assn., Inc., The.

—The Moonstone. unabr. ed. 1989. audio 112.00 (*1-55690-348-0*, 89300E7) Recorded Bks., LLC.

—The Moonstone. E-Book 5.00 (*0-7410-1426-2*) SoftBook Pr.

—The Moonstone. 1984. 13.00 (*0-606-01905-7*) Turtleback Bks.

—The Moonstone. 1999. (Penguin Classics Ser.). 528p. 8.00 (*0-14-043408-9*) Viking Penguin.

—The Moonstone. Stewart, J. I., ed. & intro. by. 1966. (Penguin Classics Ser.). 528p. pap. 6.95 o.s.i (*0-14-043014-8*, Penguin Classics) Viking Penguin.

—The Moonstone. abr. ed. 1995. (Classics on Audio Ser.). 4p. pap. 23.95 o.s.i incl. audio (*0-14-086089-4*, Penguin AudioBooks) Viking Penguin.

—The Moonstone. 2002. 436p. 39.95 (*1-59224-786-5*) Wildside Pr.

—The Moonstone. 1997. (Classics Ser.). 464p. pap. 3.95 (*1-85326-044-4*, 0444WW) Wordsworth Editions, Ltd. GBR. *Dist:* Combined Publishing.

—The New Magdalen. 1993. (Pocket Classics Ser.). pap. 8.95 (*0-7509-0455-0*) Sutton Publishing, Ltd. GBR. *Dist:* International Publishers Marketing.

—No Name. unabr. ed. Vol. 1. 1998. audio 77.95 (*1-55685-511-7*); Vol. II. audio 35.95 Audio Bk. Contractors, Inc.

—No Name. (Works of Wilkie Collins: Vol. 12). 576p. reprint ed. Pt. 1. 1999. lib. bdg. 98.00 (*1-58201-033-1*); Pt.1. 2001. pap. text 28.00 (*0-7426-5033-2*) Classic Bks.

—No Name. 2002. Vol. 1. 328p. 96.99 (*1-4043-2184-5*); Vol. 1. 328p. per. 91.99 (*1-4043-2185-3*); Vol. 2. 436p. 98.99 (*1-4043-2186-1*); Vol. 2. 436p. per. 93.99 (*1-4043-2187-X*) IndyPublish.com.

—No Name. Blain, Virginia, ed. & intro. by. 1998. (Oxford World's Classics Ser.). (Illus.). 784p. pap. 11.95 (*0-19-283388-X*) Oxford Univ. Pr., Inc.

—No Name. 1995. (Classics Ser.). 640p. pap. 14.00 (*0-14-043397-X*, Penguin Classics) Viking Penguin.

—Poor Miss Finch. Peters, Catherine, ed. 1995. (Oxford World's Classics Ser.). 470p. pap. 11.95 o.p. (*0-19-282322-1*) Oxford Univ. Pr., Inc.

—Poor Miss Finch. 1972. (Literature Ser.). (Illus.). 454p. reprint ed. 69.00 (*0-403-00559-0*) Scholarly Pr., Inc.

—The Woman in White. 1976. reprint ed. lib. bdg. 35.95 (*0-89190-242-2*, Rivercity Pr.) Amereon, Ltd.

—The Woman in White, Set. unabr. ed. 1998. 89.95 incl. audio (*1-55685-525-7*) Audio Bk. Contractors, Inc.

—The Woman in White. unabr. ed. audio 114.95 o.p. (*1-85549-918-5*, CTC 018) BBC Audiobooks America.

—The Woman in White. 1985. 576p. mass mkt. 5.95 (*0-553-21263-X*, Bantam Classics) Bantam Bks.

—The Woman in White, Pt. 1. unabr. collector's ed. 1987. audio 80.00 (*0-7366-3931-4*, 9169-A) Books on Tape, Inc.

—The Woman in White. 1990. reprint ed. lib. bdg. 30.95 (*0-89968-499-8*) Buccaneer Bks., Inc.

—The Woman in White. 1999. (Works of Wilkie Collins: Vol. 1). reprint ed. Pt. 1. 575p. lib. bdg. 98.00 (*1-58201-022-6*); Pt. 2. 556p. lib. bdg. 98.00 (*1-58201-023-4*) Classic Bks.

—The Woman in White. audio 97.95 Cover to Cover Cassettes, Ltd.

—The Woman in White, 001. Tillotson, Kathleen, ed. 1969. (C). mass mkt. 3.95 o.p. (*0-395-05211-4*, B116, Riverside Editions) Houghton Mifflin Co.

—The Woman in White. 1989. audio 89.00 Jimcin Recordings.

—The Woman in White. 1991. (Everyman's Library). 656p. 20.00 (*0-679-40563-1*, Everyman's Library) Knopf Publishing Group.

—The Woman in White. 1985. 630p. mass mkt. 5.95 o.s.i (*0-451-52437-3*, Signet Classics) NAL.

—The Woman in White. Sutherland, John, ed. & intro. by. 1998. (Oxford World's Classics Ser.). 736p. pap. 7.95 (*0-19-283429-0*) Oxford Univ. Pr., Inc.

—The Woman in White. Sucksmith, Harvey P., ed. 1981. (Oxford World's Classics Ser.). 662p. reprint ed. pap. 5.95 o.p. (*0-19-281534-2*) Oxford Univ. Pr., Inc.

—The Woman in White. Sutherland, John, ed. 2nd ed. 1996. (Oxford World's Classics Ser.). 734p. (C). pap. 6.95 o.p. (*0-19-282403-1*) Oxford Univ. Pr., Inc.

—The Woman in White. 2002. (Modern Library Classics). 704p. pap. 7.95 (*0-375-75906-9*, Modern Library) Random House Adult Trade Publishing Group.

—The Woman in White. 1998. (Works of Wilkie Collins: Vol. 1). 575p. reprint ed. lib. bdg. 90.00 (*0-7812-7716-7*) Reprint Services Corp.

—The Woman in White. (Classics Ser.). 720p. 2003. pap. 8.00 (*0-14-143961-0*, Penguin Classics); 2000. 7.95 (*0-14-043731-2*) Viking Penguin.

—The Woman in White. Symons, Julian, ed. 1982. pap. 3.95 o.p. (*0-14-005980-6*, Penguin Bks.); 1975. 656p. pap. 7.95 o.s.i (*0-14-043096-2*, Penguin Classics) Viking Penguin.

—The Woman in White. abr. ed. 1995. 4p. 23.95 o.s.i incl. audio (*0-14-086061-4*, Penguin AudioBooks) Viking Penguin.

—The Woman in White. 1998. (Wordsworth Collection). 512p. pap. 3.95 (*1-85326-077-0*, 0770WW) Wordsworth Editions, Ltd. GBR. *Dist:* Combined Publishing.

Collins, Wilkie & Farmer, Steve. The Moonstone. 1999. E-Book 9.95 (*0-585-27957-8*) netLibrary, Inc.

Collins, Wilkie & Sutherland, John. The Moonstone. 1999. E-Book 7.30 (*0-585-36165-7*) netLibrary, Inc.

Collum, Lynn. The Christmas Charm. 2000. (Zebra Regency Romance Ser.). 224p. mass mkt. 4.99 o.s.i (*0-8217-6738-0*, Zebra Bks.) Kensington Publishing Corp.

—The Valentine Charm. 2001. (Zebra Regency Romance Ser.). 224p. mass mkt. 4.99 o.s.i (*0-8217-7108-6*) Kensington Publishing Corp.

—The Wedding Charm. 2001. (Addingtons Trilogy Ser.: No. 3). 224p. mass mkt. 4.99 o.s.i (*0-8217-6804-2*, Zebra Bks.) Kensington Publishing Corp.

Compo, Susan. Malingering: Short Stories. 1993. 220p. (Orig.). pap. 13.95 o.p. (*0-571-19818-X*) Faber & Faber, Inc.

Conlon, Kathleen. The Best of Friends. 1984. 368p. 14.95 o.p. (*0-312-07714-9*) St. Martin's Pr.

Connell, Vivian. The Chinese Room. 2003. 256p. pap. 12.00 (*1-56980-264-5*) Barricade Bks., Inc.

Connolly, Cressida. The Happiest Days: Short Stories. 192p. 2001. pap. 12.00 (*0-312-28323-7*); 2000. 20.00 o.s.i (*0-312-26171-3*) Picador.

Connolly, Joseph. Winter Breaks. 1999. 336p. pap. (*0-571-19685-3*) Faber & Faber, Inc.

Connoly, Joseph. Summer Things. 1999. 336p. pap. 16.95 (*0-571-19076-6*) Faber & Faber, Inc.

Connor, Alexandra. Angel Passing Over. 2000. 552p. (*0-00-225935-4*) HarperCollins Pubs.

Conrad, Joseph. The Secret Agent. 1992. (Everyman's Library). 352p. (Orig.). 17.00 (*0-679-41723-0*) Knopf, Alfred A. Inc.

—The Secret Agent. Tennant, Roger, ed. 1996. (Oxford World's Classics Ser.). 356p. (Orig.). (C). pap. 6.95 o.p. (*0-19-281627-6*) Oxford Univ. Pr., Inc.

—The Secret Agent & Almayer's Folly. 1983. 240p. mass mkt. 3.50 o.s.i (*0-553-21134-X*, Bantam Classics) Bantam Bks.

Conway, Sara. Murder on Good Friday. 2001. (Illus.). 312p. 22.95 (*1-58182-188-3*) Cumberland Hse. Publishing.

Cook, Bob. Fire & Forget. l.t. ed. 2000. (Dales Large Print Ser.). 352p. pap. 20.99 (*1-84262-025-8*) Dales Large Print Bks. GBR. *Dist:* Ulverscroft Large Print Bks., Ltd., Ulverscroft Large Print Canada, Ltd.

—Fire & Forget. l.t. ed. 2000. pap. 20.99 (*1-84137-039-8*) Magna Large Print Bks. GBR. *Dist:* Ulverscroft Large Print Bks., Ltd.

—Fire & Forget. 1990. 15.95 o.p. (*0-312-05431-9*, Saint Martin's Minotaur) St. Martin's Pr.

Cook, Linda. Silver Wind. 2001. (Zebra Historical Romance Ser.). 352p. mass mkt. 5.99 o.s.i (*0-8217-6870-0*) Kensington Publishing Corp.

Cook, Stephen. Dead Fit. 1993. 189p. 16.95 o.p. (*0-312-08756-X*, Saint Martin's Minotaur) St. Martin's Pr.

—One Dead Tory. 1994. (Detective Sergeant Judy Best Novel Ser.). 224p. reprint ed. 20.00 o.p. (*0-88150-302-9*) Countryman Pr.

Cooke, Trish. So Much. 1994. (Illus.). 32p. (YA). (ps-3). 16.99 o.s.i (*1-56402-344-3*) Candlewick Pr.

Cookson, Catherine. The Bannaman Legacy. 1985. 528p. 18.45 o.p. (*0-671-53024-0*) Summit Bks.

—The Black Candle. 1990. 19.95 o.p. (*0-671-70176-2*, Simon & Schuster) Simon & Schuster.

—The Black Velvet Gown. l.t. ed. 1993. 22.95 o.p. (*0-7927-1674-4*); pap. 20.95 o.p. (*0-7927-1673-6*) BBC Audiobooks America.

—The Black Velvet Gown. 1984. 368p. 16.45 o.p. (*0-671-46788-3*) Summit Bks.

—The Blind Years. 2000. 264p. mass mkt. (*0-552-14609-9*); 1998. 192p. o.s.i (*0-593-04287-5*) Bantam Bks. (Corgi).

—The Branded Man. l.t. ed. 2001. 400p. lib. bdg. 29.95 (*1-58547-067-8*) Ctr. Point Large Print.

—The Branded Man. 2000. 480p. mass mkt. 11.95 (*0-552-14348-0*) Transworld Publishers Ltd. GBR. *Dist:* Trafalgar Square.

—The Desert Crop. unabr. ed. 1998. audio 69.95 (*0-7540-0151-2*, CAB 1574) BBC Audiobooks America.

—The Desert Crop. 2000. 384p. mass mkt. (*1-55166-583-2*, Harlequin Bks.) Harlequin Enterprises, Ltd.

—The Desert Crop. 1999. 320p. 23.00 (*0-684-85683-2*, Simon & Schuster) Simon & Schuster.

—The Desert Crop. 16th l.t. ed. 1999. (Basic Ser.). 483p. 29.95 (*0-7862-1830-4*) Thorndike Pr.

—The Desert Crop. 2000. 320p. 29.95 (*0-593-03476-7*); 1998. (Illus.). 512p. mass mkt. 10.95 (*0-552-14156-9*) Transworld Publishers Ltd. GBR. *Dist:* Trafalgar Square.

—Fenwick Houses. 1987. mass mkt. 3.95 o.s.i (*0-552-13165-2*) Bantam Bks.

—Fenwick Houses. 2000. 381p. pap. 9.95 (*0-552-14069-4*); 1988. mass mkt. o.s.i (*0-552-08353-4*) Transworld Publishers Ltd. GBR. *Dist:* Trafalgar Square, Random Hse. of Canada, Ltd.

—The Fifteen Streets. 1982. mass mkt. o.s.i (*0-552-08419-0*, Corgi) Bantam Bks.

—The Fifteen Streets. l.t. ed. 2003. 399p. 32.95 (*0-7862-5137-9*) Thorndike Pr.

—The Girl. l.t. ed. 1993. 20.95 o.p. (*0-7927-1438-5*); 1993. pap. o.p. (*0-7927-1439-3*); 1996. audio 69.95 (*0-7451-4143-9*, CAB826) BBC Audiobooks America.

—The Girl. 1978. pap. 2.25 o.p. (*0-553-14187-2*) Bantam Bks.

—The Girl. unabr. collector's ed. 1985. audio 56.00 (*0-7366-0948-2*, 1891) Books on Tape, Inc.

—The Girl. 1982. mass mkt. o.s.i (*0-552-10916-9*) Corgi Bks. Ltd.

—The Girl. 1998. 384p. mass mkt. 10.95 (*0-552-14468-1*) Transworld Publishers Ltd. GBR. *Dist:* Trafalgar Square.

—The Golden Straw. unabr. ed. 1994. audio 110.95 (*0-7451-4320-2*, CAB 1003) BBC Audiobooks America.

—The Golden Straw. 1995. 496p. 23.00 (*0-684-81177-4*, Simon & Schuster) Simon & Schuster.

—The Golden Straw. l.t. ed. 1996. (Basic Ser.). 805p. 26.95 o.p. (*0-7862-0588-1*) Thorndike Pr.

—The Golden Straw. 1995. 416p. mass mkt. 11.95 (*0-552-13685-9*) Transworld Publishers Ltd. GBR. *Dist:* Trafalgar Square.

—Hamilton Trilogy. 2000. 908p. pap. 12.95 (*0-552-14703-6*) Transworld Publishers Ltd. GBR. *Dist:* Trafalgar Square.

—Harold. 263p. (J). mass mkt. 9.95 o.p. (*0-552-12789-2*) Transworld Publishers Ltd. GBR. *Dist:* Trafalgar Square.

—The Harrogate Secret. l.t. ed. 1989. 536p. 21.95 o.p. (*0-8161-4667-5*, Macmillan Reference USA) Gale Group.

—The Harrogate Secret. 1988. 18.95 o.p. (*0-671-65941-3*) Summit Bks.

—Heritage of Folly. 1995. 288p. mass mkt. 10.95 (*0-552-14087-2*) Transworld Publishers Ltd. GBR. *Dist:* Trafalgar Square.

—Heritage of Folly & The Fen Tiger. 2000. 569p. pap. 11.95 (*0-552-14701-X*) Transworld Publishers Ltd. GBR. *Dist:* Trafalgar Square.

—A House Divided. l.t. ed. 2000. (Basic Ser.). 548p. 30.95 (*0-7862-2917-9*) Thorndike Pr.

—House of Men. l.t. ed. 2002. lib. bdg. 29.95 (*1-58547-070-8*, Platinum) Ctr. Point Large Print.

—House of Men. 2000. pap. 10.95 (*0-552-14088-0*) Transworld Publishers Ltd. GBR. *Dist:* Trafalgar Square.

—The Iron Facade & House of Men Omnibus. 2000. 508p. pap. 10.95 (*0-552-14700-1*) Transworld Publishers Ltd. GBR. *Dist:* Trafalgar Square.

—Justice Is a Woman. 1994. 318p. o.s.i (*0-593-01936-9*, Corgi) Bantam Bks.

—Justice Is a Woman. l.t. ed. 2001. 320p. lib. bdg. 29.95 (*1-58547-065-1*) Ctr. Point Large Print.

—Justice Is a Woman. 1995. 384p. mass mkt. 10.95 (*0-552-13622-0*) Transworld Publishers Ltd. GBR. *Dist:* Trafalgar Square.

—Kate Hannigan's Girl. 2002. 352p. mass mkt. (*0-552-14581-5*, Corgi) Bantam Bks.

—Kate Hannigan's Girl. l.t. ed. 2002. 453p. 30.95 (*0-7862-3598-5*) Gale Group.

—Kate Hannigan's Girl. 2001. 288p. 24.00 (*0-7432-1252-5*, Simon & Schuster) Simon & Schuster.

—Let Me Make Myself Plain. mass mkt. 10.95 (*0-552-13407-4*) Transworld Publishers Ltd. GBR. *Dist:* Trafalgar Square.

—The Long Corridor. 2000. 317p. pap. 9.95 (*0-552-14078-3*) Transworld Publishers Ltd. GBR. *Dist:* Trafalgar Square.

—The Maltese Angel. 1994. 480p. 23.00 o.s.i (*0-671-89649-0*, Simon & Schuster) Simon & Schuster.

—The Maltese Angel. 1994. 528p. mass mkt. 10.95 (*0-552-13684-0*) Transworld Publishers Ltd. GBR. *Dist:* Trafalgar Square.

—The Man Who Cried. l.t. ed. 1994. 23.95 o.p. (*0-7927-2052-0*) BBC Audiobooks America.

—The Moth. 1986. 17.45 o.p. (*0-671-44076-4*) Summit Bks.

—My Beloved Son. 1993. 22.00 (*0-671-75865-9*, Simon & Schuster) Simon & Schuster.

—Nice Bloke. 2000. pap. 10.95 (*0-552-14086-4*) Transworld Publishers Ltd. GBR. *Dist:* Trafalgar Square.

—Our John Willie. 1975. mass mkt. 1.50 o.p. (*0-451-06672-3*, Signet Bks.) NAL.

—Our John Willie. 2000. 17.95 (*0-385-40132-9*) Transworld Publishers Ltd. GBR. *Dist:* Trafalgar Square.

—The Parson's Daughter. l.t. ed. 1988. 594p. 21.95 o.p. (*0-8161-4389-7*, Macmillan Reference USA) Gale Group.

—The Parson's Daughter. 1987. 19.45 o.p. (*0-671-63293-0*) Summit Bks.

—Riley. l.t. ed. 2001. 480p. lib. bdg. 29.95 (*1-58547-071-6*) Ctr. Point Large Print.

—Rooney. unabr. ed. 1993. 54.95 incl. audio (*0-7451-5866-8*, CAB 163) BBC Audiobooks America.

—Rooney. l.t. ed. 1975. (Ulverscroft Large Print Ser.). 360p. 12.00 o.p. (*0-85456-362-8*, Ulverscroft) Thorpe, F. A. Pubs. GBR. *Dist:* Ulverscroft Large Print Bks., Ltd., Ulverscroft Large Print Canada, Ltd.

—Rooney. 2000. 603p. pap. 10.95 (*0-552-14706-0*); pap. 10.95 (*0-552-14074-0*) Transworld Publishers Ltd. GBR. *Dist:* Trafalgar Square.

—The Spaniard's Gift: A Novel. 1989. 392p. pap. 8.95 o.p. (*0-671-68254-7*) Summit Bks.

—The Thornman Inheritance: A Novel. 1989. 294p. pap. 8.95 o.p. (*0-671-68264-4*) Summit Bks.

—The Tide of Life. l.t. ed. 1994. pap. 22.95 o.p. (*0-7927-1889-5*); 23.95 o.p. (*0-7927-1890-9*); audio 96.95 (*0-7451-4223-0*, CAB 906) BBC Audiobooks America.

—The Tide of Life. 1993. 512p. mass mkt. 7.99 o.s.i (*0-552-10630-5*); 1977. pap. 1.75 o.p. (*0-553-10516-7*) Bantam Bks.

—The Tide of Life. l.t. ed. 1983. (Charnwood Large Print Ser.). 640p. o.p. (*0-7089-8132-1*, Charnwood) Thorpe, F. A. Pubs. GBR. *Dist:* Ulverscroft Large Print Canada, Ltd.

—The Tide of Life. 1997. mass mkt. 10.95 (*0-552-14446-0*) Transworld Publishers Ltd. GBR. *Dist:* Trafalgar Square.

—The Upstart. unabr. ed. 1997. 11p. audio 89.95 o.p. (*1-86042-137-7*) Beeler, Thomas T. Publisher.

—The Upstart. 1999. per. (*1-55166-527-1*, Mira Bks.) Harlequin Enterprises, Ltd.

—The Upstart. 1998. 352p. 23.00 (*0-684-84315-3*, Simon & Schuster) Simon & Schuster.

—The Upstart. l.t. ed. 1998. (Basic Ser.). 539p. 29.95 (*0-7862-1401-5*) Thorndike Pr.

—The Upstart. 1997. 480p. mass mkt. 10.95 (*0-552-14037-6*) Transworld Publishers Ltd. GBR. *Dist:* Trafalgar Square.

—The Whip. l.t. ed. 1994. 24.95 o.p. (*0-7927-2085-7*); pap. 22.95 o.p. (*0-7927-2084-9*) BBC Audiobooks America.

—The Whip. 1982. (Illus.). 384p. 14.50 o.p. (*0-671-43272-9*) Summit Bks.

—The Whip. 2000. 461p. mass mkt. 11.95 o.p. (*0-552-12368-4*) Transworld Publishers Ltd. GBR. *Dist:* Trafalgar Square.

—The Wingless Bird. 1991. 512p. mass mkt. 7.99 o.s.i (*0-552-13577-1*); 1990. o.s.i (*0-593-01823-0*, Corgi) Bantam Bks.

—The Wingless Bird. 1991. 384p. 19.95 o.p. (*0-671-66620-7*) Summit Bks.

—The Wingless Bird. 1998. 512p. mass mkt. 10.95 (*0-552-14515-7*) Transworld Publishers Ltd. GBR. *Dist:* Trafalgar Square.

—The Year of the Virgins. l.t. ed. 1995. 24.95 o.p. (*1-56895-247-3*, Wheeler Publishing, Inc.) Gale Group.

—The Year of the Virgins. 1995. 22.00 o.p. (*0-671-89650-4*, Simon & Schuster) Simon & Schuster.

—The Year of the Virgins. 1994. 352p. mass mkt. 11.95 (*0-552-13247-0*) Transworld Publishers Ltd. GBR. *Dist:* Trafalgar Square.

Cooper, Fiona. Blossom at the Mention of Your Name. 1996. 272p. pap. o.p. (*1-85242-399-4*) Serpent's Tail Ltd.

Cooper, Jilly. Octavia. l.t. ed. 1992. 54.95 o.p. (*0-8161-9271-5*, Macmillan Reference USA) Gale Group.

—Octavia. 2000. 189p. pap. 8.95 (*0-552-10717-4*) Transworld Publishers Ltd. GBR. *Dist:* Trafalgar Square.

—Pandora. 2004. (Illus.). 752p. mass mkt. 9.95 (*0-552-14850-4*) Corgi Bks. Ltd. GBR. *Dist:* Trafalgar Square.

Cooper, Natasha. Bitter Herbs. l.t. ed. 1995. (Ulverscroft Large Print Ser.). 528p. 29.99 o.p. (*0-7089-3291-6*, Ulverscroft) Thorpe, F. A. Pubs. GBR. *Dist:* Ulverscroft Large Print Bks., Ltd., Ulverscroft Large Print Canada, Ltd.

—Bloody Roses. 1993. 256p. 20.00 o.s.i (*0-517-59022-0*, Crown) Crown Publishing Group.

—A Common Death. l.t. ed. 1991. (Ulverscroft Large Print Ser.). Orig. Title: Festering Lillies. 29.99 o.p. (*0-7089-2458-1*, Ulverscroft) Thorpe, F. A. Pubs. GBR. *Dist:* Ulverscroft Large Print Bks., Ltd., Ulverscroft Large Print Canada, Ltd.

—Creeping Ivy. 1999. 342p. 23.95 o.p. (*0-312-20520-1*, Saint Martin's Minotaur) St. Martin's Pr.

—Creeping Ivy. l.t. ed. 1999. (Ulverscroft Large Print Ser.). 376p. 31.99 o.p. (*0-7089-4144-3*, Ulverscroft) Thorpe, F. A. Pubs. GBR. *Dist:* Ulverscroft Large Print Bks., Ltd., Ulverscroft Large Print Canada, Ltd.

—The Drowning Pool. 1998. (WWL Mystery Ser.). per. (*0-373-26271-X*, 1-26271-6, Worldwide Library) Harlequin Enterprises, Ltd.

—The Drowning Pool: A Willow King Mystery. 1997. (Willow King Mysteries Ser.). 240p. 21.95 (*0-312-15130-6*, Saint Martin's Minotaur) St. Martin's Pr.

—Fault Lines. 2000. 346p. 23.95 (*0-312-25316-8*, Saint Martin's Minotaur) St. Martin's Pr.

—Fault Lines. l.t. ed. 2000. (Ulverscroft Large Print Ser.). 480p. 31.99 (*0-7089-4276-8*, Ulverscroft) Thorpe, F. A. Pubs. GBR. *Dist:* Ulverscroft Large Print Bks., Ltd., Ulverscroft Large Print Canada, Ltd.

—A Place of Safety: A Trish Maguire Mystery. 2003. 320p. 24.95 (*0-312-31936-3*, Saint Martin's Minotaur) St. Martin's Pr.

—Poison Flowers. unabr. ed. 1998. audio 83.95 (*1-85903-128-5*) Magna Story Sound GBR. *Dist:* Ulverscroft Large Print Bks., Ltd.

—Poison Flowers. 1993. 3.99 o.p. (*0-517-09845-8*) Random Hse. Value Publishing.

—Poison Flowers. l.t. ed. 1992. (Mystery Ser.). 544p. 29.99 o.p. (*0-7089-2726-2*, Ulverscroft) Thorpe, F. A. Pubs. GBR. *Dist:* Ulverscroft Large Print Bks., Ltd., Ulverscroft Large Print Canada, Ltd.

—Rotten Apples. 1997. (WWL Mystery Ser.: No. 244). per. (*0-373-26244-2*, 1-26244-3, Worldwide Library) Harlequin Enterprises, Ltd.

—Rotten Apples. unabr. ed. 1998. audio 76.95 (*1-85903-141-2*) Magna Story Sound GBR. *Dist:* Ulverscroft Large Print Bks., Ltd.

—Rotten Apples. 1995. 288p. 21.95 o.p. (*0-312-13161-5*, Saint Martin's Minotaur) St. Martin's Pr.

—Sour Grapes. 1999. (WWL Mystery Ser.: Vol. 319). pap. (*0-373-26319-8*, Worldwide Library) Harlequin Enterprises, Ltd.

—Sour Grapes. 1998. (Willow King Mysteries Ser.). 304p. 22.95 (*0-312-18666-5*, Saint Martin's Minotaur) St. Martin's Pr.

Cooper, Natasha & Myers, Tanya. Festering Lillies. unabr. ed. 1996. audio 69.95 o.p. (*1-85903-111-0*, 31110) Magna Story Sound GBR. *Dist:* Ulverscroft Large Print Bks., Ltd.

Cooper-Posey, Tracy & Doyle, Arthur Conan. The Case of the Reluctant Agent: A Sherlock Holmes Mystery. 2001. (Illus.). 256p. pap. 12.95 (*0-88801-263-2*) Turnstone Pr. CAN. *Dist:* General Distribution Services, Inc.

Coppard, Alfred Edgar. Black Dog & Other Stories. 1977. (Short Story Index Reprint Ser.). 22.95 (*0-8369-3312-5*) Ayer Co. Pubs., Inc.

—Ninepenny Flute: Twenty-One Tales. 1977. (Short Story Index Reprint Ser.). 22.95 (*0-8369-3314-1*) Ayer Co. Pubs., Inc.

—Polly Oliver. 1977. (Short Story Index Reprint Ser.). 18.95 (*0-8369-3671-X*) Ayer Co. Pubs., Inc.

Copper, Basil. The Dossier of Solar Pons. 1987. (Academy Book Ser.). 278p. pap. 7.95 (*0-89733-252-0*) Academy Chicago Pubs., Ltd.

—Exploits of Solar Pons. 1993. (Illus.). 256p. (C). 25.00 (*1-878252-11-9*); 45.00 (*1-878252-14-3*) Fedogan & Bremer.

—The Further Adventures of Solar Pons. 1987. (Academy Book Ser.). 256p. pap. 7.95 (*0-89733-273-3*) Academy Chicago Pubs., Ltd.

—The Recollections of Solar Pons. 1995. 25.00 (*1-878252-20-8*); 75.00 (*1-878252-21-6*) Fedogan & Bremer.

—The Secret Files of Solar Pons. 1979. (Solar Pons Ser.: No. 10). pap. 1.95 o.p. (*0-523-40656-8*, Pinnacle Bks.) Kensington Publishing Corp.

Corelli, Marie. The Sorrows of Satan. 1980. (Illus.). pap. 6.95 o.p. (*0-910122-06-7*) Amherst Pr.

—The Sorrows of Satan: Or the Strange Experience of One Geoffrey Tempest, Millionaire: A Romance. 1996. (Oxford Popular Fiction Ser.). 412p. pap. 10.95 o.p. (*0-19-283220-4*) Oxford Univ. Pr., Inc.

Cork, Barry. Dead Ball. 1989. 16.95 o.p. (*0-684-19044-3*, Macmillan Reference USA) Gale Group.

Corlett, William. The Bloxworth Blue. 1985. 192p. (YA). (gr. 7 up). 12.95 (*0-06-021343-4*) HarperCollins Children's Bk. Group.

—Now & Then. 2nd ed. 1998. 300p. reprint ed. pap. 11.95 o.p. (*1-55583-424-8*) Alyson Pubns.

—Now & Then. 1996. 346p. pap. o.s.i (*0-349-10775-0*); 1995. 352p. pap. o.s.i (*0-349-10646-0*) Little Brown & Co.

Corn, Alfred Dewitt. Part of His Story. 1997. 264p. 24.00 (*0-922811-29-6*) Mid-List Pr.

Cornick, Nicola. The Blanchard Secret. 2002. (Harlequin Historicals Ser.). 304p. mass mkt. (*0-373-29230-9*, Harlequin Bks.) Harlequin Enterprises, Ltd.

—The Larkswood Legacy. 2001. 256p. mass mkt. (*0-373-51150-7*, Harlequin Bks.) Harlequin Enterprises, Ltd.

—The Larkswood Legacy. l.t. ed. 1999. (Mills & Boon Large Print Ser.). 320p. 25.99 (*0-263-16117-X*) Harlequin Mills & Boon, Ltd. GBR. *Dist:* Ulverscroft Large Print Bks., Ltd., Ulverscroft Large Print Canada, Ltd.

—True Colours. 2001. (Harlequin Regency Romance Ser.). 251p. mass mkt. (*0-373-51134-5*, Harlequin Bks.) Harlequin Enterprises, Ltd.

—True Colours. l.t. ed. 1998. (Mills & Boon Large Print Ser.). 350p. 25.99 (*0-263-15715-6*) Harlequin Mills & Boon, Ltd. GBR. *Dist:* Ulverscroft Large Print Bks., Ltd., Ulverscroft Large Print Canada, Ltd.

Cornwell, Bernard. A Crowning Mercy. 2004. 544p. mass mkt. 7.99 (*0-06-072564-8*, HarperTorch) Morrow/Avon.

—Excalibur: A Novel of Arthur. 1998. (Warlord Chronicles Ser.: Vol. 3). 448p. 24.95 o.p. (*0-312-18575-8*) St. Martin's Pr.

—Gallows Thief. 2002. (Illus.). 304p. 24.95 (*0-06-008273-9*) HarperCollins Pubs.

—Gallows Thief. l.t. ed. 2002. 29.95 (*0-7862-4596-4*) Thorndike Pr.

—Killers Wake. 1990. 432p. mass mkt. 4.95 o.s.i (*0-06-100046-9*, HarperTorch) Morrow/Avon.

—Killers Wake. 1989. 320p. 19.95 o.p. (*0-399-13458-1*, G. P. Putnam's Sons) Penguin Putnam Bks. for Young Readers.

—Sharpe's Prey: Richard Sharpe & the Expedition to Copenhagen, 1807. l.t. ed. 2002. 506p. 29.95 (*0-7862-4121-7*) Gale Group.

—Stonehenge: A Novel. 2000. (Illus.). 448p. 26.00 (*0-06-019700-5*) HarperCollins Pubs.

—Stonehenge: A Novel. l.t. ed. 2000. (Core Ser.). (Illus.). 646p. 28.95 (*0-7838-9038-9*) Thorndike Pr.

—The Winter King: A Novel of Arthur. 1996. (Warlord Chronicles Ser.: Bk. 1). 448p. text 24.95 o.p. (*0-312-14447-4*) St. Martin's Pr.

Corrick, Martin. The Navigation Log: A Novel. 2004. 304p. pap. 13.95 (*0-375-76053-9*, Random Hse. Trade Paperbacks) Random House Adult Trade Publishing Group.

—The Navigation Log: A Novel. 2003. 304p. 24.95 (*0-375-50812-0*) Random Hse., Inc.

Cottrel, Pamela. Green Saxon Darkness. 2000. E-Book 16.95 incl. cd-rom (*1-58444-026-0*) Disc-Us Bks., Inc.

Coulter, Catherine. The Aristocrat. l.t. ed. 2002. 357p. 29.95 (*0-7862-3977-8*) Gale Group.

—The Aristocrat. 1999. 251p. mass mkt. (*1-55166-513-1*, Mira Bks.); 1993. per. (*0-373-48261-2*, 5-48261-7, Harlequin Bks.); 1986. mass mkt. (*0-373-09331-4*, Harlequin Bks.) Harlequin Enterprises, Ltd.

—The Courtship. 2000. 352p. mass mkt. 7.99 (*0-515-12721-3*, Jove) Berkley Publishing Group.

—The Courtship. l.t. ed. (Core Ser.). 448p. 2001. pap. 29.95 (*0-7838-9033-8*); 2000. 31.95 (*0-7838-9032-X*) Gale Group. (Macmillan Reference USA).

—Lord Harry. 384p. 2003. mass mkt. 7.99 (*0-451-20814-5*, Signet Bks.); 1995. mass mkt. 7.99 o.s.i (*0-451-40591-9*, Topaz) NAL.

—Lord Harry. l.t. ed. 1997. (Romance Ser.). 424p. lib. bdg. 29.95 (*0-7838-2001-1*) Thorndike Pr.

—Mad Jack. 1999. 352p. mass mkt. 7.99 (*0-515-12420-6*, Jove) Berkley Publishing Group.

—Mad Jack. l.t. ed. 1999. (Wheeler Large Print Book Ser.). 394p. 27.95 o.p. (*1-56895-784-X*, Wheeler Publishing, Inc.) Gale Group.

—Moonspun Magic. 416p. 2004. mass mkt. 7.99 (*0-451-21187-1*, Signet Bks.); 1999. mass mkt. 7.99 (*0-451-40884-5*, Topaz); 1988. reprint ed. mass mkt. 6.99 o.s.i (*0-451-40090-9*, Onyx) NAL.

—Moonspun Magic. 1996. 352p. 24.00 o.p. (*0-7278-5122-5*) Severn Hse. Pubs., Ltd.

—Moonspun Magic. l.t. ed. 2000. (Romance Ser.). 559p. 28.95 (*0-7862-2349-9*) Thorndike Pr.

—The Nightingale Legacy. 1995. 464p. mass mkt. 7.99 (*0-515-11624-6*, Jove) Berkley Publishing Group.

—The Nightingale Legacy. unabr. ed. 1995. (Legacy Ser.). 13p. audio 89.25 (*1-56100-203-8*, 332, Unabridged Library Editions); audio 25.95 o.p. (*1-56100-579-7*, 1301, Bookcassette) Brilliance Audio.

—The Nightingale Legacy. 1994. 384p. 16.95 o.p. (*0-399-13970-2*, G. P. Putnam's Sons) Penguin Group (USA) Inc.

—The Nightingale Legacy. 484p. pap. 5.98 o.p. (*0-7651-0429-6*) Smithmark Pubs., Inc.

—The Valentine Legacy. 1996. 432p. mass mkt. 7.99 (*0-515-11836-2*, Jove) Berkley Publishing Group.

—The Valentine Legacy. unabr. ed. 1995. (Legacy Ser.). 12p. audio 73.25 (*1-56100-284-4*, 1114, Unabridged Library Editions); audio 23.95 o.p. (*1-56100-659-9*, 305, Bookcassette) Brilliance Audio.

—The Valentine Legacy. l.t. ed. 1995. 573p. 25.95 o.p. (*0-7838-1497-6*, Macmillan Reference USA) Gale Group.

—The Valentine Legacy. 1995. 400p. 19.95 o.p. (*0-399-14094-8*, G. P. Putnam's Sons) Penguin Group (USA) Inc.

—The Wild Baron. 1997. 384p. mass mkt. 7.99 (*0-515-12044-8*, Jove) Berkley Publishing Group.

—The Wild Baron. unabr. ed. 1998. audio 72.00 (*0-7366-4204-8*, 4700) Books on Tape, Inc.

—The Wild Baron. l.t. ed. 1997. (Basic Ser.). 26.95 (*0-7862-1117-2*) Thorndike Pr.

—The Wyndham Legacy. l.t. ed. 1994. 602p. 23.95 o.p. (*0-8161-5941-6*, Macmillan Reference USA) Gale Group.

—The Wyndham Legacy. 1994. 304p. 19.95 o.p. (*0-399-13878-1*, G. P. Putnam's Sons) Penguin Group (USA) Inc.

Counts, Wilma. The Willful Miss Winthrop. 2000. (Zebra Regency Romance Ser.). 256p. mass mkt. 4.99 o.s.i (*0-8217-6706-2*, Zebra Bks.) Kensington Publishing Corp.

Cowell, Alan S. A Walking Guide. 2003. (Illus.). 288p. 23.00 (*0-7432-4470-2*, Simon & Schuster) Simon & Schuster.

Cowell, Stephanie. The Players: A Novel of the Young Shakespeare. 1997. 352p. (C). 24.00 (*0-393-04060-7*) Norton, W. W. & Co., Inc.

Cox, Josephine. The Gilded Cage. 2001. 438p. mass mkt. 9.95 (*0-7472-5756-6*) Headline Bk. Publishing, Ltd. GBR. *Dist:* Trafalgar Square.

—The Gilded Cage. abr. ed. 1999. mass mkt. 16.95 incl. audio (*1-84032-137-7*) Hodder Headline Audiobooks GBR. *Dist:* Trafalgar Square, Ulverscroft Large Print Bks., Ltd.

Craik, Dinah Maria Mulock. Olive: And the Half-Caste. Kaplan, Cora, ed. & intro. by. 1996. (Oxford Popular Fiction Ser.). 398p. pap. 10.95 o.p. (*0-19-289262-2*) Oxford Univ. Pr., Inc.

—Unkind Word & Other Stories. 1977. (Short Story Index Reprint Ser.). 25.95 (*0-8369-3215-3*) Ayer Co. Pubs., Inc.

Crane, Hamilton. Bonjour, Miss Seeton. (Heron Carvic's Miss Seeton Ser.). 272p. 1997. 21.95 o.s.i (*0-425-15968-X*, Prime Crime); 1998. reprint ed. mass mkt. 5.99 o.s.i (*0-425-16534-5*) Berkley Publishing Group.

—Hands up, Miss Seeton. 1992. mass mkt. 5.50 o.s.i (*0-425-13132-7*) Berkley Publishing Group.

—Hands up, Miss Seeton. l.t. ed. 2001. (Heron Carvic's Miss Seeton Ser.). 335p. 28.95 (*0-7862-3544-6*); 351p. (*0-7540-4669-9*); 351p. (*0-7540-4670-2*) Thorndike Pr.

—Miss Seeton by Moonlight. 1992. mass mkt. 4.50 o.s.i (*0-425-13265-X*) Berkley Publishing Group.

—Miss Seeton by Moonlight. l.t. ed. 2000. (Mystery Ser.). 347p. 27.95 o.p. (*0-7862-2481-9*); (*0-7540-4140-9*); (*0-7540-4141-7*) Thorndike Pr.

—Miss Seeton Cracks the Case. 1991. mass mkt. 4.99 o.s.i (*0-425-12676-5*) Berkley Publishing Group.

—Miss Seeton Cracks the Case. l.t. ed. 1999. (Thorndike Mystery Ser.). o.p. (*0-7862-1766-9*, Macmillan Reference USA) Gale Group.

—Miss Seeton Goes to Bat. l.t. ed. 1999. (Mystery Ser.). 365p. 27.95 (*0-7862-2065-1*); (*0-7540-3898-X*); (*0-7540-3897-1*) Thorndike Pr.

—Miss Seeton Paints the Town. 1991. mass mkt. 4.99 o.s.i (*0-425-12848-2*) Berkley Publishing Group.

—Miss Seeton Paints the Town. l.t. ed. 2000. (Mystery Ser.). 352p. 27.95 (*0-7862-2339-1*) Thorndike Pr.

—Miss Seeton Rocks the Cradle. 1992. 208p. mass mkt. 4.99 o.s.i (*0-425-13400-8*) Berkley Publishing Group.

—Miss Seeton Rocks the Cradle. l.t. ed. 2000. (Mystery Ser.). 386p. 27.95 (*0-7862-2840-7*) Thorndike Pr.

—Miss Seeton Rules. 272p. 1995. mass mkt. 4.99 o.s.i (*0-425-15006-2*); 1994. 18.95 o.p. (*0-425-14354-6*) Berkley Publishing Group. (Prime Crime).

—Miss Seeton Undercover. 1994. 272p. mass mkt. 4.99 o.s.i (*0-425-14405-4*); 17.95 o.p. (*0-425-14137-3*) Berkley Publishing Group.

—Miss Seeton's Finest Hour. 1999. (Heron Carvic's Miss Seeton Ser.). 272p. mass mkt. 5.99 o.s.i (*0-425-17026-8*, Prime Crime) Berkley Publishing Group.

—Sold to Miss Seeton. 1996. mass mkt. 5.99 o.s.i (*0-425-15462-9*); 1995. 272p. 19.95 o.p. (*0-425-14936-6*, Prime Crime) Berkley Publishing Group.

—Sweet Miss Seeton. (Heron Carvic's Miss Seeton Ser.). 1996. 272p. 21.95 o.p. (*0-425-15471-8*); 1997. 256p. reprint ed. mass mkt. 5.99 o.s.i (*0-425-15962-0*) Berkley Publishing Group. (Prime Crime).

Crane, Hamilton & Carvic, Heron. Miss Seeton Goes to Bat. 1993. 208p. mass mkt. 4.99 o.s.i (*0-425-13576-4*) Berkley Publishing Group.

Crane, Teresa. Strange Are the Ways. 570p. 4.98 o.p. (*0-8317-4637-8*) Smithmark Pubs., Inc.

—Strange Are the Ways. 1993. 576p. 25.95 o.p. (*0-312-09919-3*) St. Martin's Pr.

Craze, Galaxy. By the Shore. 2000. 240p. pap. 12.00 (*0-8021-3687-7*, Grove Pr.); 1999. 232p. 24.00 o.p. (*0-87113-746-1*, Atlantic Monthly Pr.) Grove/Atlantic, Inc.

—By the Shore. 2000. 18.05 (*0-606-19408-8*) Turtleback Bks.

Creasey, John. A Beauty for Inspector West. 1998. 192p. 19.50 o.p. (*0-7540-8516-3*, Black Dagger) BBC Audiobooks America.

—The Beauty Queen Killer: An Inspector West Mystery. 1987. 192p. reprint ed. mass mkt. 3.95 o.p. (*0-06-080887-X*, P/887, Perennial) HarperTrade.

—The Blind Spot: An Inspector West Mystery. 1987. 224p. reprint ed. mass mkt. 3.95 o.p. (*0-06-080895-0*, P/895, Perennial) HarperTrade.

—The Case Against Paul Raeburn: An Inspector West Mystery. 1987. 192p. reprint ed. mass mkt. 3.95 o.p. (*0-06-080892-6*, P/892, Perennial) HarperTrade.

—The Creepers: An Inspector West Mystery. 1987. 224p. reprint ed. mass mkt. 3.95 o.p. (*0-06-080889-6*, P/889, Perennial) HarperTrade.

—Death of a Postman: An Inspector West Mystery. 1987. 192p. reprint ed. mass mkt. 3.95 o.p. (*0-06-080890-X*, P/890, Perennial) HarperTrade.

—The Figure in the Dusk: An Inspector West Mystery. 1987. 224p. reprint ed. mass mkt. 3.95 o.p. (*0-06-080891-8*, P/891, Perennial) HarperTrade.

—Find Inspector West. l.t. ed. 1990. pap. 15.95 o.p. (*0-7927-0323-5*, C0798) BBC Audiobooks America.

—The Gelignite Gang: An Inspector West Mystery. 1987. 182p. reprint ed. mass mkt. 3.50 o.p. (*0-06-080885-3*, P/885, Perennial) HarperTrade.

—Give a Man a Gun: An Inspector West Mystery. 1987. 224p. reprint ed. mass mkt. 3.50 o.p. (*0-06-080886-1*, P/886, Perennial) HarperTrade.

—Holiday for Inspector West. l.t. ed. 1976. 328p. 12.00 o.p. (*0-85456-490-X*, Ulverscroft) Thorpe, F. A. Pubs. GBR. *Dist:* Ulverscroft Large Print Bks., Ltd.

—Inspector West Alone. unabr. collector's ed. 1984. audio 56.00 (*0-7366-0343-3*, 1329) Books on Tape, Inc.

—Inspector West Cries Wolf. unabr. ed. 1990. audio 54.95 (*0-7451-5884-6*, CAT 4058) BBC Audiobooks America.

—Inspector West Cries Wolf. (Black Dagger Crime Ser.). 192p. 12.95 o.p. (*0-86220-738-X*) Chivers Pr. GBR. *Dist:* BBC Audiobooks America.

—Inspector West Cries Wolf. l.t. ed. 2003. lib. bdg. 24.45 (*0-7862-5212-X*) Thorndike Pr.

—Two for Inspector West. l.t. ed. 1979. 330p. 12.00 o.p. (*0-7089-0270-7*, Ulverscroft) Thorpe, F. A. Pubs. GBR. *Dist:* Ulverscroft Large Print Bks., Ltd.

Cresswell, Jasmine. The Danewood Legacy. l.t. ed. 1992. (Nightingale Ser.). 267p. 14.95 o.p. (*0-8161-5404-X*, Macmillan Reference USA) Gale Group.

Crispin, Edmund. Buried for Pleasure. 191p. reprint ed. lib. bdg. 20.95 (*0-89190-691-6*, Rivercity Pr.) Amereon, Ltd.

—Buried for Pleasure. Barzum, Jacques & Taylor, Wendell H., eds. 1976. (Crime Fiction Ser.). reprint ed. lib. bdg. 21.00 o.p. (*0-8240-2362-5*) Garland Publishing, Inc.

—Buried for Pleasure. 1980. mass mkt. 3.50 o.p. (*0-06-080506-4*, P 506, Perennial) HarperTrade.

—The Case of the Gilded Fly. l.t. ed. 1980. (YA). (gr. 7-12). lib. bdg. 13.95 o.p. (*0-8161-3018-3*, Macmillan Reference USA) Gale Group.

—The Case of the Gilded Fly. 1992. 224p. pap. 8.95 o.p. (*1-55882-108-2*) International Polygonics, Ltd.

—The Case of the Gilded Fly. 1980. pap. 2.95 o.p. (*0-380-50187-2*, 63552-6, Avon Bks.) Morrow/Avon.

—The Case of the Gilded Fly. 1979. (Walker Mystery Ser.). 223p. reprint ed. 8.95 o.s.i (*0-8027-5410-4*) Walker & Co.
—Fen Country. 18.95 (*0-89190-694-0*) Amereon, Ltd.
—Fen Country. 1987. (Classic Crime Ser.). 224p. pap. 5.95 o.p. (*0-14-008815-6*, Penguin Bks.) Viking Penguin.
—Fen Country. 1980. 176p. 9.95 o.s.i (*0-8027-5424-4*) Walker & Co.
—Frequent Hearses. l.t. ed. 1994. (General Ser.). 311p. lib. bdg. 16.95 (*0-8161-5860-6*, Macmillan Reference USA) Gale Group.
—Frequent Hearses. 1982. pap. 2.95 o.p. (*0-14-006325-0*) Penguin Group (USA) Inc.
—Frequent Hearses. 1987. (Classic Crime Ser.). 224p. pap. 5.95 o.p. (*0-14-009355-9*, Penguin Bks.) Viking Penguin.
—The Glimpses of the Moon. 23.95 (*0-89190-695-9*) Amereon, Ltd.
—The Glimpses of the Moon. 1979. pap. 2.95 o.p. (*0-380-45062-3*, 69021-7, Avon Bks.) Morrow/Avon.
—The Glimpses of the Moon. 1978. 8.95 o.s.i (*0-8027-5391-4*) Walker & Co.
—Holy Disorders. 1976. 22.95 (*0-8488-0468-6*) Amereon, Ltd.
—Holy Disorders. 1980. (General Ser.). lib. bdg. 13.95 o.p. (*0-8161-3111-2*, Macmillan Reference USA) Gale Group.
—Holy Disorders. 1980. 240p. pap. 2.95 o.p. (*0-380-51508-3*, Avon Bks.) Morrow/Avon.
—Holy Disorders. 1979. (Walker Mystery Ser.). 254p. 9.95 o.s.i (*0-8027-5411-2*) Walker & Co.
—The Long Divorce. 1981. (Crime Monthly Ser.). 256p. pap. 3.95 o.p. (*0-14-001304-0*, Penguin Bks.) Viking Penguin.
—Love Lies Bleeding. 20.95 (*0-89190-693-2*) Amereon, Ltd.
—Love Lies Bleeding. 1982. (Crime Monthly Ser.). pap. 3.95 o.p. (*0-14-000974-4*, Penguin Bks.) Viking Penguin.
—Love Lies Bleeding. 1981. 9.95 o.s.i (*0-8027-5444-9*) Walker & Co.
—The Moving Toy Shop. 20.95 (*0-8488-0104-0*) Amereon, Ltd.
—The Moving Toy Shop. 1989. (Penguin Classic Crime Ser.). 208p. pap. 6.99 (*0-14-008817-2*, Penguin Bks.) Penguin Group (USA) Inc.
—Swan Song. 1980. 192p. 16.95 (*0-8027-5420-1*) Boulevard Bks.
—Swan Song. 1993. reprint ed. lib. bdg. 16.95 (*1-56849-195-6*) Buccaneer Bks., Inc.
—Swan Song. 1982. 192p. pap. 2.50 o.p. (*0-380-55145-4*, 70020, Avon Bks.) Morrow/Avon.
—Swan Song. l.t. ed. 1987. (Linford Mystery Library). 336p. pap. 17.99 o.p. (*0-7089-6361-7*, Linford) Thorpe, F. A. Pubs. GBR. *Dist:* Ulverscroft Large Print Bks., Ltd., Ulverscroft Large Print Canada, Ltd.
Crombie, Deborah. All Shall Be Well. 1995. 272p. mass mkt. 6.99 (*0-425-14771-1*) Berkley Publishing Group.
—All Shall Be Well. 2004. 288p. mass mkt. 6.99 (*0-06-053439-7*, Avon Bks.) Morrow/Avon.
—All Shall Be Well: A Superintendent Duncan Kincaid - Sergeant Gemma James Mystery. 1994. 256p. text 20.00 (*0-684-19654-9*, Macmillan Reference USA) Gale Group.
—Dreaming of the Bones. 1998. 416p. mass mkt. 6.99 (*0-553-57931-2*) Bantam Bks.
—Dreaming of the Bones. l.t. ed. 2000. pap. 25.95 (*1-56895-899-4*, Wheeler Publishing, Inc.) Gale Group.
—Dreaming of the Bones. l.t. ed. 1998. (Magna Large Print Ser.). 480p. o.p. (*0-7505-1315-2*) Magna Large Print Bks. GBR. *Dist:* Ulverscroft Large Print Canada, Ltd.
—Dreaming of the Bones. 1997. 350p. 21.50 (*0-684-80141-8*); 21.50 (*0-684-84720-5*) Simon & Schuster. (Scribner).
—A Finer End. l.t. ed. 2001. (Illus.). 526p. 30.95 (*0-7862-3581-0*) Thorndike Pr.
—Kissed a Sad Goodbye. 2001. 400p. mass mkt. 6.99 (*0-553-57924-X*); 1999. 336p. 23.95 o.s.i (*0-553-10943-X*) Bantam Bks.
—Kissed a Sad Goodbye. l.t. ed. 1999. (Large Print Book Ser.). pap. 24.95 (*1-56895-731-9*, Wheeler Publishing, Inc.) Gale Group.
—Kissed a Sad Goodbye. l.t. ed. 2000. (Magna Large Print Ser.). 480p. (*0-7505-1541-4*) Magna Large Print Bks. GBR. *Dist:* Ulverscroft Large Print Canada, Ltd.
—Kissed a Sad Goodbye. unabr. ed. 1999. audio 87.00 (*0-7887-3751-1*, 95869E7) Recorded Bks., LLC.
—Leave the Grave Green. 1996. 304p. mass mkt. 6.50 (*0-425-15308-8*) Berkley Publishing Group.
—Leave the Grave Green. l.t. ed. 2000. pap. 23.95 (*1-56895-846-3*, Wheeler Publishing, Inc.) Gale Group.
—Leave the Grave Green. l.t. ed. 1997. (Magna Large Print Ser.). 400p. (*0-7505-1114-1*) Magna Large Print Bks. GBR. *Dist:* Ulverscroft Large Print Canada, Ltd.
—Leave the Grave Green. 1995. 224p. 20.00 o.p. (*0-684-19770-7*, Scribner) Simon & Schuster.
—Mourn Not Your Dead. 1997. 304p. reprint ed. mass mkt. 6.99 (*0-425-15778-4*, Prime Crime) Berkley Publishing Group.
—Mourn Not Your Dead. l.t. ed. 1997. (Magna Large Print Ser.). 412p. (*0-7505-1175-3*) Magna Large Print Bks. GBR. *Dist:* Ulverscroft Large Print Canada, Ltd.
—Mourn Not Your Dead: A Duncan Kincaid/Gemma James Crime Novel. l.t. ed. 1996. 25.95 (*1-56895-367-4*, Wheeler Publishing, Inc.) Gale Group.
—Mourn Not Your Dead: A Duncan Kincaid/Gemma James Crime Novel. 1996. 288p. 21.00 o.p. (*0-684-80131-0*, Scribner) Simon & Schuster.
—A Share in Death: A Mystery Introducing Superintendent Duncan Kincaid & Sergeant Gemma James. 1994. 208p. reprint ed. mass mkt. 6.50 (*0-425-14197-7*, Prime Crime) Berkley Publishing Group.
—A Share in Death: A Mystery Introducing Superintendent Duncan Kincaid & Sergeant Gemma James. l.t. ed. 1995. (Magna Large Print Ser.). 259p. (*0-7505-0833-7*) Magna Large Print Bks. GBR. *Dist:* Ulverscroft Large Print Canada, Ltd.
—A Share in Death: A Mystery Introducing Superintendent Duncan Kincaid & Sergeant Gemma James. 1993. 256p. 20.00 o.p. (*0-684-19527-5*, Scribner) Simon & Schuster.
Crow, Donna Fletcher. A Gentle Calling. rev. ed. 1994. (Cambridge Chronicles: Vol. 1). 224p. pap. 9.99 o.p. (*0-89107-806-1*) Crossway Bks.
—Glastonbury: The Novel of Christian England. 1992. 864p. pap. 17.99 o.p. (*0-89107-669-7*) Crossway Bks.
—To Be Worthy. 1986. 204p. pap. 5.95 o.p. (*0-89693-512-4*) Cook Communications Ministries.
—To Be Worthy. 1995. (Cambridge Chronicles: No. 4). 256p. reprint ed. pap. 9.99 o.p. (*0-89107-809-6*) Crossway Bks.
—To Be Worthy. l.t. ed. 2000. (Christian Fiction Ser.). (Illus.). 386p. 23.95 (*0-7862-2381-2*) Thorndike Pr.
—Treasures of the Heart. l.t. ed. 1994. (Cambridge Chronicles: Vol. 2). 224p. pap. 9.99 o.p. (*0-89107-807-X*) Crossway Bks.
—Where Love Begins. 2nd ed. 1995. (Cambridge Chronicles: Vol. 3). 224p. reprint ed. pap. 9.99 o.p. (*0-89107-808-8*) Crossway Bks.
—Where Love Begins. l.t. ed. 1997. (Christian Fiction Ser.). 319p. 23.95 (*0-7862-1231-4*) Thorndike Pr.
Culliford, Penny. Theodoras Wedding. 2003. 304p. pap. 10.99 (*0-310-25039-0*) Zondervan.
Cullman, Heather. Scandal. 2003. 352p. mass mkt. 6.50 (*0-451-20767-X*, Signet Bks.) NAL.
Curtis, Jack. Point of Impact. 1993. 400p. mass mkt. 5.50 o.s.i (*0-451-17417-8*, Signet Bks.) NAL.
—Point of Impact. 1991. 19.95 o.p. (*0-671-73640-X*, Simon & Schuster) Simon & Schuster.
Curtis, Richard. Notting Hill. 1999. (Illus.). 207p. pap. 15.00 (*0-340-73844-8*) Hodder & Stoughton, Ltd. GBR. *Dist:* Lubrecht & Cramer, Ltd., Trafalgar Square.
Curzon, Clare. All Unwary. (*0-7540-3467-4*); 1999. 340p. pap. (*0-7540-3468-2*) BBC Audiobooks America.
—All Unwary. 1998. (Thames Valley Mystery Ser.). 256p. 21.95 o.p. (*0-312-18037-3*, Saint Martin's Minotaur) St. Martin's Pr.
—All Unwary. l.t. ed. 1999. (General Ser.). 352p. pap. 23.95 (*0-7862-1544-5*) Thorndike Pr.
—The Blue-Eyed Boy. 1991. 192p. 14.95 o.s.i (*0-385-41668-7*) Doubleday Publishing.
—The Blue-Eyed Boy. l.t. ed. 1992. (Ulverscroft Large Print Ser.). 416p. 29.99 o.p. (*0-7089-2585-5*, Ulverscroft) Thorpe, F. A. Pubs. GBR. *Dist:* Ulverscroft Large Print Bks., Ltd., Ulverscroft Large Print Canada, Ltd.
—Cat's Cradle. 1994. (WWL Mystery Ser.). per. (*0-373-26151-9*, 1-26151-0, Harlequin Bks.) Harlequin Enterprises, Ltd.
—Cat's Cradle. 1992. 224p. 17.95 o.p. (*0-312-07664-9*, Saint Martin's Minotaur) St. Martin's Pr.
—Close Quarters: A Thames Valley Mystery. l.t. ed. 1997. 357p. lib. bdg. 21.95 (*0-7838-8214-9*, Macmillan Reference USA) Gale Group.
—Close Quarters: A Thames Valley Mystery. l.t. ed. 1998. 256p. per. (*0-373-26292-2*, 1-26292-2, Worldwide Library) Harlequin Enterprises, Ltd.
—Close Quarters: A Thames Valley Mystery. l.t. ed. 1996. 192p. 20.95 (*0-312-15079-2*, Saint Martin's Minotaur) St. Martin's Pr.
—Cold Hands. 218p. 26.00 o.p. (*0-7278-5462-3*) Severn Hse. Pubs., Ltd.
—Cold Hands. l.t. ed. 2001. (Ulverscroft Large Print Ser.). 376p. 31.99 (*0-7089-4329-2*) Thorpe, F. A. Pubs. GBR. *Dist:* Ulverscroft Large Print Bks., Ltd., Ulverscroft Large Print Canada, Ltd.
—Cold Hands: A Mike Yeadings Mystery. 2001. 256p. 22.95 (*0-312-20464-7*, Saint Martin's Minotaur) St. Martin's Pr.
—Death Prone. 1995. (Mystery Ser.). 251p. per. (*0-373-26189-6*, 1-26189-0, Worldwide Library) Harlequin Enterprises, Ltd.
—Death Prone. 1994. 224p. 19.95 o.p. (*0-312-10453-7*, Saint Martin's Minotaur) St. Martin's Pr.
—Don't Leave Me. 2003. 256p. mass mkt. (*0-373-26469-0*) Harlequin Enterprises, Ltd.
—Don't Leave Me. 2001. 256p. (*0-7278-5718-5*) Severn Hse. Pubs., Ltd.
—First Wife, Twice Removed. 1995. (WWL Mystery Ser.). per. (*0-373-26168-3*, 1-26168-4, Harlequin Bks.) Harlequin Enterprises, Ltd.
—First Wife, Twice Removed. 1993. (Thames Valley Mystery Ser.). 224p. 17.95 o.p. (*0-312-09289-X*, Saint Martin's Minotaur) St. Martin's Pr.
—Guilty Knowledge. 2000. 256p. 23.95 (*0-312-26169-1*, Saint Martin's Minotaur) St. Martin's Pr.
—Nice People. 1995. 246p. 20.95 o.p. (*0-312-13132-1*, Saint Martin's Minotaur) St. Martin's Pr.
—Past Mischief. 1997. per. (*0-373-26256-6*, 1-26256-7, Worldwide Library) Harlequin Enterprises, Ltd.
—Past Mischief. 1995. 280p. mass mkt. o.s.i (*0-7515-1301-6*) Little Brown & Co.
—Past Mischief. 1996. 224p. text 21.95 o.p. (*0-312-14388-5*, Saint Martin's Minotaur) St. Martin's Pr.
—Three-Core Lead. 1990. 14.95 o.s.i (*0-385-41139-1*) Doubleday Publishing.
—Three-Core Lead. l.t. ed. 1992. (Lythway Ser.). 308p. 15.95 o.p. (*0-7451-1615-9*, Macmillan Reference USA) Gale Group.
—Trojan Hearse. l.t. ed. 1986. lib. bdg. 14.95 o.p. (*0-7451-0318-9*, Macmillan Reference USA) Gale Group.
Cusk, Rachel. The Country Life. 2000. 352p. pap. 14.00 (*0-312-25280-3*); 1998. 341p. 24.00 o.s.i (*0-312-19848-5*) Picador.
—The Country Life. unabr. ed. 1997. audio 78.00 (*0-7887-3754-6*, 95444E7) Recorded Bks., LLC.
—Saving Agnes. 224p. 2001. pap. 12.00 (*0-312-27193-X*); 2000. 23.00 o.s.i (*0-312-25256-0*) Picador.
—Saving Agnes: A Novel. unabr. ed. 1998. audio 51.00 (*0-7887-2111-9*, 95436E7) Recorded Bks., LLC.
Cutler, Judith. Dying to Write. l.t. ed. 1998. (Magna Large Print Ser.). 432p. 29.99 o.p. (*0-7505-1214-8*) Magna Large Print Bks. GBR. *Dist:* Ulverscroft Large Print Bks., Ltd., Ulverscroft Large Print Canada, Ltd.
Dahl, Roald. Someone Like You. 1953. 17.95 o.s.i (*0-394-44615-1*) Knopf, Alfred A. Inc.
D'Alessandro, Jacquie. Whirlwind Wedding. 2000. (Illus.). 352p. mass mkt. 5.99 (*0-440-23551-0*, Dell Bks.) Dell Publishing.
Dams, Jeanne M. The Body in the Transept. 1996. (Dorothy Martin Mystery Ser.). 224p. mass mkt. 5.99 (*0-06-101133-9*, HarperTorch) Morrow/Avon.
—The Body in the Transept: A Dorothy Martin Mystery. unabr. collector's ed. 1996. audio 42.00 (*0-913369-23-3*, 4174) Books on Tape, Inc.
—The Body in the Transept: A Dorothy Martin Mystery. 1995. 216p. 19.95 (*0-8027-3275-5*) Walker & Co.
—Holy Terror in the Hebrides. 1999. (Dorothy Martin Mystery Ser.: Vol. 3). 272p. mass mkt. 5.99 (*0-06-101346-3*, HarperTorch) Morrow/Avon.
—Holy Terror in the Hebrides: A Dorothy Martin Mystery, , unabr. collector's ed. 1999. audio 40.00 (*0-7366-4296-X*, 4789) Books on Tape, Inc.
—Holy Terror in the Hebrides: A Dorothy Martin Mystery. l.t. ed. 2000. (Thorndike Senior Lifestyle Ser.). 333p. 27.95 o.p. (*0-7862-2407-X*, Macmillan Reference USA) Gale Group.
—Holy Terror in the Hebrides: A Dorothy Martin Mystery. 1997. (Dorothy Martin Mystery Ser.). 224p. 21.95 (*0-8027-3311-5*) Walker & Co.
—Malice in Miniature. 2000. (Dorothy Martin Mystery Ser.). 272p. mass mkt. 5.99 (*0-06-101345-5*) HarperCollins Pubs.
—Malice in Miniature: A Dorothy Martin Mystery, , unabr. collector's ed. 1999. audio 40.00 (*0-7366-4506-3*, 4919) Books on Tape, Inc.
—Malice in Miniature: A Dorothy Martin Mystery. l.t. ed. 2001. (Senior Lifestyles Ser.). 344p. 28.95 (*0-7862-2408-8*) Thorndike Pr.
—Malice in Miniature: A Dorothy Martin Mystery. 1998. (Dorothy Martin Mystery Ser.). (Illus.). 220p. (gr. 8). 22.95 (*0-8027-3322-0*) Walker & Co.
—To Perish in Penzance: A Dorothy Martin Mystery. l.t. ed. 2002. 364p. 28.95 (*0-7862-3846-1*) Gale Group.
—To Perish in Penzance: A Dorothy Martin Mystery. 2001. 240p. 23.95 (*0-8027-3367-0*) Walker & Co.
—Trouble in the Town Hall. 1998. (Dorothy Martin Mystery Ser.). 256p. mass mkt. 5.99 (*0-06-101132-0*, HarperTorch) Morrow/Avon.
—Trouble in the Town Hall: A Dorothy Martin Mystery. unabr. collector's ed. 1997. audio 42.00 (*0-7366-3834-2*, 4554) Books on Tape, Inc.
—Trouble in the Town Hall: A Dorothy Martin Mystery. l.t. ed. 2000. (Thorndike Senior Lifestyle Ser.). 315p. 27.95 (*0-7862-2406-1*) Thorndike Pr.
—Trouble in the Town Hall: A Dorothy Martin Mystery. 1996. (Dorothy Martin Mystery Ser.). 256p. 20.95 (*0-8027-3285-2*) Walker & Co.
—The Victim in Victoria Station. l.t. ed. 2001. (Dorothy Martin Mystery Ser.). (Illus.). 295p. 27.95 (*0-7862-2409-6*) Thorndike Pr.
—The Victim in Victoria Station: A Dorothy Martin Mystery. 1999. (Dorothy Martin Mystery Ser.). (Illus.). 208p. 23.95 (*0-8027-3337-9*) Walker & Co.
Daniel, Mark. The Devil to Pay. l.t. ed. 1995. 391p. pap. 20.95 o.p. (*0-7838-1351-1*, Macmillan Reference USA) Gale Group.
—The Devil to Pay. 1993. 260p. 19.95 o.p. (*0-316-17265-0*) Little Brown & Co.
—The Devil to Pay. l.t. ed. 1995. (Magna Large Print Ser.). 442p. o.p. (*0-7505-0773-X*) Magna Large Print Bks. GBR. *Dist:* Ulverscroft Large Print Canada, Ltd.
—The Devil to Pay. 1995. 256p. mass mkt. 4.99 (*0-380-72328-X*, Avon Bks.) Morrow/Avon.
—Jack the Ripper. 1988. 272p. mass mkt. 3.95 o.p. (*0-451-16018-5*, Signet Bks.) NAL.
—Pity the Sinner. l.t. ed. 1994. (Magna Large Print Ser.). 460p. 29.99 o.p. (*0-7505-0728-4*) Magna Large Print Bks. GBR. *Dist:* Ulverscroft Large Print Bks., Ltd., Ulverscroft Large Print Canada, Ltd.
—Pity the Sinner. 1996. 288p. 22.95 (*0-312-14027-4*, Saint Martin's Minotaur) St. Martin's Pr.
—Unbridled. 1990. 224p. 17.95 o.p. (*0-89919-922-4*) Houghton Mifflin Co.
—Unbridled. 1992. 256p. mass mkt. 4.99 (*0-380-71443-4*, Avon Bks.) Morrow/Avon.
Daniels, Philip. Foolproof. 1995. 175p. 19.95 o.p. (*0-312-13077-5*, Saint Martin's Minotaur) St. Martin's Pr.
—Goldmine - London W. I. 1993. 160p. 17.95 o.p. (*0-312-09821-9*, Saint Martin's Minotaur) St. Martin's Pr.
Danks, Denise. User Deadly. 1991. 208p. 17.95 o.p. (*0-312-07064-0*, Saint Martin's Minotaur) St. Martin's Pr.
Dann, Joshua. Timeshare: ATime for War. 1999. (Timeshare Trilogy Ser.). 288p. mass mkt. 5.99 o.s.i (*0-441-00638-8*) Ace Bks.
—Timeshare: Do You Believe in Yesterday? 1997. 256p. mass mkt. 5.99 o.s.i (*0-441-00457-1*) Ace Bks.
—Timeshare: Second Time Around. 1998. (Timeshare Trilogy Ser.). 256p. mass mkt. 5.99 o.s.i (*0-441-00567-5*) Ace Bks.
Dark, Alice Elliott. Think of England: A Novel. 272p. 2002. (Illus.). 24.00 (*0-684-86522-X*); 2003. reprint ed. pap. 13.00 (*0-7432-3497-9*) Simon & Schuster. (Simon & Schuster).
Darke, Majorie. A Question of Courage. 1975. 224p. (J). (gr. 6-12). 5.95 o.p. (*0-690-00789-2*) HarperCollins Children's Bk. Group.
Darrell, Elizabeth. We Will Remember. 1996. 464p. 26.95 o.p. (*0-312-14066-5*) St. Martin's Pr.
Davenport, Gwen. Time & Chance. 1993. 336p. 22.95 o.p. (*1-55611-373-0*) Fine, Donald I. Bks.
Davenport, Will. The Painter. 2003. 336p. pap. 12.95 (*0-553-38206-3*) Bantam Bks.
Davies, Andrew. B. Monkey. 1998. 224p. (J). pap. 11.95 (*0-7868-8249-2*) Hyperion Pr.
Davies, David S. Fixed Point: The Life & Death of Sherlock Holmes. 1996. audio 7.95 (*1-888728-03-5*) Classic Specialties.
Davies, David Stuart. The Scroll of the Dead: A Sherlock Holmes Adventure. 1998. 147p. o.p. (*1-899562-43-5*); pap. (*1-899562-47-8*) Ash-Tree Pr. (Calabash Pr.).
Davies, Freda. A Fine & Private Place: A Novel of Mystery. 2001. 288p. 24.00 (*0-7867-0909-X*, Carroll & Graf Pubs.) Avalon Publishing Group.
Davies, Linda. Nest of Vipers. 1995. 256p. mass mkt. 6.50 o.s.i (*0-440-22190-0*) Dell Publishing.
—Nest of Vipers. 1995. 416p. 23.00 o.s.i (*0-385-47596-9*) Doubleday Publishing.
—Nest of Vipers. l.t. ed. 1995. (Large Print Bks.). 25.95 o.p. (*1-56895-222-8*, Wheeler Publishing, Inc.) Gale Group.
Davies, Ray. Waterloo Sunset Stories. 2002. 256p. pap. 13.00 (*0-7868-8454-1*) Disney Pr.
Davies, Stevie. Four Dreamers & Emily. 1997. 272p. 21.95 (*0-312-16844-6*) St. Martin's Pr.
Davis-Goff, Annabel. The Dower House. 1999. 288p. pap. 13.95 (*0-312-20645-3*, Saint Martin's Griffin); 1998. 274p. 22.95 (*0-312-17028-9*) St. Martin's Pr.
Davis, Lindsey. A Body in the Bath House. 2003. 368p. pap. 12.95 (*0-446-69170-4*, Mysterious Pr. Paperback Bks.) Warner Bks., Inc.
Davis, Patricia K. A Midnight Carol: A Novel of How Charles Dickens Saved Christmas. 1999. 192p. 16.95 o.p. (*0-312-24523-8*); 2000. 208p. reprint ed. mass mkt. 4.99 (*0-312-97698-4*, St. Martin's Paperbacks) St. Martin's Pr.
Dawkins, Jane. Letters from Pemberley: The First Year. 1999. 200p. pap. 12.00 (*1-893337-00-6*) Chicken Soup Pr., Inc.

Dawson, Jill. Fred & Edie. l.t. ed. 2002. 324p. pap. 25.95 (*0-7862-3956-5*) Gale Group.

—Fred & Edie. 2001. 288p. 25.00 (*1-56649-222-X*) Welcome Rain Pubs.

—Fred & Edie: A Novel. 2002. 288p. pap. 13.00 (*0-618-19728-1*) Houghton Mifflin Co.

Dawson Smith, Barbara. Seduced by a Scoundrel. 1999. 320p. mass mkt. 6.50 (*0-312-97272-5*, St. Martin's Paperbacks) St. Martin's Pr.

De Botton, Alain. Kiss & Tell. 1997. 272p. pap. 13.00 (*0-312-15561-1*); 1996. 208p. 22.00 o.p. (*0-312-14282-X*) Picador.

de la Mare, Walter. Wind Blows Over. 1977. (Short Story Index Reprint Ser.). 25.95 (*0-8369-3384-2*) Ayer Co. Pubs., Inc.

De Lint, Charles. The Little Country. 2001. 544p. reprint ed. pap. 15.95 (*0-312-87649-1*, Orb Bks.) Doherty, Tom Assocs., LLC.

DeAndrea, William L. Killed in the Fog. l.t. ed. 1997. (Large Print Book Ser.). pap. 23.95 (*1-56895-434-4*, Wheeler Publishing, Inc.) Gale Group.

—Killed in the Fog. 1996. 222p. 20.50 (*0-684-83054-X*, Simon & Schuster); 20.00 (*1-883402-30-1*, Scribner) Simon & Schuster.

Defoe, Daniel. The Fortunes & Misfortunes of the Famous Moll Flanders, 2 vols., Set. (Illus.). reprint ed. (*0-404-07917-2*) AMS Pr., Inc.

—A Journal of the Plague Year. 2000. 252p. E-Book 9.95 (*0-594-02959-7*) 1873 Pr.

—A Journal of the Plague Year. (Illus.). reprint ed. (*0-404-07919-9*) AMS Pr., Inc.

—A Journal of the Plague Year. 1977. reprint ed. 11.95 o.p. (*0-460-00289-9*); 2.95 o.p. (*0-460-01289-4*) Biblio Distribution.

—A Journal of the Plague Year. 2001. per. 12.50 (*1-891355-77-5*); per. 15.50 (*1-58396-242-5*) Blue Unicorn Editions.

—A Journal of the Plague Year. (Shakespeare Head Edition of the Writings of Daniel Defoe Ser.: Vol. 6). 302p. 2001. pap. text 28.00 (*0-7426-5058-8*); 1999. reprint ed. lib. bdg. (*1-58201-058-7*) Classic Bks.

—A Journal of the Plague Year. 2001. (Dover Thrift Editions Ser.). 192p. pap. 2.50 (*0-486-41919-3*) Dover Pubns., Inc.

—A Journal of the Plague Year. 2002. 204p. 94.99 (*1-4043-1144-0*); per. 89.99 (*1-4043-1145-9*) IndyPublish.com.

—A Journal of the Plague Year. 1984. 240p. pap. 4.95 o.p. (*0-452-00689-9*, Meridian Bks.); 1984. pap. 5.95 o.p. (*0-452-01052-7*, Meridian Bks.); 1968. mass mkt. 0.75 o.p. (*0-451-50433-X*, Signet Classics); 1968. mass mkt. 0.50 o.p. (*0-451-50024-5*, Signet Classics); 1968. mass mkt. 0.60 o.p. (*0-451-50146-2*, Signet Classics); 1960. mass mkt. 0.95 o.p. (*0-451-50611-1*, Signet Classics); 1960. mass mkt. 1.25 o.p. (*0-451-50927-7*, Signet Classics); 1960. mass mkt. 1.50 o.p. (*0-451-51235-9*, CW1235, Signet Classics) NAL.

—A Journal of the Plague Year. Backsheider, Paula, ed. 1992. (Critical Editions Ser.). 361p. (C). pap. text 9.00 (*0-393-96188-5*) Norton, W. W. & Co., Inc.

—A Journal of the Plague Year. Landa, Louis, ed. (Oxford World's Classics Ser.). (Illus.). 1999. 336p. pap. 9.95 (*0-19-283618-8*); 1990. 330p. pap. 6.95 o.p. (*0-19-282682-4*) Oxford Univ. Pr., Inc.

—A Journal of the Plague Year. 2001. (Modern Library Classics). 272p. pap. 8.95 (*0-375-75789-9*, Modern Library) Random House Adult Trade Publishing Group.

—A Journal of the Plague Year. (Ebook Classic Ser.). E-Book 5.00 (*0-7410-1507-2*) SoftBook Pr.

—A Journal of the Plague Year. l.t. ed. 2000. (Perennial Bestsellers Ser.). 365p. 26.95 (*0-7838-9167-9*) Thorndike Pr.

—A Journal of the Plague Year. Man, John, ed. 1994. 336p. pap. 5.50 o.p. (*0-460-87462-4*, Everyman's Classic Library in Paperback) Tuttle Publishing.

—A Journal of the Plague Year. Burgess, Anthony & Bristow, Christopher, eds. 1966. (Penguin Classics Ser.). 256p. pap. 10.00 o.s.i (*0-14-043015-6*, Penguin Classics) Viking Penguin.

—A Journal of the Plague Year. Wall, Cynthia, ed. & intro. by. rev. ed. 2003. (Penguin Classics Ser.). (Illus.). 336p. pap. 10.00 (*0-14-043785-1*, Penguin Classics) Viking Penguin.

—Moll Flanders. 1991. (Everyman's Library: Vol. 32). 320p. 15.95 (*0-679-40548-8*, Everyman's Library) Knopf Publishing Group.

—Roxana. l.t. ed. 2000. (Perennial Bestsellers Ser.). 485p. 26.95 (*0-7838-9148-2*) Thorndike Pr.

—Roxana: The Fortunate Mistress. 2003. (Twelve-Point Ser.). lib. bdg. 25.00 (*1-58287-267-8*); lib. bdg. 26.00 (*1-58287-751-3*) North Bks.

—Roxana: The Fortunate Mistress. Jack, Jane, ed. 1971. (Oxford English Novels Ser.). pap. 7.95 o.p. (*0-19-281046-4*) Oxford Univ. Pr., Inc.

—Roxana: The Fortunate Mistress. Mullan, John, ed. 2nd ed. 1998. (Oxford World's Classics Ser.). (Illus.). 400p. pap. 11.95 (*0-19-283459-2*) Oxford Univ. Pr., Inc.

—Roxana: The Fortunate Mistress. Mullan, John, ed. & intro. by. 2nd ed. 1996. (Oxford World's Classics Ser.). (Illus.). 392p. pap. 8.95 o.p. (*0-19-282459-7*) Oxford Univ. Pr., Inc.

Defoe, Daniel & Rogers, Katherine. Roxana: The Fortunate Mistress. 1979. mass mkt. 2.25 o.p. (*0-451-51190-5*, CE1190, Signet Classics) NAL.

Deighton, Len. Ss-Gb. l.t. ed. 1993. pap. 17.95 o.p. (*0-7927-1323-0*); 1992. 19.95 o.p. (*0-7927-1324-9*) BBC Audiobooks America.

Delafield, E. M. The Provincial Lady in London. 1999. (Provincial Lady Ser.). (Illus.). 302p. pap. 16.95 (*0-89733-085-4*) Academy Chicago Pubs., Ltd.

—The Provincial Lady in London. l.t. ed. 1991. 21.95 o.p. (*0-7927-0939-X*, CH0148); pap. 19.95 o.p. (*0-7927-0940-3*, CS0245) BBC Audiobooks America.

Derleth, August. The Final Adventures of Solar Pons. 1998. (August Derleth Library ). 240p. 28.00 (*1-55246-012-6*) Battered Silicon Dispatch Box, The.

—The Return of Solar Pons. 1975. (Solar Pons Ser.: No. 6). 288p. pap. 1.50 o.p. (*0-523-23650-6*, Pinnacle Bks.) Kensington Publishing Corp.

—Solar Pons: The Chronicles of Solar Pons, No. 1. 1973. 8.95 o.p. (*0-87054-005-X*, Mycroft & Moran) Arkham Hse. Pubs.

—The Solar Pons Omnibus Edition, 2 Vols., Set. Copper, Basil, ed. 1982. (Illus.). 39.95 o.p. (*0-87054-006-8*, Mycroft & Moran) Arkham Hse. Pubs.

DesJardien, Teresa. The Reluctant Smuggler. 2001. (Signet Regency Romance Ser.). 224p. mass mkt. 4.99 o.s.i (*0-451-20220-1*) NAL.

Dessau, Joanna. All or Nothing. l.t. ed. 1998. (Ulverscroft Large Print Ser.). 320p. 29.99 (*0-7089-3964-3*, Ulverscroft) Thorpe, F. A. Pubs. GBR. *Dist:* Ulverscroft Large Print Bks., Ltd., Ulverscroft Large Print Canada, Ltd.

Deval, Jacqueline. Reckless Appetites: A Culinary Romance. 1993. 288p. text 21.00 o.p. (*0-88001-322-2*) HarperCollins Pubs.

Deveraux, Jude. The Conquest. l.t. ed. 1991. (General Ser.). 408p. 17.95 o.p. (*0-8161-5230-6*); lib. bdg. 20.95 (*0-8161-5231-4*) Gale Group. (Macmillan Reference USA).

—The Conquest. Marrow, Linda, ed. 1991. 320p. mass mkt. 7.99 (*0-671-64447-5*, Pocket) Simon & Schuster.

Devon, Marian. Miss Kendal Sets Her Cap. 1996. mass mkt. 4.50 o.s.i (*0-449-22456-2*, Fawcett) Ballantine Bks.

Dewhurst, Eileen. A Nice Little Business. 1987. (Crime Club Ser.). 192p. 12.95 o.s.i (*0-385-24313-8*) Doubleday Publishing.

—There Was a Little Girl. 1986. (Crime Club Ser.). 192p. 12.95 o.p. (*0-385-23230-6*) Doubleday Publishing.

Dexter, Colin. The Daughters of Cain. 1996. 320p. mass mkt. 6.99 (*0-8041-1364-5*) Ballantine Bks.

—The Daughters of Cain. unabr. ed. 1995. audio 49.95 (*0-7861-0714-6*, 1591) Blackstone Audio Bks., Inc.

—The Daughters of Cain. unabr. ed. 1995. (Inspector Morse Mystery Ser.: Bk. 11). audio 59.95 (*0-7451-6555-9*, CAB 1171) Chivers Audio Bks. GBR. *Dist:* BBC Audiobooks America.

—The Daughters of Cain, Set. abr. ed. 1996. (Inspector Morse Mystery Ser.). 3p. audio 16.99 (*0-88646-407-2*, 393852) Durkin Hayes Publishing Ltd.

—The Daughters of Cain. o.p. (*0-517-70153-7*) Random Hse. Value Publishing.

—The Daughters of Cain. unabr. ed. 2000. (Inspector Morse Mystery Ser.: Vol. 11). audio 70.00 (*0-7887-0297-1*, 94490E7) Recorded Bks., LLC.

—The Daughters of Cain. l.t. ed. 1995. (Charnwood Large Print Ser.). 448p. 29.99 o.p. (*0-7089-8869-5*, Charnwood) Thorpe, F. A. Pubs. GBR. *Dist:* Ulverscroft Large Print Bks., Ltd., Ulverscroft Large Print Canada, Ltd.

—The Dead of Jericho, Set. 1998. (Inspector Morse Mystery Ser.). audio 29.95 (*0-7540-7519-2*) BBC Audiobooks America.

—The Dead of Jericho. 1996. (Inspector Morse Mystery Ser.). 304p. mass mkt. 6.99 (*0-8041-1486-2*, Ivy Bks.) Ballantine Bks.

—The Dead of Jericho. 1988. 224p. mass mkt. 4.50 o.s.i (*0-553-27237-3*) Bantam Bks.

—The Dead of Jericho. unabr. ed. 2000. (Inspector Morse Mystery Ser.: Bk. 5). audio 49.95 (*0-7451-5894-3*, CAB 442) Chivers Audio Bks. GBR. *Dist:* BBC Audiobooks America.

—The Dead of Jericho. 2001. audio (*0-333-90662-4*) Macmillan U.K. GBR. *Dist:* Macmillan Publishing Co., Inc.

—The Dead of Jericho. 1981. 168p. 9.95 o.p. (*0-312-18511-1*) St. Martin's Pr.

—The Dead of Jericho. 1990. audio 53.95 o.p. (*0-8161-9623-0*) Thorndike Pr.

—The Dead of Jericho. l.t. ed. 1984. 416p. 15.95 o.p. (*0-7089-1098-X*, Ulverscroft) Thorpe, F. A. Pubs. GBR. *Dist:* Ulverscroft Large Print Bks., Ltd.

—Death Is Now My Neighbor: An Inspector Morse Novel. 1998. (Illus.). 336p. mass mkt. 6.99 (*0-8041-1572-9*, Ivy Bks.) Ballantine Bks.

—Death Is Now My Neighbor: An Inspector Morse Novel. unabr. ed. (Inspector Morse Mystery Ser.). 2000. 8p. audio compact disk 79.95 (*0-7540-5349-0*, CCD 040); 1998. audio 59.95 (*0-7451-6775-6*, CAB 1391) Chivers Audio Bks. GBR. *Dist:* BBC Audiobooks America.

—Death Is Now My Neighbor: An Inspector Morse Novel. aut. ed. 1997. 24.00 o.s.i (*0-517-70824-8*) Crown Publishing Group.

—The Jewel That Was Ours: An Inspector Morse Mystery. 1993. 256p. mass mkt. 6.99 (*0-8041-0981-8*, Ivy Bks.) Ballantine Bks.

—The Jewel That Was Ours: An Inspector Morse Mystery. unabr. ed. 1996. audio 44.95 (*0-7861-0980-7*, 1757) Blackstone Audio Bks., Inc.

—The Jewel That Was Ours: An Inspector Morse Mystery. unabr. ed. 2000. (Inspector Morse Mystery Ser.: Bk. 9). audio 59.95 (*0-7451-4090-4*, CAB 778) Chivers Audio Bks. GBR. *Dist:* BBC Audiobooks America.

—The Jewel That Was Ours: An Inspector Morse Mystery. abr. ed. 1994. audio 16.99 (*0-88646-369-6*, LFP 7369) Durkin Hayes Publishing Ltd.

—The Jewel That Was Ours: An Inspector Morse Mystery. 2001. audio (*0-333-90435-4*) Macmillan U.K. GBR. *Dist:* Macmillan Publishing Co., Inc.

—The Jewel That Was Ours: An Inspector Morse Mystery. unabr. ed. 1992. (Inspector Morse Mystery Ser.: Vol. 9). audio 60.00 (*1-55690-683-8*, 92315E7) Recorded Bks., LLC.

—Last Bus to Woodstock. 1996. 288p. mass mkt. 6.99 (*0-8041-1490-0*, Ivy Bks.) Ballantine Bks.

—Last Bus to Woodstock. 1988. 224p. mass mkt. 3.95 o.s.i (*0-553-27777-4*) Bantam Bks.

—Last Bus to Woodstock. l.t. ed. 1990. o.p. (*0-7089-2298-8*, Ulverscroft) Thorpe, F. A. Pubs.

—Last Seen Wearing: An Inspector Morse Mystery. unabr. ed. 2000. (Inspector Morse Mystery Ser.). audio 29.95 (*1-57270-145-5*, N61145u, Audio Editions Mystery Masters) Audio Partners Publishing Corp.

—Last Seen Wearing: An Inspector Morse Mystery. 1997. 336p. mass mkt. 6.99 (*0-8041-1491-9*, Ivy Bks.) Ballantine Bks.

—Last Seen Wearing: An Inspector Morse Mystery. 1988. 272p. mass mkt. 5.99 o.s.i (*0-553-28003-1*) Bantam Bks.

—Last Seen Wearing: An Inspector Morse Mystery. unabr. ed. 2000. (Inspector Morse Mystery Ser.: Bk. 2). audio 59.95 (*0-7451-4122-6*, CAB 805) Chivers Audio Bks. GBR. *Dist:* BBC Audiobooks America.

—Last Seen Wearing: An Inspector Morse Mystery. l.t. ed. 1989. 17.95 o.p. (*0-7089-2184-1*, Ulverscroft) Thorpe, F. A. Pubs. GBR. *Dist:* Ulverscroft Large Print Bks., Ltd.

—Morse's Greatest Mystery. unabr. ed. 1996. audio 39.95 (*0-7861-0957-2*, 1734) Blackstone Audio Bks., Inc.

—Morse's Greatest Mystery & Other Stories. 1996. (Inspector Morse Mystery Ser.). 304p. mass mkt. 6.99 (*0-8041-1309-2*, Ivy Bks.) Ballantine Bks.

—Morse's Greatest Mystery & Other Stories. abr. ed. 1996. audio 24.99 (*0-88646-410-2*, 7410) Durkin Hayes Publishing Ltd.

—Morse's Greatest Mystery & Other Stories. unabr. ed. 1996. audio 51.00 (*0-7887-0481-8*, 94674E7) Recorded Bks., LLC.

—The Remorseful Day. 2001. 336p. mass mkt. 6.99 (*0-8041-1954-6*, Fawcett) Ballantine Bks.

—The Remorseful Day. 2000. (Inspector Morse Mystery Ser.). 384p. 24.00 o.s.i (*0-609-60622-0*); 24.00 (*0-609-50295-6*) Crown Publishing Group. (Crown).

—The Remorseful Day. l.t. ed. 2000. (Wheeler Large Print Book Ser.). 442p. 27.95 (*1-56895-883-8*, Wheeler Publishing, Inc.) Gale Group.

—The Riddle of the Third Mile. 1997. (Inspector Morse Mystery Ser.). 272p. mass mkt. 6.99 (*0-8041-1488-9*, Ivy Bks.) Ballantine Bks.

—The Riddle of the Third Mile. 1988. 224p. mass mkt. 5.99 o.s.i (*0-553-27363-9*) Bantam Bks.

—The Riddle of the Third Mile. 1984. 224p. 11.95 o.p. (*0-312-68228-X*) St. Martin's Pr.

—The Riddle of the Third Mile. l.t. ed. 2001. 349p. 28.95 (*0-7862-3343-5*); (*0-7540-1619-6*); (*0-7540-2473-3*) Thorndike Pr.

—The Secret of Annexe 3. unabr. ed. 2000. (Inspector Morse Mystery Ser.). audio 29.95 (*1-57270-155-2*, N61155u, Audio Editions Mystery Masters) Audio Partners Publishing Corp.

—The Secret of Annexe 3. unabr. ed. 1994. (Inspector Morse Mystery Ser.). audio 54.95 (*0-7451-4321-0*, CAB 1004) BBC Audiobooks America.

—The Secret of Annexe 3, Vol. 3. 1997. (Inspector Morse Mystery Ser.). 304p. mass mkt. 6.99 (*0-8041-1489-7*, Ivy Bks.) Ballantine Bks.

—The Secret of Annexe 3. 1988. 224p. reprint ed. mass mkt. 5.99 o.s.i (*0-553-27549-6*) Bantam Bks.

—The Secret of Annexe 3. unabr. ed. 2000. (Inspector Morse Mystery Ser.: Bk. 7). audio 49.95 Chivers Audio Bks. GBR. *Dist:* BBC Audiobooks America.

—The Secret of Annexe 3. 1987. 224p. 15.95 o.p. (*0-312-01089-3*, Saint Martin's Minotaur) St. Martin's Pr.

—The Secret of Annexe 3. l.t. ed. 2000. (Mystery Ser.). 371p. pap. 26.95 (*0-7862-2676-5*); (*0-7540-4235-9*); (*0-7540-4236-7*) Thorndike Pr.

—Service of All the Dead. 1996. 304p. mass mkt. 6.99 (*0-8041-1485-4*, Ivy Bks.) Ballantine Bks.

—Service of All the Dead. 1988. 224p. mass mkt. 3.95 o.s.i (*0-553-27239-X*) Bantam Bks.

—Service of All the Dead. 1982. (Murder Ink Mystery Ser.: No. 43). pap. 2.50 o.p. (*0-440-18026-0*) Dell Publishing.

—Service of All the Dead. 1979. 9.95 o.p. (*0-312-71316-9*) St. Martin's Pr.

—Service of All the Dead. l.t. ed. 2000. (Mystery Ser.). 402p. 27.95 (*0-7862-3040-1*); (*0-7540-1531-9*); (*0-7540-2405-9*) Thorndike Pr.

—The Silent World of Nicholas Quinn. 1997. (Inspector Morse Mystery Ser.). 288p. mass mkt. 6.99 (*0-8041-1487-0*, Ivy Bks.) Ballantine Bks.

—The Silent World of Nicholas Quinn. 1988. 224p. mass mkt. 5.99 o.s.i (*0-553-27238-1*) Bantam Bks.

—The Silent World of Nicholas Quinn. (Mystery Bookshelf Selection Ser.). 1978. pap. 3.50 o.p. (*0-312-72468-3*, Saint Martin's Griffin); 1977. 7.95 o.p. (*0-312-72467-5*) St. Martin's Pr.

—The Silent World of Nicholas Quinn. l.t. ed. 1992. (Mystery Ser.). 432p. 29.99 o.p. (*0-7089-2620-7*, Ulverscroft) Thorpe, F. A. Pubs. GBR. *Dist:* Ulverscroft Large Print Bks., Ltd., Ulverscroft Large Print Canada, Ltd.

—The Way Through the Woods: An Inspector Morse Mystery. 1994. 336p. mass mkt. 6.99 (*0-8041-1142-1*, Ivy Bks.) Ballantine Bks.

—The Way Through the Woods: An Inspector Morse Mystery. unabr. ed. 1996. audio 49.95 (*0-7861-0931-9*, 1686) Blackstone Audio Bks., Inc.

—The Way Through the Woods: An Inspector Morse Mystery. abr. ed. 1993. audio 16.99 (*0-88646-352-1*, LFP 7352) Durkin Hayes Publishing Ltd.

—The Way Through the Woods: An Inspector Morse Mystery. 1995. 4.99 o.p. (*0-517-14495-6*) Random Hse. Value Publishing.

—The Way Through the Woods: An Inspector Morse Mystery. unabr. ed. 1993. (Inspector Morse Mystery Ser.: Vol. 10). audio 70.00 (*1-55690-883-0*, 93325E7) Recorded Bks., LLC.

—The Wench Is Dead. unabr. ed. 2000. (Inspector Morse Mystery Ser.). audio 29.95 (*1-57270-130-7*, N61130u, Audio Editions Mystery Masters) Audio Partners Publishing Corp.

—The Wench Is Dead. 1999. (Inspector Morse Mystery Ser.). 290p. mass mkt. 6.99 o.s.i (*0-8041-1889-2*, Ivy Bks.) Ballantine Bks.

—The Wench Is Dead. 1991. 208p. mass mkt. 5.99 o.s.i (*0-553-29120-3*) Bantam Bks.

—The Wench Is Dead. unabr. ed. 2000. (Inspector Morse Mystery Ser.: Bk. 8). audio 49.95 (*0-7451-5896-X*, CAB 582) Chivers Audio Bks. GBR. *Dist:* BBC Audiobooks America.

—The Wench Is Dead. 1992. 3.99 o.p. (*0-517-09062-7*) Random Hse. Value Publishing.

—The Wench Is Dead. 1990. 15.95 o.p. (*0-312-04444-5*, Saint Martin's Minotaur) St. Martin's Pr.

—The Wench Is Dead. l.t. ed. 1991. (Ulverscroft Large Print Ser.). 29.99 o.p. (*0-7089-2512-X*, Ulverscroft) Thorpe, F. A. Pubs. GBR. *Dist:* Ulverscroft Large Print Bks., Ltd., Ulverscroft Large Print Canada, Ltd.

—The Wench Is Dead. abr. ed. 1998. audio 15.00 (*0-333-74612-0*) Ulverscroft Audio (U.S.A.).

Dias, Dexter. Error of Judgement. 1996. 384p. 21.50 o.p. (*0-89296-651-3*) Warner Bks., Inc.

—Error of Judgment. unabr. ed. 1997. audio 69.95 (*0-7451-6751-9*, CAB 1367) BBC Audiobooks America.

—Error of Judgment. l.t. ed. 1997. (Mystery Ser.). 512p. lib. bdg. 28.95 (*0-7838-8282-3*) Thorndike Pr.

—Error of Judgment. 1997. 400p. pap. 6.50 (*0-446-40527-2*, Mysterious Pr. Paperback Bks.) Warner Bks., Inc.

—False Witness. l.t. ed. 2002. (Magna Large Print Ser.). 480p. (*0-7505-1883-9*) Magna Large Print Bks. GBR. *Dist:* Ulverscroft Large Print Canada, Ltd.

—False Witness. 1995. 82p. 19.95 o.p. (*0-89296-612-2*) Mysterious Pr.

—False Witness. 1996. 352p. mass mkt. 5.99 o.s.i (*0-446-40492-6*) Warner Bks., Inc.

Dibdin, Michael. The Dying of the Light: A Mystery. 1995. 160p. pap. 11.00 (*0-679-75310-9*, Vintage) Knopf Publishing Group.

—The Last Sherlock Holmes Story. 1978. 7.95 o.s.i (*0-394-50065-2*, Pantheon) Knopf Publishing Group.

—The Last Sherlock Holmes Story. 1996. 192p. pap. 12.00 (*0-679-76658-8*) Random Hse., Inc.

Settings

Dickens, Charles. The Annotated Christmas Carol. 1977. (Illus.). 15.00 o.s.i (*0-517-52741-3*) Crown Publishing Group.

—The Annotated Christmas Carol. 1984. (Illus.). mass mkt. 4.95 o.p. (*0-380-01722-9*, 34108-5, Avon Bks.) Morrow/Avon.

—The Annotated Christmas Carol. 2003. (Illus.). 288p. 29.95 (*0-393-05158-7*) Norton, W. W. & Co., Inc.

—The Annotated Christmas Carol. 1989. 5.99 o.s.i (*0-517-68780-1*) Random Hse. Value Publishing.

—Barnaby Rudge. Spence, G. W., ed. 1974. (Penguin English Library). (Illus.). 768p. 10.95 (*0-14-043090-3*, Penguin Classics) Viking Penguin.

—Bleak House. 1992. (Bantam Classics Ser.). 848p. mass mkt. 6.95 (*0-553-21223-0*, Bantam Classics) Bantam Bks.

—Bleak House. E-Book 5.00 (*0-7607-1428-2*) Barnes & Noble, Inc.

—Bleak House. 2000. per. 25.00 (*1-891355-95-3*) Blue Unicorn Editions.

—Bleak House. audio 220.00 Cover to Cover Cassettes, Ltd.

—Bleak House, 001. Zabel, Morton D., ed. 1956. (YA). (gr. 9 up). pap. 16.36 (*0-395-05104-5*, Riverside Editions) Houghton Mifflin Co.

—Bleak House. 1987. audio 140.00 Jimcin Recordings.

—Bleak House. 1991. (Everyman's Library: Vol. 8). 1024p. 23.00 (*0-679-40568-2*, Everyman's Library) Knopf Publishing Group.

—Bleak House. 1964. 896p. mass mkt. 6.95 o.s.i (*0-451-52402-0*, CE1739, Signet Classics); mass mkt. 3.50 o.p. (*0-451-52001-7*) NAL.

—Bleak House. Ford, George & Monod, Sylvere, eds. (Critical Editions Ser.). (Illus.). 1978. 24.95 o.p. (*0-393-04374-6*); 1977. 986p. (C). pap. text 15.50 (*0-393-09332-8*) Norton, W. W. & Co., Inc.

—Bleak House. Gill, Stephen, ed. & intro. by. (Oxford World's Classics Ser.). (Illus.). 1998. 976p. pap. 10.95 (*0-19-283401-0*); 1996. 970p. pap. 7.95 o.p. (*0-19-282985-8*) Oxford Univ. Pr., Inc.

—Bleak House. 1987. (Illus.). 908p. 17.95 (*0-19-254503-5*) Oxford Univ. Pr., Inc.

—Bleak House. 1999. E-Book 3.99 incl. cd-rom (*1-57646-073-8*) Quiet Vision Publishing.

—Bleak House. Ford, George & Monod, Sylvere, eds. 1985. 840p. 10.95 o.s.i (*0-394-60520-9*) Random Hse., Inc.

—Bleak House. 1983. (Bantam Classics Ser.). 11.05 o.p. (*0-606-03733-0*) Turtleback Bks.

—Bleak House. 1994. (Everyman Paperback Classics Ser.). 512p. pap. 6.95 (*0-460-87423-3*, Everyman's Classic Library in Paperback) Tuttle Publishing.

—Bleak House. Bradbury, Nicola, ed. & intro. by. 1997. (Penguin Classics Ser.). (Illus.). 1088p. 10.95 o.s.i (*0-14-043496-8*, Penguin Classics) Viking Penguin.

—Bleak House. Page, Norma, ed. 1971. (English Library). 976p. pap. 8.95 o.p. (*0-14-043063-6*, Penguin Classics) Viking Penguin.

—Bleak House. 1997. (Classics Ser.). 720p. pap. 3.95 (*1-85326-082-7*, 0827WW) Wordsworth Editions, Ltd. GBR. *Dist:* Casemate Pubs. & Bk. Distributors, LLC.

—The Bleak House. E-Book 2.49 (*1-58744-098-9*) Electric Umbrella Publishing.

—Bleak House. unabr. ed. Pt. 1. 1997. audio 65.95; Pt. 1, set. 1997. audio 77.95 (*1-55685-448-X*, 448-X); Pt. 2, set. 1999. audio 65.95; Pt. 2, set. 1997. audio 65.95 Audio Bk. Contractors, Inc.

—Bleak House. unabr. ed. audio 149.95 o.p. (*1-85549-961-4*, CTC 038) BBC Audiobooks America.

—Bleak House. abr. ed. 1999. audio 24.35 (*0-563-55836-9*) BBC Bk. Publishing GBR. *Dist:* Ulverscroft Large Print Bks., Ltd.

—Bleak House. 1977. reprint ed. 10.95 o.p. (*0-460-00236-8*) Biblio Distribution.

—Bleak House. unabr. ed. 1999. Pt. 1. audio 89.95 (*0-7861-1478-9*, 2330-A); Pt. 2. audio 69.95 (*0-7861-1487-8*, 2330-B) Blackstone Audio Bks., Inc.

—Bleak House. unabr. collector's ed. 1992. (J). Pt. A. audio 112.00 (*0-7366-2127-X*, 2929-A); Pt. B. audio 112.00 (*0-7366-2128-8*, 2929-B) Books on Tape, Inc.

—Bleak House. 1990. 880p. reprint ed. lib. bdg. 39.95 o.p. (*0-89966-679-5*) Buccaneer Bks., Inc.

—Bleak House. 2001. (Collected Works of Charles Dickens). (Illus.). reprint ed. pap. text 28.00 (*0-7426-7324-3*) Classic Bks.

—Bleak House. unabr. ed. 1999. Set, Pt. 1. audio 89.95; Set, Pt. 2. audio 69.95 Highsmith Inc.

—Bleak House. abr. ed. 1994. (Ultimate Classics Ser.). 16.95 o.p. (*1-55800-632-X*) NewStar Media, Inc.

—Bleak House. abr. ed. 1997. 4p. audio 23.95 o.s.i (*0-14-086177-7*, Penguin AudioBooks) Viking Penguin.

—Character Portraits from Dickens. Welsh, Charles, ed. 1972. (Studies in Dickens: No. 52). reprint ed. lib. bdg. 75.00 (*0-8383-1552-6*) M.S.G. Haskell Hse.

—Charles Dickens. 1993. 864p. 13.99 (*0-517-09339-1*) Random Hse. Value Publishing.

—Charles Dickens. unabr. ed. 1995. (Classic Author Ser.). (J). audio 16.95 (*1-55935-169-1*) Soundelux Audio Publishing.

—Charles Dickens: Three Great Novels: Hard Times; A Tale of Two Cities; Great Expectations. 1994. 836p. pap. 15.95 o.p. (*0-19-282332-9*) Oxford Univ. Pr., Inc.

—A Charles Dickens Christmas: A Christmas Carol, The Chimes & The Cricket on the Hearth. 1976. (Illus.). 19.95 o.p. (*0-19-519899-9*) Oxford Univ. Pr., Inc.

—Charles Dickens Christmas Tales. 1985. 11.99 o.p. (*0-517-47468-9*) Random Hse. Value Publishing.

—Christmas Books. 1989. (Oxford World's Classics Ser.). 520p. (J). pap. 7.95 o.p. (*0-19-281790-6*) Oxford Univ. Pr., Inc.

—Christmas Books: A Christmas Carol & The Chimes. Stater, Michael, ed. 1971. (English Library: Vol. 1). 266p. 7.95 (*0-14-043068-7*, Penguin Classics) Viking Penguin.

—Christmas Books: The Crickett on the Hearth, The Battle of Life & The Haunted Man. Stater, Michael, ed. 1971. (Penguin English Library: Vol. 2). (Illus.). 368p. pap. 9.95 o.s.i (*0-14-043069-5*, Penguin Classics) Viking Penguin.

—A Christmas Carol. 1999. E-Book 7.95 incl. cd-rom (*0-9669705-3-5*) 23 Hse.

—A Christmas Carol. Date not set. pap. text (*0-17-557046-9*) Addison-Wesley Longman, Inc.

—A Christmas Carol. 1994. pap. text 39.50 (*0-582-23664-9*) Addison-Wesley Longman, Ltd. GBR. *Dist:* Trans-Atlantic Pubns., Inc.

—A Christmas Carol. 1994. (Illustrated Classics Collection). 64p. pap. 4.95 (*0-7854-0747-2*, 40494) American Guidance Service, Inc.

—A Christmas Carol. 1999. audio Art of Hearing, Inc.

—A Christmas Carol. 1989. (Illus.). 118p. 100.00 (*0-933861-07-9*) Berliner, Harold.

—A Christmas Carol. 1992. (Illus.). 144p. 6.95 o.p. (*0-681-41606-8*) Borders Pr.

—A Christmas Carol. 2000. audio 11.99 (*0-660-17877-X*); audio compact disk 15.95 (*0-660-17878-8*) Canadian Broadcasting Corp./Societe Radio-Canada CAN. *Dist:* Georgetown Terminal Warehouse.

—A Christmas Carol. audio 4.98 Covenant Communications, Inc.

—A Christmas Carol. 1982. (Illus.). o.p. (*0-434-95857-3*) David & Charles Pubs.

—A Christmas Carol. 1996. pap. 5.95 incl. audio Dover Pubns., Inc.

—A Christmas Carol. 1931. pap. 5.60 (*0-87129-314-5*, C23) Dramatic Publishing Co.

—A Christmas Carol. 1993. 37p. pap. 5.00 (*1-57514-211-2*, 1150) Encore Performance Publishing.

—A Christmas Carol. (Focus on the Family Great Stories Ser.). 1999. (Illus.). 184p. pap. 7.99 o.p. (*1-56179-746-4*); 1997. 12.99 o.p. (*1-56179-556-9*) Focus on the Family Publishing.

—A Christmas Carol. audio 14.95 Halvorson Assocs.

—A Christmas Carol. 1996. 35.00 o.p. (*0-15-100275-4*) Harcourt Children's Bks.

—A Christmas Carol. 1995. pap. 20.00 (*0-15-200952-3*) Harcourt Trade Pubs.

—A Christmas Carol. 2001. (Illus.). 80p. (J). (gr. 1-5). 17.95 (*0-06-028577-X*) HarperCollins Children's Bk. Group.

—A Christmas Carol. 1997. (Illus.). text 8.25 (*0-03-051492-4*) Holt, Rinehart & Winston.

—A Christmas Carol. 2001. audio 12.95 Lodestone Catalog, The.

—A Christmas Carol. audio 7.95 National Recording Co.

—A Christmas Carol. Green, Frank, ed. 1995. (Thornes Classic Novels Ser.). (Illus.). 221p. pap. 14.95 (*0-7487-1832-X*) Nelson Thornes GBR. *Dist:* Trans-Atlantic Pubns., Inc.

—A Christmas Carol. 1990. (Illus.). 144p. pap. 10.00 (*0-14-007120-2*, Penguin Bks.) Penguin Group (USA) Inc.

—A Christmas Carol. 1999. E-Book 3.99 incl. cd-rom (*1-57646-075-4*) Quiet Vision Publishing.

—A Christmas Carol. 2001. (Adventures in Old-Time Radio Ser.). audio 4.98. audio compact disk 4.98 Radio Spirits, Inc.

—A Christmas Carol. 1987. (Radiobook Ser.). audio 4.98 (*0-929541-21-9*) Radiola Co.

—A Christmas Carol. 1990. (Miniature Editions Ser.). (Illus.). 160p. text 4.95 o.p. (*0-89471-854-1*) Running Pr. Bk. Pubs.

—A Christmas Carol. 1997. (Illus.). 224p. mass mkt. 3.99 (*0-671-52078-4*, Pocket) Simon & Schuster.

—A Christmas Carol. 1981. 240p. pap. 2.50 (*0-671-44199-X*, Simon Pulse) Simon & Schuster Children's Publishing.

—A Christmas Carol. 1987. (Illus.). 15.75 o.p. (*0-8446-0078-4*) Smith, Peter Pub., Inc.

—A Christmas Carol. 1979. (Illus.). 9.95 o.p. (*0-312-13403-7*) St. Martin's Pr.

—A Christmas Carol. 1991. 176p. pap. 4.95 o.p. (*0-460-87097-1*, Everyman's Classic Library in Paperback) Tuttle Publishing.

—A Christmas Carol. 1999. pap. 10.95 incl. audio (*0-14-086224-2*) Viking Penguin.

—A Christmas Carol. 1993. (Illus.). 168p. 35.00 o.p. (*0-300-05843-8*) Yale Univ. Pr.

—A Christmas Carol. Barbour Books Staff, ed. 1997. 99p. pap. text 0.99 o.p. (*1-55748-963-7*) Barbour Publishing, Inc.

—A Christmas Carol. ltd. ed. 1993. (Illus.). 116p. 685.00 (*0-910457-28-X*) Arion Pr.

—A Christmas Carol. abr. ed. audio 12.95 (*0-89926-140-X*, 828) Audio Bk. Co.

—A Christmas Carol. unabr. ed. 1999. audio 17.95 (*1-57270-115-3*, F21115u, Cover to Cover Classics) Audio Partners Publishing Corp.

—A Christmas Carol. unabr. ed. 1997. audio 18.95 o.p. (*1-85549-922-3*, C T C 125) BBC Audiobooks America.

—A Christmas Carol. 1986. (Bantam Classics Ser.). 112p. reprint ed. mass mkt. 3.95 (*0-553-21244-3*) Bantam Dell Publishing Group.

—A Christmas Carol. unabr. ed. 1989. audio 23.95 (*0-7861-0069-9*, 1065) Blackstone Audio Bks., Inc.

—A Christmas Carol. unabr. ed. 2001. audio 17.95 (*0-7366-6763-6*); audio 14.95 Books on Tape, Inc.

—A Christmas Carol. deluxe ed. 1976. 9.95 o.p. (*0-385-12816-9*) Doubleday Publishing.

—A Christmas Carol. 1991. (Thrift Editions Ser.). 80p. reprint ed. pap. 1.00 (*0-486-26865-9*) Dover Pubns., Inc.

—A Christmas Carol. abr. ed. audio 15.95 o.p. (*0-88646-035-2*, 7051) Durkin Hayes Publishing Ltd.

—A Christmas Carol. English, Martin & Warren, Bill, eds. unabr. ed. 1997. audio 12.00 (*0-9662157-0-2*) Grey Matter Productions.

—A Christmas Carol. unabr. ed. audio 14.95 Halvorson Assocs.

—A Christmas Carol, Set. unabr. ed. 1999. audio 23.95 Highsmith Inc.

—A Christmas Carol. unabr. ed. 1978. audio 7.95 Jimcin Recordings.

—A Christmas Carol. abr. ed. 1999. (Works of Charles Dickens). audio 13.98 (*962-634-682-5*, NA218214); audio compact disk 15.98 (*962-634-182-3*, NA218212) Naxos of America, Inc. (Naxos AudioBooks).

—A Christmas Carol. abr. ed. 1993. 16.95 o.p. (*1-55800-700-8*) NewStar Media, Inc.

—A Christmas Carol. unabr. ed. 2001. audio 29.95 NorthStar Audio Bks.

—A Christmas Carol. unabr. ed. 2000. audio compact disk 29.00 (*0-7887-4480-1*, C1182E7) Recorded Bks., LLC.

—A Christmas Carol. abr. ed. 2001. audio 34.95; Set. 1999. audio 34.95 Soundings, Ltd. GBR. *Dist:* Ulverscroft Large Print Bks., Ltd., ISIS Publishing.

—A Christmas Carol. abr. ed. audio 10.95 (*0-8045-0728-7*, SAC 728) Spoken Arts, Inc.

—A Christmas Carol. unabr. ed. 1993. (Audio Books Ser.). 26.95 o.p. incl. audio (*1-85496-077-6*) Thorndike Pr.

—A Christmas Carol. abr. ed. 1997. audio 16.95 (*1-85998-048-1*) Trafalgar Square.

—A Christmas Carol: A Facsimile Edition of the Autograph Manuscript in the Pierpont Morgan Library. 1993. (Illus.). 139p. (*0-87598-098-8*) Pierpont Morgan Library.

—A Christmas Carol: Adapted for Theater. 1993. (Illus.). 32p. (YA). (gr. 2-12). 14.95 (*0-8362-4507-5*) Andrews McMeel Publishing.

—A Christmas Carol: The Original Manuscript. 1971. (Illus.). 144p. reprint ed. pap. 8.95 (*0-486-20980-6*) Dover Pubns., Inc.

—A Christmas Carol: The Public Reading Version. Collins, Philip, ed. 1971. (Illus.). 232p. 20.00 (*0-87104-228-2*) New York Public Library.

—A Christmas Carol: The Radio Play. Williams, John, ed. abr. ed. 1992. audio 14.95 (*0-9634652-1-X*) Radio Theatre Productions - John L. Williams.

—A Christmas Carol & Other Christmas Stories. 1976. 21.95 (*0-8488-0796-0*) Amereon, Ltd.

—A Christmas Carol & Other Haunting Tales. 1998. (New York Public Library Collector's Edition Ser.). (Illus.). 416p. 18.50 o.s.i (*0-385-48725-8*) Doubleday Publishing.

—A Christmas Carol & Other Stories. 1995. (Modern Library Ser.). E-Book 4.95 (*1-931208-37-9*) Adobe Systems, Inc.

—A Christmas Carol & Other Stories. (Modern Library Classics). 2001. 368p. pap. 7.95 (*0-375-75888-7*); 2000. E-Book 4.95 (*0-679-64131-9*) Random House Adult Trade Publishing Group. (Modern Library).

—A Christmas Carol & Other Stories. 1995. (Modern Library Ser.). (Illus.). 368p. 14.95 (*0-679-60179-1*) Random Hse., Inc.

—A Christmas Carol & Sketches of a Young Couple. rev. ed. 2001. 150p. per. 9.90 (*1-58396-038-4*) Blue Unicorn Editions.

—A Christmas Carol Christmas Book. 9999. 16.95 o.p. (*0-316-41446-8*) Little Brown & Co.

—The Cricket on the Hearth & Other Christmas Stories. 1994. 128p. (Orig.). pap. 1.00 (*0-486-28039-X*) Dover Pubns., Inc.

—David Copperfield. 1997. (Classics Illustrated Study Guides). (Illus.). mass mkt. 4.99 (*1-57840-039-2*) Acclaim Bks.

—David Copperfield. Date not set. pap. text (*0-17-557022-1*) Addison-Wesley Longman, Inc.

—David Copperfield, Pt. 2, set. 2000. audio 65.95; 1999. 65.95 incl. audio Audio Bk. Contractors, Inc.

—David Copperfield. unabr. ed. audio 149.95 o.p. (*1-85549-960-6*, CTC 060) BBC Audiobooks America.

—David Copperfield. 1981. (Illus.). 795p. 55.00 o.p. (*0-913720-20-8*); 95.00 o.p. (*0-913720-19-4*) Beil, Frederic C. Pub., Inc.

—David Copperfield. 1975. reprint ed. 10.95 o.p. (*0-460-00242-2*) Biblio Distribution.

—David Copperfield. unabr. ed. 1992. Pt. 1. audio 85.95 (*0-7861-0381-7*, 1335-A); Pt. 2. audio 85.95 (*0-7861-0382-5*, 1335-B) Blackstone Audio Bks., Inc.

—David Copperfield. 1996. (FRE.). Vol. I. pap. 7.95 (*2-87714-325-2*); Vol. II. pap. 7.95 (*2-87714-326-0*) Bookking International FRA. *Dist:* Distribooks, Inc.

—David Copperfield. unabr. collector's ed. 1977. (J). Pt. A. audio 80.00 (*0-7366-0064-7*, 1076-A); Pt. B. audio 96.00 (*0-7366-0065-5*, 1076-B) Books on Tape, Inc.

—David Copperfield. 1982. reprint ed. lib. bdg. 45.95 (*0-89966-370-2*) Buccaneer Bks., Inc.

—David Copperfield. Fuller, Edmund, ed. abr. ed. 1958. 416p. pap. 2.50 o.p. (*0-440-31675-8*, Laurel) Dell Publishing.

—David Copperfield. 1998. (David Copperfield Ser.: Vol. 1). 1001p. pap. 4.99 (*0-8125-4404-8*, Tor Classics) Doherty, Tom Assocs., LLC.

—David Copperfield. unabr. ed. 1990. audio 16.99 (*0-88646-220-7*, 7220) Durkin Hayes Publishing Ltd.

—David Copperfield. E-Book 2.49 (*1-58744-119-5*) Electric Umbrella Publishing.

—David Copperfield. abr. ed. 1984. audio 9.95 (*1-55994-082-4*, CDL5 1706, Caedmon) HarperTrade.

—David Copperfield. 1991. (Complete Novels of Charles Dickens Ser.). (Illus.). 938p. (C). pap. 4.50 o.p. (*0-7493-0762-5*) Heinemann.

—David Copperfield. unabr. ed. 1999. Pt. 1, set. audio 85.95; Pt. 2, set. audio 85.95 Highsmith Inc.

—David Copperfield. E-Book 2.95 (*1-57799-815-4*); E-Book 2.95 (*1-57799-978-9*) Logos Research Systems, Inc.

—David Copperfield. 1996. pap. text 5.90 o.s.i (*0-582-27534-2*); 1989. pap. text 5.95 o.p. (*0-582-53501-8*, 74100) Longman Publishing Group.

—David Copperfield. abr. ed. 2000. audio 7.95 (*1-57815-114-7*, 1076, Media Bks. Audio Publishing) Media Bks., L. L. C.

—David Copperfield. E-Book 1.95 (*1-58515-053-3*) MesaView, Inc.

—David Copperfield. 1962. mass mkt. 3.75 o.p. (*0-451-52166-8*) NAL.

—David Copperfield. abr. ed. 1998. (Works of Charles Dickens). audio 22.98 (*962-634-651-5*, NA415114); audio compact disk 26.98 (*962-634-151-3*, NA415112) Naxos of America, Inc. (Naxos AudioBooks).

—David Copperfield. abr. ed. 1993. (Ultimate Classics Ser.). audio 15.95 o.p. (*1-55800-017-8*, 40080, Dove Audio) NewStar Media, Inc.

—David Copperfield. abr. ed. 1995. (Illus.). 64p. (J). (gr. 3-7). 18.88 o.p. (*1-55858-454-4*) North-South Bks., Inc.

—David Copperfield. 1999. (Critical Editions Ser.). (C). pap. text 37.00 (*0-393-98913-5*) Norton, W. W. & Co., Inc.

—David Copperfield. Buckley, Jerome H., ed. 1989. (Critical Editions Ser.). (Illus.). 854p. (C). pap. text 13.50 (*0-393-95828-0*) Norton, W. W. & Co., Inc.

—David Copperfield. (Oxford World's Classics Ser.). 2000. 1008p. 18.00 (*0-19-210043-2*); 1999. (Illus.). 944p. pap. 7.95 (*0-19-283578-5*) Oxford Univ. Pr., Inc.

—David Copperfield. Burgis, Nina, ed. 1981. (Clarendon Dickens Ser.). (Illus.). 858p. text 270.00 (*0-19-812492-9*) Oxford Univ. Pr., Inc.

—David Copperfield. 1983. (Oxford World's Classics Ser.). (Illus.). 772p. reprint ed. pap. 4.95 o.p. (*0-19-281609-8*) Oxford Univ. Pr., Inc.

—David Copperfield. Burgis, Nina, ed. 2nd ed. 1997. (Oxford World's Classics Ser.). (Illus.). 934p. pap. 6.95 o.p. (*0-19-283249-2*) Oxford Univ. Pr., Inc.

—David Copperfield. movie tie-in ed. 2000. (Illus.). 912p. pap. 8.00 (*0-14-029738-3*, Penguin Bks.) Penguin Group (USA) Inc.

—David Copperfield. 1999. E-Book 3.99 incl. cd-rom (*1-57646-076-2*) Quiet Vision Publishing.

—David Copperfield. 1987. (Radiobook Ser.). audio 4.98 (*0-929541-43-X*) Radiola Co.

—David Copperfield. 2000. E-Book 4.95 (0-679-64134-3); 896p. pap. 7.95 (0-679-78341-5) Random House Adult Trade Publishing Group. (Modern Library).
—David Copperfield. abr. unabr. ed. 1995. (BBC Radio Presents Ser.). 540p. pap. 25.95 o.s.i incl. audio (0-553-47353-0, 893004, RH Audio) Random Hse. Audio Publishing Group.
—David Copperfield. annuals 1998. (Modern Library Ser.). 928p. 22.95 o.s.i (0-679-60320-4); 1991. (Everyman's Library: Vol. 31). 1024p. 23.00 (0-679-40571-2) Random Hse., Inc.
—David Copperfield. unabr. ed. 2001. audio 186.00 (0-7887-2173-9, 95469E7); Set. 1999. audio 186.00 Recorded Bks., LLC.
—David Copperfield. 1989. 5.98 o.p. (0-86136-603-4) Smithmark Pubs., Inc.
—David Copperfield. abr. ed. (Mind's Eye Ser.). (J). audio 14.95 o.p. (0-88142-366-1) Soundelux Audio Publishing.
—David Copperfield. 1993. (Everyman Paperback Classics Ser.). 880p. pap. 6.95 (0-460-87236-2, Everyman's Classic Library in Paperback) Tuttle Publishing.
—David Copperfield. 1983. (Madhuban Abridged Classics Ser.). 118p. pap. 3.95 o.s.i (0-7069-4131-4) Vikas Publishing Hse. Private, Ltd. IND. *Dist:* South Asia Bks.
—David Copperfield. Blount, Trevor, ed. 1966. (English Library). 960p. pap. 6.95 o.s.i (0-14-043008-3, Penguin Classics) Viking Penguin.
—David Copperfield. abr. ed. 1996. 4p. audio 23.95 o.s.i (0-14-086185-8) Viking Penguin.
—David Copperfield. 1997. (Classics Library). 752p. pap. 3.95 (1-85326-024-X, 024XWW) Wordsworth Editions, Ltd. GBR. *Dist:* Combined Publishing.
—David Copperfield et de Grandes Esperances. (FRE.). 105.00 (0-8288-3432-6, M5090) French & European Pubns., Inc.
—A Dickens Christmas Collection. 1995. 176p. 14.99 o.p. (0-87788-170-7, Shaw) WaterBrook Pr.
—Dickens' Journalism Vol. 2: Sketches by Boz & Other Early Papers, 1833-39, 3 vols. Slater, Michael, ed. 1994. 580p. (C). text 50.00 (0-8142-0629-8) Ohio State Univ. Pr.
—Dombey & Son. 1994. (Everyman's Library). 960p. 23.00 (0-679-43591-3) Knopf, Alfred A. Inc.
—Dombey & Son. 1964. mass mkt. 0.95 o.p. (0-451-50261-2); mass mkt. 1.50 o.p. (0-451-50664-2); mass mkt. 2.50 o.p. (0-451-51180-8) NAL. (Signet Classics).
—Dombey & Son. Horsman, Alan, ed. (Oxford World's Classics Ser.). (Illus.). 1982. 782p. pap. 5.95 o.p. (0-19-281565-2); 1974. 79.00 o.p. (0-19-812491-0); 2nd ed. 2001. 1024p. pap. 8.95 (0-19-283990-X) Oxford Univ. Pr., Inc.
—Dombey & Son. 2003. (Modern Library Classics). (Illus.). 912p. pap. 8.95 (0-8129-6743-7, Modern Library) Random House Adult Trade Publishing Group.
—Dombey & Son. (Ebook Classic Ser.). E-Book 5.00 (0-7410-1496-3) SoftBook Pr.
—Dombey & Son. 2002. (Illus.). 992p. 9.00 (0-14-043546-8, Penguin Classics) Viking Penguin.
—Dombey & Son. Fairclough, Peter, ed. 1970. (Penguin English Library). 992p. pap. 8.95 o.s.i (0-14-043048-2, Penguin Classics) Viking Penguin.
—Great Expectations. 1996. (Longman Fiction Ser.). pap. text 7.87 o.p. (0-582-27520-2) Addison-Wesley Longman, Inc.
—Great Expectations. Date not set. 334p. 25.95 (0-8488-2527-6) Amereon, Ltd.
—Great Expectations. 1994. (Illustrated Classics Collection). 64p. pap. 4.95 (0-7854-0777-4, 40550); pap. 3.60 o.p. (1-56103-624-2) American Guidance Service, Inc.
—Great Expectations, unabr. ed. 2000. (YA). (gr. 10 up). audio 71.95 (1-55685-623-7) Audio Bk. Contractors, Inc.
—Great Expectations. unabr. ed. 1998. audio 44.95 (1-57270-063-7, F91063u, Cover to Cover Classics) Audio Partners Publishing Corp.
—Great Expectations. unabr. ed. audio 94.95 o.p. (1-85549-964-9, CTC 010) BBC Audiobooks America.
—Great Expectations. 1997. (Cyber Classics Ser.). 523p. pap. 14.95 incl. disk (1-55701-196-6) BNI Pubns., Inc.
—Great Expectations. 1982. mass mkt. 2.50 o.s.i (0-553-21113-7); mass mkt. 2.75 o.s.i (0-553-21234-6); 560p. reprint ed. mass mkt. 4.95 (0-553-21342-3) Bantam Bks. (Bantam Classics).
—Great Expectations. Carlisle, Janice, ed. 1995. (Case Studies in Contemporary Criticism). 641p. pap. text 8.50 (0-312-08082-4) Bedford/Saint Martin's.
—Great Expectations. 1979. reprint ed. 2.95 o.p. (0-460-01234-7) Biblio Distribution.
—Great Expectations. unabr. ed. 1994. audio 85.95 (0-7861-0493-7, 1444) Blackstone Audio Bks., Inc.
—Great Expectations. unabr. ed. 1990. audio 69.95 (1-55686-330-6, 330) Books in Motion.
—Great Expectations. unabr. collector's ed. 1977. (J). audio 96.00 (0-7366-4198-X, 4696) Books on Tape, Inc.
—Great Expectations. unabr. ed. 1997. (Bookcassette Classic Collection). audio 64.25 (1-56740-563-0, 883, Unabridged Library Editions); audio 21.95 o.p. (1-56100-784-6, 127, Bookcassette) Brilliance Audio.
—Great Expectations. Law, Graham & Pinnington, Adrian, eds. 1998. (Literary Texts Ser.). 654p. pap. (1-55111-174-8) Broadview Pr.
—Great Expectations. 1986. 528p. reprint ed. lib. bdg. 28.95 (0-89966-518-7) Buccaneer Bks., Inc.
—Great Expectations. 1997. (Cambridge Literature Ser.). audio 17.95 o.p. (0-521-59804-4) Cambridge Univ. Pr.
—Great Expectations. pap. 4.95 (0-7910-4123-9) Chelsea Hse. Pubs.
—Great Expectations. audio 77.95 Cover to Cover Cassettes, Ltd.
—Great Expectations. 1998. 528p. mass mkt. 3.99 (0-8125-6311-5, Tor Classics) Doherty, Tom Assocs., LLC.
—Great Expectations. unabr. ed. 2001. (Dover Thrift Editions Ser.). 400p. reprint ed. pap. 3.00 (0-486-41586-4) Dover Pubns., Inc.
—Great Expectations. 1994. 127p. (YA). (gr. 10 up). pap. 5.60 (0-87129-355-2, G56) Dramatic Publishing Co.
—Great Expectations. abr. ed. 1986. (YA). (gr. 8-10). audio 29.95 o.p. (0-88646-803-5, R 7074); 1982. audio 16.99 o.p. (0-88646-056-5, TC-LFP 7074); Set. 1992. audio 16.99 (0-88646-290-8, 7290) Durkin Hayes Publishing Ltd.
—Great Expectations. 1979. 12.95 o.p. (0-460-00234-1, Dutton) Dutton/Plume.
—Great Expectations. 2000. E-Book 2.49 (1-58744-165-9) Electric Umbrella Publishing.
—Great Expectations. 1998. audio 44.95 Filmic Archives.
—Great Expectations. 2003. 592p. pap. 4.99 (1-59308-006-9) Fine Communications.
—Great Expectations. 2nd ed. 1972. (Rinehart Editions Ser.). (C). pap. text 26.50 o.p. (0-03-077900-6) Harcourt College Pubs.
—Great Expectations. 1997. 96p. 14.95 o.p. (0-06-757478-5) HarperCollins Pubs.
—Great Expectations, Set. unabr. ed. 1999. audio 85.95 Highsmith Inc.
—Great Expectations. 1997. text 8.25 (0-03-051493-2) Holt, Rinehart & Winston.
—Great Expectations. 2002. 492p. 22.99 (1-4043-0468-1); per. 17.99 (1-4043-0469-X) IndyPublish.com.
—Great Expectations. 1999. (Cloth Bound Pocket Ser.). 7.95 (3-8290-2968-3, 521146) Konemann.
—Great Expectations. 1993. audio. audio 69.80 (1-56544-003-X, 350017) Literate Ear, Inc.
—Great Expectations. Pearce, Tim, ed. 1988. (Longman Study Texts). pap. text 5.95 (0-582-33088-2, 72040) Longman Publishing Group.
—Great Expectations. 1992. (Everyman's Library: Vol. 56). 544p. 20.00 (0-679-40579-8) McKay, David Co., Inc.
—Great Expectations. (Signet Classics). 1998. 512p. mass mkt. 4.95 (0-451-52671-6, Signet Classics); 1963. mass mkt. 1.95 o.p. (0-451-51759-8, Signet Classics); 1963. mass mkt. 1.95 o.p. (0-451-51835-7, Signet Classics); 1963. mass mkt. 2.25 o.p. (0-451-51871-3, Signet Classics); 1963. mass mkt. 1.25 o.p. (0-451-50900-5, Signet Classics); 1963. mass mkt. 2.25 o.p. (0-451-51311-8, Signet Classics); 1963. mass mkt. 2.95 o.p. (0-451-51627-3, Signet Classics); 1963. mass mkt. 2.50 o.p. (0-451-51482-3, Signet Classics); 1963. mass mkt. 0.75 o.p. (0-451-50340-6, Signet Classics); 1963. mass mkt. 0.60 o.p. (0-451-50159-4, Signet Classics); 1963. mass mkt. 1.50 o.p. (0-451-51036-4, Signet Classics); 1963. mass mkt. 1.95 o.p. (0-451-51171-9, Signet Classics); 1963. mass mkt. 0.95 o.p. (0-451-50797-5, Signet Classics); 1963. mass mkt. 2.50 o.p. (0-451-51932-9, Signet Classics); 1961. mass mkt. 2.95 o.p. (0-451-52359-8); 1961. mass mkt. 2.75 o.p. (0-451-52076-9) NAL.
—Great Expectations. abr. ed. 1996. (Works of Charles Dickens). audio 22.98 (962-634-582-9, NA408214); audio compact disk 26.98 (962-634-082-7, NA408212) Naxos of America, Inc. (Naxos AudioBooks).
—Great Expectations. abr. ed. 2004. audio compact disk 24.95 (1-59007-573-0) New Millennium Entertainment.
—Great Expectations. abr. ed. 1993. (Ultimate Classics Ser.). audio 15.95 o.p. (1-55800-138-7, 40520, Dove Audio) NewStar Media, Inc.
—Great Expectations. 2000. (Twelve-Point Ser.). 600p. reprint ed. lib. bdg. 25.00 (1-58287-127-2) North Bks.
—Great Expectations. 2000. (Critical Editions Ser.). (C). pap. text 36.50 o.p. (0-393-94868-4) Norton, W. W. & Co., Inc.
—Great Expectations. Rosenberg, Edgar, ed. 1999. (Critical Editions Ser.). (C). pap. 12.00 (0-393-96069-2, Norton Paperbacks) Norton, W. W. & Co., Inc.
—Great Expectations. 1999. (Oxford World's Classics Ser.). 544p. 16.00 o.p. (0-19-210034-3) Oxford Univ. Pr., Inc.
—Great Expectations. Cardwell, Margaret, ed. & notes by. 1998. (Oxford World's Classics Ser.). (Illus.). 544p. pap. 6.95 (0-19-283359-6) Oxford Univ. Pr., Inc.
—Great Expectations. Cardwell, Margaret & Flint, Kate, eds. 1994. (Oxford World's Classics Ser.). (Illus.). 530p. (C). pap. 5.95 o.p. (0-19-282926-2) Oxford Univ. Pr., Inc.
—Great Expectations. Cardwell, Margaret, ed. 1993. (Clarendon Dickens Ser.). (Illus.). 584p. (C). text 200.00 (0-19-818591-X, 10961) Oxford Univ. Pr., Inc.
—Great Expectations. (Illus.). 1987. 486p. 16.95 (0-19-254511-6); 1982. pap. 5.25 o.p. (0-19-638270-X) Oxford Univ. Pr., Inc.
—Great Expectations. Carlisle, Janice, ed. 1995. (Case Studies in Contemporary Criticism). 656p. 49.95 (0-312-12797-9) Palgrave Macmillan.
—Great Expectations. 1982. pap. 2.50 o.p. (0-14-006506-7) Penguin Group (USA) Inc.
—Great Expectations. 1999. 200p. E-Book 3.99 incl. audio compact disk (1-57646-115-7) Quiet Vision Publishing.
—Great Expectations. 1987. (Radiobook Ser.). audio 4.98 (0-929541-44-8) Radiola Co.
—Great Expectations. 2001. (Paperback Classics Ser.). 480p. pap. 7.95 (0-375-75701-5, Modern Library) Random House Adult Trade Publishing Group.
—Great Expectations. abr. ed. 1994. audio 21.98 o.s.i (0-553-74521-2); 340p. pap. 25.00 o.s.i incl. audio (0-553-47244-5) Random Hse. Audio Publishing Group. (RH Audio).
—Great Expectations. 1986. 3.99 o.s.i (0-517-62634-9) Random Hse. Value Publishing.
—Great Expectations. 1985. (Illus.). 432p. 12.95 o.p. (0-89577-205-1) Reader's Digest Assn., Inc., The.
—Great Expectations, unabr. ed. 1987. audio 91.00 (1-55690-204-2, 87850E7) Recorded Bks., LLC.
—Great Expectations. 560p. 2004. mass mkt. 4.95 (0-7434-8761-3); 2000. (Illus.). mass mkt. 4.99 (0-7434-0636-2) Simon & Schuster. (Pocket).
—Great Expectations. Shefter, Harry, ed. 1987. (Enriched Classics Ser.). 528p. mass mkt. 4.50 (0-671-64196-4, Pocket) Simon & Schuster.
—Great Expectations. 2000. (Aladdin Classics Ser.). 720p. (J). (gr. 4-7). pap. 5.99 (0-689-83961-8, Aladdin) Simon & Schuster Children's Publishing.
—Great Expectations. unabr. ed. 2003. audio 29.99 (1-59335-159-3, 30255) Soulmate Audio Bks., Inc.
—Great Expectations. abr. ed. 1972. (Mind's Eye Ser.). (J). pap. 11.95 o.p. incl. audio (0-88142-368-8, 368) Soundelux Audio Publishing.
—Great Expectations. 1995. pap. text 15.95 o.p. (0-312-13834-2); 1969. pap. text 6.95 o.p. (0-312-34580-1) St. Martin's Pr.
—Great Expectations. Daleski, H. M., ed. 2003. 592p. 9.95 (1-59264-010-9); pap. 7.95 (1-59264-009-5) Toby Pr.
—Great Expectations. 1999. (Signature Classics Ser.). (Illus.). 456p. 24.95 (1-58279-036-1); 29.95 (1-58279-048-5) Trident Pr. International.
—Great Expectations. 1963. 11.00 (0-606-00191-3) Turtleback Bks.
—Great Expectations. Gilmour, Robin, ed. 1994. 448p. pap. 3.95 o.s.i (0-460-87335-0, Everyman's Classic Library in Paperback) Tuttle Publishing.
—Great Expectations. 2000. 8.00 (81-85944-79-2) UBS Pubs. Distributions, Ltd. IND. *Dist:* South Asia Bks.
—Great Expectations. 2002. 544p. pap. 8.00 (0-14-143956-4, Penguin Classics); 1999. audio 10.95 (0-14-086417-2); 1997. 544p. pap. 7.95 o.s.i (0-14-043489-5, Penguin Classics) Viking Penguin.
—Great Expectations. Calder, Angus, ed. 1965. (English Library). 512p. pap. 7.95 o.p. (0-14-043003-2, Penguin Classics) Viking Penguin.
—Great Expectations. abr. ed. 1995. (Classics on Audio Ser.). 2p. pap. 16.95 o.s.i incl. audio (0-14-086041-X, Penguin AudioBooks) Viking Penguin.
—Great Expectations. 1997. (Classics Library). 432p. pap. 3.95 (1-85326-004-5, 0045WW) Wordsworth Editions, Ltd. GBR. *Dist:* Casemate Pubs. & Bk. Distributors, LLC.
—Great Expectations: New York Public Library Collector's Edition. 1997. 608p. 20.00 o.s.i (0-385-48721-5) Doubleday Publishing.
—Great Expectations & A Christmas Carol. E-Book 5.00 (0-7607-1411-8) Barnes & Noble, Inc.
—Great Expectations Readalong. 1994. (Illustrated Classics Collection). 64p. pap. 14.95 (0-7854-0793-6, 40552) American Guidance Service, Inc.
—Hard Times. 292p. 23.95 o.s.i (0-8488-2461-X) Amereon, Ltd.
—Hard Times. 1975. pap. 1.50 o.p. (0-449-30735-2, Q735, Fawcett) Ballantine Bks.
—Hard Times. 2001. per. 14.00 (1-891355-98-8) Blue Unicorn Editions.
—Hard Times. Law, Graham, ed. 1996. 464p. pap. (1-55111-075-X) Broadview Pr.
—Hard Times. Jose, Gwen, ed. 1996. (Cambridge Literature Ser.). (Illus.). 336p. pap. text 11.95 o.p. (0-521-56089-6) Cambridge Univ. Pr.
—Hard Times. 2001. reprint ed. pap. text 28.00 (0-7426-7325-1) Classic Bks.
—Hard Times. l.t. ed. 1999. 448p. pap. 22.95 (1-58855-032-X) Cyber Classics, Inc.
—Hard Times. unabr. ed. 2001. (Dover Thrift Editions Ser.). 208p. pap. 2.50 (0-486-41920-7) Dover Pubns., Inc.
—Hard Times. 1961. 2.50 o.p. (0-460-01292-4, Dutton) Dutton/Plume.
—Hard Times. Watt, William W., ed. 1958. (Rinehart Editions Ser.). 316p. (C). pap. text 25.00 o.p. (0-03-009875-0) Harcourt College Pubs.
—Hard Times. 2002. 292p. 25.99 (1-4043-0616-1); per. 20.99 (1-4043-0617-X) IndyPublish.com.
—Hard Times. 1992. (Everyman's Library: Vol. 73). 19.00 (0-679-41323-5) Knopf, Alfred A. Inc.
—Hard Times. 1970. mass mkt. 0.95 o.p. (0-451-50514-X); 1969. mass mkt. 0.75 o.p. (0-451-50473-9); 1969. mass mkt. 0.60 o.p. (0-451-50259-0); 1969. mass mkt. 0.50 o.p. (0-451-50079-2); 1961. mass mkt. 1.25 o.p. (0-451-50822-X); 1961. mass mkt. 1.50 o.p. (0-451-50909-9); 1961. mass mkt. 1.75 o.p. (0-451-51152-2) NAL. (Signet Classics).
—Hard Times. (Critical Editions Ser.). 1966. pap. 2.50 o.p. (0-393-99774-X); 3rd ed. 2000. xi, 480p. (C). pap. 8.50 (0-393-97560-6, Norton Paperbacks) Norton, W. W. & Co., Inc.
—Hard Times. Schlicke, Paul, ed. & intro. by. 1998. (Oxford World's Classics Ser.). 464p. pap. 6.95 (0-19-283367-7) Oxford Univ. Pr., Inc.
—Hard Times. 1999. 465p. E-Book 3.99 incl. cd-rom (1-57646-079-7) Quiet Vision Publishing.
—Hard Times. 2001. (Modern Library Classics). 368p. pap. 7.95 (0-679-64217-X, Modern Library) Random House Adult Trade Publishing Group.
—Hard Times. 1961. (Signet Modern Classic). 11.00 (0-606-03526-5) Turtleback Bks.
—Hard Times. 1999. 6.50 (81-86112-94-4) UBS Pubs. Distributions, Ltd. IND. *Dist:* South Asia Bks.
—Hard Times. unabr. ed. 1997. 246p. reprint ed. pap. 14.95 o.p. (1-57002-022-1) University Publishing Hse., Inc.
—Hard Times. 2003. (Classics Ser.). 368p. pap. 8.00 (0-14-143967-X, Penguin Classics) Viking Penguin.
—Hard Times. Flint, Kate, ed. & intro. by. 1996. (Penguin Classics Ser.). 368p. pap. 8.00 o.s.i (0-14-043398-8) Viking Penguin.
—Hard Times: An Authoritative Text. Kaplan, Fred & Monod, Sylvere, eds. 2001. (Norton Anthology Edition Ser.). xii, 192p. pap. (0-393-10324-2) Norton, W. W. & Co., Inc.
—The Life & Adventures of Nicholas Nickleby. (Illus.). 770p. reprint ed. 1983. 45.95 o.p. (0-8122-7873-9); 1982. pap. text 39.95 o.p. (0-8122-1135-9) Univ. of Pennsylvania Pr.
—Little Dorrit, 2 vols. rev. ed. 2000. 800p. per. 25.00 (1-58396-001-5) Blue Unicorn Editions.
—Little Dorrit. 2001. (Collected Works of Charles Dickens). (Illus.). reprint ed. pap. text 28.00 (0-7426-7328-6) Classic Bks.
—Little Dorrit. 2002. Vol. 1. 460p. 28.99 (1-4043-1324-9); Vol. 1. 460p. per. 23.99 (1-4043-1325-7); Vol. 2. 424p. 27.99 (1-4043-1326-5); Vol. 2. 424p. per. 23.99 (1-4043-1327-3) IndyPublish.com.
—Little Dorrit. 1992. (Everyman's Library: Vol. 111). 20.00 (0-679-41725-7) Knopf, Alfred A. Inc.
—Little Dorrit. Sucksmith, Harvey P., ed. (Oxford World's Classics Ser.). (Illus.). 1982. 748p. pap. 7.95 o.p. (0-19-281592-X); 1979. (C). 110.00 o.p. (0-19-812513-5) Oxford Univ. Pr., Inc.
—Little Dorrit. 2002. (Modern Library Classics). (Illus.). 912p. pap. 8.95 (0-375-75914-X, Modern Library) Random House Adult Trade Publishing Group.
—Little Dorrit. (Ebook Classic Ser.). E-Book 5.00 (0-7410-1497-1) SoftBook Pr.
—Martin Chuzzlewit. 1973. reprint ed. 10.95 o.p. (0-460-00241-4) Biblio Distribution.
—Martin Chuzzlewit. 1995. (Everyman's Library: Vol. 200). 851p. 20.00 (0-679-43884-X) Knopf, Alfred A. Inc.
—Martin Chuzzlewit. E-Book 1.95 (1-57799-816-2) Logos Research Systems, Inc.
—Martin Chuzzlewit. 1965. mass mkt. 1.50 o.p. (0-451-50907-2, CW907, Signet Classics) NAL.
—Martin Chuzzlewit. Cardwell, Margaret, ed. 1983. (Clarendon Dickens Ser.). (Illus.). 940p. text 240.00 (0-19-812488-0) Oxford Univ. Pr., Inc.
—Martin Chuzzlewit. Cardwell, Margaret, ed. & intro. by. 1998. (Oxford World's Classics Ser.). (Illus.). 768p. reprint ed. pap. 9.95 (0-19-283461-4) Oxford Univ. Pr., Inc.

—Martin Chuzzlewit. Cardwell, Margaret, ed. 1984. (Oxford World's Classics Ser.). (Illus.). 768p. reprint ed. pap. 6.95 o.p. (0-19-281676-4) Oxford Univ. Pr., Inc.
—Martin Chuzzlewit. Monod, Sylvere & Rawson, Claude, eds. 1985. (Unwin Critical Library). 192p. text 55.00 (0-04-800028-0) Routledge.
—Martin Chuzzlewit. abr. ed. 1994. mass mkt. 16.95 o.p. incl. audio (1-85998-003-1) Trafalgar Square.
—Martin Chuzzlewit. Furbank, P. N., ed. 1968. (English Library). 944p. pap. 10.95 o.s.i (0-14-043031-8, Penguin Classics) Viking Penguin.
—Martin Chuzzlewit. 1998. (Classics Library). 765p. pap. 3.95 (1-85326-205-6, 2056WW) Wordsworth Editions, Ltd. GBR. Dist: Casemate Pubs. & Bk. Distributors, LLC.
—The Mystery of Edwin Drood. 2001. (Collected Works of Charles Dickens: Vol. 33). (Illus.). reprint ed. pap. text 28.00 (0-7426-7339-1) Classic Bks.
—The Mystery of Edwin Drood. 2002. 280p. 95.99 (1-4043-1750-3); per. 90.99 (1-4043-1751-1) IndyPublish.com.
—The Mystery of Edwin Drood. 1981. (Illus.). 12.95 o.p. (0-394-51918-3, Pantheon) Knopf Publishing Group.
—The Mystery of Edwin Drood. 1974. (Studies in Dickens: No. 52). lib. bdg. 75.00 (0-8383-1962-9) M.S.G. Haskell Hse.
—The Mystery of Edwin Drood. 1970. mass mkt. 0.75 o.p. (0-451-50544-1); 1968. mass mkt. 0.60 o.p. (0-451-50430-5); 1961. mass mkt. 0.50 o.p. (0-451-50069-5); 1961. mass mkt. 1.25 o.p. (0-451-50837-8); 1961. mass mkt. 0.95 o.p. (0-451-50640-5); 1961. mass mkt. 1.50 o.p. (0-451-51062-3); 1961. mass mkt. 2.50 o.p. (0-451-51425-4, CE1425) NAL. (Signet Classics).
—The Mystery of Edwin Drood. 1999. (Oxford World's Classics Ser.). (Illus.). 272p. pap. 7.95 (0-19-283660-9) Oxford Univ. Pr., Inc.
—The Mystery of Edwin Drood. Cardwell, Margaret, ed. 1982. (Oxford World's Classics Ser.). (Illus.). 266p. pap. 6.95 o.p. (0-19-281593-8) Oxford Univ. Pr., Inc.
—The Mystery of Edwin Drood. 1972. (Illus.). 42.00 o.p. (0-19-812439-2) Oxford Univ. Pr., Inc.
—The Mystery of Edwin Drood. 1999. 436p. E-Book 3.99 incl. audio compact disk (1-57646-107-6) Quiet Vision Publishing.
—The Mystery of Edwin Drood. E-Book 5.00 (0-7410-0450-X) SoftBook Pr.
—The Mystery of Edwin Drood. 2002. (Illus.). 432p. pap. 8.00 (0-14-043926-9, Penguin Classics) Viking Penguin.
—The Mystery of Edwin Drood. Maule, Jeremy, ed. 1999. pap. 7.95 (0-14-043605-7, Penguin Classics) Viking Penguin.
—The Mystery of Edwin Drood. Cox, Arthur J., ed. 1986. pap. 3.95 o.p. (0-14-009258-7, Penguin Bks.) Viking Penguin.
—The Mystery of Edwin Drood. Cox, A., ed. 1974. (Penguin English Library). 320p. pap. 7.95 o.s.i (0-14-043092-X, Penguin Classics) Viking Penguin.
—The Mystery of Edwin Drood. 1998. (Classics Library). 432p. pap. 3.95 (1-85326-729-5, 7295WW) Wordsworth Editions, Ltd. GBR. Dist: Combined Publishing.
—Nicholas Nickleby. rev. ed. 2000. 500p. per. 25.00 (1-58396-002-3) Blue Unicorn Editions.
—Nicholas Nickleby. 1993. (Everyman's Library: Vol. 159). 914p. 20.00 (0-679-42307-9) Knopf, Alfred A. Inc.
—Nicholas Nickleby. E-Book 1.95 (1-57799-940-1) Logos Research Systems, Inc.
—Nicholas Nickleby. Schlicke, Paul, ed. 1990. (Oxford World's Classics Ser.). 916p. pap. 6.95 o.p. (0-19-281794-9) Oxford Univ. Pr., Inc.
—Nicholas Nickleby. Slater, Michael, ed. 1978. (Penguin Classics Ser.). 976p. pap. 7.95 o.s.i (0-14-043113-6, Penguin Classics) Viking Penguin.
—The Old Curiosity Shop. 2001. (Collected Works of Charles Dickens). (Illus.). reprint ed. pap. text 28.00 (0-7426-7310-3) Classic Bks.
—The Old Curiosity Shop. 1995. (Everyman's Library). 624p. 23.00 (0-679-44373-8) Knopf, Alfred A. Inc.
—The Old Curiosity Shop. Brennan, Elizabeth M., ed. & intro. by. 1998. (Oxford World's Classics Ser.). (Illus.). 672p. pap. 9.95 (0-19-282924-6); 734p. 180.00 incl. cd-rom (0-19-812493-7) Oxford Univ. Pr., Inc.
—The Old Curiosity Shop. 1988. (Illus.). 528p. 13.95 o.p. (0-89577-292-2) Reader's Digest Assn., Inc., The.
—The Old Curiosity Shop. 2001. (Classics Ser.). (Illus.). 352p. 11.00 (0-14-043742-8, Penguin Classics) Viking Penguin.
—The Old Curiosity Shop. Easson, Angus, ed. 1972. (Penguin English Library). 720p. pap. 8.95 o.s.i (0-14-043075-X, Penguin Classics) Viking Penguin.
—Our Mutual Friend. 1994. (Everyman's Library). 20.00 (0-679-42028-2) Knopf, Alfred A. Inc.
—Our Mutual Friend. Cotsell, Michael, ed. 1990. (Oxford World's Classics Ser.). (Illus.). 880p. pap. 6.95 o.p. (0-19-281795-7) Oxford Univ. Pr., Inc.
—Our Mutual Friend. 2000. E-Book 4.95 (0-679-64135-1, Modern Library) Random House Adult Trade Publishing Group.
—Our Mutual Friend. 1992. (Modern Library Ser.). 824p. 19.00 o.s.i (0-679-60022-1) Random Hse., Inc.
—The Perils of Certain English Prisoners. E-Book 1.95 (1-58515-056-8) MesaView, Inc.
—The Personal History of David Copperfield. 2001. (Collected Works of Charles Dickens). (Illus.). reprint ed. pap. text 28.00 (0-7426-7322-7) Classic Bks.
—The Personal History of David Copperfield. 1986. (Illus.). 736p. (YA). (gr. 7-12). 12.95 o.p. (0-89577-223-X) Reader's Digest Assn., Inc., The.
—The Pickwick Papers. 1968. (Classics Ser.). mass mkt. 2.95 o.p. (0-8049-0191-0, CL-191) Airmont Publishing Co., Inc.
—The Pickwick Papers. 1983. 784p. mass mkt. 6.99 (0-553-21123-4, Bantam Classics) Bantam Bks.
—The Pickwick Papers. 2000. 700p. per. 25.00 (1-58396-005-8) Blue Unicorn Editions.
—The Pickwick Papers. 1983. 495p. reprint ed. lib. bdg. 49.95 (0-89966-314-1) Buccaneer Bks., Inc.
—The Pickwick Papers. 1998. (Illus.). 925p. pap. text 5.99 (0-8125-6719-6, Tor Classics) Doherty, Tom Assocs., LLC.
—The Pickwick Papers. 1972. 5.50 o.p. (0-460-01235-5); 1954. 15.50 o.p. (0-460-00235-X) Dutton/ Plume. (Dutton).
—The Pickwick Papers. 1991. (Complete Novels of Charles Dickens Ser.). (Illus.). 916p. (C). pap. 5.50 o.p. (0-7493-0753-6, A0529) Heinemann.
—The Pickwick Papers. l.t. ed. 3920p. pap. 230.83 (0-7583-3670-5); 2591p. pap. 160.03 (0-7583-3668-3); 4547p. pap. 265.18 (0-7583-3671-3); 2024p. pap. 126.02 (0-7583-3667-5); 1582p. pap. 104.35 (0-7583-3666-7); 1154p. pap. 78.29 (0-7583-3665-9); 888p. pap. 68.26 (0-7583-3664-0); 3187p. pap. 195.33 (0-7583-3669-1); 3920p. lib. bdg. 283.81 (0-7583-3662-4); 3187p. lib. bdg. 232.41 (0-7583-3661-6); 2591p. lib. bdg. 188.06 (0-7583-3660-8); 2024p. lib. bdg. 145.22 (0-7583-3659-4); 1582p. lib. bdg. 122.35 (0-7583-3658-6); 1154p. lib. bdg. 90.29 (0-7583-3657-8); 888p. lib. bdg. 80.26 (0-7583-3656-X); 4547p. lib. bdg. 329.77 (0-7583-3663-2) Huge Print Pr.
—The Pickwick Papers. l.t. unabr. ed. 1991. (Isis Large Print Bks.: Vol. 1). 450p. 29.99 (1-85089-464-7, 894647);Vol. 2. 540p. 24.95 (1-85089-514-7, 895147) ISIS Large Print Bks. GBR. Dist: Ulverscroft Large Print Bks., Ltd., Ulverscroft Large Print Canada, Ltd., Transaction Pubs., Ulverscroft Large Print Canada, Ltd.
—The Pickwick Papers. E-Book 1.95 (1-57799-939-8) Logos Research Systems, Inc.
—The Pickwick Papers. 1968. mass mkt. 1.25 o.p. (0-451-50443-7); 1968. mass mkt. 0.95 o.p. (0-451-50200-0); 1964. 888p. mass mkt. 6.95 o.s.i (0-451-51756-3, CE1756); 1964. mass mkt. 3.95 o.p. (0-451-51620-6); 1964. mass mkt. 2.95 o.p. (0-451-51413-0); 1964. mass mkt. 2.25 o.p. (0-451-51135-2); 1964. mass mkt. 1.95 o.p. (0-451-50950-1) NAL. (Signet Classics).
—The Pickwick Papers. Kinsley, James, ed. & intro. by. (Oxford World's Classics Ser.). (Illus.). 1998. 786p. pap. 10.95 (0-19-283457-6); 1988. 772p. pap. 6.95 o.p. (0-19-281775-2) Oxford Univ. Pr., Inc.
—The Pickwick Papers. Kinsley, James, ed. 1986. (Clarendon Dickens Ser.). (Illus.). 1,002p. text 149.00 o.p. (0-19-812631-X) Oxford Univ. Pr., Inc.
—The Pickwick Papers. 1999. 1378p. E-Book 3.99 incl. audio compact disk (1-57646-106-8) Quiet Vision Publishing.
—The Pickwick Papers. 2003. (Illus.). 816p. pap. 10.95 (0-8129-6727-5, Modern Library) Random House Adult Trade Publishing Group.
—The Pickwick Papers. E-Book 5.00 (0-7410-1421-1) SoftBook Pr.
—The Pickwick Papers, 2 vols. 2000. (Signature Classics Ser.). (Illus.). 872p. (1-58279-066-3); (1-58279-072-8) Trident Pr. International.
—The Pickwick Papers. 1964. 13.00 (0-606-00941-8) Turtleback Bks.
—The Pickwick Papers. Andrews, Malcolm, ed. 1998. (Everyman Paperback Classics Ser.). (Illus.). 960p. pap. 5.95 (0-460-87664-3, Everyman's Classic Library in Paperback) Tuttle Publishing.
—The Pickwick Papers. Patten, Robert L., ed. 1973. (Penguin English Library). (Illus.). 960p. pap. 9.95 o.s.i (0-14-043078-4, Penguin Classics) Viking Penguin.
—The Pickwick Papers. 1999. E-Book 3.95 (0-8220-7163-0, Cliff Notes) Wiley, John & Sons, Inc.
—The Pickwick Papers. (Wordsworth Collection). 784p. pap. 3.95 (1-85326-052-5, 0525WW) Wordsworth Editions, Ltd. GBR. Dist: Casemate Pubs. & Bk. Distributors, LLC.
—The Posthumous Papers of the Pickwick Club. Boz, ed. 2001. (Collected Works of Charles Dickens). (Illus.). reprint ed. pap. text 28.00 (0-7426-7303-0) Classic Bks.
—The Posthumous Papers of the Pickwick Club. 1999. (Everyman's Library). 976p. 23.00 (0-375-40548-8) Knopf, Alfred A. Inc.
—The Posthumous Papers of the Pickwick Club. 1987. (Illus.). 826p. 17.95 (0-19-254501-9) Oxford Univ. Pr., Inc.
—The Posthumous Papers of the Pickwick Club. 2000. (Classics Ser.). (Illus.). 848p. pap. 11.00 (0-14-043611-1, Penguin Classics) Viking Penguin.
—The Posthumous Papers of the Pickwick Club: Digital Reprint of 1885 Philadelphia: J. B. Lippincott & Co. Edition. Exams Unlimited, Inc. Staff, ed. 2001. (Illus.). 1100p. (C). reprint ed. cd-rom 9.25 (1-885343-50-7) Exams Unlimited, Inc.
—Selected Short Fiction. Thomas, Deborah A., ed. 1976. (Penguin English Library). 368p. 8.95 (0-14-043103-9, Penguin Classics) Viking Penguin.
—Sketches by Boz: Illustrative of Everyday Life & Everyday People. 1968. 5.00 o.p. (0-460-00237-6) Biblio Distribution.
—Sketches by Boz: Illustrative of Everyday Life & Everyday People. 1999. E-Book 3.99 incl. cd-rom (1-57646-092-4) Quiet Vision Publishing.
—Sketches by Boz: Illustrative of Everyday Life & Everyday People. Walder, Dennis, ed. & intro. by. 1996. (Classics Ser.). (Illus.). 688p. pap. 15.00 (0-14-043345-7, Penguin Classics) Viking Penguin.
—A Tale of Two Cities. l.t. unabr. ed. 2001. (Large Print Classics Ser.). viii, 528p. 14.95 (0-486-41776-X) Dover Pubns., Inc.
—A Tale of Two Cities. 1993. (Everyman's Library). 480p. 20.00 (0-679-42073-8) Knopf, Alfred A. Inc.
—A Tale of Two Cities. 1996. (Modern Library Ser.). 512p. 19.95 (0-679-60208-9) Random Hse., Inc.
—A Tale of Two Cities. 1992. (Literary Classics Ser.). 272p. text 5.98 o.p. (1-56138-114-4, Courage Bks.) Running Pr. Bk. Pubs.
—Temps Difficile. 1985. (FRE.). 435p. pap. 16.95 (0-7859-2011-0, 2070376478) French & European Pubns., Inc.
—The Works of Charles Dickens. 2001. (Collected Works of Charles Dickens). reprint ed. pap. text 588.00 (0-7426-7349-9) Classic Bks.
—The Works of Charles Dickens. 1988. 11.99 o.s.i (0-517-61831-1); 1990. 864p. 19.99 (0-517-05360-8) Random Hse. Value Publishing.
—The Works of Charles Dickens. 1989. 9.98 o.p. (0-8317-9504-2) Smithmark Pubs., Inc.
—The Works of Charles Dickens. 1995. 797p. pap. o.p. (1-57215-128-5) World Pubns., Inc.
—The Works of Charles Dickens. unabr. ed. Incl. Great Expectations. audio Pickwick Papers. audio Tale of Two Cities. audio Set audio 29.75 Audio Bk. Co.
Dickens, Charles & Cardwell, Margaret. Great Expectations. 1998. E-Book 7.30 (0-585-36168-1) netLibrary, Inc.
Dickens, Charles & Chiel, Deborah. Great Expectations, Vol. 1. 1998. (Great Expectations Ser.: Vol. 1). 256p. mass mkt. 5.99 (0-312-96303-3, St. Martin's Paperbacks) St. Martin's Pr.
Dickens, Charles & Saxena, Paresh. David Copperfield. 1997. 154p. pap. 24.00 (81-209-0026-X) Pitambar Publishing IND. Dist: State Mutual Bk. & Periodical Service, Ltd.
Dickens, Charles & Sharma, V. A. Great Expectations. 1996. 144p. pap. 20.00 (81-209-0070-7) Pitambar Publishing IND. Dist: State Mutual Bk. & Periodical Service, Ltd.
Dickens, Charles, et al. A Christmas Carol & Other Victorian Fairy Tales. 1983. 368p. (Orig.). mass mkt. 2.95 o.s.i (0-553-21126-9, Bantam Classics) Bantam Bks.
—Little Dorrit. 2004. (Illus.). 1024p. pap. 9.00 (0-14-143996-3, Penguin Classics) Viking Penguin.
Dickinson, David. Goodnight Sweet Prince. 2002. (Victorian Mystery Ser.). 320p. 24.00 (0-7867-0945-6, Carroll & Graf Pubs.) Avalon Publishing Group.
Dickinson, Peter. The Glass-Sided Ant's Nest. 1991. 186p. reprint ed. pap. 7.95 o.s.i (1-55882-089-2, Library of Crime Classics) International Polygonics, Ltd.
—The Glass-Sided Ant's Nest. 1981. pap. 3.95 o.p. (0-14-005864-8, Penguin Bks.) Viking Penguin.
—Old English Peep Show. 1984. pap. 3.95 o.s.i (0-394-72602-2) Random Hse., Inc.
—One Foot in the Grave. 1980. 8.95 o.p. (0-394-50894-7, Pantheon) Knopf Publishing Group.
—One Foot in the Grave. 1981. 224p. pap. 2.95 o.p. (0-14-005779-X, Penguin Bks.) Viking Penguin.
—Perfect Gallows. 1987. 256p. 16.95 o.s.i (0-394-56311-5, Pantheon) Knopf Publishing Group.
—The Sinful Stones. 1992. 200p. pap. 8.95 o.p. (1-55882-109-0) International Polygonics, Ltd.
—Some Deaths Before Dying. l.t. ed. 2000. (G. K. Hall Core Ser.). 366p. 28.95 (0-7838-9016-8, Macmillan Reference USA) Gale Group.
—Some Deaths Before Dying. 1999. 256p. 27.00 (0-89296-696-3) Mysterious Pr.
—Some Deaths Before Dying. 256p. (0-7278-5670-7) Severn Hse. Pubs., Ltd.
—Some Deaths Before Dying. 2000. 256p. pap. 13.95 o.s.i (0-446-67612-8) Warner Bks., Inc.
Dickson, Carter, pseud. And So to Murder. l.t. ed. 18.95 o.p. (0-7451-6426-9); 1993. pap. 16.95 o.p. (0-7451-6432-3); 1989. audio 54.95 (0-7451-5902-8) BBC Audiobooks America.
—And So to Murder. 1988. mass mkt. 3.50 o.p. (0-8217-2536-X, Zebra Bks.) Kensington Publishing Corp.
—Behind the Crimson Blind. 1989. mass mkt. 3.50 o.p. (0-8217-2607-2, Zebra Bks.) Kensington Publishing Corp.
—The Cavalier's Cup. 1987. mass mkt. 3.50 o.s.i (0-8217-2170-4, Zebra Bks.) Kensington Publishing Corp.
—The Curse of the Bronze Lamp. 1997. 192p. mass mkt. 4.95 (0-7867-0440-3); 1984. 260p. pap. 3.50 o.p. (0-88184-101-3) Avalon Publishing Group. (Carroll & Graf Pubs.).
—The Curse of the Bronze Lamp. 1945. o.s.i (0-688-05616-4, Morrow, William & Co.) Morrow/Avon.
—Death in Five Boxes. 1977. reprint ed. pap. 1.50 o.s.i (0-505-51203-3) Dorchester Publishing Co., Inc.
—Death in Five Boxes. 1991. 192p. reprint ed. pap. text 5.95 o.p. (1-55882-098-1, Library of Crime Classics) International Polygonics, Ltd.
—The Gilded Man. 1988. 256p. reprint ed. pap. 4.95 o.p. (0-930330-88-9, Library of Crime Classics) International Polygonics, Ltd.
—He Wouldn't Kill Patience. 1988. 192p. pap. 4.95 o.p. (0-930330-86-2) International Polygonics, Ltd.
—The Judas Window. 1987. 192p. pap. 5.95 o.p. (0-930330-62-5) International Polygonics, Ltd.
—Merrivale Holds the Key: Two Classic Locked-Room Mysteries. 1995. 628p. pap. 14.95 (1-55882-027-2) International Polygonics, Ltd.
—My Late Wives. 1988. 288p. mass mkt. 3.50 o.p. (0-8217-2384-7, Zebra Bks.) Kensington Publishing Corp.
—Night at the Mocking Widow. 1988. 320p. mass mkt. 3.50 o.p. (0-8217-2463-0, Zebra Bks.) Kensington Publishing Corp.
—Nine & Death Makes Ten. (Black Dagger Crime Ser.). 12.95 o.p. (0-86220-797-5, BD002) Chivers Pr. GBR. Dist: BBC Audiobooks America.
—Nine & Death Makes Ten. 1987. 175p. reprint ed. pap. 5.95 (0-930330-69-2) International Polygonics, Ltd.
—The Peacock Feather Murders. 1987. 192p. reprint ed. pap. 5.95 o.p. (0-930330-68-4) International Polygonics, Ltd.
—The Plague Court Murders. 1990. 285p. reprint ed. pap. 5.95 o.p. (1-55882-062-0) International Polygonics, Ltd.
—The Punch & Judy Murders. 1988. 192p. pap. 4.95 o.p. (0-930330-85-4) International Polygonics, Ltd.
—The Reader Is Warned. 1989. 192p. pap. 5.95 o.p. (1-55882-019-1, Library of Crime Classics) International Polygonics, Ltd.
—The Red Widow Murders. 1988. 302p. reprint ed. pap. 4.95 o.p. (0-930330-87-0, Library of Crime Classics) International Polygonics, Ltd.
—Seeing Is Believing. 1990. mass mkt. 3.50 o.p. (0-8217-2928-4, Zebra Bks.) Kensington Publishing Corp.
—She Died a Lady. 1987. 256p. mass mkt. 3.50 o.p. (0-8217-2238-7, Zebra Bks.) Kensington Publishing Corp.
—The Skeleton in the Clock. 1977. reprint ed. pap. 1.50 o.s.i (0-505-51194-0) Dorchester Publishing Co., Inc.
—The Skeleton in the Clock. 1992. 303p. pap. 5.95 o.p. (1-55882-103-1) International Polygonics, Ltd.
—The Unicorn Murders. 2000. 21.95 (0-7540-8568-6, Black Dagger) BBC Audiobooks America.
—The Unicorn Murders. 1989. 192p. reprint ed. pap. 5.95 o.p. (1-55882-015-9, Library of Crime Classics) International Polygonics, Ltd.
—The White Priory Murders. 1990. 214p. reprint ed. pap. 5.95 o.s.i (1-55882-072-8) International Polygonics, Ltd.
Dickson, Carter, pseud & Melling, John K. Behind the Crimson Blind. 1990. (Black Dagger Crime Ser.). 280p. reprint ed. text 16.50 o.p. (0-86220-768-1, Black Dagger) BBC Audiobooks America.
Dickson, Gordon R. The Dragon & the Djinn. 400p. 1998. mass mkt. 6.99 o.s.i (0-441-00495-4); 1996. 21.95 o.p. (0-441-00297-8) Ace Bks.
—The Dragon & the Man of Kent. 2000. 416p. 26.95 (0-312-86160-5, Tor Bks.) Doherty, Tom Assocs., LLC.
—The Dragon & the George. 1987. 288p. mass mkt. 6.99 (0-345-35050-2, Del Rey); 1978. mass mkt. 1.95 o.p. (0-345-27201-3, Del Rey); 1976. mass mkt. 1.95 o.p. (0-345-25361-2) Ballantine Bks.

—The Dragon & the Gnarly King. 1998. 480p. mass mkt. 6.99 o.s.i (*0-8125-6270-4*); 1997. 384p. 24.95 o.p. (*0-312-86157-5*) Doherty, Tom Assocs., LLC. (Tor Bks.).

—The Dragon at War. 1993. mass mkt. 5.99 o.s.i (*0-441-16611-3*); 1992. 18.95 o.p. (*0-441-75698-0*) Ace Bks.

—The Dragon in Lyonesse. (Tor Fantasy Ser.). 1999. 608p. mass mkt. 6.99 (*0-8125-6271-2*); 1998. 381p. 25.95 (*0-312-86159-1*) Doherty, Tom Assocs., LLC. (Tor Bks.).

—The Dragon in Lyonesse. 1999. 13.04 (*0-606-17028-6*) Turtleback Bks.

—The Dragon Knight. 1991. 512p. mass mkt. 6.99 o.s.i (*0-8125-0943-9*); Vol. 1. 1990. 19.95 o.p. (*0-312-93129-8*) Doherty, Tom Assocs., LLC. (Tor Bks.).

—The Dragon on the Border. 1993. 400p. mass mkt. 6.99 o.s.i (*0-441-16657-1*); 1992. 18.95 o.p. (*0-441-34233-7*) Ace Bks.

—The Dragon, the Earl & the Troll. 448p. (Orig.). 1996. mass mkt. 6.99 o.s.i (*0-441-00282-X*); 1994. 21.95 o.p. (*0-441-00098-3*) Ace Bks.

Disch, Thomas M. & Naylor, Charles. Neighboring Lives. 1992. 368p. reprint ed. pap. text 17.95 (*0-8018-4219-0*) Johns Hopkins Univ. Pr.

—Neighboring Lives. 1981. 351p. 25.00 (*0-684-16644-5*) Ultramarine Publishing Co., Inc.

Dodd, Christina. In My Wildest Dreams. 2001. 384p. mass mkt. 6.99 (*0-380-81962-7*, Avon Bks.) Morrow/Avon.

—My Favorite Bride. 2002. 384p. mass mkt. 6.99 (*0-06-009264-5*) HarperCollins Pubs.

—My Favorite Bride. 2003. (Core Ser.). 29.95 (*0-7862-5059-3*) Thorndike Pr.

—Rules of Attraction. l.t. ed. 2002. 456p. 29.95 (*0-7838-9572-0*, Macmillan Reference USA) Gale Group.

—Rules of Attraction. 2001. 384p. mass mkt. 6.99 (*0-380-81199-5*, Avon Bks.) Morrow/Avon.

—Rules of Engagement. l.t. ed. 2001. (G.K. Hall Large Print Core Ser.). 484p. 30.95 (*0-7838-9573-9*, Macmillan Reference USA) Gale Group.

—Rules of Engagement. 2000. 384p. mass mkt. 6.99 (*0-380-81198-7*, Avon Bks.) Morrow/Avon.

—Rules of Surrender. 2000. 384p. mass mkt. 6.99 (*0-380-81197-9*, Avon Bks.) Morrow/Avon.

—Rules of Surrender. l.t. ed. 2001. 410p. 30.95 (*0-7838-9574-7*) Thorndike Pr.

—The Runaway Princess. 1999. 384p. mass mkt. 6.99 (*0-380-80292-9*, Avon Bks.) Morrow/Avon.

—Scandalous Again. l.t. ed. 2003. 369p. 30.95 (*1-58724-482-9*, Wheeler Publishing, Inc.) Gale Group.

—Scandalous Again. 2003. 384p. mass mkt. 6.99 (*0-06-009265-3*, Avon Bks.) Morrow/Avon.

Doherty, Berlie. The Vinegar Jar. 1996. 256p. 21.95 o.p. (*0-312-14442-3*) St. Martin's Pr.

Doherty, P. C. The Assassin in the Greenwood: A Medieval Mystery Featuring Hugh Corbett. unabr. ed. 1998. audio 69.95 (*1-85903-123-4*) Magna Story Sound GBR. *Dist:* Ulverscroft Large Print Bks., Ltd.

—The Assassin in the Greenwood: A Medieval Mystery Featuring Hugh Corbett. 1994. 224p. 19.95 o.p. (*0-312-11554-7*, Saint Martin's Minotaur) St. Martin's Pr.

—The Assassin in the Greenwood: A Medieval Mystery Featuring Hugh Corbett. l.t. ed. 1996. (Ulverscroft Large Print Ser.). 384p. 29.99 o.p. (*0-7089-3535-4*, Ulverscroft) Thorpe, F. A. Pubs. GBR. *Dist:* Ulverscroft Large Print Bks., Ltd., Ulverscroft Large Print Canada, Ltd.

—The Devil's Hunt. 1998. 256p. 21.95 o.p. (*0-312-18084-5*, Saint Martin's Minotaur) St. Martin's Pr.

—The Devil's Hunt. l.t. ed. 1998. (Ulverscroft Large Print Ser.). 368p. 29.99 o.p. (*0-7089-3988-0*, Ulverscroft) Thorpe, F. A. Pubs. GBR. *Dist:* Ulverscroft Large Print Bks., Ltd., Ulverscroft Large Print Canada, Ltd.

—Dove Amongst the Hawks. l.t. ed. 2001. (Linford Mystery Large Print Ser.). 280p. pap. 19.99 o.p. (*0-7089-5997-0*, Ulverscroft) Thorpe, F. A. Pubs. GBR. *Dist:* Ulverscroft Large Print Bks., Ltd., Ulverscroft Large Print Canada, Ltd.

—Murder Wears a Cowl: A Medieval Mystery Featuring Hugh Corbett. unabr. ed. 1998. audio 69.95 (*1-85903-142-0*) Magna Story Sound GBR. *Dist:* Ulverscroft Large Print Bks., Ltd.

—Murder Wears a Cowl: A Medieval Mystery Featuring Hugh Corbett. 1993. 256p. 20.95 o.p. (*0-312-10506-1*, Saint Martin's Minotaur) St. Martin's Pr.

—Murder Wears a Cowl: A Medieval Mystery Featuring Hugh Corbett. l.t. ed. 1996. (Ulverscroft Large Print Ser.). 400p. 29.99 o.p. (*0-7089-3495-1*, Ulverscroft) Thorpe, F. A. Pubs. GBR. *Dist:* Ulverscroft Large Print Bks., Ltd., Ulverscroft Large Print Canada, Ltd.

—The Prince of Darkness. 1995. (WWL Mystery Ser.). per. (*0-373-26164-0*, 1-26164-3, Harlequin Bks.) Harlequin Enterprises, Ltd.

—The Prince of Darkness. 1993. 247p. 18.95 o.p. (*0-312-08876-0*, Saint Martin's Minotaur) St. Martin's Pr.

—The Prince of Darkness. l.t. ed. 1996. (Ulverscroft Large Print Ser.). 400p. 29.99 o.p. (*0-7089-3482-X*, Ulverscroft) Thorpe, F. A. Pubs. GBR. *Dist:* Ulverscroft Large Print Bks., Ltd., Ulverscroft Large Print Canada, Ltd.

—Satan in St. Mary's. 1988. mass mkt. 3.50 (*0-312-91357-5*, St. Martin's Paperbacks); 1987. 176p. 12.95 o.p. (*0-312-00059-6*) St. Martin's Pr.

—Satan in St. Mary's. l.t. ed. 1999. (Linford Mystery Large Print Ser.). 320p. pap. 18.99 o.p. (*0-7089-5594-0*, Linford) Thorpe, F. A. Pubs. GBR. *Dist:* Ulverscroft Large Print Bks., Ltd., Ulverscroft Large Print Canada, Ltd.

—Satan's Fire: A Medieval Mystery Featuring Hugh Corbett. 1996. 256p. 21.95 (*0-312-14728-7*, Saint Martin's Minotaur) St. Martin's Pr.

—The Song of a Dark Angel: A Medieval Mystery Featuring Hugh Corbett. unabr. ed. 1998. audio 69.95 (*1-85903-104-8*) Magna Story Sound GBR. *Dist:* Ulverscroft Large Print Bks., Ltd.

—The Song of a Dark Angel: A Medieval Mystery Featuring Hugh Corbett. 1995. 249p. 21.95 o.p. (*0-312-13605-6*, Saint Martin's Minotaur) St. Martin's Pr.

—The Song of a Dark Angel: A Medieval Mystery Featuring Hugh Corbett. l.t. ed. 1996. (Large Print Ser.). 400p. 29.99 o.p. (*0-7089-3611-3*, Ulverscroft) Thorpe, F. A. Pubs. GBR. *Dist:* Ulverscroft Large Print Bks., Ltd., Ulverscroft Large Print Canada, Ltd.

—Spy in Chancery. 1989. 14.95 o.p. (*0-312-02984-5*, Saint Martin's Minotaur) St. Martin's Pr.

—Spy in Chancery. l.t. ed. 2000. (Linford Mystery Large Print Ser.). 304p. pap. 18.99 o.p. (*0-7089-5653-X*, Linford) Thorpe, F. A. Pubs. GBR. *Dist:* Ulverscroft Large Print Bks., Ltd., Ulverscroft Large Print Canada, Ltd.

Dolan, Charlotte L. The Counterfeit Gentleman. l.t. ed. 1994. 328p. (Orig.). pap. 18.95 (*0-7838-1140-3*, Macmillan Reference USA) Gale Group.

—The Counterfeit Gentleman. 1994. (Signet Regency Romance Ser.). 224p. (Orig.). mass mkt. 3.99 o.s.i (*0-451-17742-8*, Signet Bks.) NAL.

—Fallen Angel. l.t. ed. 1994. 302p. lib. bdg. 20.95 (*0-8161-5947-5*, Macmillan Reference USA) Gale Group.

Dold, Gaylord. A Penny for the Old Guy. 1991. 240p. 17.95 o.p. (*0-312-06442-X*, Saint Martin's Minotaur) St. Martin's Pr.

—The World Beat. 1993. 288p. 19.95 o.p. (*0-312-09945-2*, Saint Martin's Minotaur) St. Martin's Pr.

Domning, Denise. Autumn's Flame. 1995. 384p. mass mkt. 5.50 o.s.i (*0-451-40612-5*, Topaz) NAL.

—A Love for All Seasons. 1996. 368p. mass mkt. 5.99 o.s.i (*0-451-40704-0*, Onyx) NAL.

—Spring's Fury. 1995. 384p. (Orig.). mass mkt. 4.99 o.s.i (*0-451-40521-8*, Topaz) NAL.

—Summer's Storm. 1994. 384p. (Orig.). mass mkt. 4.99 o.s.i (*0-451-40507-2*, Topaz) NAL.

—Summer's Storm. 2000. 376p. (Orig.). pap. 17.95 (*0-595-08876-7*) iUniverse, Inc.

—Winter's Heat. 1994. 384p. (Orig.). mass mkt. 4.99 o.s.i (*0-451-40438-6*, Topaz) NAL.

Donald, Anabel. The Glass Ceiling. l.t. ed. 1995. pap. 20.95 o.p. (*0-7838-1522-0*, Macmillan Reference USA) Gale Group.

—The Glass Ceiling. 1995. 217p. 20.95 o.p. (*0-312-13501-7*, Saint Martin's Minotaur) St. Martin's Pr.

—In at the Deep End. 1994. 224p. 19.95 o.p. (*0-312-11290-4*, Saint Martin's Minotaur) St. Martin's Pr.

—An Uncommon Murder. 1993. 217p. 17.95 o.p. (*0-312-08917-1*, Saint Martin's Minotaur) St. Martin's Pr.

Donat, Peter C. & Gould, Barney. Sherlock Holmes & the Shakespeare Solution. 1997. 90p. 24.00 (*1-55246-016-9*); pap. 10.00 (*1-55246-017-7*) Battered Silicon Dispatch Box, The.

Donnelly, Shannon. A Compromising Situation. 2000. (Zebra Regency Romance Ser.). 256p. mass mkt. 4.99 o.s.i (*0-8217-6751-8*, Zebra Bks.) Kensington Publishing Corp.

—A Dangerous Compromise. 2001. (Zebra Regency Romance Ser.). 288p. mass mkt. 4.99 o.s.i (*0-8217-6752-6*, Zebra Bks.) Kensington Publishing Corp.

Donoghue, Emma. Slammerkin. 2001. 352p. 24.00 (*0-15-100672-5*) Harcourt Trade Pubs.

Dorner, Marjorie. Freeze Frame. 1992. mass mkt. 4.99 o.s.i (*0-8217-3766-X*, Zebra Bks.) Kensington Publishing Corp.

—Freeze Frame. 1990. 320p. 18.95 o.p. (*0-688-09530-5*, Morrow, William & Co.) Morrow/Avon.

Doughty, Louise. An English Murder. 2000. 240p. 23.00 (*0-7867-0757-7*, Carroll & Graf Pubs.) Avalon Publishing Group.

—An English Murder. 2001. 240p. reprint ed. mass mkt. 6.50 (*0-440-23687-8*) Dell Publishing.

—An English Murder: A Mystery. l.t. ed. 2000. (Mystery Ser.). 269p. 26.95 (*0-7862-2836-9*) Thorndike Pr.

Douglas, Carole Nelson. Good Morning, Irene. (Irene Adler Adventure Ser.). 1992. (Illus.). 374p. mass mkt. 4.99 (*0-8125-0949-8*); 1991. 19.95 o.p. (*0-312-93211-1*) Doherty, Tom Assocs., LLC. (Tor Bks.).

—Good Morning, Irene. unabr. ed. 1999. audio 80.00 (*0-7887-2487-8*, 95562E7) Recorded Bks., LLC.

—Good Night, Mr. Holmes. 1991. 408p. mass mkt. 4.99 o.s.i (*0-8125-1430-0*); 1990. 18.95 o.p. (*0-312-93210-3*) Doherty, Tom Assocs., LLC. (Tor Bks.).

—Good Night, Mr. Holmes. unabr. ed. 1998. audio 78.00 (*0-7887-2489-4*, 95564E7) Recorded Bks., LLC.

—Irene at Large. 1993. (Irene Adler Adventure Ser.). 395p. mass mkt. 5.99 (*0-8125-1702-4*, Tor Bks.) Doherty, Tom Assocs., LLC.

—Irene at Large. unabr. ed. 2000. audio 91.00 (*0-7887-2492-4*, 95567E7) Recorded Bks., LLC.

—Irene's Last Waltz. 1994. (Irene Adler Adventure Ser.). 480p. mass mkt. 4.99 (*0-8125-1703-2*); 22.95 o.p. (*0-312-85224-X*) Doherty, Tom Assocs., LLC. (Forge Bks.).

—Irene's Last Waltz. unabr. ed. 2000. audio 97.00 (*0-7887-2493-2*, 95568E7) Recorded Bks., LLC.

Downes, Frank. The Long Snake Tattoo. 1998. (Frontlines Ser.). 192p. pap. 12.95 (*1-899344-35-7*) Do-Not Pr., The GBR. *Dist:* Dufour Editions, Inc.

Doyle, Arthur Conan. The Adventure of the Beryl Coronet. E-Book 0.99 (*1-58515-033-9*) MesaView, Inc.

—The Adventure of the Blue Carbuncle. E-Book 0.99 (*1-58515-034-7*) MesaView, Inc.

—The Adventure of the Blue Carbuncle. 1983. (Radio Ser.). pap. 5.95 o.p. incl. audio (*0-88142-353-X*, 353) Soundelux Audio Publishing.

—The Adventure of the Dancing Men. 1996. (Sherlock Holmes Ser.). 18p. pap. 3.50 (*1-57514-202-3*, 3065) Encore Performance Publishing.

—The Adventure of the Dancing Men & Other Sherlock Holmes Stories. 1997. 80p. (Orig.). pap. 1.00 (*0-486-29558-3*) Dover Pubns., Inc.

—The Adventure of the Empty House. unabr. ed. 1995. (Stories from the Return of Sherlock Holmes Ser.). audio 16.99 (*0-88646-387-4*, 7387) Durkin Hayes Publishing Ltd.

—The Adventure of the Empty House. 1981. audio. audio 7.95 Jimcin Recordings.

—The Adventure of the Engineer's Thumb. E-Book 0.99 (*1-58515-036-3*) MesaView, Inc.

—The Adventure of the Musgrave Ritual. unabr. ed. 1979. audio 7.95 Jimcin Recordings.

—The Adventure of the Noble Bachelor. E-Book 0.99 (*1-58515-037-1*) MesaView, Inc.

—The Adventures of Sherlock Holmes. 1985. 304p. mass mkt. 4.99 o.s.i (*0-345-32712-8*) Ballantine Bks.

—The Adventures of Sherlock Holmes. Green, Richard Lancelyn, ed. 1993. 438p. (C). 13.95 o.p. (*0-19-212318-1*, 14613) Oxford Univ. Pr., Inc.

—The Adventures of Sherlock Holmes. Green, Richard Lancelyn, ed. & intro. by. 1995. (Oxford World's Classics Ser.). 438p. reprint ed. pap. 5.95 o.p. (*0-19-282378-7*) Oxford Univ. Pr., Inc.

—The Adventures of Sherlock Holmes. l.t. ed. 2003. (Perennial Bestsellers Ser.). 28.95 (*0-7862-5631-1*) Thorndike Pr.

—The Adventures of Sherlock Holmes. Incl. Red-Headed League. audio Scandal in Bohemia. audio Speckled Band. audio Set audio 12.95 (*0-89926-125-6*, 813) Audio Bk. Co.

—The Adventures of Sherlock Holmes: A Scandal in Bohemia. 1970. 7.95 (*0-02-732920-8*, Simon & Schuster Children's Publishing) Simon & Schuster Children's Publishing.

—The Adventures of Sherlock Holmes: BBC, Vol. 3. abr. ed. 1997. (BBC Radio Presents Ser.: Vol. 3). audio 16.99 o.s.i (*0-553-47845-1*, RH Audio) Random Hse. Audio Publishing Group.

—The Adventures of Sherlock Holmes I: The Speckled Band; the Adventure of Copper Beeches; the Stock-Broker's Clerk; the Red-Headed League. abr. ed. (Sherlock Holmes Stories). (YA). 1999. audio compact disk 19.98 (*962-634-152-1*, NA315212); 1998. audio 17.98 (*962-634-652-3*, NA315214) Naxos of America, Inc. (Naxos AudioBooks).

—The Adventures of Sherlock Holmes II: A Scandal in Bohemia; The Five Orange Pips; The Adventure of the Engineer's Thumb; Silver Blaze. unabr. ed. 1999. (Sherlock Holmes Stories). audio 17.98 (*962-634-670-1*, NA317014, Naxos AudioBooks) Naxos of America, Inc.

—The Adventures of Sherlock Holmes III: The Man with the Twisted Lip; The Musgrave Ritual; The Adventure of the Cardboard Box; The Adventure of the Blue Carbuncle. unabr. ed. 2000. (Sherlock Holmes Stories). audio 17.98 (*962-634-691-4*, NA319114, Naxos AudioBooks) Naxos of America, Inc.

—The Adventures of Sherlock Holmes III: The Man with the Twisted Lip; the Musgrave Ritual; the Adventure of the Cardboard Box; the Adventure of the Blue Carbuncle. unabr. ed. 2000. (Sherlock Holmes Stories). (YA). audio compact disk 19.98 (*962-634-191-2*, NA319112, Naxos AudioBooks) Naxos of America, Inc.

—Beyond the City. 2000. per. 12.50 (*1-58396-500-9*) Blue Unicorn Editions.

—Beyond the City. 2000. E-Book 2.49 (*1-58744-139-X*) Electric Umbrella Publishing.

—Beyond the City. 1982. (Conan Doyle Centennial Ser.). (Illus.). 187p. 28.00 (*0-934468-44-3*) Gaslight Pubns.

—The Case-Book of Sherlock Holmes. 1986. mass mkt. 3.50 o.p. (*0-425-10194-0*); 1984. mass mkt. 2.50 o.s.i (*0-425-07175-8*) Berkley Publishing Group.

—The Case-Book of Sherlock Holmes. 2001. vi, 296p. pap. 8.95 (*0-7551-0647-4*) House of Stratus, Inc. GBR. *Dist:* Midpoint Trade Bks., Inc.

—The Case-Book of Sherlock Holmes. Robson, W. W., ed. (Oxford World's Classics Ser.). 336p. 2000. pap. 10.00 (*0-19-283917-9*); 1993. (C). 13.95 o.p. (*0-19-212311-4*, 14608) Oxford Univ. Pr., Inc.

—The Case-Book of Sherlock Holmes. Robson, W. W., ed. & intro. by. 1995. (Oxford Sherlock Holmes Ser.). 334p. reprint ed. pap. 6.95 o.p. (*0-19-282374-4*) Oxford Univ. Pr., Inc.

—The Case-Book of Sherlock Holmes. 1999. 353p. E-Book 3.99 incl. cd-rom (*1-57646-185-8*) Quiet Vision Publishing.

—The Case-Book of Sherlock Holmes, Vol. 1. abr. ed. 1998. (BBC Radio Presents Ser.). 355p. 16.99 o.s.i incl. audio (*0-553-47904-0*, RH Audio) Random Hse. Audio Publishing Group.

—The Case-Book of Sherlock Holmes. l.t. ed. 1967. 12.00 o.p. (*0-85456-590-6*, Ulverscroft) Thorpe, F. A. Pubs. GBR. *Dist:* Ulverscroft Large Print Bks., Ltd.

—The Case-Book of Sherlock Holmes. unabr. ed. 2000. audio 14.95 (*0-00-105478-3*) Trafalgar Square.

—The Case-Book of Sherlock Holmes. 1998. (Classics Library). 400p. pap. 3.95 (*1-85326-070-3*, 0703WW) Wordsworth Editions, Ltd. GBR. *Dist:* Casemate Pubs. & Bk. Distributors, LLC.

—The Crooked Man. 1989. audio 7.95 Jimcin Recordings.

—The Doings of Raffles Haw. 1977. (Short Story Index Reprint Ser.). 16.95 (*0-8369-3249-8*) Ayer Co. Pubs., Inc.

—The Doings of Raffles Haw. (Collected Works of Sir Arthur Conan Doyle). 2001. 199p. pap. text 28.00 (*0-7426-7686-2*); reprint ed. lib. bdg. 98.00 (*0-7426-2686-5*) Classic Bks.

—The Doings of Raffles Haw. 2002. 144p. per. 29.95 (*1-58963-866-2*) Fredonia Bks.

—The Doings of Raffles Haw. 1981. (Conan Doyle Centennial Ser.). (Illus.). 157p. 28.00 (*0-934468-43-5*) Gaslight Pubns.

—The Doings of Raffles Haw. 1986. 256p. 15.00 o.p. (*0-947898-37-9*) Periodicals Service Co.

—A Duet, with an Occasional Chorus. reprint ed. lib. bdg. 98.00 (*0-7426-2702-0*); lib. bdg. 98.00 (*0-7426-2710-1*); 2001. (Collected Works of Sir Arthur Conan Doyle: Vol. 2). pap. text 28.00 (*0-7426-7702-8*); 2001. (Collected Works of Sir Arthur Conan Doyle: Vol. 2). pap. text 28.00 (*0-7426-7710-9*) Classic Bks.

—A Duet, with an Occasional Chorus. 2001. 340p. per. 24.95 (*1-58963-461-6*) Fredonia Bks.

—A Duet, with an Occasional Chorus. 1990. (Conan Doyle Centennial Ser.). (Illus.). 270p. 28.00 (*0-934468-48-6*) Gaslight Pubns.

—The Final Adventures of Sherlock Holmes. 2002. (Illus.). 251p. 27.50 (*0-7090-6738-0*) Hale, Robert Ltd. GBR. *Dist:* Trafalgar Square.

—The Final Problem. abr. ed. 1983. (Radio Ser.). pap. 5.95 o.p. incl. audio (*0-88142-355-6*, 355) Soundelux Audio Publishing.

—The Firm of Girdlestone. (Collected Works of Sir Arthur Conan Doyle). 2001. 381p. pap. text 28.00 (*0-7426-7682-X*); reprint ed. lib. bdg. 98.00 (*0-7426-2682-2*) Classic Bks.

—The Firm of Girdlestone. 2001. (Illus.). 380p. per. 24.95 (*1-58963-392-X*) Fredonia Bks.

—The Firm of Girdlestone. 1981. (Conan Doyle Centennial Ser.). (Illus.). 364p. 16.95 o.p. (*0-934468-42-7*) Gaslight Pubns.

—Great Works of Sir Arthur Conan Doyle: The Illustrated Sherlock Holmes Treasury. 1990. o.s.i (*0-517-05776-X*) Crown Publishing Group.

—Great Works of Sir Arthur Conan Doyle: The Illustrated Sherlock Holmes Treasury. 1987. (Illus.). 10.99 o.s.i (*0-517-64282-4*) Random Hse. Value Publishing.

—His Last Bow: Some Reminiscences of Sherlock Holmes. Date not set. (Heritage Literary Ser.). pap. text 31.50 (*0-582-34914-1*) Addison-Wesley Longman, Ltd. GBR. *Dist:* Trans-Atlantic Pubns., Inc.

—His Last Bow: Some Reminiscences of Sherlock Holmes. 1987. mass mkt. 2.50 o.p. (*0-425-10491-5*); 1986. mass mkt. 2.50 o.s.i (*0-425-09579-7*); 1984. mass mkt. 2.50 o.s.i (*0-425-07502-8*); 1981.

mass mkt. 1.95 o.s.i (*0-425-04870-5*); 1980. mass mkt. 1.75 o.s.i (*0-425-04534-X*); 1978. mass mkt. 1.50 o.s.i (*0-425-04003-8*); 1976. mass mkt. 1.25 o.s.i (*0-425-03129-2*); 1974. mass mkt. 0.95 o.s.i (*0-425-02804-6*) Berkley Publishing Group.

—His Last Bow: Some Reminiscences of Sherlock Holmes. 1990. reprint ed. lib. bdg. 18.95 o.p. (*0-89966-666-3*) Buccaneer Bks., Inc.

—His Last Bow: Some Reminiscences of Sherlock Holmes. reprint ed. lib. bdg. 98.00 (*0-7426-2735-7*); 2001. 212p. pap. text 28.00 (*0-7426-7735-4*) Classic Bks.

—His Last Bow: Some Reminiscences of Sherlock Holmes. 2001. v, 236p. pap. 8.95 (*0-7551-0646-6*) House of Stratus, Inc. GBR. *Dist:* Midpoint Trade Bks., Inc.

—His Last Bow: Some Reminiscences of Sherlock Holmes. Edwards, Owen D., ed. 1993. (Oxford Sherlock Holmes Ser.). 302p. (C). 13.95 o.p. (*0-19-212315-7*) Oxford Univ. Pr., Inc.

—His Last Bow: Some Reminiscences of Sherlock Holmes. Edwards, Owen D., ed. & intro. by. 1995. (Oxford World's Classics Ser.). 304p. reprint ed. pap. 6.95 o.p. (*0-19-282381-7*) Oxford Univ. Pr., Inc.

—His Last Bow: Some Reminiscences of Sherlock Holmes. 1993. 208p. pap. 6.95 o.p. (*0-14-005709-9*) Penguin Group (USA) Inc.

—His Last Bow: Some Reminiscences of Sherlock Holmes. collector's ed. 2002. (Illus.). im. lthr. 38.85 (*1-4115-1256-1*); pap. 19.95 (*1-4115-0526-3*); 25.95 (*1-4115-0884-X*); pap. 17.95 (*1-4115-0315-5*) Polyglot Pr., Inc.

—His Last Bow: Some Reminiscences of Sherlock Holmes. 2001. E-Book 2.95 (*1-58882-433-0*) PublishingOnline.

—His Last Bow: Some Reminiscences of Sherlock Holmes. 1999. 292p. E-Book 3.99 incl. cd-rom (*1-57646-183-1*) Quiet Vision Publishing.

—His Last Bow: Some Reminiscences of Sherlock Holmes. l.t. ed. 1977. (Ulverscroft Large Print Ser.). 29.99 o.p. (*0-7089-0076-3*, Ulverscroft) Thorpe, F. A. Pubs. GBR. *Dist:* Ulverscroft Large Print Bks., Ltd., Ulverscroft Large Print Canada, Ltd.

—The Hound of the Baskervilles. 1976. 19.95 (*0-8488-1286-7*) Amereon, Ltd.

—The Hound of the Baskervilles. 1994. (Illustrated Classics Collection). 64p. pap. 3.60 o.p. (*1-56103-528-9*); pap. 4.95 (*0-7854-0696-4*, 40450) American Guidance Service, Inc.

—The Hound of the Baskervilles. ltd. ed. 1985. (Illus.). 200p. 300.00 o.p. (*0-910457-06-9*) Arion Pr.

—The Hound of the Baskervilles. abr. ed. audio 12.95 (*0-89926-154-X*, 842) Audio Bk. Co.

—The Hound of the Baskervilles, Set. unabr. ed. 1986. audio 29.95 (*1-55685-008-5*) Audio Bk. Contractors, Inc.

—The Hound of the Baskervilles. Klinger, Leslie Hawthorne, ed. anniv. ed. 2001. (The Baker Street Irregulars Manuscript Series: Vol. 2). (Illus.). 109p. 35.00 (*0-9648788-3-6*) Baker Street Irregulars, The.

—The Hound of the Baskervilles. 1987. 192p. mass mkt. 6.50 (*0-345-35052-9*) Ballantine Bks.

—The Hound of the Baskervilles. 1986. mass mkt. 2.50 o.s.i (*0-425-09592-4*); 1984. mass mkt. 2.50 o.s.i (*0-425-08090-0*); 1983. mass mkt. 2.50 o.s.i (*0-425-06587-1*); 1982. mass mkt. 2.25 o.s.i (*0-425-05219-2*); 1980. mass mkt. 1.95 o.s.i (*0-425-04421-1*); 1979. mass mkt. 1.95 o.s.i (*0-425-04535-8*); 1978. mass mkt. 1.50 o.s.i (*0-425-04000-3*); 1977. mass mkt. 1.25 o.s.i (*0-425-03336-8*); 1974. mass mkt. 0.95 o.s.i (*0-425-02805-4*) Berkley Publishing Group.

—The Hound of the Baskervilles. Bennett, S. A., ed. 1992. (Adventures of Sherlock Holmes Ser.). (Illus.). 64p. pap. (*0-944099-17-3*) Bill Barry's Compass Bks.

—The Hound of the Baskervilles. unabr. ed. 1994. audio 32.95 (*0-7861-0499-6*, 1450) Blackstone Audio Bks., Inc.

—The Hound of the Baskervilles. unabr. ed. 1986. audio 39.95 (*1-55686-238-5*, 692234) Books in Motion.

—The Hound of the Baskervilles. unabr. collector's ed. 1993. (J). audio 36.00 (*0-7366-2454-6*, 3218) Books on Tape, Inc.

—The Hound of the Baskervilles. 2002. pap. 3.50 (*1-59109-028-8*) Booksurge, LLC.

—The Hound of the Baskervilles. 1986. lib. bdg. 19.95 (*0-89966-229-3*) Buccaneer Bks., Inc.

—The Hound of the Baskervilles. reprint ed. lib. bdg. 98.00 (*0-7426-2707-1*); lib. bdg. 48.00 (*0-7426-1122-1*); 2001. (Best Sellers of 1902 Ser.). pap. text 28.00 (*0-7426-6122-9*); 2001. (Collected Works of Sir Arthur Conan Doyle: Vol. 4). pap. text 28.00 (*0-7426-7707-9*) Classic Bks.

—The Hound of the Baskervilles. l.t. ed. 2003. (Dales Large Print Ser.). 320p. pap. 21.99 (*1-84262-219-6*) Dales Large Print Bks. GBR. *Dist:* Ulverscroft Large Print Bks., Ltd., Ulverscroft Large Print Canada, Ltd.

—The Hound of the Baskervilles. adapted ed. 1977. per. 6.50 (*0-8222-0536-X*) Dramatists Play Service, Inc.

—The Hound of the Baskervilles. abr. ed. audio 16.99 (*0-88646-005-0*, 7333); 1986. (YA). (gr. 6-8). audio 29.95 o.p. (*0-88646-809-4*, R 7007) Durkin Hayes Publishing Ltd.

—The Hound of the Baskervilles. (Illus.). 208p. 1988. pap. 10.95 o.p. (*0-86547-264-5*, North Point Pr.); 1986. 17.50 o.p. (*0-86547-263-7*) Farrar, Straus & Giroux.

—The Hound of the Baskervilles. 1976. (Crime Fiction Ser). reprint ed. lib. bdg. 21.00 o.p. (*0-8240-2364-1*) Garland Publishing, Inc.

—The Hound of the Baskervilles. abr. ed. 1996. audio 17.00 (*1-55994-073-5*, CPN 505, HarperAudio) HarperTrade.

—The Hound of the Baskervilles, unabr. ed. 1999. audio 32.95 Highsmith Inc.

—The Hound of the Baskervilles. 2001. v, 378p. pap. 8.95 (*0-7551-0642-3*) House of Stratus, Inc. GBR. *Dist:* Midpoint Trade Bks., Inc.

—The Hound of the Baskervilles. 2002. 176p. 23.99 (*1-4043-0972-1*); per. 18.99 (*1-4043-0973-X*) IndyPublish.com.

—The Hound of the Baskervilles. unabr. ed. 1979. audio 28.00 Jimcin Recordings.

—The Hound of the Baskervilles. 1975. (Illus.). 4.95 o.p. (*0-8052-3602-3*); pap. 2.95 o.p. (*0-8052-0505-5*) Knopf Publishing Group. (Schocken).

—The Hound of the Baskervilles. Goodenough, Simon, ed. 1984. (Illus.). 192p. pap. o.p. (*0-316-32002-1*) Little Brown & Co.

—The Hound of the Baskervilles. Eyre, A. G., ed. 2000. (Longman Simplified English Ser.). 72p. pap. text 5.95 o.p. (*0-582-52910-7*, 73976) Longman Publishing Group.

—The Hound of the Baskervilles. 1997. pap. 3.95 (*0-89375-410-2*); 1986. mass mkt. 2.25 o.p. (*0-451-51983-3*, Signet Classics); 1986. mass mkt. 2.50 o.p. (*0-451-52221-4*); 1967. mass mkt. 0.50 o.p. (*0-451-50337-6*, Signet Classics); 100th anniv. ed. 2001. 256p. mass mkt. 4.95 (*0-451-52801-8*) NAL.

—The Hound of the Baskervilles. unabr. ed. 34.95 incl. audio Norton Pubs., Inc., Jeffrey /Audio-Forum.

—The Hound of the Baskervilles. 2002. E-Book (*1-59342-019-6*) Outrigger Publishing.

—The Hound of the Baskervilles. Robson, W. W., ed. 1993. (Oxford Sherlock Holmes Ser.). 232p. (C). 13.95 o.p. (*0-19-212310-6*, 8954) Oxford Univ. Pr., Inc.

—The Hound of the Baskervilles. Robson, W. W., ed. & intro. by. (Oxford World's Classics Ser.). 232p. reprint ed. 1998. pap. 8.95 (*0-19-283519-X*); 1995. pap. 6.95 o.p. (*0-19-282377-9*) Oxford Univ. Pr., Inc.

—The Hound of the Baskervilles. 1981. (Sherlock Holmes Ser.). 176p. (C). pap. 5.95 (*0-14-000111-5*, Penguin Bks.) Penguin Group (USA) Inc.

—The Hound of the Baskervilles. 1996. (Sherlock Holmes Ser.). (Illus.). 120p. 9.98 (*1-879582-15-5*) Platinum Pr., Inc.

—The Hound of the Baskervilles. collector's ed. 2002. (Illus.). im. lthr. 38.85 (*1-4115-1252-9*); pap. 19.95 (*1-4115-0525-5*); 25.95 (*1-4115-0885-8*); pap. 17.95 (*1-4115-0317-1*) Polyglot Pr., Inc.

—The Hound of the Baskervilles. abr. ed. 2000. (BBC Radio Presents Ser.). audio 18.00 o.s.i (*0-553-52688-X*, RH Audio) Random Hse. Audio Publishing Group.

—The Hound of the Baskervilles. unabr. ed. 1991. (Sherlock Holmes Mystery Ser.). audio 44.00 (*1-55690-237-9*, 91333E7) Recorded Bks., LLC.

—The Hound of the Baskervilles. unabr. ed. audio 24.95 (*1-883049-79-2*, Commuters Library) Sound Room Pubs., Inc.

—The Hound of the Baskervilles. (Mind's Eye Classic Ser.). 1996. audio 10.95 o.p. (*1-55935-211-6*); 1975. pap. 5.95 o.p. incl. audio (*0-88142-334-3*) Soundelux Audio Publishing.

—The Hound of the Baskervilles. l.t. ed. 2003. (Sherlock Holmes Ser.). 259p. 29.95 (*0-7862-5870-5*) Thorndike Pr.

—The Hound of the Baskervilles. 1986. 11.00 (*0-606-01869-7*) Turtleback Bks.

—The Hound of the Baskervilles. 2002. E-Book 2.95 (*0-9712910-5-5*) Twenty Penny Pr., Inc.

—The Hound of the Baskervilles. (Illus.). 150p. pap. 8.95 (*1-57002-152-X*) University Publishing Hse., Inc.

—The Hound of the Baskervilles. (Classics Ser.). 2001. 256p. pap. 8.00 (*0-14-043786-X*, Penguin Classics); 1995. 2p. audio 16.95 o.s.i (*0-14-086164-5*, Penguin AudioBooks) Viking Penguin.

—Lasy Galley. 2001. i, 348p. pap. 8.95 (*0-7551-0655-5*) House of Stratus, Inc.

—The Man from Archangel: And Other Tales of Adventure. 1977. (Short Story Index Reprint Ser.). 19.95 (*0-8369-3189-0*) Ayer Co. Pubs., Inc.

—The Man from Archangel: And Other Tales of Adventure. 2001. 260p. per. 24.95 (*1-58963-601-5*) Fredonia Bks.

—Masterworks of Crime & Mystery. Tracy, Jack W., ed. 1982. 320p. 14.95 o.p. (*0-385-27688-5*, Dial Bks.) Dell Publishing.

—The Memoirs of Sherlock Holmes. 1986. mass mkt. 2.50 o.s.i (*0-425-09576-2*); 1984. mass mkt. 2.50 o.s.i (*0-425-07315-7*); 1976. mass mkt. 1.75 o.s.i (*0-425-04400-9*) Berkley Publishing Group.

—The Memoirs of Sherlock Holmes. 1982. reprint ed. lib. bdg. 21.95 o.p. (*0-89966-428-8*) Buccaneer Bks., Inc.

—The Memoirs of Sherlock Holmes. reprint ed. lib. bdg. 98.00 (*0-7426-2692-X*); 2001. (Collected Works of Sir Arthur Conan Doyle: Vol. 6). pap. text 28.00 (*0-7426-7692-7*) Classic Bks.

—The Memoirs of Sherlock Holmes. 2001. (Illus.). 300p. pap. 8.95 (*0-7551-0644-X*) House of Stratus, Inc. GBR. *Dist:* Midpoint Trade Bks., Inc.

—The Memoirs of Sherlock Holmes. 2002. 240p. 18.99 (*1-4043-1910-7*); per. 13.99 (*1-4043-1911-5*) IndyPublish.com.

—The Memoirs of Sherlock Holmes. 1976. (Illus.). 176p. 5.95 o.p. (*0-8052-3622-8*, Schocken) Knopf Publishing Group.

—The Memoirs of Sherlock Holmes. E-Book 2.95 (*1-57799-810-3*) Logos Research Systems, Inc.

—The Memoirs of Sherlock Holmes. l.t. ed. (Large Print Ser.). reprint ed. 1986. 421p. lib. bdg. 26.00 (*0-939495-31-7*); 1998. 270p. lib. bdg. 25.00 (*1-58287-049-7*) North Bks.

—The Memoirs of Sherlock Holmes. Roden, Christopher, ed. (Oxford World's Classics Ser.). 2000. 384p. pap. 9.95 (*0-19-283811-3*); 1993. 378p. (C). 13.95 o.p. (*0-19-212309-2*) Oxford Univ. Pr., Inc.

—The Memoirs of Sherlock Holmes. Roden, Christopher, ed. & intro. by. 1995. (Oxford World's Classics Ser.). 378p. reprint ed. pap. 6.95 o.p. (*0-19-282375-2*) Oxford Univ. Pr., Inc.

—The Memoirs of Sherlock Holmes. 1996. (Sherlock Holmes Ser.). (Illus.). 160p. 9.98 (*1-879582-14-7*) Platinum Pr., Inc.

—The Memoirs of Sherlock Holmes. collector's ed. 2002. (Illus.). im. lthr. 38.85 (*1-4115-1248-0*); pap. 19.95 (*1-4115-0518-2*); 25.95 (*1-4115-0886-6*); pap. 19.95 (*1-4115-0314-7*) Polyglot Pr., Inc.

—The Memoirs of Sherlock Holmes. 1999. 375p. E-Book 3.99 incl. cd-rom (*1-57646-178-5*) Quiet Vision Publishing.

—The Memoirs of Sherlock Holmes. 1994. audio 15.95 o.s.i (*0-553-74577-8*); 1994. audio 15.95 o.s.i (*0-553-74612-X*); 1993. audio 15.95 o.s.i (*0-553-74550-6*); 1993. audio 12.79 o.s.i (*0-553-70054-5*); Vol. 2. 1994. audio 16.99 o.s.i (*0-553-47249-6*); Vols. 1-3. 1997. 29.95 o.s.i incl. audio (*0-553-47954-7*) Random Hse. Audio Publishing Group. (RH Audio).

—The Memoirs of Sherlock Holmes. l.t. ed. 1966. (Ulverscroft Large Print Ser.). 29.99 o.p. (*0-85456-573-6*, Ulverscroft) Thorpe, F. A. Pubs. GBR. *Dist:* Ulverscroft Large Print Bks., Ltd., Ulverscroft Large Print Canada, Ltd.

—The Memoirs of Sherlock Holmes. 2001. (Classics of Mystery & Suspense Ser.). 318p. (*1-58279-190-2*) Trident Pr. International.

—The Memoirs of Sherlock Holmes. 1951. 256p. pap. 3.95 o.p. (*0-14-000785-7*, Penguin Bks.) Viking Penguin.

—The Memoirs of Sherlock Holmes. 2001. 230p. pap. 12.95 (*0-595-01467-4*) iUniverse, Inc.

—The Memoirs of Sherlock Holmes. unabr. collector's ed. Incl. Adventures of Silver Blaze. audio Crooked Man. audio Final Problem. audio Gloria Scott. audio Greek Interpreter. audio Musgrave Ritual. audio Naval Treaty. audio Reigate Squires. audio Resident Patient. audio Stockbroker's Clerk. audio Yellow Face. audio 1984. (Sherlock Holmes Ser.). 1980. Set audio 48.00 (*0-7366-0320-4*, 1308) Books on Tape, Inc.

—The Memoirs of Sherlock Holmes. unabr. ed. Incl. Adventure of the Crooked Man. audio Adventure of the Gloria Scott. audio Adventure of the Greek Interpreter. audio Adventure of the Musgrave Ritual. audio Adventure of the Naval Treaty. audio Adventure of the Reigate Squire. audio Adventure of the Resident Patient. audio Adventure of the Stockbroker's Clerk. audio Adventure of the Yellow Face. audio Adventures of Silver Blaze. audio Set audio 49.00 Jimcin Recordings.

—Micah Clarke. (Collected Works of Sir Arthur Conan Doyle). 2001. pap. text 28.00 (*0-7426-7678-1*); reprint ed. lib. bdg. 98.00 (*0-7426-2678-4*) Classic Bks.

—Micah Clarke. 2001. 408p. per. 24.95 (*1-58963-424-1*) Fredonia Bks.

—My Life with Sherlock Holmes: Conversations in Baker Street. Hamilton, J. R., ed. 1970. (Illus.). 5.75 o.p. (*0-7195-1837-7*) Transatlantic Arts, Inc.

—The Original Illustrated Sherlock Holmes: The Strand Facsimile Edition. 2001. (Illus.). 636p. 25.00 (*0-7881-9933-1*) DIANE Publishing Co.

—The Original Illustrated Strand Sherlock Holmes: The Complete Facsimile Edition. 2000. (Illus.). 1126p. reprint ed. pap. text 25.00 (*0-7881-9173-X*) DIANE Publishing Co.

—The Return of Sherlock Holmes. Date not set. (Heritage Literary Ser.). pap. text 31.50 (*0-582-34913-3*) Addison-Wesley Longman, Ltd. GBR. *Dist:* Trans-Atlantic Pubns., Inc.

—The Return of Sherlock Holmes. 1985. 320p. mass mkt. 2.95 o.s.i (*0-345-32713-6*) Ballantine Bks.

—The Return of Sherlock Holmes. unabr. ed. 1983. audio 56.95 (*0-7861-0592-5*, 2081) Blackstone Audio Bks., Inc.

—The Return of Sherlock Holmes. unabr. collector's ed. 1982. (J). audio 64.00 (*0-7366-3854-7*, 9051) Books on Tape, Inc.

—The Return of Sherlock Holmes. reprint ed. lib. bdg. 98.00 (*0-7426-2711-X*) Classic Bks.

—The Return of Sherlock Holmes. unabr. ed. 1999. audio 56.95 Highsmith Inc.

—The Return of Sherlock Holmes. 1975. (Illus.). 5.95 o.p. (*0-8052-3603-1*); pap. 2.95 o.p. (*0-8052-0506-3*) Knopf Publishing Group. (Schocken).

—The Return of Sherlock Holmes. E-Book 2.95 (*1-57799-838-3*) Logos Research Systems, Inc.

—The Return of Sherlock Holmes. 1987. (Illus.). 320p. 25.00 o.p. (*0-89296-248-8*) Mysterious Pr.

—The Return of Sherlock Holmes. Green, Richard Lancelyn, ed. 1993. (Sherlock Holmes Ser.). 474p. (C). 13.95 o.p. (*0-19-212317-3*, 8952) Oxford Univ. Pr., Inc.

—The Return of Sherlock Holmes. Green, Richard Lancelyn, ed. & intro. by. 1995. (Oxford World's Classics Ser.). 456p. reprint ed. pap. 5.95 o.p. (*0-19-282376-0*) Oxford Univ. Pr., Inc.

—The Return of Sherlock Holmes. 1996. (Sherlock Holmes Ser.). (Illus.). 200p. 9.98 (*1-879582-13-9*) Platinum Pr., Inc.

—The Return of Sherlock Holmes. 1999. 482p. E-Book 3.99 incl. cd-rom (*1-57646-179-3*) Quiet Vision Publishing.

—The Return of Sherlock Holmes. 1995. audio 16.98 o.s.i (*0-553-74557-3*); Vol. 1. 1995. audio 16.99 o.s.i (*0-553-47349-2*); Vol. 2. 1995. audio 16.98 o.s.i (*0-553-74666-9*); Vol. 3. 1996. audio 16.99 o.s.i (*0-553-47655-6*) Random Hse. Audio Publishing Group. (RH Audio).

—The Return of Sherlock Holmes. 2001. audio 29.95 (*1-931102-46-5*, CA-051) TOPICS Entertainment.

—The Return of Sherlock Holmes. l.t. ed. 1967. (Ulverscroft Large Print Ser.). 29.99 o.p. (*0-85456-574-4*, Ulverscroft) Thorpe, F. A. Pubs. GBR. *Dist:* Ulverscroft Large Print Bks., Ltd., Ulverscroft Large Print Canada, Ltd.

—The Return of Sherlock Holmes. 1987. 192p. pap. 3.50 o.p. (*0-14-010026-1*); 1982. 336p. pap. 5.95 o.p. (*0-14-005708-0*) Viking Penguin. (Penguin Bks.).

—The Return of Sherlock Holmes. 1997. (Classics Library). 320p. pap. 3.95 (*1-85326-058-4*, 0584WW) Wordsworth Editions, Ltd. GBR. *Dist:* Combined Publishing.

—The Return of Sherlock Holmes. unabr. ed. Incl. Abbey Grange. audio Adventure of Black Peter. audio Adventure of Charles Augustus Milverton. audio Adventure of the Six Napoleons. audio Dancing Men. audio Empty House. audio Golden Pince-Nez. audio Missing Three-Quarter. audio Norwood Builder. audio Priory School. audio Second Stain. audio Solitary Cyclist. audio Three Students. audio 1981. 1981. Set audio 49.00 Jimcin Recordings.

—The Return of Sherlock Holmes: The Oxford Sherlock Holmes. 1999. (Oxford World's Classics Ser.). pap. text 5.95 (*0-19-283761-3*) Oxford Univ. Pr., Inc.

—Round the Fire Stories. 35.00 (*0-8118-4162-6*); 1991. 256p. reprint ed. pap. 9.95 o.p. (*0-87701-883-9*) Chronicle Bks. LLC.

—Round the Fire Stories. reprint ed. lib. bdg. 98.00 (*0-7426-2720-9*); 2001. 356p. pap. text 28.00 (*0-7426-7720-6*) Classic Bks.

—Round the Fire Stories. 2001. 234p. pap. 8.95 (*0-7551-0654-7*) House of Stratus, Inc.

—Round the Fire Stories. unabr. ed. 2001. audio 61.95 (*1-85695-749-7*, 940409) ISIS Audio Bks. GBR. *Dist:* Ulverscroft Large Print Bks., Ltd.

—Sherlock Holmes: Selected Stories. Date not set. lib. bdg. 29.95 (*0-8488-1672-2*) Amereon, Ltd.

—Sherlock Holmes: Selected Stories. Roberts, S. C., ed. & intro. by. 1998. (Oxford World's Classics Ser.). 464p. pap. 10.95 (*0-19-283537-8*) Oxford Univ. Pr., Inc.

—Sherlock Holmes: Selected Stories. 1982. (Oxford World's Classics Ser.). 460p. pap. 7.95 o.p. (*0-19-281530-X*) Oxford Univ. Pr., Inc.

—Sherlock Holmes: The Complete Novels & Stories, Vol. II. 1986. (Bantam Classics Ser.). 768p. reprint ed. mass mkt. 6.95 (*0-553-21242-7*) Bantam Dell Publishing Group.

—Sherlock Holmes: The Complete Novels & Stories. 1986. 12.55 (*0-606-03127-8*) Turtleback Bks.

—Sherlock Holmes: The Hound of the Baskervilles. l.t. ed. 1988. 18.95 o.p. (*1-55504-538-3*) BBC Audiobooks America.

—Sherlock Holmes Reader. 1975. 3.95 o.s.i (*0-425-03010-5*) Berkley Publishing Group.

—The Sign of the Four. Date not set. 112p. 16.95 (*0-8488-2550-0*) Amereon, Ltd.

—The Sign of the Four. 1994. (Library of Congress Centennial Bestseller Ser.). 160p. 24.95 (*1-55709-301-6*) Applewood Bks.

—The Sign of the Four. unabr. ed. 1991. (Best of Sherlock Holmes Ser.). audio 26.95 o.p. (*1-55656-140-7*, DAB042) BBC Audiobooks America.

—The Sign of the Four. 1987. (Illus.). 160p. mass mkt. 3.95 o.s.i (*0-345-35290-4*) Ballantine Bks.

—The Sign of the Four. 2000. (Encore Editions Ser.). 167p. (C). pap. (*1-55111-392-9*) Broadview Pr.

—The Sign of the Four. unabr. ed. (Best of Sherlock Holmes Ser.). 1998. pap. 21.95 o.s.i incl. audio (*1-55656-228-4*); 1990. audio 21.95 o.s.i (*1-55656-139-3*) Dercum Audio.

—The Sign of the Four. 1977. 9.95 o.p. (*0-385-12285-3*) Doubleday Publishing.

—The Sign of the Four. abr. ed. 1986. (J). (gr. 5-7). audio 29.95 o.p. (*0-88646-811-6*, R 7094); 1983. audio 15.95 o.p. (*0-88646-072-7*, TC-LFP 7094) Durkin Hayes Publishing Ltd.

—The Sign of the Four. 2001. iv, 144p. pap. 8.95 (*0-7551-0639-3*) House of Stratus, Inc. GBR. *Dist:* Midpoint Trade Bks., Inc.

—The Sign of the Four. Goodenough, Simon, ed. 1985. (Illus.). 192p. pap. o.p. (*0-316-32009-9*) Little Brown & Co.

—The Sign of the Four. Roden, Christopher, ed. 1993. (Oxford Sherlock Holmes Ser.). 192p. (C). 13.95 o.p. (*0-19-212316-5*, 14614) Oxford Univ. Pr., Inc.

—The Sign of the Four. Roden, Christopher, ed. & intro. by. 1995. (Oxford World's Classics Ser.). 192p. reprint ed. pap. 5.95 o.p. (*0-19-282379-5*) Oxford Univ. Pr., Inc.

—The Sign of the Four. 1999. 185p. E-Book 3.99 incl. cd-rom (*1-57646-181-5*) Quiet Vision Publishing.

—The Sign of the Four. unabr. ed. 1986. (Sherlock Holmes Mystery Ser.). audio 26.00 (*1-55690-477-0*, 86240E7) Recorded Bks., LLC.

—The Sign of the Four. 2002. E-Book 2.95 (*0-9712910-4-7*) Twenty Penny Pr., Inc.

—The Sign of the Four. 2001. (Classics Ser.). 160p. 7.00 (*0-14-043907-2*, Penguin Classics) Viking Penguin.

—A Study in Scarlet. 1984. 192p. mass mkt. 2.50 o.s.i (*0-425-08004-8*) Ace Bks.

—A Study in Scarlet. Date not set. 121p. 17.95 (*0-8488-2554-3*) Amereon, Ltd.

—A Study in Scarlet. unabr. ed. 1998. (C). audio 24.95 (*1-55685-608-3*) Audio Bk. Contractors, Inc.

—A Study in Scarlet. unabr. ed. 1991. (Best of Sherlock Holmes Ser.: Vol. 4). audio 26.95 o.p. (*1-55656-062-1*, DAB043) BBC Audiobooks America.

—A Study in Scarlet. 1975. 160p. mass mkt. 1.25 o.p. (*0-345-24714-0*) Ballantine Bks.

—A Study in Scarlet. Bennett, S. A., ed. 1992. (Adventures of Sherlock Holmes Ser.). (Illus.). 64p. pap. (*0-944099-18-1*) Bill Barry's Compass Bks.

—A Study in Scarlet. abr. ed. 1999. audio 23.95 (*0-7861-1604-8*); audio 23.95 Blackstone Audio Bks., Inc.

—A Study in Scarlet. 2001. per. 9.90 (*1-891355-68-6*); per. 15.50 (*1-58396-234-4*) Blue Unicorn Editions.

—A Study in Scarlet. unabr. collector's ed. 1982. (J). audio 30.00 (*0-7366-3965-9*, 9504) Books on Tape, Inc.

—A Study in Scarlet. 1989. lib. bdg. 15.95 (*0-89966-231-5*) Buccaneer Bks., Inc.

—A Study in Scarlet. (Collected Works of Sir Arthur Conan Doyle). 2001. pap. text 28.00 (*0-7426-7676-5*); reprint ed. lib. bdg. 98.00 (*0-7426-2676-8*) Classic Bks.

—A Study in Scarlet. unabr. ed. audio 21.95 o.p. (*1-55656-104-0*); 1997. (Best of Sherlock Holmes Ser.: Vol. 4). pap. 21.95 o.p. incl. audio (*1-55656-229-2*) Dercum Audio.

—A Study in Scarlet. 1977. 7.95 o.p. (*0-385-12283-7*) Doubleday Publishing.

—A Study in Scarlet. abr. ed. 1986. (J). (gr. 5-7). audio 29.95 o.p. (*0-88646-784-5*, R 7011); 1984. audio 15.95 o.p. (*0-88646-087-5*, TC-LFP 7011) Durkin Hayes Publishing Ltd.

—A Study in Scarlet. E-Book 2.49 (*0-7574-0260-7*) Electric Umbrella Publishing.

—A Study in Scarlet. 2001. iv, 156p. pap. 8.95 (*0-7551-0638-5*) House of Stratus, Inc. GBR. *Dist:* Midpoint Trade Bks., Inc.

—A Study in Scarlet. 1989. audio 18.00 Jimcin Recordings.

—A Study in Scarlet. E-Book 2.95 (*1-57799-808-1*) Logos Research Systems, Inc.

—A Study in Scarlet. Edwards, Owen Dudley, ed. 2000. (Oxford World's Classics Ser.). 256p. pap. 6.95 (*0-19-283765-6*) Oxford Univ. Pr., Inc.

—A Study in Scarlet. Edwards, Owen D., ed. 1993. (Oxford Sherlock Holmes Ser.). 254p. (C). 13.95 o.p. (*0-19-212313-0*, 14615) Oxford Univ. Pr., Inc.

—A Study in Scarlet. Edwards, Dudley, ed. & intro. by. 1995. (Oxford World's Classics Ser.). 254p. reprint ed. pap. 5.95 o.p. (*0-19-282380-9*) Oxford Univ. Pr., Inc.

—A Study in Scarlet. 1982. (Classic Crime Ser.). 144p. pap. 6.95 (*0-14-005707-2*, Penguin Bks.) Penguin Group (USA) Inc.

—A Study in Scarlet. collector's ed. 2002. (Illus.). im. lthr. 38.85 (*1-4115-1254-5*); pap. 19.95 (*1-4115-0521-2*); 25.95 (*1-4115-0889-0*); pap. 17.95 (*1-4115-0319-8*) Polyglot Pr., Inc.

—A Study in Scarlet. 1999. 191p. E-Book 3.99 incl. cd-rom (*1-57646-180-7*) Quiet Vision Publishing.

—A Study in Scarlet. 2003. 160p. pap. 6.95 (*0-8129-6854-9*, Modern Library) Random House Adult Trade Publishing Group.

—A Study in Scarlet. abr. ed. 1999. (Sherlock Holmes Ser.). audio 18.00 o.s.i (*0-553-52553-0*, RH Audio) Random Hse. Audio Publishing Group.

—A Study in Scarlet. unabr. ed. 1984. (Sherlock Holmes Mystery Ser.). audio 26.00 (*1-55690-498-3*, 84071E7) Recorded Bks., LLC.

—A Study in Scarlet. E-Book 5.00 (*0-7410-1416-5*) SoftBook Pr.

—A Study in Scarlet, 1. 1998. pap. text 6.95 (*0-9666443-1-X*) Thorby Enterprises, Inc.

—A Study in Scarlet. l.t. ed. 2001. (Perennial Bestsellers Ser.). 191p. 27.95 (*0-7838-9350-7*) Thorndike Pr.

—A Study in Scarlet. E-Book 2.00 (*1-58505-984-6*) Treeless Pr.

—A Study in Scarlet. 2001. (Classics Ser.). 192p. 7.00 (*0-14-043908-0*, Penguin Classics) Viking Penguin.

—A Study in Scarlet. 2001. (New Millennium Library). 109p. pap. 9.95 (*0-595-01428-3*) iUniverse, Inc.

—A Study in Scarlet & The Sign of the Four. 1986. mass mkt. 2.50 o.s.i (*0-425-09577-0*); 1983. mass mkt. 2.25 o.s.i (*0-425-05209-5*); 1978. mass mkt. 1.75 o.s.i (*0-425-04117-4*); 1975. mass mkt. 1.25 o.s.i (*0-425-02838-0*) Berkley Publishing Group.

—A Study in Scarlet & The Sign of the Four. 2003. (Dover Thrift Editions Ser.). 208p. 2.50 (*0-486-43166-5*) Dover Pubns., Inc.

—A Study in Scarlet & The Sign of the Four. l.t. ed. 1969. o.p. (*0-7089-0190-5*, Ulverscroft) Thorpe, F. A. Pubs.

—The Valley of Fear. 1976. 17.95 (*0-8488-1288-3*) Amereon, Ltd.

—The Valley of Fear. unabr. ed. 2003. (YA). (gr. 10 up). audio 29.95 (*1-55685-676-8*, ) Audio Bk. Contractors, Inc.

—The Valley of Fear. l.t. ed. 1990. pap. 16.95 o.p. (*0-7927-0475-4*, C0775) BBC Audiobooks America.

—The Valley of Fear. 1987. 176p. mass mkt. 2.50 o.p. (*0-425-10330-7*); 1986. mass mkt. 2.50 o.s.i (*0-425-09580-0*); 1984. mass mkt. 2.50 o.s.i (*0-425-07140-5*); 1981. mass mkt. 2.25 o.s.i (*0-425-05221-4*); 1980. mass mkt. 1.95 o.s.i (*0-425-04911-6*); 1979. mass mkt. 1.75 o.s.i (*0-425-04537-4*); 1978. mass mkt. 1.50 o.s.i (*0-425-03981-1*); 1976. mass mkt. 1.25 o.s.i (*0-425-03136-5*) Berkley Publishing Group.

—The Valley of Fear. unabr. ed. 1991. audio 39.95 (*0-7861-0612-3*, 2102) Blackstone Audio Bks., Inc.

—The Valley of Fear. unabr. collector's ed. 1991. audio 36.00 (*0-7366-2030-3*, 2844) Books on Tape, Inc.

—The Valley of Fear. 1988. lib. bdg. 16.95 (*0-89966-232-3*) Buccaneer Bks., Inc.

—The Valley of Fear. 1977. 7.95 o.p. (*0-385-12284-5*) Doubleday Publishing.

—The Valley of Fear. unabr. ed. 1991. audio 16.99 (*0-88646-296-7*, 7296) Durkin Hayes Publishing Ltd.

—The Valley of Fear, Set. unabr. ed. 1999. audio 39.95 Highsmith Inc.

—The Valley of Fear. 2001. iv, 200p. pap. 8.95 (*0-7551-0645-8*) House of Stratus, Inc. GBR. *Dist:* Midpoint Trade Bks., Inc.

—The Valley of Fear. unabr. ed. 1991. (YA). (gr. 9-12). audio 29.00 Jimcin Recordings.

—The Valley of Fear. Edwards, Owen D., ed. 1993. (Oxford Sherlock Holmes Ser.). 292p. (C). 13.95 o.p. (*0-19-212314-9*, 8951) Oxford Univ. Pr., Inc.

—The Valley of Fear. Edwards, Owen D., ed. & intro. by. 1995. (Oxford World's Classics Ser.). 292p. reprint ed. pap. 6.95 o.p. (*0-19-282382-5*) Oxford Univ. Pr., Inc.

—The Valley of Fear. 1991. (Classic Crime Ser.). 192p. pap. 6.00 o.p. (*0-14-005710-2*, Penguin Bks.) Penguin Group (USA) Inc.

—The Valley of Fear. collector's ed. 2002. (Illus.). im. lthr. 38.85 (*1-4115-1255-3*); pap. 19.95 (*1-4115-0524-7*); 25.95 (*1-4115-0890-4*); pap. 17.95 (*1-4115-0320-1*) Polyglot Pr., Inc.

—The Valley of Fear. 1999. 256p. E-Book 3.99 incl. cd-rom (*1-57646-184-X*) Quiet Vision Publishing.

—The Valley of Fear. abr. ed. 1999. (BBC Radio Presents Ser.). audio 18.00 o.s.i (*0-553-52622-7*, RH Audio) Random Hse. Audio Publishing Group.

—The Valley of Fear. unabr. ed. 1986. (Sherlock Holmes Mystery Ser.). audio 35.00 (*1-55690-539-4*, 86250E7) Recorded Bks., LLC.

—The Valley of Fear. unabr. ed. 2002. audio compact disk 33.00 (*1-4001-0040-2*); audio compact disk 20.00 (*1-4001-5040-X*) Tantor Media, Inc.

—The Valley of Fear. l.t. ed. 1978. (Ulverscroft Large Print Ser.). 29.99 o.p. (*0-7089-0086-0*, Ulverscroft) Thorpe, F. A. Pubs. GBR. *Dist:* Ulverscroft Large Print Bks., Ltd., Ulverscroft Large Print Canada, Ltd.

Doyle, Arthur Conan, as told by. A Study in Scarlet. 2002. E-Book 2.95 (*0-9712910-3-9*) Twenty Penny Pr., Inc.

Doyle, Arthur Conan, ed. The Adventures of Sherlock Holmes. 1985. 288p. mass mkt. 2.95 o.s.i (*0-553-26772-8*, Bantam Classics); mass mkt. 2.50 o.s.i (*0-553-24996-7*) Bantam Bks.

—The Adventures of Sherlock Holmes, Vol. 3. l.t. ed. 2000. reprint ed. 28.00 (*1-55246-290-0*) Battered Silicon Dispatch Box, The.

—The Adventures of Sherlock Holmes. 1984. mass mkt. 2.95 o.s.i (*0-425-08089-7*); 1984. mass mkt. 2.50 o.s.i (*0-425-07501-X*); 1983. mass mkt. 2.25 o.s.i (*0-425-04869-1*); 1980. mass mkt. 1.95 o.s.i (*0-425-04337-1*); 1977. mass mkt. 1.50 o.s.i (*0-425-03518-2*); 1975. mass mkt. 0.95 o.s.i (*0-425-02802-X*) Berkley Publishing Group.

—The Adventures of Sherlock Holmes. 2002. pap. 4.95 (*1-59109-027-X*) Booksurge, LLC.

—The Adventures of Sherlock Holmes. 1982. lib. bdg. 31.95 (*0-89966-385-0*) Buccaneer Bks., Inc.

—The Adventures of Sherlock Holmes. (Collected Works of Sir Arthur Conan Doyle). 2001. pap. text 28.00 (*0-7426-7687-0*); reprint ed. lib. bdg. 98.00 (*0-7426-2687-3*); reprint ed. lib. bdg. 48.00 (*0-7426-1019-5*); 2001. (Illus.). reprint ed. pap. text 28.00 (*0-7426-6019-2*) Classic Bks.

—The Adventures of Sherlock Holmes. 1989. mass mkt. 3.25 o.s.i (*0-8125-0425-9*, Tor Classics); 1988. mass mkt. 4.95 (*0-938819-89-5*, Aerie) Doherty, Tom Assocs., LLC.

—The Adventures of Sherlock Holmes. E-Book 3.49 (*1-929120-40-0*) Electric Umbrella Publishing.

—The Adventures of Sherlock Holmes. l.t. ed. 1999. 400p. pap. 22.00 (*0-06-093322-4*); 1901. reprint ed. o.p. (*0-06-011070-8*) HarperCollins Pubs.

—The Adventures of Sherlock Holmes. unabr. ed. 1999. audio 49.95Set. audio 24.95 Highsmith Inc.

—The Adventures of Sherlock Holmes. 2001. iv, 336p. pap. 8.95 (*0-7551-0637-7*) House of Stratus, Inc. GBR. *Dist:* Midpoint Trade Bks., Inc.

—The Adventures of Sherlock Holmes. 2001. 312p. 19.99 (*1-58827-352-0*); 26.99 (*1-58827-348-2*); 126.99 (*1-58827-960-X*); per. 121.99 (*1-58827-961-8*); per. 14.99 (*1-58827-353-9*); per. 21.99 (*1-58827-349-0*) IndyPublish.com.

—The Adventures of Sherlock Holmes. 1976. (Illus.). 192p. 5.95 o.p. (*0-8052-3621-X*, Schocken) Knopf Publishing Group.

—The Adventures of Sherlock Holmes. l.t. ed. 2000. (Large Print Heritage Ser.). 502p. lib. bdg. 35.95 (*1-58118-067-5*, 23664) LRS.

—The Adventures of Sherlock Holmes, abr. ed. 1998. (National Public Radio Ser.). audio 24.95 (*1-56994-503-9*, Monterey SoundWorks) Monterey Media, Inc.

—The Adventures of Sherlock Holmes. 1997. pap. 2.95 (*0-89375-402-1*) NAL.

—The Adventures of Sherlock Holmes. l.t. ed. (Large Print Ser.). reprint ed. 1986. 494p. lib. bdg. 26.00 (*0-939495-30-9*); 1998. 308p. lib. bdg. 25.00 (*1-58287-011-X*) North Bks.

—The Adventures of Sherlock Holmes. (Oxford Progressive English Readers Ser.). (Illus.). 1982. pap. 4.95 o.p. (*0-19-581280-8*); 2nd ed. 1993. 78p. pap. text 5.95 (*0-19-585257-5*) Oxford Univ. Pr., Inc.

—The Adventures of Sherlock Holmes. 1981. (Classic Crime Ser.). 288p. pap. 6.95 (*0-14-005724-2*, Penguin Bks.) Penguin Group (USA) Inc.

—The Adventures of Sherlock Holmes. 1996. (Sherlock Holmes Ser.). (Illus.). 172p. 9.98 (*1-879582-12-0*) Platinum Pr., Inc.

—The Adventures of Sherlock Holmes. collector's ed. 2002. (Illus.). im. lthr. 38.85 (*1-4115-1249-9*); pap. 19.95 (*1-4115-0522-0*); 25.95 (*1-4115-0882-3*); pap. 17.95 (*1-4115-0313-9*) Polyglot Pr., Inc.

—The Adventures of Sherlock Holmes. 1999. 442p. E-Book 3.99 incl. cd-rom (*1-57646-177-7*) Quiet Vision Publishing.

—The Adventures of Sherlock Holmes. unabr. ed. 1985. (Cassette Bookshelf Ser.). audio 15.98 (*0-8072-3415-X*, CB 105CX, Listening Library); Vol. 1. 1996. (BBC Radio Presents Ser.). audio 16.99 o.s.i (*0-553-47763-3*, RH Audio); Vol. 2. 1997. (Adventures of Sherlock Holmes Ser.: Vol. II). audio 16.99 o.s.i (*0-553-47778-1*, RH Audio) Random Hse. Audio Publishing Group.

—The Adventures of Sherlock Holmes. 1987. (Illus.). 320p. 12.95 o.p. (*0-89577-277-9*) Reader's Digest Assn., Inc., The.

—The Adventures of Sherlock Holmes. unabr. ed. 1986. (Sherlock Holmes Mystery Ser.). audio 60.00 (*1-55690-004-X*, 86950E7) Recorded Bks., LLC.

—The Adventures of Sherlock Holmes. 1995. (Ebook Classic Ser.). E-Book 5.00 (*0-7410-1456-4*) SoftBook Pr.

—The Adventures of Sherlock Holmes. 2002. E-Book 2.95 (*0-9712910-6-3*) Twenty Penny Pr., Inc.

—The Adventures of Sherlock Holmes. 1997. (Classics Library). 464p. pap. 3.95 (*1-85326-033-9*, 0339WW) Wordsworth Editions, Ltd. GBR. *Dist:* Combined Publishing.

—The Adventures of Sherlock Holmes. 2001. 260p. per. 12.95 (*0-595-01468-2*) iUniverse, Inc.

Doyle, Arthur Conan & Earlson, Ian M. Beeton's Christmas Annual—1987: Sherlock Holmes. 1987. (Illus.). 80p. pap. 9.95 (*0-9619318-1-7*); 19.95 o.p. (*0-9619318-0-9*) Pencil Productions, Ltd.

Doyle, Arthur Conan & Green, Richard Lancelyn, eds. The Adventures of Sherlock Holmes. 1998. (Oxford World's Classics Ser.). 448p. reprint ed. pap. 9.95 (*0-19-283508-4*) Oxford Univ. Pr., Inc.

Doyle, Arthur Conan & Reyburn, Stanley. The Valley of Fear. Landes, William-Alan, ed. 1998. 55p. pap. 10.00 (*0-88734-742-8*) Players Pr., Inc.

Drabble, Margaret. The Ice Age. 1985. 304p. pap. 7.95 o.p. (*0-452-26046-9*); pap. 6.95 o.p. (*0-452-25680-1*) Dutton/Plume. (Plume).

—The Ice Age. 1985. 304p. pap. 9.95 o.p. (*0-452-26351-4*) NAL.

—The Ice Age. 1977. 10.95 o.p. (*0-394-41790-9*, Knopf Bks. for Young Readers) Random Hse. Children's Bks.

—The Ice Age. 1983. 320p. pap. 3.50 o.s.i (*0-446-31118-9*) Warner Bks., Inc.

—The Millstone. 1984. 144p. pap. 6.95 o.p. (*0-452-25976-2*); 192p. pap. 9.00 o.p. (*0-452-26456-1*); pap. 5.95 o.p. (*0-452-25516-3*); (Illus.). 144p. pap. 7.95 o.p. (*0-452-26126-0*) Dutton/Plume. (Plume).

—The Millstone. 1998. (Harvest Book Ser.). 192p. pap. 12.00 (*0-15-600619-7*, Harvest Bks.) Harcourt Trade Pubs.

—A Natural Curiosity. 320p. 1990. pap. 10.00 o.p. (*0-14-012228-1*, Penguin Bks.); 1989. 19.95 o.p. (*0-670-82837-8*) Viking Penguin.

—The Needle's Eye. 1989. 368p. mass mkt. 5.99 o.s.i (*0-8041-0364-X*, Ivy Bks.) Ballantine Bks.

—The Needle's Eye. 1972. 11.95 o.s.i (*0-394-47966-1*) Knopf, Alfred A. Inc.

—The Radiant Way. 1988. 384p. reprint ed. mass mkt. 5.99 o.s.i (*0-8041-0365-8*, Ivy Bks.) Ballantine Bks.

—The Radiant Way. 1987. 432p. 18.95 o.s.i (*0-394-56143-0*) Knopf, Alfred A. Inc.

—The Realms of Gold. 1988. 384p. reprint ed. mass mkt. 5.99 o.s.i (*0-8041-0363-1*, Ivy Bks.) Ballantine Bks.

—The Realms of Gold. 1982. 368p. pap. 3.95 o.p. (*0-553-22603-7*) Bantam Bks.

—The Waterfall. 1986. pap. 6.95 o.p. (*0-452-25825-1*); pap. 7.95 o.p. (*0-452-26017-5*); 30p. pap. 10.00 o.p. (*0-452-26192-9*) Dutton/Plume. (Plume).

—The Waterfall. l.t. ed. 1987. (Mainstream Ser.). 350p. reprint ed. 15.95 o.p. (*1-85089-138-9*) ISIS Large Print Bks. GBR. *Dist:* Transaction Pubs.

Drake, Shannon. The Lion in Glory: Last Dance, Last Chance & Other. 2003. 560p. mass mkt. 6.99 (*0-8217-7287-2*, Zebra Bks.) Kensington Publishing Corp.

Drummond, Emma. Act of Valour. 1998. 25.95 o.p. (*0-312-18521-9*) St. Martin's Pr.

Du Maurier, Daphne. The House on the Strand. 2000. 298p. pap. 15.95 (*0-8122-1726-8*) Univ. of Pennsylvania Pr.

—Rebecca: Acting Edition. l.t. ed. 1993. 688p. 25.00 o.s.i (*0-385-47197-1*) Doubleday Publishing.

Duffy, Margaret. Dressed To Kill. 1994. 240p. 19.95 o.p. (*0-312-11295-5*, Saint Martin's Minotaur) St. Martin's Pr.

—Dressed to Kill. l.t. ed. 1995. (Dales Large Print Ser.). 355p. pap. 19.99 o.p. (*1-85389-520-2*) Dales Large Print Bks. GBR. *Dist:* Ulverscroft Large Print Bks., Ltd., Ulverscroft Large Print Canada, Ltd.

—Man of Blood. l.t. ed. 1993. (Dales Mystery Ser.). 492p. pap. 19.99 o.p. (*1-85389-421-4*) Dales Large Print Bks. GBR. *Dist:* Ulverscroft Large Print Bks., Ltd., Ulverscroft Large Print Canada, Ltd.

—Man of Blood. 1992. 208p. 17.95 o.p. (*0-312-08261-4*, Saint Martin's Minotaur) St. Martin's Pr.

—Prospect of Death. 1996. 224p. 20.95 o.p. (*0-312-14396-6*, Saint Martin's Minotaur) St. Martin's Pr.

Dunant, Sarah. Birth Marks. unabr. ed. 1993. (Hannah Wolfe Mysteries Ser.). audio 69.95 (*0-7451-4034-3*, CAB 731) BBC Audiobooks America.

—Birth Marks. 1992. 240p. 17.00 o.s.i (*0-385-42318-7*) Doubleday Publishing.

—Birth Marks. l.t. ed. 1992. (Magna Large Print Ser.). 373p. o.p. (*0-7505-0270-3*) Magna Large Print Bks. GBR. *Dist:* Ulverscroft Large Print Canada, Ltd.

—Fatlands. unabr. ed. 1994. (Hannah Wolfe Mysteries Ser.). audio 54.95 (*0-7451-4297-4*, CAB 980) BBC Audiobooks America.

—Fatlands: A Hannah Wolfe Mystery. 1994. 256p. reprint ed. pap. 21.00 (*1-883402-82-4*, Scribner) Simon & Schuster.



For book reviews, descriptive annotations, tables of contents, cover images, author biographies & additional information, updated daily, subscribe to **www.booksinprint.com** 729

—Under My Skin: A Hannah Wolfe Novel. 1995. 288p. 20.00 (*0-684-81521-4*, Scribner) Simon & Schuster.

Duncker, Patricia. The Doctor. 2000. 384p. 24.00 (*0-06-019601-7*, Ecco) HarperTrade.

—Hallucinating Foucault. 2nd ed. 1996. 192p. 21.00 o.p. (*0-88001-499-7*, Ecco) HarperTrade.

—Hallucinating Foucault. 1998. 192p. pap. 12.00 (*0-375-70185-0*, Vintage) Knopf Publishing Group.

Dunmore, Helen. Ice Cream. 224p. 2004. pap. 12.00 (*0-8021-4053-X*); 2003. 23.00 (*0-8021-1733-3*) Grove/Atlantic, Inc. (Grove Pr.).

—Ice Cream. 2000. 192p. text o.p. (*0-670-88771-4*, Viking) Viking Penguin.

—A Spell of Winter. l.t. ed. 2001. 312p. 28.95 (*0-7838-9530-5*, Macmillan Reference USA) Gale Group.

—A Spell of Winter. 320p. 2002. pap. 13.00 (*0-8021-3876-4*); 2001. 24.00 o.p. (*0-87113-782-8*) Grove/Atlantic, Inc.

—A Spell of Winter. 1999. pap. (*0-316-19794-7*) Little Brown & Co.

Dunn, Alan. Payback: A Mystery. 2003. 320p. 24.95 (*0-312-31099-4*) St. Martin's Pr.

Dunn, Carola. Damsel in Distress: A Daisy Dalrymple Mystery. 2002. (Daisy Dalrymple Mystery Ser.). 256p. mass mkt. 5.99 (*1-57566-754-1*, Kensington Bks.) Kensington Publishing Corp.

—Damsel in Distress: A Daisy Dalrymple Mystery. 1997. (Daisy Dalrymple Mysteries Ser.). 234p. 21.95 o.p. (*0-312-16806-3*, Saint Martin's Minotaur) St. Martin's Pr.

—Dead in the Water. 2002. 256p. mass mkt. 5.99 (*1-57566-756-8*, Kensington Bks.) Kensington Publishing Corp.

—Dead in the Water. 1998. (Daisy Dalrymple Mysteries Ser.). 256p. 22.95 o.p. (*0-312-19181-2*, Saint Martin's Minotaur) St. Martin's Pr.

—Death at Wentwater Court. 2000. (Daisy Dalrymple Mysteries Ser.). (Illus.). 256p. (J). mass mkt. 5.99 (*1-57566-750-9*) Kensington Publishing Corp.

—Death at Wentwater Court. 1994. 240p. 19.95 o.p. (*0-312-11030-8*, Saint Martin's Minotaur) St. Martin's Pr.

—Murder on the Flying Scotsman. 1996. (Daisy Dalrymple Mysteries Ser.). 240p. 21.95 (*0-312-15175-6*, Saint Martin's Minotaur) St. Martin's Pr.

—Rattle His Bones: A Daisy Dalrymple Mystery. 2003. 256p. mass mkt. 5.99 (*0-7582-0168-0*) Kensington Publishing Corp.

—Rattle His Bones: A Daisy Dalrymple Mystery. 2000. (Daisy Dalrymple Mysteries Ser.). (Illus.). 243p. 22.95 (*0-312-20572-4*, Saint Martin's Minotaur) St. Martin's Pr.

—Rattle His Bones: A Daisy Dalrymple Mystery. l.t. ed. 2000. (Mystery Ser.). (Illus.). 355p. 26.95 (*0-7862-2913-6*) Thorndike Pr.

—Requiem for a Mezzo. 2001. 256p. mass mkt. 5.99 (*1-57566-752-5*, Kensington Bks.) Kensington Publishing Corp.

—Requiem for a Mezzo: A Daisy Dalrymple Mystery. 1996. (Daisy Dalrymple Mysteries Ser.). 240p. 20.95 (*0-312-14036-3*, Saint Martin's Minotaur) St. Martin's Pr.

—Requiem for a Mezzo: A Daisy Dalrymple Mystery. l.t. ed. 1996. 285p. pap. 23.95 (*0-7838-1857-2*) Thorndike Pr.

—Styx & Stones: A Daisy Dalrymple Mystery. 2nd ed. 1999. (Daisy Dalrymple Mysteries Ser.). 240p. 22.95 (*0-312-20592-9*, Saint Martin's Minotaur) St. Martin's Pr.

—The Winter Garden Mystery. l.t. ed. 1995. 326p. 23.95 o.p. (*0-7838-1487-9*, Macmillan Reference USA) Gale Group.

—The Winter Garden Mystery. 2001. (Daisy Dalrymple Mysteries Ser.). 256p. mass mkt. 5.99 (*1-57566-751-7*, Kensington Bks.) Kensington Publishing Corp.

—The Winter Garden Mystery. 1995. (Daisy Dalrymple Mysteries Ser.). 224p. 21.95 o.p. (*0-312-13217-4*, Saint Martin's Minotaur) St. Martin's Pr.

Dunn, Carola, et al. Once upon a Waltz. 2001. (Zebra Regency Romance Ser.). 256p. mass mkt. 4.99 o.s.i (*0-8217-6797-6*, Zebra Bks.) Kensington Publishing Corp.

Durbridge, Francis. The World of Tim Frazer. 2001. (Black Dagger Crime Ser.). 192p. 21.95 (*0-7540-8605-4*, Black Dagger) BBC Audiobooks America.

Easterman, Daniel. Maroc. 2002. 576p. (*0-00-225862-5*); pap. (*0-00-225864-1*) HarperCollins Pubs.

Eccles, Marjorie. An Accidental Shroud: An Inspector Mayo Mystery. l.t. ed. 1996. (Magna Large Print Ser.). (Illus.). 327p. 29.99 (*0-7505-0982-1*) Magna Large Print Bks. GBR. *Dist:* Ulverscroft Large Print Bks., Ltd.

—An Accidental Shroud: An Inspector Mayo Mystery. 1996. 20.95 o.p. (*0-312-15045-8*, Saint Martin's Minotaur) St. Martin's Pr.

—Cast a Cold Eye. 1999. (Constable Crime Ser.). 183p. (*0-09-479830-3*, Constable & Co. Ltd.) Constable & Robinson Ltd.

—Cast a Cold Eye. l.t. ed. 1992. (Magna Large Print Ser.). 285p. o.p. (*0-7505-0095-6*) Magna Large Print Bks. GBR. *Dist:* Ulverscroft Large Print Canada, Ltd.

—The Company She Kept. l.t. ed. 1994. (Magna Large Print Ser.). 320p. 29.99 o.p. (*0-7505-0642-3*) Magna Large Print Bks. GBR. *Dist:* Ulverscroft Large Print Bks., Ltd., Ulverscroft Large Print Canada, Ltd.

—The Company She Kept. 1996. 192p. 21.95 o.p. (*0-312-14297-8*, Saint Martin's Minotaur) St. Martin's Pr.

—Death of a Good Woman. l.t. ed. 1991. (Ulverscroft Large Print Ser.). 29.99 o.p. (*0-7089-2460-3*, Ulverscroft) Thorpe, F. A. Pubs. GBR. *Dist:* Ulverscroft Large Print Bks., Ltd., Ulverscroft Large Print Canada, Ltd.

—A Death of Distinction. l.t. ed. 1996. (Magna Large Print Ser.). 337p. (*0-7505-1021-8*) Magna Large Print Bks. GBR. *Dist:* Ulverscroft Large Print Canada, Ltd.

—A Death of Distinction. 1998. (Gil Mayo Mysteries Ser.). 192p. 20.95 o.p. (*0-312-18566-9*, Saint Martin's Minotaur) St. Martin's Pr.

—Echoes of Silence. 2003. 224p. 22.95 (*0-312-30880-9*, Saint Martin's Minotaur) St. Martin's Pr.

—Killing Me Softly. l.t. ed. 1999. (Magna Large Print Ser.). 368p. (*0-7505-1383-7*) Magna Large Print Bks. GBR. *Dist:* Ulverscroft Large Print Canada, Ltd.

—Killing Me Softly. 2000. 205p. 22.95 (*0-312-20469-8*, Saint Martin's Minotaur) St. Martin's Pr.

—Late of This Parish. l.t. ed. 1993. (Magna Large Print Ser.). 380p. 29.99 o.p. (*0-7505-0516-8*) Magna Large Print Bks. GBR. *Dist:* Ulverscroft Large Print Bks., Ltd., Ulverscroft Large Print Canada, Ltd.

—Late of This Parish. 1994. 224p. 19.95 o.p. (*0-312-11019-7*, Saint Martin's Minotaur) St. Martin's Pr.

—More Deaths Than One. 1991. 192p. 15.00 o.s.i (*0-385-41918-X*) Doubleday Publishing.

—Requiem for a Dove. l.t. ed. 1992. (Mystery Ser.). 384p. 29.99 o.p. (*0-7089-2603-7*, Ulverscroft) Thorpe, F. A. Pubs. GBR. *Dist:* Ulverscroft Large Print Bks., Ltd., Ulverscroft Large Print Canada, Ltd.

—A Species of Revenge. l.t. ed. 1998. 315p. (*0-7540-3425-9*) BBC Audiobooks America.

—A Species of Revenge. 1998. (Gil Mayo Mysteries Ser.). 224p. 20.95 o.p. (*0-312-19338-6*, Saint Martin's Minotaur) St. Martin's Pr.

—A Species of Revenge. l.t. ed. 1998. (Nightingale Ser.). 320p. pap. 20.95 (*0-7838-0288-9*) Thorndike Pr.

—A Sunset Touch: A Mystery Featuring Superintendent Gil Mayo. 2002. 208p. 22.95 (*0-312-28353-9*, Saint Martin's Minotaur) St. Martin's Pr.

Eckhardt, Jason C. & Cannon, P. H. Scream for Jeeves: A Parody. 1994. (Illus.). 86p. 20.00 (*0-940884-61-5*); pap. 7.50 (*0-940884-60-7*) Necronomicon Pr.

Eden, Marc. The Spy. 1992. 19.95 o.p. (*0-87131-703-6*) Evans, M. & Co., Inc.

Edgar, Josephine. Bright Young Thing: A Novel of London in the Twenties. 1986. 320p. 15.95 o.p. (*0-312-09627-5*) St. Martin's Pr.

—The Dark & Alien Rose. 1991. 18.95 o.p. (*0-312-05843-8*) St. Martin's Pr.

—Margaret Normanby. 1983. 448p. 13.95 o.p. (*0-312-51444-1*) St. Martin's Pr.

Edgeworth, Maria. Belinda. Kirkpatrick, Kathryn, ed. & intro. by. 1994. (Oxford World's Classics Ser.). 538p. pap. 12.95 o.p. (*0-19-283123-2*) Oxford Univ. Pr., Inc.

—The Little Dog Trusty, the Orange Man, & the Cherry Orchard: Being the Tenth Part of Early Lessons. 1990. (Augustan Reprints Ser.: Nos. 263-264). reprint ed. 21.50 (*0-404-70263-5*, PR4644) AMS Pr., Inc.

Edmonds, Janet. Sarah Camberwell Tring. 1993. 240p. 18.95 o.p. (*0-312-09907-X*) St. Martin's Pr.

Edwards, Martin. All the Lonely People. 2003. (Five Star First Edition Titles Ser.). 278p. 25.95 (*1-59414-069-3*, Five Star) Gale Group.

—Eve of Destruction: A Harry Devlin Mystery. 1998. 208p. 22.95 (*0-393-04635-4*) Norton, W. W. & Co., Inc.

—Suspicious Minds. l.t. ed. 1995. (Magna Large Print Ser.). 365p. o.p. (*0-7505-0865-5*) Magna Large Print Bks. GBR. *Dist:* Ulverscroft Large Print Canada, Ltd.

—Yesterday's Papers. l.t. ed. 1996. (Magna Large Print Ser.). 380p. (*0-7505-0867-1*) Magna Large Print Bks. GBR. *Dist:* Ulverscroft Large Print Canada, Ltd.

Edwards, Rachelle. The Duke's Dilemma. l.t. ed. 1993. 330p. lib. bdg. 15.95 o.p. (*0-8161-5726-X*, Macmillan Reference USA) Gale Group.

Edwards, Ruth Dudley. The English School of Murder. 2001. 200p. pap. 13.95 (*1-890208-78-7*) Poisoned Pen Pr.

—Murder in a Cathedral. 1997. 317 p. (*0-7540-3117-9*) BBC Audiobooks America.

—Murder in a Cathedral. l.t. ed. 1997. 192p. 20.95 (*0-312-15597-2*, Saint Martin's Minotaur) St. Martin's Pr.

—Murder in a Cathedral. l.t. ed. 1997. (Mystery Ser.). 326p. lib. bdg. 25.95 (*0-7838-8284-X*) Thorndike Pr.

—Publish & Be Murdered. l.t. unabr. ed. 2000. 282p. 25.95 (*0-7531-5975-9*, 159759) ISIS Large Print Bks. GBR. *Dist:* ISIS Publishing.

—Publish & Be Murdered. 1999. 217p. pap. 12.95 (*1-890208-13-2*) Poisoned Pen Pr.

Egleton, Clive. Cry Havoc: A Peter Ashton Novel. 2003. 352p. 24.95 (*0-312-30943-0*, Saint Martin's Minotaur) St. Martin's Pr.

Elgin, Elizabeth. Echo of a Stuart. 1998. 208p. 24.00 (*0-7278-2208-X*) Severn Hse. Pubs., Ltd.

—Echo of a Stuart. l.t. ed. 1998. (General Ser.). 256p. pap. 23.95 (*0-7862-1482-1*) Thorndike Pr.

—The House in Abercromby Square. l.t. ed. 1997. (Paperback Ser.). 234p. pap. 23.95 (*0-7838-8262-9*) Thorndike Pr.

—Whistle in the Dark. l.t. ed. 1997. pap. 20.95 o.p. (*0-7862-0921-6*) Thorndike Pr.

Eliot, George. Adam Bede. 1976. (Airmont Classics Ser.). mass mkt. 1.95 o.p. (*0-8049-0103-1*, CL 103) Airmont Publishing Co., Inc.

—Adam Bede. 1976. 29.95 (*0-8488-0481-3*) Amereon, Ltd.

—Adam Bede. 1997. audio 89.95 (*1-55685-199-5*) Audio Bk. Contractors, Inc.

—Adam Bede. unabr. ed. 1995. audio 89.95 (*0-7861-0659-X*, 1555) Blackstone Audio Bks., Inc.

—Adam Bede. 2000. Vol. 2. per. (*1-891355-21-X*); Vol.1. per. 14.00 (*1-891355-20-1*) Blue Unicorn Editions.

—Adam Bede. unabr. collector's ed. 1994. audio 120.00 (*0-7366-2803-7*, 3517) Books on Tape, Inc.

—Adam Bede. reprint ed. 1992. lib. bdg. 27.95 (*0-89968-276-6*, Lightyear Pr.); 1977. 466p. lib. bdg. 27.95 o.s.i (*0-89966-265-X*) Buccaneer Bks., Inc.

—Adam Bede. reprint ed. Pt. 1. 2001. (Writings of George Eliot Ser.: Vol. 3). 420p. pap. text 28.00 (*0-7426-5070-7*); Pt. 1. 1999. (Writings of George Eliot Ser.: Vol. 3). 420p. lib. bdg. 88.00 (*1-58201-070-6*); Pt. 2. 2001. 364p. pap. text 28.00 (*0-7426-5071-5*); Pt. 2. 1999. (Writings of George Eliot Ser.: Vol. 4). 364p. lib. bdg. 88.00 (*1-58201-071-4*) Classic Bks.

—Adam Bede. E-Book 2.49 (*1-58744-086-5*) Electric Umbrella Publishing.

—Adam Bede. 1973. (Collins Classics Ser.). 478p. (*0-00-424521-0*) HarperSanFrancisco.

—Adam Bede. Paterson, John, ed. 1968. pap. 13.16 o.p. (*0-395-05204-1*, Riverside Editions) Houghton Mifflin Co.

—Adam Bede. l.t. ed. 2000. 685p. 53.78 (*0-7583-0001-8*); 548p. 46.02 (*0-7583-0000-X*); 938p. 78.54 (*0-7583-0002-6*); 1201p. 91.44 (*0-7583-0003-4*); 1538p. 120.93 (*0-7583-0004-2*); 2698p. 193.58 (*0-7583-0007-7*); 2326p. 174.41 (*0-7583-0006-9*); 1891p. 138.36 (*0-7583-0005-0*); 2698p. pap. 159.27 (*0-7583-0015-8*); 2326p. pap. 143.57 (*0-7583-0014-X*); 1538p. pap. 102.93 (*0-7583-0012-3*); 1201p. pap. 79.44 (*0-7583-0011-5*); 938p. pap. 66.54 (*0-7583-0010-7*); 685p. pap. 47.78 (*0-7583-0009-3*); 548p. pap. 40.02 (*0-7583-0008-5*); 1891p. pap. 119.19 (*0-7583-0013-1*) Huge Print Pr.

—Adam Bede. 2001. 516p. 29.99 (*1-58827-312-1*); per. 24.99 (*1-58827-313-X*) IndyPublish.com.

—Adam Bede. 1999. (Cloth Bound Pocket Ser.). 7.95 (*3-8290-3005-3*, 521122) Konemann.

—Adam Bede. E-Book 1.95 (*1-57799-953-3*) Logos Research Systems, Inc.

—Adam Bede. 1992. (Everyman's Library: Vol. 59 0). 20.00 (*0-679-40991-2*) McKay, David Co., Inc.

—Adam Bede. 1969. mass mkt. 0.75 o.p. (*0-451-50076-8*, Signet Classics); 1969. mass mkt. 0.95 o.p. (*0-451-50483-6*, Signet Classics); 1961. mass mkt. 4.95 o.p. (*0-451-52256-7*, Signet Classics); 1961. mass mkt. 4.50 o.p. (*0-451-52110-2*); 1961. mass mkt. 2.95 o.p. (*0-451-51578-1*, Signet Classics); 1961. mass mkt. 1.95 o.p. (*0-451-51342-8*, Signet Classics); 1961. mass mkt. 1.75 o.p. (*0-451-51015-1*, Signet Classics); 1961. mass mkt. 1.50 o.p. (*0-451-50790-8*, Signet Classics); 1961. mass mkt. 3.50 o.p. (*0-451-51848-9*); 1961. 512p. mass mkt. 6.95 (*0-451-52527-2*, Signet Classics) NAL.

—Adam Bede. 2001. (Twelve-Point Ser.). lib. bdg. 27.00 (*1-58287-138-8*) North Bks.

—Adam Bede. Martin, Carol A., ed. 2001. (Clarendon Edition of the Novels of George Eliot Ser.). (Illus.). 688p. text 165.00 (*0-19-812595-X*) Oxford Univ. Pr., Inc.

—Adam Bede. (Oxford World's Classics Ser.). 1998. 656p. pap. 8.95 (*0-19-283495-9*); 1996. 646p. (C). pap. 5.95 o.p. (*0-19-283166-6*) Oxford Univ. Pr., Inc.

—Adam Bede. 2002. (Modern Library Classics). 624p. pap. 8.95 (*0-375-75901-8*, Modern Library) Random House Adult Trade Publishing Group.

—Adam Bede. 2001. 549p. E-Book 4.00 (*1-929670-68-0*) Renaissance E Bks.

—Adam Bede. 1971. pap. 0.95 o.s.i (*0-671-47190-2*, Washington Square Pr.) Simon & Schuster.

—Adam Bede. (Ebook Classic Ser.). E-Book 5.00 (*0-7410-1117-4*) SoftBook Pr.

—Adam Bede. 1985. 15.00 (*0-606-17254-8*) Turtleback Bks.

—Adam Bede. 1994. 528p. pap. 5.50 o.p. (*0-460-87461-6*, Everyman's Classic Library in Paperback) Tuttle Publishing.

—Adam Bede. Gill, Stephen, ed. 1980. (Classics Ser.). 608p. 8.95 (*0-14-043121-7*, Penguin Classics) Viking Penguin.

—Adam Bede. 1972. 4.95 o.p. (*0-460-01027-1*); 1998. audio 23.95 o.p. (*0-14-086489-X*, Penguin AudioBooks) Viking Penguin.

—Adam Bede. 1999. E-Book 5.99 (*0-8220-7250-5*, Cliff Notes) Wiley, John & Sons, Inc.

—Daniel Deronda. unabr. ed. Pt. 1, set. 1992. audio 77.95 (*1-55685-244-4*); Pt. 2. 1992. audio 59.95; Pt. 2, set. 1999. audio 59.95 Audio Bk. Contractors, Inc.

—Daniel Deronda. abr. ed. 1998. audio 16.85 (*0-563-55708-7*) BBC Bk. Publishing GBR. *Dist:* Ulverscroft Large Print Bks., Ltd.

—Daniel Deronda. unabr. ed. 1997. Pt. 1. audio 76.95 (*0-7861-1327-8*, 2224-A); Pt. 2. audio 76.95 (*0-7861-1328-6*, 2224-B) Blackstone Audio Bks., Inc.

—Daniel Deronda. (Writings of George Eliot Ser.: Vol. 15). reprint ed. Pt. 1. 1999. 400p. lib. bdg. 88.00 (*1-58201-082-X*); Pt. 2. 2001. 400p. pap. text 28.00 (*0-7426-5083-9*); Pt. 2. 1999. 400p. lib. bdg. 88.00 (*1-58201-083-8*); Pt. 3. 2001. 400p. pap. text 28.00 (*0-7426-5084-7*); Pt. 3. 1999. 88.00 (*1-58201-084-6*); Pt.1. 2001. 400p. pap. text 28.00 (*0-7426-5082-0*) Classic Bks.

—Daniel Deronda. 1999. (Everyman Paperback Classics Ser.). xxxi, 842p. pap. (*0-460-87686-4*, Everyman Paperbacks) Dent, J. M. & Sons (Canada), Ltd.

—Daniel Deronda. 2000. 928p. 23.00 (*0-375-41123-2*) Knopf, Alfred A. Inc.

—Daniel Deronda. 1979. mass mkt. 3.50 o.p. (*0-451-51204-9*, CE1204, Signet Classics) NAL.

—Daniel Deronda. Handley, Graham, ed. & intro. by. 1998. (Oxford World's Classics Ser.). 758p. pap. 9.95 (*0-19-283481-9*) Oxford Univ. Pr., Inc.

—Daniel Deronda. Handley, Graham, ed. (Oxford World's Classics Ser.). 1988. 758p. pap. 7.95 o.p. (*0-19-281787-6*); 1985. (Illus.). 792p. text 145.00 o.p. (*0-19-812557-7*) Oxford Univ. Pr., Inc.

—Daniel Deronda. abr. ed. 2000. (BBC Radio Presents Ser.). audio 18.00 o.s.i (*0-553-52686-3*, RH Audio) Random Hse. Audio Publishing Group.

—Daniel Deronda. 2002. (Modern Library Classics). 832p. pap. 9.95 (*0-375-76013-X*) Random Hse., Inc.

—Daniel Deronda. Hardy, Barbara, ed. 1967. (English Library). 912p. pap. 7.95 o.p. (*0-14-043020-2*, Penguin Classics) Viking Penguin.

—Daniel Deronda. abr. ed. 1997. audio 23.95 o.s.i (*0-14-086384-2*, Penguin AudioBooks) Viking Penguin.

—Daniel Deronda. Cave, Terence, ed. & intro. by. abr. ed. 1996. (Penguin Classics Ser.). 848p. 9.95 (*0-14-043427-5*, Penguin Classics) Viking Penguin.

—Daniel Deronda. 1998. (Classics Library). pap. 3.95 (*1-85326-176-9*, 1769WW) Wordsworth Editions, Ltd. GBR. *Dist:* Combined Publishing.

—Felix Holt, the Radical. unabr. ed. 1998. audio 71.95 (*1-55685-563-X*) Audio Bk. Contractors, Inc.

—Felix Holt, the Radical. unabr. ed. 1999. audio 85.95 (*0-7861-1727-3*, 2519) Blackstone Audio Bks., Inc.

—Felix Holt, the Radical. Baker, William & Womack, Kenneth, eds. 2000. (Literary Texts Ser.). (Illus.). 700p. pap. (*1-55111-228-0*) Broadview Pr.

—Felix Holt, the Radical. (Writings of George Eliot Ser.: Vol. 10). 400p. reprint ed. Pt. 1. 2001. pap. text 28.00 (*0-7426-5077-4*); Pt. 1. 1999. lib. bdg. 88.00 (*1-58201-077-3*); Pt. 2. 2001. pap. text 28.00 (*0-7426-5078-2*); Pt. 2. 1999. lib. bdg. 88.00 (*1-58201-078-1*) Classic Bks.

—Felix Holt, the Radical. l.t. ed. 1991. (Large Print Bks.). 537p. 24.95 (*1-85089-579-1*) ISIS Large Print Bks. GBR. *Dist:* Transaction Pubs., Ulverscroft Large Print Canada, Ltd.

—Felix Holt, the Radical. 1970. (Norton Library, N517). xxi, 487 p. (J). (*0-393-00517-8*) Norton, W. W. & Co., Inc.

—Felix Holt, the Radical. 1998. (Oxford World's Classics Ser.). 432p. pap. 12.95 (*0-19-283821-0*) Oxford Univ. Pr., Inc.

—Felix Holt, the Radical. Thompson, Fred C., ed. 1988. (Oxford World's Classics Ser.). 430p. pap. 7.95 o.p. (*0-19-281781-7*) Oxford Univ. Pr., Inc.

—Felix Holt, the Radical. Thomson, Fred C., ed. 1981. (Clarendon Edition of the Novels of George Eliot Ser.). (Illus.). 464p. text 137.00 (*0-19-812561-5*) Oxford Univ. Pr., Inc.

—Felix Holt, the Radical. 1997. (Everyman Paperback Classics Ser.). 320p. pap. 6.95 o.p. (*0-460-87687-2*, Everyman's Classic Library in Paperback) Tuttle Publishing.

—Felix Holt, the Radical. Coveney, Peter, ed. 1973. (English Library). 688p. pap. 6.95 o.p. (*0-14-043084-9*, Penguin Classics) Viking Penguin.

—Felix Holt, the Radical. Mugglestone, Lynda, ed. & intro. by. 140th ed. 1995. (Classics Ser.). 592p. pap. 14.00 (*0-14-043435-6*, Penguin Classics) Viking Penguin.

—George Eliot, Selected Works. 1995. 800p. 12.99 o.s.i (*0-517-12223-5*) Random Hse. Value Publishing.

—Impressions of Theophrastus Such. (Writings of George Eliot Ser.: Vol. 20). 400p. reprint ed. 2001. pap. text 28.00 (*0-7426-5087-1*); 1999. lib. bdg. 88.00 (*1-58201-087-0*) Classic Bks.

—Impressions of Theophrastus Such. Henry, Nancy, ed. 1995. 210p. 24.95 o.p. (*0-87745-488-4*); 1996. 232p. reprint ed. pap. text 13.95 (*0-87745-556-2*) Univ. of Iowa Pr.

—Middlemarch: A Study of English Provincial Life. 2002. (World Digital Library). E-Book 3.95 (*0-594-09735-5*) 1873 Pr.

—Middlemarch: A Study of English Provincial Life, 2 vols. 2001. 14.95 (*0-8010-1218-X*) Baker Bks.

—Middlemarch: A Study of English Provincial Life. 1985. 816p. mass mkt. 6.99 (*0-553-21180-3*, Bantam Classics) Bantam Bks.

—Middlemarch: A Study of English Provincial Life. (Writings of George Eliot Ser.: Vol. 12). 400p. reprint ed. Pt. 1. 2001. pap. text 28.00 (*0-7426-5079-0*); Pt. 1. 1999. lib. bdg. 88.00 (*1-58201-079-X*); Pt. 2. 2001. pap. text 28.00 (*0-7426-5080-4*); Pt. 2. 1999. lib. bdg. 88.00 (*1-58201-080-3*); Pt. 3. 2001. pap. text 28.00 (*0-7426-5081-2*); Pt. 3. 1999. lib. bdg. 88.00 (*1-58201-081-1*) Classic Bks.

—Middlemarch: A Study of English Provincial Life. 2002. Vol. 1. 420p. 27.99 (*1-4043-1964-6*); Vol. 1. 420p. per. 22.99 (*1-4043-1965-4*); Vol. 2. 396p. 27.99 (*1-4043-1966-2*); Vol. 2. 396p. per. 22.99 (*1-4043-1967-0*) IndyPublish.com.

—Middlemarch: A Study of English Provincial Life. Hornback, Bert G., ed. 1977. (Critical Editions Ser.). 770p. (C). pap. text o.p. (*0-393-09210-0*) Norton, W. W. & Co., Inc.

—Middlemarch: A Study of English Provincial Life. Carroll, David, ed. 1987. (Clarendon Edition of the Novels of George Eliot Ser.). (Illus.). 800p. (C). text 248.00 (*0-19-812558-5*) Oxford Univ. Pr., Inc.

—Middlemarch: A Study of English Provincial Life. Carroll, David & Bonaparte, Felicia, eds. 2nd ed. 1997. (Oxford World's Classics Ser.). 898p. pap. 6.95 o.p. (*0-19-282507-0*) Oxford Univ. Pr., Inc.

—Middlemarch: A Study of English Provincial Life. abr. ed. 1994. (Classics on Cassette). pap. 24.00 o.s.i incl. audio (*0-453-00879-8*) Penguin/HighBridge.

—Middlemarch: A Study of English Provincial Life. 1965. 3.95 (*0-671-00709-2*, Arco) Peterson's.

—Middlemarch: A Study of English Provincial Life. 2000. E-Book 4.95 (*0-679-64141-6*); 848p. pap. 9.95 (*0-679-78331-8*) Random House Adult Trade Publishing Group. (Modern Library).

—Middlemarch: A Study of English Provincial Life. abr. ed. 1994. (BBC Radio Presents Ser.). audio 22.00 o.s.i (*0-553-47342-5*, RH Audio) Random Hse. Audio Publishing Group.

—Middlemarch: A Study of English Provincial Life. 1994. o.s.i (*0-679-43517-4*); 1991. 644p. 22.00 (*0-679-40567-4*) Random Hse., Inc.

—Middlemarch: A Study of English Provincial Life. 2001. 865p. E-Book 4.00 (*1-929670-72-9*) Renaissance E Bks.

—Middlemarch: A Study of English Provincial Life. 2003. 880p. pap. 10.00 (*0-14-143954-8*, Penguin Classics) Viking Penguin.

—Middlemarch: A Study of English Provincial Life. Ashton, Rosemary, ed. & intro. by. 1994. (Penguin Classics Ser.). 880p. pap. 9.95 o.s.i (*0-14-043388-0*, Penguin Classics) Viking Penguin.

—The Mill on the Floss. 2001. reprint ed. Pt. 1. 404p. pap. text 28.00 (*0-7426-5072-3*); Pt. 2. 400p. pap. text 28.00 (*0-7426-5073-1*) Classic Bks.

—The Mill on the Floss. 2003. (Dover Thrift Editions Ser.). 416p. 3.50 (*0-486-42680-7*) Dover Pubns., Inc.

—The Mill on the Floss. 1972. 3.95 o.p. (*0-460-01325-4*); 1956. 10.50 o.p. (*0-460-00325-9*) Dutton/Plume. (Dutton).

—The Mill on the Floss. 1992. 640p. 20.00 (*0-679-41726-5*) Knopf, Alfred A. Inc.

—The Mill on the Floss. Cairns, Peter, ed. 1988. pap. 5.72 (*0-582-33169-2*, 72063) Longman Publishing Group.

—The Mill on the Floss. 2002. 560p. mass mkt. 5.95 (*0-451-52826-3*); 1968. mass mkt. 0.95 o.p. (*0-451-50438-0*); 1968. mass mkt. 0.75 o.p. (*0-451-50278-7*); 1965. mass mkt. 1.25 o.p. (*0-451-50672-3*); 1965. mass mkt. 1.50 o.p. (*0-451-50892-0*); 1965. mass mkt. 1.95 o.p. (*0-451-51055-0*); 1965. mass mkt. 2.95 o.p. (*0-451-51472-6*) NAL. (Signet Classics).

—The Mill on the Floss. 2003. (Twelve-Point Ser.). lib. bdg. 27.00 (*1-58287-240-6*); lib. bdg. 28.00 (*1-58287-724-6*) North Bks.

—The Mill on the Floss. Haight, Gordon S., ed. (Oxford World's Classics Ser.). 1998. 576p. pap. 8.95 (*0-19-283364-2*); 1980. (Illus.). 516p. (C). text 130.00 o.p. (*0-19-812560-7*); 2nd ed. 1997. 566p. pap. 5.95 o.p. (*0-19-282488-0*) Oxford Univ. Pr., Inc.

—The Mill on the Floss. 2001. (Modern Library Classics). 656p. pap. 8.95 (*0-375-75783-X*, Modern Library) Random House Adult Trade Publishing Group.

—The Mill on the Floss. Shuttleworth, Sally, ed. 1991. (English Texts Ser.). 450p. (C). pap. 19.95 o.p. (*0-415-01316-X*, A6066) Routledge.

—The Mill on the Floss. 2000. (Signature Classics Ser.). 486p. 24.95 (*1-58279-088-4*); lib. bdg. 29.95 (*1-58279-083-3*) Trident Pr. International.

—The Mill on the Floss. Skilton, David, ed. 1993. 492p. pap. 6.95 o.p. (*0-460-87286-9*, Everyman's Classic Library in Paperback) Tuttle Publishing.

—The Mill on the Floss. 2003. 704p. pap. 9.00 (*0-14-143962-9*, Penguin Classics) Viking Penguin.

—The Mill on the Floss: Authoritative Text, Backgrounds, Criticism. Christ, Carol T., ed. 1993. (Critical Editions Ser.). 613p. (C). pap. text 13.00 (*0-393-96332-2*) Norton, W. W. & Co., Inc.

—Scenes of Clerical Life. unabr. ed. 2003. audio 65.95 (*1-55685-740-3*) Audio Bk. Contractors, Inc.

—Scenes of Clerical Life. unabr. ed. 1999. audio 69.95 (*0-7861-1592-0*, 2421) Blackstone Audio Bks., Inc.

—Scenes of Clerical Life. (Writings of George Eliot Ser.: Vol. 1). reprint ed. Pt. 1. 2001. 302p. pap. text 28.00 (*0-7426-5068-5*); Pt. 1. 1999. 302p. lib. bdg. 88.00 (*1-58201-068-4*); Pt. 2. 2001. 314p. pap. text 28.00 (*0-7426-5069-3*); Pt. 2. 1999. 314p. lib. bdg. 88.00 (*1-58201-069-2*) Classic Bks.

—Scenes of Clerical Life. 1978. 8.00 o.p. (*0-460-00468-9*); 1977. 3.95 o.p. (*0-460-01468-4*) Dutton/Plume. (Dutton).

—Scenes of Clerical Life. Wolff, Robert L., ed. 1975. (Victorian Fiction Ser.). 366p. reprint ed. lib. bdg. 73.00 o.p. (*0-8240-1567-3*) Garland Publishing, Inc.

—Scenes of Clerical Life. Noble, Thomas A., ed. 2002. (Oxford World's Classics Ser.). 338p. pap. 8.95 (*0-19-283780-X*) Oxford Univ. Pr., Inc.

—Scenes of Clerical Life. 1989. (Oxford World's Classics Ser.). 328p. pap. 6.95 o.p. (*0-19-281786-8*) Oxford Univ. Pr., Inc.

—Scenes of Clerical Life. Noble, Thomas A., ed. 1985. (Clarendon Edition of the Novels of George Eliot Ser.). 374p. text 89.00 o.p. (*0-19-812559-3*) Oxford Univ. Pr., Inc.

—Scenes of Clerical Life. 1999. (Literary Classics). 340p. pap. 11.00 (*1-57392-780-5*) Prometheus Bks., Pubs.

—Scenes of Clerical Life. 1994. 304p. pap. 4.95 (*0-460-87463-2*, Everyman's Classic Library in Paperback) Tuttle Publishing.

—Scenes of Clerical Life. Gribble, Jennifer, ed. & intro. by. 1999. (Penguin Classics Ser.). (Illus.). 416p. 8.95 (*0-14-043638-3*, Penguin Classics) Viking Penguin.

—Scenes of Clerical Life. Lodge, David, ed. 1973. (Penguin Classics Ser.). 432p. pap. 8.95 o.s.i (*0-14-043087-3*, Penguin Classics) Viking Penguin.

—Silas Marner. Acclaim Comics Staff, ed. 1997. (Classics Illustrated Study Guides). (Illus.). mass mkt. 4.99 (*1-57840-050-3*) Acclaim Bks.

—Silas Marner. 1994. pap. text 39.50 (*0-582-23662-2*) Addison-Wesley Longman, Ltd. GBR. *Dist:* Trans-Atlantic Pubns., Inc.

—Silas Marner. unabr. ed. 1963. (Classics Ser.). mass mkt. 2.50 o.p. (*0-8049-0014-0*, CL-14) Airmont Publishing Co., Inc.

—Silas Marner. 20.95 (*0-88411-275-6*) Amereon, Ltd.

—Silas Marner. l.t. ed. 1992. pap. 19.95 o.p. (*0-7927-1093-2*, CS0295); 1991. 21.95 o.p. (*0-7927-1092-4*, CH0223) BBC Audiobooks America.

—Silas Marner. 1981. 192p. pap. 1.95 o.s.i (*0-553-21048-3*); mass mkt. 3.95 (*0-553-21229-X*) Bantam Bks. (Bantam Classics).

—Silas Marner. Seely, Elizabeth & Seely, John, eds. 1999. (Classic Novels ). 256p. pap. 8.95 (*0-7641-1150-7*) Barron's Educational Series, Inc.

—Silas Marner. 1987. 188p. reprint ed. lib. bdg. 21.95 (*0-89966-621-3*) Buccaneer Bks., Inc.

—Silas Marner. 1997. (Cambridge Literature Ser.). audio compact disk 18.95 o.p. (*0-521-59805-2*) Cambridge Univ. Pr.

—Silas Marner. Bousted, Mary, ed. 1995. (Literature Ser.). (Illus.). 256p. pap. text 9.95 (*0-521-48572-X*) Cambridge Univ. Pr.

—Silas Marner. (Early Best Sellers Ser.). reprint ed. lib. bdg. 48.00 (*0-7426-1022-5*); 2001. (Illus.). pap. text 28.00 (*0-7426-6022-2*) Classic Bks.

—Silas Marner. unabr. ed. 1996. (Thrift Editions Ser.). 160p. reprint ed. pap. 1.50 (*0-486-29246-0*) Dover Pubns., Inc.

—Silas Marner. 1972. 2.95 o.p. (*0-460-01121-9*); 1958. 10.50 o.p. (*0-460-00121-3*) Dutton/Plume. (Dutton).

—Silas Marner. E-Book 2.49 (*0-7574-3509-2*) Electric Umbrella Publishing.

—Silas Marner. 1980. (FRE.). pap. 11.95 (*0-7859-2434-5*, 2070371913) French & European Pubns., Inc.

—Silas Marner. l.t. ed. 2002. (Perennial Bestseller Ser.). 304p. 28.95 (*0-7838-9756-1*) Gale Group.

—Silas Marner. Clay, N. L., ed. 1986. (Guide Novel Ser.). pap. text 3.95 o.p. (*0-435-16280-2*) Heinemann.

—Silas Marner. 2000. (HRW Library). 220p. 17.90 (*0-03-056459-X*) Holt, Rinehart & Winston.

—Silas Marner. l.t. ed. 190p. pap. 19.76 (*0-7583-2312-3*); 334p. pap. 28.44 (*0-7583-2314-X*); 433p. pap. 35.33 (*0-7583-2315-8*); 561p. pap. 43.59 (*0-7583-2316-6*); 242p. pap. 22.70 (*0-7583-2313-1*); 693p. pap. 52.27 (*0-7583-2317-4*); 852p. pap. 67.81 (*0-7583-2318-2*); 1006p. pap. 77.39 (*0-7583-2319-0*); 561p. lib. bdg. 49.59 (*0-7583-2308-5*); 693p. lib. bdg. 58.27 (*0-7583-2309-3*); 242p. lib. bdg. 28.70 (*0-7583-2305-0*); 190p. lib. bdg. 25.76 (*0-7583-2304-2*); 852p. lib. bdg. 81.01 (*0-7583-2310-7*); 433p. lib. bdg. 41.33 (*0-7583-2307-7*); 334p. lib. bdg. 34.44 (*0-7583-2306-9*); 1006p. lib. bdg. 89.39 (*0-7583-2311-5*) Huge Print Pr.

—Silas Marner. l.t. unabr. ed. 1992. (Isis Large Print Bks.). 196p. 29.99 (*1-85089-538-4*, 895384) ISIS Large Print Bks. GBR. *Dist:* Ulverscroft Large Print Bks., Ltd., Ulverscroft Large Print Canada, Ltd.

—Silas Marner. 1993. (Everyman's Library). 240p. 17.00 (*0-679-42030-4*) Knopf, Alfred A. Inc.

—Silas Marner. E-Book 1.95 (*1-57799-883-9*) Logos Research Systems, Inc.

—Silas Marner. 2nd rev. ed. 1996. pap. text 5.90 o.s.i (*0-582-27531-8*); Level 3. 2000. pap. 7.66 (*0-582-41640-X*) Longman Publishing Group.

—Silas Marner. (Signet Classics). 1999. 208p. mass mkt. 3.95 (*0-451-52721-6*, Signet Classics); 1997. pap. 2.95 (*0-89375-996-1*); 1960. mass mkt. 0.60 o.p. (*0-451-50644-8*, Signet Classics); 1960. mass mkt. 0.50 o.p. (*0-451-50021-0*, Signet Classics); 1960. 192p. mass mkt. 1.95 o.p. (*0-451-52108-0*, Signet Classics); 1960. 192p. mass mkt. 3.95 o.s.i (*0-451-52427-6*, Signet Classics); 1960. mass mkt. 0.75 o.p. (*0-451-50733-9*, Signet Classics); 1960. mass mkt. 0.95 o.p. (*0-451-50999-4*, Signet Classics); 1960. mass mkt. 1.95 o.p. (*0-451-51945-0*, Signet Classics); 1960. mass mkt. 1.75 o.p. (*0-451-51678-8*, Signet Classics); 1960. mass mkt. 1.95 o.p. (*0-451-51591-9*, Signet Classics); 1960. mass mkt. 1.75 o.p. (*0-451-51418-1*, Signet Classics); 1960. mass mkt. 1.25 o.p. (*0-451-51238-3*, Signet Classics) NAL.

—Silas Marner. Seely, Elizabeth, ed. 1995. (Thornes Classic Novels Ser.). (Illus.). 247p. pap. 15.95 (*0-7487-1831-1*) Nelson Thornes GBR. *Dist:* Trans-Atlantic Pubns., Inc.

—Silas Marner. abr. ed. 1997. audio 20.00 o.p. (*0-7871-1064-7*) NewStar Media, Inc.

—Silas Marner. l.t. ed. 1998. (Large Print Ser.). reprint ed. 347p. lib. bdg. 26.00 (*0-939495-66-X*); 207p. lib. bdg. 25.00 (*1-58287-085-3*) North Bks.

—Silas Marner. Cave, Terence, ed. & intro. by. (Oxford World's Classics Ser.). 1998. 232p. pap. 6.95 (*0-19-283458-4*); 1996. 250p. pap. 4.95 o.p. (*0-19-283210-7*) Oxford Univ. Pr., Inc.

—Silas Marner. 1995. (Illus.). 94p. pap. text 5.95 (*0-19-586311-9*) Oxford Univ. Pr., Inc.

—Silas Marner. Hedge, Tricia, ed. 1995. (Illus.). 80p. pap. text 5.95 o.p. (*0-19-422708-1*) Oxford Univ. Pr., Inc.

—Silas Marner. 1986. (World's Best Reading Ser.). (Illus.). 208p. 12.95 o.p. (*0-89577-248-5*) Reader's Digest Assn., Inc., The.

—Silas Marner. 2001. 189p. E-Book 4.00 (*1-929670-73-7*) Renaissance E Bks.

—Silas Marner. E-Book 5.00 (*0-7410-0430-5*) SoftBook Pr.

—Silas Marner. 1986. (Bantam Classics Ser.). 10.00 (*0-606-02467-0*) Turtleback Bks.

—Silas Marner. Smith, Anne, ed. 1993. 256p. pap. 4.95 (*0-460-87263-X*, Everyman's Classic Library in Paperback) Tuttle Publishing.

—Silas Marner. 1998. 7.95 (*81-85944-82-2*) UBS Pubs. Distributions, Ltd. IND. *Dist:* South Asia Bks.

—Silas Marner. 2003. 240p. pap. 7.00 (*0-14-143975-0*, Penguin Classics) Viking Penguin.

—Silas Marner. Carroll, David, ed. 1997. (Penguin Classics Ser.). 240p. 6.95 (*0-14-043480-1*, Penguin Classics) Viking Penguin.

—Silas Marner. Leavis, Q. D., ed. 1968. (English Library). 272p. pap. 6.95 o.p. (*0-14-043030-X*, Penguin Classics) Viking Penguin.

—Silas Marner. 1999. E-Book 5.99 (*0-8220-7190-8*, Cliff Notes) Wiley, John & Sons, Inc.

—Silas Marner. 1998. (Classics Library). 176p. pap. 3.95 (*1-85326-221-8*, 2218WW) Wordsworth Editions, Ltd. GBR. *Dist:* Casemate Pubs. & Bk. Distributors, LLC.

—Silas Marner: The Weaver of Raveloe. 2001. (Modern Library Classics). 240p. pap. 6.95 (*0-375-75749-X*, Modern Library) Random House Adult Trade Publishing Group.

—Silas Marner, Brother Jacob. 400p. reprint ed. 2001. pap. text 28.00 (*0-7426-5074-X*); 1999. (Writings of George Eliot Ser.: Vol. 7). lib. bdg. 88.00 (*1-58201-074-9*) Classic Bks.

—Silas Marner, Brother Jacob, & The Lifted Veil. Mudford, Peter, ed. rev. ed. 1996. (Everyman Paperback Classics Ser.). 348p. (C). pap. 6.95 (*0-460-87568-X*, Everyman's Classic Library in Paperback) Tuttle Publishing.

—The Spanish Gypsy. 400p. reprint ed. 2001. pap. text 28.00 (*0-7426-5085-5*); 1999. (Writings of George Eliot Ser.: Vol. 18). lib. bdg. 88.00 (*1-58201-085-4*) Classic Bks.

Eliot, George, contrib. by. Middlemarch: A Study of English Provincial Life. 2001. (Embellished Manuscripts). 160p. 14.95 (*1-55156-198-0*) Paperblank Bk. Co.

Eliot, George & Carroll, David. Middlemarch: A Study of English Provincial Life. 1997. E-Book 9.40 (*0-585-36166-5*) netLibrary, Inc.

Eliot, George & Haight, Gordon Sherman. The Mill on the Floss. 1980. E-Book 8.35 (*0-585-36085-5*) netLibrary, Inc.

Elkins, Aaron. Murder in the Queen's Arms. 1986. 208p. mass mkt. 2.95 o.s.i (*0-553-26235-1*) Bantam Bks.

—Murder in the Queen's Arms. 1985. 195p. 14.95 o.s.i (*0-8027-5626-3*) Walker & Co.

—Murder in the Queen's Arms. 1990. 224p. mass mkt. 5.99 (*0-445-40913-4*, Mysterious Pr. Paperback Bks.) Warner Bks., Inc.

Elliott, George P. Middlemarch. 2003. 912p. mass mkt. 6.95 (*0-451-52917-0*, Signet Classics) NAL.

Ellis, Alice Thomas. The Birds of the Air. 1981. 156p. 9.95 o.p. (*0-670-16819-X*) Viking Penguin.

—Pillars of Gold. 2000. 181p. 22.95 (*1-55921-284-5*) Moyer Bell.

—Pillars of Gold. l.t. ed. 2000. (General Ser.). 236p. 24.95 (*0-7862-2805-9*); (*0-7540-4247-2*); (*0-7540-4248-0*) Thorndike Pr.

—The Summer House: A Trilogy. 2001. (Common Reader Edition Ser.). 360p. reprint ed. pap. 19.95 (*1-58579-028-1*) Akadine Pr., The.

—The Summer House: A Trilogy. 1993. 352p. pap. 11.95 o.p. (*0-14-023876-X*, Penguin Bks.) Penguin Group (USA) Inc.

—The 27th Kingdom. 1999. 220p. 22.95 (*1-55921-250-0*) Moyer Bell.

—The 27th Kingdom. l.t. ed. 2000. (General Ser.). 206p. pap. 22.95 (*0-7862-2628-5*) Thorndike Pr.

Ellis, Delia. Spa Partners. l.t. ed. 2001. (General Ser.). 297p. pap. 24.95 (*0-7862-2989-6*); (*0-7540-4342-8*) Thorndike Pr.

Ellis, Kate. The Bone Garden. 2003. 240p. 23.95 (*0-312-30037-9*, Saint Martin's Minotaur) St. Martin's Pr.

—The Merchant's House. l.t. ed. 1999. (Magna Large Print Ser.). 400p. o.p. (*0-7505-1438-8*) Magna Large Print Bks. GBR. *Dist:* Ulverscroft Large Print Canada, Ltd.

—The Merchant's House. 1999. 246p. 22.95 (*0-312-20562-7*, Saint Martin's Minotaur) St. Martin's Pr.

—An Unhallowed Grave. l.t. ed. 2001. (Magna Large Print Ser.). 400p. 31.99 (*0-7505-1627-5*) Magna Large Print Bks. GBR. *Dist:* Ulverscroft Large Print Bks., Ltd., Ulverscroft Large Print Canada, Ltd.

—An Unhallowed Grave. Date not set. E-Book 22.95 (*0-312-70164-0*) St. Martin's Pr.

—An Unhallowed Grave: Wesley Peterson Crime Novel. 2001. (Wesley Peterson Crime Novels Ser.). 240p. 22.95 (*0-312-27460-2*, Saint Martin's Minotaur) St. Martin's Pr.

Ellmann, Lucy. Man or Mango? A Lament. 1998. 224p. 22.00 o.p. (*0-374-20228-1*) Farrar, Straus & Giroux.

—Man or Mango? A Lament. 1999. 224p. pap. 12.00 o.p. (*0-312-20967-3*) Picador.

Elsberg, John. A Week in the Lake District. 1998. (Illus.). 72p. 22.00 (*1-893959-02-3*) Red Moon Pr.

Elton, Ben. Blast from the Past, Set. unabr. ed. 1999. audio 69.95 (*0-7540-0323-X*, CAB1746) Chivers Audio Bks. GBR. *Dist:* BBC Audiobooks America.

—Blast from the Past. 2000. 304p. pap. 12.95 (*0-385-33452-4*, Delta) Dell Publishing.

—Blast from the Past. l.t. unabr. ed. 1999. 331p. 25.95 (*0-7531-5998-8*, 159988) ISIS Large Print Bks. GBR. *Dist:* ISIS Publishing.

—Dead Famous. 2003. 384p. pap. (*0-552-99945-8*, Corgi) Bantam Bks.

—High Society. 2003. 389p. mass mkt. (*0-552-15053-3*, Corgi); 279p. (*0-593-04939-X*) Bantam Bks.

—High Society. 279p. pap. 19.95 (*0-593-04940-3*) Bantam Pr., Ltd. GBR. *Dist:* Trafalgar Square.

Settings

—High Society. 2003. 384p. pap. 12.00 (*0-552-99995-4*) Transworld Publishers Ltd. GBR. *Dist:* Trafalgar Square.

Emecheta, Buchi. The Family. 1990. 240p. 17.95 o.s.i (*0-8076-1245-6*); pap. 10.95 (*0-8076-1250-2*) Braziller, George Inc.

Emerson, Kathy Lynn. Face down among the Winchester Geese. 1999. (Elizabethan Mysteries Ser.). 256p. (J). 22.95 (*0-312-20542-2*, Saint Martin's Minotaur) St. Martin's Pr.

—Face down Before the Rebel Hooves. 2001. 256p. 23.95 (*0-312-28036-X*, Saint Martin's Minotaur) St. Martin's Pr.

—Face down in the Marrow-Bone Pie: An Elizabethan Mystery. 2000. 256p. mass mkt. 5.99 o.s.i (*1-57566-546-8*) Kensington Publishing Corp.

—Face down in the Marrow-Bone Pie: An Elizabethan Mystery. 1997. (Elizabethan Mysteries Ser.). 208p. 21.95 (*0-312-15123-3*, Saint Martin's Minotaur) St. Martin's Pr.

—Face down under the Wych Elm. 2002. 256p. mass mkt. 5.99 (*0-7582-0167-2*) Kensington Publishing Corp.

—Face down under the Wych Elm. 2000. (Elizabethan Mysteries Ser.: Vol. 5). 250p. 22.95 (*0-312-26589-1*, Saint Martin's Minotaur) St. Martin's Pr.

—Face down upon an Herbal. 2000. 256p. mass mkt. 5.99 (*1-57566-620-0*) Kensington Publishing Corp.

—Face down upon an Herbal. 1998. (Elizabethan Mysteries Ser.). 256p. 21.95 (*0-312-18092-6*, 874707, Saint Martin's Minotaur) St. Martin's Pr.

English, Lucy. Our Dancing Days. 256p. pap. 17.95 (*1-84115-241-2*); 2002. 213p. pap. 9.95 (*1-84115-242-0*) Fourth Estate, Ltd. GBR. *Dist:* Trafalgar Square.

—Our Dancing Days. l.t. ed. 2002. 288p. pap. 21.99 (*0-7531-6621-6*); 32.50 (*0-7531-6620-8*) ISIS Large Print Bks. GBR. *Dist:* Ulverscroft Large Print Bks., Ltd., Ulverscroft Large Print Canada, Ltd.

Enoch, Suzanne. England's Perfect Hero. 2004. 384p. mass mkt. 5.99 (*0-06-054313-2*, Avon Bks.) Morrow/Avon.

—Meet Me at Midnight: With This Ring. 2000. 384p. mass mkt. 5.99 (*0-380-80917-6*, Avon Bks.) Morrow/Avon.

Enright, Rosemary. The Walled Garden. 1993. 352p. 21.95 o.p. (*0-312-09409-4*) St. Martin's Pr.

Erickson, Steve. Days Between Stations. 1997. 288p. pap. 12.00 o.s.i (*0-8050-5070-1*, Owl Bks.) Holt, Henry & Co.

—Days Between Stations. 1986. (Vintage Contemporaries Ser.). 256p. pap. 6.95 o.s.i (*0-394-74685-6*, Vintage) Knopf Publishing Group.

—Days Between Stations: A Novel. 1985. 15.45 o.s.i (*0-671-53275-8*, Simon & Schuster) Simon & Schuster.

Erskine, Barbara. House of Echoes. abr. ed. 1996. 448p. 24.95 o.s.i (*0-525-93867-2*) Dutton/Plume.

—House of Echoes. l.t. ed. 1996. (G. K. Hall Core Ser.). 662p. 25.95 (*0-7838-1851-3*, Macmillan Reference USA) Gale Group.

—House of Echoes. 1997. 480p. mass mkt. 6.50 o.s.i (*0-451-18195-6*, Signet Bks.) NAL.

—House of Echoes. 1996. 448p. text 29.99 (*0-670-85651-7*) Viking Penguin.

—Midnight Is a Lonely Place. 1994. 352p. 20.95 o.p. (*0-525-93862-1*, Dutton) Dutton/Plume.

—Midnight Is a Lonely Place. l.t. ed. 1994. 647p. lib. bdg. 24.95 (*0-8161-7479-2*, Macmillan Reference USA) Gale Group.

Erskine, Margaret. Case with Three Husbands. l.t. ed. 1988. (Linford Mystery Library). 288p. pap. 17.99 o.p. (*0-7089-6505-9*, Linford) Thorpe, F. A. Pubs. GBR. *Dist:* Ulverscroft Large Print Bks., Ltd., Ulverscroft Large Print Canada, Ltd.

—The Ewe Lamb. 1995. 160p. 16.95 o.p. (*0-7451-8652-1*, Black Dagger) BBC Audiobooks America.

—Harriet Farewell. 1984. 176p. pap. 2.50 o.p. (*0-553-23780-2*) Bantam Bks.

—Harriet Farewell. l.t. ed. 1988. (Linford Mystery Library). 288p. pap. 17.99 o.p. (*0-7089-6513-X*, Ulverscroft) Thorpe, F. A. Pubs. GBR. *Dist:* Ulverscroft Large Print Bks., Ltd., Ulverscroft Large Print Canada, Ltd.

—The House in Hook Street. 1977. 6.95 o.p. (*0-385-13137-2*) Doubleday Publishing.

—The Woman at Belguardo. l.t. ed. 1989. (Linford Mystery Library). 371p. pap. 17.99 o.p. (*0-7089-6632-2*, Linford) Thorpe, F. A. Pubs. GBR. *Dist:* Ulverscroft Large Print Bks., Ltd., Ulverscroft Large Print Canada, Ltd.

Estleman, Loren D. Dr. Jekyll & Mr. Holmes. 2001. 224p. pap. 12.00 (*0-7434-2392-5*) ibooks, Inc.

—Dr. Jekyll & Mr. Holmes. E-Book 6.99 (*1-59019-599-X*) ipicturebooks, LLC.

Estleman, Loren D. & Watson, John H. Dr. Jekyll & Mr. Holmes. 1979. 8.95 o.p. (*0-385-15257-4*) Doubleday Publishing.

—Dr. Jekyll & Mr. Holmes. 1980. 256p. pap. 3.95 o.p. (*0-14-005665-3*, Penguin Bks.) Viking Penguin.

—Sherlock Holmes vs. Dracula or, The Adventure of the Sanguinary Count. 1978. 7.95 o.p. (*0-385-14051-7*) Doubleday Publishing.

—Sherlock Holmes vs. Dracula or, The Adventure of the Sanguinary Count. 1979. 224p. pap. 3.95 o.p. (*0-14-005262-3*, Penguin Bks.) Viking Penguin.

Eubank, Judith. Crossover. 160p. E-Book 6.99 (*1-58586-359-9*) ereads.com.

Eustace, Grant. Absolute Discretion. 1997. 189p. pap. (*1-899562-31-1*, Calabash Pr.) Ash-Tree Pr.

Evans, Geraldine. Dead Before Morning. 1995. (Mystery Ser.). 253p. per. (*0-373-26184-5*, 1-26184-1, Worldwide Library) Harlequin Enterprises, Ltd.

—Dead Before Morning. 1993. 222p. 17.95 o.p. (*0-312-08755-1*, Saint Martin's Minotaur) St. Martin's Pr.

—Down among the Dead. 1994. 192p. 18.95 o.p. (*0-312-11451-6*, Saint Martin's Minotaur) St. Martin's Pr.

—Down among the Dead Men. 1996. per. (*0-373-26208-6*, 1-26208-8, Worldwide Library) Harlequin Enterprises, Ltd.

Evans, Pamela. Town Belles. 1997. 474p. mass mkt. 13.95 (*0-7472-5166-5*) Headline Bk. Publishing, Ltd. GBR. *Dist:* Trafalgar Square.

—Town Belles. l.t. ed. 1997. (General Ser.). 544p. pap. 22.95 (*0-7862-1115-6*) Thorndike Pr.

Evans, Penelope. The Last Girl. 1997. (Last Girl Ser.: Vol. 1). 256p. mass mkt. 5.99 (*0-312-96315-7*, St. Martin's Paperbacks); 1995. 240p. text 21.95 o.p. (*0-312-13998-5*) St. Martin's Pr.

—The Last Girl. 2000. pap. 10.95 (*0-552-99602-5*) Transworld Publishers Ltd. GBR. *Dist:* Trafalgar Square.

Evans, Quinn Taylor. Merlin's Legacy: Daughter of Fire. 1998. (Merlin's Legacy Ser.: Vol. 1). 448p. pap. 12.00 o.s.i (*1-57566-306-6*, Kensington Bks.) Kensington Publishing Corp.

—Merlin's Legacy: Daughter of the Mist. (Merlin's Legacy Ser.: Vol. 2). 1999. 384p. pap. 12.00 o.s.i (*1-57566-406-2*); 1996. 480p. mass mkt. 5.50 o.s.i (*0-8217-5347-9*, Zebra Bks.) Kensington Publishing Corp.

—Merlin's Legacy: Dawn of Camelot. 1998. (Merlin's Legacy Ser.: Vol. 5). 320p. mass mkt. 5.50 o.s.i (*0-8217-6028-9*) Kensington Publishing Corp.

—Merlin's Legacy No. 3: Daughter of Light. (Merlin's Legacy Ser.). 1998. 320p. mass mkt. 5.50 o.s.i (*0-8217-6051-3*); 1997. 480p. mass mkt. 5.50 o.s.i (*0-8217-5549-8*) Kensington Publishing Corp. (Zebra Bks.).

—Merlin's Legacy No. 4: Shadows of Camelot. 1997. (Merlin's Legacy Ser.: Vol. 4). 320p. mass mkt. 5.50 o.s.i (*0-8217-5760-1*) Kensington Publishing Corp.

Ewing, Jean R. My Dark Prince. 2000. 352p. mass mkt. 6.99 o.s.i (*0-515-12883-X*, Jove) Berkley Publishing Group.

Fairchild, Elisabeth. Captain Cupid Calls the Shots. 2000. (Signet Regency Romance Ser.). 224p. mass mkt. 4.99 o.s.i (*0-451-20198-1*) NAL.

—Valentine's Change of Heart. 2003. 224p. mass mkt. 4.99 (*0-451-20772-6*, Signet Bks.) NAL.

Falconer, Elizabeth. Golden Year. 2000. 351p. pap. 12.95 (*0-552-99622-X*) Transworld Publishers Ltd. GBR. *Dist:* Trafalgar Square.

Farjeon, Eleanor, intro. Christmas Books: Including a "A Christmas Carol" 1987. (Illus.). 413p. (J). 17.95 (*0-19-254514-0*) Oxford Univ. Pr., Inc.

Farmer, Philip Jose. The Adventure of the Peerless Peer. 1974. 112p. 5.50 o.p. (*0-915230-06-2*) Rue Morgue Pr.

Farr, Diane. Once upon a Christmas. 2000. (Signet Regency Romance Ser.). 224p. mass mkt. 4.99 o.s.i (*0-451-20162-0*, Signet Bks.) NAL.

Farrell, Marjorie. Red, Red Rose. 1999. 320p. mass mkt. 6.50 o.s.i (*0-451-40817-9*, Topaz) NAL.

Farrington, Geoffrey. The Revenants. 167p. pap. o.p. (*0-946626-01-4*) Dedalus, Ltd.

—The Revenants. Newman, Kim, ed. rev. ed. 2003. 245p. pap. 11.99 (*1-903517-04-4*) Dedalus, Ltd.

Faulks, Sebastian. Charlotte Gray. l.t. ed. 1999. (Charnwood Large Print Ser.). 592p. 31.99 (*0-7089-9078-9*, Linford) Thorpe, F. A. Pubs. GBR. *Dist:* Ulverscroft Large Print Bks., Ltd., Ulverscroft Large Print Canada, Ltd.

Fawcett, Quinn. Embassy Row. (Mycroft Holmes Novels Ser.). 384p. 1999. pap. 6.99 (*0-8125-4522-2*, Tor Bks.); 1998. 24.95 o.p. (*0-312-86363-2*, Forge Bks.) Doherty, Tom Assocs., LLC.

—The Flying Scotsman. 1999. (Mycroft Holmes Novels Ser.). (Illus.). 320p. 23.95 (*0-312-86364-0*, Forge Bks.) Doherty, Tom Assocs., LLC.

—The Flying Scotsman: A Mycroft Holmes Novel Authorized by Dame Jean Conan Coyle. 2000. (Mycroft Holmes Novels Ser.). 320p. pap. 14.95 (*0-312-87689-0*, Tor Bks.) Doherty, Tom Assocs., LLC.

Feather, Jane. The Accidental Bride. l.t. ed. 2000. (Thorndike/G. K. Hall Paperback Bestsellers Ser.). 517p. 27.95 (*0-7862-2281-6*) Thorndike Pr.

—Almost Innocent. 2001. 432p. reprint ed. mass mkt. 6.99 (*0-553-57370-5*) Bantam Bks.

—Almost Innocent. l.t. ed. 2003. 691p. 25.95 (*0-375-43272-8*, Random House Large Print) Random Hse. Large Print.

—The Diamond Slipper. 1997. 416p. mass mkt. 6.99 (*0-553-57523-6*) Bantam Bks.

—The Emerald Swan. 1998. 448p. mass mkt. 6.99 (*0-553-57525-2*) Bantam Bks.

—Kissed by Shadows. 2003. E-Book 5.99 (*0-553-89732-2*) Bantam Bks.

—Kissed by Shadows. 2003. (Kiss Bks.). 480p. mass mkt. 5.99 (*0-553-58308-5*) Bantam Dell Publishing Group.

—Kissed by Shadows. l.t. ed. 2003. 31.95 (*0-7862-5421-1*) Thorndike Pr.

—Love's Charade. 2001. mass mkt. 6.99 (*0-8217-7202-3*) Kensington Publishing Corp.

—The Silver Rose. 1997. 384p. mass mkt. 6.99 (*0-553-57524-4*, Fanfare) Bantam Bks.

—Valentine. 1995. 448p. mass mkt. 6.50 (*0-553-56470-6*) Bantam Bks.

—Valentine. (Romance Ser.). 1996. lib. bdg. 24.95 (*0-7862-0860-0*, Five Star); 1995. 24.95 (*1-56895-162-0*, Wheeler Publishing, Inc.) Gale Group.

—The Widow's Kiss. 2002. 464p. reprint ed. mass mkt. 6.50 (*0-553-58187-2*) Bantam Bks.

Feherty, David. A Nasty Bit of Rough. 2002. (Illus.). 224p. 23.95 (*1-59071-000-2*) Rugged Land.

—Nasty Bit of Rough: A Novel. 2003. 256p. pap. 14.00 (*0-14-200265-8*) Penguin Group (USA) Inc.

Feinstein, Elaine. The Survivors. 1991. 320p. (Orig.). pap. 8.95 o.p. (*0-14-014848-5*) Penguin Group (USA) Inc.

Fell, Doris Elaine. Willows on the Windrush. 2000. (Sagas of a Kindred Heart Ser.: Vol. 2). 352p. (gr. 13 up). pap. 11.99 o.p. (*0-8007-5732-7*) Revell, Fleming H. Co.

Ferguson, J. A. My Lord Viking. 2001. 328p. pap. 13.00 (*1-893896-18-8*) ImaJinn Bks.

Ferguson, JamesC. Context Clues: A Basil Coventry Misadventure. 2003. pap. 17.95 o.p. (*0-595-29124-4*, iUniverse, Inc.) iUniverse, Inc.

Ferguson, Janet. Surgeon on Call. l.t. ed. 1990. 17.95 o.p. (*0-7451-9889-9*, C0618); pap. 15.95 o.p. (*0-7927-0350-2*, C0812) BBC Audiobooks America.

Ferguson, Jo Ann. His Lady Midnight. 2002. (Romance Ser.). 26.95 (*0-7862-4163-2*, Five Star) Gale Group.

—His Lady Midnight. 2001. (Zebra Regency Romance Ser.). 256p. mass mkt. 4.99 o.s.i (*0-8217-6863-8*) Kensington Publishing Corp.

Ferguson, Jo Ann, et al. A Kiss for Mama. 2000. (Zebra Regency Romance Ser.). 256p. mass mkt. 4.99 o.s.i (*0-8217-6807-7*, Zebra Bks.) Kensington Publishing Corp.

—A Kiss for Papa. 2002. (Zebra Regency Romance Ser.). 256p. mass mkt. 4.99 o.s.i (*0-8217-7286-4*) Kensington Publishing Corp.

Ferjutz, Kelly, ed. The Winter Holiday Sampler: 17 Wonderful Stories of Regency England. 2001. 232p. pap. 14.95 (*1-929085-81-8*) Regency Pr.

Ferrars, E. X. Beware of the Dog. l.t. ed. 1993. (Mystery Ser.). 304p. 29.99 o.p. (*0-7505-0490-0*) Magna Large Print Bks. GBR. *Dist:* Ulverscroft Large Print Bks., Ltd., Ulverscroft Large Print Canada, Ltd.

—A Choice of Evils. unabr. ed. 1996. audio 49.95 (*1-85695-223-1*, 951209) ISIS Audio Bks. GBR. *Dist:* Ulverscroft Large Print Bks., Ltd.

—The Crime & the Crystal. 1985. (Crime Club Ser.). 192p. 12.95 o.p. (*0-385-19996-1*) Doubleday Publishing.

—The Crime & the Crystal. l.t. ed. 1999. (Ulverscroft Large Print Ser.). 320p. 12.50 o.p. (*0-7089-1485-3*, Ulverscroft) Thorpe, F. A. Pubs. GBR. *Dist:* Ulverscroft Large Print Bks., Ltd., Ulverscroft Large Print Canada, Ltd.

—Death in Botanists Bay. l.t. ed. 1989. 17.95 o.p. (*0-7089-2070-5*, Ulverscroft) Thorpe, F. A. Pubs. GBR. *Dist:* Ulverscroft Large Print Bks., Ltd.

—Death of a Minor Character. 1983. (Crime Club Ser.). 192p. 11.95 o.p. (*0-385-18839-0*) Doubleday Publishing.

—Death of a Minor Character. l.t. ed. 1984. (Ulverscroft Large Print Ser.). 320p. 12.50 o.p. (*0-7089-1225-7*, Ulverscroft) Thorpe, F. A. Pubs. GBR. *Dist:* Ulverscroft Large Print Bks., Ltd., Ulverscroft Large Print Canada, Ltd.

—Frog in the Throat. 1981. 112p. pap. 1.95 o.p. (*0-553-20040-2*) Bantam Bks.

—Frog in the Throat. 1980. (Crime Club Ser.). 192p. 8.95 o.p. (*0-385-17207-9*) Doubleday Publishing.

—Frog in the Throat. unabr. ed. 1998. audio 54.95 (*0-7531-0239-0*, 980209) ISIS Audio Bks. GBR. *Dist:* Ulverscroft Large Print Bks., Ltd.

—Frog in the Throat. l.t. ed. 1986. (Ulverscroft Large Print Ser.). 304p. 12.50 o.p. (*0-7089-1430-6*, Ulverscroft) Thorpe, F. A. Pubs. GBR. *Dist:* Ulverscroft Large Print Bks., Ltd., Ulverscroft Large Print Canada, Ltd.

—A Hobby of Murder: An Andrew Basnett Mystery. unabr. ed. 2000. audio 49.95 (*0-7451-4359-8*, CAB 1042) Chivers Audio Bks. GBR. *Dist:* BBC Audiobooks America.

—A Hobby of Murder: An Andrew Basnett Mystery. l.t. ed. 1995. (Magna Large Print Ser.). 301p. o.p. (*0-7505-0753-5*) Magna Large Print Bks. GBR. *Dist:* Ulverscroft Large Print Canada, Ltd.

—I Met Murder. 1986. (Crime Club Ser.). 192p. 12.95 o.p. (*0-385-23367-1*) Doubleday Publishing.

—I Met Murder. unabr. ed. 1998. audio 49.95 (*0-7531-0408-3*, 970704) ISIS Audio Bks. GBR. *Dist:* Ulverscroft Large Print Bks., Ltd.

—I Met Murder. l.t. ed. 1987. (Ulverscroft Large Print Ser.). 320p. 14.50 o.p. (*0-7089-1586-8*, Ulverscroft) Thorpe, F. A. Pubs. GBR. *Dist:* Ulverscroft Large Print Bks., Ltd., Ulverscroft Large Print Canada, Ltd.

—In at the Kill. 1979. 9.95 o.p. (*0-385-14913-1*) Doubleday Publishing.

—In at the Kill. 1980. 192p. pap. 3.95 o.p. (*0-14-005644-0*, Penguin Bks.) Viking Penguin.

—Last Will & Testament. 1981. 160p. pap. 1.95 o.p. (*0-553-14795-1*) Bantam Bks.

—Last Will & Testament. 1978. 7.95 o.p. (*0-385-14455-5*) Doubleday Publishing.

—Last Will & Testament. unabr. ed. 2001. audio 39.95 (*1-85496-692-8*, 980704) Soundings, Ltd. GBR. *Dist:* Ulverscroft Large Print Bks., Ltd.

—Last Will & Testament. l.t. ed. 1980. 284p. 12.00 o.p. (*0-7089-0505-6*, Ulverscroft) Thorpe, F. A. Pubs. GBR. *Dist:* Ulverscroft Large Print Bks., Ltd.

—Milk of Human Kindness. 1997. 278 p. (*0-7451-6950-3*) BBC Audiobooks America.

—The Milk of Human Kindness. l.t. ed. 1997. (G. K. Hall Nightingale Ser.). pap. 18.95 o.p. (*0-7838-1968-4*, Macmillan Reference USA) Gale Group.

—Milk of Human Kindness. unabr. ed. 1996. audio 54.95 (*0-7451-6653-9*, CAB 1269) BBC Audiobooks America.

—Murder of a Suicide. unabr. ed. 2001. audio 54.95 ISIS Audio Bks. GBR. *Dist:* Ulverscroft Large Print Bks., Ltd.

—Murder of a Suicide. l.t. ed. 1997. (Magna Large Print Ser.). 363p. 29.99 o.p. (*0-7505-1202-4*) Magna Large Print Bks. GBR. *Dist:* Ulverscroft Large Print Bks., Ltd.

—A Murder Too Many. unabr. ed. 2001. audio 54.95 (*1-85089-773-5*, 90103) ISIS Audio Bks. GBR. *Dist:* Ulverscroft Large Print Bks., Ltd.

—A Murder Too Many. l.t. ed. 1990. (Ulverscroft Large Print Ser.). 29.99 o.p. (*0-7089-2302-X*, Ulverscroft) Thorpe, F. A. Pubs. GBR. *Dist:* Ulverscroft Large Print Bks., Ltd., Ulverscroft Large Print Canada, Ltd.

—Neck in a Noose. l.t. ed. 1995. 288p. pap. 17.95 (*0-7838-1170-5*, Macmillan Reference USA) Gale Group.

—Ninth Life. 1992. 200p. reprint ed. 14.95 o.p. (*0-86220-832-7*, Black Dagger) BBC Audiobooks America.

—Ninth Life. l.t. ed. 2001. 265p. pap. 23.95 (*0-7838-9493-7*) Thorndike Pr.

—The Other Devil's Name. 1987. (Crime Club Ser.). 192p. 12.95 o.s.i (*0-385-23553-4*) Doubleday Publishing.

—The Other Devil's Name. l.t. ed. 1988. (Ulverscroft Large Print Ser.). 336p. 29.99 o.p. (*0-7089-1833-6*, Ulverscroft) Thorpe, F. A. Pubs. GBR. *Dist:* Ulverscroft Large Print Bks., Ltd., Ulverscroft Large Print Canada, Ltd.

—Remove the Bodies. unabr. ed. 1993. audio 54.95 (*0-7451-5922-2*, CAT 4046) BBC Audiobooks America.

—Remove the Bodies. l.t. ed. 1989. (Ulverscroft Large Print Ser.). 390p. 29.99 o.p. (*0-7089-1943-X*, Ulverscroft) Thorpe, F. A. Pubs. GBR. *Dist:* Ulverscroft Large Print Bks., Ltd., Ulverscroft Large Print Canada, Ltd.

—Root of All Evil. 1984. (Crime Club Ser.). 192p. 11.95 o.p. (*0-385-19580-X*) Doubleday Publishing.

—Root of All Evil. l.t. ed. 1985. (General Ser.). 312p. 14.95 o.p. (*0-8161-3879-6*, Macmillan Reference USA) Gale Group.

—Root of All Evil. 1993. (Audio Books Ser.). 46.95 o.p. incl. audio (*0-7838-8019-7*) Thorndike Pr.

—Seeing Is Believing. 1995. 192p. 21.95 o.s.i (*0-385-47543-8*) Doubleday Publishing.

—Smoke Without Fire. unabr. ed. 2001. audio 54.95 (*1-85089-878-2*, 92085) ISIS Audio Bks. GBR. *Dist:* Ulverscroft Large Print Bks., Ltd.

—Something Wicked. unabr. ed. 1991. (Audio Ser.). audio 54.95 (*0-7451-5923-0*, CAT 4069) BBC Audiobooks America.

—Something Wicked. 1984. (Crime Club Ser.). 192p. 11.95 o.p. (*0-385-19254-1*) Doubleday Publishing.

—Something Wicked. l.t. ed. 1985. (Nightingale Ser.). 253p. pap. 9.95 o.p. (*0-8161-3763-3*, Macmillan Reference USA) Gale Group.

—A Thief in the Night. l.t. ed. 1997. (G. K. Hall Nightingale Ser.). 230p. pap. 18.95 (*0-7838-8234-3*, Macmillan Reference USA) Gale Group.

—A Thief in the Night. unabr. ed. 1997. audio 44.95 (*1-85695-296-7*, 960410) ISIS Audio Bks. GBR. *Dist:* Ulverscroft Large Print Bks., Ltd.
—Thinner Than Water. unabr. ed. 1993. 39.95 incl. audio (*0-7451-5925-7*, CAT 4063) BBC Audiobooks America.
—Thinner Than Water. 1982. (Crime Club Ser.). 192p. 10.95 o.p. (*0-385-17946-4*) Doubleday Publishing.
—Thy Brother Death. 1993. 17.00 o.s.i (*0-385-48092-X*) Doubleday Publishing.
—Thy Brother Death. l.t. ed. 1994. (Ulverscroft Large Print Ser.). 336p. 29.99 o.p. (*0-7089-3202-9*, Ulverscroft) Thorpe, F. A. Pubs. GBR. *Dist:* Ulverscroft Large Print Bks., Ltd., Ulverscroft Large Print Canada, Ltd.
—Woman Slaughter. unabr. ed. 2001. audio 49.95 (*1-85089-823-5*, 20891) ISIS Audio Bks. GBR. *Dist:* Ulverscroft Large Print Bks., Ltd.
Fforde, Jasper. The Eyre Affair. l.t. ed. 2002. 576p. 28.95 (*0-7862-4293-0*) Gale Group.
—The Eyre Affair. 2003. 384p. pap. 14.00 (*0-14-200180-5*) Penguin Group (USA) Inc.
—The Eyre Affair. 2002. 272p. 23.95 (*0-670-03064-3*, Viking) Viking Penguin.
Fforde, Katie. The Rose Revived. unabr. ed. 1996. audio 84.95 (*0-7451-6656-3*, CAB 1272) BBC Audiobooks America.
—The Rose Revived. 2003. 352p. pap. (*0-09-944666-9*) Random Hse. of Canada, Ltd. CAN. *Dist:* Random Hse., Inc.
—The Rose Revived. 1996. 352p. 23.95 (*0-312-14040-1*) St. Martin's Pr.
—The Rose Revived. l.t. ed. 1996. (Ulverscroft Large Print Ser.). 688p. 29.99 o.p. (*0-7089-3644-X*, Ulverscroft) Thorpe, F. A. Pubs. GBR. *Dist:* Ulverscroft Large Print Bks., Ltd., Ulverscroft Large Print Canada, Ltd.
—Stately Pursuits. 2000. audio 56.95 (*0-7861-1575-0*, P2404) Blackstone Audio Bks., Inc.
—Stately Pursuits. 2003. 288p. pap. (*0-09-944668-5*) Random Hse. of Canada, Ltd. CAN. *Dist:* Random Hse., Inc.
—Stately Pursuits. unabr. ed. 1998. audio 70.00 (*0-7887-2608-0*, 95446E7) Recorded Bks., LLC.
—Stately Pursuits. 288p. 1999. pap. 13.95 (*0-312-20676-3*, Saint Martin's Griffin); 1998. 22.95 o.p. (*0-312-18668-1*) St. Martin's Pr.
—Stately Pursuits. l.t. ed. 1998. (Ulverscroft Large Print Ser.). 512p. 29.99 o.p. (*0-7089-3966-X*, Ulverscroft) Thorpe, F. A. Pubs. GBR. *Dist:* Ulverscroft Large Print Bks., Ltd., Ulverscroft Large Print Canada, Ltd.
—Wild Designs. unabr. ed. 1999. audio 56.95 (*0-7861-1490-8*, 2341) Blackstone Audio Bks., Inc.
—Wild Designs. 2003. pap. (*0-09-944667-7*) Random Hse. of Canada, Ltd. CAN. *Dist:* Random Hse., Inc.
—Wild Designs. unabr. ed. 1998. audio 80.00 (*0-7887-2189-5*, 95485E7) Recorded Bks., LLC.
—Wild Designs. 1998. 320p. pap. 12.95 (*0-312-19032-8*, Saint Martin's Griffin); 1997. 308p. 22.95 (*0-312-15693-6*) St. Martin's Pr.
—Wild Designs. l.t. ed. 1997. (Ulverscroft Large Print Ser.). 624p. 29.99 o.p. (*0-7089-3845-0*, Ulverscroft) Thorpe, F. A. Pubs. GBR. *Dist:* Ulverscroft Large Print Bks., Ltd., Ulverscroft Large Print Canada, Ltd.
Fielding, Helen. Bridget Jones: The Edge of Reason. l.t. ed. 2000. (Wheeler Large Print Book Ser.). 458p. 28.95 (*1-56895-893-5*, Wheeler Publishing, Inc.) Gale Group.
—Bridget Jones: The Edge of Reason. abr. ed. 2001. audio (*0-333-74611-2*) Macmillan U.K. GBR. *Dist:* Macmillan Publishing Co., Inc.
—Bridget Jones: The Edge of Reason. 2001. 352p. pap. 14.00 (*0-14-029847-9*) Penguin Group (USA) Inc.
—Bridget Jones: The Edge of Reason. unabr. ed. 2001. audio compact disk 97.00 (*0-7887-6169-2*, C1393) Recorded Bks., LLC.
—Bridget Jones: The Edge of Reason. 2000. 352p. 24.95 (*0-670-89296-3*, Penguin Bks.) Viking Penguin.
—Bridget Jones' Diary: A Novel. l.t. ed. (Thorndike/G. K. Hall Paperback Bestsellers Ser.). 413p. 1999. pap. 26.95 (*0-7862-1637-9*); 1998. 29.95 (*0-7862-1636-0*) Thorndike Pr.
—Bridget Jones's Diary: A Novel. movie tie-in ed. 2001. 288p. pap. 12.95 (*0-14-100019-8*) Penguin Group (USA) Inc.
—Bridget Jones's Diary: A Novel. abr. ed. 1998. audio 18.00 (*0-375-40478-3*, 396075); 2001. audio compact disk 21.00 (*0-375-41681-1*) Random Hse. Audio Publishing Group. (RH Audio).
—Bridget Jones's Diary: A Novel. unabr. ed. 1999. audio 54.00 (*0-7887-2917-9*, 95709E5) Recorded Bks., LLC.
—Bridget Jones's Diary: A Novel. 1999. 288p. 14.00 (*0-14-028009-X*); 1998. 320p. 22.95 (*0-670-88072-8*) Viking Penguin.
—Diario de Bridget Jones. 2000. Tr. of Bridget Jones's Diary: A Novel. (SPA.). 320p. 10.95 (*84-01-46117-0*) Distribooks, Inc.
—Le Journal de Bridget Jones. 2000. Tr. of Bridget Jones's Diary: A Novel. (FRE.). pap. 13.95 (*2-290-30039-X*) Distribooks, Inc.
—Das Tagebuch der Bridget Jones. 2000. Tr. of Bridget Jones's Diary: A Novel. (GER.). pap. 18.95 (*3-442-44392-X*) Distribooks, Inc.
Fielding, Henry. Adventures of Joseph Andrews. 1968. (Oxford World's Classics Ser.). 6.95 o.p. (*0-19-250334-0*) Oxford Univ. Pr., Inc.
—Amelia. unabr. ed. 1998. (YA). (gr. 10 up). audio 89.95 (*1-55685-523-0*) Audio Bk. Contractors, Inc.
—Amelia. 1978. reprint ed. 16.95 o.p. (*0-460-10852-2*) Biblio Distribution.
—Amelia. (Complete Works of Henry Fielding: Vol. 6). Pt. 1. 2001. 320p. reprint ed. pap. text 28.00 (*0-7426-5099-5*); Pt. 1. 1999. 320p. reprint ed. lib. bdg. 88.00 (*1-58201-099-4*); Pt. 2. 2001. 342p. pap. text 28.00 (*0-7426-5100-2*); Pt. 2. 1999. 342p. reprint ed. lib. bdg. 88.00 (*1-58201-100-1*) Classic Bks.
—Amelia. 1902. (YA). reprint ed. pap. text 38.00 (*1-4047-7836-5*) Classic Textbooks.
—Amelia. 1978. 15.50 o.p. (*0-460-00852-8*, Dutton) Dutton/Plume.
—Amelia. Blewett, David, ed. & intro. by. 1987. (Penguin Classics Ser.). 608p. pap. 8.95 o.p. (*0-14-043229-9*, Penguin Classics) Viking Penguin.
—Amelia. Battestin, Martin C., ed. 1983. (Works of Henry Fielding Ser.). (Illus.). 693p. 50.00 o.p. (*0-8195-5084-1*); pap. 14.95 o.p. (*0-8195-6114-2*) Wesleyan Univ. Pr.
—The History of the Adventures of Joseph Andrews & His Friend Mr. Andrew Adams. (Complete Works of Henry Fielding: Vol. 1). 394p. reprint ed. 1999. lib. bdg. 88.00 (*1-58201-094-3*); Vol. 1. 2001. pap. text 28.00 (*0-7426-5094-4*) Classic Bks.
—The History of Tom Jones, a Foundling. 1987. (Illus.). 88p. pap. 4.00 o.p. (*0-88680-269-5*) Clark, I. E. Pubns.
—The History of Tom Jones, a Foundling. (Complete Works of Henry Fielding: Vol. 3). reprint ed. Pt. 1. 1999. 366p. lib. bdg. 88.00 (*1-58201-096-X*); Pt. 2. 2001. 350p. pap. text 28.00 (*0-7426-5097-9*); Pt. 2. 1999. 350p. lib. bdg. 88.00 (*1-58201-097-8*); Pt. 3. 2001. 366p. pap. text 28.00 (*0-7426-5096-0*); Pt. 3. 2001. 376p. pap. text 28.00 (*0-7426-5098-7*); Pt. 3. 1999. 376p. lib. bdg. 88.00 (*1-58201-098-6*) Classic Bks.
—The History of Tom Jones, a Foundling. Bowers, Fredson, ed. (Works of Henry Fielding Ser.). (Illus.). 1975. 1023p. pap. 29.95 (*0-8195-6048-0*); Set. 1977. 1090p. lib. bdg. 75.00 o.p. (*0-8195-4068-4*) Wesleyan Univ. Pr.
—Joseph Andrews. 1980. 401p. 40.00 o.p. (*0-913720-25-9*, Standstone Pr.); 60.00 o.p. (*0-913720-24-0*) Beil, Frederic C. Pub., Inc.
—Joseph Andrews. unabr. ed. 2001. (Dover Thrift Editions Ser.). xvii, 248p. pap. 2.50 (*0-486-41588-0*) Dover Pubns., Inc.
—Joseph Andrews, 001. Battestin, Martin C., ed. 1961. (C). pap. 13.56 o.s.i (*0-395-05157-6*) Houghton Mifflin Co.
—Joseph Andrews. 1998. (Cloth Bound Pocket Ser.). 7.95 (*3-8290-0884-8*, 520655) Konemann.
—Joseph Andrews. 1992. (York Notes Ser.). pap. text (*0-582-78174-4*) Longman Publishing Group.
—Joseph Andrews. 1976. mass mkt. 1.25 o.p. (*0-451-07379-7*, Signet Bks.); 1968. mass mkt. 0.50 o.p. (*0-451-50061-X*, Signet Classics); 1968. mass mkt. 0.60 o.p. (*0-451-50448-8*, Signet Classics); 1961. mass mkt. 1.50 o.p. (*0-451-51061-5*, Signet Classics); 1961. mass mkt. 1.95 o.p. (*0-451-51358-4*, Signet Classics); 1961. mass mkt. 2.25 o.p. (*0-451-51585-4*, Signet Classics); 1961. mass mkt. 2.75 o.p. (*0-451-51819-5*, Signet Classics); 1961. mass mkt. 0.95 o.p. (*0-451-50776-2*, Signet Classics); 1961. mass mkt. 0.75 o.p. (*0-451-50620-0*, Signet Classics) NAL.
—Joseph Andrews. 1958. (C). pap. 7.50 (*0-393-00274-8*) Norton, W. W. & Co., Inc.
—Joseph Andrews. l.t. ed. 2000. (Jane Austen Works: Vol. 3). 632p. pap. 39.99 (*1-57646-339-7*) Quiet Vision Publishing.
—Joseph Andrews. 1950. pap. 3.50 o.p. (*0-394-30916-2*, T16) Random Hse., Inc.
—Joseph Andrews. 1985. pap. 0.95 o.s.i (*0-671-47881-8*, Washington Square Pr.) Simon & Schuster.
—Joseph Andrews. Brissenden, R. E., ed. 1977. (Penguin Classics Ser.). 352p. pap. 9.95 o.s.i (*0-14-043114-4*, Penguin Classics) Viking Penguin.
—Joseph Andrews. Battestin, Martin C., ed. 1985. (Works of Henry Fielding Ser.). (Illus.). 437p. pap. 24.95 o.p. (*0-8195-6095-2*) Wesleyan Univ. Pr.
—Joseph Andrews. Battestin, Martin, ed. 1985. (Works of Henry Fielding Ser.). (Illus.). 437p. lib. bdg. 60.00 o.p. (*0-8195-3070-0*) Wesleyan Univ. Pr.
—Joseph Andrews & Shamela. 1978. 8.00 o.p. (*0-460-00467-0*); 1976. 4.50 o.p. (*0-460-01467-6*) Dutton/Plume. (Dutton).
—Joseph Andrews & Shamela. (Oxford World's Classics Ser.). 1988. 420p. pap. 6.95 o.p. (*0-19-281550-4*); 2nd ed. 1999. (Illus.). 464p. pap. 9.95 (*0-19-283343-X*) Oxford Univ. Pr., Inc.
—Joseph Andrews & Shamela. Humphreys, Arthur Raleigh, ed. 1993. 412p. pap. 7.95 (*0-460-87385-7*, Everyman's Classic Library in Paperback) Tuttle Publishing.
—Joseph Andrews & Shamela. 1992. 422p. pap. 7.95 o.p. (*0-460-87115-3*, Everyman's Classic Library in Paperback) Tuttle Publishing.
—Joseph Andrews & Shamela. 1999. (Classics Ser.). 432p. 9.95 (*0-14-043386-4*, Penguin Classics) Viking Penguin.
—Tom Jones. 1950. (Modern Library College Editions Ser.). (C). pap. text 12.75 net. o.p. (*0-07-553576-9*, T15) McGraw-Hill Cos., The.
—Tom Jones. Baker, Sheridan, ed. 1973. (Critical Editions Ser.). (C). pap. text o.p. (*0-393-09394-8*) Norton, W. W. & Co., Inc.
—Tom Jones. 2nd ed. 1994. (Critical Editions Ser.). 804p. (C). pap. text 17.05 (*0-393-96594-5*, Norton Paperbacks) Norton, W. W. & Co., Inc.
—Tom Jones. Bender, John & Stern, Simon, eds. 1996. (Oxford World's Classics Ser.). (Illus.). 960p. pap. 5.95 o.p. (*0-19-283110-0*) Oxford Univ. Pr., Inc.
—Tom Jones. 1991. (Everyman's Library: Vol. 28). 1200p. 20.00 (*0-679-40569-0*); 1985. 1003p. 10.95 o.s.i (*0-394-60519-5*) Random Hse., Inc.
—Tom Jones. Mutter, Reg, ed. 1989. (English Library). 912p. pap. 6.95 o.p. (*0-14-013117-5*, Penguin Classics) Viking Penguin.
Fielding, Henry & Bowers, Fredson. The History of Tom Jones, a Foundling. 1983. E-Book 22.95 (*0-585-38879-2*) netLibrary, Inc.
Fielding, Sarah. The Adventures of David Simple & Volume the Last. Sabor, Peter, ed. 1998. (Eighteenth-Century Novels by Women Ser.). 416p. (C). reprint ed. 45.00 o.p. (*0-8131-2055-1*); (Illus.). pap. 17.95 (*0-8131-0945-0*) Univ. Pr. of Kentucky.
Figes, Eva. Nelly's Version. 2002. 218p. pap. 12.50 (*1-56478-313-8*) Dalkey Archive Pr.
Finney, Patricia. Unicorn's Blood. 1998. 384p. pap. 14.00 (*0-312-20039-0*); pap. (*0-312-20243-1*); 384p. 25.00 o.p. (*0-312-18201-5*) Picador.
Fitt, Mary. Death & the Pleasant Voices. 1984. (Detective Stories Ser.). 224p. reprint ed. pap. 5.95 (*0-486-24603-5*) Dover Pubns., Inc.
Fitzgerald, Ellen. Ardent Apparitions. 1992. (Regency Romance Ser.). 224p. 19.95 o.p. (*0-8027-1209-6*) Walker & Co.
—The Damsels from Derbyshire. 1992. 224p. 19.95 o.s.i (*0-8027-1183-9*) Walker & Co.
Fitzgerald, Penelope. At Freddie's. 1985. 324p. 14.95 o.p. (*0-87923-439-3*) Godine, David R. Pub.
—At Freddie's. 1999. 160p. pap. 12.00 (*0-395-95618-8*, Mariner Bks.) Houghton Mifflin Co. Trade & Reference Div.
—At Freddie's. l.t. ed. 2000. 226p. (*0-7540-4074-7*); (*0-7540-4075-5*) Thorndike Pr.
—The Beginning of Spring. 1989. 192p. 18.95 o.p. (*0-8050-0981-7*) Holt, Henry & Co.
—The Beginning of Spring. l.t. ed. 1990. 240p. 19.95 o.p. (*1-85089-353-5*) ISIS Large Print Bks. GBR. *Dist:* Transaction Pubs.
—The Bookshop. 1978. 118p. (*0-7156-1320-0*) Duckworth, Gerald & Co., Ltd.
—The Bookshop. l.t. ed. 1999. (General Ser.). 168p. pap. 21.95 o.p. (*0-7862-2167-4*); (*0-7540-3910-2*); (*0-7540-3909-9*) Thorndike Pr.
—The Bookshop: A Novel. 1997. 128p. pap. 11.00 (*0-395-86946-3*, Mariner Bks.) Houghton Mifflin Co. Trade & Reference Div.
—The Gate of Angels. 1993. 352p. pap. 9.95 o.p. (*0-88184-960-X*, Carroll & Graf Pubs.) Avalon Publishing Group.
—The Gate of Angels. 1991. 176p. 19.00 o.s.i (*0-385-42150-8*) Doubleday Publishing.
—The Gate of Angels. l.t. ed. 1992. (Ulverscroft Large Print Ser.). 288p. 29.99 o.p. (*0-7089-2572-3*, Ulverscroft) Thorpe, F. A. Pubs. GBR. *Dist:* Ulverscroft Large Print Bks., Ltd., Ulverscroft Large Print Canada, Ltd.
—The Gates of Angels. unabr. ed. 2000. audio 32.95 Blackstone Audio Bks., Inc.
—The Golden Child. 1999. 192p. pap. 12.00 (*0-395-95619-6*) Houghton Mifflin Co.
—The Golden Child. l.t. ed. 2000. (General Ser.). xix, 231p. 23.95 (*0-7862-2809-1*); (Illus.). 266p. pap. 23.95 (*0-7862-2808-3*) Thorndike Pr.
—The Golden Child. l.t. ed. 2000. 266p. (*0-7540-4257-X*); (*0-7540-4258-8*) Thorndike Pr.
—The Means of Escape: Stories. 2000. 117p. 20.00 (*0-618-10455-0*) Houghton Mifflin Co.
—The Means of Escape: Stories. 2000. (Illus.). 128p. 18.00 (*0-618-07994-7*, Mariner Bks.) Houghton Mifflin Co. Trade & Reference Div.
—The Means of Escape: Stories. 2001. (Illus.). 160p. pap. 11.00 (*0-618-15450-7*, Mariner Bks.) Houghton Mifflin Co. Trade & Reference Div.
—The Means of Escape: Stories. l.t. ed. 2001. 134p. pap. 22.95 (*0-7862-3342-7*); 120p. (*0-7540-4513-7*); 120p. (*0-7540-4514-5*) Thorndike Pr.
Flagg, William G. The Clam Lover's Cookbook. 3rd ed. 1983. (Illus.). 160p. (Orig.). pap. 8.95 o.p. (*0-88427-054-8*) North River Pr. Publishing Corp., The.
Fleming, James. The Temple of Optimism. 2000. 315p. 23.95 (*0-7868-6676-4*) Hyperion Pr.
Flusfeder, D. L. Man Kills Woman. 1993. 358p. 21.00 o.p. (*0-374-20162-5*) Farrar, Straus & Giroux.
Foerster, Werner. From the Exile to Christ: Historical Introduction to Palestinian Judaism. Harris, Gordon E., ed. 1964. 264p. pap. 3.95 o.p. (*0-8006-0978-6*, 1-978, Fortress Pr.) Augsburg Fortress, Pubs.
Foley, Gaelen. The Duke. 2000. 416p. mass mkt. 6.99 (*0-449-00636-0*, Ivy Bks.) Ballantine Bks.
Follett, Ken. Paper Money. 2nd ed. 1987. 216p. reprint ed. 15.95 o.p. (*0-688-05840-X*, Morrow, William & Co.) Morrow/Avon.
—Paper Money. 1987. mass mkt. 3.95 o.p. (*0-451-15002-3*); 256p. mass mkt. 4.50 o.p. (*0-451-15904-7*); 272p. mass mkt. 7.99 (*0-451-16730-9*) NAL. (Signet Bks.).
Following Father Brown. unabr. ed. Incl. Absence of Mr. Glass. audio o.p. Blast of the Book. audio o.p. Man in the Passage. audio o.p. Oracle of the Dog. audio o.p. 1986. (Father Brown Mystery Ser.). 1986. Set audio 16.95 o.p. (*1-55656-008-7*) Dercum Audio.
Forbes, Bryan. A Spy at Twilight. 1991. 432p. reprint ed. mass mkt. 5.99 o.s.i (*0-451-40263-4*, Onyx) NAL.
—A Spy at Twilight. 1993. 3.99 o.p. (*0-517-09107-0*) Random Hse. Value Publishing.
Forbes, Leslie. Fish, Blood & Bone. 2002. 448p. pap. 13.95 (*0-553-38163-6*) Bantam Bks.
—Fish, Blood & Bone. 2000. (*0-374-92746-4*) Farrar, Straus & Giroux.
Ford, Ford Madox. Ladies Whose Bright Eyes: A Romance. 1987. 363p. pap. 9.50 o.p. (*0-88001-088-6*) HarperCollins Pubs.
Ford, Margaret L. Do Try to Speak As We Do: The Diary of an American Au Pair. 2001. 346p. 23.95 (*0-312-26866-1*) St. Martin's Pr.
Ford, Marjorie Leet. The Diary of an American Au Pair: A Novel. 2003. 352p. reprint ed. pap. 13.00 (*1-4000-3264-4*, Anchor) Knopf Publishing Group.
Forrester, Anouchka Grose. Ringing for You. l.t. ed. 2000. (Basic Ser.). 311p. 27.95 (*0-7862-2412-6*) Thorndike Pr.
—Ringing for You: A Love Story with Interruptions. 208p. 2000. pap. 15.95 (*0-671-03439-1*, Pocket); 1999. (Illus.). 22.00 o.s.i (*0-684-86292-1*, Scribner) Simon & Schuster.
Forster, E. M. Howard's End. Date not set. lib. bdg. 27.95 (*0-8488-1664-1*) Amereon, Ltd.
—Howard's End. 1985. (Bantam Classics Ser.). 288p. mass mkt. 4.99 (*0-553-21208-7*) Bantam Bks.
—Howard's End. 2002. (Thrift Editions Ser.). (Illus.). 256p. pap. 3.00 (*0-486-42454-5*) Dover Pubns., Inc.
—Howard's End. Stallybrass, Oliver, ed. 1978. (Abinger Edition of E. M. Forster Ser.). 276p. text 29.50 o.p. (*0-8419-5806-8*) Holmes & Meier Pubs., Inc.
—Howard's End. 2002. 344p. 96.99 (*1-4043-0824-5*); per. 91.99 (*1-4043-0825-3*) IndyPublish.com.
—Howard's End. 1954. pap. 4.95 o.p. (*0-394-70007-4*, Vintage) Knopf Publishing Group.
—Howard's End. (Signet Classics). 1998. 288p. mass mkt. 4.95 o.s.i (*0-451-52717-8*, Signet Classics); 1992. 288p. mass mkt. 4.99 o.s.i (*0-451-17429-1*, Signet Bks.); 1986. 464p. mass mkt. 6.95 (*0-451-52141-2*, Signet Classics) NAL.
—Howard's End. 1999. (Twelve-Point Ser.). 330p. lib. bdg. 25.00 (*1-58287-100-0*) North Bks.
—Howard's End. 2001. E-Book 4.95 (*0-679-64145-9*, Modern Library) Random House Adult Trade Publishing Group.
—Howard's End. 1991. (Everyman's Library: Vol. 25). 400p. 19.00 (*0-679-40668-9*) Random Hse., Inc.
—Howard's End. 1997. pap. text 17.95 o.p. (*0-312-15464-X*) St. Martin's Pr.
—Howard's End. 2000. (Signature Classics Ser.). 352p. (*1-58279-070-1*) Trident Pr. International.
—Howard's End. 2000. (Classics Ser.). (Illus.). 352p. 11.00 (*0-14-118213-X*, Penguin Classics) Viking Penguin.
—Howards End. 2003. (Barnes & Noble Classics Ser.). 368p. pap. 6.95 (*1-59308-022-0*) Fine Communications.
—Howards End. 1989. (Vintage International Ser.). 368p. pap. 10.00 (*0-679-72255-6*, Vintage) Knopf Publishing Group.
—Howards End. annuals 1999. (Modern Library Ser.). 368p. pap. 9.95 (*0-375-75376-1*, Modern Library) Random House Adult Trade Publishing Group.
—Howard's End, Set. unabr. ed. 1992. audio 53.95 (*1-55685-261-4*) Audio Bk. Contractors, Inc.
—Howard's End. unabr. ed. 1992. audio 56.95 (*0-7861-0376-0*, 1331) Blackstone Audio Bks., Inc.

—Howard's End. unabr. collector's ed. 1994. audio 72.00 (0-7366-2682-4, 3418) Books on Tape, Inc.

—Howard's End. 1981. 391p. reprint ed. lib. bdg. 25.95 (0-89966-301-X) Buccaneer Bks., Inc.

—Howard's End. unabr. ed. 2000. audio 69.95 (1-56054-851-7, SAB 044) Chivers Audio Bks. GBR. *Dist:* BBC Audiobooks America.

—Howard's End. reprint ed. lib. bdg. 98.00 (0-7426-3108-7); 2001. pap. text 28.00 (0-7426-8108-4) Classic Bks.

—Howard's End. l.t. ed. 1993. (General Ser.). 474p. 22.95 o.p. (0-8161-5652-2, Macmillan Reference USA) Gale Group.

—Howard's End. l.t. ed. 1999. 457p. lib. bdg. 26.00 (0-939495-74-0) North Bks.

—Howard's End. abr. ed. 1993. (Classics on Cassette). 2p. 16.00 o.p. incl. audio (0-453-00809-7, 390942) Penguin/HighBridge.

—Howard's End, unabr. ed. 1993. audio 78.00 (1-55690-888-1, 93330E7) Recorded Bks., LLC.

—Howard's End. deluxe ed. 2000. (Signature Classics Ser.). (Illus.). 352p. (1-58279-076-0) Trident Pr. International.

—Howard's End: Authoritative Text, Textual Appendix, Backgrounds & Contexts, Criticism. Armstrong, Paul B., ed. 1998. (Critical Editions Ser.). (C). pap. text 14.20 (0-393-97011-6) Norton, W. W. & Co., Inc.

—Howard's End: Case Studies. 1996. (Case Studies in Contemporary Criticism). 512p. 49.95 (0-312-16292-8) Palgrave Macmillan.

—Howard's End: Complete, Authoritative Text with Biographical & Historical Contexts, Critical History, & Essays from Five Contemporary Critical Perspectives. Duckworth, Alistair M., ed. 1996. (Case Studies in Contemporary Criticism). 499p. (C). pap. text 10.00 (0-312-11182-7) Bedford/Saint Martin's.

—Howard's End & Other Stories. 1997. (Giant Courage Classics Ser.). 444p. text 8.98 o.p. (0-7624-0176-1, Courage Bks.) Running Pr. Bk. Pubs.

—The Longest Journey. 1997. 304p. mass mkt. 4.95 o.s.i (0-553-21455-1) Bantam Bks.

—The Longest Journey. 1989. reprint ed. lib. bdg. 27.95 (0-89966-632-9) Buccaneer Bks., Inc.

—The Longest Journey. reprint ed. lib. bdg. 98.00 (0-7426-3113-3); 2001. 320p. pap. text 28.00 (0-7426-8113-0) Classic Bks.

—The Longest Journey. text (0-7131-6421-2) Hodder Arnold GBR. *Dist:* Routledge.

—The Longest Journey. Heine, Elizabeth, ed. 1985. (Abinger Edition of E. M. Forster Ser.: Vol. 2). 400p. 69.50 (0-8419-5832-7) Holmes & Meier Pubs., Inc.

—The Longest Journey. 2002. 284p. 19.99 (1-4043-1380-X); per. 14.99 (1-4043-1381-8) IndyPublish.com.

—The Longest Journey. 1993. 320p. pap. 13.00 (0-679-74815-6, Vintage) Knopf Publishing Group.

—The Longest Journey. 1962. pap. 9.00 o.p. (0-394-70040-6) Knopf, Alfred A. Inc.

—The Longest Journey. 1999. 330p. reprint ed. lib. bdg. 29.95 (0-7351-0068-3) Replica Bks.

—Maurice. 1993. 256p. pap. 13.00 (0-393-31032-9) Norton, W. W. & Co., Inc.

—A Room with a View. unabr. ed. 2000. audio compact disk 56.00 (0-7861-9926-1, z1285) Blackstone Audio Bks., Inc.

—A Room with a View. Stallybrass, Oliver, ed. 1978. (Abinger Edition of E. M. Forster Ser.). text 29.50 o.p. (0-8419-5804-1) Holmes & Meier Pubs., Inc.

—Where Angels Fear to Tread. l.t. ed. 1993. 20.95 o.p. (0-7927-1410-5); pap. 18.95 o.p. (0-7927-1409-1) BBC Audiobooks America.

—Where Angels Fear to Tread. 1993. (Thrift Editions Ser.). 128p. reprint ed. pap. 2.00 (0-486-27791-7) Dover Pubns., Inc.

—Where Angels Fear to Tread. 1992. 192p. pap. 9.95 (0-679-73634-4, Vintage) Knopf Publishing Group.

Forster, Margaret. Lady's Maid. 1992. 560p. pap. 25.00 (0-449-90715-5) Ballantine Bks.

Forsythe, Malcolm. Only Living Witness. l.t. ed. 2001. (Magna Large Print Ser.). 288p. 31.99 (0-7505-1623-2) Magna Large Print Bks. GBR. *Dist:* Ulverscroft Large Print Bks., Ltd., Ulverscroft Large Print Canada, Ltd.

—Only Living Witness. 224p. 26.00 (0-7278-5520-4) Severn Hse. Pubs., Ltd.

Fowles, John. The French Lieutenant's Woman. 1994. reprint ed. lib. bdg. 32.95 (1-56849-280-4) Buccaneer Bks., Inc.

—The French Lieutenant's Woman. 1998. pap. 13.95 (0-316-18989-8, Back Bay); 1969. 467p. 29.95 o.p. (0-316-29099-8); Vol. 1. 1998. 480p. pap. 14.95 (0-316-29116-1) Little Brown & Co.

—The French Lieutenant's Woman. 1981. mass mkt. 3.50 o.p. (0-451-11095-1, Signet Bks.); 1981. mass mkt. 3.95 o.p. (0-451-13598-9, Signet Bks.); 1981. 368p. mass mkt. 6.99 o.s.i (0-451-16375-3); 1971. mass mkt. 1.50 o.p. (0-451-04479-7, Signet Bks.); 1970. mass mkt. 2.50 o.p. (0-451-08535-3, Signet Bks.); 1970. mass mkt. 1.75 o.p. (0-451-06484-4, Signet Bks.); 1970. mass mkt. 2.25 o.p. (0-451-08066-1, Signet Bks.); 1970. mass mkt. 2.95 o.p. (0-451-09003-9, Signet Bks.) NAL.

—A Maggot. 1993. 464p. pap. 14.95 o.p. (0-452-27094-4, Meridian Bks.) Dutton/Plume.

—A Maggot. 1998. 464p. pap. 21.99 (0-316-29049-1); 1985. 19.95 o.p. (0-316-28994-9); 1985. 100.00 o.s.i (0-316-29115-3) Little Brown & Co.

—A Maggot. 1986. 25p. mass mkt. 4.50 o.p. (0-451-14476-7, Signet Bks.) NAL.

Fox, Ronald. Oaken Rings. 2000. (Illus.). 247p. pap. 17.95 o.p. (1-929925-44-1) FirstPublish.

Frame, Ronald. Sandmouth. 1988. 476p. 19.95 o.s.i (0-394-56357-3) Knopf, Alfred A. Inc.

Francis, Clare. Betrayal. 2004. 336p. pap. 14.00 (0-425-19425-6) Berkley Publishing Group.

—Betrayal. 2002. 373p. 25.00 (1-56947-290-4) Soho Pr., Inc.

—Betrayal. l.t. ed. 1996. (Charnwood Large Print Ser.). 560p. 29.99 o.p. (0-7089-8901-2, Ulverscroft) Thorpe, F. A. Pubs. GBR. *Dist:* Ulverscroft Large Print Bks., Ltd., Ulverscroft Large Print Canada, Ltd.

—A Dark Devotion: A Novel. 2003. 304p. 25.00 (1-56947-325-0) Soho Pr., Inc.

—Deceit. 2003. 384p. reprint ed. pap. 14.00 (0-425-18844-2) Berkley Publishing Group.

Francis, Dick. Blood Sport. 1995. audio 29.95 (0-7451-2831-9) BBC Audiobooks America.

—Blood Sport. 1988. mass mkt. 5.95 o.s.i (0-449-21262-9, Fawcett) Ballantine Bks.

—Blood Sport. 1999. 288p. mass mkt. 6.99 (0-515-12651-9, Jove) Berkley Publishing Group.

—Blood Sport, unabr. ed. 1996. 5p. audio 39.95 (0-7861-0941-6, 753865) Blackstone Audio Bks., Inc.

—Blood Sport. 1994. reprint ed. lib. bdg. 32.95 o.p. (1-56849-282-0) Buccaneer Bks., Inc.

—Blood Sport. unabr. ed. 2000. audio 49.95 (0-7451-5947-8, CAB 087) Chivers Audio Bks. GBR. *Dist:* BBC Audiobooks America.

—Blood Sport. l.t. ed. 1991. 16.95 o.p. (0-8161-5227-6); lib. bdg. 22.95 (0-8161-5226-8) Gale Group. (Macmillan Reference USA).

—Blood Sport. unabr. ed. 1991. audio 51.00 (1-55690-059-7, 91116E7) Recorded Bks., LLC.

—Blood Sport. 1984. mass mkt. 5.95 (0-671-55694-0); 1983. mass mkt. 3.50 o.s.i (0-671-50738-9) Simon & Schuster. (Pocket).

—Blood Sport. l.t. ed. 1972. 12.00 o.p. (0-85456-106-4, Ulverscroft) Thorpe, F. A. Pubs. GBR. *Dist:* Ulverscroft Large Print Bks., Ltd.

—Bolt. 1996. audio 29.95 (0-7451-2842-4) BBC Audiobooks America.

—Bolt. 1988. 336p. mass mkt. 5.95 o.s.i (0-449-21239-4, Fawcett) Ballantine Bks.

—Bolt. unabr. ed. 1993. (Kit Fielding Adventure Ser.: Bk. 2). audio 49.95 (0-7451-4169-2, CAB 852) Chivers Audio Bks. GBR. *Dist:* BBC Audiobooks America.

—Bolt. abr. ed. 1990. 2p. audio 16.99 (0-88646-219-3, 7219) Durkin Hayes Publishing Ltd.

—Bolt. l.t. ed. 1988. 388p. 19.95 o.p. (0-8161-4329-3); 12.95 o.p. (0-8161-4330-7) Gale Group. (Macmillan Reference USA).

—Bolt. 1987. 320p. 17.95 o.s.i (0-399-13226-0, G. P. Putnam's Sons) Penguin Putnam Bks. for Young Readers.

—Bolt. unabr. ed. 1999. audio 51.00 (0-7887-2937-3, 95719E7); audio compact disk 66.00 (0-7887-3435-0, C1041E7) Recorded Bks., LLC.

—Bonecrack. l.t. ed. 1993. pap. 16.95 o.p. (0-7927-1598-5); 18.95 o.p. (0-7927-1599-3); audio 54.95 (0-7451-5948-6) BBC Audiobooks America.

—Bonecrack. 1993. 256p. mass mkt. 6.99 o.s.i (0-449-22115-6, Fawcett) Ballantine Bks.

—Bonecrack. unabr. ed. 1991. audio 42.00 (0-7366-2039-7, 2853) Books on Tape, Inc.

—Bonecrack. 1972. (Harper Novel of Suspense Ser.). 208p. 8.95 o.p. (0-06-011319-7) HarperCollins Pubs.

—Bonecrack. 1991. mass mkt. 4.95 (0-671-74671-5); 1990. mass mkt. 4.50 (0-671-70467-2); 1983. mass mkt. 3.50 (0-671-50739-7); 1982. mass mkt. 2.95 o.s.i (0-671-45459-5) Simon & Schuster. (Pocket).

—Bonecrack. l.t. ed. 1974. 12.00 o.p. (0-85456-292-3, Ulverscroft) Thorpe, F. A. Pubs. GBR. *Dist:* Ulverscroft Large Print Bks., Ltd.

—Break In. unabr. ed. 1994. audio 69.95 (0-7451-4225-7, CAB 908); Set. 1998. (Chivers Word for Word Audio Ser.: Vol. 168). audio 34.95 (0-7540-7520-6) BBC Audiobooks America.

—Break In. 1987. 384p. mass mkt. 5.99 o.s.i (0-449-20755-2, Fawcett) Ballantine Bks.

—Break In. abr. ed. 1987. (gr. 8-10). pap. 29.99 incl. audio (0-88646-824-8, R7128); 1986. 2p. audio 16.99 (0-88646-128-6, 7128) Durkin Hayes Publishing Ltd.

—Break In. l.t. ed. 1987. (General Ser.). 18.95 o.p. (0-8161-4161-4); pap. 11.95 o.p. (0-8161-4162-2) Gale Group. (Macmillan Reference USA).

—Break In. 2001. 17.95 (0-399-13685-1) Penguin Group (USA) Inc.

—Break In. 1986. 17.95 o.p. (0-399-13121-3, G. P. Putnam's Sons) Penguin Putnam Bks. for Young Readers.

—Break In. unabr. ed. 1999. audio compact disk 73.00 (0-7887-3717-1, C1074E7) Recorded Bks., LLC.

—Come to Grief. 1996. 384p. mass mkt. 6.99 (0-515-11952-0, Jove) Berkley Publishing Group.

—Come to Grief. unabr. ed. 1996. audio 56.00 (0-7366-3274-3, 3930) Books on Tape, Inc.

—Come to Grief. 1995. 320p. 23.95 o.p. (0-399-14082-4, G. P. Putnam's Sons); o.p. (0-399-19295-6) Penguin Group (USA) Inc.

—Come to Grief. unabr. ed. audio. 2000. audio 70.00 (0-7887-0467-2, 94660E7) Recorded Bks., LLC.

—Come to Grief. abr. ed. 1999. pap. 9.98 incl. audio (0-671-04422-2); 1995. audio 18.00 (0-671-53629-X, 393277) Simon & Schuster Audio. (Simon & Schuster Audioworks).

—Come to Grief. l.t. ed. 1996. (Paperback Bestsellers Ser.). 402p. pap. 26.95 (0-7838-1509-3) Thorndike Pr.

—Come to Grief: International Edition. 1996. 6.99 o.s.i (0-515-11937-7, Jove) Berkley Publishing Group.

—Come to Grief: International Edition. l.t. ed. 1995. (Core Collection). 402p. 29.95 (0-7838-1508-5) Thorndike Pr.

—Dead Cert. 1987. mass mkt. 6.99 o.s.i (0-449-21263-7, Fawcett) Ballantine Bks.

—Dead Cert. 288p. 2004. mass mkt. 6.99 (0-425-19497-3); 2000. mass mkt. 6.99 (0-515-12726-4, Jove) Berkley Publishing Group.

—Dead Cert. unabr. ed. 2000. audio 49.95 (0-7451-6828-0, CAB 437) Chivers Audio Bks. GBR. *Dist:* BBC Audiobooks America.

—Dead Cert. l.t. ed. 1994. 365p. 22.95 (0-8161-5784-7, Macmillan Reference USA) Gale Group.

—Dead Cert. Barzun, Jacques & Taylor, W. H., eds. 1983. (Crime Fiction 1950-1975 Ser.). 220p. lib. bdg. 18.00 o.p. (0-8240-4991-8) Garland Publishing, Inc.

—Dead Cert. 1990. audio 15.95; audio 16.00 o.s.i (1-55994-142-1, CPN 2139) HarperTrade. (HarperAudio).

—Dead Cert, unabr. ed. 1996. audio 51.00 Recorded Bks., LLC.

—Dead Cert; Nerve; For Kicks. 1996. mass mkt. 7.99 o.s.i (0-449-28768-8, Fawcett) Ballantine Bks.

—Decider. 1995. 352p. mass mkt. 6.99 (0-515-11617-3, Jove) Berkley Publishing Group.

—Decider. unabr. ed. 1994. audio 56.00 (0-7366-2771-5, 3491) Books on Tape, Inc.

—Decider. l.t. ed. 1995. 399p. pap. 19.95 o.p. (0-8161-5914-9); 1994. 429p. pap. 25.95 o.p. (0-8161-5913-0) Gale Group. (Macmillan Reference USA).

—Decider. 1993. 320p. 22.95 o.p. (0-399-13871-4, G. P. Putnam's Sons) Penguin Group (USA) Inc.

—Decider. unabr. ed. 1994. audio 60.00 (0-7887-0022-7, 94221E7) Recorded Bks., LLC.

—Decider. 1999. audio 9.98 (0-671-04423-0); Set. 1993. audio 17.00 (0-671-87972-3, 390637) Simon & Schuster Audio. (Simon & Schuster Audioworks).

—Decider: Open Market Edition. 1994. mass mkt. 5.99 o.p. (0-449-22348-5, Fawcett) Ballantine Bks.

—Driving Force. 1993. 384p. mass mkt. 6.99 (0-449-22139-3, Fawcett) Ballantine Bks.

—Driving Force. unabr. ed. 1994. audio 64.00 (0-7366-2613-1, 3355) Books on Tape, Inc.

—Driving Force. abr. ed. 1992. audio 17.00 o.p. (1-55994-537-0, HarperAudio) HarperTrade.

—Driving Force. 1992. 320p. 21.95 o.p. (0-399-13776-9, G. P. Putnam's Sons) Penguin Group (USA) Inc.

—Driving Force. unabr. ed. 1993. audio 60.00 (1-55690-788-5, 93107E7) Recorded Bks., LLC.

—Enquiry. 1987. 280p. mass mkt. 6.99 o.s.i (0-449-21268-8, Fawcett) Ballantine Bks.

—Enquiry. 2000. 272p. mass mkt. 6.99 (0-515-12867-8, Jove) Berkley Publishing Group.

—Enquiry. unabr. ed. 1996. audio 32.95 (0-7861-0959-9, 1736) Blackstone Audio Bks., Inc.

—Enquiry. unabr. ed. 1993. audio 49.95 (0-7451-5949-4, CAB 051) Chivers Audio Bks. GBR. *Dist:* BBC Audiobooks America.

—Enquiry. l.t. ed. 1995. 305p. lib. bdg. 22.95 o.p. (0-7838-1142-X, Macmillan Reference USA) Gale Group.

—Enquiry. unabr. ed. 1990. audio 44.00 (1-55690-169-0, 90088E7) Recorded Bks., LLC.

—Enquiry. 1984. mass mkt. 3.50 (0-671-54362-8); 1981. pap. 2.95 o.s.i (0-671-44926-5) Simon & Schuster. (Pocket).

—Enquiry. unabr. ed. 1983. audio 53.95 o.p. (0-8161-9771-7) Thorndike Pr.

—Enquiry. l.t. ed. 1980. (Ulverscroft Large Print Ser.). 12.00 o.p. (0-7089-0399-1, Ulverscroft) Thorpe, F. A. Pubs. GBR. *Dist:* Ulverscroft Large Print Bks., Ltd., Ulverscroft Large Print Canada, Ltd.

—Flying Finish. 1997. mass mkt. 6.99 (0-449-45726-5); 1987. mass mkt. 6.99 o.s.i (0-449-21265-3) Ballantine Bks. (Fawcett).

—Flying Finish. 1999. 288p. mass mkt. 6.99 (0-515-12560-1, Jove) Berkley Publishing Group.

—Flying Finish. unabr. ed. 1994. audio 48.00 (0-7366-2676-X, 3413) Books on Tape, Inc.

—Flying Finish. unabr. ed. 2000. audio 49.95 (0-7451-6829-9, CAB 453) Chivers Audio Bks. GBR. *Dist:* BBC Audiobooks America.

—Flying Finish. l.t. ed. 1995. 349p. reprint ed. 23.95 o.p. (0-7838-1141-1, Macmillan Reference USA) Gale Group.

—Flying Finish. abr. ed. audio 15.95 o.p. (1-55994-137-5, CPN 2137, HarperAudio) HarperTrade.

—Flying Finish. unabr. ed. 1997. audio 51.00 (0-7887-0252-1, 94461E7) Recorded Bks., LLC.

—Flying Finish. 1984. mass mkt. 3.50 (0-671-50926-8); 1983. mass mkt. 2.95 (0-671-47020-5) Simon & Schuster. (Pocket).

—Flying Finish. l.t. ed. 1979. 12.00 o.p. (0-7089-0298-7, Ulverscroft) Thorpe, F. A. Pubs. GBR. *Dist:* Ulverscroft Large Print Bks., Ltd.

—For Kicks. l.t. ed. 1994. 19.95 o.p. (0-7927-1740-6); 1994. pap. 18.95 o.p. (0-7927-1739-2); 1993. audio 54.95 o.p. (0-7451-5950-8) BBC Audiobooks America.

—For Kicks. 1987. 336p. mass mkt. 5.95 o.s.i (0-449-21264-5, Fawcett) Ballantine Bks.

—For Kicks. 304p. 2004. mass mkt. 6.99 (0-425-19498-1); 1998. mass mkt. 6.99 (0-515-12386-2, Jove) Berkley Publishing Group.

—For Kicks. unabr. ed. 1991. audio 56.00 (0-7366-1918-6, 2742) Books on Tape, Inc.

—For Kicks. 1984. mass mkt. 3.50 o.s.i (0-671-53265-0); 1982. mass mkt. 2.95 o.s.i (0-671-45460-9) Simon & Schuster. (Pocket).

—For Kicks. l.t. ed. 1973. o.p. (0-85456-164-1, Ulverscroft) Thorpe, F. A. Pubs.

—For Kicks. abr. ed. 1996. 2p. audio 16.95 o.s.i (0-14-086222-6) Viking Penguin.

—Forfeit. unabr. ed. 1993. audio 54.95 o.p. (0-7451-5951-6) BBC Audiobooks America.

—Forfeit. 1987. mass mkt. 5.95 o.s.i (0-449-21272-6, Fawcett) Ballantine Bks.

—Forfeit. 1999. 256p. pap. 6.99 (0-515-12445-1, Jove) Berkley Publishing Group.

—Forfeit. unabr. ed. 1991. audio 48.00 (0-7366-1885-6, 2714) Books on Tape, Inc.

—Forfeit. l.t. ed. 1994. 22.95 (0-8161-5781-2, Macmillan Reference USA) Gale Group.

—Forfeit. 1969. (Harper Novel of Suspense Ser.). 6.95 o.p. (0-06-011328-6) HarperCollins Pubs.

—Forfeit. 1985. mass mkt. 3.50 (0-671-54692-9, Pocket) Simon & Schuster.

—Forfeit. l.t. ed. 1979. (Ulverscroft Large Print Ser.). 12.00 o.p. (0-7089-0373-8, Ulverscroft) Thorpe, F. A. Pubs. GBR. *Dist:* Ulverscroft Large Print Bks., Ltd., Ulverscroft Large Print Canada, Ltd.

—High Stakes. 1993. 272p. mass mkt. 6.99 (0-449-22114-8, Fawcett) Ballantine Bks.

—High Stakes. 2003. audio compact disk 19.95 (0-7861-9260-7); 2000. audio compact disk 40.00 (0-7861-9918-0, z1715); 1995. audio 32.95 (0-7861-0906-8, 1715) Blackstone Audio Bks., Inc.

—High Stakes. unabr. ed. 2000. audio 49.95 (0-7451-4047-5, CAB 744) Chivers Audio Bks. GBR. *Dist:* BBC Audiobooks America.

—High Stakes, abr. ed. 1980. audio 15.95 (0-88646-003-4, 390918) Durkin Hayes Publishing Ltd.

—High Stakes. 1990. mass mkt. 4.50 (0-671-70468-0); 1988. mass mkt. 3.95 (0-671-68077-3); 1985. mass mkt. 3.50 (0-671-55268-6); 1982. mass mkt. 2.95 o.s.i (0-671-46423-X) Simon & Schuster. (Pocket).

—High Stakes. l.t. ed. 1980. (Ulverscroft Large Print Ser.). 12.00 o.p. (0-7089-0412-2, Ulverscroft) Thorpe, F. A. Pubs. GBR. *Dist:* Ulverscroft Large Print Bks., Ltd., Ulverscroft Large Print Canada, Ltd.

—In the Frame. 1993. 272p. mass mkt. 6.99 (0-449-22116-4, Fawcett) Ballantine Bks.

—In the Frame. unabr. ed. 1996. audio 39.95 (0-7861-1021-X, 1799) Blackstone Audio Bks., Inc.

—In the Frame. unabr. ed. 2000. audio 49.95 (0-7451-5952-4, CAB 137) Chivers Audio Bks. GBR. *Dist:* BBC Audiobooks America.

—In the Frame. l.t. ed. 1994. 327p. lib. bdg. 22.95 o.p. (0-8161-5783-9, Macmillan Reference USA) Gale Group.

—In the Frame. unabr. ed. 1990. audio 44.00 (1-55690-253-0, 90026E7) Recorded Bks., LLC.

—In the Frame. 1989. 208p. mass mkt. 4.50 (0-671-69648-3); 1988. mass mkt. 3.95 (0-671-67429-3); 1987. mass mkt. 3.50 (0-671-55658-4); 1984. mass mkt. 3.50 (0-671-50754-0); 1982. mass mkt. 2.95 o.s.i (0-671-45461-7) Simon & Schuster. (Pocket).

—In the Frame. l.t. ed. 1977. (Ulverscroft Large Print Ser.). 12.00 o.p. (0-7089-0060-7, Ulverscroft) Thorpe, F. A. Pubs. GBR. *Dist:* Ulverscroft Large Print Bks., Ltd., Ulverscroft Large Print Canada, Ltd.

—Knockdown. l.t. ed. 1995. pap. 18.95 o.p. (*0-7927-1879-8*); 1994. 19.95 o.p. (*0-7927-1880-1*); 1995. audio 54.95 (*0-7451-6830-2*, CAB 613) BBC Audiobooks America.
—Knockdown. 1993. 256p. mass mkt. 6.99 (*0-449-22113-X*, Fawcett) Ballantine Bks.
—Knockdown. unabr. ed. 1994. audio 36.00 (*0-7366-2780-4*, 3499) Books on Tape, Inc.
—Knockdown. unabr. ed. 2000. audio 49.95 Chivers Audio Bks. GBR. *Dist:* BBC Audiobooks America.
—Knockdown. abr. ed. audio 15.95 o.p. (*1-55994-143-X*, CPN 2140, HarperAudio) HarperTrade.
—Knockdown. unabr. ed. 1994. audio 44.00 (*0-7887-0106-1*, 94347E7) Recorded Bks., LLC.
—Knockdown. 1989. mass mkt. 4.95 (*0-671-68768-9*); 1984. 208p. mass mkt. 3.50 (*0-671-50760-5*) Simon & Schuster. (Pocket).
—Knockdown. l.t. ed. 1979. 12.50 o.p. (*0-7089-0288-X*, Ulverscroft) Thorpe, F. A. Pubs. GBR. *Dist:* Ulverscroft Large Print Bks., Ltd.
—Longshot. 1999. mass mkt. (*0-449-45825-3*); 1992. 336p. mass mkt. 6.99 o.s.i (*0-449-21955-0*); 1992. mass mkt. 5.99 o.p. (*0-449-45309-X*) Ballantine Bks. (Fawcett).
—Longshot. unabr. ed. 1994. audio 56.00 (*0-7366-2739-1*, 3465) Books on Tape, Inc.
—Longshot. l.t. ed. 1992. (General Ser.). 412p. pap. 16.95 o.p. (*0-8161-5417-1*); lib. bdg. 21.95 o.p. (*0-8161-5416-3*) Gale Group. (Macmillan Reference USA).
—Longshot. abr. ed. audio 15.95 o.p. (*1-55994-345-9*, CPN 2187, HarperAudio) HarperTrade.
—Longshot. abr. ed. 2000. audio 7.95 (*1-57815-047-7*, 1019, Media Bks. Audio Publishing) Media Bks., L. L. C.
—Longshot. 1990. 324p. 19.95 o.s.i (*0-399-13581-2*, G. P. Putnam's Sons) Penguin Putnam Bks. for Young Readers.
—Longshot. 1992. 4.99 o.p. (*0-517-09581-5*) Random Hse. Value Publishing.
—Longshot: Open Market. 1991. mass mkt. 5.99 o.s.i (*0-449-22084-2*, Fawcett) Ballantine Bks.
—Nerve. l.t. ed. 1994. 18.95 o.p. (*0-7927-1755-4*); 1994. pap. o.p. (*0-7927-1754-6*); 1993. 54.95 o.p. incl. audio (*0-7451-5953-2*) BBC Audiobooks America.
—Nerve. 1987. mass mkt. 5.95 o.s.i (*0-449-21266-1*, Fawcett) Ballantine Bks.
—Nerve. 1998. 320p. reprint ed. mass mkt. 6.99 (*0-515-12346-3*, Jove) Berkley Publishing Group.
—Nerve. unabr. ed. 1991. audio 48.00 (*0-7366-1928-3*, 2751) Books on Tape, Inc.
—Nerve. 1965. mass mkt. 0.60 o.p. (*0-451-02607-1*, Signet Bks.) NAL.
—Nerve. 1984. mass mkt. 3.50 (*0-671-52522-0*); 1982. mass mkt. 2.95 (*0-671-45072-7*) Simon & Schuster. (Pocket).
—Nerve. 1987. audio 53.95 o.p. (*0-8161-9670-2*) Thorndike Pr.
—Nerve. l.t. ed. 1978. o.p. (*0-7089-0171-9*, Ulverscroft) Thorpe, F. A. Pubs.
—Odds Against. unabr. ed. audio 54.95 o.p. (*1-85549-031-5*); 1998. audio 69.95 (*0-7540-0086-9*, CAB1509) BBC Audiobooks America.
—Odds Against. 1987. 320p. mass mkt. 5.99 o.s.i (*0-449-21269-6*, Fawcett) Ballantine Bks.
—Odds Against. 2000. 288p. mass mkt. 6.99 (*0-515-12551-2*, Jove) Berkley Publishing Group.
—Odds Against. unabr. ed. 1999. audio 39.95 Blackstone Audio Bks., Inc.
—Odds Against. unabr. ed. 2000. (Sid Halley Adventure Ser.: Bk. 1). audio 59.95 Chivers Audio Bks. GBR. *Dist:* BBC Audiobooks America.
—Odds Against. l.t. ed. 1991. (General Ser.). 272p. 15.95 o.s.i (*0-8161-5034-6*); lib. bdg. 21.95 o.p. (*0-8161-5033-8*) Gale Group. (Macmillan Reference USA).
—Odds Against. abr. ed. 1991. audio 15.95 o.s.i (*1-55994-138-3*, CPN 2138, HarperAudio) HarperTrade.
—Odds Against, unabr. ed. 1999. audio 39.95 Highsmith Inc.
—Odds Against. 1982. mass mkt. 2.95 o.s.i (*0-671-45076-X*, Pocket) Simon & Schuster.
—Proof. 1999. audio 34.95 (*0-7540-7529-X*); 1993. audio 69.95 (*0-7451-4114-5*, CAB 797) BBC Audiobooks America.
—Proof. l.t. ed. 1986. 352p. mass mkt. 5.95 o.s.i (*0-449-20754-4*, Fawcett) Ballantine Bks.
—Proof. 1997. 368p. mass mkt. 6.99 (*0-515-12120-7*, Jove) Berkley Publishing Group.
—Proof. unabr. ed. 2000. audio 59.95 Chivers Audio Bks. GBR. *Dist:* BBC Audiobooks America.
—Proof. abr. ed. 1985. audio 16.99 (*0-88646-133-2*, 7134) Durkin Hayes Publishing Ltd.
—Proof. l.t. ed. 1985. (General Ser.). 465p. 17.95 o.p. (*0-8161-3927-X*); 10.95 o.p. (*0-8161-3944-X*) Gale Group. (Macmillan Reference USA).
—Proof. 1985. 324p. 16.95 o.p. (*0-399-13036-5*, G. P. Putnam's Sons) Penguin Putnam Bks. for Young Readers.
—Proof. 1993. audio 15.99 o.s.i (*0-553-47144-9*, RH Audio) Random Hse. Audio Publishing Group.
—Proof. unabr. ed. 1985. audio 60.00 (*0-7887-3485-7*, 95768E7) Recorded Bks., LLC.
—Proof. l.t. ed. 1993. 39.95 (*0-7066-1001-6*) Remploy Pr. CAN. *Dist:* State Mutual Bk. & Periodical Service, Ltd.
—Rat Race. unabr. ed. 1993. audio 39.95 (*0-7451-5954-0*, CAB 020) BBC Audiobooks America.
—Rat Race. 1993. 256p. mass mkt. 6.99 (*0-449-22112-1*, Fawcett) Ballantine Bks.
—Rat Race. unabr. ed. 2000. audio 34.95 Chivers Audio Bks. GBR. *Dist:* BBC Audiobooks America.
—Rat Race. abr. ed. audio 15.95 o.p. (*1-55994-136-7*, CPN 2136, HarperAudio) HarperTrade.
—Rat Race. 1989. 224p. mass mkt. 4.50 (*0-671-70076-6*); 1988. mass mkt. 3.95 (*0-671-67643-1*); 1984. mass mkt. 3.50 (*0-671-53026-7*) Simon & Schuster. (Pocket).
—Rat Race. l.t. ed. 1974. 12.00 o.p. (*0-85456-256-7*, Ulverscroft) Thorpe, F. A. Pubs. GBR. *Dist:* Ulverscroft Large Print Bks., Ltd.
—Reflex. unabr. ed. 2000. audio 34.95 (*1-57270-135-8*, N81135u, Audio Editions Mystery Masters) Audio Partners Publishing Corp.
—Reflex. 1997. mass mkt. (*0-449-45727-3*); 1986. 352p. mass mkt. 5.99 o.s.i (*0-449-21173-8*); 1986. mass mkt. 4.50 o.p. (*0-449-21036-7*); 1984. mass mkt. 3.95 o.p. (*0-449-20713-7*); 1982. mass mkt. 3.50 o.p. (*0-449-24500-4*) Ballantine Bks. (Fawcett).
—Reflex. 2003. 304p. mass mkt. 6.99 (*0-515-13509-7*, Jove) Berkley Publishing Group.
—Reflex. l.t. ed. 1981. (General Ser.). lib. bdg. 14.95 o.p. (*0-8161-3255-0*, Macmillan Reference USA) Gale Group.
—Reflex. 1981. 288p. 11.95 o.p. (*0-399-12598-1*) Putnam Publishing Group, The.
—Risk. 1993. 288p. mass mkt. 6.99 (*0-449-22239-X*, Fawcett) Ballantine Bks.
—Risk. unabr. ed. 1999. audio 39.95 (*0-7861-1482-7*, 2334) Blackstone Audio Bks., Inc.
—Risk. unabr. ed. 1994. audio 48.00 (*0-7366-2834-7*, 3542) Books on Tape, Inc.
—Risk. 1994. reprint ed. lib. bdg. 37.95 (*1-56849-281-2*) Buccaneer Bks., Inc.
—Risk. unabr. ed. 2000. audio 49.95 (*0-7451-5955-9*, CAB 660) Chivers Audio Bks. GBR. *Dist:* BBC Audiobooks America.
—Risk. l.t. ed. 1994. 329p. lib. bdg. 21.95 o.p. (*0-8161-5782-0*, Macmillan Reference USA) Gale Group.
—Risk. 1978. o.p. (*0-06-011302-2*) HarperCollins Pubs.
—Risk. 1990. audio 15.95; audio 17.00 o.p. (*1-55994-131-6*, CPN 2131) HarperTrade. (HarperAudio).
—Risk, Set. unabr. ed. 1999. audio 39.95 Highsmith Inc.
—Risk. abr. ed. 2000. audio 7.95 (*1-57815-048-5*, 1020, Media Bks. Audio Publishing) Media Bks., L. L. C.
—Risk. unabr. ed. 2000. audio 51.00 (*0-7887-0356-0*, 94548E7) Recorded Bks., LLC.
—Risk. 1990. mass mkt. 4.95 (*0-671-70469-9*); 1988. mass mkt. 3.95 (*0-671-68078-1*); 1984. mass mkt. 3.50 (*0-671-50755-9*); 1982. mass mkt. 2.95 o.s.i (*0-671-45074-3*) Simon & Schuster. (Pocket).
—Risk. l.t. ed. 1979. o.p. (*0-7089-0309-6*, Ulverscroft) Thorpe, F. A. Pubs.
—Second Wind. 2000. 272p. mass mkt. 6.99 (*0-515-12923-2*, Jove) Berkley Publishing Group.
—Second Wind. l.t. ed. 1999. 24.95 o.p. (*0-7838-8691-8*, Macmillan Reference USA) Gale Group.
—Second Wind. 1999. 293p. 24.95 o.s.i (*0-399-14562-1*) Penguin Group (USA) Inc.
—Second Wind. l.t. ed. 2000. 416p. pap. 11.95 (*0-375-70772-7*) Random Hse. Large Print.
—Second Wind. 2000. 13.04 (*0-606-19301-4*) Turtleback Bks.
—Shattered. 2000. 320p. 25.95 (*0-399-14660-1*) Penguin Group (USA) Inc.
—Shattered. l.t. ed. (Thorndike Press Large Print Basic Ser.). 349p. 2001. pap. 29.95 (*0-7862-2824-5*); 2000. 32.95 (*0-7862-2744-3*) Thorndike Pr.
—Straight. 1998. mass mkt. 5.99 (*0-449-45788-5*); 1991. 320p. mass mkt. 5.99 o.s.i (*0-449-21720-5*); 1991. 320p. mass mkt. 5.95 o.p. (*0-449-45310-3*) Ballantine Bks. (Fawcett).
—Straight. 2003. 320p. mass mkt. 6.99 (*0-515-13465-1*, Jove) Berkley Publishing Group.
—Straight. l.t. ed. 1990. (General Ser.). 437p. 15.95 o.p. (*0-8161-4995-X*); lib. bdg. 21.95 o.p. (*0-8161-4991-7*) Gale Group. (Macmillan Reference USA).
—Straight. abr. ed. 1989. audio 15.95 (*1-55994-118-9*, CPN 2128, Caedmon) HarperTrade.
—Straight. 1989. 324p. 18.95 o.p. (*0-399-13470-0*, G. P. Putnam's Sons) Penguin Putnam Bks. for Young Readers.
—Straight. unabr. ed. 1994. audio 70.00 (*1-55690-993-4*, 94132E7) Recorded Bks., LLC.
—Trial Run. l.t. ed. 1994. 19.95 o.p. (*0-7927-2170-5*); 1994. pap. 18.95 o.p. (*0-7927-2169-1*); 1993. 54.95 incl. audio (*0-7451-5957-5*) BBC Audiobooks America.
—Trial Run. 1987. mass mkt. 5.95 o.s.i (*0-449-21273-4*, Fawcett) Ballantine Bks.
—Trial Run. 2001. 272p. mass mkt. 6.99 (*0-515-12997-6*, Jove) Berkley Publishing Group.
—Trial Run. unabr. ed. 1991. audio 48.00 (*0-7366-2029-X*, 2843) Books on Tape, Inc.
—Trial Run. 1983. mass mkt. 3.50 o.s.i (*0-671-50732-X*); mass mkt. 2.95 (*0-671-47022-1*) Simon & Schuster. (Pocket).
—Trial Run. l.t. ed. 1980. 404p. 12.00 o.p. (*0-7089-0456-4*, Ulverscroft) Thorpe, F. A. Pubs. GBR. *Dist:* Ulverscroft Large Print Bks., Ltd.
—Twice Shy. unabr. ed. 1993. 69.95 o.p. incl. audio (*0-7451-5958-3*) BBC Audiobooks America.
—Twice Shy. 1997. mass mkt. 5.99 (*0-449-45728-1*, Fawcett); 1986. 352p. mass mkt. 5.99 o.s.i (*0-449-21314-5*, Fawcett); 1986. mass mkt. 4.50 o.p. (*0-449-21035-9*, Fawcett); 1985. mass mkt. o.s.i (*0-449-20756-0*); 1983. mass mkt. 3.50 o.p. (*0-449-20053-1*, Fawcett) Ballantine Bks.
—Twice Shy. 2003. 304p. mass mkt. 6.99 (*0-515-13488-0*, Jove) Berkley Publishing Group.
—Twice Shy. l.t. ed. 1982. 458p. lib. bdg. 14.95 o.p. (*0-8161-3445-6*, Macmillan Reference USA) Gale Group.
—Twice Shy. 1982. 13.95 o.s.i (*0-399-12707-0*) Putnam Publishing Group, The.
—Twice Shy. unabr. ed. 1998. audio 61.00 (*0-7887-2510-6*, 95582E7) Recorded Bks., LLC.
—Whip Hand. unabr. ed. 1989. audio 64.95 o.s.i (*0-8161-9460-2*) BBC Audiobooks America.
—Whip Hand. 1996. pap. 5.99 (*0-449-45617-X*); 1987. mass mkt. 5.99 o.s.i (*0-449-21274-2*) Ballantine Bks. (Fawcett).
—Whip Hand. 1999. 304p. mass mkt. 6.99 (*0-515-12504-0*, Jove) Berkley Publishing Group.
—Whip Hand. unabr. ed. 2000. (Sid Halley Adventure Ser.: Bk. 2). audio 59.95; 1993. audio 69.95 (*0-7451-5960-5*, CAB 358) Chivers Audio Bks. GBR. *Dist:* BBC Audiobooks America.
—Whip Hand. l.t. ed. 1995. 376p. 21.95 (*0-8161-5785-5*, Macmillan Reference USA) Gale Group.
—Whip Hand. 2001. (Best Mysteries of All Time Ser.). 288p. (*0-7621-8871-5*, IM Pr.) Reader's Digest Assn., Inc., The.
—Whip Hand. unabr. ed. 1991. audio 51.00 (*1-55690-560-2*, 91109E7) Recorded Bks., LLC.
—Whip Hand. 1982. 336p. mass mkt. 3.50 o.s.i (*0-671-46404-3*, Pocket) Simon & Schuster.
—Whip Hand. 1984. audio o.s.i. audio 39.95 o.s.i (*0-8161-9785-7*, 91109) Thorndike Pr.
—Whip Hand. l.t. ed. 1980. (Ulverscroft Large Print Ser.). 459p. o.p. (*0-7089-0542-0*, Ulverscroft) Thorpe, F. A. Pubs. GBR. *Dist:* Ulverscroft Large Print Canada, Ltd.
—Whip Hand. abr. ed. 1996. audio 16.95 o.s.i (*0-14-086223-4*, Penguin AudioBooks) Viking Penguin.
—Wild Horses. 352p. 2004. mass mkt. 6.99 (*0-425-19674-7*); 1995. mass mkt. 6.99 (*0-515-11723-4*, Jove); 1995. pap. 5.99 o.s.i (*0-515-11789-7*, Jove) Berkley Publishing Group.
—Wild Horses. unabr. ed. 1995. audio 56.00 (*0-7366-2970-X*, 3631) Books on Tape, Inc.
—Wild Horses. l.t. ed. 1994. (Large Print Bks.). 26.95 o.p. (*1-56895-123-X*, Wheeler Publishing, Inc.) Gale Group.
—Wild Horses. 1994. 320p. 22.95 o.p. (*0-399-13974-5*, G. P. Putnam's Sons) Penguin Group (USA) Inc.
—Wild Horses. unabr. ed. 2000. audio 60.00 (*0-7887-0265-3*, 94474E7) Recorded Bks., LLC.
—Wild Horses. 1999. pap. 9.98 (*0-671-04424-9*); Set. 1994. audio 17.00 (*0-671-87971-5*, 391913) Simon & Schuster Audio. (Simon & Schuster Audioworks).
Francis, Richard. Taking Apart the Poco Poco. 1995. 252p. 21.00 (*0-684-80337-2*, Simon & Schuster) Simon & Schuster.
Francome, John. Blood Stock. l.t. ed. 2001. (Dales Large Print Ser.). 352p. pap. (*1-84262-065-7*) Dales Large Print Bks. GBR. *Dist:* Ulverscroft Large Print Canada, Ltd.
—Blood Stock. l.t. ed. 1991. (Magna Large Print Ser.). 366p. o.p. (*1-85057-899-0*) Magna Large Print Bks. GBR. *Dist:* Ulverscroft Large Print Canada, Ltd.
—Blood Stock. 1996. 304p. mass mkt. 4.99 o.p. (*0-06-104288-9*, HarperTorch) Morrow/Avon.
—False Start. l.t. ed. 1997. (General Ser.). 384p. pap. 22.95 (*0-7862-1126-1*) Thorndike Pr.
Francome, John & MacGregor, James. Blood Stock. l.t. ed. 1991. 366p. reprint ed. lib. bdg. 11.95 o.p. (*1-85057-900-8*, Macmillan Reference USA) Gale Group.
—Blood Stock. 1991. 256p. 22.95 o.p. (*0-7472-0129-3*) Headline Bk. Publishing, Ltd. GBR. *Dist:* Trafalgar Square.
—Blood Stock. 2001. audio compact disk 71.95 (*0-7531-1347-3*); 1998. audio 54.95 (*0-7531-0280-3*, 980502) ISIS Audio Bks. GBR. *Dist:* Ulverscroft Large Print Bks., Ltd.
Fraser, Anthea. The April Rainers. 1990. 14.95 o.s.i (*0-385-41088-3*) Doubleday Publishing.
—Death Speaks Softly. 1987. (Crime Club Ser.). 192p. 12.95 o.s.i (*0-385-24147-X*) Doubleday Publishing.
—Death Speaks Softly. l.t. ed. 1988. 336p. (*0-7089-1846-8*, Ulverscroft) Thorpe, F. A. Pubs.
—The Gospel Makers. 1994. 224p. 14.99 (*0-00-232490-3*) HarperSanFrancisco.
—The Gospel Makers. 1996. 208p. 20.95 o.p. (*0-312-13979-9*, Saint Martin's Minotaur) St. Martin's Pr.
—I'll Sing You Two-O Vol. 1: An Inspector Webb Mystery. 1996. 192p. 20.95 o.p. (*0-312-14623-X*, Saint Martin's Minotaur) St. Martin's Pr.
—A Necessary End. 1986. 192p. 13.95 o.s.i (*0-8027-5641-7*) Walker & Co.
—The Nine Bright Shiners. 1988. (Crime Club Ser.). 192p. pap. 12.95 o.s.i (*0-385-24323-5*) Doubleday Publishing.
—The Nine Bright Shiners. l.t. ed. 1990. (Ulverscroft Large Print Ser.). 29.99 o.p. (*0-7089-2173-6*, Ulverscroft) Thorpe, F. A. Pubs. GBR. *Dist:* Ulverscroft Large Print Bks., Ltd., Ulverscroft Large Print Canada, Ltd.
—One Is One & All Alone. 1998. 192p. 20.95 (*0-312-19309-2*, Saint Martin's Minotaur) St. Martin's Pr.
—Presence of Mind. l.t. ed. 1997. (G. K. Hall Nightingale Ser.). 288p. pap. 18.95 o.p. (*0-7838-8254-8*, Macmillan Reference USA) Gale Group.
—Presence of Mind. 1994. reprint ed. lib. bdg. 20.00 (*0-7278-4704-X*) Severn Hse. Pubs., Ltd.
—Pretty Maids All in a Row. l.t. ed. 2001. (Dales Large Print Ser.). 272p. pap. 21.99 (*1-84262-075-4*) Dales Large Print Bks. GBR. *Dist:* Ulverscroft Large Print Bks., Ltd., Ulverscroft Large Print Canada, Ltd.
—Pretty Maids All in a Row. 1987. (Crime Club Ser.). 192p. 12.95 o.s.i (*0-385-23798-7*) Doubleday Publishing.
—Pretty Maids All in a Row. l.t. ed. 1987. (Ulverscroft Large Print Ser.). 336p. o.p. (*0-7089-1624-4*, Ulverscroft) Thorpe, F. A. Pubs. GBR. *Dist:* Ulverscroft Large Print Canada, Ltd.
—The Seven Stars. 1997. 224p. 20.95 o.p. (*0-312-15650-2*, Saint Martin's Minotaur) St. Martin's Pr.
—A Shroud for Delilah. l.t. ed. 2001. (Dales Large Print Ser.). 304p. pap. 21.99 (*1-84262-086-X*) Dales Large Print Bks. GBR. *Dist:* Ulverscroft Large Print Bks., Ltd., Ulverscroft Large Print Canada, Ltd.
—A Shroud for Delilah. 1986. (Crime Club Ser.). 192p. 12.95 o.p. (*0-385-23543-7*) Doubleday Publishing.
—A Shroud for Delilah. l.t. ed. 1985. 368p. 15.95 o.p. (*0-7089-1377-6*, Ulverscroft) Thorpe, F. A. Pubs. GBR. *Dist:* Ulverscroft Large Print Bks., Ltd.
—Six Proud Walkers. 1989. (Crime Club Ser.). 12.95 o.s.i (*0-385-24615-3*) Doubleday Publishing.
—Six Proud Walkers. l.t. ed. 1989. (Ulverscroft Large Print Ser.). 29.99 o.p. (*0-7089-2181-7*, Ulverscroft) Thorpe, F. A. Pubs. GBR. *Dist:* Ulverscroft Large Print Bks., Ltd., Ulverscroft Large Print Canada, Ltd.
—The Stone. 1980. 192p. 8.95 o.p. (*0-312-76205-4*) St. Martin's Pr.
—The Stone. l.t. ed. 2000. (General Ser.). 300p. pap. 23.95 (*0-7862-2570-X*) Thorndike Pr.
—Symbols at Your Door. 1991. 192p. 15.00 o.s.i (*0-385-41685-7*) Doubleday Publishing.
—The Ten Commandments. 2000. (DCI Webb Mysteries Ser.). 190p. 22.95 (*0-312-20915-0*); 192p. text 20.95 (*0-312-18672-X*) St. Martin's Pr. (Saint Martin's Minotaur).
—The Ten Commandments. l.t. ed. 2000. 279p. (*0-7540-4070-4*); (*0-7540-4071-2*) Thorndike Pr.
—Three, Three, the Rivals. 1992. 13.99 (*0-00-232380-X*) HarperSanFrancisco.
—Three, Three, the Rivals. 1995. 188p. 18.95 o.p. (*0-312-11902-X*, Saint Martin's Minotaur) St. Martin's Pr.
—Three, Three, the Rivals. l.t. ed. 1993. (Mystery Ser.). 368p. 29.99 o.p. (*0-7089-2984-2*, Ulverscroft) Thorpe, F. A. Pubs. GBR. *Dist:* Ulverscroft Large Print Bks., Ltd., Ulverscroft Large Print Canada, Ltd.
Fraser, Antonia. The Cavalier Case. l.t. ed. 1992. (Jemima Shore Mystery Ser.). pap. 14.95 o.p. (*0-7927-0818-0*); 18.95 o.p. (*0-7927-0817-2*, E0014); audio 69.95 (*0-7451-5967-2*, CAB 673) BBC Audiobooks America.
—The Cavalier Case. 1992. 256p. mass mkt. 4.99 o.s.i (*0-553-29544-6*) Bantam Bks.
—Cool Repentance: A Jemima Shore Mystery. unabr. ed. 1993. audio 54.95 (*0-7451-5964-8*, CSL 064) BBC Audiobooks America.
—Cool Repentance: A Jemima Shore Mystery. 1991. 240p. mass mkt. 4.50 o.s.i (*0-553-28072-4*) Bantam Bks.

Settings

Settings

—Cool Repentance: A Jemima Shore Mystery. unabr. collector's ed. 1988. audio 40.00 (0-7366-1303-X, 2210) Books on Tape, Inc.
—Cool Repentance: A Jemima Shore Mystery. 1983. 12.95 o.p. (0-393-01625-0); 1985. 224p. reprint ed. pap. 3.95 o.p. (0-393-30264-4) Norton, W. W. & Co., Inc.
—Jemima Shore at the Sunny Grave. l.t. ed. 1993. pap. 16.95 o.p. (0-7927-1348-6); 1992. 18.95 o.p. (0-7927-1349-4) BBC Audiobooks America.
—Jemima Shore's First Case & Other Stories. l.t. ed. 1988. pap. 19.95 o.p. (1-55504-654-1); lib. bdg. 21.95 o.p. (1-55504-653-3) BBC Audiobooks America.
—Jemima Shore's First Case & Other Stories. 1987. 14.95 o.p. (0-393-02453-9) Norton, W. W. & Co., Inc.
—Oxford Blood: A Jemima Shore Mystery. l.t. ed. 1986. pap. 13.95 o.p. (1-55504-037-3); 1993. 54.95 incl. audio (0-7451-5966-4, CAB 204) BBC Audiobooks America.
—Oxford Blood: A Jemima Shore Mystery. 1989. 224p. mass mkt. 3.95 o.s.i (0-553-28070-8) Bantam Bks.
—Oxford Blood: A Jemima Shore Mystery. (Jemima Shore Mystery Ser.). 1998. 224p. pap. 10.00 (0-393-31824-9, Norton Paperbacks); 1985. 13.95 o.p. (0-393-02229-3) Norton, W. W. & Co., Inc.
—Oxford Blood: A Jemima Shore Mystery. 1987. audio 49.95 o.s.i (0-8161-9661-3) Thorndike Pr.
—Political Death: A Jemima Shore Mystery. unabr. ed. 1996. audio 54.95 (0-7451-6583-4, CAB1199) BBC Audiobooks America.
—Political Death: A Jemima Shore Mystery. 1997. 240p. mass mkt. 5.99 (0-553-57203-2, Crimeline) Bantam Bks.
—Political Death: A Jemima Shore Mystery. unabr. ed. 1994. audio 40.00 Books on Tape, Inc.
—Quiet as a Nun. l.t. ed. 1993. (J). (gr. 5 up). pap. 18.95 o.p. (0-7927-1689-2); 1993. (YA). (gr. 5 up). 20.95 o.p. (0-7927-1690-6); audio 54.95 (0-7451-5971-0, CAB 397) BBC Audiobooks America.
—Quiet as a Nun. 1991. 192p. mass mkt. 4.50 o.s.i (0-553-28311-1) Bantam Bks.
—Quiet as a Nun. unabr. collector's ed. 1984. audio 42.00 (0-7366-0884-2, 1828) Books on Tape, Inc.
—Quiet as a Nun. unabr. ed. 2000. (Jemima Shore Mystery Ser.: Bk. 1). audio 49.95 Chivers Audio Bks. GBR. *Dist:* BBC Audiobooks America.
—Quiet as a Nun. (Jemima Shore Mystery Ser.). 1998. 192p. pap. 10.00 (0-393-31822-2, Norton Paperbacks); 1982. pap. 3.95 o.p. (0-393-30120-6) Norton, W. W. & Co., Inc.
—Quiet as a Nun. 1977. 8.95 o.p. (0-670-58556-4) Viking Penguin.
—A Splash of Red: A Jemina Shore Mystery, unabr. ed. 1993. 54.95 incl. audio (0-7451-5963-X, CAB 101) BBC Audiobooks America.
—A Splash of Red: A Jemima Shore Mystery. 1990. 224p. mass mkt. 3.95 o.s.i (0-553-28071-6) Bantam Bks.
—A Splash of Red: A Jemima Shore Mystery. 1984. pap. 3.50 o.p. (0-393-30213-X); 1982. 12.95 o.p. (0-393-01511-4); 1998. 240p. pap. 10.00 (0-393-31687-4) Norton, W. W. & Co., Inc.
—A Splash of Red: A Jemina Shore Mystery. unabr. ed. 1985. audio 53.95 o.s.i (0-8161-9823-3) Thorndike Pr.
—The Wild Island: A Jemima Shore Mystery. l.t. ed. 1993. 20.95 o.p. (0-7927-1486-5); 1993. pap. 18.95 o.p. (0-7927-1485-7); 1992. 54.95 incl. audio (0-7451-5968-0, CAB 522) BBC Audiobooks America.
—The Wild Island: A Jemima Shore Mystery. 1991. 224p. mass mkt. 4.50 o.s.i (0-553-29324-9) Bantam Bks.
—The Wild Island: A Jemima Shore Mystery. unabr. collector's ed. 1986. audio 42.00 (0-7366-0885-0, 1829) Books on Tape, Inc.
—The Wild Island: A Jemima Shore Mystery. 1978. 8.95 o.p. (0-393-08831-6) Norton, W. W. & Co., Inc.
—Your Royal Heritage. 1988. (Jemina Shore Mystery Ser.). 208p. 15.95 o.s.i (0-689-11954-2, Scribner) Simon & Schuster.
—Your Royal Hostage. l.t. ed. 1988. 13.95 o.p. (1-55504-394-1); Set. 1993. 54.95 incl. audio (0-7451-5969-9, CAB 261) BBC Audiobooks America.
—Your Royal Hostage. 1989. 272p. mass mkt. 3.95 o.s.i (0-553-28019-8) Bantam Bks.
Fraser, George MacDonald. Black Ajax. 256p. 1999. pap. 12.95 (0-7867-0618-X); 1998. 23.00 o.p. (0-7867-0553-1) Avalon Publishing Group. (Carroll & Graf Pubs.).
—Mr. American. 1998. 585p. pap. 15.95 (0-7867-0554-X, Carroll & Graf Pubs.) Avalon Publishing Group.
—Mr. American. 1993. 585p. pap. 16.00 o.p. (0-00-271235-0) HarperCollins Pubs. Ltd. GBR. *Dist:* HarperCollins Pubs.
—Mr. American. 1981. 16.95 o.p. (0-671-42571-4, Simon & Schuster) Simon & Schuster.
Frayn, Michael. Headlong. 2000. E-Book 14.00 (0-8050-6526-1) Holt, Henry & Co.
—Headlong. 2000. pap. 0.01 (0-312-27108-5) Picador.
Frazer, Margaret. The Bastard's Tale. 2003. 320p. mass mkt. 6.99 (0-425-19329-2) Berkley Publishing Group.
—The Bastard's Tale: A Dame Frevisse Mystery. 2003. (Dame Frevisse Mystery Ser.). 320p. 22.95 (0-425-18649-0, Prime Crime) Berkley Publishing Group.
—The Bishop's Tale. 1994. 208p. mass mkt. 6.50 (0-425-14492-5, Prime Crime) Berkley Publishing Group.
—The Boy's Tale. 1995. (Dame Frevisse Mystery Ser.). 240p. (Orig.). mass mkt. 6.50 (0-425-14899-8) Berkley Publishing Group.
—The Hunter's Tale. 2004. 336p. 23.95 (0-425-19401-9) Berkley Publishing Group.
—The Maiden's Tale. 1998. (Dame Frevisse Mystery Ser.). 256p. mass mkt. 6.99 (0-425-16407-1, Prime Crime) Berkley Publishing Group.
—The Murderer's Tale. 1996. 240p. mass mkt. 5.99 o.s.i (0-425-15406-8, Prime Crime) Berkley Publishing Group.
—The Novice's Tale. 1993. (Dame Frevisse Mystery Ser.). 240p. (Orig.). mass mkt. 6.99 (0-425-14321-X) Berkley Publishing Group.
—The Outlaw's Tale. 224p. 1995. mass mkt. 5.99 o.s.i (0-425-15119-0); 1994. mass mkt. 4.50 o.s.i (0-515-11335-2, Jove) Berkley Publishing Group.
—The Prioress' Tale. 1997. (Dame Frevisse Mystery Ser.). 256p. mass mkt. 6.99 (0-425-15944-2, Prime Crime) Berkley Publishing Group.
—The Reeve's Tale. (Dame Frevisse Mystery Ser.). 288p. 1999. 21.95 o.s.i (0-425-17232-5, Prime Crime); 2000. reprint ed. mass mkt. 6.99 (0-425-17667-3) Berkley Publishing Group.
—The Reeve's Tale. l.t. ed. 2000. (Basic Ser.). 424p. 27.95 (0-7862-2548-3) Thorndike Pr.
—The Servant's Tale. 1993. (Dame Frevisse Mystery Ser.). mass mkt. 6.99 (0-425-14389-9); 240p. mass mkt. 4.50 o.s.i (0-515-11163-5, Jove) Berkley Publishing Group.
—The Squire's Tale. 2000. (Dame Frevisse Mystery Ser.). 288p. 21.95 o.s.i (0-425-17678-9) Berkley Publishing Group.
Frazer, Margaret, et al. The Novice's Tale. 1992. (Orig.). mass mkt. 4.50 o.s.i (0-515-10900-2, Jove) Berkley Publishing Group.
Freeman, Austin R. For the Defence: Dr. Thorndyke. l.t. ed. 1992. pap. 14.95 o.p. (0-7927-1062-2) BBC Audiobooks America.
Freeman, Don. The Guard Mouse. 1974. (Seafarer Ser.). (Illus.). (J). (gr. k-2). pap. 1.50 o.p. (0-670-05092-X, Penguin Bks.) Viking Penguin.
Freeman, Mary E. Wilkins. The Copy-Cat & Other Stories. 1977. (Short Story Index Reprint Ser.). 23.95 (0-8369-3540-3) Ayer Co. Pubs., Inc.
—The Copy-Cat & Other Stories. E-Book 5.00 (0-7410-1245-6) SoftBook Pr.
Freeman, R. Austin. The Best Dr. Thorndyke Detective Stories. Bleiler, Everett F., ed. 1973. 274p. pap. 4.95 o.p. (0-486-20388-3) Dover Pubns., Inc.
—John Thorndyke's Cases. 1976. lib. bdg. 12.95 o.s.i (0-89968-169-7, Lightyear Pr.) Buccaneer Bks., Inc.
—John Thorndyke's Cases. 2000. (Illus.). 250p. pap. 9.95 (0-7551-0365-3) House of Stratus, Inc. GBR. *Dist:* Midpoint Trade Bks., Inc.
—Mr. Pottermack's Oversight. 1985. (Detective Stories Ser.). 352p. reprint ed. pap. 5.95 o.p. (0-486-24780-5) Dover Pubns., Inc.
—The Red Thumb Mark. 1986. 305p. mass mkt. 3.95 o.p. (0-88184-240-0, Carroll & Graf Pubs.) Avalon Publishing Group.
—The Red Thumb Mark. 1986. 320p. reprint ed. pap. 6.95 (0-486-25210-8) Dover Pubns., Inc.
—The Red Thumb Mark. 2001. 230p. pap. 9.95 (0-7551-0374-2) House of Stratus, Inc. GBR. *Dist:* Midpoint Trade Bks., Inc.
—The Stoneware Monkey. 1987. (Mystery Classics Ser.). 224p. reprint ed. pap. 6.95 o.p. (0-486-25471-2) Dover Pubns., Inc.
Fremlin, Celia. Possession. 1985. 158p. reprint ed. pap. 7.95 (0-89733-169-9) Academy Chicago Pubs., Ltd.
French, Marilyn. The Bleeding Heart. 1980. 12.95 o.p. (0-671-44784-X) Summit Bks.
French, Nicci. Killing Me Softly: A Novel of Obsession. 1999. (0-07-862220-4) McGraw-Hill Cos., The.
—Killing Me Softly: A Novel of Obsession. 1999. 320p. 24.00 (0-89296-697-1) Mysterious Pr.
—Killing Me Softly: A Novel of Obsession. l.t. ed. 1999. (Basic Ser.). 488p. 28.95 (0-7862-2220-4) Thorndike Pr.
—Killing Me Softly: A Novel of Obsession. movie tie-in ed. 2000. 400p. reprint ed. mass mkt. 7.50 (0-446-60838-6) Warner Bks., Inc.
—The Red Room. l.t. ed. 2001. (Hardcover Ser.). 462p. 29.95 (1-58724-064-5, Wheeler Publishing, Inc.) Gale Group.
—The Red Room. l.t. ed. 2002. (Magna Large Print Ser.). 448p. (0-7505-1847-2) Magna Large Print Bks. GBR. *Dist:* Ulverscroft Large Print Canada, Ltd.
—The Red Room. 2001. 384p. 24.45 o.p. (0-89296-730-7) Mysterious Pr.
—The Red Room. 2001. 384p. E-Book 14.95 (0-7595-8539-3); 2001. 384p. E-Book 14.95 (0-7595-9601-8); 2001. 384p. E-Book 14.95 (0-7595-4534-0); 2001. 384p. E-Book 14.95 (0-7595-6531-7); 2001. 384p. E-Book 14.95 (0-7595-0531-4); 2002. 480p. reprint ed. mass mkt. 6.99 (0-446-61137-9) Warner Bks., Inc.
Frost, Mark. The List of Seven. 1993. 368p. 20.00 o.p. (0-688-12245-0, Morrow, William & Co.) Morrow/Avon.
—The List of Seven. abr. ed. 1993. audio 16.95 o.p. (1-55800-840-3) NewStar Media, Inc.
—The List of Seven. 1994. (Super Sound Buy, Dove Ser.). 8.99 o.p. (0-7871-0238-5) Penguin Group (USA) Inc.
—The List of 7. 1994. 416p. mass mkt. 5.99 (0-380-72019-1, Avon Bks.) Morrow/Avon.
Fry, Stephen. The Hippopotamus. 2000. mass mkt. (0-09-918961-5) Arrow Bks., Ltd.
—The Hippopotamus. 1996. 294p. pap. 14.00 (1-56947-054-5) Soho Pr., Inc.
—The Liar. 277p. 1994. pap. 12.00 (1-56947-012-X); 1993. 22.00 o.s.i (0-939149-82-6) Soho Pr., Inc.
Fyfield, Frances. A Clear Conscience. unabr. ed. 1995. audio 69.95 (0-7451-6547-8, CAB 1163) BBC Audiobooks America.
—A Clear Conscience. 1996. (Helen West Mystery Ser.). mass mkt. 5.99 o.s.i (0-345-38508-X) Ballantine Bks.
—A Clear Conscience. unabr. ed. 2000. (West & Bailey Mystery Ser.). audio 59.95 Chivers Audio Bks. GBR. *Dist:* BBC Audiobooks America.
—A Clear Conscience. deluxe ed. 1995. 20.00 (0-676-50224-5, Pantheon) Knopf Publishing Group.
—A Clear Conscience. 2001. 272p. mass mkt. 6.99 (0-14-028251-3) Penguin Group (USA) Inc.
—A Clear Conscience. 1995. o.p. (0-676-50194-X) Random Hse., Inc.
—Deep Sleep. unabr. ed. 1996. (Prosecutor Helen West Mysteries Ser.). audio 54.95 (0-7451-4144-7, CAB827) BBC Audiobooks America.
—Deep Sleep. Chelius, Jane, ed. 240p. 1993. mass mkt. 4.99 o.p. (0-671-73547-0, Pocket); 1992. 18.00 o.p. (0-671-73546-2, Atria) Simon & Schuster.
—The Nature of the Beast. 2001. 280p. (0-316-85746-7); pap. (0-316-85745-9) Little Brown & Co.
—Not That Kind of Place. 1990. 224p. 17.95 o.p. (0-671-67666-0, Atria) Simon & Schuster.
—Not That Kind of Place. Chelius, Jane, ed. 1991. 256p. reprint ed. mass mkt. 5.50 (0-671-73945-X, Pocket) Simon & Schuster.
—Perfectly Pure & Good. unabr. ed. 1994. (Attorney Sarah Fortune Mysteries Ser.). audio 54.95 (0-7451-4340-7, CAB 1023) BBC Audiobooks America.
—Perfectly Pure & Good. 1995. (Mysteries Around the World Promotion Ser.). mass mkt. 5.99 o.s.i (0-345-38279-X, Ivy Bks.) Ballantine Bks.
—Perfectly Pure & Good. 1994. 224p. 20.00 o.s.i (0-679-42665-5, Pantheon) Knopf Publishing Group.
—Perfectly Pure & Good. l.t. ed. 1995. (Magna Large Print Ser.). 359p. o.p. (0-7505-0797-7) Magna Large Print Bks. GBR. *Dist:* Ulverscroft Large Print Canada, Ltd.
—Perfectly Pure & Good. 2000. 256p. pap. 5.99 (0-14-029195-4) Penguin Group (USA) Inc.
—A Question of Guilt. unabr. ed. 1993. (Prosecutor Helen West Mysteries Ser.). audio 69.95 (0-7451-5972-9, CAB 602) BBC Audiobooks America.
—A Question of Guilt. unabr. ed. 2000. (West & Bailey Mystery Ser.). audio 59.95 Chivers Audio Bks. GBR. *Dist:* BBC Audiobooks America.
—A Question of Guilt. 1990. 288p. mass mkt. 4.99 (0-671-67665-2, Pocket); 1989. 16.95 o.p. (0-671-67664-4, Atria) Simon & Schuster.
—A Question of Guilt. 1991. (Audio Books Ser.). audio 69.95 o.p. (0-8161-9227-8) Thorndike Pr.
—Shadow Play. l.t. ed. 1994. 22.95 o.p. (0-7927-1828-3); pap. 20.95 o.p. (0-7927-1827-5); audio 69.95 (0-7451-4232-X, CAB 915) BBC Audiobooks America.
—Shadow Play. 1994. mass mkt. 5.99 o.s.i (0-345-38507-1) Ballantine Bks.
—Shadow Play. unabr. ed. 2000. (West & Bailey Mystery Ser.). audio 59.95 Chivers Audio Bks. GBR. *Dist:* BBC Audiobooks America.
—Shadow Play. 1999. 288p. pap. 5.99 (0-14-028683-7, Penguin Bks.) Penguin Group (USA) Inc.
—Shadows on the Mirror. unabr. ed. 1994. audio 49.95 (0-7451-4287-7, CAB 970) Chivers Audio Bks. GBR. *Dist:* BBC Audiobooks America.
—Shadows on the Mirror. Chelius, Jane, ed. 1991. 17.95 o.p. (0-671-70161-4, Atria); 1992. 224p. reprint ed. mass mkt. 4.50 (0-671-70162-2, Pocket) Simon & Schuster.
—Staring at the Light. l.t. ed. 2000. (Basic Ser.). 511p. 27.95 (0-7862-2514-9) Thorndike Pr.
—Staring at the Light. 2000. (Attorney Sarah Fortune Mysteries Ser.). 288p. 23.95 o.s.i (0-670-88730-7) Viking Penguin.
—Trial by Fire. l.t. ed. 1992. 18.95 o.p. (0-7927-1200-5); pap. 16.95 o.p. (0-7927-1174-2); 69.95 incl. audio (0-7451-4025-4, CAB 722) BBC Audiobooks America.
—Trial by Fire. unabr. ed. 2000. (West & Bailey Mystery Ser.). audio 59.95 Chivers Audio Bks. GBR. *Dist:* BBC Audiobooks America.
—Undercurrents. 2001. 407p. (0-7838-9480-5, Macmillan Reference USA) Gale Group.
—Undercurrents. 2001. 278p. 23.95 o.p. (0-670-89636-5, Viking) Viking Penguin.
—Without Consent. unabr. ed. 1997. (West & Bailey Mystery Ser.). audio 59.95 (0-7451-6799-3, CAB 1415) Chivers Audio Bks. GBR. *Dist:* BBC Audiobooks America.
—Without Consent. 1998. 272p. mass mkt. 5.99 (0-14-027477-4) Penguin Group (USA) Inc.
—Without Consent. l.t. ed. 1998. (Mystery Ser.). 325p. 26.95 (0-7838-8437-0) Thorndike Pr.
—Without Consent. 1997. (Helen West Mystery Ser.). 224p. 21.95 o.p. (0-670-87682-8) Viking Penguin.
Fyfield, Frances, ed. Staring at the Light. 2001. 288p. mass mkt. 5.99 (0-14-029845-2) Penguin Group (USA) Inc.
Gaffney, Patricia. To Have & to Hold. 2003. 384p. pap. 13.95 (0-451-20785-8) NAL.
Gaiman, Neil. Neverwhere. abr. ed. 1997. audio 16.95 (1-56511-231-8) HighBridge Co.
—Neverwhere. 1998. 400p. mass mkt. 7.99 (0-380-78901-9, Avon Bks.); 1997. 352p. 24.00 (0-380-97363-4, Morrow, William & Co.) Morrow/Avon.
—Stardust. 1999. (Illus.). 224p. pap. 19.95 (1-56389-470-X, Vertigo) DC Comics.
—Stardust. 2001. E-Book 6.99 (0-06-001084-3) HarperCollins Pubs.
—Stardust. 2001. 272p. pap. 13.00 (0-06-093471-9, Perennial) HarperTrade.
—Stardust. 2000. 352p. mass mkt. 6.99 (0-380-80455-7, Avon Bks.); 1999. 256p. (gr. 10 up). 22.00 (0-380-97728-1, Morrow, William & Co.) Morrow/Avon.
—Stardust. l.t. ed. 2001. 291p. 22.95 (0-7862-3357-5) Thorndike Pr.
—Stardust. 1999. 13.04 (0-606-19268-9) Turtleback Bks.
Gale, Patrick. Rough Music. 2002. 384p. pap. 14.95 (0-345-44237-7) Ballantine Bks.
—Tree Surgery for Beginners. 1999. (Illus.). 275p. 25.00 (0-571-19958-5) Faber & Faber, Inc.
Galford, Ellen. The Dyke & the Dybbuk. 1994. 248p. reprint ed. pap. 10.95 o.p. (1-878067-51-6, Seal Pr.) Avalon Publishing Group.
—Moll Cutpurse: Her True History. 1985. (Illus.). 224p. (Orig.). reprint ed. pap. 7.95 (0-932379-04-4); lib. bdg. 16.95 (0-932379-05-2) Firebrand Bks.
Gallagher, Stephen. Down River. 1991. mass mkt. 4.99 (0-8125-0621-9); 1990. 18.95 o.p. (0-312-85006-9) Doherty, Tom Assocs., LLC. (Tor Bks.).
Galsworthy, John. Captures. 2001. 316p. per. 24.95 (1-58963-219-2) International Law & Taxation Pubs.
—Captures. 1971. reprint ed. 29.00 (0-403-00973-1) Scholarly Pr., Inc.
—The Complete Forsyte Saga. unabr. ed. audio 194.00 o.p. Recorded Bks., LLC.
—Flowering Wilderness. 23.95 (0-89190-659-2) Amereon, Ltd.
—Flowering Wilderness, , unabr. collector's ed. 1999. (End of Chapter Ser.: Vol. 2). audio 48.00 (0-7366-4383-4, 4849) Books on Tape, Inc.
—The Forsyte Saga. l.t. ed. 1996. (Perennial Bestseller Collection). 432p. (0-7451-3813-6, Black Dagger) BBC Audiobooks America.
—The Forsyte Saga. 1983. 540p. reprint ed. lib. bdg. 32.95 o.s.i (0-89966-443-1) Buccaneer Bks., Inc.
—The Forsyte Saga. 1982. 878p. pap. 18.00 (0-684-17653-X); 1977. 25.00 o.s.i (0-684-15368-8) Gale Group. (Macmillan Reference USA).
—The Forsyte Saga. 1999. (Oxford World's Classics Ser.). 912p. pap. 14.95 (0-19-283862-8) Oxford Univ. Pr., Inc.
—The Forsyte Saga. Harvey, Geoffrey, ed. & intro. by. 1997. (Oxford World's Classics Ser.). 902p. pap. 14.95 o.p. (0-19-282298-5) Oxford Univ. Pr., Inc.
—The Forsyte Saga. 1999. 1122p. 49.95 (0-7351-0122-1) Replica Bks.
—The Forsyte Saga. 1996. 896p. reprint ed. pap. 16.00 (0-684-81889-2, Touchstone) Simon & Schuster.
—The Forsyte Saga. 1997. (Penguin Twentieth-Century Classics Ser.). 912p. pap. 14.95 o.p. (0-14-018399-X, Penguin Classics) Viking Penguin.
—In Chancery, Vol. 2. 1996. (Forsyte Saga Ser.: Bk. II). audio 59.95 (1-55685-428-5) Audio Bk. Contractors, Inc.
—In Chancery. reprint ed. lib. bdg. 98.00 (0-7426-2777-2); 2001. 273p. pap. text 28.00 (0-7426-7777-X) Classic Bks.

—In Chancery. abr. ed. audio 15.95 o.p. *(0-88646-191-X*, 7192) Durkin Hayes Publishing Ltd.
—In Chancery, unabr. ed. 1988. (Forsyte Saga Ser.: Vol. 2). audio 70.00 *(1-55690-182-8*, 88040E7) Recorded Bks., LLC.
—In Chancery. l.t. ed. 1996. (Forsyte Saga Ser.: Vol. 2). 521p. lib. bdg. 23.95 *(0-7838-1505-0)* Thorndike Pr.
—In Chancery & Awakening, unabr. ed. 1998. (Forsyte Saga Ser.). audio 64.00 *(0-7366-4195-5*, 4693) Books on Tape, Inc.
—Maid in Waiting, unabr. collector's ed. 1999. (Forsyte Saga Ser.). audio 56.00 *(0-7366-4382-6*, 4848) Books on Tape, Inc.
—The Man of Property. E-Book 3.95 *(0-594-02239-8)* 1873 Pr.
—The Man of Property, Set. 1987. (Forsyte Saga Ser.: Bk. I). audio 53.95 *(1-55685-092-1)* Audio Bk. Contractors, Inc.
—The Man of Property. 1972. mass mkt. 1.50 o.p. *(0-345-22564-3)* Ballantine Bks.
—The Man of Property. reprint ed. lib. bdg. 98.00 *(0-7426-2747-0)*; 2001. 386p. pap. text 28.00 *(0-7426-7747-8)* Classic Bks.
—The Man of Property. abr. ed. 1986. (YA). (gr. 7-9). audio 29.95 o.p. *(0-88646-817-5*, R 7154); audio 15.95 o.p. *(0-88646-153-7*, 7154) Durkin Hayes Publishing Ltd.
—The Man of Property. 2002. 332p. 26.99 *(1-4043-1634-5)*; per. 21.99 *(1-4043-1635-3)* IndyPublish.com.
—The Man of Property, unabr. ed. 1988. (Forsyte Saga Ser.: Vol. 1). audio 85.00 *(1-55690-183-6*, 88030E7) Recorded Bks., LLC.
—The Man of Property. l.t. ed. 1995. (Forsyte Saga Ser.: Vol. 1). 500p. 24.95 *(0-7838-1504-2)* Thorndike Pr.
—The Man of Property. 1977. pap. 3.95 o.p. *(0-14-003196-0*, Penguin Bks.) Viking Penguin.
—The Man of Property & In Chancery. 2002. 896p. pap. 16.00 *(0-7432-4502-4*, Touchstone) Simon & Schuster.
—The Man of Property & Indian Summer of a Forsyte, unabr. collector's ed. 1998. audio 80.00 *(0-7366-4030-4*, 4529) Books on Tape, Inc.
—A Modern Comedy. 1920. 12.50 o.s.i *(0-684-10197-1*, Macmillan Reference USA) Gale Group.
—A Modern Comedy. 2002. 336p. pap. 32.95 *(0-7432-3774-9*, Scribner) Simon & Schuster.
—One More River, , unabr. collector's ed. 1999. (Forsyte Saga Ser.). audio 56.00 *(0-7366-4384-2*, 4850) Books on Tape, Inc.
—Salvation of a Forsyte & More. unabr. ed. 1992. (Forsyte Saga Ser.). audio 29.95 *(1-55685-224-X)* Audio Bk. Contractors, Inc.
—The Silver Spoon & Passers By. 23.95 *(0-8488-0064-8)* Amereon, Ltd.
—The Silver Spoon & Passers By. unabr. collector's ed. 1999. (Forsyte Saga Ser.). audio 56.00 *(0-7366-4385-0*, 4846) Books on Tape, Inc.
—Swan Song, unabr. collector's ed. 1999. (Forsyte Saga Ser.). audio 64.00 *(0-7366-4386-9*, 4847) Books on Tape, Inc.
—To Let, Set. 1996. (Forsyte Saga Ser.: Bk. III). audio 47.95 *(1-55685-429-3)* Audio Bk. Contractors, Inc.
—To Let. unabr. collector's ed. 1998. audio 56.00 *(0-7366-4196-3*, 4694) Books on Tape, Inc.
—To Let. reprint ed. lib. bdg. 98.00 *(0-7426-2780-2)*; 2001. 317p. pap. text 28.00 *(0-7426-7780-X)* Classic Bks.
—To Let, unabr. ed. 1988. (Forsyte Saga Ser.: Vol. 3). audio 60.00 *(1-55690-184-4*, 88050E7) Recorded Bks., LLC.
—To Let. l.t. ed. 1996. (Forsyte Saga Ser.: Vol. 3). 455p. 24.95 *(0-7838-1506-9)* Thorndike Pr.
—The White Monkey. Date not set. 336p. 25.95 *(0-8488-2271-4)* Amereon, Ltd.
—The White Monkey & A Silent Wooing, unabr. collector's ed. 1998. (Forsyte Saga Ser.). audio 56.00 *(0-7366-4349-4*, 4809) Books on Tape, Inc.
Galt, John. The Ayrshire Legatees. E-Book 2.49 *(1-58744-103-9)* Electric Umbrella Publishing.
—The Ayrshire Legatees. 2001. 120p. 22.99 *(1-58827-674-0)*; per. 18.99 *(1-58827-675-9)* IndyPublish.com.
—The Ayrshire Legatees. 1986. 168p. (C). pap. 35.00 *(0-901824-49-6)* Mercat Pr. Bks. GBR. *Dist:* State Mutual Bk. & Periodical Service, Ltd.
—The Ayrshire Legatees. (Ebook Classic Ser.). E-Book 5.00 *(0-7410-1171-9)* SoftBook Pr.
Gano, John. Arias of Blood. 2003. (Illus.). 226p. *(0-333-62963-9)* Macmillan U.K. GBR. *Dist:* Trafalgar Square.
—Arias of Blood. 1997. 240p. text 22.95 o.p. *(0-312-16775-X*, Saint Martin's Minotaur) St. Martin's Pr.
—Arias of Blood. l.t. ed. 1997. (General Ser.). 224p. pap. 22.95 *(0-7862-1114-8)* Thorndike Pr.
—Death at the Opera. l.t. ed. 1996. 267p. pap. 20.95 o.p. *(0-7838-1818-1*, Macmillan Reference USA) Gale Group.
—Death at the Opera. 1995. 208p. 20.95 o.p. *(0-312-13961-6*, Saint Martin's Minotaur) St. Martin's Pr.
—Inspector Proby's Christmas. 1994. 192p. 18.95 o.p. *(0-312-11292-0*, Saint Martin's Minotaur) St. Martin's Pr.
Gardam, Jane. The Flight of the Maidens. 2001. 288p. 25.00 *(0-7867-0879-4*, Carroll & Graf Pubs.) Avalon Publishing Group.
—The Flight of the Maidens. 2002. 288p. pap. 13.00 *(0-452-28334-5)* Dutton/Plume.
—The Flight of the Maidens. 2000. 352p. *(0-7011-6963-X)* Random Hse. of Canada, Ltd. CAN. *Dist:* Random Hse., Inc.
—The Queen of the Tambourine. 1996. 240p. pap. 11.00 o.s.i *(0-312-14398-2)* Picador.
—The Queen of the Tambourine. 1995. 240p. 20.95 o.p. *(0-312-13151-8)* St. Martin's Pr.
Gardner, John E. The Return of Moriarty. 1981. 304p. mass mkt. 3.50 o.s.i *(0-425-05093-9)* Berkley Publishing Group.
—The Revenge of Moriarty. 1981. 272p. mass mkt. 3.50 o.s.i *(0-425-05092-0)* Berkley Publishing Group.
—Win, Lose or Die. 1990. mass mkt. 4.95 o.s.i *(0-425-12261-1)* Berkley Publishing Group.
—Win, Lose or Die. l.t. ed. 1990. (Large Print Bks.). 393p. lib. bdg. 19.95 o.p. *(0-8161-4996-8*, Macmillan Reference USA) Gale Group.
—Win, Lose or Die. 1989. (James Bond Adventure Ser.). 320p. 13.95 o.p. *(0-399-13436-0*, G. P. Putnam's Sons) Penguin Putnam Bks. for Young Readers.
Garland, Alex. The Tesseract. abr. ed. 1999. audio 17.95 *(1-56740-818-4*, Nova Audio Bks.); audio 24.95 *(1-56740-097-3*, 1470, Brilliance Audio Unabridged); audio 41.25 *(1-56740-626-2*, 1471, Unabridged Library Editions) Brilliance Audio.
—The Tesseract. 2000. 288p. 13.00 *(1-57322-774-9)*; 1999. 273p. 24.95 o.p. *(1-57322-109-0)* Putnam Publishing Group, The. (Riverhead Bks. (Hardcovers)).
Garrett, George P. George Garrett. unabr. ed. 1989. audio 10.00 New Letters on Air.
Garrett, George P. & Bonetti, Kay. George Garrett. audio 13.95 *(1-55644-102-9*, 4062) American Audio Prose Library, Inc.
Garwood, Julie. Ransom. l.t. ed. 1999. (Large Print Book Ser.). 29.95 *(1-56895-722-X*, Wheeler Publishing, Inc.) Gale Group.
—Ransom. abr. ed. 1999. audio 18.00 Highsmith Inc.
—Ransom. 1999. 496p. 24.00 o.s.i *(0-671-00335-6*, Atria); (Illus.). 576p. reprint ed. mass mkt. 7.99 *(0-671-00336-4*, Pocket) Simon & Schuster.
—Ransom. 2001. audio 9.98 *(0-7435-0861-0)*; 1999. *(0-671-57685-2*, 399785) Simon & Schuster Audio. (Simon & Schuster Audioworks).
—Rebellious Desire. l.t. ed. 1992. (General Ser.). 391p. pap. 16.95 o.p. *(0-8161-5394-9)*; lib. bdg. 20.95 o.p. *(0-8161-5393-0)* Gale Group. (Macmillan Reference USA).
—Rebellious Desire. 1990. mass mkt. 4.95 *(0-671-72700-1)*; 1990. mass mkt. 4.50 *(0-671-70117-7)*; 1991. 320p. mass mkt. 7.99 *(0-671-73784-8)* Simon & Schuster. (Pocket).
Gash, Jonathan. Different Women Dancing. l.t. ed. 1997. (Large Print Book Ser.). pap. 23.95 o.p. *(1-56895-512-X*, Wheeler Publishing, Inc.) Gale Group.
—Different Women Dancing. 1998. 304p. pap. 5.99 o.s.i *(0-14-026411-6)* Penguin Group (USA) Inc.
—Different Women Dancing. 1997. 320p. 21.95 o.s.i *(0-670-87369-1)* Viking Penguin.
—Firefly Gadroon. 1985. (Lovejoy Mystery Ser.). 12.95 o.p. *(0-525-24135-3*, Dutton) Dutton/Plume.
—Firefly Gadroon. 1984. 208p. 11.95 o.p. *(0-312-29205-8)* St. Martin's Pr.
—Firefly Gadroon. l.t. ed. 1983. 352p. 15.95 o.p. *(0-7089-1012-2*, Ulverscroft) Thorpe, F. A. Pubs. GBR. *Dist:* Ulverscroft Large Print Bks., Ltd.
—Firefly Gadroon. 1985. (Lovejoy Mystery Ser.). 208p. pap. 5.95 o.s.i *(0-14-008007-4*, Penguin Bks.) Viking Penguin.
—Gold by Gemini. 1982. (Scene of the Crime Mystery Ser.: No. 36). pap. 2.25 o.p. *(0-440-12749-1)* Dell Publishing.
—Gold by Gemini. 1978. 186p. 8.95 *(0-06-011463-0)* HarperCollins Pubs.
—Gold by Gemini. 1988. (Lovejoy Mystery Ser.). 192p. mass mkt. 3.95 o.p. *(0-451-82185-8)* NAL.
—Gold by Gemini. unabr. ed. 1999. (Lovejoy Mystery Ser.). audio 53.00 *(1-84197-020-4*, H1020E7, Clipper Audio); audio compact disk 59.00 *(1-84197-090-5*, C1126E7);Set. audio 53.00 Recorded Bks., LLC.
—Gold by Gemini. l.t. ed. 1981. (Ulverscroft Large Print Ser.). 29.99 o.p. *(0-7089-0575-7*, Ulverscroft) Thorpe, F. A. Pubs. GBR. *Dist:* Ulverscroft Large Print Bks., Ltd., Ulverscroft Large Print Canada, Ltd.
—Gold by Gemini. 1988. pap. 39.50 o.p. *(0-14-778299-6)*; 224p. pap. 3.95 o.p. *(0-14-010529-8*, Penguin Bks.); 224p. pap. 5.95 o.p. *(0-14-023014-9*, Penguin Bks.) Viking Penguin.
—The Gondola Scam. 1984. 256p. 12.95 o.p. *(0-312-33828-7)* St. Martin's Pr.
—The Gondola Scam. 1985. (Lovejoy Mystery Ser.). 256p. pap. 5.99 o.p. *(0-14-007656-5*, Penguin Bks.) Viking Penguin.
—The Grace in Older Women: A Lovejoy Novel. 1996. (Lovejoy Mystery Ser.). 288p. pap. 5.95 o.p. *(0-14-024662-2*, Penguin Bks.) Penguin Group (USA) Inc.
—The Grace in Older Women: A Lovejoy Novel. 1995. (Lovejoy Mystery Ser.). 288p. 19.95 o.p. *(0-670-86128-6*, Viking) Viking Penguin.
—The Grail Tree. 21.95 *(0-88411-559-3)* Amereon, Ltd.
—The Grail Tree. 1982. (Scene of the Crime Ser.: No. 48). 288p. pap. 2.50 o.p. *(0-440-13022-0)* Dell Publishing.
—The Grail Tree. 1980. o.p. *(0-06-011462-2)* HarperCollins Pubs.
—The Grail Tree. 1988. (Lovejoy Mystery Ser.). 224p. mass mkt. 3.95 o.p. *(0-451-82186-6)* NAL.
—The Grail Tree. unabr. ed. (Lovejoy Mystery Ser.). 2001. audio compact disk 67.00 *(1-84197-098-0*, C1142E7); 1999. audio 53.00 *(1-84197-028-X*, H1027E7) Recorded Bks., LLC. (Clipper Audio).
—The Grail Tree. l.t. ed. 1983. (Ulverscroft Large Print Ser.). 368p. 29.99 o.p. *(0-7089-0958-2*, Ulverscroft) Thorpe, F. A. Pubs. GBR. *Dist:* Ulverscroft Large Print Bks., Ltd., Ulverscroft Large Print Canada, Ltd.
—The Grail Tree. 1988. pap. 39.50 o.p. *(0-14-778300-3)*; 224p. pap. 3.95 o.p. *(0-14-010530-1*, Penguin Bks.); 224p. pap. 5.95 o.s.i *(0-14-023015-7*, Penguin Bks.) Viking Penguin.
—The Great California Game. 1992. (Lovejoy Mystery Ser.). 256p. reprint ed. pap. 5.95 o.p. *(0-14-017224-6*, Penguin Bks.) Penguin Group (USA) Inc.
—The Great California Game. 1991. 288p. 19.95 o.p. *(0-312-06363-6*, Saint Martin's Minotaur) St. Martin's Pr.
—The Great California Game. l.t. ed. 1993. (Mystery Ser.). 512p. 29.99 o.p. *(0-7089-2930-3*, Ulverscroft) Thorpe, F. A. Pubs. GBR. *Dist:* Ulverscroft Large Print Bks., Ltd., Ulverscroft Large Print Canada, Ltd.
—Jade Woman. 1988. 288p. 17.95 o.p. *(0-312-02224-7*, Saint Martin's Minotaur) St. Martin's Pr.
—Jade Woman. l.t. ed. 1990. 18.95 o.p. *(0-7089-2189-2*, Ulverscroft) Thorpe, F. A. Pubs. GBR. *Dist:* Ulverscroft Large Print Bks., Ltd.
—Jade Woman. 1990. (Lovejoy Mystery Ser.). 288p. pap. 5.95 o.p. *(0-14-012280-X*, Penguin Bks.) Viking Penguin.
—The Judas Pair. 1981. (Scene of the Crime Mystery Ser.: No. 30). pap. 2.25 o.p. *(0-440-14354-3)* Dell Publishing.
—The Judas Pair. 1988. 39.50 o.p. *(0-14-778245-7)* Penguin Group (USA) Inc.
—The Judas Pair. 1999. (Lovejoy Mystery Ser.). audio 53.00 *(1-84197-004-2*, H1004E7); audio compact disk 61.00Set. audio 53.00 Recorded Bks., LLC.
—The Judas Pair. l.t. ed. 1982. (Ulverscroft Large Print Ser.). 368p. 29.99 o.p. *(0-7089-0856-X*, Ulverscroft) Thorpe, F. A. Pubs. GBR. *Dist:* Ulverscroft Large Print Bks., Ltd., Ulverscroft Large Print Canada, Ltd.
—The Judas Pair. (Lovejoy Mystery Ser.). 1989. 22p. pap. 6.95 o.p. *(0-14-012688-0)*; 1988. 224p. pap. 3.95 o.p. *(0-14-010528-X)* Viking Penguin. (Penguin Bks.).
—The Lies of Fair Ladies. 1993. (Lovejoy Mystery Ser.). 272p. pap. 5.95 o.p. *(0-14-017630-6*, Penguin Bks.) Penguin Group (USA) Inc.
—The Lies of Fair Ladies. 1992. 288p. 19.95 o.p. *(0-312-07620-7*, Saint Martin's Minotaur) St. Martin's Pr.
—The Lies of Fair Ladies. l.t. ed. 1994. (Large Print Ser.). 592p. 29.99 o.p. *(0-7089-3006-9*, Ulverscroft) Thorpe, F. A. Pubs. GBR. *Dist:* Ulverscroft Large Print Bks., Ltd., Ulverscroft Large Print Canada, Ltd.
—Moonspender. 1987. 240p. 14.95 o.p. *(0-312-00156-8)* St. Martin's Pr.
—Moonspender. (Lovejoy Mystery Ser.). 1990. 224p. pap. 5.99 o.p. *(0-14-014339-4)*; 1988. 272p. pap. 4.50 o.p. *(0-14-010646-4)* Viking Penguin. (Penguin Bks.).
—Paid & Loving Eyes. 1994. (Lovejoy Mystery Ser.). 272p. pap. 5.99 o.s.i *(0-14-023557-4*, Penguin Bks.) Penguin Group (USA) Inc.
—Paid & Loving Eyes. 1993. (Lovejoy Novel of Suspense Ser.). 288p. 19.95 o.p. *(0-312-09361-6*, Saint Martin's Minotaur) St. Martin's Pr.
—Paid & Loving Eyes. l.t. ed. 1994. (Ulverscroft Large Print Ser.). 608p. 29.99 o.p. *(0-7089-3164-2*, Ulverscroft) Thorpe, F. A. Pubs. GBR. *Dist:* Ulverscroft Large Print Bks., Ltd., Ulverscroft Large Print Canada, Ltd.
—Pearlhanger. 1985. 256p. 14.95 o.p. *(0-312-59970-6)* St. Martin's Pr.
—Pearlhanger. l.t. ed. 2000. (Mystery Ser.). 319p. 26.95 *(0-7862-2456-8)*; *(0-7540-4138-7)*; *(0-7540-4139-5)* Thorndike Pr.
—Pearlhanger. 1986. (Lovejoy Mystery Ser.). 24p. pap. 5.95 o.p. *(0-14-008468-1*, Penguin Bks.) Viking Penguin.
—The Possessions of a Lady. 1997. (Lovejoy Mystery Ser.). 336p. pap. 5.95 o.s.i *(0-14-025792-6)* Penguin Group (USA) Inc.
—The Possessions of a Lady. 1996. (Lovejoy Mystery Ser.). 332p. 21.95 o.s.i *(0-670-86933-3*, Viking) Viking Penguin.
—Prey Dancing. l.t. ed. 1999. (Dr. Clare Burtonall Mysteries Ser.). pap. 24.95 *(1-56895-626-6*, Wheeler Publishing, Inc.) Gale Group.
—Prey Dancing. 1999. (Dr. Clare Burtonall Mysteries Ser.). 288p. pap. 5.99 o.s.i *(0-14-028016-2*, Penguin Bks.) Penguin Group (USA) Inc.
—Prey Dancing. 1998. (Dr. Clare Burtonall Mysteries Ser.). 288p. 21.95 o.p. *(0-670-87764-6)* Viking Penguin.
—The Rich & the Profane. l.t. ed. 1999. pap. 23.95 *(1-56895-794-7*, Wheeler Publishing, Inc.) Gale Group.
—The Rich & the Profane. 2000. (Lovejoy Mystery Ser.). 352p. pap. 5.99 *(0-14-028622-5*, Penguin Bks.) Penguin Group (USA) Inc.
—The Rich & the Profane. 1999. (Lovejoy Mystery Ser.). 288p. 22.95 o.s.i *(0-670-88346-8)* Viking Penguin.
—The Sin Within Her Smile. l.t. ed. 1994. 385p. 20.95 *(0-8161-1115-4)*; lib. bdg. 21.95 *(0-7838-1115-2)* Gale Group. (Macmillan Reference USA).
—The Sin Within Her Smile. 1995. (Lovejoy Mystery Ser.). 240p. pap. 5.99 o.s.i *(0-14-023839-5*, Penguin Bks.) Penguin Group (USA) Inc.
—The Sin Within Her Smile. 1994. (Lovejoy Mystery Ser.). 240p. 18.95 o.p. *(0-670-85608-8*, Viking) Viking Penguin.
—The Sleepers of Erin. 1983. (Lovejoy Mystery Ser.). 228p. 13.95 o.p. *(0-525-24163-9*, 01354-410, Dutton) Dutton/Plume.
—The Sleepers of Erin. l.t. ed. 1985. 384p. 15.95 o.p. *(0-7089-1363-6*, Ulverscroft) Thorpe, F. A. Pubs. GBR. *Dist:* Ulverscroft Large Print Bks., Ltd.
—The Sleepers of Erin. 1984. (Crime Monthly Ser.). 224p. pap. 5.99 o.p. *(0-14-006970-4*, Penguin Bks.) Viking Penguin.
—Spend Game. 1981. (Joan Kahn Bk.). 204p. 9.95 o.p. *(0-89919-030-8)* Houghton Mifflin Co.
—Spend Game. unabr. ed. 2000. (Lovejoy Mystery Ser.). audio 53.00 *(1-84197-045-X*, H1050E7, Clipper Audio) Recorded Bks., LLC.
—Spend Game. l.t. ed. 1981. 360p. 12.00 o.p. *(0-7089-0673-7*, Ulverscroft) Thorpe, F. A. Pubs. GBR. *Dist:* Ulverscroft Large Print Bks., Ltd.
—Spend Game. 1982. (Crime Monthly Ser.). 208p. pap. 5.95 o.p. *(0-14-006190-8*, Penguin Bks.) Viking Penguin.
—The Tartan Sell. 1990. (Lovejoy Mystery Ser.). 24p. pap. 5.99 *(0-14-014596-6*, Penguin Bks.) Penguin Group (USA) Inc.
—The Tartan Sell. 1986. 240p. 14.95 o.p. *(0-312-78614-X)* St. Martin's Pr.
—The Tartan Sell. 1987. (Lovejoy Mystery Ser.). 240p. pap. 3.95 o.p. *(0-14-009745-7*, Penguin Bks.) Viking Penguin.
—The Vatican Rip. 1982. (Joan Kahn Bk.). 228p. 10.95 o.p. *(0-89919-080-4)* Houghton Mifflin Co.
—The Vatican Rip. l.t. ed. 1984. 368p. 15.95 o.p. *(0-7089-1101-3*, Ulverscroft) Thorpe, F. A. Pubs. GBR. *Dist:* Ulverscroft Large Print Bks., Ltd.
—The Vatican Rip. 1983. (Lovejoy Mystery Ser.). 224p. pap. 5.99 o.s.i *(0-14-006431-1*, Penguin Bks.) Viking Penguin.
—The Very Last Gambado. 1991. (Crime Monthly Ser.). 288p. reprint ed. pap. 5.95 o.p. *(0-14-014738-1*, Penguin Bks.) Penguin Group (USA) Inc.
—The Very Last Gambado. 1990. 18.95 o.p. *(0-312-05175-1)* St. Martin's Pr.
—The Very Last Gambado. l.t. ed. 1991. (Ulverscroft Large Print Ser.). 29.99 o.p. *(0-7089-2532-4*, Ulverscroft) Thorpe, F. A. Pubs. GBR. *Dist:* Ulverscroft Large Print Bks., Ltd., Ulverscroft Large Print Canada, Ltd.
Gaskell, Elizabeth. Cousin Phillis & Other Tales. 1970. 5.00 o.p. *(0-460-00615-0)* Biblio Distribution.
—Cousin Phillis & Other Tales. Easson, Angus, ed. & intro. by. 1982. (Oxford World's Classics Ser.). 384p. pap. 5.95 o.p. *(0-19-281554-7)* Oxford Univ. Pr., Inc.
—Cranford. 2003. (Dover Thrift Editions Ser.). 144p. pap. 2.00 *(0-486-42681-5)* Dover Pubns., Inc.
—Cranford. 1955. 7.00 o.p. *(0-460-00083-7*, Dutton) Dutton/Plume.
—Cranford. Watson, Elizabeth Porges, ed. 2nd ed. 1998. (Oxford World's Classics Ser.). 240p. pap. 9.95 *(0-19-283209-3)* Oxford Univ. Pr., Inc.
—Cranford/Cousin Philis. Keating, P. J., ed. 1977. (English Library). 368p. 12.00 *(0-14-043104-7*, Penguin Classics) Viking Penguin.
—A Dark Night's Work & Other Stories. Lewis, Suzanne, ed. & intro. by. 1992. (Oxford World's Classics Ser.). 352p. pap. 10.95 o.p. *(0-19-282807-X)* Oxford Univ. Pr., Inc.

Settings

—Elizabeth Gaskell: Four Short Stories. 1983. pap. 7.95 o.p. (0-86358-001-7) Pandora Pr. GBR. Dist: HarperSanFrancisco.
—Grey Woman & Other Tales. 1977. (Short Story Index Reprint Ser.). reprint ed. 19.95 (0-8369-3942-5) Ayer Co. Pubs., Inc.
—Lizzie Leigh & Other Tales. 1977. (Short Story Index Reprint Ser.). reprint ed. 19.95 (0-8369-4102-0) Ayer Co. Pubs., Inc.
—Lizzie Leigh & Other Tales. reprint ed. lib. bdg. 98.00 (0-7426-2361-0); 2001. (Collected Works of Elizabeth Gaskell: Vol. 2). (Illus.). pap. text 28.00 (0-7426-7361-8) Classic Bks.
—Mary Barton. unabr. ed. 1996. audio 65.95 (1-55685-402-1) Audio Bk. Contractors, Inc.
—Mary Barton. unabr. ed. 1997. 12p. audio 96.95 (0-7451-2772-X, SAB 136, Sterling Audio Bks.) BBC Audiobooks America.
—Mary Barton. 1971. reprint ed. 8.95 o.p. (0-460-00598-7); 2.50 o.p. (0-460-01598-2) Biblio Distribution.
—Mary Barton. Foster, Jennifer, ed. 2000. (Literary Texts Ser.). 520p. pap. (1-55111-169-1) Broadview Pr.
—Mary Barton. (Collected Works of Elizabeth Gaskell). reprint ed. lib. bdg. 196.00 (0-7426-2355-6); 2001. pap. text 56.00 (0-7426-7355-3) Classic Bks.
—Mary Barton. Easson, Angus, ed. 1998. 432p. 45.00 (1-85331-020-4) Edinburgh Univ. Pr. GBR. Dist: Columbia Univ. Pr.
—Mary Barton. 1994. (Everyman's Library). 17.00 (0-679-43494-1) Knopf, Alfred A. Inc.
—Mary Barton. Wright, Edgar, ed. & intro. by. (Oxford World's Classics Ser.). 1998. 544p. pap. 7.95 (0-19-283510-6); 1987. 530p. pap. 6.95 o.p. (0-19-281750-7) Oxford Univ. Pr., Inc.
—Mary Barton. Daly, Macdonald, ed. & intro. by. 1997. (Penguin Classics Ser.). 464p. pap. 7.95 (0-14-043464-X, Penguin Classics) Viking Penguin.
—Mary Barton. Gill, Stephen, ed. & intro. by. 1975. (English Library). 496p. pap. 8.95 o.p. (0-14-043053-9, Penguin Classics) Viking Penguin.
—Mary Barton. abr. ed. 1997. audio 23.95 o.s.i (0-14-086171-8, Penguin AudioBooks) Viking Penguin.
—The Moorland Cottage & Other Stories. Lewis, Suzanne, ed. & intro. by. 1995. (Oxford World's Classics Ser.). 348p. pap. 10.95 o.p. (0-19-282321-3) Oxford Univ. Pr., Inc.
—My Lady Ludlow & Other Stories. Wright, Edgar, ed. & intro. by. 1989. (Oxford World's Classics Ser.). 482p. pap. 10.95 o.p. (0-19-281838-4) Oxford Univ. Pr., Inc.
—North & South, 2. reprint ed. lib. bdg. 196.00 (0-7426-2363-7); 2001. pap. text 56.00 (0-7426-7363-4) Classic Bks.
—North & South. 1976. 3.25 o.p. (0-460-01680-6); 1962. 5.00 o.p. (0-460-00680-0) Dutton/Plume. (Dutton).
—North & South. 2002. 460p. 98.99 (1-4043-2172-1); per. 93.99 (1-4043-2173-X) IndyPublish.com.
—North & South. Easson, Angus, ed. & intro. by. 1982. (Oxford World's Classics Ser.). 476p. pap. 7.95 o.p. (0-19-281595-4) Oxford Univ. Pr., Inc.
—North & South. Easson, Angus, ed. 2nd ed. 1998. (Oxford World's Classics Ser.). 496p. pap. 9.95 (0-19-283194-1) Oxford Univ. Pr., Inc.
—North & South. 1988. reprint ed. lib. bdg. 49.00 (0-7812-0038-5) Reprint Services Corp.
—North & South. 1971. reprint ed. 69.00 (0-403-00985-5) Scholarly Pr., Inc.
—North & South. l.t. ed. 1982. (Charnwood Large Print Ser.). 725p. 29.99 o.p. (0-7089-8031-7, Charnwood) Thorpe, F. A. Pubs. GBR. Dist: Ulverscroft Large Print Bks., Ltd., Ulverscroft Large Print Canada, Ltd.
—North & South. Uglow, Jenny, ed. 1993. 442p. pap. 6.95 (0-460-87257-5, Everyman's Classic Library in Paperback) Tuttle Publishing.
—North & South. Ingham, Patricia, ed. & intro. by. 1996. 480p. pap. 10.00 (0-14-043424-0, Penguin Classics) Viking Penguin.
—North & South. Colin, R., ed. 1970. (English Library). 544p. pap. 6.95 o.p. (0-14-043055-5, Penguin Classics) Viking Penguin.
—North & South. 1998. (Classics Library). pap. 3.95 (1-85326-093-2, 0932WW) Wordsworth Editions, Ltd. GBR. Dist: Casemate Pubs. & Bk. Distributors, LLC.
—Sylvia's Lovers, 3. reprint ed. lib. bdg. 294.00 (0-7426-2368-8); 2001. pap. text 84.00 (0-7426-7368-5) Classic Bks.
—Sylvia's Lovers. 1964. 15.50 o.p. (0-460-00524-3, Dutton) Dutton/Plume.
—Sylvia's Lovers. 2001. (Twelve-Point Ser.). 450p. lib. bdg. 25.00 (1-58287-167-1); 681p. lib. bdg. 28.00 (1-58287-650-9) North Bks.
—Sylvia's Lovers. (Oxford World's Classics Ser.). 560p. 2000. pap. 11.95 (0-19-283731-1); 1982. pap. 9.95 o.p. (0-19-281571-7) Oxford Univ. Pr., Inc.
—Sylvia's Lovers. Handley, Graham & Henry, Nancy, eds. 1989. (Everyman Paperback Classics Ser.). 592p. pap. 8.95 (0-460-87783-6, Everyman's Classic Library in Paperback) Tuttle Publishing.
—Sylvia's Lovers. Foster, Shirley, ed. & intro. by. 1997. (Penguin Classics Ser.). 528p. pap. 11.95 o.p. (0-14-043422-4, Penguin Classics) Viking Penguin.
—Wives & Daughters. 1971. 639p. pap. 3.95 o.p. (0-586-03730-6) Academy Chicago Pubs., Ltd.
—Wives & Daughters. Easson, Angus, ed. (Oxford World's Classics Ser.). 2003. 784p. pap. 12.95 (0-19-283839-3); 1988. 768p. pap. 5.95 o.p. (0-19-281702-7) Oxford Univ. Pr., Inc.
—Wives & Daughters. 1999. (Everyman Gaskell Ser.). 816p. pap. 12.95 (0-460-87651-1) Tuttle Publishing.
—Wives & Daughters. (Penguin Classics Ser.). 720p. 2001. 13.95 (0-14-243700-X); 1997. (Illus.). pap. 13.95 (0-14-043478-X, Penguin Classics) Viking Penguin.
—Wives & Daughters. Glover-Smith, Frank, ed. 1969. (English Library). 720p. pap. 9.95 o.p. (0-14-043046-6, Penguin Classics) Viking Penguin.
Gayle, Mike. My Legendary Girlfriend. 2001. (0-385-50103-X) Doubleday Publishing.
Geary, Rick. A Treasury of Victorian Murder Vol. 2: Jack the Ripper. 1995. (Treasury of Victorian Murder Ser.). (Illus.). 64p. 15.95 (1-56163-124-8, Comics Lit) NBM Publishing Co.
Gebler, Carlo. Work & Play. 1991. 2.99 o.p. (0-517-06879-6) Random Hse. Value Publishing.
—Work & Play. 1990. pap. 7.95 o.p. (0-671-68417-5, Fireside) Simon & Schuster.
Gedney, Mona K. Lady Diana's Daring Deed. 2000. (Zebra Regency Romance Ser.). 256p. mass mkt. 4.99 o.s.i (0-8217-6721-6, Zebra Bks.) Kensington Publishing Corp.
Gedney, Mona K., et al. A Match for Mother. 1999. (Zebra Regency Romance Ser.). 254p. mass mkt. 4.99 o.s.i (0-8217-6185-4, Zebra Bks.) Kensington Publishing Corp.
Geller, Uri. Ella. 1999. (SPA.). 384p. (84-270-2430-4) Ediciones Martinez Roca.
—Ella. 1998. 438p. pap. 9.95 (0-7472-5920-8) Headline Bk. Publishing, Ltd. GBR. Dist: Trafalgar Square.
Gemmell, Nikki. Lovesong. 2001. 200p. (0-330-37292-0) Picador.
George, Elizabeth. Deception on His Mind. 1998. 752p. mass mkt. 7.99 (0-553-57509-0); mass mkt. 6.99 (0-553-84018-5) Bantam Bks.
—Deception on His Mind. l.t. ed. 1997. (Basic Ser.). 1021p. 29.95 (0-7862-1144-X) Thorndike Pr.
—For the Sake of Elena. 1993. 464p. mass mkt. 7.99 (0-553-56127-8) Bantam Bks.
—For the Sake of Elena. unabr. ed. 1993. audio 88.00 (0-7366-2385-X, 3156) Books on Tape, Inc.
—For the Sake of Elena. l.t. ed. 1993. (Magna Large Print Ser.). 659p. o.p. (0-7505-0497-8) Magna Large Print Bks. GBR. Dist: Ulverscroft Large Print Canada, Ltd.
—For the Sake of Elena. abr. ed. 1992. audio 15.99 (0-553-47034-5, 390797, RH Audio) Random Hse. Audio Publishing Group.
—A Great Deliverance. 1989. 432p. mass mkt. 7.50 (0-553-27802-9) Bantam Bks.
—A Great Deliverance. unabr. ed. 1994. audio 64.00 (0-7366-2624-7, 3364) Books on Tape, Inc.
—A Great Deliverance. abr. ed. 1992. 180p. pap. 15.99 incl. audio (0-553-47056-6, RH Audio) Random Hse. Audio Publishing Group.
—In Pursuit of the Proper Sinner. 2000. 752p. mass mkt. 7.99 (0-553-57510-4) Bantam Bks.
—In Pursuit of the Proper Sinner. 1999. Pt. 1. audio 64.00 (0-7366-4652-3, 5033-A); Pt. 2. audio 64.00 (0-7366-4722-8, 5033-B) Books on Tape, Inc.
—In Pursuit of the Proper Sinner. l.t. ed. 1999. pap. 25.95 o.p. (0-7838-8692-6, Macmillan Reference USA) Gale Group.
—In Pursuit of the Proper Sinner, Set. abr. ed. 1999. audio 25.95 Highsmith Inc.
—In Pursuit of the Proper Sinner. abr. ed. 1999. audio 25.95 (0-553-47819-2, RH Audio) Random Hse. Audio Publishing Group.
—In Pursuit of the Proper Sinner. l.t. ed. 912p. 2000. pap. 14.95 (0-375-72799-X); 1999. 25.95 (0-375-40846-0) Random Hse. Large Print.
—In the Presence of the Enemy. 1997. 656p. mass mkt. 7.99 (0-553-57608-9) Bantam Bks.
—In the Presence of the Enemy. unabr. ed. 1996. audio 120.00 (0-7366-3278-6, 3934) Books on Tape, Inc.
—In the Presence of the Enemy. unabr. ed. 2000. (Inspector Thomas Lynley Mystery Ser.: Vol. 8). audio 128.00 (0-7887-0523-7, 94718E7) Recorded Bks., LLC.
—Missing Joseph. 1994. 592p. mass mkt. 7.99 (0-553-56604-0) Bantam Bks.
—Missing Joseph. unabr. ed. 1993. audio 104.00 (0-7366-2533-X, 3285) Books on Tape, Inc.
—Missing Joseph. l.t. ed. 1993. 12.95 o.p. (1-56895-038-1, Wheeler Publishing, Inc.) Gale Group.
—Payment in Blood. 1990. 432p. mass mkt. 7.99 (0-553-28436-3) Bantam Bks.
—Payment in Blood. unabr. ed. 1994. audio 72.00 (0-7366-2637-9, 3376) Books on Tape, Inc.
—Payment in Blood. unabr. ed. 2001. audio 69.95 (1-85089-779-4, 30691) ISIS Audio Bks. GBR. Dist: Ulverscroft Large Print Bks., Ltd.
—Payment in Blood. unabr. ed. 1992. (Inspector Thomas Lynley Mystery Ser.: Vol. 2). audio 85.00 (1-55690-762-1, 92426E7) Recorded Bks., LLC.
—Playing for the Ashes. 1995. 704p. mass mkt. 7.99 (0-553-57251-2, Crimeline) Bantam Bks.
—Playing for the Ashes, Pt. 1. unabr. ed. 1994. audio 64.00 (0-7366-2885-1, 3587-A) Books on Tape, Inc.
—A Suitable Vengeance. 1992. 464p. mass mkt. 7.99 (0-553-29560-8) Bantam Bks.
—A Suitable Vengeance. unabr. ed. 1994. audio 80.00 (0-7366-2796-0, 3511) Books on Tape, Inc.
—A Suitable Vengeance. l.t. ed. 1993. (Magna Large Print Ser.). 653p. o.p. (0-7505-0456-0) Magna Large Print Bks. GBR. Dist: Ulverscroft Large Print Canada, Ltd.
—A Suitable Vengeance. abr. ed. 1991. audio 15.99 (0-553-45286-X, RH Audio) Random Hse. Audio Publishing Group.
—A Suitable Vengeance. unabr. ed. 1993. (Inspector Thomas Lynley Mystery Ser.: Vol. 4). audio 97.00 (1-55690-812-1, 93121E7) Recorded Bks., LLC.
—A Traitor to Memory. 2002. mass mkt. 7.99 (0-553-84037-1) Bantam Bks.
—A Traitor to Memory. abr. unabr. ed. 2001. audio 25.95 (0-553-52821-1); audio compact disk 29.95 (0-553-71440-6) Random Hse. Audio Publishing Group. (RH Audio).
—A Traitor to Memory. l.t. ed. 2001. 1184p. 26.95 (0-375-43113-6) Random Hse. Large Print.
—Well-Schooled in Murder. 1991. 432p. mass mkt. 7.99 (0-553-28734-6); 1990. 368p. 17.95 o.s.i (0-553-07000-2) Bantam Bks.
—Well-Schooled in Murder. unabr. ed. 1993. audio 80.00 (0-7366-2602-6, 3346) Books on Tape, Inc.
—Well-Schooled in Murder. abr. ed. 1991. audio 15.99 (0-553-45278-9, 391880, RH Audio) Random Hse. Audio Publishing Group.
George, Melanie. Devil May Care. 2001. (Zebra Historical Romance Ser.). 336p. mass mkt. 5.99 o.s.i (0-8217-7008-X, Zebra Bks.) Kensington Publishing Corp.
Gerhardie, William. Doom. 2001. 288p. pap. 13.00 (1-85375-446-3) Prion GBR. Dist: Trafalgar Square.
Gibbins, James. Searching for Johnny. 2002. (Illus.). 400p. 25.95 (0-312-28184-6) St. Martin's Pr.
Gibbons, Stella. Cold Comfort Farm, Set. unabr. ed. 1995. audio 69.95 (1-56054-905-X, SAB 039, Sterling Audio Bks.) BBC Audiobooks America.
—Cold Comfort Farm. unabr. ed. 2000. audio 59.95 Chivers Audio Bks. GBR. Dist: BBC Audiobooks America.
—Cold Comfort Farm. l.t. ed. 1987. (Mainstream Ser.). 338p. 15.95 o.p. (1-85089-093-5) ISIS Large Print Bks. GBR. Dist: Transaction Pubs.
—Cold Comfort Farm. 1999. 240p. pap. 10.95 (0-14-027414-6) Penguin Bks., Ltd. GBR. Dist: Trafalgar Square.
—Cold Comfort Farm. 1996. 240p. pap. 10.95 o.s.i (0-14-025813-2, Penguin Bks.) Penguin Group (USA) Inc.
—Cold Comfort Farm. 1985. 19.30 o.p. (0-8446-6148-1) Smith, Peter Pub., Inc.
—Cold Comfort Farm. (Twentieth Century Classics Ser.). 1996. 240p. 13.00 (0-14-018869-X, Penguin Classics); 1977. 240p. pap. 7.00 o.p. (0-14-000140-9, Penguin Bks.); 1997. audio 16.95 o.s.i (0-14-086575-6, Penguin AudioBooks) Viking Penguin.
Gibson, Elizabeth. Men of Kent. 1989. 256p. 12.95 (0-310-32220-0, 12328) Zondervan.
Gilbert, Anna. A Hint of Witchcraft. 2001. 381p. (0-7540-1568-8, Macmillan Reference USA) Gale Group.
—A Hint of Witchcraft. 2000. 256p. 23.95 (0-312-19984-8) St. Martin's Pr.
—A Hint of Witchcraft. l.t. ed. 2001. (Romance Ser.). 381p. 26.95 (0-7838-9360-4) Thorndike Pr.
—Miss Bede Is Staying. l.t. ed. 2001. (G. K. Hall Romance Ser.). 375p. 26.95 (0-7838-9454-6, Macmillan Reference USA) Gale Group.
—A Morning in Eden. l.t. ed. 2002. 379p. 27.95 (0-7862-4202-7) Gale Group.
—A Morning in Eden. 2001. 240p. 22.95 o.s.i (0-312-28438-1, Saint Martin's Minotaur) St. Martin's Pr.
—The Treachery of Time. l.t. ed. 1996. pap. 20.95 (0-7838-1663-4, Macmillan Reference USA) Gale Group.
—The Treachery of Time. 1996. 432p. 24.95 (0-312-14055-X) St. Martin's Pr.
—The Wedding Guest. 1993. 304p. 20.95 o.p. (0-312-09935-5) St. Martin's Pr.
Gilbert, Anthony. The Black Stage. unabr. ed. 1989. (C). audio 54.95 (0-7451-5982-6) BBC Audiobooks America.
—The Black Stage. (Black Dagger Crime Ser.). 232p. 12.95 o.p. (0-86220-727-4) Chivers Pr. GBR. Dist: BBC Audiobooks America.
—Death Takes a Wife. l.t. ed. 1991. pap. 16.95 o.p. (0-7927-0515-7, CS0114) BBC Audiobooks America.
—The Mouse Who Wouldn't Play Ball. l.t. ed. 1991. pap. 16.95 o.p. (0-7927-0711-7, CS0247) BBC Audiobooks America.
—Murder Comes Home. l.t. ed. 1992. pap. 14.95 o.p. (0-7927-1067-3) BBC Audiobooks America.
—A Nice Little Killing. l.t. ed. 1991. pap. 10.95 o.p. (0-7927-0146-1, C0102) BBC Audiobooks America.
—Passenger to Nowhere. l.t. ed. 1990. pap. 16.95 o.p. (0-7927-0161-5, C0253) BBC Audiobooks America.
—Snake in the Grass. (Black Dagger Crime Ser.). 1993. 192p. 16.50 o.p. (0-7451-8616-5, Black Dagger); 1994. 18.95 o.p. (0-7451-6459-5) BBC Audiobooks America.
Gilbert, Michael. Ring of Terror. 1995. 256p. 20.00 o.p. (0-7867-0193-5, Carroll & Graf Pubs.) Avalon Publishing Group.
—Ring of Terror. l.t. ed. 1996. pap. 17.95 o.p. (0-7838-1537-9, Macmillan Reference USA) Gale Group.
—Roller-Coaster. 1994. 256p. 19.95 o.p. (0-88184-996-0, Carroll & Graf Pubs.) Avalon Publishing Group.
—The Young Petrella: Stories. 1988. 224p. 15.95 o.p. (0-06-015934-0) HarperTrade.
Giles, Kenneth. A File on Death. 1985. reprint ed. pap. 2.95 o.s.i (0-8027-3103-1) Walker & Co.
—Murder Pluperfect. 1984. reprint ed. pap. 2.95 o.p. (0-8027-3094-9) Walker & Co.
Gill, A. A. Sap Rising. 2000. 317p. pap. 11.95 (0-552-99679-3) Transworld Publishers Ltd. GBR. Dist: Trafalgar Square.
Gill, John. The Tenant. 1985. 160p. 16.95 o.p. (0-89733-142-7); pap. 7.95 o.p. (0-89733-141-9) Academy Chicago Pubs., Ltd.
Gill, Stephen, ed. The Last Chronicle of Barset. 1989. 928p. 21.00 (0-19-520809-9) Oxford Univ. Pr., Inc.
Gillenwater, Sharon. Song of the Highlands. 1997. 428p. pap. 11.99 o.s.i (0-88070-946-4, Palisades) Multnomah Pubs., Inc.
—Unwilling Heart. l.t. ed. 1991. (Orig.). 21.95 o.p. (0-7927-0837-7, CH086); pap. 19.95 o.p. (0-7927-0838-5, CS0184) BBC Audiobooks America.
Gilpin, T. G. Death of a Fantasy Life. 1993. 176p. 16.95 o.p. (0-312-09270-9, Saint Martin's Minotaur) St. Martin's Pr.
—Missing Daisy. 1995. 204p. 19.95 o.p. (0-312-13564-5, Saint Martin's Minotaur) St. Martin's Pr.
Girard, Paula Tanner. Seventh Sister. 2000. (Zebra Regency Romance Ser.). 224p. mass mkt. 4.99 (0-8217-6672-4) Kensington Publishing Corp.
—The Seventh Sister. 2001. (Five Star Romance Ser.). 219p. 25.95 (0-7862-3503-9, Five Star) Gale Group.
Giroux, E. X. A Death for a Dancer: A Robert Forsythe Mystery. 1986. mass mkt. 2.95 o.s.i (0-345-33408-6) Ballantine Bks.
—A Death for a Dancer: A Robert Forsythe Mystery. 1985. 192p. 12.95 o.p. (0-312-18868-4) St. Martin's Pr.
—A Death for a Darling. 1986. 192p. mass mkt. 3.50 o.s.i (0-345-33024-2) Ballantine Bks.
—A Death for a Darling. 1985. 192p. 13.95 o.p. (0-312-18607-X) St. Martin's Pr.
—A Death for a Dietician. 1989. 192p. mass mkt. 3.95 o.s.i (0-345-35767-1) Ballantine Bks.
—A Death for a Dietitian. 1988. 176p. 13.95 o.p. (0-312-01417-1, Saint Martin's Minotaur) St. Martin's Pr.
—A Death for a Dilettante. 1987. 176p. mass mkt. 3.50 o.s.i (0-345-34758-7) Ballantine Bks.
—A Death for a Dilettante. 1987. (Robert Forsythe Mystery Ser.). 208p. 13.95 o.p. (0-312-00044-8) St. Martin's Pr.
—A Death for a Doctor: A Robert Forsythe Mystery. 1986. 208p. 13.95 o.p. (0-312-18603-7) St. Martin's Pr.
—A Death for a Dodo. 1993. 17.95 o.p. (0-312-08762-4, Saint Martin's Minotaur) St. Martin's Pr.
—A Death for a Double. 1991. 192p. mass mkt. 3.95 o.s.i (0-345-36833-9) Ballantine Bks.
—A Death for a Double. 1992. 2.99 o.p. (0-517-09039-2) Random Hse. Value Publishing.
—A Death for a Double. 1990. 208p. 15.95 o.p. (0-312-03809-7, Saint Martin's Minotaur) St. Martin's Pr.
—A Death for a Dreamer. 1990. (Death Ser.). 192p. mass mkt. 3.95 o.s.i (0-345-36528-3) Ballantine Bks.
—A Death for a Dreamer. 1989. 14.95 o.p. (0-312-02901-2, Saint Martin's Minotaur) St. Martin's Pr.
—A Death for Adonis. 1985. 160p. mass mkt. 4.95 o.s.i (0-345-32889-2) Ballantine Bks.
—A Death for Adonis. 1984. 160p. 11.95 o.p. (0-312-18610-X) St. Martin's Pr.

Giroux, E. X. & Giroux, Leo. A Death for a Doctor: A Robert Forsythe Mystery. 1987. 192p. mass mkt. 4.95 o.s.i (*0-345-34231-3*) Ballantine Bks.

Gissing, George R. Born in Exile: A Novel, 3 vols. in 1. reprint ed. 37.50 (*0-404-02786-5*) AMS Pr., Inc.

—Born in Exile: A Novel. Coustillas, Pierre, ed. 1978. (Society & the Victorians Ser.). text 22.25 o.p. (*0-85527-872-2*) Brill Academic Pubs., Inc.

—Born in Exile: A Novel. 1993. 544p. pap. 6.95 (*0-460-87241-9*, Everyman's Classic Library in Paperback) Tuttle Publishing.

—The Emancipated, 3 vols. in 1. reprint ed. 115.00 (*0-404-02785-7*) AMS Pr., Inc.

—The Emancipated. Coustillas, Pierre, ed. 1978. 469p. 22.50 o.p. (*0-8386-2171-6*) Fairleigh Dickinson Univ. Pr.

—New Grub Street. E-Book 2.49 (*0-7574-0286-0*) Electric Umbrella Publishing.

—New Grub Street. 2002. 560p. 99.99 (*1-4043-2200-0*); per. 95.99 (*1-4043-2201-9*) IndyPublish.com.

—New Grub Street. 1993. (Oxford World's Classics Ser.). (Illus.). 568p. pap. 7.95 o.p. (*0-19-282963-7*) Oxford Univ. Pr., Inc.

—New Grub Street. 2002. (Modern Library Classics). 544p. pap. 13.95 (*0-375-76110-1*) Random Hse., Inc.

—New Grub Street. E-Book 5.00 (*0-7410-1036-4*) SoftBook Pr.

—Paying Guest. reprint ed. 27.50 (*0-404-02799-7*) AMS Pr., Inc.

—The Town Traveller. reprint ed. 18.00 (*0-404-02813-6*) AMS Pr., Inc.

—The Town Traveller. Coustillas, Pierre, ed. 1981. 324p. text 21.50 o.p. (*0-85527-902-8*) Brill Academic Pubs., Inc.

—Victim of Circumstances, & Other Stories. 1977. (Short Story Index Reprint Ser.). reprint ed. 19.95 (*0-8369-4013-X*) Ayer Co. Pubs., Inc.

Gitlin, Todd. The Murder of Albert Einstein. 1994. 352p. pap. 8.95 o.s.i (*0-553-37366-8*) Bantam Bks.

Glaister, Lesley. Now You See Me. 2001. 288p. (*0-7475-5206-1*) Bloomsbury Pr.

—Trick or Treat. 1992. 192p. (J). text 19.00 (*0-689-12140-7*) Central Bureau voor Schimmelcultures NLD. *Dist:* Lubrecht & Cramer, Ltd.

Glendinning, Victoria. Electricity. unabr. ed. 1997. audio 69.95 (*0-7451-7384-5*, SAB 151, Sterling Audio Bks.) BBC Audiobooks America.

—Electricity. 1995. 250p. 22.95 o.p. (*0-316-30159-0*) Little Brown & Co.

—Electricity. 1997. 256p. pap. 12.00 o.p. (*0-312-15117-9*) Picador.

Glover, Judith. Sisters & Brothers. 1984. 288p. 12.95 o.p. (*0-312-72747-X*) St. Martin's Pr.

—Sisters & Brothers. l.t. ed. 1985. (Charnwood Large Print Ser.). 448p. 29.99 o.p. (*0-7089-8254-9*, Ulverscroft) Thorpe, F. A. Pubs. GBR. *Dist:* Ulverscroft Large Print Bks., Ltd., Ulverscroft Large Print Canada, Ltd.

—The Stallion Man. 1983. 256p. 13.95 o.p. (*0-312-75542-2*) St. Martin's Pr.

—The Stallion Man. l.t. ed. 1985. (Charnwood Large Print Ser.). 528p. 29.99 o.p. (*0-7089-8235-2*, Ulverscroft) Thorpe, F. A. Pubs. GBR. *Dist:* Ulverscroft Large Print Bks., Ltd., Ulverscroft Large Print Canada, Ltd.

Glyde, Tania. Junk DNA. 2000. 224p. pap. 12.95 (*1-899598-19-7*) Codex GBR. *Dist:* SCB Distributors.

Goddard, Robert. Caught in the Light: A Mystery. 1999. 444p. mass mkt. (*0-552-14597-1*); 1998. 352p. o.s.i (*0-593-04266-2*) Bantam Bks. (Corgi).

—Caught in the Light: A Mystery. 1999. 352p. 26.00 o.s.i (*0-8050-6155-X*) Holt, Henry & Co.

—Into the Blue. 1999. 541p. mass mkt. (*0-552-54593-7*); 1997. mass mkt. o.s.i (*0-552-13561-5*); 1993. mass mkt. o.s.i (*0-552-14030-9*); 1990. o.s.i (*0-593-01808-7*) Bantam Bks. (Corgi).

—Into the Blue. unabr. ed. 1995. audio 85.95 (*0-7861-0651-4*, 1563) Blackstone Audio Bks., Inc.

—Into the Blue. l.t. ed. 1992. (General Ser.). 630p. lib. bdg. 23.95 o.p. (*0-8161-5233-0*, Macmillan Reference USA) Gale Group.

—Into the Blue. 1991. 416p. 19.95 (*0-671-70482-6*, Simon & Schuster) Simon & Schuster.

—Into the Blue. Rubenstein, Julie, ed. 1992. 528p. reprint ed. mass mkt. 5.99 (*0-671-70483-4*, Pocket) Simon & Schuster.

—Out of the Sun. unabr. ed. 1997. audio 84.95 (*0-7451-6778-0*, CAB 1394) BBC Audiobooks America.

—Out of the Sun. 1997. 410p. mass mkt. (*0-552-14224-7*); 1996. 333p. o.s.i (*0-593-03614-X*) Bantam Bks. (Corgi).

—Out of the Sun. unabr. ed. 2000. audio 69.95 Chivers Audio Bks. GBR. *Dist:* BBC Audiobooks America.

—Out of the Sun. 352p. 1998. pap. 13.00 o.s.i (*0-8050-5836-2*, Owl Bks.); 1997. 25.00 o.s.i (*0-8050-5109-0*) Holt, Henry & Co.

—Out of the Sun. l.t. ed. 1997. (Charnwood Large Print Ser.). 496p. 29.99 o.p. (*0-7089-8967-5*, Ulverscroft) Thorpe, F. A. Pubs. GBR. *Dist:* Ulverscroft Large Print Bks., Ltd., Ulverscroft Large Print Canada, Ltd.

Godden, Rumer. China Court: The Hours of a Country House. 1993. pap. 13.00 o.p. (*0-688-11722-8*, Quill) HarperTrade.

—China Court: The Hours of a Country House. 1961. 5.00 o.p. (*0-670-21841-3*) Viking Penguin.

—An Episode of Sparrows. 1989. 256p. (YA). (gr. 7 up). pap. 4.95 o.p. (*0-14-034024-6*, Puffin Bks.) Penguin Putnam Bks. for Young Readers.

—The Kitchen Madonna. 1967. (Illus.). (J). 5.95 o.p. (*0-670-41399-2*) Viking Penguin.

Godwin, William. Caleb Williams. McCracken, David, ed. (Oxford World's Classics Ser.). 1982. (Illus.). 384p. pap. o.p. (*0-19-281621-7*); 1970. 9.95 o.p. (*0-19-255331-3*) Oxford Univ. Pr., Inc.

—Caleb Williams. Hindle, Maurice, ed. & intro. by. 1988. (Classics Ser.). 448p. pap. 14.00 (*0-14-043256-6*, Penguin Classics) Viking Penguin.

Goff, Denise. Past Continuous. 1996. 240p. 22.95 o.p. (*0-312-14025-8*) St. Martin's Pr.

Golding, William. The Pyramid. 1968. (Harvest Book Ser.). 192p. pap. 15.00 (*0-15-674703-0*, Harvest Bks.) Harcourt Trade Pubs.

Goldstein, Lisa. Walking the Labyrinth. 256p. 1998. pap. 12.95 (*0-312-85968-6*, Forge Bks.); 1996. 21.95 o.p. (*0-312-86175-3*, Tor Bks.) Doherty, Tom Assocs., LLC.

Goodall, John S. An Edwardian Summer. 1976. (Illus.). 72p. (J). (ps up). 6.95 o.p. (*0-689-50062-9*, McElderry, Margaret K.) Simon & Schuster Children's Publishing.

Gooden, Philip. Alms for Oblivion: A Shakespearean Murder Mystery. 2003. 288p. 24.00 (*0-7867-1142-6*, Carroll & Graf Pubs.) Avalon Publishing Group.

—Death of Kings: A Shakespearean Murder Mystery. 2001. 320p. pap. 12.95 (*0-7867-0875-1*, Carroll & Graf Pubs.) Avalon Publishing Group.

—Mask of Night: A Shakespearean Murder Mystery. 2004. 272p. 24.00 (*0-7867-1312-7*, Carroll & Graf Pubs.) Avalon Publishing Group.

—The Pale Companion: A Shakespearean Murder Mystery. 288p. 2002. 24.00 (*0-7867-1008-X*); 2003. reprint ed. 12.00 (*0-7867-1176-0*) Avalon Publishing Group. (Carroll & Graf Pubs.).

Gooding, Kathleen. The Festival Summer. 1984. 176p. (J). (gr. 7 up). o.p. (*0-571-13352-5*) Faber & Faber Ltd.

Goodman, Jo. My Steadfast Heart. 2000. (Five Star Romance Ser.). 478p. pap. 27.95 (*0-7862-2501-7*, Five Star) Gale Group.

Goodwin, Suzanne. The Difference. 1995. 384p. 22.95 o.p. (*0-312-13051-1*) St. Martin's Pr.

—French Leave. 2001. 256p. 25.99 (*0-7278-5691-X*); 25.99 (*0-7278-7089-0*) Severn Hse. Pubs., Ltd.

—The Rising Storm. 1993. 568p. 24.95 o.p. (*0-312-09372-1*) St. Martin's Pr.

Gordon, Abigail. The Elusive Doctor. l.t. ed. 2001. (Mills & Boon Large Print Ser.). 288p. 27.99 (*0-263-16851-4*) Harlequin Mills & Boon, Ltd. GBR. *Dist:* Ulverscroft Large Print Bks., Ltd., Ulverscroft Large Print Canada, Ltd.

—Finger on the Pulse. l.t. ed. 2001. (Mills & Boon Large Print Ser.). 288p. 27.99 (*0-263-16829-8*) Harlequin Mills & Boon, Ltd. GBR. *Dist:* Ulverscroft Large Print Bks., Ltd., Ulverscroft Large Print Canada, Ltd.

Gordon, Noah. The Physician. 1987. 640p. mass mkt. 6.99 o.s.i (*0-449-21426-5*, Fawcett) Ballantine Bks.

—The Physician. 1986. 624p. 18.45 o.p. (*0-671-47748-X*, Simon & Schuster) Simon & Schuster.

—The Physician. 2002. 720p. pap. 8.95 (*0-7515-0389-4*) Warner Bks. GBR. *Dist:* Trafalgar Square.

Gordon, Richard. Jack the Ripper. 1980. 9.95 o.p. (*0-689-11101-0*, Scribner) Simon & Schuster.

—The Private Life of Florence Nightingale. 1979. 9.95 o.p. (*0-689-10929-6*, Atheneum) Simon & Schuster Children's Publishing.

Gosling, Paula. Death Penalties. 1991. 297p. 25.00 (*0-89296-458-8*) Mysterious Pr.

—Death Penalties. 1992. 304p. mass mkt. 4.99 o.s.i (*0-446-40189-7*) Warner Bks., Inc.

—The Wychford Murders. 1986. (Crime Club Ser.). 192p. 12.95 o.p. (*0-385-23551-8*) Doubleday Publishing.

—The Wychford Murders. 1988. 224p. reprint ed. mass mkt. (*0-373-26009-1*, Harlequin Bks.) Harlequin Enterprises, Ltd.

—The Wychford Murders. unabr. ed. 1993. audio 69.95 (*1-85089-757-3*, 9008X) ISIS Audio Bks. GBR. *Dist:* Ulverscroft Large Print Bks., Ltd.

—The Wychford Murders. l.t. ed. 1987. (Ulverscroft Large Print Ser.). 528p. o.p. (*0-7089-1709-7*, Ulverscroft) Thorpe, F. A. Pubs. GBR. *Dist:* Ulverscroft Large Print Canada, Ltd.

Goudge, Elizabeth. Green Dolphin Street. 2000. 512p. 38.95 (*0-89966-113-0*) Buccaneer Bks., Inc.

—Pilgrim's Inn. 1993. Orig. Title: The Herb of Grace. 335p. reprint ed. pap. 10.99 (*0-89283-830-2*) Servant Pubns.

Gower, Iris. Arian. l.t. ed. 1995. (Magna Large Print Ser.). 592p. 29.99 (*0-7505-0810-8*) Magna Large Print Bks. GBR. *Dist:* Ulverscroft Large Print Bks., Ltd., Ulverscroft Large Print Canada, Ltd.

—Arian. 2000. 443p. (J). pap. 9.95 (*0-552-14095-3*); 26.95 (*0-593-03349-3*) Transworld Publishers Ltd. GBR. *Dist:* Trafalgar Square.

—Daughters of Rebecca. 2000. 331p. 28.00 (*0-593-04011-2*) Bantam Pr., Ltd. GBR. *Dist:* Trafalgar Square.

—The Oyster Catchers. 2000. 383p. (J). pap. 9.95 (*0-552-13688-3*) Transworld Publishers Ltd. GBR. *Dist:* Trafalgar Square.

—Proud Mary. 2000. (J). pap. 9.95 (*0-552-12637-3*) Transworld Publishers Ltd. GBR. *Dist:* Trafalgar Square.

—A Royal Ambition. 1999. 222p. 25.00 (*0-7278-5503-4*) Severn Hse. Pubs., Ltd.

—Sea Witch. 1999. 192 p. pap. (*0-7540-3678-2*) BBC Audiobooks America.

—Sea Witch. 1999. 192p. 25.00 o.p. (*0-7278-2217-9*) Severn Hse. Pubs., Ltd.

—Sea Witch. l.t. ed. 1999. (Romance Ser.). 192p. 27.95 (*0-7838-8473-7*) Thorndike Pr.

—The Wild Seed. l.t. ed. 1998. (Magna Large Print Ser.). 592p. o.p. (*0-7505-1188-5*) Magna Large Print Bks. GBR. *Dist:* Ulverscroft Large Print Canada, Ltd.

—The Wild Seed. 2000. 445p. 27.95 (*0-593-03355-8*); 444p. pap. 10.95 (*0-552-14096-1*) Transworld Publishers Ltd. GBR. *Dist:* Trafalgar Square.

Gower, Iris, contrib. by. Sea Witch. 1999. (*0-7540-3677-4*) BBC Audiobooks America.

Grabien, Deborah. The Weaver & the Factory Maid. Date not set. pap. (*0-312-31423-X*, St. Martin's Paperbacks); Date not set. mass mkt. (*0-312-98954-7*, St. Martin's Paperbacks); 2003. 192p. 22.95 (*0-312-31422-1*) St. Martin's Pr.

Grace, C. L. The Book of Shadows. 1996. 208p. 20.95 (*0-312-14287-0*, Saint Martin's Minotaur) St. Martin's Pr.

—The Eye of God. 1994. 208p. 18.95 o.p. (*0-312-10978-4*, Saint Martin's Minotaur) St. Martin's Pr.

—The Merchant of Death. 1995. 182p. (YA). 19.95 (*0-312-13124-0*, Saint Martin's Minotaur) St. Martin's Pr.

—Saintly Murders: A Medieval Mystery. 2001. 256p. 23.95 (*0-312-26993-5*, Saint Martin's Minotaur) St. Martin's Pr.

—A Shrine of Murders. 1993. 208p. 17.95 o.p. (*0-312-09388-8*, Saint Martin's Minotaur) St. Martin's Pr.

Grace, Susan. Forever & Beyond. 2001. (Zebra Historical Romance Ser.). 416p. mass mkt. 5.99 o.s.i (*0-8217-6859-X*, Zebra Bks.) Kensington Publishing Corp.

Graham, Caroline. Death in Disguise. 1993. 333p. 22.00 o.p. (*0-688-09985-8*, Morrow, William & Co.); 1994. 384p. reprint ed. mass mkt. 4.99 (*0-380-71296-2*, Avon Bks.) Morrow/Avon.

—Death of a Hollow Man: An Inspector Barnaby Mystery. unabr. ed. 1998. audio 69.95 (*0-7540-0123-7*, CAB1546) BBC Audiobooks America.

—Death of a Hollow Man: An Inspector Barnaby Mystery. 1990. 320p. mass mkt. 4.99 (*0-380-70951-1*, Avon Bks.); 360p. reprint ed. 17.95 o.p. (*0-688-09116-4*, Morrow, William & Co.) Morrow/Avon.

—Death of a Hollow Man: An Inspector Barnaby Mystery. l.t. ed. 2002. (General Ser.). 25.95 (*0-7862-4509-3*) Thorndike Pr.

—Faithful unto Death. 1998. (Chief Inspector Barnaby Mysteries Ser.). 320p. 23.95 o.p. (*0-312-18577-4*, Saint Martin's Minotaur) St. Martin's Pr.

—Faithful unto Death: A Chief Inspector Barnaby Novel. unabr. ed. 1997. audio 84.95 (*0-7540-0015-X*, CAB 1438) BBC Audiobooks America.

—Faithful unto Death: A Chief Inspector Barnaby Novel. unabr. ed. 2000. (Inspector Barnaby Mystery Ser.). audio 69.95 Chivers Audio Bks. GBR. *Dist:* BBC Audiobooks America.

—Faithful unto Death: A Chief Inspector Barnaby Novel. 2000. (Chief Inspector Barnaby Mysteries Ser.). 400p. mass mkt. 6.99 (*0-312-97295-4*, St. Martin's Paperbacks) St. Martin's Pr.

—The Killings at Badger's Drift. 1988. 264p. 16.95 o.p. (*0-917561-41-4*) Adler & Adler Pubs., Inc.

—The Killings at Badger's Drift. 2000. audio 34.95 (*0-7540-7527-3*) BBC Audiobooks America.

—The Killings at Badger's Drift. unabr. ed. 1996. audio 59.95 (*0-7451-6621-0*, CAB 1237) Chivers Audio Bks. GBR. *Dist:* BBC Audiobooks America.

—The Killings at Badger's Drift. 1989. 256p. mass mkt. 4.50 (*0-380-70563-X*, Avon Bks.) Morrow/Avon.

—The Killings at Badger's Drift. l.t. ed. 1999. (Mystery Ser.). 421p. 27.95 (*0-7862-2218-2*); (*0-7540-1376-6*); (*0-7540-2281-1*) Thorndike Pr.

—A Place of Safety: A Chief Inspector Barnaby Mystery. unabr. ed. 2000. 8p. audio 69.95 (*0-7540-0452-X*, CAB 1875) Chivers Audio Bks. GBR. *Dist:* BBC Audiobooks America.

—A Place of Safety: A Chief Inspector Barnaby Mystery. l.t. ed. 2000. (G. K. Hall Core Ser.). 434p. 29.95 (*0-7838-8968-2*, Macmillan Reference USA) Gale Group.

—A Place of Safety: A Chief Inspector Barnaby Mystery. (Chief Inspector Barnaby Mysteries Ser.). 288p. 2001. mass mkt. 6.50 (*0-312-97710-7*, St. Martin's Paperbacks); 2nd ed. 1999. 23.95 (*0-312-24419-3*, Saint Martin's Minotaur) St. Martin's Pr.

—Written in Blood: A Detective Barnaby Mystery, Set. unabr. ed. 1999. audio 96.95 (*0-7540-0351-5*, CAB1774) BBC Audiobooks America.

—Written in Blood: A Detective Barnaby Mystery. l.t. ed. 1995. (Magna Large Print Ser.). 637p. o.p. (*0-7505-0848-5*) Magna Large Print Bks. GBR. *Dist:* Ulverscroft Large Print Canada, Ltd.

—Written in Blood: A Detective Barnaby Mystery. 1996. 384p. mass mkt. 5.99 (*0-380-71297-0*, Avon Bks.); 1995. 288p. 22.00 o.p. (*0-688-10024-4*, Morrow, William & Co.) Morrow/Avon.

Graham, Laurie. The Future Homemakers of America. l.t. ed. 2003. (Core Ser.). 468p. 28.95 (*0-7862-4930-7*) Thorndike Pr.

—The Future Homemakers of America. 2002. 400p. reprint ed. pap. 14.00 (*0-446-67936-4*) Warner Bks., Inc.

—Ten O'Clock Horses. 2000. 255p. pap. 10.95 (*0-552-99656-4*) Transworld Publishers Ltd. GBR. *Dist:* Trafalgar Square.

—Ten O'clock Horses. 269p. 22.95 o.p. (*0-593-03929-7*) Transworld Publishers Ltd. GBR. *Dist:* Trafalgar Square.

Graham, Laurie, contrib. by. Perfect Meringues. 1997. 219p. 10.95 (*0-552-99657-2*) Transworld Publishers Ltd. GBR. *Dist:* Trafalgar Square.

Graham, Winston. The Angry Tide. unabr. ed. 1999. (Poldark Ser. ). Set audio 110.95; Vol. 7. audio 110.95 (*0-7540-0294-2*, CAB 1717) BBC Audiobooks America.

—The Angry Tide. 1979. mass mkt. 2.50 o.s.i (*0-345-28046-6*) Ballantine Bks.

—The Angry Tide. unabr. ed. 2000. (Poldark Ser.: Bk. 7). audio 89.95 Chivers Audio Bks. GBR. *Dist:* BBC Audiobooks America.

—The Angry Tide. 1978. 10.00 o.p. (*0-385-13682-X*) Doubleday Publishing.

—The Angry Tide. 1979. (Reader's Request Ser.). lib. bdg. 19.95 o.p. (*0-8161-6682-X*, Macmillan Reference USA) Gale Group.

—The Angry Tide: Cornwall - As the 18th Century Ebbs. 2002. (Poldark Saga Ser.: Vol. 7). (Illus.). 308p. mass mkt. 8.95 (*0-330-34500-1*) Pan Bks. Ltd. GBR. *Dist:* Trafalgar Square.

—The Black Moon. 1978. (Poldark Ser.: No.5). mass mkt. 2.25 o.s.i (*0-345-27735-X*); 1977. mass mkt. 1.95 o.s.i (*0-345-26004-X*) Ballantine Bks.

—Black Moon, 2 vols. l.t. ed. 1979. (YA). (gr. 7-12). lib. bdg. 18.95 o.p. (*0-8161-6680-3*, Macmillan Reference USA) Gale Group.

—The Black Moon. unabr. ed. 1997. (Poldark Ser. : Vol. 5). audio 96.95 (*0-7451-6753-5*, CAB 1369) BBC Audiobooks America.

—The Black Moon. unabr. ed. 2000. (Poldark Ser.: Bk. 5). audio 79.95 Chivers Audio Bks. GBR. *Dist:* BBC Audiobooks America.

—The Black Moon: Cornwall 1794. 2002. (Poldark Saga Ser.: Vol. 5). (Illus.). 324p. mass mkt. 8.95 (*0-330-34498-6*) Pan Bks. Ltd. GBR. *Dist:* Trafalgar Square.

—Demelza. unabr. ed. 1995. (Poldark Ser. : Vol. 2). audio 96.95 (*0-7451-6469-2*, CAB 1086) BBC Audiobooks America.

—Demelza. 1977. mass mkt. 1.95 o.s.i (*0-345-26001-5*) Ballantine Bks.

—Demelza. unabr. ed. 2000. (Poldark Ser.: Bk. 2). audio 79.95 Chivers Audio Bks. GBR. *Dist:* BBC Audiobooks America.

—Demelza. 1979. (Reader's Request Ser.). lib. bdg. 17.95 o.p. (*0-8161-6677-3*, Macmillan Reference USA) Gale Group.

—Four Swans. 2002. (Poldark Saga Ser.: Vol. 6). (Illus.). 581p. mass mkt. 8.95 (*0-330-34499-4*) Pan Bks. Ltd. GBR. *Dist:* Trafalgar Square.

—The Four Swans. unabr. ed. 1998. (Poldark Ser. : Vol. 6). audio 110.95 (*0-7540-0124-5*, CAB1547) BBC Audiobooks America.

—The Four Swans. 1978. mass mkt. 2.25 o.s.i (*0-345-26005-8*) Ballantine Bks.

—The Four Swans. unabr. ed. 2000. (Poldark Ser.: Bk. 6). audio 89.95 Chivers Audio Bks. GBR. *Dist:* BBC Audiobooks America.

—The Four Swans. 1977. 8.95 o.p. (*0-385-12338-8*) Doubleday Publishing.

—The Four Swans. 1979. (Reader's Request Ser.). lib. bdg. 19.95 o.p. (*0-8161-6681-1*, Macmillan Reference USA) Gale Group.

—Jeremy Poldark. unabr. ed. 1996. (Poldark Ser. : Vol. 3). audio 69.95 (*0-7451-6612-1*, CAB1228) BBC Audiobooks America.

—Jeremy Poldark. 1977. mass mkt. 1.95 o.s.i (0-345-26002-3); No. 3. 1978. mass mkt. 2.25 o.s.i (0-345-27733-3) Ballantine Bks.

—Jeremy Poldark. unabr. ed. 2000. (Poldark Ser.: Bk. 3). audio 59.95 Chivers Audio Bks. GBR. Dist: BBC Audiobooks America.

—Jeremy Poldark. l.t. ed. 1979. (YA). (gr. 7-12). lib. bdg. 14.95 o.p. (0-8161-6678-1, Macmillan Reference USA) Gale Group.

—Loving Cup. 2002. (Poldark Saga Ser.: Vol. 10). (Illus.). 580p. mass mkt. 8.95 (0-330-34503-6) Pan Bks. Ltd. GBR. Dist: Trafalgar Square.

—Loving Cup: The Tenth Poldark Novel. 1985. 456p. 17.95 o.p. (0-385-19834-5) Doubleday Publishing.

—Miller's Dance. Date not set. lib. bdg. 22.95 (0-8488-1016-3) Amereon, Ltd.

—The Miller's Dance. 1983. (Poldark Ser.: No. 9). 384p. 15.95 o.p. (0-385-18405-0) Doubleday Publishing.

—The Miller's Dance. 2002. (Poldark Saga Ser.: Vol. 9). (Illus.). 496p. mass mkt. 8.95 (0-330-34502-8) Pan Bks. Ltd. GBR. Dist: Trafalgar Square.

—Ross Poldark. unabr. ed. 1992. (Poldark Ser. : Vol. 1). audio 84.95 (0-7451-4035-1, CAB 732) BBC Audiobooks America.

—Ross Poldark. (Poldark Ser.). 1978. mass mkt. 2.25 o.s.i (0-345-27731-7); 1977. mass mkt. 1.95 o.s.i (0-345-25654-9) Ballantine Bks.

—Ross Poldark. unabr. ed. 2000. (Poldark Ser.: Bk. 1). audio 69.95 Chivers Audio Bks. GBR. Dist: BBC Audiobooks America.

—Ross Poldark, 2 vols. l.t. ed. 1979. (Reader's Request Ser.). lib. bdg. 16.95 o.p. (0-8161-6676-5, Macmillan Reference USA) Gale Group.

—Stephanie. 1993. 304p. 19.95 o.p. (0-88184-939-1, Carroll & Graf Pubs.) Avalon Publishing Group.

—Stephanie. 2002. 304p. mass mkt. 8.95 (0-330-32689-9) Pan Bks. Ltd. GBR. Dist: Trafalgar Square.

—Stephanie. l.t. ed. 1993. (Charnwood Library). 416p. 29.99 o.p. (0-7089-8731-1, Ulverscroft) Thorpe, F. A. Pubs. GBR. Dist: Ulverscroft Large Print Bks., Ltd., Ulverscroft Large Print Canada, Ltd.

—Stranger from the Sea. 22.95 (0-8488-1017-1) Amereon, Ltd.

—The Stranger from the Sea. unabr. ed. 2000. (Poldark Ser.: Vol. 8). audio 96.95 (0-7540-0437-6, CAB 1860) Chivers Audio Bks. GBR. Dist: BBC Audiobooks America.

—The Stranger from the Sea. 1982. 432p. 17.95 o.p. (0-385-17967-7) Doubleday Publishing.

—The Stranger from the Sea, Bk. 8. 2002. (Poldark Saga Ser.: Vol. 8). (Illus.). 304p. pap. 8.95 (0-330-34501-X) Pan Bks. Ltd. GBR. Dist: Trafalgar Square.

—The Twisted Sword: Cornwall - January 1815. 1991. (Poldark Novel Ser.). 512p. 21.95 o.p. (0-88184-693-7, Carroll & Graf Pubs.) Avalon Publishing Group.

—The Twisted Sword: Cornwall - January 1815, Bk. 11. 2002. (Poldark Saga Ser.: Vol. 11). (Illus.). 544p. pap. 8.95 (0-330-31749-0) Pan Bks. Ltd. GBR. Dist: Trafalgar Square.

—The Twisted Sword Pt. 1: Cornwall - January 1815. l.t. ed. 1995. (Charnwood Large Print Ser.). 496p. 29.99 o.p. (0-7089-8822-9, Charnwood) Thorpe, F. A. Pubs. GBR. Dist: Ulverscroft Large Print Bks., Ltd., Ulverscroft Large Print Canada, Ltd.

—The Twisted Sword Pt. 2: Cornwall - January 1815. l.t. ed. 1995. (Charnwood Large Print Ser.). 288p. 29.99 o.p. (0-7089-8828-8, Charnwood) Thorpe, F. A. Pubs. GBR. Dist: Ulverscroft Large Print Bks., Ltd., Ulverscroft Large Print Canada, Ltd.

—Warleggan. unabr. ed. 1996. (Poldark Ser. : Vol. 4). audio 96.95 (0-7451-6691-1, CAB1307) BBC Audiobooks America.

—Warleggan. 1978. (Poldark Ser.: No. 4). mass mkt. 2.25 o.s.i (0-345-27734-1); 1977. mass mkt. 1.95 o.s.i (0-345-26003-1) Ballantine Bks.

—Warleggan. unabr. ed. 2000. (Poldark Ser.: Bk. 4). audio 79.95 Chivers Audio Bks. GBR. Dist: BBC Audiobooks America.

—Warleggan, 2 vols. l.t. ed. 1979. (Reader's Request Ser.). lib. bdg. 17.95 o.p. (0-8161-6679-X, Macmillan Reference USA) Gale Group.

—Warleggan, Bk. 4. 2002. (Poldark Saga Ser.: Vol. 4). 471p. pap. 8.95 (0-330-34496-X) Pan Bks. Ltd. GBR. Dist: Trafalgar Square.

Grahame, Kenneth. Dream Days. 2001. (Company of Books Ser.). (Illus.). 163p. (YA). 22.95 (1-58579-018-4, Common Reader Editions) Akadine Pr., The.

—Dream Days. 1985. (Illus.). (J). (gr. 4 up). 14.95 o.p. (0-8253-0281-1) Beaufort Bks., Inc.

—Dream Days. 2000. E-Book 2.49 (1-58744-147-0) Electric Umbrella Publishing.

—Dream Days. 1976. (Classics of Children's Literature, 1621-1932: Vol. 62). (Illus.). (J). reprint ed. lib. bdg. 46.00 o.p. (0-8240-2311-0) Garland Publishing, Inc.

—Dream Days. 1975. (Illus.). mass mkt. 4.95 o.p. (0-380-00288-4, 23994, Avon Bks.) Morrow/Avon.

—Dream Days. 1993. (Illus.). 240p. (YA). (gr. 5 up). 18.95 o.s.i (0-89815-546-0) Ten Speed Pr.

—The Golden Age. 2001. (Company of Books Ser.). (Illus.). 174p. (YA). (gr. 5 up). 22.95 (1-58579-019-2, Common Reader Editions) Akadine Pr., The.

—The Golden Age. 1985. (Illus.). 288p. (J). (gr. 4 up). reprint ed. 14.95 o.p. (0-8253-0331-1) Beaufort Bks., Inc.

—The Golden Age. 1976. (Classics of Children's Literature, 1621-1932: Vol. 59). (Illus.). (J). reprint ed. lib. bdg. 46.00 o.p. (0-8240-2308-0) Garland Publishing, Inc.

—The Golden Age. 1975. (Illus.). mass mkt. 4.95 o.p. (0-380-00289-2, 23986, Avon Bks.) Morrow/Avon.

—The Golden Age. mass mkt. 0.75 o.p. (0-451-50207-8, Signet Classics) NAL.

—The Golden Age. (Ebook Classic Ser.). E-Book 5.00 (0-7410-1093-3) SoftBook Pr.

—The Golden Age. 1993. (Illus.). 264p. (YA). (gr. 5 up). 18.95 o.s.i (0-89815-545-2) Ten Speed Pr.

Grand, Sarah. The Heavenly Twins. 1993. (Ann Arbor Paperbacks Ser.). (Illus.). 736p. (C). text 60.00 (0-472-09508-0, 09508); pap. text 29.95 (0-472-06508-4, 06508) Univ. of Michigan Pr.

Granelli, Roger. Dark Edge. 1997. 200p. pap. 17.95 (1-85411-204-X) Seren Bks. GBR. Dist: Dufour Editions, Inc.

Grange, Amanda. A Most Unusual Governess. l.t. ed. 2002. 289p. pap. 23.95 (0-7862-3959-X) Gale Group.

—A Most Unusual Governess. 2002. 220p. 27.50 (0-7090-6877-8) Hale, Robert Ltd. GBR. Dist: Trafalgar Square.

Granger, Ann. Beneath These Stones. 2000. (Meredith & Markby Mysteries Ser.). 250p. 22.95 (0-312-24178-X, Saint Martin's Minotaur) St. Martin's Pr.

—Call the Dead Again. l.t. ed. 1999. 30.00 o.p. (0-7862-1817-7, Macmillan Reference USA) Gale Group.

—Call the Dead Again. 1999. (Meredith & Markby Mysteries Ser.). 256p. 22.95 (0-312-20505-8, Saint Martin's Minotaur) St. Martin's Pr.

—Candle for a Corpse. 1997. (Meredith & Markby Mysteries Ser.: Vol. 8). 288p. mass mkt. 5.99 (0-380-73012-X, Avon Bks.) Morrow/Avon.

—Candle for a Corpse. 1996. 256p. text 21.95 o.p. (0-312-14292-7, Saint Martin's Minotaur) St. Martin's Pr.

—Cold in the Earth. 1994. 256p. mass mkt. 5.50 (0-380-72213-5, Avon Bks.) Morrow/Avon.

—Cold in the Earth. 1993. 218p. 17.95 o.p. (0-312-08747-0, Saint Martin's Minotaur) St. Martin's Pr.

—Cold in the Earth. l.t. ed. 1994. (Ulverscroft Large Print Ser.). 576p. 29.99 o.p. (0-7089-3111-1, Ulverscroft) Thorpe, F. A. Pubs. GBR. Dist: Ulverscroft Large Print Bks., Ltd., Ulverscroft Large Print Canada, Ltd.

—A Fine Place for Death. 1996. (New Meredith & Markby Mystery Ser.: No. 6). 288p. mass mkt. 5.50 (0-380-72573-8, Avon Bks.) Morrow/Avon.

—A Fine Place for Death. 1994. 249p. 21.00 o.p. (0-312-11787-6, Saint Martin's Minotaur) St. Martin's Pr.

—A Fine Place for Death. l.t. ed. 1995. (Ulverscroft Large Print Ser.). 528p. 29.99 o.p. (0-7089-3346-7, Ulverscroft) Thorpe, F. A. Pubs. GBR. Dist: Ulverscroft Large Print Bks., Ltd., Ulverscroft Large Print Canada, Ltd.

—Flowers for His Funeral. 1997. mass mkt. 5.50 (0-380-72887-7, Avon Bks.) Morrow/Avon.

—Flowers for His Funeral. 1995. 250p. 21.95 o.p. (0-312-13495-9, Saint Martin's Minotaur) St. Martin's Pr.

—Keeping Bad Company. l.t. ed. 1998. (General Ser.). 352p. pap. 23.95 o.p. (0-7862-1590-9) Thorndike Pr.

—Murder among Us. 1995. (Meredith & Markby Mysteries Ser.: No. 4). 304p. mass mkt. 5.99 (0-380-72476-6, Avon Bks.) Morrow/Avon.

—Murder among Us. 1993. 224p. 18.95 o.p. (0-312-09875-8); (0-312-09343-8) St. Martin's Pr. (Saint Martin's Minotaur).

—Murder among Us. l.t. ed. 1994. (Ulverscroft Large Print Ser.). 544p. 29.99 o.p. (0-7089-3146-4, Ulverscroft) Thorpe, F. A. Pubs. GBR. Dist: Ulverscroft Large Print Bks., Ltd., Ulverscroft Large Print Canada, Ltd.

—Say It with Poison. 1993. 224p. mass mkt. 5.50 (0-380-71823-5, Avon Bks.) Morrow/Avon.

—Say It with Poison. 1991. 16.95 o.p. (0-312-05506-4, Saint Martin's Minotaur) St. Martin's Pr.

—A Season for Murder. 1993. (Meredith & Markby Mysteries Ser.: Vol. 2). 256p. mass mkt. 5.99 o.s.i (0-380-71997-5, Avon Bks.) Morrow/Avon.

—A Season for Murder. 1992. 256p. 18.95 o.p. (0-312-07079-9, Saint Martin's Minotaur) St. Martin's Pr.

—A Season for Murder. l.t. ed. 1992. (Magna Large Print Ser.). 361p. 29.99 o.p. (0-7505-0483-8, Ulverscroft) Thorpe, F. A. Pubs. GBR. Dist: Ulverscroft Large Print Bks., Ltd., Ulverscroft Large Print Canada, Ltd.

—Shades of Murder: A Mitchell & Markby Mystery. 2001. 288p. 23.95 (0-312-28445-4, Saint Martin's Minotaur) St. Martin's Pr.

—A Touch of Mortality. 1998. 288p. mass mkt. 5.99 (0-380-73087-1, Avon Bks.) Morrow/Avon.

—A Touch of Mortality. 1997. 256p. 21.95 (0-312-15231-0, Saint Martin's Minotaur) St. Martin's Pr.

—Where Old Bones Lie. 1995. (New Meredith & Markby Mystery Ser.: No. 5). 288p. mass mkt. 5.99 (0-380-72477-4, Avon Bks.) Morrow/Avon.

—Where Old Bones Lie. 1994. 224p. 19.95 o.p. (0-312-11097-9, Saint Martin's Minotaur) St. Martin's Pr.

—Where Old Bones Lie. l.t. ed. 1995. (Ulverscroft Large Print Ser.). 528p. 29.99 o.p. (0-7089-3391-2, Ulverscroft) Thorpe, F. A. Pubs. GBR. Dist: Ulverscroft Large Print Bks., Ltd., Ulverscroft Large Print Canada, Ltd.

—A Word After Dying. 1998. (Meredith & Markby Mysteries Ser.). 256p. 21.95 (0-312-17067-X, Saint Martin's Minotaur) St. Martin's Pr.

—A Word after Dying. 1999. (Meredith & Markby Mysteries Ser.). 304p. mass mkt. 5.99 (0-380-73227-0, Avon Bks.) Morrow/Avon.

—A Word after Dying. pap. 14.95 (0-312-30475-7, Saint Martin's Griffin) St. Martin's Pr.

—A Word after Dying. l.t. ed. 1997. (Ulverscroft Large Print Ser.). 560p. 29.99 o.p. (0-7089-3809-4, Ulverscroft) Thorpe, F. A. Pubs. GBR. Dist: Ulverscroft Large Print Bks., Ltd., Ulverscroft Large Print Canada, Ltd.

Granger, Pip. Not All Tarts Are Apple. l.t. ed. 2002. (Magna Large Print Ser.). 336p. (0-7505-1919-3) Magna Large Print Bks. GBR. Dist: Ulverscroft Large Print Canada, Ltd.

—Not All Tarts Are Apple. 2002. 219p. 24.95 o.s.i (1-59058-033-8) Poisoned Pen Pr.

Grant-Adamson, Lesley. Curse the Darkness. 1990. 19.95 o.p. (0-312-04291-4, Saint Martin's Minotaur) St. Martin's Pr.

—Death on Widow's Walk. 1985. 224p. 13.95 o.p. (0-684-18318-8, Macmillan Reference USA) Gale Group.

—The Face of Death. 1987. 288p. mass mkt. 2.95 o.s.i (0-449-21210-6, Fawcett) Ballantine Bks.

—The Face of Death. 1986. 304p. 14.95 o.s.i (0-684-18588-1, Macmillan Reference USA) Gale Group.

—The Face of Death. l.t. ed. 1987. (Ulverscroft Large Print Ser.). 560p. 29.99 o.p. (0-7089-1684-8, Ulverscroft) Thorpe, F. A. Pubs. GBR. Dist: Ulverscroft Large Print Bks., Ltd., Ulverscroft Large Print Canada, Ltd.

—The Face of Death, Set. 1987. audio 54.95 o.p. (1-85496-106-3, US0127) Ulverscroft Audio (U.S.A.).

—The Girl in the Case. unabr. ed. 1998. pap. text 54.95 incl. audio (0-7531-0264-1, 971206) ISIS Audio Bks. GBR. Dist: Ulverscroft Large Print Bks., Ltd.

—The Girl in the Case. l.t. ed. 1997. (Paperback Ser.). 370p. pap. 23.95 (0-7838-8279-3) Thorndike Pr.

—Too Many Questions. 1993. mass mkt. 4.50 o.s.i (0-449-22104-0, Fawcett) Ballantine Bks.

—Too Many Questions. 1991. 15.95 o.p. (0-312-05434-3, Saint Martin's Minotaur) St. Martin's Pr.

—Wild Justice. 1988. 224p. 14.95 o.p. (0-312-01845-2, Saint Martin's Minotaur) St. Martin's Pr.

Grant, Charles. Black Oak: Hunting Ground. 2000. (Black Oak Ser.: 4). 256p. mass mkt. 5.99 o.s.i (0-451-45787-0, ROC) NAL.

—Genesis. 1998. (Black Oak Ser.: Vol. 1). 272p. mass mkt. 5.99 o.s.i (0-451-45677-7, ROC) NAL.

—Winter Knight. 1999. (Black Oak Ser.: Vol. 3). 240p. (Orig.). mass mkt. 5.99 o.s.i (0-451-45762-5, ROC) NAL.

Grant, Charles L. The Hush of Dark Wings. 1999. (Black Oak Ser.: Vol. 2). 256p. mass mkt. 5.99 o.s.i (0-451-45733-1, ROC) NAL.

—Stunts. 1992. mass mkt. 4.99 (0-8125-0698-7); 1990. 19.95 o.p. (0-312-85013-1) Doherty, Tom Assocs., LLC. (Tor Bks.).

Grant, Linda. Still Here. 2001. 320p. (0-316-85995-8); pap. (0-316-85993-1) Little Brown & Co.

—Still Here. l.t. ed. 2003. (Charnwood Large Print Ser.). 480p. 32.50 (0-7089-9421-0) Thorpe, F. A. Pubs. GBR. Dist: Ulverscroft Large Print Bks., Ltd., Ulverscroft Large Print Canada, Ltd.

Gray, Vanessa. Best-Laid Plans. l.t. ed. 1993. (Orig.). 21.95 o.p. (0-7927-1568-3); pap. 19.95 o.p. (0-7927-1567-5) BBC Audiobooks America.

Grayson, Emily. Waterloo Station. 2004. 304p. mass mkt. 6.99 (***0-06-001398-2**, HarperTorch); 2003. 208p. 21.95 (0-06-001397-4, Morrow, William & Co.) Morrow/Avon.

—Waterloo Station. l.t. ed. 2003. 232p. 29.95 (0-7862-5789-X) Thorndike Pr.

Green, Christina. The Turning Wheel. l.t. ed. 2000. (G. K. Hall Nightingale Ser.). 130p. pap. 20.95 (0-7838-9000-1, Macmillan Reference USA) Gale Group.

Green, Denis & Boucher, Anthony. The New Adventures of Sherlock Holmes Vol. 2: The Viennese Strangler & The Notorious Canary Trainer. abr. ed. 1988. 9.95 incl. audio (0-671-66433-6, Simon & Schuster Audioworks) Simon & Schuster Audio.

Green, Jane. Mr. Maybe. 2001. 368p. 19.95 o.s.i (0-7679-0519-9) Broadway Bks.

Green, Roger Lancelyn. King Arthur & His Knights of the Round Table. 1980. pap. 2.95 o.p. (0-14-005589-4) Penguin Group (USA) Inc.

—King Arthur & His Knights of the Round Table. 2002. (Perennial Bestsellers Ser.). 28.95 (0-7862-4839-4) Thorndike Pr.

—King Arthur & His Knights of the Round Table. 1980. 11.04 (0-606-01627-9) Turtleback Bks.

Green, Simon. Robin Hood: Prince of Thieves. 1991. mass mkt. 4.50 o.s.i (0-425-13089-4) Berkley Publishing Group.

Green, Simon R. Drinking Midnight Wine. 2003. 352p. mass mkt. 6.50 (0-451-45935-0); 2002. 320p. pap. 14.00 (0-451-45867-2) NAL. (ROC).

Greenberg, Joanne. The King's Persons. 1985. 288p. pap. o.p. (0-03-005623-3, Owl Bks.) Holt, Henry & Co.

Greenberg, Martin H., et al, eds. Holmes for the Holidays. 304p. 1996. 21.95 o.s.i (0-425-15473-4); 1998. reprint ed. pap. 13.00 o.s.i (0-425-16754-2) Berkley Publishing Group. (Prime Crime).

—More Holmes for the Holidays. 1999. 272p. 21.95 o.s.i (0-425-17033-0, Prime Crime) Berkley Publishing Group.

Greenberg, Martin H. & Rossel-Waugh, Carol-Lynn, eds. The New Adventures of Sherlock Holmes. 1987. (Illus.). 18.95 o.p. (0-88184-344-X, Carroll & Graf Pubs.) Avalon Publishing Group.

Greenberg, Martin H. & Waugh, Carol-Lynn Rossel, eds. The New Adventures of Sherlock Holmes. 1999. (Illus.). 344p. pap. 13.95 (0-7867-0698-8, Carroll & Graf Pubs.) Avalon Publishing Group.

Greene, Graham. The Captain & the Enemy. 1991. pap. text 22.25 (0-582-06024-9) Addison-Wesley Longman, Ltd. GBR. Dist: Trans-Atlantic Pubns., Inc.

—The Captain & the Enemy. l.t. ed. 1989. (General Ser.). 256p. 13.95 o.p. (0-8161-4932-1); lib. bdg. 19.95 o.p. (0-8161-4799-X) Gale Group. (Macmillan Reference USA).

—The Captain & the Enemy. 1992. 2.99 o.p. (0-517-07986-0) Random Hse. Value Publishing.

—The Captain & the Enemy. 192p. 1989. pap. 7.95 o.s.i (0-14-012418-7, Penguin Bks.); 1988. 17.95 o.p. (0-670-82405-4) Viking Penguin.

—The End of the Affair. 1999. 192p. pap. 11.95 (0-14-029109-1, Penguin Bks.) Penguin Group (USA) Inc.

—The End of the Affair. 9999. 14.95 o.p. (0-559-35055-4) Putnam Publishing Group, The.

—The End of the Affair. 1975. 240p. mass mkt. 2.95 o.s.i (0-671-44535-9, Pocket) Simon & Schuster.

—The End of the Affair. (Penguin Twentieth-Century Classics Ser.). 1991. 192p. 13.00 (0-14-018495-3, Penguin Classics); 1977. 256p. pap. 6.95 o.p. (0-14-004696-8, Penguin Bks.); 1951. 16.95 o.p. (0-670-29457-8) Viking Penguin.

Greene, Maria. Midnight Mask: A Lover's Kiss. 2000. (Ballad Romances Ser.). 352p. mass mkt. 5.50 o.s.i (0-8217-6869-7) Kensington Publishing Corp.

Greenlaw, Lavinia. Mary George of Allnorthover. 2003. 320p. pap. 12.00 (0-00-710594-0) HarperCollins Pubs. Ltd. GBR. Dist: Trafalgar Square.

—Mary George of Allnorthover. 2001. 288p. tchr. ed. 24.00 (0-618-09523-3) Houghton Mifflin Co.

Greenwood, D. M. Idol Bones. 1993. 224p. 18.95 o.p. (0-312-09829-4, Saint Martin's Minotaur) St. Martin's Pr.

—Unholy Ghosts. 1992. 224p. 17.95 o.p. (0-312-08515-X, Saint Martin's Minotaur) St. Martin's Pr.

—Unholy Ghosts. l.t. ed. 2001. 288p. pap. 23.95 (0-7838-9596-8) Thorndike Pr.

Greenwood, John. The Mind of Mr. Mosley. 1987. 15.95 o.p. (0-8027-5680-8) Walker & Co.

—The Missing Mr. Mosley. 1985. (Mosley Mystery Ser.). 192p. 13.95 (0-8027-5618-2) Walker & Co.

—Mists over Mosley. 1986. 192p. 15.95 (0-8027-5642-5) Walker & Co.

—Mosley by Moonlight. 1985. 12.95 o.s.i (0-8027-5606-9) Walker & Co.

—Murder, Mr. Mosley. 1983. (Mysteries Ser.). 192p. 12.95 o.p. (0-8027-5574-7) Walker & Co.

—What, Me, Mr. Mosley? 1987. 15.95 o.p. (0-8027-5692-1) Walker & Co.

Greenwood, L. B. Sherlock Holmes & the Case of Sabina Hall. 1988. 16.95 o.p. (0-671-65914-6, Simon & Schuster) Simon & Schuster.

Gregory, Deborah. The Cornflake House. 240p. 2000. pap. 12.00 (0-312-25271-4); 1999. 21.95 o.p. (0-312-20290-3) Picador.

Gregory, Philippa. Bread & Chocolate. 2000. 247p. (0-00-225761-0) HarperCollins Pubs.

—The Little House. l.t. ed. 1997. pap. 23.95 o.p. (1-56895-422-0, Wheeler Publishing, Inc.) Gale Group.

—The Little House. 1996. 304p. 25.00 o.s.i (*0-06-017670-9*) HarperCollins Pubs.
—The Little House. unabr. ed. 1998. audio 69.95 (*0-7531-0288-9*, 971102) ISIS Audio Bks. GBR. *Dist:* Ulverscroft Large Print Bks., Ltd.
—The Other Boleyn Girl. 2002. 672p. pap. 15.00 (*0-7432-2744-1*, Touchstone) Simon & Schuster.
—A Respectable Trade. l.t. ed. 1995. 682p. 26.95 o.p. (*0-7838-1477-1*, Macmillan Reference USA) Gale Group.
—A Respectable Trade. 1995. 512p. 25.00 o.p. (*0-06-017663-6*) HarperCollins Pubs.
—A Respectable Trade. unabr. ed. 1999. audio 94.95 (*0-7531-0478-4*, 981113) ISIS Audio Bks. GBR. *Dist:* Ulverscroft Large Print Bks., Ltd.
—A Respectable Trade. 1996. 480p. mass mkt. 5.99 o.p. (*0-06-109433-1*, HarperTorch) Morrow/Avon.
Gregory, Susanna. A Plague on Both Your Houses. 1996. (Illus.). 406p. mass mkt. o.s.i (*0-7515-1695-3*) Little Brown & Co.
—A Plague on Both Your Houses. 1998. (Chronicle of Matthew Bartholomew Ser.: Vol. 3). 416p. 24.95 o.p. (*0-312-19318-1*) St. Martin's Pr.
Gregson, J. M. Body Politic. l.t. ed. 2003. 306p. pap. 24.45 (*0-7862-5414-9*) Thorndike Pr.
—Murder at the Lodge. 2003. 224p. 26.99 (*0-7278-5813-0*) Severn Hse. Pubs., Ltd.
—Sherlock Holmes & the Frightened Golfer. 1999. (Sherlock Holmes... Ser.). (*0-947533-68-0*) Breese Bks., Ltd.
—Sherlock Holmes & the Frightened Golfer. 2000. (Sherlock Holmes Ser.). 176p. pap. 12.95 (*0-947533-63-X*) Breese Bks., Ltd. GBR. *Dist:* Midpoint Trade Bks., Inc.
—Stranglehold. l.t. ed. 2002. (Nightingale Ser.). 24.45 (*0-7862-4250-7*) Thorndike Pr.
Greyle, Katherine. Rules for a Lady. 2001. 320p. mass mkt. 4.99 (*0-8439-4818-3*, Leisure Bks.) Dorchester Publishing Co., Inc.
Griffiths, Niall. Kelly & Victor. 224p. 2003. pap. 12.00 (*0-09-942205-0*); 2002. pap. 16.95 (*0-224-06166-6*) Random Hse. UK, Ltd. GBR. *Dist:* Trafalgar Square.
Grimes, Martha. The Anodyne Necklace. 1990. 256p. reprint ed. mass mkt. 5.99 o.s.i (*0-440-10280-4*) Dell Publishing.
—The Anodyne Necklace. 1983. 252p. 15.95 o.p. (*0-316-32882-0*) Little Brown & Co.
—The Anodyne Necklace. 2004. 320p. mass mkt. 7.99 (*0-451-41089-0*, Onyx) NAL.
—The Anodyne Necklace. abr. ed. 1999. audio 9.98 (*0-671-04429-X*, Simon & Schuster Audioworks) Simon & Schuster Audio.
—The Anodyne Necklace. l.t. ed. 1983. 420p. reprint ed. 13.95 o.p. (*0-89621-486-9*) Thorndike Pr.
—The Blue Last: A Richard Jury Mystery. 16th l.t. ed. 2002. 472p. lib. bdg. 29.95 (*1-58547-166-6*) Ctr. Point Large Print.
—The Blue Last: A Richard Jury Mystery. 2001. 384p. 24.95 o.p. (*0-670-03004-X*, Viking) Viking Penguin.
—The Case Has Altered: A Richard Jury Mystery. unabr. ed. 1998. audio 72.00 (*0-7366-4072-X*, 4581) Books on Tape, Inc.
—The Case Has Altered: A Richard Jury Mystery. l.t. ed. 1998. (Wheeler Large Print Book Ser.). 515p. 27.95 o.p. (*1-56895-546-4*, Wheeler Publishing, Inc.) Gale Group.
—The Case Has Altered: A Richard Jury Mystery. 1997. 384p. 24.00 o.s.i (*0-8050-5620-3*) Holt, Henry & Co.
—The Case Has Altered: A Richard Jury Mystery. 1998. 432p. mass mkt. 7.99 (*0-451-40868-3*, Onyx) NAL.
—The Case Has Altered: A Richard Jury Mystery. abr. ed. 1997. audio 24.00 (*0-671-57756-5*, 595585, Simon & Schuster Audioworks) Simon & Schuster Audio.
—The Deer Leap. 1986. 256p. mass mkt. 6.99 o.s.i (*0-440-11938-3*) Dell Publishing.
—The Deer Leap. 1985. 15.95 o.p. (*0-316-32886-3*) Little Brown & Co.
—The Dirty Duck. 1990. 256p. mass mkt. 6.99 o.s.i (*0-440-12050-0*) Dell Publishing.
—The Dirty Duck. 1984. 252p. 14.95 o.s.i (*0-316-32883-9*) Little Brown & Co.
—The Dirty Duck. abr. ed. 1993. (Inspector Richard Jury Ser.). audio 16.00 (*0-671-75989-2*, 390661, Simon & Schuster Audioworks) Simon & Schuster Audio.
—The Five Bells & Bladebone. 1988. 384p. mass mkt. 6.99 o.s.i (*0-440-20133-0*) Dell Publishing.
—The Five Bells & Bladebone. 1987. 15.95 o.p. (*0-316-32889-8*) Little Brown & Co.
—The Five Bells & Bladebone. 2002. 352p. reprint ed. mass mkt. 6.99 (*0-451-41038-6*, Onyx) NAL.
—Help the Poor Struggler. 1986. 240p. mass mkt. 6.99 o.s.i (*0-440-13584-2*) Dell Publishing.
—Help the Poor Struggler. 1985. 288p. 15.95 o.p. (*0-316-32884-7*) Little Brown & Co.
—I Am the Only Running Footman. 1990. 320p. mass mkt. 5.99 o.s.i (*0-440-13924-4*) Dell Publishing.
—I Am the Only Running Footman. 1986. 15.95 o.s.i (*0-316-32887-1*) Little Brown & Co.
—I Am the Only Running Footman. 2001. 320p. mass mkt. 6.99 (*0-451-41002-5*, Onyx) NAL.
—I Am the Only Running Footman. 1992. 4.99 o.p. (*0-517-09217-4*) Random Hse. Value Publishing.
—Jerusalem Inn. 1990. 288p. reprint ed. mass mkt. 6.99 o.s.i (*0-440-14181-8*) Doubleday Publishing.
—Jerusalem Inn. 1984. 288p. 15.95 o.s.i (*0-316-32879-0*) Little Brown & Co.
—The Lamorna Wink: A Richard Jury Mystery. 2000. 432p. reprint ed. mass mkt. 6.99 (*0-451-40936-1*, Onyx) NAL.
—The Lamorna Wink: A Richard Jury Mystery. l.t. ed. 2000. (Basic Ser.). 515p. 29.95 (*0-7862-2324-3*) Thorndike Pr.
—The Lamorna Wink: A Richard Jury Mystery. 1999. 3384p. 22.95 o.s.i (*0-670-88870-2*, Viking) Viking Penguin.
—The Man with a Load of Mischief. 1990. 320p. mass mkt. 5.99 o.s.i (*0-440-15327-1*) Dell Publishing.
—The Man with a Load of Mischief. 1981. 255p. 15.95 o.s.i (*0-316-32880-4*) Little Brown & Co.
—The Man with a Load of Mischief. 2003. 288p. mass mkt. 6.99 (*0-451-41081-5*, Onyx) NAL.
—The Man with a Load of Mischief. abr. ed. 1992. audio 16.00 (*0-671-75960-4*, Simon & Schuster Audioworks) Simon & Schuster Audio.
—The Man with a Load of Mischief. l.t. ed. 1984. 455p. reprint ed. 13.95 o.p. (*0-89621-514-8*) Thorndike Pr.
—The Old Contemptibles. 1992. 304p. mass mkt. 6.99 (*0-345-37456-8*); 1991. mass mkt. 5.99 o.s.i (*0-345-37515-7*) Ballantine Bks.
—The Old Contemptibles. unabr. ed. 1991. audio 56.00 (*0-7366-1954-2*, 2775) Books on Tape, Inc.
—The Old Contemptibles. 1991. 22.95 o.s.i (*0-316-32898-7*); 19.95 o.s.i (*0-316-32894-4*) Little Brown & Co.
—The Old Contemptibles. l.t. ed. 1995. (Magna Large Print Ser.). 531p. o.p. (*0-7505-0835-3*) Magna Large Print Bks. GBR. *Dist:* Ulverscroft Large Print Canada, Ltd.
—The Old Contemptibles. abr. ed. 1999. audio 9.98 (*0-671-04500-8*); 1991. audio 15.95 (*0-671-73569-1*, 391301) Simon & Schuster Audio. (Simon & Schuster Audioworks).
—The Old Fox Deceiv'd. 1991. 304p. mass mkt. 5.99 o.s.i (*0-440-16747-7*) Dell Publishing.
—The Old Fox Deceiv'd. 1982. 288p. 16.95 o.p. (*0-316-32881-2*) Little Brown & Co.
—The Old Fox Deceiv'd. 2003. 320p. mass mkt. 7.99 (*0-451-41068-8*) NAL.
—The Old Fox Deceiv'd. 1999. pap. 9.98 (*0-671-04430-3*); 1992. audio 16.00 (*0-671-75991-4*, 391302) Simon & Schuster Audio. (Simon & Schuster Audioworks).
—The Old Silent. unabr. ed. 1990. audio 72.00 (*0-7366-1833-3*, 2668) Books on Tape, Inc.
—The Old Silent. 448p. 1993. mass mkt. 3.99 o.s.i (*0-440-21519-6*); 1990. mass mkt. 6.99 o.s.i (*0-440-20492-5*) Dell Publishing.
—The Old Silent. 1989. 296p. 18.95 o.p. (*0-316-32318-7*) Little Brown & Co.
—The Old Silent. 1992. 5.99 o.p. (*0-517-07973-9*) Random Hse. Value Publishing.
—The Old Silent. abr. ed. 1992. audio 16.00 (*0-671-73617-5*, Simon & Schuster Audioworks) Simon & Schuster Audio.
—Rainbow's End. 1996. 448p. mass mkt. 7.50 (*0-345-39426-7*) Ballantine Bks.
—Rainbow's End. unabr. ed. 1995. audio 60.00 (*0-7366-3138-0*, 3813) Books on Tape, Inc.
—Rainbow's End. l.t. ed. 1995. 22.00 o.s.i (*0-679-76228-0*) Random Hse. Large Print.
—Rainbow's End. abr. ed. 1995. (Inspector Richard Jury Ser.). audio 17.00 (*0-671-53450-5*, 392985, Simon & Schuster Audioworks) Simon & Schuster Audio.
—The Stargazey: A Richard Jury Mystery. unabr. ed. 1999. audio 64.00 (*0-7366-4463-6*, 4908) Books on Tape, Inc.
—The Stargazey: A Richard Jury Mystery. 1998. 384p. 25.00 o.s.i (*0-8050-5622-X*) Holt, Henry & Co.
—The Stargazey: A Richard Jury Mystery. 1999. 432p. reprint ed. mass mkt. 7.99 (*0-451-40897-7*, Onyx) NAL.
—The Stargazey: A Richard Jury Mystery. l.t. ed. (Thorndike/G. K. Hall Paperback Bestsellers Ser.). 2000. 647p. pap. 27.95 (*0-7862-1789-8*); 1999. 581p. 30.95 (*0-7862-1788-X*) Thorndike Pr.
Grossman, Judith. Her Own Terms. 1988. 224p. reprint ed. mass mkt. 3.95 o.s.i (*0-8041-0394-1*, Ivy Bks.) Ballantine Bks.
—Her Own Terms. 2002. 277p. pap. 14.00 (*1-56947-289-0*); 1987. 256p. 16.95 o.p. (*0-939149-11-7*) Soho Pr., Inc.
Grossmith, George. The Diary of a Nobody. 1978. 3.50 o.p. (*0-460-01963-5*); 1962. 8.00 o.p. (*0-460-00963-X*) Dutton/Plume. (Dutton).
—The Diary of a Nobody. 2000. E-Book 2.49 (*1-58744-142-X*) Electric Umbrella Publishing.
Grossmith, George & Grossmith, Weedom. Diary of a Nobody: The Essential Library Edition. 2001. 142p. pap. 20.99 (*0-7388-1228-5*) Xlibris Corp.
Grossmith, George & Grossmith, Weedon. The Diary of a Nobody. unabr. ed. 1992. audio 32.95 (*0-7861-0309-4*, 1271) Blackstone Audio Bks., Inc.
—The Diary of a Nobody. l.t. ed. 1987. (Mainstream Ser.). (Illus.). 296p. 16.95 o.p. (*1-85089-040-4*) ISIS Large Print Bks. GBR. *Dist:* Transaction Pubs.
—The Diary of a Nobody. Flint, Kate, ed. & intro. by. 1998. (Oxford World's Classics Ser.). (Illus.). 176p. pap. 8.95 (*0-19-283327-8*) Oxford Univ. Pr., Inc.
—The Diary of a Nobody. Trotter, David, ed. 1995. (Oxford Popular Fiction Ser.). (Illus.). 158p. pap. 7.95 o.p. (*0-19-282404-X*) Oxford Univ. Pr., Inc.
—The Diary of a Nobody. (Illus.). 240p. pap. (*0-14-028556-3*) Penguin Bks. Canada, Ltd.
—The Diary of a Nobody. 1945. 240p. pap. 12.95 (*0-14-000510-2*) Penguin Bks., Ltd. GBR. *Dist:* Trafalgar Square.
—The Diary of a Nobody. abr. ed. 2015. audio 16.95 (*0-14-086276-5*) Penguin Group (USA) Inc.
—The Diary of a Nobody. 2000. (Humour Classics Ser.). (Illus.). 194p. 14.95 (*1-85375-364-5*) Prion GBR. *Dist:* Trafalgar Square.
—The Diary of a Nobody. 1993. (Illus.). 288p. pap. 8.95 o.p. (*0-460-87227-3*); pap. 8.95 o.p. (*0-460-87264-8*) Tuttle Publishing. (Everyman's Classic Library in Paperback).
Gupta, Sunetra. Memories of Rain: A Novel. 1992. 17.95 o.p. (*0-8021-1448-2*) Grove/Atlantic, Inc.
Gurnah, Abdulrazak. By the Sea: A Novel. 2001. 256p. text 22.95 (*1-56584-658-3*) New Pr., The.
Gurney, Jane. Gone Tomorrow. 2000. 573p. pap. 10.95 (*0-553-40408-3*) Transworld Publishers Ltd. GBR. *Dist:* Trafalgar Square.
—The Green of the Spring. 1993. 24.95 o.p. (*0-312-09023-4*) St. Martin's Pr.
Guthrie, A. B., Jr. Murder in the Cotswolds. l.t. ed. 1990. (General Ser.). 304p. lib. bdg. 19.95 o.p. (*0-8161-4977-1*, Macmillan Reference USA) Gale Group.
—Murder in the Cotswolds, 001. 1989. 16.95 o.p. (*0-395-41456-3*) Houghton Mifflin Co.
Haddon, Mark. The Curious Incident of the Dog in the Night-Time: A Novel. 2004. 224p. pap. (*0-385-65980-6*, Anchor Canada); 2003. 240p. (*0-385-65979-2*) Doubleday Canada, Ltd. CAN. *Dist:* Random Hse., Inc.
—The Curious Incident of the Dog in the Night-Time: A Novel. 2003. (Illus.). 240p. 22.95 (*0-385-50945-6*) Doubleday Publishing.
—The Curious Incident of the Dog in the Night-Time: A Novel. 2004. 240p. pap. 12.00 (*1-4000-3271-7*, Vintage) Knopf Publishing Group.
Hadley, Tessa. Everything Will Be All Right. 2003. 320p. 24.00 (*0-8050-7065-6*) Holt, Henry & Co.
Haines, Pamela. The Golden Lion. 1986. 500p. 18.95 o.s.i (*0-684-18731-0*, Macmillan Reference USA) Gale Group.
Haire-Sargeant, Lin. Heathcliff: The Return to Wuthering Heights. Zion, Clarie, ed. 1992. 304p. 20.00 (*0-671-77700-9*, Atria) Simon & Schuster.
Hale, Deborah. Beauty & the Baron. 2003. (Harlequin Historicals Ser.: No. 655). 304p. mass mkt. (*0-373-29255-4*, Harlequin Bks.) Harlequin Enterprises, Ltd.
—Lady Lyte's Little Secret. 2003. (Harlequin Historicals Ser.: No. 639). 304p. mass mkt. (*0-373-29239-2*, Harlequin Bks.) Harlequin Enterprises, Ltd.
Hall, John. Sherlock Holmes & the Disgraced Inspector. 1998. 140p. pap. 14.95 (*0-947533-88-5*) Breese Bks., Ltd. GBR. *Dist:* Midpoint Trade Bks., Inc.
—Sherlock Holmes & the Disgraced Inspector. l.t. ed. 2000. (Linford Mystery Large Print Ser.). 248p. pap. 18.99 (*0-7089-5783-8*, Linford) Thorpe, F. A. Pubs. GBR. *Dist:* Ulverscroft Large Print Bks., Ltd., Ulverscroft Large Print Canada, Ltd.
—Sherlock Holmes & the Telephone Murder Mystery. 1998. 189p. pap. 14.95 (*0-947533-47-8*) Breese Bks., Ltd. GBR. *Dist:* Midpoint Trade Bks., Inc.
Hall, John, ed. The Abominable Wife & Other Unrecorded Cases of Mr. Sherlock Holmes. 1998. 114p. pap. (*1-899562-61-3*, Calabash Pr.) Ash-Tree Pr.
Hall, Patricia. The Dead of Winter. 1996. (Yorkshire Mystery Ser.). 21.95 o.p. (*0-312-15148-9*, Saint Martin's Minotaur) St. Martin's Pr.
—Dead on Arrival. l.t. ed. 2000. (Dales Large Print Ser.). 400p. pap. (*1-84262-012-6*) Dales Large Print Bks. GBR. *Dist:* Ulverscroft Large Print Canada, Ltd.
—Dead on Arrival. 2001. (Yorkshire Mystery Ser.). 224p. 22.95 (*0-312-26572-7*, Saint Martin's Minotaur) St. Martin's Pr.
—Death by Election. l.t. ed. 1994. (Dales Large Print Ser.). 418p. pap. o.p. (*1-85389-519-9*) Dales Large Print Bks. GBR. *Dist:* Ulverscroft Large Print Canada, Ltd.
—Death by Election. 1994. (Yorkshire Mystery Ser.). 256p. 20.95 o.p. (*0-312-11461-3*, Saint Martin's Minotaur) St. Martin's Pr.
—Death in Dark Waters: A Yorkshire Mystery. 2004. 272p. 23.95 (*0-312-32155-4*, Saint Martin's Minotaur) St. Martin's Pr.
—Deep Freeze. l.t. ed. 2002. (Magna Large Print Ser.). 416p. (*0-7505-1880-4*) Magna Large Print Bks. GBR. *Dist:* Ulverscroft Large Print Canada, Ltd.
—Deep Freeze: A Yorkshire Mystery. 2003. (Yorkshire Mystery Ser.). 272p. 23.95 (*0-312-28212-5*, Saint Martin's Minotaur) St. Martin's Pr.
—Dying Fall. l.t. ed. 1995. (Dales Large Print Ser.). 432p. pap. o.p. (*1-85389-561-X*) Dales Large Print Bks. GBR. *Dist:* Ulverscroft Large Print Canada, Ltd.
—Dying Fall. 1996. 248p. mass mkt. o.s.i (*0-7515-1204-4*) Little Brown & Co.
—Dying Fall. 1995. (Yorkshire Mystery Ser.). 248p. 21.95 o.p. (*0-312-13477-0*, Saint Martin's Minotaur) St. Martin's Pr.
—The Italian Girl. 2000. 208p. 21.95 (*0-312-26489-5*, Saint Martin's Minotaur) St. Martin's Pr.
—Perils of the Night. 1998. (Yorkshire Mystery Ser.). 224p. 22.95 (*0-312-19996-1*, Saint Martin's Minotaur) St. Martin's Pr.
—The Poison Pool. 1993. 256p. 19.95 o.p. (*0-312-09894-4*, Saint Martin's Minotaur) St. Martin's Pr.
—Skeleton at the Feast. l.t. ed. 2001. (Magna Large Print Ser.). 368p. (*0-7505-1728-X*) Magna Large Print Bks. GBR. *Dist:* Ulverscroft Large Print Canada, Ltd.
—Skeleton at the Feast. 2002. (Yorkshire Mystery Ser.). 256p. 23.95 (*0-312-28208-7*, Saint Martin's Minotaur) St. Martin's Pr.
Hall, Robert L. Ben Franklin Takes the Case: The American Agent Investigates Murder in the Dark Byways of London. 1988. 256p. 16.95 o.p. (*0-312-01735-9*, Saint Martin's Minotaur) St. Martin's Pr.
—Benjamin Franklin & a Case of Artful Murder. 1995. mass mkt. 4.99 (*0-312-95419-0*, St. Martin's Paperbacks) St. Martin's Pr.
—Benjamin Franklin & a Case of Christmas Murder. l.t. ed. 1998. 413p. reprint ed. text 15.00 (*0-7881-5175-4*) DIANE Publishing Co.
—Benjamin Franklin & a Case of Christmas Murder. 1991. 288p. mass mkt. 3.99 o.p. (*0-312-92670-7*, St. Martin's Paperbacks); 1990. 17.95 o.p. (*0-312-05383-5*, Saint Martin's Minotaur) St. Martin's Pr.
—Benjamin Franklin & the Case of the Artful Murder. 1994. 304p. 20.95 o.p. (*0-312-10936-9*, Saint Martin's Minotaur) St. Martin's Pr.
—Benjamin Franklin Takes the Case: The American Agent Investigates Murder in the Dark Byways of London. 1993. mass mkt. 3.99 o.p. (*0-312-95047-0*, St. Martin's Paperbacks) St. Martin's Pr.
—London Blood: Further Adventures of the American Agent Abroad: A Benjamin Franklin Mystery. 1997. (Benjamin Franklin Mystery Ser.). 256p. 21.95 (*0-312-16908-6*, Saint Martin's Minotaur) St. Martin's Pr.
—Murder at Drury Lane: Further Adventures of the American Agent in London. 1993. mass mkt. 4.50 (*0-312-95112-4*, St. Martin's Paperbacks); 1992. 288p. 18.95 o.p. (*0-312-08266-5*, Saint Martin's Minotaur) St. Martin's Pr.
—Murder by the Waters: A Benjamin Franklin Mystery. pap. 15.95 (*0-312-30104-9*, Saint Martin's Griffin); 1995. 272p. 21.95 (*0-312-13568-8*, Saint Martin's Minotaur) St. Martin's Pr.
Hall, Roy. A Perfect Gentleman. 1999. (Illus.). 256p. 26.00 (*1-85782-376-1*) Blake Publishing, Inc.
—A Perfect Gentleman. 1999. (Illus.). 256p. pap. text 26.00 (*1-85782-307-9*) Blake, John Publishing, Ltd. GBR. *Dist:* 7 Hills Bk. Distributors.
Halliday, Sylvia. The Ring. 1996. 320p. 21.95 o.p. (*1-57566-014-8*) Kensington Publishing Corp.
—Summer Darkness, Winter Light. 1996. 384p. mass mkt. 4.99 o.s.i (*0-8217-5260-X*); 1995. mass mkt. 18.95 o.p. (*0-8217-4922-6*, Pinnacle Bks.) Kensington Publishing Corp.
Halliwell, Anthea. Cuckoos Parting Cry. 2000. 303p. (J). pap. 10.95 (*0-552-99774-9*) Transworld Publishers Ltd. GBR. *Dist:* Trafalgar Square.
Halpern, Chaiky. The House on Kyverdale Road. 1995. 16.95 (*0-87306-737-1*); pap. 12.95 (*0-87306-738-X*) Feldheim, Philipp Inc.
Hamburger, Jean. Diary of William Harvey. Wright, Barbara, tr. from FRE. 1992. 224p. (C). 35.00 o.p. (*0-8135-1825-3*); pap. 14.95 (*0-8135-1826-1*) Rutgers Univ. Pr.
Hamilton. Paradise Lane. 2000. 429p. 27.95 (*0-593-03466-X*) Transworld Publishers Ltd. GBR. *Dist:* Trafalgar Square.
Hamilton, Andrew. A Taste of His Own Medicine. 1993. 160p. pap. 7.99 o.p. (*0-89107-755-3*) Crossway Bks.
Hamilton-Paterson, James. Gerontius. 264p. 1992. 10.95 (*0-939149-69-9*); 1991. 19.95 (*0-939149-48-6*) Soho Pr., Inc.

Settings

Hamilton, Peter F. Mindstar Rising. (Greg Mandel Ser.). 1997. 423p. mass mkt. 6.99 (0-8125-9056-2); 1996. 384p. 23.95 o.p. (0-312-85955-4) Doherty, Tom Assocs., LLC. (Tor Bks.).
—Mindstar Rising. 1993. 438p. pap. 16.95 (0-330-32376-8) Pan Bks. Ltd. GBR. *Dist:* Trans-Atlantic Pubns., Inc.
—The Nano Flower. 1999. (Greg Mandel Ser.: Vol. 3). 602p. mass mkt. 6.99 (0-8125-7769-8); 1998. 448p. 25.95 (0-312-86580-5) Doherty, Tom Assocs., LLC. (Tor Bks.).
—A Quantum Murder. 1998. 375p. mass mkt. 6.99 (0-8125-5524-4); 1997. 384p. 24.95 (0-312-85954-6) Doherty, Tom Assocs., LLC. (Tor Bks.).
Hamilton, Ruth. The Bells of Scotland Road. 1997. 572p. 10.95 (0-552-14385-5) Transworld Publishers Ltd. GBR. *Dist:* Trafalgar Square.
Hammer, David L., et al. My Dear Watson: Being the Annals of Sherlock Holmes. 1995. (Illus.). 104p. (Orig.). pap. 12.95 (0-938501-22-4) Wessex Pr.
Hampton, Denise. The Warrior's Damsel. 2001. (Illus.). 384p. mass mkt. 5.99 (0-380-81546-X, Avon Bks.) Morrow/Avon.
Hampton, Maisie. Time of Wonder. l.t. ed. 2001. (Thorndike General Ser.). 319p. pap. 24.95 o.p. (0-7862-3003-7); (0-7540-4341-X); (0-7540-4340-1) Thorndike Pr.
Hanna, Edward B. The Whitechapel Horrors. 1993. 400p. pap. 10.95 (0-7867-0019-X, Carroll & Graf Pubs.) Avalon Publishing Group.
Hannah, Sophie. The Superpower of Love. 2003. 440p. pap. 14.00 (1-56947-320-X); 2002. 336p. 25.00 (1-56947-281-5) Soho Pr., Inc.
Harbaugh, Karen. Cupid's Bow. 1998. 224p. mass mkt. 4.99 o.s.i (0-451-19471-3, Signet Bks.) NAL.
—Cupid's Kiss. 1999. (Signet Regency Romance Ser.). 224p. mass mkt. 4.99 o.s.i (0-451-19535-3) NAL.
—Cupid's Mistake. 1997. 224p. mass mkt. 5.50 o.s.i (0-451-19239-7, Signet Bks.) NAL.
—The Devil's Bargain. 1995. (Regency Romance Ser.). 224p. (Orig.). mass mkt. 3.99 o.s.i (0-451-18318-5, Signet Bks.) NAL.
—Reluctant Cavalier. 1996. (Signet Regency Romance Ser.). 224p. mass mkt. 5.50 o.s.i (0-451-19020-3, Signet Bks.) NAL.
Harding, Paul T., pseud. The House of Crows: The Sorrowful Mysteries of Brother Athelstan. 1996. (Illus.). 280p. pap. 13.95 (0-7472-4918-0) Headline Bk. Publishing, Ltd. GBR. *Dist:* Trafalgar Square.
—The Nightingale Gallery: Being the First of the Sorrowful Mysteries of Brother Athelstan. 1993. 256p. mass mkt. 4.99 (0-380-71751-4, Avon Bks.); 1992. 20.00 o.p. (0-688-11225-0, Morrow, William & Co.) Morrow/Avon.
Hardwick, Mollie. The Bandersnatch. 1994. mass mkt. 4.50 o.s.i (0-449-22029-X, Fawcett) Ballantine Bks.
—The Bandersnatch. 1989. 15.95 o.p. (0-312-02865-2, Saint Martin's Minotaur) St. Martin's Pr.
—The Bandersnatch. l.t. ed. 1991. (Ulverscroft Large Print Ser.). 29.99 o.p. (0-7089-2534-0, Ulverscroft) Thorpe, F. A. Pubs. GBR. *Dist:* Ulverscroft Large Print Bks., Ltd., Ulverscroft Large Print Canada, Ltd.
—Come Away, Death. 1997. 214p. mass mkt. 5.50 (0-449-22421-X, Fawcett) Ballantine Bks.
—The Dreaming Damozel. 1995. mass mkt. 4.99 o.s.i (0-449-22073-7, Fawcett) Ballantine Bks.
—The Dreaming Damozel. l.t. ed. 1992. (Nightingale Series Large Print Bks.). 337p. pap. 14.95 o.p. (0-8161-5323-X, Macmillan Reference USA) Gale Group.
—The Dreaming Damozel. 1991. 15.95 o.p. (0-312-05421-1, Saint Martin's Minotaur) St. Martin's Pr.
—Malice Domestic. 1992. mass mkt. 4.50 o.s.i (0-449-22032-X, Fawcett) Ballantine Bks.
—Malice Domestic. 1989. mass mkt. o.s.i (0-552-13235-7, Corgi) Bantam Bks.
—Malice Domestic. 1986. 208p. 13.95 o.p. (0-312-50940-5) St. Martin's Pr.
—Malice Domestic. l.t. ed. 1988. 400p. o.p. (0-7089-1835-2, Ulverscroft) Thorpe, F. A. Pubs.
—Parson's Pleasure. 1992. mass mkt. 4.50 o.s.i (0-449-22031-1, Fawcett) Ballantine Bks.
—Parson's Pleasure. 1989. mass mkt. o.s.i (0-552-13236-5, Corgi) Bantam Bks.
—Parson's Pleasure. 1987. 208p. 14.95 o.p. (0-312-00642-X) St. Martin's Pr.
—Parson's Pleasure. l.t. ed. 1989. 332p. 17.95 o.p. (0-7089-1932-4, Ulverscroft) Thorpe, F. A. Pubs. GBR. *Dist:* Ulverscroft Large Print Bks., Ltd.
—Perish in July. 1994. mass mkt. 4.99 o.s.i (0-449-22028-1, Fawcett) Ballantine Bks.
—Perish in July. 1991. mass mkt. o.s.i (0-552-13664-6, Corgi) Bantam Bks.
—Perish in July. 1990. 15.95 o.p. (0-312-04402-X, Saint Martin's Minotaur) St. Martin's Pr.
—Uneaseful Death. 1993. mass mkt. 5.99 o.s.i (0-449-22030-3, Fawcett) Ballantine Bks.
—Uneaseful Death. 1989. mass mkt. o.s.i (0-552-13411-2, Corgi) Bantam Bks.
—Uneaseful Death. 1988. 192p. 14.95 o.p. (0-312-01842-8, Saint Martin's Minotaur) St. Martin's Pr.
—Uneaseful Death. l.t. ed. 1990. (Ulverscroft Large Print Ser.). 29.99 o.p. (0-7089-2252-X, Ulverscroft) Thorpe, F. A. Pubs. GBR. *Dist:* Ulverscroft Large Print Bks., Ltd., Ulverscroft Large Print Canada, Ltd.
Hardwicke, Edward, reader. The Adventures of Sherlock Holmes. abr. ed. 1994. audio 12.00 (1-878427-38-5, XC422) Cimino Publishing Group.
Hardy, Thomas. The Bedside Thomas Hardy. Leeson, Edward, ed. 1979. 15.00 o.p. (0-312-07131-0) St. Martin's Pr.
—A Changed Man & Other Stories. 1984. (Pocket Classics Ser.). 336p. pap. 8.95 (0-86299-149-8) Sutton Publishing.
—Desperate Remedies, 3. reprint ed. lib. bdg. 294.00 (0-7426-2783-7); 2001. pap. text 84.00 (0-7426-7783-4) Classic Bks.
—Desperate Remedies. 1975. 448 p. (J). 12.50 (0-333-17760-6) Macmillan U.K. GBR. *Dist:* Trans-Atlantic Pubns., Inc.
—Desperate Remedies. Ingham, Patricia, ed. 2003. (Oxford World's Classics Ser.). 464p. pap. 12.95 (0-19-284070-3) Oxford Univ. Pr., Inc.
—Desperate Remedies. 1977. (Hardy New Wessex Editions Ser.). pap. 3.95 o.p. (0-312-19494-3, Saint Martin's Griffin) St. Martin's Pr.
—Desperate Remedies. Rimmer, Mary, ed. & intro. by. 1998. (Classics Ser.). (Illus.). 512p. 15.00 (0-14-043523-9, Penguin Classics) Viking Penguin.
—Far from the Madding Crowd: Penguin Readers Level 4. 1998. pap. 7.00 (0-14-081531-7) Longman Publishing Group.
—The Fiddler of the Reels & Other Stories. Blaisdell, Bob, ed. & intro. by. 1997. (Dover Thrift Editions Ser.). (Illus.). 80p. pap. 1.50 (0-486-29960-0) Dover Pubns., Inc.
—The Hand of Ethelberta. 2002. 392p. 27.99 (1-4043-0606-4); per. 22.99 (1-4043-0607-2) IndyPublish.com.
—The Hand of Ethelberta. 1978. (Hardy New Wessex Editions Ser.). pap. 3.95 o.p. (0-312-35736-2, Saint Martin's Griffin) St. Martin's Pr.
—The Hand of Ethelberta. 1998. pap. 7.50 (0-460-87645-7) Tuttle Publishing.
—The Hand of Ethelberta. 1998. (Classics Ser.). (Illus.). 512p. 13.95 (0-14-043502-6, Penguin Classics) Viking Penguin.
—The Hand of Ethelberta: A Comedy in Chapters. reprint ed. lib. bdg. 196.00 (0-7426-2787-X) Classic Bks.
—The Hand of Ethelberta: A Comedy in Chapters. 1990. (New Wessex Edition Ser.). 362p. 42.50 (0-333-17767-3) Macmillan U.K. GBR. *Dist:* Trans-Atlantic Pubns., Inc.
—An Indiscretion in the Life of an Heiress & Other Stories. Dalziel, Pamela, ed. 1999. (Oxford World's Classics Ser.). (Illus.). 320p. pap. 9.95 (0-19-283685-4) Oxford Univ. Pr., Inc.
—An Indiscretion in the Life of an Heiress & Other Stories. Dalziel, Pamela, ed. & intro. by. 1995. (Oxford World's Classics Ser.). (Illus.). 312p. pap. 9.95 o.p. (0-19-282344-2) Oxford Univ. Pr., Inc.
—Jude the Obscure. 1966. (Airmont Classics Ser.). (YA). (gr. 11 up). mass mkt. 1.95 o.p. (0-8049-0108-2, CL-108) Airmont Publishing Co., Inc.
—Jude the Obscure. 1976. 27.95 (0-8488-0515-1) Amereon, Ltd.
—Jude the Obscure. 1985. 448p. (gr. 8-12). mass mkt. 5.95 (0-553-21191-9, Bantam Classics) Bantam Bks.
—Jude the Obscure. Watts, Cedric, ed. 1999. (Literary Texts Ser.). text (1-55111-313-9); (Illus.). 517p. pap. (1-55111-171-3) Broadview Pr.
—Jude the Obscure. 1990. 400p. reprint ed. lib. bdg. 25.95 (0-89966-665-5) Buccaneer Bks., Inc.
—Jude the Obscure. reprint ed. lib. bdg. 98.00 (0-7426-2798-5); 2001. pap. text 28.00 (0-7426-7798-2) Classic Bks.
—Jude the Obscure. Howe, Irving, ed. 1972. (YA). (gr. 9 up). pap. 16.36 (0-395-05191-6, Riverside Editions) Houghton Mifflin Co.
—Jude the Obscure. 1996. 522p. 20.00 (0-676-51620-3); 1992. 560p. 20.00 (0-679-40993-9) Knopf, Alfred A. Inc.
—Jude the Obscure. 2000. (Cloth Bound Pocket Ser.). (Illus.). 7.95 (3-8290-3007-X, 521123) Konemann.
—Jude the Obscure. 1998. 144p. (C). pap. 7.66 (0-582-40264-6) Longman Publishing Group.
—Jude the Obscure. 1961. mass mkt. 2.95 o.p. (0-451-51783-0); 1961. 416p. mass mkt. 5.95 o.s.i (0-451-52370-9, Signet Classics); 1999. 448p. mass mkt. 5.95 (0-451-52725-9, Signet Classics) NAL.
—Jude the Obscure. l.t. ed. 1998. (Large Print Ser.). reprint ed. 575p. lib. bdg. 26.00 (0-939495-69-4); 457p. lib. bdg. 25.00 (1-58287-092-6) North Bks.
—Jude the Obscure. Page, Norman, ed. 1978. (Critical Editions Ser.). (Illus.). (C). o.p. (0-393-04473-4); 468p. pap. text o.p. (0-393-09089-2) Norton, W. W. & Co., Inc.
—Jude the Obscure. Ingham, Patricia, ed. 1985. (Oxford World's Classics Ser.). (Illus.). 492p. pap. 5.95 o.p. (0-19-281670-5) Oxford Univ. Pr., Inc.
—Jude the Obscure. 2003. o.p. (0-333-16897-6) Pan Macmillan.
—Jude the Obscure. Slack, Robert C., ed. 1978. 6.95 o.s.i (0-394-60462-8) Random Hse., Inc.
—Jude the Obscure. 1992. (BCL1-PR English Literature Ser.). 503p. reprint ed. lib. bdg. 99.00 (0-7812-7547-4) Reprint Services Corp.
—Jude the Obscure. 1977. (Hardy New Wessex Editions Ser.). pap. 2.95 o.p. (0-312-44661-6, Saint Martin's Griffin) St. Martin's Pr.
—Jude the Obscure. 1995. (Sun & Moon Classics Ser.: No. 77). 496p. pap. 12.95 o.p. (1-55713-203-8) Sun & Moon Pr.
—Jude the Obscure. l.t. ed. 1982. (Charnwood Large Print Ser.). 640p. 29.99 o.p. (0-7089-8067-8, Ulverscroft) Thorpe, F. A. Pubs. GBR. *Dist:* Ulverscroft Large Print Bks., Ltd., Ulverscroft Large Print Canada, Ltd.
—Jude the Obscure. 1961. (Signet Classics Ser.). 12.00 (0-606-03696-2) Turtleback Bks.
—Jude the Obscure. Hands, Timothy, ed. 1995. (Everyman Paperback Classics Ser.). 528p. (C). pap. 5.95 (0-460-87567-1, Everyman's Classic Library in Paperback) Tuttle Publishing.
—Jude the Obscure. Taylor, Dennis, ed. & intro. by. 1998. (Classics Ser.). 528p. pap. 7.95 (0-14-043538-7, Penguin Classics) Viking Penguin.
—Jude the Obscure. Sisson, C. H., ed. 1978. (Penguin Classics Ser.). 512p. (C). pap. 7.95 o.s.i (0-14-043131-4, Penguin Classics) Viking Penguin.
—Jude the Obscure. abr. ed. 1997. pap. 23.95 o.s.i incl. audio (0-14-086455-5, Penguin AudioBooks) Viking Penguin.
—Jude the Obscure. 1998. (Classics Library). pap. 3.95 (1-85326-261-7, 2617WW) Wordsworth Editions, Ltd. GBR. *Dist:* Casemate Pubs. & Bk. Distributors, LLC.
—Jude the Obscure. Hands, Timothy, ed. rev. ed. 1993. 528p. pap. 5.95 (0-460-87413-6, Everyman's Classic Library in Paperback) Tuttle Publishing.
—Jude the Obscure, Set. 1995. audio 65.95 (1-55685-364-5) Audio Bk. Contractors, Inc.
—Jude the Obscure, Set. unabr. ed. 1995. audio 96.95 (1-56054-914-9, SAB 028, Sterling Audio Bks.) BBC Audiobooks America.
—Jude the Obscure. unabr. ed. 1997. audio 76.95 (0-7861-1249-2, 2158) Blackstone Audio Bks., Inc.
—Jude the Obscure. unabr. collector's ed. 1983. (YA). audio 96.00 (0-7366-3978-0, 9526) Books on Tape, Inc.
—Jude the Obscure. Ingham, Patricia, ed. & intro. by. 2nd ed. 1998. (Oxford World's Classics Ser.). (Illus.). 496p. pap. 6.95 o.p. (0-19-283379-0) Oxford Univ. Pr., Inc.
—A Laodicean, 3. (Collected Works of Thomas Hardy). reprint ed. lib. bdg. 294.00 (0-7426-2790-X); 2001. pap. text 84.00 (0-7426-7790-7) Classic Bks.
—A Laodicean. 2002. 428p. 21.99 (1-4043-1290-0); per. 16.99 (1-4043-1291-9) IndyPublish.com.
—A Laodicean. 2003. o.p. (0-333-17765-7) Macmillan U.K. GBR. *Dist:* Trafalgar Square.
—A Laodicean. Gatewood, Jane, ed. 1992. (Oxford World's Classics Ser.). 506p. pap. 9.95 o.p. (0-19-282783-9) Oxford Univ. Pr., Inc.
—A Laodicean. 1978. (Hardy New Wessex Editions Ser.). pap. 3.95 o.p. (0-312-46936-5, Saint Martin's Griffin) St. Martin's Pr.
—A Laodicean. Stape, J. H., ed. 1997. (Everyman Paperback Classics Ser.). 432p. pap. 8.50 (0-460-87637-6, Everyman's Classic Library in Paperback) Tuttle Publishing.
—A Laodicean: A Story of Today. 1975. (New Wessex Ser.). 461p. (J). 12.50 (0-333-17759-2) Macmillan U.K. GBR. *Dist:* Trans-Atlantic Pubns., Inc.
—Life's Little Ironies. 2002. 244p. 18.99 (1-4043-1388-5); per. 13.99 (1-4043-1389-3) IndyPublish.com.
—Life's Little Ironies. Manford, Alan, ed. 2000. (Oxford World's Classics Ser.). (Illus.). 304p. pap. 9.95 (0-19-283663-3) Oxford Univ. Pr., Inc.
—Life's Little Ironies. Manford, Alan & Page, Norman, eds. 1996. (Oxford World's Classics Ser.). (Illus.). 294p. (C). pap. 7.95 o.p. (0-19-283177-1) Oxford Univ. Pr., Inc.
—Life's Little Ironies. 1998. 224p. pap. 6.95 o.p. (0-86299-069-6) Sutton Publishing.
—A Pair of Blue Eyes. 2001. per. 25.00 (1-891355-57-0) Blue Unicorn Editions.
—A Pair of Blue Eyes. E-Book 2.49 (1-58627-431-7) Electric Umbrella Publishing.
—A Pair of Blue Eyes. 2003. o.p. (0-333-17764-9) Macmillan U.K. GBR. *Dist:* Trafalgar Square.
—A Pair of Blue Eyes. Manford, Alan, ed. & intro. by. 1998. (Oxford World's Classics Ser.). (Illus.). 432p. pap. 7.95 (0-19-283482-7) Oxford Univ. Pr., Inc.
—A Pair of Blue Eyes. Manford, Alan, ed. 1985. (Oxford World's Classics Ser.). 426p. pap. 5.95 o.p. (0-19-281684-5) Oxford Univ. Pr., Inc.
—A Pair of Blue Eyes. 1979. (Hardy New Wessex Editions Ser.). pap. 3.95 o.p. (0-312-59466-6, Saint Martin's Griffin) St. Martin's Pr.
—A Pair of Blue Eyes. Dalziel, Pamela, ed. & intro. by. 1998. (Penguin Classics Ser.). 448p. pap. 10.00 (0-14-043529-8, Penguin Classics) Viking Penguin.
—A Pair of Blue Eyes. Ebbatson, Roger, ed. & intro. by. 1986. (Penguin Classics Ser.). 480p. pap. 7.95 o.s.i (0-14-043266-3, Penguin Classics) Viking Penguin.
—Pair of Blue Eyes. 1998. (Classics Library). pap. 3.95 (1-85326-277-3, 2773WW) Wordsworth Editions, Ltd. GBR. *Dist:* Casemate Pubs. & Bk. Distributors, LLC.
—A Pair of Blue Eyes. l.t. ed. 2000. per. 15.50 (1-58396-224-7) Blue Unicorn Editions.
—The Penguin Thomas Hardy. 1984. Vol. 1. 928p. pap. 8.95 o.p. (0-14-009010-X); Vol. 2. 1216p. pap. 8.95 o.p. (0-14-009011-8) Viking Penguin. (Penguin Bks.).
—The Return of Native. 1994. (Modern Library Ser.). 448p. 13.00 o.s.i (0-679-44108-5) Knopf, Alfred A. Inc.
—The Return of the Native. reprint ed. lib. bdg. 28.95 (0-88411-561-5) Amereon, Ltd.
—The Return of the Native. 1994. (Illustrated Classics Collection). 64p. pap. 4.95 (0-7854-0753-7, 40512); pap. 3.60 o.p. (1-56103-600-5) American Guidance Service, Inc.
—The Return of the Native. 1982. 384p. mass mkt. 1.95 o.s.i (0-553-21080-7) Bantam Bks.
—The Return of the Native. 1992. reprint ed. lib. bdg. 24.95 (0-89968-264-2, Lightyear Pr.) Buccaneer Bks., Inc.
—The Return of the Native. Milne, John, ed. 1980. (Heinemann Guided Readers Ser.). pap. text 3.00 o.p. (0-435-27061-3) Heinemann.
—The Return of the Native. 1997. text 8.25 (0-03-051494-0) Holt, Rinehart & Winston.
—The Return of the Native. 1992. (Everyman's Library). 20.00 (0-679-41730-3) Knopf, Alfred A. Inc.
—The Return of the Native. 2003. o.p. (0-333-16894-1) Macmillan U.K. GBR. *Dist:* Trafalgar Square.
—The Return of the Native. 1959. 416p. mass mkt. 4.95 o.s.i (0-451-52471-3, Signet Classics); 1959. 414p. mass mkt. 2.50 o.p. (0-451-52307-5, Signet Classics); 1999. 416p. mass mkt. 5.95 (0-451-52738-0) NAL.
—The Return of the Native. l.t. ed. (Large Print Ser.). reprint ed. 1992. 573p. lib. bdg. 26.00 (0-939495-36-8); 1998. 433p. lib. bdg. 25.00 (1-58287-064-0) North Bks.
—The Return of the Native. Gindin, James, ed. 1969. (Critical Editions Ser.). (Illus.). 7.00 o.p. (0-393-04300-2) Norton, W. W. & Co., Inc.
—The Return of the Native. Gatrell, Simon, ed. & intro. by. 1998. (Oxford World's Classics Ser.). (Illus.). 512p. pap. 8.95 (0-19-283406-1) Oxford Univ. Pr., Inc.
—The Return of the Native. 1990. (Oxford World's Classics Ser.). (Illus.). 510p. pap. 6.95 o.p. (0-19-282717-0) Oxford Univ. Pr., Inc.
—The Return of the Native. 1992. (BCL1-PR English Literature Ser.). 485p. reprint ed. lib. bdg. 99.00 (0-7812-7548-2) Reprint Services Corp.
—The Return of the Native. 1979. (Hardy New Wessex Editions Ser.). pap. 2.95 o.p. (0-312-67901-7, Saint Martin's Griffin) St. Martin's Pr.
—The Return of the Native. 1959. 12.00 (0-606-03347-5) Turtleback Bks.
—The Return of the Native. Hodgson, Amanda, ed. 1995. pap. 4.95 o.p. (0-460-87531-0, Everyman's Classic Library in Paperback) Tuttle Publishing.
—The Return of the Native. 1999. (Classics Ser.). (Illus.). 496p. pap. 8.95 (0-14-043518-2, Penguin Classics) Viking Penguin.
—The Return of the Native. Woodcock, George, ed. 1978. (Penguin Classics Ser.). 496p. pap. 8.95 o.s.i (0-14-043122-5, Penguin Classics) Viking Penguin.
—The Return of the Native. 1998. (Classics Library). 510p. pap. 3.95 (1-85326-238-2, 2382WW) Wordsworth Editions, Ltd. GBR. *Dist:* Casemate Pubs. & Bk. Distributors, LLC.
—The Return of the Native Readalong. 1994. (Illustrated Classics Collection). 64p. pap. 13.50 o.p. incl. audio (1-56103-602-1); pap. 14.95 incl. audio (0-7854-0769-3, 40514) American Guidance Service, Inc.
—Selected Stories of Thomas Hardy. 1980. pap. 3.95 (0-312-71119-0, Saint Martin's Griffin) St. Martin's Pr.
—Tess of the d'Urbervilles. 1991. 560p. 20.00 (0-679-40586-0, Everyman's Library) Knopf Publishing Group.
—Tess of the d'Urbervilles. 1979. 8.95 o.s.i (0-394-60484-9) Random Hse., Inc.
—Tess of the d'Urbervilles: A Pure Woman. 1999. (Signet Classics). 432p. mass mkt. 4.95 (0-451-52722-4, Signet Classics) NAL.
—Tess of the d'Urbervilles: A Pure Woman. 1998. (Modern Library Ser.). 544p. 16.95 o.s.i (0-679-60318-2) Random Hse., Inc.

—Tess of the d'Urbervilles: A Pure Woman. 1985. (Illus.). 368p. 12.95 o.p. (0-89577-215-9) Reader's Digest Assn., Inc., The.
—Tess of the d'Urbervilles: A Pure Woman. 1995. (Literary Classics Giant Ser.). 528p. text 8.98 o.p. (1-56138-653-7, Courage Bks.) Running Pr. Bk. Pubs.
—Tess of the d'Urbervilles: A Pure Woman. 1998. 9.00 (81-85944-57-1) UBS Pubs. Distributions, Ltd. IND. Dist: South Asia Bks.
—Tess of the d'Urbervilles: A Pure Woman Faithfully Presented. reprint ed. lib. bdg. 294.00 (0-7426-2796-9); 2001. pap. text 84.00 (0-7426-7796-6) Classic Bks.
—Thomas Hardy: Three Complete Novels. 1995. 704p. 12.99 o.s.i (0-517-12419-X) Random Hse., Inc.
—Thomas Hardy: Three Great Novels: Far from the Madding Crowd, The Mayor of Casterbridge, Tess of the D'Urbervilles. 1994. (Oxford World's Classics Ser.). (Illus.). 848p. pap. 15.95 o.p. (0-19-282286-1) Oxford Univ. Pr., Inc.
—The Thomas Hardy Omnibus. 1979. 15.00 o.p. (0-312-80157-2) St. Martin's Pr.
—The Trumpet-Major. l.t. unabr. ed. 1992. (Isis Large Print Bks.). 384p. 29.99 (1-85089-387-X, 89387X) ISIS Large Print Bks. GBR. Dist: Ulverscroft Large Print Bks., Ltd., Ulverscroft Large Print Canada, Ltd.
—The Trumpet-Major. 2003. o.p. (0-333-16890-9) Macmillan U.K. GBR. Dist: Trafalgar Square.
—The Trumpet-Major. Nemesvari, Richard, ed. & intro. by. 1999. (Oxford World's Classics Ser.). (Illus.). 416p. pap. 5.95 o.p. (0-19-283635-8) Oxford Univ. Pr., Inc.
—The Trumpet-Major. (Oxford World's Classics Ser.). 1998. pap. 5.95 (0-19-283135-6); 1991. (Illus.). 410p. pap. 5.95 o.p. (0-19-282718-9) Oxford Univ. Pr., Inc.
—The Trumpet-Major. 1977. (Hardy New Wessex Editions Ser.). pap. 3.95 (0-312-82146-8, Saint Martin's Griffin) St. Martin's Pr.
—The Trumpet-Major. Rimmer, Mary, ed. 2000. 432p. pap. 6.95 (0-460-87790-9, Everyman's Classic Library in Paperback) Tuttle Publishing.
—The Trumpet-Major. Shires, Linda M., ed. 1998. (Penguin Classics Ser.). 416p. pap. 7.95 o.p. (0-14-043540-9, Penguin Classics) Viking Penguin.
—The Trumpet-Major. 1989. 400p. pap. 6.95 o.s.i (0-14-043273-6, Penguin Classics) Viking Penguin.
—The Trumpet-Major. 1998. (Classics Library). 410p. pap. 3.95 (1-85326-246-3, 2463WW) Wordsworth Editions, Ltd. GBR. Dist: Casemate Pubs. & Bk. Distributors, LLC.
—The Trumpet-Major & Robert His Brother. 1975. pap. text 10.95 o.p. (0-312-82145-X) St. Martin's Pr.
—The Trumpet-Major & Robert his Brother. 1985. (Nonfiction Ser.). 320p. pap. 4.95 o.p. (0-14-043142-X, Penguin Classics) Viking Penguin.
—Two on a Tower. 1999. (Everyman Paperback Classics Ser.). 288p. pap. (0-460-87784-4) Dent, J.M. & Sons.
—Two on a Tower. 1990. (New Wessex Edition Ser.). 264p. text 42.50 o.s.i (0-333-17763-0) Macmillan U.K. GBR. Dist: Trans-Atlantic Pubns., Inc.
—Two on a Tower. Ahmad, Suleiman M., ed. 1999. (Oxford World's Classics Ser.). 352p. pap. 10.95 (0-19-283641-2) Oxford Univ. Pr., Inc.
—Two on a Tower. 1993. (Oxford World's Classics Ser.). 350p. pap. 9.95 o.p. (0-19-282919-X) Oxford Univ. Pr., Inc.
—Two on a Tower. 1977. (Hardy New Wessex Editions Ser.). pap. 3.95 o.p. (0-312-82742-3, Saint Martin's Griffin) St. Martin's Pr.
—Two on a Tower. 2000. (Classics Ser.). (Illus.). 336p. 10.95 (0-14-043536-0, Penguin Classics) Viking Penguin.
—Under the Greenwood Tree. 1976. 22.95 (0-8488-0517-8) Amereon, Ltd.
—Under the Greenwood Tree. l.t. ed. 2003. 302p. 29.95 (0-7862-6007-6) Gale Group.
—Under the Greenwood Tree. 1998. (Penguin Readers Ser.: Level 2 ). 144p. (J). pap. 7.66 (0-582-40161-5) Longman Publishing Group.
—Under the Greenwood Tree. 2003. (Twelve-Point Ser.). lib. bdg. 25.00 (1-58287-235-X); lib. bdg. 26.00 (1-58287-719-X) North Bks.
—Under the Greenwood Tree. Gatrell, simon, ed. & intro. by. 1999. (Oxford World's Classics Ser.). (Illus.). 256p. pap. 4.95 (0-19-283517-3) Oxford Univ. Pr., Inc.
—Under the Greenwood Tree. Gatrell, Simon, ed. & intro. by. 1985. (Oxford World's Classics Ser.). (Illus.). 250p. pap. 4.95 o.p. (0-19-281706-X) Oxford Univ. Pr., Inc.
—Under the Greenwood Tree. 1977. (Hardy New Wessex Editions Ser.). pap. 3.95 o.p. (0-312-82987-6, Saint Martin's Griffin) St. Martin's Pr.
—Under the Greenwood Tree. 1999. (Penguin Classics Ser.). 288p. pap. 5.95 o.s.i (0-14-043553-0) Viking Penguin.
—Under the Greenwood Tree. Wright, David, ed. 1978. (Penguin Classics Ser.). 256p. pap. 5.95 o.s.i (0-14-043123-3, Penguin Classics) Viking Penguin.
—Under the Greenwood Tree. 1998. (Classics Library). 250p. pap. 3.95 (1-85326-227-7, 2277WW) Wordsworth Editions, Ltd. GBR. Dist: Casemate Pubs. & Bk. Distributors, LLC.
—Under the Greenwood Tree, Our Exploits at West Poley & Short Stories. Gibson, James, ed. 1997. (Everyman Paperback Classics Ser.). 296p. pap. 5.95 o.p. (0-460-87575-2, Everyman's Classic Library in Paperback) Tuttle Publishing.
—The Well-Beloved. Hetherington, Tom, ed. & intro. by. 1998. (Oxford World's Classics Ser.). (Illus.). 328p. pap. 8.95 (0-19-283560-2) Oxford Univ. Pr., Inc.
—The Well-Beloved. 1987. (Oxford World's Classics Ser.). (Illus.). 316p. pap. 6.95 o.p. (0-19-281721-3) Oxford Univ. Pr., Inc.
—Wessex Tales. l.t. ed. 1987. (Mainstream Ser.). 242p. 15.95 o.p. (1-85089-148-6) ISIS Large Print Bks. GBR. Dist: Transaction Pubs.
—Wessex Tales. 1998. 288p. pap. 7.95 (0-19-283558-0); 1991. (Illus.). 280p. pap. 6.95 o.p. (0-19-282720-0, 6498) Oxford Univ. Pr., Inc.
—Wessex Tales. 1978. (Hardy New Wessex Editions Ser.). pap. 3.95 o.p. (0-312-86276-8, Saint Martin's Griffin) St. Martin's Pr.
—The Woodlanders, 3. reprint ed. lib. bdg. 294.00 (0-7426-2793-4) Classic Bks.
—The Woodlanders. 1998. (Everyman's Library: Vol. 233). 20.00 (0-375-40082-6) Knopf, Alfred A. Inc.
—The Woodlanders. Pinion, F. B., ed. 1975. (Students' Hardy Ser.). 494p. (J). 12.50 (0-333-17265-5) Macmillan U.K. GBR. Dist: Trans-Atlantic Pubns., Inc.
—The Woodlanders. 1974. 416p. (J). 12.50 (0-333-16883-6) Macmillan U.K. GBR. Dist: Trans-Atlantic Pubns., Inc.
—The Woodlanders. Kramer, Dale, ed. (Oxford World's Classics Ser.). 2001. (Illus.). 448p. pap. 7.95 (0-19-283504-1); 1985. 342p. pap. 6.95 o.p. (0-19-281600-4); 1981. 506p. text 98.00 o.p. (0-19-812504-6) Oxford Univ. Pr., Inc.
—The Woodlanders. abr. ed. pap. 23.95 incl. audio (0-14-086576-4, Penguin AudioBooks) Penguin Group (USA) Inc.
—The Woodlanders. 1998. 20.00 (0-375-40319-1) Random Hse., Inc.
—The Woodlanders. 1978. (Hardy New Wessex Editions Ser.). pap. 3.95 o.p. (0-312-88901-1, Saint Martin's Griffin) St. Martin's Pr.
—The Woodlanders. 1995. pap. 5.50 o.p. (0-460-87459-4) Tuttle Publishing.
—The Woodlanders. Ingham, Patricia, ed. & intro. by. 1998. (Classics Ser.). (Illus.). 464p. pap. 7.95 (0-14-043547-6, Penguin Classics) Viking Penguin.
—The Woodlanders. Gibson, James, ed. 1981. (English Library). 464p. pap. 7.95 o.s.i (0-14-043145-4, Penguin Classics) Viking Penguin.
—The Woodlanders. 1998. (Classics Library). 352p. pap. 3.95 (1-85326-293-5, 2935WW) Wordsworth Editions, Ltd. GBR. Dist: Combined Publishing.
Hardy, Thomas, ed. Far from the Madding Crowd. l.t. ed. 2000. 576p. pap. 24.00 (0-06-095696-8, HarperCollins) HarperTrade.
—Tess of the d'Urbervilles. 1993. (Longman Literature Ser.). pap. text 7.00 (0-582-09715-0) Addison-Wesley Longman, Ltd. GBR. Dist: Trans-Atlantic Pubns., Inc.
—Tess of the d'Urbervilles. 1963. (Airmont Classics Ser.). (gr. 11 up). mass mkt. 3.50 (0-8049-0082-5, CL-82) Airmont Publishing Co., Inc.
—Tess of the d'Urbervilles. 1976. 29.95 (0-8488-0516-X) Amereon, Ltd.
—Tess of the d'Urbervilles. 1984. (Bantam Classics Ser.). 448p. (gr. 9-12). mass mkt. 4.95 (0-553-21168-4, Bantam Classics) Bantam Bks.
—Tess of the d'Urbervilles. 1987. 432p. reprint ed. lib. bdg. 35.95 (0-89966-624-8) Buccaneer Bks., Inc.
—Tess of the d'Urbervilles. pap. 4.95 (0-7910-4167-0) Chelsea Hse. Pubs.
—Tess of the d'Urbervilles. 1980. pap. 1.50 o.p. (0-440-38626-8) Dell Publishing.
—Tess of the d'Urbervilles. 2001. (Dover Thrift Editions Ser.). xiii, 321p. pap. 3.00 (0-486-41589-9) Dover Pubns., Inc.
—Tess of the d'Urbervilles. abr. ed. 2000. audio (0-00-104681-0) HarperCollins Pubs. Ltd.
—Tess of the d'Urbervilles. 1999. (Cloth Bound Pocket Ser.). (Illus.). 7.95 (3-8290-3008-8, 521260) Konemann.
—Tess of the d'Urbervilles. E-Book 1.95 (1-57799-944-4) Logos Research Systems, Inc.
—Tess of the d'Urbervilles. 1988. (Study Texts Ser.). pap. text 5.95 (0-582-01978-8) Longman Publishing Group.
—Tess of the d'Urbervilles. 2003. (0-333-16896-8) Macmillan U.K. GBR. Dist: Trafalgar Square.
—Tess of the d'Urbervilles. 1964. mass mkt. 3.50 o.p. (0-451-52429-2); mass mkt. 2.95 o.p. (0-451-51924-8, CE1686, Signet Classics); 432p. mass mkt. 4.95 o.s.i (0-451-52546-9, Signet Classics) NAL.
—Tess of the d'Urbervilles, Set. abr. ed. 1996. (Ultimate Classics Ser.). 19.95 o.p. (0-7871-0899-5, 694329) NewStar Media, Inc.
—Tess of the d'Urbervilles. 1978. (Hardy New Wessex Editions Ser.). pap. 2.95 o.p. (0-312-79346-4, Saint Martin's Griffin) St. Martin's Pr.
—Tess of the d'Urbervilles. l.t. ed. 1982. (Classics Ser.). 649p. 13.95 o.p. (0-7089-8038-4, Charnwood) Thorpe, F. A. Pubs. GBR. Dist: Ulverscroft Large Print Bks., Ltd.
—Tess of the d'Urbervilles. 1973. (Washington Square Press Enriched Classic Ser.). 11.00 (0-606-01449-7) Turtleback Bks.
—Tess of the d'Urbervilles. 1984. 447p. pap. 3.95 o.p. (0-460-87122-6, Everyman's Classic Library in Paperback) Tuttle Publishing.
—Tess of the d'Urbervilles. 2003. 592p. pap. 8.00 (0-14-143959-9, Penguin Classics); 1996. 4p. 23.95 incl. audio (0-14-086040-1, Penguin AudioBooks) Viking Penguin.
—Tess of the d'Urbervilles. 384p. 2001. pap. 9.95 incl. cd-rom (1-903342-02-3); 1997. pap. 3.95 (1-85326-005-3, 0053WW) Wordsworth Editions, Ltd. GBR. Dist: Combined Publishing, Casemate Pubs. & Bk. Distributors, LLC.
Hardy, Thomas, et al, eds. Tess of the d'Urbervilles. (Oxford World's Classics Ser.). (Illus.). 1988. 450p. pap. 5.95 o.p. (0-19-281826-0); 1983. 754p. text 194.50 o.p. (0-19-812495-3); 1998. 456p. reprint ed. pap. 6.95 (0-19-283362-6) Oxford Univ. Pr., Inc.
Hardy, Thomas & Buckler, William E., eds. Tess of the d'Urbervilles. 1960. (YA). (gr. 9 up). pap. 16.36 (0-395-05144-4, Riverside Editions) Houghton Mifflin Co.
Hardy, Thomas & Dolin, Tim, eds. Tess of the d'Urbervilles. 1999. (Classics Ser.). (Illus.). 592p. 7.95 (0-14-043514-X, Penguin Classics) Viking Penguin.
Hardy, Thomas & Elledge, Scott, eds. Tess of the d'Urbervilles. (Critical Editions Ser.). 1978. (Illus.). (C). pap. o.p. (0-393-09044-2); 2nd ed. 1979. (Illus.). 14.95 o.p. (0-393-04507-2); 3rd ed. 1990. 492p. (C). pap. text 11.50 (0-393-95903-1) Norton, W. W. & Co., Inc.
Hardy, Thomas & Gibson, James, eds. Tess of the d'Urbervilles. 1993. 447p. pap. 4.95 o.p. (0-460-87344-X, Everyman's Classic Library in Paperback) Tuttle Publishing.
Hardy, Thomas & Gibson, Rex, eds. Tess of the d'Urbervilles. 1996. (Cambridge Literature Ser.). (Illus.). 448p. pap. text 11.95 o.p. (0-521-56714-9) Cambridge Univ. Pr.
Hardy, Thomas & Maier, Sarah, eds. Tess of the d'Urbervilles. 1996. (Illus.). 280p. pap. (1-55111-066-0) Broadview Pr.
Hardy, Thomas & Page, Norman. Jude the Obscure: An Authoritative Text: Backgrounds & Contexts Criticism. 2nd ed. 1999. (Critical Editions Ser.). (Illus.). xii, 468p. pap. 11.00 (0-393-97278-X) Norton, W. W. & Co., Inc.
Hardy, Thomas & Riquelme, John P., eds. Tess of the d'Urbervilles. 1998. 528p. (C). pap. text 9.50 (0-312-10688-2) Bedford/Saint Martin's.
—Tess of the d'Urbervilles. 1998. (Case Studies in Contemporary Criticism). 528p. (C). 35.00 (0-312-16375-4) Palgrave Macmillan.
Hardy, Thomas & Skilton, David, eds. Tess of the d'Urbervilles. 1978. (Penguin Classics Ser.). 544p. pap. 7.95 o.s.i (0-14-043135-7, Penguin Classics) Viking Penguin.
Hardy, Thomas & Widdowson, Peter, eds. Tess of the d'Urbervilles. 1993. (New Casebooks Ser.). 528p. 49.95 o.p. (0-312-09092-7) Palgrave Macmillan.
Hare, Cyril. Death Is No Sportsman: An Inspector Mallett Mystery. 1991. 320p. pap. 5.95 o.p. (0-06-080555-2, Perennial) HarperTrade.
—Death Walks the Woods: A Francis Pettigrew Mystery. 1991. 288p. reprint ed. pap. 8.00 o.p. (0-06-092136-6, Perennial) HarperTrade.
—He Should Have Died Hereafter. 2000. (Black Dagger Crime Ser.). 21.95 (0-7540-8569-4, Black Dagger) BBC Audiobooks America.
—Suicide Excepted: An Inspector Mallett Mystery. 1982. (Illus.). 219p. (C). pap. 4.95 (0-486-24245-5) Dover Pubns., Inc.
—Suicide Excepted: An Inspector Mallett Mystery. 1983. 288p. pap. 5.95 o.p. (0-06-080636-2, Perennial) HarperTrade.
—Tenant for Death: An Inspector Mallet Mystery. 1981. 200p. reprint ed. pap. 4.95 o.p. (0-486-24103-3) Dover Pubns., Inc.
—Tenant for Death: An Inspector Mallet Mystery. 1991. 304p. pap. 5.95 o.p. (0-06-080570-6, Perennial) HarperTrade.
—Tragedy at Law: An Inspector Mallett & Francis Pettigrew Mystery. 1986. mass mkt. 9.95 o.p. (0-553-06518-1) Bantam Bks.
—Tragedy at Law: An Inspector Mallett & Francis Pettigrew Mystery. 1991. 400p. pap. 5.95 o.p. (0-06-080522-6, Perennial) HarperTrade.
—Untimely Death: An Inspector Mallett & Francis Pettigrew Mystery. 1992. 192p. reprint ed. pap. 8.00 o.p. (0-06-092252-4, Perennial) HarperTrade.
—When the Wind Blows. l.t. ed. 2001. (Dales Large Print Ser.). 304p. pap. 21.99 (1-84262-104-1) Dales Large Print Bks. GBR. Dist: Ulverscroft Large Print Bks., Ltd., Ulverscroft Large Print Canada, Ltd.
—When the Wind Blows. 1976. (Crime Fiction Ser.). reprint ed. lib. bdg. 21.00 o.p. (0-8240-2373-0) Garland Publishing, Inc.
—When the Wind Blows. 1978. reprint ed. pap. 1.95 o.p. (0-06-080454-8, P 454) HarperCollins Pubs.
—The Wind Blows Death: A Francis Pettigrew Mystery. 1991. 272p. reprint ed. pap. 8.00 o.p. (0-06-092138-2, Perennial) HarperTrade.
—With a Bare Bodkin: A Francis Pettigrew Mystery. 1991. 256p. reprint ed. pap. 8.00 o.p. (0-06-092139-0, Perennial) HarperTrade.
Harkness, Lucy. The Happy Pigs. 2001. 160p. pap. 16.95 (0-85640-656-2) Blackstaff Pr., The IRL. Dist: Dufour Editions, Inc.
—The Happy Pigs. 2002. 256p. 23.95 (0-312-28286-9) St. Martin's Pr.
Harley, Don. Stranger in the Wings. E-Book (1-84045-051-7) Online Originals.
Harmon, Danelle. The Defiant One. 2000. 384p. mass mkt. 5.99 (0-380-80908-7, Avon Bks.) Morrow/Avon.
Harnett, Cynthia. The Merchant's Mark. 1984. (Cynthia Harnett's Adventure Novels Ser.). (Illus.). 192p. (J). (gr. 5 up). 13.50 o.p. (0-8225-0891-5, Lerner Pubns.) Lerner Publishing Group.
Harper, Karen. The Baby Farm. unabr. ed. 1999. audio 7.99 (1-55204-185-9, MIR-1185) Durkin Hayes Publishing Ltd.
—The Poyson Garden: An Elizabethan Mystery. 2000. (Elizabeth I Mysteries Ser.). 320p. mass mkt. 6.99 (0-440-22592-2) Dell Publishing.
—The Tidal Poole: An Elizabeth I Mystery. (Elizabeth I Mysteries Ser.). 2001. 336p. mass mkt. 6.50 (0-440-22593-0); 2000. (Illus.). 304p. 22.95 o.s.i (0-385-33284-X, Delacorte Pr.) Dell Publishing.
—The Tidal Poole: An Elizabeth I Mystery. l.t. ed. 2000. (Wheeler Large Print Book Ser.). 306p. 28.95 (1-56895-894-3, Wheeler Publishing, Inc.) Gale Group.
—The Twylight Tower: An Elizabeth I Mystery. 2002. (Elizabeth I Mysteries Ser.). (Illus.). 352p. mass mkt. 6.99 (0-440-23592-8) Dell Publishing.
Harries, Ann. Manly Pursuits. 2000. 339p. pap. 13.95 (1-58234-073-0); 1999. 24.95 (1-58234-019-6) Bloomsbury Publishing.
Harris, Don R. Foggy Night Murders. 1998. 239p. pap. 9.95 (0-9656811-4-9) Four Seasons Pubs.
Harris, Rosemary. Zed. 1984. 192p. (YA). (gr. 7 up). o.p. (0-571-11947-6) Faber & Faber Ltd.
Harrison, Carey. Richard's Feet. 1990. 672p. 22.95 o.p. (0-8050-1404-7) Holt, Henry & Co.
Harrison, Ray. Akin to Murder. l.t. ed. 1995. (Magna Large Print Ser.). 468p. (0-7505-0873-6) Magna Large Print Bks. GBR. Dist: Ulverscroft Large Print Canada, Ltd.
—Counterfeit of Murder. 1989. mass mkt. 3.95 o.p. (0-425-11645-X) Berkley Publishing Group.
—Counterfeit of Murder. 1987. 320p. 15.95 o.p. (0-312-00585-7) St. Martin's Pr.
—Death of a Dancing Lady. 1988. mass mkt. 2.95 o.s.i (0-425-11047-8) Berkley Publishing Group.
—Death of a Dancing Lady: A Sargent Bragg-Constable Morton Mystery. 1986. 256p. 13.95 o.p. (0-684-18581-4, Macmillan Reference USA) Gale Group.
—Death of an Honourable Member. 1988. mass mkt. 3.50 o.p. (0-425-11189-X) Berkley Publishing Group.
—Death of an Honourable Member. 1985. 160p. 11.95 o.p. (0-684-18245-9, Macmillan Reference USA) Gale Group.
—Deathwatch. 1989. mass mkt. 3.50 o.p. (0-425-11392-2) Berkley Publishing Group.
—Deathwatch. 1986. 176p. 13.95 o.p. (0-684-18425-7, Macmillan Reference USA) Gale Group.
—Draught of Death. l.t. ed. 2000. (Dales Large Print Ser.). 352p. pap. (1-84137-009-6) Magna Large Print Bks. GBR. Dist: Ulverscroft Large Print Bks., Ltd., Ulverscroft Large Print Canada, Ltd.
—Facets of Murder. l.t. ed. 1998. (Ulverscroft Large Print Ser.). 368p. 29.99 (0-7089-3952-X, Ulverscroft) Thorpe, F. A. Pubs. GBR. Dist: Ulverscroft Large Print Bks., Ltd., Ulverscroft Large Print Canada, Ltd.
—Hallmark of Murder. l.t. ed. 1996. (Dales Large Print Ser.). (Illus.). 403p. pap. 19.99 (1-85389-663-2) Dales Large Print Bks. GBR. Dist: Ulverscroft Large Print Bks., Ltd.
—Harvest of Death. 1990. mass mkt. 3.95 o.s.i (0-425-11979-3) Berkley Publishing Group.
—Harvest of Death. 1988. 288p. 16.95 o.p. (0-312-02218-2, Saint Martin's Minotaur) St. Martin's Pr.

Settings

—Murder by Design. l.t. ed. 1997. (Linford Mystery Library). 416p. pap. 17.99 o.p. (0-7089-5071-X, Linford) Thorpe, F. A. Pubs. GBR. Dist: Ulverscroft Large Print Bks., Ltd., Ulverscroft Large Print Canada, Ltd.
—Patently Murder. l.t. ed. 1996. (Magna Large Print Ser.). 492p. 29.99 (0-7505-0922-8) Magna Large Print Bks. GBR. Dist: Ulverscroft Large Print Bks., Ltd.
—Patently Murder: A Sergeant Bragg & Constable Morton Mystery. 1991. 256p. 18.95 o.p. (0-312-07058-6, Saint Martin's Minotaur) St. Martin's Pr.
—A Season for Death. 1988. 288p. 15.95 o.p. (0-312-01815-0, Saint Martin's Minotaur) St. Martin's Pr.
—Sphere of Death. 1990. 17.95 o.p. (0-312-05161-1, Saint Martin's Minotaur) St. Martin's Pr.
—Tincture of Death. 1991. mass mkt. 3.95 o.p. (0-425-12550-5) Berkley Publishing Group.
—Tincture of Death. 1989. 240p. 15.95 o.p. (0-312-03442-3, Saint Martin's Minotaur) St. Martin's Pr.
—Why Kill Arthur Potter? 1984. 160p. 11.95 o.s.i (0-684-18131-2, Scribner) Simon & Schuster.
—Why Kill Arthur Potter? 1985. mass mkt. 2.95 o.s.i (0-445-20053-7) Warner Bks., Inc.
Harrison, Sarah. The Grass Memorial. 2002. 400p. 26.95 (0-312-29086-1) St. Martin's Pr.
Harrod-Eagles, Cynthia. Blood Lines. 1996. 281p. o.s.i (0-316-91420-7) Little Brown & Co.
—Blood Lines. 1997. (Inspector Bill Slider Mysteries Ser.). mass mkt. 5.50 (0-380-73052-9, Avon Bks.) Morrow/Avon.
—Blood Lines. 1996. 281p. 20.50 o.p. (0-684-80047-0, Scribner) Simon & Schuster.
—Blood Sinister. l.t. ed. 2001. (Magna Large Print Ser.). 384p. (0-7505-1599-6) Magna Large Print Bks. GBR. Dist: Ulverscroft Large Print Canada, Ltd.
—Blood Sinister. E-Book 23.95 (0-312-70251-5); 2001. 308p. 23.95 (0-312-27485-8, Saint Martin's Minotaur) St. Martin's Pr.
—Dead End. 1996. 234p. mass mkt. o.s.i (0-7515-1354-7) Little Brown & Co.
—Dead End. unabr. ed. 2000. audio 79.95 (1-86042-433-3, 24333) Soundings, Ltd. GBR. Dist: Ulverscroft Large Print Bks., Ltd.
—Death to Go. l.t. ed. 1994. 413p. reprint ed. pap. 18.95 (0-8161-5977-7, Macmillan Reference USA) Gale Group.
—Death to Go. 1995. 288p. mass mkt. 4.99 o.s.i (0-380-72346-8, Avon Bks.) Morrow/Avon.
—Death to Go: An Inspector Bill Slider Mystery. 1994. 288p. 20.00 (0-684-19650-6, Macmillan Reference USA) Gale Group.
—Death Watch. 1994. 288p. mass mkt. 4.99 (0-380-72065-5, Avon Bks.) Morrow/Avon.
—Death Watch: An Inspector Bill Slider Mystery. 1993. 288p. 20.00 o.p. (0-684-19519-4, Macmillan Reference USA) Gale Group.
—Grave Music. 1996. 256p. mass mkt. 5.50 o.s.i (0-380-72636-X, Avon Bks.) Morrow/Avon.
—Grave Music: An Inspector Bill Slider Mystery. l.t. ed. 1995. 370p. 23.95 o.p. (0-7838-1469-0, Macmillan Reference USA) Gale Group.
—Grave Music: An Inspector Bill Slider Mystery. 1995. 234p. 20.00 (0-684-80046-2, Scribner) Simon & Schuster.
—Killing Time. 1996. 313p. o.s.i (0-316-88103-1) Little Brown & Co.
—Killing Time. l.t. ed. 2000. (Magna Large Print Ser.). 464p. (0-7505-1597-X) Magna Large Print Bks. GBR. Dist: Ulverscroft Large Print Canada, Ltd.
—Killing Time: An Inspector Bill Slider Mystery. 1998. (Inspector Bill Slider Mysteries Ser.). 320p. 22.00 (0-684-83776-5, Scribner) Simon & Schuster.
—Necrochip. l.t. ed. 1994. (Magna Large Print Ser.). 462p. o.p. (0-7505-0638-5) Magna Large Print Bks. GBR. Dist: Ulverscroft Large Print Canada, Ltd.
—Orchestrated Death. 1993. 272p. mass mkt. 5.50 o.s.i (0-380-71967-3, Avon Bks.) Morrow/Avon.
—Orchestrated Death: A Mystery Introducing Inspector Bill Slider. 1992. 256p. text 19.95 (0-684-19388-4, Macmillan Reference USA) Gale Group.
—Real Life. l.t. ed. 2000. (0-7540-3917-X); (0-7540-3918-8) Thorndike Pr.
—Shallow Grave. l.t. ed. 2001. (Magna Large Print Ser.). 464p. (0-7505-1598-8) Magna Large Print Bks. GBR. Dist: Ulverscroft Large Print Canada, Ltd.
—Shallow Grave. 1999. (Inspector Bill Slider Mysteries Ser.). 320p. 22.00 (0-684-83777-3, Scribner) Simon & Schuster.
—Shallow Grave. unabr. ed. 2000. audio 84.95 (1-86042-521-6, 25216) Soundings, Ltd. GBR. Dist: Ulverscroft Large Print Bks., Ltd.
Harry, Lilian. A Girl Called Thursday. 2003. 480p. mass mkt. (0-7528-4950-6) Orion Publishing Group, Ltd. GBR. Dist: Trafalgar Square.
Hart, Josephine. The Reconstructionist. 2001. 288p. 26.95 (1-58567-170-3) Overlook Pr., The.
—The Stillest Day. l.t. ed. 1999. 192p. 32.50 (0-7531-5974-0); pap. (0-7531-5987-2, 159872) ISIS Large Print Bks. GBR. Dist: Ulverscroft Large Print Bks., Ltd., Ulverscroft Large Print Canada, Ltd., Ulverscroft Large Print Canada, Ltd.
—The Stillest Day. 224p. 1999. 13.95 (0-87951-727-1); 1998. 23.95 (0-87951-894-4) Overlook Pr., The.
Hart, Roy. Blood Kin. 1991. 208p. 17.95 o.p. (0-312-06909-X, Saint Martin's Minotaur) St. Martin's Pr.
—Breach of Promise. 1990. 15.95 o.p. (0-312-05393-2, Saint Martin's Minotaur) St. Martin's Pr.
—A Deadly Schedule. 1996. (WWL Mystery Ser.). per. (0-373-26205-1, 1-26205-4, Worldwide Library) Harlequin Enterprises, Ltd.
—A Deadly Schedule. 1995. mass mkt. o.s.i (0-7515-1034-3) Little Brown & Co.
—A Deadly Schedule: An Inspector Roper Mystery. 1994. 224p. 19.95 o.p. (0-312-10964-4, Saint Martin's Minotaur) St. Martin's Pr.
—Final Appointment. 1993. 248p. 17.95 o.p. (0-312-08777-2, Saint Martin's Minotaur) St. Martin's Pr.
—A Fox in the Night. 1998. (WWL Mystery Ser.). per. (0-373-26280-9, 1-26280-7, Worldwide Library) Harlequin Enterprises, Ltd.
—A Fox in the Night. 1988. 224p. 15.95 o.p. (0-312-02212-3, Saint Martin's Minotaur) St. Martin's Pr.
—A Fox in the Night. l.t. ed. 1990. (Ulverscroft Large Print Ser.). 29.99 (0-7089-2218-X, Ulverscroft) Thorpe, F. A. Pubs. GBR. Dist: Ulverscroft Large Print Bks., Ltd., Ulverscroft Large Print Canada, Ltd.
—Remains to Be Seen. 1989. 15.95 o.p. (0-312-02971-3, Saint Martin's Minotaur) St. Martin's Pr.
—Remains to Be Seen. l.t. ed. 1991. (Ulverscroft Large Print Ser.). 29.99 (0-7089-2535-9, Ulverscroft) Thorpe, F. A. Pubs. GBR. Dist: Ulverscroft Large Print Bks., Ltd., Ulverscroft Large Print Canada, Ltd.
—Robbed Blind. 1998. (WWL Mystery Ser.: Vol. 289). per. (0-373-26289-2, 1-26289-8, Worldwide Library) Harlequin Enterprises, Ltd.
—Robbed Blind. 1990. 15.95 o.p. (0-312-04414-3, Saint Martin's Minotaur) St. Martin's Pr.
—Robbed Blind. l.t. ed. 1992. (Linford Mystery Library). 416p. 29.99 o.p. (0-7089-2769-6, Linford) Thorpe, F. A. Pubs. GBR. Dist: Ulverscroft Large Print Bks., Ltd., Ulverscroft Large Print Canada, Ltd.
—Seascape with Dead Figures. 1987. 192p. 13.95 o.p. (0-312-01088-5, Saint Martin's Minotaur) St. Martin's Pr.
—Seascape with Dead Figures. l.t. ed. 1989. (Ulverscroft Large Print Ser.). 29.99 o.p. (0-7089-2105-1, Ulverscroft) Thorpe, F. A. Pubs. GBR. Dist: Ulverscroft Large Print Bks., Ltd., Ulverscroft Large Print Canada, Ltd.
—Seascape with Dead Figures: A Detective Superintendent Roper Mystery. 1998. (WWL Mystery Ser.). per. (0-373-26268-X, 1-26268-2, Worldwide Library) Harlequin Enterprises, Ltd.
Harte, Kelly. Guilty Feet. 2003. (Red Dress Ink Ser.: No. 16). 320p. pap. (0-373-25026-6, Red Dress Ink) Harlequin Enterprises, Ltd.
Hartley, L. P. The Go-Between. 1978. reprint ed. text 27.50 o.p. (0-241-90208-8) Dufour Editions, Inc.
—The Go-Between. 2002. (New York Review Books Classics Ser.). xiii, 326p. pap. 14.95 (0-940322-99-4) New York Review of Bks., Inc., The.
—The Go-Between. 1997. (Twentieth Century Classics Ser.). 336p. pap. 13.95 o.p. (0-14-018852-5, Penguin Classics) Viking Penguin.
Hartnett, P. Call Me. 1997. (Stonewall Inn Editions Ser.). 192p. pap. 11.95 (0-312-18063-2, Saint Martin's Griffin) St. Martin's Pr.
Hartnett, P. -P. Call Me. 1997. 184p. (Orig.). pap. 16.95 (1-901072-00-2) Pulp Faction GBR. Dist: AK Pr. Distribution.
Harvey, Caroline, pseud. The Best of Friends. 1998. 304p. 23.95 o.p. (0-670-87973-8, Viking) Viking Penguin.
—Legacy of Love. l.t. ed. 1995. (Charnwood Large Print Ser.). 720p. 29.99 o.p. (0-7089-8823-7, Charnwood) Thorpe, F. A. Pubs. GBR. Dist: Ulverscroft Large Print Bks., Ltd., Ulverscroft Large Print Canada, Ltd.
—Legacy of Love. 2000. 544p. 24.95 o.s.i (0-670-89181-9, Viking) Viking Penguin.
Harvey, John. Cold Light. 1994. 370p. 22.00 o.p. (0-8050-2046-2) Holt, Henry & Co.
—Cold Light. unabr. ed. 1997. audio 69.95 (1-85695-970-8, 950507) ISIS Audio Bks. GBR. Dist: Ulverscroft Large Print Bks., Ltd.
—Cold Light. unabr. ed. 2000. (Charlie Resnick Mystery Ser.: Vol. 6). audio 70.00 (0-7887-0483-4, 94676E7) Recorded Bks., LLC.
—Cold Light. 1995. 370p. pap. text 4.99 (0-312-95603-7, St. Martin's Paperbacks) St. Martin's Pr.
—Cutting Edge. 1998. (Cutting Edge Ser.: Vol. 1). 288p. pap. 13.00 o.s.i (0-8050-5497-9, Owl Bks.) Holt, Henry & Co.
—Cutting Edge. 1992. 352p. mass mkt. 4.99 (0-380-71615-1, Avon Bks.) Morrow/Avon.
—Cutting Edge: A Charlie Resnick Mystery. 1991. 288p. 18.95 o.p. (0-8050-1264-8) Holt, Henry & Co.
—Easy Meat. 1997. 400p. pap. 11.00 o.s.i (0-8050-5495-2, Owl Bks.); 1996. 384p. 23.00 o.p. (0-8050-4148-6) Holt, Henry & Co.
—Easy Meat. unabr. ed. 1997. (Charlie Resnick Mystery Ser.: Vol. 8). audio 78.00 (0-7887-0818-X, 94968E7) Recorded Bks., LLC.
—Last Rites: A Novel. l.t. ed. 1999. (Core Ser.). 396p. 27.95 (0-7838-8674-8, Macmillan Reference USA) Gale Group.
—Last Rites: A Novel. 1999. (Charles Resnick Novels Ser.). 312p. 25.00 o.s.i (0-8050-4150-8) Holt, Henry & Co.
—Last Rites: A Novel. unabr. ed. 2000. audio 71.00 (1-84197-042-5, H1056E7, Clipper Audio) Recorded Bks., LLC.
—Living Proof. 1995. 283p. 22.50 o.p. (0-8050-2045-4) Holt, Henry & Co.
—Living Proof. unabr. ed. 1996. (Charlie Resnick Mystery Ser.: Vol. 7). audio 51.00 (0-7887-0507-5, 94700E7) Recorded Bks., LLC.
—Living Proof. 1996. mass mkt. 5.99 (0-312-95863-3, St. Martin's Paperbacks) St. Martin's Pr.
—Lonely Hearts. 288p. 1997. pap. 11.00 o.s.i (0-8050-5494-4, Owl Bks.); 1989. 16.95 o.p. (0-8050-0982-5) Holt, Henry & Co.
—Lonely Hearts. 1990. 320p. pap. 4.99 (0-380-71006-4, Avon Bks.) Morrow/Avon.
—Off Minor. 288p. 1998. pap. 11.00 o.s.i (0-8050-5498-7, Owl Bks.); 1992. 18.95 o.p. (0-8050-1265-6) Holt, Henry & Co.
—Off Minor. 1993. 288p. mass mkt. 4.99 (0-380-72009-4, Avon Bks.) Morrow/Avon.
—Rough Treatment. unabr. ed. 1992. 69.95 incl. audio (0-7451-4062-9) BBC Audiobooks America.
—Rough Treatment. 1997. 288p. pap. 11.00 o.s.i (0-8050-5496-0, Owl Bks.) Holt, Henry & Co.
—Rough Treatment. 1991. 304p. mass mkt. 3.99 (0-380-71171-0, Avon Bks.) Morrow/Avon.
—Rough Treatment: A Charlie Resnick Mystery. 1990. 288p. 17.95 o.p. (0-8050-0983-3) Holt, Henry & Co.
—Still Waters. unabr. ed. 2000. (Charlie Resnick Mystery Ser.: Vol. 9). audio 70.00 (0-7887-3057-6, 95751E7) Recorded Bks., LLC.
—Still Waters: A Crime Novel. 1997. 320p. 23.00 o.s.i (0-8050-4149-4) Holt, Henry & Co.
—Wasted Years. unabr. ed. 1998. audio 69.95 (1-85695-764-0, 951004) ISIS Audio Bks. GBR. Dist: Ulverscroft Large Print Bks., Ltd.
—Wasted Years. 1994. 352p. mass mkt. 4.99 (0-380-72182-1, Avon Bks.) Morrow/Avon.
—Wasted Years. unabr. ed. 1995. (Charlie Resnick Mystery Ser.: Vol. 5). audio. audio 70.00 (0-7887-0450-8, 94640E7) Recorded Bks., LLC.
—Wasted Years: A Charlie Resnick Mystery. 1993. 352p. 19.95 o.p. (0-8050-2044-6) Holt, Henry & Co.
—Wasted Years: A Crime Novel. 1999. 348p. pap. 13.00 o.s.i (0-8050-5499-5, Owl Bks.) Holt, Henry & Co.
Hastings, Juliet. Waiting Game. 1997. (Crime & Passion Ser.). 255p. mass mkt. 5.95 (0-7535-0109-0) Virgin Bks. GBR. Dist: London Bridge.
Hatfield, Kate. Drowning in Honey. 1996. 288p. text 23.95 o.p. (0-312-14590-X) St. Martin's Pr.
—Drowning in Honey. 2000. 347p. 27.50 (0-385-40594-4) Transworld Publishers Ltd. GBR. Dist: Trafalgar Square.
Hattersley, Ray, told to. Buster's Diaries: The True Story of a Dog & His Man. 2001. 192p. reprint ed. pap. 11.95 (0-446-67781-7) Warner Bks., Inc.
Hattersley, Roy. The Maker's Mark. 1991. 608p. 22.00 o.p. (0-671-73493-8, Simon & Schuster) Simon & Schuster.
Hattersley, Roy, told to. Buster's Diaries: A True Story of a Dog & His Man. l.t. ed. 2000. (Basic Ser.). 184p. 27.95 (0-7862-2869-5) Thorndike Pr.
—Buster's Diaries: The True Story of a Dog & His Man. 2000. (Illus.). 192p. 15.95 o.p. (0-446-52662-2) Warner Bks., Inc.
Hawes, James. A White Merc with Fins. 1997. 304p. pap. 12.00 o.s.i (0-679-77615-X) Random Hse., Inc.
Hawkesworth, John. In My Lady's Chamber. 1980. (Reader's Request Ser.). lib. bdg. 11.95 o.p. (0-8161-6795-8, Macmillan Reference USA) Gale Group.
Hawks, Kate. Watch by Moonlight. 2001. 240p. 24.00 (0-380-81465-X, Morrow, William & Co.) Morrow/Avon.
Hayder, Mo. Birdman. 2000. 448p. mass mkt. 6.99 (0-440-23616-9) Dell Publishing.
—The Treatment: A Novel. 2002. 416p. mass mkt. 7.50 (0-440-23617-7, Delta) Dell Publishing.
—The Treatment: A Novel. 2002. 368p. 23.95 (0-385-49695-8, Image) Doubleday Publishing.
Haymon, S. T. A Beautiful Death. 1993. 19.95 o.p. (0-312-10420-0, Saint Martin's Minotaur) St. Martin's Pr.
—Death & the Pregnant Virgin. 208p. 1991. mass mkt. 2.50 o.s.i (0-553-18513-6); 1984. pap. text 2.95 o.p. (0-553-23703-9) Bantam Bks.
—Death & the Pregnant Virgin. unabr. ed. 1993. audio 61.95 (1-85089-848-0, 40791) ISIS Audio Bks. GBR. Dist: Ulverscroft Large Print Bks., Ltd.
—Death & the Pregnant Virgin. 1980. 224p. 9.95 o.p. (0-312-18592-8) St. Martin's Pr.
—Death of a God. 1990. 256p. mass mkt. 3.95 o.s.i (0-553-27266-7) Bantam Bks.
—Death of a God. 1992. 1.99 o.p. (0-517-08388-4) Random Hse. Value Publishing.
—Death of a God. 1987. 224p. 14.95 o.p. (0-312-00119-3) St. Martin's Pr.
—Death of a Hero. l.t. ed. 2000. pap. 21.99 (0-7531-6225-3) ISIS Large Print Bks. GBR. Dist: Ulverscroft Large Print Bks., Ltd., Ulverscroft Large Print Canada, Ltd.
—Death of a Hero. 1996. 256p. 21.95 o.p. (0-312-14582-9, Saint Martin's Minotaur) St. Martin's Pr.
—Death of a Warrior Queen. l.t. ed. 1996. 352p. 24.95 (1-85695-334-3) ISIS Large Print Bks. GBR. Dist: Transaction Pubs.
—Death of a Warrior Queen. 1991. 224p. 17.95 o.p. (0-312-06950-2, Saint Martin's Minotaur) St. Martin's Pr.
—Ritual Murder. 1991. 256p. mass mkt. 4.50 o.s.i (0-553-29385-0) Bantam Bks.
—Ritual Murder. 1984. 256p. pap. 2.50 o.p. (0-523-42175-3, Pinnacle Bks.) Kensington Publishing Corp.
—Ritual Murder. 1982. 224p. 11.95 o.p. (0-312-68478-9) St. Martin's Pr.
—Stately Homicide. 1984. 11.95 o.p. (0-312-75708-5) St. Martin's Pr.
—Stately Homicide. 1985. 256p. mass mkt. 3.50 o.s.i (0-445-20161-4) Warner Bks., Inc.
—A Very Particular Murder. 1991. 288p. mass mkt. 4.50 o.s.i (0-553-28880-6) Bantam Bks.
—A Very Particular Murder. 1992. 2.99 o.p. (0-517-09061-9) Random Hse. Value Publishing.
—A Very Particular Murder. 1989. 16.95 o.p. (0-312-02998-5) St. Martin's Pr.
Hays, Mary. Memoirs of Emma Courtney. Brooks, Marilyn L., ed. 2000. (Literary Texts Ser.). 340p. (1-55111-314-7) Broadview Pr.
—Memoirs of Emma Courtney. Brooks, Marilyn, ed. 2000. (Literary Texts Ser.). 340p. pap. (1-55111-155-1) Broadview Pr.
—Memoirs of Emma Courtney. 1974. (Feminist Controversy in England, 1788-1810 Ser.). lib. bdg. 121.00 o.p. (0-8240-0870-7) Garland Publishing, Inc.
—Memoirs of Emma Courtney. Ty, Eleanor, ed. (Oxford World's Classics Ser.). 2001. 272p. pap. 12.95 (0-19-283729-X); 1996. 266p. (C). pap. 11.95 o.p. (0-19-282306-X) Oxford Univ. Pr., Inc.
—The Victim of Prejudice. Ty, Eleanor, ed. 1994. 280p. pap. (0-921149-37-9) Broadview Pr.
—The Victim of Prejudice. 1990. 468p. reprint ed. 75.00 (0-8201-1446-4) Scholars' Facsimiles & Reprints.
Hays, Mary & Brooks, Marilyn L. Memoirs of Emma Courtney. 2000. E-Book 24.95 (0-585-23649-6) netLibrary, Inc.
Hays, Tony. Murder on the Twelfth Night. 1993. 168p. (Orig.). pap. 10.95 o.p. (0-916078-30-2) Bell Buckle Pr.
Haywood, Eliza. The History of Miss Betsy Thoughtless. Blouch, Christine, ed. 1998. (Literary Texts Ser.). 620p. (C). pap. (1-55111-147-0) Broadview Pr.
—The History of Miss Betsy Thoughtless, 4 vols. Paulson, Ronald, ed. 1979. (Novel 1720-1805 Ser.: Vol. 4). lib. bdg. 150.00 o.p. (0-8240-3653-0) Garland Publishing, Inc.
—The History of Miss Betsy Thoughtless. 1997. (Oxford World's Classics Ser.). (Illus.). 624p. pap. 14.95 o.p. (0-19-282490-2) Oxford Univ. Pr., Inc.
Hazard, Barbara. Wary Widow. 2000. (Signet Regency Romance Ser.). 240p. mass mkt. 4.99 o.s.i (0-451-20131-0, Signet Bks.) NAL.
Hazzard, Shirley. The Transit of Venus. 1981. 368p. 3.95 o.p. (0-425-07511-7) Berkley Publishing Group.
—The Transit of Venus. 1990. 352p. pap. 13.95 (0-14-010747-9, Penguin Bks.) Penguin Group (USA) Inc.
—The Transit of Venus. 1980. 11.95 o.p. (0-670-72426-2) Viking Penguin.
Headley, Victor. Yardie. 1993. 192p. 18.00 o.p. (0-87113-550-7, Atlantic Monthly Pr.) Grove/Atlantic, Inc.
Heald, Tim. Business Unusual. 1990. 14.95 o.s.i (0-385-41337-8) Doubleday Publishing.
—Business Unusual, Set. unabr. ed. 1998. audio 63.95 o.p. (1-872672-99-X) Magna Story Sound GBR. Dist: Ulverscroft Large Print Bks., Ltd.
Heath, Sandra. Hide & Seek. 2001. (Signet Regency Romance Ser.). 224p. mass mkt. 4.99 o.s.i (0-451-20345-3) NAL.

—Mistletoe Mischief. 2000. (Signet Regency Romance Ser.). 240p. mass mkt. 4.99 o.s.i (*0-451-20147-7*, Signet Bks.) NAL.
—Second Thoughts. 2002. (Signet Regency Romance Ser.). 224p. mass mkt. 4.99 o.s.i (*0-451-20589-8*) NAL.
Heaven, Constance. The Wildcliffe Bird. 1985. 288p. mass mkt. 2.95 o.s.i (*0-345-32119-7*) Ballantine Bks.
—The Wildcliffe Bird. 1983. (General Ser.). 450p. lib. bdg. 14.95 o.p. (*0-8161-3608-4*, Macmillan Reference USA) Gale Group.
—The Wildcliffe Bird. 1983. 256p. 13.95 o.p. (*0-698-11235-0*) Putnam Publishing Group, The.
—The Wind from the Sea. 1993. 23.95 o.p. (*0-312-08921-X*) St. Martin's Pr.
Heber, R. W. Murder at Wittenham Park. 1997. 224p. 22.95 o.p. (*0-312-16938-8*, Saint Martin's Minotaur) St. Martin's Pr.
Hegarty, Frances. Half Light. Chelius, Jane, ed. 1993. 288p. 20.00 o.p. (*0-671-78967-8*, Atria) Simon & Schuster.
Heley, Veronica. Eden Hall. 2004. 304p. pap. 12.99 (*0-310-24963-5*) Zondervan.
—Murder at the Altar. 2001. 290p. mass mkt. (*0-00-274074-5*) HarperCollins Pubs. Canada, Ltd.
Heller, Keith. Man's Storm: A Novel of Crime Set in London, 1703. 1986. 196p. 13.95 o.p. (*0-684-18653-5*, Macmillan Reference USA) Gale Group.
—The Woman Who Knew Gandhi: A Novel. 2004. 224p. pap. 12.00 (*0-618-33545-5*) Houghton Mifflin Co. Trade & Reference Div.
Hemstock, Patricia. Rosalie. l.t. ed. 1996. (Romance Ser.). 288p. pap. 17.95 (*0-7838-1543-3*, Macmillan Reference USA) Gale Group.
Henderson, Lauren. Chained! 2000. 249p. (*0-09-180045-5*) Hutchinson, Fred Cancer Research Ctr.
—Chained! 2000. 256p. pap. o.p. (*0-09-180050-1*) Random Hse. of Canada, Ltd. CAN. *Dist:* Random Hse., Inc.
—Chained! A Novel. 2002. 336p. pap. 12.95 (*0-609-80865-6*, Three Rivers Pr.) Crown Publishing Group.
—Pretty Boy: A Novel. 2002. 352p. pap. 12.95 (*0-609-80866-4*) Random Hse., Inc.
Hendrickson, Emily. Lord Nick's Folly. 2002. 240p. mass mkt. 4.99 o.s.i (*0-451-20696-7*) NAL.
Henley, Virginia. Desired. 1995. 448p. mass mkt. 6.99 (*0-440-21703-2*) Dell Publishing.
—Desired. l.t. ed. 1995. 625p. 21.95 o.p. (*0-7838-1359-7*, Macmillan Reference USA) Gale Group.
—Dream Lover. 1997. 432p. mass mkt. 6.50 (*0-440-22422-5*) Dell Publishing.
—Dream Lover. l.t. ed. 2000. (Wheeler Large Print Book Ser.). 522p. 27.95 (*1-56895-824-2*, Wheeler Publishing, Inc.) Gale Group.
—Enslaved. 1995. 448p. mass mkt. 6.99 (*0-440-21706-7*) Dell Publishing.
—The Pirate & the Pagan. 1990. 464p. mass mkt. 6.99 (*0-440-20623-5*) Dell Publishing.
—The Raven & the Rose. 1987. 400p. (Orig.). mass mkt. 6.99 (*0-440-17161-X*) Dell Publishing.
—A Woman of Passion. 2000. 544p. mass mkt. 6.99 (*0-440-22208-7*) Dell Publishing.
—A Woman of Passion. l.t. ed. 1999. (Wheeler Large Print Book Ser.). 605p. 26.95 (*1-56895-762-9*, Wheeler Publishing, Inc.) Gale Group.
Henry, Marguerite. King of the Wind. unabr. ed. 2000. (J). (gr. 4-6). audio 32.00 (*0-8072-8696-6*, YA239CX, Listening Library) Random Hse. Audio Publishing Group.
Hensher, Philip, contrib. by. The Bedroom of the Mister's Wife. 1999. 200p. (*0-7011-6729-7*) Chatto & Windus.
Henty, G. A. Bonnie Prince Charlie: A Tale of Fontenoy & Culloden. 2000. (J). pap. 14.99 (*1-887159-55-X*); (Illus.). 290p. 20.99 (*1-887159-54-1*) Preston-Speed Pubns.
—By England's Aid: The Freeing of the Netherlands, 1585-1604. 2000. 252p. (J). E-Book 3.95 (*0-594-02371-8*) 1873 Pr.
—In the Reign of Terror: The Adventures of a Westminster Boy. 2000. (J). 20.99 (*1-887159-50-9*); pap. 14.99 (*1-887159-51-7*) Preston-Speed Pubns.
Herbert, A. P. Uncommon Law. 1997. 500p. pap. 10.95 o.p. (*1-55882-107-4*) International Polygonics, Ltd.
Herbert, James. The Fog. 2003. vi, 345p. (*0-333-76119-7*) Macmillan U.K. GBR. *Dist:* Trafalgar Square.
—The Fog. l.t. ed. 1993. (Magna Large Print Ser.). 487p. o.p. (*0-7505-0586-9*) Magna Large Print Bks. GBR. *Dist:* Ulverscroft Large Print Canada, Ltd.
—The Fog. 1975. mass mkt. 3.95 o.p. (*0-451-15541-6*); mass mkt. 1.50 o.p. (*0-451-06708-8*); mass mkt. 1.75 o.p. (*0-451-08174-9*); mass mkt. 1.95 o.p. (*0-451-09193-0*); mass mkt. 3.50 o.p. (*0-451-12937-7*); mass mkt. 4.50 o.p. (*0-451-15769-9*) NAL. (Signet Bks.).
—'48. 1997. 280p. 22.00 o.p. (*0-06-105293-0*, Eos) Morrow/Avon.
Hern, Candice. Miss Lacey's Final Fling. 2001. (Signet Regency Romance Ser.). 224p. mass mkt. 4.99 o.s.i (*0-451-20161-2*) NAL.
Herries, Anne. The Abducted Bride. l.t. ed. 2001. (Mills & Boon Large Print Ser.). 320p. 27.99 (*0-263-17196-5*) Harlequin Mills & Boon, Ltd. GBR. *Dist:* Ulverscroft Large Print Bks., Ltd., Ulverscroft Large Print Canada, Ltd.
—Rosalyn & the Scoundrel. l.t. ed. 2001. (Mills & Boon Large Print Ser.). 320p. 27.99 (*0-263-17188-4*) Harlequin Mills & Boon, Ltd. GBR. *Dist:* Ulverscroft Large Print Bks., Ltd., Ulverscroft Large Print Canada, Ltd.
Herriot, James. Bonny's Big Day. 1991. (Illus.). 32p. (J). (gr. 1-2). pap. 6.95 (*0-312-06571-X*, Saint Martin's Griffin) St. Martin's Pr.
Hessayon. Capel Bells. 2000. 393p. 26.95 (*0-593-03608-5*); pap. 8.95 (*0-552-14220-4*) Transworld Publishers Ltd. GBR. *Dist:* Trafalgar Square.
Hessayon, Joan. Helmingham Rose. 2000. 379p. pap. 10.95 (*0-552-14535-1*) Transworld Publishers Ltd. GBR. *Dist:* Trafalgar Square.
Hewitt, Edward. Emma: The Cartwright Saga. l.t. ed. 2000. (Cartwright Saga Ser.: Vol. 4). 384p. 31.99 (*0-7089-4254-7*, Ulverscroft) Thorpe, F. A. Pubs. GBR. *Dist:* Ulverscroft Large Print Bks., Ltd., Ulverscroft Large Print Canada, Ltd.
—The Harbinger of Doom. l.t. ed. 2000. (Cartwright Saga Ser.: 2). 312p. 31.99 (*0-7089-4168-0*, Ulverscroft) Thorpe, F. A. Pubs. GBR. *Dist:* Ulverscroft Large Print Bks., Ltd., Ulverscroft Large Print Canada, Ltd.
—The Miller's Daughters. l.t. ed. 2000. (Cartwright Saga Ser.: 3). 248p. 31.99 (*0-7089-4205-9*, Ulverscroft) Thorpe, F. A. Pubs. GBR. *Dist:* Ulverscroft Large Print Bks., Ltd., Ulverscroft Large Print Canada, Ltd.
—Where Waters Meet. l.t. ed. 1999. (Cartwright Saga Ser.: Vol. 1). 368p. 31.99 (*0-7089-4148-6*, Ulverscroft) Thorpe, F. A. Pubs. GBR. *Dist:* Ulverscroft Large Print Bks., Ltd., Ulverscroft Large Print Canada, Ltd.
Heyer, Georgette. Behold, Here's Poison. reprint ed. lib. bdg. 24.95 (*0-89190-639-8*, Rivercity Pr.) Amereon, Ltd.
—Behold, Here's Poison. 2001. 284p. pap. 8.95 (*0-7551-0894-9*) House of Stratus, Inc. GBR. *Dist:* Midpoint Trade Bks., Inc.
—A Blunt Instrument. 1976. (Crime Fiction Ser.). reprint ed. lib. bdg. 21.00 o.p. (*0-8240-2375-7*) Garland Publishing, Inc.
Higgins, Jack. Angel of Death. 1996. 352p. mass mkt. 7.99 (*0-425-15223-5*) Berkley Publishing Group.
—Angel of Death. unabr. ed. 1995. 24.95 o.p. (*0-7871-0391-8*, 692879) NewStar Media, Inc.
—Angel of Death. 2001. 23.95 (*0-399-14274-6*); 1995. 311p. 23.95 (*0-399-14042-5*, G. P. Putnam's Sons) Penguin Group (USA) Inc.
—Angel of Death. l.t. ed. 1996. (Paperback Bestsellers Ser.). 402p. lib. bdg. 24.95 (*0-7862-0465-6*) Thorndike Pr.
—The Graveyard Shift. l.t. ed. 1994. 18.95 o.p. (*0-7927-1991-3*); pap. 17.95 o.p. (*0-7927-1990-5*) BBC Audiobooks America.
—Memoirs of a Dance-Hall Romeo. 1989. 17.95 o.p. (*0-671-67843-4*, Simon & Schuster) Simon & Schuster.
Highsmith, Patricia. A Suspension of Mercy. 2001. 235p. pap. 11.00 (*0-393-32197-5*) Norton, W. W. & Co., Inc.
—A Suspension of Mercy. l.t. ed. 2002. (Mystery Ser.). 376p. 28.95 (*0-7862-3903-4*) Thorndike Pr.
—A Suspension of Mercy. 1982. 208p. pap. 3.95 o.p. (*0-14-003470-6*, Penguin Bks.) Viking Penguin.
Hildick, E. W. Ghost Squad Flies Concorde. 1986. 192p. mass mkt. 2.50 (*0-8125-6854-0*, Tor Bks.) Doherty, Tom Assocs., LLC.
Hill, Harry. Last Flight from Deathrow. 2003. 224p. pap. (*0-7515-3329-7*) Warner Bks. GBR. *Dist:* Trafalgar Square.
Hill, Pamela. The Gods Return. l.t. ed. 2001. 224p. (*0-7540-4389-4*); (*0-7540-4390-8*) Gale Group. (Macmillan Reference USA).
—The Gods Return. l.t. ed. 2001. (Nightingale Ser.). 224p. pap. 22.95 (*0-7838-9339-6*) Thorndike Pr.
Hill, Reginald. An Advancement of Learning. unabr. ed. 2000. (Dalziel & Pascoe Mystery Ser.). audio 59.95 (*0-7451-6688-1*, CAB 1304) Chivers Audio Bks. GBR. *Dist:* BBC Audiobooks America.
—An Advancement of Learning. 1985. 254p. 14.95 o.s.i (*0-88150-053-4*) Countryman Pr.
—An Advancement of Learning. 1987. 256p. mass mkt. 4.50 o.p. (*0-451-14656-5*, Signet Bks.) NAL.
—An April Shroud. 1986. 256p. 15.95 o.p. (*0-88150-065-8*) Countryman Pr.
—An April Shroud. 1987. mass mkt. 3.50 o.p. (*0-451-14783-9*, Signet Bks.) NAL.
—An April Shroud. l.t. ed. 1999. (Charnwood Large Print Ser.). 320p. 31.99 o.p. (*0-7089-9084-3*, Ulverscroft) Thorpe, F. A. Pubs. GBR. *Dist:* Ulverscroft Large Print Bks., Ltd., Ulverscroft Large Print Canada, Ltd.
—Arms & the Women. (Dalziel & Pascoe Mystery Ser.). 2000. 512p. mass mkt. 6.99 (*0-440-22594-9*); 1999. 416p. 23.95 o.s.i (*0-385-33279-3*, Delacorte Pr.) Dell Publishing.
—Asking for the Moon. 1998. (Dalziel & Pascoe Mystery Ser.). 336p. reprint ed. mass mkt. 6.50 (*0-440-22583-3*) Doubleday Publishing.
—Asking for the Moon. l.t. ed. 1997. (Charnwood Large Print Ser.). 384p. 29.99 o.p. (*0-7089-8974-8*, Ulverscroft) Thorpe, F. A. Pubs. GBR. *Dist:* Ulverscroft Large Print Bks., Ltd., Ulverscroft Large Print Canada, Ltd.
—Blood Sympathy. 1996. (WWL Mystery Ser.). per. (*0-373-26210-8*, 1-26210-4, Worldwide Library) Harlequin Enterprises, Ltd.
—Blood Sympathy, Set. unabr. ed. 1998. audio 69.95 (*1-85903-203-6*) Magna Story Sound GBR. *Dist:* Ulverscroft Large Print Bks., Ltd.
—Blood Sympathy. 1994. 224p. 19.95 o.p. (*0-312-11249-1*, Saint Martin's Minotaur) St. Martin's Pr.
—Blood Sympathy. l.t. ed. 1995. (Ulverscroft Large Print Ser.). 464p. 29.99 o.p. (*0-7089-3368-8*, Ulverscroft) Thorpe, F. A. Pubs. GBR. *Dist:* Ulverscroft Large Print Bks., Ltd., Ulverscroft Large Print Canada, Ltd.
—Bones & Silence. 1991. (Dalziel & Pascoe Mystery Ser.). 448p. mass mkt. 6.99 (*0-440-20935-8*) Dell Publishing.
—Bones & Silence. l.t. ed. 1992. (Mystery Ser.). 528p. 29.99 o.p. (*0-7089-8673-0*, Ulverscroft) Thorpe, F. A. Pubs. GBR. *Dist:* Ulverscroft Large Print Bks., Ltd., Ulverscroft Large Print Canada, Ltd.
—Born Guilty. 1996. mass mkt. (*0-373-26226-4*, 1-26226-0, Worldwide Library) Harlequin Enterprises, Ltd.
—Born Guilty. unabr. ed. 1998. audio 69.95 (*1-85903-234-6*) Magna Story Sound GBR. *Dist:* Ulverscroft Large Print Bks., Ltd.
—Born Guilty. 1995. 240p. 20.95 o.p. (*0-312-13032-5*, Saint Martin's Minotaur) St. Martin's Pr.
—Born Guilty. l.t. ed. 1996. (Ulverscroft Large Print Ser.). 416p. 29.99 o.p. (*0-7089-3571-0*, Ulverscroft) Thorpe, F. A. Pubs. GBR. *Dist:* Ulverscroft Large Print Bks., Ltd., Ulverscroft Large Print Canada, Ltd.
—Child's Play. l.t. ed. 1988. (Ulverscroft Large Print Ser.). 560p. 29.99 o.p. (*0-7089-1912-X*, Ulverscroft) Thorpe, F. A. Pubs. GBR. *Dist:* Ulverscroft Large Print Bks., Ltd., Ulverscroft Large Print Canada, Ltd.
—Child's Play. 1988. mass mkt. 3.95 (*0-446-34533-4*) Warner Bks., Inc.
—A Clubbable Woman. unabr. ed. 2000. (Dalziel & Pascoe Mystery Ser.). audio 59.95 (*0-7451-6613-X*, CAB 1230) Chivers Audio Bks. GBR. *Dist:* BBC Audiobooks America.
—A Clubbable Woman. 1985. mass mkt. 2.95 o.p. (*0-451-13810-4*, Signet Bks.) NAL.
—Deadheads, Set unabr. ed. 1999. (Superintendent Daiziel & Sergeant Pascoe Mysteries Ser.). audio 69.95 BBC Audiobooks America.
—Deadheads. 1985. mass mkt. 3.95 o.p. (*0-451-15895-4*, Signet Bks.); mass mkt. 3.50 o.p. (*0-451-13559-8*, ROC) NAL.
—Deadheads. l.t. ed. 1985. 512p. o.p. (*0-7089-1312-1*, Ulverscroft) Thorpe, F. A. Pubs.
—Deadheads: A Dalziel & Pascoe Mystery, Set unabr. ed. 1999. audio 69.95 (*0-7540-0286-1*, CAB 1709) BBC Audiobooks America.
—Death's Jest Book. 2003. 576p. 25.95 (*0-06-052805-2*) HarperCollins Pubs.
—Exit Lines. 1986. mass mkt. 3.50 o.p. (*0-451-14252-7*, Signet Bks.); 256p. mass mkt. 3.99 o.s.i (*0-451-16166-1*) NAL.
—Exit Lines. l.t. ed. 1985. (Charnwood Large Print Ser.). 400p. 29.99 o.p. (*0-7089-8266-2*, Ulverscroft) Thorpe, F. A. Pubs. GBR. *Dist:* Ulverscroft Large Print Bks., Ltd., Ulverscroft Large Print Canada, Ltd.
—A Killing Kindness. 1989. 269p. reprint ed. pap. 5.95 o.s.i (*1-55882-003-5*, Library of Crime Classics) International Polygonics, Ltd.
—A Killing Kindness. 1981. 10.95 o.p. (*0-394-51910-8*, Pantheon) Knopf Publishing Group.
—A Killing Kindness: A Dalziel & Pascoe Mystery, Set. unabr. ed. 1999. audio 69.95 (*0-7540-0382-5*, CAB1805) BBC Audiobooks America.
—Killing the Lawyers. 1998. per. (*0-373-26298-1*, 1-26298-9, Mira Bks.) Harlequin Enterprises, Ltd.
—Killing the Lawyers. unabr. ed. 1998. audio 83.95 (*1-85903-235-4*) Magna Story Sound GBR. *Dist:* Ulverscroft Large Print Bks., Ltd.
—Killing the Lawyers. 1997. (Joe Sixsmith Mysteries Ser.). 336p. 23.95 o.p. (*0-312-16877-2*, Saint Martin's Minotaur) St. Martin's Pr.
—On Beulah Height. 1999. (Dalziel & Pascoe Mystery Ser.). 560p. mass mkt. 6.99 (*0-440-22590-6*) Dell Publishing.
—On Beulah Height. 1998. 384p. o.s.i (*0-385-25734-1*) Doubleday Canada, Ltd. CAN. *Dist:* Random Hse., Inc.
—On Beulah Height. l.t. ed. 1999. (Charnwood Large Print Ser.). 624p. 31.99 o.p. (*0-7089-9056-8*, Charnwood) Thorpe, F. A. Pubs. GBR. *Dist:* Ulverscroft Large Print Bks., Ltd., Ulverscroft Large Print Canada, Ltd.
—On Beulah Height: A Dalziel-Pascoe Murder Mystery. 1998. 384p. 22.95 o.s.i (*0-385-33278-5*) Doubleday Publishing.
—Pictures of Perfection. 1995. (Dalziel & Pascoe Mystery Ser.). 352p. mass mkt. 6.99 (*0-440-21800-4*) Dell Publishing.
—Pictures of Perfection. l.t. ed. 1995. (Charnwood Large Print Ser.). 432p. 29.99 o.p. (*0-7089-8845-8*, Charnwood) Thorpe, F. A. Pubs. GBR. *Dist:* Ulverscroft Large Print Bks., Ltd., Ulverscroft Large Print Canada, Ltd.
—A Pinch of Snuff. 1990. 336p. mass mkt. 6.99 (*0-440-16912-7*) Dell Publishing.
—A Pinch of Snuff. 1978. (Harper Novel of Suspense Ser.). 9.95 o.p. (*0-06-011876-8*) HarperCollins Pubs.
—Recalled to Life. 1993. (Dalziel & Pascoe Mystery Ser.). 400p. mass mkt. 6.99 (*0-440-21573-0*) Dell Publishing.
—Ruling Passion. unabr. ed. 2000. (Dalziel & Pascoe Mystery Ser.). audio 69.95 (*0-7540-0042-7*, CAB 1465) Chivers Audio Bks. GBR. *Dist:* BBC Audiobooks America.
—Ruling Passion. 1990. 336p. mass mkt. 6.99 (*0-440-16889-9*) Dell Publishing.
—Ruling Passion. l.t. ed. 2001. (Charnwood Large Print Ser.). 376p. 31.99 o.p. (*0-7089-9230-7*, Ulverscroft) Thorpe, F. A. Pubs. GBR. *Dist:* Ulverscroft Large Print Bks., Ltd., Ulverscroft Large Print Canada, Ltd.
—Singing the Sadness. 2001. (WWL Mystery Ser.: No. 371). 251p. mass mkt. (*0-373-26371-6*, 1-26371-4, Worldwide Library) Harlequin Enterprises, Ltd.
—Singing the Sadness. 2nd ed. 1999. 352p. 23.95 (*0-312-24238-7*, Saint Martin's Minotaur) St. Martin's Pr.
—Singing the Sadness. l.t. ed. 2000. (Charnwood Large Print Ser.). 392p. 31.99 (*0-7089-9143-2*, Ulverscroft) Thorpe, F. A. Pubs. GBR. *Dist:* Ulverscroft Large Print Bks., Ltd., Ulverscroft Large Print Canada, Ltd.
—Underworld: A New Dalziel-Pascoe Murder Mystery. 1988. 288p. 14.95 o.s.i (*0-684-18931-3*, Scribner) Simon & Schuster.
—The Wood Beyond. 1997. (Dalziel & Pascoe Mystery Ser.). 448p. mass mkt. 6.99 (*0-440-21803-9*) Dell Publishing.
—The Wood Beyond, Set. unabr. ed. 1997. audio 94.95 Eye in the Ear Inc.
—The Wood Beyond. l.t. ed. 1996. 25.95 o.p. (*0-7838-1864-5*, Macmillan Reference USA) Gale Group.
Hill, Rosa. House of Green Dragons. 1983. 224p. 12.95 o.p. (*0-312-39261-3*) St. Martin's Pr.
Hill, Susan. Mrs. De Winter. abr. ed. 1993. audio 24.95 (*1-55927-250-3*, 102649) Audio Renaissance.
—Mrs. De Winter. unabr. ed. audio 64.00 (*0-7366-2884-3*, 3586) Books on Tape, Inc.
—Mrs. De Winter. 1993. 349p. 20.00 o.p. (*0-688-12707-X*, Morrow, William & Co.) Morrow/Avon.
—Mrs. de Winter: Library Edition. unabr. ed. 1994. audio 79.95 (*1-55927-273-2*, 102802) Audio Renaissance.
Hilton, John B. The Anathema Stone. 1980. 8.95 o.p. (*0-312-03351-6*) St. Martin's Pr.
—The Asking Price. 1983. 160p. 10.95 o.p. (*0-312-05660-5*) St. Martin's Pr.
—Corridors of Guilt. 1984. 160p. 10.95 o.p. (*0-312-17003-3*) St. Martin's Pr.
—Displaced Person. l.t. ed. 1988. (Nightingale Ser.). 298p. 12.95 o.p. (*0-8161-4493-1*, Macmillan Reference USA) Gale Group.
—Displaced Person. 1988. 192p. 13.95 o.p. (*0-312-01421-X*, Saint Martin's Minotaur) St. Martin's Pr.
—The Green Frontier. 1982. 196p. 9.95 o.p. (*0-312-35006-6*) St. Martin's Pr.
—Hangman's Tide. 1975. 6.95 o.p. (*0-312-35945-4*) St. Martin's Pr.
—The Hobbema Prospect. 1984. 192p. 10.95 o.p. (*0-312-38828-4*) St. Martin's Pr.
—The Innocents at Home: A Superintendent Kenworthy Mystery. 1986. 224p. 14.95 o.p. (*0-312-00014-6*) St. Martin's Pr.
—Passion in the Peak: A Superintendent Kenworthy Novel. 1985. 184p. 11.95 o.p. (*0-312-59781-9*) St. Martin's Pr.
—The Sunset Law. 1982. 192p. 9.95 o.p. (*0-312-77576-8*) St. Martin's Pr.
—Surrender Value. 1981. 224p. 9.95 o.p. (*0-312-77710-8*) St. Martin's Pr.
Hinshaw, Victoria. Cordelia's Corinthian. 2004. 224p. mass mkt. 4.99 (*0-8217-7673-8*, Kensington Bks.) Kensington Publishing Corp.
Hitt, Jack, et al. Perfect Murder: Five Great Mystery Writers Create the Perfect Crime, Set. abr. ed. 1992. audio 16.99 (*0-88646-317-3*, 7317) Durkin Hayes Publishing Ltd.

Hoban, Russell. Riddley Walker. exp. ed. 1998. (Illus.). 256p. 29.95 (*0-253-33448-9*); pap. 12.95 (*0-253-21234-0*) Indiana Univ. Pr.

—Riddley Walker. mass mkt. 2.95 (*0-671-60777-4*, Pocket); 1990. pap. 10.00 o.s.i (*0-671-70127-4*, Touchstone) Simon & Schuster.

Hocker, Karla. The Impertinent Miss Bancroft. 2002. (Zebra Regency Romance Ser.). 256p. mass mkt. 4.99 o.s.i (*0-8217-7360-7*) Kensington Publishing Corp.

—The Impertinent Miss Bancroft. 1991. 224p. 18.95 (*0-8027-1164-2*) Walker & Co.

—The Incorrigible Sophia: A Regency Intrigue. 1992. 208p. 19.95 o.p. (*0-8027-1208-8*) Walker & Co.

—A Madcap Scheme. 2000. 350p. E-Book 6.00 (*1-58200-546-X*) Hard Shell Word Factory.

Hodge, Jane Aiken. Escapade. 1993. 240p. 18.95 o.p. (*0-312-09799-9*) St. Martin's Pr.

Hoeg, Peter. The Woman & the Ape. 1997. 272p. mass mkt. 7.50 (*0-7704-2756-1*) Bantam Bks.

—The Woman & the Ape. Haveland, Barbara, tr. l.t. ed. 1996. 256p. 23.00 o.p. (*0-374-29203-5*) Farrar, Straus & Giroux.

—The Woman & the Ape. Haveland, Barbara, tr. l.t. ed. 1997. (G. K. Hall Core Ser.). 364p. 25.95 (*0-7838-8068-5*, Macmillan Reference USA) Gale Group.

—The Woman & the Ape. l.t. ed. 1997. 272p. pap. 12.95 o.s.i (*0-14-026844-8*) Penguin Group (USA) Inc.

—The Woman & the Ape, unabr. ed. 1997. audio 56.00 (*0-7887-0856-2*, 95002E7) Recorded Bks., LLC.

Holbrok, Cindy. Lord Sayer's Ghost. 1996. 416p. mass mkt. 4.99 o.s.i (*0-8217-5320-7*) Kensington Publishing Corp.

Holbrook, Cindy. The Missing Brides. 2001. (Zebra Regency Romance Ser.). 256p. mass mkt. 4.99 o.s.i (*0-8217-6812-3*, Zebra Bks.) Kensington Publishing Corp.

—The Missing Grooms. 2001. (Zebra Regency Romance Ser.). 288p. mass mkt. 4.99 o.s.i (*0-8217-6769-0*, Zebra Bks.) Kensington Publishing Corp.

Holbrook, Cindy, et al. Valentine Rogues. 2000. (Zebra Regency Romance Ser.). 256p. mass mkt. 4.99 o.s.i (*0-8217-6772-0*, Zebra Bks.) Kensington Publishing Corp.

Holden, Alice, et al. My Sweet Valentine. 2002. (Zebra Regency Romance Ser.). 288p. mass mkt. 4.99 o.s.i (*0-8217-7184-1*, Zebra Bks.) Kensington Publishing Corp.

Holden, Wendy. Bad Heir Day. 2001. 352p. pap. 13.00 (*0-452-28178-4*, Plume) Dutton/Plume.

—Bad Heir Day. l.t. ed. 384p. 2002. pap. 21.99 o.p. (*0-7531-6405-1*); 2001. 32.50 (*0-7531-6404-3*) ISIS Large Print Bks. GBR. *Dist:* Ulverscroft Large Print Bks., Ltd., Ulverscroft Large Print Canada, Ltd.

—Farm Fatale: A Comedy of Country Manors. 2002. 352p. pap. 13.00 (*0-452-28302-7*, Plume) Dutton/Plume.

Holland, Cecelia. The Pillar of the Sky. 1986. pap. 9.95 o.s.i (*0-345-33336-5*) Ballantine Bks.

—The Pillar of the Sky. 2000. 544p. pap. 14.95 (*0-312-86887-1*, Forge Bks.) Doherty, Tom Assocs., LLC.

—The Pillar of the Sky. 1985. (Illus.). 544p. 17.95 o.s.i (*0-394-53538-3*) Knopf, Alfred A. Inc.

Holland, David. Murcheston: The Wolf's Tale. E-Book 23.95 (*0-312-87699-8*, Tor Bks.); 2000. 349p. 23.95 (*0-312-87213-5*, Forge Bks.) Doherty, Tom Assocs., LLC.

Hollick, Helen. Pendragon's Banner. 1996. 560p. 25.95 o.p. (*0-312-14699-X*) St. Martin's Pr.

—Shadow of the King. 1998. 400p. mass mkt. o.p. (*0-7493-2058-3*) Random Hse. of Canada, Ltd. CAN. *Dist:* Random Hse., Inc.

—Shadow of the King. 1997. (Pendragon's Banner Ser.: Vol. 3). 560p. 27.95 o.p. (*0-312-17000-9*) St. Martin's Pr.

Holliday, Liz & McGovern, Jimy. Cracker: One Day a Lemming Will Fly. 1997. (Cracker Ser.). 272p. 22.95 o.p. (*0-312-18072-1*, Saint Martin's Minotaur) St. Martin's Pr.

Hollinghurst, Alan. The Spell. 1998. 257p. o.p. (*0-7011-6519-7*) Random Hse. of Canada, Ltd. CAN. *Dist:* Random Hse., Inc.

—The Spell. 2000. 272p. 12.95 (*0-14-028637-3*); 1999. 288p. 24.95 o.p. (*0-670-88356-5*) Viking Penguin.

—The Swimming-Pool Library. 1989. (Vintage International Ser.). 352p. pap. 14.00 (*0-679-72256-4*, Vintage) Knopf Publishing Group.

Holman, Sheri. The Dress Lodger. 2001. (Reader's Circle Ser.). 320p. pap. 14.00 (*0-345-43691-1*, Ballantine Bks.) Ballantine Bks.

—The Dress Lodger. l.t. ed. 2000. (Wheeler Large Print Book Ser.). 471p. 28.95 (*1-56895-880-3*, Wheeler Publishing, Inc.) Gale Group.

—The Dress Lodger. 2000. 291p. 24.00 o.p. (*0-87113-753-4*, Atlantic Monthly Pr.) Grove/Atlantic, Inc.

Holmes, Clare F. The Burning Quest. l.t. ed. 1994. 270p. lib. bdg. 16.95 (*0-8161-5843-6*, Macmillan Reference USA) Gale Group.

—The Turning Blade. l.t. ed. 1996. (Nightingale Ser.). pap. 17.95 o.p. (*0-7838-1624-3*, Macmillan Reference USA) Gale Group.

Holt, Cheryl. Total Surrender. 2002. 384p. mass mkt. 6.50 o.s.i (*0-312-97841-3*, St. Martin's Paperbacks) St. Martin's Pr.

Holt, Hazel. The Cruellest Month. l.t. ed. 1992. 240p. 14.95 o.p. (*0-7451-1491-1*, Macmillan Reference USA) Gale Group.

—The Cruellest Month. 1992. (Mrs. Malory Mystery Ser.). 224p. mass mkt. 4.50 o.s.i (*0-451-40313-4*, Onyx) NAL.

—The Cruellest Month. 1991. 15.95 o.p. (*0-312-05840-3*, Saint Martin's Minotaur) St. Martin's Pr.

—Death among Friends, 1 vol. 1999. (Sheila Malory Mysteries Ser.). 256p. mass mkt. 5.99 o.s.i (*0-451-19691-0*) NAL.

—Death among Friends. l.t. ed. 1999. (General Ser.). 232p. pap. 24.95 (*0-7862-1979-3*); (*0-7540-3816-5*); (*0-7540-3815-7*) Thorndike Pr.

—Mrs. Malory: Death of a Dean. l.t. ed. 1996. (Mrs. Malory Mystery Ser.). 194p. 22.95 o.s.i (*0-525-94150-9*, Dutton) Dutton/Plume.

—Mrs. Malory: Death of a Dean. l.t. ed. 1996. pap. 23.95 (*1-56895-392-5*, Wheeler Publishing, Inc.) Gale Group.

—Mrs. Malory: Death of a Dean. 1997. (Sheila Malory Mysteries Ser.). 176p. mass mkt. 5.99 o.s.i (*0-451-19109-9*) NAL.

—Mrs. Malory: Detective in Residence. 1994. (Mrs. Malory Mystery Ser.). 192p. 18.95 o.p. (*0-525-93903-2*) Dutton/Plume.

—Mrs. Malory: Detective in Residence. 1995. (Sheila Malory Mysteries Ser.). 256p. mass mkt. 4.99 o.s.i (*0-451-18017-8*, Signet Bks.) NAL.

—Mrs. Malory & Death by Water. 2003. 256p. mass mkt. 5.99 (*0-451-20809-9*, Signet Bks.) NAL.

—Mrs. Malory & the Delay of Execution. l.t. ed. 2002. (Mystery Ser.). 273p. 28.95 (*0-7862-4910-2*) Gale Group.

—Mrs. Malory & the Delay of Execution. 2002. 256p. mass mkt. 5.99 (*0-451-20627-4*) NAL.

—Mrs. Malory & the Fatal Legacy: A Sheila Malory Mystery. 2000. (Sheila Malory Mysteries Ser.). 256p. mass mkt. 5.99 (*0-451-20002-0*, Signet Bks.) NAL.

—Mrs. Malory & the Fatal Legacy: A Sheila Malory Mystery. l.t. ed. 2000. (Mystery Ser.). 344p. 27.95 (*0-7862-2842-3*) Thorndike Pr.

—Mrs. Malory & the Festival Murders. 1994. (Mrs. Malory Mystery Ser.). 224p. mass mkt. 3.99 o.s.i (*0-451-18015-1*, Signet Bks.) NAL.

—Mrs. Malory & the Festival Murders. 1993. 171p. 17.95 o.p. (*0-312-08852-3*, Saint Martin's Minotaur) St. Martin's Pr.

—Mrs. Malory & the Lilies That Fester. 2001. (Sheila Malory Mysteries Ser.). 256p. mass mkt. 5.99 o.s.i (*0-451-20354-2*, Signet Bks.) NAL.

—Mrs. Malory & the Lilies That Fester. 2001. 303p. 28.95 (*0-7862-3675-2*) Thorndike Pr.

—Mrs. Malory & the Only Good Lawyer. 1997. (Mrs. Malory Mystery Ser.). 192p. 22.95 o.p. (*0-525-94151-7*) Dutton/Plume.

—Mrs. Malory & the Only Good Lawyer. 1998. (Sheila Malory Mysteries Ser.). 256p. mass mkt. 5.99 o.s.i (*0-451-19264-8*, Signet Bks.) NAL.

—Mrs. Malory Investigates. 1991. (Mrs. Malory Mystery Ser.). 224p. mass mkt. 5.50 o.s.i (*0-451-40269-3*, Onyx) NAL.

—Mrs. Malory Investigates. 1990. 192p. 14.95 o.p. (*0-312-03894-1*, Saint Martin's Minotaur) St. Martin's Pr.

—Mrs. Malory Wonders Why. 1995. (Mrs. Malory Mystery Ser.). 192p. 20.95 o.s.i (*0-525-93932-6*, Dutton) Dutton/Plume.

—Mrs. Malory Wonders Why. 1996. (Sheila Malory Mysteries Ser.). 256p. mass mkt. 5.50 o.s.i (*0-451-18286-3*) NAL.

—Mrs. Malory's Shortest Journey. 1995. (Mrs. Malory Mystery Ser.). 256p. mass mkt. 4.99 o.s.i (*0-451-18395-9*, Signet Bks.) NAL.

—The Shortest Journey: A Mrs. Malory Mystery. l.t. ed. 1995. 232p. pap. 17.95 o.p. (*0-7838-1138-1*, Macmillan Reference USA) Gale Group.

—The Shortest Journey: A Mrs. Malory Mystery. 1994. 224p. 19.95 o.p. (*0-312-11140-1*, Saint Martin's Minotaur) St. Martin's Pr.

Holt, Tom. Lucia in Wartime. 1986. 192p. 12.95 o.p. (*0-06-055003-1*) HarperTrade.

—Lucia Triumphant. 2004. (Lucia Ser.). 224p. pap. 12.95 (*1-55921-310-8*) Moyer Bell.

—Lucia Triumphant: Based on the Character Created by E. F. Benson. 1988. 224p. (Orig.). pap. 6.95 o.p. (*0-06-096196-1*, PL-6196, Perennial) HarperTrade.

—Nothing but Blue Skies. 2002. 336p. mass mkt. 7.95 (*1-84149-058-X*) Orbit GBR. *Dist:* Trafalgar Square.

Holt, Victoria. The House of a Thousand Lanterns. 1974. 336p. 9.95 o.s.i (*0-385-00817-1*) Doubleday Publishing.

—The Legend of the Seventh Virgin. 1993. mass mkt. 5.99 o.s.i (*0-449-45251-4*); 1986. 288p. mass mkt. 5.99 o.s.i (*0-449-21123-1*) Ballantine Bks. (Fawcett).

—The Legend of the Seventh Virgin. 1965. 13.95 o.p. (*0-385-00609-8*) Doubleday Publishing.

—The Legend of the Seventh Virgin. l.t. ed. 2001. (Thorndike Press Large Print Famous Authors Ser.). 519p. 28.95 (*0-7862-3460-1*) Thorndike Pr.

—Paragon Revels. l.t. ed. 1994. 22.95 o.p. (*0-7927-1923-9*) BBC Audiobooks America.

—Paragon Revels. l.t. ed. 1972. (Ulverscroft Large Print Ser.). 12.00 o.p. (*0-85456-141-2*, Ulverscroft) Thorpe, F. A. Pubs. GBR. *Dist:* Ulverscroft Large Print Bks., Ltd., Ulverscroft Large Print Canada, Ltd.

—Seven for a Secret. l.t. ed. 1992. 560p. 25.00 o.p. (*0-385-46800-8*, Doubleday Large Type) Bantam Doubleday Dell Large Print Group, Inc.

—Seven for a Secret. l.t. ed. 1994. 500p. pap. 18.95 o.p. (*0-8161-5804-5*, Macmillan Reference USA) Gale Group.

—The Silk Vendetta. unabr. ed. 1993. 84.95 incl. audio (*0-7451-4063-7*, CAB 760) BBC Audiobooks America.

—The Silk Vendetta. 1997. mass mkt. 3.50 (*0-449-00054-0*); 1988. mass mkt. 5.99 o.s.i (*0-449-21548-2*) Ballantine Bks. (Fawcett).

—The Silk Vendetta. l.t. ed. (General Ser.). 507p. 1988. 20.95 o.p. (*0-8161-4638-1*); 1989. 13.95 o.p. (*0-8161-4639-X*) Gale Group. (Macmillan Reference USA).

Home, Stewart. Slow Death. 1996. (High Risk Ser.). 296p. (Orig.). (*1-85242-519-9*) Serpent's Tail Ltd.

Hope, Christopher. Darkest England. 1996. 304p. 25.00 o.p. (*0-393-04040-2*) Norton, W. W. & Co., Inc.

—The Hottentot Room. 1987. 218p. 16.95 o.p. (*0-374-17284-6*) Farrar, Straus & Giroux.

Hope-Hawkins, Anthony. Dolly Dialogues. 2000. E-Book 2.49 (*1-58744-124-1*) Electric Umbrella Publishing.

Hornby, Nick. About a Boy. l.t. ed. 1998. 424p. (*0-7540-1206-9*) BBC Audiobooks America.

—About a Boy. movie tie-in ed. 320p. 2002. pap. 12.95 (*1-57322-957-1*); 1999. reprint ed. pap. 12.95 (*1-57322-733-1*) Berkley Publishing Group. (Riverhead Trade (Paperbacks)).

—About a Boy. 2002. pap. (*1-57322-961-X*) Penguin Group (USA) Inc.

—About a Boy. 1998. 288p. 22.95 o.s.i (*1-57322-087-6*, Riverhead Bks. (Hardcovers)); audio 17.95 o.p. (*1-57322-101-5*) Putnam Publishing Group, The.

—About a Boy. l.t. ed. 1998. (Basic Ser.). 424p. 28.95 (*0-7862-1606-9*) Thorndike Pr.

—High Fidelity. 336p. 2000. pap. 14.00 (*1-57322-821-4*); 1996. pap. 14.00 (*1-57322-551-7*) Berkley Publishing Group. (Riverhead Trade (Paperbacks)).

—High Fidelity. 1995. 304p. 21.95 o.p. (*1-57322-016-7*, Riverhead Bks. (Hardcovers)) Putnam Publishing Group, The.

Hornby, Nick, contrib. by. High Fidelity, abr. ed. 1998. audio 17.95 o.p. (*1-57322-102-3*) Putnam Publishing Group, The.

Hornung, E. W. The Collected Raffles Stories. 1996. (Oxford Popular Fiction Ser.). (Illus.). 424p. pap. 11.95 o.p. (*0-19-282324-8*) Oxford Univ. Pr., Inc.

—Raffles: The Amateur Cracksman. l.t. ed. 1990. pap. 10.95 o.p. (*0-7927-0157-7*, C0154) BBC Audiobooks America.

—Raffles: The Amateur Cracksman. unabr. ed. 1992. audio 32.95 (*0-7861-0632-8*, 2122) Blackstone Audio Bks., Inc.

—Raffles: The Amateur Cracksman. unabr. collector's ed. 1989. audio 36.00 (*0-7366-3953-5*, 9199) Books on Tape, Inc.

—Raffles: The Amateur Cracksman. 1975. 154p. 16.95 (*0-241-89168-X*) Boulevard Bks.

—Raffles: The Amateur Cracksman. l.t. unabr. ed. 1991. 204p. 32.50 (*1-85089-468-X*, 89468X) ISIS Large Print Bks. GBR. *Dist:* Ulverscroft Large Print Bks., Ltd.

—Raffles: The Amateur Cracksman. 1976. (Illus.). x, 244p. pap. 5.95 o.p. (*0-8032-5836-4*, Bison Bks.) Univ. of Nebraska Pr.

—Raffles: The Amateur Cracksman. 2003. 240p. pap. 13.00 (*0-14-143933-5*, Penguin Classics) Viking Penguin.

—Raffles, the Amateur Cracksman. 1976. (Illus.). 268p. reprint ed. pap. 83.10 (*0-608-02671-9*, 206332400004) Bks. on Demand.

—Raffles, the Amateur Cracksman: The Complete Stories of E. W. Hornung. (Spies & Intrigues Ser.: No. 7). 478p. reprint ed. pap. 8.95 (*0-918172-20-9*) Leete's Island Bks.

—Stingaree. 1977. (Short Story Index Reprint Ser.). 28.95 (*0-8369-3351-6*) Ayer Co. Pubs., Inc.

—Stingaree. 2002. 300p. per. 29.95 (*1-58963-833-6*) Fredonia Bks.

Hornung, E. W. & Covell, Walter. Raffles: The Amateur Cracksman. unabr. ed. 1989. audio 26.00 Jimcin Recordings.

Horvath, Brooke & Malin, Irving, eds. George Garrett: The Elizabethan Trilogy. 1998. 200p. 26.00 (*1-881515-13-3*); pap. 15.00 (*1-881515-14-1*) Texas Review Pr.

Hosier, Sydney. Game's Afoot, Mrs. Hudson. 1998. mass mkt. 5.99 (*0-380-79217-6*, Avon Bks.) Morrow/Avon.

Howard, Elizabeth J. Confusion. Grose, Bill, ed. 1995. 352p. pap. 14.00 (*0-671-52796-7*, Washington Square Pr.) Simon & Schuster.

—Confusion. 1994. 352p. 22.00 o.p. (*0-671-70911-9*, Atria) Simon & Schuster.

—The Light Years. Grose, Bill, ed. 1990. (Cazalet Chronicles Ser.). 464p. 18.95 (*0-671-70907-0*, Atria) Simon & Schuster.

Howard, Elizabeth Jane. Confusion. l.t. ed. 1994. (Cazalet Chronicle Ser.: Vol. 3). 596p. lib. bdg. 23.95 (*0-8161-7475-X*, Macmillan Reference USA) Gale Group.

—Mr. Wrong. l.t. ed. 2001. 263p. pap. 22.95 (*0-7862-3337-0*) Thorndike Pr.

Howard, Linda. Almost Forever. 2002. 256p. mass mkt. (*1-55166-934-X*, Mira Bks.) Harlequin Enterprises, Ltd.

Howard, Liz. Elizabeth Fytton of Gawsworth Hall. l.t. ed. 1994. (Ulverscroft Large Print Ser.). 416p. 29.99 o.p. (*0-7089-3093-X*, Ulverscroft) Thorpe, F. A. Pubs. GBR. *Dist:* Ulverscroft Large Print Bks., Ltd., Ulverscroft Large Print Canada, Ltd.

Howatch, Susan. Absolute Truths. 1996. mass mkt. 6.50 o.s.i (*0-449-22392-2*); 1996. 640p. mass mkt. 7.50 (*0-449-22555-0*); 1996. mass mkt. o.p. (*0-449-22121-0*); 1995. mass mkt. 6.99 o.s.i (*0-449-22417-1*) Ballantine Bks. (Fawcett).

—Absolute Truths. l.t. ed. 1995. (G. K. Hall Core Ser.). 967p. lib. bdg. 26.95 (*0-7838-1219-1*, Macmillan Reference USA) Gale Group.

—Cashelmara. 1984. 672p. mass mkt. 7.99 (*0-449-20623-8*); 1983. mass mkt. 3.50 o.p. (*0-449-20327-1*) Ballantine Bks. (Fawcett).

—Glamorous Powers. l.t. ed. 1990. (General Ser.). 674p. 20.95 o.p. (*0-8161-4863-5*, Macmillan Reference USA) Gale Group.

—Glamorous Powers. 1990. 4.99 o.p. (*0-517-05075-7*) Random Hse. Value Publishing.

—Glittering Images. l.t. ed. 1989. 680p. lib. bdg. 20.95 o.p. (*0-8161-4668-3*, Macmillan Reference USA) Gale Group.

—Mystical Paths. 1993. 512p. mass mkt. 6.99 (*0-449-22122-9*, Fawcett) Ballantine Bks.

—Mystical Paths. l.t. ed. 1993. (General Ser.). 800p. lib. bdg. 23.95 o.p. (*0-8161-5671-9*, Macmillan Reference USA) Gale Group.

—Mystical Paths. 1994. 5.99 o.p. (*0-517-11629-4*) Random Hse. Value Publishing.

—A Question of Integrity. 1997. (*0-316-64297-5*) Little Brown & Co.

—Ultimate Prizes. 1990. mass mkt. 5.95 o.s.i (*0-449-21913-5*) Ballantine Bks.

—Ultimate Prizes. l.t. ed. 1990. (General Ser.). 668p. 21.95 o.p. (*0-8161-4994-1*, Macmillan Reference USA) Gale Group.

—Ultimate Prizes. 1991. 4.99 o.p. (*0-517-06772-2*) Random Hse. Value Publishing.

—The Wonder Worker. 1998. 560p. pap. 14.00 (*0-449-00150-4*, Fawcett) Ballantine Bks.

—The Wonder Worker. 1997. 544p. 25.95 o.s.i (*0-375-40102-4*) Knopf, Alfred A. Inc.

Hucker, Hazel. Cousin Susannah. 1996. 384p. 23.95 (*0-312-13950-0*) St. Martin's Pr.

—A Dangerous Happiness. 1996. pap. o.s.i (*0-7515-1625-2*); o.s.i (*0-7515-1648-1*) Little Brown & Co.

—A Dangerous Happiness. 1996. 272p. 21.95 (*0-312-14307-9*) St. Martin's Pr.

—A Dangerous Happiness. l.t. ed. 1996. (Ulverscroft Large Print Ser.). 560p. 29.99 o.p. (*0-7089-3487-0*, Ulverscroft) Thorpe, F. A. Pubs. GBR. *Dist:* Ulverscroft Large Print Bks., Ltd., Ulverscroft Large Print Canada, Ltd.

—Trials of Friendship. 1998. 293p. pap. text o.s.i (*0-7515-1825-5*) Little Brown & Co.

—Trials of Friendship. 1997. 268p. 22.95 o.p. (*0-312-17051-3*) St. Martin's Pr.

Hughes, F. M. The Girl on the Shore: Adventures at Beacon House - A Care Home with a Difference. 2002. (Illus.). 128p. (C). pap. 14.95 (*1-84310-111-4*) Kingsley, Jessica Pubs. GBR. *Dist:* Taylor & Francis, Inc.

Hughes, Glyn. Bronte. 1996. 432p. 24.95 o.p. (*0-312-14816-X*) St. Martin's Pr.

—Bronte. 2000. 431p. 27.95 (*0-593-03549-6*) Transworld Publishers Ltd. GBR. *Dist:* Trafalgar Square.

—The Rape of the Rose: A Novel. 1993. 320p. 21.00 (*0-671-72516-5*, Simon & Schuster) Simon & Schuster.

Hughes, Richard. Lost in London. Wheeler, Jill, ed. 1988. (Great Cities Adventures Ser.). (Illus.). 48p. (J). (gr. 4). lib. bdg. 10.95 o.p. (*0-939179-47-4*) ABDO Publishing Co.

Hughes, Shirley. An Evening at Alfie's. 1985. (Illus.). 32p. (J). (ps-1). 16.00 o.p. (*0-688-04122-1*); lib. bdg. 15.93 o.p. (*0-688-04123-X*) HarperCollins Children's Bk. Group.

Hughes, Thomas P. Tom Brown's Schooldays. Sanders, Andrew, ed. 1989. (Oxford World's Classics Ser.). (Illus.). 456p. (YA). pap. 6.95 o.p. (*0-19-282198-9*) Oxford Univ. Pr., Inc.

Hull, Richard. Keep It Quiet. 1983. (Detective Stories Ser.). 192p. reprint ed. pap. 5.95 (*0-486-24520-9*) Dover Pubns., Inc.

Humphreys, Helen. Afterimage. 2000. 247p. (*0-00-225499-9*) HarperCollins Pubs.

—Afterimage. 2001. (Illus.). 256p. 23.00 o.s.i (*0-8050-6666-7*, Metropolitan Bks.) Holt, Henry & Co.

—The Lost Garden: A Novel. 2003. 23.95 (*0-393-05183-8*); 192p. pap. 13.95 (*0-393-32491-5*) Norton, W. W. & Co., Inc.

Hunt, Angela Elwell. The Case of the Birthday Bracelet. 1994. pap. 4.99 o.p. (*0-8407-6303-4*) Nelson, Thomas Inc.

Hunt, Kyle, pseud. As Merry as Hell. 1974. 192p. 13.95 o.p. (*0-8128-1662-5*, Scarborough Hse.) Madison Bks., Inc.

—This Man Did I Kill? 1985. 256p. pap. 2.95 o.p. (*0-8128-8133-8*, Scarborough Hse.) Madison Bks., Inc.

Hunt, Richard. Dead Man's Shoes. 1999. 224p. 25.00 (*0-7278-2255-1*) Severn Hse. Pubs., Ltd.

—Deadlocked. 1995. 192p. 19.95 o.p. (*0-312-13461-4*, Saint Martin's Minotaur) St. Martin's Pr.

—Death of a Merry Widow, Set. unabr. ed. 1998. audio 69.95 o.p. (*1-85903-048-3*) Magna Story Sound GBR. *Dist:* Ulverscroft Large Print Bks., Ltd.

—Death of a Merry Widow. 1994. 191p. 18.95 o.p. (*0-312-11773-6*, Saint Martin's Minotaur) St. Martin's Pr.

—The Man Trap. l.t. ed. 1998. (Dales Large Print Ser.). 336p. pap. 19.99 o.p. (*1-85389-866-X*) Dales Large Print Bks. GBR. *Dist:* Ulverscroft Large Print Bks., Ltd., Ulverscroft Large Print Canada, Ltd.

—Murder Benign. l.t. ed. 1997. (Dales Large Print Ser.). 305p. pap. 19.99 (*1-85389-721-3*) Dales Large Print Bks. GBR. *Dist:* Ulverscroft Large Print Bks., Ltd.

—Murder Benign. 1996. 192p. 20.95 o.p. (*0-312-14684-1*, Saint Martin's Minotaur) St. Martin's Pr.

Hunter, Alan. Death on the Broadlands: A Superintendent Gently Novel. 192p. 1986. pap. 2.95 o.p. (*0-8027-3156-2*); 1984. 12.95 o.s.i (*0-8027-5590-9*) Walker & Co.

—Death on the Heath. 1983. (Scene of the Crime Ser.: No. 58). pap. 2.75 o.p. (*0-440-11686-4*) Dell Publishing.

—Death on the Heath. 1982. 160p. 10.95 o.s.i (*0-8027-5468-6*) Walker & Co.

—Gently Between the Tides. 1985. (Walker's British Paperback Mysteries Ser.). pap. 2.95 o.p. (*0-8027-3145-7*) Walker & Co.

—Gently Between Tides. l.t. ed. 1986. lib. bdg. 14.95 o.p. (*0-7451-0321-9*, Macmillan Reference USA) Gale Group.

—Gently Between Tides. 1982. 11.95 o.s.i (*0-8027-5480-5*) Walker & Co.

—Gently by the Shore. l.t. ed. 1996. 304p. pap. 20.95 o.p. (*0-7862-0881-3*) Thorndike Pr.

—Gently Does It. l.t. ed. 1996. (G. K. Hall Nightingale Ser.). 287p. 17.95 (*0-7838-1879-3*, Macmillan Reference USA) Gale Group.

—Gently Floating. (Black Dagger Crime Ser.). 1992. 192p. 16.50 o.p. (*0-86220-848-3*, Black Dagger); 1993. 18.95 o.p. (*0-7451-6450-1*) BBC Audiobooks America.

—Gently Mistaken: An Inspector Gently Mystery, Set. unabr. ed. 1999. audio 39.95 (*0-7540-0369-8*, CAB1792) BBC Audiobooks America.

—Gently Scandalous. l.t. ed. 1992. 240p. 15.95 o.p. (*0-7451-1558-6*, Macmillan Reference USA) Gale Group.

—Gently Through the Woods. 1982. (Scene of the Crime Mystery Ser.: No. 46). pap. 2.25 o.p. (*0-440-13055-7*) Dell Publishing.

—Gently to the Summit. 1999. 208p. 21.95 (*0-7540-8553-8*, Black Dagger) BBC Audiobooks America.

—Gently with the Innocents. 1981. (Scene of the Crime Mystery Ser.: No. 28). pap. 2.25 o.p. (*0-440-12834-X*) Dell Publishing.

—Gently with the Millions. unabr. ed. 2001. audio 49.95 (*1-85695-472-2*, 92104) ISIS Audio Bks. GBR. *Dist:* Ulverscroft Large Print Bks., Ltd.

—Gently with the Painters. 1996. 208p. 19.50 (*0-7451-8675-0*, Black Dagger) BBC Audiobooks America.

—The Honfleur Decision. 1984. 182p. pap. 2.95 o.p. (*0-8027-3084-1*); 1981. 9.95 o.s.i (*0-8027-5437-6*) Walker & Co.

—Landed Gently. 1995. 224p. 19.50 o.p. (*0-7451-8663-7*, Black Dagger) BBC Audiobooks America.

—Landed Gently. 1982. (Scene of the Crime Ser.: No. 38). pap. 2.25 o.p. (*0-440-14711-5*) Dell Publishing.

—The Scottish Decision. 1981. 145p. 9.95 o.s.i (*0-8027-5456-2*); 1985. 192p. reprint ed. pap. 2.95 o.s.i (*0-8027-3113-9*) Walker & Co.

—The Unhanged Man. 1984. 192p. 12.95 o.s.i (*0-8027-5602-6*) Walker & Co.

Hunter, Jillian. Indiscretion. 2000. (Sonnet Bks.). 336p. pap. 6.50 (*0-671-02683-6*, Pocket) Simon & Schuster.

Hunter, Madeline. By Arrangement. 2000. 416p. mass mkt. 5.99 (*0-553-58222-4*) Bantam Bks.

Hunter, Madeline C. By Possession. 2000. 400p. mass mkt. 4.99 (*0-553-58221-6*) Bantam Bks.

Hutchinson, Meg. No Place for a Woman. 2002. 534p. mass mkt. (*0-340-73860-X*) Coronet GBR. *Dist:* Trafalgar Square.

—No Place for a Woman. l.t. ed. 2002. (Magna Large Print Ser.). 496p. 32.50 (*0-7505-1753-0*) Magna Large Print Bks. GBR. *Dist:* Ulverscroft Large Print Bks., Ltd., Ulverscroft Large Print Canada, Ltd.

—The Peppercorn Woman. 2002. 416p. mass mkt. (*0-340-73864-2*) Coronet GBR. *Dist:* Trafalgar Square.

—Peppercorn Woman. l.t. ed. 2002. (Magna Large Print Ser.). 464p. 32.50 (*0-7505-1915-0*) Magna Large Print Bks. GBR. *Dist:* Ulverscroft Large Print Bks., Ltd., Ulverscroft Large Print Canada, Ltd.

Huth, Angela. Invitation to the Married Life: A Novel. 1992. 304p. 19.95 o.p. (*0-8021-1465-2*) Grove/Atlantic, Inc.

—Land Girls. unabr. ed. 1999. audio compact disk 99.95 (*0-7531-0699-X*, 10699X) ISIS Audio Bks. GBR. *Dist:* Ulverscroft Large Print Bks., Ltd.

—Land Girls. 1995. 378p. pap. o.s.i (*0-349-10601-0*) Little Brown & Co.

—Land Girls. 378p. 1998. pap. 13.95 (*0-312-17195-1*, Saint Martin's Griffin); 1996. 23.95 o.p. (*0-312-14296-X*) St. Martin's Pr.

—Land Girls: Film Tie-In. 1998. 378p. pap. text o.s.i (*0-349-10993-1*) Little Brown & Co.

Huxley, Aldous. Antic Hay. 1997. 208p. reprint ed. pap. 12.50 (*1-56478-149-6*) Dalkey Archive Pr.

—Crome Yellow. 2002. (Coleman Dowell Ser.). 152p. reprint ed. pap. 11.95 (*1-56478-304-9*) Dalkey Archive Pr.

—Point Counter Point. 1996. 448p. reprint ed. pap. 13.95 (*1-56478-131-3*) Dalkey Archive Pr.

—Point Counter Point. 1939. o.p. (*0-06-012105-X*) HarperCollins Pubs.

—Point Counter Point. 1942. mass mkt. 4.95 o.p. (*0-06-083048-4*, P3048, Perennial) HarperTrade.

Hyde, Christopher. A Gathering of Saints. 1997. 438p. per. 6.99 (*0-671-87581-7*, Pocket); 1996. 432p. 24.00 (*0-671-87580-9*, Atria) Simon & Schuster.

Hylton, Sara. The Chosen Ones. l.t. ed. 1993. (Magna Large Print Ser.). 491p. 29.99 o.p. (*0-7505-0465-X*) Magna Large Print Bks. GBR. *Dist:* Ulverscroft Large Print Bks., Ltd., Ulverscroft Large Print Canada, Ltd.

—The Chosen Ones. 1992. 322p. 19.95 o.p. (*0-312-07669-X*) St. Martin's Pr.

—Footsteps in the Rain. l.t. ed. 1999. (Magna Large Print Ser.). 512p. (*0-7505-1313-6*) Magna Large Print Bks. GBR. *Dist:* Ulverscroft Large Print Canada, Ltd.

—Footsteps in the Rain. 1998. 368p. 23.95 o.p. (*0-312-19413-7*) St. Martin's Pr.

—Fragile Heritage. 1990. 464p. 19.95 o.p. (*0-312-04849-1*) St. Martin's Pr.

—The Last Reunion. l.t. ed. 1995. (Magna Large Print Ser.). 585p. 29.99 o.p. (*0-7505-0723-3*) Magna Large Print Bks. GBR. *Dist:* Ulverscroft Large Print Bks., Ltd., Ulverscroft Large Print Canada, Ltd.

—The Last Reunion. 1993. 480p. 23.95 o.p. (*0-312-09842-1*) St. Martin's Pr.

—Reckmire Marsh. l.t. ed. 1996. lib. bdg. 20.00 (*0-7838-1697-9*, Macmillan Reference USA) Gale Group.

—Reckmire Marsh. l.t. ed. 1996. (Magna Large Print Ser.). 608p. o.p. (*0-7505-0948-1*) Magna Large Print Bks. GBR. *Dist:* Ulverscroft Large Print Canada, Ltd.

—Reckmire Marsh. 1995. 432p. 24.95 o.p. (*0-312-13595-5*) St. Martin's Pr.

Inklings: A Novel. 2001. (Oxford Chronicles: Bk. 1). 240p. pap. 13.99 (*1-931232-84-9*) Xulon Pr., Inc.

Innes, Michael. The Ampersand Papers. 2000. 174p. pap. 9.95 (*1-84232-871-9*) House of Stratus, Inc. GBR. *Dist:* Midpoint Trade Bks., Inc.

—The Ampersand Papers. 1980. (Crime Monthly Ser.). 192p. pap. 3.95 o.p. (*0-14-005163-5*, Penguin Bks.) Viking Penguin.

—Appleby & Honeybath. l.t. ed. 2003. (Dales Large Print Ser.). 304p. pap. 21.99 (*1-84262-221-8*) Dales Large Print Bks. GBR. *Dist:* Ulverscroft Large Print Bks., Ltd., Ulverscroft Large Print Canada, Ltd.

—Appleby & Honeybath. 2000. 176p. pap. 9.95 (*1-84232-718-6*) House of Stratus, Inc. GBR. *Dist:* Midpoint Trade Bks., Inc.

—Appleby & Honeybath. 1984. 160p. pap. 3.95 o.p. (*0-14-007307-8*, Penguin Bks.) Viking Penguin.

—Appleby & the Ospreys. 2001. 170p. pap. 9.95 (*1-84232-719-4*) House of Stratus, Inc. GBR. *Dist:* Midpoint Trade Bks., Inc.

—Appleby & the Ospreys. 1988. 39.50 o.p. (*0-14-778337-2*) Penguin Group (USA) Inc.

—Appleby & the Ospreys. 1988. (Crime Ser.). 192p. pap. 3.95 o.p. (*0-14-011092-5*, Penguin Bks.) Viking Penguin.

—The Appleby File. 2001. 204p. pap. 9.95 (*1-84232-717-8*) House of Stratus, Inc. GBR. *Dist:* Midpoint Trade Bks., Inc.

—The Appleby File. l.t. ed. 1978. (Ulverscroft Large Print Ser.). 29.99 o.p. (*0-7089-0224-3*, Ulverscroft) Thorpe, F. A. Pubs. GBR. *Dist:* Ulverscroft Large Print Bks., Ltd., Ulverscroft Large Print Canada, Ltd.

—Appleby on Ararat: A Sir John Appleby Mystery. 1971. 254p. reprint ed. 69.95 (*0-8371-3377-7*, STAO, Greenwood Pr.) Greenwood Publishing Group, Inc.

—Appleby on Ararat: A Sir John Appleby Mystery. 1983. 288p. reprint ed. pap. 5.95 o.p. (*0-06-080648-6*, Perennial) HarperTrade.

—Appleby on Ararat: A Sir John Appleby Mystery. 2001. 192p. pap. 9.95 (*1-84232-715-1*) House of Stratus, Inc. GBR. *Dist:* Midpoint Trade Bks., Inc.

—Appleby Talks Again. 1977. (Short Story Index Reprint Ser.). 19.95 (*0-8369-3029-0*) Ayer Co. Pubs., Inc.

—Appleby Talks Again. 2001. 185p. pap. 9.95 (*1-84232-723-2*) House of Stratus, Inc. GBR. *Dist:* Midpoint Trade Bks., Inc.

—Appleby's Answer. 2000. 190p. pap. 9.95 (*1-84232-714-3*) House of Stratus, Inc. GBR. *Dist:* Midpoint Trade Bks., Inc.

—Appleby's Answer. 1985. (Crime Monthly Ser.). 160p. pap. 3.95 o.p. (*0-14-003981-3*, Penguin Bks.) Viking Penguin.

—Appleby's End. 1975. 224p. mass mkt. 1.25 o.s.i (*0-345-24409-5*) Ballantine Bks.

—Appleby's End. 1970. 211p. reprint ed. 69.95 (*0-8371-3376-9*, STAE, Greenwood Pr.) Greenwood Publishing Group, Inc.

—Appleby's End. 1983. 224p. pap. 2.95 o.p. (*0-06-080649-4*, P 649, Perennial) HarperTrade.

—Appleby's End. 2001. 218p. pap. 9.95 (*1-84232-716-X*) House of Stratus, Inc. GBR. *Dist:* Midpoint Trade Bks., Inc.

—Appleby's Other Story: A Sir John Appleby Mystery. 1975. 192p. mass mkt. 1.25 o.s.i (*0-345-24505-9*) Ballantine Bks.

—Appleby's Other Story: A Sir John Appleby Mystery. 2001. 179p. pap. 9.95 (*1-84232-720-8*) House of Stratus, Inc. GBR. *Dist:* Midpoint Trade Bks., Inc.

—Appleby's Other Story: A Sir John Appleby Mystery. 1993. (Classic Crime Ser.). 208p. pap. 6.00 o.p. (*0-14-014679-2*, Penguin Bks.) Penguin Group (USA) Inc.

—Appleby's Other Story: A Sir John Appleby Mystery. 1986. (Crime Ser.). 208p. pap. 3.95 o.p. (*0-14-004159-1*, Penguin Bks.) Viking Penguin.

—An Awkward Lie. 2001. 180p. pap. 9.95 (*1-84232-724-0*) House of Stratus, Inc. GBR. *Dist:* Midpoint Trade Bks., Inc.

—An Awkward Lie. 1991. (Classic Crime Ser.). 176p. reprint ed. pap. 4.95 o.p. (*0-14-012785-2*, Penguin Bks.) Penguin Group (USA) Inc.

—An Awkward Lie. 1974. (Crime Ser.). 176p. pap. 3.95 o.p. (*0-14-003664-4*, Penguin Bks.) Viking Penguin.

—The Bloody Wood. 1986. 224p. reprint ed. pap. 4.95 o.p. (*0-06-080811-X*, P 811, Perennial) HarperTrade.

—The Bloody Wood. 2001. 182p. pap. (*1-84232-725-9*) House of Stratus, Inc.

—The Bloody Wood. 1990. 192p. (C). reprint ed. lib. bdg. 19.95 o.p. (*0-8095-9028-X*) Millefleurs.

—Carson's Conspiracy: A Sir John Appleby Mystery Novel. 2001. 174p. pap. 9.95 (*1-84232-726-7*) House of Stratus, Inc. GBR. *Dist:* Midpoint Trade Bks., Inc.

—Carson's Conspiracy: A Sir John Appleby Mystery Novel. 1986. (Crime Monthly Ser.). 192p. pap. 3.95 o.p. (*0-14-008444-4*, Penguin Bks.) Viking Penguin.

—A Comedy of Terrors. 1989. pap. 4.95 o.p. (*0-14-012919-7*); 1987. 256p. mass mkt. 3.95 o.p. (*0-14-010090-3*, Penguin Bks.) Viking Penguin.

—A Connoisseur's Case. 2001. 180p. pap. 9.95 (*1-84232-729-1*) House of Stratus, Inc. GBR. *Dist:* Midpoint Trade Bks., Inc.

—A Connoisseur's Case. l.t. ed. 1980. (Ulverscroft Large Print Ser.). 29.99 o.p. (*0-7089-0421-1*, Ulverscroft) Thorpe, F. A. Pubs. GBR. *Dist:* Ulverscroft Large Print Bks., Ltd., Ulverscroft Large Print Canada, Ltd.

—The Crabtree Affair: A Sir John Appleby Mystery. 1984. 240p. reprint ed. pap. 5.95 o.p. (*0-06-080706-7*, Perennial) HarperTrade.

—The Daffodil Affair. 1976. (Crime Fiction Ser.). reprint ed. lib. bdg. 21.00 o.p. (*0-8240-2378-1*) Garland Publishing, Inc.

—The Daffodil Affair. 2001. 230p. pap. 9.95 (*1-84232-730-5*) House of Stratus, Inc. GBR. *Dist:* Midpoint Trade Bks., Inc.

—The Daffodil Affair. (Crime Ser.). 1990. 208p. pap. 5.00 o.p. (*0-14-011498-X*, Penguin Bks.); 1984. 208p. pap. 3.95 o.p. (*0-14-002202-3*, Penguin Bks.); 1983. Viking Penguin.

—Death at the Chase. 2000. 186p. pap. 9.95 (*1-84232-731-3*) House of Stratus, Inc. GBR. *Dist:* Midpoint Trade Bks., Inc.

—Death at the Chase. 1986. (Crime Monthly Ser.). 192p. pap. 3.95 o.p. (*0-14-003243-6*); reprint ed. pap. 6.00 o.p. (*0-14-017242-4*) Viking Penguin. (Penguin Bks.).

—Death at the President's Lodging. 2000. (Illus.). 254p. pap. 9.95 (*1-84232-732-1*) House of Stratus, Inc. GBR. *Dist:* Midpoint Trade Bks., Inc.

—Death at the President's Lodging. 1992. (Penguin Crime Fiction Ser.). 288p. pap. 6.95 o.s.i (*0-14-010555-7*, Penguin Bks.) Penguin Group (USA) Inc.

—Death at the President's Lodging. l.t. ed. 1989. (Ulverscroft Large Print Ser.). 448p. 29.99 o.p. (*0-7089-2012-8*, Ulverscroft) Thorpe, F. A. Pubs. GBR. *Dist:* Ulverscroft Large Print Bks., Ltd., Ulverscroft Large Print Canada, Ltd.

—Death at the President's Lodging. 1983. Viking Penguin.

—Death by Water: A Sir John Appleby Mystery. 1982. 224p. reprint ed. pap. 5.95 o.p. (*0-06-080574-9*, Perennial) HarperTrade.

—Death on a Quiet Day: A Sir John Appleby Mystery. 1983. 224p. pap. o.p. (*0-06-080677-X*, P677) HarperCollins Pubs.

—Death on a Quiet Day: A Sir John Appleby Mystery. 1991. 288p. reprint ed. pap. 8.00 o.p. (*0-06-092137-4*, Perennial) HarperTrade.

—Death on a Quiet Day: A Sir John Appleby Mystery. 1994. 2.99 o.p. (*0-517-12586-2*) Random Hse. Value Publishing.

—The Gay Phoenix. 2001. 184p. pap. 9.95 (*1-84232-735-6*) House of Stratus, Inc. GBR. *Dist:* Midpoint Trade Bks., Inc.

—The Gay Phoenix. l.t. ed. 1992. (Adventure Suspense Ser.). 279p. 29.99 o.p. (*0-7505-0048-4*) Magna Large Print Bks. GBR. *Dist:* Ulverscroft Large Print Bks., Ltd., Ulverscroft Large Print Canada, Ltd.

—The Gay Phoenix. 1981. 192p. pap. 3.50 o.p. (*0-14-004701-8*, Penguin Bks.) Viking Penguin.

—Hamlet, Revenge! 2001. 316p. pap. 9.95 (*1-84232-737-2*) House of Stratus, Inc. GBR. *Dist:* Midpoint Trade Bks., Inc.

—Hamlet, Revenge! l.t. ed. 1994. (Magna Large Print Ser.). 498p. 29.99 o.p. (*0-7505-0493-5*) Magna Large Print Bks. GBR. *Dist:* Ulverscroft Large Print Bks., Ltd., Ulverscroft Large Print Canada, Ltd.

—Hamlet, Revenge! (Classic Crime Ser.). 1990. 288p. pap. 6.00 o.p. (*0-14-011497-1*, Penguin Bks.); 1983.; 1976. 288p. pap. 3.50 o.p. (*0-14-001640-6*, Penguin Bks.) Viking Penguin.

—Hare Sitting Up: A Sir John Appleby Mystery. 1982. 256p. reprint ed. pap. 5.95 o.p. (*0-06-080590-0*, Perennial) HarperTrade.

—Hare Sitting Up: A Sir John Appleby Mystery. 2001. 182p. pap. (*1-84232-738-0*) House of Stratus, Inc.

—Hare Sitting Up: A Sir John Appleby Mystery. l.t. ed. 1992. (Magna Large Print Ser.). 280p. 29.99 (*0-7505-0276-2*) Magna Large Print Bks. GBR. *Dist:* Ulverscroft Large Print Bks., Ltd., Ulverscroft Large Print Canada, Ltd.

—Lament for a Maker: A Sir John Appleby Mystery. 1985. 256p. mass mkt. 9.95 o.p. (*0-553-06514-9*) Bantam Bks.

—Lament for a Maker: A Sir John Appleby Mystery. 1985. 288p. mass mkt. 3.50 o.p. (*0-06-080729-6*, P729); 1990. 272p. reprint ed. pap. 4.95 o.p. (*0-06-081041-6*) HarperTrade. (Perennial).

—Lament for a Maker: A Sir John Appleby Mystery. 2001. 286p. pap. 9.95 (*1-84232-741-0*) House of Stratus, Inc. GBR. *Dist:* Midpoint Trade Bks., Inc.

—Lament for a Maker: A Sir John Appleby Mystery. 1990. 272p. (C). reprint ed. lib. bdg. 19.95 o.p. (*0-8095-9029-8*) Millefleurs.

—The Long Farewell. l.t. ed. 1991. pap. 17.95 o.p. (*0-7927-0142-9*, C0012) BBC Audiobooks America.

—The Long Farewell. 1982. (Sir John Appleby Mystery Ser.). 240p. reprint ed. pap. 5.95 o.p. (*0-06-080575-7*, Perennial) HarperTrade.

—The Long Farewell. 2001. 190p. pap. 9.95 (*1-84232-742-9*) House of Stratus, Inc. GBR. *Dist:* Midpoint Trade Bks., Inc.

—A Night of Errors: A Sir John Appleby Mystery. 1989. 304p. reprint ed. pap. 3.95 o.p. (*0-06-080877-2*, P 877, Perennial) HarperTrade.

—A Night of Errors: A Sir John Appleby Mystery. 2000. 234p. pap. 9.95 (*1-84232-748-8*) House of Stratus, Inc. GBR. *Dist:* Midpoint Trade Bks., Inc.

—One Man Show. Barzun, Jacques & Taylor, W. H., eds. 1983. (Crime Fiction 1950-1975 Ser.). 192p. lib. bdg. 18.00 o.p. (0-8240-4994-2) Garland Publishing, Inc.

—One Man Show. 1983. 400p. pap. 5.95 o.p. (0-06-080672-9, Perennial) HarperTrade.

—Open House. 1982. pap. 2.95 o.p. (0-14-003663-6, Penguin Bks.) Viking Penguin.

—Operation Pax. 2001. 346p. pap. 9.95 (1-84232-751-8) House of Stratus, Inc. GBR. Dist: Midpoint Trade Bks., Inc.

—The Paper Thunderbolt. 1987. 352p. mass mkt. 3.95 o.p. (0-14-010089-X, Penguin Bks.) Viking Penguin.

—Picture of Guilt: A Sir John Appleby Mystery. 1988. 224p. reprint ed. pap. 3.95 o.p. (0-06-080878-0, P-878, Perennial) HarperTrade.

—The Secret Vanguard: A Sir John Appleby Mystery. 1982. 288p. reprint ed. pap. 4.95 o.p. (0-06-080584-6, Perennial) HarperTrade.

—The Secret Vanguard: A Sir John Appleby Mystery. l.t. ed. 1991. (Magna Large Print Ser.). 284p. o.p. (1-85057-864-8) Magna Large Print Bks. GBR. Dist: Ulverscroft Large Print Canada, Ltd.

—The Secret Vanguard: A Sir John Appleby Mystery. 2001. 190p. pap. 9.95 (1-84232-753-4) Midpoint Trade Bks., Inc.

—Seven Suspects. 1984. (Crime Ser.). 288p. pap. 3.95 o.p. (0-14-006886-4, Penguin Bks.) Viking Penguin.

—Sheiks & Adders: A Sir John Appleby Mystery Novel. 1983. 160p. pap. 2.95 o.p. (0-14-006520-2, Penguin Bks.) Viking Penguin.

—Silence Observed: A Sir John Appleby Mystery. 1988. 224p. reprint ed. pap. 3.95 o.p. (0-06-080879-9, P-879, Perennial) HarperTrade.

—There Came Both Mist & Snow. 2001. 198p. pap. 9.95 (1-84232-757-7) House of Stratus, Inc. GBR. Dist: Midpoint Trade Bks., Inc.

—There Came Both Mist & Snow. l.t. ed. 1991. (Magna Large Print Ser.). 302p. o.p. (1-85057-862-1) Magna Large Print Bks. GBR. Dist: Ulverscroft Large Print Canada, Ltd.

Ireland, Perrin. Ana Imagined. 2000. vii, 195p. 22.95 (1-55597-300-0) Graywolf Pr.

Irving, Washington. Bracebridge Hall. Smith, Herbert F., ed. 1977. (Critical Editions Program Ser.). lib. bdg. 26.00 o.p. (0-8057-8506-X, Macmillan Reference USA) Gale Group.

—Bracebridge Hall. reprint ed. 24.00 o.p. (0-404-03508-6) AMS Pr., Inc.

—Bracebridge Hall. (Illus.). 320p. reprint ed. 12.00 o.p. (0-912882-35-2) Sleepy Hollow Pr.

—Bracebridge Hall, Or the Humorists. 1992. (BCL1-PS American Literature Ser.). 561p. reprint ed. lib. bdg. 99.00 (0-7812-6753-6) Reprint Services Corp.

—Bracebridge Hall, Or the Humorists. 1902. reprint ed. 10.00 (0-403-00239-7) Scholarly Pr., Inc.

—Bracebridge Hall, Tales of a Traveller & the Alhambra. Myers, Andrew B., ed. 1991. (Library of America: Vol. 52). 1104p. 35.00 (0-940450-59-3) Library of America, The.

—Hearthside Tales: Selections from the Sketch Book, Bracebridge Hall & Tales of a Traveller. Gado, Frank, ed. 1995. (Signature Ser.). 280p. (C). pap. 8.95 (0-912756-10-1) Union College Pr.

—Hearthside Tales: Selections from the Sketch Book, Bracebridge Hall & Tales of a Traveller. 1983. (Signature Ser.). 215p. (C). 19.75 o.p. (0-912756-13-6) Union College Pr.

—The Sketch Book of Geoffrey Crayon, Vol. 19. 1973. (Works of Washington Irving Ser.). 532 p. (0-404-03529-9) AMS Pr., Inc.

—The Sketch Book of Geoffrey Crayon. reprint ed. lib. bdg. 48.00 (0-7426-1034-9); 2001. (Illus.). pap. text 28.00 (0-7426-6034-6) Classic Bks.

—The Sketch Book of Geoffrey Crayon. 1961. (Signet Classics). 384p. mass mkt. 5.95 (0-451-52495-0); mass mkt. 0.60 o.p. (0-451-50101-2); mass mkt. 0.75 o.p. (0-451-50282-5); mass mkt. 0.95 o.p. (0-451-50599-9); mass mkt. 1.50 o.p. (0-451-51094-1); mass mkt. 1.75 o.p. (0-451-51263-4); mass mkt. 2.95 o.p. (0-451-51614-1) NAL. (Signet Classics).

—The Sketch Book of Geoffrey Crayon. 1992. (BCL1-PS American Literature Ser.). 487p. reprint ed. lib. bdg. 99.00 (0-7812-6755-2) Reprint Services Corp.

—The Sketch Book of Geoffrey Crayon. 1981. (Illus.). 512p. reprint ed. 23.95 (0-912882-47-6) Sleepy Hollow Pr.

—The Sketch Book of Geoffrey Crayon. Bradbury, Malcolm & Bigsby, Christopher, eds. 1993. 400p. pap. 6.95 (0-460-87151-X, Everyman's Classic Library in Paperback) Tuttle Publishing.

—The Sketch Book of Geoffrey Crayon. 1988. 368p. pap. 7.95 o.p. (0-14-039032-4, Penguin Classics) Viking Penguin.

—The Sketch Book of Geoffrey Crayon. 24.95 o.p. (0-8488-0539-9); 1998. lib. bdg. 26.95 (1-56723-063-6) Yestermorrow, Inc.

Irving, Washington, et al. The Sketch Book of Geoffrey Crayon. 1981. xii, 465p. (0-912882-51-4) Sleepy Hollow Pr.

Irwin, Robert. Exquisite Corpse. 1999. pap. (0-679-77916-7, Vintage) Knopf Publishing Group.

—Exquisite Corpse. 2003. 235p. 14.95 (1-58567-386-2) Overlook Pr., The.

Isherwood, Christopher. The Memorial: Portrait of a Family. 1988. (Michael di Capua Bks.). 288p. pap. 8.95 o.s.i (0-374-52067-4) Farrar, Straus & Giroux.

—The Memorial: Portrait of a Family. 294p. reprint ed. lib. bdg. 32.00 (0-8371-3544-3) Irvington Pubs.

—The Memorial: Portrait of a Family. 1977. pap. 2.25 o.p. (0-380-01814-4, 53983-7, Avon Bks.) Morrow/Avon.

—The Memorial: Portrait of a Family. 1999. 296p. reprint ed. pap. 15.95 (0-8166-3369-X) Univ. of Minnesota Pr.

Isherwood, Christopher & Upward, Edward. The Mortmere Stories. 1995. (Illus.). 206p. pap. 15.95 (1-870612-69-8) Enitharmon Pr. GBR. Dist: Dufour Editions, Inc.

Ishiguro, Kazuo. The Remains of the Day. 1993. pap. 11.00 (0-394-25134-2); 1990. 256p. pap. 13.00 (0-679-73172-5) Knopf Publishing Group. (Vintage).

—The Remains of the Day. 1989. 22.00 o.s.i (0-394-57343-9) Knopf, Alfred A. Inc.

—The Remains of the Day. l.t. ed. 1990. (Charnwood Large Print Ser.). 29.99 o.p. (0-7089-8564-5, Ulverscroft) Thorpe, F. A. Pubs. GBR. Dist: Ulverscroft Large Print Bks., Ltd., Ulverscroft Large Print Canada, Ltd.

—The Remains of the Day. 1990. 19.05 (0-606-14304-1) Turtleback Bks.

Iunes, Michael. Silence Observed. 1975. 160p. mass mkt. 1.25 o.s.i (0-345-24627-6) Ballantine Bks.

Ivory, Judith. Untie My Heart. 2002. 384p. mass mkt. 6.99 (0-380-81297-5, Avon Bks.) Morrow/Avon.

Jack, Colin. The Strange Case of Mrs. Hudson's Cat: And Other Science Mysteries Solved by Sherlock Holmes. 1997. 272p. (C). text 23.00 o.p. (0-201-46139-0) Perseus Bks. Group.

Jackson, Melanie N. Manon. 2000. 320p. mass mkt. 4.99 (0-8439-4737-3, Leisure Bks.) Dorchester Publishing Co., Inc.

Jackson, Mick. Five Boys: A Novel. 2001. 239p. (0-571-21401-0); 248p. pap. (0-571-20613-1) Faber & Faber, Inc.

—Five Boys: A Novel. 2002. 288p. 24.95 (0-06-001394-X, Morrow, William & Co.) Morrow/Avon.

—The Underground Man. abr. ed. 2001. audio (0-333-73749-0) Macmillan U.K. GBR. Dist: Macmillan Publishing Co., Inc.

—The Underground Man. unabr. ed. 1997. 272p. 22.00 (0-688-15449-2, Morrow, William & Co.) Morrow/Avon.

—The Underground Man. 1998. 272p. pap. 12.95 o.s.i (0-14-027437-5) Penguin Group (USA) Inc.

Jacobs, Anna. Mistress of Marymoor. 2002. 256p. 26.99 (0-7278-5862-9); 28.99 (0-7278-7234-6) Severn Hse. Pubs., Ltd.

Jacobs, William W. Captains All. 1977. (Short Story Index Reprint Ser.). 19.95 (0-8369-3051-7) Ayer Co. Pubs., Inc.

—Lady of the Barge. 1977. (Short Story Index Reprint Ser.). 23.95 (0-8369-3203-X) Ayer Co. Pubs., Inc.

—Light Freights. 1977. (Short Story Index Reprint Ser.). 26.95 (0-8369-3407-5) Ayer Co. Pubs., Inc.

—Many Cargoes. 1977. (Short Story Index Reprint Ser.). 22.95 (0-8369-3262-5) Ayer Co. Pubs., Inc.

—More Cargoes. 1977. (Short Story Index Reprint Ser.). 19.95 (0-8369-3005-3) Ayer Co. Pubs., Inc.

Jaffe, Michele. The Water Nymph. 2000. 336p. 22.95 o.s.i (0-671-02741-7, Atria); 2001. 432p. reprint ed. pap. 7.50 (0-671-02742-5, Pocket Star) Simon & Schuster.

Jagger, Brenda. Days of Grace. 1984. 480p. 15.95 o.p. (0-688-02728-8, Morrow, William & Co.) Morrow/Avon.

—Distant Choices. 1987. 488p. 19.95 o.p. (0-688-07102-3, Morrow, William & Co.) Morrow/Avon.

—A Song Twice Over. 1987. 544p. mass mkt. 4.50 o.s.i (0-449-21040-5, Fawcett) Ballantine Bks.

—A Song Twice Over. 1986. 504p. 18.95 o.p. (0-688-06169-9, Morrow, William & Co.) Morrow/Avon.

James, Bill. Kill Me. 2001. 272p. pap. 7.95 (0-393-32166-5) Norton, W. W. & Co., Inc.

—Split. 2002. 221p. 29.95 (1-899344-72-1); pap. 14.95 (1-899344-73-X) Do-Not Pr., The GBR. Dist: Dufour Editions, Inc.

James, Bill, pseud. Astride a Grave. 1996. (Detective Colin Harpur Novel Ser.). 208p. reprint ed. 21.00 o.p. (0-88150-361-4, Foul Play) Norton, W. W. & Co., Inc.

—Club. 1995. (Detective Colin Harpur Novel Ser.). 224p. 20.00 o.p. (0-88150-331-2, Foul Play) Norton, W. W. & Co., Inc.

—Come Clean. 1992. (Detective Colin Harpur Novel Ser.). 256p. 20.00 (0-88150-243-X, Foul Play) Norton, W. W. & Co., Inc.

—The Detective Is Dead. 2001. (Harpur & Iles Ser.). 215p. 22.95 (0-393-05019-X) Norton, W. W. & Co., Inc.

—Eton Crop: A Harpur & Iles Mystery. (Harpur & Iles Ser.). 2000. 288p. pap. 7.95 (0-393-32098-7, Norton Paperbacks); 1999. 284p. 22.95 (0-393-04761-X) Norton, W. W. & Co., Inc.

—Gospel. l.t. ed. 1997. (G. K. Hall Core Ser.). 384p. lib. bdg. 25.95 (0-7838-8236-X, Macmillan Reference USA) Gale Group.

—Gospel. l.t. ed. (Harpur & Iles Ser.). 1998. 208p. pap. 10.00 (0-393-31781-1); 1997. 206p. 22.95 (0-88150-383-5) Norton, W. W. & Co., Inc.

—Halo Parade: A Harpur & Iles Mystery. (Harpur & Iles Ser.). 176p. 1998. pap. 10.00 (0-393-31831-1); 1991. reprint ed. 17.95 o.p. (0-88150-204-9) Norton, W. W. & Co., Inc. (Foul Play).

—In Good Hands. 2000. (Harpur & Iles Ser.). 214p. 22.95 (0-393-05005-X) Norton, W. W. & Co., Inc.

—Kill Me. (Harpur & Iles Ser.). 2001. (Illus.). 352p. pap. 15.95 (0-393-32165-7); 2000. 267p. 22.95 (0-393-04920-5) Norton, W. W. & Co., Inc.

—The Lolita Man. (Harpur & Iles Ser.). 1998. 160p. pap. 10.00 (0-393-31782-X); 1991. 158p. 17.95 (0-88150-198-0, Foul Play) Norton, W. W. & Co., Inc.

—Lovely Mover: A Harpur & Iles Mystery. (Harpur & Iles Ser.). 2000. 272p. pap. 7.95 (0-393-32034-0); 1999. 264p. 23.00 o.p. (0-393-04763-6, Foul Play) Norton, W. W. & Co., Inc.

—Lovely Mover: A Harpur & Iles Mystery. l.t. ed. 1998. (Mystery Ser.). 343p. 26.95 (0-7862-1680-8) Thorndike Pr.

—Naked at the Window: A Harpur & Iles Mystery. 2002. 224p. 23.95 (0-393-05198-6) Norton, W. W. & Co., Inc.

—Panicking Ralph. 2002. pap. 8.95 (0-393-32306-4); 2001. 288p. 24.95 (0-393-04762-8) Norton, W. W. & Co., Inc.

—Pay Days: A Harpur & Iles Mystery. 2001. 256p. 24.00 (0-393-04214-6) Norton, W. W. & Co., Inc.

—Protection. 1992. (Detective Colin Harpur Novel Ser.). 188p. 18.95 o.p. (0-88150-231-6) Norton, W. W. & Co., Inc.

—Roses, Roses: A Harpur & Iles Mystery. (Harpur & Iles Ser.). 1999. 208p. pap. 7.95 (0-393-31925-3); 1998. 216p. 23.00 o.p. (0-393-04637-0) Norton, W. W. & Co., Inc.

—Take. 1994. (Harpur & Iles Ser.). 240p. reprint ed. 20.00 (0-88150-294-4, Foul Play) Norton, W. W. & Co., Inc.

—Top Banana: A Harpur & Iles Mystery. l.t. ed. 1999. (Core Ser.). 306p. 27.95 (0-7838-8717-5, Macmillan Reference USA) Gale Group.

—Top Banana: A Harpur & Iles Mystery. (Harpur & Iles Ser.). 2000. 288p. pap. 7.95 (0-393-31969-5, Norton Paperbacks); 1999. 284p. 23.00 o.p. (0-393-04718-0) Norton, W. W. & Co., Inc.

—You'd Better Believe It. 1991. (Detective Chief Superintendent Colin Harper Novels / By Bill Ser.). 158p. pap. 4.95 (0-88150-197-2, Foul Play) Norton, W. W. & Co., Inc.

—You'd Better Believe It. 1985. 192p. pap. 12.95 o.p. (0-312-89683-2) St. Martin's Pr.

James, Dean. Faked to Death: A Simon Kirby-Jones Mystery. 2003. 288p. 22.00 (1-57566-887-4) Kensington Publishing Corp.

James, Henry. The Awkward Age. 1971. (Novels & Tales of Henry James Ser.: Vol. 9). xxiii, 544p. reprint ed. lib. bdg. 45.00 (0-678-02809-5) Kelley, Augustus M. Pubs.

—The Golden Bowl. (YA). reprint ed. pap. 99.00 (1-4047-3440-6) Classic Textbooks.

—The Golden Bowl. 2000. 432p. (J). pap. 12.95 (0-7868-8608-0) Talk Miramax Bks.

—The Portrait of a Lady. unabr. ed. 1999. audio 53.95; Pt. 1. 1989. audio 53.95 (1-55685-131-6) Audio Bk. Contractors, Inc.

—The Portrait of a Lady. 1983. (Bantam Classics Ser.). 560p. mass mkt. 4.95 (0-553-21127-7, Bantam Classics) Bantam Bks.

—The Portrait of a Lady. unabr. ed. 1995. audio 99.95 (0-7861-0899-1, 1675) Blackstone Audio Bks., Inc.

—The Portrait of a Lady. unabr. ed. 1998. (Bookcassette Classic Collection). 22p. audio 66.25 (1-56740-622-X, 1525, Unabridged Library Editions); audio 22.95 (1-56740-093-0, 1524, Bookcassette) Brilliance Audio.

—The Portrait of a Lady. 1990. reprint ed. lib. bdg. 21.95 (0-89966-651-5) Buccaneer Bks., Inc.

—The Portrait of a Lady. 1998. (Bloom's Notes Ser.). pap. 4.95 (0-7910-4567-6) Chelsea Hse. Pubs.

—The Portrait of a Lady. 1908. 495p. (YA). reprint ed. pap. text 28.00 (1-4047-3379-5) Classic Textbooks.

—The Portrait of a Lady. abr. ed. 1995. (Classics Ser.). audio 16.95 (1-56511-126-5) HighBridge Co.

—The Portrait of a Lady. 1977. (Novels & Tales of Henry James Ser.: Vol. 3). reprint ed. Vol. 1. 437p. lib. bdg. 37.50 (0-678-02803-6); Vol. 2. xx, 427p. lib. bdg. 37.50 (0-678-02804-4) Kelley, Augustus M. Pubs.

—The Portrait of a Lady. 1992. 640p. pap. 12.50 o.s.i (0-679-73635-2, Vintage); 1991. 672p. 18.95 (0-679-40562-3, Everyman's Library) Knopf Publishing Group.

—The Portrait of a Lady. 1998. (Cloth Bound Pocket Ser.). 240p. 7.95 (3-89508-454-9, 520035) Konemann.

—The Portrait of a Lady. 1966. (Modern Library College Editions Ser.). 591p. (C). pap. 11.25 (0-07-553637-4, T47, McGraw-Hill Humanities, Social Sciences & World Languages) McGraw-Hill Higher Education.

—The Portrait of a Lady. 1996. 560p. mass mkt. 5.99 o.s.i (0-451-19130-7); 1995. 560p. mass mkt. 5.95 (0-451-52597-3); 1963. mass mkt. 2.25 o.p. (0-451-51174-3); 1963. mass mkt. 2.95 o.p. (0-451-51362-2); 1963. mass mkt. 3.50 o.p. (0-451-51605-2); 1963. mass mkt. 1.75 o.p. (0-451-51000-3); 1963. 560p. mass mkt. 4.95 o.p. (0-451-52288-5); 1963. mass mkt. 1.25 o.p. (0-451-50738-X); 1963. mass mkt. 0.95 o.p. (0-451-50358-9); 1963. mass mkt. 0.75 o.p. (0-451-50195-0) NAL. (Signet Classics).

—The Portrait of a Lady. abr. ed. 1996. audio 22.98 (962-634-600-0, NA410014); audio compact disk 26.98 (962-634-100-9, NA410012) Naxos of America, Inc. (Naxos AudioBooks).

—The Portrait of a Lady. 1996. 19.95 o.p. (0-7871-0353-5, NewStar Pr.) NewStar Media, Inc.

—The Portrait of a Lady. Bamberg, Robert D., ed. 1975. (Critical Editions Ser.). (C). pap. o.p. (0-393-09259-3) Norton, W. W. & Co., Inc.

—The Portrait of a Lady. 1999. 704p. 17.00 (0-19-210038-6) Oxford Univ. Pr., Inc.

—The Portrait of a Lady. Bradbury, Nicola, ed. & intro. by. 1998. (Oxford World's Classics Ser.). 672p. pap. 8.95 (0-19-283369-3) Oxford Univ. Pr., Inc.

—The Portrait of a Lady. 1982. (Oxford World's Classics Ser.). pap. 4.95 o.p. (0-19-281514-8) Oxford Univ. Pr., Inc.

—The Portrait of a Lady. Bradbury, Nicola, ed. & intro. by. 2nd rev. ed. 1995. (Oxford World's Classics Ser.). 668p. pap. 6.95 o.p. (0-19-282362-0) Oxford Univ. Pr., Inc.

—The Portrait of a Lady. 1975. pap. 3.95 o.p. (0-14-001921-9) Penguin Group (USA) Inc.

—The Portrait of a Lady. Dixson, Robert James, ed. rev. ed. 1987. (American Classics: Bk. 7). (gr. 9 up). audio 72.75 o.p. (0-13-024746-4, 58229) Prentice Hall, ESL Dept.

—The Portrait of a Lady. 2002. (Modern Library Classics). 640p. pap. 9.95 (0-375-75919-0, Modern Library) Random House Adult Trade Publishing Group.

—The Portrait of a Lady. 2nd ed. 1983. 9.95 o.s.i (0-394-60432-6) Random Hse., Inc.

—The Portrait of a Lady. 1992. (Notable American Authors Ser.). reprint ed. lib. bdg. 75.00 (0-7812-3379-8) Reprint Services Corp.

—The Portrait of a Lady. l.t. ed. 1997. (Perennial Bestsellers Ser.). 465p. lib. bdg. 25.95 (0-7838-8266-1);Vol. II. 469p. lib. bdg. 25.95 (0-7838-8268-8) Thorndike Pr.

—The Portrait of a Lady. Watson, Priscilla L., ed. 1995. 640p. pap. 4.95 (0-460-87588-4, Everyman's Classic Library in Paperback) Tuttle Publishing.

—The Portrait of a Lady. 2003. 656p. pap. 10.00 (0-14-143963-7, Penguin Classics); 1996. 610p. 17.95 o.s.i (0-670-87139-7) Viking Penguin.

—The Portrait of a Lady. Moore, Geoffrey, ed. & intro. by. 1984. (Penguin Classics Ser.). 688p. 9.95 (0-14-043223-X) Viking Penguin.

—The Portrait of a Lady. abr. ed. 1996. audio 23.95 o.s.i (0-14-086287-0, Penguin AudioBooks) Viking Penguin.

—The Portrait of a Lady. 1997. (Classics Ser.). 528p. pap. 3.95 (1-85326-177-7, 1777WW) Wordsworth Editions, Ltd. GBR. Dist: Combined Publishing.

—The Portrait of a Lady. 1998. E-Book 9.40 (0-585-35135-X) netLibrary, Inc.

—The Portrait of a Lady: An Authoritative Text, Henry James & the Novel, Reviews & Criticism. Bamberg, Robert D., ed. 2nd ed. 1995. (Critical Editions Ser.). (C). pap. text 13.00 (0-393-96646-1) Norton, W. W. & Co., Inc.

—The Princess Casamassima. 1991. (Everyman's Library). 640p. 20.00 (0-679-40672-7) Random Hse., Inc.

—The Sacred Fount. 2000. 252p. E-Book 9.95 (0-594-05443-5) 1873 Pr.

—The Sacred Fount. 2000. audio 35.95 (1-55685-605-9) Audio Bk. Contractors, Inc.

—The Sacred Fount. 1979. reprint ed. pap. 4.95 o.p. (0-394-17081-4, B418, Grove Pr.) Grove/Atlantic, Inc.

—The Sacred Fount. 1995. (Revived Modern Classic Ser.: Vol. 790). 236p. pap. 11.95 (0-8112-1279-3, NDP790) New Directions Publishing Corp.

—The Sacred Fount. 1992. (Notable American Authors Ser.). reprint ed. lib. bdg. 75.00 (0-7812-3428-X) Reprint Services Corp.

—The Sacred Fount. Lyon, John, ed. & intro. by. 1995. (Penguin Classics Ser.). 240p. pap. 10.95 o.p. (*0-14-043350-3*, Penguin Classics) Viking Penguin.
—The Spoils of Poynton. (YA). reprint ed. pap. 75.00 (*1-4047-3413-9*); 1897. 323p. pap. text 28.00 (*1-4047-6928-5*) Classic Textbooks.
—The Spoils of Poynton. Richards, Bernard, ed. 2000. (Oxford World's Classics Ser.). 256p. pap. 10.95 (*0-19-283779-6*) Oxford Univ. Pr., Inc.
—The Turn of the Screw. 1994. (Case Studies in Contemporary Criticism: Vol. 1). 313p. pap. text 8.50 (*0-312-08083-2*) Bedford/Saint Martin's.
—The Turn of the Screw. 1991. (Dover Thrift Editions Ser.). 96p. (J). pap. 1.50 (*0-486-26684-2*) Dover Pubns., Inc.
—The Turn of the Screw. Kimbrough, Robert, ed. 1966. (Critical Editions Ser.). (C). pap. text o.p. (*0-393-09669-6*) Norton, W. W. & Co., Inc.
—The Turn of the Screw. Lloyd-Smith, Alan, ed. 1993. 139p. pap. 7.95 (*0-460-87299-0*, Everyman's Classic Library in Paperback) Tuttle Publishing.
—The Turn of the Screw, Beidler, Peter G., ed. 1994. (Case Studies in Contemporary Criticism: Vol. 1). 313p. 55.00 (*0-312-12260-8*) Palgrave Macmillan.
—The Turn of the Screw & In the Cage. 2001. (Modern Library Classics). 256p. pap. 5.95 (*0-375-75740-6*, Modern Library) Random House Adult Trade Publishing Group.
—The Turn of the Screw & The Aspern Papers. 1998. (Classics Library). 224p. pap. 3.95 (*1-85326-069-X*, 069XWW) Wordsworth Editions, Ltd. GBR. *Dist:* Combined Publishing.
—The Turn of the Screw & The Lesson of the Master. 1996. (Literary Classics). 211p. pap. 10.00 (*1-57392-099-1*) Prometheus Bks., Pubs.
—The Wings of the Dove. abr. ed. 1992. audio 15.95 o.p. (*0-88646-333-5*, 7333) Durkin Hayes Publishing Ltd.
—The Wings of the Dove. 1997. (Illus.). 528p. (J). pap. 12.95 (*0-7868-8251-4*) Hyperion Pr.
—The Wings of the Dove. 1997. (Everyman's Library). 544p. 20.00 (*0-679-45512-4*) Knopf, Alfred A. Inc.
—The Wings of the Dove. 2000. (Cloth Bound Pocket Ser.). 7.95 (*3-8290-5387-8*, 522085) Konemann.
—The Wings of the Dove. (Signet Classics). 1999. 512p. mass mkt. 6.95 (*0-451-52728-3*, Signet Classics); 1964. pap. 4.50 o.p. (*0-452-00858-1*, Meridian Bks.); 1964. mass mkt. 3.95 o.p. (*0-451-51872-1*, CE1872, Signet Classics) NAL.
—The Wings of the Dove. Crowley, Joseph Donald & Hocks, Richard A., eds. 1978. (Critical Editions Ser.). (C). o.p. (*0-393-04478-5*); 583p. pap. text 12.00 (*0-393-09088-4*) Norton, W. W. & Co., Inc.
—The Wings of the Dove. Brooks, Peter, ed. & intro. by. 1998. (Oxford World's Classics Ser.). 592p. pap. 8.95 (*0-19-283861-X*) Oxford Univ. Pr., Inc.
—The Wings of the Dove. Brooks, Peter, ed. 1985. (Oxford World's Classics Ser.). 584p. pap. 6.95 o.p. (*0-19-281631-4*) Oxford Univ. Pr., Inc.
—The Wings of the Dove. 1974. pap. 3.95 o.p. (*0-14-002320-8*) Penguin Group (USA) Inc.
—The Wings of the Dove. 1993. (Modern Library Ser.). 712p. 19.00 o.s.i (*0-679-60067-1*) Random Hse., Inc.
—The Wings of the Dove. 1997. (Everyman Paperback Classics Ser.). 464p. pap. 5.95 (*0-460-87617-1*, Everyman's Classic Library in Paperback) Tuttle Publishing.
—The Wings of the Dove. Bayley, John, ed. & intro. by. 1986. (Penguin Classics Ser.). 528p. pap. 9.95 (*0-14-043263-9*, Penguin Classics) Viking Penguin.
—The Wings of the Dove. abr. ed. 1997. (Classic Fiction Ser.). audio 17.98 o.p. (*962-634-612-4*, NA311214); audio compact disk 19.98 o.p. (*962-634-112-2*, NA311212) Naxos of America, Inc. (Naxos AudioBooks).
—The Wings of the Dove, Set. unabr. ed. 1993. audio 77.95 (*1-55685-286-X*) Audio Bk. Contractors, Inc.
—The Wings of the Dove. unabr. ed. 1999. audio 89.95 (*0-7861-1525-4*, 2375) Blackstone Audio Bks., Inc.
—The Wings of the Dove, Vol. 2. 1977. (Novels & Tales of Henry James Ser.: Vol. 20). 404p. reprint ed. lib. bdg. 37.50 (*0-678-02820-6*) Kelley, Augustus M. Pubs.
—The Wings of the Dove. (BCL1-PS American Literature Ser.). reprint ed. 1993. 329p. lib. bdg. 89.00 (*0-7812-6978-4*); 1992. lib. bdg. 75.00 (*0-7812-3429-8*) Reprint Services Corp.
James, Henry & Curtis, Anthony. The Turn of the Screw & The Aspern Papers. 2003. 272p. pap. 6.00 (*0-14-143990-4*, Penguin Classics) Viking Penguin.
James, Margaret. The Snake Stone. l.t. ed. 1994. (Dales Large Print Ser.). 488p. pap. 19.99 o.p. (*1-85389-516-4*) Dales Large Print Bks. GBR. *Dist:* Ulverscroft Large Print Bks., Ltd., Ulverscroft Large Print Canada, Ltd.
—The Snake Stone. 1994. 304p. 20.00 (*0-7278-4566-7*) Severn Hse. Pubs., Ltd.
James, P. D. The Black Tower. unabr. ed. 1993. audio 72.00 (*0-7366-2509-7*, 3265) Books on Tape, Inc.
—The Black Tower. (Paperback Ser.). 1990. 464p. 13.95 o.p. (*0-8161-4983-6*); 1981. 14.95 o.p. (*0-8161-6789-3*) Gale Group. (Macmillan Reference USA).
—The Black Tower. 2001. 352p. pap. 12.00 (*0-7432-1961-9*, Touchstone) Simon & Schuster.
—The Black Tower. 1990. audio 69.95 o.p. (*0-8161-9622-2*) Thorndike Pr.
—The Black Tower. 1988. 288p. mass mkt. 6.99 o.p. (*0-446-31502-8*) Warner Bks., Inc.
—A Certain Justice: An Adam Dalgliesh Mystery. 2003. 448p. pap. 13.95 (*0-345-42532-4*); 1999. 7.99 (*0-345-91605-0*); 1998. mass mkt. 5.99 (*0-345-42533-2*); 1998. 448p. mass mkt. 7.99 (*0-345-43057-3*); 1998. mass mkt. 6.99 (*0-345-42564-2*, Del Rey) Ballantine Bks.
—A Certain Justice: An Adam Dalgliesh Mystery. unabr. ed. 1998. audio 104.00 (*0-7366-4067-3*, 4578) Books on Tape, Inc.
—A Certain Justice: An Adam Dalgliesh Mystery. unabr. ed. 2000. audio 79.95 (*0-7540-0079-6*, CAB 1502) Chivers Audio Bks. GBR. *Dist:* BBC Audiobooks America.
—A Certain Justice: An Adam Dalgliesh Mystery. 1997. 390p. (*0-571-19164-9*) Faber & Faber, Inc.
—A Certain Justice: An Adam Dalgliesh Mystery. l.t. ed. pap. 25.00 o.p. (*0-7838-8251-3*, Macmillan Reference USA) Gale Group.
—A Certain Justice: An Adam Dalgliesh Mystery. 1997. 364p. 25.00 o.s.i (*0-375-40109-1*) Knopf, Alfred A. Inc.
—A Certain Justice: An Adam Dalgliesh Mystery. unabr. ed. 1997. audio 44.95 (*0-679-46085-3*, 115588, RH Audio) Random Hse. Audio Publishing Group.
—A Certain Justice: An Adam Dalgliesh Mystery. l.t. ed. 1997. 640p. pap. 25.00 (*0-679-77452-1*) Random Hse. Large Print.
—A Certain Justice: An Adam Dalgliesh Mystery. 1999. (Remainder Ser.). 5.99 o.s.i (*0-517-46309-1*) Random Hse. Value Publishing.
—A Certain Justice: An Adam Dalgliesh Mystery. unabr. ed. 1998. (Inspector Dalgliesh Mystery Ser.: Vol. 10). audio 97.00 (*0-7887-1966-1*, 95354E7) Recorded Bks., LLC.
—A Certain Justice: An Adam Dalgliesh Mystery. 2003. E-Book 8.99 (*0-7953-2798-6*) RosettaBooks.
—The Children of Men. 1992. 239p. (*0-571-16741-1*) Faber & Faber Ltd.
—The Children of Men. 1994. 368p. mass mkt. 6.99 (*0-446-36462-2*); 2002. 320p. reprint ed. pap. 13.95 (*0-446-67920-8*) Warner Bks., Inc.
—Cover Her Face. unabr. ed. 1993. audio 56.00 (*0-7366-2330-2*, 3110) Books on Tape, Inc.
—Cover Her Face. unabr. ed. 2000. audio 49.95 (*0-7451-6065-4*, CAB 138) Chivers Audio Bks. GBR. *Dist:* BBC Audiobooks America.
—Cover Her Face. 1979. (General Ser.). lib. bdg. 12.95 o.p. (*0-8161-6793-1*, Macmillan Reference USA) Gale Group.
—Cover Her Face. Barzun, Jacques & Taylor, W. H., eds. 1982. (Crime Fiction 1950-1975 Ser.). 254p. lib. bdg. 18.00 o.p. (*0-8240-4983-7*) Garland Publishing, Inc.
—Cover Her Face. unabr. ed. 1992. (Inspector Dalgliesh Mystery Ser.: Vol. 1). audio 51.00 (*1-55690-676-5*, 92329E7) Recorded Bks., LLC.
—Cover Her Face. 2001. 256p. pap. 12.00 (*0-7432-1957-0*, Touchstone) Simon & Schuster.
—Cover Her Face. 1990. 18.05 (*0-606-22453-X*) Turtleback Bks.
—Cover Her Face. 1989. 256p. mass mkt. 6.99 o.p. (*0-446-31221-5*); 1987. mass mkt. 3.50 (*0-446-31437-4*) Warner Bks., Inc.
—Death in Holy Orders. l.t. ed. 2001. 640p. 25.00 (*0-375-43117-9*) Random Hse. Large Print.
—Death of An Expert Witness. 1978. lib. bdg. 13.95 o.p. (*0-8161-6600-5*, Macmillan Reference USA) Gale Group.
—Death of An Expert Witness. 2003. 496p. mass mkt. (*0-7704-2915-7*) Seal Bks. CAN. *Dist:* Random Hse. of Canada, Ltd.
—Death of An Expert Witness. 2001. 368p. pap. 12.00 (*0-7432-1962-7*, Touchstone) Simon & Schuster.
—Death of An Expert Witness. 1988. 352p. mass mkt. 6.99 o.p. (*0-446-31472-2*) Warner Bks., Inc.
—Death of an Expert Witness. l.t. ed. 1992. (General Ser.). 443p. pap. 18.95 (*0-8161-5575-5*, Macmillan Reference USA) Gale Group.
—Death of An Expert Witness. unabr. ed. 1993. audio 72.00 (*0-7366-2569-0*, 3318) Books on Tape, Inc.
—Death of An Expert Witness. unabr. ed. 2000. audio 59.95 (*0-7451-6066-2*, CAB 311) Chivers Audio Bks. GBR. *Dist:* BBC Audiobooks America.
—Death of An Expert Witness. unabr. ed. 1993. (Inspector Dalgliesh Mystery Ser.: Vol. 6). audio 70.00 (*1-55690-884-9*, 93326E7) Recorded Bks., LLC.
—Devices & Desires. unabr. collector's ed. 1990. audio 96.00 (*0-7366-1819-8*, 2655) Books on Tape, Inc.
—Devices & Desires. l.t. ed. 1990. (General Ser.). 608p. pap. 15.95 o.p. (*0-8161-5045-1*); lib. bdg. 14.95 o.p. (*0-8161-5044-3*) Gale Group. (Macmillan Reference USA).
—Devices & Desires. 2004. 480p. pap. 12.95 (*1-4000-7624-2*, Vintage) Knopf Publishing Group.
—Devices & Desires. 1992. 5.99 o.p. (*0-517-08846-0*); 1991. 4.99 o.p. (*0-517-07898-8*) Random Hse. Value Publishing.
—Devices & Desires. unabr. ed. 1990. (Inspector Dalgliesh Mystery Ser.: Vol. 8). audio 97.00 (*1-55690-141-0*, 90089E7) Recorded Bks., LLC.
—Devices & Desires. 1992. audio 96.95 o.p. (*0-8161-3212-7*, 90089) Thorndike Pr.
—Devices & Desires. 480p. 1991. mass mkt. 7.99 (*0-446-35975-0*); 2002. reprint ed. pap. 13.95 (*0-446-67919-4*) Warner Bks., Inc.
—Innocent Blood. 1980. 10.95 o.s.i (*0-684-16591-0*); 1981. 14.95 o.p. (*0-8161-3180-5*) Gale Group. (Macmillan Reference USA).
—Innocent Blood. 2001. 400p. pap. 12.00 (*0-7432-1963-5*, Touchstone) Simon & Schuster.
—A Mind to Murder. unabr. ed. 1993. audio 56.00 (*0-7366-2396-5*, 3165) Books on Tape, Inc.
—A Mind to Murder. (General Ser.). 1980. lib. bdg. 12.95 o.p. (*0-8161-3057-4*); 1994. 304p. pap. 17.95 (*0-8161-5645-X*) Gale Group. (Macmillan Reference USA).
—A Mind to Murder. 2001. 256p. pap. 12.00 (*0-7432-1958-9*, Touchstone) Simon & Schuster.
—A Mind to Murder. 1986. audio 49.95 o.s.i (*0-8161-9903-5*) Thorndike Pr.
—A Mind to Murder. 1991. 18.05 (*0-606-22454-8*) Turtleback Bks.
—A Mind to Murder. 1988. 256p. mass mkt. 6.99 o.p. (*0-446-31480-3*); 1987. mass mkt. 3.95 (*0-446-34828-7*); 1985. mass mkt. 3.50 (*0-446-31395-5*) Warner Bks., Inc.
—Original Sin. unabr. ed. 1995. audio 120.00 (*0-7366-3044-9*, 3726) Books on Tape, Inc.
—Original Sin. unabr. ed. 2000. 14p. audio compact disk 115.95 (*0-7540-5357-1*, CCD 048) Chivers Audio Bks. GBR. *Dist:* BBC Audiobooks America.
—Original Sin. l.t. ed. 1995. 23.00 o.s.i (*0-679-76033-4*) Random Hse., Inc.
—Original Sin. unabr. ed. audio. 2000. (Inspector Dalgliesh Mystery Ser.: Vol. 9). audio 97.00 (*0-7887-0273-4*, 94484E7) Recorded Bks., LLC.
—Original Sin. 1996. 560p. mass mkt. 7.99 (*0-446-60234-5*) Warner Bks., Inc.
—P. D. James: Three Complete Novels. 1988. 9.99 o.s.i (*0-517-64111-9*) Random Hse. Value Publishing.
—P. D. James in Murderous Company: Unnatural Causes, An Unsuitable Job for a Woman, The Black Tower. 1992. 688p. reprint ed. 13.99 o.s.i (*0-517-07228-9*) Random Hse. Value Publishing.
—Shroud for a Nightingale. unabr. ed. 1993. audio 72.00 (*0-7366-2443-0*, 3208) Books on Tape, Inc.
—Shroud for a Nightingale. unabr. ed. 2000. audio 59.95 (*0-7451-6069-7*, CAB 388) Chivers Audio Bks. GBR. *Dist:* BBC Audiobooks America.
—Shroud for a Nightingale. (Paperback Ser.). 1991. 448p. pap. 15.95 o.p. (*0-8161-5032-X*); 1982. lib. bdg. 14.95 o.p. (*0-8161-6791-5*) Gale Group. (Macmillan Reference USA).
—Shroud for a Nightingale. 2002. (Best Mysteries of All Time Ser.). 310p. (*0-7621-8879-0*, Impress) Scriptorium Pr., The.
—Shroud for a Nightingale. 2001. 368p. pap. 13.00 (*0-7432-1960-0*, Touchstone) Simon & Schuster.
—Shroud for a Nightingale. 1988. 288p. mass mkt. 6.99 o.p. (*0-446-31303-3*) Warner Bks., Inc.
—The Skull Beneath the Skin. unabr. ed. 1994. audio 88.00 (*0-7366-2647-6*, 3384) Books on Tape, Inc.
—The Skull Beneath the Skin. unabr. ed. 2000. (Cordelia Gray Mystery Ser.: Bk. 2). audio 69.95 (*0-7451-6838-8*, CAB 330) Chivers Audio Bks. GBR. *Dist:* BBC Audiobooks America.
—The Skull Beneath the Skin. l.t. ed. (Wheeler Large Print Book Ser.). 2001. 517p. 29.95 (*1-58724-122-6*, Wheeler Publishing, Inc.); 1983. 571p. 18.95 o.p. (*0-8161-3508-8*, Macmillan Reference USA); 1983. 9.95 o.p. (*0-8161-3569-X*, Macmillan Reference USA) Gale Group.
—The Skull Beneath the Skin. 1988. mass mkt. 4.95 (*0-446-35272-1*) Little Brown & Co.
—The Skull Beneath the Skin, Set. abr. ed. 1994. audio 15.99 o.s.i (*0-553-47223-2*, 391595, RH Audio) Random Hse. Audio Publishing Group.
—The Skull Beneath the Skin. (Classics Ser.). 2001. 352p. 25.00 (*0-7432-2205-9*, Scribner); 2001. 448p. pap. 12.00 (*0-7432-1956-2*, Touchstone); 1982. 352p. 13.95 o.s.i (*0-684-17773-0*, Scribner) Simon & Schuster.
—The Skull Beneath the Skin. 2001. 18.05 (*0-606-22452-1*) Turtleback Bks.
—The Skull Beneath the Skin. 1988. 432p. mass mkt. 7.99 o.p. (*0-446-35372-8*) Warner Bks., Inc.
—A Taste for Death. audio 8.95 American Audio Prose Library, Inc.
—A Taste for Death. 2003. 480p. pap. 13.95 (*0-345-46938-0*); 1999. mass mkt. 6.99 (*0-345-42916-8*); 1998. 480p. mass mkt. 7.99 (*0-345-43058-1*) Ballantine Bks.
—A Taste for Death, Pt. 1. unabr. ed. 1994. audio 64.00 (*0-7366-2703-0*, 3437-A) Books on Tape, Inc.
—A Taste for Death. l.t. ed. 1987. 713p. 20.95 o.p. (*0-8161-4265-3*); 12.95 o.p. (*0-8161-4266-1*) Gale Group. (Macmillan Reference USA).
—A Taste for Death. 1987. 512p. mass mkt. 6.50 (*0-446-32352-7*) Warner Bks., Inc.
—Unnatural Causes. unabr. ed. 1993. 54.95 incl. audio (*0-7451-6071-9*, CAB 072) BBC Audiobooks America.
—Unnatural Causes. unabr. ed. 1992. audio 56.00 (*0-7366-2318-3*, 3098) Books on Tape, Inc.
—Unnatural Causes. l.t. ed. 1993. 340p. pap. 16.95 o.p. (*0-8161-5646-8*, Macmillan Reference USA) Gale Group.
—Unnatural Causes. unabr. ed. 1993. (Inspector Dalgliesh Mystery Ser.: Vol. 3). audio 51.00 (*1-55690-832-6*, 93128E7) Recorded Bks., LLC.
—Unnatural Causes. 2003. 352p. mass mkt. (*0-7704-2912-2*) Seal Bks. CAN. *Dist:* Random Hse. of Canada, Ltd.
—Unnatural Causes. 2001. 272p. pap. 12.00 (*0-7432-1959-7*, Touchstone) Simon & Schuster.
—Unnatural Causes. 2001. 18.05 (*0-606-22455-6*) Turtleback Bks.
—Unnatural Causes. 1988. 256p. mass mkt. 7.50 o.p. (*0-446-31219-3*) Warner Bks., Inc.
—An Unsuitable Job for a Woman. unabr. ed. 1993. audio 56.00 (*0-7366-2497-X*, 3255) Books on Tape, Inc.
—An Unsuitable Job for a Woman. unabr. ed. 2000. (Cordelia Gray Mystery Ser.: Bk. 1). audio 49.95 (*0-7451-6064-6*, CAB 180) Chivers Audio Bks. GBR. *Dist:* BBC Audiobooks America.
—An Unsuitable Job for a Woman. 1980. (General Ser.). lib. bdg. 13.95 o.p. (*0-8161-6788-5*, Macmillan Reference USA) Gale Group.
—An Unsuitable Job for a Woman. unabr. ed. 1992. audio 51.00 (*1-55690-737-0*, 92110E7) Recorded Bks., LLC.
—An Unsuitable Job for a Woman. 2001. (Classic Ser.). 208p. 25.00 (*0-7432-2204-0*, Scribner); 256p. pap. 12.00 (*0-7432-1955-4*, Touchstone); 320p. 25.00 o.p. (*0-7432-2492-2*, Scribner) Simon & Schuster.
—An Unsuitable Job for a Woman. 1988. 288p. reprint ed. mass mkt. 6.99 o.p. (*0-446-31517-6*) Warner Bks., Inc.
James, Peter. Twilight. 1993. 316p. 19.95 o.p. (*0-312-08914-7*) St. Martin's Pr.
James, Russell. The Annex. l.t. ed. 2002. (Five Star First Edition Mystery Ser.). 240p. 25.95 (*0-7862-3931-X*, Five Star) Gale Group.
—The Annex. l.t. ed. 2002. (Mystery Ser.). 338p. 29.95 (*0-7862-4470-4*) Thorndike Pr.
—Count Me Out. 368p. 1998. pap. 10.00 (*0-393-31832-X*, Foul Play); 1997. 22.95 o.p. (*0-88150-384-3*) Norton, W. W. & Co., Inc.
—Payback: A Novel of Suspense. 1993. 224p. 19.00 o.p. (*0-88150-267-7*) Countryman Pr.
Jansen, Sheila. Becky Ryan. 2002. 320p. 26.99 (*0-7278-5897-1*) Severn Hse. Pubs., Ltd.
Jarman, Rosemary H. We Speak No Treason, Bk. 2. 1986. 336p. mass mkt. 3.95 o.s.i (*0-515-08567-7*, Jove) Berkley Publishing Group.
Jarrett, Miranda. Star Bright. 2000. 336p. pap. 6.50 (*0-7434-0356-8*, Pocket) Simon & Schuster.
—Starlight. 2000. (Illus.). 384p. pap. 6.50 (*0-7434-0355-X*, Pocket) Simon & Schuster.
Jarrett, Miranda, et al. Gifts of the Season: A Gift Most Rare/Christmas Charade/The Virtuous Widow. 2002. (Harlequin Historicals Ser.). 304p. mass mkt. (*0-373-29231-7*, Harlequin Bks.) Harlequin Enterprises, Ltd.
Jecks, Michael. The Devil's Acolyte. 2002. 416p. mass mkt. 9.95 (*0-7472-6725-1*); 320p. 28.00 (*0-7472-6920-3*) Headline Bk. Publishing, Ltd. GBR. *Dist:* Trafalgar Square.
—Sticklepath Strangler. 2002. 366p. 28.00 (*0-7472-6919-X*) Headline Bk. Publishing, Ltd. GBR. *Dist:* Trafalgar Square.
—The Tournament of Blood. 2001. (Medieval West Country Mysteries Ser.). 320p. mass mkt. 9.95 (*0-7472-6612-3*) Headline Bk. Publishing, Ltd. GBR. *Dist:* Trafalgar Square.
Jefferies, Richard. After London. l.t. ed. 225p. pap. 21.74 (*0-7583-3584-9*); 1152p. pap. 83.98 (*0-7583-3591-1*); 293p. pap. 25.21 (*0-7583-3585-7*); 401p. pap. 31.45 (*0-7583-3586-5*); 513p. pap. 38.94 (*0-7583-3587-3*); 657p. pap. 47.93 (*0-7583-3588-1*); 808p. pap. 65.36 (*0-7583-3589-X*); 993p. pap. 74.87 (*0-7583-3590-3*); 401p. lib. bdg. 37.45 (*0-7583-3578-4*); 513p. lib. bdg. 44.94 (*0-7583-3579-2*); 657p. lib. bdg. 53.93 (*0-7583-3580-6*);

808p. lib. bdg. 77.36 (*0-7583-3581-4*); 993p. lib. bdg. 86.87 (*0-7583-3582-2*); 1152p. lib. bdg. 95.98 (*0-7583-3583-0*); 293p. lib. bdg. 31.21 (*0-7583-3577-6*); 225p. lib. bdg. 27.74 (*0-7583-3576-8*) Huge Print Pr.

—Bevis. Hunt, Peter, ed. 1989. (Oxford World's Classics Ser.). 464p. pap. 7.95 o.p. (*0-19-282229-2*) Oxford Univ. Pr., Inc.

—Bevis. 1974. 384p. pap. 1.50 o.p. (*0-14-030677-3*, Puffin Bks.) Penguin Putnam Bks. for Young Readers.

Jensen, Emma. Best Laid Schemes. 1998. mass mkt. 4.99 o.s.i (*0-449-00234-9*, Fawcett) Ballantine Bks.

—A Grand Design. 2000. (Signet Regency Romance Ser.). 224p. mass mkt. 4.99 o.s.i (*0-451-20121-3*) NAL.

—His Grace Endures. 1998. (Regency Romance Ser.). 213p. mass mkt. 4.99 o.s.i (*0-449-00233-0*, Fawcett) Ballantine Bks.

Jerome, Jerome K. The Diary of a Pilgrimage. E-Book 2.49 (*1-58627-999-8*) Electric Umbrella Publishing.

—John Ingerfield, & Other Stories. 1977. (Short Story Index Reprint Ser.). 19.95 (*0-8369-3052-5*) Ayer Co. Pubs., Inc.

—Observations of Henry. 1977. (Short Story Index Reprint Ser.). 19.95 (*0-8369-3114-9*) Ayer Co. Pubs., Inc.

—Three Men in a Boat. 1976. 19.95 (*0-8488-1388-X*) Amereon, Ltd.

—Three Men in a Boat, Set. audio 35.95 (*1-55685-169-3*) Audio Bk. Contractors, Inc.

—Three Men in a Boat. l.t. ed. 1993. 21.95 o.p. (*0-7927-1448-2*); pap. 19.95 o.p. (*0-7927-1449-0*) BBC Audiobooks America.

—Three Men in a Boat. unabr. ed. 1993. audio 39.95 (*0-7861-0220-9*, 1194) Blackstone Audio Bks., Inc.

—Three Men in a Boat. unabr. collector's ed. 1990. (J). audio 42.00 (*0-7366-1874-0*, 2705) Books on Tape, Inc.

—Three Men in a Boat. 1986. reprint ed. lib. bdg. 18.95 (*0-89966-541-1*) Buccaneer Bks., Inc.

—Three Men in a Boat. unabr. ed. 2000. audio compact disk 64.95 (*0-7540-5358-X*, CCD 049); audio 34.95 (*0-7862-9947-9*, SAB 064) Chivers Audio Bks. GBR. *Dist:* BBC Audiobooks America.

—Three Men in a Boat. reprint ed. lib. bdg. 48.00 (*0-7426-1035-7*); 2001. (Illus.). pap. text 28.00 (*0-7426-6035-4*) Classic Bks.

—Three Men in a Boat. Jasen, David A., ed. 1980. (Continuum Classic of Humor Bk.). 208p. 11.95 o.p. (*0-8264-0018-3*) Continuum International Publishing Group, Inc.

—Three Men in a Boat. 2001. 256p. mass mkt. 5.99 (*0-7653-4161-1*, Tor Classics) Doherty, Tom Assocs., LLC.

—Three Men in a Boat. 1972. 4.95 o.p. (*0-460-01118-9*); 1957. 5.00 o.p. (*0-460-00118-3*) Dutton/Plume. (Dutton).

—Three Men in a Boat. 1999. E-Book 2.49 (*1-58627-954-8*) Electric Umbrella Publishing.

—Three Men in a Boat. abr. ed. 1984. audio 12.95 (*0-694-50361-4*, SWC 1711, Caedmon) HarperTrade.

—Three Men in a Boat. (Illus.). 2000. 240p. pap. 8.95 (*1-86205-221-2*); 1992. 215p. pap. 22.95 o.p. (*1-85145-778-X*); 1991. 224p. 34.95 o.p. (*1-85145-362-8*) Pavilion Bks., Ltd. GBR. *Dist:* Trafalgar Square.

—Three Men in a Boat. 2000. (Humour Classics Ser.). 224p. 13.95 (*1-85326-051-7*); ix, 245p. 15.95 (*1-85375-371-8*) Prion GBR. *Dist:* Trafalgar Square.

—Three Men in a Boat. unabr. ed. 1989. audio 44.00 (*1-55690-513-0*, 89910E7) Recorded Bks., LLC.

—Three Men in a Boat. E-Book 5.00 (*0-7410-0459-3*) SoftBook Pr.

—Three Men in a Boat. 1989. (Jerome K. Jerome Ser.). (Illus.). 224p. (J). (gr. 6-9). pap. 8.00 o.s.i (*0-86299-028-9*) Sutton Publishing, Ltd. GBR. *Dist:* International Publishers Marketing.

—Three Men in a Boat. 1978. (Illus.). 14.00 o.p. (*0-600-38767-4*) Transatlantic Arts, Inc.

—Three Men in a Boat. 1991. (Illus.). 192p. pap. 6.95 o.p. (*0-460-87028-9*, Everyman's Classic Library in Paperback) Tuttle Publishing.

—Three Men in a Boat. abr. ed. 1998. audio 16.85 (*1-901768-15-5*) Ulverscroft Audio (U.S.A.).

—Three Men in a Boat. 192p. 1989. 19.95 o.p. (*1-85145-357-1*, Joseph, Michael); 1978. pap. 6.95 o.s.i (*0-14-001213-3*, Penguin Bks.) Viking Penguin.

—Three Men in a Boat & Three Men on the Bummel. Harvey, Geoffrey, ed. & intro. by. 1998. (Oxford World's Classics Ser.). (Illus.). 368p. pap. 9.95 (*0-19-288033-0*) Oxford Univ. Pr., Inc.

—Three Men in a Boat & Three Men on the Bummel. 2000. (Classics Ser.). 400p. 9.95 (*0-14-043750-9*, Penguin Classics) Viking Penguin.

Jevons, Marshall. A Deadly Indifference: A Henry Spearman Mystery. 1995. 192p. 19.95 o.p. (*0-7867-0200-1*, Carroll & Graf Pubs.) Avalon Publishing Group.

Jewell, Lisa. A Friend of the Family: A Novel. 2003. 336p. 23.95 (*0-525-94734-5*, Plume) Dutton/Plume.

—One-Hit Wonder. 464p. (*0-7278-5910-2*) Severn Hse. Pubs., Ltd.

Jewsbury, Geraldine E. The Half Sisters. Wilkes, Joanne, ed. & intro. by. 1999. (Oxford World's Classics Ser.). 448p. pap. 12.95 (*0-19-283757-5*) Oxford Univ. Pr., Inc.

—The Half Sisters. Wilkes, Joanne, ed. 1994. (Oxford World's Classics Ser.). 442p. pap. 11.95 o.p. (*0-19-283114-3*) Oxford Univ. Pr., Inc.

—The Half-Sisters: A Tale, 2 vols., 1 bk. reprint ed. 44.50 (*0-404-61945-2*) AMS Pr., Inc.

John, Katherine. By Any Other Name. 1998. 288p. 23.95 o.p. (*0-312-18547-2*, Saint Martin's Minotaur) St. Martin's Pr.

—By Any Other Name. l.t. ed. 1997. (Ulverscroft Large Print Ser.). 576p. 29.99 o.p. (*0-7089-3849-3*, Ulverscroft) Thorpe, F. A. Pubs. GBR. *Dist:* Ulverscroft Large Print Bks., Ltd., Ulverscroft Large Print Canada, Ltd.

—Murder of a Dead Man. 1996. 314p. 23.95 o.p. (*0-312-15369-4*, Saint Martin's Minotaur) St. Martin's Pr.

—Six Foot Under. 1996. 384p. 23.95 o.p. (*0-312-14416-4*, Saint Martin's Minotaur) St. Martin's Pr.

—Six Foot Under. l.t. ed. 1996. (Large Print Ser.). 752p. 29.99 o.p. (*0-7089-3554-0*, Ulverscroft) Thorpe, F. A. Pubs. GBR. *Dist:* Ulverscroft Large Print Bks., Ltd., Ulverscroft Large Print Canada, Ltd.

—Without Trace. 1995. 426p. 24.95 o.p. (*0-312-13218-2*, Saint Martin's Minotaur) St. Martin's Pr.

Johnson, Jeannie. Penny for Tomorrow. 2003. 320p. (*0-7528-4669-8*); pap. 17.95 (*0-7528-5382-1*) Orion Publishing Group, Ltd. GBR. *Dist:* Trafalgar Square.

—A Penny for Tomorrow. l.t. ed. 2003. (Magna Large Print Ser.). 592p. (*0-7505-2070-1*) Magna Large Print Bks. GBR. *Dist:* Ulverscroft Large Print Canada, Ltd.

—A Penny for Tomorrow. 2003. 400p. pap. 11.00 (*0-7528-4282-X*) Orion Publishing Group, Ltd. GBR. *Dist:* Trafalgar Square.

Johnson, Susan. Temporary Mistress. 2000. (St. John-Duras Ser.). 368p. mass mkt. 6.99 (*0-553-58253-4*) Bantam Bks.

Johnstone, Iain. Fierce Creatures. 1997. 256p. mass mkt. 5.99 o.s.i (*1-57297-196-7*) Boulevard Bks.

Jolley, Elizabeth. Cabin Fever: A Novel. 1991. 224p. 19.95 o.p. (*0-06-016622-3*) HarperTrade.

—My Father's Moon. 1989. 15.95 o.p. (*0-06-016062-4*) HarperTrade.

Jones, Dylan. Outside the Rules. l.t. ed. 2003. (Magna Large Print Ser.). 448p. 32.50 (*0-7505-2053-1*) Magna Large Print Bks. GBR. *Dist:* Ulverscroft Large Print Bks., Ltd., Ulverscroft Large Print Canada, Ltd.

—Outside the Rules. 1995. 21.00 o.p. (*0-312-11873-2*, Saint Martin's Minotaur) St. Martin's Pr.

—Thicker Than Water. 1994. 208p. 18.95 o.p. (*0-312-10558-4*, Saint Martin's Minotaur) St. Martin's Pr.

Jones, Elwyn. Barlow Exposed. 1977. 7.95 o.p. (*0-312-06685-6*) St. Martin's Pr.

Jones, Susanna. Water Lily. 2003. 224p. 23.95 (*0-89296-776-5*) Mysterious Pr.

—Water Lily. 2004. 224p. pap. 12.95 (*0-446-69168-2*, Mysterious Pr. Paperback Bks.) Warner Bks., Inc.

Jones, Tanya. Ophelia O. & the Antenatal Mysteries. 1996. 416p. pap. 13.95 (*0-7472-4912-1*) Headline Bk. Publishing, Ltd. GBR. *Dist:* Trafalgar Square.

—Ophelia O. & the Mortgage Bandits. 1996. 448p. pap. 13.95 (*0-7472-4867-2*) Headline Bk. Publishing, Ltd. GBR. *Dist:* Trafalgar Square.

Jong, Erica. Fanny: Being the True History of the Adventures of Fanny Hackabout-Jones. 1981. pap. 6.95 o.p. (*0-452-25273-3*, Z5273, Plume) Dutton/Plume.

Jordan, Jennifer. Murder under Mistletoe. 1990. 2.99 o.p. (*0-517-05939-8*) Random Hse. Value Publishing.

—Murder under the Mistletoe. 1989. 192p. 16.95 o.p. (*0-312-02354-5*, Saint Martin's Minotaur) St. Martin's Pr.

—Murder under the Mistletoe: A Dee & Barry Vaughan Mystery. 1998. (WWL Mystery Ser.: No. 295). per. (*0-373-26295-7*, 1-26295-5, Worldwide Library) Harlequin Enterprises, Ltd.

Jordan, Lee. The Deadly Side of the Square. l.t. ed. 1990. (Ulverscroft Large Print Ser.). 29.99 o.p. (*0-7089-2222-8*, Ulverscroft) Thorpe, F. A. Pubs. GBR. *Dist:* Ulverscroft Large Print Bks., Ltd., Ulverscroft Large Print Canada, Ltd.

—The Deadly Side of the Square. Hutchings, Janet, ed. 1991. 189p. 17.95 o.p. (*0-8027-5794-4*) Walker & Co.

Jordan, Nicole. The Passion. 2000. 384p. mass mkt. 6.99 (*0-449-00485-6*, Ivy Bks.) Ballantine Bks.

Jordan, Penny. Now or Never. 2003. 448p. mass mkt. (*1-55166-671-5*, Mira Bks.) Harlequin Enterprises, Ltd.

—Power Play. 2000. mass mkt. (*1-55166-587-5*, 1-66587-6, Mira Bks.); 1990. mass mkt. o.s.i (*0-373-97108-7*, Harlequin Bks.) Harlequin Enterprises, Ltd.

Joseph, Alison. The Hour of Our Death: A Sister Agnes Mystery. 1997. 288p. text 23.95 o.p. (*0-312-15142-X*, Saint Martin's Minotaur) St. Martin's Pr.

—Sacred Hearts: A Mystery Introducing Sister Agnes. 1996. 256p. 22.95 o.p. (*0-312-14405-9*, Saint Martin's Minotaur) St. Martin's Pr.

Joseph, Jenny. Extended Similes. 1997. 224p. pap. 19.95 (*1-85224-302-3*) Bloodaxe Bks. GBR. *Dist:* Dufour Editions, Inc.

Joyce, Brenda. House of Dreams. l.t. ed. 2001. (Large Print Book Ser.). 624p. 26.95 (*1-58724-036-X*, Wheeler Publishing, Inc.) Gale Group.

—House of Dreams. mass mkt. 3.99 (*0-312-99885-6*, St. Martin's Paperbacks); E-Book 23.95 (*0-312-27166-2*); 2001. 416p. mass mkt. 6.99 (*0-312-97740-9*, St. Martin's Paperbacks); 2000. 416p. 23.95 o.p. (*0-312-26247-7*) St. Martin's Pr.

—The Third Heiress. l.t. ed. 2000. 27.95 (*1-56895-838-2*, Wheeler Publishing, Inc.) Gale Group.

—The Third Heiress. 2000. 512p. mass mkt. 6.99 (*0-312-97419-1*, St. Martin's Paperbacks); 1999. 416p. 19.95 o.p. (*0-312-20387-X*) St. Martin's Pr.

Joyce, Graham. The Tooth Fairy. 1998. 320p. pap. 14.95 (*0-312-86833-2*); 22.95 o.p. (*0-312-86261-X*) Doherty, Tom Assocs., LLC. (Tor Bks.).

—The Tooth Fairy. 1996. 342 p. o.p. (*0-451-18435-1*) NAL.

Judd, Alan. Legacy. 2003. 256p. 24.00 (*0-375-41484-3*) Knopf, Alfred A. Inc.

June, Kathryn. The Marrying Man. 2001. (Zebra Regency Romance Ser.). 256p. mass mkt. 4.99 o.s.i (*0-8217-6784-4*, Zebra Bks.) Kensington Publishing Corp.

Kaewert, Julie. Unbound. 1997. (Booklover's Mystery Ser.). 448p. mass mkt. 5.99 (*0-553-57715-8*, Crimeline) Bantam Bks.

Kaewert, Julie W. Unsolicited: A Mystery. 1994. 320p. 20.95 o.p. (*0-312-11088-X*, Saint Martin's Minotaur) St. Martin's Pr.

Kalmar, Stephen S. Goodbye, Vienna! 1987. (Illus.). 252p. (Orig.). pap. 9.95 (*0-89407-074-6*) Strawberry Hill Pr.

Kanan, Nabiel. Lost Girl. 1999. (Illus.). 96p. pap. 9.95 (*1-56163-229-5*, Comics Lit) NBM Publishing Co.

Kaufman, Pamela. Banners of Gold: A Novel. 2002. 416p. pap. 9.95 (*0-609-80947-4*) Crown Publishing Group.

Kavan, Anna. A Stranger Still. 1996. 320p. 30.00 (*0-7206-0955-0*) Owen, Peter Ltd. GBR. *Dist:* Dufour Editions, Inc.

Kaye, Gillian. The Enigmatic Mr. Farrar. l.t. ed. 2003. 225p. pap. 24.45 (*0-7862-5408-4*) Thorndike Pr.

Kaye, Marvin. The Confidential Casebook of Sherlock Holmes. 1999. E-Book 23.95 o.s.i (*0-312-20713-1*) St. Martin's Pr.

—The Resurrected Holmes. 1997. 352p. pap. 14.95 (*0-312-15639-1*, Saint Martin's Griffin) St. Martin's Pr.

Kaye, Marvin, ed. The Confidential Casebook of Sherlock Holmes. 368p. 1999. (Illus.). pap. 14.95 (*0-312-20638-0*, Saint Martin's Griffin); 1997. 23.95 (*0-312-18071-3*, Saint Martin's Minotaur) St. Martin's Pr.

—The Resurrected Holmes: New Cases from the Notes of John H. Watson, M. D. 1996. 353p. 24.95 o.p. (*0-312-14037-1*, Saint Martin's Minotaur) St. Martin's Pr.

Keating, H. R. F. The Bad Detective. unabr. ed. 1997. audio 54.95 Eye in the Ear Inc.

—The Bad Detective. l.t. ed. 1997. (Magna Large Print Ser.). 313p. 29.99 o.p. (*0-7505-1147-8*) Magna Large Print Bks. GBR. *Dist:* Ulverscroft Large Print Bks., Ltd., Ulverscroft Large Print Canada, Ltd.

—The Bad Detective. 1999. 288p. 23.95 o.p. (*0-312-24371-5*, Saint Martin's Minotaur) St. Martin's Pr.

—The Good Detective. unabr. ed. 1995. audio 32.95 (*0-7861-0823-1*, 1646) Blackstone Audio Bks., Inc.

—The Good Detective. l.t. ed. 1996. pap. 21.95 (*1-56895-294-5*, Wheeler Publishing, Inc.) Gale Group.

—The Good Detective. 1995. 208p. 21.00 (*0-684-81522-2*); 20.00 (*1-883402-81-6*) Simon & Schuster. (Scribner).

—The Hard Detective. l.t. ed. 2000. (G. K. Hall Nightingale Ser.). 263p. pap. 20.95 (*0-7838-9256-X*); (*0-7540-4297-9*); (*0-7540-4298-7*) Gale Group. (Macmillan Reference USA).

—The Hard Detective. 2000. 236p. 21.95 o.p. (*0-312-24648-X*, Saint Martin's Minotaur) St. Martin's Pr.

—A Long Walk to Wimbledon. l.t. ed. 2002. 300p. pap. 24.95 (*0-7862-3960-3*) Gale Group.

—The Rich Detective. l.t. ed. 1994. (Magna Large Print Ser.). 349p. o.p. (*0-7505-0623-7*) Magna Large Print Bks. GBR. *Dist:* Ulverscroft Large Print Canada, Ltd.

—The Rich Detective. 1993. 256p. 18.95 (*0-89296-506-1*) Mysterious Pr.

—The Rich Detective. 1994. 256p. mass mkt. 5.50 (*0-446-40382-2*, Mysterious Pr. Paperback Bks.) Warner Bks., Inc.

—The Soft Detective. 1998. 272p. 22.95 o.p. (*0-312-19335-1*, Saint Martin's Minotaur) St. Martin's Pr.

—The Soft Detective. l.t. ed. 1998. (Mystery Ser.). 343p. 26.95 (*0-7862-1565-8*) Thorndike Pr.

Keegan, Alex. Cuckoo: A Caz Flood Mystery. 1995. 410p. 23.95 o.p. (*0-312-13043-0*, Saint Martin's Minotaur) St. Martin's Pr.

Kelly, Carla Sue. The Lady's Companion. 1996. 224p. mass mkt. 4.99 o.s.i (*0-451-18684-2*, Signet Bks.) NAL.

Kelly, Nora. Bad Chemistry, Vol. 21. 2000. (Missing Mysteries Ser.: Vol. 21). 240p. pap. 14.95 (*1-890208-34-5*) Poisoned Pen Pr.

—Bad Chemistry. 1994. 256p. 20.95 o.p. (*0-312-10934-2*, Saint Martin's Minotaur) St. Martin's Pr.

—In the Shadow of Kings. 2000. (Missing Mysteries Ser.: Vol. 12). 189p. pap. 14.95 (*1-890208-22-1*) Poisoned Pen Pr.

—In the Shadow of Kings. 1984. 12.95 o.p. (*0-312-41171-5*) St. Martin's Pr.

—In the Shadow of Kings. l.t. ed. 1995. (Linford Mystery Library). 400p. pap. 17.99 o.p. (*0-7089-7733-2*, Linford) Thorpe, F. A. Pubs. GBR. *Dist:* Ulverscroft Large Print Bks., Ltd., Ulverscroft Large Print Canada, Ltd.

Kelly, Susan. Killing the Fatted Calf: A Gregory Summers Mystery. 2001. 224p. 26.95 (*0-7490-0511-4*) Allison & Busby, Ltd. GBR. *Dist:* International Publishers Marketing.

—Little Girl Lost: A Gregory Summers Mystery. 2002. (Gregory Summers Mystery Ser.). 282p. 24.95 (*0-7490-0533-5*) Allison & Busby, Ltd. GBR. *Dist:* International Publishers Marketing.

—Little Girl Lost: A Gregory Summers Mystery. l.t. ed. 2003. (Magna Large Print Ser.). 400p. 32.50 (*0-7505-2001-9*) Magna Large Print Bks. GBR. *Dist:* Ulverscroft Large Print Bks., Ltd., Ulverscroft Large Print Canada, Ltd.

Kelly, Susan B. Hope Against Hope. 1991. 256p. 19.95 o.s.i (*0-684-19387-6*, Macmillan Reference USA) Gale Group.

—Hope Against Hope. 1993. per. (*0-373-26118-7*, 1-26118-9, Harlequin Bks.) Harlequin Enterprises, Ltd.

—Hope Against Hope. l.t. ed. 1991. (Magna Large Print Ser.). 345p. o.p. (*0-7505-0163-4*) Magna Large Print Bks. GBR. *Dist:* Ulverscroft Large Print Canada, Ltd.

—Hope Will Answer: An Inspector Nick Trevellyan - Alison Hope Mystery. 1993. 256p. 20.00 o.p. (*0-684-19523-2*, Macmillan Reference USA) Gale Group.

—Hope Will Answer: An Inspector Nick Trevellyan - Alison Hope Mystery. l.t. ed. 1994. (Magna Large Print Ser.). 428p. 29.99 o.p. (*0-7505-0594-X*) Magna Large Print Bks. GBR. *Dist:* Ulverscroft Large Print Bks., Ltd., Ulverscroft Large Print Canada, Ltd.

—Kids' Stuff. 1994. 256p. 20.00 (*0-684-19649-2*, Macmillan Reference USA) Gale Group.

—Time of Hope. 1994. (WWL Mystery Ser.). mass mkt. (*0-373-26141-1*, 1-26141-1, Harlequin Bks.) Harlequin Enterprises, Ltd.

—Time of Hope. 1992. 224p. 20.00 o.s.i (*0-684-19423-6*, Scribner) Simon & Schuster.

—A Time of Hope. l.t. ed. 1993. (Magna Large Print Ser.). 346p. 29.99 o.p. (*0-7505-0487-0*) Magna Large Print Bks. GBR. *Dist:* Ulverscroft Large Print Bks., Ltd., Ulverscroft Large Print Canada, Ltd.

Kemp, Gene. The Well. 1984. (Illus.). 90p. (J). (gr. 4-8). o.p. (*0-571-13284-7*) Faber & Faber Ltd.

Kennealy-Morrison, Patricia. The Hedge of Mist. 1996. (Tales of Arthur Ser.: Vol. 3). 528p. mass mkt. 22.00 o.p. (*0-06-105230-2*) HarperTrade.

Kennedy, Adam. No Place to Cry. 1989. 24.95 o.p. (*0-312-02955-1*) St. Martin's Pr.

Kennedy, Shirley. The Irish Upstart. 2001. (Signet Regency Romance Ser.). 224p. mass mkt. 4.99 o.s.i (*0-451-20280-5*) NAL.

—Selfless Sister. 2000. (Signet Regency Romance Ser.). 224p. mass mkt. 4.99 o.s.i (*0-451-20138-8*, Signet Bks.) NAL.

Kenworthy, Christopher. The Winter Inside. 2001. 288p. pap. 15.00 (*1-85242-637-3*) Serpent's Tail Ltd. GBR. *Dist:* Consortium Bk. Sales & Distribution.

Kenyon, Michael. The Elgar Variation. 1981. 360p. 13.95 o.p. (*0-698-11057-9*) Putnam Publishing Group, The.

—A Free-Range Wife. 1988. 208p. pap. 3.50 o.p. (*0-380-70382-3*, Avon Bks.) Morrow/Avon.

—A Free Range Wife. 1983. (Crime Club Ser.). (Illus.). 192p. 11.95 o.p. (*0-385-18838-2*) Doubleday Publishing.

—A Healthy Way to Die. 1986. (Crime Club Ser.). 192p. 12.95 o.p. (*0-385-23355-8*) Doubleday Publishing.

—A Healthy Way to Die. 1987. 192p. pap. 2.95 o.p. (*0-380-70380-7*, Avon Bks.) Morrow/Avon.

—Kill the Butler. 1993. 221p. 17.95 o.p. (*0-312-08833-7*, Saint Martin's Minotaur) St. Martin's Pr.
—Man at the Wheel. 1982. (Crime Club Ser.). 11.95 o.p. (*0-385-18299-6*) Doubleday Publishing.
—Man at the Wheel. 1988. 192p. pap. 3.50 (*0-380-70381-5*, Avon Bks.) Morrow/Avon.
—Peckover & the Bog Man: An Inspector Peckover Mystery. 1995. 208p. 20.95 o.p. (*0-312-13582-3*, Saint Martin's Minotaur) St. Martin's Pr.
—Peckover Holds the Baby. 1988. (Crime Club Ser.). 192p. pap. 12.95 o.s.i (*0-385-24324-3*) Doubleday Publishing.
—Peckover Holds the Baby. 1988. pap. 3.50 (*0-380-70636-9*, Avon Bks.) Morrow/Avon.
—Peckover Joins the Choir. 1994. 224p. 19.95 o.p. (*0-312-10523-1*, Saint Martin's Minotaur) St. Martin's Pr.
Kernick, Simon. The Business of Dying. 2003. 416p. mass mkt. (*0-552-14970-5*, Corgi) Bantam Bks.
—The Business of Dying. Date not set. pap. (*0-312-31402-7*, St. Martin's Paperbacks); Date not set. mass mkt. (*0-312-98933-4*, St. Martin's Paperbacks); 2003. 336p. 24.95 (*0-312-31401-9*, Saint Martin's Minotaur) St. Martin's Pr.
Kerr, Peg. The Wild Swans. 1999. 400p. pap. 13.99 (*0-446-67366-8*) Warner Bks., Inc.
Kerr, Philip. A Philosophical Investigation. 1995. 384p. mass mkt. 8.99 o.s.i (*0-7704-2592-5*) Bantam Bks.
—A Philosophical Investigation. 1994. 336p. pap. 14.00 o.s.i (*0-452-27140-1*, Plume) Dutton/Plume.
—A Philosophical Investigation. 1993. 329p. 20.00 o.p. (*0-374-23176-1*) Farrar, Straus & Giroux.
Kerridge, Roy. Subjects of the Queen. 2003. 192p. 24.95 (*0-7156-3020-2*) Duckworth, Gerald & Co., Ltd. GBR. *Dist:* International Publishers Marketing.
Kerstan, Lynn. Celia's Grand Passion. 1998. (Regency Romance Ser.). 214p. mass mkt. 5.99 o.s.i (*0-449-00183-0*, Fawcett) Ballantine Bks.
—The Golden Leopard. 2002. 384p. mass mkt. 6.50 (*0-451-41057-2*, Onyx) NAL.
—Lucy in Disguise. 1998. 213p. mass mkt. 4.99 o.s.i (*0-449-00184-9*, Fawcett) Ballantine Bks.
Kihlstrom, April. An Honorable Rogue. 1997. 224p. mass mkt. 4.99 o.s.i (*0-451-18817-9*, Signet Bks.) NAL.
—The Wicked Groom. 1996. (Regency Romance Ser.). 224p. mass mkt. 4.99 o.s.i (*0-451-18750-4*, Signet Bks.) NAL.
—Widowed Bride. 1996. 224p. mass mkt. 5.50 o.s.i (*0-451-18816-0*, Signet Bks.) NAL.
King, Betty. The Lady Margaret. l.t. ed. 2000. (Ulverscroft Large Print Ser.). 392p. 31.99 (*0-7089-4309-8*, Ulverscroft) Thorpe, F. A. Pubs. GBR. *Dist:* Ulverscroft Large Print Bks., Ltd., Ulverscroft Large Print Canada, Ltd.
King, Gabriel. The Wild Road. 1999. 480p. mass mkt. 6.99 (*0-345-42303-8*, Del Rey) Ballantine Bks.
King, John. White Trash. 2001. 256p. pap. o.p. (*0-224-06049-X*) Random Hse. UK, Ltd.
King, Laurie R. The Beekeeper's Apprentice. 1996. 448p. reprint ed. mass mkt. 6.99 (*0-553-57165-6*) Bantam Bks.
—The Beekeeper's Apprentice. abr. ed. 1996. 6p. audio 16.99 (*0-88646-388-2*, 7388) Durkin Hayes Publishing Ltd.
—The Beekeeper's Apprentice. l.t. ed. 1996. 574p. 24.95 (*0-7838-1932-3*, Macmillan Reference USA) Gale Group.
—The Beekeeper's Apprentice. unabr. ed. (Mary Russell Mystery Ser.: Vol. 1). 2001. audio compact disk 124.00; 1995. audio 85.00 (*0-7887-0319-6*, 94511E7) Recorded Bks., LLC.
—The Beekeeper's Apprentice. 1994. xvii, 347p. 23.95 (*0-312-10423-5*, Saint Martin's Minotaur) St. Martin's Pr.
—Justice Hall. 2003. 464p. mass mkt. 6.99 (*0-553-58111-2*); 2002. 352p. 23.95 (*0-553-11113-2*) Bantam Bks.
—Justice Hall. l.t. ed. 2002. 625p. 30.95 (*0-7862-3953-0*) Thorndike Pr.
—A Letter of Mary. 1998. (Mary Russell Novels Ser.). 336p. reprint ed. mass mkt. 6.99 (*0-553-57780-8*) Bantam Bks.
—A Letter of Mary. abr. ed. 1997. audio 16.99 (*0-88646-420-X*, 7420) Durkin Hayes Publishing Ltd.
—A Letter of Mary. l.t. ed. 1997. (G. K. Hall Mystery Ser.). 384p. lib. bdg. 26.95 o.p. (*0-7838-8067-7*, Macmillan Reference USA) Gale Group.
—A Letter of Mary. 1999. E-Book 23.95 (*0-312-20728-X*); 1996. viii, 276p. 23.95 (*0-312-14670-1*, Saint Martin's Minotaur) St. Martin's Pr.
—A Monstrous Regiment of Women. 1996. (Mary Russell Ser.: No. 2). 368p. mass mkt. 6.99 (*0-553-57456-6*, Crimeline) Bantam Bks.
—A Monstrous Regiment of Women. abr. ed. 1995. audio 16.99 (*0-88646-390-4*, 7390) Durkin Hayes Publishing Ltd.
—A Monstrous Regiment of Women. unabr. ed. 1996. (Mary Russell Mystery Ser.: Vol. 2). audio 78.00 (*0-7887-0493-1*, 94685E7) Recorded Bks., LLC.
—A Monstrous Regiment of Women. 1995. viii, 326p. 22.95 (*0-312-13565-3*, Saint Martin's Minotaur) St. Martin's Pr.
—The Moor. 1999. (Mary Russell Novels Ser.). 400p. (gr. 5 up). mass mkt. 6.99 (*0-553-57952-5*) Bantam Bks.
—The Moor. l.t. ed. 1998. (G. K. Hall Mystery Ser.). 419p. 27.95 (*0-7838-0162-9*, Macmillan Reference USA) Gale Group.
—The Moor. unabr. ed. 1998. (Mary Russell Mystery Ser.: Vol. 4). audio 75.00 (*0-7887-1979-3*, 95366E7 ) Recorded Bks., LLC.
—The Moor. 1999. E-Book 23.95 (*0-312-20731-X*); 1997. (Illus.). 307p. 23.95 o.p. (*0-312-16934-5*, Saint Martin's Minotaur) St. Martin's Pr.
—O Jerusalem. 2000. (Mary Russell Novels Ser.). 464p. mass mkt. 6.99 (*0-553-58105-8*) Bantam Bks.
—O Jerusalem. 1999. (Mary Russell Novels Ser.). (Illus.). 384p. 23.95 o.s.i (*0-553-11093-4*) Broadway Bks.
—O Jerusalem. unabr. ed. 1999. (Mary Russell Mystery Ser.: Vol. 5). audio 83.00 (*0-7887-3746-5*, 95781E7) Recorded Bks., LLC.
King, Peter. Death Al Dente: A Gourmet Detective Mystery. 2000. (Culinary Mysteries Ser.). 256p. mass mkt. 5.99 (*0-312-97038-2*, St. Martin's Paperbacks); 1999. (Gourmet Detective Mystery Ser.: Vol. 4). 240p. 22.95 o.p. (*0-312-19891-4*, Saint Martin's Minotaur) St. Martin's Pr.
—Death & the Celestial Spice. 1997. (*0-312-15137-3*) St. Martin's Pr.
—Dying on the Vine: A Further Adventure of the Gourmet Detective. (Culinary Mysteries Ser.). 1999. 288p. mass mkt. 5.99 (*0-312-96683-0*, St. Martin's Paperbacks); 1998. 304p. 22.95 o.p. (*0-312-18090-X*, Saint Martin's Minotaur) St. Martin's Pr.
—The Gourmet Detective. 256p. 1996. 22.95 (*0-312-14346-X*, Saint Martin's Minotaur); Vol. 1. 1997. mass mkt. 5.99 o.s.i (*0-312-96260-6*, St. Martin's Paperbacks) St. Martin's Pr.
—A Healthy Place to Die: A Gourmet Detective Mystery. (Gourmet Detective Mystery Ser.). 2001. 240p. mass mkt. 5.99 (*0-312-97683-6*, St. Martin's Paperbacks); 2000. 230p. 22.95 (*0-312-24269-7*, Saint Martin's Minotaur) St. Martin's Pr.
—Spiced to Death. (Culinary Mysteries Ser.). 1998. 304p. mass mkt. 5.99 (*0-312-96500-1*, St. Martin's Paperbacks); 1997. 352p. text 23.95 o.p. (*0-312-15661-8*, Saint Martin's Minotaur) St. Martin's Pr.
King-Smith, Dick. Harriet's Hare. 1997. (Illus.). 112p. (J). (gr. 3-5). pap. 4.99 (*0-679-88551-X*) Knopf, Alfred A. Inc.
King, Stephen, et al. The New Adventures of Sherlock Holmes. Greenberg, Martin H. & Rossel Waugh, Carol-Lynn, eds. 1988. (Illus.). 344p. pap. 11.95 o.p. (*0-88184-435-7*, Carroll & Graf Pubs.) Avalon Publishing Group.
King, Valerie. A Brighton Flirtation. 2000. (Zebra Regency Romance Ser.). 256p. mass mkt. 4.99 o.s.i (*0-8217-6737-2*, Zebra Bks.) Kensington Publishing Corp.
—A London Flirtation. 2000. (Zebra Regency Romance Ser.). 256p. mass mkt. 4.99 o.s.i (*0-8217-6535-3*) Kensington Publishing Corp.
—My Lord Highwayman. 2001. (Zebra Regency Romance Ser.). 256p. mass mkt. 4.99 o.s.i (*0-8217-6794-1*, Zebra Bks.) Kensington Publishing Corp.
—A Rogue's Deception. 2002. (Zebra Regency Romance Ser.). 256p. mass mkt. 4.99 o.s.i (*0-8217-7178-7*) Kensington Publishing Corp.
Kingsbury, Kate. A Bicycle Built for Murder. 2001. 224p. mass mkt. 5.99 o.s.i (*0-425-17856-0*) Berkley Publishing Group.
—Check-Out Time. 1995. 224p. (Orig.). mass mkt. 5.50 o.s.i (*0-425-14640-5*, Prime Crime) Berkley Publishing Group.
—Chivalry Is Dead. 1996. mass mkt. 5.50 o.s.i (*0-425-15515-3*) Berkley Publishing Group.
—Death with Reservations: A Pennyfoot Hotel Mystery. 1998. (Pennyfoot Hotel Mystery Ser.). 224p. mass mkt. 5.99 o.s.i (*0-425-16144-7*, Prime Crime) Berkley Publishing Group.
—Do Not Disturb. 1994. (Orig.). mass mkt. 4.99 o.s.i (*0-425-14914-5*); 208p. mass mkt. 4.50 o.s.i (*0-515-11282-8*) Berkley Publishing Group. (Jove).
—Dying Room Only. 1998. (Pennyfoot Hotel Mystery Ser.). 224p. mass mkt. 5.99 o.s.i (*0-425-16568-X*, Prime Crime) Berkley Publishing Group.
—Eat, Drink, & Be Buried. 1994. 208p. mass mkt. 4.50 o.p. (*0-425-14352-X*, Prime Crime) Berkley Publishing Group.
—Grounds for Murder. 1995. (Pennyfoot Hotel Mystery Ser.). 240p. (Orig.). mass mkt. 5.50 o.s.i (*0-425-14901-3*) Berkley Publishing Group.
—Maid to Murder, 1 vol. 1999. (Pennyfoot Hotel Mystery Ser.: Vol.12). 224p. mass mkt. 5.99 o.s.i (*0-425-16967-7*) Berkley Publishing Group.
—Paint by Murder. 2003. 224p. mass mkt. 5.99 (*0-425-19215-6*, Prime Crime) Berkley Publishing Group.
—Pay the Piper. 1996. 224p. (Orig.). mass mkt. 5.50 o.s.i (*0-425-15231-6*) Berkley Publishing Group.
—Ring for Tomb Service: In Edwardian England Murder Rings a Bell. 1997. 240p. mass mkt. 5.99 o.s.i (*0-425-15857-8*, Prime Crime) Berkley Publishing Group.
—Room with a Clue. 1993. 208p. (Orig.). mass mkt. 3.99 o.s.i (*0-515-11188-0*, Jove) Berkley Publishing Group.
—A Room with a Clue. 1993. 208p. (Orig.). mass mkt. 5.50 o.s.i (*0-425-14326-0*) Berkley Publishing Group.
—Service for Two. 1994. 208p. (Orig.). mass mkt. 4.99 o.s.i (*0-425-14223-X*, Prime Crime) Berkley Publishing Group.
Kingsley, Katherine. In the Presence of Angels. 2000. 352p. mass mkt. 6.50 (*0-440-23599-5*) Bantam Dell Publishing Group.
—Song from the Sea. 2003. 352p. mass mkt. 6.50 (*0-440-23744-0*) Dell Publishing.
Kingsley, Mary. In a Pirate's Arms. 1996. 352p. mass mkt. 5.50 o.s.i (*0-451-40644-3*, Onyx) NAL.
—Masquerade. 1997. 384p. mass mkt. 5.99 o.s.i (*0-451-40701-6*, Onyx) NAL.
Kingston, Beryl. Gemma's Journey. l.t. ed. 1998. (Basic Ser.). 679p. 28.95 (*0-7862-1648-4*) Thorndike Pr.
Kingston, Christina. The Night the Stars Fell. 2001. 304p. mass mkt. 5.99 o.s.i (*0-515-13041-9*, Jove) Berkley Publishing Group.
—Ride for the Roses. 2000. 336p. mass mkt. 5.99 o.s.i (*0-515-12785-X*, Jove) Berkley Publishing Group.
Kinsella, Sophie. Can You Keep a Secret? 2004. 368p. 21.95 (*0-385-33681-0*, Dial Bks.) Dell Publishing.
—Confessions of a Shopaholic. 2003. 384p. mass mkt. 6.99 (*0-440-24141-3*, Dell Bks.); 2001. (Illus.). 320p. pap. 11.95 (*0-385-33548-2*, Delta) Dell Publishing.
—Confessions of a Shopaholic. audio 29.99 (*1-4025-3603-8*) Recorded Bks., LLC.
Kirk, Cynthia. The Lady & the Lion. 2001. 320p. mass mkt. 4.99 (*0-8439-4856-6*, Leisure Bks.) Dorchester Publishing Co., Inc.
Kirkland, Martha. His Lordship's Swan. 2001. (Zebra Regency Romance Ser.). 24p. mass mkt. 4.99 o.s.i (*0-8217-6722-4*, Zebra Bks.) Kensington Publishing Corp.
—An Inconvenient Heir. 2003. 224p. mass mkt. 4.99 (*0-451-20771-8*, Signet Bks.) NAL.
—Miss Wilson's Reputation. 2002. (Signet Regency Romance Ser.). 224p. mass mkt. 4.99 o.s.i (*0-451-20587-1*, Signet Bks.) NAL.
—The Rake's Fiancee. 2001. (Signet Regency Romance Ser.). 224p. mass mkt. 4.99 o.s.i (*0-451-20260-0*) NAL.
—The Ruby Necklace. 1996. 224p. mass mkt. 4.99 o.s.i (*0-451-18720-2*, Signet Bks.) NAL.
—Seductive Spy. 1999. (Zebra Regency Romance Ser.). 221p. mass mkt. 4.99 o.s.i (*0-8217-6123-4*) Kensington Publishing Corp.
—The Seductive Spy. 2000. (Five Star Romance Ser.). 200p. 25.95 (*0-7862-2725-7*, Five Star) Gale Group.
—Uncommon Courtship. 2003. (Signet Regency Romance Ser.). 224p. mass mkt. 4.99 o.s.i (*0-451-20132-9*, Signet Bks.) NAL.
Kirwan, Larry. Liverpool Fantasy. 2003. 256p. pap. 14.95 (*1-56025-497-1*) Avalon Publishing Group.
Klavan, Andrew. The Uncanny. abr. ed. 1998. audio 17.95 o.p. (*1-56740-759-5*, 513, Nova Audio Bks.); audio 23.95 (*1-56100-782-X*, 303, Bookcassette); audio 73.25 (*1-56740-561-4*, 1112, Unabridged Library Editions);Set. audio 7.99 o.s.i (*1-56740-278-X*, 1690, Nova Audio Bks.) Brilliance Audio.
—The Uncanny. 1998. 416p. reprint ed. mass mkt. 6.99 (*0-440-22577-9*) Dell Publishing.
Kleypas, Lisa. Suddenly You. 2001. 384p. mass mkt. 7.50 (*0-380-80232-5*, Avon Bks.) Morrow/Avon.
Kneale, Matthew. Sweet Thames. 2000. pap. 11.95 (*0-552-99542-8*) Transworld Publishers Ltd. GBR. *Dist:* Trafalgar Square.
Knight. The Secret Woman. 2001. 274p. 14.95 (*1-85381-630-2*) Virago Pr., Ltd. GBR. *Dist:* Trafalgar Square.
Kohl, Candice. The Kinsmen: A Knight's Passion. 2000. (Ballad Romances Ser.). 320p. mass mkt. 5.50 o.s.i (*0-8217-6714-3*) Kensington Publishing Corp.
—Kinsmen: A Knight's Vow. 2000. (Ballad Romances Ser.). 32p. mass mkt. 5.50 o.s.i (*0-8217-6681-3*, Zebra Bks.) Kensington Publishing Corp.
Krahn, Betina. The Husband Test. 2001. 400p. mass mkt. 6.99 (*0-553-58386-7*) Bantam Bks.
—The Husband Test. l.t. ed. 2002. 597p. 29.95 (*0-7862-4129-2*) Gale Group.
—The Perfect Mistress. 1995. 464p. mass mkt. 6.99 (*0-553-56523-0*, Fanfare) Bantam Bks.
Krahn, Betina M. The Last Bachelor. 1994. 528p. mass mkt. 6.50 (*0-553-56522-2*) Bantam Bks.
—The Last Bachelor. l.t. ed. 1995. (Large Print Bks.). 23.95 o.p. (*1-56895-170-1*, Wheeler Publishing, Inc.) Gale Group.
—The Perfect Mistress. l.t. ed. 1995. pap. 21.95 o.p. (*1-56895-274-0*, Wheeler Publishing, Inc.) Gale Group.
Kruger, Mary. Wagered Hearts. 2001. (Zebra Regency Romance Ser.). 256p. mass mkt. 4.99 o.s.i (*0-8217-6997-9*, Zebra Bks.) Kensington Publishing Corp.
Kunzru, Hari. The Impressionist. 2002. 416p. 24.95 o.s.i (*0-525-94642-X*, Dutton); 2003. 480p. reprint ed. pap. 14.00 (*0-452-28397-3*) Dutton/Plume.
Kureishi, Hanif. The Black Album. 288p. 1996. pap. 13.00 (*0-684-82540-6*); 1995. 22.00 (*0-684-81342-4*) Simon & Schuster. (Scribner).
—The Black Album. abr. ed. 1997. (Audio Ser.). pap. 16.95 o.s.i incl. audio (*0-14-086414-8*, Penguin AudioBooks) Viking Penguin.
—Intimacy. 1999. 128p. 16.00 (*0-684-85275-6*, Scribner) Simon & Schuster.
Kurland, Lynn. Another Chance to Dream. 1998. 432p. mass mkt. 7.50 (*0-425-16514-0*) Berkley Publishing Group.
—From This Moment On. 2002. 432p. mass mkt. 7.99 (*0-425-18685-7*) Berkley Publishing Group.
—If I Had You. 2000. 448p. mass mkt. 7.99 (*0-425-17694-0*, Jove) Berkley Publishing Group.
Kurland, Michael, ed. My Sherlock Holmes: Untold Stories of the Great Detective. 2004. 384p. pap. 14.95 (*0-312-32595-9*); 2003. 368p. 24.95 (*0-312-28093-9*) St. Martin's Pr.
La Plante, Lynda. Prime Suspect, No. 3. 1994. 320p. mass mkt. 4.99 o.s.i (*0-440-21496-3*) Dell Publishing.
Lacey, Sarah. File under Arson. unabr. ed. 1998. audio 63.95 (*1-85903-172-2*) Magna Story Sound GBR. *Dist:* Ulverscroft Large Print Bks., Ltd.
—File under Arson. 1996. 224p. 20.95 o.p. (*0-312-13972-1*, Saint Martin's Minotaur) St. Martin's Pr.
—File under Deceased. l.t. ed. 1994. (Dales Large Print Ser.). 321p. pap. 19.99 o.p. (*1-85389-475-3*) Dales Large Print Bks. GBR. *Dist:* Ulverscroft Large Print Bks., Ltd., Ulverscroft Large Print Canada, Ltd.
—File under Deceased. unabr. ed. 1998. audio 57.95 (*1-85903-171-4*) Magna Story Sound GBR. *Dist:* Ulverscroft Large Print Bks., Ltd.
—File under Deceased. 1993. 192p. 17.95 o.p. (*0-312-09807-3*, Saint Martin's Minotaur) St. Martin's Pr.
—File under Jeopardy. unabr. ed. audio 63.95 (*1-85903-173-0*) Magna Story Sound GBR. *Dist:* Ulverscroft Large Print Bks., Ltd.
—File under Jeopardy. 1997. 21.95 o.p. (*0-312-15127-6*, Saint Martin's Minotaur) St. Martin's Pr.
—File under Missing. l.t. ed. 1994. (Dales Large Print Ser.). 393p. pap. 19.99 o.p. (*1-85389-499-0*) Dales Large Print Bks. GBR. *Dist:* Ulverscroft Large Print Bks., Ltd., Ulverscroft Large Print Canada, Ltd.
—File under Missing, Set. unabr. ed. 1998. audio 63.95 (*1-85903-176-5*) Magna Story Sound GBR. *Dist:* Ulverscroft Large Print Bks., Ltd.
—File under Missing. 1994. 224p. 19.95 o.p. (*0-312-10982-2*, Saint Martin's Minotaur) St. Martin's Pr.
Lackey, Mercedes. The Serpent's Shadow, Vol. 1. 2002. 400p. reprint ed. mass mkt. 6.99 (*0-7564-0061-9*) DAW Bks., Inc.
Laden, Janis. Bewitching Minx. 1993. 512p. mass mkt. 3.99 o.s.i (*0-8217-4233-7*, Zebra Bks.) Kensington Publishing Corp.
Lake, Amy. The Carriagemaker's Daughter. l.t. ed. 2002. (Five Star First Edition Romance Ser.). 300p. 26.95 (*0-7862-4013-X*, Five Star) Gale Group.
—The Earl's Wife. l.t. ed. 2001. (First Edition Romance Ser.). 285p. 26.95 (*0-7862-3035-5*, Five Star) Gale Group.
—Lady Pamela. l.t. ed. 2003. 287p. 26.95 (*0-7862-4232-9*, Five Star) Gale Group.
Lake, Deryn. Death in the West Wind. 2001. 224p. 26.95 (*0-7490-0501-7*); 2002. 282p. reprint ed. pap. 9.95 (*0-7490-0588-2*) Allison & Busby, Ltd. GBR. *Dist:* International Publishers Marketing.
—Death in the West Wind. l.t. ed. 2003. (Ulverscroft Large Print Ser.). 464p. 32.50 (*0-7089-4738-7*) Thorpe, F. A. Pubs. GBR. *Dist:* Ulverscroft Large Print Bks., Ltd., Ulverscroft Large Print Canada, Ltd.
Laker, Rosalind, pseud. Gilded Splendour. l.t. ed. 1982. (General Ser.). lib. bdg. 17.95 o.p. (*0-8161-3476-6*, Macmillan Reference USA) Gale Group.
—The Silver Touch. 1990. mass mkt. 4.50 o.s.i (*0-553-28336-7*) Bantam Bks.
—The Silver Touch. 1987. 360p. 16.95 o.s.i (*0-385-23745-6*) Doubleday Publishing.
—The Silver Touch. l.t. ed. 1989. (Magna Large Print Ser.). 551p. o.p. (*1-85057-461-8*) Magna Large Print Bks. GBR. *Dist:* Ulverscroft Large Print Canada, Ltd.
Lamb, Charlotte. In the Still of the Night. l.t. ed. 1997. 431p. 24.95 o.p. (*0-7838-1944-7*, Macmillan Reference USA) Gale Group.



For book reviews, descriptive annotations, tables of contents, cover images, author biographies & additional information, updated daily, subscribe to **www.booksinprint.com** 751

Lancaster, Osbert. The Littlehampton Saga: Comprising the Saracen's Head, Drayneflete Revealed, the Littlehampton Bequest. 1992. (Illus.). 253p. reprint ed. o.p. (*0-7126-5248-5*) Random Hse. of Canada, Ltd. CAN. *Dist:* Random Hse., Inc.

Landsdowne, Judith A. Lord Nightingale's Love Song. 2000. (Zebra Regency Romance Ser.). 256p. mass mkt. 4.99 o.s.i (*0-8217-6688-0*, Zebra Bks.) Kensington Publishing Corp.

Lane, Allison. A Bird in Hand. 1999. (Signet Regency Romance Ser.). 224p. mass mkt. 4.99 o.s.i (*0-451-19790-9*, Signet Bks.) NAL.

—The Notorious Widow. 2000. (Signet Regency Romance Ser.). 240p. mass mkt. 4.99 o.s.i (*0-451-20166-3*) NAL.

Lane, Joel. From Blue to Black. 2001. 224p. pap. 15.00 (*1-85242-618-7*) Serpent's Tail Ltd. GBR. *Dist:* Consortium Bk. Sales & Distribution.

Langton, Jane. Dead as a Dodo: A Homer Kelly Mystery. 1997. (Homer Kelly Mystery Ser.). (Illus.). 256p. pap. 6.95 o.s.i (*0-14-024795-5*) Penguin Group (USA) Inc.

—Dead as a Dodo: A Homer Kelly Mystery. 1996. (Homer Kelly Mystery Ser.). 352p. 21.95 o.s.i (*0-670-86221-5*) Viking Penguin.

—Dead As a Dodo: A Homer Kelly Mystery. unabr. ed. 1997. audio 56.00 (*0-913369-62-4*, 4295) Books on Tape, Inc.

Lansdowne, Judith. Just in Time. 2003. (Zebra Historical Romance Ser.). 32p. mass mkt. 5.99 (*0-8217-7421-2*) Kensington Publishing Corp.

Lansdowne, Judith A. Annabella's Diamond. 1999. (Zebra Regency Romance Ser.). 224p. mass mkt. 4.99 o.s.i (*0-8217-6228-1*) Kensington Publishing Corp.

—Lord Nightingale's Christmas. 2000. (Zebra Regency Romance Ser.). 256p. mass mkt. 4.99 o.s.i (*0-8217-6908-1*) Kensington Publishing Corp.

—Lord Nightingale's Debut. 2000. (Zebra Regency Romance Ser.). 256p. mass mkt. 4.99 o.s.i (*0-8217-6671-6*) Kensington Publishing Corp.

—Lord Nightingale's Triumph. 2000. (Zebra Regency Romance Ser.). 256p. mass mkt. 4.99 o.s.i (*0-8217-6704-6*, Zebra Bks.) Kensington Publishing Corp.

—Mutiny at Almack's. 1999. (Zebra Regency Romance Ser.). 256p. mass mkt. 4.99 o.s.i (*0-8217-6388-1*, Zebra Bks.) Kensington Publishing Corp.

—The Mystery Kiss. 2001. (Zebra Historical Romance Ser.). 352p. mass mkt. 5.99 o.s.i (*0-8217-7016-0*) Kensington Publishing Corp.

Larabee, Kim. Behind the Mask. 1989. 200p. (Orig.). pap. 6.95 o.p. (*1-55583-151-6*) Alyson Pubns.

Laurence, Janet. Death & the Epicure. l.t. ed. 1994. (Magna Large Print Ser.). 384p. (*0-7505-0702-0*) Magna Large Print Bks. GBR. *Dist:* Ulverscroft Large Print Canada, Ltd.

—Death & the Epicure. 1993. 208p. 18.95 o.p. (*0-312-10451-0*, Saint Martin's Minotaur) St. Martin's Pr.

—Death at the Table. l.t. ed. 1997. (Paperback Ser.). 360p. lib. bdg. 21.95 (*0-7838-8255-6*, Macmillan Reference USA) Gale Group.

—Death at the Table. 1999. (Mystery Ser.: Bk. 316). per. (*0-373-26316-3*, 1-26316-9, Worldwide Library) Harlequin Enterprises, Ltd.

—Death at the Table. l.t. ed. 1997. 224p. 20.95 o.p. (*0-312-15105-5*, Saint Martin's Minotaur) St. Martin's Pr.

—A Deep Coffyn. 1989. 14.95 o.s.i (*0-385-26626-X*) Doubleday Publishing.

—Recipe for Death. l.t. ed. 1994. (Magna Large Print Ser.). 415p. (*0-7505-0640-7*) Magna Large Print Bks. GBR. *Dist:* Ulverscroft Large Print Canada, Ltd.

—A Tasty Way to Die. 1991. 192p. 14.95 o.s.i (*0-385-41491-9*) Doubleday Publishing.

—To Kill the Past. 1995. 215p. 19.95 o.p. (*0-312-11906-2*, Saint Martin's Minotaur) St. Martin's Pr.

Laurens, Stephanie. All about Love. l.t. ed. 2001. (G. K. Hall Romance Ser.). 407p. 29.95 (*0-7838-9497-X*, Macmillan Reference USA) Gale Group.

—All about Love. 2001. E-Book 6.99 (*0-06-050190-1*); E-Book 6.99 (*0-06-050189-8*); E-Book 6.99 (*0-06-050187-1*); E-Book 6.99 (*0-06-050188-X*) HarperCollins General Bks. Group. (PerfectBound).

—All about Love. 2001. 416p. mass mkt. 7.50 (*0-380-81201-0*, Avon Bks.) Morrow/Avon.

—A Comfortable Wife. l.t. ed. 1997. (Mills & Boon Large Print Ser.). 350p. 25.99 o.p. (*0-263-15148-4*) Harlequin Mills & Boon, Ltd. GBR. *Dist:* Ulverscroft Large Print Bks., Ltd., Ulverscroft Large Print Canada, Ltd.

—A Gentleman's Honor. 2003. E-Book 7.99 (*0-06-057596-4*); E-Book 7.99 (*0-06-057672-3*); E-Book 7.99 (*0-06-057673-1*); E-Book 7.99 (*0-06-057671-5*); mass mkt. 143.82 (*0-06-056819-4*) HarperCollins Pubs.

—A Gentleman's Honor. 2003. 464p. mass mkt. 7.99 (*0-06-000207-7*, Avon Bks.) Morrow/Avon.

—Gentleman's Honor, 24 Copies. 2003. mass mkt. 191.76 (*0-06-056820-8*); mass mkt. 191.76 (*0-06-056821-6*) HarperCollins Pubs.

—The Lady Chosen. 2003. (Bastion Club Ser.: Bk. 1). E-Book 7.99 (*0-06-057668-5*, PerfectBound) HarperCollins General Bks. Group.

—The Lady Chosen. 2003. E-Book 7.99 (*0-06-057667-7*); E-Book 7.99 (*0-06-057669-3*); E-Book 7.99 (*0-06-057670-7*) HarperCollins Pubs.

—The Lady Chosen. 2003. (Bastion Club Ser.: Bk. 1). 464p. mass mkt. 7.99 (*0-06-000206-9*, Avon Bks.) Morrow/Avon.

—The Perfect Lover. 2003. 368p. 22.95 (*0-06-050571-0*) Morrow/Avon.

Law, Elizabeth. The Sealed Knot. l.t. ed. 1992. 19.95 o.p. (*0-7927-1169-6*); pap. 17.95 o.p. (*0-7927-1168-8*) BBC Audiobooks America.

—The Sealed Knot. 1989. 224p. 18.95 (*0-8027-1085-9*) Walker & Co.

Lawrence, D. H. Collected Stories. 1994. 25.00 o.s.i (*0-679-43135-7*, Everyman's Library) Knopf Publishing Group.

—Complete Short Stories of D. H. Lawrence, 3 vols. 28p. Vol. 1. 1976. pap. 8.95 o.p. (*0-14-004382-9*); Vol. 3. 1977. pap. 8.00 o.p. (*0-14-004383-7*) Viking Penguin. (Penguin Bks.).

—D. H. Lawrence: The Complete Short Stories, 3 vols., Vol. 2. 1976. 596p. pap. 11.00 o.s.i (*0-14-004255-5*, Penguin Bks.) Viking Penguin.

—D. H. Lawrence: The Lost Girl. Worthen, John, ed. 1981. (Cambridge Edition of the Works of D. H. Lawrence). (Illus.). 483p. 99.95 o.p. (*0-521-22263-X*) Cambridge Univ. Pr.

—D.H. Lawrence: The Prussian Officer & Other Stories. Worthen, John, ed. 1983. (Cambridge Edition of the Works of D. H. Lawrence). (Illus.). 360p. 59.50 o.p. (*0-521-24822-1*) Cambridge Univ. Pr.

—England, My England. 1980. (Short Story Index Reprint Ser.). reprint ed. 23.95 (*0-8369-4153-5*) Ayer Co. Pubs., Inc.

—England, My England & Other Stories. Steele, Bruce, ed. 1990. (Cambridge Edition of the Works of D. H. Lawrence). 340p. 90.00 o.s.i (*0-521-35267-3*); 337p. pap. 33.00 (*0-521-35814-0*) Cambridge Univ. Pr.

—England, My England & Other Stories. Steele, Bruce, ed. 1996. (Penguin Twentieth-Century Classics Ser.). 288p. pap. 11.95 o.s.i (*0-14-018791-X*) Viking Penguin.

—Lady Chatterley's Lover. 1976. 20.95 (*0-8488-0559-3*) Amereon, Ltd.

—Lady Chatterley's Lover. abr. ed. audio 12.95 (*0-89926-156-6*, 844) Audio Bk. Co.

—Lady Chatterley's Lover. Kay, Marilyn, ed. abr. ed. 1986. audio 12.95 (*1-882071-10-7*, 012) B&B Audio, Inc.

—Lady Chatterley's Lover. 1983. (Classics Ser.). 384p. mass mkt. 2.95 o.s.i (*0-553-21272-9*, Bantam Classics) Bantam Bks.

—Lady Chatterley's Lover. Durrell, Lawrence, ed. 1983. (Bantam Classics Ser.). 384p. mass mkt. 4.95 (*0-553-21262-1*) Bantam Bks.

—Lady Chatterley's Lover. unabr. collector's ed. 1987. audio 72.00 (*0-7366-1127-4*, 2050) Books on Tape, Inc.

—Lady Chatterley's Lover. 1981. reprint ed. lib. bdg. 23.95 (*0-89966-375-3*) Buccaneer Bks., Inc.

—Lady Chatterley's Lover. abr. ed. audio 15.95 o.p. (*0-88646-044-1*, 7061) Durkin Hayes Publishing Ltd.

—Lady Chatterley's Lover. l.t. ed. 1993. (General Ser.). 474p. lib. bdg. 19.95 o.p. (*0-8161-5651-4*, Macmillan Reference USA) Gale Group.

—Lady Chatterley's Lover. 1993. 384p. pap. 12.00 (*0-8021-3334-7*, Grove Pr.); 1987. 384p. pap. 3.95 o.p. (*0-8021-3068-2*); 1969. pap. 3.95 o.p. (*0-394-62424-6*, B479) Grove/Atlantic, Inc.

—Lady Chatterley's Lover. abr. ed. 2000. audio 7.95 (*1-57815-121-X*, 1083, Media Bks. Audio Publishing) Media Bks., L. L. C.

—Lady Chatterley's Lover. 1959. mass mkt. 2.95 o.p. (*0-451-52247-8*); 304p. mass mkt. 5.95 o.p. (*0-451-52498-5*, CE1787) NAL. (Signet Classics).

—Lady Chatterley's Lover. 2000. (Modern Library Ser.). E-Book 4.95 (*0-679-64164-5*, Modern Library) Random House Adult Trade Publishing Group.

—Lady Chatterley's Lover. 1986. 5.99 o.s.i (*0-517-38587-2*) Random Hse. Value Publishing.

—Lady Chatterley's Lover. (Modern Library Ser.). 1993. 560p. 17.95 o.s.i (*0-679-60065-5*); 1960. 3.95 o.s.i (*0-394-60148-3*); 2nd ed. 1983. 7.95 o.s.i (*0-394-60430-X*) Random Hse., Inc.

—Lady Chatterley's Lover, unabr. ed. 1988. audio 78.00 (*1-55690-292-1*, 88100E7) Recorded Bks., LLC.

—Lady Chatterley's Lover. Squires, Michael, ed. & intro. by. 1995. (Twentieth Century Classics Ser.). 400p. 12.00 (*0-14-018786-3*, Penguin Classics) Viking Penguin.

—Lady Chatterley's Lover & a Propos of "Lady Chatterley's Lover" Squires, Michael, ed. 1993. (Cambridge Edition of the Works of D. H. Lawrence). (Illus.). 522p. 120.00 (*0-521-22266-4*) Cambridge Univ. Pr.

—The Lost Girl. 26.95 (*0-89190-611-8*) Amereon, Ltd.

—The Lost Girl. 1996. 416p. mass mkt. 5.95 o.s.i (*0-553-21448-9*, Bantam Classics) Bantam Bks.

—The Lost Girl. Worthen, John, ed. 1981. (Cambridge Edition of the Works of D. H. Lawrence). (Illus.). 484p. pap. 45.00 (*0-521-29423-1*) Cambridge Univ. Pr.

—The Lost Girl. reprint ed. lib. bdg. 98.00 (*0-7426-3143-5*); 2001. pap. text 28.00 (*0-7426-8143-2*) Classic Bks.

—The Lost Girl. 1968. pap. 2.75 o.p. (*0-670-00226-7*) Penguin Group (USA) Inc.

—The Lost Girl. 2003. (Modern Library Classics). 400p. pap. 13.95 (*0-8129-6997-9*, Modern Library) Random House Adult Trade Publishing Group.

—The Lost Girl. Worthen, John, ed. 1996. (Penguin Twentieth-Century Classics Ser.). 416p. pap. 11.95 o.s.i (*0-14-018808-8*) Viking Penguin.

—The Lost Girl. 1990. 400p. pap. 7.95 o.p. (*0-14-018206-3*, Penguin Classics) Viking Penguin.

—The Lost Girl. Worthen, John, ed. 1982. 432p. 22.95 o.p. (*0-670-44101-5*) Viking Penguin.

—The Lost Girl. 1978. 400p. pap. 5.95 o.p. (*0-14-000752-0*, Penguin Bks.) Viking Penguin.

—Love among the Haystacks. reprint ed. lib. bdg. 20.95 (*0-88411-676-X*) Amereon, Ltd.

—Love among the Haystacks. 1995. 64p. pap. 0.95 o.p. (*0-14-600091-9*) Penguin Group (USA) Inc.

—Love among the Haystacks & Other Pieces. 1977. (Select Bibliographies Reprint Ser.). reprint ed. 19.95 (*0-518-19074-9*) Ayer Co. Pubs., Inc.

—Love among the Haystacks & Other Stories. Worthen, John, ed. 1987. (Cambridge Edition of the Works of D. H. Lawrence). (Illus.). 340p. 94.95 o.p. (*0-521-26836-2*); 339p. pap. 33.00 (*0-521-33674-0*) Cambridge Univ. Pr.

—Love among the Haystacks & Other Stories. Worthen, John, ed. 1996. (Penguin Twentieth-Century Classics Ser.). 256p. pap. 10.95 o.s.i (*0-14-018818-5*) Viking Penguin.

—Love among the Haystacks & Other Stories. 1991. 176p. pap. 8.95 o.p. (*0-14-018203-9*, Penguin Classics); 1989. 192p. 16.95 o.p. (*0-670-82586-7*) Viking Penguin.

—A Modern Lover: And Other Stories. 1977. (Short Story Index Reprint Ser.). reprint ed. 18.95 (*0-8369-4135-7*) Ayer Co. Pubs., Inc.

—A Modern Lover: And Other Stories. 1969. mass mkt. 1.25 o.s.i (*0-345-21501-X*) Ballantine Bks.

—Paul Morel. Baron, Helen, ed. 2003. (Cambridge Edition of the Works of D. H. Lawrence Ser.). (Illus.). 382p. 100.00 (*0-521-56009-8*) Cambridge Univ. Pr.

—The Prussian Officer & Other Stories. 1977. (Short Story Index Reprint Ser.). reprint ed. 25.95 (*0-8369-3918-2*) Ayer Co. Pubs., Inc.

—The Prussian Officer & Other Stories. Worthen, John, ed. 1987. (Cambridge Edition of the Works of D. H. Lawrence). (Illus.). 359p. pap. 38.00 (*0-521-28985-8*) Cambridge Univ. Pr.

—The Prussian Officer & Other Stories. reprint ed. lib. bdg. 98.00 (*0-7426-3134-6*); 2001. 310p. pap. text 28.00 (*0-7426-8134-3*) Classic Bks.

—The Prussian Officer & Other Stories. Atkins, Antony, ed. 1995. (Oxford World's Classics Ser.). 308p. pap. 8.95 o.p. (*0-19-283181-X*) Oxford Univ. Pr., Inc.

—The Prussian Officer & Other Stories. Worthen, John, ed. (Penguin Twentieth-Century Classics Ser.). 1995. 304p. pap. 20.00 (*0-14-018780-4*, Penguin Classics); 1985. 272p. 18.95 o.p. (*0-670-58053-8*) Viking Penguin.

—The Rainbow. Kinkead-Weekes, Mark, ed. 1989. (Cambridge Edition of the Works of D. H. Lawrence). (Illus.). (C). 748p. 125.00 o.p. (*0-521-22869-7*); 752p. pap. 39.95 o.p. (*0-521-29689-7*) Cambridge Univ. Pr.

—The Rainbow. 1993. (Everyman's Library). 496p. 20.00 (*0-679-42305-2*) Knopf, Alfred A. Inc.

—The Rainbow. Flint, Kate, ed. & intro. by. 1997. (Oxford World's Classics Ser.). 542p. pap. 7.95 o.p. (*0-19-283080-5*) Oxford Univ. Pr., Inc.

—The Rainbow. Kinkead-Weekes, Mark, ed. 1995. (Twentieth Century Classics Ser.). (Illus.). 528p. pap. 10.00 (*0-14-018813-4*, Penguin Classics) Viking Penguin.

—The Rainbow & Women in Love. Beynon, Richard, ed. 2003. (Readers' Guides to Essential Criticism Ser.). 192p. pap. 14.99 o.s.i (*1-874166-69-2*) Palgrave Macmillan.

—Selected Short Stories. Lockwood, Michael, ed. 1997. (Literature Ser.). (Illus.). 336p. pap. text, stu. ed. 11.95 (*0-521-57505-2*) Cambridge Univ. Pr.

—Selected Short Stories. 1993. 128p. reprint ed. pap. text 1.00 (*0-486-27794-1*) Dover Pubns., Inc.

—Selected Short Stories of D. H. Lawrence. annuals Wood, James, ed. 1999. (Modern Library Ser.). 512p. 21.95 o.s.i (*0-679-60327-1*) Random Hse., Inc.

—Sons & Lovers. Trotter, David, ed. 1995. (Oxford World's Classics Ser.). 522p. pap. 7.95 o.p. (*0-19-283107-0*) Oxford Univ. Pr., Inc.

—Sons & Lovers. 1998. pap. text o.p. (*0-17-556631-3*); 1930. 124p. pap. text 5.95 (*0-582-52634-5*) Addison-Wesley Longman, Inc.

—Sons & Lovers. 1976. 23.95 (*0-8488-0561-5*) Amereon, Ltd.

—Sons & Lovers. 1985. (Classics Ser.). 432p. mass mkt. 5.95 (*0-553-21192-7*) Bantam Bks.

—Sons & Lovers. 1982. reprint ed. lib. bdg. 28.95 (*0-89966-400-8*) Buccaneer Bks., Inc.

—Sons & Lovers. Baron, Helen & Baron, Carl, eds. 1992. (Cambridge Edition of the Works of D. H. Lawrence). 466p. (C). 34.95 o.p. (*0-521-43221-9*); (Illus.). 757p. 125.00 o.p. (*0-521-24276-2*) Cambridge Univ. Pr.

—Sons & Lovers. 2002. (Dover Thrift Editions Ser.). 384p. pap. 3.50 (*0-486-42121-X*) Dover Pubns., Inc.

—Sons & Lovers. 2003. (Barnes & Noble Classics Ser.). 512p. pap. 7.95 (*1-59308-013-1*) Fine Communications.

—Sons & Lovers. 1988. (Study Texts Ser.). pap. text 5.95 (*0-582-33166-8*, 72062) Longman Publishing Group.

—Sons & Lovers. mass mkt. 0.50 o.p. (*0-451-01509-6*, Signet Bks.); mass mkt. 0.50 o.p. (*0-451-01829-X*, Signet Bks.); mass mkt. 0.50 o.p. (*0-451-01039-6*, Signet Bks.); 1985. 416p. mass mkt. 5.95 (*0-451-51882-9*, Signet Classics) NAL.

—Sons & Lovers. 1998. (Twelve-Point Ser.). 463p. reprint ed. lib. bdg. 25.00 (*1-58287-072-1*) North Bks.

—Sons & Lovers. 1997. (Critical Editions Ser.). (C). pap. (*0-393-95758-6*, Norton Paperbacks) Norton, W. W. & Co., Inc.

—Sons & Lovers. Trotter, David, ed. & intro. by. 1998. (Oxford World's Classics Ser.). 528p. pap. 10.95 (*0-19-283860-1*) Oxford Univ. Pr., Inc.

—Sons & Lovers. 1983. pap. 3.95 o.p. (*0-14-006682-9*); 1968. pap. 3.95 o.p. (*0-670-01804-X*); 1958. pap. 2.25 o.p. (*0-670-00037-X*) Penguin Group (USA) Inc.

—Sons & Lovers. 2000. E-Book 4.95 (*0-679-64165-3*); 1999. 752p. pap. 10.95 (*0-375-75373-7*) Random House Adult Trade Publishing Group. (Modern Library).

—Sons & Lovers. (Modern Library Ser.). 1997. 616p. 18.50 o.s.i (*0-679-60268-2*); 1991. 432p. 17.00 (*0-679-40572-0*); 1978. 8.95 o.s.i (*0-394-60452-0*) Random Hse., Inc.

—Sons & Lovers. Baron, Helen & Baron, Carl, eds. 1995. (Twentieth Century Classics Ser.). 544p. 10.95 (*0-14-018832-0*, Penguin Classics) Viking Penguin.

—Sons & Lovers. 1989. 512p. pap. 8.95 o.p. (*0-14-018215-2*, 462, Penguin Classics); 1982. 512p. pap. 4.95 o.p. (*0-14-043154-3*, Penguin Bks.); 1976. 432p. pap. 6.95 o.p. (*0-14-004217-2*, Viking); 1968. pap. 12.95 o.p. (*0-670-65765-4*); 1913. 10.00 o.p. (*0-670-65764-6*) Viking Penguin.

—Sons & Lovers. 1997. (Classics Library). 400p. pap. 3.95 (*1-85326-047-9*, 0479WW) Wordsworth Editions, Ltd. GBR. *Dist:* Casemate Pubs. & Bk. Distributors, LLC.

—Sons & Lovers, Level 5. 2000. (Illus.). vi, 72p. pap. 7.93 (*0-582-41696-5*) Addison-Wesley Longman, Inc.

—Sons & Lovers: A Facsimile of the Manuscript. Schorer, Mark, ed. 1978. 200.00 o.p. (*0-520-03190-3*) Univ. of California Pr.

—Sons & Lovers: Text & Criticism. Moynahan, Julian, ed. 1977. (Critical Studies: No. 4). 640p. pap. 14.95 o.p. (*0-14-015504-X*, Viking) Viking Penguin.

—St. Mawr & Other Stories. Finney, Brian, ed. (Cambridge Edition of the Works of D. H. Lawrence). 314p. 1987. pap. 33.00 (*0-521-29425-8*); 1983. 74.95 o.p. (*0-521-22265-6*) Cambridge Univ. Pr.

—The Trespasser. Mansfield, Elizabeth, ed. 1982. (Cambridge Edition of the Works of D. H. Lawrence). (Illus.). 343p. pap. 38.00 (*0-521-29424-X*) Cambridge Univ. Pr.

—The Trespasser. reprint ed. lib. bdg. 98.00 (*0-7426-3148-6*); 2001. pap. text 28.00 (*0-7426-8148-3*) Classic Bks.

—The Trespasser. 1988. reprint ed. lib. bdg. 49.00 (*0-7812-0179-9*) Reprint Services Corp.

—The Trespasser. 1971. reprint ed. 49.00 (*0-403-01067-5*) Scholarly Pr., Inc.

—The Trespasser. Mansfield, Elizabeth, ed. 1983. (Cambridge Edition Texts Ser.). 256p. 20.00 o.p. (*0-670-72991-4*) Viking Penguin.

—The White Peacock. Robertson, Andrew, ed. (Cambridge Edition of the Works of D. H. Lawrence). (Illus.). 1987. 507p. pap. 46.00 (*0-521-29427-4*); 1983. 512p. 49.50 o.p. (*0-521-22267-2*) Cambridge Univ. Pr.

—The White Peacock. reprint ed. lib. bdg. 98.00 (*0-7426-3147-8*) Classic Bks.

—The White Peacock. 2000. (Oxford World's Classics Ser.). 410p. pap. 9.95 (*0-19-283639-0*) Oxford Univ. Pr., Inc.

—The White Peacock. Bradshaw, David, ed. 1997. (Oxford World's Classics Ser.). 410p. pap. 9.95 o.p. (*0-19-283087-2*) Oxford Univ. Pr., Inc.

—The White Peacock. Robertson, Andrew, ed. 1995. (Penguin Twentieth-Century Classics Ser.). 416p. pap. 12.95 o.s.i (*0-14-018778-2*, Penguin Classics) Viking Penguin.

—The White Peacock. 1990. 432p. pap. 9.95 o.p. (*0-14-018219-5*, Penguin Classics) Viking Penguin.

—The White Peacock. Robertson, Andrew, ed. 1985. (Cambridge Edition Texts Ser.). 416p. 22.50 o.p. (*0-670-76358-6*) Viking Penguin.

—The Woman Who Rode Away & Other Stories. Mehl, Dieter & Jansohn, Christa, eds. 1995. (Cambridge Edition of the Works of D. H. Lawrence). 554p. 130.00 o.s.i (*0-521-22270-2*) Cambridge Univ. Pr.

—The Woman Who Rode Away & Other Stories. 2002. 316p. per. 29.95 (*1-58963-758-5*) Fredonia Bks.

—The Woman Who Rode Away & Other Stories. Mehl, Dieter & Jansohn, Christa, eds. 1997. (Penguin Twentieth-Century Classics Ser.). 224p. pap. 12.95 o.s.i (*0-14-018806-1*) Viking Penguin.

—The Woman Who Rode Away & Other Stories. 1993. 256p. pap. 9.95 o.p. (*0-14-018212-8*, Penguin Classics) Viking Penguin.

—Women in Love. E-Book 4.95 (*1-931208-66-2*) Adobe Systems, Inc.

—Women in Love. 30.95 (*0-89190-612-6*) Amereon, Ltd.

—Women in Love. 1996. 560p. reprint ed. mass mkt. 4.95 (*0-553-21454-3*, Bantam Classics) Bantam Bks.

—Women in Love. E-Book 5.00 (*0-7607-1338-3*) Barnes & Noble, Inc.

—Women in Love. 1984. 421p. reprint ed. lib. bdg. 27.95 (*0-89966-496-2*) Buccaneer Bks., Inc.

—Women in Love. Farmer, David H. et al, eds. 1987. (Cambridge Edition of the Works of D. H. Lawrence). (Illus.). 706p. 115.00 o.p. (*0-521-23565-0*); 705p. pap. 55.00 (*0-521-28041-9*) Cambridge Univ. Pr.

—Women in Love. reprint ed. lib. bdg. 98.00 (*0-7426-3142-7*); 2001. 548p. pap. text 28.00 (*0-7426-8142-4*) Classic Bks.

—Women in Love. 2002. (Thrift Editions Ser.). 400p. pap. 3.50 (*0-486-42458-8*) Dover Pubns., Inc.

—Women in Love. 1992. 20.00 (*0-679-41326-X*, Everyman's Library) Knopf Publishing Group.

—Women in Love. 1992. (Everyman's Library). 20.00 (*0-679-40995-5*) Knopf, Alfred A. Inc.

—Women in Love. 1995. 544p. mass mkt. 6.95 (*0-451-52591-4*, Signet Bks.) NAL.

—Women in Love. 2002. (Twelve-Point Ser.). lib. bdg. 25.00 (*1-58287-180-9*); 722p. lib. bdg. 28.00 (*1-58287-663-0*) North Bks.

—Women in Love. Bradshaw, David, ed. 1998. (Oxford World's Classics Ser.). 576p. pap. 9.95 (*0-19-282995-5*) Oxford Univ. Pr., Inc.

—Women in Love. (Penguin Great Books of the 20th Century Ser.). 2000. (Illus.). 512p. pap. 12.95 o.s.i (*0-14-028337-4*); 1960. pap. 2.75 o.p. (*0-670-00065-5*) Penguin Group (USA) Inc.

—Women in Love. 2000. E-Book 4.95 (*0-679-64166-1*); 576p. pap. 8.95 (*0-375-75488-1*) Random House Adult Trade Publishing Group. (Modern Library).

—Women in Love. 1978. 6.95 o.s.i (*0-394-60442-3*) Random Hse., Inc.

—Women in Love. l.t. ed. 1982. (Charnwood Large Print Ser.). 769p. 29.99 o.p. (*0-7089-8049-X*, Ulverscroft) Thorpe, F. A. Pubs. GBR. *Dist:* Ulverscroft Large Print Bks., Ltd., Ulverscroft Large Print Canada, Ltd.

—Women in Love. 1998. 15.00 (*0-606-21001-6*) Turtleback Bks.

—Women in Love. Farmer, David H. et al, eds. 1995. (Twentieth Century Classics Ser.). (Illus.). 592p. 10.95 (*0-14-018816-9*, Penguin Classics) Viking Penguin.

—Women in Love. 1990. 608p. pap. 8.95 o.p. (*0-14-018221-7*, Penguin Bks.); 1989. 464p. 18.95 o.p. (*0-670-82585-9*) Viking Penguin.

—Women in Love. Ross, Charles L., ed. 1982. (English Library). 608p. pap. 4.95 o.p. (*0-14-043156-X*, Penguin Classics) Viking Penguin.

—Women in Love. 1976. 496p. pap. 7.95 o.p. (*0-14-004260-1*, Penguin Bks.) Viking Penguin.

—Women in Love. 1995. (Classics Ser.). 464p. pap. 3.95 (*1-85326-007-X*, 007XWW) Wordsworth Editions, Ltd. GBR. *Dist:* Casemate Pubs. & Bk. Distributors, LLC.

Lawrence, Kim. Passionate Retribution. 2002. (Harlequin Presents Ser.). 192p. mass mkt. (*0-373-80524-1*, Harlequin Bks.) Harlequin Enterprises, Ltd.

Lawrence, Margaret. The Iceweaver. 2001. 416p. pap. 14.00 (*0-380-79613-9*, Perennial) HarperTrade.

—The Iceweaver. 2000. 416p. 24.00 (*0-380-97621-8*, Morrow, William & Co.) Morrow/Avon.

Lawrence, Nancy. An Intimate Arrangement. 2000. (Zebra Regency Romance Ser.). 224p. mass mkt. 4.99 o.s.i (*0-8217-6740-2*, Zebra Bks.) Kensington Publishing Corp.

Layton, Edith. Duke's Wager: Lord of Dishonor. 2000. (Signet Regency Romance Ser.). 448p. mass mkt. 5.50 o.s.i (*0-451-20139-6*, Signet Bks.) NAL.

Le Carré, John. The Night Manager. (George Smiley Ser.). 1997. pap. 12.00 o.p. (*0-345-41830-1*); 1994. 480p. mass mkt. 6.99 (*0-345-38576-4*) Ballantine Bks.

—The Night Manager. unabr. collector's ed. 1994. (George Smiley Novels Ser.). audio 104.00 (*0-7366-2789-8*, 3505) Books on Tape, Inc.

—The Night Manager. 1993. (George Smiley Novels Ser.). 24.00 o.s.i (*0-679-42513-6*) Knopf, Alfred A. Inc.

—The Night Manager. l.t. ed. 1993. (George Smiley Ser.). 22.00 o.s.i (*0-679-74728-1*) Random Hse. Large Print.

—Single & Single. l.t. ed. (Wheeler Press Paperback Ser.). 2000. 11.95 (*1-56895-969-9*); 1999. 28.95 (*1-56895-748-3*) Gale Group. (Wheeler Publishing, Inc.).

—Single & Single. 1999. (SPA.). 352p. (*84-01-01220-1*) Plaza & Janés Editories, S.A.

—Single & Single. 2000. (SPA.). pap. 13.95 (*84-01-01350-X*) Plaza & Janés Editories, S.A. ESP. *Dist:* Distribooks, Inc.

—Single & Single. 1999. 352p. 26.00 o.s.i (*0-684-86305-7*, Scribner); 1999. (Illus.). 352p. 26.00 o.s.i (*0-684-85926-2*, Scribner); 2003. 368p. reprint ed. pap. 14.00 (*0-7434-5806-0*, Scribner); 2000. 400p. reprint ed. mass mkt. 7.99 (*0-671-02797-2*, Pocket) Simon & Schuster.

Le Fanu, J. Sheridan. Uncle Silas. 1998. (Twelve-Point Ser.). 515p. reprint ed. lib. bdg. 25.00 (*1-58287-001-2*) North Bks.

—Uncle Silas. 1986. 9.00 o.p. (*0-8446-2444-6*) Smith, Peter Pub., Inc.

—Uncle Silas. 2002. 432p. 39.95 (*1-58715-886-8*) Wildside Pr.

—Uncle Silas: A Tale of Bartram-Haugh, 3 vols. 1977. (Collected Works). reprint ed. 90.95 (*0-405-09237-7*) Ayer Co. Pubs., Inc.

—Uncle Silas: A Tale of Bartram-Haugh, 3 vols. Varma, Devendra P., ed. 1977. (Collected Works). reprint ed. 1. 30.95 (*0-405-09238-5*); Vol. 2. 30.95 (*0-405-09239-3*); Vol. 3. 30.95 (*0-405-09240-7*) Ayer Co. Pubs., Inc.

—Uncle Silas: A Tale of Bartram-Haugh. 1992. 400p. reprint ed. lib. bdg. 34.95 (*0-89968-311-8*, Lightyear Pr.) Buccaneer Bks., Inc.

—Uncle Silas: A Tale of Bartram-Haugh. 1966. 436p. reprint ed. pap. 11.95 (*0-486-21715-9*) Dover Pubns., Inc.

—Uncle Silas: A Tale of Bartram-Haugh. l.t. ed. 1992. (Large Print Ser.). 655p. reprint ed. lib. bdg. 28.00 (*0-939495-37-6*) North Bks.

—Uncle Silas: A Tale of Bartram-Haugh. McCormack, W. J., ed. 1982. (Oxford World's Classics Ser.). 464p. pap. 9.95 o.p. (*0-19-281541-5*) Oxford Univ. Pr., Inc.

Le Feuvre, Amy. Probable Sons, No. 2. 1996. (Golden Inheritance Ser.). (J). pap. 5.90 (*0-921100-81-7*) Inheritance Pubns.

—Probable Sons. 1997. (Classic Ser.). 128p. (J). (gr. 4-7). pap. 6.00 (*0-7188-2818-6*) Lutherworth Pr., The GBR. *Dist:* Parkwest Pubns., Inc.

Leach, Christopher. Rosalinda. 1978. (J). (gr. 5 up). 6.95 o.p. (*0-7232-6153-9*, Warne, Frederick) Penguin Putnam Bks. for Young Readers.

Leaman, Celia Ann. Mary's Child. 2002. pap. 15.95 (*1-58749-201-6*); 2000. 300p. E-Book 4.75 (*1-58749-001-3*); 2000. 300p. E-Book 4.75 (*1-58749-000-5*) Awe-Struck E-Bks.

Leather, Stephen. The Chinaman. Grose, Bill, ed. 1992. 320p. 20.00 (*0-671-74301-5*, Atria) Simon & Schuster.

Leavitt, David. While England Sleeps. rev. ed. 1995. 324p. 24.95 o.p. (*0-395-75937-4*); 304p. pap. 11.95 o.s.i (*0-395-75286-8*) Houghton Mifflin Co.

—While England Sleeps. 320p. 9999. pap. 10.95 o.s.i (*0-14-013361-5*, Penguin Bks.); 1993. (Illus.). 22.00 o.p. (*0-670-83349-5*, Viking) Viking Penguin.

Lee, Bernie. Murder Takes Two. 1992. 240p. 18.95 o.p. (*1-55611-280-7*) Fine, Donald I. Bks.

Lee, Earl. Drakulya: The Lost Journal of Mircea Drakulya, Lord of the Undead. 1994. 224p. pap. 10.95 o.p. (*1-884365-02-7*) See Sharp Pr.

Lee, Sandra. Falling for Her. 2000. 304p. pap. 19.00 (*0-553-76276-1*, Fanfare); mass mkt. 5.50 o.s.i (*0-553-58011-6*) Bantam Bks.

Lefebure, Molly. Blitz! 1989. 18.95 o.p. (*0-312-02873-3*) St. Martin's Pr.

Leigh-Austen, Joan & Austen, Jane. Visit to Highbury: Another View of Emma. 1995. 182p. 18.95 o.p. (*0-312-11860-0*) St. Martin's Pr.

Leigh, James. Hangdog Hall. E-Book (*1-84045-038-X*) Online Originals.

Leigh, Tamara. Blackheart. 2001. 400p. mass mkt. 5.99 (*0-8439-4855-8*, Leisure Bks.) Dorchester Publishing Co., Inc.

Leith, Prue. Leaving Patrick. 2001. 320p. 23.95 (*0-312-28258-3*) St. Martin's Pr.

Lemarchand, Elizabeth. Alibi for a Corpse. l.t. ed. 1985. 368p. 15.95 o.p. (*0-7089-1350-4*, Ulverscroft) Thorpe, F. A. Pubs. GBR. *Dist:* Ulverscroft Large Print Bks., Ltd.

—Alibi for a Corpse. 1986. 192p. 14.95 o.p. (*0-8027-5638-7*) Walker & Co.

—Cyanide with Compliments. 1992. (Black Dagger Crime Ser.). 184p. reprint ed. 16.50 o.p. (*0-86220-829-7*, Black Dagger) BBC Audiobooks America.

—Cyanide with Compliments. l.t. ed. 1977. (Ulverscroft Large Print Ser.). 29.99 o.p. (*0-85456-507-8*, Ulverscroft) Thorpe, F. A. Pubs. GBR. *Dist:* Ulverscroft Large Print Bks., Ltd., Ulverscroft Large Print Canada, Ltd.

—Cyanide with Compliments. 1984. (British Mystery Ser.). 175p. reprint ed. pap. 2.95 o.p. (*0-8027-3075-2*) Walker & Co.

—Death of an Old Girl: A Tom Pollard Mystery. 1985. 192p. 13.95 o.p. (*0-8027-5615-8*) Walker & Co.

—The Glade Manor Murders. 1989. 192p. 17.95 (*0-8027-5741-3*) Walker & Co.

—Light Through the Glass. 1986. 192p. 15.95 o.s.i (*0-8027-5649-2*) Walker & Co.

—The Wheel Turns. l.t. ed. 1985. (Ulverscroft Large Print Ser.). 368p. o.p. (*0-7089-1283-4*, Ulverscroft) Thorpe, F. A. Pubs. GBR. *Dist:* Ulverscroft Large Print Canada, Ltd.

—The Wheel Turns. 1986. pap. 2.95 o.p. (*0-8027-3146-5*); 1984. 192p. 12.95 o.s.i (*0-8027-5598-4*) Walker & Co.

—Who Goes Home? l.t. ed. 1987. (Ulverscroft Large Print Ser.). 320p. 29.99 o.p. (*0-7089-1599-X*, Ulverscroft) Thorpe, F. A. Pubs. GBR. *Dist:* Ulverscroft Large Print Bks., Ltd., Ulverscroft Large Print Canada, Ltd.

—Who Goes Home? 1987. 192p. 15.95 (*0-8027-5675-1*) Walker & Co.

Lemarchard, Elizabeth. The Affacombe Affair. 1985. 214p. 13.95 o.p. (*0-8027-5622-0*) Walker & Co.

Lennox, Charlotte. The Life of Harriot Stuart, Written by Herself. Kubica, Susan, ed. & intro. by. 1995. 328p. 45.00 (*0-8386-3579-2*) Fairleigh Dickinson Univ. Pr.

Lennox, Judith. Some Old Lover's Ghost. 1999. 480p. reprint ed. pap. 14.00 (*0-688-17219-9*, Quill) HarperTrade.

—Some Old Lover's Ghost. 2000. 479p. 29.95 (*0-385-40675-4*); 571p. pap. 10.95 (*0-552-14333-2*) Transworld Publishers Ltd. GBR. *Dist:* Trafalgar Square.

Lessing, Doris. The Golden Notebook. 1984. 24.45 o.p. (*0-671-28770-2*, Simon & Schuster) Simon & Schuster.

—The Golden Notebook: A Novel. 1994. 656p. reprint ed. pap. 14.00 o.p. (*0-06-097590-3*, Perennial) HarperTrade.

—Love, Again. l.t. ed. 1996. (Large Print Bks.). 25.95 o.p. (*1-56895-341-0*, Wheeler Publishing, Inc.) Gale Group.

—Love, Again. 1996. 352p. 24.00 o.p. (*0-06-017687-3*) HarperCollins Pubs.

—Love, Again: A Novel. 1997. 368p. pap. 13.00 (*0-06-092796-8*, Perennial) HarperTrade.

—The Real Thing. 1992. 214p. 20.00 o.p. (*0-06-016853-6*) HarperTrade.

Lewin, Michael Z. Family Business: A Novel of Detection. 1995. (Lunghi Family Mystery Ser.). 176p. reprint ed. 20.00 o.p. (*0-88150-348-7*, Foul Play) Norton, W. W. & Co., Inc.

—Family Planning. 1999. 272p. 23.95 (*0-312-24391-X*, Saint Martin's Minotaur) St. Martin's Pr.

Lewis, Roy. Angel of Death. l.t. ed. 1997. (Magna Large Print Ser.). 335p. o.p. (*0-7505-1204-0*) Magna Large Print Bks. GBR. *Dist:* Ulverscroft Large Print Canada, Ltd.

—Angel of Death. unabr. ed. 1999. audio 69.95 (*1-85903-264-8*) Ulverscroft Audio (U.S.A.).

—Bloodeagle. l.t. ed. 1994. 22.95 o.p. (*0-7927-1928-X*); pap. 20.95 o.p. (*0-7927-1927-1*) BBC Audiobooks America.

—Cock of the Walk: A Mid Victorian Rumpus. 1996. (Illus.). 154p. 32.00 (*0-7206-0942-9*) Owen, Peter Ltd. GBR. *Dist:* Dufour Editions, Inc.

—The Cross Bearer. l.t. ed. 1995. (Magna Large Print Ser.). 378p. o.p. (*0-7505-0846-9*) Magna Large Print Bks. GBR. *Dist:* Ulverscroft Large Print Canada, Ltd.

—Cross Bearer: An Arnold Landon Mystery. 1994. 205p. 18.95 o.p. (*0-312-11765-5*, Saint Martin's Minotaur) St. Martin's Pr.

—Dead Secret: An Arnold Landon Mystery. 2001. 256p. 24.00 (*0-7867-0885-9*, Carroll & Graf Pubs.) Avalon Publishing Group.

—The Devil Is Dead. l.t. ed. 1990. 17.95 o.p. (*0-7451-9920-8*, C0638); pap. 15.95 o.p. (*0-7927-0370-7*, C0832) BBC Audiobooks America.

—The Devil Is Dead. 1990. 208p. 15.95 o.p. (*0-312-04851-3*, Saint Martin's Minotaur) St. Martin's Pr.

—A Gathering of Ghosts. 1983. 192p. 10.95 o.p. (*0-312-31788-3*) St. Martin's Pr.

—Men of Subtle Craft. 1988. 192p. 13.95 (*0-312-81789-4*) St. Martin's Pr.

—Most Cunning Workmen. 1986. (Atlantic Ser.). 274 p. (*0-89340-966-9*) BBC Audiobooks America.

—Most Cunning Workmen. 1985. 182 p. 10.95 o.p. (*0-312-54907-5*) St. Martin's Pr.

—A Secret Dying: An Arthur Landon Mystery. l.t. ed. 1993. 21.95 o.p. (*0-7927-1546-2*); pap. 19.95 o.p. (*0-7927-1545-4*) BBC Audiobooks America.

—A Secret Dying: An Arthur Landon Mystery. 1993. 17.95 o.p. (*0-312-08887-6*, Saint Martin's Minotaur) St. Martin's Pr.

—A Wisp of Smoke. 1991. 208p. 17.95 o.p. (*0-312-07123-X*, Saint Martin's Minotaur) St. Martin's Pr.

Lewis, Roy H. Bloodeagle: An Arnold Landon Mystery. 1993. 224p. 19.95 o.p. (*0-312-10431-6*, Saint Martin's Minotaur) St. Martin's Pr.

—A Blurred Reality. 1985. 192p. 12.95 o.p. (*0-312-08725-X*) St. Martin's Pr.

—Dwell in Danger. 1982. 192p. 10.95 o.p. (*0-312-22286-6*) St. Martin's Pr.

—Men of Subtle Craft. l.t. ed. 1988. pap. 14.95 o.p. (*1-55504-661-4*, 462) BBC Audiobooks America.

—Once Dying, Twice Dead. l.t. ed. 1985. 12.95 o.p. (*0-8166-0110-0*, Macmillan Reference USA) Gale Group.

—Once Dying, Twice Dead. 1984. 192p. 10.95 o.p. (*0-312-58476-8*) St. Martin's Pr.

—Premium on Death: An Eric Ward Novel. 1987. 208p. 13.95 o.p. (*0-312-00019-7*) St. Martin's Pr.

—The Salamander Chill. l.t. ed. 1991. 8.95 o.p. (*0-7451-9504-0*, 73); pap. 10.95 o.p. (*1-55504-903-6*, 359) BBC Audiobooks America.

—The Salamander Chill. 1988. 192p. 14.95 o.p. (*0-312-02637-4*, Saint Martin's Minotaur) St. Martin's Pr.

—A Trout in the Milk: An Arnold Landon Novel. l.t. ed. 1988. (Atlantic Large Print Ser.). 285 p. (*1-55504-562-6*) BBC Audiobooks America.

—A Trout in the Milk: An Arnold Landon Novel. 1986. 208p. 13.95 o.p. (*0-312-82009-7*) St. Martin's Pr.

—A Wisp of Smoke. l.t. ed. 1992. (Magna Large Print Ser.). 326p. 29.99 (*0-7505-0355-6*) Magna Large Print Bks. GBR. *Dist:* Ulverscroft Large Print Bks., Ltd.

Lewis, Wyndham. The Apes of God. 1992. (Illus.). 642p. reprint ed. 25.00 o.p. (*0-87685-513-3*, Black Sparrow Pr.) Godine, David R. Pub.

—The Apes of God. 1992. (Illus.). 642p. reprint ed. pap. 17.50 (*0-87685-512-5*) HarperCollins Pubs.

Lide, Mary. Polmena Cove. l.t. ed. 1995. 323p. pap. 19.95 o.p. (*0-7838-1203-5*, Macmillan Reference USA) Gale Group.

—Polmena Cove. 1994. 230p. 19.95 o.p. (*0-312-11877-5*) St. Martin's Pr.

—The Sea Scape. 1992. 256p. 17.95 o.p. (*0-312-07799-8*) St. Martin's Pr.

Lightfoot, Freda. Manchester Pride. l.t. ed. 2000. (Magna Large Print Ser.). 448p. (*0-7505-1478-7*) Magna Large Print Bks. GBR. *Dist:* Ulverscroft Large Print Bks., Ltd., Ulverscroft Large Print Canada, Ltd.

Lillington, Kenneth. Josephine. 1989. (Children's Paperbacks Ser.). 148p. (J). (gr. 3-6). pap. 4.95 o.p. (*0-571-16118-9*) Faber & Faber, Inc.

—The Mad Detective. 1992. 160p. (YA). (gr. 7 up). 15.95 o.p. (*0-571-16593-1*) Faber & Faber, Inc.

—The Real Live Dinosaur & Other Stories. 1990. (Illus.). 96p. (J). (gr. 3-7). bds. 10.95 o.p. (*0-571-14144-7*) Faber & Faber, Inc.

—Selkie. 1985. 145p. (YA). (gr. 7-10). o.p. (*0-571-13421-1*) Faber & Faber Ltd.

Lindsey, Johanna. Joining. abr. ed. 2000. audio 7.99 o.s.i (*1-56740-346-8*, 2107, Paperback Nova Audio Bks.); 1999. audio 17.95 o.p. (*1-56740-858-3*, 1795, Nova Audio Bks.); 1999. 9p. audio 57.25 (*1-56740-674-2*, 1794, Unabridged Library Editions); 1999. audio 35.95 (*1-56740-448-0*, 1793, Brilliance Audio Unabridged) Brilliance Audio.

—Joining. l.t. ed. 1999. 27.95 o.p. (*1-56895-771-8*, Wheeler Publishing, Inc.) Gale Group.

—Joining. unabr. ed. 1999. audio 57.25 Highsmith Inc.

—Joining. 2000. 400p. mass mkt. 7.99 (*0-380-79333-4*); 1999. 384p. 24.00 o.p. (*0-380-97535-1*) Morrow/Avon. (Avon Bks.).

—Say You Love Me. abr. ed. (Malory Family Ser.). 1997. audio 7.99 o.p. (*1-56740-196-1*, 696, Paperback Nova Audio Bks.); 1996. audio 16.95 o.p. (*1-56100-921-0*, 1429, Nova Audio Bks.); 1996. 10p. audio 73.25 o.p. (*1-56100-336-0*, 1026, Unabridged Library Editions); 1996. audio 23.95 o.p. (*1-56100-711-0*, 248, Bookcassette) Brilliance Audio.

—Say You Love Me. l.t. ed. 1997. (Core Ser.). 477p. lib. bdg. 26.95 (*0-7838-1928-5*, Macmillan Reference USA) Gale Group.

—Say You Love Me. l.t. ed. 1997. (Malory Novels Ser.). 432p. mass mkt. 7.99 (*0-380-72571-1*, Avon Bks.) Morrow/Avon.

Settings

—Say You Love Me. l.t. ed. 1998. (Paperback Bestsellers Ser.). 454p. pap. 25.95 (*0-7838-1927-7*) Thorndike Pr.
—Secret Fire. l.t. ed. 1996. (Americana Ser.). 505p. lib. bdg. 26.95 o.p. (*0-7862-0725-6*) Thorndike Pr.
—When Love Awaits. l.t. ed. 1987. 374p. 17.95 o.p. (*0-8161-4176-2*, Macmillan Reference USA) Gale Group.
—When Love Awaits. 1991. reprint ed. 19.95 o.p. (*0-7278-4168-8*) Severn Hse. Pubs., Ltd.
Linney, Romulus. A Christmas Carol. 1996. per. 6.50 (*0-8222-1539-X*) Dramatists Play Service, Inc.
Linscott, Gillian. Absent Friends. l.t. ed. 2000. (Magna Large Print Ser.). 368p. (*0-7505-1488-4*) Magna Large Print Bks. GBR. *Dist:* Ulverscroft Large Print Bks., Ltd., Ulverscroft Large Print Canada, Ltd.
—Absent Friends. 1999. 288p. 22.95 (*0-312-20765-4*, Saint Martin's Minotaur) St. Martin's Pr.
—Crown Witness. l.t. ed. 1997. (Dales Large Print Ser.). 383p. pap. 19.99 (*1-85389-712-4*) Dales Large Print Bks. GBR. *Dist:* Ulverscroft Large Print Bks., Ltd.
—Crown Witness. 1996. 218p. mass mkt. o.s.i (*0-7515-1657-0*); 1995. 256p. o.s.i (*0-316-91419-3*) Little Brown & Co.
—Crown Witness. 1995. 224p. 20.95 o.p. (*0-312-13456-8*, Saint Martin's Minotaur) St. Martin's Pr.
—Dance on Blood. l.t. ed. 1999. (Magna Large Print Ser.). 384p. (*0-7505-1385-3*) Magna Large Print Bks. GBR. *Dist:* Ulverscroft Large Print Canada, Ltd.
—Dance on Blood. 1998. (Nell Bray Mystery Ser.). 256p. 22.95 o.p. (*0-312-18075-6*, 853567, Saint Martin's Minotaur) St. Martin's Pr.
—Dance on Blood. 1998. 250p. pap. o.s.i (*1-86049-312-2*) Virago Pr., Ltd. GBR. *Dist:* Little Brown & Co.
—Dead Man Riding. Date not set. (Nell Bray Mystery Ser.). (*0-312-30747-0*, Saint Martin's Minotaur); mass mkt. (*0-312-98990-3*, St. Martin's Paperbacks) St. Martin's Pr.
—Dead Man Riding: A Nell Bray Mystery. 2003. (Nell Bray Mystery Ser.). 320p. 24.95 (*0-312-30824-8*, Saint Martin's Minotaur) St. Martin's Pr.
—Dead Man's Sweetheart. 1996. 272p. 21.95 o.p. (*0-312-14579-9*, Saint Martin's Minotaur) St. Martin's Pr.
—An Easy Day for a Lady. 1995. 210p. 19.95 o.p. (*0-312-11811-2*, Saint Martin's Minotaur) St. Martin's Pr.
—Stage Fright. l.t. ed. 1994. 20.95 o.p. (*0-7927-2044-X*); pap. 19.95 o.p. (*0-7927-2043-1*) BBC Audiobooks America.
—Stage Fright. 1993. 192p. 17.95 o.p. (*0-312-09812-X*, Saint Martin's Minotaur) St. Martin's Pr.
Liss, David. A Conspiracy of Paper. E-Book 19.95 (*1-58945-562-2*) Adobe Systems, Inc.
—A Conspiracy of Paper. 2001. (Reader's Circle Ser.). 464p. pap. 14.95 (*0-8041-1912-0*, Ballantine Bks.) Ballantine Bks.
—A Conspiracy of Paper. 2000. E-Book 19.95 (*0-375-50504-0*) Random Hse., Inc.
—A Conspiracy of Paper. l.t. ed. 2000. (Basic Ser.). 781p. pap. 28.95 (*0-7862-2665-X*) Thorndike Pr.
Littlejohn, Richard. Reasonable Force. 2001. 425p. mass mkt. (*0-00-710613-0*) HarperCollins Pubs.
Litton, Josie. Dream of Me/Believe in Me. 2001. 816p. mass mkt. 5.99 (*0-553-58436-7*) Bantam Bks.
Lively, Penelope. City of the Mind: A Novel. 1991. 240p. 20.00 o.p. (*0-06-016666-5*) HarperTrade.
—Passing On. 224p. 1990. 17.95 o.p. (*0-8021-1155-6*); 1999. reprint ed. pap. 12.00 (*0-8021-3626-5*, Grove Pr.) Grove/Atlantic, Inc.
—Passing On. 1991. 224p. reprint ed. pap. 12.00 o.s.i (*0-06-097370-6*, Perennial) HarperTrade.
—Passing On. unabr. ed. 2001. audio 61.95 (*1-85089-786-7*, 9007X); 2000. audio compact disk 59.95 (*0-7531-0701-5*, 107015) ISIS Audio Bks. GBR. *Dist:* Ulverscroft Large Print Bks., Ltd.
—Passing On. l.t. ed. 1990. 342p. 19.95 (*1-85089-329-2*) ISIS Large Print Bks. GBR. *Dist:* Transaction Pubs.
—The Photograph. 2003. 240p. 24.95 (*0-670-03205-0*, Viking) Viking Penguin.
—The Road to Lichfield. 224p. 1991. 17.95 o.p. (*0-8021-1134-3*); 1999. reprint ed. pap. 12.00 (*0-8021-3625-7*, Grove Pr.) Grove/Atlantic, Inc.
—The Road to Lichfield. 1992. 224p. reprint ed. pap. 12.00 o.p. (*0-06-097461-3*, Perennial) HarperTrade.
—Spiderweb. l.t. ed. 240p. 2000. pap. 21.99 (*0-7531-6057-9*); 1999. 32.50 (*0-7531-5996-1*, 159961) ISIS Large Print Bks. GBR. *Dist:* Ulverscroft Large Print Bks., Ltd., Ulverscroft Large Print Canada, Ltd.
—Spiderweb. unabr. ed. 2000. audio 54.95 (*1-86042-512-7*, 25127) Soundings, Ltd. GBR. *Dist:* Ulverscroft Large Print Bks., Ltd.
—Spiderweb: A Novel. 1999. 224p. o.s.i (*0-06-019233-X*, HarperFlamingo) HarperCollins Pubs. Canada, Ltd.
—Spiderweb: A Novel. 2000. 224p. pap. 13.00 (*0-06-092972-3*, Perennial) HarperTrade.
Livingston, Nancy. Death in a Distant Land. l.t. ed. 1989. 15.95 o.p. (*0-7451-9454-0*, 252); pap. 14.95 o.p. (*1-55504-807-2*, 692) BBC Audiobooks America.
—Death in a Distant Land. 1989. 192p. 14.95 o.p. (*0-312-02565-3*, Saint Martin's Minotaur) St. Martin's Pr.
—Death in Close-Up. l.t. ed. 1990. 16.95 o.p. (*0-7451-9844-9*, C0325); pap. 15.95 o.p. (*0-7927-0303-0*) BBC Audiobooks America.
—Death in Close-Up. 1990. 15.95 o.p. (*0-312-04296-5*, Saint Martin's Minotaur) St. Martin's Pr.
—The Far Side of the Hill. 1988. 480p. 19.95 o.p. (*0-312-02207-7*) St. Martin's Pr.
—Fatality at Bath & Wells: A G. D. H. Pringle Mystery. 1986. 224p. 14.95 o.p. (*0-312-00004-9*) St. Martin's Pr.
—Incident at Parga. 1989. mass mkt. (*0-373-28001-7*, 1-28001-5, Harlequin Bks.) Harlequin Enterprises, Ltd.
—Incident at Parga. 1999. mass mkt. 2.95 (*0-312-91389-3*, St. Martin's Paperbacks); 1987. 224p. 15.95 o.p. (*0-312-01446-5*, Saint Martin's Minotaur) St. Martin's Pr.
—The Land of Our Dreams. 1989. 384p. 18.95 o.p. (*0-312-03374-5*) St. Martin's Pr.
—Mayhem in Parva. l.t. ed. 1992. 18.95 o.p. (*0-7451-8307-7*, AH0286); pap. 16.95 o.p. (*0-7927-0963-2*, AS0322) BBC Audiobooks America.
—Mayhem in Parva. 1991. 192p. 16.95 o.p. (*0-312-06410-1*, Saint Martin's Minotaur) St. Martin's Pr.
—Never Were Such Times. l.t. ed. 1992. (Magna Large Print Ser.). 763p. o.p. (*0-7505-0195-2*) Magna Large Print Bks. GBR. *Dist:* Ulverscroft Large Print Canada, Ltd.
—Never Were Such Times. 1991. 19.95 o.p. (*0-312-05902-7*) St. Martin's Pr.
—Quiet Murder. l.t. ed. 1993. 23.95 o.p. (*0-7927-1797-X*); pap. 21.95 o.p. (*0-7927-1796-1*) BBC Audiobooks America.
—Quiet Murder. 1995. 253p. per. (*0-373-26186-1*, 1-26186-6, Worldwide Library) Harlequin Enterprises, Ltd.
—Quiet Murder. l.t. ed. 1993. (Magna Large Print Ser.). 388p. o.p. (*0-7505-0582-6*) Magna Large Print Bks. GBR. *Dist:* Ulverscroft Large Print Canada, Ltd.
—Quiet Murder. 1993. 17.95 o.p. (*0-312-08878-7*, Saint Martin's Minotaur) St. Martin's Pr.
—The Trouble at Aquitaine. 1985. 192p. 12.95 o.p. (*0-312-81975-7*) St. Martin's Pr.
—Two Sisters. 1994. 592p. 25.95 o.p. (*0-312-11346-3*) St. Martin's Pr.
—Unwillingly to Vegas. l.t. ed. 1993. 21.95 o.p. (*0-7927-1488-1*); pap. 19.95 o.p. (*0-7927-1487-3*) BBC Audiobooks America.
—Unwillingly to Vegas. l.t. ed. 1993. (Magna Large Print Ser.). 354p. (*0-7505-0495-1*) Magna Large Print Bks. GBR. *Dist:* Ulverscroft Large Print Canada, Ltd.
—Unwillingly to Vegas. 1992. 192p. 16.95 o.p. (*0-312-08329-7*, Saint Martin's Minotaur) St. Martin's Pr.
Llewellyn, Caroline. False Light. l.t. ed. 1997. (Large Print Bks.). pap. 23.95 (*1-56895-403-4*, Wheeler Publishing, Inc.) Gale Group.
—False Light. 1996. 315p. 21.50 o.p. (*0-684-82460-4*, Scribner) Simon & Schuster.
—Life Blood. 1994. mass mkt. 5.99 o.s.i (*0-8041-1263-0*, Ivy Bks.) Ballantine Bks.
—Life Blood. 1993. 352p. 20.00 o.p. (*0-684-19402-3*); 1994. 571p. lib. bdg. 21.95 (*0-8161-5940-8*) Gale Group. (Macmillan Reference USA).
Llewellyn, Sam. Death Roll. unabr. ed. 1990. audio 69.95 (*0-7451-6108-1*) BBC Audiobooks America.
—Death Roll. Chelius, Jane, ed. 1991. 256p. reprint ed. bds. 3.95 (*0-671-67043-3*, Pocket) Simon & Schuster.
—Death Roll. 1990. 247p. 18.95 o.p. (*0-671-67045-X*) Summit Bks.
—Maelstrom. 1996. 384p. mass mkt. 5.99 (*0-671-78997-X*, Pocket) Simon & Schuster.
—Maelstrom. Chelius, Jane, ed. 1994. 416p. 20.00 o.p. (*0-671-78995-3*, Atria) Simon & Schuster.
Lloyd, A. R. The Farm Dog. l.t. ed. 2002. (Ulverscroft Large Print Ser.). 304p. 32.50 (*0-7089-4763-8*, Ulverscroft) Thorpe, F. A. Pubs. GBR. *Dist:* Ulverscroft Large Print Bks., Ltd., Ulverscroft Large Print Canada, Ltd.
—The Farm Dog. 1986. 260p. 18.95 o.p. (*0-7126-9513-3*) Trafalgar Square.
Lloyd, Jeremy. The Are You Being Served? Stories: "Camping In" & Other Fiascoes. 1997. Orig. Title: Are You Being Served?. (Illus.). 224p. reprint ed. pap. 12.95 (*0-912333-02-2*) Bay Soma Publishing.
Lodge, David. The British Museum Is Falling Down. 1989. (King Penguin Ser.). 182p. pap. 14.00 (*0-14-012419-5*, Penguin Bks.) Penguin Group (USA) Inc.
—Nice Work. l.t. ed. 1989. 432p. reprint ed. lib. bdg. 19.95 o.p. (*1-85089-293-8*) ISIS Large Print Bks. GBR. *Dist:* Transaction Pubs.
—Nice Work. 1990. (King Penguin Ser.). 288p. pap. 14.00 (*0-14-013396-8*, Penguin Bks.) Penguin Group (USA) Inc.
—Nice Work. 1989. 288p. 18.95 o.p. (*0-670-82806-8*) Viking Penguin.
—Therapy. unabr. ed. 1998. audio 84.95 (*1-85089-879-0*, 951106) ISIS Audio Bks. GBR. *Dist:* Ulverscroft Large Print Bks., Ltd.
—Therapy. 1996. 336p. 14.00 (*0-14-024900-1*); 1995. 368p. 22.95 o.p. (*0-670-86358-0*, Viking); 1996. 2p. audio 16.95 o.s.i (*0-14-086356-7*, Penguin AudioBooks) Viking Penguin.
—Thinks... 2001. 320p. (*0-436-44502-6*) Secker, Martin & Warburg, Ltd. GBR. *Dist:* Random Hse. of Canada, Ltd.
—Thinks... 2002. 352p. 14.00 (*0-14-200086-8*) Viking Penguin.
—Thinks. . . A Novel. 2001. 288p. 24.95 o.p. (*0-670-89984-4*, Viking) Viking Penguin.
Lodge, Thomas. Rosalynd. Nellist, Brian, ed. 1998. (Renaissance Texts & Studies). 128p. pap. 18.50 (*1-85331-106-5*) Edinburgh Univ. Pr. GBR. *Dist:* Columbia Univ. Pr.
—Rosalynde, Being the Original of Shakespeare's As You Like It. Greg, W. W., ed. 1977. (Select Bibliographies Reprint Ser.). reprint ed. 19.95 (*0-8369-5510-2*) Ayer Co. Pubs., Inc.
Long, James. Ferney. 2000. 464p. mass mkt. 6.50 (*0-553-58141-4*) Bantam Bks.
Loring, Emilie Baker. High of Heart, No. 30. 1981. 224p. pap. 1.95 o.p. (*0-553-20112-3*) Bantam Bks.
Lovesey, Peter. Abracadaver. 1994. 224p. 16.95 o.p. (*0-7451-8645-9*, Black Dagger); 1996. audio 54.95 (*0-7451-6110-3*, CAB294) BBC Audiobooks America.
—Abracadaver. 1989. 256p. reprint ed. pap. 4.50 o.p. (*0-06-081000-9*, Perennial) HarperTrade.
—Abracadaver. l.t. ed. 2000. (General Ser.). 284p. 24.95 (*0-7862-2802-4*) Thorndike Pr.
—Abracadaver. 1981. 224p. pap. 3.95 o.p. (*0-14-005803-6*, Penguin Bks.) Viking Penguin.
—Bertie & the Crime of Passion. 1995. 256p. 19.95 o.s.i (*0-89296-550-9*) Mysterious Pr.
—Bertie & the Crime of Passion. 1995. 240p. mass mkt. 5.50 o.s.i (*0-446-40368-7*) Warner Bks., Inc.
—Bertie & the Seven Bodies. Set. unabr. ed. 1993. (Detective Memoirs of King Edward the Eighth Ser.). 54.95 incl. audio (*0-7451-6111-1*, CAB 623) BBC Audiobooks America.
—Bertie & the Seven Bodies. 1990. 208p. 16.95 o.p. (*0-89296-399-9*) Mysterious Pr.
—Bertie & the Seven Bodies. 1991. (Audio Books Ser.). audio 53.95 o.p. (*0-8161-9247-2*) Thorndike Pr.
—Bertie & the Seven Bodies. 1991. mass mkt. 4.95 o.s.i (*0-445-40858-8*) Warner Bks., Inc.
—Bertie & the Tin Man, from the Detective Memoirs of King Edward the Seventh. unabr. ed. 1990. audio 54.95 (*0-7451-6113-8*) BBC Audiobooks America.
—Bertie & the Tinman. 1988. 15.95 o.p. (*0-89296-196-1*) Mysterious Pr.
—Bertie & the Tinman. 1989. mass mkt. 3.95 (*0-445-40592-9*, Mysterious Pr. Paperback Bks.) Warner Bks., Inc.
—Bloodhounds. l.t. ed. 1997. (G. K. Hall Mystery Ser.). 509p. 26.95 o.p. (*0-7838-8097-9*, Macmillan Reference USA) Gale Group.
—Bloodhounds. (Peter Diamond Mystery Ser.). 368p. 1997. mass mkt. 5.99 o.p. (*0-446-40535-3*); 1996. 22.00 o.p. (*0-89296-645-9*) Warner Bks., Inc.
—The Bloodhounds. unabr. ed. 1999. audio 84.95 (*1-86042-283-7*, 22837) Soundings, Ltd. GBR. *Dist:* Ulverscroft Large Print Bks., Ltd.
—A Case of Spirits. 1977. (Crime Ser.). 192p. pap. 3.95 o.p. (*0-14-004333-0*, Penguin Bks.) Viking Penguin.
—The Detective Wore Silk Drawers. 1988. audio 35.95 o.p. (*0-8161-9452-1*) Thorndike Pr.
—The Detective Wore Silk Drawers. 1980. (Crime Monthly Ser.). pap. 3.95 o.p. (*0-14-005558-4*, Penguin Bks.) Viking Penguin.
—The Detective Wore Silk Drawers: A Sergeant Cribb Adventure. unabr. ed. 1995. audio 39.95 (*0-7451-6112-X*, CAB 338) BBC Audiobooks America.
—The Detective Wore Silk Drawers: A Sergeant Cribb Mystery. 1989. 208p. reprint ed. pap. 4.50 o.p. (*0-06-080999-X*, Perennial) HarperTrade.
—The Detective Wore Silk Drawers: A Sergeant Cribb Mystery. l.t. ed. 2000. (General Ser.). 268p. pap. 23.95 (*0-7862-2426-6*) Thorndike Pr.
—Diamond Dust. unabr. ed. 2002. 10p. audio 84.95 (*0-7540-0877-0*) Chivers Audio Bks. GBR. *Dist:* BBC Audiobooks America.
—Diamond Dust. 2003. 356p. pap. 13.00 (*1-56947-322-6*); 2002. 296p. 24.00 (*1-56947-291-2*); 2002. 304p. 23.00 (*1-56947-300-5*) Soho Pr., Inc.
—Diamond Dust. 2002. (Basic Ser.). 27.95 (*0-7862-4894-7*) Thorndike Pr.
—Diamond Solitaire. 2002. 327p. pap. 13.00 (*1-56947-292-0*) Soho Pr., Inc.
—Diamond Solitaire. 1994. 336p. mass mkt. 5.50 o.p. (*0-446-40347-4*, Mysterious Pr. Paperback Bks.) Warner Bks., Inc.
—The House Sitter. 2003. 304p. 25.00 (*1-56947-326-9*) Soho Pr., Inc.
—The House Sitter. l.t. ed. 2003. (Peter Diamond Mystery Ser.). 560p. 28.95 (*0-7862-5807-1*) Thorndike Pr.
—Invitation to a Dynamite Party. 1981. 176p. pap. 3.95 o.p. (*0-14-004029-3*, Penguin Bks.) Viking Penguin.
—The Last Detective. 1992. 416p. mass mkt. 4.99 o.s.i (*0-553-29619-1*) Bantam Bks.
—The Last Detective. 2000. 368p. pap. 13.00 (*1-56947-209-2*) Soho Pr., Inc.
—Mad Hatter's Holiday. 1990. 256p. reprint ed. pap. 4.50 o.p. (*0-06-081022-X*, Perennial) HarperTrade.
—Mad Hatter's Holiday. 1990. 256p. (C). reprint ed. lib. bdg. 20.00 o.p. (*0-8095-9022-0*) Millefleurs.
—Mad Hatter's Holiday. l.t. ed. 2001. 246p. pap. 25.95 (*0-7862-3498-9*); 259p. (*0-7540-4593-5*); 259p. (*0-7540-4594-3*) Thorndike Pr.
—Mad Hatter's Holiday. 1981. 192p. pap. 3.95 o.p. (*0-14-005804-4*, Penguin Bks.) Viking Penguin.
—The Reaper. 2002. 304p. pap. 12.00 (*1-56947-308-0*); 2001. 295p. 23.00 (*1-56947-227-0*) Soho Pr., Inc.
—The Reaper. l.t. ed. 2001. 368p. 28.95 o.p. (*0-7862-3438-5*) Thorndike Pr.
—The Summons. 1995. (Peter Diamond Mystery Ser.). 352p. 21.95 o.p. (*0-89296-551-7*) Mysterious Pr.
—The Summons. 1996. 352p. mass mkt. 5.99 o.s.i (*0-446-40369-5*) Warner Bks., Inc.
—Swing, Swing Together. 1976. 21.95 (*0-89190-093-4*) Amereon, Ltd.
—Swing, Swing Together. 1990. 352p. (C). reprint ed. lib. bdg. 20.00 o.p. (*0-8095-9023-9*) Millefleurs.
—Swing, Swing Together. 1978. (Crime Ser.). pap. 3.95 o.p. (*0-14-004618-6*, Penguin Bks.) Viking Penguin.
—Swing, Swing Together: A Sergeant Cribb Mystery. 1990. 352p. reprint ed. pap. 4.50 o.p. (*0-06-081023-8*, Perennial) HarperTrade.
—Swing, Swing Together: A Sergeant Cribb Mystery. 2002. (General Ser.). 24.95 (*0-7862-4408-9*) Thorndike Pr.
—Upon a Dark Night. 1998. 384p. 23.00 o.p. (*0-89296-669-6*) Mysterious Pr.
—Upon a Dark Night. l.t. ed. 1998. (Mystery Ser.). 583p. 27.95 (*0-7862-1530-5*) Thorndike Pr.
—The Vault. 2000. 331p. 23.00 (*1-56947-208-4*); 2001. 332p. reprint ed. pap. 13.00 (*1-56947-256-4*) Soho Pr., Inc.
—The Vault. l.t. ed. 2001. (Basic Ser.). 496p. 28.95 (*0-7862-3063-0*) Thorndike Pr.
—Waxwork. l.t. ed. 1978. 12.95 o.p. (*0-8161-6651-X*, Macmillan Reference USA) Gale Group.
—Waxwork. 1978. 7.95 o.p. (*0-394-50066-0*, Pantheon) Knopf Publishing Group.
—Waxwork. 1980. (Crime Monthly Ser.). pap. 3.95 o.p. (*0-14-004887-1*, Penguin Bks.) Viking Penguin.
—Wobble to Death. l.t. ed. 1999. (General Ser.). 272p. pap. 23.95 (*0-7862-1868-1*) Thorndike Pr.
—Wobble to Death. 1980. pap. 3.95 o.p. (*0-14-005557-6*, Penguin Bks.) Viking Penguin.
Lowndes, Marie B. The Lodger. Marcus, Laura, ed. 1996. (Oxford Popular Fiction Ser.). 228p. pap. 8.95 o.p. (*0-19-282371-X*) Oxford Univ. Pr., Inc.
Lumley, Brian. Necroscope: The Lost Years. 1995. (Necroscope Ser.: Vol. 9). 384p. 23.95 o.p. (*0-312-85947-3*, Tor Bks.) Doherty, Tom Assocs., LLC.
—Necroscope II: Vamphyri! 1996. (Necroscope Ser.: Vol. 2). 384p. 24.95 o.p. (*0-312-86212-1*, Tor Bks.) Doherty, Tom Assocs., LLC.
Lyall, Francis. Death in the Winter Garden. l.t. ed. 2001. (Dales Large Print Ser.). 288p. pap. 21.99 (*1-84262-079-7*) Dales Large Print Bks. GBR. *Dist:* Ulverscroft Large Print Bks., Ltd., Ulverscroft Large Print Canada, Ltd.
Lynnford, Janet. Lady Shadowhawk. 1997. 352p. mass mkt. 5.99 o.s.i (*0-451-40764-4*, Onyx) NAL.
—Lord of Lightning. 1996. 384p. mass mkt. 5.50 o.s.i (*0-451-40685-0*, Topaz) NAL.
—Pirate's Rose. 1995. 384p. (Orig.). mass mkt. 4.99 o.s.i (*0-451-40597-8*, Topaz) NAL.
Lytton, Edward Bulwer & Ainsworth, William Harrison. Cult Criminals: The Newgate Novels, 1830-1847, 6 vols. John, Juliet, ed. 1998. (Subcultures & Subversions: 1750-1850 Ser.). 2712p. (C). lib. bdg. 715.00 (*0-415-14383-7*) Routledge.
MacDonald, George. Home Again. Hamilton, Dan, ed. 1988. 192p. pap. text 5.95 o.p. (*0-89693-464-0*) Cook Communications Ministries.
—Home Again. 2003. (George MacDonald Original Works Ser.: Series II). 373p. reprint ed. 24.00 (*1-881084-11-6*) Johannesen Printing & Publishing.
MacDonald, George & Phillips, Michael R. The Poet's Homecoming. 1990. 192p. pap. 7.99 o.p. (*1-55661-135-8*) Bethany Hse. Pubs.

MacDonald, George, et al. The Curate of Glaston. 2002. 624p. pap. 12.99 (*0-7642-2591-X*) Bethany Hse. Pubs.
MacDonald, John F. Tribe. 2002. 279p. 22.00 (*1-931561-06-0*) MacAdam/Cage Publishing, Inc.
MacDonald, Malcolm. Kernow & Daughter. 1996. 400p. 23.95 o.p. (*0-312-13995-0*) St. Martin's Pr.
Macdonald, Malcolm. Tessa D'Arblay. 1985. 320p. 15.95 o.p. (*0-312-79350-2*) St. Martin's Pr.
—To the End of Her Days. 1994. 384p. 23.95 o.p. (*0-312-11080-4*) St. Martin's Pr.
—The Trevarton Inheritance. 1996. 400p. 24.95 o.p. (*0-312-14748-1*) St. Martin's Pr.
MacDonald, Malcolm. Woman Alone. 1991. 18.95 o.p. (*0-312-06000-9*) St. Martin's Pr.
Macdonald, Malcolm. A Woman Possessed. 1993. 384p. 21.95 o.p. (*0-312-09416-7*) St. Martin's Pr.
MacDonald, Malcolm, et al. Like a Diamond. 2nd ed. 1999. 377p. 23.95 o.p. (*0-312-20557-0*) St. Martin's Pr.
MacDonald, Marianne. Death's Autograph. abr. ed. 1998. audio 54.95 (*0-7540-0089-3*, CAB1512) BBC Audiobooks America.
—Death's Autograph: A Mystery. 1999. (Antiquarian Book Mysteries Ser.). 352p. mass mkt. 5.99 (*0-06-109742-X*, HarperTorch) Morrow/Avon.
—Death's Autograph: A Mystery. 1997. (Dido Hoare Mysteries Ser.). 224p. 22.95 o.p. (*0-312-16815-2*, Saint Martin's Minotaur) St. Martin's Pr.
—Ghost Walk. 2000. (Antiquarian Book Mysteries Ser.). 304p. mass mkt. 5.99 (*0-06-101426-5*) HarperCollins Pubs.
—Ghost Walk. 1998. (Dido Hoare Mysteries Ser.). 256p. 21.95 o.p. (*0-312-19417-X*, Saint Martin's Minotaur) St. Martin's Pr.
—Smoke Screen. 1999. 255p. 23.95 o.p. (*0-312-24243-3*, Saint Martin's Minotaur) St. Martin's Pr.
Macdonald, Peter. X V-DA. E-Book (*1-84045-028-2*) Online Originals.
MacDonald, Shari. Forget-Me-Not. 1996. 274p. pap. 9.99 o.s.i (*0-88070-769-0*, Palisades) Multnomah Pubs., Inc.
MacGregor, Kinley. Master of Desire. 2001. 384p. mass mkt. 5.99 (*0-06-108713-0*, Avon Bks.) Morrow/Avon.
MacInnes, Colin. Absolute Beginners. 2001. 203p. pap. 10.95 (*0-7490-0540-8*) Allison & Busby, Ltd. GBR. *Dist:* International Publishers Marketing.
—Absolute Beginners. 1980. 208p. 13.95 o.p. (*0-8052-8039-1*); pap. 5.95 o.p. (*0-8052-8038-3*) Knopf Publishing Group. (Schocken).
—Absolute Beginners. 1985. pap. 7.95 o.p. (*0-525-48189-3*, Obelisk) NAL.
—City of Spades. 1985. pap. 8.95 o.p. (*0-525-48188-5*, Obelisk) NAL.
MacInnes, Mairi. Quondam Wives. Novel. 1993. 128p. 19.95 o.p. (*0-8071-1810-9*) Louisiana State Univ. Pr.
Macintyre, F. Gwynplaine. The Woman Between the Worlds. 2000. (Illus.). 324p. pap. 19.95 (*0-595-08884-8*, Backinprint.com) iUniverse, Inc.
Mack, William P. Captain Kilburnie: A Novel. 1999. 367p. 25.95 (*1-55750-586-1*) Naval Institute Pr.
Mackay, Sheena. Dunedin. 1993. 296p. reprint ed. 21.95 o.p. (*1-55921-093-1*) Moyer Bell.
Mackay, Shena. An Advent Calendar. 1997. 160p. 19.95 (*1-55921-211-X*) Moyer Bell.
—Dunedin. 1994. pap. 5.95 o.p. (*1-55921-119-9*) Moyer Bell.
—Old Crow. 2002. 158p. reprint ed. pap. 10.95 (*1-55921-318-3*) Moyer Bell.
—Old Crow. 1992. o.s.i (*1-85381-193-9*) Random Hse., Inc.
—The Orchard Fire. 1997. (Harvest Book Ser.). 224p. pap. 12.00 o.s.i (*0-15-600532-8*, Harvest Bks.) Harcourt Trade Pubs.
—The Orchard on Fire. l.t. unabr. ed. 2000. 288p. 32.50 (*0-7531-6026-9*, 160269) ISIS Large Print Bks. GBR. *Dist:* Ulverscroft Large Print Bks., Ltd.
—The Orchard on Fire. 1996. 215p. 19.95 (*1-55921-175-X*) Moyer Bell.
MacKenzie, Donald. Loose Cannon: A John Raven Mystery. 1993. 160p. 17.95 o.p. (*0-312-09863-4*, Saint Martin's Minotaur) St. Martin's Pr.
—Raven after Dark, 001. 1979. 7.95 o.p. (*0-395-28209-8*) Houghton Mifflin Co.
—Raven & the Paperhangers, 001. 1980. 204p. 9.95 o.p. (*0-395-29450-9*) Houghton Mifflin Co.
—Raven Settles a Score, 001. 1978. 7.95 o.p. (*0-395-27100-2*) Houghton Mifflin Co.
Mackenzie, Donald. Raven's Revenge, 001. 1982. 192p. 10.95 o.p. (*0-395-32050-X*) Houghton Mifflin Co.
Mackey, Maureen. Lord Peter's Page. 2000. 200p. E-Book 4.75 incl. disk (*1-58749-015-3*); E-Book 4.75 (*1-58749-016-1*) Awe-Struck E-Bks.
MacLeod, Ian. The Light Ages. 2003. 416p. 23.95 (*0-441-01055-5*) Ace Bks.
MacLeod, Ian R. The Light Ages. 2004. 464p. pap. 14.00 (*0-441-01149-7*) Ace Bks.
Madden, Sandra. A Princess Born. 2002. 32p. mass mkt. 5.99 o.s.i (*0-8217-7250-3*) Kensington Publishing Corp.
Madison, Carolyn. The Sinister Spinster. 2001. (Zebra Regency Romance Ser.). 256p. mass mkt. 4.99 o.s.i (*0-8217-6826-3*, Zebra Bks.) Kensington Publishing Corp.
Maitland, Barry. The Chalon Heads. 1999. (Brock & Kolla Ser.: Bk. 4). 326p. (*1-86508-047-0*) Allen & Unwin Pty., Ltd.
—The Chalon Heads. 2002. 336p. 6.99 (*0-14-200082-5*) Viking Penguin.
Maitland, Joanna. A Penniless Prospect. l.t. ed. 2001. (Mills & Boon Large Print Ser.). 320p. 27.99 (*0-263-17193-0*) Harlequin Mills & Boon, Ltd. GBR. *Dist:* Ulverscroft Large Print Bks., Ltd., Ulverscroft Large Print Canada, Ltd.
Maitland, Sara. Daughter of Jerusalem: A Novel. 1995. 88p. pap. 12.00 o.p. (*0-8050-3810-8*, Owl Bks.) Holt, Henry & Co.
Malcolm, John. A Back Room in Somers Town. 1986. 160p. mass mkt. 2.95 o.s.i (*0-345-33032-3*) Ballantine Bks.
—A Back Room in Somers Town. 1985. 160p. 12.95 o.s.i (*0-684-18301-3*, Macmillan Reference USA) Gale Group.
—A Deceptive Appearance. (Tim Simpson Mystery Ser.). 1992. 224p. text 20.00 o.s.i (*0-684-19508-9*); 1993. 318p. lib. bdg. 15.95 (*0-8161-5780-4*) Gale Group. (Macmillan Reference USA).
—The Godwin Sideboard. 1986. mass mkt. 2.95 o.s.i (*0-345-33371-3*) Ballantine Bks.
—The Godwin Sideboard. 1985. (Tim Simpson Mystery Ser.). 176p. 13.95 o.s.i (*0-684-18398-6*, Macmillan Reference USA) Gale Group.
—Gothic Pursuit. 1987. (Tim Simpson Mystery Ser.). 208p. 14.95 o.p. (*0-684-18833-3*, Macmillan Reference USA) Gale Group.
—Hung Over. 1995. 240p. 19.95 o.p. (*0-312-13514-9*, Saint Martin's Minotaur) St. Martin's Pr.
—Into the Vortex, Vol. 1. 1997. (Into the Vortex Ser.: Vol. 1). 240p. 21.95 o.p. (*0-312-15555-7*, Saint Martin's Minotaur) St. Martin's Pr.
—Mortal Ruin. 1988. 208p. 15.95 o.s.i (*0-684-18958-5*, Macmillan Reference USA) Gale Group.
—Sheep, Goats & Soap: A Tim Simpson Mystery. l.t. ed. 1992. 275p. pap. 14.95 o.p. (*0-8161-5475-9*, Macmillan Reference USA) Gale Group.
—Sheep, Goats & Soap: A Tim Simpson Mystery. 1992. 224p. 19.95 o.s.i (*0-684-19384-1*, Scribner) Simon & Schuster.
—Whistler in the Dark. 1988. mass mkt. 3.50 o.s.i (*0-345-34292-5*) Ballantine Bks.
—Whistler in the Dark. 1987. 160p. 14.95 o.p. (*0-684-18701-9*, Scribner) Simon & Schuster.
—The Wrong Impression: A Tim Simpson Mystery. 1990. 224p. 18.95 o.p. (*0-684-19252-7*, Scribner) Simon & Schuster.
Mallory, James. The End of Magic. 2000. (Merlin Ser.: Vol. 3). 304p. mass mkt. 6.99 (*0-446-60792-4*) Warner Bks., Inc.
—The King's Wizard. 1999. (Merlin Ser.: Vol. 2). 304p. mass mkt. 6.99 (*0-446-60791-6*) Warner Bks., Inc.
—Merlin Pt. I: The Old Magic. l.t. ed. 1999. (G. K. Hall Science Fiction Ser.). 283p. 23.95 (*0-7838-8772-8*) Thorndike Pr.
—The Old Magic. 1999. (Merlin Ser.: Vol. 1). 288p. mass mkt. 6.99 (*0-446-60766-5*) Warner Bks., Inc.
Malory, Thomas. Le Morte D'Arthur. E-Book 2.49 (*1-58627-784-7*); E-Book 2.49 (*1-58627-783-9*) Electric Umbrella Publishing.
—Le Morte D'Arthur. Lumiansky, Robert M., ed. 1982. (Illus.). 784p. 100.00 o.s.i (*0-684-17673-4*, Macmillan Reference USA) Gale Group.
—Le Morte D'Arthur. 1970. lib. bdg. 75.00 (*0-8383-0619-5*) M.S.G. Haskell Hse.
—Le Morte D'Arthur. 2001. 512p. mass mkt. 7.95 (*0-451-52816-6*) NAL.
—Le Morte D'Arthur. 1996. (Classic Ser.). 64p. pap. 0.95 o.p. (*0-14-600142-7*) Penguin Group (USA) Inc.
—Le Morte D'Arthur. 2000. E-Book 4.95 (*0-679-64169-6*); 1999. 992p. pap. 14.95 (*0-375-75322-2*) Random House Adult Trade Publishing Group. (Modern Library).
—Le Morte D'Arthur. 1972. (Illus.). 6000p. 50.00 o.p. (*0-312-47600-0*) St. Martin's Pr.
Malvey, Victoria. Enchanted. 1999. 320p. mass mkt. 6.50 (*0-671-02071-4*, Pocket) Simon & Schuster.
—Fortune's Bride. 2000. 320p. pap. 6.50 (*0-7434-0334-7*, Pocket) Simon & Schuster.
—A Merry Chase. 2000. 320p. pap. 6.50 (*0-671-77525-1*, Pocket) Simon & Schuster.
—A Proper Affair. 2001. 320p. pap. 6.50 (*0-7434-1883-2*, Pocket) Simon & Schuster.
Mann, Jessica. Telling Only Lies. 1993. 256p. 19.95 o.p. (*0-88184-943-X*, Carroll & Graf Pubs.) Avalon Publishing Group.
—Under a Dark Sun. l.t. ed. 2001. (Thorndike General Ser.). 271p. pap. 22.95 o.p. (*0-7862-3221-8*); (*0-7540-4422-X*); (*0-7540-4423-8*) Thorndike Pr.
Mantel, Hilary. An Experiment in Love. unabr. ed. 1996. audio 54.95 (*0-7451-2761-4*, SAB 127, Sterling Audio Bks.) BBC Audiobooks America.
—An Experiment in Love. 1997. 256p. pap. 13.00 (*0-8050-5202-X*, Owl Bks.); 1996. 88p. 23.00 o.p. (*0-8050-4427-2*) Holt, Henry & Co.
—Fludd. 2000. 181p. pap. 13.00 (*0-8050-6273-4*, Owl Bks.) Holt, Henry & Co.
—Fludd. l.t. ed. 2001. (Thorndike General Ser.). 256p. pap. 25.95 (*0-7862-2993-4*); (*0-7540-4337-1*); (*0-7540-4336-3*) Thorndike Pr.
—The Giant, O'Brien. 1998. 208p. o.s.i (*0-385-25832-1*) Doubleday Canada, Ltd. CAN. *Dist:* Random Hse., Inc.
—The Giant O'Brien. 1999. (Illus.). 208p. (gr. 9). pap. (*0-385-25895-X*) Doubleday Canada, Ltd. CAN. *Dist:* Random Hse., Inc.
—The Giant, O'Brien: A Novel. 1999. 208p. pap. 13.00 (*0-8050-6295-5*, Owl Bks.); 1998. 192p. 22.00 o.s.i (*0-8050-4428-0*) Holt, Henry & Co.
—The Giant, O'Brien: A Novel. l.t. ed. 1999. (Basic Ser.). 296p. 29.95 (*0-7862-1797-9*) Thorndike Pr.
March, Caeia. Three Ply Yarn. 2nd ed. 1997. 240p. pap. 14.95 (*0-7043-4007-0*) Women's Pr., Ltd., The GBR. *Dist:* Trafalgar Square.
March, Hannah. The Complaint of the Dove. 2003. 272p. mass mkt. 5.99 (*0-451-20880-3*, Signet Bks.) NAL.
—The Devil's Highway. 2003. 320p. mass mkt. 5.99 (*0-451-21071-9*, Signet Bks.) NAL.
March, Stella. Mistress of Lamberly Grange. l.t. ed. 2001. 298p. pap. 22.95 (*0-7862-3499-7*); 184p. (*0-7540-4589-7*); 184p. (*0-7540-4590-0*) Thorndike Pr.
Marchant, Catherine, pseud. The Bailey Chronicles. l.t. ed. 1990. (General Ser.). 55.95 o.p. (*0-8161-4972-0*, Macmillan Reference USA) Gale Group.
—The Bailey Chronicles. 1989. 600p. 19.95 o.p. (*0-671-62387-7*) Summit Bks.
—Bill Bailey. unabr. ed. 1993. audio 54.95 (*0-7451-5846-3*, CAB 241) BBC Audiobooks America.
—Bill Bailey, Vol. 1. l.t. ed. 1990. (General Ser.). 387p. lib. bdg. 20.95 o.p. (*0-8161-4485-0*, Macmillan Reference USA) Gale Group.
—Bill Bailey. l.t. ed. 1987. (Ulverscroft Large Print Ser.). 432p. 14.50 o.p. (*0-7089-1698-8*, Ulverscroft) Thorpe, F. A. Pubs. GBR. *Dist:* Ulverscroft Large Print Bks., Ltd., Ulverscroft Large Print Canada, Ltd.
—Bill Bailey Omnibus. 2000. 299p. pap. 13.95 (*0-552-14624-2*) Transworld Publishers Ltd. GBR. *Dist:* Trafalgar Square.
—Bill Bailey's Daughter. unabr. ed. 1989. audio 54.95 (*0-7451-5847-1*, CAB 377) BBC Audiobooks America.
—Bill Bailey's Daughter, Vol. 3. l.t. ed. 1990. (General Ser.). 321p. lib. bdg. 20.95 o.p. (*0-8161-4768-X*, Macmillan Reference USA) Gale Group.
—Bill Bailey's Lot. unabr. ed. 1993. audio 69.95 (*0-7451-5848-X*, CAB 273) BBC Audiobooks America.
—Bill Bailey's Lot, Vol. 2. l.t. ed. 1990. (General Ser.). 406p. lib. bdg. 21.95 o.p. (*0-8161-4767-1*, Macmillan Reference USA) Gale Group.
—The Mallen Girl. 1981. 288p. pap. 2.50 o.p. (*0-553-13933-9*) Bantam Bks.
—The Mallen Girl. l.t. ed. 2000. (Romance Ser.). 447p. 28.95 (*0-7862-2140-2*) Thorndike Pr.
—The Mallen Girl. l.t. ed. 1981. (Ulverscroft Large Print Ser.). 458p. 12.50 o.p. (*0-7089-0641-9*, Ulverscroft) Thorpe, F. A. Pubs. GBR. *Dist:* Ulverscroft Large Print Bks., Ltd., Ulverscroft Large Print Canada, Ltd.
—The Mallen Girl. 1988. 288p. mass mkt. 11.95 (*0-552-09896-5*) Transworld Publishers Ltd. GBR. *Dist:* Trafalgar Square.
—The Mallen Litter. l.t. ed. 2000. (Romance Ser.). 504p. 28.95 (*0-7862-2139-9*, Macmillan Reference USA) Gale Group.
—The Mallen Litter. l.t. ed. 2000. 504p. (*0-7540-1502-5*); (*0-7540-2383-4*) Thorndike Pr.
—The Mallen Litter. l.t. ed. 1981. 529p. 12.00 o.p. (*0-7089-0669-9*, Ulverscroft) Thorpe, F. A. Pubs. GBR. *Dist:* Ulverscroft Large Print Bks., Ltd.
—The Mallen Litter. 1988. 320p. mass mkt. 11.95 (*0-552-10151-6*) Transworld Publishers Ltd. GBR. *Dist:* Trafalgar Square.
—The Mallen Lot. 1981. 320p. pap. 2.75 o.p. (*0-553-13934-7*) Bantam Bks.
—The Mallen Streak. 1981. 288p. pap. 2.50 o.p. (*0-553-13932-0*) Bantam Bks.
—The Mallen Streak. unabr. ed. 1997. audio 79.95 (*1-85496-267-1*, 62671) Soundings, Ltd. GBR. *Dist:* Ulverscroft Large Print Bks., Ltd.
—The Mallen Streak. l.t. ed. 1999. (Romance Ser.). 456p. 28.95 (*0-7862-2141-0*) Thorndike Pr.
—The Mallen Streak. 2000. 999p. (J). pap. 13.95 o.p. (*0-552-14699-4*); 1984. 256p. mass mkt. 10.95 (*0-552-09720-9*) Transworld Publishers Ltd. GBR. *Dist:* Trafalgar Square.
Margam, Kate. Milch Cow. 2001. 184p. pap. 15.00 (*1-85242-601-2*) Serpent's Tail Ltd. GBR. *Dist:* Consortium Bk. Sales & Distribution.
Marian, Babson. The Cat Next Door. 2003. 192p. mass mkt. 5.99 (*0-312-98300-X*, St. Martin's Paperbacks) St. Martin's Pr.
Marion, Chesney. Zen in the Martial Arts. 1988. pap. 2.95 o.p. (*0-312-91036-3*, St. Martin's Paperbacks) St. Martin's Pr.
Mark, Jan. Something in the Air. 2003. 209p. (*0-385-60539-0*) Doubleday Canada, Ltd. CAN. *Dist:* Random Hse. of Canada, Ltd., Random Hse., Inc.
—Zeno Was Here. 1988. 284p. 19.95 o.s.i (*0-374-29664-2*) Farrar, Straus & Giroux.
Marquis, Max. The Twelfth Man: A Detective Timberlake Mystery. 1992. 240p. 17.95 o.p. (*0-312-07874-9*, Saint Martin's Minotaur) St. Martin's Pr.
—Undignified Death: A Detective Inspector Harry Timberlake Mystery. 1994. 192p. 18.95 o.p. (*0-312-11087-1*) St. Martin's Pr.
Marric, J. J. Gideon's Art. 1990. mass mkt. 3.50 o.s.i (*0-8217-3149-1*, Zebra Bks.) Kensington Publishing Corp.
—Gideon's Badge. l.t. ed. 1980. (Ulverscroft Large Print Ser.). 354p. 29.99 o.p. (*0-7089-0535-8*, Ulverscroft) Thorpe, F. A. Pubs. GBR. *Dist:* Ulverscroft Large Print Bks., Ltd., Ulverscroft Large Print Canada, Ltd.
—Gideon's Day. 1989. mass mkt. 3.95 o.p. (*0-8217-2721-4*, Zebra Bks.) Kensington Publishing Corp.
—Gideon's Day. 1985. 304p. pap. 2.95 o.p. (*0-8128-8197-4*, Scarborough Hse.) Madison Bks., Inc.
—Gideon's Day. l.t. ed. 1972. (Ulverscroft Large Print Ser.). 29.99 o.p. (*0-85456-138-2*, Ulverscroft) Thorpe, F. A. Pubs. GBR. *Dist:* Ulverscroft Large Print Bks., Ltd., Ulverscroft Large Print Canada, Ltd.
—Gideon's Drive. 2003. 192p. 21.95 (*0-7540-8640-2*, Black Dagger) BBC Audiobooks America.
—Gideon's Drive. 1976. (Harper Novel of Suspense Ser.). 7.95 o.p. (*0-06-012821-6*) HarperCollins Pubs.
—Gideon's Drive. 1991. 224p. mass mkt. 3.50 o.p. (*0-8217-3322-2*, Zebra Bks.) Kensington Publishing Corp.
—Gideon's Drive. l.t. ed. 1978. (Ulverscroft Large Print Ser.). 29.99 o.p. (*0-7089-0164-6*, Ulverscroft) Thorpe, F. A. Pubs. GBR. *Dist:* Ulverscroft Large Print Bks., Ltd., Ulverscroft Large Print Canada, Ltd.
—Gideon's Fire. (Black Dagger Crime Ser.). 16.50 o.p. (*0-86220-814-9*, BD013, Black Dagger); 1992. audio 54.95 (*0-7451-2405-4*, CD 006) BBC Audiobooks America.
—Gideon's Fire. 1989. mass mkt. 3.50 o.s.i (*0-8217-2845-8*, Zebra Bks.) Kensington Publishing Corp.
—Gideon's Fire. l.t. ed. 1974. (Ulverscroft Large Print Ser.). 29.99 o.p. (*0-85456-264-8*, Ulverscroft) Thorpe, F. A. Pubs. GBR. *Dist:* Ulverscroft Large Print Bks., Ltd., Ulverscroft Large Print Canada, Ltd.
—Gideon's Fog. 1974. (Harper Novel of Suspense Ser.). 188p. 7.95 o.p. (*0-06-012798-8*) HarperCollins Pubs.
—Gideon's Fog. 1991. 224p. mass mkt. 3.50 o.s.i (*0-8217-3276-5*, Zebra Bks.) Kensington Publishing Corp.
—Gideon's Fog. l.t. ed. 1976. o.p. (*0-85456-422-5*, Ulverscroft) Thorpe, F. A. Pubs.
—Gideon's Force. 1985. 192p. 12.95 o.p. (*0-8128-3027-X*) Holt, Henry & Co.
—Gideon's Force. l.t. ed. 1980. (Ulverscroft Large Print Ser.). 29.99 o.p. (*0-7089-0422-X*, Ulverscroft) Thorpe, F. A. Pubs. GBR. *Dist:* Ulverscroft Large Print Bks., Ltd., Ulverscroft Large Print Canada, Ltd.
—Gideon's Law. 1991. 192p. 14.95 o.p. (*0-8128-3042-3*) Holt, Henry & Co.
—Gideon's Lot. 1990. mass mkt. 3.50 o.s.i (*0-8217-2927-6*, Zebra Bks.) Kensington Publishing Corp.
—Gideon's March. 1994. 192p. 16.95 o.p. (*0-7451-8640-8*, Black Dagger) BBC Audiobooks America.
—Gideon's March. 1990. mass mkt. 3.50 o.s.i (*0-8217-2876-8*, Zebra Bks.) Kensington Publishing Corp.
—Gideon's Men. 1990. mass mkt. 3.50 o.s.i (*0-8217-3219-6*, Zebra Bks.) Kensington Publishing Corp.
—Gideon's Men. l.t. ed. 1975. (Ulverscroft Large Print Ser.). 29.99 o.p. (*0-85456-325-3*, Ulverscroft) Thorpe, F. A. Pubs. GBR. *Dist:* Ulverscroft Large Print Bks., Ltd., Ulverscroft Large Print Canada, Ltd.
—Gideon's Month. 1989. mass mkt. 3.95 o.s.i (*0-8217-2766-4*, Zebra Bks.) Kensington Publishing Corp.
—Gideon's Month. pap. 2.95 o.p. (*0-8128-8207-5*, Scarborough Hse.) Madison Bks., Inc.
—Gideon's Month. l.t. ed. 1975. (Ulverscroft Large Print Ser.). 29.99 o.p. (*0-85456-313-X*, Ulverscroft) Thorpe, F. A. Pubs. GBR. *Dist:* Ulverscroft Large Print Bks., Ltd., Ulverscroft Large Print Canada, Ltd.
—Gideon's Night. 1989. mass mkt. 3.50 o.s.i (*0-8217-2734-6*, Zebra Bks.) Kensington Publishing Corp.
—Gideon's Night. 1985. 192p. pap. 2.95 o.p. (*0-8128-8198-2*, Scarborough Hse.) Madison Bks., Inc.
—Gideon's Power. 1990. mass mkt. 3.50 o.p. (*0-8217-3105-X*, Zebra Bks.) Kensington Publishing Corp.

—Gideon's Power. 1986. pap. 2.95 o.p. (*0-8128-8307-1*, Scarborough Hse.) Madison Bks., Inc.

—Gideon's Press. 1973. (Harper Novel of Suspense Ser.). 192p. 7.95 o.p. (*0-06-012787-2*) HarperCollins Pubs.

—Gideon's Press. 1990. mass mkt. 3.50 o.s.i (*0-8217-3243-9*, Zebra Bks.) Kensington Publishing Corp.

—Gideon's Press. l.t. ed. 1977. (Ulverscroft Large Print Ser.). 29.99 o.p. (*0-7089-0031-3*, Ulverscroft) Thorpe, F. A. Pubs. GBR. *Dist:* Ulverscroft Large Print Bks., Ltd., Ulverscroft Large Print Canada, Ltd.

—Gideon's Ride. 1990. mass mkt. 3.50 o.s.i (*0-8217-2900-4*, Zebra Bks.) Kensington Publishing Corp.

—Gideon's Ride. l.t. ed. 1974. (Ulverscroft Large Print Ser.). 29.99 o.p. (*0-85456-234-6*, Ulverscroft) Thorpe, F. A. Pubs. GBR. *Dist:* Ulverscroft Large Print Bks., Ltd., Ulverscroft Large Print Canada, Ltd.

—Gideon's Risk. 1989. mass mkt. 3.50 o.s.i (*0-8217-2823-7*, Zebra Bks.) Kensington Publishing Corp.

—Gideon's Risk. pap. 2.95 o.p. (*0-8128-8226-1*, Scarborough Hse.) Madison Bks., Inc.

—Gideon's River. 1995. 224p. 18.50 o.p. (*0-7451-8654-8*, Black Dagger) BBC Audiobooks America.

—Gideon's River. Barzun, Jacques & Taylor, W. H., eds. 1983. (Crime Fiction 1950-1975 Ser.). 143p. lib. bdg. 18.00 o.p. (*0-8240-4956-X*) Garland Publishing, Inc.

—Gideon's River. 1990. mass mkt. 3.50 o.s.i (*0-8217-3079-7*, Zebra Bks.) Kensington Publishing Corp.

—Gideon's River. 1986. pap. 2.95 o.p. (*0-8128-8286-5*, Scarborough Hse.) Madison Bks., Inc.

—Gideon's River. l.t. ed. 1973. (Ulverscroft Large Print Ser.). 29.99 o.p. (*0-85456-179-X*, Ulverscroft) Thorpe, F. A. Pubs. GBR. *Dist:* Ulverscroft Large Print Bks., Ltd., Ulverscroft Large Print Canada, Ltd.

—Gideon's Sport. 1990. mass mkt. 3.50 o.p. (*0-8217-3128-9*, Zebra Bks.) Kensington Publishing Corp.

—Gideon's Sport. 1987. pap. 2.95 o.p. (*0-8128-8331-4*, Scarborough Hse.) Madison Bks., Inc.

—Gideon's Sport. l.t. ed. 1980. (Ulverscroft Large Print Ser.). 334p. 29.99 o.p. (*0-7089-0462-9*, Ulverscroft) Thorpe, F. A. Pubs. GBR. *Dist:* Ulverscroft Large Print Bks., Ltd., Ulverscroft Large Print Canada, Ltd.

—Gideon's Staff. l.t. ed. 1991. pap. 16.95 o.p. (*0-7927-0628-5*, CS052); 1990. 18.95 o.p. (*0-7927-0627-7*, C0589) BBC Audiobooks America.

—Gideon's Staff. 1989. mass mkt. 3.50 o.s.i (*0-8217-2797-4*, Zebra Bks.) Kensington Publishing Corp.

—Gideon's Vote. 1990. mass mkt. 3.50 o.s.i (*0-8217-2971-3*, Zebra Bks.) Kensington Publishing Corp.

—Gideon's Vote. l.t. ed. 1982. 360p. 15.95 o.p. (*0-7089-0745-8*, Ulverscroft) Thorpe, F. A. Pubs. GBR. *Dist:* Ulverscroft Large Print Bks., Ltd.

—Gideon's Way. 1991. 192p. 14.95 o.p. (*0-8128-3075-X*) Holt, Henry & Co.

—Gideon's Way. 1987. pap. 3.50 o.s.i (*0-8128-8329-2*, Scarborough Hse.) Madison Bks., Inc.

—Gideon's Week. 1989. mass mkt. 3.95 o.s.i (*0-8217-2722-2*, Zebra Bks.) Kensington Publishing Corp.

—Gideon's Week. 1985. 192p. pap. 2.95 o.p. (*0-8128-8199-0*, Scarborough Hse.) Madison Bks., Inc.

—Gideon's Week. l.t. ed. 1969. (Ulverscroft Large Print Ser.). 29.99 o.p. (*0-85456-659-7*, Ulverscroft) Thorpe, F. A. Pubs. GBR. *Dist:* Ulverscroft Large Print Bks., Ltd., Ulverscroft Large Print Canada, Ltd.

—Gideon's Wrath. 1990. mass mkt. 3.50 o.p. (*0-8217-3050-9*, Zebra Bks.) Kensington Publishing Corp.

—Gideon's Wrath. l.t. ed. 1975. (Ulverscroft Large Print Ser.). 29.99 o.p. (*0-85456-342-3*, Ulverscroft) Thorpe, F. A. Pubs. GBR. *Dist:* Ulverscroft Large Print Bks., Ltd., Ulverscroft Large Print Canada, Ltd.

Marsh, Jean. Fiennders Keepers. unabr. ed. 1997. audio 84.95 (*0-7540-0045-1*) BBC Audiobooks America.

—Fiennders Keepers. l.t. ed. 1998. (Magna Large Print Ser.). 545p. o.p. (*0-7505-1185-0*) Magna Large Print Bks. GBR. *Dist:* Ulverscroft Large Print Canada, Ltd.

—Fiennders Keepers. 1997. 416p. text 24.95 o.p. (*0-312-15528-X*) St. Martin's Pr.

Marsh, Ngaio. Artists in Crime. 1976. reprint ed. lib. bdg. 24.95 (*0-88411-471-6*) Amereon, Ltd.

—Artists in Crime. 1994. 256p. mass mkt. 4.50 o.p. (*0-425-14331-7*, Prime Crime); 1984. 256p. mass mkt. 3.99 o.p. (*0-515-07534-5*, Jove); 1982. mass mkt. 2.50 o.s.i (*0-515-06341-X*, Jove); 1980. mass mkt. 1.95 o.s.i (*0-515-05414-3*, Jove) Berkley Publishing Group.

—Artists in Crime. unabr. ed. 1994. audio 49.95 (*0-7861-0692-1*, 1477) Blackstone Audio Bks., Inc.

—Artists in Crime. 1997. (Dead Letter Mysteries Ser.). 256p. mass mkt. 5.99 (*0-312-96359-9*, St. Martin's Paperbacks) St. Martin's Pr.

—Black As He's Painted. 1976. reprint ed. lib. bdg. 23.95 (*0-88411-472-4*) Amereon, Ltd.

—Black As He's Painted. (Mystery Ser.). 1984. 224p. mass mkt. 3.99 o.s.i (*0-515-07627-9*); 1982. mass mkt. 2.50 o.s.i (*0-515-06818-7*); 1981. mass mkt. 2.25 o.s.i (*0-515-05871-8*); 1978. mass mkt. 1.50 o.s.i (*0-515-04611-6*) Berkley Publishing Group. (Jove).

—Black As He's Painted. 1994. reprint ed. lib. bdg. 27.95 (*1-56849-307-X*) Buccaneer Bks., Inc.

—Black As He's Painted. 1999. 256p. mass mkt. 5.99 (*0-312-97279-2*, St. Martin's Paperbacks) St. Martin's Pr.

—Clutch of Constables. 1976. reprint ed. lib. bdg. 22.95 (*0-88411-473-2*) Amereon, Ltd.

—Clutch of Constables. 1986. 224p. mass mkt. 3.99 o.s.i (*0-515-08775-0*); 1983. mass mkt. 2.50 o.s.i (*0-515-07105-6*); 1981. mass mkt. 2.25 o.s.i (*0-515-06013-5*) Berkley Publishing Group. (Jove).

—Clutch of Constables. 1994. reprint ed. lib. bdg. 27.95 (*1-56849-308-8*) Buccaneer Bks., Inc.

—Clutch of Constables. unabr. ed. 2000. (Inspector Alleyn Mystery Ser.). audio 49.95 (*0-7451-6138-3*, CAB 355) Chivers Audio Bks. GBR. *Dist:* BBC Audiobooks America.

—Clutch of Constables. 1999. 224p. mass mkt. 5.99 (*0-312-97084-6*, St. Martin's Paperbacks) St. Martin's Pr.

—The Collected Short Fiction of Ngaio Marsh. 1989. 252p. 19.95 o.p. (*1-55882-050-7*); 1991. 242p. reprint ed. pap. 9.95 o.p. (*1-55882-086-8*) International Polygonics, Ltd. (Library of Crime Classics).

—Colour Scheme. 1976. reprint ed. lib. bdg. 24.95 (*0-88411-474-0*) Amereon, Ltd.

—Colour Scheme. 1995. mass mkt. 5.99 o.p. (*0-425-14651-0*); 1984. 288p. mass mkt. 3.99 o.s.i (*0-515-07881-6*, Jove); 1982. mass mkt. 2.50 o.s.i (*0-515-06014-3*, Jove); 1978. mass mkt. 1.75 o.s.i (*0-425-03859-9*) Berkley Publishing Group.

—Colour Scheme. 1998. (Colour Scheme Ser.: Vol. 1). 288p. mass mkt. 5.99 (*0-312-96603-2*, St. Martin's Paperbacks) St. Martin's Pr.

—Dead Water. 1976. reprint ed. lib. bdg. 23.95 (*0-88411-475-9*) Amereon, Ltd.

—Dead Water. 1994. mass mkt. 4.50 o.p. (*0-425-14486-0*); 1983. 288p. mass mkt. 3.99 o.s.i (*0-515-07440-3*, Jove); 1982. mass mkt. 2.50 o.s.i (*0-515-06017-8*, Jove); 1978. mass mkt. 1.75 o.s.i (*0-425-03857-2*) Berkley Publishing Group.

—Dead Water. unabr. ed. 2000. (Inspector Alleyn Mystery Ser.). audio 49.95 (*0-7451-6139-1*, CAB 280) Chivers Audio Bks. GBR. *Dist:* BBC Audiobooks America.

—Dead Water. 1999. 224p. mass mkt. 5.99 (*0-312-96990-2*, St. Martin's Paperbacks) St. Martin's Pr.

—Dead Water. (G. K. Hall Audio Bks.). 1988. audio 53.95 o.s.i (*0-8161-7752-X*); 1999. 368p. 26.95 o.p. (*0-7862-2050-3*) Thorndike Pr.

—Dead Water. l.t. ed. 2000. (Ulverscroft Large Print Ser.). 368p. o.p. (*0-7089-4197-4*, Ulverscroft) Thorpe, F. A. Pubs. GBR. *Dist:* Ulverscroft Large Print Bks., Ltd., Ulverscroft Large Print Canada, Ltd.

—Death at the Bar. 1976. reprint ed. lib. bdg. 25.95 (*0-88411-476-7*) Amereon, Ltd.

—Death at the Bar. 1995. mass mkt. 4.99 o.s.i (*0-425-14654-5*); 1982. mass mkt. 2.50 o.s.i (*0-515-06700-8*, Jove); 1981. mass mkt. 2.25 o.s.i (*0-515-05998-6*, Jove); 1980. mass mkt. 1.95 o.s.i (*0-515-05641-3*, Jove) Berkley Publishing Group.

—Death at the Bar. unabr. ed. 1997. audio 44.95 (*0-7861-1075-9*, 1845) Blackstone Audio Bks., Inc.

—Death at the Bar. 1998. (Dead Letter Mysteries Ser.). 272p. mass mkt. 5.99 (*0-312-96426-9*, St. Martin's Paperbacks) St. Martin's Pr.

—Death at the Dolphin. unabr. ed. 2000. (Inspector Alleyn Mystery Ser.). 8p. audio 59.95 (*0-7451-6681-4*, CAB 1297) Chivers Audio Bks. GBR. *Dist:* BBC Audiobooks America.

—Death in a White Tie. 1976. reprint ed. lib. bdg. 24.95 (*0-88411-479-1*) Amereon, Ltd.

—Death in a White Tie. 1994. 352p. mass mkt. 4.50 o.p. (*0-425-14408-9*); 1986. mass mkt. 3.99 o.s.i (*0-515-08591-X*, Jove); 1983. mass mkt. 2.50 o.s.i (*0-515-06224-3*, Jove); 1980. mass mkt. 2.25 o.s.i (*0-515-05896-3*, Jove); 1980. mass mkt. 1.95 o.s.i (*0-515-05628-6*, Jove); 1977. mass mkt. 1.50 o.s.i (*0-515-04391-5*, Jove) Berkley Publishing Group.

—Death in a White Tie. 1997. 352p. mass mkt. 5.99 (*0-312-96361-0*, St. Martin's Paperbacks) St. Martin's Pr.

—Died in the Wool. 1976. reprint ed. lib. bdg. 22.95 (*0-88411-482-1*) Amereon, Ltd.

—Died in the Wool. 1994. 256p. mass mkt. 5.99 o.s.i (*0-425-14469-0*, Prime Crime); 1983. 256p. mass mkt. 3.99 o.s.i (*0-515-07506-X*, Jove); 1981. mass mkt. 2.50 o.s.i (*0-515-06019-4*, Jove); 1981. mass mkt. 2.25 o.s.i (*0-425-05050-5*); 1978. mass mkt. 1.75 o.s.i (*0-425-03860-2*) Berkley Publishing Group.

—Died in the Wool. unabr. ed. 1996. audio 44.95 (*0-7861-0999-8*, 1776) Blackstone Audio Bks., Inc.

—Died in the Wool. 1998. (Inspector Roderick Alleyn Mysteries Ser.). 256p. mass mkt. 5.99 (*0-312-96604-0*, St. Martin's Paperbacks) St. Martin's Pr.

—Died in the Wool. l.t. ed. 1999. (Mystery Ser.). 437p. 26.95 o.p. (*0-7862-1772-3*) Thorndike Pr.

—Enter a Murderer. 1976. reprint ed. lib. bdg. 22.95 (*0-88411-483-X*) Amereon, Ltd.

—Enter a Murderer. 1982. mass mkt. 2.50 o.s.i (*0-515-06819-5*); 1981. mass mkt. 2.25 o.s.i (*0-515-05943-9*); 1984. 192p. reprint ed. mass mkt. 3.99 o.s.i (*0-515-07447-0*); Vol. 2. 1982. pap. Berkley Publishing Group.

—Enter a Murderer. unabr. ed. 2000. (Inspector Alleyn Mystery Ser.). audio 49.95 (*0-7451-6574-5*, CAB 1190) Chivers Audio Bks. GBR. *Dist:* BBC Audiobooks America.

—Enter a Murderer. 1998. (Dead Letter Mysteries Ser.). 245p. mass mkt. 5.99 (*0-312-96670-9*, St. Martin's Paperbacks) St. Martin's Pr.

—False Scent. 1976. reprint ed. lib. bdg. 23.95 (*0-88411-484-8*) Amereon, Ltd.

—False Scent. (Ngaio Marsh Mystery Ser.). 1984. 224p. mass mkt. 3.99 o.s.i (*0-515-08056-X*); 1981. mass mkt. 2.50 o.s.i (*0-515-06007-0*) Berkley Publishing Group. (Jove).

—False Scent. unabr. ed. 2000. (Inspector Alleyn Mystery Ser.). 8p. audio 59.95 (*0-7451-6609-1*, CAB 1225) Chivers Audio Bks. GBR. *Dist:* BBC Audiobooks America.

—False Scent. 1999. 224p. mass mkt. 5.99 (*0-312-96898-1*, St. Martin's Paperbacks) St. Martin's Pr.

—Final Curtain. 1976. reprint ed. lib. bdg. 26.95 (*0-88411-485-6*) Amereon, Ltd.

—Final Curtain. 1997. (Inspector Roderick Alleyn Mysteries Ser.). audio 34.95 (*0-7540-7501-X*) BBC Audiobooks America.

—Final Curtain. 1993. mass mkt. 4.99 o.p. (*0-425-14320-1*); 1983. mass mkt. 2.50 o.s.i (*0-515-07074-2*, Jove); 1981. mass mkt. 2.25 o.s.i (*0-515-06118-2*, Jove); 1980. mass mkt. 1.95 o.s.i (*0-515-05554-9*, Jove) Berkley Publishing Group.

—Final Curtain. unabr. ed. 1994. audio 49.95 (*0-7861-0676-X*, 1464) Blackstone Audio Bks., Inc.

—Final Curtain. unabr. ed. 2000. (Inspector Alleyn Mystery Ser.). audio 59.95 (*0-7451-6484-6*, CAB 1100) Chivers Audio Bks. GBR. *Dist:* BBC Audiobooks America.

—Grave Mistake. 1976. 22.95 (*0-8488-0577-1*) Amereon, Ltd.

—Grave Mistake. unabr. ed. 1993. (Inspector Roderick Alleyn Mysteries Ser.). 69.95 incl. audio (*0-7451-6141-3*, CAB 144) BBC Audiobooks America.

—Grave Mistake. 1994. mass mkt. 4.50 o.p. (*0-425-14243-4*); 1987. 256p. mass mkt. 3.50 o.s.i (*0-515-08847-1*, Jove); 1983. mass mkt. 2.95 o.s.i (*0-515-07549-3*, Jove); 1981. mass mkt. 2.50 o.s.i (*0-515-06178-6*, Jove); 1980. mass mkt. 1.95 o.s.i (*0-515-05369-4*, Jove) Berkley Publishing Group.

—Hand in Glove. 1976. reprint ed. lib. bdg. 22.95 (*0-88411-486-4*) Amereon, Ltd.

—Hand in Glove. 1992. mass mkt. 4.50 o.p. (*0-425-14485-2*); 1983. 240p. mass mkt. 3.99 o.s.i (*0-515-07502-7*, Jove); 1982. mass mkt. 2.50 o.s.i (*0-515-06309-6*, Jove); 1981. mass mkt. 2.25 o.s.i (*0-515-06136-0*, Jove); 1980. mass mkt. 1.95 o.s.i (*0-515-05763-0*, Jove); 1979. mass mkt. 1.75 o.s.i (*0-515-05202-7*, Jove) Berkley Publishing Group.

—Hand in Glove. unabr. ed. 2000. (Inspector Alleyn Mystery Ser.). audio 49.95 (*0-7451-6142-1*, CAB 196) Chivers Audio Bks. GBR. *Dist:* BBC Audiobooks America.

—Hand in Glove. 1999. (Dead Letter Mysteries Ser.). 256p. mass mkt. 5.99 (*0-312-96908-2*, St. Martin's Paperbacks) St. Martin's Pr.

—Hand in Glove. l.t. ed. 1983. (Ulverscroft Large Print Ser.). 368p. 12.50 o.p. (*0-7089-1029-7*, Ulverscroft) Thorpe, F. A. Pubs. GBR. *Dist:* Ulverscroft Large Print Bks., Ltd., Ulverscroft Large Print Canada, Ltd.

—Killer Dolphin. 1976. reprint ed. lib. bdg. 25.95 (*0-88411-487-2*) Amereon, Ltd.

—Killer Dolphin. 1995. mass mkt. 4.99 o.p. (*0-425-14657-X*); 1986. 256p. mass mkt. 3.99 o.s.i (*0-515-08590-1*, Jove); 1983. mass mkt. 2.50 o.s.i (*0-515-06820-9*, Jove); 1981. mass mkt. 2.25 o.s.i (*0-515-06071-2*, Jove); 1980. mass mkt. 1.95 o.s.i (*0-515-05435-6*, Jove) Berkley Publishing Group.

—Killer Dolphin. 1999. 288p. mass mkt. 5.99 (*0-312-97010-2*, St. Martin's Paperbacks) St. Martin's Pr.

—Last Ditch. 1976. 23.95 (*0-8488-0578-X*) Amereon, Ltd.

—Last Ditch. 1986. 288p. mass mkt. 3.99 o.p. (*0-515-08798-X*); 1983. mass mkt. 2.50 o.s.i (*0-515-06821-7*); 1981. mass mkt. 2.25 o.s.i (*0-515-05966-8*) Berkley Publishing Group. (Jove).

—Last Ditch. l.t. ed. 1977. lib. bdg. 13.50 o.p. (*0-8161-6537-8*, Macmillan Reference USA) Gale Group.

—Last Ditch. 2000. 288p. mass mkt. 5.99 (*0-312-97286-5*, St. Martin's Paperbacks) St. Martin's Pr.

—Light Thickens. 1976. 21.95 (*0-8488-0579-8*) Amereon, Ltd.

—Light Thickens. 240p. 1994. mass mkt. 4.99 o.p. (*0-425-14529-8*, Prime Crime); 1985. mass mkt. 3.99 o.s.i (*0-515-07359-8*, Jove) Berkley Publishing Group.

—Light Thickens. 2002. 8p. audio compact disk 79.95 (*0-7540-5528-0*, CCD 219); 1998. audio 59.95 (*0-7540-0231-4*, CAB 1654) Chivers Audio Bks. GBR. *Dist:* BBC Audiobooks America.

—Light Thickens. l.t. ed. 1983. 394p. lib. bdg. 16.95 o.p. (*0-8161-3509-6*, Macmillan Reference USA) Gale Group.

—Light Thickens. 2000. 5.99p. mass mkt. 5.99 (*0-312-97314-4*, St. Martin's Paperbacks) St. Martin's Pr.

—A Man Lay Dead. lib. bdg. 20.95 (*0-8488-2104-1*); 1976. reprint ed. lib. bdg. 21.95 (*0-88411-488-0*) Amereon, Ltd.

—A Man Lay Dead. 1993. mass mkt. 4.50 o.p. (*0-425-14319-8*); 1981. mass mkt. 2.50 o.s.i (*0-515-06496-3*, Jove); 1980. mass mkt. 1.95 o.s.i (*0-515-05729-0*, Jove); 1978. mass mkt. 1.50 o.s.i (*0-515-04529-2*, Jove) Berkley Publishing Group.

—A Man Lay Dead. 1997. (Dead Letter Mysteries Ser.). 192p. mass mkt. 5.99 (*0-312-96358-0*, St. Martin's Paperbacks) St. Martin's Pr.

—New Zealand. 1976. reprint ed. lib. bdg. 24.95 (*0-88411-489-9*) Amereon, Ltd.

—Ngaio Marsh, 5 vols. Incl. Vol. 1. Black As He's Painted. Vol. 2. Enter a Murderer. pap. Vol. 3. Killer Dolphin. pap. Vol. 4. Last Ditch. Vol. 5. Overture to Death. pap. 1982. 12.50 o.s.i (*0-515-06816-0*, Jove) Berkley Publishing Group.

—Ngaio Marsh: Five Complete Novels. 1990. 784p. 11.99 o.s.i (*0-517-41017-6*) Random Hse. Value Publishing.

—The Nursing Home Murder. 1976. reprint ed. lib. bdg. 22.95 (*0-88411-491-0*) Amereon, Ltd.

—The Nursing Home Murder. 1994. 240p. mass mkt. 4.50 o.p. (*0-425-14242-6*, Prime Crime) Berkley Publishing Group.

—The Nursing Home Murder. unabr. ed. 1992. (Inspector Alleyn Mystery Ser.). audio 49.95 (*0-7451-6145-6*, CAB 691) Chivers Audio Bks. GBR. *Dist:* BBC Audiobooks America.

—The Nursing Home Murder. 1999. 192p. mass mkt. 5.99 (*0-312-96999-6*, St. Martin's Paperbacks) St. Martin's Pr.

—Opening Night. unabr. ed. 2000. (Inspector Alleyn Mystery Ser.). audio 49.95 (*0-7451-6143-X*, CAB 530) Chivers Audio Bks. GBR. *Dist:* BBC Audiobooks America.

—Overture to Death. 1976. reprint ed. lib. bdg. 24.95 (*0-88411-492-9*) Amereon, Ltd.

—Overture to Death. 1982. mass mkt. 2.50 o.s.i (*0-515-06822-5*); 1981. mass mkt. 2.25 o.s.i (*0-515-06011-9*); 1978. mass mkt. 1.75 o.s.i (*0-515-04531-4*) Berkley Publishing Group. (Jove).

—Overture to Death. 1998. (Dead Letter Mysteries Ser.). 320p. mass mkt. 5.99 (*0-312-96425-0*, St. Martin's Paperbacks) St. Martin's Pr.

—Photo Finish. 1976. 21.95 (*0-8488-0580-1*) Amereon, Ltd.

—Photo Finish. (Ngaio Marsh Mystery Ser.). 1983. 224p. mass mkt. 3.99 o.s.i (*0-515-07505-1*); 1981. mass mkt. 2.50 o.s.i (*0-515-05995-1*) Berkley Publishing Group. (Jove).

—Photo Finish. l.t. ed. 1981. (General Ser.). lib. bdg. 14.95 o.p. (*0-8161-3192-9*, Macmillan Reference USA) Gale Group.

—Photo Finish. 2000. 224p. mass mkt. 5.99 (*0-312-97301-2*, St. Martin's Paperbacks) St. Martin's Pr.

—Scales of Justice. 1976. reprint ed. lib. bdg. 24.95 (*0-88411-493-7*) Amereon, Ltd.

—Scales of Justice. 1994. mass mkt. 4.99 o.p. (*0-425-14487-9*); 1984. 256p. mass mkt. 3.99 o.s.i (*0-515-07917-0*, Jove); 1982. mass mkt. 2.50 o.s.i (*0-515-06497-1*, Jove); 1980. mass mkt. 1.95 o.s.i (*0-515-05436-4*, Jove) Berkley Publishing Group.

—Scales of Justice. unabr. ed. 1996. audio 44.95 (*0-7861-0927-0*, 893480) Blackstone Audio Bks., Inc.

—Scales of Justice. 1999. (Inspector Roderick Alleyn Mysteries Ser.). 256p. mass mkt. 5.99 (*0-312-96671-7*, St. Martin's Paperbacks) St. Martin's Pr.

—Singing in the Shrouds. 1976. reprint ed. lib. bdg. 23.95 (*0-88411-494-5*) Amereon, Ltd.

—Singing in the Shrouds. l.t. ed. 1993. 22.95 o.p. (*0-7927-1780-5*); pap. 20.95 o.p. (*0-7927-1781-3*) BBC Audiobooks America.

—Singing in the Shrouds. 1984. 240p. mass mkt. 3.99 o.s.i (*0-515-07735-6*, Jove) Berkley Publishing Group.

—Spinsters in Jeopardy. 1976. reprint ed. lib. bdg. 23.95 (*0-88411-495-3*) Amereon, Ltd.

—Spinsters in Jeopardy. 1986. 256p. mass mkt. 3.99 o.p. (*0-515-08718-1*); 1981. mass mkt. 2.50 o.s.i (*0-515-06179-4*); 1980. mass mkt. 1.95 o.s.i (*0-515-05716-9*) Berkley Publishing Group. (Jove).

—Spinsters in Jeopardy. 1998. (Inspector Roderick Alleyn Mysteries Ser.). 256p. mass mkt. 5.99 (*0-312-96669-5*, St. Martin's Paperbacks) St. Martin's Pr.

—Tied up in Tinsel. 1976. reprint ed. lib. bdg. 23.95 (*0-88411-496-1*) Amereon, Ltd.

—Tied up in Tinsel. 1983. 288p. mass mkt. 3.99 o.s.i (0-515-07443-8); 1982. mass mkt. 2.50 o.s.i (0-515-06015-1); 1981. mass mkt. 2.25 o.s.i (0-515-06285-5); 1978. mass mkt. 1.75 o.s.i (0-515-04533-0) Berkley Publishing Group. (Jove).
—Tied up in Tinsel. unabr. ed. 1994. audio 44.95 (0-7861-0683-2, 1470) Blackstone Audio Bks., Inc.
—Tied up in Tinsel. unabr. ed. 2000. (Inspector Alleyn Mystery Ser.). audio 49.95 (0-7451-6146-4, CAB 412) Chivers Audio Bks. GBR. *Dist:* BBC Audiobooks America.
—Tied up in Tinsel. 1989. audio 53.95 o.s.i (0-8161-9488-2) Thorndike Pr.
—Vintage Murder. 1976. reprint ed. lib. bdg. 22.95 (0-88411-497-X) Amereon, Ltd.
—Vintage Murder. 1985. 272p. mass mkt. 3.99 o.s.i (0-515-08084-5); 1982. mass mkt. 2.50 o.s.i (0-515-06012-7); 1981. mass mkt. 2.25 o.s.i (0-515-06164-6); 1978. mass mkt. 1.75 o.s.i (0-515-04534-9) Berkley Publishing Group. (Jove).
—Vintage Murder, Set. unabr. ed. 2000. (Roderick Alleyn Mystery Ser.). audio 69.95 (0-7540-0412-0, CAB 1835) Chivers Audio Bks. GBR. *Dist:* BBC Audiobooks America.
—Vintage Murder. 1999. 256p. mass mkt. 5.99 (0-312-97179-6, St. Martin's Paperbacks) St. Martin's Pr.
—When in Rome. 1976. lib. bdg. 23.95 (0-88411-498-8) Amereon, Ltd.
—When in Rome. 1983. 224p. mass mkt. 3.99 o.s.i (0-515-07504-3); 1981. mass mkt. 2.50 o.s.i (0-515-06180-8); 1980. mass mkt. 1.95 o.s.i (0-515-05627-8) Berkley Publishing Group. (Jove).
—When in Rome. unabr. ed. 1998. audio 44.95 Blackstone Audio Bks., Inc.
—When in Rome. unabr. ed. 2000. (Inspector Alleyn Mystery Ser.). audio 49.95 (0-7451-6147-2, CAB 466) Chivers Audio Bks. GBR. *Dist:* BBC Audiobooks America.
—When in Rome. 1999. 242p. mass mkt. 5.99 (0-312-97097-8, St. Martin's Paperbacks) St. Martin's Pr.
—A Wreath for Rivera. 1994. 336p. mass mkt. 4.50 o.p. (0-425-14247-7); 1984. mass mkt. 3.50 o.s.i (0-515-07501-9, Jove); 1982. mass mkt. 2.50 o.s.i (0-515-06016-X, Jove) Berkley Publishing Group.
—Wreath for Rivera. 1998. (Wreath for Rivera Ser.: Vol. 1). 336p. mass mkt. 5.99 (0-312-96606-7, St. Martin's Paperbacks) St. Martin's Pr.
—A Wreath for Rivera. 1976. reprint ed. lib. bdg. 25.95 (0-88411-499-6) Amereon, Ltd.
—A Wreath for Rivera. unabr. ed. 1994. 30p. audio 49.95 (0-7861-0829-0, 1534) Blackstone Audio Bks., Inc.
—A Wreath for Rivera. 1976. (Crime Fiction Ser.). reprint ed. lib. bdg. 21.00 o.p. (0-8240-2385-4) Garland Publishing, Inc.
Marshall, Archibald. Clinton Twins, & Other Stories. 1977. (Short Story Index Reprint Ser.). 19.95 (0-8369-3661-2) Ayer Co. Pubs., Inc.
Marshall, Paula. The Dollar Prince's Wife. l.t. ed. 2001. (Mills & Boon Large Print Ser.). 320p. 27.99 (0-263-17192-2) Harlequin Mills & Boon, Ltd. GBR. *Dist:* Ulverscroft Large Print Bks., Ltd., Ulverscroft Large Print Canada, Ltd.
—Miss Jesmond's Heir. 2001. 256p. mass mkt. (0-373-51151-5, Harlequin Bks.) Harlequin Enterprises, Ltd.
Marshall, Sybil. A Nest of Magpies. pap. 15.95 (0-312-31070-6, Saint Martin's Griffin); 1994. 476p. 24.95 (0-312-11034-0) St. Martin's Pr.
Marston, Edward. The Bawdy Basket. 2002. (An Elizabethan Theater Mystery Featuring Nicholas Bracewell Ser.). 288p. 23.95 (0-312-28501-9, Saint Martin's Minotaur) St. Martin's Pr.
—The Dragons of Archenfield. 1996. mass mkt. 5.99 o.s.i (0-449-22545-3, Fawcett) Ballantine Bks.
—The Dragons of Archenfield. 1995. 256p. 14.30 o.p. (0-312-13472-X, Saint Martin's Minotaur) St. Martin's Pr.
—The Fair Maid of Bohemia: A Novel. 2002. 271p. pap. 14.95 o.s.i (1-59058-005-2) Poisoned Pen Pr.
—The Fair Maid of Bohemia: A Novel. 1997. 229p. 21.95 o.p. (0-312-15606-5, Saint Martin's Minotaur) St. Martin's Pr.
—The Hawks of Delamere. 2000. (Domesday Bks.: Vol. 7). (Illus.). 246p. 22.95 (0-312-20948-7, Saint Martin's Minotaur) St. Martin's Pr.
—The Laughing Hangman. 2002. (Missing Mystery Ser.: Vol. 50). 200p. pap. 14.95 o.s.i (1-59058-023-0) Poisoned Pen Pr.
—The Laughing Hangman. 1996. 320p. 21.95 o.p. (0-312-14305-2, Saint Martin's Minotaur) St. Martin's Pr.
—The Lions of the North. 1996. 227p. 21.95 (0-312-14671-X, Saint Martin's Minotaur) St. Martin's Pr.
—The Mad Courtesan. 1994. reprint ed. mass mkt. 4.99 o.s.i (0-449-22246-2, Fawcett) Ballantine Bks.
—The Mad Courtesan. 2002. (Missing Mystery Ser.: Vol. 39). 200p. pap. 13.95 (1-890208-83-3) Poisoned Pen Pr.
—The Mad Courtesan. 1992. 240p. 18.95 o.p. (0-312-08259-2, Saint Martin's Minotaur) St. Martin's Pr.
—The Merry Devils. 1991. (Elizabethan Mystery Ser.). 240p. mass mkt. 3.95 o.s.i (0-449-21880-5, Fawcett) Ballantine Bks.
—The Merry Devils. 1990. mass mkt. o.s.i (0-552-13293-4, Corgi) Bantam Bks.
—The Merry Devils. 2001. (Missing Mystery Ser.: Vol. 30). 200p. pap. 14.95 o.s.i (1-890208-55-8) Poisoned Pen Pr.
—The Merry Devils. 1989. 240p. 16.95 o.p. (0-312-03863-1, Saint Martin's Minotaur) St. Martin's Pr.
—The Nine Giants. 1993. mass mkt. 4.50 o.s.i (0-449-22128-8, Fawcett) Ballantine Bks.
—The Nine Giants. 2001. (Missing Mystery Ser.: Vol. 34). 220p. pap. 13.95 (1-890208-68-X) Poisoned Pen Pr.
—The Nine Giants. 1991. 224p. 17.95 o.p. (0-312-06426-8, Saint Martin's Minotaur) St. Martin's Pr.
—The Owls of Gloucester, Vol. V. 2003. (Doomsday Ser.). (Illus.). 288p. 23.95 (0-312-28542-6, Saint Martin's Minotaur) St. Martin's Pr.
—The Queen's Head. 1990. 224p. mass mkt. 3.95 o.s.i (0-449-21791-4, Fawcett) Ballantine Bks.
—The Queen's Head. 1989. mass mkt. o.s.i (0-552-13292-6, Corgi) Bantam Bks.
—The Queen's Head. 2000. (Missing Mysteries Ser.: No. 19). 300p. pap. 14.95 (1-890208-45-0) Poisoned Pen Pr.
—The Queen's Head. 1989. 16.95 o.p. (0-312-02970-5, Saint Martin's Minotaur) St. Martin's Pr.
—The Ravens of Blackwater. 1996. mass mkt. 5.99 o.s.i (0-449-22410-4, Fawcett) Ballantine Bks.
—The Ravens of Blackwater. 1994. 20.95 o.p. (0-312-11330-7, Saint Martin's Minotaur) St. Martin's Pr.
—The Roaring Boy. 1996. 296p. mass mkt. 5.99 o.s.i (0-449-22431-7, Fawcett) Ballantine Bks.
—The Roaring Boy. 2002. 250p. pap. 14.95 o.s.i (1-59058-001-X) Poisoned Pen Pr.
—The Roaring Boy. 1995. 272p. 14.99 o.p. (0-312-13155-0, Saint Martin's Minotaur) St. Martin's Pr.
—The Serpents of Harbledown: A Novel. 1998. (Domesday Bks.: Vol. 5). 288p. 22.95 (0-312-18021-7, Saint Martin's Minotaur) St. Martin's Pr.
—The Silent Woman. 1995. mass mkt. 5.99 o.s.i (0-449-22375-2, Fawcett) Ballantine Bks.
—The Silent Woman. 2002. 240p. pap. 14.95 o.s.i (1-59058-000-1) Poisoned Pen Pr.
—The Silent Woman. 1994. 320p. 21.95 o.p. (0-312-11115-0, Saint Martin's Minotaur) St. Martin's Pr.
—The Stallions of Woodstock. 1998. (Domesday Bks.: Vol. 6). 288p. 22.95 (0-312-20021-8, Saint Martin's Minotaur) St. Martin's Pr.
—The Trip to Jerusalem: An Elizabethan Whodunit. 1991. 240p. mass mkt. 3.99 o.s.i (0-449-21987-9, Fawcett) Ballantine Bks.
—The Trip to Jerusalem: An Elizabethan Whodunit. 1991. mass mkt. o.s.i (0-552-13294-2, Corgi) Bantam Bks.
—The Trip to Jerusalem: An Elizabethan Whodunit. 2001. (Missing Mystery Ser.: Vol. 32). 200p. pap. 14.95 o.s.i (1-890208-60-4) Poisoned Pen Pr.
—The Trip to Jerusalem: An Elizabethan Whodunit. 1990. 224p. 15.95 o.p. (0-312-05174-3, Saint Martin's Minotaur) St. Martin's Pr.
—The Vagabond Clown: An Elizabethan Theater Mystery Featuring Nicholas Bracewell. Date not set. pap. (0-312-30790-X, Saint Martin's Griffin); mass mkt. (0-312-98612-2, St. Martin's Paperbacks); E-Book (0-312-70591-3); 2003. 352p. 24.95 (0-312-30789-6, Saint Martin's Minotaur) St. Martin's Pr.
—The Wanton Angel. 2nd ed. 1999. 288p. 23.95 (0-312-20391-8, Saint Martin's Minotaur) St. Martin's Pr.
—The Wolves of Savernake. 1995. mass mkt. 5.99 o.s.i (0-449-22310-8, Fawcett) Ballantine Bks.
—The Wolves of Savernake. 1993. 256p. 19.95 o.p. (0-312-09942-8, Saint Martin's Minotaur) St. Martin's Pr.
Martin, J. Wallis. A Likeness in Stone. 1998. 288p. 22.95 (0-312-18626-6) St. Martin's Pr.
—A Likeness in Stone. l.t. ed. 1998. (Mystery Ser.). 376p. 26.95 (0-7862-1684-0) Thorndike Pr.
—A Likeness in Stone. l.t. ed. 1998. (Ulverscroft Large Print Ser.). 448p. 29.99 o.p. (0-7089-3895-7, Ulverscroft) Thorpe, F. A. Pubs. GBR. *Dist:* Ulverscroft Large Print Bks., Ltd., Ulverscroft Large Print Canada, Ltd.
Martin, Julia Wallis. A Likeness in Stone. 1999. 282p. mass mkt. 6.50 (0-312-97077-3, St. Martin's Paperbacks) St. Martin's Pr.
Martin, Kat. Heartless. 2001. 336p. mass mkt. 6.99 (0-312-97944-4, St. Martin's Paperbacks) St. Martin's Pr.
—Heartless. l.t. ed. 2001. (Thorndike Press Large Print Romance Ser.). 529p. 28.95 (0-7862-3585-3) Thorndike Pr.
—Silk & Steel. (Orig.). mass mkt. 3.99 (0-312-99886-4); 2000. 368p. mass mkt. 6.99 (0-312-97281-4) St. Martin's Pr. (St. Martin's Paperbacks).
Martin, Malia. Much Ado about Love. 2000. 384p. mass mkt. 5.99 (0-380-81517-6, Avon Bks.) Morrow/Avon.
Martin, Michelle. The Butler Who Laughed. 1997. mass mkt. 4.50 o.s.i (0-449-22528-3, Fawcett) Ballantine Bks.
—The Queen of Hearts. 1994. mass mkt. 3.99 o.s.i (0-449-22203-9, Fawcett) Ballantine Bks.
Martin, Valerie. Mary Reilly. 1990. 272p. 18.95 o.s.i (0-385-24968-3) Doubleday Publishing.
Martyn, Isolde. The Maiden & the Unicorn. 1999. 448p. reprint ed. mass mkt. 5.99 (0-553-58168-6) Bantam Bks.
Mason, Connie. A Taste of Sin. 2000. (Avon Romantic Treasure Ser.). 384p. mass mkt. 5.99 (0-380-80801-3, Avon Bks.) Morrow/Avon.
Mason, Richard. The Drowning People. unabr. ed. 2000. audio 84.95 (0-7540-0413-9, CAB 1836) Chivers Audio Bks. GBR. *Dist:* BBC Audiobooks America.
—The Drowning People. 1999. 352p. o.s.i (0-385-25830-5) Doubleday Canada, Ltd. CAN. *Dist:* Random Hse., Inc.
—The Drowning People. abr. ed. 1999. audio 24.98 (1-57042-691-0, 696881) Time Warner AudioBooks.
—The Drowning People. 1999. 288p. 24.00 o.p. (0-446-52524-3); 2000. 400p. reprint ed. mass mkt. 7.50 (0-446-60800-9) Warner Bks., Inc.
Mason, Sarah J. Corpse in the Kitchen. 1993. 224p. (Orig.). mass mkt. 4.50 o.p. (0-425-14006-7) Berkley Publishing Group.
—Dying Breath. 1994. 240p. (Orig.). mass mkt. 4.50 o.p. (0-425-14245-0, Prime Crime) Berkley Publishing Group.
—Frozen Stiff. 1993. 224p. (Orig.). mass mkt. 4.50 o.p. (0-425-13837-2) Berkley Publishing Group.
—Murder in the Maze. 1993. 224p. mass mkt. 4.99 o.s.i (0-425-13795-3) Berkley Publishing Group.
—Murder in the Maze. l.t. ed. 1999. (Linford Mystery Large Print Ser.). 448p. pap. 18.99 (0-7089-5561-4, Linford) Thorpe, F. A. Pubs. GBR. *Dist:* Ulverscroft Large Print Bks., Ltd., Ulverscroft Large Print Canada, Ltd.
—Seeing Is Deceiving. 1997. 208p. mass mkt. 5.99 o.s.i (0-425-15901-9, Prime Crime) Berkley Publishing Group.
—Seeing Is Deceiving. l.t. ed. 2000. (Linford Mystery Large Print Ser.). 384p. pap. 18.99 (0-7089-5673-4, Linford) Thorpe, F. A. Pubs. GBR. *Dist:* Ulverscroft Large Print Bks., Ltd., Ulverscroft Large Print Canada, Ltd.
—Sew Easy to Kill. 1996. 208p. mass mkt. 5.99 o.s.i (0-425-15310-X) Berkley Publishing Group.
—Sew Easy to Kill. l.t. ed. 2000. (Linford Mystery Large Print Ser.). 392p. pap. 18.99 o.p. (0-7089-5656-4, Linford) Thorpe, F. A. Pubs. GBR. *Dist:* Ulverscroft Large Print Bks., Ltd., Ulverscroft Large Print Canada, Ltd.
Masters, Priscilla. Embroidering Shrouds. 2002. (Joanna Piercy Mystery Ser.). 288p. pap. 9.95 (0-7490-0587-4) Allison & Busby, Ltd. GBR. *Dist:* International Publishers Marketing.
Materer, Timothy. Wyndham Lewis: The Novelist. 1976. 189p. text 21.50 o.p. (0-8143-1544-5) Wayne State Univ. Pr.
Mather, Linda. Blood of an Aries: A Zodiac Mystery. 1994. 208p. 18.95 o.p. (0-312-10429-4, Saint Martin's Minotaur) St. Martin's Pr.
—Gemini Doublecross. l.t. ed. 1997. (Nightingale Ser.). 17.95 o.p. (0-7838-1869-6, Macmillan Reference USA) Gale Group.
Matthews, John. Secret Camelot. 1997. (Illus.). 176 p. 29.95 (0-7137-2646-6) Blandford Pr. GBR. *Dist:* Sterling Publishing Co., Inc.
—The Unknown Arthur: Forgotten Tales of the Round Table. 1996. (Illus.). 172p. 27.95 o.p. (0-7137-2476-5) Blandford Pr. GBR. *Dist:* Sterling Publishing Co., Inc.
Maugham, W. Somerset. Cakes & Ale. 2000. 320p. pap. 13.00 (0-375-72502-4, Vintage) Knopf Publishing Group.
—Of Human Bondage. 1999. E-Book 4.95 (1-931208-71-9) Adobe Systems, Inc.
—Of Human Bondage. 1977. (Works of W. Somerset Maugham). reprint ed. 27.95 o.p. (0-405-07819-6) Ayer Co. Pubs., Inc.
—Of Human Bondage. 2002. Vol. 1. 352p. 96.99 (1-4043-2254-X); Vol. 1. 352p. per. 91.99 (1-4043-2255-8); Vol. 2. 400p. 97.99 (1-4043-2256-6); Vol. 2. 400p. per. 92.99 (1-4043-2257-4) IndyPublish-.com.
—Of Human Bondage. 2000. E-Book 4.95 (0-679-64170-X, Modern Library) Random House Adult Trade Publishing Group.
Maxted, Anna. Getting over It. 2001. 416p. pap. 14.00 (0-06-098824-X); 2000. 288p. 25.00 (0-06-039320-3) HarperTrade. (ReganBooks).
—Running in Heels. 432p. 2002. pap. 13.95 (0-06-098825-8); 2001. (Illus.). 25.00 (0-06-039321-1) HarperTrade. (ReganBooks).
Maxwell, Cathy. Because of You. 1999. (Avon Romantic Treasure Ser.). 384p. mass mkt. 6.99 (0-380-79710-0, Avon Bks.) Morrow/Avon.
—The Seduction of an English Lady. 2004. 384p. mass mkt. 6.99 (0-06-009297-1, Avon Bks.) Morrow/Avon.
Maxwell, Robin. The Queen's Bastard. 1999. 448p. 24.95 (1-55970-475-6) Arcade Publishing, Inc.
—The Queen's Bastard. 2000. 448p. pap. 13.00 (0-684-85760-X, Touchstone) Simon & Schuster.
May, Gideon S. Gideon's Way. 1980. pap. 30.00 (0-907526-61-6) Alloway Publishing, Ltd. GBR. *Dist:* State Mutual Bk. & Periodical Service, Ltd.
Mayhew, Margaret. Bluebirds. 2000. pap. 12.95 (0-552-13910-6) Transworld Publishers Ltd. GBR. *Dist:* Trafalgar Square.
Maynard, Nan. Between the Waters. l.t. ed. 1998. (Romance Ser.). 211p. pap. (0-7540-3417-8) BBC Audiobooks America.
—Pageant. l.t. ed. 1997. pap. 17.95 o.p. (0-7838-2011-9, Macmillan Reference USA) Gale Group.
Maynard, Nan, contrib. by. Between the Waters. (0-7540-3418-6) BBC Audiobooks America.
Mayo, J. K. Wolf's Head. 1988. mass mkt. 3.50 o.s.i (0-449-21549-0, Fawcett) Ballantine Bks.
—Wolf's Head. 1987. 256p. 16.95 o.p. (0-87113-138-2) Grove/Atlantic, Inc.
McAlpine, Gordon. The Persistence of Memory. 1998. 176p. 29.95 (0-7206-1047-8) Owen, Peter Ltd. GBR. *Dist:* Dufour Editions, Inc.
McCabe, Amanda. Scandal in Venice. 2001. (Signet Regency Romance Ser.). 224p. mass mkt. 4.99 o.s.i (0-451-20286-4) NAL.
McCall, Wendell. Concerto in Dead Flat. l.t. ed. 2002. lib. bdg. 28.95 (1-58547-157-7, Premier) Ctr. Point Large Print.
—Concerto in Dead Flat. 2000. pap. 12.95 (1-890208-52-3); 1999. 277p. 23.95 (1-890208-18-3) Poisoned Pen Pr.
McCarver, Sam. The Case of the Ripper's Revenge. 2001. 224p. mass mkt. 5.99 o.s.i (0-451-20458-1, Signet Bks.) NAL.
—The Case of the 2nd Seance. 2000. (John Darnell Mysteries Ser.: Vol. 3). 224p. mass mkt. 5.99 o.s.i (0-451-20160-4) NAL.
—The Case of the 2nd Seance: A John Darnell Mystery. l.t. ed. 2001. 344p. 27.95 (0-7862-3331-1) Thorndike Pr.
—To Die, or Not to Die- A John Darnell Mystery. l.t. ed. 2003. (Five Star First Edition Mystery Ser.). 215p. 25.95 (0-7862-5444-0, Five Star) Gale Group.
McCaslin, Nellie. The Crowning of Arthur. 1996. 55p. (Orig.). (gr. 1-8). pap. 5.00 (0-88734-450-X) Players Pr., Inc.
McClymer, Kelly. Once upon a Wedding: The Fairy Tale Bride. 2000. (Once Upon a Wedding Ser.). 32p. mass mkt. 5.50 o.s.i (0-8217-6699-6, Zebra Bks.) Kensington Publishing Corp.
McCraw, JoAnne. The Viscount's Journey. 2001. E-Book 4.75 incl. disk (1-58749-012-9); E-Book 4.75 (1-58749-013-7) Awe-Struck E-Bks.
McCrery, Nigel. Silent Witness. pap. (0-312-30022-0, Saint Martin's Griffin); 2001. 324p. per. 15.95 (0-312-29197-3, Dunne, Thomas Bks.); 1998. 320p. 23.95 (0-312-18178-7, Saint Martin's Minotaur) St. Martin's Pr.
—Silent Witness. l.t. ed. 1999. (Charnwood Large Print Ser.). 344p. 31.99 o.p. (0-7089-9116-5, Ulverscroft) Thorpe, F. A. Pubs. GBR. *Dist:* Ulverscroft Large Print Bks., Ltd., Ulverscroft Large Print Canada, Ltd.
—The Spider's Web. 1999. 320p. 22.95 o.p. (0-312-20017-X, Saint Martin's Minotaur) St. Martin's Pr.
—Strange Screams of Death. l.t. ed. 2001. (Charnwood Large Print Ser.). 408p. 32.50 (0-7089-9191-2) Ulverscroft Large Print Bks., Ltd.
McCrum, Robert. Suspicion: A Novel. 1997. 256p. 23.00 o.p. (0-393-04046-1) Norton, W. W. & Co., Inc.
McCullough, Colleen. Morgan's Run. E-Book 28.00 (1-930161-95-6) Adobe Systems, Inc.
—Morgan's Run. 2000. E-Book 28.00 (0-7432-1467-6, Simon & Schuster); 2000. (Illus.). 608p. 28.00 (0-684-85329-9, Simon & Schuster); 2001. 848p. reprint ed. mass mkt. 7.99 (0-7434-1719-4, Pocket) Simon & Schuster.
—Morgan's Run. l.t. ed. 2001. 918p. 30.95 (0-7862-3083-5); 31.95 (0-7862-3082-7) Thorndike Pr.
McCutchan, Philip. Halfhyde & the Admiral. l.t. ed. 1991. (Lythway Ser.). 288p. 21.95 (0-7451-1259-5, Macmillan Reference USA) Gale Group.
McDermid, Val. Blue Genes: A Kate Brannigan Mystery. l.t. ed. 1997. (G. K. Hall Mystery Ser.). 358p. lib. bdg. 24.95 o.p. (0-7838-8141-X, Macmillan Reference USA) Gale Group.
—Blue Genes: A Kate Brannigan Mystery. 1997. 304p. 21.50 (0-684-83398-0, Scribner) Simon & Schuster.
—Blue Genes: A Kate Brannigan Mystery. unabr. ed. 2000. audio 54.95 (0-7531-0620-5, 990703); 8p. audio compact disk 64.95 (0-7531-0899-2, 108992) Ulverscroft Large Print Bks., Ltd.
—Booked for Murder. 2nd ed. 2000. (Lindsay Gordon Mystery Ser.). 260p. pap. 12.00 (1-883523-37-0) Spinsters Ink Bks.

Settings

For book reviews, descriptive annotations, tables of contents, cover images, author biographies & additional information, updated daily, subscribe to **www.booksinprint.com** 757

—Clean Break. 2002. 12.95 (*1-883523-51-6*) Spinsters Ink Bks.
—Clean Break: A Kate Brannigan Mystery. 1996. 288p. mass mkt. 4.99 o.p. (*0-06-104393-1*, Harper-Torch) Morrow/Avon.
—Clean Break: A Kate Brannigan Mystery. 1995. 288p. 20.00 o.s.i (*0-684-80461-1*, Scribner) Simon & Schuster.
—Common Murder. 2nd ed. 1995. 264p. pap. 10.95 (*1-883523-08-7*) Spinsters Ink Bks.
—Common Murder. l.t. ed. 2001. 286p. 32.50 (*0-7531-6538-4*) Thorpe, F. A. Pubs. GBR. *Dist:* Ulverscroft Large Print Bks., Ltd., Ulverscroft Large Print Canada, Ltd.
—Conferences Are Murder: A Lindsay Gordon Mystery. 1999. (Lindsay Gordon Mystery Ser.: Vol. 4). (Illus.). 264p. pap. 12.00 (*1-883523-30-3*) Spinsters Ink Bks.
—Crack Down. 1994. 288p. 20.00 (*0-684-19756-1*, Macmillan Reference USA) Gale Group.
—Crack Down. 1996. 256p. mass mkt. 4.99 o.s.i (*0-06-104394-X*) HarperCollins Pubs.
—Crack Down. 2002. 12.95 (*1-883523-50-8*) Spinsters Ink Bks.
—Dead Beat. 1993. 207p. 16.95 o.p. (*0-312-08754-3*, Saint Martin's Minotaur) St. Martin's Pr.
—Dead Beat. l.t. ed. 1997. pap. 20.95 o.p. (*0-7862-0929-1*) Thorndike Pr.
—Deadline for Murder: A Lindsay Gordon Mystery. 2nd ed. 1997. (Kate Brannigan Mystery Ser.). 264p. (Orig.). pap. 10.95 (*1-883523-17-6*) Spinsters Ink Bks.
—Final Edition. l.t. ed. 2001. 288p. 32.50 (*0-7531-6540-6*) Thorpe, F. A. Pubs. GBR. *Dist:* Ulverscroft Large Print Bks., Ltd., Ulverscroft Large Print Canada, Ltd.
—Kickback. 1993. 192p. 17.95 o.p. (*0-312-09836-7*, Saint Martin's Minotaur) St. Martin's Pr.
—Killing the Shadows. unabr. ed. 2001. audio 107.25 (*1-58788-625-1*, 2921, Unabridged Library Editions) Brilliance Audio.
—Killing the Shadows. l.t. ed. 2002. (Wheeler Large Print Book Ser.). 28.95 (*1-58724-184-6*, Wheeler Publishing, Inc.) Gale Group.
—Killing the Shadows. 2000. 422p. (*0-00-226108-1*) HarperCollins Pubs.
—Killing the Shadows. E-Book 24.95 (*0-312-70297-3*); 2002. 496p. mass mkt. 6.99 (*0-312-98338-7*, St. Martin's Paperbacks); 2001. 432p. 24.95 (*0-312-26615-4*, Saint Martin's Minotaur) St. Martin's Pr.
—The Mermaids Singing. unabr. ed. 1999. 14p. audio compact disk 104.95 (*0-7531-0710-4*, 107104); audio 84.95 (*0-7531-0075-4*, 960808) ISIS Audio Bks. GBR. *Dist:* Ulverscroft Large Print Bks., Ltd.
—The Mermaids Singing. 1997. 480p. mass mkt. 6.50 o.p. (*0-06-101175-4*); 1996. 288p. mass mkt. 22.00 o.p. (*0-06-101174-6*) Morrow/Avon. (HarperTorch).
—A Place of Execution. l.t. ed. 2001. (Large Print Book Ser.). 659p. 29.95 (*1-58724-125-0*, Wheeler Publishing, Inc.) Gale Group.
—A Place of Execution. 2000. 403p. 24.95 (*0-312-26632-4*, Saint Martin's Minotaur); 2001. 480p. reprint ed. mass mkt. 6.99 (*0-312-97953-3*, St. Martin's Paperbacks) St. Martin's Pr.
—Report for Murder. l.t. ed. 2001. (Magna Large Print Ser.). 400p. 32.50 (*0-7505-1699-2*) Magna Large Print Bks. GBR. *Dist:* Ulverscroft Large Print Bks., Ltd., Ulverscroft Large Print Canada, Ltd.
—Report for Murder. 224p. 25.00 (*0-7278-5554-9*) Severn Hse. Pubs., Ltd.
—Report for Murder. 2nd ed. 1998. 264p. pap. 10.95 (*1-883523-24-9*) Spinsters Ink Bks.
—Report for Murder. 1989. 208p. 16.95 o.p. (*0-312-03888-7*, Saint Martin's Minotaur) St. Martin's Pr.
—The Wire in the Blood. unabr. ed. 1998. audio 94.95 (*0-7531-0350-8*, 980504) ISIS Audio Bks. GBR. *Dist:* Ulverscroft Large Print Bks., Ltd.
—The Wire in the Blood. ltd. ed. 1998. xii, 372p. 50.00 (*1-890208-21-3*) Poisoned Pen Pr.
—The Wire in the Blood. 2002. 528p. mass mkt. 6.99 (*0-312-98365-4*, St. Martin's Paperbacks) St. Martin's Pr.
McEwan, Ian. Amsterdam: A Novel. unabr. ed. 1999. audio 24.00 (*0-7366-4451-2*, 4896) Books on Tape, Inc.
—Amsterdam: A Novel. Oeser, Hans-Christian, tr. from ENG. 1999. (GER.). 224p. (*3-257-06220-6*) Diogenes Verlag AG CHE. *Dist:* International Bk. Import Service, Inc.
—Amsterdam: A Novel. 1998. 208p. 21.00 o.s.i (*0-385-49423-8*, Talese, Nan A.) Doubleday Publishing.
—Amsterdam: A Novel. unabr. ed. 1999. audio 24.95 (*1-57511-060-1*) Publishing Mills, Inc., The.
—Amsterdam: A Novel. 1999. 208p. pap. 13.00 (*0-385-49424-6*, Knopf Bks. for Young Readers) Random Hse. Children's Bks.
—Amsterdam: A Novel. l.t. ed. 1999. (Basic Ser.). 232p. 29.95 (*0-7862-1796-0*) Thorndike Pr.
—Amsterdam: A Novel. abr. ed. 1999. audio 18.70 (*0-00-105566-6*) Ulverscroft Audio (U.S.A.).
—Atonement: A Novel. 2002. E-Book 12.00 (*1-4014-4204-8*) Barnes & Noble Digital.
—Atonement: A Novel. 368p. 2002. 26.00 (*0-385-50395-4*, Talese, Nan A.); 2003. reprint ed. pap. 14.00 (*0-385-72179-X*) Doubleday Publishing.
—Atonement: A Novel. l.t. ed. 2002. 624p. 29.95 (*0-7862-3921-2*) Gale Group.
—Atonement: A Novel. pap. (*1-4000-3514-7*) Knopf Publishing Group.
—Atonement: A Novel. unabr. ed. 2002. audio 34.99 (*1-4025-1178-7*, 01234) Recorded Bks., LLC.
—Black Dogs. 1994. 192p. pap. 9.95 o.s.i (*0-553-37367-6*) Bantam Bks.
—Black Dogs. 1998. 176p. pap. 14.00 (*0-385-49432-7*) Doubleday Publishing.
—Black Dogs. 1992. o.p. (*0-224-03572-X*) Random Hse. UK, Ltd.
—Black Dogs. 1994. 3.99 o.p. (*0-517-12909-4*) Random Hse. Value Publishing.
—Black Dogs. l.t. ed. 2003. (General Ser.). lib. bdg. 25.95 (*0-7862-5132-8*) Thorndike Pr.
—The Cement Garden. 1980. mass mkt. 2.25 o.p. (*0-425-04496-3*) Berkley Publishing Group.
—The Cement Garden. 1994. 160p. pap. 11.00 (*0-679-75018-5*, Villard Bks.) Random House Adult Trade Publishing Group.
—The Cement Garden. 1978. 8.95 o.s.i (*0-671-24288-1*, Simon & Schuster) Simon & Schuster.
—Enduring Love. unabr. ed. 2000. audio 59.95 (*0-7540-0200-4*, CAB 1623) Chivers Audio Bks. GBR. *Dist:* BBC Audiobooks America.
—Enduring Love. 1998. 272p. 23.95 o.s.i (*0-385-49112-3*, Talese, Nan A.) Doubleday Publishing.
—Enduring Love, Set. abr. ed. 1997. audio 24.95 (*1-57511-040-7*) Publishing Mills, Inc., The.
—Enduring Love. 1998. 272p. pap. 13.00 (*0-385-49414-9*, Knopf Bks. for Young Readers) Random Hse. Children's Bks.
—Enduring Love. unabr. ed. 1998. audio 51.00 (*0-7887-2176-3*, 95472E7) Recorded Bks., LLC.
—Enduring Love. l.t. ed. 1998. (Basic Ser.). 395p. 29.95 (*0-7862-1447-3*) Thorndike Pr.
—Enduring Love. abr. ed. 1999. audio 16.85 (*0-00-105565-8*) Ulverscroft Audio (U.S.A.).
—First Love, Last Rites. l.t. ed. 2003. (General Ser.). lib. bdg. 25.95 (*0-7862-5720-2*) Thorndike Pr.
—First Love, Last Rites: Stories. 1994. 176p. pap. 12.00 (*0-679-75019-3*) Knopf, Alfred A. Inc.
—In Between the Sheets. 1994. 160p. pap. 12.00 (*0-679-74983-7*, Vintage) Knopf Publishing Group.
—In Between the Sheets. 1979. 8.95 o.s.i (*0-671-24290-3*, Simon & Schuster) Simon & Schuster.
—In Between the Sheets. 1990. 176p. pap. 6.95 o.p. (*0-14-011281-2*, Penguin Bks.) Viking Penguin.
McFarland, Dennis. A Face at the Window. 1998. 320p. pap. 19.00 (*0-7679-0130-4*) Broadway Bks.
McGovern, Jimmy. Cracker to Be a Somebody. 2000. mass mkt. (*0-312-96998-8*, St. Martin's Paperbacks) St. Martin's Pr.
McGovern, Jimmy & Holliday, Liz. Cracker: One Day a Lemming Will Fly. 1999. (Cracker Ser.). 272p. mass mkt. 5.99 (*0-312-96817-5*, St. Martin's Paperbacks) St. Martin's Pr.
McGowan, Heather. Schooling. l.t. ed. 2001. (Hardcover Ser.). 428p. 28.95 o.p. (*1-58724-048-3*, Wheeler Publishing, Inc.) Gale Group.
—Schooling. 2002. 320p. pap. 13.00 (*0-375-71432-4*) Knopf, Alfred A. Inc.
McGown, Jill. Death in the Family. 2004. 336p. mass mkt. 6.99 (*0-345-45849-4*, Fawcett); 2003. 320p. 22.95 (*0-345-45848-6*, Ballantine Bks.) Ballantine Bks.
—Death in the Family. l.t. ed. 2003. 30.45 (*0-7862-5380-0*) Thorndike Pr.
—An Evil Hour. 1987. 256p. 16.95 o.p. (*0-312-00592-X*) St. Martin's Pr.
—Picture of Innocence. (British Mystery Ser.). 1999. 352p. mass mkt. 6.99 (*0-449-00251-9*); 1998. 336p. 22.00 o.p. (*0-449-00250-0*) Ballantine Bks. (Fawcett).
—Picture of Innocence. l.t. ed. 1998. (Mystery Ser.). 560p. 27.95 (*0-7862-1670-0*) Thorndike Pr.
—Plots & Errors. 2000. (Detective Chief Inspector Lloyd & Judy Hill Mysteries Ser.). 384p. mass mkt. 6.99 (*0-449-00253-5*, Fawcett) Ballantine Bks.
—Scene of Crime. l.t. ed. 2001. 391p. 29.95 (*0-7862-3647-7*) Thorndike Pr.
—Verdict Unsafe. 1997. 327p. 22.00 o.p. (*0-449-91067-9*, Fawcett) Ballantine Bks.
McGrath, Patrick. Asylum. l.t. ed. 1997. 25.95 (*1-56895-439-5*, Wheeler Publishing, Inc.) Gale Group.
—Asylum. 1998. 272p. pap. 13.00 (*0-679-78138-2*, Vintage) Knopf Publishing Group.
—Dr. Haggard's Disease. 1994. (Vintage Contemporaries Ser.). 192p. pap. 12.00 (*0-679-75261-7*) Random Hse., Inc.
—Dr. Haggard's Disease. 1993. 192p. 20.00 o.p. (*0-671-72733-8*, Simon & Schuster) Simon & Schuster.
—The Grotesque: A Novel. 1990. 256p. mass mkt. 4.95 o.s.i (*0-345-36407-4*) Ballantine Bks.
—The Grotesque: A Novel. 1997. (Vintage Contemporaries Ser.). 192p. pap. 12.00 (*0-679-77621-4*) Random Hse., Inc.
—The Grotesque: A Novel. 1989. 17.95 o.p. (*0-671-66509-X*, Simon & Schuster) Simon & Schuster.
McGregor, Jon. If Nobody Speaks of Remarkable Things. 2003. 288p. pap. 13.00 (*0-618-34458-6*, Mariner Bks.) Houghton Mifflin Co. Trade & Reference Div.
McHugh, Stuart D. Knock on the Nursery Door: Tales of the Dickens Children. 1973. 9.95 o.p. (*0-7181-1031-5*) Transatlantic Arts, Inc.
McKinney, Blanaid. The Ledge. 2002. 249p. 24.95 (*1-86159-167-5*) Weidenfeld & Nicolson, Ltd. GBR. *Dist:* Trafalgar Square.
McKinney, Meagan. Gentle from the Night. l.t. ed. 1998. 397p. 25.95 (*1-57490-136-2*, Beeler Large Print Bks.) Beeler, Thomas T. Publisher.
—Gentle from the Night. 1997. 352p. mass mkt. 5.99 o.s.i (*0-8217-5803-9*, Zebra Bks.); 1997. 352p. 21.95 o.s.i (*1-57566-136-5*); 1995. 384p. mass mkt. 18.95 o.p. (*0-8217-4825-4*) Kensington Publishing Corp.
McLeay, Alison. Summer House. l.t. ed. 1998. (Romance Ser.). 432p. 28.95 (*0-7838-0164-5*) Thorndike Pr.
—The Summer House. unabr. ed. 1999. audio 84.95; 1998. audio 84.95 (*0-7540-0143-1*, CAB1566) BBC Audiobooks America.
McLeay, Allison. The Summer House. 1997. 320p. 23.95 (*0-312-15666-9*) St. Martin's Pr.
McMaster, Michelle. The Marriage Bargain. 2000. 320p. mass mkt. 4.99 (*0-8439-4750-0*, Leisure Bks.) Dorchester Publishing Co., Inc.
McMinn, Suzanne. My Lady Imposter. 2001. (Sword & the Ring Ser.). 336p. mass mkt. 5.50 o.s.i (*0-8217-6875-1*) Kensington Publishing Corp.
McNaught, Judith. Until You. l.t. ed. 1994. 26.95 o.p. (*1-56895-160-4*, Wheeler Publishing, Inc.) Gale Group.
—Until You. 1994. 448p. 22.00 o.p. (*0-671-88059-4*, Atria) Simon & Schuster.
—Until You. Marrow, Linda, ed. 1995. 448p. reprint ed. mass mkt. 7.99 (*0-671-88060-8*, Pocket) Simon & Schuster.
—Until You. 1999. audio 9.98 (*0-671-04634-9*); Set. 1994. audio 17.00 (*0-671-89476-5*, 391839) Simon & Schuster Audio. (Simon & Schuster Audioworks).
—Whitney, My Love. l.t. ed. 1994. 25.95 o.p. (*1-56895-107-8*, Wheeler Publishing, Inc.) Gale Group.
—Whitney, My Love. 1989. reprint ed. 19.95 o.p. (*0-7278-1694-2*) Severn Hse. Pubs., Ltd.
—Whitney, My Love. 1990. mass mkt. 4.95 (*0-671-70861-9*); 2000. 736p. reprint ed. pap. 7.99 (*0-671-77609-6*) Simon & Schuster. (Pocket).
McNeil, Gil. The Only Boy for Me. 2002. 276p. 23.95 (*1-58234-223-7*) Bloomsbury Publishing.
McRae, Melinda. Miss Chadwick's Companion. 2000. (Regency Romance Ser.). 240p. mass mkt. 4.99 o.s.i (*0-451-19857-3*, Signet Bks.) NAL.
Medeiros, Teresa. Charming the Prince. 1999. 352p. mass mkt. 6.99 (*0-553-57502-3*) Bantam Bks.
Meek, M. R. D. Hang the Consequences. 1985. (Lennox Kemp Mystery Ser.). 160p. 12.95 o.s.i (*0-684-18465-6*, Macmillan Reference USA) Gale Group.
—A House to Die For. l.t. ed. 2000. (Dales Large Print Ser.). 368p. pap. 20.99 o.p. (*1-84262-044-4*) Dales Large Print Bks. GBR. *Dist:* Ulverscroft Large Print Bks., Ltd., Ulverscroft Large Print Canada, Ltd.
—A House to Die For. l.t. ed. 2000. pap. 20.99 (*1-84137-069-X*) Magna Large Print Bks. GBR. *Dist:* Ulverscroft Large Print Bks., Ltd.
—A House to Die For. 1999. 219p. 25.00 (*0-7278-5442-9*) Severn Hse. Pubs., Ltd.
—In Remembrance of Rose: A Lennox Kemp Mystery. 1987. 14.95 o.p. (*0-684-18832-5*, Macmillan Reference USA) Gale Group.
—A Mouthful of Sand. 1989. 16.95 o.s.i (*0-684-19067-2*, Macmillan Reference USA) Gale Group.
—A Mouthful of Sand. 1990. 224p. mass mkt. (*0-373-26060-1*, Harlequin Bks.) Harlequin Enterprises, Ltd.
—A Mouthful of Sand. l.t. ed. 1990. (Magna Large Print Ser.). 343p. o.p. (*1-85057-795-1*) Magna Large Print Bks. GBR. *Dist:* Ulverscroft Large Print Canada, Ltd.
—Postscript to Murder, Vol. 1. 1997. (PostScript to Murder Ser.: Vol. 1). 224p. text 21.95 o.p. (*0-312-15626-X*, Saint Martin's Minotaur) St. Martin's Pr.
—The Split Second: A Lennox Kemp Mystery. 1987. 170p. 13.95 o.p. (*0-684-18734-5*, Scribner) Simon & Schuster.
—A Worm of Doubt: A Lennox Kemp Mystery. l.t. ed. 1988. lib. bdg. 11.95 o.p. (*1-85057-487-1*, Macmillan Reference USA) Gale Group.
—A Worm of Doubt: A Lennox Kemp Mystery. 1990. mass mkt. (*0-373-26048-2*, Harlequin Bks.) Harlequin Enterprises, Ltd.
—A Worm of Doubt: A Lennox Kemp Mystery. 1988. 208p. 14.95 o.s.i (*0-684-18939-9*, Scribner) Simon & Schuster.
Meiser, Edith. The Adventures of Sherlock Holmes. abr. collector's ed. 1998. (Smithsonian Historical Performances Ser.). 60p. pap. 24.98 incl. audio (*1-57019-034-8*, 5016); (Illus.). pap. 39.98 incl. audio compact disk (*1-57019-035-6*, 5017) Radio Spirits, Inc.
Melville, Jennie. Dead Again: A Charmian Daniels Mystery. l.t. ed. 2000. 281p. (*0-7540-4212-X*); (*0-7540-4213-8*) Gale Group. (Macmillan Reference USA).
—Dead Again: A Charmian Daniels Mystery. l.t. ed. 2000. (Nightingale Ser.). 281p. pap. 20.95 (*0-7838-9099-0*) Thorndike Pr.
—Dead Set: A Charmian Daniels Mystery. 1995. (WWL Mystery Ser.). 252p. per. (*0-373-26174-8*, 1-26174-2, Harlequin Bks.) Harlequin Enterprises, Ltd.
—Dead Set: A Charmian Daniels Mystery. 1992. 17.95 (*0-312-08757-8*, Saint Martin's Minotaur) St. Martin's Pr.
—Death in the Family. 1995. 277p. 21.00 (*0-312-11772-8*, Saint Martin's Minotaur) St. Martin's Pr.
—A Different Kind of Summer. l.t. ed. 1993. 18.95 o.p. (*0-7451-6437-4*); 1992. audio 39.95 (*0-7451-2401-1*, CD 002) BBC Audiobooks America.
—A Different Kind of Summer. (Black Dagger Crime Ser.). 12.95 o.p. (*0-86220-800-9*, BD005) Chivers Pr. GBR. *Dist:* BBC Audiobooks America.
—Footsteps in the Blood. pap. 15.95 (*0-312-29187-6*, Saint Martin's Griffin); 1993. 192p. 17.95 (*0-312-09813-8*, Saint Martin's Minotaur) St. Martin's Pr.
—Making Good Blood. 1990. 15.95 o.p. (*0-312-04344-9*, Saint Martin's Minotaur) St. Martin's Pr.
—The Morbid Kitchen. 208p. 1996. 20.95 (*0-312-14681-7*, Saint Martin's Minotaur); 1995. per. 15.95 (*0-312-29172-8*, Saint Martin's Griffin) St. Martin's Pr.
—Murder Has a Pretty Face. 1991. reprint ed. per. (*0-373-26079-2*, Harlequin Bks.) Harlequin Enterprises, Ltd.
—Murder Has a Pretty Face. l.t. ed. 1996. (Magna Large Print Ser.). 400p. 29.99 (*0-7505-1047-1*) Magna Large Print Bks. GBR. *Dist:* Ulverscroft Large Print Bks., Ltd., Ulverscroft Large Print Canada, Ltd.
—Murder Has a Pretty Face. 1989. 256p. 16.95 o.p. (*0-312-03405-9*, Saint Martin's Minotaur) St. Martin's Pr.
—Murder in the Garden. 1991. 2.99 o.p. (*0-517-07814-7*) Random Hse. Value Publishing.
—Murder in the Garden. pap. 15.95 (*0-312-29185-X*, Saint Martin's Griffin); 1990. 224p. 15.95 (*0-312-03895-X*, Saint Martin's Minotaur) St. Martin's Pr.
—Revengeful Death. l.t. ed. 1998. (Magna Large Print Ser.). 272p. (*0-7505-1232-6*) Magna Large Print Bks. GBR. *Dist:* Ulverscroft Large Print Canada, Ltd.
—Tarot's Tower. 1979. mass mkt. 1.75 o.s.i (*0-449-24001-0*, Fawcett) Ballantine Bks.
—Tarot's Tower. 1978. 8.95 o.s.i (*0-671-22905-2*, Simon & Schuster) Simon & Schuster.
—Whoever Has the Heart. 218p. 3.95 o.p. (*0-8317-5152-5*) Smithmark Pubs., Inc.
—Whoever Has the Heart. pap. 15.95 (*0-312-29175-2*, Saint Martin's Griffin); 1994. 224p. 19.95 (*0-312-11099-5*, Saint Martin's Minotaur) St. Martin's Pr.
—Windsor Red. pap. 9.95 (*1-902002-01-6*) CT Publishing GBR. *Dist:* Trafalgar Square.
—Windsor Red. 1990. mass mkt. (*0-373-26051-2*, Harlequin Bks.) Harlequin Enterprises, Ltd.
—Windsor Red. 1988. 256p. 16.95 o.p. (*0-312-01846-0*, Saint Martin's Minotaur) St. Martin's Pr.
—Witching Murder. 1991. (Lythway Adult Ser.). 280p. 20.50 o.p. (*0-7451-1374-5*) Chivers Pr. GBR. *Dist:* BBC Audiobooks America.
—Witching Murder. pap. 15.95 (*0-312-29186-8*, Saint Martin's Griffin); 1991. 15.95 (*0-312-05999-X*, Saint Martin's Minotaur) St. Martin's Pr.
Meredith, George. The Egoist. Set. unabr. ed. 1992. audio 83.95 (*1-55685-248-7*) Audio Bk. Contractors, Inc.
—The Egoist. audio HarperTrade.
—The Egoist. 1999. E-Book 1.95 (*1-58515-098-3*) MesaView, Inc.
—The Egoist. mass mkt. 0.75 o.p. (*0-451-50191-8*, Signet Classics); 1986. pap. 5.95 o.p. (*0-452-00820-4*, Meridian Bks.) NAL.
—The Egoist. Adams, Robert M., ed. 1979. (Critical Editions Ser.). (C). o.p. (*0-393-04431-9*); 561p. pap. text 12.00 (*0-393-09171-6*) Norton, W. W. & Co., Inc.
—The Egoist. 1968. (Oxford World's Classics Ser.). 12.95 o.p. (*0-19-250508-4*) Oxford Univ. Pr., Inc.
—The Egoist. Wilson, Angus, ed. 1979. (Penguin Classics Ser.). 608p. pap. 12.95 o.p. (*0-14-043034-2*, Penguin Classics) Viking Penguin.
—The Egoist. 448p. pap. 3.95 (*1-85326-266-8*) Wordsworth Editions, Ltd. GBR. *Dist:* Combined Publishing.

—The Egoist: A Comedy in Narrative. Harris, Margaret, ed. 1992. (Oxford World's Classics Ser.). 610p. pap. 9.95 o.p. (*0-19-281817-1*) Oxford Univ. Pr., Inc.

Metzger, Barbara. Lord Heartless. 1998. mass mkt. 4.99 o.s.i (*0-449-00171-7*, Fawcett) Ballantine Bks.

—Miss Westlake's Windfall. 2001. (Signet Regency Romance Ser.). 224p. mass mkt. 4.99 o.s.i (*0-451-20279-1*) NAL.

Meyer, Nicholas. The Seven-Percent Solution. l.t. ed. 1977. (Ulverscroft Large Print Ser.). 29.99 o.p. (*0-7089-0052-6*, Ulverscroft) Thorpe, F. A. Pubs. GBR. *Dist:* Ulverscroft Large Print Bks., Ltd., Ulverscroft Large Print Canada, Ltd.

Meyer, Nicholas, ed. The Seven-Percent Solution: Being a Reprint from the Reminiscences of John H. Watson, M. D. 1993. 256p. pap. 13.00 (*0-393-31119-8*) Norton, W. W. & Co., Inc.

Meynell, Laurence. The Fairly Innocent Little Man. (Jubilee Mystery Ser.). 192p. 7.95 o.s.i (*0-8128-2421-0*, Scarborough Hse.) Madison Bks., Inc.

—The Lost Half Hour. (Jubilee Mystery Ser.). 224p. 14.95 o.s.i (*0-8128-2420-2*, Scarborough Hse.) Madison Bks., Inc.

Michaels, Barbara, pseud. The Dancing Floor. 1997. 352p. 23.00 o.p. (*0-06-017764-0*) HarperCollins Pubs.

—The Dancing Floor. abr. ed. 1997. 3p. pap. 18.00 o.s.i incl. audio (*0-694-51783-6*, CPN 2625, HarperAudio) HarperTrade.

—The Dancing Floor. l.t. ed. 1998. 464p. mass mkt. 7.99 (*0-06-109254-1*, HarperTorch) Morrow/Avon.

—The Dancing Floor, unabr. ed. 1998. audio 75.00 (*0-7887-0806-6*, 94955E7) Recorded Bks., LLC.

—The Dancing Floor. l.t. ed. 1998. (Paperback Bestsellers Ser.). 557p. pap. 27.95 (*0-7862-1059-1*) Thorndike Pr.

—Greygallows. l.t. ed. 1994. pap. 19.95 o.p. (*0-7927-1741-4*); 20.95 o.p. (*0-7927-1742-2*) BBC Audiobooks America.

—Greygallows. l.t. ed. 1986. 462p. 12.50 o.p. (*0-7089-1405-5*, Ulverscroft) Thorpe, F. A. Pubs. GBR. *Dist:* Ulverscroft Large Print Bks., Ltd.

—The Wizard's Daughter. 1981. (General Ser.). lib. bdg. 13.95 o.p. (*0-8161-3248-8*, Macmillan Reference USA) Gale Group.

Michaels, Fern. Split Second. 1999. 248p. 25.00 (*0-7278-5431-3*); 2001. 320p. 25.00 (*0-7278-7025-4*) Severn Hse. Pubs., Ltd.

Michaels, Kasey. Come Near Me. 2000. 384p. reprint ed. mass mkt. 6.50 (*0-446-60583-2*, Warner Romance) Warner Bks., Inc.

—Indiscreet. l.t. ed. 2000. (Wheeler Large Print Book Ser.). 413p. 26.95 (*1-56895-843-9*, Wheeler Publishing, Inc.) Gale Group.

—Indiscreet. 1998. 400p. reprint ed. mass mkt. 6.50 (*0-446-60582-4*, Warner Romance) Warner Bks., Inc.

—Someone to Love. l.t. ed. 2001. 495p. 27.95 (*0-7862-3491-1*) Thorndike Pr.

—Someone to Love. 2001. 368p. reprint ed. mass mkt. 6.99 (*0-446-60585-9*, Warner Romance) Warner Bks., Inc.

—Waiting for You. l.t. ed. 2001. (Large Print Bks.). pap. 23.95 o.p. (*1-58724-113-7*, Wheeler Publishing, Inc.) Gale Group.

—Waiting for You. 2000. 368p. E-Book 4.95 (*0-7595-8003-0*) Little Brown & Co.

—Waiting for You. 2000. 368p. E-Book 4.95 (*0-7595-9003-6*); 368p. E-Book 4.95 (*0-7595-0003-7*); 384p. reprint ed. mass mkt. 6.99 o.s.i (*0-446-60584-0*, Warner Romance) Warner Bks., Inc.

Middleton, Stanley. Changes & Chances. 1991. 252p. 18.95 (*1-56131-004-2*, New Amsterdam Bks) Dee, Ivan R. Pub.

—Live & Learn. 1996. 248p. o.p. (*0-09-179220-7*) Random Hse. of Canada, Ltd. CAN. *Dist:* Random Hse., Inc.

—Toward the Sea. 1995. 217p. o.p. (*0-09-179158-8*) Random Hse. of Canada, Ltd. CAN. *Dist:* Random Hse., Inc.

—Toward the Sea. l.t. ed. 1997. (General Ser.). 352p. pap. 22.95 (*0-7862-1128-8*) Thorndike Pr.

Mieville, China. King Rat. 1999. 320p. 23.95 (*0-312-89073-7*); 2nd ed. 2000. 318p. pap. 14.95 (*0-312-89072-9*, CPB1120) Doherty, Tom Assocs., LLC. (Tor Bks.).

Mildmay, Eroica. Lucker & Tiffany Peel Out. 1994. 192p. pap. (*1-85242-285-8*) Serpent's Tail Ltd.

Miles, Rosalind. Guenevere, Queen of the Summer Country. (Guenevere Ser.: Bk. 1). 2000. (Illus.). 528p. pap. 11.95 (*0-609-80650-5*, Crown); 1999. 432p. 24.00 o.s.i (*0-609-60362-0*) Crown Publishing Group.

Miller, Andrew. Ingenious Pain: A Novel. 352p. 1998. pap. 13.00 (*0-15-600600-6*, Harvest Bks.); 1997. 24.00 o.s.i (*0-15-100258-4*) Harcourt Trade Pubs.

—Oxygen. 2003. 352p. pap. 14.00 (*0-15-602740-2*, Harvest Bks.); 2002. 336p. 24.00 (*0-15-100721-7*) Harcourt Trade Pubs.

Miller, Barbara. Dearest Max. 2000. (Sonnet Bks.). (Illus.). 416p. pap. 6.50 (*0-671-77452-2*, Pocket) Simon & Schuster.

—The Guardian. 2001. 368p. pap. 6.50 (*0-7434-1229-X*, Pocket) Simon & Schuster.

—My Phillipe. 2000. (Sonnet Bks.). 416p. pap. 6.50 (*0-671-77453-0*, Pocket) Simon & Schuster.

Miller, Hugh. Skin Deep. 1992. 192p. 16.95 o.p. (*0-312-08293-2*, Saint Martin's Minotaur) St. Martin's Pr.

Miller, Julie. The Duke's Covert Mission. 2002. (Harlequin Intrigue Ser.: No. 666). 251p. mass mkt. (*0-373-22666-7*, 1-22666-1, Harlequin Bks.) Harlequin Enterprises, Ltd.

Miller, Linda Lael. Knights. l.t. ed. 1996. 25.95 o.p. (*1-56895-391-7*, Wheeler Publishing, Inc.) Gale Group.

—Knights. 1996. 400p. mass mkt. 6.99 (*0-671-87317-2*, Pocket); 304p. 22.00 o.p. (*0-671-52850-5*, Atria) Simon & Schuster.

Miller, Nadine. The Yorkshire Lady. 2001. (Signet Regency Romance Ser.). 240p. mass mkt. 4.99 o.s.i (*0-451-20146-9*) NAL.

Millington, Mil. Things My Girlfriend & I Have Argued About: A Novel. 2003. 384p. pap. 12.95 (*0-8129-6666-X*, Villard Bks.) Random House Adult Trade Publishing Group.

Mills, Magnus. The Restraint of Beasts. 1998. 224p. 22.95 (*1-55970-437-3*) Arcade Publishing, Inc.

—The Restraint of Beasts. 1999. 224p. pap. 11.00 (*0-684-86511-4*, Touchstone) Simon & Schuster.

—The Restraint of Beasts. abr. ed. 1999. audio 16.85 (*0-00-105567-4*) Ulverscroft Audio (U.S.A.).

Mindel, Jenna. Blessing in Disguise. 2001. (Signet Regency Romance Ser.). 224p. mass mkt. 4.99 o.s.i (*0-451-20370-4*) NAL.

Miss Read. Affairs at Thrush Green. 2002. (Illus.). 256p. pap. 12.00 (*0-618-23857-3*, Mariner Bks.) Houghton Mifflin Co. Trade & Reference Div.

—At Home in Thrush Green. 2002. (Illus.). 272p. pap. 12.00 (*0-618-23858-1*, Mariner Bks.) Houghton Mifflin Co. Trade & Reference Div.

—Friends at Thrush Green. 2002. (Illus.). 256p. pap. 12.00 (*0-618-23888-3*, Mariner Bks.) Houghton Mifflin Co. Trade & Reference Div.

Mitchell, Gladys. Cold, Lone & Still. l.t. ed. 1987. (Nightingale Paperbacks Ser.). 304p. 11.95 o.p. (*0-8161-4374-9*, Macmillan Reference USA) Gale Group.

—The Dancing Druids. 1986. 239p. 14.95 o.p. (*0-312-18207-4*) St. Martin's Pr.

—Death at the Opera. 1992. 248p. reprint ed. 14.95 o.p. (*0-86220-835-1*, Black Dagger) BBC Audiobooks America.

—The Death-Cap Dancers. (Fingerprint Mysteries Ser.). 192p. 1983. pap. 5.95 o.p. (*0-312-18609-6*, Saint Martin's Griffin); 1981. 9.95 o.p. (*0-312-18608-8*) St. Martin's Pr.

—Faintley Speaking. 1986. 224p. 14.95 o.p. (*0-312-27957-4*) St. Martin's Pr.

—Here Lies Gloria Mundy. 1983. 192p. 9.95 o.p. (*0-312-36986-7*) St. Martin's Pr.

—Late, Late in the Evening. 1995. 192p. reprint ed. 19.00 o.p. (*0-7278-4793-7*) Severn Hse. Pubs., Ltd.

—Late, Late in the Evening. l.t. ed. 1996. (Linford Mystery Library). 400p. pap. 17.99 o.p. (*0-7089-7941-6*, Ulverscroft) Thorpe, F. A. Pubs. GBR. *Dist:* Ulverscroft Large Print Bks., Ltd., Ulverscroft Large Print Canada, Ltd.

—No Winding-Sheet. l.t. ed. 1989. (Popular Ser.). lib. bdg. 11.95 o.p. (*1-85057-319-0*, Macmillan Reference USA) Gale Group.

—The Rising of the Moon. 1984. 11.95 o.p. (*0-312-68442-8*) St. Martin's Pr.

—Speedy Death. 1999. 21.95 (*0-7540-8547-3*, Black Dagger) BBC Audiobooks America.

—Spotted Hemlock: A Murder Mystery. 1985. 240p. 14.95 o.p. (*0-312-75350-0*) St. Martin's Pr.

—St. Peter's Finger. 1986. 352p. 15.95 (*0-312-00192-4*) St. Martin's Pr.

—Three Quick & Five Dead, Set. unabr. ed. 1999. audio 47.95 (*1-86015-418-2*) Beeler, Thomas T. Publisher.

—Uncoffin'd Clay. 1982. 189p. 9.95 o.p. (*0-312-82857-8*) St. Martin's Pr.

—Watson's Choice. 1976. 6.95 o.p. (*0-679-50658-6*) McKay, David Co., Inc.

—Winking at the Brim. 1977. (McKay-Washburn Mystery Ser.). 6.95 o.p. (*0-679-50732-9*) McKay, David Co., Inc.

Mitchell, Kay. In Stony Places. 1993. mass mkt. (*0-373-26126-8*, 1-26126-2, Harlequin Bks.) Harlequin Enterprises, Ltd.

—In Stony Places. 1992. 208p. 17.95 o.p. (*0-312-07001-2*, Saint Martin's Minotaur) St. Martin's Pr.

—In Stony Places. l.t. ed. 1994. (Ulverscroft Large Print Ser.). 336p. 29.99 o.p. (*0-7089-3115-4*, Ulverscroft) Thorpe, F. A. Pubs. GBR. *Dist:* Ulverscroft Large Print Bks., Ltd., Ulverscroft Large Print Canada, Ltd.

—A Lively Form of Death. 1992. (WWL Mystery Ser.). mass mkt. (*0-373-26106-3*, 1-26106-4, Harlequin Bks.) Harlequin Enterprises, Ltd.

—A Lively Form of Death. 1991. 15.95 o.p. (*0-312-05464-5*, Saint Martin's Minotaur) St. Martin's Pr.

—A Lively Form of Death. l.t. ed. 1993. (General Ser.). 336p. 29.99 o.p. (*0-7089-2864-1*, Ulverscroft) Thorpe, F. A. Pubs. GBR. *Dist:* Ulverscroft Large Print Bks., Ltd., Ulverscroft Large Print Canada, Ltd.

—A Portion for Foxes. 1997. per. (*0-373-26235-3*, 1-26235-1, Worldwide Library) Harlequin Enterprises, Ltd.

—A Portion for Foxes. 1995. 240p. 21.95 o.p. (*0-312-13589-0*, Saint Martin's Minotaur) St. Martin's Pr.

—A Rage of Innocents. 1999. (Chief Inspector Morrissey Mysteries Ser.: Vol. 318). 252p. per. (*0-373-26318-X*, Worldwide Library) Harlequin Enterprises, Ltd.

—A Rage of Innocents. 1998. (Chief Inspector Morrissey Mysteries Ser.). 224p. 20.95 (*0-312-18656-8*, Saint Martin's Minotaur) St. Martin's Pr.

—Roots of Evil. 1995. (WWL Mystery Ser.). per. (*0-373-26162-4*, 1-26162-7, Harlequin Bks.) Harlequin Enterprises, Ltd.

—Roots of Evil. 1993. (Chief Inspector Morrissey Mysteries Ser.). 176p. 17.95 o.p. (*0-312-09374-8*, Saint Martin's Minotaur) St. Martin's Pr.

—A Strange Desire. l.t. ed. 1995. (Ulverscroft Large Print Ser.). 432p. 29.99 o.p. (*0-7089-3244-4*, Ulverscroft) Thorpe, F. A. Pubs. GBR. *Dist:* Ulverscroft Large Print Bks., Ltd., Ulverscroft Large Print Canada, Ltd.

Mitchell, Sally, ed. East Lynne: Mrs. Henry Wood. 1984. 545p. reprint ed. 50.00 o.p. (*0-8135-1041-4*); pap. 17.00 o.p. (*0-8135-1042-2*) Rutgers Univ. Pr.

Mitchell, Sara. Trial of the Innocent. 1995. (Shadowcatchers Ser.: Bk. 1). 336p. pap. 9.99 o.p. (*1-55661-497-7*) Bethany Hse. Pubs.

—Trial of the Innocent. l.t. ed. 2000. (Christian Mystery Ser.: Vol. 1). 479p. 24.95 (*0-7862-2726-5*) Thorndike Pr.

Mitchelson, Austin. The Baker Street Irregular: The Unauthorized Biography of Sherlock Holmes. 1994. 35.00 (*0-88734-905-6*) Players Pr., Inc.

Mitchelson, Austin & Utechin, Nicholas. Sherlock Holmes & the Earthquake Machine. 1994. 25.00 (*0-86025-283-3*) Henry, Ian Pubns. GBR. *Dist:* Empire Publishing Service.

—Sherlock Holmes & the Earthquake Machine. 1994. 25.00 (*0-88734-903-X*) Players Pr., Inc.

—Sherlock Holmes & the Hellbirds. 1995. 35.00 (*0-86025-284-1*); 35.00 (*0-88734-916-1*) Players Pr., Inc.

Mitford, Mary R. Belford Regis: or Sketches of a Country Town, 3 vols, Vol. 1. 1977. (Short Story Index Reprint Ser.). reprint ed. 66.95 (*0-8369-4185-3*) Ayer Co. Pubs., Inc.

—Country Stories. 1977. (Short Story Index Reprint Ser.). 22.95 (*0-8369-3359-1*) Ayer Co. Pubs., Inc.

—Our Village. l.t. unabr. ed. 1991. (Isis Large Print Bks.). 170p. 24.95 (*1-85089-489-2*, 894892) ISIS Large Print Bks. GBR. *Dist:* Transaction Pubs., Ulverscroft Large Print Canada, Ltd.

—Our Village. 1987. (Illus.). 224p. 19.95 o.p. (*0-13-644923-9*) Prentice Hall PTR.

—Our Village. 1988. 336p. pap. 6.95 o.p. (*0-14-010278-7*, Penguin Bks.) Viking Penguin.

—Our Village, 1824. 2003. (Revolution & Romanticism, 1789-1834 Ser.). 310p. (*1-85477-185-X*) Woodstock Books.

Mitford, Mary Russell. Our Village. E-Book 3.95 (*0-594-02661-X*) 1873 Pr.

Mitford, Nancy. Love in a Cold Climate. l.t. ed. 1985. (Mainstream Ser.). 342p. 14.95 o.p. (*1-85089-003-X*) ISIS Large Print Bks. GBR. *Dist:* Transaction Pubs.

—The Pursuit of Love & Love in a Cold Climate. 1979. 15.00 o.s.i (*0-394-60481-4*); 19th ed. 1994. 656p. 19.95 (*0-679-60090-6*) Random Hse., Inc.

—The Pursuit of Love & Love in a Cold Climate: Two Novels. 2001. 480p. reprint ed. pap. 14.00 (*0-375-71899-0*, Vintage) Knopf Publishing Group.

Moggach, Deborah. Close to Home. 1998. 249p. mass mkt. o.p. (*0-7493-1229-7*) Random Hse. of Canada, Ltd.

—The Ex-Wives. l.t. ed. 2001. (Thorndike General Ser.). 354p. 25.95 (*0-7862-3199-8*) Thorndike Pr.

Moline, Karen. Lunch. 1994. 287p. 22.00 o.p. (*0-688-13320-7*, Morrow, William & Co.) Morrow/Avon.

Monahan, Brent. The Sceptered Isle Club. 2002. 288p. 24.95 (*0-312-28803-4*, Saint Martin's Minotaur) St. Martin's Pr.

Monsarrat, Nicholas. The Ship That Died of Shame, & Other Stories. 1977. (Short Story Index Reprint Ser.). reprint ed. 19.95 (*0-8369-3958-1*) Ayer Co. Pubs., Inc.

Moody, Susan. Death Takes a Hand. 1995. 240p. mass mkt. 4.99 o.s.i (*0-425-14639-1*, Prime Crime) Berkley Publishing Group.

—Death Takes a Hand. 1994. 288p. 20.00 (*1-883402-00-X*, Scribner) Simon & Schuster.

—Doubled in Spades. l.t. ed. 1997. pap. 23.95 o.p. (*1-56895-494-8*, Wheeler Publishing, Inc.) Gale Group.

—Doubled in Spades. 1997. 313p. 21.50 (*0-684-80259-7*, Scribner) Simon & Schuster.

—Dummy Hand. l.t. ed. 1999. (Ulverscroft Large Print Ser.). 368p. 31.99 o.p. (*0-7089-4088-9*, Ulverscroft) Thorpe, F. A. Pubs. GBR. *Dist:* Ulverscroft Large Print Bks., Ltd., Ulverscroft Large Print Canada, Ltd.

—Grand Slam. 1996. 272p. mass mkt. 5.99 o.s.i (*0-425-15229-4*, Prime Crime) Berkley Publishing Group.

—Grand Slam. unabr. ed. 1998. audio 83.95 (*1-85903-229-X*) Magna Story Sound GBR. *Dist:* Ulverscroft Large Print Bks., Ltd.

—Grand Slam. 1995. 310p. 20.50 (*1-883402-32-8*, Scribner) Simon & Schuster.

—King of Hearts: A Cassandra Swann Bridge Mystery. 1997. 304p. reprint ed. mass mkt. 5.99 o.s.i (*0-425-15725-3*, Prime Crime) Berkley Publishing Group.

—King of Hearts: A Cassandra Swann Bridge Mystery. unabr. ed. 1998. audio 76.95 (*1-85903-230-3*) Magna Story Sound GBR. *Dist:* Ulverscroft Large Print Bks., Ltd.

—King of Hearts: A Cassandra Swann Bridge Mystery. 1996. 320p. 21.00 o.s.i (*0-684-80258-9*, Scribner) Simon & Schuster.

—Mosaic. 1992. 432p. mass mkt. 4.99 o.s.i (*0-440-21260-X*) Dell Publishing.

—Mosaic. l.t. ed. 1992. (General Ser.). 563p. lib. bdg. 21.95 o.p. (*0-8161-5367-1*, Macmillan Reference USA) Gale Group.

—Penny Black. 1986. 272p. mass mkt. 2.95 o.s.i (*0-449-12864-4*, Fawcett) Ballantine Bks.

—Penny Black. 1997. (Missing Mysteries Ser.: Vol. 1). pap. 7.95 (*1-890208-01-9*) Poisoned Pen Pr.

—Penny Black. l.t. ed. 1985. (Ulverscroft Large Print Ser.). 464p. 29.99 o.p. (*0-7089-1391-1*, Ulverscroft) Thorpe, F. A. Pubs. GBR. *Dist:* Ulverscroft Large Print Bks., Ltd., Ulverscroft Large Print Canada, Ltd.

—Penny Dreadful. 1986. mass mkt. 2.95 o.s.i (*0-449-12865-2*, Fawcett) Ballantine Bks.

—Penny Dreadful. unabr. ed. 2000. (Penny Wanawake Mystery Ser.). audio 59.95 (*0-7451-4183-8*, CAB 866) Chivers Audio Bks. GBR. *Dist:* BBC Audiobooks America.

—Penny Dreadful. l.t. ed. 1987. (Ulverscroft Large Print Ser.). 432p. 29.99 o.p. (*0-7089-1603-1*, Ulverscroft) Thorpe, F. A. Pubs. GBR. *Dist:* Ulverscroft Large Print Bks., Ltd., Ulverscroft Large Print Canada, Ltd.

—Penny Pinching. 1989. 240p. mass mkt. 3.50 o.s.i (*0-449-13237-4*, Fawcett) Ballantine Bks.

—Penny Pinching. l.t. ed. 1991. (Ulverscroft Large Print Ser.). 29.99 o.p. (*0-7089-2374-7*, Ulverscroft) Thorpe, F. A. Pubs. GBR. *Dist:* Ulverscroft Large Print Bks., Ltd., Ulverscroft Large Print Canada, Ltd.

—Penny Post. 1986. mass mkt. 2.95 o.s.i (*0-449-12866-0*, Fawcett) Ballantine Bks.

—Penny Post. l.t. ed. 1987. (Ulverscroft Large Print Ser.). 416p. 29.99 o.p. (*0-7089-1703-8*, Ulverscroft) Thorpe, F. A. Pubs. GBR. *Dist:* Ulverscroft Large Print Bks., Ltd., Ulverscroft Large Print Canada, Ltd.

—Penny Royal. 1987. 304p. mass mkt. 2.95 o.s.i (*0-449-12867-9*, Fawcett) Ballantine Bks.

—Penny Royal. l.t. ed. 1988. (Ulverscroft Large Print Ser.). 464p. 29.99 o.p. (*0-7089-1763-1*, Ulverscroft) Thorpe, F. A. Pubs. GBR. *Dist:* Ulverscroft Large Print Bks., Ltd., Ulverscroft Large Print Canada, Ltd.

—Penny Saving. unabr. ed. 2000. (Penny Wanawake Mystery Ser.). audio 59.95 (*0-7451-4007-6*, CAB 704) Chivers Audio Bks. GBR. *Dist:* BBC Audiobooks America.

—Penny Saving. l.t. ed. 1993. (Mystery Ser.). 464p. 29.99 o.p. (*0-7089-2938-9*, Ulverscroft) Thorpe, F. A. Pubs. GBR. *Dist:* Ulverscroft Large Print Bks., Ltd., Ulverscroft Large Print Canada, Ltd.

—Penny Wise. unabr. ed. 1992. (Penny Wanawake Mysteries Ser.). 69.95 incl. audio (*0-7451-4066-1*, CAB 763) BBC Audiobooks America.

—Penny Wise, No. 5. 1989. mass mkt. 3.50 o.s.i (*0-449-13236-6*, Fawcett) Ballantine Bks.

—Return to the Secret Garden. l.t. ed. 1998. (Core Ser.). 600p. 29.95 (*0-7838-0279-X*) Thorndike Pr.

—Takeout Double, Set. unabr. ed. 1998. audio 69.95 (*1-85903-204-4*) Magna Story Sound GBR. *Dist:* Ulverscroft Large Print Bks., Ltd.

Mooney, Ted. Traffic & Laughter. 1992. pap. 23.00 (*0-679-73884-3*, Vintage) Knopf Publishing Group.

Moorcock, Michael. King of the City. 2002. 432p. pap. 14.95 (*0-380-79503-5*, Perennial) HarperTrade.

—King of the City. 2001. 432p. 26.00 (*0-380-97589-0*, Morrow, William & Co.) Morrow/Avon.

—Mother London. 1990. 496p. reprint ed. pap. 8.95 o.p. (*0-06-097309-9*, Perennial) HarperTrade.

Moorcraft, Paul L. Anchoress of Shere. 2003. 368p. pap. 14.95 o.s.i (*1-59058-028-1*); 2002. 320p. 24.95 (*1-59058-011-7*) Poisoned Pen Pr.

Moore, George. Esther Waters. 1977. 377p. reprint ed. pap. 11.00 o.p. (*0-915864-53-3*) Academy Chicago Pubs., Ltd.

—Esther Waters. 1942. (Black & Gold Library). 7.95 o.p. (*0-87140-872-4*) Liveright Publishing Corp.
—Esther Waters. Skilton, David, ed. 1983. (Oxford World's Classics Ser.). 424p. pap. 9.95 o.p. (*0-19-281578-4*) Oxford Univ. Pr., Inc.
—Esther Waters. Laurie, Hilary, ed. 1993. 384p. pap. 9.95 (*0-460-87326-1*, Everyman's Classic Library in Paperback) Tuttle Publishing.
Moore, Oscar. A Matter of Life & Sex. 1993. 336p. pap. 11.95 o.p. (*0-452-27006-5*, Plume) Dutton/Plume.
Moorings. Baker St. Mysteries, Vol. 4. 1996. (Baker St. Mysteries Ser.). pap. 5.99 o.s.i (*0-345-39558-1*) Ballantine Bks.
Moran, Alec F. A Matter of Life & Sex. 1992. 336p. 20.00 o.p. (*0-525-93484-7*, Dutton) Dutton/Plume.
Morgan, Fidelis. Unnatural Fire. 2001. 368p. 24.00 (*0-688-17683-6*, Morrow, William & Co.) Morrow/Avon.
Morgan, Robert. All Things under the Moon. 1994. 224p. (Orig.). mass mkt. 4.99 o.p. (*0-425-14302-3*, Prime Crime) Berkley Publishing Group.
—The Only Thing to Fear. 1994. 256p. mass mkt. 4.99 o.s.i (*0-425-14468-2*, Prime Crime) Berkley Publishing Group.
—Some Things Come Back. 1995. 256p. (Orig.). mass mkt. 4.99 o.s.i (*0-425-14690-1*, Prime Crime) Berkley Publishing Group.
—Some Things Never Die. 1993. 208p. (Orig.). 3.99 o.p. (*1-55773-887-4*, Diamond Bks.) Ace Bks.
—Thing That Darkness Hides. 1993. 4.50 o.p. (*1-55773-960-9*, Diamond Bks.) Ace Bks.
—Things That Are Not There. 1992. 208p. (Orig.). 3.99 o.p. (*1-55773-827-0*, Diamond Bks.) Ace Bks.
Morice, Anne. Dead on Cue. l.t. ed. 1986. (Nightingale Ser.). 291p. 11.95 o.p. (*0-8161-4118-5*, Macmillan Reference USA) Gale Group.
—Death in the Round. 1980. 192p. 8.95 o.p. (*0-312-18616-9*) St. Martin's Pr.
—Death in the Round. 1981. (Crime Monthly Ser.). 192p. pap. 2.95 o.p. (*0-14-005997-0*, Penguin Bks.) Viking Penguin.
—Death of a Wedding Guest. 1976. 7.95 o.p. (*0-312-18830-7*) St. Martin's Pr.
—Design for Dying. unabr. ed. 1991. (Audio Ser.). audio 39.95 (*0-7451-6174-X*, CAT 4070) BBC Audiobooks America.
—Design for Dying. 1988. 192p. 14.95 o.p. (*0-312-01759-6*, Saint Martin's Minotaur) St. Martin's Pr.
—Fatal Charm. l.t. ed. 1990. (Nightingale Ser.). 276p. pap. 13.95 o.p. (*0-8161-4925-9*, Macmillan Reference USA) Gale Group.
—Fatal Charm. 1989. 192p. 14.95 o.p. (*0-312-03338-9*, Saint Martin's Minotaur) St. Martin's Pr.
—Getting Away with Murder? l.t. ed. 1985. (Nightingale Ser.). 304p. 10.95 o.p. (*0-8161-3865-6*, Macmillan Reference USA) Gale Group.
—Getting Away with Murder? 1984. 11.95 o.p. (*0-312-32633-5*) St. Martin's Pr.
—Hollow Vengeance. 1982. 196p. 10.95 o.p. (*0-312-38834-9*) St. Martin's Pr.
—The Men in Her Death. 1981. 224p. 9.95 o.p. (*0-312-52939-2*) St. Martin's Pr.
—Murder by Proxy. 1978. 7.95 o.p. (*0-312-55292-0*) St. Martin's Pr.
—Murder in Outline. 1986. 176p. mass mkt. 2.95 o.s.i (*0-553-25647-5*) Bantam Bks.
—Murder in Outline. 1979. 8.95 o.p. (*0-312-55303-X*) St. Martin's Pr.
—Murder Post-Dated. 1986. 208p. mass mkt. 2.95 o.s.i (*0-553-25652-1*) Bantam Bks.
—Murder Post-Dated. l.t. ed. 1985. (Nightingale Ser.). 396p. pap. 11.95 o.p. (*0-8161-3769-2*, Macmillan Reference USA) Gale Group.
—Murder Post-Dated. 1984. 192p. 10.95 o.p. (*0-312-55321-8*) St. Martin's Pr.
—Nursery Tea & Poison, Vol. 1. 1975. 6.95 o.p. (*0-312-58030-4*) St. Martin's Pr.
—Planning for Murder. l.t. ed. 1991. (Nightingale Ser.). 267p. pap. 14.95 o.p. (*0-8161-5246-2*, Macmillan Reference USA) Gale Group.
—Planning for Murder. 1991. 15.95 o.p. (*0-312-04869-6*, Saint Martin's Minotaur) St. Martin's Pr.
—Publish & Be Killed. l.t. ed. 1988. (Nightingale Ser.). 294p. 12.95 o.p. (*0-8161-4394-3*, Macmillan Reference USA) Gale Group.
—Publish & Be Killed. 1986. 192p. 12.95 o.p. (*0-312-00178-9*) St. Martin's Pr.
—Scared to Death. 1986. mass mkt. 2.95 o.s.i (*0-553-25628-9*) Bantam Bks.
—Scared to Death. 1978. (General Ser.). lib. bdg. 10.95 o.p. (*0-8161-6584-X*, Macmillan Reference USA) Gale Group.
—Scared to Death. 1977. 7.95 o.p. (*0-312-70043-1*) St. Martin's Pr.
—Sleep of Death. 1986. mass mkt. 2.95 o.s.i (*0-553-25877-X*) Bantam Bks.
—Sleep of Death. 1982. 176p. 10.95 o.p. (*0-312-72863-8*) St. Martin's Pr.
—Treble Exposure. l.t. ed. 1988. (Nightingale Ser.). 312p. 12.95 o.p. (*0-8161-4622-5*, Macmillan Reference USA) Gale Group.
—Treble Exposure. 1988. 192p. 13.95 o.p. (*0-312-01525-9*, Saint Martin's Minotaur) St. Martin's Pr.
Morpurgo, Michael. Escape from Shangri-La. 1998. 192p. (J). (gr. 5-8). 16.99 o.s.i (*0-399-23311-3*, Philomel) Penguin Putnam Bks. for Young Readers.
Morris, Bernie & Singer, M. R. Bobby's Girl. 2000. 208p. pap. 12.95 (*0-595-00712-0*) iUniverse, Inc.
Morris, Gilbert. White Hunter. 1999. (House of Winslow Ser.: Vol. 22). (Illus.). 320p. pap. 11.99 (*1-55661-909-X*) Bethany Hse. Pubs.
Morrison, Arthur. A Child of the Jago. (Academy Book Ser.). 208p. 1995. pap. 12.00 (*0-89733-392-6*); 1983. pap. 8.95 o.p. (*0-85115-203-1*) Academy Chicago Pubs., Ltd.
—The Hole in the Wall. 1994. 179p. reprint ed. pap. 10.00 o.p. (*0-89733-393-4*) Academy Chicago Pubs., Ltd.
—Tales of Mean Streets. 1997. (Academy Book Ser.). 175p. pap. text 12.00 (*0-89733-440-X*) Academy Chicago Pubs., Ltd.
—Tales of Mean Streets. 1977. (Short Story Index Reprint Ser.). 19.95 (*0-8369-3633-7*) Ayer Co. Pubs., Inc.
Morrissey, J. P. A Weekend at Blenheim: A Novel. (Illus.). 320p. 2003. pap. 13.95 (*0-312-31138-9*, Saint Martin's Griffin); 2002. 24.95 (*0-312-28268-0*, Saint Martin's Minotaur) St. Martin's Pr.
Morse, David E. The Iron Bridge. 1998. 448p. 25.00 o.s.i (*0-15-100259-2*) Harcourt Trade Pubs.
Morson, Ian. A Psalm for Falconer, Vol. 1. Date not set. mass mkt. (*0-312-96534-6*, St. Martin's Paperbacks) St. Martin's Pr.
—A Psalm for Falconer: A William Falconer Medieval Mystery. 1997. 220p. 21.95 o.p. (*0-312-16833-0*, Saint Martin's Minotaur) St. Martin's Pr.
Mortimer, John. The Best of Rumpole. 1994. (Rumpole Ser.). 288p. reprint ed. pap. 14.00 (*0-14-017684-5*, Penguin Bks.) Penguin Group (USA) Inc.
—The Best of Rumpole. 1993. (Rumpole Ser.). 288p. 21.00 o.p. (*0-670-84978-2*, Viking) Viking Penguin.
—Felix in the Underworld. l.t. ed. 1997. 308p. pap. 21.95 o.p. (*0-7838-8307-2*, Macmillan Reference USA) Gale Group.
—Felix in the Underworld. 1997. 247p. 22.95 o.s.i (*0-670-86079-4*); 2p. pap. 16.95 o.s.i incl. audio (*0-14-086151-3*, Penguin AudioBooks) Viking Penguin.
—A First Rumpole Omnibus. 1984. (Crime Monthly Ser.). 560p. pap. 18.00 (*0-14-006768-X*, Penguin Bks.) Penguin Group (USA) Inc.
—Like Men Betrayed. l.t. ed. 1994. 21.95 o.p. (*0-7927-1930-1*); pap. 19.95 o.p. (*0-7927-1929-8*) BBC Audiobooks America.
—Like Men Betrayed. 1990. 208p. pap. 8.95 o.p. (*0-14-009268-4*, Penguin Bks.) Viking Penguin.
—Paradise Postponed. unabr. ed. 2000. (Leslie Titmuss Trilogy Ser.: Bk. 1). audio 69.95 (*0-7451-6175-8*, CAB 504) Chivers Audio Bks. GBR. *Dist:* BBC Audiobooks America.
—Paradise Postponed. abr. ed. audio 15.95 o.p. (*0-88646-209-6*, 7209) Durkin Hayes Publishing Ltd.
—Paradise Postponed. l.t. ed. 1987. 555p. 18.95 o.p. (*0-8161-4247-5*, Macmillan Reference USA) Gale Group.
—Paradise Postponed. 1986. 384p. pap. 12.95 (*0-14-009864-X*, Penguin Bks.) Penguin Group (USA) Inc.
—Paradise Postponed. 1986. 400p. 17.95 o.p. (*0-670-80094-5*); 448p. reprint ed. pap. 11.95 o.s.i (*0-14-006928-3*) Viking Penguin.
—The Rapstone Chronicles: Paradise Postponed & Titmuss Regained. 1993. 704p. pap. 14.00 o.p. (*0-14-017595-4*, Penguin Bks.) Penguin Group (USA) Inc.
—The Second Rumpole Omnibus: Rumpole & the Golden Thread, Rumpole for the Defence & Rumpole's Last Case. 1988. (Rumpole Ser.). 672p. pap. 16.95 (*0-14-008958-6*, Penguin Bks.) Penguin Group (USA) Inc.
—The Second Rumpole Omnibus: Rumpole & the Golden Thread, Rumpole for the Defence & Rumpole's Last Case. 1987. (Rumpole Ser.). 672p. 18.95 o.p. (*0-670-81125-4*) Viking Penguin.
—The Sound of Trumpets. unabr. ed. 2000. (Leslie Titmuss Trilogy Ser.: Bk. 3). audio 59.95 (*0-7540-0315-9*, CAB 1738) Chivers Audio Bks. GBR. *Dist:* BBC Audiobooks America.
—The Sound of Trumpets. l.t. ed. 1999. (Core Ser.). 359p. 27.95 (*0-7838-8716-7*, Macmillan Reference USA) Gale Group.
—The Sound of Trumpets. 1999. 288p. pap. 12.95 o.s.i (*0-14-028851-1*) Penguin Group (USA) Inc.
—The Sound of Trumpets. 1999. (Rapstone Chronicles Ser.). 256p. 23.95 o.p. (*0-670-87861-8*) Viking Penguin.
—The Third Rumpole Omnibus: Rumpole a la Carte, Rumpole on Trial, Rumpole & the Angel of Death. 150th ed. 1998. (Rumpole Ser.). 752p. pap. 18.00 (*0-14-025741-1*, Penguin Bks.) Penguin Group (USA) Inc.
—Titmuss Regained. l.t. ed. 1992. pap. 15.95 o.p. (*0-7927-0666-8*); 1991. 17.95 o.p. (*0-7927-0665-X*, E0007) BBC Audiobooks America.
—Titmuss Regained. l.t. ed. 1992. 70.95 o.p. (*0-8161-3213-5*, Macmillan Reference USA) Gale Group.
—Titmuss Regained. 1991. 288p. pap. 12.95 o.s.i (*0-14-014921-X*, Penguin Bks.) Penguin Group (USA) Inc.
—Titmuss Regained. 1990. 288p. 19.95 o.p. (*0-670-82333-3*, Viking) Viking Penguin.
—Titmuss Regained: Movie-TV Tie-In. 1992. 272p. pap. 10.00 o.p. (*0-14-017185-1*, Penguin Bks.) Penguin Group (USA) Inc.
—The Trials of Rumpole. 20.95 (*0-89190-276-7*) Amereon, Ltd.
—The Trials of Rumpole. unabr. ed. 1993. audio 39.95 (*0-7861-0422-8*, 1374) Blackstone Audio Bks., Inc.
—The Trials of Rumpole. abr. ed. 1986. audio 16.99 (*0-88646-118-9*, TC-LFP 7118) Durkin Hayes Publishing Ltd.
—The Trials of Rumpole. unabr. ed. 1993. (Rumpole of the Bailey Ser.: Vol. 2). audio 51.00 (*1-55690-825-3*, 93126E7) Recorded Bks., LLC.
—The Trials of Rumpole. 1981. (Rumpole Ser.). 208p. pap. 6.00 o.p. (*0-14-005162-7*); pap. 9.95 o.s.i (*0-14-024697-5*) Viking Penguin. (Penguin Bks.).
Mortimore, Jim. Cracker: The Mad Woman in the Attic. 1996. 256p. 21.95 o.p. (*0-312-14576-4*, Saint Martin's Minotaur); Vol. 1. 1998. (Cracker Ser.: Vol. 1). mass mkt. 5.99 (*0-312-96337-8*, St. Martin's Paperbacks) St. Martin's Pr.
Mosco, Maisie. Between Two Worlds. 1984. 480p. pap. 3.95 o.p. (*0-553-23421-8*) Bantam Bks.
—For Love & Duty. l.t. ed. 1992. pap. 15.95 o.p. (*0-7927-0820-2*); 18.95 o.p. (*0-7927-0819-9*, E0015) BBC Audiobooks America.
—From the Bitter Land. 1985. 336p. pap. 3.95 o.p. (*0-553-25086-8*) Bantam Bks.
—Glittering Harvest: From the Bitter Land, No. 3. 1985. 352p. pap. 3.50 o.p. (*0-553-20664-8*) Bantam Bks.
—The Price of Fame. 1994. 400p. mass mkt. 5.50 o.p. (*0-06-100625-4*, HarperTorch) Morrow/Avon.
—The Price of Fame. l.t. ed. 1986. (Charnwood Large Print Ser.). 464p. 15.45 o.p. (*0-7089-8346-4*, Charnwood) Thorpe, F. A. Pubs. GBR. *Dist:* Ulverscroft Large Print Bks., Ltd., Ulverscroft Large Print Canada, Ltd.
—Scattered Seed. 1991. 608p. mass mkt. 4.95 o.p. (*0-06-100185-6*, HarperTorch) Morrow/Avon.
—A Sense of Place. 1994. 432p. mass mkt. 5.50 o.p. (*0-06-100624-6*, HarperTorch) Morrow/Avon.
—A Sense of Place. l.t. ed. 1985. (Charnwood Large Print Ser.). 512p. 13.95 o.p. (*0-7089-8279-4*, Charnwood) Thorpe, F. A. Pubs. GBR. *Dist:* Ulverscroft Large Print Bks., Ltd., Ulverscroft Large Print Canada, Ltd.
Mosley, Nicholas. Children of Darkness & Light. 1997. 248p. pap. 13.95 (*1-56478-151-8*) Dalkey Archive Pr.
Mount, Ferdinand. Fairness. 306p. 2001. 26.00 (*0-7867-0850-6*); 2002. reprint ed. pap. 13.00 (*0-7867-0992-8*) Avalon Publishing Group. (Carroll & Graf Pubs.).
—Jem (& Sam) 2000. 432p. pap. 13.95 (*0-7867-0745-3*); 1999. 425p. 25.95 o.p. (*0-7867-0649-X*) Avalon Publishing Group. (Carroll & Graf Pubs.).
—Jem (& Sam) 1998. 425p. o.p. (*0-7011-6815-3*) Random Hse. of Canada, Ltd. CAN. *Dist:* Random Hse., Inc.
Moyes, Patricia. Angel Death. 1982. (Henry Tibbett Mystery Ser.). 240p. pap. 5.95 o.s.i (*0-8050-0505-6*, Owl Bks.) Holt, Henry & Co.
—Angel Death. l.t. ed. 1982. (Henry Tibbett Mystery Ser.). 457p. 12.50 o.p. (*0-7089-0746-6*, Ulverscroft) Thorpe, F. A. Pubs. GBR. *Dist:* Ulverscroft Large Print Bks., Ltd., Ulverscroft Large Print Canada, Ltd.
—Black Girl, White Girl. unabr. ed. 1993. (Henry Tibbett Mystery Ser.). audio 36.00 (*0-7366-2327-2*, 3107) Books on Tape, Inc.
—Black Girl, White Girl. l.t. ed. 1991. (Henry Tibbett Mystery Ser.). 326p. lib. bdg. 19.95 o.p. (*0-8161-5011-7*, Macmillan Reference USA) Gale Group.
—Black Girl, White Girl. (Henry Tibbett Mystery Ser.). 224p. 1990. pap. 5.95 o.s.i (*0-8050-1149-8*, Owl Bks.); 1989. 15.95 o.p. (*0-8050-1148-X*) Holt, Henry & Co.
—Black Widower. unabr. ed. 1992. (Henry Tibbett Mystery Ser.). audio 42.00 (*0-7366-2272-1*, 3060) Books on Tape, Inc.
—Black Widower. 1985. (Henry Tibbett Mystery Ser.). 224p. pap. 5.95 o.s.i (*0-8050-0243-X*, Owl Bks.) Holt, Henry & Co.
—Black Widower. 1977. (Henry Tibbett Mystery Ser.). 224p. pap. 2.95 o.p. (*0-14-004334-9*, Penguin Bks.) Viking Penguin.
—The Coconut Killings. (Henry Tibbett Mystery Ser.). 1985. 224p. pap. 5.95 o.s.i (*0-8050-0754-7*, Owl Bks.); 1985. pap. o.p. (*0-03-005608-X*, Owl Bks.); 1977. o.p. (*0-03-018481-9*) Holt, Henry & Co.
—The Coconut Killings. 1979. (Henry Tibbett Mystery Ser.). pap. 1.95 o.p. (*0-14-004593-7*, Penguin Bks.) Viking Penguin.
—The Curious Affair of the Third Dog. unabr. ed. 1993. (Henry Tibbett Mystery Ser.). audio 44.95 (*0-7861-0428-7*, 1380) Blackstone Audio Bks., Inc.
—The Curious Affair of the Third Dog. 1986. (Henry Tibbett Mystery Ser.). 224p. pap. 5.95 o.s.i (*0-8050-0503-X*); pap. o.p. (*0-03-009534-4*) Holt, Henry & Co. (Owl Bks.).
—The Curious Affair of the Third Dog. 1976. (Henry Tibbett Mystery Ser.). 208p. pap. 1.95 o.p. (*0-14-004027-7*, Penguin Bks.) Viking Penguin.
—Dead Men Don't Ski. 1984. (Henry Tibbett Mystery Ser.). 288p. pap. 5.95 o.s.i (*0-8050-0705-9*, Owl Bks.) Holt, Henry & Co.
—Dead Men Don't Ski. l.t. ed. 1983. (Ulverscroft Large Print Ser.). 496p. 29.99 o.p. (*0-7089-1006-8*, Ulverscroft) Thorpe, F. A. Pubs. GBR. *Dist:* Ulverscroft Large Print Bks., Ltd., Ulverscroft Large Print Canada, Ltd.
—Death & the Dutch Uncle. 1983. (Henry Tibbett Mystery Ser.). 256p. pap. 5.95 o.s.i (*0-8050-0506-4*, Owl Bks.) Holt, Henry & Co.
—Death on the Agenda. 1984. (Henry Tibbett Mystery Ser.). 192p. pap. 5.95 o.s.i (*0-8050-0507-2*, Owl Bks.) Holt, Henry & Co.
—Down among the Dead Men. (Henry Tibbett Mystery Ser.). 18.50 o.p. (*0-86220-823-8*, BD022, Black Dagger); 1994. 18.95 o.p. (*0-7451-6461-7*) BBC Audiobooks America.
—Down among the Dead Men. 1982. (Henry Tibbett Mystery Ser.). 240p. pap. 2.50 o.p. (*0-440-11627-9*) Dell Publishing.
—Down among the Dead Men. 1986. (Henry Tibbett Mystery Ser.). 240p. pap. 5.95 o.s.i (*0-8050-0117-4*, Owl Bks.) Holt, Henry & Co.
—Falling Star. 1982. (Henry Tibbett Mystery Ser.). (Orig.). 256p. pap. 5.95 o.s.i (*0-8050-0755-5*); pap. o.p. (*0-03-059784-6*) Holt, Henry & Co. (Owl Bks.).
—Johnny under Ground. (Henry Tibbett Mystery Ser.). 18.50 o.p. (*0-86220-789-4*, C1029, Black Dagger); 1993. 18.95 o.p. (*0-7451-6441-2*); 1996. audio 54.95 (*0-7451-2414-3*, CDA015) BBC Audiobooks America.
—Johnny under Ground. 1983. (Henry Tibbett Mystery Ser.). pap. 2.95 o.p. (*0-440-14211-3*) Dell Publishing.
—Johnny under Ground. Barzun, Jacques & Taylor, W. H., eds. 1983. (Henry Tibbett Mystery Ser.). 253p. lib. bdg. 18.00 o.p. (*0-8240-4987-X*) Garland Publishing, Inc.
—Johnny under Ground: An Inspector Henry Tibbett Mystery. 1987. (Henry Tibbett Mystery Ser.). 256p. pap. 5.95 o.s.i (*0-8050-0270-7*, Owl Bks.) Holt, Henry & Co.
—Many Deadly Returns. unabr. ed. 1994. (Henry Tibbett Mystery Ser.). audio 49.95 (*0-7861-0433-3*, 1385) Blackstone Audio Bks., Inc.
—Many Deadly Returns. 1981. (Henry Tibbett Mystery Ser.). pap. 2.25 o.p. (*0-440-16172-X*) Dell Publishing.
—Many Deadly Returns: An Inspector Henry Tibbett Mystery. 1987. (Henry Tibbett Mystery Ser.). 256p. pap. 5.95 o.s.i (*0-8050-0598-6*, Owl Bks.) Holt, Henry & Co.
—Murder a la Mode. 1983. (Henry Tibbett Mystery Ser.). 224p. pap. 5.95 o.s.i (*0-8050-0706-7*, Owl Bks.) Holt, Henry & Co.
—Murder Fantastical. (Henry Tibbett Mystery Ser.). 189p. 12.95 o.p. (*0-86220-722-3*) Chivers Pr. GBR. *Dist:* BBC Audiobooks America.
—Murder Fantastical. 1984. (Henry Tibbett Mystery Ser.). 256p. pap. 5.95 o.s.i (*0-8050-0504-8*, Owl Bks.) Holt, Henry & Co.
—Night Ferry to Death. (Henry Tibbett Mystery Ser.). 192p. 1986. pap. 5.95 o.s.i (*0-8050-0116-6*, Owl Bks.); 1985. o.p. (*0-03-004477-4*) Holt, Henry & Co.
—Night Ferry to Death. l.t. ed. 1987. (Henry Tibbett Mystery Ser.). 336p. 29.99 o.p. (*0-7089-1615-5*, Ulverscroft) Thorpe, F. A. Pubs. GBR. *Dist:* Ulverscroft Large Print Bks., Ltd., Ulverscroft Large Print Canada, Ltd.
—Season of Snows & Sins. (Henry Tibbett Mystery Ser.). 1988. 224p. pap. 6.95 o.s.i (*0-8050-0849-7*); 1983. pap. o.p. (*0-03-063542-X*) Holt, Henry & Co. (Owl Bks.).
—A Six-Letter Word for Death. 1985. (Henry Tibbett Mystery Ser.). 256p. pap. 5.95 o.s.i (*0-8050-0244-8*, Owl Bks.) Holt, Henry & Co.
—A Six-Letter Word for Death. l.t. ed. 1984. (Henry Tibbett Mystery Ser.). 432p. 29.99 o.p. (*0-7089-1163-3*, Ulverscroft) Thorpe, F. A. Pubs. GBR. *Dist:* Ulverscroft Large Print Bks., Ltd., Ulverscroft Large Print Canada, Ltd.

—To Kill a Coconut. l.t. ed. 1981. (Ulverscroft Large Print Ser.). 336p. 29.99 o.p. (*0-7089-0632-X*, Ulverscroft) Thorpe, F. A. Pubs. GBR. *Dist:* Ulverscroft Large Print Bks., Ltd., Ulverscroft Large Print Canada, Ltd.
—Twice in a Blue Moon. (Henry Tibbett Mystery Ser.). 1994. pap. 5.95 o.s.i (*0-8050-2948-6*, Owl Bks.); 1993. 192p. 19.95 o.p. (*0-8050-2823-4*) Holt, Henry & Co.
—Who Is Simon Warwick? (Henry Tibbett Mystery Ser.). 1982. pap. o.p. (*0-03-059783-8*, Owl Bks.); 1982. 176p. pap. 5.95 o.s.i (*0-8050-0719-9*, Owl Bks.); 1979. 180p. o.p. (*0-03-044726-7*) Holt, Henry & Co.
Mullarkey, Gabrielle. Hush, Hush. 1999. (*1-86059-103-5*) Town Hse.
Murdoch, Iris. The Book & the Brotherhood. 1989. 624p. pap. 16.00 (*0-14-010470-4*, Penguin Bks.) Penguin Group (USA) Inc.
—The Book & the Brotherhood. 1989. 4.99 o.p. (*0-517-02631-7*) Random Hse. Value Publishing.
—The Book & the Brotherhood. 1988. 19.95 o.p. (*0-670-81912-3*) Viking Penguin.
—The Good Apprentice. 1987. 528p. pap. 10.95 o.p. (*0-14-009815-1*, Penguin Bks.); 1986. 522p. 18.95 o.p. (*0-670-80940-3*) Viking Penguin.
—The Green Knight. 1994. 480p. 23.95 o.p. (*0-670-85229-5*, Viking) Viking Penguin.
—Henry & Cato. 1977. 12.95 o.p. (*0-670-36697-8*) Viking Penguin.
—Jackson's Dilemma. 1996. 256p. 22.95 o.p. (*0-670-86815-9*) Viking Penguin.
—20th Century Bell. 2001. (Penguin Twentieth-Century Classics Ser.). 320p. pap. 15.00 (*0-14-118669-0*) Viking Penguin.
Murray, Katharine. Jake. 1995. 186p. 9.99 o.p. (*0-7852-8095-2*) Nelson, Thomas Inc.
Murray, Max. The Voice of the Corpse. 1985. 224p. reprint ed. pap. 5.95 o.p. (*0-486-24905-0*) Dover Pubns., Inc.
Murray, Rachel. Thread of Scarlet. l.t. ed. 2001. 250p. pap. 22.95 (*0-7862-3572-1*); 243p. (*0-7540-4625-7*); 243p. (*0-7540-4626-5*) Thorndike Pr.
Murray, Stephen. Fatal Opinions. 1992. 256p. 18.95 o.p. (*0-312-08193-6*, Saint Martin's Minotaur) St. Martin's Pr.
Musser, Joe. The Infidel: A Novel. 2001. 368p. 12.99 (*0-8054-2480-6*) Broadman & Holman Pubs.
Myers, Amy. Murder at Plum's. pap. 9.95 (*0-7472-3397-7*) Headline Bk. Publishing, Ltd. GBR. *Dist:* Trafalgar Square.
—Murder at Plum's. 1993. 224p. mass mkt. 4.50 (*0-380-76586-1*, Avon Bks.) Morrow/Avon.
—Murder at Plum's. l.t. ed. 1993. (General Ser.). 432p. 29.99 o.p. (*0-7089-2847-1*, Ulverscroft) Thorpe, F. A. Pubs. GBR. *Dist:* Ulverscroft Large Print Bks., Ltd., Ulverscroft Large Print Canada, Ltd.
—Murder at the Masque. 1993. 256p. mass mkt. 4.99 (*0-380-76584-5*, Avon Bks.) Morrow/Avon.
—Murder at the Music Hall. 1999. 345p. pap. 11.00 (*0-7472-4843-5*) Headline Bk. Publishing, Ltd. GBR. *Dist:* Trafalgar Square.
—Murder in Pug's Parlour. 1992. 256p. mass mkt. 4.50 (*0-380-76587-X*, Avon Bks.) Morrow/Avon.
—Murder in Pug's Parlour. l.t. ed. 1992. (Ulverscroft Large Print Ser.). 432p. 29.99 o.p. (*0-7089-2732-7*, Ulverscroft) Thorpe, F. A. Pubs. GBR. *Dist:* Ulverscroft Large Print Bks., Ltd., Ulverscroft Large Print Canada, Ltd.
—Murder in the Limelight. 1992. 224p. mass mkt. 4.50 (*0-380-76585-3*, Avon Bks.) Morrow/Avon.
—Murder in the Limelight. l.t. ed. 1991. (General Ser.). 29.99 o.p. (*0-7089-2435-2*, Ulverscroft) Thorpe, F. A. Pubs. GBR. *Dist:* Ulverscroft Large Print Bks., Ltd., Ulverscroft Large Print Canada, Ltd.
—Murder in the Motor Stable. 1999. 311p. pap. 11.00 (*0-7472-4844-3*) Headline Bk. Publishing, Ltd. GBR. *Dist:* Trafalgar Square.
—Murder in the Queen's Boudoir. l.t. ed. 28.99 (*0-7278-7159-5*); 2000. 256p. 26.00 (*0-7278-5561-1*) Severn Hse. Pubs., Ltd.
—Murder in the Smokehouse: An Auguste Didier Whodunit. 1997. 312p. 23.95 o.p. (*0-312-15598-0*, Saint Martin's Minotaur) St. Martin's Pr.
—Murder Makes an Entree. 1996. 288p. 21.95 o.p. (*0-312-14376-1*, Saint Martin's Minotaur) St. Martin's Pr.
—Murder with Majesty. 1999. 288p. 25.00 (*0-7278-5415-1*) Severn Hse. Pubs., Ltd.
Myerson, Julie. Laura Blundy. 2000. 272p. 22.95 o.s.i (*1-57322-168-6*, Riverhead Bks. (Hardcovers)) Putnam Publishing Group, The.
—Me & the Fat Man. 1999. 224p. o.p. (*0-88001-649-3*, Ecco) HarperTrade.
—Something Might Happen. 2003. 336p. 23.95 (*0-316-77984-9*) Little Brown & Co.
—The Touch. 1996. 320p. 21.95 o.s.i (*0-385-47507-1*, Talese, Nan A.) Doubleday Publishing.
Naef, Adam. The Barbury Hall Murders: A Mystery Set in the England of Jane Austen. 1997. 216p. (Orig.). pap. 12.95 (*0-9633494-8-1*) Picardy Pr.
Naipaul, V. S. The Enigma of Arrival. 1988. 368p. reprint ed. pap. 15.00 (*0-394-75760-2*, Vintage) Knopf Publishing Group.
—Vintage Naipaul. 2004. 208p. pap. 9.95 (*1-4000-3400-0*, Vintage) Knopf Publishing Group.
Naslund, Sena J. Sherlock in Love. 1993. 240p. 21.95 (*0-87923-977-8*) Godine, David R. Pub.
Nattel, Lilian. The Theater of Consolation. 2005. 320p. pap. 14.00 (*0-7432-4967-4*); 2004. 336p. 25.00 (*0-7432-4966-6*) Simon & Schuster. (Scribner).
Naughton, Bill. Spit Nolan. 1993. (Creative Short Stories Ser.). 32p. (YA). (gr. 3-12). lib. bdg. 18.60 (*0-88682-122-3*, Creative Education) Creative Co., The.
Naylor, Clare. Love: A User's Guide. 1999. 288p. pap. 13.95 (*0-449-00556-9*, Fawcett) Ballantine Bks.
Neale, Jonathan. Laughter of Heroes. 1993. 128p. pap. (*1-85242-279-3*) Serpent's Tail Ltd.
Neel, Janet. Death among the Dons. l.t. ed. 1994. 369p. lib. bdg. 21.95 (*0-8161-7439-3*, Macmillan Reference USA) Gale Group.
—Death among the Dons. 1995. (Illus.). 272p. (J). mass mkt. 5.50 (*0-671-89952-X*, Pocket) Simon & Schuster.
—Death among the Dons. 1993. 240p. 19.95 o.p. (*0-312-10450-2*, Saint Martin's Minotaur) St. Martin's Pr.
—Death of a Partner. l.t. ed. 1996. 384p. pap. 20.95 (*0-7838-1641-3*, Macmillan Reference USA) Gale Group.
—Death of a Partner. Chelius, Jane, ed. 1994. 256p. reprint ed. mass mkt. 4.99 (*0-671-74839-4*, Pocket) Simon & Schuster.
—Death of a Partner. 1991. 16.95 o.p. (*0-312-05411-4*, Saint Martin's Minotaur) St. Martin's Pr.
—Death on Site. l.t. ed. 1996. 363p. pap. 20.95 o.p. (*0-7838-1640-5*, Macmillan Reference USA) Gale Group.
—Death on Site. Chelius, Jane, ed. 1993. 288p. reprint ed. mass mkt. 4.99 (*0-671-73581-0*, Pocket) Simon & Schuster.
—Death on Site. 1990. 256p. 16.95 o.p. (*0-312-04298-1*, Saint Martin's Minotaur) St. Martin's Pr.
—Death's Bright Angel. Chelius, Jane, ed. 1991. 288p. reprint ed. mass mkt. 4.99 (*0-671-73579-9*, Pocket) Simon & Schuster.
—Death's Bright Angel. 1988. 224p. 15.95 o.p. (*0-312-02568-8*, Saint Martin's Minotaur) St. Martin's Pr.
—Death's Bright Angel. l.t. ed. 1998. (General Ser.). 365p. pap. 23.95 (*0-7862-1289-6*) Thorndike Pr.
—O Gentle Death. 2001. 240p. 22.95 (*0-312-28052-1*, Saint Martin's Minotaur) St. Martin's Pr.
—A Timely Death. l.t. ed. 1997. 382p. pap. 21.95 (*0-7838-8140-1*, Macmillan Reference USA) Gale Group.
—A Timely Death. 1996. 219p. text 21.95 o.p. (*0-312-15223-X*, Saint Martin's Minotaur) St. Martin's Pr.
—To Die for: A Mystery. 1999. 240p. 21.95 o.p. (*0-312-20598-8*, Saint Martin's Minotaur) St. Martin's Pr.
Newark, Elizabeth. Consequence: Or, Whatever Became of Charlotte Lucas. 1997. (Illus.). 135p. pap. 12.50 (*0-9659147-0-4*) New Ark Productions.
Newman, Kim. Anno Dracula. 1993. 400p. 21.00 o.p. (*0-88184-967-7*, Carroll & Graf Pubs.) Avalon Publishing Group.
—Jago. 1993. 536p. 22.00 o.p. (*0-88184-868-9*, Carroll & Graf Pubs.) Avalon Publishing Group.
—The Quorum. 1994. 310p. 21.00 o.p. (*0-7867-0132-3*, Carroll & Graf Pubs.) Avalon Publishing Group.
Nicholl, Charles. The Reckoning: The Murder of Christopher Marlowe. 1994. 413p. (C). 24.95 o.s.i (*0-15-175981-2*) Harcourt Trade Pubs.
—The Reckoning: The Murder of Christopher Marlowe. 1995. 424p. pap. 17.00 (*0-226-58024-5*) Univ. of Chicago Pr.
Nicholls, David. A Question of Attraction: A Novel. 2004. 352p. 23.95 (*1-4000-6181-4*, Villard Bks.) Random House Adult Trade Publishing Group.
Nicholson, Geoff. Bedlam Burning. 298p. 2003. pap. 15.95 (*1-58567-453-2*); 2002. 26.95 (*1-58567-239-4*) Overlook Pr., The.
—Bleeding London. 320p. 1998. 13.95 (*0-87951-886-3*); 1997. 23.95 (*0-87951-807-3*) Overlook Pr., The.
—Still Life with Volkswagens. 1996. 240p. pap. 12.95 (*0-87951-694-1*); 1995. pap. 19.95 (*0-87951-633-X*); 1995. 240p. 21.95 (*0-87951-616-X*) Overlook Pr., The.
Noon, Jeff. Vurt. 2000. (SPA.). 336p. pap. 10.47 (*84-397-0538-7*) AIMS International Bks., Inc.
—Vurt. abr. ed. 1995. audio 22.00 (*0-671-52532-8*, 492057, Simon & Schuster Audioworks) Simon & Schuster Audio.
—Vurt, Vol. 1. 1996. (Vurt Ser.: Vol. 1). 384p. pap. 14.95 (*0-312-14144-0*, Saint Martin's Griffin) St. Martin's Pr.
Norman, Hilary. Laura. 1994. 570p. 22.95 o.p. (*0-525-93783-8*) Dutton/Plume.
Nuernberg, Leslie S. Only Glory Awaits. 2003. pap. 11.99 (*1-889893-95-1*, Ambassador-Emerald, International) Emerald Hse. Group, Inc.
Nunez, Sigrid. Mitz: The Marmoset of Bloomsbury. unabr. ed. 1999. audio 19.95 (*0-7861-1533-5*); 1998. audio 23.95 (*0-7861-1436-3*, 2322) Blackstone Audio Bks., Inc.
—Mitz: The Marmoset of Bloomsbury. 1998. 128p. 18.00 o.s.i (*0-06-017407-2*) HarperCollins Pubs.
Nye, Robert. Falstaff: A Novel. 2003. 464p. reprint ed. pap. 14.95 (*1-55970-649-X*) Arcade Publishing, Inc.
—Falstaff: A Novel. 1976. 8.95 o.p. (*0-316-61738-5*) Little Brown & Co.
—Falstaff: A Novel. 1976. 450p. o.p. (*0-241-89429-8*, Hamilton, Hamish) Viking Penguin.
Oakleaf, David, ed. Love in Excess or the Fatal Enquiry: Eliza Haywood. 1994. (Literary Texts Ser.). 240p. pap. (*1-55111-016-4*) Broadview Pr.
O'Brian, Patrick. The Surgeon's Mate. l.t. ed. 2001. (Thorndike Press Large Print Famous Authors Ser.). (Illus.). 624p. (*0-7540-1662-5*); (*0-7540-9076-0*) Thorndike Pr.
O'Brien, Charles. Black Gold. 2002. (Illus.). 396p. 24.95 o.s.i (*1-59058-010-9*); 384p. pap. (*1-59058-021-4*) Poisoned Pen Pr.
O'Brien, Edna. Nights. 1987. 15.95 o.p. (*0-374-22198-7*); pap. 12.00 o.s.i (*0-374-52051-8*) Farrar, Straus & Giroux.
—Nights. 2001. 120p. pap. 11.00 (*0-618-12689-9*, Mariner Bks.) Houghton Mifflin Co. Trade & Reference Div.
O'Brien, Edward J., ed. Elizabethan Tales. 1977. (Short Story Index Reprint Ser.). reprint ed. 23.95 (*0-8369-4053-9*) Ayer Co. Pubs., Inc.
O'Brien, Patrick. The Making of a Knight: How Sir James Earned His Armor. 1998. (Illus.). 32p. (J). (gr. 1-4). 15.95 (*0-88106-354-1*); pap. 6.95 (*0-88106-355-X*) Charlesbridge Publishing, Inc.
O'Connor, Gemma. Farewell to the Flesh. 2000. 444p. pap. 10.95 (*0-553-50586-6*) Transworld Publishers Ltd. GBR. *Dist:* Trafalgar Square.
—Time to Remember. l.t. ed. 2000. (Magna Large Print Ser.). 400p. (*0-7505-1512-0*) Magna Large Print Bks. GBR. *Dist:* Ulverscroft Large Print Bks., Ltd., Ulverscroft Large Print Canada, Ltd.
—Time to Remember. 2000. 350p. pap. 10.95 (*0-553-50587-4*) Transworld Publishers Ltd. GBR. *Dist:* Trafalgar Square.
Oke, Janette. The Birthright. ltd. ed. 2001. (Song of Acadia Ser.). 288p. pap. 10.99 o.p. (*0-7642-8801-6*) Bethany Hse. Pubs.
Oke, Janette & Bunn, T. Davis. The Birthright. 2001. (Song of Acadia Ser.). 288p. pap. 11.99 (*0-7642-2229-5*); 1p. pap. 15.99 o.p. (*0-7642-2231-7*); 288p. text 16.99 o.p. (*0-7642-2230-9*) Bethany Hse. Pubs.
Oldfield, Jenny. All Fall Down. 1998. 551 p. (*0-7540-2120-3*, Macmillan Reference USA) Gale Group.
—All Fall Down. 2003. 392p. pap. (*0-330-34843-4*) Pan Macmillan.
—All Fall Down. l.t. ed. 1998. (Romance Ser.). 552p. 26.95 (*0-7862-1393-0*) Thorndike Pr.
—Paradise Court. l.t. ed. 1997. 603 p. (*0-7540-2011-8*, Galaxy Children's Large Print) BBC Audiobooks America.
—Paradise Court. 2003. 421p. pap. (*0-330-33886-2*) Macmillan Children's Bks.
Oldfield, Pamela. Golden Tally. 1986. mass mkt. o.s.i (*0-7515-0375-4*) Little Brown & Co.
—Golden Tally. l.t. ed. 1997. (Magna Large Print Ser.). 515p. 29.99 (*0-7505-1177-X*) Magna Large Print Bks. GBR. *Dist:* Ulverscroft Large Print Bks., Ltd.
—Golden Tally. 1988. 383p. pap. 19.95 o.p. (*0-7126-0987-3*) Trafalgar Square.
—Green Harvest. 1988. 379p. 19.95 o.p. (*0-7126-0077-9*) Trafalgar Square.
—New Beginnings. 2002. 224p. 25.99 (*0-7278-5865-3*); 29.99 (*0-7278-7236-2*) Severn Hse. Pubs., Ltd.
—Pieces of Silver. l.t. ed. 2000. (Romance Ser.). 478p. 27.95 (*0-7838-9146-6*) Thorndike Pr.
—A Woman Alone. l.t. ed. 2001. 428p. (*0-7540-1569-6*); (*0-7540-2431-8*) Gale Group. (Macmillan Reference USA).
—A Woman Alone. l.t. ed. 2001. (G. K. Hall Romance Ser.). 428p. 26.95 (*0-7838-9364-7*) Thorndike Pr.
—Yesterday's Shadow. l.t. ed. 2001. (Magna Large Print Ser.). 432p. 31.99 (*0-7505-1635-6*) Magna Large Print Bks. GBR. *Dist:* Ulverscroft Large Print Bks., Ltd., Ulverscroft Large Print Canada, Ltd.
Oldham, Nick. Backlash. 2001. 384p. 25.99 (*0-7278-5700-2*) Severn Hse. Pubs., Ltd.
—Substantial Threat. 2003. 256p. 26.99 (*0-7278-5874-2*) Severn Hse. Pubs., Ltd.
Oliphant, Margaret. Miss Marjoribanks. Wolff, Robert L., ed. 1985. (Victorian Fiction Ser.). lib. bdg. 66.00 o.p. (*0-8240-1615-7*) Garland Publishing, Inc.
—Miss Marjoribanks. (Classics Ser.). 1999. 592p. 15.00 (*0-14-043630-8*, Penguin Classics); 1989. 496p. pap. 8.95 o.p. (*0-14-016189-9*, Penguin Bks.) Viking Penguin.
Oliver, Patricia. Lady in Gray. 1999. (Signet Regency Romance Ser.). 224p. mass mkt. 4.99 o.s.i (*0-451-19500-0*) NAL.
Orde, Lewis. The Proprietor's Daughter. 1988. 18.95 (*0-316-67340-4*) Little Brown & Co.
Ormerod, Roger. The Second Jeopardy. 1988. (Crime Club Ser.). 12.95 o.s.i (*0-385-24613-7*) Doubleday Publishing.
—The Second Jeopardy. l.t. ed. 2001. (General Ser.). 313p. pap. 22.95 o.p. (*0-7862-2986-1*); (*0-7540-4347-9*); (*0-7540-4346-0*) Thorndike Pr.
Outlet Book Company Staff. Agatha Christie Detective: 5 Complete Cwl. 1985. 11.99 o.s.i (*0-517-48150-2*) Random Hse. Value Publishing.
Owen, Ruth. Midnight Mistress. 2000. (Meet Me at Midnight Ser.). 320p. mass mkt. 5.99 o.s.i (*0-553-57746-8*) Bantam Bks.
Oxley, Dorothy. Winter Song. 1984. 140p. (J). (gr. 6-10). reprint ed. pap. 3.95 o.p. (*0-89107-320-5*) Crossway Bks.
Page, Lorna. Nurse in Charge. l.t. ed. 2001. (Dales Large Print Ser.). 304p. pap. 21.99 (*1-84262-067-3*) Dales Large Print Bks. GBR. *Dist:* Ulverscroft Large Print Bks., Ltd., Ulverscroft Large Print Canada, Ltd.
Paige, Lori A. Passion's Legacy. 1991. 256p. (Orig.). pap. 8.95 (*0-941483-81-9*) Naiad Pr., Inc.
Paige, Robin. Death at Bishop's Keep: A Victorian Mystery. 1998. 304p. mass mkt. 6.50 (*0-425-16435-7*, Prime Crime) Berkley Publishing Group.
—Death at Bishop's Keep: A Victorian Mystery. 1994. pap. 4.99 (*0-380-77498-4*, Avon Bks.) Morrow/Avon.
—Death at Daisy's Folly. 1997. 288p. mass mkt. 6.50 (*0-425-15671-0*, Prime Crime) Berkley Publishing Group.
—Death at Dartmoor: A Victorian Mystery. 336p. 2003. mass mkt. 6.50 (*0-425-18909-0*, Prime Crime); 2002. 21.95 (*0-425-18342-4*) Berkley Publishing Group.
—Death at Devil's Bridge. 1998. (Prime Crime Mysteries Ser.). 288p. mass mkt. 6.50 (*0-425-16195-1*, Prime Crime) Berkley Publishing Group.
—Death at Epsom Downs. 2001. 304p. 21.95 o.s.i (*0-425-17807-2*, Prime Crime) Berkley Publishing Group.
—Death at Gallows Green. 1998. 288p. mass mkt. 6.50 (*0-425-16399-7*) Berkley Publishing Group.
—Death at Gallows Green. 1995. (Victorian Mystery Ser.). pap. 4.99 (*0-380-77499-2*, Avon Bks.) Morrow/Avon.
—Death at Rottingdean. 1999. (Victorian Mystery Ser.). 304p. mass mkt. 6.50 (*0-425-16782-8*, Prime Crime) Berkley Publishing Group.
—Death at Whitechapel. 2000. (Victorian Mystery Ser.: Vol. 6). 288p. mass mkt. 6.50 (*0-425-17341-0*, Prime Crime) Berkley Publishing Group.
Palin, Michael. Hemingway's Chair. 288p. 1998. 23.95 o.p. (*0-312-18593-6*); 2nd ed. 1999. pap. 12.95 (*0-312-20550-3*, Saint Martin's Griffin) St. Martin's Pr.
Paling, Chris. Morning All Day. 1997. 193p. (*0-224-04446-X*) Cape, Jonathan Ltd. GBR. *Dist:* National Geographic Society, Trafalgar Square.
Palliser, Charles. The Unburied. 1999. 400p. 24.00 (*0-374-28035-5*) Farrar, Straus & Giroux.
—The Unburied. 2000. 432p. reprint ed. pap. 13.95 (*0-7434-1051-3*, Washington Square Pr.) Simon & Schuster.
—The Unburied. l.t. ed. 2000. (Basic Ser.). 655p. 29.95 (*0-7862-2543-2*) Thorndike Pr.
Palmer, Catherine. English Ivy. 2002. (HeartQuest Ser.). 336p. pap. 9.99 (*0-8423-1927-1*) Tyndale Hse. Pubs.
—Love's Proof. 2003. (HeartQuest Ser.). 336p. pap. 9.99 (*0-8423-7032-3*) Tyndale Hse. Pubs.
—Victorian Rose. 2002. 144p. 12.99 (*0-8423-1957-3*) Tyndale Hse. Pubs.
—Wild Heather. 2004. (HeartQuest Ser.). (*0-8423-1928-X*) Tyndale Hse. Pubs.
Palmer, Elizabeth. Flowering Judas. unabr. ed. 1997. audio 69.95 (*0-7540-0058-3*, CAB 1481) BBC Audiobooks America.
—Flowering Judas. 2000. 408p. mass mkt. (*1-55166-593-X*, 1-66593-4, Mira Bks.) Harlequin Enterprises, Ltd.
—Flowering Judas. 1997. 280p. 22.95 o.p. (*0-312-16843-8*) St. Martin's Pr.
—Flowering Judas. l.t. ed. 1998. (Core Ser.). 442p. 28.95 (*0-7838-8401-X*) Thorndike Pr.
—Old Money. 1999. mass mkt. (*1-55166-547-6*, 1-66547-0, Mira Bks.) Harlequin Enterprises, Ltd.
—Old Money. 1996. 288p. 21.95 o.p. (*0-312-14020-7*) St. Martin's Pr.
—Plucking the Apple. l.t. ed. 1999. 396p. 27.95 (*0-7838-8624-1*, Macmillan Reference USA) Gale Group.
—Plucking the Apple. 1999. (Mira Bks.). 378p. mass mkt. (*1-55166-493-3*, 1-66493-7, Mira Bks.) Harlequin Enterprises, Ltd.
—Plucking the Apple. 1994. 272p. 20.95 o.p. (*0-312-11326-9*) St. Martin's Pr.
—Scarlet Angel. 1998. per. (*1-55166-456-9*, Harlequin Bks.) Harlequin Enterprises, Ltd.
—Scarlet Angel. 3.98 o.p. (*0-8317-4618-1*) Smithmark Pubs., Inc.

Settings

—Scarlet Angel. 1993. 19.95 o.p. (*0-312-09917-7*) St. Martin's Pr.
Palmer, Elizabeth, contrib. by. Plucking the Apple. 1999. (*0-7540-1300-6*) BBC Audiobooks America.
Palmer, Frank. Nightwatch. 1996. 208p. 20.95 o.p. (*0-312-14381-8*, Saint Martin's Minotaur) St. Martin's Pr.
—Unfit to Plead: A Detective Inspector Jacko Jackson Mystery. 1994. 224p. 19.95 o.p. (*0-312-10569-X*, Saint Martin's Minotaur) St. Martin's Pr.
Palmer, William J. The Detective & Mr. Dickens: A Secret Victorian Journal. 1992. reprint ed. mass mkt. 3.99 o.s.i (*0-345-37471-1*) Ballantine Bks.
—The Dons & Mr. Dickens: The Strange Case of the Oxford Christmas Plot. 2000. ix, 244p. 23.95 (*0-312-26576-X*, Saint Martin's Minotaur) St. Martin's Pr.
—The Highwayman & Mr. Dickens: A Secret Victorian Journal, Attributed to Wilkie Collins. 1993. reprint ed. mass mkt. 4.99 o.s.i (*0-345-38252-8*) Ballantine Bks.
—The Hoydens & Mr. Dickens. 1996. 256p. 21.95 o.p. (*0-312-15145-4*) St. Martin's Pr.
Palmer, William J., ed. The Detective & Mr. Dickens: A Secret Victorian Journal. 1990. 320p. 17.95 o.p. (*0-312-05073-9*) St. Martin's Pr.
—The Highwayman & Mr. Dickens: A Secret Victorian Journal, Attributed to Wilkie Collins. 1992. 288p. text 18.95 o.p. (*0-312-08207-X*, Saint Martin's Minotaur) St. Martin's Pr.
Paquet, Laura. Lord Langdon's Tutor. 2000. (Zebra Regency Romance Ser.). 224p. mass mkt. 4.99 o.s.i (*0-8217-6675-9*, Zebra Bks.) Kensington Publishing Corp.
Pargeter, Edith. The Marriage of Meggotta. 2001. (Common Reader Edition Ser.). 304p. pap. 16.95 (*1-58579-029-X*, Common Reader Editions) Akadine Pr., The.
—The Marriage of Meggotta. l.t. ed. 1994. (Magna Large Print Ser.). 520p. 29.99 o.p. (*0-7505-0713-6*) Magna Large Print Bks. GBR. *Dist:* Ulverscroft Large Print Bks., Ltd., Ulverscroft Large Print Canada, Ltd.
Parkin, Frank. The Mind & Body Shop. 1987. 224p. 14.95 o.p. (*0-689-11895-3*, Scribner) Simon & Schuster.
Parkinson, C. Northcote. Jeeves: A Gentleman's Personal Gentleman. 1981. 191p. 8.95 o.p. (*0-312-44144-4*) St. Martin's Pr.
Parks, Tim. Loving Roger. 1987. 160p. 15.95 o.p. (*0-8021-0016-3*) Grove/Atlantic, Inc.
—Loving Roger. 1989. 160p. pap. 6.95 o.p. (*0-14-011459-9*, Penguin Bks.) Viking Penguin.
Parsell, Roger E. CliffsNotes TM the Way of All Flesh. 1999. E-Book 1.95 (*0-8220-7292-0*, Cliff Notes) Wiley, John & Sons, Inc.
Paton Walsh, Jill. A Piece of Justice. pap. 15.95 (*0-312-29252-X*, Saint Martin's Griffin); 1995. 208p. 19.95 o.p. (*0-312-13145-3*, Saint Martin's Minotaur) St. Martin's Pr.
—A Presumption of Death. E-Book 24.95 (*0-312-70987-0*) St. Martin's Pr.
—The Wyndham Case. pap. 14.95 (*0-312-28747-X*, Saint Martin's Griffin); 1993. 224p. 17.95 (*0-312-09420-5*, Saint Martin's Minotaur) St. Martin's Pr.
—The Wyndham Case. l.t. ed. 1994. (Ulverscroft Large Print Ser.). 384p. 29.99 o.p. (*0-7089-3176-6*, Ulverscroft) Thorpe, F. A. Pubs. GBR. *Dist:* Ulverscroft Large Print Bks., Ltd., Ulverscroft Large Print Canada, Ltd.
Paton Walsh, Jill & Sayers, Dorothy L. A Presumption of Death. l.t. ed. 2003. (New Lord Peter Wimsey/Harriet Vane Mystery Ser.). 449p. 28.95 (*0-7862-5561-7*) Thorndike Pr.
Paul, Paula. Half a Mind to Murder. 2003. 208p. mass mkt. 5.99 (*0-425-19282-2*, Prime Crime) Berkley Publishing Group.
Pavese, Cesare. Among Women Only. Paige, D. D., tr. from ITA. 1979. 168p. 24.00 (*0-7206-0350-1*) Dufour Editions, Inc.
—Among Women Only. Paige, D. D., tr. from ITA. 1997. 198p. pap. 14.95 (*0-7206-1030-3*) Owen, Peter Ltd. GBR. *Dist:* Dufour Editions, Inc.
—Among Women Only. 1996. 168p. pap. 14.95 (*0-7206-1005-2*) Owen, Peter Ltd. GBR. *Dist:* Dufour Editions, Inc.
Payne, Carol. A Pinch of Rosemary: Country Tales of Lust & Passion. 1993. (Illus.). 64p. 12.95 o.p. (*0-88184-568-X*, Carroll & Graf Pubs.) Avalon Publishing Group.
Peace, David. Nineteen Eighty. 2001. (Red Riding Quartet Ser.: Bk. 3). 382p. 24.00 (*1-85242-683-7*) Serpent's Tail Ltd. GBR. *Dist:* Consortium Bk. Sales & Distribution.
—Nineteen Eighty Three. 2003. (Red Riding Quartet Ser.: Vol. 4). 416p. pap. 16.00 (*1-85242-684-5*) Serpent's Tail Ltd. GBR. *Dist:* Consortium Bk. Sales & Distribution.
—Nineteen Seventy-Four. 2000. 295p. pap. o.p. (*1-85242-634-9*) Serpent's Tail Ltd.
—Nineteen Seventy Four. 2000. (Red Riding Quartet Ser.: Bk. 1). 320p. pap. (*1-85242-741-8*) Serpent's Tail Ltd.
—Nineteen Seventy Seven. 2001. (Red Riding Quartet Ser.: Bk. 2). 344p. pap. 14.00 (*1-85242-639-X*) Serpent's Tail Ltd. GBR. *Dist:* Consortium Bk. Sales & Distribution.
Peacock, Thomas Love. Maid Marion. E-Book 2.49 (*1-58627-729-4*) Electric Umbrella Publishing.
—Nightmare Abbey, Crotchet Castle. Wright, Raymond, ed. 1982. (Penguin English Library). 284p. 17.00 (*0-14-043045-8*, Penguin Classics) Viking Penguin.
Peake, Lilian. Love in Moonlight. l.t. ed. 1994. 18.95 o.p. (*0-7927-2130-6*); pap. 17.95 o.p. (*0-7927-2129-2*) BBC Audiobooks America.
Pearce, Mary E. The Old House at Railes. l.t. ed. 1994. 595p. lib. bdg. 24.95 (*0-8161-5989-0*, Macmillan Reference USA) Gale Group.
—The Old House at Railes. 410p. 3.98 o.p. (*0-8317-5247-5*) Smithmark Pubs., Inc.
—The Old House at Railes. 1993. 416p. 23.95 o.p. (*0-312-10514-2*) St. Martin's Pr.
Pearlman, Gilbert. The Adventures of Sherlock Holmes' Smarter Brother. Wilder, Gene, ed. 1975. pap. 1.75 o.p. (*0-345-25282-9*) Ballantine Bks.
Pears, Iain. An Instance of the Fingerpost. abr. ed. 1998. audio 24.95 (*1-55927-491-3*, 695651) Audio Renaissance.
—An Instance of the Fingerpost. 2000. 704p. pap. 14.95 (*1-57322-795-1*, Riverhead Trade (Paperbacks)); 1999. 752p. reprint ed. mass mkt. 7.99 (*0-425-16772-0*) Berkley Publishing Group.
—An Instance of the Fingerpost. l.t. ed. 1998. (G. K. Hall Core Ser.). 995p. 28.95 (*0-7838-0280-3*, Macmillan Reference USA) Gale Group.
—An Instance of the Fingerpost. 1998. 800p. 27.00 o.p. (*1-57322-082-5*, Riverhead Bks. (Hardcovers)) Putnam Publishing Group, The.
—An Instance of the Fingerpost. 1999. 14.04 (*0-606-16940-7*) Turtleback Bks.
Pears, Tim. In a Land of Plenty. 1999. 612p. pap. o.s.i (*0-552-99718-8*, Corgi) Bantam Bks.
—In a Land of Plenty. 544p. 1999. pap. 15.00 o.s.i (*0-312-20412-4*); 1998. 25.00 o.s.i (*0-312-18112-4*) Picador.
—In the Place of Fallen Leaves. 1994. 347p. pap. o.s.i (*0-552-99536-3*, Corgi) Bantam Bks.
—In the Place of Fallen Leaves. 320p. 1995. 21.95 o.s.i (*1-55611-423-0*); 2nd ed. 1996. reprint ed. pap. 11.95 o.s.i (*1-55611-472-9*, Fine, Donald I.) Fine, Donald I. Bks.
Pearson, Diane. The Summer of the Barshinskeys. 1985. 448p. mass mkt. 4.50 o.s.i (*0-449-20783-8*, Fawcett) Ballantine Bks.
—The Summer of the Barshinskeys. 1984. 480p. 1.99 o.p. (*0-517-55520-4*) Random Hse. Value Publishing.
—The Summer of the Barshinskeys. 2000. pap. 8.95 (*0-552-12641-1*) Transworld Publishers Ltd. GBR. *Dist:* Trafalgar Square.
Peart, Jane. Thread of Suspicion. l.t. ed. 1999. 332p. 23.95 o.p. (*0-7862-2142-9*, Macmillan Reference USA) Gale Group.
—Thread of Suspicion. 1998. (Edgecliffe Manor Mysteries Ser.: Vol. 4). 224p. (gr. 13 up). pap. 10.99 o.p. (*0-8007-5676-2*) Revell, Fleming H. Co.
—Web of Deception. l.t. ed. 2000. (G. K. Hall Inspirational Ser.). 261p. 26.95 o.p. (*0-7838-8942-9*, Macmillan Reference USA) Gale Group.
—Web of Deception. 1996. (Edgecliffe Manor Mystery Ser.: No. 2). 208p. (gr. 10). pap. 9.99 o.p. (*0-8007-5598-7*) Revell, Fleming H. Co.
Pemberton, Margaret. Coronation Summer. 2000. 428p. 29.95 (*0-593-03412-0*); pap. 10.95 (*0-552-14125-9*) Transworld Publishers Ltd. GBR. *Dist:* Trafalgar Square.
Penman, Sharon Kay. Cruel As the Grave: A Medieval Mystery. 1999. (Reader's Circle Ser.). 272p. pap. 12.00 (*0-345-43422-6*, Ballantine Bks.) Ballantine Bks.
—Cruel As the Grave: A Medieval Mystery. 1998. 304p. (YA). (gr. 6 up). 22.00 o.s.i (*0-8050-5608-4*) Holt, Henry & Co.
—The Queen's Man: A Medieval Mystery. (Medieval Mysteries Ser.). 2000. 288p. mass mkt. 6.50 (*0-345-42316-X*, Fawcett); 1998. 320p. pap. 12.00 (*0-345-41718-6*) Ballantine Bks.
—The Queen's Man: A Medieval Mystery. 1996. 304p. 20.00 o.s.i (*0-8050-3885-X*) Holt, Henry & Co.
—Time & Chance. 2003. 544p. pap. 15.95 (*0-345-39672-3*) Ballantine Bks.
—Time & Chance. 2002. (Illus.). 512p. 27.95 o.s.i (*0-399-14785-3*, Wood, Marian Bks.) Putnam Publishing Group, The.
Penn, John. A Legacy of Death. l.t. ed. 1993. 19.95 o.p. (*0-7927-1632-9*); pap. 17.95 o.p. (*0-7927-1631-0*) BBC Audiobooks America.
Perowne. Raffles of Albany. 1977. 8.95 o.p. (*0-312-66220-3*) St. Martin's Pr.
Perriam, Wendy. Devils for a Change. 1990. 480p. 19.95 o.p. (*0-312-04300-7*) St. Martin's Pr.
Perry, Anne. Ashworth Hall. 1998. 384p. mass mkt. 7.50 (*0-449-00086-9*, Fawcett) Ballantine Bks.
—Bedford Square. 2000. 336p. mass mkt. 6.99 (*0-449-00582-8*, Ballantine Bks.); 1995. o.p. (*0-449-90633-7*, Fawcett) Ballantine Bks.
—Bedford Square. l.t. ed. 1999. (Basic Ser.). 571p. 30.95 (*0-7862-2018-X*) Thorndike Pr.
—Belgrave Square. 1993. 384p. mass mkt. 6.99 (*0-449-22227-6*, Fawcett) Ballantine Bks.
—Belgrave Square. 1994. 4.99 o.p. (*0-517-12853-5*) Random Hse. Value Publishing.
—Bethlehem Road. 1991. 320p. mass mkt. 5.99 o.p. (*0-449-45316-2*); mass mkt. 6.99 (*0-449-21914-3*) Ballantine Bks. (Fawcett).
—Bethlehem Road. l.t. ed. 2001. (Dales Large Print Ser.). 464p. pap. (*1-84262-093-2*) Dales Large Print Bks. GBR. *Dist:* Ulverscroft Large Print Canada, Ltd.
—Bethlehem Road. 1990. 17.95 o.p. (*0-312-04266-3*, Saint Martin's Minotaur) St. Martin's Pr.
—Bethlehem Road. l.t. ed. 1993. (Mystery Ser.). 592p. 29.99 o.p. (*0-7089-2939-7*, Ulverscroft) Thorpe, F. A. Pubs. GBR. *Dist:* Ulverscroft Large Print Bks., Ltd., Ulverscroft Large Print Canada, Ltd.
—Bluegate Fields. 1985. 288p. mass mkt. 5.99 o.p. (*0-449-45317-0*); mass mkt. 6.99 (*0-449-20766-8*) Ballantine Bks. (Fawcett).
—Bluegate Fields. l.t. ed. 2000. 398p. lib. bdg. 28.95 (*1-58547-017-1*) Ctr. Point Large Print.
—Bluegate Fields. l.t. ed. 2001. (Magna Large Print Ser.). 384p. (*0-7505-1709-3*) Magna Large Print Bks. GBR. *Dist:* Ulverscroft Large Print Canada, Ltd.
—Bluegate Fields. unabr. ed. 2002. audio 72.00 (*1-4025-3604-6*, Clipper Audio) Recorded Bks., LLC.
—Bluegate Fields. 1984. 320p. 13.95 o.p. (*0-312-08718-7*) St. Martin's Pr.
—A Breach of Promise. (William Monk Novels Ser.). 1999. 384p. mass mkt. 6.99 (*0-8041-1855-8*, Ivy Bks.); 1998. 384p. 25.00 o.s.i (*0-449-90849-6*, Fawcett); 1998. mass mkt. 6.99 (*0-8041-1888-4*, Ivy Bks.) Ballantine Bks.
—A Breach of Promise. abr. ed. 1998. audio 18.00 o.s.i (*0-375-40275-6*, 396111, RH Audio) Random Hse. Audio Publishing Group.
—A Breach of Promise. l.t. ed. 1998. (Basic Ser.). 639p. 29.95 (*0-7862-1465-1*) Thorndike Pr.
—Brunswick Gardens. 1999. 416p. mass mkt. 7.50 (*0-449-00318-3*, Fawcett) Ballantine Bks.
—Brunswick Gardens. l.t. ed. 1998. (Basic Ser.). 656p. 30.95 (*0-7862-1464-3*) Thorndike Pr.
—Cain His Brother. 1996. 416p. mass mkt. 7.50 (*0-8041-1507-9*); mass mkt. 6.99 o.s.i (*0-8041-1504-4*) Ballantine Bks. (Ivy Bks.).
—Cain His Brother. abr. ed. 1997. (William Monk Mystery Ser.). audio 8.99 o.s.i (*0-679-46025-X*, 393145, RH Audio) Random Hse. Audio Publishing Group.
—Cain His Brother. l.t. ed. 1996. (Cloak & Dagger Ser.). 629p. 26.95 (*0-7862-0607-1*) Thorndike Pr.
—Callander Square. 1998. mass mkt. 3.99 o.s.i (*0-449-00461-9*); 1985. 256p. mass mkt. 6.99 (*0-449-20999-7*); 1981. mass mkt. 2.25 o.p. (*0-449-24365-6*) Ballantine Bks. (Fawcett).
—Callander Square. 1980. 10.00 o.p. (*0-312-11430-3*) St. Martin's Pr.
—Callander Square. l.t. ed. 1981. 447p. 12.00 o.p. (*0-7089-0718-0*, Ulverscroft) Thorpe, F. A. Pubs. GBR. *Dist:* Ulverscroft Large Print Bks., Ltd.
—Cardington Crescent. 1988. 304p. reprint ed. mass mkt. 6.99 (*0-449-21442-7*, Fawcett) Ballantine Bks.
—Cardington Crescent. l.t. ed. 2001. 375p. lib. bdg. 28.95 (*1-58547-015-5*) Ctr. Point Large Print.
—Cardington Crescent. unabr. ed. 1998. audio 83.95 (*1-85903-217-6*) Magna Story Sound GBR. *Dist:* Ulverscroft Large Print Bks., Ltd.
—Cardington Crescent. 1987. 304p. 15.95 o.p. (*0-312-00113-4*) St. Martin's Pr.
—The Cater Street Hangman. 1998. mass mkt. 3.99 o.s.i (*0-449-00460-0*); 1985. 288p. mass mkt. 6.99 (*0-449-20867-2*); 1980. mass mkt. 2.25 o.s.i (*0-449-24327-3*) Ballantine Bks. (Fawcett).
—The Cater Street Hangman. l.t. ed. 2000. 364p. lib. bdg. 27.95 (*1-58547-002-3*) Ctr. Point Large Print.
—The Cater Street Hangman. 1979. 8.95 o.p. (*0-312-12385-X*) St. Martin's Pr.
—A Dangerous Mourning. 1992. 352p. mass mkt. 6.99 (*0-8041-1037-9*, Ivy Bks.) Ballantine Bks.
—A Dangerous Mourning. unabr. ed. 1995. (Inspector Monk Ser.: Vol. 2). audio 91.00 (*0-7887-0417-6*, 94609E7) Recorded Bks., LLC.
—Death in the Devil's Acre. 1987. 272p. mass mkt. 6.99 (*0-449-21095-2*, Fawcett) Ballantine Bks.
—Death in the Devil's Acre. l.t. ed. 2001. lib. bdg. 27.95 (*1-58547-016-3*) Ctr. Point Large Print.
—Death in the Devil's Acre. 1985. 288p. 14.95 o.p. (*0-312-18869-2*) St. Martin's Pr.
—Defend & Betray. 1993. 448p. mass mkt. 7.50 (*0-8041-1188-X*, Ivy Bks.); 1992. 18.00 o.p. (*0-449-90555-1*, Fawcett); 1992. 368p. 18.00 o.p. (*0-449-90755-4*, Fawcett) Ballantine Bks.
—Defend & Betray. unabr. ed. 2000. (Inspector Monk Ser.: Vol. 3). audio 97.00 (*0-7887-0403-6*, 94595E7) Recorded Bks., LLC.
—The Face of a Stranger. 1998. mass mkt. 3.99 o.s.i (*0-8041-1885-X*); 1991. 352p. mass mkt. 6.99 (*0-8041-0858-7*) Ballantine Bks. (Ivy Bks.).
—The Face of a Stranger. unabr. ed. 1995. (Inspector Monk Ser.: Vol. 1). audio 78.00 (*0-7887-0321-8*, 94513E7) Recorded Bks., LLC.
—Farriers' Lane. 1994. 432p. mass mkt. 7.50 (*0-449-21961-5*, Fawcett) Ballantine Bks.
—Highgate Rise. 1992. 352p. mass mkt. 7.50 (*0-449-21959-3*, Fawcett) Ballantine Bks.
—Highgate Rise. l.t. ed. 1994. (Ulverscroft Ser.). 672p. 21.95 o.p. (*0-7089-3013-1*, Ulverscroft) Thorpe, F. A. Pubs. GBR. *Dist:* Ulverscroft Large Print Bks., Ltd., Ulverscroft Large Print Canada, Ltd.
—The Hyde Park Headsman. 1995. 352p. mass mkt. 7.50 (*0-449-22350-7*); 1994. 432p. 21.00 o.s.i (*0-449-90636-1*) Ballantine Bks. (Fawcett).
—No Graves As Yet: A Novel of World War I. 2003. 352p. 25.95 (*0-345-45652-1*, Ballantine Bks.) Ballantine Bks.
—No Graves As Yet: A Novel of World War I. abr. ed. (World War One Ser.). 2004. audio 12.99 (*1-59355-050-2*, 4640, Brilliance Audio Paperback Audiobooks); 2003. audio 24.95 (*1-59355-047-2*, 4637); 2003. audio 87.25 (*1-59355-046-4*, 4636, Brilliance Audio Unabridged Lib Ed); 2003. audio 32.95 (*1-59355-045-6*, 4635, Brilliance Audio Unabridged); 2003. audio compact disk 102.25 (*1-59355-049-9*, 4639, Brilliance Audio on CD Unabridged Lib Ed); 2003. audio compact disk 36.95 (*1-59355-048-0*, 4638, Brilliance Audio on CD Unabridged) Brilliance Audio.
—Paragon Walk. 1986. 256p. mass mkt. 6.99 (*0-449-21168-1*); 1986. mass mkt. 5.99 (*0-449-45319-7*); 1982. mass mkt. 2.50 o.p. (*0-449-20110-4*); 1982. 224p. mass mkt. 2.50 o.p. (*0-449-24497-0*) Ballantine Bks. (Fawcett).
—Paragon Walk. l.t. ed. 2000. 308p. lib. bdg. 27.95 (*1-58547-005-8*) Ctr. Point Large Print.
—Paragon Walk. 1981. 224p. 9.95 o.p. (*0-312-59598-0*) St. Martin's Pr.
—Pentecost Alley. 1997. (Charlotte & Thomas Pitt Novel Ser.). 416p. mass mkt. 6.99 (*0-449-22566-6*, Fawcett) Ballantine Bks.
—Pentecost Alley. l.t. ed. 1996. (Cloak & Dagger Ser.). 708p. 27.95 (*0-7862-0812-0*) Thorndike Pr.
—Resurrection Row. 1986. 224p. mass mkt. 6.99 (*0-449-21067-7*, Fawcett) Ballantine Bks.
—Resurrection Row. l.t. ed. 2000. 312p. lib. bdg. 27.95 (*1-58547-009-0*) Ctr. Point Large Print.
—Resurrection Row. 1981. 224p. 9.95 o.p. (*0-312-67797-9*) St. Martin's Pr.
—Rutland Place. 1986. 224p. mass mkt. 6.99 (*0-449-21285-8*); 1986. 224p. mass mkt. 5.99 o.p. (*0-449-45318-9*); 1984. mass mkt. 2.50 o.p. (*0-449-20474-X*) Ballantine Bks. (Fawcett).
—Rutland Place. l.t. ed. 2000. 319p. lib. bdg. 27.95 (*1-58547-013-9*) Ctr. Point Large Print.
—Rutland Place. 224p. (*0-7278-5864-5*) Severn Hse. Pubs., Ltd.
—Rutland Place. 1983. 256p. 12.95 o.p. (*0-312-69621-3*) St. Martin's Pr.
—The Silence in Hanover Close. 1989. 352p. mass mkt. 7.50 (*0-449-21686-1*, Fawcett) Ballantine Bks.
—The Silence in Hanover Close. 1988. 384p. 17.95 o.p. (*0-312-01824-X*, Saint Martin's Minotaur) St. Martin's Pr.
—The Silence in Hanover Close. l.t. ed. 1990. (Mystery Ser.). 29.99 o.p. (*0-7089-2324-0*, Ulverscroft) Thorpe, F. A. Pubs. GBR. *Dist:* Ulverscroft Large Print Bks., Ltd., Ulverscroft Large Print Canada, Ltd.
—The Silent Cry. 368p. 1998. (William Monk Novels Ser.: Vol. 8). mass mkt. 6.99 (*0-8041-1793-4*, Ivy Bks.); 1997. 24.95 o.s.i (*0-449-90848-8*, Fawcett) Ballantine Bks.
—The Silent Cry. l.t. ed. 1998. (Basic Ser.). 616p. 30.95 (*0-7862-1301-9*) Thorndike Pr.
—The Sins of the Wolf. 1995. 448p. mass mkt. 6.99 (*0-8041-1383-1*, Ivy Bks.) Ballantine Bks.
—The Sins of the Wolf. unabr. ed. 2000. (Inspector Monk Ser.: Vol. 5). audio 91.00 (*0-7887-0272-6*, 94481E7) Recorded Bks., LLC.
—A Sudden, Fearful Death. 1994. 464p. mass mkt. 6.99 (*0-8041-1283-5*, Ivy Bks.) Ballantine Bks.
—A Sudden, Fearful Death. unabr. ed. 2000. (Inspector Monk Ser.: Vol. 4). audio 97.00 (*0-7887-0499-0*, 94692E7) Recorded Bks., LLC.
—Traitor's Gate. 1996. 432p. mass mkt. 7.50 (*0-449-22439-2*, Fawcett) Ballantine Bks.
—The Twisted Root. 2000. (William Monk Novels Ser.). 368p. mass mkt. 7.50 (*0-8041-1936-8*, Ballantine Bks.) Ballantine Bks.
—The Twisted Root. l.t. ed. 1999. pap. 25.00 o.p. (*0-7838-8698-5*, Macmillan Reference USA) Gale Group.
—The Twisted Root, Set. abr. ed. 1999. audio 25.00 Highsmith Inc.

—The Twisted Root. Set. abr. ed. 1999. audio 25.00 o.s.i (*0-375-40810-X*, RH Audio) Random Hse. Audio Publishing Group.

—The Twisted Root. l.t. ed. 1999. 496p. 25.00 (*0-375-40857-6*) Random Hse. Large Print.

—Weighed in the Balance. 1996. mass mkt. 6.99 o.s.i (*0-8041-1619-9*, Ivy Bks.) Ballantine Bks.

Peters, Elizabeth, pseud. The Camelot Caper. unabr. ed. 1995. audio 39.95 (*0-7861-0908-4*, 1713) Blackstone Audio Bks., Inc.

—The Camelot Caper. 1990. 320p. mass mkt. 5.99 (*0-8125-1241-3*, Tor Bks.) Doherty, Tom Assocs., LLC.

—The Camelot Caper. l.t. ed. 1991. 352p. pap. 19.95 o.p. (*0-8161-5165-2*, Macmillan Reference USA) Gale Group.

—The Camelot Caper. 2001. 352p. mass mkt. 6.99 (*0-380-73113-4*, Avon Bks.) Morrow/Avon.

—The Camelot Caper. 1996. 320p. reprint ed. 24.00 (*0-7278-4936-0*) Severn Hse. Pubs., Ltd.

—The Deeds of the Disturber. l.t. ed. 1989. (Amelia Peabody Mystery Ser.: No. 5). 512p. 20.95 o.p. (*0-8161-4694-2*, Macmillan Reference USA) Gale Group.

—The Deeds of the Disturber. 2000. (Amelia Peabody Mystery Ser.: No. 5). 400p. mass mkt. 7.50 (*0-380-73195-9*, Avon Bks.) Morrow/Avon.

—The Deeds of the Disturber. 1988. (Amelia Peabody Mystery Ser.: No. 5). 320p. 16.95 o.s.i (*0-689-11907-0*, Scribner) Simon & Schuster.

—The Deeds of the Disturber. 1989. (Amelia Peabody Mystery Ser.: No. 5). 304p. mass mkt. 5.99 (*0-446-35333-7*) Warner Bks., Inc.

Peters, Ellis, pseud. The Benediction of Brother Cadfael. 1992. (Chronicles of Brother Cadfael Ser.). 364p. 35.00 o.p. (*0-89296-449-9*) Mysterious Pr.

—Black is the Colour of My True Love's Heart. 2002. (Inspector George Felse Mystery Ser.: Vol. 6). 220p. mass mkt. 7.95 (*0-7515-1233-8*) Warner Bks. GBR. *Dist:* Trafalgar Square.

—Black is the Colour of My True Love's Heart. 1992. (Inspector George Felse Mystery Ser.: Vol. 6). 208p. mass mkt. 5.99 o.p. (*0-446-40072-6*) Warner Bks., Inc.

—Black Is the Colour of My True Love's Heart. unabr. ed. 1993. (Inspector George Felse Mystery Ser.: Vol. 6 ). audio 41.00 (*1-55690-894-6*, 93336E7) Recorded Bks., LLC.

—Brother Cadfael's Penance. l.t. ed. 1995. (Chronicles of Brother Cadfael Ser.: Vol. 20). 352p. 21.95 o.p. (*0-7838-1175-6*, Macmillan Reference USA) Gale Group.

—Brother Cadfael's Penance. 1994. (Chronicles of Brother Cadfael Ser.: Vol. 20). 292p. 18.95 (*0-89296-599-1*) Mysterious Pr.

—Brother Cadfael's Penance. abr. ed. 1994. (Chronicles of Brother Cadfael Ser.: Vol. 20). audio 17.95 o.p. (*0-7871-0376-4*, 393552) NewStar Media, Inc.

—Brother Cadfael's Penance. 1996. (Chronicles of Brother Cadfael Ser.: Vol. 20). 272p. mass mkt. 6.99 (*0-446-40453-5*) Warner Bks., Inc.

—City of Gold & Shadows. unabr. ed. 1991. (Inspector George Felse Mystery Ser.: Vol. 12). audio 51.00 (*1-55690-104-6*, 91207E7) Recorded Bks., LLC.

—City of Gold & Shadows. l.t. ed. 1979. (Inspector George Felse Mystery Ser.: Vol. 12). 12.00 o.p. (*0-7089-0354-1*, Ulverscroft) Thorpe, F. A. Pubs. GBR. *Dist:* Ulverscroft Large Print Bks., Ltd.

—The Confession of Brother Haluin. unabr. ed. 1995. (Chronicles of Brother Cadfael Ser.: Vol. 15). audio 54.95 (*0-7451-4380-6*, CAB 1064) BBC Audiobooks America.

—The Confession of Brother Haluin. l.t. ed. 1990. (Chronicles of Brother Cadfael Ser.: Vol. 15). 282p. lib. bdg. 20.95 (*0-8161-4859-7*, Macmillan Reference USA) Gale Group.

—The Confession of Brother Haluin. 1990. (Chronicles of Brother Cadfael Ser.: Vol. 15). 15.95 o.p. (*0-89296-349-2*) Mysterious Pr.

—The Confession of Brother Haluin. unabr. ed. (Chronicles of Brother Cadfael Ser.: Vol. 15). audio 51.00 (*0-7887-0322-6*, 94514E7) Recorded Bks., LLC.

—The Confession of Brother Haluin. l.t. ed. 1989. (Ulverscroft Large Print Ser.). 336p. 17.95 o.p. (*0-7089-2032-2*, Ulverscroft) Thorpe, F. A. Pubs. GBR. *Dist:* Ulverscroft Large Print Bks., Ltd., Ulverscroft Large Print Canada, Ltd.

—The Confession of Brother Haluin. 1989. (Chronicles of Brother Cadfael Ser.: Vol. 15). 208p. mass mkt. 6.99 (*0-445-40855-3*) Warner Bks., Inc.

—Dead Man's Ransom. 1986. (Chronicles of Brother Cadfael Ser.: Vol. 9). mass mkt. 4.95 o.s.i (*0-449-20819-2*, Fawcett) Ballantine Bks.

—Dead Man's Ransom. 2003. audio compact disk 19.95 (*0-7861-9657-2*) Blackstone Audio Bks., Inc.

—Dead Man's Ransom. unabr. ed. 2000. (Chronicles of Brother Cadfael Ser.: Vol. 9). audio 49.95 (*0-7451-4039-4*, CAB 736) Chivers Audio Bks. GBR. *Dist:* BBC Audiobooks America.

—Dead Man's Ransom. abr. ed. 1998. (Chronicles of Brother Cadfael Ser.: Vol. 9). audio 16.85 (*1-84032-155-5*) Hodder Headline Audiobooks GBR. *Dist:* Ulverscroft Large Print Bks., Ltd.

—Dead Man's Ransom. 1995. (Chronicles of Brother Cadfael Ser.: Vol. 9). 271p. mass mkt. o.s.i (*0-7515-1109-9*) Little Brown & Co.

—Dead Man's Ransom. Williams, Jennifer, ed. 1985. (Chronicles of Brother Cadfael Ser.: Vol. p). 224p. reprint ed. 13.95 o.p. (*0-688-04194-9*, Morrow, William & Co.) Morrow/Avon.

—Dead Man's Ransom. unabr. ed. 1993. (Chronicles of Brother Cadfael Ser.: Vol. 9). audio 51.00 (*1-55690-931-4*, 93427E7) Recorded Bks., LLC.

—Dead Man's Ransom. l.t. ed. 1999. (Chronicles of Brother Cadfael Ser.: Vol. 9). 304p. pap. 24.95 (*0-7862-1829-0*) Thorndike Pr.

—Dead Man's Ransom. l.t. ed. 1986. (Chronicles of Brother Cadfael Ser.: Vol. 9). 384p. 12.50 o.p. (*0-7089-1407-1*, Ulverscroft) Thorpe, F. A. Pubs. GBR. *Dist:* Ulverscroft Large Print Bks., Ltd.

—Dead Man's Ransom. 1997. (Chronicles of Brother Cadfael Ser.: Vol. 9). 288p. mass mkt. 6.99 (*0-446-40516-7*) Warner Bks., Inc.

—Death & the Joyful Woman. l.t. ed. (Insoector George Felse Mystery Ser.: Vol. 2). 1993. pap. 16.95 o.p. (*0-7927-1403-2*); 1992. 18.95 o.p. (*0-7927-1404-0*) BBC Audiobooks America.

—Death & the Joyful Woman. unabr. ed. 1992. (Inspector George Felse Mystery Ser.: Vol. 2). audio 44.00 (*1-55690-657-9*, 92227E7) Recorded Bks., LLC.

—Death & the Joyful Woman. 1995. (Inspector George Felse Mystery Ser.: Vol. 2). 224p. mass mkt. 5.50 (*0-446-40068-8*) Warner Bks., Inc.

—Death to the Landlords! l.t. ed. 1992. (Inspector George Felse Mystery Ser.: Vol. 11). 256p. lib. bdg. 20.95 o.p. (*0-7451-7324-1*, Macmillan Reference USA) Gale Group.

—Death to the Landlords! unabr. ed. (Inspector George Felse Mystery Ser.: Vol. 11). 2000. audio compact disk 64.95 (*0-7531-0905-0*, 109050); 1996. audio 54.95 (*1-85695-994-5*, 960309) ISIS Audio Bks. GBR. *Dist:* Ulverscroft Large Print Bks., Ltd.

—Death to the Landlords! l.t. ed. 1979. (Inspector George Felse Mystery Ser.: Vol. 11). 12.00 o.p. (*0-7089-0304-5*, Ulverscroft) Thorpe, F. A. Pubs. GBR. *Dist:* Ulverscroft Large Print Bks., Ltd.

—The Devil's Novice. 1985. (Chronicles of Brother Cadfael Ser.: Vol. 8). 224p. mass mkt. 3.95 o.s.i (*0-449-20701-3*, Fawcett) Ballantine Bks.

—The Devil's Novice. unabr. ed. 1999. (Chronicles of Brother Cadfael Ser.: Vol. 8). audio 44.95 Blackstone Audio Bks., Inc.

—The Devil's Novice. unabr. ed. 2000. (Chronicles of Brother Cadfael Ser.: Vol. 8). audio 49.95 (*0-7451-4104-8*, CAB 787) Chivers Audio Bks. GBR. *Dist:* BBC Audiobooks America.

—The Devil's Novice. 1995. (Chronicles of Brother Cadfael Ser.: Vol. 8). (Illus.). 286p. mass mkt. o.s.i (*0-7515-1399-7*) Little Brown & Co.

—The Devil's Novice. Williams, Jennifer, ed. 1984. (Chronicles of Brother Cadfael Ser.: Vol. 8). 192p. 13.95 o.p. (*0-688-03247-8*, Morrow, William & Co.) Morrow/Avon.

—The Devil's Novice. unabr. ed. 1993. (Chronicles of Brother Cadfael Ser.: Vol. 8). audio 51.00 (*1-55690-885-7*, 93327E7) Recorded Bks., LLC.

—The Devil's Novice. l.t. ed. 1999. (Chronicles of Brother Cadfael Ser.: Vol. 8). 304p. pap. 24.95 (*0-7862-1668-9*) Thorndike Pr.

—The Devil's Novice. l.t. ed. 1985. (Chronicles of Brother Cadfael Ser.: Vol. 8). 368p. 12.50 o.p. (*0-7089-1342-3*, Ulverscroft) Thorpe, F. A. Pubs. GBR. *Dist:* Ulverscroft Large Print Bks., Ltd.

—The Devil's Novice. 1997. (Chronicles of Brother Cadfael Ser.: Vol. 8). 288p. mass mkt. 6.99 (*0-446-40515-9*) Warner Bks., Inc.

—An Excellent Mystery. unabr. ed. 2000. (Chronicles of Brother Cadfael Ser.: Vol. 11). audio 29.95 (*1-57270-140-4*, N61140u, Audio Editions Mystery Masters) Audio Partners Publishing Corp.

—An Excellent Mystery. 1987. mass mkt. 4.95 o.s.i (*0-449-21224-6*, Fawcett) Ballantine Bks.

—An Excellent Mystery. unabr. ed. 2000. (Chronicles of Brother Cadfael Ser.: Bk. 11 ). audio 49.95 (*0-7451-4184-6*, CAB 867) Chivers Audio Bks. GBR. *Dist:* BBC Audiobooks America.

—An Excellent Mystery. 1995. (Chronicles of Brother Cadfael Ser.). 253p. pap. text o.s.i (*0-7515-1111-0*) Little Brown & Co.

—An Excellent Mystery. Williams, Jennifer, ed. 1986. (Chronicles of Brother Cadfael Ser.: Vol. 11). 224p. reprint ed. 15.95 o.p. (*0-688-06250-4*, Morrow, William & Co.) Morrow/Avon.

—An Excellent Mystery. unabr. ed. 1994. (Chronicles of Brother Cadfael Ser.: Vol. 11). audio 51.00 (*0-7887-0112-6*, 94353E7) Recorded Bks., LLC.

—An Excellent Mystery. l.t. ed. 2000. (General Ser.). 299p. pap. 24.95 (*0-7862-2269-7*) Thorndike Pr.

—An Excellent Mystery. l.t. ed. 1987. 384p. 14.50 o.p. (*0-7089-1660-0*, Ulverscroft) Thorpe, F. A. Pubs. GBR. *Dist:* Ulverscroft Large Print Bks., Ltd.

—An Excellent Mystery. 1997. (Chronicles of Brother Cadfael Ser.: Vol. 11). 224p. mass mkt. 6.99 (*0-446-40532-9*) Warner Bks., Inc.

—Fallen into the Pit. l.t. ed. 1994. (Inspector George Felse Mystery Ser.: Vol. 1). 24.95 (*1-56895-116-7*, Wheeler Publishing, Inc.) Gale Group.

—Fallen into the Pit. 1994. (Inspector George Felse Mystery Ser.: Vol. 1). 336p. 17.95 o.s.i (*0-89296-519-3*) Mysterious Pr.

—Fallen into the Pit. unabr. ed. 1991. (Inspector George Felse Mystery Ser.: Vol. 1). audio 70.00 (*1-55690-623-4*, 91419E7) Recorded Bks., LLC.

—Fallen into the Pit. 1996. (Inspector George Felse Mystery Ser.: Vol. 1). 336p. mass mkt. 6.99 (*0-446-40318-0*) Warner Bks., Inc.

—Flight of a Witch. l.t. ed. 1992. (Inspector George Felse Mystery Ser.: Vol. 3). 320p. lib. bdg. 19.95 o.p. (*0-8161-5315-9*, Macmillan Reference USA) Gale Group.

—Flight of a Witch. unabr. ed. 1997. (Inspector George Felse Mystery Ser.: Vol. 3). audio 54.95 (*1-85695-993-7*, 960509) ISIS Audio Bks. GBR. *Dist:* Ulverscroft Large Print Bks., Ltd.

—Flight of a Witch. 1991. (Inspector George Felse Mystery Ser.: Vol. 3). 16.95 o.p. (*0-89296-404-9*) Mysterious Pr.

—Flight of a Witch. 1992. (Inspector George Felse Mystery Ser.: Vol. 3). 240p. mass mkt. 5.99 o.s.i (*0-446-40146-3*) Warner Bks., Inc.

—The Grass Widow's Tale. unabr. ed. (Inspector George Felse Mystery Ser.: Vol. 7). 2000. audio compact disk 64.95 (*0-7531-0707-4*, 107074); 1995. audio 54.95 (*1-85695-989-9*, 950709) ISIS Audio Bks. GBR. *Dist:* Ulverscroft Large Print Bks., Ltd.

—The Heretic's Apprentice. l.t. ed. 2001. (Chronicles of Brother Cadfael Ser.: Vol. 16). 342p. lib. bdg. 25.95 (*1-58547-138-0*) Ctr. Point Large Print.

—The Heretic's Apprentice. 1990. (Chronicles of Brother Cadfael Ser.: Vol. 16). 16.95 o.p. (*0-89296-381-6*) Mysterious Pr.

—The Heretic's Apprentice. 1991. (Chronicles of Brother Cadfael Ser.: Vol. 16). 256p. mass mkt. 6.99 (*0-446-40000-9*) Warner Bks., Inc.

—The Hermit of Eyton Forest. 1998. (Chronicles of Brother Cadfael Ser.: Vol. 14). audio 29.95 (*0-7540-7521-4*) BBC Audiobooks America.

—The Hermit of Eyton Forest. l.t. ed. 1989. (Chronicles of Brother Cadfael Ser.: Vol. 14). 329p. lib. bdg. 19.95 o.p. (*0-8161-4677-2*, Macmillan Reference USA) Gale Group.

—The Hermit of Eyton Forest. 1987. (Chronicles of Brother Cadfael Ser.: Vol. 14). 224p. (*0-7472-0037-8*) Headline Bk. Publishing, Ltd.

—The Hermit of Eyton Forest. 1988. (Chronicles of Brother Cadfael Ser.: Vol. 14). 15.45 o.p. (*0-89296-290-9*) Mysterious Pr.

—The Hermit of Eyton Forest. unabr. ed. (Chronicles of Brother Cadfael Ser.: Vol. 14). audio 51.00 (*0-7887-0308-0*, 94501E7) Recorded Bks., LLC.

—The Hermit of Eyton Forest. 1989. (Chronicles of Brother Cadfael Ser.: Vol. 14). 240p. mass mkt. 6.50 (*0-445-40347-0*) Warner Bks., Inc.

—The Holy Thief. l.t. ed. 1994. (Chronicles of Brother Cadfael Ser.: Vol. 19). 19.95 o.p. (*0-7927-1744-9*); pap. 18.95 o.p. (*0-7927-1743-0*) BBC Audiobooks America.

—The Holy Thief, Set. abr. ed. 1993. (Chronicles of Brother Cadfael Ser.: Vol. 19). 58p. audio 16.99 (*0-88646-357-2*, 390926) Durkin Hayes Publishing Ltd.

—The Holy Thief. 1993. (Chronicles of Brother Cadfael Ser.: Vol. 19). 256p. 17.95 (*0-89296-524-X*) Mysterious Pr.

—The Holy Thief. 1994. (Chronicles of Brother Cadfael Ser.: Vol. 19). 256p. mass mkt. 6.99 (*0-446-40363-6*) Warner Bks., Inc.

—The House of Green Turf. l.t. ed. 1993. (Inspector George Felse Mystery Ser.: Vol. 8). pap. 16.95 o.p. (*0-7927-1582-9*); 18.95 o.p. (*0-7927-1583-7*) BBC Audiobooks America.

—The House of Green Turf. unabr. ed. 1993. (Inspector George Felse Mystery Ser.: Vol. 8). audio 44.00 (*1-55690-922-5*, 93418E7) Recorded Bks., LLC.

—The Knocker on Death's Door, unabr. ed. 1994. (Inspector George Felse Mystery Ser.: Vol. 10). audio 44.00 (*1-55690-991-8*, 94130E7) Recorded Bks., LLC.

—The Knocker on Death's Door. 2003. (Inspector George Felse Mystery Ser.: Vol. 10). lib. bdg. 25.95 (*0-7862-4744-4*) Thorndike Pr.

—The Knocker on Death's Door. l.t. ed. 1981. (Inspector George Felse Mystery Ser.: Vol. 10). 331p. 12.00 o.p. (*0-7089-0633-8*, Ulverscroft) Thorpe, F. A. Pubs. GBR. *Dist:* Ulverscroft Large Print Bks., Ltd.

—The Knocker on Death's Door. 1992. (Inspector George Felse Mystery Ser.: Vol. 10). 208p. mass mkt. 5.99 o.p. (*0-446-40016-5*) Warner Bks., Inc.

—The Knocker on Death's Door. 1997. (Inspector George Felse Mystery Ser.: Vol. 10). 221p. mass mkt. o.s.i (*0-7515-2079-9*) Warner Futura GBR. *Dist:* Little Brown & Co.

—Monk's Hood. 1999. (Chronicles of Brother Cadfael Ser.: Vol. 3). audio 9.95 (*1-56938-266-2*, AMP-2662) Acorn Media Publishing, Inc.

—Monk's Hood. (Chronicles of Brother Cadfael Ser.: Vol. 3). 1999. audio 29.95 (*0-7451-2828-9*); 1990. audio 54.95 (*0-7451-6189-8*, CAB 524) BBC Audiobooks America.

—Monk's Hood. 1986. (Chronicles of Brother Cadfael Ser.: Vol. 3). 224p. mass mkt. 4.95 o.s.i (*0-449-20699-8*, Fawcett) Ballantine Bks.

—Monk's Hood, unabr. ed. 1999. (Chronicles of Brother Cadfael Ser.: Vol. 3). audio 44.95 Blackstone Audio Bks., Inc.

—Monk's Hood. unabr. ed. 2000. (Chronicles of Brother Cadfael Ser.: Vol. 3). audio 49.95 Chivers Audio Bks. GBR. *Dist:* BBC Audiobooks America.

—Monk's Hood. 1995. (Chronicles of Brother Cadfael Ser.: Vol. 3). (Illus.). 268p. mass mkt. o.s.i (*0-7515-1103-X*) Little Brown & Co.

—Monk's Hood. abr. ed. 1995. (Chronicles of Brother Cadfael Ser.: Vol. 3). 17.95 o.p. (*0-7871-0254-7*, 391199) NewStar Media, Inc.

—Monk's Hood. unabr. ed. 1991. (Chronicles of Brother Cadfael Ser.: Vol. 3). audio 60.00 (*1-55690-630-7*, 91409E7) Recorded Bks., LLC.

—Monk's Hood. l.t. ed. 1982. (Chronicles of Brother Cadfael Ser.: Vol. 3). 368p. 12.50 o.p. (*0-7089-0829-2*, Ulverscroft) Thorpe, F. A. Pubs. GBR. *Dist:* Ulverscroft Large Print Bks., Ltd.

—Monk's Hood. 1992. (Chronicles of Brother Cadfael Ser.: Vol. 3). 224p. mass mkt. 6.99 (*0-446-40300-8*) Warner Bks., Inc.

—A Morbid Taste for Bones. 1985. (Chronicles of Brother Cadfael Ser.: Vol. 1). 224p. mass mkt. 4.95 o.s.i (*0-449-20700-5*, Fawcett) Ballantine Bks.

—A Morbid Taste for Bones. unabr. ed. 1997. (Chronicles of Brother Cadfael Ser.: Vol. 1). audio 39.95 (*0-7861-1099-6*, 1863) Blackstone Audio Bks., Inc.

—A Morbid Taste for Bones, unabr. ed. 1991. (Chronicles of Brother Cadfael Ser.: Vol. 1). audio 16.99 (*0-88646-275-4*, 391202) Durkin Hayes Publishing Ltd.

—A Morbid Taste for Bones. 1995. (Chronicles of Brother Cadfael Ser.: Vol. 1). pap. o.s.i (*0-7515-1101-3*) Little Brown & Co.

—A Morbid Taste for Bones. unabr. ed. 1991. (Chronicles of Brother Cadfael Ser.: Vol. 1). audio 51.00 (*1-55690-349-9*, 91206E7) Recorded Bks., LLC.

—A Morbid Taste for Bones. l.t. ed. 1981. (Chronicles of Brother Cadfael Ser.: Vol. 1). 344p. 12.00 o.p. (*0-7089-0659-1*, Ulverscroft) Thorpe, F. A. Pubs. GBR. *Dist:* Ulverscroft Large Print Bks., Ltd.

—A Morbid Taste for Bones. 1994. (Chronicles of Brother Cadfael Ser.: Vol. 1). 208p. mass mkt. 6.99 (*0-446-40015-7*) Warner Bks., Inc.

—Mourning Raga. unabr. ed. 1996. (Inspector George Felse Mystery Ser.: Vol. 9). audio 54.95 (*1-85695-992-9*, 951210) ISIS Audio Bks. GBR. *Dist:* Ulverscroft Large Print Bks., Ltd.

—Mourning Raga. l.t. ed. 1981. (Inspector George Felse Mystery Ser.: Vol. 9). o.p. (*0-7089-0576-5*, Ulverscroft) Thorpe, F. A. Pubs.

—A Nice Derangement of Epitaphs. 2003. (Inspector George Felse Mystery Ser.: Vol. 4). 192p. 21.95 (*0-7540-8632-1*, Black Dagger) BBC Audiobooks America.

—A Nice Derangement of Epitaphs. l.t. ed. 1992. (Inspector George Felse Mystery Ser.: Vol. 4). 316p. 18.95 (*0-7505-0311-4*) Magna Large Print Bks. GBR. *Dist:* Ulverscroft Large Print Bks., Ltd.

—A Nice Derangement of Epitaphs. unabr. ed. 1991. (Inspector George Felse Mystery Ser.: Vol. 4). audio 44.00 (*1-55690-374-X*, 91226E7) Recorded Bks., LLC.

—A Nice Derangement of Epitaphs. 1992. (Inspector George Felse Mystery Ser.: Vol. 4). 208p. mass mkt. 6.00 o.p. (*0-446-40069-6*) Warner Bks., Inc.

—One Corpse Too Many. 1999. (Chronicles of Brother Cadfael Ser.: Vol. 2). audio 9.95 (*1-56938-265-4*, AMP-2654) Acorn Media Publishing, Inc.

—One Corpse Too Many. 1985. (Chronicles of Brother Cadfael Ser.: Vol. 2). 224p. mass mkt. 4.95 o.s.i (*0-449-20702-1*, Fawcett) Ballantine Bks.

—One Corpse Too Many. unabr. ed. 1997. (Chronicles of Brother Cadfael Ser.: Vol. 2). audio 44.95 Blackstone Audio Bks., Inc.

—One Corpse Too Many, abr. ed. 1994. (Chronicles of Brother Cadfael Ser.: Vol. 2). audio 16.99 (*0-88646-350-5*, 391312) Durkin Hayes Publishing Ltd.

—One Corpse Too Many. 1998. (Chronicles of Brother Cadfael Ser.: Vol. 2). audio 16.85 (*1-84032-150-4*) Hodder Headline Audiobooks GBR. *Dist:* Ulverscroft Large Print Bks., Ltd.

—One Corpse Too Many. 1995. (Chronicles of Brother Cadfael Ser.: Vol. 2). (Illus.). 254p. mass mkt. o.s.i (*0-7515-1102-1*) Little Brown & Co.

—One Corpse Too Many. unabr. ed. 1991. (Chronicles of Brother Cadfael Ser.: Vol. 2). audio 60.00 (*1-55690-392-8*, 91302E7) Recorded Bks., LLC.

—One Corpse Too Many. 1994. (Chronicles of Brother Cadfael Ser.: Vol. 2). 224p. mass mkt. 6.99 (*0-446-40051-3*) Warner Bks., Inc.

—The Pilgrim of Hate. unabr. ed. 2000. (Chronicles of Brother Cadfael Ser.: Vol. 10). audio 29.95 (*1-57270-127-7*, N61127u, Audio Editions Bks. on Cassette) Audio Partners Publishing Corp.

—The Pilgrim of Hate. 1986. (Chronicles of Brother Cadfael Ser.: Vol. 10). mass mkt. 4.95 o.s.i (*0-449-21223-8*, Fawcett) Ballantine Bks.

—The Pilgrim of Hate. (Chronicles of Brother Cadfael Ser.: Vol. 10). 1999. mass mkt. o.s.i (*0-7515-0220-0*); 1995. 271p. mass mkt. o.s.i (*0-7515-1110-2*) Little Brown & Co.

—The Pilgrim of Hate. Williams, Jennifer, ed. 1985. (Chronicles of Brother Cadfael Ser.: Vol. 10). 190p. reprint ed. 14.95 o.p. (*0-688-04964-8*, Morrow, William & Co.) Morrow/Avon.

—The Pilgrim of Hate. unabr. ed. 1994. (Chronicles of Brother Cadfael Ser.: No. 10). audio 51.00 (*0-7887-0005-7*, 94144E7) Recorded Bks., LLC.

—The Pilgrim of Hate. l.t. ed. 1999. (General Ser.). 288p. pap. 24.95 (*0-7862-1945-9*) Thorndike Pr.

—The Pilgrim of Hate. l.t. ed. 1986. (Chronicles of Brother Cadfael Ser.: Vol. 10). 368p. o.p. (*0-7089-1535-3*, Ulverscroft) Thorpe, F. A. Pubs.

—The Pilgrim of Hate. 1997. (Chronicles of Brother Cadfael Ser.: Vol. 10). 256p. mass mkt. 6.99 (*0-446-40531-0*) Warner Bks., Inc.

—The Piper on the Mountain. l.t. ed. 1993. (Magna Large Print Ser.). 342p. 29.99 o.p. (*0-7505-0584-2*) Magna Large Print Bks. GBR. *Dist:* Ulverscroft Large Print Bks., Ltd., Ulverscroft Large Print Canada, Ltd.

—The Piper on the Mountain. unabr. ed. (Inspector George Felse Mystery Ser.: Vol. 5). audio 44.00 (*1-55690-716-8*, 92344E7) Recorded Bks., LLC.

—The Piper on the Mountain. 1996. (Inspector George Felse Mystery Ser.: Vol. 5). 208p. mass mkt. 5.99 (*0-446-40071-8*) Warner Bks., Inc.

—The Potter's Field. unabr. ed. 2003. audio 29.95 (*1-57270-298-2*) Audio Partners Publishing Corp.

—The Potter's Field. unabr. ed. 2000. (Chronicles of Brother Cadfael Ser.: Vol. 17). audio 49.95 (*0-7451-6513-3*, CAB 1129) Chivers Audio Bks. GBR. *Dist:* BBC Audiobooks America.

—The Potter's Field. l.t. ed. 1991. (Chronicles of Brother Cadfael Ser.: Vol. 17). 303p. lib. bdg. 19.95 o.p. (*0-8161-5194-6*, Macmillan Reference USA) Gale Group.

—The Potter's Field. 1990. (Chronicles of Brother Cadfael Ser.: Vol. 17). 240p. 16.95 o.p. (*0-89296-419-7*) Mysterious Pr.

—The Potter's Field. abr. ed. 1996. (Chronicles of Brother Cadfael Ser.: Vol. 17). 17.95 o.p. (*0-7871-0375-6*) NewStar Media, Inc.

—The Potter's Field. unabr. ed. 1997. (Chronicles of Brother Cadfael Ser.: Vol. 17). audio 51.00 (*0-7887-1089-3*, 95092E7) Recorded Bks., LLC.

—The Potter's Field. 1991. (Chronicles of Brother Cadfael Ser.: Vol. 17). 224p. mass mkt. 6.99 (*0-446-40058-0*) Warner Bks., Inc.

—Rainbow's End. unabr. ed. 1991. (Inspector George Felse Mystery Ser.: Vol. 13). audio 44.00 (*1-55690-433-9*, 91232E7) Recorded Bks., LLC.

—Rainbow's End. l.t. ed. 1992. (Inspector George Felse Mystery Ser.: Vol. 13). 368p. 29.99 o.p. (*0-7089-2733-5*, Ulverscroft) Thorpe, F. A. Pubs. GBR. *Dist:* Ulverscroft Large Print Bks., Ltd., Ulverscroft Large Print Canada, Ltd.

—Rainbow's End. 1992. (Inspector George Felse Mystery Ser.: Vol. 13). 208p. mass mkt. 5.99 o.p. (*0-446-40017-3*) Warner Bks., Inc.

—The Raven in the Foregate. 1987. (Chronicles of Brother Cadfael Ser.: Vol. 12). 208p. mass mkt. 4.95 o.s.i (*0-449-21225-4*, Fawcett) Ballantine Bks.

—The Raven in the Foregate. unabr. ed. 1998. (Chronicles of Brother Cadfael Ser.: Vol. 12). audio 39.95 Blackstone Audio Bks., Inc.

—The Raven in the Foregate. unabr. ed. 2000. (Chronicles of Brother Cadfael Ser.: Vol. 12). audio 49.95 (*0-7451-4229-X*, CAB 912) Chivers Audio Bks. GBR. *Dist:* BBC Audiobooks America.

—The Raven in the Foregate, Bk 12. 1995. (Chronicles of Brother Cadfael Ser.: Vol. 12). (Illus.). 252p. mass mkt. o.s.i (*0-7515-1740-2*) Little Brown & Co.

—The Raven in the Foregate. Williams, Jennifer, ed. 1986. (Chronicles of Brother Cadfael Ser.: Vol 12). 204p. reprint ed. 15.95 o.p. (*0-688-06558-9*, Morrow, William & Co.) Morrow/Avon.

—The Raven in the Foregate. unabr. ed. 1995. (Chronicles of Brother Cadfael Ser.: Vol. 12). audio 51.00 (*0-7887-0163-0*, 94388E7) Recorded Bks., LLC.

—The Raven in the Foregate. l.t. ed. 1987. (Chronicles of Brother Cadfael Ser.: Vol. 12). 368p. 16.95 o.p. (*0-7089-1731-3*, Ulverscroft) Thorpe, F. A. Pubs. GBR. *Dist:* Ulverscroft Large Print Bks., Ltd.

—The Raven in the Foregate. 1997. (Chronicles of Brother Cadfael Ser.: Vol. 12). 240p. mass mkt. 6.99 (*0-446-40534-5*) Warner Bks., Inc.

—The Rose Rent. 1988. (Chronicles of Brother Cadfael Ser.: Vol. 13). mass mkt. 4.95 o.s.i (*0-449-21495-8*, Fawcett) Ballantine Bks.

—The Rose Rent. 1995. (Chronicles of Brother Cadfael Ser.: Vol. 13). mass mkt. o.s.i (*0-7515-1113-7*); (Illus.). 270p. mass mkt. o.s.i (*0-7515-1741-0*) Little Brown & Co.

—The Rose Rent. Williams, Jennifer, ed. 1987. (Chronicles of Brother Cadfael Ser.: Vol. 13). 201p. 15.95 o.p. (*0-688-06982-7*, Morrow, William & Co.) Morrow/Avon.

—The Rose Rent. 1990. (Chronicles of Brother Cadfael Ser.: Vol. 13). 2.99 o.p. (*0-517-05798-0*) Random Hse. Value Publishing.

—The Rose Rent. l.t. ed. 2000. (Chronicles of Brother Cadfael Ser.: Vol. 13). (Illus.). 289p. pap. 24.95 (*0-7862-2569-6*); (*0-7540-4168-9*); (*0-7540-4169-7*) Thorndike Pr.

—The Rose Rent. l.t. ed. 1988. (Chronicles of Brother Cadfael Ser.: Vol. 13). 368p. 15.95 o.p. (*0-7089-1776-3*, Ulverscroft) Thorpe, F. A. Pubs. GBR. *Dist:* Ulverscroft Large Print Bks., Ltd.

—The Rose Rent. 1997. (Chronicles of Brother Cadfael Ser.: Vol. 13). 240p. mass mkt. 6.99 (*0-446-40533-7*) Warner Bks., Inc.

—The Sanctuary Sparrow. (Chronicles of Brother Cadfael Ser.: Vol. 7). 1999. mass mkt. o.s.i (*0-7515-0217-0*); 1995. 271p. mass mkt. o.s.i (*0-7515-1107-2*) Little Brown & Co.

—The Sanctuary Sparrow. 1995. (Chronicles of Brother Cadfael Ser.: Vol. 7). 224p. mass mkt. 6.99 (*0-446-40429-2*) Warner Bks., Inc.

Peterson, Audrey. Dartmoor Burial. Isaacson, Dana, ed. 1992. 256p. (Orig.). mass mkt. 5.50 o.s.i (*0-671-72970-5*, Pocket) Simon & Schuster.

—Death Too Soon. Isaacson, Dana, ed. 1994. 288p. (Orig.). mass mkt. 4.99 o.s.i (*0-671-79509-0*, Pocket) Simon & Schuster.

—Murder in Burgundy. 1989. mass mkt. 3.95 o.s.i (*0-671-65737-2*, Pocket) Simon & Schuster.

—Nocturne Murder. 1987. 14.95 o.p. (*0-87795-862-9*, Morrow, William & Co.) Morrow/Avon.

—Nocturne Murder. 1989. 2.99 o.p. (*0-517-69456-5*) Random Hse. Value Publishing.

—Shroud for a Scholar. 1995. 272p. mass mkt. 5.50 o.s.i (*0-671-79510-4*, Pocket) Simon & Schuster.

—An Unmourned Death. 2002. (Five Star First Edition Mystery Ser.). 224p. 25.95 (*0-7862-3934-4*, Five Star) Gale Group.

Petit, Chris. Robinson. 1994. 208p. 20.95 o.p. (*0-670-84925-1*, Viking) Viking Penguin.

Peyton, K. M. The Edge of the Cloud. 1992. (YA). (gr. 7 up). 16.50 o.p. (*0-8446-6566-5*) Smith, Peter Pub., Inc.

—Flambards. 1983. 9.95 o.p. (*0-399-20925-5*) Penguin Putnam Bks. for Young Readers.

—Flambards. 1992. 16.50 o.p. (*0-8446-6533-9*) Smith, Peter Pub., Inc.

—Flambards. 1989. (Flambards Ser.). (Illus.). 512p. pap. 3.95 o.p. (*0-14-005461-8*, Penguin Bks.) Viking Penguin.

Phillips, Caryl. A Distant Shore. 2003. 288p. 23.95 (*1-4000-4109-0*, Knopf) Knopf, Alfred A. Inc.

—The Final Passage. 1990. 208p. pap. 7.95 o.p. (*0-14-012796-8*, Penguin Bks.) Viking Penguin.

Phillips, Jill M. Walford's Oak. 1992. 3.99 o.p. (*0-517-09410-X*) Random Hse. Value Publishing.

Phillips, Michael. Wayward Winds. 1999. (Secrets of Heathersleigh Hall Ser.: Vol. 2). (Illus.). 432p. pap. 13.99 (*0-7642-2044-6*); text 16.99 o.p. (*0-7642-2082-9*) Bethany Hse. Pubs.

Phillips, Michael R. A New Dawn over Devon. 2001. (Secrets of Heathersleigh Hall Ser.: Vol. 4). (Illus.). 448p. pap. 13.99 (*0-7642-2440-9*); text 17.99 o.s.i (*0-7642-2441-7*) Bethany Hse. Pubs.

Phillips, Pat. Lady of the Moor. l.t. ed. 2001. (Thorndike Candlelight Romance Ser.). 238p. 22.95 (*0-7862-3139-4*); (*0-7540-4431-9*) Thorndike Pr.

Phillips, Patricia. The Sword & the Flame. 2000. 320p. mass mkt. 4.99 (*0-8439-4726-8*, Leisure Bks.) Dorchester Publishing Co., Inc.

Pianka, Phyllis T. Heather Wild. l.t. ed. 1990. pap. 17.95 o.p. (*0-7927-0395-2*, C0482); 19.95 o.p. (*0-7927-0394-4*, C0254) BBC Audiobooks America.

Pickens, Andrea. A Diamond in the Rough. 2001. (Signet Regency Romance Ser.). 224p. mass mkt. 4.99 o.p. (*0-451-20385-2*) NAL.

—Lady of Letters. 2000. (Signet Regency Romance Ser.). 224p. mass mkt. 4.99 o.s.i (*0-451-20170-1*, Signet Bks.) NAL.

—Major's Mistake. 2000. (Signet Regency Romance Ser.). 224p. mass mkt. 4.99 o.s.i (*0-451-20096-9*, Signet Bks.) NAL.

Pilcher, Rosamunde. Coming Home. unabr. ed. 1997. Vol. 1. audio 110.95 (*0-7451-6638-5*, CAB 1254); Vol. 2. audio 96.95 (*0-7451-6639-3*, CAB 1255) BBC Audiobooks America.

—Coming Home. 1995. audio 96.00 (*0-7366-3194-1*);Pt. A. audio 104.00 (*0-7366-3193-3*, 3859 A);Pt. B. audio 96.00 Books on Tape, Inc.

—Coming Home. 1995. 752p. 35.00 (*0-7710-7011-X*) McClelland & Stewart/Tundra Bks.

—Coming Home. 1995. audio 25.98 o.s.i (*0-553-74648-0*); audio 25.95 (*0-553-47175-9*) Random Hse. Audio Publishing Group. (RH Audio).

—Coming Home. 1996. 977p. mass mkt. 7.99 (*0-312-95812-9*, St. Martin's Paperbacks); 1995. 736p. 25.95 o.p. (*0-312-13451-7*) St. Martin's Pr.

—Coming Home. l.t. ed. 1995. (Basic Ser.). 1217p. 31.95 (*0-7862-0531-8*) Thorndike Pr.

—The Shell Seekers. 1989. 592p. reprint ed. mass mkt. 7.50 o.s.i (*0-440-20204-3*) Dell Publishing.

—The Shell Seekers. l.t. ed. 1989. (Magna Large Print Ser.). 909p. o.p. (*1-85057-530-4*) Magna Large Print Bks. GBR. *Dist:* Ulverscroft Large Print Canada, Ltd.

—The Shell Seekers. abr. ed. 1989. 180p. pap. 18.00 incl. audio (*0-553-45183-9*, 391558, RH Audio) Random Hse. Audio Publishing Group.

—The Shell Seekers. 2004. 544p. 11.99 (*0-517-22285-X*, Gramercy) Random Hse. Value Publishing.

—The Shell Seekers. 1987. 560p. 23.95 o.p. (*0-312-01058-3*); 10th anniv. ed. 1997. 560p. 30.00 (*0-312-17023-8*); 10th annot. ed. 1997. (Shell Seekers Ser.: Vol. 1). 582p. mass mkt. 7.99 (*0-312-96132-4*, St. Martin's Paperbacks) St. Martin's Pr.

—Voices in Summer. l.t. ed. 1985. (Nightingale Ser.). 454p. 11.95 o.p. (*0-8161-3792-7*, Macmillan Reference USA) Gale Group.

—Voices in Summer. 1989. pap. 3.95 o.s.i (*0-312-91474-1*, St. Martin's Paperbacks); 1984. 288p. 13.95 o.p. (*0-312-85076-X*) St. Martin's Pr.

Pinter, Harold. The Dwarfs. 1991. 224p. 17.95 o.p. (*0-8021-1385-0*); 1991. 192p. pap. 11.95 (*0-8021-3266-9*, Grove Pr.); 1962. Grove/Atlantic, Inc.

Pirie, David. The Patient's Eyes Murder Rooms: The Dark Beginnings of Sherlock Holmes. unabr. ed. 2001. audio 40.00 (*0-7366-8482-4*) Books on Tape, Inc.

—The Patient's Eyes Murder Rooms: The Dark Beginnings of Sherlock Holmes. 2002. (Illus.). 252p. 23.95 (*0-312-29095-0*, Saint Martin's Minotaur) St. Martin's Pr.

Pirkis, Catherine L. The Experiences of Loveday Brooke, Lady Detective. 1986. 112p. reprint ed. pap. 4.95 o.p. (*0-486-25164-0*) Dover Pubns., Inc.

—The Murder at Troyte's Hill. 1981. audio Jimcin Recordings.

Plaidy, Jean. The Wandering Prince. 1971. 6.95 o.p. (*0-399-10850-5*) Putnam Publishing Group, The.

Plante, David. Annunciation. 1994. 346p. 21.95 o.p. (*0-395-68091-3*) Houghton Mifflin Co.

Plass, Adrian. Ghosts: The Story of a Reunion. 2003. 206p. pap. 11.99 (*0-551-03110-7*); 224p. pap. 10.99 (*0-310-24917-1*) Zondervan.

Plute, Patricia. The Sword & the Rose. 2001. 278p. pap. 15.95 (*1-931391-72-6*) Booklocker.com, Inc.

Pohl, Frederik & Kornbluth, C. M. Gladiator-at-Law. 1986. 256p. (Orig.). pap. 2.95 o.s.i (*0-671-65566-3*) Baen Bks.

Porter, Henry. Remembrance Day: A Novel. 2000. 368p. 25.00 o.s.i (*0-684-86549-1*, Simon & Schuster) Simon & Schuster.

Porter, Joyce. Dead Easy for Dover. 1991. (Inspector Dover of Scotland Yard Ser.). 176p. reprint ed. pap. 6.50 (*0-88150-212-X*, Foul Play) Norton, W. W. & Co., Inc.

—Dead Easy for Dover. 1978. 7.95 o.p. (*0-312-18492-1*) St. Martin's Pr.

—Dover: The Collected Short Stories. 1995. (Inspector Dover of Scotland Yard Ser.). 304p. 20.00 (*0-88150-342-8*, Foul Play) Norton, W. W. & Co., Inc.

—Dover & the Claret Tappers. 1989. (Inspector Dover of Scotland Yard Ser.). 203p. 16.95 o.s.i (*0-88150-148-4*) Countryman Pr.

—Dover & the Claret Tappers. 1989. (Chief Inspector Dover Mysteries Ser.). 208p. pap. 6.00 (*0-88150-245-6*, Foul Play) Norton, W. W. & Co., Inc.

—Dover & the Unkindest Cut of All. 1990. (Inspector Dover of Scotland Yard Ser.). 188p. reprint ed. pap. 5.95 (*0-88150-174-3*, Foul Play) Norton, W. W. & Co., Inc.

—Dover Beats the Band. 1991. 169p. 17.95 o.p. (*0-88150-195-6*) Countryman Pr.

—Dover Beats the Band. 1993. (Inspector Dover of Scotland Yard Ser.). 170p. pap. 6.00 (*0-88150-268-5*, Foul Play) Norton, W. W. & Co., Inc.

—Dover Goes to Pott. 1990. (Inspector Dover of Scotland Yard Ser.). 192p. reprint ed. pap. 5.95 (*0-88150-173-5*, Foul Play) Norton, W. W. & Co., Inc.

—Dover One. 1989. (Inspector Dover of Scotland Yard Ser.). 176p. reprint ed. pap. 6.95 (*0-88150-134-4*, Foul Play) Norton, W. W. & Co., Inc.

—Dover Strikes Again. 1991. (Inspector Dover of Scotland Yard Ser.). 202p. reprint ed. pap. 5.95 (*0-88150-211-1*, Foul Play) Norton, W. W. & Co., Inc.

—Dover Three. 1989. (Inspector Dover of Scotland Yard Ser.). 188p. reprint ed. pap. 6.50 (*0-88150-147-6*, Foul Play) Norton, W. W. & Co., Inc.

—Dover Two. 1989. (Inspector Dover of Scotland Yard Ser.). 192p. reprint ed. pap. 7.95 (*0-88150-135-2*, Foul Play) Norton, W. W. & Co., Inc.

—It's Murder with Dover. 2002. (Crime ser.). 192p. 21.95 (*0-7540-8625-9*, Black Dagger) BBC Audiobooks America.

—It's Murder with Dover. 1992. (Inspector Dover of Scotland Yard Ser.). 192p. pap. 6.00 (*0-88150-233-2*, Foul Play) Norton, W. W. & Co., Inc.

—A Meddler & Her Murder. 1992. 176p. pap. 7.95 o.p. (*0-89733-328-4*); pap. 7.95 (*0-89733-322-5*) Academy Chicago Pubs., Ltd.

Porter, Margaret E. Dangerous Diversions. 1994. (Signet Regency Romance Ser.). 224p. mass mkt. 3.99 o.p. (*0-451-18069-0*) NAL.

—Dangerous Diversions. l.t. ed. 2000. (Romance Ser.). 381p. 26.95 (*0-7862-3020-7*) Thorndike Pr.

—Road to Ruin. 1992. (Signet Regency Romance Ser.). 224p. mass mkt. 3.99 o.s.i (*0-451-17508-5*, Signet Bks.) NAL.

—Road to Ruin. 1991. 224p. 18.95 (*0-8027-1129-4*) Walker & Co.

—Toast of the Town. l.t. ed. 2001. 395p. (Orig.). 27.95 (*0-7862-3345-1*) Thorndike Pr.

Powell, Anthony. Dance to Music Time First Movement. 1995. 732p. pap. 22.00 (*0-226-67714-1*) Univ. of Chicago Pr.

—Dance to the Music of Time. 2002. pap. 27.95 (*0-09-944547-6*) Arrow Bks., Ltd. GBR. *Dist:* Random Hse. of Canada, Ltd.

—Dance to the Music of Time. 2000. 0.00 (*0-375-40318-3*) Random Hse., Inc.

—A Dance to the Music of Time. unabr. collector's ed. 1996. Vol. 1. audio 88.00 (*0-7366-3458-4*, 4102); Vol. 2. audio 80.00 (*0-7366-3459-2*, 4103); Vol. 3. audio 88.00 (*0-7366-3460-6*, 4104); Vol. 4. audio 80.00 (*0-7366-3461-4*, 4105); Vol. 5. audio 88.00 (*0-7366-3462-2*, 4106); Vol. 6. audio 96.00 (*0-7366-3463-0*, 4107) Books on Tape, Inc.

—A Dance to the Music of Time: All Four Movements, 4 vols. Incl. Dance to Music Time First Movement. 732p. pap. 22.00 (*0-226-67714-1*); Dance to Music Time Fourth Movement. 804p. pap. 22.00 (*0-226-67718-4*); Dance to Music Time Second Movement. 724p. pap. 21.00 (*0-226-67716-8*); Dance to Music Time Third Movement. 736p. pap. 21.00 (*0-226-67717-6*); 1995. 1998. Set pap. 72.80 o.s.i (*0-226-67719-2*) Univ. of Chicago Pr.

—A Dance to the Music of Time: First Movement. Incl. Acceptance World. Buyer's Market. Question of Upbringing. 1962. 24.95 (*0-316-71535-2*) Little Brown & Co.

—A Dance to the Music of Time: Fourth Movement. Incl. Books Do Furnish a Room. Temporary Kings. Hearing Secret Harmonies. 1976. 24.95 o.s.i (*0-316-71548-4*) Little Brown & Co.

—A Dance to the Music of Time: Second Movement. Incl. At Lady Molly's. o.s.i Casanova's Chinese Restaurant. o.s.i Kindly Ones. o.s.i 1964. 24.95 o.s.i (*0-316-71536-0*) Little Brown & Co.

—A Dance to the Music of Time: Third Movement. Incl. Military Philosophers. Soldier's Art. Valley of Bones. 1971. 24.95 (*0-316-71546-8*) Little Brown & Co.

—The Soldier's Art. l.t. unabr. ed. 1999. (Dance to the Music of Time Ser.). 253p. 25.95 (*0-7531-5821-3*, 158213) ISIS Large Print Bks. GBR. *Dist:* ISIS Publishing.

—The Soldier's Art. 1985. mass mkt. 3.95 o.s.i (*0-445-20126-6*) Warner Bks., Inc.

Powell, Elizabeth. A Reckless Bargain. 2002. 224p. mass mkt. 4.99 o.s.i (*0-451-20551-0*) NAL.

Power, Jo-Ann. Allure. 1999. (Sonnet Bks.). 352p. per. 6.50 (*0-671-03408-1*, Pocket) Simon & Schuster.

Power, M. S. Nathan Crosby's Fan Mail. 2001. 304p. pap. 13.00 (*0-7528-3694-3*) Orion Publishing Group, Ltd. GBR. *Dist:* Trafalgar Square.

Powys, John Cowper. A Glastonbury Romance. 1987. 1120p. reprint ed. 35.00 (*0-87951-282-2*) Overlook Pr., The.

—Wolf Solent. 614p. text 35.95 (*0-912568-09-7*) Colgate Univ. Pr.

—Wolf Solent. 1984. 640p. reprint ed. pap. 9.95 o.p. (*0-06-091163-8*, CN 1163, Perennial) HarperTrade.

—Wolf Solent. 1998. 636p. pap. 17.00 (*0-375-70307-1*, Vintage) Knopf Publishing Group.

—Wolf Solent, 2 vols., Set. 1971. reprint ed. 79.00 (*0-403-01159-0*) Scholarly Pr., Inc.

Prentice-Hall Staff. Pride & Prejudice. 2nd ed. text, stu. ed. (*0-13-716978-7*) Prentice Hall (Schl. Div.).

Preston, Fayrene. In Guilty Night. 1998. 352p. mass mkt. 5.99 o.s.i (*0-553-57582-1*) Bantam Bks.

Prevel, Mona. Educating Emily. 2000. (Zebra Regency Romance Ser.). 224p. mass mkt. 4.99 o.s.i (*0-8217-6995-2*) Kensington Publishing Corp.

Priest, Christopher. Prestige. 1997. 416p. reprint ed. pap. 14.95 (*0-312-85886-8*, NPB 0236, Tor Bks.) Doherty, Tom Assocs., LLC.

—Prestige. 1999. 404p. 36.00 (*0-671-71924-6*, Simon Pulse) Simon & Schuster Children's Publishing.
—Prestige. 1996. 416p. 24.95 o.p. (*0-312-14705-8*) St. Martin's Pr.
Priestley, J. B. The Good Companions. 1992. (Phoenix Fiction Ser.). 640p. pap. 9.95 o.s.i (*0-226-68223-4*) Univ. of Chicago Pr.
Prince, Maggie. The House on Hound Hill. (YA). 2003. 256p. (gr. 5). pap. 6.95 (*0-618-33124-7*); 1998. 242p. (gr. 7-9). tchr. ed. 16.00 (*0-395-90702-0*) Houghton Mifflin Co.
—Rachel on the Run. 1988. 96p. (J). (gr. 5-7). 15.95 o.p. (*0-340-33806-7*) Hodder & Stoughton, Ltd. GBR. *Dist:* Lubrecht & Cramer, Ltd., Trafalgar Square.
Pritchett, V. S. The Camberwell Beauty, & Other Stories. 1974. 9.95 o.s.i (*0-394-49222-6*) Random Hse., Inc.
Pryse, Marjorie. Selected Stories of Freeman. 1991. (C). pap. 18.15 (*0-393-30106-0*, Norton Paperbacks) Norton, W. W. & Co., Inc.
Pullinger, Kate. My Life as a Girl in a Men's Prison. 1997. 222p. (*1-86159-024-5*) Phoenix Hse.
—Weird Sister. 2000. 308p. pap. (*0-7538-1064-6*) Phoenix.
Purser, Ann. Orphan Lamb. 1997. 320p. 26.00 o.p. (*1-85797-761-0*); pap. 8.95 o.p. (*0-7528-0245-3*) Orion Publishing Group, Ltd. GBR. *Dist:* Trafalgar Square.
—Terror on Tuesday. 2004. 288p. mass mkt. 5.99 (*0-425-19753-0*) Berkley Publishing Group.
—Terror on Tuesday. 2003. 288p. 26.99 (*0-7278-5956-0*) Severn Hse. Pubs., Ltd.
Putney, Mary Jo. The Bargain. 1999. 384p. mass mkt. 6.99 (*0-451-19864-6*, Signet Bks.) NAL.
—The Bargain. l.t. ed. 2000. (Basic Ser.). 493p. pap. 29.95 (*0-7862-2462-2*) Thorndike Pr.
—Shattered Rainbows. 1996. (Fallen Angels Ser.). 384p. mass mkt. 6.99 o.s.i (*0-451-40614-1*, Topaz) NAL.
—Silk & Shadows. l.t. ed. 2001. (Large Print Bks.). 555p. 28.95 o.p. (*1-56895-132-9*, Wheeler Publishing, Inc.) Gale Group.
—Silk & Shadows. 432p. 2000. mass mkt. 6.99 (*0-451-20206-6*, Signet Bks.); 1991. mass mkt. 6.99 o.s.i (*0-451-40277-4*, Onyx) NAL.
—The Wild Child. 2000. 384p. mass mkt. 6.99 (*0-449-00584-4*, Ballantine Bks.) Ballantine Bks.
—The Wild Child. l.t. ed. 1999. (Large Print Book Ser.). 28.95 (*1-56895-791-2*, Wheeler Publishing, Inc.) Gale Group.
—The Wild Child. unabr. ed. 1999. audio 87.00 (*0-7887-4048-2*, 96158E7) Recorded Bks., LLC.
Pykare, Nina Coombs. Death Comes for Desdemona. 1999. (First Edition Romance Ser.). 136p. 24.95 (*0-7862-2042-2*, Five Star) Gale Group.
—The Haunting of Grey Cliffs. 1992. 192p. 4.50 o.p. (*1-55773-830-0*, Diamond Bks.) Ace Bks.
—The Haunting of Grey Cliffs. l.t. ed. 2000. (Romance Ser.). 234p. 24.95 (*0-7862-2350-2*) Thorndike Pr.
Pym, Barbara. An Academic Question. 1987. 192p. pap. 9.00 o.p. (*0-452-25996-7*, Plume); 1986. 15.95 o.p. (*0-525-24441-7*, Dutton) Dutton/Plume.
—An Academic Question. l.t. ed. 1987. 250p. 17.95 o.p. (*0-8161-4226-2*, Macmillan Reference USA) Gale Group.
—Crampton Hodnet. unabr. ed. 1997. audio 54.95 (*0-7451-6209-6*, CAB 150) BBC Audiobooks America.
—Crampton Hodnet. 1986. 224p. pap. 8.95 o.p. (*0-452-25816-2*, Plume); 1986. 22p. pap. 9.00 o.p. (*0-452-26492-8*, Plume); 1985. 224p. 14.95 o.p. (*0-525-24333-X*, Dutton) Dutton/Plume.
—Crampton Hodnet. l.t. ed. 1986. (General Ser.). 345p. 14.95 o.p. (*0-8161-3968-7*, Macmillan Reference USA) Gale Group.
—Crampton Hodnet. 2000. viii, 216p. pap. 12.95 (*1-55921-243-8*) Moyer Bell.
—Excellent Women. l.t. ed. 1985. (General Ser.). 14.95 o.p. (*0-8161-3839-7*, Macmillan Reference USA) Gale Group.
—A Few Green Leaves. 1980. 256p. 13.95 o.p. (*0-525-10450-X*, Dutton) Dutton/Plume.
—A Few Green Leaves. l.t. ed. 1985. (General Ser.). 336p. 15.95 o.p. (*0-8161-3840-0*, Macmillan Reference USA) Gale Group.
—A Few Green Leaves. 1986. 256p. reprint ed. pap. 6.95 o.p. (*0-06-097032-4*, PL/7032, Perennial) HarperTrade.
—A Glass of Blessings. l.t. ed. 1986. (General Ser.). 427p. 17.95 o.p. (*0-8161-3841-9*, Macmillan Reference USA) Gale Group.
—A Glass of Blessings. 1987. 272p. reprint ed. pap. 6.95 o.p. (*0-06-097074-X*, PL 7074, Perennial) HarperTrade.
—Jane & Prudence. unabr. ed. 2000. audio 49.95 (*0-7451-2728-2*, SAB 094) Chivers Audio Bks. GBR. *Dist:* BBC Audiobooks America.
—Jane & Prudence. 1990. 22p. pap. 10.00 o.p. (*0-452-26895-8*, Plume); 1981. 13.95 o.p. (*0-525-13640-1*, Dutton) Dutton/Plume.
—Jane & Prudence. l.t. ed. 1985. (General Ser.). 384p. 15.95 o.p. (*0-8161-3861-3*, Macmillan Reference USA) Gale Group.
—Jane & Prudence. 1982. mass mkt. 3.50 o.p. (*0-06-080594-3*, P 594); 1987. 224p. reprint ed. pap. 6.95 o.p. (*0-06-097101-0*, PL 7101) HarperTrade. (Perennial).
—Jane & Prudence. 1999. 256p. pap. 12.95 (*1-55921-226-8*) Moyer Bell.
—Jane & Prudence. 1990. 22p. pap. 8.95 o.p. (*0-525-48570-8*, Obelisk) NAL.
—Less Than Angels. 1981. 256p. 13.95 o.p. (*0-525-14440-4*, Dutton) Dutton/Plume.
—Less Than Angels. l.t. ed. 1986. (General Ser.). 432p. 15.95 o.p. (*0-8161-3842-7*, Macmillan Reference USA) Gale Group.
—Less Than Angels. 1987. 256p. pap. 6.95 o.p. (*0-06-097117-7*, Perennial) HarperTrade.
—No Fond Return of Love. 2003. 256p. reprint ed. pap. 12.95 (*1-55921-306-X*) Moyer Bell.
—Quartet in Autumn. l.t. ed. 1993. 20.95 o.p. (*0-7927-1634-5*); pap. 18.95 o.p. (*0-7927-1633-7*) BBC Audiobooks America.
—Quartet in Autumn. 1992. 224p. pap. 12.95 o.s.i (*0-452-26934-2*, Plume); 1978. 13.95 o.p. (*0-525-18665-4*, Dutton) Dutton/Plume.
—Quartet in Autumn. 1979. (General Ser.). lib. bdg. 10.95 o.p. (*0-8161-6661-7*, Macmillan Reference USA) Gale Group.
—Quartet in Autumn. reprint ed. 1986. 224p. pap. 6.95 o.p. (*0-06-097031-6*, PL/7031); 1980. 218p. mass mkt. 3.50 o.p. (*0-06-080513-7*, P 513) HarperTrade. (Perennial).
—Quartet in Autumn. unabr. ed. 1995. audio 54.95 (*1-85089-553-8*, 91122) ISIS Audio Bks. GBR. *Dist:* Ulverscroft Large Print Bks., Ltd.
—Quartet in Autumn. 1988. 228p. pap. 7.95 o.p. (*0-525-48379-9*, Obelisk) NAL.
—An Unsuitable Attachment. 1982. 224p. 13.95 o.p. (*0-525-24117-5*, Dutton) Dutton/Plume.
—An Unsuitable Attachment. 256p. 1983. mass mkt. o.p. (*0-06-080653-2*, P 653); 1986. reprint ed. pap. 7.95 o.p. (*0-06-097055-3*, PL/7055) HarperTrade. (Perennial).
—An Unsuitable Attachment. unabr. ed. 1996. audio 61.95 (*1-85695-687-3*, 89116) ISIS Audio Bks. GBR. *Dist:* Ulverscroft Large Print Bks., Ltd.
Queen, Ellery. A Study in Terror. l.t. ed. 2001. 192p. (*0-7540-4586-2*); (*0-7540-4585-4*) Gale Group. (Macmillan Reference USA).
Quest, Erica. Model Murder. l.t. ed. 1992. 18.95 o.p. (*0-7451-8408-1*) BBC Audiobooks America.
Quick, Amanda, pseud. I Thee Wed. 2000. 384p. reprint ed. mass mkt. 7.50 (*0-553-57410-8*) Bantam Bks.
—I Thee Wed. unabr. ed. 1999. audio 56.00 (*0-7366-4564-0*, 4971) Books on Tape, Inc.
—I Thee Wed. abr. ed. 1999. audio 18.00 Highsmith Inc.
—I Thee Wed. unabr. ed. 1999. audio compact disk 79.00 (*0-7887-3978-6*, C1097E7); audio 60.00 (*0-7887-3474-1*, 95876E7) Recorded Bks., LLC.
—I Thee Wed. l.t. ed. (Thorndike/G. K. Hall Paperback Bestsellers Ser.). 503p. 2000. pap. 27.95 (*0-7862-1941-6*); 1999. 30.95 (*0-7862-1940-8*) Thorndike Pr.
—Late for the Wedding. 2003. 336p. 24.95 (*0-553-80271-2*); E-Book 19.95 (*0-553-89756-X*) Bantam Bks.
—Late for the Wedding. l.t. ed. 2003. 544p. 26.95 (*0-375-43206-X*) Random Hse. Large Print.
—Mischief. l.t. ed. 1997. 384p. mass mkt. 7.50 (*0-553-57190-7*) Bantam Bks.
—Mischief. abr. ed. 2000. pap. 9.99 o.s.i incl. audio (*0-553-52707-X*, RH Audio) Random Hse. Audio Publishing Group.
—Mischief. unabr. ed. audio 78.00 (*0-7887-0631-4*, 94806E7); audio Recorded Bks., LLC.
—Mischief. l.t. ed. 1997. (Paperback Bestsellers Ser.). 532p. pap. 26.95 (*0-7862-0782-5*) Thorndike Pr.
—Slightly Shady. l.t. ed. 2001. (Large Print Book Ser.). 391p. 31.95 (*1-58724-026-2*, Wheeler Publishing, Inc.) Gale Group.
—Surrender. l.t. ed. 1994. 25.95 (*1-56895-103-5*, Wheeler Publishing, Inc.) Gale Group.
—Surrender. l.t. ed. 1995. (Magna Large Print Ser.). 382p. o.p. (*0-7505-0842-6*) Magna Large Print Bks. GBR. *Dist:* Ulverscroft Large Print Canada, Ltd.
—Wicked Widow. 2001. 352p. reprint ed. mass mkt. 7.50 (*0-553-57411-6*, Spectra) Bantam Bks.
—Wicked Widow. abr. ed. 2000. audio 18.00 (*0-553-52682-0*, RH Audio) Random Hse. Audio Publishing Group.
—Wicked Widow. l.t. ed. 2000. (Basic Ser.). 453p. 31.95 (*0-7862-2596-3*) Thorndike Pr.
Quinn, Julia. The Duke & I. l.t. ed. 2003. (Romance Ser.). 28.95 (*1-58724-378-4*, Wheeler Publishing, Inc.) Gale Group.
—The Duke & I. 2000. (Avon Romantic Treasure Ser.). 384p. mass mkt. 6.99 (*0-380-80082-9*, Avon Bks.) Morrow/Avon.
—How to Marry a Marquis. 1999. (Avon Romantic Treasure Ser.). 384p. mass mkt. 6.99 (*0-380-80081-0*, Avon Bks.) Morrow/Avon.
—An Offer from a Gentleman. 2001. 384p. mass mkt. 6.99 (*0-380-81558-3*, Avon Bks.) Morrow/Avon.
—To Sir Phillip, with Love. 2003. 384p. mass mkt. 6.99 (*0-380-82085-4*, Avon Bks.) Morrow/Avon.
Raban, Jonathan. Foreign Land. 352p. 1986. pap. 6.95 o.p. (*0-14-008266-2*, Penguin Bks.); 1985. 16.95 o.p. (*0-670-80767-2*) Viking Penguin.
—Foreign Land: A Novel. 2001. 352p. pap. 14.00 (*0-375-72594-6*, Vintage) Knopf Publishing Group.
Radcliffe, Robert. Under an English Heaven. 2001. (Illus.). 448p. (*0-316-85990-7*) Little Brown & Co.
Radley, Sheila. Blood on the Happy Highway. l.t. ed. 1984. 384p. 16.95 o.p. (*0-7089-1316-4*, Ulverscroft) Thorpe, F. A. Pubs. GBR. *Dist:* Ulverscroft Large Print Bks., Ltd.
—The Chief Inspector's Daughter. 1987. (Mystery Ser.). 224p. mass mkt. 3.50 o.s.i (*0-553-26942-9*) Bantam Bks.
—The Chief Inspector's Daughter. 1982. (Nightingale Ser.). pap. 9.95 o.p. (*0-8161-3413-8*, Macmillan Reference USA) Gale Group.
—The Chief Inspector's Daughter. l.t. ed. 1982. (Ulverscroft Large Print Ser.). 432p. 29.99 o.p. (*0-7089-1033-5*, Ulverscroft) Thorpe, F. A. Pubs. GBR. *Dist:* Ulverscroft Large Print Bks., Ltd., Ulverscroft Large Print Canada, Ltd.
—Cross My Heart & Hope to Die: An Inspector Quantrill Mystery. 1992. (Quantrill Ser.: No. 8). 288p. text 19.00 (*0-684-19410-4*, Macmillan Reference USA) Gale Group.
—Cross My Heart & Hope to Die: An Inspector Quantrill Mystery. l.t. ed. 1998. (Ulverscroft Large Print Ser.). 416p. 29.99 o.p. (*0-7089-3956-2*, Ulverscroft) Thorpe, F. A. Pubs. GBR. *Dist:* Ulverscroft Large Print Bks., Ltd., Ulverscroft Large Print Canada, Ltd.
—Death in the Morning. 1987. 224p. reprint ed. mass mkt. 3.50 o.s.i (*0-553-26857-0*) Bantam Bks.
—Death in the Morning. 1980. pap. 3.50 o.p. (*0-440-11785-2*) Dell Publishing.
—Death in the Morning. 1981. (General Ser.). lib. bdg. 13.95 o.p. (*0-8161-3199-6*, Macmillan Reference USA) Gale Group.
—Fair Game. l.t. ed. 1999. (Ulverscroft Large Print Ser.). 416p. 31.99 o.p. (*0-7089-4028-5*, Ulverscroft) Thorpe, F. A. Pubs. GBR. *Dist:* Ulverscroft Large Print Bks., Ltd., Ulverscroft Large Print Canada, Ltd.
—Fate Worse Than Death. 1987. 208p. mass mkt. 2.95 o.s.i (*0-553-26538-5*) Bantam Bks.
—Fate Worse Than Death. 1986. 224p. 13.95 o.p. (*0-684-18582-2*, Macmillan Reference USA) Gale Group.
—Fate Worse Than Death. l.t. ed. 1986. (Mystery Ser.). 448p. 29.99 o.p. (*0-7089-1630-9*, Ulverscroft) Thorpe, F. A. Pubs. GBR. *Dist:* Ulverscroft Large Print Bks., Ltd., Ulverscroft Large Print Canada, Ltd.
—New Blood from Old Bones. l.t. ed. 2000. (Ulverscroft Large Print Ser.). 352p. 31.99 (*0-7089-4199-0*, Ulverscroft) Thorpe, F. A. Pubs. GBR. *Dist:* Ulverscroft Large Print Bks., Ltd., Ulverscroft Large Print Canada, Ltd.
—The Quiet Road to Death. 1984. 176p. 11.95 o.s.i (*0-684-18124-X*, Scribner) Simon & Schuster.
—The Quiet Road to Death. 1985. (Crime Monthly Ser.). 192p. pap. 3.95 o.p. (*0-14-007746-4*, Penguin Bks.) Viking Penguin.
—A Talent for Destruction. 1984. mass mkt. 2.50 o.s.i (*0-345-31250-3*) Ballantine Bks.
—A Talent for Destruction. 1982. 224p. 10.95 o.p. (*0-684-17663-7*, Scribner) Simon & Schuster.
—This Way Out. 1992. 2.99 o.p. (*0-517-08033-8*) Random Hse. Value Publishing.
—This Way Out. 1989. 256p. 16.95 o.s.i (*0-684-19125-3*, Scribner) Simon & Schuster.
—This Way Out. 1990. 224p. reprint ed. pap. 4.50 o.p. (*0-14-014453-6*, Penguin Bks.) Viking Penguin.
—Who Saw Him Die? 1988. 224p. mass mkt. 3.50 o.s.i (*0-553-27607-7*) Bantam Bks.
—Who Saw Him Die? 1988. (Inspector Douglas Quantrill Mystery Ser.). 224p. 14.95 o.s.i (*0-684-18883-X*, Scribner) Simon & Schuster.
Rae, Catherine M. Julia's Story. 1990. 2.99 o.p. (*0-517-05817-0*) Random Hse. Value Publishing.
—Julia's Story. 1989. 15.95 o.p. (*0-312-02935-7*) St. Martin's Pr.
Raine, Jerry. Smalltime. 1997. (Bloodlines Ser.). 184p. pap. 12.95 (*1-899344-13-6*) Dufour Editions, Inc.
Raison, Jennifer & Goldie, Michael. Caraboo: The Servant Girl Princess: The Real Story of the Grand Hoax. 1995. (Illus.). 220p. pap. 13.95 (*1-56656-179-5*) Interlink Publishing Group, Inc.
Raleigh, Debbie. A Bride for Lord Brasleigh. 2001. (Zebra Regency Romance Ser.). 224p. mass mkt. 4.99 o.s.i (*0-8217-6814-X*, Zebra Bks.) Kensington Publishing Corp.
—A Bride for Lord Challmond. 2001. (Zebra Regency Romance Ser.). 256p. mass mkt. 4.99 o.s.i (*0-8217-6771-2*, Zebra Bks.) Kensington Publishing Corp.
—A Bride for Lord Wickton. 2001. (Zebra Regency Romance Ser.). 224p. mass mkt. 4.99 o.s.i (*0-8217-6796-8*, Zebra Bks.) Kensington Publishing Corp.
—The Valentine Wish. 2002. (Zebra Regency Romance Ser.). 224p. mass mkt. 4.99 o.s.i (*0-8217-7170-1*) Kensington Publishing Corp.
—The Valentine Wish. 2002. (Romance Ser.). 27.95 (*0-7862-4813-0*) Thorndike Pr.
Ramsay, Eileen. Never Call It Loving. 2001. 250p. 25.99 (*0-7278-5704-5*) Severn Hse. Pubs., Ltd.
Randall, Lindsay. Dangerous Courtship. 1999. (Zebra Regency Romance Ser.). 224p. mass mkt. 4.99 o.s.i (*0-8217-6184-6*, Zebra Bks.) Kensington Publishing Corp.
Rankin. Book of Ultimate Truths. 2000. pap. 13.00 (*0-552-13922-X*) Transworld Publishers Ltd. GBR. *Dist:* Trafalgar Square.
—Dance of the Vodoo Handbag. 2000. 335p. pap. 12.00 (*0-552-14580-7*) Transworld Publishers Ltd. GBR. *Dist:* Trafalgar Square.
Ranney, Karen. After the Kiss. 2000. 384p. mass mkt. 5.99 (*0-380-81298-3*, Avon Bks.) Morrow/Avon.
Ransley, Peter. The Hawk. 272p. 1990. pap. 4.50 o.p. (*0-14-012141-2*, Penguin Bks.); 1989. 17.95 o.p. (*0-670-82796-7*) Viking Penguin.
Ransome, Arthur. Bohemia in London. 1984. (Oxford Paperbacks Ser.). (Illus.). pap. 5.95 o.p. (*0-19-281412-5*) Oxford Univ. Pr., Inc.
—Coot Club. 1990. (Swallows & Amazons Ser.). (Illus.). 352p. (J). (gr. 4-6). reprint ed. pap. 14.95 (*0-87923-787-2*) Godine, David R. Pub.
Rathbone, Basil & Bruce, Nigel. The New Adventures of Sherlock Holmes. 1998. Vol. 1 24.98 incl. audio; Vol. 2 24.98 incl. audio; Vol. 3 24.98 incl. audio; Vol. 4. 24.98 incl. audio; Vol. 5. 24.98 incl. audio; Vol. 6. 24.98 incl. audio Radio Spirits, Inc.
Rathbone, Julian. The Last English King. 1998. 416p. o.s.i (*0-316-64139-1*) Little Brown & Co.
—The Last English King. 1999. 400p. 24.95 (*0-312-24213-1*) St. Martin's Pr.
Raven, Simon. Fielding Gray. 1985. (Alms for Oblivion Ser.: No. 1). 208p. reprint ed. 13.95 o.p. (*0-8253-0310-9*) Beaufort Bks., Inc.
Rawlinson, Peter. Indictment for Murder. 2000. 251p. 22.95 (*0-312-25325-7*, Saint Martin's Minotaur) St. Martin's Pr.
Ray, Rebecca. Pure. 2000. 416p. pap. 13.50 (*0-8021-3700-8*, Grove Pr.) Grove/Atlantic, Inc.
Rayner, Claire. First Blood. l.t. ed. 1995. (Charnwood Large Print Ser.). 480p. 29.99 o.p. (*0-7089-8825-3*, Charnwood) Thorpe, F. A. Pubs. GBR. *Dist:* Ulverscroft Large Print Bks., Ltd., Ulverscroft Large Print Canada, Ltd.
—Fourth Attempt. l.t. ed. 1997. (Charnwood Large Print Ser.). 496p. 29.99 o.p. (*0-7089-8975-6*, Ulverscroft) Thorpe, F. A. Pubs. GBR. *Dist:* Ulverscroft Large Print Bks., Ltd., Ulverscroft Large Print Canada, Ltd.
—Second Opinion. unabr. ed. 1995. audio 84.95 (*0-7451-6539-7*, CAB 1155) BBC Audiobooks America.
—Second Opinion. l.t. ed. 1996. (Charnwood Large Print Ser.). 528p. 29.99 o.p. (*0-7089-8897-0*, Ulverscroft) Thorpe, F. A. Pubs. GBR. *Dist:* Ulverscroft Large Print Bks., Ltd., Ulverscroft Large Print Canada, Ltd.
Read, Martha M. Tiggy & the Fairacre Festival. l.t. ed. 2000. (General Ser.). 200p. pap. 24.95 (*0-7862-2314-6*) Thorndike Pr.
Read, Miss. Affairs at Thrush Green. 1984. 13.95 o.p. (*0-395-36554-6*) Houghton Mifflin Co.
—Affairs at Thrush Green. l.t. ed. 1993. (General Fiction Ser.). 258p. 19.95 o.p. (*0-7505-0205-3*) Magna Large Print Bks. GBR. *Dist:* Ulverscroft Large Print Bks., Ltd.
—At Home in Thrush Green, 001. 1986. 16.95 o.p. (*0-395-41224-2*) Houghton Mifflin Co.
—Celebrations at Thrush Green. l.t. ed. 1994. 18.95 o.p. (*0-7927-1921-2*); pap. o.p. (*0-7927-1920-4*) BBC Audiobooks America.
—Celebrations at Thrush Green. 1993. (Illus.). 151p. 19.95 o.p. (*0-395-65030-5*) Houghton Mifflin Co.
—Celebrations at Thrush Green. 1993. pap. 11.00 (*0-14-015798-0*) Penguin Bks., Ltd. GBR. *Dist:* Trafalgar Square.
—Changes at Fairacre. l.t. ed. 1993. 20.95 o.p. (*0-7927-1593-4*) BBC Audiobooks America.
—Changes at Fairacre. 2001. 252p. pap. 12.00 (*0-618-15457-4*); 1992. (Illus.). 256p. 19.95 o.p. (*0-395-63126-2*) Houghton Mifflin Co.
—Chronicles of Fairacre, 3 vols. 1977. 10.95 o.p. (*0-395-25181-8*) Houghton Mifflin Co.
—Encounters at Thrush Green. (Illus.). 448p. 29.95 o.p. (*0-7181-4334-5*) Joseph, Michael Ltd. GBR. *Dist:* Trafalgar Square.
—The Fairacre Festival. 1990. (Illus.). 104p. reprint ed. pap. 12.00 (*0-89733-333-0*) Academy Chicago Pubs., Ltd.

Settings

—The Fairacre Festival. Date not set. lib. bdg. 21.95 (*0-8488-1698-6*) Amereon, Ltd.
—The Fairacre Festival. 2002. lib. bdg. 27.95 (*1-58547-235-2*, Premier) Ctr. Point Large Print.
—The Fairacre Festival: And Tiggy. l.t. ed. 2000. (*0-7540-3996-X*); (*0-7540-3997-8*) Thorndike Pr.
—Farewell to Fairacre. 2001. 224p. pap. 12.00 (*0-618-15456-6*); 1994. 192p. 19.95 o.p. (*0-395-68994-5*) Houghton Mifflin Co.
—Fresh from the Country. 1995. (Illus.). 219p. reprint ed. pap. 12.00 (*0-89733-417-5*) Academy Chicago Pubs., Ltd.
—Fresh from the Country. 21.95 (*0-8488-1453-3*) Amereon, Ltd.
—Fresh from the Country. l.t. ed. 2002. lib. bdg. 27.95 (*1-58547-220-4*, Premier) Ctr. Point Large Print.
—Friends at Thrush Green. 1991. (Illus.). 256p. 21.95 o.p. (*0-395-57381-5*) Houghton Mifflin Co.
—Gossip from Thrush Green. l.t. ed. 1993. pap. 16.95 o.p. (*0-7927-1375-3*); 1992. 18.95 o.p. (*0-7927-1376-1*) BBC Audiobooks America.
—Gossip from Thrush Green, 001. 1982. 13.50 o.p. (*0-395-32215-4*) Houghton Mifflin Co.
—The Market Square. Date not set. lib. bdg. 21.95 (*0-8488-1696-X*) Amereon, Ltd.
—The Market Square. l.t. ed. 1992. pap. 14.95 o.p. (*0-7927-0560-2*); 1991. 17.95 o.p. (*0-7927-0559-9*, E0002) BBC Audiobooks America.
—Miss Clare Remembers. 1988. (Illus.). 238p. reprint ed. pap. 9.00 o.p. (*0-89733-308-X*) Academy Chicago Pubs., Ltd.
—Miss Clare Remembers. l.t. ed. 1996. (Core Collection). 275p. 26.95 (*0-7838-1658-8*) Thorndike Pr.
—Miss Read's Christmas. 1990. (Miss Read Ser.). (Illus.). 220p. 20.00 o.p. (*0-89733-352-7*) Academy Chicago Pubs., Ltd.
—Miss Read's Christmas Tales: Village Christmas; The Christmas Mouse. 1995. (Illus.). 256p. (J). 24.95 o.s.i (*0-395-75289-2*); pap. 11.95 o.p. (*0-395-74131-9*) Houghton Mifflin Co.
—Mrs. Pringle of Fairacre. 2001. 176p. pap. 12.00 (*0-618-15588-0*) Houghton Mifflin Co.
—News from Thrush Green. 1990. (Illus.). 240p. reprint ed. pap. 12.00 (*0-89733-334-9*) Academy Chicago Pubs., Ltd.
—News from Thrush Green. lib. bdg. 21.95 (*0-8488-1455-X*) Amereon, Ltd.
—News from Thrush Green. 1983. 291p. reprint ed. lib. bdg. 16.95 o.p. (*0-89966-465-2*) Buccaneer Bks., Inc.
—News from Thrush Green. l.t. ed. (General Ser.). 1993. (Illus.). 325p. lib. bdg. 21.95 (*0-8161-5503-8*); 1993. 22.00 (*0-8161-5504-6*); 1976. reprint ed. lib. bdg. 10.95 o.p. (*0-8161-6432-0*) Gale Group. (Macmillan Reference USA).
—Over the Gate. 1988. (Illus.). 238p. reprint ed. pap. 9.00 o.p. (*0-89733-298-9*) Academy Chicago Pubs., Ltd.
—Over the Gate. l.t. ed. 1996. (Core Collection). (Illus.). 300p. 27.95 (*0-7838-1656-1*) Thorndike Pr.
—A Peaceful Retirement. l.t. ed. 1997. 189p. 26.95 o.p. (*0-7838-8276-9*, Macmillan Reference USA) Gale Group.
—A Peaceful Retirement. 1997. 160p. 22.00 o.p. (*0-395-85062-2*) Houghton Mifflin Co.
—Return to Thrush Green. l.t. ed. 1993. pap. 15.95 o.p. (*0-7927-1266-8*); 1992. 18.95 o.p. (*0-7927-1267-6*) BBC Audiobooks America.
—Return to Thrush Green, 001. 1979. 8.95 o.p. (*0-395-27627-6*) Houghton Mifflin Co.
—The School at Thrush Green. 1988. (Illus.). 272p. 17.95 o.p. (*0-395-46108-1*) Houghton Mifflin Co.
—Storm in the Village. 1987. (Illus.). 247p. pap. 9.00 o.p. (*0-89733-244-X*) Academy Chicago Pubs., Ltd.
—Storm in the Village. Date not set. lib. bdg. 22.95 (*0-8488-1691-9*) Amereon, Ltd.
—Storm in the Village, Set. unabr. ed. 1998. audio 69.95 o.p. (*1-872672-14-0*) Magna Story Sound GBR. *Dist:* Ulverscroft Large Print Bks., Ltd.
—Storm in the Village. (G. K. Hall Audio Bks.). 1992. audio 53.95 o.p. (*0-8161-7608-6*); 1996. (Illus.). 305p. 27.95 (*0-7838-1655-3*) Thorndike Pr.
—Summer at Fairacre. unabr. ed. 2000. (Fairacre Chronicles). audio 49.95 (*0-7451-6220-7*, CAB 139) Chivers Audio Bks. GBR. *Dist:* BBC Audiobooks America.
—Summer at Fairacre. (Fairacre Chronicles ). (Illus.). 2001. 240p. pap. 12.00 (*0-618-12704-6*); 1985. 256p. 14.95 o.p. (*0-395-38016-2*) Houghton Mifflin Co.
—Tales from a Village School. 1996. audio 24.95 (*0-7451-2844-0*) BBC Audiobooks America.
—Tales from a Village School. unabr. ed. 2000. (Fairacre Chronicles). audio 34.95 (*0-7451-6540-0*, CAB 1156) Chivers Audio Bks. GBR. *Dist:* BBC Audiobooks America.
—Tales from a Village School. l.t. ed. 1995. 226p. 24.95 o.p. (*0-7838-1441-0*, Macmillan Reference USA) Gale Group.
—Tales from a Village School. 1995. (Illus.). 176p. 19.95 o.p. (*0-395-71762-0*) Houghton Mifflin Co.
—Tales from a Village School. l.t. ed. 1996. (Paperback Bestsellers Ser.). 190p. pap. 23.95 (*0-7838-1442-9*) Thorndike Pr.
—Thrush Green. 1987. (Illus.). 226p. pap. 9.00 o.s.i (*0-89733-263-6*) Academy Chicago Pubs., Ltd.
—Thrush Green. Date not set. lib. bdg. 21.95 (*0-8488-1692-7*) Amereon, Ltd.
—Thrush Green. l.t. ed. 1992. pap. 14.95 o.p. (*0-7927-0867-9*); 18.95 o.p. (*0-7927-0866-0*, E0019) BBC Audiobooks America.
—Thrush Green. 1982. reprint ed. lib. bdg. 25.95 (*0-89966-435-0*) Buccaneer Bks., Inc.
—Thrush Green. 1988. 10.95 o.p. (*0-7181-0370-X*) Viking Penguin.
—Tylers Row. 1990. (Illus.). 240p. pap. 12.00 (*0-89733-339-X*) Academy Chicago Pubs., Ltd.
—Tyler's Row. l.t. ed. 1993. (General Ser.). 312p. lib. bdg. 20.95 (*0-8161-5509-7*, Macmillan Reference USA) Gale Group.
—Village Affairs, 001. 1978. 7.95 o.p. (*0-395-26482-0*) Houghton Mifflin Co.
—Village Centenary. (Fairacre Chronicles ). 240p. 2001. (Illus.). pap. 12.00 (*0-618-12703-8*); 1981. 11.20 o.p. (*0-395-31262-0*) Houghton Mifflin Co.
—Village Christmas & the Christmas Mouse. l.t. ed. 1993. (Large Print Bks.). 172p. 23.95 o.p. (*0-8161-5501-1*, Macmillan Reference USA) Gale Group.
—Village Christmas & The Christmas Mouse. l.t. ed. 1994. (Large Print Bks.). 172p. pap. 17.95 o.p. (*0-8161-5502-X*, Macmillan Reference USA) Gale Group.
—Village Diary. 1986. (Illus.). 255p. pap. 9.00 o.p. (*0-89733-212-1*) Academy Chicago Pubs., Ltd.
—Village Diary. Date not set. lib. bdg. 22.95 (*0-8488-1690-0*) Amereon, Ltd.
—Village Diary. l.t. ed. 1993. 19.95 o.p. (*0-7927-1536-5*); 1993. pap. o.p. (*0-7927-1535-7*); 1991. audio 54.95 (*0-7451-6223-1*, CAB 558) BBC Audiobooks America.
—Village School. 1986. (Illus.). 239p. pap. 9.00 o.p. (*0-89733-211-3*) Academy Chicago Pubs., Ltd.
—Village School. Date not set. lib. bdg. 21.95 (*0-8488-1689-7*) Amereon, Ltd.
—Village School. l.t. ed. 1994. 18.95 o.p. (*0-7927-1763-5*); 1994. pap. 17.95 o.p. (*0-7927-1762-7*); 1993. 54.95 incl. audio (*0-7451-6224-X*, CSL 057) BBC Audiobooks America.
—Winter in Thrush Green. 1987. (Illus.). 226p. pap. 9.00 o.p. (*0-89733-264-4*) Academy Chicago Pubs., Ltd.
—Winter in Thrush Green. 1982. reprint ed. lib. bdg. 25.95 (*0-89966-436-9*) Buccaneer Bks., Inc.
—The World of Thrush Green. l.t. ed. 1993. (Illus.). 326p. lib. bdg. 17.95 o.p. (*0-8161-5508-9*); 22.95 (*0-8161-5507-0*) Gale Group. (Macmillan Reference USA).
—The World of Thrush Green. 1989. (Illus.). 208p. 24.95 o.p. (*0-395-50228-4*) Houghton Mifflin Co.
—The World of Thrush Green. l.t. ed. 1992. (Magna Large Print Ser.). 350p. o.p. (*0-7505-0179-0*) Magna Large Print Bks. GBR. *Dist:* Ulverscroft Large Print Canada, Ltd.
—The Year at Thrush Green. 1996. 272p. 21.95 o.p. (*0-395-79570-2*) Houghton Mifflin Co.
Read, Miss & Goodall, J. S. Winter in Thrush Green. 1999. (J). 21.95 (*0-8488-1456-8*) Amereon, Ltd.
Read, Miss & Grimley, Harry. The Market Square. 1988. (Illus.). 224p. reprint ed. pap. 9.00 o.p. (*0-89733-318-7*) Academy Chicago Pubs., Ltd.
Read Staff. The White Robin, 001. 1980. 8.95 o.p. (*0-395-29452-5*) Houghton Mifflin Co.
Reah, Danuta. Silent Playgrounds. 2000. 325p. (*0-00-232683-3*) HarperCollins Pubs.
Redmond, Patrick. Something Dangerous. 2000. 416p. mass mkt. 7.50 (*0-7868-8957-8*) Disney Pr.
—Something Dangerous. l.t. ed. 2000. (J). 26.95 (*1-56895-832-3*, Wheeler Publishing, Inc.) Gale Group.
—Something Dangerous. abr. ed. 1999. audio 17.95 (*1-55935-325-2*) Soundelux Audio Publishing.
—Something Dangerous: A Novel. 2000. mass mkt. (*0-7868-8972-1*) Disney Pr.
—Something Dangerous: A Novel. 1999. 320p. 23.95 (*0-7868-6552-0*) Hyperion Pr.
Reed, Eden. Valley of Hemlock. 1999. 194p. pap. 12.95 (*1-930076-25-8*) WigWam Publishing Co.
Reed, Joy. Anne's Wish: The Wishing Well. 2001. 352p. mass mkt. 5.50 o.s.i (*0-8217-6810-7*) Kensington Publishing Corp.
—Lord Yates & the Yankee. 2003. 256p. mass mkt. 4.99 (*0-8217-7476-X*) Kensington Publishing Corp.
—The Wishing Well: Emily's Wish. 2000. (Ballad Romances Ser.). 352p. mass mkt. 5.50 o.s.i (*0-8217-6713-5*) Kensington Publishing Corp.
Reeve, Clara, et al. The Old English Baron/the Castle of Otranto. 2001. (Eighteenth Century Literature Ser.: Vol. 1). (Illus.). 273p. per. 11.20 net. (*0-9679121-2-1*) College Publishing.
Rendell, Ruth. The Babes in the Wood. 2003. 336p. 25.00 (*1-4000-4930-X*, Crown) Crown Publishing Group.
—Barker VC. 1997. (Chief Inspector Wexford Novel Ser.). (Illus.). 320p. 29.95 o.s.i (*0-385-25682-5*) Doubleday Publishing.
—The Best Man to Die. reprint ed. lib. bdg. 20.95 (*0-89190-887-0*, American Reprint Co.) Amereon, Ltd.
—The Best Man to Die. 1987. 208p. mass mkt. 6.99 (*0-345-34530-4*) Ballantine Bks.
—The Bridesmaid. 1990. 272p. mass mkt. 7.99 (*0-7704-2383-3*) Bantam Bks.
—The Bridesmaid. 1989. 272p. 22.95 o.p. (*0-385-25223-4*) Doubleday Publishing.
—The Bridesmaid. 1989. 259p. 17.95 o.s.i (*0-89296-388-3*) Mysterious Pr.
—The Bridesmaid. 1990. mass mkt. 4.95 o.s.i (*0-445-40912-6*) Warner Bks., Inc.
—The Crocodile Bird, Set. abr. ed. 1993. audio 16.95 (*1-55927-258-9*, 390580) Audio Renaissance.
—The Crocodile Bird. 1997. 368p. mass mkt. 7.99 (*0-7704-2598-4*) Bantam Bks.
—The Crocodile Bird. unabr. collector's ed. 1994. audio 56.00 (*0-7366-2670-0*, 3407) Books on Tape, Inc.
—The Crocodile Bird. 1994. 384p. mass mkt. 6.99 (*0-440-21865-9*) Dell Publishing.
—The Crocodile Bird. 1993. 368p. 25.95 o.s.i (*0-385-25429-6*) Doubleday Publishing.
—The Crocodile Bird, unabr. ed. 1994. audio 78.00 (*1-55690-944-6*, 93440E7) Recorded Bks., LLC.
—Death Notes. (Chief Inspector Wexford Ser.). 1986. 224p. mass mkt. 6.99 (*0-345-34198-8*); 1982. mass mkt. 2.50 o.p. (*0-345-30272-9*) Ballantine Bks.
—Death Notes. l.t. ed. 1982. (General Ser.). 352p. lib. bdg. 13.95 o.p. (*0-8161-3335-2*, Macmillan Reference USA) Gale Group.
—Death Notes. 1981. 207p. 9.95 o.p. (*0-394-52078-5*, Pantheon) Knopf Publishing Group.
—From Doon with Death. (Chief Inspector Wexford Ser.). 1988. 208p. mass mkt. 6.99 (*0-345-34817-6*); 1985. mass mkt. 2.95 o.s.i (*0-345-32414-5*); 1980. mass mkt. 1.95 o.p. (*0-345-29287-1*); 1975. mass mkt. 1.25 o.p. (*0-345-24799-X*) Ballantine Bks.
—Going Wrong. l.t. ed. 1992. pap. 15.95 o.p. (*0-7927-0822-9*); 302p. 19.95 o.p. (*0-7927-0821-0*, E0016) BBC Audiobooks America.
—Going Wrong. 1991. 272p. mass mkt. 6.99 (*0-7704-2435-X*) Bantam Bks.
—Going Wrong. unabr. collector's ed. 1991. audio 48.00 (*0-7366-1920-8*, 2744) Books on Tape, Inc.
—Going Wrong. 1990. 256p. 24.95 o.p. (*0-385-25281-1*) Doubleday Publishing.
—Going Wrong. 1990. 304p. 18.95 o.p. (*0-89296-389-1*) Mysterious Pr.
—Going Wrong. 1993. 3.99 o.p. (*0-517-09872-5*) Random Hse. Value Publishing.
—Going Wrong. 1991. mass mkt. 4.99 o.s.i (*0-446-40028-9*) Warner Bks., Inc.
—A Guilty Thing Surprised. Date not set. 174p. 19.95 (*0-8488-2381-8*) Amereon, Ltd.
—A Guilty Thing Surprised. 1987. (Chief Inspector Wexford Mysteries Ser.). 208p. mass mkt. 6.99 (*0-345-34811-7*) Ballantine Bks.
—Harm Done. l.t. ed. 1999. (Inspector Reginald Wexford Mystery Novel Ser.). 26.95 o.p. (*1-56895-805-6*, Wheeler Publishing, Inc.) Gale Group.
—Harm Done: A New Inspector Wexford Mystery. 2000. (Inspector Reginald Wexford Mystery Novel Ser.). 368p. pap. 12.00 (*0-375-72484-2*, Vintage) Knopf Publishing Group.
—The Killing Doll. 1985. 288p. mass mkt. 4.95 o.s.i (*0-345-31199-X*) Ballantine Bks.
—The Killing Doll. l.t. ed. 1984. (General Ser.). 354p. 15.95 o.p. (*0-8161-3720-X*, Macmillan Reference USA) Gale Group.
—The Killing Doll. 1984. 258p. 12.95 o.s.i (*0-394-53097-7*, Pantheon) Knopf Publishing Group.
—Kissing the Gunner's Daughter. 1997. (Inspector Reginald Wexford Mystery Novel Ser.). 368p. mass mkt. 6.99 (*0-7704-2515-1*) Bantam Bks.
—Kissing the Gunner's Daughter. 1992. (Inspector Reginald Wexford Mystery Novel Ser.). 378p. 19.95 o.p. (*0-89296-390-5*) Mysterious Pr.
—Kissing the Gunner's Daughter. 1993. (Inspector Reginald Wexford Mystery Novel Ser.). 384p. mass mkt. 6.99 (*0-446-40334-2*) Warner Bks., Inc.
—Murder Being Once Done. 1998. (Wexford Mystery Ser.). 21.95 (*0-89190-372-0*) Amereon, Ltd.
—Murder Being Once Done. 1999. (Wexford Mystery Ser.). 224p. pap. 11.00 (*0-679-70488-4*); pap. 11.00 (*0-375-70488-4*) Knopf Publishing Group. (Vintage).
—Murder Being Once Done. 1992. pap. o.p. (*0-09-174313-3*) Random Hse. of Canada, Ltd.
—A New Lease of Death. Barzun, Jacques & Taqylor, W. H., eds. 1982. 214p. lib. bdg. 18.00 o.p. (*0-8240-4998-5*) Garland Publishing, Inc.
—No More Dying Then. 21.95 (*0-89190-373-9*) Amereon, Ltd.
—No More Dying Then. 1999. 224p. pap. 11.00 (*0-679-70489-2*); pap. 12.00 (*0-375-70489-2*) Knopf Publishing Group. (Vintage).
—Put on by Cunning. 1992. 208p. mass mkt. o.p. (*0-09-927730-1*) Random Hse. of Canada, Ltd. CAN. *Dist:* Random Hse., Inc.
—Road Rage. 1998. (Chief Inspector Wexford Novel Ser.). 400p. mass mkt. 6.99 (*0-440-22602-3*); mass mkt. 5.99 (*0-440-29558-0*) Dell Publishing.
—Road Rage. l.t. ed. 1997. (Chief Inspector Wexford Novel Ser.). pap. 25.00 o.p. (*0-7838-8243-2*, Macmillan Reference USA) Gale Group.
—Road Rage: An Inspector Wexford Novel. 1997. 384p. 29.95 o.s.i (*0-385-25681-7*) Bantam Bks.
—Shake Hands Forever. 1980. 208p. mass mkt. 3.50 o.s.i (*0-553-25970-9*) Bantam Bks.
—Shake Hands Forever. 2000. (Crime - Black Lizard Ser.). 192p. pap. 11.00 (*0-375-70495-7*, Vintage) Knopf Publishing Group.
—A Sight for Sore Eyes. unabr. collector's ed. 1999. audio 72.00 (*0-7366-4504-7*, 4939) Books on Tape, Inc.
—A Sight for Sore Eyes. aut. ed. 1999. 24.00 (*0-609-50208-5*) Crown Publishing Group.
—A Sight for Sore Eyes. 2000. 384p. reprint ed. mass mkt. 6.99 (*0-440-23544-8*) Dell Publishing.
—A Sight for Sore Eyes. 1999. 340p. o.s.i (*0-385-25855-0*) Doubleday Canada, Ltd. CAN. *Dist:* Random Hse., Inc.
—A Sight for Sore Eyes. 1999. o.p. (*0-7838-8484-2*, Macmillan Reference USA) Gale Group.
—A Sight for Sore Eyes, Set. abr. ed. 1999. audio 18.00 Highsmith Inc.
—A Sight for Sore Eyes, Set. abr. ed. 1999. audio 18.00 o.s.i (*0-375-40570-4*, 396145, RH Audio) Random Hse. Audio Publishing Group.
—A Sight for Sore Eyes. l.t. ed. 1999. 352p. 24.00 (*0-375-70573-2*) Random Hse. Large Print.
—A Sight for Sore Eyes, unabr. ed. 1999. audio 91.00 (*0-7887-2505-X*, 95577E7) Recorded Bks., LLC.
—Simisola. 1997. (Inspector Reginald Wexford Mystery Novel Ser.). 336p. mass mkt. 6.50 (*0-7704-2714-6*) Bantam Bks.
—Simisola. 1996. (Chief Inspector Wexford Novel Ser.). 384p. mass mkt. 6.99 (*0-440-22202-8*) Dell Publishing.
—Simisola. l.t. ed. 1995. (Inspector Reginald Wexford Mystery Novel Ser.). 512p. 22.00 o.p. (*0-7838-1588-3*, Macmillan Reference USA) Gale Group.
—Simisola. l.t. ed. 1995. (Inspector Reginald Wexford Mystery Novel Ser.). 488p. 22.00 o.s.i (*0-679-76502-6*) Random Hse. Large Print.
—Sins of the Fathers. 1985. mass mkt. 2.95 o.p. (*0-345-32740-3*); 1980. mass mkt. 1.95 o.p. (*0-345-29283-9*); 1976. mass mkt. 1.25 o.p. (*0-345-24862-7*) Ballantine Bks.
—Sins of the Fathers. 1994. reprint ed. lib. bdg. 29.95 (*1-56849-322-3*) Buccaneer Bks., Inc.
—A Sleeping Life. lib. bdg. 19.95 (*0-8488-2019-3*) Amereon, Ltd.
—A Sleeping Life. 1998. (Chief Inspector Wexford Mysteries Ser.). audio 29.95 (*0-7540-7523-0*) BBC Audiobooks America.
—A Sleeping Life. 1986. 192p. mass mkt. 3.50 o.s.i (*0-553-25969-5*) Bantam Bks.
—A Sleeping Life. 1978. 180p. 7.95 o.p. (*0-385-13224-7*) Doubleday Publishing.
—A Sleeping Life. 1979. (General Ser.). 344p. lib. bdg. 11.95 o.p. (*0-8161-6711-7*, Macmillan Reference USA) Gale Group.
—A Sleeping Life. 2000. (Crime - Black Lizard Ser.). 192p. pap. 11.00 (*0-375-70493-0*, Vintage) Knopf Publishing Group.
—Some Lie & Some Die. lib. bdg. 20.95 (*0-8488-2020-7*) Amereon, Ltd.
—Some Lie & Some Die. 1999. (Vintage Crime/Black Lizard Ser.). (Illus.). 192p. pap. 11.00 (*0-375-70490-6*, Vintage) Knopf Publishing Group.
—Speaker of Mandarin. lib. bdg. 21.95 (*0-8488-2016-9*) Amereon, Ltd.
—Speaker of Mandarin. 1984. (Chief Inspector Wexford Ser.). 224p. mass mkt. 5.99 o.s.i (*0-345-30274-5*) Ballantine Bks.
—Speaker of Mandarin. 1983. 223p. 12.95 o.s.i (*0-394-52272-9*, Pantheon) Knopf Publishing Group.
—An Unkindness of Ravens. 1986. 352p. mass mkt. 6.99 (*0-345-32746-2*) Ballantine Bks.
—An Unkindness of Ravens. 1992. mass mkt. o.p. (*0-09-174862-3*) Random Hse. of Canada, Ltd.
—The Veiled One. 1989. (Inspector Reginald Wexford Mystery Novel Ser.). 320p. mass mkt. 6.99 (*0-345-35994-1*) Ballantine Bks.
—The Veiled One. l.t. ed. 1989. (Inspector Reginald Wexford Mystery Novel Ser.). 450p. lib. bdg. 19.95 o.p. (*0-8161-4804-X*, Macmillan Reference USA) Gale Group.
—The Veiled One. 1990. 4.99 o.p. (*0-517-05108-7*) Random Hse. Value Publishing.

—Wolf to the Slaughter. 1987. 224p. mass mkt. 6.99 (*0-345-34520-7*); 1983. mass mkt. 2.25 o.p. (*0-345-31744-0*); 1980. mass mkt. 1.95 o.p. (*0-345-29284-7*); 1976. mass mkt. 1.25 o.p. (*0-345-24817-1*) Ballantine Bks.

Reynolds. Autobiography of a Thief. 2000. (Illus.). xi, 398p. 27.95 (*0-593-03779-0*); 525p. pap. 10.95 (*0-552-14275-1*) Transworld Publishers Ltd. GBR. *Dist:* Trafalgar Square.

Rhea, Nicholas. Garland for a Dead Maiden. l.t. ed. 2003. (Magna Large Print Ser.). 368p. 32.50 (*0-7505-2054-X*) Magna Large Print Bks. GBR. *Dist:* Ulverscroft Large Print Bks., Ltd., Ulverscroft Large Print Canada, Ltd.

Rhode, John & Dickson, Carter. Fatal Descent. 1987. (Mystery Classics Ser.). 160p. reprint ed. pap. 5.95 o.p. (*0-486-25409-7*) Dover Pubns., Inc.

Rhodes, Dan. Anthropology. 2000. 224p. pap. 15.00 o.s.i (*0-8129-9223-7*) Random House Adult Trade Publishing Group.

Rhodes, Elvi. The Bright One. 2000. 476p. pap. 9.95 (*0-552-14057-0*) Transworld Publishers Ltd. GBR. *Dist:* Trafalgar Square.

—Doctor Rose. 2000. 313p. (J). pap. 9.95 (*0-552-12607-1*) Transworld Publishers Ltd. GBR. *Dist:* Trafalgar Square.

—The Mountain. 2000. 317p. 27.95 (*0-593-03932-7*); 381p. pap. 10.95 (*0-552-14400-2*) Transworld Publishers Ltd. GBR. *Dist:* Trafalgar Square.

—Opal. l.t. ed. 1985. 432p. o.p. (*0-7089-1289-3*, Ulverscroft) Thorpe, F. A. Pubs.

—Opal. 2000. pap. 8.95 (*0-552-12367-6*) Transworld Publishers Ltd. GBR. *Dist:* Trafalgar Square.

Rice, Patricia. All a Woman Wants. 2001. (Signet Historical Romance Ser.). 384p. mass mkt. 6.99 (*0-451-20289-9*, Signet Bks.) NAL.

—Merely Magic. l.t. ed. 2000. (Romance Ser.). 591p. 26.95 (*0-7862-3024-X*) Thorndike Pr.

Richardson, Dorothy. Pilgrimage Vol. 1: Pointed Roofs, Backwater, Honeycomb. 1989. 496p. reprint ed. pap. text 12.50 (*0-252-06076-8*) Univ. of Illinois Pr.

Richardson, Robert. The Lazarus Tree. l.t. ed. 1996. (G. K. Hall Nightingale Ser.). 303p. pap. 17.95 o.p. (*0-7838-1483-6*, Macmillan Reference USA) Gale Group.

—The Lazarus Tree. 1992. 208p. 17.95 o.p. (*0-312-08232-0*, Saint Martin's Minotaur) St. Martin's Pr.

Richardson, Samuel. Clarissa: Or the History of a Young Lady. Ross, Angus, ed. & intro. by. 1986. (Classics Ser.). 1536p. 24.95 (*0-14-043215-9*, Penguin Classics) Viking Penguin.

—Pamela. 1976. 3.25 o.p. (*0-460-01683-0*); 1955. 10.50 o.p. (*0-460-00683-5*); 1955. 6.00 o.p. (*0-460-00684-3*); Vol. 2. 1976. 3.25 o.p. (*0-460-01684-9*) Dutton/Plume. (Dutton).

—Pamela. Duncan-Eaves, T. C. & Kimpel, B. D., eds. 1971. (C). pap. 16.36 (*0-395-11152-8*, Riverside Editions) Houghton Mifflin Co.

—Pamela. 1991. 453p. pap. 7.95 (*0-460-87064-5*, Everyman's Classic Library in Paperback) Tuttle Publishing.

—Pamela. Sabor, Petr, ed. 1981. (Penguin Classics Ser.). 544p. 9.00 (*0-14-043140-3*) Viking Penguin.

—Pamela: Or Virtue Rewarded. 2001. (Complete Novels of Mr. Samuel Richardson Ser. : Vol. 1). (Illus.). (Orig.). reprint ed. Pt. 1. 280p. pap. text 28.00 (*0-7426-5127-4*); Pt. 3. 332p. pap. text 28.00 (*0-7426-5129-0*); Pt. 4. 346p. pap. text 28.00 (*0-7426-5130-4*) Classic Bks.

—Pamela: Or Virtue Rewarded. Keymer, Thomas & Wakely, Alice, eds. 2001. (Oxford World's Classics Ser.). (Illus.). 592p. (Orig.). pap. 7.95 (*0-19-282960-2*) Oxford Univ. Pr., Inc.

Richmond, Grace. The Doctor's Secret. l.t. ed. 1994. 19.95 o.p. (*0-7927-1911-5*); pap. 17.95 o.p. (*0-7927-1910-7*) BBC Audiobooks America.

Rickman, Phil. The Cure of Souls. 2003. 496p. pap. 7.95 (*0-330-48756-6*) Pan Bks. Ltd. GBR. *Dist:* Trafalgar Square.

—The Cure of Souls. 2002. (Illus.). 485p. 28.00 (*0-333-90623-3*) Trafalgar Square.

Ridpath, Michael. Free to Trade: A Novel of Suspense. 1994. 346p. 23.00 o.p. (*0-06-017630-X*) HarperTrade.

Riley, Gwendolyn. Cold Water. 2003. 176p. 20.00 (*0-7867-1109-4*, Carroll & Graf Pubs.) Avalon Publishing Group.

Riley, Joan. Romance. 1998. 240p. pap. 14.95 (*0-7043-4508-0*) Women's Pr., Ltd., The GBR. *Dist:* Trafalgar Square.

Ripley, Mike. Angel City. 1995. 192p. 18.95 o.p. (*0-312-11742-6*, Saint Martin's Minotaur) St. Martin's Pr.

Rizzolo, S. K. The Rose in the Wheel. 226p. 2003. pap. 14.95 o.s.i (*1-890208-89-2*); 2002. 24.95 (*1-890208-85-X*) Poisoned Pen Pr.

Robards, Karen. Scandalous. 2001. 368p. pap. 7.99 (*0-7434-1059-9*, Pocket) Simon & Schuster.

Robb, Candace. The Apothecary Rose. unabr. ed. 1999. audio compact disk 99.95 (*0-7531-0706-6*, 107066); 1997. (Owen Archer Mystery Ser.: Vol. 1). audio 69.95 ISIS Audio Bks. GBR. *Dist:* Ulverscroft Large Print Bks., Ltd.

—A Gift of Sanctuary: An Owen Archer Mystery. 2000. (Owen Archer Mystery Ser.: Vol. 6). 320p. mass mkt. 6.99 (*0-312-97477-9*, St. Martin's Paperbacks); 1998. 304p. 22.95 o.p. (*0-312-19266-5*, Saint Martin's Minotaur) St. Martin's Pr.

—A Gift of Sanctuary: An Owen Archer Mystery. l.t. ed. 1999. (Mystery Ser.). 475p. 28.95 (*0-7862-1910-6*); (*0-7540-1302-2*); (*0-7540-2226-9*) Thorndike Pr.

—The King's Bishop. unabr. ed. 1997. audio 69.95 (*0-7531-0084-3*, 970704) ISIS Audio Bks. GBR. *Dist:* Ulverscroft Large Print Bks., Ltd.

—The King's Bishop. l.t. unabr. ed. 1999. (Illus.). 416p. 32.50 (*0-7531-5951-1*, 159511) ISIS Large Print Bks. GBR. *Dist:* Ulverscroft Large Print Bks., Ltd.

—The King's Bishop. 384p. 1996. 23.95 (*0-312-14638-8*, Saint Martin's Minotaur); Vol. 1. 1997. mass mkt. 6.99 (*0-312-96282-7*, St. Martin's Paperbacks) St. Martin's Pr.

—The Lady Chapel. unabr. ed. 1997. audio 84.95 (*0-7531-0086-X*, 970107) ISIS Audio Bks. GBR. *Dist:* Ulverscroft Large Print Bks., Ltd.

—The Lady Chapel. 1995. 287p. mass mkt. 6.99 (*0-312-95460-3*, St. Martin's Paperbacks); 1994. 304p. 20.95 o.p. (*0-312-11409-5*, Saint Martin's Minotaur) St. Martin's Pr.

—The Nun's Tale. unabr. ed. 1997. audio 69.95 ISIS Audio Bks. GBR. *Dist:* Ulverscroft Large Print Bks., Ltd.

—The Nun's Tale: An Owen Archer Mystery. 1996. (Nun's Tale Ser.: Vol. 1). 355p. mass mkt. 6.50 (*0-312-95982-6*, St. Martin's Paperbacks); 1995. 288p. 23.95 o.p. (*0-312-13573-4*, Saint Martin's Minotaur) St. Martin's Pr.

—The Riddle of St. Leonard's: An Owen Archer Mystery. 1997. 256p. (YA). 21.95 (*0-312-16983-3*, Saint Martin's Minotaur); Vol. 1. 1998. 304p. mass mkt. 6.99 (*0-312-96651-2*, St. Martin's Paperbacks) St. Martin's Pr.

Roberson, Jennifer. Lady of the Forest. 1999. 608p. pap. 14.00 o.s.i (*1-57566-400-3*, Kensington Bks.); 1995. 608p. mass mkt. 12.00 o.s.i (*0-8217-4891-2*, Kensington Bks.); 1993. 768p. mass mkt. 5.99 o.s.i (*0-8217-4284-1*, Zebra Bks.); 1992. 608p. mass mkt. 22.00 o.s.i (*0-8217-3919-0*, Zebra Bks.) Kensington Publishing Corp.

Roberts, Barrie. Sherlock Holmes & the Crosby Murder. 2002. 224p. 24.00 (*0-7867-1016-0*, Carroll & Graf Pubs.) Avalon Publishing Group.

Roberts, G. Cracker Best Boys. 2000. 247p. 22.95 (*0-312-20498-1*, Saint Martin's Minotaur) St. Martin's Pr.

Robinson, Pamela. Pride & Prejudice: Dramatic Reading. 1968. audio 11.95 Norton Pubs., Inc., Jeffrey /Audio-Forum.

Robinson, Peter. Aftermath: An Inspector Banks Novel. 2001. 384p. 25.00 (*0-380-97832-6*, Morrow, William & Co.) Morrow/Avon.

—Blood at the Root. 1998. (Inspector Banks Mystery Ser.: No. 9). 320p. mass mkt. 5.99 (*0-380-79476-4*, Avon Bks.) Morrow/Avon.

—Blood at the Root: An Inspector Banks Mystery. 1997. 352p. mass mkt. 22.00 o.p. (*0-380-97580-7*, Avon Bks.) Morrow/Avon.

—Cold Is the Grave: A Novel of Suspense. 2001. 448p. mass mkt. 6.99 (*0-380-80935-4*, Avon Bks.); 2000. 384p. 24.00 (*0-380-97808-3*, Morrow, William & Co.) Morrow/Avon.

—Dead Right. 320p. mass mkt. (*0-14-026716-6*) Penguin Group (USA) Inc.

—A Dedicated Man. 1991. 272p. 18.95 o.s.i (*0-684-19265-9*, Macmillan Reference USA) Gale Group.

—A Dedicated Man. l.t. ed. 1991. (Magna Large Print Ser.). 396p. o.p. (*1-85057-831-1*) Magna Large Print Bks. GBR. *Dist:* Ulverscroft Large Print Canada, Ltd.

—A Dedicated Man. 1992. (Inspector Banks Mystery Ser.). 352p. mass mkt. 7.50 (*0-380-71645-3*, Avon Bks.) Morrow/Avon.

—A Dedicated Man. 272p. pap. (*0-14-009665-5*) Penguin Group (USA) Inc.

—Final Account: An Inspector Banks Mystery. (Inspector Banks Mystery Ser.). 1995. 320p. 21.95 o.s.i (*0-425-14935-8*, Prime Crime); 1996. 352p. reprint ed. mass mkt. 5.99 o.s.i (*0-425-15382-7*) Berkley Publishing Group.

—Final Account: An Inspector Banks Mystery. 336p. mass mkt. (*0-14-024185-X*) Penguin Group (USA) Inc.

—Final Account: An Inspector Banks Mystery, Set. abr. ed. 1995. (Inspector Banks Mystery Ser.). audio 17.00 (*1-56876-045-0*, 393291) Soundlines Entertainment, Inc.

—Gallows View. 2000. (Inspector Banks Mystery Ser.). 336p. mass mkt. 7.50 (*0-380-71400-0*, Avon Bks.) Morrow/Avon.

—Gallows View: An Inspector Banks Mystery. 1997. 320p. mass mkt. 5.99 o.s.i (*0-425-15672-9*, Prime Crime) Berkley Publishing Group.

—Gallows View: An Inspector Banks Mystery. 1990. 224p. 17.95 o.s.i (*0-684-19266-7*); 1991. 415p. reprint ed. lib. bdg. 11.95 o.p. (*1-85057-940-7*) Gale Group. (Macmillan Reference USA).

—Gallows View: An Inspector Banks Mystery. l.t. ed. 1991. (Magna Large Print Ser.). 415p. o.p. (*1-85057-939-3*) Magna Large Print Bks. GBR. *Dist:* Ulverscroft Large Print Canada, Ltd.

—Gallows View: An Inspector Banks Mystery. 240p. pap. (*0-14-009663-9*) Penguin Group (USA) Inc.

—The Hanging Valley. 1994. (Inspector Banks Mystery Ser.). 272p. mass mkt. 5.99 o.s.i (*0-425-14196-9*) Berkley Publishing Group.

—The Hanging Valley. 1992. (Chief Inspector Banks Ser.: No. 4). 288p. 20.00 o.p. (*0-684-19393-0*, Macmillan Reference USA) Gale Group.

—The Hanging Valley. l.t. ed. 1992. (Mystery Ser.). 406p. 29.99 o.p. (*0-7505-0345-9*) Magna Large Print Bks. GBR. *Dist:* Ulverscroft Large Print Bks., Ltd., Ulverscroft Large Print Canada, Ltd.

—The Hanging Valley. 288p. pap. (*0-14-011544-7*) Penguin Group (USA) Inc.

—In a Dry Season. 2000. 480p. mass mkt. 7.50 (*0-380-79477-2*); 1999. 422p. 24.00 (*0-380-97581-5*) Morrow/Avon. (Avon Bks.).

—In a Dry Season. 456p. pap. (*0-330-39201-8*) Pan Bks. Ltd.

—In a Dry Season. 352p. pap. (*0-14-028177-0*) Penguin Bks. Canada, Ltd.

—Innocent Graves: An Inspector Banks Mystery. 400p. 1996. 21.95 o.p. (*0-425-15315-0*); 1997. reprint ed. mass mkt. 5.99 o.s.i (*0-425-15779-2*) Berkley Publishing Group. (Prime Crime).

—Innocent Graves: An Inspector Banks Mystery. 384p. mass mkt. (*0-14-025689-X*) Penguin Group (USA) Inc.

—Innocent Graves: An Inspector Banks Mystery, Set. abr. ed. 1997. (Inspector Banks Mystery Ser.). audio 17.00 (*1-56876-060-4*, 394919) Soundlines Entertainment, Inc.

—A Necessary End. 1992. 320p. text 19.95 (*0-684-19385-X*, Macmillan Reference USA) Gale Group.

—A Necessary End. l.t. ed. 1992. (Magna Large Print Ser.). 466p. 29.99 (*0-7505-0343-2*) Magna Large Print Bks. GBR. *Dist:* Ulverscroft Large Print Bks., Ltd., Ulverscroft Large Print Canada, Ltd.

—A Necessary End. 1993. (Inspector Banks Mystery Ser.). 352p. mass mkt. 6.99 (*0-380-71946-0*, Avon Bks.) Morrow/Avon.

—A Necessary End. pap. (*0-14-011545-5*) Penguin Group (USA) Inc.

—Past Reason Hated: An Inspector Banks Mystery. 1994. (Inspector Banks Mystery Ser.). 320p. mass mkt. 5.99 o.s.i (*0-425-14489-5*, Prime Crime) Berkley Publishing Group.

—Past Reason Hated: An Inspector Banks Mystery. 1993. 352p. 20.00 o.p. (*0-684-19529-1*, Macmillan Reference USA) Gale Group.

—Past Reason Hated: An Inspector Banks Mystery. 2000. 384p. mass mkt. 6.99 (*0-380-73328-5*, Avon Bks.) Morrow/Avon.

—Past Reason Hated: An Inspector Banks Mystery. 352p. mass mkt. (*0-14-014842-6*) Penguin Group (USA) Inc.

—Playing with Fire. 2004. 368p. 23.95 (*0-06-019877-X*, Morrow, William & Co.) Morrow/Avon.

—Wednesday's Child. 1995. 320p. mass mkt. 5.99 o.s.i (*0-425-14834-3*, Prime Crime) Berkley Publishing Group.

—Wednesday's Child. 2002. 352p. mass mkt. 6.99 (*0-380-82049-8*) Morrow/Avon.

—Wednesday's Child. 2001. (Inspector Banks Mystery Ser.). 357p. pap. (*0-330-48219-X*) Pan Bks. Ltd.

—Wednesday's Child. 352p. mass mkt. (*0-14-017474-5*) Penguin Group (USA) Inc.

—Wednesday's Child. 1994. 352p. 20.00 (*0-684-19644-1*, Scribner) Simon & Schuster.

Robinson, Roxana. Summer Light. 1991. 208p. pap. 9.00 o.p. (*0-06-097407-9*, Perennial) HarperTrade.

—Summer Light. 1995. 211p. reprint ed. pap. 14.95 (*0-87451-738-9*, Hardscrabble Bks.) Univ. Pr. of New England.

—Summer Light. 1988. 16.95 o.p. (*0-670-82248-5*) Viking Penguin.

Robinson, Suzanne. Just Before Midnight. 2000. (Meet Me at Midnight Ser.). 336p. mass mkt. 5.99 o.s.i (*0-553-57961-4*) Bantam Bks.

Roe, Jill. Angels Flying Slowly. l.t. ed. 1996. 270p. pap. 20.95 o.p. (*0-7838-1820-3*, Macmillan Reference USA) Gale Group.

—Angels Flying Slowly. 1995. 224p. 20.95 o.p. (*0-312-13427-4*) St. Martin's Pr.

—A New Leaf. 1997. 224p. 20.95 o.p. (*0-312-15603-0*) St. Martin's Pr.

—A New Leaf. l.t. ed. 1997. (Romance Ser.). 310p. 24.95 (*0-7862-1070-2*) Thorndike Pr.

—A New Leaf. l.t. ed. 1997. (Ulverscroft Large Print Ser.). 368p. 29.99 o.p. (*0-7089-3817-5*, Ulverscroft) Thorpe, F. A. Pubs. GBR. *Dist:* Ulverscroft Large Print Bks., Ltd., Ulverscroft Large Print Canada, Ltd.

—A Well Kept Secret. l.t. ed. 1999. 256p. 32.50 (*0-7531-6075-7*) ISIS Large Print Bks. GBR. *Dist:* Ulverscroft Large Print Bks., Ltd., Ulverscroft Large Print Canada, Ltd.

Rogers, Evelyn. Devil in the Dark. 2001. 400p. mass mkt. 5.99 (*0-505-52407-4*, Love Spell) Dorchester Publishing Co., Inc.

—Raven. 1995. 384p. mass mkt. 4.99 o.s.i (*0-8217-4800-9*, Zebra Bks.) Kensington Publishing Corp.

Rogers, Jane. Mr. Wroe's Virgins. 1992. 256p. 21.95 o.p. (*0-571-16194-4*) Faber & Faber, Inc.

—Mr. Wroe's Virgins. 2000. 288p. pap. 13.00 (*0-618-06613-6*, Mariner Bks.) Houghton Mifflin Co. Trade & Reference Div.

—Mr. Wroe's Virgins. 1999. 288p. 24.95 (*0-87951-702-6*) Overlook Pr., The.

Rogers, Rosemary. A Reckless Encounter. abr. ed. 2001. audio 9.99 (*1-55204-288-X*, MIR-1288) Durkin Hayes Publishing Ltd.

—A Reckless Encounter. 2001. 408p. mass mkt. (*1-55166-852-1*, Mira Bks.) Harlequin Enterprises, Ltd.

Rogow, Roberta. The Problem of the Evil Editor: A Charles Dodgson/Arthur Conan Doyle Mystery. 2000. (Charles Dodgson/Arthur Conan Doyle Mysteries Ser.). 298p. 23.95 (*0-312-20903-7*, Saint Martin's Minotaur) St. Martin's Pr.

—Problem of the Spiteful Spiritualist. 1999. (Charles Dodgson/Arthur Conan Doyle Mysteries Ser.). 282p. 23.95 (*0-312-20570-8*, Saint Martin's Minotaur) St. Martin's Pr.

—The Problem of the Surly Servant. 2001. (Charles Dodgson/Arthur Conan Doyle Mysteries Ser.). 288p. 24.95 (*0-312-26638-3*, Saint Martin's Minotaur) St. Martin's Pr.

Roiphe, Katie. Still She Haunts Me. 2002. 240p. pap. 12.95 (*0-385-33530-X*, Delta) Dell Publishing.

—Still She Haunts Me: A Novel of Lewis Carroll & Alice Liddell. 2002. E-Book 11.50 (*0-440-33385-7*, Delta) Dell Publishing.

Ross, Jonathan. Daphne Dead & Done For. l.t. ed. 1992. (Lythway Ser.). 320p. lib. bdg. 20.50 o.p. (*0-7451-1440-7*, Macmillan Reference USA) Gale Group.

—Daphne Dead & Done For. 1991. 15.95 o.p. (*0-312-05408-4*, Saint Martin's Minotaur) St. Martin's Pr.

—Dead Eye. 1984. 192p. 11.95 o.p. (*0-312-18495-6*) St. Martin's Pr.

—Dead Eye. l.t. ed. 1985. (Ulverscroft Large Print Ser.). 384p. 29.99 o.p. (*0-7089-1394-6*, Ulverscroft) Thorpe, F. A. Pubs. GBR. *Dist:* Ulverscroft Large Print Bks., Ltd., Ulverscroft Large Print Canada, Ltd.

—Death's Head. 1983. 256p. 11.95 o.p. (*0-312-18882-X*) St. Martin's Pr.

—Dropped Dead. 1985. 176p. 11.95 o.p. (*0-312-21973-3*) St. Martin's Pr.

—Fate Accomplished. 1987. 192p. 13.95 o.p. (*0-312-00597-0*) St. Martin's Pr.

—Murder Be Hanged. 1993. 192p. 17.95 o.p. (*0-312-08857-4*, Saint Martin's Minotaur) St. Martin's Pr.

—Murder! Murder! Burning Bright. 1997. 176p. text 20.95 o.p. (*0-312-15599-9*, Saint Martin's Minotaur) St. Martin's Pr.

—None the Worse for a Hanging. 1995. 192p. 19.95 o.p. (*0-312-13572-6*, Saint Martin's Minotaur) St. Martin's Pr.

—Sudden Departures. 1988. 192p. 14.95 o.p. (*0-312-02292-1*, Saint Martin's Minotaur) St. Martin's Pr.

—This Too, Too Sullied Flesh. 1998. 299 p. pap. (*0-7540-3429-1*); audio 54.95 (*0-7540-0233-0*, CAB 1656) BBC Audiobooks America.

—This Too, Too Sullied Flesh. l.t. ed. 1998. (Nightingale Ser.). 304p. pap. 20.95 (*0-7838-0290-0*) Thorndike Pr.

—A Time for Dying. l.t. ed. 1990. 328p. lib. bdg. 20.95 o.p. (*0-7451-1131-9*, Macmillan Reference USA) Gale Group.

—A Time for Dying. 1989. 192p. 14.95 o.p. (*0-312-03441-5*, Saint Martin's Minotaur) St. Martin's Pr.

Ross, Kate. A Broken Vessel. 1995. (Crime Ser.). 304p. pap. 6.99 (*0-14-023453-5*, Penguin Bks.) Penguin Group (USA) Inc.

—A Broken Vessel. 1994. (Julian Kestrel Mystery Ser.). 304p. 18.95 o.p. (*0-670-84999-5*, Viking) Viking Penguin.

—Cut to the Quick. 1994. (Crime Ser.). 352p. pap. 6.99 (*0-14-023394-6*, Penguin Bks.) Penguin Group (USA) Inc.

—Cut to the Quick. 1993. 352p. 19.00 o.p. (*0-670-84847-6*, Viking) Viking Penguin.

—The Devil in Music. 1998. (Julian Kestrel Mystery Ser.). 480p. pap. 6.99 (*0-14-026364-0*) Penguin Group (USA) Inc.

—The Devil in Music. 1997. (Julian Kestrel Mystery Ser.). 464p. 24.95 o.s.i (*0-670-86359-9*) Viking Penguin.

For book reviews, descriptive annotations, tables of contents, cover images, author biographies & additional information, updated daily, subscribe to **www.booksinprint.com** 767

—Whom the Gods Love. 1996. (Julian Kestrel Mystery Ser.). 400p. pap. 6.99 (*0-14-024767-X*, Penguin Bks.) Penguin Group (USA) Inc.
—Whom the Gods Love. 1995. (Julian Kestrel Mystery Ser.). 400p. 20.95 o.p. (*0-670-86207-X*, Viking) Viking Penguin.
Ross-Russell, Noel, contrib. by. A Voice Within. 1998. (*1-871871-39-5*) Open Gate Pr. GBR. *Dist:* Paul & Co. Pubs. Consortium, Inc.
Rossiter, Clare. Orphanage Miss. l.t. ed. 1996. (Nightingale Ser.). pap. 17.95 (*0-7838-1623-5*, Macmillan Reference USA) Gale Group.
Roth, Philip. The Professor of Desire. 1977. 263p. 8.95 o.p. (*0-374-23756-5*) Farrar, Straus & Giroux.
—The Professor of Desire. 1994. 272p. pap. 13.00 (*0-679-74900-4*, Vintage) Knopf Publishing Group.
Rowell, Patricia Frances. A Perilous Attraction. 2002. (Harlequin Historicals Ser.: No. 621). 296p. mass mkt. (*0-373-29221-X*, Harlequin Bks.) Harlequin Enterprises, Ltd.
Rowland, Peter. The Disappearance of Edwin Drood. 1992. 176p. 16.95 o.p. (*0-312-06953-7*, Saint Martin's Minotaur) St. Martin's Pr.
Rowlands, Betty. Exhaustive Enquiries: A Melissa Craig Mystery. 1995. 240p. mass mkt. 4.99 o.p. (*0-425-14689-8*, Prime Crime) Berkley Publishing Group.
—Exhaustive Enquiries: A Melissa Craig Mystery. 1994. 252p. 19.95 o.p. (*0-8027-3180-5*) Walker & Co.
—Finishing Touch: A Melissa Craig Mystery. 1993. 256p. mass mkt. 4.50 o.s.i (*0-515-11059-0*, Jove) Berkley Publishing Group.
—Finishing Touch: A Melissa Craig Mystery. 1992. 253p. 19.95 (*0-8027-3209-7*) Walker & Co.
—A Little Gentle Sleuthing. 1992. 240p. mass mkt. 3.99 o.s.i (*0-515-10878-2*, Jove) Berkley Publishing Group.
—A Little Gentle Sleuthing. l.t. ed. 1992. (Mystery Ser.). 512p. 29.99 o.p. (*0-7089-2736-X*, Ulverscroft) Thorpe, F. A. Pubs. GBR. *Dist:* Ulverscroft Large Print Bks., Ltd., Ulverscroft Large Print Canada, Ltd.
—A Little Gentle Sleuthing. 1991. 272p. 18.95 o.s.i (*0-8027-5781-2*) Walker & Co.
Rowntree, Kathleen. Mr. Brightly's Evening Off. 1997. (Illus.). 270p. (J). (*0-385-40879-X*) Doubleday Publishing.
—Mr. Brightly's Evening Off. l.t. unabr. ed. 1998. 24.95 (*0-7531-5856-6*, 158566) ISIS Large Print Bks. GBR. *Dist:* ISIS Publishing.
—Mr. Brightly's Evening Off. 2000. 271p. (J). pap. 10.95 (*0-552-99733-1*) Transworld Publishers Ltd. GBR. *Dist:* Trafalgar Square.
—Quiet War of Rebecca Sheldon. 2000. (J). pap. 12.95 (*0-552-99325-5*) Transworld Publishers Ltd. GBR. *Dist:* Trafalgar Square.
—Tell Mrs. Poole I'm Sorry. 1995. 416p. 23.95 o.p. (*0-312-11882-1*) St. Martin's Pr.
—Tell Mrs. Poole I'm Sorry. 2000. (J). pap. 12.95 (*0-552-99561-4*) Transworld Publishers Ltd. GBR. *Dist:* Trafalgar Square.
Roy, Jacqueline. The Fat Lady Sings. 2002. 184p. pap. 14.95 (*0-7043-4711-3*); 2001. 288p. pap. 16.95 (*0-7043-4647-8*) Women's Pr., Ltd., The GBR. *Dist:* Trafalgar Square.
Royal, Lauren. Amethyst. 2000. 416p. mass mkt. 6.99 (*0-451-19951-0*, Signet Bks.) NAL.
—Emerald. 2000. 416p. mass mkt. 6.99 (*0-451-20142-6*, Signet Bks.) NAL.
—Violet. 2002. 384p. mass mkt. 6.99 (*0-451-20688-6*, Signet Bks.) NAL.
Royce, Kenneth. Shadows. 1996. 288p. 22.00 (*0-7278-4878-X*); 384p. 26.00 o.p. (*0-7278-7006-8*) Severn Hse. Pubs., Ltd.
Royle, Nicholas. The Matter of the Heart. 1998. 256p. pap. o.s.i (*0-349-10956-7*) Little Brown & Co.
Rushdie, Salman. The Ground Beneath Her Feet: A Novel. l.t. ed. 2000. (Thorndike/G. K. Hall Paperback Bestsellers Ser.). 816p. pap. 30.95 (*0-7838-8712-4*, Macmillan Reference USA) Gale Group.
—The Ground Beneath Her Feet: A Novel. 1999. 592p. 27.50 o.s.i (*0-8050-5308-5*) Holt, Henry & Co.
—The Ground Beneath Her Feet: A Novel. abr. ed. 1999. audio 25.00 (*0-7871-1917-2*, Dove Audio) NewStar Media, Inc.
—The Ground Beneath Her Feet: A Novel. 2000. 592p. pap. 16.00 (*0-312-25499-7*) Picador.
—The Ground Beneath Her Feet: A Novel. unabr. ed. 1999. audio 104.00 (*0-7887-3747-3*, 95939E5); audio 163.00 (*0-7887-4350-3*, 95939E7) Recorded Bks., LLC.
—The Ground Beneath Her Feet: A Novel. l.t. ed. 1999. (G. K. Hall Core Ser.). 816p. 31.95 (*0-7838-8713-2*) Thorndike Pr.
—The Satanic Verses. 1992. 546p. pap. 14.00 (*0-9632707-0-2*) Consortium, Inc.
—The Satanic Verses. 1997. 576p. pap. 16.00 o.s.i (*0-8050-5309-3*, Owl Bks.) Holt, Henry & Co.
—The Satanic Verses. 2000. 576p. pap. 16.00 (*0-312-27082-8*) Picador.
—The Satanic Verses. 1989. 496p. 27.95 (*0-670-82537-9*) Viking Penguin.
Rushforth, Peter. Kindergarten. 1989. 208p. pap. 10.95 (*0-87923-701-5*) Godine, David R. Pub.
—Kindergarten. 1980. 8.95 o.p. (*0-394-50917-X*) Knopf, Alfred A. Inc.
—Kindergarten. 1983. pap. 2.95 o.p. (*0-380-56150-6*, 56150, Avon Bks.) Morrow/Avon.
Rutherford, Edward. The Forest. l.t. ed. 2000. (Illus.). 1136p. 26.95 (*0-375-41037-6*) Random Hse. Large Print.
Rutherfurd, Edward. The Forest. 2001. 784p. mass mkt. o.s.i (*0-345-44722-0*); (Illus.). mass mkt. 7.99 (*0-345-44178-8*, Ballantine Bks.) Ballantine Bks.
—The Forest. abr. ed. 2000. audio 25.00 o.s.i (*0-375-40960-2*, RH Audio) Random Hse. Audio Publishing Group.
—London. 1152p. 2002. pap. 18.95 (*0-345-45568-1*); 1998. mass mkt. 7.99 (*0-449-00263-2*, Fawcett) Ballantine Bks.
—Sarum: The Novel of England. 1997. 912p. pap. 17.95 (*0-449-00072-9*, Fawcett); 1988. 1056p. mass mkt. 7.99 (*0-8041-0298-8*, Ivy Bks.) Ballantine Bks.
—Sarum: The Novel of England. 1993. reprint ed. lib. bdg. 45.95 (*1-56849-114-X*) Buccaneer Bks., Inc.
—Sarum: The Novel of England. 1987. o.p. (*5-550-21740-6*) Nairi.
—Sarum: The Novel of England. 2004. 912p. 11.99 (*0-517-22354-6*, Gramercy) Random Hse. Value Publishing.
—Sarum: The Novel of England. 1994. (*0-09-952730-8*) Random Hse. of Canada, Ltd. CAN. *Dist:* Random Hse., Inc.
Rutherfurd, Edward & Outlet Book Company Staff. Sarum: The Novel of England. 1990. 5.99 o.p. (*0-517-03389-5*) Random Hse. Value Publishing.
Ryan, Patricia. Silken Threads. 1999. 352p. mass mkt. 5.99 o.s.i (*0-451-40827-6*, Topaz) NAL.
Saberhagen, Fred & Hart, James V. Bram Stoker's Dracula. 1992. 304p. mass mkt. 4.99 o.p. (*0-451-17575-1*, Signet Bks.) NAL.
Sallis, Susan. Choices. 2000. 411p. pap. 10.95 (*0-552-14549-1*) Transworld Publishers Ltd. GBR. *Dist:* Trafalgar Square.
—A Scattering of Daisies. l.t. ed. 1989. (General Ser.). lib. bdg. 11.95 o.p. (*1-85057-493-6*, Macmillan Reference USA) Gale Group.
—A Scattering of Daisies. 1999. 347p. 26.00 (*0-7278-5500-X*) Severn Hse. Pubs., Ltd.
—A Scattering of Daisies. 2000. pap. 10.95 (*0-552-12375-7*) Transworld Publishers Ltd. GBR. *Dist:* Trafalgar Square.
—Touched by Angels. l.t. ed. 1997. (Magna Large Print Ser.). 523p. 29.99 o.p. (*0-7505-1121-4*) Magna Large Print Bks. GBR. *Dist:* Ulverscroft Large Print Bks., Ltd., Ulverscroft Large Print Canada, Ltd.
—Touched by Angels. 2000. 351p. 27.95 (*0-593-04035-X*); 411p. pap. 10.95 (*0-552-14466-5*) Transworld Publishers Ltd. GBR. *Dist:* Trafalgar Square.
—Water under the Bridge. l.t. ed. 1996. (Magna Large Print Ser.). 624p. 29.99 (*0-7505-0980-5*) Magna Large Print Bks. GBR. *Dist:* Ulverscroft Large Print Bks., Ltd.
—Water under the Bridge. 2000. (Illus.). 475p. pap. 9.95 (*0-552-14318-9*) Transworld Publishers Ltd. GBR. *Dist:* Trafalgar Square.
Sampson, Kevin. Clubland. 2003. 224p. pap. (*0-09-944885-8*) Random Hse. of Canada, Ltd.
—Powder: A Rock 'n' Roll Novel. 2002. 505p. pap. 15.00 (*1-84195-371-7*) Canongate Bks. GBR. *Dist:* Grove/Atlantic, Inc., Publishers Group West.
Sand, George. The Mammoth Book of New Sherlock Holmes Adventures. Ashley, Mike, ed. 1997. (Mammoth Bks.). 512p. pap. 11.95 (*0-7867-0477-2*, Carroll & Graf Pubs.) Avalon Publishing Group.
Sanderson, Mark. Audacious Perversion. 1999. 236p. pap. 14.95 (*1-899344-32-2*) DuFour, Howard.
Sansom, C. J. Dissolution: A Novel. 2003. 400p. 24.95 (*0-670-03203-4*, Viking) Viking Penguin.
Satinwood, Deborah. English Rose. 2000. 352p. mass mkt. 5.99 o.s.i (*0-8217-6662-7*) Kensington Publishing Corp.
Satterthwait, Walter. Escapade. 1996. 355p. mass mkt. 5.99 (*0-312-95920-6*, St. Martin's Paperbacks); 1995. 336p. 22.95 o.p. (*0-312-13068-6*, Saint Martin's Minotaur) St. Martin's Pr.
Sattler, Veronica. A True Prince. 2000. 352p. mass mkt. 5.99 o.s.i (*0-8217-7031-4*) Kensington Publishing Corp.
Saunders, Kate. Night Shall Overtake Us. 1994. 512p. 22.95 o.p. (*0-525-93764-1*, Dutton) Dutton/Plume.
Savarin, Julian J. Naja: A "Gallagher" Novel. 1993. 336p. mass mkt. 4.99 o.p. (*0-06-100475-8*, HarperTorch) Morrow/Avon.
—Naja: A "Gallagher" Novel. 1989. 256p. 16.95 o.p. (*0-312-03969-7*) St. Martin's Pr.
—Wolf Run. 1992. 464p. mass mkt. 4.50 o.p. (*0-06-100474-X*, HarperTorch) Morrow/Avon.
—Wolf Run. 1994. 2.99 o.p. (*0-517-12527-7*) Random Hse. Value Publishing.
—Wolf Run. 1991. 288p. 19.95 (*0-8027-1148-0*) Walker & Co.
Savery, Jeanne. The Last of the Winter Roses. 1991. 224p. 18.95 o.s.i (*0-8027-1162-6*) Walker & Co.
—The Perfect Husband. 2001. (Zebra Regency Romance Ser.). 288p. mass mkt. 4.99 o.s.i (*0-8217-7064-0*) Kensington Publishing Corp.
Saville, Diana. Marriage Bed. 1996. 320p. 23.95 o.p. (*0-312-14012-6*) St. Martin's Pr.
Saxton, Judith. Still Waters. 1998. 504p. 26.95 o.p. (*0-312-18185-X*) St. Martin's Pr.
Saxton, Judith A. All My Fortunes. 1988. 592p. 22.95 o.p. (*0-312-02159-3*) St. Martin's Pr.
—A Family Affair. 1990. 432p. 19.95 o.p. (*0-312-03966-2*) St. Martin's Pr.
—Family Feeling. l.t. ed. 1994. (Magna Large Print Ser.). 704p. 29.99 o.p. (*0-7505-0716-0*) Magna Large Print Bks. GBR. *Dist:* Ulverscroft Large Print Bks., Ltd., Ulverscroft Large Print Canada, Ltd.
—Family Feeling. 1987. 576p. 19.95 o.p. (*0-312-01024-9*) St. Martin's Pr.
—Harvest Moon. 1996. 536p. 26.95 o.p. (*0-312-15138-1*) St. Martin's Pr.
Sayers, Dorothy L. Busman's Honeymoon. unabr. ed. 2002. audio 34.95 (*1-57270-317-2*) Audio Partners Publishing Corp.
—Busman's Honeymoon. l.t. ed. (Lord Peter Wimsey Mystery Ser.). 1993. pap. 17.95 o.p. (*0-7927-1366-4*); 1992. 21.95 o.p. (*0-7927-1367-2*) BBC Audiobooks America.
—Busman's Honeymoon. unabr. ed. 2000. (Lord Peter Wimsey Mysteries Ser.: Bk. 13). audio 69.95 (*0-7451-4313-X*, CAB 996) Chivers Audio Bks. GBR. *Dist:* BBC Audiobooks America.
—Busman's Honeymoon. 1981. (Lord Peter Wimsey Mystery Ser.). lib. bdg. 16.95 o.p. (*0-8161-3041-8*, Macmillan Reference USA) Gale Group.
—Busman's Honeymoon. 1960. (Lord Peter Wimsey Mystery Ser.). 12.95 o.p. (*0-06-013765-7*) HarperCollins Pubs.
—Busman's Honeymoon. (Lord Peter Wimsey Mystery Ser.). 1986. 17.95 o.p. (*0-06-055021-X*); 1986. pap. 6.00 o.p. (*0-06-080823-3*, Perennial); 1993. 400p. reprint ed. pap. 8.00 o.p. (*0-06-092393-8*, Perennial) HarperTrade.
—Busman's Honeymoon. (Lord Peter Wimsey Mystery Ser.). 1995. 416p. mass mkt. 6.99 (*0-06-104351-6*, HarperTorch); 1978. pap. 2.75 o.p. (*0-380-01076-3*, 62489-3, Avon Bks.) Morrow/Avon.
—Clouds of Witness. l.t. ed. 1993. (Lord Peter Wimsey Mystery Ser.). 21.95 o.p. (*0-7927-1435-0*); pap. o.p. (*0-7927-1434-2*) BBC Audiobooks America.
—Clouds of Witness. unabr. ed. 2000. (Lord Peter Wimsey Mysteries Ser.: Bk. 2). audio 59.95 (*0-7451-4008-4*, CAB 705) Chivers Audio Bks. GBR. *Dist:* BBC Audiobooks America.
—Clouds of Witness, Set. abr. ed. 1992. (Lord Peter Wimsey Mystery Ser.). 30p. audio 16.99 (*0-88646-310-6*, 390538) Durkin Hayes Publishing Ltd.
—Clouds of Witness. l.t. ed. 1979. (Lord Peter Wimsey Mystery Ser.). (YA). lib. bdg. 15.95 o.p. (*0-8161-6721-4*, Macmillan Reference USA) Gale Group.
—Clouds of Witness. 1987. (Lord Peter Wimsey Mystery Ser.). 288p. 17.95 o.p. (*0-06-055035-X*); pap. 6.50 o.p. (*0-06-080835-7*, PL835, Perennial) HarperTrade.
—Clouds of Witness. (Lord Peter Wimsey Mystery Ser.). 1995. 288p. mass mkt. 5.99 (*0-06-104353-2*, HarperTorch); 1976. 224p. pap. 2.75 o.p. (*0-380-01107-7*, 64394-4, Avon Bks.) Morrow/Avon.
—Clouds of Witness. 1973. mass mkt. 1.25 o.p. (*0-451-05594-2*); 1969. mass mkt. 0.75 o.p. (*0-451-03970-X*) NAL. (Signet Bks.).
—Dorothy L. Sayers: Four Complete Lord Peter Wimsey Novels. 1990. 752p. reprint ed. 9.99 o.s.i (*0-517-39575-4*) Random Hse. Value Publishing.
—Dorothy L. Sayers: On the Case with Lord Peter Wimsey: Three Complete Novels. 1992. 576p. reprint ed. 6.99 o.s.i (*0-517-07243-2*) Random Hse. Value Publishing.
—Dorothy L. Sayers: The Complete Stories. 2002. 816p. pap. 17.95 (*0-06-008461-8*, Perennial) HarperTrade.
—Dorothy L. Sayers: Three Complete Lord Peter Wimsey Novels. 1992. 586p. 7.99 o.s.i (*0-517-07777-9*) Random Hse. Value Publishing.
—The Five Red Herrings. 1994. (Lord Peter Wimsey Mystery Ser.). reprint ed. lib. bdg. 32.95 (*1-56849-332-0*) Buccaneer Bks., Inc.
—The Five Red Herrings. unabr. ed. 2000. (Lord Peter Wimsey Mysteries Ser.: Bk. 7). audio 69.95 (*0-7451-6259-2*, CAB 607) Chivers Audio Bks. GBR. *Dist:* BBC Audiobooks America.
—The Five Red Herrings. l.t. ed. (Lord Peter Wimsey Mystery Ser.). 1991. pap. 15.95 o.p. (*0-8161-5225-X*); 1980. 525p. lib. bdg. 15.95 o.p. (*0-8161-3044-2*) Gale Group. (Macmillan Reference USA).
—The Five Red Herrings. (Lord Peter Wimsey Mystery Ser.). 1995. 368p. mass mkt. 6.99 (*0-06-104363-X*); 1958. o.p. (*0-06-013775-4*) HarperCollins Pubs.
—The Five Red Herrings. (Lord Peter Wimsey Mystery Ser.). 1993. 320p. pap. 8.00 o.p. (*0-06-092387-3*); 1986. pap. 6.00 o.p. (*0-06-080830-6*) HarperTrade. (Perennial).
—The Five Red Herrings. 1976. (Lord Peter Wimsey Mystery Ser.). pap. 2.75 o.p. (*0-380-01187-5*, 62109-6, Avon Bks.) Morrow/Avon.
—The Five Red Herrings. 1974. mass mkt. 0.95 o.p. (*0-451-05887-9*); mass mkt. 0.75 o.p. (*0-451-03346-9*) NAL. (Signet Bks.).
—Four Classic Dorothy L. Sayers Mysteries: Strong Poison; Have His Carcase; Gaudy Night; Busman's Honeymoon, 4 vols. 1990. 1504p. reprint ed. pap. 22.95 o.p. (*0-06-081051-3*, Perennial) HarperTrade.
—Gaudy Night. unabr. ed. 1993. (Lord Peter Wimsey Mysteries Ser.: Bk. 12). audio 79.95 (*0-7451-4106-4*, CAB 789) Chivers Audio Bks. GBR. *Dist:* BBC Audiobooks America.
—Gaudy Night. abr. ed. 1996. (Lord Peter Wimsey Mystery Ser.). audio 16.99 (*0-88646-284-3*, 7284) Durkin Hayes Publishing Ltd.
—Gaudy Night. l.t. ed. 1981. (Lord Peter Wimsey Mystery Ser.). lib. bdg. 18.95 o.p. (*0-8161-3040-X*, Macmillan Reference USA) Gale Group.
—Gaudy Night. (Lord Peter Wimsey Mystery Ser.). 1986. 17.95 o.p. (*0-06-055022-8*); 1986. pap. 6.50 o.p. (*0-06-080824-1*); 1993. 480p. reprint ed. pap. 9.00 o.p. (*0-06-092392-X*, Perennial); 1987. 464p. reprint ed. pap. 5.50 o.p. (*0-06-080907-8*, P-907, Perennial) HarperTrade.
—Gaudy Night. (Lord Peter Wimsey Mystery Ser.). 1995. 512p. mass mkt. 6.99 (*0-06-104349-4*, HarperTorch); 1976. pap. 3.50 o.p. (*0-380-01207-3*, 65037, Avon Bks.) Morrow/Avon.
—Hangman's Holiday. unabr. ed. 1993. (Lord Peter Wimsey Mystery Ser.). audio 39.95 (*0-7861-0405-8*, 752397) Blackstone Audio Bks., Inc.
—Hangman's Holiday. 1979. (Lord Peter Wimsey Mystery Ser.). (gr. 7-12). lib. bdg. 12.95 o.p. (*0-8161-6783-4*, Macmillan Reference USA) Gale Group.
—Hangman's Holiday. (Lord Peter Wimsey Mystery Ser.). 1987. 288p. 21.95 o.p. (*0-06-055033-3*); 1987. 288p. pap. 6.00 o.p. (*0-06-080837-3*, P837, Perennial); 1993. 368p. reprint ed. pap. 13.00 (*0-06-092396-2*, Perennial) HarperTrade.
—Hangman's Holiday. 1979. (Lord Peter Wimsey Mystery Ser.). pap. 2.50 o.p. (*0-380-01240-5*, 60048-X, Avon Bks.) Morrow/Avon.
—Have His Carcase. l.t. ed. 1993. (Lord Peter Wimsey Mystery Ser.). 24.95 o.p. (*0-7927-1589-6*); pap. 22.95 o.p. (*0-7927-1588-8*) BBC Audiobooks America.
—Have His Carcase. unabr. ed. 2000. (Lord Peter Wimsey Mystery Ser.). 12p. audio compact disk 110.95 (*0-7540-5367-9*, CCD 058); (Lord Peter Wimsey Mysteries Ser.: Bk. 8). audio 79.95 (*0-7540-0355-8*, CAB 1778) Chivers Audio Bks. GBR. *Dist:* BBC Audiobooks America.
—Have His Carcase, Set. abr. ed. 1990. (Lord Peter Wimsey Mystery Ser.). 29p. audio 16.99 (*0-88646-270-3*, 390905) Durkin Hayes Publishing Ltd.
—Have His Carcase. l.t. ed. 1980. (Lord Peter Wimsey Mystery Ser.). 17.95 o.p. (*0-8161-3043-4*, Macmillan Reference USA) Gale Group.
—Have His Carcase. 1959. (Lord Peter Wimsey Mystery Ser.). 12.95 o.p. (*0-06-013785-1*) HarperCollins Pubs.
—Have His Carcase. (Lord Peter Wimsey Mystery Ser.). 1987. 416p. pap. 5.50 o.p. (*0-06-080909-4*, P-909); 1986. pap. 6.50 o.p. (*0-06-080827-6*); 1993. 448p. reprint ed. pap. 8.00 o.p. (*0-06-092391-1*) HarperTrade. (Perennial).
—Have His Carcase. (Lord Peter Wimsey Mystery Ser.). 1995. 448p. mass mkt. 7.99 (*0-06-104352-4*, HarperTorch); 1976. pap. 2.75 o.p. (*0-380-00939-0*, 58305-4, Avon Bks.) Morrow/Avon.
—In the Teeth of the Evidence: And Other Mysteries. 1997. (Lord Peter Wimsey Mysteries Ser.). audio 34.95 (*0-7540-7504-4*) BBC Audiobooks America.
—In the Teeth of the Evidence: And Other Mysteries. 1987. 320p. 17.95 o.p. (*0-06-055031-7*); 1987. 320p. pap. 6.00 o.p. (*0-06-080838-1*, P838, Perennial); 2001. 352p. reprint ed. pap. 13.00 (*0-06-092397-0*, Perennial) HarperTrade.
—In the Teeth of the Evidence: And Other Mysteries. (Lord Peter Wimsey Mystery Ser.). 1995. 272p. mass mkt. 5.99 (*0-06-104356-7*, HarperTorch); 1976. pap. 2.50 o.p. (*0-380-01280-4*, 62943-7, Avon Bks.) Morrow/Avon.
—In the Teeth of the Evidence: And Other Mysteries. 1974. mass mkt. 0.95 o.p. (*0-451-05885-2*); mass mkt. 0.75 o.p. (*0-451-03321-3*) NAL. (Signet Bks.).
—Lord Peter: A Collection of All the Lord Peter Wimsey Stories. (Lord Peter Wimsey Mystery Ser.). 31.95 (*0-8488-1153-4*) Amereon, Ltd.
—Lord Peter: A Collection of All the Lord Peter Wimsey Stories. 1995. (Lord Peter Wimsey Mystery Ser.). 496p. mass mkt. 5.99 o.s.i (*0-06-104361-3*) HarperCollins Pubs.

—Lord Peter: A Collection of All the Lord Peter Wimsey Stories. Sandoe, James, ed. 1972. (Lord Peter Wimsey Mystery Ser.). o.p. *(0-06-013788-6)* HarperCollins Pubs.

—Lord Peter: A Collection of All the Lord Peter Wimsey Stories. 1986. (Lord Peter Wimsey Mystery Ser.). 512p. 18.95 o.p. *(0-06-055039-2)*; 496p. pap. 16.00 *(0-06-091380-0*, Perennial) HarperTrade.

—Lord Peter: A Collection of All the Lord Peter Wimsey Stories. Sandoe, James, ed. 1991. (Lord Peter Wimsey Mystery Ser.). 501p. reprint ed. lib. bdg. 27.00 o.p. *(0-8095-9129-4)* Millefleurs.

—Lord Peter: A Collection of All the Lord Peter Wimsey Stories. 1976. (Lord Peter Wimsey Mystery Ser.). mass mkt. 6.95 o.p. *(0-380-01694-X*, 59683-0, Avon Bks.) Morrow/Avon.

—Lord Peter Views the Body. (Lord Peter Wimsey Mystery Ser.). 1986. pap. 6.50 o.p. *(0-06-080839-X)*; 1993. 336p. reprint ed. pap. 8.00 o.p. *(0-06-092395-4)* HarperTrade. (Perennial).

—Lord Peter Views the Body. (Lord Peter Wimsey Mystery Ser.). 1995. 320p. mass mkt. 5.99 o.s.i *(0-06-104359-1*, HarperTorch); 1976. pap. 2.50 o.p. *(0-380-00946-3*, 63503-8, Avon Bks.) Morrow/Avon.

—Murder Must Advertise. unabr. ed. audio 29.95 *(1-57270-300-8)* Audio Partners Publishing Corp.

—Murder Must Advertise. unabr. ed. 1997. (Lord Peter Wimsey Mystery Ser.). audio 56.95 *(0-7861-1165-8*, 1936) Blackstone Audio Bks., Inc.

—Murder Must Advertise. unabr. ed. 2000. (Lord Peter Wimsey Mysteries Ser.: Bk. 10). audio 69.95 *(0-7451-6862-0*, CAB 331) Chivers Audio Bks. GBR. *Dist:* BBC Audiobooks America.

—Murder Must Advertise. l.t. ed. 1980. (Lord Peter Wimsey Mystery Ser.). 508p. lib. bdg. 15.95 o.p. *(0-8161-3045-0*, Macmillan Reference USA) Gale Group.

—Murder Must Advertise. (Lord Peter Wimsey Mystery Ser.). 352p. 1993. pap. 8.00 o.p. *(0-06-092388-1*, Perennial); 1986. 17.95 o.p. *(0-06-055024-4)*; 1986. pap. 6.50 o.p. *(0-06-080825-X*, P825, Perennial) HarperTrade.

—Murder Must Advertise. (Lord Peter Wimsey Mystery Ser.). 1995. 368p. mass mkt. 6.99 *(0-06-104355-9*, HarperTorch); 1985. pap. 2.25 o.p. *(0-380-00916-1*, 60913-4, Avon Bks.) Morrow/Avon.

—Murder Must Advertise. 1974. mass mkt. 0.95 o.p. *(0-451-06170-5)*; 1968. mass mkt. 0.75 o.p. *(0-451-03369-8)* NAL. (Signet Bks.).

—Murder Must Advertise, unabr. ed. 1997. (Lord Peter Wimsey Mystery Ser.). audio 78.00 *(0-7887-1289-6*, 95145E7) Recorded Bks., LLC.

—The Nine Tailors. Date not set. (Lord Peter Wimsey Mystery Ser.). 320p. 24.95 *(0-8488-2388-5)* Amereon, Ltd.

—The Nine Tailors. l.t. ed. 1981. (Lord Peter Wimsey Mystery Ser.). lib. bdg. 15.95 o.p. *(0-8161-3036-1*, Macmillan Reference USA) Gale Group.

—The Nine Tailors. (Lord Peter Wimsey Mystery Ser.). 1989. 331p. 15.95 o.s.i *(0-15-165897-8)*; 1966. 420p. pap. 12.00 *(0-15-665899-2*, Harvest Bks.) Harcourt Trade Pubs.

—Striding Folly. unabr. ed. 1994. (Lord Peter Wimsey Mystery Ser.). audio 24.95 *(0-7451-4265-6*, CAB 948) BBC Audiobooks America.

—Striding Folly. (Lord Peter Wimsey Mystery Ser.). text 34.95 *(0-450-54973-9)* Hodder & Stoughton, Ltd. GBR. *Dist:* Lubrecht & Cramer, Ltd., Trafalgar Square.

—Strong Poison. (Lord Peter Wimsey Mystery Ser.). 20.95 *(0-8488-1154-2)* Amereon, Ltd.

—Strong Poison. unabr. ed. 2001. (Lord Peter Wimsey Mystery Ser.). audio 29.95 *(1-57270-124-2*, N61124u, Audio Editions Mystery Masters) Audio Partners Publishing Corp.

—Strong Poison. unabr. ed. 2000. (Lord Peter Wimsey Mysteries Ser.: Bk. 6). audio 49.95 *(0-7451-6258-4*, CAB 400) Chivers Audio Bks. GBR. *Dist:* BBC Audiobooks America.

—Strong Poison, Set. abr. ed. 1990. (Lord Peter Wimsey Mystery Ser.). audio 16.99 *(0-88646-257-6*, 391702) Durkin Hayes Publishing Ltd.

—Strong Poison. l.t. ed. 1980. (Lord Peter Wimsey Mystery Ser.). 450p. lib. bdg. 15.95 o.p. *(0-8161-3042-6*, Macmillan Reference USA) Gale Group.

—Strong Poison. 1976. (Lord Peter Wimsey Mystery Ser.). reprint ed. lib. bdg. 21.00 o.p. *(0-8240-2392-7)* Garland Publishing, Inc.

—Strong Poison. (Lord Peter Wimsey Mystery Ser.). 1987. 256p. 17.95 o.p. *(0-06-055025-2)*; 1987. pap. 6.00 o.p. *(0-06-080826-8*, Perennial); 1993. 256p. reprint ed. pap. 8.00 o.p. *(0-06-092390-3*, Perennial); 1987. 240p. reprint ed. pap. 4.95 o.p. *(0-06-080908-6*, P-908, Perennial) HarperTrade.

—Strong Poison. (Lord Peter Wimsey Mystery Ser.). 1995. 272p. mass mkt. 6.99 *(0-06-104350-8*, HarperTorch); 1978. pap. 2.75 o.p. *(0-380-01567-6*, 69401-8, Avon Bks.) Morrow/Avon.

—Strong Poison. 1974. mass mkt. 0.60 o.p. *(0-451-03264-0)*; mass mkt. 0.75 o.p. *(0-451-05748-1)* NAL. (Signet Bks.).

—Strong Poison. 2001. (Best Mysteries of All Time Ser.). 320p. *(0-7621-8865-0*, IM Pr.) Reader's Digest Assn., Inc., The.

—Unnatural Death. unabr. ed. 2001. (Lord Peter Wimsey Mystery Ser.). audio 29.95 *(1-57270-144-7*, N61144u, Audio Editions Mystery Masters) Audio Partners Publishing Corp.

—Unnatural Death. l.t. ed. 1992. (Lord Peter Wimsey Mystery Ser.). pap. 17.95 o.p. *(0-7927-1264-1)*; 20.95 o.p. *(0-7927-1265-X*, E0039) BBC Audiobooks America.

—Unnatural Death. unabr. ed. 2000. (Lord Peter Wimsey Mysteries Ser.: Bk. 3). audio 49.95 *(0-7451-6262-2*, CAB 496) Chivers Audio Bks. GBR. *Dist:* BBC Audiobooks America.

—Unnatural Death. 1979. (Lord Peter Wimsey Mystery Ser.). lib. bdg. 15.95 o.p. *(0-8161-6723-0*, Macmillan Reference USA) Gale Group.

—Unnatural Death. 1956. (Lord Peter Wimsey Mystery Ser.). 12.95 o.p. *(0-06-013800-9)* HarperCollins Pubs.

—Unnatural Death. (Lord Peter Wimsey Mystery Ser.). 1993. 256p. pap. 8.00 o.p. *(0-06-092386-5*, Perennial); 1987. 288p. 17.95 o.p. *(0-06-055032-5)* HarperTrade.

—Unnatural Death. (Lord Peter Wimsey Mystery Ser.). 1995. 288p. mass mkt. 6.99 *(0-06-104358-3*, HarperTorch); 1978. pap. 2.50 o.p. *(0-380-00794-0*, 68353-9, Avon Bks.) Morrow/Avon.

—The Unpleasantness at the Bellona Club. (Lord Peter Wimsey Mystery Ser.). 256p. 22.95 o.s.i *(0-8488-2463-6)* Amereon, Ltd.

—The Unpleasantness at the Bellona Club. unabr. ed. 2000. (Lord Peter Wimsey Mysteries Ser.: Bk. 5 ). audio 49.95 *(0-7451-6261-4*, CAB 448) Chivers Audio Bks. GBR. *Dist:* BBC Audiobooks America.

—The Unpleasantness at the Bellona Club. l.t. ed. 1979. (Lord Peter Wimsey Mystery Ser.). (YA). lib. bdg. 14.95 o.p. *(0-8161-6724-9*, Macmillan Reference USA) Gale Group.

—The Unpleasantness at the Bellona Club. 1957. (Lord Peter Wimsey Mystery Ser.). 12.95 o.p. *(0-06-013805-X)* HarperCollins Pubs.

—The Unpleasantness at the Bellona Club. (Lord Peter Wimsey Mystery Ser.). 1993. 240p. pap. 8.00 o.p. *(0-06-092389-X*, Perennial); 1987. 352p. 17.95 o.p. *(0-06-055026-0)*; 1987. 192p. reprint ed. pap. 6.00 o.p. *(0-06-080828-4*, P-828, Perennial) HarperTrade.

—The Unpleasantness at the Bellona Club. 1995. 256p. mass mkt. 6.99 *(0-06-104354-0*, HarperTorch); 1978. pap. 2.50 o.p. *(0-380-01597-8*, 67132-8, Avon Bks.) Morrow/Avon.

—Whose Body?, unabr. ed. 1998. (Lord Peter Wimsey Mystery Ser.). audio 29.95 *(1-55685-503-6)* Audio Bk. Contractors, Inc.

—Whose Body?, unabr. ed. 2001. (Lord Peter Wimsey Mystery Ser.). audio 22.95 *(1-57270-018-1*, N51018u, Audio Editions Bks. on Cassette) Audio Partners Publishing Corp.

—Whose Body? unabr. ed. (Lord Peter Wimsey Mystery Ser.). 2000. audio compact disk 48.00 *(0-7861-9940-7*, z2391); 1999. audio 39.95 *(0-7861-1561-0*, 2391) Blackstone Audio Bks., Inc.

—Whose Body? 1979. (Lord Peter Wimsey Mystery Ser.). lib. bdg. 12.95 o.p. *(0-8161-6722-2*, Macmillan Reference USA) Gale Group.

—Whose Body? (Lord Peter Wimsey Mystery Ser.). 1993. 176p. pap. 9.00 o.p. *(0-06-092385-7*, Perennial); 1987. 256p. 17.95 o.p. *(0-06-055036-8)*; 1987. 256p. pap. 5.50 o.p. *(0-06-080829-2*, P829, Perennial) HarperTrade.

—Whose Body? (Lord Peter Wimsey Mystery Ser.). 1995. 224p. mass mkt. 6.99 *(0-06-104357-5*, HarperTorch); 1978. pap. 2.50 o.p. *(0-380-00897-1*, 69781-5, Avon Bks.) Morrow/Avon.

Sayers, Dorothy L., et al. Double Death. 1986. (Lord Peter Wimsey Mystery Ser.). 160p. 18.95 o.p. *(0-575-03679-6)* Gollancz, Victor GBR. *Dist:* Trafalgar Square.

Scammell, W. M. The Stability of the International Monetary System. 1987. 176p. pap. 22.00 *(0-8476-7541-6)* Rowman & Littlefield Pubs., Inc.

Schaff, Donna. Priceless. 2002. (Five Star Romance Ser.). 374p. 26.95 *(0-7862-3845-3*, Five Star) Gale Group.

Schleimer, Sarah M. One Good Turn. 1990. 10.95 o.p. *(0-87306-527-1)* Feldheim, Philipp Inc.

Scholefield, Alan. Burn Out. 1995. 346p. 22.95 o.p. *(0-312-13035-X*, Saint Martin's Minotaur) St. Martin's Pr.

—Dirty Weekend. 1990. 15.95 o.p. *(0-312-05415-7*, Saint Martin's Minotaur) St. Martin's Pr.

—Never Die in January. 1993. 192p. 16.95 o.p. *(0-312-09351-9*, Saint Martin's Minotaur) St. Martin's Pr.

—Night Child. 1993. 256p. 19.95 o.p. *(0-312-08863-9*, Saint Martin's Minotaur) St. Martin's Pr.

—Night Child. l.t. ed. 1994. (Ulverscroft Large Print Ser.). 480p. 29.99 o.p. *(0-7089-3082-4*, Ulverscroft) Thorpe, F. A. Pubs. GBR. *Dist:* Ulverscroft Large Print Bks., Ltd., Ulverscroft Large Print Canada, Ltd.

—Thief Taker. 1992. 272p. 17.95 o.p. *(0-312-08320-3*, Saint Martin's Minotaur) St. Martin's Pr.

—Thief Taker. l.t. ed. 1994. (Ulverscroft Ser.). 400p. 29.99 o.p. *(0-7089-3029-8*, Ulverscroft) Thorpe, F. A. Pubs. GBR. *Dist:* Ulverscroft Large Print Bks., Ltd., Ulverscroft Large Print Canada, Ltd.

Schullery, Paul. Shupton's Fancy: A Tale of the Fly-Fishing Obsession. 1996. (Illus.). 64p. 15.00 *(0-8117-1534-5)* Stackpole Bks.

Schunk, Laurel. Death in Exile. 1999. 310p. 24.99 *(0-9661879-2-X)* St Kitts Pr.

Schwartz, Irwin. Piltdown Confession. 1994. vi, 210p. 20.95 o.p. *(0-312-11043-X)* St. Martin's Pr.

Scott, Barbara A. Pay Out & Pay Back. 1999. 222p. pap. 12.50 *(0-9637134-2-6)* Zenar Bks.

Scott, Jack S. All the Pretty People. 1984. 256p. 14.95 o.p. *(0-312-02006-6)* St. Martin's Pr.

—A Death in Irish Town: A Novel of Suspense. 1985. 192p. 12.95 o.p. *(0-312-18870-6)* St. Martin's Pr.

—A Knife Between the Ribs: A Novel of Suspense. 1986. 192p. 12.95 o.p. *(0-312-00015-4)* St. Martin's Pr.

—A Little Darling, Dead. 1986. 224p. 14.95 o.p. *(0-312-48845-9)* St. Martin's Pr.

—The Local Lads: A Novel of Suspense. 1983. 12.95 o.p. *(0-525-24159-0*, 01258-370, Dutton) Dutton/Plume.

—An Uprush of Mayhem. 1982. (Joan Kahn Bk.). 192p. 10.95 o.p. *(0-89919-095-2)* Houghton Mifflin Co.

—The View from Deacon Hill. 1981. (Joan Kahn Bk.). 204p. 9.95 o.p. *(0-89919-033-2)* Houghton Mifflin Co.

Scott, Lawrence. Aelred's Sin. 2001. 445p. pap. 11.95 *(0-7490-0374-X)* Allison & Busby, Ltd. GBR. *Dist:* International Publishers Marketing.

Scott, Paul. The Birds of Paradise. 290p. pap. 89.90 *(0-598-49716-1*, OP6031600052) Bks. on Demand.

Scott, Regina. The Incomparable Miss Compton. 2001. (Zebra Regency Romance Ser.). 224p. mass mkt. 4.99 o.s.i *(0-8217-6991-X)* Kensington Publishing Corp.

—Lord Borin's Secret Love. 2003. 191p. 26.95 *(1-59414-019-7*, Five Star) Gale Group.

—Lord Borin's Secret Love. 2002. (Zebra Regency Romance Ser.). 224p. mass mkt. 4.99 o.s.i *(0-8217-7279-1)* Kensington Publishing Corp.

—The Marquis' Kiss. 2000. (Zebra Regency Romance Ser.). 256p. mass mkt. 4.99 o.s.i *(0-8217-6705-4*, Zebra Bks.) Kensington Publishing Corp.

Scott, Regina, et al. His Blushing Bride. 2001. (Zebra Regency Romance Ser.). 256p. mass mkt. 4.99 o.s.i *(0-8217-6815-8*, Zebra Bks.) Kensington Publishing Corp.

Scott, Sarah. The History of Sir George Ellison. Rizzo, Betty, ed. 1995. (Eighteenth-Century Novels by Women Ser.). 288p. (C). pap. 16.95 *(0-8131-0849-7)*; (Illus.). 45.00 *(0-8131-1938-3)* Univ. Pr. of Kentucky.

Scott, Valerie. Mysterious Nurse. l.t. ed. 1998. (Nightingale Ser.). 287p. pap. 20.95 *(0-7838-8289-0)* Thorndike Pr.

Scott, Walter, Sr. Ivanhoe. 2001. (Wishbone Classics Ser.: No. 12). 512p. (J). (gr. 3-7). mass mkt. 5.95 *(0-451-52799-2)* NAL.

Sedley, Kate. Brothers of Glastonbury. 279p. text 29.95 *(0-7472-2087-5)*; 1998. pap. 11.95 *(0-7472-5877-5)* Headline Bk. Publishing, Ltd. GBR. *Dist:* Trafalgar Square.

—Brothers of Glastonbury. 2001. 288p. 23.95 *(0-312-27282-0*, Saint Martin's Minotaur) St. Martin's Pr.

—Death & the Chapman. l.t. ed. 1992. (Mystery Ser.). 315p. 29.99 o.p. *(0-7505-0420-X)* Magna Large Print Bks. GBR. *Dist:* Ulverscroft Large Print Bks., Ltd., Ulverscroft Large Print Canada, Ltd.

—Death & the Chapman. 1994. 272p. mass mkt. 4.50 o.p. *(0-06-104319-2*, HarperTorch) Morrow/Avon.

—Death & the Chapman. 1991. 224p. 17.95 o.p. *(0-312-06945-6*, Saint Martin's Minotaur) St. Martin's Pr.

—Eve of Saint Hyacinth. 1996. 288p. 21.95 o.p. *(0-312-14331-1*, Saint Martin's Minotaur) St. Martin's Pr.

—The Hanged Man. unabr. ed. 2000. (Chapman Mystery Ser.). audio 54.95 *(0-7540-0241-1*, CAB 1664) Chivers Audio Bks. GBR. *Dist:* BBC Audiobooks America.

—The Holy Innocents, Set. unabr. ed. 1999. audio 69.95 *(0-7540-0330-2*, CAB1753) Chivers Audio Bks. GBR. *Dist:* BBC Audiobooks America.

—The Holy Innocents. 1996. 304p. mass mkt. 4.99 o.s.i *(0-06-104379-6*, HarperTorch) Morrow/Avon.

—The Holy Innocents. 1995. 21.00 o.p. *(0-312-11823-6*, Saint Martin's Minotaur) St. Martin's Pr.

—The Plymouth Cloak. unabr. ed. 1998. audio 54.95 *(0-7540-0188-1*, CAB 1611) BBC Audiobooks America.

—The Plymouth Cloak. l.t. ed. 1994. (Magna Large Print Ser.). 317p. 29.99 o.p. *(0-7505-0614-8)* Magna Large Print Bks. GBR. *Dist:* Ulverscroft Large Print Bks., Ltd., Ulverscroft Large Print Canada, Ltd.

—The Plymouth Cloak. 1994. 224p. mass mkt. 4.50 o.p. *(0-06-104320-6*, HarperTorch) Morrow/Avon.

—The Plymouth Cloak. 1993. 192p. 16.95 o.p. *(0-312-08875-2*, Saint Martin's Minotaur) St. Martin's Pr.

—The Saint John's Fern: A Roger the Chapman Medieval Mystery. 1999. 246p. 29.95 o.s.i *(0-7472-7496-7)* Headline Bk. Publishing, Ltd. GBR. *Dist:* Trafalgar Square.

—The Saint John's Fern: A Roger the Chapman Medieval Mystery. Date not set. *(0-312-27883-7)*; 2002. 256p. 23.95 *(0-312-27683-4)* St. Martin's Pr. (Saint Martin's Minotaur).

—The Weaver's Inheritance. 247p. 29.95 *(0-7472-2277-0)*; 1999. pap. 11.95 *(0-7472-6128-8)* Headline Bk. Publishing, Ltd. GBR. *Dist:* Trafalgar Square.

—The Weaver's Inheritance. 2001. 256p. 23.95 *(0-312-27684-2*, Saint Martin's Minotaur) St. Martin's Pr.

—The Weaver's Tale. 1995. 224p. mass mkt. 4.50 o.p. *(0-06-104336-2*, HarperTorch) Morrow/Avon.

—The Weaver's Tale. 1994. 256p. 20.95 o.p. *(0-312-10474-X*, Saint Martin's Minotaur) St. Martin's Pr.

—The Wicked Winter. 1997. 282p. pap. 11.95 *(0-7472-5631-4)* Headline Bk. Publishing, Ltd. GBR. *Dist:* Trafalgar Square.

—The Wicked Winter. 2nd ed. 1999. 288p. 22.95 *(0-312-20625-9*, Saint Martin's Minotaur) St. Martin's Pr.

Selby, Bettina. Two Cats Walking. l.t. ed. 2001. (Illus.). ix, 229p. pap. 24.95 *(0-7862-3346-X)*; *(0-7540-4507-2)*; *(0-7540-4508-0)* Thorndike Pr.

Self, Will. Grey Area: And Other Stories. 1996. 287p. 22.00 o.p. *(0-87113-620-1*, Atlantic Monthly Pr.) Grove/Atlantic, Inc.

—Tough, Tough Toys for Tough, Tough Boys. 1998. 244p. *(0-7475-3906-5)* Bloomsbury Publishing, Ltd.

—Tough, Tough Toys for Tough, Tough Boys. 256p. 2000. pap. 12.00 *(0-8021-3702-4)*; 1999. 23.00 o.p. *(0-8021-1644-2)* Grove/Atlantic, Inc. (Grove Pr.).

Self, Will & Wilde, Oscar. Dorian: An Imitation. 2003. 288p. 23.00 *(0-8021-1729-5*, Grove Pr.) Grove/Atlantic, Inc.

Selvon, Samuel. The Lonely Londoners. 1989. (Longman Caribbean Writers Ser.). 141p. (C). pap. 16.00 *(0-582-64264-7*, TG7161) Longman Publishing Group.

—The Lonely Londoners. 1991. pap. *(0-920661-16-5)* TSAR Pubns.

Selwyn, Francis. Cracksman on Velvet. 1974. 25.00 o.p. *(0-8128-1729-X*, Scarborough Hse.) Madison Bks., Inc.

—Sergeant Verity & the Blood Royal. 1979. 2.95 o.s.i *(0-8128-2608-6)*; pap. 2.50 o.s.i *(0-8128-7072-7)* Madison Bks., Inc. (Scarborough Hse.).

—Sergeant Verity & the Imperial Diamond. 1976. 252p. 7.95 o.p. *(0-8128-1917-9)*; No. 1. 1984. 256p. pap. 2.95 o.p. *(0-8128-8038-2)* Madison Bks., Inc. (Scarborough Hse.).

—Sergeant Verity & the Swell Mob. 1980. 288p. 10.95 o.p. *(0-8128-2727-9*, Scarborough Hse.) Madison Bks., Inc.

—Sergeant Verity Presents His Compliments. 1977. 7.95 o.p. *(0-8128-2148-3*, Scarborough Hse.) Madison Bks., Inc.

Sennett, Richard. Palais-Royal. 1994. pap. 11.95 *(0-393-31251-8)* Norton, W. W. & Co., Inc.

Seymour, Gerald. A Line in the Sand. 2000. (Illus.). 469p. mass mkt. *(0-552-14682-X*, Corgi) Bantam Bks.

—A Line in the Sand. 2000. (Illus.). 400p. 25.00 *(0-684-85477-5*, Simon & Schuster); 2001. 464p. reprint ed. mass mkt. 7.99 *(0-671-02530-9*, Pocket) Simon & Schuster.

—A Line in the Sand. l.t. ed. 2000. (Charnwood Large Print Ser.). 480p. o.p. *(0-7089-9131-9*, Ulverscroft) Thorpe, F. A. Pubs. GBR. *Dist:* Ulverscroft Large Print Bks., Ltd., Ulverscroft Large Print Canada, Ltd.

Shakespeare, L. M. Question of Risk. 1990. 17.95 o.p. *(0-312-04407-0*, Saint Martin's Minotaur) St. Martin's Pr.

Sharp, Allen. Shadow over the Marsh. 1985. (Storytrails Ser.). 89p. (gr. 6-9). pap. text 6.50 o.p. *(0-521-31704-5)* Cambridge Univ. Pr.

Sharp, Paula. The Woman Who Was Not All There. 1988. 17.95 o.p. *(0-06-015989-8)* HarperTrade.

Sharpe, Tom. The Midden. 1999. 245p. 13.95 *(0-87951-928-2)*; 1997. 256p. 23.95 *(0-87951-801-4)* Overlook Pr., The.

—Porterhouse Blue. 1989. 224p. pap. 12.00 *(0-87113-279-6*, Atlantic Monthly Pr.) Grove/Atlantic, Inc.

—Porterhouse Blue. l.t. unabr. ed. 1998. 344p. reprint ed. 19.95 *(1-85089-308-X*, 89308X) ISIS Large Print Bks. GBR. *Dist:* Transaction Pubs.

—The Throwback. 1984. pap. 3.95 o.s.i *(0-394-72439-9*, Vintage) Knopf Publishing Group.

—Vintage Stuff. 1984. pap. 3.95 o.s.i (*0-394-72417-8*, Vintage) Knopf Publishing Group.
—Wilt. 1984. pap. 9.00 o.s.i (*0-394-72418-6*) Random Hse., Inc.
—The Wilt Alternative. 1984. 224p. pap. 3.95 o.s.i (*0-394-72621-9*, Vintage) Knopf Publishing Group.
—The Wilt Alternative. 1980. 9.95 o.p. (*0-312-88212-2*) St. Martin's Pr.
—Wilt on High. 1985. 13.95 o.p. (*0-394-54480-3*) Random Hse., Inc.
—Wilt on High: Being the Further Misadventures of One Henry Wilt. 1986. 224p. pap. 4.95 o.s.i (*0-394-74321-0*, Vintage) Knopf Publishing Group.
Shaw, Debra Benita. Women, Science & Fiction: The Frankenstein Inheritance. 2000. (Illus.). 309p. 26.95 (*0-7862-2747-8*, Five Star) Gale Group.
Shaw, Simon. The Company of Knaves. 1997. (Philip Fletcher Mystery Ser.). 224p. 22.95 (*0-312-18069-1*, Saint Martin's Minotaur) St. Martin's Pr.
—Dead for a Ducat. 1996. 224p. 20.95 o.p. (*0-312-14309-5*, Saint Martin's Minotaur) St. Martin's Pr.
—Killing Grace. 2000. 280p. (*0-00-710627-0*) HarperCollins Pubs. Canada, Ltd.
—Murder Out of Tune. unabr. ed. 1993. audio 54.95 (*0-7451-4094-7*, CAB 782) BBC Audiobooks America.
—Murder Out of Tune. 1992. 256p. mass mkt. 4.50 o.s.i (*0-553-29592-6*) Bantam Bks.
—Murder Out of Tune. 1988. 192p. o.s.i (*0-385-24602-1*) Doubleday Publishing.
—The Villain of the Earth. 1995. 189p. 19.95 o.p. (*0-312-13201-8*, Saint Martin's Minotaur) St. Martin's Pr.
Sheepshanks, Mary. Facing the Music. 1997. 320p. 22.95 o.p. (*0-312-16832-2*) St. Martin's Pr.
—Picking up the Pieces. 1998. 304p. 23.95 o.p. (*0-312-19997-X*) St. Martin's Pr.
—Picking Up the Pieces. 1999. 336p. mass mkt. 5.99 (*0-312-97037-4*, St. Martin's Paperbacks) St. Martin's Pr.
—A Price for Everything. 1996. 256p. 21.95 o.p. (*0-312-14394-X*) St. Martin's Pr.
—A Price for Everything: Rosamunde Pilcher's Bookshelf, Vol. 1. 1998. (Rosamunde Pilcher's Bookshelf Ser.). 306p. mass mkt. 5.99 (*0-312-96478-1*, St. Martin's Paperbacks) St. Martin's Pr.
Shefter, Harry. Tess of the d'Urbervilles. Hardy, Thomas, ed. 1973. (Enriched Classics Ser.). pap. 0.95 o.s.i (*0-671-47905-9*, Washington Square Pr.) Simon & Schuster.
Sheldon, Mary. The Blue Unicorn. 2000. 208p. (YA). pap. 12.95 (*0-595-00120-3*) iUniverse, Inc.
Shepherd, Stella. Embers of Death: An Inspector Montgomery Mystery. l.t. ed. 1997. (Dales Large Print Ser.). 272p. pap. 19.99 (*1-85389-757-4*) Dales Large Print Bks. GBR. *Dist:* Ulverscroft Large Print Bks., Ltd.
—Embers of Death: An Inspector Montgomery Mystery. 1996. 224p. text 20.95 o.p. (*0-312-15097-0*, Saint Martin's Minotaur) St. Martin's Pr.
—Nurse Dawes Is Dead. l.t. ed. 1995. (Magna Large Print Ser.). 422p. 29.99 o.p. (*0-7505-0792-6*) Magna Large Print Bks. GBR. *Dist:* Ulverscroft Large Print Bks., Ltd., Ulverscroft Large Print Canada, Ltd.
—Nurse Dawes Is Dead. 1994. 222p. 18.95 o.p. (*0-312-11867-8*, Saint Martin's Minotaur) St. Martin's Pr.
Sherrod, Barbara. The Players. 2001. (Five Star Romance Ser.). 248p. 26.95 (*0-7862-3709-0*, Five Star) Gale Group.
—The Players. 1989. 256p. mass mkt. 3.95 (*0-446-35870-3*) Warner Bks., Inc.
Sherwood, John. A Bouquet of Thorns. 1991. mass mkt. 3.95 o.s.i (*0-345-36525-9*) Ballantine Bks.
—A Bouquet of Thorns. 1989. 224p. 16.95 o.s.i (*0-684-19091-5*, Macmillan Reference USA) Gale Group.
—Creeping Jenny: A Celia Grant Mystery. 1993. 256p. 20.00 o.p. (*0-684-19613-1*, Macmillan Reference USA) Gale Group.
—Flowers of Evil. 1990. 224p. mass mkt. 3.95 o.s.i (*0-345-35342-0*) Ballantine Bks.
—Flowers of Evil. 1988. (Celia Grant Mystery Ser.). 204p. 14.95 o.p. (*0-684-18867-8*, Macmillan Reference USA) Gale Group.
—Flowers of Evil. l.t. ed. 1989. (Ulverscroft Large Print Ser.). 379p. 29.99 o.p. (*0-7089-1980-4*, Ulverscroft) Thorpe, F. A. Pubs. GBR. *Dist:* Ulverscroft Large Print Bks., Ltd., Ulverscroft Large Print Canada, Ltd.
—Green Trigger Finger. 1986. 176p. mass mkt. 2.95 o.s.i (*0-345-32890-6*) Ballantine Bks.
—The Mantrap Garden. 1987. 192p. mass mkt. 2.95 o.s.i (*0-345-34306-9*) Ballantine Bks.
—The Mantrap Garden. 1986. 224p. 13.95 o.p. (*0-684-18726-4*, Macmillan Reference USA) Gale Group.
—The Mantrap Garden. l.t. ed. 1990. (Magna Large Print Ser.). 327p. o.p. (*1-85057-560-6*) Magna Large Print Bks. GBR. *Dist:* Ulverscroft Large Print Canada, Ltd.
—A Shot in the Arm: Death at the BBC. 1983. 176p. 12.95 o.s.i (*0-684-17990-3*, Macmillan Reference USA) Gale Group.
—A Shot in the Arm: Death at the BBC. 1985. 172p. pap. 4.95 (*0-930330-25-0*) International Polygonics, Ltd.
—The Sunflower Plot. l.t. ed. 1992. 18.95 o.p. (*0-7451-8332-8*); pap. 16.95 o.p. (*0-7927-1018-5*) BBC Audiobooks America.
—The Sunflower Plot. 1991. 256p. 18.95 o.s.i (*0-684-19270-5*, Scribner) Simon & Schuster.
Shillingburg, Peter L., ed. Vanity Fair: A Novel Without a Hero. 1989. (Thackeray Edition Project Ser.). 848p. 96.00 o.p. (*0-8240-4291-3*, H864) Garland Publishing, Inc.
Shipway, George. The Paladin. 1973. 7.95 o.p. (*0-15-170740-5*) Harcourt Trade Pubs.
Shirley, Edna I. As I Like It: A Tale of Shakespeare & His Associates. 1996. 196p. pap. 16.95 o.p. (*1-85756-295-X*) Janus Publishing Co. GBR. *Dist:* Paul & Co. Pubs. Consortium, Inc.
Short, Luke. The Whip. 1980. (General Ser.). lib. bdg. 10.95 o.p. (*0-8161-3087-6*, Macmillan Reference USA) Gale Group.
Sillitoe, Alan. Birthday. 2002. 249p. (*0-00-710781-1*) HarperCollins Pubs.
—Birthday. 2002. 256p. pap. 12.00 (*0-00-710883-4*) HarperCollins Pubs. Ltd. GBR. *Dist:* HarperCollins Pubs. Canada, Ltd., Trafalgar Square.
—The Loneliness of the Long-Distance Runner. 1986. mass mkt. 3.50 o.p. (*0-451-16026-6*, AE3214, Signet Bks.); 1986. 144p. mass mkt. 3.99 o.p. (*0-451-16831-3*); 1969. mass mkt. 0.50 o.p. (*0-451-01928-8*, Signet Bks.); 1969. mass mkt. 0.60 o.p. (*0-451-02629-2*, Signet Bks.); 1969. mass mkt. 0.75 o.p. (*0-451-03960-2*, Signet Bks.); 1961. mass mkt. 1.25 o.p. (*0-451-06620-0*, Signet Bks.); 1961. mass mkt. 1.50 o.p. (*0-451-07908-6*, Signet Bks.); 1961. mass mkt. 1.75 o.p. (*0-451-09747-5*, Signet Bks.); 1961. mass mkt. 1.95 o.p. (*0-451-11436-1*, Signet Bks.); 1961. mass mkt. 2.25 o.p. (*0-451-13214-9*, Signet Bks.); 1961. mass mkt. 2.50 o.p. (*0-451-14328-0*, Signet Bks.); 1961. mass mkt. 0.95 o.p. (*0-451-06049-0*, Signet Bks.) NAL.
—Loneliness of the Long Distance Runner. 1986. mass mkt. 2.95 o.p. (*0-451-14835-5*, Signet Bks.) NAL.
—The Loneliness of the Long Distance Runner. abr. ed. 1981. audio 15.95 o.p. (*0-88646-060-3*, TC-LFP 7078) Durkin Hayes Publishing Ltd.
—The Loneliness of the Long-Distance Runner. 1992. (Plume Contemporary Fiction Ser.). 176p. reprint ed. pap. 13.00 (*0-452-26908-3*, Plume) Dutton/Plume.
Silva, Daniel. The Unlikely Spy. 2000. mass mkt. 6.99 (*0-449-45938-1*); 1998. 544p. mass mkt. 7.99 o.s.i (*0-449-00264-0*) Ballantine Bks. (Fawcett).
—The Unlikely Spy. 2003. 544p. mass mkt. 7.99 (*0-451-20930-3*, Signet Bks.) NAL.
Simmons, Deborah. The Devil Earl. 1996. (Harlequin Historicals Ser.). mass mkt. (*0-373-28917-0*, 1-28917-2, Harlequin Bks.) Harlequin Enterprises, Ltd.
Simmons, Steven J. Percy to the Rescue. 1998. (Illus.). 32p. (J). (ps-3). 15.95 (*0-88106-390-8*, Talewinds) Charlesbridge Publishing, Inc.
Simmons, Suzanne. You & No Other. 1998. (Topaz Historical Romance Ser.). 352p. mass mkt. 6.50 o.s.i (*0-451-40865-9*, Topaz) NAL.
Simpson, Donna. Lady Delafont's Dilemma. 2002. (Five Star Romance Ser.). 264p. 25.95 (*0-7862-3911-5*, Five Star) Gale Group.
—Miss Truelove Beckons. 2001. (Zebra Regency Romance Ser.). 288p. mass mkt. 4.99 o.s.i (*0-8217-7039-X*) Kensington Publishing Corp.
—A Rake's Redemption. 2002. (Five Star Romance Ser.). 240p. 26.95 (*0-7862-4444-5*, Five Star) Gale Group.
Simpson, Donna J. Lady Delafont's Dilemma. 2000. (Zebra Regency Romance Ser.). 256p. mass mkt. 4.99 o.s.i (*0-8217-6674-0*) Kensington Publishing Corp.
—Lady May's Folly. 2001. (Zebra Regency Romance Ser.). 256p. mass mkt. 4.99 o.s.i (*0-8217-6805-0*, Zebra Bks.) Kensington Publishing Corp.
Simpson, Dorothy. Close Her Eyes. 1990. 208p. mass mkt. 2.25 o.s.i (*0-553-18518-7*); mass mkt. 4.50 o.s.i (*0-553-29826-7*) Bantam Bks.
—Close Her Eyes. 1984. 224p. 12.95 o.p. (*0-684-18197-5*, Macmillan Reference USA) Gale Group.
—Close Her Eyes. l.t. ed. 1986. 448p. 15.95 o.p. (*0-7089-1450-0*, Ulverscroft) Thorpe, F. A. Pubs. GBR. *Dist:* Ulverscroft Large Print Bks., Ltd.
—A Day for Dying. l.t. ed. 1996. (G. K. Hall Mystery Ser.). 339p. 24.95 o.p. (*0-7838-1930-7*, Macmillan Reference USA) Gale Group.
—A Day for Dying. 1996. 280p. mass mkt. o.s.i (*0-7515-1377-6*) Little Brown & Co.
—A Day for Dying. 1996. 288p. 21.00 (*0-684-81568-0*, Scribner) Simon & Schuster.
—Dead by Morning. 1990. 256p. mass mkt. 3.95 o.s.i (*0-553-28606-4*) Bantam Bks.
—Dead by Morning. 1989. 224p. 16.95 o.s.i (*0-684-19123-7*, Macmillan Reference USA) Gale Group.
—Dead by Morning. l.t. ed. 1990. (Ulverscroft Large Print Ser.). 29.99 o.p. (*0-7089-2342-9*, Ulverscroft) Thorpe, F. A. Pubs. GBR. *Dist:* Ulverscroft Large Print Bks., Ltd., Ulverscroft Large Print Canada, Ltd.
—Dead on Arrival. 1989. 224p. mass mkt. 3.50 o.s.i (*0-553-27000-1*) Bantam Bks.
—Dead on Arrival. 1987. 208p. 14.95 o.p. (*0-684-18732-9*, Macmillan Reference USA) Gale Group.
—Dead on Arrival. l.t. ed. 1987. 400p. 14.95 o.p. (*0-7089-1716-X*, Ulverscroft) Thorpe, F. A. Pubs. GBR. *Dist:* Ulverscroft Large Print Bks., Ltd.
—Dead on Arrival. 1995. mass mkt. o.s.i (*0-7515-1411-X*) Virago Pr., Ltd.
—Doomed to Die. 1992. 288p. mass mkt. 4.50 o.s.i (*0-553-29694-9*) Bantam Bks.
—Doomed to Die. 1991. 288p. 19.95 o.s.i (*0-684-19381-7*, Macmillan Reference USA) Gale Group.
—Element of Doubt. 1989. 240p. mass mkt. 3.50 o.s.i (*0-553-28175-5*) Bantam Bks.
—Element of Doubt. 1988. 256p. 14.95 o.s.i (*0-684-18885-6*, Macmillan Reference USA) Gale Group.
—Element of Doubt. l.t. ed. 1989. 469p. 17.95 o.p. (*0-7089-1949-9*, Ulverscroft) Thorpe, F. A. Pubs. GBR. *Dist:* Ulverscroft Large Print Bks., Ltd.
—Last Seen Alive: A Luke Thanet Mystery. 1986. 224p. mass mkt. 3.95 o.s.i (*0-553-27773-1*) Bantam Bks.
—Last Seen Alive: A Luke Thanet Mystery. 1985. (Luke Thanet Mystery Ser.). 224p. 13.95 (*0-684-18435-4*, Macmillan Reference USA) Gale Group.
—Last Seen Alive: A Luke Thanet Mystery. l.t. ed. 1986. (Ulverscroft Large Print Ser.). 416p. 29.99 o.p. (*0-7089-1508-6*, Ulverscroft) Thorpe, F. A. Pubs. GBR. *Dist:* Ulverscroft Large Print Bks., Ltd., Ulverscroft Large Print Canada, Ltd.
—The Night She Died. 1985. (Mystery Ser.). 208p. mass mkt. 3.50 o.s.i (*0-553-27772-3*) Bantam Bks.
—The Night She Died. 1981. 192p. 9.95 o.s.i (*0-684-16869-3*); 1982. pap. 9.95 o.p. (*0-8161-3329-8*) Gale Group. (Macmillan Reference USA).
—The Night She Died. 1998. (Missing Mysteries Ser.: Vol. 4). 206p. reprint ed. pap. 8.95 (*1-890208-06-X*) Poisoned Pen Pr.
—No Laughing Matter. 1993. (Inspector Luke Thanet Ser.). 256p. 20.00 o.p. (*0-684-19626-3*, Macmillan Reference USA) Gale Group.
—Once Too Often. 1998. (Inspector Luke Thanet Ser.). 224p. 20.50 o.s.i (*0-684-84578-4*, Scribner) Simon & Schuster.
—Puppet for a Corpse: A Luke Thanet Mystery. 1983. 192p. 11.95 o.s.i (*0-684-17909-1*, Scribner) Simon & Schuster.
—Puppet for a Corpse: A Luke Thanet Mystery. l.t. ed. 1984. (Ulverscroft Large Print Ser.). 384p. 12.50 o.p. (*0-7089-1206-0*, Ulverscroft) Thorpe, F. A. Pubs. GBR. *Dist:* Ulverscroft Large Print Bks., Ltd., Ulverscroft Large Print Canada, Ltd.
—Six Feet Under. 176p. 1989. mass mkt. 2.25 o.s.i (*0-553-18506-3*); 1985. mass mkt. 3.95 o.s.i (*0-553-25192-9*) Bantam Bks.
—Six Feet Under. 1982. 192p. 10.95 o.p. (*0-684-17665-3*, Scribner) Simon & Schuster.
—Suspicious Death: A Luke Thanet Mystery. 1990. 240p. mass mkt. 3.95 o.s.i (*0-553-28459-2*) Bantam Bks.
—Suspicious Death: A Luke Thanet Mystery. 1988. 272p. 16.95 o.s.i (*0-684-19026-5*, Scribner) Simon & Schuster.
—Suspicious Death: A Luke Thanet Mystery. l.t. ed. 1990. (Ulverscroft Large Print Ser.). 29.99 o.p. (*0-7089-2246-5*, Ulverscroft) Thorpe, F. A. Pubs. GBR. *Dist:* Ulverscroft Large Print Bks., Ltd., Ulverscroft Large Print Canada, Ltd.
—Wake the Dead. 1993. 272p. mass mkt. 4.99 o.s.i (*0-553-56252-5*) Bantam Bks.
—Wake the Dead. 1992. (Inspector Luke Thanet Ser.). 256p. text 19.00 (*0-684-19507-0*, Scribner) Simon & Schuster.
Sinclair, May. Life & Death of Harriett Frean. 2003. 112p. pap. 10.95 (*0-8129-6995-2*, Modern Library) Random House Adult Trade Publishing Group.
Sisson, Rosemary A. The Bretts. 1987. 256p. pap. 4.50 o.p. (*0-14-010513-1*, Penguin Bks.) Viking Penguin.
Skeggs, Douglas. The Triumph of Bacchus. 1993. 288p. 19.95 o.p. (*0-312-09927-4*, Saint Martin's Minotaur) St. Martin's Pr.
Skinner, Melynda Beth. The Blue Devil. 2001. 256p. mass mkt. 4.99 o.s.i (*0-8217-7049-7*) Kensington Publishing Corp.
Slaughter, Carolyn. The Banquet. 1984. 192p. 13.95 o.p. (*0-89919-274-2*) Houghton Mifflin Co.
—The Banquet. 1987. 208p. pap. 4.95 o.p. (*0-14-006662-4*, Penguin Bks.) Viking Penguin.
Slovo, Gillian. Catnap. 1996. 288p. 23.95 o.p. (*0-312-14561-6*, Saint Martin's Minotaur) St. Martin's Pr.
—Catnap. 1995. 276p. pap. o.s.i (*1-85381-815-1*) Virago Pr., Ltd. GBR. *Dist:* Little Brown & Co.
—Close Call: A Kate Baeier Mystery. 1996. 314p. mass mkt. o.s.i (*1-85381-816-X*) Virago Pr., Ltd. GBR. *Dist:* Little Brown & Co.
—Death Comes Staccato. 1988. 12.95 o.s.i (*0-385-24609-9*) Doubleday Publishing.
Small, Bertrice. Hellion. (Orig.). 1997. mass mkt. 5.99 (*0-345-40925-6*); 1997. mass mkt. 6.99 (*0-449-15041-0*, Fawcett); 1997. 448p. mass mkt. 6.99 (*0-449-15038-0*, Fawcett); 1996. 448p. pap. 10.00 o.s.i (*0-345-38599-3*) Ballantine Bks.
—Hellion. l.t. ed. 1996. (Orig.). pap. 22.95 o.p. (*1-56895-354-2*, Wheeler Publishing, Inc.) Gale Group.
—The Innocent. 2001. 416p. mass mkt. 6.99 (*0-449-00672-7*, Ivy Bks.); 1999. 384p. pap. 12.95 (*0-449-00180-6*, Fawcett) Ballantine Bks.
—A Love for All Time. 2001. 528p. pap. 14.00 (*0-451-20474-3*, Signet Bks.) NAL.
Smart, Ariel. Stolen Moments: And Other Stories. 2003. 160p. pap. 12.95 (*1-56474-422-1*) Fithian Pr.
Smith, A. C. Lady Jane. 1986. 192p. o.p. (*0-03-006168-7*); pap. o.p. (*0-03-005968-2*, Owl Bks.) Holt, Henry & Co.
Smith, Barbara Dawson. Too Wicked to Love. 1999. 352p. mass mkt. 5.99 (*0-312-96893-0*, St. Martin's Paperbacks) St. Martin's Pr.
Smith, Carol. Friends for Life. 480p. 2001. pap. 4.95 (*0-446-52004-7*); 1997. mass mkt. 6.50 (*0-446-60445-3*) Warner Bks., Inc.
Smith, Cynthia. Silver & Guilt. 1998. (Emma Rhodes Mysteries Ser.). 256p. mass mkt. 5.99 o.s.i (*0-425-16382-2*, Prime Crime) Berkley Publishing Group.
Smith, Dodie. I Capture the Castle. 2003. (Illus.). 352p. pap. 13.95 (*0-312-31616-X*); 2000. pap. 69.75 (*0-312-26533-6*) St. Martin's Pr. (Saint Martin's Griffin).
Smith, Frank. Acts of Vengeance: A Mystery. 2003. 368p. 24.95 (*0-312-30739-X*, Saint Martin's Minotaur) St. Martin's Pr.
—Fatal Flaw, No. 331. 1999. (WWL Mystery Ser.: Vol. 331). mass mkt. (*0-373-26331-7*, Worldwide Library) Harlequin Enterprises, Ltd.
—Fatal Flaw. 1996. 256p. 20.95 o.p. (*0-312-14332-X*, Saint Martin's Minotaur) St. Martin's Pr.
—Stone Dead. 1999. (WWL Mystery Ser.: No. 20). per. (*0-373-26320-1*, 1-26320-1, Worldwide Library) Harlequin Enterprises, Ltd.
—Stone Dead. 1998. 192p. 20.95 o.p. (*0-312-18186-8*, Saint Martin's Minotaur) St. Martin's Pr.
—Stone Dead. l.t. ed. 1998. (Mystery Ser.). 373p. 26.95 (*0-7862-1664-6*) Thorndike Pr.
—Thread of Evidence. E-Book 24.95 (*0-312-70124-1*); 2001. 309p. 24.95 (*0-312-26947-1*, Saint Martin's Minotaur) St. Martin's Pr.
Smith, Haywood. Border Lord. 2001. 384p. mass mkt. 6.50 (*0-312-97859-6*, St. Martin's Paperbacks) St. Martin's Pr.
—Dangerous Gifts. Enderlin, J., ed. 1999. 320p. mass mkt. 5.99 o.s.i (*0-312-96883-3*, St. Martin's Paperbacks) St. Martin's Pr.
Smith, Janet Elaine. Dunnottar. FirstPublish, Inc. Staff, ed. 2000. (Illus.). 191p. pap. 19.95 o.p. (*1-929925-04-2*) FirstPublish.
—Dunnottar. 2002. 232p. per. 17.95 (*1-930252-80-3*) PageFree Publishing, Inc.
Smith, Joan. Behold, a Mystery! 1994. 256p. 20.95 o.p. (*0-312-10424-3*, Saint Martin's Minotaur) St. Martin's Pr.
—Kissing Cousins. 1995. mass mkt. 4.50 o.s.i (*0-449-22381-7*, Fawcett) Ballantine Bks.
—A Masculine Ending. 1989. 224p. mass mkt. 5.99 o.s.i (*0-449-21688-8*, Fawcett) Ballantine Bks.
—A Masculine Ending. 1988. 186p. 15.95 o.s.i (*0-684-18938-0*, Macmillan Reference USA) Gale Group.
—Murder & Misdeeds. 1997. mass mkt. 4.50 o.s.i (*0-449-28791-2*, Fawcett) Ballantine Bks.
—Murder Comes to Mind. 1998. mass mkt. 4.99 o.s.i (*0-449-00287-X*, Fawcett) Ballantine Bks.
—Murder While I Smile. 1997. mass mkt. 4.99 o.s.i (*0-449-22494-5*, Fawcett) Ballantine Bks.
—Murder Will Speak. 1997. mass mkt. 4.50 o.s.i (*0-449-22465-1*, Fawcett) Ballantine Bks.
—Murder Will Speak. 1996. 208p. 21.95 o.p. (*0-312-14378-8*, Saint Martin's Minotaur) St. Martin's Pr.
—What Men Say. 1995. mass mkt. 5.99 o.s.i (*0-449-22297-7*, Fawcett) Ballantine Bks.
—What Men Say: A Loretta Lawson Mystery. 1994. 224p. 20.00 o.s.i (*0-449-90920-4*, Fawcett) Ballantine Bks.
Smith, Martin Cruz. Rose. 2000. 416p. mass mkt. 7.99 (*0-345-42252-X*); 1997. 384p. pap. 14.00 (*0-345-39044-X*); 1997. mass mkt. 7.99 o.s.i (*0-345-41232-X*) Ballantine Bks.
—Rose. unabr. collector's ed. 1997. audio 64.00 (*0-913369-68-3*, 4319) Books on Tape, Inc.
—Rose. l.t. ed. 1996. 588p. 25.00 o.p. (*0-7838-1681-2*, Macmillan Reference USA) Gale Group.
—Rose. 1998. (Coleccion Bestseller Mundial). (SPA., Illus.). 410p. (*84-08-02445-0*) GeoPlaneta, Editorial, S. A.
—Rose, unabr. ed. 1997. audio 85.00 (*0-7887-0918-6*, 95058E7) Recorded Bks., LLC.

Smith, Stevie. Novel on Yellow Paper. 1994. (Revived Modern Classic Ser.: Vol. 778). 256p. reprint ed. pap. 10.95 (*0-8112-1239-4*, NDP778) New Directions Publishing Corp.

Smith, Zadie. White Teeth. E-Book 19.95 (*1-58945-566-5*) Adobe Systems, Inc.

—White Teeth. l.t. ed. 2000. 717p. 28.95 o.p. (*1-56895-950-8*, Wheeler Publishing, Inc.) Gale Group.

—White Teeth. 2001. E-Book 19.95 (*0-375-50561-X*) Random Hse., Inc.

—White Teeth: A Novel. 2001. (International Ser.). 464p. reprint ed. pap. 14.00 (*0-375-70386-1*, Vintage) Knopf Publishing Group.

—White Teeth: A Novel. 2000. (Illus.). 464p. 24.95 (*0-375-50185-1*) Random Hse., Inc.

Smithers, David W. Dicken's Doctors. 1979. 68.00 o.p. (*0-08-023386-4*) Pergamon Pr. Reprint GBR. *Dist:* Franklin Bk. Co., Inc.

Sole, Linda. The Last Summer of Innocence. 1991. 336p. 19.95 o.p. (*0-312-07015-2*) St. Martin's Pr.

—Shadow Players. 1992. 320p. 19.95 o.p. (*0-312-08292-4*) St. Martin's Pr.

—This Land This Love. 1998. 320p. 23.95 (*0-312-18195-7*) St. Martin's Pr.

—This Land, This Love. l.t. ed. 1997. (Ulverscroft Large Print Ser.). 704p. 29.99 o.p. (*0-7089-3871-X*, Ulverscroft) Thorpe, F. A. Pubs. GBR. *Dist:* Ulverscroft Large Print Bks., Ltd., Ulverscroft Large Print Canada, Ltd.

Solmssen, Arthur R. G. The Wife of Shore: A Search. 2000. (Illus.). vi, 284p. (Orig.). pap. 20.00 (*0-9705336-0-8*) Mill Creek Pr.

Solomon, Hayley Ann. By Way of a Wager. 2000. (Zebra Regency Romance Ser.). 256p. mass mkt. 4.99 o.s.i (*0-8217-6723-2*, Zebra Bks.) Kensington Publishing Corp.

—Raven's Ransom. 2001. (Zebra Regency Romance Ser.). 288p. mass mkt. 4.99 o.s.i (*0-8217-6782-8*, Zebra Bks.) Kensington Publishing Corp.

—A Scandalous Connection. 2002. (Zebra Regency Romance Ser.). 256p. mass mkt. 4.99 o.s.i (*0-8217-7235-X*) Kensington Publishing Corp.

Somers, Jane. The Diary of a Good Neighbor. 1983. 12.95 o.s.i (*0-394-52970-7*) Knopf, Alfred A. Inc.

South, Sheri Cobb. Miss Darby's Duenna. l.t. ed. 2001. (G. K. Hall Romance Ser.). 217p. 26.95 (*0-7838-9532-1*, Macmillan Reference USA) Gale Group.

—The Weaver Takes A Wife. 1999. 234p. pap. 12.95 (*0-9668005-0-8*) PrinnyWorld Pr.

—The Weaver Takes a Wife. l.t. ed. 2000. (G. K. Hall Romance Ser.). 237p. 27.95 (*0-7838-9304-3*, Macmillan Reference USA) Gale Group.

Spark, Muriel. The Abbess of Crewe. 1995. (Bibelots Ser.). 116p. pap. 6.00 (*0-8112-1296-3*, 805) New Directions Publishing Corp.

—The Abbess of Crewe. 1984. 128p. pap. 6.95 o.p. (*0-399-50952-6*) Putnam Publishing Group, The.

—The Abbess of Crewe. 1977. 112p. pap. 1.95 o.p. (*0-14-004074-9*, Penguin Bks.); 1974. 6.95 o.p. (*0-670-10029-3*) Viking Penguin.

—Aiding & Abetting. 2001. E-Book 10.00 (*1-58945-957-1*) Adobe Systems, Inc.

—Aiding & Abetting. 2002. 176p. pap. 11.00 (*0-385-72090-4*, Knopf Bks. for Young Readers) Random Hse. Children's Bks.

—Aiding & Abetting. l.t. ed. 2001. (Thorndike Basic Ser.). 192p. 29.95 (*0-7862-3184-X*); (*0-7540-4515-3*) Thorndike Pr.

—A Far Cry from Kensington. 1988. 192p. 17.95 o.p. (*0-395-47694-1*) Houghton Mifflin Co.

—A Far Cry from Kensington. 1990. 192p. pap. 7.95 (*0-380-70786-1*, Avon Bks.) Morrow/Avon.

—A Far Cry from Kensington. 2000. (Classics Ser.). 189p. pap. 12.95 (*0-8112-1457-5*) New Directions Publishing Corp.

—A Far Cry from Kensington. 1990. 3.99 o.p. (*0-517-05284-9*) Random Hse. Value Publishing.

—The Girls of Slender Means. l.t. ed. 1986. (Mainstream Ser.). 148p. reprint ed. lib. bdg. 15.50 o.p. (*1-85089-053-6*) ISIS Large Print Bks. GBR. *Dist:* Transaction Pubs.

—The Girls of Slender Means. 1990. 128p. pap. 7.95 (*0-380-70937-6*, Avon Bks.) Morrow/Avon.

—The Girls of Slender Means. 1998. (Classics Ser.). 144p. pap. 10.95 (*0-8112-1379-X*, NDP859) New Directions Publishing Corp.

—The Girls of Slender Means. 1982. 192p. pap. 5.95 o.p. (*0-399-50659-4*) Putnam Publishing Group, The.

—The Girls of Slender Means. 1963. 4.95 o.p. (*0-394-42637-1*, Knopf Bks. for Young Readers) Random Hse. Children's Bks.

Spencer, Sally. Death of a Cave Dweller. l.t. ed. 2001. (Magna Large Print Ser.). 336p. (*0-7505-1704-2*) Magna Large Print Bks. GBR. *Dist:* Ulverscroft Large Print Canada, Ltd.

—Death of a Cave Dweller. 256p. 26.00 (*0-7278-5543-3*) Severn Hse. Pubs., Ltd.

Spring, Michelle. Every Breath You Take. 1999. (Laura Principal Mysteries Ser.). 256p. mass mkt. 5.99 (*0-345-43548-6*) Ballantine Bks.

—Every Breath You Take. 256p. 1995. mass mkt. 5.50 (*0-671-87092-0*, Pocket); 1994. 20.00 o.p. (*0-671-87091-2*, Atria) Simon & Schuster.

—In the Midnight Hour. 2002. 304p. mass mkt. 6.99 (*0-345-43747-0*) Random Hse., Inc.

—Nights in White Satin: A Laura Principal Novel. 2000. 336p. mass mkt. 6.99 (*0-345-42494-8*, Fawcett); 1999. 288p. 23.00 o.s.i (*0-345-42493-X*) Ballantine Bks.

—Running for Shelter. 2000. (Laura Principal Mysteries Ser.). 256p. mass mkt. 6.50 (*0-345-43549-4*, Fawcett) Ballantine Bks.

—Running for Shelter: A Laura Principal Mystery. 1997. per. 5.99 (*0-671-87094-7*, Pocket); 1996. 288p. 21.00 o.p. (*0-671-87093-9*, Atria) Simon & Schuster.

—Standing in the Shadows. 1999. 336p. mass mkt. 5.99 (*0-345-42492-1*) Ballantine Bks.

—Standing in the Shadows. l.t. ed. 1999. (Ulverscroft Large Print Ser.). 464p. 31.99 o.p. (*0-7089-4053-6*, Ulverscroft) Thorpe, F. A. Pubs. GBR. *Dist:* Ulverscroft Large Print Bks., Ltd., Ulverscroft Large Print Canada, Ltd.

Springer, Nancy. Rowan Hood. 2002. 176p. (J). pap. 5.99 (*0-698-11972-X*, PaperStar) Penguin Putnam Bks. for Young Readers.

St. John, Madeleine. A Pure Clear Light. 2000. 240p. 22.00 (*0-7867-0756-9*, Carroll & Graf Pubs.) Avalon Publishing Group.

—A Pure Clear Light. 1996. 233p. (*1-85702-387-0*) Fourth Estate, Ltd.

—A Stairway to Paradise. 1999. 185p. 22.00 o.p. (*0-7867-0662-7*); 2000. 192p. reprint ed. pap. 11.95 (*0-7867-0795-X*) Avalon Publishing Group. (Carroll & Graf Pubs.).

—A Stairway to Paradise. 1999. 185p. pap. (*1-85702-881-3*) Fourth Estate, Ltd.

Stableford, Brian M. The Angel of Pain. 1993. 396p. 21.00 o.p. (*0-88184-932-4*, Carroll & Graf Pubs.) Avalon Publishing Group.

Stacey, Susannah. Body of Opinion. 1990. mass mkt. o.s.i (*0-552-13470-8*, Corgi) Bantam Bks.

—Body of Opinion. 1990. 17.95 o.p. (*0-671-69170-8*, Simon & Schuster) Simon & Schuster.

—Body of Opinion. Chelius, Jane, ed. 1991. 224p. reprint ed. mass mkt. 4.99 (*0-671-73427-X*, Pocket) Simon & Schuster.

—Bone Idle. 320p. 1996. mass mkt. 5.99 (*0-671-51062-2*, Pocket); 1995. 21.00 o.p. (*0-671-73531-4*, Atria) Simon & Schuster.

—Dead Serious. 1997. (Superintendent Bone Mystery Ser.). 320p. per. 5.99 (*0-671-00118-3*, Pocket) Simon & Schuster.

—Goodbye, Nanny Gray. 1989. mass mkt. 4.50 (*0-671-65779-8*, Pocket) Simon & Schuster.

—Goodbye, Nanny Gray. 1988. 16.95 o.p. (*0-671-65778-X*) Summit Bks.

—Grave Responsibility: A Superintendent Bone Mystery. l.t. ed. 1992. 20.95 o.p. (*0-7927-1054-1*); pap. 18.95 o.p. (*0-7927-1055-X*) BBC Audiobooks America.

—Grave Responsibility: A Superintendent Bone Mystery. Chelius, Jane, ed. 1992. 224p. reprint ed. mass mkt. 4.50 (*0-671-77827-7*, Pocket) Simon & Schuster.

—Grave Responsibility: A Superintendent Bone Mystery. 1991. 160p. 17.95 o.p. (*0-671-69171-6*) Summit Bks.

—Hunters Quarry. 1998. 352p. mass mkt. 6.50 (*0-671-00119-1*, Pocket) Simon & Schuster.

—A Knife at the Opera: An Inspector Bone Mystery. 1990. 224p. mass mkt. 4.99 (*0-671-70508-3*, Pocket) Simon & Schuster.

—A Knife at the Opera: An Inspector Bone Mystery. 1989. 17.95 o.p. (*0-671-65780-1*) Summit Bks.

—The Late Lady. l.t. ed. 1993. 23.95 o.p. (*0-7927-1692-2*); pap. 21.95 o.p. (*0-7927-1691-4*) BBC Audiobooks America.

—The Late Lady. 1994. 256p. mass mkt. 4.99 (*0-671-73895-X*, Pocket) Simon & Schuster.

—The Late Lady. Chelius, Jane, ed. 1993. 256p. 20.00 (*0-671-73530-6*, Atria) Simon & Schuster.

Staincliffe, Cath. Stone Cold Red Hot. (Sal Kilkenny Myerstery Ser.). 2002. 263p. pap. 9.95 (*0-7490-0522-X*); 2001. 254p. 24.95 (*0-7490-0515-7*) Allison & Busby, Ltd. GBR. *Dist:* International Publishers Marketing.

—Stone Cold Red Hot. l.t. ed. 2002. (Magna Large Print Ser.). 320p. 32.50 (*0-7505-1875-8*) Magna Large Print Bks. GBR. *Dist:* Ulverscroft Large Print Bks., Ltd., Ulverscroft Large Print Canada, Ltd.

Stallwood, Veronica. Death & the Oxford Box: A Mystery Introducing Kate Ivory. 1994. 224p. 20.00 o.p. (*0-684-19596-8*, Macmillan Reference USA) Gale Group.

—Deathspell. l.t. ed. 1994. 21.95 o.p. (*0-7927-1989-1*); pap. 19.95 o.p. (*0-7927-1988-3*) BBC Audiobooks America.

—Deathspell. 1992. 224p. text 20.00 (*0-684-19517-8*, Macmillan Reference USA) Gale Group.

—Oxford Exit. 1995. 192p. 20.00 o.s.i (*0-684-19729-4*, Scribner) Simon & Schuster.

—Oxford Mourning: A Kate Ivory Mystery. 1996. 208p. 20.00 o.p. (*0-684-19730-8*, Scribner) Simon & Schuster.

—Oxford Mourning: A Kate Ivory Mystery. l.t. ed. 1997. (Ulverscroft Large Print Ser.). 448p. 31.50 o.p. (*0-7089-3710-1*, Ulverscroft) Thorpe, F. A. Pubs. GBR. *Dist:* Ulverscroft Large Print Bks., Ltd., Ulverscroft Large Print Canada, Ltd.

Stanhope. Dear Boy. 2000. 16.95 (*0-593-01790-0*) Transworld Publishers Ltd. GBR. *Dist:* Trafalgar Square.

Staples, John. Camberwell Raid. 2000. (Illus.). 318p. pap. 8.95 (*0-552-14469-X*) Transworld Publishers Ltd. GBR. *Dist:* Trafalgar Square.

—Echoes of Yesterday. 2000. 348p. pap. 8.95 (*0-552-14375-8*) Transworld Publishers Ltd. GBR. *Dist:* Trafalgar Square.

—Ghost of Whitechapel. 2000. 316p. (J). pap. 10.95 (*0-552-14548-3*) Transworld Publishers Ltd. GBR. *Dist:* Trafalgar Square.

Staples, Mary Jane. Camberwell Road. 2000. (Illus.). 318p. 27.95 (*0-593-04043-0*) Transworld Publishers Ltd. GBR. *Dist:* Trafalgar Square.

—Fire over London. l.t. ed. 2000. (Magna Large Print Ser.). 448p. (*0-7505-1466-3*) Magna Large Print Bks. GBR. *Dist:* Ulverscroft Large Print Bks., Ltd., Ulverscroft Large Print Canada, Ltd.

—Ghost Whitechapel. 2000. 316p. 27.95 (*0-593-04146-1*) Transworld Publishers Ltd. GBR. *Dist:* Trafalgar Square.

—King of Camberwell. 2000. pap. 8.95 (*0-552-13573-9*) Transworld Publishers Ltd. GBR. *Dist:* Trafalgar Square.

—Missing Person. 2000. 25.95 (*0-593-03641-7*); pap. 8.95 (*0-552-14230-1*) Transworld Publishers Ltd. GBR. *Dist:* Trafalgar Square.

—On Mother Brown's Doorstep. 2000. (J). pap. 9.95 (*0-552-13975-0*) Transworld Publishers Ltd. GBR. *Dist:* Trafalgar Square.

—Our Emily. 2000. (J). pap. 10.95 (*0-552-13444-9*) Transworld Publishers Ltd. GBR. *Dist:* Trafalgar Square.

—The Pearly Queen. 2000. 379p. (J). pap. 7.95 (*0-552-13856-8*) Transworld Publishers Ltd. GBR. *Dist:* Trafalgar Square.

—The Trap. l.t. ed. 1994. (Magna Large Print Ser.). 474p. 29.99 o.p. (*0-7505-0707-1*) Magna Large Print Bks. GBR. *Dist:* Ulverscroft Large Print Bks., Ltd., Ulverscroft Large Print Canada, Ltd.

—The Trap. 2000. 381p. pap. 8.95 (*0-552-14106-2*) Transworld Publishers Ltd. GBR. *Dist:* Trafalgar Square.

—The Young Ones. 2000. 331p. pap. 9.95 (*0-552-14418-5*) Transworld Publishers Ltd. GBR. *Dist:* Trafalgar Square.

Starr, Sarah A. Lady-Lessons. 2000. 256p. E-Book 4.95 (*1-929085-18-4*); 256p. 19.95 (*1-929085-17-6*); 256p. mass mkt. 4.95 (*1-929085-16-8*); 356p. E-Book incl. disk, cd-rom (*1-929085-19-2*); 356p. per. 19.95 (*1-929085-20-6*) Regency Pr.

Staynes, Jill. Goodbye, Nanny Gray. l.t. ed. 1990. (Ulverscroft Large Print Ser.). 29.99 o.p. (*0-7089-2261-9*, Ulverscroft) Thorpe, F. A. Pubs. GBR. *Dist:* Ulverscroft Large Print Bks., Ltd., Ulverscroft Large Print Canada, Ltd.

Steed, Neville. Boxed In. 1992. 256p. 18.95 o.p. (*0-312-07662-2*, Saint Martin's Minotaur) St. Martin's Pr.

Steel, Danielle. The Kiss. 2001. 360p. 26.95 (*0-385-33540-7*, Delacorte Pr.) Dell Publishing.

Stephens, Kay. Dark Before Dawn. 288p. 24.00 (*0-7278-4988-3*) Severn Hse. Pubs., Ltd.

—Felstead. l.t. ed. 1997. 223p. pap. 21.95 o.p. (*0-7838-8076-6*, Macmillan Reference USA) Gale Group.

—Felstead. 1996. 192p. 22.00 (*0-7278-4961-1*) Severn Hse. Pubs., Ltd.

Sterne, Laurence. The Florida Edition of the Works of Laurence Sterne, 2 vols., Vol. 1. New, Melvyn & New, Joan, eds. 1978. (Florida Edition of the Works of Laurence Sterne). 487p. 49.95 (*0-8130-0580-9*) Univ. Pr. of Florida.

—The Life & Opinions of Tristram Shandy, Gentleman. 1979. 7.00 o.p. (*0-460-00617-7*); 1975. 4.95 o.p. (*0-460-01617-2*) Dutton/Plume. (Dutton).

—The Life & Opinions of Tristram Shandy, Gentleman, 001. Watt, Ian, ed. 1965. (C). pap. 14.76 o.p. (*0-395-05145-2*, Riverside Editions) Houghton Mifflin Co.

—The Life & Opinions of Tristram Shandy, Gentleman. 2002. 452p. 21.99 (*1-4043-1470-9*); per. 17.99 (*1-4043-1471-7*) IndyPublish.com.

—The Life & Opinions of Tristram Shandy, Gentleman. 1962. mass mkt. 1.50 o.p. (*0-451-50857-2*); mass mkt. 0.75 o.p. (*0-451-50142-X*); mass mkt. 0.95 o.p. (*0-451-50607-3*); mass mkt. 1.95 o.p. (*0-451-51051-8*); mass mkt. 2.95 o.p. (*0-451-51424-6*); mass mkt. 3.95 o.p. (*0-451-51778-4*) NAL. (Signet Classics).

—The Life & Opinions of Tristram Shandy, Gentleman. Ross, Ian C., ed. & intro. by. 1998. (Oxford World's Classics Ser.). (Illus.). 626p. pap. 9.95 (*0-19-283470-3*) Oxford Univ. Pr., Inc.

—The Life & Opinions of Tristram Shandy, Gentleman. Ross, Ian C., ed. 1983. 624p. pap. 7.95 o.p. (*0-19-281566-0*) Oxford Univ. Pr., Inc.

—The Life & Opinions of Tristram Shandy, Gentleman, 3 vols. New, Melvyn, ed. 1978. (Florida Edition of the Works of Laurence Sterne). 75.00 o.p. (*0-8130-0819-0*) Univ. Pr. of Florida.

—The Life & Opinions of Tristram Shandy, Gentleman. New, Melvyn & New, Joan, eds. 1998. (Penguin Classics Ser.). (Illus.). 720p. 11.00 (*0-14-043505-0*) Viking Penguin.

—The Life & Opinions of Tristram Shandy, Gentleman. Ricks, Christopher & Petrie, Graham, eds. 1967. (English Library). 656p. pap. 9.95 o.s.i (*0-14-043019-9*, Penguin Classics) Viking Penguin.

—The Life & Opinions of Tristram Shandy, Gentleman. 1998. (Classics Library). 464p. pap. 3.95 (*1-85326-291-9*, 2919WW) Wordsworth Editions, Ltd. GBR. *Dist:* Combined Publishing.

—The Life & Opinions of Tristram Shandy, Gentleman: The Notes. New, Melvyn, ed. 1984. (Florida Edition of the Works of Laurence Sterne: Vol. 3). (Illus.). 572p. 49.95 (*0-8130-0738-0*) Univ. Pr. of Florida.

—The Life & Opinions of Tristram Shandy, Gentleman: The Text, 2 vols., 2. New, Melvyn & New, Joan, eds. 1978. (Florida Edition of the Works of Laurence Sterne). 475p. 49.95 (*0-8130-0599-X*) Univ. Pr. of Florida.

—The Life & Opinions of Tristram Shandy, Gentleman & a Sentimental Journey. 1999. E-Book 4.95 (*0-679-64007-X*, Modern Library) Random House Adult Trade Publishing Group.

—Tristram Shandy. 1991. (Everyman's Library: Vol. 7). 752p. 23.00 (*0-679-40560-7*, Everyman's Library) Knopf Publishing Group.

—Tristram Shandy. 1992. 512p. pap. 6.95 o.p. (*0-460-87130-7*, Everyman's Classic Library in Paperback) Tuttle Publishing.

Steven, William, et al. Looking for the Down Tale. Thompson, Dorothy, ed. 1987. (Chartism, Working-Class Politics in the Industrial Revolution Ser.). 392p. lib. bdg. 31.00 o.p. (*0-8240-5582-9*) Garland Publishing, Inc.

Stevens, David. Waters of Babylon: A Novel about Lawrence after Arabia. 2000. 320p. 24.00 o.s.i (*0-684-86210-7*, Simon & Schuster) Simon & Schuster.

Stevens, Rosemary. Death on a Silver Tray. (Beau Brummell Mysteries Ser.). 288p. 2001. mass mkt. 6.50 (*0-425-17946-X*); 2000. 21.95 o.s.i (*0-425-17468-9*) Berkley Publishing Group. (Prime Crime).

—The Tainted Snuff Box: A Beau Brummell Mystery. 2001. 304p. text 21.95 o.s.i (*0-425-17948-6*, Prime Crime) Berkley Publishing Group.

Stevens, Serita & Moore, Rayanne. Bagels for Tea. 2002. 212p. pap. 10.95 (*0-7599-0374-3*); 2nd ed. 2000. (Fanny Zendel Mystery Ser.: Vol. 2). E-Book 6.00 (*1-58200-506-0*) Hard Shell Word Factory.

—Bagels for Tea. 1993. 272p. 18.95 o.p. (*0-312-09348-9*, Saint Martin's Minotaur) St. Martin's Pr.

Stevenson, Jane. London Bridges: A Novel. 2002. 304p. pap. 13.00 (*0-618-25773-X*, Mariner Bks.) Houghton Mifflin Co. Trade & Reference Div.

Stevenson, Robert Louis. Dr. Jekyll & Mr. Hyde. (Illus.). lib. bdg. 19.95 (*0-88411-994-7*, Aeonian Pr.) Amereon, Ltd.

—Dr. Jekyll & Mr. Hyde. 1992. (Everyman's Library). 272p. 17.00 (*0-679-40538-0*) McKay, David Co., Inc.

—Dr. Jekyll & Mr. Hyde. 1987. (Running Press Classics Ser.). 63p. pap. 2.95 o.p. (*0-89471-491-0*); lib. bdg. 12.90 o.p. (*0-89471-492-9*) Running Pr. Bk. Pubs.

—Dr. Jekyll & Mr. Hyde. 1998. 135p. text 27.95 (*1-56000-517-3*) Transaction Pubs.

—Dr. Jekyll & Mr. Hyde & Other Stories. E-Book 5.00 (*0-7607-1297-2*) Barnes & Noble, Inc.

—Dr. Jekyll & Mr. Hyde & Other Stories. 1982. (Oxford Progressive English Readers Ser.). (Illus.). pap. 4.95 o.p. (*0-19-581056-2*) Oxford Univ. Pr., Inc.

—Dr. Jekyll & Mr. Hyde & Other Stories. 1994. (Literary Classics Ser.). 221p. (YA). text 5.98 o.p. (*1-56138-474-7*, Courage Bks.) Running Pr. Bk. Pubs.

—Dr. Jekyll & Mr. Hyde & Other Stories. Calder, Jenni, ed. 1981. (English Library). pap. 2.95 o.p. (*0-14-005776-5*) Viking Penguin.

—Dr. Jekyll & Mr. Hyde & Other Stories. Calder, Jenni, ed. & intro. by. 1980. (Penguin English Library). 304p. pap. 6.95 o.s.i (*0-14-043117-9*, Penguin Classics) Viking Penguin.

—Dr. Jekyll & Mr. Hyde & Weir of Hermiston. Letley, Emma, ed. & intro. by. 1987. (Oxford World's Classics Ser.). 256p. pap. 5.95 o.p. (*0-19-281740-X*) Oxford Univ. Pr., Inc.

—The Strange Case of Dr. Jekyll & Mr. Hyde. 1991. (Dover Thrift Editions Ser.). 64p. pap. 1.00 (*0-486-26688-5*) Dover Pubns., Inc.

—The Strange Case of Dr. Jekyll & Mr. Hyde. Qualls, Barry V., ed. & intro. by. 1995. 144p. mass mkt. 3.99 (0-671-53210-3, Pocket) Simon & Schuster.
—The Strange Case of Dr. Jekyll & Mr. Hyde. 1990. (Illus.). 164p. reprint ed. 25.00 o.p. (0-8032-4212-3) Univ. of Nebraska Pr.
Stewart, Marcy. The Daring Miss Lassiter. 2001. (Zebra Regency Romance Ser.). 256p. mass mkt. 4.99 o.s.i (0-8217-6813-1, Zebra Bks.) Kensington Publishing Corp.
Stewart, Mary. The Crystal Cave. 1996. (Book I of the Arthurian Saga Ser.). 544p. pap. 12.95 o.s.i (0-449-91161-6, Fawcett) Ballantine Bks.
—The Crystal Cave. 1983. 19.00 (0-606-18993-9) Turtleback Bks.
—The Prince & the Pilgrim. 1996. 292p. 23.00 o.p. (0-688-14538-8, Morrow, William & Co.) Morrow/Avon.
—Rose Cottage. l.t. ed. 1998. 26.95 (1-56895-550-2, Wheeler Publishing, Inc.) Gale Group.
—Rose Cottage. abr. ed. 1997. mass mkt. incl. audio (1-85998-876-8) Hodder Audiobooks.
—Rose Cottage. 1997. 208p. 24.00 (0-688-15584-7, Morrow, William & Co.) Morrow/Avon.
—Rose Cottage. abr. ed. 1997. 18.00 o.p. (0-7871-1662-9) NewStar Media, Inc.
—Rose Cottage: A Novel. 1998. (Illus.). 272p. mass mkt. 6.99 (0-449-00061-3, Fawcett) Ballantine Bks.
—The Wicked Day. 1996. (Arthurian Saga Ser.: Vol. 4). 464p. pap. 14.00 o.s.i (0-449-91185-3, Fawcett) Ballantine Bks.
Stewart, Sally. Postcards from a Stranger. l.t. ed. 2000. (Magna Large Print Ser.). 320p. 31.99 (0-7505-1468-X) Magna Large Print Bks. GBR. *Dist:* Ulverscroft Large Print Bks., Ltd., Ulverscroft Large Print Canada, Ltd.
Stickland, Caroline. An Ancient Hope. l.t. ed. 1994. 392p. lib. bdg. 21.95 (0-8161-7469-5, Macmillan Reference USA) Gale Group.
—An Ancient Hope. 1994. 272p. 20.95 o.p. (0-312-10929-6) St. Martin's Pr.
—The Darkening Leaf. l.t. ed. 1997. (Ulverscroft Large Print Ser.). 464p. 29.99 o.p. (0-7089-3675-X, Ulverscroft) Thorpe, F. A. Pubs. GBR. *Dist:* Ulverscroft Large Print Bks., Ltd., Ulverscroft Large Print Canada, Ltd.
—The Darkening Leaf. 2000. 286p. 27.95 (0-385-40539-1) Transworld Publishers Ltd. GBR. *Dist:* Trafalgar Square.
—Darkness of Corn. 1991. 16.95 o.p. (0-312-05844-6) St. Martin's Pr.
Stinto, Judith. Tom's Tale. 1983. (Illus.). (J). (gr. k-3). 5.95 o.p. (0-531-04606-0, Watts, Franklin) Scholastic Library Publishing.
Stirling. Drums of Time. 1979. 12.95 o.p. (0-312-22019-7) St. Martin's Pr.
Stirling, Jessica. The Gates of Midnight. 1983. 256p. 13.95 o.p. (0-312-31763-8) St. Martin's Pr.
Stoker, Bram. Dracula. 2000. 252p. E-Book 9.95 (0-594-05212-2) 1873 Pr.
—Dracula. Date not set. pap. text (0-17-557040-X) Addison-Wesley Longman, Inc.
—Dracula. Date not set. reprint ed. lib. bdg. 27.95 (0-88411-131-8, Aeonian Pr.) Amereon, Ltd.
—Dracula. 2000. (SPA.). 496p. 10.95 (84-406-5500-2) B Ediciones S.A. ESP. *Dist:* Distribooks, Inc.
—Dracula. abr. ed. 1995. audio 19.95 (1-882071-36-0) B&B Audio, Inc.
—Dracula. 1983. mass mkt. 1.95 o.s.i (0-553-21148-X, Bantam Classics) Bantam Bks.
—Dracula. E-Book 5.00 (0-7607-1358-8) Barnes & Noble, Inc.
—Dracula. Bennett, S. A., ed. 1992. (Illus.). 64p. pap. (0-944099-20-3) Bill Barry's Compass Bks.
—Dracula. 2002. pap. 4.50 (1-59109-321-X) Booksurge, LLC.
—Dracula. 1992. 320p. reprint ed. pap. 9.95 (0-86322-143-2) Brandon Bk. Pubs., Ltd. IRL. *Dist:* Irish Bks. & Media, Inc.
—Dracula. Byron, Glennis, ed. 1997. (Literary Texts Ser.). 400p. (C). pap. (1-55111-136-5) Broadview Pr.
—Dracula. 1990. reprint ed. lib. bdg. 26.95 (0-89966-692-2) Buccaneer Bks., Inc.
—Dracula. ed. 1999. (J). (gr. 2). spiral bd. (0-616-01788-X) Canadian National Institute for the Blind/Institut National Canadien pour les Aveugles.
—Dracula. reprint ed. lib. bdg. 98.00 (0-7426-2890-6); 2001. pap. text 28.00 (0-7426-7890-3) Classic Bks.
—Dracula. 1997. 384p. 21.95 (0-312-86358-6, Tor Bks.); 1992. 384p. mass mkt. 4.99 (0-8125-2301-6, Tor Classics); 1988. mass mkt. 4.95 (1-55902-006-7, Aerie) Doherty, Tom Assocs., LLC.
—Dracula. 1959. 7.95 o.p. (0-385-00383-8) Doubleday Publishing.
—Dracula. 2000. 320p. pap. 2.00 (0-486-41109-5) Dover Pubns., Inc.
—Dracula. 1980. 82p. (YA). (gr. 7 up). pap. 5.60 (0-87129-308-0, D35) Dramatic Publishing Co.
—Dracula. l.t. ed. 2079p. pap. 123.00 (0-7583-3191-6); 1792p. pap. 110.00 (0-7583-3190-8); 406p. pap. 32.00 (0-7583-3184-3); 528p. pap. 37.00 (0-7583-3185-1); 723p. pap. 45.00 (0-7583-3186-X); 926p. pap. 64.00 (0-7583-3187-8); 1185p. pap. 76.00 (0-7583-3188-6); 528p. lib. bdg. 43.00 (0-7583-3177-0); 1792p. lib. bdg. 133.00 (0-7583-3182-7); 406p. lib. bdg. 38.00 (0-7583-3176-2); 723p. lib. bdg. 51.00 (0-7583-3178-9); 926p. lib. bdg. 76.00 (0-7583-3179-7); 1185p. lib. bdg. 88.00 (0-7583-3180-0); 1457p. lib. bdg. 102.00 (0-7583-3181-9); 2079p. lib. bdg. 148.00 (0-7583-3183-5) Huge Print Pr.
—Dracula. 1998. (Cloth Bound Pocket Ser.). 240p. 7.95 (3-89508-096-9, 520018) Konemann.
—Dracula. 2002. (Classics for Young Readers Ser.). (SPA.). (YA). 14.95 (84-392-0934-7, EV30652) Lectorum Pubns., Inc.
—Dracula. 2000. (English As a Second Language Bk.). pap. text 5.95 o.p. (0-582-53523-9) Longman Publishing Group.
—Dracula. 1989. 368p. 19.95 o.p. (0-87226-189-1, Bedrick, Peter Bks.) McGraw-Hill Children's Publishing.
—Dracula. 1992. 392p. mass mkt. 3.99 o.p. (0-451-17581-6, Signet Classics); 1986. mass mkt. 2.50 o.p. (0-451-52097-1); 1973. mass mkt. 0.60 o.p. (0-451-02793-0, Signet Bks.); 1973. mass mkt. 0.95 o.p. (0-451-05438-5, Signet Bks.); 1965. mass mkt. 1.75 o.p. (0-451-51129-8, Signet Classics); 1965. mass mkt. 2.50 o.p. (0-451-51670-2, Signet Classics); 1965. mass mkt. 1.50 o.p. (0-451-51030-5, Signet Classics); 1965. mass mkt. 1.95 o.p. (0-451-51889-6, Signet Classics); 1965. mass mkt. 1.25 o.p. (0-451-50717-7, Signet Classics) NAL.
—Dracula. l.t. ed. (Large Print Ser.). 1993. 558p. lib. bdg. 26.00 (0-939495-43-0); 1998. 435p. reprint ed. lib. bdg. 25.00 (1-58287-024-1) North Bks.
—Dracula. l.t. ed. 2003. 448p. E-Book 2.99 (1-932681-17-5) NuVision Pubns.
—Dracula. Ellmann, Maud, ed. & intro. by. 1998. (Oxford World's Classics Ser.). 432p. pap. 9.95 (0-19-283386-3) Oxford Univ. Pr., Inc.
—Dracula. 1995. (Illus.). 126p. pap. text 5.95 (0-19-586322-4); 1984. 408p. pap. 4.95 o.p. (0-19-281598-9) Oxford Univ. Pr., Inc.
—Dracula. Ellman, Maud, ed. & intro. by. 2nd ed. 1996. (Oxford World's Classics Ser.). 428p. pap. 6.95 o.p. (0-19-282462-7) Oxford Univ. Pr., Inc.
—Dracula. Teresa Agnes, ed. Heller, Rudolf, tr. 1979. (SPA., Illus.). 64p. stu. ed. 1.50 (0-88301-566-8); pap. text 3.95 (0-88301-446-7) Pendulum Pr., Inc.
—Dracula. abr. ed. 1992. (Classics on Cassette). 15.95 o.p. incl. audio (0-453-00786-4) Penguin/HighBridge.
—Dracula. 1993. (SPA.). 464p. (84-01-49200-9) Plaza & Janés Editories, S.A.
—Dracula. (Paperback Classics Ser.). 2001. 432p. pap. 10.95 (0-375-75670-1); 2000. E-Book 4.95 (0-679-64197-1) Random House Adult Trade Publishing Group. (Modern Library).
—Dracula. (Modern Library Ser.). 1996. 448p. 17.95 o.s.i (0-679-60229-1); 1978. 6.95 o.s.i (0-394-60447-4) Random Hse., Inc.
—Dracula. 2002. E-Book 4.95 (0-9712207-1-9) Riverdale Electronic Bks.
—Dracula. unabr. ed. 1995. 528p. text 8.98 o.p. (1-56138-515-8, Courage Bks.) Running Pr. Bk. Pubs.
—Dracula. 2003. 528p. mass mkt. 5.99 (0-7434-7736-7, Pocket) Simon & Schuster.
—Dracula. l.t. ed. 1993. 592p. lib. bdg. 22.95 (0-8161-5692-1) Thorndike Pr.
—Dracula. Johnson, Beth, ed. & afterword by by. 2003. 428p. mass mkt. 2.00 (1-59194-003-6) Townsend Pr.
—Dracula. 2001. (Classics of Mystery & Suspense Ser.). 334p. (1-58279-187-2) Trident Pr. International.
—Dracula. 1965. (Signet Classics Ser.). 11.00 (0-606-00578-1) Turtleback Bks.
—Dracula. 1993. 432p. pap. 5.95 o.p. (0-460-87189-7, Everyman's Classic Library in Paperback) Tuttle Publishing.
—Dracula. Howes, Marjorie, ed. rev. ed. 1995. 400p. pap. 5.95 (0-460-87598-1, Everyman's Classic Library in Paperback) Tuttle Publishing.
—Dracula. (Penguin Classics Ser.). 560p. 2003. pap. 11.00 (0-14-143984-X, Penguin Classics); 1999. pap. (0-14-043381-3) Viking Penguin.
—Dracula. annuals Hindle, Maurice, ed. & intro. by. 1993. (Classics Ser.). 560p. 10.95 (0-14-043406-2, Penguin Classics) Viking Penguin.
—Dracula. 1979. 448p. pap. 4.95 o.p. (0-14-005280-1, Penguin Bks.) Viking Penguin.
—Dracula. 2002. 324p. pap. 18.95 (1-58715-588-5); lib. bdg. 29.95 (1-58715-589-3) Wildside Pr.
—Dracula. 1997. (Classics Library). 336p. pap. 3.95 (1-85326-086-X, 086XWW) Wordsworth Editions, Ltd. GBR. *Dist:* Casemate Pubs. & Bk. Distributors, LLC.
—Dracula. l.t. ed. 1994. 592p. pap. 14.95 o.p. (0-8161-5817-7) World Pubns., Inc.
Stoker, Bram & Byron, Glennis. Dracula. 1998. E-Book 9.95 (0-585-29380-5) netLibrary, Inc.
Stoker, Bram & Outlet Book Company Staff. Dracula. 1992. 9.99 o.s.i (0-517-06973-3) Random Hse. Value Publishing.
Stone, Irving. The Origin: A Biographical Novel of Charles Darwin. 1980. 744p. 17.95 o.s.i (0-385-12064-8) Doubleday Publishing.
Stone, Lyn. My Lady's Choice. 2000. (Harlequin Historicals Ser.: Vol. 511). 296p. mass mkt. (0-373-29111-6, Harlequin Bks.) Harlequin Enterprises, Ltd.
Stowe, Harriet Beecher. Betty's Bright Idea. 1977. (Short Story Index Reprint Ser.). reprint ed. 18.95 (0-8369-4121-7) Ayer Co. Pubs., Inc.
Stranger, Joyce. The Call of the Sea. 2003. 192p. 25.99 (0-7278-5938-2) Severn Hse. Pubs., Ltd.
Stratton, Penelope, pseud. The Unromantic Lady. 1996. mass mkt. 4.50 o.s.i (0-449-22386-8, Fawcett) Ballantine Bks.
Streatfeild, Noel. Thursday's Child. 1971. (Illus.). (Orig.). (J). (gr. 4-7). 4.50 o.p. (0-394-82096-7, Random Hse. Bks. for Young Readers) Random Hse. Children's Bks.
Stretton, Hesba. Pilgrim Street. 1996. (Golden Inheritance Ser.). (J). 7.90 (0-921100-91-4) Inheritance Pubns.
Strickland, Caroline. The Darkening Leaf. 1996. 288p. 21.95 o.p. (0-312-14308-7) St. Martin's Pr.
Strong, Tony. The Poison Tree. 1998. 400p. pap. 23.00 (0-440-61402-3); mass mkt. 6.50 o.s.i (0-440-22498-5) Dell Publishing.
—The Poison Tree. 1998. 400p. mass mkt. o.s.i (0-7704-2793-6) Seal Bks. CAN. *Dist:* Random Hse. of Canada, Ltd.
Stuart, Anne. Prince of Swords. 1997. (Romance Ser.). 270p. lib. bdg. 22.95 (0-7862-1116-4, Five Star) Gale Group.
—Prince of Swords. 1996. 384p. mass mkt. 5.99 o.s.i (0-8217-5397-5, Zebra Bks.) Kensington Publishing Corp.
Stubbs, Jean. Family Games. 1995. mass mkt. 4.99 o.p. (0-312-95479-4, St. Martin's Paperbacks); 1994. 320p. 21.95 o.p. (0-312-10437-5) St. Martin's Pr.
—Imperfect Joy. 1982. mass mkt. 3.50 o.p. (0-451-11613-5, AE1613, Signet Bks.) NAL.
—Kelly Park: A Novel. 1992. 320p. 19.95 o.p. (0-312-07850-1) St. Martin's Pr.
—Light in Summer. 1991. 18.95 o.p. (0-312-05462-9) St. Martin's Pr.
—The Witching Time. l.t. ed. 1999. (Core Ser.). 597p. 28.95 (0-7838-8558-X) Thorndike Pr.
Sturtevant, Katherine. A Mistress Moderately Fair. 1988. 249p. (Orig.). pap. 8.95 o.p. (1-55583-137-0) Alyson Pubns.
Sully, Sue. The Bluebell Pool. 1994. 320p. 22.95 o.p. (0-312-11281-5) St. Martin's Pr.
—The Bluebell Pool. l.t. ed. 1995. (Ulverscroft Large Print Ser.). 736p. 29.99 o.p. (0-7089-3355-6, Ulverscroft) Thorpe, F. A. Pubs. GBR. *Dist:* Ulverscroft Large Print Bks., Ltd., Ulverscroft Large Print Canada, Ltd.
—The Dovecote. 1995. 352p. 23.95 o.p. (0-312-13471-1) St. Martin's Pr.
Summerson, Rachel. Belgrave Square. 1981. 300p. 11.95 o.p. (0-312-07427-1) St. Martin's Pr.
Sumner, Penny. Crosswords: The 2nd Victoria Cross Mystery. 1994. 256p. pap. 9.95 (1-56280-064-7) Naiad Pr., Inc.
—The End of April. 1992. (Victoria Cross Mystery Ser.). 256p. pap. 8.95 o.p. (1-56280-007-8) Naiad Pr., Inc.
Sutcliffe, Katherine. Notorious. 2000. 368p. mass mkt. 7.50 o.s.i (0-515-12948-8, Jove) Berkley Publishing Group.
Sutherland. Jelly Roll. 2000. 413p. pap. 11.95 (1-86230-030-5) Transworld Publishers Ltd. GBR. *Dist:* Trafalgar Square.
Swan, Thomas. The Final Faberge: A Novel of Suspense. 2001. 416p. mass mkt. 6.50 o.s.i (0-451-40964-7, Onyx) NAL.
—The Final Faberge: A Novel of Suspense. 2004. 320p. 24.95 (1-55704-382-5) Newmarket Pr.
Sweeney, Eamonn. Waiting for the Healer. 1998. 308p. 23.00 (0-312-18206-6) Picador.
Swift, Graham. Last Orders. unabr. ed. 2000. audio 59.95 (0-7451-7368-3, SAB 143) Chivers Audio Bks. GBR. *Dist:* BBC Audiobooks America.
—Last Orders. unabr. ed. 2003. 510p. audio 34.95 (1-56511-764-6); audio compact disk 34.95 (1-56511-765-4) HighBridge Co.
—Last Orders. movie tie-in ed. 1997. 304p. pap. 13.00 (0-679-76662-6, Vintage) Knopf Publishing Group.
—Shuttlecock. 1992. 220p. pap. 11.00 (0-679-73933-5, Vintage) Knopf Publishing Group.
—Waterland. 1992. 368p. pap. 13.00 (0-679-73979-3, Vintage) Knopf Publishing Group.
—Waterland. 1992. (0-679-74033-3) McKay, David Co., Inc.
—Waterland. 1991. pap. 10.00 o.p. (0-671-73758-9, Simon & Schuster); 1987. 288p. pap. 7.95 o.s.i (0-671-65948-0, Pocket); 1985. mass mkt. 6.95 o.s.i (0-671-55457-3, Pocket); 1984. 15.50 o.s.i (0-671-49863-0, Simon & Schuster) Simon & Schuster.
Swindells, Madge. Winners & Losers. l.t. ed. 2001. (Charnwood Large Print Ser.). 480p. 32.50 (0-7089-9239-0, Ulverscroft) Thorpe, F. A. Pubs. GBR. *Dist:* Ulverscroft Large Print Bks., Ltd., Ulverscroft Large Print Canada, Ltd.
Swindells, Robert. Fallout. 1993. (J). (gr. 7 up). 17.25 (0-8446-6669-6) Smith, Peter Pub., Inc.
Syal, Meera. Anita & Me. 1999. 336p. 23.00 (1-56584-372-X); 366p. pap. text 13.95 (1-56584-529-3) New Pr., The.
—Life Isn't All Ha Ha Hee Hee. 2000. 336p. text 22.95 (1-56584-614-1) New Pr., The.
Symons, Julian. Playing Happy Families. unabr. ed. 1996. audio 69.95 (0-7451-2747-9, SAB 113, Sterling Audio Bks.) BBC Audiobooks America.
—Playing Happy Families. 1995. 320p. 28.00 (0-89296-578-9) Mysterious Pr.
—Playing Happy Families. 1995. 288p. mass mkt. 5.50 (0-446-40412-8, Mysterious Pr. Paperback Bks.) Warner Bks., Inc.
Talbot, Michael. The Bog. 1987. mass mkt. 3.95 o.s.i (0-515-09049-2, Jove) Berkley Publishing Group.
—The Bog. 1986. 320p. 17.95 o.p. (0-688-05952-X, Morrow, William & Co.) Morrow/Avon.
Tallis, Raymond. Absence. 192p. 2000. pap. 15.95 (1-902881-16-8); 1999. 19.95 (1-902881-00-1) Toby Pr.
Tambling, Jeremy, ed. Bleak House: Charles Dickens. 1998. (New Casebooks Ser.). 272p. 59.95 (0-312-21120-1) Palgrave Macmillan.
Tarkington, Booth. Monsieur Beaucaire. reprint ed. lib. bdg. 18.95 (0-88411-703-0) Amereon, Ltd.
—Monsieur Beaucaire. unabr. ed. 1989. (J). (gr. 6 up). audio 19.95 (1-55685-157-X) Audio Bk. Contractors, Inc.
—Monsieur Beaucaire. 1999. (Works of Booth Tarkington). 127p. reprint ed. lib. bdg. 88.00 (1-58201-863-4) Classic Bks.
—Monsieur Beaucaire. 1992. (BCL1-PS American Literature Ser.). 127p. reprint ed. lib. bdg. 69.00 (0-7812-6875-3) Reprint Services Corp.
Tarr, Judith. Pride of Kings. 2001. 464p. pap. 14.95 (0-451-45847-8, ROC) NAL.
Tarrant, Desmond. Priceless Souls. 1996. 192p. 16.95 (0-913720-85-2) Beil, Frederic C. Pub., Inc.
Taylor, Andrew. An Air That Kills. 1995. 266p. 19.95 o.p. (0-312-11739-6, Saint Martin's Minotaur) St. Martin's Pr.
—The American Boy. 2004. 24.95 (1-4013-0102-9) Hyperion Pr.
—Blood Relation. 1991. 192p. 14.95 o.s.i (0-385-41761-6) Doubleday Publishing.
—Caroline Minuscule. l.t. ed. 2002. 289p. pap. 24.95 (0-7862-4008-3) Gale Group.
—Caroline Minuscule. 2001. 200p. pap. 13.95 (1-890208-71-X) Poisoned Pen Pr.
—The Four Last Things. 1997. (Roth Trilogy Ser.: Vol. 1). 304p. 22.95 (0-312-16845-4, Saint Martin's Minotaur) St. Martin's Pr.
—Judgement of Strangers. pap. 14.95 (0-312-28730-5, Saint Martin's Griffin); 1998. (Roth Trilogy Ser.: Vol. 2). 304p. 22.95 o.p. (0-312-19292-4, Saint Martin's Minotaur) St. Martin's Pr.
—The Lover of the Grave. 1997. 309p. 22.95 o.p. (0-312-15573-5, Saint Martin's Minotaur) St. Martin's Pr.
—The Mortal Sickness. 1996. 304p. 22.95 o.p. (0-312-14371-0, Saint Martin's Minotaur) St. Martin's Pr.
—The Office of the Dead. 2000. (Roth Trilogy Ser.: Vol. 3). 352p. 24.95 (0-312-20348-9, Saint Martin's Minotaur) St. Martin's Pr.
—An Old School Tie. 1987. 224p. pap. 3.50 o.p. (0-14-010087-3, Penguin Bks.) Viking Penguin.
—Our Fathers Lies. 1986. 240p. pap. 3.50 o.p. (0-14-008838-5, Penguin Bks.) Viking Penguin.
—Our Father's Lies. 1986. 35.00 o.p. (0-14-778054-3) Penguin Group (USA) Inc.
—The Suffocating Night. l.t. ed. 2000. (Ulverscroft Large Print Ser.). 392p. 31.99 (0-7089-4188-5, Ulverscroft) Thorpe, F. A. Pubs. GBR. *Dist:* Ulverscroft Large Print Bks., Ltd., Ulverscroft Large Print Canada, Ltd.
Taylor, D. J. The Comedy Man. 2002. 352p. pap. 9.95 (0-7156-3157-8) Duckworth, Gerald & Co., Ltd. GBR. *Dist:* International Publishers Marketing.
Taylor, Domini. Teacher's Pet. 1989. mass mkt. 3.95 o.s.i (0-515-10029-3, Jove) Berkley Publishing Group.
—Teacher's Pet. 1987. 288p. 18.95 o.p. (0-689-11933-X, Scribner) Simon & Schuster.
Taylor, Elizabeth. At Mrs. Lippincote's. 2001. (Modern Classics). 214p. 13.00 (0-86068-538-1) Virago Pr., Ltd. GBR. *Dist:* Trafalgar Square.
Templeton, Aline. The Last Act of All. 1996. 224p. 21.95 o.p. (0-312-14303-6, Saint Martin's Minotaur) St. Martin's Pr.

—Shades of Death. 2002. 352p. 24.95 (*0-312-29024-1*, Saint Martin's Minotaur) St. Martin's Pr.

Tennant, Emma. Adele: Jane Eyre's Hidden Story. 2002. 240p. 25.95 (*0-06-000454-1*, Morrow, William & Co.) Morrow/Avon.

—Adele: Jane Eyre's Hidden Story. l.t. ed. 2003. (Women's Fiction Ser.). 29.95 (*0-7862-5326-6*) Thorndike Pr.

—Emma in Love: Jane Austen's Emma Continued. 229p. 1997. pap. 11.00 o.p. (*1-85702-663-2*); 1996. pap. (*1-85702-527-X*) Fourth Estate, Ltd. GBR. *Dist:* Trafalgar Square.

—Pemberley: Or Pride & Prejudice Continued. l.t. ed. 1995. (Charnwood Large Print Ser.). 272p. 29.99 o.p. (*0-7089-8826-1*, Charnwood) Thorpe, F. A. Pubs. GBR. *Dist:* Ulverscroft Large Print Bks., Ltd., Ulverscroft Large Print Canada, Ltd.

Tennant, Emma & Austen, Jane. Pemberley: Or Pride & Prejudice Continued. 1993. 184p. pap. 18.95 (*0-312-10793-5*) St. Martin's Pr.

—An Unequal Marriage: Or Pride & Prejudice Twenty Years Later. 1994. 224p. 18.95 o.p. (*0-312-11533-4*) St. Martin's Pr.

Tettmar, Elizabeth. Trial Love. 1998. 255p. pap. (*0-7540-3421-6*) BBC Audiobooks America.

—Trial Love. 192p. 22.00 (*0-7278-5234-5*) Severn Hse. Pubs., Ltd.

—Trial Love. l.t. ed. 1998. (Nightingale Ser.). 264p. pap. 20.95 (*0-7838-0249-8*) Thorndike Pr.

Tey, Josephine. Brat Farrar. 1981. reprint ed. lib. bdg. 16.00 (*0-8376-0445-1*) Bentley Pubs.

—Brat Farrar. 1997. 288p. pap. 12.00 (*0-684-80385-2*, Touchstone); 1982. mass mkt. 2.95 o.s.i (*0-671-44190-6*, Pocket) Simon & Schuster.

—Brat Farrar. l.t. ed. 2000. (Mystery Ser.). 437p. 27.95 o.p. (*0-7862-2554-8*) Thorndike Pr.

—Miss Pym Disposes. Date not set. 223p. 21.95 (*0-8488-2408-3*) Amereon, Ltd.

—Miss Pym Disposes. 1981. 200p. reprint ed. lib. bdg. 16.00 (*0-8376-0447-8*) Bentley Pubs.

—Miss Pym Disposes. 1998. 240p. per. 12.00 (*0-684-84751-5*, Touchstone); 1983. 224p. mass mkt. 3.95 o.s.i (*0-671-49413-9*, Pocket) Simon & Schuster.

—Miss Pym Disposes. l.t. ed. 1999. (Mystery Ser.). 375p. 26.95 (*0-7862-1778-2*) Thorndike Pr.

Thackeray, William Makepeace. The Memoirs of Mr. Charles J. Yellowplush. 2002. 184p. 23.99 (*1-4043-2088-1*); per. 19.99 (*1-4043-2089-X*) IndyPublish.com.

—The Memoirs of Mr. Charles J. Yellowplush. 1997. (Pocket Classics Ser.). 128p. pap. 10.95 (*0-7509-1558-7*) Sutton Publishing, Ltd. GBR. *Dist:* International Publishers Marketing.

—The Newcomes. unabr. ed. Pt. 1. 1998. audio 77.95 (*1-55685-527-3*); Pt. II. audio 65.95 Audio Bk. Contractors, Inc.

—The Newcomes. (Complete Works of William Makepeace Thackeray: Vol. 14). reprint ed. 2001. (Illus.). 1054p. pap. text 28.00 (*0-7426-5395-1*); 1999. lib. bdg. 98.00 (*1-58201-395-0*) Classic Bks.

—The Newcomes. Sanders, Andrew, ed. 1995. (Oxford World's Classics Ser.). (Illus.). 1149p. pap. 13.95 o.p. (*0-19-283173-9*) Oxford Univ. Pr., Inc.

—The Newcomes. 1994. 416p. pap. 8.50 (*0-460-87495-0*, Everyman's Classic Library in Paperback) Tuttle Publishing.

—The Newcomes. Shillinsburg, Peter L., ed. 1996. (Thackeray Edition Ser.). (Illus.). 1104p. (C). text 95.00 (*0-472-10675-9*, 10675) Univ. of Michigan Pr.

—The Newcomes. Pascoe, David, ed. & intro. by. 1996. (Penguin Classics Ser.). 880p. pap. 13.95 o.p. (*0-14-043481-X*, Viking) Viking Penguin.

—Pendennis: His Fortunes & Misfortunes, His Friends & His Greatest Enemy. 1994. (Oxford World's Classics Ser.). (Illus.). 1,118p. pap. 7.95 o.p. (*0-19-283168-2*) Oxford Univ. Pr., Inc.

—Vanity Fair. Sutherland, John, ed. 1983. (Oxford World's Classics Ser.). (Illus.). 1,006p. pap. 7.95 o.p. (*0-19-281642-X*) Oxford Univ. Pr., Inc.

—Vanity Fair. 2001. (Modern Library Classics). 768p. pap. 7.95 (*0-375-75726-0*, Modern Library) Random House Adult Trade Publishing Group.

—Vanity Fair. 1991. 752p. 20.00 (*0-679-40566-6*) Random Hse., Inc.

—Vanity Fair. 1948. 16.00 (*0-606-03031-X*) Turtleback Bks.

—Vanity Fair. Stewart, J. I., ed. & intro. by. 1969. (Penguin Classics Ser.). 816p. pap. 9.95 o.s.i (*0-14-043035-0*, Penguin Classics) Viking Penguin.

—Vanity Fair: Authoritative Text, Backgrounds & Contents, Criticism. Shillingsburg, Peter L., ed. 1994. (Critical Editions Ser.). 876p. (C). pap. text 14.00 (*0-393-96595-3*) Norton, W. W. & Co., Inc.

Thane, Elswyth. Ever After. 1976. reprint ed. lib. bdg. 26.95 (*0-88411-958-0*) Amereon, Ltd.

—Ever After. 1983. mass mkt. 3.50 o.s.i (*0-553-22933-8*) Bantam Bks.

—Ever After. 1993. reprint ed. lib. bdg. 31.95 (*1-56849-230-8*) Buccaneer Bks., Inc.

—Ever After. 1981. (Reader's Request Ser.). lib. bdg. 17.95 o.p. (*0-8161-3165-1*, Macmillan Reference USA) Gale Group.

—Homing. 272p. reprint ed. lib. bdg. 23.95 (*0-88411-969-6*) Amereon, Ltd.

—Homing. 1994. lib. bdg. 29.95 (*1-56849-479-3*) Buccaneer Bks., Inc.

—Homing. l.t. ed. 1981. lib. bdg. 15.95 o.p. (*0-8161-3164-3*, Macmillan Reference USA) Gale Group.

—This Was Tomorrow. 1976. reprint ed. lib. bdg. 24.95 (*0-88411-962-9*) Amereon, Ltd.

—This Was Tomorrow. 1994. lib. bdg. 29.95 (*1-56849-478-5*) Buccaneer Bks., Inc.

—This Was Tomorrow. 1981. (Williamsburg Ser.: No. 6). lib. bdg. 14.95 o.p. (*0-8161-3161-9*, Macmillan Reference USA) Gale Group.

Thaw, John. Deceived by Flight. 1998. (Inspector Morse Mystery Ser.). audio 14.95 o.p. (*1-56938-257-3*, AMP-2573) Acorn Media Publishing, Inc.

—The Ghost in the Machine. 1998. (Inspector Morse Mystery Ser.). audio 14.95 o.p. (*1-56938-256-5*, AMP-2565) Acorn Media Publishing, Inc.

—Infernal Serpent. 1998. (Inspector Morse Mystery Ser.). audio 14.95 o.p. (*1-56938-258-1*, AMP-2581) Acorn Media Publishing, Inc.

—Inspector Morse Series, 4 vols. 1998. audio 59.80 (*1-56938-255-7*, AMP-2557) Acorn Media Publishing, Inc.

—Masonic Mysteries. 1998. (Inspector Morse Mystery Ser.). audio 14.95 o.p. (*1-56938-259-X*, AMP-8259) Acorn Media Publishing, Inc.

Theroux, Paul. The Family Arsenal. 1977. mass mkt. 2.25 o.s.i (*0-345-25751-0*) Ballantine Bks.

—The Family Arsenal, 001. 1976. 8.95 o.p. (*0-395-24400-5*) Houghton Mifflin Co.

—The Family Arsenal. 1996. 288p. pap. 14.00 (*0-14-004465-5*, Penguin Bks.) Penguin Group (USA) Inc.

—The Family Arsenal. 1984. mass mkt. 4.95 o.s.i (*0-671-49824-X*, Pocket) Simon & Schuster.

—Half Moon Street. 1984. 14.95 o.p. (*0-395-36511-2*) Houghton Mifflin Co.

Thimpson, Flora. The Illustrated Still Glides the Stream. 1985. 7.99 o.p. (*0-517-55841-6*) Random Hse. Value Publishing.

Thirkell, Angela. Close Quarters. 2001. (Angela Thirkell Barsetshire Ser.: Vol. 17). (Illus.). 285p. pap. 12.95 (*1-55921-290-X*) Moyer Bell.

—Love at All Ages. 2001. (Illus.). 336p. pap. 12.95 (*1-55921-297-7*) Moyer Bell.

Thirkell, Angela M. Ankle Deep. lib. bdg. 20.95 (*0-8488-1879-2*) Amereon, Ltd.

—August Folly. 1995. 272p. pap. 11.95 (*0-7867-0272-9*); 1988. 297p. pap. 4.95 o.p. (*0-88184-421-7*) Avalon Publishing Group. (Carroll & Graf Pubs.).

—August Folly. 1980. 312p. reprint ed. pap. o.p. (*0-06-080525-0*, P 525) HarperCollins Pubs.

—August Folly. l.t. ed. 1993. (Magna Large Print Ser.). 406p. o.p. (*0-7505-0500-1*) Magna Large Print Bks. GBR. *Dist:* Ulverscroft Large Print Canada, Ltd.

—Before Lunch. 1988. (Barsetshire Novels Ser.). 336p. mass mkt. 5.95 o.p. (*0-88184-397-0*, Carroll & Graf Pubs.) Avalon Publishing Group.

—Before Lunch. 1979. pap. o.p. (*0-06-080498-X*, P 498) HarperCollins Pubs.

—Before Lunch. l.t. ed. 1994. (Magna Large Print Ser.). 414p. o.p. (*0-7505-0703-9*) Magna Large Print Bks. GBR. *Dist:* Ulverscroft Large Print Canada, Ltd.

—The Brandons. 1997. 368p. pap. 12.95 o.p. (*0-7867-0362-8*); 1987. 358p. reprint ed. pap. 4.95 o.p. (*0-88184-361-X*) Avalon Publishing Group. (Carroll & Graf Pubs.).

—The Brandons. 1979. pap. o.p. (*0-06-080497-1*, P 497) HarperCollins Pubs.

—Cheerfulness Breaks In: A Barsetshire Novel. 1996. 320p. pap. 11.95 o.p. (*0-7867-0318-0*, Carroll & Graf Pubs.) Avalon Publishing Group.

—Cheerfulness Breaks In: A Barsetshire Novel. l.t. ed. 1999. (Magna Large Print Ser.). 448p. 31.99 o.p. (*0-7505-1339-X*) Magna Large Print Bks. GBR. *Dist:* Ulverscroft Large Print Bks., Ltd., Ulverscroft Large Print Canada, Ltd.

—County Chronicle. 1998. 352p. pap. 12.95 (*1-55921-213-6*) Moyer Bell.

—The Demon in the House: A Novel. 1996. 254p. pap. 12.95 (*1-55921-159-8*) Moyer Bell.

—A Double Affair. 2000. 290p. pap. 12.95 (*1-55921-249-7*) Moyer Bell.

—The Duke's Daughter. 1998. 355p. pap. 12.95 (*1-55921-214-4*) Moyer Bell.

—Enter Sir Robert. 2000. (Angela Thirkell Barsetshire Ser.). (Illus.). 265p. pap. 12.95 (*1-55921-236-5*) Moyer Bell.

—Growing Up. 1995. 272p. pap. 12.95 (*1-55921-149-0*) Moyer Bell.

—Happy Returns. 1998. (Angela Thirkell Barsetshire Ser.). 324p. pap. 12.95 (*1-55921-255-1*) Moyer Bell.

—The Headmistress. 1996. 296p. reprint ed. pap. 12.95 (*1-55921-150-4*) Moyer Bell.

—Jutland Cottage. 1999. (Angela Thirkell Barsetshire Ser.). 298p. pap. 12.95 (*1-55921-273-X*) Moyer Bell.

—Love among the Ruins. 1997. 464p. pap. 13.95 (*1-55921-204-7*) Moyer Bell.

—Marling Hall. 1995. 400p. pap. 11.95 (*0-7867-0273-7*); 1990. 319p. pap. 4.95 o.p. (*0-88184-676-7*) Avalon Publishing Group. (Carroll & Graf Pubs.).

—Miss Bunting: A Novel. l.t. ed. 1999. (Magna Large Print Ser.). 432p. 31.99 o.p. (*0-7505-1341-1*) Magna Large Print Bks. GBR. *Dist:* Ulverscroft Large Print Bks., Ltd., Ulverscroft Large Print Canada, Ltd.

—Miss Bunting: A Novel. 1996. (Illus.). 336p. reprint ed. pap. 12.95 (*1-55921-174-1*) Moyer Bell.

—Never Too Late. 2000. 285p. pap. 12.95 (*1-55921-235-7*) Moyer Bell.

—Northbridge Rectory. (Barsetshire Ser.). 320p. 1991. pap. 5.95 o.p. (*0-88184-718-6*); 2nd ed. 1997. pap. 12.95 o.p. (*0-7867-0380-6*) Avalon Publishing Group. (Carroll & Graf Pubs.).

—Northbridge Rectory. l.t. ed. 1999. (Magna Large Print Ser.). 480p. 31.99 (*0-7505-1340-3*) Magna Large Print Bks. GBR. *Dist:* Ulverscroft Large Print Bks., Ltd., Ulverscroft Large Print Canada, Ltd.

—O, These Men, These Men: A Novel. 1996. (Illus.). 224p. reprint ed. pap. 12.95 (*1-55921-173-3*) Moyer Bell.

—The Old Bank House. 1997. 400p. pap. 12.95 (*1-55921-205-5*) Moyer Bell.

—Peace Breaks Out. 1997. (Angela Thirkell Barsetshire Ser.). 328p. pap. 12.95 (*1-55921-188-1*) Moyer Bell.

—Pomfret Towers. 1986. 272p. mass mkt. 4.95 o.p. (*0-88184-276-1*, Carroll & Graf Pubs.) Avalon Publishing Group.

—Pomfret Towers. 1979. pap. o.p. (*0-06-080496-3*, P 496) HarperCollins Pubs.

—Pomfret Towers. l.t. ed. 1992. (Magna Large Print Ser.). 425p. o.p. (*0-7505-0458-7*) Magna Large Print Bks. GBR. *Dist:* Ulverscroft Large Print Canada, Ltd.

—Private Enterprise. 1997. 381p. pap. 13.95 (*1-55921-189-X*) Moyer Bell.

—Summer Half, Set. unabr. ed. 1998. audio 76.95 o.p. (*1-85903-012-2*) Magna Story Sound GBR. *Dist:* Ulverscroft Large Print Bks., Ltd.

—Summer Half: A Barsetshire Novel. 1996. 256p. pap. 10.95 (*0-7867-0331-8*, Carroll & Graf Pubs.) Avalon Publishing Group.

—What Did It Mean? 1999. 318p. pap. 12.95 (*1-55921-274-8*) Moyer Bell.

—Wild Strawberries. 1989. 265p. pap. 4.95 o.p. (*0-88184-555-8*); 2nd ed. 1996. 272p. pap. 11.95 (*0-7867-0438-1*) Avalon Publishing Group. (Carroll & Graf Pubs.).

—Wild Strawberries. 1980. (Barsetshire Ser.). 280p. reprint ed. pap. o.p. (*0-06-080526-9*, P526) HarperCollins Pubs.

—Wild Strawberries. l.t. ed. 1992. 288p. 18.95 o.p. (*1-85089-294-6*) ISIS Large Print Bks. GBR. *Dist:* Transaction Pubs.

Thirkell, Angela Mackail. Pomfret Towers. 2004. (Angela Thirkell Barsetshire Ser.). 288p. pap. 13.95 (*1-55921-302-7*) Moyer Bell.

Thoene, Jake. The Mystery of the Yellow Hands. 1997. (Baker Street Ser.: Vol. 1). pap. 5.99 o.p. (*0-8499-4005-2*) W Publishing Group.

Thoene, Jake & Luke. The Eyes of Justice: A Novel. 2003. pap. 9.99 (*0-7852-6384-5*) Nelson, Thomas Inc.

Thoene, Jake & Thoene, Luke. The Mystery of the Yellow Hands. 1995. (Baker Street Brigade Ser.: No. 1). 160p. pap. 5.99 o.s.i (*0-345-39561-1*, Ballantine Bks.) Ballantine Bks.

Thomas, D. M. Charlotte Bronte Revelations: Bronte Revelations: The Final Journey of Jane Eyre. 2001. (Duck Editions). (Illus.). 288p. 26.95 (*0-7156-3004-0*) Duckworth, Gerald & Co., Ltd. GBR. *Dist:* International Publishers Marketing.

—Eating Pavlova. 1995. 240p. pap. 10.95 (*0-7867-0270-2*); 1994. 231p. 21.00 o.p. (*0-7867-0142-0*) Avalon Publishing Group. (Carroll & Graf Pubs.).

—Pictures at an Exhibition. 1994. 278p. pap. 10.95 (*0-7867-0147-1*, Carroll & Graf Pubs.) Avalon Publishing Group.

—Pictures at an Exhibition. 1993. (Robert Stewart Bk.). 272p. 22.00 o.p. (*0-684-19586-0*, Scribner) Simon & Schuster.

Thomas, Graham. Malice Downstream. 2002. 240p. mass mkt. 6.99 (*0-449-00709-X*) Ballantine Bks.

—Malice in Cornwall. 1998. (Erskine Powell Mysteries Ser.: Vol. 2). 240p. mass mkt. 6.50 (*0-8041-1656-3*, Ivy Bks.) Ballantine Bks.

—Malice in Cornwall. l.t. ed. 2000. (Ulverscroft Large Print Ser.). 312p. 31.99 (*0-7089-4324-1*, Ulverscroft) Thorpe, F. A. Pubs. GBR. *Dist:* Ulverscroft Large Print Bks., Ltd., Ulverscroft Large Print Canada, Ltd.

—Malice in London: An Erskine Powell Mystery. 2000. (Erskine Powell Mysteries Ser.). 240p. mass mkt. 6.50 (*0-8041-1840-X*, Fawcett) Ballantine Bks.

Thomas, Jerry D. Detective Zack Trapped in Darkmoor Manor. 1997. (Detective Zack Ser.: Vol. 9). (J). pap. 6.99 (*0-8163-1394-6*) Pacific Pr. Publishing Assn.

Thomas, Rosie. Strangers. 1987. 324p. 17.45 o.s.i (*0-671-62875-5*, Simon & Schuster) Simon & Schuster.

Thomas, Ross. Voodoo, Ltd. l.t. ed. 1993. (General Ser.). 367p. lib. bdg. 21.95 (*0-8161-5679-4*, Macmillan Reference USA) Gale Group.

—Voodoo, Ltd. 1992. 288p. 19.95 (*0-89296-451-0*) Mysterious Pr.

—Voodoo, Ltd., unabr. ed. 1993. (Durant & Wu Ser.). audio 51.00 (*1-55690-785-0*, 93105E7) Recorded Bks., LLC.

—Voodoo, Ltd. 1993. 320p. mass mkt. 5.99 (*0-446-40030-0*, Mysterious Pr. Paperback Bks.) Warner Bks., Inc.

Thomas, Scarlett. Dead Clever: A Lily Pascale Mystery. 2004. 296p. pap. 13.99 (*1-932112-19-7*); 2003. 288p. 24.95 (*1-932112-01-4*, Kate's Mystery Bks.) Justin, Charles & Co. Pubs.

Thompson, Flora. Candleford Green. l.t. ed. 2001. 224p. pap. 21.99 (*0-7531-5782-9*) Thorpe, F. A. Pubs. GBR. *Dist:* Ulverscroft Large Print Bks., Ltd., Ulverscroft Large Print Canada, Ltd.

—The Illustrated Lark Rise to Candleford: A Trilogy. 1984. 7.99 o.p. (*0-517-55187-X*) Random Hse. Value Publishing.

—Still Glides the Stream. (Illus.). reprint ed. 1981. 19.95 o.p. (*0-19-217414-2*); 1976. 240p. pap. 10.95 o.p. (*0-19-281192-4*) Oxford Univ. Pr., Inc.

Thomson, June. The Secret Chronicles of Sherlock Holmes. 1994. 208p. reprint ed. 20.00 (*1-883402-37-9*, Scribner) Simon & Schuster.

—The Secret Files of Sherlock Holmes. l.t. ed. 1994. 21.95 o.p. (*0-7927-2042-3*); pap. 20.95 o.p. (*0-7927-2041-5*) BBC Audiobooks America.

—The Secret Files of Sherlock Holmes. 1994. 224p. 20.00 (*1-883402-36-0*, Scribner) Simon & Schuster.

—The Unquiet Grave. l.t. ed. 2002. (General Ser.). 288p. pap. 22.95 (*0-7862-3727-9*) Gale Group.

Thomson, Rupert. Dreams of Leaving. 1988. 448p. 19.95 o.p. (*0-689-11957-7*, Scribner) Simon & Schuster.

Thorne, Nicola. My Name Is Martha Brown. 2000. 312p. (*0-00-225949-4*) HarperCollins Pubs.

—Repossession. 1996. 320p. 26.00 o.p. (*0-7278-7004-1*); 216p. 22.00 o.p. (*0-7278-4931-X*) Severn Hse. Pubs., Ltd.

—Repossession. l.t. ed. 1998. (General Ser.). 296p. pap. 23.95 (*0-7862-1483-X*) Thorndike Pr.

Thornton, Elizabeth. Whisper His Name. 1999. 400p. mass mkt. 6.50 (*0-553-57427-2*) Bantam Bks.

Thornton, Margaret. Sunset View. l.t. ed. 2003. (Magna Large Print Ser.). 512p. (*0-7505-2071-X*) Magna Large Print Bks. GBR. *Dist:* Ulverscroft Large Print Canada, Ltd.

Thorpe, Adam. Ulverton. 1993. 390p. 23.00 o.p. (*0-374-28031-2*) Farrar, Straus & Giroux.

Three Nineteenth-Century Novels. Incl. Pride & Prejudice. Austen, Jane. 9999. o.p. Wuthering Heights. Bronte, Emily. 1979. o.p. 1979. Set mass mkt. 2.95 o.p. (*0-451-51241-3*, CE 1241, Signet Classics) NAL.

Tiffany, Grace. My Father Had a Daughter: Judith Shakespeare's Tale. 2003. 304p. 21.95 (*0-425-19003-X*) Berkley Publishing Group.

Titchmarsh, Alan. The Last Lighthouse Keeper. 1999. (Illus.). 242p. (*0-684-81990-2*, Simon & Schuster) Simon & Schuster.

Tobin, Betsy. Bone House: A Novel. 224p. 2002. pap. 13.00 (*0-7434-0616-8*); 2001. 23.00 o.s.i (*0-7432-0196-5*) Simon & Schuster. (Scribner).

Todd, Charles. Search the Dark. unabr. ed. 2001. audio compact disk 94.00 (*1-84197-099-9*, C1144E7); 1999. audio 79.00 (*1-84197-039-5*, H1039E7) Recorded Bks., LLC. (Clipper Audio).

—Search the Dark. E-Book 5.99 (*0-312-26467-4*); 1999. 336p. 24.95 o.p. (*0-312-20000-5*, Saint Martin's Minotaur) St. Martin's Pr.

—A Test of Wills. l.t. ed. 1998. 336p. mass mkt. 6.99 (*0-553-57759-X*) Bantam Bks.

—A Test of Wills. unabr. ed. 1999. audio compact disk 81.00 (*1-84197-092-1*, C1128E7, Clipper Audio); audio 71.00 (*1-84197-006-9*, H1006E7);Set. audio 71.00 Recorded Bks., LLC.

—A Test of Wills. 4th l.t. ed. 1996. 320p. 22.95 o.p. (*0-312-14431-8*, Saint Martin's Minotaur) St. Martin's Pr.

—A Test of Wills. l.t. ed. 1997. (Mystery Ser.). 416p. lib. bdg. 25.95 o.p. (*0-7838-2023-2*) Thorndike Pr.

—Watchers of Time: An Inspector Ian Rutledge Mystery. 2002. 448p. reprint ed. mass mkt. 6.99 (*0-553-58316-6*) Bantam Bks.

—Wings of Fire. unabr. ed. 1999. audio 71.00 (*1-84197-023-9*, H1023E7);Set. audio 71.00 Recorded Bks., LLC.

—Wings of Fire. 1999. (Wings of Fire Ser.: Vol. 1). 320p. mass mkt. 6.99 (*0-312-96568-0*, St. Martin's Paperbacks); 1999. E-Book 23.95 (*0-312-20751-4*);

1998. (Inspector Ian Rutledge Mysteries Ser.). 294p. (gr. 5 up). 23.95 (*0-312-17064-5*, Saint Martin's Minotaur) St. Martin's Pr.

Toksvig, S. Flying under Bridges. 2001. 310p. (*0-316-85635-5*) Little Brown & Co.

Tonkin, Peter. The Point of Death. 2002. 256p. 25.99 (*0-7278-5723-1*); 29.99 (*0-7278-7215-X*) Severn Hse. Pubs., Ltd.

Tope, Rebecca. Dark Undertakings. l.t. ed. 2001. (Magna Large Print Ser.). 432p. 31.99 (*0-7505-1624-0*) Magna Large Print Bks. GBR. *Dist:* Ulverscroft Large Print Bks., Ltd., Ulverscroft Large Print Canada, Ltd.

—Dark Undertakings. Date not set. (*0-312-27780-6*); 2001. 304p. 23.95 (*0-312-26570-0*, Saint Martin's Minotaur) St. Martin's Pr.

—A Dirty Death. l.t. ed. 2000. (Magna Large Print Ser.). 432p. (*0-7505-1498-1*) Magna Large Print Bks. GBR. *Dist:* Ulverscroft Large Print Bks., Ltd., Ulverscroft Large Print Canada, Ltd.

—A Dirty Death. 2000. 308p. 23.95 (*0-312-26144-6*, Saint Martin's Minotaur) St. Martin's Pr.

—Grave Concerns. l.t. ed. 2001. (Magna Large Print Ser.). 432p. 32.50 (*0-7505-1696-8*) Magna Large Print Bks. GBR. *Dist:* Ulverscroft Large Print Bks., Ltd., Ulverscroft Large Print Canada, Ltd.

—Grave Concerns. 2002. 352p. 24.95 (*0-312-28127-7*, Saint Martin's Minotaur) St. Martin's Pr.

Topley, Donald. The Break. 2000. 272p. 22.95 (*1-58345-593-0*); 259p. pap. 15.95 (*1-58345-574-4*) Domhan Bks.

—Horse Passing. 2001. 320p. 19.95 (*1-58345-633-3*); pap. 15.95 (*1-58345-570-1*) Domhan Bks.

Tourney, Leonard. The Bartholomew Fair Murders. 1987. 256p. reprint ed. mass mkt. 4.99 o.s.i (*0-345-34370-0*) Ballantine Bks.

—The Bartholomew Fair Murders. 1986. 240p. 14.95 o.p. (*0-312-06710-0*) St. Martin's Pr.

—Familiar Spirits. 1989. 240p. mass mkt. 3.50 o.s.i (*0-345-34372-7*) Ballantine Bks.

—Familiar Spirits. 1984. 224p. 13.95 o.p. (*0-312-28025-4*) St. Martin's Pr.

—Frobisher's Savage. 1994. 304p. 20.95 o.p. (*0-312-11437-0*, Saint Martin's Minotaur) St. Martin's Pr.

—Knaves Templar. 1992. mass mkt. 3.99 o.s.i (*0-345-37335-9*) Ballantine Bks.

—Knaves Templar. 1991. 17.95 o.p. (*0-312-04961-7*, Saint Martin's Minotaur) St. Martin's Pr.

—Low Treason. 1989. mass mkt. 3.50 o.s.i (*0-345-34368-9*) Ballantine Bks.

—Low Treason. 1983. 228p. 12.95 o.p. (*0-525-24153-1*, 01258-370, Dutton) Dutton/Plume.

—Old Saxon Blood. 1989. 288p. mass mkt. 4.95 o.s.i (*0-345-35765-5*) Ballantine Bks.

—Old Saxon Blood. 1988. 240p. 15.95 o.p. (*0-312-01799-5*, Saint Martin's Minotaur) St. Martin's Pr.

—The Player's Boy Is Dead. 1988. mass mkt. 4.99 o.s.i (*0-345-34371-9*) Ballantine Bks.

—The Player's Boy Is Dead. 1980. 208p. o.p. (*0-06-014341-X*) HarperCollins Pubs.

—Witness of Bones. 1993. reprint ed. mass mkt. 4.99 o.s.i (*0-345-38319-2*) Ballantine Bks.

—Witness of Bones. 1992. 256p. 18.95 o.p. (*0-312-08339-4*, Saint Martin's Minotaur) St. Martin's Pr.

Townsend, Sue. Adrian Mole: The Cappuccino Years. unabr. ed. 2000. audio compact disk 82.00 (*1-84197-136-7*, C1246E7); 1999. audio 60.00 (*0-7887-4054-7*, 96160E7) Recorded Bks., LLC.

—Adrian Mole: The Cappuccino Years. 2001. 400p. pap. 14.00 (*1-56947-247-5*); 2000. xv, 390p. 24.00 (*1-56947-204-1*) Soho Pr., Inc.

—Adrian Mole: The Cappuccino Years. abr. ed. 2000. 3p. audio compact disk (*0-14-180188-3*); 1999. audio (*0-14-180090-9*) Viking Penguin. (Penguin AudioBooks).

—Adrian Mole: The Lost Years. 309p. 1996. pap. 14.00 (*1-56947-055-3*); 1994. 22.00 (*1-56947-014-6*) Soho Pr., Inc.

—Adrian Mole: The Wilderness Years. unabr. ed. 1994. (Mini-CAB Audio Bks.). audio 39.95 (*0-7451-4281-8*, CAB 964) BBC Audiobooks America.

—Adrian Mole Diaries. 1986. 368p. 14.95 o.p. (*0-394-55298-9*) Grove/Atlantic, Inc.

—Adrian Mole Diaries. 1997. 304p. pap. 12.95 (*0-380-73044-8*, Perennial) HarperTrade.

—Rebuilding Coventry. 1993. 2.99 o.p. (*0-517-11035-0*) Random Hse. Value Publishing.

—Rebuilding Coventry. 1997. 160p. pap. 11.00 (*1-56947-090-1*) Soho Pr., Inc.

—Rebuilding Coventry: A Tale of Two Cities. 1990. 158p. 16.95 o.p. (*0-8021-1115-7*) Grove/Atlantic, Inc.

Tranter, Nigel. Crusader. 1998. 356p. mass mkt. 11.95 (*0-340-57927-7*); 1992. 352p. 27.50 (*0-340-55897-0*) Hodder & Stoughton, Ltd. GBR. *Dist:* Lubrecht & Cramer, Ltd., Trafalgar Square.

—Flowers of Chivalry. 1998. 402p. mass mkt. 11.95 (*0-340-52028-0*); 1989. 398p. 22.95 o.p. (*0-340-40698-4*) Hodder & Stoughton, Ltd. GBR. *Dist:* Lubrecht & Cramer, Ltd., Trafalgar Square.

—Kenneth. 1998. 356p. mass mkt. 11.95 (*0-340-56638-8*) Hodder & Stoughton, Ltd. GBR. *Dist:* Lubrecht & Cramer, Ltd., Trafalgar Square.

Trapido, Barbara. The Travelling Hornplayer. 2000. 256p. pap. 12.95 o.s.i (*0-14-028190-8*, Penguin Bks.) Penguin Group (USA) Inc.

—The Travelling Hornplayer. 1999. 256p. 24.95 o.p. (*0-670-88357-3*) Viking Penguin.

Trease, Geoffrey. A Flight of Angels. 1989. (Mystery Ser.). 120p. (YA). (gr. 5-8). lib. bdg. 14.95 (*0-8225-0731-5*, Lerner Pubns.) Lerner Publishing Group.

Tremain, Rose. Music & Silence. (*0-374-96028-3*) Farrar, Straus & Giroux.

—Music & Silence. 2001. 512p. reprint ed. pap. 14.95 (*0-7434-1826-3*, Washington Square Pr.) Simon & Schuster.

—Restoration: A Novel of Seventeenth-Century England. 384p. 1994. pap. 14.00 (*0-14-024488-3*, Penguin Bks.); 1991. pap. 9.95 o.p. (*0-14-012893-X*) Penguin Group (USA) Inc.

—Restoration: A Novel of Seventeenth-Century England. 1997. 384p. o.p. (*1-85619-583-X*) Random Hse. of Canada, Ltd. CAN. *Dist:* Random Hse., Inc.

—Restoration: A Novel of Seventeenth-Century England. 1990. 384p. 19.95 o.p. (*0-670-83109-3*, Viking) Viking Penguin.

—Sacred Country. 1993. 352p. text 21.00 (*0-689-12170-9*) Central Bureau voor Schimmelcultures NLD. *Dist:* Lubrecht & Cramer, Ltd.

—Sacred Country. Rubenstein, Julie, ed. 1995. 336p. reprint ed. pap. 14.00 (*0-671-88609-6*, Washington Square Pr.) Simon & Schuster.

—Sadler's Birthday. 1976. v, 190 p. o.p. (*0-356-08387-X*) Jane's Information Group, Inc.

—Sadler's Birthday. 1991. 208p. pap. 7.95 o.p. (*0-14-014771-3*) Penguin Group (USA) Inc.

—Sadler's Birthday. 1977. 7.95 o.p. (*0-312-69650-7*) St. Martin's Pr.

Tremaine, Jennie, pseud. Maggie. 1984. 192p. 11.95 o.p. (*0-312-50406-3*) St. Martin's Pr.

Trevor, William. The Children of Dynmouth. 1995. 192p. pap. 12.00 (*0-14-004718-2*, Penguin Bks.) Penguin Group (USA) Inc.

—The Children of Dynmouth. 1978. pap. 1.95 o.s.i (*0-671-81892-9*, Pocket) Simon & Schuster.

—The Children of Dynmouth. 1977. 11.95 o.p. (*0-670-21665-8*) Viking Penguin.

—Death in Summer. l.t. ed. 1999. (Core Ser.). 255p. 28.95 (*0-7838-0426-1*) Thorndike Pr.

—Death in Summer. l.t. ed. 1999. (Charnwood Large Print Ser.). 256p. 31.99 (*0-7089-9091-6*, Linford) Thorpe, F. A. Pubs. GBR. *Dist:* Ulverscroft Large Print Bks., Ltd., Ulverscroft Large Print Canada, Ltd.

—Death in Summer. 1999. 240p. 12.95 (*0-14-028782-5*); 1999. 213p. pap. 12.95 (*0-14-027720-X*, Penguin Bks.); 1998. 240p. 23.95 o.p. (*0-670-88202-X*) Viking Penguin.

—Felicia's Journey. unabr. ed. 1995. audio 54.95 (*0-7451-2735-5*, SAB 101, Sterling Audio Bks.) BBC Audiobooks America.

—Felicia's Journey. unabr. collector's ed. 1995. audio 48.00 (*0-7366-3120-8*, 3796) Books on Tape, Inc.

—Felicia's Journey. l.t. ed. 1995. (Large Print Bks.). pap. 20.95 o.p. (*1-56895-098-5*, Wheeler Publishing, Inc.) Gale Group.

—Felicia's Journey. 1999. 224p. pap. 12.95 (*0-14-029021-4*) Penguin Group (USA) Inc.

—Felicia's Journey. unabr. ed. 1999. audio 51.00 (*0-7887-0323-4*, 94515E7) Recorded Bks., LLC.

—Felicia's Journey. 224p. 1995. 21.95 o.p. (*0-670-85745-9*, Viking); 1996. reprint ed. 12.95 (*0-14-025360-2*) Viking Penguin.

—Miss Gomez & the Brethren. 1997. 256p. pap. 11.95 (*0-14-025264-9*, Penguin Bks.) Penguin Group (USA) Inc.

Trollope, Anthony. The American Senator. unabr. ed. (Classic Books on Cassette). Pt. 1. 1988. audio 53.95 (*1-55685-107-3*); Pt. 2. 1988. audio 35.95; Pts. 1 & 2. audio 82.95 Audio Bk. Contractors, Inc.

—The American Senator, 3 vols. reprint ed. lib. bdg. 294.00 (*0-7426-2475-7*); 2001. pap. text 84.00 (*0-7426-7475-4*) Classic Bks.

—The American Senator. 1979. 561p. reprint ed. pap. 8.95 o.p. (*0-486-23801-6*) Dover Pubns., Inc.

—The American Senator. Halperin, John, ed. & intro. by. 1999. (Oxford's World Classics Ser.). 608p. pap. 9.95 (*0-19-283714-1*) Oxford Univ. Pr., Inc.

—Ayala's Angel. Thompson-Furnival, Julian, ed. & intro. by. 1986. (Oxford World's Classics Ser.). 688p. pap. 9.95 o.p. (*0-19-281747-7*) Oxford Univ. Pr., Inc.

—Ayala's Angel. 1994. (Trollope Ser.). 640p. pap. 8.95 o.p. (*0-14-043845-9*, Penguin Classics) Viking Penguin.

—Barchester Towers. 1992. (Everyman's Library). 20.00 (*0-679-40587-9*) McKay, David Co., Inc.

—Barchester Towers. Page, Frederick & Sadleir, Michael, eds. 1989. 308p. 21.00 (*0-19-520813-7*); 1981. (Illus.). 586p. pap. 4.95 o.p. (*0-19-281507-5*) Oxford Univ. Pr., Inc.

—Barchester Towers. Sadleir, Michael & Page, Frederick, eds. 2nd ed. 1997. (Oxford World's Classics Ser.). (Illus.). 656p. pap. 5.95 o.p. (*0-19-282393-0*) Oxford Univ. Pr., Inc.

—The Belton Estate. 1985. (Literature Ser.). 396p. reprint ed. pap. 7.50 (*0-486-24815-1*) Dover Pubns., Inc.

—The Belton Estate. Halperin, John, ed. & intro. by. 1986. (Oxford World's Classics Ser.). 462p. pap. 8.95 o.p. (*0-19-281725-6*) Oxford Univ. Pr., Inc.

—The Bertrams, 3 vols. Hall, N. John, ed. 1981. (Selected Works of Anthony Trollope). reprint ed. lib. bdg. 115.95 (*0-405-14130-0*) Ayer Co. Pubs., Inc.

—The Bertrams. 1986. 487p. reprint ed. pap. 9.95 o.p. (*0-486-25119-5*) Dover Pubns., Inc.

—The Bertrams. Harvey, Geoffrey, ed. 1991. (Oxford World's Classics Ser.). 628p. pap. 11.95 o.p. (*0-19-282645-X*) Oxford Univ. Pr., Inc.

—The Bertrams. 1993. (Trollope Ser.). 496p. pap. 8.95 o.p. (*0-14-043807-6*, Penguin Classics) Viking Penguin.

—Can You Forgive Her? 1994. (Everyman's Library). 960p. 23.00 (*0-679-43595-6*) Knopf, Alfred A. Inc.

—Can You Forgive Her? Swarbrick, Andrew, ed. (Palliser Novels Ser.). (Illus.). 1991. 928p. 21.00 o.p. (*0-19-520895-1*); 1984. 916p. pap. 8.95 o.p. (*0-19-281585-7*) Oxford Univ. Pr., Inc.

—Can You Forgive Her? Wail, Stephen, ed. 1975. (English Library). 848p. 11.95 (*0-14-043086-5*, Penguin Classics) Viking Penguin.

—Doctor Thorne. 1993. (Everyman's Library). 20.00 (*0-679-42304-4*) Knopf, Alfred A. Inc.

—Doctor Thorne. 1989. (Barsetshire Novels Ser.). 672p. 21.00 o.p. (*0-19-520812-9*) Oxford Univ. Pr., Inc.

—Dr. Wortle's School, 2 vols. reprint ed. lib. bdg. 196.00 (*0-7426-2487-0*); 2001. 273p. pap. text 56.00 (*0-7426-7487-8*) Classic Bks.

—Dr. Wortle's School. Halperin, John, ed. 1984. (Oxford World's Classics Ser.). 304p. pap. 8.95 o.p. (*0-19-281673-X*) Oxford Univ. Pr., Inc.

—Dr. Wortle's School. Imlah, Mick, ed. & intro. by. 1999. (Classics Ser.). 240p. pap. 10.00 (*0-14-043404-6*, Penguin Classics) Viking Penguin.

—Dr. Wortle's School. 1994. (Trollope Ser.). 288p. pap. 6.95 o.s.i (*0-14-043844-0*, Penguin Classics) Viking Penguin.

—The Duke's Children. 1991. (Palliser Novels Ser.). (Illus.). 704p. 21.00 o.p. (*0-19-520900-1*) Oxford Univ. Pr., Inc.

—The Duke's Children. Lee, Hermione, ed. 1984. (Oxford World's Classics Ser.). (Illus.). 704p. pap. 6.95 o.p. (*0-19-281586-5*) Oxford Univ. Pr., Inc.

—The Duke's Children. Birch, Dinah, ed. & intro. by. 1996. (Penguin Classics Ser.). 560p. pap. 10.95 o.p. (*0-14-043344-9*) Viking Penguin.

—The Eustace Diamonds. unabr. ed. Pt. 1. 1994. audio 53.95 (*1-55685-313-0*); Pt. 2. 1999. audio 59.95 Audio Bk. Contractors, Inc.

—The Eustace Diamonds. unabr. ed. (Palliser Novels: Vol. 3). audio 124.95 o.p. (*1-85549-938-X*, CTC 129) BBC Audiobooks America.

—The Eustace Diamonds, Pt. 1. unabr. collector's ed. 1993. audio 72.00 (*0-7366-2638-7*, 3377-A ) Books on Tape, Inc.

—The Eustace Diamonds, 3. reprint ed. lib. bdg. 294.00 (*0-7426-2468-4*); 2001. pap. text 84.00 (*0-7426-7468-1*) Classic Bks.

—The Eustace Diamonds. 1992. (Everyman's Library). 20.00 (*0-679-41745-1*) Knopf, Alfred A. Inc.

—The Eustace Diamonds. McCormack, W. J., ed. (Palliser Novels Ser.). (Illus.). 1991. 830p. 21.00 (*0-19-520897-8*); 1984. 818p. pap. 7.95 o.p. (*0-19-281588-1*) Oxford Univ. Pr., Inc.

—The Eustace Diamonds. 1973. pap. 5.95 o.p. (*0-19-281145-2*); 1968. (Oxford World's Classics Ser.: No. 357). 15.95 o.p. (*0-19-250357-X*) Oxford Univ. Pr., Inc.

—The Eustace Diamonds. McCormack, W. J., ed. & intro. by. 1998. (Oxford World's Classics Ser.). (Illus.). 832p. reprint ed. pap. 8.95 (*0-19-283466-5*) Oxford Univ. Pr., Inc.

—The Eustace Diamonds. (Trollope Ser.). 1994. 624p. pap. 8.95 o.p. (*0-14-043832-7*); 1976. lib. bdg. 14.95 (*0-89968-140-9*) Viking Penguin. (Penguin Classics).

—The Eustace Diamonds. Gillers, Stephen & Sutherland, John, eds. 1969. (Penguin English Library). 784p. pap. 10.00 (*0-14-043041-5*, Penguin Classics) Viking Penguin.

—Framley Parsonage. 1989. 624p. 21.00 o.p. (*0-19-520811-0*) Oxford Univ. Pr., Inc.

—Framley Parsonage. Edwards, P. D., ed. 1981. 620p. reprint ed. pap. 7.95 o.p. (*0-19-281545-8*) Oxford Univ. Pr., Inc.

—Framley Parsonage. Skilton, David & Miles, Peter, eds. 1985. (English Library). 516p. 9.95 (*0-14-043213-2*, Penguin Classics) Viking Penguin.

—He Knew He Was Right. reprint ed. lib. bdg. 98.00 (*0-7426-2459-5*) Classic Bks.

—He Knew He Was Right. 1983. (Literature Ser.). 832p. pap. 10.95 o.p. (*0-486-24531-4*) Dover Pubns., Inc.

—He Knew He Was Right. Sutherland, John, ed. & intro. by. 1998. (Oxford World's Classics Ser.). 992p. pap. 10.95 (*0-19-283540-8*) Oxford Univ. Pr., Inc.

—He Knew He Was Right. Sutherland, John, ed. 1985. (Oxford World's Classics Ser.). (Illus.). 980p. pap. 9.95 o.p. (*0-19-281692-6*) Oxford Univ. Pr., Inc.

—He Knew He Was Right. Skilton, David, ed. 1993. 960p. pap. 5.95 (*0-460-87249-4*, Everyman's Classic Library in Paperback) Tuttle Publishing.

—He Knew He Was Right. Kermode, Frank, ed. & intro. by. 1996. (Classics Ser.). 864p. 11.95 (*0-14-043391-0*, Penguin Classics) Viking Penguin.

—He Knew He Was Right. 1994. (Trollope Ser.). 944p. pap. 9.95 o.p. (*0-14-043826-2*, Penguin Classics) Viking Penguin.

—Is He Popenjoy?, 3. reprint ed. lib. bdg. 294.00 (*0-7426-2478-1*); 2001. pap. text 84.00 (*0-7426-7478-9*) Classic Bks.

—Is He Popenjoy? Sutherland, John, ed. 1986. (Oxford World's Classics Ser.). 690p. pap. 9.95 o.p. (*0-19-281716-7*) Oxford Univ. Pr., Inc.

—Is He Popenjoy? 1994. (Trollope Ser.). 656p. pap. 8.95 o.p. (*0-14-043839-4*, Penguin Classics) Viking Penguin.

—John Caldigate. reprint ed. 38.50 o.p. (*0-404-15327-5*) AMS Pr., Inc.

—John Caldigate, 3. reprint ed. lib. bdg. 294.00 (*0-7426-2482-X*) Classic Bks.

—John Caldigate. 1993. (Oxford World's Classics Ser.). 654p. (C). pap. 8.95 o.p. (*0-19-282817-7*) Oxford Univ. Pr., Inc.

—John Caldigate. 1994. (Trollope Ser.). 624p. pap. 8.95 o.p. (*0-14-043841-6*, Penguin Classics) Viking Penguin.

—Kept in the Dark. 1978. (Illus.). pap. 3.95 o.p. (*0-486-23609-9*) Dover Pubns., Inc.

—Kept in the Dark. Pigman, G. W., III, ed. 1992. (Oxford World's Classics Ser.). 250p. pap. 9.95 o.p. (*0-19-282740-5*) Oxford Univ. Pr., Inc.

—Kept in the Dark. l.t. ed. 1999. (Perennial Bestsellers Ser.). 291p. 24.95 (*0-7838-8767-1*) Thorndike Pr.

—Kept in the Dark. 1994. (Trollope Ser.). 512p. pap. 8.95 o.p. (*0-14-043847-5*, Penguin Classics) Viking Penguin.

—Lady Anna. 1984. (Literature Ser.). 384p. reprint ed. pap. 8.95 o.p. (*0-486-24669-8*) Dover Pubns., Inc.

—Lady Anna. 1991. (Oxford World's Classics Ser.). 550p. pap. 8.95 o.p. (*0-19-282134-2*) Oxford Univ. Pr., Inc.

—The Last Chronicle of Barset. Gill, Stephen, ed. 1981. (Oxford World's Classics Ser.). (Illus.). 924p. pap. 6.95 o.p. (*0-19-281544-X*) Oxford Univ. Pr., Inc.

—Mr. Scarborough's Family, 3. reprint ed. lib. bdg. 294.00 (*0-7426-2496-X*); 2001. pap. text 84.00 (*0-7426-7496-7*) Classic Bks.

—Mr. Scarborough's Family. Harvey, Geoffrey, ed. 1989. (Oxford World's Classics Ser.). 672p. pap. 9.95 o.p. (*0-19-281808-2*) Oxford Univ. Pr., Inc.

—Phineas Finn. unabr. ed. 1993. audio 101.95 (*1-55685-267-3*) Audio Bk. Contractors, Inc.

—Phineas Finn. unabr. ed. audio 114.95 o.p. (*1-85549-937-1*, CTC 102) BBC Audiobooks America.

—Phineas Finn. unabr. ed. 2000. audio 99.95 (*0-7861-1782-6*, 2581) Blackstone Audio Bks., Inc.

—Phineas Finn, Pt. 1. unabr. collector's ed. 1994. audio 72.00 (*0-7366-2618-2*, 3359-A) Books on Tape, Inc.

—Phineas Finn. 1973. pap. 5.95 o.p. (*0-19-281144-4*); 1968. 17.95 o.p. (*0-19-250447-9*) Oxford Univ. Pr., Inc.

—Phineas Finn. MacCormack, Bill, ed. 1997. (Everyman Paperback Classics Ser.). (Illus.). 432p. pap. 6.95 (*0-460-87497-7*, Everyman's Classic Library in Paperback) Tuttle Publishing.

—Phineas Finn. Sutherland, John, ed. 1975. (Penguin Classics Ser.). 752p. pap. 8.95 o.p. (*0-14-043085-7*, Penguin Classics) Viking Penguin.

—Phineas Finn: The Irish Member, 2. reprint ed. lib. bdg. 98.00 (*0-7426-2460-9*); 2001. pap. text 28.00 (*0-7426-7460-6*) Classic Bks.

—Phineas Finn: The Irish Member. 1991. (Palliser Novels Ser.). (Illus.). 323p. 21.00 o.p. (*0-19-520896-X*) Oxford Univ. Pr., Inc.

—Phineas Finn: The Irish Member. Berthoud, Jacques, ed. 1984. (Oxford World's Classics Ser.). (Illus.). 776p. pap. 6.95 o.p. (*0-19-281587-3*) Oxford Univ. Pr., Inc.

—Phineas Finn: The Irish Member. Berthoud, Jacques, ed. & intro. by. 1999. (Oxford World's Classics Ser.). (Illus.). 776p. reprint ed. pap. 7.95 (*0-19-283533-5*) Oxford Univ. Pr., Inc.

—Phineas Finn: The Irish Member. 1994. (Trollope Ser.). 688p. pap. 8.95 o.p. (*0-14-043825-4*, Penguin Classics) Viking Penguin.

—Phineas Redux. unabr. ed. Pt. 1. 1994. audio 59.95 (*1-55685-312-2*); Pt. 2. 1999. audio 59.95 Audio Bk. Contractors, Inc.

—Phineas Redux. unabr. ed. (Palliser Novels: Vol. 4). audio 114.95 o.p. (*1-85549-939-8*, CTC 130) BBC Audiobooks America.

—Phineas Redux, Pt. 1. unabr. collector's ed. 1994. audio 72.00 (*0-7366-2790-1*, 3506-A) Books on Tape, Inc.

—Phineas Redux, 2. reprint ed. lib. bdg. 196.00 (*0-7426-2471-4*); 2001. pap. text 56.00 (*0-7426-7471-1*) Classic Bks.

—Phineas Redux. 2002. (Oxford World's Classics Ser.). (Illus.). 768p. pap. 8.95 (*0-19-283559-9*) Oxford Univ. Pr., Inc.

—Phineas Redux. Whale, John C., ed. (Palliser Novels Ser.). (Illus.). 1991. 784p. 21.00 o.p. (*0-19-520898-6*); 1984. 768p. pap. 7.95 o.p. (*0-19-281589-X*) Oxford Univ. Pr., Inc.

—Phineas Redux. 1968. (Oxford World's Classics Ser.: No. 450). 14.95 o.p. (*0-19-250450-9*) Oxford Univ. Pr., Inc.

—Phineas Redux. 1994. (Trollope Ser.). 896p. pap. 8.95 o.s.i (*0-14-043833-5*) Penguin Group (USA) Inc.

—Phineas Redux. 2003. (Illus.). 688p. pap. 11.00 (*0-14-043762-2*, Penguin Classics) Viking Penguin.

—The Prime Minister. Uglow, Jennifer, ed. (Palliser Novels Ser.). (Illus.). 1991. 864p. 21.00 o.p. (*0-19-520899-4*); 1984. 852p. pap. 8.95 o.p. (*0-19-281590-3*) Oxford Univ. Pr., Inc.

—The Prime Minister. Skilton, David, ed. & intro. by. 1996. (Classics Ser.). 736p. 14.00 (*0-14-043349-X*, Penguin Classics) Viking Penguin.

—Rachel Ray, 2 vols. Hall, N. John, ed. 1981. (Selected Works of Anthony Trollope). reprint ed. lib. bdg. 71.95 (*0-405-14140-8*) Ayer Co. Pubs., Inc.

—Rachel Ray. 1980. 391p. reprint ed. pap. 7.95 (*0-486-23930-6*) Dover Pubns., Inc.

—Rachel Ray. 1989. (Oxford World's Classics Ser.). 450p. pap. 9.95 o.p. (*0-19-281809-0*) Oxford Univ. Pr., Inc.

—Rachel Ray. Sutherland, John, ed. & intro. by. 1996. (Penguin Classics Ser.). 368p. pap. 9.95 o.p. (*0-14-043410-0*) Viking Penguin.

—Ralph the Heir. 1978. (Illus.). 434p. pap. 7.95 (*0-486-23642-0*) Dover Pubns., Inc.

—Ralph the Heir. Sutherland, John, ed. 1990. (Oxford World's Classics Ser.). 414p. pap. 9.95 o.p. (*0-19-281805-8*) Oxford Univ. Pr., Inc.

—Sir Harry Hotspur of Humblethwaite. Hall, N. John, ed. 1981. (Selected Works of Anthony Trollope). reprint ed. lib. bdg. 38.95 (*0-405-14158-0*) Ayer Co. Pubs., Inc.

—Sir Harry Hotspur of Humblethwaite. 1985. 250p. reprint ed. pap. 6.95 (*0-486-24953-0*) Dover Pubns., Inc.

—Sir Harry Hotspur of Humblethwaite. Hall, N. John, ed. 1992. (Oxford World's Classics Ser.). 288p. pap. 7.95 o.p. (*0-19-282205-5*, 12513) Oxford Univ. Pr., Inc.

—The Small House at Allington. 1997. (Everyman's Library: Vol. 237). 784p. 23.00 (*0-375-40067-2*) Knopf, Alfred A. Inc.

—The Small House at Allington. Kincaid, James R., ed. 1989. 704p. 21.00 (*0-19-520810-2*) Oxford Univ. Pr., Inc.

—The Three Clerks. 1981. 497p. reprint ed. pap. 8.95 (*0-486-24099-1*) Dover Pubns., Inc.

—The Three Clerks. Handley, Graham, ed. 1990. (Oxford World's Classics Ser.). (Illus.). 646p. pap. 9.95 o.p. (*0-19-281829-5*) Oxford Univ. Pr., Inc.

—The Vicar of Bullhampton. 1979. (Illus.). pap. 7.50 o.p. (*0-486-23824-5*) Dover Pubns., Inc.

—The Vicar of Bullhampton. Skilton, David, ed. 1988. (Oxford World's Classics Ser.). 566p. pap. 9.95 o.p. (*0-19-282163-6*) Oxford Univ. Pr., Inc.

—The Warden. 1998. (Thrift Editions Ser.). 176p. pap. 2.00 (*0-486-40076-X*) Dover Pubns., Inc.

—The Warden. 1980. (Oxford World's Classics Ser.). (Illus.). 318p. pap. 5.95 o.p. (*0-19-281506-7*) Oxford Univ. Pr., Inc.

—The Warden. 1991. (Everyman's Library). 240p. 15.00 (*0-679-40551-8*) Random Hse., Inc.

—The Way We Live Now. 1982. (Illus.). 416p. reprint ed. pap. 8.95 o.p. (*0-486-24360-5*) Dover Pubns., Inc.

—The Way We Live Now. Sutherland, John, ed. 1982. (Oxford World's Classics Ser.). 1,024p. pap. 10.95 o.p. (*0-19-281576-8*) Oxford Univ. Pr., Inc.

—The Way We Live Now. (Paperback Classics Ser.). 2001. 896p. pap. 11.95 (*0-375-75731-7*); 2000. E-Book 4.95 (*0-679-64203-X*) Random House Adult Trade Publishing Group. (Modern Library).

—The Way We Live Now. 1996. (Modern Library Ser.). 832p. 21.00 o.s.i (*0-679-60183-X*) Random Hse., Inc.

Trollope, Frances M. The Vicar of Wrexhill. (Bentley's Standard Novels Ser.: No. 78). reprint ed. 27.50 o.p. (*0-404-54478-9*) AMS Pr., Inc.

—The Vicar of Wrexhill. Wolff, Robert L., ed. 1975. (Victorian Fiction Ser.). reprint ed. lib. bdg. 66.00 o.p. (*0-8240-1563-0*) Garland Publishing, Inc.

Trollope, Joanna. The Best of Friends. 1996. 315p. pap. (*0-552-99643-2*, Corgi) Bantam Bks.

—The Best of Friends. l.t. ed. 1998. 366p. 26.95 (*1-56895-674-6*, Wheeler Publishing, Inc.) Gale Group.

—The Best of Friends. unabr. ed. 1998. audio 66.00 (*0-7887-2162-3*, 95458E7) Recorded Bks., LLC.

—The Best of Friends. abr. ed. 1998. 3p. audio 17.95 o.p. (*0-14-086780-5*, Penguin AudioBooks) Viking Penguin.

—The Choir. l.t. ed. 1994. 322p. 20.95 o.p. (*0-7927-2089-X*); pap. 19.95 o.p. (*0-7927-2088-1*) BBC Audiobooks America.

—The Choir. 2002. 320p. pap. 14.00 (*0-425-18457-9*); 1997. 336p. reprint ed. mass mkt. 7.50 (*0-425-15718-0*) Berkley Publishing Group.

—The Choir, unabr. ed. audio 49.95 (*0-7861-1030-9*, 894401) Blackstone Audio Bks., Inc.

—The Choir. 1995. 261p. 22.00 o.s.i (*0-679-44454-8*) Random Hse., Inc.

—Next of Kin. 2002. 352p. pap. 14.00 (*0-425-18474-9*) Berkley Publishing Group.

—Next of Kin. l.t. ed. 2001. (Thorndike Press Large Print Women's Fiction Ser.). 533p. 29.95 (*0-7862-3666-3*) Thorndike Pr.

—Next of Kin. 2001. 304p. 23.95 o.p. (*0-670-89999-2*, Viking) Viking Penguin.

—Other People's Children. 2000. 368p. pap. 14.00 (*0-425-17437-9*) Berkley Publishing Group.

—Other People's Children. l.t. ed. 1999. 380p. 27.95 o.p. (*1-56895-753-X*, Wheeler Publishing, Inc.) Gale Group.

—Other People's Children. 1999. 294p. 23.95 o.s.i (*0-670-88513-4*, Viking) Viking Penguin.

—A Passionate Man. 2000. 304p. pap. 12.95 (*0-425-17653-3*) Berkley Publishing Group.

—The Rector's Wife. l.t. ed. 1993. pap. 16.95 o.p. (*0-7927-1362-1*); 1992. 316p. 18.95 o.p. (*0-7927-1363-X*) BBC Audiobooks America.

—The Rector's Wife. 1993. 288p. pap. 10.95 (*0-552-99470-7*) Bantam Bks.

—The Rector's Wife. 1999. 368p. pap. 14.00 (*0-425-17055-1*); 1996. 336p. mass mkt. 6.99 (*0-425-15529-3*) Berkley Publishing Group.

—The Rector's Wife. l.t. ed. 1995. (Large Print Bks.). 364p. 22.95 o.p. (*1-56895-200-7*, Wheeler Publishing, Inc.) Gale Group.

—A Village Affair, 1 vol. 304p. 1999. mass mkt. 6.99 (*0-425-17109-4*); 2002. reprint ed. pap. 14.00 (*0-425-18605-9*) Berkley Publishing Group.

—A Village Affair. 1989. 231p. 17.95 o.p. (*0-06-039102-2*) HarperCollins Pubs.

Trow, M. J. The Adventures of Inspector Lestrade. (Lestrade Mysteries Ser.: Vol. 1). 2000. 224p. pap. 9.95 (*0-89526-291-6*); 1998. 208p. 19.95 (*0-89526-343-2*) Regnery Publishing, Inc., An Eagle Publishing Co. (Gateway Editions).

—Brigade: The Further Adventures of Lestrade. (Lestrade Mystery Ser.: Vol. 2). 2000. 219p. pap. 9.95 (*0-89526-290-8*); 1998. 208p. 19.95 (*0-89526-342-4*) Regnery Publishing, Inc., An Eagle Publishing Co. (Gateway Editions).

—Maxwell's House. 1995. 222p. 20.95 o.p. (*0-312-13123-2*, Saint Martin's Minotaur) St. Martin's Pr.

—The Supreme Adventure of Inspector Lestrade. 1987. pap. 3.95 o.s.i (*0-8128-8313-6*); 1985. 224p. 14.95 o.p. (*0-8128-3036-9*) Madison Bks., Inc. (Scarborough Hse.).

Tully, James. The Crimes of Charlotte Bronte. 2000. 288p. pap. 12.95 (*0-7867-0742-9*, Carroll & Graf Pubs.) Avalon Publishing Group.

—The Crimes of Charlotte Bronte: The Secrets of a Mysterious Family. 1999. (Illus.). 284p. 24.00 o.p. (*0-7867-0646-5*, Carroll & Graf Pubs.) Avalon Publishing Group.

Turnbull, Peter. After the Flood. 29.99 (*0-7278-7220-6*); 2002. 224p. 25.99 (*0-7278-5745-2*) Severn Hse. Pubs., Ltd.

—Fear of Drowning. 2002. (WWL Mystery Ser.: No. 423). 256p. mass mkt. (*0-373-26423-2*, Worldwide Library) Harlequin Enterprises, Ltd.

—Fear of Drowning. 2000. 176p. 22.95 (*0-312-26158-6*, Saint Martin's Minotaur) St. Martin's Pr.

—Fear of Drowning. l.t. ed. 2001. (Ulverscroft Large Print Ser.). 288p. 31.99 o.p. (*0-7089-4369-1*, Ulverscroft) Thorpe, F. A. Pubs. GBR. *Dist:* Ulverscroft Large Print Bks., Ltd., Ulverscroft Large Print Canada, Ltd.

Turtledove, Harry. Ruled Britannia. 2003. 576p. mass mkt. 7.50 (*0-451-45915-6*, ROC) NAL.

Twain, Mark. A Connecticut Yankee in King Arthur's Court. 2001. (Dover Thrift Editions Ser.). 311p. pap. 3.00 (*0-486-41591-0*) Dover Pubns., Inc.

Twigger, Robert. The Extinction Club: A Mostly True Story about Two Men, a Deer & a Writer. 2002. (Illus.). 240p. 23.95 (*0-688-17539-2*, Morrow, William & Co.) Morrow/Avon.

—The Extinction Club: A Mostly True Story about Two Men, a Deer & a Writer. 2001. 179p. (*0-241-14067-6*, Hamilton, Hamish) Viking Penguin.

Tyson, Donald. The Tortuous Serpent: An Occult Adventure. 480p. pap. 12.95 (*1-56718-743-9*) Llewellyn Pubns.

Underwood, Michael. A Compelling Case. 1994. audio 49.95 (*1-85496-592-1*, 65921); Set. 1999. audio 39.95 Soundings, Ltd. GBR. *Dist:* Ulverscroft Large Print Bks., Ltd., ISIS Publishing.

—A Compelling Case. 1989. 14.95 o.p. (*0-312-02887-3*, Saint Martin's Minotaur) St. Martin's Pr.

—A Compelling Case. l.t. ed. 1991. (Ulverscroft Large Print Ser.). 29.99 (*0-7089-2381-X*, Ulverscroft) Thorpe, F. A. Pubs. GBR. *Dist:* Ulverscroft Large Print Bks., Ltd., Ulverscroft Large Print Canada, Ltd.

—Crime upon Crime. 1980. 224p. 9.95 o.p. (*0-312-17204-4*) St. Martin's Pr.

—A Dangerous Business. 1991. 15.95 o.p. (*0-312-05842-X*, Saint Martin's Minotaur) St. Martin's Pr.

—A Dangerous Business. l.t. ed. 1993. (Mystery Ser.). 368p. 29.99 o.p. (*0-7089-2923-0*, Ulverscroft) Thorpe, F. A. Pubs. GBR. *Dist:* Ulverscroft Large Print Bks., Ltd., Ulverscroft Large Print Canada, Ltd.

—Death at Deepwood Grange. 1986. 192p. 12.95 o.p. (*0-312-18604-5*) St. Martin's Pr.

—Death at Deepwood Grange. 1993. (Audio Books Ser.). 39.95 o.p. incl. audio (*0-7838-8012-X*) Thorndike Pr.

—Death at Deepwood Grange. l.t. ed. 1987. (Ulverscroft Large Print Ser.). 336p. 29.99 o.p. (*0-7089-1673-2*, Ulverscroft) Thorpe, F. A. Pubs. GBR. *Dist:* Ulverscroft Large Print Bks., Ltd., Ulverscroft Large Print Canada, Ltd.

—Death in Camera. l.t. ed. 1985. (Nightingale Ser.). 288p. 10.95 o.p. (*0-8161-3811-7*, Macmillan Reference USA) Gale Group.

—Death in Camera. 1984. 192p. 11.95 o.p. (*0-312-18612-6*) St. Martin's Pr.

—Double Jeopardy. 1981. 224p. 9.95 o.p. (*0-312-21814-1*) St. Martin's Pr.

—Double Jeopardy. l.t. ed. 1982. (Ulverscroft Large Print Ser.). 336p. 29.99 o.p. (*0-7089-0885-3*, Ulverscroft) Thorpe, F. A. Pubs. GBR. *Dist:* Ulverscroft Large Print Bks., Ltd., Ulverscroft Large Print Canada, Ltd.

—Dual Enigma. 1988. 192p. 15.95 o.p. (*0-312-02197-6*, Saint Martin's Minotaur) St. Martin's Pr.

—Dual Enigma. l.t. ed. 1990. (Ulverscroft Large Print Ser.). 29.99 o.p. (*0-7089-2263-5*, Ulverscroft) Thorpe, F. A. Pubs. GBR. *Dist:* Ulverscroft Large Print Bks., Ltd., Ulverscroft Large Print Canada, Ltd.

—Goddess of Death. 1982. 224p. 10.95 o.p. (*0-312-33056-1*) St. Martin's Pr.

—Guilty Conscience. 1999. audio 54.95 Soundings, Ltd. GBR. *Dist:* Ulverscroft Large Print Bks., Ltd.

—Guilty Conscience. 1993. 208p. 18.95 o.p. (*0-312-09824-3*, Saint Martin's Minotaur) St. Martin's Pr.

—Guilty Conscience. l.t. ed. 1994. (Ulverscroft Large Print Ser.). 432p. 29.99 o.p. (*0-7089-3103-0*, Ulverscroft) Thorpe, F. A. Pubs. GBR. *Dist:* Ulverscroft Large Print Bks., Ltd., Ulverscroft Large Print Canada, Ltd.

—The Hidden Man. 1999. audio 49.95 Soundings, Ltd. GBR. *Dist:* Ulverscroft Large Print Bks., Ltd.

—The Hidden Man. 1985. 196p. 10.95 o.p. (*0-312-37196-9*) St. Martin's Pr.

—The Hidden Man. l.t. ed. 1986. (Ulverscroft Large Print Ser.). 352p. 29.99 o.p. (*0-7089-1536-1*, Ulverscroft) Thorpe, F. A. Pubs. GBR. *Dist:* Ulverscroft Large Print Bks., Ltd., Ulverscroft Large Print Canada, Ltd.

—The Injudicious Judge. unabr. ed. 1993. audio 49.95 (*1-85496-682-0*, 66820) Soundings, Ltd. GBR. *Dist:* Ulverscroft Large Print Bks., Ltd.

—The Injudicious Judge. 1988. 224p. 15.95 o.p. (*0-312-01447-3*, Saint Martin's Minotaur) St. Martin's Pr.

—The Injudicious Judge. l.t. ed. 1989. (Ulverscroft Large Print Ser.). 29.99 o.p. (*0-7089-2083-7*, Ulverscroft) Thorpe, F. A. Pubs. GBR. *Dist:* Ulverscroft Large Print Bks., Ltd., Ulverscroft Large Print Canada, Ltd.

—A Party to Murder. unabr. ed. 1993. audio 49.95 (*1-85496-667-7*, 66677) Soundings, Ltd. GBR. *Dist:* Ulverscroft Large Print Bks., Ltd.

—A Party to Murder. 1984. 200p. 10.95 o.p. (*0-312-59768-1*) St. Martin's Pr.

—A Party to Murder. l.t. ed. 1985. (Ulverscroft Large Print Ser.). 320p. 12.50 o.p. (*0-7089-1246-X*, Ulverscroft) Thorpe, F. A. Pubs. GBR. *Dist:* Ulverscroft Large Print Bks., Ltd., Ulverscroft Large Print Canada, Ltd.

—Rosa's Dilemma. 1992. 1.99 o.p. (*0-517-08491-0*) Random Hse. Value Publishing.

—Rosa's Dilemma. 1990. 15.95 o.p. (*0-312-04416-X*, Saint Martin's Minotaur) St. Martin's Pr.

—Rosa's Dilemma. l.t. ed. 1992. (Romance Ser.). 368p. 29.99 o.p. (*0-7089-2780-7*, Ulverscroft) Thorpe, F. A. Pubs. GBR. *Dist:* Ulverscroft Large Print Bks., Ltd., Ulverscroft Large Print Canada, Ltd.

—The Seeds of Murder. 1992. 224p. 17.95 o.p. (*0-312-07800-5*, Saint Martin's Minotaur) St. Martin's Pr.

—The Seeds of Murder. l.t. ed. 1993. (Mystery Ser.). 416p. 29.99 o.p. (*0-7089-2979-6*, Ulverscroft) Thorpe, F. A. Pubs. GBR. *Dist:* Ulverscroft Large Print Bks., Ltd., Ulverscroft Large Print Canada, Ltd.

—The Uninvited Corpse. unabr. ed. 1993. 49.95 incl. audio (*1-85496-712-6*, 67126) Soundings, Ltd. GBR. *Dist:* Ulverscroft Large Print Bks., Ltd.

—The Uninvited Corpse. 1987. 224p. 15.95 o.p. (*0-312-00023-5*) St. Martin's Pr.

—The Uninvited Corpse. l.t. ed. 1988. 336p. 17.95 o.p. (*0-7089-1889-1*, Ulverscroft) Thorpe, F. A. Pubs. GBR. *Dist:* Ulverscroft Large Print Bks., Ltd.

Unsworth, Barry. The Hide. 192p. 1997. pap. 11.00 (*0-393-31632-7*); 1996. 22.00 (*0-393-03955-2*) Norton, W. W. & Co., Inc.

—The Partnership. 2001. 256p. pap. 13.00 (*0-393-32147-9*, Norton Paperbacks) Norton, W. W. & Co., Inc.

—Sugar & Rum. 1999. (Norton Paperback Fiction Ser.). 256p. pap. 13.00 (*0-393-31890-7*) Norton, W. W. & Co., Inc.

Upcher, Caroline. The Visitors' Book. 2002. 352p. mass mkt. 6.99 (*1-57566-906-4*); 256p. pap. 14.00 (*1-57566-905-6*) Kensington Publishing Corp.

Van Ash, Cay. Ten Years Beyond Baker Street: Sherlock Holmes Matches Wits with the Diabolical Dr. Fu Manchu. 1984. (Illus.). 352p. 14.95 o.p. (*0-06-015171-4*) HarperTrade.

Vanneman, Alan. Sherlock Holmes & the Hapsburg Tiara. 2004. 320p. 25.00 (*0-7867-1297-X*, Carroll & Graf Pubs.) Avalon Publishing Group.

Vernon, Claire. The Doctor Went A'roaming. l.t. ed. 1999. (*0-7540-3633-2*) BBC Audiobooks America.

—New Life for the Doctor. l.t. ed. 1993. 19.95 o.p. (*0-7927-1636-1*); pap. 17.95 o.p. (*0-7927-1635-3*) BBC Audiobooks America.

Vernon, Claire, contrib. by. The Doctor Went A'roaming. 1999. pap. (*0-7540-3634-0*) BBC Audiobooks America.

Veryan, Patricia. Had We Never Loved: A Novel of Georgian England. 1992. 320p. 19.95 o.p. (*0-312-07769-6*) St. Martin's Pr.

—Lanterns. 1997. mass mkt. 4.99 o.s.i (*0-449-00131-8*, Fawcett) Ballantine Bks.

—Lanterns. 1996. 352p. 23.95 (*0-312-14640-X*) St. Martin's Pr.

—Never Doubt I Love. 1996. mass mkt. 4.99 o.s.i (*0-449-22412-0*, Fawcett) Ballantine Bks.

—Never Doubt I Love. 1995. 21.95 o.p. (*0-312-11864-3*) St. Martin's Pr.

—The Riddle of Alabaster Royal. 1997. 325p. 23.95 (*0-312-17121-8*) St. Martin's Pr.

—The Riddle of the Reluctant Rake. 2001. (Zebra Regency Romance Ser.). 288p. mass mkt. 4.99 o.s.i (*0-8217-6741-0*, Zebra Bks.) Kensington Publishing Corp.

—The Riddle of the Reluctant Rake. 1999. 320p. 23.95 (*0-312-20474-4*) St. Martin's Pr.

—Riddle of the Shipwrecked Spinster. E-Book 24.95 (*0-312-70142-X*); 2001. 330p. 24.95 (*0-312-26942-0*) St. Martin's Pr.

—Time's Fool. 1991. 19.95 o.p. (*0-312-05978-7*) St. Martin's Pr.

Vickers, Salley. Mr. Golightly's Holiday. 2004. 368p. 24.00 (*0-374-21489-1*) Farrar, Straus & Giroux.

Victor, Cynthia. Consequences. l.t. ed. 2000. (Wheeler Large Print Book Ser.). 435p. 27.95 (*1-56895-904-4*, Wheeler Publishing, Inc.) Gale Group.

—Consequences. 2000. 352p. mass mkt. 6.99 o.s.i (*0-451-40901-9*, Onyx) NAL.

—Consequences. 1989. 320p. mass mkt. 5.50 (*0-671-66886-2*, Pocket) Simon & Schuster.

Vine, Barbara, pseud. Anna's Book. 1994. 384p. mass mkt. 6.99 (*0-451-40549-8*, Onyx) NAL.

—The Brimstone Wedding. unabr. ed. 1996. audio 84.95 (*0-7451-6701-2*, CAB1317) BBC Audiobooks America.

—The Brimstone Wedding. abr. ed. 1997. audio 7.99 o.p. (*1-56740-151-1*, 1746, Paperback Nova Audio Bks.); 1996. audio 16.95 o.p. (*1-56100-865-6*, 815, Nova Audio Bks.); 1996. audio 73.25 o.p. (*1-56100-294-1*, 1138, Unabridged Library Editions); 1996. audio 23.95 o.p. (*1-56100-669-6*, 52, Bookcassette) Brilliance Audio.

—The Brimstone Wedding. 1997. 384p. mass mkt. 5.99 o.s.i (*0-451-19195-1*, Signet Bks.) NAL.

—The Chimney Sweeper's Boy. unabr. collector's ed. 1998. audio 72.00 (*0-7366-4533-0*, 4719) Books on Tape, Inc.

—The Chimney Sweeper's Boy. l.t. ed. 1998. 24.00 o.p. (*0-7838-0156-4*, Macmillan Reference USA) Gale Group.

—The Chimney Sweeper's Boy, unabr. ed. 1998. audio 91.00 (*0-7887-2171-2*, 95467E7) Recorded Bks., LLC.

—The Chimney Sweeper's Boy. 1999. per. (*0-671-03430-8*); 352p. pap. 14.95 (*0-671-03429-4*) Simon & Schuster. (Pocket).

—The Chimney Sweeper's Boy. 1999. 20.05 (*0-606-19048-1*) Turtleback Bks.

Settings

—The Chimney Sweeper's Boy. 1998. 352p. text o.p. (*0-670-87927-4*, Viking) Viking Penguin.

—A Dark-Adapted Eye. 1993. 288p. pap. 7.95 (*0-452-27064-2*, Plume) Dutton/Plume.

—King Solomon's Carpet. l.t. ed. 1992. pap. 15.95 o.p. (*0-7927-1059-2*); 396p. 19.95 o.p. (*0-7927-1058-4*, E0026) BBC Audiobooks America.

—King Solomon's Carpet. 1993. 384p. mass mkt. 5.99 o.s.i (*0-451-40388-6*, Onyx) NAL.

—No Night Is Too Long. abr. ed. 1995. audio 16.95 (*0-945353-97-9*, N20397, Audio Editions Bks. on Cassette) Audio Partners Publishing Corp.

—No Night Is Too Long. unabr. ed. 2000. audio 69.95 (*0-7451-4375-X*, CAB 1058) Chivers Audio Bks. GBR. *Dist:* BBC Audiobooks America.

—No Night Is Too Long. l.t. ed. 1995. 518p. 24.95 o.p. (*0-7838-1145-4*, Macmillan Reference USA) Gale Group.

—No Night Is Too Long. abr. ed. 2000. audio 7.95 (*1-57815-184-8*, 1124, Media Bks. Audio Publishing) Media Bks., L. L. C.

—No Night Is Too Long. 1996. 352p. mass mkt. 5.99 o.p. (*0-451-40634-6*, Onyx) NAL.

Vine, Barbara, pseud, contrib. by. The Chimney Sweeper's Boy. 1998. (*0-670-87937-1*) Viking Penguin.

Vogiel, Eva. A Weed among the Roses. 1993. 14.95 (*0-87306-635-9*); pap. 11.95 (*0-87306-637-5*) Feldheim, Philipp Inc.

Vollmann, William T. Argall. 2002. (Illus.). 768p. 18.00 (*0-14-200150-3*) Viking Penguin.

Von Arnim, Elizabeth. The Caravaners. 1990. 352p. pap. 7.95 o.p. (*0-14-016201-1*, Penguin Bks.) Viking Penguin.

Voss, Louise. To Be Someone: A Novel. 2001. 400p. 23.00 o.s.i (*0-609-60892-4*, Crown) Crown Publishing Group.

Waddell, Patricia. A Stylish Marriage. 2002. (Zebra Historical Romance Ser.). 352p. mass mkt. 5.99 (*0-8217-7324-0*) Kensington Publishing Corp.

Wade, Don. Take Dead Aim. 2002. 272p. 24.95 (*1-58536-037-6*) Clock Tower Pr. LLC.

Waide, Peggy. Duchess for a Day. 1999. 320p. pap. 4.99 (*0-8439-4554-0*, Leisure Bks.) Dorchester Publishing Co., Inc.

Wainwright. Square Dance. 1975. 6.95 o.p. (*0-312-75425-6*) St. Martin's Pr.

Wainwright, John. Dominoes. 1980. 224p. 8.95 o.p. (*0-312-21668-8*) St. Martin's Pr.

—Duty Elsewhere. 1979. 7.95 o.p. (*0-312-22280-7*) St. Martin's Pr.

—Duty Elsewhere. l.t. ed. 1981. (Ulverscroft Large Print Ser.). 303p. 29.99 o.p. (*0-7089-0563-3*, Ulverscroft) Thorpe, F. A. Pubs. GBR. *Dist:* Ulverscroft Large Print Bks., Ltd., Ulverscroft Large Print Canada, Ltd.

—The Forest. 1984. 192p. 11.95 o.p. (*0-312-29871-4*) St. Martin's Pr.

—Forest. l.t. ed. 1986. (Nightingale Ser.). 317p. 10.95 o.p. (*0-8161-3902-4*, Macmillan Reference USA) Gale Group.

—Pool of Tears. 1977. 7.95 o.p. (*0-312-63008-5*) St. Martin's Pr.

—A Ripple of Murders. 1979. 7.95 o.p. (*0-312-68243-3*) St. Martin's Pr.

—Take Murder. 1981. 176p. 9.95 o.p. (*0-312-78357-4*) St. Martin's Pr.

Waites, Martyn. Candleland. 2001. 300p. pap. 10.95 (*0-7490-0494-0*) Allison & Busby, Ltd. GBR. *Dist:* International Publishers Marketing.

—Mary's Prayer. 2002. 233p. pap. 9.95 (*0-7490-0585-8*) Allison & Busby, Ltd. GBR. *Dist:* International Publishers Marketing.

Wakefield, Tom. War Paint. pap. 14.95 (*0-312-28732-1*, Saint Martin's Griffin); 1994. 240p. 19.95 (*0-312-11094-4*) St. Martin's Pr.

Walker, Elizabeth. Court. 1990. 19.95 o.p. (*0-446-51596-5*) Warner Bks., Inc.

Walker, Jan. The Singular Case of the Duplicate Holmes. 1994. text 30.00 (*0-86025-278-7*) Henry, Ian Pubns. GBR. *Dist:* Empire Publishing Service.

Walker, Nick. Blackbox. 2003. 320p. pap. 12.95 (*0-06-053224-6*, Perennial) HarperTrade.

Walker, Robert W. Blind Instinct: A Jessica Coren Novel. 2000. 369p. 21.95 o.s.i (*0-425-17234-1*) Berkley Publishing Group.

Wall, Alan. The Lightning Cage. 1999. 300p. (*0-436-20491-6*) Secker, Martin & Warburg, Ltd.

—The Lightning Cage: A Novel. 2003. 320p. 24.95 (*0-312-28772-0*) St. Martin's Pr.

Wallace, Brian. Labyrinth of Chaos. 2000. 288p. pap. 16.95 (*1-56184-148-X*) New Falcon Pubns.

Wallace, Doreen Eileen Agnew. Latter Howe. 1935. o.p. (*0-00-221474-1*) HarperSanFrancisco.

Waller, Leslie. Embassy. 1988. 432p. pap. text 5.95 o.p. (*0-07-067944-4*); 1987. 256p. 15.95 o.p. (*0-07-067941-X*) McGraw-Hill Cos., The.

Walsh, Sheila. The Lady from Lisbon. 2001. (Signet Regency Romance Ser.). 224p. mass mkt. 4.99 o.s.i (*0-451-20095-0*) NAL.

Walters, Minette. Acid Row. 2002. (Illus.). 384p. 24.95 (*0-399-14862-0*) Penguin Group (USA) Inc.

—Acid Row. l.t. ed. 2002. (Core Collection). 488p. 29.95 (*0-7862-4635-9*) Thorndike Pr.

—The Breaker. unabr. ed. 1999. audio (*0-7540-0373-6*); audio compact disk 94.95 (*0-7540-5315-6*, CCD006) BBC Audiobooks America. (Chivers Sound Library).

—The Breaker. 2000. 384p. mass mkt. 7.99 (*0-515-12882-1*, Jove) Berkley Publishing Group.

—The Breaker. l.t. ed. 1999. 464p. 27.95 (*1-56895-727-0*, Wheeler Publishing, Inc.) Gale Group.

—The Breaker. abr. ed. 1998. audio 15.00 (*0-333-74614-7*) Macmillan U.K. GBR. *Dist:* Macmillan Publishing Co., Inc.

—The Breaker. 1999. (Illus.). 351p. 23.95 o.s.i (*0-399-14492-7*, G. P. Putnam's Sons) Penguin Group (USA) Inc.

—The Breaker. 1999. 368p. 23.95 (*0-7710-8755-1*, G. P. Putnam's Sons) Penguin Putnam Bks. for Young Readers.

—The Breaker. unabr. ed. 2000. audio compact disk 90.00 (*0-7887-4208-6*, C1137E7); 1999. audio 70.00 (*0-7887-3897-6*, 96077E7) Recorded Bks., LLC.

—The Echo. 1998. 368p. mass mkt. 7.99 (*0-515-12256-4*, Jove) Berkley Publishing Group.

—The Echo. l.t. ed. 1997. (Large Print Book Ser.). (Illus.). 449p. 25.95 o.p. (*1-56895-471-9*, Wheeler Publishing, Inc.) Gale Group.

—The Echo. 1998. 424p. mass mkt. 8.99 o.s.i (*0-7710-8754-3*) McClelland & Stewart/Tundra Bks.

—The Echo. 1997. (Illus.). 338p. 23.95 o.s.i (*0-399-14251-7*, G. P. Putnam's Sons) Penguin Group (USA) Inc.

—The Echo, unabr. ed. 1997. audio 70.00 (*0-7887-4044-X*, 96153E7) Recorded Bks., LLC.

—Fox Evil. 2004. 400p. mass mkt. 7.99 (*0-425-19450-7*) Berkley Publishing Group.

—Fox Evil. 2003. (Illus.). 384p. 24.95 (*0-399-15054-4*, Putnam & Grosset) Putnam Publishing Group, The.

—The Ice House. 2003. (Illus.). 304p. o.p. (*0-333-73367-3*) Macmillan U.K. GBR. *Dist:* Trafalgar Square.

—The Ice House. l.t. ed. 1993. (Magna Large Print Ser.). 453p. 29.99 o.p. (*0-7505-0589-3*) Magna Large Print Bks. GBR. *Dist:* Ulverscroft Large Print Bks., Ltd., Ulverscroft Large Print Canada, Ltd.

—The Ice House. 1993. 306p. mass mkt. 6.50 (*0-312-95142-6*, St. Martin's Paperbacks); 1992. 240p. 18.95 o.p. (*0-312-07801-3*, Saint Martin's Minotaur) St. Martin's Pr.

—The Scold's Bridle. abr. ed. 1996. audio 7.99 o.p. (*1-56740-102-3*, 697, Paperback Nova Audio Bks.); 1994. audio 17.00 o.p. (*1-56100-397-2*, 1361, Nova Audio Bks.); 1994. audio 73.25 o.p. (*1-56100-231-3*, 1029, Unabridged Library Editions); 1994. audio 23.95 o.p. (*1-56100-606-8*, 251, Bookcassette) Brilliance Audio.

—The Scold's Bridle. l.t. ed. 1995. 494p. 22.95 (*0-7838-1131-4*, Macmillan Reference USA) Gale Group.

—The Scold's Bridle. 1994. 327p. 21.95 o.p. (*0-312-11377-3*, Saint Martin's Minotaur); 1995. 384p. reprint ed. mass mkt. 7.99 (*0-312-95612-6*, St. Martin's Paperbacks) St. Martin's Pr.

—The Sculptress. l.t. ed. 1994. (Magna Large Print Ser.). 488p. 29.99 o.p. (*0-7505-0625-3*) Magna Large Print Bks. GBR. *Dist:* Ulverscroft Large Print Bks., Ltd., Ulverscroft Large Print Canada, Ltd.

—The Sculptress. 1993. (Illus.). 308p. 21.95 o.p. (*0-312-09909-6*, Saint Martin's Minotaur); Vol. 1. 1994. mass mkt. 7.99 (*0-312-95361-5*, St. Martin's Paperbacks) St. Martin's Pr.

Walters, Minette, contrib. by. The Breaker. 1998. (Illus.). 356p. (*0-333-74712-7*) Macmillan Pr.

Warady, Phylis A. The Earl's Comeuppance. 1991. 224p. 18.95 (*0-8027-1186-3*) Walker & Co.

—Scandal's Daughter. 1993. 2.99 o.p. (*0-517-09677-3*) Random Hse. Value Publishing.

—Scandal's Daughter. 1990. 172p. 17.95 o.p. (*0-8027-1133-2*) Walker & Co.

Warmington, Mary Jane. Pyramid of Love. l.t. ed. 1997. (Nightingale Ser.). 245p. lib. bdg. 17.95 o.p. (*0-7838-8110-X*, Macmillan Reference USA) Gale Group.

Warner, Janet. Other Sorrows, Other Joys: The Marriage of Catherine Sophia Boucher & William Blake. 2003. (Illus.). 368p. 25.95 (*0-312-31440-X*) St. Martin's Pr.

Warner, Sylvia Townsend. Music at the Long Verney: Twenty Stories. Steinman, Michael, ed. 2000. 224p. text 24.00 (*1-58243-112-4*, Counterpoint Pr.) Basic Bks.

Warrington, Freda. A Taste of Blood Wine. 2001. pap. 16.00 (*1-892065-48-7*) Meisha Merlin Publishing, Inc.

Waters, Sarah. Affinity. 2000. 352p. 24.95 o.s.i (*1-57322-156-2*, Riverhead Bks. (Hardcovers)) Putnam Publishing Group, The.

—Tipping the Velvet. 2000. 480p. pap. 13.95 (*1-57322-788-9*, Riverhead Trade (Paperbacks)) Berkley Publishing Group.

—Tipping the Velvet. 1999. 480p. 25.95 o.s.i (*1-57322-136-8*, Riverhead Bks. (Hardcovers)) Putnam Publishing Group, The.

Watson, Colin. Charity Ends at Home. l.t. ed. 2003. (Dales Large Print Ser.). 272p. pap. 21.99 (*1-84262-160-2*) Dales Large Print Bks. GBR. *Dist:* Ulverscroft Large Print Bks., Ltd., Ulverscroft Large Print Canada, Ltd.

—Charity Ends at Home. 1983. (Murder Ink Mystery Ser.: No. 59). pap. 2.75 o.p. (*0-440-11187-0*) Dell Publishing.

—Coffin Scarcely Used. 1981. (Murder Ink Mystery Ser.: No. 29). pap. 2.25 o.p. (*0-440-11511-6*) Dell Publishing.

—Coffin Scarcely Used. unabr. ed. 1994. audio 54.95 (*1-85089-724-7*, 90093) ISIS Audio Bks. GBR. *Dist:* Ulverscroft Large Print Bks., Ltd.

—Hopjoy Was Here. 2002. (Crime ser.). 160p. 21.95 (*0-7540-8626-7*, Black Dagger) BBC Audiobooks America.

—Hopjoy Was Here. 1982. (Scene of the Crime Ser.: No. 53). pap. 2.50 o.p. (*0-440-13625-3*) Dell Publishing.

—It Shouldn't Happen to a Dog. 1977. (J). 7.95 o.p. (*0-399-11881-0*) Putnam Publishing Group, The.

—Just What the Doctor Ordered. 1982. (Murder Ink Mystery Ser.: No. 37). pap. 2.25 o.p. (*0-440-14242-3*) Dell Publishing.

—Just What the Doctor Ordered. 1983. (Crime Fiction 1950-1975 Ser.). 192p. lib. bdg. 5.00 o.p. (*0-8240-4952-7*) Garland Publishing, Inc.

—Lonelyheart 4122. 160p. pap. 5.95 o.p. (*0-89733-076-5*) Academy Chicago Pubs., Ltd.

—Lonelyheart 4122. (Black Dagger Crime Ser.). 1990. 18.50 o.p. (*0-86220-723-1*, Black Dagger); 18.95 o.p. (*0-7451-6429-3*); 1994. pap. 16.95 o.p. (*0-7451-6435-8*) BBC Audiobooks America.

—Plaster Sinners. 1981. (Crime Club Ser.). 192p. 10.95 o.p. (*0-385-17338-5*) Doubleday Publishing.

—Six Nuns & a Shotgun. 1983. (Murder Ink Mystery Ser.: No. 65). 192p. pap. 3.25 o.p. (*0-440-17871-1*) Dell Publishing.

—Whatever's Been Going on at Mumblesby? l.t. ed. 2002. (Dales Large Print Ser.). 272p. pap. 21.99 (*1-84262-161-0*) Dales Large Print Bks. GBR. *Dist:* Ulverscroft Large Print Bks., Ltd., Ulverscroft Large Print Canada, Ltd.

—Whatever's Been Going on at Mumblesby? 1983. (Crime Club Ser.). 192p. 11.95 o.p. (*0-385-18382-8*) Doubleday Publishing.

Watson, Elsa. Maid Marian. 2004. 304p. 23.95 (*1-4000-5041-3*) Crown Publishing Group.

Watson, Jessie. The Country Mouse. 2000. (Zebra Regency Romance Ser.). 256p. mass mkt. 4.99 o.s.i (*0-8217-6689-9*, Zebra Bks.) Kensington Publishing Corp.

Watson, John H. & Meyer, Nicholas. The Seven-Percent Solution. 1985. mass mkt. 3.95 o.s.i (*0-345-33156-7*) Ballantine Bks.

Watson, Rob. Frail Flesh. 2002. pap. 13.95 (*1-85411-289-9*) Seren Bks. GBR. *Dist:* Dufour Editions, Inc.

Watts, Alan S. The Confessions of Charles Dickens: A Very Factual Fiction. 1992. (Dickens' Universe Ser.: Vol. 1). 179p. (C). text 24.00 o.p. (*0-8204-1533-2*) Lang, Peter Publishing, Inc.

Waugh, Evelyn. Brideshead Revisited. l.t. ed. 1982. 15.95 o.p. (*0-8161-3400-6*, Macmillan Reference USA) Gale Group.

—Brideshead Revisited. 1993. (Everyman's Library: Vol. 172). 368p. 17.00 (*0-679-42300-1*) Knopf, Alfred A. Inc.

—Charles Ryder's Schooldays & Other Stories. 1982. 15.95 o.s.i (*0-316-92638-8*); 292p. pap. 16.99 (*0-316-92639-6*) Little Brown & Co.

—The Complete Stories of Evelyn Waugh. 2000. 640p. pap. 19.95 (*0-316-92660-4*, Back Bay); 624p. E-Book 9.95 (*0-446-92270-6*); E-Book 9.95 (*0-446-93144-6*); 624p. E-Book 9.95 (*0-446-91455-X*) Little Brown & Co.

—The Complete Stories of Evelyn Waugh. 2000. 624p. E-Book 9.95 (*0-446-92407-5*); E-Book 9.95 (*0-446-96030-6*) Mysterious Pr.

—The Complete Stories of Evelyn Waugh. 2000. 624p. E-Book 9.95 (*0-446-92876-3*) Warner Bks., Inc.

—Decline & Fall. 1993. (Everyman's Library). 224p. 17.00 (*0-679-42041-X*) Knopf, Alfred A. Inc.

—Decline & Fall. 1977. 15.95 (*0-316-92619-1*) Little Brown & Co.

—A Handful of Dust. 2002. 256p. 18.00 (*0-375-41420-7*) Knopf, Alfred A. Inc.

Waugh, Evelyn, intro. The Complete Stories of Evelyn Waugh. 1999. 536p. (gr. 8). 29.95 (*0-316-92546-2*) Little Brown & Co.

Weale, Anne. All My Worldly Goods. 1989. 542p. 22.95 o.p. (*0-312-03965-4*) St. Martin's Pr.

—Foundation of Delight. 1990. 21.95 o.p. (*0-312-05090-9*) St. Martin's Pr.

Webster, Elizabeth A. Dolphin Sunrise. 1993. 368p. 21.95 o.p. (*0-312-09276-8*) St. Martin's Pr.

Weeks-Pearson, Tony. Dodo. 1986. 14.95 o.p. (*0-948681-00-4*) Viking Penguin.

Weldon, Fay. The Hearts & Lives of Men. 1989. 384p. reprint ed. mass mkt. 4.95 o.s.i (*0-440-20322-8*) Dell Publishing.

—The Hearts & Lives of Men. 1990. 4.99 o.p. (*0-517-03020-9*) Random Hse. Value Publishing.

—The Hearts & Lives of Men. 1988. 36p. 18.95 o.p. (*0-670-82098-9*) Viking Penguin.

—Trouble. 1993. 240p. 21.00 o.p. (*0-670-84148-X*, Viking) Viking Penguin.

Weldon, Fay, et al. So Very English. Rowe, Marsha, ed. 1992. 224p. (Orig.). pap. o.p. (*1-85242-179-7*) Serpent's Tail Ltd.

Welles, Orson, et al. The Adventures of Sherlock Holmes: The Napoleon of Crime. audio 7.95 National Recording Co.

Wells, Dee. Jane. 1987. 288p. reprint ed. pap. 7.95 o.p. (*0-06-097078-2*, PL 7078, Perennial) HarperTrade.

Wells, H. G. The Invisible Man. 3rd ed. 1992. (Longman Simplified English Ser.). (Illus.). 78p. pap. text 5.95 o.p. (*0-582-53697-9*) Addison-Wesley Longman, Inc.

—The Invisible Man. 1964. (Airmont Classics Ser.). (YA). (gr. 8 up). mass mkt. 2.95 o.p. (*0-8049-0040-X*, CL-40) Airmont Publishing Co., Inc.

—The Invisible Man. 19.95 (*0-89190-423-9*) Amereon, Ltd.

—The Invisible Man. 1994. (Illustrated Classics Collection). 64p. pap. 3.60 o.p. (*1-56103-488-6*) American Guidance Service, Inc.

—The Invisible Man. unabr. ed. 1991. audio 26.95 o.p. (*1-55656-068-0*, DAB069) BBC Audiobooks America.

—The Invisible Man. 1984. 144p. mass mkt. 2.25 o.s.i (*0-553-21155-2*); 1983. mass mkt. 1.95 o.s.i (*0-553-21207-9*); 1983. 160p. mass mkt. 4.95 (*0-553-21353-9*, Bantam Classics); 1983. 160p. mass mkt. 2.50 o.s.i (*0-553-21253-2*, Bantam Classics) Bantam Bks.

—The Invisible Man. unabr. ed. 1998. audio 39.95 (*1-86015-452-2*) Beeler, Thomas T. Publisher.

—The Invisible Man. 1981. 279p. reprint ed. lib. bdg. 14.00 o.s.i (*0-8376-0457-5*) Bentley Pubs.

—The Invisible Man. 1991. (Illus.). 3.95 (*0-425-12663-3*); 1982. 1.95 o.s.i (*0-425-05352-0*); 1980. 1.75 o.s.i (*0-425-04728-8*); 1978. 1.50 o.s.i (*0-425-04069-0*); 1976. 1.25 o.s.i (*0-425-03438-0*); 1975. 0.75 o.s.i (*0-425-02989-1*); 1968. 0.60 o.p. (*0-425-02124-6*) Berkley Publishing Group.

—The Invisible Man. unabr. ed. 2000. audio 32.95 (*0-7861-1737-0*, 2542); 1986. audio 32.95 (*0-7861-0583-6*, 2072) Blackstone Audio Bks., Inc.

—The Invisible Man. unabr. ed. audio 26.95 (*1-55686-158-3*, 158) Books in Motion.

—The Invisible Man. 1982. reprint ed. lib. bdg. 21.95 (*0-89966-377-X*) Buccaneer Bks., Inc.

—The Invisible Man. l.t. ed. 2000. 314p. pap. 19.95 (*1-58855-000-1*) Cyber Classics, Inc.

—The Invisible Man. unabr. ed. audio 21.95 o.s.i (*1-55656-112-1*); 1998. pap. 21.95 o.p. incl. audio (*1-55656-261-6*) Dercum Audio.

—The Invisible Man. 1988. mass mkt. 4.95 (*1-55902-001-6*, Aerie) Doherty, Tom Assocs., LLC.

—The Invisible Man. 1992. (Thrift Editions Ser.). 112p. reprint ed. pap. 1.00 (*0-486-27071-8*) Dover Pubns., Inc.

—The Invisible Man. abr. ed. 1994. audio 4.99 (*0-88646-707-1*) Durkin Hayes Publishing Ltd.

—The Invisible Man. l.t. ed. 182p. pap. 18.00 (*0-7583-3297-1*); 249p. pap. 23.00 (*0-7583-3298-X*); 140p. pap. 15.00 (*0-7583-3296-3*); 319p. pap. 29.00 (*0-7583-3299-8*); 409p. pap. 36.00 (*0-7583-3300-5*); 502p. pap. 43.00 (*0-7583-3301-3*); 618p. pap. 50.00 (*0-7583-3302-1*); 717p. pap. 57.00 (*0-7583-3303-X*); 409p. lib. bdg. 42.00 (*0-7583-3292-0*); 502p. lib. bdg. 49.00 (*0-7583-3293-9*); 618p. lib. bdg. 56.00 (*0-7583-3294-7*); 717p. lib. bdg. 63.00 (*0-7583-3295-5*); 249p. lib. bdg. 29.00 (*0-7583-3290-4*); 140p. lib. bdg. 21.00 (*0-7583-3288-2*); 182p. lib. bdg. 24.00 (*0-7583-3289-0*); 319p. lib. bdg. 35.00 (*0-7583-3291-2*) Huge Print Pr.

—The Invisible Man. unabr. ed. 1979. audio 27.00 Jimcin Recordings.

—The Invisible Man. l.t. ed. 2000. (LRS Large Print Heritage Ser.). 238p. (YA). (gr. 6-12). lib. bdg. 28.95 (*1-58118-077-2*, 23671) LRS.

—The Invisible Man. abr. ed. 1996. (Ultimate Classics Ser.). audio 19.95 o.p. (*1-55800-940-X*, 694289, Dove Audio) NewStar Media, Inc.

—The Invisible Man. Lake, David et al, eds. 1996. (Oxford World's Classics Ser.). 208p. (C). pap. 6.95 o.p. (*0-19-283195-X*) Oxford Univ. Pr., Inc.

—The Invisible Man. 2000. 120p. pap. 10.99 (*1-57646-278-1*); 2000. 120p. lib. bdg. 24.99 (*1-57646-529-2*); 1999. E-Book 3.99 o.p. incl. cd-rom (*1-57646-051-7*) Quiet Vision Publishing.

—The Invisible Man. 2002. (Modern Library Classics). 192p. pap. 5.95 (*0-8129-6645-7*) Random House Adult Trade Publishing Group.

—The Invisible Man. unabr. ed. 1986. audio 35.00 (*1-55690-257-3*, 86590E7) Recorded Bks., LLC.

—The Invisible Man. abr. ed. 1984. (Mind's Eye Ser.). audio 7.95 o.p. (0-88142-370-X) Soundelux Audio Publishing.
—The Invisible Man. l.t. ed. 1996. (Large Print Perennial Bestseller Ser.). 220p. 21.95 (0-7838-1545-X) Thorndike Pr.
—The Invisible Man. Daly, Macdonald, ed. rev. ed. 1995. (Everyman Paperback Classics Ser.). 320p. (C). pap. 5.95 (0-460-87628-7, Everyman's Classic Library in Paperback) Tuttle Publishing.
—The Invisible Man. unabr. ed. 1997. 175p. reprint ed. pap. 14.95 o.p. (1-57002-052-3) University Publishing Hse., Inc.
—The Invisible Man. abr. ed. 1996. (Classic Ser.). audio 16.95 o.s.i (0-14-086175-0, Penguin AudioBooks) Viking Penguin.
—Kipps. 2001. (Works of H. G. Wells: Vol. 8). (Illus.). 364p. reprint ed. pap. text 28.00 (0-7426-5407-9) Classic Bks.
—Kipps. 1986. (Twentieth Century Classics Ser.). (C). pap. 6.95 o.p. (0-19-281477-X) Oxford Univ. Pr., Inc.
—Kipps. Hughes, David, ed. 1993. 192p. pap. 7.95 (0-460-87277-X, Everyman's Classic Library in Paperback) Tuttle Publishing.
Wendorf, Patricia. The Marriage Menders. l.t. ed. 2000. (G. K. Hall Romance Ser.). 535p. 27.95 (0-7838-9021-4, Macmillan Reference USA) Gale Group.
Wentworth, Patricia. The Alington Inheritance. 21.95 (0-88411-730-8) Amereon, Ltd.
—The Alington Inheritance. unabr. ed. 1992. audio 39.95 (0-7861-0318-3, 1279) Blackstone Audio Bks., Inc.
—The Alington Inheritance. 1992. 320p. reprint ed. pap. 8.00 o.p. (0-06-092297-4, Perennial) HarperTrade.
—The Alington Inheritance. 1990. 256p. (C). reprint ed. lib. bdg. 19.95 o.p. (0-8095-9024-7) Millefleurs.
—The Alington Inheritance. 1996. 272p. mass mkt. 4.99 o.p. (0-06-104408-3, HarperTorch) Morrow/Avon.
—The Alington Inheritance. l.t. ed. 1983. (Ulverscroft Large Print Ser.). 448p. 29.99 o.p. (0-7089-1051-3, Ulverscroft) Thorpe, F. A. Pubs. GBR. Dist: Ulverscroft Large Print Bks., Ltd., Ulverscroft Large Print Canada, Ltd.
—Anna, Where Are You? 21.95 (0-88411-728-6) Amereon, Ltd.
—Anna, Where Are You?, unabr. ed. 1992. audio 44.95 (0-7861-0317-5, 1278) Blackstone Audio Bks., Inc.
—Anna, Where Are You? (Miss Silver Mystery Ser.). 352p. 1992. pap. 8.00 o.p. (0-06-092335-0); 1991. reprint ed. pap. 5.95 o.p. (0-06-081057-2) HarperTrade. (Perennial).
—The Benevent Treasure. 1976. reprint ed. lib. bdg. 23.95 (0-88411-731-6) Amereon, Ltd.
—The Benevent Treasure. 1992. 224p. pap. 8.00 o.p. (0-06-092336-9); 1990. 256p. reprint ed. mass mkt. 4.95 o.p. (0-06-081225-7) HarperTrade. (Perennial).
—The Benevent Treasure. 1996. 288p. mass mkt. 4.99 o.s.i (0-06-104406-7, HarperTorch) Morrow/Avon.
—The Benevent Treasure. l.t. ed. 1982. 448p. 15.95 o.p. (0-7089-0886-1, Ulverscroft) Thorpe, F. A. Pubs. GBR. Dist: Ulverscroft Large Print Bks., Ltd.
—The Brading Collection. 22.95 (0-88411-729-4) Amereon, Ltd.
—The Brading Collection. 256p. 1992. pap. 8.00 o.p. (0-06-092337-7); 1990. reprint ed. mass mkt. 4.95 o.p. (0-06-081226-5) HarperTrade. (Perennial).
—The Brading Collection. l.t. ed. 1978. (Ulverscroft Large Print Ser.). 29.99 o.p. (0-7089-0108-5, Ulverscroft) Thorpe, F. A. Pubs. GBR. Dist: Ulverscroft Large Print Bks., Ltd., Ulverscroft Large Print Canada, Ltd.
—The Case Is Closed. 22.95 (0-8488-0326-4) Amereon, Ltd.
—The Case Is Closed. 1986. 256p. mass mkt. 3.99 o.s.i (0-446-34471-0) Warner Bks., Inc.
—The Case of William Smith. 24.95 (0-88411-746-4) Amereon, Ltd.
—The Case of William Smith. (Miss Silver Mystery Ser.). 352p. 1992. pap. 8.00 o.p. (0-06-092340-7); 1991. reprint ed. pap. 5.95 o.p. (0-06-081058-0) HarperTrade. (Perennial).
—The Catherine Wheel. 22.95 (0-88411-747-2) Amereon, Ltd.
—The Catherine Wheel. 1991. 352p. reprint ed. pap. 9.00 o.p. (0-06-097441-9, Perennial) HarperTrade.
—The Catherine Wheel. l.t. ed. 1977. (Ulverscroft Large Print Ser.). 12.00 o.p. (0-85456-534-5, Ulverscroft) Thorpe, F. A. Pubs. GBR. Dist: Ulverscroft Large Print Bks., Ltd., Ulverscroft Large Print Canada, Ltd.
—The Chinese Shawl. l.t. ed. 1992. (General Ser.). 305p. lib. bdg. 14.95 o.p. (0-8161-5314-0, Macmillan Reference USA) Gale Group.
—The Chinese Shawl. 1996. 272p. mass mkt. 4.99 o.p. (0-06-104397-4) HarperCollins Pubs.
—The Chinese Shawl. (Miss Silver Mystery Ser.). 256p. 1992. pap. 8.00 o.p. (0-06-092339-3); 1990. reprint ed. 5.95 o.p. (0-06-081047-5) HarperTrade. (Perennial).
—The Clock Strikes Twelve. 21.95 (0-89190-923-0) Amereon, Ltd.
—The Clock Strikes Twelve. 1996. 288p. mass mkt. 4.99 o.p. (0-06-104400-8) HarperCollins Pubs.
—The Clock Strikes Twelve. 1993. 256p. pap. 8.00 o.p. (0-06-092408-X, Perennial) HarperTrade.
—The Clock Strikes Twelve. l.t. ed. 1981. (Ulverscroft Large Print Ser.). 424p. o.p. (0-7089-0604-4, Ulverscroft) Thorpe, F. A. Pubs. GBR. Dist: Ulverscroft Large Print Canada, Ltd.
—The Clock Strikes Twelve. 1988. 295p. mass mkt. 3.95 o.s.i (0-446-34905-4) Warner Bks., Inc.
—Danger Point. l.t. ed. 1975. 12.00 o.p. (0-85456-320-2, Ulverscroft) Thorpe, F. A. Pubs. GBR. Dist: Ulverscroft Large Print Bks., Ltd.
—The Eternity Ring. 22.95 (0-88411-748-0) Amereon, Ltd.
—The Eternity Ring. 1991. 336p. reprint ed. pap. 9.00 o.p. (0-06-097442-7, Perennial) HarperTrade.
—The Fingerprint. 23.95 (0-88411-727-8) Amereon, Ltd.
—The Fingerprint. 1985. 240p. pap. 2.95 o.p. (0-553-24986-X) Bantam Bks.
—The Fingerprint. l.t. ed. 1990. (Ulverscroft Large Print Ser.). 29.99 o.p. (0-7089-2265-1, Ulverscroft) Thorpe, F. A. Pubs. GBR. Dist: Ulverscroft Large Print Bks., Ltd., Ulverscroft Large Print Canada, Ltd.
—The Fingerprint. 1988. 240p. mass mkt. 3.95 o.s.i (0-446-34859-7) Warner Bks., Inc.
—The Gazebo. 20.95 (0-88411-725-1) Amereon, Ltd.
—The Gazebo. (Miss Silver Mystery Ser.). 304p. 1992. pap. 8.00 o.p. (0-06-092338-5); 1990. reprint ed. 5.95 o.p. (0-06-081048-3) HarperTrade. (Perennial).
—The Gazebo. 1996. 288p. mass mkt. 4.99 o.p. (0-06-104405-9, HarperTorch) Morrow/Avon.
—The Girl in the Cellar. 20.95 (0-89190-920-6) Amereon, Ltd.
—The Girl in the Cellar. 1992. 192p. reprint ed. pap. 8.00 o.p. (0-06-097445-1, Perennial) HarperTrade.
—Grey Mask. 24.95 (0-88411-726-X) Amereon, Ltd.
—Grey Mask. 1996. 272p. mass mkt. 4.99 o.p. (0-06-104398-2) HarperCollins Pubs.
—Grey Mask. 1993. 224p. pap. 8.00 o.p. (0-06-092364-4, Perennial) HarperTrade.
—Grey Mask. l.t. ed. 1984. 432p. 12.50 o.p. (0-7089-1221-4, Ulverscroft) Thorpe, F. A. Pubs. GBR. Dist: Ulverscroft Large Print Bks., Ltd.
—Grey Mask. 1986. 256p. mass mkt. 3.95 o.s.i (0-446-30135-3) Warner Bks., Inc.
—The Ivory Dagger. 1976. reprint ed. lib. bdg. 21.95 (0-88411-735-9) Amereon, Ltd.
—The Ivory Dagger. 1981. 240p. mass mkt. 2.95 o.s.i (0-553-25128-7) Bantam Bks.
—The Ivory Dagger. 1992. 352p. reprint ed. pap. 8.00 o.p. (0-06-092299-0, Perennial) HarperTrade.
—The Ivory Dagger. 1996. 272p. mass mkt. 4.99 o.s.i (0-06-104403-2, HarperTorch) Morrow/Avon.
—The Ivory Dagger. l.t. ed. 1977. 12.00 o.p. (0-85456-525-6, Ulverscroft) Thorpe, F. A. Pubs. GBR. Dist: Ulverscroft Large Print Bks., Ltd.
—The Key. 1992. 224p. reprint ed. pap. 8.00 o.p. (0-06-097446-X, Perennial) HarperTrade.
—Ladies' Bane. 1976. reprint ed. lib. bdg. 21.95 (0-88411-737-5) Amereon, Ltd.
—Ladies' Bane. (Miss Silver Mystery Ser.). 1991. 368p. reprint ed. mass mkt. 5.95 o.p. (0-06-081059-9); 2nd ed. 1993. 336p. pap. 8.00 o.p. (0-06-092361-X) HarperTrade. (Perennial).
—Latter End. 25.95 (0-89190-924-9) Amereon, Ltd.
—Latter End. (Miss Silver Mystery Ser.). 272p. 1992. pap. 8.00 o.p. (0-06-092334-2); 1990. reprint ed. 5.95 o.p. (0-06-081049-1) HarperTrade. (Perennial).
—Latter End. l.t. ed. 1974. (Ulverscroft Large Print Ser.). 29.99 o.p. (0-85456-252-4, Ulverscroft) Thorpe, F. A. Pubs. GBR. Dist: Ulverscroft Large Print Bks., Ltd., Ulverscroft Large Print Canada, Ltd.
—The Listening Eye. 1976. reprint ed. lib. bdg. 23.95 (0-88411-738-3) Amereon, Ltd.
—The Listening Eye. 1985. mass mkt. 2.95 o.s.i (0-553-24885-5) Bantam Bks.
—The Listening Eye. l.t. ed. 1981. 405p. o.p. (0-7089-0661-3, Ulverscroft) Thorpe, F. A. Pubs.
—The Listening Eye. 1990. mass mkt. 4.50 (0-446-34857-0) Warner Bks., Inc.
—Lonesome Road. 1993. 320p. pap. 8.00 o.p. (0-06-092406-3, Perennial) HarperTrade.
—Lonesome Road. 1988. 208p. mass mkt. 3.50 o.s.i (0-446-31466-8) Warner Bks., Inc.
—Miss Silver Comes to Stay. 22.95 (0-88411-749-9) Amereon, Ltd.
—Miss Silver Comes to Stay. 1985. (Mystery Ser.). 208p. mass mkt. 2.95 o.s.i (0-553-25362-X) Bantam Bks.
—Miss Silver Comes to Stay. 320p. reprint ed. 1992. pap. 8.00 o.p. (0-06-092300-8); 1989. mass mkt. 3.95 o.p. (0-06-080978-7, P 978) HarperTrade. (Perennial).
—Miss Silver Comes to Stay. 1996. 288p. mass mkt. 4.99 o.p. (0-06-104404-0, HarperTorch) Morrow/Avon.
—Miss Silver Comes to Stay. l.t. ed. 1977. (Ulverscroft Large Print Ser.). 12.00 o.p. (0-7089-0064-X, Ulverscroft) Thorpe, F. A. Pubs. GBR. Dist: Ulverscroft Large Print Bks., Ltd., Ulverscroft Large Print Canada, Ltd.
—Miss Silver Deals with Death. 21.95 (0-8488-1218-2) Amereon, Ltd.
—Miss Silver Deals with Death. 1991. 336p. reprint ed. pap. 8.00 o.p. (0-06-097443-5, Perennial) HarperTrade.
—Out of the Past. 21.95 (0-89190-922-2) Amereon, Ltd.
—Out of the Past. (Miss Silver Mystery Ser.). 1991. 320p. reprint ed. mass mkt. 5.95 o.p. (0-06-081060-2); 2nd ed. 1993. 336p. pap. 8.00 o.p. (0-06-092363-6) HarperTrade. (Perennial).
—Out of the Past. l.t. ed. 1974. (Ulverscroft Large Print Ser.). 12.00 o.p. (0-85456-235-4, Ulverscroft) Thorpe, F. A. Pubs. GBR. Dist: Ulverscroft Large Print Bks., Ltd., Ulverscroft Large Print Canada, Ltd.
—Pilgrim's Rest. 25.95 (0-88411-721-9) Amereon, Ltd.
—Pilgrim's Rest. 1993. 256p. pap. 8.00 o.p. (0-06-092407-1, Perennial) HarperTrade.
—Pilgrim's Rest. 1996. 288p. mass mkt. 4.99 o.p. (0-06-104402-4, HarperTorch) Morrow/Avon.
—Pilgrim's Rest. l.t. ed. 1983. (Ulverscroft Large Print Ser.). 464p. 29.99 o.p. (0-7089-0938-8, Ulverscroft) Thorpe, F. A. Pubs. GBR. Dist: Ulverscroft Large Print Bks., Ltd., Ulverscroft Large Print Canada, Ltd.
—Pilgrim's Rest. 1988. 240p. mass mkt. 3.50 o.s.i (0-446-31463-3) Warner Bks., Inc.
—Poison in the Pen. 1976. reprint ed. lib. bdg. 23.95 (0-88411-739-1) Amereon, Ltd.
—Poison in the Pen. 1985. 208p. mass mkt. 2.95 o.s.i (0-553-25067-1) Bantam Bks.
—Poison in the Pen, unabr. ed. 1992. audio 39.95 (0-7861-0320-5, 752375) Blackstone Audio Bks., Inc.
—Poison in the Pen. l.t. ed. 1991. (Paperback Ser.). 315p. pap. 15.95 o.p. (0-8161-5137-7, Macmillan Reference USA) Gale Group.
—Poison in the Pen. 1992. 320p. reprint ed. pap. 8.00 o.p. (0-06-092302-4, Perennial) HarperTrade.
—Poison in the Pen. 1990. 352p. (C). reprint ed. lib. bdg. 20.00 o.p. (0-8095-9025-5) Millefleurs.
—Poison in the Pen. 1996. 79p. mass mkt. 4.99 o.p. (0-06-104407-5, HarperTorch) Morrow/Avon.
—She Came Back. 20.95 (0-88411-744-8) Amereon, Ltd.
—She Came Back. 1985. 208p. pap. 2.95 o.p. (0-553-25173-2) Bantam Bks.
—She Came Back, unabr. ed. 1993. audio 39.95 (0-7861-0319-1, 752406) Blackstone Audio Bks., Inc.
—She Came Back. 1996. 256p. mass mkt. 4.99 o.p. (0-06-104399-0) HarperCollins Pubs.
—She Came Back. 1992. 320p. reprint ed. pap. 8.00 o.p. (0-06-092301-6, Perennial) HarperTrade.
—The Silent Pool. 1980. reprint ed. lib. bdg. 20.95 (0-88411-740-5) Amereon, Ltd.
—The Silent Pool. (Miss Silver Mystery Ser.). 288p. 1992. pap. 8.00 o.p. (0-06-092333-4); 1990. reprint ed. 5.95 o.p. (0-06-081050-5) HarperTrade. (Perennial).
—The Silent Pool. l.t. ed. 1980. (Ulverscroft Large Print Ser.). 424p. 12.00 o.p. (0-7089-0549-8, Ulverscroft) Thorpe, F. A. Pubs. GBR. Dist: Ulverscroft Large Print Bks., Ltd., Ulverscroft Large Print Canada, Ltd.
—Spotlight. 22.95 (0-88411-722-7) Amereon, Ltd.
—Through the Wall. 22.95 (0-88411-723-5) Amereon, Ltd.
—Through the Wall. 1982. 240p. mass mkt. 2.95 o.s.i (0-553-25255-0) Bantam Bks.
—Through the Wall, unabr. ed. 1992. audio 44.95 (0-7861-0321-3, 892528) Blackstone Audio Bks., Inc.
—Through the Wall. reprint ed. 1992. 368p. pap. 8.00 o.p. (0-06-092298-2); 1989. 352p. mass mkt. 3.95 o.p. (0-06-080979-5, P979) HarperTrade. (Perennial).
—Through the Wall. l.t. ed. 1988. (Ulverscroft Large Print Ser.). 496p. 29.99 o.p. (0-7089-1826-3, Ulverscroft) Thorpe, F. A. Pubs. GBR. Dist: Ulverscroft Large Print Bks., Ltd., Ulverscroft Large Print Canada, Ltd.
—The Traveller Returns. 21.95 (0-89190-921-4) Amereon, Ltd.
—The Traveller Returns. l.t. ed. 1993. 21.95 o.p. (0-7927-1638-8); pap. 19.95 o.p. (0-7927-1637-X) BBC Audiobooks America.
—Vanishing Point. 1976. reprint ed. lib. bdg. 22.95 (0-88411-742-1) Amereon, Ltd.
—Vanishing Point. 1991. 368p. reprint ed. pap. 8.00 o.p. (0-06-097444-3, Perennial) HarperTrade.
—The Watersplash. 1976. reprint ed. lib. bdg. 22.95 (0-88411-741-3, 741) Amereon, Ltd.
—The Watersplash. 1994. reprint ed. lib. bdg. 32.95 (1-56849-359-2) Buccaneer Bks., Inc.
—The Watersplash. l.t. ed. 1976. o.p. (0-85456-489-6, Ulverscroft) Thorpe, F. A. Pubs.
—The Watersplash. 1989. 256p. mass mkt. 4.50 o.s.i (0-446-35699-9); 1987. mass mkt. 3.50 (0-446-34448-6) Warner Bks., Inc.
—Wicked Uncle. 22.95 (0-88411-724-3) Amereon, Ltd.
—Wicked Uncle. 1993. 288p. pap. 8.00 o.p. (0-06-092362-8, Perennial) HarperTrade.
—Wicked Uncle. 1996. 288p. mass mkt. 4.99 o.s.i (0-06-104401-6, HarperTorch) Morrow/Avon.
—Wicked Uncle. 1986. 272p. mass mkt. 3.99 o.s.i (0-446-30083-7) Warner Bks., Inc.
Wesley, Mary. Harnessing Peacocks. 1987. 380p. pap. 10.95 o.p. (0-552-99210-0) Bantam Bks.
—Harnessing Peacocks. 1986. 288p. 16.95 o.p. (0-684-18637-3); 1994. 391p. pap. 18.95 (0-8161-7490-3) Gale Group. (Macmillan Reference USA).
—Harnessing Peacocks. unabr. ed. 1994. audio 61.95 (1-85089-660-7, 91041) ISIS Audio Bks. GBR. Dist: Ulverscroft Large Print Bks., Ltd.
—Harnessing Peacocks. 1990. 288p. pap. 14.00 (0-14-012393-8, Penguin Bks.) Penguin Group (USA) Inc.
—An Imaginative Experience. 1995. 376p. mass mkt. 10.95 o.p. (0-552-99592-4) Bantam Bks.
—An Imaginative Experience. unabr. ed. 2000. audio 49.95 (0-7451-4383-0, CAB 1067) Chivers Audio Bks. GBR. Dist: BBC Audiobooks America.
—An Imaginative Experience. 1996. 224p. pap. 10.95 o.s.i (0-14-024749-1, Penguin Bks.) Penguin Group (USA) Inc.
—An Imaginative Experience. l.t. ed. 1995. (Charnwood Large Print Ser.). 304p. 29.99 o.p. (0-7089-8848-2, Charnwood) Thorpe, F. A. Pubs. GBR. Dist: Ulverscroft Large Print Bks., Ltd., Ulverscroft Large Print Canada, Ltd.
—An Imaginative Experience. abr. ed. 1997. mass mkt. 16.95 incl. audio (1-85998-022-8) Trafalgar Square.
—An Imaginative Experience. 1995. 224p. 21.95 o.p. (0-670-85649-5, Viking) Viking Penguin.
—Part of the Furniture. 1997. 255p. o.p. (0-593-04115-1, Corgi) Bantam Bks.
—Part of the Furniture. 1998. 288p. pap. o.s.i (0-552-99723-4) Corgi Bks. Ltd. GBR. Dist: Doubleday Publishing.
—Part of the Furniture. l.t. ed. 1997. (G. K. Hall Core Ser.). 351p. lib. bdg. 25.95 (0-7838-8223-8, Macmillan Reference USA) Gale Group.
—Part of the Furniture. l.t. ed. 1998. 256p. pap. 12.95 o.s.i (0-14-026628-3) Penguin Group (USA) Inc.
—Part of the Furniture. abr. ed. 1997. mass mkt. 16.95 incl. audio (1-85998-863-6) Trafalgar Square.
—Part of the Furniture. l.t. ed. 1997. 256p. 22.95 o.s.i (0-670-87363-2) Viking Penguin.
—A Sensible Life. l.t. ed. 1991. (General Ser.). 350p. lib. bdg. 21.95 (0-8161-5127-X, Macmillan Reference USA) Gale Group.
—A Sensible Life. 1990. 320p. 18.95 o.p. (0-670-83338-X, Viking) Viking Penguin.
West, Pamela. Yours Truly, Jack the Ripper. 1987. 320p. 17.95 o.p. (0-312-00868-6, Saint Martin's Minotaur) St. Martin's Pr.
West, Paul. The Women of Whitechapel & Jack the Ripper. 1992. 428p. pap. 14.95 (0-87951-478-7) Overlook Pr., The.
West, Rebecca. The Fountain Overflows. 2003. (New York Review Books Classics Ser.). 408p. pap. 16.95 (1-59017-034-2) New York Review of Bks., Inc., The.
—The Return of the Soldier. 2002. (Thrift Editions Ser.). 128p. pap. 5.95 (0-486-42207-0) Dover Pubns., Inc.
Westmacott, Mary, pseud. Absent in the Spring: And Other Novels. 2001. (Mary Westmacott Omnibus Ser.: No. 1). 576p. pap. 18.95 (0-312-27322-3, Saint Martin's Griffin) St. Martin's Pr.
Wharton, Edith. The Buccaneers, Set. 1996. audio 41.95 (1-55685-427-7) Audio Bk. Contractors, Inc.
—The Buccaneers. unabr. ed. 1994. audio 72.00 (0-7366-2717-0, 3447) Books on Tape, Inc.
—The Buccaneers. 2000. (Illus.). 414p. reprint ed. 16.00 (0-7881-9371-6) DIANE Publishing Co.
—The Buccaneers. Mainwaring, Marion, ed. l.t. ed. 1994. 26.95 (1-56895-062-4, Wheeler Publishing, Inc.) Gale Group.
—The Buccaneers. 1995. (Illus.). 448p. 15.95 o.p. (0-670-86645-8, Viking); 1969. pap. 3.50 o.p. (0-14-044212-X, Penguin Classics); 1994. 384p. reprint ed. 13.00 (0-14-023202-8) Viking Penguin.
Wharton, Edith & Mainwaring, Marion. The Buccaneers. abr. ed. 1993. (Classics on Cassette). 16.00 o.p. incl. audio (0-453-00854-2, 390454) Penguin/HighBridge.
—The Buccaneers. 1993. 416p. 22.00 o.p. (0-670-85219-8, Viking) Viking Penguin.

Settings

Wheatcroft, John. Catherine, Her Book. 1983. 13.95 (*0-8453-4742-X*, Cornwall Bks.) Associated Univ. Presses.
—Killer Swan. 1992. 168p. 18.95 (*0-8453-4836-1*, Cornwall Bks.) Associated Univ. Presses.
White, Alan. Ravenswyke, 001. 1980. 12.95 o.p. (*0-395-28589-5*) Houghton Mifflin Co.
White, Patricia Lucas. P. S. I've Taken a Lover. 2000. 394p. mass mkt. 7.99 (*1-57343-004-8*) LionHearted Publishing, Inc.
White, T. H. The Once & Future King. 1996. 688p. pap. 17.95 (*0-441-00383-4*); 1987. 640p. mass mkt. 7.99 (*0-441-62740-4*) Ace Bks.
—The Once & Future King. 1985. 640p. 4.95 o.s.i (*0-425-09116-3*); 1985. 4.50 o.s.i (*0-425-08196-6*); 1983. 3.95 o.s.i (*0-425-06310-0*); 1982. o.s.i; 1982. 3.50 o.s.i (*0-425-05614-7*); 1981. 3.25 o.s.i (*0-425-05076-9*); 1979. 2.95 o.s.i (*0-425-04490-4*); 1977. 2.75 o.s.i (*0-425-03796-7*); 1976. 2.25 o.s.i (*0-425-03174-8*); 1974. 1.95 o.s.i (*0-425-02678-7*); 1971. 1.25 o.p. (*0-425-02077-0*) Berkley Publishing Group.
—The Once & Future King. 1958. 688p. 25.95 (*0-399-10597-2*, G. P. Putnam's Sons) Penguin Group (USA) Inc.
—The Once & Future King. 1966. (Berkley Medallion Book Ser.). 13.04 (*0-606-01195-1*) Turtleback Bks.
White, Terence. What Happened to Sherlock Holmes? As Set to Rest In . . . The Legend of Wilson - The Amazing Athlete. Blackburn, Francis et al, eds. 1984. (Illus.). 102p. (J). 9.95 (*0-9612698-0-4*) Seagull Publishing Co.
Whitechurch, Victor L. Murder at the Pageant. 1987. (Mystery Classics Ser.). 160p. reprint ed. pap. 6.95 (*0-486-25528-X*) Dover Pubns., Inc.
Whitehead, Barbara. The Dean It Was That Died. 1991. 208p. 17.95 o.p. (*0-312-06333-4*, Saint Martin's Minotaur) St. Martin's Pr.
—Sweet Death Come Softly. 1993. 189p. 16.95 o.p. (*0-312-08900-7*, Saint Martin's Minotaur) St. Martin's Pr.
Whitmee, Jeanne. The Eagle & the Wren. l.t. ed. 2000. (General Ser.). 221p. pap. 22.95 o.p. (*0-7862-2470-3*); (*0-7540-4079-8*); (*0-7540-4078-X*) Thorndike Pr.
—A Lobster & a Lady. 1980. 8.95 o.p. (*0-312-49410-6*) St. Martin's Pr.
—A Lobster & a Lady. l.t. ed. 2000. (General Ser.). 304p. pap. 22.95 (*0-7862-2810-5*); (*0-7540-4253-7*); (*0-7540-4254-5*) Thorndike Pr.
Whitnell, Barbara. Charmed Circle. 1993. 352p. 21.95 o.p. (*0-312-10438-3*) St. Martin's Pr.
—A Clear Blue Sky. 1995. 320p. 23.95 o.p. (*0-312-13945-4*) St. Martin's Pr.
Whitney, Phyllis A. Silverhill. 1981. 192p. pap. o.p. (*0-449-44782-0*); 1981. 192p. mass mkt. 5.99 o.s.i (*0-449-24094-0*); 1978. mass mkt. 1.75 o.s.i (*0-449-23592-0*) Ballantine Bks. (Fawcett).
—Silverhill. unabr. ed. 2000. audio 54.95 (*0-7540-0431-7*, CAB 1854) Chivers Audio Bks. GBR. *Dist:* BBC Audiobooks America.
—Silverhill. 1967. 6.95 o.p. (*0-385-03797-X*) Doubleday Publishing.
—Silverhill. l.t. ed. 1979. 12.00 o.p. (*0-7089-0340-1*, Ulverscroft) Thorpe, F. A. Pubs. GBR. *Dist:* Ulverscroft Large Print Bks., Ltd.
Whyte, Jack. The Eagles' Brood. 1997. (Camulod Chronicles: Bk. 3). 416p. 25.95 (*0-312-85289-4*, Forge Bks.) Doherty, Tom Assocs., LLC.
—The Saxon Shore. 1998. (Camulod Chronicles: Bk. 4). (Illus.). 496p. 26.95 o.p. (*0-312-86596-1*, Forge Bks.) Doherty, Tom Assocs., LLC.
—The Sorcerer: Metamorphosis. 1999. (Camulod Chronicles: Bk. 6). (Illus.). 352p. 23.95 (*0-312-86598-8*, Forge Bks.) Doherty, Tom Assocs., LLC.
Wick, Lori. The Hawk & the Jewel. (Kensington Chronicles Ser.: Bk. 1). 1993. 347p. pap. 9.99 (*1-56507-101-8*); 2nd ed. 2004. reprint ed. pap. 10.99 (*0-7369-1320-3*) Harvest Hse. Pubs.
—The Hawk & the Jewel. l.t. ed. 2000. (Christian Fiction Ser.). 542p. 26.95 (*0-7862-2724-9*) Thorndike Pr.
—The Visitor. l.t. ed. 424p. 2004. pap. 16.95 (*1-59415-000-1*, Walker Large Print); 2003. 27.95 (*0-7862-5641-9*) Gale Group.
—The Visitor. 2003. (English Garden Ser.). 300p. pap. 10.99 (*0-7369-0913-3*) Harvest Hse. Pubs.
—Who Brings Forth the Wind? 1994. (Kensington Chronicles Ser.). 396p. pap. 9.99 (*1-56507-229-4*) Harvest Hse. Pubs.
—Who Brings Forth the Wind? l.t. ed. 2001. (Thorndike Christian Fiction Ser.). 568p. 26.95 (*0-7862-2957-8*) Thorndike Pr.
Wickham, Madeleine. A Desirable Residence. (Rosamunde Pilcher's Bookshelf Ser.). 1999. 288p. mass mkt. 5.99 (*0-312-96815-9*, St. Martin's Paperbacks); 1997. 224p. 21.95 (*0-312-15108-X*) St. Martin's Pr.
—A Desirable Residence. 1996. 286p. pap. 12.95 (*0-552-99641-6*) Transworld Publishers Ltd. GBR. *Dist:* Trafalgar Square.
—The Gatecrasher. 1998. 288p. pap. o.s.i (*0-552-99761-7*, Corgi) Bantam Bks.
—The Gatecrasher. 2000. 301p. 23.95 (*0-312-24398-7*) St. Martin's Pr.
—The Tennis Party. 1996. 256p. text 22.95 o.p. (*0-312-14053-3*) St. Martin's Pr.
Wickham, Madeline. The Tennis Party. 1996. 256p. pap. 10.95 (*0-552-99639-4*) Transworld Publishers Ltd. GBR. *Dist:* Trafalgar Square.
Wiggin, Helene. Dancing at the Victory Cafe. 1995. 256p. 21.95 o.p. (*0-312-13954-3*) St. Martin's Pr.
Wilbourne, David. Summers Diary. 2001. 288p. 21.99 (*0-00-710006-X*) Zondervan.
Wilde, Jennifer. Angel in Scarlet. 1986. 608p. mass mkt. 4.95 (*0-380-89782-2*, Avon Bks.) Morrow/Avon.
Wilkins, Christopher. The Measure of Love. 2000. 208p. 21.00 (*0-7867-0758-5*, Carroll & Graf Pubs.) Avalon Publishing Group.
Williams, David. Advertise for Treasure: A Mark Treasure Novel. 1984. 256p. 12.95 o.p. (*0-312-00724-8*) St. Martin's Pr.
—Copper, Gold & Treasure: A Mark Treasure Novel. 1982. 210p. 9.95 o.p. (*0-312-16967-1*) St. Martin's Pr.
—Divided Treasure. 1988. (Mark Treasure Mystery Ser.). 224p. 15.95 o.p. (*0-312-01422-8*, Saint Martin's Minotaur) St. Martin's Pr.
—Holy Treasure! l.t. ed. 1991. (Lythway Ser.). 304p. 23.95 (*0-7451-1264-1*, Macmillan Reference USA) Gale Group.
—Holy Treasure! 1989. 224p. 15.95 o.p. (*0-312-03362-1*, Saint Martin's Minotaur) St. Martin's Pr.
—Murder for Treasure. 2000. 216p. 21.95 (*0-7540-8559-7*, Black Dagger) BBC Audiobooks America.
—Murder for Treasure. l.t. ed. 1988. lib. bdg. 13.95 o.p. (*1-85057-302-6*, Macmillan Reference USA) Gale Group.
—Murder for Treasure. 1980. 224p. 9.95 o.p. (*0-312-55296-3*) St. Martin's Pr.
—Murder in Advent. l.t. ed. 2002. (Magna Large Print Ser.). 304p. 32.50 (*0-7505-1871-5*) Magna Large Print Bks. GBR. *Dist:* Ulverscroft Large Print Bks., Ltd., Ulverscroft Large Print Canada, Ltd.
—Murder in Advent. 1987. 192p. pap. 2.95 o.p. (*0-380-70257-6*, Avon Bks.) Morrow/Avon.
—Murder in Advent. 1986. 224p. 14.95 o.p. (*0-312-55297-1*) St. Martin's Pr.
—Prescription for Murder. 1991. 15.95 o.p. (*0-312-05009-7*, Saint Martin's Minotaur) St. Martin's Pr.
—Treasure by Degrees. l.t. ed. 1990. 280p. 20.95 (*0-7451-1134-3*, Macmillan Reference USA) Gale Group.
—Treasure by Degrees. 1984. reprint ed. pap. 3.95 o.s.i (*0-89296-093-0*) Mysterious Pr.
—Treasure by Degrees. 1977. 7.95 o.p. (*0-312-81643-X*) St. Martin's Pr.
—Treasure by Post. l.t. ed. 1992. pap. 16.95 o.p. (*0-7927-1161-0*) BBC Audiobooks America.
—Treasure by Post: A Mark Treasure Mystery. l.t. ed. 1992. 18.95 o.p. (*0-7451-8409-X*) BBC Audiobooks America.
—Treasure by Post: A Mark Treasure Mystery. 1992. mass mkt. 4.99 (*0-00-647253-2*) HarperCollins Pubs. Ltd. GBR. *Dist:* HarperCollins Pubs.
—Treasure by Post: A Mark Treasure Mystery. 1992. 192p. 16.95 o.p. (*0-312-07101-9*, Saint Martin's Minotaur) St. Martin's Pr.
—Treasure in Oxford: A Mark Treasure Mystery. 1988. 224p. 15.95 o.p. (*0-312-02662-5*, Saint Martin's Minotaur) St. Martin's Pr.
—Treasure in Roubles: A Mark Treasure Mystery. l.t. ed. 1987. pap. 13.95 o.p. (*1-55504-358-5*) BBC Audiobooks America.
—Treasure in Roubles: A Mark Treasure Mystery. 1988. 224p. pap. 2.95 (*0-380-70546-X*, Avon Bks.) Morrow/Avon.
—Treasure in Roubles: A Mark Treasure Mystery. 1987. 208p. 14.95 o.p. (*0-312-00697-7*) St. Martin's Pr.
—Treasure Preserved: A Mark Treasure Novel. 1987. 224p. pap. 2.95 o.p. (*0-380-70256-8*, Avon Bks.) Morrow/Avon.
—Treasure Preserved: A Mark Treasure Novel. 1983. 224p. 10.95 o.p. (*0-312-81647-2*) St. Martin's Pr.
—Treasure up in Smoke. 2003. 200p. 21.95 (*0-7540-8638-0*, Black Dagger) BBC Audiobooks America.
—Treasure up in Smoke. 1978. 7.95 o.p. (*0-312-81648-0*) St. Martin's Pr.
—Wedding Treasure. l.t. ed. 1986. pap. 13.95 o.p. (*1-55504-041-1*) BBC Audiobooks America.
—Wedding Treasure. 1987. 224p. pap. 2.95 o.p. (*0-380-70258-4*, Avon Bks.) Morrow/Avon.
—Wedding Treasure. 1985. 240p. 10.95 o.p. (*0-312-86002-1*) St. Martin's Pr.
Williams, Dee. Annie of Albert Mews. 2001. mass mkt. 9.95 (*0-7472-4113-9*) Headline Bk. Publishing, Ltd. GBR. *Dist:* Trafalgar Square.
Williams, Gerard. Dr. Mortimer & the Aldgate Mystery. 2001. 224p. 22.95 (*0-312-26920-X*, Saint Martin's Minotaur) St. Martin's Pr.
—Dr. Mortimer & the Barking Man Mystery. 2001. 256p. 24.00 (*0-7867-0859-X*, Carroll & Graf Pubs.) Avalon Publishing Group.
Williams, Mary. Trenhawk. l.t. ed. 1993. (Magna Large Print Ser.). 558p. 29.99 o.p. (*0-7505-0528-1*) Magna Large Print Bks. GBR. *Dist:* Ulverscroft Large Print Bks., Ltd., Ulverscroft Large Print Canada, Ltd.
—Trenhawk. 1982. 322p. 13.95 o.p. (*0-312-81766-5*) St. Martin's Pr.
Williams, Nigel. Hatchett & Lycett: A Comedy of Love, Betrayal, & Murder. 2002. 288p. pap. (*0-670-91255-7*, Viking) Viking Penguin.
—Wimbledon Poisoner. 1991. 320p. 19.95 o.p. (*0-571-14242-7*) Faber & Faber, Inc.
Willingham, Bess. A Scandalous Wager. 2001. (Zebra Regency Romance Ser.). 24p. mass mkt. 4.99 o.s.i (*0-8217-6770-4*, Zebra Bks.) Kensington Publishing Corp.
Willis, Connie. To Say Nothing of the Dog. (Bantam Spectra Book Ser.). 1998. 512p. mass mkt. 7.50 (*0-553-57538-4*); 1997. 448p. 23.95 o.s.i (*0-553-09995-7*, Spectra) Bantam Bks.
Willis, Ted. The Bells of Autumn. 1993. 2.99 o.p. (*0-517-09906-3*) Random Hse. Value Publishing.
—The Bells of Autumn. 1991. 256p. 18.95 o.p. (*0-312-06303-2*) St. Martin's Pr.
—The Bells of Autumn. l.t. ed. 1993. (General Ser.). 464p. 29.99 o.p. (*0-7089-2888-9*, Ulverscroft) Thorpe, F. A. Pubs. GBR. *Dist:* Ulverscroft Large Print Bks., Ltd., Ulverscroft Large Print Canada, Ltd.
—The Green Leaves of Summer: The Second Season of Rosie Carr. 1989. 17.95 o.p. (*0-312-03354-0*) St. Martin's Pr.
—The Green Leaves of Summer: The Second Season of Rosie Carr. l.t. ed. 1989. (Ulverscroft Large Print Ser.). 29.99 o.p. (*0-7089-2113-2*, Ulverscroft) Thorpe, F. A. Pubs. GBR. *Dist:* Ulverscroft Large Print Bks., Ltd., Ulverscroft Large Print Canada, Ltd.
—Spring at The Winged Horse: The First Season of Rosie Carr. 1983. 288p. 12.95 o.p. (*0-688-02135-2*, Morrow, William & Co.) Morrow/Avon.
Willman, Marianne. The Wish. 2000. 320p. mass mkt. 6.50 (*0-312-97577-5*, St. Martin's Paperbacks) St. Martin's Pr.
Willsher, Audrey. The Sower Went Forth. l.t. ed. 2000. (Magna Large Print Ser.). 384p. 31.99 (*0-7505-1570-8*) Magna Large Print Bks. GBR. *Dist:* Ulverscroft Large Print Bks., Ltd., Ulverscroft Large Print Canada, Ltd.
—The Sower Went Forth. 1999. 281p. 25.00 (*0-7278-5420-8*) Severn Hse. Pubs., Ltd.
Wilson, A. N. A Bottle in the Smoke. 1991. 288p. pap. 8.95 o.p. (*0-14-013165-5*, Penguin Bks.) Penguin Group (USA) Inc.
—A Bottle in the Smoke. 1990. 288p. 18.95 o.p. (*0-670-83221-9*, Viking) Viking Penguin.
—Daughters of Albion. 1993. 304p. pap. 10.00 o.p. (*0-14-013166-3*, Penguin Bks.); pap. 10.00 o.p. (*0-14-017509-1*) Penguin Group (USA) Inc.
—Daughters of Albion. 1992. 304p. 21.00 o.p. (*0-670-83959-0*, Viking) Viking Penguin.
—Dream Children. 2000. 224p. pap. 13.00 (*0-393-31993-8*) Norton, W. W. & Co., Inc.
—Dream Children: A Novel. 1998. 224p. 23.95 (*0-393-02740-6*) Norton, W. W. & Co., Inc.
—Incline Our Hearts. 1992. 2.99 o.p. (*0-517-08020-6*) Random Hse. Value Publishing.
—Incline Our Hearts. 256p. 1990. pap. 9.95 o.p. (*0-14-011337-1*, Penguin Bks.); 1989. 17.95 o.p. (*0-670-82358-9*) Viking Penguin.
—The Vicar of Sorrows. unabr. ed. 1996. audio 76.95 (*0-7861-0972-6*, 1749) Blackstone Audio Bks., Inc.
—The Vicar of Sorrows. 1995. 400p. pap. 12.00 (*0-393-31294-1*, Norton Paperbacks); 1994. 384p. 23.00 o.p. (*0-393-03610-3*) Norton, W. W. & Co., Inc.
—A Watch in the Night. 1998. 224p. pap. 12.00 (*0-393-31725-0*); 1996. 256p. 23.00 o.p. (*0-393-04042-9*) Norton, W. W. & Co., Inc.
Wilson, Adrian. The Righteous Brother. 1997. (Illus.). (*1-901927-00-8*) Route.
Wilson, Angus. Anglo-Saxon Attitudes. 1963. mass mkt. 0.75 o.p. (*0-451-50151-9*, Signet Classics) NAL.
—Anglo-Saxon Attitudes. 1960. pap. 1.85 o.p. (*0-670-00062-0*) Penguin Group (USA) Inc.
—Anglo-Saxon Attitudes. 1996. 352p. pap. 14.95 o.p. (*0-312-14275-7*, Saint Martin's Griffin) St. Martin's Pr.
—Anglo-Saxon Attitudes. 1978. 352p. pap. 4.95 o.p. (*0-14-001311-3*, Penguin Bks.); 1956. 4.50 o.p. (*0-670-12635-7*) Viking Penguin.
—No Laughing Matter. 1983. 479p. pap. 5.95 o.p. (*0-586-04897-9*) Academy Chicago Pubs., Ltd.
—No Laughing Matter. 2001. 608p. pap. 9.95 (*1-84232-444-6*) House of Stratus, Inc. GBR. *Dist:* Midpoint Trade Bks., Inc.
—No Laughing Matter. 1967. 6.95 o.p. (*0-670-51421-7*) Viking Penguin.
Wilson, Barbara. Gaudi Afternoon: A Cassandra Reilly Mystery. 1990. (Cassandra Reilly Mysteries Ser.). 172p. pap. 11.95 (*0-931188-89-X*, Seal Pr.) Avalon Publishing Group.
Wilson, Gayle. Lady Sarah's Son. 1999. (Harlequin Historicals Ser.: No. 483). per. (*0-373-29083-7*, 1-29083-2, Harlequin Bks.) Harlequin Enterprises, Ltd.
Wilson, Laura. Dying Voices. 2001. 320p. mass mkt. 5.99 (*0-553-58282-8*) Bantam Bks.
—My Best Friend. 2003. 336p. mass mkt. 6.99 (*0-440-23710-6*) Dell Publishing.
—Telling Lies to Alice. 2004. 304p. 22.95 (*0-385-33580-6*, Delacorte Pr.) Dell Publishing.
Wilson, T. R. Beauty for Ashes. 1992. 320p. 19.95 o.p. (*0-312-08143-X*) St. Martin's Pr.
—The Straw Tower. 1991. 18.95 o.p. (*0-312-05969-8*) St. Martin's Pr.
Wimer, Genevieve R. Honour & Humility. 2002. (Illus.). 592p. 19.95 (*0-915010-46-1*) Hemlock Hill Bk. Distributors.
Windsor, Joyce. Arriving in Snowy Weather. 2000. 238p. pap. 10.95 (*0-552-99797-8*) Transworld Publishers Ltd. GBR. *Dist:* Trafalgar Square.
—A Mislaid Magic. 1994. 240p. 19.95 o.p. (*0-312-11316-1*) St. Martin's Pr.
Wingfield, R. D. Frost at Christmas. 1995. 288p. mass mkt. 6.50 (*0-553-57168-0*, Crimeline) Bantam Bks.
—Frost at Christmas. unabr. ed. 1997. audio 69.95 ISIS Audio Bks. GBR. *Dist:* Ulverscroft Large Print Bks., Ltd.
—Frost at Christmas. l.t. ed. 1993. (Magna Large Print Ser.). 433p. o.p. (*0-7505-0564-8*) Magna Large Print Bks. GBR. *Dist:* Ulverscroft Large Print Canada, Ltd.
—Frost at Christmas. 2000. (J). pap. 10.95 (*0-552-13981-5*) Transworld Publishers Ltd. GBR. *Dist:* Trafalgar Square.
—Hard Frost. 1995. (Jack Frost Mystery Ser.). 464p. mass mkt. 6.50 (*0-553-57170-2*, Crimeline) Bantam Bks.
—Hard Frost. unabr. ed. 1997. audio 94.95 (*0-7531-0099-1*, 970613) ISIS Audio Bks. GBR. *Dist:* Ulverscroft Large Print Bks., Ltd.
—Hard Frost. l.t. ed. 1997. (Magna Large Print Ser.). 560p. o.p. (*0-7505-1072-2*) Magna Large Print Bks. GBR. *Dist:* Ulverscroft Large Print Canada, Ltd.
—Night Frost. 1995. 368p. mass mkt. 6.99 (*0-553-57167-2*) Bantam Bks.
—Night Frost. l.t. ed. 1993. (Magna Large Print Ser.). 583p. o.p. (*0-7505-0566-4*) Magna Large Print Bks. GBR. *Dist:* Ulverscroft Large Print Canada, Ltd.
—A Touch of Frost. 1995. 368p. mass mkt. 6.50 (*0-553-57169-9*) Bantam Bks.
—A Touch of Frost. unabr. ed. 1997. audio 84.95 ISIS Audio Bks. GBR. *Dist:* Ulverscroft Large Print Bks., Ltd.
—A Touch of Frost. l.t. ed. 1993. (Magna Large Print Ser.). 597p. o.p. (*0-7505-0565-6*) Magna Large Print Bks. GBR. *Dist:* Ulverscroft Large Print Canada, Ltd.
—A Touch of Frost. 2000. 426p. pap. 10.95 (*0-552-14555-6*) Transworld Publishers Ltd. GBR. *Dist:* Trafalgar Square.
Winslow, Pauline G. The Brandenburg Hotel. 1976. 200p. 7.95 o.p. (*0-312-09450-7*) St. Martin's Pr.
—Coppergold. 1978. 8.95 o.p. (*0-312-16966-3*) St. Martin's Pr.
—The Counsellor Heart. 1980. 224p. 8.95 o.p. (*0-312-17014-9*) St. Martin's Pr.
—The Rockefeller Gift. 1981. 288p. 12.95 o.p. (*0-312-68795-8*) St. Martin's Pr.
—The Witch Hill Murder. 1983. 256p. pap. 5.95 o.p. (*0-312-88428-1*, Saint Martin's Griffin); 1977. 7.95 o.p. (*0-312-88427-3*) St. Martin's Pr.
Winterson, Jeanette. Oranges Are Not the Only Fruit. 1997. 192p. 12.00 (*0-8021-3516-1*) Grove/Atlantic, Inc.
—Oranges Are Not the Only Fruit. Fisketjon, Gary, ed. 1995. (Fiction Ser.). 90p. reprint ed. pap. 12.00 o.p. (*0-87113-163-3*, Grove Pr.) Grove/Atlantic, Inc.
—Written on the Body. 1994. 192p. pap. 12.00 (*0-679-74447-9*) Knopf, Alfred A. Inc.
Wittich, Justine. Chloe & the Spy. 2002. (Five Star First Edition Romance Ser.). 250p. 26.95 (*0-7862-3749-X*, Five Star) Gale Group.
—The Shocking Miss Shaw. 2003. (Five Star First Edition Romance Ser.). 296p. 26.95 (*0-7862-4767-3*, Five Star) Gale Group.
Wodehouse, P. G. Aunts Aren't Gentlemen. unabr. ed. 2000. (Wooster & Jeeves Comedy Ser.). audio 34.95 (*0-7451-4098-X*, CAB 786) Chivers Audio Bks. GBR. *Dist:* BBC Audiobooks America.
—Bertie Wooster Sees It Through. 18.95 (*0-8488-0671-9*) Amereon, Ltd.
—Bertie Wooster Sees It Through. 2000. 240p. pap. 13.00 (*0-7432-0361-5*, Touchstone) Simon & Schuster.
—Carry On, Jeeves! 19.95 (*0-89190-296-1*) Amereon, Ltd.
—Carry On, Jeeves! unabr. ed. 2000. audio compact disk 48.00 (*0-7861-9949-0*, z2442) Blackstone Audio Bks., Inc.

—Carry On, Jeeves! 1990. reprint ed. lib. bdg. 15.95 (0-89968-559-5) Buccaneer Bks., Inc.
—Carry On, Jeeves! 2003. 17.95 (1-58567-392-7) Overlook Pr., The.
—Carry On, Jeeves! 240p. 2000. 7.95 (0-14-028408-7); 1975. pap. 8.95 o.s.i (0-14-001174-9, Penguin Bks.) Viking Penguin.
—Carry on, Jeeves! 8 Complete Stories. unabr. ed. 1999. audio 22.95 (1-57270-109-9, C41109u, Audio Editions Bks. on Cassette) Audio Partners Publishing Corp.
—The Cat-Nappers. unabr. ed. 2001. audio compact disk 19.95; 2000. audio compact disk 32.00 (0-7861-6897-8, z1783); 1996. audio 23.95 (0-7861-1006-6, 1783); 1996. audio 23.95 (0-7861-1393-6, 1783) Blackstone Audio Bks., Inc.
—The Cat-Nappers. reprint ed. 1990. 240p. pap. 11.00 o.p. (0-06-097250-5); 1985. 192p. mass mkt. 3.95 o.p. (0-06-080769-5, P 769) HarperTrade. (Perennial).
—The Cat-Nappers. 1975. 192p. 7.95 o.s.i (0-671-21972-3, Simon & Schuster) Simon & Schuster.
—The Code of the Woosters. reprint ed. lib. bdg. 21.95 (0-89190-291-0, Rivercity Pr.) Amereon, Ltd.
—The Code of the Woosters. unabr. ed. 2000. (Wooster & Jeeves Comedy Ser.). audio 49.95 (0-7451-6372-6, CAB 497) Chivers Audio Bks. GBR. Dist: BBC Audiobooks America.
—The Code of the Woosters. 1975. 240p. mass mkt. 9.00 (0-394-72028-8, Vintage) Knopf Publishing Group.
—The Code of the Woosters. unabr. ed. 1997. (Wodehouse's Bertie & Jeeves Ser.). audio 22.95 (1-58081-060-8, CTA60) L. A. Theatre Works.
—The Code of the Woosters. 2000. (Collector's Wodehouse Ser.). 224p. 17.95 (1-58567-057-X) Overlook Pr., The.
—The Code of the Woosters, unabr. ed. 1989. audio 51.00 (1-55690-109-7, 89600E7) Recorded Bks., LLC.
—Enter Jeeves: 15 Early Stories. 1997. 288p. reprint ed. pap. 8.95 (0-486-29717-9) Dover Pubns., Inc.
—Heavy Weather. 2002. (Illus.). 321p. 16.95 (1-58567-230-0) Overlook Pr., The.
—How Right You Are, Jeeves. reprint ed. lib. bdg. 21.95 (0-89190-293-7, Rivercity Pr.) Amereon, Ltd.
—How Right You Are, Jeeves. 1990. reprint ed. lib. bdg. 17.95 (0-89968-560-9) Buccaneer Bks., Inc.
—How Right You Are, Jeeves. 1985. 192p. reprint ed. pap. 3.95 o.p. (0-06-080770-9, P 770, Perennial) HarperTrade.
—How Right You Are, Jeeves. 2000. 208p. pap. 12.00 (0-7432-0359-3, Touchstone); 1960. 3.50 o.p. (0-671-32460-8, Simon & Schuster) Simon & Schuster.
—How Right You Are, Jeeves: A Jeeves & Bertie Novel. 1990. 205p. reprint ed. pap. 11.00 o.p. (0-06-096499-5, Perennial) HarperTrade.
—Jeeves & the Tie That Binds. 20.95 (0-8488-0674-3) Amereon, Ltd.
—Jeeves & the Tie That Binds. audio 24.95 (0-7861-1398-7); 1992. audio 32.95 (0-7861-0291-8, 1255) Blackstone Audio Bks., Inc.
—Jeeves & the Tie That Binds. 1983. 192p. mass mkt. 3.95 o.p. (0-06-080667-2, P667); 1990. 79p. reprint ed. pap. 10.00 o.p. (0-06-097283-1) HarperTrade. (Perennial).
—Jeeves & the Tie That Binds, Set. unabr. ed. 1999. audio 32.95 Highsmith Inc.
—Jeeves & the Tie That Binds. 1971. 5.95 o.s.i (0-671-21038-6, Simon & Schuster) Simon & Schuster.
—Jeeves in the Morning. unabr. ed. 2000. audio compact disk 69.99 (0-7861-9941-5, z1740); 1996. audio 39.95 (0-7861-0963-7, 1740) Blackstone Audio Bks., Inc.
—Jeeves in the Morning. 1983. reprint ed. pap. 3.95 o.p. (0-06-080658-3, P 658, Perennial) HarperTrade.
—Jeeves in the Offing. 2002. 16.95 (1-58567-325-0) Penguin Group (USA) Inc.
—Jeeves in the Offing. 1984. audio 53.95 o.p. (0-8161-9784-9) Thorndike Pr.
—Life with Jeeves. 1983. 560p. pap. 15.95 (0-14-005902-4, Penguin Bks.) Penguin Group (USA) Inc.
—Luck of the Bodkins. 2002. 16.95 (1-58567-336-6) Overlook Pr., The.
—Mating Season. 22.95 (0-8488-0677-8) Amereon, Ltd.
—The Mating Season. unabr. ed. 1995. audio 44.95 (0-7861-0761-8, 1610) Blackstone Audio Bks., Inc.
—The Mating Season. 1989. 224p. reprint ed. pap. 10.00 o.p. (0-06-097248-3, Perennial) HarperTrade.
—P. G. Wodehouse: Five Complete Novels. annuals 1995. (Avenel Readers Library). 688p. 12.99 o.s.i (0-517-40538-5) Random Hse. Value Publishing.
—Piccadilly Jim. 1995. (Penguin Bks.). 240p. pap. 8.00 (0-14-003039-5, Penguin Bks.) Penguin Group (USA) Inc.
—The Return of Jeeves. 21.95 (0-8488-0332-9) Amereon, Ltd.
—The Return of Jeeves. 1985. 240p. reprint ed. pap. 3.95 o.p. (0-06-080768-7, P 768, Perennial) HarperTrade.
—The Return of Jeeves. mass mkt. 0.50 o.p. (0-451-02843-0, Signet Bks.) NAL.
—The Return of Jeeves: A Jeeves & Bertie Novel. 1990. 231p. reprint ed. pap. 11.00 o.p. (0-06-096502-9, Perennial) HarperTrade.
—Right Ho, Jeeves. 22.95 (0-8488-0680-8) Amereon, Ltd.
—Right Ho, Jeeves. 1999. audio 29.95 (0-7451-2814-9) BBC Audiobooks America.
—Right Ho, Jeeves. unabr. ed. 1992. audio 44.95 (0-7861-0363-9, 1320) Blackstone Audio Bks., Inc.
—Right Ho, Jeeves. unabr. ed. 2000. (Wooster & Jeeves Comedy Ser.). audio 49.95 (0-7451-6371-8, CAB 414) Chivers Audio Bks. GBR. Dist: BBC Audiobooks America.
—Right Ho, Jeeves. 2000. (Collector's Wodehouse Ser.). 224p. 17.95 (1-58567-058-8) Overlook Pr., The.
—Right Ho, Jeeves. 2000. 272p. pap. 7.95 (0-14-028409-5) Penguin Group (USA) Inc.
—Right Ho, Jeeves, unabr. ed. 1988. audio 44.00 (1-55690-444-4, 88070E7) Recorded Bks., LLC.
—Right Ho, Jeeves. 2001. 2p. audio (0-14-180315-0, Penguin AudioBooks); 1975. 256p. pap. 9.95 o.s.i (0-14-000934-5, Penguin Bks.) Viking Penguin.
—Something New. 2000. 192p. pap. 6.95 (0-486-41404-3) Dover Pubns., Inc.
—Stiff Upper Lip, Jeeves. 20.95 (0-8488-0682-4) Amereon, Ltd.
—Stiff Upper Lip, Jeeves. unabr. ed. 1991. audio 39.95 (0-7861-0279-9, 1245) Blackstone Audio Bks., Inc.
—Stiff Upper Lip, Jeeves. unabr. ed. 2000. (Wooster & Jeeves Comedy Ser.). audio 49.95 (0-7451-4043-2, CAB 740) Chivers Audio Bks. GBR. Dist: BBC Audiobooks America.
—Stiff Upper Lip, Jeeves. 192p. 1983. mass mkt. 3.95 o.p. (0-06-080668-0, P668); 1990. reprint ed. pap. 10.00 o.p. (0-06-097284-X) HarperTrade. (Perennial).
—Stiff Upper Lip, Jeeves. mass mkt. 0.50 o.p. (0-451-02841-4, Signet Bks.) NAL.
—Stiff Upper Lip, Jeeves. 2000. 224p. pap. 12.00 (0-7432-0360-7, Touchstone); (Illus.). 24.00 (0-7432-0410-7, Simon & Schuster) Simon & Schuster.
—Tales from the Drones Club. reprint ed. 1992. 360p. pap. 14.95 o.p. (1-55882-118-X); 1991. 352p. 21.95 o.p. (1-55882-088-4) International Polygonics, Ltd. (Library of Crime Classics).
—Thank You, Jeeves. reprint ed. lib. bdg. 23.95 (0-89190-294-5, Rivercity Pr.) Amereon, Ltd.
—Thank You, Jeeves. unabr. ed. 1989. audio 39.95 (0-7861-0174-1, 1155) Blackstone Audio Bks., Inc.
—Thank You, Jeeves. 1983. 480p. mass mkt. 3.95 o.p. (0-06-080657-5) HarperCollins Pubs.
—Thank You, Jeeves. 1989. 288p. reprint ed. pap. 10.00 o.p. (0-06-097249-1, Perennial) HarperTrade.
—Thank You, Jeeves. unabr. ed. 1998. audio 19.95 (1-58081-119-1, TPT117) L. A. Theatre Works.
—Thank You, Jeeves. 2003. 288p. 17.95 (1-58567-434-6) Overlook Pr., The.
—Thank You, Jeeves, unabr. ed. 1984. audio 35.00 (1-55690-509-2, 84130E7) Recorded Bks., LLC.
—Uneasy Money. reprint ed. lib. bdg. 98.00 (0-7426-3253-9); 2001. pap. text 28.00 (0-7426-8253-6) Classic Bks.
—Uneasy Money. 1992. 192p. pap. 8.95 o.s.i (0-14-001273-7, Penguin Bks.) Penguin Group (USA) Inc.
—Very Good, Jeeves. 1998. (Bertie Wooster & Jeeves Ser.). audio 34.95 (0-7540-7524-9) BBC Audiobooks America.
—Very Good, Jeeves. 1975. (ACE.). 256p. pap. 8.95 o.s.i (0-14-001173-0, Penguin Bks.) Viking Penguin.
—Very Good, Jeeves! 2000. 288p. 7.95 (0-14-028410-9) Viking Penguin.
—Very Good, Jeeves. reprint ed. lib. bdg. 22.95 (0-89190-295-3, Rivercity Pr.) Amereon, Ltd.
—Very Good, Jeeves. unabr. ed. 1992. audio 44.95 (0-7861-0310-8, 1272) Blackstone Audio Bks., Inc.
—Very Good, Jeeves. 1990. reprint ed. lib. bdg. 18.95 (0-89968-561-7) Buccaneer Bks., Inc.
—The World of Jeeves. 672p. 1988. 25.00 o.p. (0-06-015968-5); 1989. reprint ed. pap. 18.00 o.s.i (0-06-097244-0, Perennial) HarperTrade.
Wolf, Joan. Golden Girl. 1999. 336p. reprint ed. mass mkt. 6.50 (0-446-60693-6) Warner Bks., Inc.
—Someday Soon. 2000. 368p. reprint ed. mass mkt. 6.50 (0-446-60694-4, Warner Romance) Warner Bks., Inc.
Wolf, Joan & McRae, Melinda. His Lordship's Mistress/Married by Mistake. 2000. (Signet Regency Romance Ser.). 448p. mass mkt. 5.50 o.s.i (0-451-20268-6) NAL.
Wolf, Leonard, ed. The Essential Dr. Jekyll & Mr. Hyde: The Definitive, Annotated Edition of Robert Louis Stevenson's Classic Novel. annot. ed. 1995. (Essentials Ser.). (Illus.). 304p. (Orig.). pap. 14.95 o.p. (0-452-26969-5, Plume) Dutton/Plume.
Wolf, Leonard & Stoker, Bram. The Essential Dracula. 1993. (Essentials Ser.). (Illus.). 512p. pap. 16.95 o.p. (0-452-26943-1, Plume) Dutton/Plume.
Wolff, Isabel. The Trials of Tiffany Trott. 1999. 416p. mass mkt. 7.99 (0-451-40888-8, Onyx) NAL.
Wood. East Lynne. 1993. (Pocket Classics Ser.). pap. text 13.95 (0-7509-0446-1) Sutton Publishing, Ltd. GBR. Dist: International Publishers Marketing.
—East Lynne. 656p. 1994. 8.95 (0-460-87430-6); 1984. pap. 9.95 o.p. (0-460-11402-6) Tuttle Publishing. (Everyman's Classic Library in Paperback).
—Hungry Tide. 2000. 477p. pap. 9.95 (0-552-14118-6) Transworld Publishers Ltd. GBR. Dist: Trafalgar Square.
—Romany Girl. 2000. 536p. 29.95 (0-593-04365-0) Transworld Publishers Ltd. GBR. Dist: Trafalgar Square.
Wood, Henry. East Lynne. Maunder, Andrew, ed. 2000. (Literary Texts Ser.). (Illus.). 700p. pap. (1-55111-234-5) Broadview Pr.
Wood, Valerie. Annie. 2000. pap. 8.95 (0-552-14263-8) Transworld Publishers Ltd. GBR. Dist: Trafalgar Square.
—Middle Court. 2002. 448p. 29.95 o.s.i (0-593-05073-8) Bantam Bks.
—Romany Girl. 2000. 536p. pap. 8.95 (0-552-14640-4) Transworld Publishers Ltd. GBR. Dist: Trafalgar Square.
Woodbury, Francine G. Shade & Shadow. 1996. 313p. mass mkt. 4.99 o.s.i (0-345-39428-3) Ballantine Bks.
Woodhouse, Sarah. Enchanted Ground. 1993. 256p. 21.95 o.p. (0-312-09795-6) St. Martin's Pr.
—My Summer with Julia. 2000. 256p. 23.95 (0-312-26622-7) St. Martin's Pr.
—My Summer with Julia. l.t. ed. 2001. (Thorndike General Ser.). 261p. 24.95 (0-7862-3028-2) Thorndike Pr.
—The Native Air. 1991. 17.95 o.p. (0-312-05901-9) St. Martin's Pr.
Woodman, Richard. Arctic Treachery. 1987. 232p. 15.95 o.p. (0-8027-0948-6) Walker & Co.
Woods, Sara. Away with Them to Prison. 1989. 224p. pap. 3.50 (0-380-70589-3, Avon Bks.) Morrow/Avon.
—Away with Them to Prison. 1985. 12.95 o.p. (0-312-06311-3) St. Martin's Pr.
—Away with Them to Prison. l.t. ed. 1988. 464p. 17.95 o.p. (0-7089-1811-5, Ulverscroft) Thorpe, F. A. Pubs. GBR. Dist: Ulverscroft Large Print Bks., Ltd.
—Bloody Instructions. 1986. pap. 2.95 (0-380-69858-7, Avon Bks.) Morrow/Avon.
—Call Back Yesterday. 1983. 224p. 10.95 o.p. (0-312-11424-9) St. Martin's Pr.
—Call Back Yesterday. l.t. ed. 1985. (Ulverscroft Large Print Ser.). 368p. 12.50 o.p. (0-7089-1358-X, Ulverscroft) Thorpe, F. A. Pubs. GBR. Dist: Ulverscroft Large Print Bks., Ltd., Ulverscroft Large Print Canada, Ltd.
—Cry Guilty. 1981. 192p. 9.95 o.p. (0-312-17802-6) St. Martin's Pr.
—Dearest Enemy. 1981. 196p. 9.95 o.p. (0-312-18546-4) St. Martin's Pr.
—Dearest Enemy. l.t. ed. 1984. (Ulverscroft Large Print Ser.). 416p. 12.50 o.p. (0-7089-1235-4, Ulverscroft) Thorpe, F. A. Pubs. GBR. Dist: Ulverscroft Large Print Bks., Ltd., Ulverscroft Large Print Canada, Ltd.
—Defy the Devil. 1984. 304p. 11.95 o.p. (0-312-19121-9) St. Martin's Pr.
—Defy the Devil. l.t. ed. 1986. 328p. 15.95 o.p. (0-7089-1481-0, Ulverscroft) Thorpe, F. A. Pubs. GBR. Dist: Ulverscroft Large Print Bks., Ltd.
—Error of the Moon. 1986. 176p. pap. 2.95 (0-380-69859-5, Avon Bks.) Morrow/Avon.
—Exit Murderer. (Fingerprint Mysteries Ser.). 1983. 192p. pap. 5.95 o.p. (0-312-27588-9, Saint Martin's Griffin); 1978. 7.95 o.p. (0-312-27587-0) St. Martin's Pr.
—The Law's Delay. 1977. 7.95 o.p. (0-312-47565-9) St. Martin's Pr.
—Let's Choose Executors. 1986. (Anthony Maitland Detective Ser.). 224p. pap. 2.95 o.p. (0-380-69860-9, Avon Bks.) Morrow/Avon.
—The Lie Direct. 1989. 160p. pap. 3.95 (0-380-70588-5, Avon Bks.) Morrow/Avon.
—The Lie Direct. 1983. 192p. 10.95 o.p. (0-312-48369-4) St. Martin's Pr.
—The Lie Direct. l.t. ed. 1986. 336p. o.p. (0-7089-1551-5, Ulverscroft) Thorpe, F. A. Pubs.
—Most Deadly Hate. 1987. 240p. pap. 3.50 (0-380-70477-3, Avon Bks.) Morrow/Avon.
—Most Deadly Hate. 1986. 224p. 13.95 o.p. (0-312-54914-8) St. Martin's Pr.
—Most Deadly Hate. l.t. ed. 1987. 496p. 14.95 o.p. (0-7089-1663-5, Ulverscroft) Thorpe, F. A. Pubs. GBR. Dist: Ulverscroft Large Print Bks., Ltd.
—Most Grievous Murder. 1982. 192p. 10.95 o.p. (0-312-54908-3) St. Martin's Pr.
—Most Grievous Murder. l.t. ed. 1984. (Ulverscroft Large Print Ser.). 288p. o.p. (0-7089-1179-X, Ulverscroft) Thorpe, F. A. Pubs. GBR. Dist: Ulverscroft Large Print Canada, Ltd.
—Murder's Out of Tune. l.t. ed. 1986. (Nightingale Ser.). 314p. pap. 10.95 o.p. (0-8161-4002-2, Macmillan Reference USA) Gale Group.
—Murder's Out of Tune. 1988. 192p. pap. 3.50 (0-380-70586-9, Avon Bks.) Morrow/Avon.
—Murder's Out of Tune. 1984. 208p. 11.95 o.p. (0-312-55345-5) St. Martin's Pr.
—Naked Villainy. l.t. ed. 1988. (General Ser.). 379p. 17.95 o.p. (0-8161-4395-1, Macmillan Reference USA) Gale Group.
—Naked Villainy. 1988. 288p. pap. 3.50 (0-380-70479-X, Avon Bks.) Morrow/Avon.
—Naked Villainy. 1987. 256p. 14.95 o.p. (0-312-00163-0) St. Martin's Pr.
—Nor Live So Long. l.t. ed. 1987. (Nightingale Ser.). 331p. 10.95 o.p. (0-8161-4225-4, Macmillan Reference USA) Gale Group.
—Nor Live So Long. 1988. 224p. pap. 3.50 (0-380-70478-1, Avon Bks.) Morrow/Avon.
—Nor Live So Long. 1986. 208p. 13.95 o.p. (0-312-57740-0) St. Martin's Pr.
—An Obscure Grave. 1985. 11.95 o.p. (0-312-58053-3) St. Martin's Pr.
—An Obscure Grave. l.t. ed. 1987. 384p. 14.95 o.p. (0-7089-1607-4, Ulverscroft) Thorpe, F. A. Pubs. GBR. Dist: Ulverscroft Large Print Bks., Ltd.
—Proceed to Judgment. 1980. 8.95 o.p. (0-312-64776-X) St. Martin's Pr.
—A Show of Violence. l.t. ed. 1980. 238p. o.p. (0-7089-0436-X, Ulverscroft) Thorpe, F. A. Pubs.
—They Stay for Death. 1988. 192p. mass mkt. 3.50 (0-380-70587-7, Avon Bks.) Morrow/Avon.
—They Stay for Death. 1980. 8.95 o.p. (0-312-79983-7) St. Martin's Pr.
—Third Encounter. 1986. pap. 3.50 (0-380-69863-3, Avon Bks.) Morrow/Avon.
—This Fatal Writ. 1979. 7.95 o.p. (0-312-80050-9) St. Martin's Pr.
—This Fatal Writ. l.t. ed. 1983. (Ulverscroft Large Print Ser.). 336p. 29.99 o.p. (0-7089-0967-1, Ulverscroft) Thorpe, F. A. Pubs. GBR. Dist: Ulverscroft Large Print Bks., Ltd., Ulverscroft Large Print Canada, Ltd.
—This Little Measure. 1986. (Anthony Maitland Detective Ser.). 192p. mass mkt. 2.95 (0-380-69862-5, Avon Bks.) Morrow/Avon.
—Villains by Necessity. 1982. 224p. 10.95 o.p. (0-312-84683-5) St. Martin's Pr.
—Villains by Necessity. l.t. ed. 1988. (Ulverscroft Large Print Ser.). 384p. 29.99 o.p. (0-7089-1781-X, Ulverscroft) Thorpe, F. A. Pubs. GBR. Dist: Ulverscroft Large Print Bks., Ltd., Ulverscroft Large Print Canada, Ltd.
—Weep for Her. 1981. 224p. 9.95 o.p. (0-312-86019-6) St. Martin's Pr.
—Where Should He Die? 1983. 224p. 10.95 o.p. (0-312-86702-6) St. Martin's Pr.
Woods, Sara, ed. Malice Domestic. 1986. pap. 3.50 (0-380-69861-7, Avon Bks.) Morrow/Avon.
Woods, Stuart. Imperfect Strangers. l.t. ed. 1995. 26.95 o.p. (1-56895-203-1, Wheeler Publishing, Inc.) Gale Group.
—Imperfect Strangers. 1994. 320p. 23.00 o.p. (0-06-017775-6) HarperCollins Pubs.
—Imperfect Strangers. abr. ed. audio 17.00 o.p. (1-55994-673-3, CPN 2472, HarperAudio) HarperTrade.
—Imperfect Strangers. 1995. 368p. mass mkt. 7.99 (0-06-109404-8, HarperTorch) Morrow/Avon.
Woodward, Lilian. Nurse to the Maharajah. l.t. ed. 1994. 19.95 o.p. (0-7927-1817-8); pap. 17.95 o.p. (0-7927-1816-X) BBC Audiobooks America.
Woolf, Virginia. Between the Acts. 1970. 228p. (C). reprint ed. pap. 12.00 (0-15-611870-X, Harvest Bks.) Harcourt Trade Pubs.
—Between the Acts. Kermode, Frank, ed. 1992. (Oxford World's Classics Ser.). 244p. pap. o.p. (0-19-281814-7) Oxford Univ. Pr., Inc.
—Flush. 1976. (Harvest Book Ser.). 204p. pap. 12.00 (0-15-631952-7, Harvest Bks.) Harcourt Trade Pubs.
—Jacob's Room. 1998. 240p. mass mkt. 5.95 o.s.i (0-553-21490-X) Bantam Bks.
—Jacob's Room. 1998. (Thrift Editions Ser.). 144p. pap. 1.50 (0-486-40109-X) Dover Pubns., Inc.
—Jacob's Room. 1950. (Harvest Book Ser.). 180p. pap. 12.00 (0-15-645742-3, Harvest Bks.) Harcourt Trade Pubs.
—Jacob's Room. 1998. (Signet Classics). 224p. mass mkt. 5.95 (0-451-52665-1) NAL.
—Jacob's Room. 2002. (Twelve-Point Ser.). lib. bdg. 24.00 (1-58287-182-5); 285p. lib. bdg. 25.00 (1-58287-665-7) North Bks.
—Jacob's Room. Flint, Kate, ed. 1992. (Oxford World's Classics Ser.). 306p. pap. o.p. (0-19-281819-8) Oxford Univ. Pr., Inc.

Settings

—Jacob's Room. l.t. ed. 2001. (Perennial Bestsellers Ser.). 245p. 28.95 (*0-7838-9380-9*) Thorndike Pr.
—Jacob's Room. Roe, Sue, ed. & notes by. 1998. (Penguin Twentieth-Century Classics Ser.). 192p. (C). pap. 9.95 (*0-14-018570-4*) Viking Penguin.
—Monday or Tuesday. 1921. E-Book (*1-58734-067-4*) Bartleby.com.
—Monday or Tuesday. reprint ed. lib. bdg. 98.00 (*0-7426-3272-5*); 2001. 116p. pap. text 28.00 (*0-7426-8272-2*) Classic Bks.
—Monday or Tuesday. unabr. ed. 1997. (Thrift Editions Ser.). 64p. reprint ed. pap. text 1.00 (*0-486-29453-6*) Dover Pubns., Inc.
—Monday or Tuesday. 2004. 112p. pap. 12.00 (*1-84391-059-4*) Hesperus Pr. GBR. *Dist:* Trafalgar Square.
—Monday or Tuesday, Kew Gardens & More. unabr. ed. 1996. audio 20.95 (*1-55685-414-5*) Audio Bk. Contractors, Inc.
—Mrs. Dalloway. 1998. 216p. pap. 12.00 (*0-15-600555-7*) Harcourt Trade Pubs.
—Mrs. Dalloway. l.t. ed. 1996. lib. bdg. 23.95 (*0-7838-1824-6*) Thorndike Pr.
—Night & Day. reprint ed. lib. bdg. 98.00 (*0-7426-3271-7*); 2001. 538p. pap. text 28.00 (*0-7426-8271-4*) Classic Bks.
—Night & Day. 1999. E-Book 2.49 (*1-58627-475-9*) Electric Umbrella Publishing.
—Night & Day. 1973. (Harvest Book Ser.). 516p. reprint ed. pap. 16.00 o.s.i (*0-15-665600-0*, HB263, Harvest Bks.) Harcourt Trade Pubs.
—Night & Day. Raitt, Suzanne, ed. 1992. (Oxford World's Classics Ser.). 582p. pap. (*0-19-281842-2*) Oxford Univ. Pr., Inc.
—Night & Day. l.t. ed. 2000. 590p. 37.95 (*0-7658-0782-3*) Transaction Pubs.
—Night & Day. Briggs, Julia, ed. & intro. by. 1996. (Twentieth Century Classics Ser.). (Illus.). 496p. 13.95 (*0-14-018568-2*, Penguin Classics) Viking Penguin.
—Orlando. 1973. (Harvest Book Ser.). (Illus.). 352p. reprint ed. pap. 12.00 (*0-15-670160-X*, Harvest Bks.) Harcourt Trade Pubs.
—To the Lighthouse. 24.95 (*0-88411-849-5*) Amereon, Ltd.
—To the Lighthouse. (HBJ Book Ser.). 1990. 236p. 18.00 (*0-15-190737-4*); 1989. 228p. pap. 12.00 (*0-15-690739-9*, Harvest Bks.); 1981. 209p. 17.95 o.p. (*0-15-190736-6*); 1964. pap. 5.95 o.p. (*0-15-690738-0*, Harvest Bks.) Harcourt Trade Pubs.
—To the Lighthouse. abr. ed. 1995. (Classic Fiction Ser.). audio compact disk 15.98 (*962-634-036-3*, NA203612, Naxos AudioBooks) Naxos of America, Inc.
—To the Lighthouse. Drabble, Margaret, ed. 1992. (Oxford World's Classics Ser.). 328p. pap. (*0-19-281816-3*) Oxford Univ. Pr., Inc.
—To the Lighthouse. Kemp, Sandra, ed. 1995. (English Texts Ser.). 227p. (C). pap. 19.99 o.p. (*0-415-01663-0*, A7125) Routledge.
—To the Lighthouse. 1990. 18.80 o.p. (*0-8446-6210-0*) Smith, Peter Pub., Inc.
—To the Lighthouse. l.t. ed. 1997. (Perennial Ser.). 278p. 24.95 (*0-7838-8137-1*) Thorndike Pr.
—To the Lighthouse. Dick, Susan, ed. 1982. 366p. o.p. (*0-8020-5524-9*) Univ. of Toronto Pr.
Woolf, Virginia & Bishop, Edward. Jacob's Room. 2004. (*0-631-17722-1*) Blackwell Publishing.
Woolf, Virginia & Cather, Willa. O Pioneers! & Other Tales of the Praire: New York Public Library Collector's Edition. 1999. (New York Public Library Collector's Edition Ser.). (Illus.). 432p. 18.95 o.s.i (*0-385-48720-7*) Doubleday Publishing.
Woolf, Virginia & Everyman's Library Staff. To the Lighthouse. 1992. (Everyman's Library). 272p. 17.00 (*0-679-40537-2*) Knopf, Alfred A. Inc.
Worcester, Wayne. The Jewel of Covent Garden. 2000. 336p. mass mkt. 5.99 o.s.i (*0-451-20195-7*) NAL.
Wrede, Patricia C. Magician's Ward. 1997. 320p. 22.95 (*0-312-85369-6*, Tor Bks.) Doherty, Tom Assocs., LLC.
—The Magician's Ward. 1998. (Tor Fantasy Ser.). 288p. mass mkt. 5.99 o.s.i (*0-8125-2085-8*, Tor Bks.) Doherty, Tom Assocs., LLC.
Wright, Eric. Death in the Old Country. l.t. ed. 1986. (Nightingale Ser.). 265p. 10.95 o.p. (*0-8161-3966-0*, Macmillan Reference USA) Gale Group.
—Death in the Old Country: An Inspector Charlie Salter Mystery. 1985. 192p. 12.95 o.s.i (*0-684-18384-6*, Macmillan Reference USA) Gale Group.
—Death in the Old Country: An Inspector Charlie Salter Mystery. 1986. 256p. mass mkt. 3.99 o.p. (*0-451-14450-3*, Signet Bks.) NAL.
Wright, Laura. Charming the Prince. 2003. (Silhouette Desire Ser.: No. 1492). 192p. mass mkt. (*0-373-76492-8*, Silhouette) Harlequin Enterprises, Ltd.
Wright, Patricia. I Am England. 1988. mass mkt. o.s.i (*0-552-13423-6*, Corgi) Bantam Bks.
—I Am England. 1987. 480p. 18.95 o.p. (*0-312-01045-1*) St. Martin's Pr.
—I Am England. l.t. ed. 1988. (Charnwood Large Print Ser.). 736p. 29.99 o.p. (*0-7089-8491-6*, Charnwood) Thorpe, F. A. Pubs. GBR. *Dist:* Ulverscroft Large Print Bks., Ltd., Ulverscroft Large Print Canada, Ltd.
—That Near & Distant Place: A Novel of England. 1988. 432p. 18.95 o.p. (*0-312-02297-2*) St. Martin's Pr.
Wynne, Diana. Step into My World. l.t. ed. 2000. (G. K. Hall Nightingale Ser.). 184p. pap. 20.95 o.p. (*0-7838-8999-2*, Macmillan Reference USA) Gale Group.
Yorke, Margaret. Act of Violence. 1997. 282p. o.s.i (*0-316-88254-2*) Little Brown & Co.
—Act of Violence. 1998. 288p. 22.95 o.p. (*0-312-18522-7*, Saint Martin's Minotaur) St. Martin's Pr.
—Act of Violence. 1998. 282p. mass mkt. o.s.i (*0-7515-2024-1*) Warner Futura GBR. *Dist:* Little Brown & Co.
—Almost the Truth. 1995. 294p. mass mkt. o.s.i (*0-7515-1216-8*) Little Brown & Co.
—Almost the Truth. 1995. (Cloak & Dagger Ser.). 278p. 18.95 o.p. (*0-89296-582-7*) Mysterious Pr.
—Almost the Truth. 1996. 240p. mass mkt. 5.99 o.s.i (*0-446-40479-9*) Warner Bks., Inc.
—A Case to Answer. unabr. ed. 2001. 8p. audio 69.95 (*0-7540-0659-X*, CAB 2081) Chivers Audio Bks. GBR. *Dist:* BBC Audiobooks America.
—A Case to Answer. 2000. 326p. (*0-316-85192-2*) Little Brown & Co.
—A Case to Answer. 2002. 336p. 24.95 (*0-312-28430-6*, Saint Martin's Minotaur) St. Martin's Pr.
—Cast for Death. 1996. 18.50 o.p. (*0-7451-8685-8*, Black Dagger) BBC Audiobooks America.
—Cast for Death. 1983. pap. 2.25 o.p. (*0-553-22828-5*) Bantam Bks.
—Cast for Death. l.t. unabr. ed. 1999. 214p. 25.95 (*0-7531-6029-3*, 160293) ISIS Large Print Bks. GBR. *Dist:* ISIS Publishing.
—Cast for Death. l.t. ed. 1980. 12.00 o.p. (*0-7089-0408-4*, Ulverscroft) Thorpe, F. A. Pubs. GBR. *Dist:* Ulverscroft Large Print Bks., Ltd.
—Cast for Death. 1976. 6.95 o.p. (*0-8027-5353-1*) Walker & Co.
—Crime in Question. l.t. ed. 272p. 2003. pap. 21.99 (*0-7531-6778-6*); 2002. 32.50 (*0-7531-6777-8*) ISIS Large Print Bks. GBR. *Dist:* Ulverscroft Large Print Bks., Ltd., Ulverscroft Large Print Canada, Ltd.
—Crime in Question. 240p. 1990. pap. 3.95 o.p. (*0-14-012435-7*, Penguin Bks.); 1989. 16.95 o.p. (*0-670-82932-3*) Viking Penguin.
—Dangerous to Know. 1994. 272p. 17.95 o.p. (*0-89296-500-2*); 1995. pap. 21.95 o.p. (*0-7927-2055-5*); 1994. 23.95 o.p. (*0-7927-2056-3*) BBC Audiobooks America.
—Dangerous to Know. 1995. 256p. mass mkt. 5.50 o.s.i (*0-446-40198-6*) Warner Bks., Inc.
—Dead in the Morning. 2000. 224p. 21.95 (*0-7540-8560-0*, Black Dagger) BBC Audiobooks America.
—Dead in the Morning. 1982. pap. 2.25 (*0-553-22858-7*) Bantam Bks.
—Dead in the Morning. unabr. ed. 2000. audio 34.95 (*0-7451-6378-5*, CSL 079) Chivers Audio Bks. GBR. *Dist:* BBC Audiobooks America.
—Dead in the Morning. l.t. ed. 2000. (G. K. Hall Nightingale Ser.). 253p. 30.00 (*0-7838-8760-4*, Macmillan Reference USA) Gale Group.
—Dead in the Morning. l.t. ed. 1975. (Ulverscroft Large Print Ser.). 29.99 o.p. (*0-85456-390-3*, Ulverscroft) Thorpe, F. A. Pubs. GBR. *Dist:* Ulverscroft Large Print Bks., Ltd., Ulverscroft Large Print Canada, Ltd.
—Evidence to Destroy. l.t. ed. 1994. 22.95 o.p. (*0-7927-1964-6*); pap. o.p. (*0-7927-1963-8*) BBC Audiobooks America.
—Evidence to Destroy. l.t. ed. 1988. 464p. 15.95 o.p. (*0-7089-1827-1*, Ulverscroft) Thorpe, F. A. Pubs. GBR. *Dist:* Ulverscroft Large Print Bks., Ltd.
—Evidence to Destroy. (Crime Ser.). 288p. 1988. pap. 3.95 o.p. (*0-14-010250-7*, Penguin Bks.); 1987. 15.95 o.p. (*0-670-81776-7*) Viking Penguin.
—False Pretences, Set unabr. ed. 1999. audio 69.95 (*0-7540-0304-3*, CAB 1727) BBC Audiobooks America.
—False Pretences. 1998. 310p. o.s.i (*0-316-64438-2*) Little Brown & Co.
—False Pretences. 1999. 320p. 23.95 o.p. (*0-312-19975-9*, Saint Martin's Minotaur) St. Martin's Pr.
—False Pretences. l.t. ed. 1999. (Charnwood Large Print Ser.). 384p. 31.99 o.p. (*0-7089-9081-9*, Linford) Thorpe, F. A. Pubs. GBR. *Dist:* Ulverscroft Large Print Bks., Ltd., Ulverscroft Large Print Canada, Ltd.
—Grave Matters. 1983. pap. 2.50 (*0-553-22914-1*) Bantam Bks.
—Grave Matters. l.t. ed. 1975. (Ulverscroft Large Print Ser.). 29.99 o.p. (*0-85456-333-4*, Ulverscroft) Thorpe, F. A. Pubs. GBR. *Dist:* Ulverscroft Large Print Bks., Ltd., Ulverscroft Large Print Canada, Ltd.
—Mortal Remains. l.t. ed. 1990. 18.95 o.p. (*0-7089-2163-9*, Ulverscroft) Thorpe, F. A. Pubs. GBR. *Dist:* Ulverscroft Large Print Bks., Ltd.
—The Price of Guilt. unabr. ed. 2000. 8p. audio 69.95 (*0-7540-0517-8*, CAB1940) BBC Audiobooks America.
—The Price of Guilt. 2000. 336p. 24.95 (*0-312-25332-X*, Saint Martin's Minotaur) St. Martin's Pr.
—The Price of Guilt. l.t. ed. 2000. (Charnwood Large Print Ser.). 360p. 31.99 o.p. (*0-7089-9183-1*, Charnwood) Thorpe, F. A. Pubs. GBR. *Dist:* Ulverscroft Large Print Bks., Ltd., Ulverscroft Large Print Canada, Ltd.
—A Question of Belief. 1997. 288p. 23.00 o.p. (*0-89296-649-1*) Mysterious Pr.
—Serious Intent. 280p. 1996. mass mkt. o.s.i (*0-7515-1596-5*); 1995. o.s.i (*0-316-91280-8*) Little Brown & Co.
—Serious Intent. 1996. 82p. 21.95 o.s.i (*0-89296-583-5*) Mysterious Pr.
—Serious Intent. 1997. 288p. mass mkt. 5.99 (*0-446-40514-0*) Warner Bks., Inc.
—Silent Witness. l.t. unabr. ed. 1999. 208p. 32.50 o.p. (*0-7531-6028-5*, 160285) ISIS Large Print Bks. GBR. *Dist:* Ulverscroft Large Print Bks., Ltd., Ulverscroft Large Print Canada, Ltd.
—Silent Witness. l.t. ed. 1976. o.p. (*0-85456-455-1*, Ulverscroft) Thorpe, F. A. Pubs.
—Silent Witness. 1975. 5.95 (*0-8027-5318-3*) Walker & Co.
Young, Elizabeth. Asking for Trouble: A Novel. 2001. 416p. pap. 14.00 (*0-380-81897-3*, Avon Bks.) Morrow/Avon.
—Asking for Trouble: A Novel. 2000. (Illus.). 400p. o.p. (*0-434-00944-X*) Random Hse. of Canada, Ltd. CAN. *Dist:* Random Hse., Inc.
Zahavi, Helen. Dirty Weekend: A Novel of Revenge. 1994. 188p. pap. 10.95 o.p. (*0-939416-85-9*) Cleis Pr.
—The Weekend. 1991. 17.95 o.p. (*1-55611-241-6*) Fine, Donald I. Bks.
Zangwill, Israel. Children of the Ghetto. 1977. (Victorian Library Ser.). (Illus.). 448p. reprint ed. text 15.75 o.p. (*0-7185-5028-5*) Brill Academic Pubs., Inc.
—Children of the Ghetto. 2001. (Works of Israel Zangwill). pap. text 56.00 (*0-7426-8780-5*) Classic Bks.
—Children of the Ghetto. 1998. 512p. reprint ed. pap. 27.95 (*0-8143-2593-9*) Wayne State Univ. Pr.
Zipes, Jack D., ed. Don't Bet on the Prince: Contemporary Feminist Fairy Tales in North America & England. 1986. 277p. (C). pap. 22.95 (*0-415-90263-0*, 9902) Routledge.

## ERDE (IMAGINARY PLACE)—FICTION

Modesitt, L. E., Jr. Darksong Rising. (Spellsong Cycle Ser.: Bk. 3). 2001. 501p. mass mkt. 6.99 (*0-8125-6668-8*); 1999. 507p. 27.95 (*0-312-86822-7*) Doherty, Tom Assocs., LLC. (Tor Bks.).
—The Soprano Sorceress. (Spellsong Cycle Ser.: Bk. 1). 1998. 672p. mass mkt. 6.99 (*0-8125-4559-1*); 1997. 509p. 25.95 (*0-312-86022-6*) Doherty, Tom Assocs., LLC. (Tor Bks.).
—The Spellsong War. (Spellsong Cycle Ser.: 2). 1999. 657p. pap. text 6.99 (*0-8125-4002-6*); 1997. 464p. 25.95 o.p. (*0-312-86492-2*) Doherty, Tom Assocs., LLC. (Tor Bks.).
—The Spellsong War. 1999. (Spellsong Cycle Ser.: No. 2). E-Book 6.99 (*0-312-87151-1*) St. Martin's Pr.

## ERIADOR (IMAGINARY PLACE)—FICTION

Salvatore, R. A. The Dragon King. 1996. 352p. 19.95 o.p. (*0-446-51728-3*); 1997. 384p. reprint ed. mass mkt. 6.99 (*0-446-60485-2*, Aspect) Warner Bks., Inc.
—Luthien's Gamble. 1996. (Crimson Shadow Ser.: Bk. 2). 82p. 18.95 o.s.i (*0-446-51727-5*); 336p. reprint ed. mass mkt. 6.99 (*0-446-60361-9*) Warner Bks., Inc. (Aspect).
—The Sword of Bedwyr. 1995. (Crimson Shadow Ser.: Bk. 1). 256p. 18.95 o.s.i (*0-446-51726-7*); 1996. 320p. reprint ed. mass mkt. 6.99 (*0-446-60272-8*) Warner Bks., Inc. (Aspect).

## ERNA (IMAGINARY PLACE)—FICTION

Friedman, C. S. Black Sun Rising. (Daw Book Collectors Ser.: Bk. I). 1992. 592p. mass mkt. 7.99 (*0-88677-527-2*); 1991. 496p. 18.95 o.p. (*0-88677-485-3*) DAW Bks., Inc.
—Crown of Shadows. 1996. (Daw Book Collectors Ser.: 3). 528p. mass mkt. 7.99 (*0-88677-717-8*) DAW Bks., Inc.
—Crown of Shadows: The Final Volume of the Coldfire Trilogy. 1995. (Coldfire Trilogy Ser.: Vol. 3). 448p. 21.95 o.p. (*0-88677-664-3*) DAW Bks., Inc.
—When True Night Falls. (Coldfire Trilogy Ser.: Bk. II). 1993. 592p. 22.00 o.p. (*0-88677-569-8*); Vol. 2. 1994. 624p. mass mkt. 7.99 (*0-88677-615-5*) DAW Bks., Inc.

## ETHIOPIA—FICTION

Bright, Bill & Dekker, Ted. A Man Called Blessed. 2002. vii, 356p. pap. 14.99 (*0-8499-4380-9*) W Publishing Group.
Bull, Bartle. A Cafe on the Nile. (Illus.). 1999. 480p. 13.95 (*0-7867-0675-9*); 1998. 465p. 26.00 (*0-7867-0556-6*) Avalon Publishing Group. (Carroll & Graf Pubs.).
Caputo, Philip. Horn of Africa: A Novel. 1983. 544p. mass mkt. 4.95 o.s.i (*0-440-33675-9*, Laurel) Dell Publishing.
—Horn of Africa: A Novel. 1991. 544p. pap. 11.00 o.p. (*0-06-098605-0*, Perennial) HarperTrade.
—Horn of Africa: A Novel. 1980. 528p. 12.95 o.p. (*0-03-042136-5*) Holt, Henry & Co.
—Horn of Africa: A Novel. 2002. (Vintage Contemporaries Ser.). 496p. pap. 15.00 (*0-375-72511-3*, Vintage) Knopf Publishing Group.
Cobb, Melvin. Vessel of Honor. 2004. 12.99 (*0-8024-1365-X*) Moody Pr.
Cody, Liza. Rift: A Novel of Suspense. 1988. 224p. 15.95 o.s.i (*0-684-18959-3*, Scribner) Simon & Schuster.
—Rift: A Novel of Suspense. 1989. 240p. pap. 3.95 o.p. (*0-14-012420-9*, Penguin Bks.) Viking Penguin.
Du Brul, Jack. The Medusa Stone. abr. ed. 2000. audio 24.95 o.p. (*1-56740-898-2*, 2069, Nova Audio Bks.); audio 89.25 (*1-56740-721-8*, 2068, Unabridged Library Editions) Brilliance Audio.
—The Medusa Stone. 2000. 464p. mass mkt. 6.99 (*0-451-40922-1*, Onyx) NAL.
Due, Tananarive. The Living Blood. 2001. 528p. 25.95 o.s.i (*0-671-04083-9*, Atria) Simon & Schuster.
Farah, Nuruddin. Gifts. 1999. 246p. 23.95 (*1-55970-484-5*) Arcade Publishing, Inc.
—Gifts. 2000. 256p. 13.00 (*0-14-029642-5*) Viking Penguin.
—Maps. 1999. 288p. 23.95 (*1-55970-485-3*) Arcade Publishing, Inc.
—Maps. 1987. 256p. 11.95 o.s.i (*0-394-56325-5*, Pantheon) Knopf Publishing Group.
—Maps. 2000. 288p. pap. 14.00 (*0-14-029643-3*) Penguin Group (USA) Inc.
Llewellyn, Sam. Clawhammer. l.t. ed. 1994. 516p. pap. 19.95 (*0-8161-7401-6*, Macmillan Reference USA) Gale Group.
—Clawhammer. l.t. ed. 1994. (Magna Large Print Ser.). 548p. 29.99 o.p. (*0-7505-0684-9*) Magna Large Print Bks. GBR. *Dist:* Ulverscroft Large Print Bks., Ltd., Ulverscroft Large Print Canada, Ltd.
—Clawhammer. Chelius, Jane, ed. 1995. 384p. mass mkt. 5.50 (*0-671-78994-5*, Pocket) Simon & Schuster.
Mezlekia, Nega. The God Who Begat a Jackal. 2001. (Illus.). 288p. pap. (*0-14-100662-5*) Penguin Group (USA) Inc.
—The God Who Begat a Jackal. 2002. (Illus.). 256p. 23.00 (*0-312-28701-1*) Picador.
—The God Who Begat a Jackal: A Novel. 2003. 256p. pap. 13.00 (*0-312-30996-1*) Picador.
Worku, Daniachew. The Thirteenth Sun: A Novel. 2000. pap. 16.95 (*1-56902-123-6*); 184p. 49.95 (*1-56902-122-8*) Red Sea Pr.

## EUGENE (OR.)—FICTION

Vukcevich, Ray. Man of Maybe Half-a-Dozen Faces. 2000. 245p. 22.95 (*0-312-24652-8*, Saint Martin's Minotaur) St. Martin's Pr.

## EUROPE—FICTION

Alcock, Deborah. By Far Euphrates. 2002. 274p. pap. 12.90 (*1-894666-00-3*) Inheritance Pubns.
Alcott, Louisa May. A Long Fatal Love Chase. l.t. ed. 1996. 368p. mass mkt. 6.99 (*0-440-22301-6*) Dell Publishing.
—A Long Fatal Love Chase. l.t. ed. 1997. (Thorndike/G. K. Hall Paperback Bestsellers Ser.). 356p. pap. 25.95 (*0-7862-0623-3*) Thorndike Pr.
Ambler, Eric. A Coffin for Dimitrios. 1983. mass mkt. 2.25 o.s.i (*0-345-31695-9*, Ballantine Bks.); 1979. mass mkt. 1.95 o.s.i (*0-345-28323-6*) Ballantine Bks.
—A Coffin for Dimitrios. 2001. 304p. pap. 12.00 (*0-375-72671-3*, Vintage) Knopf Publishing Group.
Auel, Jean M. Los Cazadores de Mamuts. 2002. (ENG & SPA., Illus.). 672p. pap. 13.00 (*0-7432-3604-1*, Fireside) Simon & Schuster.
—El Clan del Oso Cavernario. 2002. (Libros en Espanol Ser.). Orig. Title: Clan of the Cave Bear. 512p. pap. 12.00 (*0-7432-3358-1*, Fireside) Simon & Schuster.
—The Clan of the Cave Bear. 1984. (Earth's Children Ser.: Vol. 1). 528p. mass mkt. 7.99 (*0-553-25042-6*) Bantam Bks.
—The Clan of the Cave Bear. unabr. ed. (Earth's Children Ser.: Vol. 1). 2002. audio compact disk 49.95 (*1-59086-086-1*, 3635, CD Unabridged); 1999. audio 44.95 (*1-56740-471-5*, 1918, Brilliance Audio Unabridged); 1986. audio 26.95 (*0-930435-22-2*, 64, Bookcassette); 1986. audio 105.25 (*1-56100-017-5*, 1142, Unabridged Library Editions) Brilliance Audio.

—The Clan of the Cave Bear. unabr. ed. 2001. audio 99.95 (*0-7451-4001-7*, CAB 698) Chivers Audio Bks. GBR. *Dist:* BBC Audiobooks America.
—The Clan of the Cave Bear. 1980. 480p. 19.95 o.s.i (*0-517-54202-1*, Crown) Crown Publishing Group.
—The Clan of the Cave Bear, Set. unabr. ed. 1999. audio 105.25 Highsmith Inc.
—The Clan of the Cave Bear. audio New Letters on Air.
—The Clan of the Cave Bear. 1998. (Earth's Children Ser.). 480p. 12.99 o.s.i (*0-517-18918-6*) Random Hse. Value Publishing.
—The Clan of the Cave Bear. unabr. ed. 2003. (Earth's Children Ser.). audio 29.99 (*1-59335-105-4*, 30199) Soulmate Audio Bks., Inc.
—The Clan of the Cave Bear. 1980. (Earth's Children Ser.). (J). 14.04 (*0-606-00288-X*) Turtleback Bks.
—Las Llanuras del Transito. 2002. (Illus.). 1024p. pap. 14.00 (*0-7432-3605-X*, Fireside) Simon & Schuster.
—The Mammoth Hunters. 1986. 784p. mass mkt. 4.95 o.s.i (*0-553-26096-0*); 1986. mass mkt. o.s.i (*0-553-26592-X*); 1986. (Earth's Children Ser.: No. 3). 752p. mass mkt. 7.99 (*0-553-28094-5*, Bantam Classics); 2002. 656p. pap. 14.95 (*0-553-38164-4*) Bantam Bks.
—The Mammoth Hunters. unabr. collector's ed. 1986. (Earth's Children Ser.). Pt. 1. audio 88.00 (*0-7366-0814-1*, 1764A ); Pt. 2. audio 80.00 (*0-7366-0815-X*, 1764-B) Books on Tape, Inc.
—The Mammoth Hunters. unabr. ed. (Earth's Children Ser.: Bk. 3). 1999. audio 49.95 (*1-56740-472-3*, 1919, Brilliance Audio Unabridged); 1986. audio 28.95 o.p. (*0-930435-28-1*, 169, Bookcassette); 1986. audio 162.55 (*1-56100-023-X*, 935, Unabridged Library Editions) Brilliance Audio.
—The Mammoth Hunters. 1985. (Earth's Children Ser.). 656p. 25.00 o.s.i (*0-517-55627-8*, Crown) Crown Publishing Group.
—The Mammoth Hunters. unabr. ed. 1999. audio 162.55 Highsmith Inc.
—The Mammoth Hunters. l.t. ed. 2002. 1152p. 26.95 (*0-375-43177-2*) Random Hse., Inc.
—The Mammoth Hunters. 1985. (Earth's Children Ser.). (J). 14.04 (*0-606-03115-4*) Turtleback Bks.
—The Plains of Passage. 1991. 880p. mass mkt. 6.99 o.s.i (*0-553-18047-9*); 1991. 896p. mass mkt. 7.99 (*0-553-28941-1*); 2002. 768p. pap. 14.95 (*0-553-38165-2*) Bantam Bks.
—The Plains of Passage, Pt. 1. unabr. collector's ed. 1991. (Earth's Children Ser.). audio 96.00 (*0-7366-1941-0*, 2763-A ) Books on Tape, Inc.
—The Plains of Passage. unabr. ed. (Earth's Children Ser.: Bk. 4). 1999. audio 59.95 (*1-56740-474-X*, 1921, Brilliance Audio Unabridged); 1991. 34p. audio 189.55 (*1-56100-074-4*, 986, Unabridged Library Editions); 1991. audio 39.95 (*0-930435-80-X*, 213, Bookcassette) Brilliance Audio.
—The Plains of Passage. 2001. 768p. 24.95 (*0-609-61100-3*, Crown) Crown Publishing Group.
—The Plains of Passage, Set. unabr. ed. 1999. audio 189.55 Highsmith Inc.
—The Plains of Passage. l.t. ed. 2002. 1328p. 26.95 (*0-375-43178-0*) Random Hse., Inc.
—The Plains of Passage. unabr. ed. 1991. Pt. 1. audio 100.00 (*1-55690-416-9*, 91212E7); Pt. 2. audio 82.00 (*1-55690-417-7*, 91213E7) Recorded Bks., LLC.
—The Shelters of Stone. (Earth's Children Ser.). (Illus.). 2003. 912p. mass mkt. 7.99 (*0-553-28942-X*, Crown); 2002. 768p. 28.95 (*0-609-61059-7*) Crown Publishing Group.
—El Valle de los Caballos. 2002. (Illus.). 560p. pap. 12.00 (*0-7432-3603-3*, Fireside) Simon & Schuster.
—The Valley of Horses, Set. unabr. ed. 1999. audio 130.55 Highsmith Inc.
Auel, Jean M. & Burr, Sandra. The Valley of Horses. unabr. ed. 1999. (Earth's Children Ser.: Bk. 2). audio 44.95 (*1-56740-473-1*, 1920, Brilliance Audio Unabridged) Brilliance Audio.
Bainbridge, Beryl. Master Georgie. 190p. 1999. pap. 11.95 (*0-7867-0697-X*); 1998. 21.00 o.p. (*0-7867-0563-9*) Avalon Publishing Group. (Carroll & Graf Pubs.).
—Master Georgie. l.t. ed. 1999. (General Ser.). 224p. pap. 23.95 (*0-7862-1681-6*) Thorndike Pr.
Baudino, Gael. Strands of Starlight. 1989. 384p. mass mkt. 4.50 o.p. (*0-451-16371-0*, 015, Signet Bks.) NAL.
Beauman, Sally. Danger Zones. 1997. mass mkt. 6.99 o.s.i (*0-449-22561-5*, Fawcett) Ballantine Bks.
—Danger Zones. l.t. ed. 1996. pap. 22.95 o.p. (*1-56895-343-7*, Wheeler Publishing, Inc.) Gale Group.
Bedford, Sybille. Jigsaw: An Unsentimental Education. 1991. 352p. pap. 10.00 o.p. (*0-14-011388-6*, Penguin Bks.) Penguin Group (USA) Inc.
—Jigsaw: An Unsentimental Education, a Biographical Novel. 2001. 368p. pap. text 15.00 (*1-58243-143-4*, Counterpoint Pr.) Basic Bks.
—Quicksands. 2004. text 24.00 (*1-58243-169-8*, Counterpoint Pr.) Basic Bks.
Begiebing, Robert J. The Adventures of Allegra Fullerton: Or a Memoir of Startling & Amusing Episodes from Itinerant Life - A Novel. 1999. (Illus.). 326p. text 30.00 (*0-87451-947-0*, Hardscrabble Bks.) Univ. Pr. of New England.
Bemelmans, Ludwig. How to Travel Incognito. 2001. (Humour Classics Ser.). (Illus.). 192p. 14.95 (*1-85375-419-6*) Prion GBR. *Dist:* Trafalgar Square.
—How to Travel Incognito. 1952. 3.00 o.p. (*0-670-38489-5*) Viking Penguin.
Boccaccio, Giovanni. The Decameron. 1992. (SPA.). 608p. (*84-320-7822-0*) GeoPlaneta, Editorial, S. A.
—The Decameron. 2002. 848p. mass mkt. 7.95 (*0-451-52866-2*, Signet Bks.); 1982. 736p. mass mkt. 7.99 o.s.i (*0-451-62746-6*) NAL.
—The Decameron. Musa, Mark & Bondanella, Peter E., trs. 1982. mass mkt. 5.95 o.p. (*0-451-62134-4*, ME2134, Mentor) NAL.
—The Decameron. Musa, Mark & Bondanella, Peter E., trs. from ITA. 1983. (Critical Editions Ser.). 29.95 o.s.i (*0-393-01754-0*) Norton, W. W. & Co., Inc.
—The Decameron. Musa, Mark & Bondanella, Peter E., eds. 1977. (Critical Editions Ser.). 15.95 o.p. (*0-393-04458-0*); 334p. (C). pap. text 14.20 (*0-393-09132-5*) Norton, W. W. & Co., Inc.
—The Decameron. Usher, Jonathan, ed. Waldman, Guideo, tr. 1999. (Oxford World's Classics Ser.). 752p. pap. 13.95 (*0-19-283691-9*) Oxford Univ. Pr., Inc.
—The Decameron. Waldman, Guido, tr. from ITA. 1993. (Oxford World's Classics Ser.). 738p. pap. 10.95 o.p. (*0-19-282712-X*) Oxford Univ. Pr., Inc.
—The Decameron. McWilliam, G. H., tr. from ITA. 1972. (Penguin Classics Ser.). 848p. pap. 11.95 o.p. (*0-14-044269-3*, Penguin Classics) Viking Penguin.
—Decameron. 1953. 10.50 o.p. (*0-460-00845-5*, Dutton) Dutton/Plume.
—The Decameron, Bk. I. 1996. audio 65.95 (*1-55685-425-0*) Audio Bk. Contractors, Inc.
—The Decameron, Vol. II. 1973. reprint ed. o.p. (*0-460-00846-3*) Biblio Distribution.
—The Decameron. unabr. ed. 1999. Pt. 1. audio 76.95 (*0-7861-1657-9*, 2485-A); Pt. 2. audio 69.95 (*0-7861-1708-7*, 2485-B) Blackstone Audio Bks., Inc.
—The Decameron, Vol. I. 2002. 308p. 19.99 (*1-4043-0130-5*); per. 14.99 (*1-4043-0131-3*) IndyPublish-.com.
—The Decameron. Aldington, Richard, tr. abr. ed. 2000. (YA). audio 22.98 (*962-634-709-0*, NA420914); audio compact disk 26.98 (*962-634-209-9*, NA420912) Naxos of America, Inc. (Naxos AudioBooks).
—The Decameron. McWilliam, G. H., tr. from ITA. & intro. by. 2nd ed. (Illus.). 1072p. 2003. pap. 14.00 (*0-14-044930-2*, Penguin Classics); 1996. pap. 13.95 o.s.i (*0-14-044629-X*) Viking Penguin.
—The Decameron: A Diplomatic Edition. Singleton, Charles S., ed. 1988. (ITA., Illus.). 688p. text 165.00 o.p. (*0-8018-1465-0*) Johns Hopkins Univ. Pr.
—The Decameron: A Selection. Speight, Kathleen, ed. 1988. (Italian Texts Ser.). 250p. text 11.95 o.s.i (*0-7190-0934-0*) Manchester Univ. Pr. GBR. *Dist:* Holtzbrinck Pubs.
—Decameron: Preserved to Posterity, 4 vols. Hutton, Edward, tr. (Tudor Translations, First Ser.: Nos. 41-44). reprint ed. 230.00 (*0-404-51960-1*);Vol. 1. 57.50 o.p. (*0-404-51961-X*);Vol. 2. 57.50 o.p. (*0-404-51962-8*);Vol. 3. 57.50 o.p. (*0-404-51963-6*);Vol. 4. 57.50 o.p. (*0-404-51964-4*) AMS Pr., Inc.
—The Decameron: Selected Tales. 2000. (Thrift Editions Ser.). 192p. pap. 2.00 (*0-486-41113-3*) Dover Pubns., Inc.
—Decameron: The John Payne Translation, 3 vols. Payne, John, tr. from ITA. 1983. (Illus.). 444p. pap. text 47.50 o.p. (*0-520-05872-0*);Set. 195.00 o.p. (*0-520-03557-7*) Univ. of California Pr.
—Il Decamerone - Ferondo in Purgatorio, Il Canto dell'Usignuolo. 1996. (ITA.). 17.50 incl. audio (*1-58085-456-7*) Interlingua Foreign Language AudioBooks.
Borthwick, J. S. The Garden Plot. (Dead Letter Mysteries Ser.). 1998. 336p. pap. 6.50 (*0-312-96291-6*, St. Martin's Paperbacks); 1997. 352p. 23.95 (*0-312-15131-4*, Saint Martin's Minotaur) St. Martin's Pr.
Boyd, W. Y. The Gentle Infantryman. 3rd ed. 2003. 360p. per. 12.99 (*1-58619-048-2*) Elton-Wolf Publishing.
—A Rendezvous with Death. 2003. 204p. 21.95 (*1-58619-046-6*) Elton-Wolf Publishing.
Bunn, T. Davis. Florian's Gate. 1992. (Priceless Collection). 352p. (ps up). pap. 9.99 o.p. (*1-55661-244-3*) Bethany Hse. Pubs.
—Florian's Gate. l.t. ed. 2000. (Christian Mystery Ser.). 563p. 24.95 (*0-7862-2877-6*) Thorndike Pr.
Burroughs, Edgar Rice. Beyond Thirty: The Lost Continent. 2001. (Bison Frontiers of Imagination Ser.). 124p. reprint ed. pap. 9.95 (*0-8032-6184-5*, Bison Bks.) Univ. of Nebraska Pr.
Canetti, Elias. Auto Da Fe. Wedgewood, D. V., tr. from GER. 1984. 464p. pap. 16.00 (*0-374-51879-3*) Farrar, Straus & Giroux.
Chase-Riboud, Barbara. Hottentot Venus: A Novel. 2003. 336p. 24.00 (*0-385-50856-5*) Doubleday Publishing.
Christie, Agatha. Destination Unknown. 1985. mass mkt. 3.50 o.s.i (*0-671-54213-3*); 1983. mass mkt. 2.95 o.s.i (*0-671-47308-5*) Simon & Schuster. (Pocket).
—Destination Unknown. l.t. ed. 1968. (Ulverscroft Large Print Ser.). 355p. o.p. (*0-85456-473-X*, Ulverscroft) Thorpe, F. A. Pubs. GBR. *Dist:* Ulverscroft Large Print Canada, Ltd.
—Murder on the Orient Express. unabr. ed. 1996. audio 54.95 o.p. (*0-7451-6819-1*, CAB 315) BBC Audiobooks America.
—Murder on the Orient Express. 2000. (Hercule Poirot Mystery Ser.). 256p. mass mkt. 5.99 (*0-425-17375-5*) Berkley Publishing Group.
—Murder on the Orient Express. (Hercule Poirot Mystery Ser.). 19.95 (*0-399-13708-4*) Penguin Group (USA) Inc.
—Murder on the Orient Express. 1985. (Agatha Christie Ser.). 12.95 o.s.i (*0-396-08575-X*, G. P. Putnam's Sons) Penguin Putnam Bks. for Young Readers.
—Murder on the Orient Express. abr. ed. 1993. (BBC Radio Presents Ser.). audio 16.99 o.s.i (*0-553-47215-1*, 390218, RH Audio) Random Hse. Audio Publishing Group.
—Murder on the Orient Express. 1999. 295p. (*0-7621-0255-1*) Reader's Digest Assn., Inc., The.
—Murder on the Orient Express. 1984. 256p. mass mkt. 3.50 o.s.i (*0-671-52368-6*); 1982. mass mkt. 2.95 o.s.i (*0-671-46894-4*) Simon & Schuster. (Pocket).
—Murder on the Orient Express. l.t. ed. 1983. (Ulverscroft Large Print Ser.). 384p. 32.50 o.p. (*0-7089-0188-3*, Ulverscroft) Thorpe, F. A. Pubs. GBR. *Dist:* Ulverscroft Large Print Bks., Ltd., Ulverscroft Large Print Canada, Ltd.
—Murder on the Orient Express. 1991. (Hercule Poirot Mystery Ser.). 12.04 (*0-606-12439-X*) Turtleback Bks.
—Murder on the Orient Express: A Hercule Poirot Novel. 2000. (Hercule Poirot Ser.). 256p. pap. 12.00 (*0-425-17393-3*) Berkley Publishing Group.
—So Many Steps to Death. 1986. (Mystery Ser.). 224p. mass mkt. 9.95 o.p. (*0-553-35052-8*) Bantam Bks.
—So Many Steps to Death. l.t. ed. (Agatha Christie Ser.). 330p. 1992. pap. 13.95 o.p. (*0-8161-4602-0*); 1991. lib. bdg. 20.95 o.p. (*0-8161-4601-2*) Gale Group. (Macmillan Reference USA).
—So Many Steps to Death. 1982. mass mkt. 2.75 o.s.i (*0-671-46151-6*, Pocket) Simon & Schuster.
Clancy, Tom. The Teeth of the Tiger. 2003. 448p. 27.95 (*0-399-15079-X*); 640p. 150.00 (*0-399-15136-2*) Putnam Publishing Group, The.
Coffman, Virginia. Pacific Cavalcade. 1982. 560p. mass mkt. 3.50 o.s.i (*0-449-20002-7*, Fawcett) Ballantine Bks.
—Pacific Cavalcade. l.t. ed. 2001. 728p. (*0-7540-1584-X*, Macmillan Reference USA) Gale Group.
—Pacific Cavalcade. 1981. 12.95 o.p. (*0-87795-277-9*, Morrow, William & Co.) Morrow/Avon.
—Pacific Cavalcade. l.t. ed. 2001. (G. K. Hall Core Ser.). 728p. 29.95 (*0-7838-9397-3*) Thorndike Pr.
Cortázar, Julio. Sixty-Two: A Model Kit. Rabassa, Gregory, tr. 1972. 6.95 o.s.i (*0-394-46822-8*, Pantheon) Knopf Publishing Group.
—Sixty-Two: A Model Kit. Rabassa, Gregory, tr. from SPA. 2000. (Classics Ser.). 288p. pap. 14.00 (*0-8112-1437-0*) New Directions Publishing Corp.
Crawford, Judy A. Alpine Dove. 2001. 160p. pap. 12.95 (*1-55517-560-0*, Bonneville Bks.) Cedar Fort, Inc./CFI Distribution.
Cummings, J. A. Nightchild: A Clans Novel. 1999. (Vampire Clans Ser.). 328p. pap. 15.95 (*0-9670668-0-8*) Kresnak Pr., Ltd.
De Moor, Margriet. Duke of Egypt: A Novel. 2002. 288p. 24.95 (*1-55970-546-9*); 2003. 256p. reprint ed. pap. 13.95 (*1-55970-661-9*) Arcade Publishing, Inc.
Deighton, Len. Hope. l.t. ed. 1996. (Bernard Samson Ser.). 27.95 (*1-56895-315-1*, Wheeler Publishing, Inc.) Gale Group.
—Hope. 1995. 320p. 24.00 o.p. (*0-06-017696-2*) HarperTrade.
—Hope. 1996. 320p. mass mkt. 6.99 o.s.i (*0-06-109555-9*, Eos) Morrow/Avon.
Dunnett, Dorothy. Gemini: The Eighth Book of the House of Niccolo. 2000. (Illus.). 720p. 27.50 (*0-375-41083-X*) Knopf, Alfred A. Inc.
Edwards, Wilma M. Shandor. 2003. 544p. per. 15.95 (*1-58275-078-5*) Black Forest Pr.
Fawcett, Quinn. Against the Brotherhood. (Mycroft Holmes Novels Ser.). 1998. 320p. mass mkt. 6.99 (*0-8125-4523-0*, Tor Bks.); 1997. 352p. 23.95 (*0-312-86362-4*, Forge Bks.) Doherty, Tom Assocs., LLC.
—Against the Brotherhood. 2001. audio compact disk 94.00 (*0-7887-3981-6*, C1143E7); 1999. audio 71.00 (*0-7887-4079-2*, H1073E7, Clipper Audio) Recorded Bks., LLC.
Fischer, Tibor. I Like Being Killed: Stories. 2000. 272p. 24.00 o.s.i (*0-8050-6601-2*, Metropolitan Bks.) Holt, Henry & Co.
Follett, Ken. The Big Needle. 1996. mass mkt. 5.99 o.s.i (*0-8217-5675-3*); 1993. 176p. mass mkt. 3.99 o.s.i (*0-8217-4516-6*, Zebra Bks.); 1989. 176p. mass mkt. 3.50 o.p. (*0-8217-2776-1*); 1982. mass mkt. 2.50 o.p. (*0-8217-1076-1*); 1901. mass mkt. 2.25 o.p. (*0-89083-787-2*) Kensington Publishing Corp.
Frederick, K. C. Accomplices. 2003. 240p. 22.00 (*1-57962-091-4*) Permanent Pr., The.
Furst, Alan. Dark Star. (Illus.). 390p. pap. 13.00 (*0-00-651131-7*) HarperCollins Pubs. Ltd. GBR. *Dist:* Trafalgar Square.
—Dark Star. 1991. 288p. 22.95 o.p. (*0-395-51064-3*) Houghton Mifflin Co.
—Dark Star. 1992. mass mkt. 6.99 o.p. (*0-312-92845-9*, St. Martin's Paperbacks) St. Martin's Pr.
Gabor, Marta S. In Pursuit of Balance: A Novel. 2000. 446p. 24.95 (*0-9700207-0-8*) Optyon Bks.
Gallant, Mavis. Paris Stories. 2002. (New York Review Books Classics Ser.). 350p. pap. 14.95 (*1-59017-022-9*) New York Review of Bks., Inc., The.
Garwood, Haley Elizabeth. Swords across the Thames. 1999. pap. text 17.95 (*0-9659721-8-6*) Writers Block, The.
Gentle, Mary. The Wild Machines. Gill, D. C. G., ed. 2000. (Book of Ash Ser.: 3). (Illus.). 400p. mass mkt. 6.99 (*0-380-81113-8*, Eos) Morrow/Avon.
Gerritsen, Tess. Call after Midnight. l.t. ed. 2002. 380p. 29.95 (*0-7862-3970-0*) Gale Group.
—Call after Midnight. 2001. 256p. mass mkt. (*1-55166-834-3*); 1991. pap. (*0-373-15153-5*); 1987. pap. (*0-373-22078-2*) Harlequin Enterprises, Ltd. (Harlequin Bks.).
Gilman, Dorothy. Uncertain Voyage. 1988. 192p. mass mkt. 6.99 (*0-449-21628-4*, Fawcett) Ballantine Bks.
—Uncertain Voyage. l.t. ed. 2001. (Illus.). (J). lib. bdg. 25.95 (*1-58547-075-9*) Ctr. Point Large Print.
Glandfield, J. The Cuckoo Wood. 1999. 488p. mass mkt. 13.95 (*0-575-60311-9*) Gollancz, Victor GBR. *Dist:* Trafalgar Square.
Glanfield, Jenny. The Cuckoo Wood. 1999. 446p. (*0-575-06498-6*) Gollancz, Victor.
Goulden, Gordon. Put Your Hands Here. . . 2002. 210p. pap. (*1-55369-556-9*) Trafford Publishing.
Greenhall, Ken. Lenoir. (GER.). (*3-612-27475-9*) Econ-Verlag GmbH DEU. *Dist:* International Bk. Import Service, Inc.
—Lenoir. 1999. 246p. pap. o.p. (*1-58195-013-6*); 1998. 272p. 24.00 o.p. (*0-944072-93-3*) Steerforth Pr. (Zoland Bks., Inc.).
Grundy, Stephan. Attila's Treasure. 1997. 528p. mass mkt. 6.99 o.s.i (*0-553-57531-7*) Bantam Bks.
Guttmann, B. J. Magdalene. 1996. 231 p. (*1-85863-742-2*) Minerva Pr. GBR. *Dist:* Unity Distribution.
Hansen, Erik F. Psalm at Journey's End. Tate, Joan, tr. 1996. 388p. 24.00 o.p. (*0-374-23868-5*) Farrar, Straus & Giroux.
—Psalm at Journey's End. Tate, Joana, tr. 1997. (Harvest Book Ser.). 384p. pap. 13.00 o.s.i (*0-15-600527-1*, Harvest Bks.) Harcourt Trade Pubs.
Harrington. Auto da Fe. Date not set. (*0-312-06153-6*) St. Martin's Pr.
Haslam, Chris. Twelve-Step Fandango. 2004. 352p. pap. 13.95 (*0-06-058539-0*) HarperTrade.
Ishiguro, Kazuo. The Unconsoled. unabr. collector's ed. 1997. audio 112.00 (*0-7366-4040-1*, 4539) Books on Tape, Inc.
—The Unconsoled. 1996. 544p. pap. 15.95 (*0-679-73587-9*) Knopf, Alfred A. Inc.
—The Unconsoled. 1999. pap. 2.99 (*0-517-48426-9*) Random Hse. Value Publishing.
James, Henry. Daisy Miller. l.t. ed. 2001. per. 15.50 (*1-58396-130-5*) Blue Unicorn Editions.
—Daisy Miller. 1988. mass mkt. 4.95 (*1-55902-007-5*, Aerie) Doherty, Tom Assocs., LLC.
—Daisy Miller. l.t. ed. 2002. 172p. 28.95 (*0-7862-4386-4*) Gale Group.
—Daisy Miller. mass mkt. 0.25 o.p. (*0-451-00625-9*, Signet Bks.) NAL.
—Daisy Miller. l.t. ed. 2002. (Large Print Ser.). 213p. lib. bdg. 25.00 (*1-58287-661-4*) North Bks.
—Daisy Miller. 2002. (Modern Library Classics). 112p. pap. 5.95 (*0-375-75966-2*, Modern Library) Random House Adult Trade Publishing Group.
—Daisy Miller. (Ebook Classic Ser.). E-Book 3.00 (*0-7410-0413-5*) SoftBook Pr.
Kay, Guy Gavriel. Last Light of the Sun. 2004. 24.95 (*0-451-45965-2*) NAL.

Kemske, Floyd. The Third Lion: A Novel about Talleyrand. 1997. 224p. pap. 22.95 (0-945774-37-0, PS3561.E4226T48) Catbird Pr.

Keyes, J. Gregory. A Calculus of Angels. (Age of Unreason Ser.: 2). 2000. 448p. mass mkt. 6.99 (0-345-40608-7, Del Rey); 1999. (Illus.). 416p. pap. 14.00 o.s.i (0-345-40607-9) Ballantine Bks.

King, Ross. Ex-Libris. 2002. 400p. reprint ed. 13.00 (0-14-200080-9) Viking Penguin.

—Ex-Libris: A Novel. 2001. (Dorothy Martin Mystery Ser.). 400p. reprint ed. 24.95 (0-8027-3357-3) Walker & Co.

Kinrade, Kim. Rockets of the Reich: A WWII Action Novel. 2000. (New Millennium Writers Ser.). 300p. 24.95 (1-891696-14-9) BainBridgeBooks.

Leviant, Curt. Ladies & Gentlemen, the Original Music of the Hebrew Alphabet; & Weekend in Mustara: Two Novellas. 2002. (Library of American Fiction). 156p. 21.95 (0-299-17950-8) Univ. of Wisconsin Pr.

Massie, Allan. The Evening of the World. 2002. xiii, 286p. (0-297-81697-7) Weidenfeld & Nicolson, Ltd. GBR. *Dist:* Trafalgar Square.

Maugham, W. Somerset. The Magician. 1977. (Works of W. Somerset Maugham). reprint ed. 23.95 o.p. (0-405-07814-5) Ayer Co. Pubs., Inc.

—The Magician. unabr. ed. 1999. audio 44.95 (0-7861-1654-4, 2482) Blackstone Audio Bks., Inc.

—The Magician. reprint ed. lib. bdg. 98.00 (0-7426-3188-5); 2001. 310p. pap. text 28.00 (0-7426-8188-2) Classic Bks.

—The Magician. 1974. 233p. reprint ed. spiral bd. 11.80 (0-7873-0589-8) Health Research.

—The Magician. 1999. 288p. lib. bdg. 26.95 (0-7351-0175-2) Replica Bks.

—The Magician. (Twentieth Century Classics Ser.). 208p. 1992. pap. 12.95 (0-14-018595-X, Penguin Classics); 1978. pap. 5.95 o.p. (0-14-002668-1, Penguin Bks.) Viking Penguin.

McBride, Mary. Sarah's Knight. 2002. (Silhouette Intimate Moments Ser.). mass mkt. (0-373-27248-0, Silhouette) Harlequin Enterprises, Ltd.

McKay, Donald N. DOMO 17. 2003. (Dr. Jamazi: No. 1). 512p. (C). pap. 12.95 (1-932053-03-4) Nonetheless Pr.

Neider, Charles, ed. A Tramp Abroad. abr. ed. 1977. (Illus.). 319p. o.p. (0-06-014428-9) HarperCollins Pubs.

Nerval, Gérard de. Aurelia Followed by Sylvie. Lappin, Kendall, tr. from FRE. 2nd rev. ed. 1993. 160p. pap. 14.00 (1-878580-07-8) Asylum Arts.

Patterson, James. Cat & Mouse. unabr. ed. 1998. audio 56.00 (0-7366-4138-6, 4643) Books on Tape, Inc.

—Cat & Mouse. 1997. 400p. 24.95 o.p. (0-316-69329-4) Little Brown & Co.

—Cat & Mouse. unabr. ed. 1999. audio compact disk 69.00 (0-7887-3411-3, C1017E7); 1998. audio 70.00 (0-7887-2022-8, 95395E7) Recorded Bks., LLC.

—Cat & Mouse. l.t. ed. (Paperback Bestsellers Ser.). 472p. 1999. pap. 27.95 (0-7838-8345-5); 1998. 30.95 (0-7838-8344-7) Thorndike Pr.

—Cat & Mouse. abr. ed. 1999. audio (1-57042-737-2); 1997. audio 24.00 (1-57042-577-9, 695410) Time Warner AudioBooks.

—Cat & Mouse. 2003. E-Book 5.95 (0-7595-4742-4) Time Warner Bk. Group.

—Cat & Mouse. 2003. 432p. pap. 13.95 (0-446-69264-6); 1998. 480p. reprint ed. mass mkt. 7.99 (0-446-60618-9) Warner Bks., Inc.

Prose, Francine. Guided Tours of Hell: Novellas. 2002. 256p. pap. 12.95 (0-06-008085-X, Perennial) HarperTrade.

—Guided Tours of Hell: Novellas. 1998. 224p. pap. 12.00 o.p. (0-8050-5586-X, Owl Bks.); 1997. 256p. 23.00 o.p. (0-8050-4861-8, Metropolitan Bks.) Holt, Henry & Co.

Ragen, Naomi. The Ghost of Hannah Mendes. 5th ed. 2001. (Illus.). 384p. reprint ed. pap. 14.95 (0-312-28125-0, CPB1198, Saint Martin's Griffin) St. Martin's Pr.

Rathbone, Julian. Blame Hitler. 288p. (0-575-06284-3) Gollancz, Victor.

—Blame Hitler. 288p. mass mkt. 10.95 (0-575-40094-3) Gollancz, Victor GBR. *Dist:* Trafalgar Square.

—Blame Hitler. l.t. ed. 1998. 24.95 (0-7531-5582-6) ISIS Large Print Bks. GBR. *Dist:* Transaction Pubs.

—The Brandenburg Concerto. 1998. (Mask Noir Ser.). 224p. pap. (1-85242-525-3) Serpent's Tail Ltd.

—The Brandenburg Concerto. 256p. 25.99 (0-7278-5716-9) Severn Hse. Pubs., Ltd.

Riviere, Kate Caterina. 2003. pap. 14.00 (0-8021-3973-6) Grove/Atlantic, Inc.

Roberts, Nora. Three Fates. 2003. 496p. mass mkt. 7.99 (0-515-13506-2, Jove) Berkley Publishing Group.

—Three Fates. l.t. ed. 2002. 742p. 32.95 (0-7862-3835-6) Gale Group.

—Three Fates. 2002. 432p. 25.95 o.s.i (0-399-14840-X) Penguin Group (USA) Inc.

—Three Fates. l.t. ed. 2003. 733p. pap. 14.95 (1-4104-0098-0, Large Print Pr.); 2002. pap. 29.95 (0-7862-3839-9) Thorndike Pr.

Salter, James. Cassada. 224p. 2001. pap. text 14.00 (1-58243-186-8); 2000. text 25.00 o.p. (1-887178-89-9) Basic Bks. (Counterpoint Pr.).

Savarin, Julian J. Wolf Run. 1992. 464p. mass mkt. 4.50 o.p. (0-06-100474-X, HarperTorch) Morrow/Avon.

—Wolf Run. 1994. 2.99 o.p. (0-517-12527-7) Random Hse. Value Publishing.

—Wolf Run. 1991. 288p. 19.95 (0-8027-1148-0) Walker & Co.

Sebald, W. G. Vertigo. Hulse, Michael, tr. from GER. 2000. (Illus.). 224p. 23.95 (0-8112-1430-3); 2001. 272p. reprint ed. pap. 14.95 (0-8112-1485-0) New Directions Publishing Corp.

Skinner, Richard. The Red Dancer: The Life & Times of Mata Hari. 2002. 272p. 24.95 (0-06-621366-5, Ecco) HarperTrade.

Slater, Harrison Gradwell. Night Music. 2003. 576p. pap. 14.95 (0-451-20972-9) NAL.

Solmssen, Arthur R. G. The Wife of Shore: A Search. 2000. (Illus.). vi, 284p. (Orig.). pap. 20.00 (0-9705336-0-8) Mill Creek Pr.

Sovakova, Lidmila. Tender Cruelties. 2001. (Goldfish Saga Ser.: Vol. 2). 191p. 19.95 (1-58345-761-5); pap. 13.95 (1-58345-438-1) Domhan Bks.

Stroyar, J. N. The Children's War. 2002. (Illus.). 1168p. pap. 16.00 (0-7434-0740-7, Washington Square Pr.); 2001. (Illus.). 1168p. 29.95 (0-7434-0739-3, Atria); 2001. reprint ed. E-Book 29.95 (0-7434-1928-6, Atria) Simon & Schuster.

Temcov, Joanne L. Marika - A Bulgarian Odyssey: Adventures of Bulgarian Dreamers. 1999. (Illus.). 216p. 28.00 (0-9651935-2-7); pap. 28.00 (0-9651935-1-9) Fisher Enterprises, Inc. (Prometheus Pr.).

Thoene, Bodie. The Twilight of Courage. 1999. 324p. pap. text 9.97 (0-7852-6923-1) Nelson, Thomas Pubs.

Thoene, Bodie & Thoene, Brock. The Twilight of Courage. audio o.p. (0-7852-7726-9); 1995. 528p. pap. 12.99 (0-7852-7596-7); 1994. 524p. 22.99 o.p. (0-7852-8196-7) Nelson, Thomas Inc.

Thomas, Ross. Protocol for a Kidnapping. 1993. 224p. mass mkt. 4.99 o.p. (0-446-40176-5) Warner Bks., Inc.

Tubach, Sally Patterson. Memoirs of a Terrorist. 1996. (SUNY Series, The Margins of Literature). 174p. (C). pap. text 19.95 (0-7914-3006-5); text 20.50 (0-7914-3005-7) State Univ. of New York Pr.

Twain, Mark. A Tramp Abroad. 1880. 631p. reprint ed. 128.00 (0-7222-2227-0) Best Bks.

—A Tramp Abroad. 2001. per. 14.00 (1-891355-65-1); per. 15.50 (1-58396-231-X) Blue Unicorn Editions.

—A Tramp Abroad. 2003. (Illus.). 336p. 9.95 (0-486-42445-6) Dover Pubns., Inc.

—A Tramp Abroad. E-Book 2.49 (1-58627-135-0) Electric Umbrella Publishing.

—A Tramp Abroad. 1978. pap. 1.95 o.p. (0-06-080453-X, P 453) HarperCollins Pubs.

—A Tramp Abroad. 2001. pap. (1-57646-256-0); 1999. 200p. E-Book 8.99 o.s.i incl. audio compact disk (1-57646-156-4) Quiet Vision Publishing.

—A Tramp Abroad. 2003. (Modern Library Classics). (Illus.). 400p. pap. 14.95 (0-8129-7003-9, Modern Library) Random House Adult Trade Publishing Group.

—A Tramp Abroad. 1988. (Works of Mark Twain). reprint ed. 1. (0-7812-1108-5); 2. (0-7812-1109-3) Reprint Services Corp.

—A Tramp Abroad. l.t. ed. 2003. (Perennial Bestsellers Ser.). 29.95 (0-7862-5637-0) Thorndike Pr.

—A Tramp Abroad. 1997. (Classics Ser.). (Illus.). 640p. 14.95 (0-14-043608-1, Penguin Classics) Viking Penguin.

Van Dijk, Lutz. Damned Strong Love: The True Story of Willi G. & Stephan K., ERS. Crawford, Elizabeth D., tr. from GER. 1995. 144p. (YA). (gr. 9 up). 15.95 o.s.i (0-8050-3770-5, Holt, Henry & Co. Bks. For Young Readers) Holt, Henry & Co.

Von Sacher-Masoch, Leopold. Jewish Life: Tales from Nineteenth-Century Europe. Lewis, Virginia, tr. from GER. & afterword by. by. 2002. (Studies in Austrian Literature, Culture, & Thought). (Illus.). 216p. 24.50 (1-57241-114-7) Ariadne Pr.

Wegner, Hart. Houses of Ivory. 1988. 241p. 15.95 o.p. (0-939149-13-3) Soho Pr., Inc.

Weiner, Steve. The Yellow Sailor. 2002. 220p. pap. 13.95 (1-58567-324-2); 2001. 256p. 26.95 (1-58567-169-X) Overlook Pr., The.

Weinstein, Lewis. The Heretic: A Novel. 2003. (Library of American Fiction). 388p. pap. 17.95 (0-299-18794-2) Univ. of Wisconsin Pr.

Weiss, Ernst. Jarmila. 2003. 128p. pap. 12.00 (1-901285-29-4) Pushkin Pr., Ltd. GBR. *Dist:* Consortium Bk. Sales & Distribution.

Wharton, Thomas. Salamander. 2002. 400p. pap. 14.00 (0-7434-4415-9, Washington Square Pr.) Simon & Schuster.

Wolf, Joan. The Reindeer Hunters. 1994. 384p. 20.95 o.p. (0-525-93848-6, Dutton) Dutton/Plume.

—The Reindeer Hunters. 1995. 464p. mass mkt. 5.99 o.s.i (0-451-17878-5, Onyx) NAL.

Woodman, Richard. The Shadow of the Eagle Bk. 13: A Nathaniel Drinkwater Novel. 1997. (Illus.). 372p. pap. o.s.i (0-7515-2051-9) Warner Futura GBR. *Dist:* Little Brown & Co.

Zangwill, Israel. The King of Schnorrers. E-Book 3.95 (0-594-01478-6) 1873 Pr.

—The King of Schnorrers. 2003. (Judaica Ser.). 128p. pap. 6.95 (0-486-42872-9) Dover Pubns., Inc.

—The King of Schnorrers. 1987. (Illus.). 156p. 14.95 (0-915361-98-1) Lambda Pubs., Inc.

—King of Schnorrers. 1983. pap. 1.50 o.p. (0-486-21354-4) Dover Pubns., Inc.

—King of Schnorrers. 1981. 5.00 o.p. (0-8446-3228-7) Smith, Peter Pub., Inc.

Zweig, Stefan. Twenty-Four Hours in the Life of a Woman. 2003. 112p. pap. 12.00 (1-901285-48-0) Pushkin Pr., Ltd. GBR. *Dist:* Consortium Bk. Sales & Distribution.

## EUROPE, EASTERN—FICTION

Albahari, David. Tsing. 1997. (Writings from an Unbound Europe). 100p. pap. 14.95 (0-8101-1568-9) Northwestern Univ. Pr.

Appelfeld, Aharon. The Iron Tracks. 1999. 208p. pap. 12.00 (0-8052-1099-7, Schocken) Knopf Publishing Group.

Bernstein, Michael Andre. Conspirators. 2004. 512p. 24.00 (0-374-23754-9) Farrar, Straus & Giroux.

Bradbury, Malcolm. Rates of Exchange. 1983. 320p. 13.95 o.p. (0-394-53268-6) Knopf, Alfred A. Inc.

—Rates of Exchange. 1985. 320p. pap. 11.95 o.p. (0-14-017534-2); pap. 10.00 o.p. (0-14-007631-X, Penguin Bks.) Viking Penguin.

Bunn, T. Davis. The Amber Room. 1992. (Priceless Collection). 336p. pap. 9.99 o.p. (1-55661-285-0) Bethany Hse. Pubs.

Coelho, Paulo. Veronika Decides to Die. Costa, Margaret Jull, tr. from POR. 2000. 224p. 24.00 (0-06-019612-2) HarperCollins Pubs.

Dilke, Annabel. Present from the Past. 1994. 240p. 23.95 (0-233-98800-9) Andre Deutsch GBR. *Dist:* Trafalgar Square, Trans-Atlantic Pubns., Inc.

Egleton, Clive. Cry Havoc: A Peter Ashton Novel. 2003. 352p. 24.95 (0-312-30943-0, Saint Martin's Minotaur) St. Martin's Pr.

Esrati, Stephen G. Comrades, Avenge Us. 1996. 404p. per. 5.99 (1-896329-24-1) Esrati Co.

—Comrades, Avenge Us. 2000. 420p. pap. 24.99 (0-7388-2441-0) Xlibris Corp.

Fahri, Moris. Children of the Rainbow. 2002. (Illus.). 390p. pap. 14.95 (0-86356-306-6) I.B.Tauris & Co., Ltd. GBR. *Dist:* Holtzbrinck Pubs., Palgrave Macmillan.

Farhi, Moris. Children of the Rainbow. 1999. 389p. pap. (0-86356-059-8) Saqi Bks.

Frederick, K. C. Country of Memory. 1998. 240p. pap. 16.00 (1-57962-056-6); 176p. 22.00 o.p. (1-57962-013-2) Permanent Pr., The.

Germain, Sylvie. Invitation to a Journey: Eclat du Sel. 2003. (Dedalus Europe 2003 Ser.). (FRE.). 196p. pap. 12.99 (1-903517-16-8) Dedalus, Ltd.

Haig, Brian. Secret Sanction. 2001. 416p. 24.95 o.p. (0-446-52743-2) Warner Bks., Inc.

Hansson, Carola. Steinhof. Scobbie, Irene, tr. from SWE. 2002. 288p. pap. 13.95 (1-900850-66-4) Arcadia Bks. GBR. *Dist:* Consortium Bk. Sales & Distribution.

Higgins, Jack. The Keys of Hell. 1981. 160p. mass mkt. 1.95 o.s.i (0-449-14298-1, Fawcett); 1978. mass mkt. 1.50 o.s.i (0-449-13673-6) Ballantine Bks.

—The Keys of Hell. l.t. ed. 2000. 255p. lib. bdg. 28.95 o.p. (1-58547-036-8) Ctr. Point Large Print.

Hoch, Edward D. The Iron Angel: And Other Tales of the Gypsy Sleuth. 2003. 232p. 42.00 (1-885941-90-0); pap. 17.00 (1-885941-91-9) Crippen & Landru, Pubs.

Kadare, Ismail. Spring Flowers, Spring Frost: A Novel. Date not set. Tr. of Lulet e Ftohta te Marsit. (Illus.). 192p. pap. 12.95 (1-55970-669-4) Arcade Publishing, Inc.

—Spring Flowers, Spring Frost: A Novel. Belios, David, tr. from ALB. 2002. Tr. of Lulet e Ftohta te Marsit. 192p. pap. 23.95 (1-55970-635-X) Arcade Publishing, Inc.

Lawrence, Starling. Montenegro. 1998. 368p. reprint ed. pap. 6.99 o.s.i (0-425-16446-2) Berkley Publishing Group.

—Montenegro. 1997. 320p. 23.00 o.p. (0-374-21407-7) Farrar, Straus & Giroux.

Mankell, Henning. The Dogs of Riga. 2004. 336p. pap. 13.00 (1-4000-3152-4, Vintage) Knopf Publishing Group.

—The Dogs of Riga: A Kurt Wallander Mystery. Thompson, Laurie, tr. from SWE. 2003. 336p. pap. 24.95 (1-56584-787-3) New Pr., The.

Marcus, Shmuel M. Chicken Kiev. 2002. 12p. 14.00 (1-880880-70-9) Israeli Trading Co.

Mazzini, Miha. Guarding Hanna. 2002. 272p. pap. 16.00 (0-9720287-1-4) Scala Hse. Pubs., LLC.

McNab, Andy. Firewall. 2001. 384p. mass mkt. 7.99 (0-7434-3515-X, Pocket); 24.95 (0-7434-0626-5, Atria) Simon & Schuster.

Mewshaw, Michael. Shelter from the Storm. 288p. 2004. pap. 14.00 (0-425-19375-6); 2003. 23.95 (0-399-14988-0) Putnam Publishing Group, The. (BlueHen Bks.).

Queffelec, Yann. Happy Birthday Sara. l.t. ed. 1998. (French Ser.). 228p. pap. 30.99 (2-84011-252-3) Feryane, SA, Editions FRA. *Dist:* Ulverscroft Large Print Bks., Ltd., Ulverscroft Large Print Canada, Ltd.

Sienkiewicz, Henryk. The Deluge Vol. II: An Historical Novel of Poland, Sweden & Russia, 2 vols., Set. 2001. reprint ed. 196.00 (0-7426-4131-7) Classic Bks.

—The Deluge Vol. II: An Historical Novel of Poland, Sweden & Russia. Curtin, Jeremiah, tr. 2001. 585p. pap. 37.50 (1-58963-021-1); 673p. pap. 24.95 (1-58963-019-X) Fredonia Bks.

—Pan Michael: An Historical Novel of Poland, the Ukraine & Turkey. 2001. xvi, 527p. reprint ed. 168.00 (0-7426-4132-5) Classic Bks.

Simecka, Martin M. The Year of the Frog. 1996. 256p. pap. 12.00 o.s.i (0-684-81367-X, Touchstone) Simon & Schuster.

Steinhauer, Olen. The Bridge of Sighs: A Novel. 288p. 2004. pap. 13.95 (0-312-32601-7, Saint Martin's Griffin); 2003. 23.95 (0-312-30245-2, Saint Martin's Minotaur) St. Martin's Pr.

Tomsits, Julius. Gyuszika: Promises Kept. 2001. 156p. pap. 17.95 (0-7596-2835-1) 1stBooks Library.

Ulitskaya, Ludmila. Medea & Her Children. 2004. Tr. of Medeeiia i ee Deti. 320p. pap. 13.00 (0-8052-1144-6, Schocken) Knopf Publishing Group.

—Medea & Her Children. Tait, Arch, tr. from RUS. 2002. Tr. of Medeeiia i ee Deti. (Illus.). 320p. 24.00 (0-8052-4196-5, Schocken) Knopf Publishing Group.

## EVERIEN (IMAGINARY PLACE)—FICTION

Leith, Valery. The Company of Glass. 2000. (Everien Ser.: Vol. 1). 544p. mass mkt. 5.99 (0-553-57899-5) Bantam Bks.

—The Riddled Night. 2000. (Everien Ser.: Vol. 2). 528p. pap. 27.00 (0-553-37939-9, Spectra) Bantam Bks.

# F

## FARBERVILLE (ARK.: IMAGINARY PLACE)—FICTION

Hess, Joan. Busy Bodies. 1995. (Claire Malloy Mystery Ser.). 256p. 19.95 o.p. (0-525-93910-5) Dutton/Plume.

—Busy Bodies. 1996. (Claire Malloy Mystery Ser.). 272p. mass mkt. 5.50 o.s.i (0-451-40560-9, Onyx) NAL.

—Closely Akin to Murder. 1996. (Claire Malloy Mystery Ser.). 240p. 21.95 o.s.i (0-525-93911-3, Dutton) Dutton/Plume.

—Closely Akin to Murder. 1997. (Claire Malloy Mysteries Ser.). 272p. mass mkt. 5.99 o.s.i (0-451-40561-7, Onyx) NAL.

—A Conventional Corpse. l.t. ed. 2000. (Wheeler Softcover Ser.). 293p. pap. 24.95 (1-56895-995-8, Wheeler Publishing, Inc.) Gale Group.

—A Conventional Corpse. 2001. 304p. mass mkt. 6.50 o.s.i (0-312-97726-3, St. Martin's Paperbacks); 2000. 275p. 23.95 (0-312-24662-5, Saint Martin's Minotaur) St. Martin's Pr.

—Dear Miss Demeanor. 1990. (Claire Malloy Ser.: No. 3). 195p. mass mkt. 4.99 o.s.i (0-345-34911-3) Ballantine Bks.

—Dear Miss Demeanor. (Claire Malloy Mysteries Ser.). 2000. 208p. mass mkt. 5.99 (0-312-97313-6, St. Martin's Paperbacks); 1987. 192p. 13.95 o.p. (0-312-00702-7, Saint Martin's Minotaur) St. Martin's Pr.

—Death by the Light of the Moon. 208p. 1995. pap. 15.00 (0-345-47171-7); 1994. mass mkt. 6.50 (0-345-37838-5) Ballantine Bks.

—Death by the Light of the Moon. (Claire Malloy Mystery Ser.). 240p. 2003. mass mkt. 6.99 (0-312-99101-0, St. Martin's Paperbacks); 1992. 18.95 o.p. (0-312-06949-9, Saint Martin's Minotaur) St. Martin's Pr.

—A Diet to Die For. 1992. (Claire Mallory Mystery Ser.). reprint ed. mass mkt. 5.50 o.s.i (0-345-36654-9) Ballantine Bks.

—A Diet to Die For. 1989. 192p. 14.95 o.p. (0-312-03326-5, Saint Martin's Minotaur) St. Martin's Pr.

—A Holly, Jolly Murder. l.t. ed. 2003. (Mystery Ser.). 27.95 (1-57490-531-7) Beeler, Thomas T. Publisher.

—A Holly, Jolly Murder. 1997. (Claire Malloy Mystery Ser.). 272p. 22.95 o.s.i (0-525-94240-8) Dutton/Plume.

—A Holly, Jolly Murder. 1998. (Claire Malloy Mystery Ser.). 288p. mass mkt. 5.99 o.s.i (0-451-40728-8, Onyx) NAL.

—The Murder at the Murder at the Mimosa Inn. 1987. mass mkt. 4.99 o.s.i (0-345-34324-7) Ballantine Bks.
—The Murder at the Murder at the Mimosa Inn. 1999. 192p. mass mkt. 5.99 (0-312-97178-8, St. Martin's Paperbacks); 1986. 208p. 13.95 o.p. (0-312-55293-9) St. Martin's Pr.
—Poisoned Pins. 1993. (Claire Malloy Mystery Ser.). 256p. 18.00 o.p. (0-525-93591-6) Dutton/Plume.
—Poisoned Pins. 1994. (Claire Malloy Mystery Ser.). 256p. mass mkt. 5.99 o.s.i (0-451-40390-8, Onyx) NAL.
—A Really Cute Corpse. 1988. 192p. 14.95 o.p. (0-312-02271-9, Saint Martin's Minotaur) St. Martin's Pr.
—Roll over & Play Dead. 1992. reprint ed. mass mkt. 5.50 o.s.i (0-345-37586-6) Ballantine Bks.
—Roll over & Play Dead. (Claire Mallory Mystery Ser.). 2003. 208p. mass mkt. 5.99 (0-312-98828-1, St. Martin's Paperbacks); 1991. 17.95 o.p. (0-312-05956-6, Saint Martin's Minotaur) St. Martin's Pr.
—Strangled Prose. 1987. mass mkt. 5.99 o.s.i (0-345-34059-0) Ballantine Bks.
—Strangled Prose. 192p. 1998. mass mkt. 5.99 (0-312-96864-7, St. Martin's Paperbacks); 1985. 12.95 o.p. (0-312-76428-6) St. Martin's Pr.
—Tickled to Death. 1994. (Claire Malloy Mystery Ser.). 224p. 18.95 o.p. (0-525-93810-9) Dutton/Plume.
—Tickled to Death. l.t. ed. 1994. pap. 19.95 o.p. (1-56895-079-9, Wheeler Publishing, Inc.) Gale Group.
—Tickled to Death. 1995. (Claire Malloy Mystery Ser.). 304p. mass mkt. 5.99 o.s.i (0-451-40550-1, Onyx) NAL.

**FELICITY GROVE (N.Y.: IMAGINARY PLACE)—FICTION**

Piccirilli, Tom. The Dead Past, Vol. 1. 1999. (Felicity Grove Mysteries Ser.). 208p. reprint ed. mass mkt. 5.99 o.s.i (0-425-16696-1, Prime Crime) Berkley Publishing Group.
—The Dead Past. l.t. ed. 1999. (Thorndike Senior Lifestyle Ser.). 285p. 26.95 (0-7862-1833-9) Thorndike Pr.
—The Dead Past. 1997. (Felicity Grove Mysteries Ser.). 212p. 21.95 o.p. (1-885173-28-8) Write Way Publishing.
—Sorrow's Crown. 1999. (Felicity Grove Mysteries Ser.). 208p. mass mkt. 5.99 o.s.i (0-425-17028-4, Prime Crime) Berkley Publishing Group.
—Sorrow's Crown. 1999. 240p. 21.95 o.p. (1-885173-53-9) Write Way Publishing.

**FIJI—FICTION**

Gaarder, Jostein. Maya. 2nd ed. 2001. (SPA., Illus.). 415p. 25.95 (84-7844-498-X) Siruela, Ediciones S.A. ESP. *Dist:* Lectorum Pubns., Inc.
Morris, Marion E. The Sand Crabs. 1999. 192p. 16.00 (1-891954-30-X) Russell Dean & Co.

**FINLAND—FICTION**

Carpelan, Bo. Urwind. McDuff, David, tr. from FIN. 1997. 220p. pap. 24.95 (1-85754-250-9) Carcanet Pr., Ltd. GBR. *Dist:* Paul & Co. Pubs. Consortium, Inc.
—Urwind. McDuff, David, tr. from SWE. 807th ed. 1998. 200p. 33.00 (0-8101-1618-9, Hydra Bks.) Northwestern Univ. Pr.
Finnish Short Stories. 1990. 238p. 12.95 o.p. (0-941016-82-X) Penfield Pr.
Gunn, Robin Jones. Sisterchicks on the Loose. 2003. (Sister Chicks Series, Book One Ser.). 325p. pap. 12.99 (1-59052-198-6) Multnomah Pubs., Inc.
Hart, Francis. Love Is a Secret. l.t. ed. 1999. (Paperback Ser.). 223p. 24.95 o.p. (0-7838-8794-9) Thorndike Pr.
Joensuu, Matti. The Stone Murders. Taylor, Raili, tr. from FIN. 1987. 160p. 13.95 o.p. (0-312-00689-6) St. Martin's Pr.
Kihlman, Christer. The Blue Mother. 1990. (Modern Scandinavian Literature in Translation Ser.). 315p. reprint ed. pap. 97.70 (0-608-02383-3, 206302500004) Bks. on Demand.
—The Blue Mother. Tate, Joan, tr. from FIN. 1990. (Modern Scandinavian Literature in Translation Ser.). vi, 308p. text 29.95 o.p. (0-8032-2721-3); pap. 11.95 o.p. (0-8032-7769-5, Bison Bks.) Univ. of Nebraska Pr.
Kilpi, Eva. Tamara. Binham, Philip, tr. 1978. pap. 8.95 o.s.i (0-440-08494-6, Delacorte Pr.) Dell Publishing.
Lehtinen, Lasse. Blood, Sweat & Bears. Parsons, Jeremy, tr. 1990. 256p. 15.95 o.p. (0-08-040350-6) Brassey's, UK Ltd. GBR. *Dist:* Brassey's, Inc.
Sillanpaa, Frans Eemil. The Maid Silja. 1984. 320p. reprint ed. 36.00 (0-87797-174-9) Cherokee Publishing Co.
Trotter, William R. Winter Fire. 2003. 464p. pap. 14.00 (0-7867-1257-0) Avalon Publishing Group.
—Winter Fire. 1993. 496p. 22.00 o.p. (0-525-93581-9) Dutton/Plume.
—Winter Fire. 1994. 464p. mass mkt. 4.99 o.p. (0-451-17718-5, Signet Bks.) NAL.
Wisuri, Leslie W. Jonas of Kiivijarvi: Finnish Freedom Fighter. 1996. 240p. (Orig.). pap. 12.95 (0-87839-104-5) North Star Pr. of St. Cloud.
Ylimusi, Tauno. Hand in Hand: A Novel. Impola, Richard A., tr. from FIN. & intro. by. 1992. (Illus.). 176p. 17.95 (0-8397-3156-6) Eriksson, Paul S. Pub.

**FIONAVAR (IMAGINARY PLACE)—FICTION**

Kay, Guy Gavriel. The Darkest Road. 1986. (Fionavar Tapestry Ser.: Bk. 3). 352p. 22.45 o.p. (0-87795-822-X, Morrow, William & Co.) Morrow/Avon.
—The Darkest Road. (Fionavar Tapestry Ser.: Vol. 3). 448p. 1992. mass mkt. 6.99 o.s.i (0-451-45180-5); 2001. (Illus.). reprint ed. pap. 13.95 (0-451-45833-8) NAL. (ROC).
—The Summer Tree. 1986. (Fionavar Tapestry Ser.: Bk. 1). 320p. 3.50 o.p. (0-425-09294-1) Berkley Publishing Group.
—The Summer Tree. 1985. (Fionavar Tapestry Ser.: Bk. 1). 324p. 15.95 o.p. (0-87795-760-6, Morrow, William & Co.) Morrow/Avon.
—The Summer Tree. (Fionavar Tapestry Ser.: Vol. 1). 400p. 1992. mass mkt. 6.99 o.s.i (0-451-45138-4); 2001. (Illus.). reprint ed. mass mkt. 15.00 (0-451-45822-2) NAL. (ROC).
—The Wandering Fire. 1987. (Fionavar Tapestry Ser.: Bk. 2). mass mkt. 3.50 o.s.i (0-441-87046-5) Ace Bks.
—The Wandering Fire. 1986. (Fionavar Tapestry Ser.: Bk. 2). 15.95 o.p. (0-87795-785-1, Morrow, William & Co.) Morrow/Avon.
—The Wandering Fire. (Fionavar Tapestry Ser.: Bk. 2). 400p. 1992. mass mkt. 6.99 o.s.i (0-451-45156-2); 2001. (Illus.). reprint ed. pap. 15.00 (0-451-45826-5) NAL. (ROC).

**FISHERSVILLE (N.J.: IMAGINARY PLACE)—FICTION**

Gallison, Kate. Grave Misgivings: A Mother Lavinia Grey Mystery. 1999. (Mother Lavinia Grey Mysteries Ser.). 256p. mass mkt. 5.99 o.s.i (0-440-22413-6) Dell Publishing.
—Hasty Retreat: A Mother Lavinia Grey Mystery. 1998. (Mother Lavinia Grey Mysteries Ser.). 256p. mass mkt. 5.99 o.s.i (0-440-22410-1, Dell Bks.) Dell Publishing.
—Unholy Angels: A Mother Lavinia Grey Mystery. 1996. (Mother Lavinia Grey Mysteries Ser.). 272p. mass mkt. 5.99 o.s.i (0-440-22220-6) Dell Publishing.

**FLAT SKUNK (CALIF.: IMAGINARY PLACE)—FICTION**

Warner, Penny. Dead Body Language. 1997. (Connor Westphal Mystery Ser.). 288p. mass mkt. 5.50 o.s.i (0-553-57586-4, Crimeline) Bantam Bks.
—A Quiet Undertaking. 2000. 272p. mass mkt. 5.50 o.s.i (0-553-57965-7) Bantam Bks.
—Right to Remain Silent. 1998. 288p. mass mkt. 5.50 o.s.i (0-553-57962-2, Crimeline) Bantam Bks.
—Sign of Foul Play: A Connor Westphal Mystery. 1997. (Connor Westphal Mystery Ser.). 288p. mass mkt. 5.50 o.s.i (0-553-57587-2, Crimeline) Bantam Bks.

**FLORIDA—FICTION**

Abreu-Felippe, Nicolas. Miami en Brumas. 2000. (Coleccion Caniqui).Tr. of Miami in Fog. (SPA.). 205p. pap. 16.00 (0-89729-919-1) Ediciones Universal.
Adams, Pepper. The Bachelor Cure. l.t. ed. 1995. 200p. per. 20.95 o.p. (0-7838-1488-7, Macmillan Reference USA) Gale Group.
Adler, Warren. Mourning Glory. l.t. ed. 2001. (Wheeler Large Print Book Ser.). 498p. 28.95 o.p. (1-58724-115-3, Wheeler Publishing, Inc.) Gale Group.
—Mourning Glory. 352p. 2002. mass mkt. 6.99 o.s.i (0-7582-0044-7); 2001. 23.00 o.s.i (1-57566-898-X) Kensington Publishing Corp.
—Mourning Glory. E-Book 9.95 (1-59006-071-7); E-Book 9.95 (1-931304-23-8) Stonehouse Pr., Inc.
—Never Too Late for Love. 1995. 288p. 22.95 (0-943972-44-2); pap. 14.95 (0-943972-45-0) Homestead Publishing.
Aiken, Ginny, et al. Strings of the Heart: Members of a String Quartet Find Love under a Miami Moon in Four Novellas. 2003. (Contemporary Collection). 352p. pap. 6.97 (1-58660-967-X) Barbour Publishing, Inc.
Alam, Glynn Marsh. Cold Water Corpse: A Luanne Fogarty Mystery. 2003. (Illus.). 254p. 12.95 (0-9725078-0-9) Avocet Pr., Inc.
—Deep Water Death. 2001. (Luanne Fogarty Mystery Ser.: Vol. 2). 304p. pap. 12.95 (0-9705049-1-8) Avocet Pr., Inc.
—Dive Deep & Deadly. 2000. 236p. pap. 12.95 (0-9661072-9-2) Avocet Pr., Inc.
—River Whispers. 2002. (Illus.). 127p. pap. 12.95 (0-9705049-5-0) Avocet Pr., Inc.
Albanese, Laurie Lico. Lynelle by the Sea. 240p. 2000. (Illus.). 22.95 o.p. (0-525-94536-9, Dutton); 2001. reprint ed. pap. 13.00 o.s.i (0-452-28218-7, Plume) Dutton/Plume.
—Lynelle by the Sea. l.t. ed. 2000. (Americana Ser.). 371p. 26.95 (0-7862-2916-0) Thorndike Pr.
Alberto, Eliseo. Caracol Beach. 1998. (SPA., Illus.). 360p. 11.95 (84-204-8370-2) Alfaguara, Ediciones, S.A.- Grupo Santillana ESP. *Dist:* Lectorum Pubns., Inc., Santillana USA Publishing Co., Inc.
Amberg, Jay. Doubloon. mass mkt. (0-7653-4036-4); 2003. 320p. 24.95 (0-7653-0100-8) Doherty, Tom Assocs., LLC. (Tor Bks.).
—Doubloon. 2003. (Adventure Ser.). 307p. 28.95 (0-7862-5399-1) Thorndike Pr.
Anderson, Kevin J. Ignition. abr. ed. 1997. audio 7.99 o.p. (1-56740-232-1, 661, Nova Audio Bks.) Brilliance Audio.
Anderson, Kevin J. & Beason, Doug. Ignition. abr. ed. 1997. audio 16.95 o.p. (1-56100-910-5, 1263, Nova Audio Bks.); audio 57.25 o.p. (1-56100-328-X, 906, Unabridged Library Editions); audio 23.95 o.p. (1-56100-702-1, 143, Bookcassette) Brilliance Audio.
—Ignition. 1998. 402p. mass mkt. 6.99 o.p. (0-8125-4548-6, Tor Bks.); 1997. 304p. 23.95 (0-312-86270-9, Forge Bks.) Doherty, Tom Assocs., LLC.
Anderson, Virginia S. Storm Front. 1992. 448p. 16.50 o.s.i (0-385-42232-6) Doubleday Publishing.
Andrews, Sarah. Killer Dust: A Mystery Featuring Forensic Geologist Em Hansen. 2003. 320p. 24.95 (0-312-30196-0, Saint Martin's Minotaur) St. Martin's Pr.
Apple, Max. The Propheteers. 1987. 288p. 16.95 o.p. (0-06-055056-2); pap. 7.95 o.p. (0-06-096158-9, PL6158, Perennial) HarperTrade.
Arnold, Catherine. Due Process. 1996. 368p. mass mkt. 5.99 o.s.i (0-451-18614-1, Signet Bks.) NAL.
Arnold, Eugene. Big Water: Revenge - Bounty. 1998. (Illus.). 150p. pap. 6.95 (1-891118-26-9) Wind Canyon Bks., Inc.
Asher, Steven. The Undercover Single Man. 1998. 126p. 14.95 o.p. (0-533-12452-2) Vantage Pr., Inc.
Ayres, E. C. Eye of the Gator. 1995. 320p. 22.95 o.p. (0-312-13490-8, Saint Martin's Minotaur) St. Martin's Pr.
—Night of the Panther. 1997. (Tony Lowell Mysteries Ser.). 272p. 22.95 o.p. (0-312-15607-3, Saint Martin's Minotaur) St. Martin's Pr.
Bailey, Mitchell. Fair Injustice: Sic Semper Tyranus. 2000. 220p. pap. 21.99 (0-7388-2992-7) Xlibris Corp.
Baker, Larry. Flamingo Rising. 1998. 336p. pap. 12.95 (0-345-42702-5) Ballantine Bks.
—The Flamingo Rising. abr. ed. 1997. audio 18.00 o.s.i (0-679-46054-3, RH Audio) Random Hse. Audio Publishing Group.
Bandy, Franklin. Athena. 1988. 320p. pap. 3.95 o.p. (0-8125-8050-8); 1987. 15.95 o.p. (0-312-93018-6) Doherty, Tom Assocs., LLC. (Tor Bks.).
Banks, Russell. Continental Drift. 1986. 432p. mass mkt. 5.99 o.s.i (0-345-33021-8) Ballantine Bks.
—Continental Drift. (Perennial Classics Ser.). 2000. 432p. pap. 15.00 (0-06-095673-9, Perennial); 1994. (Illus.). 384p. pap. 13.50 (0-06-092574-4); 1985. 416p. 17.95 o.p. (0-06-015383-0) HarperTrade.
—Gegenstroemung. 2003. (GER.). 508p. pap. 27.00 (1-4000-5511-3) Random Hse. Information Group.
Barr, Nevada. Flashback. 2004. 416p. mass mkt. 7.99 (0-425-19449-3) Berkley Publishing Group.
—Flashback. 2004. 543p. pap. 13.95 (1-4104-0172-3); 2003. 32.95 (1-58724-380-6) Gale Group. (Wheeler Publishing, Inc.).
—Flashback. 2003. (Illus.). 400p. 24.95 (0-399-14975-9, Putnam & Grosset) Putnam Publishing Group, The.
—Flashback. audio 34.99 (1-4025-3633-X) Recorded Bks., LLC.
Barry, Dave. Big Trouble. 2001. 336p. mass mkt. 7.50 (0-425-17810-2); mass mkt. 7.50 o.s.i (0-425-18412-9) Berkley Publishing Group.
—Big Trouble. abr. ed. 1999. audio 17.95 o.p. (1-56740-864-8, 1892, Nova Audio Bks.); audio 27.95 o.p. (1-56740-459-6, 1890, Brilliance Audio Unabridged); audio 57.25 (1-56740-686-6, 1891, Unabridged Library Editions) Brilliance Audio.
—Big Trouble. l.t. ed. 2000. (G. K. Hall Core Ser.). 329p. 30.95 (0-7838-8924-0, Macmillan Reference USA) Gale Group.
—Big Trouble, Set. abr. ed. 1999. audio 17.95 Highsmith Inc.
—Big Trouble. 1999. 320p. 23.95 o.p. (0-399-14567-2, G. P. Putnam's Sons) Penguin Group (USA) Inc.
—Big Trouble. l.t. ed. 2001. (Paperback Bestsellers Ser.). 311p. pap. 28.95 (0-7838-8930-5) Thorndike Pr.
—Tricky Business. 2003. 304p. mass mkt. 7.99 (0-425-19274-1) Berkley Publishing Group.
—Tricky Business. 2003. 390p. pap. 12.95 (1-4104-0158-8, Wheeler Publishing, Inc.) Gale Group.
—Tricky Business. 2002. 256p. 24.95 o.s.i (0-399-14924-4) Penguin Group (USA) Inc.
—Tricky Business. 2003. (Core Ser.). 31.95 (0-7862-5037-2) Thorndike Pr.
Barry, Dave, et al. Naked Came the Manatee: A Novel. Hiaasen, Carl, ed. 1998. 208p. pap. 12.95 (0-449-00124-5, Fawcett) Ballantine Bks.
Barthelme, Frederick. Tracer. 2001. 128p. pap. text 13.00 (1-58243-129-9, Counterpoint Pr.) Basic Bks.
—Tracer. 1985. 104p. 13.70 o.p. (0-671-54253-2, Simon & Schuster) Simon & Schuster.
—Tracer. 1986. 128p. pap. 4.95 o.p. (0-14-008969-1, Penguin Bks.) Viking Penguin.
Bartholomew, Nancy. Drag Strip. 1999. (Sierra Lavotini Mysteries Ser.). 272p. 23.95 (0-312-20295-4, Saint Martin's Minotaur) St. Martin's Pr.
—Drag Strip: A Sierra Lavotini Mystery. 2000. 288p. mass mkt. 5.99 (0-312-97579-1, St. Martin's Paperbacks) St. Martin's Pr.
—Film Strip: A Sierra Lavotini Mystery. 2000. 262p. 23.95 o.p. (0-312-26161-6, Saint Martin's Minotaur) St. Martin's Pr.
—The Miracle Strip. 1998. (Sierra Lavotini Mysteries Ser.). 256p. 22.95 (0-312-19299-1, Saint Martin's Minotaur) St. Martin's Pr.
—The Miracle Strip: A Sierra Lavotini Mystery. 1999. (Sierra Lavotini Mysteries Ser.). 256p. mass mkt. 5.99 (0-312-97095-1, St. Martin's Paperbacks) St. Martin's Pr.
—Strip Poker: A Sierra Lavotini Mystery. 2001. 272p. 23.95 (0-312-26259-0, Saint Martin's Minotaur) St. Martin's Pr.
Bausch, Robert. On the Way Home. 2000. (Voices of the South Ser.). 224p. pap. 15.95 (0-8071-2638-1) Louisiana State Univ. Pr.
—On the Way Home. 1983. 240p. pap. 3.50 (0-380-63131-8, 63131-8, Avon Bks.) Morrow/Avon.
—On the Way Home. 1982. 260p. 13.95 o.p. (0-312-58459-8) St. Martin's Pr.
Belgrave, Laura. Deadly Associations. 2003. (Claudia Hershey Mysteries Ser.). 220p. 23.95 (1-57072-247-1); 208p. pap. 13.95 (1-57072-248-X) Overmountain Pr. (Silver Dagger Mysteries).
—Quietly Dead. 2001. (Claudia Hershey Mysteries Ser.: Vol. 2). v, 200p. 23.95 (1-57072-172-6); pap. 13.95 (1-57072-173-4) Overmountain Pr. (Silver Dagger Mysteries).
Bell, Christine. The Perez Family: A Novel. 1991. 256p. reprint ed. pap. 11.00 o.p. (0-06-097401-X, Perennial) HarperTrade.
—The Perez Family: A Novel. 1990. 19.95 o.p. (0-393-02798-8) Norton, W. W. & Co., Inc.
—Saint. 1985. 256p. 14.95 o.p. (0-910923-21-3) Pineapple Pr., Inc.
—Saint. 1987. 272p. pap. 6.95 o.s.i (0-671-63847-5, Pocket) Simon & Schuster.
Bernardo, Anilu. Jumping off to Freedom. 1996. 198p. (YA). (gr. 4-7). pap. 9.95 (1-55885-088-0); (gr. 6-12). 14.95 o.p. (1-55885-087-2) Arte Publico Pr. (Piñata Books).
—Jumping off to Freedom. 1996. 16.00 (0-606-13547-2) Turtleback Bks.
Bierce, Jane. Funny Business. 2001. E-Book 4.75 incl. disk (1-58749-040-4); E-Book 4.75 (1-58749-041-2) Awe-Struck E-Bks.
Bishop, Claudia. Death Dines Out. 1997. (Hemlock Falls Mysteries Ser.). 256p. mass mkt. 5.99 (0-425-16111-0, Prime Crime) Berkley Publishing Group.
Blackstock, Terri. Seaside: A Novella. l.t. ed. 2001. 137p. 26.95 (0-7838-9511-9, Macmillan Reference USA) Gale Group.
Booth, Pat. All for Love. l.t. ed. 1995. pap. 22.95 o.p. (0-7927-2061-X); 1994. 23.95 o.p. (0-7927-2062-8) BBC Audiobooks America.
—All for Love. 1993. 404p. 21.00 o.s.i (0-517-58416-6, Crown) Crown Publishing Group.
—Miami. 1992. mass mkt. 5.99 o.s.i (0-345-38165-3) Ballantine Bks.
—Miami. 1991. 384p. 20.00 o.s.i (0-517-58415-8, Crown) Crown Publishing Group.
—Miami. 1994. 4.99 o.p. (0-517-11672-3) Random Hse. Value Publishing.
—Palm Beach. 1986. pap. o.p. (0-345-00738-7); mass mkt. 5.99 o.s.i (0-345-33357-8) Ballantine Bks.
—Palm Beach. 1985. 400p. 4.99 o.p. (0-517-55844-0) Random Hse. Value Publishing.
Born, James O. Walking Money. 2004. 23.95 (0-399-15169-9, Putnam & Grosset) Putnam Publishing Group, The.
Bothum, Ken Coffman and Mark. Alligator Alley. 2002. 372p. pap. 22.99 (1-4010-6218-0); text 32.99 (1-4010-6219-9); E-Book 8.00 (1-4010-6220-2) Xlibris Corp.
Bowden, Jesse Earle. Look & Tremble: A Novel of West Florida. 2000. (Illus.). 295p. 21.95 (0-942407-53-9) Father & Son Publishing.
Bowman, Eric. Before I Wake. 1998. 336p. reprint ed. mass mkt. 6.99 o.s.i (0-515-12353-6, Jove) Berkley Publishing Group.
—Before I Wake, Set. abr. ed. 1997. 25.00 o.p. (0-7871-1463-4, 695277) NewStar Media, Inc.
—Before I Wake. 1997. 320p. 24.95 o.p. (0-399-14263-0, G. P. Putnam's Sons) Penguin Group (USA) Inc.
Bradow, Stuart N. Daytona Dirt. 1999. (Illus.). 234p. per. 6.95 (0-9668159-0-4) Red Quill Publishing.

Brady, Steve & Roderus, Frank. Murder Revisited. 1996. 296p. (Orig.). mass mkt. 5.99 (*0-380-77489-5*, Avon Bks.) Morrow/Avon.

Brooks, Walter R. Freddy Goes to Florida. 1987. (Knopf Children's Paperbacks Ser.). (Illus.). 208p. (J). (gr. 3-7). 3.95 o.s.i (*0-394-88886-3*, Knopf Bks. for Young Readers) Random Hse. Children's Bks.

Bruce, Annette J. & Brooks, J. Stephen, eds. Sandspun: Florida Tales by Florida Tellers. 2001. xix, 149p. 16.95 (*1-56164-242-8*); pap. 9.95 (*1-56164-243-6*) Pineapple Pr., Inc.

Bruns, Donn. Jamaica Blue. Date not set. pap. (*0-312-30491-9*, Saint Martin's Griffin); E-Book 24.95 (*0-312-70486-0*); E-Book 18.95 (*0-312-70853-X*); 2003. 336p. mass mkt. 6.99 (*0-312-98506-1*, St. Martin's Paperbacks); 2002. 320p. 24.95 (*0-312-30490-0*, Saint Martin's Minotaur) St. Martin's Pr.

Buchanan, Edna. Act of Betrayal. unabr. collector's ed. 1996. (Britt Montero Ser.). audio 56.00 (*0-7366-3306-5*, 3960) Books on Tape, Inc.

—Act of Betrayal. abr. ed. (Britt Montero Mystery Ser.). 1997. 3p. audio 7.99 o.p. (*1-56740-148-1*, 617, Paperback Nova Audio Bks.); 1996. audio 17.95 o.p. (*1-56100-868-0*, 454, Nova Audio Bks.); 1996. 7p. audio 57.25 o.p. (*1-56100-296-8*, 786, Unabridged Library Editions); 1996. audio 23.95 o.p. (*1-56100-671-8*, 24, Bookcassette) Brilliance Audio.

—Act of Betrayal, Set. unabr. ed. 1999. audio 57.25 Highsmith Inc.

—Act of Betrayal. 1997. 448p. mass mkt. 5.99 (*0-7868-8923-3*); 1996. 320p. 21.95 o.p. (*0-7868-6098-7*) Hyperion Pr.

—Act of Betrayal. unabr. ed. 2000. (Britt Montero Mystery Ser.: Vol. 4). audio 60.00 (*0-7887-0488-5*, 94681E7) Recorded Bks., LLC.

—Contents under Pressure. unabr. collector's ed. 1993. (Britt Montero Ser.). audio 56.00 (*0-7366-2378-7*, 3150) Books on Tape, Inc.

—Contents under Pressure. 1992. 304p. (YA). 21.95 o.p. (*1-56282-932-7*) Hyperion Pr.

—Contents under Pressure. 1994. (Britt Montero Mysteries Ser.). 368p. mass mkt. 6.99 (*0-380-72260-7*, Avon Bks.) Morrow/Avon.

—Contents under Pressure. l.t. ed. 472p. pap. 2.99 o.s.i (*0-7669-1026-1*) World Pubns., Inc.

—Garden of Evil. (Britt Montero Mysteries Ser.). 2000. 320p. mass mkt. 6.99 (*0-380-79841-7*); 1999. 319p. 24.00 (*0-380-97654-4*) Morrow/Avon. (Avon Bks.).

—Garden of Evil. l.t. ed. 2000. (Mystery Ser.). 437p. 29.95 (*0-7862-2331-6*) Thorndike Pr.

—Margin of Error. unabr. collector's ed. 1997. (Britt Montero Ser.). audio 56.00 (*0-7366-3832-6*, 4552) Books on Tape, Inc.

—Margin of Error. abr. ed. 1998. audio 7.99 o.p. (*1-56740-253-4*, 675, Paperback Nova Audio Bks.); 1997. 8p. audio 57.25 o.p. (*1-56100-822-2*, 937, Unabridged Library Editions); 1997. audio 23.95 (*1-56100-747-1*, 171) Brilliance Audio.

—Margin of Error. l.t. ed. 1998. pap. 24.95 (*1-56895-563-4*, Wheeler Publishing, Inc.) Gale Group.

—Margin of Error. 1997. 304p. 22.95 o.p. (*0-7868-6232-7*); 1998. 384p. reprint ed. mass mkt. 5.99 (*0-7868-8931-4*) Hyperion Pr.

—Margin of Error. unabr. ed. (Britt Montero Mystery Ser.: Vol. 5). 1999. audio compact disk 79.00 (*0-7887-3424-5*, C1030E7); 1997. audio 75.00 (*0-7887-1777-4*, 95251E7) Recorded Bks., LLC.

—Margin of Error. l.t. ed. 2000. (Ulverscroft Large Print Ser.). 488p. (*0-7089-4189-3*, Ulverscroft) Thorpe, F. A. Pubs. GBR. *Dist:* Ulverscroft Large Print Bks., Ltd., Ulverscroft Large Print Canada, Ltd.

—Miami, It's Murder. unabr. collector's ed. 1994. (Britt Montero Ser.). audio 48.00 (*0-7366-2740-5*, 3466) Books on Tape, Inc.

—Miami, It's Murder. unabr. ed. 1994. audio 57.25 o.p. (*1-56100-175-9*, 941, Unabridged Library Editions); audio 21.95 o.p. (*1-56100-548-7*, 175, Bookcassette) Brilliance Audio.

—Miami, It's Murder. abr. ed. audio 17.00 o.p. (*1-55994-794-2*, CPN 2383, HarperAudio) HarperTrade.

—Miami, It's Murder. 1994. 256p. 21.95 o.p. (*1-56282-802-9*) Hyperion Pr.

—Miami, It's Murder. 1995. (Britt Montero Mysteries Ser.). 320p. mass mkt. 6.99 (*0-380-72261-5*, Avon Bks.) Morrow/Avon.

—Suitable for Framing. unabr. collector's ed. 1995. (Britt Montero Ser.). audio 56.00 (*0-7366-3072-4*, 3754) Books on Tape, Inc.

—Suitable for Framing. abr. ed. 1995. audio 16.95 o.p. (*1-56100-401-4*, 1383, Nova Audio Bks.); 9p. audio 57.25 o.p. (*1-56100-234-8*, 1062, Unabridged Library Editions); audio 23.95 o.p. (*1-56100-609-2*, 281, Bookcassette) Brilliance Audio.

—Suitable for Framing. l.t. ed. 1995. 25.95 o.p. (*1-56895-210-4*, Wheeler Publishing, Inc.) Gale Group.

—Suitable for Framing. 1996. 368p. mass mkt. 4.99 (*0-7868-8901-2*); 1995. 256p. 21.95 (*0-7868-6047-2*) Hyperion Pr.

—Suitable for Framing. abr. ed. 2000. audio 7.95 (*1-57815-028-0*, 1033, Media Bks. Audio Publishing) Media Bks., L. L. C.

—Suitable for Framing. unabr. ed. 2000. (Britt Montero Mystery Ser.: Vol. 3). audio 60.00 (*0-7887-0296-3*, 94489E7) Recorded Bks., LLC.

—You Only Die Twice. 2002. 368p. mass mkt. 6.99 (*0-380-79842-5*) Morrow/Avon.

Buechner, Frederick. The Storm. 208p. 2002. pap. 13.95 (*0-06-061145-6*); 1998. 18.00 (*0-06-061144-8*) HarperSanFrancisco.

—The Storm. l.t. ed. 1999. (Inspirational Ser.). 223p. 25.95 (*0-7838-8605-5*) Thorndike Pr.

Burns, Virginia Law. Gentle Hunter: Biography of Alice Evans, Bacteriologist. 1993. (Illus.). 224p. (J). (gr. 5-12). lib. bdg. 22.00 (*0-9604726-5-7*) Enterprise Pr.

Cameron, Stella. Key West. l.t. ed. 2000. 27.95 (*1-56895-851-X*, Wheeler Publishing, Inc.) Gale Group.

—Key West. 2000. 48p. mass mkt. 6.99 (*0-8217-6595-7*); 1999. 392p. 23.00 o.s.i (*1-57566-454-2*) Kensington Publishing Corp.

Cannell, Stephen J. Final Victim. 1997. 384p. mass mkt. 7.99 (*0-380-72816-8*, Avon Bks.); 1996. 416p. 25.00 o.p. (*0-688-14775-5*, Morrow, William & Co.) Morrow/Avon.

—Final Victim. abr. ed. 1996. 24.95 o.p. (*0-7871-1111-2*, 694124) NewStar Media, Inc.

Carballo, Arles, et al. In the Shadow of Gleam. Koenigsberg, Linda, ed. 2nd ed. 2000. 218p. 23.95 (*0-9672603-1-0*) Carbapr.

Casemore, Robert F. Splendid Morning. l.t. ed. 1999. (Romance Ser.). 439p. 26.95 (*0-7838-8474-5*) Thorndike Pr.

Casey, Barbara. Shyla's Initiative. 2002. 149p. pap. (*1-890109-78-9*, Cross Time) Crossquarter Publishing Group.

Chapman, Herb & Chapman, Muncy. Wiregrass Country. 1998. (Pioneer Series of Westerns Ser.). 370p. 16.95 (*1-56164-164-2*); pap. 9.95 (*1-56164-156-1*) Pineapple Pr., Inc.

Chiarella, Tom. Foley's Luck. 1994. 3.99 o.p. (*0-517-11620-0*) Random Hse. Value Publishing.

Child, Lee. Tripwire. 2000. 432p. mass mkt. 7.99 (*0-515-12863-5*, Jove) Berkley Publishing Group.

—Tripwire. l.t. ed. 2000. (Wheeler Softcover Ser.). pap. 25.95 (*1-56895-912-5*, Wheeler Publishing, Inc.) Gale Group.

—Tripwire. 1999. 343p. 23.95 o.p. (*0-399-14467-6*, G. P. Putnam's Sons) Penguin Group (USA) Inc.

—Tripwire, unabr. ed. 2000. 12p. audio 94.95 (*1-86042-691-3*, 26913) Soundings, Ltd. GBR. *Dist:* Ulverscroft Large Print Bks., Ltd.

Civil-Brown, Sue. Breaking All the Rules. 2002. 384p. mass mkt. 5.99 (*0-06-050231-2*) HarperCollins Pubs.

—Next Stop, Paradise. 2001. 384p. mass mkt. 5.99 (*0-380-81180-4*, Avon Bks.) Morrow/Avon.

—Tempting Mr. Wright. 2000. 384p. mass mkt. 5.99 (*0-380-81179-0*, Avon Bks.) Morrow/Avon.

Clark, Carol Higgins. Snagged. l.t. ed. 1994. 22.95 o.p. (*0-7927-1915-8*); pap. 20.95 o.p. (*0-7927-1914-X*) BBC Audiobooks America.

—Snagged. abr. ed. 1993. (Regan Reilly Mystery Ser.). audio 16.95 o.p. (*1-55800-787-3*, 391606) NewStar Media, Inc.

—Snagged. 1994. 320p. mass mkt. 7.99 (*0-446-60076-8*); 1993. 227p. 28.00 (*0-446-51548-5*) Warner Bks., Inc.

Cochrun, Tom. Sanibel Arcanum. 1994. 250p. pap. 15.95 (*1-878208-41-1*) Emmis Bks.

Coe, Marian. Legacy. 1993. (Illus.). 373p. pap. 14.95 (*0-9633341-0-7*); reprint ed. 19.95 (*0-9633341-1-5*) SouthLore Pr.

Cohen, Nancy J. Body Wave: A Bad Hair Day Mystery. 2002. (Bad Hair Day Mysteries Ser.: Vol. 4). 304p. 22.00 (*0-7582-0068-4*) Kensington Publishing Corp.

—Hair Raiser. (Bad Hair Day Mysteries Ser.). 2001. 288p. mass mkt. 5.99 o.s.i (*1-57566-688-X*); 2000. 34p. 20.00 o.s.i (*1-57566-622-7*) Kensington Publishing Corp.

—Murder by Manicure. (Bad Hair Day Mysteries Ser.). 2002. 34p. mass mkt. 5.99 (*1-57566-741-X*); 2001. 24p. 22.00 o.s.i (*1-57566-687-1*) Kensington Publishing Corp.

—Permed to Death. (Bad Hair Day Mysteries Ser.). 2000. 32p. mass mkt. 5.99 (*1-57566-624-3*); 1999. 293p. 20.00 o.s.i (*1-57566-482-8*, Kensington Bks.) Kensington Publishing Corp.

Cohen, Paula Marantz. Jane Austen in Boca. l.t. ed. 2003. (Thorndike Press Large Print Women's Fiction Ser.). 388p. 28.95 (*0-7862-4973-0*) Thorndike Pr.

Coleman, Lynn A. Key West: Four Complete Novels of Building Community & Love. 2003. (Historical Collections). 464p. pap. 6.97 (*1-58660-962-9*) Barbour Publishing, Inc.

Conley, Robert J. War Woman: A Novel of the Real People. 1998. 368p. pap. 15.95 (*0-312-19361-0*, Saint Martin's Griffin); 1997. 384p. 25.95 o.p. (*0-312-17058-0*) St. Martin's Pr.

—War Woman: A Novel of the Real People. 2001. 357p. pap. 17.95 (*0-8061-3369-4*) Univ. of Oklahoma Pr.

Cook, Ann Turner. Shadow over Cedar Key: A Brandy O'Bannon Mystery. 2003. 258p. pap. 16.95 (*0-595-27843-4*) iUniverse, Inc.

Cook, Robin. Terminal. 384p. 1996. mass mkt. 7.99 (*0-425-15506-4*); 1994. mass mkt. 6.99 o.s.i (*0-425-14094-6*) Berkley Publishing Group.

—Terminal. 1993. 400p. 21.95 o.p. (*0-399-13771-8*, G. P. Putnam's Sons) Penguin Group (USA) Inc.

—Terminal. pap. 6.98 o.p. (*0-8317-4385-9*) Smithmark Pubs., Inc.

—Terminal. 1994. 14.04 (*0-606-06051-0*) Turtleback Bks.

Corcoran, Tom. Gumbo Limbo. 1999. 293p. 23.95 (*0-312-24194-1*, Saint Martin's Minotaur) St. Martin's Pr.

—Gumbo Limbo: An Alex Rutledge Mystery. 2000. 304p. mass mkt. 6.50 (*0-312-97570-8*, St. Martin's Paperbacks) St. Martin's Pr.

—The Mango Opera. 304p. 1999. mass mkt. 6.99 (*0-312-96988-0*, St. Martin's Paperbacks); Vol. 1. 1998. (Mango Opera Ser.: Vol. 1). 22.95 (*0-312-18628-2*, Saint Martin's Minotaur) St. Martin's Pr.

Cornwell, Patricia. Blow Fly: A Scarpetta Novel. l.t. ed. 2003. 674p. 32.95 (*0-7862-5690-7*) Gale Group.

—Blow Fly: A Scarpetta Novel. ltd. ed. 2003. 400p. (*0-399-15135-4*, G. P. Putnam's Sons) Penguin Putnam Bks. for Young Readers.

—Blow Fly: A Scarpetta Novel. 2003. E-Book 26.95 (*0-7865-4293-4*) Penguin Putnam, Inc E-Books.

—Blow Fly: A Scarpetta Novel. 2003. 480p. 26.95 (*0-399-15089-7*); audio 25.95 (*0-399-15117-6*, Putnam Berkley Audio); audio compact disk 29.95 (*0-399-15118-4*, Putnam Berkley Audio); 404.25 (*0-399-19755-9*); 508.05 (*0-399-19756-7*); audio 44.95 (*0-399-15119-2*, Putnam Berkley Audio) Putnam Publishing Group, The.

Coupland, Douglas. All Families Are Psychotic. 288p. 2002. pap. 13.95 (*1-58234-215-6*); 2001. 24.95 (*1-58234-165-6*) Bloomsbury Publishing.

Coyle, Beverly. In Troubled Waters. 1993. 224p. 19.95 o.p. (*0-395-57437-4*) Houghton Mifflin Co.

—In Troubled Waters. 1994. 336p. pap. 19.00 (*0-14-023301-6*, Penguin Bks.) Penguin Group (USA) Inc.

Craig, Kit. Twice Burned. 1995. 352p. mass mkt. 5.99 o.s.i (*0-425-14877-7*) Berkley Publishing Group.

—Twice Burned. 286p. 3.98 o.p. (*0-8317-7063-5*) Smithmark Pubs., Inc.

—Twice Burned: A Novel. 1993. 19.95 o.p. (*0-316-15933-6*) Little Brown & Co.

Cresswell, Jasmine. The Inheritance. 2000. 408p. mass mkt. (*1-55166-511-5*, 1-66511-6, Mira Bks.) Harlequin Enterprises, Ltd.

Crews, Harry. All We Need of Hell: A Novel. 1987. 160p. 14.95 o.p. (*0-06-015680-5*) HarperTrade.

—Celebration: A Novel. 1999. 272p. pap. 13.00 (*0-684-84810-4*, Touchstone); 1998. 256p. 22.50 (*0-684-83758-7*, Simon & Schuster) Simon & Schuster.

—The Mulching of America: A Novel. 1996. 272p. pap. 12.00 (*0-684-82541-4*, Touchstone); 1995. 256p. 22.00 (*0-684-80934-6*, Simon & Schuster) Simon & Schuster.

Crump, David. Conflict of Interest: A Novel about Trial Lawyers, Greed, Passion, Power, Revenge...& Justice. 1997. 288p. (Orig.). pap. 14.95 (*0-89407-122-X*, 122X) Strawberry Hill Pr.

Curtis, James R. Shango. 1996. 197p. (Orig.). pap. 11.95 (*1-55885-096-1*) Arte Publico Pr.

Daniels, Sarah. The Woman with Qualities. 2002. 272p. pap. 14.95 (*1-893302-11-3*) Dandelion Bks., LLC.

Darty, Peggy. Seascape. 1996. (Palisades Pure Romance Ser.). 272p. pap. 9.99 o.s.i (*0-88070-927-8*, Palisades) Multnomah Pubs., Inc.

Date, S. V. Black Sunshine. 2003. 320p. mass mkt. 6.99 (*0-425-19216-4*) Berkley Publishing Group.

—Black Sunshine. 2002. 24.95 o.s.i (*0-399-14946-5*) Putnam Publishing Group, The.

—Deep Water. 2002. 304p. mass mkt. 6.99 o.s.i (*0-425-18692-X*) Berkley Publishing Group.

—Deep Water. 2001. 240p. 23.95 o.s.i (*0-399-14815-9*) Penguin Group (USA) Inc.

—Smokeout. 2001. 288p. reprint ed. mass mkt. 6.50 o.s.i (*0-425-18275-4*, Prime Crime) Berkley Publishing Group.

—Smokeout. 2000. 240p. 23.95 o.s.i (*0-399-14649-0*) Penguin Group (USA) Inc.

—Speed Week. 1999. 224p. 22.95 o.p. (*0-399-14513-3*, G. P. Putnam's Sons) Penguin Group (USA) Inc.

Davis, Corbett A., Jr. The Deadly Reef. 2000. (Illus.). 172p. 19.95 (*1-56167-554-7*) Noble Hse.

Davis, Don. Death Cruise. 1996. (Illus.). 304p. mass mkt. 6.50 (*0-312-95786-6*, St. Martin's Paperbacks) St. Martin's Pr.

Delacorta. The Rap Factor: Novel. Texier, Catherine, tr. from FRE. 1993. 208p. pap. 11.00 (*0-87113-617-1*, Atlantic Monthly Pr.); 200p. 18.00 o.p. (*0-87113-529-9*) Grove/Atlantic, Inc.

Deleva, John. Hours Like Diamonds. 2000. 169p. (Orig.). pap. 11.77 (*0-9701668-0-X*) Johnsbook.com.

Deveraux, Jude. High Tide. l.t. ed. 1999. 25.95 (*1-56895-800-5*, Wheeler Publishing, Inc.) Gale Group.

—High Tide. 2003. (Illus.). 368p. mass mkt. 5.99 (*0-7434-6713-2*, Pocket); 2000. (Illus.). 368p. mass mkt. 7.99 (*0-671-01417-X*, Pocket); 1999. 320p. 24.00 o.s.i (*0-671-01416-1*, Atria) Simon & Schuster.

Dexter, Pete. The Paperboy. 1996. 336p. pap. 19.00 (*0-385-31572-4*) Dell Publishing.

—The Paperboy. l.t. ed. 1995. (Large Print Bks.). pap. 23.95 (*1-56895-217-1*, Wheeler Publishing, Inc.) Gale Group.

—The Paperboy. unabr. ed. 1999. audio compact disk 75.00 (*0-7887-3714-7*, C1071E7); 1997. audio 60.00 (*0-7887-0659-4*, 94836E7) Recorded Bks., LLC.

Dorsey, Tim. Cadillac Beach. 2004. 352p. 24.95 (*0-06-052046-9*, Morrow, William & Co.) Morrow/Avon.

—Florida Roadkill. 2000. 384p. mass mkt. 6.99 (*0-380-73233-5*, HarperTorch); 1999. 273p. 24.00 o.p. (*0-688-16782-9*, Morrow, William & Co.) Morrow/Avon.

—Hammerhead Ranch Motel. 2001. 384p. mass mkt. 6.99 (*0-380-73234-3*, HarperTorch); 2000. 304p. 24.00 (*0-688-16783-7*, Morrow, William & Co.) Morrow/Avon.

—Orange Crush. 2002. 384p. mass mkt. 6.99 (*0-06-103154-2*) HarperCollins Pubs.

—Orange Crush. 2001. 304p. 25.00 (*0-06-018577-5*, Morrow, William & Co.) Morrow/Avon.

—The Stingray Shuffle. 2004. 400p. mass mkt. 7.50 (*0-06-055693-5*, HarperTorch); 2003. 320p. 24.95 (*0-06-052045-0*, Morrow, William & Co.) Morrow/Avon.

—Triggerfish Twist. 2003. 400p. mass mkt. 6.99 (*0-06-103155-0*, HarperTorch); 2002. 320p. 24.95 (*0-06-018571-6*, Morrow, William & Co.) Morrow/Avon.

Douglas, Marjory S. Nine Florida Stories: A Florida Sand Dollar Book. E-Book 17.95 (*0-8130-1847-1*) Univ. Pr. of Florida.

—Nine Florida Stories: A Florida Sand Dollar Book. McCarthy, Kevin M., ed. 1990. 216p. 22.95 (*0-8130-0988-X*); pap. 17.95 (*0-8130-0994-4*) Univ. Pr. of Florida.

Douglass, Thea C. Royal Poinciana. 1988. 448p. 18.95 o.p. (*1-55611-048-0*) Fine, Donald I. Bks.

Eberhart, Mignon G. The White Dress. 1997. (Romance Ser.). 225p. lib. bdg. 23.95 (*0-7862-1131-8*, Five Star) Gale Group.

Elbrecht, Joyce & Fakundiny, Lydia. The Restorationist: Text One: A Collaborative Fiction by Jael B. Juba. (SUNY Series, The Margins of Literature). 429p. (C). 1994. pap. text 17.95 (*0-7914-1532-5*); 1993. text 18.50 (*0-7914-1531-7*) State Univ. of New York Pr.

Elkin, Stanley. Mrs. Ted Bliss. 2002. (American Literature Ser.). 294p. reprint ed. pap. 14.95 (*1-56478-322-7*) Dalkey Archive Pr.

—Mrs. Ted Bliss. l.t. ed. 1996. pap. 22.95 o.p. (*1-56895-314-3*, Wheeler Publishing, Inc.) Gale Group.

—Mrs. Ted Bliss. 1995. 304p. 22.95 (*0-7868-6104-5*) Hyperion Pr.

—Mrs. Ted Bliss. 1996. pap. 12.00 (*0-380-72896-6*, Avon Bks.) Morrow/Avon.

—Mrs. Ted Bliss. unabr. ed. 1997. audio 78.00 (*0-7887-1073-7*, 95086E7) Recorded Bks., LLC.

Eringer, Robert. Lo Mein. 2000. 224p. 19.95 (*1-929175-14-0*); pap. 14.95 (*1-929175-22-1*) Cote Literary Group, The. (Corinthian Bks.).

Evans, Elizabeth. Carter Clay: A Novel. 1999. 416p. o.s.i (*0-06-019265-8*, HarperFlamingo) HarperCollins Pubs. Canada, Ltd.

—Carter Clay: A Novel. 2000. 416p. pap. 14.00 (*0-06-092982-0*, Perennial) HarperTrade.

Fairchild, Sally. Orchid Isle. 2000. 384p. mass mkt. (*1-55166-604-9*, 1-66604-9, Mira Bks.) Harlequin Enterprises, Ltd.

Fernandez, Roberto G. Holy Radishes. 1995. 298p. 17.95 (*1-55885-075-9*); pap. 9.95 (*1-55885-076-7*) Arte Publico Pr.

Ferrigno, Robert. Heartbreaker. 2000. 368p. mass mkt. 7.50 (*0-446-60891-2*) Warner Bks., Inc.

—Heartbreaker Signed Edition. 1999. 24.00 o.s.i (*0-676-58995-2*) Knopf, Alfred A. Inc.

Files, Lolita. Scenes from a Sistah. 1998. 288p. pap. 13.99 (*0-446-67442-7*); 1998. 320p. mass mkt. 6.50 (*0-446-60539-5*); 1997. 288p. 22.00 o.p. (*0-446-52100-0*) Warner Bks., Inc.

Fisher, David E. Hostage One. 1990. mass mkt. 4.95 o.p. (*0-312-92144-6*, St. Martin's Paperbacks) St. Martin's Pr.

Fo, Dario. Johan Padan & the Discovery of the Americas. Jenkins, Ron, tr. from ITA. 2001. (Illus.). xii, 131p. pap. 15.00 (*0-8021-3777-6*, Grove Pr.) Grove/Atlantic, Inc.

Foley, Thomas. Measuring Lives: A Thriller. 1996. 352p. 24.00 (*1-56980-091-X*) Barricade Bks., Inc.

Fowler, Connie M. River of Hidden Dreams. 1994. 320p. 22.95 o.p. (*0-399-13912-5*, G. P. Putnam's Sons) Penguin Group (USA) Inc.

—River of Hidden Dreams. abr. ed. 1994. audio 17.00 o.s.i (*1-57042-062-9*, 4-520629) Time Warner AudioBooks.

—Sugar Cage. l.t. ed. 1993. (General Ser.). 487p. lib. bdg. 20.95 o.p. (*0-8161-5577-1*, Macmillan Reference USA) Gale Group.

—Sugar Cage. 1992. 320p. 19.95 o.p. (*0-399-13681-9*, G. P. Putnam's Sons) Penguin Group (USA) Inc.

—Sugar Cage. Sacco, Maryanne, ed. 1993. 320p. pap. 12.95 (*0-671-74809-2*, Washington Square Pr.) Simon & Schuster.

Fowler, Connie May. Before Women Had Wings. 1999. 320p. mass mkt. 6.99 (*0-8041-1890-6*, Ivy Bks.); 1997. 268p. pap. 12.00 (*0-449-91144-6*, Fawcett) Ballantine Bks.

—Before Women Had Wings. l.t. ed. 1996. 23.95 o.p. (*1-56895-377-1*, Wheeler Publishing, Inc.) Gale Group.

—Before Women Had Wings. 1996. 288p. 22.95 o.s.i (*0-399-14129-4*, G. P. Putnam's Sons) Penguin Group (USA) Inc.

—Remembering Blue. l.t. ed. 2000. (Large Print Book Ser.). 416p. 27.95 (*1-56895-942-7*, Wheeler Publishing, Inc.) Gale Group.

—Remembering Blue: A Novel. 2001. (Reader's Circle Ser.). 320p. pap. 14.00 (*0-345-43924-4*, Ballantine Bks.) Ballantine Bks.

—River of Hidden Dreams. 1995. 336p. pap. 14.00 (*0-449-98363-3*, Fawcett) Ballantine Bks.

—River of Hidden Dreams. l.t. ed. 1994. 305p. reprint ed. lib. bdg. 23.95 (*0-8161-5954-8*, Macmillan Reference USA) Gale Group.

Fox, Ronald. Oaken Rings. 2000. (Illus.). 247p. pap. 17.95 o.p. (*1-929925-44-1*) FirstPublish.

Francis, Dorothy Brenner. Keys to Love. l.t. ed. 2002. 185p. 26.95 (*0-7862-4036-9*) Gale Group.

Freundlich, Jeffrey. Tropical Depression. 1994. 256p. 20.95 o.p. (*1-55611-401-X*) Fine, Donald I. Bks.

Friedman, Mickey. Magic Mirror. l.t. ed. 1990. (General Ser.). 354p. lib. bdg. 18.95 o.p. (*0-8161-4823-6*, Macmillan Reference USA) Gale Group.

—Magic Mirror. 256p. 1989. pap. 3.95 o.p. (*0-14-010847-5*, Penguin Bks.); 1988. 16.95 o.p. (*0-670-82132-2*) Viking Penguin.

—Riptide. 1993. 256p. 20.95 o.p. (*0-312-10417-0*, Saint Martin's Minotaur) St. Martin's Pr.

—A Temporary Ghost. l.t. ed. 1991. (General Ser.). 285p. lib. bdg. 18.95 o.p. (*0-8161-5012-5*, Macmillan Reference USA) Gale Group.

—A Temporary Ghost. (Georgia Lee Maxwell Mystery Ser.). 224p. 1990. pap. 4.50 o.p. (*0-14-010848-3*, Penguin Bks.); 1989. 16.95 o.p. (*0-670-82133-0*) Viking Penguin.

Gaddis, Peggy. Love Is Enough. l.t. ed. 1992. 18.95 o.p. (*0-7927-1226-9*, CH0255) BBC Audiobooks America.

—Second Chance at Love. l.t. ed. 1993. 18.95 o.p. (*0-7927-1791-0*); pap. 17.95 o.p. (*0-7927-1790-2*) BBC Audiobooks America.

Gannon, Michael V. Secret Missions: A Novel. 1994. 320p. 22.00 o.p. (*0-06-017733-0*) HarperTrade.

Garcia-Aguilera, Carolina. Bitter Sugar. 2001. (Lupe Solano Mystery Ser.). 336p. 24.00 (*0-380-97781-8*, Morrow, William & Co.) Morrow/Avon.

—Bloody Secrets. 1999. 336p. reprint ed. mass mkt. 6.50 o.s.i (*0-425-16779-8*, Prime Crime) Berkley Publishing Group.

—Bloody Secrets. 1998. 274p. 23.95 o.p. (*0-399-14386-6*, G. P. Putnam's Sons) Penguin Group (USA) Inc.

—Bloody Shame: A Lupe Solano Mystery. 1998. 320p. mass mkt. 6.50 o.s.i (*0-425-16140-4*, Prime Crime) Berkley Publishing Group.

—Bloody Shame: A Lupe Solano Mystery. 1997. 288p. 22.95 o.p. (*0-399-14256-8*, G. P. Putnam's Sons) Penguin Group (USA) Inc.

—Bloody Waters: A Lupe Solano Mystery. 1997. (Lupo Solano Mystery Ser.). 304p. mass mkt. 5.99 o.s.i (*0-425-15670-2*, Prime Crime) Berkley Publishing Group.

—Bloody Waters: A Lupe Solano Mystery. 1996. 256p. 21.95 o.p. (*0-399-14157-X*, G. P. Putnam's Sons) Penguin Group (USA) Inc.

—A Miracle in Paradise. (Lupe Solano Mystery Ser.). 2000. 352p. mass mkt. 5.99 o.s.i (*0-380-80738-6*); 1999. viii, 277p. 23.00 (*0-380-97779-6*) Morrow/Avon. (Avon Bks.).

Garcia, Cristina. The Aguero Sisters. 1998. 103.60 o.s.i (*0-345-91389-2*); 103.60 o.s.i (*0-345-91390-6*); 336p. pap. 14.00 (*0-345-40651-6*, Ballantine Bks.) Ballantine Bks.

—Las Hermanas Aguero: Una Novela. 1997. (SPA.). 320p. pap. 13.95 (*0-679-78145-5*, RH9081, Vintage) Knopf Publishing Group.

Garrett, George P. The King of Babylon Shall Not Come Against You. 352p. 1998. pap. 13.00 (*0-15-600553-0*, Harvest Bks.); 1996. 24.00 o.s.i (*0-15-157554-1*) Harcourt Trade Pubs.

Gear, Kathleen O'Neal & Gear, W. Michael. People of the Lightning. (First North Americans Ser.). 1996. 587p. mass mkt. 7.99 (*0-8125-1556-0*, Tor Bks.); 1995. 480p. 16.25 o.p. (*0-312-85852-3*, Forge Bks.) Doherty, Tom Assocs., LLC.

—People of the Lightning. 1996. 13.04 (*0-606-11733-4*) Turtleback Bks.

George, Anne. Murder Makes Waves. l.t. ed. 2000. (Beeler Large Print Mystery Ser.). 246p. 26.95 (*1-57490-274-1*, Beeler Large Print Bks.) Beeler, Thomas T. Publisher.

—Murder Makes Waves. (Southern Sisters Mysteries Ser.). 1998. 272p. mass mkt. 6.99 (*0-380-78450-5*); 1997. 256p. 20.00 o.p. (*0-380-97527-0*) Morrow/Avon. (Avon Bks.).

Gischler, Victor. Gun Monkeys. 2003. 304p. mass mkt. 6.99 (*0-440-24128-6*) Dell Publishing.

—Gun Monkeys. 2001. 280p. pap. 15.00 (*0-9663473-6-6*) UglyTown.

Glassman, Steve. Blood on the Moon: A Novel of Old Florida. 1990. 324p. (Orig.). pap. 9.95 o.p. (*0-934040-16-8*) Pathway Bk. Service.

—Blood on the Moon: A Novel of Old Florida. 2002. 325p. (Orig.). pap. 22.95 (*0-595-22636-1*, Mystery Writers of America Presents) iUniverse, Inc.

—The Near Death Experiment. 2001. 280p. pap. 16.95 (*0-9666173-7-1*) Tropical Pr., Inc.

Goingback, Owl. Breed. 2002. 352p. mass mkt. 6.99 o.s.i (*0-451-20567-7*) NAL.

Gordon, Alison. Night Game. 1993. 269p. 18.95 o.p. (*0-312-09062-5*, Saint Martin's Minotaur) St. Martin's Pr.

—Night Games: A Kate Henry Mystery. 1993. 271p. mass mkt. 6.99 (*0-7710-3424-5*) McClelland & Stewart/Tundra Bks.

Graham, Heather. Captive. l.t. ed. 2000. (Large Print Book Ser.). 580p. 28.95 (*1-56895-889-7*, Wheeler Publishing, Inc.) Gale Group.

—Captive. 1996. 464p. mass mkt. 6.99 o.s.i (*0-451-40687-7*, Topaz) NAL.

—Drop Dead Gorgeous. l.t. ed. 1999. 27.95 (*1-56895-667-3*, Wheeler Publishing, Inc.) Gale Group.

—Drop Dead Gorgeous. 1998. 352p. mass mkt. 6.99 (*0-451-40846-2*, Onyx) NAL.

—Hurricane Bay. 2003. 400p. mass mkt. (*1-55166-665-0*, Mira Bks.) Harlequin Enterprises, Ltd.

—Hurricane Bay. l.t. ed. 2003. (Romance Ser.). 29.95 (*0-7862-5532-3*) Thorndike Pr.

—Night Heat. 2001. 588p. pap. (*1-55166-787-8*, 1-66787-2, Mira Bks.) Harlequin Enterprises, Ltd.

—Runaway. 1995. 512p. mass mkt. 6.99 (*0-440-21688-5*) Dell Publishing.

—Runaway. l.t. ed. 1994. pap. 21.95 o.p. (*1-56895-080-2*, Wheeler Publishing, Inc.) Gale Group.

—Runaway. abr. ed. 1994. audio 16.95 (*1-879371-83-9*, 40300) Publishing Mills, Inc., The.

—A Season for Love. l.t. ed. 2000. (Famous Authors Ser.). 303p. 27.95 (*0-7862-2425-8*) Thorndike Pr.

—Surrender. 1998. (Star-Romance Ser.). 450p. 26.95 (*0-7862-1602-6*, Five Star); 26.95 (*1-56895-579-0*, Wheeler Publishing, Inc.) Gale Group.

—Surrender. 1998. 386p. mass mkt. 6.99 o.s.i (*0-451-40690-7*, Onyx) NAL.

—Tall, Dark & Deadly. l.t. ed. (Wheeler Press Paperback Ser.). 2000. pap. 11.95 (*1-56895-971-0*); 1999. 27.95 (*1-56895-799-8*) Gale Group. (Wheeler Publishing, Inc.).

—Tender Taming. l.t. ed. 2000. (Famous Authors Ser.). 287p. 26.95 (*0-7862-2521-1*) Thorndike Pr.

—Triumph. l.t. ed. 2000. (Wheeler Romance Ser.). 664p. 25.95 (*1-56895-131-0*, Wheeler Publishing, Inc.) Gale Group.

—Triumph. 2000. 496p. mass mkt. 6.99 o.s.i (*0-451-40849-7*, Signet Bks.) NAL.

—When Next We Love. l.t. ed. 1991. 19.95 o.p. (*0-7927-0833-4*, CH084); pap. 17.95 o.p. (*0-7927-0834-2*, CS0182) BBC Audiobooks America.

—When Next We Love. 1983. (Candlelight Regency Romance Ser.: No. 117). pap. 1.95 o.s.i (*0-440-19588-8*) Dell Publishing.

—When Next We Love. l.t. ed. 2000. (Famous Authors Ser.). 311p. 27.95 (*0-7862-2522-X*, MML06400-171944) Thorndike Pr.

Gramling, Lee. Ghosts of the Green Swamp: A Cracker Western. 1996. (Cracker Western Ser.). 296p. 14.95 (*1-56164-120-0*); (gr. 4-7). pap. 8.95 o.s.i (*1-56164-126-X*) Pineapple Pr., Inc.

—Ninety-Mile Praire. 2002. (Cracker Western Ser.). (Illus.). 280p. pap. 8.95 (*1-56164-257-6*); 279p. 14.95 (*1-56164-255-X*) Pineapple Pr., Inc.

—Riders of the Suwannee. 1993. 292p. 14.95 (*1-56164-046-8*); (gr. 4-7). pap. 8.95 o.s.i (*1-56164-043-3*) Pineapple Pr., Inc.

—Thunder on the St. Johns. 1994. 260p. 14.95 (*1-56164-064-6*); (gr. 4-7). pap. 8.95 (*1-56164-080-8*) Pineapple Pr., Inc.

—Trail from St. Augustine. 1993. 264p. 14.95 (*1-56164-047-6*); (gr. 4-7). pap. 8.95 o.s.i (*1-56164-042-5*) Pineapple Pr., Inc.

Green, Tim. The Red Zone. abr. ed. 1998. audio 17.98 (*1-57042-594-9*) Time Warner AudioBooks.

—The Red Zone. 1999. 384p. mass mkt. 7.50 (*0-446-60756-8*); 1998. 325p. 24.00 o.p. (*0-446-52298-8*) Warner Bks., Inc.

Grey, Harper. Fast Ride with the Top Down. 160p. 1997. pap. text 9.95 o.p. (*1-55583-416-7*); 2nd ed. 1996. reprint ed. 19.95 o.p. (*1-55583-370-5*) Alyson Pubns.

Grippando, James M. The Informant. l.t. ed. 1997. lib. bdg. 24.95 (*1-57490-079-X*, Beeler Large Print Bks.) Beeler, Thomas T. Publisher.

—The Informant. 1996. 368p. 23.00 o.p. (*0-06-017693-8*) HarperCollins Pubs.

—The Pardon. l.t. ed. 1994. 24.95 o.p. (*1-56895-159-0*, Wheeler Publishing, Inc.) Gale Group.

—The Pardon. 1994. 320p. 22.00 o.p. (*0-06-017782-9*) HarperTrade.

Hailey, Arthur. Detective. 1998. 608p. reprint ed. mass mkt. 7.99 (*0-425-16386-5*) Berkley Publishing Group.

—Detective. l.t. ed. 1997. pap. 24.00 o.p. (*0-7838-8132-0*, Macmillan Reference USA) Gale Group.

—Detective. 1999. (SPA.). (*84-08-02910-X*) GeoPlaneta, Editorial, S. A.

Haldeman, Joe. The Coming. 2001. 288p. reprint ed. mass mkt. 6.99 (*0-441-00876-3*) Ace Bks.

Hall, James W. Blackwater Sound. abr. ed. 2002. audio 24.95 o.p. (*1-58788-894-7*, 3413, Nova Audio Bks.); audio 32.95 (*1-58788-892-0*, 3411, Brilliance Audio Unabridged) Brilliance Audio.

—Blackwater Sound. E-Book 24.95 (*0-312-70384-8*); 2002. 368p. mass mkt. 6.99 (*0-312-98628-9*, St. Martin's Paperbacks); 2002. (Illus.). 352p. 24.95 (*0-312-20384-5*) St. Martin's Pr.

—Bones of Coral. 1993. 400p. mass mkt. 7.50 (*0-440-21453-X*) Dell Publishing.

—Bones of Coral. 1992. 3.99 o.p. (*0-517-08828-2*) Random Hse. Value Publishing.

—Bones of Coral, unabr. ed. audio 85.00 (*1-55690-668-4*, 92316E7) Recorded Bks., LLC.

—Buzz Cut. 1997. 464p. mass mkt. 7.50 (*0-440-21782-2*) Dell Publishing.

—Buzz Cut. abr. ed. 1999. audio 9.99 o.s.i (*0-553-70207-6*, RH Audio) Random Hse. Audio Publishing Group.

—Buzz Cut. unabr. ed. 1999. audio compact disk 99.00 (*0-7887-3413-X*, C1019E7); 1996. audio 85.00 (*0-7887-0628-4*, 94802E7) Recorded Bks., LLC.

—Gone Wild. 1996. 464p. mass mkt. 7.50 (*0-440-21781-4*) Dell Publishing.

—Gone Wild. l.t. ed. 1995. 607p. 25.95 o.p. (*0-7838-1368-6*, Macmillan Reference USA) Gale Group.

—Gone Wild, unabr. ed. 1995. audio 85.00 (*0-7887-0264-5*, 94473E7) Recorded Bks., LLC.

—Hard Aground. 1994. 464p. mass mkt. 7.50 (*0-440-21357-6*) Dell Publishing.

—Hard Aground. l.t. ed. 1993. 89.95 o.p. incl. audio (*0-7838-1113-6*, Macmillan Reference USA) Gale Group.

—Mean High Tide. 1995. 448p. mass mkt. 7.50 (*0-440-21355-X*) Dell Publishing.

—Mean High Tide. l.t. ed. 1994. 545p. lib. bdg. 23.95 (*0-8161-7441-5*, Macmillan Reference USA) Gale Group.

—Mean High Tide. abr. ed. 1999. audio 9.99 o.s.i (*0-553-70191-6*, RH Audio) Random Hse. Audio Publishing Group.

—Mean High Tide, unabr. ed. 1994. audio 78.00 (*0-7887-0026-X*, 94225E7) Recorded Bks., LLC.

—Mean High Tide. 372p. 4.98 o.p. (*0-8317-5431-1*) Smithmark Pubs., Inc.

—Off the Chart. 2003. (Illus.). audio compact disk 30.00 (*1-55927-825-0*); pap. 25.95 incl. audio (*1-55927-883-8*) Audio Renaissance.

—Off the Chart. 2003. 8p. 69.95 (*0-7927-2890-4*); 10p. pap. 94.95 (*0-7927-2891-2*) BBC Audiobooks America.

—Off the Chart. E-Book 20.95 (*0-312-71013-5*) St. Martin's Pr.

—Off the Chart. l.t. ed. 2003. 586p. 30.95 (*0-7862-5796-2*, Large Print Pr.) Thorndike Pr.

—Red Sky at Night. 1998. 400p. reprint ed. mass mkt. 6.99 (*0-440-22574-4*) Doubleday Publishing.

—Red Sky at Night, unabr. ed. 1997. audio 75.00 (*0-7887-1294-2*, 95128E7) Recorded Bks., LLC.

—Tropical Freeze. l.t. ed. 2003. lib. bdg. 28.95 (*1-58547-288-3*, Premier) Ctr. Point Large Print.

—Tropical Freeze. 1999. 446p. pap. 9.00 (*0-393-31895-8*); 1989. 18.95 o.p. (*0-393-02694-9*) Norton, W. W. & Co., Inc.

—Tropical Freeze. 1991. 320p. mass mkt. 6.50 o.p. (*0-446-36062-7*) Warner Bks., Inc.

—Under Cover of Daylight. 1997. 352p. pap. 9.95 o.s.i (*0-385-31867-7*, Delta) Dell Publishing.

—Under Cover of Daylight. l.t. ed. 2001. (Large Print Book Ser.). 358p. 26.95 (*1-58724-028-9*, Wheeler Publishing, Inc.) Gale Group.

—Under Cover of Daylight. 2001. 272p. pap. 10.00 (*0-393-32125-8*); 1987. 16.95 o.p. (*0-393-02484-9*) Norton, W. W. & Co., Inc.

—Under Cover of Daylight. 1988. 384p. mass mkt. 6.50 o.s.i (*0-446-35231-4*) Warner Bks., Inc.

Hamill, Pete. Loving Women. 2003. mass mkt. 6.99 o.p. (*0-7582-0678-X*, Kensington Bks.); 2003. mass mkt. 6.99 (*0-7860-1638-8*, Pinnacle Bks.); 1990. mass mkt. 5.50 o.s.i (*1-55817-385-4*, Pinnacle Bks.) Kensington Publishing Corp.

Hanlon, Julia. The Wedding Wager. 2000. 352p. mass mkt. 5.99 o.s.i (*0-8217-6524-8*, Zebra Bks.) Kensington Publishing Corp.

Harper, Brian. Deadly Pursuit. 1995. 400p. (Orig.). mass mkt. 5.99 o.s.i (*0-451-18198-0*, Signet Bks.) NAL.

Harper, Karen. Black Orchid. l.t. ed. 1997. lib. bdg. 25.95 (*1-57490-099-4*, Beeler Large Print Bks.) Beeler, Thomas T. Publisher.

—Black Orchid. 1996. 384p. mass mkt. 5.99 o.s.i (*0-451-18866-7*, Signet Bks.) NAL.

—The Wings of Morning. 1993. 384p. 20.00 o.p. (*0-525-93614-9*, Dutton) Dutton/Plume.

—The Wings of Morning. l.t. ed. 1993. 100.95 (*0-7862-9995-9*, Macmillan Reference USA) Gale Group.

—The Wings of Morning. 1994. 432p. mass mkt. 5.99 o.s.i (*0-451-18065-8*, Signet Bks.) NAL.

Harrison, Sam. Birdsong Ascending. 1992. 382p. 21.95 (*0-15-100060-3*) Harcourt Trade Pubs.

Heller, Jane. Infernal Affairs, Set. abr. ed. 1999. audio 16.99 (*0-88646-417-X*, 393986) Durkin Hayes Publishing Ltd.

—Infernal Affairs. 2002. 32p. mass mkt. 6.99 (*0-7582-0306-3*); 1997. 320p. mass mkt. 5.99 o.s.i (*1-57566-154-3*, Kensington Bks.); 1996. 304p. 21.95 o.s.i (*1-57566-021-0*) Kensington Publishing Corp.

—Sis Boom Bah: Having a Sister Means Always Having To Say You're Sorry. 2nd ed. 1999. 320p. 23.95 (*0-312-20312-8*) St. Martin's Pr.

Heller, Jean. Handyman. 1995. 316p. 23.95 o.p. (*0-312-85818-3*, Forge Bks.) Doherty, Tom Assocs., LLC.

Henderson, William M. I Killed Hemingway. 1993. 313p. 18.95 o.p. (*0-312-08816-7*) St. Martin's Pr.

—I Killed Hemingway: A Novel. 1995. 320p. pap. 12.00 (*0-312-11925-9*) Picador.

Hendricks, Vicki. Iguana Love. 2000. (Illus.). 192p. (J). reprint ed. pap. 11.95 (*0-312-26752-5*, NPB 0292, Saint Martin's Griffin) St. Martin's Pr.

—Miami Purity. 1996. pap. 10.00 o.s.i (*0-679-76800-9*, Vintage) Knopf Publishing Group.

—Sky Blues. Date not set. pap. (*0-312-30313-0*, Saint Martin's Griffin); E-Book 16.95 (*0-312-70431-3*); 2002. 224p. 22.95 (*0-312-28346-6*, Saint Martin's Minotaur) St. Martin's Pr.

—Voluntary Madness. 2000. 215p. o.p. (*1-85242-666-7*) Serpent's Tail Ltd.

—Voluntary Madness. 2002. 224p. pap. 13.00 (*1-85242-751-5*) Serpent's Tail Ltd. GBR. *Dist:* Consortium Bk. Sales & Distribution.

Hersey, John. Key West Tales. 1993. 227p. 23.00 o.s.i (*0-679-42992-1*) Knopf, Alfred A. Inc.

—Key West Tales: Stories. 1996. 240p. pap. 12.00 (*0-679-77263-4*) McKay, David Co., Inc.

Hest, Amy. Travel Tips from Harry: A Guide to Family Vacations in the Sun. 1989. (Illus.). 64p. (J). (gr. 2 up). lib. bdg. 11.88 o.p. (*0-688-09291-8*, Morrow, William & Co.) Morrow/Avon.

Hiaasen, Carl. Basket Case. 2002. E-Book 20.95 (*1-59061-759-2*) Adobe Systems, Inc.

—Basket Case. 2002. 336p. 25.95 (*0-375-41107-0*) Knopf, Alfred A. Inc.

—Basket Case. abr. ed. 2002. audio 25.00 (*0-553-71485-6*) Random Hse. Audio Publishing Group.

—Basket Case. l.t. ed. 2003. 13.95 (*1-4104-0083-2*, Large Print Pr.) Thorndike Pr.

—Basket Case. 2003. 432p. mass mkt. 7.99 (*0-446-61193-X*) Warner Bks., Inc.

—Double Whammy. l.t. ed. 1996. 554p. 24.95 o.p. (*0-7838-1645-6*, Macmillan Reference USA) Gale Group.

—Double Whammy. 1988. 304p. 16.95 o.p. (*0-399-13297-X*, G. P. Putnam's Sons) Penguin Putnam Bks. for Young Readers.

—Double Whammy. 1989. 320p. reprint ed. mass mkt. 7.99 (*0-446-35276-4*) Warner Bks., Inc.

—Lucky You. aut. ed. 1997. 24.00 o.s.i (*0-676-54009-0*) Random Hse., Inc.

—Lucky You. deluxe ltd. ed. 1997. 368p. 150.00 (*1-890885-01-0*) Trice, B.E. Publishing.

—Lucky You. 1998. 496p. reprint ed. mass mkt. 7.99 (*0-446-60465-8*) Warner Bks., Inc.

—Naked Came the Manatee: A Novel. abr. ed. 1997. audio 16.99 (*0-88646-431-5*, 7431) Durkin Hayes Publishing Ltd.

—Native Tongue. 1992. (Florida Mysteries Ser.). 416p. mass mkt. 7.50 o.s.i (*0-449-22118-0*, Fawcett) Ballantine Bks.

—Native Tongue. l.t. ed. 1996. (Large Print Bks.). pap. 21.95 o.p. (*1-56895-344-5*, Wheeler Publishing, Inc.) Gale Group.

Settings

Settings

—Native Tongue. Set. abr. ed. 1991. audio 16.00 o.s.i (0-394-58966-1, 391249, RH Audio) Random Hse. Audio Publishing Group.

—Native Tongue. 1993. 4.99 o.p. (0-517-10755-4) Random Hse. Value Publishing.

—Native Tongue, unabr. ed. 1992. audio 91.00 (1-55690-761-3, 92421E7) Recorded Bks., LLC.

—Native Tongue. 2003. mass mkt. 7.99 (0-446-61320-7) Warner Bks., Inc.

—Powder Burn. 1998. 288p. pap. 12.00 (0-375-70068-4, Vintage) Knopf Publishing Group.

—Sick Puppy. l.t. ed. 1999. 27.95 (1-56895-869-2, Wheeler Publishing, Inc.) Gale Group.

—Sick Puppy. aut. ed. 2000. 352p. 25.00 o.s.i (0-676-54099-6) Knopf, Alfred A. Inc.

—Sick Puppy. 2001. 528p. reprint ed. mass mkt. 7.99 (0-446-60466-6) Warner Bks., Inc.

—Skin Tight. 1990. (Florida Mysteries Ser.). 384p. mass mkt. 6.99 o.s.i (0-449-21941-0, Fawcett) Ballantine Bks.

—Skin Tight. l.t. ed. 1996. (G. K. Hall Mystery Ser.). 599p. 24.95 o.p. (0-7838-1648-0, Macmillan Reference USA) Gale Group.

—Skin Tight. 1989. 320p. 18.95 o.p. (0-399-13489-1, G. P. Putnam's Sons) Penguin Putnam Bks. for Young Readers.

—Stormy Weather. l.t. ed. 1996. 26.95 (1-56895-276-7, Wheeler Publishing, Inc.) Gale Group.

—Stormy Weather. 1995. 352p. 24.00 o.s.i (0-679-41982-9) Knopf, Alfred A. Inc.

—Stormy Weather. reprint ed. 2001. 416p. pap. 14.95 (0-446-67716-7); 1996. 400p. mass mkt. 7.99 (0-446-60342-2) Warner Bks., Inc.

—Tourist Season. l.t. ed. 1996. (G. K. Hall Mystery Ser.). 524p. lib. bdg. 23.95 o.p. (0-7838-1647-2, Macmillan Reference USA) Gale Group.

—Tourist Season. 1986. 295p. 15.95 o.p. (0-399-13145-0, G. P. Putnam's Sons) Penguin Putnam Bks. for Young Readers.

—Tourist Season. 1989. mass mkt. 3.95 (0-446-73857-3); 1987. 384p. reprint ed. mass mkt. 7.99 (0-446-34345-5) Warner Bks., Inc.

Hirschfeld, Corson. Freeze Dry. Date not set. pap. (0-7653-0801-0); Date not set. mass mkt. (0-7653-4709-1); 2003. 464p. 26.95 (0-7653-0800-2) Doherty, Tom Assocs., LLC. (Forge Bks.).

Hoag, Tami. Dark Horse. 2004. 592p. mass mkt. 7.99 (0-553-58357-3); 2002. E-Book 21.95 (0-553-89706-3); 2002. 448p. 26.95 (0-553-80192-9) Bantam Bks.

—Dark Horse. l.t. ed. 2002. 768p. 28.95 (0-375-43182-9) Random Hse., Inc.

Hodgman, D. A. The Color of Blood. 1995. (Stakeout Ser.: Vol. 3). per. (0-373-63412-9, Harlequin Bks.) Harlequin Enterprises, Ltd.

—Miami Heat. 1995. (Stakeout Ser.). per. (0-373-63411-0, 1-63411-2, Harlequin Bks.) Harlequin Enterprises, Ltd.

Hoffman, Alice. Turtle Moon. 1993. 304p. mass mkt. 7.99 (0-425-13699-X); 1997. 288p. reprint ed. pap. 13.00 (0-425-16128-5) Berkley Publishing Group.

—Turtle Moon. unabr. ed. 1992. audio 22.95 o.s.i (1-56100-465-0, 302, Bookcassette); audio 57.25 (1-56100-099-X, 1111, Unabridged Library Editions) Brilliance Audio.

—Turtle Moon. 1992. 256p. 21.95 o.p. (0-399-13720-3, G. P. Putnam's Sons) Penguin Group (USA) Inc.

Hogan, Linda. Power. (Norton Paperback Fiction Ser.). 1999. 248p. pap. 13.00 (0-393-31968-7, Norton Paperbacks); 1998. 192p. 23.00 (0-393-04636-2) Norton, W. W. & Co., Inc.

Hood, Mary. Familiar Heat. 1995. 416p. 25.00 o.s.i (0-394-58658-1) Knopf, Alfred A. Inc.

—Familiar Heat. 1996. 464p. pap. 19.99 (0-446-67274-2) Warner Bks., Inc.

Horne, J. S. Willard Jerhom. 2003. 139p. pap. 8.00 (0-9740335-0-2) Smith, Kenneth.

Howard, Mildred T. Brave the Wild Trail. 1987. 122p. (J). (gr. 4-7). pap. 6.49 (0-89084-384-8, 031492) Jones, Bob Univ. Pr.

—The Treasure of Pelican Cove. 1988. 104p. (J). (gr. 2-4). pap. 6.49 (0-89084-464-X, 043182) Jones, Bob Univ. Pr.

Hoyt, Richard. Marimba. 1993. 352p. mass mkt. 4.99 o.p. (0-8125-1563-3); 1992. 288p. 18.95 o.p. (0-312-85193-6) Doherty, Tom Assocs., LLC. (Tor Bks.).

Hubbard, Susan & Wilson, Robley, eds. 100% Pure Florida Fiction: An Anthology. 2000. xvi, 203p. 49.95 (0-8130-1752-1); pap. 16.95 (0-8130-1753-X) Univ. Pr. of Florida.

Huber, Fred. Axx Goes South. 1989. 293p. 18.95 o.s.i (0-8027-5740-5) Walker & Co.

Hudson, Joyce Rockwood. Apalachee. 416p. 2002. pap. 18.95 (0-8203-2402-7); 2000. 27.95 (0-8203-2190-7) Univ. of Georgia Pr.

Hunt, Angela. Gentle Touch. 1997. (Portraits Ser.). 256p. pap. 8.99 o.p. (1-55661-944-8) Bethany Hse. Pubs.

Hunt, E. Howard. Islamorada. 1995. 240p. 20.95 o.s.i (1-55611-438-9) Fine, Donald I. Bks.

Hunter, Jack D. Slingshot, unabr. ed. 1995. 5p. audio 62.95 (0-7861-0872-X, 113377) Blackstone Audio Bks., Inc.

—Slingshot. 1996. 432p. pap. text 6.99 o.p. (0-8125-2457-8); 1994. 384p. 22.95 o.p. (0-312-85500-1) Doherty, Tom Assocs., LLC. (Forge Bks.).

—Slingshot. 2000. 29.95 (0-7351-0450-6) Replica Bks.

Hurston, Zora Neale. Seraph on the Suwanee. reprint ed. 24.50 o.p. (0-404-11391-5) AMS Pr., Inc.

—Seraph on the Suwanee. 1991. 400p. reprint ed. pap. 14.00 (0-06-097359-5, Perennial) HarperTrade.

—Seraph on the Suwanee. 1991. 320p. (C). reprint ed. lib. bdg. 35.00 o.p. (0-8095-9032-8) Millefleurs.

—Seraph on the Suwanee. l.t. ed. 1997. (Perennial Bestsellers Ser.). 519p. 25.95 (0-7838-8126-6) Thorndike Pr.

—Their Eyes Were Watching God, Vol. 2. 2nd ed. 1994. (C). pap. text 52.65 (0-06-502316-1) Addison-Wesley Educational Pubs., Inc.

—Their Eyes Were Watching God. 1998. (Perennial Classics Ser.). 240p. pap. 13.95 (0-06-093141-8, Perennial) HarperTrade.

—Their Eyes Were Watching God. 1978. 296p. (gr. 10-12). 6.95 o.p. (0-252-00686-0) Univ. of Illinois Pr.

Hury, Hadley. The Edge of the Gulf. 2003. 324p. 24.95 (1-59058-083-4) Poisoned Pen Pr.

Jackson, Hialeah. The Alligator's Farewell. 1998. (Annabelle Hardy Mystery Ser.: No. 1). 368p. mass mkt. 5.99 o.s.i (0-440-22660-0) Dell Publishing.

—Farewell, Conch Republic. 1999. 368p. mass mkt. 5.99 o.s.i (0-440-22663-5) Dell Publishing.

Jakubowski, Maxim. It's You That I Want to Kiss. 1997. 222p. pap. 16.95 (1-899344-15-2) Do-Not Pr., The GBR. Dist: Dufour Editions, Inc.

Johnston, Coleen L. Guardians. 1994. (Gairden Legacy Ser.: No. 2). mass mkt. 4.99 o.p. (0-312-95125-6, St. Martin's Paperbacks) St. Martin's Pr.

Johnston, Joan. Marriage by the Book. l.t. ed. 2003. 184p. 28.95 (1-58724-496-9, Wheeler Publishing, Inc.) Gale Group.

—Marriage by the Book. 2003. 256p. mass mkt. (1-55166-698-7, Mira Bks.) Harlequin Enterprises, Ltd.

Jones, John P., Jr. Cold Before Morning: A Heart-Warming Novel of Pioneer Life in Florida. 1992. 240p. 19.95 (0-942407-18-0) Father & Son Publishing.

Jordan, Pat. A. K. A. Sheila Weinstein: A Novel of Crime. 2003. (Otto Penzler Book Ser.). 272p. 24.00 (0-7867-1191-4, Carroll & Graf Pubs.) Avalon Publishing Group.

Kaminsky, Stuart M. Retribution. mass mkt. 6.99 (0-8125-4036-0); 2001. 272p. 24.95 (0-312-87452-9) Doherty, Tom Assocs., LLC. (Forge Bks.).

—Vengeance. 2000. 288p. mass mkt. 6.99 (0-8125-7518-0); 2nd ed. 1999. 256p. 22.95 (0-312-86927-4) Doherty, Tom Assocs., LLC. (Forge Bks.).

—Vengeance. l.t. ed. 2000. 26.95 (1-56895-870-6, Wheeler Publishing, Inc.) Gale Group.

Katzenbach, John. In the Heat of the Summer. 1982. 13.95 o.p. (0-689-11269-6, Scribner) Simon & Schuster.

—The Shadow Man. 1996. mass mkt. 6.99 o.s.i (0-345-38630-2); 1995. 480p. 22.00 o.p. (0-345-38629-9) Ballantine Bks.

—The Shadow Man. l.t. ed. 1995. 655p. 24.95 o.p. (0-7838-1357-0, Macmillan Reference USA) Gale Group.

—State of Mind. 1998. 544p. mass mkt. 6.99 (0-345-42253-8); 1997. 409p. 24.00 o.s.i (0-345-38631-0, Ballantine Bks.) Ballantine Bks.

—State of Mind. l.t. ed. 1998. (Large Print Book Ser.). 26.95 o.p. (1-56895-528-6, Wheeler Publishing, Inc.) Gale Group.

Kaufelt, David A. American Tropic. 1988. 624p. mass mkt. 4.50 o.s.i (0-671-52883-1, Pocket); 1987. 464p. 17.45 (0-671-52882-3, Simon & Schuster) Simon & Schuster.

Keasler, John. Surrounded on Three Sides. 1999. (Florida Sand Dollar Book Ser.). 219p. pap. 14.95 (0-8130-1710-6) Univ. Pr. of Florida.

Keene, Carolyn. Dangerous Relations. Greenberg, Anne, ed. 1993. (Nancy Drew Files: No. 82). 160p. (YA). (gr. 6 up). mass mkt. 3.99 (0-671-73086-X, Simon Pulse) Simon & Schuster Children's Publishing.

King, Jonathon. The Blue Edge of Midnight. 2003. 54.95 (0-7927-2876-9); 74.95 (0-7927-2877-7) BBC Audiobooks America.

—The Blue Edge of Midnight. 2002. 320p. 22.95 (0-525-94643-8, Dutton) Dutton/Plume.

—The Blue Edge of Midnight. 2004. 288p. mass mkt. 6.99 (0-451-41078-5, Onyx) NAL.

—The Blue Edge of Midnight. l.t. ed. 2002. (Mystery Ser.). 415p. 30.45 (0-7862-4698-7) Thorndike Pr.

—Shadow Men. unabr. ed. 2004. (Max Freeman Ser.). audio 27.95 (1-59355-306-4, 4918, Brilliance Audio Unabridged); audio 69.25 (1-59355-307-2, 4919, Brilliance Audio Unabridged Lib Ed); audio compact disk 29.95 (1-59355-308-0, 4920, Brilliance Audio on CD Unabridged); audio compact disk 82.25 (1-59355-309-9, 4921, Brilliance Audio on CD Unabridged Lib Ed) Brilliance Audio.

—Shadow Men. 2004. 288p. 23.95 (0-525-94807-4, Dutton) Dutton/Plume.

—A Visible Darkness. 2003. 49.95 (0-7927-2868-8); 64.95 (0-7927-2869-6) BBC Audiobooks America.

—A Visible Darkness. l.t. ed. 2003. lib. bdg. 28.95 (1-58547-349-9, Platinum) Ctr. Point Large Print.

—A Visible Darkness. 2003. 256p. 23.95 (0-525-94714-0) Dutton/Plume.

—A Visible Darkness. 2004. 288p. mass mkt. 6.99 (0-451-41135-8, Onyx) NAL.

Klein, Dave. Kilos in the Keys. 2000. 256p. 23.95 (0-312-86371-3, Forge Bks.) Doherty, Tom Assocs., LLC.

Kling, Christine. Surface Tension. 2003. mass mkt. 6.99 (0-345-44827-8); 2002. 304p. 23.95 (0-345-44828-6, Ballantine Bks.) Ballantine Bks.

—Surface Tension. 2003. 28.95 (0-7862-5213-8) Thorndike Pr.

Kotker, Norman. Billy in Love. 1996. 160p. (Orig.). pap. 13.95 o.p. (0-944072-68-2, Zoland Bks., Inc.) Steerforth Pr.

Kreps, Penelope B. Carnivores. 1993. 352p. mass mkt. 4.50 o.s.i (0-8217-4225-6, Zebra Bks.) Kensington Publishing Corp.

—Demon's Fright. 1992. mass mkt. 4.50 o.s.i (0-8217-3775-9, Zebra Bks.) Kensington Publishing Corp.

Lamazares, Ivonne. The Sugar Island. 2000. 224p. tchr. ed. 23.00 (0-395-86040-7, Mariner Bks.) Houghton Mifflin Co. Trade & Reference Div.

Lamb, Fay. Tatted Angels. 2000. 108p. pap. 14.95 o.p. (1-929925-50-6) FirstPublish.

Lamb, Joyce. Caught in the ACT. 2003. 333p. 26.95 (0-7862-5335-5, Five Star) Gale Group.

—Relative Strangers. 2003. 272p. pap. 13.95 (1-4104-0110-3, Five Star Trade); 2002. 250p. 26.95 (0-7862-3730-9, Five Star) Gale Group.

Lardo, Vincent. McNally's Chance. l.t. ed. (Paperback Bestsellers Ser.). 2003. 416p. pap. 13.95 (0-7862-3361-3); 2001. 447p. 31.95 (0-7862-3360-5); 2001. 416p. (0-7540-1697-8) Thorndike Pr.

—McNally's Folly. l.t. ed. 431p. 2001. pap. 29.95 (0-7862-2644-7); 2000. (0-7540-1532-7) Thorndike Pr.

Lardo, Vincent & Sanders, Lawrence. McNally's Alibi. 2003. 304p. mass mkt. 7.99 (0-425-19119-2) Berkley Publishing Group.

—McNally's Chance. 2001. 320p. 24.95 o.p. (0-399-14732-2) Penguin Group (USA) Inc.

Largo, Michael. Lies Within. 1999. 438p. pap. 14.95 (0-9666173-0-4) Tropical Pr., Inc.

—Welcome to Miami: A Novel. 2000. (Illus.). 250p. pap. 14.95 (0-9666173-4-7) Tropical Pr., Inc.

Latour, Jose. Outcast. 1999. 217p. pap. 13.95 o.p. (1-888451-07-6, AKB04) Akashic Bks.

—Outcast. 2001. 304p. 24.00 (0-06-018488-4, Morrow, William & Co.) Morrow/Avon.

Law, Janice. Cross-Check. 1998. (WWL Mystery Ser.). 256p. per. (0-373-26291-4, 1-26291-4, Worldwide Library) Harlequin Enterprises, Ltd.

—Cross-Check. 1997. 224p. 20.95 (0-312-15504-2, Saint Martin's Minotaur) St. Martin's Pr.

Leddick, David. My Worst Date. pap. 15.95 (0-312-29990-7, Saint Martin's Griffin); 1996. 288p. 22.95 (0-312-14689-2); 3rd ed. 1998. 272p. pap. 12.95 (0-312-18138-8, Saint Martin's Griffin) St. Martin's Pr.

Lee, Edward. Monstrosity. 2002. 350p. 40.00 (1-58767-060-7) Cemetery Dance Pubns.

—Monstrosity. 2003. 384p. mass mkt. 6.99 (0-8439-5075-7) Dorchester Publishing Co., Inc.

Lee, Rachel. After I Dream. l.t. ed. 2000. 377p. 27.95 (1-57490-278-4, Beeler Large Print Bks.) Beeler, Thomas T. Publisher.

—After I Dream. 2000. 400p. reprint ed. mass mkt. 6.50 (0-446-60654-5, Warner Romance) Warner Bks., Inc.

—Before I Sleep. l.t. ed. 2000. 28.95 (1-57490-302-0, Beeler Large Print Bks.) Beeler, Thomas T. Publisher.

—Before I Sleep. 1999. 400p. reprint ed. mass mkt. 6.50 (0-446-60653-7, Warner Romance) Warner Bks., Inc.

—With Malice. 2003. 384p. mass mkt. (1-55166-658-8, Mira Bks.) Harlequin Enterprises, Ltd.

Leek, Alfred. God's Fool: A Novel. 2001. xiii, 222p. 21.95 (0-9709554-0-5, 113-001) Black Skimmer Pr.

Leonard, Elmore. Cat Chaser. unabr. collector's ed. 1995. audio 48.00 (0-7366-3117-8, 3793) Books on Tape, Inc.

—Cat Chaser. abr. ed. (Audio Favorites Ser.). audio 9.99 (1-55204-011-9, 390491); 1989. audio 16.99 (0-88646-239-8) Durkin Hayes Publishing Ltd.

—Cat Chaser. l.t. ed. 1986. (General Ser.). 364p. 16.95 o.p. (0-8161-3947-4, Macmillan Reference USA) Gale Group.

—Cat Chaser. 1998. (Elmore Leonard Library). 288p. pap. 12.00 (0-688-16341-6, Perennial) HarperTrade.

—Cat Chaser. 2003. 384p. mass mkt. 7.50 (0-06-051222-9, HarperTorch); 1983. 288p. mass mkt. 6.50 (0-380-64642-0, Avon Bks.); 1982. 13.50 o.p. (0-87795-398-8, Morrow, William & Co.) Morrow/Avon.

—Cat Chaser, unabr. ed. 1995. audio 51.00 (0-7887-0256-4, 94465E7) Recorded Bks., LLC.

—Gold Coast. 1985. mass mkt. 3.95 o.s.i (0-553-27627-1); 224p. mass mkt. 3.50 o.s.i (0-553-26267-X) Bantam Bks.

—Gold Coast. 1999. mass mkt. (0-553-13321-7) Bantam Dell Publishing Group.

—Gold Coast. unabr. collector's ed. 1995. audio 42.00 (0-7366-3160-7, 3831) Books on Tape, Inc.

—Gold Coast. 1999. mass mkt. (0-553-25006-X); 1990. 224p. mass mkt. 7.50 o.s.i (0-440-20832-7) Dell Publishing.

—Gold Coast. 2002. 352p. mass mkt. 7.50 (0-06-008405-7) Morrow/Avon.

—Gold Coast, unabr. ed. 1995. audio 44.00 (0-7887-0257-2, 94466E7) Recorded Bks., LLC.

—Jackie Brown. 1997. 352p. mass mkt. 6.50 o.s.i (0-440-22606-6) Dell Publishing.

—Maximum Bob. 1998. 304p. pap. 10.95 o.s.i (0-385-32396-4, Delta); 1992. 352p. mass mkt. 6.99 o.s.i (0-440-21218-9); 1991. 304p. 100.00 o.s.i (0-385-30493-5, Delacorte Pr.) Dell Publishing.

—Maximum Bob. l.t. ed. 1994. 335p. pap. 18.95 o.p. (0-8161-5808-8, Macmillan Reference USA) Gale Group.

—Maximum Bob: International Edition. 1992. 352p. mass mkt. 5.99 o.s.i (0-440-29520-3) Dell Publishing.

—Pronto. 1994. 384p. mass mkt. 6.50 o.s.i (0-440-21443-2) Dell Publishing.

—Pronto. 1998. 272p. pap. 9.95 o.s.i (0-385-33290-4) Doubleday Publishing.

—Riding the Rap. 1998. 304p. pap. 10.95 o.s.i (0-385-32417-0, Delta); 1996. 352p. mass mkt. 6.50 o.s.i (0-440-21441-6); 1995. 336p. mass mkt. 6.50 (0-440-29539-4) Dell Publishing.

—Riding the Rap. l.t. ed. 1995. (Large Print Bks.). 27.95 (1-56895-224-4, Wheeler Publishing, Inc.) Gale Group.

—Riding the Rap. 2002. 352p. mass mkt. 7.50 (0-06-008218-6) HarperCollins Pubs.

—Rum Punch. unabr. ed. 1992. audio 48.00 (0-7366-2306-X, 3089) Books on Tape, Inc.

—Rum Punch. 1998. 304p. pap. 9.95 o.s.i (0-385-33280-7, Dell Bks.); 1993. 368p. mass mkt. 6.99 o.s.i (0-440-21415-7); 1993. 304p. mass mkt. 5.99 o.s.i (0-440-29524-6) Dell Publishing.

—Rum Punch. l.t. ed. 1994. (General Ser.). 376p. pap. 18.95 (0-8161-5807-X, Macmillan Reference USA) Gale Group.

—Rum Punch. 1992. audio 15.95 o.s.i (0-553-74537-9); audio 15.99 o.s.i (0-553-47074-4, 391496) Random Hse. Audio Publishing Group. (RH Audio).

—Stick. unabr. collector's ed. 1996. audio 48.00 (0-7366-3360-X, 4010) Books on Tape, Inc.

—Stick. l.t. ed. 1985. (General Ser.). 360p. 15.95 o.p. (0-8161-3908-3, Macmillan Reference USA) Gale Group.

—Stick. 1998. (Elmore Leonard Library). 304p. pap. 12.00 (0-688-16340-8, Perennial) HarperTrade.

—Stick. 1984. 304p. mass mkt. 6.50 (0-380-67652-4, Avon Bks.); 1983. 14.50 o.p. (0-87795-436-4, Morrow, William & Co.) Morrow/Avon.

—Stick, unabr. ed. audio 51.00 (0-7887-0359-5, 94551E7) Recorded Bks., LLC.

Leonard, Elmore, et al. Naked Came the Manatee: A Novel. Hiaasen, Carl, ed. 1997. 224p. 22.95 o.p. (0-399-14192-8, G. P. Putnam's Sons) Penguin Group (USA) Inc.

Leslie, John. Blue Moon. 1998. (Gideon Lowry Mystery Ser.: Vol. 4). 256p. 23.00 o.s.i (0-671-53514-5, Atria) Simon & Schuster.

—Killing Me Softly. Grose, Bill, ed. (Orig.). 1995. 272p. mass mkt. 5.50 (0-671-86421-1, Pocket); 1994. 256p. 20.00 (0-671-86420-3, Atria) Simon & Schuster.

—Love for Sale. 1997. (Gideon Lowry Mystery Ser.). 272p. pap. 6.50 (0-671-51126-2, Pocket) Simon & Schuster.

—Love for Sale: A Gideon Lowry Mystery. 1997. 272p. 22.00 (0-671-51127-0, Atria) Simon & Schuster.

—Night & Day. 256p. 2002. pap. 17.95 (0-7434-7025-7); 1996. mass mkt. 5.99 (0-671-86423-8) Simon & Schuster. (Pocket).

—Night & Day: A Gideon Lowry Mystery. Grose, William, ed. 1995. 256p. (Orig.). pap. 20.00 o.p. (0-671-86422-X, Atria) Simon & Schuster.

Leunem, Christine. Primordial Soup. 2002. 196p. pap. 12.99 (1-873982-19-4) Dedalus, Ltd.

Levine, Paul. False Dawn. 1993. 320p. 21.95 o.s.i (0-553-08995-1) Bantam Bks.

—False Dawn. 1993. audio 15.99 o.s.i (0-553-47136-8, RH Audio) Random Hse. Audio Publishing Group.

—The False Dawn. 1994. 368p. mass mkt. 5.99 o.s.i (*0-553-56504-4*) Bantam Bks.
—Flesh & Bones. 1998. (Jake Lassiter Mystery Ser.). 352p. mass mkt. 5.99 (*0-380-72591-6*, Avon Bks.) Morrow/Avon.
—Flesh & Bones: A Jake Lassiter Novel. l.t. ed. 1997. 336p. 23.00 (*0-688-14305-9*, Morrow, William & Co.) Morrow/Avon.
—Fool Me Twice. 1996. 352p. mass mkt. 5.99 (*0-380-72590-8*, Avon Bks.) Morrow/Avon.
—Fool Me Twice: A Jake Lassiter Novel. 1996. 356p. 22.00 o.p. (*0-688-14304-0*, Morrow, William & Co.) Morrow/Avon.
—Mortal Sin. 1995. 352p. mass mkt. 5.50 (*0-380-72161-9*, Avon Bks.); 1994. 20.00 o.p. (*0-688-12717-7*, Morrow, William & Co.) Morrow/Avon.
—Night Vision. 1992. 448p. mass mkt. 5.99 o.s.i (*0-553-29762-7*); 1991. 352p. 20.00 o.s.i (*0-553-07796-1*) Bantam Bks.
—Slashback. abr. ed. 1995. audio 16.95 o.p. (*1-56100-415-4*, 1375, Nova Audio Bks.); audio 57.25 o.p. (*1-56100-246-1*, 1049, Unabridged Library Editions) Brilliance Audio.
—Slashback. abr. ed. 2000. audio 7.95 (*1-57815-144-9*, 1103, Media Bks. Audio Publishing) Media Bks., L. L. C.
—Slashback. 1995. pap. 5.99 o.p. (*0-380-72162-7*, Avon Bks.) Morrow/Avon.
—Slashback: A Jake Lassiter Novel. 1995. 350p. 22.00 o.p. (*0-688-12718-5*, Morrow, William & Co.) Morrow/Avon.
—To Speak for the Dead. 1991. 400p. mass mkt. 5.99 o.s.i (*0-553-29172-6*) Bantam Bks.
Levine, Paul J. To Speak for the Dead. 1990. 304p. 17.95 o.s.i (*0-553-05747-2*) Bantam Bks.
Lewbart, Greg. Ivory Hunters. 1996. 224p. reprint ed. 17.50 (*1-57524-009-2*) Krieger Publishing Co.
—Ivory Hunters: A Novel of Extinction. 1996. 211p. pap. 9.95 (*1-884570-40-2*) Research Triangle Publishing.
Lewis, Catherine. Dry Fire: A Novel. 1996. 288p. 21.00 (*0-393-03835-1*) Norton, W. W. & Co., Inc.
Lewis, Terry. Conflict of Interest. 1998. 352p. mass mkt. 5.99 o.s.i (*0-7860-0539-4*, Pinnacle Bks.) Kensington Publishing Corp.
—Conflict of Interest. 1997. 328p. 18.95 (*1-56164-132-4*) Pineapple Pr., Inc.
—Privileged Information. 2003. 337p. 19.95 (*1-56164-287-8*) Pineapple Pr., Inc.
Lilliefors, Jim. Bananaville. 1996. 288p. text 22.95 o.p. (*0-312-14548-9*, Saint Martin's Minotaur) St. Martin's Pr.
Lisicky, Paul. Lawnboy. 1999. 386p. pap. 14.95 (*1-885983-40-9*) Turtle Point Pr.
Lister, Michael. Power in the Blood: A John Jordan Mystery. 1997. (John Jordan Mystery Ser.). 326p. 18.95 o.p. (*1-56164-137-5*) Pineapple Pr., Inc.
Locke, Thomas. The Omega Network. 1995. (Thomas Locke Ser.: Bk. 2). 256p. pap. 8.99 o.p. (*1-55661-502-7*) Bethany Hse. Pubs.
—The Omega Network. l.t. ed. 2001. (Christian Mystery Ser.). 363p. 24.95 (*0-7862-3579-9*) Thorndike Pr.
Lutz, John. Blood Fire. 1991. 17.95 o.p. (*0-8050-0969-8*) Holt, Henry & Co.
—Blood Fire. 1992. (Fred Carver Mystery Ser.). 224p. reprint ed. mass mkt. 3.99 (*0-380-71446-9*, Avon Bks.) Morrow/Avon.
—Burn: A Fred Carver Mystery. 1995. (Henry Holt Mystery Ser.). 278p. 22.50 o.p. (*0-8050-3480-3*) Holt, Henry & Co.
—Flame. unabr. ed. 1990. audio 57.25 o.p. (*1-56100-050-7*, 1197, Unabridged Library Editions); Set. audio 19.95 o.p. (*0-930435-56-7*, 344, Bookcassette) Brilliance Audio.
—Flame. 1996. 88p. pap. 5.95 o.p. (*0-8050-4567-8*, Owl Bks.) Holt, Henry & Co.
—Flame. 1991. 272p. pap. 3.95 (*0-380-71070-6*, Avon Bks.) Morrow/Avon.
—Hot: A Fred Carver Mystery. 1992. 288p. 18.95 o.p. (*0-8050-1584-1*) Holt, Henry & Co.
—Hot: A Fred Carver Mystery. 1993. 256p. mass mkt. 4.99 (*0-380-71447-7*, Avon Bks.) Morrow/Avon.
—Kiss. unabr. ed. 1990. audio 57.25 o.p. (*1-56100-056-6*, 920, Unabridged Library Editions); audio 19.95 o.p. (*0-930435-62-1*, 2030, Bookcassette) Brilliance Audio.
—Kiss. (Fred Carver Mystery Ser.). 1996. 88p. pap. 5.95 o.p. (*0-8050-4566-X*, Owl Bks.); 1988. 17.95 o.p. (*0-8050-0412-2*) Holt, Henry & Co.
—Kiss. 1990. 272p. pap. 3.95 (*0-380-70934-1*, Avon Bks.) Morrow/Avon.
—Lightning: A Fred Carver Mystery. unabr. ed. 1996. (P. I. Fred Carver Mystery Ser.). audio 48.00 (*0-7366-3519-X*, 4156) Books on Tape, Inc.
—Lightning: A Fred Carver Mystery. 1996. 88p. 22.50 o.p. (*0-8050-4379-9*) Holt, Henry & Co.
—Scorcher. unabr. ed. 1990. audio 57.25 o.p. (*1-56100-060-4*, 1030, Unabridged Library Editions); audio 19.95 o.p. (*0-930435-66-4*, 252, Bookcassette) Brilliance Audio.
—Scorcher. 272p. 1995. pap. 5.95 o.p. (*0-8050-3829-9*, Owl Bks.); 1987. 16.95 o.p. (*0-8050-0411-4*) Holt, Henry & Co.
—Scorcher. 1988. 256p. pap. 3.95 (*0-380-70526-5*, Avon Bks.) Morrow/Avon.
—Spark: A Fred Carver Mystery. 1993. 288p. 19.95 o.p. (*0-8050-1993-6*) Holt, Henry & Co.
—Torch. 1994. (Henry Holt Mystery Ser.). 290p. 22.00 o.p. (*0-8050-2610-X*) Holt, Henry & Co.
—Tropical Heat. l.t. ed. 1991. 21.95 o.p. (*1-55504-579-0*); pap. 6.95 o.p. (*1-55504-550-2*, 456) BBC Audiobooks America.
—Tropical Heat. unabr. ed. 1989. (P. I. Fred Carver Mystery Ser.). audio 19.95 o.p. (*0-930435-53-2*, 359, Bookcassette); audio 57.25 o.p. (*1-56100-047-7*, 1107, Unabridged Library Editions) Brilliance Audio.
—Tropical Heat. 1995. 252p. pap. 5.95 o.p. (*0-8050-3828-0*, Owl Bks.); 1986. 224p. o.p. (*0-03-006958-0*) Holt, Henry & Co.
—Tropical Heat. 1987. 256p. pap. 3.95 (*0-380-70309-2*, Avon Bks.) Morrow/Avon.
MacDonald, John D. Area of Suspicion. 1986. (Travis McGee Novel Ser.). 208p. mass mkt. 5.99 o.s.i (*0-449-13099-1*, Fawcett) Ballantine Bks.
—Bright Orange for the Shroud. (Travis McGee Novel Ser.). 1987. 224p. mass mkt. 5.99 o.s.i (*0-449-13358-3*, Fawcett); 1996. reprint ed. mass mkt. 5.99 (*0-449-45615-3*, Fawcett); 1996. 352p. reprint ed. mass mkt. 6.99 (*0-449-22444-9*, Ballantine Bks.) Ballantine Bks.
—Bright Orange for the Shroud. unabr. collector's ed. 1978. (Travis McGee Ser.: No. 6). audio 48.00 (*0-7366-0174-0*, 1176) Books on Tape, Inc.
—Bright Orange for the Shroud. l.t. ed. 1985. 14.95 o.p. (*0-8161-3979-2*, Macmillan Reference USA) Gale Group.
—Cinnamon Skin. (Travis McGee Novel Ser.). 1996. 336p. mass mkt. 7.50 (*0-449-22484-8*); 1986. 288p. mass mkt. 5.95 o.s.i (*0-449-12873-3*) Ballantine Bks. (Fawcett).
—Cinnamon Skin. unabr. collector's ed. 1982. (Travis McGee Ser.: No. 20). audio 48.00 (*0-7366-0689-0*, 1649) Books on Tape, Inc.
—Cinnamon Skin. 1983. (General Ser.). lib. bdg. 14.95 o.p. (*0-8161-3504-5*, Macmillan Reference USA) Gale Group.
—Cinnamon Skin. 1982. 288p. o.p. (*0-06-014990-6*) HarperCollins Pubs.
—Cinnamon Skin. abr. ed. 2000. (Travis McGee Ser.). audio 9.99 (*0-375-41014-7*, RH Audio) Random Hse. Audio Publishing Group.
—Cinnamon Skin. 1990. 3.99 o.p. (*0-517-05439-6*) Random Hse. Value Publishing.
—Condominium. 1985. 480p. mass mkt. 6.99 (*0-449-20737-4*, Fawcett) Ballantine Bks.
—Condominium. unabr. collector's ed. 1977. audio 80.00 (*0-7366-0066-3*, 1077) Books on Tape, Inc.
—The Damned. 1985. (Travis McGee Novel Ser.). mass mkt. 3.95 o.s.i (*0-449-12887-3*, Fawcett) Ballantine Bks.
—Darker Than Amber. 1997. mass mkt. 5.99 (*0-449-45637-4*); 1996. 320p. mass mkt. 6.99 (*0-449-22446-5*); 1987. 192p. mass mkt. 5.99 o.s.i (*0-449-13339-7*); 1984. 192p. mass mkt. 2.95 o.p. (*0-449-12752-4*) Ballantine Bks. (Fawcett).
—Darker Than Amber. unabr. collector's ed. 1978. (Travis McGee Ser.: No. 7). audio 42.00 (*0-7366-0216-X*, 1214) Books on Tape, Inc.
—Darker Than Amber. l.t. ed. 1988. (General Ser.). 319p. 16.95 o.p. (*0-8161-4008-1*, Macmillan Reference USA) Gale Group.
—A Deadly Shade of Gold. (Travis McGee Novel Ser.). 1996. 448p. mass mkt. 6.99 (*0-449-22442-2*); 1987. 288p. mass mkt. 5.99 o.s.i (*0-449-13313-3*) Ballantine Bks. (Fawcett).
—A Deadly Shade of Gold. unabr. collector's ed. 1978. (Travis McGee Ser.: No. 5). audio 64.00 (*0-7366-0106-6*, 1114) Books on Tape, Inc.
—A Deadly Shade of Gold. l.t. ed. 1987. 447p. 16.95 o.p. (*0-8161-4004-9*, Macmillan Reference USA) Gale Group.
—The Deep Blue Goodbye. 1995. 320p. mass mkt. 6.99 (*0-449-22383-3*); 1986. 256p. mass mkt. 4.95 o.s.i (*0-449-13252-8*); 1984. mass mkt. 2.95 o.p. (*0-449-12673-0*) Ballantine Bks. (Fawcett).
—The Deep Blue Goodbye. l.t. ed. 1984. (General Ser.). 296p. 12.95 o.p. (*0-8161-3626-2*); 8.95 o.p. (*0-8161-3740-4*) Gale Group. (Macmillan Reference USA).
—The Dreadful Lemon Sky. (Travis McGee Novel Ser.). 1996. 320p. mass mkt. 6.99 (*0-449-22479-1*); 1987. 272p. mass mkt. 5.99 o.s.i (*0-449-13404-0*); 1985. 272p. mass mkt. 3.50 o.p. (*0-449-12964-0*) Ballantine Bks. (Fawcett).
—Dress Her in Indigo. 1997. pap. text 5.99 (*0-449-45716-8*); 1996. 336p. mass mkt. 7.50 (*0-449-22462-7*); 1987. 256p. mass mkt. 5.99 o.s.i (*0-449-13293-5*); 1985. mass mkt. 3.50 o.p. (*0-449-12984-5*) Ballantine Bks. (Fawcett).
—Dress Her in Indigo. unabr. collector's ed. 1980. (Travis McGee Ser.: No. 11). audio 56.00 (*0-7366-0243-7*, 1239) Books on Tape, Inc.
—Dress Her in Indigo. l.t. ed. 1985. (General Ser.). 360p. 13.95 o.p. (*0-8161-3822-2*); 9.95 o.p. (*0-8161-3820-6*) Gale Group. (Macmillan Reference USA).
—The Empty Copper Sea. 21.95 (*0-89190-778-5*) Amereon, Ltd.
—The Empty Copper Sea. 1996. 320p. mass mkt. 7.50 (*0-449-22480-5*); 1987. 256p. mass mkt. 4.99 o.s.i (*0-449-13333-8*); 1985. mass mkt. 3.50 o.p. (*0-449-12913-6*) Ballantine Bks. (Fawcett).
—The Empty Copper Sea. unabr. collector's ed. 1979. (Travis McGee Ser.: No. 17). audio 48.00 (*0-7366-0331-X*, 1318) Books on Tape, Inc.
—The Empty Copper Sea. 1979. lib. bdg. 13.50 o.p. (*0-8161-6702-8*, Macmillan Reference USA) Gale Group.
—The Empty Copper Sea. abr. ed. 1987. audio 15.95 o.s.i (*0-394-56085-X*, RH Audio) Random Hse. Audio Publishing Group.
—Five Complete Travis McGee Novels. 1988. 8.99 o.s.i (*0-517-47671-1*) Random Hse. Value Publishing.
—A Flash of Green. 1984. (Travis McGee Novel Ser.). 336p. mass mkt. 6.99 (*0-449-12692-7*, Fawcett) Ballantine Bks.
—A Flash of Green. 1962. 5.50 o.p. (*0-671-26183-5*) Simon & Schuster.
—Free Fall in Crimson. 1996. 320p. mass mkt. 7.50 (*0-449-22482-1*); 1987. 288p. mass mkt. 4.95 o.s.i (*0-449-13253-6*); 1985. 288p. mass mkt. 3.50 o.p. (*0-449-12894-6*) Ballantine Bks. (Fawcett).
—Free Fall in Crimson. unabr. collector's ed. 1981. (Travis McGee Ser.: No. 19). audio 48.00 (*0-7366-0632-7*, 1593) Books on Tape, Inc.
—Free Fall in Crimson. l.t. ed. 1981. 13.50 o.p. (*0-8161-3272-0*, Macmillan Reference USA) Gale Group.
—Free Fall in Crimson. 1981. 224p. 15.00 o.p. (*0-06-014833-0*) HarperTrade.
—Free Fall in Crimson. 1992. audio 16.00 o.s.i (*0-394-55989-4*, RH Audio) Random Hse. Audio Publishing Group.
—The Girl in the Plain Brown Wrapper. 1997. mass mkt. 5.99 (*0-449-45715-X*); 1996. 352p. mass mkt. 7.50 (*0-449-22461-9*); 1987. 256p. mass mkt. 5.99 o.s.i (*0-449-13341-9*); 1985. mass mkt. 3.50 o.p. (*0-449-12915-2*) Ballantine Bks. (Fawcett).
—The Girl in the Plain Brown Wrapper. unabr. collector's ed. 1984. (Travis McGee Ser.: No. 10). audio 56.00 (*0-7366-0704-8*, 1667) Books on Tape, Inc.
—The Girl in the Plain Brown Wrapper. l.t. ed. 1984. (General Ser.). lib. bdg. 12.95 o.p. (*0-8161-3627-0*, Macmillan Reference USA) Gale Group.
—The Green Ripper. 21.95 (*0-89190-779-3*) Amereon, Ltd.
—The Green Ripper. (Travis McGee Novel Ser.). 1996. 320p. mass mkt. 7.50 (*0-449-22481-3*); 1987. 288p. mass mkt. 5.99 o.s.i (*0-449-13246-3*); 1985. 228p. mass mkt. 3.50 o.p. (*0-449-13042-8*) Ballantine Bks. (Fawcett).
—The Green Ripper. unabr. collector's ed. 1980. (Travis McGee Ser.: No. 18). audio 42.00 (*0-7366-0474-X*, 1449) Books on Tape, Inc.
—The Green Ripper. 1980. (General Ser.). lib. bdg. 12.95 o.p. (*0-8161-3023-X*, Macmillan Reference USA) Gale Group.
—The Green Ripper. 1979. 15.00 o.p. (*0-397-01362-0*) HarperCollins Pubs.
—The Green Ripper. abr. ed. (Travis McGee Ser.). 1994. audio 8.99 o.s.i (*0-679-43407-0*); 1991. audio 16.00 o.p. (*0-394-55988-6*); Set. 2000. audio 9.99 o.s.i (*0-375-41581-5*) Random Hse. Audio Publishing Group. (RH Audio).
—The Lonely Silver Rain. 1996. 320p. mass mkt. 7.50 (*0-449-22485-6*); 1986. 256p. mass mkt. 5.95 o.s.i (*0-449-12509-2*) Ballantine Bks. (Fawcett).
—The Lonely Silver Rain. unabr. collector's ed. 1986. (Travis McGee Ser.: No. 21). audio 42.00 (*0-7366-0476-6*, 1451) Books on Tape, Inc.
—The Long Lavender Look. (Travis McGee Novel Ser.). 1998. mass mkt. 5.99 (*0-449-45717-6*); 1996. 352p. mass mkt. 6.99 (*0-449-22474-0*); 1987. 256p. mass mkt. 4.95 o.s.i (*0-449-13334-6*) Ballantine Bks. (Fawcett).
—The Long Lavender Look. unabr. collector's ed. 1984. (Travis McGee Ser.: No. 12). audio 48.00 (*0-7366-0705-6*, 1668) Books on Tape, Inc.
—The Long Lavender Look. l.t. ed. 1986. (General Ser.). 363p. 15.95 o.p. (*0-8161-4007-3*, Macmillan Reference USA) Gale Group.
—The Long Lavender Look. abr. ed. (Travis McGee Ser.). 1994. audio 8.99 o.s.i (*0-679-43406-2*); 1990. audio 15.95 o.p. (*0-394-55982-7*) Random Hse. Audio Publishing Group. (RH Audio).
—Nightmare in Pink. (Travis McGee Novel Ser.). 1995. 304p. mass mkt. 6.99 (*0-449-22414-7*); 1987. 144p. mass mkt. 4.95 o.s.i (*0-449-13312-5*) Ballantine Bks. (Fawcett).
—Nightmare in Pink. unabr. collector's ed. 1983. (Travis McGee Ser.: No. 2). audio 36.00 (*0-7366-0700-5*, 1663) Books on Tape, Inc.
—Nightmare in Pink. 1976. (Adult Ser.). reprint ed. lib. bdg. 9.95 o.p. (*0-8161-6382-0*, Macmillan Reference USA) Gale Group.
—One Fearful Yellow Eye. 1997. mass mkt. 5.99 (*0-449-45639-0*); 1996. 336p. mass mkt. 7.50 (*0-449-22458-9*); 1987. 244p. mass mkt. 4.95 o.s.i (*0-449-13292-7*); 1985. mass mkt. 3.50 o.p. (*0-449-12933-0*) Ballantine Bks. (Fawcett).
—One Fearful Yellow Eye. 1983. (General Ser.). lib. bdg. 14.95 o.p. (*0-8161-3380-8*, Macmillan Reference USA) Gale Group.
—Pale Gray for Guilt. 1997. mass mkt. 5.99 (*0-449-45721-4*); 1996. 320p. mass mkt. 6.99 (*0-449-22460-0*); 1987. 224p. mass mkt. 5.99 o.s.i (*0-449-13331-1*); 1985. mass mkt. 3.95 o.p. (*0-449-12897-0*) Ballantine Bks. (Fawcett).
—Pale Gray for Guilt. unabr. collector's ed. 1984. (Travis McGee Ser.: No. 9). audio 48.00 (*0-7366-0703-X*, 1666) Books on Tape, Inc.
—Pale Gray for Guilt. l.t. ed. 1986. (Large Print Bks.). 357p. lib. bdg. 15.95 o.p. (*0-8161-4006-5*, Macmillan Reference USA) Gale Group.
—A Purple Place for Dying. 1995. 320p. mass mkt. 7.50 (*0-449-22438-4*); 1987. 160p. mass mkt. 5.99 o.s.i (*0-449-13336-2*); 1980. mass mkt. 2.25 o.p. (*0-449-14219-1*) Ballantine Bks. (Fawcett).
—A Purple Place for Dying. unabr. collector's ed. 1977. (Travis McGee Ser.: No. 3). audio 36.00 (*0-7366-0052-3*, 1064) Books on Tape, Inc.
—A Purple Place for Dying. l.t. ed. 1984. (General Ser.). 312p. 9.95 o.p. (*0-8161-3690-4*); lib. bdg. 13.95 o.p. (*0-8161-3625-4*) Gale Group. (Macmillan Reference USA).
—A Purple Place for Dying. 1976. 15.00 o.p. (*0-397-01166-0*) HarperCollins Pubs.
—The Quick Red Fox. 1996. mass mkt. 5.99 (*0-449-45613-7*); 1995. 320p. mass mkt. 7.50 (*0-449-22440-6*); 1987. 160p. mass mkt. 4.95 o.s.i (*0-449-13403-2*); 1981. mass mkt. 2.50 o.p. (*0-449-14264-7*) Ballantine Bks. (Fawcett).
—The Quick Red Fox. l.t. ed. 1993. 12.95 o.p. (*0-8161-3382-4*, Macmillan Reference USA) Gale Group.
—The Scarlet Ruse. 1996. 352p. mass mkt. 7.50 (*0-449-22477-5*); 1987. 320p. mass mkt. 4.95 o.s.i (*0-449-13247-1*); 1985. mass mkt. 3.50 o.p. (*0-449-13040-1*) Ballantine Bks. (Fawcett).
—The Scarlet Ruse. unabr. collector's ed. 1985. (Travis McGee Ser.: No. 14). audio 48.00 (*0-7366-0707-2*, 1670) Books on Tape, Inc.
—The Scarlet Ruse. 1980. (General Ser.). lib. bdg. 13.95 o.p. (*0-8161-3118-X*, Macmillan Reference USA) Gale Group.
—The Scarlet Ruse. abr. ed. 1994. (Travis McGee Ser.). audio 8.99 o.s.i (*0-679-43405-4*, RH Audio) Random Hse. Audio Publishing Group.
—Slam the Big Door. 1987. 272p. mass mkt. 4.95 o.s.i (*0-449-13275-7*, Fawcett) Ballantine Bks.
—Slam the Big Door. 1987. 208p. 16.45 o.p. (*0-89296-190-2*) Mysterious Pr.
—Slam the Big Door. 1989. 3.99 o.p. (*0-517-00478-X*) Random Hse. Value Publishing.
—A Tan & Sandy Silence. (Travis McGee Novel Ser.). 1996. 336p. mass mkt. 7.50 (*0-449-22476-7*, Fawcett); 1986. 256p. mass mkt. 4.95 o.s.i (*0-449-13250-1*, Fawcett); 1985. 256p. mass mkt. 3.50 o.p. (*0-449-12969-1*, Fawcett); 1984. mass mkt. 2.95 o.p. (*0-449-12707-9*); 1983. mass mkt. 2.95 o.p. (*0-449-12677-3*); 1982. mass mkt. 2.75 o.p. (*0-449-12404-5*); 1981. mass mkt. 2.50 o.p. (*0-449-14220-5*); 1978. mass mkt. 1.75 o.p. (*0-449-13635-3*) Ballantine Bks.
—A Tan & Sandy Silence. unabr. collector's ed. 1984. (Travis McGee Ser.: No. 13). audio 48.00 (*0-7366-0706-4*, 1669) Books on Tape, Inc.
—A Tan & Sandy Silence. l.t. ed. 1982. 360p. lib. bdg. 13.95 o.p. (*0-8161-3381-6*, Macmillan Reference USA) Gale Group.
—A Tan & Sandy Silence. abr. ed. 1994. audio 8.99 o.s.i (*0-679-43408-9*); 1993. audio 16.00 o.p. (*0-394-55983-5*) Random Hse. Audio Publishing Group. (RH Audio).
—The Turquoise Lament. 1996. 320p. mass mkt. 6.99 (*0-449-22478-3*); 1987. 256p. mass mkt. 5.99 o.s.i (*0-449-13249-8*); 1982. 256p. mass mkt. 2.95 o.p. (*0-449-14200-0*) Ballantine Bks. (Fawcett).
—The Turquoise Lament. unabr. collector's ed. 1983. (Travis McGee Ser.: No. 15). audio 48.00 (*0-7366-0708-0*, 1671) Books on Tape, Inc.
—The Turquoise Lament. l.t. ed. 1982. lib. bdg. 13.95 o.p. (*0-8161-3383-2*, Macmillan Reference USA) Gale Group.
—The Turquoise Lament. 1973. 15.00 (*0-397-00987-9*, Lippincott) Lippincott Williams & Wilkins.
—The Turquoise Lament. abr. ed. 1991. (Travis McGee Ser.). audio 16.00 o.s.i (*0-394-55985-1*, RH Audio) Random Hse. Audio Publishing Group.
MacGregor, T. J. Blue Pearl. 1994. 384p. 21.95 (*0-7868-6061-8*) Hyperion Pr.
—Dark Fields. 9999. 4.95 o.p. (*0-345-22756-5*); 1986. mass mkt. 5.99 o.s.i (*0-345-33756-5*) Ballantine Bks.

Settings

—Death Flats. 1991. (Florida Mysteries Ser.). (Orig.). mass mkt. 4.99 o.s.i (*0-345-35768-X*) Ballantine Bks.

—Death Sweet. 1988. 384p. mass mkt. 4.99 o.s.i (*0-345-33753-0*) Ballantine Bks.

—Kill Flash. 1987. pap. 3.95 o.p. (*0-345-00751-4*); mass mkt. 4.99 o.s.i (*0-345-33754-9*) Ballantine Bks.

—Kin Dread. 1990. 320p. (Orig.). mass mkt. 4.95 o.s.i (*0-345-35766-3*) Ballantine Bks.

—Mistress of the Bones. 1995. 352p. 21.95 (*0-7868-6106-1*) Hyperion Pr.

—On Ice. 1989. mass mkt. 4.99 o.s.i (*0-345-35045-6*) Ballantine Bks.

—The Seventh Sense. 1999. 272p. 23.00 o.s.i (*1-57566-411-9*) Kensington Publishing Corp.

—Seventh Sense. 2000. 352p. mass mkt. 6.99 (*0-7860-1083-5*, Pinnacle Bks.) Kensington Publishing Corp.

—Spree. 1992. (Florida Mysteries Ser.). (Orig.). mass mkt. 4.99 o.s.i (*0-345-37346-4*) Ballantine Bks.

—Storm Surge. 1993. 336p. (YA). 19.95 o.p. (*1-56282-789-8*) Hyperion Pr.

—Vanished. 2001. 384p. mass mkt. 6.99 (*0-7860-1162-9*, Pinnacle Bks.) Kensington Publishing Corp.

Mackle, Elliott. It Takes Two: A Novel. 2003. 280p. pap. 13.95 (*1-55583-754-9*) Alyson Pubns.

Macomber, Robert N. At the Edge of Honor: A Novel of the Naval Civil War. 2002. (Illus.). 278p. 19.95 (*1-56164-252-5*) Pineapple Pr., Inc.

Mansell, Patrick J. The Fathers Club. 2002. 268p. pap. 23.50 (*0-9676853-8-9*); 2001. 276p. 23.50 (*0-9676853-2-X*) Bimini Twist Adventures, Inc.

Marcus, Martin L. Freedom Land. 2003. 352p. 24.95 (*0-7653-0482-1*, Forge Bks.) Doherty, Tom Assocs., LLC.

Marlowe, Toby. Beyond a Reasonable Doubt. 1997. 352p. mass mkt. 5.99 o.s.i (*0-7860-0429-0*, Pinnacle Bks.) Kensington Publishing Corp.

Martin, Clayton M. El Destino. 2001. Tr. of Destination. 194p. per. 16.95 o.p. (*1-929925-92-1*) First-Publish.

Mathews, Richard & Wilber, Rick, eds. Subtropical Speculations: An Anthology of Florida Science Fiction. 1991. 304p. pap. 12.95 o.p. (*0-910923-82-5*) Pineapple Pr., Inc.

Matteson, Stefanie. Murder under the Palms. l.t. ed. 1998. (Beeler Large Print Mystery Ser.). 25.95 (*1-57490-137-0*, Beeler Large Print Bks.) Beeler, Thomas T. Publisher.

—Murder under the Palms. 1997. 256p. (Charlotte Graham Mystery Ser.: Vol. 3). 21.95 o.s.i (*0-425-15628-1*); reprint ed. mass mkt. 5.99 o.s.i (*0-425-16035-1*) Berkley Publishing Group. (Prime Crime).

—Murder under the Palms. unabr. ed. 1999. audio 44.95 (*0-7861-1653-6*, 2481) Blackstone Audio Bks., Inc.

Matthiessen, Peter. Killing Mister Watson. 1991. 384p. pap. 14.00 (*0-679-73405-8*, Vintage) Knopf Publishing Group.

—Killing Mister Watson. 1992. 3.99 o.p. (*0-517-08671-9*) Random Hse. Value Publishing.

—Lost Man's River. 1998. 560p. pap. 15.00 (*0-679-73564-X*) Random Hse., Inc.

Mayerson, Evelyn W. Dade County Pine. 1994. 464p. 22.95 o.p. (*0-525-93646-7*, Dutton) Dutton/Plume.

—Miami. 1995. 496p. mass mkt. 5.99 o.s.i (*0-451-18147-6*, Signet Bks.) NAL.

McBain, Ed, pseud. Beauty & the Beast. unabr. ed. 1985. (Matthew Hope Ser.). audio 42.00 (*0-7366-1034-0*, 1964) Books on Tape, Inc.

—Beauty & the Beast. 1983. 228p. o.p. (*0-03-062198-4*) Holt, Henry & Co.

—Beauty & the Beast. 1988. 256p. mass mkt. 3.99 o.s.i (*1-55817-662-4*); mass mkt. 3.95 o.p. (*1-55817-134-7*) Kensington Publishing Corp. (Pinnacle Bks.).

—Beauty & the Beast. 1994. 224p. mass mkt. 5.99 o.s.i (*0-446-60131-4*) Warner Bks., Inc.

—Cinderella. unabr. ed. 1992. (Matthew Hope Ser.). audio 48.00 (*0-7366-2245-4*, 3035) Books on Tape, Inc.

—Cinderella. 1986. (Matthew Hope Ser.). 256p. (J). o.p. (*0-03-004959-8*) Holt, Henry & Co.

—Cinderella. 1993. 15.95 o.p. (*1-55800-396-7*); audio 8.95 o.p. (*1-55800-494-7*, Dove Audio) NewStar Media, Inc.

—Cinderella. 272p. 1994. mass mkt. 5.99 o.s.i (*0-446-60134-9*); 1989. mass mkt. 4.99 (*0-445-40898-7*, Mysterious Pr. Paperback Bks.); 1988. mass mkt. 3.95 o.s.i (*0-445-40618-6*) Warner Bks., Inc.

—Gladly the Cross-Eyed Bear. unabr. ed. 1997. (Matthew Hope Ser.). audio 48.00 (*0-913369-38-1*, 4214) Books on Tape, Inc.

—Gladly the Cross-Eyed Bear. Set. abr. ed. 1996. (Matthew Hope Mystery Ser.). 3p. audio 16.99 (*0-88646-423-4*, 394439) Durkin Hayes Publishing Ltd.

—Gladly the Cross-Eyed Bear. l.t. ed. 1996. (G. K. Hall Core Ser.). 424p. 25.95 (*0-7838-1899-8*, Macmillan Reference USA) Gale Group.

—Gladly the Cross-Eyed Bear. l.t. ed. 1998. (Paperback Bestsellers Ser.). 424p. pap. 25.95 (*0-7838-1900-5*) Thorndike Pr.

—Gladly the Cross-Eyed Bear. (Matthew Hope Novels Ser.). 336p. 1998. mass mkt. 6.50 o.s.i (*0-446-60494-1*); 1996. 22.50 o.p. (*0-446-51989-8*) Warner Bks., Inc.

—Goldilocks. 1979. pap. 2.25 o.p. (*0-553-12158-8*, 13158-3) Bantam Bks.

—Goldilocks. unabr. ed. 1985. (Matthew Hope Ser.). audio 36.00 (*0-7366-1032-4*, 1962) Books on Tape, Inc.

—Goldilocks. 224p. 1988. mass mkt. 3.95 o.s.i (*1-55817-108-8*); 1985. pap. 3.50 o.p. (*0-523-42452-3*) Kensington Publishing Corp. (Pinnacle Bks.).

—Goldilocks. 1978. 8.95 o.p. (*0-87795-177-2*, Morrow, William & Co.) Morrow/Avon.

—Goldilocks. 1996. 224p. mass mkt. 5.99 o.s.i (*0-446-60305-8*) Warner Bks., Inc.

—The House That Jack Built. unabr. ed. 1992. (Matthew Hope Ser.). audio 48.00 (*0-7366-2177-6*, 2974) Books on Tape, Inc.

—The House That Jack Built. l.t. ed. 1989. (General Ser.). 320p. 13.95 o.p. (*0-8161-4934-8*); lib. bdg. 20.95 (*0-8161-4758-2*) Gale Group. (Macmillan Reference USA).

—The House That Jack Built. 1988. 16.95 o.p. (*0-8050-0787-3*) Holt, Henry & Co.

—The House That Jack Built. 256p. 1994. mass mkt. 5.99 o.s.i (*0-446-60136-5*); 1989. mass mkt. 4.99 (*0-445-40623-2*, Mysterious Pr. Paperback Bks.) Warner Bks., Inc.

—Jack & the Beanstalk. unabr. ed. 1985. (Matthew Hope Ser.). audio 48.00 Books on Tape, Inc.

—Jack & the Beanstalk. 1984. o.p. (*0-03-062197-6*) Holt, Henry & Co.

—Jack & the Beanstalk. 288p. 1992. mass mkt. 3.99 o.s.i (*1-55817-663-2*); 1985. pap. 3.50 o.p. (*0-523-42559-7*) Kensington Publishing Corp. (Pinnacle Bks.).

—Jack & the Beanstalk. 1994. 256p. mass mkt. 5.99 (*0-446-60132-2*) Warner Bks., Inc.

—The Last Best Hope. unabr. ed. 1998. (Matthew Hope Ser.). audio 40.00 (*0-7366-4215-3*, 4713) Books on Tape, Inc.

—The Last Best Hope. l.t. ed. 1998. (Basic Ser.). 397p. pap. 29.95 (*0-7862-1605-0*) Thorndike Pr.

—The Last Best Hope. (Matthew Hope Novels Ser.). 1999. 304p. mass mkt. 7.50 o.s.i (*0-446-60673-1*); 1998. 320p. 24.00 o.p. (*0-446-51990-1*) Warner Bks., Inc.

—Mary, Mary. l.t. ed. 1993. 24.95 o.p. (*0-7927-1662-0*); pap. 22.95 o.p. (*0-7927-1661-2*) BBC Audiobooks America.

—Mary, Mary. unabr. ed. 1993. (Matthew Hope Ser.). audio 72.00 (*0-7366-2480-5*, 3242) Books on Tape, Inc.

—Mary, Mary. unabr. ed. 1993. 73.25 o.p. incl. audio (*1-56100-137-6*, 1280, Unabridged Library Editions); audio 23.95 o.p. (*1-56100-508-8*, 173, Bookcassette) Brilliance Audio.

—Mary, Mary. 384p. 1994. mass mkt. 5.99 o.s.i (*0-446-60054-7*); 1993. 19.95 o.s.i (*0-446-51738-0*) Warner Bks., Inc.

—Puss in Boots. unabr. ed. 1992. (Matthew Hope Ser.). audio 48.00 (*0-7366-2193-8*, 2988) Books on Tape, Inc.

—Puss in Boots. 1987. 15.95 o.p. (*0-8050-0371-1*) Holt, Henry & Co.

—Puss in Boots. 1993. audio 15.95 o.p. (*1-55800-259-6*) NewStar Media, Inc.

—Puss in Boots. 1994. 224p. mass mkt. 5.99 o.s.i (*0-446-60135-7*); 1988. mass mkt. 4.95 o.s.i (*0-445-40621-6*) Warner Bks., Inc.

—Rumpelstiltskin. 1985. 240p. mass mkt. 4.95 o.s.i (*0-345-33149-4*); 1982. mass mkt. 2.50 o.p. (*0-345-30436-5*) Ballantine Bks.

—Rumpelstiltskin. 1981. (Matthew Hope Mystery Ser.). 12.95 o.p. (*0-670-61059-3*) Viking Penguin.

—Rumpelstiltskin. 1994. 240p. mass mkt. 5.99 o.s.i (*0-446-60130-6*) Warner Bks., Inc.

—Snow White & Rose Red. unabr. ed. 1995. audio 54.95 (*0-7451-6155-3*, CAB 162) BBC Audiobooks America.

—Snow White & Rose Red. unabr. ed. 1986. (Matthew Hope Ser.). audio 48.00 (*0-7366-1036-7*, 1966) Books on Tape, Inc.

—Snow White & Rose Red. 1985. o.p. (*0-03-002603-2*) Holt, Henry & Co.

—Snow White & Rose Red. abr. ed. 1993. audio 15.95 o.p. (*1-55800-256-1*, Dove Audio) NewStar Media, Inc.

—Snow White & Rose Red. 256p. 1994. mass mkt. 5.99 o.p. (*0-446-60133-0*); 1986. reprint ed. mass mkt. 4.99 o.s.i (*0-445-40513-9*) Warner Bks., Inc.

—There Was a Little Girl. l.t. ed. 1995. 424p. pap. 19.95 o.p. (*0-7838-1181-0*); 480p. 24.95 o.p. (*0-7838-1180-2*) Gale Group. (Macmillan Reference USA).

—There Was a Little Girl. 1995. 352p. mass mkt. 6.50 (*0-446-60214-0*); 1994. 336p. 21.95 o.s.i (*0-446-51739-9*) Warner Bks., Inc.

—Three Blind Mice. unabr. ed. 1991. (Matthew Hope Ser.). audio 56.00 (*0-7366-1963-1*, 2784) Books on Tape, Inc.

—Three Blind Mice. l.t. ed. 1991. (General Ser.). 396p. lib. bdg. 21.95 (*0-8161-5169-5*, Macmillan Reference USA) Gale Group.

—Three Blind Mice. abr. ed. (Super Sound Buy, Dove Ser.). 1994. audio 8.99 o.p. (*0-7871-0233-4*); 1993. 15.95 o.p. (*1-55800-392-4*, 41460) NewStar Media, Inc.

—Three Blind Mice. 1994. 304p. mass mkt. 5.99 o.s.i (*0-446-60137-3*); 1991. mass mkt. 4.99 o.s.i (*0-446-40035-1*) Warner Bks., Inc.

McCarthy, Kevin. More Florida Stories. 1996. (Illus.). 326p. pap. 17.95 (*0-8130-1485-9*) Univ. Pr. of Florida.

McCarthy, Kevin, ed. Florida Stories. 1989. (Illus.). 300p. pap. 17.95 (*0-8130-0910-3*) Univ. Pr. of Florida.

—More Florida Stories. 1996. (Illus.). 326p. 29.95 (*0-8130-1468-9*) Univ. Pr. of Florida.

McCarthy, Susan Carol. Lay That Trumpet in Our Hands. 288p. 2003. pap. 12.95 (*0-553-38103-2*); 2002. 23.95 (*0-553-80169-4*) Bantam Bks.

McCunn, Ruthanne Lum. Wooden Fish Songs. 2000. (Blue Streak Ser.). 384p. pap. 14.00 (*0-8070-6229-4*) Beacon Pr.

—Wooden Fish Songs. 400p. 1996. pap. 12.95 o.p. (*0-452-27346-3*, Plume); 1995. 22.95 o.p. (*0-525-93927-X*, Dutton) Dutton/Plume.

McDonald, Cherokee P. Summer's Reason. 1994. 256p. 19.95 o.p. (*1-55611-409-5*) Fine, Donald I. Bks.

McElroy, Paul E. Treasure Coast Deceit. 2002. (Treasure Coast Mystery Ser.). (Illus.). 306p. pap. 18.45 (*0-9715136-0-0*) Treasure Coast Mysteries, Inc.

McFarland, Dennis. School for the Blind. 1995. 272p. mass mkt. 6.99 o.s.i (*0-8041-1350-5*, Ivy Bks.) Ballantine Bks.

—School for the Blind. 1994. 304p. 21.95 o.p. (*0-395-64497-6*) Houghton Mifflin Co.

—School for the Blind. unabr. ed. 1995. audio 29.95 (*1-879371-84-7*, 70030) Publishing Mills, Inc., The.

McGuane, Thomas. Ninety-Two in the Shade. 1973. 224p. 8.95 o.p. (*0-374-22259-2*) Farrar, Straus & Giroux.

—Ninety-Two in the Shade. 1980. pap. 4.95 o.p. (*0-14-005319-0*) Penguin Group (USA) Inc.

—Ninety-Two in the Shade. 1995. (Vintage Contemporaries Ser.). 208p. pap. 13.00 (*0-679-75289-7*) Random Hse., Inc.

—Ninety-Two in the Shade. 1987. 208p. pap. 10.00 o.p. (*0-14-009907-7*, Penguin Bks.) Viking Penguin.

McKinney, Michael. A Thousand Bridges: A Novel. 1992. 153p. 19.95 o.p. (*0-8027-1223-1*) Walker & Co.

McLeod, Loren. Abandoned in Wysteria. 2003. 192p. pap. 13.95 (*0-595-29787-0*) iUniverse, Inc.

—Settling in Sandspur. 2003. 160p. pap. 12.95 (*0-595-29853-2*) iUniverse, Inc.

McNaught, Judith. Night Whispers. l.t. ed. (Wheeler Press Paperback Ser.). 2000. 11.95 (*1-56895-968-0*); 1999. 27.95 o.p. (*1-56895-647-9*) Gale Group. (Wheeler Publishing, Inc.).

—Night Whispers. 1999. (Illus.). 464p. pap. 7.99 (*0-671-52574-3*, Pocket); 1998. mass mkt. 7.99 (*0-671-02834-0*, Pocket); 1998. (Illus.). 400p. 24.00 o.s.i (*0-671-00085-3*, Atria) Simon & Schuster.

—Night Whispers. 2001. audio 9.98 (*0-7435-0863-7*, Simon & Schuster Audioworks) Simon & Schuster Audio.

Medina, C. C. A Little Love. 2000. 368p. 18.95 (*0-446-52448-4*) Warner Bks., Inc.

Michener, James A. Recessional. 1995. 544p. mass mkt. 7.99 (*0-449-22345-0*, Fawcett) Ballantine Bks.

—Recessional. unabr. ed. 1995. audio 136.00 (*0-7366-2956-4*, 3650A/B) Books on Tape, Inc.

—Recessional. abr. ed. 1994. audio 17.00 o.s.i (*0-679-43717-7*, RH Audio) Random Hse. Audio Publishing Group.

—Recessional. l.t. ed. 1994. 640p. 24.00 o.s.i (*0-679-75691-4*) Random Hse. Large Print.

Miller, Carlene. Killing at the Cat: A Lexy Hyatt Mystery. 1998. 200p. pap. 10.95 (*0-934678-95-2*) New Victoria Pubs., Inc.

—Mayhem at the Marina: A Lexy Hyatt Mystery. 1999. (Lexy Hyatt Mysteries Ser.). 220p. pap. 11.95 (*1-892281-05-8*) New Victoria Pubs., Inc.

Miller, Craig Miles. Chester Stubbs. 2001. 288p. 30.00 (*0-939767-36-8*) McMillan, Dennis Pubns.

Mink, Charles. Princess of the Everglades. 1991. 212p. 16.95 o.p. (*0-910923-98-1*) Pineapple Pr., Inc.

Mixon, Laura J. & Gould, Steven. Greenwar. 1998. 608p. mass mkt. 6.99 (*0-8125-7116-9*, Tor Bks.); 1997. 384p. 25.95 (*0-312-85261-4*, Forge Bks.) Doherty, Tom Assocs., LLC.

Monroe, Mary. The Upper Room. 1986. 304p. mass mkt. 3.95 o.s.i (*0-345-32913-9*) Ballantine Bks.

—The Upper Room. 2002. 32p. pap. 15.00 (*0-7582-0023-4*); 2001. 352p. 24.00 o.s.i (*1-57566-910-2*); 2001. 15.00 (*0-7582-0000-5*, Dafina) Kensington Publishing Corp.

—The Upper Room. 1985. 272p. 14.95 o.p. (*0-312-83402-0*) St. Martin's Pr.

—The Upper Room. 2002. (African American Ser.). 28.95 (*0-7862-4864-5*) Thorndike Pr.

Montalbano, William D. & Hiaasen, Carl. Trap Line. 1982. 256p. 13.95 o.p. (*0-689-11307-2*, Scribner) Simon & Schuster.

Morris, Scott M. Waiting for April: A Novel. 2003. 352p. tchr. ed. 24.95 (*1-56512-370-0*, 72370) Algonquin Bks. of Chapel Hill.

Mukherjee, Bharati. Jasmine. audio 8.95 American Audio Prose Library, Inc.

—Jasmine. 1990. 244p. mass mkt. 6.99 o.s.i (*0-449-21923-2*, Fawcett) Ballantine Bks.

—Jasmine. 1989. 228p. 17.95 o.p. (*0-8021-1032-0*); 1999. 256p. reprint ed. pap. 12.00 (*0-8021-3630-3*, Grove Pr.) Grove/Atlantic, Inc.

Munn, Vella. Seminole Song. 1997. 352p. 23.95 (*0-312-85896-5*, Forge Bks.) Doherty, Tom Assocs., LLC.

—The Seminole Song. 1998. 306p. mass mkt. 5.99 (*0-8125-3883-8*, Forge Bks.) Doherty, Tom Assocs., LLC.

Nagel, Edward A. No Entry. 1995. 184p. 20.00 (*1-56858-025-8*) Four Walls Eight Windows.

Nehrbass, Arthur F. Dead Easy. 1992. 240p. 19.00 o.p. (*0-525-93513-4*, Dutton) Dutton/Plume.

—Dead Heat. 1994. 336p. 19.95 o.p. (*0-525-93664-5*, Dutton) Dutton/Plume.

Nelson, Liza. Playing Botticelli. 2001. 288p. pap. 12.95 o.s.i (*0-425-17818-8*) Berkley Publishing Group.

Noone, John J. The Barrys of Key West & Annapolis. 1996. 450p. pap. 24.00 (*1-57197-008-8*) Pentland Pr., Inc.

Norman, Geoffrey. Blue Chipper. 1992. 256p. 20.00 o.p. (*0-688-11654-X*, Morrow, William & Co.) Morrow/Avon.

—Deep End. 1994. 302p. 20.00 o.p. (*0-688-11655-8*, Morrow, William & Co.) Morrow/Avon.

O'Sullivan, Maurice J. & Glassman, Steve, eds. Orange Pulp: Stories of Mayhem, Murder & Mystery. 2000. viii, 311p. 24.95 (*0-8130-1803-X*) Univ. Pr. of Florida.

Owens, Janis. My Brother Michael. 1997. 304p. 18.95 (*1-56164-124-3*) Pineapple Pr., Inc.

—Myra Sims. 1999. 480p. 22.95 (*1-56164-177-4*) Pineapple Pr., Inc.

—The Schooling of Claybird Catts. 2003. 304p. 24.95 (*0-06-009062-6*) HarperCollins Pubs.

—The Schooling of Claybird Catts. 2004. 304p. pap. 12.95 (*0-06-009063-4*, Perennial) HarperTrade.

Pairo, Preston. Winner's Cut. 1988. 256p. pap. (*0-373-97069-2*, Harlequin Bks.) Harlequin Enterprises, Ltd.

Pairo, Preston A., III. Angel's Crime. 1998. 416p. mass mkt. 6.50 o.s.i (*0-451-40710-5*, Onyx) NAL.

Parker, Barbara. Blood Relations. 1996. 384p. 22.95 o.s.i (*0-525-93976-8*) Dutton/Plume.

—Blood Relations. 1997. 448p. mass mkt. 6.99 (*0-451-18473-4*, Signet Bks.) NAL.

—Blood Relations. abr. ed. 1996. audio 16.95 o.p. (*0-14-086285-4*, Penguin AudioBooks) Viking Penguin.

—Criminal Justice. 1997. 320p. 22.95 o.p. (*0-525-93977-6*) Dutton/Plume.

—Criminal Justice. l.t. ed. 1997. 26.95 (*1-56895-498-0*, Wheeler Publishing, Inc.) Gale Group.

—Criminal Justice. 1998. 448p. mass mkt. 6.99 (*0-451-18474-2*, Signet Bks.) NAL.

—Suspicion of Betrayal. 2000. 432p. mass mkt. 6.99 (*0-451-19838-7*, Signet Bks.) NAL.

—Suspicion of Deceit. unabr. ed. 1998. audio 78.00 (*0-7887-3572-1*, 95937E7) Recorded Bks., LLC.

—Suspicion of Guilt. 1995. 400p. 22.95 o.p. (*0-525-93769-2*, Dutton) Dutton/Plume.

—Suspicion of Guilt. l.t. ed. 1995. 26.95 (*1-56895-232-5*, Wheeler Publishing, Inc.) Gale Group.

—Suspicion of Guilt. 1996. 432p. mass mkt. 6.99 (*0-451-17703-7*, Signet Bks.) NAL.

—Suspicion of Guilt. unabr. ed. 1995. audio 91.00 (*0-7887-0353-6*, 94545E7) Recorded Bks., LLC.

—Suspicion of Innocence. 1994. 352p. 20.95 o.p. (*0-525-93744-7*); 20.95 (*0-525-93747-1*) Dutton/Plume. (Dutton).

—Suspicion of Innocence. 1994. 448p. mass mkt. 6.99 (*0-451-17340-6*, Signet Bks.) NAL.

—Suspicion of Innocence. unabr. ed. 1994. audio 85.00 (*0-7887-0024-3*, 94223E7) Recorded Bks., LLC.

—Suspicion of Innocence. 344p. 4.98 o.p. (*0-8317-4569-X*) Smithmark Pubs., Inc.

—Suspicion of Malice. 2000. 352p. 22.95 o.s.i (*0-525-94542-3*) Dutton/Plume.

—Suspicion of Malice. 2001. 432p. reprint ed. mass mkt. 6.99 (*0-451-20125-6*, Signet Bks.) NAL.

—Suspicion of Malice. l.t. ed. 2000. (Mystery Ser.). 565p. 29.95 (*0-7862-2655-2*) Thorndike Pr.

Settings

Parrish, P. J. Paint It Black. 2002. 416p. mass mkt. 6.99 (*0-7860-1419-9*, Pinnacle Bks.) Kensington Publishing Corp.

Patti, Paul. Silhouettes. 1991. 256p. mass mkt. 3.99 (*0-312-92672-3*, St. Martin's Paperbacks); 1990. 16.95 o.p. (*0-312-04684-7*, Saint Martin's Minotaur) St. Martin's Pr.

Peck, Robert Newton. Hallapoosa. 1988. 215p. (gr. 4-7). 16.95 o.p. (*0-8027-1016-6*) Walker & Co.

—The Horse Hunters. 1988. (Illus.). 160p. 15.95 o.s.i (*0-394-56980-6*) Random Hse., Inc.

Pedrazas, Allan. Angel's Cove: A Harry Rice Mystery. 1999. (WWL Mystery Ser.: No. 302). per. (*0-373-26302-3*, 1-26302-9, Worldwide Library) Harlequin Enterprises, Ltd.

—Angel's Cove: A Harry Rice Mystery. 1997. (Harry Rice Mystery Ser.). 272p. 21.95 (*0-312-16773-3*, Saint Martin's Minotaur) St. Martin's Pr.

—The Harry Chronicles: A Mystery. 1997. 256p. mass mkt. 4.99 o.p. (*0-06-104435-0*, HarperTorch) Morrow/Avon.

—The Harry Chronicles: A Mystery. 1995. 256p. 21.95 o.p. (*0-312-13506-8*, Saint Martin's Minotaur) St. Martin's Pr.

Pickard, Nancy. Ring of Truth. l.t. ed. 2002. (Marie Lightfoot Mysteries Ser.). 29.95 (*0-7862-3743-0*) Gale Group.

—Ring of Truth. (Marie Lightfoot Mysteries Ser.). 2001. 23.95 (*0-7434-1205-2*, Atria); 2001. (Illus.). 272p. 23.95 (*0-671-88797-1*, Atria); 2002. (Illus.). 384p. reprint ed. pap. 6.99 (*0-671-88796-3*, Pocket); 2001. reprint ed. E-Book 23.95 (*0-7434-1805-0*, Atria) Simon & Schuster.

—The Truth Hurts. (Marie Lightfoot Mysteries Ser.). 2003. 400p. mass mkt. 6.99 (*0-7434-1204-4*, Pocket); 2002. 336p. 24.00 (*0-7434-1203-6*, Atria) Simon & Schuster.

—The Truth Hurts. l.t. ed. 2002. (Marie Lightfoot Mysteries Ser.). 29.95 (*0-7862-4675-8*) Thorndike Pr.

—The Whole Truth. (Marie Lightfoot Mysteries Ser.). E-Book 22.95 (*1-58945-297-6*) Adobe Systems, Inc.

—The Whole Truth. (Marie Lightfoot Mysteries Ser.). 2000. 272p. 22.95 o.s.i (*0-671-88795-5*, Atria); 2001. reprint ed. E-Book 22.95 (*0-7434-1804-2*, Atria); 2001. (Illus.). 368p. reprint ed. mass mkt. 6.99 o.s.i (*0-671-88794-7*, Pocket) Simon & Schuster.

—The Whole Truth. l.t. ed. 2000. (Marie Lightfoot Mysteries Ser.). 439p. 29.95 (*0-7862-2577-7*) Thorndike Pr.

Pistone, Joseph D. Donnie Brasco: Deep Cover. 1999. 368p. mass mkt. 6.99 o.s.i (*0-451-40881-0*, Onyx) NAL.

Poyer, David. Down to a Sunless Sea: A Tiller Galloway Underwater Thriller. 1998. (Down to a Sunless Sea Ser.: Vol. 1). 368p. mass mkt. 5.99 (*0-312-96407-2*, St. Martin's Paperbacks); 1996. 352p. 23.95 o.p. (*0-312-14589-6*) St. Martin's Pr.

Pozzessere, Heather G. If Looks Could Kill. 1997. 48p. mass mkt. (*1-55166-285-X*, 0-66285-8, Mira Bks.) Harlequin Enterprises, Ltd.

Price, Eugenia. Don Juan McQueen. 416p. 1993. mass mkt. 5.99 o.s.i (*0-553-22853-6*); 1975. pap. 1.75 o.p. (*0-553-06485-1*) Bantam Bks.

—Don Juan McQueen. 1992. 416p. mass mkt. 5.50 o.s.i (*0-515-10554-6*, Jove); 1986. mass mkt. 4.95 o.s.i (*0-425-09451-0*); 1984. mass mkt. 3.95 o.s.i (*0-425-07108-1*) Berkley Publishing Group.

—Don Juan McQueen. 1997. reprint ed. lib. bdg. 39.95 (*1-56849-598-6*) Buccaneer Bks., Inc.

—Don Juan McQueen. 2000. pap. 14.95 (*1-57736-213-6*, Hillsboro Pr.) Providence Hse. Pubs.

—Margaret's Story. 1999. mass mkt. (*0-553-22583-9*); 1984. 432p. mass mkt. 6.50 o.s.i (*0-553-26559-8*) Bantam Bks.

—Margaret's Story. 1980. 416p. 13.50 o.p. (*0-690-01939-4*) HarperCollins Pubs.

—Margaret's Story. 2001. pap. 14.95 (*1-57736-214-4*, Hillsboro Pr.) Providence Hse. Pubs.

—Maria. 1999. mass mkt. (*0-553-14089-2*); 1999. mass mkt. (*0-553-23476-5*); 1999. mass mkt. (*0-553-26241-5*); 1984. 432p. mass mkt. 6.99 o.s.i (*0-553-26362-5*) Bantam Bks.

Price, Eugenia, ed. Maria. 1999. (First Novel in the Florida Trilogy Ser.: Vol. 1). 408p. pap. 14.95 (*1-57736-152-0*) Providence Hse. Pubs.

Prospero, Ann. Almost Night. 2001. 320p. mass mkt. 6.99 (*0-451-20226-0*, Signet Bks.) NAL.

—Almost Night: A Novel. 2000. 256p. 23.95 o.s.i (*0-525-94532-6*, Dutton) Dutton/Plume.

Puig Zaldivar, Raquel, et al. Women Don't Need to Write. 1998. 352p. pap. 13.95 (*1-55885-257-3*) Arte Publico Pr.

Pulitzer, Roxanne. Facade. 1992. 256p. 20.00 o.p. (*0-671-74332-5*, Simon & Schuster) Simon & Schuster.

—The Palm Beach Story. 1997. 288p. mass mkt. 5.99 o.s.i (*1-57566-167-5*) Kensington Publishing Corp.

—The Palm Beach Story. 1995. 256p. 22.00 o.p. (*0-684-80190-6*, Simon & Schuster) Simon & Schuster.

Quesada, Roberto. Never Through Miami. Duncan, Patricia J., tr. from SPA. 2002. 192p. pap. 12.95 (*1-55885-366-9*) Arte Publico Pr.

Quindlen, Anna. Black & Blue: A Novel. 2000. 288p. pap. 13.95 (*0-385-33313-7*, Delta); 1999. 384p. mass mkt. 7.99 (*0-440-22610-4*) Dell Publishing.

—Black & Blue: A Novel. l.t. ed. 1998. 27.95 o.p. (*1-56895-565-0*, Wheeler Publishing, Inc.) Gale Group.

—Black & Blue: A Novel, abr. ed. 1998. audio 24.00 (*0-375-40190-3*, RH Audio) Random Hse. Audio Publishing Group.

—Black & Blue: A Novel. 1998. 296p. 23.00 (*0-375-50051-0*) Random Hse., Inc.

—Black & Blue: A Novel. 1999. 13.55 (*0-606-16456-1*) Turtleback Bks.

Quindlen, Anna, contrib. by. Black & Blue: A Novel. 1998. (*0-679-43539-5*, Random Hse. Bks. for Young Readers) Random Hse. Children's Bks.

Rainey, John C. The Thang That Ate My Grandaddy's Dog. 1997. 368p. 18.95 o.p. (*1-56164-130-8*) Pineapple Pr., Inc.

Ramus, David. The Gravity of Shadows. 1998. 304p. 24.00 o.s.i (*0-06-018779-4*) HarperCollins Pubs.

—The Gravity of Shadows: A Novel. 1999. 432p. mass mkt. 6.50 o.s.i (*0-06-109626-1*, HarperTorch) Morrow/Avon.

Rawlings, Marjorie Kinnan. Short Stories by Marjorie Kinnan Rawlings. Tarr, Rodger L., ed. 1994. (Illus.). 392p. (C). 49.95 (*0-8130-1252-X*); pap. 24.95 (*0-8130-1253-8*) Univ. Pr. of Florida.

Richards, Judith. Summer Lightning. l.t. ed. 1993. 13.50 o.p. (*0-8161-6647-1*, Macmillan Reference USA) Gale Group.

—Summer Lightning. 1987. 272p. reprint ed. pap. 6.95 o.p. (*0-934601-18-6*) Peachtree Pubs., Ltd.

—Summer Lightning. 6th ed. 1998. 271p. reprint ed. pap. 13.95 (*0-9668579-0-9*) Pierian Quality Reprints.

—Summer Lightning. 1978. 8.95 o.p. (*0-312-77544-X*) St. Martin's Pr.

Rivera, Beatriz. Playing with Light. 2000. 245p. pap. 12.95 (*1-55885-310-3*) Arte Publico Pr.

Roberts, T. A. Shy Moon. 1989. 260p. 16.95 o.p. (*0-910923-73-6*) Pineapple Pr., Inc.

Robinson, Kevin. Mall Rats: A Stick Foster Mystery. 1992. 202p. 19.95 o.p. (*0-8027-3215-1*) Walker & Co.

—A Matter of Perspective. 1993. (Stick Foster Mystery Ser.). 217p. 19.95 o.p. (*0-8027-3242-9*) Walker & Co.

—Split Seconds. 1991. 208p. 18.95 (*0-8027-5785-5*) Walker & Co.

Roby, Kinley. Death in a Hammock. 2003. 266p. 25.95 (*0-7862-5396-7*, Five Star) Gale Group.

Rodi, Robert. The Bird Cage. 1996. pap. 10.95 o.s.i (*0-452-27668-3*, Plume) Dutton/Plume.

Rosenbaum, Thane. Second Hand Smoke. 320p. 2000. pap. 13.95 (*0-312-25418-0*, Saint Martin's Griffin); 1999. 24.95 (*0-312-19954-6*) St. Martin's Pr.

Rosenfeld, Arthur. Diamond Eye: A Max Diamond Novel. 2001. 320p. 23.95 (*0-312-87871-0*, Forge Bks.) Doherty, Tom Assocs., LLC.

Rust, Ann O. Kissimmee. 1990. (Floridians Ser.: Vol. III). (Orig.). 250p. pap. 12.95 (*0-9620556-2-X*); 225p. pap. 17.50 (*0-9620556-3-8*) Amaro Bks.

—Monticello, Vol. IV. 1991. (Floridians Ser.). 250p. 17.50 (*0-9620556-6-2*); pap. 12.95 (*0-9620556-5-4*) Amaro Bks.

—Pahokee, Vol. V. 1992. (Floridians Ser.). 275p. 17.50 (*0-9620556-8-9*); pap. 12.95 (*0-9620556-9-7*) Amaro Bks.

—Palatka. (Floridians Ser.). (Orig.). 1989. 235p. pap. 12.95 (*0-9620556-1-1*); Vol. II. 1994. 231p. pap. text 17.50 (*1-883203-00-7*) Amaro Bks.

—Punta Rassa. (Floridians Ser.). 275p. (Orig.). 1991. pap. text 17.50 (*0-9620556-7-0*); 1988. pap. 12.95 (*0-9620556-0-3*) Amaro Bks.

Rutledge, Leigh W. The Lighthouse, the Cat & the Sea: A Tropical Tale. 1999. (Illus.). 128p. 17.95 o.p. (*0-525-94349-8*, Dutton Children's Bks.) Dutton/Plume.

—The Lighthouse, the Cat, & the Sea: A Tropical Tale. l.t. ed. 2000. (Americana Ser.). 175p. 26.95 (*0-7862-2528-9*) Thorndike Pr.

Sabatino, James R. Trilogy on South Beach: So Be, South Beach, Miami Beach; Full Moon over SoBe; And Away We Go. 2002. 257p. pap. 21.99 (*0-7388-5644-4*); text 31.99 (*0-7388-5643-6*) Xlibris Corp.

Salvatore, Diane. Paxton Court. 2003. 256p. reprint ed. pap. 10.95 (*1-931513-41-4*) Bella Bks., Inc.

—Paxton Court. 1996. 240p. pap. 10.95 (*1-56280-114-7*); 1995. 256p. 21.95 (*1-56280-109-0*) Naiad Pr., Inc.

Sanchez, Thomas. Mile Zero. audio 13.95 (*1-55644-354-4*, 10031) American Audio Prose Library, Inc.

—Mile Zero. 1990. (Vintage Contemporaries Ser.). 368p. pap. 14.00 (*0-679-73260-8*, Vintage) Knopf Publishing Group.

—Mile Zero. 1993. 4.99 o.p. (*0-517-10902-6*) Random Hse. Value Publishing.

Sanders, Glenda. Home Again. 2001. (Five Star Romance Ser.). 163p. 26.95 (*0-7862-3128-9*, Five Star) Gale Group.

—The Things We Do for Love. 2001. (Romances Ser.). 158p. 26.95 (*0-7862-3130-0*, Five Star) Gale Group.

Sanders, Lawrence. Guilty Pleasures. 1998. 352p. mass mkt. 7.50 o.s.i (*0-425-16639-2*) Berkley Publishing Group.

—Guilty Pleasures. l.t. ed. 1999. 27.95 (*1-56895-634-7*, Wheeler Publishing, Inc.) Gale Group.

—Guilty Pleasures. 1998. 320p. 24.95 o.p. (*0-399-14365-3*, G. P. Putnam's Sons); 24.95 o.s.i (*0-399-14690-3*) Penguin Group (USA) Inc.

—McNally's Caper. 1995. (Archy McNally Mystery Ser.). 352p. mass mkt. 7.99 (*0-425-14530-1*) Berkley Publishing Group.

—McNally's Caper. l.t. ed. 384p. reprint ed. 1995. pap. 18.95 o.p. (*0-8161-5975-0*); 1994. lib. bdg. 24.95 (*0-8161-5974-2*) Gale Group. (Macmillan Reference USA).

—McNally's Caper. l.t. ed. 1995. (Magna Large Print Ser.). 403p. o.p. (*0-7505-0837-X*) Magna Large Print Bks. GBR. *Dist:* Ulverscroft Large Print Canada, Ltd.

—McNally's Caper. 1994. 320p. 22.95 o.p. (*0-399-13919-2*, G. P. Putnam's Sons) Penguin Group (USA) Inc.

—McNally's Dilemma. 2000. (Archy McNally Mystery Ser.). 336p. mass mkt. 7.99 (*0-425-17536-7*) Berkley Publishing Group.

—McNally's Dilemma. 1999. 320p. 24.95 o.s.i (*0-399-14490-0*) Penguin Group (USA) Inc.

—McNally's Dilemma. l.t. ed. (Thorndike/G. K. Hall Paperback Bestsellers Ser.). 2000. 407p. 28.95 (*0-7862-2247-6*); 1999. 432p. 31.95 (*0-7862-2246-8*) Thorndike Pr.

—McNally's Gamble. 1998. (Archy McNally Mystery Ser.). 368p. mass mkt. 7.50 (*0-425-16259-1*) Berkley Publishing Group.

—McNally's Gamble. l.t. ed. 1997. 26.95 o.p. (*1-56895-487-5*, Wheeler Publishing, Inc.) Gale Group.

—McNally's Gamble. 1997. 307p. 24.95 o.s.i (*0-399-14248-7*, G. P. Putnam's Sons) Penguin Group (USA) Inc.

—McNally's Gamble. 24.95 o.s.i (*0-399-14560-5*) Putnam Publishing Group, The.

—McNally's Gamble. 1998. audio 9.98 (*0-671-58153-8*); 1997. audio 18.00 (*0-671-53793-8*, 394532) Simon & Schuster Audio. (Simon & Schuster Audioworks).

—McNally's Luck. 1993. (Archy McNally Mystery Ser.). 336p. mass mkt. 7.99 (*0-425-13745-7*) Berkley Publishing Group.

—McNally's Luck. l.t. ed. (G. K. Hall Large Print Book Ser.). 350p. 1994. pap. 19.95 o.p. (*0-8161-5678-6*); 1993. 24.95 (*0-8161-5677-8*) Gale Group. (Macmillan Reference USA).

—McNally's Luck. l.t. ed. 1994. (Magna Large Print Ser.). 406p. o.p. (*0-7505-0679-2*) Magna Large Print Bks. GBR. *Dist:* Ulverscroft Large Print Canada, Ltd.

—McNally's Luck. 1992. 320p. 22.95 o.p. (*0-399-13762-9*, G. P. Putnam's Sons) Penguin Group (USA) Inc.

—McNally's Luck. 1994. 5.99 o.p. (*0-517-12590-0*) Random Hse. Value Publishing.

—McNally's Luck, abr. ed. 1992. (Archy McNally Mystery Ser.). audio 17.00 (*0-671-76989-8*, Simon & Schuster Audioworks) Simon & Schuster Audio.

—McNally's Puzzle. l.t. ed. 1997. (Archy McNally Mystery Ser.). 352p. mass mkt. 7.99 (*0-425-15746-6*) Berkley Publishing Group.

—McNally's Puzzle. l.t. ed. 1996. 26.95 o.p. (*0-7838-1712-6*, Macmillan Reference USA) Gale Group.

—McNally's Puzzle. 1996. 320p. 24.95 o.p. (*0-399-14135-9*, G. P. Putnam's Sons) Penguin Group (USA) Inc.

—McNally's Puzzle, abr. ed. 1996. (Archy McNally Mystery Ser.). audio 18.00 (*0-671-53792-X*, 393484, Simon & Schuster Audioworks) Simon & Schuster Audio.

—McNally's Puzzle. l.t. ed. 1997. (Paperback Bestsellers Ser.). pap. 26.95 (*0-7838-1713-4*) Thorndike Pr.

—McNally's Risk. 1994. (Archy McNally Mystery Ser.). 336p. reprint ed. pap. 7.99 (*0-425-14286-8*) Berkley Publishing Group.

—McNally's Risk. l.t. ed. 1993. 322p. 26.95 o.p. (*1-56895-042-X*, Wheeler Publishing, Inc.) Gale Group.

—McNally's Risk. l.t. ed. 1994. (Magna Large Print Ser.). 420p. (*0-7505-0680-6*) Magna Large Print Bks. GBR. *Dist:* Ulverscroft Large Print Canada, Ltd.

—McNally's Risk. 1993. 320p. 22.95 o.p. (*0-399-13816-1*, G. P. Putnam's Sons) Penguin Group (USA) Inc.

—McNally's Risk, abr. ed. 1993. (Archy McNally Mystery Ser.). audio 17.00 (*0-671-79743-3*, 391159, Simon & Schuster Audioworks) Simon & Schuster Audio.

—McNally's Secret. 1993. (Archy McNally Mystery Ser.). 352p. pap. 7.99 (*0-425-13572-1*) Berkley Publishing Group.

—McNally's Secret. l.t. ed. 1993. (General Ser.). 381p. pap. 17.95 o.p. (*0-8161-5540-2*); lib. bdg. 22.95 o.p. (*0-8161-5539-9*) Gale Group. (Macmillan Reference USA).

—McNally's Secret. 1992. 320p. 21.95 o.p. (*0-399-13675-4*, G. P. Putnam's Sons) Penguin Group (USA) Inc.

—McNally's Secret. abr. ed. 1992. (Archy McNally Mystery Ser.). audio 17.00 (*0-671-74472-0*, 391160, Simon & Schuster Audioworks) Simon & Schuster Audio.

—McNally's Trial. 1996. (Archy McNally Mystery Ser.). 352p. pap. 7.99 (*0-425-14755-X*) Berkley Publishing Group.

—McNally's Trial. l.t. ed. 1995. (Large Print Bks.). 26.95 o.p. (*1-56895-208-2*, Wheeler Publishing, Inc.) Gale Group.

—McNally's Trial. 1995. 309p. 23.95 o.p. (*0-399-14006-9*) Penguin Group (USA) Inc.

—McNally's Trial. 1999. pap. 12.98 (*0-671-04455-9*, Simon & Schuster Audioworks) Simon & Schuster Audio.

—Sullivan's Sting. 1991. 368p. mass mkt. 7.99 (*0-425-12845-8*); 1990. 384p. 19.95 o.s.i (*0-399-13542-1*) Berkley Publishing Group.

—Sullivan's Sting. l.t. ed. 1991. (General Ser.). 428p. 18.95 (*0-8161-5088-5*); lib. bdg. 22.95 o.p. (*0-8161-5087-7*) Gale Group. (Macmillan Reference USA).

—Three Complete Novels: McNally's Caper; McNally's Trial; McNally's Puzzle. 1998. 800p. 12.98 o.p. (*0-399-14435-8*, G. P. Putnam's Sons) Penguin Group (USA) Inc.

—Three Complete Novels: McNally's Secret; McNally's Luck; McNally's Risk. 1997. 576p. 12.98 o.p. (*0-399-14307-6*, G. P. Putnam's Sons) Penguin Group (USA) Inc.

Sanders, Lawrence & Lardo, Vincent. McNally's Dare. 2003. 304p. 24.95 (*0-399-15055-2*) Penguin Group (USA) Inc.

—McNally's Folly. 2000. (Archy McNally Ser.). 320p. 24.95 o.s.i (*0-399-14618-0*) Penguin Group (USA) Inc.

—McNally's Folly. l.t. ed. 2000. (Basic Ser.). 431p. 31.95 (*0-7862-2643-9*) Thorndike Pr.

Saul, John. Darkness. 1992. 400p. mass mkt. 7.99 (*0-553-29726-0*) Bantam Bks.

—Darkness. 1991. audio 12.79 o.s.i (*0-553-70029-4*); 1999. audio 9.99 o.s.i (*0-553-70202-5*) Random Hse. Audio Publishing Group. (RH Audio).

—Darkness. 1992. 13.55 (*0-606-00760-1*) Turtleback Bks.

Sawyer, Meryl. Every Waking Moment. 2002. 384p. mass mkt. 6.99 (*0-8217-7212-0*) Kensington Publishing Corp.

—Every Waking Moment. 2003. 29.95 (*0-7862-5192-1*) Thorndike Pr.

Sayles, John. Los Gusanos. 1999. (SPA.). 536p. (*84-8306-223-2*) Debate, Editorial.

—Los Gusanos. (SPA.). 536p. 30.95 (*84-8306-224-0*, DB11247) Debate, Editorial ESP. *Dist:* Lectorum Pubns., Inc.

—Los Gusanos. 480p. 1992. pap. 12.00 o.p. (*0-06-092159-5*, Perennial); 1991. 22.95 o.p. (*0-06-016653-3*) HarperTrade.

—Los Gusanos. 1992. 4.99 o.p. (*0-517-09228-X*) Random Hse. Value Publishing.

Schmitt, Richard. The Aerialist: A Novel. 2002. 300p. pap. 13.00 (*0-15-600717-7*, Harvest Bks.) Harcourt Trade Pubs.

Schumacher, Aileen. Rosewood's Ashes: A Travers/Alvarez Mystery. 2001. (Tory Travers/David Alvarez Mysteries Ser.). 272p. 23.95 (*1-890768-32-4*, Intrigue Pr.) Corvus Publishing.

Sellers, Heather. Georgia under Water: Stories. 2001. 217p. pap. 13.95 (*1-889330-56-6*) Sarabande Bks., Inc.

Shames, Laurence. The Naked Detective. 2001. 304p. mass mkt. 6.99 (*0-345-43219-3*, Fawcett) Ballantine Bks.

—Sunburn. unabr. collector's ed. 1998. audio 48.00 (*0-7366-4167-X*, 4669) Books on Tape, Inc.

—Sunburn. 1996. 384p. mass mkt. 4.99 (*0-7868-8903-9*); 1995. 288p. 21.95 (*0-7868-6068-5*) Hyperion Pr.

—Sunburn, unabr. ed. 1998. audio 60.00 (*0-7887-1882-7*, 95304E7) Recorded Bks., LLC.

Shepard, Lucius. Valentine. 2003. 181p. pap. 11.95 (*1-56858-251-X*); 2002. 208p. 18.00 (*1-56858-215-3*) Four Walls Eight Windows.

Sher, Ira. Gentlemen of Space: A Novel. 304p. 2004. pap. 13.00 (*0-7432-4219-X*); 2003. 23.00 (*0-7432-4218-1*) Simon & Schuster. (Free Pr.).

Shetterly, Will. Dogland. 2002. mass mkt. 5.99 (*0-7653-4233-2*, Starscape); 1998. 448p. pap. 15.95 (*0-312-86605-4*, Tor Bks.); 1997. 488p. 25.95 o.p. (*0-312-85171-5*, Tor Bks.) Doherty, Tom Assocs., LLC.

Shriner, Larry. Epilogue for Murder. 1994. 264p. 21.95 (*0-8027-3182-1*) Walker & Co.

Shropshire, Mike. The Pro: A Golf Novel. 2001. 265p. 23.95 (*0-312-24231-X*) St. Martin's Pr.
Shulman, Sondra. Moon People. 1994. 353p. 20.00 (*1-880909-18-9*) Baskerville Pubs., Inc.
Singerman, Philip. Bobby Bagel & the Roadmasters. 2003. (*0-312-87505-3*, Forge Bks.) Doherty, Tom Assocs., LLC.
—The Prancing Tiger. 1995. 384p. mass mkt. 6.99 o.s.i (*0-8041-1428-5*, Ivy Bks.) Ballantine Bks.
—Prancing Tiger: A Thriller. 1995. 396p. 20.00 o.p. (*0-688-13049-6*, Morrow, William & Co.) Morrow/Avon.
—Proof Positive. 2001. 352p. 24.95 (*0-312-87686-6*, Forge Bks.) Doherty, Tom Assocs., LLC.
Smith, Debra White. Let's Begin Again. 2003. (Seven Sisters Ser.). 350p. pap. 10.99 (*0-7369-0663-0*) Harvest Hse. Pubs.
Smith, Edwin R. Blue Star Highway Vol. 1: A Tale of Redemption from North Florida. unabr. ed. 1997. 288p. (YA). (gr. 9 up). pap. 9.95 (*0-9659054-0-3*) Mile Marker 12 Publishing.
Smith, Mitchell. Sacrifice. 1997. 368p. 23.95 o.p. (*0-525-93978-4*) Dutton/Plume.
—Sacrifice. 1997. 432p. mass mkt. 6.99 o.s.i (*0-451-18475-0*, Signet Bks.) NAL.
Smith, Patrick. The River Is Home & Angel City: A Patrick Smith Reader. 1989. 400p. reprint ed. 18.95 (*0-910923-64-7*) Pineapple Pr., Inc.
Smith, Patrick D. Forever Island & Allapattah: A Patrick Smith Reader. 1987. 386p. reprint ed. 17.95 (*0-910923-42-6*) Pineapple Pr., Inc.
—A Land Remembered. 1986. mass mkt. 3.95 o.p. (*0-451-14037-0*); 432p. mass mkt. 5.99 o.p. (*0-451-15897-0*) NAL. (Signet Bks.).
—A Land Remembered. 1996. 403p. pap. 12.95 (*1-56164-116-2*); 1984. 404p. 18.95 (*0-910923-12-4*) Pineapple Pr., Inc.
Smith, Robert Kimmel. Sadie Shapiro in Miami. 1978. (General Ser.). lib. bdg. 9.95 o.p. (*0-8161-6551-3*, Macmillan Reference USA) Gale Group.
—Sadie Shapiro in Miami. 1977. 7.95 o.s.i (*0-671-22607-X*, Simon & Schuster) Simon & Schuster.
Spindler, Erica. Dead Run. l.t. ed. 2003. 576p. 28.95 (*1-58724-508-6*, Wheeler Publishing, Inc.) Gale Group.
—Dead Run. 2003. 480p. mass mkt. (*1-55166-683-9*, Mira Bks.) Harlequin Enterprises, Ltd.
Standiford, Les. Bone Key: A John Deal Novel. 2002. 320p. 24.95 (*0-399-14874-4*) Putnam Publishing Group, The.
—Deal on Ice. 1997. 256p. 23.00 o.p. (*0-06-017620-2*) HarperCollins Pubs.
—Deal on Ice. 1998. 400p. mass mkt. 6.50 o.s.i (*0-06-109338-6*, HarperTorch) Morrow/Avon.
—Deal to Die For. 1995. 352p. 22.00 o.p. (*0-06-017621-0*) HarperTrade.
—Deal to Die For. 1996. 352p. mass mkt. 5.99 o.p. (*0-06-109337-8*, HarperTorch) Morrow/Avon.
—Done Deal. 1993. 288p. 20.00 o.p. (*0-06-017731-4*) HarperTrade.
—Done Deal. 1994. 336p. mass mkt. 5.50 o.s.i (*0-06-109143-X*, HarperTorch) Morrow/Avon.
—Done Deal. 2002. 299p. pap. 14.95 o.s.i (*1-59058-002-8*) Poisoned Pen Pr.
—Done Deal, unabr. ed. 1998. audio 60.00 (*0-7887-1887-8*, 95309E7) Recorded Bks., LLC.
—Havana Run. 2004. 288p. mass mkt. 7.99 (*0-425-19717-4*) Berkley Publishing Group.
—Havana Run. l.t. ed. 2003. (John Deal Novel Ser.). 422p. 29.95 (*0-7862-5565-X*) Thorndike Pr.
—The Havana Run: A John Deal Novel. 2003. 320p. 24.95 (*0-399-15059-5*, Putnam & Grosset) Putnam Publishing Group, The.
—Presidential Deal. 1998. 304p. 24.00 o.s.i (*0-06-018655-0*) HarperCollins Pubs.
—Presidential Deal. 1999. 432p. mass mkt. 6.50 o.s.i (*0-06-109553-2*, HarperTorch) Morrow/Avon.
—Presidential Deal, 1998. audio 80.00 (*0-7887-2503-3*, 95575E7) Recorded Bks., LLC.
—Raw Deal. 1994. 288p. 22.00 o.p. (*0-06-017732-2*) HarperCollins Pubs.
—Raw Deal. 1995. 384p. mass mkt. 5.50 o.s.i (*0-06-109144-8*, HarperTorch) Morrow/Avon.
—Raw Deal. 2003. 320p. pap. 14.95 o.s.i (*1-59058-106-7*) Poisoned Pen Pr.
—Raw Deal, unabr. ed. 1998. audio 70.00 (*0-7887-1318-3*, 95176E7) Recorded Bks., LLC.
Stark, Richard. Comeback. 1997. 304p. 18.00 o.p. (*0-89296-661-0*) Mysterious Pr.
—Comeback. l.t. ed. 1998. (Cloak & Dagger Ser.). 315p. 27.95 (*0-7862-1348-5*) Thorndike Pr.
—Comeback. 1998. 304p. pap. 12.95 (*0-446-67465-6*) Warner Bks., Inc.
—Flashfire. 2000. 288p. 22.95 o.p. (*0-89296-710-2*); 304p. E-Book 14.95 (*0-7595-8032-4*); 304p. E-Book 14.95 (*0-7595-9036-2*); 304p. E-Book 14.95 (*0-7595-4031-4*); E-Book 14.95 (*0-7595-6031-5*) Mysterious Pr.
—Flashfire. l.t. ed. 2001. (Mystery Ser.). 328p. 29.95 (*0-7862-2940-3*) Thorndike Pr.
—Flashfire. 2001. 288p. reprint ed. pap. 12.95 (*0-446-67790-6*) Warner Bks., Inc.
Stewart, Mary. My Brother Michael. 1985. mass mkt. 4.95 o.s.i (*0-449-20735-8*, Fawcett); 1978. mass mkt. 1.75 o.s.i (*0-449-22974-2*) Ballantine Bks.
—My Brother Michael. 1960. 9.95 o.p. (*0-688-02140-9*, Morrow, William & Co.) Morrow/Avon.
—My Brother Michael. 1981. (Keith Jennison Large Type Bks.). (gr. 7 up). lib. bdg. 8.95 o.p. (*0-531-00243-8*, Watts, Franklin) Scholastic Library Publishing.
Stinemetz, Morgan. Bubba Whartz Stories. 2002. 128p. pap. 12.95 (*1-58980-013-3*) Pelican Publishing Co., Inc.
Stream, Arnold C. Until Proven Guilty. 1992. 320p. mass mkt. 4.99 o.p. (*0-425-13373-7*) Berkley Publishing Group.
—Until Proven Guilty. 1991. 272p. 19.95 o.p. (*0-8128-4010-0*, Scarborough Hse.) Madison Bks., Inc.
Stroud, Carsten. Cuba Strait. 2003. 624p. mass mkt. 7.99 (*0-7434-6393-5*, Pocket); 432p. 25.00 (*0-7432-4389-7*, Simon & Schuster) Simon & Schuster.
Suarez, Virgil. Going Under. 1996. 159p. 18.95 (*1-55885-159-3*) Arte Publico Pr.
Sullivan, Thomas. The Martyring. 2000. 256p. pap. 13.95 (*0-312-87498-7*, Tor Bks.); 1999. mass mkt. (*0-8125-4543-5*, Tor Bks.); 1998. 256p. 22.95 (*0-312-86361-6*, Forge Bks.) Doherty, Tom Assocs., LLC.
Sullivan, Winona. Dead South: A Sister Cecile Mystery. 1997. (Sister Cecile Mystery Ser.). 275p. mass mkt. 5.99 o.s.i (*0-8041-1513-3*, Ivy Bks.) Ballantine Bks.
—Dead South: A Sister Cecile Mystery. 1996. 288p. 21.95 o.p. (*0-312-13959-4*, Saint Martin's Minotaur) St. Martin's Pr.
—Death's a Beach: A Sister Cecile Mystery. 1997. (Sister Cecile Mystery Ser.). 276p. mass mkt. 5.99 o.s.i (*0-8041-1568-0*, Ivy Bks.) Ballantine Bks.
—Saving Death: A Sister Cecile Mystery. 2000. 256p. mass mkt. 6.50 (*0-8041-1899-X*, Ivy Bks.) Ballantine Bks.
Taylor, Matt & Taylor, Bonnie. Neon Dancers. 1991. 208p. 19.95 o.s.i (*0-8027-3207-0*) Walker & Co.
Templeton, Catherine C. The Righteous Rebel: Adam Cloud & the Natchez Intrigues, 1790-1795: A Novel. ltd. ed. 1997. 404p. 35.00 (*1-57168-163-9*) Eakin Pr.
—The Righteous Rebel: Adam Cloud & the Natchez Intrigues, 1790-1795: A Novel. 1997. 404p. pap. 19.95 (*1-57168-164-7*) Eakin Pr.
Tesler, Nancy. Sharks, Jellyfish & Other Deadly Things. 1998. (Carrie Carlin Mystery Ser.). 224p. mass mkt. 5.99 o.s.i (*0-440-22409-8*, Dell Bks.) Dell Publishing.
Thompson, Lee B. Addie. 2001. (Five Star First Edition Romance Ser.). 305p. 25.95 (*0-7862-3364-8*, Five Star) Gale Group.
Tonyan, Rick. Guns of the Palmetto Plains. 1994. (Cracker Western Ser.). 406p. 16.95 (*1-56164-061-1*); (gr. 4-7). pap. 9.95 (*1-56164-070-0*) Pineapple Pr., Inc.
Trocheck, Kathy Hogan. Crash Course. 1997. 272p. 22.50 o.p. (*0-06-017642-3*) HarperCollins Pubs.
—Crash Course. 1998. (Truman Kicklighter Mysteries Ser.). 320p. mass mkt. 5.99 o.s.i (*0-06-109172-3*, HarperTorch) Morrow/Avon.
—Lickety-Split. 1996. 288p. 22.00 o.p. (*0-06-017641-5*) HarperCollins Pubs.
—Lickety-Split. 1997. 272p. mass mkt. 5.99 o.s.i (*0-06-109361-0*, HarperTorch) Morrow/Avon.
Truluck, Bob. Saw Red. 2003. 230p. 30.00 (*0-939767-45-7*) McMillan, Dennis Pubns.
—Street Level. E-Book 22.95 (*0-312-27616-8*); 2000. 218p. 22.95 (*0-312-26626-X*, Saint Martin's Minotaur) St. Martin's Pr.
Unsworth, Barry. Sacred Hunger. 1992. 640p. 25.00 o.s.i (*0-385-26530-1*) Doubleday Publishing.
—Sacred Hunger. 1993. (Norton Paperback Fiction Ser.). 629p. pap. 14.95 (*0-393-31114-7*) Norton, W. W. & Co., Inc.
Van Lustbader, Eric. Dark Homecoming, 4 cass. abr. ed. 1997. audio 25.00 o.p. (*0-7871-0912-6*, 695113) NewStar Media, Inc.
—Dark Homecoming. 1998. per. 6.99 (*0-671-00330-5*, Pocket Star); 1998. per. 6.99 (*0-671-01742-X*, Pocket); 1997. 368p. 23.00 (*0-671-00329-1*, Atria) Simon & Schuster.
Van Wert, William. What's It All About? A Novel of Life, Love, & Key Lime Pie. 1996. 240p. 19.50 o.p. (*0-684-81872-8*, Simon & Schuster) Simon & Schuster.
Veciana-Suarez, Ana. The Chin Kiss King. 1998. 320p. pap. 12.95 o.s.i (*0-452-28009-5*, Plume) Dutton/Plume.
—The Chin Kiss King. 1997. 496p. 24.00 o.p. (*0-374-12130-3*) Farrar, Straus & Giroux.
Verne, Jules. From the Earth to the Moon. 1967. (Airmont Classics Ser.). (YA). (gr. 8 up). mass mkt. 1.75 (*0-8049-0142-2*, CL-142) Airmont Publishing Co., Inc.
—From the Earth to the Moon. (Illus.). reprint ed. lib. bdg. 21.95 (*0-88411-901-7*) Amereon, Ltd.
—From the Earth to the Moon. 1993. 208p. mass mkt. 5.95 (*0-553-21420-9*, Bantam Classics) Bantam Bks.
—From the Earth to the Moon. 1975. (Dent's Illustrated Children's Classics Ser.). (Illus.). 192p. (YA). reprint ed. 9.00 o.p. (*0-460-05088-5*) Biblio Distribution.
—From the Earth to the Moon. l.t. ed. 2000. (LRS Large Print Heritage Ser.). 223p. (YA). (gr. 7-12). lib. bdg. 27.95 (*1-58118-070-5*) LRS.
—From the Earth to the Moon. E-Book 2.95 (*1-57799-848-0*) Logos Research Systems, Inc.
—From the Earth to the Moon. E-Book 1.95 (*1-58515-183-1*) MesaView, Inc.
—From the Earth to the Moon. 1999. (Twelve-Point Ser.). 245p. lib. bdg. 25.00 (*1-58287-103-5*); 400p. lib. bdg. 26.00 (*0-939495-96-1*) North Bks.
—From the Earth to the Moon. l.t. ed. 2000. (Science Fiction Ser.). 245p. 25.95 (*0-7838-9075-3*) Thorndike Pr.
—From the Earth to the Moon & a Trip Round It! E-Book 2.49 (*1-58627-446-5*) Electric Umbrella Publishing.
—From the Earth to the Moon & a Trip Round It! 1998. (Pocket Classics). xi, 208p. pap. 10.95 (*0-7509-0824-6*) Sutton Publishing, Ltd. GBR. *Dist:* International Publishers Marketing.
Viets, Elaine. Murder between the Covers: A Dead-End Job Mystery. 2003. 288p. mass mkt. 5.99 (*0-451-21081-6*, Signet Bks.) NAL.
Vilmure, Daniel. Toby's Lie: A Novel. 1996. 272p. pap. 12.00 o.p. (*0-06-097694-2*) HarperCollins Pubs.
—Toby's Lie: A Novel. 1995. 272p. 21.00 o.p. (*0-684-80204-X*, Simon & Schuster) Simon & Schuster.
Vogt, M. Diane. Silicone Solution: A Novel of Mystery & Suspense. 1999. 174p. pap. 11.95 (*1-56315-171-5*) SterlingHouse Pubs., Inc.
—Six Bills: A Wilhelmina Carson Novel. 2003. 256p. 24.95 (*1-932407-02-2*, New Millennium Pr.) New Millennium Entertainment.
Wainscott, Tina. Back in Baby's Arms. 2001. 368p. mass mkt. 5.99 (*0-312-97688-7*, St. Martin's Paperbacks) St. Martin's Pr.
—Now You See Me. 2002. 384p. mass mkt. 6.99 (*0-312-97909-6*, St. Martin's Paperbacks) St. Martin's Pr.
Ward, Jon, illus. Big Deal & the Fountain of Youth. 2000. (J). (*1-892339-09-9*) Beachfront Publishing.
Watson, Sterling. Deadly Sweet. Grose, Bill, ed. 1994. 384p. 22.00 o.p. (*0-671-87135-8*, Atria) Simon & Schuster.
Webb, Cynthia. No Daughter of the South. 1997. 200p. (Orig.). pap. 10.95 (*0-934678-82-0*) New Victoria Pubs., Inc.
Weinman, Irving. Stealing Home: A Novel. 2003. 224p. pap. 14.95 (*1-880284-72-3*) Daniel, John & Co., Pubs.
West, Richard F. As Crime Goes by. 1998. (Old Gang of Mine Mysteries Ser.). 240p. mass mkt. 5.99 o.s.i (*0-425-16536-1*) Berkley Publishing Group.
—Ghoul of My Dreams. 1999. (Old Gang of Mine Mysteries Ser.). 256p. mass mkt. 5.99 o.s.i (*0-425-16983-9*) Berkley Publishing Group.
—Old Gang of Mine. 1997. 224p. mass mkt. 5.99 o.s.i (*0-425-15964-7*, Prime Crime) Berkley Publishing Group.
Wetlaufer, Suzy. Judgement Call: A Novel. 1992. 20.00 o.p. (*0-688-10930-6*, Morrow, William & Co.) Morrow/Avon.
White, Randy Wayne. Captiva. 1997. 336p. reprint ed. mass mkt. 6.99 (*0-425-15854-3*, Prime Crime) Berkley Publishing Group.
—Captiva. 1996. 256p. 21.95 o.s.i (*0-399-14140-5*, G. P. Putnam's Sons) Penguin Group (USA) Inc.
—Everglades. l.t. ed. 2003. 469p. 30.95 (*1-58724-468-3*, Wheeler Publishing, Inc.) Gale Group.
—Everglades. 2003. 352p. 21.95 (*0-399-15058-7*, Putnam & Grosset) Putnam Publishing Group, The.
—The Heat Islands. (Doc Ford Novel Ser.). 1993. 307p. mass mkt. 6.99 (*0-312-92977-3*, St. Martin's Paperbacks); 1992. 336p. 19.95 (*0-312-06993-6*, Saint Martin's Minotaur) St. Martin's Pr.
—The Man Who Invented Florida. 1993. 288p. 20.95 o.p. (*0-312-09866-9*, Saint Martin's Minotaur); 1997. 294p. reprint ed. pap. 6.99 (*0-312-95398-4*, St. Martin's Paperbacks) St. Martin's Pr.
—The Mangrove Coast. 1999. (Prime Crime Mysteries Ser.). 336p. reprint ed. mass mkt. 6.99 (*0-425-17194-9*, Prime Crime) Berkley Publishing Group.
—The Mangrove Coast. 1998. 256p. 22.95 o.p. (*0-399-14372-6*, G. P. Putnam's Sons) Penguin Group (USA) Inc.
—Sanibel Flats. 320p. 1990. 17.95 (*0-312-03926-3*, Saint Martin's Minotaur); 1991. reprint ed. mass mkt. 6.99 (*0-312-92602-2*, St. Martin's Paperbacks) St. Martin's Pr.
—Shark River. l.t. ed. 2002. 332p. lib. bdg. 28.95 (*1-58547-160-7*) Ctr. Point Large Print.
—Shark River. 2001. 320p. 24.95 o.p. (*0-399-14729-2*, Putnam & Grosset) Penguin Group (USA) Inc.
—Ten Thousand Islands. 2001. 320p. reprint ed. mass mkt. 6.99 (*0-425-18043-3*, Prime Crime) Berkley Publishing Group.
—Ten Thousand Islands. l.t. ed. 2001. xiv, 331p. 29.95 (*1-58724-110-2*, Wheeler Publishing, Inc.) Gale Group.
—Ten Thousand Islands. 2000. xvi, 320p. 23.95 o.s.i (*0-399-14620-2*) Penguin Group (USA) Inc.
—Twelve Mile Limit. 2002. 304p. 24.95 o.s.i (*0-399-14873-6*) Penguin Group (USA) Inc.
Whiteley, L. S. Snakes in the Garden. 1990. 280p. 19.95 o.p. (*0-8027-1113-8*) Walker & Co.
Wilkerson, William R. Forty Years Later: Florida: After the Takeover. 1991. 96p. pap. 9.95 (*0-942963-13-X*) Distinctive Publishing Corp.
Willeford, Charles. The Burnt Orange Heresy. 2000. 192p. mass mkt. 5.95 (*0-7867-0668-6*, Carroll & Graf Pubs.) Avalon Publishing Group.
—Burnt Orange Heresy. 1990. (Vintage Crime/Black Lizard Ser.). 160p. pap. 7.95 o.s.i (*0-679-73252-7*, Vintage) Knopf Publishing Group.
—The Burnt Orange Heresy. 1987. 160p. reprint ed. pap. 3.95 o.p. (*0-88739-025-0*, Black Mask) Creative Arts Bk. Co.
—The Difference. rev. ed. 1999. Orig. Title: The Hombre from Sonora. 156p. 30.00 (*0-939767-33-3*) McMillan, Dennis Pubns.
—Miami Blues. 1984. 208p. 12.95 o.p. (*0-312-53171-0*) St. Martin's Pr.
—The Shark-Infested Custard. 1993. 272p. 20.95 o.p. (*0-88733-163-7*) Underwood Bks., Inc.
—The Shark Infested Custard. 1996. 320p. mass mkt. 4.99 o.s.i (*0-440-21881-0*) Dell Publishing.
—Sideswipe. 1987. 272p. 15.95 o.p. (*0-312-00188-6*) St. Martin's Pr.
Willey, Gordon R. Selena. 1995. (Mystery Ser.). 250p. per. (*0-373-26190-X*, 1-26190-8, Harlequin Bks.) Harlequin Enterprises, Ltd.
—Selena. 1993. 208p. 19.95 (*0-8027-3227-5*) Walker & Co.
Williams, Carol Lynch. Christmas in Heaven. 2000. 171p. (J). (gr. 5-9). 16.99 o.s.i (*0-399-23436-5*, G. P. Putnam's Sons) Penguin Group (USA) Inc.
Wilson, F. Paul. Gateways: A Repairman Jack Novel. 2003. (Repairman Jack Ser.). 368p. 25.95 (*0-7653-0690-5*, Forge Bks.) Doherty, Tom Assocs., LLC.
—Gateways: A Repairman Jack Novel. 2003. 436p. 60.00 (*1-887368-67-1*) Gauntlett Pr.
Wilson, Jon. Bridger's Run: A Cracker Western. 1999. (Cracker Ser.). 256p. 14.95 (*1-56164-170-7*); (gr. 4-7). pap. 8.95 (*1-56164-174-X*) Pineapple Pr., Inc.
Wimberley, Darryl. A Rock & a Hard Place. 1999. 260p. 22.95 o.p. (*0-312-20504-X*, Saint Martin's Minotaur) St. Martin's Pr.
—Strawman's Hammock. 2001. 288p. 23.95 (*0-312-27187-5*) St. Martin's Pr.
Woods, Sherryl. Flamingo Diner. 2003. 400p. mass mkt. (*1-55166-722-3*, Mira Bks.) Harlequin Enterprises, Ltd.
—Hot Money. 1993. 288p. mass mkt. 4.99 o.s.i (*0-440-21485-8*) Dell Publishing.
—Hot Money. l.t. ed. 1995. 231p. pap. 19.95 o.p. (*0-7838-1192-6*, Macmillan Reference USA) Gale Group.
—Hot Property. 1992. 272p. mass mkt. 4.50 o.s.i (*0-440-21003-8*) Dell Publishing.
—Hot Schemes. 1994. 288p. mass mkt. 4.99 o.s.i (*0-440-21486-6*) Dell Publishing.
—Hot Schemes. l.t. ed. 1995. 248p. pap. 19.95 (*0-7838-1193-4*, Macmillan Reference USA) Gale Group.
—Hot Secret. 1992. 256p. mass mkt. 4.99 o.s.i (*0-440-21004-6*) Dell Publishing.
Woods, Stuart. Blood Orchid. l.t. ed. 2003. 32.95 (*1-58724-395-4*, Wheeler Publishing, Inc.) Gale Group.
—Blood Orchid. 2003. 368p. reprint ed. mass mkt. 7.99 (*0-451-20881-1*, Signet Bks.) NAL.
—Blood Orchid. 2002. (Holly Barker Ser.: No. 3). 304p. 25.95 o.s.i (*0-399-14929-5*); 4p. 24.95 incl. audio (*0-399-14953-8*, Putnam Berkley Audio) Putnam Publishing Group, The.
—Blood Orchid. unabr. ed. 2003. (Holly Barker Ser.). audio 19.99 (*1-59335-059-7*, 30144) Soulmate Audio Bks., Inc.
—Choke. unabr. ed. 1995. audio 56.00 (*0-7366-3192-5*, 3858) Books on Tape, Inc.
—Choke. l.t. ed. 1995. (Large Print Bks.). 25.95 o.p. (*1-56895-265-1*, Wheeler Publishing, Inc.) Gale Group.
—Choke. 1995. 320p. 23.00 o.p. (*0-06-017667-9*, Perennial); audio 17.00 o.p. (*0-694-51603-1*, HarperAudio) HarperTrade.
—Choke. 1996. 352p. mass mkt. 7.99 (*0-06-109422-6*, HarperTorch) Morrow/Avon.
—Choke, unabr. ed. audio 60.00 (*0-7887-0446-X*, 94642E7) Recorded Bks., LLC.
—Orchid Beach. l.t. ed. 1999. (Wheeler Large Print Book Ser.). 408p. 27.95 o.p. (*1-56895-774-2*, Wheeler Publishing, Inc.) Gale Group.

—Orchid Beach. 1999. 416p. mass mkt. 7.50 (*0-06-101341-2*); 1998. 336p. (YA). (gr. 10 up). 25.00 o.s.i (*0-06-019181-3*) HarperCollins Pubs.
—Orchid Blues. unabr. ed. 2001. (Holly Barker Ser.). audio 29.95 (*1-58788-784-3*, 3099, Brilliance Audio Unabridged) Brilliance Audio.
—Orchid Blues. 2002. 400p. reprint ed. mass mkt. 7.99 (*0-451-20671-1*, Signet Bks.) NAL.
—Orchid Blues. 2001. 350p. 24.95 o.s.i (*0-399-14777-2*) Penguin Group (USA) Inc.
—Orchid Blues. abr. ed. 2001. 4p. audio 24.95 o.s.i (*0-399-14820-5*, Putnam Berkley Audio) Putnam Publishing Group, The.
—Orchid Blues. unabr. ed. 2003. audio 19.99 (*1-59335-001-5*, 30085) Soulmate Audio Bks., Inc.
—Orchid Blues. l.t. ed. 2003. (Paperback Bestsellers Ser.). pap. 29.95 (*0-7838-9747-2*) Thorndike Pr.
Wyle, Dirk. Biotechnology Is Murder: A Ben Candidi Mystery. 2000. 271p. pap. 14.95 (*1-56825-045-2*, 045-2) Rainbow Bks., Inc.
—Pharmacology Is Murder: A Novel. 1998. 388p. pap. 16.95 (*1-56825-038-X*, 038X) Rainbow Bks., Inc.
Yancey, Richard. A Burning in Homeland. 2003. 352p. 25.00 (*0-7432-3013-2*, Simon & Schuster) Simon & Schuster.
Yglesias, Jose. The Truth about Them. 1999. (Pioneer Ser.). 272p. pap. 12.95 (*1-55885-273-5*) Arte Publico Pr.
—A Wake in Ybor City. 1998. (Pioneer Ser.). 212p. pap. 14.95 (*1-55885-248-4*) Arte Publico Pr.
—A Wake in Ybor City. 1981. 31.95 (*0-405-13172-0*) Ayer Co. Pubs., Inc.
Young, Douglas H. Jack-O-Lantern. 2003. 474p. 24.95 (*0-9606510-4-7*) Writer's Publishing Hse.
Young, Karen. Heat of the Night: Debt of Love, Touch the Dawn, The Silence of Midnight, 4 bks. in 1. 1999. 768p. per. (*0-373-20169-9*, 1-20169-8, Harlequin Bks.) Harlequin Enterprises, Ltd.
Ziegler, Irene. Rules of the Lake: Stories. 1999. 208p. 19.95 (*0-87074-447-X*) Southern Methodist Univ. Pr.

### FOREST COUNTY (IMAGINARY PLACE)—FICTION

Forrest, Leon. Divine Days. 1995. 1144p. pap. 18.00 (*0-393-31221-6*); 1993. 135p. 32.00 o.p. (*0-393-03612-X*) Norton, W. W. & Co., Inc.
—There Is a Tree More Ancient Than Eden. 2001. 213p. pap. 13.00 (*0-226-25721-5*) Univ. of Chicago Pr.

### FOREST KINGDOM (IMAGINARY PLACE: GREEN)—FICTION

Green, Simon R. Beyond the Blue Moon. 2000. (Hawk & Fisher Ser.). 496p. mass mkt. 6.99 (*0-451-45805-2*) DAW Bks., Inc.
—Blood & Honor. 1993. 336p. (Orig.). mass mkt. 4.99 o.s.i (*0-451-45242-9*, ROC) NAL.
—Blue Moon Rising. 1991. (Hawk & Fisher Ser.). 480p. mass mkt. 6.99 o.s.i (*0-451-45095-7*, ROC) NAL.
—Down among the Dead Men. 1993. 288p. (Orig.). mass mkt. 4.50 o.s.i (*0-451-45301-8*, ROC) NAL.

### FORGOTTEN REALMS (IMAGINARY PLACE)—FICTION

Anthony, Mark. Curse of the Shadowmage. 1995. (Forgotten Realms Harpers Ser.: 9). 320p. (Orig.). pap. 5.99 o.p. (*0-7869-0191-8*) Wizards of the Coast.
—Escape from the Undermountain. 1996. (Forgotten Realms Nobles Ser.: Bk. 3). 316p. pap. 5.99 (*0-7869-0477-1*) Wizards of the Coast.
—Forgotten Realms: Crypt of the Shadowking. 1993. (Harpers Ser.: Bk. 6). 320p. (Orig.). pap. 4.95 o.p. (*1-56076-594-1*) Wizards of the Coast.
Athans, Philip. Baldur's Gate. 1999. (Forgotten Realms Ser.). (Illus.). 246p. mass mkt. 6.99 (*0-7869-1525-0*) Wizards of the Coast.
—Baldur's Gate 2: Shadows of Amn. 2000. (Forgotten Realms Novel Ser.: Vol. II). (Illus.). 245p. mass mkt. 6.99 (*0-7869-1569-2*) Wizards of the Coast.
—Realms of the Deep. 2000. (Forgotten Realms Anthology Ser.). (Illus.). 342p. mass mkt. 5.99 (*0-7869-1568-4*) Wizards of the Coast.
Awlinson, Richard. Shadowdale. 1989. (Forgotten Realms Avatar Trilogy Ser.: Bk. 1). 335p. pap. 6.99 (*0-88038-730-0*) Wizards of the Coast.
—Tantras. 1989. (Forgotten Realms Avatar Trilogy Ser.: Bk. 2). 338p. mass mkt. 6.99 (*0-88038-748-3*) Wizards of the Coast.
—Waterdeep. 1989. (Forgotten Realms Avatar Trilogy Ser.: Bk. 3). 341p. mass mkt. 7.99 (*0-88038-759-9*) Wizards of the Coast.
Borowitz, Jeri B. Roscoe I. 1995. 159p. 7.50 (*0-9645624-0-5*) Clinton Publishing.
Boyd, Eric L. Powers & Pantheons Lorebook. 1997. (Forgotten Realms Game World Ser.). 21.95 (*0-7869-0657-X*) Wizards of the Coast.
Byers, Richard Lee. The Shattered Mask. 2001. (Forgotten Realms Ser.). 320p. mass mkt. 6.99 (*0-7869-1862-4*) Wizards of the Coast.
Ciencin, Scott. Forgotten Realms: The Night Parade. 1992. (Harpers Ser.: Bk. 4). 320p. (Orig.). pap. 4.95 o.p. (*1-56076-323-X*) Wizards of the Coast.
Cook, David. Forgotten Realms: Soldiers of Ice. 1993. (Harpers Ser.: Bk. 7). 320p. (Orig.). pap. 4.95 o.p. (*1-56076-641-7*) Wizards of the Coast.
Cook, Monte. Glass Prison. 1999. (Forgotten Realms Ser.). (Illus.). 292p. pap. 5.99 o.s.i (*0-7869-1343-6*) Wizards of the Coast.
Cunningham, Elaine. Elfshadow. 2000. (Forgotten Realms Ser.). (Illus.). 312p. mass mkt. 6.99 (*0-7869-1660-5*, TSR21660) Wizards of the Coast.
—Elfsong. 1994. (Forgotten Realms Harpers Ser.: No. 8). 310p. pap. 4.95 (*1-56076-679-4*) Wizards of the Coast.
—Forgotten Realms: Elfshadow. 1991. (Harpers Ser.: Bk. 2). 312p. pap. 5.99 (*1-56076-117-2*) Wizards of the Coast.
—The Magehound. 2000. (Forgotten Realms Ser.: Bk I). (Illus.). 312p. mass mkt. 5.99 (*0-7869-1561-7*) Wizards of the Coast.
—Silver Shadows. 1996. (Forgotten Realms Ser.). (Illus.). 374p. pap. 5.99 (*0-7869-0498-4*) Wizards of the Coast.
—Tangled Webs: Forgotten Realms Daughter of the Drow. 1996. 314p. pap. 19.99 o.p. (*0-7869-0516-6*) Wizards of the Coast.
Denning, Troy. Crucible: The Trial of Cyric the Mad, Vol. 5. 1998. (Forgotten Realms Novel Ser.). (Illus.). 378p. mass mkt. 6.99 (*0-7869-0724-X*) Wizards of the Coast.
—Dark Sun: The Verdant Passage. 1991. (Prism Pentad Ser.: Bk. 1). 320p. (Orig.). pap. 4.95 o.p. (*1-56076-121-0*) Wizards of the Coast.
—Forgotten Realms: The Parched Sea. 1991. (Harpers Ser.: Bk. 1). 320p. (Orig.). pap. 4.95 o.p. (*1-56076-067-2*) Wizards of the Coast.
—The Ogre's Pact. 1994. (Forgotten Realms Twilight Giants Ser.). 320p. (Orig.). pap. 4.95 o.p. (*1-56076-891-6*) Wizards of the Coast.
—The Veiled Dragon. 1996. (Forgotten Realms Harpers Ser.: Bk. 3). 320p. pap. 5.99 o.p. (*0-7869-0482-8*) Wizards of the Coast.
Dundee. Murder in Ravens Bluff. 1997. (Forgotten Realms Ser.). 16.99 o.s.i (*0-7869-0685-5*) TSR, Inc.
Greenwood, Ed. City of Splendor. 1994. (Advanced Dungeons & Dragons, 2nd Edition). 25.00 (*1-56076-868-1*) Wizards of the Coast.
—Crown of Fire. (Orig.). 2002. (Illus.). 384p. pap. 14.95 (*0-7869-2749-6*); 1994. 375p. pap. 6.99 (*1-56076-839-8*) Wizards of the Coast.
—Elminster: The Making of a Mage. (Forgotten Realms Ser.). 1995. 331p. pap. 7.99 (*0-7869-0203-5*); 1994. 320p. 16.95 o.p. (*1-56076-936-X*) Wizards of the Coast.
—Pages from the Mages: Forgotten Realms Accessory. 1995. 15.00 (*0-7869-0183-7*) Wizards of the Coast.
—Prayers from the Faithful. 1997. (Forgotten Realms Game World Ser.). 19.95 o.p. (*0-7869-0682-0*) Wizards of the Coast.
—Silverfall: Stories of the Seven Sisters. 1999. (Forgotten Realms Ser.). (Illus.). 376p. pap. 14.95 (*0-7869-1365-7*) Wizards of the Coast.
—Spellfire. 1988. (Forgotten Realms Novel Ser.). 382p. (Orig.). pap. 5.99 (*0-88038-587-1*) Wizards of the Coast.
—Volo's Guide to the Sword Coast. 1994. (Forgotten Realms). 9.95 (*1-56076-904-1*) TSR, Inc.
Greenwood, Ed & Denning, Troy. Death of the Dragon Bk. III: Cormyr Saga. 2001. (Forgotten Realms Ser.). 416p. reprint ed. pap. 7.99 (*0-7869-1863-2*, WTC21863) Wizards of the Coast.
Greenwood, Ed & Grubb, Jeff. Cormyr. 1994. 9.95 o.p. (*1-56076-818-5*) TSR, Inc.
—Cormyr: A Novel. 1998. (Forgotten Realms). 486p. pap. 7.99 (*0-7869-0710-X*) Wizards of the Coast.
Greenwood, Ed, et al. The Halls of Stormweather: A Novel in Seven Parts. 2000. (Forgotten Realms Ser.). (Illus.). 341p. mass mkt. 10.99 (*0-7869-1560-9*) Wizards of the Coast.
Grubb, Jeff. Forgotten Realms Campaign, 3 vols. 1993. (Advanced Dungeons & Dragons). 64p. 30.00 (*1-56076-617-4*) Wizards of the Coast.
Lowder, James. Forgotten Realms: Prince of Lies. 1993. (Finder's Stone Trilogy Ser.). 376p. (Orig.). pap. 6.99 (*1-56076-626-3*) Wizards of the Coast.
—Forgotten Realms: The Ring of Winter. 1992. (Harpers Ser.: Bk. 5). 320p. (Orig.). pap. 4.95 o.p. (*1-56076-330-2*) Wizards of the Coast.
—Ravenloft: Knight of the Black Rose. 1991. 313p. (Orig.). pap. 5.99 (*1-56076-156-3*) Wizards of the Coast.
—Realms of Infamy. 1995. (Forgotten Realms Ser.). 346p. pap. 5.99 (*1-56076-911-4*) Wizards of the Coast.
Meyers, Richard S. Murder in Halruaa. 1996. (Forgotten Realms Ser.). 280p. 18.99 (*0-7869-0521-2*, 8657) Wizards of the Coast.
Milan, Victor. Sword Play. 1996. (Forgotten Realms Ser.: Bk. 1). 313p. mass mkt. 5.99 o.s.i (*0-7869-0492-5*, TSR08569) Wizards of the Coast.
Niles, Douglas. Forgotten Realms: Black Wizards. 1988. (Moonshae Trilogy Ser.: Bk. 2). (Illus.). 352p. (Orig.). pap. 4.95 o.p. (*0-88038-563-4*) Wizards of the Coast.
—Forgotten Realms: Darkwell. 1989. (Moonshae Trilogy Ser.: Bk. 3). pap. 4.95 o.p. (*0-88038-717-3*) Wizards of the Coast.
—Forgotten Realms: The Coral Kingdom. 1992. (Druidhome Trilogy Ser.: Bk. 2). 320p. (Orig.). pap. 4.95 o.p. (*1-56076-332-9*) Wizards of the Coast.
—Forgotten Realms: The Druid Queen. 1993. (Druidhome Trilogy Ser.: Bk. 3). 320p. (Orig.). pap. 4.95 o.p. (*1-56076-568-2*) Wizards of the Coast.
—Forgotten Realms: The Prophet of Mooshae, Bk. 1. 1992. (Druidhome Trilogy Ser.). 320p. (Orig.). pap. 4.95 o.p. (*1-56076-319-1*) Wizards of the Coast.
Novak, Kate & Grubb, Jeff. Finder's Bane. 1997. (Forgotten Realms Novel Ser.). (Illus.). 314p. pap. 5.99 (*0-7869-0658-8*) Wizards of the Coast.
—Forgotten Realms: Azure Bonds. 1988. (Finder's Stone Trilogy Ser.: Bk. 1). 352p. (Orig.). pap. 4.95 o.p. (*0-88038-612-6*) Wizards of the Coast.
—Forgotten Realms: Song of the Saurials. 1991. (Finder's Stone Trilogy Ser.: Bk. 3). 320p. (Orig.). pap. 4.95 o.p. (*1-56076-060-5*) Wizards of the Coast.
—Forgotten Realms: The Wyvern's Spur. 1990. (Finder's Stone Trilogy Ser.: Bk. 2). (Illus.). 320p. (Orig.). pap. 4.95 o.p. (*0-88038-902-8*) Wizards of the Coast.
Odom, Mel. Under Fallen Stars Bk. II: The Threat from the Sea. 1999. (Forgotten Realms Ser.). (Illus.). 344p. pap. 5.99 (*0-7869-1378-9*) Wizards of the Coast.
Rabe, Jean. Forgotten Realms: Red Magic. 1991. (Harpers Ser.: Bk. 3). 320p. (Orig.). pap. 4.95 o.p. (*1-56076-118-0*) Wizards of the Coast.
Salvatore, R. A. Canticle. 1991. (Cleric Quintet Ser.: Bk. 1). 320p. pap. 5.99 o.p. (*1-56076-119-9*) TSR, Inc.
—Canticle. 2000. (Forgotten Realms Ser.). (Illus.). 314p. pap. 6.99 (*0-7869-1604-4*) Wizards of the Coast.
—The Chaos Curse. 2000. (Forgotten Realms Cleric Quintet Ser.: Vol. 5). (Illus.). 312p. mass mkt. 7.99 (*0-7869-1608-7*) Wizards of the Coast.
—The Crystal Shard. 1988. (Forgotten Realms Ser.: Bk. 1). (Illus.). 333p. pap. 7.99 (*0-88038-535-9*, TSR08411) Wizards of the Coast.
—The Dark Elf Trilogy. (Illus.). 1998. 805p. 24.99 o.p. (*0-7869-1176-X*); 2000. 808p. pap. 19.95 (*0-7869-1588-9*) Wizards of the Coast.
—The Dark Elf Trilogy Gift Set: Homeland; Exile; Sojourn, 3 bks., Set. gif. ed. 2001. (Forgotten Realms Ser.). 960p. reprint ed. mass mkt. 23.97 (*0-7869-2683-X*) Wizards of the Coast.
—Exile. rev. ed. 1990. (Forgotten Realms Dark Elf Trilogy Bks.: Vol. 2). (Illus.). 306p. mass mkt. 7.99 (*0-88038-920-6*) Wizards of the Coast.
—The Halfling's Gem. 1990. (Forgotten Realms Ser.: Bk. 3). (Illus.). 314p. mass mkt. 7.99 (*0-88038-901-X*) Wizards of the Coast.
—Homeland. (Illus.). (Orig.). 2004. 352p. 25.95 (*0-7869-3123-X*); 1990. (Forgotten Realms Dark Elf Trilogy Bks.: Bk. 1). 314p. pap. 7.99 (*0-88038-905-2*) Wizards of the Coast.
—The Icewind Dale Trilogy. collector's ed. (Forgotten Realms Ser.). (Illus.). 2000. 1040p. 27.95 (*0-7869-1557-9*); Set. 2002. mass mkt. 23.97 (*0-7869-2720-8*) Wizards of the Coast.
—In Sylvan Shadows. 1992. (Cleric Quintet Ser.: Bk. 2). 320p. (Orig.). pap. 5.99 o.p. (*1-56076-321-3*) TSR, Inc.
—Night Masks. 1992. (Cleric Quintet Ser.: Bk. 3). 320p. pap. 5.99 (*1-56076-328-0*) TSR, Inc.
—The Silent Blade. (Forgotten Realms Ser.). (Illus.). 1999. 394p. pap. 7.99 (*0-7869-1388-6*); 1998. 347p. 23.99 (*0-7869-1180-8*) Wizards of the Coast.
—Sojourn. 1991. (Forgotten Realms Dark Elf Trilogy Bks.: Bk. 3). (Illus.). 309p. mass mkt. 7.99 (*1-56076-047-8*) Wizards of the Coast.
—The Spine of the World. (Forgotten Realms Ser.). 1999. 345p. 23.99 (*0-7869-1418-1*); 2000. (Illus.). 381p. reprint ed. mass mkt. 7.99 (*0-7869-1404-1*) Wizards of the Coast.
—Streams of Silver. 1989. (Forgotten Realms Ser.: Bk. 2). 342p. mass mkt. 7.99 (*0-88038-672-X*) Wizards of the Coast.
—Sylvan Shadows, 2000. (Forgotten Realms Cleric Quintet Ser.: Vol. 2). (Illus.). 314p. mass mkt. 6.99 (*0-7869-1605-2*) Wizards of the Coast.
Schend, S., et al. Cloak & Dagger. 2000. (Forgotten Realms Ser.). 158p. pap. 26.95 (*0-7869-1627-3*) Wizards of the Coast.
Terra, John. Four from Cormyr. 1997. (Forgotten Realms Game World Ser.). 20.00 (*0-7869-0646-4*) Wizards of the Coast.
Thomsen, Brian M. Realms of Magic. 1995. (Forgotten Realms Anthology Ser.). 348p. (Orig.). pap. 6.99 (*0-7869-0303-1*) Wizards of the Coast.
—Realms of the Arcane. 1997. (Forgotten Realms Novel Ser.). 312p. mass mkt. 5.99 (*0-7869-0647-2*) Wizards of the Coast.
TSR Hobbies Staff. Port of Ravens Bluff. 1991. (Forgotten Realms Game World Ser.). 9.95 o.p. (*1-56076-120-2*) TSR, Inc.
TSR Inc. Staff. AD&D Forgotten Realms Interact. 1999. 28.00 (*0-7869-1451-3*) Wizards of the Coast.
—Adventures Drawn from Dungeon Magazine. 1999. (Forgotten Realms Game World Ser.). 32p. 9.95 o.p. (*0-7869-1337-1*) Wizards of the Coast.
—Demihumans of the Realms. 1999. (Forgotten Realms Game World Ser.). 96p. pap. 18.95 o.p. (*0-7869-1316-9*) Wizards of the Coast.
—Dream Spheres. 1999. (Forgotten Realms Novel Ser.). 375p. 5.99 (*0-7869-1342-8*) Wizards of the Coast.
—Elminster's Ecologies Appendix: The Battle of Bones & the Hill of Lost Souls. 1995. (TSR Forgotten Realms Game World Ser.). 9.95 (*0-7869-0115-2*) Wizards of the Coast.
—Elminster's Ecologies Appendix: The High Moor & the Serpent Hills, Vol. 2. 1995. (TSR Forgotten Realms Game World Ser.: Vol. 2). 9.95 (*0-7869-0171-3*) Wizards of the Coast.
—The Return of Randal Morn. 1995. (Advanced Dungeons & Dragons, 2nd Edition). 6.95 o.p. (*0-7869-0170-5*) TSR, Inc.
—Spellbound: Thay, Rashemen & Aglarond. 1995. (TSR Forgotten Realms Game World Ser.). 25.00 (*0-7869-0139-X*) Wizards of the Coast.
—Star of Cursrah. 1999. (Forgotten Realms Ser.). 310p. mass mkt. 5.99 o.s.i (*0-7869-1322-3*) Wizards of the Coast.
Ward, James M. Forgotten Realms: Pools of Darkness. 1992. (Pools Ser.: Bk. 2). pap. 4.95 o.p. (*1-56076-318-3*) Wizards of the Coast.
Ward, James M. & Brown, Anne K. Forgotten Realms. 1993. (Pools Ser.: Bk. 3). 320p. (Orig.). pap. 4.95 o.p. (*1-56076-582-8*) Wizards of the Coast.
Ward, James M. & Hong, Jane C. Forgotten Realms: Pool of Radiance. 1989. (Pools Ser.: Bk. 1). 316p. (Orig.). (J). pap. 4.95 o.p. (*0-88038-735-1*) Wizards of the Coast.

### FORT LAUDERDALE (FLA.)—FICTION

Files, Lolita. Scenes from a Sistah. 1998. 288p. pap. 13.99 (*0-446-67442-7*); 1998. 320p. mass mkt. 6.50 (*0-446-60539-5*); 1997. 288p. 22.00 o.p. (*0-446-52100-0*) Warner Bks., Inc.
MacDonald, John D. Bright Orange for the Shroud. (Travis McGee Novel Ser.). 1987. 224p. mass mkt. 5.99 o.s.i (*0-449-13358-3*, Fawcett); 1996. reprint ed. mass mkt. 5.99 (*0-449-45615-3*, Fawcett); 1996. 352p. reprint ed. mass mkt. 6.99 (*0-449-22444-9*, Ballantine Bks.) Ballantine Bks.
—Bright Orange for the Shroud. unabr. collector's ed. 1978. (Travis McGee Ser.: No. 6). audio 48.00 (*0-7366-0174-0*, 1176) Books on Tape, Inc.
—Bright Orange for the Shroud. l.t. ed. 1985. 14.95 o.p. (*0-8161-3979-2*, Macmillan Reference USA) Gale Group.
—Cinnamon Skin. (Travis McGee Novel Ser.). 1996. 336p. mass mkt. 7.50 (*0-449-22484-8*); 1986. 288p. mass mkt. 5.95 o.s.i (*0-449-12873-3*) Ballantine Bks. (Fawcett).
—Cinnamon Skin. unabr. collector's ed. 1982. (Travis McGee Ser.: No. 20). audio 48.00 (*0-7366-0689-0*, 1649) Books on Tape, Inc.
—Cinnamon Skin. 1983. (General Ser.). lib. bdg. 14.95 o.p. (*0-8161-3504-5*, Macmillan Reference USA) Gale Group.
—Cinnamon Skin. 1982. 288p. o.p. (*0-06-014990-6*) HarperCollins Pubs.
—Cinnamon Skin. abr. ed. 2000. (Travis McGee Ser.). audio 9.99 (*0-375-41014-7*, RH Audio) Random Hse. Audio Publishing Group.
—Cinnamon Skin. 1990. 3.99 o.p. (*0-517-05439-6*) Random Hse. Value Publishing.
—The Damned. 1985. (Travis McGee Novel Ser.). mass mkt. 3.95 o.s.i (*0-449-12887-3*, Fawcett) Ballantine Bks.
—Darker Than Amber. 1997. mass mkt. 5.99 (*0-449-45637-4*); 1996. 320p. mass mkt. 6.99 (*0-449-22446-5*); 1987. 192p. mass mkt. 5.99 o.s.i (*0-449-13339-7*); 1984. 192p. mass mkt. 2.95 o.p. (*0-449-12752-4*) Ballantine Bks. (Fawcett).
—Darker Than Amber. unabr. collector's ed. 1978. (Travis McGee Ser.: No. 7). audio 42.00 (*0-7366-0216-X*, 1214) Books on Tape, Inc.
—Darker Than Amber. l.t. ed. 1988. (General Ser.). 319p. 16.95 o.p. (*0-8161-4008-1*, Macmillan Reference USA) Gale Group.
—A Deadly Shade of Gold. (Travis McGee Novel Ser.). 1996. 448p. mass mkt. 6.99 (*0-449-22442-2*); 1987. 288p. mass mkt. 5.99 o.s.i (*0-449-13313-3*) Ballantine Bks. (Fawcett).
—A Deadly Shade of Gold. unabr. collector's ed. 1978. (Travis McGee Ser.: No. 5). audio 64.00 (*0-7366-0106-6*, 1114) Books on Tape, Inc.
—A Deadly Shade of Gold. l.t. ed. 1987. 447p. 16.95 o.p. (*0-8161-4004-9*, Macmillan Reference USA) Gale Group.

—The Deep Blue Goodbye. 1995. 320p. mass mkt. 6.99 (*0-449-22383-3*); 1986. 256p. mass mkt. 4.95 o.s.i (*0-449-13252-8*); 1984. mass mkt. 2.95 o.p. (*0-449-12673-0*) Ballantine Bks. (Fawcett).

—The Deep Blue Goodbye. unabr. collector's ed. 1983. (Travis McGee Ser.: No. 1). audio 36.00 (*0-7366-0699-8*, 1662) Books on Tape, Inc.

—The Deep Blue Goodbye. l.t. ed. 1984. (General Ser.). 296p. 12.95 o.p. (*0-8161-3626-2*); 8.95 o.p. (*0-8161-3740-4*) Gale Group. (Macmillan Reference USA).

—The Dreadful Lemon Sky. (Travis McGee Novel Ser.). 1996. 320p. mass mkt. 6.99 (*0-449-22479-1*); 1987. 272p. mass mkt. 5.99 o.s.i (*0-449-13404-0*); 1985. 272p. mass mkt. 3.50 o.p. (*0-449-12964-0*) Ballantine Bks. (Fawcett).

—Dress Her in Indigo. 1997. pap. text 5.99 (*0-449-45716-8*); 1996. 336p. mass mkt. 7.50 (*0-449-22462-7*); 1987. 256p. mass mkt. 5.99 o.s.i (*0-449-13293-5*); 1985. mass mkt. 3.50 o.p. (*0-449-12984-5*) Ballantine Bks. (Fawcett).

—Dress Her in Indigo. unabr. collector's ed. 1980. (Travis McGee Ser.: No. 11). audio 56.00 (*0-7366-0243-7*, 1239) Books on Tape, Inc.

—Dress Her in Indigo. l.t. ed. 1985. (General Ser.). 360p. 13.95 o.p. (*0-8161-3822-2*); 9.95 o.p. (*0-8161-3820-6*) Gale Group. (Macmillan Reference USA).

—The Empty Copper Sea. 21.95 (*0-89190-778-5*) Amereon, Ltd.

—The Empty Copper Sea. 1996. 320p. mass mkt. 7.50 (*0-449-22480-5*); 1987. 256p. mass mkt. 4.99 o.s.i (*0-449-13333-8*); 1985. mass mkt. 3.50 o.p. (*0-449-12913-6*) Ballantine Bks. (Fawcett).

—The Empty Copper Sea. unabr. collector's ed. 1979. (Travis McGee Ser.: No. 17). audio 48.00 (*0-7366-0331-X*, 1318) Books on Tape, Inc.

—The Empty Copper Sea. 1979. lib. bdg. 13.50 o.p. (*0-8161-6702-8*, Macmillan Reference USA) Gale Group.

—The Empty Copper Sea. abr. ed. 1987. audio 15.95 o.s.i (*0-394-56085-X*, RH Audio) Random Hse. Audio Publishing Group.

—Five Complete Travis McGee Novels. 1988. 8.99 o.s.i (*0-517-47671-1*) Random Hse. Value Publishing.

—Free Fall in Crimson. 1996. 320p. mass mkt. 7.50 (*0-449-22482-1*); 1987. 288p. mass mkt. 4.95 o.s.i (*0-449-13253-6*); 1985. 288p. mass mkt. 3.50 o.p. (*0-449-12894-6*) Ballantine Bks. (Fawcett).

—Free Fall in Crimson. unabr. collector's ed. 1981. (Travis McGee Ser.: No. 19). audio 48.00 (*0-7366-0632-7*, 1593) Books on Tape, Inc.

—Free Fall in Crimson. l.t. ed. 1981. 13.50 o.p. (*0-8161-3272-0*, Macmillan Reference USA) Gale Group.

—Free Fall in Crimson. 1981. 224p. 15.00 o.p. (*0-06-014833-0*) HarperTrade.

—Free Fall in Crimson. 1992. audio 16.00 o.s.i (*0-394-55989-4*, RH Audio) Random Hse. Audio Publishing Group.

—The Girl in the Plain Brown Wrapper. 1997. mass mkt. 5.99 (*0-449-45715-X*); 1996. 352p. mass mkt. 7.50 (*0-449-22461-9*); 1987. 256p. mass mkt. 5.99 o.s.i (*0-449-13341-9*); 1985. mass mkt. 3.50 o.p. (*0-449-12915-2*) Ballantine Bks. (Fawcett).

—The Girl in the Plain Brown Wrapper. unabr. collector's ed. 1984. (Travis McGee Ser.: No. 10). audio 56.00 (*0-7366-0704-8*, 1667) Books on Tape, Inc.

—The Girl in the Plain Brown Wrapper. l.t. ed. 1984. (General Ser.). lib. bdg. 12.95 o.p. (*0-8161-3627-0*, Macmillan Reference USA) Gale Group.

—The Green Ripper. 21.95 (*0-89190-779-3*) Amereon, Ltd.

—The Green Ripper. (Travis McGee Novel Ser.). 1996. 320p. mass mkt. 7.50 (*0-449-22481-3*); 1987. 288p. mass mkt. 5.99 o.s.i (*0-449-13246-3*); 1985. 228p. mass mkt. 3.50 o.p. (*0-449-13042-8*) Ballantine Bks. (Fawcett).

—The Green Ripper. unabr. collector's ed. 1980. (Travis McGee Ser.: No. 18). audio 42.00 (*0-7366-0474-X*, 1449) Books on Tape, Inc.

—The Green Ripper. 1980. (General Ser.). lib. bdg. 12.95 o.p. (*0-8161-3023-X*, Macmillan Reference USA) Gale Group.

—The Green Ripper. 1979. 15.00 o.p. (*0-397-01362-0*) HarperCollins Pubs.

—The Green Ripper. abr. ed. (Travis McGee Ser.). 1994. audio 8.99 o.s.i (*0-679-43407-0*); 1991. audio 16.00 o.p. (*0-394-55988-6*); Set. 2000. audio 9.99 o.s.i (*0-375-41581-5*) Random Hse. Audio Publishing Group. (RH Audio).

—The Lonely Silver Rain. 1996. 320p. mass mkt. 7.50 (*0-449-22485-6*); 1986. 256p. mass mkt. 5.95 o.s.i (*0-449-12509-2*) Ballantine Bks. (Fawcett).

—The Lonely Silver Rain. unabr. collector's ed. 1986. (Travis McGee Ser.: No. 21). audio 42.00 (*0-7366-0476-6*, 1451) Books on Tape, Inc.

—The Long Lavender Look. (Travis McGee Novel Ser.). 1998. mass mkt. 5.99 (*0-449-45717-6*); 1996. 352p. mass mkt. 6.99 (*0-449-22474-0*); 1987. 256p. mass mkt. 4.95 o.s.i (*0-449-13334-6*) Ballantine Bks. (Fawcett).

—The Long Lavender Look. unabr. collector's ed. 1984. (Travis McGee Ser.: No. 12). audio 48.00 (*0-7366-0705-6*, 1668) Books on Tape, Inc.

—The Long Lavender Look. l.t. ed. 1986. (General Ser.). 363p. 15.95 o.p. (*0-8161-4007-3*, Macmillan Reference USA) Gale Group.

—The Long Lavender Look. abr. ed. (Travis McGee Ser.). 1994. audio 8.99 o.s.i (*0-679-43406-2*); 1990. audio 15.95 o.p. (*0-394-55982-7*) Random Hse. Audio Publishing Group. (RH Audio).

—Nightmare in Pink. (Travis McGee Novel Ser.). 1995. 304p. mass mkt. 6.99 (*0-449-22414-7*); 1987. 144p. mass mkt. 4.95 o.s.i (*0-449-13312-5*) Ballantine Bks. (Fawcett).

—Nightmare in Pink. unabr. collector's ed. 1983. (Travis McGee Ser.: No. 2). audio 36.00 (*0-7366-0700-5*, 1663) Books on Tape, Inc.

—Nightmare in Pink. 1976. (Adult Ser.). reprint ed. lib. bdg. 9.95 o.p. (*0-8161-6382-0*, Macmillan Reference USA) Gale Group.

—One Fearful Yellow Eye. 1997. mass mkt. 5.99 (*0-449-45639-0*); 1996. 336p. mass mkt. 7.50 (*0-449-22458-9*); 1987. 244p. mass mkt. 4.95 o.s.i (*0-449-13292-7*); 1985. mass mkt. 3.50 o.p. (*0-449-12933-0*) Ballantine Bks. (Fawcett).

—One Fearful Yellow Eye. 1983. (General Ser.). lib. bdg. 14.95 o.p. (*0-8161-3380-8*, Macmillan Reference USA) Gale Group.

—Pale Gray for Guilt. 1997. mass mkt. 5.99 (*0-449-45721-4*); 1996. 320p. mass mkt. 6.99 (*0-449-22460-0*); 1987. 224p. mass mkt. 5.99 o.s.i (*0-449-13331-1*); 1985. mass mkt. 3.50 o.p. (*0-449-12897-0*) Ballantine Bks. (Fawcett).

—Pale Gray for Guilt. unabr. collector's ed. 1984. (Travis McGee Ser.: No. 9). audio 48.00 (*0-7366-0703-X*, 1666) Books on Tape, Inc.

—Pale Gray for Guilt. l.t. ed. 1986. (Large Print Bks.). 357p. lib. bdg. 15.95 o.p. (*0-8161-4006-5*, Macmillan Reference USA) Gale Group.

—A Purple Place for Dying. 1995. 320p. mass mkt. 7.50 (*0-449-22438-4*); 1987. 160p. mass mkt. 5.99 o.s.i (*0-449-13336-2*); 1980. mass mkt. 2.25 o.p. (*0-449-14219-1*) Ballantine Bks. (Fawcett).

—A Purple Place for Dying. unabr. collector's ed. 1977. (Travis McGee Ser.: No. 3). audio 36.00 (*0-7366-0052-3*, 1064) Books on Tape, Inc.

—A Purple Place for Dying. l.t. ed. 1984. (General Ser.). 312p. 9.95 o.p. (*0-8161-3690-4*); lib. bdg. 13.95 o.p. (*0-8161-3625-4*) Gale Group. (Macmillan Reference USA).

—A Purple Place for Dying. 1976. 15.00 o.p. (*0-397-01166-0*) HarperCollins Pubs.

—The Quick Red Fox. 1996. mass mkt. 5.99 (*0-449-45613-7*); 1995. 320p. mass mkt. 7.50 (*0-449-22440-6*); 1987. 160p. mass mkt. 4.95 o.s.i (*0-449-13403-2*); 1981. mass mkt. 2.50 o.p. (*0-449-14264-7*) Ballantine Bks. (Fawcett).

—The Quick Red Fox. unabr. collector's ed. 1983. (Travis McGee Ser.: No. 4). audio 36.00 (*0-7366-0701-3*, 1664) Books on Tape, Inc.

—The Quick Red Fox. l.t. ed. 1993. 12.95 o.p. (*0-8161-3382-4*, Macmillan Reference USA) Gale Group.

—The Quick Red Fox. abr. ed. 1999. audio 9.99 o.s.i (*0-375-41593-9*, RH Audio) Random Hse. Audio Publishing Group.

—The Scarlet Ruse. 1996. 352p. mass mkt. 7.50 (*0-449-22477-5*); 1987. 320p. mass mkt. 4.95 o.s.i (*0-449-13247-1*); 1985. mass mkt. 3.50 o.p. (*0-449-13040-1*) Ballantine Bks. (Fawcett).

—The Scarlet Ruse. unabr. collector's ed. 1985. (Travis McGee Ser.: No. 14). audio 48.00 (*0-7366-0707-2*, 1670) Books on Tape, Inc.

—The Scarlet Ruse. 1980. (General Ser.). lib. bdg. 13.95 o.p. (*0-8161-3118-X*, Macmillan Reference USA) Gale Group.

—The Scarlet Ruse. abr. ed. 1994. (Travis McGee Ser.). audio 8.99 o.s.i (*0-679-43405-4*, RH Audio) Random Hse. Audio Publishing Group.

—A Tan & Sandy Silence. (Travis McGee Novel Ser.). 1996. 336p. mass mkt. 7.50 (*0-449-22476-7*, Fawcett); 1986. 256p. mass mkt. 4.95 o.s.i (*0-449-13250-1*, Fawcett); 1985. 256p. mass mkt. 3.50 o.p. (*0-449-12969-1*, Fawcett); 1984. mass mkt. 2.95 o.p. (*0-449-12707-9*); 1983. mass mkt. 2.95 o.p. (*0-449-12677-3*); 1982. mass mkt. 2.75 o.p. (*0-449-12404-5*); 1981. mass mkt. 2.50 o.p. (*0-449-14220-5*); 1978. mass mkt. 1.75 o.p. (*0-449-13635-3*) Ballantine Bks.

—A Tan & Sandy Silence. unabr. collector's ed. 1984. (Travis McGee Ser.: No. 13). audio 48.00 (*0-7366-0706-4*, 1669) Books on Tape, Inc.

—A Tan & Sandy Silence. l.t. ed. 1982. 360p. lib. bdg. 13.95 o.p. (*0-8161-3381-6*, Macmillan Reference USA) Gale Group.

—A Tan & Sandy Silence. abr. ed. 1994. audio 8.99 o.s.i (*0-679-43408-9*); 1993. audio 16.00 o.p. (*0-394-55983-5*) Random Hse. Audio Publishing Group. (RH Audio).

—The Turquoise Lament. 1996. 320p. mass mkt. 6.99 (*0-449-22478-3*); 1987. 256p. mass mkt. 5.99 o.s.i (*0-449-13249-8*); 1982. 256p. mass mkt. 2.95 o.p. (*0-449-14200-0*) Ballantine Bks. (Fawcett).

—The Turquoise Lament. unabr. collector's ed. 1983. (Travis McGee Ser.: No. 15). audio 48.00 (*0-7366-0708-0*, 1671) Books on Tape, Inc.

—The Turquoise Lament. l.t. ed. 1982. lib. bdg. 13.95 o.p. (*0-8161-3383-2*, Macmillan Reference USA) Gale Group.

—The Turquoise Lament. 1973. 15.00 (*0-397-00987-9*, Lippincott) Lippincott Williams & Wilkins.

—The Turquoise Lament. abr. ed. 1991. (Travis McGee Ser.). audio 16.00 o.s.i (*0-394-55985-1*, RH Audio) Random Hse. Audio Publishing Group.

Viets, Elaine. Shop Till You Drop: A Dead-End Job Mystery. 2003. 288p. mass mkt. 5.99 (*0-451-20855-2*, Signet Bks.) NAL.

## FORT WORTH (TEX.)—FICTION

Martin, Lee. Bird in a Cage. 1996. per. (*0-373-26225-6*, 1-26225-2, Worldwide Library) Harlequin Enterprises, Ltd.

—A Conspiracy of Strangers. 1986. 208p. 13.95 o.p. (*0-312-16433-5*) St. Martin's Pr.

—The Day that Dusty Died. 1994. 304p. 20.95 o.p. (*0-312-09779-4*, Saint Martin's Minotaur) St. Martin's Pr.

—Death Warmed Over. 1991. mass mkt. (*0-373-26065-2*, Harlequin Bks.) Harlequin Enterprises, Ltd.

—Death Warmed Over. 1988. 224p. 15.95 o.p. (*0-312-02221-2*, Saint Martin's Minotaur) St. Martin's Pr.

—Deficit Ending. 1992. (Mystery Ser.: No. 101). mass mkt. (*0-373-26101-2*, Harlequin Bks.) Harlequin Enterprises, Ltd.

—Deficit Ending. 1990. 208p. 15.95 o.p. (*0-312-03813-5*, Saint Martin's Minotaur) St. Martin's Pr.

—Genealogy of Murder. 1997. (WWL Mystery Ser.: No. 239). per. (*0-373-26239-6*, 1-26239-3, Worldwide Library) Harlequin Enterprises, Ltd.

—Genealogy of Murder. 1996. 240p. 22.95 o.p. (*0-312-13975-6*, Saint Martin's Minotaur) St. Martin's Pr.

—Hacker. 1993. (WWL Mystery Ser.). per. (*0-373-26135-7*, 1-26135-3, Harlequin Bks.) Harlequin Enterprises, Ltd.

—Hacker: A Deb Ralston Mystery. 1992. 192p. 16.95 o.p. (*0-312-06990-1*, Saint Martin's Minotaur) St. Martin's Pr.

—Hal's Own Murder Case. 1991. mass mkt. (*0-373-26087-3*, Harlequin Bks.) Harlequin Enterprises, Ltd.

—Hal's Own Murder Case. 1989. 14.95 o.p. (*0-312-02925-X*, Saint Martin's Minotaur) St. Martin's Pr.

—Inherited Murder. 1994. (Deb Ralston Mystery Ser.). 304p. 19.95 o.p. (*0-312-11415-X*, Saint Martin's Minotaur) St. Martin's Pr.

—The Mensa Murders. 1993. mass mkt. (*0-373-26115-2*, 1-26115-5, Harlequin Bks.) Harlequin Enterprises, Ltd.

—The Mensa Murders. 1990. 192p. 15.95 o.p. (*0-312-05126-3*, Saint Martin's Minotaur) St. Martin's Pr.

—Murder at the Blue Owl. 1990. mass mkt. (*0-373-26054-7*, Harlequin Bks.) Harlequin Enterprises, Ltd.

—Murder at the Blue Owl. 1988. 208p. 14.95 o.p. (*0-312-01795-2*) St. Martin's Pr.

—Too Sane a Murder. 1984. 192p. 12.95 o.p. (*0-312-80901-8*) St. Martin's Pr.

Moseley, Margaret. Grinning in His Mashed Potatoes. 1999. 304p. mass mkt. 6.50 o.s.i (*0-425-16982-0*, Prime Crime) Berkley Publishing Group.

Orcutt, Jane. The Living Stone. 2000. 352p. pap. 10.95 (*1-57856-292-9*) WaterBrook Pr.

## FORTY-THREE LIGHT STREET (IMAGINARY PLACE)—FICTION

York, Rebecca. Cradle & All. 1993. (Harlequin Intrigue Ser.: 233). 245p. mass mkt. (*0-373-22233-5*, 1-22233-0, Harlequin Bks.) Harlequin Enterprises, Ltd.

—Face to Face. 1996. (Forty-Third Light Street Ser.). per. (*0-373-83323-7*, 1-83323-5, Harlequin Bks.) Harlequin Enterprises, Ltd.

—Father & Child. 1997. 244p. per. (*0-373-22437-0*, 1-22437-7, Harlequin Bks.) Harlequin Enterprises, Ltd.

—For Your Eyes Only. 1997. (Harlequin Intrigue Ser.). 251p. per. (*0-373-22407-9*, 1-22407-0, Harlequin Bks.) Harlequin Enterprises, Ltd.

—Hopscotch. 1993. (Harlequin Intrigue Ser.: 213). 252p. per. (*0-373-22213-0*, 1-22213-2, Harlequin Bks.) Harlequin Enterprises, Ltd.

—Life Line. 1990. (Harlequin Intrigue Ser.: 143). pap. (*0-373-22143-6*, Harlequin Bks.) Harlequin Enterprises, Ltd.

—Midnight Kiss. 1994. (Harlequin Intrigue Ser.: 273). 246p. per. (*0-373-22273-4*, Harlequin Bks.) Harlequin Enterprises, Ltd.

—Only Skin Deep. 1992. (Harlequin Intrigue Ser.: 179). 252p. pap. (*0-373-22179-7*, 1-22179-5, Harlequin Bks.) Harlequin Enterprises, Ltd.

—Prince of Time. 1999. (Promo Ser.). per. (*0-373-21952-0*, 1-21952-6, Harlequin Bks.) Harlequin Enterprises, Ltd.

—Prince of Time: 43 Light Street. 1995. 251p. per. (*0-373-22338-2*, Harlequin Bks.) Harlequin Enterprises, Ltd.

—Shattered Vows. 1991. (Harlequin Intrigue Ser.: 155). pap. (*0-373-22155-X*, Harlequin Bks.) Harlequin Enterprises, Ltd.

—Tangled Vows. 1994. (Harlequin Intrigue Ser.). 253p. per. (*0-373-22289-0*, 1-22289-2, Harlequin Bks.) Harlequin Enterprises, Ltd.

—Till Death Us Do Part: (43 Light St.) 1995. (Harlequin Intrigue Ser.). 249p. per. (*0-373-22318-8*, 1-22318-9, Harlequin Bks.) Harlequin Enterprises, Ltd.

—Trial by Fire. 1992. (Harlequin Intrigue Ser.: 193). 250p. pap. (*0-373-22193-2*, 1-22193-6, Harlequin Bks.) Harlequin Enterprises, Ltd.

—What Child Is This? 1993. (Harlequin Intrigue Ser.: 253). 249p. per. (*0-373-22253-X*, 1-22253-8, Harlequin Bks.) Harlequin Enterprises, Ltd.

—Whispers in the Night. 1991. (Harlequin Intrigue Ser.: 167). pap. (*0-373-22167-3*, Harlequin Bks.) Harlequin Enterprises, Ltd.

## FRANCE—FICTION

Abro, Ben. Assassination! July 14. 2001. 256p. pap. 16.95 (*0-8032-5939-5*, Bison Bks.) Univ. of Nebraska Pr.

Absire, Alain. God's Equal. 1989. 272p. 21.95 (*0-15-136070-7*) Harcourt Trade Pubs.

Achard, Amedee. Belle Rose. 2000. 252p. E-Book 9.95 (*0-594-04213-5*) 1873 Pr.

Adamson, Lydia. A Cat with No Regrets. 1994. (Alice Nestleton Mystery Ser.: No. 8). 208p. mass mkt. 3.99 o.s.i (*0-451-18055-0*, Signet Bks.) NAL.

—A Cat with No Regrets. 1999. pap. (*0-525-93811-7*) Viking Penguin.

Adler, Elizabeth A. The Hotel Riviera. 2003. (Illus.). 320p. 24.95 (*0-312-30809-4*) St. Martin's Pr.

—The Last Time I Saw Paris. E-Book 23.95 (*0-312-70197-7*); 2002. 352p. mass mkt. 6.99 (*0-312-98030-2*, St. Martin's Paperbacks); 2001. (Illus.). 304p. 23.95 (*0-312-26982-X*) St. Martin's Pr.

—The Last Time I Saw Paris. (Illus.). 2001. 423p. (*0-7540-1684-6*); 2002. 423p. 28.95 (*0-7862-3437-7*); 2001. 390p. 31.95 (*0-7862-3436-9*); 2001. 423p. (*0-7540-9084-1*) Thorndike Pr.

Adnan, Etel. Paris, When It's Naked. 1993. 115p. (Orig.). pap. 13.50 (*0-942996-20-8*) Post-Apollo Pr., The.

Albert, Marvin. The Riviera Contract. 1992. mass mkt. 3.99 o.s.i (*0-449-14625-1*, Fawcett) Ballantine Bks.

Allain, Marcel. Fantomas, le Paravent Chinois, Set. 1996. (FRE.). audio 28.95 Olivia & Hill Pr., The.

—The Silent Executioner: Being the Second in the Series of Fantomas Adventures. 1987. (Fantomas Ser.: No. 2). (Illus.). 288p. 15.95 o.p. (*0-688-07265-8*, Morrow, William & Co.) Morrow/Avon.

—La Vengeance de Fantomas, Set. adapted ed. 1996. (FRE.). audio 28.95 Olivia & Hill Pr., The.

Allain, Marcel & Souvestre, Pierre. Fantomas: The Legendary French Thriller. Ashbery, John, tr. 1987. mass mkt. 3.95 o.s.i (*0-345-34421-9*) Ballantine Bks.

—Fantomas: The Legendary French Thriller. Ashbery, John, tr. 1986. 320p. 17.95 o.p. (*0-688-04360-7*, Morrow, William & Co.) Morrow/Avon.

Allbeury, Ted. The Lantern Network. 1989. 208p. 17.95 (*0-89296-185-6*) Mysterious Pr.

—The Lantern Network. l.t. ed. 1982. (Ulverscroft Large Print Ser.). 352p. 29.99 o.p. (*0-7089-0864-0*, Ulverscroft) Thorpe, F. A. Pubs. GBR. *Dist:* Ulverscroft Large Print Bks., Ltd., Ulverscroft Large Print Canada, Ltd.

—The Lantern Network. 1990. mass mkt. 4.95 o.s.i (*0-445-40875-8*, Mysterious Pr. Paperback Bks.) Warner Bks., Inc.

Alleyn, Susanne. A Far Better Rest. 2000. 353p. 25.00 (*1-56947-197-5*) Soho Pr., Inc.

Anderson, David Martin. The Truth about Snipe. Abreau, Kevin, ed. 2000. 128p. pap. 9.99 (*1-892617-12-9*) Conroca Publishing.

Angelica, J. Fermentation. 1997. 128p. 20.00 o.p. (*0-8021-1614-0*, Grove Pr.) Grove/Atlantic, Inc.

Anonymous, Anderson A. School Life in Paris. 2000. 128p. mass mkt. 7.95 (*1-56201-172-3*, Blue Moon Bks.) Avalon Publishing Group.

Anson-Weber, Joan. Snuffles. 1994. (Illus.). 32p. (J). (ps-7). 14.95 (*0-87797-262-1*) Cherokee Publishing Co.

Anthony, Evelyn. Sleeping with the Enemy. 2003. 288p. 25.99 (*0-7278-5947-1*) Severn Hse. Pubs., Ltd.

Arnaud, Rayne. The Paternoster Bead. E-Book (*1-84045-011-8*) Online Originals.

Ashour, Linda P. Speaking in Tongues. 1988. 17.95 o.p. (*0-671-64090-9*, Simon & Schuster) Simon & Schuster.

Asimov, Janet & Asimov, Isaac. Norby & the Queen's Necklace. 1986. (Norby Ser.). 144p. (J). (gr. 4-9). 11.95 (*0-8027-6659-5*); lib. bdg. 12.85 (*0-8027-6660-9*) Walker & Co.

Aubert, Brigitte. Death from the Woods. Koral, David A., tr. from FRE. 2001. 288p. pap. 12.00 o.s.i (*0-425-17905-2*, Prime Crime) Berkley Publishing Group.
—Death from the Woods. l.t. ed. 2001. 328p. 32.50 (*0-7531-6577-5*) ISIS Large Print Bks. GBR. *Dist:* Ulverscroft Large Print Bks., Ltd., Ulverscroft Large Print Canada, Ltd.
Baker, Donna. Firestorm. 2000. 224p. 25.00 (*0-7278-5436-4*) Severn Hse. Pubs., Ltd.
—Firestorm. l.t. ed. 2000. (Romance Ser.). 272p. 25.95 (*0-7862-2838-5*); (*0-7540-4319-3*); (*0-7540-4320-7*) Thorndike Pr.
Baker, Leslie A. Paris Cat. 1999. (Illus.). 32p. (J). (ps-3). 15.95 o.p. (*0-316-07309-1*) Little Brown & Co.
—Paris Cat. 1999. E-Book (*1-58824-663-9*); E-Book (*1-58824-888-7*); E-Book (*1-58824-662-0*) ipicturebooks, LLC.
Baldwin, Michael. The Rape of OC. 1996. 656p. pap. 13.95 o.p. (*0-7515-0624-9*) Trafalgar Square.
Ball, Margaret. The Duchess of Aquitaine. 2001. 432p. 27.95 (*0-312-20533-3*) St. Martin's Pr.
Balzac, Honoré de. About Catherine De' Medici. 2000. 252p. E-Book 3.95 (*0-594-01853-6*) 1873 Pr.
—Another Study of Woman. E-Book 2.49 (*1-58627-016-8*) Electric Umbrella Publishing.
—Another Study of Woman. E-Book 2.00 (*0-7410-0677-4*) SoftBook Pr.
—The Black Sheep. Adamson, Donald, tr. 1976. (Penguin Classics Ser.). 344p. 13.95 (*0-14-044237-5*, Penguin Classics) Viking Penguin.
—Bureaucracy. 2002. per. 9.90 (*1-58396-375-8*); 2001. per. 15.50 (*1-58396-463-0*) Blue Unicorn Editions.
—Bureaucracy. E-Book 2.49 (*1-58627-100-8*) Electric Umbrella Publishing.
—Bureaucracy. Wormeley, Katharine Prescott, tr. 2002. 204p. per. 89.99 (*1-58827-111-0*); 94.99 (*1-58827-110-2*) IndyPublish.com.
—Bureaucracy. E-Book 5.00 (*0-7410-1119-0*) SoftBook Pr.
—The Bureaucrats. Foulkes, Charles, tr. from FRE. 1993. (European Classics Ser.). 300p. 52.00 (*0-8101-0973-5*) Northwestern Univ. Pr.
—The Bureaucrats. Foulkes, Charles, tr. from FRE. 1993. (European Classics Ser.). 300p. pap. 14.95 (*0-8101-0987-5*) Northwestern Univ. Pr.
—The Chouans. E-Book 2.49 (*1-58627-007-9*) Electric Umbrella Publishing.
—The Collection of Antiquities. 2000. per. 9.90 (*1-58396-308-1*); per. 15.50 (*1-58396-396-0*) Blue Unicorn Editions.
—The Collection of Antiquities. E-Book 2.49 (*1-58627-006-0*) Electric Umbrella Publishing.
—The Collection of Antiquities. 1999. E-Book 1.95 (*1-58515-045-2*) MesaView, Inc.
—Colonel Chabert. 2000. per. 9.90 (*1-58396-309-X*); per. 15.50 (*1-58396-397-9*) Blue Unicorn Editions.
—Colonel Chabert. E-Book 2.49 (*1-58627-004-4*) Electric Umbrella Publishing.
—Colonel Chabert. 2003. 88p. pap. 12.00 (*1-84391-037-3*) Hesperus Pr. GBR. *Dist:* Trafalgar Square.
—Colonel Chabert. pap. 6.95 (*2-253-03404-5*, LP0010E) Librairie Generale Francaise, LGF FRA. *Dist:* Continental Bk. Co., Inc.
—Colonel Chabert. Cosman, Carol, tr. from FRE. 1997. 128p. pap. 9.95 (*0-8112-1359-5*, NDP847) New Directions Publishing Corp.
—Colonel Chabert, Set. 1995. (FRE.). audio 26.95 Olivia & Hill Pr., The.
—Colonel Chabert. (FRE.). pap. 6.95 (*2-266-08330-9*) Presses Pocket FRA. *Dist:* Distribooks, Inc.
—Colonel Chabert. 1964. (Folio Ser.: No. 593). (FRE.). pap. 9.95 (*2-07-036593-X*) Schoenhof's Foreign Bks., Inc.
—Colonel Chabert. E-Book 3.00 (*0-7410-0875-0*) SoftBook Pr.
—Colonel Chabert: Suivi de le Contrat de Mariage. 1984. (FRE.). pap. 10.95 (*0-7859-3119-8*) French & European Pubns., Inc.
—Colonel Chabert: Suivi de le Contrat de Mariage. 1974. (FRE.). (C). pap. 11.95 (*0-8442-1827-8*, VF1827-8) McGraw-Hill/Contemporary.
—Colonel Chabert, el Verdugo, Adieu, le Requisitionnaire. 1974. (FRE.). 320p. pap. 11.95 (*0-7859-2207-5*, 207036593X) French & European Pubns., Inc.
—Colonel Chabert, les Peines de Coeur... unabr. ed. (FRE.). pap. 5.95 (*2-87714-199-3*) Bookking International FRA. *Dist:* Distribooks, Inc.
—The Commission in Lunacy. 2000. per. 9.90 (*1-58396-341-3*); per. 15.50 (*1-58396-429-0*) Blue Unicorn Editions.
—The Commission in Lunacy. E-Book 2.49 (*1-58627-001-X*) Electric Umbrella Publishing.
—The Commission in Lunacy. E-Book 3.00 (*0-7410-1075-5*) SoftBook Pr.
—Le Cousin Pons. 2000. per. 9.90 (*1-58396-371-5*); per. 15.50 (*1-58396-459-2*) Blue Unicorn Editions.
—Le Cousin Pons. unabr. ed. (FRE.). pap. 7.95 (*2-87714-190-X*) Bookking International FRA. *Dist:* Distribooks, Inc.
—Le Cousin Pons. E-Book 2.49 (*1-58627-029-X*) Electric Umbrella Publishing.
—Le Cousin Pons. Allem, Maurice, ed. (Coll. Prestige). 1977. pap. 12.95 (*0-7859-3468-5*); 1962. pap. 10.95 o.p. (*0-8288-9338-1*) French & European Pubns., Inc.
—Le Cousin Pons. 1962. (Folio Ser.: No. 380). pap. 9.95 (*2-07-036380-5*, 989) Schoenhof's Foreign Bks., Inc.
—Le Cousin Pons. E-Book 5.00 (*0-7410-1169-7*) SoftBook Pr.
—Le Cousin Pons. Hunt, Herbert J., tr. 1978. (Classics Ser.). 336p. 14.00 (*0-14-044205-7*, Penguin Classics) Viking Penguin.
—La Cousine Bette. Allem, Maurice, ed. 1984. (Coll. Prestige). (FRE.). pap. 10.95 (*0-7859-3466-9*, 2070361381) French & European Pubns., Inc.
—La Cousine Bette. 8.95 (*2-253-01067-7*, LO0009E) Librairie Generale Francaise, LGF FRA. *Dist:* Continental Bk. Co., Inc.
—La Cousine Bette. Raphael, Sylvia & Bellos, David, eds. 1992. (Illus.). 518p. pap. 7.95 o.p. (*0-19-282606-9*) Oxford Univ. Pr., Inc.
—La Cousine Bette. 1955. (Folio Ser.: No. 138). (FRE.). pap. 10.95 (*2-07-036138-1*, 952) Schoenhof's Foreign Bks., Inc.
—La Cousine Bette. Crawford, Marion A., tr. 1965. (Classics Ser.). 448p. 10.95 (*0-14-044160-3*, Penguin Classics) Viking Penguin.
—La Cousine Bette. unabr. ed. (FRE.). pap. 7.95 (*2-87714-154-3*) Bookking International FRA. *Dist:* Distribooks, Inc.
—The Deserted Woman. E-Book 2.49 (*1-58627-137-7*) Electric Umbrella Publishing.
—The Deserted Woman. E-Book 3.00 (*0-7410-0669-3*) SoftBook Pr.
—Domestic Peace. E-Book 2.49 (*1-58744-214-0*) Electric Umbrella Publishing.
—Eugenie Grandet. 1994. 256p. mass mkt. 4.95 o.s.i (*0-553-21429-2*, Bantam Classics) Bantam Bks.
—Eugenie Grandet. 2000. per. 12.50 (*1-58396-525-4*); per. 14.00 (*1-58396-543-2*) Blue Unicorn Editions.
—Eugenie Grandet. unabr. ed. 1999. (World Classics Ser.). (FRE.). pap. 5.95 (*2-87714-129-2*) Bookking International FRA. *Dist:* Distribooks, Inc.
—Eugenie Grandet. 1972. 1.95 o.p. (*0-460-01169-3*); 1956. 7.95 o.p. (*0-460-00169-8*) Dutton/Plume. (Dutton).
—Eugenie Grandet. E-Book 1.79 (*1-929120-75-3*) Electric Umbrella Publishing.
—Eugenie Grandet. (FRE.). 6.50 (*2-08-070003-0*) Flammarion et Cie FRA. *Dist:* Continental Bk. Co., Inc.
—Eugenie Grandet. Castex, ed. 1979. (Coll. Prestige). (FRE.). 432p. 24.95 (*0-7859-4661-6*, F55628) French & European Pubns., Inc.
—Eugenie Grandet. Caster, Pierre-Georges, ed. 1964. (Class. Garnier Ser.). (FRE.). pap. 10.95 (*0-7859-3544-4*, F55639) French & European Pubns., Inc.
—Eugenie Grandet. 1992. (Everyman's Library). 288p. 15.00 (*0-679-41716-8*) Knopf, Alfred A. Inc.
—Eugenie Grandet. 1983. (FRE.). (C). pap. 7.95 (*0-8442-1958-4*, VF1958-4) McGraw-Hill/Contemporary.
—Eugenie Grandet. mass mkt. 0.60 o.p. (*0-451-50199-3*, Signet Classics) NAL.
—Eugenie Grandet. 2002. (Twelve-Point Ser.). 221p. lib. bdg. 25.00 (*1-58287-193-0*); 367p. lib. bdg. 26.00 (*1-58287-676-2*) North Bks.
—Eugenie Grandet, Set. 1991. (FRE.). audio 31.95 Olivia & Hill Pr., The.
—Eugenie Grandet. Prendergast, Christopher, ed. Raphael, Sylvia, tr. from FRE. 2003. (Oxford World's Classics Ser.). 240p. pap. 11.95 (*0-19-280474-X*) Oxford Univ. Pr., Inc.
—Eugenie Grandet. Raphael, Sylvia, tr. 1991. (Oxford World's Classics Ser.). 240p. pap. 10.95 o.p. (*0-19-282605-0*) Oxford Univ. Pr., Inc.
—Eugenie Grandet. (FRE.). pap. 7.95 (*2-266-03337-9*) Presses Pocket FRA. *Dist:* Distribooks, Inc.
—Eugenie Grandet. 1965. (Folio Ser.: No. 31). (FRE.). pap. 8.95 (*2-07-036031-8*) Schoenhof's Foreign Bks., Inc.
—Eugenie Grandet. E-Book 5.00 (*0-7410-1017-8*) SoftBook Pr.
—Eugenie Grandet. Crawford, Marion A., tr. 1955. (Classics Ser.). 256p. 12.00 (*0-14-044050-X*, Penguin Classics) Viking Penguin.
—Eugenie Grandet: A Comedie Humaine. unabr. ed. 1998. audio 47.95 (*1-86015-440-9*) Beeler, Thomas T. Publisher.
—Four Novellas: Gobseck; The Commission in Lunacy; The Cure of Tour; Secrets of the Princess de Cadignan. Bell, Clara & Marriage, Ellen, trs. from FRE. 2002. 312p. (C). pap. 13.00 (*0-86527-439-8*) Fertig, Howard Inc.
—A Harlot High & Low. Heppenstall, Rayner, tr. 1970. (Classics Ser.). 558p. 15.00 (*0-14-044232-4*, Penguin Classics) Viking Penguin.
—Lost Illusions. 2001. (Modern Library Classics). 752p. pap. 13.95 (*0-375-75790-2*, Modern Library) Random House Adult Trade Publishing Group.
—Lost Illusions. Raine, Kathleen, tr. 1997. (Modern Library Ser.). 760p. 21.00 o.s.i (*0-679-60264-X*, Modern Library) Random House Adult Trade Publishing Group.
—Lost Illusions. Hunt, Herbert J., tr. 1976. (Classics Ser.). 704p. pap. 15.00 (*0-14-044251-0*, Penguin Classics) Viking Penguin.
—Old Goriot. 1991. 272p. 15.00 (*0-679-40535-6*, Vintage) Knopf Publishing Group.
—Old Goriot. Crawford, Marion A., tr. from FRE. 1951. (Classics Ser.). 304p. pap. 10.95 (*0-14-044017-8*, Penguin Classics) Viking Penguin.
—Le Pere Goriot. Raffel, Burton, tr. 1994. (Critical Editions Ser.). (FRE.). 29.95 o.p. (*0-393-03620-0*) Norton, W. W. & Co., Inc.
—Le Pere Goriot. Krailsheimer, Alban J., ed. 1992. (Oxford World's Classics Ser.). (Illus.). 298p. pap. 8.95 o.p. (*0-19-282858-4*) Oxford Univ. Pr., Inc.
—Selected Short Stories: A Dual-Language Book. 1999. 256p. pap. text 9.95 (*0-486-40895-7*) Dover Pubns., Inc.
—Seraphita. 3rd ed. 1986. (Spiritual Fiction Ser.). 214p. reprint ed. pap. 11.50 o.p. (*0-8334-0015-0*, Spiritual Literature Library) Garber Communications, Inc.
—The Unknown Masterpiece. Neff, Michael, tr. from FRE. 1983. (Illus.). 72p. pap. 4.95 o.p. (*0-916870-55-3*) Creative Arts Bk. Co.
—The Unknown Masterpiece. Howard, Richard, tr. from FRE. 2001. (New York Review Books Classics Ser.). xxvii, 135p. pap. 12.95 (*0-940322-74-9*) New York Review of Bks., Inc., The.
—Ursule Mirouet. 1981. (FRE.). pap. 12.95 (*0-7859-1937-6*, 2070373002) French & European Pubns., Inc.
—Ursule Mirouet. (Folio Ser.: No. 1300). (FRE.). pap. 9.95 (*2-07-037300-2*) Schoenhof's Foreign Bks., Inc.
—Ursule Mirouet. Adamson, Donald, tr. 1976. (Penguin Classics Ser.). 272p. pap. 9.95 o.p. (*0-14-044316-9*, Penguin Classics) Viking Penguin.
Balzac, Honoré de & Castex, Pierre Georges, eds. Eugenie Grandet. 1965. (Coll. Prestige). 39.95 o.p. (*0-8288-9342-X*, F55628) French & European Pubns., Inc.
Balzac, Honoré de & Everyman's Library Staff. Cousin Bette. 1991. 496p. 20.00 (*0-679-40671-9*) Random Hse., Inc.
Baricco, Alessandro. Ocean Sea. 2000. (International Ser.). 256p. pap. 12.00 (*0-375-70395-0*, Vintage) Knopf Publishing Group.
Barnes, Julian. Cross Channel. 1997. 224p. pap. 12.00 (*0-679-76755-X*) Random Hse., Inc.
—Flaubert's Parrot. unabr. ed. 1994. audio 54.95 (*1-85089-726-3*, 89066) ISIS Audio Bks. GBR. *Dist:* Ulverscroft Large Print Bks., Ltd.
—Flaubert's Parrot. 1985. 190p. 13.95 o.s.i (*0-394-54272-X*) Knopf, Alfred A. Inc.
—Flaubert's Parrot. 1986. 224p. pap. text 4.95 o.p. (*0-07-003748-5*) McGraw-Hill Cos., The.
—Flaubert's Parrot. 1990. (Vintage International Ser.). 192p. pap. 12.00 (*0-679-73136-9*) Random Hse., Inc.
Bassett, Jennifer. The Phantom of the Opera. 1993. (Illus.). 48p. pap. text 5.95 o.p. (*0-19-422707-3*) Oxford Univ. Pr., Inc.
Bataille, Christophe. Absinthe. Howard, Richard, tr. from FRE. 1999. 96p. 25.00 (*0-8101-6042-0*, Marlboro Pr., The) Northwestern Univ. Pr.
Bayley, John. The Red Hat. 1998. 224p. 21.95 (*0-312-18658-4*) St. Martin's Pr.
—The Red Hat. 2001. 196p. pap. 14.00 (*1-56649-194-0*) Welcome Rain Pubs.
Bazaldua, Barbara, et al. Quasimodo the Hero. 1997. (Golden Book Ser.). (Illus.). 24p. (J). (ps-k). o.p. (*0-307-98797-3*, Golden Bks.) Random Hse. Children's Bks.
Bedford, Sybille. Compass Error. 2001. 240p. pap. text 16.00 (*1-58243-159-0*, Counterpoint Pr.) Basic Bks.
—Favorite of the Gods. 2001. 320p. pap. text 16.00 (*1-58243-158-2*, Counterpoint Pr.) Basic Bks.
Belletto, Rene. Machine: A Novel. 1993. 368p. 21.00 o.p. (*0-8021-1437-7*, Grove Pr.) Grove/Atlantic, Inc.
Bellow, Saul. Ravelstein. l.t. ed. 2000. (Compass Press Large Print Book Ser.). 286p. 26.95 (*1-56895-127-2*, Wheeler Publishing, Inc.) Gale Group.
—Ravelstein. unabr. ed. 2000. 29.95 (*1-56511-428-0*) HighBridge Co.
—Ravelstein. 240p. 2000. 24.95 o.p. (*0-670-84134-X*); 50th ed. 2001. reprint ed. 13.00 (*0-14-100176-3*) Viking Penguin.
Benson, Ann. The Burning Road. 2000. 720p. mass mkt. 6.50 (*0-440-22591-4*) Dell Publishing.
Berger, John. King: A Street Story. (International Ser.). 2000. 208p. pap. 12.00 (*0-375-70534-1*, Vintage); 1999. 200p. 20.00 (*0-375-40556-9*, Pantheon) Knopf Publishing Group.
—Once in Europa. 2000. (Illus.). 288p. 27.50 (*1-58234-070-6*) Bloomsbury Publishing.
—Once in Europa: Into Their Labors Trilogy. (Into Their Labours Ser.). 1992. 176p. pap. 14.00 (*0-679-73716-2*, Vintage); Vol. II. 1988. 208p. pap. 8.95 o.s.i (*0-394-75164-7*, Pantheon) Knopf Publishing Group.
—Pig Earth. 1992. 208p. pap. 13.00 (*0-679-73715-4*, Vintage); 1981. pap. 6.95 o.p. (*0-394-73989-2*, Pantheon); 1980. 9.95 o.p. (*0-394-51268-5*, Pantheon) Knopf Publishing Group.
—Pig Earth: Into Their Labors Trilogy, Vol. I. 1988. 224p. pap. 11.00 o.s.i (*0-394-75739-4*, Pantheon) Knopf Publishing Group.
Bernanos, Georges. The Impostor. Whitehouse, J. C., tr. from FRE. 1999. 250p. pap. 20.00 (*0-8032-6153-5*); text 50.00 (*0-8032-1290-9*) Univ. of Nebraska Pr.
Bernheim, Emmanuele. Sa Femme: Or the Other Woman. 1995. 128p. pap. 9.95 o.p. (*0-14-024178-7*) Penguin Group (USA) Inc.
Besson, Philippe. In the Absence of Men. Wynne, Frank, tr. 2003. 176p. 21.00 (*0-7867-1161-2*, Carroll & Graf Pubs.) Avalon Publishing Group.
Beyala, Calixthe. Loukoum: The Little Prince of Belleville. 1995. (African Writers Ser.). 177p. pap. 10.95 (*0-435-90968-1*) Heinemann.
Bibesco, Marthe. The Green Parrot. Cowley, Malcolm, tr. 1995. 250p. (Orig.). pap. 12.95 (*0-9627987-9-7*) Turtle Point Pr.
Bichelberger, Roger. An Ordinary Exodus. Garfitt, Toby, tr. from FRE. 1991. 384p. 19.95 o.p. (*0-7459-2101-9*) Lion Publishing.
Bingham, Mindy. Minou. 1987. (Illus.). 64p. (J). (ps up). 14.95 (*0-911655-36-0*) Advocacy Pr.
Bishop, Claire Huchet. Twenty & Ten. 76p. (J). (gr. 3-5). pap. 4.99 (*0-8072-1418-3*, Listening Library) Random Hse. Audio Publishing Group.
—Twenty & Ten. 1984. (Illus.). (J). (gr. 5-9). 18.75 (*0-8446-6168-6*) Smith, Peter Pub., Inc.
Blake, Jennifer. Royal Passion. 384p. 1991. mass mkt. 5.99 o.s.i (*0-449-14790-8*); 1986. pap. 8.95 o.p. (*0-449-90101-7*) Ballantine Bks. (Fawcett).
—Royal Passion. 1993. 20.00 o.p. (*0-7278-4419-9*) Severn Hse. Pubs., Ltd.
Blank, Hannah. Brave Man Dead: An Alphonse Dantan. 2000. (Alphonse Dantan Mystery Ser.: No. 2). 300p. (*0-9652778-3-6*, Hightrees Bks.) Prism Corp.
—A Murder of Convenience. 1999. 24.95 (*0-9652778-1-X*, Hightrees Bks.) Prism Corp.
Blickensdorfer, Hans. North Wind in Your Spokes: A Novel of the Tour de France. 2003. Tr. of Salz im Kaffee. 320p. pap. 13.00 (*1-891369-39-3*) Breakaway Bks.
—North Wind in Your Spokes: A Novel of the Tour de France. Cambon, Marlis, tr. from GER. 2000. Tr. of Salz im Kaffee. 304p. 23.00 (*1-891369-18-0*) Breakaway Bks.
Boeser, Knut. Nostradamus. Brownjohn, John, tr. from GER. 1996. 256p. 7.99 o.s.i (*0-517-14910-9*) Random Hse. Value Publishing.
—Nostradamus: Based on the Screenplay & Motion Picture. 1994. 248p. pap. 11.00 o.p. (*0-06-251245-5*) HarperSanFrancisco.
Bogner, Norman. The Deadliest Art. 2001. 384p. 25.95 (*0-312-86856-1*, Forge Bks.) Doherty, Tom Assocs., LLC.
—To Die in Provence. 1999. 391p. mass mkt. 6.99 (*0-8125-9044-9*); 1998. 382p. 24.95 o.p. (*0-312-86628-3*) Doherty, Tom Assocs., LLC. (Forge Bks.).
Bond, Michael. Monsieur Pamplemousse. 1986. 192p. mass mkt. 4.99 o.s.i (*0-449-20956-3*, Fawcett) Ballantine Bks.
—Monsieur Pamplemousse. 1985. 192p. 13.95 o.p. (*0-8253-0267-6*) Beaufort Bks., Inc.
—Monsieur Pamplemousse. l.t. ed. 1991. (Nightingale Series Large Print Bks.). 240p. pap. 14.95 o.p. (*0-8161-5111-3*, Macmillan Reference USA) Gale Group.
—Monsieur Pamplemousse. unabr. ed. 1991. (Monsieur Pamplemousse Mystery Ser.: Vol. 1). (YA). (gr. 10 up). audio 35.00 (*1-55690-346-4*, 91225E7) Recorded Bks., LLC.
—Monsieur Pamplemousse Afloat. 1999. 214p. pap. 9.95 (*0-7490-0347-2*) Allison & Busby, Ltd. GBR. *Dist:* International Publishers Marketing.
—Monsieur Pamplemousse Aloft. 1990. mass mkt. 4.99 o.s.i (*0-449-21673-X*, Fawcett) Ballantine Bks.
—Monsieur Pamplemousse Aloft. 1991. 2.99 o.p. (*0-517-07165-7*) Random Hse. Value Publishing.
—Monsieur Pamplemousse & the Secret Mission. 1987. mass mkt. 4.95 o.s.i (*0-449-21128-2*, Fawcett) Ballantine Bks.
—Monsieur Pamplemousse & the Secret Mission. 1986. 208p. 13.95 o.p. (*0-8253-0301-X*) Beaufort Bks., Inc.
—Monsieur Pamplemousse & the Secret Mission. l.t. ed. 1991. (Nightingale Ser.). 280p. pap. 14.95 o.p. (*0-8161-5110-5*, Macmillan Reference USA) Gale Group.

Settings

—Monsieur Pamplemousse & the Secret Mission. unabr. ed. 1991. (Monsieur Pamplemousse Mystery Ser.: Vol. 3). audio 35.00 (1-55690-327-8, 91311E7) Recorded Bks., LLC.

—Monsieur Pamplemousse Investigates. 1991. mass mkt. 3.99 o.s.i (0-449-21899-6, Fawcett) Ballantine Bks.

—Monsieur Pamplemousse Investigates. unabr. ed. 1991. (Monsieur Pamplemousse Mystery Ser.: Vol. 7 ). audio 44.00 (1-55690-698-6, 91408E7) Recorded Bks., LLC.

—Monsieur Pamplemousse Omnibus. 1999. Vol. 1. 191p. 16.95 o.p. (0-7490-0352-9); Vol. 2. 592p. pap. text 16.95 (0-7490-0410-X); Vol. 3. 704p. pap. 16.95 (0-7490-0442-8) Allison & Busby, Ltd. GBR. *Dist:* International Publishers Marketing.

—Monsieur Pamplemousse on Probation. 2000. 160p. pap. 9.95 (0-7490-0463-0, London Hse.) Allison & Busby, Ltd. GBR. *Dist:* International Publishers Marketing.

—Monsieur Pamplemousse on the Spot. 1988. reprint ed. mass mkt. 3.95 o.s.i (0-449-21338-2, Fawcett) Ballantine Bks.

—Monsieur Pamplemousse on the Spot. 1987. 160p. 14.95 o.p. (0-8253-0389-3) Beaufort Bks., Inc.

—Monsieur Pamplemousse on the Spot. l.t. unabr. ed. 1989. (Nightingale Ser.). 277p. 13.95 o.p. (0-8161-4695-0, Macmillan Reference USA) Gale Group.

—Monsieur Pamplemousse Rests His Case. 1993. mass mkt. 4.50 o.p. (0-449-22045-1); 1991. 176p. 17.00 o.s.i (0-449-90639-6) Ballantine Bks. (Fawcett).

—Monsieur Pamplemousse Rests His Case. l.t. ed. 1993. (Nightingale Ser.). 285p. lib. bdg. 15.95 o.p. (0-8161-5768-5, Macmillan Reference USA) Gale Group.

—Monsieur Pamplemousse Rests His Case. 1993. mass mkt. 3.99 o.p. (0-517-09781-8) Random Hse. Value Publishing.

—Monsieur Pamplemousse Rests His Case. unabr. ed. 1992. (Monsieur Pamplemousse Mystery Ser.: Vol. 8). audio 35.00 (1-55690-759-1, 92415E7) Recorded Bks., LLC.

—Monsieur Pamplemousse Stands Firm. 1994. mass mkt. 4.99 o.s.i (0-449-22201-2, Fawcett) Ballantine Bks.

—Monsieur Pamplemousse Takes the Cure. 1989. mass mkt. 3.95 o.s.i (0-449-21674-8, Fawcett) Ballantine Bks.

—Monsieur Pamplemousse Takes the Cure. l.t. ed. 1990. (Nightingale Ser.). 288p. pap. 14.95 o.p. (0-8161-4893-7, Macmillan Reference USA) Gale Group.

Bonner, Cindy. Right from Wrong: A Novel. 1999. 336p. tchr. ed. 19.95 (1-56512-104-X, 72104) Algonquin Bks. of Chapel Hill.

Borchardt, Alice. Beguiled. abr. ed. 1997. audio 7.99 o.p. (1-56740-200-3, 625, Paperback Nova Audio Bks.); 1997. audio 16.95 o.p. (1-56100-965-2, 1177, Nova Audio Bks.); 1997. audio 121.25 o.p. (1-56100-802-8, 806, Unabridged Library Editions); 1997. audio 29.95 o.p. (1-56100-727-7, 41, Bookcassette); 1996. audio 27.95 o.p. Brilliance Audio.

—Beguiled. 1997. 432p. 24.95 o.s.i (0-525-94272-6) Dutton/Plume.

—Beguiled. 1998. mass mkt. 6.99 o.s.i (0-451-19188-9, Signet Bks.) NAL.

—Devoted. 1995. 480p. 23.95 o.p. (0-525-94046-4, Dutton) Dutton/Plume.

Bosquet, Alain. A Russian Mother. Bray, Barbara, tr. from FRE. 1996. (French Expressions Ser.). 284p. 26.00 (0-8419-1329-3) Holmes & Meier Pubs., Inc.

Bourget, Paul Charles Joseph. Monica & Other Stories. Marchant, William, tr. 1977. (Short Story Index Reprint Ser.). 22.95 (0-8369-3286-2) Ayer Co. Pubs., Inc.

Bove, Emmanuel. A Man Who Knows. 1989. 25.00 o.p. (0-85635-804-5) Carcanet Pr., Ltd. GBR. *Dist:* Paul & Co. Pubs. Consortium, Inc.

—A Man Who Knows. Louth, Janet, tr. from FRE. 1999. 136p. pap. 15.95 (0-8101-6057-9, Marlboro Pr., The) Northwestern Univ. Pr.

—Quicksand. Di Bernardi, Dominic, tr. from FRE. 1993. 192p. pap. 11.95 (0-910395-70-5) Marlboro Pr., Inc., The.

—Quicksand. Di Bernado, Dominic, tr. from FRE. 1991. 192p. 29.95 (0-910395-69-1) Marlboro Pr., Inc., The.

Boyle, Kay. Plagued by the Nightingale. 1990. 192p. pap. 7.95 o.p. (0-14-016212-7, Penguin Bks.) Viking Penguin.

Braddon, M. E. Eleanor's Victory. 1996. (Pocket Classics Ser.). 416p. pap. 12.95 (0-7509-1118-2) Sutton Publishing, Ltd. GBR. *Dist:* International Publishers Marketing.

Bradford, Barbara Taylor. A Sudden Change of Heart. 1999. mass mkt. (0-440-29567-X); 400p. mass mkt. 7.99 (0-440-23514-6) Dell Publishing.

—A Sudden Change of Heart. l.t. ed. 1999. 11.95 (1-56895-965-6); 29.95 o.p. (1-56895-735-1) Gale Group. (Wheeler Publishing, Inc.).

—A Sudden Change of Heart. l.t. ed. 2000. (Charnwood Large Print Ser.). 440p. o.p. (0-7089-9134-3, Ulverscroft) Thorpe, F. A. Pubs. GBR. *Dist:* Ulverscroft Large Print Bks., Ltd., Ulverscroft Large Print Canada, Ltd.

Bradshaw, Gillian. The Wolf Hunt. E-Book 14.95 (0-312-70657-X, Tor Bks.); 2001. 384p. 24.95 (0-312-87332-8, Forge Bks.); 2002. 384p. reprint ed. pap. 14.95 (0-312-87595-9, Tor Bks.) Doherty, Tom Assocs., LLC.

Brink, André. The Wall of the Plague. 1985. 447p. 17.45 o.p. (0-671-54189-7) Summit Bks.

Bromfield, Louis. The Green Bay Tree. 2002. 390p. pap. 14.00 (1-888683-64-3) Wooster Bk. Co., The.

Brooke, Gabriella. The Words of Bernfrieda: A Chronicle of Hauteville. 2002. 258p. reprint ed. per. 18.95 (0-9719988-0-9, Malgari Pr.) Brooke, Gabriella.

—The Words of Bernfrieda: A Chronicle of Hauteville. 1998. (Illus.). 258p. (0-910055-50-5); 304p. pap. 18.95 (0-910055-49-1) Eastern Washington Univ. Pr.

Brookner, Anita. The Bay of Angels. E-Book 9.95 (1-58945-826-5) Adobe Systems, Inc.

—The Bay of Angels. 2002. 208p. pap. 12.00 (0-375-72760-4) Knopf, Alfred A. Inc.

—The Bay of Angels. E-Book 19.00 (1-58836-006-7) Random Hse., Inc.

—The Bay of Angels. 2001. (Thorndike Press Large Print Women's Fiction Ser.). 335p. 29.95 (0-7862-3654-X) Thorndike Pr.

—Incidents in the Rue Laugier. l.t. ed. 1996. 25.95 (1-56895-301-1, Wheeler Publishing, Inc.) Gale Group.

—Incidents in the Rue Laugier. unabr. ed. 2001. audio 54.95 (1-85695-232-0, 951002) ISIS Audio Bks. GBR. *Dist:* Ulverscroft Large Print Bks., Ltd.

—Incidents in the Rue Laugier. 1997. 240p. pap. 13.00 (0-679-76512-3, Vintage) Knopf Publishing Group.

Brunel, Sigrid. Woman with Red Hair. 1991. 200p. (Orig.). pap. 8.95 (0-934678-30-8) New Victoria Pubs., Inc.

Bullis, Douglas. Not by Bread Alone: The Thousand Years of the French Revolution. 1989. (Illus.). 160p. (Orig.). pap. 14.95 o.p. (0-87905-345-3) Smith, Gibbs Pub.

Bunner, Henry C. Made in France. 1977. (Short Story Index Reprint Ser.). (Illus.). 18.95 (0-8369-3085-1) Ayer Co. Pubs., Inc.

Burney, Fanny. The Wanderer: Or, Female Difficulties. Doody, Margaret Anne et al, eds. 2001. (Oxford World's Classics Ser.). 1008p. pap. 16.95 (0-19-283758-3) Oxford Univ. Pr., Inc.

—The Wanderer: Or, Female Difficulties. 1991. (Oxford World's Classics Ser.). 1,004p. pap. 15.95 o.p. (0-19-282133-4) Oxford Univ. Pr., Inc.

Burnham, Sophy. The Treasure of Montsegur: A Novel of the Cathars. 2003. 304p. pap. 13.95 (0-06-000080-5); 2002. 288p. 23.95 (0-06-000079-1) HarperSanFrancisco.

Cadell, Elizabeth. I Love a Lass. 22.95 (0-88411-394-9) Amereon, Ltd.

Calaferte, Louis. C'est la Guerre: A Novel. Wainhouse, Austryn, tr. from FRE. 1999. 130p. 66.00 (0-8101-6032-3); pap. 14.95 (0-8101-6068-4) Northwestern Univ. Pr. (Marlboro Pr., The).

Calasso, Roberto. The Ruin of Kasch. Weaver, William & Sartarelli, Stephen, trs. 1996. Orig. Title: Rovina di Kasch. 400p. pap. 14.95 (0-674-78029-9) Harvard Univ. Pr.

—The Ruin of Kasch. Weaver, William & Sartorelli, Stephen, trs. from ITA. 1996. Orig. Title: Rovina di Kasch. 400p. pap. text 24.95 (0-674-78026-4, Belknap Pr.) Harvard Univ. Pr.

Caldwell, Taylor. Arm & Darkness. 1983. mass mkt. 3.50 o.s.i (0-449-20321-2); 1975. mass mkt. 1.95 o.s.i (0-449-22627-1) Ballantine Bks. (Fawcett).

—The Arm & the Darkness. 1974. reprint ed. lib. bdg. 34.95 (0-88411-151-2) Amereon, Ltd.

Carlile, Clancy. The Paris Pilgrims. 2000. 464p. pap. 14.00 (0-7867-0753-4); 1999. 496p. 25.00 o.p. (0-7867-0615-5) Avalon Publishing Group. (Carroll & Graf Pubs.).

Carole, Douglas. Another Scandal in Bohemia. 2003. (Irene Adler Ser.). 480p. mass mkt. 6.99 (0-7653-4325-8, Forge Bks.) Doherty, Tom Assocs., LLC.

Carr, John Dickson. Captain Cut-Throat. 1980. 232p. 1.95 o.s.i (0-441-09134-2) Ace Bks.

—Captain Cut-Throat. 1998. 240p. mass mkt. 4.95 (0-7867-0547-7); 1988. 306p. pap. 3.95 o.p. (0-88184-437-3) Avalon Publishing Group. (Carroll & Graf Pubs.).

—Captain Cut-Throat. 1996. 21.50 o.p. (0-7451-8689-0, Black Dagger) BBC Audiobooks America.

—The Corpse in the Waxworks: A Monsieur Bencolin Mystery. 1990. 192p. reprint ed. mass mkt. 4.95 o.p. (0-06-081039-4, Perennial) HarperTrade.

—The Corpse in the Waxworks: A Monsieur Bencolin Mystery. 1990. 192p. (C). reprint ed. lib. bdg. 20.00 o.p. (0-8095-9026-3) Millefleurs.

—It Walks by Night. 1997. 19.50 o.p. (0-7451-8698-X, Black Dagger) BBC Audiobooks America.

—It Walks by Night. 1986. 256p. mass mkt. 3.50 o.p. (0-8217-1931-9, Zebra Bks.) Kensington Publishing Corp.

Carroll, Lewis, pseud, ed. The Works of Charles Dickens, 21 vols. reprint ed. lib. bdg. 2058.00 (0-7426-2349-1) Classic Bks.

Carter, Vincent O. Such Sweet Thunder: A Novel. 2003. (Illus.). 560p. 25.95 (1-58642-058-5) Steerforth Pr.

Cartland, Barbara. The Captive Heart. 1980. 1.75 o.s.i (0-515-05566-2, Jove) Berkley Publishing Group.

Cather, Willa. Shadows on the Rock. 1995. (Vintage Bks.). 240p. pap. 12.00 (0-679-76404-6, Vintage) Knopf Publishing Group.

—Shadows on the Rock. 1995. 18.05 (0-606-22207-3) Turtleback Bks.

Celine, Louis-Ferdinand. Castle to Castle. 1987. Tr. of D'un Chateau l'autre. 352p. pap. 8.95 o.p. (0-88184-360-1, Carroll & Graf Pubs.) Avalon Publishing Group.

—Castle to Castle. Manheim, Ralph, tr. from FRE. 1997. Tr. of D'un Chateau l'autre. 360p. reprint ed. pap. 13.95 (1-56478-150-X) Dalkey Archive Pr.

—Castle to Castle. Manheim, Ralph, tr. from FRE. 1976. Tr. of D'un Chateau l'autre. pap. 2.95 o.p. (0-14-004341-1, Penguin Bks.) Viking Penguin.

—Fable for Another Time. Hudson, Mary, tr. from FRE. 2003. (French Modernist Library Ser.). (Illus.). 288p. pap. 25.00 (0-8032-6424-0, Bison Bks.); text 55.00 (0-8032-1520-7) Univ. of Nebraska Pr.

—Romans. Godard, Henri, ed. 1988. lib. bdg. 140.00 (0-7859-3885-0); 1981. lib. bdg. 125.00 (0-7859-3875-3) French & European Pubns., Inc.

—Romans, Vol. 2. Godard, J., ed. 1974. (FRE.). lib. bdg. 110.00 (0-7859-3827-3) French & European Pubns., Inc.

—Romans, 3 tomes. deluxe ed. (Pleiade Ser.). (FRE.). Vol. 1: Voyage au Bout de la Nuit. 83.95 (2-07-011000-1); Vol. 3. 89.95 (2-07-011155-5) Schoenhof's Foreign Bks., Inc.

—Romans: D'un Chateau l'Autre; Nord; Rigodon, Tome 2. deluxe ed. 1974. (Pleiade Ser.). (FRE.). 1272p. 71.95 (2-07-010797-3) Schoenhof's Foreign Bks., Inc.

Cendrars, Blaise. To the End of the World. (Peter Owen Modern Classics Ser.). 2002. 253p. pap. 19.95 (0-7206-1097-4); 1991. 251p. reprint ed. 30.00 (0-7206-0819-8) Owen, Peter Ltd. GBR. *Dist:* Dufour Editions, Inc.

Center for Learning Network Staff & Hugo, Victor. Les Miserables: Curriculum Unit. 1992. (Novel Ser.). 98p. reprint ed. tchr. ed., spiral bd. 18.95 (1-56077-255-7) Ctr. for Learning, The.

Cerasini, Marc A. The Hunchback of Notre Dame. 1995. (Bullseye Step into Classics Ser.). 9.09 o.p. (0-606-09442-3) Turtleback Bks.

Ch, Weir. Madame Bovary. 1948. (C). pap. text 4.50 o.p. (0-03-009895-5) Harcourt College Pubs.

Chamberlin, Ann. The Merlin of the Oak Wood. 2001. (Joan of Arc Tapestries Ser.: Vol. 2). (Illus.). 352p. 24.95 (0-312-87284-4, Tor Bks.) Doherty, Tom Assocs., LLC.

Champlin, Tim. The Survivor. 2002. 272p. mass mkt. 4.99 (0-8439-4981-3, Leisure Bks.) Dorchester Publishing Co., Inc.

—The Survivor. 1996. (Western Ser.). 264p. 17.95 (0-7862-0661-6, Five Star) Gale Group.

—The Survivor. l.t. ed. 1997. (Western Ser.). 309p. 24.95 (0-7838-1672-3) Thorndike Pr.

Chandernagor, Francoise. The King's Way: The Life of Madame de Maintenon. Bray, Barbara, tr. 1984. (Helen & Kurt Wolff Bk.). 512p. 15.95 o.p. (0-15-147274-2) Harcourt Trade Pubs.

Chevalier, Tracy. The Virgin Blue. 2002. 312p. pap. (0-00-710827-3) HarperCollins Pubs.

—The Virgin Blue. l.t. ed. 2003. 443p. 29.95 (0-7862-5772-5) Thorndike Pr.

—The Virgin Blue: A Novel. 2003. 320p. pap. 14.00 (0-452-28444-9, Plume) Dutton/Plume.

Chevallier, Gabriel. Clochemerle. 2004. 320p. pap. (0-09-945388-6) Vintage UK GBR. *Dist:* Random Hse. of Canada, Ltd., Random Hse., Inc.

Chraibi, Driss. Heirs to the Past. 1971. (African Writers Ser.). 107p. (C). pap. 8.95 (0-435-90079-X, 90079) Heinemann.

—Passe Simple. 1986. (FRE.). 273p. pap. 11.95 (0-7859-2031-5, 2070377288) French & European Pubns., Inc.

—Passe Simple. 1987. (Folio Ser.: No. 1728). (FRE.). 272p. pap. 10.95 (2-07-037728-8) Schoenhof's Foreign Bks., Inc.

—Succession Ouverte. 1979. (FRE.). 192p. pap. 10.95 (0-7859-1900-7, 2070371360) French & European Pubns., Inc.

Christie, Agatha. The Mystery of the Blue Train. Date not set. lib. bdg. 20.95 (0-8488-2138-6) Amereon, Ltd.

—The Mystery of the Blue Train. 1987. (Hardcover Collection). 9.95 o.s.i (0-553-35068-4) Bantam Bks.

—The Mystery of the Blue Train. 1991. (Hercule Poirot Mystery Ser.). 288p. reprint ed. mass mkt. 5.99 (0-425-13026-6) Berkley Publishing Group.

—The Mystery of the Blue Train. l.t. ed. 1992. 391p. 13.95 o.p. (0-8161-4580-6); 1991. 350p. 19.95 o.p. (0-8161-4579-2) Gale Group. (Macmillan Reference USA).

—The Mystery of the Blue Train. abr. ed. 1993. (BBC Radio Presents Ser.). audio 18.00 o.s.i (0-553-47181-3, RH Audio) Random Hse. Audio Publishing Group.

—The Mystery of the Blue Train. 1989. 224p. mass mkt. 4.99 o.p. (0-671-70264-5); 1985. mass mkt. 3.50 o.s.i (0-671-60637-9) Simon & Schuster. (Pocket).

—The Mystery of the Blue Train. l.t. ed. 1976. 423p. 12.00 o.p. (0-85456-438-1, Ulverscroft) Thorpe, F. A. Pubs. GBR. *Dist:* Ulverscroft Large Print Bks., Ltd.

—The Mystery of the Blue Train. 1991. 12.04 (0-606-12445-4) Turtleback Bks.

Coelho, Paulo. By the River Piedra I Sat down & Wept. Clarke, Alan R., tr. from POR. 1996. 224p. 20.00 o.s.i (0-06-251398-2) HarperSanFrancisco.

—By the River Piedra I Sat down & Wept. 1997. 192p. pap. 13.00 (0-06-097726-4, Perennial) HarperTrade.

—By the River Piedra I Sat down & Wept, Set. unabr. ed. 1996. 24.95 o.p. (0-7871-1176-7, 494322) NewStar Media, Inc.

Coffman, Virginia. Veronique. 1975. 8.95 o.p. (0-87795-107-1, Morrow, William & Co.) Morrow/Avon.

Cokal, Susann. Mirabilis. 2002. 400p. pap. 14.00 (0-425-18532-X) Berkley Publishing Group.

—Mirabilis. 2001. 304p. 25.95 o.p. (0-399-14753-5, BlueHen Bks.) Putnam Publishing Group, The.

Colette, Sidonie-Gabrielle. Bella-Vista. 1974. (FRE.). pap. 11.95 (0-8288-9137-0, M3321) French & European Pubns., Inc.

—Bella-Vista. 1996. pap. 1.99 o.s.i (0-679-77097-6) Random Hse., Inc.

—Cheri. 1958. (FRE.). pap. 10.95 (0-8288-9154-0, F97041) French & European Pubns., Inc.

—Cheri. (FRE.). pap. 9.95 (2-253-01333-1) Librairie Generale Francaise, LGF FRA. *Dist:* Distribooks, Inc.

—Cheri & the Last of Cheri. 1995. (Penguin Twentieth-Century Classics Ser.). 256p. pap. 11.95 o.s.i (0-14-018317-5, Penguin Bks.) Viking Penguin.

—Cheri & the Last of Cheri. 1986. 240p. mass mkt. 4.95 o.s.i (0-345-34017-5) Ballantine Bks.

—Cheri & the Last of Cheri. Senhouse, Roger, tr. from FRE. 1976. 304p. 7.95 o.p. (0-374-12102-8); 1976. 304p. pap. 5.95 o.p. (0-374-51314-7); 2nd ed. 2001. 320p. pap. 15.00 (0-374-52801-2) Farrar, Straus & Giroux.

—Cheri & the Last of Cheri. 1994. 263p. 7.99 o.s.i (0-517-12260-X) Random Hse. Value Publishing.

—Cheri & the Last of Cheri. 1974. 256p. pap. 2.50 o.p. (0-14-001020-3, Penguin Bks.) Viking Penguin.

—Gigi: Julie De Carneilhan: Chance Acquaintances. Senhouse, Roger & Fermor, Patrick, trs. from FRE. 1976. 320p. pap. 8.95 o.p. (0-374-51317-1) Farrar, Straus & Giroux.

—The Other One. Tait, Elizabeth & Senhouse, Roger, trs. 1972. 160p. reprint ed. 62.95 (0-8371-6295-5, COTO, Greenwood Pr.) Greenwood Publishing Group, Inc.

—Retreat from Love. Crosland, Margaret, tr. 1980. (Harvest Book Ser.). 240p. reprint ed. pap. 10.00 (0-15-676588-8, Harvest Bks.) Harcourt Trade Pubs.

—The Ripening Seed. Senhouse, Roger, tr. from FRE. 1975. 186p. 7.95 o.p. (0-374-25069-3) Farrar, Straus & Giroux.

—The Vagabond. 1982. 224p. mass mkt. 4.99 o.s.i (0-345-30061-0) Ballantine Bks.

—The Vagabond. McLeod, Enid, tr. from FRE. 1974. 223p. 8.95 o.p. (0-374-28233-1); 1974. 223p. pap. 12.00 o.p. (0-374-51175-6); 2nd ed. 2001. 224p. pap. 12.00 (0-374-52804-7) Farrar, Straus & Giroux.

—The Vagabond. 1995. 7.99 o.s.i (0-517-12259-6) Random Hse. Value Publishing.

—The Vagabond. McLeod, Enid, tr. 1995. (Penguin Twentieth-Century Classics Ser.). 192p. pap. 10.95 o.p. (0-14-018325-6, Penguin Classics) Viking Penguin.

—La Vagabonde. 1993. 256p. mass mkt. 3.50 o.s.i (0-553-21423-3, Bantam Classics) Bantam Bks.

—La Vagabonde. 1958. (FRE.). 256p. pap. (0-7859-4722-1); pap. 11.95 o.p. (0-8288-9164-8, F97341) French & European Pubns., Inc.

Collins, Max Allan. Saving Private Ryan. 1998. 319p. mass mkt. 6.50 o.s.i (0-451-19727-5, Signet Bks.) NAL.

Combaz, Christian. Jours de France. 1999. (FRE.). 324p. reprint ed. pap. 15.95 (1-58348-192-3) iUniverse, Inc.

Conde, Maryse. Desirada. 1998. (FRE.). pap. 11.95 (2-266-08697-9) Presses Pocket FRA. *Dist:* Distribooks, Inc.
—Desirada. Philcox, Richard, tr. from FRE. 2000. 260p. 24.00 (1-56947-215-7) Soho Pr., Inc.
—Desirada: A Novel. Philcox, Richard, tr. from FRE. 2001. 262p. reprint ed. pap. 14.00 (1-56947-263-7) Soho Pr., Inc.
Connery, Tom. Honour Redeemed. 2003. 336p. pap. 13.00 (0-425-18972-4) Berkley Publishing Group.
—Honour Redeemed. 2000. (Markham of the Marines Ser.: Vol. 2). 328p. 21.95 (0-89526-255-X) Regnery Publishing, Inc., An Eagle Publishing Co.
Constant, Benjamin. Adolphe. Coleman, Patrick, ed. Mauldon, Margaret, tr. from FRE. 2001. (Oxford World's Classics Ser.). 128p. pap. 10.95 (0-19-283927-6) Oxford Univ. Pr., Inc.
Cornwell, Bernard. Vagabond. 2002. (Illus.). 416p. 25.95 (0-06-621080-1, HarperCollins); 688p. pap. 25.95 (0-06-051743-3, HarperLargePrint) HarperTrade.
—Vagabond. 2003. 480p. mass mkt. 7.99 (0-06-053268-8, HarperTorch) Morrow/Avon.
Cosse, Laurence. A Corner of the Veil. Asher, Linda, tr. from FRE. 1999. 272p. 23.00 (0-684-84667-5, Scribner) Simon & Schuster.
Courtine, Robert J. Madame Maigret's Recipes. Manheim, Mary, tr. 1987. pap. 5.95 o.p. (0-15-650172-4, Harvest Bks.) Harcourt Trade Pubs.
Cowley, Marjorie. Anooka's Answer. 1998. (Illus.). 152p. (J). (gr. 5-9). tchr. ed. 16.00 (0-395-88530-2, Clarion Bks.) Houghton Mifflin Co. Trade & Reference Div.
Crackanthorpe, David. Horseman, Pass By. 2001. 320p. pap. 12.50 (0-7472-6086-9); 313p. pap. 17.95 (0-7472-2250-9) Headline Bk. Publishing, Ltd. GBR. *Dist:* Trafalgar Square.
Craig, Charmaine. The Good Men: A Novel of Heresy. 2003. 480p. reprint ed. pap. 14.00 (1-57322-973-3, Riverhead Trade (Paperbacks)) Berkley Publishing Group.
—The Good Men: A Novel of Heresy. 2002. (Illus.). 448p. 24.95 o.s.i (1-57322-197-X, Riverhead Bks. (Hardcovers)) Putnam Publishing Group, The.
Crawford, Marion A., tr. The Chouans. 1972. (Penguin Classics Ser.). 400p. pap. 11.95 o.p. (0-14-044260-X, Penguin Classics) Viking Penguin.
Cru, Jean N. War Books. 1988. 210p. pap. 12.50 (0-916304-22-1) San Diego State Univ. Pr.
cummings, e e. The Enormous Room. 2002. (Dover Thrift Editions Ser.). (Illus.). 224p. pap. 3.00 (0-486-42120-1) Dover Pubns., Inc.
Daeninckx, Didier. Meurtres pour Memoire. 1988. Tr. of Murder in Memoriam. (FRE.). 215p. pap. 10.95 (0-7859-2094-3, 2070380491) French & European Pubns., Inc.
—Murder in Memoriam. Heron, Liz, tr. from FRE. 1992. (Mask Noir Ser.). Orig. Title: Meurtres pour Memoire. 176p. (Orig.). pap. (1-85242-206-8) Serpent's Tail Ltd.
Daley, Robert. The Dangerous Edge. 1984. pap. 3.95 o.p. (0-440-11809-3) Dell Publishing.
—The Dangerous Edge. 1983. 16.50 o.p. (0-671-47057-4, Simon & Schuster) Simon & Schuster.
—The Dangerous Edge. 1995. 480p. mass mkt. 5.99 o.s.i (0-446-60278-7) Warner Bks., Inc.
—The Innocents Within. 2001. 480p. mass mkt. 7.50 (0-449-00415-5, Ballantine Bks.) Ballantine Bks.
—The Innocents Within. 2001. 13.55 (0-606-20497-0) Turtleback Bks.
—The Innocents Within: A Novel. 1999. 448p. 25.95 o.s.i (0-375-50178-9, Villard Bks.) Random House Adult Trade Publishing Group.
—Nowhere to Run. abr. ed. 1997. audio 7.99 o.p. (1-56740-191-0, 685, Paperback Nova Audio Bks.); 1996. audio 16.95 o.p. (1-56100-920-2, 1309, Nova Audio Bks.); 1996. audio 25.95 o.p. (1-56100-710-2, 200, Bookcassette); 1996. audio 89.25 o.p. (1-56100-335-2, 968, Unabridged Library Editions) Brilliance Audio.
—Nowhere to Run. l.t. ed. 1997. (G. K. Hall Mystery Ser.). 631p. lib. bdg. 26.95 o.p. (0-7838-2012-7, Macmillan Reference USA) Gale Group.
—Nowhere to Run. 1997. 480p. mass mkt. 6.99 o.p. (0-446-60470-4); 1997. mass mkt. 188.73 (0-446-16416-X); 1996. 464p. 24.00 o.p. (0-446-52063-2) Warner Bks., Inc.
Darrieussecq, Marie. Undercurrents. Coverdale, Linda, tr. from FRE. 2001. 114p. 21.95 (1-56584-627-3) New Pr., The.
Daudet, Alphonse. Les Contes du Lundi. 1962. (FRE.). pap. 10.95 (0-8288-9188-5, F59800) French & European Pubns., Inc.
—Contes du Lundi. 1991. (FRE.). audio 19.95 Olivia & Hill Pr., The.
—Les Contes du Lundi. unabr. ed. (FRE.). pap. 5.95 (2-87714-290-6) Bookking International FRA. *Dist:* Distribooks, Inc.
—Letters from My Mill & Letters to an Absent One. 1980. (Short Story Index Reprint Ser.). reprint ed. 22.95 (0-8369-4077-6) Ayer Co. Pubs., Inc.
—Monday Tales. 1977. (Short Story Index Reprint Ser.). 23.95 (0-8369-3383-4) Ayer Co. Pubs., Inc.
—The Nabob. E-Book 3.95 (0-594-02079-4) 1873 Pr.
—The Nabob. Trent, William P., tr. from FRE. 1976. reprint ed. 40.00 o.p. (0-86527-282-4) Fertig, Howard Inc.
—The Nabob. 2002. 368p. 96.99 (1-4043-2134-9); per. 92.99 (1-4043-2135-7) IndyPublish.com.
Davis, Kathryn. Versailles: A Novel. 2002. 224p. tchr. ed. 21.00 (0-618-22136-0) Houghton Mifflin Co.
Davis, William Stearns. Falaise of the Blessed Voice. 2000. 252p. pap. 9.95 (0-594-00057-2); E-Book 3.95 (0-594-02081-6) 1873 Pr.
Davison, Liam. The Betrayal. 1999. 273p. (0-670-88652-1, Viking) Viking Penguin.
De Bastide, Jean-Francois. The Little House: An Architectural Seduction. El-Khoury, Rodolfe, tr. from FRE. 1996. (Illus.). 112p. (Orig.). pap. 14.95 (1-56898-017-5) Princeton Architectural Pr.
De Duras, Claire. Ourika: An English Translation. Fowles, John, tr. from FRE. & frwd. by. 1994. (MLA Texts & Translations Ser.: No. 3b). xxxiii, 47p. (Orig.). pap. 7.95 (0-87352-780-1, P003P) Modern Language Assn. of America.
—Ourika: The Original French Text. DeJean, Joan, ed. & intro. by. Waller, Margaret, intro. 1994. (MLA Texts & Translations Ser.: No. 3a). (FRE.). xxviii, 45p. (Orig.). pap. 6.95 (0-87352-779-8, Q003P) Modern Language Assn. of America.
De Duras, Madame. Ourika: Madame de Duras. Little, Roger, ed. 2nd rev. ed. 1998. (Exeter French Texts). (FRE., Illus.). 136p. pap. 25.95 (0-85989-573-4) Univ. of Exeter Pr. GBR. *Dist:* Brown, David Bk. Co.
De Kretser, Michelle. The Rose Grower. 2000. 448p. 25.00 (0-7867-0733-X, Carroll & Graf Pubs.) Avalon Publishing Group.
—The Rose Grower. 2001. 336p. pap. 12.95 (0-553-38121-0) Bantam Bks.
De La Fayette, Marie-Madeleine. La Princesse de Cleves. unabr. ed. (FRE.). pap. 7.95 (2-87714-160-8) Bookking International FRA. *Dist:* Distribooks, Inc.
—La Princesse de Cleves. 1958. (Folio Ser.: No. 778). pap. 9.95 (2-07-036778-9) Schoenhof's Foreign Bks., Inc.
—La Princesse de Cleves. audio Spoken Arts, Inc.
De La Valdene, Guy. Red Stag. 2003. 272p. 22.95 (1-59228-134-6, Lyons Pr.) Globe Pequot Pr., The.
De Laclos, Choderlos. Les Liaisons Dangereuses. 1991. Tr. of Dangerous Liaisons. (FRE.). audio 64.95 Olivia & Hill Pr., The.
—Les Liaisons Dangereuses. Coward, David, ed. Parmee, Douglas, tr. 1995. (Oxford World's Classics Ser.).Tr. of Dangerous Liaisons. (ENG & FRE.). 442p. pap. 7.95 o.p. (0-19-282921-1) Oxford Univ. Pr., Inc.
—Les Liaisons Dangereuses.Tr. of Dangerous Liaisons. (FRE.). pap. 12.95 (2-266-08303-1) Presses Pocket FRA. *Dist:* Distribooks, Inc.
—Les Liaisons Dangereuses. 1987. Tr. of Dangerous Liaisons. 448p. (C). pap. 19.95 (0-415-09447-X) Routledge.
De, Laclos Choderlos. Les Liaisons Dangereuses. 1988. mass mkt. 3.95 o.s.i (0-671-67528-1, Pocket) Simon & Schuster.
De Lafayette, Madame. The Princesse de Cleves. Mitfod, Nancy, tr. from FRE. 1978. (Penguin Classics Ser.). pap. 5.95 o.p. (0-14-044337-1) Viking Penguin.
—La Princesse de Cleves, Set. 1991. (FRE.). audio 38.95 Olivia & Hill Pr., The.
—The Princesse de Cleves: The Princesse de Montpensier, The Comtesse de Tende. Cave, Terence, ed. & tr. by. 1992. (Oxford World's Classics Ser.). 272p. pap. 8.95 o.p. (0-19-282687-5) Oxford Univ. Pr., Inc.
—The Princesse de Cleves: The Princesse de Montpensier; The Comtesse de Tende. 1999. (Oxford World's Classics Ser.). 288p. pap. 10.95 (0-19-283726-5) Oxford Univ. Pr., Inc.
De Lafayette, Madame, et al. The Princesse de Cleves. Buss, Robin, tr. & intro. by. 8th ed. 1992. (Classics Ser.). 192p. pap. 10.95 (0-14-044587-0, Penguin Classics) Viking Penguin.
de Sade, Marquis. Juliette. Wainhouse, Austryn, tr. from FRE. 1968. pap. 14.95 o.p. (0-394-17131-4, E676) Grove/Atlantic, Inc.
DeAndrea, William L. The Werewolf Murders. 1992. 240p. 16.50 o.s.i (0-385-42089-7) Doubleday Publishing.
Debreczeny, Paul. Temptations of the Past. 1982. 110p. (C). pap. 6.50 o.p. (0-938920-17-0) Hermitage Pubs.
Delacorta. Alba. 1990. 208p. pap. 7.95 o.p. (0-87113-387-3, Atlantic Monthly Pr.) Grove/Atlantic, Inc.
—Alba. Texier, Catherine, tr. 1989. 288p. 17.95 o.p. (0-87113-324-5) Grove/Atlantic, Inc.
—Diva. 1984. 192p. mass mkt. 3.50 o.s.i (0-345-31265-1, Ballantine Bks.) Ballantine Bks.
—Diva. Bair, Lowell, tr. from FRE. 1983. 9.50 o.p. (0-671-47056-6) Summit Bks.
—Lola. 1985. 176p. mass mkt. 2.95 o.s.i (0-345-31268-6, Ballantine Bks.) Ballantine Bks.
—Lola. 1985. 9.70 o.p. (0-671-47752-8) Summit Bks.
—Luna. 1985. 176p. mass mkt. 2.95 o.s.i (0-345-31266-X, Ballantine Bks.) Ballantine Bks.
—Luna. Reiter, Victoria, tr. 1984. (Gorodish-Alba Ser.). 128p. 9.70 o.p. (0-671-49379-5) Summit Bks.
—Nana. 1984. 192p. mass mkt. 2.75 o.s.i (0-345-31267-8, Ballantine Bks.) Ballantine Bks.
—Nana. Reiter, Victoria, tr. from FRE. 1984. (Gorodish-Alba Ser.: No. 2). 128p. 9.50 o.p. (0-671-49210-1) Summit Bks.
—Vida. Reiter, Victoria, tr. from FRE. 1985. 12.70 o.p. (0-671-60424-4) Summit Bks.
Delderfield, R. F. Seven Men of Gascony. 2001. (Military Fiction Classics Ser.). (Illus.). 366p. pap. 16.95 (0-935526-97-8) McBooks Pr., Inc.
—Seven Men of Gascony. 1975. 8.95 o.s.i (0-671-21794-1, Simon & Schuster) Simon & Schuster.
—Too Few for Drums. 2001. (Military Fiction Classics Ser.). (Illus.). 254p. pap. 14.95 (0-935526-96-X) McBooks Pr., Inc.
—Too Few for Drums. l.t. ed. 1988. (Ulverscroft Large Print Ser.). 368p. 29.99 o.p. (0-7089-1756-9, Ulverscroft) Thorpe, F. A. Pubs. GBR. *Dist:* Ulverscroft Large Print Bks., Ltd., Ulverscroft Large Print Canada, Ltd.
Delelis, Philippe. The Last Cantata. 2000. 352p. pap. 15.95 (1-902881-31-1); (1-902881-30-3) Toby Pr.
D'Eon, Leonard J. The Cavalier. 1987. 256p. 18.95 o.p. (0-399-13227-9, G. P. Putnam's Sons) Penguin Putnam Bks. for Young Readers.
Desjarlais, John J. Relics. 1993. pap. 10.99 o.p. (0-8407-6735-8) Nelson, Thomas Inc.
Devlin, Wende & Devlin, Harry. The Trouble with Henriette. 1995. (J). 15.00 o.s.i (0-02-729937-6, Simon & Schuster Children's Publishing) Simon & Schuster Children's Publishing.
Dickens, Charles. Charles Dickens. 1993. 864p. 13.99 (0-517-09339-1) Random Hse. Value Publishing.
—Charles Dickens. unabr. ed. 1995. (Classic Author Ser.). (J). audio 16.95 (1-55935-169-1) Soundelux Audio Publishing.
—Charles Dickens: Three Great Novels: Hard Times; A Tale of Two Cities; Great Expectations. 1994. 836p. pap. 15.95 o.p. (0-19-282332-9) Oxford Univ. Pr., Inc.
—A Tale of Two Cities. 1982. reprint ed. lib. bdg. 20.95 (0-89966-371-0) Buccaneer Bks., Inc.
—A Tale of Two Cities. 1989. 384p. (YA). mass mkt. 3.99 (0-8125-0506-9, Tor Classics) Doherty, Tom Assocs., LLC.
—A Tale of Two Cities. l.t. unabr. ed. 2001. (Large Print Classics Ser.). viii, 528p. 14.95 (0-486-41776-X) Dover Pubns., Inc.
—A Tale of Two Cities. 1990. (Vintage Bks.). 400p. pap. 10.00 (0-679-72965-8, Vintage) Knopf Publishing Group.
—A Tale of Two Cities. 1993. (Everyman's Library). 480p. 20.00 (0-679-42073-8) Knopf, Alfred A. Inc.
—A Tale of Two Cities. 1998. (Cloth Bound Pocket Ser.). 7.95 (3-8290-0880-5, 520656) Konemann.
—A Tale of Two Cities. Sanders, Andrew, ed. & intro. by. 1998. (Oxford World's Classics Ser.). 560p. pap. 5.95 (0-19-283390-1) Oxford Univ. Pr., Inc.
—A Tale of Two Cities. 1987. (Illus.). 380p. (J). 15.95 (0-19-254504-3) Oxford Univ. Pr., Inc.
—A Tale of Two Cities. 1999. 620p. E-Book 3.99 incl. audio compact disk (1-57646-108-4) Quiet Vision Publishing.
—A Tale of Two Cities. 2000. E-Book 4.95 (0-679-64132-7, Modern Library) Random House Adult Trade Publishing Group.
—A Tale of Two Cities. 1996. (Modern Library Ser.). 512p. 19.95 (0-679-60208-9) Random Hse., Inc.
—A Tale of Two Cities. 1984. (Illus.). 400p. 12.95 o.p. (0-89577-179-9) Reader's Digest Assn., Inc., The.
—A Tale of Two Cities. (Literary Classics Ser.). 1992. 272p. text 5.98 o.p. (1-56138-114-4, Courage Bks.); 1986. 256p. pap. 4.95 o.p. (0-89471-478-3) Running Pr. Bk. Pubs.
—A Tale of Two Cities. 1996. (Enriched Classics Ser.). 528p. reprint ed. mass mkt. 5.99 (0-671-00274-0, Pocket) Simon & Schuster.
—A Tale of Two Cities. 1989. 416p. pap. 6.95 o.p. (0-14-013218-X, Penguin Bks.) Viking Penguin.
—A Tale of Two Cities. Woodcock, George, ed. 1970. (English Library). (Illus.). 416p. pap. 6.95 o.s.i (0-14-043054-7, Penguin Classics) Viking Penguin.
—The Works of Charles Dickens. 2001. (Collected Works of Charles Dickens). reprint ed. pap. text 588.00 (0-7426-7349-9) Classic Bks.
—The Works of Charles Dickens. 1988. 11.99 o.s.i (0-517-61831-1); 1990. 864p. 19.99 (0-517-05360-8) Random Hse. Value Publishing.
—The Works of Charles Dickens. 1989. 9.98 o.p. (0-8317-9504-2) Smithmark Pubs., Inc.
—The Works of Charles Dickens. 1995. 797p. pap. o.p. (1-57215-128-5) World Pubns., Inc.
—The Works of Charles Dickens. unabr. ed. Incl. Great Expectations. audio Pickwick Papers. audio Tale of Two Cities. audio Set audio 29.75 Audio Bk. Co.
Diwo, Jean. Les Dames du Fauborg. 1987. (FRE.). pap. 16.95 (0-7859-2064-1, 2070378349) French & European Pubns., Inc.
Doherty, P. C. The Masked Man. 1991. 176p. 16.95 o.p. (0-312-06409-8, Saint Martin's Minotaur) St. Martin's Pr.
Dorrie, Doris. Where Do We Go from Here? Brownjohn, John, tr. 2002. 256p. pap. 14.95 (1-58234-319-5); 2001. 242p. 24.95 (1-58234-151-6) Bloomsbury Publishing.
Douglas, Carole Nelson. Irene's Last Waltz. 1994. (Irene Adler Adventure Ser.). 480p. mass mkt. 4.99 (0-8125-1703-2); 22.95 o.p. (0-312-85224-X) Doherty, Tom Assocs., LLC. (Forge Bks.).
Douglas, L. Warren. The Sacred Pool. 2001. (Illus.). 416p. 24.00 (0-671-31956-6) Baen Bks.
Doyle, Peter R. Stalked in the Catacombs. 1993. (Daring Adventure Ser.: Vol. 3). (J). (gr. 4). pap. 5.99 o.p. (1-56179-144-X) Focus on the Family Publishing.
Drieu La Rochelle, Pierre. La Comedie de Charleroi. 1982. (FRE.). pap. 10.95 (0-7859-1955-4, 2070373665) French & European Pubns., Inc.
Drummond, Hamilton. The Justice of the King. 2000. 252p. E-Book 3.95 (0-594-02129-4) 1873 Pr.
Du Maurier, George Louis Palmella Busson. Trilby. 1976. 26.95 (0-8488-0265-9) Amereon, Ltd.
—Trilby. unabr. ed. 1998. (YA). (gr. 9 up). audio 47.95 (1-55685-567-2) Audio Bk. Contractors, Inc.
—Trilby. unabr. ed. 1998. audio 56.95 (0-7861-1298-0, 2194) Blackstone Audio Bks., Inc.
—Trilby. 1994. reprint ed. lib. bdg. 32.95 (1-56849-527-7) Buccaneer Bks., Inc.
—Trilby. (Early Best Sellers Ser.). reprint ed. lib. bdg. 48.00 (0-7426-1020-9); 2001. (Illus.). pap. text 28.00 (0-7426-6020-6) Classic Bks.
—Trilby. unabr. ed. 1994. (Illus.). 384p. pap. text 9.95 (0-486-28319-4) Dover Pubns., Inc.
—Trilby. 1956. 7.50 o.p. (0-460-00863-3, Dutton) Dutton/Plume.
—Trilby. Showalter, Elaine, ed. 1999. (Oxford World's Classics Ser.). (Illus.). 368p. pap. 7.95 (0-19-283351-0) Oxford Univ. Pr., Inc.
—Trilby. Showalter, Elaine & Trotter, David, eds. 1995. (Oxford Popular Fiction Ser.). (Illus.). 316p. pap. 8.95 o.p. (0-19-282323-X) Oxford Univ. Pr., Inc.
—Trilby. 1998. 447p. reprint ed. lib. bdg. 75.00 (0-7812-7712-4) Reprint Services Corp.
—Trilby. 1994. 390p. pap. 7.50 (0-460-87447-0, Everyman's Classic Library in Paperback) Tuttle Publishing.
—Trilby. Pick, Daniel, ed. & intro. by. 1995. (Penguin Classics Ser.). 336p. pap. 7.95 o.p. (0-14-043403-8, Penguin Classics) Viking Penguin.
—Trilby. 368p. pap. 4.00 o.p. (1-85326-233-1) Wordsworth Editions, Ltd. GBR. *Dist:* Casemate Pubs. & Bk. Distributors, LLC.
Du Plessix Gray, Francine. Lovers & Tyrants. 1988. pap. 7.95 (0-393-30547-3) Norton, W. W. & Co., Inc.
—Lovers & Tyrants. 1976. 8.95 o.s.i (0-671-22338-0, Simon & Schuster) Simon & Schuster.
Ducornet, Rikki. The Stain. 1995. 230p. reprint ed. pap. 11.95 (1-56478-085-6) Dalkey Archive Pr.
—The Stain. 1984. 192p. 12.95 o.p. (0-394-54284-3, GP-955) Grove/Atlantic, Inc.
Duffy, James. The Christmas Gang. 1989. (Illus.). 80p. (J). (gr. 3-6). 12.95 o.s.i (0-684-19008-7, Atheneum) Simon & Schuster Children's Publishing.
—The Revolt of the Teddy Bears: A May Gray Mystery. 1985. (Illus.). 80p. (J). (gr. 5 up). 1.00 o.p. (0-517-55533-6) Random Hse. Value Publishing.
Dukthas, Ann. The Prince Lost to Time. 1996. 229p. mass mkt. 5.99 (0-312-95843-9, St. Martin's Paperbacks); 1995. 240p. 21.95 o.p. (0-312-13592-0, Saint Martin's Minotaur) St. Martin's Pr.
Dumas, Alexandre. Aerie Three Musketeers. 1995. mass mkt. 4.99 (1-55902-919-6, Aerie) Doherty, Tom Assocs., LLC.
—Le Comte de Monte-Cristo. 1981. (FRE.). 99.50 o.p. (0-8288-3442-3, F120780); 1. 1988. pap. 12.95 o.p. (0-7859-3089-2); 2. 1988. pap. 12.95 o.p. (0-7859-3090-6); 3. 1988. pap. 12.95 o.p. (0-7859-3092-2) French & European Pubns., Inc.
—Le Comte de Monte-Cristo. 7.95 (2-01-018349-5, LF056E) Hachette Groupe Livre FRA. *Dist:* Continental Bk. Co., Inc.
—Le Comte de Monte-Cristo. (FRE.). No. I. 13.95 (2-253-01436-2, LP084AE); No. II. 13.25 (2-253-01437-0, LP084BE) Librairie Generale Francaise, LGF FRA. *Dist:* Continental Bk. Co., Inc.
—Le Comte de Monte-Cristo. 2001. (FRE., Illus.). 136p. (C). pap. 11.25 (0-8442-1232-6, VF1232-6) McGraw-Hill/Contemporary.
—Le Comte de Monte-Cristo. (FRE.). Vol. I. pap. 13.95 (2-266-08319-8); Vol. II. pap. 14.95 (2-266-08320-1) Presses Pocket FRA. *Dist:* Distribooks, Inc.
—Le Comte de Monte-Cristo. 1981. (Pleiade Ser.). (FRE.). 1476p. pap. 75.95 o.p. (2-07-010979-8) Schoenhof's Foreign Bks., Inc.

—Le Comte de Monte-Cristo: Level 2. (FRE.). 6.25 (*2-09-031884-8*, Cl8848E) Cle International FRA. *Dist:* Continental Bk. Co., Inc.

—The Count of Monte Cristo. 1976. 29.95 (*0-8488-0478-3*) Amereon, Ltd.

—The Count of Monte Cristo. 1984. mass mkt. 3.95 o.s.i (*0-553-21230-3*, Bantam Classics) Bantam Bks.

—The Count of Monte Cristo. 1990. (Illus.). 3.75 o.s.i (*0-425-12028-7*, Classics Illustrated) Berkley Publishing Group.

—The Count of Monte Cristo. 1998. 580p. mass mkt. 4.99 (*0-8125-6568-1*, Tor Classics) Doherty, Tom Assocs., LLC.

—The Count of Monte Cristo. E-Book 2.49 (*1-58744-204-3*) Electric Umbrella Publishing.

—The Count of Monte Cristo. pap. 7.95 (*0-8359-0989-1*) Globe Fearon Educational Publishing.

—The Count of Monte Cristo. E-Book 2.95 (*1-57799-973-8*); 2001. E-Book 2.95 (*1-57799-945-2*) Logos Research Systems, Inc.

—The Count of Monte Cristo. 1991. (Oxford World's Classics Ser.). 1,162p. pap. 12.95 o.p. (*0-19-282715-4*) Oxford Univ. Pr., Inc.

—The Count of Monte Cristo. (Modern Library Classics). 1488p. 2002. pap. 12.95 (*0-375-76030-X*); 1996. 25.95 (*0-679-60199-6*) Random Hse., Inc.

—The Count of Monte Cristo. (Saddleback Classics). 2001. (Illus.). 13.10 (*0-606-21548-4*); 1956. 12.00 (*0-606-00491-2*) Turtleback Bks.

—The Count of Monte Cristo. Buss, Robin, tr. from FRE. & intro. by. 1997. (Penguin Classics Ser.). 1136p. 12.95 (*0-14-044615-X*, Penguin Classics) Viking Penguin.

—The Count of Monte Cristo. 1999. E-Book 5.99 (*0-8220-7042-1*, Cliff Notes) Wiley, John & Sons, Inc.

—The Count of Monte Cristo. 1998. (Classics Ser.). 896p. pap. 3.95 (*1-85326-733-3*, 7333WW) Wordsworth Editions, Ltd. GBR. *Dist:* Combined Publishing.

—The Count of Monte Cristo. Coward, David, ed. & intro. by. 1998. (Oxford World's Classics Ser.). 1168p. pap. 13.95 (*0-19-283395-2*) Oxford Univ. Pr., Inc.

—The Count of Monte Cristo. 1976. lib. bdg. 42.95 (*0-89968-147-6*, Lightyear Pr.) Buccaneer Bks., Inc.

—The Count of Monte Cristo. 2004. 512p. mass mkt. 6.50 (*0-7434-8755-9*, Pocket) Simon & Schuster.

—The Count of Monte Cristo. Buss, Robin, tr. from FRE. & intro. by. 2003. (Penguin Classics Ser.). 1312p. pap. 13.00 (*0-14-044926-4*, Penguin Classics) Viking Penguin.

—The Count of Monte Cristo. Bair, Lowell, tr. from FRE. abr. ed. 1981. (Bantam Classics Ser.). 446p. pap. 3.95 o.s.i (*0-553-21187-0*) Bantam Bks.

—The Count of Monte Cristo. Blair, Lowell, tr. & abr. by. abr. ed. 1984. (Bantam Classics Ser.). 544p. reprint ed. mass mkt. 6.50 (*0-553-21350-4*) Bantam Dell Publishing Group.

—The Count of Monte Cristo. l.t. ed. 1358p. pap. 94.86 (*0-7583-0648-2*); 2419p. pap. 163.95 (*0-7583-0650-4*); 4874p. pap. 308.33 (*0-7583-0653-9*); 6954p. pap. 410.79 (*0-7583-0655-5*); 1765p. pap. 126.96 (*0-7583-0649-0*); 5995p. pap. 360.48 (*0-7583-0654-7*); 3096p. pap. 206.74 (*0-7583-0651-2*); 3963p. pap. 256.49 (*0-7583-0652-0*); 1765p. lib. bdg. 144.96 (*0-7583-0641-5*); 2419p. lib. bdg. 187.95 (*0-7583-0642-3*); 3096p. lib. bdg. 236.74 (*0-7583-0643-1*); 3963p. lib. bdg. 292.49 (*0-7583-0644-X*); 4874p. lib. bdg. 350.33 (*0-7583-0645-8*); 5995p. lib. bdg. 417.98 (*0-7583-0646-6*); 6954p. lib. bdg. 481.04 (*0-7583-0647-4*); 1358p. lib. bdg. 106.86 (*0-7583-0640-7*) Huge Print Pr.

—The Count of Monte Cristo, Level 3. 2001. pap. 7.67 (*0-582-42701-0*) Longman Publishing Group.

—The Count of Monte Cristo. abr. ed. 1988. 528p. mass mkt. 6.95 (*0-451-52195-1*, Signet Classics) NAL.

—The Count of Monte Cristo. movie tie-in ed. 2001. 528p. pap. 11.00 (*0-14-200073-6*) Penguin Group (USA) Inc.

—The Count of Monte Cristo. 1998. (Count of Monte Cristo Ser.: Vol. 1). 448p. Vol. I. pap. 14.95 o.p. (*0-89526-347-5*); Vol. II. pap. 14.95 o.p. (*0-89526-346-7*) Regnery Publishing, Inc., An Eagle Publishing Co. (Gateway Editions).

—The Knight of Maison-Rouge: A Novel of Marie Antoinette. 2003. (Illus.). 448p. 24.95 (*0-679-64298-6*) Random Hse., Inc.

—Louise de la Valliere. 1994. reprint ed. lib. bdg. 37.95 (*1-56849-274-X*) Buccaneer Bks., Inc.

—Louise de la Valliere. 2002. 492p. 22.99 (*1-4043-1446-6*); per. 17.99 (*1-4043-1447-4*) IndyPublish-.com.

—Louise de la Valliere. Coward, David, ed. & intro. by. (Oxford World's Classics Ser.). 1998. 768p. pap. 15.95 (*0-19-283465-7*); 1995. 764p. pap. 14.95 o.p. (*0-19-282389-2*) Oxford Univ. Pr., Inc.

—The Man in the Iron Mask. 1976. 27.95 (*0-8488-1293-X*) Amereon, Ltd.

—The Man in the Iron Mask. 1994. (Illustrated Classics Collection). 64 p. pap. 4.95 (*0-7854-0750-2*, 40503) American Guidance Service, Inc.

—The Man in the Iron Mask. unabr. ed. 1994. Pt. 1. audio 69.95 (*0-7861-0487-2*, 1439-A); Pt. 2. audio 62.95 (*0-7861-0641-7*, 1439-B) Blackstone Audio Bks., Inc.

—The Man in the Iron Mask. unabr. collector's ed. 1985. (J). audio 48.00 (*0-7366-3904-7*, 895784) Books on Tape, Inc.

—The Man in the Iron Mask. unabr. ed. 1999. (Bookcassette Classic Collection). 16p. audio 66.25 (*1-56740-680-7*, 1818, Unabridged Library Editions) Brilliance Audio.

—The Man in the Iron Mask. 1976. lib. bdg. 35.95 (*0-89968-146-8*, Lightyear Pr.) Buccaneer Bks., Inc.

—The Man in the Iron Mask. 1998. 574p. pap. text 4.99 (*0-8125-6499-5*, Tor Classics) Doherty, Tom Assocs., LLC.

—The Man in the Iron Mask. 2002. 504p. 29.99 (*1-4043-1632-9*); per. 24.99 (*1-4043-1633-7*) IndyPublish.com.

—The Man in the Iron Mask. abr. ed. 1985. audio 42.00 Jimcin Recordings.

—The Man in the Iron Mask. rev. ed. 1998. (Signet Regency Romance Ser.: Vol. 9700). 496p. mass mkt. 6.99 (*0-451-19700-3*, Signet Bks.) NAL.

—The Man in the Iron Mask. Rogers, Jacqueline, tr. rev. ed. 1992. 496p. mass mkt. 6.95 (*0-451-52564-7*, Signet Classics) NAL.

—The Man in the Iron Mask. abr. ed. (Works of Alexandre Dumas). 1996. audio 13.98 (*962-634-569-1*, NA206914); 1995. audio compact disk 15.98 (*962-634-069-X*, NA206912) Naxos of America, Inc. (Naxos AudioBooks).

—The Man in the Iron Mask. abr. ed. 1994. (Classic, Ultimate, Dove Ser.). audio 19.95 o.p. (*0-7871-0155-9*, 693103) NewStar Media, Inc.

—The Man in the Iron Mask. Coward, David, ed. & intro. by. 1998. (Oxford World's Classics Ser.). 656p. pap. 13.95 (*0-19-283842-3*) Oxford Univ. Pr., Inc.

—The Man in the Iron Mask. 1992. (Oxford World's Classics Ser.). 654p. pap. 11.95 o.p. (*0-19-282752-9*) Oxford Univ. Pr., Inc.

—The Man in the Iron Mask. 2003. (Penguin Classics Ser.). 496p. pap. 13.00 (*0-14-043924-2*) Penguin Group (USA) Inc.

—The Man in the Iron Mask. 1998. (Gateway Movie Classics Ser.). 448p. pap. 14.95 o.p. (*0-89526-348-3*, Gateway Editions) Regnery Publishing, Inc., An Eagle Publishing Co.

—The Man in the Iron Mask. abr. ed. 1998. audio 17.95 (*1-55935-267-1*) Soundelux Audio Publishing.

—The Man in the Iron Mask. 2000. (Signature Classics Ser.). 456p. 24.95 (*1-58279-067-1*); (*1-58279-073-6*) Trident Pr. International.

—The Musketeer. 2001. 608p. mass mkt. 6.99 (*0-7653-4344-4*, Tor Bks.) Doherty, Tom Assocs., LLC.

—La Reine Margot. unabr. ed. (FRE.). pap. 8.95 (*2-87714-188-8*) Bookking International FRA. *Dist:* Distribooks, Inc.

—La Reine Margot. 1992. (FRE.). pap. 16.95 (*0-7859-3287-9*, 2277232793); 1935. pap. 11.90 o.p. French & European Pubns., Inc.

—La Reine Margot. Coward, David, ed. (Oxford World's Classics Ser.). (Illus.). 1999. 560p. pap. 14.95 (*0-19-283844-X*); 1998. 558p. pap. 13.95 o.p. (*0-19-283302-2*) Oxford Univ. Pr., Inc.

—La Reine Margot. (FRE.). pap. 13.95 (*2-266-04336-6*) Presses Pocket FRA. *Dist:* Distribooks, Inc.

—La Reine Margot: Dame De Monsoreau: Les Quarante-Cinq. 1988. (FRE.). 1680p. pap. 65.00 (*0-7859-2192-3*, 2715213638) French & European Pubns., Inc.

—Ten Years Later. abr. ed. 1996. 19.95 o.p. (*0-7871-0501-5*, 693547) NewStar Media, Inc.

—The Three Musketeers. 1997. (Classics Illustrated Study Guides). (Illus.). mass mkt. 4.99 (*1-57840-029-5*) Acclaim Bks.

—The Three Musketeers. 1976. 29.95 (*0-8488-1295-6*) Amereon, Ltd.

—The Three Musketeers, unabr. ed. 1997. audio 77.95 (*1-55685-477-3*, 477-3) Audio Bk. Contractors, Inc.

—The Three Musketeers. 1977. 1.75 o.p. (*0-515-03492-4*, V3492, Jove) Berkley Publishing Group.

—The Three Musketeers. 1977. reprint ed. 14.95 o.p. (*0-460-00081-0*) Biblio Distribution.

—The Three Musketeers. unabr. ed. 1990. Pt. 1. audio 69.95 (*0-7861-0577-1*, 2067-A); Pt. 2. audio 62.95 (*0-7861-0578-X*, 2067-B) Blackstone Audio Bks., Inc.

—The Three Musketeers, Pt. A. unabr. collector's ed. 1991. (J). audio 80.00 (*0-7366-3957-8*, 9209-A) Books on Tape, Inc.

—The Three Musketeers, unabr. ed. 1998. (Bookcassette Classic Collection). audio 22.95 (*1-56740-053-1*, 12, Bookcassette); audio 66.25 (*1-56740-582-7*, 1074, Unabridged Library Editions) Brilliance Audio.

—The Three Musketeers. adapted ed. 1976. per. 6.50 (*0-8222-1140-8*) Dramatists Play Service, Inc.

—The Three Musketeers. abr. ed. (Read-Along Ser.). 1994. pap. 29.99 incl. audio (*0-88646-845-0*, LSR 7208); Set. 1987. audio 16.99 (*0-88646-208-8*, 7208) Durkin Hayes Publishing Ltd.

—The Three Musketeers. E-Book 2.49 (*1-58744-092-X*) Electric Umbrella Publishing.

—The Three Musketeers. abr. ed. audio 8.98 o.p. (*0-89845-115-9*, CPN 1692, HarperAudio) HarperTrade.

—The Three Musketeers, Set. abr. ed. 1999. audio 16.95 Highsmith Inc.

—The Three Musketeers. unabr. ed. 1991. (YA). (gr. 9-12). audio 104.00 Jimcin Recordings.

—The Three Musketeers. 1999. (Everyman's Library Children's Classics). (Illus.). 720p. (gr. 8-12). 17.95 (*0-375-40657-3*) Knopf, Alfred A. Inc.

—The Three Musketeers. E-Book 2.95 (*1-57799-942-8*) Logos Research Systems, Inc.

—The Three Musketeers. abr. ed. 2000. audio 7.95 (*1-57815-126-0*, 1088, Media Bks. Audio Publishing) Media Bks., L. L. C.

—The Three Musketeers. E-Book 1.95 (*1-58515-020-7*) MesaView, Inc.

—The Three Musketeers. abr. ed. 1999. (Adventure Theatre Ser.). audio 16.95 (*1-56994-520-9*, 345344, Monterey SoundWorks) Monterey Media, Inc.

—The Three Musketeers. 1993. 648p. mass mkt. 6.95 o.s.i (*0-451-52594-9*, Signet Classics) NAL.

—The Three Musketeers. audio 7.95 National Recording Co.

—The Three Musketeers. abr. ed. 1996. (Works of Alexandre Dumas). audio compact disk 19.98 (*962-634-089-4*, NA308912); audio 17.98 (*962-634-589-6*, NA308914) Naxos of America, Inc. (Naxos AudioBooks).

—The Three Musketeers. abr. ed. 1993. (Ultimate Classics Ser.). audio 19.95 o.p. (*1-55800-788-1*, 692322) NewStar Media, Inc.

—The Three Musketeers. 2001. pap., tchr. ed., wbk. ed. (*1-58130-700-4*); pap., stu. ed. (*1-58130-701-2*) Novel Units, Inc.

—The Three Musketeers. Coward, David, ed. & intro. by. 1999. (Oxford World's Classics Ser.). 704p. pap. 8.95 (*0-19-283575-0*) Oxford Univ. Pr., Inc.

—The Three Musketeers. 1987. (Classics for Young Readers Ser.). 400p. pap. 4.99 o.p. (*0-14-035054-3*, Puffin Bks.) Penguin Putnam Bks. for Young Readers.

—The Three Musketeers. (Paperback Classics Ser.). 2001. 640p. pap. 9.95 (*0-375-75674-4*); 1999. E-Book 4.95 (*0-679-64140-8*) Random House Adult Trade Publishing Group. (Modern Library).

—The Three Musketeers. 1998. (Gateway Movie Classics Ser.). 416p. pap. 14.95 o.p. (*0-89526-349-1*, Gateway Editions) Regnery Publishing, Inc., An Eagle Publishing Co.

—The Three Musketeers. 1999. (Signature Classics Ser.). (Illus.). 776p. 24.95 (*1-58279-035-3*); 29.95 (*1-58279-047-7*) Trident Pr. International.

—The Three Musketeers. 1984. (Bantam Classics Ser.). 12.00 (*0-606-02468-9*) Turtleback Bks.

—The Three Musketeers. Sudley, Lord, tr. from FRE. 1982. (Penguin Classics Ser.). 720p. 11.00 (*0-14-044025-9*, Penguin Classics) Viking Penguin.

—The Three Musketeers. abr. ed. 1996. (Classic Ser.). audio 10.95 o.s.i (*0-14-086348-6*, Penguin Audio-Books) Viking Penguin.

—The Three Musketeers. 1997. (Classics Ser.). 576p. pap. 3.95 (*1-85326-040-1*, j0401WW) Wordsworth Editions, Ltd. GBR. *Dist:* Combined Publishing.

—Les Trois Mousquetaires. unabr. ed. 1999. (World Classics Ser.). (FRE.). pap. 7.95 (*2-87714-198-5*) Bookking International FRA. *Dist:* Distribooks, Inc.

—Les Trois Mousquetaires. 1962. (FRE.). 1800p. 95.00 (*0-7859-1098-0*, 2070101800); 1962. (FRE.). 115.00 (*0-8288-3443-1*, F60650); 1935. pap. 11.90 o.p.; Tome I. 1973. (FRE.). 448p. pap. 11.95 (*0-7859-1771-3*, 2070365263); Tome II. 1973. (FRE.). 448p. pap. 11.95 (*0-7859-1772-1*, 2070365271) French & European Pubns., Inc.

—Les Trois Mousquetaires. 2001. (FRE., Illus.). 168p. (C). pap. 11.25 (*0-8442-1229-6*, VF1229-6) McGraw-Hill/Contemporary.

—Les Trois Mousquetaires. (FRE.). pap. 12.95 (*2-266-08579-4*) Presses Pocket FRA. *Dist:* Distribooks, Inc.

—Les Trois Mousquetaires. deluxe ed. (Pleiade Ser.). (FRE.). 82.95 (*2-07-010180-0*) Schoenhof's Foreign Bks., Inc.

—Twenty Years After. 1999. pap. 4.99 o.p. (*1-57840-192-5*) Acclaim Bks.

—Twenty Years After. 1976. 28.95 (*0-8488-1296-4*) Amereon, Ltd.

—Twenty Years After. 1979. reprint ed. 14.95 o.p. (*0-460-00175-2*) Biblio Distribution.

—Twenty Years After. unabr. ed. 1999. Pt. 1. audio 76.95 (*0-7861-1308-1*, 2218-A); Pt. 2. audio 62.95 Blackstone Audio Bks., Inc.

—Twenty Years After. 1981. 467p. reprint ed. lib. bdg. 31.95 (*0-89968-229-4*, Lightyear Pr.) Buccaneer Bks., Inc.

—Twenty Years After. 2001. 508p. per. 29.95 (*1-58963-225-7*) International Law & Taxation Pubs.

—Twenty Years After. E-Book 1.95 (*1-58515-019-3*); E-Book 1.95 (*1-58515-021-5*) MesaView, Inc.

—Twenty Years After. (Oxford World's Classics Ser.). 1998. (Illus.). 880p. pap. 15.95 (*0-19-283843-1*); 1993. 872p. (C). pap. 13.95 o.p. (*0-19-283074-0*) Oxford Univ. Pr., Inc.

—Le Vicomte de Bragelonne. Coward, David, ed. & intro. by. (Oxford World's Classics Ser.). 768p. 1998. pap. 15.95 (*0-19-283463-0*); 1995. pap. 14.95 o.p. (*0-19-282390-6*) Oxford Univ. Pr., Inc.

—Vingt Ans Apres. Samaran, Charles, ed. 1989. (Class. Garnier Ser.). pap. 20.95 (*0-7859-3150-3*, 2253050520) French & European Pubns., Inc.

—Vingt Ans Apres, 2 tomes. 1935. pap. 11.90 o.p.; Tome I. 1975. (FRE.). 544p. pap. 11.95 (*0-7859-1803-5*, 2070366820); Tome II. 1975. (FRE.). 544p. pap. 12.95 (*0-7859-1804-3*, 2070366839) French & European Pubns., Inc.

—Vingt Ans Apres. (FRE.). pap. 23.95 (*2-07-040478-1*) Gallimard, Editions FRA. *Dist:* Distribooks, Inc.

—Vingt Ans Apres, 2 vols. 1975. (Folio Ser.: Nos. 682 & 683). 1. pap. 7.95 o.p. (*2-07-036682-0*); 2. pap. 9.95 o.p. (*2-07-036683-9*) Schoenhof's Foreign Bks., Inc.

Dumas, Alexandre & Page, Michael. The Man in the Iron Mask. unabr. ed. 1999. (Bookcassette Classic Collection). audio 22.95 (*1-56740-454-5*, 1816, Bookcassette) Brilliance Audio.

Dumas, Alexandre & Rizvi, S. N. The Three Musketeers. 1997. 156p. pap. 20.00 (*81-209-0218-1*) Pitambar Publishing IND. *Dist:* State Mutual Bk. & Periodical Service, Ltd.

Dunn, Samantha. Failing Paris. 2000. 169p. pap. 12.95 (*1-902881-17-6*); 1999. 146p. 19.95 (*1-902881-01-X*) Toby Pr.

Dunnett, Dorothy. Checkmate. 1976. 34.95 (*0-8488-1292-1*) Amereon, Ltd.

—Checkmate. 1983. 425p. lib. bdg. 39.95 (*0-89966-319-2*) Buccaneer Bks., Inc.

—Checkmate. 1997. (Legendary Lymond Chronicles: Vol. 6). (Illus.). 608p. pap. 15.95 (*0-679-77748-2*, Vintage) Knopf Publishing Group.

—Checkmate. 1984. 736p. mass mkt. 4.95 o.s.i (*0-446-31301-7*) Warner Bks., Inc.

—Queen's Play. 1976. 21.95 (*0-8488-1301-4*) Amereon, Ltd.

—Queen's Play. 1983. 425p. reprint ed. lib. bdg. 39.95 (*0-89966-320-6*) Buccaneer Bks., Inc.

—Queen's Play. 1997. (Legendary Lymond Chronicles: Vol. 2). 448p. pap. 15.00 (*0-679-77744-X*, Vintage) Knopf Publishing Group.

—Queen's Play. 1984. 512p. mass mkt. 3.95 o.s.i (*0-446-31288-6*) Warner Bks., Inc.

Durand, Loup. Daddy. l.t. ed. 1990. (Large Print Books General Ser.). 571p. lib. bdg. 21.95 (*0-8161-4862-7*, Macmillan Reference USA) Gale Group.

—Daddy. 1990. 4.99 o.p. (*0-517-05619-4*) Random Hse. Value Publishing.

—Daddy. 1988. pap. o.s.i (*0-679-72124-X*) Random Hse., Inc.

—Daddy. 1990. mass mkt. 5.95 o.s.i (*0-446-35917-3*) Warner Bks., Inc.

Duras, Marguerite. Summer Rain. Bray, Barbara, tr. from FRE. 1992. 128p. 18.00 o.s.i (*0-684-19403-1*, Scribner) Simon & Schuster.

Durfort, Claire de. Ourika. Fowles, John, tr. ltd. ed. 1977. 110.00 o.p. (*0-935072-01-2*) Taylor, W. Thomas Inc.

Dyer, Geoff. Paris Trance: A Romance. 272p. 2000. pap. 13.00 (*0-86547-600-4*, North Point Pr.); 1999. 23.00 o.p. (*0-374-22981-3*) Farrar, Straus & Giroux.

—Paris Trance: A Romance. 1998. 274p. o.s.i (*0-349-11020-4*) Little Brown & Co.

Eberhart, Mignon G. The White Cockatoo. 1976. reprint ed. lib. bdg. 24.95 (*0-88411-766-9*) Amereon, Ltd.

Echnoz, Jean. I'm Gone: A Novel. Polizzotti, Mark, tr. from FRE. 2001. 208p. 22.95 (*1-56584-628-1*) New Pr., The.

Edgeworth, Maria. Ormond. 1972. reprint ed. 13.00 o.p. (*0-7165-1799-X*) Biblio Distribution.

—Ormond. 2001. (Tales & Novels Ser.). reprint ed. pap. text 28.00 (*0-7426-8398-2*) Classic Bks.

—Ormond. 2001. (Penguin Classics Ser.). 352p. 12.00 (*0-14-043644-8*) Viking Penguin.

Edwards, Amelia B. Hand & Glove: A Novel. 2000. 294p. pap. 15.95 (*0-948695-63-3*) Rubicon Pr., The GBR. *Dist:* Brown, David Bk. Co.

Eisner, William. The Sevigne Letters. Putnam, Jeff, ed. 1994. 201p. 18.00 (*1-880909-27-8*) Baskerville Pubs., Inc.

Elkins, Aaron. Old Bones: A Gideon Oliver Mystery. l.t. ed. 1991. pap. 8.95 o.p. (*1-55504-804-8*, 533) BBC Audiobooks America.

—Old Bones: A Gideon Oliver Mystery. 1987. 208p. 15.45 o.p. (*0-89296-262-3*) Mysterious Pr.

—Old Bones: A Gideon Oliver Mystery. 1988. 256p. mass mkt. 6.50 o.s.i (*0-445-40687-9*) Warner Bks., Inc.

—Skeleton Dance. (Gideon Oliver Mystery Ser.). 2001. 352p. mass mkt. 6.99 (*0-380-73163-0*, Avon Bks.); 2000. 256p. 23.00 (*0-688-15928-1*, Morrow, William & Co.) Morrow/Avon.

—Skeleton Dance: A Novel. l.t. ed. 2000. (G. K. Hall Core Ser.). 343p. 30.95 (*0-7838-9190-3*, Macmillan Reference USA) Gale Group.

—Turncoat: A Novel of Suspense. 2002. 304p. 24.95 (*0-06-019770-6*, Morrow, William & Co.) Morrow/ Avon.

Ellis, Bret Easton. Glamorama. 2000. (Vintage Contemporaries Ser.). 560p. pap. 14.95 (*0-375-70384-5*, Vintage) Knopf Publishing Group.

—Glamorama. abr. ed. 2001. audio (*0-333-78165-1*) Macmillan U.K. GBR. *Dist:* Macmillan Publishing Co., Inc.

Endore, Guy. The Werewolf of Paris. 1993. reprint ed. lib. bdg. 18.95 (*0-89968-425-4*, Lightyear Pr.) Buccaneer Bks., Inc.

—The Werewolf of Paris. 1976. pap. 1.95 o.s.i (*0-671-80584-3*, Pocket) Simon & Schuster.

Engel, Howard. Murder in Montparnasse. 304p. 2000. 14.95 (*1-58567-094-4*); 1999. 23.95 (*0-87951-701-8*) Overlook Pr., The.

Erckmann, E. & Chatrain, A. Waterloo. 2000. 252p. pap. 9.95 (*0-594-00456-X*); E-Book 3.95 (*0-594-02189-8*) 1873 Pr.

Erckmann, E. & Erckmann, Chatrian. The Conscript. E-Book 3.95 (*0-594-02187-1*) 1873 Pr.

Ernaux, Annie. Cleaned Out. Sanders, Carol, tr. from FRE. 1990. 127p. 19.95 o.p. (*0-916583-65-1*) Dalkey Archive Pr.

—A Man's Place. 1993. 112p. pap. 15.00 o.s.i (*0-345-37895-4*) Ballantine Bks.

—A Man's Place. 1992. 99p. 15.95 o.p. (*0-941423-75-1*) Four Walls Eight Windows.

—A Man's Place. Leslie, Tanya, tr. 1992. 99p. 15.95 (*1-888363-19-3*) Seven Stories Pr.

—Passion Simple. 1992. (Folio Ser.: No. 2545). Tr. of Simple Passions. (FRE.). 77p. pap. 12.95 (*2-07-038840-9*) Schoenhof's Foreign Bks., Inc.

—Simple Passion. 1994. 80p. reprint ed. pap. 8.50 o.s.i (*0-345-38254-4*) Ballantine Bks.

—Simple Passion. 1993. 80p. 15.00 o.p. (*1-56858-003-7*) Four Walls Eight Windows.

—Simple Passion. Leslie, Tanya, tr. from FRE. 1993. 72p. 14.95 (*1-888363-26-6*) Seven Stories Pr.

—A Simple Passion. Leslie, Tanya, tr. from FRE. 2003. 72p. reprint ed. pap. 8.95 (*1-58322-574-9*) Seven Stories Pr.

Espinosa, Maria. Longing. 1995. 298p. pap. 9.95 (*1-55885-145-3*) Arte Publico Pr.

Falconer, Elizabeth. Golden Year. 2000. 351p. pap. 12.95 (*0-552-99622-X*) Transworld Publishers Ltd. GBR. *Dist:* Trafalgar Square.

Faulks, Sebastian. Charlotte Gray. unabr. ed. 1999. audio 110.95 (*0-7540-0395-7*, CAB1818) BBC Audiobooks America.

—Charlotte Gray. 2001. 14p. audio compact disk 115.95 (*0-7540-5438-1*, CCD 129) Chivers Audio Bks. GBR. *Dist:* BBC Audiobooks America.

—Charlotte Gray. abr. ed. 1999. audio 25.95 (*0-375-40598-4*, RH Audio) Random Hse. Audio Publishing Group.

—Charlotte Gray. l.t. ed. 1999. (Charnwood Large Print Ser.). 592p. 31.99 (*0-7089-9078-9*, Linford) Thorpe, F. A. Pubs. GBR. *Dist:* Ulverscroft Large Print Bks., Ltd., Ulverscroft Large Print Canada, Ltd.

—The Girl at the Lion d'Or. l.t. ed. 2000. (General Ser.). 365p. pap. 23.95 (*0-7862-2645-5*) Thorndike Pr.

—The Girl at the Lion d'Or. l.t. ed. 1991. (Ulverscroft Large Print Ser.). 29.99 o.p. (*0-7089-2443-3*, Ulverscroft) Thorpe, F. A. Pubs. GBR. *Dist:* Ulverscroft Large Print Bks., Ltd., Ulverscroft Large Print Canada, Ltd.

Fell, Doris Elaine. Always in September. 1993. (Seasons of Intrigue Ser.: Vol. 1). 288p. pap. 9.99 o.p. (*0-89107-760-X*) Crossway Bks.

—The Race for Autumn's Glory. 1997. (Seasons of Intrigue Ser.: Vol. 6). 272p. pap. 9.99 o.p. (*0-89107-926-2*) Crossway Bks.

—The Race for Autumn's Glory. l.t. ed. 1999. (Christian Mystery Ser.). 615p. 24.95 (*0-7862-1954-8*) Thorndike Pr.

Ferguson, Jo Ann. Daughter's Destiny. 2000. (Shadow of the Bastille Ser.). 320p. mass mkt. 5.50 o.s.i (*0-8217-6664-3*) Kensington Publishing Corp.

—Shadow of the Bastille: A Brother's Honor. 2000. (Shadow of the Bastille Ser.). 32p. mass mkt. 5.50 o.s.i (*0-8217-6729-1*, Zebra Bks.) Kensington Publishing Corp.

—Shadow of the Bastille: A Sister's Quest. 2000. (Shadow of the Bastille Ser.). 32p. mass mkt. 5.50 o.s.i (*0-8217-6788-7*) Kensington Publishing Corp.

Fermine, Maxence. L' Apiculteur. l.t. ed. 2001. (French Ser.). pap. 30.99 (*2-84011-414-3*) Feryane, SA, Editions FRA. *Dist:* Ulverscroft Large Print Bks., Ltd., Ulverscroft Large Print Canada, Ltd.

Fiechter, J. J. A Masterpiece of Revenge: A Novel. 1998. 192p. 21.95 (*1-55970-430-6*) Arcade Publishing, Inc.

Fischer, Tibor. The Thought Gang. 1995. 320p. text 18.95 (*1-56584-286-3*) New Pr., The.

—The Thought Gang. 1994. 18.00 (*0-7486-6160-3*) Polygon GBR. *Dist:* Subterranean Co.

—The Thought Gang. 1997. 320p. pap. 13.00 (*0-684-83079-5*, Touchstone) Simon & Schuster.

Fisher, Alan. The Rage of Angels. 1997. 224p. 21.00 o.p. (*0-7867-0409-8*, Carroll & Graf Pubs.) Avalon Publishing Group.

Fisher, M. F. K. The Boss Dog: A Story of Provence. 2001. 118p. pap. 14.00 o.p. (*0-86547-630-6*); 1991. 128p. reprint ed. 16.95 o.p. (*0-86547-465-6*) Farrar, Straus & Giroux. (North Point Pr.).

Fitzgerald, F. Scott. Tender Is the Night. (Longman Literature Ser.). 1993. pap. text 7.00 (*0-582-09716-9*); 1992. pap. text 9.95 (*0-582-78275-9*) Addison-Wesley Longman, Ltd. GBR. *Dist:* Trans-Atlantic Pubns., Inc.

—Tender Is the Night. 25.95 (*0-89190-600-2*) Amereon, Ltd.

—Tender Is the Night, Set. unabr. ed. 2000. audio 69.95 (*1-56054-969-6*, SAB 009) Chivers Audio Bks. GBR. *Dist:* BBC Audiobooks America.

—Tender Is the Night. 1991. (F. Scott Fitzgerald Manuscripts: Vol. 4B). 3214p. text 236.00 (*0-8240-5960-3*) Garland Publishing, Inc.

—Tender Is the Night, Pt. I, Vols. 1-2. Bruccoli, Matthew J., ed. 1990. (F. Scott Fitzgerald Manuscripts: Vol. 4A). 654p. text 54.00 (*0-8240-5958-1*) Garland Publishing, Inc.

—Tender Is the Night, unabr. ed. 1997. audio 78.00 (*0-7887-0727-2*, 94904E7) Recorded Bks., LLC.

—Tender Is the Night. (Scribner Classics). 1996. 320p. 25.00 (*0-684-83050-7*, Scribner); 1995. (Illus.). 320p. pap. 12.00 (*0-684-80154-X*, Scribner); 1985. pap. 4.95 o.s.i (*0-684-18611-X*, Scribner Paper Fiction); 1982. 320p. pap. 5.95 o.s.i (*0-684-17817-6*, Scribner Paper Fiction); 1977. 315p. 40.00 (*0-684-15151-0*, Scribner); 1960. 320p. pap. 12.00 o.s.i (*0-684-71763-8*, SL2, Scribner Paper Fiction) Simon & Schuster.

—Tender Is the Night. l.t. ed. 1994. 470p. lib. bdg. 23.95 (*0-8161-5960-2*) Thorndike Pr.

—Tender Is the Night. 1995. 17.05 (*0-606-01446-2*) Turtleback Bks.

—Tender Is the Night. 1999. 16.95 (*0-14-086167-X*, Penguin Classics) Viking Penguin.

Flaubert, Gustave. Madame Bovary. 2000. 252p. E-Book 9.95 (*0-594-03963-0*) 1873 Pr.

—Madame Bovary. 1965. (Airmont Classics Ser.). (YA). (gr. 11 up). mass mkt. 2.50 o.p. (*0-8049-0089-2*, CL-89) Airmont Publishing Co., Inc.

—Madame Bovary. unabr. ed. 1988. (Classic Books on Cassettes Ser.). audio 53.95 (*1-55685-099-9*) Audio Bk. Contractors, Inc.

—Madame Bovary. unabr. ed. 1997. (Illus.). audio 39.95 (*1-57270-056-4*, F91056u, Cover to Cover Classics) Audio Partners Publishing Corp.

—Madame Bovary. unabr. ed. audio 94.95 o.p. (*1-85549-946-0*, CTC 120) BBC Audiobooks America.

—Madame Bovary. Bair, Lowell, tr. 1982. (Bantam Classics Ser.). 448p. mass mkt. 5.95 (*0-553-21341-5*); (gr. 9-12). mass mkt. 2.50 o.s.i (*0-553-21101-3*) Bantam Bks. (Bantam Classics).

—Madame Bovary. 1985. (Barron's Book Notes Ser.). (Illus.). 122p. (YA). (gr. 10-12). pap. 3.95 (*0-8120-3524-0*) Barron's Educational Series, Inc.

—Madame Bovary. unabr. ed. 1983. audio 62.95 (*0-7861-0569-0*, 2059) Blackstone Audio Bks., Inc.

—Madame Bovary. unabr. ed. (FRE.). pap. 7.95 (*2-87714-130-6*) Bookking International FRA. *Dist:* Distribooks, Inc.

—Madame Bovary. 1983. (Illus.). 320p. reprint ed. lib. bdg. 27.95 (*0-89966-324-9*) Buccaneer Bks., Inc.

—Madame Bovary. (Early Best Sellers Ser.). reprint ed. lib. bdg. 48.00 (*0-7426-1025-X*); 2001. (Illus.). pap. text 28.00 (*0-7426-6025-7*) Classic Bks.

—Madame Bovary. Marmur, Mildred, tr. 1997. (New York Public Library Collector's Edition Ser.). (Illus.). 384p. 18.50 (*0-385-48719-3*) Doubleday Publishing.

—Madame Bovary. unabr. ed. 1996. (Thrift Editions Ser.). 256p. reprint ed. pap. 2.50 (*0-486-29257-6*) Dover Pubns., Inc.

—Madame Bovary. Aveling, Eleanor Marx, tr. 2004. (Barnes & Noble Classics Ser.). 400p. pap. 5.95 (*1-59308-052-2*) Fine Communications.

—Madame Bovary. (FRE.). 11.25 (*2-08-070464-8*, GF0086E) Flammarion et Cie FRA. *Dist:* Continental Bk. Co., Inc.

—Madame Bovary. Gothot-Mesch, ed. 1961. (FRE.). pap. 11.95 (*0-8288-9748-4*, 2266033581) French & European Pubns., Inc.

—Madame Bovary. Steegmuller, Francis, tr. l.t. ed. 1993. 499p. lib. bdg. 20.95 o.p. (*0-8161-5680-8*, Macmillan Reference USA) Gale Group.

—Madame Bovary. l.t. ed. 1999. (SPA.). 512p. 32.50 (*84-397-0569-7*) Grijalbo Mondadori, S.A.-Junior ESP. *Dist:* Continental Bk. Co., Inc.

—Madame Bovary. l.t. ed. 2000. 544p. pap. 22.00 (*0-06-095695-X*, HarperCollins) HarperTrade.

—Madame Bovary, 001. Bree, Germaine, ed. Lawrence, Merloyd, tr. 1969. (C). pap. 15.16 o.p. (*0-395-05210-6*, Riverside Editions) Houghton Mifflin Co.

—Madame Bovary. 2002. 336p. 26.99 (*1-4043-1578-0*); per. 21.99 (*1-4043-1579-9*) IndyPublish.com.

—Madame Bovary. 1989. audio 59.00 Jimcin Recordings.

—Madame Bovary. Steegmuller, Francis, tr. 1991. (Vintage Bks.). (Illus.). 432p. pap. 12.00 (*0-679-73636-0*, Vintage) Knopf Publishing Group.

—Madame Bovary. Steegmuller, Francis, tr. 1993. (Everyman's Library). (Illus.). 368p. 17.00 (*0-679-42031-2*) Knopf, Alfred A. Inc.

—Madame Bovary. 2000. 7.95 (*3-89508-252-X*, 520219) Konemann.

—Madame Bovary. Hardy, Thomas, ed. 1999. (Cloth Bound Pocket Ser.). (Illus.). 7.95 (*3-8290-3006-1*) Konemann.

—Madame Bovary. (FRE.). pap. 8.95 (*2-253-00486-3*, LP0088E) Librairie Generale Francaise, LGF FRA. *Dist:* Continental Bk. Co., Inc.

—Madame Bovary. 1982. 396p. (C). pap. 11.25 (*0-07-554378-8*, McGraw-Hill Humanities, Social Sciences & World Languages) McGraw-Hill Higher Education.

—Madame Bovary. 1972. (FRE.). (C). pap. 13.95 (*0-8442-1758-1*, VF1758-1) McGraw-Hill/ Contemporary.

—Madame Bovary. Marmur, Mildred, tr. from FRE. 2001. 408p. mass mkt. 5.95 (*0-451-52820-4*, Signet Classics) NAL.

—Madame Bovary. 1970. mass mkt. 0.50 o.p. (*0-451-50234-5*, Signet Classics); 1970. mass mkt. 0.60 o.p. (*0-451-50511-5*, Signet Classics); 1964. mass mkt. 0.95 o.p. (*0-451-50692-8*, Signet Classics); 1964. mass mkt. 0.75 o.p. (*0-451-50592-1*, Signet Classics); 1964. mass mkt. 2.75 o.p. (*0-451-52240-0*); 1964. mass mkt. 2.25 o.p. (*0-451-51365-7*, Signet Classics); 1964. mass mkt. 2.75 o.p. (*0-451-51487-4*, Signet Classics); 1964. mass mkt. 1.95 o.p. (*0-451-51681-8*, Signet Classics); 1964. mass mkt. 2.25 o.p. (*0-451-51805-5*, Signet Classics); 1964. mass mkt. 2.50 o.p. (*0-451-51914-0*, Signet Classics); 1964. mass mkt. 1.50 o.p. (*0-451-51008-9*, Signet Classics); 1964. mass mkt. 1.75 o.p. (*0-451-51214-6*, Signet Classics) NAL.

—Madame Bovary. Marmur, Mildred, tr. 1964. (Illus.). 400p. mass mkt. 5.95 o.s.i (*0-451-52387-3*, Signet Classics) NAL.

—Madame Bovary. abr. ed. 1999. (Classic Fiction Ser.). audio 22.98 (*962-634-678-7*, NA216814); audio compact disk 26.98 (*962-634-178-5*, NA417814) Naxos of America, Inc. (Naxos Audio-Books).

—Madame Bovary. abr. ed. 1994. (Classic, Ultimate, Dove Ser.). audio 19.95 o.p. (*1-55800-946-9*, 693105, Dove Audio) NewStar Media, Inc.

—Madame Bovary. l.t. ed. 2001. 519p. 26.00 (*1-58287-634-7*) North Bks.

—Madame Bovary. (C). pap. 15.75 (*0-393-94860-9*); 1965. (Illus.). xvi, 462p. pap. text 10.50 (*0-393-09608-4*, 9608) Norton, W. W. & Co., Inc.

—Madame Bovary. De Man, Paul, ed. & tr. by. 2nd ed. 2004. pap. (*0-393-97917-2*) Norton, W. W. & Co., Inc.

—Madame Bovary. audio 89.95 o.p. 1991. audio 59.95Pts. 1 & 2. audio 34.95Pts. 1 & 2. audio 34.95 Olivia & Hill Pr., The.

—Madame Bovary. Mauldon, Margaret, tr. 2004. (Oxford World's Classics Hardcovers Ser.). 384p. 26.00 (*0-19-280549-5*) Oxford Univ. Pr., Inc.

—Madame Bovary. 1999. (Oxford World's Classics Ser.). 400p. 15.00 (*0-19-210025-4*) Oxford Univ. Pr., Inc.

—Madame Bovary. Cave, Terence, ed. 1989. (Oxford World's Classics Ser.). 390p. pap. 6.95 o.p. (*0-19-281564-4*) Oxford Univ. Pr., Inc.

—Madame Bovary. abr. ed. 1992. (Classics on Cassette). audio 15.95 (*0-453-00784-8*) Penguin/ HighBridge.

—Madame Bovary. (FRE.). pap. 11.95 (*2-266-08314-7*) Presses Pocket FRA. *Dist:* Distribooks, Inc.

—Madame Bovary. Steegmuller, Francis, tr. 1992. 476p. 16.95 o.s.i (*0-679-60013-2*) Random Hse., Inc.

—Madame Bovary. Steegmuller, Francis, tr. & intro. by. 1952. 396p. 3.95 o.s.i (*0-394-60028-2*, T17) Random Hse., Inc.

—Madame Bovary, unabr. ed. 1989. audio 78.00 (*1-55690-328-6*, 89393E7) Recorded Bks., LLC.

—Madame Bovary. Brombert, Victor, ed. 1985. (ENG & FRE.). 440p. 6.95 (*0-88332-467-9*) Schoenhof's Foreign Bks., Inc.

—Madame Bovary. 1976. (Folio Ser.: No. 804). (FRE.). pap. 10.95 (*2-07-036804-1*) Schoenhof's Foreign Bks., Inc.

—Madame Bovary. audio Spoken Arts, Inc.

—Madame Bovary. 2003. 28.95 (*0-7862-5602-8*) Thorndike Pr.

—Madame Bovary. 1964. 12.00 (*0-606-00911-6*) Turtleback Bks.

—Madame Bovary. 2002. 384p. pap. 10.00 (*0-14-044912-4*, Penguin Classics) Viking Penguin.

—Madame Bovary. Wall, Geoffrey, tr. & intro. by. 1993. (Penguin Classics Ser.). (Illus.). 320p. pap. 10.00 o.s.i (*0-14-044526-9*, Penguin Classics) Viking Penguin.

—Madame Bovary. Russell, Alan, tr. 1951. (Penguin Classics Ser.). 368p. pap. 3.95 o.p. (*0-14-044015-1*, Penguin Classics) Viking Penguin.

—Madame Bovary. 1998. (Classics Library). (Illus.). 288p. pap. 3.95 (*1-85326-078-9*, 0789WW) Wordsworth Editions, Ltd. GBR. *Dist:* Casemate Pubs. & Bk. Distributors, LLC.

—Madame Bovary. 2000. (SPA.). 420p. pap. 18.95 (*1-58348-813-8*) iUniverse, Inc.

—Madame Bovary Level 4. (FRE.). 7.25 (*2-09-031993-3*, CL9933E) Cle International FRA. *Dist:* Continental Bk. Co., Inc.

—Madame Bovary Level 4. 1998. (Oxford World's Classics Ser.). 400p. pap. 8.95 (*0-19-283399-5*) Oxford Univ. Pr., Inc.

Flaubert, Gustave, et al. Madame Bovary. 1998. E-Book 8.35 (*0-585-36395-1*) netLibrary, Inc.

Fletcher, Jessica. Murder She Wrote: Provence to Die For. 2002. 272p. mass mkt. 6.50 (*0-451-20566-9*, Signet Bks.) NAL.

Flokos, Nicholas. Nike: A Romance. 2000. (Illus.). 192p. pap. 10.00 (*0-618-00207-3*); 1998. 179p. tchr. ed. 20.00 o.s.i (*0-395-88396-2*) Houghton Mifflin Co.

Florde, Katie. Dot to Dot. 2002. 320p. 24.95 (*0-312-27571-4*) St. Martin's Pr.

Follett, Ken. Jackdaws. 2001. 464p. 26.95 o.s.i (*0-525-94628-4*, Dutton) Dutton/Plume.

—Jackdaws. 2002. 496p. pap. 7.99 (*0-451-20559-6*); 512p. reprint ed. mass mkt. 7.99 (*0-451-20752-1*, Signet Bks.) NAL.

—Jackdaws. 2003. E-Book 7.99 (*0-7865-3809-0*) Penguin Putnam, Inc E-Books.

—Jackdaws. l.t. ed. 2001. 688p. 26.95 (*0-375-43159-4*) Random Hse. Large Print.

—Jackdaws. abr. ed. 2001. 4p. audio 24.95 o.s.i (*0-14-280001-5*); 5p. audio compact disk 29.95 (*0-14-280002-3*); 8p. audio 44.95 o.s.i (*0-14-280003-1*) Viking Penguin. (Penguin AudioBooks).

Ford, Ford Madox. Parade's End. 2001. 864p. pap. 19.00 (*0-14-118661-5*, Penguin Classics) Viking Penguin.

Forsyth, Frederick. The Day of the Jackal. l.t. ed. 1992. pap. 17.95 o.p. (*0-7927-1004-5*); 20.95 o.p. (*0-7927-1003-7*, E0024) BBC Audiobooks America.

—The Day of the Jackal. 1999. mass mkt. (*0-553-14765-X*); 1999. mass mkt. (*0-553-23535-4*); 1992. 384p. mass mkt. 3.99 o.s.i (*0-553-19980-3*); 1985. mass mkt. o.s.i (*0-552-09121-9*, Corgi); 1982. 384p. mass mkt. 7.99 (*0-553-26630-6*) Bantam Bks.

—The Day of the Jackal. 1994. reprint ed. lib. bdg. 32.95 (*1-56849-279-0*) Buccaneer Bks., Inc.

—The Day of the Jackal. 2002. (Best Mysteries of All Time Ser.). 400p. (*0-7621-8866-9*, IM Pr.) Reader's Digest Assn., Inc., The.

—The Day of the Jackal. l.t. ed. 2000. (Famous Authors Ser.). 653p. 28.95 (*0-7862-2634-X*) Thorndike Pr.

—The Day of the Jackal. abr. l.t. ed. 1976. (Ulverscroft Large Print Ser.). 12.50 o.p. (*0-85456-565-5*, Ulverscroft) Thorpe, F. A. Pubs. GBR. *Dist:* Ulverscroft Large Print Bks., Ltd., Ulverscroft Large Print Canada, Ltd.

Four on Maigret. unabr. ed. Incl. Drowned Men's Inn. audio o.s.i Maigret's Mistake. audio o.s.i Maigret's Pipe. audio o.s.i Mr. Monday. audio o.s.i 1985. 1985. Set audio 16.95 o.s.i (*1-55656-002-8*) Dercum Audio.

Frame, Ronald. Permanent Violet. 2002. 160p. pap. 12.95 (*0-7486-6321-5*) Polygon GBR. *Dist:* Interlink Publishing Group, Inc.

France, Anatole. Clio. Stephens, Winifred, tr. 1977. (Short Story Index Reprint Ser.). 19.95 (*0-8369-3537-3*) Ayer Co. Pubs., Inc.

—The Crime of Sylvestre Bonnard. l.t. ed. 2000. 245p. 29.95 (*1-56000-449-5*) Transaction Pubs.

—The Crime of Sylvestre Bonnard. 2002. 236p. pap. 19.95 (*1-58715-683-0*); lib. bdg. 29.95 (*1-58715-682-2*) Wildside Pr.

—The Merrie Tales of Jacques Tournebroche & Child life in town & country. Allinson, Alfred, tr. 1977. (Short Story Index Reprint Ser.). reprint ed. 19.95 (*0-8369-3504-7*) Ayer Co. Pubs., Inc.

—Mother of Pearl. Chapman, Frederic, tr. 1977. (Short Story Index Reprint Ser.). 22.95 (*0-8369-3746-5*) Ayer Co. Pubs., Inc.

—Tales from a Mother-of-Pearl Casket. Pene Du Bois, Henri, tr. from FRE. 1977. (Short Story Index Reprint Ser.). reprint ed. 18.95 (*0-8369-4101-2*) Ayer Co. Pubs., Inc.

Freeling, Nicolas. A City Solitary. 2001. 236p. pap. 9.95 (*1-84232-860-3*) House of Stratus, Inc. GBR. *Dist:* Midpoint Trade Bks., Inc.

—A City Solitary. 1986. 35.00 o.p. (*0-14-778032-2*) Penguin Group (USA) Inc.

—A City Solitary. 1986. 208p. pap. 3.50 o.p. (*0-14-009402-4*, Penguin Bks.); 1985. 224p. 14.95 o.p. (*0-670-80607-2*) Viking Penguin.

—City Solitary. l.t. ed. 1986. pap. 13.95 o.p. (*1-55504-026-8*) BBC Audiobooks America.

French, Allen. The Red Keep: A Story of Burgundy in the Year 1165. 1997. (Adventure Library). (Illus.). 380p. (Orig.). (J). (gr. 5-12). pap. 14.95 (*1-883937-29-9*, 29-9) Bethlehem Bks.

Friedman, Mickey. Magic Mirror. l.t. ed. 1990. (General Ser.). 354p. lib. bdg. 18.95 o.p. (*0-8161-4823-6*, Macmillan Reference USA) Gale Group.

—Magic Mirror. 256p. 1989. pap. 3.95 o.p. (*0-14-010847-5*, Penguin Bks.); 1988. 16.95 o.p. (*0-670-82132-2*) Viking Penguin.

—A Temporary Ghost. l.t. ed. 1991. (General Ser.). 285p. lib. bdg. 18.95 o.p. (*0-8161-5012-5*, Macmillan Reference USA) Gale Group.

—A Temporary Ghost. (Georgia Lee Maxwell Mystery Ser.). 224p. 1990. pap. 4.50 o.p. (*0-14-010848-3*, Penguin Bks.); 1989. 16.95 o.p. (*0-670-82133-0*) Viking Penguin.

Fuller, Dean. A Death in Paris: An Alex Grismolet Mystery. 1992. 352p. 19.95 o.p. (*0-316-29603-1*) Little Brown & Co.

—Death of a Critic: An Alex Grismolet Mystery. 1996. 304p. 21.95 o.p. (*0-316-29601-5*) Little Brown & Co.

—Death of a Critic Vol. 1: An Alex Grismolet Mystery. 1996. 21.95 (*0-316-92601-9*) Little Brown & Co.

Fullerton, Alexander. Return to the Field. l.t. ed. 1998. 544 p. (*0-7540-2128-9*) BBC Audiobooks America.

—Return to the Field. 1997. (Illus.). 378p. o.s.i (*0-316-88293-3*) Little Brown & Co.

—Return to the Field. l.t. ed. 1998. (Paperback Ser.). 544p. (gr. 7). pap. 24.95 (*0-7838-0205-6*) Thorndike Pr.

—Single to Paris. l.t. ed. 2002. (Charnwood Large Print Ser.). 456p. 32.50 (*0-7089-9364-8*) Thorpe, F. A. Pubs. GBR. *Dist:* Ulverscroft Large Print Bks., Ltd., Ulverscroft Large Print Canada, Ltd.

Furst, Alan. Kingdom of Shadows: A Novel. E-Book 19.95 (*1-58945-591-6*) Adobe Systems, Inc.

—Kingdom of Shadows: A Novel. l.t. ed. 2001. (Illus.). 359p. 28.95 (*0-7838-9427-9*); (*0-7540-1587-4*); pap. (*0-7540-2448-2*) Gale Group. (Macmillan Reference USA).

—Kingdom of Shadows: A Novel. 2001. 272p. pap. 11.95 (*0-375-75826-7*) Random House Adult Trade Publishing Group.

—Red Gold. 2000. 283p. reprint ed. pap. 13.00 (*0-00-649903-1*) HarperCollins Pubs. Ltd. GBR. *Dist:* Trafalgar Square.

—Red Gold. l.t. ed. 2000. (Ulverscroft Large Print Ser.). 432p. 31.99 (*0-7089-4253-9*, Ulverscroft) Thorpe, F. A. Pubs. GBR. *Dist:* Ulverscroft Large Print Bks., Ltd., Ulverscroft Large Print Canada, Ltd.

—Red Gold: A Novel. 2002. 288p. pap. 11.95 (*0-375-75859-3*) Random House Adult Trade Publishing Group.

—Red Gold: A Novel. 1999. (Illus.). 288p. 23.95 o.s.i (*0-679-45186-2*) Random Hse., Inc.

—The World at Night. 2000. 320p. pap. 13.00 (*0-00-651097-3*) HarperCollins Pubs. Ltd. GBR. *Dist:* Trafalgar Square.

—The World at Night, abr. ed. 2000. audio compact disk 79.95 (*0-7531-0704-X*, 10704X); 1998. audio 69.95 (*0-7531-0383-4*, 980508) ISIS Audio Bks. GBR. *Dist:* Ulverscroft Large Print Bks., Ltd.

—The World at Night. l.t. ed. 1999. (Ulverscroft Large Print Ser.). 448p. 31.99 o.p. (*0-7089-4024-2*, Ulverscroft) Thorpe, F. A. Pubs. GBR. *Dist:* Ulverscroft Large Print Bks., Ltd., Ulverscroft Large Print Canada, Ltd.

—The World at Night: A Novel. 2002. (Illus.). 288p. pap. 11.95 (*0-375-75858-5*) Random House Adult Trade Publishing Group.

Gadol, Peter. Light at Dusk. 2000. 288p. 24.00 (*0-312-20336-5*) Picador.

Gallant, Mavis. Overhead in a Balloon: Twelve Short Stories of Paris. 1988. pap. 7.95 o.p. (*0-393-30546-5*) Norton, W. W. & Co., Inc.

Galloway, Janice. Foreign Parts. 1995. 262p. pap. 12.95 (*1-56478-082-1*) Dalkey Archive Pr.

—Foreign Parts. 1999. 21.95 o.p. (*0-87951-578-3*) Overlook Pr., The.

Gandy, Alain. Les Corneilles de Toulonjac. l.t. ed. 2001. (French Ser.). pap. 30.99 (*2-84011-391-0*) Feryane, SA, Editions FRA. *Dist:* Ulverscroft Large Print Bks., Ltd., Ulverscroft Large Print Canada, Ltd.

Garfield, Leon. The Prisoners of September. 1975. 280p. (J). 7.95 o.p. (*0-670-57843-6*) Viking Penguin.

Gellis, Roberta. The English Heiress. 1980. (Orig.). mass mkt. 2.50 o.s.i (*0-440-12141-8*) Dell Publishing.

Genet, Jean. Miracle of the Rose. Frechtman, Bernard, tr. from FRE. 1971. pap. 7.95 o.p. (*0-394-17470-4*, B322) Grove/Atlantic, Inc.

Gerritsen, Tess. In Their Footsteps. 1999. mass mkt. (*1-55166-532-8*, Mira Bks.); 1994. (Illus.). 251p. mass mkt. (*0-373-22278-5*, 1-22278-5, Harlequin Bks.) Harlequin Enterprises, Ltd.

—In Their Footsteps. l.t. ed. 2001. (Thorndike Famous Authors Ser.). 344p. 29.95 (*0-7862-3154-8*) Thorndike Pr.

Gille, Elisabeth. Shadows of a Childhood: A Novel of War & Friendship. Coverdale, Linda, tr. 1999. (Illus.). 144p. pap. text 12.95 (*1-56584-528-5*) New Pr., The.

Gille, Elisabeth. Shadows of a Childhood: A Novel of War & Friendship. Coverdale, Linda, tr. from FRE. 1998. 144p. text 23.00 (*1-56584-388-6*) New Pr., The.

Gillenwater, Sharon. Highland Call. 2003. (Alabaster Bks.). 352p. pap. 11.99 (*1-57673-275-4*) Multnomah Pubs., Inc.

Giono, Jean. To the Slaughterhouse. 1969. 28.00 (*0-7206-3602-7*) Dufour Editions, Inc.

Globe-Fearon Staff. A Tale of Two Cities. 1985. (Globe Ser.). pap. 6.95 o.p. (*0-671-55585-5*) Alpha Bks.

Goddard, Robert. A Debt of Dishonour. 1992. 432p. 21.00 (*0-671-70484-2*, Simon & Schuster) Simon & Schuster.

—Hand in Glove. 1994. mass mkt. o.s.i (*0-552-14165-8*, Corgi); 528p. mass mkt. 7.99 (*0-552-13839-8*) Bantam Bks.

—Hand in Glove. unabr. ed. 2000. audio 89.95 (*0-7451-4362-8*, CAB 1045) Chivers Audio Bks. GBR. *Dist:* BBC Audiobooks America.

—Hand in Glove. 1993. 432p. 22.00 o.p. (*0-671-75070-4*, Simon & Schuster) Simon & Schuster.

—Hand in Glove. Rosenman, Jane, ed. 1994. 432p. reprint ed. pap. (*0-671-89037-9*, Washington Square Pr.) Simon & Schuster.

—Hand in Glove. l.t. ed. 1994. (Charnwood Large Print Ser.). 720p. 29.99 o.p. (*0-7089-8773-7*, Ulverscroft) Thorpe, F. A. Pubs. GBR. *Dist:* Ulverscroft Large Print Bks., Ltd., Ulverscroft Large Print Canada, Ltd.

Godden, Rumer. Five for Sorrow, Ten for Joy. 1979. 10.95 o.p. (*0-670-31701-2*) Viking Penguin.

—The Greengage Summer. 1999. 272p. (*0-7540-3686-3*); 1993. audio 54.95 (*0-7451-5986-9*, CSL 065) BBC Audiobooks America.

—The Greengage Summer. 1981. 218p. pap. o.p. (*0-06-080561-7*, P 561) HarperCollins Pubs.

—The Greengage Summer. 208p. 1990. pap. 3.95 o.p. (*0-14-032622-7*); 1986. (YA). (gr. 7 up). pap. 3.95 o.p. (*0-14-031982-4*) Penguin Putnam Bks. for Young Readers. (Puffin Bks.).

—The Greengage Summer. l.t. ed. 1999. (Perennial Bestsellers Ser.). 272p. (J). (gr. 4-7). 25.95 (*0-7838-8496-6*) Thorndike Pr.

—The Greengage Summer. l.t. ed. 1986. 352p. 12.50 o.p. (*0-7089-1458-6*, Ulverscroft) Thorpe, F. A. Pubs. GBR. *Dist:* Ulverscroft Large Print Bks., Ltd.

—The Greengage Summer. 1958. 5.75 o.p. (*0-670-35441-4*) Viking Penguin.

Godden, Rumer, contrib. by. The Greengage Summer. 1999. 272p. (*0-7540-3685-5*) BBC Audiobooks America.

Godwin, William. St. Leon: A Tale of the Sixteenth Century. (Illus.). reprint ed. 45.00 (*0-404-54405-3*) AMS Pr., Inc.

—St. Leon: A Tale of the Sixteenth Century. 1976. (Gothic Novels Ser.). reprint ed. 51.95 (*0-405-00802-3*) Ayer Co. Pubs., Inc.

—St. Leon: A Tale of the Sixteenth Century, 4 vols. 1974. (Feminist Controversy in England, 1788-1810 Ser.). lib. bdg. 242.00 o.p. (*0-8240-0862-6*) Garland Publishing, Inc.

—St. Leon: A Tale of the Sixteenth Century. 1994. (World's Classics Ser.). 528p. (C). pap. 12.95 o.p. (*0-19-282833-9*) Oxford Univ. Pr., Inc.

Goldberg, Lucianne. Madame Cleo's Girls. Zion, Claire, ed. 1992. 416p. 21.00 (*0-671-69524-X*, Atria) Simon & Schuster.

Goldstein, Lisa. The Dream Years. 1986. mass mkt. 2.95 o.s.i (*0-553-25693-9*); 1985. 192p. 13.95 o.p. (*0-553-05090-7*, Spectra) Bantam Bks.

Golon, Anne & Golon, Serge. Angelique: The Marquise of the Angels. l.t. ed. 1995. 800p. 23.95 o.p. (*0-7838-1392-9*, Macmillan Reference USA) Gale Group.

—Angelique: The Road to Versailles. l.t. ed. 1997. (Romance-Hall Ser.). 512p. 24.95 o.p. (*0-7838-1393-7*, Macmillan Reference USA) Gale Group.

Gorrara, Claire. The Roman Noir in Post-War French Culture: Dark Fictions. 2003. (Oxford Studies in Modern European Culture). 144p. text 45.00 (*0-19-924609-2*) Oxford Univ. Pr., Inc.

Gracq, Julien. Chateau d'Argol. Varese, Louise, tr. 148p. pap. 14.00 (*1-901285-14-6*) Pushkin Pr., Ltd. GBR. *Dist:* Consortium Bk. Sales & Distribution.

—Chateau d'Argol. Varese, Louise, tr. from FRE. 2000. 160p. pap. 13.95 (*1-885586-06-X*) Turtle Point Pr.

Graffigny, Francoise De. Letters from a Peruvian Woman. Kornacker, David, tr. from FRE. 1993. (Texts & Translations Ser.: No. 2b). Orig. Title: Letters of a Peruvian Princess. xxviii, 174p. (Orig.). pap. 8.95 (*0-87352-778-X*, P002P) Modern Language Assn. of America.

Grant-Adamson, Lesley. Guilty Knowledge. 1988. 272p. 16.95 o.p. (*0-312-01438-4*, Saint Martin's Minotaur) St. Martin's Pr.

Gras, Felix. The Reds of the Midi: An Episode of the French Revolution. E-Book 3.95 (*0-594-02291-6*) 1873 Pr.

—The Terror. E-Book 3.95 (*0-594-02293-2*) 1873 Pr.

—The White Terror. 2000. 252p. E-Book 9.95 (*0-594-02295-9*) 1873 Pr.

Gray, Francine D. Lovers & Tyrants. 1977. (gr. 10 up). pap. 2.25 o.p. (*0-671-82446-5*, Pocket) Simon & Schuster.

Gray, Francine du Plessix. Lovers & Tyrants. 1982. 320p. 3.50 (*0-86721-126-1*) Berkley Publishing Group.

Grayson, Richard. Death au Gratin. 1995. 192p. 19.95 o.p. (*0-312-13047-3*, Saint Martin's Minotaur) St. Martin's Pr.

—Death off Stage. 1992. 192p. 16.95 o.p. (*0-312-06951-0*, Saint Martin's Minotaur) St. Martin's Pr.

—Death on the Cards. 2001. audio 54.95 (*1-85496-746-0*, 67460) Soundings, Ltd. GBR. *Dist:* Ulverscroft Large Print Bks., Ltd.

—Death on the Cards. 1988. 176p. 13.95 o.p. (*0-312-01758-8*, Saint Martin's Minotaur) St. Martin's Pr.

—Death on the Cards. l.t. ed. 1990. (Ulverscroft Large Print Ser.). 29.99 (*0-7089-2190-6*, Ulverscroft) Thorpe, F. A. Pubs. GBR. *Dist:* Ulverscroft Large Print Bks., Ltd., Ulverscroft Large Print Canada, Ltd.

Greene, Liz. The Dreamer of the Vine: A Novel About Nostradamus. 1981. 12.95 o.p. (*0-393-01434-7*) Norton, W. W. & Co., Inc.

Grenier, Roger. Piano Music for Four Hands. Kaplan, Alice, tr. from FRE. 2001. 153p. pap. 15.00 (*0-8032-7087-9*) Univ. of Nebraska Pr.

—Piano Music for Four Hands. Kaplan, Alice, tr. from FRE. & pref. by. 2001. 153p. text 45.00 (*0-8032-2181-9*) Univ. of Nebraska Pr.

Griffin, John Howard. Street of the Seven Angels. Bonazzi, Robert, ed. & intro. by. 2003. 172p. 22.95 (*0-930324-74-9*) Wings Pr.

Gross, Joel. Sarah. 1987. 384p. 18.95 o.p. (*0-688-06703-4*, Morrow, William & Co.) Morrow/Avon.

—Sarah. 1989. 3.99 o.p. (*0-517-69426-3*) Random Hse. Value Publishing.

Grunwald, Henry A. A Saint, More or Less: A Novel. 2003. 256p. 23.95 (*1-4000-6149-0*) Random Hse., Inc.

Guedj, Denis. The Measure of the World: A Novel. Goldhammer, Arthur, tr. from FRE. 2001. (Illus.). 312p. 27.00 (*0-226-31030-2*) Univ. of Chicago Pr.

—The Parrots Thereom: A Novel. 2002. 352p. pap. 14.95 (*0-312-30302-5*, Saint Martin's Griffin) St. Martin's Pr.

Guerard, Albert. Gabrielle. 1992. 224p. 20.00 o.p. (*1-55611-288-2*) Fine, Donald I. Bks.

Guerard, Albert J. Maquisard: A Christmas Tale. 1995. 192p. 17.95 o.p. (*0-89141-585-8*, Presidio Pr.) Ballantine Bks.

Guibert, Herve. The Compassion Protocol. Kirkup, James, tr. 1994. 200p. 20.00 (*0-8076-1352-5*) Braziller, George Inc.

—Protocole Compassionnel. 1991. (Folio Ser.: No. 2481). (FRE.). 226p. pap. 29.95 (*2-07-038731-3*) Schoenhof's Foreign Bks., Inc.

—To the Friend Who Did Not Save My Life. Coverdale, Linda, tr. from FRE. 1991. 272p. text 18.95 (*0-689-12120-2*) Central Bureau voor Schimmelcultures NLD. *Dist:* Lubrecht & Cramer, Ltd.

—To the Friend Who Did Not Save My Life. Coverdale, Linda, tr. from FRE. 1994. (High Risk Ser.). 240p. reprint ed. pap. (*1-85242-328-5*) Serpent's Tail Ltd.

Gulland, Sandra. The Josephine Bonaparte Collection: The Many Lives & Secret Sorrows of Josephine B - Tales of Passion, Tales of Woe, & the Last Great Dance on Earth. 2002. 1216p. pap. 35.00 (*0-7432-4621-7*, Touchstone) Simon & Schuster.

—The Last Great Dance on Earth. 2000. (Illus.). 372p. (*0-00-224387-3*); pap. (*0-00-648562-6*, HarperPerennial) HarperCollins Pubs. Canada, Ltd.

—The Last Great Dance on Earth. 2000. 384p. pap. 14.00 (*0-684-85608-5*); E-Book 14.00 (*0-7432-1359-9*) Simon & Schuster. (Touchstone).

—The Many Lives & Secret Sorrows of Josephine B. A Novel. 1999. 448p. pap. 14.00 (*0-684-85606-9*, Touchstone) Simon & Schuster.

—Tales of Passion, Tales of Woe. 1999. 384p. pap. 14.00 (*0-684-85607-7*, Touchstone) Simon & Schuster.

Haig, Kathryn. Apple Blossom Time. 1998. 464p. 26.95 o.p. (*0-312-18313-5*) St. Martin's Pr.

—Apple Blossom Time. 2000. 458p. pap. 9.95 (*0-552-14537-8*) Transworld Publishers Ltd. GBR. *Dist:* Trafalgar Square.

Hall, John. Sherlock Holmes & the Boulevard Assassin. 1998. 174p. pap. 14.95 (*0-947533-52-4*) Breese Bks., Ltd. GBR. *Dist:* Midpoint Trade Bks., Inc.

Harkness, Clare. Monsieur De Brillancourt: A Novel. 1995. 208p. 18.95 o.p. (*0-312-11854-6*) St. Martin's Pr.

Harris, Joanne. Blackberry Wine. 336p. 2002. pap. (*0-385-65945-8*); 2001. (Illus.). pap. (*0-385-25776-7*) Doubleday Canada, Ltd. CAN. *Dist:* Random Hse., Inc.

—Blackberry Wine. l.t. ed. 2001. (G. K. Hall Core Ser.). 416p. 28.95 (*0-7838-9453-8*, Macmillan Reference USA) Gale Group.

—Blackberry Wine. 2001. 368p. pap. 13.00 (*0-380-81592-3*, Perennial) HarperTrade.

—Blackberry Wine. 2000. 368p. 24.00 (*0-380-97872-5*, Morrow, William & Co.) Morrow/Avon.

—Chocolat. 2000. 320p. pap. o.s.i (*0-385-25773-2*) Doubleday Canada, Ltd. CAN. *Dist:* Random Hse., Inc.

—Chocolat: A Novel. 2000. 320p. pap. (*0-385-65811-7*) Doubleday Canada, Ltd. CAN. *Dist:* Random Hse., Inc.

—Chocolat: A Novel. l.t. ed. 1999. 26.95 o.p. (*0-7862-2079-1*, Macmillan Reference USA) Gale Group.

—Chocolat: A Novel. movie tie-in ed. 2000. 320p. pap. 12.95 (*0-14-100018-X*, Penguin Bks.) Penguin Group (USA) Inc.

—Chocolat: A Novel. 2000. (Illus.). 19.00 (*0-606-18395-7*) Turtleback Bks.

—Chocolat: A Novel. 2000. 320p. 12.95 (*0-14-028203-3*); 1999. 304p. 22.95 (*0-670-88179-1*) Viking Penguin.

—The Coastliners. l.t. ed. 2003. lib. bdg. 29.95 (*1-58547-287-5*, Platinum) Ctr. Point Large Print.

—Coastliners: A Novel. 2003. 368p. pap. 13.95 (*0-06-095801-4*, Perennial) HarperTrade.

—Coastliners: A Novel. 2002. 368p. 24.95 (*0-06-019812-5*, Morrow, William & Co.) Morrow/Avon.

—Five Quarters of the Orange. l.t. ed. 2001. 420p. lib. bdg. 28.95 (*1-58547-137-2*) Ctr. Point Large Print.

—Five Quarters of the Orange. 2002. 320p. pap. 13.95 (*0-06-095802-2*, Perennial) HarperTrade.

—Five Quarters of the Orange. 2001. 320p. 25.00 (*0-06-019813-3*, Morrow, William & Co.) Morrow/Avon.

—Holy Fools. 2004. 368p. 24.95 (*0-06-055912-8*, Morrow, William & Co.) Morrow/Avon.

Harris, Sarah, adapted by. La Belle et la Bete - Beauty & the Beast. 1995. (Comes to Life Bks.). (ENG & FRE.). 16p. (J). (ps-2). (*1-57234-045-2*) YES! Entertainment Corp.

Harrison, Kathryn. The Binding Chair: or A Visit from the Foot Emancipation Society. l.t. ed. 2000. (Compass Press Large Print Book Ser.). 419p. 26.95 (*1-56895-139-6*, Wheeler Publishing, Inc.) Gale Group.

—The Binding Chair: or A Visit from the Foot Emancipation Society. 2001. 336p. pap. 13.00 (*0-06-093442-5*, Perennial) HarperTrade.

Hart, Mallory Dorn. A Glass Full of Stars. unabr. ed. 1999. 544p. pap. 12.00 (*0-9675915-0-3*) John James Co.

Harwood, Ronald. Cesar & Augusta. 1980. 10.95 o.p. (*0-316-34991-7*) Little Brown & Co.

Hayes, Karen. Summer Poem. 1994. 256p. 20.95 o.p. (*0-312-11076-6*) St. Martin's Pr.

—Summer Poem. l.t. ed. 1995. (Ulverscroft Large Print Ser.). 512p. 29.99 o.p. (*0-7089-3430-7*, Ulverscroft) Thorpe, F. A. Pubs. GBR. *Dist:* Ulverscroft Large Print Bks., Ltd., Ulverscroft Large Print Canada, Ltd.

Hebden, Mark. Death Set to Music. 1979. o.p. (*0-241-10085-2*) David & Charles Pubs.

—Death Set to Music. 1983. 192p. 12.95 o.p. (*0-8027-3117-1*) Walker & Co.

—Pel among the Pueblos. 1988. 16.95 o.p. (*0-8027-5690-5*) Walker & Co.

—Pel & the Bombers. 1986. pap. 2.95 o.p. (*0-8027-3169-4*); 1985. 13.95 o.p. (*0-8027-5608-5*) Walker & Co.

—Pel & the Faceless Corpse. 1984. 192p. pap. 2.95 o.p. (*0-8027-3100-7*); 1982. 190p. 11.95 o.s.i (*0-8027-5473-2*) Walker & Co.

—Pel & the Missing Persons. 1991. 208p. 17.95 o.p. (*0-312-06441-1*, Saint Martin's Minotaur) St. Martin's Pr.

—Pel & the Party Spirit. 1990. 15.95 o.p. (0-312-05491-2, Saint Martin's Minotaur) St. Martin's Pr.
—Pel & the Picture of Innocence. 1989. 192p. 14.95 o.p. (0-312-02628-5, Saint Martin's Minotaur) St. Martin's Pr.
—Pel & the Pirates. 1987. 192p. 15.95 o.p. (0-8027-5672-7) Walker & Co.
—Pel & the Predators. 1985. 192p. 14.95 o.p. (0-8027-5624-7) Walker & Co.
—Pel & the Promised Land. 1992. 17.95 o.p. (0-312-08872-8, Saint Martin's Minotaur) St. Martin's Pr.
—Pel & the Prowler. 1986. 208p. 15.95 o.p. (0-8027-5658-1) Walker & Co.
—Pel & the Sepulchre Job. 1993. 160p. 17.95 o.p. (0-312-09893-6, Saint Martin's Minotaur) St. Martin's Pr.
—Pel & the Staghound. 1984. 192p. 12.95 o.s.i (0-8027-5580-1) Walker & Co.
—Pel & the Touch of Pitch. 1988. 16.95 o.p. (0-8027-5720-0) Walker & Co.
—Pel under Pressure. 1983. 192p. 12.95 o.s.i (0-8027-5566-6) Walker & Co.
Heffernan, William. The Corsican. 1983. 448p. 16.50 o.p. (0-671-44909-5, Simon & Schuster) Simon & Schuster.
—Corsican Honor. 1992. 464p. 22.00 o.p. (0-525-93465-0, Dutton) Dutton/Plume.
Hemingway, Ernest. The Garden of Eden. unabr. collector's ed. 1990. audio 48.00 (0-7366-1822-8, 2658) Books on Tape, Inc.
—The Garden of Eden. 1987. 251p. pap. 9.95 o.s.i (0-684-18871-6); 1986. 250p. 18.95 o.s.i (0-684-18693-4); 1987. 300p. 19.95 o.p. (0-8161-4152-5); 1987. 300p. 11.95 o.p. (0-8161-4153-3) Gale Group. (Macmillan Reference USA).
—The Garden of Eden. 1995. 256p. pap. 12.00 (0-684-80452-2, Scribner) Simon & Schuster.
Hendricks, Virginia H. Girl in the Tapestry. 1998. 212p. pap. 10.95 (0-9661605-0-9) Heartwood Pr.
Herring, Peggy J. Love's Harvest. 1996. 224p. pap. 10.95 o.p. (1-56280-117-1) Naiad Pr., Inc.
Highsmith, Patricia. The Boy Who Followed Ripley. 1993. (Mr. Ripley Ser.). 304p. pap. 12.00 (0-679-74567-X, Vintage) Knopf Publishing Group.
—The Boy Who Followed Ripley. 1985. (Mr. Ripley Ser.). 336p. pap. 3.95 o.p. (0-14-005739-0, Penguin Bks.) Viking Penguin.
—The Mysterious Mr. Ripley. 1985. (Crime Ser.). 656p. pap. 10.95 o.p. (0-14-007196-2, Penguin Bks.) Viking Penguin.
—Ripley under Ground. unabr. ed. 1993. (Mr. Ripley Ser.). audio 69.95 (1-85088-853-1, 91094) Eye in the Ear Inc.
—Ripley under Ground. l.t. ed. 1990. (Mr. Ripley Ser.). 416p. 19.95 (1-85089-304-7) ISIS Large Print Bks. GBR. Dist: Transaction Pubs.
—Ripley under Ground. 1992. (Mr. Ripley Ser.). 320p. pap. 12.95 (0-679-74230-1, Vintage) Knopf Publishing Group.
—Ripley under Water. unabr. ed. 2001. (Mr. Ripley Series). audio 69.95 (1-85089-888-X, 92061) ISIS Audio Bks. GBR. Dist: Ulverscroft Large Print Bks., Ltd.
—Ripley under Water. 1993. (Mr. Ripley Ser.). 320p. pap. 12.00 (0-679-74809-1, Vintage) Knopf Publishing Group.
—Ripley under Water. 1994. (Mr. Ripley Ser.). 4.99 o.p. (0-517-11787-8) Random Hse. Value Publishing.
—Ripley's Game. l.t. ed. 1991. (Mr. Ripley Ser.). 376p. 32.50 o.p. (1-85089-423-X) ISIS Large Print Bks. GBR. Dist: Ulverscroft Large Print Bks., Ltd.
—Ripley's Game. 1993. (Mr. Ripley Ser.). 288p. pap. 12.95 (0-679-74568-8, Vintage) Knopf Publishing Group.
Hill, Reginald. The Collaborators. 1989. 448p. 19.95 o.p. (0-88150-138-7) Countryman Pr.
—The Collaborators. l.t. ed. 1988. (Charnwood Large Print Ser.). 656p. 15.95 o.p. (0-7089-8488-6, Charnwood) Thorpe, F. A. Pubs. GBR. Dist: Ulverscroft Large Print Bks., Ltd., Ulverscroft Large Print Canada, Ltd.
Hilton, John B. Moondrop to Murder: A Superintendent Kenworthy Novel. 1986. 176p. 12.95 o.p. (0-312-54699-8) St. Martin's Pr.
Holden, Wendy. Azur Like It. 2004. 368p. pap. 13.00 (0-452-28517-8, Plume) Dutton/Plume.
Holland, Cecelia. The Angel & the Sword. 2000. 304p. 23.95 o.p. (0-312-86890-1, Forge Bks.) Doherty, Tom Assocs., LLC.
—The Lords of Vaumartin. 1988. 352p. 18.95 o.p. (0-395-48828-1) Houghton Mifflin Co.
—The Lords of Vaumartin. 1990. 4.99 o.p. (0-517-02966-9) Random Hse. Value Publishing.
Holland, Sharon. The Hunchback of Notre Dame. 1996. 96p. mass mkt. 3.50 o.p. (0-06-106434-3, HarperTorch) Morrow/Avon.
Holt, Victoria. The Queen's Confession: The Story of Marie Antoinette. unabr. ed. 1999. audio 96.95 (0-7540-0312-4, CAB 1735) BBC Audiobooks America.
—The Queen's Confession: The Story of Marie Antoinette. 498p. 1992. mass mkt. 5.99 o.p. (0-449-45103-8); 1986. mass mkt. 6.99 o.s.i (0-449-21229-7) Ballantine Bks. (Fawcett).
—The Queen's Confession: The Story of Marie Antoinette. unabr. collector's ed. 1995. audio 96.00 (0-7366-2988-2, 3677) Books on Tape, Inc.
—The Queen's Confession: The Story of Marie Antoinette. 1968. 14.95 o.p. (0-385-08276-2) Doubleday Publishing.
—The Queen's Confession: The Story of Marie Antoinette. unabr. ed. 1998. audio 112.00 (0-7887-1925-4, 95346E7) Recorded Bks., LLC.
Hopkinson, Nalo. The Salt Roads. 2003. 400p. 22.95 (0-446-53302-5) Warner Bks., Inc.
Houellebecq, Michel. The Elementary Particles. E-Book 19.95 (1-58945-586-X) Adobe Systems, Inc.
—The Elementary Particles. 2001. 272p. pap. 13.00 (0-375-72701-9, Vintage) Knopf Publishing Group.
—Whatever. Hammond, Paul, tr. from FRE. 1999. Tr. of Extension du Domaine de la Lutte. 155p. pap. 12.99 (1-85242-584-9) Serpent's Tail Ltd. GBR. Dist: Consortium Bk. Sales & Distribution.
Hughes, David. The Pork Butcher. 1988. 277p. (C). reprint ed. pap. 9.95 (0-941533-49-2, New Amsterdam Bks) Dee, Ivan R. Pub.
Hugo, Victor. The Hunchback of Notre-Dame. Cobb, Walter J., tr. from FRE. 2001. (Signet Classics). 512p. mass mkt. 5.95 (0-451-52788-7) NAL.
—The Hunchback of Notre-Dame. 1995. (Literary Classics Giant Ser.). 696p. text 8.98 o.p. (1-56138-602-2, Courage Bks.) Running Pr. Bk. Pubs.
—The Hunchback of Notre Dame. 1997. (Classics Illustrated Notes). pap. text 4.99 (1-57840-067-8) Acclaim Bks.
—The Hunchback of Notre Dame. 1976. 24.95 (0-8488-0534-8) Amereon, Ltd.
—The Hunchback of Notre Dame, Set. 1995. audio 71.95 (1-55685-390-4) Audio Bk. Contractors, Inc.
—The Hunchback of Notre Dame. 1981. mass mkt. 2.50 o.s.i (0-553-21224-9) Bantam Bks.
—The Hunchback of Notre Dame. Bair, Lowell, tr. 1981. 320p. mass mkt. 5.95 (0-553-21370-9, Bantam Classics) Bantam Bks.
—The Hunchback of Notre Dame. 1991. 3.95 (0-425-12667-6) Berkley Publishing Group.
—The Hunchback of Notre Dame. 1991. audio 73.95 (0-7861-0570-4); 1996. audio 85.95 (0-7861-0988-2, 1765) Blackstone Audio Bks., Inc.
—The Hunchback of Notre Dame. unabr. collector's ed. 1992. (J). audio 104.00 (0-7366-2281-0, 3068) Books on Tape, Inc.
—The Hunchback of Notre Dame. 1981. reprint ed. lib. bdg. 31.95 (0-89966-382-6) Buccaneer Bks., Inc.
—The Hunchback of Notre Dame. 1996. 458p. mass mkt. 3.99 (0-8125-6312-3, Tor Classics) Doherty, Tom Assocs., LLC.
—The Hunchback of Notre Dame. 1995. (Illus.). 96p. pap. text 1.00 (0-486-28564-2) Dover Pubns., Inc.
—The Hunchback of Notre Dame. abr. ed. audio 15.95 o.p. (0-88646-139-1, 7140); 1986. (YA). (gr. 7-9). audio 29.95 o.p. (0-88646-808-6, R 7140);Set. 1996. audio 9.99 (1-55204-005-4, 9005) Durkin Hayes Publishing Ltd.
—The Hunchback of Notre Dame. 1996. (Illus.). 584p. reprint ed. 17.95 (0-7868-6235-1) Hyperion Pr.
—The Hunchback of Notre Dame. 1986. (Illus.). (J). pap. 8.95 o.p. (0-86685-142-9) International Bk. Ctr., Inc.
—The Hunchback of Notre Dame. unabr. ed. 1991. audio 89.00 Jimcin Recordings.
—The Hunchback of Notre Dame. 1989. (English As a Second Language Bk.). pap. text 4.46 net. o.p. (0-582-53494-1, 74095) Longman Publishing Group.
—The Hunchback of Notre Dame. Cobb, Walter J., tr. 1965. 512p. mass mkt. 5.95 o.s.i (0-451-52222-2, Signet Classics) NAL.
—The Hunchback of Notre Dame. abr. ed. 1996. 37p. audio 13.98 (962-634-506-3, NA200614); 1994. audio compact disk 15.98 o.p. (962-634-006-1, NA200612) Naxos of America, Inc. (Naxos AudioBooks).
—The Hunchback of Notre Dame. abr. ed. 1996. (Ultimate Classics Ser.). 19.95 o.p. (0-7871-0526-0, 628385) NewStar Media, Inc.
—The Hunchback of Notre Dame. unabr. ed. 34.95 incl. audio Norton Pubs., Inc., Jeffrey /Audio-Forum.
—The Hunchback of Notre Dame. 1991. pap. 4.95 o.p. (0-8114-6827-5) Raintree Pubs.
—The Hunchback of Notre Dame. 1996. (Modern Library Ser.). 416p. 15.00 o.s.i (0-679-60255-0) Random Hse., Inc.
—The Hunchback of Notre Dame, unabr. ed. 1991. audio 128.00 (1-55690-241-7, 91224E7) Recorded Bks., LLC.
—The Hunchback of Notre Dame. 1989. 5.98 o.p. (0-86136-602-6) Smithmark Pubs., Inc.
—The Hunchback of Notre Dame. 1996. 9.60 o.p. (0-606-09443-1); 1956. 12.00 (0-606-00835-7) Turtleback Bks.
—The Hunchback of Notre Dame. 1998. (Classics Library). 448p. pap. 3.95 (1-85326-068-1, 0681WW) Wordsworth Editions, Ltd. GBR. Dist: Casemate Pubs. & Bk. Distributors, LLC.
—Les Miserables. 1997. (Classics Illustrated Study Guides). (Illus.). 64p. (YA). (gr. 7 up). mass mkt., stu. ed. 4.99 o.p. (1-57840-017-1) Acclaim Bks.
—Les Miserables. 1976. (J). 25.95 (0-8488-0535-6) Amereon, Ltd.
—Les Miserables. 1998. (J). mass mkt. 5.99 (0-449-45834-2) Ballantine Bks.
—Les Miserables. Wilbour, Charles E., tr. 1996. 336p. pap. 12.95 (0-449-91167-5, Fawcett) Ballantine Bks.
—Les Miserables. 1987. (J). mass mkt. 3.95 o.s.i (0-449-30057-9); 1982. (Illus.). 416p. mass mkt. 5.99 (0-449-30002-1) Ballantine Bks. (Fawcett).
—Les Miserables. abr. ed. audio 62.95 Blackstone Audio Bks., Inc.
—Les Miserables. unabr. collector's ed. 1993. (J). audio 72.00 (0-7366-2339-6, 116013) Books on Tape, Inc.
—Les Miserables. 1990. 528p. (J). reprint ed. lib. bdg. 49.95 (0-89966-452-0) Buccaneer Bks., Inc.
—Les Miserables. 1987. (J). pap. 5.60 (0-87129-287-4, L57) Dramatic Publishing Co.
—Les Miserables. Allem, Maurice, ed. 1976. (FRE.). 1808p. (J). lib. bdg. 125.00 (0-7859-3757-9, 2070102645) French & European Pubns., Inc.
—Les Miserables. Wilbour, Charles E., tr. 1998. (Everyman's Library). 1472p. (J). 23.00 (0-375-40317-5) Knopf, Alfred A. Inc.
—Les Miserables. E-Book 2.95 (1-57799-952-5) Logos Research Systems, Inc.
—Les Miserables. abr. ed. 2000. audio 7.95 (1-57815-117-1, 1079, Media Bks. Audio Publishing) Media Bks., L. L. C.
—Les Miserables. E-Book 1.95 (1-58515-009-6) MesaView, Inc.
—Les Miserables. 1987. 19.95 o.p. (0-453-00579-9); 1408p. (J). mass mkt. 7.95 (0-451-52526-4, Signet Classics); (J). mass mkt. 6.95 o.p. (0-451-52157-9, Signet Classics); mass mkt. 5.95 o.p. (0-451-52082-3) NAL.
—Les Miserables. audio 23.85 National Recording Co.
—Les Miserables. abr. ed. 1996. audio 22.98 (962-634-605-1, NA410514); audio compact disk 26.98 (962-634-105-X, NA410512) Naxos of America, Inc. (Naxos AudioBooks).
—Les Miserables. abr. ed. 1993. audio 16.95 o.p. (1-55800-036-4, Dove Audio) NewStar Media, Inc.
—Les Miserables. Fahnestock, Lee & MacAfee, Norman, trs. abr. ed. (Classics on Cassette). 1998. audio compact disk 34.95 (0-453-00966-2); 1992. 23.95 incl. audio (0-453-00785-6, 693468) Penguin/HighBridge.
—Les Miserables. 1987. (Radiola 3-CMR 5). audio 16.95 (0-929541-48-0); audio 4.98 (0-929541-22-7) Radiola Co.
—Les Miserables. 2000. E-Book 4.95 (0-679-64155-6, Modern Library) Random House Adult Trade Publishing Group.
—Les Miserables. Wilbour, Charles E., tr. 1992. (Modern Library Ser.). 1280p. 22.95 (0-679-60012-4) Random Hse., Inc.
—Les Miserables. deluxe ed. (Pleiade Ser.). (FRE.). (J). 84.95 (2-07-010264-5) Schoenhof's Foreign Bks., Inc.
—Les Miserables. Benichou, Paul, ed. Wilbour, Charles E., tr. abr. ed. 1983. 544p. (gr. 11 up). mass mkt. 5.99 (0-671-50439-8, Pocket) Simon & Schuster.
—Les Miserables. abr. ed. 1998. audio 22.95 (1-55935-273-6) Soundelux Audio Publishing.
—Les Miserables. audio Spoken Arts, Inc.
—Les Miserables. 1964. (J). 12.04 (0-606-02836-6) Turtleback Bks.
—Les Miserables. abr. ed. 1997. (Penguin Classics Ser.). 4p. (J). pap. 18.95 o.p. incl. audio (0-14-086261-7, Penguin AudioBooks) Viking Penguin.
—Les Miserables. Denny, Norman, tr. from FRE. & intro. by. rev. ed. 1982. (Classics Ser.). 1232p. (J). pap. 11.95 (0-14-044430-0, Penguin Classics) Viking Penguin.
—Les Miserables. 1997. (Classics Ser.: Vol. 2). (J). 512p. pap. 3.95 (1-85326-050-9, 0509WW); 496p. pap. 3.95 (1-85326-085-1, 0851WW) Wordsworth Editions, Ltd. GBR. Dist: Casemate Pubs. & Bk. Distributors, LLC.
—Los Miserables. 6th ed. 1998. (Clasicos Universales Ser.: Vol. 18). (SPA., Illus.). 1392p. 23.95 (84-08-01939-2) Planeta Publishing Corp.
—Les Miserables. unabr. ed. Pt. 1. 1996. audio 99.95 (0-7861-0534-8, 1810-A); Pt. 2. 1996. audio 85.95 (0-7861-0535-6, 1810-B); Pt. 3. audio 83.95 Blackstone Audio Bks., Inc.
—Les Miserables. unabr. ed. 1996. (FRE.). (J). Vol. I. pap. 8.95 (2-87714-296-5); Vol. II. pap. 7.95 (2-87714-301-5); Vol. III. pap. 7.95 (2-87714-302-3) Bookking International FRA. Dist: Distribooks, Inc.
—Les Miserables. Vol. 1. 1990. pap. 12.95 (0-7859-2876-6); Vol. 1. 1973. (FRE.). pap. 11.95 (0-7859-2306-3, 2070363481); Vol. 2. 1990. (FRE.). (J). pap. 12.95 (0-7859-3385-9); Vol. 2. 1973. (FRE.). pap. 11.95 (0-7859-2633-X, 207036349X); Vol. 3. 1973. (FRE.). pap. 11.95 (0-7859-2307-1, 2070363503) French & European Pubns., Inc.
—Les Miserables, Set. abr. ed. 1998. audio compact disk 29.95; 1995. 29.95 o.p. (0-7871-0289-X) NewStar Media, Inc.
—Les Miserables, 3 tomes. 1951. (Folio Ser.: Nos. 348, 349, & 350). (FRE.). I. (J). pap. 10.95 (2-07-036348-1); II. (J). pap. 10.95 (2-07-036349-X); III. pap. 10.95 (2-07-036350-3) Schoenhof's Foreign Bks., Inc.
—Les Miserables, 5 vols., Set. Hapgood, Isabel F., tr. from FRE. 1993. (Illus.). reprint ed. o.p. (1-877767-87-5) University Publishing Hse., Inc.
—Les Miserables: Parts I & II. abr. ed. 1989. audio 120.00 Jimcin Recordings.
—Ninety-Three. 1976. 27.95 (0-8488-0820-7) Amereon, Ltd.
—Ninety-Three. 1998. 400p. pap. 11.95 (0-7867-0590-6); 1988. 8.95 o.p. (0-88184-405-5) Avalon Publishing Group. (Carroll & Graf Pubs.).
—Ninety-Three. unabr. ed. 2000. audio 69.95 (0-7861-1768-0, 2571) Blackstone Audio Bks., Inc.
—Ninety-Three. 2001. (Illus.). 392p. per. 27.95 (1-58963-198-6) International Law & Taxation Pubs.
—Ninety-Three. Bair, Lowell, tr. 2002. 352p. 39.95 (1-889439-31-2) Paper Tiger, The.
—Ninety-Three. Bair, Lowell, tr. 1998. reprint ed. pap. (1-56114-264-6) Second Renaissance Bks.
—Notre-Dame de Paris. Krailsheimer, Alban J., tr. & intro. by. 1993. (Oxford World's Classics Ser.). 592p. pap. 7.95 o.p. (0-19-282911-4) Oxford Univ. Pr., Inc.
—Notre-Dame of Paris. Sturrock, John, tr. from FRE. & intro. by. 1978. (Classics Ser.). 496p. 11.95 (0-14-044353-3, Penguin Classics) Viking Penguin.
—Romans Complets: Les Miserables, Vol. 2. 1970. (FRE.). pap. 49.95 (0-7859-3933-4) French & European Pubns., Inc.
—Victor Hugo's Les Miserables. 1998. pap. (0-345-42502-2); mass mkt. (0-345-42503-0) Ballantine Bks.
—Works of Victor Hugo: The Hunchback of Notre-Dame, Les Miserables. 1991. (Classics - Bonded Leather Fibers Ser.). 763p. 24.95 o.p. (0-681-41056-6) Borders Pr.
Hugo, Victor & Dawson, Michael. Les Miserables. adapted collector's ed. 1998. (Smithsonian Historical Performances Ser.). 29p. (Illus.). pap. 24.98 incl. audio compact disk (1-57019-066-6, 4035); pap. 9.99 incl. audio (1-57019-065-8, 4034) Radio Spirits, Inc.
Hugo, Victor & Kulling, Monica. Les Miserables. 1995. (Step into Classics Ser.). (Illus.). 112p. (gr. 3-5). pap. text 3.99 (0-679-86668-X) Random Hse., Inc.
Hugo, Victor & Reimann, Jim. Les Miserables. 2001. (Reimann Classic Ser.). (Illus.). 304p. pap. 19.99 (0-8499-1687-9) W Publishing Group.
Hull, Jonathan. Losing Julia. 2001. 400p. mass mkt. 6.99 (0-440-23485-9, Delta) Dell Publishing.
—Losing Julia. l.t. ed. 2000. 26.95 o.p. (1-56895-827-7, Wheeler Publishing, Inc.) Gale Group.
Hunt, E. Howard. The Paris Edge. 1995. 329p. 22.95 o.p. (0-312-13138-0, Saint Martin's Minotaur) St. Martin's Pr.
Hunt, Herbert J., tr. from FRE. History of the Thirteen. 1975. (Classics Ser.). 392p. 13.95 (0-14-044301-0, Penguin Classics) Viking Penguin.
Hunter, Madeline. The Protector. 2001. 368p. mass mkt. 4.99 (0-553-58354-9) Bantam Bks.
Hylton, Sara. The Sunflower Girl. l.t. ed. 1997. (Magna Large Print Ser.). 526p. (0-7505-1136-2) Magna Large Print Bks. GBR. Dist: Ulverscroft Large Print Canada, Ltd.
—The Sunflower Girl. unabr. ed. 1998. audio 98.95 (1-85903-199-4) Magna Story Sound GBR. Dist: Ulverscroft Large Print Bks., Ltd.
—The Sunflower Girl. 1997. 339p. 23.95 o.p. (0-312-15667-7) St. Martin's Pr.
Hyvrard, Jeanne. Mother Death. Edson, Laurie, tr. 1988. (European Women Writers Ser.). viii, 124p. text 20.00 o.p. (0-8032-2339-0) Univ. of Nebraska Pr.
Ingman, Heather. The Dance of the Muses: A Novel on the Life of Pierre Ronsard. 1988. 197p. 24.95 (0-7206-0679-9) Owen, Peter Ltd. GBR. Dist: Dufour Editions, Inc.
Irwin, Margaret E. Royal Flush. 1983. 368p. 13.95 o.p. (0-312-69471-7) St. Martin's Pr.

Settings

—Royal Flush. l.t. ed. 1974. (Shadows of the Crown Ser.). 29.99 o.p. (*0-85456-617-1*, Ulverscroft) Thorpe, F. A. Pubs. GBR. *Dist:* Ulverscroft Large Print Bks., Ltd., Ulverscroft Large Print Canada, Ltd.

Jakeman, Jane. Death in the South of France. 2001. 274p. 24.95 (*0-7490-0555-6*) Allison & Busby, Ltd. GBR. *Dist:* International Publishers Marketing.

Janes, J. Robert. Carousel. 1993. 20.00 o.p. (*1-55611-357-9*) Fine, Donald I. Bks.

—Carousel. 1999. (St-Cyr & Kohler Ser.). 288p. pap. 12.00 (*1-56947-175-4*) Soho Pr., Inc.

—Dollmaker. 2003. pap. 12.00 (*1-56947-346-3*); 2002. 258p. 23.00 (*1-56947-285-8*) Soho Pr., Inc.

—Kaleidoscope. 2002. 294p. pap. 13.00 (*1-56947-286-6*); 2001. 304p. 22.00 (*1-56947-253-X*) Soho Pr., Inc.

—Mannequin. (St-Cyr & Kohler Ser.). 1999. 272p. pap. 12.00 (*1-56947-176-2*); 1998. 266p. 22.00 (*1-56947-129-0*) Soho Pr., Inc.

—Mayhem. 1999. 272p. pap. 12.00 (*1-56947-158-4*) Soho Pr., Inc.

—Mirage. 1992. 272p. 20.00 o.p. (*1-55611-340-4*) Fine, Donald I. Bks.

—Salamander. (Crime Ser.). 1999. 314p. pap. 12.00 (*1-56947-157-6*); 1998. 322p. 22.00 (*1-56947-119-3*) Soho Pr., Inc.

—Sandman. (St-Cyr & Kohler Ser.). 272p. 1998. pap. 12.00 (*1-56947-120-7*); 1997. 22.00 (*1-56947-106-1*) Soho Pr., Inc.

—Stonekiller. 1997. 261p. pap. 12.00 (*1-56947-107-X*); 22.00 o.p. (*1-56947-083-9*) Soho Pr., Inc.

Japisot, Sebastian. One Deadly Summer. Sheridan, Alan, tr. 1997. 288p. pap. 11.95 o.p. (*0-452-27780-9*, Plume) Dutton/Plume.

Japrisot, Sebastien. One Deadly Summer. Sheridan, Alan, tr. 1980. (Helen & Kurt Wolff Bk.). 288p. 9.95 o.p. (*0-15-169381-1*) Harcourt Trade Pubs.

—One Deadly Summer. 1981. 320p. pap. 3.95 o.p. (*0-14-005846-X*, Penguin Bks.) Viking Penguin.

—Piege pour Cendrillon. 1972. (FRE.). 224p. pap. 10.95 (*0-7859-2282-2*, 2070362167) French & European Pubns., Inc.

—The Sleeping Car Murders. 1997. Orig. Title: The Ten-Thirty from Marseille. 192p. reprint ed. pap. 11.95 (*0-452-27778-7*, Plume) Dutton/Plume.

—The Sleeping Car Murders. 1978. (Crime Ser.). Orig. Title: The Ten-Thirty from Marseille. pap. 1.95 o.p. (*0-14-004992-4*, Penguin Bks.) Viking Penguin.

—A Very Long Engagement. Coverdale, Linda, tr. from FRE. 1994. Tr. of Long Dimanche de Finacailles. 336p. pap. 14.00 (*0-452-27297-1*, Plume) Dutton/Plume.

—A Very Long Engagement. 1993. Tr. of Long Dimanche de Finacailles. 327p. 23.00 o.p. (*0-374-28335-4*) Farrar, Straus & Giroux.

—Visages de l'Amour et de la Haine. 1989. (FRE.). 120p. pap. 10.95 (*0-7859-2658-5*, 207038179X) French & European Pubns., Inc.

Jardin, Alexandre. Fanfan. (FRE.). pap. 13.95 (*2-07-038513-2*) Gallimard, Editions FRA. *Dist:* Distribooks, Inc.

—Fanfan. 1994. 176p. 18.95 o.p. (*0-312-10981-4*) St. Martin's Pr.

Jinks, Catherine. The Inquisitor. 1999. 393p. (*0-7329-0972-4*) Macmillan Education Australia.

—The Inquisitor. mass mkt. (*0-312-98644-0*, St. Martin's Paperbacks); E-Book 25.95 (*0-312-70852-1*) St. Martin's Pr.

—The Inquisitor: A Novel. 2002. 400p. 25.95 (*0-312-30815-9*, Saint Martin's Minotaur) St. Martin's Pr.

Johnson, Diana M. Destiny's Godchild: A Novel of Intrigue & Enchantment in Frankish Gaul. 1998. 272p. per. 12.00 (*0-9661504-0-6*) Superior Bk. Publishing Co.

—Pepin's Bastard: The Story of Charles Martel. 1999. (Illus.). 296p. pap. 14.95 (*0-9661504-1-4*) Superior Bk. Publishing Co.

—Quest for the Crown: The Story of Pepin the Short. 2002. 384p. per. 15.95 (*0-9661504-2-2*) Superior Bk. Publishing Co.

Johnson, Diane. L' Affaire. 2003. 352p. 24.95 (*0-525-94740-X*, Dutton) Dutton/Plume.

—L' Affaire. l.t. ed. 2004. 544p. 31.95 (*1-58724-586-8*, Wheeler Publishing, Inc.) Gale Group.

—Le Divorce. (William Abrahams Book Ser.). 320p. 1998. pap. 14.00 (*0-452-27733-7*, Plume); 1997. 23.95 (*0-525-94238-6*); 2003. pap. 12.95 (*0-452-28448-1*, Plume) Dutton/Plume.

—Le Divorce. l.t. ed. 2004. 482p. pap. 25.95 (*1-58724-591-4*, Wheeler Publishing, Inc.) Gale Group.

—Le Mariage. 2000. 320p. 23.95 o.s.i (*0-525-94518-0*, Dutton) Dutton/Plume.

—Le Mariage. l.t. ed. 2000. 457p. 27.95 (*1-56895-936-2*, Wheeler Publishing, Inc.) Gale Group.

Johnson, Eyvind. Dreams of Roses & Fire. Friis, Erik J., ed. 1984. (Library of Nordic Literature). 384p. 14.95 o.p. (*0-88254-897-2*) Hippocrene Bks., Inc.

Jonath, Leslie. Postmark Paris: A Little Album of Memories. 1995. (Illus.). 108p. 12.95 o.p. (*0-8118-0555-7*) Chronicle Bks. LLC.

Jordan, Evora. Twenty-One Days with a Vulture. Jordan, Evora, ed. unabr. ed. 2000. 210p. pap. 7.95 (*0-9725071-1-6*) EvoraBooks, LLC.

—Twenty-One Days with a Vulture. 2000. 210p. pap. 7.95 (*1-928782-02-7*) Publishing Directions, LLC.

Jordan, Lee. Chain Reaction. 1993. 207p. 19.95 o.p. (*0-8027-1249-5*) Walker & Co.

Jouve, Pierre J. Helene. Davis, Lydia, tr. from FRE. 1993. 104p. 29.95 (*0-910395-92-6*) Marlboro Pr., Inc., The.

—Helene. Davis, Lydia, tr. 1995. 104p. (C). pap. 16.00 (*0-8101-6003-X*, Marlboro Pr., The) Northwestern Univ. Pr.

Just, Ward. The Translator. 1991. 313p. 21.95 o.p. (*0-395-57168-5*) Houghton Mifflin Co.

Kafka, Paul. Love Enter. 1993. 288p. 19.95 o.p. (*0-395-60478-8*) Houghton Mifflin Co.

Kalogridis, Jeanne. The Burning Times: A Novel. 2002. 400p. pap. 14.00 (*0-684-86924-1*, Simon & Schuster) Simon & Schuster.

—The Burning Times: A Novel of Medieval France. 2001. (Illus.). 400p. 25.00 (*0-684-86923-3*, Simon & Schuster) Simon & Schuster.

Kalpakian, Laura. Cosette: The Sequel to "Les Miserables" 1995. 640p. 24.00 o.p. (*0-06-017222-3*) HarperCollins Pubs.

Kartun, Derek. The Courier. 1985. 248p. 14.95 o.p. (*0-312-17044-0*) St. Martin's Pr.

Kay, Guy Gavriel. The Song for Arbonne. Chizmar, Richard & Morrish, Robert, eds. 2002. 512p. reprint ed. pap. 15.00 (*0-451-45897-4*) NAL.

Kelby, N. M. In the Company of Angels: A Novel. 2002. (Illus.). 192p. pap. 12.00 (*0-7868-8583-1*); 2001. 164p. 21.00 (*0-7868-6666-7*) Hyperion Pr.

Keller, J. R. La Belle Agnes. 1988. 13.95 o.p. (*0-533-07616-1*) Vantage Pr., Inc.

Kellogg, Marne Davis. Brilliant. l.t. ed. 2003. 444p. 30.95 (*1-58724-543-4*, Wheeler Publishing, Inc.) Gale Group.

—Brilliant. 2003. 352p. 24.95 (*0-312-30347-5*) St. Martin's Pr.

Kells, Susannah. The Fallen Angels. 1985. pap. 3.95 o.p. (*0-312-90192-5*, St. Martin's Paperbacks); 1985. pap. 3.95 o.p. (*0-312-90193-3*, St. Martin's Paperbacks); 1984. 384p. 14.95 o.p. (*0-312-28007-6*) St. Martin's Pr.

Kelly, Carla Sue. The Lady's Companion. 1996. 224p. mass mkt. 4.99 o.s.i (*0-451-18684-2*, Signet Bks.) NAL.

Kelly, Susan. The Ghosts of Albi. 1998. 256p. 25.00 (*0-7278-5350-3*) Severn Hse. Pubs., Ltd.

—The Ghosts of Albi. l.t. ed. 1999. (Ulverscroft Large Print Ser.). 432p. 31.99 (*0-7089-4035-8*, Ulverscroft) Thorpe, F. A. Pubs. GBR. *Dist:* Ulverscroft Large Print Bks., Ltd., Ulverscroft Large Print Canada, Ltd.

Kemp, Shirley. Ete Magique en Provence. 1997. (Harlequin Azur Ser.). (FRE.). pap. (*0-373-34654-9*, 1-34654-3, Harlequin Bks.) Harlequin Enterprises, Ltd.

Kemske, Floyd. The Third Lion: A Novel about Talleyrand. 1997. 224p. pap. 22.95 (*0-945774-37-0*, PS3561.E4226T48) Catbird Pr.

Kendrick, Jeana. St. Abient Run. 2002. 188p. pap. 14.95 (*0-9678343-8-4*) Panther Creek Pr.

Kercheval, Jesse L. The Museum of Happiness. 1993. 276p. 22.95 o.s.i (*0-571-19821-X*) Faber & Faber, Inc.

Kercheval, Jesse Lee. The Museum of Happiness: A Novel. 2003. (Library of American Fiction). 277p. pap. 17.95 (*0-299-18734-9*) Univ. of Wisconsin Pr.

Keyes, J. Gregory. Empire of Unreason. 2001. (Age of Unreason Ser.: Vol. 3). 416p. mass mkt. 6.99 (*0-345-40610-9*, Del Rey) Ballantine Bks.

—Newton's Cannon. (Age of Unreason Ser.: Vol. 1). 1999. 384p. mass mkt. 6.99 (*0-345-43378-5*, Del Rey); 1998. 480p. pap. 14.00 o.s.i (*0-345-40605-2*) Ballantine Bks.

King, Barrington. All Through the Night. 2001. (First Edition Romance Ser.). 370p. 26.95 (*0-7862-3287-0*, Five Star) Gale Group.

King, Lily. The Pleasing Hour. 1999. 237p. (YA). 24.00 o.p. (*0-87113-754-2*, Atlantic Monthly Pr.) Grove/Atlantic, Inc.

—The Pleasing Hour. 2000. 256p. pap. 12.00 (*0-7432-0164-7*, Touchstone) Simon & Schuster.

King, Peter. Death & the Celestial Spice. 1997. (*0-312-15137-3*) St. Martin's Pr.

—Dying on the Vine: A Further Adventure of the Gourmet Detective. (Culinary Mysteries Ser.). 1999. 288p. mass mkt. 5.99 (*0-312-96683-0*, St. Martin's Paperbacks); 1998. 304p. 22.95 o.p. (*0-312-18090-X*, Saint Martin's Minotaur) St. Martin's Pr.

Kolpen, Jana. The Legend of the Villa Della Luna. 1997. (Illus.). 90p. 19.95 o.p. (*1-55670-628-6*) Stewart, Tabori & Chang.

—The Secrets of Pistoulet. 2003. (Illus.). 86p. 22.50 (*1-55670-440-2*) Stewart, Tabori & Chang.

Koning, Hans. Zeeland: or Elective Concurrences: A Novel of War, Death, Love & Loss. 2001. 256p. (*1-58838-050-5*) NewSouth, Inc.

Koren, Elaine Todd. Suzanne: Of Love & Art. Date not set. 21.95 (*0-9672355-3-7*); 2001. 377p. pap. 14.95 (*0-9672355-2-9*) Maverick Bks.

Kristeva, Julia. The Samurai: A Novel. Bray, Barbara, tr. from FRE. 1992. 341p. (C). 40.50 (*0-231-07542-1*) Columbia Univ. Pr.

Kruger, Michael. The Man in the Tower. 1993. 176p. 19.95 (*0-8076-1297-9*) Braziller, George Inc.

Kundera, Milan. Slowness. unabr. collector's ed. 1997. audio 18.00 (*0-7366-3579-3*, 4232) Books on Tape, Inc.

—Slowness. Asher, Linda, tr. 1996. 160p. 21.00 o.p. (*0-06-017369-6*) HarperCollins Pubs.

—Slowness. Asher, Linda, tr. 1997. 176p. pap. 12.95 (*0-06-092841-7*, Perennial) HarperTrade.

Kurzweil, Allen. A Case of Curiosities. 1993. 368p. pap. 10.00 o.s.i (*0-345-38057-6*) Ballantine Bks.

—A Case of Curiosities. 1992. 19.95 (*0-15-115793-6*); 2001. 384p. reprint ed. pap. 14.00 (*0-15-601289-8*, Harvest Bks.) Harcourt Trade Pubs.

La Rochelle, Pierre Drieu. The Comedy of Charleroi & Other Stories. 1980. (Illus.). 236p. 9.95 (*0-903747-03-0*) Writers & Readers Publishing, Inc.

Labro, Philippe. Le Petit Garcon. Coverdale, Linda, tr. 1992. 320p. 23.00 o.p. (*0-374-18448-8*) Farrar, Straus & Giroux.

—Le Petit Garcon. (Folio Ser.: No. 2389). (FRE.). pap. 13.95 (*2-07-038526-4*) Schoenhof's Foreign Bks., Inc.

Laclos, Choderlos de. Les Liaisons Dangereuses. 1992. (Everyman's Library). 17.00 (*0-679-41325-1*) Knopf, Alfred A. Inc.

Lafayette, Marie J. The Princess of Cleves. 1977. 210p. reprint ed. 38.50 o.s.i (*0-8371-9729-5*, LAFPC, Greenwood Pr.) Greenwood Publishing Group, Inc.

Laker, Rosalind, pseud. The Sugar Pavilion. unabr. ed. 1996. 12p. audio 96.95 (*0-7451-6591-5*, CAB 1207) BBC Audiobooks America.

—To Dance with Kings. 1989. mass mkt. 4.95 o.s.i (*0-553-28284-0*) Bantam Bks.

Lambdin, Dewey. H.M.S. Cockerel: An Alan Lewrie Naval Adventure. 1997. (Alan Lewrie Naval Adventures Ser.). 416p. mass mkt. 6.50 (*0-449-22448-1*, Fawcett) Ballantine Bks.

—H.M.S. Cockerel: An Alan Lewrie Naval Adventure. 1995. (Alan Lewrie Ser.). 368p. 23.95 o.s.i (*1-55611-446-X*) Fine, Donald I. Bks.

—H.M.S. Cockerel: An Alan Lewrie Naval Adventure. 1996. text 23.95 (*0-07-036237-8*) McGraw-Hill Cos., The.

Lambrichs, Louise. Hannah's Diary. Reynolds, Sian, tr. from FRE. 1999. 220p. pap. 12.95 (*0-7043-8081-1*) Interlink Publishing Group, Inc.

Lamorisse, Albert. The Red Balloon. 1990. (Short Story Library). (Illus.). 32p. (YA). (gr. 5 up). lib. bdg. 13.95 o.p. (*0-88682-304-8*, Creative Education) Creative Co., The.

Lampitt, Dianah. The King's Women. 1993. 560p. (Orig.). mass mkt. 5.99 o.p. (*0-451-40389-4*, Signet Bks.) NAL.

Lanchester, John. The Debt to Pleasure. abr. ed. 1996. audio 17.95 (*1-57453-025-9*, 330093) Audio Literature.

—The Debt to Pleasure. unabr. collector's ed. 1997. audio 48.00 (*0-7366-3724-9*, 4405) Books on Tape, Inc.

—The Debt to Pleasure. 1997. 272p. pap. 13.00 o.s.i (*0-8050-5130-9*, Owl Bks.); 1996. (Illus.). 88p. 20.00 o.p. (*0-8050-4388-8*) Holt, Henry & Co.

—The Debt to Pleasure. 1996. 256p. 26.99 (*0-7710-4585-9*) McClelland & Stewart/Tundra Bks.

—The Debt to Pleasure. 1998. 272p. pap. 14.99 (*0-7710-4587-5*) St. Martin's Pr.

—The Debt to Pleasure: A Novel. 2001. 256p. pap. 13.00 (*0-312-42036-6*) Picador.

—The Debt to Pleasure: Reader Group. 1997. 0.01 o.s.i (*0-8050-5378-6*, Owl Bks.) Holt, Henry & Co.

Lane, Simon. Fear: A Novel. 1998. 211p. 21.95 (*1-882593-22-7*) Bridge Works Publishing Co., Inc.

—Still Life with Books: A Novel. 1993. 176p. 17.95 (*1-882593-02-2*) Bridge Works Publishing Co., Inc.

Larson, Elyse. The Hope Before Us. 2002. (Women of Valor Ser.: Vol. 3). 352p. pap. 12.99 (*0-7642-2376-3*) Bethany Hse. Pubs.

Law, Janice. All the King's Ladies. 1986. 320p. 16.95 o.p. (*0-312-01966-1*) St. Martin's Pr.

—All the King's Ladies. 1999. 324p. pap. 14.95 (*1-58348-730-1*) iUniverse, Inc.

Le Fort, Gertrud von. Song at the Scaffold: A Novel of Horror & Holiness in the Reign of Terror. 2001. 176p. pap. 12.95 (*1-928832-34-2*) Sophia Institute Pr.

Lee, Simon, ed. French Short Stories Two. 1993. (Penguin Parallel Texts). 256p. 13.00 (*0-14-003414-5*) Viking Penguin.

Leefeldt, Ed. The Woman Who Rode the Wind. Carroll, Kent, ed. 2001. (Illus.). 320p. pap. 14.95 (*0-9679535-1-0*) Lighter Than Air, L.P.

Lennox, Judith. The Glittering Strand. 1994. 480p. 24.95 o.p. (*0-312-10469-3*) St. Martin's Pr.

Leroux, Gaston. Le Fantome de l'Opera. 1992. (FRE., Illus.). 152p. pap. 14.64 (*0-8442-1233-4*, 12334) Glencoe/McGraw-Hill.

—The Phantom of the Opera. Date not set. lib. bdg. 26.95 (*0-8488-1652-8*) Amereon, Ltd.

—The Phantom of the Opera, Set. unabr. ed. 1988. (Classic Books on Cassettes Ser.). audio 41.95 (*1-55685-118-9*) Audio Bk. Contractors, Inc.

—The Phantom of the Opera. 1986. 269p. reprint ed. pap. 3.95 o.p. (*0-88184-249-4*, Carroll & Graf Pubs.) Avalon Publishing Group.

—The Phantom of the Opera. 1990. (Bantam Classics Ser.). 288p. mass mkt. 4.95 (*0-553-21376-8*) Bantam Bks.

—The Phantom of the Opera. E-Book 5.00 (*0-7607-1322-7*) Barnes & Noble, Inc.

—The Phantom of the Opera. unabr. ed. 1988. audio 49.95 (*0-7861-0565-8*, 2057) Blackstone Audio Bks., Inc.

—The Phantom of the Opera. unabr. collector's ed. 2000. audio 56.00 (*0-7366-5139-X*, 9188); 1998. audio 48.00 (*0-7366-4154-8*, 4657) Books on Tape, Inc.

—The Phantom of the Opera. 1975. lib. bdg. 28.95 (*0-89966-136-X*) Buccaneer Bks., Inc.

—The Phantom of the Opera. abr. ed. audio 15.95 o.p. (*0-88646-216-9*, 7216) Durkin Hayes Publishing Ltd.

—The Phantom of the Opera. E-Book 2.49 (*1-58627-839-8*) Electric Umbrella Publishing.

—The Phantom of the Opera, Set. abr. ed. 1998. audio 18.00 (*0-89845-776-9*, CPN 2108, HarperAudio) HarperTrade.

—The Phantom of the Opera. 1990. 300p. pap. 9.95 o.s.i (*0-87052-937-4*) Hippocrene Bks., Inc.

—The Phantom of the Opera. l.t. ed. 710p. pap. 54.00 (*0-7583-1804-9*); 551p. pap. 44.00 (*0-7583-1803-0*); 249p. pap. 23.80 (*0-7583-1800-6*); 313p. pap. 28.72 (*0-7583-1801-4*); 1262p. pap. 93.20 (*0-7583-1807-3*); 1075p. pap. 83.07 (*0-7583-1806-5*); 874p. pap. 69.34 (*0-7583-1805-7*); 429p. pap. 35.66 (*0-7583-1802-2*); 249p. lib. bdg. 29.80 (*0-7583-1792-1*); 313p. lib. bdg. 34.72 (*0-7583-1793-X*); 874p. lib. bdg. 84.50 (*0-7583-1797-2*); 1262p. lib. bdg. 105.20 (*0-7583-1799-9*); 1075p. lib. bdg. 95.07 (*0-7583-1798-0*); 429p. lib. bdg. 41.66 (*0-7583-1794-8*); 710p. lib. bdg. 60.00 (*0-7583-1796-4*); 551p. lib. bdg. 50.00 (*0-7583-1795-6*) Huge Print Pr.

—The Phantom of the Opera. l.t. ed. 1988. (Mainstream Ser.). 432p. reprint ed. lib. bdg. 18.95 o.p. (*1-85089-234-2*) ISIS Large Print Bks. GBR. *Dist:* Transaction Pubs.

—The Phantom of the Opera. 1989. audio 36.00 Jimcin Recordings.

—The Phantom of the Opera. 1988. (Illus.). 25.00 o.p. (*0-89296-279-8*) Mysterious Pr.

—The Phantom of the Opera. (Signet Classics). 1989. 288p. mass mkt. 4.95 o.s.i (*0-451-52482-9*, Signet Classics); 1987. mass mkt. 4.50 o.p. (*0-451-52432-2*, Signet Classics); 1987. mass mkt. 3.95 o.p. (*0-451-52173-0*) NAL.

—The Phantom of the Opera. abr. ed. 1997. audio 13.98 (*962-634-618-3*, NA211814); audio compact disk 15.98 o.p. (*962-634-118-1*, NA211812) Naxos of America, Inc. (Naxos AudioBooks).

—The Phantom of the Opera. abr. ed. 1993. (Classic, Ultimate, Dove Ser.). audio 29.95 o.p. (*0-7871-0110-9*);Set. audio 15.95 o.p. (*1-55800-007-0*, 390236, Dove Audio) NewStar Media, Inc.

—The Phantom of the Opera, unabr. ed. 1988. audio 60.00 (*1-55690-410-X*, 88991E7) Recorded Bks., LLC.

—The Phantom of the Opera. 1938. 10.60 o.p. (*0-606-03258-4*) Turtleback Bks.

—The Phantom of the Opera. 1995. mass mkt. 5.95 (*0-352-31716-7*) Virgin Bks. GBR. *Dist:* London Bridge.

—The Phantom of the Opera. 1986. 272p. mass mkt. 5.99 (*0-446-30120-5*) Warner Bks., Inc.

—The Phantom of the Opera. 1998. (Classics Library). 224p. pap. 3.95 (*1-85326-273-0*, 2730WW) Wordsworth Editions, Ltd. GBR. *Dist:* Combined Publishing.

—The Phantom of the Opera: The Original Novel. 1988. 368p. reprint ed. mass mkt. 7.00 (*0-06-080924-8*, PL-7140, Perennial) HarperTrade.

—The Phantom of the Opera: The Play. 1979. pap. 5.60 (*0-87129-363-3*, P45) Dramatic Publishing Co.

Levy, Justine. The Rendezvous: A Novel. Davis, Lydia, tr. 1999. 144p. pap. 11.00 (*0-684-84632-2*, Scribner Paper Fiction); 1997. 142p. 21.50 (*0-684-82579-1*, Scribner) Simon & Schuster.

Ley, Alice C. The Intrepid Miss Haydon. 1983. mass mkt. 2.25 o.s.i (*0-449-20274-7*, Fawcett) Ballantine Bks.

—The Intrepid Miss Haydon. l.t. ed. 1995. (Nightingale Ser.). 364p. pap. 17.95 (*0-8161-7491-1*, Macmillan Reference USA) Gale Group.

Lindsey, Johanna. So Speaks the Heart. 1983. 384p. mass mkt. 7.99 (*0-380-81471-4*, Avon Bks.) Morrow/Avon.

Linscott, Gillian. Sister Beneath the Sheet. l.t. ed. 1992. 18.95 o.p. (*0-7451-8355-7*); pap. 16.95 o.p. (*0-7927-1103-3*) BBC Audiobooks America.

—Sister Beneath the Sheet. 1991. 224p. 17.95 o.p. (*0-312-06464-0*, Saint Martin's Minotaur) St. Martin's Pr.

Llywelyn, Morgan. The Druids. 1992. 416p. mass mkt. 6.99 (*0-8041-0844-7*, Ivy Bks.) Ballantine Bks.

—The Druids. 1991. (Illus.). 416p. 19.95 o.p. (*0-688-08819-8*, Morrow, William & Co.) Morrow/Avon.

Lomer, Mary. Robert of Normandy. l.t. ed. 1992. (Magna Large Print Ser.). 490p. 29.99 (*0-7505-0308-4*) Magna Large Print Bks. GBR. *Dist:* Ulverscroft Large Print Bks., Ltd.

Lordon, Randye. East of Nice. 2002. 288p. pap. 13.95 (*0-312-28714-3*, Saint Martin's Griffin) St. Martin's Pr.

—East of Niece. 2001. (Sydney Sloane Mystery Ser.). 288p. 23.95 (*0-312-27114-X*, Saint Martin's Minotaur) St. Martin's Pr.

Lorrimer, Claire. Relentless Storm. 1981. 224p. pap. 2.25 o.p. (*0-553-13658-5*) Bantam Bks.

—Relentless Storm. 2001. 242p. pap. 12.95 (*0-7551-0336-X*) House of Stratus, Inc.

—Relentless Storm. 1979. mass mkt. 0.95 o.p. (*0-380-00417-8*, 25163, Avon Bks.) Morrow/Avon.

—Relentless Storm. l.t. ed. 1984. (Ulverscroft Large Print Ser.). 384p. 29.99 o.p. (*0-7089-1104-8*, Ulverscroft) Thorpe, F. A. Pubs. GBR. *Dist:* Ulverscroft Large Print Bks., Ltd., Ulverscroft Large Print Canada, Ltd.

Lorrimer, Clarie. Relentless Storm. 1994. 19.00 (*0-7278-4580-2*) Severn Hse. Pubs., Ltd.

Loughery, David. The Three Musketeers: The Screenplay. 2000. pap. 19.95 o.p. (*1-929750-05-6*) Harvest Moon Publishing.

Louis-Napoleon, Geoffroy-Chateau & Geoffroy-Chateau, Louis-Napoleon. Napoleon & the Conquest of the World: A Fictional Account of Napoleon's Escape from Russia, Invasion of England, & Conquest of Asia & America. 1994. (Illus.). 440p. reprint ed. lib. bdg. 39.95 (*0-9642115-3-X*) Campaign Pr. Pubns.

Lyons, Genevieve. Alice's Awakening. l.t. ed. 2000. 248p. (*0-7540-4205-7*, Macmillan Reference USA) Gale Group.

—Alice's Awakening. 224p. 26.00 (*0-7278-5506-9*) Severn Hse. Pubs., Ltd.

—Alice's Awakening. l.t. ed. 2000. (Nightingale Ser.). 248p. pap. 20.95 (*0-7838-9109-1*) Thorndike Pr.

Lytton, Edward Bulwer. The Parisians. E-Book 3.95 (*0-594-02585-0*) 1873 Pr.

—The Parisians. 2001. (Works of Edward George Bulwer-Lytton ). reprint ed. pap. text 28.00 (*0-7426-8357-5*) Classic Bks.

Mack, William P. Christopher & the Quasi War with France. 2002. 22.95 (*1-877853-65-8*) Nautical & Aviation Publishing Co. of America, Inc., The.

MacKenzie, Henry. Julia de Roubigne, Vol. 4. 1976. reprint ed. 30.00 (*0-404-04094-2*) AMS Pr., Inc.

—Julia de Roubigne. 2000. 192p. pap. 16.95 (*1-86232-047-0*) Tuckwell Pr. Ltd. GBR. *Dist:* General Distribution Services, Inc.

Macklin, Alys E., ed. Twenty-Nine Tales from the French. Herrick, Robert, tr. & intro. by. 1977. (Short Story Index Reprint Ser.). reprint ed. 23.95 (*0-8369-3897-6*) Ayer Co. Pubs., Inc.

MacLeod, Robert. The Money Mountain. l.t. ed. 1988. (Ulverscroft Large Print Ser.). 400p. 29.99 o.p. (*0-7089-1838-7*, Ulverscroft) Thorpe, F. A. Pubs. GBR. *Dist:* Ulverscroft Large Print Bks., Ltd., Ulverscroft Large Print Canada, Ltd.

Maguire, Gregory. The Good Liar. 1999. 144p. (J). (gr. 5-9). tchr. ed. 15.00 (*0-395-90697-0*, Clarion Bks.) Houghton Mifflin Co. Trade & Reference Div.

Major, Kevin. No Man's Land. 264p. 2001. (Illus.). pap. (*0-385-65886-9*, Anchor Canada); 1997. pap. o.s.i (*0-385-25579-9*) Doubleday Canada, Ltd. CAN. *Dist:* Random Hse., Inc.

Malraux, André. The Walnut Trees of Altenburg. Fielding, A. W., tr. from FRE. 1989. 224p. lib. bdg. 35.00 (*0-86527-392-8*) Fertig, Howard Inc.

—The Walnut Trees of Altenburg. Fielding, A. W., tr. 1992. (Phoenix Fiction Ser.). 226p. pap. 14.00 (*0-226-50289-9*) Univ. of Chicago Pr.

Manchette, Jean-Patrick. Three to Kill. Nicholson-Smith, Donald, tr. from FRE. 2002. 185p. pap. 11.95 (*0-87286-395-6*) City Lights Bks.

Mann, Heinrich. Henry King of France. 1985. 800p. 35.00 (*0-87951-999-1*) Overlook Pr., The.

—Young Henry of Navarre. 2003. 585p. pap. 24.95 (*1-58567-487-7*); 1986. pap. 14.95 o.p. (*0-87951-978-9*) Overlook Pr., The.

—Young Henry of Navarre. Sutton, Eric, tr. from GER. 585p. reprint ed. 1986. pap. 24.95 (*0-87951-206-7*); 1985. 25.00 (*0-87951-981-9*) Overlook Pr., The.

Manton, Richard. La Vie Parisienne. 2001. 256p. pap. 7.95 (*1-56201-239-8*, Blue Moon Bks.) Avalon Publishing Group.

The Many Lives & Secret Sorrows of Josephine B: A Novel. 2000. E-Book 14.00 (*0-7432-1357-2*, Scribner Paper Fiction) Simon & Schuster.

Marcantel, Pamela. An Army of Angels: A Novel of Joan of Arc. 592p. 1998. (Illus.). pap. 15.95 (*0-312-18042-X*, Saint Martin's Griffin); 1997. 24.95 o.p. (*0-312-15030-X*) St. Martin's Pr.

Marquis, Max. Undignified Death: A Detective Inspector Harry Timberlake Mystery. 1994. 192p. 18.95 o.p. (*0-312-11087-1*) St. Martin's Pr.

Marshall, Paule. The Fisher King: A Novel. l.t. ed. 2001. 256p. lib. bdg. 27.95 (*1-58547-074-0*) Ctr. Point Large Print.

—The Fisher King: A Novel. 224p. 2000. 23.00 o.s.i (*0-684-87283-8*); 2001. reprint ed. pap. 12.00 (*0-684-86970-5*) Simon & Schuster. (Scribner).

Marton, Sandra. Until You. 1997. 416p. mass mkt. 5.50 o.s.i (*0-7860-0372-3*, Pinnacle Bks.) Kensington Publishing Corp.

Maso, Carole. The American Woman in the Chinese Hat. 1994. 200p. 19.95 (*1-56478-045-7*) Dalkey Archive Pr.

—The American Woman in the Chinese Hat. 1995. 224p. pap. 13.00 o.s.i (*0-452-27507-5*, Plume) Dutton/Plume.

Matalon, Ronit. Bliss: A Novel. Cohen, Jessica, tr. from HEB. 2003. 272p. 23.00 (*0-8050-6602-0*, Metropolitan Bks.) Holt, Henry & Co.

Maugham, W. Somerset. Christmas Holiday. 2000. (Vintage International Ser.). 320p. pap. 13.00 (*0-375-72461-3*, Vintage) Knopf Publishing Group.

Maughon, Robert M. Elvis Is Alive. Maughon, Donna, ed. 1997. 24.95 (*0-9650366-1-8*); 2nd ed. 1999. 254p. pap. 19.95 (*0-9650366-2-6*) Cinnamon Moon.

Maupassant, Guy de. Maupassant: Contes. Jotcham, N., ed. 1984. (FRE.). 176p. pap. text 19.95 o.p. (*0-521-27135-5*) Cambridge Univ. Pr.

Maxwell, William. All the Days & Nights: The Collected Stories of William Maxwell. 1995. 432p. pap. 15.00 (*0-679-76102-0*, Vintage) Knopf Publishing Group.

—The Chateau. 1985. 416p. pap. 12.95 o.p. (*0-87923-600-0*) Godine, David R. Pub.

—The Chateau. 1995. (Vintage Bks.). 416p. pap. 19.00 (*0-679-76156-X*) Knopf, Alfred A. Inc.

Mayle, Peter. Anything Considered. abr. ed. 1996. audio 16.95 (*1-55927-390-9*, 394125) Audio Renaissance.

—Anything Considered. unabr. ed. 1996. audio 48.00 (*0-7366-3453-3*, 4097) Books on Tape, Inc.

—Anything Considered. l.t. ed. 1996. 614p. 23.00 o.p. (*0-7838-1685-5*, Macmillan Reference USA) Gale Group.

—Anything Considered. 1996. 352p. 23.00 (*0-679-44123-9*) Random Hse., Inc.

—Anything Considered: A Novel. 1997. 320p. pap. 13.00 (*0-679-76268-X*, Vintage) Knopf Publishing Group.

—Chasing Cezanne. l.t. ed. 1997. pap. 23.00 o.p. (*0-7838-8133-9*, Macmillan Reference USA) Gale Group.

—Chasing Cezanne. 1997. 295p. 23.00 (*0-679-45511-6*) Knopf, Alfred A. Inc.

—Chasing Cezanne. l.t. ed. 1997. 23.00 o.s.i (*0-679-77440-8*) Random Hse. Large Print.

—Chasing Cezanne. aut. ed. 1997. 23.00 o.p. (*0-676-53421-X*) Random Hse., Inc.

—Chasing Cezanne: A Novel. 1998. 304p. reprint ed. pap. 12.00 (*0-679-78120-X*, Vintage) Knopf Publishing Group.

—Chasing Cezanne: A Novel. l.t. ed. 1997. (Large Print Ser.). pap. 23.00 o.s.i (*0-679-77432-7*) Random Hse., Inc.

—A Dog's Life. unabr. collector's ed. 1997. audio 24.00 (*0-913369-75-6*, 4330) Books on Tape, Inc.

—A Dog's Life. 1996. (Illus.). 208p. pap. 12.00 (*0-679-76267-1*, Vintage) Knopf Publishing Group.

—A Dog's Life. 1995. 192p. 20.00 o.s.i (*0-679-44122-0*) Knopf, Alfred A. Inc.

—A Dog's Life, Set. abr. ed. 1995. audio 16.00 o.s.i (*0-679-44328-2*, RH Audio) Random Hse. Audio Publishing Group.

—Hotel Pastis: A Novel of Provence. 2000. (FRE.). pap. 15.95 (*2-02-030743-X*) Editions du Seuil FRA. *Dist:* Distribooks, Inc.

—Hotel Pastis: A Novel of Provence. 1994. 400p. pap. 14.00 (*0-679-75111-4*, Vintage) Knopf Publishing Group.

—Hotel Pastis: A Novel of Provence. 1993. 389p. 23.00 o.s.i (*0-679-40229-2*) Knopf, Alfred A. Inc.

—Hotel Pastis: A Novel of Provence, Set. abr. ed. 1993. audio 17.00 o.s.i (*0-679-42713-9*, 390938, RH Audio) Random Hse. Audio Publishing Group.

—Hotel Pastis: A Novel of Provence. unabr. ed. 1995. audio 78.00 (*0-7887-0087-1*, 94327E7) Recorded Bks., LLC.

McCann, Lee. Nostradamus: The Man Who Saw Through Time. 1982. (Illus.). 421p. 22.50 o.p. (*0-374-22317-3*); pap. 32.00 (*0-374-51754-1*) Farrar, Straus & Giroux.

—Nostradamus: The Man Who Saw Through Time. 1994. (Illus.). 448p. reprint ed. 9.99 (*0-517-43693-0*) Random Hse. Value Publishing.

McHugh, Frances Y. High on a Hill. l.t. ed. 2000. (G. K. Hall Paperback Ser.). 170p. pap. 23.95 (*0-7838-8938-0*, Macmillan Reference USA) Gale Group.

—Window on the Seine. l.t. ed. 2001. (Paperback Ser.). 191p. 23.95 (*0-7838-9345-0*) Thorndike Pr.

McIntyre, Vonda N. The Moon & the Sun. unabr. ed. 1999. audio 76.95 (*0-7861-1637-4*, 2465) Blackstone Audio Bks., Inc.

—The Moon & the Sun. 1998. 480p. pap. 6.99 (*0-671-56766-7*, Pocket); 1997. 432p. 23.00 o.s.i (*0-671-56765-9*, Atria) Simon & Schuster.

—The Moon & the Sun. l.t. ed. 1998. (Basic Ser.). 709p. 27.95 (*0-7862-1591-7*) Thorndike Pr.

—The Moon & the Sun. 1998. 13.04 (*0-606-19500-9*) Turtleback Bks.

McNab, Andy. Liberation Day. 2003. 368p. 25.00 (*0-7434-0630-3*); 25.00 (*0-7434-7717-0*) Simon & Schuster. (Atria).

—Liberation Day: A Nick Stone Mission. 400p. 2004. mass mkt. 7.99 (*0-7434-0631-1*); 2003. mass mkt. 7.99 (*0-7434-7437-6*) Simon & Schuster. (Pocket).

Meade, Marion. Stealing Heaven. 1985. 448p. pap. 2.95 o.p. (*0-380-50674-2*, 50674-2, Avon Bks.) Morrow/Avon.

—Stealing Heaven. 1994. (Hera Ser.). 415p. pap. 16.00 (*1-56947-011-1*) Soho Pr., Inc.

Medeiros, Teresa. Charming the Prince. 1999. 352p. mass mkt. 6.99 (*0-553-57502-3*) Bantam Bks.

Mehdi, Charef. Tea in the Harem. Emery, Ed, tr. from FRE. 1991. 160p. (Orig.). (*1-85242-151-7*) Serpent's Tail Ltd.

Meir Bar-Am. The Fateful Mission. 1986. 180p. 10.95 o.p. (*0-87306-420-8*) Feldheim, Philipp Inc.

Mendoza, George. Henri Mouse. 1986. (Picture Puffin Ser.). (Illus.). 32p. (J). (ps-3). pap. 3.95 o.p. (*0-14-050636-5*, Puffin Bks.) Penguin Putnam Bks. for Young Readers.

Merwin, W. S. The Lost Upland: Stories of Southwest France. 1993. 320p. pap. 14.95 o.p. (*0-8050-2593-6*, Owl Bks.) Holt, Henry & Co.

Messud, Claire. The Last Life. 2000. 400p. pap. 14.00 (*0-15-601165-4*, Harvest Bks.) Harcourt Trade Pubs.

—The Last Life: A Novel. 1999. 368p. 24.00 (*0-15-100471-4*, Harvest Bks.) Harcourt Trade Pubs.

Meyer, Nicholas. Canary Trainer: From the Memoirs of John H. Watson. 1995. 224p. pap. 10.95 (*0-393-31241-0*) Norton, W. W. & Co., Inc.

Meyer, Nicholas, ed. The Canary Trainer: From the Memoirs of John H. Watson. 1993. 224p. 19.95 o.p. (*0-393-03608-1*) Norton, W. W. & Co., Inc.

Miller, Alex. Conditions of Faith. 2002. 400p. reprint ed. pap. 13.95 (*0-425-18177-4*) Berkley Publishing Group.

—Conditions of Faith. 2000. (Illus.). 352p. 25.00 o.s.i (*0-684-86935-7*, Scribner) Simon & Schuster.

Millner, Denene & Chiles, Nick. Love Don't Live Here Anymore. 2002. 324p. 23.95 o.s.i (*0-525-94641-1*, Dutton) Dutton/Plume.

Minshull, Evelyn W. Madame Pastry & Meow. 1975. (Illus.). 176p. (J). (gr. 4-8). 5.95 o.p. (*0-664-32573-4*) Westminster John Knox Pr.

Modiano, Patrick. Honeymoon. Wright, Barbara, tr. from FRE. 1995. (Verba Mundi Ser.). 128p. 19.95 (*0-87923-947-6*) Godine, David R. Pub.

—Out of the Dark. Stump, Jordan, tr. from FRE. 1998. Orig. Title: Du Plus Loin de L'Oubli. 139p. text 50.00 (*0-8032-3196-2*) Univ. of Nebraska Pr.

Moinot, Pierre. As Night Follows Day. Gladding, Jody & Deshays, Elizabeth, trs. 2003. 224p. pap. 15.00 (*1-56649-257-2*) Welcome Rain Pubs.

—As Night Follows Day. Gladding, Jody, tr. from FRE. 2001. 224p. 24.95 o.p. (*1-56649-154-1*) Welcome Rain Pubs.

Mokeddem, Malika. Of Dreams & Assassins. Marcus, K. Melissa, tr. from FRE. 2000. (Caraf Bks.). 128p. 45.00 (*0-8139-1933-9*); pap. 16.95 (*0-8139-1994-0*) Univ. Pr. of Virginia.

Monarch Staff & Hugo, Victor. Les Miserables. (C). 3.95 (*0-671-00844-7*, Arco) Peterson's.

Monbrun, Estelle. Murder Chez Proust. 1996. 240p. pap. 10.95 (*1-55970-341-5*) Arcade Publishing, Inc.

—Murder Chez Proust. Martyn, David, tr. 1995. (ENG & FRE.). 240p. 19.95 (*1-55970-283-4*) Arcade Publishing, Inc.

Moody, Gregory A. Perfect Circles. 1998. 400p. pap. 12.95 (*1-884737-44-7*) VeloPress.

Moore, Brian. Cold Heaven. 1984. 256p. mass mkt. 2.95 o.s.i (*0-449-20602-5*, Fawcett) Ballantine Bks.

—The Statement. 2003. 224p. pap. 19.95 (*0-394-28199-3*, Plume); 1997. 256p. pap. 13.00 (*0-452-27632-2*, Plume); 1996. 256p. 22.95 o.p. (*0-525-94128-2*, Dutton) Dutton/Plume.

—The Statement. unabr. ed. 1998. audio 44.00 (*0-7887-1311-6*, 95085E7) Recorded Bks., LLC.

Moore, Madeline. As You Desire. 1993. 180p. (Orig.). pap. 9.95 (*0-933216-95-5*) Spinsters Ink Bks.

Moore, Viviane. A Black Romance. 2002. (Illus.). 197p. mass mkt. 7.95 (*0-7528-4417-2*) Trafalgar Square.

—Blue Blood. 2002. (Illus.). v, 215p. mass mkt. 7.95 (*0-575-40319-5*) Trafalgar Square.

—The Darkest Red. 2002. (Illus.). 230p. mass mkt. 7.95 (*0-7528-4475-X*) Trafalgar Square.

—The White Path. Hunter, Adriana, tr. from FRE. 2003. (Illus.). 226p. pap. 13.95 (*0-575-07327-6*) Orion Publishing Group, Ltd. GBR. *Dist:* Trafalgar Square.

Morand, Paul. Green Shoots. 1977. (Short Story Index Reprint Ser.). reprint ed. 17.95 (*0-8369-3850-X*) Ayer Co. Pubs., Inc.

Morazzoni, Marta. The Invention of Truth. 1995. Tr. of Invenzione della Verita. pap. 10.00 o.p. (*0-88001-376-1*) HarperCollins Pubs.

—The Invention of Truth. Fitzgerald, M. J., tr. from ITA. 1993. Tr. of Invenzione della Verita. 99p. 18.00 o.s.i (*0-394-58088-5*) Knopf, Alfred A. Inc.

Morgenstern, Susie. Secret Letters from 0 to 10. Rosner, Gill, tr. 1998. 208p. (J). (gr. 4-7). 16.99 (*0-670-88007-8*, Viking) Penguin Putnam Bks. for Young Readers.

Morris, Gilbert. Flying Cavalier. 1999. (House of Winslow Ser.: Vol. 23). 320p. pap. 11.99 (*0-7642-2115-9*) Bethany Hse. Pubs.

Moseley, Margaret. Bonita Faye. 1997. 240p. mass mkt. 5.99 o.s.i (*0-06-101189-4*, HarperTorch) Morrow/Avon.

—Bonita Faye. l.t. ed. 2001. (G. K. Hall Paperback Ser.). 307p. 24.95 (*0-7838-9378-7*) Thorndike Pr.

—Bonita Faye. 1996. 178p. 20.00 (*0-9637629-4-X*) Three Forks Pr.

Musser, Elizabeth. Two Testaments. 1997. 450p. pap. 11.99 o.p. (*1-56476-610-1*) Cook Communications Ministries.

Myers, Tamar. The Crepes of Wrath. 2002. 272p. mass mkt. 5.99 (*0-451-20322-4*) NAL.

Newman, Sharan. Death Comes As Epiphany. 1995. 322p. mass mkt. 5.99 (*0-8125-2293-1*, Forge Bks.); 1993. 320p. 19.95 (*0-312-85419-6*, Tor Bks.); 2002. reprint ed. pap. 14.95 (*0-7653-0374-4*, Forge Bks.) Doherty, Tom Assocs., LLC.

—The Devil's Door. 1995. 416p. mass mkt. 6.99 (*0-8125-2295-8*); 1994. 384p. 21.95 o.p. (*0-312-85420-X*) Doherty, Tom Assocs., LLC. (Forge Bks.).

—Strong As Death. unabr. collector's ed. 1999. (Catherine LeVendeur Ser.: 4). audio 72.00 (*0-7366-4862-3*, 5189) Books on Tape, Inc.

—Strong As Death. (Catherine Levendeur Mystery Ser.). 384p. 1997. mass mkt. 5.99 (*0-8125-3935-4*); 1996. 23.95 o.p. (*0-312-86179-6*) Doherty, Tom Assocs., LLC. (Forge Bks.).

—The Wandering Arm. 2001. pap. 14.95 (*0-312-87733-1*); 1996. 372p. mass mkt. 5.99 (*0-8125-5089-7*); 1995. 352p. 23.95 o.p. (*0-312-85829-9*) Doherty, Tom Assocs., LLC. (Forge Bks.).

Nimier, Marie. The Giraffe. Feeney, Mary, tr. 1995. 208p. 18.00 (*1-56858-026-6*) Four Walls Eight Windows.

Noah, Robert. The Man Who Stole the Mona Lisa. 1998. 256p. 22.95 o.p. (*0-312-16916-7*) St. Martin's Pr.

Nordhoff, Charles & Hall, James Norman. Falcons of France. 21.95 (*0-89190-232-5*) Amereon, Ltd.

—Falcons of France. Gilbert, James B., ed. 1980. (Flight). (Illus.). reprint ed. lib. bdg. 33.95 (*0-405-12198-9*) Ayer Co. Pubs., Inc.

Nothomb, Amelie. The Stranger Next Door. Volk, Carol, tr. 1998. Tr. of Catilinaires. 160p. 20.00 o.s.i (*0-8050-4841-3*) Holt, Henry & Co.

O'Brien, Charles. Mute Witness. 2002. pap. 14.95 (*1-890208-75-2*); 2001. (Illus.). 325p. 23.95 (*1-890208-62-0*) Poisoned Pen Pr.

O'Faolain, Julia. Women in the Wall. 1988. pap. 8.95 o.p. (*0-88184-442-X*, Carroll & Graf Pubs.) Avalon Publishing Group.

—Women in the Wall. 1981. pap. 1.75 o.p. (*0-380-00592-1*, 28811, Avon Bks.) Morrow/Avon.

—Women in the Wall. 1987. o.s.i (*0-86068-442-3*) Random Hse., Inc.

—Women in the Wall. 1975. 7.95 o.p. (*0-670-77853-2*) Viking Penguin.

O'Grady, Myles. Colonfay. 2000. 263p. 25.00 (*1-57962-068-X*) Permanent Pr., The.

Ollier, Claude. Disconnection. Di Bernardi, Dominic, tr. from FRE. 1989. 130p. 19.95 (*0-916583-47-3*) Dalkey Archive Pr.

Orczy, Baroness Emmuska. Adventures of the Scarlet Pimpernel. 1983. 321p. reprint ed. lib. bdg. 35.95 (*0-89966-459-8*) Buccaneer Bks., Inc.

—Eldorado. lib. bdg. 22.95 (*0-8488-2010-X*) Amereon, Ltd.

—Eldorado. 1980. 435p. reprint ed. lib. bdg. 35.95 (*0-89968-195-6*, Lightyear Pr.) Buccaneer Bks., Inc.

—The Elusive Pimpernel. 288p. 23.95 (*0-8488-2521-7*) Amereon, Ltd.

—The Elusive Pimpernel. unabr. ed. 1998. audio 49.95 (*0-7861-1279-4*, 2169) Blackstone Audio Bks., Inc.

—The Elusive Pimpernel. 1984. 419p. lib. bdg. 35.95 (*0-89966-488-1*); 1976. lib. bdg. 31.95 o.p. (*0-89968-073-9*, Lightyear Pr.) Buccaneer Bks., Inc.

—I Will Repay. unabr. ed. 1994. audio 44.95 (*0-7861-0778-2*, 1506) Blackstone Audio Bks., Inc.

Settings

Settings

—I Will Repay. 2000. 192p. reprint ed. 29.95 (*1-56849-732-6*) Buccaneer Bks., Inc.
—The League of the Scarlet Pimpernel. Date not set. 282p. 23.95 (*0-8488-2377-X*) Amereon, Ltd.
—The League of the Scarlet Pimpernel. 1981. 238p. reprint ed. lib. bdg. 35.95 (*0-89966-286-2*) Buccaneer Bks., Inc.
—Lord Tony's Wife. 1986. (gr. 4-7). reprint ed. lib. bdg. 37.95 (*0-89966-553-5*) Buccaneer Bks., Inc.
—Pimpernel & Rosemary. 312p. 24.95 (*0-8488-2543-8*) Amereon, Ltd.
—Pimpernel & Rosemary. 1996. 37.95 (*0-89966-462-8*) Buccaneer Bks., Inc.
—The Scarlet Pimpernel. 1964. (Airmont Classics Ser.). (J). (gr. 7 up). mass mkt. 2.95 o.p. (*0-8049-0028-0*, CL-28) Airmont Publishing Co., Inc.
—The Scarlet Pimpernel. 20.95 (*0-8488-0601-8*) Amereon, Ltd.
—The Scarlet Pimpernel. 1994. (Illustrated Classics Collection). 64p. pap. 3.60 o.p. (*1-56103-606-4*); pap. 4.95 (*0-7854-0755-3*, 40518) American Guidance Service, Inc.
—The Scarlet Pimpernel. 1987. audio 41.95 (*1-55685-110-3*) Audio Bk. Contractors, Inc.
—The Scarlet Pimpernel. 1992. (Bantam Classics Ser.). 272p. mass mkt. 4.95 (*0-553-21402-0*, Bantam Classics) Bantam Bks.
—The Scarlet Pimpernel, unabr. ed. 1982. audio 49.95 (*0-7861-0524-0*, 2023) Blackstone Audio Bks., Inc.
—The Scarlet Pimpernel. unabr. ed. 1983. (J). audio 56.00 (*0-7366-3882-2*, 9106) Books on Tape, Inc.
—The Scarlet Pimpernel. unabr. ed. 1999. (Bookcassette Classic Collection). audio 57.25 (*1-56740-678-5*, 1807, Unabridged Library Editions); audio 17.95 (*1-56740-452-9*, 1806, Bookcassette) Brilliance Audio.
—The Scarlet Pimpernel. 1976. lib. bdg. 21.95 o.p. (*0-89968-072-0*, Lightyear Pr.); 1984. 256p. reprint ed. lib. bdg. 21.95 (*0-89966-508-X*) Buccaneer Bks., Inc.
—The Scarlet Pimpernel. abr. ed. (Read-Along Ser.). 1994. pap. 29.99 incl. audio (*0-88646-844-2*, LSR 7268); 1990. audio 16.99 (*0-88646-268-1*, 7268) Durkin Hayes Publishing Ltd.
—The Scarlet Pimpernel. E-Book 2.49 (*1-58627-775-8*) Electric Umbrella Publishing.
—The Scarlet Pimpernel. (Reader's Request Ser.). 1984. lib. bdg. 12.95 o.p. (*0-8161-3077-9*, Macmillan Reference USA); 2002. 437p. 28.95 (*0-7862-4012-1*) Gale Group.
—The Scarlet Pimpernel. abr. ed. audio 12.95 o.p. (*0-694-50950-7*, SWC 1647, Caedmon) HarperTrade.
—The Scarlet Pimpernel. unabr. ed. 1984. audio 56.00 Jimcin Recordings.
—The Scarlet Pimpernel. 1999. 320p. (gr. 8-12). 14.95 (*0-375-40658-1*) Knopf, Alfred A. Inc.
—The Scarlet Pimpernel. l.t. ed. 2002. (LRS Large Print Heritage Ser.). lib. bdg. 34.95 (*1-58118-093-4*) LRS.
—The Scarlet Pimpernel. E-Book 1.95 (*1-58515-047-9*) MesaView, Inc.
—The Scarlet Pimpernel. 2000. (Signet Classics). 288p. mass mkt. 4.95 (*0-451-52762-3*, Signet Bks.) NAL.
—The Scarlet Pimpernel. abr. ed. 1995. (Classic, Ultimate, Dove Ser.). (gr. 4-7). audio 19.95 o.p. (*1-55800-924-8*, 692917, Dove Audio) NewStar Media, Inc.
—The Scarlet Pimpernel. 2000. (Twelve-Point Ser.). 245p. reprint ed. lib. bdg. 24.00 o.p. (*1-58287-122-1*) North Bks.
—The Scarlet Pimpernel. 1985. 11.95 (*0-396-08690-X*, G. P. Putnam's Sons) Penguin Putnam Bks. for Young Readers.
—The Scarlet Pimpernel, 2000. (YA). pap., stu. ed. 73.20 incl. audio (*0-7887-3191-2*, 40926X4) Recorded Bks., LLC.
—The Scarlet Pimpernel. 1998. 304p. pap. 12.95 (*0-89526-365-3*, Gateway Editions) Regnery Publishing, Inc., An Eagle Publishing Co.
—The Scarlet Pimpernel. abr. ed. 1982. (Radio Ser.). audio 7.95 o.p. (*0-88142-412-9*) Soundelux Audio Publishing.
—The Scarlet Pimpernel. abr. ed. 1998. mass mkt. 16.95 incl. audio (*1-85998-958-6*) Trafalgar Square.
—The Scarlet Pimpernel. 1974. 11.00 (*0-606-00955-8*) Turtleback Bks.
—The Scarlet Pimpernel & Other Tales. Wellborn, Sandra, ed. 2000. cd-rom 9.95 (*1-930430-02-7*) Waltsan Publishing, LLC.
—Sir Percy Hits Back. 2000. 320p. reprint ed. 37.95 (*1-56849-733-4*) Buccaneer Bks., Inc.
—Sir Percy Leads the Band. 2002. reprint ed. lib. bdg. 35.95 (*1-56849-737-7*) Buccaneer Bks., Inc.
—The Triumph of the Scarlet Pimpernel. 320p. 24.95 (*0-8488-2557-8*) Amereon, Ltd.
—The Triumph of the Scarlet Pimpernel. 1983. 321p. reprint ed. lib. bdg. 35.95 (*0-89966-460-1*) Buccaneer Bks., Inc.
—The Triumph of the Scarlet Pimpernel. abr. ed. pap. incl. audio (*1-85998-959-4*) Hodder Children's Audio.
—The Triumph of the Scarlet Pimpernel. abr. ed. 1999. audio 16.85 (*1-84032-118-0*) Hodder Headline Audiobooks GBR. *Dist:* Ulverscroft Large Print Bks., Ltd.
—The Way of the Scarlet Pimpernel. 24.95 (*0-8488-1442-8*) Amereon, Ltd.
—The Way of the Scarlet Pimpernel. 1983. 318p. reprint ed. lib. bdg. 37.95 (*0-89966-461-X*) Buccaneer Bks., Inc.
Pagano, Emma Maria. Heart of a Girl. 2003. Orig. Title: Si Accade Il 2 Gennaio. (ITA.). 21.95 (*0-9729518-1-4*, Olive Tree Bks.) El Paso City Bks., LLC.
Page, Katherine Hall. The Body in the Vestibule. l.t. ed. 2000. (Beeler Large Print Mystery Ser.). 223p. 26.95 (*1-57490-318-7*, Beeler Large Print Bks.) Beeler, Thomas T. Publisher.
—The Body in the Vestibule. 1993. 352p. mass mkt. 6.99 (*0-380-72079-5*, Avon Bks.) Morrow/Avon.
—The Body in the Vestibule. 1992. 234p. 17.95 o.p. (*0-312-08148-0*, Saint Martin's Minotaur) St. Martin's Pr.
Pagnol, Marcel. Jean de Florette, Level C. 2000. (FRE.). (YA). (gr. 7-12). text 8.95 (*0-8219-1851-6*, 40338) EMC/Paradigm Publishing.
—Jean de Florette. (FRE.). pap. 16.50 (*2-87706-054-3*) Editions de Fallois FRA. *Dist:* Distribooks, Inc.
—Jean de Florette. 1988. (FRE.). 318p. pap. 13.95 (*0-7859-1668-7*, 2877060543); 1976. (FRE.). 320p. 13.95 (*0-8288-9893-6*, F117460); Tome I. 19.95 French & European Pubns., Inc.
—Jean de Florette & Manon des Sources. abr. ed. 1995. audio 29.95 o.p. (*1-85998-299-9*) Trafalgar Square.
—Jean de Florette & Manon of the Springs. Van Heyningen, W. E., tr. from FRE. 1988. (Illus.). 448p. pap. 16.00 o.s.i (*0-86547-312-9*, North Point Pr.) Farrar, Straus & Giroux.
—Jean de Florette & Manon of the Springs: Two Novels. Van Heyningen, W. E., tr. from FRE. 1988. 448p. 30.00 o.p. (*0-86547-311-0*, North Point Pr.) Farrar, Straus & Giroux.
—Manon des Sources. (FRE.). pap. 16.50 (*2-87706-055-1*) Editions de Fallois FRA. *Dist:* Distribooks, Inc.
—Manon des Sources. 1988. (FRE.). 318p. pap. 13.95 (*0-7859-1657-1*, 2877060551); 1976. (FRE.). 320p. 13.95 (*0-8288-9894-4*, F117461); Tome II. 19.95 French & European Pubns., Inc.
Palmer, Diana. Once in Paris. unabr. ed. 1998. audio 7.99 (*1-55204-159-X*, MIR-1159) Durkin Hayes Publishing Ltd.
—Once in Paris. l.t. ed. 2002. pap. 24.95 (*1-58724-233-8*, Wheeler Publishing, Inc.) Gale Group.
—Once in Paris. 1998. 377p. mass mkt. o.s.i (*1-55166-470-4*, 1-66470-5, Mira Bks.) Harlequin Enterprises, Ltd.
Palmer, Frank. Blood Brother. l.t. ed. 1995. 282p. pap. 20.95 o.p. (*0-7838-1544-1*, Macmillan Reference USA) Gale Group.
—Blood Brother: An Inspector "Jacko" Jackson Mystery. 1995. 192p. 19.95 o.p. (*0-312-13435-5*, Saint Martin's Minotaur) St. Martin's Pr.
Patterson, James & Gross, Andrew. The Jester. 2003. 464p. 27.95 (*0-316-60205-1*); 656p. 27.95 (*0-316-14787-7*) Little Brown & Co.
—The Jester. abr. ed. 2003. audio 31.98 (*1-58621-536-1*) Time Warner AudioBooks.
—The Jester. 2003. E-Book 15.95 (*0-7595-8751-5*); E-Book 15.95 (*0-7595-4744-0*) Time Warner Bk. Group.
—The Jester. 2003. 464p. pap. 16.00 (*0-446-69051-1*) Warner Bks., Inc.
Paul, Elliot. Hugger-Mugger in the Louvre: A Homer Evans Murder Mystery. 1986. viii, 328p. reprint ed. pap. 5.95 o.p. (*0-486-25185-3*) Dover Pubns., Inc.
—Mayhem in B-Flat: A Homer Evans Murder Mystery. 1988. 320p. reprint ed. pap. 6.95 (*0-486-25621-9*) Dover Pubns., Inc.
—The Mysterious Mickey Finn. 1984. 256p. reprint ed. pap. 5.95 o.p. (*0-486-24751-1*) Dover Pubns., Inc.
Paulson, Michael G. & Alvarez-Detrell, Tamara. Madame de la Fayette's The Princess of Cleves: A New Translation. 1994. 196p. (Orig.). 41.00 (*0-8191-9732-7*) Univ. Pr. of America.
Pavillon, Fernand. The Stones of the Abbey. 1976. pap. 1.95 o.p. (*0-380-00737-1*, 30106, Avon Bks.) Morrow/Avon.
Pawel, Rebecca. Law of Return. 2004. 288p. 24.00 (*1-56947-343-9*) Soho Pr., Inc.
Pears, Iain. The Dream of Scipio. 2003. 400p. pap. (*0-676-97292-6*, Vintage) Knopf Publishing Group.
—The Dream of Scipio. 2002. (Illus.). 608p. 27.99 o.s.i (*1-57322-202-X*, Riverhead Bks. (Hardcovers)) Putnam Publishing Group, The.
Pemberton, Margaret. Lion of Languedoc. l.t. ed. 2001. (Dales Large Print Ser.). 228p. pap. 21.99 (*1-84262-099-1*) Dales Large Print Bks. GBR. *Dist:* Ulverscroft Large Print Bks., Ltd., Ulverscroft Large Print Canada, Ltd.
Petsinis, Tom. The French Mathematician. 2000. 426p. pap. 13.95 o.s.i (*0-425-17291-0*) Berkley Publishing Group.
—The French Mathematician. 1998. 400p. reprint ed. 24.00 (*0-8027-1345-9*) Walker & Co.
The Phantom of the Opera. 1998. 16p. pap. 6.95 (*0-7935-9664-5*) Leonard, Hal Corp.
Piercy, Marge. City of Darkness, City of Light. 1997. 496p. pap. 14.95 (*0-449-91275-2*, Fawcett) Ballantine Bks.
Pineiro, R. J. Breakthrough. unabr. ed. 1999. audio 56.95 (*0-7861-1283-2*, 2178) Blackstone Audio Bks., Inc.
—Breakthrough. 1999. 381p. mass mkt. 6.99 (*0-8125-4390-4*, Tor Bks.); 1997. 384p. 23.95 o.p. (*0-312-85983-X*, Forge Bks.) Doherty, Tom Assocs., LLC.
Plaidy, Jean. Mary, Queen of France. 2003. 304p. pap. 12.95 (*0-609-81021-9*, Three Rivers Pr.) Crown Publishing Group.
Poe, Edgar Allan. The Murders in the Rue Morgue. 1985. audio Dercum Audio.
—The Murders in the Rue Morgue. 1984. audio; 1977. audio 7.95 Jimcin Recordings.
—The Murders in the Rue Morgue. 1998. (Cloth Bound Pocket Ser.). 240p. 7.95 (*3-89508-090-X*, 520019) Konemann.
—The Murders in the Rue Morgue. 1977. (American Classics). (gr. 9-12). pap. 9.08 o.p. (*0-88343-404-0*) McDougal Littell Inc.
—The Murders in the Rue Morgue. 1996. (Classic Ser.). 64p. pap. 0.95 o.p. (*0-14-600191-5*) Penguin Group (USA) Inc.
—The Murders in the Rue Morgue. 1981. audio Recorded Bks., LLC.
—The Murders in the Rue Morgue. (Radio Ser.). audio 7.95 o.p. (*0-88142-430-7*, 126) Soundelux Audio Publishing.
—The Murders in the Rue Morgue & Other Stories. unabr. collector's ed. 1992. audio 30.00 (*0-7366-2189-X*, 2984) Books on Tape, Inc.
—The Murders in the Rue Morgue & Other Stories. 1999. 322p. pap. 7.95 (*1-902058-02-X*) Pulp Fictions GBR. *Dist:* 7 Hills Bk. Distributors.
—The Murders in the Rue Morgue & Other Tales. l.t. ed. 1997. (Murders in the Rue Morgue & Other Tales Ser.: Vol. 2). 240p. text 22.95 (*1-56000-535-1*) Transaction Pubs.
—The Purloined Letter. 1985. audio Dercum Audio.
—The Purloined Letter. 1984. audio; 1977. audio Jimcin Recordings.
—The Purloined Letter. 1980. audio Random Hse. Audio Publishing Group.
Pouillon, Fernand. The Stones of the Abbey. Gillot, Edward, tr. from FRE. 1985. (Illus.). 218p. pap. 15.00 (*0-15-685100-8*, Harvest Bks.); 1970. 5.95 o.p. (*0-15-185075-5*) Harcourt Trade Pubs.
Proctor, Candice E. The Last Knight. 2000. 416p. mass mkt. 6.99 (*0-8041-1930-9*, Ivy Bks.) Ballantine Bks.
—The Last Knight. l.t. ed. 2001. (Large Print Book Ser.). 475p. pap. 23.95 (*1-58724-019-X*, Wheeler Publishing, Inc.) Gale Group.
Proust, Marcel. A la Recherche du Temps Perdu, 4 vols. Tadie, Jean-Yves, ed. Vol. 1. 1987. lib. bdg. 145.00 (*0-7859-3879-6*); Vol. 2. 1988. (FRE.). lib. bdg. 145.00 (*0-7859-3882-6*); Vol. 3. 1988. (FRE.). lib. bdg. 150.00 (*0-7859-3884-2*); Vol. 4. 1989. (FRE.). lib. bdg. 155.00 (*0-7859-3886-9*) French & European Pubns., Inc.
— A la Recherche du Temps Perdu. Brookes, H. F. & Fraenkel, C. E., eds. 1954. pap. text 3.25 o.p. (*0-435-37100-2*) Heinemann.
— A la Recherche du Temps Perdu. 2000. (FRE.). 41p. (*0-330-37576-8*) Picador.
— A la Recherche du Temps Perdu. deluxe ed. (Pleiade Ser.). (FRE.). Vol. 1. 1969. 400p. 89.95 (*2-07-011126-1*); Vol. 2. 1969. 376p. 89.95 (*2-07-011136-9*); Vol. 3. 1969. 488p. 89.95 (*2-07-011143-1*); Vol. 4. 1989. 504p. 89.95 (*2-07-011164-4*) Schoenhof's Foreign Bks., Inc.
—The Captive. 1987. reprint ed. lib. bdg. 22.95 o.p. (*0-89966-582-9*) Buccaneer Bks., Inc.
—The Captive. Moncrieff, C. Scott, tr. 1970. pap. 4.95 o.p. (*0-394-70598-X*) Random Hse., Inc.
—The Captive & the Fugitive. (Modern Library Ser.). E-Book 7.95 (*1-931208-84-0*) Adobe Systems, Inc.
—The Captive & the Fugitive. 1999. (In Search of Lost Time Ser.: Vol. V). 992p. pap. 13.95 (*0-375-75311-7*, Modern Library) Random House Adult Trade Publishing Group.
—Cities of the Plain. 1988. reprint ed. lib. bdg. 23.95 o.p. (*0-89966-583-7*) Buccaneer Bks., Inc.
—Cities of the Plain. Scott-Moncrieff, C. K., tr. 1970. pap. 4.95 o.p. (*0-394-70597-1*, Vintage) Knopf Publishing Group.
—Combray. Bree, Germaine & Lynes, Carlos, Jr., eds. 1952. (FRE.). 252p. (Orig.). (C). pap. 25.60 (*0-13-152439-9*, Prentice Hall) Prentice Hall PTR.
—Combray. Hodson, L., ed. 1996. (French Texts). (FRE.). pap. 20.95 (*1-85399-456-1*) Bristol Classical Pr. GBR. *Dist:* Focus Publishing/R. Pullins Co., Inc.
—La Fugitive. 1986. (FRE.). pap. 16.95 (*0-7859-3399-9*) French & European Pubns., Inc.
—The Guermantes Way. (Modern Library Ser.). E-Book 7.95 (*1-931208-82-4*) Adobe Systems, Inc.
—The Guermantes Way. Scott-Moncrieff, C. K., tr. 1970. pap. 5.95 o.p. (*0-394-70596-3*, Vintage) Knopf Publishing Group.
—The Guermantes Way. Moncrieff, C. K. Scott, tr. abr. ed. (Remembrance of Things Past Ser.: Vol. V). 1997. audio 17.98 (*962-634-616-7*, NA311614); 1997. audio compact disk 19.98 (*962-634-116-5*, NA311612); Pt. 2. 1998. audio 17.98 (*962-634-641-8*, NA314114); Pt. 2. 1997. audio compact disk 19.98 (*962-634-141-6*, NA314112) Naxos of America, Inc. (Naxos AudioBooks).
—The Guermantes Way. Treharne, Mark, tr. 2004. 640p. 29.95 (*0-670-03317-0*) Viking Penguin.
—In Search of Lost Time. 2000. Vol. I. E-Book 7.95 (*0-679-64178-5*); Vol. III. E-Book 7.95 (*0-679-64180-7*); Vol. IV. E-Book 7.95 (*0-679-64181-5*) Random House Adult Trade Publishing Group. (Modern Library).
—In Search of Lost Time, 6 vols., Set. Incl. Captive & the Fugitive. 992p. 1999. pap. 13.95 (*0-375-75311-7*); Guermantes Way. 864p. 1998. pap. 13.95 (*0-375-75233-1*); Sodom & Gomorrah. 784p. 1999. pap. 13.95 (*0-375-75310-9*); Swann's Way. 656p. 1998. pap. 11.95 (*0-375-75154-8*); Time Regained. 784p. 1999. pap. 14.95 (*0-375-75312-5*); . Within a Budding Grove. 784p. 1998. pap. 13.95 (*0-375-75219-6*); 2003. 75.00 (*0-8129-6964-2*, Modern Library) Random House Adult Trade Publishing Group.
—In Search of Lost Time: The Captive & the Fugitive. 1993. (Modern Library Ser.: Vol. V). 976p. 24.95 (*0-679-42477-6*, Modern Library) Random House Adult Trade Publishing Group.
—In Search of Lost Time: Time Regained-The Guide to Proust. Mayor, Andreas & Kilmartin, Terence, trs. 1993. (Modern Library Ser.: No. VI). 768p. 26.95 (*0-679-42476-8*, Modern Library) Random House Adult Trade Publishing Group.
—In Search of Lost Time Vol. 1: Swann's Way. Scott-Moncrieff, C. K. & Kilmartin, Terence, trs. from FRE. 1992. (Modern Library Ser.: Vol. 1). 640p. 21.95 (*0-679-60005-1*) Random Hse., Inc.
—In Search of Lost Time Vol. 2: Within a Budding Grove. Scott-Moncrieff, C. K. & Kilmartin, Terence, trs. from FRE. 1992. (Modern Library Ser.: ). 768p. 24.95 (*0-679-60006-X*) Random Hse., Inc.
—In Search of Lost Time Vol. II: Within a Budding Grove. 2000. E-Book 7.95 (*0-679-64179-3*, Modern Library) Random House Adult Trade Publishing Group.
—In Search of Lost Time Vol. III: The Guermantes Way. Scott-Moncrieff, C. K. & Kilmartin, Terence, trs. 1993. (Modern Library Ser.: ). (Illus.). 864p. 24.95 (*0-679-60028-0*) Random Hse., Inc.
—In Search of Lost Time Vol. IV: Sodom & Gomorrah. Scott-Moncrieff, C. K. & Kilmartin, Terence, trs. 1993. (Modern Library Ser.: Vol. 4). 768p. 24.95 (*0-679-60029-9*) Random Hse., Inc.
—In the Shadow of Young Girls in Flower. Grieve, James, tr. 2004. 576p. 27.95 (*0-670-03277-8*) Viking Penguin.
—Past Recaptured. Mayor, Andreas, tr. 1971. pap. 5.95 o.p. (*0-394-74600-7*); 1970. 10.00 o.p. (*0-394-43989-9*) Random Hse., Inc.
—Remembrance of Things Past, Vol. 2. 1982. 1216p. pap. 22.00 (*0-394-71183-1*, Vintage) Knopf Publishing Group.
—Remembrance of Things Past, 3 vols., Vol. 3. Scott-Moncrieff, C. K. et al, trs. from FRE. 1982. (Remembrance of Things Past Boxed Set Ser.: Vol. 3). (C). 64.00 (*0-394-71243-9*, Vintage) Knopf Publishing Group.
—Remembrance of Things Past. 1934. 50.00 o.p. (*0-394-44254-7*); 2. 1981. 25.00 o.s.i (*0-394-50645-6*) Random Hse., Inc.
—Remembrance of Things Past. Scott-Moncrieff, C. K., tr. 1981. 3. 25.00 o.s.i (*0-394-50646-4*); Set. 75.00 o.s.i (*0-394-50643-X*) Random Hse., Inc.
—Remembrance of Things Past. 1934. Vol. 1. o.p. (*0-394-44255-5*); Vol. 2. o.p. (*0-394-44256-3*) Random Hse., Inc.
—Remembrance of Things Past Vol. III: The Captive, The Fugitive, Time Regained. 1982. (Captive the Fugitive Time Ser.: Vol. III). 1152p. pap. 22.00 (*0-394-71184-X*, Vintage) Knopf Publishing Group.
—Sodom & Gomorrah: Cities of the Plain. Moncrieff, C. K. Scott, tr. abr. ed. (Remembrance of Things Past Ser.: Vol. VII). 1998. audio 17.98 (*962-634-661-2*, NA316114); 1998. audio compact disk 19.98 (*962-634-161-0*, NA316112); Pt. 2. 1999. audio 17.98 (*962-634-667-1*, NA316714); Pt. 2. 1999. audio compact disk 19.98 (*962-634-167-X*, NA316712) Naxos of America, Inc. (Naxos AudioBooks).

—Swann's Way. (Modern Library Ser.). E-Book 7.95 (*1-931208-80-8*); E-Book 7.95 (*1-931208-81-6*) Adobe Systems, Inc.
—Swann's Way. unabr. ed. 1999. (Remembrance of Things Past Ser.: Pt. 1). (C). audio 77.95 (*1-55685-607-5*) Audio Bk. Contractors, Inc.
—Swann's Way, Vol. 1. Moncrieff, C. K. Scott & Moncrieff, Mona, trs. from FRE. unabr. ed. 1999. (Remembrance of Things Past Ser.). audio 49.95 (*1-57270-092-0*, F91092u, Cover to Cover Classics) Audio Partners Publishing Corp.
—Swann's Way. 1986. reprint ed. lib. bdg. 21.95 (*0-89966-581-0*) Buccaneer Bks., Inc.
—Swann's Way. Scott-Moncrieff, C. K., tr. from FRE. 2002. (Dover Thrift Editions Ser.). vi, 377p. pap. 3.50 (*0-486-42123-6*) Dover Pubns., Inc.
—Swann's Way. Scott-Moncrieff, C. K. & Kilmartin, Terence, trs. 1989. (Vintage International Ser.). 496p. pap. 12.00 (*0-679-72009-X*, Vintage) Knopf Publishing Group.
—Swann's Way. Scott-Moncrieff, C. K., tr. 1964. 551p. (C). pap. 11.25 (*0-07-553647-1*, T67, McGraw-Hill Humanities, Social Sciences & World Languages) McGraw-Hill Higher Education.
—Swann's Way. Moncrieff, C. K. Scott, tr. abr. ed. (Remembrance of Things Past Ser.: Vol. I). 1996. audio 17.98 (*962-634-553-5*, NA305314); 1995. audio compact disk 19.98 (*962-634-053-3*, NA305312) Naxos of America, Inc. (Naxos AudioBooks).
—Swann's Way. Scott-Moncrieff, C. K. & Kilmartin, Terence, trs. 1982. 1056p. pap. 20.00 (*0-394-71182-3*) Random Hse., Inc.
—Swann's Way. 1978. 6.95 o.s.i (*0-394-60429-6*) Random Hse., Inc.
—Swann's Way. Moncrieff, C. Scott, tr. 1970. pap. 4.95 o.p. (*0-394-70594-7*) Random Hse., Inc.
—Swann's Way, Scott-Moncrieff, C. K. & Kilmartin, Torence, trs. unabr. ed. 1999. audio 128.00 (*0-7887-2186-0*, 95482E7) Recorded Bks., LLC.
—Swann's Way. abr. ed. 2000. audio 22.95 (*0-00-105213-6*) Trafalgar Square.
—Swann's Way. Davis, Lydia, tr. from FRE. 2003. 496p. 27.95 (*0-670-03245-X*) Viking Penguin.
—Swann's Way. Kilmartin, Terence & Mancrief, C. K. Scott, trs. from FRE. 1998. (Twentieth Century Classics Ser.). 224p. 12.95 (*0-14-118058-7*, Penguin Classics) Viking Penguin.
—Swann's Way. abr. ed. 2015. audio 24.95 (*0-14-086751-1*, Penguin AudioBooks) Viking Penguin.
—Swann's Way: Within a Budding Grove. 1981. (Remembrance of Things Past Ser.: Vol. 1). 25.00 o.s.i (*0-394-50644-8*) Random Hse., Inc.
—The Sweet Cheat Gone. Moncrieff, C. Scott, tr. 1970. pap. 4.65 o.s.i (*0-394-70599-8*) Random Hse., Inc.
—Time Regained. 1999. (In Search of Lost Time Ser.: Vol. VI). 784p. pap. 14.95 (*0-375-75312-5*, Modern Library) Random House Adult Trade Publishing Group.
—Within a Budding Grove. Moncrieff, C. K. Scott, tr. abr. ed. 1996. (Remembrance of Things Past Ser.: Vol. III). audio 17.98 (*962-634-588-8*, NA308814); audio compact disk 19.98 (*962-634-088-6*, NA308812);Pt. 2. audio 17.98 (*962-634-606-X*, NA310614);Pt. 2. audio compact disk 19.98 (*962-634-106-8*, NA310612) Naxos of America, Inc. (Naxos AudioBooks).
—Within a Budding Grove. Moncrieff, C. Scott, tr. 1970. pap. 5.95 o.p. (*0-394-70595-5*) Random Hse., Inc.
The Purloined Letter & Other Works. abr. ed. Incl. Dream Within a Dream. audio Ulalume. audio Valley of Unrest. audio 1984. Set audio 9.95 (*1-55994-101-4*, CPN 1288, Caedmon) HarperTrade.
Raczymow, Henri. Writing the Book of Esther. Katz, Dori, tr. from FRE. 1995. (French Expressions Ser.). 220p. 24.00 (*0-8419-1335-8*) Holmes & Meier Pubs., Inc.
Radiguet, Raymond. Count d'Orgel. 1970. pap. 1.25 o.p. (*0-394-17448-8*, B214, Grove Pr.) Grove/Atlantic, Inc.
—Count D'Orgel's Ball. Cancogni, Annapaola, tr. from FRE. 1989. 174p. reprint ed. 20.00 o.p. (*0-941419-31-2*); pap. 11.00 (*0-941419-30-4*) Marsilio Pubs. (Eridanos Library).
—Count D'Orgel's Ball. Schiff, Violet, tr. from FRE. 2001. 160p. pap. 14.00 (*1-901285-03-0*) Pushkin Pr., Ltd. GBR. *Dist:* Consortium Bk. Sales & Distribution.
Radiquet, Raymond. Count d'Orgel. Schiff, Violet, tr. from FRE. 2000. 160p. pap. 12.95 (*1-885586-02-7*) Turtle Point Pr.
Randall, Rona. The Doctor Falls in Love. l.t. ed. 235p. 2001. (*0-7540-4289-8*); 2001. (*0-7540-4290-1*); 2000. pap. 20.95 (*0-7838-9191-1*) Gale Group. (Macmillan Reference USA).
Raphael, Frederic. A Double Life. 2000. 374p. 24.00 (*0-945774-46-X*) Catbird Pr.
Raspail, Jean. Blue Island. Leggatt, Jeremy, tr. from FRE. 1991. 208p. 17.95 (*0-916515-99-0*) Mercury Hse.
Raymond, Grace. How They Kept the Faith: A Tale of the Huguenots of Languedoc. 1996. (Huguenots Inheritance Ser.). (J). 12.90 (*0-921100-64-7*) Inheritance Pubns.
Redonnet, Marie. Candy Story. Quinn, Alexandra, tr. from FRE. 1995. (European Women Writers Ser.). 99p. text 20.00 o.p. (*0-8032-3915-7*); pap. 10.00 (*0-8032-8958-8*) Univ. of Nebraska Pr.
—Forever Valley. Stump, Jordan, tr. 1994. (European Women Writers Ser.). 117p. pap. 10.00 (*0-8032-8951-0*, Bison Bks.) Univ. of Nebraska Pr.
—Rose Mellie Rose. Stump, Jordan, tr. 1994. (European Women Writers Ser.). 123p. pap. 10.00 (*0-8032-8952-9*, Bison Bks.) Univ. of Nebraska Pr.
Reece, Colleen L. The Hills of Hope. l.t. ed. 2001. (Christian Fiction Ser.). 259p. 25.95 (*0-7862-3071-1*) Thorndike Pr.
Reese, James. The Book of Shadows. 2002. 640p. mass mkt. 7.99 (*0-06-103184-4*, Avon Bks.) Morrow/Avon.
—The Book of Shadows: A Novel. 2002. 480p. 25.95 (*0-06-621015-1*, Morrow, William & Co.) Morrow/Avon.
Reza, Yasmina. Hammerklavier: A Memoir. Cosman, Carol, tr. from FRE. 2000. 128p. 20.00 (*0-8076-1451-3*) Braziller, George Inc.
Rhys, Jean. Good Morning, Midnight. 1982. 192p. pap. o.p. (*0-06-080580-3*, P 580) HarperCollins Pubs.
—Good Morning, Midnight. 1999. (Shoreline Bks.). 192p. pap. 12.00 (*0-393-30394-2*) Norton, W. W. & Co., Inc.
—Good Morning, Midnight. 1974. pap. 2.95 o.p. (*0-394-71042-8*) Random Hse., Inc.
—Quartet. l.t. ed. 1994. reprint ed. 19.95 o.p. (*0-7927-2101-2*); pap. 18.95 o.p. (*0-7927-2100-4*) BBC Audiobooks America.
Rice, Luanne. Secrets of Paris. l.t. ed. 1992. (General Ser.). 393p. 20.95 o.p. (*0-8161-5329-9*, Macmillan Reference USA) Gale Group.
—Secrets of Paris. 1991. 336p. 19.95 o.p. (*0-670-82773-8*) Viking Penguin.
Richaud, Frederic. Gardener to the King: A Novel. Bray, Barbara, tr. from FRE. 2001. (Illus.). 128p. 19.95 (*1-55970-583-3*) Arcade Publishing, Inc.
Riley, Judith M. The Master of All Desires. 1999. 480p. 26.95 o.s.i (*0-670-88450-2*, Viking) Viking Penguin.
—The Oracle Glass. 1995. 528p. pap. 14.00 (*0-449-91006-7*, Fawcett) Ballantine Bks.
—The Oracle Glass. 1994. 544p. 22.95 o.p. (*0-670-85054-3*, Penguin Bks.) Viking Penguin.
Riley, Philip J. The Phantom of the Opera: The Original Shooting Script. Conforti, John, ed. 1999. (Universal Filmscript Series: Classic Silents: 1). (Illus.). pap. text 24.95 (*1-882127-33-1*) Magicimage Filmbooks.
Riley, Wilma. Cut-Out. 1993. 256p. pap. 12.95 (*1-55050-053-8*) Coteau Bks. CAN. *Dist:* General Distribution Services, Inc.
Rivele, Stephen J. A Booke of Days: A Journal of the Crusades. 1997. 448p. 24.00 o.p. (*0-7867-0348-2*, Carroll & Graf Pubs.) Avalon Publishing Group.
—A Booke of Days: A Novel of the Crusades. 1998. 448p. pap. 13.95 (*0-7867-0462-4*, Carroll & Graf Pubs.) Avalon Publishing Group.
Rizzo, Claude. Au Temps du Jasmine. l.t. ed. 2002. (French Ser.). (FRE.). 408p. pap. 30.99 (*2-84011-454-2*) Feryane, SA, Editions FRA. *Dist:* Ulverscroft Large Print Bks., Ltd., Ulverscroft Large Print Canada, Ltd.
Robbins, Adreana. Paris Never Leaves You. unabr. ed. 1999. audio 83.95 (*0-7861-1630-7*, 2458) Blackstone Audio Bks., Inc.
—Paris Never Leaves You. 2000. 468p. mass mkt. 6.99 (*0-8125-7078-2*); 2nd ed. 1999. 384p. 25.95 (*0-312-86755-7*) Doherty, Tom Assocs., LLC. (Forge Bks.).
Roberts, Michele. Daughters of the House. 1993. 223p. 18.00 o.p. (*0-688-04610-X*, Morrow, William & Co.); 1994. 224p. reprint ed. pap. 10.00 (*0-380-72139-2*, Avon Bks.) Morrow/Avon.
—Daughters of the House. 2001. (Illus.). 176p. pap. 12.00 (*0-312-42038-2*) Picador.
—Daughters of the House. 1993. 208p. o.s.i (*1-85381-600-0*) Random Hse., Inc.
—Daughters of the House. 1992. o.s.i (*1-85381-637-X*); o.s.i (*1-85381-550-0*) Virago Pr., Ltd. GBR. *Dist:* Random Hse. of Canada, Ltd.
—Fair Exchange. 2002. 256p. pap. 13.00 (*0-312-42037-4*) Picador.
—The Looking Glass: A Novel. 2000. 277p. (*0-316-85456-5*) Little Brown & Co.
—The Looking Glass: A Novel. 2002. 304p. pap. 13.00 (*0-312-42083-8*) Picador.
Robinette, Joseph & Chauls, Robert. The Phantom of the Opera: Musical. 1992. pap. 5.95 (*0-87129-173-8*, P08) Dramatic Publishing Co.
Roe, Caroline. A Draught for a Dead Man. 336p. 2003. mass mkt. 6.50 (*0-425-19308-X*); 2002. (Illus.). 22.95 (*0-425-18648-2*, Prime Crime) Berkley Publishing Group.
Rohmer, Eric. Six Moral Tales. D'Estree, Sabine, tr. 1980. (Richard Seaver Bks.). 12.95 o.p. (*0-670-64732-2*) Viking Penguin.
Romains, Jules. Verdun. 1964. (FRE.). 376p. pap. 17.95 (*0-7859-1598-2*, 208060211X) French & European Pubns., Inc.
—Verdun. 2000. (Lost Treasures Ser.). 500p. pap. 17.95 (*1-85375-358-0*) Prion GBR. *Dist:* Trafalgar Square.
Roosevelt, Elliott. Murder in the Chateau. l.t. ed. 1999. (Wheeler Large Print Bks.). pap. 23.95 o.p. (*1-56895-769-6*, Wheeler Publishing, Inc.) Gale Group.
—Murder in the Chateau. 1996. 276p. mass mkt. 5.99 (*0-312-96050-6*, St. Martin's Paperbacks); 192p. 19.95 o.p. (*0-312-14375-3*, Saint Martin's Minotaur) St. Martin's Pr.
Roscoe, Theodore. Toughest in the Legion. 1989. (Starmont Facsimile Fiction Ser.: No. 3). 19.95 o.p. (*1-55742-099-8*); pap. 9.95 o.p. (*1-55742-098-X*); 144p. (C). reprint ed. lib. bdg. 19.95 o.p. (*0-8095-5452-6*) Millefleurs.
Ross, Clarissa. Secret of the Pale Lover. 2000. 196p. pap. 25.95 (*0-7862-2636-6*, Five Star) Gale Group.
Rouaud, Jean. Fields of Glory. Manheim, Ralph, tr. from FRE. 1992. 160p. 18.95 o.p. (*1-55970-165-X*) Arcade Publishing, Inc.
—Of Illustrious Men. Wright, Barbara, tr. from FRE. 160p. 1995. pap. 10.95 (*1-55970-319-9*); 1994. 19.95 (*1-55970-265-6*) Arcade Publishing, Inc.
—The World More or Less. Wright, Barbara, tr. from FRE. 1998. Tr. of Monde, Plus ou Monis. 192p. 22.95 (*1-55970-405-5*) Arcade Publishing, Inc.
Rowlands, Betty. Over the Edge: A Melissa Craig Mystery. 1994. 240p. reprint ed. mass mkt. 4.50 o.p. (*0-425-14329-5*, Prime Crime) Berkley Publishing Group.
—Over the Edge: A Melissa Craig Mystery. 1993. 252p. 19.95 (*0-8027-3228-3*) Walker & Co.
Rufin, Jean-Christophe. The Abyssinian: A Novel. 1999. 422p. 25.95 o.p. (*0-393-04716-4*); 2000. 448p. reprint ed. pap. 14.95 (*0-393-32109-6*) Norton, W. W. & Co., Inc.
Russell-Taylor, Elisabeth, et al. Pillion Riders. 1993. 165p. 29.00 (*0-7206-0890-2*) Owen, Peter Ltd. GBR. *Dist:* Dufour Editions, Inc.
Sabatini, Rafael. Scaramouche. 1976. reprint ed. lib. bdg. 25.95 (*0-89190-744-0*, Rivercity Pr.) Amereon, Ltd.
—Scaramouche. unabr. ed. 2003. audio 59.95 (*1-55685-688-1*, ) Audio Bk. Contractors, Inc.
—Scaramouche. 1976. mass mkt. 1.75 o.s.i (*0-345-25162-8*) Ballantine Bks.
—Scaramouche. unabr. ed. 1998. audio 62.95 Blackstone Audio Bks., Inc.
—Scaramouche. unabr. collector's ed. 1983. (J). audio 80.00 (*0-7366-0365-4*, 1349) Books on Tape, Inc.
—Scaramouche. 1990. reprint ed. lib. bdg. 31.95 (*0-89968-547-1*) Buccaneer Bks., Inc.
—Scaramouche. E-Book 2.49 (*1-58627-421-X*) Electric Umbrella Publishing.
—Scaramouche, 001. 9999. 10.95 o.p. (*0-395-08142-4*) Houghton Mifflin Co.
—Scaramouche. 2001. 384p. mass mkt. 5.95 (*0-451-52797-6*) NAL.
—Scaramouche. 2002. (Twelve-Point Ser.). 400p. lib. bdg. 25.00 (*1-58287-189-2*); 500p. lib. bdg. 26.00 (*1-58287-672-X*) North Bks.
—Scaramouche. 2002. 406p. pap. 13.95 (*0-393-32330-7*) Norton, W. W. & Co., Inc.
—Scaramouche. 1999. (Gateway Movie Classics Ser.). 384p. pap. 14.95 o.s.i (*0-89526-310-6*, Gateway Editions) Regnery Publishing, Inc., An Eagle Publishing Co.
—Scaramouche. (Ebook Classic Ser.). E-Book 5.00 (*0-7410-1054-2*) SoftBook Pr.
—Scaramouche: A Historical Romance of the French Revolution. 1992. 320p. reprint ed. pap. 10.95 o.p. (*0-8118-0190-X*) Chronicle Bks. LLC.
Sagan, Francoise. Dear Sarah Bernhardt. Desiree, Sabine, tr. from FRE. 1988. (Illus.). 240p. 18.95 o.p. (*0-8050-0845-4*) Holt, Henry & Co.
—Evasion. l.t. ed. 1993. 19.95 o.p. (*0-7927-1803-8*); pap. 17.95 o.p. (*0-7927-1802-X*) BBC Audiobooks America.
—Evasion. 1993. 20.00 (*0-7278-4392-3*) Severn Hse. Pubs., Ltd.
Salter, James. A Sport & a Pastime. 1985. 192p. reprint ed. pap. 13.00 (*0-86547-210-6*, North Point Pr.) Farrar, Straus & Giroux.
—A Sport & a Pastime. 1995. (Modern Library Ser.). 196p. reprint ed. 14.95 o.s.i (*0-679-60156-2*) Random Hse., Inc.
—A Sport & a Pastime. 1980. (Contemporary American Fiction Ser.). pap. 3.50 o.p. (*0-14-005638-6*, Penguin Bks.) Viking Penguin.
Sanchez, Thomas. Day of the Bees. 2001. 320p. pap. 13.00 (*0-375-70177-X*, Vintage) Knopf Publishing Group.
Sand, George. Horace. Rogow, Zack, tr. from FRE. 1995. (Illus.). 352p. pap. 15.95 (*1-56279-082-X*) Mercury Hse.
—Indiana. Ives, George B., tr. from FRE. 1992. (Illus.). 327p. reprint ed. pap. 16.95 (*0-915864-57-6*) Academy Chicago Pubs., Ltd.
—Indiana. lib. bdg. 23.95 (*0-8488-2024-X*) Amereon, Ltd.
—Indiana. Ives, G. B., tr. 1975. xxi, 327p. reprint ed. 21.50 o.p. (*0-86527-260-3*) Fertig, Howard Inc.
—Indiana. 1984. (FRE.). pap. 16.95 (*0-7859-2907-X*, 2070376044) French & European Pubns., Inc.
—Indiana. Hochman, Eleanor, tr. 1993. 272p. mass mkt. 5.95 o.s.i (*0-451-52572-8*, Signet Classics) NAL.
—Indiana. Schor, Naomi, ed. Raphael, Sylvia, tr. from FRE. 2001. (Oxford World's Classics Ser.). 320p. pap. 10.95 (*0-19-283797-4*) Oxford Univ. Pr., Inc.
—Indiana. Raphael, Silvia, tr. 1995. (Oxford World's Classics Ser.). 306p. (C). pap. 10.95 o.p. (*0-19-283075-9*) Oxford Univ. Pr., Inc.
—Indiana. (Folio Ser.: No. 1604). (FRE.). 13.95 (*2-07-037604-4*) Schoenhof's Foreign Bks., Inc.
—The Master Pipers. Lloyd, Rosemary, tr. 1994. (Oxford World's Classics Ser.). (Illus.). 356p. pap. 10.95 o.p. (*0-19-283097-X*) Oxford Univ. Pr., Inc.
—The Miller of Angibault. 1995. (Oxford World's Classics Ser.). 342p. pap. 10.95 o.p. (*0-19-283084-8*) Oxford Univ. Pr., Inc.
Sanders, Louis. Death in the Dordogne. Hunter, Adriana, tr. from FRE. 2002. 192p. pap. 13.00 (*1-85242-673-X*) Serpent's Tail Ltd. GBR. *Dist:* Consortium Bk. Sales & Distribution.
Sartre, Jean-Paul. The Age of Reason. Sutton, Eric, tr. 1992. (Roads To Freedom = les Chemins de la Liberte Ser.: Vol. 1). 416p. pap. 15.00 (*0-679-73895-9*, Vintage) Knopf Publishing Group.
—The Age of Reason. 1972. pap. 8.00 o.p. (*0-394-71838-0*) Random Hse., Inc.
—Troubled Sleep. 1972. pap. 9.95 o.p. (*0-394-71840-2*, Vintage) Knopf Publishing Group.
—Troubled Sleep: A Novel. Hopkins, Gerard Manley, tr. 1992. (Chemins de la Liberte = The Roads To Freedom Ser.: Vol. 3). 432p. pap. 16.00 (*0-679-74079-1*, Vintage) Knopf Publishing Group.
Satterthwait, Walter. Masquerade. 1999. 336p. mass mkt. 5.99 (*0-312-96989-9*, St. Martin's Paperbacks); Vol. 1. 1998. (Masquerade Ser.: Vol. 1). 272p. 22.95 (*0-312-18629-0*, Saint Martin's Minotaur) St. Martin's Pr.
Sayers, Dorothy L. & Paton Walsh, Jill. Thrones, Dominations. unabr. ed. 2001. (Lord Peter Wimsey Mystery Ser.). audio 34.95 (*1-57270-129-3*, N81129u, Audio Editions Mystery Masters) Audio Partners Publishing Corp.
—Thrones, Dominations. unabr. ed. 1998. (Lord Peter Wimsey Mysteries Ser.: Bk. 15). audio 59.95 (*0-7540-0203-9*, CAB 1626) Chivers Audio Bks. GBR. *Dist:* BBC Audiobooks America.
Sayers, Dorothy L. & Walsh, J. P. Thrones, Dominations, unabr. collector's ed. 1999. (Lord Peter Wimsey Mystery Ser.). audio 56.00 (*0-7366-4299-4*, 4791) Books on Tape, Inc.
Sayers, Dorothy L., et al. Thrones, Dominations. 1999. 322p. mass mkt. 6.50 (*0-312-96830-2*, St. Martin's Paperbacks); 1998. 312p. (gr. 5-6). 23.95 o.p. (*0-312-18196-5*, Saint Martin's Minotaur) St. Martin's Pr.
—Thrones, Dominations. l.t. ed. 1998. (Lord Peter Wimsey Mystery Ser.). 439p. 29.95 (*0-7838-8438-9*) Thorndike Pr.
Saylor, Steven. Last Seen in Massilia. 2000. 277p. 23.95 (*0-312-20928-2*, Saint Martin's Minotaur); 2001. 288p. reprint ed. mass mkt. 6.50 (*0-312-97787-5*, St. Martin's Paperbacks) St. Martin's Pr.
Schwartz, John Burnham. Claire Marvel. 2002. 336p. 25.00 (*0-385-50344-X*, Talese, Nan A.) Doubleday Publishing.
—Claire Marvel. l.t. ed. 2002. 27.95 (*1-58724-202-8*, Wheeler Publishing, Inc.) Gale Group.
Scott, Gail. My Paris: A Novel. 1999. 180p. pap. 14.50 (*1-55128-068-X*) Mercury Pr., The CAN. *Dist:* SPD-Small Pr. Distribution.
Scott, Walter, Sr. Quentin Durward. 2001. (Works of Sir Walter Scott: Vol. 31). (Illus.). 406p. reprint ed. Pt. 1. pap. text 28.00 (*0-7426-5263-7*); Pt. 2. pap. text 28.00 (*0-7426-5264-5*) Classic Bks.
—Quentin Durward. Alexander, J. H. & Wood, G. A. M., eds. 2001. (Waverley Novels Ser.). (Illus.). 592p. text 52.50 (*0-7486-0579-7*) Edinburgh Univ. Pr. GBR. *Dist:* Columbia Univ. Pr.
—Quentin Durward. Eno, Arthur L., ed. 2001. (Illus.). 564p. per. 32.50 (*1-58963-489-6*) Fredonia Bks.
—Quentin Durward. Manning, Susan A., ed. 1993. (Oxford World's Classics Ser.). (Illus.). 606p. pap. 12.95 o.p. (*0-19-282658-1*) Oxford Univ. Pr., Inc.
Sebbar, Leila. Silence on the Shores. Mortimer, Mildred, tr. from FRE. 2000. 79p. pap. 15.00 (*0-8032-9276-7*, Bison Bks.); text 40.00 (*0-8032-4285-9*) Univ. of Nebraska Pr.
Semprun, Jorge. The Long Voyage. 1999. pap. (*0-14-026262-8*) Viking Penguin.
—The Long Voyage. Seaver, Richard, tr. 1997. (Penguin Twentieth-Century Classics Ser.). 240p. pap. 11.95 o.s.i (*0-14-118029-3*) Viking Penguin.

Sennett, Richard. Palais-Royal. 1994. pap. 11.95 (*0-393-31251-8*) Norton, W. W. & Co., Inc.

Settle, Mary Lee. Charley Bland. 1991. 208p. pap. 8.95 o.p. (*0-88184-709-7*, Carroll & Graf Pubs.) Avalon Publishing Group.

—Charley Bland. 1989. 18.95 o.p. (*0-374-12078-1*) Farrar, Straus & Giroux.

—Charley Bland. 1996. (Mary Lee Settle Collection). 208p. pap. 12.95 (*1-57003-149-5*) Univ. of South Carolina Pr.

Sheckley, Robert. Soma Blues. 224p. 1998. pap. 13.95 (*0-312-86579-1*); 1997. 20.95 o.p. (*0-312-86273-3*) Doherty, Tom Assocs., LLC. (Forge Bks.).

Shelby, Philip. Gatekeeper. l.t. ed. 1997. 27.95 o.p. (*1-56895-660-6*, Wheeler Publishing, Inc.) Gale Group.

—Gatekeeper. 2000. E-Book 25.00 (*0-684-86476-2*, Simon & Schuster); 1999. 448p. pap. 7.50 (*0-671-01392-0*, Pocket); 1998. 336p. 25.00 (*0-684-84260-2*, Simon & Schuster) Simon & Schuster.

Sherman, Delia. The Porcelain Dove: Constancy's Reward. 416p. 1994. pap. 11.95 o.p. (*0-452-27226-2*, Plume); 1993. 22.00 o.p. (*0-525-93608-4*, Dutton) Dutton/Plume.

Sherwood, John. Bones Gather No Moss. 1994. 256p. 20.00 (*0-684-19738-3*); 1995. 288p. pap. 18.95 o.p. (*0-7838-1349-X*) Gale Group. (Macmillan Reference USA).

Shone, Anna. Mr. Donaghue Investigates. 1997. per. (*0-373-26238-8*, 0-26238-6, Worldwide Library) Harlequin Enterprises, Ltd.

—Mr. Donaghue Investigates. 1995. 256p. 21.95 o.p. (*0-312-13127-5*, Saint Martin's Minotaur) St. Martin's Pr.

—Secrets in Stone. 1996. 208p. 21.95 (*0-312-14043-6*, Saint Martin's Minotaur) St. Martin's Pr.

—Secrets in Stones. 1997. 48p. per. (*0-373-26247-7*, 1-26247-6, Worldwide Library) Harlequin Enterprises, Ltd.

Shrayer-Petrov, David. Frantsuzskii Kottedzh: Roman. 1999. Tr. of French Cottage: Novel. (RUS.). 400p. pap. 10.95 (*1-888244-02-X*) APKA Pubs., Translators & Bk. Distributors.

Siciliano, Sam. The Angel of the Opera: Sherlock Holmes Meets the Phantom of the Opera. 1994. 272p. 21.95 (*1-883402-46-8*, Scribner) Simon & Schuster.

Siler, Jenny. Flashback. 2004. 272p. 24.00 (*0-8050-7211-X*) Holt, Henry & Co.

Simenon. Maigret & the Wine Merchant. 2003. pap. 8.00 (*0-15-602844-1*) Harcourt Trade Pubs.

Simenon, Georges. The Accomplices. Frechtman, Bernard, tr. 1977. pap. 2.25 o.p. (*0-15-602670-8*, Harvest Bks.) Harcourt Trade Pubs.

—The Accomplices. mass mkt. 0.50 o.p. (*0-451-02751-5*, Signet Bks.) NAL.

—Across the Street. 1992. 18.95 (*0-15-103266-1*) Harcourt Trade Pubs.

—African Trio: Talatala, Tropic Moon, Aboard the Aquitaine. 1979. 9.95 o.p. (*0-15-103955-0*) Harcourt Trade Pubs.

—Aine des Ferchaux. 1985. (Folio Ser.: No. 930). (FRE.). 4332p. (Orig.). pap. 10.95 o.p. (*2-07-036930-7*) Schoenhof's Foreign Bks., Inc.

—L' Aine des Ferchaux. 1977. (FRE.). pap. 13.95 (*0-7859-4076-6*) French & European Pubns., Inc.

—L' Ami d'Enfance de Maigret. pap. 10.95 (*0-8288-6099-8*, F126480) French & European Pubns., Inc.

—L' Ami d'Enfance de Maigret. 2000. (Maigret Mystery Ser.). (FRE.). pap. 12.95 (*2-253-14213-1*) Librairie Generale Francaise, LGF FRA. *Dist:* Distribooks, Inc.

—L' Amie de Madame Maigret. (FRE.). pap. 10.95 (*0-8288-6156-0*, F126404) French & European Pubns., Inc.

—L' Amie de Madame Maigret. 2000. (Maigret Mystery Ser.). (FRE.). pap. 12.95 (*2-253-14225-5*) Librairie Generale Francaise, LGF FRA. *Dist:* Distribooks, Inc.

—Aunt Jeanne. Sainsbury, Geoffrey, tr. from FRE. 1983. 160p. 13.95 o.p. (*0-15-109792-5*) Harcourt Trade Pubs.

—Les Autres. 1992. (FRE.). pap. 11.95 (*0-7859-3261-5*, 2266053019) French & European Pubns., Inc.

—Betty. 1992. (FRE.). pap. 11.95 (*0-7859-3255-0*, 2266049801) French & European Pubns., Inc.

—Big Bob. Lowe, Eileen M., tr. 1981. 180p. 11.95 o.p. (*0-15-112075-7*) Harcourt Trade Pubs.

—Le Blanc a Lunettes. 1978. (FRE.). pap. 10.95 (*0-7859-4093-6*) French & European Pubns., Inc.

—The Blue Room. Ellenbogen, Eileen, tr. 1978. 141p. reprint ed. pap. 2.95 o.s.i (*0-15-613267-2*, Harvest Bks.) Harcourt Trade Pubs.

—Le Bourgmestre de Fumes, Malempin, les Inconnus Dans la Masion. 1992. (FRE.). 1148p. 49.95 (*0-7859-0494-8*, 2258035279) French & European Pubns., Inc.

—Le Bourgmestre de Furnes. 1977. (FRE.). pap. 10.95 (*0-7859-4077-4*) French & European Pubns., Inc.

—The Cat. Frechtman, Bernard, tr. from FRE. 1976. (Helen & Kurt Wolff Bk.). 182p. pap. 2.95 o.s.i (*0-15-615549-4*, Harvest Bks.) Harcourt Trade Pubs.

—Le Cercle des Mahe. 1981. (FRE.). pap. 10.95 (*0-7859-4161-4*) French & European Pubns., Inc.

—Ceux de la Soif. 1978. (FRE.). pap. 10.95 (*0-7859-4098-7*) French & European Pubns., Inc.

—Le Chat. 1992. (FRE.). pap. 11.95 (*0-7859-3254-2*, 2266049798) French & European Pubns., Inc.

—Chemin sans Issue. 1979. (FRE.). pap. 10.95 (*0-7859-4118-5*) French & European Pubns., Inc.

—Le Chien Jaune. Katz, Eve & Hall, Donald R., eds. 1967. (FRE.). (C). pap. text 18.12 o.p. (*0-06-046163-2*) Addison-Wesley Educational Pubs., Inc.

—Le Chien Jaune. 1967. (College French Ser.). (FRE.). pap. 21.95 o.p. (*0-8384-3771-0*) Heinle.

—Choix De Simenon. Lindsay, Frank W. & Nazzaro, Anthony M., eds. 1972. (Illus.). pap. o.p. (*0-13-133033-0*) Prentice-Hall.

—Les Clients d'Avrenos. 1966. (FRE.). pap. 11.95 (*0-7859-3962-8*) French & European Pubns., Inc.

—The Clockmaker. Benny, Norman, tr. 1977. 124p. pap. 2.95 o.s.i (*0-15-618170-3*, Harvest Bks.) Harcourt Trade Pubs.

—Colere de Maigret. 1963. (FRE.). 192p. pap. 11.95 (*0-7859-1472-2*, 2258001730) French & European Pubns., Inc.

—Confidence de Maigret. 1992. (FRE.). 192p. pap. 11.95 (*0-7859-1605-9*, 226604978X) French & European Pubns., Inc.

—Le Coup de Vague. 1978. (FRE.). pap. 10.95 (*0-7859-4100-2*) French & European Pubns., Inc.

—The Couple from Poitiers. Ellenbogen, Eileen, tr. 1986. 144p. 13.95 (*0-15-122700-4*) Harcourt Trade Pubs.

—La Dansuese Du Gai-Moulin, la Guinguette a Deux Sous, l'Ombre Chinoise. 1991. (FRE.). 928p. 49.95 (*0-7859-0486-7*, 2258032725) French & European Pubns., Inc.

—The Delivery. Ellenbogen, Eileen, ed. 1981. (Helen & Kurt Wolff Bk.). 10.95 o.p. (*0-15-124655-6*) Harcourt Trade Pubs.

—Demoiselles de Concarneau. 1936. (Folio Ser.: No. 933). (FRE.). 148p. pap. 6.95 (*2-07-036933-1*) Schoenhof's Foreign Bks., Inc.

—Les Demoiselles de Concarneau. 1977. (FRE.). pap. 10.95 (*0-7859-4078-2*) French & European Pubns., Inc.

—The Disappearance of Odile. 1972. (Helen & Kurt Wolff Bk.). 6.95 o.p. (*0-15-125720-5*) Harcourt Trade Pubs.

—Donadieu's Will. Gilbert, Stuart, tr. 2nd ed. 1991. 343p. 22.95 (*0-15-126310-8*) Harcourt Trade Pubs.

—The Door. Woodward, Daphne, tr. 1990. 138p. 18.95 o.s.i (*0-15-126370-1*) Harcourt Trade Pubs.

—Echec de Maigret. 1990. (FRE.). 192p. pap. 11.95 (*0-7859-1494-3*, 2285002475) French & European Pubns., Inc.

—Enigmes, Level B. (FRE.). text 8.95 (*0-88436-058-X*, 40269) EMC/Paradigm Publishing.

—The Family Lie. Hillier, Caroline & Quigly, Isabel, trs. 1978. (Helen & Kurt Wolff Bk.). 7.95 o.p. (*0-15-156247-4*) Harcourt Trade Pubs.

—Les Fantomes du Chapelier. 1992. (FRE.). pap. 11.95 (*0-7859-3256-9*, 2266050877) French & European Pubns., Inc.

—Faubourg. 1978. (FRE.). pap. 8.95 (*0-7859-4094-4*) French & European Pubns., Inc.

—Fils Cardinaud. 1943. (Folio Ser.: No. 1047). (FRE.). 148p. pap. 6.95 (*2-07-037047-X*) Schoenhof's Foreign Bks., Inc.

—Le Fils, le Negre, Maigret Voyage, Strip-Tease, les Scruples de Maigret, le President, le Passage de la Ligne, 23 vols., Set. 1989. (FRE.). 832p. 49.95 (*0-7859-0555-3*, 225803003X) French & European Pubns., Inc.

—La Folle de Maigret. 1990. (FRE.). 186p. pap. 11.95 (*0-7859-1495-1*, 2285003846) French & European Pubns., Inc.

—Four on Maigret. unabr. ed. (Inspector Maigret Mystery Ser.). audio 21.95 o.p. (*1-55656-077-X*, DAB056) BBC Audiobooks America.

—Four on Maigret. unabr. ed. 1997. (Mystery Library). pap. 16.95 o.p. incl. audio (*1-55656-254-3*) Dercum Audio.

—The Girl with a Squint. Thomson, Helen, tr. 1978. 7.95 o.p. (*0-15-135692-0*) Harcourt Trade Pubs.

—The Glass Cage. 1973. (Helen & Kurt Wolff Bk.). 5.50 o.p. (*0-15-135800-1*) Harcourt Trade Pubs.

—The Grandmother. Stewart, Jean, tr. 1980. (Helen & Kurt Wolff Bk.). 192p. reprint ed. 8.95 o.p. (*0-15-136738-8*) Harcourt Trade Pubs.

—The Hatter's Phantoms. 19.95 (*0-89190-428-X*) Amereon, Ltd.

—The Hatter's Phantoms. Trask, Willard R., tr. (Helen & Kurt Wolff Bk.). 1981. 176p. pap. 3.95 o.s.i (*0-15-639342-5*, Harvest Bks.); 1976. 6.95 o.p. (*0-15-139270-6*) Harcourt Trade Pubs.

—L' Homme Qui Regardait Passer les Trains. 1967. (FRE.). pap. 15.95 (*0-7859-3963-6*) French & European Pubns., Inc.

—L' Horloger d'Everton. 1992. (FRE.). pap. 16.95 (*0-7859-3304-2*, 2804007790) French & European Pubns., Inc.

—The House on the Quai Notre-Dame. Hamilton, Alastair, tr. 1975. (Helen & Kurt Wolff Bk.). 160p. 6.95 o.p. (*0-15-142181-1*) Harcourt Trade Pubs.

—Inconnus Dans la Maison. 1975. (Folio Ser.: No. 664). (FRE.). pap. 8.95 (*2-07-036664-2*) Schoenhof's Foreign Bks., Inc.

—Les Inconnus dans la Maison. 1975. (FRE.). pap. 10.95 (*0-7859-4041-3*) French & European Pubns., Inc.

—The Innocents. 1974. (Helen & Kurt Wolff Bk.). 6.50 o.p. (*0-15-144430-7*) Harcourt Trade Pubs.

—Inspector Maigret & the Strangled Stripper. unabr. collector's ed. 1983. audio 30.00 (*0-7366-0533-9*, 1507) Books on Tape, Inc.

—Inspector Maigret's Case Files: Murder a la Carte. 1992. 9.98 (*0-88365-810-0*, Galahad Bks.) BBS Publishing Corp.

—Intimate Memoirs: Including Marie-Jo's Book. Salemson, Harold J., tr. 1984. 800p. 22.95 o.s.i (*0-15-144892-2*) Harcourt Trade Pubs.

—Intimate Memoirs: Including Marie-Jo's Book. Salemson, Harold J., tr. 1984. 815 p. o.p. (*0-241-11219-2*, Hamilton, Hamish) Viking Penguin.

—The Iron Staircase. Date not set. lib. bdg. 18.95 (*0-8488-2161-0*) Amereon, Ltd.

—The Iron Staircase. Ellenbogen, Eileen, tr. 1981. 192p. pap. 2.95 o.s.i (*0-15-645484-X*, Harvest Bks.) Harcourt Trade Pubs.

—Justice. Sainsbury, Geoffrey, tr. from FRE. 1985. (Helen & Kurt Wolff Bk.). 176p. reprint ed. 13.95 (*0-15-146585-1*) Harcourt Trade Pubs.

—Letter to My Mother. Manheim, Ralph, tr. 1976. (Helen & Kurt Wolff Bk.). 96p. 5.95 o.p. (*0-15-150445-8*) Harcourt Trade Pubs.

—The Little Doctor. Stewart, Jean, tr. from FRE. 1981. (Helen & Kurt Wolff Bk.). 10.95 o.p. (*0-15-152768-7*) Harcourt Trade Pubs.

—Le Locataire. 1978. (FRE.). pap. 10.95 (*0-7859-4091-X*, 2070369986) French & European Pubns., Inc.

—Le Locataire. 1934. (Folio Ser.: No. 998). (FRE.). 181p. pap. 6.95 (*2-07-036998-6*) Schoenhof's Foreign Bks., Inc.

—Le Locataire, les Suicides, les Pitard. 1992. (FRE.). 990p. 49.95 (*0-7859-0491-3*, 2258035244) French & European Pubns., Inc.

—The Lodger. Gilbert, Stuart, tr. from FRE. 1983. (Helen & Kurt Wolff Bk.). 176p. reprint ed. 12.95 o.p. (*0-15-152960-4*) Harcourt Trade Pubs.

—The Long Exile. Ellenbogen, Eileen, tr. 1983. (Helen & Kurt Wolff Bk.). 372p. 15.95 o.s.i (*0-15-152997-3*) Harcourt Trade Pubs.

—Madame Maigret's Own Case. 2003. 180p. pap. 8.00 (*0-15-602849-2*); 2nd ed. 1991. 182p. (C). pap. 6.00 o.s.i (*0-15-655106-3*, Harvest Bks.); 2nd ed. 1990. 192p. 17.95 o.s.i (*0-15-154968-0*) Harcourt Trade Pubs.

—Maigret a New York. 1996. (FRE.). audio 21.95 Olivia & Hill Pr., The.

—Maigret a Vichy. 2000. (Maigret Mystery Ser.). (FRE.). pap. 12.95 (*2-253-14216-6*) Librairie Generale Francaise, LGF FRA. *Dist:* Distribooks, Inc.

—Maigret a Vichy. 1992. (FRE.). audio 32.95 Olivia & Hill Pr., The.

—Maigret Afraid. Duff, Margaret, tr. (Helen & Kurt Wolff Bk.). 1996. 170p. pap. 6.00 o.s.i (*0-15-655142-X*, Harvest Bks.); 1983. 176p. 13.95 o.s.i (*0-15-155560-5*) Harcourt Trade Pubs.

—Maigret among the Rich. 1978. mass mkt. 5.95 o.p. (*0-671-79051-X*, Pocket) Simon & Schuster.

—Maigret & the Apparition. Ellenbogen, Eileen, tr. 1978. (Adult Ser.). lib. bdg. 9.95 o.p. (*0-8161-6503-3*, Macmillan Reference USA) Gale Group.

—Maigret & the Apparition. 168p. 2003. pap. 8.00 (*0-15-602838-7*); 1991. pap. 6.00 o.s.i (*0-15-655127-6*) Harcourt Trade Pubs. (Harvest Bks.).

—Maigret & the Apparition. Ellenbogen, Eileen, tr. 1976. (Helen & Kurt Wolff Bk.). 6.95 o.p. (*0-15-155125-1*) Harcourt Trade Pubs.

—Maigret & the Black Sheep. l.t. ed. 2001. (Dales Large Print Ser.). 208p. pap. 21.99 (*1-84262-061-4*) Dales Large Print Bks. GBR. *Dist:* Ulverscroft Large Print Bks., Ltd., Ulverscroft Large Print Canada, Ltd.

—Maigret & the Black Sheep. Thompson, Helen, tr. 1976. (Helen & Kurt Wolff Bk.). 168p. 6.95 o.p. (*0-15-155146-4*) Harcourt Trade Pubs.

—Maigret & the Black Sheep. Thomson, Helen, tr. 1983. 168p. reprint ed. pap. 3.95 o.s.i (*0-15-655138-1*, Harvest Bks.) Harcourt Trade Pubs.

—Maigret & the Bum. unabr. collector's ed. 1984. audio 24.00 (*0-7366-0540-1*, 1514) Books on Tape, Inc.

—Maigret & the Bum. 2003. 160p. pap. 8.00 (*0-15-602839-5*, Harvest Bks.) Harcourt Trade Pubs.

—Maigret & the Bum. Stewart, Jean, tr. 1996. 156p. (C). pap. 3.95 o.s.i (*0-15-655130-6*, Harvest Bks.) Harcourt Trade Pubs.

—Maigret & the Bum. 1995. pap. 6.00 (*0-15-600249-3*) Harcourt Trade Pubs.

—Maigret & the Burglar's Wife. 2003. 176p. pap. 8.00 (*0-15-602840-9*); 1992. 167p. pap. 5.95 o.s.i (*0-15-655167-5*, Harvest Bks.) Harcourt Trade Pubs.

—Maigret & the Burglar's Wife. Maclaren-Ross, J., tr. 1990. 18.95 o.s.i (*0-15-155572-9*) Harcourt Trade Pubs.

—Maigret & the Calame Report. Budberg, Moura, tr. 1996. 192p. pap. 6.00 (*0-15-655153-5*, Harvest Bks.) Harcourt Trade Pubs.

—Maigret & the Calame Report. 1995. pap. o.s.i (*0-15-600248-5*) Harcourt Trade Pubs.

—Maigret & the Death of a Harbor-Master. Gilbert, Stuart, tr. 1989. 182p. pap. 6.00 (*0-15-655161-6*, Harvest Bks.) Harcourt Trade Pubs.

—Maigret & the Enigmatic Letter. 1964. pap. 2.95 o.p. (*0-14-002023-3*, Penguin Bks.) Viking Penguin.

—Maigret & the Flemish Shop. Sainsbury, Geoffrey, tr. 1990. 182p. pap. 5.95 o.p. (*0-15-655118-7*) Harcourt Trade Pubs.

—Maigret & the Fortuneteller. 1990. 140p. pap. 5.95 o.s.i (*0-15-655163-2*) Harcourt Trade Pubs.

—Maigret & the Fortuneteller. Sainsbury, Geoffrey, tr. 1989. 144p. 16.95 o.s.i (*0-15-155571-0*) Harcourt Trade Pubs.

—Maigret & the Gangsters. Varese, Louise, tr. from FRE. 1986. 162p. 14.95 (*0-15-155565-6*) Harcourt Trade Pubs.

—Maigret & the Gangsters. Varese, Louise, tr. 1988. 160p. pap. 3.50 (*0-380-70414-5*, Avon Bks.) Morrow/Avon.

—Maigret & the Headless Corpse. Ellenbogen, Eileen, tr. l.t. ed. 1989. (Nightingale Ser.). 274p. 13.95 o.p. (*0-8161-4664-0*, Macmillan Reference USA) Gale Group.

—Maigret & the Headless Corpse. Ellenbogen, Eileen, tr. 1985. (Helen & Kurt Wolff Bk.). 196p. (C). pap. 6.00 (*0-15-655144-6*, Harvest Bks.) Harcourt Trade Pubs.

—Maigret & the Hotel Majestic. Hillier, Caroline, tr. 1991. 182p. pap. 6.00 o.s.i (*0-15-655133-0*, Harvest Bks.) Harcourt Trade Pubs.

—Maigret & the Hundred Gibbets. 1963. pap. 2.95 o.p. (*0-14-002025-X*, Penguin Bks.) Viking Penguin.

—Maigret & the Informer. lib. bdg. 18.95 (*0-8488-2033-9*) Amereon, Ltd.

—Maigret & the Informer. 1973. 5.95 o.p. (*0-15-155140-5*) Harcourt Trade Pubs.

—Maigret & the Killer. lib. bdg. 19.95 (*0-8488-2034-7*) Amereon, Ltd.

—Maigret & the Killer. unabr. ed. 1993. (Inspector Maigret Mystery Ser.). audio 39.95 (*0-7451-6284-3*, CAB 600) BBC Audiobooks America.

—Maigret & the Killer. unabr. ed. 2000. (Inspector Maigret Mystery Ser.). audio 34.95 Chivers Audio Bks. GBR. *Dist:* BBC Audiobooks America.

—Maigret & the Killer. abr. ed. 1997. (Maigret Ser.). audio 16.99 (*0-88646-452-8*, 7452) Durkin Hayes Publishing Ltd.

—Maigret & the Killer. Moir, Lyn, tr. l.t. ed. 1991. (Nightingale Ser.). 239p. pap. 14.95 o.p. (*0-8161-5117-2*, Macmillan Reference USA) Gale Group.

—Maigret & the Killer. 2003. 168p. pap. 8.00 (*0-15-602841-7*, Harvest Bks.) Harcourt Trade Pubs.

—Maigret & the Killer. Moir, Lyn, tr. 1991. (Helen & Kurt Wolff Bk.). 165p. pap. 5.95 o.s.i (*0-15-655124-1*, Harvest Bks.) Harcourt Trade Pubs.

—Maigret & the Loner. 166p. 19.95 (*0-89190-429-8*) Amereon, Ltd.

—Maigret & the Loner. 1983. 168p. pap. 3.95 o.s.i (*0-15-655139-X*, Harvest Bks.) Harcourt Trade Pubs.

—Maigret & the Madwoman. unabr. ed. 1999. audio 21.95 (*1-57270-125-0*, N31125u, Audio Editions Mystery Masters) Audio Partners Publishing Corp.

—Maigret & the Madwoman. unabr. ed. 1995. (Inspector Maigret Mystery Ser.). audio 31.95 (*0-7451-6520-6*, CAB 1136) BBC Audiobooks America.

—Maigret & the Madwoman. 2003. 180p. pap. 8.00 (*0-15-602850-6*, Harvest Bks.) Harcourt Trade Pubs.

—Maigret & the Madwoman. Ellenbogen, Eileen, tr. 1992. (Helen & Kurt Wolff Bk.). 176p. pap. 5.95 o.s.i (*0-15-655122-5*, Harvest Bks.) Harcourt Trade Pubs.

—Maigret & the Man on the Bench. 2003. 192p. pap. 8.00 (*0-15-602837-9*, Harvest Bks.) Harcourt Trade Pubs.

—Maigret & the Man on the Bench. Ellenbogen, Eileen, tr. from FRE. (Helen & Kurt Wolff Bk.). 1993. 181p. pap. 5.95 o.s.i (*0-15-655123-3*, Harvest Bks.); 1975. 9.95 o.p. (*0-15-155145-6*) Harcourt Trade Pubs.

—Maigret & the Millionaires. l.t. ed. 2002. (Dales Large Print Ser.). 224p. pap. 21.99 (*1-84262-097-5*) Dales Large Print Bks. GBR. *Dist:* Ulverscroft Large Print Bks., Ltd., Ulverscroft Large Print Canada, Ltd.

—Maigret & the Millionaires. Stewart, Jean, tr. 1992. 182p. pap. 5.95 o.s.i (*0-15-655150-0*, Harvest Bks.); 1974. 168p. 5.95 o.p. (*0-15-155143-X*) Harcourt Trade Pubs.

—Maigret & the Nahour Case. Hamilton, Alastair, tr. l.t. ed. 1992. (Nightingale Ser.). 229p. pap. 14.95 o.p. (*0-8161-5274-8*, Macmillan Reference USA) Gale Group.

—Maigret & the Nahour Case. Hamilton, Alastair, tr. 1993. 168p. pap. 5.95 (*0-15-655149-7*, Harvest Bks.) Harcourt Trade Pubs.

—Maigret & the Nahour Case. 1983. (Helen & Kurt Wolff Bk.). 168p. 10.95 o.p. (*0-15-155559-1*) Harcourt Trade Pubs.

—Maigret & the Pickpocket. unabr. ed. 1992. (Inspector Maigret Mystery Ser.). 39.95 incl. audio (*0-7451-4030-0*, CAB 727) BBC Audiobooks America.

—Maigret & the Pickpocket. unabr. ed. 2000. (Inspector Maigret Mystery Ser.). audio 34.95 Chivers Audio Bks. GBR. *Dist:* BBC Audiobooks America.

—Maigret & the Pickpocket. Ryan, Nigel, tr. l.t. ed. 1990. (Nightingale Ser.). 13.95 o.p. (*0-8161-4666-7*, Macmillan Reference USA) Gale Group.

—Maigret & the Pickpocket. Ryan, Nigel, tr. from FRE. 1995. (Helen & Kurt Wolff Bk.). 156p. pap. 6.00 (*0-15-655145-4*, Harvest Bks.) Harcourt Trade Pubs.

—Maigret & the Reluctant Witness. abr. ed. 1998. audio 16.99 (*0-88646-458-7*, 7458) Durkin Hayes Publishing Ltd.

—Maigret & the Saturday Caller. 2003. 128p. pap. 8.00 (*0-15-602842-5*); 1992. 132p. pap. 6.00 o.s.i (*0-15-655175-6*, Harvest Bks.) Harcourt Trade Pubs.

—Maigret & the Saturday Caller. White, Tony, tr. 1991. 124p. 17.95 (*0-15-155566-4*) Harcourt Trade Pubs.

—Maigret & the Spinster. 2003. 168p. pap. 8.00 (*0-15-602843-3*, Harvest Bks.) Harcourt Trade Pubs.

—Maigret & the Spinster. Ellenbogen, Eileen, tr. 1996. 168p. (C). pap. 6.00 o.s.i (*0-15-655129-2*, Harvest Bks.); 1977. reprint ed. 6.95 o.p. (*0-15-155550-8*) Harcourt Trade Pubs.

—Maigret & the Tavern by the Seine. Sainsbury, Geoffrey, tr. 1990. 182p. pap. 6.00 (*0-15-655164-0*, Harvest Bks.) Harcourt Trade Pubs.

—Maigret & the Toy Village. unabr. ed. 1992. (Inspector Maigret Mystery Ser.). audio 39.95 (*0-7451-6283-5*, CAB 666) BBC Audiobooks America.

—Maigret & the Toy Village. Ellenbogen, Eileen, tr. l.t. ed. 1989. 216p. pap. 12.95 o.p. (*0-8161-4427-3*, Macmillan Reference USA) Gale Group.

—Maigret & the Toy Village. Ellenbogen, Eileen, tr. 1994. pap. 5.95 (*0-15-655154-3*, Harvest Bks.); 1979. 7.95 o.p. (*0-15-155554-0*) Harcourt Trade Pubs.

—Maigret & the Wine Merchant. unabr. collector's ed. 1984. audio 30.00 (*0-7366-0544-4*, 1518) Books on Tape, Inc.

—Maigret & the Wine Merchant. Ellenbogen, Eileen, tr. 1993. 187p. pap. 6.00 o.s.i (*0-15-655125-X*, Harvest Bks.) Harcourt Trade Pubs.

—Maigret & the Yellow Dog. 1995. (Helen & Kurt Wolff Bk.). 140p. pap. 6.00 (*0-15-655157-8*) Harcourt Trade Pubs.

—Maigret & the Yellow Dog. Asher, Linda, tr. 1987. 15.95 o.s.i (*0-15-155564-8*) Harcourt Trade Pubs.

—Maigret at the Coroner's. Keene, Frances, tr. (Helen & Kurt Wolff Bk.). 1992. 176p. (C). pap. 5.95 o.s.i (*0-15-655143-8*, Harvest Bks.); 1980. 180p. reprint ed. 8.95 o.p. (*0-15-155556-7*) Harcourt Trade Pubs.

—Maigret at the Crossroads. 1963. pap. 2.95 o.p. (*0-14-002028-4*, Penguin Bks.) Viking Penguin.

—Maigret at the Crossroads (Omnibus) 1984. (Crime Ser.). 320p. pap. 6.95 o.p. (*0-14-006652-7*, Penguin Bks.) Viking Penguin.

—Maigret at the Gai-Moulin.Tr. of Danseuse du Gai-Moulin. 2003. 176p. pap. 8.00 (*0-15-602845-X*); 1993. 182p. pap. 6.00 (*0-15-655176-4*) Harcourt Trade Pubs.

—Maigret at the Gai-Moulin. Sainsbury, Geoffrey, tr. 2nd ed. 1991. Tr. of Danseuse du Gai-Moulin. 166p. 17.95 o.s.i (*0-15-155568-0*) Harcourt Trade Pubs.

—Maigret au Picratt's. 2000. (Maigret Mystery Ser.). (FRE.). pap. 12.95 (*2-253-14219-0*) Librairie Generale Francaise, LGF FRA. *Dist:* Distribooks, Inc.

—Maigret Bides His Time. Hamilton, Alastair, tr. 160p. 1992. pap. 5.95 (*0-15-655151-9*, Harvest Bks.); 1985. 12.95 o.p. (*0-15-155563-X*) Harcourt Trade Pubs.

—Maigret et la Grande Perche. 2000. (Maigret Mystery Ser.). (FRE.). pap. 12.95 (*2-253-14223-9*) Librairie Generale Francaise, LGF FRA. *Dist:* Distribooks, Inc.

—Maigret et l'Affaire Nahour. 2000. (Maigret Mystery Ser.). (FRE.). pap. 12.95 (*2-253-14220-4*) Librairie Generale Francaise, LGF FRA. *Dist:* Distribooks, Inc.

—Maigret et le Clochard, Level B. (FRE.). text 8.95 (*0-88436-047-4*, 40270) EMC/Paradigm Publishing.

—Maigret et le Clochard. l.t. ed. 1997. (French Ser.). (FRE.). 236p. pap. 30.99 o.p. (*2-84011-186-1*) Feryane, SA, Editions FRA. *Dist:* Ulverscroft Large Print Bks., Ltd., Ulverscroft Large Print Canada, Ltd.

—Maigret et le Clochard. 2000. (Maigret Mystery Ser.). (FRE.). pap. 12.95 (*2-253-14228-X*) Librairie Generale Francaise, LGF FRA. *Dist:* Distribooks, Inc.

—Maigret et le Clochard. 1995. (FRE.). audio 28.95 Olivia & Hill Pr., The.

—Maigret et le Corps Sans Tete. 1992. (FRE.). pap. 11.95 (*0-7859-3257-7*, 2266051032) French & European Pubns., Inc.

—Maigret et le Corps Sans Tete, La Boule Noire, Maigret Tend un Piege, Les Complices, En Cas de Malheur, Un Echec de Maigret, Le Petit Homme d'Arkhangelsh, Maigret S'Amuse. 1989. (FRE.). 49.95 (*0-7859-0482-4*, 2258027977) French & European Pubns., Inc.

—Maigret et le Fantome, Level B. 2000. (FRE.). text 8.95 (*0-8219-1470-7*, 40271) EMC/Paradigm Publishing.

—Maigret et le Fantome. l.t. ed. 1996. (French Ser.). (FRE.). 224p. pap. 30.99 o.p. (*2-84011-152-7*) Feryane, SA, Editions FRA. *Dist:* Ulverscroft Large Print Bks., Ltd., Ulverscroft Large Print Canada, Ltd.

—Maigret et les Braves Gens. l.t. ed. 2002. (French Ser.). 221p. pap. 30.99 o.p. (*2-84011-459-3*) Feryane, SA, Editions FRA. *Dist:* Ulverscroft Large Print Bks., Ltd., Ulverscroft Large Print Canada, Ltd.

—Maigret et les Braves Gens: Student Edition. Daudon, Rene, ed. 1969. (FRE.). (Orig.). (C). pap. text, stu. ed. 4.95 o.p. (*0-15-551287-0*) Harcourt College Pubs.

—Maigret et les Temoins Recalcitrants, La Vielle, L'Ours en Peluche, Une Confidence de Maigret, Le Veuf, Maigret aux Assises, Maigret et les Viellards, Betty. 1990. (FRE.). 830p. 49.95 (*0-7859-0483-2*, 2258031532) French & European Pubns., Inc.

—Maigret et l'Inspecteur Maigrecieux, la Passager Clandestin, le Temoignage de l'Enfant Du Choeur, le Client le Plus Obstine Du Monde, On Ne Tue Pas les Pauvres Types, la Jument Perdue, Maigret et Son Mort, Pedigree. 1988. (FRE.). 49.95 (*0-7859-0477-8*, 2258021154) French & European Pubns., Inc.

—Maigret Goes Home. Baldick, Robert, tr. 1992. 144p. pap. 5.95 o.s.i (*0-15-655165-9*, Harvest Bks.); 1989. 16.95 (*0-15-155150-2*) Harcourt Trade Pubs.

—Maigret Goes Home. Baldick, Robert, tr. 1967. 139p. pap. 1.95 o.p. (*0-14-001901-4*, Penguin Bks.) Viking Penguin.

—Maigret Goes to School. Woodward, Daphne, tr. 1992. Tr. of Maigret a l'Ecole. 196p. pap. 5.95 o.s.i (*0-15-655156-X*) Harcourt Trade Pubs.

—Maigret Has Doubts. Moir, Lyn, tr. 1982. 144p. 10.95 o.p. (*0-15-155558-3*) Harcourt Trade Pubs.

—Maigret Has Doubts. 1988. 160p. pap. 3.50 (*0-380-70410-2*, Avon Bks.) Morrow/Avon.

—Maigret Has Scruples. Eglesfield, Robert, tr. 1996. (Helen & Kurt Wolff Bk.). 192p. pap. 6.00 (*0-15-655160-8*) Harcourt Trade Pubs.

—Maigret Has Scruples. 1995. pap. 6.00 (*0-15-600247-7*) Harcourt Trade Pubs.

—Maigret Hesitates. Moir, Lyn, tr. 1993. 182p. pap. 5.95 (*0-15-655152-7*, Harvest Bks.) Harcourt Trade Pubs.

—Maigret in Court. Brain, Robert, tr. 1983. (Helen & Kurt Wolff Bk.). 160p. reprint ed. 11.95 o.s.i (*0-15-155561-3*) Harcourt Trade Pubs.

—Maigret in Court. Brain, Robert, tr. 1988. 160p. pap. 3.50 (*0-380-70411-0*, Avon Bks.) Morrow/Avon.

—Maigret in Exile. Ellenbogen, Eileen, tr. from FRE. (Harvest Book Ser.). 1994. 168p. pap. 5.95 (*0-15-655136-5*, Harvest Bks.); 1979. 7.95 o.p. (*0-15-155147-2*) Harcourt Trade Pubs.

—Maigret in Holland. 2003. 180p. pap. 8.00 (*0-15-602852-2*); 2nd ed. 1994. 182p. pap. 5.95 o.s.i (*0-15-600084-9*) Harcourt Trade Pubs. (Harvest Bks.).

—Maigret in Holland. Sainsbury, Geoffrey, tr. 2nd ed. 1993. 165p. 18.95 o.s.i (*0-15-155159-6*) Harcourt Trade Pubs.

—Maigret in Montmartre. Woodward, Daphne, tr. 1989. 202p. pap. 6.00 (*0-15-655162-4*) Harcourt Trade Pubs.

—Maigret in Vichy. Ellenbogen, Eileen, tr. 1995. (Harvest Book Ser.). 182p. pap. 6.00 o.s.i (*0-15-655140-3*, Harvest Bks.) Harcourt Trade Pubs.

—Maigret Loses His Temper. 2003. 144p. pap. 8.00 (*0-15-602847-6*, Harvest Bks.) Harcourt Trade Pubs.

—Maigret Loses His Temper. Eglesfield, Robert, tr. 1993. (Helen & Kurt Wolff Bk.). 144p. pap. 5.95 o.s.i (*0-15-655128-4*, Harvest Bks.) Harcourt Trade Pubs.

—Maigret Meets a Milord. 1963. pap. 2.95 o.p. (*0-14-002027-6*, Penguin Bks.) Viking Penguin.

—Maigret Meets a Milord (Omnibus) 1983. pap. 6.95 o.p. (*0-14-006651-9*, Penguin Bks.) Viking Penguin.

—Maigret Mystified. 1964. Orig. Title: Shadow in the Courtyard. pap. 1.95 o.p. (*0-14-002024-1*, Penguin Bks.) Viking Penguin.

—Maigret on the Defensive. Hamilton, Alastair, tr. 1981. (Helen & Kurt Wolff Bk.). 144p. 10.95 o.p. (*0-15-155557-5*) Harcourt Trade Pubs.

—Maigret on the Defensive. 1987. 160p. pap. 3.50 (*0-380-70409-9*, Avon Bks.) Morrow/Avon.

—Maigret on the Riviera. 1989. 140p. pap. 6.00 o.s.i (*0-15-655158-6*, Harvest Bks.) Harcourt Trade Pubs.

—Maigret on the Riviera. Sainsbury, Geoffrey, tr. 1988. 144p. 14.95 o.s.i (*0-15-155149-9*) Harcourt Trade Pubs.

—Maigret S'Amuse. l.t. ed. 1999. (French Ser.). (FRE.). 275p. pap. 30.99 (*2-84011-329-5*) Feryane, SA, Editions FRA. *Dist:* Ulverscroft Large Print Bks., Ltd., Ulverscroft Large Print Canada, Ltd.

—Maigret Se Trompe. 2000. (Maigret Mystery Ser.). (FRE.). pap. 12.95 (*2-253-14227-1*) Librairie Generale Francaise, LGF FRA. *Dist:* Distribooks, Inc.

—Maigret Se Trompe, Crime Impuni, Maigret a l'Ecole, Maigret et la Jeun Morte. 1990. (FRE.). 860p. 49.95 (*0-7859-0480-8*, 2258025966) French & European Pubns., Inc.

—Maigret Sets a Trap. 20.95 (*0-89190-427-1*) Amereon, Ltd.

—Maigret Sets a Trap. unabr. ed. 2000. audio 21.95 (*1-57270-152-8*, N31152u, Audio Editions Mystery Masters) Audio Partners Publishing Corp.

—Maigret Sets a Trap. (Black Dagger Crime Ser.). 16.50 o.p. (*0-86220-825-4*, BD024, Black Dagger) BBC Audiobooks America.

—Maigret Sets a Trap. unabr. collector's ed. 1983. audio 30.00 (*0-7366-0534-7*, 1508) Books on Tape, Inc.

—Maigret Sets a Trap. unabr. ed. 2000. (Inspector Maigret Mystery Ser.). audio 34.95 (*0-7451-4118-8*, CAB 801) Chivers Audio Bks. GBR. *Dist:* BBC Audiobooks America.

—Maigret Sets a Trap. Woodward, Daphne, tr. l.t. ed. 1990. (Nightingale Ser.). 230p. pap. 13.95 o.p. (*0-8161-4665-9*, Macmillan Reference USA) Gale Group.

—Maigret Sets a Trap. 2003. 192p. pap. 8.00 (*0-15-602848-4*, Harvest Bks.) Harcourt Trade Pubs.

—Maigret Sets a Trap. Woodward, Daphne, tr. 1992. (Helen & Kurt Wolff Bk.). 182p. pap. 5.95 o.s.i (*0-15-655126-8*, Harvest Bks.) Harcourt Trade Pubs.

—Maigret Stonewalled. 1963. pap. 2.95 o.p. (*0-14-002026-8*, Penguin Bks.) Viking Penguin.

—Maigret Tend un Piege. l.t. ed. 1994. (French Ser.). (FRE.). pap. 30.99 o.p. (*2-84011-095-4*) Feryane, SA, Editions FRA. *Dist:* Ulverscroft Large Print Bks., Ltd., Ulverscroft Large Print Canada, Ltd.

—A Maigret Trio: Maigret's Failure, Maigret in Society, & Maigret & the Lazy Burglar. 23.95 (*0-89190-425-5*) Amereon, Ltd.

—A Maigret Trio: Maigret's Failure, Maigret in Society, & Maigret & the Lazy Burglar. Woodward, Daphne & Eglesfield, Robert, trs. 1994. (Harvest Book Ser.). 288p. pap. 10.00 o.s.i (*0-15-655137-3*, Harvest Bks.) Harcourt Trade Pubs.

—Maigret's Boyhood Friend. 19.95 (*0-89190-426-3*) Amereon, Ltd.

—Maigret's Boyhood Friend. unabr. collector's ed. 1984. audio 36.00 (*0-7366-0543-6*, 1517) Books on Tape, Inc.

—Maigret's Boyhood Friend. Ellenbogen, Eileen, tr. l.t. ed. 1991. (Nightingale Ser.). 260p. pap. 14.95 o.p. (*0-8161-5116-4*, Macmillan Reference USA) Gale Group.

—Maigret's Boyhood Friend. 2003. 192p. pap. 8.00 (*0-15-602851-4*, Harvest Bks.) Harcourt Trade Pubs.

—Maigret's Boyhood Friend. Ellenbogen, Eileen, tr. (Harvest Book Ser.). 1996. 196p. pap. 6.00 o.s.i (*0-15-655131-4*, Harvest Bks.); 1970. 4.95 o.p. (*0-15-155135-9*) Harcourt Trade Pubs.

—Maigret's Christmas. unabr. collector's ed. 1979. audio 80.00 (*0-7366-0226-7*, 1223) Books on Tape, Inc.

—Maigret's Christmas: 9 Stories. Stewart, Jean, tr. (Helen & Kurt Wolff Bk.). 1992. 336p. pap. 12.00 o.s.i (*0-15-655132-2*, Harvest Bks.); 1977. 8.95 o.p. (*0-15-155551-6*) Harcourt Trade Pubs.

—Maigret's Memoirs. Stewart, Jean, tr. from FRE. 1985. (Helen & Kurt Wolff Bk.). 160p. reprint ed. 13.95 (*0-15-155148-0*) Harcourt Trade Pubs.

—Maigret's Memoirs. Stewart, Jean, tr. 1989. 144p. reprint ed. pap. 3.50 (*0-380-70412-9*, Avon Bks.) Morrow/Avon.

—Maigret's Mistake. Hodge, Alan, tr. 1988. 188p. pap. 6.00 (*0-15-655155-1*) Harcourt Trade Pubs.

—Maigret's Pipe. Stewart, Jean, tr. from FRE. (Harvest Book Ser.). 1994. 336p. pap. 11.00 (*0-15-655146-2*, Harvest Bks.); 1978. 8.95 o.p. (*0-15-155553-2*) Harcourt Trade Pubs.

—Maigret's Revolver. Ryan, Nigel, tr. from FRE. l.t. ed. 1992. (Nightingale Ser.). 241p. pap. 14.95 o.p. (*0-8161-5316-7*, Macmillan Reference USA) Gale Group.

—Maigret's Revolver. Ryan, Nigel, tr. from FRE. (Helen & Kurt Wolff Bk.). 1991. 182p. (C). pap. 5.95 o.s.i (*0-15-659556-7*, Harvest Bks.); 1984. (FRE.). 176p. 12.95 o.s.i (*0-15-155562-1*) Harcourt Trade Pubs.

—Maigret's Rival. Thomson, Helen, tr. l.t. ed. 1988. (Nightingale Ser.). 244p. 12.95 o.p. (*0-8161-4426-5*, Macmillan Reference USA) Gale Group.

—Maigret's Rival. Thomson, Helen, tr. 1994. 182p. pap. 5.95 (*0-15-655141-1*, Harvest Bks.); 1980. 180p. reprint ed. 7.95 o.p. (*0-15-155555-9*) Harcourt Trade Pubs.

—Maigret's War of Nerves. Sainsbury, Geoffrey, tr. l.t. ed. 1987. (Nightingale Ser.). 280p. 10.95 o.p. (*0-8161-4309-9*, Macmillan Reference USA) Gale Group.

—Maigret's War of Nerves. Sainsbury, Geoffrey, tr. 1986. (Helen & Kurt Wolff Bk.). 180p. 13.95 (*0-15-155570-2*) Harcourt Trade Pubs.

—Maigret's War of Nerves. Sainsbury, Geoffrey, tr. 1989. 160p. pap. 3.50 (*0-380-70413-7*, Avon Bks.) Morrow/Avon.

—The Man on the Bench in the Barn. Budberg, Moura, tr. 1970. (Helen & Kurt Wolff Bk.). 188p. 5.95 o.p. (*0-15-156928-2*) Harcourt Trade Pubs.

—The Man with the Little Dog. Stewart, Jean, tr. 1989. 176p. 16.95 (*0-15-156933-9*) Harcourt Trade Pubs.

—Le Meurtre d'un Etudiant. Ernst, ed. 1971. (FRE.). 240p. (C). pap. text 39.00 o.p. (*0-03-084993-4*) Harcourt College Pubs.

—Mon Ami Maigret, 1996. (FRE.). audio 28.95 Olivia & Hill Pr., The.

—Monsieur Gallet, Decede, le Pendu De Saint-Pholien, le Charretier De la Providence. 1991. (FRE.). 924p. 49.95 (*0-7859-0485-9*, 2258032458) French & European Pubns., Inc.

—Monsieur Monde Vanishes. Stewart, Jean, tr. 1977. (Helen & Kurt Wolff Bk.). 6.95 o.p. (*0-15-162098-9*) Harcourt Trade Pubs.

—Monsieur Monde Vanishes. 2004. 144p. pap. 12.95 (*1-59017-096-2*) New York Review of Bks., Inc., The.

—La Mort de Belle, le Revolver de Maigret, les Freres Rico, Maigret et l'Homme du Banc, Antoine et Julie, Maigret a Peur, l'Escalier de Fer, Feux Rouges. 1989. (FRE.). 49.95 (*0-7859-0481-6*, 2258027098) French & European Pubns., Inc.

—La Morte d'August. 1991. (FRE.). pap. 11.95 (*0-7859-3249-6*, 2266045911) French & European Pubns., Inc.

—The Murderer. Sainsbury, Geoffrey, tr. 1986. 144p. 15.95 (*0-15-163270-7*) Harcourt Trade Pubs.

—Mystery: Four Great Inspector Maigret Novels. 1996. 12.98 o.p. (*0-88365-948-4*, Galahad Bks.) BBS Publishing Corp.

—The Nightclub. Stewart, Jean, tr. 1979. (Helen & Kurt Wolff Bk.). 7.95 o.p. (*0-15-165589-8*) Harcourt Trade Pubs.

—None of Maigret's Business. unabr. collector's ed. 1983. audio 30.00 (*0-7366-0535-5*, 1509) Books on Tape, Inc.

—Un Nouveau Dans la Ville, Maigret et la Vielle Dame, l'Amie de Madame Maigret, l'Enterrement de Monsieur Bouvet, Maigret et les Petits Cochons Sans Queue, les Voles Verts, Tante Jeanne, les Memoires de Maigret, 23 vols., Set. 1988. (FRE.). 860p. 49.95 (*0-7859-0554-5*, 225802353X) French & European Pubns., Inc.

—November. Stewart, Jean, tr. 1978. 185p. pap. 2.95 o.s.i (*0-15-667582-X*, Harvest Bks.); 1970. 9.95 o.p. (*0-15-167560-0*) Harcourt Trade Pubs.

—Oncle Charles S'est Enferme, la Veuve Couderc, Cecile Est Morte. 1992. (FRE.). 1018p. 49.95 (*0-7859-0495-6*, 2258035287) French & European Pubns., Inc.

—The Outlaw. Curtis, Howard, tr. 1987. 15.95 (*0-15-170509-7*) Harcourt Trade Pubs.

—La Patience de Maigret. 2000. (Maigret Mystery Ser.). (FRE.). pap. 12.95 (*2-253-14221-2*) Librairie Generale Francaise, LGF FRA. *Dist:* Distribooks, Inc.

—La Patience de Maigret, le Confessional, la Morte d'Auguste. 1990. (FRE.). 896p. 49.95 (*0-7859-0488-3*, 2258033039) French & European Pubns., Inc.

—The Patience of Maigret. unabr. ed. 1996. (Inspector Maigret Mystery Ser.). audio 31.95 (*0-7451-6564-8*, CAB1180) BBC Audiobooks America.

—Il Peut Bergere. 1966. (FRE.). pap. 11.95 (*0-7859-3964-4*) French & European Pubns., Inc.

—La Pipe de Maigret. Goodall, Geoffrey, ed. 1969. (FRE.). 70p. pap. text 6.95 o.p. (*0-312-46235-2*) St. Martin's Pr.

Settings

—La Pipe de Maigret, Maigret Se Fache, Maigret a New York, Lettre a Mon Juge, le Destin Des Malou. 1988. (FRE.). 49.95 (*0-7859-0476-X*, 2258020980) French & European Pubns., Inc.

—La Porte. 1993. (FRE.). pap. 11.95 (*0-7859-3258-5*, 2266052683) French & European Pubns., Inc.

—La Premiere Enquete de Maigret, Les Fantomes du Chapelier, Mon Ami Maigret, Les Quatres Jours du Pauvre Homme, Maigret Chez le Coroner, Un Nouveau dans la Ville, La Neige Etait Sale, Le Fond de la Bouteille. (FRE.). 49.95 (*0-7859-0478-6*, 2258021421) French & European Pubns., Inc.

—La Prison, Maigret Hesite, la Main. 1991. (FRE.). 896p. 49.95 (*0-7859-0489-1*, 2258033047) French & European Pubns., Inc.

—The Reckoning. Read, Emily, tr. 1984. (Helen & Kurt Wolff Bk.). 128p. 12.95 o.p. (*0-15-175980-4*) Harcourt Trade Pubs.

—The Rich Man. Stewart, Jean, tr. from FRE. 1971. (Helen & Kurt Wolff Bk.). 5.95 o.p. (*0-15-177162-6*) Harcourt Trade Pubs.

—Le Riche Homme, la Folie de Maigret, la Disparition D'Odile. 1991. (FRE.). 864p. 49.95 (*0-7859-0490-5*, 2258033055) French & European Pubns., Inc.

—La Rue aux Trois Poussins. 1992. (FRE.). pap. 11.95 (*0-7859-3260-7*, 2266052993) French & European Pubns., Inc.

—La Rue aux Trois Poussins: Le Mari de Melie, Level A. (FRE.). text 7.95 (*0-88436-985-4*, 40301) EMC/Paradigm Publishing.

—The Rules of the Game. l.t. ed. 1991. 212p. reprint ed. lib. bdg. 11.95 o.p. (*1-85057-869-9*, Macmillan Reference USA) Gale Group.

—The Rules of the Game. Curtis, Howard, tr. 1988. (Helen & Kurt Wolff Bk.). 160p. 18.95 o.p. (*0-15-169475-3*) Harcourt Trade Pubs.

—The Rules of the Game. l.t. ed. 1991. (Magna Large Print Ser.). 212p. o.p. (*1-85057-868-0*) Magna Large Print Bks. GBR. *Dist:* Ulverscroft Large Print Canada, Ltd.

—Sailors' Rendezvous. 1970. pap. 1.95 o.p. (*0-14-003136-7*, Penguin Bks.) Viking Penguin.

—Soeurs Lacroix. (Folio Ser.: No. 1209). (FRE.). pap. 8.95 (*2-07-037209-X*) Schoenhof's Foreign Bks., Inc.

—Striptease. 1993. (FRE.). pap. 11.95 (*0-7859-3259-3*, 2266052691) French & European Pubns., Inc.

—Striptease. Brain, Robert, tr. 1989. 17.95 (*0-15-185910-8*) Harcourt Trade Pubs.

—Sunday. Ryan, Nigel, tr. 1976. (Helen & Kurt Wolff Bk.). pap. 2.50 o.p. (*0-15-686301-4*, Harvest Bks.) Harcourt Trade Pubs.

—The Survivors. Gilbert, Stuart, tr. from FRE. 1985. (Helen & Kurt Wolff Bk.). 180p. 14.95 o.s.i (*0-15-187047-0*) Harcourt Trade Pubs.

—The Suspect. Gilbert, Stuart, tr. 1991. 17.95 o.s.i (*0-15-137057-5*) Harcourt Trade Pubs.

—Tante Jeanne. 1991. (FRE.). pap. 11.95 (*0-7859-3244-5*, 2266045202) French & European Pubns., Inc.

—Le Temps de Anais, un Noel de Maigret, Maigret Au Picratt's, Maigret en Meuble, une Vie Comme Neuve, Maigret et la Grande Perche, Marie Qui Louche, Miagret Lognon et les Gangsters. 1988. (FRE.). 49.95 (*0-7859-0479-4*, 2258023564) French & European Pubns., Inc.

—Le Testament Donadieu, l'Assassin, le Blanc a Lunettes. 1992. (FRE.). 1000p. 49.95 (*0-7859-0492-1*, 2258035252) French & European Pubns., Inc.

—Le Train. 1991. (FRE.). pap. 11.95 (*0-7859-3248-8*, 2266045849) French & European Pubns., Inc.

—Les Treize Enigmes, la Folle d'Itteville, les Treize Mysteres. 1992. (FRE.). 1047p. 49.95 (*0-7859-0487-5*, 2258032733) French & European Pubns., Inc.

—Trois Crimes de Mes Amis. (Folio Ser.: No. 1112). (FRE.). pap. 8.95 (*2-07-037112-3*) Schoenhof's Foreign Bks., Inc.

—Les Trois Crimes de Mes Amis, le Suspect, les Soeurs Lacroix. 1992. (FRE.). 1021p. 49.95 (*0-7859-0493-X*, 2258035260) French & European Pubns., Inc.

—Trois Nouvelles de Georges Simenon. Lindsay, Frank W. & Nazzaro, Anthony M., eds. 1966. (gr. 10-12). pap. text o.p. (*0-13-930917-9*) Prentice-Hall.

—The Truth about Bebe Donge. Varese, Louise, tr. 2nd ed. 1992. 176p. 18.95 (*0-15-191319-6*) Harcourt Trade Pubs.

—Uncle Charles. l.t. unabr. ed. 1998. (Keating's Choice Ser.). 202p. 22.95 (*1-85089-418-3*, 894183) ISIS Large Print Bks. GBR. *Dist:* Transaction Pubs.

—Uncle Charles Has Locked Himself In. Curtis, Howard, tr. 1987. 19.95 o.s.i (*0-15-192685-9*) Harcourt Trade Pubs.

—The Venice Train. Hamilton, Alastair, tr. (Helen & Kurt Wolff Bk.). 1983. 160p. pap. 3.95 o.s.i (*0-15-693523-6*, Harvest Bks.); 1974. 168p. 6.50 o.p. (*0-15-193506-8*) Harcourt Trade Pubs.

—La Vieille. 1991. (FRE.). pap. 11.95 (*0-7859-3245-3*, 2266045210) French & European Pubns., Inc.

—Le Voleur de Maigret. 2000. (Maigret Mystery Ser.). (FRE.). pap. 12.95 (*2-253-14218-2*) Librairie Generale Francaise, LGF FRA. *Dist:* Distribooks, Inc.

—Voyageur de la Toussaint. 1941. (Folio Ser.: No. 932). (FRE.). 360p. pap. 9.95 (*2-07-036932-3*) Schoenhof's Foreign Bks., Inc.

—When I Was Old. 1971. (Helen & Kurt Wolff Bk.). (Illus.). 343p. 8.50 o.p. (*0-15-195950-1*) Harcourt Trade Pubs.

—The White Horse Inn. Denny, Norman, tr. 1980. (Helen & Kurt Wolff Bk.). 144p. 7.95 o.p. (*0-15-196240-5*) Harcourt Trade Pubs.

—The Widower. Baldick, Robert, tr. from FRE. 1982. 10.95 o.p. (*0-15-196644-3*) Harcourt Trade Pubs.

Simon, Claude. The Flanders Road. 1961. Orig. Title: La Route des Flandres. (Orig.). 4.00 o.p. (*0-8076-0146-2*) Braziller, George Inc.

—The Flanders Road. Howard, Richard, tr. from FRE. 1986. Orig. Title: La Route des Flandres. 224p. (Orig.). (C). pap. 11.95 o.s.i (*0-7145-3994-5*) Riverrun Pr., Inc.

Smith, Haywood. Shadows on Velvet. 1996. 424p. mass mkt. 5.99 (*0-312-95873-0*, St. Martin's Paperbacks) St. Martin's Pr.

Smith, Jane S. Fool's Gold. 2000. 288p. 24.00 o.p. (*1-58195-019-5*); 2001. 352p. reprint ed. pap. 13.00 o.p. (*1-58195-035-7*) Steerforth Pr. (Zoland Bks., Inc.).

Smith, Sarah. The Knowledge of Water. 2000. 416p. mass mkt. 6.99 (*0-345-43946-5*, Ballantine Bks.); 1997. 496p. pap. 12.00 (*0-345-40963-9*) Ballantine Bks.

Sobin, Gustaf. The Fly-Truffler: A Novel. 160p. 2001. pap. 12.00 (*0-393-32179-7*, Norton Paperbacks); 2000. text 19.95 (*0-393-04832-2*) Norton, W. W. & Co., Inc.

Sohmers, Barbara. The Fox & the Puma. 1997. 148p. pap. 10.00 (*1-58345-486-1*) Domhan Bks.

—The Fox & the Pussycat. 2000. 163p. pap. 10.00 (*1-58345-491-8*) Domhan Bks.

Sole, Linda. The Rose Arch. 2001. 256p. 25.99 (*0-7278-5651-0*); 29.99 (*0-7278-7179-X*) Severn Hse. Pubs., Ltd.

Soliman, Patricia B. Coco, the Novel. 1990. 448p. 21.95 o.p. (*0-399-13516-2*, G. P. Putnam's Sons) Penguin Putnam Bks. for Young Readers.

Souvestre, Pierre. Silent Executioner. 1989. mass mkt. 3.95 o.s.i (*0-345-35297-1*) Ballantine Bks.

Steel, Danielle. Five Days in Paris. 1997. 304p. mass mkt. 7.50 (*0-440-22284-2*); 1995. 288p. 15.95 (*0-385-31530-9*, Delacorte Pr.) Dell Publishing.

—Five Days in Paris. 1996. pap. 6.50 (*0-440-29548-3*) Doubleday Publishing.

—Five Days in Paris. unabr. ed. 1995. audio 25.95 (*0-553-47429-4*, 693303, RH Audio) Random Hse. Audio Publishing Group.

—Five Days in Paris. l.t. ed. 1998. (Core Ser.). 288p. 29.95 (*0-7838-0181-5*) Thorndike Pr.

—Jewels. l.t. ed. 1992. 832p. 27.50 o.s.i (*0-385-30515-X*, Delacorte Large Type) Bantam Doubleday Dell Large Print Group, Inc.

—Jewels. 480p. 1993. mass mkt. 6.99 (*0-440-21422-X*); 1992. 23.00 (*0-385-30490-0*, Delacorte Pr.) Dell Publishing.

—Jewels. 1993. audio 13.59 o.s.i (*0-553-70079-0*); audio 18.00 o.s.i (*0-553-47172-4*) Random Hse. Audio Publishing Group. (RH Audio).

—Jewels. 1992. 12.09 o.p. (*0-606-05385-9*) Turtleback Bks.

—The Kiss. 2002. 448p. mass mkt. 7.99 (*0-440-23669-X*); 2001. 360p. 200.00 (*0-385-33589-X*, Delacorte Pr.); 2001. 360p. 26.95 (*0-385-33540-7*, Delacorte Pr.) Dell Publishing.

—The Kiss. abr. ed. 2001. audio 26.95 (*0-553-52786-X*); audio compact disk 29.95 (*0-553-71229-2*) Random Hse. Audio Publishing Group. (RH Audio).

—The Kiss. l.t. ed. 544p. 2002. pap. 14.95 (*0-375-72817-1*); 2001. 26.95 (*0-375-43132-2*) Random Hse. Large Print.

—Sunset in St. Tropez. l.t. ed. 2002. 336p. 19.95 (*0-375-43169-1*) Random Hse., Inc.

Steiner, Peter, illus. A French Country Murder: A Novel. 2003. 256p. 23.95 (*0-312-30687-3*, Saint Martin's Minotaur) St. Martin's Pr.

Stendhal. The Red & the Black. 1970. mass mkt. 0.95 o.p. (*0-451-50492-5*); mass mkt. 1.25 o.p. (*0-451-50821-1*); mass mkt. 1.50 o.p. (*0-451-50993-5*); mass mkt. 1.75 o.p. (*0-451-51175-1*); mass mkt. 1.95 o.p. (*0-451-51398-3*); mass mkt. 3.50 o.p. (*0-451-51607-9*) NAL. (Signet Classics).

—The Red & the Black. Raffel, Burton, tr. from FRE. 2003. 560p. 24.95 (*0-679-64284-6*, Modern Library) Random House Adult Trade Publishing Group.

—The Red & the Black. Raffel, Burton, tr. from FRE. 2003. 19.95 (*1-58836-305-8*) Random Hse., Inc.

—The Red & the Black: A Chronicle of 1830. 32.95 (*0-8488-0635-2*) Amereon, Ltd.

—The Red & the Black: A Chronicle of 1830. 1989. 464p. mass mkt. 3.95 o.s.i (*0-553-21357-1*, Bantam Classics) Bantam Bks.

—The Red & the Black: A Chronicle of 1830. unabr. collector's ed. 1990. audio 104.00 (*0-7366-1813-9*, 2649) Books on Tape, Inc.

—The Red & the Black: A Chronicle of 1830. 1987. 532p. reprint ed. lib. bdg. 35.95 (*0-89966-619-1*) Buccaneer Bks., Inc.

—The Red & the Black: A Chronicle of 1830. Scott-Moncrieff, C. K., tr. 1954. (Black & Gold Library). 8.95 o.p. (*0-87140-833-3*) Liveright Publishing Corp.

—The Red & the Black: A Chronicle of 1830, Level 6. 2001. pap. 7.66 (*0-582-34368-2*) Longman Publishing Group.

—The Red & the Black: A Chronicle of 1830. 2003. 352p. pap. 11.95 (*0-87140-148-7*) Norton, W. W. & Co., Inc.

—The Red & the Black: A Chronicle of 1830. Slater, Catherine, ed. & tr. by. 1998. (Oxford World's Classics Ser.). 592p. pap. 8.95 (*0-19-283871-7*) Oxford Univ. Pr., Inc.

—The Red & the Black: A Chronicle of 1830. Slater, Catherine, tr. 1991. (Oxford World's Classics Ser.). 588p. pap. 6.95 o.p. (*0-19-281715-9*) Oxford Univ. Pr., Inc.

—The Red & the Black: A Chronicle of 1830. Scott-Moncrieff, C. K., tr. (Modern Library Ser.). 1995. 770p. 17.50 o.s.i (*0-679-60162-7*); 1984. 633p. 9.95 o.s.i (*0-394-60511-X*) Random Hse., Inc.

—The Red & the Black: A Chronicle of 1830. unabr. ed. 1988. audio 120.00 (*1-55690-436-3*, 88900E7) Recorded Bks., LLC.

—The Red & the Black: A Chronicle of 1830. La Farge, Phyllis, ed. Turgie, Charles, tr. rev. ed. 1970. reprint ed. mass mkt. 0.95 o.s.i (*0-671-47870-2*, Pocket) Simon & Schuster.

—The Red & the Black: A Chronicle of 1830. Jefferson, Ann, ed. 1995. (Everyman Paperback Classics Ser.). 608p. pap. 6.50 (*0-460-87643-0*, Everyman's Classic Library in Paperback) Tuttle Publishing.

—The Red & the Black: A Chronicle of 1830. 2002. (Penguin Classics Ser.). 607p. pap. 9.00 (*0-14-044764-4*) Viking Penguin.

—The Red & the Black: A Chronicle of 1830. Shaw, Margaret R., tr. 1953. (Penguin Classics Ser.). 512p. pap. 8.95 (*0-14-044030-5*, Penguin Classics) Viking Penguin.

—The Red & the Black: A Chronicle of 1830. 2001. (World Literature Ser.). 576p. pap. 5.95 (*1-84022-127-5*) Wordsworth Editions, Ltd. GBR. *Dist:* Advanced Global Distribution Services.

—The Red & the Black: An Annotated Text with Critical Essays. Adams, Robert M., ed. annot. ed. 1969. (Critical Editions Ser.). (C). pap. text 12.00 (*0-393-09821-4*) Norton, W. W. & Co., Inc.

—Scarlet & Black: A Chronicle of 1830. Scott-Moncrieff, C. K., tr. 1991. (Everyman's Library). 656p. 20.00 o.s.i (*0-679-40565-8*) Random Hse., Inc.

Stendhal, et al. The Red & the Black: A Chronicle of 1830. Parks, Lloyd C., tr. 1970. (Illus.). 536p. mass mkt. 6.95 (*0-451-51793-8*, CE1793, Signet Classics) NAL.

Stephenson, Neal. The Confusion. 2004. 816p. 27.95 (*0-06-052386-7*, Morrow, William & Co.) Morrow/Avon.

Sterne, Laurence. A Sentimental Journey. 2000. per. 9.90 (*1-891355-67-8*); per. 15.50 (*1-58396-233-6*) Blue Unicorn Editions.

—A Sentimental Journey. 2004. 112p. pap. 2.50 (*0-486-43473-7*) Dover Pubns., Inc.

—A Sentimental Journey. E-Book 2.49 (*1-58627-640-9*) Electric Umbrella Publishing.

—A Sentimental Journey. mass mkt. 0.60 o.p. (*0-451-50254-X*, Signet Classics) NAL.

—A Sentimental Journey. (Ebook Classic Ser.). E-Book 5.00 (*0-7410-1326-6*) SoftBook Pr.

—A Sentimental Journey. 1995. 282p. 5.50 (*0-460-87336-9*, Everyman's Classic Library in Paperback) Tuttle Publishing.

—A Sentimental Journey. Goring, Paul, ed. & intro. by. 2002. (Classics Ser.). 160p. pap. 7.00 (*0-14-043779-7*) Viking Penguin.

—A Sentimental Journey. Alvarez, A. & Petrie, Graham, eds. 1967. (Penguin Classics Ser.). 160p. pap. 5.95 o.s.i (*0-14-043026-1*, Penguin Classics) Viking Penguin.

—A Sentimental Journey Through France & Italy. 2002. E-Book 3.95 (*0-594-08623-X*) 1873 Pr.

—A Sentimental Journey Through France & Italy. 1983. 19.50 o.p. (*0-913720-29-1*); ring bd. 37.50 o.p. (*0-913720-28-3*) Beil, Frederic C. Pub., Inc.

—A Sentimental Journey Through France & Italy. 1975. reprint ed. 11.95 o.p. (*0-460-00796-3*); 2.50 o.p. (*0-460-01796-9*) Biblio Distribution.

—A Sentimental Journey Through France & Italy. reprint ed. lib. bdg. 196.00 (*0-7426-2068-9*); 2001. (Collected Works of Laurence Sterne: Vol. 4). pap. text 56.00 (*0-7426-7068-6*) Classic Bks.

—A Sentimental Journey Through France & Italy. 1968. (Oxford World's Classics Ser.). 8.95 o.p. (*0-19-250333-2*) Oxford Univ. Pr., Inc.

—A Sentimental Journey Through France & Italy by Mr. Yorick. Stout, Gardner D., ed. rev. ed. 1967. (Illus.). 42.00 o.p. (*0-520-01228-3*) Univ. of California Pr.

—A Sentimental Journey Through France & Italy by Mr. Yorick: With the Journal to Eliza & a Political Romance. Jack, Ian, ed. & intro. by. 1998. (Oxford World's Classics Ser.). 272p. pap. 6.95 (*0-19-283522-X*) Oxford Univ. Pr., Inc.

—A Sentimental Journey Through France & Italy by Mr. Yorick: With the Journal to Eliza & a Political Romance. Jack, Ian, ed. 1984. (Oxford World's Classics Ser.). 270p. pap. 4.95 o.p. (*0-19-281685-3*) Oxford Univ. Pr., Inc.

Steward, Samuel M. Parisian Lives. 1984. 192p. 5.99 o.p. (*0-312-59666-9*) St. Martin's Pr.

Stewart, Mary. Madam, Will You Talk? 2003. 368p. mass mkt. 7.99 (*0-06-009356-0*, HarperTorch); 1956. 8.95 o.p. (*0-688-02017-8*, Morrow, William & Co.) Morrow/Avon.

Stockwin, Julian. Artemis. 2003. 352p. pap. 13.00 (*0-7432-1461-7*); 2002. 336p. 24.00 (*0-7432-1460-9*) Simon & Schuster. (Scribner).

—Artemis. l.t. ed. 2002. 28.95 (*0-7862-4588-3*) Thorndike Pr.

Stokes, Lawrence D. & Brown, James W., eds. Silence of the Sea: A Novel of French Resistance During the Second World War by "Vercors" 1992. Tr. of Silence de la Mer. (ENG & FRE.). 112p. (*0-85496-671-4*) Berg Pubs.

Stone, Irving. Depths of Glory: A Biographical Novel of Camille Pissarro, Pt. 1. unabr. ed. 1988. audio 80.00 (*0-7366-1262-9*, 2175-A) Books on Tape, Inc.

—Depths of Glory: A Biographical Novel of Camille Pissarro. 1995. 624p. pap. 14.95 o.p. (*0-452-27501-6*, Plume) Dutton/Plume.

—Depths of Glory: A Biographical Novel of Camille Pissarro. 1987. mass mkt. 2.95 o.p. (*0-451-15790-7*); 624p. mass mkt. 5.95 o.p. (*0-451-16497-0*); mass mkt. 4.95 o.p. (*0-451-14602-6*) NAL. (Signet Bks.).

Stream, Arnold C. Until Proven Guilty. 1992. 320p. mass mkt. 4.99 o.p. (*0-425-13373-7*) Berkley Publishing Group.

—Until Proven Guilty. 1991. 272p. 19.95 o.p. (*0-8128-4010-0*, Scarborough Hse.) Madison Bks., Inc.

Strom, Carolyn & Bernheim, Emmanuele. Sa Femme: Or the Other Woman. 1995. 128p. 14.95 o.p. (*0-670-85811-0*) Viking Penguin.

Sullivan, Jean. Eternity, My Beloved (Car Jet'aime, O Eternite) Riordan, Francis Ellen, tr. from FRE. 1998. 160p. pap. 15.00 (*0-9654756-2-X*) River Boat Bks.

Suskind, Patrick. El Perfume: Historia de la Asesino. (SPA.). 240p. 1998. 10.50 (*84-322-1500-7*); 1997. 7.95 (*84-322-0531-1*); 8th ed. 1998. (Illus.). 10.50 (*84-322-1524-4*) Editorial Seix Barral ESP. *Dist:* Continental Bk. Co., Inc.

—Perfume: The Story of a Murderer. 2001. 272p. reprint ed. pap. 13.00 (*0-375-72584-9*, Vintage) Knopf Publishing Group.

—Perfume: The Story of a Murderer. 1991. 320p. pap. (*0-671-74960-9*, Washington Square Pr.); 1990. mass mkt. 4.95 (*0-671-72595-5*, Pocket) Simon & Schuster.

—Perfume: The Story of a Murderer. Woods, John E., tr. 1987. mass mkt. 4.50 (*0-671-64370-3*, Pocket) Simon & Schuster.

—Perfume: The Story of a Murderer. abr. unabr. ed. 1997. 6p. pap. 29.95 o.s.i incl. audio (*0-14-086291-9*, Penguin AudioBooks) Viking Penguin.

Suthren, Victor. The Black Cockade. 1986. 256p. reprint ed. pap. 2.95 o.p. (*0-8125-8862-2*, Tor Bks.) Doherty, Tom Assocs., LLC.

—The Black Cockade: Paul Gallant's Louisburg Command. 1982. 256p. 10.95 o.p. (*0-312-08303-3*) St. Martin's Pr.

—In Perilous Seas. 1987. 224p. reprint ed. pap. 3.50 o.p. (*0-8125-8868-1*, Tor Bks.) Doherty, Tom Assocs., LLC.

—In Perilous Seas. 1984. 224p. 11.95 o.p. (*0-312-41105-7*) St. Martin's Pr.

—A King's Ransom. 1981. 224p. 9.95 o.p. (*0-312-45610-7*) St. Martin's Pr.

Swan, Mary. The Deep & Other Stories. 2004. 240p. pap. 12.95 (*0-8129-6650-3*, Random Hse. Trade Paperbacks) Random House Adult Trade Publishing Group.

—The Deep & Other Stories. 2003. 240p. 23.95 (*0-375-50851-1*) Random Hse., Inc.

Sylvester, Martin. Rough Red. l.t. ed. 1991. (Ulverscroft Large Print Ser.). 29.99 o.p. (*0-7089-2354-2*, Ulverscroft) Thorpe, F. A. Pubs. GBR. *Dist:* Ulverscroft Large Print Bks., Ltd., Ulverscroft Large Print Canada, Ltd.

Symons, Allene. Vagabond Prophet: A Novel of Nostradamus. 1987. 187p. 2.99 o.s.i (*0-517-64116-X*) Random Hse. Value Publishing.

—Vagabond Prophet: A Novel of Nostradamus & His Time. 1983. 160p. pap. 2.95 o.p. (*0-380-84459-1*, 84459, Avon Bks.) Morrow/Avon.
Tales of Passion, Tales of Woe. 2000. E-Book 14.00 (*0-7432-1358-0*, Touchstone) Simon & Schuster.
Tansley, David. Puppet Master. 1988. 320p. pap. 7.95 o.p. (*0-14-019050-3*, Penguin Bks.) Viking Penguin.
Tapon, Philippe. The Mistress: A Novel. 192p. 2000. pap. 12.95 o.s.i (*0-452-28058-3*, Plume); 1999. 23.95 o.p. (*0-525-94461-3*, Abrahams, William Bks.) Dutton/Plume.
—The Mistress: A Novel. l.t. ed. 1999. (Wheeler Large Print Book Ser.). 213p. 26.95 (*1-56895-725-4*, Wheeler Publishing, Inc.) Gale Group.
—Parisian from Kansas. (William Abrahams Book Ser.). 336p. 1998. pap. 13.95 o.s.i (*0-452-27735-3*, Plume); 1997. 23.95 o.s.i (*0-525-94239-4*) Dutton/Plume.
Tate, Ellalice. The Scarlet Cloak. 1992. 336p. 21.95 o.p. (*0-399-13783-1*, G. P. Putnam's Sons) Penguin Group (USA) Inc.
Taylor, Domini. Siege. l.t. ed. 1992. pap. 14.95 o.p. (*0-7927-0672-2*); 1991. 17.95 o.p. (*0-7927-0671-4*, E0012) BBC Audiobooks America.
—Siege. 1990. 240p. 17.95 o.p. (*0-06-016284-8*) HarperTrade.
—Siege. 1991. 2.99 o.p. (*0-517-06904-0*) Random Hse. Value Publishing.
Taylor, Georgia. Lamia: A Witch. 1994. 304p. 21.95 o.p. (*0-525-93745-5*, Dutton) Dutton/Plume.
Taylor, John. Mysteries of the Body & the Mind. 1998. 130p. pap. text 12.95 (*1-885266-53-7*) Story Line Pr.
Thackara, James. The Book of Kings. 2000. 773p. 16.95 (*1-58567-050-2*); 1999. 800p. 28.95 (*0-87951-923-1*) Overlook Pr., The.
Thomas, Chantal. Farewell, My Queen. Black, Moishe, tr. from FRE. 2003. 256p. 22.50 (*0-8076-1514-5*) Braziller, George Inc.
Tindall, Gillian. Fly Away Home. 1971. 222p. (*0-340-15039-4*) St. Martin's Pr.
Tremain, Rose. The Swimming Pool Season. 1985. 16.45 o.p. (*0-671-50464-9*) Summit Bks.
—The Way I Found Her. Set. unabr. ed. 1999. audio 84.95 (*0-7540-0343-4*, CAB1766, Sterling Audio Bks.) BBC Audiobooks America.
—The Way I Found Her. l.t. ed. 1998. 24.95 (*1-57490-165-6*, Beeler Large Print Bks.) Beeler, Thomas T. Publisher.
—The Way I Found Her. 1998. 368p. 25.00 o.s.i (*0-374-28666-3*) Farrar, Straus & Giroux.
—The Way I Found Her. 1999. 368p. pap. 14.00 (*0-671-03570-3*, Washington Square Pr.) Simon & Schuster.
Triolet, Elsa. A Fine of Two Hundred Francs. 1986. (Virago Modern Classics Ser.). 240p. pap. 6.95 o.p. (*0-14-016134-1*, Penguin Bks.) Viking Penguin.
Trollope, Anthony. The Golden Lion of Granpere. fac. ed. 2002. 317p. per. 8.95 (*1-4021-0055-8*, Elibron Classics) Adamant Media.
—The Golden Lion of Granpere. Hall, N. John, ed. 1981. (Selected Works of Anthony Trollope). reprint ed. lib. bdg. 44.95 (*0-405-14159-9*) Ayer Co. Pubs., Inc.
—The Golden Lion of Granpere. reprint ed. lib. bdg. 98.00 (*0-7426-2467-6*); 2001. 353p. pap. text 28.00 (*0-7426-7467-3*) Classic Bks.
—The Golden Lion of Granpere. 1993. (Oxford World's Classics Ser.). 296p. pap. 9.95 o.p. (*0-19-282843-6*) Oxford Univ. Pr., Inc.
—The Golden Lion of Granpere. 1994. (Trollope Ser.). 272p. pap. 6.95 o.p. (*0-14-043831-9*, Penguin Classics) Viking Penguin.
—La Vendee: An Historical Romance, 3 vols. Hall, N. John, ed. 1981. (Selected Works of Anthony Trollope). reprint ed. 115.95 (*0-405-14122-X*) Ayer Co. Pubs., Inc.
—La Vendee: An Historical Romance, 3. reprint ed. lib. bdg. 294.00 (*0-7426-2433-1*); 2001. pap. text 84.00 (*0-7426-7433-9*) Classic Bks.
—La Vendee: An Historical Romance. McCormack, W. J., ed. 1994. (Oxford World's Classics Ser.). (Illus.). 500p. (C). pap. 10.95 o.p. (*0-19-282838-X*) Oxford Univ. Pr., Inc.
—La Vendee: An Historical Romance, 1850. 1993. (Trollope Ser.). 992p. pap. 9.95 o.p. (*0-14-043802-5*, Penguin Classics) Viking Penguin.
Trott, Susan. Sightings. 1988. 224p. reprint ed. pap. 6.95 o.p. (*0-06-097158-4*, PL-7158, Perennial) HarperTrade.
—Sightings. 1987. 16.45 o.p. (*0-671-63804-1*, Simon & Schuster) Simon & Schuster.
Troyan, Sasha. Angels in the Morning. 2003. 256p. 26.00 (*1-57962-083-3*) Permanent Pr., The.
Truscott, Lucian K., IV. The Boys of St. Julien, Set. abr. ed. 2000. audio 17.95 (*1-56740-846-X*, Nova Audio Bks.); Date not set. audio 73.25 (*1-56740-661-0*, Unabridged Library Editions); audio 26.95 (*1-56740-435-9*, Bookcassette) Brilliance Audio.
—The Boys of St. Julien. 2000. 336p. 25.00 (*0-688-16896-5*, Morrow, William & Co.) Morrow/Avon.
Tuten, Frederic. Tallien: A Brief Romance. 1994. 152p. pap. 13.95 o.p. (*0-7145-2990-7*) Boyars, Marion Pubs., Inc.
—Tallien: A Brief Romance. 1988. 230p. 17.95 o.p. (*0-374-27249-2*) Farrar, Straus & Giroux.
Twain, Mark. Personal Recollections of Joan of Arc. 1917. 461p. reprint ed. 98.00 (*0-7222-2337-4*) Best Bks.
—Personal Recollections of Joan of Arc. 2002. (Thrift Editions Ser.). 336p. pap. 3.50 (*0-486-42459-6*) Dover Pubns., Inc.
—Personal Recollections of Joan of Arc. o.p. (*0-06-014385-1*) HarperCollins Pubs.
—Personal Recollections of Joan of Arc. 1980. (Illus.). 34p. reprint ed. pap. 8.95 o.p. (*0-917482-16-6*) Stowe-Day Foundation.
Van Lustbader, Eric. The Kaisho. abr. ed. 1993. audio 16.95 o.p. (*1-55800-889-6*) NewStar Media, Inc.
—The Kaisho. Zion, Claire, ed. 1993. 496p. 22.00 (*0-671-86806-3*, Atria); 1994. 592p. reprint ed. mass mkt. 6.99 (*0-671-86807-1*, Pocket Star) Simon & Schuster.
Vansittart, Peter. Hermes in Paris. 2001. 234p. 33.95 (*0-7206-1106-7*) Owen, Peter Ltd. GBR. *Dist:* Dufour Editions, Inc.
Vercel, Roger. Tides of Mont St. Michel. Wells, Warre B., tr. 1971. 305p. reprint ed. 35.00 o.s.i (*0-8371-4052-8*, VEMM, Greenwood Pr.) Greenwood Publishing Group, Inc.
Verne, Jules. Paris in the Twentieth Century. Howard, Richard, tr. from FRE. 1997. (Illus.). 256p. pap. 12.95 (*0-345-42039-X*, Del Rey) Ballantine Bks.
Vian, Boris. Blues for a Black Cat & Other Stories. Older, Julia, ed. & tr. by. 1992. (French Modernist Library Ser.). 118p. pap. 12.95 (*0-8032-9609-6*, Bison Bks.); text 30.00 o.p. (*0-8032-4661-7*) Univ. of Nebraska Pr.
Villefranche, Anne-Marie. Plaisir D'Amour: An Erotic Memoir of Paris in the 1920s. 1984. 252p. 12.95 o.p. (*0-88184-022-X*, Carroll & Graf Pubs.) Avalon Publishing Group.
Vlerick, Colette. Le Brodeur de Pont-l'Abbe. l.t. ed. 2000. (French Ser.). (FRE.). 414p. pap. 30.99 (*2-84011-333-3*) Feryane, SA, Editions FRA. *Dist:* Ulverscroft Large Print Bks., Ltd., Ulverscroft Large Print Canada, Ltd.
Wainhouse, Austryn, tr. from FRE. Juliette. 1988. 1216p. pap. 21.95 (*0-8021-3085-2*, Grove Pr.) Grove/Atlantic, Inc.
Ward, Just S. Ambition & Love. 1994. 277p. 22.95 o.p. (*0-395-68196-0*) Houghton Mifflin Co.
Watkins, Paul. In the Blue Light of African Dreams. 1990. 256p. 18.95 o.p. (*0-395-55136-6*) Houghton Mifflin Co.
—In the Blue Light of African Dreams. 1992. 320p. pap. 10.00 (*0-380-71640-2*, Avon Bks.) Morrow/Avon.
—In the Blue Light of African Dreams. 1998. 320p. pap. 13.00 o.s.i (*0-312-18113-2*) Picador.
—In the Blue Light of African Dreams. unabr. ed. 1991. audio 78.00 (*1-55690-625-0*, 91410E7) Recorded Bks., LLC.
Webster, Noah. Flight from Paris. 1987. (Crime Club Ser.). 192p. 12.95 o.s.i (*0-385-23560-7*) Doubleday Publishing.
Weismiller, Edward. The Serpent Sleeping. 2nd ed. 1998. (Classics of Espionage Ser.: Vol. 4). 368p. 49.50 o.s.i (*0-7146-4729-2*); pap. 24.50 o.s.i (*0-7146-4279-7*) Cass, Frank Pubs. GBR. *Dist:* International Specialized Bk. Services.
Welch, James. The Heartsong of Charging Elk. pap. (*0-385-72880-8*) Knopf Publishing Group.
—The Heartsong of Charging Elk: A Novel. 2001. 448p. pap. 14.95 (*0-385-49675-3*, Knopf Bks. for Young Readers) Random Hse. Children's Bks.
Werber, Bernard. An Empire of the Ants. 1999. 320p. reprint ed. mass mkt. 5.99 (*0-553-57352-7*) Bantam Bks.
Werfel, Franz. The Song of Bernadette. Lewisohn, Ludwig, tr. reprint ed. lib. bdg. 32.95 (*0-88411-720-0*) Amereon, Ltd.
—The Song of Bernadette. 1990. reprint ed. lib. bdg. 28.95 (*0-89968-558-7*) Buccaneer Bks., Inc.
—The Song of Bernadette. 1956. pap. 1.95 o.p. (*0-670-00012-4*) Penguin Group (USA) Inc.
—The Song of Bernadette. 1989. (Religious Miracle Fiction Ser.). 576p. reprint ed. pap. 17.95 (*0-312-03429-6*, Saint Martin's Griffin) St. Martin's Pr.
Werfel, Franz, et al. The Song of Bernadette. 1944. 108p. pap. 5.60 (*1-58342-007-X*) Dramatic Publishing Co.
West, Yvonne. Rosemary for Remembrance: A Novel. 1997. 192p. 19.95 (*1-56474-202-4*) Fithian Pr.
Weyman, Stanley J. Count Hannibal. 2000. 252p. E-Book 9.95 (*0-594-06106-7*) 1873 Pr.
—Count Hannibal. 1977. 326p. reprint ed. lib. bdg. 14.95 o.p. (*0-89966-278-1*) Buccaneer Bks., Inc.
—From the Memoirs of a Minister of France. 1977. (Short Story Index Reprint Ser.). 28.95 (*0-8369-3423-7*) Ayer Co. Pubs., Inc.
Wharton, Edith. The Mother's Recompense. (Collected Works of Edith Wharton). 341p. reprint ed. 2001. (Illus.). pap. text 28.00 (*0-7426-5988-7*); 1998. lib. bdg. 98.00 (*1-58201-988-6*) Classic Bks.
—The Mother's Recompense. 1986. 342p. 15.95 o.s.i (*0-684-18771-X*); pap. 12.00 (*0-684-18737-X*) Gale Group. (Macmillan Reference USA).
—The Mother's Recompense. 1996. 288p. pap. 13.00 (*0-684-82531-7*, Scribner) Simon & Schuster.
—The Reef, unabr. ed. 1988. (Classic Books on Cassettes Ser.). audio 47.95 (*1-55685-105-7*) Audio Bk. Contractors, Inc.
—The Reef. unabr. ed. 2000. 8p. audio 69.95 (*0-7540-0471-6*, CAB 1894, Sterling Audio Bks.) BBC Audiobooks America.
—The Reef, unabr. ed. 1996. audio 56.95 (*0-7861-0981-5*, 1758) Blackstone Audio Bks., Inc.
—The Reef. 1998. (Collected Works of Edith Wharton). 366p. reprint ed. lib. bdg. 88.00 (*1-58201-991-6*) Classic Bks.
—The Reef. 2000. 304p. mass mkt. 4.99 (*0-380-81549-4*, Avon Bks.) Morrow/Avon.
—The Reef. Orgel, Stephen, ed. 1998. (Oxford World's Classics Ser.). 236p. pap. 9.95 o.p. (*0-19-282319-1*) Oxford Univ. Pr., Inc.
—The Reef. 1996. 336p. 16.00 (*0-679-44724-5*) Random Hse., Inc.
—The Reef. 1996. 336p. pap. 12.00 (*0-684-82444-2*, Scribner); 1984. 384p. pap. 9.95 o.s.i (*0-684-18249-1*, Scribner Paper Fiction); 1977. 384p. 20.00 (*0-684-15557-5*, Scribner) Simon & Schuster.
—The Reef. 1995. (Penguin Great Books of the 20th Century Ser.). 368p. pap. 10.95 o.s.i (*0-14-018731-6*, Penguin Classics) Viking Penguin.
—A Son at the Front. (Collected Works of Edith Wharton). 426p. reprint ed. 2001. (Illus.). pap. text 28.00 (*0-7426-5993-3*); 1998. lib. bdg. 98.00 (*1-58201-993-2*) Classic Bks.
—A Son at the Front. rev. ed. 2003. 280p. (C). pap. 16.00 (*0-87580-568-X*); lib. bdg. 38.00 (*0-87580-203-6*) Northern Illinois Univ. Pr.
Wharton, William. Last Lovers. unabr. ed. 1991. 23.95 o.p. incl. audio (*0-930435-87-7*, 158, Bookcassette); audio 73.25 o.p. (*1-56100-081-7*, 923, Unabridged Library Editions) Brilliance Audio.
—Last Lovers. 1991. 288p. 22.00 o.s.i (*0-374-18389-9*) Farrar, Straus & Giroux.
—A Midnight Clear. 1983. 256p. mass mkt. 4.99 o.s.i (*0-345-31291-0*) Ballantine Bks.
—A Midnight Clear. 2004. 288p. pap. 14.95 (*1-55704-257-8*) Newmarket Pr.
—Scumbler. 1985. 288p. pap. 3.95 o.p. (*0-88184-135-8*, Carroll & Graf Pubs.) Avalon Publishing Group.
—Scumbler. 1984. 288p. 14.95 o.p. (*0-394-53574-X*) Knopf, Alfred A. Inc.
—Scumbler. 2004. 288p. pap. 12.95 (*1-55704-258-6*) Newmarket Pr.
—Tidings. 1987. 320p. 17.95 o.p. (*0-8050-0532-3*) Holt, Henry & Co.
—Tidings. 1989. 276p. pap. text 5.95 o.p. (*0-07-069504-0*) McGraw-Hill Cos., The.
Whelan, Hilary. A Shoulder to Die On. 1995. 192p. 18.95 o.p. (*0-312-11889-9*, Saint Martin's Minotaur) St. Martin's Pr.
Widdecombe, Ann. The Act of Treachery. 2002. 257p. 24.95 (*0-297-64573-0*) Weidenfeld & Nicolson, Ltd. GBR. *Dist:* Trafalgar Square.
Winterson, Jeanette. The Passion. 1997. 176p. pap. 12.00 (*0-8021-3522-6*, Grove Pr.); 1988. 180p. 16.95 o.p. (*0-87113-183-8*) Grove/Atlantic, Inc.
—The Passion. 1990. (Vintage International Ser.). pap. 10.00 o.s.i (*0-679-72437-0*, Vintage) Knopf Publishing Group.
Wolf, Joan. Daughter of the Red Deer. 1991. 432p. 19.95 o.p. (*0-525-93379-4*, Dutton) Dutton/Plume.
—Daughter of the Red Deer. 1992. 480p. mass mkt. 5.99 o.s.i (*0-451-40334-7*, Onyx) NAL.
—The Horsemasters. 1993. 416p. 22.00 o.p. (*0-525-93589-4*, Dutton) Dutton/Plume.
—The Horsemasters. 1994. 448p. mass mkt. 5.50 o.s.i (*0-451-40505-6*, Onyx) NAL.
Wood. East Lynne. 1993. (Pocket Classics Ser.). pap. text 13.95 (*0-7509-0446-1*) Sutton Publishing, Ltd. GBR. *Dist:* International Publishers Marketing.
—East Lynne. 656p. 1994. 8.95 (*0-460-87430-6*); 1984. pap. 9.95 o.p. (*0-460-11402-6*) Tuttle Publishing. (Everyman's Classic Library in Paperback).
Wood, Graham R. Death in Provence: Detective Lauriant Mysteries. 2003. (WorldKrime Ser.). 320p. 24.95 (*1-890768-52-9*, Intrigue Pr.) Corvus Publishing.
—Detective Lauriant Investigates: Death in a Ditch; Murder in the Vendee. 2002. 340p. 21.95 (*1-890768-44-8*, Intrigue Pr.) Corvus Publishing.
Wood, Henry. East Lynne. Maunder, Andrew, ed. 2000. (Literary Texts Ser.). (Illus.). 700p. pap. (*1-55111-234-5*) Broadview Pr.
Yarbro, Chelsea Quinn. Blood Roses: A Novel of Saint-Germain. 1999. 382p. pap. 15.95 (*0-312-87248-8*); 1998. 384p. 24.95 (*0-312-86529-5*) Doherty, Tom Assocs., LLC. (Tor Bks.).
—A Candle for d'Artagnan. 1994. 485p. pap. 15.95 (*0-312-89019-2*, Orb Bks.); 1989. (Illus.). ix,485p. pap. 22.95 o.p. (*0-312-93202-2*, Tor Bks.) Doherty, Tom Assocs., LLC.
—Night Blooming. (Illus.). 2003. 672p. mass mkt. 6.99 (*0-446-61102-6*); 2002. 448p. 24.95 (*0-446-52981-8*, Aspect) Warner Bks., Inc.
Youngblood, Shay. Black Girl in Paris. 2001. (Illus.). 256p. pap. 12.00 (*1-57322-851-6*, Riverhead Trade (Paperbacks)) Berkley Publishing Group.
—Black Girl in Paris. 2000. (Illus.). 300p. 23.95 o.p. (*1-57322-151-1*, Riverhead Bks. (Hardcovers)) Putnam Publishing Group, The.
Zackheim, Michele. Violette's Embrace. 1997. 224p. reprint ed. 12.00 o.s.i (*1-57322-608-4*, Riverhead Trade (Paperbacks)) Berkley Publishing Group.
—Violette's Embrace. 1996. 256p. 23.95 o.s.i (*1-57322-036-1*, Riverhead Bks. (Hardcovers)) Putnam Publishing Group, The.
Zencey, Eric. Panama. 1997. 400p. reprint ed. mass mkt. 6.99 o.s.i (*0-425-15602-8*) Berkley Publishing Group.
—Panama. 1995. 384p. 24.00 o.p. (*0-374-22943-0*) Farrar, Straus & Giroux.
—Panama. unabr. ed. 1995. audio 91.00 (*0-7887-0454-0*, 94646E7) Recorded Bks., LLC.
—Panama. abr. ed. 1995. audio 23.00 (*0-671-54922-7*, 494361, Simon & Schuster Audioworks) Simon & Schuster Audio.
—Panama. l.t. ed. 1996. (Niagara Large Print Ser.). 514p. 29.50 o.p. (*0-7089-5833-8*, Ulverscroft) Thorpe, F. A. Pubs. GBR. *Dist:* Ulverscroft Large Print Bks., Ltd.
—Panama: A Novel. 2001. 400p. pap. 14.00 (*0-425-17833-1*) Berkley Publishing Group.
Zola, Emile. L' Assommoir. unabr. ed. 1999. (FRE.). pap. 5.95 (*2-87714-127-6*) Bookking International FRA. *Dist:* Distribooks, Inc.
—L' Assommoir. Dubois, Jacques, ed. 1990. (FRE.). 568p. pap. 11.95 (*0-7859-1486-2*, 2266033646) French & European Pubns., Inc.
—L' Assommoir. 1983. (FRE.). (C). pap. 11.95 (*0-8442-1748-4*, VF1748-4) McGraw-Hill/Contemporary.
—L' Assommoir. Tancock, Leonard, tr. & intro. by. mass mkt. 0.75 o.p. (*0-451-50128-4*, Signet Classics) NAL.
—L' Assommoir. Lethbridge, Robert, ed. Mauldon, Margaret, tr. from FRE. 1999. (Oxford World's Classics Ser.). (Illus.). 528p. pap. 10.95 (*0-19-283813-X*) Oxford Univ. Pr., Inc.
—L' Assommoir. Mauldon, Margaret, tr. 1995. (Oxford World's Classics Ser.). (Illus.). 514p. pap. 6.95 o.p. (*0-19-282983-1*) Oxford Univ. Pr., Inc.
—L' Assommoir. 1955. (Folio Ser.: No. 1051). pap. 12.95 (*2-07-037051-8*) Schoenhof's Foreign Bks., Inc.
—L' Assommoir. audio Spoken Arts, Inc.
—L' Assommoir. White, Nicholas, ed. rev. ed. 1995. (Everyman Paperback Classics Ser.). 288p. pap. 7.50 (*0-460-87576-0*, Everyman's Classic Library in Paperback) Tuttle Publishing.
—L' Assommoir. 2001. (Classics Ser.). (Illus.). 480p. pap. 11.00 (*0-14-044753-9*, Penguin Classics) Viking Penguin.
—L' Assommoir. Tancock, Leonard W., tr. 1970. (Penguin Classics Ser.). 432p. pap. 10.95 o.s.i (*0-14-044231-6*, Penguin Classics) Viking Penguin.
—The Belly of Paris. unabr. ed. 1999. audio 62.95 Blackstone Audio Bks., Inc.
—The Belly of Paris. Vizetelly, Ernest A., tr. 2003. (Green Integer Bks.: Vol. 57). 400p. pap. 15.95 (*1-892295-99-7*) Green Integer.
—The Belly of Paris. Vizetelly, Ernest Alfred, tr. from FRE. 1995. (Sun & Moon Classics Ser.: No. 70). 397p. pap. 14.95 o.p. (*1-55713-066-3*) Sun & Moon Pr.
—The Belly of Paris. Vizetelly, Ernest Alfred, tr. from FRE. 1993. (Pocket Classics Ser.). pap. 10.95 (*0-7509-0449-6*) Sutton Publishing, Ltd. GBR. *Dist:* International Publishers Marketing.
—Germinal. Ellis, Havelock, tr. 1964. 5.00 o.p. (*0-460-00897-8*); pap. o.p. (*0-460-01897-3*, EP1897) Biblio Distribution.
—Germinal. unabr. ed. 1996. audio 85.95 (*0-7861-0955-6*, 1732);Set. audio 85.95 Blackstone Audio Bks., Inc.
—Germinal. unabr. ed. 1999. (FRE.). pap. 5.95 (*2-87714-139-X*) Bookking International FRA. *Dist:* Distribooks, Inc.
—Germinal. Guillmin, Henri, ed. 1975. (FRE.). pap. 13.95 (*0-7859-1422-6*, 2080701916) French & European Pubns., Inc.
—Germinal. Ellis, Havelock, tr. from FRE. 1994. 558p. pap. 9.00 o.s.i (*0-679-75430-X*, Vintage) Knopf Publishing Group.
—Germinal. (FRE.). pap. 11.25 (*2-253-00422-7*, LP0206E) Librairie Generale Francaise, LGF FRA. *Dist:* Continental Bk. Co., Inc.
—Germinal. 1970. mass mkt. 2.95 o.p. (*0-451-51577-3*); mass mkt. 3.50 o.p. (*0-451-51809-8*); mass mkt. 1.75 o.p. (*0-451-50731-2*); mass mkt. 2.50 o.p. (*0-451-51331-2*); mass mkt. 2.25 o.p. (*0-451-*

Settings

51056-9); mass mkt. 1.50 o.p. (0-451-50499-2); mass mkt. 1.95 o.p. (0-451-50897-1); 448p. mass mkt. 6.95 o.s.i (0-451-51975-2, CE1809) NAL. (Signet Classics).

—Germinal. 1995. (FRE.). Pt. 1, set. audio 31.95; Pt. 2, set. audio 34.95; Pt. 3, set. audio 34.95; Pt. 4, set. audio 31.95; Pts. 1-4, set. audio 119.95 Olivia & Hill Pr., The.

—Germinal. Collier, Peter, tr. 1998. (Oxford World's Classics Ser.). (Illus.). 576p. pap. 7.95 (0-19-283702-8) Oxford Univ. Pr., Inc.

—Germinal. Lethbridge, Robert, ed. Collier, Peter, tr. from FRE. 1994. (Oxford World's Classics Ser.). (Illus.). 574p. pap. 6.95 o.p. (0-19-282701-4) Oxford Univ. Pr., Inc.

—Germinal. 1999. (FRE.). pap. 12.95 (2-266-08262-0) Presses Pocket FRA. Dist: Distribooks, Inc.

—Germinal. Tancock, Leonard W., tr. 1991. xxxi, 498p. 17.00 o.s.i (0-679-40556-9, Modern Library) Random House Adult Trade Publishing Group.

—Germinal. 1956. (Folio Ser.: No. 1001). (FRE.). 12.95 (2-07-037001-1) Schoenhof's Foreign Bks., Inc.

—Germinal. Ellis, Havelock, tr. 1980. 4.75 o.p. (0-8446-1488-2) Smith, Peter Pub., Inc.

—Germinal. Baguley, David, ed. rev. ed. 1996. (Everyman Paperback Classics Ser.). 432p. pap. 7.50 (0-460-87581-7, Everyman's Classic Library in Paperback) Tuttle Publishing.

—Germinal. Tancock, Leonard W., tr. & intro. by. 1954. (Classics Ser.). 512p. pap. 8.95 (0-14-044045-3, Penguin Classics) Viking Penguin.

—Lourdes. 7.95 French & European Pubns., Inc.

—Lourdes. 2000. (Literary Classics). 504p. pap. 11.00 (1-57392-828-3) Prometheus Bks., Pubs.

—Lourdes. Vizetelly, Ernest Alfred, tr. from FRE. 1993. (Pocket Classics Ser.). xii, 492p. pap. 10.95 (0-7509-0452-6) Sutton Publishing, Ltd. GBR. Dist: International Publishers Marketing.

—Paris. Vizetelly, Ernest Alfred, tr. 1993. (Pocket Classics Ser.). pap. text 10.95 (0-7509-0450-X) Sutton Publishing.

—Les Rougon-Macquart, Vol. 1. Lanoux, Armand, ed. 1964. (FRE.). lib. bdg. 150.00 (0-7859-3807-9) French & European Pubns., Inc.

—Les Rougon-Macquart, Vol. 2. Lanoux, Rene, ed. 1961. 130.00 (0-7859-3806-0) French & European Pubns., Inc.

—Les Rougon-Macquart. Lanoux, Armand, ed. (FRE.). Vol. 2. 1960. lib. bdg. 150.00 (0-7859-3923-7); Vol. 4. 1966. lib. bdg. 150.00 (0-7859-3924-5) French & European Pubns., Inc.

—Les Rougon-Macquart, Vol. 5. 1967. (FRE.). lib. bdg. 150.00 (0-7859-3808-7) French & European Pubns., Inc.

—Les Rougon-Macquart, 5 tomes. Mitterand & Lanoux, Armand, eds. deluxe ed. 1968. (Pleiade Ser.). (FRE.). Vol. 1. 84.95 (2-07-010589-X); Vol. 2. 75.95 (2-07-010590-3); Vol. 3. 84.95 (2-07-010591-1); Vol. 4. 85.95 (2-07-010592-X); Vol. 5. 84.95 (2-07-010593-8) Schoenhof's Foreign Bks., Inc.

Zollo, Burt. Prisoners. 2003. 22.50 (0-89733-515-5) Academy Chicago Pubs., Ltd.

## G

### GAINESVILLE (FLA.)—FICTION

Crews, Harry. All We Need of Hell: A Novel. 1987. 160p. 14.95 o.p. (0-06-015680-5); 1988. 162p. reprint ed. pap. 6.95 o.p. (0-06-091460-2, PL-1460, Perennial) HarperTrade.

### GALACTIC MILIEU (IMAGINARY PLACE)—FICTION

May, Julian. The Adversary. 1987. (Saga of the Pliocene Exile Ser.: Vol. 4). 512p. mass mkt. 6.99 o.s.i (0-345-35244-0, Del Rey) Ballantine Bks.

—The Adversary. 1984. (Saga of Pliocene Exile Ser.: 4). 480p. 16.95 o.p. (0-395-34410-7) Houghton Mifflin Co.

—Diamond Mask. 1995. 448p. pap. 23.00 (0-345-47034-6); (Galactic Milieu Trilogy Ser.: Bk. 2). mass mkt. 6.99 (0-345-36248-9) Ballantine Bks. (Del Rey).

—Diamond Mask. 1994. (Galactic Milieu Trilogy Ser.: Vol. 2). 461p. 22.00 o.s.i (0-679-43310-4); o.s.i (0-679-43577-8) Knopf, Alfred A. Inc.

—The Golden Torc. 1985. (Saga of the Pliocene Exile Ser.: Vol. II). 416p. mass mkt. 6.99 o.s.i (0-345-32419-6); 1983. mass mkt. 2.95 o.p. (0-345-30838-7) Ballantine Bks. (Del Rey).

—The Golden Torc, 001. 1982. (Saga of Pliocene Exile Ser.: Vol. II). 448p. 13.95 o.p. (0-395-31261-2) Houghton Mifflin Co.

—Impressionists Side by Side: Their Friendships, Rivalries, & Artistic Exchanges. 1996. (Galactic Milieu Trilogy Ser.: 3). 416p. 25.00 o.s.i (0-679-44177-8) Random Hse., Inc.

—Intervention. 1987. 400p. 18.95 o.p. (0-395-43782-2) Houghton Mifflin Co.

—Jack the Bodiless. 1993. (Galactic Milieu Trilogy Ser.: 1). 480p. mass mkt. 6.99 (0-345-36247-0, Del Rey); mass mkt. (0-345-38573-X, Ballantine Bks.) Ballantine Bks.

—Jack the Bodiless. 1994. (Galactic Milieu Trilogy Ser.: 1). 4.99 o.p. (0-517-11644-8) Random Hse. Value Publishing.

—Magnificat, Vol. 3. 1997. (Galactic Milieu Trilogy Ser.: Vol. 3). 432p. mass mkt. 6.99 o.s.i (0-345-36249-7, Del Rey) Ballantine Bks.

—The Many-Colored Land. 1985. 480p. mass mkt. 6.99 o.s.i (0-345-32444-7, Del Rey) Ballantine Bks.

—The Many-Colored Land, 001. 1981. (Saga of Pliocene Exile Ser.). 432p. 12.95 o.p. (0-395-30230-7) Houghton Mifflin Co.

—The Metaconcert. 1989. (Intervention Ser.: Bk. 2). 320p. mass mkt. 5.99 o.s.i (0-345-35524-5, Del Rey) Ballantine Bks.

—The Nonborn King. 1987. (Saga of the Pliocene Exile Ser.: Vol. 3). 480p. mass mkt. 6.99 o.s.i (0-345-34749-8, Del Rey) Ballantine Bks.

—The Nonborn King, 001. 1983. (Saga of Pliocene Exile Ser.: 3). (Illus.). 395p. 16.95 o.p. (0-395-32211-1) Houghton Mifflin Co.

—The Surveillance. 1988. (Intervention Ser.: 1). 368p. mass mkt. 6.99 o.s.i (0-345-35523-7, Del Rey) Ballantine Bks.

### GALVESTON (TEX.)—FICTION

Blake, James Carlos. Under the Skin: A Novel. 2003. 304p. 25.95 (0-380-97751-6) Morrow/Avon.

Crider, Bill. Dead on the Island. unabr. ed. 1995. audio 17.00 (1-883268-19-2) Spellbinders, Inc.

—Dead on the Island. 1991. 193p. 18.95 (0-8027-5787-1) Walker & Co.

—Gator Kill. Haywood, Richard, ed. unabr. ed. 1995. (Truman Smith Trilogy Ser.). audio 17.00 (1-883268-27-3) Spellbinders, Inc.

—Gator Kill: A Truman Smith. 1992. 202p. 18.95 (0-8027-3213-5) Walker & Co.

—Murder Takes a Break: A Truman Smith Mystery. 1997. (Truman Smith Mystery Ser.). 246p. 21.95 (0-8027-3308-5) Walker & Co.

—The Prairie Chicken Kill: A Truman Smith Mystery. 1996. (Truman Smith Mystery Ser.). 216p. 20.95 (0-8027-3282-8) Walker & Co.

—When Old Men Die. abr. ed. 1997. audio 17.00 (1-883268-33-8) Spellbinders, Inc.

—When Old Men Die. 1994. 192p. 19.95 (0-8027-3195-3) Walker & Co.

Grissom, Ken. Drop-Off: A John Rodrigue Novel. 1989. mass mkt. 3.95 (0-312-91617-5, Tor Bks.) Doherty, Tom Assocs., LLC.

—Drop-Off: A John Rodrigue Novel. 1989. mass mkt. 3.95 (0-312-91616-7, St. Martin's Paperbacks); 1988. 224p. 15.95 o.p. (0-312-02196-8, Saint Martin's Minotaur) St. Martin's Pr.

Leavenworth, Geoffrey. Isle of Misfortune: A Novel. 2003. (Illus.). 256p. 26.50 (0-87565-269-7) Texas Christian Univ. Pr.

Nagle, P. G. Galveston. E-Book 24.95 (0-312-70631-6, Tor Bks.); 2002. (Illus.). 384p. 24.95 (0-312-87614-9, Forge Bks.) Doherty, Tom Assocs., LLC.

Ryan, Nan. Naughty Marietta. 2003. 384p. mass mkt. (1-55166-676-6, Mira Bks.) Harlequin Enterprises, Ltd.

—Naughty Marietta. l.t. ed. 2003. 429p. 27.95 (0-7862-5844-6) Thorndike Pr.

### GANDALARA (IMAGINARY PLACE)—FICTION

Garrett, Randall. The River Wall. 1986. (Orig.). mass mkt. 3.95 o.s.i (0-553-27671-9, Spectra) Bantam Bks.

Garrett, Randall & Heydron, Vicki A. The Glass of Dyskornis. 1982. 144p. pap. 2.95 o.p. (0-553-25230-5) Bantam Bks.

—Return to Eddarta. 1985. (Gandalara Cycle Ser.: No. 6). 160p. pap. 2.75 o.p. (0-553-24709-3) Bantam Bks.

—The River Wall. 1986. 288p. (Orig.). mass mkt. 3.50 o.s.i (0-553-25565-7, Spectra) Bantam Bks.

—The Search for Ka. 1984. 192p. pap. 2.50 o.p. (0-553-24120-6) Bantam Bks.

—The Steel of Raithskar. 1981. 192p. pap. 2.75 o.p. (0-553-24911-8) Bantam Bks.

—The Well of Darkness. 1983. (Gandalara Cycle Ser.: No. 4). pap. 2.75 o.p. (0-553-24505-8) Bantam Bks.

### GARILLON (IMAGINARY PLACE)—FICTION

Harris, Deborah T. The Burning Stone. 320p. (Orig.). 1988. mass mkt. 3.50 (0-8125-3958-3); 1987. pap. 7.95 o.p. (0-8125-3950-8) Doherty, Tom Assocs., LLC. (Tor Bks.).

—Gauntlet of Malice, Vol. 2. 1988. 352p. pap. 3.50 o.p. (0-8125-3956-7, Tor Bks.) Doherty, Tom Assocs., LLC.

—Spiral of Fire Bk. III: The Mages of Garillon, Vol. 3. 1989. pap. 3.95 o.p. (0-8125-3954-0, Tor Bks.) Doherty, Tom Assocs., LLC.

### GENEVA (SWITZERLAND)—FICTION

Cohen, Albert. Belle du Seigneur. 1986. (FRE.). 110.00 (0-8288-3464-4, F73582) French & European Pubns., Inc.

—Belle du Seigneur. 2000. (FRE.). pap. 23.95 (2-07-040402-1) Gallimard, Editions FRA. Dist: Distribooks, Inc.

—Belle du Seigneur. 1968. (Gallimard Ser.). (FRE.). pap. 44.95 (2-07-026917-5) Schoenhof's Foreign Bks., Inc.

—Belle du Seigneur. Coward, David, tr. from FRE. & intro. by. 1998. (Penguin Twentieth-Century Classics Ser.). (SPA.). 992p. pap. 15.95 o.s.i (0-14-018871-1, Penguin Classics) Viking Penguin.

—Belle du Seigneur. 1996. 992p. 34.95 o.s.i (0-670-82187-X) Viking Penguin.

Darcy, Emma. A Marriage Betrayed. 1999. (Harlequin Presents Ser.: Vol. 2069). mass mkt. (0-373-12069-9, Harlequin Bks.) Harlequin Enterprises, Ltd.

—A Marriage Betrayed. l.t. ed. 2000. (Harlequin I Romance Ser.). 22.95 (0-263-16406-3) Harlequin Mills & Boon, Ltd. GBR. Dist: Thorndike Pr.

Harcourt, Palma. Limited Options. 1987. 224p. 15.95 o.p. (0-8253-0419-9) Beaufort Bks., Inc.

—Limited Options. l.t. ed. 1988. (Ulverscroft Large Print Ser.). 400p. 29.99 o.p. (0-7089-1847-6, Ulverscroft) Thorpe, F. A. Pubs. GBR. Dist: Ulverscroft Large Print Bks., Ltd., Ulverscroft Large Print Canada, Ltd.

Moorhouse, Frank. Dark Palace. 2000. 678p. (0-09-183676-X) Hutchinson Children's Bks, Ltd.

Shelley, Mary Wollstonecraft. Frankenstein. 2000. (SPA.). 320p. 8.95 (84-406-1953-7) B Ediciones S.A. ESP. Dist: Distribooks, Inc.

—Frankenstein. E-Book (0-7607-1308-1) Barnes & Noble, Inc.

—Frankenstein. 2001. per. 14.00 (1-891355-53-8); per. 15.50 (1-58396-220-4) Blue Unicorn Editions.

—Frankenstein. 1997. (Cambridge Literature Ser.). audio 14.95 o.p. (0-521-59793-5) Cambridge Univ. Pr.

—Frankenstein. 1999. (Bloom's Reviews Comprehensive Research & Study Guides). 72p. pap. 4.95 (0-7910-4121-2) Chelsea Hse. Pubs.

—Frankenstein. l.t. ed. 1998. 343p. pap. 19.95 (1-58855-029-X) Cyber Classics, Inc.

—Frankenstein. 1988. mass mkt. 4.95 (0-938819-80-1, Aerie) Doherty, Tom Assocs., LLC.

—Frankenstein. l.t. unabr. ed. 2001. (Large Print Classics Ser.). xv, 283p. pap. 9.95 (0-486-41562-7) Dover Pubns., Inc.

—Frankenstein. 2003. (Barnes & Noble Classics Ser.). 288p. pap. 3.95 (1-59308-005-0) Fine Communications.

—Frankenstein. l.t. ed. 2001. 315p. 27.95 (0-7838-9622-0, Hall, G. K. & Co.) Gale Group.

—Frankenstein. 2003. pap. 6.50 (1-59456-236-9) GreatUNpublished.com.

—Frankenstein. 1965. mass mkt. 0.50 o.p. (0-451-50329-5); mass mkt. 0.75 o.p. (0-451-50695-2); mass mkt. 0.95 o.p. (0-451-50839-4); mass mkt. 1.50 o.p. (0-451-51132-8); mass mkt. 0.60 o.p. (0-451-50618-9); mass mkt. 1.25 o.p. (0-451-50975-7) NAL. (Signet Classics).

—Frankenstein. (C). pap. (0-393-97938-5) Norton, W. W. & Co., Inc.

—Frankenstein. 2003. (Penguin Classics Ser.). 336p. pap. 8.00 (0-14-143947-5) Penguin Group (USA) Inc.

—Frankenstein. 1995. (SPA.). 304p. (84-01-46253-3) Plaza & Janés Editories, S.A.

—Frankenstein. (FRE.). pap. 10.95 (2-266-00354-2) Presses Pocket FRA. Dist: Distribooks, Inc.

—Frankenstein. 2004. 304p. mass mkt. 3.95 (0-7434-8758-3, Pocket) Simon & Schuster.

—Frankenstein: Or, the Modern Prometheus. 2001. (Oxford World's Classics Ser.). 224p. 15.00 (0-19-514901-7) Oxford Univ. Pr., Inc.

Szczypiorski, Andrzej. Self-Portrait with Woman. Johnson, Bill, tr. 1996. 224p. 21.00 o.p. (0-8021-1567-5, Grove Pr.) Grove/Atlantic, Inc.

—Self-Portrait with Woman. Johnston, Bill, tr. from POL. 1997. 256p. reprint ed. pap. 12.00 (0-8021-3488-2, Grove Pr.) Grove/Atlantic, Inc.

Weber, Katherine. Objects in Mirror Are Closer Than They Appear. 1996. 272p. pap. 12.00 (0-312-14383-4) Picador.

Williams, Amanda K. A Singular Spy. 1992. 192p. pap. 8.95 o.p. (1-56280-008-6) Naiad Pr., Inc.

### GEORGIA—FICTION

Adair, Frances E. A Little Leaven. Burgess, J. R., ed. 1984. 352p. reprint ed. 19.95 o.p. (0-87797-065-3) Cherokee Publishing Co.

Adler, John M. Hunt Out of the Thicket. 1990. 208p. 15.95 o.p. (0-945575-06-8) Algonquin Bks. of Chapel Hill.

Allison, Dorothy. Cavedweller. abr. ed. 1998. audio 7.99 o.s.i (1-56740-280-1, 1681, Paperback Nova Audio Bks.); audio 17.95 o.p. (1-56740-763-3, 463, Nova Audio Bks.); audio 28.95 (1-56100-788-9, 60, Bookcassette); 15p. audio 89.25 (1-56740-567-3, 822, Unabridged Library Editions) Brilliance Audio.

—Cavedweller. 448p. 1999. pap. 13.95 (0-452-27969-0, Plume); 1998. 24.95 o.s.i (0-525-94167-3) Dutton/Plume.

—Cavedweller. l.t. ed. 1998. (Basic Ser.). 683p. 28.95 (0-7862-1503-8) Thorndike Pr.

Andrews, Mary Kay. Savannah Blues. 2002. 23.95 (0-06-008611-4) HarperCollins Pubs.

Andrews, Raymond. Jessie & Jesus & Cousin Claire. (Illus.). 208p. 1991. 16.95 o.s.i (1-56145-032-4); 1993. reprint ed. pap. 11.95 (1-56145-090-1) Peachtree Pubs., Ltd.

Ansa, Tina McElroy. The Hand I Fan With. unabr. ed. 1997. audio 96.00 (0-7366-3660-9, 4334) Books on Tape, Inc.

—The Hand I Fan With. 1997. 496p. pap. 14.00 (0-385-47601-9) Doubleday Publishing.

—The Hand I Fan With, Set. abr. ed. 1996. 360p. audio 23.95 o.s.i (0-553-47804-4, 694513, RH Audio) Random Hse. Audio Publishing Group.

—Ugly Ways. 1993. 277p. 19.95 o.s.i (0-15-192553-4) Harcourt Trade Pubs.

—Ugly Ways: A Novel. 1995. (Harvest American Writing Ser.). 288p. pap. 14.00 (0-15-600077-6, Harvest Bks.) Harcourt Trade Pubs.

Bacon, Eugenia J. Lyddy. 1977. (Black Heritage Library Collection). reprint ed. 22.95 (0-8369-8958-9) Ayer Co. Pubs., Inc.

Bacon, Eugenia J. & MacKethan, Lucinda H. Lyddy: A Tale of the Old South. 1998. (Illus.). iix, 287p. pap. 17.00 (0-8203-1967-8) Univ. of Georgia Pr.

Ballard, F. Mignon. An Angel to Die For. E-Book 22.95 (0-312-27632-X); 2000. 307p. 23.95 o.p. (0-312-24174-7, Saint Martin's Minotaur) St. Martin's Pr.

Ballard-Jones, Anita. Rehoboth Road. 2003. 248p. 28.95 (0-9729455-1-2); per. 19.95 (0-9729455-0-4) Black Deer Bks.

Ballard, Mignon F. An Angel to Die For. l.t. ed. 2001. (Beeler Large Print Mystery Ser.). 246p. 26.95 (1-57490-337-3, Beeler Large Print Bks.) Beeler, Thomas T. Publisher.

—An Angel to Die For. 2001. 208p. mass mkt. 5.99 o.s.i (0-425-18208-8) Berkley Publishing Group.

—Deadly Promise. 1989. 16.95 o.p. (0-88184-515-9, Carroll & Graf Pubs.) Avalon Publishing Group.

—The War in Sallie's Station. 275p. 2003. pap. 13.95 (1-4104-0117-0, Five Star Trade); 2001. 25.95 (0-7862-3377-X, Five Star) Gale Group.

Bambara, Toni Cade. The Salt Eaters. (Vintage Contemporaries Ser.). 304p. 1992. pap. 13.00 (0-679-74076-7); 1981. pap. 8.00 o.p. (0-394-75050-0) Knopf Publishing Group. (Vintage).

—The Salt Eaters. 1980. 9.95 o.p. (0-394-50712-6) Random Hse., Inc.

—Those Bones Are Not My Child. 2000. (Illus.). 688p. pap. 16.00 (0-679-77408-4, Vintage) Knopf Publishing Group.

Barclay, Max. Red Mercury. 1997. pap. 5.99 o.p. (0-7871-1416-2, NewStar Pr.); 1996. 17.95 o.p. (0-7871-0972-X, 394019) NewStar Media, Inc.

—Red Mercury. 1996. 416p. 22.95 o.p. (0-7871-0920-7, Signet Bks.) Penguin Group (USA) Inc.

Barr, Nevada. Endangered Species. l.t. ed. 1997. 25.95 (1-57490-108-7, Beeler Large Print Bks.) Beeler, Thomas T. Publisher.

—Endangered Species. 1998. (Anna Pigeon Mysteries Ser.). 400p. mass mkt. 7.99 (0-380-72583-5, Avon Bks.) Morrow/Avon.

—Endangered Species, Set. abr. ed. 1997. 18.00 o.p. (0-7871-1373-5, 395114) NewStar Media, Inc.

—Endangered Species. 1997. 320p. 22.95 o.p. (0-399-14246-0, G. P. Putnam's Sons) Penguin Group (USA) Inc.

Battle, Lois. Southern Women. 1984. 384p. 14.95 o.p. (0-312-74747-0) St. Martin's Pr.

Bernhardt, William. Final Round. 2003. 336p. mass mkt. 7.50 (0-345-44963-0); 2002. 256p. 23.95 (0-345-44962-2) Ballantine Bks. (Ballantine Bks.).

—Final Round. l.t. ed. 2003. 307p. 25.95 (0-375-43276-0, Random House Large Print) Random Hse. Large Print.

Berry, Linda. Death & the Easter Bunny. 1999. (WWL Mystery Ser.: Vol. 326). per. (0-373-26326-0, Worldwide Library) Harlequin Enterprises, Ltd.

—Death & the Easter Bunny. 1998. 224p. 20.95 (1-885173-44-X) Write Way Publishing.

—Death & the Hubcap. 2002. (WWL Mystery Ser.: No. 409). 252p. mass mkt. (0-373-26409-7, 1-26409-2, Worldwide Library) Harlequin Enterprises, Ltd.

—Death & the Ice Box: A Trudy Roundtree Mystery. 2003. 248p. 25.95 (0-7862-5233-2, Five Star) Gale Group.

Bigelow, Lydia Tilden. The Live Oak Motel. 2000. 158p. per. (0-9676053-4-2) Athena Pr.

Biggle, Lloyd, Jr. Where Dead Soldiers Walk: A Pletcher & Lambert Mystery. 1994. 288p. 20.95 o.p. (0-312-11011-1, Saint Martin's Minotaur) St. Martin's Pr.

Birmingham, Ruth. Atlanta Graves. 1998. (Sunny Childs Mysteries Ser.). 288p. mass mkt. 5.99 o.s.i (*0-425-16267-2*) Berkley Publishing Group.
—Fulton County Blues. 1999. (Fulton County Blues Ser.: Vol. 2). 288p. mass mkt. 5.99 o.s.i (*0-425-16697-X*, Prime Crime) Berkley Publishing Group.
—Fulton County Blues. 2000. 12.04 (*0-606-19296-4*) Turtleback Bks.
—Sweet Georgia. 2000. (Sunny Childs Mysteries Ser.). 320p. mass mkt. 5.99 o.s.i (*0-425-17671-1*, Prime Crime) Berkley Publishing Group.
Bishop, Michael. Ancient of Days. 1995. 354p. pap. 13.95 (*0-312-89027-3*); 1986. 416p. reprint ed. mass mkt. 3.95 (*0-8125-3197-3*) Doherty, Tom Assocs., LLC. (Tor Bks.).
—Ancient of Days. 1985. 310p. 16.95 o.p. (*0-87795-724-X*, Morrow, William & Co.) Morrow/Avon.
—Brittle Innings. 1995. 528p. mass mkt. 5.99 o.s.i (*0-553-56943-0*) Bantam Bks.
Blackburn, Joyce K. The Bloody Summer of Seventeen Forty-Two: A Colonial Boy's Journal. 1985. (Illus.). 64p. (J). (gr. 5-8). pap. 7.95 (*0-930803-00-0*) Fort Frederica Assn., Inc.
Blackstock, Terri. Cape Refuge Bk #1. 2002. 400p. pap. 12.99 (*0-310-23592-8*) Zondervan.
—Southern Storm. l.t. ed. 2004. 633p. pap. 16.95 (*1-59415-008-7*, Walker Large Print) Gale Group.
—Southern Storm. 2003. (Cape Refuge Ser.). (Illus.). 384p. pap. 12.99 (*0-310-23593-6*) Zondervan.
Blake, Jennifer, et al. With a Southern Touch: Adam; A Night in Paradise; Garden Cop. 2002. 384p. mass mkt. (*1-55166-876-9*, 1-66876-3, Mira Bks.) Harlequin Enterprises, Ltd.
Blakeney, Reed. A Mulberry Summer. 2002. 158p. pap. (*1-55369-092-3*) Trafford Publishing.
Bolton, Clyde. The Lost Sunshine. 1994. 192p. 20.00 (*1-881320-06-5*, Black Belt Pr.) River City Publishing.
Bottoms, David. Any Cold Jordan. 1987. 263p. 14.95 o.p. (*0-934601-12-7*) Peachtree Pubs., Ltd.
—Any Cold Jordan. 1988. bds. 6.95 (*0-671-65987-1*, Washington Square Pr.) Simon & Schuster.
Braselton, Jeanne. A False Sense of Well Being. 2001. 352p. 23.95 (*0-345-44311-X*, Ballantine Bks.) Ballantine Bks.
—A False Sense of Well Being. 2002. 400p. pap. 13.95 (*0-345-44312-8*) Random Hse., Inc.
—The Other Side of Air. 2004. 352p. 23.95 (*0-345-44309-8*, Ballantine Bks.) Ballantine Bks.
Brown, Linda Beatrice. Crossing over Jordan. 1995. 320p. 22.00 o.p. (*0-345-37857-1*) Ballantine Bks.
Brown, Sandra. Envy. 2001. 496p. 25.95 o.p. (*0-446-52713-0*) Warner Bks., Inc.
Burns, Olive Ann. Cold Sassy Tree. l.t. ed. 1992. 720p. 15.00 o.s.i (*0-385-30842-6*, Delacorte Large Type) Bantam Doubleday Dell Large Print Group, Inc.
—Cold Sassy Tree. unabr. ed. 2000. audio compact disk 88.00 (*0-7861-9924-5*, z1354); 1993. audio 62.95 (*0-7861-0402-3*, 112687) Blackstone Audio Bks., Inc.
—Cold Sassy Tree. unabr. collector's ed. 1987. audio 88.00 (*0-7366-1207-6*, 2125) Books on Tape, Inc.
—Cold Sassy Tree. 1992. 480p. mass mkt. 5.99 o.s.i (*0-440-21272-3*); 1986. 400p. pap. 5.95 o.s.i (*0-440-51442-8*, Laurel); 1986. 400p. pap. 14.95 (*0-385-31258-X*, Delta) Dell Publishing.
—Cold Sassy Tree. l.t. ed. 1985. (General Ser.). 18.95 o.p. (*0-8161-3880-X*, Macmillan Reference USA) Gale Group.
—Cold Sassy Tree, Set. unabr. ed. 1999. audio 62.95 Highsmith Inc.
—Cold Sassy Tree. 1984. 400p. tchr. ed. 26.00 (*0-89919-309-9*) Houghton Mifflin Co.
—Cold Sassy Tree. abr. ed. 1989. audio 18.00 (*0-553-45166-9*, 390540, RH Audio) Random Hse. Audio Publishing Group.
—Cold Sassy Tree. 1984. (J). 20.00 (*0-606-02606-1*) Turtleback Bks.
—Leaving Cold Sassy: The Unfinished Sequel to Cold Sassy Tree. 1994. 320p. pap. 13.95 (*0-385-31220-2*, Delta) Dell Publishing.
—Leaving Cold Sassy: The Unfinished Sequel to Cold Sassy Tree. l.t. ed. (General Ser.). 336p. 1994. lib. bdg. 22.95 (*0-8161-5702-2*); 1993. lib. bdg. 16.95 o.p. (*0-8161-5703-0*) Gale Group. (Macmillan Reference USA).
—Leaving Cold Sassy: The Unfinished Sequel to Cold Sassy Tree. 1992. (Illus.). 256p. 21.00 o.p. (*0-89919-908-9*) Houghton Mifflin Co.
—Leaving Cold Sassy: The Unfinished Sequel to Cold Sassy Tree. 1992. 19.00 (*0-606-06523-7*) Turtleback Bks.
Busby, Mark. Fort Benning Blues. 2001. 206p. 24.50 (*0-87565-238-7*) Texas Christian Univ. Pr.
Caldwell, Erskine. Georgia Boy. 1975. mass mkt. 1.25 o.p. (*0-451-06908-0*, Signet Bks.); 1971. mass mkt. 0.75 o.p. (*0-451-04531-9*, Signet Bks.); 1971. mass mkt. 0.50 o.p. (*0-451-50057-1*, Signet Classics); 1971. mass mkt. 0.25 o.p. (*0-451-00760-3*, Signet Bks.); 1971. mass mkt. 0.35 o.p. (*0-451-01666-1*, Signet Bks.) NAL.
—Georgia Boy. 1995. (Brown Thrasher Bks.). 248p. pap. 12.95 (*0-8203-1736-5*) Univ. of Georgia Pr.
—God's Little Acre. 18.95 (*0-88411-456-2*) Amereon, Ltd.
—God's Little Acre. 1977. (Illus.). 212p. 25.00 (*0-88322-024-5*) Beehive Pr., The.
—God's Little Acre. unabr. ed. 1999. audio 27.95 (*0-7861-1541-6*); 1996. audio 39.95 (*0-7861-0926-2*, 1681) Blackstone Audio Bks., Inc.
—God's Little Acre. unabr. ed. 1996. (Bookcassette Classic Collection). audio 17.95 o.p. (*1-56100-655-6*, 123, Bookcassette); 6p. audio 57.25 o.p. (*1-56100-280-1*, 1218, Unabridged Library Editions) Brilliance Audio.
—God's Little Acre. 1993. 300p. reprint ed. lib. bdg. 25.95 (*0-89966-869-0*) Buccaneer Bks., Inc.
—God's Little Acre. 1976. 6.95 o.p. (*0-453-00367-2*, Dutton) Dutton/Plume.
—God's Little Acre, Set. unabr. ed. 1999. audio 39.95 Highsmith Inc.
—God's Little Acre. 2015. mass mkt. 3.50 o.p. (*0-451-51996-5*, Signet Classics); 1969. mass mkt. 0.75 o.p. (*0-451-03969-6*, Signet Bks.); 1946. mass mkt. 0.60 o.p. (*0-451-03246-2*, Signet Bks.); 1946. mass mkt. 2.95 o.p. (*0-451-12155-4*, Signet Bks.); 1946. mass mkt. 0.50 o.p. (*0-451-02289-0*, Signet Bks.); 1946. mass mkt. 0.35 o.p. (*0-451-00581-3*, Signet Bks.); 1946. mass mkt. 2.95 o.p. (*0-451-51802-0*, Signet Classics); 1946. mass mkt. 1.75 o.p. (*0-451-51167-0*, Signet Classics); 1946. mass mkt. 1.50 o.p. (*0-451-50984-6*, Signet Classics) NAL.
—God's Little Acre. abr. ed. 1997. (Ultimate Classics Ser.). 3p. 18.00 o.p. (*0-7871-0910-X*, 396100) NewStar Media, Inc.
—God's Little Acre. unabr. ed. 1995. audio 51.00 (*0-7887-0420-6*, 94612E7) Recorded Bks., LLC.
—God's Little Acre. l.t. ed. 1982. 335p. reprint ed. 12.95 o.p. (*0-89621-329-3*) Thorndike Pr.
—God's Little Acre. 1995. (Brown Thrasher Bks.). 232p. 25.00 o.p. (*0-8203-1662-8*); pap. 12.95 (*0-8203-1663-6*) Univ. of Georgia Pr.
—Le Petit Arpent du Bon Dieu. 1983. (FRE.). pap. 10.95 (*0-7859-1751-9*, 2070364194) French & European Pubns., Inc.
—Un Petit Gars de Georgie. 1978. (FRE.). 182p. pap. 10.95 (*0-7859-1881-7*, 2070370593) French & European Pubns., Inc.
—La Route au Tabac. 1973. (FRE.). 256p. pap. 10.95 (*0-7859-1753-5*, 2070364380) French & European Pubns., Inc.
—Tobacco Road. 1978. reprint ed. lib. bdg. 14.00 (*0-8376-0422-2*) Bentley Pubs.
—Tobacco Road. 1970. mass mkt. 0.75 o.p. (*0-451-04140-2*, Signet Bks.); 1947. mass mkt. 1.75 o.p. (*0-451-51133-6*, Signet Classics); 1947. mass mkt. 1.95 o.p. (*0-451-51509-9*, Signet Classics); 1947. mass mkt. 0.35 o.p. (*0-451-00627-5*, Signet Bks.); 1947. mass mkt. 0.25 o.p. (*0-451-00978-9*, Signet Bks.); 1947. mass mkt. 0.50 o.p. (*0-451-02086-3*, Signet Bks.); 1947. mass mkt. 0.60 o.p. (*0-451-03300-0*, Signet Bks.); 1947. mass mkt. 1.50 o.p. (*0-451-50985-4*, Signet Classics) NAL.
—Tobacco Road. l.t. ed. 1995. 236p. lib. bdg. 20.95 (*0-7838-1365-1*) Thorndike Pr.
—Tobacco Road. 1995. (Brown Thrasher Bks.). 200p. reprint ed. 25.00 o.p. (*0-8203-1660-1*); pap. 12.95 (*0-8203-1661-X*) Univ. of Georgia Pr.
Cannon, Julie. Truelove & Homegrown Tomatoes. l.t. ed. 2001. (Thorndike Press Large Print Americana Ser.). 352p. 28.95 (*0-7862-3762-7*) Thorndike Pr.
—TrueLove & Homegrown Tomatoes: A Novel. 2001. 224p. 19.95 (*1-892514-87-7*) Hill Street Pr., LLC.
—Truelove Homegrown Tomatoes. 2003. 288p. pap. 13.00 (*0-7432-4588-1*, Touchstone) Simon & Schuster.
Carter, William. The Search for Savin' Sam. 1998. 186p. 20.00 (*1-56352-468-6*) Longstreet Pr., Inc.
Champlin, Tim. Raiders of the Western & Atlantic. 2004. mass mkt. 4.99 (*0-8439-5304-7*) Dorchester Publishing Co., Inc.
—Raiders of the Western & Atlantic. 2002. (Five Star Western Ser.). (Illus.). 244p. 24.95 (*0-7862-3538-1*, Five Star) Gale Group.
Child, Lee. Killing Floor. 1998. 432p. mass mkt. 7.99 (*0-515-12344-7*, Jove) Berkley Publishing Group.
—Killing Floor. abr. ed. (Jack Reacher Ser.). 2004. audio compact disk 14.99 (*1-59355-558-X*, 5182, Brilliance Audio on CD Value Priced); 1997. audio 7.99 o.s.i (*1-56740-234-8*, 668, Paperback Nova Audio Bks.); 1997. audio 16.95 o.p. (*1-56100-969-5*, 1261, Nova Audio Bks.); 2004. audio 29.95 (*1-59355-557-1*, 5183, Brilliance Audio Unabridged); 1997. audio 27.95 (*1-56100-732-3*, 153, Bookcassette); 1997. audio 105.25 (*1-56100-806-0*, 918, Unabridged Library Editions) Brilliance Audio.
—Killing Floor. l.t. ed. 1998. pap. 23.95 (*1-56895-690-8*, Wheeler Publishing, Inc.) Gale Group.
—Killing Floor. 1997. 368p. 23.95 o.p. (*0-399-14253-3*, G. P. Putnam's Sons) Penguin Group (USA) Inc.
Cold Sassy Tree. 1999. (YA). 11.95 (*1-56137-509-8*) Novel Units, Inc.
Coleman, Evelyn. What a Woman's Gotta Do. 1999. 400p. mass mkt. 6.99 (*0-440-23500-6*) Dell Publishing.
—What a Woman's Gotta Do. 1998. 320p. 23.00 (*0-684-83175-9*, Simon & Schuster) Simon & Schuster.
Connor, Beverly. Dressed to Die: A Lindsay Chamberlain Novel. 1998. (Lindsay Chamberlain Mysteries Ser.). 320p. 20.95 (*1-888952-89-X*) Cumberland Hse. Publishing.
—One Grave Too Many. 2003. 400p. mass mkt. 6.99 (*0-451-41119-6*, Onyx) NAL.
—Questionable Remains. 1997. (Lindsay Chamberlain Mysteries Ser.). 288p. 20.95 (*1-888952-53-9*) Cumberland Hse. Publishing.
—A Rumor of Bones. 1996. (Lindsay Chamberlain Mysteries Ser.: Vol. 1). (Illus.). 254p. 20.95 o.p. (*1-888952-08-3*) Cumberland Hse. Publishing.
—Skeleton Crew. 1999. (Lindsay Chamberlain Mysteries Ser.: Vol. 3). (Illus.). 352p. 20.95 (*1-58182-042-9*, Cumberland Hearthside) Cumberland Hse. Publishing.
Cook, Thomas H. Evidence of Blood. 1998. 400p. reprint ed. mass mkt. 5.99 (*0-553-57836-7*) Bantam Bks.
—Evidence of Blood. 1993. 384p. mass mkt. 5.99 o.s.i (*0-8217-4123-3*, Zebra Bks.) Kensington Publishing Corp.
—Evidence of Blood. 1991. 320p. 19.95 o.p. (*0-399-13668-1*, G. P. Putnam's Sons) Penguin Group (USA) Inc.
Coram, Robert. Atlanta Heat. 1997. 368p. mass mkt. 5.99 o.s.i (*0-451-19391-1*, Signet Bks.) NAL.
—Dead South. 1999. 336p. mass mkt. 5.99 o.s.i (*0-451-19688-0*, Signet Bks.) NAL.
Cox, Elizabeth. Night Talk. 1997. 267p. 23.95 (*1-55597-267-5*) Graywolf Pr.
—Night Talk. 1998. 272p. pap. 13.95 (*0-312-19516-8*, Saint Martin's Griffin) St. Martin's Pr.
Crane, Teresa. Freedom's Banner. 1995. 23.95 o.p. (*0-312-11793-0*) St. Martin's Pr.
Crews, Harry. Body. 1990. 240p. 18.95 o.p. (*0-671-69576-2*, Simon & Schuster) Simon & Schuster.
Darnton, John. The Experiment. 1999. 416p. 24.95 o.p. (*0-525-94517-2*) Dutton/Plume.
—The Experiment. l.t. ed. 2000. 26.95 (*1-56895-819-6*, Wheeler Publishing, Inc.) Gale Group.
—The Experiment. 2000. 496p. mass mkt. 6.99 (*0-451-20010-1*, Signet Bks.) NAL.
Daugharty, Janice. Dark of the Moon. Howle, Jane, ed. 1994. 275p. 19.00 (*1-880909-17-0*) Baskerville Pubs., Inc.
—Dark of the Moon: A Novel. 1995. 288p. pap. 12.00 o.s.i (*0-06-097655-1*, Perennial) HarperTrade.
—Earl in the Yellow Shirt: A Novel. 1997. 272p. 22.00 (*0-06-018750-6*) HarperCollins Pubs.
—Going Through the Change: Stories. 1994. 200p. 19.95 (*0-86538-081-3*) Ontario Review Pr.
—Necessary Lies. 1995. 176p. 20.00 o.p. (*0-06-017177-4*) HarperCollins Pubs.
—The Pawpaw Patch. 1996. 79p. 22.00 o.p. (*0-06-017379-3*) HarperCollins Pubs.
Davis, Don. Appointment with the Squire: A Novel. 1995. 333p. 24.95 (*1-55750-157-2*) Naval Institute Pr.
Davis, Jerry Lee. Twin City. 2000. 300p. pap. 14.95 o.p. (*1-928704-13-1*, Authorlink Pr.) Authorlink.
Davis, Thomas A. The Christmas Quilt. 2000. xi, 272p. 18.99 (*1-55853-814-3*) Rutledge Hill Pr.
Deitz, Tom. Darkthunder's Way. 1989. pap. 3.95 (*0-380-75508-4*, Avon Bks.) Morrow/Avon.
—Dreamseeker's Road. 2000. 20.00 (*0-380-97254-9*); 1996. 368p. mass mkt. 5.99 (*0-380-77484-4*, Avon Bks.); 1995. 356p. 20.00 o.p. (*0-688-14155-2*, Morrow, William & Co.) Morrow/Avon.
—Fireshaper's Doom. 1987. 320p. pap. 3.95 (*0-380-75329-4*, Avon Bks.) Morrow/Avon.
—Ghostcountry's Wrath. 1995. 400p. (Orig.). mass mkt. 5.50 o.p. (*0-380-76838-0*, Avon Bks.) Morrow/Avon.
—Landslayer's Law. 1997. 304p. mass mkt. 5.99 (*0-380-78649-4*, Avon Bks.) Morrow/Avon.
—Stoneskin's Revenge. 1991. 320p. pap. 3.95 (*0-380-76063-0*, Avon Bks.) Morrow/Avon.
—Sunshaker's War. 1990. 368p. mass mkt. 3.95 (*0-380-76062-2*, Avon Bks.) Morrow/Avon.
—Warstalker's Track. 1999. 384p. mass mkt. 6.50 o.s.i (*0-380-78650-8*, Eos) Morrow/Avon.
—Windmaster's Bane. 1986. (Orig.). pap. 4.99 (*0-380-75029-5*, Avon Bks.) Morrow/Avon.
DePoy, Phillip. Dancing Made Easy. 1999. (Flap Tucker Mysteries Ser.). 304p. mass mkt. 5.99 o.s.i (*0-440-22618-X*) Dell Publishing.
—Dead Easy. 2000. (Flap Tucker Mysteries Ser.). 288p. mass mkt. 5.99 o.s.i (*0-440-23643-6*) Dell Publishing.
—The Devil's Hearth: A Fever Devilin Mystery. 2003. 272p. 23.95 (*0-312-28485-3*, Saint Martin's Minotaur) St. Martin's Pr.
—Easy. 1997. (Flap Tucker Mysteries Ser.). 288p. mass mkt. 5.99 o.s.i (*0-440-22494-2*) Dell Publishing.
—Easy: A Flap Tucker Mystery. 1999. E-Book 5.99 (*0-440-33375-X*) Random Hse., Inc.
—Easy as One, Two, Three: A Flap Tucker Mystery. 1999. (Flap Tucker Mysteries Ser.: Bk. 3). 288p. mass mkt. 5.99 o.s.i (*0-440-22617-1*) Dell Publishing.
—Easy as One, Two, Three: A Flap Tucker Mystery. 1999. E-Book 5.99 (*0-440-33381-4*) Random Hse., Inc.
—Too Easy. 1998. (Flap Tucker Mysteries Ser.). 288p. mass mkt. 5.99 o.s.i (*0-440-22495-0*) Dell Publishing.
Dieguez, Sharlee. The Bearded Lady: A Novel. 1999. 308p. 3.95 o.p. (*1-892514-15-X*) Hill Street Pr., LLC.
Diehl, Stanford. Angel in the Front Room, Devil Out Back. 2001. 428p. 25.00 (*1-56352-643-3*) Longstreet Pr., Inc.
Diehl, William. Hooligans. 1996. mass mkt. 5.99 (*0-345-90987-9*); 1985. 448p. mass mkt. 7.99 (*0-345-31201-5*, Ballantine Bks.) Ballantine Bks.
—Hooligans. 1984. 15.95 o.p. (*0-394-53049-7*) Random Hse., Inc.
—27. 1993. 4.99 o.p. (*0-517-10689-2*); 1992. 5.99 o.p. (*0-517-08082-6*) Random Hse. Value Publishing.
Doster, Paul. Mind Set. 1997. 416p. mass mkt. 5.99 o.s.i (*0-451-19042-4*, Signet Bks.) NAL.
Doster, Stephen. Lord Baltimore. 2002. (Salem Selections Ser.). 360p. 22.95 (*0-89587-264-1*) Blair, John F. Pub.
Doxey, William. Cousins to the Kudzu. 1985. 255p. 18.95 (*0-8071-1225-9*) Louisiana State Univ. Pr.
Elliott, Michael. Running with the Dolphins & Other Tybee Tales. 1995. 152p. pap. 14.00 (*1-57312-006-5*) Smyth & Helwys Publishing, Inc.
Ellis, Julie. Savage Oaks. 1981. mass mkt. 2.25 o.s.i (*0-449-23996-9*, Fawcett) Ballantine Bks.
—Savage Oaks. l.t. ed. 2000. (G. K. Hall Romance Ser.). 453p. 26.95 (*0-7838-9158-X*, Macmillan Reference USA) Gale Group.
Everson, Eva Marie & Chadwick, G. W. Shadow of Dreams: A Novel. 2001. 199p. pap. 10.99 (*1-58660-143-1*) Barbour Publishing, Inc.
Everson, Eva Marie & Chadwick, G. W. Francis. Shadow of Dreams. l.t. ed. 2003. (Christian Mystery Ser.). 28.95 (*0-7862-4565-4*) Thorndike Pr.
Faith & the Good Thing. 2001. E-Book 12.00 (*0-7432-1534-6*, Scribner) Simon & Schuster.
Farley, Benjamin W. Hero of St. Lo & Other Stories. 1986. Orig. Title: The Hero of St. Lo: Stories of Abbeville & the Upcountry. (Illus.). 124p. reprint ed. 13.95 (*0-87797-121-8*) Cherokee Publishing Co.
—Mercy Road & Other Stories. 1986. (Illus.). 136p. 13.95 (*0-87797-122-6*) Cherokee Publishing Co.
Farris, John. Sacrifice. 1995. 379p. pap. text 5.99 (*0-8125-0956-0*); 1994. 320p. 15.50 o.p. (*0-312-85067-0*) Doherty, Tom Assocs., LLC. (Tor Bks.).
Fields, Gina, et al. Georgia: Love Is Just Peachy in Four Complete Novels. 2003. (Contemporary Collection). 464p. pap. 6.97 (*1-58660-969-6*) Barbour Publishing, Inc.
Fields, Jeff. Cry of Angels. 1974. 8.95 o.p. (*0-689-10593-2*, Atheneum) Simon & Schuster Children's Publishing.
Ford-Williamson, Estelle. Abbeville Farewell: A Novel of Early Atlanta & North Georgia. 2001. 264p. pap. 18.00 (*0-9708320-0-1*); 2nd ed. per. 18.00 (*0-9708320-1-X*) Other Voices.
Forkner, Ben, ed. Georgia Stories: Major Georgia Short Fiction of the Nineteenth & Twentieth Centuries. 1992. o.p. (*1-56145-066-9*) Peachtree Pubs., Ltd.
—Georgia Stories: Major Georgia Short Fiction of the 19th & 20th Centuries. 1992. 285p. pap. 13.95 (*1-56145-067-7*) Peachtree Pubs., Ltd.
Fuhrman, Chris. The Dangerous Lives of Altar Boys: A Novel. Ng, Donna, ed. 1996. 192p. pap. 12.00 (*0-671-52903-X*, Washington Square Pr.) Simon & Schuster.
—The Dangerous Lives of Altar Boys: A Novel. 1994. 176p. 19.95 (*0-8203-1632-6*); 2001. 200p. reprint ed. 14.95 (*0-8203-2338-1*) Univ. of Georgia Pr.
Fuller, Richard. Escape from Savannah. 2001. 397p. 27.95 (*1-931055-40-8*) SuperiorBooks.com, Inc.
Gearino, G. D. Counting Coup. 1997. 224p. 22.00 (*0-684-83726-9*, Simon & Schuster) Simon & Schuster.
—What the Deaf-Mute Heard, Set. abr. ed. 1996. audio 16.95 o.p. (*1-55927-380-1*, 393311) Audio Renaissance.
—What the Deaf-Mute Heard. unabr. ed. 1996. audio 42.00 (*0-7366-3366-9*, 4016) Books on Tape, Inc.
—What the Deaf-Mute Heard. 1997. per. 14.00 (*0-671-02073-0*, Pocket); 1996. 224p. 21.00 (*0-684-81337-8*, Simon & Schuster) Simon & Schuster.
Gilmore, Monique. Soul Deep. 1997. 256p. mass mkt. 4.99 o.s.i (*0-7860-0395-2*, Pinnacle Bks.) Kensington Publishing Corp.
Gover, Paula. White Boys & River Girls: Stories. 1995. 238p. tchr. ed. 17.95 o.p. (*1-56512-049-3*) Algonquin Bks. of Chapel Hill.



For book reviews, descriptive annotations, tables of contents, cover images, author biographies & additional information, updated daily, subscribe to **www.booksinprint.com** 809

Gover, Paula K. White Boys & River Girls. 1996. 240p. pap. 11.00 o.s.i (0-684-82518-X, Scribner) Simon & Schuster.

Grant, Charles. Black Oak Vol. 5: When the Cold Wind Blows. 2001. 256p. mass mkt. 5.99 o.s.i (0-451-45811-7, Onyx) NAL.

Green, Betsy Brannon. Hearts in Hiding. 2001. (Illus.). 299p. 14.95 (1-57734-823-0) Covenant Communications.

Griffith, Nicola. The Blue Place: A Novel of Suspense. 1999. 320p. pap. 13.00 (0-380-79088-2, Perennial) HarperTrade.

—The Blue Place: A Novel of Suspense. 1998. 320p. pap. 23.00 (0-380-97446-0, Avon Bks.) Morrow/Avon.

Grindle, Lucretia W. The Nightspinners: A Novel. 2003. 304p. 23.95 (0-375-50776-0) Random Hse., Inc.

Guhrke, Laura L. Breathless. 1999. (Sonnet Bks.). (Illus.). 416p. pap. 6.50 (0-671-02368-3, Pocket) Simon & Schuster.

Haeger, Diane. My Dearest Cecelia: A Novel of the Southern Belle Who Stole General Sherman's Heart. 2004. 320p. pap. 14.95 (0-312-32594-0, Saint Martin's Griffin); 2003. 288p. 24.95 (0-312-28200-1) St. Martin's Pr.

Hall, Karen. Dark Debts. 1997. 501p. mass mkt. 6.99 o.s.i (0-8041-1655-5, Ivy Bks.) Ballantine Bks.

Harben, William N. Northern Georgia Sketches. 1977. (Short Story Index Reprint Ser.). 23.95 (0-8369-3345-1) Ayer Co. Pubs., Inc.

Harper, Jon. Blue Ridge. 1995. (Illus.). 160p. (J). pap. 8.95 (0-9611872-7-1) Our Child Pr.

Harrell, Sara G. Mallory's Island: Puppy Love. 1986. (Christian Reader Ser.). (Illus.). 80p. (Orig.). (J). (gr. 4-7). pap. 3.95 o.s.i (0-570-03637-2, 39-1099) Concordia Publishing Hse.

Harris, Charlaine. A Bone to Pick. 1993. (WWL Mystery Ser.). per. (0-373-26136-5, 1-26136-1, Harlequin Bks.) Harlequin Enterprises, Ltd.

—A Bone to Pick. 1992. 168p. 18.95 o.s.i (0-8027-1245-2) Walker & Co.

—Dead over Heels. 1997. per. (0-373-26260-4, 1-26260-9, Worldwide Library) Harlequin Enterprises, Ltd.

—Dead over Heels. 1996. 208p. 20.50 o.p. (0-684-80429-8, Scribner) Simon & Schuster.

—A Fool & His Honey. 2001. (WWL Mystery Ser.: No. 384). 253p. mass mkt. (0-373-26384-8, 1-26384-7, Worldwide Library) Harlequin Enterprises, Ltd.

—A Fool & His Honey. 1999. 224p. 22.95 (0-312-20306-3, Saint Martin's Minotaur) St. Martin's Pr.

—A Fool & His Honey. l.t. ed. 2000. (Mystery Ser.). 304p. 28.95 (0-7862-2467-3) Thorndike Pr.

—The Julius House. 1996. per. (0-373-26217-5, 1-26217-9, Worldwide Library) Harlequin Enterprises, Ltd.

—The Julius House. 1995. 221p. 20.00 (0-684-19640-9, Scribner) Simon & Schuster.

—Last Scene Alive. l.t. ed. 2002. (Wheeler Hardcover Ser.). 320p. 28.95 (1-58724-364-4, Wheeler Publishing, Inc.) Gale Group.

—Last Scene Alive. 2003. (WWL Mystery Ser.: No. 476). 256p. mass mkt. (0-373-26476-3, Worldwide Library) Harlequin Enterprises, Ltd.

—Last Scene Alive. 2002. (Aurora Teagarden Mystery Ser.). 224p. 22.95 (0-312-26246-9, Saint Martin's Minotaur) St. Martin's Pr.

—Real Murders. l.t. ed. 1991. 17.95 o.p. (0-7451-8204-6, AH0240) BBC Audiobooks America.

—Real Murders. 1992. mass mkt. (0-373-26104-7, 1-26104-9, Harlequin Bks.) Harlequin Enterprises, Ltd.

—Real Murders. 1990. 192p. 18.95 o.s.i (0-8027-5769-3) Walker & Co.

—Three Bedrooms, One Corpse. 1995. per. (0-373-26177-2, Harlequin Bks.) Harlequin Enterprises, Ltd.

—Three Bedrooms, One Corpse. 2001. 224p. pap. 14.95 o.p. (0-7432-2891-X); 1994. 256p. 20.00 (0-684-19643-3) Simon & Schuster. (Scribner).

Harris, Joel Chandler. Nights with Uncle Remus: Myths & Legends of the Old Plantation. Bickley, Bruce, ed. 2003. (Penguin Classics Ser.). 384p. pap. 14.00 (0-14-243766-2, Penguin Classics) Viking Penguin.

—On the Plantation: A Story of a Georgia Boy's Adventures During the War. Seagrave, Pia S., ed. 1997. (Illus.). 280p. pap. 19.95 (1-887901-16-7) Sergeant Kirkland's Pr.

—On the Plantation: A Story of a Georgia Boy's Adventures During the War. 1980. (Illus.). 248p. per. 15.95 (0-8203-2373-X); reprint ed. 17.00 o.p. (0-8203-0494-8); reprint ed. pap. 12.95 (0-8203-0495-6) Univ. of Georgia Pr.

Harris, William Charles, Jr. Delirium of the Brave. 2nd ed. 1999. xi, 366p. 24.95 (0-312-25495-4) St. Martin's Pr.

Hodge, Jane Aiken. Savannah Purchase. unabr. ed. 1998. audio 54.95 (0-7540-0178-4, CAB 1601) BBC Audiobooks America.

—Savannah Purchase. 1979. mass mkt. 1.95 o.s.i (0-449-24097-5, Fawcett) Ballantine Bks.

Holbrook, Teri. The Grass Widow. 1996. 320p. mass mkt. 5.99 o.s.i (0-553-56860-4, Crimeline) Bantam Bks.

Hooper, Kay. Hiding in the Shadows. 2000. (Shadows Trilogy Ser.). 368p. mass mkt. 7.50 (0-553-57692-5) Bantam Bks.

Iakovou, Takis & Iakovou, Judy. Go Close Against the Enemy. 1999. (WWL Mystery Ser.: Bk. 314). 256p. per. (0-373-26314-7, 1-26314-4, Worldwide Library) Harlequin Enterprises, Ltd.

—Go Close Against the Enemy. 1998. 288p. 23.95 o.p. (0-312-18587-1, Saint Martin's Minotaur) St. Martin's Pr.

—So Dear to Wicked Men. 1998. (WWL Mystery Ser.). per. (0-373-26277-9, 1-26277-3, Worldwide Library) Harlequin Enterprises, Ltd.

—So Dear to Wicked Men, Vol. 1. 1996. (So Dear to Wicked Men Ser.: Vol. 1). 320p. 22.95 (0-312-14740-6, Saint Martin's Minotaur) St. Martin's Pr.

Inman, Robert. Dairy Queen Days. 1998. 288p. reprint ed. pap. 13.95 (0-316-41837-4, Back Bay) Little Brown & Co.

—Dairy Queen Days: A Novel. 1998. pap. 12.95 (0-316-18997-9, Back Bay); 1997. 288p. (YA). (gr. 8 up). 21.95 o.p. (0-316-41873-0) Little Brown & Co.

Jekel, Pamela. River Without End. 1998. (Illus.). 576p. mass mkt. 6.50 o.s.i (1-57566-307-4); 1997. 448p. 22.95 o.p. (1-57566-172-1, Kensington Bks.) Kensington Publishing Corp.

Johansen, Roy. The Answer Man. 2001. 336p. mass mkt. 5.99 (0-553-58191-0, Spectra) Bantam Bks.

—Answer Man, unabr. ed. 1999. audio 66.00 (0-7887-3134-3, 95826E7) Recorded Bks., LLC.

Johnson, Charles. Faith & the Good Thing. 1991. (Contemporary Fiction Ser.). 208p. pap. 8.95 o.p. (0-452-26690-4, Plume) Dutton/Plume.

—Faith & the Good Thing. 2001. 240p. pap. 12.00 (0-7432-1254-1, Scribner); 2001. (Illus.). 240p. pap. 22.00 (0-7432-1250-9, Scribner); 1987. 208p. pap. 9.95 o.s.i (0-689-70720-7, 351, Scribner Paper Fiction) Simon & Schuster.

—Faith & the Good Thing. 1974. 7.95 o.p. (0-670-30569-3) Viking Penguin.

Johnston, Richard M. Mr. Absalom Billingslea & Other Georgia Folk. 1977. (Short Story Index Reprint Ser.). 28.95 (0-8369-3354-0) Ayer Co. Pubs., Inc.

—Primes & Their Neighbors: Ten Tales of Middle Georgia. 1977. (Short Story Index Reprint Ser.). 23.95 (0-8369-3222-6) Ayer Co. Pubs., Inc.

Johnston, Richard Malcolm. Old Times in Middle Georgia. E-Book 3.95 (0-594-05618-7) 1873 Pr.

—Old Times in Middle Georgia. 2002. lib. bdg. (1-4035-0429-6) Brookhaven Pr.

Johnstone, William W. What the Heart Knows. 1996. 256p. mass mkt. 4.99 (1-57566-028-8); 1995. 304p. mass mkt. 17.95 o.p. (0-8217-5028-3, Zebra Bks.) Kensington Publishing Corp.

Jones, Jack P. The Third Season. 224p. 1999. 21.95 (0-9666721-4-3); 2000. reprint ed. pap. 21.95 (0-9666721-9-4) GoldenIsle Pubs., Inc.

Jones, Tayari. Leaving Atlanta. 2002. 272p. 23.95 (0-446-52830-7) Warner Bks., Inc.

Joseph, Henry. Bloodwork: The New Rugged Cross. 1994. 224p. 19.95 o.p. (0-87905-628-2) Smith, Gibbs Pub.

Joseph, Sheri. Bear Me Safely Over. 272p. 2003. pap. 13.00 (0-8021-3984-1); 2002. 23.00 o.p. (0-87113-841-7, Atlantic Monthly Pr.) Grove/Atlantic, Inc.

Kanner, S. Lee. The Ripple Effect. 2001. pap. 15.00 (0-8059-5199-7) Dorrance Publishing Co., Inc.

Kay, Terry. The Kidnapping of Aaron Greene. 1999. 288p. 25.00 (0-688-15034-9, Morrow, William & Co.) Morrow/Avon.

—The Runaway. 2000. 416p. pap. 13.00 (0-380-81342-4, Perennial) HarperTrade.

—Taking Lottie Home. 2001. 320p. pap. 13.00 (0-06-093701-7, Perennial) HarperTrade.

—Taking Lottie Home. 2000. viii, 294p. 25.00 (0-688-17646-1, Morrow, William & Co.) Morrow/Avon.

Kellum, Rose. A Storm of Passion. 1999. 230p. pap. 10.95 (1-929416-11-3) Magner Publishing & American Binding & Publishing.

Kelly, Lelia. False Witness. 2000. 416p. mass mkt. 6.99 o.s.i (0-7860-1193-9); 312p. 23.00 o.s.i (1-57566-490-9, Kensington Bks.) Kensington Publishing Corp.

—Presumption of Guilt. 1998. 352p. mass mkt. 5.99 (0-7860-0584-X, Pinnacle Bks.); 224p. 22.95 o.s.i (1-57566-249-3) Kensington Publishing Corp.

Kendal. Something about Cecily. 2001. (Avon Romance Ser.). 400p. mass mkt. 5.99 (0-380-81852-3, Avon Bks.) Morrow/Avon.

Killens, John O. Youngblood. 2000. 488p. pap. text 17.95 (0-8203-2201-6); 1982. 512p. reprint ed. 20.00 o.p. (0-8203-0601-0) Univ. of Georgia Pr.

King, Barrington. The Way Upcountry. 2002. (Five Star First Edition Romance Ser.). 260p. 26.95 (0-7862-4407-0, Five Star) Gale Group.

King, Stephen. The Bad Death of Eduard Delacroix. 1996. (Green Mile Ser.: Vol. 4). 96p. mass mkt. 2.99 o.s.i (0-451-19055-6, Signet Bks.) NAL.

—The Bad Death of Eduard Delacroix. 1996. 8.09 (0-606-09366-4) Turtleback Bks.

—Coffey on the Mile. 1996. (Green Mile Ser.: Vol. 6). 144p. mass mkt. 3.99 o.s.i (0-451-19057-2, Signet Bks.) NAL.

—Coffey on the Mile. 1996. 10.04 (0-606-09368-0) Turtleback Bks.

—Coffey on the Mile. abr. ed. 1996. (Green Mile Ser.). audio 7.95 o.p. (0-14-086382-6, Penguin AudioBooks) Viking Penguin.

—Coffey's Hands. 1996. (Green Mile Ser.: Vol. 3). 96p. mass mkt. 2.99 o.s.i (0-451-19054-8, Signet Bks.) NAL.

—Coffey's Hands. 1996. 8.09 (0-606-09365-6) Turtleback Bks.

—The Green Mile. unabr. ed. 1999. audio 39.95 (0-671-04721-3); audio compact disk 49.95 (0-671-04725-6) Simon & Schuster Audio. (Simon & Schuster Audioworks).

—The Green Mile. unabr. ed. 1996. (Green Mile Ser.). 39.95 o.p. (0-14-771135-5, Penguin AudioBooks) Viking Penguin.

—The Green Mile: The Complete Serial Novel. 1997. (Illus.). 480p. pap. 14.95 o.p. (0-452-27890-2, Plume) Dutton/Plume.

—The Green Mile: The Complete Serial Novel. 1996. 18.94 o.s.i (0-451-93302-8, Signet Bks.) NAL.

—The Green Mile: The Complete Serial Novel. (Illus.). 2000. 400p. 25.00 (0-7432-1089-1, Scribner); 1999. 544p. pap. 7.99 (0-671-04178-9, Pocket); 1999. 536p. reprint ed. mass mkt. 7.99 (0-671-03265-8, Pocket) Simon & Schuster.

—The Green Mile: The Complete Serial Novel. 1999. 14.04 (0-606-17409-5) Turtleback Bks.

—Der Grune Meile. 1999. Tr. of Green Mile. (GER.). pap. 22.95 (3-404-13958-5) Lubbe, Gustav Verlag GmbH DEU. *Dist:* Distribooks, Inc.

—The Mouse on the Mile. 1996. (Green Mile Ser.: Vol. 2). 96p. mass mkt. 2.99 o.s.i (0-451-19052-1, Signet Bks.) NAL.

—The Mouse on the Mile. 1996. 8.09 (0-606-09364-8) Turtleback Bks.

—The Night Journey. 1996. (Green Mile Ser.: Vol. 5). 96p. mass mkt. 2.99 o.s.i (0-451-19056-4, Signet Bks.) NAL.

—The Night Journey. 1996. 9.04 (0-606-09367-2) Turtleback Bks.

—The Two Dead Girls. 1996. (Green Mile Ser.: Vol. 1). (Illus.). 96p. mass mkt. 2.99 o.s.i (0-451-19049-1, Signet Bks.) NAL.

—The Two Dead Girls. 1996. 8.09 o.p. (0-606-09363-X) Turtleback Bks.

—The Two Dead Girls. abr. ed. 1996. (Green Mile Ser.: Vol. 1). audio 7.95 o.p. (0-14-086377-X, Penguin AudioBooks) Viking Penguin.

Lanier, Virginia. Blind Bloodhound Justice: A Jo Beth Sidden Mystery. unabr. ed. 2000. (Bloodhound Ser.). audio 59.95 (0-7927-2261-2, CSL 150) Chivers Audio Bks. GBR. *Dist:* BBC Audiobooks America.

—Blind Bloodhound Justice: A Jo Beth Sidden Mystery. 1998. 288p. 24.00 o.s.i (0-06-017547-8) HarperCollins Pubs.

—Blind Bloodhound Justice: A Jo Beth Sidden Mystery. 1999. (Bloodhound Ser.). 352p. mass mkt. 6.99 (0-06-109971-6, HarperTorch) Morrow/Avon.

—A Bloodhound to Die For. 2003. 240p. 23.95 (0-06-019388-3) HarperCollins Pubs.

—A Bloodhound to Die For. 2004. 320p. mass mkt. 6.99 (0-06-109840-X, Avon Bks.) Morrow/Avon.

—A Brace of Bloodhounds. (Bloodhound Ser.). 1998. 448p. mass mkt. 6.50 (0-06-101087-1); 1997. 336p. 23.00 o.p. (0-06-101089-8) HarperCollins Pubs.

—Death in Bloodhound Red. 1996. (Bloodhound Ser.). 544p. mass mkt. 6.50 (0-06-101025-1, HarperTorch) Morrow/Avon.

—Death in Bloodhound Red. 1995. (Bloodhound Ser.). 462p. 19.95 (1-56164-076-X) Pineapple Pr., Inc.

—House on Bloodhound Lane. 1996. 352p. mass mkt. 20.00 o.p. (0-06-101088-X, HarperTorch) Morrow/Avon.

—The House on Bloodhound Lane. 1997. (Bloodhound Ser.). 384p. mass mkt. 5.99 (0-06-101086-3, HarperTorch) Morrow/Avon.

—Ten Little Bloodhounds: A Jo Beth Sidden Mystery, Set. unabr. ed. 1999. audio 69.95 (0-7927-2335-X, CSL 224, Chivers Sound Library) BBC Audiobooks America.

—Ten Little Bloodhounds: A Jo Beth Sidden Mystery. 1999. (Bloodhound Ser.). 288p. 24.00 (0-06-017548-6) HarperCollins Pubs.

—Ten Little Bloodhounds: A Jo Beth Sidden Mystery. 2000. (Bloodhound Ser.). 352p. mass mkt. 6.50 (0-06-109066-2, Avon Bks.) Morrow/Avon.

Longstreet, Augustus Baldwin. Georgia Scenes. 1990. 224p. reprint ed. pap. 12.95 o.p. (0-87797-213-3) Cherokee Publishing Co.

Mamet, David. The Old Religion: A Novel. 1997. 288p. 24.00 o.p. (0-684-84119-3, Free Pr.) Simon & Schuster.

Manley, Frank. Within the Ribbons. 1989. 240p. 17.95 o.p. (0-86547-379-X, North Point Pr.) Farrar, Straus & Giroux.

Martin, Clayton M. El Destino. 2001. Tr. of Destination. 194p. per. 16.95 o.p. (1-929925-92-1) First-Publish.

Martin, Douglas A. Outline of My Lover: A Novel. 2000. 166p. pap. 12.00 (1-887128-47-6) Soft Skull Pr., Inc.

Mayes, Frances. Swan: A Novel. 2003. 336p. pap. 11.95 (0-7679-0286-6); 2002. 336p. 25.00 (0-7679-0285-8); 2002. 319p. 15.00 (0-7679-1436-8) Broadway Bks.

—Swan: A Novel. 2002. (Americana Ser.). 31.95 (0-7862-4853-X) Thorndike Pr.

McCullers, Carson. The Heart Is a Lonely Hunter. 1999. mass mkt. (0-553-22698-3); 1999. mass mkt. (0-553-23911-2); 1994. mass mkt. 6.99 (0-553-54173-0); 1983. 320p. mass mkt. 6.50 (0-553-26963-1, Bantam Classics); 1983. (YA). (gr. 10-12). mass mkt. 3.50 o.s.i (0-553-25481-2) Bantam Bks.

—The Heart Is a Lonely Hunter. 1994. lib. bdg. 19.95 (1-56849-462-9) Buccaneer Bks., Inc.

—The Heart Is a Lonely Hunter, 001. 9999. 18.95 o.p. (0-395-07978-0) Houghton Mifflin Co.

—The Heart Is a Lonely Hunter. 2000. 320p. pap. 12.00 (0-618-08474-6, Mariner Bks.) Houghton Mifflin Co. Trade & Reference Div.

—The Heart Is a Lonely Hunter. mass mkt. 0.25 o.p. (0-451-00596-1, Signet Bks.) NAL.

—The Heart Is a Lonely Hunter. 1993. (Modern Library Ser.). 448p. 18.95 (0-679-42474-1, Modern Library) Random House Adult Trade Publishing Group.

—The Heart Is a Lonely Hunter. l.t. ed. 1999. (Perennial Bestsellers Ser.). 474p. 27.95 (0-7838-8773-6) Thorndike Pr.

—The Heart Is a Lonely Hunter. 1953. 12.04 (0-606-00786-5) Turtleback Bks.

McElroy-Ansa, Tina. Ugly Ways. unabr. ed. 1994. audio 48.00 (0-7366-2800-2, 3515) Books on Tape, Inc.

McRee, Jannelle J. Down on Cooter's Creek & Other Stories. Selph, Alexa M., ed. 1986. (Illus.). 160p. 14.95 (0-87797-127-7) Cherokee Publishing Co.

Mee, Susie. Girl Who Loved Elvis. 1993. 224p. 18.95 o.p. (1-56145-080-4) Peachtree Pubs., Ltd.

Michaels, Fern. About Face. 2003. 352p. mass mkt. 7.99 (0-8217-7020-9, Zebra Bks.) Kensington Publishing Corp.

—About Face. l.t. ed. 2003. 643p. 30.95 (0-7862-5495-5) Thorndike Pr.

Miles, J. L. Roseflower Creek: A Novel. 2003. 240p. pap. 12.95 (1-58182-377-0); 2001. 256p. 20.95 (1-58182-240-5) Cumberland Hse. Publishing.

Miller, Caroline. Lamb in His Bosom. 1991. lib. bdg. 35.95 (1-56849-057-7) Buccaneer Bks., Inc.

—Lamb in His Bosom. 1993. (Modern Southern Classics Ser.). 368p. 24.95 (1-56145-074-X); pap. 14.95 (1-56145-075-8) Peachtree Pubs., Ltd.

Minnick, Wayne. The Crossbow Murder. 2000. 208p. pap. 13.95 (0-88739-301-2) Creative Arts Bk. Co.

Mitcham, Judson. Sabbath Creek: A Novel. 2004. 22.95 (0-8203-2577-5) Univ. of Georgia Pr.

—The Sweet Everlasting: A Novel. 1997. pap. 6.99 (0-380-73027-8, Avon Bks.) Morrow/Avon.

—The Sweet Everlasting: A Novel. 1996. 200p. 22.95 (0-8203-1807-8) Univ. of Georgia Pr.

Mitchell, Margaret. Gone with the Wind. l.t. unabr. ed. 1992. lib. bdg. (0-8161-5531-3);Set. 37.95 o.p. (0-8161-5529-1);Set. pap. 25.95 (0-8161-5530-5);Vol. 2. 19.95 (0-8161-5532-1) Gale Group. (Macmillan Reference USA).

—Gone with the Wind. 1976. 1024p. reprint ed. mass mkt. 6.50 (0-380-00109-8, Avon Bks.) Morrow/Avon.

—Gone with the Wind, 28 cass., Set. 2002. audio 79.99 (0-7887-8957-0, 00414) Recorded Bks., LLC.

—Gone with the Wind. 1936. 1048p. reprint ed. 26.00 (0-684-83068-X, Scribner) Simon & Schuster.

—Gone with the Wind. 1993. 1024p. mass mkt. 7.99 (0-446-36538-6); 1999. 1056p. reprint ed. pap. 15.95 (0-446-67553-9) Warner Bks., Inc.

—Gone with the Wind: 60th Anniversary Edition. 60th anniv. ed. 1996. 960p. 40.00 o.s.i (0-684-82625-9, Scribner) Simon & Schuster.

Mitchell, Sara. In the Midst of Lions. 1996. (Shadowcatchers Ser.: No. 2). 320p. pap. 9.99 o.p. (1-55661-498-5) Bethany Hse. Pubs.

—In the Midst of Lions. l.t. ed. 2000. (Christian Mystery Ser.). 485p. 23.95 (0-7862-2878-4) Thorndike Pr.

Mobley, Mims. Sleep Well, Hippocrates. 2000. 302p. pap. (1-55212-506-8) Trafford Publishing.

Monahan, Brent. The Sceptered Isle Club. 2002. 288p. 24.95 (0-312-28803-4, Saint Martin's Minotaur) St. Martin's Pr.

Moore, James A. Fireworks. 2001. 384p. pap. 16.00 (*1-892065-40-1*) Meisha Merlin Publishing, Inc.
Morgan, Julian. Roller: A Dirt Road Sport. 2000. x, 221p. 19.95 (*0-942407-48-2*) Father & Son Publishing.
Olshaker, Mark. Unnatural Causes. 1986. 480p. 18.95 o.p. (*0-688-05896-5*, Morrow, William & Co.) Morrow/Avon.
—Unnatural Causes. 1989. mass mkt. 4.50 o.s.i (*0-671-64435-1*, Pocket) Simon & Schuster.
O'Neal, Charles. Three Wishes for Jamie. 1976. 22.95 (*0-8488-0184-9*) Amereon, Ltd.
—Three Wishes for Jamie. 1991. 256p. reprint ed. pap. 5.95 (*1-56129-066-1*) Knightsbridge Publishing.
—Three Wishes for Jamie. 1980. 256p. reprint ed. 26.00 (*0-933256-08-6*); pap. text 16.00 (*0-933256-09-4*) Second Chance Pr.
Osborne, Anne R. Reap the Whirlwind: Augusta & the Revolution. 1990. 4.95 o.p. (*0-87844-087-9*) Sandlapper Publishing Co., Inc.
Parker, Robert B. Hugger Mugger. 2001. (Spenser Mystery Ser.: Bk. 27). 336p. reprint ed. mass mkt. 7.99 (*0-425-17955-9*) Berkley Publishing Group.
—Hugger Mugger. unabr. ed. 2000. audio 34.95 (*0-7366-4915-8*, 5222) Books on Tape, Inc.
—Hugger Mugger. l.t. ed. 2000. (Spenser Mystery Ser.). 309p. 27.95 (*1-56895-865-X*, Wheeler Publishing, Inc.) Gale Group.
—Hugger Mugger. 2000. (Spenser Mystery Ser.). 320p. 23.95 o.s.i (*0-399-14587-7*) Penguin Group (USA) Inc.
—Hugger Mugger. unabr. ed. 2000. (Spenser Mystery Ser.). audio 29.95 (*0-553-50246-8*); audio compact disk 34.99 (*0-553-45673-3*) Random Hse. Audio Publishing Group. (RH Audio).
Parshall, Craig. Custody of the State. 2003. (Chambers of Justice Ser.). 400p. pap. 11.99 (*0-7369-1026-3*) Harvest Hse. Pubs.
Phillips, Delores. The Darkest Child: A Novel. 2004. 388p. 26.00 (*1-56947-345-5*) Soho Pr., Inc.
Price, Eugenia. Beauty from Ashes. l.t. ed. 1995. 1008p. 28.50 o.s.i (*0-385-42314-4*);Vol. 3. (Beauty from Ashes Ser.: Vol. 3). 640p. 23.50 o.s.i (*0-385-26703-7*) Doubleday Publishing.
—Beauty from Ashes. 1996. 631p. mass mkt. 7.50 (*0-312-95917-6*, St. Martin's Paperbacks) St. Martin's Pr.
—Before the Darkness Falls. 1990. mass mkt. 7.99 o.s.i (*0-515-10538-4*, Jove); 1988. mass mkt. 4.95 o.s.i (*0-425-11092-3*) Berkley Publishing Group.
—Before the Darkness Falls. 1987. 480p. 17.95 o.s.i (*0-385-23068-0*) Doubleday Publishing.
—Bright Captivity. 1992. 704p. mass mkt. 6.50 o.s.i (*0-553-29523-3*) Bantam Bks.
—Bright Captivity. l.t. ed. 1991. 960p. 25.00 o.s.i (*0-385-41823-X*, Doubleday Large Type) Bantam Doubleday Dell Large Print Group, Inc.
—Bright Captivity. 1991. 640p. 20.00 o.s.i (*0-385-26701-0*) Doubleday Publishing.
—Bright Captivity. 1996. 613p. mass mkt. 6.99 (*0-312-95968-0*, St. Martin's Paperbacks) St. Martin's Pr.
—Savannah. 1990. mass mkt. 6.99 o.p. (*0-515-10486-8*, Jove); 1986. 608p. mass mkt. 4.95 o.s.i (*0-425-10004-9*); 1985. mass mkt. 4.50 o.s.i (*0-425-08973-8*); 1984. mass mkt. 3.95 o.s.i (*0-425-06829-3*); 1984. mass mkt. 4.50 o.s.i (*0-425-07293-2*) Berkley Publishing Group.
—Savannah. 1983. 608p. 19.95 o.s.i (*0-385-15274-4*) Doubleday Publishing.
—Savannah. 1997. 608p. mass mkt. 7.99 (*0-312-96232-0*, St. Martin's Paperbacks) St. Martin's Pr.
—Stranger in Savannah. 1989. 768p. 19.95 o.s.i (*0-385-23069-9*) Doubleday Publishing.
—To See Your Face Again. 1985. 552p. 21.95 o.s.i (*0-385-15275-2*) Doubleday Publishing.
—The Waiting Time. l.t. ed. 1998. (Waiting Time Ser.: Vol. 1). 352p. pap. 6.99 (*0-312-96506-0*, St. Martin's Paperbacks) St. Martin's Pr.
—The Waiting Time. l.t. ed. 1998. (Bestsellers Ser.). 547p. pap. 27.95 (*0-7862-1065-6*) Thorndike Pr.
—Where Shadows Go. l.t. ed. 1993. 1024p. 26.00 o.s.i (*0-385-42313-6*, Doubleday Large Type) Bantam Doubleday Dell Large Print Group, Inc.
Rachels, David, ed. Augustus Baldwin Longstreet's Georgia Scenes Completed. 1998. 392p. (C). text 50.00 (*0-8203-1978-3*); (Illus.). pap. 19.95 (*0-8203-2019-6*) Univ. of Georgia Pr.
Racine, David. Floating in a Most Peculiar Way. 1999. 230p. 24.00 (*0-9657639-3-5*) Van Neste Bks.
Rawlings, William. The Lazard Legacy. 2003. 24.95 (*1-891799-23-1*) Harbor Hse.
Ray, Jeanne. Step-Ball-Change: A Novel. unabr. ed. 2002. audio 62.25 (*1-59086-083-7*, 3632, Unabridged Library Editions) Brilliance Audio.
—Step-Ball-Change: A Novel. 2002. 240p. 22.95 (*0-609-61003-1*, Shaye Areheart Bks.) Crown Publishing Group.
Reasoner, James. Chickamauga: A Novel. 2002. (Civil War Battle Ser.: Vol. 7). 432p. 22.95 (*1-58182-253-7*) Cumberland Hse. Publishing.
Roberts, Nora. Sanctuary. l.t. ed. 1998. 528p. mass mkt. 7.99 (*0-515-12273-4*, Jove) Berkley Publishing Group.
—Sanctuary. abr. ed. 1998. audio 7.99 o.p. (*1-56740-247-X*, 695, Paperback Nova Audio Bks.); 1997. audio 89.25 o.p. (*1-56100-804-4*, 1025, Unabridged Library Editions); 1997. audio 25.95 o.p. (*1-56100-729-3*, 247, Bookcassette) Brilliance Audio.
—Sanctuary. 1997. 438p. 23.95 o.s.i (*0-399-14240-1*, G. P. Putnam's Sons) Penguin Group (USA) Inc.
—Sanctuary. 23.95 o.s.i (*0-399-14549-4*) Putnam Publishing Group, The.
—Three Complete Novels. 2001. 852p. 14.98 (*0-399-14731-4*, Putnam & Grosset) Penguin Group (USA) Inc.
Rogers, Evelyn. Raven. 1995. 384p. mass mkt. 4.99 o.s.i (*0-8217-4800-9*, Zebra Bks.) Kensington Publishing Corp.
Rosen, Charles. The Cockroach Basketball League. 1992. 288p. 21.00 o.p. (*1-55611-329-3*) Fine, Donald I. Bks.
—The Cockroach Basketball League: A Novel. 1998. 240p. pap. 13.95 (*1-888363-78-9*) Seven Stories Pr.
Ruppersburg, Hugh, ed. After O'Connor: Stories from Contemporary Georgia. 2003. (Illus.). xvi, 375p. 49.95 (*0-8203-2556-2*); pap. 19.95 (*0-8203-2557-0*) Univ. of Georgia Pr.
Rutland, Eva. No Crystal Stair. 2003. 368p. pap. (*1-55166-662-6*); 2000. 480p. per. (*1-55166-519-0*, 1-66519-9) Harlequin Enterprises, Ltd. (Mira Bks.).
Salem, Jon. The Perfect Mother. 2000. 352p. mass mkt. 5.99 o.s.i (*0-7860-1130-0*, Pinnacle Bks.) Kensington Publishing Corp.
Sammons, Sonny. The Keepers of Echowah. Selph, Alexa M., ed. 1995. 240p. 18.95 (*0-87797-269-9*) Cherokee Publishing Co.
Scott, Leonard B. Solemn Duty. 1998. 5.99 (*0-345-39186-1*); 1997. 320p. mass mkt. 5.99 (*0-345-41997-9*) Ballantine Bks.
Shaffer, Louise. The Three Miss Margarets. l.t. ed. 2003. 496p. 28.95 (*0-7862-5547-1*) Thorndike Pr.
—The Three Miss Margarets: A Novel. 2004. 336p. pap. 13.95 (*0-375-76088-1*) Ballantine Bks.
—The Three Miss Margarets: A Novel. 2003. 320p. 23.95 (*0-375-50852-X*) Random Hse., Inc.
Shankman, Sarah. First Kill All the Lawyers. 1991. mass mkt. 5.99 (*0-671-74893-9*); 1988. 224p. mass mkt. 3.50 (*0-671-64529-3*) Simon & Schuster. (Pocket).
Shriner, Larry. Epilogue for Murder. 1994. 264p. 21.95 (*0-8027-3182-1*) Walker & Co.
Sibley, Celestine. Ah, Sweet Mystery: A Kate Mulcay Novel of Suspense. 1991. 224p. 19.00 o.p. (*0-06-016304-6*) HarperTrade.
—Ah, Sweet Mystery: A Kate Mulcay Novel of Suspense. 1992. 272p. mass mkt. 4.50 o.p. (*0-06-109083-2*, HarperTorch) Morrow/Avon.
—Christmas in Georgia. 1964. 10.95 o.p. (*0-385-08495-1*) Doubleday Publishing.
—Christmas in Georgia. 2nd ed. 1985. 112p. (gr. 4-7). 12.95 (*0-931948-83-5*) Peachtree Pubs., Ltd.
—Dire Happenings at Scratch Ankle: A Kate Mulcay Mystery. 1993. 224p. 19.00 o.p. (*0-06-017703-9*) HarperTrade.
—Dire Happenings at Scratch Ankle: A Kate Mulcay Mystery. 1994. 224p. mass mkt. 4.50 o.p. (*0-06-109050-6*, HarperTorch) Morrow/Avon.
—A Plague of Kinfolks: A Kate Mulcay Mystery. 1996. 224p. mass mkt. 4.99 o.s.i (*0-06-109049-2*); 1995. 208p. 20.00 o.p. (*0-06-017704-7*) HarperCollins Pubs.
—Spider in the Sink: A Kate Mulcay Mystery. 1997. (Kate Mulcay Mystery Ser.). 208p. 22.50 o.p. (*0-06-017515-X*) HarperCollins Pubs.
—Spider in the Sink: A Kate Mulcay Mystery. 1998. (Kate Mulcay Mystery Ser.). 256p. reprint ed. mass mkt. 5.99 o.s.i (*0-06-109518-4*, HarperTorch) Morrow/Avon.
—Straight As an Arrow: A Kate Mulcay Mystery. 1992. 256p. 19.00 o.p. (*0-06-016305-4*) HarperTrade.
—Straight As an Arrow: A Kate Mulcay Mystery. 1994. 224p. mass mkt. 4.50 o.p. (*0-06-109190-1*, HarperTorch) Morrow/Avon.
Siddons, Anne Rivers. Downtown. 1995. 512p. mass mkt. 7.99 (*0-06-109968-6*, HarperTorch) Morrow/Avon.
—Fox's Earth. 1982. 416p. mass mkt. 6.99 o.s.i (*0-345-30461-6*) Ballantine Bks.
—Fox's Earth. l.t. ed. 1998. 26.95 (*1-57490-150-8*, Beeler Large Print Bks.) Beeler, Thomas T. Publisher.
—Fox's Earth. 1996. 464p. mass mkt. 7.99 (*0-06-101065-0*, HarperTorch) Morrow/Avon.
—Fox's Earth. unabr. ed. 1995. audio 112.00 (*0-7887-0316-1*, 94508E7) Recorded Bks., LLC.
—Nora, Nora. 2000. 272p. 25.00 (*0-06-017613-X*); 384p. pap. 25.00 (*0-06-019718-8*) HarperCollins Pubs.
—Nora, Nora. 2001. 480p. mass mkt. 7.99 (*0-06-109333-5*, HarperTorch) Morrow/Avon.
—Peachtree Road. 1989. 608p. mass mkt. 6.99 o.s.i (*0-345-36272-1*) Ballantine Bks.
—Peachtree Road. l.t. ed. 1995. 969p. lib. bdg. 19.95 o.p. (*0-8161-7413-X*, Macmillan Reference USA) Gale Group.
—Peachtree Road. 1988. 18.95 o.p. (*0-06-015799-2*) HarperTrade.
—Peachtree Road. 10th anniv. ed. 1998. 832p. mass mkt. 7.99 (*0-06-109723-3*, HarperTorch) Morrow/Avon.
—Peachtree Road. 1996. 576p. reprint ed. 27.50 (*0-937036-05-6*) Old New York Bk. Shop Pr.
—Peachtree Road. abr. ed. 1989. audio 16.00 o.s.i (*0-394-58044-3*, RH Audio) Random Hse. Audio Publishing Group.
—Peachtree Road. l.t. ed. 1994. (Core Collection). 969p. lib. bdg. 28.95 (*0-8161-7412-1*) Thorndike Pr.
Simms, William Gilmore. Guy Rivers. 2000. 252p. E-Book 3.95 (*0-594-04248-8*) 1873 Pr.
—Guy Rivers: A Tale of Georgia. Guilds, John Caldwell, ed. rev. ed. reprint ed. 31.50 (*0-404-06034-X*) AMS Pr., Inc.
—Guy Rivers: A Tale of Georgia, 2 vols. 1834. (YA). reprint ed. pap. text 28.00 (*1-4047-6859-9*) Classic Textbooks.
—Guy Rivers: A Tale of Georgia, 2 vols., Set. Guilds, John Caldwell, ed. 1992. (BCL1-PS American Literature Ser.). reprint ed. lib. bdg. 180.00 (*0-7812-6859-1*) Reprint Services Corp.
—Guy Rivers: A Tale of Georgia. Guilds, John Caldwell, ed. 1993. (Simms Ser.: Vol. 9). 544p. text 49.95 (*1-55728-274-9*) Univ. of Arkansas Pr.
—Joscelyn: A Tale of the Revolution. Butterworth, Keen, ed. 1975. (Centennial Edition of the Writings of William Gilmore Simms). xxx, 338p. 34.95 o.s.i (*0-87249-322-9*) Univ. of South Carolina Pr.
Skinner, Gloria Dale. Passion's Choice. 2001. (Five Star Romance Ser.). 282p. 26.95 (*0-7862-3463-6*, Five Star) Gale Group.
—Passion's Choice. 1990. mass mkt. 4.50 (*0-445-21062-1*, Mysterious Pr. Paperback Bks.) Warner Bks., Inc.
Skoryna, Stanley C. Atlanta on My Mind, Vol. 1. Mullen, Joseph A., ed. 1996. (Illus.). 335p. 38.95 (*0-943100-01-1*, 100-03) Home Museum Pr.
Slaughter, Karin. Blindsighted: A Novel. 2001. 320p. 25.00 (*0-688-17457-4*, Morrow, William & Co.) Morrow/Avon.
—A Faint Cold Fear. abr. ed. 2003. audio 25.95 (*0-06-051468-X*, HarperAudio) HarperTrade.
—A Faint Cold Fear. 2003. mass mkt. 7.99 (*0-06-053405-2*, Morrow, William & Co.) Morrow/Avon.
—Kisscut. 2003. E-Book 7.99 (*0-06-057880-7*); E-Book 7.99 (*0-06-057881-5*); E-Book 7.99 (*0-06-057882-3*); E-Book 7.99 (*0-06-057883-1*) HarperCollins Pubs.
—Kisscut. 2003. 448p. mass mkt. 7.99 (*0-06-053404-4*, HarperTorch) Morrow/Avon.
Smith, Charlie. Shine Hawk. 1988. 368p. 17.95 o.s.i (*0-945167-01-6*) British American Publishing, Ltd.
—Shine Hawk. 1990. 384p. reprint ed. pap. (*0-671-68498-1*, Washington Square Pr.) Simon & Schuster.
—Shine Hawk: A Novel by Charlie Smith. 1998. 384p. pap. 16.95 (*0-8203-1997-X*) Univ. of Georgia Pr.
Smith, Deborah. On Bear Mountain. l.t. ed. 2001. (Large Print Book Ser.). 446p. 26.95 (*1-58724-010-6*, Wheeler Publishing, Inc.) Gale Group.
—On Bear Mountain: A Novel. 2001. 352p. 23.95 o.p. (*0-316-80077-5*) Little Brown & Co.
Smith, Faye M. Flight of the Blackbird. 1996. 348p. 22.50 (*0-684-82971-1*, Scribner) Simon & Schuster.
—The Flight of the Blackbird. 1997. 464p. reprint ed. mass mkt. 6.50 (*0-446-60561-1*) Warner Bks., Inc.
Smith, Haywood. Miss Mamie's Porch. mass mkt. (*0-312-98043-4*, St. Martin's Paperbacks) St. Martin's Pr.
—Queen Bee of Mimosa Branch: A Novel. 2002. 352p. 24.95 (*0-312-30056-5*) St. Martin's Pr.
Smith, Zane. Wicked Stop, Georgia. 2003. 315p. pap. 10.99 (*1-932162-12-7*) Benoy Publishing.
Sorrells, Walter. Will to Murder. 1996. 304p. (Orig.). mass mkt. 5.50 (*0-380-78020-8*, Avon Bks.) Morrow/Avon.
Spencer, LaVyrle. Morning Glory. mass mkt. 5.99 o.s.i (*0-515-11303-4*); 1990. 448p. mass mkt. 7.50 (*0-515-10263-6*) Berkley Publishing Group. (Jove).
—Morning Glory. l.t. ed. 1990. (Magna Large Print Ser.). 637p. o.p. (*1-85057-842-7*) Magna Large Print Bks. GBR. *Dist:* Ulverscroft Large Print Canada, Ltd.
—Morning Glory. 14.95 o.s.i (*0-399-13641-X*) Putnam Publishing Group, The.
—Morning Glory. 1991. 5.99 o.p. (*0-517-07426-5*) Random Hse. Value Publishing.
Sprinkle, Patricia. But Why Shoot the Magistrate? l.t. ed. 1999. (Christian Mystery Ser.). 456p. 23.95 (*0-7862-2060-0*) Thorndike Pr.
—But Why Shoot the Magistrate? 1998. (MacLaren Yarbrough Mysteries Ser.: Vol. 2). 320p. pap. 9.99 (*0-310-21324-X*) Zondervan.
—Who Let That Killer in the House? 2003. 272p. mass mkt. 5.99 (*0-451-21019-0*, Signet Bks.) NAL.
Sprinkle, Patricia H. Death of a Dunwoody Matron. 1993. 272p. 17.00 o.s.i (*0-385-42485-X*) Doubleday Publishing.
—Murder on Peachtree Street. 1991. 17.95 o.p. (*0-312-05476-9*, Saint Martin's Minotaur) St. Martin's Pr.
—Somebody's Dead in Snellville. 1992. 256p. 18.95 o.p. (*0-312-07809-9*, Saint Martin's Minotaur) St. Martin's Pr.
Staats, Marilyn D. Looking for Atlanta. 1999. 232p. pap. 12.95 (*0-8203-2120-6*); 1992. 240p. 19.95 (*0-8203-1470-6*) Univ. of Georgia Pr.
—Looking for Atlanta. 1993. 240p. mass mkt. 5.99 (*0-446-36574-2*) Warner Bks., Inc.
Starnes, Henry G. Summer at the Resort: Remembering the 50s. Epps, Robert, ed. rev. ed. 1997. 250p. pap. 12.00 (*0-9657613-0-4*) Starnes Publishing Co.
Statham, Frances P. The Roswell Women. 1987. (Orig.). pap. 7.95 o.p. (*0-449-90182-3*, Fawcett) Ballantine Bks.
Statham, Frances Patton. Call the River Home. 1991. 320p. (Orig.). pap. 9.00 o.s.i (*0-449-90340-0*, Fawcett) Ballantine Bks.
Steadman, Mark. McAfee County: A Chronicle. 1998. 320p. pap. 16.95 (*0-8203-2014-5*) Univ. of Georgia Pr.
Steadman, Mark S., Jr. McAfee County: A Chronicle. reprint ed. 37.50 (*0-404-19941-0*) AMS Pr., Inc.
Stephens, Martha. Children of the World: A Novel. 1994. 416p. (Orig.). pap. 22.50 (*0-87074-378-3*); pap. 10.95 (*0-87074-379-1*) Southern Methodist Univ. Pr.
Stores, Teresa. Getting to the Point. 1995. 240p. pap. 10.95 o.p. (*1-56280-100-7*) Naiad Pr., Inc.
Sumner, Melanie. The School of Beauty & Charm. 2002. 320p. reprint ed. pap. 13.00 (*0-7434-4644-5*, Washington Square Pr.) Simon & Schuster.
—The School of Beauty & Charm: A Novel. 2001. 320p. tchr. ed. 23.95 (*1-56512-286-0*, Shannon Ravenel Bks.) Algonquin Bks. of Chapel Hill.
Talley, Linda. Jackson's Plan. 1998. (Key Concepts in Personal Development Ser.). (Illus.). 32p. (J). (gr. k-4). 16.95 (*1-55942-104-5*, 7665) Marsh Media.
Tan, Maureen. A. K. A. Jane. 1999. 336p. mass mkt. 6.50 (*0-446-60667-7*) Warner Bks., Inc.
—AKA Jane. 1997. 304p. 22.00 o.p. (*0-89296-658-0*) Mysterious Pr.
—AKA Jane. abr. ed. 1998. audio 23.00 (*1-56876-070-1*) Soundlines Entertainment, Inc.
—Run Jane Run. 1999. 274p. 22.00 o.s.i (*0-89296-659-9*) Mysterious Pr.
—Run Jane Run. 2000. 304p. mass mkt. 6.50 (*0-446-60904-8*); 1999. E-Book 4.95 (*0-446-91276-X*) Warner Bks., Inc.
Taylor, Janelle. Promise Me Forever. l.t. ed. 1997. (Romance Ser.). 554p. 24.95 (*0-7862-0905-4*, Five Star) Gale Group.
—Promise Me Forever. 1992. mass mkt. 5.99 o.s.i (*0-8217-3764-3*); 1991. mass mkt. 20.00 o.p. (*0-8217-3553-5*) Kensington Publishing Corp. (Zebra Bks.).
—Promise Me Forever. abr. ed. 1994. audio 5.99 (*1-57096-007-0*, RAZ 908) Romance Alive Audio.
Thomas, Jacquelin. Singsation. 352p. 2003. pap. 13.95 (*0-446-67886-4*, Walk Worthy Pr.); 2001. 21.95 o.p. (*0-446-52798-X*); 2001. E-Book 14.95 (*0-7595-4244-9*); 2001. E-Book 14.95 (*0-7595-9273-X*); 2001. E-Book 14.95 (*0-7595-6241-5*); 2001. E-Book 14.95 (*0-7595-8247-5*); 2001. E-Book 14.95 (*0-7595-0241-2*) Warner Bks., Inc.
Trobaugh, Augusta. Sophie & the Rising Sun. 2002. 224p. pap. 13.00 (*0-452-28349-3*, Plume); 2001. 208p. 22.95 o.s.i (*0-525-94627-6*, Dutton) Dutton/Plume.
—Sophie & the Rising Sun. l.t. ed. 2002. (Women's Fiction Ser.). 291p. 28.95 (*0-7862-4052-0*) Gale Group.
Trocheck, Kathy Hogan. Every Crooked Nanny. 1992. 208p. 19.00 o.p. (*0-06-017923-6*) HarperTrade.
—Every Crooked Nanny. 1993. (Callahan Garrity Mystery Ser.). 336p. mass mkt. 6.50 (*0-06-109170-7*, HarperTorch) Morrow/Avon.
—Every Crooked Nanny. l.t. ed. 1997. (Ulverscroft Large Print Ser.). 544p. 29.99 o.p. (*0-7089-3748-9*, Ulverscroft) Thorpe, F. A. Pubs. GBR. *Dist:* Ulverscroft Large Print Bks., Ltd., Ulverscroft Large Print Canada, Ltd.
—Happy Never After. 1995. 306p. 22.00 o.p. (*0-06-017637-7*) HarperCollins Pubs.
—Happy Never After. 1996. (Callahan Garrity Mystery Ser.). 320p. mass mkt. 5.99 (*0-06-109360-2*, HarperTorch) Morrow/Avon.
—Heart Trouble. 1996. (Callahan Garrity Mystery Ser.). 304p. 22.00 o.p. (*0-06-017638-5*) HarperCollins Pubs.
—Heart Trouble. 1997. 304p. mass mkt. 5.99 (*0-06-109585-0*, HarperTorch) Morrow/Avon.

Settings

—Heart Trouble. l.t. ed. 1998. (Ulverscroft Large Print Ser.). 448p. 29.99 (*0-7089-3947-3*, Ulverscroft) Thorpe, F. A. Pubs. GBR. *Dist:* Ulverscroft Large Print Bks., Ltd., Ulverscroft Large Print Canada, Ltd.

—Homemade Sin. l.t. ed. 1994. 379p. pap. 19.95 (*0-7838-1163-2*, Macmillan Reference USA) Gale Group.

—Homemade Sin. 1994. 256p. 20.00 o.p. (*0-06-017765-9*) HarperTrade.

—Homemade Sin. 1995. (Callahan Garrity Mystery Ser.). 304p. mass mkt. 5.99 (*0-06-109256-8*, HarperTorch) Morrow/Avon.

—Irish Eyes. 2000. (Callahan Garrity Mystery Ser.). 304p. 24.00 (*0-06-019421-9*) HarperCollins Pubs.

—Irish Eyes. 2001. (Callahan Garrity Mystery Ser.). 320p. mass mkt. 5.99 (*0-06-109869-8*, Avon Bks.) Morrow/Avon.

—Irish Eyes. l.t. ed. 2000. (Mystery Ser.). 473p. 28.95 (*0-7862-2837-7*) Thorndike Pr.

—Midnight Clear. l.t. ed. 2000. 360p. 26.95 (*1-57490-323-3*, Beeler Large Print Bks.) Beeler, Thomas T. Publisher.

—Midnight Clear. 1998. (Callahan Garrity Mystery Ser.). 288p. 23.00 o.s.i (*0-06-017543-5*) HarperCollins Pubs.

—Midnight Clear. 1999. (Callahan Garrity Mystery Ser.). 416p. mass mkt. 5.99 (*0-06-109800-0*, HarperTorch) Morrow/Avon.

—Strange Brew. l.t. ed. 1999. 24.95 (*1-57490-219-9*, Beeler Large Print Bks.) Beeler, Thomas T. Publisher.

—Strange Brew. 1997. (Callahan Garrity Mystery Ser.). 288p. 23.00 o.s.i (*0-06-017542-7*) HarperCollins Pubs.

—Strange Brew. 1998. (Callahan Garrity Mystery Ser.). 336p. reprint ed. mass mkt. 5.99 (*0-06-109173-1*, HarperTorch) Morrow/Avon.

—To Live & Die in Dixie. 1993. 288p. 20.00 o.p. (*0-06-017924-4*) HarperTrade.

—To Live & Die in Dixie. 1994. (Callahan Garrity Mystery Ser.). 320p. mass mkt. 5.99 (*0-06-109171-5*, HarperTorch) Morrow/Avon.

—To Live & Die in Dixie. l.t. ed. 1997. (Ulverscroft Large Print Ser.). 496p. 29.99 o.p. (*0-7089-3837-X*, Ulverscroft) Thorpe, F. A. Pubs. GBR. *Dist:* Ulverscroft Large Print Bks., Ltd., Ulverscroft Large Print Canada, Ltd.

Truscott, Lucian K., IV. Heart of War. 1997. 400p. 23.95 o.p. (*0-525-94117-7*) Dutton/Plume.

—Heart of War. 1998. 432p. mass mkt. 6.99 o.s.i (*0-451-18770-9*, Signet Bks.) NAL.

—Heart of War. abr. ed. 1997. 25.00 o.p. (*0-7871-1512-6*) NewStar Media, Inc.

Veron, J. Michael. The Greatest Course That Never Was. 2001. 384p. 22.95 (*1-886947-92-9*) Clock Tower Pr. LLC.

—The Greatest Course That Never Was: A Novel. 2002. 384p. reprint ed. pap. 12.95 (*0-7679-0717-5*) Broadway Bks.

Walker, Alice. The Third Life of Grange Copeland. Bernard, Andre, ed. 2003. 328p. pap. 14.00 (*0-15-602836-0*, Harvest Bks.) Harcourt Trade Pubs.

Warner, Jack. Shikar. 2003. (Illus.). 368p. 24.95 (*0-7653-0343-4*, Forge Bks.) Doherty, Tom Assocs., LLC.

White, Bailey. Quite a Year for Plums: A Novel. l.t. ed. 1999. 368p. 22.00 o.p. (*0-7838-0159-9*, Macmillan Reference USA) Gale Group.

—Quite a Year for Plums: A Novel. 1999. pap. (*0-375-70276-8*, Vintage) Knopf Publishing Group.

—Quite a Year for Plums: A Novel. 1999. 240p. pap. 12.95 (*0-679-76492-5*) Knopf, Alfred A. Inc.

—Quite a Year for Plums: A Novel. abr. unabr. ed. 1998. audio 25.00 (*0-375-40301-9*, BW04Z, RH Audio) Random Hse. Audio Publishing Group.

—Quite a Year for Plums: A Novel. l.t. ed. 1998. pap. 22.00 o.s.i (*0-375-70292-X*) Random Hse., Inc.

White, Karen. Falling Home. 2002. 356p. mass mkt. 5.99 (*0-8217-7338-0*) Kensington Publishing Corp.

White, Walter. The Fire in the Flint. 1995. 312p. pap. 19.95 (*0-8203-1742-X*) Univ. of Georgia Pr.

White, Walter F. Fire in the Flint. 1969. 300p. reprint ed. 35.00 o.s.i (*0-8371-0945-0*, WFF&) Greenwood Publishing Group, Inc.

Wieland, Liza. The Names of the Lost: A Novel. 1992. 312p. 19.95 (*0-87074-337-6*) Southern Methodist Univ. Pr.

Wilcox, Patricia. Shaped Notes: Stories of Twentieth Century Georgia. 2001. xvi, 160p. pap. 24.95 (*0-9703743-6-4*, 129) Pageant Pr.

Wilkins, Gina F. Yesterday's Scandal. 2000. (Promo Ser.). 304p. mass mkt. (*0-373-83439-X*, 1-83439-9, Harlequin Bks.) Harlequin Enterprises, Ltd.

Willard, Fred. Down on Ponce. 1997. 288p. (Orig.). pap. 12.00 (*1-56352-431-7*) Longstreet Pr., Inc.

Windham, Donald. The Dog Star: A Novel. 1999. (Hill Street Classics Ser.). 224p. reprint ed. pap. 14.95 (*1-892514-09-5*, Hill Street Classics) Hill Street Pr., LLC.

Wolfe, Tom. A Man in Full. 1999. 800p. mass mkt. 8.50 (*0-553-58093-0*) Bantam Bks.

—A Man in Full, Pt. 1. unabr. ed. 1999. audio 104.00 (*0-7366-4373-7*, 4814-A) Books on Tape, Inc.

—A Man in Full. 1998. 742p. 28.95 (*0-374-27032-5*); 528p. 200.00 o.p. (*0-374-27030-9*) Farrar, Straus & Giroux.

—A Man in Full. l.t. ed. 1998. 33.95 o.p. (*1-56895-694-0*, Wheeler Publishing, Inc.) Gale Group.

—A Man in Full. abr. ed. 1999. audio 27.50 Highsmith Inc.

—A Man in Full. abr. ed. 1998. audio 27.50 (*0-553-47890-7*, 756001); audio compact disk 39.95 (*0-553-45619-9*) Random Hse. Audio Publishing Group. (RH Audio).

Woods, Sherryl. Bank on It. 2000. 235p. 26.95 (*0-7351-0306-2*); pap. 16.95 (*0-7351-0307-0*) Replica Bks.

—Bank on It. 1993. 240p. mass mkt. 4.99 o.s.i (*0-446-36404-5*) Warner Bks., Inc.

—Body & Soul. 2000. 254p. 26.95 (*0-7351-0310-0*); pap. 16.95 (*0-7351-0311-9*) Replica Bks.

—Body & Soul. 1990. 19.00 o.p. (*0-7278-4111-4*) Severn Hse. Pubs., Ltd.

—Body & Soul. 1994. 256p. mass mkt. 5.50 o.s.i (*0-446-60155-1*, Mysterious Pr. Paperback Bks.); 1989. 3.95 (*0-445-20900-3*) Warner Bks., Inc.

—Deadly Obsession. 2000. 236p. 26.95 (*0-7351-0314-3*); pap. 16.95 (*0-7351-0315-1*) Replica Bks.

—Deadly Obsession. 1995. 256p. mass mkt. 5.50 (*0-446-60091-1*) Warner Bks., Inc.

—Hide & Seek. unabr. collector's ed. 1994. audio 36.00 (*0-7366-2778-2*, 3497) Books on Tape, Inc.

—Hide & Seek. 2000. 339p. 28.95 (*0-7351-0304-6*); pap. 18.95 (*0-7351-0305-4*) Replica Bks.

—Hide & Seek. 1993. 240p. mass mkt. 4.99 o.s.i (*0-446-36405-3*) Warner Bks., Inc.

—Reckless. 2000. 240p. 26.95 (*0-7351-0312-7*); 235p. pap. 16.95 (*0-7351-0313-5*) Replica Bks.

—Reckless. 1990. reprint ed. 18.00 o.p. (*0-7278-4048-7*) Severn Hse. Pubs., Ltd.

—Reckless. 1993. 240p. mass mkt. 4.99 o.s.i (*0-446-36549-1*); 1989. pap. 3.95 (*0-445-20819-8*) Warner Bks., Inc.

—Stolen Moments. 2000. 253p. 26.95 (*0-7351-0300-3*); pap. 16.95 (*0-7351-0301-1*) Replica Bks.

—Stolen Moments. 1991. reprint ed. 18.95 o.p. (*0-7278-4174-2*) Severn Hse. Pubs., Ltd.

—Stolen Moments. 1995. 256p. mass mkt. 5.99 o.s.i (*0-446-60163-2*); 1990. mass mkt. 4.95 (*0-445-21010-9*, Mysterious Pr. Paperback Bks.) Warner Bks., Inc.

—Ties That Bind. 2000. 255p. 26.95 (*0-7351-0308-9*); 16.95 (*0-7351-0309-7*) Replica Bks.

—Ties That Bind. 1991. 256p. reprint ed. 19.00 o.p. (*0-7278-4245-5*) Severn Hse. Pubs., Ltd.

—Ties That Bind. 1991. 256p. mass mkt. 4.99 (*0-446-36117-8*) Warner Bks., Inc.

—White Lightning. 2000. 316p. 28.95 (*0-7351-0302-X*); pap. 18.95 (*0-7351-0303-8*) Replica Bks.

—White Lightning. 1995. 320p. mass mkt. 5.99 o.p. (*0-446-60090-3*) Warner Bks., Inc.

Woods, Stuart. Chiefs. 1982. pap. 3.95 o.p. (*0-553-24080-3*) Bantam Bks.

—Chiefs. 1999. 432p. mass mkt. 7.99 (*0-380-70347-5*, Avon Bks.) Morrow/Avon.

—Chiefs. 1981. 14.95 o.s.i (*0-393-01461-4*) Norton, W. W. & Co., Inc.

—Chiefs. l.t. ed. 2001. (Thorndike Basic Ser.). 701p. 30.95 (*0-7862-3150-5*) Thorndike Pr.

—Grass Roots. l.t. ed. 1990. (General Ser.). 548p. 24.95 (*0-8161-4993-3*, Macmillan Reference USA) Gale Group.

—Grass Roots. 2002. 496p. mass mkt. 7.99 (*0-06-101422-2*); 1990. pap. 6.99 (*0-380-71169-9*) Morrow/Avon. (Avon Bks.).

—Grass Roots. 1989. 19.95 o.p. (*0-671-66739-4*, Simon & Schuster) Simon & Schuster.

—Palindrome. l.t. ed. 1998. pap. 24.95 (*1-56895-688-6*, Wheeler Publishing, Inc.) Gale Group.

—Palindrome. 1991. 352p. 239.40 o.p. (*0-06-017913-9*) HarperCollins Pubs.

—Palindrome. 1991. (Illus.). 368p. 19.95 o.p. (*0-06-017911-2*) HarperTrade.

—Palindrome. 1995. 79p. mass mkt. 3.99 o.p. (*0-06-109482-X*); 1991. 464p. mass mkt. 7.99 (*0-06-109936-8*) Morrow/Avon. (HarperTorch).

—Run Before the Wind. 1999. 320p. mass mkt. 7.99 (*0-380-70507-9*, Avon Bks.) Morrow/Avon.

—Run Before the Wind. 1983. 16.50 o.p. (*0-393-01651-X*) Norton, W. W. & Co., Inc.

—Run Before the Wind. l.t. ed. 1989. (Ulverscroft Large Print Ser.). 624p. 29.99 o.p. (*0-7089-2003-9*, Ulverscroft) Thorpe, F. A. Pubs. GBR. *Dist:* Ulverscroft Large Print Bks., Ltd., Ulverscroft Large Print Canada, Ltd.

—Under the Lake. 1999. 368p. mass mkt. 7.99 (*0-06-101417-6*) HarperCollins Pubs.

—Under the Lake. 1988. 288p. pap. 6.50 (*0-380-70519-2*, Avon Bks.) Morrow/Avon.

—Under the Lake. unabr. ed. audio 60.00 (*0-7887-0496-6*, 94688E7) Recorded Bks., LLC.

—Under the Lake. 1987. 17.45 o.p. (*0-671-63332-5*, Simon & Schuster) Simon & Schuster.

—Under the Lake. l.t. ed. 1988. (Charnwood Large Print Ser.). 416p. 19.95 o.p. (*0-7089-8490-8*, Charnwood) Thorpe, F. A. Pubs. GBR. *Dist:* Ulverscroft Large Print Bks., Ltd., Ulverscroft Large Print Canada, Ltd.

Woolson, Constance F. Jupiter Lights, a Novel. reprint ed. 29.50 (*0-404-07037-X*) AMS Pr., Inc.

Wyrick, E. L. Power in the Blood. 1996. 336p. 22.95 o.p. (*0-312-13590-4*, Saint Martin's Minotaur) St. Martin's Pr.

—A Strange & Bitter Crop. 1994. 304p. 20.95 o.p. (*0-312-11075-8*, Saint Martin's Minotaur) St. Martin's Pr.

York, Rebecca. Witching Moon. 2003. 352p. mass mkt. 5.99 (*0-425-19278-4*) Berkley Publishing Group.

Youngblood, Shay. Soul Kiss. 1998. 224p. 13.00 (*1-57322-658-0*, Riverhead Trade (Paperbacks)) Berkley Publishing Group.

—Soul Kiss. 1997. 224p. 21.00 o.s.i (*1-57322-063-9*, Riverhead Bks. (Hardcovers)) Putnam Publishing Group, The.

Zubro, Mark Richard. Rust on the Razor. (Tom & Scott Mystery Ser.). 224p. 1997. pap. 11.95 (*0-312-15644-8*, Saint Martin's Griffin); 1996. text 20.95 o.p. (*0-312-14404-0*, Saint Martin's Minotaur) St. Martin's Pr.

## GERMANY—FICTION

Aaron, David. Crossing by Night. 1994. 416p. mass mkt. 5.99 (*0-380-72191-0*, Avon Bks.); 1993. 22.00 o.p. (*0-688-09296-9*, Morrow, William & Co.) Morrow/Avon.

Abbott, Margot. The Last Innocent Hour. 1993. 553p. mass mkt. 5.99 (*0-312-92942-0*, St. Martin's Paperbacks); 1991. 512p. 21.95 o.p. (*0-312-06377-6*) St. Martin's Pr.

Abish, Walter. How German Is It=Wie Deutsch Ist Es. 1982. 195p. text 15.25 o.p. (*0-85635-396-5*) Brill Academic Pubs., Inc.

—How German Is It=Wie Deutsch Ist Es. 1980. 256p. pap. 10.95 (*0-8112-0776-5*, NDP508); 14.95 o.p. (*0-8112-0775-7*) New Directions Publishing Corp.

Aichinger, Ilse. Bound Man, & Other Stories. Mosbacher, Eric, tr. 1977. (Short Story Index Reprint Ser.). reprint ed. 13.95 (*0-8369-3766-X*) Ayer Co. Pubs., Inc.

Ali, Tariq. Fear of Mirrors. 1998. 240p. pap. 24.95 (*1-900850-10-9*) Arcadia Bks. GBR. *Dist:* Dufour Editions, Inc.

Allbeury, Ted. Children of Tender Years. 1985. 240p. 14.95 o.p. (*0-8253-0306-0*) Beaufort Bks., Inc.

—Mission Berlin. 1988. 224p. pap. 3.95 o.p. (*0-380-70444-7*, Avon Bks.) Morrow/Avon.

—Mission Berlin. 1986. 15.95 (*0-8027-0892-7*) Walker & Co.

Altman, John. A Game of Spies. 2003. 304p. reprint ed. mass mkt. 6.99 (*0-515-13463-5*, Jove) Berkley Publishing Group.

—A Game of Spies. l.t. ed. 2002. 373p. 28.95 (*0-7862-4104-7*) Gale Group.

—A Game of Spies. 2002. 320p. 25.95 o.s.i (*0-399-14837-X*) Putnam Publishing Group, The.

Andersch, Alfred. The Father of a Murderer. Vennewitz, Leila, tr. from GER. 1994. 128p. 17.95 (*0-8112-1261-0*) New Directions Publishing Corp.

Andrews, Robert. Last Spy Out. 1991. 384p. mass mkt. 4.99 o.s.i (*0-553-29126-2*) Bantam Bks.

Arjouni, Jakob. Happy Birthday, Turk! 191p. pap. 9.95 o.p. (*1-874061-37-8*) Oldcastle Bks., Ltd. GBR. *Dist:* Trafalgar Square.

Bachmann, Ingeborg. The Thirtieth Year. Bullock, Michael, tr. from GER. (Portico Paperbacks Ser.). 200p. 1995. pap. 12.95 (*0-8419-1069-3*); 1987. 19.95 o.s.i (*0-8419-1068-5*) Holmes & Meier Pubs., Inc.

—The Thirtieth Year. 1996. 11.99 o.s.i (*0-7486-6142-5*) Polygon GBR. *Dist:* Subterranean Co.

—Three Paths to the Lake. Gilbert, Mary F. & Anderson, Mark, trs. from GER. 1989. (Modern German Voices Ser.). Orig. Title: Simultan. 212p. (C). 29.95 (*0-8419-1070-7*) Holmes & Meier Pubs., Inc.

—Three Paths to the Lake. Gilbert, Mary F., tr. from GER. 1997. (Portico Paperbacks Ser.). Orig. Title: Simultan. 212p. (C). reprint ed. pap. 14.00 (*0-8419-1071-5*) Holmes & Meier Pubs., Inc.

Baddock, James. Emerald. 1991. 208p. 17.95 o.s.i (*0-8027-1144-8*) Walker & Co.

Banville, John. Kepler. 1983. 208p. 14.95 o.p. (*0-87923-438-5*); pap. 8.95 o.p. (*0-87923-527-6*) Godine, David R. Pub.

—Kepler. 1993. 208p. pap. 12.00 (*0-679-74370-7*, Vintage) Knopf Publishing Group.

Bar Am, Meir. The Parnas. Van Handel, Esther, tr. 1986. 10.95 o.p. (*0-87306-393-7*); pap. 6.95 (*0-87306-400-3*) Feldheim, Philipp Inc.

Barnard, Richard & Hertogs, Sam. The Price of Ashes. Field, Barbara, ed. 1999. (Jacob's Star Trilogy Ser.: Vol. 1). ix, 502p. pap. 7.50 (*0-9644751-3-8*) Hubbard, Louis Publishing.

—The Price of Ashes. 1995. 625p. 21.95 (*0-9644751-1-1*); pap. (*0-9644751-0-3*) Hubbard, Louis Publishing.

Becker, Jurek. Jacob the Liar. 1997. pap. 12.95 o.p. (*1-55970-374-1*) Arcade Publishing, Inc.

—Jacob the Liar. Vennewitz, Leila, tr. from GER. 1996. (Illus.). 256p. 21.95 (*1-55970-315-6*) Arcade Publishing, Inc.

—Jacob the Liar. Vennewitz, Leila, tr. from GER. 1997. 256p. pap. 11.95 o.s.i (*0-452-27903-8*, Plume) Dutton/Plume.

—Jacob the Liar. Kornfeld, Melvin, tr. 1975. (Helen & Kurt Wolff Bk.). 256p. 7.95 o.p. (*0-15-145975-4*) Harcourt Trade Pubs.

—Jacob the Liar. 1990. 19.95 o.p. (*0-8052-4097-7*, Schocken) Knopf Publishing Group.

Bedford, Sybille. Jigsaw: An Unsentimental Education. 1991. 352p. pap. 10.00 o.p. (*0-14-011388-6*, Penguin Bks.) Penguin Group (USA) Inc.

—Jigsaw: An Unsentimental Education, a Biographical Novel. 2001. 368p. pap. text 15.00 (*1-58243-143-4*, Counterpoint Pr.) Basic Bks.

—Legacy. 2001. 384p. pap. text 15.00 (*1-58243-142-6*, Counterpoint Pr.) Basic Bks.

—Legacy. 1984. (Neglected Books of the 20th Century Ser.). 380p. reprint ed. pap. 8.50 o.p. (*0-912946-26-1*, Ecco) HarperTrade.

Benary-Isbert, Margot. The Ark. 1991. (J). (gr. 5-9). 19.50 o.p. (*0-8446-6295-X*) Smith, Peter Pub., Inc.

Benjamin, Lewis S. & Hargreaves, Reginald, eds. Great German Short Stories. 1977. (Short Story Index Reprint Ser.). reprint ed. 51.95 (*0-8369-4001-6*) Ayer Co. Pubs., Inc.

Berkewicz, Ulla. Angels Are Black & White. Willson, A. Leslie, tr. from GER. 1997. 300p. 39.95 (*1-57113-112-4*) Camden Hse.

Berliner, Janet. Children of the Dusk, Bk. 3. 1997. (Madagascar Manifesto Ser.). 447p. mass mkt. 5.99 (*1-56504-932-2*, Borealis) White Wolf Publishing, Inc.

Berliner, Janet & Guthridge, George. Child of the Journey. 1996. (Child of the Journey Ser.: Bk. II). 471p. pap. 5.99 (*1-56504-942-X*, Borealis) White Wolf Publishing, Inc.

—Child of the Light. 1996. (Madagascar Manifesto Ser.: Bk. 1). (Illus.). 440p. (Orig.). pap. 5.99 (*1-56504-931-4*, 12100, Borealis) White Wolf Publishing, Inc.

Bernau, George. Black Phoenix. 304p. 1995. mass mkt. 5.99 o.s.i (*0-446-60182-9*); 1994. (Illus.). 22.95 o.s.i (*0-446-51610-4*) Warner Bks., Inc.

Blum, Jenna. Those Who Save Us. 2004. 496p. (*0-15-101019-6*) Harcourt Trade Pubs.

Bobrowski, Johannes. Levin's Mill. Cropper, Janet, tr. from GER. 1988. Orig. Title: Levins Muhle. 240p. 16.95 (*0-7145-0020-8*) Boyars, Marion Pubs., Inc.

—Levin's Mill. Cropper, Janet, tr. from GER. 1996. (Classics Ser.). Orig. Title: Levins Muhle. 230p. pap. 12.00 (*0-8112-1329-3*) New Directions Publishing Corp.

Bock, Dennis. Olympia. 1999. 272p. 22.95 (*1-58234-023-4*) Bloomsbury Publishing.

—Olympia. 1998. 256p. pap. o.s.i (*0-385-25698-1*) Doubleday Publishing.

Bock, Dennis, contrib. by. Olympia. 1998. 252p. (*0-7475-3680-5*) Bloomsbury Publishing, Ltd. GBR. *Dist:* Trafalgar Square.

Boetius, Henning. The Phoenix: A Novel about the Hindenburg. Cullen, John, tr. from GER. 2001. 352p. 24.95 (*0-385-50183-8*, Talese, Nan A.) Doubleday Publishing.

Boll, Heinrich. The Silent Angel. Mitchell, Breon, tr. 1994. 176p. 19.95 o.p. (*0-312-11064-2*) St. Martin's Pr.

—The Silent Angel. 2002. (Cassell Military Paperbacks Ser.). 288p. pap. 9.95 (*0-304-35974-2*) Sterling Publishing Co., Inc.

—The Silent Angel: A Novel. Mitchell, Breon, tr. from GER. 1995. 192p. pap. 12.00 (*0-312-13171-2*) Picador.

Broner, Peter. Night of the Broken Glass. 1997. 336p. pap. text 10.95 (*1-886449-43-0*) Barrytown, Ltd.

—Night of the Broken Glass. 1991. 304p. 19.95 (*0-88268-132-X*); 316p. pap. 10.95 (*0-88268-141-9*) Station Hill Pr.

Browne, Marshall. Eye of the Abyss. Date not set. pap. (*0-312-31157-5*, St. Martin's Paperbacks); Date not set. mass mkt. (*0-312-98835-4*, St. Martin's Paperbacks); 2003. 304p. 23.95 (*0-312-31156-7*) St. Martin's Pr.

Buchan, James. The Golden Plough: A Novel. 1995. 240p. 21.00 o.p. (*0-374-16873-3*) Farrar, Straus & Giroux.

Buckley, William F., Jr. Nuremberg: The Reckoning. 2002. (Illus.). 384p. 25.00 (*0-15-100679-2*) Harcourt Trade Pubs.

Bukiet, Melvin J. After. 1997. 400p. pap. 14.00 o.s.i (*0-312-16760-1*) Picador.

—After. 1996. 400p. 24.95 o.p. (*0-312-14536-5*) St. Martin's Pr.

—Signs & Wonders. 1999. 384p. 26.00 o.p. (*0-312-20009-9*) Picador.

Bunn, T. Davis. Berlin Encounter. 1995. (Rendezvous with Destiny Ser.: Bk. 4). 192p. pap. 8.99 o.p. (*1-55661-382-2*) Bethany Hse. Pubs.

—Berlin Encounter. l.t. ed. 1997. (Christian Mystery Ser.). 227p. 22.95 o.p. (0-7862-1234-9) Thorndike Pr.

—Gibraltar Passage. l.t. ed. 1994. (Rendezvous with Destiny Ser.: No. 2). 192p. pap. 8.99 o.p. (1-55661-380-6) Bethany Hse. Pubs.

—Rhineland Inheritance. 1993. (Rendezvous with Destiny Ser.: No. 1). 224p. pap. 8.99 o.p. (1-55661-347-4) Bethany Hse. Pubs.

—Rhineland Inheritance. l.t. ed. 1995. 285p. 29.95 (0-7838-1388-0, Macmillan Reference USA) Gale Group.

Burke, James. Fun F Mann: A Prisoner of War Story. 1994. (Illus.). 168p. (Orig.). reprint ed. pap. 10.00 (0-9640884-0-1) Meredith Pr.

Butor, Michel. Portrait of the Artist as a Young Ape. 1995. pap. 10.95 (1-56478-089-9) Dalkey Archive Pr.

—Portrait of the Artist as a Young Ape. Di Bernardi, Dominic, tr. from FRE. 1995. 128p. 19.95 (1-56478-077-5) Dalkey Archive Pr.

Carlyle, Thomas. Sartor Resartus. 1954. 8.95 o.p. (0-460-00278-3); 3.50 o.p. (0-460-01278-9) Biblio Distribution.

—Sartor Resartus. E-Book 2.49 (1-58627-097-4) Electric Umbrella Publishing.

—Sartor Resartus. McSweeney, Kerry & Sabor, Peter, eds. (Oxford World's Classics Ser.). 2000. 320p. pap. 11.95 (0-19-283673-0); 1987. 314p. pap. 10.95 o.p. (0-19-281757-4) Oxford Univ. Pr., Inc.

—Sartor Resartus. 1977. reprint ed. 29.00 o.p. (0-403-07182-8) Scholarly Pr., Inc.

—Sartor Resartus: The Life & Opinions of Herr Teufelsdrockh. (Works of Thomas Carlyle: Vol. 1). 500p. reprint ed. 2001. (Illus.). pap. text 28.00 (0-7426-5310-2); 1999. lib. bdg. 88.00 (1-58201-310-1) Classic Bks.

Carlyle, Thomas, et al. Sartor Resartus: The Life & Opinions of Herr Teufelsdrockh, 3 bks. 1998. (Norman & Charlotte Strouse Edition of the Writings of Thomas Carlyle: Vol. 2). (Illus.). 774p. text 85.00 (0-520-20928-1) Univ. of California Pr.

Cartland, Barbara. Bewildered in Berlin, No. 47. 1987. mass mkt. 2.75 o.s.i (0-515-09054-9, Jove) Berkley Publishing Group.

—Bewildered in Berlin. l.t. ed. 2000. (G. K. Hall Paperback Ser.). 205p. pap. 23.95 (0-7838-9103-2, Macmillan Reference USA) Gale Group.

Cavanaugh, Jack. While Mortals Sleep. 2001. (Songs in the Night Ser.: Vol. 1). 384p. pap. 12.99 (0-7642-2307-0) Bethany Hse. Pubs.

Cerda, Carlos. To Die in Berlin. Labinger, Andrea G., tr. from SPA. 1999. (Series Discoveries Ser.).Tr. of Morir en Berlin. 176p. pap. 15.95 (1-891270-02-8) Latin American Literary Review Pr.

Charles, Elizabeth R. Luther: By Those Who Knew Him. 1983. pap. 5.95 o.p. (0-8024-0314-X) Moody Pr.

Christie, Agatha. Passenger to Frankfurt. 23.95 (0-88411-384-1) Amereon, Ltd.

—Passenger to Frankfurt. 1985. mass mkt. 3.50 o.s.i (0-671-60062-1); 1983. mass mkt. 2.95 o.s.i (0-671-47346-8) Simon & Schuster. (Pocket).

—Passenger to Frankfurt. 2003. 288p. mass mkt. 5.99 (0-312-98170-8, St. Martin's Paperbacks) St. Martin's Pr.

—Passenger to Frankfurt. 1992. 12.04 (0-606-12474-8) Turtleback Bks.

—Passenger to Frankfurt: An Extravaganza. 1987. (Agatha Christie Ser.). 14.95 o.s.i (0-396-09164-4, G. P. Putnam's Sons) Penguin Putnam Bks. for Young Readers.

Clancy, Tom & Pieczenik, Steve, creators. The Games of State. 1996. (Tom Clancy's Op Center Ser.: Vol. 3 ). 512p. mass mkt. 7.99 (0-425-15187-5) Berkley Publishing Group.

—Games of State. l.t. ed. 1997. (Op-Center Ser.: No. 3). 662p. lib. bdg. 28.95 (0-7862-0912-7) Thorndike Pr.

Clement, Catherine. Martin & Hannah: A Novel. Smith, Julia Shirek, tr. from FRE. 2001. 304p. 27.00 (1-57392-906-9) Prometheus Bks., Pubs.

Clifford, Alan N. The Fatherland Files. 1994. 288p. 22.00 (1-56881-034-2) AK Peters, Ltd.

Colbert, Larry L. Songs of Zion. 2001. 448p. 23.99 (1-887399-03-8) Colbert Hse., The.

Conroy, Robert. 1901: A Novel. 1995. 384p. 21.95 o.p. (0-89141-537-8, Presidio Pr.) Ballantine Bks.

Constantine, David, ed. German Short Stories 2. 1976. (Penguin Parallel Texts). 288p. 12.95 (0-14-004119-2) Viking Penguin.

Coppel, Alfred. Wars & Winters. 1993. 256p. 21.95 o.p. (1-55611-377-3) Fine, Donald I. Bks.

Cowell, Stephanie. Marrying Mozart: A Novel. 2004. 368p. 24.95 (0-670-03268-9, Viking) Viking Penguin.

Crayon, Geoffrey, pseud. Tales of a Traveller. Haig, Judith G., ed. 1987. (Twayne's Critical Editions Program - The Works of Washington Irving). 500p. 65.00 o.s.i (0-8057-8515-9, Macmillan Reference USA) Gale Group.

—Tales of a Traveller. 1977. (Short Story Index Reprint Ser.). reprint ed. 19.95 (0-8369-4110-1) Ayer Co. Pubs., Inc.

Crespi, Francesca, illus. A Treasure Box of Fairy Tales: Hansel & Gretel, Rapunzel, Jack & the Beanstalk, & Aladdin, 4 bks. 1984. (J). (ps-3). 8.95 o.p. (0-8037-0079-2, 0869-260, Dial Bks. for Young Readers) Penguin Putnam Bks. for Young Readers.

Currer-Briggs, Noel. Young Men at War. 1996. 240p. pap. 14.95 (0-85449-236-4) Millivres Prowler Group GBR. *Dist:* LPC Group.

Dalmas, John. The Bavarian Gate. 1997. 352p. mass mkt. 5.99 o.s.i (0-671-87764-X) Baen Bks.

Darton, Eric. Free City: A Novel. 1996. 176p. 18.00 o.p. (0-393-03980-3) Norton, W. W. & Co., Inc.

Davis, J. Madison. The Murder of Frau Schutz. 1988. 18.95 (0-8027-1055-7) Walker & Co.

Degens, T. Transport Seven-Forty One-R. l.t. ed. 1976. (Young Adult Ser.). lib. bdg. 9.95 o.p. (0-8161-6357-X, Macmillan Reference USA) Gale Group.

Deighton, Len. Berlin Game. 1997. 344p. pap. 19.00 (0-345-41834-4); 1984. 352p. mass mkt. 5.95 o.s.i (0-345-31498-0, Ballantine Bks.) Ballantine Bks.

—Charity. l.t. ed. 1997. (Large Print Book Ser.). 27.95 (1-56895-436-0, Wheeler Publishing, Inc.) Gale Group.

—Charity. 1996. 288p. 25.00 o.p. (0-06-018728-X) HarperCollins Pubs.

—Winter. 1997. pap. 14.00 o.p. (0-345-42018-7) Ballantine Bks.

—Winter. l.t. ed. 1988. (General Ser.). 816p. 21.95 o.p. (0-8161-4659-4, Macmillan Reference USA) Gale Group.

—Winter. 1989. 5.99 o.p. (0-517-69931-1) Random Hse. Value Publishing.

—Winter: A Novel of a Berlin Family. 1988. 544p. mass mkt. 6.99 o.s.i (0-345-35931-3) Ballantine Bks.

Dische, Irene. Sad Strains of a Gay Waltz: A Novel. 1997. 288p. 23.00 o.p. (0-8050-5357-3, Metropolitan Bks.) Holt, Henry & Co.

Dodd, Susan M. The Silent Woman: A Novel. 2001. 336p. 25.00 (0-688-17000-5, Morrow, William & Co.) Morrow/Avon.

Dorrie, Doris. Love, Pain & the Whole Damn Thing. 1991. pap. 9.00 o.s.i (0-679-72992-5) Random Hse., Inc.

Doyle, Peter R. Launched from the Castle. 1995. (Daring Adventure Ser.: Vol. 7). (J). (gr. 4). pap. 5.99 o.p. (1-56179-368-X) Focus on the Family Publishing.

Duve, Karen. Rain: A Novel. Bell, Anthea, tr. from GER. 2003. 221p. pap. 14.95 (1-58234-179-6) Bloomsbury Publishing.

Egleton, Clive. In the Red. 1991. 3.99 o.p. (0-517-07811-2) Random Hse. Value Publishing.

—In the Red. 1990. 17.95 o.p. (0-312-04677-4) St. Martin's Pr.

—In the Red. l.t. ed. 1991. (Ulverscroft Large Print Ser.). 624p. 29.99 o.p. (0-7089-2461-1, Ulverscroft) Thorpe, F. A. Pubs. GBR. *Dist:* Ulverscroft Large Print Bks., Ltd., Ulverscroft Large Print Canada, Ltd.

Elkins, Aaron. Fellowship of Fear. 1982. 256p. 11.95 o.s.i (0-8027-5478-3) Walker & Co.

—Fellowship of Fear. 1994. 216p. mass mkt. 5.99 o.s.i (0-446-40402-0); 1989. pap. 4.99 (0-445-20953-4) Warner Bks., Inc.

Elrod, Robert. Didrick. 2000. (Illus.). 80p. pap. 9.00 (0-8059-4854-6) Dorrance Publishing Co., Inc.

Elwood, Roger. Wolf's Lair. 1995. mass mkt. 5.99 o.p. (0-8499-3884-8); 1993. 224p. pap. 8.99 o.p. (0-8499-3386-2) W Publishing Group.

Fast, Howard. The Bridge Builder's Story. l.t. ed. 1995. o.p. (0-15-749003-3); 184p. lib. bdg. 22.95 (1-57490-033-1) Beeler, Thomas T. Publisher. (Beeler Large Print Bks.).

—The Bridge Builder's Story. 1995. 224p. (C). (gr. 13). 29.95 (1-56324-691-0) Sharpe, M.E. Inc.

Fedin, Konstantin. Cities & Years. Scammell, Michael, tr. from RUS. 1993. (European Classics Ser.). 350p. reprint ed. pap. 21.00 (0-8101-1066-0) Northwestern Univ. Pr.

—Cities & Years: A Novel. Scammell, Michael, tr. 1975. (ENG & RUS.). 415p. reprint ed. lib. bdg. 45.00 o.p. (0-8371-8029-5, FECY) Greenwood Publishing Group, Inc.

Fielding, Gabriel. The Birthday King. 1995. (Phoenix Fiction Ser.). 320p. pap. 11.95 o.s.i (0-226-24848-8) Univ. of Chicago Pr.

Fitzgerald, Penelope. The Blue Flower. l.t. ed. 1998. (Large Print Bks.). 26.95 (1-56895-670-3, Wheeler Publishing, Inc.) Gale Group.

—The Blue Flower. 1997. 240p. pap. 12.00 (0-395-85997-2) Houghton Mifflin Co.

Follett, Ken. Eye of the Needle. 2000. 384p. mass mkt. 7.99 (0-380-73335-8); 1978. 17.95 o.p. (0-87795-186-1, Morrow, William & Co.) Morrow/Avon.

—Eye of the Needle. 1981. mass mkt. 3.50 o.p. (0-451-09913-3); 1980. mass mkt. 3.50 o.p. (0-451-09550-2); 1979. mass mkt. 2.95 o.p. (0-451-08746-1); 1979. mass mkt. 3.50 o.p. (0-451-11444-2); 1979. mass mkt. 3.95 o.p. (0-451-11970-3); 1979. mass mkt. 4.50 o.p. (0-451-14141-5); 1979. (Illus.). 352p. mass mkt. 7.99 o.s.i (0-451-16348-6); 1979. (Illus.). 360p. mass mkt. 4.95 o.p. (0-451-15524-6) NAL. (Signet Bks.).

—Eye of the Needle. 2001. (Best Mysteries of All Time Ser.). 15.99 (0-7621-8861-8) Reader's Digest Assn., Inc., The.

Fontane, Theodor. Before the Storm. Hollingdale, R. J., ed. 1985. (Oxford World's Classics Ser.). (C). pap. 6.95 o.p. (0-19-281649-7) Oxford Univ. Pr., Inc.

—Delusions, Confusions & the Poggenpuhl Family. Demetz, Peter, ed. 1989. (German Library Ser.: Vol. 47). 292p. 39.50 (0-8264-0325-5); (C). pap. 19.95 (0-8264-0326-3) Continuum International Publishing Group, Inc.

—Effi Briest. Rorrison, Hugh & Chambers, Helen, trs. from GER. 1996. 246p. pap. 16.95 (0-946162-44-1) Angel Bks. GBR. *Dist:* Dufour Editions, Inc.

—Effi Briest. unabr. ed. 1999. (World Classic Literature Ser.). (GER.). pap. 6.95 (3-89507-004-1) Bookking International FRA. *Dist:* Distribooks, Inc.

—Effi Briest. (GER.). audio 69.95 o.p. Olivia & Hill Pr., The.

—Effi Briest. Cooper, W. A., tr. abr. ed. 1966. pap. 7.50 o.p. (0-8044-6156-2) Ungar, Frederick A Bk.

—Effi Briest. Parmee, Douglas, tr. 1976. (Penguin Classics Ser.). 272p. pap. 11.95 o.s.i (0-14-044190-5, Penguin Classics) Viking Penguin.

Ford, Ford Madox. The Good Soldier: A Tale of Passion. 1990. reprint ed. lib. bdg. 23.95 (0-89966-669-8) Buccaneer Bks., Inc.

—The Good Soldier: A Tale of Passion. 1998. 236p. pap. 12.95 (1-85754-300-9) Carcanet Pr., Ltd. GBR. *Dist:* Paul & Co. Pubs. Consortium, Inc.

—The Good Soldier: A Tale of Passion. 1980. 256p. reprint ed. lib. bdg. 24.50 o.p. (0-374-92773-1) Hippocrene Bks., Inc.

—The Good Soldier: A Tale of Passion. 2002. 180p. 23.99 (1-4043-0588-2); per. 19.99 (1-4043-0589-0) IndyPublish.com.

—The Good Soldier: A Tale of Passion. Schorer, Mark, tr. 1989. (Vintage International Ser.). 304p. pap. 12.00 (0-679-72218-1, Vintage) Knopf Publishing Group.

—The Good Soldier: A Tale of Passion. l.t. ed. 1995. 330p. lib. bdg. 26.00 (0-939495-88-0); 1998. 212p. reprint ed. lib. bdg. 25.00 (1-58287-031-4) North Bks.

—The Good Soldier: A Tale of Passion. Stannard, Martin, ed. 1995. (Critical Editions Ser.). 401p. (C). pap. text 9.00 (0-393-96634-8) Norton, W. W. & Co., Inc.

—The Good Soldier: A Tale of Passion. 1999. (Great Books of the 20th Century Ser.). (Illus.). 192p. pap. 13.00 (0-14-028331-5) Penguin Group (USA) Inc.

—The Good Soldier: A Tale of Passion. (Everyman's Library). 1991. 864p. 17.00 (0-679-40665-4); 1957. pap. 3.95 o.p. (0-394-70045-7) Random Hse., Inc.

—The Good Soldier: A Tale of Passion. 1992. 21.50 o.p. (0-8446-6637-8) Smith, Peter Pub., Inc.

—The Good Soldier: A Tale of Passion. 1998. lib. bdg. 21.95 (1-56723-040-7) Yestermorrow, Inc.

Ford, Robert. The Student Conductor. 2003. 304p. 24.95 (0-399-15037-4, Putnam & Grosset) Putnam Publishing Group, The.

Freemantle, Brian. Little Grey Mice. 1992. 368p. 21.95 o.p. (0-312-07625-8) St. Martin's Pr.

Frenssen, Gustow. Jornuhl. 2000. 252p. E-Book 3.95 (0-594-02225-8) 1873 Pr.

Freud, Esther. Summer at Gaglow. 1999. 256p. pap. 15.00 (0-88001-672-8); reprint ed. o.p. (0-88001-585-3) HarperTrade. (Ecco).

Furst, Peter. Don Quixote in Exile. 1996. (Jewish Lives Ser.). 210p. (C). 64.00 (0-8101-1447-X); pap. 21.00 (0-8101-1448-8) Northwestern Univ. Pr.

Gabbard, Alex. Blood of the Roses. 2002. 256p. 22.95 (0-9622608-7-8) Gabbard Pubns.

Gallizier, Nathan. The Sorceress of Rome. 2000. 252p. E-Book 3.95 (0-594-02237-1) 1873 Pr.

Galloway, Janice. Clara. 2003. (Illus.). 432p. 25.00 (0-684-84449-4, Simon & Schuster) Simon & Schuster.

Gault, Rebecca. Into the Blue. l.t. ed. 2001. (Romance Ser.). 272p. 25.95 (0-7862-2929-2, Five Star) Gale Group.

Gercke, Doris. How Many Miles to Babylon. Hamilton, Anna, tr. from GER. 1991. 100p. (Orig.). pap. 8.95 o.p. (1-879679-02-7) Women In Translation.

Gerson, Jack. Death's Head Berlin. 1988. 224p. 15.95 o.p. (0-312-02569-6, Saint Martin's Minotaur) St. Martin's Pr.

Gifford, Thomas. The First Sacrifice. l.t. ed. 1995. (Large Print Bks.). pap. 22.95 o.p. (1-56895-097-7, Wheeler Publishing, Inc.) Gale Group.

Gillespie, Donna. The Light Bearer. 1996. 1024p. mass mkt. 8.50 o.s.i (0-515-11966-0, Jove); 1994. pap. 15.00 o.p. (0-425-14368-6) Berkley Publishing Group.

Godwin-Jones, Robert, tr. from GER. Tales of Courtship by Jeremias Gotthelf. 1984. (American University Studies: Ser. I, Vol. 35). 241p. (C). text 28.00 o.p. (0-8204-0177-3) Lang, Peter Publishing, Inc.

Goebbels, Joseph. Michael. Nevgroschell, Joachim, tr. from GER. 1987. 160p. (Orig.). pap. 6.95 o.p. (0-941693-00-7) Amok Pr., Inc.

Gold, Alison Leslie. The Devil's Mistress: The Diary of Eva Braun, the Woman Who Lived & Died with Hitler. 1997. 226p. 24.95 (0-571-19923-2) Faber & Faber, Inc.

Gom, Leona. After-Image: A Vicky Bauer Mystery. 310p. pap. 14.95 (0-929005-91-0) Second Story Pr. CAN. *Dist:* Orca Bk. Pubs.

—After-Image: A Vicky Bauer Mystery. 1996. 256p. 22.95 o.p. (0-312-14537-3, Saint Martin's Minotaur) St. Martin's Pr.

—Double Negative: A Vicky Bauer Mystery. 1998. 476p. pap. 12.95 (1-896764-07-X) Second Story Pr. CAN. *Dist:* LPC/InBook.

Grab, Hermann. The Town Park & Other Stories. Hoare, Quintin, tr. 1988. 256p. 18.95 o.p. (0-86091-189-6) Verso.

Gramm, Kent. Clare. 1991. (Northcote Bks.). 432p. (Orig.). pap. 11.99 o.p. (0-87788-124-3, Shaw) WaterBrook Pr.

Grant, Reg. The Storm. 2001. (Illus.). 416p. pap. 10.95 (1-57856-189-2) WaterBrook Pr.

Grass, Gunter. Cat & Mouse.Tr. of Katz & Maus. 17.95 (0-8488-0112-1) Amereon, Ltd.

—Cat & Mouse. Manheim, Ralph, tr. from GER. Tr. of Katz & Maus. 1991. 192p. pap. 13.00 (0-15-615551-6, Harvest Bks.); 1963. 189p. 10.95 o.p. (0-15-116100-3) Harcourt Trade Pubs.

—Crabwalk. Winston, Krishna, tr. from GER. 2003. 240p. 25.00 (0-15-100764-0) Harcourt Trade Pubs.

—The Danzig Trilogy.Tr. of Danziger Trilogie. 1999. 16.98 (1-56731-374-4); 1996. 1030p. reprint ed. 16.98 o.p. (1-56731-098-2) Fine Communications. (MJF Bks.).

—The Danzig Trilogy. Manheim, Ralph, tr. from GER. 1987. Tr. of Danziger Trilogie. 290p. 35.00 (0-15-123816-2) Harcourt Trade Pubs.

—Dog Years. Manheim, Ralph, tr. from GER. 1965. Tr. of Hundejahre. 570p. 6.95 o.p. (0-15-126222-5) Harcourt Trade Pubs.

—The Tin Drum. 1999. Tr. of Blechtrommel. 592p. 20.00 (0-375-42057-6, Pantheon) Knopf Publishing Group.

—The Tin Drum. Manheim, Ralph, tr. from GER. 1990. (Vintage International Ser.).Tr. of Blechtrommel. 592p. pap. 15.95 (0-679-72575-X, Vintage) Knopf Publishing Group.

—The Tin Drum. 1964. Tr. of Blechtrommel. pap. 5.95 o.p. (0-394-70300-6, Vintage) Knopf Publishing Group.

—The Tin Drum. Manheim, Ralph, tr. from GER. 1993. (Everyman's Library).Tr. of Blechtrommel. xxxvii, 551p. 20.00 (0-679-42033-9) Knopf, Alfred A. Inc.

—The Tin Drum. 1963. Tr. of Blechtrommel. 10.95 o.s.i (0-394-44902-9) Random Hse., Inc.

Greeley, Andrew M. The Bishop & the Three Kings: A Blackie Ryan Mystery. 1998. (Blackie Ryan Novels Ser.). (Illus.). 320p. mass mkt. 6.99 (0-425-16617-1) Berkley Publishing Group.

—A Midwinter's Tale. 1999. 448p. mass mkt. 6.99 (0-8125-9025-2); No. 1. 1998. (Midwinter's Tale Ser.: Vol. 1). 383p. 24.95 (0-312-86571-6) Doherty, Tom Assocs., LLC. (Forge Bks.).

—A Midwinter's Tale. l.t. ed. 2000. 542p. 26.95 (1-56895-949-4, Wheeler Publishing, Inc.) Gale Group.

Grzimek, Martin. Heartstop. Mitchell, Breon, tr. from GER. 1984. Orig. Title: Stillstand des Herzens. 192p. 17.95 (0-8112-0921-0); pap. 8.95 (0-8112-0922-9, NDP583) New Directions Publishing Corp.

Hacker, Katherina. The Lifeguard. Atkins, Helen, tr. 2002. 216p. 24.95 (1-902881-45-1) Toby Pr.

Hagberg, David. Desert Fire. 1993. 384p. 13.99 o.p. (0-312-85496-X, Tor Bks.) Doherty, Tom Assocs., LLC.

—Desert Fire. 4.98 o.s.i (0-8317-5537-7) Smithmark Pubs., Inc.

Halpert, Sam. A Real Good War. 1999. 288p. pap. 12.95 (0-385-49618-4) Doubleday Publishing.

—A Real Good War. Kennedy, Byron, ed. 1997. (Illus.). 330p. (C). 19.95 (0-941072-30-4) Southern Heritage Pr., Inc.

Hansen, Ron. Hitler's Niece: A Novel. 1999. 320p. 25.00 (0-06-019419-7) HarperCollins Pubs.

—Hitler's Niece: A Novel. 2000. 320p. pap. 14.00 (0-06-093220-1, Perennial) HarperTrade.

—Hitler's Niece: A Novel. l.t. ed. 2000. (Basic Ser.). 539p. 28.95 (0-7862-2305-7) Thorndike Pr.

Harrington, William. Endgame in Berlin. 1991. 320p. 19.95 o.p. (1-55611-313-7) Fine, Donald I. Bks.

Harris, Robert. Fatherland. unabr. ed. 2000. audio 59.95 (0-7451-4115-3, CAB 798) Chivers Audio Bks. GBR. *Dist:* BBC Audiobooks America.

Settings

—Fatherland. 400p. 1994. mass mkt. 6.50 o.p. (*0-06-100881-8*); 1993. mass mkt. 7.99 (*0-06-100662-9*) Morrow/Avon. (HarperTorch).

—Fatherland. abr. ed. 2002. audio 9.99 (*0-553-70229-7*); 1993. audio 8.99 o.s.i (*0-679-42955-7*); 1992. audio 16.00 o.p. (*0-679-41413-4*) Random Hse. Audio Publishing Group. (RH Audio).

Harrison, Carey. Richard's Feet. 1990. 672p. 22.95 o.p. (*0-8050-1404-7*) Holt, Henry & Co.

Harrison, Dorothy L. Operation Morningstar. 1997. (Chronicles of Courage Ser.). 128p. (J). (gr. 3-7). pap. 4.99 o.p. (*0-7814-0242-5*) Cook Communications Ministries.

Hegi, Ursula. Floating in My Mother's Palm. 1991. 192p. pap. 11.00 o.s.i (*0-679-73115-6*) Random Hse., Inc.

—Floating in My Mother's Palm. 1998. 192p. pap. 11.00 (*0-684-85475-9*, Touchstone) Simon & Schuster.

—Stones from the River. (Reading Group Guides Ser.). 1997. pap. (*0-684-00597-2*, Touchstone); 1997. 528p. pap. 14.00 (*0-684-84477-X*, Touchstone); 1995. 528p. pap. 12.00 (*0-684-80035-7*, Scribner); 1994. 507p. 25.50 o.s.i (*0-671-78075-1*, Simon & Schuster); 1997. 26.00 (*0-684-84472-9*, Simon & Schuster) Simon & Schuster.

—Stones from the River. 1994. 20.05 (*0-606-19627-7*) Turtleback Bks.

—Unearned Pleasures & Other Stories. 1988. 130p. (C). 14.95 o.p. (*0-89301-125-8*) Univ. of Idaho Pr.

—The Vision of Emma Blau. 2000. 432p. 25.00 (*0-7432-0012-8*); (Illus.). 25.00 (*0-684-82997-5*) Simon & Schuster. (Simon & Schuster).

—The Vision of Emma Blau. abr. ed. 2000. audio compact disk 32.00 (*0-684-87407-5*, Simon & Schuster Audioworks) Simon & Schuster Audio.

Hein, Christoph. The Tango Player. Boehm, Philip, tr. from GER. 1992. 224p. 20.00 o.p. (*0-374-27252-2*) Farrar, Straus & Giroux.

—The Tango Player. Boehm, Philip, tr. from GER. 1994. (Writings from an Unbound Europe). 224p. (C). reprint ed. pap. 17.00 (*0-8101-1116-0*) Northwestern Univ. Pr.

Hensher, Philip. Pleasured. 1998. 373p. o.p. (*0-7011-6728-9*) Random Hse. of Canada, Ltd. CAN. *Dist:* Random Hse., Inc.

Hermann, Judith. Summerhouse, Later: Stories. 224p. 2003. pap. 13.95 (*0-06-000687-0*); 2002. 22.95 (*0-06-000686-2*) HarperTrade. (Ecco).

Hershman, Marcie. Tales of the Master Race: A Novel. 1992. 240p. pap. 14.00 (*0-06-092353-9*, Perennial); 1991. 224p. 20.00 o.p. (*0-06-016644-4*) HarperTrade.

Hettche, Thomas. The Arbogast Case. 2003. E-Book (*0-374-70313-2*); E-Book (*0-374-70314-0*); E-Book (*0-374-70315-9*); E-Book (*0-374-70316-7*) Farrar, Straus & Giroux.

—Der Fall Arbogast. 2003. 336p. 25.00 (*0-374-13812-5*) Farrar, Straus & Giroux.

Heym, Georg. The Thief: And Other Stories. Bennett, Susan, tr. 1994. 112p. 29.95 (*1-870352-68-8*); pap. 9.95 (*1-870352-48-3*) Libris, Ltd. GBR. *Dist:* Independent Pubs. Group, Paul & Co. Pubs. Consortium, Inc.

Heym, Stefan. Queen Against Defoe & Other Stories. 1974. (Illus.). 128p. 6.95 o.p. (*0-88208-041-5*, Hill, Lawrence Bks.) Chicago Review Pr., Inc.

Higgins, Jack. The Eagle Has Flown. l.t. ed. 1992. (General Ser.). 373p. lib. bdg. 22.95 (*0-8161-5363-9*, Macmillan Reference USA) Gale Group.

—The Eagle Has Flown. 2002. 336p. mass mkt. 7.99 (*0-7434-5650-5*, Pocket); 1991. 336p. mass mkt. 7.99 (*0-671-74669-3*, Pocket); 1991. 352p. 21.95 o.p. (*0-671-72458-4*, Simon & Schuster) Simon & Schuster.

—The Eagle Has Flown. abr. ed. 1991. audio 15.95 (*0-671-72465-7*, 296620, Simon & Schuster Audioworks) Simon & Schuster Audio.

—The Eagle Has Flown. l.t. ed. 1992. (G. K. Hall Large Print Book Ser.). 373p. pap. 19.95 (*0-8161-5364-7*) Thorndike Pr.

—The Eagle Has Landed. 1946. pap. text o.p. (*0-17-556767-0*) Addison-Wesley Longman, Inc.

—The Eagle Has Landed. 1982. 368p. mass mkt. 3.95 o.s.i (*0-553-23345-9*); mass mkt. 4.50 o.s.i (*0-553-27042-7*) Bantam Bks.

—The Eagle Has Landed. 2000. 368p. mass mkt. 7.99 (*0-425-17718-1*) Berkley Publishing Group.

—The Eagle Has Landed. 1995. reprint ed. lib. bdg. 26.95 (*1-56849-593-5*) Buccaneer Bks., Inc.

—The Eagle Has Landed. abr. ed. audio 15.95 o.p. (*0-88646-027-1*, 7040) Durkin Hayes Publishing Ltd.

—The Eagle Has Landed. l.t. ed. 1992. 17.95 o.p. (*0-8161-5474-0*); 1975. reprint ed. lib. bdg. 14.95 o.p. (*0-8161-6330-8*) Gale Group. (Macmillan Reference USA).

—The Eagle Has Landed. 1975. o.p. (*0-03-013746-2*) Holt, Henry & Co.

—The Eagle Has Landed. abr. ed. 1996. 24.95 o.p. (*0-7871-0960-6*); 39.95 o.p. (*0-7871-0959-2*, 103449) NewStar Media, Inc.

—The Eagle Has Landed. 1993. audio 15.99 o.s.i (*0-553-47143-0*, RH Audio) Random Hse. Audio Publishing Group.

—The Eagle Has Landed. 1997. 400p. pap. 19.95 o.p. (*0-671-01934-1*); 1989. bds. 4.95 (*0-671-66529-4*) Simon & Schuster. (Pocket).

—The Eagle Has Landed. Rubenstein, Julie, ed. 1990. 336p. reprint ed. mass mkt. 7.99 (*0-671-72773-7*, Pocket) Simon & Schuster.

—The Eagle Has Landed. rev. ed. 1991. 368p. 21.95 o.p. (*0-671-73310-9*, Simon & Schuster) Simon & Schuster.

—The Eagle Has Landed. l.t. ed. 1983. 528p. 12.50 o.p. (*0-7089-0973-6*, Ulverscroft) Thorpe, F. A. Pubs. GBR. *Dist:* Ulverscroft Large Print Bks., Ltd.

—The Valhalla Exchange. 1981. mass mkt. 2.95 o.s.i (*0-449-23449-5*, Fawcett) Ballantine Bks.

—The Valhalla Exchange. 1977. lib. bdg. 12.50 o.p. (*0-8161-6496-7*, Macmillan Reference USA) Gale Group.

—The Valhalla Exchange. 1977. 8.95 o.s.i (*0-8128-1932-2*, Scarborough Hse.) Madison Bks., Inc.

Highsmith, Patricia. The Boy Who Followed Ripley. 1993. (Mr. Ripley Ser.). 304p. pap. 12.00 (*0-679-74567-X*, Vintage) Knopf Publishing Group.

—The Boy Who Followed Ripley. 1985. (Mr. Ripley Ser.). 336p. pap. 3.95 o.p. (*0-14-005739-0*, Penguin Bks.) Viking Penguin.

Hitchcock, Raymond. The Canaris Legacy. 1980. 196p. 10.95 o.p. (*0-312-11817-1*) St. Martin's Pr.

Hoffmann, Yoel. Katschen & The Book of Joseph. Kriss, David et al, trs. from HEB. 1998. 160p. 17.95 (*0-8112-1373-0*); 1999. 161p. reprint ed. pap. 11.95 (*0-8112-1405-2*, NDP875) New Directions Publishing Corp.

Hofmann, Gert. The Film Explainer: A Novel. Hofmann, Michael, tr. from GER. 1996. 256p. 33.00 (*0-8101-1293-0*, Hydra Bks.) Northwestern Univ. Pr.

—Luck. Hoffman, Michael, tr. from GER. 2002. 256p. 23.95 (*0-8112-1502-4*) New Directions Publishing Corp.

Hughes, Richard Arthur Warren. The Fox in the Attic. 1962. o.p. (*0-06-011985-3*) HarperCollins Pubs.

—The Fox in the Attic. 2000. (New York Review Books Classics Ser.). 326p. reprint ed. pap. 12.95 (*0-940322-29-3*) New York Review of Bks., Inc., The.

—The Wooden Shepherdess. 1973. 389 p. (*0-7011-1946-2*) Chatto & Windus GBR. *Dist:* Trafalgar Square.

—The Wooden Shepherdess. 2000. (New York Review Books Classics Ser.). 419p. pap. 14.95 (*0-940322-30-7*) New York Review of Bks., Inc., The.

Iles, Greg. Black Cross. l.t. ed. 1995. 528p. 19.95 o.p. (*0-525-93829-X*, Dutton) Dutton/Plume.

—Black Cross. l.t. ed. 1995. pap. 23.95 (*1-56895-225-2*, Wheeler Publishing, Inc.) Gale Group.

—Black Cross. 1995. 576p. mass mkt. 7.99 (*0-451-18519-6*); pap. 5.99 (*0-451-18746-6*) NAL. (Signet Bks.).

—Black Cross. abr. ed. 1995. pap. 23.95 o.p. incl. audio (*0-453-00935-2*, 692155) Penguin/HighBridge.

Irving, Washington. Bracebridge Hall. Smith, Herbert F., ed. 1977. (Critical Editions Program Ser.). lib. bdg. 26.00 o.p. (*0-8057-8506-X*, Macmillan Reference USA) Gale Group.

—Bracebridge Hall. reprint ed. 24.00 o.p. (*0-404-03508-6*) AMS Pr., Inc.

—Bracebridge Hall. (Illus.). 320p. reprint ed. 12.00 o.p. (*0-912882-35-2*) Sleepy Hollow Pr.

—Bracebridge Hall, Or the Humorists. 1992. (BCL1-PS American Literature Ser.). 561p. reprint ed. lib. bdg. 99.00 (*0-7812-6753-6*) Reprint Services Corp.

—Bracebridge Hall, Or the Humorists. 1902. reprint ed. 10.00 (*0-403-00239-7*) Scholarly Pr., Inc.

—Bracebridge Hall, Tales of a Traveller & the Alhambra. Myers, Andrew B., ed. 1991. (Library of America: Vol. 52). 1104p. 35.00 (*0-940450-59-3*) Library of America, The.

—Hearthside Tales: Selections from the Sketch Book, Bracebridge Hall & Tales of a Traveller. Gado, Frank, ed. 1995. (Signature Ser.). 280p. (C). pap. 8.95 (*0-912756-10-1*) Union College Pr.

—Hearthside Tales: Selections from the Sketch Book, Bracebridge Hall & Tales of a Traveller. 1983. (Signature Ser.). 215p. (C). 19.75 o.p. (*0-912756-13-6*) Union College Pr.

Isherwood, Christopher. The Berlin of Sally Bowles. 1975. 583 p. (*0-7012-0407-9*) Hogarth Pr., The.

—The Berlin Stories. 1963. pap. 11.95 (*0-8112-0070-1*, NDP134) New Directions Publishing Corp.

—Mr. Norris Changes Trains. l.t. ed. 1985. (Mainstream Ser.). 271p. 14.95 o.p. (*1-85089-018-8*) ISIS Large Print Bks. GBR. *Dist:* Transaction Pubs.

Isherwood, Christopher, intro. The Berlin Stories. 1979. reprint ed. lib. bdg. 18.00 (*0-8376-0449-4*) Bentley Pubs.

Jackson, Felix. Secrets of the Blood. 1980. 10.95 o.p. (*0-689-11076-6*, Scribner) Simon & Schuster.

Jerome, Jerome K. Three Men in a Boat & Three Men on the Bummel. Harvey, Geoffrey, ed. & intro. by. 1998. (Oxford World's Classics Ser.). (Illus.). 368p. pap. 9.95 (*0-19-288033-0*) Oxford Univ. Pr., Inc.

—Three Men in a Boat & Three Men on the Bummel. 2000. (Classics Ser.). 400p. 9.95 (*0-14-043750-9*, Penguin Classics) Viking Penguin.

—Three Men on the Bummel. 1991. (Jerome K. Jerome Ser.). (Illus.). 240p. pap. 8.00 o.p. (*0-86299-029-7*) Sutton Publishing, Ltd. GBR. *Dist:* International Publishers Marketing.

Junger, Ernst. The Glass Bees. Bogan, Louise & Mayer, Elizabeth, trs. from GER. 1991. 160p. pap. 9.95 o.p. (*0-374-52173-5*) Farrar, Straus & Giroux.

Just, Ward. The American Ambassador. 1987. 320p. 17.95 o.p. (*0-395-42694-4*) Houghton Mifflin Co.

Kafka, Franz. The Trial. Date not set. lib. bdg. 24.95 (*0-8488-1392-8*) Amereon, Ltd.

—The Trial. 1983. 179p. reprint ed. lib. bdg. 25.95 (*0-89966-453-9*) Buccaneer Bks., Inc.

—The Trial. Mitchell, Breon, tr. from ENG. & pref. by. 1998. 304p. 24.00 o.s.i (*0-8052-4165-5*, Schocken) Knopf Publishing Group.

—The Trial. Muir, Willa et al, trs. 1995. (Illus.). 312p. pap. 13.50 (*0-8052-1040-7*, Schocken) Knopf Publishing Group.

—The Trial. 1987. (Illus.). 288p. pap. 6.95 o.p. (*0-8052-0416-4*, Schocken) Knopf Publishing Group.

—The Trial. 1992. 336p. 17.00 (*0-679-40994-7*); 1937. 16.95 o.p. (*0-394-44955-X*) Knopf, Alfred A. Inc.

Kaminsky, Stuart M. & Thomas, Ross. The Cold War Swap. 2003. 208p. pap. 13.95 (*0-312-31581-3*, Saint Martin's Griffin) St. Martin's Pr.

Kaschnitz, Marie L. Long Shadows: Stories. Whissen, Anni, tr. & intro. by. 1995. (GERM Ser.). 168p. 45.00 (*1-57113-021-7*) Camden Hse.

Katzenbach, John. Hart's War. 2002. E-Book 7.99 (*1-59061-829-7*) Adobe Systems, Inc.

—Hart's War. movie tie-in ed. 2000. 576p. mass mkt. 7.99 (*0-345-42625-8*, Ballantine Bks.) Ballantine Bks.

Kaye, M. M. Death in Berlin. unabr. ed. 2000. audio 49.95 (*0-7451-6080-8*, CAB 237) Chivers Audio Bks. GBR. *Dist:* BBC Audiobooks America.

—Death in Berlin. 2000. 272p. pap. 12.95 (*0-312-26308-2*, Saint Martin's Griffin); 1986. 320p. mass mkt. 3.95 (*0-312-90103-8*, St. Martin's Paperbacks); 1985. 288p. 14.95 o.p. (*0-312-18621-5*) St. Martin's Pr.

Keller, Gottfried. People of Seldwyla & Seven Legends. Hottinger, M. D., tr. 1977. (Short Story Index Reprint Ser.). 30.95 (*0-8369-3723-6*) Ayer Co. Pubs., Inc.

—Seldwyla Folks: Three Singular Tales by the Swiss Poet. Von Schierbrand, Wolf, tr. from GER. 1977. (Short Story Index Reprint Ser.). reprint ed. 19.95 (*0-8369-3842-9*) Ayer Co. Pubs., Inc.

Kelly, Mary A. Keeper of the Mill. 1995. 320p. 21.95 o.p. (*0-312-13530-0*, Saint Martin's Minotaur) St. Martin's Pr.

Kempowski, Walter. Dog Days. Davis, Norma et al, trs. from GER. 1991. (GERM Ser.: Vol. 53). (Illus.). 338p. 35.00 (*0-938100-78-5*) Camden Hse.

Kennedy, Raymond. The Bitterest Age. 1994. 224p. tchr. ed. 22.95 o.p. (*0-395-68629-6*) Houghton Mifflin Co.

Kerr, Philip. Berlin Noir: March Violets - The Pale Criminal - A German Requiem. 1994. (Penguin Crime/Mystery Ser.). 848p. 15.95 (*0-14-023170-6*) Viking Penguin.

—A German Requiem. 1993. (Crime Ser.). 320p. pap. 4.95 o.p. (*0-14-017561-X*, Penguin Bks.) Penguin Group (USA) Inc.

—A German Requiem. 1991. 320p. 19.95 o.p. (*0-670-83516-1*, Viking) Viking Penguin.

—March Violets. (Crime Ser.). 256p. 1990. pap. 4.95 o.p. (*0-14-011466-1*, Penguin Bks.); 1989. 17.95 o.p. (*0-670-82431-3*) Viking Penguin.

—The Pale Criminal. 1991. (Crime Monthly Ser.). 288p. reprint ed. pap. 4.95 o.p. (*0-14-015393-4*, Penguin Bks.) Penguin Group (USA) Inc.

—The Pale Criminal. 1990. 288p. 18.95 o.p. (*0-670-82433-X*) Viking Penguin.

Keun, Irmgard. The Artificial Silk Girl. van Ankum, Kathie, tr. from GER. 2002. 216p. 22.00 (*1-892746-81-6*) Other Pr., LLC.

Kirk, Susan Van. CliffsNotes TM All Quiet on the Western Front. 1999. E-Book 5.99 (*0-8220-7005-7*, Cliff Notes) Wiley, John & Sons, Inc.

Kirkwood, Thomas. The Quiet Assassin. 1985. 288p. 16.95 o.p. (*0-917657-14-4*) Fine, Donald I. Bks.

Kirsch, Sarah. The Panther Woman: Five Tales from the Cassette Recorder. Faber, Marion, tr. & intro. by. 1989. (European Women Writers Ser.). 128p. reprint ed. pap. 39.70 (*0-608-01858-9*, 206250800003) Bks. on Demand.

—The Panther Woman: Five Tales from the Cassette Recorder. Faber, Marion, tr. from GER. & intro. by. 1989. (European Women Writers Ser.). xviii, 109p. text 20.00 o.p. (*0-8032-2722-1*); pap. 9.95 o.p. (*0-8032-7768-7*, Bison Bks.) Univ. of Nebraska Pr.

Kirshenbaum, Binnie. Hester among the Ruins: A Novel. 2003. 304p. pap. 14.00 (*0-15-602750-X*, Harvest Bks.) Harcourt Trade Pubs.

—Hester among the Ruins: A Novel. 2002. 288p. 24.95 (*0-393-04152-2*) Norton, W. W. & Co., Inc.

Klein, Olaf G. Aftertime. Dembo, Margot B., tr. from GER. 1999. 124p. 28.00 (*0-8101-1504-2*, Hydra Bks.) Northwestern Univ. Pr.

Kluge, Alexander. Case Histories. Vennewitz, Leila, tr. from GER. (Modern German Voices Ser.). 200p. 1991. pap. 10.95 (*0-8419-1045-6*); 1988. 19.95 (*0-8419-1044-8*) Holmes & Meier Pubs., Inc.

Knauss, Sibylle. Eva's Cousin. 2003. 352p. pap. 13.95 (*0-345-44906-1*, Ballantine Bks.) Ballantine Bks.

—Eva's Cousin: A Novel. Bell, Anthea, tr. from GER. 2002. 336p. 24.95 (*0-345-44905-3*, Ballantine Bks.) Ballantine Bks.

—Eva's Cousin: A Novel. Bell, Anthea, tr. 2002. (Women's Fiction Ser.). 28.95 (*0-7862-4902-1*) Thorndike Pr.

Koch, Eric. Earrings. 2002. (Illus.). 200p. pap. 15.00 (*0-88962-775-4*) Mosaic Pr.

—The Man Who Knew Charlie Chaplin: A Novel about the Weimar Republic. 2000. (Illus.). xxiv, 150p. pap. 15.00 (*0-88962-718-5*); pap. 15.00 (*0-88962-719-3*) Mosaic Pr.

Koeppen, Wolfgang. The Hothouse. Hofmann, Michael, tr. from GER. & intro. by. 2001. 224p. 23.95 (*0-393-04902-7*) Norton, W. W. & Co., Inc.

—The Hothouse: A Novel. Hofmann, Michael, tr. 2002. 224p. pap. 13.95 (*0-393-32326-9*) Norton, W. W. & Co., Inc.

Kolmar, Gertrud. A Jewish Mother from Berlin & Susanna. Goldstein, Brigitte, tr. from GER. 1997. (Modern German Voices Ser.).Tr. of Judische Mutter, Susanna. 225p. 24.00 (*0-8419-1345-5*) Holmes & Meier Pubs., Inc.

Krell, David Farrell. Nietzsche: A Novel. 1996. (SUNY Series in Contemporary Continental Philosophy). 364p. (C). text 20.50 (*0-7914-2999-7*); pap. text 19.95 (*0-7914-3000-6*) State Univ. of New York Pr.

La Plante, Lynda. Entwined. 1993. 22.00 o.p. (*0-688-09243-8*, Morrow, William & Co.) Morrow/Avon.

Lachman, Barbara. Hildegard, the Last Year. 1998. pap. 13.00 (*1-57062-393-7*); 1997. 160p. 20.00 o.s.i (*1-57062-315-5*) Shambhala Pubns., Inc.

Landis, J. D. Longing: A Novel. 2000. 464p. 26.00 o.s.i (*0-15-100453-6*) Harcourt Trade Pubs.

Lange, Bruno W. Born into Turmoil. 2001. 260p. 26.95 (*0-7596-4254-0*) 1stBooks Library.

Lawrence, D. H. D.H. Lawrence: Mr. Noon. Vasey, Lindeth, ed. 1984. (Cambridge Edition of the Works of D. H. Lawrence). (Illus.). 416p. 49.95 o.p. (*0-521-25251-2*) Cambridge Univ. Pr.

—Mr. Noon. Vasey, Lindeth, ed. 1987. (Cambridge Edition of the Works of D. H. Lawrence). (Illus.). 416p. pap. 40.00 (*0-521-27247-5*) Cambridge Univ. Pr.

—Mr. Noon. Vasey, Lindeth, ed. (Penguin Twentieth-Century Classics Ser.). (Illus.). 1997. 368p. pap. 21.00 (*0-14-018973-4*); 1985. 384p. 22.50 o.p. (*0-670-80818-0*) Viking Penguin.

Le Carré, John. The Looking Glass War. (George Smiley Ser.). 1997. pap. 12.00 o.s.i (*0-345-41829-8*); 1992. 272p. mass mkt. 6.99 o.s.i (*0-345-37736-2*) Ballantine Bks.

—A Small Town in Germany. 2002. 352p. reprint ed. pap. 14.00 (*0-7434-3171-5*, Scribner) Simon & Schuster.

Lebert, Benjamin. Crazy: A Novel. Janeway, Carol Brown, tr. from GER. 2000. 192p. 17.95 o.s.i (*0-375-40913-0*) Knopf, Alfred A. Inc.

Leffland, Ella. The Knight, Death & the Devil. 1990. 864p. 22.95 o.p. (*0-688-05836-1*, Morrow, William & Co.) Morrow/Avon.

—The Knight, Death & the Devil. 1991. 72p. pap. 10.95 o.p. (*0-14-014537-0*) Penguin Group (USA) Inc.

Lindquist, Donald. Berlin Tunnel, Twenty-One. 1978. pap. 2.95 o.p. (*0-380-01843-8*, 78394-0, Avon Bks.) Morrow/Avon.

Ludlum, Robert. The Scarlatti Inheritance. 1982. 368p. mass mkt. 7.99 (*0-553-27146-6*) Bantam Bks.

Ludwig, Charles. Queen of the Reformation. 1986. 224p. pap. 7.99 o.p. (*0-87123-652-4*) Bethany Hse. Pubs.

Lustiger, Gila. The Inventory. Morrison, Rebecca, tr. from GER. 2001. 294p. 24.95 (*1-55970-549-3*) Arcade Publishing, Inc.

Mackie, Mary. A Season for Singing. l.t. ed. 1993. 19.95 o.p. (*0-7927-1550-0*); pap. 17.95 o.p. (*0-7927-1524-1*) BBC Audiobooks America.

MacLeod, Robert. A Witchdance in Bavaria. l.t. ed. 1977. (Ulverscroft Large Print Ser.). 29.99 o.p. (*0-7089-0010-0*, Ulverscroft) Thorpe, F. A. Pubs. GBR. *Dist:* Ulverscroft Large Print Bks., Ltd., Ulverscroft Large Print Canada, Ltd.

Mann, Thomas. The Black Swan. 1954. 11.50 o.s.i (*0-394-41708-9*) Knopf, Alfred A. Inc.

—The Black Swan. Trask, Willard R., tr. 1990. 155p. pap. 15.95 (*0-520-07009-7*); text 30.00 (*0-520-07008-9*) Univ. of California Pr.

—Buddenbrooks: The Decline of a Family. Woods, John E., tr. (Everyman's Library). 1994. 784p. 20.00 (*0-679-41737-0*); 1993. 648p. 35.00 o.s.i (*0-679-41994-2*) Knopf, Alfred A. Inc.

—Buddenbrooks: The Decline of a Family. Woods, John E., tr. 1994. 736p. pap. 17.00 (*0-679-75260-9*) Random Hse., Inc.

—Doctor Faustus: The Life of the German Composer, Adrian Leverkuhn, As Told by a Friend. 1992. 20.00 (*0-679-41328-6*, Everyman's Library) Knopf Publishing Group.

—Doctor Faustus: The Life of the German Composer, Adrian Leverkuhn, As Told by a Friend. Lowe-Porter, H. T., tr. 1992. 510p. pap. 15.00 o.p. (*0-679-73905-X*, Vintage) Knopf Publishing Group.

—Doctor Faustus: The Life of the German Composer, Adrian Leverkuhn, As Told by a Friend. 1971. pap. 11.00 o.p. (*0-394-71297-8*, Vintage) Knopf Publishing Group.

—Doctor Faustus: The Life of the German Composer, Adrian Leverkuhn, As Told by a Friend. Woods, John E., tr. 1997. 496p. 35.00 o.s.i (*0-375-40054-0*) Knopf, Alfred A. Inc.

—Doctor Faustus: The Life of the German Composer, Adrian Leverkuhn, As Told by a Friend. Lowe-Porter, H. T., tr. 1992. 580p. 20.00 (*0-679-40996-3*) Knopf, Alfred A. Inc.

—Doctor Faustus: The Life of the German Composer, Adrian Leverkuhn, As Told by a Friend. 1948. 15.00 o.s.i (*0-394-42224-4*, Knopf Bks. for Young Readers) Random Hse. Children's Bks.

—Doctor Faustus: The Life of the German Composer, Adrian Leverkuhn, As Told by a Friend. Lowe-Porter, Helen T., tr. from GER. 1992. 980p. 18.50 o.s.i (*0-679-60042-6*) Random Hse., Inc.

—Doctor Faustus: The Life of the German Composer, Adrian Leverkuhn, As Told by a Friend. 1966. 3.95 o.s.i (*0-394-60365-6*, M365) Random Hse., Inc.

—The Magic Mountain. 1976. 33.95 (*0-8488-0576-3*) Amereon, Ltd.

—The Magic Mountain. 1983. 340p. reprint ed. lib. bdg. 28.95 (*0-89966-454-7*) Buccaneer Bks., Inc.

—The Magic Mountain. 1966. 35.00 o.s.i (*0-394-43458-7*) Knopf, Alfred A. Inc.

—The Magic Mountain. Woods, John E., tr. 1995. 720p. reprint ed. 50.00 (*0-679-44183-2*) Knopf, Alfred A. Inc.

—The Magic Mountain. Lowe-Porter, Helen T., tr. 1967. (C). pap. text 6.50 net. o.p. (*0-07-553665-X*, 30993) McGraw-Hill Cos., The.

—The Magic Mountain. 1996. 720p. pap. 17.00 (*0-679-77287-1*) McKay, David Co., Inc.

—The Magic Mountain. Lowe-Porter, Helen T., tr. from GER. 1992. 784p. 19.00 o.s.i (*0-679-60041-8*) Random Hse., Inc.

—The Magic Mountain. 1969. 740p. pap. 10.95 o.p. (*0-394-70497-5*) Random Hse., Inc.

Mann, Thomas & Woods, John E. Doctor Faustus: The Life of the German Composer, Adrian Leverkuhn, As Told by a Friend. 1999. (Vintage International Ser.). 544p. pap. 16.00 (*0-375-70116-8*, Vintage) Knopf Publishing Group.

Mansfield, Katherine. In a German Pension. 1991. 128p. mass mkt. 3.50 o.s.i (*0-553-21398-9*, Bantam Classics) Bantam Bks.

—In a German Pension. unabr. ed. 1995. (Thrift Editions Ser.). 112p. reprint ed. pap. text 1.50 (*0-486-28719-X*) Dover Pubns., Inc.

—In a German Pension. 2003. pap. 12.00 (*1-84391-041-1*) Hesperus Pr. GBR. *Dist:* Trafalgar Square.

—In a German Pension. 2002. 112p. 22.99 (*1-4043-0982-9*); per. 17.99 (*1-4043-0983-7*) IndyPublish-.com.

—In a German Pension. 128p. pap. 13.95 (*0-14-018875-4*) Penguin Bks., Ltd. GBR. *Dist:* Trafalgar Square.

—In a German Pension. (Ebook Classic Ser.). E-Book 5.00 (*0-7410-0415-1*) SoftBook Pr.

—In a German Pension. 1990. (Penguin Twentieth-Century Classics Ser.). 128p. pap. 10.95 o.p. (*0-14-018149-0*, Penguin Classics) Viking Penguin.

Marcum, Robert. The Return: A Novel. 2002. 437p. 22.95 (*1-59156-067-5*) Covenant Communications.

Marks, John. The Wall. 1999. 448p. reprint ed. 14.00 (*1-57322-757-9*, Riverhead Trade (Paperbacks)) Berkley Publishing Group.

—The Wall. unabr. ed. 2000. audio 79.95 (*0-7927-2277-9*, CSL 166) Chivers Audio Bks. GBR. *Dist:* BBC Audiobooks America.

—The Wall. 1998. 384p. 24.95 o.p. (*1-57322-122-8*, Riverhead Bks. (Hardcovers)) Putnam Publishing Group, The.

Maron, Monika. Animal Triste. Goldstein, Brigitte M., tr. from GER. 2000. (European Women Writers Ser.). 135p. pap. 15.00 (*0-8032-8255-9*, Bison Bks.); text 45.00 (*0-8032-3206-3*) Univ. of Nebraska Pr.

Mason, Anita. Perfection. 2003. (*1-883523-63-X*); pap. 14.00 (*1-883523-54-0*) Spinsters Ink Bks.

—Reich Angel. (Hera Ser.). 373p. 1997. pap. 13.00 o.p. (*1-56947-071-5*); 1995. 24.00 o.p. (*1-56947-033-2*) Soho Pr., Inc.

Maurensig, Paolo. The Luneburg Variation. Rothschild, Jon, tr. from ITA. 1997. 160p. 19.00 o.p. (*0-374-19435-1*) Farrar, Straus & Giroux.

McDermid, Val. The Last Temptation. 2002. (Illus.). 431p. (*0-00-226109-X*) HarperCollins Pubs.

—The Last Temptation. 2003. 496p. mass mkt. 6.99 (*0-312-98631-9*, St. Martin's Paperbacks) St. Martin's Pr.

McDonald, Cherokee P. Blue Truth. 1992. 272p. pap. text 4.99 o.p. (*0-312-92773-8*, St. Martin's Paperbacks) St. Martin's Pr.

McEwan, Ian. The Innocent. 1995. 288p. mass mkt. 6.99 o.s.i (*0-553-56554-0*); 1991. 320p. pap. 6.99 o.s.i (*0-553-55000-4*) Bantam Bks.

—The Innocent. 288p. 1998. pap. 14.00 (*0-385-49433-5*); 1990. 18.95 o.p. (*0-385-41370-X*) Doubleday Publishing.

Meador, D. J. His Father's House. 1994. 384p. (YA). (gr. 10-12). 25.00 (*1-56554-032-8*) Pelican Publishing Co., Inc.

Meckel, Christoph. Zund & Other Stories. Bedwell, Carol, tr. from GER. 1991. (Studies in German Language & Literature: Vol. 2). (Illus.). 120p. lib. bdg. 59.95 (*0-88946-580-0*) Mellen, Edwin Pr., The.

Mekler, Eva. Sunrise Shows Late: A Novel. 1997. 321p. 21.95 (*1-882593-17-0*); 2002. 224p. reprint ed. 13.95 (*1-882593-58-8*) Bridge Works Publishing Co., Inc.

Meredith, George. The Tragic Comedians. 2000. 252p. pap. 9.95 (*0-594-01759-9*); E-Book 3.95 (*0-594-02639-3*) 1873 Pr.

—The Tragic Comedians: A Study in a Well-Known Story. (Revised Edition) 1975. (Modern Jewish Experience Ser.). reprint ed. 18.95 (*0-405-06735-6*) Ayer Co. Pubs., Inc.

Minatra, MaryAnn. Before Night Falls. 1996. (Legacy of Honor Ser.: Vol. 1). 420p. pap. 10.99 o.s.i (*1-56507-432-7*) Harvest Hse. Pubs.

—Jewel in the Evening Sky. 1997. (Legacy of Honor Ser.: No. 2). 400p. pap. 9.99 o.p. (*1-56507-668-0*) Harvest Hse. Pubs.

Montague, Terry. Fireweed. 1992. pap. 10.95 (*1-55503-407-1*, 01111078) Covenant Communications, Inc.

Moore, Philip N. What If Hitler Won the War: Where Would We Be Today. 1998. (Illus.). 190p. pap. 19.95 (*1-57915-996-6*) Rams Head Pr., International, The.

Morley, John D. Feast of Fools. 1994. ix, 443p. 23.95 o.p. (*0-312-11786-8*) St. Martin's Pr.

—The Feast of Fools. 1995. 464p. pap. 13.95 o.p. (*0-312-13493-2*, Saint Martin's Griffin) St. Martin's Pr.

Morrison, Blake. The Justification of Johann Gutenberg. 2000. 259p. (*0-7011-6965-6*) Chatto & Windus GBR. *Dist:* Trafalgar Square.

—The Justification of Johann Gutenberg. 2002. 272p. pap. (*0-385-25985-9*, Anchor Canada) Doubleday Canada, Ltd. CAN. *Dist:* Random Hse., Inc.

—The Justification of Johann Gutenberg. 2003. 272p. pap. 13.95 (*0-06-093571-5*) HarperTrade.

—The Justification of Johann Gutenberg. 2002. 272p. 23.95 (*0-06-621088-7*, Morrow, William & Co.) Morrow/Avon.

Mulisch, Harry. Siegfried. 2003. 192p. 22.95 (*0-670-03253-0*) Viking Penguin.

Nebenzal, Harold. Cafe Berlin. 1992. 290p. 22.95 o.p. (*0-87951-458-2*) Overlook Pr., The.

Nelson, Lee. A Thousand Souls: A Young Man's Improbable Journey Begins with a Prophet's Promise. 2002. 200p. 18.95 (*1-55517-653-4*, Council Pr.) Cedar Fort, Inc./CFI Distribution.

Nelson, Penelope. Beyond Berlin. 1996. 256p. (Orig.). pap. 11.95 o.p. (*1-86373-847-9*) Allen & Unwin Pty., Ltd. AUS. *Dist:* Independent Pubs. Group.

O'Connor, Robert. Buffalo Soldiers: A Novel. 1994. (Vintage Contemporaries Ser.). 336p. pap. 13.95 (*0-679-74203-4*, Vintage) Knopf Publishing Group.

—Buffalo Soldiers: A Novel. 1993. 323p. 22.00 o.s.i (*0-679-41508-4*) Knopf, Alfred A. Inc.

Ohanna, Karin. Star Crossed: A Novel. 1999. pap. 12.95 o.p. (*0-533-12976-1*) Vantage Pr., Inc.

Oren, Aras. Please, No Police: A Novella. Sipahigil, Teoman, tr. from TUR. 1992. (Modern Middle Eastern Literature in Translation Ser.). 174p. pap. 8.95 (*0-292-76038-8*) Ctr. for Middle Eastern Studies.

Page, Carole G. Bouquet of Good-Byes. 1992. (Kasey Carlone Ser.). (YA). pap. 4.99 o.p. (*0-8024-8180-9*) Moody Pr.

Parrinder, Patrick & Rolfe, Christopher, eds. H. G. Wells under Revision: Proceedings of the International H. G. Wells Symposium, London, July 1986. 1990. 264p. 40.00 (*0-945636-05-9*) Susquehanna Univ. Pr.

Peters, Elizabeth, pseud. Borrower of the Night. l.t. ed. 1992. 15.95 o.p. (*0-7927-0652-8*); 1991. 17.95 o.p. (*0-7927-0651-X*, E0008) BBC Audiobooks America.

—Borrower of the Night. 1992. mass mkt. 4.99 (*0-8125-2355-5*); 1990. pap. 3.95 o.s.i (*0-8125-0752-5*) Doherty, Tom Assocs., LLC. (Tor Bks.).

—Borrower of the Night. 2000. (Vicky Bliss Mysteries Ser.). 336p. mass mkt. 6.99 (*0-380-73339-0*, Avon Bks.) Morrow/Avon.

—Borrower of the Night. 1994. reprint ed. lib. bdg. 20.00 o.p. (*0-7278-4664-7*) Severn Hse. Pubs., Ltd.

—Night Train to Memphis. unabr. ed. 1997. (Vicky Bliss Mysteries Ser.). audio 28.00 (*1-885608-26-8*) Airplay.

—Night Train to Memphis. unabr. ed. 1996. audio 62.95 (*0-7861-1065-1*, 1836) Blackstone Audio Bks., Inc.

—Night Train to Memphis. unabr. ed. 1995. (Vicky Bliss Mystery Ser.: Vol. 5). audio 85.00 (*0-7887-0109-6*, 94372E7) Recorded Bks., LLC.

—Night Train to Memphis. 354p. pap. 5.98 o.p. (*0-7651-0300-1*) Smithmark Pubs., Inc.

—Night Train to Memphis. 368p. 1995. mass mkt. 7.50 (*0-446-60248-5*); 1994. 21.95 o.s.i (*0-446-51586-8*) Warner Bks., Inc.

—Silhouette in Scarlet. 1990. mass mkt. 4.50 (*0-8125-0940-4*, Tor Bks.) Doherty, Tom Assocs., LLC.

—Silhouette in Scarlet. l.t. ed. 1986. 10.00 o.p. (*0-8161-3592-4*, Macmillan Reference USA) Gale Group.

—Silhouette in Scarlet. 2000. (Vicky Bliss Mysteries Ser.). 320p. mass mkt. 6.99 (*0-380-73337-4*, Avon Bks.) Morrow/Avon.

—Silhouette in Scarlet. unabr. ed. (Vicky Bliss Mystery Ser.: Vol. 3). audio 44.00 (*0-7887-0160-6*, 94385E7) Recorded Bks., LLC.

—Silhouette in Scarlet. l.t. ed. 1985. (Ulverscroft Large Print Ser.). 29.99 o.p. (*0-7089-1315-6*, Ulverscroft) Thorpe, F. A. Pubs. GBR. *Dist:* Ulverscroft Large Print Bks., Ltd., Ulverscroft Large Print Canada, Ltd.

—Silhouette in Scarlet. 1994. 224p. mass mkt. 5.50 o.p. (*0-446-36482-7*) Warner Bks., Inc.

—Street of the Five Moons. 1979. pap. 1.95 o.s.i (*0-449-23897-0*, Fawcett) Ballantine Bks.

—Street of the Five Moons. 1990. 256p. mass mkt. 5.99 (*0-8125-1244-8*); 1988. pap. 3.95 o.s.i (*0-8125-0795-9*); 1987. 256p. pap. 3.50 o.s.i (*0-8125-0766-5*) Doherty, Tom Assocs., LLC. (Tor Bks.).

—Street of the Five Moons. l.t. ed. 1991. (General Ser.). 350p. pap. 18.95 o.p. (*0-8161-4906-2*, Macmillan Reference USA) Gale Group.

—Street of the Five Moons. 2000. (Vicky Bliss Mysteries Ser.). 384p. mass mkt. 6.99 (*0-380-73121-5*, Avon Bks.) Morrow/Avon.

—Street of the Five Moons. unabr. ed. 1994. (Vicky Bliss Mystery Ser.: Vol. 2). audio 51.00 (*0-7887-0040-5*, 94239E7) Recorded Bks., LLC.

—Trojan Gold. 1992. mass mkt. 5.99 o.p. (*0-8125-2357-1*); 1988. 416p. pap. 3.95 o.s.i (*0-8125-0758-4*) Doherty, Tom Assocs., LLC. (Tor Bks.).

—Trojan Gold. 2000. (Vicky Bliss Mysteries Ser.). 368p. mass mkt. 6.99 (*0-380-73123-1*, Avon Bks.) Morrow/Avon.

—Trojan Gold. 1987. 288p. 15.95 o.p. (*0-689-11621-7*, Scribner) Simon & Schuster.

Phillips, Michael. The Eleventh Hour. 2000. (Secret of the Rose Ser.). 496p. mass mkt. 6.99 (*0-8423-4289-3*, Living Bks.); 1994. (Secret of the Rose Ser.: No. 1). 504p. 8.99 o.p. (*0-8423-3932-9*); 1993. (Secret of the Rose Ser.: Vol. 1). 504p. pap. 8.99 (*0-8423-3933-7*) Tyndale Hse. Pubs.

—Escape to Freedom. (Secret of the Rose Ser.: No. 3). 1995. 16.99 o.p. (*0-8423-5951-6*); 1994. 487p. pap. 11.99 (*0-8423-5942-7*) Tyndale Hse. Pubs.

—A Rose Remembered. (Secret of the Rose Ser.: Vol. 2). 2001. 528p. mass mkt. 7.99 (*0-8423-4291-5*, Living Bks.); 1994. 576p. pap. 11.99 o.p. (*0-8423-5929-X*) Tyndale Hse. Pubs.

Plain, Belva. Legacy of Silence. unabr. ed. 2000. audio 84.95 (*0-7540-0329-9*, CAB 1752) Chivers Audio Bks. GBR. *Dist:* BBC Audiobooks America.

—Legacy of Silence. 1999. mass mkt. 7.99 o.s.i (*0-440-29557-2*); 432p. mass mkt. 7.99 (*0-440-22640-6*) Dell Publishing.

—Legacy of Silence. l.t. ed. (Paperback Bestsellers Ser.). 471p. 1999. pap. 27.95 (*0-7862-1512-7*); 1998. 30.95 (*0-7862-1511-9*) Thorndike Pr.

Pressler, Mirjam. Halinka. ERS. Crawford, Elizabeth D., tr. from GER. 1998. (Illus.). 214p. (YA). (gr. 4-7). 16.95 o.s.i (*0-8050-5861-3*, Holt, Henry & Co. Bks. For Young Readers) Holt, Henry & Co.

—Halinka. Crawford, Elizabeth D., tr. 2000. 224p. (YA). (gr. 5-7). reprint ed. mass mkt. 5.50 o.s.i (*0-440-22857-3*, Laurel Leaf) Random Hse. Children's Bks.

Price, Anthony. A New Kind of War. 1988. 272p. 17.95 (*0-89296-281-X*); pap. 4.95 o.p. (*0-445-40338-1*) Mysterious Pr.

Rahlens, Holly-Jane. Becky Bernstein Goes Berlin. 1997. 256p. 22.95 (*1-55970-381-4*) Arcade Publishing, Inc.

Ransmayr, Christoph. The Dog King. Woods, John, tr. 1997. 355p. 24.00 o.s.i (*0-679-45057-2*) Knopf, Alfred A. Inc.

—The Kitahara Syndrome. Woods, John, tr. from GER. 1998. 368p. pap. 19.00 (*0-679-76860-2*, Vintage) Knopf Publishing Group.

Rathbone, Julian. Accidents Will Happen. 1997. (Mask Noir Ser.). 256p. pap. text (*1-85242-312-9*) Serpent's Tail Ltd.

—Accidents Will Happen. 296p. 26.00 (*0-7278-5619-7*) Severn Hse. Pubs., Ltd.

Reeman, Douglas. The White Guns. 1989. 326p. (C). 19.95 o.p. (*0-434-62634-1*, 00635) Heinemann.

Reich, Christopher. The Runner. l.t. ed. 2000. (Trade Editions Ser.). 688p. 26.95 (*0-375-40973-4*) Random Hse. Large Print.

Reinhart, Robert C. Walk the Night: A Novel of Gays in the Holocaust. 1994. 240p. pap. 9.95 o.p. (*1-55583-267-9*) Alyson Pubns.

Remarque, Erich-Maria. All Quiet on the Western Front. 1998. (Classics Illustrated Study Guides). (Illus.). mass mkt. 4.99 (*1-57840-056-2*) Acclaim Bks.

—All Quiet on the Western Front. 20.95 (*0-8488-1459-2*) Amereon, Ltd.

—All Quiet on the Western Front. 1999. mass mkt. 2.22 o.s.i (*0-449-45942-X*); 1996. 304p. pap. 13.95 (*0-449-91149-7*, Fawcett); 1987. 304p. mass mkt. 6.99 (*0-449-21394-3*, Ballantine Bks.) Ballantine Bks.

—All Quiet on the Western Front. 1929. 248p. (gr. 8). 24.95 (*0-316-73992-8*) Little Brown & Co.

—All Quiet on the Western Front. 9999. pap. 2.50 o.s.i (*0-590-02981-9*) Scholastic, Inc.

—All Quiet on the Western Front. 1975. 13.04 (*0-606-00101-8*) Turtleback Bks.

—All Quiet on the Western Front: The Illustrated Edition. Wheen, A. W., tr. from GER. 1996. (Illus.). 208p. 29.95 o.p. (*0-8212-2312-7*) Little Brown & Co.

Rhenisch, Harold. Carnival. 2000. 208p. pap. (*0-88984-213-2*) Porcupine's Quill, Inc.

Ridley, Ruth Ann. Bach's Passion: The Life of Johann Sebastian Bach - a Novel. 1999. 400p. pap. 16.99 o.p. (*1-57921-170-4*) WinePress Publishing.

Roth, Joseph. Right & Left: The Legend of the Holy Drinker. Hoffman, Michael, tr. 1993. 304p. pap. 15.95 (*0-87951-456-6*) Overlook Pr., The.

—Right & Left & The Legend of the Holy Drinker. Hofmann, Michael, tr. 1992. 320p. 23.95 (*0-87951-448-5*) Overlook Pr., The.

Rothmann, Ralf. Knife Edge. Mitchell, Breon, tr. from GER. 1992. 128p. 19.95 (*0-8112-1204-1*); pap. 9.95 (*0-8112-1210-6*, NDP744) New Directions Publishing Corp.

Said, Kurban. The Girl from the Golden Horn. 2003. 288p. pap. 13.00 (*1-4000-3082-X*) Knopf Publishing Group.

—The Girl from the Golden Horn. 2001. 256p. 25.95 (*1-58567-173-8*) Overlook Pr., The.

Savarin, Julian J. A Cold Rain in Berlin. 2002. 256p. 26.99 (*0-7278-5892-0*) Severn Hse. Pubs., Ltd.

—Romeo Summer. 2003. 256p. 26.99 (*0-7278-5957-9*) Severn Hse. Pubs., Ltd.

Schlink, Bernhard. The Reader. 2001. E-Book 11.95 (*1-58945-800-1*) Adobe Systems, Inc.

—The Reader. Janeway, Carol Brown, tr. from GER. (Oprah's Book Club Ser.). 224p. 1999. 22.00 o.s.i (*0-375-40826-6*, Pantheon); 1999. pap. 11.95 (*0-375-70797-2*, Vintage); 1998. pap. 11.00 o.s.i (*0-679-78130-7*, Vintage); 1997. 21.00 o.p. (*0-679-44279-0*, Pantheon) Knopf Publishing Group.

—The Reader. l.t. ed. 1999. 216p. pap. 24.95 (*0-7838-8646-2*) Thorndike Pr.

—The Reader. l.t. ed. 1999. (Ulverscroft Large Print Ser.). 240p. 31.99 (*0-7089-4064-1*, Linford) Thorpe, F. A. Pubs. GBR. *Dist:* Ulverscroft Large Print Bks., Ltd., Ulverscroft Large Print Canada, Ltd.

Schneider, Peter. Couplings. Boehm, Philip, tr. 1996. 300p. 24.00 o.p. (*0-374-13053-1*) Farrar, Straus & Giroux.

—Couplings. 1998. (Phoenix Fiction Ser.). 294p. pap. 15.00 (*0-226-73939-2*) Univ. of Chicago Pr.

—The Wall Jumper: A Berlin Story. Hafrey, Leigh, tr. 1985. pap. 9.95 o.s.i (*0-394-72882-3*, Pantheon) Knopf Publishing Group.

Schulze, Ingo. Simple Stories: A Novel from the East German Provinces. 2002. 304p. pap. 13.00 (*0-375-70512-0*, Vintage) Knopf Publishing Group.

Schwaiger, Brigitte. Why Is There Salt in the Sea? Lug, Sieglinde, tr. from GER. 1988. (European Women Writers Ser.). vi, 128p. text 15.95 o.p. (*0-8032-4174-7*) Univ. of Nebraska Pr.

Sebastian, Tim. The Memory Church: A Novel. 1993. 288p. 20.00 o.p. (*0-688-11447-4*, Morrow, William & Co.) Morrow/Avon.

Seiffert, Rachel. The Dark Room: A Novel. 2002. 288p. pap. 13.00 (0-375-72632-2) Knopf, Alfred A. Inc.

Semprun, Jorge. The Long Voyage. 1999. pap. (0-14-026262-8) Viking Penguin.

—The Long Voyage. Seaver, Richard, tr. 1997. (Penguin Twentieth-Century Classics Ser.). 240p. pap. 11.95 o.s.i (0-14-118029-3) Viking Penguin.

Seymour, Gerald. Dead Ground. 2001. E-Book 9.99 (1-58945-771-4) Adobe Systems, Inc.

—Dead Ground. 2000. E-Book 25.00 (0-684-87218-8, Simon & Schuster); 1999. (Illus.). 368p. 25.00 (0-684-85476-7, Simon & Schuster); 2000. 464p. reprint ed. mass mkt. 6.99 (0-671-02529-5, Pocket) Simon & Schuster.

—Dead Ground. l.t. ed. 1999. (Basic Ser.). 675p. 28.95 (0-7862-1917-3) Thorndike Pr.

Shea, Michael. The Iron Veil. 192p. 25.00 (0-7278-5465-8) Severn Hse. Pubs., Ltd.

—The Iron Veil. l.t. ed. 2000. (General Ser.). viii, 220p. 22.95 (0-7862-2806-7); (0-7540-4249-9); (0-7540-4250-2) Thorndike Pr.

Simon, Frank. Trial by Fire. 1999. 320p. pap. 12.99 (1-58134-075-3) Crossway Bks.

—Trial by Fire. l.t. ed. 1999. (Christian Mystery Ser.). 539p. 24.95 o.p. (0-7862-2143-7) Thorndike Pr.

Slider, John W. A Soldier of the King. 2001. pap. 11.95 (0-595-17607-0) iUniverse, Inc.

Steinhauer, Harry, ed. & tr. from GER. Twelve German Novellas. 1977. 648p. pap. text 25.00 (0-520-03002-8) Univ. of California Pr.

Stone, Todd. Kriegspiel: A Novel of Tomorrow's Europe. 1993. 292p. 19.95 o.p. (0-89141-466-5, Presidio Pr.) Ballantine Bks.

Storm, Theodor. The Dykemaster. Jackson, Denis, tr. from GER. 1996. 196p. pap. 14.95 (0-946162-54-9) Angel Bks. GBR. Dist: Dufour Editions, Inc.

Strauss, Botho. Living, Glimmering, Lying. Theobald, Roslyn, tr. from GER. 1999. 176p. 26.95 (0-8101-1283-3, Hydra Bks.) Northwestern Univ. Pr.

Swanwick, Michael. Jack Faust. 1998. pap. 12.50 o.p. (0-380-79070-X); 1997. 352p. 23.00 (0-380-97444-4) Morrow/Avon. (Avon Bks.).

Szeman, Sherri. The Kommandant's Mistress. 2000. 273p. pap. 13.95 (1-55970-542-6) Arcade Publishing, Inc.

—The Kommandant's Mistress. 1993. 224p. 17.50 o.p. (0-06-017011-5); 1994. 288p. reprint ed. pap. 12.50 o.p. (0-06-092497-7, Perennial) HarperTrade.

Taylor, Frederick. The Kinder Garden. 1991. 432p. 21.95 o.p. (0-88184-697-X, Carroll & Graf Pubs.) Avalon Publishing Group.

Taylor, Kathrine Kressmann. Address Unknown. 2001. (Illus.). 64p. reprint ed. pap. 8.95 (0-7434-1271-0, Washington Square Pr.) Simon & Schuster.

Taylor, Kressmann. Address Unknown. 1995. 64p. 12.99 o.p. (1-884910-17-3, Story Pr.) F&W Pubns., Inc.

Thoene, Bodie. Munich Signature. 1990. (Zion Covenant Ser.: Vol. 3). 400p. pap. 12.99 (1-55661-079-3) Bethany Hse. Pubs.

Thomas, Ross. The Cold War Swap. mass mkt. (0-312-99036-7, St. Martin's Paperbacks) St. Martin's Pr.

—The Cold War Swap. l.t. ed. 2003. 356p. 29.95 (0-7862-5576-5) Thorndike Pr.

—The Cold War Swap: A McCorkle & Padillo Novel. 224p. 1984. pap. 2.95 o.p. (0-06-080686-9, P686); 1986. reprint ed. mass mkt. 3.50 o.p. (0-06-080834-9, P 834) HarperTrade. (Perennial).

—The Cold War Swap: A McCorkle & Padillo Novel. 1978. pap. 1.75 o.p. (0-671-81898-8, Pocket) Simon & Schuster.

—The Cold War Swap: A McCorkle & Padillo Novel. 1992. mass mkt. 5.99 o.p. (0-446-40168-4) Warner Bks., Inc.

Timm, Uwe. The Invention of Curried Sausage. Vennewitz, Leila, tr. from GER. 1997. pap. 9.95 (0-8112-1368-4, NDP854); 1995. 224p. 19.95 o.p. (0-8112-1297-1) New Directions Publishing Corp.

Townsend, Tom. Trader Wooly & the Secret of the Lost Nazi Treasure. Roberts, Melissa, ed. 1987. (Illus.). 120p. (J). (gr. 6-7). 13.95 o.p. (0-89015-602-6) Eakin Pr.

Trollope, Anthony. Linda Tressel, 2 vols. 1982. (Selected Works of Anthony Trollope). reprint ed. lib. bdg. 49.95 (0-405-14152-1) Ayer Co. Pubs., Inc.

—Nina Balatka & Linda Tressel. 1991. (Oxford World's Classics Ser.). (Illus.). 434p. pap. 8.95 o.p. (0-19-282723-5) Oxford Univ. Pr., Inc.

Tuccille, Jerome & Jacobs, Philip S. The Mission: A Novel about the Flight of Rudolf Hess. 1991. 18.95 o.p. (1-55611-199-1) Fine, Donald I. Bks.

Ugresic, Dubravka. The Museum of Unconditional Surrender. Hawkesworth, Celia, tr. from CRO. 1999. 256p. 24.95 o.s.i (0-8112-1421-4) New Directions Publishing Corp.

Uhlman, Fred. Reunion. 112p. 1997. pap. 10.00 (0-374-52515-3); 1977. 6.95 o.p. (0-374-24951-2) Farrar, Straus & Giroux.

Vansittart, Peter. A Safe Conduct. 1996. 184p. pap. 29.95 (0-7206-0977-1); 30.00 (0-7206-0953-4) Owen, Peter Ltd. GBR. Dist: Dufour Editions, Inc.

Von Arnim, Elizabeth. Elizabeth & Her German Garden. 2001. (Modern Classics). (Illus.). 208p. 13.95 (0-86068-423-7) Virago Pr., Ltd. GBR. Dist: Trafalgar Square.

—The Solitary Summer. 2001. (Modern Classics). 190p. pap. 13.95 (1-85381-553-5) Virago Pr., Ltd. GBR. Dist: Trafalgar Square.

Von Drogas, Johann. As Once We Were: A Love Story. Wade, Virginia, ed. unabr. ed. 1999. 438p. 23.50 (0-9620016-2-7) Great Lakes Publishing Co.

von La Roche, Sophie. The History of Lady Sophia Sternheim: Extracted by a Woman Friend of the Same from Original Documents & Other Reliable Sources. Britt, Christa Baguss, tr. from GER. 1991. (SUNY Series, Women Writers in Translation). 246p. (C). pap. text 23.95 (0-7914-0533-8) State Univ. of New York Pr.

—The History of Lady Sophia Sternheim: Extracted by a Woman Friend of the Same from Original Documents & Other Reliable Sources. Britt, Christa Baguss, tr. from GER. 1991. (SUNY Series, Women Writers in Translation). 246p. (C). text 64.50 o.p. (0-7914-0532-X) State Univ. of New York Pr.

—The History of Lady Sophie Sternheim. Lynn, James, ed. (Women's Classics Ser.). 250p. (C). 1993. pap. text 19.50 o.p. (0-8147-8775-4); 1992. text 55.00 o.p. (0-8147-8774-6) New York Univ. Pr.

Von Rezzori, Gregor. Oedipus at Stalingrad. 1994. 304p. 25.00 o.p. (0-374-22426-9) Farrar, Straus & Giroux.

Wagner, Ray C. Delayed Justice: A Mystery Novel. 1999. 340p. (0-9670744-2-8, 0325); 282p. pap. (0-9670744-1-X, 0324) MC Pr.

Waidson, H. M. German Short Stories, 3. 1969. 160p. pap. text 7.95 o.p. (0-521-07180-1) Cambridge Univ. Pr.

Waldrop, Rosmarie. The Hanky of Pippin's Daughter. 2001. xviii, 248p. reprint ed. pap. 17.95 (0-8101-1834-3) Northwestern Univ. Pr.

—The Hanky of Pippin's Daughter. 1987. 152p. 19.95 (0-88268-038-2) Station Hill Pr.

Wallace, Irving. The Seventh Secret. 1986. 436p. 17.95 o.p. (0-525-24382-8, Dutton) Dutton/Plume.

—The Seventh Secret. l.t. ed. 1986. 515p. 19.95 o.p. (0-8161-4148-7, Macmillan Reference USA) Gale Group.

—The Seventh Secret. 1986. mass mkt. 4.95 o.s.i (0-451-14557-7, Signet Bks.) NAL.

Walser, Martin. The Swan Villa. Vennewitz, Leila, tr. 1982. 14.95 o.p. (0-03-059372-7) Holt, Henry & Co.

Wasserman, Jakob. Caspar Hauser. Hulse, Michael, tr. & intro. by. 1993. (Penguin Twentieth-Century Classics Ser.). 416p. pap. 11.95 o.p. (0-14-018195-4, Penguin Classics) Viking Penguin.

Welt, Elly. Berlin Wild. 1988. 400p. mass mkt. 4.50 o.p. (0-451-40028-3, Onyx) NAL.

—Berlin Wild. 1986. 384p. 17.95 o.p. (0-670-80925-X) Viking Penguin.

Wickram, Jorg. The Golden Thread: An Agreeable & Entertaining Tale of Lionel, Son of a Poor Shepherd. Kaufke, Pierre, tr. from GER. 1991. 192p. 49.95 (0-8130-1045-4) Univ. Pr. of Florida.

Williams, John A. Clifford's Blues. 1999. 272p. pap. 14.95 (1-56689-080-2) Coffee Hse. Pr.

Wiseman, T. The Day Before Sunrise. 1976. o.p. (0-03-015206-2) Holt, Henry & Co.

Wiseman, Thomas. Children of the Ruins. 1986. 17.95 o.p. (0-316-94857-8) Little Brown & Co.

Yale, Dorothea. Angelshut Again: A Novel. 2001. (0-9652784-1-7) Entis Publishing.

—The Fall & Rise of Angelshut: A Novel. 1996. 480p. 18.00 (0-9652784-0-9) Entis Publishing.

Yarbro, Chelsea Quinn. Better in the Dark. 1995. 412p. pap. 14.95 (0-312-85978-3, Orb Bks.); 1993. (Illus.). 416p. 23.95 o.p. (0-312-85504-4, Tor Bks.) Doherty, Tom Assocs., LLC.

Yoder, James D. Black Spider over Tiegenhof. 1995. 232p. pap. 11.99 o.p. (0-8361-9012-2) Herald Pr.

—Black Spider over Tiegenhof. l.t. ed. 2000. (Christian Mystery Ser.). 335p. 23.95 (0-7862-2709-5) Thorndike Pr.

—Black Spider over Tiegenhof. 1995. E-Book 11.99 (0-585-22785-3) netLibrary, Inc.

Zimmerman, R. D. Deadfall in Berlin. 1990. 18.95 o.p. (1-55611-222-X) Fine, Donald I. Bks.

## GIBBSVILLE (PA.: IMAGINARY PLACE)—FICTION

O'Hara, John. Appointment in Samarra. (Modern Library Ser.). 1994. 364p. 14.95 o.s.i (0-679-60110-4); 1982. 256p. mass mkt. 10.00 o.s.i (0-394-71192-0); 1934. 3.00 o.p. (0-394-41542-6) Random Hse., Inc.

—Appointment in Samarra. 1993. reprint ed. lib. bdg. 89.00 (0-7812-5481-7) Reprint Services Corp.

—Appointment in Samarra. l.t. ed. 1998. (Perennial Bestsellers Ser.). 331p. 25.95 (0-7838-0376-1) Thorndike Pr.

## GOR (IMAGINARY PLACE)—FICTION

Norman, John. Assassin of Gor. 1986. mass mkt. 4.95 o.s.i (0-345-34502-9); 1984. mass mkt. 2.95 o.s.i (0-345-31922-2, Del Rey); 1981. mass mkt. 2.75 o.s.i (0-345-30282-6, Del Rey); 1980. mass mkt. 2.50 o.s.i (0-345-29417-3, Del Rey); 1978. mass mkt. 1.95 o.s.i (0-345-28133-0, Del Rey); 1975. mass mkt. 1.50 o.s.i (0-345-24686-1); 1973. mass mkt. 0.95 o.s.i (0-345-22489-2) Ballantine Bks.

—Beasts of Gor. 1978. (Gor Ser.). mass mkt. 1.95 o.p. (0-87997-363-3); mass mkt. 2.25 o.p. (0-87997-471-0); mass mkt. 2.95 o.p. (0-87997-677-2); mass mkt. 3.50 o.p. (0-87997-903-8); mass mkt. 3.95 o.p. (0-88677-028-9, UE2028) DAW Bks., Inc.

—Blood Brothers of Gor. 1982. (Gor Ser.: No. 18). mass mkt. 3.95 o.p. (0-88677-157-9); mass mkt. 3.50 o.p. (0-87997-777-9) DAW Bks., Inc.

—Captive of Gor. 1981. mass mkt. 2.75 o.s.i (0-345-30281-8, Del Rey); 1980. mass mkt. 2.50 o.s.i (0-345-29414-9, Del Rey); No. 7. 1986. (Gor Ser.: No. 7). mass mkt. 4.95 o.s.i (0-345-34199-6) Ballantine Bks.

—Captive of Gor. 1997. (Gor Ser.: No. 7). 408p. mass mkt. 6.95 (1-56333-581-6) Masquerade Bks., Inc.

—Dancer of Gor. 1985. (Gor Ser.). mass mkt. 3.95 o.p. (0-88677-100-5); mass mkt. 4.50 o.p. (0-88677-301-6) DAW Bks., Inc.

—Explorers of Gor. 1979. (Gor Ser.). mass mkt. 2.25 o.p. (0-87997-449-4); mass mkt. 2.50 o.p. (0-87997-607-1); mass mkt. 2.95 o.p. (0-87997-685-3); mass mkt. 3.50 o.p. (0-87997-905-4, UE1905) DAW Bks., Inc.

—Fighting Slave of Gor. 1980. (Gor Ser.). mass mkt. 2.25 o.p. (0-87997-522-9); mass mkt. 2.95 o.p. (0-87997-681-0); mass mkt. 3.50 o.p. (0-87997-882-1) DAW Bks., Inc.

—Guardsman of Gor. 1981. (Gor Ser.). mass mkt. 2.95 o.p. (0-87997-664-0); mass mkt. 3.50 o.p. (0-87997-890-2, UE 1890) DAW Bks., Inc.

—Hunters of Gor. 1974. (Gor Ser.). mass mkt. 1.50 o.p. (0-87997-102-9); mass mkt. 1.75 o.p. (0-87997-294-7); mass mkt. 1.95 o.p. (0-87997-368-4); mass mkt. 2.25 o.p. (0-87997-472-9); mass mkt. 2.75 o.p. (0-87997-678-0); mass mkt. 2.95 o.p. (0-88677-010-6); mass mkt. 3.95 o.p. (0-88677-205-2) DAW Bks., Inc.

—Hunters of Gor. 1998. (Gor Ser.: No. 8). 352p. reprint ed. mass mkt. 6.95 (1-56333-592-1) Masquerade Bks., Inc.

—Hunters of Gor. E-Book 6.99 (1-58586-495-1) ereads.com.

—Kajira of Gor. 1983. (Gor Ser.: No. 19). 448p. mass mkt. 3.50 o.p. (0-87997-807-4) DAW Bks., Inc.

—Magicians of Gor. 1988. (Gor Ser.: No. 25). mass mkt. 4.95 o.p. (0-88677-279-6) DAW Bks., Inc.

—Marauders of Gor. 1975. (Gor Ser.). mass mkt. 1.50 o.p. (0-87997-160-6); mass mkt. 1.75 o.p. (0-87997-295-5); mass mkt. 1.95 o.p. (0-87997-369-2); mass mkt. 2.25 o.p. (0-87997-465-6); mass mkt. 2.75 o.p. (0-87997-676-4); mass mkt. 2.95 o.p. (0-87997-901-1); mass mkt. 3.50 o.p. (0-88677-025-4, UE2025) DAW Bks., Inc.

—Marauders of Gor. 1998. (Gor Ser.: No. 9). reprint ed. mass mkt. 6.95 (1-56333-662-6, Masquerade SF) Masquerade Bks., Inc.

—Mercenaries of Gor. 1985. (Gor Ser.). mass mkt. 3.95 o.p. (0-88677-018-1); mass mkt. 4.95 o.p. (0-88677-369-5) DAW Bks., Inc.

—Nomads of Gor. 1981. mass mkt. 2.50 o.s.i (0-345-29722-9, Del Rey); 1978. mass mkt. 1.95 o.s.i (0-345-27795-3, Del Rey); 1975. mass mkt. 1.50 o.s.i (0-345-24784-1); 1969. mass mkt. 0.75 o.s.i (0-345-21765-9) Ballantine Bks.

—Nomads of Gor. 1997. (Gor Ser.: No. 4). mass mkt. 6.95 (1-56333-527-1, Masquerade SF) Masquerade Bks., Inc.

—Nomads of Gor. 2002. 482p. mass mkt. 9.95 (1-58586-200-2) ereads.com.

—The Nomads of Gor, No. 4. 1985. (Gor Ser.: No. 4). mass mkt. 3.95 o.s.i (0-345-33421-3) Ballantine Bks.

—Outlaw of Gor. (Gor Ser.: No. 2). E-Book 6.99 (1-58586-498-6) ereads.com.

—The Outlaw of Gor. 1984. (Gor Ser.: No. 2). mass mkt. 3.95 o.s.i (0-345-32394-7) Ballantine Bks.

—Outlaw of Gor. 1997. (Gor Ser.: No. 2). reprint ed. mass mkt. 6.95 (1-56333-487-9, Masquerade SF) Masquerade Bks., Inc.

—Priest Kings of Gor. 1980. (Gor Ser.: No. 3). mass mkt. 3.95 o.s.i (0-345-29539-0); 1978. mass mkt. 1.95 o.s.i (0-345-28132-2, Del Rey); 1977. mass mkt. 1.75 o.s.i (0-345-27199-8, Del Rey); 1976. mass mkt. 1.50 o.s.i (0-345-25181-4); 1975. mass mkt. 1.50 o.s.i (0-345-24783-3); 1973. mass mkt. 0.95 o.s.i (0-345-22487-6); 1969. mass mkt. 0.75 o.s.i (0-345-21832-9); 1968. mass mkt. 0.75 o.s.i (0-345-21096-4) Ballantine Bks.

—Priest Kings of Gor. 1996. (Gor Ser.: No. 3). mass mkt. 6.95 (1-56333-488-7) Masquerade Bks., Inc.

—Priest Kings of Gor. 2002. 419p. mass mkt. 9.95 (0-7592-0036-X); 2000. (Gor Ser.: No. 3). E-Book 6.99 (1-58586-133-2); 2000. (Gor Ser.: No. 3). E-Book 6.99 (1-58586-134-0); 2000. (Gor Ser.: No. 3). E-Book 6.99 (1-58586-266-5) ereads.com.

—Raiders of Gor. 1985. (Gor Ser.: No. 6). mass mkt. 3.95 o.s.i (0-345-33109-5); 1980. mass mkt. 2.50 o.s.i (0-345-29538-2, Del Rey); 1978. mass mkt. 1.95 o.s.i (0-345-28134-9, Del Rey); 1975. mass mkt. 1.50 o.s.i (0-345-24701-9) Ballantine Bks.

—Raiders of Gor. 1997. (Gor Ser.: No. 6). mass mkt. 6.95 (1-56333-558-1) Masquerade Bks., Inc.

—Renegades of Gor. 1986. (Gor Ser.). mass mkt. 3.95 o.p. (0-88677-112-9); mass mkt. 4.95 o.p. (0-88677-382-2) DAW Bks., Inc.

—Rogue of Gor. 1981. (Gor Ser.). mass mkt. 2.50 o.p. (0-87997-602-0); mass mkt. 2.95 o.p. (0-87997-710-8); mass mkt. 3.50 o.p. (0-87997-892-9) DAW Bks., Inc.

—Savages of Gor. 1982. (Gor Ser.: No. 17). mass mkt. 3.95 o.p. (0-88677-191-9); mass mkt. 3.50 o.p. (0-87997-715-9) DAW Bks., Inc.

—Slave Girl of Gor. 1977. (Gor Ser.). mass mkt. 1.95 o.p. (0-87997-285-8); mass mkt. 2.25 o.p. (0-87997-474-5); mass mkt. 3.95 o.p. (0-88677-027-0); mass mkt. 4.95 o.p. (0-88677-370-9); mass mkt. 2.95 o.p. (0-87997-679-9); mass mkt. 3.50 o.p. (0-87997-904-6) DAW Bks., Inc.

—Tansman of Gor. 1981. (Gor Ser.: No. 1). mass mkt. 2.75 o.s.i (0-345-30284-2) Ballantine Bks.

—Tansman of Gor. 1997. (Gor Ser.: No. 1). mass mkt. 6.95 (1-56333-486-0, Masquerade SF) Masquerade Bks., Inc.

—Tarnsmen of Gor. E-Book 6.99 (1-58586-224-X) ereads.com.

—Tribesmen of Gor. 1976. (Gor Ser.). mass mkt. 1.50 o.p. (0-87997-223-8); mass mkt. 1.75 o.p. (0-87997-296-3); mass mkt. 1.95 o.p. (0-87997-370-6); mass mkt. 2.25 o.p. (0-87997-473-7); mass mkt. 2.95 o.p. (0-87997-720-5); mass mkt. 3.50 o.p. (0-87997-893-7) DAW Bks., Inc.

—Tribesmen of Gor. annuals 1998. (Gor Ser.: No. 10). mass mkt. 6.95 (1-56333-677-4, Masquerade SF) Masquerade Bks., Inc.

—Vagabonds of Gor. 1987. (Gor Ser.: No. 24). mass mkt. 3.95 o.p. (0-88677-188-9) DAW Bks., Inc.

## GORMENGHAST CASTLE (IMAGINARY PLACE)—FICTION

Peake, Mervyn. Gormenghast. 1978. mass mkt. 2.50 o.s.i (0-345-27699-X); 1973. mass mkt. 1.25 o.s.i (0-345-23519-3); 1970. mass mkt. 0.95 o.s.i (0-345-21118-9) Ballantine Bks.

—Gormenghast. 2000. 24.95 (1-58567-082-0); 1982. (Gormenghast Trilogy: Vol. II). (Illus.). 524p. 30.00 (0-87951-144-3) Overlook Pr., The.

—The Gormenghast Novels: Titus Groan, Gormenghast, Titus Alone. 2000. 1168p. 28.95 (0-87951-628-3) Overlook Pr., The.

—The Gormenghast Trilogy. 1991. (Gormenghast Trilogy: Vol. II). (Illus.). 264p. pap. 16.95 (0-87951-426-4); 1988. 1032p. 40.00 (0-87951-974-6); Vol. III. 1991. (Illus.). 262p. pap. 16.95 (0-87951-427-2) Overlook Pr., The.

—Titus Alone. 1978. mass mkt. 2.50 o.s.i (0-345-28193-4); 1977. mass mkt. 1.95 o.s.i (0-345-25791-X); 1974. mass mkt. 1.50 o.s.i (0-345-24323-4); 1973. mass mkt. 1.25 o.s.i (0-345-23520-7); 1970. mass mkt. 0.95 o.s.i (0-345-21119-7) Ballantine Bks.

—Titus Alone. 1982. (Gormenghast Trilogy: Vol. III). (Illus.). 264p. 30.00 (0-87951-145-1) Overlook Pr., The.

—Titus Groan. 1977. mass mkt. 2.25 o.s.i (0-345-27096-7); 1973. mass mkt. 1.25 o.s.i (0-345-23518-5) Ballantine Bks.

—Titus Groan. (Gormenghast Trilogy: Vol. I). (Illus.). 1991. 408p. pap. 16.95 (0-87951-425-6); 1982. 512p. 30.00 (0-87951-143-5) Overlook Pr., The.

## GRAISTAN (ENGLAND: IMAGINARY PLACE)—FICTION

Domning, Denise. Autumn's Flame. 1995. 384p. mass mkt. 5.50 o.s.i (0-451-40612-5, Topaz) NAL.

—A Love for All Seasons. 1996. 368p. mass mkt. 5.99 o.s.i (0-451-40704-0, Onyx) NAL.

—Spring's Fury. 1995. 384p. (Orig.). mass mkt. 4.99 o.s.i (0-451-40521-8, Topaz) NAL.

—Summer's Storm. 1994. 384p. (Orig.). mass mkt. 4.99 o.s.i (0-451-40507-2, Topaz) NAL.

—Summer's Storm. 2000. 376p. (Orig.). pap. 17.95 (0-595-08876-7) iUniverse, Inc.

—Winter's Heat. 1994. 384p. (Orig.). mass mkt. 4.99 o.s.i (0-451-40438-6, Topaz) NAL.

## GREAT BRITAIN—FICTION

Abbey, Margaret. The Flight of the Kestrel. 1978. pap. 1.75 o.p. (0-345-25424-4) Ballantine Bks.

—The Son of York. l.t. ed. 1995. (Large Print Romance Ser.). 248p. pap. 17.95 o.p. (0-8161-7498-9, Macmillan Reference USA) Gale Group.

—The Warwick Heiress. l.t. ed. 1995. (Nightingale Ser.). 269p. pap. 16.95 (0-8161-7497-0, Macmillan Reference USA) Gale Group.

Ackerley, Joe R. We Think the World of You. 1981. 190p. pap. 5.95 o.p. (*0-916870-36-7*) Creative Arts Bk. Co.
—We Think the World of You. 2000. (New York Review Books Classics Ser.). 211p. pap. 12.95 (*0-940322-26-9*) New York Review of Bks., Inc., The.
—We Think the World of You. 1988. pap. 12.95 o.p. (*0-14-011554-4*) Penguin Group (USA) Inc.
—We Think the World of You. 1989. pap. 7.95 o.s.i (*0-671-67811-6*, Simon & Schuster) Simon & Schuster.
Adams, Bronte & Tate, Trudi, eds. That Kind of Woman. 1993. 304p. pap. 10.95 o.p. (*0-88184-963-4*, Carroll & Graf Pubs.) Avalon Publishing Group.
—That Kind of Woman. 1997. o.s.i (*1-85381-196-3*) Virago Pr., Ltd. GBR. *Dist:* Little Brown & Co.
Airth, Rennie. River of Darkness: A Novel of Suspense in the Shadow of World War I. 1999. 400p. 24.95 o.s.i (*0-670-88595-9*) Viking Penguin.
Aitken, Rosemary. The Granite Cliffs. 2002. 224p. 25.99 (*0-7278-5854-8*) Severn Hse. Pubs., Ltd.
Allbeury, Ted. The Reckoning. l.t. ed. 2000. (Mystery Ser.). 392p. 26.95 (*0-7862-2664-1*); (*0-7540-2356-7*); (*0-7540-1471-1*) Thorndike Pr.
—Shadow of a Doubt. l.t. ed. 1999. (Mystery Ser.). 469p. 26.95 (*0-7862-1906-8*) Thorndike Pr.
Alphin, Elaine Marie. Tournament of Time. 1994. 125p. (Orig.). (J). (gr. 4-6). pap. 3.95 (*0-9643683-0-7*) Bluegrass Bks.
Ambler, Eric. The Intercom Conspiracy. 1986. 256p. pap. 3.95 o.p. (*0-374-51968-4*) Farrar, Straus & Giroux.
—The Intercom Conspiracy. l.t. ed. 1974. (Ulverscroft Large Print Ser.). 351p. 29.99 o.p. (*0-85456-246-X*, Ulverscroft) Thorpe, F. A. Pubs. GBR. *Dist:* Ulverscroft Large Print Bks., Ltd., Ulverscroft Large Print Canada, Ltd.
—Journey into Fear. 1988. 22.95 (*0-8488-0191-1*) Amereon, Ltd.
—Journey into Fear. l.t. ed. 1993. 22.95 o.p. (*0-7927-1451-2*); pap. 20.95 o.p. (*0-7927-1450-4*) BBC Audiobooks America.
—Journey into Fear. 1977. mass mkt. 1.75 o.s.i (*0-345-25913-0*) Ballantine Bks.
—Journey into Fear. 2002. (Vintage Crime/Black Lizard Ser.). 288p. pap. 12.00 (*0-375-72672-1*) Knopf, Alfred A. Inc.
Amis, Martin. The Information. unabr. ed. 1998. audio 88.00 (*0-7366-4163-7*, 4666) Books on Tape, Inc.
—The Information. ltd. ed. 1995. 150.00 o.s.i (*0-517-70155-3*, Harmony) Crown Publishing Group.
—The Information. 1996. 384p. pap. 14.00 (*0-679-73573-9*, Vintage) Knopf Publishing Group.
—The Information. audio o.p. National Humanities Ctr.
—Yellow Dog. 2003. (Illus.). 24.95 (*1-4013-5203-0*) Hyperion Pr.
—Yellow Dog. 2003. 352p. (*0-676-97616-6*) Knopf Canada CAN. *Dist:* Random Hse. of Canada, Ltd., Random Hse., Inc.
Anand, Valerie. Crown of Roses. 1989. 416p. 19.95 o.p. (*0-312-03315-X*) St. Martin's Pr.
—The Disputed Crown. 1982. 320p. 14.95 o.p. (*0-684-17629-7*, Macmillan Reference USA) Gale Group.
—The Faithful Lovers. 1994. (Bridges over Time Ser.: Bk. 4). 384p. 22.95 o.p. (*0-312-10979-2*) St. Martin's Pr.
—King of the Wood. 1989. 18.95 o.p. (*0-312-02939-X*) St. Martin's Pr.
—The Proud Villeins. 1992. 320p. 19.95 o.p. (*0-312-08282-7*) St. Martin's Pr.
—The Ruthless Yeomen. 1993. (Bridges over Time Ser.: Bk. 2). 19.95 o.p. (*0-312-08884-1*) St. Martin's Pr.
—Women of Ashdon. 1993. (Bridges over Time Ser.: Bk. 3). 384p. 21.95 o.p. (*0-312-09417-5*) St. Martin's Pr.
Anthony, Evelyn. Albatross, Set. unabr. ed. 1993. 54.95 incl. audio (*0-7451-5740-8*, CAB 129) BBC Audiobooks America.
—Albatross. 1984. mass mkt. 3.95 o.s.i (*0-515-07644-9*, Jove) Berkley Publishing Group.
—Albatross. l.t. ed. 1997. 24.95 o.p. (*0-7838-8071-5*, Macmillan Reference USA) Gale Group.
—Albatross. 1983. 240p. 14.95 o.p. (*0-399-12773-9*, G. P. Putnam's Sons) Penguin Putnam Bks. for Young Readers.
—Albatross. 1996. 288p. reprint ed. 24.00 o.p. (*0-7278-5135-7*) Severn Hse. Pubs., Ltd.
—Albatross. l.t. ed. 1983. 452p. reprint ed. 16.95 o.p. (*0-89621-484-2*) Thorndike Pr.
—Bloodstones. 1996. 384p. mass mkt. 7.99 o.p. (*0-552-14241-7*); 1995. 352p. o.s.i (*0-593-03656-5*, Corgi) Bantam Bks.
—Bloodstones. 1995. 288p. 23.00 o.p. (*0-06-017221-5*) HarperCollins Pubs.
—Bloodstones. 336p. pap. 4.98 o.p. (*0-7651-0378-8*) Smithmark Pubs., Inc.
—The Company of Saints. 1984. 240p. 15.95 o.p. (*0-399-12895-6*, G. P. Putnam's Sons) Penguin Putnam Bks. for Young Readers.
—The Defector. 1982. mass mkt. 3.95 o.p. (*0-451-15186-0*, AE1765); mass mkt. 3.50 o.p. (*0-451-11765-4*); mass mkt. 3.95 o.p. (*0-451-13588-1*) NAL. (Signet Bks.).
—The Defector. 1981. 12.95 o.p. (*0-698-11064-1*) Putnam Publishing Group, The.
—A Place to Hide. 1987. 256p. 17.95 o.p. (*0-399-13207-4*, G. P. Putnam's Sons) Penguin Putnam Bks. for Young Readers.
—Victoria. l.t. ed. 1994. pap. 20.95 o.p. (*0-7927-1606-X*); 1993. 22.95 o.p. (*0-7927-1607-8*) BBC Audiobooks America.
—Voices on the Wind. 1985. 288p. 16.95 o.p. (*0-399-13067-5*, G. P. Putnam's Sons) Penguin Putnam Bks. for Young Readers.
Archer, Geoffrey. Skydancer. unabr. ed. 2000. 8p. audio 69.95 (*0-7540-0475-9*, CAB1898) BBC Audiobooks America.
—Skydancer. 1989. mass mkt. 4.95 o.p. (*0-8125-0025-3*, Tor Bks.) Doherty, Tom Assocs., LLC.
—Skydancer. l.t. ed. 1999. (Mystery Ser.). 424p. 26.95 (*0-7862-2226-3*); (*0-7540-1377-4*); (*0-7540-2282-X*) Thorndike Pr.
Austen, Jane. Persuasion. (SPA.). 286p. 9.95 (*84-89691-80-0*, AB11393) A.B. Espanola, Editorial S.L. ESP. *Dist:* Lectorum Pubns., Inc.
—Persuasion. 1977. 2.95 o.p. (*0-460-01894-9*, Dutton) Dutton/Plume.
—Persuasion. 2003. (Barnes & Noble Classics Ser.). 288p. mass mkt. 4.95 (*1-59308-048-4*) Fine Communications.
—Persuasion. 1969. mass mkt. 0.50 o.p. (*0-451-50256-6*); 1969. mass mkt. 0.60 o.p. (*0-451-50455-0*); 1964. mass mkt. 0.95 o.p. (*0-451-50803-3*); 1964. mass mkt. 1.25 o.p. (*0-451-50887-4*); 1964. mass mkt. 1.75 o.p. (*0-451-51273-1*); 1964. mass mkt. 2.25 o.p. (*0-451-51555-2*); 1964. mass mkt. 2.95 o.p. (*0-451-51715-6*) NAL. (Signet Classics).
—Persuasion. abr. ed. 1994. (Classic, Ultimate, Dove Ser.). 19.95 o.p. (*0-7871-0104-4*) NewStar Media, Inc.
—Persuasion. Kinsley, James, ed. 2nd ed. 2004. (Oxford World's Classics Ser.). 304p. pap. 4.95 (*0-19-280263-1*) Oxford Univ. Pr., Inc.
—Persuasion. collector's ed. 2002. (Illus.). im. lthr. 38.85 (*1-931927-38-3*); pap. 19.95 (*1-931927-19-7*); 25.95 (*1-931927-37-5*); pap. 17.95 (*1-931927-39-1*) Polyglot Pr., Inc.
—Persuasion. E-Book 5.00 (*0-7410-0530-1*) SoftBook Pr.
—Persuasion. l.t. ed. 2002. (Perennial Bestsellers Ser.). 386p. 28.95 (*0-7862-4624-3*) Thorndike Pr.
Austen, Jane & Beer, Gillian. Persuasion. 2003. 272p. pap. 6.00 (*0-14-143968-8*, Penguin Classics) Viking Penguin.
Bacon, Jack & Ratigan, Hugh. My Grandfathers' Clock. 2001. (Illus.). 448p. 31.97 (*0-9708319-0-0*) Normandy Hse. Pubs.
Baddock, James. Piccolo. 1992. 252p. 19.95 (*0-8027-1201-0*) Walker & Co.
Badenoch, Lindsay. Crosscurrents. 1989. 20.00 (*1-85063-114-X*, Viking Compass) Viking Penguin.
Balling, L. Christian. Champion. 1988. 324p. 18.95 o.p. (*0-87113-198-6*) Grove/Atlantic, Inc.
Baltuck, Naomi. Keeper of the Crystal Spring. 1999. 448p. pap. 12.95 o.s.i (*0-14-027611-4*) Penguin Group (USA) Inc.
—Keeper of the Crystal Spring. 1998. 448p. 24.95 o.p. (*0-670-87963-0*, Viking) Viking Penguin.
Bantock, Nick. The Golden Mean: In Which the Extraordinary Correspondence of Griffin & Sabine Concludes. 1993. (Illus.). 48p. 17.95 (*0-8118-0298-1*) Chronicle Bks. LLC.
—The Golden Mean: In Which the Extraordinary Correspondence of Griffin & Sabine Concludes. unabr. ed. 1993. (Griffin & Sabine Trilogy). 40p. audio 10.95 (*1-879371-49-9*) Publishing Mills, Inc., The.
—Griffin & Sabine: An Extraordinary Correspondence. (Illus.). 48p. 1991. 19.95 (*0-87701-788-3*); 10th anniv. ltd. ed. 2001. 19.95 o.p. (*0-8118-3200-7*) Chronicle Bks. LLC.
—Griffin & Sabine: An Extraordinary Correspondence. 1991. audio 10.95 (*1-879371-42-1*, 30000) Publishing Mills, Inc., The.
—The Griffin & Sabine Trilogy, 3 bks. 1994. (Illus.). 49.95 (*0-8118-0696-0*) Chronicle Bks. LLC.
—Sabine's Notebook: In Which the Extraordinary Correspondence of Griffin & Sabine Continues. 1992. (Illus.). 48p. 17.95 (*0-8118-0180-2*) Chronicle Bks. LLC.
—Sabine's Notebook: In Which the Extraordinary Correspondence of Griffin & Sabine Continues. 1992. audio 10.95 (*1-879371-41-3*, 30010) Publishing Mills, Inc., The.
Banville, John. The Untouchable. 1998. 384p. pap. 13.00 (*0-679-76747-9*, Vintage) Knopf Publishing Group.
—The Untouchable. 1997. 368p. 25.00 o.s.i (*0-679-45108-0*) Knopf, Alfred A. Inc.
Barker, Pat. The Eye in the Door, Vol. 2. unabr. ed. 2001. audio 59.95 (*0-7451-2765-7*, SAB 129) Chivers Audio Bks. GBR. *Dist:* BBC Audiobooks America.
—The Eye in the Door. 288p. 1995. pap. 14.00 (*0-452-27272-6*, Abrahams, William Bks.); 1994. 20.95 o.p. (*0-525-93808-7*, Dutton) Dutton/Plume.
—The Eye in the Door. l.t. ed. 1996. 25.95 o.p. (*1-56895-350-X*, Wheeler Publishing, Inc.) Gale Group.
—The Ghost Road. 1995. 256p. 21.95 o.p. (*0-525-94191-6*, Abrahams, William Bks.) Dutton/Plume.
—The Ghost Road. 1996. o.p. (*0-452-15520-7*) NAL.
—Ghost Road. 1996. 288p. pap. 14.00 (*0-452-27672-1*, Plume) Dutton/Plume.
—The Ghost Road, Vol. 3. unabr. ed. 2001. audio 59.95 (*0-7451-2766-5*, SAB 130) Chivers Audio Bks. GBR. *Dist:* BBC Audiobooks America.
—The Ghost Road, Vol. 3. l.t. ed. 1996. 26.95 (*1-56895-380-1*, Wheeler Publishing, Inc.) Gale Group.
—The Ghost Road. unabr. ed. 1996. audio 51.00 (*0-7887-0583-0*, 94761E7) Recorded Bks., LLC.
—Regeneration, Vol. 1. unabr. ed. 2001. audio 59.95 (*0-7451-2758-4*, SAB 124) Chivers Audio Bks. GBR. *Dist:* BBC Audiobooks America.
—Regeneration. (William Abrahams Book Ser.). 256p. 1993. pap. 14.00 (*0-452-27007-3*); 1992. 20.00 o.p. (*0-525-93427-8*) Dutton/Plume. (Abrahams, William Bks.).
—Regeneration. l.t. ed. 1996. 26.95 (*1-56895-320-8*, Wheeler Publishing, Inc.) Gale Group.
—Regeneration. unabr. ed. 1996. audio 60.00 (*0-7887-0658-6*, 94835E7) Recorded Bks., LLC.
Barlow, Jane. Maureen's Fairing. 1977. (Short Story Index Reprint Ser.). (Illus.). reprint ed. 23.95 (*0-8369-4169-1*) Ayer Co. Pubs., Inc.
Barnacle, Hugo. Day One. 2000. 288p. 12.95 (*0-7043-8114-1*) Quartet Bks., Ltd. GBR. *Dist:* Interlink Publishing Group, Inc.
Barnacle, Hugo, contrib. by. Day One. 1998. (*0-7043-8085-4*) Quartet Bks., Ltd. GBR. *Dist:* Interlink Publishing Group, Inc.
Barnes, Margaret C. Brief Gaudy Hour. l.t. ed. 1973. (Shadows of the Crown Ser.). 689p. 12.00 o.p. (*0-85456-632-5*, Ulverscroft) Thorpe, F. A. Pubs. GBR. *Dist:* Ulverscroft Large Print Bks., Ltd., Ulverscroft Large Print Canada, Ltd.
—Brief Gaudy Hour: A Novel of Anne Boleyn. 25.95 (*0-8488-0423-6*) Amereon, Ltd.
Barnett, Jill. Wonderful. l.t. ed. 2001. (Wheeler Large Print Book Ser.). 389p. 28.95 (*1-58724-102-1*, Wheeler Publishing, Inc.) Gale Group.
—Wonderful. 1997. 352p. pap. 6.99 (*0-671-00412-3*, Pocket) Simon & Schuster.
Barr, Amelia E. The Lion's Whelp. 2000. 252p. E-Book 9.95 (*0-594-01859-5*) 1873 Pr.
Barrie, J. M. Holiday in Bed, & Other Sketches: With a Short Biographical Sketch of the Author. 1977. (Short Story Index Reprint Ser.). reprint ed. 18.95 (*0-8369-3909-3*) Ayer Co. Pubs., Inc.
Bates, H. E. Day's End & Other Stories. 1971. reprint ed. 39.00 (*0-403-00504-3*) Scholarly Pr., Inc.
Bayer, Valerie T. Forbidden Objects. 1995. 336p. 22.95 (*0-312-10986-5*); 22.95 o.p. (*0-312-11790-6*) St. Martin's Pr.
Becnel, Rexanne. Knight of Rosecliffe. 1999. 336p. mass mkt. 6.50 (*0-312-96905-8*, St. Martin's Paperbacks) St. Martin's Pr.
Bedell, Geraldine. Party Tricks. 1998. 288p. 22.95 o.p. (*0-312-18154-X*, Saint Martin's Minotaur) St. Martin's Pr.
Beer, Eileene, Harrison. The Blood Axe: Story of Viking Kings Knut & Olav. 2001. (Illus.). 191p. pap. 12.95 (*1-888106-56-5*) Agreka Bks., LLC.
Belle, Pamela. The Chains of Fate. 1986. 432p. mass mkt. 3.95 o.p. (*0-425-09218-6*); 1984. pap. 6.95 o.p. (*0-425-07367-X*) Berkley Publishing Group.
—The Chains of Fate. 1991. o.p. (*1-55836-000-X*) Chain Sales Marketing, Inc.
—A Falling Star. 1990. 544p. 22.95 o.p. (*0-312-05084-4*) St. Martin's Pr.
—Herald of Joy. 1990. 22.95 o.p. (*0-312-04327-9*) St. Martin's Pr.
—Treason's Gift. 1993. 24.95 o.p. (*0-312-08913-9*) St. Martin's Pr.
Bennett, Nigel & Elrod, P. N. Keeper of the King. 1997. 384p. 21.00 o.s.i (*0-671-87759-3*, Starline); 2002. 416p. reprint ed. pap. 6.99 (*0-671-87862-X*) Baen Bks.
Benson, E. F. Mapp & Lucia. 1986. pap. o.s.i (*0-552-99084-1*, Corgi) Bantam Bks.
—Mapp & Lucia. 2000. (Humour Classics Ser.). 315p. 14.95 (*1-85375-390-4*) Prion GBR. *Dist:* Trafalgar Square.
Benson, Raymond. Double Shot. l.t. ed. 2000. (Basic Ser.). 427p. 27.95 (*0-7862-2870-9*) Thorndike Pr.
—The Facts of Death. 1999. 304p. reprint ed. mass mkt. 6.99 o.s.i (*0-515-12550-4*, Jove) Berkley Publishing Group.
—The Facts of Death: The New James Bond Adventure. 1998. 288p. 23.95 o.p. (*0-399-14405-6*, G. P. Putnam's Sons) Penguin Group (USA) Inc.
—High Time to Kill. 2000. (James Bond Ser.). 304p. mass mkt. 6.99 o.s.i (*0-515-12833-3*, Jove) Berkley Publishing Group.
—High Time to Kill. 1999. (James Bond Adventure Ser.). 272p. 23.95 o.p. (*0-399-14500-1*, G. P. Putnam's Sons) Penguin Group (USA) Inc.
—High Time to Kill. l.t. ed. 2000. 496p. (*0-7540-1389-8*); (*0-7540-2293-5*); 28.95 (*0-7862-2338-3*) Thorndike Pr.
—Never Dream of Dying. 2002. 320p. reprint ed. mass mkt. 7.50 (*0-515-13307-8*, Jove) Berkley Publishing Group.
—Never Dream of Dying. l.t. ed. 2001. 407p. 28.95 (*0-7838-9624-7*, Hall, G. K. & Co.) Gale Group.
—Never Dream of Dying. 2001. 272p. 23.95 o.p. (*0-399-14746-2*) Penguin Group (USA) Inc.
—Zero Minus Ten. 1997. 288p. 22.95 o.p. (*0-399-14257-6*, G. P. Putnam's Sons) Penguin Group (USA) Inc.
Bermant, Chaim. Dancing Bear. 1985. 256p. 13.95 o.p. (*0-312-18211-2*) St. Martin's Pr.
—The House of Women. 1983. 304p. 12.95 o.p. (*0-312-39306-7*) St. Martin's Pr.
Besant, Walter. For Faith & Freedom. E-Book 3.95 (*0-594-06461-9*) 1873 Pr.
—In Deacon's Orders, & Other Stories. 1977. (Short Story Index Reprint Ser.). 19.95 (*0-8369-3611-6*) Ayer Co. Pubs., Inc.
—The World Went Very Well Then. E-Book 3.95 (*0-594-05558-X*) 1873 Pr.
Billington, Rachel. The Garish Day. 1986. 304p. 17.95 o.p. (*0-688-06167-2*, Morrow, William & Co.) Morrow/Avon.
—The Garish Day. l.t. ed. 1986. (Charnwood Large Print Ser.). 560p. 29.99 o.p. (*0-7089-8361-8*, Ulverscroft) Thorpe, F. A. Pubs. GBR. *Dist:* Ulverscroft Large Print Bks., Ltd., Ulverscroft Large Print Canada, Ltd.
Binding, Tim. Lying with the Enemy. 1999. 360p. 24.00 (*0-7867-0657-0*); 2000. 368p. reprint ed. pap. 12.95 (*0-7867-0809-3*) Avalon Publishing Group. (Carroll & Graf Pubs.).
Birkhead, Margaret. Trust & Treason. 1990. 19.95 (*0-312-05525-0*) St. Martin's Pr.
Blackwell, Lawana. The Widow of Larkspur Inn. 1998. (Gresham Chronicles Ser.: Vol. 1). 432p. pap. 12.99 (*1-55661-947-2*) Bethany Hse. Pubs.
Blackwood, Gary L. The Lion & the Unicorn. 1983. 291p. (Orig.). pap. 6.95 (*0-910971-00-5*) Eagle Bks.
Blythe, Ronald. The Visitors: The Stories of Ronald Blythe. 1985. (Helen & Kurt Wolff Bk.). 256p. 16.95 (*0-15-193912-8*) Harcourt Trade Pubs.
Bolen, Cheryl. With His Ring. 2002. 32p. mass mkt. 5.99 o.s.i (*0-8217-7248-1*) Kensington Publishing Corp.
Bolitho, Janie. Exposure of Evil. l.t. ed. 1999. (Magna Large Print Ser.). 384p. o.p. (*0-7505-1430-2*) Magna Large Print Bks. GBR. *Dist:* Ulverscroft Large Print Canada, Ltd.
Boucheron, Rose. Inverness Square. l.t. ed. 2002. (Magna Large Print Ser.). 320p. 32.50 (*0-7505-1779-4*) Magna Large Print Bks. GBR. *Dist:* Ulverscroft Large Print Bks., Ltd., Ulverscroft Large Print Canada, Ltd.
Bowen, Elizabeth. Eva Trout. 2003. 320p. pap. 13.00 (*0-385-72131-5*) Doubleday Canada, Ltd. CAN. *Dist:* Random Hse., Inc.
—Eva Trout. 1987. 272p. pap. 6.95 o.p. (*0-14-008542-4*, Penguin Bks.) Viking Penguin.
—Eva Trout or Changing Scenes. 1991. (Penguin Twentieth-Century Classics Ser.). 272p. pap. 10.95 o.p. (*0-14-018298-5*, Penguin Classics) Viking Penguin.
Bowen, Marjorie. For God & the King. 1995. (William & Mary Trilogy Ser.: Vol. 3). (Illus.). 351p. (Orig.). pap. 15.90 (*0-921100-44-2*) Inheritance Pubns.
—The Governor of England: A Novel on Oliver Cromwell. 2000. 252p. E-Book 3.95 (*0-594-01887-0*) 1873 Pr.
—I Will Maintain. 2000. 252p. pap. 9.95 (*0-594-00636-8*); E-Book 3.95 (*0-594-01888-9*) 1873 Pr.
—I Will Maintain. 1993. (William & Mary Trilogy Ser.: Vol. 1). 383p. pap. 15.90 (*0-921100-42-6*) Inheritance Pubns.
Boyd, William. Armadillo: A Novel. 2000. 352p. pap. 14.00 (*0-375-70216-4*) Knopf, Alfred A. Inc.
Bradbury, Malcolm. Cuts. 1987. (Harper Short Novel Ser.). (Illus.). 96p. 10.95 o.p. (*0-06-015845-X*) HarperTrade.
Bradley, Marion Zimmer. The Forest House. unabr. ed. 1994. audio 105.25 o.p. (*1-56100-186-4*, 1200, Unabridged Library Editions); audio 27.95 o.p. (*1-56100-560-6*, 112, Bookcassette);Set. audio 16.95 o.p. (*1-56100-367-0*, 1308, Nova Audio Bks.) Brilliance Audio.
—The Forest House. abr. ed. 2000. audio 7.95 (*1-57815-009-4*, 1062, Media Bks. Audio Publishing) Media Bks., L. L. C.
—The Forest House. 1995. 432p. pap. 15.95 (*0-451-45424-3*, ROC) NAL.

—The Forest House. 1994. 432p. 21.95 o.p. (*0-670-84454-3*, Viking) Viking Penguin.
—Lady of Avalon. 1998. 480p. pap. 15.95 (*0-451-45652-1*, ROC) NAL.
—Lady of Avalon. unabr. ed. 1998. audio 97.00 (*0-7887-2039-2*, 95403E7) Recorded Bks., LLC.
—Lady of Avalon. 1997. 480p. 24.95 o.s.i (*0-670-85783-1*); 4p. pap. 23.95 o.s.i incl. audio (*0-14-086608-6*, Penguin AudioBooks) Viking Penguin.
—Priestess of Avalon. 2002. 416p. pap. 15.95 (*0-451-45862-1*); 2001. pap. (*0-451-45735-8*); 2001. 448p. pap. 7.99 (*0-451-45853-2*) NAL. (ROC).
Bradley, Marion Zimmer & Paxson, Diana L. Priestess of Avalon. l.t. ed. 2001. 682p. 27.95 (*0-7862-3653-1*) Thorndike Pr.
—Priestess of Avalon. 2001. (Illus.). 480p. 25.95 o.s.i (*0-670-91023-6*, Viking) Viking Penguin.
Bradshaw, Gillian. Hawk of May. 1992. 336p. mass mkt. 4.99 o.s.i (*0-553-29922-0*, Spectra) Bantam Bks.
—Hawk of May. 1981. mass mkt. 2.75 o.p. (*0-451-09765-3*, E9765, Signet Bks.) NAL.
—Hawk of May. 1980. 10.95 o.p. (*0-671-25093-0*, Simon & Schuster) Simon & Schuster.
—Island of Ghosts. 1998. 319p. 22.95 o.p. (*0-312-86439-6*, Forge Bks.) Doherty, Tom Assocs., LLC.
—Island of Ghosts. 1999. 22.95 (*0-312-87075-2*) St. Martin's Pr.
—The Island of Ghosts. 1999. 384p. mass mkt. 5.99 (*0-8125-4514-1*, Tor Bks.) Doherty, Tom Assocs., LLC.
Brandewyne, Rebecca. Rose of Rapture. 1991. (Orig.). reprint ed. pap. 22.95 o.p. (*0-7278-4244-7*) Severn Hse. Pubs., Ltd.
—Rose of Rapture. 1988. 480p. (Orig.). mass mkt. 5.95 o.s.i (*0-446-35652-2*) Warner Bks., Inc.
Brandis, Marianne. Elizabeth, Duchess of Somerset. 1989. 376p. pap. (*0-88984-093-8*);Vol. II. pap. (*0-88984-095-4*) Porcupine's Quill, Inc.
Brenner, Joseph Hayyim. Out of the Depths. 1992. 101p. (C). pap. 16.00 o.p. (*0-8133-1427-5*); text 21.95 (*0-8133-8446-X*) Westview Pr.
British Parliamentary Papers: The Great Famine Volumes, Vol. 8. 1996. 496p. 107.00 (*0-7165-1117-7*) Irish Academic Pr. IRL. *Dist:* International Specialized Bk. Services.
Bronte, Charlotte, et al. Bronte Set. l.t. ed. 1997. (Charnwood Large Print Ser.). 54.00 (*0-7089-8964-0*, Linford) Thorpe, F. A. Pubs. GBR. *Dist:* Ulverscroft Large Print Bks., Ltd., Ulverscroft Large Print Canada, Ltd.
Brooks, Geraldine. Year of Wonders: A Novel of the Plague. l.t. ed. 2001. (Illus.). 403p. 30.95 (*0-7838-9682-4*) Thorndike Pr.
—Year of Wonders: A Novel of the Plague. 2001. (Illus.). 400p. 24.95 o.s.i (*0-670-91021-X*, Viking); 2002. 320p. reprint ed. pap. 14.00 (*0-14-200143-0*) Viking Penguin.
Brownjohn, Alan, contrib. by. The Long Shadows. 1997. 382p. (*1-899235-21-3*) Lewis, Dewi Publishing GBR. *Dist:* Distributed Art Pubs./D.A.P.
Brust, Steven & Bull, Emma. Freedom & Necessity. 1997. 589p. pap. 6.99 (*0-8125-6261-5*); 448p. 25.95 (*0-312-85974-0*) Doherty, Tom Assocs., LLC. (Tor Bks.).
Bryers, Paul. Coming First. 1988. 252p. pap. 7.95 o.p. (*0-87113-224-9*) Grove/Atlantic, Inc.
Buchan, James. High Latitudes: A Romance. 1997. 192p. pap. text 13.95 o.p. (*1-56924-734-X*, Marlowe & Co.) Avalon Publishing Group.
—High Latitudes: A Romance. 1996. 192p. 22.00 o.p. (*0-374-16999-3*) Farrar, Straus & Giroux.
Buchan, John. Greenmantle. lib. bdg. 20.95 (*0-8488-0925-4*) Amereon, Ltd.
—Greenmantle. unabr. ed. 1997. audio 69.95 (*0-7451-5813-7*, CAB 229) BBC Audiobooks America.
—Greenmantle. unabr. ed. 1996. audio 49.95 (*0-7861-1015-5*, 1793) Blackstone Audio Bks., Inc.
—Greenmantle. 1999. E-Book 2.49 (*1-58627-246-2*) Electric Umbrella Publishing.
—Greenmantle. 1986. pap. 9.95 o.p. (*0-87923-598-5*); 1988. 345p. reprint ed. 19.95 o.p. (*0-933852-84-3*) Godine, David R. Pub.
—Greenmantle. 2002. 244p. 24.99 (*1-4043-0500-9*); per. 20.99 (*1-4043-0501-7*) IndyPublish.com.
—Greenmantle. Macdonald, Kate, ed. (Oxford World's Classics Ser.). 320p. 1999. pap. 9.95 (*0-19-283684-6*); 1994. pap. 8.95 o.p. (*0-19-282953-X*) Oxford Univ. Pr., Inc.
—Greenmantle. 1992. (Classic Crime Ser.). (Illus.). 272p. pap. 5.95 o.p. (*0-14-001132-3*, Penguin Bks.) Penguin Group (USA) Inc.
—Greenmantle. (Ebook Classic Ser.). E-Book 5.00 (*0-7410-0825-4*) SoftBook Pr.
—Greenmantle. 1998. (Classics Library). 225p. pap. 3.95 (*1-85326-204-8*, 2048WW) Wordsworth Editions, Ltd. GBR. *Dist:* Casemate Pubs. & Bk. Distributors, LLC.
—Mr. Standfast. 19.95 (*0-8488-0927-0*) Amereon, Ltd.
—Mr. Standfast. 1994. (Oxford World's Classics Ser.). 384p. pap. 11.95 o.p. (*0-19-283116-X*) Oxford Univ. Pr., Inc.
—Mr. Standfast. 1928. 374p. reprint ed. 69.00 (*0-403-00879-4*) Scholarly Pr., Inc.
—Mr. Standfast. 1998. (Classics Library). 400p. pap. 3.95 (*1-85326-225-0*, 2250WW) Wordsworth Editions, Ltd. GBR. *Dist:* Casemate Pubs. & Bk. Distributors, LLC.
—The Thirty-Nine Steps. Date not set. (Nelson Readers Ser.). (J). pap. text (*0-17-557053-1*) Addison-Wesley Longman, Inc.
—The Thirty-Nine Steps. 1967. pap. text 61.25 (*0-582-53752-5*) Addison-Wesley Longman, Ltd. GBR. *Dist:* Trans-Atlantic Pubns., Inc.
—The Thirty-Nine Steps. 1976. reprint ed. lib. bdg. 19.95 (*0-89190-243-0*, Rivercity Pr.) Amereon, Ltd.
—The Thirty-Nine Steps. 1915. E-Book (*1-58734-003-8*) Bartleby.com.
—The Thirty-Nine Steps. 1990. reprint ed. lib. bdg. 13.95 (*0-89968-487-4*) Buccaneer Bks., Inc.
—The Thirty-Nine Steps. unabr. ed. 1994. (Illus.). 96p. pap. text 1.50 (*0-486-28201-5*) Dover Pubns., Inc.
—The Thirty-Nine Steps. E-Book 2.49 (*1-58627-240-3*) Electric Umbrella Publishing.
—The Thirty-Nine Steps. 1991. 160p. reprint ed. pap. 6.95 o.s.i (*0-87923-838-0*) Godine, David R. Pub.
—The Thirty-Nine Steps. 1995. (Fiction Ser.). (YA). pap. text 7.88 o.p. (*0-582-08467-9*, 79834) Longman Publishing Group.
—The Thirty-Nine Steps. Harvie, Christopher, ed. 1999. (Oxford World's Classics Ser.). 160p. pap. 8.95 (*0-19-283931-4*) Oxford Univ. Pr., Inc.
—The Thirty-Nine Steps. Hedge, Tricia, ed. 1995. (Illus.). 80p. pap. text 5.95 o.p. (*0-19-421677-2*) Oxford Univ. Pr., Inc.
—The Thirty-Nine Steps. 1994. (Oxford World's Classics Ser.). 150p. pap. 8.95 o.p. (*0-19-282991-2*) Oxford Univ. Pr., Inc.
—The Thirty-Nine Steps, Level 4. Hedge, Tricia, ed. 2000. (Bookworms Ser.). (Illus.). 96p. (J). pap. text 5.95 (*0-19-423048-1*) Oxford Univ. Pr., Inc.
—The Thirty-Nine Steps. 1993. (Pocket Classics Ser.). pap. 4.95 (*0-7509-0482-8*) Sutton Publishing, Ltd. GBR. *Dist:* International Publishers Marketing.
—The Thirty-Nine Steps. l.t. ed. 1998. 132p. text 27.95 (*1-56000-497-5*) Transaction Pubs.
—The Thirty-Nine Steps. 1991. (World's Classics Ser.). 132p. 6.95 (*0-14-001130-7*) Viking Penguin.
—The Thirty-Nine Steps. 1998. (Classics Library). 100p. pap. 3.95 (*1-85326-080-0*, 0800WW) Wordsworth Editions, Ltd. GBR. *Dist:* Casemate Pubs. & Bk. Distributors, LLC.
Buckley, Fiona. The Fugitive Queen: An Ursula Blanchard Mystery at Queen Elizabeth I's Court. 2003. 288p. 24.00 (*0-7432-3751-X*, Scribner) Simon & Schuster.
—Queen's Ransom. 2003. 336p. reprint ed. mass mkt. 6.99 (*0-671-03293-3*, Pocket) Simon & Schuster.
—Queen's Ransom: A Mystery at Queen Elizabeth I's Court Featuring Ursula Blanchard. 2000. E-Book 23.00 (*0-7432-1362-9*); 352p. 23.00 o.s.i (*0-684-86267-0*) Simon & Schuster. (Scribner).
—To Ruin a Queen: An Ursula Blanchard Mystery at Queen Elizabeth I's Court. 2000. E-Book 23.00 (*0-7432-1365-3*); (Illus.). 288p. 23.00 o.s.i (*0-684-86268-9*) Simon & Schuster. (Scribner).
Buckley, Roger N. Congo Jack: A Novel. 1997. 312p. 22.95 (*0-9632476-5-4*) Pinto Pr.
Burgess, Anthony. Nothing Like the Sun: A Story of Shakespeare's Love-Life. 1996. 240p. pap. 12.00 (*0-393-31507-X*) Norton, W. W. & Co., Inc.
Burton, Hester. Beyond the Weir Bridge. 1970. (Illus.). (J). (gr. 6 up). 4.95 o.p. (*0-690-14052-5*) HarperCollins Children's Bk. Group.
Bushnell, O. A. The Return of Lono: A Novel of Captain Cook's Last Voyage. 1979. (Pacific Classics Ser.: Vol. 1). 300p. reprint ed. pap. 14.95 (*0-87022-931-1*) Univ. of Hawaii Pr.
Caggiano, Phyllis. Love's Fragile Flame. 1984. 144p. (Orig.). pap. 4.99 o.p. (*0-87123-582-X*) Bethany Hse. Pubs.
Caldecott, Moyra. Etheldreda. E-Book (*1-899142-53-3*) Mushroom Publishing.
—Etheldreda. 1988. 224p. pap. 7.95 o.p. (*0-14-019021-X*, Penguin Bks.) Viking Penguin.
Canning, Victor. Raven's Wind. 1983. 192p. 11.95 o.p. (*0-688-02133-6*, Morrow, William & Co.) Morrow/Avon.
Carr, Philippa. The Changeling. l.t. ed. 1990. (General Ser.). 552p. 21.95 o.p. (*0-8161-4894-5*, Macmillan Reference USA) Gale Group.
—The Changeling. 1989. 368p. 19.95 o.p. (*0-399-13419-0*, G. P. Putnam's Sons) Penguin Putnam Bks. for Young Readers.
Carr, Robyn. The Everlasting Covenant. 1987. 17.95 o.p. (*0-316-12979-8*) Little Brown & Co.
Cartland, Barbara. Barbara Cartland's Etiquette for Love & Romance. l.t. ed. 1986. lib. bdg. 13.95 o.p. (*0-7451-0282-4*, Macmillan Reference USA) Gale Group.
—Five Complete Novels of Dukes & Their Ladies. 1995. (Wings Bestsellers Ser.). 672p. 13.99 o.s.i (*0-517-14679-7*) Random Hse., Inc.
—Three Complete Novels of Dukes & Their Ladies: Never Laugh at Love, The Disgraceful Duke, A Touch of Love. 1996. 448p. 7.99 o.s.i (*0-517-15046-8*) Random Hse. Value Publishing.
—Three Complete Novels of Earls & Their Ladies. 1996. 432p. 7.99 o.s.i (*0-517-14772-6*) Crown Publishing Group.
—Three Complete Novels of Royalty & Romance. 1995. 432p. 7.99 o.s.i (*0-517-14678-9*) Crown Publishing Group.
Cary, Joyce. Not Honour More. 1976. 24.95 (*0-88411-312-4*, Queens Hse., Inc.) Amereon, Ltd.
—Not Honour More. 1985. (Classics Ser.: ). 320p. reprint ed. pap. 7.95 (*0-8112-0966-0*, NDP608) New Directions Publishing Corp.
—Spring Song & Other Stories. 1970. 285p. 19.95 (*0-8369-3448-2*) Ayer Co. Pubs., Inc.
Caskoden, Edwin. When Knighthood Was in Flower: or The Love Story of Charles & Mary Tudor the King's Sister & Happening in the Reign of His August Majesty, King Henry VIII. 1972. (Illus.). 310p. reprint ed. 39.00 o.p. (*0-403-01088-8*) Scholarly Pr., Inc.
Castle, Linda Lea. Surrender the Stars. 2002. 32p. mass mkt. 5.99 o.s.i (*0-8217-7267-8*) Kensington Publishing Corp.
Cecil, Henry. According to the Evidence. 1988. 160p. pap. 7.95 (*0-89733-295-4*) Academy Chicago Pubs., Ltd.
—According to the Evidence. 1996. 200p. reprint ed. 60.00 (*1-56169-294-8*) Gaunt, Inc.
—Alibi for a Judge. 1997. (Henry Cecil Reprint Ser.). 206p. reprint ed. 61.00 (*1-56169-285-9*) Gaunt, Inc.
—The Asking Price. 1990. (Academy Book Ser.). 143p. reprint ed. pap. 7.95 (*0-89733-355-1*) Academy Chicago Pubs., Ltd.
—The Asking Price. 1996. (Henry Cecil Reprint Ser.). 190p. reprint ed. 60.00 (*1-56169-297-2*) Gaunt, Inc.
—Brief Tales from the Bench: Eight Courtroom Vignettes. 1997. (Henry Cecil Reprint Ser.). 180p. reprint ed. 54.00 (*1-56169-286-7*) Gaunt, Inc.
—Brothers in Law. 1997. (Henry Cecil Reprint Ser.). 192p. reprint ed. 57.00 (*1-56169-292-1*) Gaunt, Inc.
—Brothers in Law. 2000. 249p. pap. 11.50 (*1-84232-046-7*) House of Stratus, Inc.
—The Buttercup Spell. 1997. (Henry Cecil Reprint Ser.). 164p. reprint ed. 48.00 (*1-56169-267-0*) Gaunt, Inc.
—The Buttercup Spell. 2000. 162p. pap. 11.50 (*1-84232-047-5*) House of Stratus, Inc.
—Cross Purposes. 1997. (Henry Cecil Reprint Ser.). 186p. reprint ed. 55.00 (*1-56169-272-7*) Gaunt, Inc.
—Cross Purposes. 2000. 199p. pap. 11.50 (*1-84232-045-9*) House of Stratus, Inc.
—Cross Purposes. 1976. 186 p. 3.75 (*0-7181-1442-6*, Joseph, Michael) Viking Penguin.
—Daughters in Law. 1997. (Henry Cecil Reprint Ser.). 206p. reprint ed. 61.00 (*1-56169-273-5*) Gaunt, Inc.
—Daughters in Law. 2000. 213p. pap. 11.50 (*1-84232-049-1*) House of Stratus, Inc.
—Daughters in Law. 1991. 187p. pap. 8.95 o.p. (*1-55882-105-8*) International Polygonics, Ltd.
—The English Judge. 1997. (Henry Cecil Reprint Ser.). 190p. reprint ed. 57.00 (*1-56169-258-1*) Gaunt, Inc.
—Friends at Court. 1997. (Henry Cecil Reprint Ser.). 208p. reprint ed. 62.00 (*1-56169-290-5*) Gaunt, Inc.
—Friends at Court. 2000. 224p. pap. 11.50 (*1-84232-053-X*) House of Stratus, Inc.
—Full Circle. 1997. (Henry Cecil Reprint Ser.). 236p. reprint ed. 70.00 (*1-56169-262-X*) Gaunt, Inc.
—Full Circle. 2000. 226p. pap. 11.50 (*1-84232-054-8*) House of Stratus, Inc.
—Hunt the Slipper. 1997. (Henry Cecil Reprint Ser.). 152p. reprint ed. 45.00 (*1-56169-276-X*) Gaunt, Inc.
—Hunt the Slipper. 2000. 149p. pap. 11.50 (*1-84232-055-6*) House of Stratus, Inc.
—Hunt the Slipper. 1977. 151 p. 3.75 (*0-7181-1578-3*, Joseph, Michael) Viking Penguin.
—I Married the Girl. 1997. (Henry Cecil Reprint Ser.). 174p. reprint ed. 52.00 (*1-56169-277-8*) Gaunt, Inc.
—Independent Witness. 1989. 172p. reprint ed. pap. 7.95 (*0-89733-325-X*) Academy Chicago Pubs., Ltd.
—Independent Witness. 1997. (Henry Cecil Reprint Ser.). 190p. reprint ed. 56.00 (*1-56169-274-3*) Gaunt, Inc.
—Independent Witness. 2000. 195p. pap. 11.50 (*1-84232-056-4*) House of Stratus, Inc.
—Much in Evidence. 1997. (Henry Cecil Reprint Ser.). 192p. reprint ed. 57.00 (*1-56169-289-1*) Gaunt, Inc.
—Much in Evidence. 2000. 203p. pap. 11.50 (*1-84232-057-2*) House of Stratus, Inc.
—No Bail for the Judge. 1997. (Henry Cecil Reprint Ser.). 205p. reprint ed. 61.00 (*1-56169-291-3*) Gaunt, Inc.
—No Bail for the Judge. 2000. 193p. pap. 11.50 (*1-84232-059-9*) House of Stratus, Inc.
—No Fear or Favour. 1997. (Henry Cecil Reprint Ser.). 184p. reprint ed. 54.00 (*1-56169-259-X*) Gaunt, Inc.
—No Fear or Favour. 2000. 184p. pap. 11.50 (*1-84232-060-2*) House of Stratus, Inc.
—Not Such an Ass. 1997. (Henry Cecil Reprint Ser.). 208p. reprint ed. 62.00 (*1-56169-260-3*) Gaunt, Inc.
—The Painswick Line. 1997. (Henry Cecil Reprint Ser.). 224p. reprint ed. 66.00 (*1-56169-279-4*) Gaunt, Inc.
—The Painswick Line. 2000. 218p. pap. 11.50 (*1-84232-061-0*) House of Stratus, Inc.
—Portrait of a Judge: And Other Stories. 1997. (Henry Cecil Reprint Ser.). 202p. reprint ed. 60.00 (*1-56169-264-6*) Gaunt, Inc.
—Settled Out of Court. 1997. (Henry Cecil Reprint Ser.). 190p. reprint ed. 57.00 (*1-56169-288-3*) Gaunt, Inc.
—Settled Out of Court. 2000. 198p. pap. 11.50 (*1-84232-063-7*) House of Stratus, Inc.
—Settled Out of Court. 1992. (Library of Crime Classics). 184p. pap. 8.95 (*1-55882-104-X*) International Polygonics, Ltd.
—Sober As a Judge. 1997. (Henry Cecil Reprint Ser.). 206p. reprint ed. 61.00 (*1-56169-263-8*) Gaunt, Inc.
—Sober As a Judge. 2000. 195p. pap. 11.50 (*1-84232-064-5*) House of Stratus, Inc.
—Tell You What I'll Do. 1997. (Henry Cecil Reprint Ser.). 216p. reprint ed. 64.00 (*1-56169-275-1*) Gaunt, Inc.
—Tell You What I'll Do. 2000. 220p. pap. 11.50 (*1-84232-065-3*) House of Stratus, Inc.
—Tell You What I'll Do. 1969. 216 p. (*0-7181-0354-8*, Joseph, Michael) Viking Penguin.
—Tipping the Scales. 1997. (Henry Cecil Reprint Ser.). 272p. reprint ed. 81.00 (*1-56169-265-4*) Gaunt, Inc.
—Truth with Her Boots on. 1974. 191 p. 2.20 (*0-7181-1167-2*, Joseph, Michael) Viking Penguin.
—Truth with Her Boots On. 1997. (Henry Cecil Reprint Ser.). 192p. reprint ed. 57.00 (*1-56169-268-9*) Gaunt, Inc.
—Truth with Her Boots On. 2000. 161p. pap. 11.50 (*1-84232-066-1*) House of Stratus, Inc.
—Unlawful Occasions. 1997. (Henry Cecil Reprint Ser.). 182p. reprint ed. 54.00 (*1-56169-261-1*) Gaunt, Inc.
—Unlawful Occasions. 2000. 186p. pap. 11.50 (*1-84232-067-X*) House of Stratus, Inc.
—The Wanted Man. 1997. (Henry Cecil Reprint Ser.). 189p. reprint ed. 56.00 (*1-56169-271-9*) Gaunt, Inc.
—The Wanted Man. 2000. 163p. pap. 11.50 (*1-84232-068-8*) House of Stratus, Inc.
—The Wanted Man. 1972. 189 p. o.p. (*0-7181-1011-0*, Joseph, Michael) Viking Penguin.
—Ways & Means. 1997. (Henry Cecil Reprint Ser.). 192p. reprint ed. 57.00 (*1-56169-284-0*) Gaunt, Inc.
—Ways & Means. 2000. 188p. pap. 11.50 (*1-84232-069-6*) House of Stratus, Inc.
—A Woman Named Anne. 1993. 261p. reprint ed. pap. 7.95 (*0-89733-338-1*) Academy Chicago Pubs., Ltd.
—A Woman Named Anne. 1997. (Henry Cecil Reprint Ser.). 218p. reprint ed. 66.00 (*1-56169-293-X*) Gaunt, Inc.
—A Woman Named Anne. 2000. 200p. pap. 11.50 (*1-84232-070-X*) House of Stratus, Inc.
Cecil, Henry & BBC Staff. Brief Tales from the Bench: Eight Courtroom Vignettes. 1972. (Inner Sanctum Mystery Ser.). 180 p. o.p. (*0-671-21145-5*) Simon & Schuster.
Chadwick, Elizabeth. The Conquest. 1997. 568p. pap. text o.s.i (*0-7515-1177-3*) Little Brown & Co.
—The Conquest. 1997. 464p. 25.95 (*0-312-15497-6*) St. Martin's Pr.
—Conquest. 1996. 458p. o.s.i (*0-316-91222-0*) Little Brown & Co.
—The Leopard Unleashed. 1993. 336p. 19.95 o.p. (*0-312-09323-3*) St. Martin's Pr.
—Lords of the White Castle. 2002. 614p. 27.95 (*0-312-28827-1*) St. Martin's Pr.
—Shields of Pride. 1994. mass mkt. 4.99 o.s.i (*0-345-38839-9*) Ballantine Bks.
—Shields of Pride. l.t. ed. 1995. 471p. 22.95 (*0-7838-1154-3*, Macmillan Reference USA) Gale Group.
—The Winter Mantle. 2001. 416p. (*0-316-85151-5*) Little Brown & Co.
—The Winter Mantle. 2003. 512p. 27.95 (*0-312-31291-1*) St. Martin's Pr.
Chance, John Newton. The Bad Circle. l.t. ed. 1999. 163p. (*0-7540-3547-6*) BBC Audiobooks America.
Chaplin, Elizabeth. Hostage to Fortune. 1993. 272p. 17.95 (*0-89296-504-5*) Mysterious Pr.

—Hostage to Fortune. l.t. ed. 2001. (Ulverscroft Large Print Ser.). 408p. 32.50 (*0-7089-4427-2*) Ulverscroft Large Print Bks., Ltd.

—Hostage to Fortune. 1994. 256p. mass mkt. 4.99 (*0-446-40306-7*, Mysterious Pr. Paperback Bks.) Warner Bks., Inc.

Chapman, Vera. The Enchantresses. 223p. 1999. mass mkt. 8.95 (*0-575-60325-9*); 1998. 27.00 (*0-575-06524-9*) Gollancz, Victor GBR. *Dist:* Trafalgar Square.

Charles, Paul. The Ballad of Sean & Wilko. 2000. (Inspector Christy Kennedy Mystery Ser.: No. 4). 284p. 31.00 (*1-899344-58-6*); 283p. pap. 15.95 (*1-899344-57-8*) Do-Not Pr., The GBR. *Dist:* Dufour Editions, Inc.

—The Ballad of Sean & Wilko. 2000. 283p. (*1-902602-02-1*) New Island Bks. IRL. *Dist:* Dufour Editions, Inc.

—Last Boat to Camden Town: An Inspector Christy Kennedy Mystery. 1998. (Illus.). 168p. pap. 15.95 (*1-899344-30-6*); 34.95 (*1-899344-29-2*) Do-Not Pr., The GBR. *Dist:* Dufour Editions, Inc.

Chase, Nicholas. Locksley. 1983. 288p. 12.95 o.p. (*0-312-49428-9*) St. Martin's Pr.

Chesney, Marion. Snobbery with Violence: A Mystery. 2003. 224p. 22.95 (*0-312-30451-X*, Saint Martin's Minotaur) St. Martin's Pr.

Childers, Erskine. The Riddle of the Sands. 1976. reprint ed. lib. bdg. 24.95 (*0-89190-240-6*, River-city Pr.) Amereon, Ltd.

—The Riddle of the Sands. unabr. ed. 1997. audio 53.95 (*1-55685-509-5*, 509-5) Audio Bk. Contractors, Inc.

—The Riddle of the Sands. unabr. ed. 1999. audio 34.95 (*1-57270-103-X*, F81103u, Cover to Cover Classics) Audio Partners Publishing Corp.

—The Riddle of the Sands. unabr. ed. 1997. audio 56.95 (*0-7861-1082-1*, 1901) Blackstone Audio Bks., Inc.

—The Riddle of the Sands. unabr. collector's ed. 1981. audio 64.00 (*0-7366-3853-9*, 9049) Books on Tape, Inc.

—The Riddle of the Sands. 1977. (Mariners Library). reprint ed. text 15.00 o.p. (*0-246-11041-4*) Brill Academic Pubs., Inc.

—The Riddle of the Sands. 1990. 310p. reprint ed. lib. bdg. 23.95 (*0-89966-743-0*) Buccaneer Bks., Inc.

—The Riddle of the Sands. (Thrift Editions Ser.). 1999. (Illus.). xv, 229p. pap. text 2.00 (*0-486-40879-5*); 1976. 284p. pap. 5.95 (*0-486-23280-8*) Dover Pubns., Inc.

—The Riddle of the Sands. unabr. ed. 1989. audio 36.00 Jimcin Recordings.

—The Riddle of the Sands. 1977. (Illus.). 12.50 o.p. (*0-679-50772-8*) McKay, David Co., Inc.

—The Riddle of the Sands. Sweetman, Jack, ed. 1991. (Classics of Naval Literature Ser.). 320p. 34.95 (*0-87021-601-5*) Naval Institute Pr.

—The Riddle of the Sands. abr. ed. 1995. audio compact disk 15.98 o.p. (*962-634-055-X*, NA205512, Naxos AudioBooks) Naxos of America, Inc.

—The Riddle of the Sands. 1998. 420p. reprint ed. lib. bdg. 25.00 (*1-58287-008-X*) North Bks.

—The Riddle of the Sands, unabr. ed. 1989. audio 78.00 (*1-55690-442-8*, 89180E7) Recorded Bks., LLC.

—The Riddle of the Sands. (Illus.). 1986. 280p. pap. 14.95 o.p. (*0-246-13039-3*); 1998. 272p. reprint ed. pap. 14.95 (*1-57409-015-1*) Sheridan Hse., Inc.

—The Riddle of the Sands. (Classics Ser.). 336p. 2000. (Illus.). pap. 7.95 (*0-14-118165-6*, Penguin Classics); 1978. pap. 7.95 o.s.i (*0-14-000905-1*, Penguin Bks.) Viking Penguin.

—The Riddle of the Sands. 1998. (Classics Library). pap. 3.95 (*1-85326-038-X*, 038XWW) Wordsworth Editions, Ltd. GBR. *Dist:* Combined Publishing.

—The Riddle of the Sands: A Record of Secret Service. abr. ed. 1995. audio 13.98 o.p. (*962-634-555-1*, NA205514, Naxos AudioBooks) Naxos of America, Inc.

—The Riddle of the Sands: A Record of Secret Service. Trotter, David & Snaith, Anna, eds. 1998. (Oxford World's Classics Ser.). (Illus.). 304p. pap. 14.00 (*0-19-283347-2*) Oxford Univ. Pr., Inc.

—The Riddle of the Sands: A Record of Secret Service. Trotter, David, ed. 1995. (Oxford Popular Fiction Ser.). (Illus.). 290p. pap. 7.95 o.p. (*0-19-282318-3*) Oxford Univ. Pr., Inc.

Childers, Erskine, et al, contrib. by. The Riddle of the Sands. 1998. (Illus.). (*0-85036-476-0*) Merlin Pr. Ltd.

Chisholm, P. F. A Famine of Horses: A Sir Robert Carey Mystery. unabr. ed. 1997. audio 61.95 Eye in the Ear Inc.

—A Famine of Horses: A Sir Robert Carey Mystery. l.t. ed. 1995. (Magna Large Print Ser.). 447p. 29.99 (*0-7505-0838-8*) Magna Large Print Bks. GBR. *Dist:* Ulverscroft Large Print Bks., Ltd., Ulverscroft Large Print Canada, Ltd.

—A Famine of Horses: A Sir Robert Carey Mystery. 2000. (Sir Robert Carey Mysteries Ser.: Vol. 14). 400p. pap. 14.95 (*1-890208-27-2*) Poisoned Pen Pr.

—A Famine of Horses: A Sir Robert Carey Mystery. 1995. 270p. text 20.95 (*0-8027-3252-6*) Walker & Co.

—A Plague of Angels: A Sir Robert Carey Mystery. 2000. 252p. pap. 14.95 (*1-890208-43-4*) Poisoned Pen Pr.

—A Season of Knives: A Sir Robert Carey Mystery. 2000. (Missing Mysteries Ser.: No. 18). 250p. pap. 14.95 (*1-890208-32-9*) Poisoned Pen Pr.

—A Season of Knives: A Sir Robert Carey Mystery. 1996. (Sir Robert Carey Mystery Ser.). 240p. 19.95 (*0-8027-3276-3*) Walker & Co.

—A Surfeit of Guns: A Sir Robert Carey Mystery, Vol. 20. 2000. (Missing Mysteries Ser.: Vol. 20). pap. 14.95 (*1-890208-35-3*) Poisoned Pen Pr.

—A Surfeit of Guns: A Sir Robert Carey Mystery. 1997. (Sir Robert Carey Mysteries Ser.). 233p. 20.95 (*0-8027-3304-2*) Walker & Co.

Cholmondeley, Mary. Romance of His Life, & Other Romances. 1977. (Short Story Index Reprint Ser.). reprint ed. 19.95 (*0-8369-4099-7*) Ayer Co. Pubs., Inc.

Christie, Agatha. The Secret Adversary. 1983. mass mkt. 2.95 o.s.i (*0-553-24035-8*) Bantam Bks.

—The Secret Adversary. E-Book 2.49 (*0-7574-0450-2*) Electric Umbrella Publishing.

—The Secret Adversary. 2002. 264p. pap. 19.95 (*1-59224-846-2*); lib. bdg. 29.95 (*1-59224-847-0*) Wildside Pr.

Clewlow, Carol. Keeping the Faith. 1990. 16.95 o.p. (*0-671-67117-0*, Simon & Schuster) Simon & Schuster.

Clifford, Lucy. Eve's Lover, & Other Stories. 1977. (Short Story Index Reprint Ser.). 19.95 (*0-8369-3615-9*) Ayer Co. Pubs., Inc.

Clowes, W. Laird. The Captain of the "Mary Rose" A Tale of Tomorrow, 8 vols., Vol. 2. 1999. (Sources of Science Fiction: Future War Novels of the 1890s Ser.). (Illus.). 328p. (C). lib. bdg. 150.00 (*0-415-19290-0*) Routledge.

Cockrell, Amanda. The Legions of the Mist. 1979. 12.95 o.p. (*0-689-10989-X*, Atheneum) Simon & Schuster Children's Publishing.

Cocquyt, Kathryn M. The Celtic Heart. Henkel, Pamela, ed. 1971. (Illus.). 592p. pap. 14.95 o.p. (*1-56718-156-2*) Llewellyn Pubns.

Colegate, Isabel. Winter Journey. 2000. 208p. text 23.00 o.p. (*1-58243-122-1*, Counterpoint Pr.) Basic Bks.

Collenette, Eric J. The Gemini Plot. 1986. 192p. 15.95 o.s.i (*0-8027-0930-3*) Walker & Co.

—Ninety Feet to the Sun: A Sea Novel of World War II. 1986. 192p. 15.95 o.s.i (*0-8027-0893-5*) Walker & Co.

Collett, Bill. The Last Mutiny: The Further Adventures of Captain Bligh. 1995. 304p. 23.00 o.p. (*0-393-03877-7*) Norton, W. W. & Co., Inc.

Connolly, Cressida. The Rare & the Beautiful. 2004. 288p. 25.95 (*0-06-621247-2*, Ecco) HarperTrade.

Connor, Alexandra. Midnight's Smiling. unabr. ed. 1999. audio 69.95 (*0-7531-0517-9*, 990309) ISIS Audio Bks. GBR. *Dist:* Ulverscroft Large Print Bks., Ltd.

—Midnight's Smiling. l.t. ed. 1999. (Ulverscroft Large Print Ser.). 400p. 31.99 o.p. (*0-7089-4096-X*, Linford) Thorpe, F. A. Pubs. GBR. *Dist:* Ulverscroft Large Print Bks., Ltd., Ulverscroft Large Print Canada, Ltd.

Conran, Shirley. Crimson. l.t. ed. 1993. 23.95 o.p. (*0-7927-1402-4*); pap. o.p. (*0-7927-1401-6*) BBC Audiobooks America.

—Crimson. 1992. 544p. 23.00 o.p. (*0-671-50149-6*, Simon & Schuster) Simon & Schuster.

—Crimson. Rubenstein, Julie, ed. 1992. 544p. reprint ed. mass mkt. 5.99 (*0-671-79161-3*, Pocket) Simon & Schuster.

—Crimson, Set. abr. ed. 1992. audio 17.00 (*0-671-75959-0*, Simon & Schuster Audioworks) Simon & Schuster Audio.

Conway, Sara. Daughters of Summmer. 2003. (Illus.). 208p. 22.95 (*1-58182-340-1*) Cumberland Hse. Publishing.

Cook, Judith. The Slicing Edge of Death: Who Killed Christopher Marlowe? 1993. 224p. 18.95 o.p. (*0-312-10011-6*, Saint Martin's Minotaur) St. Martin's Pr.

Cookson, Catherine. The Love Child. 1991. 20.00 o.p. (*0-671-72836-9*) Summit Bks.

Cooper, James Fenimore. The Two Admirals. 1842. 504p. (YA). reprint ed. pap. text 34.00 (*1-4047-2388-9*) Classic Textbooks.

—The Two Admirals. 1990. (Works of James Fenimore Cooper). reprint ed. lib. bdg. 79.00 (*0-7812-2388-1*) Reprint Services Corp.

—The Two Admirals: A Tale. 1990. 511p. (C). (gr. 9-12). text 59.50 (*0-88706-905-3*); pap. text 20.95 (*0-88706-907-X*) State Univ. of New York Pr.

—The Wing & Wing. 1998. (Heart of Oak Sea Classics Ser.). 448p. 30.00 o.s.i (*0-8050-5987-3*);No. 4. 412p. pap. 15.00 o.s.i (*0-8050-5567-3*, Owl Bks.);No. 5. 470p. pap. 15.00 (*0-8050-5568-1*, Owl Bks.) Holt, Henry & Co.

—The Wing & Wing. 1990. (Works of James Fenimore Cooper). reprint ed. lib. bdg. 79.00 (*0-7812-2389-X*) Reprint Services Corp.

Cooper, Susan. Dawn of Fear. 1988. (Illus.). 157p. (YA). (gr. 5 up). 14.95 o.s.i (*0-15-266201-4*) Harcourt Children's Bks.

Coppard, Alfred Edgar. Adam & Eve & Pinch Me: Tales. 1976. 23.95 (*0-8488-0971-8*) Amereon, Ltd.

—Adam & Eve & Pinch Me: Tales. 1977. (Short Story Index Reprint Ser.). 23.95 (*0-8369-3451-2*) Ayer Co. Pubs., Inc.

Corelli, Marie. The Sorrows of Satan. Keating, Peter, ed. 1999. (Oxford World's Classics Ser.). 426p. pap. 10.95 o.p. (*0-19-283324-3*) Oxford Univ. Pr., Inc.

—The Sorrows of Satan (1896) 1998. 450p. reprint ed. pap. 27.00 (*0-7661-0146-0*) Kessinger Publishing Co.

Corlett, William. Two Gentlemen Sharing. 1999. 392p. pap. 12.95 o.p. (*1-55583-527-9*) Alyson Pubns.

—Two Gentlemen Sharing. 1998. 391p. pap. o.s.i (*0-349-10830-7*); 1997. 352p. o.s.i (*0-316-88170-8*) Little Brown & Co.

Cornwell, Bernard. The Archer's Tale. l.t. ed. 2002. 643p. 29.95 (*0-7862-3898-4*) Gale Group.

—The Archer's Tale. 2001. 384p. 26.00 (*0-06-621084-4*) HarperCollins Pubs.

—The Archer's Tale. 2002. 464p. mass mkt. 7.99 (*0-06-050525-7*) Morrow/Avon.

—Heretic. 2003. 368p. 24.95 (*0-06-053049-9*) HarperCollins Pubs.

—Heretic. l.t. ed. 2003. 592p. pap. 24.95 (*0-06-056998-0*, HarperLargePrint) HarperTrade.

—Sharpe's Battle: Richard Sharpe & the Battle of Fuentes de Onoro, May 1811. 1995. (Richard Sharpe Adventure Ser.: No. 7). 320p. 20.00 o.p. (*0-06-017677-6*) HarperTrade.

—Sharpe's Battle: Richard Sharpe & the Battle of Fuentes de Onoro, May 1811. 1996. (Richard Sharpe Adventure Ser.: No. 7). 432p. mass mkt. 6.50 o.s.i (*0-06-109537-0*, HarperTorch) Morrow/Avon.

—Sharpe's Battle: Richard Sharpe & the Battle of Fuentes de Onoro, May 1811. 1999. 18.05 (*0-606-21712-6*) Turtleback Bks.

—Sharpe's Battle: Spain 1811. 1999. (Richard Sharpe Adventure Ser.: No. 7). (Illus.). 368p. pap. 12.95 (*0-06-093228-7*, Perennial) HarperTrade.

—Sharpe's Company: Richard Sharpe & the Siege of Badajoz, January to April 1812. 1982. (Richard Sharpe Adventure Ser.: No. 8). 288p. 14.95 o.p. (*0-670-63942-7*) Viking Penguin.

—Sharpe's Devil: Chile 1820. 1999. (Richard Sharpe Adventure Ser.). 336p. pap. 12.95 (*0-06-093229-5*, Perennial) HarperTrade.

—Sharpe's Devil: Richard Sharpe & the Emperor, 1820-1821. l.t. ed. 1993. pap. 17.95 o.p. (*0-7927-1466-0*); 19.95 o.p. (*0-7927-1467-9*) BBC Audiobooks America.

—Sharpe's Devil: Richard Sharpe & the Emperor, 1820-1821. 1992. 256p. 20.00 o.p. (*0-06-017977-5*) HarperTrade.

—Sharpe's Eagle: Richard Sharpe & the Talavera Campaign, July 1809. 1982. (Richard Sharpe Adventure Ser.: No. 5). (Illus.). 352p. 3.25 o.s.i (*0-441-76091-0*) Ace Bks.

—Sharpe's Eagle: Richard Sharpe & the Talavera Campaign, July 1809, unabr. ed. 1993. (Richard Sharpe Adventure Ser.: No. 5). 69.95 incl. audio (*0-7451-5879-X*, CAB 429) BBC Audiobooks America.

—Sharpe's Eagle: Richard Sharpe & the Talavera Campaign, July 1809, unabr. ed. 1995. (Richard Sharpe Adventure Ser.: No. 5). 5p. audio 49.95 (*0-7861-0662-X*, 1564) Blackstone Audio Bks., Inc.

—Sharpe's Eagle: Richard Sharpe & the Talavera Campaign, July 1809. unabr. ed. 2000. (Richard Sharpe Adventure Ser.: No. 5). audio 42.00 Books on Tape, Inc.

—Sharpe's Eagle: Richard Sharpe & the Talavera Campaign, July 1809. 1991. (Richard Sharpe Adventure Ser.: No. 5). reprint ed. lib. bdg. 29.95 (*1-56849-076-3*) Buccaneer Bks., Inc.

—Sharpe's Eagle: Richard Sharpe & the Talavera Campaign, July 1809. 1989. (Richard Sharpe Adventure Ser.: No. 5). audio 64.95 o.p. (*0-8161-9664-8*) Thorndike Pr.

—Sharpe's Eagle: Richard Sharpe & the Talavera Campaign, July 1809. l.t. ed. 1983. (Richard Sharpe Adventure Ser.: No. 5). 480p. 29.99 o.p. (*0-7089-0945-0*, Ulverscroft) Thorpe, F. A. Pubs. GBR. *Dist:* Ulverscroft Large Print Bks., Ltd., Ulverscroft Large Print Canada, Ltd.

—Sharpe's Eagle: Richard Sharpe & the Talavera Campaign, July 1809. (Richard Sharpe Adventure Ser.: No. 5). 1987. 288p. pap. 10.95 o.s.i (*0-14-009921-2*, Penguin Bks.); 1981. 264p. 12.95 o.p. (*0-670-63944-3*) Viking Penguin.

—Sharpe's Enemy: Richard Sharpe & the Defense of Portugal, Christmas 1812. 1987. (Richard Sharpe Adventure Ser.: No. 10). 352p. pap. 11.95 o.s.i (*0-14-010430-5*, Penguin Bks.) Viking Penguin.

—Sharpe's Gold: Richard Sharpe & the Destruction of Almeida August, 1810. (Richard Sharpe Adventure Ser.: No. 6). 1987. 256p. pap. 3.50 o.p. (*0-14-010028-8*, Penguin Bks.); 1982. 252p. 13.95 o.p. (*0-670-63943-5*) Viking Penguin.

—Sharpe's Honour: Richard Sharpe & the Vitoria Campaign, February to June, 1813. l.t. ed. 1989. (Richard Sharpe Adventure Ser.: No. 11). lib. bdg. 11.95 o.p. (*1-85057-421-9*, Macmillan Reference USA) Gale Group.

—Sharpe's Honour: Richard Sharpe & the Vitoria Campaign, February to June, 1813. 1985. (Richard Sharpe Adventure Ser.: No. 11). 324p. 16.95 o.p. (*0-670-80389-8*) Viking Penguin.

—Sharpe's Prey: Richard Sharpe & the Expedition to Copenhagen, 1807. 2002. (Illus.). 272p. 24.95 (*0-06-000252-2*) HarperCollins Pubs.

—Sharpe's Regiment: Richard Sharpe & the Invasion of France, June to November 1913. 1986. (Sharpe Ser.). 304p. 16.95 o.p. (*0-670-81148-3*) Viking Penguin.

—Sharpe's Revenge: Richard Sharpe & the Peace of 1814. 1989. (Sharpe Ser.). 352p. 17.95 o.p. (*0-670-80867-9*); No. 10. 1990. (Richard Sharpe Adventure Ser.: Vol. 10). 320p. pap. 11.95 o.s.i (*0-14-008472-X*, Penguin Bks.) Viking Penguin.

—Sharpe's Rifles: Richard Sharpe & the French Invasion of Galicia, January 1809. l.t. ed. 1990. (Richard Sharpe Adventure Ser.: No. 4). 479p. 29.99 o.p. (*1-85057-547-9*) Magna Large Print Bks. GBR. *Dist:* Ulverscroft Large Print Bks., Ltd., Ulverscroft Large Print Canada, Ltd.

—Sharpe's Rifles: Richard Sharpe & the French Invasion of Galicia, January 1809. (Richard Sharpe Adventure Ser.: No. 4). 304p. 1989. pap. 11.95 o.s.i (*0-14-011014-3*, Penguin Bks.); 1988. 17.95 o.p. (*0-670-82222-1*) Viking Penguin.

—Sharpe's Siege: Richard Sharpe & the Winter Campaign, 1814. 320p. 1987. (Sharpe Ser.). 17.95 o.p. (*0-670-80866-0*); No. 9. 1990. (Richard Sharpe Adventure Ser.: Vol. 9). pap. 11.95 o.s.i (*0-14-014442-0*, Penguin Bks.) Viking Penguin.

—Sharpe's Sword: Richard Sharpe & the Salamanca Campaign, June & July, 1812. l.t. ed. 1989. (Richard Sharpe Adventure Ser.: No. 9). lib. bdg. 11.95 o.p. (*1-85057-380-8*, Macmillan Reference USA) Gale Group.

—Sharpe's Sword: Richard Sharpe & the Salamanca Campaign, June & July, 1812. 1983. (Richard Sharpe Adventure Ser.: No. 9). 324p. 15.75 o.p. (*0-670-63941-9*) Viking Penguin.

—Sharpe's Tiger: Richard Sharpe & the Siege of Seringapatam, 1799. 1997. (Richard Sharpe Adventure Ser.: No. 1). (Illus.). 303p. o.p. (*0-00-225010-1*) HarperSanFrancisco.

—Sharpe's Tiger: Richard Sharpe & the Siege of Seringapatam, 1799. 1999. (Richard Sharpe Adventure Ser.: No. 1). 400p. pap. 13.00 (*0-06-093230-9*, Perennial) HarperTrade.

—Sharpe's Tiger: Richard Sharpe & the Siege of Seringapatam, 1799. 1997. (Richard Sharpe Adventure Ser.: No. 1). 496p. mass mkt. 6.50 o.s.i (*0-06-101269-6*, HarperTorch) Morrow/Avon.

—Sharpe's Tiger: Richard Sharpe & the Siege of Seringapatam, 1799. 1999. (Richard Sharpe Adventures Ser.). (Illus.). 19.05 (*0-606-21714-2*) Turtleback Bks.

—Sharpe's Trafalgar: Richard Sharpe & the Battle of Trafalgar, 21 October 1805. 2001. 19.95 (*0-06-621326-6*) HarperCollins Pubs.

—Sharpe's Trafalgar: Richard Sharpe & the Battle of Trafalgar, 21 October 1805. l.t. ed. 2001. (Thorndike Press Large Print Adventure Ser.). (Illus.). 571p. 29.95 (*0-7862-3699-X*) Thorndike Pr.

—Waterloo: Sharpe's Final Adventure. 1990. (Sharpe Ser.). 288p. 18.95 o.p. (*0-670-80868-7*) Viking Penguin.

—Waterloo No. 11: Sharpe's Final Adventure. unabr. ed. 1996. audio 69.95 Blackstone Audio Bks., Inc.

—Waterloo No. 11: Sharpe's Final Adventure. 1991. (Sharpe Ser.). 384p. pap. 11.95 o.s.i (*0-14-008473-8*, Penguin Bks.) Penguin Group (USA) Inc.

Coulter, Catherine. Fire Song. 2002. 464p. mass mkt. 7.99 (*0-451-20928-1*, Signet Bks.) NAL.

—Fire Song. 1991. 19.95 o.p. (*0-7278-4041-X*) Severn Hse. Pubs., Ltd.

—Fire Song. l.t. ed. 2000. (Basic Ser.). 634p. 29.95 o.p. (*0-7862-2355-3*) Thorndike Pr.

—Rosehaven. 1997. 384p. reprint ed. mass mkt. 7.99 (*0-515-12088-X*, Jove) Berkley Publishing Group.

—Rosehaven. unabr. ed. 1996. (Song Novels Ser.). audio 23.95 (*1-56100-696-3*, 240, Bookcassette); audio 73.25 o.p. (*1-56100-321-2*, 1018, Unabridged Library Editions) Brilliance Audio.

—Rosehaven. l.t. ed. 1997. (Large Print Bks.). 26.95 o.p. (*1-56895-405-0*, Wheeler Publishing, Inc.) Gale Group.

—Rosehaven. 1996. 384p. 21.95 o.s.i (*0-399-14143-X*, G. P. Putnam's Sons) Penguin Group (USA) Inc.

—Secret Song. 384p. 2003. mass mkt. 7.99 (*0-451-20929-X*, Signet Bks.); 1991. mass mkt. 7.99 o.s.i (*0-451-40234-0*, Onyx) NAL.

—Secret Song. 1991. 21.95 o.p. (*0-7278-4185-8*) Severn Hse. Pubs., Ltd.

—Secret Song. l.t. ed. 2000. (Basic Ser.). 567p. 29.95 (*0-7862-2357-X*) Thorndike Pr.

Counts, Wilma. Rules of Marriage. 2002. (Zebra Historical Romance Ser.). 34p. mass mkt. 5.99 o.s.i (*0-8217-7043-8*) Kensington Publishing Corp.

Coward, Noel. Star Quality: Six Stories. 1970. reprint ed. lib. bdg. 24.75 o.p. (*0-8371-3831-0*, COSQ, Greenwood Pr.) Greenwood Publishing Group, Inc.

Cowell, Stephanie. Nicholas Cooke: Actor, Soldier, Physician, Priest. 1994. 448p. reprint ed. pap. 12.00 o.s.i (*0-345-39016-4*) Ballantine Bks.

—Nicholas Cooke: Actor, Soldier, Physician, Priest. 1993. 442p. 24.00 o.p. (*0-393-03543-3*) Norton, W. W. & Co., Inc.

—The Physician of London: The 2nd Part of the Seventeenth-Century Trilogy of Nicholas Cooke. 1995. 416p. 23.00 o.p. (*0-393-03873-4*) Norton, W. W. & Co., Inc.

Crace, Jim. Arcadia. 1997. 311p. pap. 13.00 (*0-88001-530-6*, Ecco) HarperTrade.

—Arcadia. 1992. 320p. 20.00 o.s.i (*0-689-12158-X*, Scribner) Simon & Schuster.

Cressell, H. B., et al. The Honeywood File: An Adventure in Building. 1999. 230p. pap. 14.95 (*0-89733-473-6*) Academy Chicago Pubs., Ltd.

Crofts, Andrew & Freeman-Keel, Tom. The Disappearing Duke: The Improbable Tale of an English Family. 2003. 272p. 26.00 (*0-7867-1045-4*, Carroll & Graf Pubs.) Avalon Publishing Group.

Cronin, A. J. The Citadel. 1983. (J). 16.95 (*0-316-16158-6*) Little Brown & Co.

Crosby, Caroline. The Haldanes. 1993. 352p. 21.95 o.p. (*0-312-09303-9*) St. Martin's Pr.

Crow, Donna Fletcher. Encounter the Light. 1997. 240p. pap. 10.99 o.p. (*0-89107-876-2*) Crossway Bks.

—Encounter the Light. 1999. (Five Star Christian Fiction Ser.). 253p. 22.95 (*0-7862-1949-1*, Five Star) Gale Group.

Crumey, Andrew. Music in a Foreign Language. 1997. 256p. pap. 12.00 o.s.i (*0-312-16946-9*) Picador.

—Music in a Foriegn Language. 1996. 256p. 22.00 o.p. (*0-312-14688-4*) Picador.

Cusk, Rachel. The Temporary. Date not set. (*0-312-26999-4*) Picador.

Cutler, Judith. Dying on Principle. l.t. ed. 1999. (Magna Large Print Ser.). 448p. (*0-7505-1423-X*) Magna Large Print Bks. GBR. *Dist:* Ulverscroft Large Print Canada, Ltd.

Daniels, Philip. Nice Knight for Murder. l.t. ed. 2001. 203p. pap. 23.95 (*0-7838-9486-4*) Thorndike Pr.

—Nice Knight for Murder. l.t. ed. 1988. (Linford Mystery Library). 240p. pap. 17.99 o.p. (*0-7089-6625-X*, Linford) Thorpe, F. A. Pubs. GBR. *Dist:* Ulverscroft Large Print Bks., Ltd., Ulverscroft Large Print Canada, Ltd.

Darby, Catherine. Love Knot. 1991. 16.95 o.p. (*0-312-04996-X*) St. Martin's Pr.

Darling, Julia. Crocodile Soup: A Novel. 2000. 352p. 25.00 (*0-06-019602-5*, Ecco) HarperTrade.

Davies, Carol Anne. Noise Abatement. 2001. 244p. 29.95 (*1-899344-65-9*); 240p. pap. 15.95 (*1-899344-64-0*) Do-Not Pr., The GBR. *Dist:* Dufour Editions, Inc.

Davis, Lindsey. A Body in the Bath House. 2002. 368p. 24.95 (*0-89296-771-4*) Mysterious Pr.

—The Jupiter Myth. 2003. (Illus.). 336p. 24.95 (*0-89296-777-3*) Mysterious Pr.

De La Ramee, Louise. Cecil Castlemaine's Gage, Lady Marabout's Troubles & Other Stories. 1977. (Short Story Index Reprint Ser.). 25.95 (*0-8369-3490-3*) Ayer Co. Pubs., Inc.

De La Torre, Lillian. Dr. Sam Johnson, Detector. 1983. (Compleat Adventures of Dr. Sam Johnson, Detector Ser.). 257p. pap. 6.95 o.p. (*0-930330-08-0*) International Polygonics, Ltd.

Defoe, Daniel. Memoirs of a Cavalier. (Illus.). reprint ed. (*0-404-07915-6*) AMS Pr., Inc.

Deighton, Len. Berlin Game. l.t. ed. 1984. 16.95 o.p. (*0-8161-3685-8*, Macmillan Reference USA) Gale Group.

—Berlin Game. 1983. 289p. 15.95 o.s.i (*0-394-53407-7*) Knopf, Alfred A. Inc.

—Faith. 1994. 384p. 24.00 o.p. (*0-06-017622-9*) HarperTrade.

—Faith. 1995. 352p. mass mkt. 6.99 o.p. (*0-06-109419-6*, HarperTorch) Morrow/Avon.

—London Match. 1997. pap. 12.95 o.p. (*0-345-41835-2*); 1989. mass mkt. 4.95 o.p. (*0-345-01073-6*); 1986. mass mkt. 5.95 o.s.i (*0-345-33268-7*) Ballantine Bks.

—London Match. l.t. ed. 1987. 586p. 11.95 o.p. (*0-8161-4106-1*); 19.95 o.p. (*0-8161-4105-3*) Gale Group. (Macmillan Reference USA).

—Mexico Set. l.t. ed. 1985. (General Ser.). 528p. 17.95 o.p. (*0-8161-3955-5*, Macmillan Reference USA) Gale Group.

—Mexico Set. Gottlieb, Robert, ed. 1985. 384p. 16.95 o.s.i (*0-394-53525-1*) Knopf, Alfred A. Inc.

—Spy Line. 1990. 336p. reprint ed. mass mkt. 6.99 o.s.i (*0-345-37006-6*, Ballantine Bks.) Ballantine Bks.

—Spy Sinker. 1990. 374p. 21.95 o.p. (*0-06-039118-9*) HarperTrade.

Deis, Elizabeth J., ed. George Meredith's 1895 Collection of Three Stories: Explorations of Gender & Power. 1997. (Studies in British Literature: Vol. 26). 316p. text 99.95 (*0-7734-8779-4*) Mellen, Edwin Pr., The.

Del Wollert, Edwin. Dreamers of the Grail. 2002. 540p. pap. 29.95 (*0-940121-71-9*) Cross Cultural Pubns., Inc.

Delafield, E. M. The Provincial Lady in Wartime. 1986. (Cassandra Editions Ser.). (Illus.). 349p. pap. 16.95 (*0-89733-210-5*) Academy Chicago Pubs., Ltd.

Delderfield, R. F. God Is an Englishman. 1998. 704p. pap. 15.95 (*0-7867-0528-0*, Carroll & Graf Pubs.) Avalon Publishing Group.

—God Is an Englishman. unabr. collector's ed. 1983. Pt. 1. audio 104.00 (*0-7366-0487-1*, 1462-A); Pt. 2. audio 72.00 (*0-7366-0488-X*, 1462-B) Books on Tape, Inc.

—God Is an Englishman. 1986. 832p. mass mkt. 4.95 o.s.i (*0-671-62722-8*, Pocket) Simon & Schuster.

—Theirs Was the Kingdom. 1999. (Illus.). 798p. pap. 15.95 (*0-7867-0637-6*, Carroll & Graf Pubs.) Avalon Publishing Group.

—Theirs Was the Kingdom, Pt. 1. unabr. collector's ed. 1996. (Swann Family Trilogy). audio 88.00 (*0-7366-3401-0*, 4048-A) Books on Tape, Inc.

—Theirs Was the Kingdom. 1987. mass mkt. 4.95 (*0-671-63734-7*, Pocket) Simon & Schuster.

—Too Few for Drums. 2001. (Military Fiction Classics Ser.). (Illus.). 254p. pap. 14.95 (*0-935526-96-X*) McBooks Pr., Inc.

—Too Few for Drums. l.t. ed. 1988. (Ulverscroft Large Print Ser.). 368p. 29.99 o.p. (*0-7089-1756-9*, Ulverscroft) Thorpe, F. A. Pubs. GBR. *Dist:* Ulverscroft Large Print Bks., Ltd., Ulverscroft Large Print Canada, Ltd.

Dell, Ethel M. House of Happiness: And Other Stories. 1977. (Short Story Index Reprint Ser.). reprint ed. 25.95 (*0-8369-4209-4*) Ayer Co. Pubs., Inc.

—The Passerby: And Other Stories. 1977. (Short Story Index Reprint Ser.). reprint ed. 25.95 (*0-8369-4210-8*) Ayer Co. Pubs., Inc.

—Swindler & Other Stories. 1977. (Short Story Index Reprint Ser.). 25.95 (*0-8369-3721-X*) Ayer Co. Pubs., Inc.

Denham, Bertie. Foxhunt. 1988. 208p. 15.95 o.p. (*0-312-02323-5*, Saint Martin's Minotaur) St. Martin's Pr.

Dennys, Joyce. Henrietta Sees It Through: More News from the Home Front 1942-1945. 1987. (Illus.). 176p. 15.95 o.p. (*0-233-97970-0*) Andre Deutsch GBR. *Dist:* Trafalgar Square, Trans-Atlantic Pubns., Inc.

Dibdin, Michael. Dirty Tricks. 2003. (Vintage Crime/Black Lizard Ser.). 256p. pap. 12.00 (*0-375-70009-9*, Vintage) Knopf Publishing Group.

—Dirty Tricks. Chelius, Jane, ed. 1992. 256p. reprint ed. mass mkt. 4.99 (*0-671-69546-0*, Pocket) Simon & Schuster.

—Dirty Tricks. 1991. 241p. pap. 18.00 (*0-671-69545-2*) Summit Bks.

Dickens, Charles. Great Expectations. 2003. (Perennial Bestsellers Ser.). 29.95 (*0-7862-5405-X*) Thorndike Pr.

Dickinson, David. Death & the Jubilee. 2003. 352p. 24.00 (*0-7867-1110-8*, Carroll & Graf Pubs.) Avalon Publishing Group.

Dickinson, Peter. Skeleton-in-Waiting. 1990. 16.95 o.s.i (*0-394-58002-8*, Pantheon) Knopf Publishing Group.

—The Yellow Room Conspiracy. 1994. 272p. 18.95 o.s.i (*0-89296-556-8*) Mysterious Pr.

—The Yellow Room Conspiracy. 1995. 256p. mass mkt. 5.99 (*0-446-40373-3*) Warner Bks., Inc.

Dietrich, William. Hadrian's Wall. 2004. 384p. 24.95 (*0-06-056371-0*, HarperCollins) HarperTrade.

Disraeli, Benjamin. Coningsby: Or, the New Generation. Smith, Sheila M., ed. 1982. (Oxford World's Classics Ser.). pap. 6.95 o.p. (*0-19-281580-6*) Oxford Univ. Pr., Inc.

Dobbs, Michael. At the Right Hand. 2002. 320p. (*0-00-225414-X*); pap. (*0-00-713018-X*) HarperCollins Pubs.

Doherty, P. C. An Ancient Evil: The Knight's Tale of Mystery & Murder as He Goes on Pilgrimage from London to Canterbury. unabr. ed. 1998. audio 69.95 (*1-85903-149-8*) Magna Story Sound GBR. *Dist:* Ulverscroft Large Print Bks., Ltd.

—An Ancient Evil: The Knight's Tale of Mystery & Murder as He Goes on Pilgrimage from London to Canterbury. 1995. 248p. 21.00 o.p. (*0-312-11740-X*, Saint Martin's Minotaur) St. Martin's Pr.

—An Ancient Evil: The Knight's Tale of Mystery & Murder as He Goes on Pilgrimage from London to Canterbury. l.t. ed. 1995. (Ulverscroft Large Print Ser.). 432p. 29.99 o.p. (*0-7089-3409-9*, Ulverscroft) Thorpe, F. A. Pubs. GBR. *Dist:* Ulverscroft Large Print Bks., Ltd., Ulverscroft Large Print Canada, Ltd.

—Angel of Death. 1990. 176p. 14.95 o.p. (*0-312-03791-0*, Saint Martin's Minotaur) St. Martin's Pr.

—Corpse Candle: A Medieval Mystery Featuring Hugh Corbett. 2002. 320p. 24.95 (*0-312-30087-5*, Saint Martin's Minotaur) St. Martin's Pr.

—The Crown in Darkness. 1988. 192p. 13.95 o.p. (*0-312-01754-5*, Saint Martin's Minotaur) St. Martin's Pr.

—The Crown in Darkness. l.t. ed. 1999. (Linford Mystery Large Print Ser.). 304p. pap. 18.99 o.p. (*0-7089-5601-7*, Linford) Thorpe, F. A. Pubs. GBR. *Dist:* Ulverscroft Large Print Bks., Ltd., Ulverscroft Large Print Canada, Ltd.

—The Death of a King. 1987. 208p. mass mkt. 2.95 o.s.i (*0-553-26333-1*) Bantam Bks.

—The Death of a King. 1998. (Missing Mysteries Ser.: Vol. 5). 150p. pap. 14.95 (*1-890208-11-6*) Poisoned Pen Pr.

—The Death of a King. 1985. 176p. 12.95 o.p. (*0-312-18651-7*) St. Martin's Pr.

—The Demon Archer: A Medieval Mystery Featuring Hugh Corbett. l.t. ed. 2000. (Magna Large Print Ser.). 384p. (*0-7505-1553-8*) Magna Large Print Bks. GBR. *Dist:* Ulverscroft Large Print Canada, Ltd.

—The Demon Archer: A Medieval Mystery Featuring Hugh Corbett. 2001. 256p. 22.95 (*0-312-27287-1*, Saint Martin's Minotaur) St. Martin's Pr.

—The Devil's Domain. l.t. ed. 1999. (Magna Large Print Ser.). (Illus.). 416p. o.p. (*0-7505-1458-2*) Magna Large Print Bks. GBR. *Dist:* Ulverscroft Large Print Canada, Ltd.

—The Fate of Princes. 1991. 15.95 o.p. (*0-312-05429-7*) St. Martin's Pr.

—Ghostly Murders: The Priest's Tale of Mystery & Murder as He Goes on Pilgrimage from London to Canterbury. 1998. 256p. 21.95 (*0-312-19418-8*, Saint Martin's Minotaur) St. Martin's Pr.

—Ghostly Murders: The Priest's Tale of Mystery & Murder as He Goes on Pilgrimage from London to Canterbury. l.t. ed. 1999. (Ulverscroft Large Print Ser.). 368p. 31.99 o.p. (*0-7089-4059-5*, Ulverscroft) Thorpe, F. A. Pubs. GBR. *Dist:* Ulverscroft Large Print Bks., Ltd., Ulverscroft Large Print Canada, Ltd.

—A Tapestry of Murders: The Lawyer's Tale of Mystery & Murder as He Goes on a Pilgrimage from London to Canterbury. unabr. ed. 1998. audio 69.95 (*1-85903-165-X*) Magna Story Sound GBR. *Dist:* Ulverscroft Large Print Bks., Ltd.

—A Tapestry of Murders: The Lawyer's Tale of Mystery & Murder as He Goes on a Pilgrimage from London to Canterbury. 1996. 256p. 21.95 (*0-312-14052-5*, Saint Martin's Minotaur) St. Martin's Pr.

—A Tapestry of Murders: The Lawyer's Tale of Mystery & Murder as He Goes on a Pilgrimage from London to Canterbury. l.t. ed. 1996. (Ulverscroft Large Print Ser.). 416p. 29.99 o.p. (*0-7089-3446-3*, Ulverscroft) Thorpe, F. A. Pubs. GBR. *Dist:* Ulverscroft Large Print Bks., Ltd., Ulverscroft Large Print Canada, Ltd.

—A Tournament of Murders: The Franklin's Tale of Mystery & Murder As He Goes on Pilgrimage from London to Canterbury. 1997. 256p. 21.95 (*0-312-17048-3*, Saint Martin's Minotaur) St. Martin's Pr.

—A Tournament of Murders: The Franklin's Tale of Mystery & Murder As He Goes on Pilgrimage from London to Canterbury. l.t. ed. 1998. (Ulverscroft Large Print Ser.). 384p. 29.99 o.p. (*0-7089-3938-4*, Ulverscroft) Thorpe, F. A. Pubs. GBR. *Dist:* Ulverscroft Large Print Bks., Ltd., Ulverscroft Large Print Canada, Ltd.

—The Whyte Harte. 1988. 256p. 16.95 o.p. (*0-312-02318-9*, Saint Martin's Minotaur) St. Martin's Pr.

Donachie, David. The Devil's Own Luck. l.t. ed. 1995. (Magna Large Print Ser.). 537p. o.p. (*0-7505-0811-6*) Magna Large Print Bks. GBR. *Dist:* Ulverscroft Large Print Canada, Ltd.

—The Devil's Own Luck. 2001. (Privateersman Mysteries Ser.: Vol. 1). 320p. 23.95 (*1-59013-003-0*) McBooks Pr., Inc.

—A Game of Bones. 2003. (Privateersman Mysteries Ser.: No. 6). 352p. pap. 15.95 (*1-59013-032-4*) McBooks Pr., Inc.

—A Hanging Matter. l.t. ed. 1995. (Magna Large Print Ser.). 655p. o.p. (*0-7505-0805-1*) Magna Large Print Bks. GBR. *Dist:* Ulverscroft Large Print Canada, Ltd.

—A Hanging Matter. 1995. 389p. pap. 16.95 o.p. (*0-330-32862-X*) Pan Bks. Ltd. GBR. *Dist:* Trans-Atlantic Pubns., Inc.

—On a Making Tide. 2003. (Nelson & Emma Trilogy Ser.: No. 1). 416p. pap. 17.95 (*1-59013-041-3*) McBooks Pr., Inc.

—The Scent of Betrayal. 2003. (Privateersman Mysteries Ser.: No. 5). 448p. pap. 17.95 (*1-59013-031-6*) McBooks Pr., Inc.

Donoghue, Emma. Slammerkin. 2001. 352p. 24.00 (*0-15-100672-5*); 2002. 408p. reprint ed. pap. 14.00 (*0-15-600747-9*, Harvest Bks.) Harcourt Trade Pubs.

Dorsch, T. S., ed. Charmed Lives: Classic English Short Stories. 1988. 256p. pap. 7.95 o.p. (*0-19-282150-4*) Oxford Univ. Pr., Inc.

Douglass, Sara. Hades' Daughter. 2003. (Troy Game Ser.: Bk. 1). (Illus.). 672p. mass mkt. 7.99 (*0-7653-4442-4*); 592p. 27.95 (*0-7653-0540-2*) Doherty, Tom Assocs., LLC. (Tor Bks.).

Dowson, Ernest C. Dilemmas: Stories & Studies in Sentiment. 1977. (Short Story Index Reprint Ser.). reprint ed. 17.95 (*0-8369-3886-0*) Ayer Co. Pubs., Inc.

Doyle, Arthur Conan. The Adventure of the Copper Beeches. E-Book 0.99 (*1-58515-035-5*) MesaView, Inc.

—The Captain of the Polestar & Other Tales. 1977. (Short Story Index Reprint Ser.). 13.95 (*0-8369-3453-9*) Ayer Co. Pubs., Inc.

—The Green Flag & Other Stories of War & Sport. 1977. (Short Story Index Reprint Ser.). 21.95 (*0-8369-3201-3*) Ayer Co. Pubs., Inc.

—The Green Flag & Other Stories of War & Sport. reprint ed. lib. bdg. 98.00 (*0-7426-2704-7*); 2001. (Collected Works of Sir Arthur Conan Doyle: Vol. 13). pap. text 28.00 (*0-7426-7704-4*) Classic Bks.

—The Hound of the Baskervilles. 2002. (Modern Library Classics). 208p. pap. 7.95 (*0-8129-6606-6*) Random House Adult Trade Publishing Group.

Drake, Shannon. Princess of Fire. 1989. 4.95 (*1-55773-202-7*, Diamond Bks.) Berkley Publishing Group.

—Princess of Fire. 1998. (Romance Ser.). 25.95 (*0-7862-1386-8*, Five Star) Gale Group.

—Princess of Fire. 1994. 512p. mass mkt. 5.99 o.s.i (*0-8217-4796-7*, Zebra Bks.) Kensington Publishing Corp.

—Princess of Fire. 1990. reprint ed. 20.00 o.p. (*0-7278-4034-7*) Severn Hse. Pubs., Ltd.

Dreyfuss, Richard & Turtledove, Harry. The Two Georges. 1996. 384p. 23.95 o.p. (*0-312-85969-4*); Vol. 1. 1997. 596p. pap. 6.99 o.s.i (*0-8125-4459-5*) Doherty, Tom Assocs., LLC. (Tor Bks.).

Du Maurier, Daphne. Mary Anne. 1971. 352p. reprint ed. lib. bdg. 20.00 (*0-8376-0411-7*) Bentley Pubs.

Duffy, Bruce. The World As I Found It. 1988. 550p. pap. 16.00 (*0-89919-808-2*); 1987. 19.95 o.p. (*0-89919-456-7*) Houghton Mifflin Co.

Duffy, Margaret. Brass Eagle. 1990. 256p. mass mkt. 3.95 o.s.i (*0-449-21887-2*, Fawcett) Ballantine Bks.

—Brass Eagle. unabr. ed. 1998. audio 83.95 (*1-85903-017-3*) Magna Story Sound GBR. *Dist:* Ulverscroft Large Print Bks., Ltd.

—Brass Eagle. 1989. 15.95 o.p. (*0-312-02880-6*, Saint Martin's Minotaur) St. Martin's Pr.

—Brass Eagle. l.t. ed. 1991. (Ulverscroft Large Print Ser.). 29.99 o.p. (*0-7089-2347-X*, Ulverscroft) Thorpe, F. A. Pubs. GBR. *Dist:* Ulverscroft Large Print Bks., Ltd., Ulverscroft Large Print Canada, Ltd.

—Death of a Raven. 1989. 240p. mass mkt. 3.50 o.s.i (*0-449-21741-8*, Fawcett) Ballantine Bks.

—Death of a Raven. 1988. 224p. 15.95 o.p. (*0-312-02567-X*, Saint Martin's Minotaur) St. Martin's Pr.

—Death of a Raven. l.t. ed. 1990. (Ulverscroft Large Print Ser.). 29.99 o.p. (*0-7089-2202-3*, Ulverscroft) Thorpe, F. A. Pubs. GBR. *Dist:* Ulverscroft Large Print Bks., Ltd., Ulverscroft Large Print Canada, Ltd.

—A Murder of Crows. 1988. mass mkt. 3.50 o.s.i (*0-449-21563-6*, Fawcett) Ballantine Bks.

—A Murder of Crows. 1988. 240p. 15.95 o.p. (*0-312-01483-X*, Saint Martin's Minotaur) St. Martin's Pr.

—A Murder of Crows. l.t. ed. 1989. (Ulverscroft Large Print Ser.). 531p. 29.99 o.p. (*0-7089-1929-4*, Ulverscroft) Thorpe, F. A. Pubs. GBR. *Dist:* Ulverscroft Large Print Bks., Ltd., Ulverscroft Large Print Canada, Ltd.

—Rook-Shoot. l.t. ed. 1993. (Dales Mystery Ser.). 392p. pap. 19.99 (*1-85389-399-4*) Dales Large Print Bks. GBR. *Dist:* Ulverscroft Large Print Bks., Ltd.

—Rook-Shoot. 1991. 240p. 17.95 o.p. (*0-312-06456-X*, Saint Martin's Minotaur) St. Martin's Pr.

—Who Killed Cock Robin? 1990. 224p. 16.95 o.p. (*0-312-04988-9*, Saint Martin's Minotaur) St. Martin's Pr.

Dukthas, Ann. In the Time of the Poisoned Queen. 1998. (Nicholas Segalla Time-Travel Mystery Ser.). 273p. 22.95 o.p. (*0-312-18030-6*, Saint Martin's Minotaur) St. Martin's Pr.

Duncker, Patricia. The Doctor. 2000. 384p. 24.00 (*0-06-019601-7*, Ecco) HarperTrade.

Dunnett, Dorothy. Dolly & the Nanny Bird. 1983. pap. 3.95 o.p. (*0-394-71723-6*, Vintage) Knopf Publishing Group.

Dupont, Desiree. Love Me Forever. 1996. 142p. pap. 12.95 (*81-7328-065-7*) International Specialized Bk. Services.

Eccles, Frank. The Mutiny Run. 1994. 288p. 21.95 o.p. (*0-312-10507-X*) St. Martin's Pr.

—The Mutiny Run. l.t. ed. 1998. (Ulverscroft Large Print Ser.). 496p. 29.99 (*0-7089-3975-9*, Ulverscroft) Thorpe, F. A. Pubs. GBR. *Dist:* Ulverscroft Large Print Bks., Ltd., Ulverscroft Large Print Canada, Ltd.

Eccles, Marjorie. Superintendent's Daughter. 2000. (Gil Mayo Mysteries Ser.). 240p. 22.95 (*0-312-25338-9*, Saint Martin's Minotaur) St. Martin's Pr.

Edelman, Maurice. Disraeli Rising. 1984. 282p. pap. 3.95 o.p. (*0-8128-8058-7*); 1978. 282p. 1.95 o.p. (*0-8128-7007-7*); 1975. 3.95 o.p. (*0-8128-1675-7*) Madison Bks., Inc. (Scarborough Hse.).

Edghill, Rosemary & Norton, Andre. Leopard in Exile. 2001. (Carolus Rex Ser.: Vol. 2). 352p. 24.95 (*0-312-86428-0*, Tor Bks.) Doherty, Tom Assocs., LLC.

—The Shadow of Albion. 1999. (Carolus Rex Ser.: Vol. 1). 352p. 23.95 (*0-312-86427-2*, Tor Bks.) Doherty, Tom Assocs., LLC.

Edwards, Anne. Wallis: The Novel. 1991. 480p. 22.00 o.p. (*0-688-08835-X*, Morrow, William & Co.) Morrow/Avon.

Edwards, Ruth Dudley. Clubbed to Death. 1992. 208p. 17.95 o.p. (*0-312-08163-4*, Saint Martin's Minotaur) St. Martin's Pr.

—Corridors of Death. l.t. ed. 2001. 21.95 (*0-7540-8581-3*, Black Dagger); 1983. 335 p. (*0-89340-591-4*) BBC Audiobooks America.

—Corridors of Death. l.t. ed. 2000. (G. K. Hall Nightingale Ser.). 288p. pap. 21.95 (*0-7838-9261-6*); (*0-7540-4301-0*); (*0-7540-4302-9*) Gale Group. (Macmillan Reference USA).

—Corridors of Death. 1982. 196p. 10.95 o.p. (*0-312-17012-2*) St. Martin's Pr.

—The English School of Murder. 1990. 15.95 o.p. (*0-312-04311-2*, Saint Martin's Minotaur) St. Martin's Pr.

—Matricide at St. Martha's. 1995. 192p. 19.95 o.p. (*0-312-13122-4*, Saint Martin's Minotaur) St. Martin's Pr.

—Publish & Be Murdered. unabr. ed. 1999. audio 54.95 (*0-7540-0238-1*, CAB1661) Chivers Audio Bks. GBR. *Dist:* BBC Audiobooks America.

—The Saint Valentine's Day Murders. 1985. 192p. 12.95 o.p. (*0-312-69732-5*) St. Martin's Pr.

—The School of English Murder. l.t. ed. 1992. (Mystery Ser.). 432p. 29.99 o.p. (*0-7089-2765-3*, Ulverscroft) Thorpe, F. A. Pubs. GBR. *Dist:* Ulverscroft Large Print Bks., Ltd., Ulverscroft Large Print Canada, Ltd.

—Ten Lords A-Leaping. Wallis, Bill, ed. unabr. ed. 1999. audio 54.95 (*0-7540-0389-2*, CAB1812) Chivers Audio Bks. GBR. *Dist:* BBC Audiobooks America.

—Ten Lords A-Leaping. 1996. 272p. 21.95 o.p. (*0-312-14430-X*, Saint Martin's Minotaur) St. Martin's Pr.

—Ten Lords A-Leaping. l.t. ed. 1997. (Ulverscroft Large Print Ser.). 432p. 29.99 o.p. (*0-7089-3718-7*, Ulverscroft) Thorpe, F. A. Pubs. GBR. *Dist:* Ulverscroft Large Print Bks., Ltd., Ulverscroft Large Print Canada, Ltd.

Elgin, Elizabeth. Scapegoat for a Stuart. 1999. 208p. 24.00 (*0-7278-5385-6*) Severn Hse. Pubs., Ltd.

—Scapegoat for a Stuart. l.t. ed. 1999. (General Ser.). 258p. pap. 22.95 (*0-7862-1819-3*) Thorndike Pr.

Emerson, Kathy Lynn. Face down among the Winchester Geese. 2001. 272p. mass mkt. 5.99 o.s.i (*1-57566-655-3*, Kensington Bks.) Kensington Publishing Corp.

Farnol, Jeffrey. Shadow, & Other Stories. 1977. (Short Story Index Reprint Ser.). 19.95 (*0-8369-3529-2*) Ayer Co. Pubs., Inc.

Feather, Jane. To Kiss a Spy. (Kiss Bks.). 2003. 432p. mass mkt. 5.99 (*0-553-58307-7*); 2002. 320p. 19.95 (*0-553-80172-4*) Bantam Dell Publishing Group.

—To Kiss a Spy. l.t. ed. 2002. 544p. 31.95 (*0-7838-9739-1*) Gale Group.

—To Kiss a Spy. l.t. ed. (Core Ser.). 2003. 544p. 13.95 (*0-7838-9746-4*); 2002. (*0-7862-9748-4*) Thorndike Pr.

—The Widow's Kiss. l.t. ed. 2001. (Romance Ser.). 548p. 29.95 o.p. (*1-58724-087-4*, Wheeler Publishing, Inc.) Gale Group.

Ferguson, Jo Ann. His Unexpected Bride. 2002. (Zebra Regency Romance Ser.). 256p. mass mkt. 4.99 o.s.i (*0-8217-7175-2*) Kensington Publishing Corp.

—His Unexpected Bride. 2002. (Romance Ser.). 27.95 (*0-7862-4866-1*) Thorndike Pr.

Ferrier, Susan. Marriage. Set. unabr. ed. 1994. (Orig.). audio 65.95 (*1-55685-322-X*) Audio Bk. Contractors, Inc.

—Marriage. Foltinek, Herbert, ed. & intro. by. 1986. (Oxford World's Classics Ser.). 528p. (Orig.). pap. 6.95 o.p. (*0-19-281743-4*) Oxford Univ. Pr., Inc.

—Marriage. 2nd ed. 1998. (Oxford World's Classics Ser.). 524p. (Orig.). pap. 10.95 o.p. (*0-19-282524-0*) Oxford Univ. Pr., Inc.

—Marriage. 1986. (Virago Modern Classics Ser.). 512p. (Orig.). pap. 6.95 o.p. (*0-14-016126-0*, Penguin Bks.) Viking Penguin.

Ferrier, Susan, et al. Marriage. Foltinek, Herbert, ed. 2nd ed. 2002. (Oxford World's Classics Ser.). 528p. (Orig.). pap. 10.95 (*0-19-283893-8*) Oxford Univ. Pr., Inc.

Fforde, Jasper. The Well of Lost Plots: A Thursday Next Novel. 2004. 400p. 24.95 (*0-670-03289-1*) Viking Penguin.

Ffrode, Katie. Second Thyme Around. 2001. 384p. 24.95 (*0-312-27304-5*) St. Martin's Pr.

Fiechler, J. J. Death by Publication: An Arcade Mystery. 1996. 176p. pap. 9.95 (*1-55970-337-7*) Arcade Publishing, Inc.

Fiechter, J. J. Death by Publication. 1995. 176p. 19.95 (*1-55970-285-0*) Arcade Publishing, Inc.

Fischer, Tibor. The Thought Gang. 1995. 320p. text 18.95 (*1-56584-286-3*) New Pr., The.

—The Thought Gang. 1994. 18.00 (*0-7486-6160-3*) Polygon GBR. *Dist:* Subterranean Co.

—The Thought Gang. 1997. 320p. pap. 13.00 (*0-684-83079-5*, Touchstone) Simon & Schuster.

Fishkin, Shelley Fisher, ed. 1601 & Is Shakespeare Dead? (1882, 1909) 1996. (Illus.). 256p. 22.00 o.p. (*0-19-510160-X*) Oxford Univ. Pr., Inc.

Fitzgerald, Penelope. Human Voices. 1980. 176p. 5.25 (*0-00-222280-9*) HarperSanFrancisco.

—Human Voices. 1999. 143p. pap. 12.00 (*0-395-95617-X*, Mariner Bks.) Houghton Mifflin Co. Trade & Reference Div.

—Human Voices. l.t. ed. 2000. (General Ser.). 202p. pap. 22.95 o.p. (*0-7862-2306-5*) Thorndike Pr.

—Offshore, Human Voices: The Beginning of Spring. 2003. 480p. 23.00 (*1-4000-4125-2*, Everyman's Library) Knopf Publishing Group.

Fleming, Ian. Goldfinger. l.t. ed. 1993. pap. 17.95 o.p. (*0-7927-1319-2*); 1993. pap. 17.95 o.p. (*0-7927-1472-5*); 1992. 19.95 o.p. (*0-7927-1320-6*) BBC Audiobooks America.

—James Bond 007: Five Complete Novels. 1988. 2.00 o.s.i (*0-517-65352-4*) Random Hse. Value Publishing.

Foley, Winifred. Village Fates. 16th l.t. ed. 2001. 192p. pap. 21.99 o.p. (*0-7531-6343-8*) Thorpe, F. A. Pubs. GBR. *Dist:* Ulverscroft Large Print Bks., Ltd., Ulverscroft Large Print Canada, Ltd.

Follett, Ken. A Dangerous Fortune. unabr. ed. 1994. audio 105.25 (*1-56100-177-5*, 853, Unabridged Library Editions); audio 27.95 o.p. (*1-56100-551-7*, 80, Bookcassette) Brilliance Audio.

—A Dangerous Fortune. 1994. 576p. mass mkt. 7.99 (*0-440-21749-0*); 1994. 576p. mass mkt. 8.99 (*0-440-22078-5*); 1993. 896p. 28.95 o.s.i (*0-385-31188-5*, Delacorte Pr.) Dell Publishing.

—A Dangerous Fortune. unabr. ed. 1994. audio 112.00 (*1-55690-965-9*, 94108E7); Set. 1999. audio 85.00 Recorded Bks., LLC.

—Jackdaws. 2001. 464p. 26.95 o.s.i (*0-525-94628-4*, Dutton) Dutton/Plume.

—Jackdaws. 2002. 496p. pap. 7.99 (*0-451-20559-6*); 512p. reprint ed. mass mkt. 7.99 (*0-451-20752-1*, Signet Bks.) NAL.

—Jackdaws. 2003. E-Book 7.99 (*0-7865-3809-0*) Penguin Putnam, Inc E-Books.

—Jackdaws. l.t. ed. 2001. 688p. 26.95 (*0-375-43159-4*) Random Hse. Large Print.

—Jackdaws. abr. ed. 2001. 4p. audio 24.95 o.s.i (*0-14-280001-5*); 5p. audio compact disk 29.95 (*0-14-280002-3*); 8p. audio 44.95 o.s.i (*0-14-280003-1*) Viking Penguin. (Penguin AudioBooks).

—The Man from St. Petersburg. l.t. ed. 1993. 23.95 o.p. (*0-7927-1473-3*) BBC Audiobooks America.

—The Man from St. Petersburg. l.t. ed. 1982. lib. bdg. 15.95 o.p. (*0-8161-3412-X*, Macmillan Reference USA) Gale Group.

—The Man from St. Petersburg. 1982. 320p. 19.95 o.p. (*0-688-01150-0*, Morrow, William & Co.) Morrow/Avon.

—The Man from St. Petersburg. 2003. 320p. pap. 13.95 (*0-451-20870-6*); 1983. 352p. mass mkt. 4.95 o.p. (*0-451-15494-0*, Signet Bks.); 1983. 384p. mass mkt. 7.99 (*0-451-16351-6*, Signet Bks.); 1983. mass mkt. 3.95 o.p. (*0-451-12438-3*, Signet Bks.); 1983. mass mkt. 4.50 o.p. (*0-451-14327-2*, Signet Bks.) NAL.

—The Pillars of the Earth. unabr. ed. 1989. audio 216.00 Books on Tape, Inc.

—The Pillars of the Earth. unabr. ed. 1989. audio 39.95 o.p. (*0-930435-52-4*, 212, Bookcassette); audio 178.50 (*1-56100-046-9*, 985, Unabridged Library Editions); audio 39.95 Brilliance Audio.

—The Pillars of the Earth. Golbitz, Pat, ed. 1989. (Illus.). 1000p. 22.95 o.p. (*0-688-04659-2*, Morrow, William & Co.) Morrow/Avon.

—The Pillars of the Earth. 2002. 976p. pap. 19.00 (*0-451-20714-9*); 1990. 992p. mass mkt. 7.99 (*0-451-16689-2*, Signet Bks.) NAL.

—The Pillars of the Earth, Set. abr. ed. 1989. audio 22.95 (*0-671-69084-1*, 692288, Simon & Schuster Audioworks) Simon & Schuster Audio.

Ford, Ford Madox. The Fifth Queen Crowned: A Romance. 2000. 252p. E-Book 3.95 (*0-594-02477-3*) 1873 Pr.

—The Fifth Queen Crowned: A Romance. reprint ed. lib. bdg. 98.00 (*0-7426-3077-3*); 2001. 314p. pap. text 28.00 (*0-7426-8077-0*) Classic Bks.

—No More Parades: A Novel. 1999. 305p. text 29.95 (*1-56000-468-1*) Transaction Pubs.

—Parade's End. 1997. 600p. pap. 27.95 (*1-85754-342-4*) Carcanet Pr., Ltd. GBR. *Dist:* Paul & Co. Pubs. Consortium, Inc.

—Parade's End. 1992. 20.00 (*0-679-41728-1*); 1961. 18.95 o.s.i (*0-394-43972-4*) Knopf, Alfred A. Inc.

—Parade's End: Consisting of "Some Do Not", "No More Parades", "A Man Could Stand up", & "The Last Post" 1979. pap. 20.00 o.s.i (*0-394-74108-0*, Vintage) Knopf Publishing Group.

—The Young Lovell: A Romance. 2000. 252p. E-Book 9.95 (*0-594-03094-3*) 1873 Pr.

—The Young Lovell: A Romance. reprint ed. lib. bdg. 98.00 (*0-7426-3094-3*); 2001. 93p. pap. text 28.00 (*0-7426-8094-0*) Classic Bks.

—The Young Lovell: A Romance. 320p. reprint ed. lib. bdg. (*0-7734-9990-3*) Mellen, Edwin Pr., The.

Forester, C. S. Hornblower & the Atropos. 1953. 17.95 o.p. (*0-316-28911-6*); 1985. (Hornblower Ser.: No. 5). 352p. reprint ed. pap. 13.00 (*0-316-28929-9*, Back Bay) Little Brown & Co.

—Hornblower & the Hotspur. 1976. (Hornblower Ser.: No. 3). 25.95 (*0-8488-0488-0*, Queens Hse., Inc.) Amereon, Ltd.

—Hornblower & the Hotspur. 1981. (Hornblower Ser.: No. 3). 352p. pap. 2.75 o.p. (*0-523-41790-X*, Pinnacle Bks.) Kensington Publishing Corp.

—Hornblower & the Hotspur. 1998. (Hornblower Ser.: No. 3). 400p. pap. 13.00 (*0-316-29046-7*, Back Bay); 1985. 344p. pap. 14.95 o.p. (*0-316-28928-0*, Back Bay); 1962. 17.95 o.p. (*0-316-28899-3*) Little Brown & Co.

—Hornblower During the Crisis. 1967. (Illus.). 162p. 17.95 o.p. (*0-316-28915-9*); 1990. (Hornblower Ser.: No. 4). 176p. reprint ed. pap. 13.00 (*0-316-28944-2*, Back Bay) Little Brown & Co.

—Lieutenant Hornblower. 1976. (Hornblower Ser.: No. 2). 24.95 (*0-8488-0489-9*, Queens Hse., Inc.) Amereon, Ltd.

—Lieutenant Hornblower. (Hornblower Ser.: No. 2). 1980. 320p. pap. 2.50 o.p. (*0-523-41387-4*); 1974. pap. 1.50 o.p. (*0-523-00382-X*) Kensington Publishing Corp. (Pinnacle Bks.).

—Lieutenant Hornblower. 1998. (Hornblower Ser.: No. 2). 320p. pap. 13.00 (*0-316-29063-7*, Back Bay) Little Brown & Co.

—Mr. Midshipman Hornblower. 1991. (Hornblower Ser.: No. 1). lib. bdg. 21.95 (*1-56849-053-4*) Buccaneer Bks., Inc.

—Mr. Midshipman Hornblower. (Hornblower Ser.: No. 1). 1981. 172p. pap. 2.50 o.p. (*0-523-41672-5*); 1974. pap. 1.50 o.p. (*0-523-23381-7*) Kensington Publishing Corp. (Pinnacle Bks.).

—Mr. Midshipman Hornblower. 320p. 1998. 18.95 o.p. (*0-316-29060-2*); 1984. (Hornblower Ser.: No. 1). reprint ed. pap. 13.00 (*0-316-28912-4*, Back Bay) Little Brown & Co.

—Mr. Midshipman Hornblower. abr. ed. 1998. (Hornblower Ser.: No. 1). audio 16.95 (*1-85998-975-6*) Trafalgar Square.

Forrest, Anthony. A Balance of Dangers: A Captain Justice Story. 1984. 240p. 14.95 o.p. (*0-8090-2800-X*, Hill & Wang) Farrar, Straus & Giroux.

Forster, E. M. Eternal Moment & Other Stories. 1970. 132p. reprint ed. pap. 14.00 (*0-15-629125-8*, Harvest Bks.) Harcourt Trade Pubs.

Foster, Stephen. It Cracks Like Breaking Skin. 1999. 150p. pap. (*0-571-19506-7*) Faber & Faber, Inc.

Francis, Clare. Deceit. 2001. 425p. 24.00 (*1-56947-239-4*) Soho Pr., Inc.

—Deceit. l.t. ed. 1995. (Charnwood Large Print Ser.). 608p. 29.99 o.p. (*0-7089-8813-X*, Charnwood) Thorpe, F. A. Pubs. GBR. *Dist:* Ulverscroft Large Print Bks., Ltd., Ulverscroft Large Print Canada, Ltd.

—The Killing Winds: A Novel. 1992. 23.00 o.p. (*0-671-76939-1*, Simon & Schuster) Simon & Schuster.

Frankau, Gilbert. Men, Maids & Mustard-Pot: A Collection of Tales. 1977. (Short Story Index Reprint Ser.). reprint ed. 25.95 (*0-8369-3939-5*) Ayer Co. Pubs., Inc.

Fraser, George MacDonald. Flash for Freedom! unabr. ed. 1993. audio 69.95 o.p. (*0-7451-4208-7*, CAB 891) BBC Audiobooks America.

—Flash for Freedom! unabr. ed. 1994. (Flashman Ser.). audio 64.00 (*0-7366-2724-3*, 3454) Books on Tape, Inc.

—Flash for Freedom! 1985. (Flashman Ser.). pap. 6.95 o.p. (*0-452-25677-1*); 304p. pap. 14.00 (*0-452-26089-2*) Dutton/Plume. (Plume).

—Flash for Freedom! 1973. (Flashman Ser.). mass mkt. 1.50 o.p. (*0-451-06933-1*); mass mkt. 1.25 o.p. (*0-451-05491-1*) NAL. (Signet Bks.).

—Flashman. unabr. ed. 1994. (Flashman Ser.). audio 56.00 (*0-7366-2675-1*, 3412) Books on Tape, Inc.

—Flashman. 1984. (Flashman Ser.). 256p. pap. 14.00 (*0-452-25961-4*); pap. 6.95 o.p. (*0-452-25588-0*) Dutton/Plume. (Plume).

—Flashman. (Flashman Ser.). 1974. mass mkt. 1.25 o.p. (*0-451-06116-0*); 1970. mass mkt. 0.95 o.p. (*0-451-04264-6*); 1970. mass mkt. 1.50 o.p. (*0-451-06932-3*); 1970. mass mkt. 1.75 o.p. (*0-451-08009-2*); 1970. mass mkt. 2.50 o.p. (*0-451-11658-5*) NAL. (Signet Bks.).

—Flashman. l.t. ed. 1982. (Ulverscroft Large Print Ser.). 476p. 29.99 o.p. (*0-7089-0810-1*, Ulverscroft) Thorpe, F. A. Pubs. GBR. *Dist:* Ulverscroft Large Print Bks., Ltd., Ulverscroft Large Print Canada, Ltd.

—Flashman & the Mountain of Light. unabr. ed. 1995. (Flashman Ser.). audio 80.00 (*0-7366-3096-1*, 3772) Books on Tape, Inc.

—Flashman & the Mountain of Light. 1992. (Flashman Ser.). 368p. reprint ed. pap. 13.95 (*0-452-26785-4*, Plume) Dutton/Plume.

—Flashman's Lady. unabr. collector's ed. 1995. (Flashman Ser.). audio 72.00 (*0-7366-3008-2*, 3694) Books on Tape, Inc.

—Flashman's Lady. 1988. (Flashman Ser.). pap. 8.95 o.p. (*0-452-26080-9*); 336p. pap. 13.95 (*0-452-26489-8*) Dutton/Plume. (Plume).

—Flashman's Lady. 1979. (Flashman Ser.). mass mkt. 2.95 o.p. (*0-451-11660-7*, AE1660); mass mkt. 2.25 o.p. (*0-451-08514-0*) NAL. (Signet Bks.).

—Flashman's Lady. 1978. 8.95 o.p. (*0-394-50135-7*, Knopf Bks. for Young Readers) Random Hse. Children's Bks.

Frazer, Margaret. The Clerk's Tale. 2002. (Dame Frevisse Mystery Ser.). 320p. 22.95 (*0-425-18324-6*, Prime Crime) Berkley Publishing Group.

Freemantle, Brian. Charlie Muffin U. S. A. 1982. 208p. mass mkt. 2.50 o.s.i (*0-345-29440-8*) Ballantine Bks.

—Charlie's Apprentice. l.t. ed. 1994. 577p. lib. bdg. 22.95 (*0-8161-7489-X*, Macmillan Reference USA) Gale Group.

—Charlie's Apprentice: A Charlie Muffin Mystery. 1994. 320p. 21.95 o.p. (*0-312-10951-2*, Saint Martin's Minotaur) St. Martin's Pr.

—Charlie's Choice: The First Charlie Muffin Omnibus. 1998. 415p. pap. 18.95 (*1-899344-26-8*) Do-Not Pr., The GBR. *Dist:* Dufour Editions, Inc.

—Comrade Charlie: A Charlie Muffin Novel. 1992. 448p. 22.95 o.p. (*0-312-08166-9*) St. Martin's Pr.

Friends at Court. 1988. 2.50 o.p. (*0-938822-77-2*) U.S. Tennis Assn.

Fritchley, Alma. Chicken Feed. 138p. pap. 11.95 (*0-7043-4692-3*); 1999. 222p. pap. 13.95 (*0-7043-4570-6*) Women's Pr., Ltd., The GBR. *Dist:* Trafalgar Square.

—Chicken Out. 2000. (Letty Campbell Mystery Ser.: No. 3). 164p. pap. 13.95 (*0-7043-4619-2*) Women's Pr., Ltd., The GBR. *Dist:* Trafalgar Square.

—Chicken Run: A Letty Campbell Mystery. 1998. 136p. pap. 13.95 (*0-7043-4515-3*) Women's Pr., Ltd., The GBR. *Dist:* Trafalgar Square.

Fullerton, Alexander. Sixty Minutes for St. George. 2003. 320p. pap. 13.00 (*1-56947-321-8*); 2002. 308p. 24.00 (*1-56947-293-9*) Soho Pr., Inc.

—Sixty Minutes for St. George. l.t. ed. 1988. (Ulverscroft Large Print Ser.). 480p. 29.99 o.p. (*0-7089-1761-5*, Ulverscroft) Thorpe, F. A. Pubs. GBR. *Dist:* Ulverscroft Large Print Bks., Ltd., Ulverscroft Large Print Canada, Ltd.

Gardner, John E. Cold Fall. 1997. 304p. mass mkt. 6.99 o.s.i (*0-425-15902-7*) Berkley Publishing Group.

—Cold Fall, Set. abr. ed. 1996. audio 17.95 o.p. (*0-7871-0544-9*, 393873, Dove Audio) NewStar Media, Inc.

—Cold Fall. 1996. 240p. 22.95 o.p. (*0-399-14149-9*, G. P. Putnam's Sons) Penguin Group (USA) Inc.

—Confessor. l.t. ed. 1995. 25.95 (*1-56895-280-5*, Wheeler Publishing, Inc.) Gale Group.

—Confessor. 1995. 560p. 22.50 (*1-883402-25-5*, Scribner) Simon & Schuster.

—For Special Services. l.t. ed. 1982. (General Ser.). 13.95 o.p. (*0-8161-3477-4*, Macmillan Reference USA) Gale Group.

—Ian Fleming's James Bond: Three Complete Novels. 1988. 592p. 11.99 o.s.i (*0-517-67250-2*); 1987. 672p. 7.99 o.s.i (*0-517-64293-X*) Random Hse. Value Publishing.

—Icebreaker. 1986. 304p. mass mkt. 4.95 o.s.i (*0-425-08758-1*) Berkley Publishing Group.

Settings

—Maestro. 1993. 280p. 23.00 (1-883402-24-7, Scribner) Simon & Schuster.

—Maestro. 1995. 656p. mass mkt. 6.50 o.s.i (0-446-60168-3) Warner Bks., Inc.

—The Man from Barbarossa. l.t. ed. 1993. pap. 17.95 o.p. (0-7927-1350-8); 1992. 19.95 o.p. (0-7927-1351-6) BBC Audiobooks America.

—The Man from Barbarossa. 1992. mass mkt. 5.50 o.s.i (0-425-13234-X) Berkley Publishing Group.

—The Man from Barbarossa. 1991. (James Bond Adventure Ser.). 304p. 14.95 o.p. (0-399-13625-8, G. P. Putnam's Sons) Penguin Group (USA) Inc.

—Never Send Flowers. 1994. pap. 19.95 o.p. (0-7927-1924-7) BBC Audiobooks America.

—No Deals, Mr. Bond. 1987. 320p. 13.95 o.p. (0-399-13254-6, G. P. Putnam's Sons) Penguin Putnam Bks. for Young Readers.

—Nobody Lives Forever. unabr. ed. 1992. (James Bond Ser.). audio 54.95 (0-7451-4048-3, CAB 745) BBC Audiobooks America.

—Nobody Lives Forever. 1990. (James Bond Ser.). mass mkt. 4.99 o.s.i (0-425-12320-0) Berkley Publishing Group.

—Nobody Lives Forever. 1986. 13.95 o.p. (0-399-13151-5) Putnam Publishing Group, The.

—Role of Honor. 1987. 4.50 o.s.i (0-441-73437-5) Ace Bks.

—Role of Honor. 1988. 4.50 (1-55773-125-X, Diamond Bks.); 1986. 304p. pap. 3.95 o.s.i (0-425-09497-9); 1985. mass mkt. 4.95 o.s.i (0-425-07671-7) Berkley Publishing Group.

—Role of Honor. l.t. ed. 1985. (General Ser.). 15.95 o.p. (0-8161-3850-8, Macmillan Reference USA) Gale Group.

—Role of Honor. 1984. (James Bond Adventure Ser.). 304p. 11.95 o.p. (0-399-12912-X, G. P. Putnam's Sons) Penguin Putnam Bks. for Young Readers.

—Seafire. 1995. 304p. mass mkt. 6.99 o.s.i (0-425-14775-4) Berkley Publishing Group.

—Seafire. 1994. 288p. 18.95 o.p. (0-399-13938-9, G. P. Putnam's Sons) Penguin Group (USA) Inc.

—The Secret Houses. 1987. 384p. 18.95 o.p. (0-399-13311-9, G. P. Putnam's Sons) Penguin Putnam Bks. for Young Readers.

Garrett, George P. Entered from the Sun: The Murder of Marlowe. 1990. 349p. 19.95 o.s.i (0-385-19095-6) Doubleday Publishing.

—Entered from the Sun: The Murder of Marlowe. 1991. 372p. pap. 20.00 (0-15-628795-1, Harvest Bks.) Harcourt Trade Pubs.

Garwood, Haley E. The Forgotten Queen. 1998. (Warrior Queen Ser.). (Illus.). x, 465p. pap. 17.95 (0-9659721-9-4, 1998-3-1-1) Writers Block, The.

Garwood, Julie. Saving Grace. l.t. ed. 593p. 1994. lib. bdg. 17.95 (0-8161-5891-6); 1993. lib. bdg. 22.95 (0-8161-5890-8) Gale Group. (Macmillan Reference USA).

—Saving Grace. 1993. 384p. 22.00 (0-671-74422-4, Atria) Simon & Schuster.

—Saving Grace. Marrow, Linda, ed. 1994. (Illus.). 432p. reprint ed. mass mkt. 7.99 (0-671-87011-4, Pocket) Simon & Schuster.

—Saving Grace. 1999. pap. 9.98 (0-671-04495-8); 1993. audio 17.00 (0-671-86966-3, 391512) Simon & Schuster Audio. (Simon & Schuster Audioworks).

Gaskin, Catherine. The Ambassador's Women. 1986. 512p. 18.95 o.p. (0-684-18661-6, Macmillan Reference USA) Gale Group.

Geisler, Barbara R. Other Gods: The Averillan Chronicles. 2002. (Illus.). 304p. pap. 16.95 (1-882897-64-1) Lost Coast Pr.

Gellis, Roberta. Bone of Contention: A Magdalene la Batarde Mystery. mass mkt. (0-7653-4007-0, Tor Bks.); 2002. 432p. 25.95 (0-7653-0019-2, Forge Bks.) Doherty, Tom Assocs., LLC.

—Masques of Gold. 1988. pap. 7.95 o.p. (0-515-09816-7, Jove) Berkley Publishing Group.

—A Silver Mirror. 1994. 512p. mass mkt. 5.99 o.s.i (0-425-14237-X) Berkley Publishing Group.

George, Melanie. The Mating Game. 2002. 336p. mass mkt. 5.99 (0-8217-7120-5) Kensington Publishing Corp.

Giardina, Denise. Fallam's Secret: A Novel. 2003. 356p. 24.95 (0-393-05206-0) Norton, W. W. & Co., Inc.

Gibbs, Tony. Shadow Queen. 1992. 336p. 17.95 o.p. (0-89296-473-1) Mysterious Pr.

—Shadow Queen. 1993. 336p. mass mkt. 4.99 (0-446-40108-0, Mysterious Pr. Paperback Bks.) Warner Bks., Inc.

Gidley, Charles. Armada. 1988. 19.95 o.p. (0-670-81807-0) Viking Penguin.

Gilbert, Michael. Into Battle. 1997. 224p. 21.00 o.p. (0-7867-0398-9, Carroll & Graf Pubs.) Avalon Publishing Group.

—Mr. Calder & Mr. Behrens. 1982. 224p. 12.45 o.p. (0-06-014932-9) HarperCollins Pubs.

—Mr. Calder & Mr. Behrens. 1983. 256p. pap. 3.95 o.p. (0-14-006637-3, Penguin Bks.) Viking Penguin.

Gissing, George R. The House of Cobwebs. 1977. (Short Story Index Reprint Ser.). reprint ed. 25.95 (0-8369-3911-5) Ayer Co. Pubs., Inc.

—Human Odds & Ends. Fletcher, Ian & Stokes, John, eds. 1977. (Decadent Consciousness Ser.). lib. bdg. 46.00 o.p. (0-8240-2759-0) Garland Publishing, Inc.

Godwin, Parke. Invitation to Camelot. 1988. mass mkt. 3.50 o.s.i (0-441-37200-7) Ace Bks.

—Lord of Sunset. 1999. 576p. mass mkt. 6.99 o.s.i (0-380-81064-6, Eos); 1998. pap. 13.00 o.s.i (0-380-72675-0, Avon Bks.) Morrow/Avon.

—Robin & the King. 1993. 366p. 21.00 o.p. (0-688-05274-6, Morrow, William & Co.) Morrow/Avon.

—Sherwood. 1991. 384p. 20.00 o.p. (0-688-05264-9, Morrow, William & Co.) Morrow/Avon.

Golding, William. Darkness Visible. 1981. (Windstone Ser.). 304p. pap. 3.95 o.p. (0-553-14704-8) Bantam Bks.

—Darkness Visible. 1994. lib. bdg. 21.95 o.p. (1-56849-470-X) Buccaneer Bks., Inc.

—Darkness Visible. 1999. 272p. pap. 21.00 (0-374-52560-9); 1979. 265p. 14.95 o.s.i (0-374-13502-9) Farrar, Straus & Giroux.

—Darkness Visible. 1985. 276p. pap. 8.95 (0-15-623931-0, Harvest Bks.) Harcourt Trade Pubs.

Goodman, Joan Elizabeth. The Winter Hare. 1998. 276p. (J). (gr. 4-8). pap. 5.95 o.s.i (0-7868-1242-7) Disney Pr.

Goodwin, Suzanne. A Change of Season. 1992. 576p. 24.95 o.p. (0-312-06923-5) St. Martin's Pr.

—While the Music Lasts. 1993. 384p. 21.95 o.p. (0-312-09937-1) St. Martin's Pr.

—While the Music Lasts. l.t. ed. 1994. (Ulverscroft Large Print Ser.). 752p. 29.99 o.p. (0-7089-3024-7, Ulverscroft) Thorpe, F. A. Pubs. GBR. Dist: Ulverscroft Large Print Bks., Ltd., Ulverscroft Large Print Canada, Ltd.

Gower, Iris. A Royal Ambition. l.t. ed. 2000. (Romance Ser.). 293p. 25.95 (0-7862-2647-1) Thorndike Pr.

Gower, Iris, contrib. by. A Royal Ambition. l.t. ed. 2000. 293p. (0-7540-4233-2); (0-7540-4234-0) Thorndike Pr.

Grace, C. L. A Maze of Murders: A Medieval Mystery Featuring Kathryn Swinbrooke. 2003. 256p. 23.95 (0-312-29016-0, Saint Martin's Minotaur) St. Martin's Pr.

Grand, Sarah. Our Manifold Nature. 1977. (Short Story Index Reprint Ser.). 19.95 (0-8369-3255-2) Ayer Co. Pubs., Inc.

Grange, Amanda. Marriage at the Manor. l.t. ed. 2003. 288p. pap. 25.95 (0-7862-5419-X) Thorndike Pr.

Granger, Ann. A Restless Evil: A Mitchell & Markby Mystery. Date not set. pap. (0-312-30656-3, Saint Martin's Griffin); Date not set. E-Book (0-312-70514-X); mass mkt. (0-312-98553-3, St. Martin's Paperbacks); 2002. (Illus.). 256p. 23.95 (0-312-30655-5, Saint Martin's Minotaur) St. Martin's Pr.

—A Restless Evil: A Mitchell & Markby Mystery. l.t. ed. 2003. lib. bdg. 25.95 (0-7862-5096-8) Thorndike Pr.

Grasso, Patricia. To Tempt an Angel. 2002. (Zebra Historical Romance Ser.). 384p. mass mkt. 5.99 o.s.i (0-8217-6872-7) Kensington Publishing Corp.

Greene, Graham. Collected Stories. 1973. 16.95 o.p. (0-670-22911-3) Viking Penguin.

Greene, Maria. The Ghost & Mrs. Wenthaven. 2003. 196p. 26.95 (1-59414-022-7, Five Star) Gale Group.

—The Ghost & Mrs. Wenthaven. 2002. (Zebra Regency Romance Ser.). 256p. mass mkt. 4.99 o.s.i (0-8217-7237-6) Kensington Publishing Corp.

Gregory, Philippa. Earthly Joys, Set. unabr. ed. 1999. audio 116.00 Recorded Bks., LLC.

—Earthly Joys. 1998. 448p. 25.95 (0-312-19262-2) St. Martin's Pr.

—Fallen Skies. l.t. ed. 1996. 25.95 o.p. (0-7838-1692-8, Macmillan Reference USA) Gale Group.

—Fallen Skies. 1995. 512p. 25.00 o.p. (0-06-017639-3) HarperTrade.

—Fallen Skies. 1995. 640p. mass mkt. 5.99 o.p. (0-06-109378-5, HarperTorch) Morrow/Avon.

—The Favored Child. 2003. 624p. pap. 14.00 (0-7432-4930-5, Touchstone); 1989. 18.95 o.p. (0-671-67910-4, Atria) Simon & Schuster.

—The Wise Woman. 1994. 528p. mass mkt. 5.99 (0-671-79275-X, Pocket) Simon & Schuster.

—The Wise Woman. Zion, Claire, ed. 1993. 448p. 22.00 (0-671-79274-1, Atria) Simon & Schuster.

Gregory, Susanna. A Bone of Contention. 1998. (Illus.). 506p. mass mkt. 7.95 o.s.i (0-7515-2022-5) Warner Futura GBR. Dist: Trafalgar Square.

—A Bone of Contention: The Second Chronicle of Matthew Bartholomew. 1997. (Illus.). 288p. o.s.i (0-316-88280-1) Little Brown & Co.

—A Bone of Contention: The Second Chronicle of Matthew Bartholomew. 1997. (Chronicle of Matthew Bartholomew Ser.: Vol. 2). 288p. 23.95 (0-312-16792-X, Saint Martin's Minotaur) St. Martin's Pr.

—An Unholy Alliance. 1996. (Illus.). 310p. o.s.i (0-316-87911-8) Little Brown & Co.

—An Unholy Alliance. 1998. (Matthew Bartholomew Mysteries Ser.). 336p. mass mkt. 5.99 o.p. (0-312-96631-8, St. Martin's Paperbacks); 1996. (Chronicle of Matthew Bartholomew Ser.: Vol. 1). 288p. 23.95 o.p. (0-312-14752-X, Saint Martin's Minotaur) St. Martin's Pr.

—A Wicked Deed. 2003. (Illus.). 506p. pap. 7.95 (0-7515-2544-8) Warner Bks. GBR. Dist: Trafalgar Square.

Guler, Kathleen C. Into the Path of Gods. 1998. (Macsen's Treasure Ser.). (Illus.). 413p. 22.95 (0-9660371-0-3) Bardsong Pr.

Haggard, William. The Martello Tower. l.t. ed. 1987. pap. 13.95 o.p. (1-55504-453-0) BBC Audiobooks America.

—The Martello Tower. 1987. 160p. 18.95 o.p. (0-340-39213-4) Hodder & Stoughton, Ltd. GBR. Dist: Lubrecht & Cramer, Ltd., Trafalgar Square.

—Meritocrats. l.t. ed. 1987. pap. 13.95 o.p. (1-55504-217-1) BBC Audiobooks America.

—Need to Know. l.t. ed. 1986. pap. 13.95 o.p. (1-55504-038-1) BBC Audiobooks America.

—Teleman Touch. l.t. ed. 1988. pap. 13.95 o.p. (1-55504-446-8) BBC Audiobooks America.

Haig, Kathryn. Apple Blossom Time. 1998. 464p. 26.95 o.p. (0-312-18313-5) St. Martin's Pr.

—Apple Blossom Time. 2000. 458p. pap. 9.95 (0-552-14537-8) Transworld Publishers Ltd. GBR. Dist: Trafalgar Square.

Hale, Edward E., ed. English Stories. 1977. (Short Story Index Reprint Ser.). 19.95 (0-8369-3145-9) Ayer Co. Pubs., Inc.

Hall, Adam. The Kobra Manifesto. 1986. 256p. (J). mass mkt. 3.50 o.s.i (0-515-08698-3, Jove) Berkley Publishing Group.

—The Kobra Manifesto. unabr. collector's ed. 1984. (Quiller Ser.). audio 48.00 (0-7366-0604-1, 1570) Books on Tape, Inc.

—The Kobra Manifesto. 1978. pap. 1.95 o.p. (0-440-14406-X) Dell Publishing.

—The Kobra Manifesto. 1977. lib. bdg. 13.50 o.p. (0-8161-6454-1, Macmillan Reference USA) Gale Group.

—The Kobra Manifesto. 1993. 352p. mass mkt. 4.50 o.p. (0-06-100532-0, HarperTorch) Morrow/Avon.

—The Mandarin Cypher. 1986. 240p. mass mkt. 3.50 o.s.i (0-515-08623-1, Jove) Berkley Publishing Group.

—The Mandarin Cypher. unabr. collector's ed. 1987. (Quiller Ser.). audio 48.00 (0-7366-1164-9, 2089) Books on Tape, Inc.

—The Mandarin Cypher. 1975. reprint ed. lib. bdg. 11.95 o.p. (0-8161-6333-2, Macmillan Reference USA) Gale Group.

—The Mandarin Cypher. 1993. 320p. mass mkt. 4.50 o.p. (0-06-100531-2, HarperTorch) Morrow/Avon.

—The Peking Target. 1988. mass mkt. 3.95 o.s.i (0-515-09680-6); 1983. 290p. 2.95 (0-86721-188-1) Berkley Publishing Group. (Jove).

—The Peking Target. 1994. (Quiller Ser.). 336p. mass mkt. 4.50 o.p. (0-06-100535-5, HarperTorch) Morrow/Avon.

—The Peking Target. 1982. 13.50 o.p. (0-87223-755-9) Playboy Enterprises, Inc.

—Quiller Bamboo. unabr. collector's ed. 1992. (Quiller Ser.). audio 56.00 (0-7366-2117-2, 2920) Books on Tape, Inc.

—Quiller Bamboo. 1992. 320p. mass mkt. 4.99 (0-380-71161-3, Avon Bks.); 1991. 288p. 20.00 o.p. (0-688-09696-4, Morrow, William & Co.) Morrow/Avon.

—Quiller Barracuda. unabr. collector's ed. 1991. (Quiller Ser.). audio 56.00 (0-7366-2023-0, 2838) Books on Tape, Inc.

—Quiller Barracuda. l.t. ed. 1992. 356p. 24.95 (1-85089-594-5) ISIS Large Print Bks. GBR. Dist: Transaction Pubs.

—Quiller Barracuda. 1991. 304p. mass mkt. 4.95 (0-380-70814-0, Avon Bks.); 1990. 18.95 o.p. (0-688-08784-1, Morrow, William & Co.) Morrow/Avon.

—Quiller Meridian. unabr. collector's ed. 1994. (Quiller Ser.). audio 48.00 (0-7366-2641-7, 3379) Books on Tape, Inc.

—Quiller Meridian. 1994. 288p. mass mkt. 4.99 (0-380-71534-1, Avon Bks.); 1993. 287p. 22.00 o.p. (0-688-11797-X, Morrow, William & Co.) Morrow/Avon.

—Quiller Salamander. unabr. collector's ed. 1995. (Quiller Ser.). audio 48.00 (0-7366-2955-6, 3649) Books on Tape, Inc.

—Quiller Salamander. 1994. 272p. 23.00 (1-883402-40-9, Scribner) Simon & Schuster.

—Quiller Solitaire. unabr. collector's ed. 1992. (Quiller Ser.). audio 48.00 (0-7366-2304-3, 3087) Books on Tape, Inc.

—Quiller Solitaire. 288p. 1992. 20.00 o.p. (0-688-10730-3, Morrow, William & Co.); 1993. reprint ed. pap. 4.99 (0-380-71921-5, Avon Bks.) Morrow/Avon.

—The Scorpion Signal. 1988. mass mkt. 3.95 o.s.i (0-515-09645-8); 1981. 288p. 2.95 (0-87216-831-X) Berkley Publishing Group. (Jove).

—The Scorpion Signal. unabr. collector's ed. 1982. (Quiller Ser.). audio 48.00 (0-7366-0603-3, 1569) Books on Tape, Inc.

—The Scorpion Signal. 1980. 10.00 o.p. (0-385-12277-2) Doubleday Publishing.

—The Scorpion Signal. 1993. (Quiller Ser.: No. 9). 79p. mass mkt. 4.50 o.p. (0-06-100534-7, HarperTorch) Morrow/Avon.

—The Sinkiang Executive. 1986. 240p. mass mkt. 3.50 o.s.i (0-515-08678-9, Jove) Berkley Publishing Group.

—The Sinkiang Executive. unabr. collector's ed. 1985. (Quiller Ser.). audio 48.00 (0-7366-0605-X, 1571) Books on Tape, Inc.

—The Sinkiang Executive. 1978. 7.95 o.p. (0-385-12276-4) Doubleday Publishing.

—The Sinkiang Executive. 1993. 352p. mass mkt. 4.50 o.p. (0-06-100533-9, HarperTorch) Morrow/Avon.

—The Striker Portfolio. 1988. mass mkt. 3.50 o.s.i (0-515-09569-9, Jove) Berkley Publishing Group.

—The Striker Portfolio. unabr. collector's ed. 1990. (Quiller Ser.). audio 42.00 (0-7366-1804-X, 2641) Books on Tape, Inc.

—The Striker Portfolio. 1993. 256p. mass mkt. 4.50 o.p. (0-06-100528-2, HarperTorch) Morrow/Avon.

—The Tango Briefing. 1986. 224p. mass mkt. 3.50 o.s.i (0-515-08505-7, Jove) Berkley Publishing Group.

—The Tango Briefing. unabr. collector's ed. 1990. (Quiller Ser.). audio 48.00 (0-7366-1873-2, 2704) Books on Tape, Inc.

—The Tango Briefing. 1993. 336p. mass mkt. 4.50 o.p. (0-06-100530-4, HarperTorch) Morrow/Avon.

—The Warsaw Document. 1988. mass mkt. 3.50 o.s.i (0-515-09768-3, Jove) Berkley Publishing Group.

—The Warsaw Document. unabr. collector's ed. 1990. (Quiller Ser.). audio 48.00 (0-7366-1808-2, 2645) Books on Tape, Inc.

—The Warsaw Document. 1993. 320p. mass mkt. 4.50 o.p. (0-06-100529-0, HarperTorch) Morrow/Avon.

Hall, James Norman. Doctor Dogbody's Leg. 1998. (Heart of Oak Sea Classics Ser.). 272p. 25.00 o.s.i (0-8050-5564-9); 258p. pap. 13.00 o.s.i (0-8050-5831-1, Owl Bks.) Holt, Henry & Co.

Hall, Patricia. In the Bleak Midwinter. 1997. 250p. mass mkt. o.s.i (0-7515-1712-7); 1995. 256p. o.s.i (0-316-91279-4) Little Brown & Co.

Halloran, James D., et al. Television & Delinquency. 1970. (Television Research Committee Working Paper Ser.: No. 3). pap. text 13.00 o.p. (0-7185-1088-7) St. Martin's Pr.

Hamalian, Leo & Karl, Frederick R. The Shape of Fiction: British & American Short Stories. 2nd ed. 1978. (C). (gr. 10-12). text 27.50 net. o.p. (0-07-025699-3) McGraw-Hill Cos., The.

Harding, Paul T., pseud. Red Slayer: Being the Second of the Sorrowful Mysteries of Brother Athelstan. 1995. 288p. mass mkt. 4.99 (0-380-72106-6, Avon Bks.); 1994. 283p. 20.00 o.p. (0-688-12569-7, Morrow, William & Co.) Morrow/Avon.

Hardwick, Mollie. Blood Royal. 1989. 320p. 17.95 o.p. (0-312-02548-3) St. Martin's Pr.

—By the Sword Divided. 1986. (Fiction Ser.). 192p. pap. 3.95 o.p. (0-14-008867-9, Penguin Bks.) Viking Penguin.

Harper, Karen. The Poyson Garden: An Elizabethan Mystery. l.t. ed. 1999. (1-57490-191-5, Beeler Large Print Bks.) Beeler, Thomas T. Publisher.

—The Poyson Garden: An Elizabethan Mystery. 1999. (Bess Tudor Mystery Ser.). 320p. 21.95 o.s.i (0-385-33283-1, Delacorte Pr.) Dell Publishing.

—The Queene's Cure: An Elizabeth I Mystery. 2003. 368p. mass mkt. 6.99 (0-440-23595-2); 2002. (Illus.). 288p. 23.95 (0-385-33478-8) Dell Publishing.

—The Thorne Maze: An Elizabeth I Mystery. 2003. (Elizabeth I Mystery Ser.). 320p. mass mkt. 6.99 (0-312-99349-8, St. Martin's Paperbacks); (Illus.). 288p. 23.95 (0-312-30176-6, Saint Martin's Minotaur) St. Martin's Pr.

Harris, Robert. Enigma, Set. abr. ed. 1995. audio 3.99 o.s.i (0-679-44549-8, 693150, RH Audio) Random Hse. Audio Publishing Group.

—Enigma: A Novel. 1996. 384p. mass mkt. 6.99 (0-8041-1548-6, Ivy Bks.) Ballantine Bks.

—Enigma: A Novel. l.t. ed. 1996. (Large Print Bks.). 27.95 (1-56895-275-9, Wheeler Publishing, Inc.) Gale Group.

—Enigma: A Novel. 1995. pap. 22.00 o.p. (0-679-76505-0) Random Hse., Inc.

Harrison, Harry. The Hammer & the Cross. 1994. 470p. mass mkt. 7.99 (0-8125-2348-2); 1993. 416p. 23.95 o.p. (0-312-85439-0) Doherty, Tom Assocs., LLC. (Tor Bks.).

—King & Emperor. 1997. (Berserker Ser.: Vol. 3). 467p. mass mkt. 6.99 (0-8125-3646-0); 1996. (Hammer & the Cross Ser.: Bk. 3). 384p. 24.95 o.p. (0-312-85692-X) Doherty, Tom Assocs., LLC. (Tor Bks.).

—One King's Way. 1995. 400p. (YA). 23.95 o.p. (0-312-85691-1, Tor Bks.) Doherty, Tom Assocs., LLC.

—Stars & Stripes Triumphant. 2003. 304p. mass mkt. 6.99 (0-345-40938-8); (Illus.). 256p. 24.95 (0-345-40937-X) Ballantine Bks. (Del Rey).
Harrod-Eagles, Cynthia. The Flood-Tide. 1995. (Morland Dynasty Ser.: No. 9). 428p. mass mkt. 6.95 (0-7515-0646-X) Warner Futura GBR. Dist: Trafalgar Square.
—I, Victoria. 1995. 432p. 24.95 o.p. (0-312-13516-5) St. Martin's Pr.
Harry, Lilian. A Girl Called Thursday. l.t. ed. 2003. (Magna Large Print Ser.). 576p. (0-7505-2136-8) Magna Large Print Bks. GBR. Dist: Ulverscroft Large Print Canada, Ltd.
Harvey, John. Last Rites. 1998. 280p. (0-434-00328-X) Heinemann.
Hatfield, Kate. Drowning in Honey. 1996. 288p. text 23.95 o.p. (0-312-14590-X) St. Martin's Pr.
—Drowning in Honey. 2000. 347p. 27.50 (0-385-40594-4) Transworld Publishers Ltd. GBR. Dist: Trafalgar Square.
Hawke, Simon. Much Ado about Murder. E-Book 23.95 (0-312-70933-1, Tor Bks.); 2004. 240p. pap. 13.95 (0-7653-0836-3, Forge Bks.); 2002. 304p. 23.95 (0-7653-0241-1, Forge Bks.) Doherty, Tom Assocs., LLC.
—The Slaying of the Shrew. 2001. 255p. 23.95 (0-312-87894-X, Forge Bks.) Doherty, Tom Assocs., LLC.
Hawkes, Ellen & Manso, Peter. The Shadow of the Moth: A Novel of Espionage with Virginia Woolf. 1984. (Crime Ser.). 288p. pap. 3.95 o.p. (0-14-007060-5, Penguin Bks.) Viking Penguin.
Hawksley, Elizabeth. The Belvedere Tower. 2003. 242p. 29.95 (0-7090-7306-2) Hale, Robert Ltd. GBR. Dist: Trafalgar Square.
—Lysander's Lady. 1996. 192p. 19.95 o.p. (0-312-14008-8) St. Martin's Pr.
—Lysander's Lady. l.t. ed. 1995. (Ulverscroft Large Print Ser.). 400p. 29.99 o.p. (0-7089-3415-3, Ulverscroft) Thorpe, F. A. Pubs. GBR. Dist: Ulverscroft Large Print Bks., Ltd., Ulverscroft Large Print Canada, Ltd.
Hayton, Sian. Cells of Knowledge. 1992. 168p. pap. 9.95 (1-56131-031-X); 1990. 123p. 16.95 (1-56131-000-X) Dee, Ivan R. Pub. (New Amsterdam Bks).
Haywood, Ian. The Literature of Struggle: An Anthology of Chartist Fiction. 1995. (Nineteenth Century Ser.). 224p. 99.95 (1-85928-032-3) Ashgate Publishing, Ltd. GBR. Dist: Ashgate Publishing Co.
Heald, Tim. Blue Blood Will Out. 1980. 192p. mass mkt. 2.25 o.s.i (0-345-28904-8) Ballantine Bks.
—Blue Blood Will Out. 1974. 192p. 15.95 o.p. (0-8128-1688-9, Scarborough Hse.) Madison Bks., Inc.
—Caroline R. 1980. 11.95 o.p. (0-87795-285-X, Morrow, William & Co.) Morrow/Avon.
—Deadline. 1980. mass mkt. 2.25 o.s.i (0-345-28905-6) Ballantine Bks.
—Deadline. 1975. 192p. 6.95 o.p. (0-8128-1757-5, Scarborough Hse.) Madison Bks., Inc.
—Let Sleeping Dogs Die. 1981. 192p. mass mkt. 2.25 o.p. (0-345-28903-X) Ballantine Bks.
—Murder at Moosejaw. 1981. (Crime Club Ser.). 192p. 10.95 o.p. (0-385-17754-2) Doubleday Publishing.
—Red Herrings. 1986. (Crime Club Ser.). 192p. 12.95 o.p. (0-385-23354-X) Doubleday Publishing.
—Red Herrings. l.t. ed. 1987. lib. bdg. 18.50 o.p. (0-7451-0581-5, Macmillan Reference USA) Gale Group.
—A Small Masterpiece. 1982. (Crime Club Ser.). 192p. 10.95 o.p. (0-385-17942-1) Doubleday Publishing.
Hensher, Philip. The Mulberry Empire: A Novel. 2003. 496p. pap. 15.00 (1-4000-3089-7) Doubleday Publishing.
Herbert, Kathleen. Bride of the Spear. 1988. 304p. 17.95 o.p. (0-312-02173-9) St. Martin's Pr.
—The Ghost in the Sunlight. 1986. 335p. 16.95 o.p. (0-312-00126-6) St. Martin's Pr.
—Queen of the Lightning. 1983. 256p. 12.95 o.p. (0-312-65996-2) St. Martin's Pr.
Herley, Richard. The Stone Arrow, Bk. 1. 1987. 288p. mass mkt. 3.50 o.s.i (0-345-34326-3) Ballantine Bks.
—The Stone Arrow. 1985. 209p. 12.95 o.p. (0-688-02920-5, Morrow, William & Co.) Morrow/Avon.
—The Stone Arrow. 1978. 8.95 o.p. (0-312-76207-0) St. Martin's Pr.
Hiatt, Brenda. Scandalous Virtue. 1999. 384p. mass mkt. 5.99 (0-06-101379-X) HarperCollins Pubs.
Highsmith, Domini. Keeper at the Shrine: A Medieval Mystery. 1995. 512p. 25.95 o.p. (0-312-13102-X, Saint Martin's Minotaur) St. Martin's Pr.
Highsmith, Patricia. The Talented Mr. Ripley. unabr. ed. 2001. (Mr. Ripley Series). audio 69.95 (1-85089-775-1, 89102) ISIS Audio Bks. GBR. Dist: Ulverscroft Large Print Bks., Ltd.
—The Talented Mr. Ripley. l.t. ed. 1988. (Mr. Ripley Ser.). 392p. reprint ed. lib. bdg. 18.95 o.p. (1-85089-184-2) ISIS Large Print Bks. GBR. Dist: Transaction Pubs.
—The Talented Mr. Ripley. (Mr. Ripley Ser.). 304p. 1999. pap. 13.00 (0-676-58972-3); 1992. pap. 13.00 (0-679-74229-8) Knopf Publishing Group. (Vintage).
—The Talented Mr. Ripley, Set. unabr. ed. 1999. (Mr. Ripley Ser.). audio 39.95 (0-375-40511-9, RH Audio) Random Hse. Audio Publishing Group.
—The Talented Mr. Ripley. 2000. (Mr. Ripley Ser.). 287p. (0-7621-8856-1) Reader's Digest Assn., Inc., The.
—The Talented Mr. Ripley. 1982. (Mr. Ripley Ser.). 256p. pap. 4.95 o.p. (0-14-004020-X, Penguin Bks.) Viking Penguin.
Hil, Richard. Shoot the Piper: A Randall Gatsby Sierra Mystery. 1994. 224p. 18.95 o.p. (0-312-10549-5, Saint Martin's Minotaur) St. Martin's Pr.
Hill, Pamela. Knock at a Star. l.t. ed. 1998. (Nightingale Ser.). 342p. pap. 20.95 (0-7838-8319-6) Thorndike Pr.
Hill, Porter. The Bombay Marines. 2000. 288p. mass mkt. 5.99 o.s.i (0-425-17786-6) Berkley Publishing Group.
—The Bombay Marines. 1988. (Adam Horne Adventure Ser.). 228p. 17.95 (0-8027-1048-4) Walker & Co.
—The War Chest: An Adam Horne Adventure. 1989. 224p. 17.95 (0-8027-1049-2) Walker & Co.
Hill, Reginald. Singleton's Law. l.t. ed. 1997. (Myst-Hall Ser.). 295p. lib. bdg. 24.95 o.p. (0-7838-8106-1, Macmillan Reference USA) Gale Group.
—Singleton's Law. 1997. 224p. 24.00 o.p. (0-7278-4994-8) Severn Hse. Pubs., Ltd.
Hitchcock, Alfred & Buchan, John. The Thirty-Nine Steps. 1984. (Masterworks Collections). pap. 8.95 o.p. (0-8044-6267-4) Continuum International Publishing Group, Inc.
Hodge, Jane Aiken. Windover. 1992. 224p. 17.95 o.p. (0-312-07884-6) St. Martin's Pr.
Holbrook, Cindy, et al. Flowers for Mama. 2002. (Zebra Regency Romance Ser.). 256p. mass mkt. 4.99 o.s.i (0-8217-7283-X, Zebra Bks.) Kensington Publishing Corp.
Holmes, Kate. The Wild Swans. 2000. (Faerie Tale Romance Ser.). 400p. mass mkt. 5.99 (0-505-52383-3, Love Spell) Dorchester Publishing Co., Inc.
Housman, Laurence. House of Joy. 1977. (Short Story Index Reprint Ser.). 18.95 (0-8369-3020-7) Ayer Co. Pubs., Inc.
Howard, Elizabeth J. Marking Time. Grose, Bill, ed. 1992. 416p. 22.00 (0-671-70909-7, Atria) Simon & Schuster.
Hoyland, John, ed. Fathers & Sons. 1992. 224p. pap. o.p. (1-85242-203-3) Serpent's Tail Ltd.
Hoyt, Sarah A. Ill Met by Moonlight. 2001. 288p. 21.95 (0-441-00860-7); 2002. 304p. reprint ed. mass mkt. 5.99 (0-441-00983-2) Ace Bks.
Hunt, Caroline Rose. Primrose Past. 2000. 256p. 26.00 (0-06-039413-7, ReganBooks) HarperTrade.
Hunt, Chris. Gaveston. 2nd ed. 1997. 317p. reprint ed. pap. 14.95 (0-85449-262-3) Millivres Prowler Group GBR. Dist: LPC Group.
Hussein, Abdullah. Emigre Journeys. 2001. 250p. pap. 15.00 (1-85242-638-1) Serpent's Tail Ltd. GBR. Dist: Consortium Bk. Sales & Distribution.
Hyatt, Angela C. N. The James Bond Internet Guide. 2000. 40p. pap. 10.00 o.p. (1-883573-41-6, Lightning Rod Limited) Windstorm Creative Ltd.
Hylton, Sara. Melissa. l.t. ed. 493p. (0-7505-1019-6) Magna Large Print Bks. GBR. Dist: Ulverscroft Large Print Bks., Ltd.
—Melissa. 1996. 304p. 22.95 (0-312-14677-9) St. Martin's Pr.
Iles, Greg. Black Cross. l.t. ed. 1995. 528p. 19.95 o.p. (0-525-93829-X, Dutton) Dutton/Plume.
—Black Cross. l.t. ed. 1995. pap. 23.95 (1-56895-225-2, Wheeler Publishing, Inc.) Gale Group.
—Black Cross. 1995. 576p. mass mkt. 7.99 (0-451-18519-6); pap. 5.99 (0-451-18746-6) NAL. (Signet Bks.).
—Black Cross. abr. ed. 1995. pap. 23.95 o.p. incl. audio (0-453-00935-2, 692155) Penguin/HighBridge.
Iparraguirre, Sylvia. La Tierra del Fuego. 1999. (SPA., Illus.). 286p. 21.95 (950-511-414-1) Alfaguara S.A. de Ediciones ARG. Dist: Libros Sin Fronteras, Santillana USA Publishing Co., Inc.
Irving, Clive. Axis. 1980. 12.95 o.p. (0-689-11044-8, Scribner) Simon & Schuster.
Irwin, Margaret E. Elizabeth, Captive Princess. 1948. (Illus.). 7.50 o.p. (0-15-128361-3) Harcourt Trade Pubs.
—Elizabeth, Captive Princess. l.t. ed. 1974. (Shadows of the Crown Ser.). 29.99 o.p. (0-85456-640-6, Ulverscroft) Thorpe, F. A. Pubs. GBR. Dist: Ulverscroft Large Print Bks., Ltd., Ulverscroft Large Print Canada, Ltd.
—Elizabeth, Captive Princess: A Novel. 2000. 320p. pap. text 14.95 (0-7490-0389-8) Allison & Busby, Ltd. GBR. Dist: International Publishers Marketing.
—The Stranger Prince. 1985. 18.95 o.p. (0-312-76425-1) St. Martin's Pr.
Ivanhoe. 1988. (Short Classics Ser.). (Illus.). 48p. (J). (gr. 4 up). pap. 9.27 o.p. (0-8172-2769-5) Raintree Pubs.
Jacobs, Anna. High Street. l.t. ed. 1996. (Magna Large Print Ser.). (Illus.). 590p. 29.99 o.p. (0-7505-0913-9) Magna Large Print Bks. GBR. Dist: Ulverscroft Large Print Bks., Ltd., Ulverscroft Large Print Canada, Ltd.
—High Street. 1996. 352p. 24.95 (0-312-14614-0) St. Martin's Pr.
James, Sally. Otherwise Engaged. l.t. ed. 2001. (Linford Romance Large Print Ser.). 200p. pap. 19.99 (0-7089-4551-1, Ulverscroft) Thorpe, F. A. Pubs. GBR. Dist: Ulverscroft Large Print Bks., Ltd., Ulverscroft Large Print Canada, Ltd.
Jecks, Michael. The Boy-Bishop's Glovemaker. 2001. (Medieval West Country Mysteries Ser.: Vol. 10). 320p. (J). mass mkt. 9.95 (0-7472-6611-5); 331p. 28.00 (0-7472-7247-6) Headline Bk. Publishing, Ltd. GBR. Dist: Trafalgar Square.
—The Mad Monk of Gidleigh. 2003. 480p. mass mkt. 9.95 (0-7553-0169-2); 2002. 320p. 27.50 (0-7553-0168-4) Headline Bk. Publishing, Ltd. GBR. Dist: Trafalgar Square.
—The Traitor of St. Giles. 2001. (Medieval West Country Mysteries Ser.: No. 9). 320p. (YA). mass mkt. 9.95 (0-7472-6362-0); 2000. 328p. 28.00 (0-7472-7403-7) Headline Bk. Publishing, Ltd. GBR. Dist: Trafalgar Square.
Jensen, Liz. Ark Baby. 288p. 1999. 13.95 (0-87951-729-8); 1998. 24.95 (0-87951-833-2) Overlook Pr., The.
Johnson, Mary E. The Lion & the Leopard: A Novel of Plantagenet England. 1985. 320p. 2.99 o.p. (0-517-55727-4) Random Hse. Value Publishing.
Jones, Ellen. The Fatal Crown. 1992. 592p. reprint ed. pap. 5.99 (0-380-71707-7, Avon Bks.) Morrow/Avon.
—The Fatal Crown: A Novel. 1991. 608p. 19.95 o.p. (0-671-72464-9, Simon & Schuster) Simon & Schuster.
Kaewert, Julie. Unsolicited. 2000. (Booklover's Mystery Ser.). 336p. mass mkt. 5.99 (0-553-58209-7) Bantam Bks.
Kalechofsky, Roberta. Bodmin, 1349: An Epic Novel of the Middle Ages, of Christians, Jews in the Plague Years. 1988. 448p. (Orig.). pap. 14.95 (0-916288-24-2) Micah Pubns.
Kaufman, Pamela. Banners of Gold. 1986. 2.99 o.p. (0-517-56133-6) Random Hse. Value Publishing.
Kay, Jackie. Trumpet: A Novel. 2000. (Contemporaries Ser.). 288p. pap. 13.00 (0-375-70463-9, Vintage) Knopf Publishing Group.
Keane, Molly. Good Behaviour. 1983. pap. 6.95 o.p. (0-525-48051-X, Dutton) Dutton/Plume.
—Good Behaviour. 1981. 245p. 10.95 o.s.i (0-394-51818-7) Knopf, Alfred A. Inc.
—Good Behaviour. 2001. (Modern Classics). 245p. pap. 13.00 (1-86049-834-5) Virago Pr., Ltd. GBR. Dist: Trafalgar Square.
Kells, Susannah. A Crowning Mercy. 480p. 1987. pap. 3.95 o.p. (0-14-010148-9, Penguin Bks.); 1983. 16.95 o.p. (0-670-20068-9) Viking Penguin.
Kelman, James. Greyhound for Breakfast. 1988. 232p. 15.95 o.s.i (0-374-16687-0) Farrar, Straus & Giroux.
Kent, Alexander. Beyond the Reef. 2000. (Richard Bolitho Ser.: Vol. 19). 349p. pap. 14.95 (0-935526-82-X) McBooks Pr., Inc.
—Colors Aloft! 1987. mass mkt. 3.50 o.s.i (0-425-10264-5) Berkley Publishing Group.
—Colors Aloft! 1999. 288p. reprint ed. 31.95 (1-56849-728-8) Buccaneer Bks., Inc.
—Colors Aloft! 1986. 16.95 o.p. (0-399-12988-X) Putnam Publishing Group, The.
—Colours Aloft. 2000. (Richard Bolitho Ser.: Vol. 16). 300p. reprint ed. pap. 14.95 (0-935526-72-2) McBooks Pr., Inc.
—Colours Aloft. l.t. ed. 1987. (Charnwood Large Print Ser.). 432p. 29.99 o.p. (0-7089-8380-4, Charnwood) Thorpe, F. A. Pubs. GBR. Dist: Ulverscroft Large Print Bks., Ltd., Ulverscroft Large Print Canada, Ltd.
—Command a King's Ship. 1984. 320p. mass mkt. 3.50 o.s.i (0-515-07866-2, Jove); 1979. 1.95 o.p. (0-425-04083-6) Berkley Publishing Group.
—Command a King's Ship. 1993. reprint ed. lib. bdg. 25.95 (1-56849-028-3) Buccaneer Bks., Inc.
—Command a King's Ship. 1998. (Richard Bolitho Ser.: Vol. 6). 352p. pap. 14.95 (0-935526-50-1) McBooks Pr., Inc.
—Command a King's Ship. l.t. ed. 1987. (Charnwood Large Print Ser.). 528p. 29.99 o.p. (0-7089-8440-1, Ulverscroft) Thorpe, F. A. Pubs. GBR. Dist: Ulverscroft Large Print Bks., Ltd., Ulverscroft Large Print Canada, Ltd.
—The Darkening Sea. unabr. ed. 1998. audio 84.95 (0-7540-0222-5, CAB 1645) BBC Audiobooks America.
—The Darkening Sea. 2000. (Richard Bolitho Ser.: Vol. 20). 351p. pap. 14.95 (0-935526-83-8) McBooks Pr., Inc.
—Enemy in Sight! 1976. 25.95 (0-8488-0550-X) Amereon, Ltd.
—Enemy in Sight! 1985. mass mkt. 3.50 o.s.i (0-515-08177-9, Z2609, Jove) Berkley Publishing Group.
—Enemy in Sight! 1999. (Richard Bolitho Ser.: Vol. 10). 352p. reprint ed. pap. 14.95 (0-935526-60-9) McBooks Pr., Inc.
—The Flag Captain. 1984. 352p. mass mkt. 3.50 o.s.i (0-515-07749-6, Jove) Berkley Publishing Group.
—The Flag Captain. 1999. (Richard Bolitho Ser.: Vol. 11). 384p. reprint ed. pap. 15.95 (0-935526-66-8) McBooks Pr., Inc.
—For My Country's Freedom. 2000. (Richard Bolitho Ser.: Vol. 21). 300p. pap. 15.95 (0-935526-84-6) McBooks Pr., Inc.
—Form Line of Battle. 1985. mass mkt. 3.50 o.s.i (0-515-07699-6, Jove); 1984. mass mkt. 3.50 o.s.i (0-515-07500-0, Jove); 1983. mass mkt. 2.95 o.s.i (0-515-06804-7, Jove); 1979. mass mkt. 1.95 o.s.i (0-425-04113-1); 1977. mass mkt. 1.75 o.s.i (0-425-03645-6); 1975. mass mkt. 1.50 o.s.i (0-425-03100-4) Berkley Publishing Group.
—Form Line of Battle. 1993. reprint ed. lib. bdg. 37.95 (1-56849-027-5) Buccaneer Bks., Inc.
—Form Line of Battle. 1999. (Richard Bolitho Ser.: Vol. 9). 416p. pap. 14.95 (0-935526-59-5) McBooks Pr., Inc.
—Honor This Day. 1990. mass mkt. 3.95 o.s.i (0-515-10285-7, Jove) Berkley Publishing Group.
—Honor This Day. 1988. (Richard Bolitho Ser.). 304p. 17.95 o.p. (0-399-13348-8) Putnam Publishing Group, The.
—Honour This Day. 1987. 287 p. (0-434-38834-3, Butterworth-Heinemann) Elsevier Science & Technology Bks.
—Honour This Day. 2000. (Richard Bolitho Ser.: Vol. 17). 316p. reprint ed. pap. 15.95 (0-935526-73-0) McBooks Pr., Inc.
—Honour This Day. l.t. ed. 1988. (Ulverscroft Large Print Ser.). 560p. 29.99 o.p. (0-7089-1880-8, Ulverscroft) Thorpe, F. A. Pubs. GBR. Dist: Ulverscroft Large Print Bks., Ltd., Ulverscroft Large Print Canada, Ltd.
—In Gallant Company. 1984. mass mkt. 3.50 o.s.i (0-515-07856-5, Jove); 1983. mass mkt. 2.95 o.s.i (0-515-07064-5, Jove); 1978. mass mkt. 1.95 o.s.i (0-425-03987-0) Berkley Publishing Group.
—In Gallant Company. 1992. reprint ed. lib. bdg. 21.95 (0-89966-973-5) Buccaneer Bks., Inc.
—In Gallant Company. 1977. 287 p. (0-09-128830-4) Hutchinson.
—In Gallant Company. 1998. (Richard Bolitho Ser.: Vol. 3). 320p. pap. 13.95 (0-935526-43-9) McBooks Pr., Inc.
—In Gallant Company. 1977. 8.95 o.p. (0-399-11987-6) Putnam Publishing Group, The.
—The Inshore Squadron. 1984. 256p. mass mkt. 3.50 o.s.i (0-515-07984-7, Jove) Berkley Publishing Group.
—The Inshore Squadron. 1999. (Richard Bolitho Ser.: Vol. 13). 288p. pap. 13.95 (0-935526-68-4) McBooks Pr., Inc.
—The Inshore Squadron. l.t. ed. 1983. (Ulverscroft Large Print Ser.). 480p. 29.99 o.p. (0-7089-0905-1, Ulverscroft) Thorpe, F. A. Pubs. GBR. Dist: Ulverscroft Large Print Bks., Ltd., Ulverscroft Large Print Canada, Ltd.
—Midshipman Bolitho. 1998. (Richard Bolitho Ser.: Vol. 1). 240p. pap. 11.95 (0-935526-41-2) McBooks Pr., Inc.
—Midshipman Bolitho & the Avenger. 1976. 19.95 (0-8488-1398-7) Amereon, Ltd.
—Midshipman Bolitho & the Avenger. 1990. 144p. reprint ed. lib. bdg. 25.95 (0-89966-732-5) Buccaneer Bks., Inc.
—Midshipman Bolitho & the Avenger. 1978. (J). (gr. 6-8). 6.95 o.p. (0-399-20652-3) Putnam Publishing Group, The.
—The Only Victor. 2000. (Richard Bolitho Ser.: Vol. 18). 384p. reprint ed. pap. 15.95 (0-935526-74-9) McBooks Pr., Inc.
—Passage to Mutiny. 1985. mass mkt. 3.50 o.s.i (0-515-08261-9); 1984. mass mkt. 3.50 o.s.i (0-515-07445-4); 1983. mass mkt. 2.95 o.s.i (0-515-06746-6); 1980. mass mkt. 1.95 o.s.i (0-515-05437-2) Berkley Publishing Group. (Jove).
—Passage to Mutiny. 1993. reprint ed. lib. bdg. 37.95 (1-56849-029-1) Buccaneer Bks., Inc.
—Passage to Mutiny. 1999. (Richard Bolitho Ser.: Vol. 7). 352p. reprint ed. pap. 14.95 (0-935526-58-7) McBooks Pr., Inc.
—Second to None. 2001. (Richard Bolitho Novels Ser.: Vol. 24). 350p. pap. 16.95 (0-935526-94-3) McBooks Pr., Inc.
—Signal-Close Action. 1984. 352p. mass mkt. 3.50 o.s.i (0-515-07437-3); 1983. mass mkt. 2.95 o.s.i (0-515-06883-7) Berkley Publishing Group. (Jove).
—Signal-Close Action. 1999. (Richard Bolitho Ser.: Vol. 12). 368p. reprint ed. pap. 15.95 (0-935526-67-6) McBooks Pr., Inc.

—Sloop of War. 1984. mass mkt. 3.50 o.s.i (0-515-07975-8); 1982. mass mkt. 2.95 o.s.i (0-515-06726-1); 1979. mass mkt. 1.95 o.s.i (0-515-05370-8) Berkley Publishing Group. (Jove).

—Sloop of War. 1992. reprint ed. lib. bdg. 37.95 (0-89966-974-3) Buccaneer Bks., Inc.

—Sloop of War. 1998. (Richard Bolitho Ser.: Vol. 4). 352p. pap. 15.95 (0-935526-48-X) McBooks Pr., Inc.

—Sloop of War. l.t. ed. 1987. (Charnwood Large Print Ser.). 512p. 29.99 o.p. (0-7089-8405-3, Charnwood) Thorpe, F. A. Pubs. GBR. *Dist:* Ulverscroft Large Print Bks., Ltd., Ulverscroft Large Print Canada, Ltd.

—Stand into Danger. 1984. mass mkt. 3.50 o.s.i (0-515-07641-4); 1983. mass mkt. 2.95 o.s.i (0-515-06888-8) Berkley Publishing Group. (Jove).

—Stand into Danger. 1992. reprint ed. lib. bdg. 37.95 (0-89966-972-7) Buccaneer Bks., Inc.

—Stand into Danger. 1998. (Richard Bolitho Ser.: Vol. 2). 288p. pap. 13.95 (0-935526-42-0) McBooks Pr., Inc.

—Stand into Danger. 1981. 300p. 10.95 o.p. (0-399-12539-6) Putnam Publishing Group, The.

—Stand into Danger. l.t. ed. 1982. 481p. 15.95 o.p. (0-7089-0753-9, Ulverscroft) Thorpe, F. A. Pubs. GBR. *Dist:* Ulverscroft Large Print Bks., Ltd.

—Success to the Brave. 1984. mass mkt. 3.50 o.s.i (0-515-08052-7, Jove) Berkley Publishing Group.

—Success to the Brave. 2000. (Richard Bolitho Ser.: Vol. 15). 287p. reprint ed. pap. 13.95 (0-935526-71-4) McBooks Pr., Inc.

—Success to the Brave. 1983. 284p. 13.95 o.p. (0-399-12878-6, G. P. Putnam's Sons) Penguin Putnam Bks. for Young Readers.

—Success to the Brave. l.t. ed. 1985. (Ulverscroft Large Print Ser.). 512p. 29.99 o.p. (0-7089-1255-9, Ulverscroft) Thorpe, F. A. Pubs. GBR. *Dist:* Ulverscroft Large Print Bks., Ltd., Ulverscroft Large Print Canada, Ltd.

—To Glory We Steer. 1976. 23.95 (0-8488-0551-8) Amereon, Ltd.

—To Glory We Steer. 1984. mass mkt. 3.50 o.s.i (0-515-07636-8, Jove); 1983. mass mkt. 2.95 o.s.i (0-515-06892-6, Jove); 1980. mass mkt. 2.25 o.s.i (0-515-05732-0, Jove); 1976. mass mkt. 1.75 o.s.i (0-425-03371-6) Berkley Publishing Group.

—To Glory We Steer. 1993. reprint ed. lib. bdg. 32.95 (1-56849-026-7) Buccaneer Bks., Inc.

—To Glory We Steer. 1998. (Richard Bolitho Ser.: Vol. 5). 352p. pap. 15.95 (0-935526-49-8) McBooks Pr., Inc.

—To Glory We Steer. l.t. ed. 1987. (Charnwood Large Print Ser.). 528p. 29.99 o.p. (0-7089-8423-1, Charnwood) Thorpe, F. A. Pubs. GBR. *Dist:* Ulverscroft Large Print Bks., Ltd., Ulverscroft Large Print Canada, Ltd.

—A Tradition of Victory. 296p. mass mkt. (0-09-928370-0) Arrow Bks., Ltd.

—A Tradition of Victory. 1984. 304p. mass mkt. 3.50 o.s.i (0-515-07871-9, Jove) Berkley Publishing Group.

—A Tradition of Victory. 1982. 304p. 12.95 o.p. (0-399-12706-2) Putnam Publishing Group, The.

—Tradition of Victory. 1983. mass mkt. 2.95 o.s.i (0-515-07116-1, Jove) Berkley Publishing Group.

—A Tradition of Victory. l.t. ed. 1985. (Ulverscroft Large Print Ser.). 528p. 29.99 o.p. (0-7089-1367-9, Ulverscroft) Thorpe, F. A. Pubs. GBR. *Dist:* Ulverscroft Large Print Bks., Ltd., Ulverscroft Large Print Canada, Ltd.

—Tradition of Victory. 2000. (Richard Bolitho Ser.: Vol. 14). 302p. reprint ed. pap. 14.95 (0-935526-70-6) McBooks Pr., Inc.

—With All Despatch. 1993. (Illus.). reprint ed. lib. bdg. 37.95 (1-56849-030-5) Buccaneer Bks., Inc.

—With All Despatch. 1988. 272 p. (0-434-38836-X, Butterworth-Heinemann) Elsevier Science & Technology Bks.

—With All Despatch. 1999. (Richard Bolitho Ser.: Vol. 8). 352p. reprint ed. pap. 14.95 (0-935526-61-7) McBooks Pr., Inc.

—With All Despatch. 1989. 288p. 18.95 o.p. (0-399-13430-1, G. P. Putnam's Sons) Penguin Putnam Bks. for Young Readers.

Kent, Chris. The Boys of Swithins Hall. 1998. 189p. pap. 13.95 (1-879194-25-2) GLB Pubs.

Kerr, Philip. Dark Matter: The Private Life of Sir Isaac Newton: A Novel. 2002. (Illus.). 352p. 24.00 (0-609-60981-5, Crown) Crown Publishing Group.

Kerr, William. The Red Hand. 200p. 2002. 23.35 (0-7596-4748-8); 2001. pap. 15.54 (0-7596-3378-9) 1stBooks Library.

King, Peter. Eat Drink & Be Dead: A Gourmet Detective Mystery. 2001. 215p. 22.95 (0-312-24270-0, Saint Martin's Minotaur) St. Martin's Pr.

Kingsley, Charles. Westward Ho. 1968. (Airmont Classics Ser.). (J). (gr. 8 up). mass mkt. 1.25 o.p. (0-8049-0184-8, CL-184) Airmont Publishing Co., Inc.

—Westward Ho! deluxe ltd. ed. 1992. (Scribner Illustrated Classics Ser.). (Illus.). 432p. (YA). (gr. 7 up). 26.95 (0-684-19444-9, Atheneum) Simon & Schuster Children's Publishing.

Kinsolving, William. Mister Christian: The Further Adventures of Fletcher Christian, the Ledgendary Leader of the Bounty Mutiny. 1996. 384p. 23.00 o.p. (0-684-81303-3, Simon & Schuster) Simon & Schuster.

—Mr. Christian. l.t. ed. 1996. (Large Print Bks.). 26.95 (1-56895-339-9, Wheeler Publishing, Inc.) Gale Group.

—Mr. Christian. 1997. 23.00 (0-07-158770-5) McGraw-Hill Cos., The.

Kipling, Rudyard. Puck of Pook's Hill. 1988. 272p. mass mkt. 3.50 o.p. (0-451-52168-4, Signet Classics) NAL.

—Puck of Pook's Hill & Rewards & Fairies. MacKenzie, Donald, ed. 1993. (Oxford World's Classics Ser.). 492p. (J). (gr. 4 up). pap. 7.95 o.p. (0-19-282575-5) Oxford Univ. Pr., Inc.

Kirby, Kate. Scapegoat for a Stuart. 1977. 7.95 o.p. (0-312-70035-0) St. Martin's Pr.

Klaus, Gustav, ed. Tramps, Workmates, & Revolutionaries: Working-Class Stories of the 1920s. 1993. (C). text 44.00 (0-85172-030-7); pap. text 16.95 (0-85172-031-5) Westview Pr.

—Tramps, Workmates & Revolutionaries: Working Class Stories of the 1920's. 1993. 182p. (C). text 49.00 (1-85172-030-8) Westview Pr.

Kluger, Richard. The Sheriff of Nottingham. 1992. 544p. 23.00 o.s.i (0-670-84022-X, Viking) Viking Penguin.

Kneale, Matthew. English Passengers. 2001. 464p. pap. (0-385-65866-4, Anchor Canada) Doubleday Canada, Ltd. CAN. *Dist:* Random Hse., Inc.

—English Passengers. pap. (0-385-72876-X) Knopf Publishing Group.

—English Passengers. 2001. 20.05 (0-606-20652-3) Turtleback Bks.

Koen, Karleen. Now Face to Face. unabr. ed. 1996. audio 31.95 o.p. (1-56100-648-3, 199, Bookcassette) Brilliance Audio.

—Now Face to Face. 1997. 608p. mass mkt. 6.99 o.s.i (1-57566-177-2) Kensington Publishing Corp.

Kureishi, Hanif. Intimacy & Midnight All Day: A Novel & Stories. 2001. 336p. pap. 13.00 (0-7432-1714-4, Scribner) Simon & Schuster.

—Midnight All Day. 1999. 217p. (0-571-19456-7) Faber & Faber, Inc.

Kyle, Barbara. A Dangerous Devotion. 1995. 480p. (Orig.). mass mkt. 5.99 o.s.i (0-451-17933-1, Onyx) NAL.

—A Dangerous Temptation. 1994. 512p. (Orig.). mass mkt. 4.99 o.p. (0-451-17932-3, Onyx) NAL.

Lacy, Al & Lacy, JoAnna. A Prince among Them. 2003. (Shadow of Liberty Ser.). 336p. pap. 10.99 (1-57673-880-9) Multnomah Pubs., Inc.

Laker, Rosalind, pseud. Circle of Pearls. l.t. ed. 1991. (General Ser.). 830p. 22.95 o.p. (0-8161-5098-2, Macmillan Reference USA) Gale Group.

Lamb, Arnette. Chieftain. l.t. ed. 1995. 402p. pap. 19.95 (0-7838-1279-5, Macmillan Reference USA) Gale Group.

—Chieftain. 1994. 320p. mass mkt. 6.50 (0-671-77937-0, Pocket) Simon & Schuster.

Lambdin, Dewey. For King & Country: The Naval Adventures of Alan Lewrie. 1994. 1088p. pap. 19.95 o.s.i (1-55611-413-3, Fine, Donald I.) Fine, Donald I. Bks.

—The French Admiral. 1999. mass mkt. (0-449-00359-0, Fawcett) Ballantine Bks.

—The French Admiral. 1990. (Midshipman Alan Lewrie Adventure Ser.). 19.95 o.p. (1-55611-208-4) Fine, Donald I. Bks.

—The French Admiral. l.t. ed. 1999. (G. K. Hall Core Ser.). 637p. 27.95 (0-7838-8788-4, Macmillan Reference USA) Gale Group.

—The French Admiral. 1991. mass mkt. 4.95 o.s.i (1-55817-491-5, Pinnacle Bks.) Kensington Publishing Corp.

—The Gun Ketch: An Alan Lewrie Naval Adventure. 1996. (Alan Lewrie Navel Adventures Ser.). 336p. mass mkt. 6.99 (0-449-22450-3, Fawcett) Ballantine Bks.

—The Gun Ketch: An Alan Lewrie Naval Adventure. 1993. 21.95 o.s.i (1-55611-356-0) Fine, Donald I. Bks.

—Havoc's Sword: An Alan Lewrie Naval Adventure. 2003. (Illus.). 384p. 25.95 (0-312-28688-0) St. Martin's Pr.

—H.M.S. Cockerel: An Alan Lewrie Naval Adventure. 1997. (Alan Lewrie Navel Adventures Ser.). 416p. mass mkt. 6.50 (0-449-22448-1, Fawcett) Ballantine Bks.

—H.M.S. Cockerel: An Alan Lewrie Naval Adventure. 1995. (Alan Lewrie Ser.). 368p. 23.95 o.s.i (1-55611-446-X) Fine, Donald I. Bks.

—H.M.S. Cockerel: An Alan Lewrie Naval Adventure. 1996. text 23.95 (0-07-036237-8) McGraw-Hill Cos., The.

—Jester's Fortune. 2002. (Naval Adventures of Alan Lewrie: No. 8). 432p. pap. 17.95 (1-59013-034-0) McBooks Pr., Inc.

—Jester's Fortune: An Alan Lewrie Naval Adventure. 1999. (Alan Lewrie Navel Adventures Ser.). (Illus.). 384p. 26.95 o.p. (0-525-94482-6) Dutton/Plume.

—Jester's Fortune: An Alan Lewrie Naval Adventure. l.t. ed. 1999. (Core Ser.). (Illus.). 618p. pap. 27.95 (0-7838-8681-0, Macmillan Reference USA) Gale Group.

—King's Captain. 2000. (Alan Lewrie Navel Adventures Ser.). 358p. 25.95 (0-312-26885-8) St. Martin's Pr.

—The King's Coat. 1998. (Alan Lewrie Navel Adventures Ser.: Vol. 1). 384p. mass mkt. 6.99 (0-449-00360-4, Fawcett) Ballantine Bks.

—The King's Coat. 1989. 384p. 19.95 o.s.i (1-55611-142-8) Fine, Donald I. Bks.

—The King's Coat. 1990. mass mkt. 3.95 o.p. (1-55817-389-7, Pinnacle Bks.) Kensington Publishing Corp.

—The King's Coat. 1991. 3.99 o.p. (0-517-07481-8) Random Hse. Value Publishing.

—The King's Coat. l.t. ed. 1999. (G. K. Hall Core Ser.). 573p. 28.95 (0-7838-0440-7) Thorndike Pr.

—A King's Commander. 1998. (Alan Lewrie Navel Adventures Ser.). (Illus.). 384p. mass mkt. 6.99 (0-449-00022-2, Fawcett) Ballantine Bks.

—A King's Commander. 1997. (Alan Lewrie Ser.). 384p. 24.95 o.s.i (1-55611-504-0) Fine, Donald I. Bks.

—The King's Commission. 1996. (Alan Lewrie Navel Adventures Ser.). 384p. mass mkt. 6.99 (0-449-22452-X, Fawcett) Ballantine Bks.

—The King's Commission. 1991. 21.95 o.p. (1-55611-187-8) Fine, Donald I. Bks.

—The King's Privateer: An Alan Lewrie Naval Adventure. 1996. (Alan Lewrie Navel Adventures Ser.). 368p. mass mkt. 5.99 (0-449-22451-1, Fawcett) Ballantine Bks.

—The King's Privateer: An Alan Lewrie Naval Adventure. 1992. 21.95 o.s.i (1-55611-324-2) Fine, Donald I. Bks.

—Sea of Grey. (Alan Lewrie Navel Adventures Ser.). 2003. 400p. pap. 14.95 (0-312-32016-7, Saint Martin's Griffin); 2002. (Illus.). 416p. 25.95 (0-312-28685-6) St. Martin's Pr.

—Sea of Grey. 2002. (Alan Lewrie Naval Adventure Ser.: Bk. 10). 29.95 (0-7862-4891-2) Thorndike Pr.

Lamming, George. The Emigrants. 1987. 274p. pap. 6.95 (0-8052-8036-7, Schocken) Knopf Publishing Group.

—The Emigrants. 1994. (Ann Arbor Paperback Ser.). (Illus.). 280p. (C). reprint ed. pap. text 17.95 (0-472-06470-3, 06470) Univ. of Michigan Pr.

Lang, Jennifer H. The Peacock & the Pearl. 1992. 22.95 o.p. (0-312-08871-X) St. Martin's Pr.

Langan, Ruth R. Blackthorne. abr. ed. 1999. (Harlequin Romance Ser.). audio 7.99 o.p. (1-56740-537-1, 1836, Harlequin Romance Audio) Brilliance Audio.

—Blackthorne. 1998. (Harlequin Historicals Ser.: Vol. 435). per. (0-373-29035-7, 1-29035-2, Harlequin Bks.) Harlequin Enterprises, Ltd.

Langley, Lee. Persistent Rumours. 304p. 1998. pap. 14.95 (1-57131-014-2); 1994. 21.95 (1-57131-001-0) Milkweed Editions.

Le Carré, John. The Honourable Schoolboy: A Novel. 1985. (George Smiley Novels Ser.). mass mkt. 4.50 o.s.i (0-553-25197-X); 576p. mass mkt. 6.99 o.s.i (0-553-27437-6) Bantam Bks.

—The Honourable Schoolboy: A Novel. unabr. ed. 1991. audio 99.95 (0-7861-0270-5, 1236) Blackstone Audio Bks., Inc.

—The Honourable Schoolboy: A Novel. unabr. collector's ed. 1978. audio 120.00 (0-7366-0112-0, 1119) Books on Tape, Inc.

—The Honourable Schoolboy: A Novel. 1977. (General Ser.). lib. bdg. 18.95 o.p. (0-8161-6539-4, Macmillan Reference USA) Gale Group.

—The Honourable Schoolboy: A Novel. reprint ed. 2002. 608p. pap. 14.00 (0-7434-5791-9, Scribner); 2000. 688p. mass mkt. 7.99 (0-671-04274-2, Pocket) Simon & Schuster.

—John Le Carre: A New Collection of Three Complete Novels. 1996. 864p. 13.99 o.s.i (0-517-15019-0) Random Hse., Inc.

—John Le Carre: Three Complete Novels. 1995. 704p. 13.99 o.p. (0-517-14697-5); 1995. 12.99 o.s.i (0-517-14899-4); 1988. 9.99 o.s.i (0-517-42284-0) Random Hse. Value Publishing.

—The John Le Carre Value Collection, Set. abr. ed. 2000. audio 39.95 (0-375-41589-0, RH Audio) Random Hse. Audio Publishing Group.

—A Murder of Quality. 1990. (George Smiley Novels Ser.). 176p. mass mkt. 4.95 o.s.i (0-553-26443-5) Bantam Bks.

—A Murder of Quality. unabr. ed. 1991. (George Smiley Ser.). audio 32.95 (0-7861-0272-1, 1238) Blackstone Audio Bks., Inc.

—A Murder of Quality. unabr. ed. 1986. (George Smiley Novels Ser.). audio 36.00 (0-7366-0456-1, 1428) Books on Tape, Inc.

—A Murder of Quality. unabr. ed. 2000. (George Smiley Ser.: Bk. 2). audio 34.95 (0-7451-4013-0, CAB 710) Chivers Audio Bks. GBR. *Dist:* BBC Audiobooks America.

—A Murder of Quality. abr. ed. 1986. (George Smiley Novels Ser.). audio 15.95 (0-88646-160-X) Durkin Hayes Publishing Ltd.

—A Murder of Quality. abr. ed. 1999. (George Smiley Ser.). audio 16.85 (1-84032-103-2) Hodder Headline Audiobooks GBR. *Dist:* Ulverscroft Large Print Bks., Ltd.

—A Murder of Quality. 1968. mass mkt. 0.75 o.p. (0-451-03667-0); 1964. mass mkt. 0.50 o.p. (0-451-02529-6) NAL. (Signet Bks.).

—A Murder of Quality. 1989. 2.99 o.p. (0-517-68437-3) Random Hse. Value Publishing.

—A Murder of Quality, unabr. ed. 1990. (George Smiley Novels Ser.). audio 35.00 (1-55690-361-8, 90063E7) Recorded Bks., LLC.

—A Murder of Quality. 2002. 160p. pap. 13.00 (0-7434-3168-5, Scribner) Simon & Schuster.

—A Perfect Spy: A Novel. 2003. 608p. reprint ed. pap. 14.00 (0-7434-5792-7, Scribner) Simon & Schuster.

—Smiley's People: A Novel. 2002. 416p. reprint ed. pap. 14.00 (0-7434-5580-0, Scribner) Simon & Schuster.

—Tinker Tailor Soldier Spy. 1984. (George Smiley Novels Ser.). 384p. mass mkt. 6.99 o.s.i (0-553-26778-7) Bantam Bks.

—Tinker Tailor Soldier Spy. unabr. ed. 1991. (George Smiley Ser.). audio 62.95 (0-7861-0278-0, 1244) Blackstone Audio Bks., Inc.

—Tinker Tailor Soldier Spy. unabr. ed. 1984. (George Smiley Novels Ser.). audio 64.00 (0-7366-0966-0, 1908) Books on Tape, Inc.

—Tinker Tailor Soldier Spy. unabr. ed. 2000. (George Smiley Ser.: Bk. 5). audio 79.95 (0-7451-6744-6, CAB 1360) Chivers Audio Bks. GBR. *Dist:* BBC Audiobooks America.

—Tinker Tailor Soldier Spy. abr. ed. 1981. (George Smiley Novels Ser.). audio 16.99 o.p. (0-88646-064-6, TC-LFP 7082) Durkin Hayes Publishing Ltd.

—Tinker Tailor Soldier Spy. Date not set. (George Smiley Novels Ser.). 14.95 (0-559-35018-X) Putnam Publishing Group, The.

—Tinker Tailor Soldier Spy. reprint ed. 2002. 400p. pap. 14.00 (0-7434-5790-0, Scribner); 2000. 448p. per. 7.99 o.s.i (0-671-04273-4, Pocket) Simon & Schuster.

Le Queux, William. The Great War in England in 1897, 8 vols., Vol. 3. 1999. (Sources of Science Fiction: Future War Novels of the 1890s Ser.). (Illus.). 276p. (C). lib. bdg. 150.00 (0-415-19291-9) Routledge.

Lennox-Smith, Judith. Till the Day Goes Down. 1992. 368p. 21.95 o.p. (0-312-07096-9) St. Martin's Pr.

Lewis, Roy. Nothing but Foxes. 1978. 7.95 o.p. (0-312-57964-0) St. Martin's Pr.

—A Secret Dying: An Arthur Landon Mystery. 1993. 17.95 o.p. (0-312-08887-6, Saint Martin's Minotaur) St. Martin's Pr.

Lewis, Roy H. Dwell in Danger. 1982. 192p. 10.95 o.p. (0-312-22286-6) St. Martin's Pr.

—A Limited Vision. 1983. 208p. 10.95 o.p. (0-312-48679-0) St. Martin's Pr.

—Premium on Death: An Eric Ward Novel. 1987. 208p. 13.95 o.p. (0-312-00019-7) St. Martin's Pr.

—The Salamander Chill. l.t. ed. 1991. pap. 10.95 o.p. (1-55504-903-6, 359) BBC Audiobooks America.

—The Salamander Chill. 1988. 192p. 14.95 o.p. (0-312-02637-4, Saint Martin's Minotaur) St. Martin's Pr.

Lide, Mary. Command of the King. 1991. 288p. 18.95 o.p. (0-312-06319-9) St. Martin's Pr.

Lindsey, Johanna. Love Me Forever. unabr. ed. 1996. audio 56.00 (0-7366-3308-1, 3962) Books on Tape, Inc.

—Love Me Forever. abr. ed. (Sherring Cross Ser.). 1996. audio 7.99 o.s.i (1-56740-136-8, 673, Paperback Nova Audio Bks.); 1995. audio 16.95 o.p. (1-56100-864-8, 1281, Nova Audio Bks.); 1995. audio 57.25 (1-56100-293-3, 931, Unabridged Library Editions); 1995. audio 23.95 (1-56100-668-8, 165, Bookcassette) Brilliance Audio.

—Love Me Forever. l.t. ed. 1995. 480p. 25.95 o.p. (0-7838-1501-8, Macmillan Reference USA) Gale Group.

—Love Me Forever. 2000. 22.00 (0-380-97263-8); 1996. 400p. mass mkt. 7.99 (0-380-72570-3, Avon Bks.); 1995. 356p. 22.00 o.p. (0-688-14286-9, Morrow, William & Co.) Morrow/Avon.

—Love Me Forever. 1997. 5.98 o.p. (0-7651-0785-6) Smithmark Pubs., Inc.

—Surrender My Love. l.t. ed. 1994. 403p. 23.95 o.p. (0-7838-1124-1, Macmillan Reference USA) Gale Group.

—Surrender My Love. 1994. 416p. mass mkt. 7.99 (0-380-76256-0, Avon Bks.) Morrow/Avon.

Linton, E. Lynn. The Rebel of the Family. Meem, Deborah T., ed. 2002. (Broadview Literary Texts Ser.). 487p. (*1-55111-293-0*) Broadview Pr.

Little, Mary E. Julian's Cat: An Imaginary History of a Cat of Destiny. 1989. 96p. 12.95 o.p. (*0-8192-1430-2*); 1993. 132p. reprint ed. pap. 8.95 o.p. (*0-8192-1609-7*) Morehouse Publishing.

Lofts, Norah. Madselin. 1983. (Illus.). 216p. 13.95 o.p. (*0-385-18103-5*) Doubleday Publishing.

—Madselin. l.t. ed. 1984. (General Ser.). 14.95 o.p. (*0-8161-3678-5*, Macmillan Reference USA) Gale Group.

—Madselin. l.t. ed. 1971. 12.00 o.p. (*0-85456-045-9*, Ulverscroft) Thorpe, F. A. Pubs. GBR. *Dist:* Ulverscroft Large Print Bks., Ltd.

London, Mary. La Double Mort de Thomas Stuart. Baudricourt, J. P., tr. 1999. (FRE., Illus.). 308p. reprint ed. pap. 14.95 (*1-58348-146-X*) iUniverse, Inc.

—Un Meurtre Chez les Francs-Macons. 1999. (FRE.). 220p. reprint ed. pap. 12.95 (*1-58348-153-2*) iUniverse, Inc.

London Mercury Staff. Second Mercury Story Book. 1977. (Short Story Index Reprint Ser.). reprint ed. 27.95 (*0-8369-4112-8*) Ayer Co. Pubs., Inc.

Lorna Doone. 2001. mass mkt. 5.99 (*0-8125-9000-7*, Tor Bks.) Doherty, Tom Assocs., LLC.

Lovesey, Peter. Abracadaver. 1994. 224p. 16.95 o.p. (*0-7451-8645-9*, Black Dagger) BBC Audiobooks America.

—Abracadaver. 1989. 256p. reprint ed. pap. 4.50 o.p. (*0-06-081000-9*, Perennial) HarperTrade.

—Abracadaver. 1981. 224p. pap. 3.95 o.p. (*0-14-005803-6*, Penguin Bks.) Viking Penguin.

Lynnford, Janet. Firebrand Bride. 1999. 320p. mass mkt. 5.99 o.s.i (*0-451-40830-6*, Topaz) NAL.

Macaulay, Rose. The Shadow Flies. 1972. (Literature Ser.). 484p. reprint ed. 59.00 (*0-403-01082-9*) Scholarly Pr., Inc.

—They Were Defeated. 1986. (Twentieth Century Classics Ser.). 445p. pap. 6.95 o.p. (*0-19-281316-1*) Oxford Univ. Pr., Inc.

Mack, William P. Captain Kilburnie: An Age-of-Sail Novel of Triumph over Adversity in Nelson's Navy. 2001. 384p. reprint ed. pap. 13.95 o.s.i (*0-425-17826-9*) Berkley Publishing Group.

Mackin, Jeanne. Queens War. 1991. 22.95 o.p. (*0-312-04960-9*) St. Martin's Pr.

MacLeod, Ken. The Star Fraction. 320p. 2001. 25.95 (*0-7653-0084-2*); 2002. reprint ed. pap. 14.95 (*0-7653-0156-3*) Doherty, Tom Assocs., LLC. (Tor Bks.).

MacNeil, Duncan. The Train at Bundarbar. 1986. 192p. 15.95 o.s.i (*0-8027-0895-1*) Walker & Co.

MacWilliams, Margaret. Toria. l.t. ed. 1991. 18.95 o.p. (*0-7927-0682-X*, CH004); pap. 16.95 o.p. (*0-7927-0683-8*, CS0106) BBC Audiobooks America.

Magrs, Paul. All the Rage: Two Boys, Two Girls, & a Dream of Pop Stardom... 2002. pap. 14.95 (*0-7490-0536-X*) Allison & Busby, Ltd. GBR. *Dist:* International Publishers Marketing.

Mahon, Brid. A Time to Love. 1992. 484p. pap. 13.95 (*1-85371-221-3*) Poolbeg Pr. IRL. *Dist:* Dufour Editions, Inc.

Major, Charles. When Knighthood Was in Flower. reprint ed. 45.00 (*0-404-04169-8*) AMS Pr., Inc.

—When Knighthood Was in Flower. reprint ed. lib. bdg. 23.95 (*0-88411-095-8*) Amereon, Ltd.

—When Knighthood Was in Flower. reprint ed. lib. bdg. 48.00 (*0-7426-1102-7*); 2001. pap. text 28.00 (*0-7426-6102-4*) Classic Bks.

—When Knighthood Was in Flower. 1899. 295p. (YA). reprint ed. pap. text 28.00 (*1-4047-6792-4*) Classic Textbooks.

—When Knighthood Was in Flower. 1992. (BCL1-PS American Literature Ser.). 295p. reprint ed. lib. bdg. 79.00 (*0-7812-6792-7*) Reprint Services Corp.

Mallinson, Allan. A Close Run Thing: A Novel of Wellington's Army of 1815. 2000. 320p. pap. 19.00 (*0-553-38043-5*, Spectra) Bantam Bks.

Mandeville, Joyce. Careful Mistakes. 1996. 184p. o.s.i (*0-316-87899-5*) Little Brown & Co.

—Careful Mistakes: A Novel. 1997. 432p. 21.95 (*0-316-87999-1*) Little Brown & Co.

Manning, Anne. The Maiden & Married Life of Mary Powell, Afterwards Mistress Milton, 2 vols., 1 bk. reprint ed. 44.50 (*0-404-62021-3*) AMS Pr., Inc.

Manning, Rosemary. The Chinese Garden. 2000. 192p. pap. 12.95 (*1-55861-216-5*); 208p. 29.00 (*1-55861-215-7*) Feminist Pr. at The City Univ. of New York.

Mansbridge, Paul. Kitchen Sink Dramas. 2001. 108p. pap. 20.99 (*0-7388-5997-4*) Xlibris Corp.

Margolis, Sue. Breakfast at Stephanie's. 2004. 336p. pap. 12.00 (*0-385-33733-7*, Delta) Dell Publishing.

—Spin Cycle. 2001. 288p. pap. 11.95 (*0-440-50923-8*, Delta) Dell Publishing.

Marks, Annie. An Enchanted Place. 2003. 242p. 29.95 (*0-7090-7148-5*) Hale, Robert Ltd. GBR. *Dist:* Trafalgar Square.

Marryat, Frederick. Frank Mildmay or the Naval Officer. 2000. 252p. E-Book 3.95 (*0-594-02605-9*) 1873 Pr.

—Frank Mildmay or the Naval Officer. 1997. (Classics of Nautical Fiction Ser.). 352p. reprint ed. pap. 14.95 (*0-935526-39-0*) McBooks Pr., Inc.

—Mr. Midshipman Easy. 2000. 252p. pap. 9.95 (*0-594-01690-8*); E-Book 3.95 (*0-594-02609-1*) 1873 Pr.

—Mr. Midshipman Easy. Date not set. lib. bdg. 24.95 (*0-8488-1678-1*) Amereon, Ltd.

—Mr. Midshipman Easy. unabr. collector's ed. 1996. audio 88.00 (*0-7366-3499-1*, 4139) Books on Tape, Inc.

—Mr. Midshipman Easy. 1972. 2.95 o.p. (*0-460-01082-4*, Dutton) Dutton/Plume.

—Mr. Midshipman Easy. 1998. (Heart of Oak Sea Classics Ser.). 368p. 30.00 o.s.i (*0-8050-5988-1*) Holt, Henry & Co.

—Mr. Midshipman Easy. 1997. (Classics of Nautical Fiction Ser.). 352p. reprint ed. pap. 14.95 (*0-935526-40-4*) McBooks Pr., Inc.

—Mr. Midshipman Easy. 2001. (Signet Classics). 384p. mass mkt. 5.95 (*0-451-52796-8*) NAL.

—Mr. Midshipman Easy. 1990. (Classics of Naval Literature Ser.). 448p. reprint ed. 34.95 (*0-87021-590-6*) Naval Institute Pr.

—Mr. Midshipman Easy. 1983. pap. 4.95 o.p. (*0-14-005295-X*, Penguin Bks.) Viking Penguin.

—Newton Forster or the Merchant Service. 1998. (Classics of Nautical Fiction Ser.). 352p. pap. 13.95 (*0-935526-44-7*) McBooks Pr., Inc.

—Peter Simple. unabr. ed. 2000. audio 85.95 (*0-7861-1753-2*, 2557) Blackstone Audio Bks., Inc.

—Peter Simple. 1970. 5.00 o.p. (*0-460-00232-5*, Dutton) Dutton/Plume.

—Peter Simple. 1998. (Heart of Oak Sea Classics Ser.). 483p. 30.00 o.s.i (*0-8050-5830-3*) Holt, Henry & Co.

—Peter Simple: Heart of Oak Sea Classics. 1998. (Heart of Oak Sea Classics Ser.). 480p. pap. 15.00 o.s.i (*0-8050-5565-7*, Owl Bks.) Holt, Henry & Co.

Mars-Jones, Adam. Monopolies of Loss. 1994. pap. 11.00 o.s.i (*0-679-74415-0*, Vintage) Knopf Publishing Group.

Maugham, W. Somerset. Of Human Bondage. 1999. (Modern Library Ser.). 656p. pap. 11.95 (*0-375-75315-X*) Random Hse., Inc.

Maxwell, Robin. The Queen's Bastard. 1999. 448p. 24.95 (*1-55970-475-6*) Arcade Publishing, Inc.

—The Queen's Bastard. 2000. 448p. pap. 13.00 (*0-684-85760-X*, Touchstone) Simon & Schuster.

—The Secret Diary of Anne Boleyn: A Novel. 1997. 288p. 23.95 (*1-55970-375-X*) Arcade Publishing, Inc.

—The Secret Diary of Anne Boleyn: A Novel. 1998. 288p. pap. 14.00 (*0-684-84969-0*, Touchstone) Simon & Schuster.

—The Secret Diary of Anne Boleyn: A Novel. l.t. ed. 2000. (Ulverscroft Large Print Ser.). 512p. (*0-7089-4198-2*, Ulverscroft) Thorpe, F. A. Pubs. GBR. *Dist:* Ulverscroft Large Print Bks., Ltd., Ulverscroft Large Print Canada, Ltd.

—The Secret Diary of Anne Boleyn: A Novel. 2001. 18.05 (*0-606-20494-6*) Turtleback Bks.

—Virgin: A Novel. 2001. 256p. 24.95 (*1-55970-563-9*) Arcade Publishing, Inc.

—The Wild Irish: A Novel. 2003. 400p. 24.95 (*0-06-009142-8*, Morrow, William & Co.) Morrow/Avon.

Maynard, Kenneth. First Lieutenant. 1985. 224p. 13.95 o.p. (*0-312-29244-9*) St. Martin's Pr.

—Lamb in Command. 1986. mass mkt. 3.50 (*0-312-90618-8*, St. Martin's Paperbacks); 208p. 13.95 o.p. (*0-312-46435-5*) St. Martin's Pr.

—Lieutenant Lamb. 1984. 176p. 10.95 o.p. (*0-312-48371-6*) St. Martin's Pr.

McCann, Maria. As Meat Loves Salt. 2003. 584p. pap. 15.00 (*0-15-601226-X*, Harvest Bks.) Harcourt Trade Pubs.

McCrumb, Sharyn. The Windsor Knot. 2000. mass mkt. 6.50 (*0-345-91577-1*); 1991. 224p. mass mkt. 6.99 (*0-345-36427-9*) Ballantine Bks.

—The Windsor Knot. l.t. ed. 2001. 267p. 29.95 (*0-7838-9407-4*, Macmillan Reference USA) Gale Group.

—The Windsor Knot. unabr. ed. 1993. audio 44.00 (*1-55690-890-3*, 93332E7) Recorded Bks., LLC.

McCutchan, Philip. Apprentice to the Sea. 1995. 17.95 o.p. (*0-312-11743-4*) St. Martin's Pr.

—Cameron & the Kaiserhof. 1984. 192p. 10.95 o.p. (*0-312-11443-5*) St. Martin's Pr.

—Cameron Comes Through. 1986. 160p. 12.95 o.p. (*0-312-11444-3*) St. Martin's Pr.

—Cameron in Command. 1986. pap. 3.50 o.p. (*0-312-90468-1*, St. Martin's Paperbacks); 1984. 176p. 10.95 o.p. (*0-312-11446-X*) St. Martin's Pr.

—Cameron in the Gap. 1999. audio 44.95 Soundings, Ltd. GBR. *Dist:* Ulverscroft Large Print Bks., Ltd.

—Cameron in the Gap. 1983. 160p. 9.95 o.p. (*0-312-11448-6*) St. Martin's Pr.

—Cameron in the Gap. l.t. ed. 1999. (General Ser.). 232p. pap. 23.95 (*0-7862-1964-5*); (*0-7540-3810-6*); (*0-7540-3809-2*) Thorndike Pr.

—Cameron of the Castle Bay. unabr. ed. 2001. audio 44.95 (*1-85496-708-8*, 67088) Soundings, Ltd. GBR. *Dist:* Ulverscroft Large Print Bks., Ltd.

—Cameron's Chase. unabr. ed. 1997. audio 49.95 (*1-85496-934-X*, 6934X) Soundings, Ltd. GBR. *Dist:* Ulverscroft Large Print Bks., Ltd.

—Cameron's Chase. 1987. pap. 3.50 o.p. (*0-312-90703-6*, St. Martin's Paperbacks); 1986. 182p. 12.95 o.p. (*0-312-11450-8*) St. Martin's Pr.

—Cameron's Commitment. 1989. 192p. 14.95 o.p. (*0-312-02532-7*) St. Martin's Pr.

—Cameron's Convoy. 156p. 14.99 o.p. (*0-7278-4771-6*) Severn Hse. Pubs., Ltd.

—Cameron's Convoy. 2001. audio 44.95 (*1-85496-138-1*, 61381) Soundings, Ltd. GBR. *Dist:* Ulverscroft Large Print Bks., Ltd.

—Cameron's Convoy. l.t. ed. 1999. (General Ser.). 240p. pap. 23.95 (*0-7862-1821-5*) Thorndike Pr.

—Cameron's Crossing. 1993. 176p. 17.95 o.p. (*0-312-09762-X*) St. Martin's Pr.

—Cameron's Raid. unabr. ed. 1999. audio 54.95 (*1-86042-388-4*, 23884) Soundings, Ltd. GBR. *Dist:* Ulverscroft Large Print Bks., Ltd.

—Cameron's Raid. 1986. pap. 3.50 o.p. (*0-312-90081-3*, St. Martin's Paperbacks); 1985. 11.95 o.p. (*0-312-11452-4*) St. Martin's Pr.

—Cameron's Troop Lift. 1987. 208p. 13.95 o.p. (*0-312-01008-7*) St. Martin's Pr.

—Captain at Arms, 1. 1999. 286p. 25.00 o.p. (*0-7278-2231-4*) Severn Hse. Pubs., Ltd.

—Captain at Arms. l.t. ed. 1999. (General Ser.). 426p. pap. 23.95 (*0-7862-2094-5*); (*0-7540-3922-6*); (*0-7540-3921-8*) Thorndike Pr.

—The Convoy Commodore. 1986. 192p. 12.95 o.p. (*0-312-00116-9*) St. Martin's Pr.

—Convoy East. 1997. pap. 11.95 o.p. (*0-312-15499-2*, Saint Martin's Griffin); 1989. 192p. 14.95 o.p. (*0-312-03310-9*) St. Martin's Pr.

—Convoy Homeward. 1992. 224p. 17.95 o.p. (*0-312-08168-5*) St. Martin's Pr.

—Convoy North. 1988. 192p. 13.95 o.p. (*0-312-01405-8*) St. Martin's Pr.

—Convoy of Fear. l.t. ed. 1992. (Lythway Ser.). 273p. 15.95 o.p. (*0-7451-1617-5*, Macmillan Reference USA) Gale Group.

—Convoy of Fear. 1997. 192p. pap. 11.95 o.p. (*0-312-16607-9*, Saint Martin's Griffin); 1990. 15.95 o.p. (*0-312-05065-8*) St. Martin's Pr.

—Convoy South. 192p. 1996. pap. 8.95 o.p. (*0-312-14299-4*, Saint Martin's Griffin); 1988. 14.95 o.p. (*0-312-02178-X*) St. Martin's Pr.

—Halfhyde & the Admiral. l.t. ed. 1991. (Lythway Ser.). 288p. 21.95 (*0-7451-1259-5*, Macmillan Reference USA) Gale Group.

—Halfhyde & the Admiral. 1990. 14.95 o.p. (*0-312-04323-6*) St. Martin's Pr.

—Halfhyde & the Chain Gangs. l.t. ed. 1986. lib. bdg. 17.50 o.p. (*0-7451-0406-1*, Macmillan Reference USA) Gale Group.

—Halfhyde & the Chain Gangs. 1985. 192p. 12.95 o.p. (*0-312-35662-5*) St. Martin's Pr.

—Halfhyde & the Flag Captain. 1981. 183p. 9.95 o.p. (*0-312-35684-6*) St. Martin's Pr.

—Halfhyde & the Fleet Review. l.t. ed. 1998. (Dales Large Print Ser.). 385p. pap. 19.99 o.p. (*1-85389-835-X*) Dales Large Print Bks. GBR. *Dist:* Ulverscroft Large Print Bks., Ltd., Ulverscroft Large Print Canada, Ltd.

—Halfhyde & the Fleet Review. 1991. 224p. 17.95 o.p. (*0-312-06991-X*) St. Martin's Pr.

—Halfhyde for the Queen. 1978. 7.95 o.p. (*0-312-35687-0*) St. Martin's Pr.

—Halfhyde Goes to War. l.t. ed. 1998. (Dales Large Print Ser.). 304p. pap. 19.99 o.p. (*1-85389-834-1*) Dales Large Print Bks. GBR. *Dist:* Ulverscroft Large Print Bks., Ltd., Ulverscroft Large Print Canada, Ltd.

—Halfhyde Goes to War. 1987. 176p. 12.95 o.p. (*0-312-00603-9*) St. Martin's Pr.

—Halfhyde on the Amazon. l.t. ed. 1990. 288p. lib. bdg. 22.95 o.p. (*0-7451-1164-5*, Macmillan Reference USA) Gale Group.

—Halfhyde on the Amazon. 1988. 224p. 14.95 o.p. (*0-312-01769-3*) St. Martin's Pr.

—Halfhyde on Zanatu. l.t. ed. 2002. (Magna Large Print Ser.). 288p. 32.50 (*0-7505-1856-1*) Magna Large Print Bks. GBR. *Dist:* Ulverscroft Large Print Bks., Ltd., Ulverscroft Large Print Canada, Ltd.

—Halfhyde on Zanatu. 1982. 176p. 10.95 o.p. (*0-312-35688-9*) St. Martin's Pr.

—Halfhyde Ordered South. 1979. 9.95 o.p. (*0-312-35689-7*) St. Martin's Pr.

—Halfhyde Outward Bound. 1984. 176p. 10.95 o.p. (*0-312-35691-9*) St. Martin's Pr.

—Halfhyde to the Narrows. 1977. 7.95 o.p. (*0-312-35690-0*) St. Martin's Pr.

—Halfhyde's Island. 1976. 184p. 7.95 o.p. (*0-312-35700-1*) St. Martin's Pr.

—Halfhyde's Island. l.t. ed. 1978. (Ulverscroft Large Print Ser.). 29.99 o.p. (*0-7089-0159-X*, Ulverscroft) Thorpe, F. A. Pubs. GBR. *Dist:* Ulverscroft Large Print Bks., Ltd., Ulverscroft Large Print Canada, Ltd.

—Halfhyde's Island. 1985. 240p. mass mkt. 2.95 o.s.i (*0-446-32940-1*) Warner Bks., Inc.

—Lieutenant Cameron RNVR. unabr. ed. 1998. audio 63.95 (*1-85903-068-8*) Magna Story Sound GBR. *Dist:* Ulverscroft Large Print Bks., Ltd.

—Lieutenant Cameron RNVR. 1987. pap. 3.50 o.p. (*0-312-90691-9*, St. Martin's Paperbacks); 1985. 160p. 11.95 o.p. (*0-312-48373-2*) St. Martin's Pr.

—The New Lieutenant. 1997. 192p. 20.95 (*0-312-15604-9*) St. Martin's Pr.

—The New Lieutenant. l.t. ed. 1997. (General Ser.). 266p. pap. 22.95 (*0-7862-1127-X*) Thorndike Pr.

—Orders for Cameron. l.t. ed. 1985. lib. bdg. 14.50 o.p. (*0-7451-0246-8*); 13.50 o.p. (*0-8166-0246-8*) Gale Group. (Macmillan Reference USA).

—Orders for Cameron. unabr. ed. 1996. audio 49.95 (*1-86042-123-7*, 21237) Soundings, Ltd. GBR. *Dist:* Ulverscroft Large Print Bks., Ltd.

—Orders for Cameron. 1983. 160p. 10.95 o.p. (*0-312-58722-8*) St. Martin's Pr.

—The Second Mate. 1996. 192p. 19.95 o.p. (*0-312-14410-5*) St. Martin's Pr.

McDonald, Eva. The Rebel Bride. l.t. ed. 1997. 233p. pap. 23.95 (*0-7838-8274-2*) Thorndike Pr.

McDonough, James. The Limits of Glory: A Novel of Waterloo. 1991. (Illus.). 312p. 19.95 o.p. (*0-89141-384-7*, Presidio Pr.) Ballantine Bks.

McGown, Jill. Gone to Her Death. 1991. mass mkt. 4.99 (*0-449-21966-6*, Fawcett) Ballantine Bks.

—Gone to Her Death. l.t. ed. 1991. (General Ser.). 330p. lib. bdg. 22.95 o.p. (*0-8161-5094-X*, Macmillan Reference USA) Gale Group.

—Gone to Her Death. 1989. 256p. 16.95 o.p. (*0-312-03839-9*, Saint Martin's Minotaur) St. Martin's Pr.

—Murder . . . Now & Then. 1993. 304p. 20.95 o.p. (*0-312-10006-X*, Saint Martin's Minotaur) St. Martin's Pr.

—Murder at the Old Vicarage. 1991. (Mysteries Around the World Promotion Ser.). 256p. mass mkt. 6.50 (*0-449-21819-8*, Ivy Bks.) Ballantine Bks.

—Murder at the Old Vicarage. l.t. ed. 1990. (General Ser.). 348p. lib. bdg. 18.95 o.p. (*0-8161-4838-4*, Macmillan Reference USA) Gale Group.

—Murder at the Old Vicarage. 1988. 256p. 16.95 o.p. (*0-312-02615-3*, Saint Martin's Minotaur) St. Martin's Pr.

—Murder... Now & Then. 1995. (Mysteries Around the World Promotion). mass mkt. 5.99 o.s.i (*0-449-22311-6*, Fawcett) Ballantine Bks.

—Murder... Now & Then. 1993. 407p. pap. 13.95 (*0-330-33243-0*) Pan Bks. Ltd. GBR. *Dist:* Trans-Atlantic Pubns., Inc.

—The Murders of Mrs. Austin & Mrs. Beale. 1993. 256p. reprint ed. mass mkt. 6.50 (*0-449-22162-8*, Fawcett) Ballantine Bks.

—The Murders of Mrs. Austin & Mrs. Beale. 1991. 224p. 17.95 o.p. (*0-312-06422-5*, Saint Martin's Minotaur) St. Martin's Pr.

—The Other Woman. 1994. mass mkt. 5.99 (*0-449-22272-1*, Fawcett) Ballantine Bks.

—The Other Woman. l.t. ed. 1997. 477p. (*0-7505-1065-X*) Magna Large Print Bks. GBR. *Dist:* Ulverscroft Large Print Bks., Ltd.

—The Other Woman. 1993. 236p. 17.95 o.p. (*0-312-08868-X*, Saint Martin's Minotaur) St. Martin's Pr.

—A Perfect Match. 1990. 192p. mass mkt. 6.50 (*0-449-21820-1*, Fawcett) Ballantine Bks.

—A Perfect Match. 1983. 192p. 11.95 o.p. (*0-312-60069-0*) St. Martin's Pr.

McGraw, Milena. After Dunkirk. 1999. 468p. pap. 13.00 (*0-395-97780-0*) Houghton Mifflin Co.

—After Dunkirk: A Novel. 1998. 480p. tchr. ed. 24.00 o.p. (*0-395-86885-8*) Houghton Mifflin Co.

Medwin, Thomas. Lady Singleton. 2000. (*0-8201-1529-0*) Scholars' Facsimiles & Reprints.

Meredith, George. Diana of the Crossways: A Novel. 2001. (Works of George Meredith: Vol. 17). (Illus.). reprint ed. Pt. 1. 282p. pap. text 28.00 (*0-7426-5202-5*); Pt. 2. 279p. pap. text 28.00 (*0-7426-5203-3*) Classic Bks.

—Diana of the Crossways: A Novel. 1897. (YA). reprint ed. pap. text 38.00 (*1-4047-7817-9*); pap. text 28.00 (*1-4047-7818-7*) Classic Textbooks.

—Diana of the Crossways: A Novel. 2001. (Illus.). 448p. 49.95 (*0-8143-2976-4*); 365p. pap. 19.95 (*0-8143-2894-6*) Wayne State Univ. Pr.

Merritt, Stephanie. Gaveston. 2002. 320p. pap. (*0-571-21055-4*) Faber & Faber, Inc.

Metcalfe, John. Smoking Leg, & Other Stories. 1977. (Short Story Index Reprint Ser.). reprint ed. 22.95 (*0-8369-3828-3*) Ayer Co. Pubs., Inc.

Miller, Linda Lael. My Lady Beloved. l.t. ed. 2002. lib. bdg. 28.95 (*1-58547-194-1*, Premier) Ctr. Point Large Print.

Mills, Magnus. All Quiet on the Orient Express: A Novel. 1999. 224p. 23.95 (*1-55970-495-0*) Arcade Publishing, Inc.



For book reviews, descriptive annotations, tables of contents, cover images, author biographies & additional information, updated daily, subscribe to **www.booksinprint.com** 825

—All Quiet on the Orient Express: A Novel. 2000. 224p. pap. 12.00 (*0-684-87168-8*, Touchstone) Simon & Schuster.

Mitchison, Naomi M. When the Bough Breaks, & Other Stories. 1977. (Short Story Index Reprint Ser.). reprint ed. 22.95 (*0-8369-3923-9*) Ayer Co. Pubs., Inc.

Morgan, Cynthia. Court of Shadows. 1992. 672p. pap. 27.00 (*0-345-36651-4*, Ballantine Bks.) Ballantine Bks.

Morris, Gilbert. Command the Sun. 2000. (Liberty Bell Ser.: 7). 288p. pap. 10.99 o.p. (*1-55661-571-X*) Bethany Hse. Pubs.

—Fields of Glory. 1996. (Wakefield Dynasty Ser.: Vol. 4). 376p. pap. 11.99 o.p. (*0-8423-6229-0*) Tyndale Hse. Pubs.

—The Honorable Imposter. 1987. (House of Winslow Ser.: No. 1). 336p. pap. 11.99 (*0-87123-933-7*) Bethany Hse. Pubs.

—The Honorable Imposter. l.t. ed. 1993. (General Ser.). 464p. lib. bdg. 20.95 o.p. (*0-8161-5672-7*, Macmillan Reference USA) Gale Group.

—The Ramparts of Heaven. 1997. (Wakefield Dynasty Ser.: No. 5). 361p. pap. 11.99 o.p. (*0-8423-6233-9*) Tyndale Hse. Pubs.

—The Shield of Honor. 1995. (Wakefield Dynasty Ser.: Vol. 3). 394p. pap. 11.99 o.p. (*0-8423-5930-3*) Tyndale Hse. Pubs.

—The Song of Princes. 1997. (Wakefield Dynasty Ser.). 386p. pap. 11.99 o.p. (*0-8423-6234-7*) Tyndale Hse. Pubs.

—The Winds of God. 1994. (Wakefield Dynasty Ser.: No. 2). 380p. pap. 11.99 o.p. (*0-8423-7953-3*) Tyndale Hse. Pubs.

Morris, Gilbert, ed. The Sword of Truth. 1994. (Wakefield Dynasty Ser.). 409p. pap. 8.99 (*0-8423-6228-2*) Tyndale Hse. Pubs.

Morson, Ian. Falconer & the Face of God. 1997. 208p. mass mkt. 5.99 (*0-312-96410-2*, St. Martin's Paperbacks) St. Martin's Pr.

—Falconer & the Face of God: A William Falconer Medieval Mystery. 1997. 192p. text 21.95 o.p. (*0-312-15124-1*, Saint Martin's Minotaur) St. Martin's Pr.

—Falconer & the Great Beast. l.t. unabr. ed. 1998. (Illus.). 272p. 32.50 (*0-7531-5938-4*, 159384) ISIS Large Print Bks. GBR. *Dist:* Ulverscroft Large Print Bks., Ltd., Ulverscroft Large Print Canada, Ltd.

—Falconer & the Great Beast: A Medieval Oxford Mystery. 1999. (Medieval Oxford Mysteries Ser.). (Illus.). 220p. (YA). 21.95 (*0-312-20543-0*, Saint Martin's Minotaur) St. Martin's Pr.

—Falconer's Crusade. 1996. mass mkt. 4.99 (*0-312-95697-5*, St. Martin's Paperbacks); 1995. 190p. 18.95 o.p. (*0-312-11784-1*, Saint Martin's Minotaur) St. Martin's Pr.

—Falconer's Judgement. (Dead Letter Mysteries Ser.). 1997. 224p. mass mkt. 5.99 (*0-312-96151-0*, St. Martin's Paperbacks); 1996. 192p. 20.95 o.p. (*0-312-13971-3*, Saint Martin's Minotaur) St. Martin's Pr.

Mosley, Nicholas. Natalie Natalia. 2nd rev. ed. 1996. 278p. pap. 12.95 (*1-56478-086-4*) Dalkey Archive Pr.

Motley, Annette. The Quickenberry Tree. 1984. 704p. 17.95 o.p. (*0-312-66069-3*) St. Martin's Pr.

Mullin, Chris. A Very British Coup. 2001. 220p. pap. 12.95 (*1-902301-92-7*) Politico's Publishing Ltd. GBR. *Dist:* International Specialized Bk. Services.

Myers, Amy. Murder Makes an Entree. 1996. 288p. 21.95 o.p. (*0-312-14376-1*, Saint Martin's Minotaur) St. Martin's Pr.

Naipaul, V. S. In a Free State. 1984. 256p. mass mkt. 10.00 o.s.i (*0-394-72205-1*, Vintage) Knopf Publishing Group.

—In a Free State. 1977. 256p. pap. 3.95 o.p. (*0-14-003711-X*, Penguin Bks.) Viking Penguin.

Needle, Jan. A Fine Boy for Killing. 1983. 256p. (gr. 9 up). 10.95 o.p. (*0-233-97106-8*) Blackwell Publishing.

—A Fine Boy for Killing. 2000. (Sea Officer William Bentley Ser.: Vol. 1). 320p. pap. 15.95 (*0-935526-86-2*) McBooks Pr., Inc.

Neville, Jim. Swimming the Channel. 1994. 192p. 18.95 o.p. (*0-312-11337-4*) St. Martin's Pr.

Nicole, Christopher. The Regiment. 1989. 382p. 19.95 o.p. (*0-312-03418-0*) St. Martin's Pr.

Nobbs, David. The Better World of Reginald Perrin. l.t. unabr. ed. 1998. 400p. 32.50 (*0-7531-5506-0*, 155060) ISIS Large Print Bks. GBR. *Dist:* Ulverscroft Large Print Bks., Ltd., Ulverscroft Large Print Canada, Ltd.

—The Fall & Rise of Reginald Perrin. l.t. unabr. ed. 1998. 368p. 24.95 (*0-7531-5504-4*, 155044) Ulverscroft Large Print Bks., Ltd.

—The Legacy of Reginald Perrin. l.t. unabr. ed. 1999. 336p. 25.95 (*0-7531-5507-9*, 155079) ISIS Large Print Bks. GBR. *Dist:* ISIS Publishing.

—The Return of Reginald Perrin. l.t. unabr. ed. 1999. 342p. 26.95 (*0-7531-5505-2*, 155052) ISIS Large Print Bks. GBR. *Dist:* ISIS Publishing.

Nordhoff, Charles. Mutiny on the Bounty. 1976. 26.95 (*0-8488-0597-6*) Amereon, Ltd.

Nordhoff, Charles & Hall, James Norman. Men Against the Sea. 20.95 (*0-89190-564-2*) Amereon, Ltd.

—Men Against the Sea. 2003. 272p. pap. 13.95 (*0-316-73888-3*, Back Bay); 1989. pap. 8.95 o.p. (*0-316-61163-8*); 1934. (Illus.). 16.95 o.p. (*0-316-61156-5*) Little Brown & Co.

—Men Against the Sea. 1985. pap. 1.75 o.p. (*0-671-83200-X*, Pocket) Simon & Schuster.

—Mutiny on the Bounty. 1998. pap. 4.99 o.p. (*1-57840-197-6*) Acclaim Bks.

—Mutiny on the Bounty. 1989. 400p. pap. 13.95 (*0-316-61168-9*, Back Bay) Little Brown & Co.

—Mutiny on the Bounty. 2002. 375p. 38.95 (*1-57002-198-8*); pap. 19.95 (*1-57002-200-3*) University Publishing Hse., Inc.

Norman, Diana. The Morning Gift. 1986. 288p. 15.95 o.p. (*0-312-00159-2*) St. Martin's Pr.

—The Morning Gift. l.t. ed. 1987. (Ulverscroft Large Print Ser.). 544p. 29.99 o.p. (*0-7089-1629-5*, Ulverscroft) Thorpe, F. A. Pubs. GBR. *Dist:* Ulverscroft Large Print Bks., Ltd., Ulverscroft Large Print Canada, Ltd.

Nye, Robert. The Late Mr. Shakespeare. 1999. 400p. 25.95 (*1-55970-469-1*) Arcade Publishing, Inc.

—The Late Mr. Shakespeare. 2000. 416p. 13.95 (*0-14-028952-6*) Viking Penguin.

—The Voyage of the Destiny: A Novel. 400p. 2004. pap. 13.95 (*1-55970-695-3*); 2003. 24.95 (*1-55970-646-5*) Arcade Publishing, Inc.

—The Voyage of the Destiny: A Novel. 1982. 400p. 15.95 o.p. (*0-399-12760-7*) Putnam Publishing Group, The.

O'Brian, Patrick. Aubrey & Maturin, 18 vols. 1996. 432.00 (*0-393-04117-4*) Norton, W. W. & Co., Inc.

—The Aubrey-Maturin Series, 17 vols. (Aubrey-Maturin Ser.). (C). 1995. 408.00 (*0-393-03975-7*); Set. 1994. 384.00 (*0-393-03749-5*) Norton, W. W. & Co., Inc.

—Blue at the Mizzen. unabr. ed. 1999. (Aubrey-Maturin Ser.). audio 48.00 (*0-7366-4737-6*, 5075) Books on Tape, Inc.

—Blue at the Mizzen. (Aubrey-Maturin Ser.). 1999. (Illus.). 288p. 24.00 (*0-393-04844-6*); 250.00 (*0-393-04874-8*); 2000. (Illus.). 272p. reprint ed. pap. 13.95 (*0-393-32107-X*, Norton Paperbacks) Norton, W. W. & Co., Inc.

—Blue at the Mizzen. abr. ed. 1999. (Aubrey-Maturin Ser.). audio 25.00 (*0-375-40876-2*, RH Audio) Random Hse. Audio Publishing Group.

—Blue at the Mizzen. unabr. ed. (Aubrey-Maturin Ser.). 2000. audio compact disk 81.00 (*0-7887-4204-3*, C1133E7); 1999. audio 60.00 (*0-7887-3769-4*, 95986E7) Recorded Bks., LLC.

—Blue at the Mizzen. l.t. ed. 2000. (Aubrey-Maturin Ser.). 393p. 27.95 (*0-7862-2047-3*); 435p. 30.95 (*0-7862-2046-5*) Thorndike Pr.

—The Commodore. l.t. ed. 1995. (Aubrey-Maturin Ser.). 25.95 (*1-56895-271-6*, Wheeler Publishing, Inc.) Gale Group.

—The Commodore. (Aubrey-Maturin Ser.). 1996. 288p. pap. 13.95 (*0-393-31459-6*, Norton Paperbacks); 1995. 288p. 24.00 (*0-393-03760-6*); 1995. 150.00 o.p. (*0-393-03886-6*) Norton, W. W. & Co., Inc.

—Desolation Island. 1979. (Aubrey-Maturin Ser.). 276p. 9.95 o.s.i (*0-8128-2590-X*); pap. 2.50 o.p. (*0-8128-7066-2*) Madison Bks., Inc. (Scarborough Hse.).

—Desolation Island. (Aubrey-Maturin Ser.). 1994. 24.00 (*0-393-03705-3*); 1991. (Illus.). 325p. pap. 13.95 (*0-393-30812-X*) Norton, W. W. & Co., Inc.

—The Far Side of the World. l.t. ed. 2002. (Aubrey-Maturin Ser.). 538p. 29.95 (*0-7862-1930-0*, Macmillan Reference USA) Gale Group.

—The Far Side of the World. 2003. 366p. pap. 13.95 (*0-393-32476-1*); 1994. 24.00 (*0-393-03710-X*); 1992. 368p. pap. 13.95 (*0-393-30862-6*) Norton, W. W. & Co., Inc.

—The Fortune of War. (Aubrey-Maturin Ser.). 1994. 24.00 (*0-393-03706-1*); 1991. 329p. pap. 13.95 (*0-393-30813-8*) Norton, W. W. & Co., Inc.

—The Fortune of War. l.t. ed. 2001. (Illus.). 311p. (*0-7540-1588-2*); (*0-7540-2449-0*) Thorndike Pr.

—The Golden Ocean. unabr. ed. 1995. audio 56.00 (*0-7366-2912-2*, 3609) Books on Tape, Inc.

—The Golden Ocean. 1994. 22.50 o.p. (*0-07-048056-7*) McGraw-Hill Cos., The.

—The Golden Ocean. 1996. 288p. pap. 13.95 (*0-393-31537-1*); 1994. 256p. 24.00 (*0-393-03630-8*) Norton, W. W. & Co., Inc.

—The Golden Ocean. unabr. ed. 1995. audio 70.00 (*0-7887-0388-9*, 94579E7) Recorded Bks., LLC.

—HMS Surprise. (Aubrey-Maturin Ser.). 1994. 24.00 (*0-393-03703-7*); 1991. 379p. pap. 13.95 (*0-393-30761-1*) Norton, W. W. & Co., Inc.

—HMS Surprise. l.t. ed. 2000. (Famous Authors Ser.). 608p. 28.95 (*0-7862-1934-3*, MML06400-170754); (*0-7540-1460-6*); (*0-7540-2350-8*) Thorndike Pr.

—The Hundred Days. (Aubrey-Maturin Ser.). 288p. 1999. pap. 13.95 (*0-393-31979-2*); 1998. 24.00 (*0-393-04674-5*) Norton, W. W. & Co., Inc.

—The Hundred Days. l.t. ed. (Aubrey-Maturin Ser.). 461p. 2000. 26.95 (*0-7862-1749-9*); 1999. 29.95 (*0-7862-1748-0*) Thorndike Pr.

—The Ionian Mission. unabr. ed. 1993. (Aubrey-Maturin Ser.). audio 80.00 (*0-7366-2336-1*, 3115) Books on Tape, Inc.

—The Ionian Mission. (Aubrey-Maturin Ser.). 1994. 24.00 (*0-393-03708-8*); 1992. 368p. pap. 13.95 (*0-393-30821-9*) Norton, W. W. & Co., Inc.

—The Ionian Mission. abr. ed. 2000. (Aubrey-Maturin Ser.). audio 25.00 (*0-375-41577-7*, RH Audio) Random Hse. Audio Publishing Group.

—The Ionian Mission. unabr. ed. 1994. (Aubrey-Maturin Ser.: No. 8). audio 91.00 (*1-55690-985-3*, 94124E7) Recorded Bks., LLC.

—The Ionian Mission. l.t. ed. 2001. (Aubrey-Maturin Ser.). (Illus.). 572p. 28.95 (*0-7862-1928-9*); 576p. (*0-7540-1700-1*); 576p. (*0-7540-9100-7*) Thorndike Pr.

—The Letter of Marque. (Aubrey-Maturin Ser.). 1992. 288p. pap. 13.95 (*0-393-30905-3*); 1990. 284p. 24.00 (*0-393-02874-7*) Norton, W. W. & Co., Inc.

—The Letter of Marque. l.t. ed. 1999. (Aubrey-Maturin Ser.). 495p. 29.95 (*0-7862-1925-4*) Thorndike Pr.

—Master & Commander. l.t. ed. 1999. (*0-7540-1334-0*); (*0-7540-2248-X*) BBC Audiobooks America.

—Master & Commander. 2003. 412p. pap. 13.95 (*0-393-32517-2*); 1994. 24.00 (*0-393-03701-0*); 1990. (Illus.). 411p. pap. 13.95 (*0-393-30705-0*) Norton, W. W. & Co., Inc.

—Master & Commander. l.t. ed. 1999. (Aubrey-Maturin Ser.). 696p. 28.95 o.p. (*0-7862-1932-7*) Thorndike Pr.

—The Mauritius Command. l.t. ed. 2000. (Aubrey-Maturin Ser.). (Illus.). 530p. 28.95 (*0-7862-1935-1*, Macmillan Reference USA) Gale Group.

—The Mauritius Command. 1978. (Aubrey-Maturin Ser.). 8.95 o.p. (*0-8128-2476-8*); pap. 2.50 o.p. (*0-8128-7046-8*) Madison Bks., Inc. (Scarborough Hse.).

—The Mauritius Command. (Aubrey-Maturin Ser.). 1994. 24.00 (*0-393-03704-5*); 1991. 348p. pap. 13.95 (*0-393-30762-X*) Norton, W. W. & Co., Inc.

—The Mauritius Command. l.t. ed. 2000. (Illus.). 530p. (*0-7540-1519-X*); (*0-7540-2398-2*) Thorndike Pr.

—The Nutmeg of Consolation. (Aubrey-Maturin Ser.). 320p. 1993. pap. 13.95 (*0-393-30906-1*); 1991. 24.00 (*0-393-03032-6*) Norton, W. W. & Co., Inc.

—The Nutmeg of Consolation. l.t. ed. 2002. (Famous Authors Ser.). 516p. 29.95 (*0-7862-1938-6*) Thorndike Pr.

—Post Captain. (Aubrey-Maturin Ser.). 1994. 24.00 (*0-393-03702-9*); 1990. 496p. pap. 13.95 (*0-393-30706-9*) Norton, W. W. & Co., Inc.

—Post Captain. l.t. ed. 2000. (Aubrey-Maturin Ser.). (Illus.). 721p. 27.95 (*0-7862-1933-5*, MML06400-17053); (*0-7540-1423-1*); (*0-7540-2320-6*) Thorndike Pr.

—The Reverse of the Medal. l.t. ed. 2002. (Aubrey-Maturin Ser.). 419p. 29.95 (*0-7862-1931-9*, Macmillan Reference USA) Gale Group.

—The Reverse of the Medal. (Aubrey-Maturin Ser.). 1994. 24.00 (*0-393-03711-8*); 1992. 288p. pap. 13.95 (*0-393-30960-6*) Norton, W. W. & Co., Inc.

—The Surgeon's Mate. l.t. ed. 2001. (Aubrey-Maturin Ser.). (Illus.). 569p. 28.95 (*0-7862-1936-X*, Macmillan Reference USA) Gale Group.

—The Surgeon's Mate. (Aubrey-Maturin Ser.). 1994. 24.00 (*0-393-03707-X*); 1992. 384p. pap. 13.95 (*0-393-30820-0*) Norton, W. W. & Co., Inc.

—The Surgeon's Mate. abr. ed. 2000. (Aubrey-Maturin Ser.). audio 25.00 (*0-375-41020-1*, RH Audio) Random Hse. Audio Publishing Group.

—The Thirteen-Gun Salute. (Aubrey-Maturin Ser.). 1992. 336p. pap. 13.95 (*0-393-30907-X*); 1991. 24.00 (*0-393-02974-3*) Norton, W. W. & Co., Inc.

—The Thirteen-Gun Salute. l.t. ed. 2002. (Famous Authors Ser.). 510p. 29.95 (*0-7862-1937-8*) Thorndike Pr.

—Treason's Harbour. (Aubrey-Maturin Ser.). 1994. 24.00 (*0-393-03709-6*); 1992. 334p. pap. 13.95 (*0-393-30863-4*) Norton, W. W. & Co., Inc.

—The Truelove. (Aubrey-Maturin Ser.). 1993. 256p. pap. 13.95 (*0-393-31016-7*); 1992. 192p. 24.00 (*0-393-03109-8*) Norton, W. W. & Co., Inc.

—The Wine-Dark Sea. (Aubrey-Maturin Ser.). 1994. 272p. pap. 13.95 (*0-393-31244-5*); 1993. 261p. 24.00 (*0-393-03558-1*) Norton, W. W. & Co., Inc.

—The Yellow Admiral. l.t. ed. 1997. (Aubrey-Maturin Ser.). 27.95 o.p. (*1-56895-430-1*, Wheeler Publishing, Inc.) Gale Group.

—The Yellow Admiral. (Aubrey-Maturin Ser.). 1997. (Illus.). 272p. pap. 13.95 (*0-393-31704-8*); 1996. 262p. 24.00 (*0-393-04044-5*) Norton, W. W. & Co., Inc.

—The Yellow Admiral. 1999. (Aubrey-Maturin Ser.). pap. 12.98 (*0-671-04444-3*, Simon & Schuster Audioworks) Simon & Schuster Audio.

O'Brien, Kate. Without My Cloak. 1987. (Virago Modern Classics Ser.). 490p. pap. 7.95 o.p. (*0-14-016155-4*, Penguin Bks.) Viking Penguin.

—Without My Cloak. 2001. (Modern Classics). 200p. pap. 13.95 (*0-86068-760-0*) Virago Pr., Ltd. GBR. *Dist:* Trafalgar Square.

O'Brien, Maureen. Mask of Betrayal. l.t. ed. 1999. (Magna Large Print Ser.). 480p. (*0-7505-1437-X*) Magna Large Print Bks. GBR. *Dist:* Ulverscroft Large Print Canada, Ltd.

O'Donoghue, Maureen. Winner. 1990. 3.99 o.p. (*0-517-05547-3*) Random Hse. Value Publishing.

—Winner. 1988. 19.95 o.p. (*0-671-53198-0*, Simon & Schuster) Simon & Schuster.

Oppenheim, E. Phillips. Advice Limited. 1977. (Short Story Index Reprint Ser.). 22.95 (*0-8369-3703-1*) Ayer Co. Pubs., Inc.

Orczy, Baroness Emmuska. The Scarlet Pimpernel. 2002. (Modern Library Classics). 304p. pap. 7.95 (*0-8129-6611-2*) Random House Adult Trade Publishing Group.

O'Rourke, William. Notts: A Striking Novel. 1996. 250p. 22.95 o.p. (*1-56924-806-0*, Marlowe & Co.) Avalon Publishing Group.

Orton, Joe & Halliwell, Kenneth. The Boy Hairdresser: And, Lord Cucumber: Two Novels. 1999. xxxvi, 279p. (*1-85459-414-1*) Hern, Nick Bks. GBR. *Dist:* Consortium Bk. Sales & Distribution.

Padfield, Peter. Salt & Steel. 1986. 384p. 24.95 o.p. (*0-7126-9489-7*) Trafalgar Square.

Palmer, William. Good Republic. 1991. 19.95 o.p. (*0-670-83571-4*) Viking Penguin.

Pargeter, Edith. A Bloody Field by Shrewsbury. 1991. 378p. mass mkt. 12.95 o.p. (*0-7472-3366-7*) Headline Bk. Publishing, Ltd. GBR. *Dist:* Trafalgar Square.

—The Green Branch. l.t. ed. 1991. (Magna Large Print Ser.). 469p. o.p. (*0-7505-0051-4*) Magna Large Print Bks. GBR. *Dist:* Ulverscroft Large Print Canada, Ltd.

—The Heaven Tree. l.t. ed. 1991. (Magna Large Print Ser.). 604p. 29.99 o.p. (*0-7505-0049-2*) Magna Large Print Bks. GBR. *Dist:* Ulverscroft Large Print Bks., Ltd., Ulverscroft Large Print Canada, Ltd.

—The Heaven Tree Trilogy, 3. 1993. 912p. 24.95 o.p. (*0-446-51708-9*) Warner Bks., Inc.

—The Marriage of Meggotta. 1979. 10.95 o.p. (*0-670-45873-2*) Viking Penguin.

—The Scarlet Seed. l.t. ed. 1991. (Magna Large Print Ser.). 467p. o.p. (*0-7505-0053-0*) Magna Large Print Bks. GBR. *Dist:* Ulverscroft Large Print Canada, Ltd.

Parker, Mark. X-Calibre: The Absurd Legend of Cantiger the Wizard. 2000. 320p. pap. 11.95 (*0-7867-0802-6*, Carroll & Graf Pubs.) Avalon Publishing Group.

Parkes, Patricia. Queen's Lady. 1981. 504p. 14.95 o.p. (*0-312-66008-1*) St. Martin's Pr.

Parkinson, C. Northcote. Dead Reckoning, 001. 1978. 10.95 o.p. (*0-395-27115-0*) Houghton Mifflin Co.

—Dead Reckoning. 2003. (Richard Delancey Novels: 6). 320p. pap. 15.95 (*1-59013-038-3*) McBooks Pr., Inc.

—Dead Reckoning. 1978. 276p. (J). (*0-7195-3484-4*) Murray, John Pubs., Ltd. GBR. *Dist:* Trafalgar Square.

—Devil to Pay. 2001. (Richard Delancey Novels: Vol. 2). 288p. pap. 14.95 (*1-59013-002-2*) McBooks Pr., Inc.

—Devil to Pay. 1973. 278p. text (*0-7195-2838-0*) Murray, John Pubs., Ltd. GBR. *Dist:* Trafalgar Square.

—The Fireship. 1980. (Parkinson Hist Sea Adventure Ser.: No. 2). 208p. 2.25 (*0-87216-685-6*, Jove) Berkley Publishing Group.

—The Fireship, 001. 1975. 192p. 6.95 o.p. (*0-395-20428-3*) Houghton Mifflin Co.

—The Fireship. 1975. 187p. (J). (*0-7195-3175-6*) Murray, John Pubs., Ltd. GBR. *Dist:* Trafalgar Square.

—The Guernseyman. 2001. (Richard Delancey Novels: Vol. 1). 224p. pap. 13.95 (*1-59013-001-4*) McBooks Pr., Inc.

—The Life & Times of Horatio Hornblower. 1994. reprint ed. lib. bdg. 32.95 (*1-56849-318-5*) Buccaneer Bks., Inc.

—The Life & Times of Horatio Hornblower. l.t. ed. 2000. (Charnwood Large Print Ser.). 432p. 31.99 (*0-7089-9193-9*, Ulverscroft) Thorpe, F. A. Pubs. GBR. *Dist:* Ulverscroft Large Print Bks., Ltd., Ulverscroft Large Print Canada, Ltd.

—The Life & Times of Horatio Hornblower. 1970. 304p. (*0-7181-0787-X*, Joseph, Michael) Viking Penguin.

—The Life & Times of Horatio Hornblower: A Fictional Biography. 1998. 320p. pap. 10.95 (*0-7509-2109-9*) Sutton Publishing.

—So Near So Far. 2003. (Richard Delancey Novels: No. 5). 272p. pap. 13.95 (*1-59013-037-5*) McBooks Pr., Inc.

—Touch & Go. 1980. 272p. 2.25 (*0-87216-713-5*, Jove) Berkley Publishing Group.

—Touch & Go. 1978. (General Ser.). lib. bdg. 13.50 o.p. (*0-8161-6592-0*, Macmillan Reference USA) Gale Group.

—Touch & Go, 001. 1977. (Illus.). 230p. 8.95 o.p. (0-395-25592-9) Houghton Mifflin Co.
—Touch & Go. 2003. (Richard Delancey Novels: No. 4). 224p. pap. 13.95 (1-59013-025-1) McBooks Pr., Inc.
—Touch & Go. 1977. 230p. (J). (0-7195-3371-6) Murray, John Pubs., Ltd. GBR. Dist: Trafalgar Square.
Parks, Tim. Judge Savage. 2003. 456p. 22.95 (1-55970-691-0) Arcade Publishing, Inc.
Paton Walsh, Jill. The Huffler, RS. 1975. (Illus.). 96p. (J). (gr. 4 up). 9.95 o.p. (0-374-33505-2, Farrar, Straus & Giroux (BYR)) Farrar, Straus & Giroux.
Paxson, Diana. The White Raven. 1988. 320p. 18.95 o.p. (0-688-07496-0, Morrow, William & Co.) Morrow/Avon.
Paxson, Diana L. The Book of the Spear. l.t. ed. 2002. 307p. 27.95 (0-7838-9556-9, Macmillan Reference USA) Gale Group.
—The Book of the Spear. 1999. (Hallowed Isle Ser.: 2). 208p. pap. 10.00 (0-380-80546-4, Eos) Morrow/Avon.
Peachment, Christopher. The Green & the Gold. 2003. 200p. (0-330-48733-7) Picador.
Penman, Sharon Kay. Dragon's Lair: A Medieval Mystery. 2003. 336p. 23.95 (0-399-15077-3, Putnam & Grosset) Putnam Publishing Group, The.
—Falls the Shadow. 1988. 580p. 19.95 o.p. (0-8050-0300-2) Holt, Henry & Co.
—The Reckoning. 1992. 608p. pap. 14.95 (0-345-37888-1) Ballantine Bks.
—The Reckoning. 1991. 592p. 24.95 o.p. (0-8050-1014-9) Holt, Henry & Co.
—The Sunne in Splendour. 1990. 944p. pap. 15.95 (0-345-36313-2) Ballantine Bks.
—The Sunne in Splendour. 1982. o.p. (0-03-061368-X) Holt, Henry & Co.
—The Sunne in Splendour. 1984. 896p. pap. 8.95 o.p. (0-14-006764-7, Penguin Bks.) Viking Penguin.
Perkins, Wilder. Hoare & the Headless Captains: A Maritime Mystery Featuring Captain Bartholomew Hoare. 2000. 247p. 22.95 (0-312-25248-X, Saint Martin's Minotaur) St. Martin's Pr.
—Hoare & the Matter of Treason. 2001. 215p. 22.95 (0-312-27291-X, Saint Martin's Minotaur) St. Martin's Pr.
—Hoare & the Portsmouth Atrocities. 1998. 224p. 21.95 (0-312-19283-5, Saint Martin's Minotaur) St. Martin's Pr.
Peters, Ellis, pseud. The Leper of St. Giles. 1999. (Chronicles of Brother Cadfael Ser.: Vol. 5). audio 9.95 (1-56938-267-0, AMP-2670) Acorn Media Publishing, Inc.
—The Leper of St. Giles. unabr. ed. 1996. (Chronicles of Brother Cadfael Ser.: Vol. 5). audio 20.97 o.p. (0-7451-2843-2) BBC Audiobooks America.
—The Leper of St. Giles. 1985. (Chronicles of Brother Cadfael Ser.: Vol. 5). 208p. mass mkt. 4.95 o.s.i (0-449-20541-X, Fawcett) Ballantine Bks.
—The Leper of St. Giles. unabr. ed. 1999. (Chronicles of Brother Cadfael Ser.: Vol. 5). audio 39.95 (0-7861-1260-3, 2181) Blackstone Audio Bks., Inc.
—The Leper of St. Giles. 1995. (Chronicles of Brother Cadfael Ser.: Vol. 5). (Illus.). 223p. mass mkt. o.s.i (0-7515-1105-6) Little Brown & Co.
—The Leper of St. Giles. 1982. (Chronicles of Brother Cadfael Ser.: Vol. 5). 224p. 11.50 o.p. (0-688-01097-0, Morrow, William & Co.) Morrow/Avon.
—The Leper of St. Giles. unabr. ed. 1992. (Chronicles of Brother Cadfael Ser.: Vol. 5). audio 60.00 (1-55690-686-2, 92339E7) Recorded Bks., LLC.
—The Leper of St. Giles. l.t. ed. 1998. (Chronicles of Brother Cadfael Ser.: Vol. 5). 296p. pap. 24.95 (0-7862-1375-2) Thorndike Pr.
—The Leper of St. Giles. l.t. ed. 1983. (Chronicles of Brother Cadfael Ser.: Vol. 5). 352p. 29.99 o.p. (0-7089-1020-3, Ulverscroft) Thorpe, F. A. Pubs. GBR. Dist: Ulverscroft Large Print Bks., Ltd.
—The Sanctuary Sparrow. 1984. (Chronicles of Brother Cadfael Ser.: Vol. 7). 224p. mass mkt. 3.95 o.s.i (0-449-20613-0, Fawcett) Ballantine Bks.
—The Sanctuary Sparrow. 1983. (Chronicles of Brother Cadfael Ser.: Vol. 7). 12.50 o.p. (0-688-02252-9, Morrow, William & Co.) Morrow/Avon.
—The Sanctuary Sparrow. l.t. ed. 1999. (Chronicles of Brother Cadfael Ser.: Vol. 7). 312p. pap. 24.95 (0-7862-1599-2) Thorndike Pr.
—The Sanctuary Sparrow. l.t. ed. 1985. (Chronicles of Brother Cadfael Ser.: Vol. 7). 384p. o.p. (0-7089-1288-5, Ulverscroft) Thorpe, F. A. Pubs.
—St. Peter's Fair. 1981. (Chronicles of Brother Cadfael Ser.: Vol. 4). 220p. 19.95 (0-333-31050-0) Macmillan U.K. GBR. Dist: Trans-Atlantic Pubns., Inc.
—St. Peter's Fair. l.t. ed. 1998. (Chronicles of Brother Cadfael Ser.: Vol. 4). 302p. pap. 24.95 (0-7862-1074-5) Thorndike Pr.
—St. Peter's Fair. l.t. ed. 1983. (Chronicles of Brother Cadfael Ser.: Vol. 4). 416p. 15.95 o.p. (0-7089-0933-7, Ulverscroft) Thorpe, F. A. Pubs. GBR. Dist: Ulverscroft Large Print Bks., Ltd.
—The Summer of the Danes. 1991. (Chronicles of Brother Cadfael Ser.: Vol. 18). 256p. 16.95 o.p. (0-89296-448-0) Mysterious Pr.
—The Summer of the Danes. abr. ed. 1996. (Chronicles of Brother Cadfael Ser.: Vol. 18). 17.95 o.p. (0-7871-0278-4, 394020) NewStar Media, Inc.
—The Summer of the Danes. l.t. ed. 1993. (Ulverscroft Large Print Ser.). 480p. 29.99 o.p. (0-7089-2941-9, Ulverscroft) Thorpe, F. A. Pubs. GBR. Dist: Ulverscroft Large Print Bks., Ltd., Ulverscroft Large Print Canada, Ltd.
—The Summer of the Danes. 1992. (Chronicles of Brother Cadfael Ser.: Vol. 18). 256p. mass mkt. 6.99 (0-446-40018-1) Warner Bks., Inc.
—The Virgin in the Ice. 1986. (Chronicles of Brother Cadfael Ser.: Vol. 6). mass mkt. 4.95 o.s.i (0-449-21121-5); 1984. mass mkt. 2.50 o.s.i (0-449-20537-1) Ballantine Bks. (Fawcett).
—The Virgin in the Ice. 1995. (Chronicles of Brother Cadfael Ser.: Vol. 6). (Illus.). 271p. mass mkt. o.s.i (0-7515-1401-2) Little Brown & Co.
—The Virgin in the Ice. l.t. ed. 1998. (General Ser.). 320p. pap. 24.95 (0-7862-1479-1) Thorndike Pr.
—The Virgin in the Ice. l.t. ed. 1985. (Chronicles of Brother Cadfael Ser.: Vol. 6). 400p. o.p. (0-7089-1258-3, Ulverscroft) Thorpe, F. A. Pubs.
—The Virgin in the Ice. 1995. (Chronicles of Brother Cadfael Ser.: Vol. 6). 208p. mass mkt. 6.99 (0-446-40428-4) Warner Bks., Inc.
Peterson, Tracie. Framed. 1998. (Portraits Ser.). 240p. pap. 8.99 o.p. (1-55661-992-8) Bethany Hse. Pubs.
—Framed. l.t. ed. 2000. (Christian Mystery Ser.). 367p. 24.95 (0-7862-2696-X) Thorndike Pr.
Phillips, Caryl. The Final Passage. 1985. 208p. o.p. (0-571-13437-8) Faber & Faber Ltd.
—The Final Passage. 1985. 208p. pap. 8.95 o.p. (0-571-13438-6) Faber & Faber, Inc.
—The Final Passage. 1995. 208p. pap. 15.00 (0-679-75931-X, Vintage) Knopf Publishing Group.
Phillpotts, Eden. The Torch, & Other Tales. 1977. (Short Story Index Reprint Ser.). reprint ed. 19.95 (0-8369-3782-1) Ayer Co. Pubs., Inc.
Pilcher, Rosamunde. The Blue Bedroom & Other Stories. 1985. 288p. 15.95 o.p. (0-312-08527-3) St. Martin's Pr.
—Wild Mountain Thyme. l.t. ed. 1994. 19.95 o.p. (0-7927-1724-4); pap. 17.95 o.p. (0-7927-1723-6); audio 69.95 (0-7451-4067-X, CAB 764) BBC Audiobooks America.
—Wild Mountain Thyme. unabr. ed. 1992. audio 48.00 (0-7366-2199-7, 2994) Books on Tape, Inc.
—Wild Mountain Thyme. 1989. 304p. reprint ed. mass mkt. 5.50 o.s.i (0-440-20250-7) Dell Publishing.
—Wild Mountain Thyme. 1991. audio 12.79 o.s.i (0-553-70030-8); 1991. audio 15.95 o.s.i (0-553-74546-8); 2001. audio 9.99 (0-553-70186-X) Random Hse. Audio Publishing Group. (RH Audio).
—Wild Mountain Thyme. 1996. mass mkt. 6.50 (0-312-96123-5, St. Martin's Paperbacks); 1979. 8.95 o.p. (0-312-87981-4) St. Martin's Pr.
—Wild Mountain Thyme. l.t. ed. 1981. (Ulverscroft Large Print Ser.). 456p. 29.99 o.p. (0-7089-0621-4, Ulverscroft) Thorpe, F. A. Pubs. GBR. Dist: Ulverscroft Large Print Bks., Ltd., Ulverscroft Large Print Canada, Ltd.
Plaidy, Jean. The Bastard King. 24.95 (0-8488-0605-0) Amereon, Ltd.
—The Bastard King. 1980. mass mkt. 2.25 o.s.i (0-449-24273-0, Fawcett) Ballantine Bks.
—The Bastard King. 1979. 10.00 o.p. (0-399-12322-9) Putnam Publishing Group, The.
—The Courts of Love. 1989. 496p. mass mkt. 4.95 o.s.i (0-449-21657-8, Fawcett) Ballantine Bks.
—The Courts of Love. 1988. (Queens of England Ser.: Vol. 5). 416p. 18.95 o.p. (0-399-13294-5, G. P. Putnam's Sons) Penguin Putnam Bks. for Young Readers.
—Epitaph for Three Women. 1985. 352p. mass mkt. 3.95 o.s.i (0-449-20631-9, Fawcett) Ballantine Bks.
—Epitaph for Three Women. 1983. (Plantagenet Saga Ser.: Vol. 12). 336p. 12.95 o.p. (0-399-12782-8) Putnam Publishing Group, The.
—Goddess of the Green Room. 1991. mass mkt. 4.99 o.s.i (0-449-21983-6, Fawcett) Ballantine Bks.
—Goddess of the Green Room. 1989. (Georgian Saga Ser.: Vol. 10). 352p. 19.95 o.p. (0-399-13476-X, G. P. Putnam's Sons) Penguin Putnam Bks. for Young Readers.
—A Health unto His Majesty. 253p. reprint ed. lib. bdg. 23.95 (0-88411-894-0) Amereon, Ltd.
—A Health unto His Majesty. 1973. 288p. mass mkt. 1.75 o.p. (0-449-22019-2, P2019, Fawcett) Ballantine Bks.
—A Health unto His Majesty. 1972. 288p. 6.95 o.p. (0-399-10982-X) Putnam Publishing Group, The.
—Indiscretions of the Queen. 1988. (Georgian Saga Ser.: Vol. 8). 352p. 17.95 o.p. (0-399-13389-5, G. P. Putnam's Sons) Penguin Putnam Bks. for Young Readers.
—Katharine, the Virgin Widow. 1993. 224p. 22.95 o.p. (0-399-13873-0, G. P. Putnam's Sons) Penguin Group (USA) Inc.
—Katharine the Virgin Widow. 1995. mass mkt. 5.99 o.s.i (0-449-22286-1, Fawcett) Ballantine Bks.
—Myself, My Enemy. 1985. 352p. mass mkt. 3.95 o.s.i (0-449-20648-3, Fawcett) Ballantine Bks.
—Myself, My Enemy. l.t. ed. 1984. (General Ser.). 19.95 o.p. (0-8161-3686-6, Macmillan Reference USA) Gale Group.
—Myself, My Enemy. 1984. (Queens of England Ser.). 396p. 13.95 o.p. (0-399-12877-8, G. P. Putnam's Sons) Penguin Putnam Bks. for Young Readers.
—The Passionate Enemies. 24.95 (0-8488-0606-9) Amereon, Ltd.
—The Passionate Enemies. 1981. 320p. mass mkt. 2.50 o.s.i (0-449-24390-7, Fawcett) Ballantine Bks.
—The Passionate Enemies. 1979. 10.00 o.p. (0-399-12413-6) Putnam Publishing Group, The.
—The Plantagenet Prelude. 24.95 (0-8488-0607-7) Amereon, Ltd.
—The Plantagenet Prelude, No. 1. 1985. 320p. mass mkt. 2.95 o.s.i (0-449-21102-9, Fawcett) Ballantine Bks.
—The Plantagenet Prelude. 1980. 10.95 o.p. (0-399-12448-9) Putnam Publishing Group, The.
—The Pleasures of Love. l.t. ed. 1993. pap. 17.95 o.p. (0-7927-1381-8); 1992. 19.95 o.p. (0-7927-1382-6) BBC Audiobooks America.
—The Pleasures of Love. 1993. reprint ed. mass mkt. 4.99 o.s.i (0-449-22212-8, Fawcett) Ballantine Bks.
—The Pleasures of Love. 1992. (Queens of England Ser.). 336p. 21.95 o.p. (0-399-13731-9, G. P. Putnam's Sons) Penguin Group (USA) Inc.
—The Princess of Celle. (Georgian Saga Ser.). 27.95 (0-8488-0608-5) Amereon, Ltd.
—The Princess of Celle. 1986. (Georgian Saga Ser.). mass mkt. 3.95 o.s.i (0-449-21004-9, Fawcett) Ballantine Bks.
—The Princess of Celle. l.t. ed. 1986. (Georgian Saga Ser.). 597p. 18.95 o.p. (0-8161-3973-3, Macmillan Reference USA) Gale Group.
—The Princess of Celle. 1985. (Georgian Saga Ser.: No. 1). 336p. 15.95 o.p. (0-399-13070-5, G. P. Putnam's Sons) Penguin Putnam Bks. for Young Readers.
—The Princess of Celle. l.t. ed. 1974. (Shadows of the Crown Ser.). 29.99 o.p. (0-85456-594-9, Ulverscroft) Thorpe, F. A. Pubs. GBR. Dist: Ulverscroft Large Print Bks., Ltd., Ulverscroft Large Print Canada, Ltd.
—The Queen & Lord M. 268p. reprint ed. lib. bdg. 22.95 (0-88411-895-9) Amereon, Ltd.
—The Queen & Lord M. 1978. mass mkt. 1.75 o.s.i (0-449-23605-6, Fawcett) Ballantine Bks.
—The Queen & Lord M. 1977. 7.95 o.p. (0-399-11994-9) Putnam Publishing Group, The.
—The Queen & Lord M. l.t. ed. 1975. (Shadows of the Crown Ser.). 29.99 o.p. (0-85456-600-7, Ulverscroft) Thorpe, F. A. Pubs. GBR. Dist: Ulverscroft Large Print Bks., Ltd., Ulverscroft Large Print Canada, Ltd.
—Queen in Waiting. 26.95 (0-8488-0609-3) Amereon, Ltd.
—Queen in Waiting. 1987. mass mkt. 3.95 o.s.i (0-449-21096-0, Fawcett) Ballantine Bks.
—Queen in Waiting. 1985. 400p. 16.95 o.p. (0-399-13101-9) Putnam Publishing Group, The.
—Queen of This Realm. 1986. mass mkt. 4.99 o.s.i (0-449-20979-2, Fawcett) Ballantine Bks.
—Queen of This Realm. 2004. 448p. pap. 14.95 (0-609-81020-0, Three Rivers Pr.) Crown Publishing Group.
—Queen of This Realm. 1985. (Queens of England Ser.: Vol. 2). 576p. 16.95 o.p. (0-399-12985-5, G. P. Putnam's Sons) Penguin Putnam Bks. for Young Readers.
—The Queen's Secret. 1992. mass mkt. 4.99 o.s.i (0-449-22008-7, Fawcett) Ballantine Bks.
—The Queen's Secret. 1990. 320p. 19.95 o.p. (0-399-13531-6, G. P. Putnam's Sons) Penguin Putnam Bks. for Young Readers.
—The Reluctant Queen. 1993. (Queens of England Ser.). mass mkt. 4.99 o.s.i (0-449-22161-X, Fawcett) Ballantine Bks.
—The Reluctant Queen. 1994. 3.66 o.p. (0-8161-2837-5); 468p. lib. bdg. 22.95 (0-8161-7426-1) Gale Group. (Macmillan Reference USA).
—The Reluctant Queen. unabr. ed. 1994. audio 69.95 (1-85695-830-2, 940908) ISIS Audio Bks. GBR. Dist: Ulverscroft Large Print Bks., Ltd.
—The Reluctant Queen. 1991. (Queens of England Ser.). 304p. 21.95 o.p. (0-399-13609-6, G. P. Putnam's Sons) Penguin Group (USA) Inc.
—The Rose Without a Thorn. 1995. mass mkt. 5.99 o.s.i (0-449-22326-4, Fawcett) Ballantine Bks.
—The Rose Without a Thorn. 2003. 288p. pap. 12.95 (0-609-81017-0, Three Rivers Pr.) Crown Publishing Group.
—The Rose Without a Thorn. l.t. ed. 1994. 23.95 o.p. (1-56895-161-2, Wheeler Publishing, Inc.) Gale Group.
—The Rose Without a Thorn. l.t. ed. 1994. (Magna Large Print Ser.). 420p. o.p. (0-7505-0658-X) Magna Large Print Bks. GBR. Dist: Ulverscroft Large Print Canada, Ltd.
—The Rose Without a Thorn. 1994. (Queens of England Ser.). 256p. 22.95 o.p. (0-399-13930-3, G. P. Putnam's Sons) Penguin Group (USA) Inc.
—St. Thomas's Eve. 22.95 (0-8488-0610-7) Amereon, Ltd.
—St. Thomas's Eve. 1970. 6.95 o.p. (0-399-10717-7) Putnam Publishing Group, The.
—Victoria in the Wings. 1992. reprint ed. mass mkt. 4.99 o.s.i (0-449-22025-7, Fawcett) Ballantine Bks.
—Victoria in the Wings. 1990. 352p. 19.95 o.p. (0-399-13539-1, G. P. Putnam's Sons) Penguin Putnam Bks. for Young Readers.
—Victoria in the Wings. l.t. ed. 1974. (Shadows of the Crown Ser.). 29.99 o.p. (0-85456-598-1, Ulverscroft) Thorpe, F. A. Pubs. GBR. Dist: Ulverscroft Large Print Bks., Ltd., Ulverscroft Large Print Canada, Ltd.
—Victoria Victorious. 1987. 560p. reprint ed. mass mkt. 4.95 o.s.i (0-449-21251-3, Fawcett) Ballantine Bks.
—Victoria Victorious. 1986. 560p. 17.95 o.p. (0-399-13102-7) Putnam Publishing Group, The.
—William's Wife. 1995. mass mkt. 5.99 o.s.i (0-449-22284-5, Fawcett) Ballantine Bks.
—William's Wife. 1993. (Queens of England Ser.). 288p. 22.95 o.p. (0-399-13807-2, G. P. Putnam's Sons) Penguin Group (USA) Inc.
—William's Wife. l.t. ed. 1994. (Ulverscroft Large Print Ser.). 592p. 29.99 o.p. (0-7089-3066-2, Ulverscroft) Thorpe, F. A. Pubs. GBR. Dist: Ulverscroft Large Print Bks., Ltd., Ulverscroft Large Print Canada, Ltd.
Plunkett, Robert L. A California Dreamer in King Henry's Court. 1989. 213p. lib. bdg. 16.95 (0-9623139-4-7) Silver Dawn Media.
Pope, Dudley. Buccaneer. 2001. (Illus.). 320p. pap. 9.95 (0-7551-0437-4) House of Stratus, Inc. GBR. Dist: Midpoint Trade Bks., Inc.
—Buccaneer. 1984. 288p. 12.95 o.p. (0-8027-0783-1) Walker & Co.
—Galleon. 2001. (Illus.). 330p. pap. 9.95 (0-7551-0439-0) House of Stratus, Inc. GBR. Dist: Midpoint Trade Bks., Inc.
—Galleon. 1988. 17.95 o.s.i (0-8027-0989-3) Walker & Co.
—Ramage & the Dido. 2002. (Lord Ramage Novels Ser.: No. 18). (Illus.). 288p. pap. 15.95 (1-59013-024-3) McBooks Pr., Inc.
—Ramage & the Renegades Book #12. 2001. (Lord Ramage Novels Ser.: Vol. 12). 320p. pap. 15.95 (1-59013-009-X) McBooks Pr., Inc.
—Ramage at Trafalgar. 2002. (Lord Ramage Novels: 16). (Illus.). 256p. pap. 14.95 (1-59013-022-7) McBooks Pr., Inc.
—The Ramage Touch Book #10. 2001. (Lord Ramage Novels Ser.: Vol. 10). 272p. pap. 15.95 (1-59013-007-3) McBooks Pr., Inc.
—Ramage's Devil. 2002. (Lord Ramage Novels Ser.: Vol. 13). (Illus.). 320p. pap. 15.95 (1-59013-010-3) McBooks Pr., Inc.
—Ramage's Signal Book #11. 2001. (Lord Ramage Novels Ser.: Vol. 11). 320p. pap. 15.95 (1-59013-008-1) McBooks Pr., Inc.
Porter, Henry. A Spy's Life. 402p. (0-7528-4321-4); 2001. (0-7528-3859-8) Orion Publishing Group, Ltd. GBR. Dist: Trafalgar Square.
—A Spy's Life: A Novel. 2002. 400p. 25.00 (0-7432-1560-5, Simon & Schuster) Simon & Schuster.
Powell, Anthony. The Fisher King. 1986. 15.95 o.p. (0-393-02363-X) Norton, W. W. & Co., Inc.
—The Fisher King: A Novel. 1987. pap. 7.95 o.p. (0-393-30502-3) Norton, W. W. & Co., Inc.
—Hearing Secret Harmonies. l.t. unabr. ed. 1999. 324p. 25.95 (0-7531-5825-6, 158256) ISIS Large Print Bks. GBR. Dist: ISIS Publishing.
—The Valley of Bones. l.t. unabr. ed. 1999. (Dance to the Music of Time Ser.). 284p. 25.95 (0-7531-5820-5, 158205) ISIS Large Print Bks. GBR. Dist: ISIS Publishing.
Powers, Anne. Queen's Ransom. 1986. 400p. reprint ed. mass mkt. 3.95 o.s.i (0-8439-2352-0) Dorchester Publishing Co., Inc.
Preston, Peter. 51st State. 1998. 278p. (0-670-88107-4); pap. (0-670-88326-3) Viking Penguin. (Viking).
Price, Susan. From Where I Stand. 1984. 128p. (J). (gr. 6 up). o.p. (0-571-13247-2) Faber & Faber Ltd.
Pyle, Howard. Men of Iron. l.t. ed. 190p. pap. 19.76 (0-7583-3912-7); 973p. pap. 78.13 (0-7583-3919-4); 247p. pap. 22.98 (0-7583-3913-5); 338p. pap. 28.78 (0-7583-3914-3); 433p. pap. 35.73 (0-7583-3915-1); 554p. pap. 44.08 (0-7583-3916-X); 682p. pap. 52.84 (0-7583-3917-8); 839p. pap. 69.67 (0-7583-3918-6); 338p. lib. bdg. 34.78 (0-7583-3906-2); 433p. lib. bdg. 41.73 (0-7583-3907-0); 554p. lib. bdg. 50.08 (0-7583-3908-9); 682p. lib.

bdg. 58.84 (*0-7583-3909-7*); 839p. lib. bdg. 81.67 (*0-7583-3910-0*); 973p. lib. bdg. 90.13 (*0-7583-3911-9*); 247p. lib. bdg. 28.98 (*0-7583-3905-4*); 190p. lib. bdg. 25.76 (*0-7583-3904-6*) Huge Print Pr.

Quick, Amanda, pseud. Desire. 1993. 400p. mass mkt. 7.50 (*0-553-56153-7*, Fanfare) Bantam Bks.

—Desire. l.t. ed. 1994. 25.95 o.p. (*1-56895-067-5*, Wheeler Publishing, Inc.) Gale Group.

—Mystique. 1996. 352p. mass mkt. 7.50 (*0-553-57159-1*) Bantam Bks.

—Mystique. l.t. ed. 1995. 25.95 o.p. (*0-7838-1630-8*, Macmillan Reference USA) Gale Group.

—Mystique. 1995. audio 16.98 o.s.i (*0-553-74590-5*, RH Audio) Random Hse. Audio Publishing Group.

—Mystique. unabr. ed. 1999. audio 78.00 (*0-7887-0415-X*, 94607E7) Recorded Bks., LLC.

Rackham, Jeff. The Rag & Bone Shop. 2001. 320p. 25.00 o.p. (*1-58195-105-1*, Zoland Bks., Inc.) Steerforth Pr.

—The Rag & Bone Shop. 2002. 320p. 14.00 (*0-14-200225-9*) Viking Penguin.

Radcliffe, Ann. Gaston de Blondeville, or, The Court of Henry 3rd, Keeping Festival in Ardenne, 2 vols., Set. 1979. (Gothic Novels Ser.). reprint ed. 53.95 (*0-405-00815-5*) Ayer Co. Pubs., Inc.

Raleigh, Debbie. The Wedding Wish. 2003. 185p. 26.95 (*1-59414-024-3*, Five Star) Gale Group.

—The Wedding Wish. 2002. 224p. mass mkt. 4.99 o.s.i (*0-8217-7171-X*) Kensington Publishing Corp.

Raphael, Frederic. Coast to Coast. 1999. 240p. 22.95 (*0-945774-42-7*, PR6068.A6C63) Catbird Pr.

Rawlinson, Peter. The Richmond Diary. 2001. 288p. 23.95 (*0-312-27553-6*, Saint Martin's Minotaur) St. Martin's Pr.

Read, Miss. Howards of Caxley. 1988. (Illus.). pap. 9.00 o.p. (*0-89733-319-5*) Academy Chicago Pubs., Ltd.

Rebecca. Rose of Rapture. 1984. mass mkt. 6.95 (*0-446-37613-2*) Warner Bks., Inc.

Reeman, Douglas. Battlecruiser. 2003. (Douglas Reeman Modern Naval Library). 320p. pap. 15.95 (*1-59013-043-X*) McBooks Pr., Inc.

—The White Guns. 1989. 326p. (C). 19.95 o.p. (*0-434-62634-1*, 00635) Heinemann.

Reid, Jamie. Easy Money. 1987. 17.95 (*0-8027-0999-0*) Walker & Co.

Reilly, Judith M. A Vision of Light. 1990. 480p. mass mkt. 4.95 o.s.i (*0-440-20520-4*) Dell Publishing.

Renault, Mary. The Charioteer. 2003. 352p. pap. 14.00 (*0-375-71418-9*, Vintage); 1983. pap. 6.95 o.s.i (*0-394-71480-6*, Pantheon) Knopf Publishing Group.

—Charioteer. 1994. (Harvest Book Ser.). 348p. pap. 10.95 o.s.i (*0-15-616768-9*, Harvest Bks.) Harcourt Trade Pubs.

—The Charioteer. unabr. ed. 1988. audio 85.00 (*1-55690-097-X*, 88760E7) Recorded Bks., LLC.

Rice, Sile. The Saxon Tapestry. 1992. 400p. 21.95 o.p. (*1-55970-158-7*) Arcade Publishing, Inc.

Riley, Judith M. The Serpent Garden. 1997. 480p. pap. 13.95 o.s.i (*0-14-025880-9*) Penguin Group (USA) Inc.

—The Serpent Garden. 1996. (Illus.). 480p. 24.95 o.p. (*0-670-86661-X*) Viking Penguin.

Ripley, Mike & Jakubowski, Maxim, eds. Fresh Blood II. 1998. (Bloodlines Ser.). 200p. pap. 16.95 (*1-899344-20-9*) Do-Not Pr., The GBR. *Dist:* Dufour Editions, Inc.

—Fresh Blood III. 2000. 191p. pap. 16.95 (*1-899344-52-7*) Do-Not Pr., The GBR. *Dist:* Dufour Editions, Inc.

Robb, Candace. The Apothecary Rose. 1994. 319p. mass mkt. 6.99 (*0-312-95360-7*, St. Martin's Paperbacks); 1993. 256p. 19.95 o.p. (*0-312-09782-4*, Saint Martin's Minotaur) St. Martin's Pr.

—The Cross-Legged Knight. 2003. (An/Owen Archer Mystery Ser.). (Illus.). 336p. 23.95 (*0-89296-772-2*) Mysterious Pr.

—The Cross-Legged Knight. l.t. ed. 2003. (Owen Archer Mystery Ser.). 517p. 28.95 (*0-7862-5611-7*) Thorndike Pr.

—The Cross-Legged Knight. 2004. 336p. pap. 12.95 (*0-446-69166-6*, Mysterious Pr. Paperback Bks.) Warner Bks., Inc.

—A Spy for the Redeemer. 2003. 320p. pap. 12.95 (*0-446-67965-8*, Mysterious Pr. Paperback Bks.) Warner Bks., Inc.

Robbins, Alan. On the Trail of Blood: A Participatory Mystery. 1988. (Illus.). 256p. pap. 7.95 o.p. (*0-8050-0538-2*, Owl Bks.) Holt, Henry & Co.

Roberts, Ann V. Morning's Gate: A Novel. 1992. 620p. 22.00 o.p. (*0-688-11074-6*, Morrow, William & Co.) Morrow/Avon.

Roberts, David. Hollow Crown. 2002. (Lord Edward Corinth & Verity Browne Mystery Ser.: Bk. 3). 320p. 24.00 (*0-7867-1052-7*, Carroll & Graf Pubs.) Avalon Publishing Group.

Roberts, J. M. Without Sanction. 1993. 320p. (Orig.). pap. 8.95 o.p. (*1-55583-215-6*) Alyson Pubns.

Robertson, Denise. Strength for the Morning. l.t. ed. 1994. (Magna Large Print Ser.). 640p. 29.99 o.p. (*0-7505-0616-4*) Magna Large Print Bks. GBR. *Dist:* Ulverscroft Large Print Bks., Ltd., Ulverscroft Large Print Canada, Ltd.

Robinson, Bruce. The Peculiar Memories of Thomas Penman. 1998. 256p. 29.95 (*0-7475-3614-7*) Chronicle Bks. LLC.

—The Peculiar Memories of Thomas Penman. 2000. 288p. pap. 13.00 (*0-06-095540-6*, Perennial) HarperTrade.

—The Peculiar Memories of Thomas Penman. 1999. 278p. 24.95 (*0-87951-914-2*) Overlook Pr., The.

Ross, Robert. Colonial & Post-Colonial Fiction in English: An Anthology. 1999. (Reference Library of the Humanities: Vol. 1770). ix, 457p. reprint ed. 75.00 (*0-8153-1431-0*) Garland Publishing, Inc.

Royce, Kenneth. Man on a Short Leash. 1974. 228p. 25.00 o.p. (*0-8128-1684-6*, Scarborough Hse.) Madison Bks., Inc.

Ruell, Patrick. The Only Game: A Novel of Suspense. 1993. 288p. 20.00 o.p. (*0-88150-253-7*) Countryman Pr.

Sabatini, Rafael. Captain Blood. unabr. ed. 2000. audio compact disk 80.00 (*0-7861-9862-1*, ZP2606) Blackstone Audio Bks., Inc.

—Captain Blood. unabr. collector's ed. 1981. (J). audio 64.00 (*0-7366-0580-0*, 1550) Books on Tape, Inc.

—Captain Blood. 1990. reprint ed. lib. bdg. 25.95 (*0-89968-546-3*) Buccaneer Bks., Inc.

—Captain Blood. 1998. (Classics of Nautical Fiction Ser.). 288p. reprint ed. pap. 13.95 (*0-935526-45-5*) McBooks Pr., Inc.

—Captain Blood. 1998. (Gateway Movie Classics Ser.). 304p. pap. 12.95 (*0-89526-379-3*, Gateway Editions) Regnery Publishing, Inc., An Eagle Publishing Co.

—Captain Blood: His Odyssey. 2000. (Common Reader Edition Ser.). pap. 19.95 (*1-888173-44-0*) Akadine Pr., The.

—Captain Blood: His Odyssey. 24.95 (*0-8488-1147-X*) Amereon, Ltd.

—Captain Blood: His Odyssey. 1990. 442p. reprint ed. 19.95 o.s.i (*0-87797-197-8*) Cherokee Publishing Co.

—Captain Blood: His Odyssey. 2003. 325p. E-Book 4.95 (*0-9679159-9-6*) Hidden Knowledge.

—Captain Blood Returns. 1976. reprint ed. lib. bdg. 23.95 (*0-89190-742-4*, Rivercity Pr.) Amereon, Ltd.

—Captain Blood Returns. 1976. mass mkt. 1.50 o.s.i (*0-345-24963-1*) Ballantine Bks.

—Captain Blood Returns. 1994. lib. bdg. 27.95 (*1-56849-481-5*) Buccaneer Bks., Inc.

Sampson, John. The Demoniacs of Downing Street. 1992. (Illus.). 261p. 8.95 (*0-9613075-4-4*) Thornfield Pr.

—Little Miss Magi. 1997. (Illus.). 195p. 7.95 (*0-9613075-6-0*) Thornfield Pr.

Samson, Lisa. Love's Ransom. 1997. (Abbey Ser.). 350p. (Orig.). pap. 9.99 o.p. (*1-56507-529-3*) Harvest Hse. Pubs.

—The Warrior's Bride. 1997. (Abbey Ser.: No. 3). 400p. pap. 9.99 o.p. (*1-56507-636-2*) Harvest Hse. Pubs.

Sansom, William. The Stories of William Sansom. 1977. (Short Story Index Reprint Ser.). reprint ed. 28.95 (*0-8369-3786-4*) Ayer Co. Pubs., Inc.

Sauers, Victoria. Lionhearted Queen: Berengaria of Navarre. 2000. 242p. pap. 14.95 (*0-9666294-2-6*) Blue Bear Pr.

Savery, Jeanne. Smuggler's Heart. 2002. (Zebra Regency Romance Ser.). 288p. mass mkt. 4.99 o.s.i (*0-8217-7066-7*) Kensington Publishing Corp.

Saxton, Judith A. Someone Special. 1995. 25.95 o.p. (*0-312-13173-9*) St. Martin's Pr.

Scarrow, Simon. Under the Eagle: A Tale of Military Adventure & Reckless Heroism with the Roman Legions. l.t. ed. 2002. 578p. 28.95 (*0-7862-4076-8*) Gale Group.

Schneiderman, Beth K., ed. By & about Women: An Anthology of Short Fiction. 1973. (C). pap. text 8.75 o.p. (*0-15-505665-4*) Harcourt College Pubs.

Scott, Amanda. Border Storm. 2001. mass mkt. 3.99 (*0-8217-7730-0*); 336p. mass mkt. 5.99 (*0-8217-6762-3*) Kensington Publishing Corp. (Zebra Bks.).

—The Rose at Twilight. 1992. 400p. mass mkt. 4.99 o.s.i (*0-440-20725-8*) Dell Publishing.

Scott, Manda. Dreaming the Eagle. 2004. 496p. pap. 14.00 (*0-385-33773-6*, Delta) Dell Publishing.

—Dreaming the Eagle. 2003. E-Book 19.50 (*0-440-33410-1*) Random Hse., Inc.

—Dreaming the Eagle: A Novel of Boudica, The Warrior Queen. 2003. (Illus.). 480p. 23.95 (*0-385-33670-5*, Delacorte Pr.) Dell Publishing.

Scott, Walter, Sr. Ivanhoe. 1997. (Classics Illustrated Notes). (Illus.). pap. text 4.99 (*1-57840-063-5*) Acclaim Bks.

—Ivanhoe. 1964. (Airmont Classics Ser.). (YA). (gr. 9 up). pap. 2.95 o.p. (*0-8049-0034-5*, CL-34) Airmont Publishing Co., Inc.

—Ivanhoe. 36.75 (*0-8488-0857-6*) Amereon, Ltd.

—Ivanhoe. 1994. (Illustrated Classics Collection). 64p. pap. 4.95 (*0-7854-0749-9*, 40500) American Guidance Service, Inc.

—Ivanhoe. 1988. 480p. mass mkt. 5.95 (*0-553-21326-1*, Bantam Classics) Bantam Bks.

—Ivanhoe. 1991. (Illus.). 3.95 (*0-425-12526-2*, Classics Illustrated) Berkley Publishing Group.

—Ivanhoe. Tulloch, Graham, ed. 1998. 560p. 50.00 (*0-7486-0573-8*) Edinburgh Univ. Pr. GBR. *Dist:* Columbia Univ. Pr.

—Ivanhoe. 1998. (Clasicos Universales Ser.: Vol. 203). (SPA.). 560p. (*84-320-6975-2*) GeoPlaneta, Editorial, S. A.

—Ivanhoe. 1986. audio 69.00 Jimcin Recordings.

—Ivanhoe. 1999. E-Book 1.95 (*1-58515-246-3*) MesaView, Inc.

—Ivanhoe. 1962. 512p. (J). (gr. 7). mass mkt. 5.95 o.s.i (*0-451-52194-3*, CE1876, Signet Classics) NAL.

—Ivanhoe. Duncan, Ian, ed. & intro. by. (Oxford World's Classics Ser.). 1998. 622p. pap. 8.95 (*0-19-283499-1*); 1996. 618p. (C). pap. 6.95 o.p. (*0-19-283172-0*) Oxford Univ. Pr., Inc.

—Ivanhoe. 1990. (gr. 4-7). pap. 6.95 o.p. (*0-8114-6829-1*) Raintree Pubs.

—Ivanhoe. (Modern Library Classics). 2001. 592p. pap. 8.95 (*0-679-64223-4*); 2000. E-Book 4.95 (*0-679-64187-4*) Random House Adult Trade Publishing Group. (Modern Library).

—Ivanhoe. 1997. (Modern Library Ser.). 576p. 16.95 o.s.i (*0-679-60263-1*) Random Hse., Inc.

—Ivanhoe. Wilson, A. N., ed. & intro. by. 1984. (Penguin Classics Ser.). 624p. (C). pap. 8.95 o.s.i (*0-14-043143-8*, Penguin Classics) Viking Penguin.

—Ivanhoe. 1972. 9.25 o.p. (*0-460-01016-6*) Viking Penguin.

—Ivanhoe. 1998. (Classics Library). 400p. pap. 3.95 (*1-85326-202-1*, 2021WW) Wordsworth Editions, Ltd. GBR. *Dist:* Casemate Pubs. & Bk. Distributors, LLC.

—Ivanhoe. abr. ed. 1997. audio 16.95 o.p. (*1-56511-211-3*) HighBridge Co.

—Ivanhoe, Set. 1997. (YA). (gr. 4-10). audio 77.95 (*1-55685-455-2*) Audio Bk. Contractors, Inc.

—Ivanhoe. unabr. ed. 1999. audio 89.95 (*0-7861-1486-X*, 2338); 1986. audio 89.95 (*0-7861-0605-0*, 2095) Blackstone Audio Bks., Inc.

—Ivanhoe, Pt. A. unabr. collector's ed. 1986. (Jimcin Recording Ser.). (J). audio 56.00 (*0-7366-3921-7*, 9160-A) Books on Tape, Inc.

—Ivanhoe. unabr. ed. 1999. (Bookcassette Classic Collection). audio 66.25 (*1-56740-681-5*, 1809, Unabridged Library Editions); audio 22.95 (*1-56740-455-3*, 1808, Bookcassette) Brilliance Audio.

—Ivanhoe. 1989. 1982p. reprint ed. lib. bdg. 37.95 (*0-89967-043-1*, Harmony Raine & Co.) Buccaneer Bks., Inc.

—Ivanhoe. 1999. (Works of Sir Walter Scott: Vol. 16). 398p. reprint ed. Pt. 1. lib. bdg. 90.00 (*1-58201-248-2*); Pt. 2. lib. bdg. 90.00 (*1-58201-249-0*) Classic Bks.

—Ivanhoe. abr. ed. 1977. audio 19.95 (*0-694-50430-0*, SWC 2076, Caedmon) HarperTrade.

—Ivanhoe. l.t. ed. 1992. (Clear Type Classics Ser.). 510p. 29.95 (*1-85089-494-9*) ISIS Large Print Bks. GBR. *Dist:* Transaction Pubs., Ulverscroft Large Print Canada, Ltd.

—Ivanhoe. abr. ed. 1994. audio 13.98 (*962-634-525-X*, NA202514); audio compact disk 15.98 (*962-634-025-8*, NA202512) Naxos of America, Inc. (Naxos AudioBooks).

—Ivanhoe. abr. ed. 1997. (Ultimate Classics Ser.). 19.95 o.p. (*0-7871-1063-9*, 694870) NewStar Media, Inc.

—Ivanhoe. 1998. (Twelve-Point Ser.). 547p. reprint ed. lib. bdg. 25.00 (*1-58287-088-8*) North Bks.

—Kenilworth. 1968. (Airmont Classics Ser.). (J). (gr. 10 up). mass mkt. 2.95 o.p. (*0-8049-0193-7*, CL-193) Airmont Publishing Co., Inc.

—Kenilworth. 1955. 10.95 o.p. (*0-460-00135-3*) Biblio Distribution.

—Kenilworth. reprint ed. lib. bdg. 48.00 (*0-7426-1041-1*); 2001. (Early Best Sellers Ser.). (Illus.). pap. text 28.00 (*0-7426-6041-9*);Pt. 1. 2001. (Works of Sir Walter Scott: Vol. 22). (Illus.). 368p. pap. text 28.00 (*0-7426-5254-8*);Pt. 1. 1999. (Works of Sir Walter Scott: Vol. 22). 368p. lib. bdg. 90.00 (*1-58201-254-7*);Pt. 2. 2001. (Works of Sir Walter Scott: Vol. 23). (Illus.). 408p. pap. text 28.00 (*0-7426-5255-6*);Pt. 2. 1999. (Works of Sir Walter Scott: Vol. 23). 408p. lib. bdg. 90.00 (*1-58201-255-5*) Classic Bks.

—Kenilworth. Alexander, John H., ed. 1993. 541p. 52.50 (*0-231-08472-2*) Columbia Univ. Pr.

—Kenilworth. 2002. 472p. 98.99 (*1-4043-1194-7*); per. 93.99 (*1-4043-1195-5*) IndyPublish.com.

—Kenilworth. (Ebook Classic Ser.). E-Book 5.00 (*0-7410-1022-4*) SoftBook Pr.

—Kenilworth. l.t. ed. 1982. (Classics Ser.). 746p. 29.99 o.p. (*0-7089-8028-7*, Ulverscroft) Thorpe, F. A. Pubs. GBR. *Dist:* Ulverscroft Large Print Bks., Ltd., Ulverscroft Large Print Canada, Ltd.

—Kenilworth. 1999. (Classics Ser.). (Illus.). 528p. 13.95 (*0-14-043654-5*, Penguin Classics) Viking Penguin.

Sedley, Kate. Nine Men Dancing. 2003. 224p. 26.99 (*0-7278-5977-3*) Severn Hse. Pubs., Ltd.

Seton, Anya. Avalon. 1977. mass mkt. 1.95 o.s.i (*0-449-23308-1*, Fawcett) Ballantine Bks.

—Avalon. 1965. 10.00 o.p. (*0-395-08170-X*) Houghton Mifflin Co.

—Avalon. l.t. ed. 1982. (Ulverscroft Large Print Ser.). 587p. 12.50 o.p. (*0-7089-0750-4*, Ulverscroft) Thorpe, F. A. Pubs. GBR. *Dist:* Ulverscroft Large Print Bks., Ltd., Ulverscroft Large Print Canada, Ltd.

Shapiro, Fred R. & Garry, Jane, eds. Trial & Error: An Oxford Anthology of Legal Stories. 1998. 496p. 35.00 (*0-19-509547-2*) Oxford Univ. Pr., Inc.

Sharpe, Tom. Blott on the Landscape. unabr. ed. 1992. audio 48.00 (*0-7366-2241-1*, 3031) Books on Tape, Inc.

—Blott on the Landscape. unabr. ed. 2000. audio 59.95 (*0-7451-4203-6*, CAB 886) Chivers Audio Bks. GBR. *Dist:* BBC Audiobooks America.

—Blott on the Landscape. l.t. ed. 1988. (Mainstream Ser.). 347p. reprint ed. 16.95 o.p. (*1-85089-169-9*) ISIS Large Print Bks. GBR. *Dist:* Transaction Pubs.

—Blott on the Landscape. 1984. 224p. pap. 3.95 o.s.i (*0-394-72419-4*, Vintage) Knopf Publishing Group.

—Blott on the Landscape. 1999. 256p. 13.95 (*0-87951-927-4*) Overlook Pr., The.

Shelley, Mary Wollstonecraft. The Fortunes of Perkin Warbeck: A Romance, 3 vols. 2nd ed. (Illus.). reprint ed. 84.50 (*0-404-62114-7*);1. o.p. (*0-404-62115-5*);2. o.p. (*0-404-62116-3*) AMS Pr., Inc.

Sherwood, Frances. Vindication. 1993. 435p. 22.00 o.p. (*0-374-28390-7*) Farrar, Straus & Giroux.

—Vindication. 2004. 448p. pap. 14.95 (*0-393-32538-5*) Norton, W. W. & Co., Inc.

—Vindication. 1994. 448p. pap. 12.95 o.p. (*0-14-023668-6*, Penguin Bks.) Penguin Group (USA) Inc.

Shipway, George. Imperial Governor: The Great Novel of Boudicca's Revolt. 2003. (Cassell Military Paperbacks Ser.). (Illus.). 408p. pap. 9.95 o.s.i (*0-304-36324-3*) Cassell P L C GBR. *Dist:* Sterling Publishing Co., Inc.

Shwartz, Susan. The Grail of Hearts. 1992. 352p. 21.95 o.p. (*0-312-85176-6*, Tor Bks.) Doherty, Tom Assocs., LLC.

Sigal, Clancy. The Secret Defector: A Novel. 1992. 288p. 22.00 o.p. (*0-06-019011-6*) HarperTrade.

Sillitoe, Alan. Long-Distance Runner. 1960. 18.95 o.s.i (*0-394-43389-0*) Knopf, Alfred A. Inc.

Sinclair, James. Warrior Queen. 1978. 8.95 o.p. (*0-312-85626-1*) St. Martin's Pr.

Skilton. Castle Richmond: (trollope 1994) 1994. 43.00 (*1-870587-35-9*) Ashgate Publishing Co.

—Orley Farm: (trollope 1993) 1993. 48.00 (*1-870587-27-8*) Ashgate Publishing Co.

Slaughter, Carolyn. The Black Englishman. 2004. (*0-374-11399-8*) Farrar, Straus & Giroux.

Small, Bertrice. Love, Remember Me. 1996. 448p. mass mkt. 6.99 (*0-345-40926-4*) Ballantine Bks.

—Rosamund. l.t. ed. 2003. (Thorndike Romance Ser.). 683p. 28.95 (*0-7862-4987-0*) Gale Group.

—Rosamund. 2004. 448p. mass mkt. 6.99 (*0-451-21168-5*, Signet Bks.); 2002. 384p. pap. 14.00 (*0-451-20637-1*) NAL.

Smollett, Tobias George. The Expedition of Humphry Clinker. lib. bdg. 26.95 (*0-8488-1887-3*) Amereon, Ltd.

—The Expedition of Humphry Clinker. Knapp, Lewis M., ed. & intro. by. 1998. (Oxford World's Classics Ser.). (Illus.). 400p. pap. 9.95 (*0-19-283594-7*) Oxford Univ. Pr., Inc.

—The Expedition of Humphry Clinker. Knapp, Lewis M., ed. 1984. (Oxford World's Classics Ser.). (Illus.). 400p. pap. 6.95 o.p. (*0-19-281664-0*) Oxford Univ. Pr., Inc.

—The Expedition of Humphry Clinker. Brack, O. M., Jr. & Preston, Thomas R., eds. 1979. (Works of Tobias Smollett Ser.: Vol. 1). 18.00 (*0-87413-121-9*) Univ. of Delaware Pr.

—The Expedition of Humphry Clinker. Preston, Thomas R., ed. (Works of Tobias Smollett). (Illus.). 544p. 1993. pap. 20.00 (*0-8203-1537-0*); 1991. 50.00 (*0-8203-1203-7*) Univ. of Georgia Pr.

—The Expedition of Humphry Clinker. (Shakespeare Head Edition of Smollett's Novels Ser.: Vol. 3). reprint ed. Pt. 1. lib. bdg. 88.00 (*1-58201-149-4*); Pt. 2. 1999. 192p. lib. bdg. 88.00 (*1-58201-150-8*) Classic Bks.

—The Expedition of Humphry Clinker. 1992. (BCL1-PR English Literature Ser.). 433p. reprint ed. lib. bdg. 99.00 (*0-7812-7403-6*) Reprint Services Corp.

Solomon, Andrew. A Stone Boat. 1996. 256p. pap. 13.00 (*0-452-27498-2*, Plume) Dutton/Plume.

Spark, Muriel. All the Stories of Muriel Spark. 2001. 416p. pap. 19.95 (*0-8112-1494-X*) New Directions Publishing Corp.

—The Comforters. 1994. (Revived Modern Classic Ser.: Vol. 796). 208p. reprint ed. pap. 11.95 (0-8112-1285-8, NDP796) New Directions Publishing Corp.
—The Comforters. 1984. 224p. 6.95 o.p. (0-399-50931-3) Putnam Publishing Group, The.
—Symposium. 1990. 160p. 18.95 o.p. (0-395-51101-1) Houghton Mifflin Co.
Spencer, Sally. The Golden Mile to Murder. 2001. 256p. 25.99 (0-7278-5710-X); 29.99 (0-7278-7118-8) Severn Hse. Pubs., Ltd.
—South of the River. l.t. ed. 1999. (Magna Large Print Ser.). 400p. (0-7505-1378-0) Magna Large Print Bks. GBR. *Dist:* Ulverscroft Large Print Canada, Ltd.
Spicer, Michael. Cotswold Manners. 1990. 2.99 o.p. (0-517-05812-X) Random Hse. Value Publishing.
—Cotswold Manners. 1989. 192p. 14.95 o.p. (0-312-02562-9, Saint Martin's Minotaur) St. Martin's Pr.
—Cotswold Mistress: A Mystery. 1992. 208p. 16.95 o.p. (0-312-07683-5, Saint Martin's Minotaur) St. Martin's Pr.
—The Cotswold Murder. 1990. 15.95 o.p. (0-312-04285-X, Saint Martin's Minotaur) St. Martin's Pr.
—The Cotswold Murders. l.t. ed. 1992. 248p. 15.95 o.p. (0-7451-1543-8, Macmillan Reference USA) Gale Group.
Steed, Neville. Black Eye. 1990. 256p. 16.95 o.p. (0-312-03797-X, Saint Martin's Minotaur) St. Martin's Pr.
Stephen, Martin. The Desperate Remedy: Henry Gresham & the Gunpowder Plot. 2001. 324p. (0-316-85970-2) Little Brown & Co.
—The Desperate Remedy: Henry Gresham & the Gunpowder Plot. Date not set. pap. (0-312-30720-9, Saint Martin's Griffin); mass mkt. (0-312-98581-9, St. Martin's Paperbacks); E-Book (0-312-70568-9) St. Martin's Pr.
—The Desperate Remedy: Henry Gresham & the Gunpowder Plot. l.t. ed. 2002. (Ulverscroft Large Print Ser.). 544p. 32.50 (0-7089-4766-2, Ulverscroft) Thorpe, F. A. Pubs. GBR. *Dist:* Ulverscroft Large Print Bks., Ltd., Ulverscroft Large Print Canada, Ltd.
—The Desperate Remedy: Henry Gresham & the Gunpowder Plot; A Novel. 2003. 336p. 24.95 (0-312-30719-5) St. Martin's Pr.
Stern, Gladys Bronwyn. Smoke Rings. 1977. (Short Story Index Reprint Ser.). reprint ed. 25.95 (0-8369-4229-9) Ayer Co. Pubs., Inc.
Stevens, Rosemary. Murder in the Pleasure Gardens. 2003. 256p. 22.95 (0-425-19051-X, Prime Crime) Berkley Publishing Group.
Stevenson, Robert Louis. The Black Arrow. 21.95 (0-8488-1182-8) Amereon, Ltd.
—The Black Arrow. 2001. per. 14.00 (1-891355-81-3) Blue Unicorn Editions.
—The Black Arrow. E-Book 2.49 (1-58627-549-6) Electric Umbrella Publishing.
—The Black Arrow. 2002. 252p. 24.99 (1-58827-850-6); per. 20.99 (1-58827-851-4) IndyPublish.com.
—The Black Arrow. 1981. (English As a Second Language Bk.). pap. text 5.95 o.p. (0-582-53503-4, 74102) Longman Publishing Group.
—The Black Arrow. 2003. 272p. mass mkt. 6.95 (0-451-52916-2, Signet Classics) NAL.
—The Black Arrow. 2002. (Twelve-Point Ser.). 235p. lib. bdg. 25.00 (1-58287-194-9); 377p. lib. bdg. 26.00 (1-58287-677-0) North Bks.
—The Black Arrow: A Tale of the Two Roses. 2001. 224p. pap. 9.95 (1-873631-12-X) B & W Publishing GBR. *Dist:* Interlink Publishing Group, Inc.
—The Black Arrow: A Tale of the Two Roses. deluxe ed. 1987. (Scribners Illustrated Classics Ser.). (Illus.). xii, 328p. 75.00 o.s.i (0-684-18897-X, Atheneum) Simon & Schuster Children's Publishing.
—The Black Arrow, the Misadventures of John Nicholson. (Works of Robert Louis Stevenson Valima Edition Ser.: Vol. 13). 484p. reprint ed. 2001. (Illus.). pap. text 28.00 (0-7426-5171-1); 1999. lib. bdg. 88.00 (1-58201-171-0) Classic Bks.
Stockwin, Julian. Artemis. 2003. 352p. pap. 13.00 (0-7432-1461-7); 2002. 336p. 24.00 (0-7432-1460-9) Simon & Schuster. (Scribner).
—Artemis. l.t. ed. 2002. 28.95 (0-7862-4588-3) Thorndike Pr.
—Seaflower. l.t. ed. 2003. (Kydd Novel Ser.). 518p. 28.95 (0-7862-5514-5) Thorndike Pr.
—Seaflower: A Kydd Novel. 2004. 352p. pap. 13.00 (0-7432-1463-3); 2003. 336p. 24.00 (0-7432-1462-5) Simon & Schuster. (Scribner).
Stollery, Martin. Trainspotting. 2001. 88p. pap. 9.99 o.p. (0-582-45258-9) Longman Publishing Group.
Stuart, V. A. The Heroic Garrison. 2003. (Alexander Sheridan Novels: No. 5). 256p. pap. 13.95 (1-59013-030-8) McBooks Pr., Inc.
Sutherland, John, ed. The Oxford Book of English Love Stories. 2003. 452p. pap. 16.95 (0-19-280467-7) Oxford Univ. Pr., Inc.
Suthren, Victor. Admiral of Fear. 1991. 15.95 o.p. (0-312-05377-0) St. Martin's Pr.
—Captain Monsoon. 1993. 16.95 o.p. (0-312-08728-4) St. Martin's Pr.
—The Golden Galleon. 1988. 224p. 15.95 o.p. (0-312-02216-6) St. Martin's Pr.
—Royal Yankee. 1987. 192p. 13.95 o.p. (0-312-01084-2) St. Martin's Pr.
Tannahill, Reay. Return of the Stranger. 1996. 384p. 24.95 o.p. (0-312-14038-X) St. Martin's Pr.
Taylor, Don. Dirty Laundry. 1999. 232p. pap. o.p. (1-85242-593-8) Serpent's Tail Ltd.
Tey, Josephine. The Daughter of Time. unabr. ed. 2000. audio 24.95 (1-57270-138-2, N41138u, Audio Editions Mystery Masters) Audio Partners Publishing Corp.
—The Daughter of Time. 1985. 224p. mass mkt. 9.95 o.p. (0-553-06510-6) Bantam Bks.
—The Daughter of Time. 1976. 1.50 o.s.i (0-425-03223-X) Berkley Publishing Group.
—The Daughter of Time. 1976. 220p. lib. bdg. 27.95 (0-89966-184-X) Buccaneer Bks., Inc.
—The Daughter of Time. l.t. ed. 1984. (General Ser.). 320p. 12.95 o.p. (0-8161-3634-3); 9.95 o.p. (0-8161-3688-2) Gale Group. (Macmillan Reference USA).
—The Daughter of Time. 2003. 224p. (0-434-76670-4) Heinemann, William Ltd. GBR. *Dist:* Random Hse. of Canada, Ltd.
—The Daughter of Time. 2003. (Best Mysteries of All Time Ser.). ix, 224p. (0-7621-8888-X, Impress) Scriptorium Pr., The.
—The Daughter of Time. 1995. 208p. pap. 12.00 (0-684-80386-0, Touchstone) Simon & Schuster.
—The Daughter of Time. 1986. audio 49.95 o.p. (0-8161-9726-1) Thorndike Pr.
—The Franchise Affair. 1981. reprint ed. lib. bdg. 16.00 (0-8376-0446-X) Bentley Pubs.
—The Franchise Affair. unabr. ed. 2000. (Inspector Grant Mystery Ser.: Bk. 3). audio 59.95 (0-7451-6324-6, CAB 578) Chivers Audio Bks. GBR. *Dist:* BBC Audiobooks America.
—The Franchise Affair. 1993. pap. 5.95 o.p. (0-87129-257-2, F52) Dramatic Publishing Co.
—The Franchise Affair. 1998. 304p. pap. 11.00 (0-684-84256-4, Touchstone); 1988. 289p. pap. 6.00 o.s.i (0-02-008823-X, Scribner Paper Fiction); 1983. reprint ed. mass mkt. 3.95 o.s.i (0-671-50812-1, Pocket) Simon & Schuster.
—The Man in the Queue. 1981. reprint ed. lib. bdg. 16.00 (0-8376-0450-8) Bentley Pubs.
—The Man in the Queue. 1976. 1.25 o.p. (0-425-03220-5) Berkley Publishing Group.
—The Man in the Queue. unabr. ed. 2000. (Inspector Grant Mystery Ser.: Bk. 1). audio 49.95 (0-7451-4161-7, CAB 844) Chivers Audio Bks. GBR. *Dist:* BBC Audiobooks America.
—The Man in the Queue. 1995. 256p. pap. 12.00 (0-684-81502-8, Touchstone); 1986. 224p. mass mkt. 3.95 o.s.i (0-671-41493-3, Pocket); 1982. mass mkt. 2.95 o.s.i (0-671-43524-8, Pocket) Simon & Schuster.
—A Shilling for Candles. 22.95 (0-8488-1203-4) Amereon, Ltd.
—A Shilling for Candles. 1976. 1.25 o.p. (0-425-03221-3) Berkley Publishing Group.
—A Shilling for Candles. unabr. ed. 1991. audio 39.95 (0-7861-0224-1, 1197) Blackstone Audio Bks., Inc.
—A Shilling for Candles. 1998. 240p. pap. 11.00 (0-684-84238-6, Touchstone); 1988. 240p. pap. 6.00 (0-02-054530-4, Scribner Paper Fiction); 1984. mass mkt. 3.95 o.s.i (0-671-55179-5, Pocket); 1983. mass mkt. 2.95 o.s.i (0-671-47625-4, Pocket) Simon & Schuster.
—The Singing Sands. l.t. ed. 1975. 1.25 o.p. (0-425-02948-4) Berkley Publishing Group.
—The Singing Sands. Barzun, Jacques & Taylor, W. H., eds. 1982. (Crime Fiction 1950-1975 Ser.). 192p. lib. bdg. 5.00 o.p. (0-8240-5000-2) Garland Publishing, Inc.
—The Singing Sands. 1996. 224p. pap. 12.00 (0-684-81892-2, Touchstone); 1988. 240p. pap. 6.00 o.s.i (0-02-008825-6, Scribner Paper Fiction); 1983. 224p. mass mkt. 3.95 o.s.i (0-671-49456-2, Pocket) Simon & Schuster.
—The Singing Sands. l.t. ed. 1999. (Mystery Ser.). 341p. 27.95 (0-7862-1916-5) Thorndike Pr.
—To Love & Be Wise. l.t. ed. 1975. 1.25 o.s.i (0-425-02898-4) Berkley Publishing Group.
—To Love & Be Wise. unabr. ed. 2000. (Inspector Grant Mystery Ser.: Bk. 4). audio 49.95 (0-7451-4259-1, CAB 942) Chivers Audio Bks. GBR. *Dist:* BBC Audiobooks America.
—To Love & Be Wise. 1998. 224p. per. 12.00 (0-684-00631-6, Touchstone); 1987. mass mkt. 3.95 (0-671-64547-1, Pocket); 1984. mass mkt. 3.95 o.s.i (0-671-50979-9, Pocket); 1982. mass mkt. 2.95 o.s.i (0-671-44191-4, Pocket) Simon & Schuster.
Thackeray, William Makepeace. The History of Henry Esmond. Harden, Edgar F., ed. 1989. 688p. 80.00 o.p. (0-8240-4292-1, H863) Garland Publishing, Inc.
—The History of Henry Esmond. 1991. (Oxford World's Classics Ser.). 526p. pap. 7.95 o.p. (0-19-282727-8, 4866) Oxford Univ. Pr., Inc.
—The History of Pendennis. Shillingsburg, Peter L., ed. 1991. (Thackeray Edition Project Ser.). 976p. 100.00 o.p. (0-8240-5098-3, H1325) Garland Publishing, Inc.
—The History of Pendennis. Hawes, Donald, ed. 1972. (Penguin Classics Ser.). 816p. pap. 7.95 o.p. (0-14-043076-8, Penguin Classics) Viking Penguin.
—Pendennis: His Fortunes & Misfortunes, His Friends & His Greatest Enemy. Sutherland, John, ed. 1999. (Oxford World's Classics Ser.). (Illus.). 1120p. pap. 7.95 o.p. (0-19-283959-4) Oxford Univ. Pr., Inc.
Thayer, James S. S Day. 1990. 19.95 o.p. (0-312-04148-9) St. Martin's Pr.
Thomas, Craig. A Different War. unabr. ed. 2000. (Mitchell Gant Adventure Ser.). audio 79.95 (0-7540-0075-3, CAB 1498) Chivers Audio Bks. GBR. *Dist:* BBC Audiobooks America.
—A Different War. l.t. ed. 1997. (G. K. Hall Mystery Ser.). 601p. lib. bdg. 25.95 (0-7838-8281-5) Thorndike Pr.
Thorne, Nicola. Oh, Happy Day! 2002. 224p. 25.99 (0-7278-5903-X) Severn Hse. Pubs., Ltd.
Thornton, Margaret. Wish upon a Star. l.t. ed. 1999. (Magna Large Print Ser.). 448p. o.p. (0-7505-1377-2) Magna Large Print Bks. GBR. *Dist:* Ulverscroft Large Print Canada, Ltd.
Todd, Catherine. Bond of Honor. 1981. 224p. 11.95 o.p. (0-312-08763-2) St. Martin's Pr.
Tonkin, Peter. The Hound of the Borders. 2003. 256p. 26.99 (0-7278-5935-8) Severn Hse. Pubs., Ltd.
Townsend, Sue. Adrian Mole: The Cappuccino Years. 2000. xv, 390p. 24.00 (1-56947-204-1) Soho Pr., Inc.
—The Queen & I. unabr. ed. 2000. audio 59.95 (0-7451-4206-0, CAB 889) Chivers Audio Bks. GBR. *Dist:* BBC Audiobooks America.
—The Queen & I. 1995. 96p. pap. 11.95 (0-413-68970-0, A0729, Methuen Drama) Heinemann.
—The Queen & I. unabr. ed. 1993. audio 51.00 (1-55690-906-3, 93402E7) Recorded Bks., LLC.
—The Queen & I. 239p. 1994. pap. 12.00 (1-56947-015-4); 1993. 22.00 o.s.i (0-939149-97-4) Soho Pr., Inc.
Tremain, Rose. Restoration: A Novel of Seventeenth-Century England. 1994. 384p. pap. 14.00 (0-14-024488-3, Penguin Bks.) Penguin Group (USA) Inc.
Tremayne, Peter. Valley of the Shadow. 2001. (Sister Fidelma Mysteries Ser.). 320p. mass mkt. 5.99 (0-451-20330-5) NAL.
Trevor, William. Angels at the Ritz & Other Stories. 1976. 253p. 10.95 o.p. (0-670-12594-6) Viking Penguin.
—Ballroom of Romance & Other. 1972. 6.95 o.p. (0-670-14681-1) Viking Penguin.
—The Old Boys. 1996. 192p. pap. 12.95 o.s.i (0-14-002428-X, Penguin Bks.) Penguin Group (USA) Inc.
—The Old Boys. 1964. 3.95 o.p. (0-670-52210-4) Viking Penguin.
Trollope, Anthony. The American Senator, 3 vols. 1981. (Selected Works of Anthony Trollope). reprint ed. lib. bdg. 115.95 (0-405-14164-5) Ayer Co. Pubs., Inc.
—The American Senator. Halperin, John, ed. & intro. by. 1986. (Oxford World's Classics Ser.). 592p. pap. 8.95 o.p. (0-19-281739-6) Oxford Univ. Pr., Inc.
—The American Senator. 1994. (Trollope Ser.). 576p. pap. 8.95 o.p. (0-14-043838-6, Penguin Classics) Viking Penguin.
—Anthony Trollope: The Complete Short Stories - Tourists & Colonials, Vol. III. Breyer, Betty J., ed. 1981. 260p. 17.50 o.p. (0-912646-62-4) Texas Christian Univ. Pr.
—Castle Richmond, unabr. ed. 1997. audio 77.95 (1-55685-489-7, 489-7) Audio Bk. Contractors, Inc.
—Castle Richmond, 3 vols. Hall, N. John, ed. 1981. (Selected Works of Anthony Trollope). reprint ed. lib. bdg. 115.95 (0-405-14134-3) Ayer Co. Pubs., Inc.
—Castle Richmond, 3. (Collected Works of Anthony Trollope). reprint ed. lib. bdg. 294.00 (0-7426-2440-4); 2001. pap. text 84.00 (0-7426-7440-1) Classic Bks.
—Castle Richmond. 1984. 440p. reprint ed. pap. 8.50 (0-486-24760-0) Dover Pubns., Inc.
—Castle Richmond. Wolff, Robert L., ed. 1979. (Ireland Nineteenth Century Fiction Ser.: Vol. 55). 912p. lib. bdg. 152.00 o.p. (0-8240-3504-6) Garland Publishing, Inc.
—Castle Richmond. Hamer, Mary, ed. 1989. (Oxford World's Classics Ser.). (Illus.). 530p. pap. 10.95 o.p. (0-19-282173-3) Oxford Univ. Pr., Inc.
—Castle Richmond, 1860. 1993. (Trollope Ser.). 912p. pap. 9.95 o.p. (0-14-043808-4, Penguin Classics) Viking Penguin.
—The Claverings, Set. 1995. audio 89.95 (1-55685-366-1) Audio Bk. Contractors, Inc.
—The Claverings, 2. (Collected Works of Anthony Trollope). reprint ed. lib. bdg. 196.00 (0-7426-2454-4); 2001. 514p. pap. text 56.00 (0-7426-7454-1) Classic Bks.
—The Claverings. 1977. (Illus.). 412p. pap. 8.50 (0-486-23464-9) Dover Pubns., Inc.
—The Claverings. Skilton, David, ed. & intro. by. (Oxford World's Classics Ser.). 1999. 560p. pap. 11.95 (0-19-283707-9); 1986. 546p. pap. 8.95 o.p. (0-19-281727-2) Oxford Univ. Pr., Inc.
—The Claverings. 1994. (Trollope Ser.). 528p. pap. 8.95 o.p. (0-14-043822-X, Penguin Classics) Viking Penguin.
—Collected Short Stories. Hampden, John, ed. 1987. (Illus.). 397p. pap. text 8.95 o.p. (0-486-25484-4) Dover Pubns., Inc.
—Collected Short Stories: Anthony Trollope. Hall, N. John, ed. 1981. (Selected Works of Anthony Trollope). lib. bdg. 33.95 (0-405-14117-3) Ayer Co. Pubs., Inc.
—The Complete Short Stories, Vol. I. Breyer, Betty J., ed. 1979. 248p. 17.50 o.p. (0-912646-56-X) Texas Christian Univ. Pr.
—Early Short Stories. Sutherland, John, ed. & intro. by. 1995. (Oxford World's Classics Ser.). 524p. (C). pap. 9.95 o.p. (0-19-282987-4) Oxford Univ. Pr., Inc.
—An Editor's Tales. 1994. (Trollope Ser.). 384p. pap. 7.95 o.p. (0-14-043828-9, Penguin Classics) Viking Penguin.
—Later Short Stories. Sutherland, John, ed. 1995. (Oxford World's Classics Ser.). 628p. pap. 10.95 o.p. (0-19-282988-2) Oxford Univ. Pr., Inc.
—Lotta Schmidt & Other Stories. Hall, N. John, ed. 1981. (Selected Works of Anthony Trollope). reprint ed. lib. bdg. 49.95 (0-405-14151-3) Ayer Co. Pubs., Inc.
—Lotta Schmidt & Other Stories. 1994. (Trollope Ser.). 384p. pap. 7.95 o.p. (0-14-043823-8, Penguin Classics) Viking Penguin.
—Marion Fay, 3 vols. 1981. (Selected Works of Anthony Trollope). reprint ed. lib. bdg. 99.95 (0-405-14191-2) Ayer Co. Pubs., Inc.
—Marion Fay. Super, R. H., ed. 1982. (Illus.). 465p. pap. 15.95 (0-932282-18-0) Caledonia Pr.
—Marion Fay, 3 vols. reprint ed. lib. bdg. 294.00 (0-7426-2492-7); 2001. pap. text 84.00 (0-7426-7492-4) Classic Bks.
—Marion Fay. Harvey, Geoffrey, ed. 1992. (Oxford World's Classics Ser.). 592p. pap. 11.95 o.p. (0-19-282855-X) Oxford Univ. Pr., Inc.
—Marion Fay. 1982. (Illus.). 492p. (C). pap. text 22.95 o.p. (0-472-08136-5, 08136) Univ. of Michigan Pr.
—Marion Fay. Super, R. H., ed. 1982. (Illus.). 464p. text 25.00 o.p. (0-472-10023-8) Univ. of Michigan Pr.
—Marion Fay. 1994. (Trollope Ser.). 880p. pap. 9.95 o.p. (0-14-043848-3, Penguin Classics) Viking Penguin.
—Miss Mackenzie, unabr. ed. 1997. audio 53.95 (1-55685-482-X, 482-X) Audio Bk. Contractors, Inc.
—Miss Mackenzie, 2 vols. Hall, N. John, ed. 1981. (Selected Works of Anthony Trollope). reprint ed. lib. bdg. 71.95 (0-405-14143-2) Ayer Co. Pubs., Inc.
—Miss Mackenzie. unabr. collector's ed. 1995. audio 72.00 (0-7366-2994-7, 3683) Books on Tape, Inc.
—Miss Mackenzie, 2. reprint ed. lib. bdg. 196.00 (0-7426-2450-1); 2001. pap. text 56.00 (0-7426-7450-9) Classic Bks.
—Miss Mackenzie. 1986. 388p. reprint ed. pap. 8.95 o.p. (0-486-25201-9) Dover Pubns., Inc.
—Miss Mackenzie. Cockshut, A. O. J., ed. 1988. (Oxford World's Classics Ser.). 432p. pap. 9.95 o.p. (0-19-281846-5) Oxford Univ. Pr., Inc.
—Miss Mackenzie. 1994. (Trollope Ser.). 416p. pap. 8.95 o.p. (0-14-043818-1, Penguin Classics) Viking Penguin.
—An Old Man's Love, 2 vols. Hall, N. John, ed. 1981. (Selected Works of Anthony Trollope). reprint ed. lib. bdg. 55.95 (0-405-14202-1) Ayer Co. Pubs., Inc.
—An Old Man's Love, 2. reprint ed. lib. bdg. 196.00 (0-7426-2502-8); 2001. pap. text 56.00 (0-7426-7502-5) Classic Bks.
—An Old Man's Love. Sutherland, John, ed. 1991. (Oxford World's Classics Ser.). 328p. pap. 8.95 o.p. (0-19-282646-8) Oxford Univ. Pr., Inc.
—An Old Man's Love, 1884. 1994. (Penguin Trollope Ser.). 272p. pap. 6.95 o.p. (0-14-043852-1, Penguin Classics) Viking Penguin.
—Orley Farm. reprint ed. lib. bdg. 98.00 (0-7426-2443-9); 2001. 729p. pap. text 28.00 (0-7426-7443-6) Classic Bks.
—Orley Farm. 1981. (Illus.). 736p. reprint ed. pap. 11.95 (0-486-24181-5) Dover Pubns., Inc.
—Orley Farm. Skilton, David, ed. (Oxford World's Classics Ser.). 2001. 864p. pap. 11.95 (0-19-283856-3); 1985. 860p. pap. 9.95 o.p. (0-19-281713-2) Oxford Univ. Pr., Inc.

Settings

—Orley Farm, 1862. 1993. (Trollope Ser.). 848p. pap. 9.95 o.p. (*0-14-043812-2*, Penguin Classics) Viking Penguin.
—The Struggles of Brown, Jones & Robinson: By One of the Firm. Hall, N. John, ed. 1981. (Selected Works of Anthony Trollope). reprint ed. lib. bdg. 31.95 (*0-405-14156-4*) Ayer Co. Pubs., Inc.
—The Struggles of Brown, Jones & Robinson: By One of the Firm. reprint ed. lib. bdg. 98.00 (*0-7426-2444-7*) Classic Bks.
—The Struggles of Brown, Jones & Robinson: By One of the Firm. 1993. (Oxford World's Classics Ser.). 216p. pap. 7.95 o.p. (*0-19-282860-6*) Oxford Univ. Pr., Inc.
—The Struggles of Brown, Jones & Robinson: By One of the Firm, 1862. 1993. (Trollope Ser.). 272p. pap. 7.95 o.p. (*0-14-043813-0*, Penguin Classics) Viking Penguin.
Twain, Mark. A Connecticut Yankee in King Arthur's Court. 1994. (Illustrated Classics Collection: No. 3). 64p. pap. 3.60 o.p. (*1-56103-525-4*); pap. 4.95 (*0-7854-0695-6*, 40447) American Guidance Service, Inc.
—A Connecticut Yankee in King Arthur's Court. 1983. 288p. mass mkt. 4.95 (*0-553-21143-9*, Bantam Classics) Bantam Bks.
—A Connecticut Yankee in King Arthur's Court. 2000. (Stratford Festival Ser.). audio 12.92 (*0-660-18178-9*) Canadian Broadcasting Corp./Societe Radio-Canada CAN. *Dist:* Georgetown Terminal Warehouse.
—A Connecticut Yankee in King Arthur's Court. E-Book 2.95 (*1-57799-844-8*) Logos Research Systems, Inc.
—A Connecticut Yankee in King Arthur's Court. E-Book 1.95 (*1-58515-199-8*) MesaView, Inc.
—A Connecticut Yankee in King Arthur's Court. 1963. 334p. mass mkt. 2.25 o.p. (*0-451-52353-9*, Signet Classics); mass mkt. 1.95 o.p. (*0-451-51874-8*) NAL.
—A Connecticut Yankee in King Arthur's Court. Ensor, Allison E., ed. 1982. (Critical Editions Ser.). (Illus.). (C). 455p. 24.95 o.p. (*0-393-01378-2*); 450p. pap. text 16.35 (*0-393-95137-5*) Norton, W. W. & Co., Inc.
—A Connecticut Yankee in King Arthur's Court. Inge, M. Thomas, ed. (Oxford World's Classics Ser.). (Illus.). 1999. 400p. pap. 7.95 (*0-19-283902-0*); 1997. 386p. pap. 5.95 o.p. (*0-19-282721-9*) Oxford Univ. Pr., Inc.
—A Connecticut Yankee in King Arthur's Court. 1987. (Regents Illustrated Classics Ser.). 62p. pap. text 4.65 net. o.p. (*0-13-167701-2*, 20468) Prentice Hall, ESL Dept.
—A Connecticut Yankee in King Arthur's Court. 2000. (Illus.). 260p. pap. 19.99 (*1-57646-258-7*) Quiet Vision Publishing.
—A Connecticut Yankee in King Arthur's Court. 2001. (Modern Library Classics). (Illus.). 512p. pap. 7.95 (*0-375-75780-5*, Modern Library) Random House Adult Trade Publishing Group.
—A Connecticut Yankee in King Arthur's Court. 1984. (Illus.). 334p. 12.95 o.p. (*0-89577-185-3*) Reader's Digest Assn., Inc., The.
—A Connecticut Yankee in King Arthur's Court. 1979. 368p. pap. 2.50 (*0-671-41017-2*, Simon Pulse) Simon & Schuster Children's Publishing.
—A Connecticut Yankee in King Arthur's Court. 1960. (Signet Classics Ser.). 11.00 (*0-606-01831-X*) Turtleback Bks.
—A Connecticut Yankee in King Arthur's Court. 1983. (Mark Twain Library: No. 4). (Illus.). 482p. (C). 30.00 o.p. (*0-520-05089-4*); pap. 14.95 (*0-520-05109-2*) Univ. of California Pr.
—A Connecticut Yankee in King Arthur's Court. Stein, Bernard L., ed. 1979. (Iowa-California Edition of the Works of Mark Twain: No. 9). (Illus.). 847p. text 75.00 (*0-520-03621-2*) Univ. of California Pr.
—A Connecticut Yankee in King Arthur's Court. Kaplan, Justin, ed. & intro. by. 1972. (Classics Ser.). 416p. 7.95 (*0-14-043064-4*, Penguin Classics) Viking Penguin.
—A Connecticut Yankee in King Arthur's Court. Fishkin, Shelley Fisher, ed. 1996. (Oxford Mark Twain Ser.). (Illus.). 656p. 22.00 o.p. (*0-19-510141-3*) Oxford Univ. Pr., Inc.
—A Connecticut Yankee in King Arthur's Court. unabr. ed. 1991. audio 34.95 o.p. (*1-55656-089-3*, DAB015) BBC Audiobooks America.
—A Connecticut Yankee in King Arthur's Court, unabr. ed. 2000. audio 56.95 (*0-7861-1721-4*, 2525) Blackstone Audio Bks., Inc.
—A Connecticut Yankee in King Arthur's Court. 1982. reprint ed. lib. bdg. 19.95 (*0-89966-381-8*) Buccaneer Bks., Inc.
—A Connecticut Yankee in King Arthur's Court. unabr. ed. audio 29.95 o.s.i (*1-55656-034-6*); 1997. pap. 29.95 incl. audio (*1-55656-200-4*) Dercum Audio.
—A Connecticut Yankee in King Arthur's Court. abr. ed. 1992. audio 16.99 (*0-88646-324-6*, 7324) Durkin Hayes Publishing Ltd.
—A Connecticut Yankee in King Arthur's Court. 1980. (Holiday Editions). (Illus.). reprint ed. 7.95 o.p. (*0-06-014445-9*) HarperCollins Pubs.
—A Connecticut Yankee in King Arthur's Court. abr. ed. 1989. audio 21.00 Jimcin Recordings.
—A Connecticut Yankee in King Arthur's Court. abr. ed. (Ultimate Classics Ser.). 1994. 29.95 o.p. incl. audio compact disk (*0-7871-0059-5*); 1993. 16.95 o.p. incl. audio (*1-55800-739-3*) NewStar Media, Inc.
—A Connecticut Yankee in King Arthur's Court. 2000. (Twelve-Point Ser.). 245p. reprint ed. lib. bdg. 25.00 (*1-58287-118-3*) North Bks.
—A Connecticut Yankee in King Arthur's Court. 1988. (Works of Mark Twain). reprint ed. lib. bdg. 79.00 (*0-7812-1121-2*) Reprint Services Corp.
—A Connecticut Yankee in King Arthur's Court: 1889. 1988. mass mkt. 4.95 (*0-938819-79-8*, Aerie) Doherty, Tom Assocs., LLC.
—A Connecticut Yankee in King Arthur's Court: 1889. Fishkin, Shelley Fisher, ed. 1997. (Oxford Mark Twain Ser.). (Illus.). 656p. text 28.00 (*0-19-511410-8*) Oxford Univ. Pr., Inc.
—A Connecticut Yankee in King Arthur's Court Readalong. 1994. (Illustrated Classics Collection: No. 3). 64p. pap. 14.95 incl. audio (*0-7854-0736-7*, 40449) American Guidance Service, Inc.
Unsworth, Barry. Losing Nelson. 1999. 352p. 23.95 o.s.i (*0-385-48652-9*, Talese, Nan A.) Doubleday Publishing.
—Losing Nelson. 2000. 352p. pap. 14.00 (*0-393-32117-7*, Norton Paperbacks) Norton, W. W. & Co., Inc.
—Morality Play. l.t. ed. 1996. 23.95 o.p. (*1-56895-297-X*, Wheeler Publishing, Inc.) Gale Group.
—Morality Play. 1996. 208p. pap. 13.95 (*0-393-31560-6*) Norton, W. W. & Co., Inc.
Veryan, Patricia. The Mandarin of Mayfair. 1996. mass mkt. 4.99 o.s.i (*0-449-22522-4*, Fawcett) Ballantine Bks.
—The Mandarin of Mayfair. 1995. 352p. 23.95 o.p. (*0-312-13562-9*) St. Martin's Pr.
—A Shadow's Bliss. l.t. ed. 1994. 486p. lib. bdg. 22.95 o.p. (*0-8161-7481-4*, Macmillan Reference USA) Gale Group.
—A Shadow's Bliss. 1994. (Tales of the Jewelled Men Ser.: Vol. 4). 336p. 21.95 o.p. (*0-312-10543-6*) St. Martin's Pr.
Vine, Barbara, pseud. The Blood Doctor. 2003. 384p. pap. 13.00 (*1-4000-3252-0*, Vintage) Knopf Publishing Group.
Vivian, Daisy. Rose White, Rose Red. 1983. 192p. 12.95 o.p. (*0-8027-0750-5*) Walker & Co.
Wainwright, John. The Life & Times of Christmas Calvert . . . Assassin. l.t. ed. 1996. (Nightingale Ser.). 270p. pap. 17.95 o.p. (*0-7838-1473-9*, Macmillan Reference USA) Gale Group.
—The Life & Times of Christmas Calvert . . . Assassin. 1995. 185p. 19.95 o.p. (*0-316-91757-5*); o.s.i (*0-316-91252-2*) Little Brown & Co.
Wallace, Robert C. Mons Graupius. Kincade-Clifton, Rena, ed. (Illus.). 1993. 600p. 24.00 (*0-9634992-1-1*); 1996. 578p. pap. text 12.00 (*0-9634992-9-7*) Pretani.
Warner, Sylvia Townsend. The Corner That Held Them. 1996. (Virago Modern Classics Ser.). 320p. reprint ed. pap. 9.95 o.p. (*0-14-016214-3*, Penguin Bks.) Viking Penguin.
Watson, I. K. Manor: A Novel of Suspense. 1996. 224p. reprint ed. 20.00 o.p. (*0-88150-362-2*, Foul Play) Norton, W. W. & Co., Inc.
Wells, H. G. Joan & Peter: The Story of an Education, Pt. 1. 2001. (Works of H. G. Wells: Vol. 23). (Illus.). 1060p. reprint ed. pap. text 28.00 (*0-7426-5422-2*) Classic Bks.
—Tono-Bungay. 32.95 (*0-89190-698-3*) Amereon, Ltd.
—Tono-Bungay. rev. ed. 2000. 400p. per. 14.00 (*1-58396-062-7*) Blue Unicorn Editions.
—Tono-Bungay. 1990. reprint ed. lib. bdg. 19.95 o.p. (*0-89966-691-4*) Buccaneer Bks., Inc.
—Tono-Bungay. 1999. (Works of H. G. Wells: Vol. 12). reprint ed. lib. bdg. 88.00 (*1-58201-411-6*) Classic Bks.
—Tono-Bungay. Cheyette, Bryan, ed. 1997. (Oxford World's Classics Ser.). (Illus.). 480p. pap. 11.95 o.p. (*0-19-282829-0*) Oxford Univ. Pr., Inc.
—Tono-Bungay. Hammond, John, ed. 1994. 416p. pap. 7.95 (*0-460-87259-1*); pap. text 7.95 o.p. (*0-460-87421-7*) Tuttle Publishing. (Everyman's Classic Library in Paperback).
—Tono-Bungay. 1978. 317p. text 27.50 o.p. (*0-8032-4702-8*); pap. text 9.95 o.p. (*0-8032-9701-7*, Bison Bks.) Univ. of Nebraska Pr.
West, Paul. The Fifth of November: Novel. 2001. 362p. 25.95 (*0-8112-1467-2*) New Directions Publishing Corp.
Weyman, Stanley J. King's Stratagem & Other Stories. 1977. (Short Story Index Reprint Ser.). 22.95 (*0-8369-3424-5*) Ayer Co. Pubs., Inc.
Whitney, Phyllis A. Hunters Green. l.t. ed. 1993. 13.95 o.p. (*0-8161-3296-8*, Macmillan Reference USA) Gale Group.
Whyte, Jack. The Skystone. (Illus.). 2002. 352p. pap. 14.95 (*0-7653-0372-8*, Forge Bks.); 1996. (Camulod Chronicles: Bk. 1). 498p. mass mkt. 6.99 (*0-8125-5138-9*, Tor Bks.); 1996. (Camulod Chronicles: Bk. 1). 352p. 22.95 o.p. (*0-312-86091-9*, Forge Bks.) Doherty, Tom Assocs., LLC.
Wichelns, Lee. The Shadow of the Earth. 1987. (Illus.). 300p. (Orig.). 18.95 (*0-941692-07-8*) Elysian Pr.
Wick, Lori. The Knight & the Dove. (Kensington Chronicles Ser.). 1995. 345p. pap. 9.99 (*1-56507-289-8*); 2nd ed. 2004. reprint ed. pap. 10.99 (*0-7369-1324-6*) Harvest Hse. Pubs.
—The Knight & the Dove. l.t. ed. 2001. (Kensington Chronicles Ser.). 543p. 28.95 (*0-7862-2955-1*) Thorndike Pr.
Willard, Barbara. The Eldest Son. 1989. 192p. (J). (gr. k-12). mass mkt. 3.25 o.s.i (*0-440-20412-7*, Laurel Leaf) Random Hse. Children's Bks.
—A Flight of Swans. 1989. (Mantlemass Ser.: No. 6). 192p. (J). (gr. k up). mass mkt. 3.25 o.s.i (*0-440-20458-5*, Laurel Leaf) Random Hse. Children's Bks.
Williams, Alan. Gentleman Traitor. 1975. 312p. 8.95 o.p. (*0-15-135015-9*) Harcourt Trade Pubs.
Willis, Clint, ed. High Seas: Stories of Life & Death from the Age of Sail. 2002. (Adrenaline Ser.). (Illus.). 364p. pap. 17.95 (*1-56025-434-3*, Thunder's Mouth Pr.) Avalon Publishing Group.
Wilson, A. N. Gentlemen in England: A Vision. 1986. 320p. 17.95 o.p. (*0-670-80971-3*) Viking Penguin.
Wodehouse, P. G. Joy in the Morning. 2002. 296p. 16.95 (*1-58567-276-9*) Overlook Pr., The.
—Lord Emsworth. 2002. 268p. 16.95 (*1-58567-277-7*) Overlook Pr., The.
Wolf, Joan. Born of the Sun. 1989. 400p. 18.95 o.p. (*0-453-00666-3*); 1991. 512p. reprint ed. mass mkt. 5.50 o.p. (*0-451-40225-1*, Onyx) NAL.
—The Edge of Light. 1990. 416p. 18.95 o.p. (*0-453-00738-4*) NAL.
Woodman, Richard. Arctic Treachery. 1987. 232p. 15.95 o.p. (*0-8027-0948-6*) Walker & Co.
—Baltic Mission. 1996. 320p. mass mkt. o.s.i (*0-7515-1495-0*) Little Brown & Co.
—Baltic Mission. l.t. ed. 2001. (Magna Large Print Ser.). 384p. (*0-7505-1735-2*) Magna Large Print Bks. GBR. *Dist:* Ulverscroft Large Print Canada, Ltd.
—Baltic Mission. 2000. (Mariner's Library Fiction Classics). 211p. pap. 14.95 (*1-57409-097-6*) Sheridan Hse., Inc.
—The Bomb Vessel. 1995. mass mkt. o.s.i (*0-7515-1018-1*) Little Brown & Co.
—The Bomb Vessel, Set. unabr. ed. 1994. (Nathaniel Drinkwater Ser.: No. 4). audio 42.00 (*0-7887-0002-2*, 94141) Recorded Bks., LLC.
—The Bomb Vessel. 1986. 215p. 15.95 o.p. (*0-8027-0886-2*) Walker & Co.
—A Brig of War. 1984. 224p. pap. 2.95 o.p. (*0-523-41978-3*, Pinnacle Bks.) Kensington Publishing Corp.
—A Brig of War. 1995. mass mkt. o.s.i (*0-7515-1304-0*) Little Brown & Co.
—A Brig of War. 1998. 320p. mass mkt. 5.99 o.p. (*0-446-60463-1*) Warner Bks., Inc.
—A Brig of War: A Nathaniel Drinkwater Novel. 2001. (Mariner's Library Fiction Classics). (Illus.). 240p. reprint ed. pap. 14.95 (*1-57409-125-5*) Sheridan Hse., Inc.
—The Corvette, Set. unabr. ed. 1992. audio 49.00 (*1-55690-679-X*, 92331) Recorded Bks., LLC.
—Decision at Trafalgar. 1987. 16.95 o.p. (*0-8027-0993-1*) Walker & Co.
—Ebb Tide. l.t. ed. 1999. (Magna Large Print Ser.). 448p. (*0-7505-1441-8*) Magna Large Print Bks. GBR. *Dist:* Ulverscroft Large Print Canada, Ltd.
—Ebb Tide Bk. 14: A Nathaniel Drinkwater Novel. 2002. (Mariner's Library Fiction Classics: Vol. 14). 240p. pap. 14.95 (*1-57409-104-2*) Sheridan Hse., Inc.
—An Eye of the Fleet. 1997. 288p. mass mkt. 5.99 o.p. (*0-446-60461-5*) Warner Bks., Inc.
—An Eye of the Fleet: A Nathaniel Drinkwater Novel. 2001. (Mariner's Library Fiction Classics: Bk. 1). 192p. reprint ed. pap. 14.95 (*1-57409-123-9*) Sheridan Hse., Inc.
—In Distant Waters. 1996. 320p. mass mkt. o.s.i (*0-7515-1491-8*) Little Brown & Co.
—In Distant Waters. l.t. ed. 2002. (Magna Large Print Ser.). 400p. (*0-7505-1736-0*) Magna Large Print Bks. GBR. *Dist:* Ulverscroft Large Print Canada, Ltd.
—In Distant Waters. 1988. 256p. 16.95 o.p. (*0-312-02586-6*) St. Martin's Pr.
—In Distant Waters: A Nathaniel Drinkwater Novel. 2000. (Mariner's Library Fiction Classics). (Illus.). 256p. pap. 14.95 (*1-57409-098-4*) Sheridan Hse., Inc.
—A King's Cutter. 1984. 224p. pap. 2.50 o.p. (*0-523-41977-5*, Pinnacle Bks.) Kensington Publishing Corp.
—A King's Cutter. 1995. (Illus.). 273p. mass mkt. o.s.i (*0-7515-0895-0*) Little Brown & Co.
—A King's Cutter. 1997. (Nathan DrinkWater Ser.: Bk. 2). 224p. mass mkt. 5.99 o.p. (*0-446-60462-3*) Warner Bks., Inc.
—A King's Cutter: A Nathaniel Drinkwater Novel. 2001. (Captain Drinkwater Ser.: Bk. 2). (Illus.). 176p. reprint ed. pap. 14.95 (*1-57409-124-7*) Sheridan Hse., Inc.
—A Private Revenge. 1996. (Illus.). 247p. mass mkt. o.s.i (*0-7515-0724-5*) Little Brown & Co.
—A Private Revenge. l.t. ed. 2002. (Magna Large Print Ser.). 384p. (*0-7505-1737-9*) Magna Large Print Bks. GBR. *Dist:* Ulverscroft Large Print Canada, Ltd.
—A Private Revenge. 1990. 16.95 o.p. (*0-312-04405-4*) St. Martin's Pr.
—A Private Revenge: A Nathaniel Drinkwater Novel. 1999. (Mariner's Library). 256p. pap. 14.95 (*1-57409-078-X*) Sheridan Hse., Inc.
—Under False Colours: A Nathaniel Drinkwater Novel. 1999. (Illus.). 256p. pap. 14.95 (*1-57409-079-8*) Sheridan Hse., Inc.
—Wager. 1999. (Mariner's Library Fiction Classics). 272p. pap. 14.95 (*1-57409-080-1*) Sheridan Hse., Inc.
—1805. 1996. (Illus.). 306p. mass mkt. o.s.i (*0-7515-1479-9*) Little Brown & Co.
—1805. unabr. ed. 1993. (Nathaniel Drinkwater Ser.: No. 6). audio 49.00 (*1-55690-946-2*, 93428) Recorded Bks., LLC.
Wynn, Patricia. The Birth of Blue Satan: Featuring Blue Satan & Mrs. Kean. 2001. (Blue Satan Mystery Ser.: Vol. 1). 328p. 25.95 (*0-9702727-0-7*, 108501) Pemberley Pr.
—The Spider's Touch: Featuring Blue Satan & Mrs. Kean. ltd. ed. 2002. (Blue Satan Mystery Ser.: Vol. 2). 386p. 25.95 (*0-9702727-4-X*) Pemberley Pr.
Yonge, Charlotte M. The Armourer's Prentices. E-Book 3.95 (*0-594-00716-X*) 1873 Pr.
Zelitch, Simone. The Confession of Jack Straw. 1991. 260p. pap. 12.00 (*0-930773-18-7*); text 19.95 (*0-930773-17-9*) Black Heron Pr.

**GREAT BRITAIN—SOCIAL LIFE AND CUSTOMS—FICTION**

Austen, Jane. Emma. 2002. (World Digital Library). E-Book 3.95 (*0-594-08158-0*) 1873 Pr.
—Emma. 1997. (Modern Library Ser.). E-Book 4.95 (*1-931208-08-5*) Adobe Systems, Inc.
—Emma. 1966. (Airmont Classics Ser.). mass mkt. 2.95 o.p. (*0-8049-0102-3*, CL-102) Airmont Publishing Co., Inc.
—Emma. Date not set. 232p. 21.95 (*0-8488-2522-5*) Amereon, Ltd.
—Emma. l.t. ed. 1999. 630p. pap. 24.95 (*1-55701-279-2*) BNI Pubns., Inc.
—Emma. 1984. mass mkt. 1.95 o.s.i (*0-553-21159-5*, Bantam Classics); 432p. mass mkt. 4.95 (*0-553-21273-7*) Bantam Bks.
—Emma. 2002. audio compact disk 120.00 (*0-7366-8766-1*) Books on Tape, Inc.
—Emma. 1986. lib. bdg. 19.95 (*0-89966-242-0*) Buccaneer Bks., Inc.
—Emma, 3 Vols. (Collected Works of Jane Austen). reprint ed. lib. bdg. 294.00 (*0-7426-2073-5*); 2001. pap. text 84.00 (*0-7426-7073-2*) Classic Bks.
—Emma. l.t. ed. 1999. 630p. pap. 24.95 (*1-58855-018-4*) Cyber Classics, Inc.
—Emma. unabr. ed. 1999. 384p. pap. text 2.50 (*0-486-40648-2*) Dover Pubns., Inc.
—Emma. 1956. 10.50 o.p. (*0-460-00024-1*, Dutton) Dutton/Plume.
—Emma. E-Book 2.49 (*1-58744-220-5*) Electric Umbrella Publishing.
—Emma. 1998. (SPA.). 416p. (*84-320-3877-6*) GeoPlaneta, Editorial, S. A.
—Emma. l.t. ed. 2000. 624p. pap. 22.00 (*0-06-095693-3*, HarperCollins) HarperTrade.
—Emma. 2003. audio 14.95 (*1-84032-771-5*) Hodder Headline Audiobooks GBR. *Dist:* Trafalgar Square.
—Emma. Trilling, Lionel, ed. 1972. (C). pap. 16.36 (*0-395-05115-0*) Houghton Mifflin Co.
—Emma. l.t. ed. 555p. pap. 41.61 (*0-7583-0811-6*); 436p. pap. 33.67 (*0-7583-0810-8*); 319p. pap. 27.06 (*0-7583-0809-4*); 254p. pap. 23.38 (*0-7583-0808-6*); 708p. pap. 51.13 (*0-7583-0812-4*); 1233p. pap. 88.84 (*0-7583-0815-9*); 1063p. pap. 79.19 (*0-7583-0814-0*); 865p. pap. 68.70 (*0-7583-0813-2*); 254p. lib. bdg. 29.38 (*0-7583-0800-0*); 319p. lib. bdg. 33.06 (*0-7583-0801-9*); 1233p. lib. bdg. 100.84 (*0-7583-0807-8*); 436p. lib. bdg. 39.67 (*0-7583-0802-7*); 1063p. lib. bdg. 91.19 (*0-7583-0806-X*); 865p. lib. bdg. 81.13 (*0-7583-0805-1*); 555p. lib. bdg. 47.61 (*0-7583-0803-5*); 708p. lib. bdg. 57.13 (*0-7583-0804-3*) Huge Print Pr.
—Emma. 1996. (Illus.). 464p. reprint ed. pap. 9.95 (*0-7868-8183-6*) Hyperion Pr.
—Emma. 1991. (Everyman's Library). 484p. (*1-85715-036-8*, Everyman's Library) Knopf Publishing Group.
—Emma. 1999. (Cloth Bound Pocket Ser.). 7.95 (*3-8290-0827-9*, 520519) Konemann.

—Emma. E-Book 2.95 (*1-57799-980-0*); E-Book 2.95 (*1-57799-846-4*) Logos Research Systems, Inc.
—Emma. Cheetham, Paul, ed. 1984. (Study Texts Ser.). pap. text 4.29 (*0-582-33153-6*, 72058) Longman Publishing Group.
—Emma. E-Book 1.95 (*1-58515-171-8*) MesaView, Inc.
—Emma. (Signet Classics). 1996. 416p. mass mkt. 4.95 (*0-451-52627-9*, Signet Classics); 1968. mass mkt. 0.50 o.p. (*0-451-50216-7*, Signet Classics); 1968. mass mkt. 0.75 o.p. (*0-451-50388-0*, Signet Classics); 1964. mass mkt. 2.25 o.p. (*0-451-51941-8*); 1964. 400p. mass mkt. 4.95 o.p. (*0-451-52306-7*, Signet Classics); 1964. mass mkt. 1.95 o.p. (*0-451-51524-2*, Signet Classics); 1964. mass mkt. 1.25 o.p. (*0-451-50798-3*, Signet Classics); 1964. mass mkt. 0.95 o.p. (*0-451-50705-3*, Signet Classics); 1964. mass mkt. 1.75 o.p. (*0-451-51357-6*, Signet Classics); 1943. mass mkt. 1.50 o.p. (*0-451-51010-0*, Signet Classics) NAL.
—Emma. l.t. ed. reprint ed. 1997. 610p. lib. bdg. 26.00 (*0-939495-08-2*); 1998. 478p. lib. bdg. 25.00 (*1-58287-025-X*) North Bks.
—Emma. Parrish, Stephen M., ed. (Critical Editions Ser.). 430p. (C). 1972. pap. o.p. (*0-393-09667-X*); 2nd ed. 1993. pap. text o.p. (*0-393-96014-5*) Norton, W. W. & Co., Inc.
—Emma. 1999. (Oxford World's Classics Ser.). 464p. 13.00 o.p. (*0-19-210030-0*) Oxford Univ. Pr., Inc.
—Emma. Kinsley, James, ed. (Oxford World's Classics Ser.). 1998. 488p. pap. 6.95 o.p. (*0-19-283357-X*); 1990. 482p. pap. 4.50 o.p. (*0-19-282756-1*) Oxford Univ. Pr., Inc.
—Emma. Kinsley, James & Lodge, David, eds. 1980. (Oxford World's Classics Ser.). pap. 2.50 o.p. (*0-19-281504-0*) Oxford Univ. Pr., Inc.
—Emma. Pinch, Adela, ed. 2nd ed. 2003. (Oxford World's Classics Ser.). 672p. pap. 6.95 (*0-19-280237-2*) Oxford Univ. Pr., Inc.
—Emma. Kinsley, James, ed. 2nd ed. 1995. (Oxford World's Classics Ser.). 484p. pap. 4.95 o.p. (*0-19-282432-5*) Oxford Univ. Pr., Inc.
—Emma, Vol. IV. Chapman, R. W., ed. 3rd ed. 1988. (Illus.). 536p. reprint ed. 20.00 (*0-19-254704-6*) Oxford Univ. Pr., Inc.
—Emma. collector's ed. 2002. (Illus.). im. lthr. 38.85 (*1-931927-22-7*); pap. 19.95 (*1-931927-23-5*); 25.95 (*1-931927-21-9*); pap. 17.95 (*1-931927-14-6*) Polyglot Pr., Inc.
—Emma. (Jane Austen Works). 2000. 364p. lib. bdg. 41.99 (*1-57646-332-X*); 2000. 364p. pap. 19.99 o.p. (*1-57646-261-7*); 1999. 200p. E-Book 3.99 incl. audio compact disk (*1-57646-144-0*); 2000. 646p. pap. 39.99 (*1-57646-333-8*); 2000. 646p. lib. bdg. 49.99 (*1-57646-334-6*) Quiet Vision Publishing.
—Emma. (Modern Library Classics). 2001. 384p. pap. 7.95 (*0-375-75742-2*); 2001. E-Book 4.95 (*0-679-64108-4*); 1995. 14.95 o.s.i (*0-679-60193-7*) Random House Adult Trade Publishing Group. (Modern Library).
—Emma. 1988. (Zodiac Press Ser.). 520p. o.p. (*0-7011-1232-8*) Random Hse. of Canada, Ltd. CAN. *Dist:* Random Hse., Inc.
—Emma. 2002. (SPA.). 600p. mass mkt. 9.95 (*1-4000-0083-1*); 1997. 13.00 o.s.i (*0-679-60257-7*); 1991. 560p. 18.00 (*0-679-40581-X*); 1989. o.s.i (*1-85381-096-7*) Random Hse., Inc.
—Emma. 1994. (World's Best Reading Ser.). 391p. (*0-89577-582-4*) Reader's Digest Assn., Inc., The.
—Emma. 2000. E-Book 2.95 incl. cd-rom (*1-58853-011-6*) Sensory Publishing, Inc.
—Emma. E-Book 5.00 (*0-7410-0560-3*) SoftBook Pr.
—Emma. unabr. ed. 2003. audio 19.99 (*1-59335-041-4*, 30126) Soulmate Audio Bks., Inc.
—Emma. l.t. ed. 1985. (Charnwood Large Print Ser.). 547p. 29.99 (*0-7089-8258-1*, Charnwood) Thorpe, F. A. Pubs. GBR. *Dist:* Ulverscroft Large Print Bks., Ltd., Ulverscroft Large Print Canada, Ltd.
—Emma. Daleski, H. M., ed. 2003. 9.95 (*1-59264-004-4*); 510p. pap. 9.95 (*1-59264-003-6*) Toby Pr.
—Emma. 2000. (Signature Classics Ser.). 459p. 24.95 (*1-58279-090-6*); lib. bdg. 29.95 (*1-58279-081-7*) Trident Pr. International.
—Emma. 1997. 19.00 (*0-606-17578-4*); 1980. 11.00 (*0-606-03147-2*) Turtleback Bks.
—Emma. 1994. 464p. pap. 3.95 o.p. (*0-460-87467-5*); 1964. 432p. pap. 5.95 o.p. (*0-460-15024-3*) Tuttle Publishing. (Everyman's Classic Library in Paperback).
—Emma. 2000. 9.00 (*81-85944-76-8*) UBS Pubs. Distributions, Ltd. IND. *Dist:* South Asia Bks.
—Emma. (Classics Ser.). 2003. 512p. pap. 8.00 (*0-14-143958-0*, Penguin Classics); 1997. 448p. 7.95 (*0-14-043415-1*); 1971. 4.50 o.p. (*0-460-01024-7*) Viking Penguin.
—Emma. Blythe, Ronald, ed. 1966. (English Library). 480p. pap. 6.95 o.s.i (*0-14-043010-5*, Penguin Classics) Viking Penguin.
—Emma. 1999. E-Book 5.99 (*0-8220-7063-4*, Cliff Notes) Wiley, John & Sons, Inc.
—Emma. 1997. (Classics Library). 384p. pap. 3.95 (*1-85326-028-2*, 0282WW) Wordsworth Editions, Ltd. GBR. *Dist:* Casemate Pubs. & Bk. Distributors, LLC.
—Emma: Critical Edition. Parrish, Stephen M., ed. 3rd ed. 2000. (Critical Editions Ser.). (Illus.). ix, 449p. pap. 11.00 (*0-393-97284-4*) Norton, W. W. & Co., Inc.
—Emma, Northanger Abbey & Persuasion, Vol. 2. 1976. pap. 8.95 o.p. (*0-394-71892-5*, V-892) Random Hse., Inc.
Austen, Jane, et al. Emma. 1998. E-Book 7.30 (*0-585-36169-X*) netLibrary, Inc.
Bennett, Alan. The Laying on of Hands. 15.00 (*0-312-70655-3*) Picador.
—The Laying on of Hands: Stories. 208p. 2003. pap. 11.00 (*0-312-42225-3*); 2002. 15.00 (*0-312-29051-9*) Picador.
—The Laying on of Hands: Stories. 2001. 120p. 14.00 (*1-86197-374-8*) Profile Bks. Ltd. GBR. *Dist:* Renouf Publishing Co., Ltd.
Chappell, Margaret. Cookley Green. l.t. ed. 2003. (Magna Large Print Ser.). 496p. (*0-7505-2094-9*) Magna Large Print Bks. GBR. *Dist:* Ulverscroft Large Print Canada, Ltd.
—Cookley Green. 2003. 369p. pap. 13.00 (*0-552-14974-8*) Transworld Publishers Ltd. GBR. *Dist:* Trafalgar Square.
Coe, Amanda. A Whore in Your Kitchen. 2002. 213p. pap. (*1-86049-813-2*) Virago Pr., Ltd. GBR. *Dist:* Trafalgar Square.
Cox, J. Somewhere, Someday. 2001. 437p. mass mkt. 9.95 (*0-7472-5757-4*) Headline Bk. Publishing, Ltd. GBR. *Dist:* Trafalgar Square.
Edric, Robert. Peacetime. 2002. 384p. (*0-385-60297-9*) Doubleday Publishing.
Hall, Donald. Willow Temple: New & Selected Stories. 2003. 224p. tchr. ed. 24.00 (*0-618-32981-1*) Houghton Mifflin Co.
—Willow Temple: New & Selected Stories. 2004. 224p. pap. 12.00 (*0-618-44661-3*, Mariner Bks.) Houghton Mifflin Co. Trade & Reference Div.
Lee, Maureen. House by Princes Park. 2002. 512p. pap. (*0-7528-4835-6*); 406p. (*0-7528-3803-2*) Orion Publishing Group, Ltd. GBR. *Dist:* Trafalgar Square.
MacLean, A. D., ed. Winter's Tales. No. 19. 1973. 270p. 6.95 o.p. (*0-312-88305-6*); No. 24. 1978. 8.95 o.p. (*0-312-88412-5*); No. 26. 1981. 224p. 11.95 o.p. (*0-312-88414-1*); No. 28. 1983. 224p. 11.95 o.p. (*0-312-88421-4*) St. Martin's Pr.
Sutherland, John, ed. The Oxford Book of English Love Stories. 2003. 452p. pap. 16.95 (*0-19-280467-7*); 1996. 464p. (C). text 40.00 (*0-19-214237-2*); 1997. 464p. reprint ed. pap. 15.95 o.p. (*0-19-283268-9*) Oxford Univ. Pr., Inc.
Wilson, James. Dark Clue. 2003. 320p. pap. (*0-385-65806-0*, Anchor Canada) Doubleday Canada, Ltd. CAN. *Dist:* Random Hse., Inc.
—The Dark Clue: A Novel of Suspense. 2001. 400p. 25.00 o.p. (*0-87113-831-X*, Atlantic Monthly Pr.) Grove/Atlantic, Inc.

**GREECE—FICTION**

Aiken, Joan. A Cluster of Separate Sparks. 1972. 8.95 o.p. (*0-385-02906-3*) Doubleday Publishing.
—A Cluster of Separate Sparks. l.t. ed. 1992. 387p. pap. 15.95 o.p. (*0-8161-5513-5*, Macmillan Reference USA) Gale Group.
Apostolou, Anna. A Murder in Macedon. 1998. 272p. mass mkt. 5.99 (*0-312-96792-6*, St. Martin's Paperbacks); 1997. 256p. 21.95 (*0-312-16939-6*, Saint Martin's Minotaur) St. Martin's Pr.
—A Murder in Thebes. 1998. 240p. 21.95 o.p. (*0-312-19585-0*, Saint Martin's Minotaur) St. Martin's Pr.
—A Murder in Thebes: A Mystery of Alexander the Great. 1999. (St. Martin's Minotaur Mysteries Ser.). 240p. mass mkt. 5.99 (*0-312-97278-4*, St. Martin's Paperbacks) St. Martin's Pr.
Arnold, Margot, pseud. Exit Actors, Dying. 1982. 176p. 2.50 (*0-86721-181-4*, Jove) Berkley Publishing Group.
—Exit Actors, Dying. 1988. (Penny Spring & Sir Toby Glendower Mystery Ser.). 176p. reprint ed. pap. 7.95 (*0-88150-115-8*, Foul Play) Norton, W. W. & Co., Inc.
—The Midas Murders. 1995. (Penny Spring & Sir Toby Glendower Mystery Ser.). 224p. 20.00 (*0-88150-340-1*, Foul Play) Norton, W. W. & Co., Inc.
—The Midas Murders: A Penny Spring & Sir Toby Glendower Mystery. 1997. (Penny Spring & Sir Toby Glendower Mystery Ser.). 224p. pap. 7.95 (*0-88150-394-0*) Norton, W. W. & Co., Inc.
Ashley, Mike, ed. Classical Whodunits. 1997. 384p. pap. 9.95 (*0-7867-0418-7*, Carroll & Graf Pubs.) Avalon Publishing Group.
Axler, Leo. Grave Matters: A Bill Hawley Undertaking. 1995. 256p. (Orig.). mass mkt. 4.99 o.s.i (*0-425-14581-6*, Prime Crime) Berkley Publishing Group.
Beaton, Roderick. Ariadne's Children. pap. 15.95 (*0-312-30457-9*, Saint Martin's Griffin); 1996. 384p. 24.95 o.p. (*0-312-13923-3*) St. Martin's Pr.
Belanger, Sean. Gods & Spears. 2003. 192p. 21.95 (*1-59209-011-7*) USA Bks.
Benedict, Helen. The Sailor's Wife. 2000. 224p. 24.00 o.p. (*1-58195-024-1*, Zoland Bks., Inc.) Steerforth Pr.
Boneparth, Ellen. Death at the Olive Press. 2000. 212p. pap. 21.99 (*0-7388-2034-2*); text 31.99 (*0-7388-2033-4*) Xlibris Corp.
Booky, Albert R. Remember Us. 1992. 168p. (Orig.). pap. 9.00 (*1-56002-032-6*, University Editions) Aegina Pr., Inc.
Boylan, Carle. Last Resorts: A Novel. 1986. 288p. 16.45 o.p. (*0-671-54998-7*) Summit Bks.
Bradshaw, Gillian. The Sand-Reckoner. 2000. 348p. 23.95 (*0-312-87340-9*, Forge Bks.) Doherty, Tom Assocs., LLC.
Brindel, June R. Ariadne. 1981. 246p. pap. 7.95 o.p. (*0-312-04912-9*, Saint Martin's Griffin); 1980. 272p. 10.95 o.p. (*0-312-04911-0*) St. Martin's Pr.
Brown, James W. Blood Dance. 1993. 258p. 22.95 o.s.i (*0-15-113214-3*) Harcourt Trade Pubs.
Bunting, Eve. I Have an Olive Tree. 1999. (Joanna Cotler Bks.). (Illus.). 32p. (J). (ps-3). lib. bdg. 15.89 (*0-06-027574-X*, Cotler, Joanna Bks.) HarperCollins Children's Bk. Group.
Burnham, Carol. Attic Light. 1997. 192p. 24.00 (*1-877946-88-5*) Permanent Pr., The.
Byers, Richard M. Andromache Beneath the Load of Life. 1989. (Illus.). 240p. 15.00 (*0-9602048-4-9*) Fairfield Hse.
—Andromache's Hector & Helenus. 1989. (Illus.). 279p. 16.00 (*0-9602048-3-0*) Fairfield Hse.
Cahill, Jane. Her Kind: Women from Greek Mythology. 1995. 275p. (C). pap. (*1-55111-042-3*) Broadview Pr.
Caldecott, Moyra. The Lily & the Bull. 1979. 192p. 9.95 o.p. (*0-8090-6572-X*, Hill & Wang) Farrar, Straus & Giroux.
—The Lily & the Bull. E-Book (*1-899142-54-1*) Mushroom Publishing.
Caunitz, William J. Black Sand. 1994. 20.95 o.p. (*0-7927-1757-0*); pap. 18.95 o.p. (*0-7927-1756-2*) BBC Audiobooks America.
—Black Sand. 1991. mass mkt. 2.99 o.s.i (*0-553-19643-X*); 1990. 384p. mass mkt. 6.50 o.s.i (*0-553-28359-6*); 1989. 384p. mass mkt. 4.95 o.s.i (*0-553-17336-7*) Bantam Bks.
—Black Sand. 1988. 18.95 o.p. (*0-517-57226-5*, Crown) Crown Publishing Group.
—Black Sand. 1991. 3.99 o.p. (*0-517-06438-3*) Random Hse. Value Publishing.
Chaikin, Linda L. Thursday's Child. 2001. (Day to Remember Ser.: Vol. 4). 358p. 10.99 (*0-7369-0070-5*) Harvest Hse. Pubs.
Chavarria, Daniel. The Eye of Cybele. Lopez, Carlos, tr. from SPA. 2002. 400p. 27.00 (*1-888451-25-4*) Akashic Bks.
Cook, Elizabeth. Achilles. 2002. 128p. 16.00 (*0-312-28884-0*) Picador.
—Achilles: A Novel. 2003. 128p. pap. 11.00 (*0-312-31110-9*) Picador.
Cory, Desmond. The Mask of Zeus. 1993. 256p. 19.95 o.p. (*0-312-09873-1*, Saint Martin's Minotaur) St. Martin's Pr.
Craven, Sara. Smokescreen Marriage. 2002. (Harlequin Presents Ser.). 192p. mass mkt. (*0-373-12287-X*, Harlequin Bks.) Harlequin Enterprises, Ltd.
—Smokescreen Marriage. l.t. ed. 2002. (Mills & Boon Large Print Ser.). 288p. 27.99 (*0-263-17294-5*) Harlequin Mills & Boon, Ltd. GBR. *Dist:* Thorndike Pr., Ulverscroft Large Print Bks., Ltd., Ulverscroft Large Print Canada, Ltd.
Davidson, Catherine Temma. The Priest Fainted. unabr. ed. 1998. audio 60.00 (*0-7887-2606-4*, 95450E7 ) Recorded Bks., LLC.
—The Priest Fainted: A Novel. 272p. 1999. pap. 13.00 o.s.i (*0-8050-6109-6*, Owl Bks.); 1998. 23.00 o.s.i (*0-8050-5539-8*) Holt, Henry & Co.
Davis, William Stearns. A Victor of Salamis. E-Book 3.95 (*0-594-05045-6*) 1873 Pr.
—A Victor of Salamis. 1907. 20.00 o.p. (*0-8196-1208-1*) Biblo & Tannen Booksellers & Pubs., Inc.
De Bernieres, Louis. Corelli's Mandolin: A Novel. 1994. 24.00 o.s.i (*0-679-43644-8*, Pantheon) Knopf Publishing Group.
—Corelli's Mandolin: A Novel. Desser, Robin, ed. 1995. 448p. reprint ed. pap. 14.00 (*0-679-76397-X*, Vintage) Knopf Publishing Group.
De Fenelon, Marquis. The Adventures of Telemachus, the Son of Ulysses. Brack, O. M., Jr., ed. Smollett, Tobias George, tr. 1997. (Works of Tobias Smollett). (Illus.). xxxv, 383p. 50.00 (*0-8203-1820-5*) Univ. of Georgia Pr.
Demetrios, George. When Greek Meets Greek. 1977. (Short Story Index Reprint Ser.). (Illus.). 22.95 (*0-8369-3452-0*) Ayer Co. Pubs., Inc.
DiFazio, Charles P. Apollonius the Divine Magician: The Divine Magician. 2002. (Orig.). pap. 17.95 (*1-930410-05-0*) Zilch Publishing, Inc.
Doody, Margaret Anne. Aristotle Detective. 1996. 19.50 o.p. (*0-7451-8697-1*, Black Dagger) BBC Audiobooks America.
—Aristotle Detective. 1980. (Harper Novel of Suspense Ser.). 288p. o.p. (*0-06-011086-4*) Harper-Collins Pubs.
—Aristotle Detective. 1981. (Crime Monthly Ser.). pap. 2.95 o.p. (*0-14-005753-6*, Penguin Bks.) Viking Penguin.
Edwards, Gene. The Titus Diary: The Story of an Incredible Adventure That Changed the World. 1999. (First Century Diaries). (Illus.). 280p. pap. 9.99 (*0-8423-7162-1*) Tyndale Hse. Pubs.
Edwards, Jane. Dangerous Odyssey. unabr. ed. 1993. audio 26.95 (*1-55686-467-1*, 467) Books in Motion.
—Dangerous Odyssey. 1990. 192p. 13.95 o.p. (*0-8034-8803-3*) Bouregy, Thomas & Co., Inc.
—Dangerous Odyssey. l.t. ed. 1996. (G. K. Hall Nightingale Ser.). pap. 17.95 o.p. (*0-7838-1620-0*, Macmillan Reference USA) Gale Group.
Edwards, Michael B. Murder at the Panionic Games. 2001. 260p. 23.50 (*0-89733-500-7*) Academy Chicago Pubs., Ltd.
Elsink, Henk. Confession of a Hired Killer. Smittenaar, H. G., tr. from DUT. 1993. 273p. pap. 8.95 (*1-881164-53-5*) Intercontinental Publishing, Inc.
Fakinos, Aris. The Marked Men. 288p. 1972. pap. 2.45 (*0-87140-263-7*); 1971. 6.95 (*0-87140-516-4*) Liveright Publishing Corp.
Faust, Ron. Lord of the Dark Lake. 2000. 320p. pap. 13.95 (*0-312-87510-X*, Forge Bks.); 1998. mass mkt. 6.99 (*0-8125-3023-3*, Tor Bks.); 1996. 320p. 22.95 o.p. (*0-312-85535-4*, Forge Bks.) Doherty, Tom Assocs., LLC.
Fenelon, Francois S. Finelon: Telemachus. Riley, Patrick, ed. Wiley, Patrick, tr. from FRE. 1994. (Texts in the History of Political Thought ). 378p. (C). pap. text 26.00 (*0-521-45662-2*) Cambridge Univ. Pr.
—Telemachus. Riley, Patrick, ed. Wiley, Patrick, tr. from FRE. 1994. (Texts in the History of Political Thought ). 378p. (C). text 70.00 (*0-521-45042-X*) Cambridge Univ. Pr.
Flokos, Nicholas. Nike: A Romance. 2000. (Illus.). 192p. pap. 10.00 (*0-618-00207-3*); 1998. 179p. tchr. ed. 20.00 o.s.i (*0-395-88396-2*) Houghton Mifflin Co.
Ford, Michael Curtis. The Last King: A Novel of Mithridates the Great. 2004. (Illus.). 384p. 24.95 (*0-312-27539-0*) St. Martin's Pr.
—The Ten Thousand: A Novel of Ancient Greece. 2002. 448p. mass mkt. 6.99 (*0-312-98032-9*, St. Martin's Paperbacks); 2001. 384p. 24.95 (*0-312-26946-3*) St. Martin's Pr.
Fowles, John. The Magus. 1978. mass mkt. 2.50 o.s.i (*0-440-15162-7*); 1985. 672p. mass mkt. 7.99 (*0-440-35162-6*) Dell Publishing.
—The Magus. 2001. 656p. pap. 16.95 (*0-316-29619-8*, Back Bay); 1978. 19.95 o.s.i (*0-316-29092-0*) Little Brown & Co.
—The Magus. annuals 1998. (Modern Library Ser.). 736p. 23.95 o.s.i (*0-679-60283-6*) Random Hse., Inc.
—The Magus. 1997. 656p. (*0-09-974391-4*) Trafalgar Square.
Fox, Paula. Lily & the Lost Boy. l.t. unabr. ed. 1989. 230p. (J). (gr. 5-7). lib. bdg. 13.95 o.p. (*0-8161-4725-6*, Macmillan Reference USA) Gale Group.
Fragoulis, Tess. Ariadne's Dream. 2002. 368p. pap. (*1-894345-30-4*) Thistledown Pr., Ltd.
Freedman, Nancy. Sappho: The Tenth Muse. 1998. 352p. 25.95 (*0-312-18660-6*) St. Martin's Pr.
Frye, Ellen. Amazon Story Bones. 1994. 208p. 10.95 o.p. (*1-883523-00-1*) Spinsters Ink Bks.
—Amazon Story Bones Library. 1994. 208p. 21.95 o.p. (*1-883523-01-X*) Spinsters Ink Bks.
—The Other Sappho. 1989. 218p. (Orig.). pap. 8.95 (*0-932379-68-0*); pap. text 18.95 (*0-932379-69-9*) Firebrand Bks.
Frye, Harriet & Frye, John. North to Thule: An Imagined Narrative of the Famous "Lost" Sea Voyage of Pytheas of Massalia in the 4th Century B.C. 1985. (Illus.). 232p. 16.95 o.p. (*0-912697-20-2*) Algonquin Bks. of Chapel Hill.
Gemmell, David. Lion of Macedon. 1992. 560p. pap. 8.00 o.p. (*0-345-37911-X*, Del Rey) Ballantine Bks.
Gerritsen, Tess. In Their Footsteps. 1999. mass mkt. (*1-55166-532-8*, Mira Bks.); 1994. (Illus.). 251p. mass mkt. (*0-373-22278-5*, 1-22278-5, Harlequin Bks.) Harlequin Enterprises, Ltd.
—In Their Footsteps. l.t. ed. 2001. (Thorndike Famous Authors Ser.). 344p. 29.95 (*0-7862-3154-8*) Thorndike Pr.
Gilchrist, Ellen. Anabasis: A Journey to the Interior. 192p. 1995. pap. 15.95 (*0-87805-821-4*); 1994. 23.00 (*0-87805-726-9*) Univ. Pr. of Mississippi.
Goddard, Robert. Into the Blue. 1999. 541p. mass mkt. (*0-552-54593-7*); 1997. mass mkt. o.s.i (*0-552-13561-5*); 1993. mass mkt. o.s.i (*0-552-14030-9*); 1990. o.s.i (*0-593-01808-7*) Bantam Bks. (Corgi).
—Into the Blue. unabr. ed. 1995. audio 85.95 (*0-7861-0651-4*, 1563) Blackstone Audio Bks., Inc.

—Into the Blue. l.t. ed. 1992. (General Ser.). 630p. lib. bdg. 23.95 o.p. (*0-8161-5233-0*, Macmillan Reference USA) Gale Group.

—Into the Blue. 1991. 416p. 19.95 (*0-671-70482-6*, Simon & Schuster) Simon & Schuster.

—Into the Blue. Rubenstein, Julie, ed. 1992. 528p. reprint ed. mass mkt. 5.99 (*0-671-70483-4*, Pocket) Simon & Schuster.

Golding, William. The Double Tongue. 165p. 1999. pap. 16.00 (*0-374-52637-0*); 1995. 20.00 o.p. (*0-374-14329-3*) Farrar, Straus & Giroux.

Goodman, Anthony A. The Shadow of God: A Novel of the Siege of Rhodes. 2002. 500p. 24.00 o.p. (*1-57071-904-7*, Sourcebooks Landmark) Sourcebooks, Inc.

Gould, Judith. The Greek Villa. 2003. 352p. 23.95 (*0-451-21047-6*) NAL.

Graham, Lynne. The Heiress Bride. 2002. (Harlequin Presents Ser.). 192p. mass mkt. (*0-373-12283-7*, Harlequin Bks.) Harlequin Enterprises, Ltd.

—The Heiress Bride. 2003. (Harlequin II Romance Ser.). 25.95 (*0-263-17868-4*) Harlequin Mills & Boon, Ltd. GBR. *Dist:* Thorndike Pr.

Green, Peter. The Laughter of Aphrodite: A Novel about Sappho of Lesbos. 274p. 1995. pap. 25.00 (*0-520-20340-2*); 1993. text 40.00 (*0-520-07966-3*) Univ. of California Pr.

Grossman, David. The Zigzag Kid. Rosenberg, Betsy, tr. from HEB. 1998. 320p. pap. 13.00 o.p. (*0-374-52563-3*) Farrar, Straus & Giroux.

Haris, Petros. The Longest Night: Chronicle of a Dead City. Stavrou, Theofanis G., ed. Sampson, Theodore, tr. from GRE. 1985. (Modern Greek History & Culture Ser.). (Illus.). 128p. 20.00 (*0-932963-02-1*) Nostos Bks.

Harrison, Don. The Spartan. 1992. 175p. reprint ed. pap. 7.95 o.p. (*0-932870-20-1*) Alyson Pubns.

Hart, Roy. A Deadly Schedule. 1996. (WWL Mystery Ser.). per. (*0-373-26205-1*, 1-26205-4, Worldwide Library) Harlequin Enterprises, Ltd.

—A Deadly Schedule. 1995. mass mkt. o.s.i (*0-7515-1034-3*) Little Brown & Co.

—A Deadly Schedule: An Inspector Roper Mystery. 1994. 224p. 19.95 o.p. (*0-312-10964-4*, Saint Martin's Minotaur) St. Martin's Pr.

Harvey, John. Coup d'Etat. 1985. 480p. 16.95 o.p. (*0-689-11484-2*, Scribner) Simon & Schuster.

Haviaras, Stratis. The Heroic Age. 1985. 352p. pap. 6.95 o.p. (*0-14-007976-9*, Penguin Bks.) Viking Penguin.

Henty, G. A. In Greek Waters: A Story of the Greek War of Independance, 1821-1827. 2000. 252p. E-Book 9.95 (*0-594-05564-4*) 1873 Pr.

—In Greek Waters: A Story of the Greek War of Independance, 1821-1827. 2002. 432p. 29.95 (*1-59087-069-7*, GAH069); per. 19.95 (*1-59087-068-9*, GAH068) Althouse Pr.

—In Greek Waters: A Story of the Greek War of Independance, 1821-1827. collector's ed. 2002. (Illus.). im. lthr. 38.85 (*1-4115-1312-6*); pap. 19.95 (*1-4115-0564-6*); 25.95 (*1-4115-0943-9*); pap. 17.95 (*1-4115-0191-8*) Polyglot Pr., Inc.

Holland, Tom. The Lord of the Dead. 1998. 336p. pap. 14.00 (*0-671-02411-6*, Pocket) Simon & Schuster.

—The Lord of the Dead: Slave of My Thirst. 1997. 368p. per. 6.99 (*0-671-53426-2*, Pocket) Simon & Schuster.

—Lord of the Dead: The Secret History of Byron. Chernoff, Dona, ed. 1996. 336p. 23.00 o.p. (*0-671-53425-4*, Atria) Simon & Schuster.

Holt, Tom. Goatsong. 1990. 256p. 16.95 o.p. (*0-312-03838-0*) St. Martin's Pr.

—Walled Orchard. 1991. 17.95 o.p. (*0-312-05990-6*) St. Martin's Pr.

Howard, Linda. All That Glitters. (Mira Bks.). 1998. 248p. per. (*1-55166-432-1*, 1-66432-5, Mira Bks.); 1993. mass mkt. (*0-373-48270-1*, Silhouette) Harlequin Enterprises, Ltd.

—All That Glitters. l.t. ed. 2001. (Romance Ser.). 341p. 28.95 (*0-7862-2622-6*) Thorndike Pr.

James, Chris K. Fling with a Demon Lover. 1997. 256p. pap. 12.00 o.p. (*0-06-092827-1*, Perennial) HarperTrade.

James, Kelvin C. A Fling with a Demon Lover: A Novel. 1996. 79p. 22.00 o.p. (*0-06-017350-5*) HarperCollins Pubs.

Jong, Erica. Sappho's Leap: A Novel. 2003. (Illus.). 320p. 24.95 (*0-393-05761-5*); 256p. 24.95 (*0-393-05762-3*) Norton, W. W. & Co., Inc.

Karnezis, Panos. Little Infamies: Stories. 2003. 296p. 24.00 (*0-374-18937-4*) Farrar, Straus & Giroux.

—Little Infamies: Stories. 2004. 288p. pap. 14.00 (*0-312-42154-0*) Picador.

Kazantzakis, Nikos. Alexander the Great: A Novel. Vasils, Theodora, tr. from GRE. 1982. (Illus.). x, 222p. pap. 12.95 (*0-8214-0663-9*) Ohio Univ. Pr.

—The Fratricides. 1985. (C). pap. 7.95 o.p. (*0-671-27221-7*, Touchstone) Simon & Schuster.

—Freedom or Death. 1983. 320p. pap. 8.50 o.p. (*0-671-49260-8*); 1982. pap. 6.95 o.p. (*0-671-27251-9*) Simon & Schuster. (Touchstone).

—Zorba the Greek. 1993. reprint ed. lib. bdg. 26.95 (*1-56849-178-6*) Buccaneer Bks., Inc.

—Zorba the Greek. unabr. ed. 1999. audio 78.00 (*0-7887-0471-0*, 94664E7) Recorded Bks., LLC.

—Zorba the Greek. 1996. 320p. pap. 13.00 (*0-684-82554-6*); 1971. 314p. pap. 11.00 o.s.i (*0-671-21132-3*) Simon & Schuster. (Touchstone).

Keeley, Edmund. School for Pagan Lovers. 1993. (Rutgers Press Fiction Ser.). 302p. (C). 19.95 (*0-8135-1935-7*) Rutgers Univ. Pr.

—Some Wine for Remembrance. 2002. pap. 15.00 (*1-893996-15-8*) White Pine Pr.

Kirkman, M. M. Iskander. 2000. 252p. E-Book 3.95 (*0-594-02551-6*) 1873 Pr.

La Tourrette, Jacqueline. The Pompeii Scroll. 1975. 256p. pap. 7.95 o.p. (*0-440-06091-5*, Delacorte Pr.) Dell Publishing.

Lattimore, Deborah Nourse. The Prince & the Golden Ax: A Minoan Tale. 1988. (Illus.). 40p. (J). (gr. k-3). lib. bdg. 12.89 o.p. (*0-06-023716-3*) HarperCollins Children's Bk. Group.

LeClair, Tom. Passing Off. 1996. 176p. 24.00 (*1-877946-77-X*) Permanent Pr., The.

Leontis, Artemis, ed. Greece: A Traveler's Literary Companion. 1997. (Travelers' Literary Companions Ser.: Vol. 5). (Illus.). 256p. pap. 13.95 (*1-883513-04-9*) Whereabouts.

MacInnes, Helen. The Double Image. 1966. 7.50 o.s.i (*0-15-126411-2*) Harcourt Trade Pubs.

Madison, Miriam. Secret Passages of the Heart. 1989. pap. o.p. (*0-938645-22-6*) In His Steps Publishing.

Majkut, Paul. Asterion, the Minotaur: A Book of Suspicion, Resentment, Confusion, Regret, Poor Memory, Tales, Poetry, & Conversation. 1993. (*0-9632702-3-0*) Lightning Pubns.

Makepeace, Joanna. Not in Our Stars. l.t. ed. 2001. (Thorndike General Ser.). 237p. pap. 22.95 (*0-7862-2991-8*); (*0-7540-4329-0*); (*0-7540-4328-2*) Thorndike Pr.

McCullough, Colleen. The Song of Troy. 2001. (Illus.). 483p. pap. 7.95 (*0-7528-1763-9*) Orion Publishing Group, Ltd. GBR. *Dist:* Trafalgar Square.

Merrill, James. The Diblos Notebook. 1994. 160p. reprint ed. pap. 9.95 (*1-56478-064-3*) Dalkey Archive Pr.

—The Diblos Notebook. 1975. (C). pap. 2.95 (*0-689-70519-0*, 209, Scribner Paper Fiction) Simon & Schuster.

Michaels, Barbara, pseud. The Sea King's Daughter. l.t. ed. 1993. pap. 16.95 o.p. (*0-7927-1301-X*); 1992. 18.95 o.p. (*0-7927-1302-8*) BBC Audiobooks America.

—The Sea King's Daughter. 1976. mass mkt. 1.75 o.s.i (*0-449-23023-6*) Ballantine Bks.

Molinaro, Ursule. The New Moon with the Old Moon in Her Arms. 1993. 119p. (Orig.). pap. 22.00 (*0-7043-5057-2*); pap. 10.00 (*0-929701-29-1*) McPherson & Co.

Neophyte, K. S., contrib. by. Cypriotica. 1997. (*0-620-20838-4*) Kwagga Pubs.

Neville, Pauline. Double Vision. 2002. 216p. 22.50 (*0-86356-360-0*) I.B.Tauris & Co., Ltd. GBR. *Dist:* Holtzbrinck Pubs., Palgrave Macmillan.

Norfolk, Lawrence. In the Shape of a Boar. 2001. 336p. 25.00 o.p. (*0-8021-1701-5*) Grove/Atlantic, Inc.

Papandreou, Nicholas. A Crowded Heart. 192p. 1999. pap. 12.00 o.s.i (*0-312-20400-0*); 1998. 21.00 o.p. (*0-312-18685-1*) Picador.

Parks, Tim. Shear. 224p. 1995. pap. 11.00 (*0-8021-3360-6*); 1994. 21.00 o.p. (*0-8021-1552-7*) Grove/Atlantic, Inc. (Grove Pr.).

Parotti, Phillip. The Greek Generals Talk: Memoirs of the Trojan War Stories. 1986. (Illinois Short Fiction Ser.). 190p. 14.95 o.p. (*0-252-01304-2*) Univ. of Illinois Pr.

—The Trojan Generals Talk: Memoirs of the Greek War - Stories. 1988. (Illinois Short Fiction Ser.). 184p. 14.95 o.p. (*0-252-01510-X*) Univ. of Illinois Pr.

Pendleton, Don. Ring of Retaliation. 2002. (Executioner Ser.: No. 283). 224p. mass mkt. (*0-373-64283-0*, 1-64283-4, Worldwide Library) Harlequin Enterprises, Ltd.

Petrakis, Harry Mark. The Hour of the Bell. 1984. 384p. 19.95 o.p. (*0-385-04877-7*) Lake View Pr.

Petrou, Sophia. In the Shadow of the Green Line. l.t. ed. 2002. (Five Star First Edition Romance Ser.). 309p. 25.95 (*0-7862-4116-0*, Five Star) Gale Group.

Pressfield, Steven. Gates of Fire: An Epic Novel of the Battle of Thermopylae. 1999. 480p. mass mkt. 7.99 (*0-553-58053-1*) Bantam Bks.

—Gates of Fire: An Epic Novel of the Battle of Thermopylae. 1998. 400p. 29.95 (*0-385-49251-0*) Doubleday Publishing.

—Gates of Fire: An Epic Novel of the Battle of Thermopylae. abr. ed. 1999. audio 23.95 Highsmith Inc.

—Gates of Fire: An Epic Novel of the Battle of Thermopylae. unabr. ed. 1999. audio 93.00 (*0-7887-3771-6*, 95988E7) Recorded Bks., LLC.

—Last of the Amazons: A Novel. 2002. (Illus.). 416p. 24.95 (*0-385-50098-X*) Doubleday Publishing.

—Tides of War: A Novel of Alcibiades & the Peloponnesian War. 2001. 448p. reprint ed. pap. 13.95 (*0-553-38139-3*, Spectra) Bantam Bks.

—Tides of War: A Novel of Alcibiades & the Peloponnesian War. abr. ed. 2000. audio 25.95 (*0-553-52731-2*, RH Audio) Random Hse. Audio Publishing Group.

Preuss, Paul. Secret Passages. 1998. 352p. mass mkt. 6.99 o.p. (*0-8125-7148-7*); 1997. 384p. 24.95 (*0-312-86346-2*) Doherty, Tom Assocs., LLC. (Tor Bks.).

Prevelakis, Pandelis. The Cretan. Rick, Abbott & Mackridge, Peter, trs. from GRE. 1991. xvii, 480p. 35.00 (*0-932963-06-4*) Nostos Bks.

Price, Anthony. A New Kind of War. 1988. 272p. 17.95 (*0-89296-281-X*); pap. 4.95 o.p. (*0-445-40338-1*) Mysterious Pr.

Redmon, Anne. The Head of Dionysos. 1997. ix, 229p. (*1-85619-677-1*) Sinclair-Stevenson, Ltd. GBR. *Dist:* Trafalgar Square.

Renault, Mary. The Bull from the Sea. Date not set. 351p. 25.95 (*0-8488-2380-X*) Amereon, Ltd.

—The Bull from the Sea. l.t. ed. 1987. (Mainstream Ser.). 362p. reprint ed. 16.95 o.p. (*1-85089-123-0*) ISIS Large Print Bks. GBR. *Dist:* Transaction Pubs.

—The Bull from the Sea. 1975. (Illus.). 352p. mass mkt. 10.00 o.p. (*0-394-71504-7*, Vintage); 1962. 10.00 o.s.i (*0-394-41805-0*, Pantheon); 2nd ed. 2001. (Illus.). 352p. pap. 14.00 (*0-375-72680-2*, Vintage) Knopf Publishing Group.

—The Bull from the Sea. l.t. ed. 2000. 340p. 32.95 (*0-7658-0783-1*) Transaction Pubs.

—The Last of the Wine. (Illus.). 1975. 464p. mass mkt. 12.00 o.p. (*0-394-71653-1*); 2nd ed. 2001. 400p. pap. 14.00 (*0-375-72681-0*) Knopf Publishing Group. (Vintage).

—The Mask of Apollo: A Novel. 1988. 384p. pap. 14.00 (*0-394-75105-1*, Vintage) Knopf Publishing Group.

—The Persian Boy. 1984. mass mkt. 4.50 o.s.i (*0-553-24294-6*) Bantam Bks.

—The Persian Boy. 1988. 432p. pap. 14.00 (*0-394-75101-9*, Vintage) Knopf Publishing Group.

—The Praise Singer. 1988. 304p. pap. 6.95 o.s.i (*0-394-75102-7*, Vintage) Knopf Publishing Group.

Ross, David A. Xenos: A Romantic Novel of Travel & Self-Discovery in the Grecian Isles. 1998. 232p. pap. 12.95 (*0-9661861-1-7*) Escape Media.

Roth, Philip. Operation Shylock: A Confession. unabr. ed. 1993. audio 49.95 o.p. (*1-55800-795-4*, 112910) NewStar Media, Inc.

Saberhagen, Fred. God of the Golden Fleece. (Book of the Gods Ser.). 2003. 368p. mass mkt. 6.99 o.s.i (*0-8125-7002-2*); 2001. 378p. 24.95 (*0-312-87037-X*) Doherty, Tom Assocs., LLC. (Tor Bks.).

Sheldon, Sidney. The Other Side of Midnight. 1974. 21.95 o.p. (*0-688-00220-X*, Morrow, William & Co.) Morrow/Avon.

Somoza, Jose Carlos. The Athenian Murders. Soto, Sonia, tr. from SPA. 2002. 272p. 24.00 (*0-374-10677-0*) Farrar, Straus & Giroux.

Spanidou, Irini. Fear: A Novel. 2000. (International Ser.). 192p. pap. 15.00 (*0-679-73048-6*, Vintage) Knopf Publishing Group.

—God's Snake. 1998. 256p. pap. 13.00 (*0-375-70286-5*, Vintage) Knopf Publishing Group.

—God's Snake. 1986. 15.95 o.p. (*0-393-02320-6*) Norton, W. W. & Co., Inc.

—God's Snake. 1987. 256p. pap. 6.95 o.p. (*0-14-010360-0*, Penguin Bks.) Viking Penguin.

Spencer, Sharon. Dance of the Ariadnes. 1999. (Illus.). 14.95p. pap. 14.95 (*0-9652364-2-0*) Sky Blue Pr.

St. James, Ian. Vengeance. 1992. 79p. mass mkt. 5.99 o.p. (*0-06-109078-6*, HarperTorch) Morrow/Avon.

Stewart, Mary. The Moon-Spinners. unabr. ed. 1993. audio 69.95 (*0-7451-6307-6*, CAB 197) BBC Audiobooks America.

—The Moon-Spinners. 1989. pap. 3.95 o.p. (*0-449-44824-X*); 1984. mass mkt. 4.95 o.s.i (*0-449-20609-2*) Ballantine Bks. (Fawcett).

—The Moon-Spinners. l.t. ed. 1968. (Ulverscroft Large Print Ser.). 12.00 o.p. (*0-85456-708-9*, Ulverscroft) Thorpe, F. A. Pubs. GBR. *Dist:* Ulverscroft Large Print Bks., Ltd., Ulverscroft Large Print Canada, Ltd.

—This Rough Magic. 1987. mass mkt. 3.95 o.s.i (*0-449-21577-6*, Fawcett) Ballantine Bks.

Stratton, Eugene Aubrey. Fit for Fate: A Tale of Byzantine Intrigue in Modern Athens. 2003. pap. 17.95 (*0-595-28754-9*, iUniverse, Inc.) iUniverse, Inc.

Sundell, Thomas. A Bloodline of Kings Vol. 1: A Novel of Philip of Macedon. 2002. (Illus.). 496p. 28.50 (*0-9665871-8-9*) Crow Woods Publishing.

Thieblot, Robert J. Telemachus or the Memoirs of an Immortal God. 1997. 777p. 31.95 (*0-9659465-0-9*) Pozzi Pr. Corp.

Tillman, Lynne. Cast in Doubt. 1993. (Masks Ser.). 244p. reprint ed. pap. (*1-85242-340-4*) Serpent's Tail Ltd.

—Cast in Doubt. 1992. 20.00 o.p. (*0-671-78814-0*, Simon & Schuster) Simon & Schuster.

Turteltaub, H. N. Over the Wine-Dark Sea. 2001. E-Book 25.95 (*1-59061-136-5*) Adobe Systems, Inc.

—Over the Wine-Dark Sea. 2002. mass mkt. 6.99 (*0-7653-4451-3*, Tor Bks.) Doherty, Tom Assocs., LLC.

—The Sacred Land. 3rd ed. 2003. 384p. 25.95 (*0-7653-0037-0*, Tor Bks.) Doherty, Tom Assocs., LLC.

Unsworth, Barry. Pascali's Island. 1997. 192p. pap. 11.00 (*0-393-31721-8*) Norton, W. W. & Co., Inc.

—Pascali's Island. 1988. 192p. pap. 5.95 o.p. (*0-14-011537-4*, Penguin Bks.) Viking Penguin.

—The Songs of the Kings. 2003. (Illus.). 352p. 26.00 (*0-385-50114-5*, Talese, Nan A.) Doubleday Publishing.

Valencak, Hannelore. When Half-Gods Go. Crampton, Patricia, tr. from GER. 1976. 192p. (Orig.). (J). (gr. 7 up). 9.50 o.p. (*0-688-22077-0*, Morrow, William & Co.) Morrow/Avon.

Varlow, Andy. Just Another Man: A Story of the Nazi Massacre of Kalavryta. 1998. 25.00 (*1-883319-72-2*) Frog, Ltd.

Vasilikos, Vasilis. The Coroner's Assistant. Pappas, Peter, tr. from GRE. 1990. 188p. pap. text 10.00 (*0-918618-41-X*) Pella Publishing Co., Inc.

Wolfe, Gene. Soldier of Arete. 1989. 17.95 o.p. (*0-312-93185-9*, Tor Bks.) Doherty, Tom Assocs., LLC.

Woodhouse, Sarah. Other Lives. 1996. 21.95 o.p. (*0-312-15185-3*) St. Martin's Pr.

—Other Lives. l.t. ed. 1997. (Charnwood Large Print Ser.). 336p. 29.99 o.p. (*0-7089-8972-1*, Ulverscroft) Thorpe, F. A. Pubs. GBR. *Dist:* Ulverscroft Large Print Bks., Ltd., Ulverscroft Large Print Canada, Ltd.

Worby, Anne. High Hostage. l.t. ed. 1994. 19.95 o.p. (*0-7927-2026-1*); pap. 17.95 o.p. (*0-7927-2025-3*) BBC Audiobooks America.

Wright, Frances. A Few Days in Athens: Being the Translation of a Greek Manuscript Discovered in Herculaneum. 1972. (Romantic Tradition in American Literature Ser.). 218p. reprint ed. 20.95 (*0-405-04653-7*) Ayer Co. Pubs., Inc.

Yorke, Margaret. Grave Matters. 1983. pap. 2.50 (*0-553-22914-1*) Bantam Bks.

—Grave Matters. l.t. ed. 1975. (Ulverscroft Large Print Ser.). 29.99 o.p. (*0-85456-333-4*, Ulverscroft) Thorpe, F. A. Pubs. GBR. *Dist:* Ulverscroft Large Print Bks., Ltd., Ulverscroft Large Print Canada, Ltd.

## GREENLAND—FICTION

Bandy, Franklin. Athena. 1988. 320p. pap. 3.95 o.p. (*0-8125-8050-8*); 1987. 15.95 o.p. (*0-312-93018-6*) Doherty, Tom Assocs., LLC. (Tor Bks.).

Griesemer, John. No One Thinks of Greenland. 2002. 320p. pap. 14.00 (*0-312-28336-9*); 2001. 352p. 24.00 (*0-312-27457-2*) Picador.

Haugaard, Erik Christian. Leif the Unlucky, 001. 1982. (J). (gr. 7 up). 9.95 o.p. (*0-395-32156-5*) Houghton Mifflin Co.

MacLean, Alistair. Night Without End. reprint ed. lib. bdg. 21.95 (*0-89190-174-4*, Rivercity Pr.) Amereon, Ltd.

—Night Without End. 1984. mass mkt. 3.50 o.s.i (*0-449-20627-0*, Fawcett); 1981. mass mkt. 2.75 o.p. (*0-449-14129-2*, Fawcett); 1978. mass mkt. 1.75 o.s.i (*0-449-13710-4*) Ballantine Bks.

—Night Without End. 1960. 6.95 (*0-385-00546-6*) Doubleday Publishing.

—Night Without End. l.t. ed. 1969. (Ulverscroft Large Print Ser.). 12.50 o.p. (*0-85456-691-0*, Ulverscroft) Thorpe, F. A. Pubs. GBR. *Dist:* Ulverscroft Large Print Bks., Ltd., Ulverscroft Large Print Canada, Ltd.

Smiley, Jane. The Greenlanders. 608p. 1996. pap. 15.00 (*0-449-91089-X*, Fawcett); 1989. mass mkt. 6.99 o.s.i (*0-8041-0453-0*, Ivy Bks.) Ballantine Bks.

—The Greenlanders. 1989. 4.99 o.p. (*0-517-69939-7*) Random Hse. Value Publishing.

Spinka, Penina Keen. Dream Weaver. 2003. (Illus.). 464p. 26.95 (*0-525-94684-5*, Dutton) Dutton/Plume.

—Dream Weaver. 2004. 512p. mass mkt. 7.99 (*0-451-41111-0*, Onyx) NAL.

Vollmann, William T. The Ice-Shirt. 1993. (Seven Dreams Ser.: Vol. 1). 432p. pap. 15.00 (*0-14-013196-5*) Penguin Group (USA) Inc.

—The Ice-Shirt. 1993. 3.99 o.p. (*0-517-09877-6*) Random Hse. Value Publishing.

—The Ice-Shirt. 1990. (Seven Dreams Ser.). (Illus.). 432p. 19.95 o.p. (*0-670-83239-1*) Viking Penguin.

Woodman, Richard. The Corvette. 1996. (Illus.). 310p. mass mkt. o.s.i (*0-7515-1303-2*) Little Brown & Co.

## GREENWICH (CONN.)—FICTION

Fast, Howard. Greenwich. 2002. 240p. reprint ed. mass mkt. 6.99 (*0-515-13346-9*, Jove) Berkley Publishing Group.

—Greenwich. 2000. 304p. 25.00 o.s.i (*0-15-100620-2*) Harcourt Trade Pubs.

—Greenwich. l.t. ed. 2002. (General Ser.). 320p. pap. 24.95 (*0-7862-4229-9*) Thorndike Pr.

**GRENADA—FICTION**

Brand, Dionne. In Another Place, Not Here. 1997. 256p. 24.00 o.p. (*0-8021-1622-1*); 247p. 24.00 o.p. (*0-8021-1615-9*) Grove/Atlantic, Inc. (Grove Pr.).

Buffong, Jean. Snowflakes in the Sun. 1997. 180p. pap. 14.95 (*0-7043-4423-8*) Women's Pr., Ltd., The GBR. *Dist:* Trafalgar Square.

—Under the Silk Cotton Tree. 1993. (Emerging Voices Ser.). 144p. 22.95 (*1-56656-126-4*); pap. 9.95 (*1-56656-122-1*) Interlink Publishing Group, Inc.

Collins, Merle. Angel. 1988. 294p. reprint ed. pap. 9.95 o.p. (*0-931188-64-4*); 2nd ed. 1998. 304p. pap. 12.95 (*1-58005-014-X*) Avalon Publishing Group. (Seal Pr.).

**GREYSTONE BAY (IMAGINARY PLACE)—FICTION**

Grant, Charles L. In the Fog, Vol. 1. 1958. 20.95 o.p. (*0-312-09703-4*, Tor Bks.) Doherty, Tom Assocs., LLC.

Grant, Charles L., ed. Greystone Bay. 1985. 288p. (Orig.). mass mkt. 2.95 (*0-8125-1852-7*, Tor Bks.) Doherty, Tom Assocs., LLC.

—In the Fog. 1994. 300p. mass mkt. 4.99 (*0-8125-1874-8*); 1993. 304p. 20.95 o.p. (*0-312-85674-1*) Doherty, Tom Assocs., LLC. (Tor Bks.).

**GRYYLTH (IMAGINARY PLACE)—FICTION**

Baudino, Gael. Dragon Death. 1992. (Dragonsword Ser.: No. 3). 384p. (Orig.). mass mkt. 4.99 o.s.i (*0-451-45147-3*, ROC) NAL.

—Dragonsword. 1991. (Dragonsword Ser.: 1). 384p. (Orig.). mass mkt. 4.99 o.p. (*0-451-45081-7*, ROC) NAL.

—The Duel of Dragons. 1991. (Dragonsword Ser.: No. 2). 384p. (Orig.). mass mkt. 4.99 o.s.i (*0-451-45097-3*, ROC) NAL.

**GUATEMALA—FICTION**

Brazaitis, Mark. The River of Lost Voices: Stories from Guatemala. 1998. (Iowa Short Fiction Award Ser.). 202p. pap. 16.95 (*0-87745-642-9*) Univ. of Iowa Pr.

Graham, Norman. Death in Guatemala: A Novel. 2000. 336p. E-Book 8.00 (*0-7388-8669-6*) Xlibris Corp.

Graves, Richard L. Quicksilver. l.t. ed. 1990. pap. 17.95 o.p. (*0-7927-0393-6*, C0422); 12.95 o.p. (*0-7927-0392-8*, C0042) BBC Audiobooks America.

—Quicksilver. 1976. 224p. pap. 2.95 o.p. (*0-8128-7075-1*, Scarborough Hse.) Madison Bks., Inc.

Henley, Patricia. The Hummingbird House. 2000. pap. 13.00 (*1-878448-98-6*); 1999. 399p. 22.00 (*1-878448-87-0*) MacMurray & Beck, Inc.

Morales, Mario R. Face of the Earth, Heart of the Sky. Hood, Edward W., tr. from SPA. 2000. Tr. of Senores Bajo los Arboles. 128p. pap. 11.00 (*0-927534-88-6*) Bilingual Pr./Editorial Bilingue.

Reichs, Kathy. Grave Secrets. 2003. mass mkt. (*0-7434-5738-2*, Pocket Star); 2002. 336p. 25.00 o.s.i (*0-7432-4414-1*, Scribner); 2002. (Illus.). 336p. 25.00 (*0-684-85973-4*, Scribner); 2002. 624p. 25.00 (*0-7432-3364-6*, Scribner) Simon & Schuster.

—Grave Secrets. l.t. ed. 2002. (Core Collection). 516p. 32.95 (*0-7862-4664-2*) Thorndike Pr.

Rice, Anne. Merrick. 2001. 400p. reprint ed. mass mkt. 7.99 (*0-345-42240-6*, Ballantine Bks.) Ballantine Bks.

Schweidel, David. Confidence of the Heart. 1995. 224p. pap. 12.95 (*1-57131-004-5*) Milkweed Editions.

Seymour, Gerald. The Fighting Man. l.t. ed. 1994. 24.95 (*1-56895-151-5*, Wheeler Publishing, Inc.) Gale Group.

—The Fighting Man. 1994. 352p. 23.00 o.p. (*0-06-017770-5*) HarperTrade.

—The Fighting Man. 1995. 416p. mass mkt. 5.99 o.p. (*0-06-109257-6*, HarperTorch) Morrow/Avon.

Tobar, Hector. Tattooed Soldier: A Novel. 2000. 320p. 23.00 (*1-883285-15-1*) Delphinium Bks., Inc.

—Tattooed Soldier: A Novel. 2000. 320p. 12.95 (*0-14-028861-9*) Viking Penguin.

Unger, David. Life in the Damn Tropics: A Novel. 2002. (Library of Modern Jewish Literature). 308p. 34.95 (*0-8156-0737-7*) Syracuse Univ. Pr.

Wood, Philip. Xultun. 2000. 349p. pap. 23.95 (*0-9677983-0-2*) Sun & Shore Pubns.

**GUYANA—FICTION**

Harris, Wilson. The Eye of the Scarecrow. 1974. 108p. pap. o.p. (*0-571-10557-2*) Faber & Faber Ltd.

—The Guyana Quartet. 1985. 480p. o.p. (*0-571-13679-6*) Faber & Faber Ltd.

—The Guyana Quartet. 1985. 480p. pap. 16.95 o.p. (*0-571-13451-3*) Faber & Faber, Inc.

—Whole Armor & the Secret Ladder. 1973. 260p. pap. o.p. (*0-571-10231-X*) Faber & Faber Ltd.

Heath, Roy A. The Armstrong Trilogy: From the Heat of Day, One Generation, Genetha. 1994. 552p. (Orig.). pap. 15.00 (*0-89255-199-2*) Persea Bks., Inc.

—From the Heat of the Day. 1980. 160p. 9.95 o.p. (*0-8052-8003-0*, Schocken) Knopf Publishing Group.

—From the Heat of the Day: A Novel. 1992. 160p. 19.95 o.p. (*0-89255-175-5*) Persea Bks., Inc.

—Kwaku: Or, The Man Who Could Not Keep His Mouth Shut. 1997. 254p. pap. 14.95 (*0-7145-3023-9*) Boyars, Marion Pubs., Inc.

—The Ministry of Hope. 1996. 320p. 24.95 (*0-7145-3015-8*) Boyars, Marion Pubs., Inc.

—The Murderer. 190p. 1992. 19.95 o.p. (*0-89255-168-2*); 1986. (C). reprint ed. pap. text 9.95 (*0-89255-169-0*) Persea Bks., Inc.

—The Shadow Bride. 1995. 428p. 24.95 (*0-89255-213-1*) Persea Bks., Inc.

Kempadoo, Oonya. Buxton Spice. 2004. 176p. pap. 13.00 (*0-8070-8371-2*) Beacon Pr.

—Buxton Spice. 176p. 2000. pap. 11.95 o.s.i (*0-452-28099-0*); 1999. 21.95 o.p. (*0-525-94506-7*) Dutton/Plume.

Kempadoo, Peter Lauchmonen. Guyana Boy. 2nd ed. 2002. 190p. pap. 14.95 (*1-900715-56-2*) Peepal Tree Pr., Ltd. GBR. *Dist:* Independent Pubs. Group.

Knowles, Yereth K. The Town Is Aaron. 1989. 279p. (Orig.). pap. 10.00 (*0-916383-79-2*) Aegina Pr., Inc.

Mandiela. Guyana Betrayal. 1994. 466p. pap. (*0-920813-80-1*) Sister Vision Pr.

Monar, Rooplall. Backdam People. 1985. 96p. (Orig.). pap. 9.00 o.p. (*0-948833-00-9*, Three Continents) Rienner, Lynne Pubs., Inc.

Munroe, Andrew A. Caribbean Stories: Supernatural Tales of Guyana. 1994. 145p. (Orig.). pap. 9.95 (*0-9643010-0-8*) Golden Grove Publishing.

Nagamootoo, Moses. Hendree's Cure. 2001. 148p. pap. 14.95 (*1-900715-45-7*) Peepal Tree Pr., Ltd. GBR. *Dist:* Paul & Co. Pubs. Consortium, Inc.

Shinebourne, Jan Lo. The Last English Plantation. 2nd ed. 2002. 182p. pap. 13.95 (*1-900715-33-3*) Peepal Tree Pr., Ltd. GBR. *Dist:* Independent Pubs. Group, Paul & Co. Pubs. Consortium, Inc.

Wilson, Gar. Terror in Guyana. 1990. (Phoenix Force Ser.: No. 47). pap. (*0-373-61347-4*, Harlequin Bks.) Harlequin Enterprises, Ltd.

## H

**HAGERVILLE (MD.: IMAGINARY PLACE)—FICTION**

D'Amuk, Nanisi B. Outside In: A Cameron Andrews Mystery. 1996. 200p. (Orig.). pap. 10.95 (*0-934678-75-8*) New Victoria Pubs., Inc.

**HAITI—FICTION**

Bell, Madison Smartt. All Souls' Rising. 1995. 25.00 (*0-394-18350-9*); 530p. 25.95 o.s.i (*0-679-43989-7*) Knopf Publishing Group. (Pantheon).

—All Souls' Rising. 1996. 544p. pap. 15.00 (*0-14-025947-3*) Penguin Group (USA) Inc.

Buchmeyer, Dean & Gardner, Peter. A Touch of Voodoo. 2000. 316p. pap. 22.99 (*0-7388-2622-7*); text 32.99 (*0-7388-2621-9*) Xlibris Corp.

Carnes, Nat. Frozen Empire. Carnes, Nat, ed. 1998. 482p. E-Book 20.00 (*0-9650053-1-3*) News Center Pubns.

Cave, Hugh B. The Evil Returns. 2001. 368p. mass mkt. 5.99 (*0-8439-4893-0*, Leisure Bks.) Dorchester Publishing Co., Inc.

Danticat, Edwidge. Breath, Eyes, Memory. 1995. (Vintage Contemporaries Ser.). pap. 11.00 o.p. (*0-679-75661-2*); 2nd ed. 1998. (Breath, Eyes, Memory Ser.: Vol. 16). 256p. pap. 12.00 (*0-375-70504-X*) Knopf Publishing Group. (Vintage).

—Breath, Eyes, Memory. 1994. 230p. 20.00 o.p. (*1-56947-005-7*) Soho Pr., Inc.

—Breath, Eyes, Memory. l.t. ed. (Paperback Bestsellers Ser.). 301p. 1999. pap. 26.95 (*0-7862-1655-7*); 1998. 29.95 (*0-7862-1654-9*) Thorndike Pr.

—The Dew Breaker. 2004. 256p. 22.00 (*1-4000-4114-7*) Knopf Publishing Group.

—The Farming of Bones. 1999. 320p. pap. 14.00 (*0-14-028049-9*, Penguin Bks.) Penguin Group (USA) Inc.

—The Farming of Bones. 1998. 312p. 23.00 (*1-56947-126-6*) Soho Pr., Inc.

—The Farming of Bones. l.t. ed. 1999. (Basic Ser.). 416p. 29.95 (*0-7862-1732-4*) Thorndike Pr.

Danticat, Edwidge, et al. Breath, Eyes, Memory. 2nd ed. 1994. (Breath, Eyes, Memory Ser.: Vol. 16). 230p. 20.00 (*1-56947-142-8*) Soho Pr., Inc.

Depestre, Rene. The Festival of the Greasy Pole. Arnold, A. J. & Dranne, K., eds. Coates, Carrol F., tr. from FRE. & intro. by. 1990. (CARAF Bks.). 142p. text 30.00 (*0-8139-1281-4*); pap. text 15.50 o.p. (*0-8139-1282-2*) Univ. Pr. of Virginia.

Dold, Gaylord. Samedi's Backpack: Mitch Robert's Mystery. 2001. 313p. 23.95 (*0-312-26643-X*, Saint Martin's Minotaur) St. Martin's Pr.

Easterman, Daniel. Night of the Seventh Darkness: A Novel. 1991. 480p. 23.00 o.p. (*0-06-017928-7*) HarperTrade.

Guy, Rosa. The Sun, the Sea, a Touch of the Wind. 1995. 320p. 22.95 o.p. (*0-525-24780-7*, Dutton) Dutton/Plume.

Henty, G. A. A Roving Commission: Through the Black Insurrection of Haiti. 2000. 252p. pap. 9.95 (*0-594-03470-1*); E-Book 3.95 (*0-594-03473-6*) 1873 Pr.

—A Roving Commission: Through the Black Insurrection of Haiti. 2002. 408p. 29.95 (*1-59087-013-1*, GAH013); per. 19.95 (*1-59087-012-3*, GAH012) Althouse Pr.

—A Roving Commission: Through the Black Insurrection of Haiti. collector's ed. 2002. (Illus.). im. lthr. 38.85 (*1-4115-1364-9*); pap. 19.95 (*1-4115-0616-2*); 25.95 (*1-4115-0896-3*); pap. 17.95 (*1-4115-0130-6*) Polyglot Pr., Inc.

Lambdin, Dewey. Sea of Grey. (Alan Lewrie Navel Adventures Ser.). 2003. 400p. pap. 14.95 (*0-312-32016-7*, Saint Martin's Griffin); 2002. (Illus.). 416p. 25.95 (*0-312-28685-6*) St. Martin's Pr.

—Sea of Grey. 2002. (Alan Lewrie Naval Adventure Ser.: Bk. 10). 29.95 (*0-7862-4891-2*) Thorndike Pr.

Montero, Mayra. In the Palm of Darkness. Grossman, Edith, tr. from SPA. 1997. 181p. 21.00 o.p. (*0-06-018703-4*) HarperCollins Pubs.

Orem, William. Zombi, You My Love. 1999. 225p. pap. 12.00 (*0-9644348-2-2*) La Questa Pr.

Williams, Karen L. Painted Dreams. 1998. (Illus.). 40p. (J). (gr. k-3). 16.99 (*0-688-13901-9*) HarperCollins Children's Bk. Group.

—Painted Dreams. 1998. (Illus.). 40p. (J). (gr. k-3). 15.89 (*0-688-13902-7*, Morrow, William & Co.) Morrow/Avon.

**HALRUAA (IMAGINARY PLACE)—FICTION**

Cunningham, Elaine. The Magehound. 2000. (Forgotten Realms Ser.: Bk I). (Illus.). 312p. mass mkt. 5.99 (*0-7869-1561-7*) Wizards of the Coast.

Meyers, Richard S. Murder in Halruaa. 1996. (Forgotten Realms Ser.). 280p. 18.99 (*0-7869-0521-2*, 8657) Wizards of the Coast.

**HAMPSTEAD (KAN.: IMAGINARY PLACE)—FICTION**

Weir, Charlene. Consider the Crows. 1995. (WWL Mystery Ser.). 251p. per. (*0-373-26172-1*, 1-26172-6, Harlequin Bks.) Harlequin Enterprises, Ltd.

—Consider the Crows. 1993. 272p. 19.95 o.p. (*0-312-09772-7*, Saint Martin's Minotaur) St. Martin's Pr.

—Family Practice. 1997. (Susan Wren Mystery Ser.). 301p. per. (*0-373-26236-1*, 0-26236-0, Worldwide Library) Harlequin Enterprises, Ltd.

—Family Practice. 1995. 320p. 22.95 (*0-312-13492-4*, Saint Martin's Minotaur) St. Martin's Pr.

—Murder Take Two. pap. 15.95 (*0-312-29193-0*, Saint Martin's Griffin); pap. 16.95 o.p. (*0-312-30029-8*, Saint Martin's Griffin); 1998. 336p. 23.95 (*0-312-18136-1*, Saint Martin's Minotaur) St. Martin's Pr.

—The Winter Widow. 1993. per. (*0-373-26128-4*, 1-26128-8, Harlequin Bks.) Harlequin Enterprises, Ltd.

—The Winter Widow. 1992. 256p. 18.95 o.p. (*0-312-07009-8*, Saint Martin's Minotaur) St. Martin's Pr.

**HARDLUCK (ALASKA: IMAGINARY PLACE)—FICTION**

Macomber, Debbie. Because of the Baby. 1996. (Harlequin Romance Ser.). 185p. per. (*0-373-03395-8*, 1-03395-0, Harlequin Bks.) Harlequin Enterprises, Ltd.

—Because of the Baby. l.t. ed. 1997. (Harlequin Romance Ser.). 20.95 (*0-263-15007-0*) Harlequin Mills & Boon, Ltd. GBR. *Dist:* Ulverscroft Large Print Bks., Ltd.

—Brides for Brothers. 1995. 187p. per. (*0-373-03379-6*, 1-03379-4, Harlequin Bks.) Harlequin Enterprises, Ltd.

—Brides for Brothers. l.t. ed. 1997. 20.95 o.s.i (*0-263-14919-6*) Harlequin Mills & Boon, Ltd. GBR. *Dist:* Ulverscroft Large Print Bks., Ltd.

—Daddy's Little Helper. 1995. 185p. per. (*0-373-03387-7*, 1-03387-7, Harlequin Bks.) Harlequin Enterprises, Ltd.

—Ending in Marriage. 1996. (Harlequin Romance Ser.). 186p. per. (*0-373-03403-2*, 1-03403-2, Harlequin Bks.) Harlequin Enterprises, Ltd.

—Falling for Him (Midnight Sons) 1996. (Harlequin Romance Ser.). 184p. per. (*0-373-03399-0*, 1-03399-2, Harlequin Bks.) Harlequin Enterprises, Ltd.

—Falling for Him (Midnight Sons) l.t. ed. 1997. (Harlequin Romance Ser.). 20.95 o.s.i (*0-263-15044-5*) Harlequin Mills & Boon, Ltd. GBR. *Dist:* Ulverscroft Large Print Bks., Ltd.

—Family Men: Daddy's Little Helper & Because of the Baby, 2 bks. in 1. 2000. (Harlequin Midnight Sons Ser.). 384p. mass mkt. (*0-373-83435-7*, 1-83435-7, Harlequin Bks.) Harlequin Enterprises, Ltd.

—Mail-Order Marriages. 2000. (Harlequin Midnight Sons Ser.: Vol. 1). 384p. mass mkt. (*0-373-83434-9*, Harlequin Bks.) Harlequin Enterprises, Ltd.

—The Marriage Risk. 1995. (Harlequin Romance Ser.: Vol. 3383). 189p. per. (*0-373-03383-4*, Harlequin Bks.) Harlequin Enterprises, Ltd.

Macomber, Debbie & Wisdom, Linda Randall. The Last Two Bachelors. 2000. (Harlequin Midnight Sons Ser.: Vol. 3). 384p. mass mkt. (*0-373-83436-5*, 1-83436-5, Harlequin Bks.) Harlequin Enterprises, Ltd.

**HARPER'S HALL (IMAGINARY PLACE)—FICTION**

McCaffrey, Anne. Dragondrums. 1997. (Harper Hall Trilogy Ser.: Vol. 3). 208p. mass mkt. 7.50 o.s.i (*0-553-25855-9*, Spectra) Bantam Bks.

—Dragondrums. 1993. (Dragon Ser.: Vol. 3). audio 44.20 (*1-56544-041-2*, 550012); audio Literate Ear, Inc.

—Dragondrums. 1993. (Super Sound Buy, Dove Ser.). 8.99 o.p. (*0-7871-0067-6*) Penguin Group (USA) Inc.

—Dragondrums, unabr. ed. 1992. (YA). (gr. 7). audio 53.00 (*1-55690-618-8*, 92311E7) Recorded Bks., LLC.

—Dragondrums. (Illus.). 256p. 2003. (J). pap. 5.99 (*0-689-86006-4*, Aladdin); 2003. (YA). mass mkt. 6.99 (*0-689-86025-0*, Simon Pulse); 1979. (YA). (gr. 6 up). lib. bdg. 16.95 o.s.i (*0-689-30685-7*, Atheneum) Simon & Schuster Children's Publishing.

—Dragondrums. l.t. ed. 1999. (Science Fiction Ser.). 304p. 24.95 o.p. (*0-7838-8506-7*) Thorndike Pr.

—Dragondrums. 1980. (Harper Hall Trilogy Ser.). (J). 13.04 (*0-606-01413-6*) Turtleback Bks.

—Dragonsinger. 1997. (Harper Hall Trilogy Ser.: Vol. 2). 256p. mass mkt. 7.50 o.s.i (*0-553-25854-0*, Spectra) Bantam Bks.

—Dragonsinger. 1994. (Super Sound Buy, Dove Ser.). 8.99 o.p. (*0-7871-0080-3*) Penguin Group (USA) Inc.

—Dragonsinger, unabr. ed. 1992. (Harper Hall Trilogy: Vol. 2). (YA). (gr. 7 up). audio 60.00 (*1-55690-617-X*, 92310) Recorded Bks., LLC.

—Dragonsinger. 2003. (Illus.). 288p. (J). pap. 5.99 (*0-689-86007-2*, Aladdin); 2003. (Illus.). 288p. (YA). mass mkt. 6.99 (*0-689-86024-2*, Simon Pulse); 1977. (Dragon Singer Ser.: Vol. 1). 276p. (J). 18.00 (*0-689-30570-2*, Atheneum) Simon & Schuster Children's Publishing.

—Dragonsinger. l.t. ed. 1999. (Science Fiction Ser.). 347p. 24.95 (*0-7838-8499-0*) Thorndike Pr.

—Dragonsinger. 1977. (Harper Hall Trilogy Ser.). (J). 13.04 (*0-606-01501-9*) Turtleback Bks.

—Dragonsong. 1994. mass mkt. 6.99 (*0-553-54176-5*); 1986. 192p. pap. 3.50 o.s.i (*0-553-23460-9*, Spectra); 1977. (Harper Hall Trilogy Ser.: Vol. 1). 192p. mass mkt. 7.50 o.s.i (*0-553-25852-4*, Bantam Classics) Bantam Bks.

—Dragonsong. 1993. (Dragon Ser.: Vol. 1). audio 41.00 (*1-56544-029-3*, 550010); audio Literate Ear, Inc.

—Dragonsong, Set. abr. ed. 1994. (Super Sound Buy, Dove Ser.). audio 8.99 o.p. (*0-7871-0075-7*, Dove Audio) NewStar Media, Inc.

—Dragonsong, unabr. ed. 1992. (Harper Hall Trilogy: Vol. 1). (YA). (gr. 7). audio 46.00 (*1-55690-588-2*, 92125E7) Recorded Bks., LLC.

—Dragonsong. (Illus.). 2003. 208p. (J). pap. 5.99 (*0-689-86008-0*, Aladdin); 2003. 208p. (YA). mass mkt. 6.99 (*0-689-86023-4*, Simon Pulse); 1976. 224p. (gr. 5-9). text 16.95 o.s.i (*0-689-30507-9*, Atheneum) Simon & Schuster Children's Publishing.

—Dragonsong. l.t. ed. 1998. (Science Fiction Ser.). 255p. 24.95 (*0-7838-8422-2*) Thorndike Pr.

—Dragonsong. 1977. (Harper Hall Trilogy Ser.). 13.04 (*0-606-01138-2*) Turtleback Bks.

—Dragonsong & Dragonsinger. abr. ed. 1993. 22.95 o.p. (*1-55800-638-9*) NewStar Media, Inc.

**HATTERAS, CAPE (N.C.)—FICTION**

Poyer, David. Hatteras Blue: A Tiller Gallaway Underwater Thriller. 1992. 288p. mass mkt. 5.99 (*0-312-92749-5*, St. Martin's Paperbacks); 1989. 16.95 o.p. (*0-312-02926-8*) St. Martin's Pr.

**HAVANA (CUBA)—FICTION**

Bernardo, Raul Jose. The Wise Women of Havana. 2003. 336p. pap. 13.95 (*0-06-093615-0*, Rayo) HarperTrade.

Buckley, William F., Jr. Mongoose R. I. P. A Blackford Oakes Novel. 1998. (Blackford Oakes Novel Ser.). 376p. reprint ed. pap. 12.95 (*1-888952-72-5*) Cumberland Hse. Publishing.

—Mongoose R. I. P. A Blackford Oakes Novel. 1989. 384p. reprint ed. mass mkt. 4.50 o.s.i (*0-440-20231-0*) Dell Publishing.

—Mongoose R. I. P. A Blackford Oakes Novel. 1993. 4.99 o.p. (*0-517-10701-5*) Random Hse. Value Publishing.

Chavarria, Daniel. Adios Muchachos. Lopez, Carlos, tr. from SPA. 2001. 245p. (Orig.). pap. 13.95 (*1-888451-16-5*) Akashic Bks.

Greene, Graham. Our Man in Havana. l.t. ed. 2002. (Perennial Bestseller Ser.). 320p. 28.95 (*0-7838-9757-X*) Gale Group.

Gutierrez, Pedro Juan. Dirty Havana Trilogy. Wimmer, Natasha, tr. from SPA. 2001. 392p. 25.00 o.p. (*0-374-14016-2*) Farrar, Straus & Giroux.

—Dirty Havana Trilogy: A Novel in Stories. Wimmer, Natasha, tr. from SPA. 2002. 400p. pap. 13.95 (*0-06-000689-7*, Ecco) HarperTrade.

Iyer, Pico. Cuba & the Night. unabr. collector's ed. 1995. audio 48.00 (*0-7366-3169-0*, 3839) Books on Tape, Inc.

—Cuba & the Night. 1996. 256p. pap. 13.00 (*0-679-76075-X*, Vintage) Knopf Publishing Group.

Sanchez, Thomas. King Bongo: A Novel of Havana. 2004. 320p. pap. 13.95 (*0-679-73746-4*, Vintage) Knopf Publishing Group.

—King Bongo: A Novel of Havana. 2003. 320p. 25.00 (*0-679-40696-4*) Random Hse., Inc.

Standiford, Les. Havana Run. 2004. 288p. mass mkt. 7.99 (*0-425-19717-4*) Berkley Publishing Group.

—Havana Run. l.t. ed. 2003. (John Deal Novel Ser.). 422p. 29.95 (*0-7862-5565-X*) Thorndike Pr.

—The Havana Run: A John Deal Novel. 2003. 320p. 24.95 (*0-399-15059-5*, Putnam & Grosset) Putnam Publishing Group, The.

Truman, Margaret. Murder in Havana. 2001. E-Book 19.95 (*1-59061-170-5*) Adobe Systems, Inc.

—Murder in Havana. l.t. ed. 2002. 617p. 31.95 (*0-7862-3849-6*) Gale Group.

—Murder in Havana. 2002. 384p. mass mkt. 7.50 (*0-449-00668-9*, Laurel Leaf) Random Hse. Children's Bks.

—Murder in Havana. 2001. E-Book 19.95 (*1-58836-019-9*) Random Hse., Inc.

White, Randy Wayne. North of Havana. 1998. 272p. mass mkt. 6.99 (*0-425-16294-X*, Prime Crime) Berkley Publishing Group.

—North of Havana. 1997. 256p. 22.95 o.p. (*0-399-14242-8*, G. P. Putnam's Sons) Penguin Group (USA) Inc.

**HAVEN (IMAGINARY PLACE: GREEN)—FICTION**

Green, Simon R. Bones of Haven. 1992. (Hawk & Fisher Ser.: 6). mass mkt. 3.99 o.s.i (*0-441-31837-1*) Ace Bks.

—God Killer. 1991. (Hawk & Fisher Ser.: 3). mass mkt. 3.95 o.s.i (*0-441-29460-X*) Ace Bks.

—Guard Against Dishonor. 1991. (Hawk & Fisher Ser.: 5). mass mkt. 3.99 o.s.i (*0-441-31836-3*) Ace Bks.

—Guards of Haven: The Adventures of Hawk & Fisher, Bk. 2. 1999. 576p. reprint ed. mass mkt. 7.99 (*0-451-45755-2*, ROC) NAL.

—Hawk & Fisher. 1990. (Hawk & Fisher Ser.: 1). mass mkt. 4.50 o.s.i (*0-441-58417-9*) Ace Bks.

—Swords of Haven. 1999. (Hawk & Fisher Omnibus Ser.: No. 1). 512p. reprint ed. mass mkt. 7.99 (*0-451-45750-1*, ROC) NAL.

—Winner Takes All. 1991. (Hawk & Fisher Ser.: 2). mass mkt. 3.95 o.s.i (*0-441-14291-5*) Ace Bks.

—Wolf in the Fold. 1991. (Hawk & Fisher Ser.: 4). mass mkt. 3.95 o.s.i (*0-441-31835-5*) Ace Bks.

**HAVEN (ME.: IMAGINARY PLACE)—FICTION**

King, Stephen. The Tommyknockers. 752p. 1993. mass mkt. 6.99 o.p. (*0-451-17842-4*, Signet Bks.); 1988. reprint ed. mass mkt. 7.99 (*0-451-15660-9*) NAL.

—The Tommyknockers. 19.95 (*0-399-13699-1*) Penguin Group (USA) Inc.

—The Tommyknockers. 1987. 544p. 19.95 o.p. (*0-399-13314-3*, G. P. Putnam's Sons) Penguin Putnam Bks. for Young Readers.

—The Tommyknockers. 2nd ed. 1999. (Nevedomoe, Neobiasnimoe, Neveroitnoe Ser.: Vol. 102). (SPA., Illus.). 968p. (*84-01-47465-5*) Plaza & Janés Editories, S.A.

—The Tommyknockers. 1992. (SPA.). 704p. 15.50 (*84-01-49998-4*) Plaza & Janés Editories, S.A. ESP. *Dist:* Distribooks, Inc.

—The Tommyknockers. 1987. 14.04 (*0-606-04113-3*) Turtleback Bks.

**HAWAII—FICTION**

Adair, Dick. Aloha Bear & the Meaning of Aloha. 1987. (Illus.). 24p. (J). (ps). 10.95 (*0-89610-077-4*) Island Heritage Publishing.

Adams, David. Of Angels & Vipers: A Hawaiian Mystery. 2000. 296p. E-Book 8.00 (*0-7388-8410-3*) Xlibris Corp.

Adrienne, Dawn. The Hawaiian Christmas Tree. 1999. (Illus.). 31p. (J). (gr. 2-5). 14.95 (*0-9667484-1-7*) Tamarind.

Allen, Steve. Murder in Hawaii. 2000. 352p. mass mkt. 5.99 o.s.i (*1-57566-529-8*); 1999. (Illus.). 320p. 22.00 o.s.i (*1-57566-375-9*) Kensington Publishing Corp.

Ambrose, David. Song of the Exile. unabr. ed. 1999. audio 93.00 (*0-7887-3772-4*, 95989E7) Recorded Bks., LLC.

Ball, Pamela. The Floating City. 2002. 272p. 23.95 (*0-670-89472-9*, Viking) Viking Penguin.

—The Floating City: A Novel of 19th Century Hawaii. 2003. 272p. pap. 14.00 (*0-14-200187-2*) Viking Penguin.

—Lava. 1998. 192p. pap. 12.00 o.p. (*0-8050-5776-5*, Owl Bks.) Holt, Henry & Co.

—Lava: A Novel. 1997. 192p. 21.00 (*0-393-04024-0*) Norton, W. W. & Co., Inc.

Barclay, Robert. Melal: A Novel of the Pacific. 2002. (Illus.). viii, 300p. (C). pap. 14.95 (*0-8248-2591-8*) Univ. of Hawaii Pr.

Barry, Maxine. Dark Desire. 1998. 388p. text 19.95 (*1-85487-547-7*); 400p. mass mkt. 3.99 (*1-85487-566-3*) Scarlet Bks. GBR. *Dist:* London Bridge.

Beechcroft, William. Pursuit of Fear. 1990. 17.95 o.p. (*0-88184-510-8*, Carroll & Graf Pubs.) Avalon Publishing Group.

—Pursuit of Fear. l.t. ed. 1991. 17.95 o.p. (*0-7451-8094-9*, AH0155); pap. 15.95 o.p. (*0-7927-0600-5*, AS0191) BBC Audiobooks America.

Biggers, Earl Derr. Behind that Curtain. 1987. 240p. reprint ed. mass mkt. 3.95 o.s.i (*0-445-40214-8*, Mysterious Pr. Paperback Bks.) Warner Bks., Inc.

—The Black Camel. Date not set. 224p. 21.95 (*0-8488-2211-0*) Amereon, Ltd.

—The Black Camel. 1978. reprint ed. lib. bdg. 27.95 (*0-89966-077-0*) Buccaneer Bks., Inc.

—The Black Camel. 1987. 224p. reprint ed. mass mkt. 3.95 o.s.i (*0-445-40215-6*, Mysterious Pr. Paperback Bks.) Warner Bks., Inc.

—Charlie Chan Carries On. 1976. (Charlie Chan Mysteries Ser.). reprint ed. lib. bdg. 23.95 o.p. (*0-89966-073-8*) Buccaneer Bks., Inc.

—Charlie Chan Carries On. 1987. 224p. mass mkt. 3.95 o.s.i (*0-445-40221-0*, Mysterious Pr. Paperback Bks.) Warner Bks., Inc.

—The Chinese Parrot. 1990. mass mkt. 3.95 o.p. (*0-445-40212-1*); 1987. 224p. reprint ed. mass mkt. 3.95 o.s.i (*0-445-40211-3*, Mysterious Pr. Paperback Bks.) Warner Bks., Inc.

—The House Without a Key. Date not set. lib. bdg. 24.95 (*0-8488-1956-X*) Amereon, Ltd.

—The House Without a Key. 1979. reprint ed. lib. bdg. 35.95 (*0-89966-081-9*) Buccaneer Bks., Inc.

—The House Without a Key. 2003. 316p. pap. 14.95 (*1-891936-65-4*, D'Asia Vu Reprint Library) EastBridge.

—The House Without a Key. 1994. 316p. 35.00 (*1-883402-23-9*, Scribner) Simon & Schuster.

—The House Without a Key. 1986. 240p. mass mkt. 3.95 o.s.i (*0-445-40219-9*, Mysterious Pr. Paperback Bks.) Warner Bks., Inc.

—Keeper of the Keys. 1988. 224p. mass mkt. 3.95 o.s.i (*0-445-40217-2*, Mysterious Pr. Paperback Bks.) Warner Bks., Inc.

Brennert, Alan. Moloka'i. 2003. (Illus.). 384p. 24.95 (*0-312-30434-X*) St. Martin's Pr.

Bridgman, C. A. My Hawaiian Smile. (J). 14.95 (*0-681-32826-6*) Booklines Hawaii, Ltd.

Brown, Mark. Game Face. 1992. (Ben McMillen Hawaiian Mystery Ser.). 302p. 19.95 (*0-918024-92-7*) Ox Bow Pr.

—The Puna Kahuna: A Ben McMillen Hawaiian Mystery. 1993. 19.95 (*1-881987-02-7*) Ox Bow Pr.

—Yellowfin. 1992. (Ben McMillen Hawaiian Mystery Ser.). 256p. 19.95 (*0-918024-93-5*) Ox Bow Pr.

Buck, John L. The Kahoolawe Project. 2000. viii, 284p. (*1-887471-11-1*); (*1-887471-12-X*) Dr. Leisure.

—No Crime Committed: Hawaiian Romance Novel. 2002. (*1-887471-17-0*) Dr. Leisure.

Burrows, Geraldine. Stranger in Paradise. 2003. 198p. 26.95 (*1-59414-025-1*, Five Star) Gale Group.

Bushnell, O. A. The Stone of Kannon. 1979. 448p. 12.95 o.p. (*0-8248-0663-8*) Univ. of Hawaii Pr.

—The Water of Kane. 1980. 472p. 12.95 o.p. (*0-8248-0714-6*) Univ. of Hawaii Pr.

Christensen, Mark. Aloha. 1994. 21.00 (*0-671-87023-8*, Simon & Schuster) Simon & Schuster.

Chun, Pam. The Money Dragon. 352p. 2003. pap. 14.00 (*1-57071-867-9*); 2002. (Illus.). 24.00 (*1-57071-866-0*) Sourcebooks, Inc. (Sourcebooks Landmark).

Coffman, Virginia. The House at Sandalwood. 1977. mass mkt. 1.75 o.s.i (*0-449-23155-0*, Fawcett) Ballantine Bks.

—The House at Sandalwood. l.t. ed. 2001. 240p. 28.95 o.p. (*0-7838-9422-8*, Macmillan Reference USA) Gale Group.

—The House at Sandalwood. 1974. 7.95 o.p. (*0-87795-075-X*, Morrow, William & Co.) Morrow/Avon.

—Pacific Cavalcade. 1982. 560p. mass mkt. 3.50 o.s.i (*0-449-20002-7*, Fawcett) Ballantine Bks.

—Pacific Cavalcade. l.t. ed. 2001. 728p. (*0-7540-1584-X*, Macmillan Reference USA) Gale Group.

—Pacific Cavalcade. 1981. 12.95 o.p. (*0-87795-277-9*, Morrow, William & Co.) Morrow/Avon.

—Pacific Cavalcade. l.t. ed. 2001. (G. K. Hall Core Ser.). 728p. 29.95 (*0-7838-9397-3*) Thorndike Pr.

Collins, Max Allan. Pearl Harbor Murders. 2001. 272p. mass mkt. 6.99 o.s.i (*0-425-17943-5*, Prime Crime) Berkley Publishing Group.

Colvin, D. A. Hawaiian Eyes: The Quest for True Health. 2000. 200p. pap. 21.99 (*0-7388-2394-5*) Xlibris Corp.

Converse, Jane. Surf Safari Nurse. l.t. ed. 2002. 185p. pap. 23.95 (*0-7862-4626-X*) Thorndike Pr.

Corum, Ann K. Aunty Pua's Dilemma. 1994. (Illus.). 32p. 7.95 (*1-56647-086-2*) Mutual Publishing LLC.

Courtney, Dayle. Escape from Eden. 1981. (Thorne Twins Adventure Bks.). (Illus.). 192p. (Orig.). (J). (gr. 5 up). pap. 2.98 o.p. (*0-87239-467-0*, 2712) Standard Publishing.

Craig, Mary S. Dark Paradise. 1986. 384p. (Orig.). mass mkt. 4.50 o.s.i (*0-446-32205-9*) Warner Bks., Inc.

Crouch, Howard E. Damien & Dutton, Two Josephs on Molokai. 1998. 336p. 18.00 (*0-9606330-4-9*) Damien-Dutton Society for Leprosy Aid, Inc.

Crouch, Howard E. & Augustine, Mary. After Damien - Dutton: Yankee Soldier at Molokai. 1981. (Illus.). 144p. pap. 5.95 (*0-9606330-0-6*) Damien-Dutton Society for Leprosy Aid, Inc.

Dave, Robert. Run to the Sun. 2001. 256p. pap. 16.95 (*1-882897-59-5*) Lost Coast Pr.

Davenport, Kiana. Shark Dialogues. Goerner, Lee, ed. 1994. 512p. 22.00 (*0-689-12191-1*) Central Bureau voor Schimmelcultures NLD. *Dist:* Lubrecht & Cramer, Ltd.

—Shark Dialogues. 1995. 512p. pap. 15.00 (*0-452-27458-3*, Plume) Dutton/Plume.

—Song of the Exile. 2000. 384p. pap. 14.95 (*0-345-43494-3*) Ballantine Bks.

—Song of the Exile. abr. ed. 1999. audio 25.00 (*0-7871-1994-6*, Dove Audio) NewStar Media, Inc.

Davids, Hollace & Davids, Paul. The Fires of Pele: Mark Twain's Legendary Lost Journal. 1986. (Illus.). 56p. (Orig.). (YA). pap. 9.95 (*0-939031-00-0*) Pictorial Legends.

Davis, Gloria. In December. 2003. (*0-936389-93-1*) Tudor Pubs., Inc.

Dean, Nicola & Dean, Cloisjean N. Fever: A Novel Set in Hana, Maui. 1998. 179p. pap. 12.95 (*0-9662021-0-4*) Puuiki Pr.

Deford, Frank. Love & Infamy. 1995. 576p. mass mkt. 5.99 (*0-8217-0122-3*, Zebra Bks.); mass mkt. 5.99 o.s.i (*0-7860-0122-4*, Pinnacle Bks.) Kensington Publishing Corp.

—Love & Infamy. 1993. 576p. 24.00 o.p. (*0-670-82995-1*) Viking Penguin.

Du Brul, Jack. Vulcan's Forge. unabr. ed. 1998. audio 56.95 (*0-7861-1314-6*, 106031) Blackstone Audio Bks., Inc.

—Vulcan's Forge. abr. ed. 1998. audio 7.99 o.s.i (*1-56740-281-X*, 1691, Paperback Nova Audio Bks.); audio 17.95 o.p. (*1-56740-772-2*, 515, Nova Audio Bks.); audio 26.95 (*1-56100-798-6*, 312, Bookcassette); audio 73.25 (*1-56740-577-0*, 1091, Unabridged Library Editions) Brilliance Audio.

—Vulcan's Forge. 1999. 378p. mass mkt. 6.99 (*0-8125-6461-8*); 1998. 352p. 24.95 (*0-312-86481-7*) Doherty, Tom Assocs., LLC. (Forge Bks.).

Dukore, Margaret M. Bloom: A Novel. 1985. 304p. 17.95 o.p. (*0-531-09708-0*, Watts, Franklin) Scholastic Library Publishing.

Eberhardt, Michael C. Against the Law. 1995. 320p. 21.95 o.p. (*0-525-93994-6*) Dutton/Plume.

—Against the Law. unabr. ed. 1998. audio 103.95 (*1-85903-122-6*) Magna Story Sound GBR. *Dist:* Ulverscroft Large Print Bks., Ltd.

—Against the Law. 1996. 432p. mass mkt. 6.99 o.s.i (*0-451-18549-8*) NAL.

—Against the Law. 316p. pap. 3.98 o.p. (*0-7651-0600-0*) Smithmark Pubs., Inc.

—Against the Law. l.t. ed. 1997. (Niagara Large Print Ser.). 454p. 29.50 o.p. (*0-7089-5834-6*, Ulverscroft) Thorpe, F. A. Pubs. GBR. *Dist:* Ulverscroft Large Print Bks., Ltd., Ulverscroft Large Print Canada, Ltd.

Eisemann, Henry. Hump-Free Heads for Hawaii. 1989. (Illus.). 24p. (Orig.). (J). (gr. k-6). pap. 8.95 o.p. (*0-938129-02-3*) Emprise Pubns.

Flora, Kate. Death in Paradise. 2000. (Thea Kozak Mystery Ser.). 352p. mass mkt. 6.99 (*0-8125-7157-6*, Tor Bks.); 24.95 (*0-312-86398-5*, Forge Bks.) Doherty, Tom Assocs., LLC.

Francis, Dorothy Brenner. Murder in Hawaii. l.t. ed. 2002. (Romance Ser.). 246p. 27.95 (*0-7862-4530-1*) Thorndike Pr.

Friedman, Kinky. Steppin' on a Rainbow. 2001. 208p. 23.00 (*0-684-86487-8*, Simon & Schuster); 2002. 288p. reprint ed. mass mkt. 6.99 (*0-671-04744-2*, Pocket) Simon & Schuster.

Fuentes, Erica. Hearts Ahoy. 2002. 256p. mass mkt. 4.99 o.s.i (*0-7860-1182-3*) Kensington Publishing Corp.

—Window to Paradise. 2001. 256p. mass mkt. 4.99 o.s.i (*0-7860-1181-5*, Encanto) Kensington Publishing Corp.

Gerritsen, Tess. Under the Knife. 2000. 256p. mass mkt. (*1-55166-611-1*, 1-66611-4, Mira Bks.); 1990. (Harlequin Intrigue Ser.: No. 136). (Illus.). 253p. pap. (*0-373-22136-3*, Harlequin Bks.) Harlequin Enterprises, Ltd.

—Under the Knife. l.t. ed. 2001. (Thorndike Famous Authors Ser.). 376p. 29.95 (*0-7862-3133-5*) Thorndike Pr.

Gerritsen, Tess, et al. Suspense & Adventure: Under the Knife; Adam's Story; Return to Yesterday; Everything but Time; Marriage, Diamond Style. 2001. (Harlequin Special Releases Ser.: No. 4). 266p. mass mkt. (*0-373-83495-0*, 1-83495-1, Harlequin Bks.) Harlequin Enterprises, Ltd.

Goldsberry, Steven. Maui the Demigod: An Epic Novel of Mythical Hawaii. 1984. (Illus.). 400p. 18.45 o.s.i (*0-671-47788-9*, Simon & Schuster) Simon & Schuster.

—Maui the Demigod: An Epic Novel of Mythical Hawai'i. 1989. (Illus.). pap. 16.95 o.p. (*0-8248-1274-3*) Univ. of Hawaii Pr.

Goodman, Allegra. Paradise Park. 2002. 368p. pap. 12.95 (*0-385-33418-4*, Delta) Dell Publishing.

—Total Immersion: Stories. 1989. 16.95 o.p. (*0-06-015998-7*) HarperTrade.

Goonan, Kathleen A. The Bones of Time. 1997. 401p. mass mkt. 6.99 (*0-8125-5746-8*); 1996. 384p. 23.95 o.p. (*0-312-85916-3*) Doherty, Tom Assocs., LLC. (Tor Bks.).

Gordon, Dan. Just Play Dead. 1997. 288p. 22.95 o.p. (*0-312-16876-4*) St. Martin's Pr.

Gordon Staff. Just Play Dead, Vol. 1. 1999. (Elmore Leonard Library). 240p. mass mkt. 5.99 (*0-312-96567-2*, St. Martin's Paperbacks) St. Martin's Pr.

Gunn, Robin J. Whispers. 1998. 22.95 (*0-7862-1650-6*, Macmillan Reference USA) Gale Group.

—Whispers. 1995. 262p. pap. 9.99 o.p. (*0-88070-755-0*, Palisades) Multnomah Pubs., Inc.

Gunn, Robin Jones. Sisterchicks Do the Hula. 2004. pap. (*1-59052-226-5*) Multnomah Pubs., Inc.

—Whispers. 2003. (Glenbrooke Ser.: Vol. 2). 288p. pap. 10.99 (*1-57673-327-0*) Multnomah Pubs., Inc.

Hale, Bruce. Moki & the Magic Surfboard: A Hawaiian Fantasy. 1996. 32p. (J). (gr. k-4). 8.95 (*0-9621280-5-8*) Words & Pictures Publishing, Inc.

Hall, Oakley M. Ambrose Bierce & the Death of Kings. 2001. 288p. 22.95 o.s.i (*0-670-03007-4*, Viking) Viking Penguin.

Hansen-Young, Diana. Mango Hill. 1988. pap. 6.95 o.p. (*0-89610-150-9*) Island Heritage Publishing.

Hara, Marie. Bananaheart & Other Stories. 1994. (Bamboo Ridge Ser.: Nos. 61-62). 172p. pap. 8.00 (*0-910043-33-7*); pap. incl. audio. audio 8.00 (*0-910043-34-5*) Bamboo Ridge Pr.

Hart, Carolyn G. Death in Paradise. unabr. ed. 1998. (Henrie O Mysteries Ser.). audio 48.00 (*0-7366-4263-3*, 4762) Books on Tape, Inc.

—Death in Paradise. 1999. 304p. mass mkt. 6.50 (*0-380-79003-3*); 1998. 288p. 20.00 (*0-380-97414-2*) Morrow/Avon. (Avon Bks.).

—Death in Paradise, Set. abr. ed. 1998. audio 18.00 (*0-7871-1704-8*, Dove Audio) NewStar Media, Inc.

—Death in Paradise. l.t. ed. 2000. (Mystery Ser.). 415p. 29.95 (*0-7862-2679-X*) Thorndike Pr.

Hawkes, G. W. Gambler's Rose. 2000. 260p. 26.95 (*1-878448-96-X*) MacMurray & Beck, Inc.

Heller, Steve. The Man Who Drank a Thousand Beers. 1984. 109p. pap. 10.00 (*0-933428-03-0*) Chariton Review Pr.

Hirschfeld, Corson. Aloha, Mr. Lucky. 2001. 384p. reprint ed. pap. 14.95 (*0-312-87601-7*, Forge Bks.) Doherty, Tom Assocs., LLC.

Holt, John D. Princess of the Night Rides. 1977. 4.95 (*0-914916-21-1*); pap. 2.50 (*0-914916-22-X*) Ku Pa'a Publishing.

Houston, James D. The Last Paradise. (Literature of the American West Ser.). 384p. 2000. pap. 17.95 (*0-8061-3290-6*); 1998. 24.95 (*0-8061-3033-4*) Univ. of Oklahoma Pr.

Hughes, Dean. Lucky in Love. 1993. (Lucky Ladd Ser.: No. 9). 161p. (Orig.). (J). (gr. 3-7). pap. 4.95 (*0-87579-805-5*, Cinnamon Tree) Deseret Bk. Co.

Iida, Deborah. Middle Son: A Novel. 1996. 228p. tchr. ed. 18.95 (*1-56512-119-8*, 72119) Algonquin Bks. of Chapel Hill.

—Middle Son: A Novel. 224p. 2000. pap. 12.95 (*0-425-17443-3*); 1998. mass mkt. 6.99 o.s.i (*0-425-16151-X*) Berkley Publishing Group.

Jackson, Marian J. A. Diamond Head: A Miss Danforth Mystery. 1992. 167p. 18.95 (*0-8027-1247-9*) Walker & Co.

Johnson, Kay. Island Snatchers. 1997. 384p. 24.95 o.p. (*0-312-86232-6*, Forge Bks.) Doherty, Tom Assocs., LLC.

—The Island Snatchers. 2000. 384p. mass mkt. 6.99 (*0-8125-5527-9*, Tor Bks.) Doherty, Tom Assocs., LLC.

Jones, James. The Pistol. 2003. 158p. pap. 12.00 (*0-226-39186-8*) Univ. of Chicago Pr.

Kaopuiki, Stacey S. Bring Me What I Ask: A Hawaiian Story about Numbers. Despins, Cindy R., ed. 1991. (Peter Panini Keiki Reader Ser.). (Illus.). 32p. (J). (ps-3). 12.95 (*1-878498-03-7*) Hawaiian Island Concepts.

—Peter Panini & the Search for the Menehune. 1990. (Peter Panini Adventure Ser.). (Illus.). 44p. (J). (ps-5). 10.95 (*1-878498-00-2*) Hawaiian Island Concepts.

—The Secret of the Hawaiian Rainbow: A Hawaiian Story about Colors. Despins, Cindy R., ed. 1991. (Peter Panini Keiki Reader Ser.). (Illus.). 32p. (J). (ps-3). 12.95 (*1-878498-02-9*) Hawaiian Island Concepts.

Katkov, Norman. Blood & Orchids. 1983. 544p. 15.95 o.p. (*0-312-08395-5*) St. Martin's Pr.

Kawano, Doris. Harue, Child of Hawaii. 1984. pap. 11.95 o.p. (*0-914916-64-5*) Ku Pa'a Publishing.

Keller, Nora O. Comfort Woman. 1998. 224p. pap. 12.95 (*0-14-026335-7*) Penguin Group (USA) Inc.

—Comfort Woman. 1997. 224p. 21.95 o.s.i (*0-670-87269-5*, Viking) Viking Penguin.

Kingston, Maxine Hong. The Fifth Book of Peace. 2003. 416p. 26.00 (*0-679-44075-5*) Knopf, Alfred A. Inc.

Knief, Charles. Diamond Head. (John Caine Mysteries Ser.). 1998. 240p. mass mkt. 6.50 (*0-312-96547-8*, St. Martin's Paperbacks); 1996. 256p. 21.95 o.p. (*0-312-14558-6*, Saint Martin's Minotaur) St. Martin's Pr.

—Emerald Flash. (John Caine Mysteries Ser.). 2000. 304p. mass mkt. 5.99 (*0-312-97058-7*, St. Martin's Paperbacks); 1999. 292p. 23.95 (*0-312-19866-3*, Saint Martin's Minotaur) St. Martin's Pr.

—Sand Dollars. (John Caine Mysteries Ser.). 1999. 304p. mass mkt. 5.99 (*0-312-96682-2*, St. Martin's Paperbacks); 1998. 336p. 23.95 (*0-312-18170-1*, 874700, Saint Martin's Minotaur) St. Martin's Pr.

—Silversword. mass mkt. (*0-312-98025-6*, St. Martin's Paperbacks); 2001. 400p. 24.95 (*0-312-27302-9*, Saint Martin's Minotaur) St. Martin's Pr.

Koretsky, J. Lea. Wall of Darkness. 2002. 119p. pap. 14.95 (*1-58790-020-3*) Regent Pr.

Lapka, Fay S. The Sea, the Song & the Trumpetfish. 1991. (Young Adult Fiction Ser.). 160p. (Orig.). (YA). (gr. 7-12). pap. 6.99 o.p. (*0-87788-754-3*, Shaw) WaterBrook Pr.

Lodge, David. Paradise News. unabr. ed. 1998. audio 69.95 (*1-85695-775-6*, 931006) ISIS Audio Bks. GBR. *Dist:* Ulverscroft Large Print Bks., Ltd.

—Paradise News. 1993. 304p. pap. 14.00 (*0-14-016521-5*, Penguin Bks.) Penguin Group (USA) Inc.

—Paradise News. 1992. 352p. 21.00 o.p. (*0-670-84228-1*, Viking) Viking Penguin.

London, Jack. Jack London's Tales of Hawaii. 1984. 80p. pap. 4.95 (*0-916630-25-0*) Press Pacifica, Ltd.

Loomis, Albertine. Grapes of Canaan: Hawaii, 1820. 1999. xvi, 334p. reprint ed. pap. 19.95 (*1-881987-12-4*) Ox Bow Pr.

Lowell, Elizabeth. Eden Burning: A Classic Love Story. abr. ed. 2002. audio 19.95 o.p. (*1-58788-263-9*, 2526, Nova Audio Bks.); audio 29.95 (*1-58788-261-2*, 2524, Brilliance Audio Unabridged); audio 69.25 (*1-58788-262-0*, 2525, Unabridged Library Editions) Brilliance Audio.

—Eden Burning: A Classic Love Story. 2002. E-Book 16.95 (*0-06-008526-6*); E-Book 16.95 (*0-06-008525-8*); E-Book 16.95 (*0-06-009781-7*); E-Book 16.95 (*0-06-008527-4*) HarperCollins General Bks. Group. (PerfectBound).

—Eden Burning: A Classic Love Story. l.t. ed. 2002. 448p. pap. 20.95 (*0-06-008330-1*) HarperCollins Pubs.

—Eden Burning: A Classic Love Story. 2002. 352p. 20.95 (*0-06-621274-X*) Morrow/Avon.

MacMillan, Ian. Exiles from Time - Stories of Hawaii. 1998. 150p. pap. 12.95 (*0-9653971-6-5*) Anoai Pr.

—Ullambana: And Other Stories of Hawaii. 2002. 164p. 14.95 (*0-9702618-4-5*) Anoai Pr.

Mahon, Annette. The Secret Wedding. 2002. 183p. text 19.95 (*0-8034-9535-8*, Avalon Bks.) Bouregy, Thomas & Co., Inc.

Mainning, Liza. The Garland Girl. l.t. ed. 1996. 280p. pap. 17.95 o.p. (*0-7838-1625-1*, Macmillan Reference USA) Gale Group.

Martin, Dorothy. Mystery of the Stolen Flight Bag. 1983. (Vicki Adventure Ser.). 128p. (Orig.). (J). (gr. 6). pap. 2.95 o.p. (*0-8024-0273-9*) Moody Pr.

Matsuura, Richard & Matsuura, Ruth. Ali'i Kai. (Illus.). (J). 7.95 (*1-887916-05-9*) Orchid Isle Publishing Co.

—Birthday Wish. (Illus.). (J). 8.95 (*1-887916-04-0*) Orchid Isle Publishing Co.

—Hawaiian Christmas Story. (Illus.). (J). 8.95 (*1-887916-01-6*) Orchid Isle Publishing Co.

McBarnet, Gill. Gift of Aloha. 1996. (Illus.). 32p. (J). (gr. k-2). 8.95 (*0-9615102-9-3*) Ruwanga Trading.

McKay, Rena. The Singing Stone. 2003. 180p. 25.95 (*1-59414-023-5*, Five Star) Gale Group.

McLane, Gretel B. Kailia & the King's Horse. 1982. (Illus.). 96p. (J). (gr. 4-6). 7.95 o.p. (*0-916630-28-5*) Press Pacifica, Ltd.

Michener, James A. Hawaii. 1994. mass mkt. 6.95 o.p. (*0-449-45268-9*); 1986. (Illus.). 1056p. mass mkt. 7.99 (*0-449-21335-8*); 1984. mass mkt. 4.95 o.p. (*0-449-20711-0*); 1982. mass mkt. 3.95 o.p. (*0-449-20286-0*); 1982. mass mkt. 3.95 o.p. (*0-449-23761-3*) Ballantine Bks. (Fawcett).

—Hawaii, Pt. 1. unabr. ed. 1991. audio 96.00 (*0-7366-2056-7*, 2867A) Books on Tape, Inc.

—Hawaii. 1995. reprint ed. lib. bdg. 39.95 (*1-56849-612-5*) Buccaneer Bks., Inc.

—Hawaii. 1959. 45.00 o.s.i (*0-394-42797-1*, Vintage) Knopf Publishing Group.

—Hawaii, Set. abr. ed. 1990. audio 18.00 o.s.i (*0-394-58282-9*, 390906, RH Audio) Random Hse. Audio Publishing Group.

—Hawaii: A Novel. 2002. (Illus.). 960p. pap. 14.95 (*0-375-76037-7*) Random House Adult Trade Publishing Group.

—James Michener: Two Complete Novels. 1994. 14.99 o.s.i (*0-517-14683-5*) Random Hse. Value Publishing.

Miller, Janice. The Jade Crucible. 1995. 324p. pap. 10.99 o.p. (*0-7852-7706-4*) Nelson, Thomas Inc.

—Plum Blossoms: Alexis Albright—Private Investigator. 1994. pap. 10.99 o.p. (*0-7852-8208-4*) Nelson, Thomas Inc.

Moore, B. Clay. Byrd of Paradise. 2003. (Hawaiian Dick Ser.: Vol. 1). (Illus.). 136p. pap. 14.95 (*1-58240-317-1*) Image Comics.

Moore, Christopher. Fluke, or, I Know Why the Winged Whale Sings: A Novel. 2003. 336p. 23.95 (*0-380-97841-5*, Morrow, William & Co.) Morrow/Avon.

Moore, Susanna. Sleeping Beauties. 1994. 240p. pap. 13.00 (*0-679-75539-X*, Vintage) Knopf Publishing Group.

Morales, Rodney. When the Shark Bites. 2002. 352p. (C). pap. text 17.00 (*0-8248-2565-9*) Univ. of Hawaii Pr.

Morris, Lynn & Morris, Gilbert. Island of the Innocent. 1998. (Cheney Duvall, M. D. Ser.: Bk. 7). 320p. pap. 11.99 (*1-55661-698-8*) Bethany Hse. Pubs.

—Island of the Innocent. 2000. 395p. 24.95 (*0-7862-2442-8*, Five Star) Gale Group.

Morrison, Susan. Kamehameha: The Warrior King of Hawai'i. Kiefer, Karen, tr. & illus. by. 2003. xi, 85p. pap. 12.95 (*0-8248-2700-7*, Latitude 20 Bks.) Univ. of Hawaii Pr.

Mower, Nancy A. Tutu Kane & Granpa. 1989. (Illus.). 32p. (J). (ps). 8.95 (*0-916630-66-8*) Press Pacifica, Ltd.

Muller, Marcia. A Walk Through the Fire. 1999. 362p. 23.00 o.s.i (*0-89296-688-2*) Mysterious Pr.

Murayama, Milton. All I'm Asking for Is My Body. 1988. (Kolowalu Bks.). 120p. reprint ed. pap. 9.95 (*0-8248-1172-0*, Kolowalu Bk.) Univ. of Hawaii Pr.

—Five Years on a Rock. 1994. 160p. (C). 17.95 (*0-8248-1647-1*); pap. 9.95 (*0-8248-1677-3*) Univ. of Hawaii Pr.

—Plantation Boy. 1998. 180p. 24.95 (*0-8248-1965-9*); pap. 14.95 (*0-8248-2007-X*) Univ. of Hawaii Pr.

Nelson, Curt. Darkstar. 2001. 390p. pap. 22.99 (*0-7388-1825-9*); text 32.99 (*0-7388-1824-0*) Xlibris Corp.

Nordquist, Kay. Dark Gods. Costa, Gwen, ed. 1992. 166p. (Orig.). pap. 13.95 (*0-87949-322-4*) Ashley Bks., Inc.

Novak, Walt. The Haole Substitute. 1994. 160p. (Orig.). pap. 12.95 (*1-879384-19-1*) Cypress Hse.

O'Brien, Meg. Take My Breath Away. 1997. 306p. mass mkt. 5.99 (*0-312-96158-8*, St. Martin's Paperbacks) St. Martin's Pr.

O'Connor, Dan. Spice: An Island Intrigue. 2002. 348p. 14.95 (*0-9667235-5-4*) Waterton Pr.

—Sugar: A Hawaiian Novel. (Illus.). 320p. 2001. 18.95 (*0-9667235-2-X*); 2000. pap. 12.95 (*0-9667235-1-1*) Waterton Pr.

Pak, Gary. A Ricepaper Airplane. 1998. (Intersections Ser.). 264p. pap. 18.95 (*0-8248-1301-4*) Univ. of Hawaii Pr.

—The Watcher of Waipuna & Other Stories. 1992. (Bamboo Ridge Ser.: Nos. 55-56). 180p. pap. 8.00 (*0-910043-28-0*) Bamboo Ridge Pr.

Palamarek, Ernie. Thundersea. 1999. 348p. pap. (*1-55212-251-4*, Trade Winds Productions) Trafford Publishing.

Patterson, Rosemary I. An End to Innocence. 2000. 175p. pap. 20.99 (*0-7388-1173-4*); text 20.00 (*0-7388-1172-6*) Xlibris Corp.

—Kunina Nui: A Novel Based on the Life of Ka'ahumanu, the Queen Regent of Hawaii (1819-1832) 1998. 188p. pap. 14.95 (*1-880836-21-1*) Pine Island Pr.

Pella, Judith. Somewhere a Song. 2002. (Daughters of Fortune Ser.). 432p. 18.99 (*0-7642-2720-3*) Bethany Hse. Pubs.

Perkins, Leialoha A. The Firemakers & Other Stories about Hawaii, the Samoas, & Tonga. 1987. 107p. (*1-892174-05-7*) Kamalu'uluolele Pubs.

—Natural: And Other Stories about Contemporary Hawaiians. 1995. 43p. reprint ed. pap. (*1-892174-07-3*) Kamalu'uluolele Pubs.

—Natural: Short Stories of Contemporary Hawaiians. 1979. iv, 43p. pap. (*1-892174-08-1*) Kamalu'uluolele Pubs.

Perry, Yvonne N. The Other Side of the Island: Stories. 1994. (Illus.). 112p. (Orig.). pap. 10.00 (*1-880284-06-5*) Daniel, John & Co., Pubs.

Random House Staff, ed. Hawaiian Shirt. 1998. (J). lib. bdg. 8.99 (*0-679-99413-0*, Random Hse. Bks. for Young Readers) Random Hse. Children's Bks.

Rapozo, Douglas E. Escape from Management's America. 1998. 462p. 21.95 o.p. (*0-533-12184-1*) Vantage Pr., Inc.

Roberts, Nora. Island of Flowers. 1992. (NR Flowers Ser.: No. 10). per. (*0-373-51010-1*, 5-51010-2, Harlequin Bks.) Harlequin Enterprises, Ltd.

—Island of Flowers. l.t. ed. 2002. (Core Collection). 167p. 31.95 (*0-7862-4218-3*) Thorndike Pr.

Roddy, Lee. Eye of the Hurricane. 1994. (Ladd Family Adventure Ser.: Vol. 9). 170p. (J). (gr. 3-7). pap. 5.99 o.p. (*1-56179-220-9*) Focus on the Family Publishing.

Roop, Peter. The Cry of the Conch. 1984. (Treasury of Children's Hawaiian Stories Ser.). (Illus.). (J). (gr. 3-5). 8.95 o.p. (*0-916630-39-0*) Press Pacifica, Ltd.

Saiki, Jessica. From the Lanai & Other Hawaii Stories. 1991. (Minnesota Voices Project Ser.: Vol. 48). 115p. pap. 10.95 (*0-89823-127-2*) New Rivers Pr.

—Once, a Lotus Garden. 1987. pap. 7.95 o.p. (*0-89823-087-X*) New Rivers Pr.

Samuels, Barbara. Aloha, Dolores. 2000. (Melanie Kroupa Bks.). (Illus.). 32p. (J). (ps-2). pap. 15.95 (*0-7894-2508-4*, D K Ink) Dorling Kindersley Publishing, Inc.

Saul, John. The Presence. 1998. 432p. mass mkt. 7.99 (*0-449-00241-1*, Fawcett) Ballantine Bks.

—The Presence. l.t. ed. 1997. (G. K. Hall Core Ser.). 580p. 26.95 (*0-7838-8361-7*, Macmillan Reference USA) Gale Group.

—The Presence, unabr. ed. 1998. audio 75.00 (*0-7887-1868-1*, 95290E7) Recorded Bks., LLC.

—The Presence. 1998. 14.04 (*0-606-16479-0*) Turtleback Bks.

Schweizer, Niklaus R. His Hawaiian Excellency. 1988. 267p. 24.00 o.p. (*0-8204-0622-8*) Lang, Peter Publishing, Inc.

Scoville, Shelagh. Ulu's Dog: And Other Stories. 2003. 320p. pap. 14.95 (*1-56474-415-9*) Fithian Pr.

Sheehan, Ed. The Guns of Eden: A Novel of Hawaii When the White Man Came. 1995. 280p. (Orig.). pap. 15.95 (*0-914916-98-X*); pap. text 21.95 (*0-914916-99-8*) Ku Pa'a Publishing.

Shelton, Connie. Deadly Gamble. unabr. ed. 1996. (Charlie Parker Ser.: Bk. 1). audio 39.95 (*1-55686-653-4*) Books in Motion.

—Deadly Gamble: The First Charlie Parker Mystery. Lenz, Leslie, ed. 1995. 216p. 21.95 o.p. (*0-9643161-0-2*, Intrigue Pr.) Corvus Publishing.

—Deadly Gamble: The First Charlie Parker Mystery. 1997. (The Charlie Parker Mystery Ser.: Vol. 1). 288p. reprint ed. mass mkt. 5.50 (*1-890768-00-6*, Intrigue Pr.) Corvus Publishing.

—Vacations Can Be Murder. unabr. ed. 1996. (Charlie Parker Ser.: Bk. 2). audio 39.95 (*1-55686-660-7*) Books in Motion.

—Vacations Can Be Murder: The Second Charlie Parker Mystery. Lenz, Leslie, ed. 1995. (Charlie Parker Mysteries Ser.). 216p. 21.95 o.p. (*0-9643161-1-0*, Intrigue Pr.) Corvus Publishing.

—Vacations Can Be Murder: The Second Charlie Parker Mystery. 1997. (The Charlie Parker Mystery Ser.: Vol. 2). 272p. reprint ed. mass mkt. 5.50 (*1-890768-01-4*, Intrigue Pr.) Corvus Publishing.

Sheridan, Juanita. The Mamo Murders. 2002. 154p. reprint ed. pap. 14.00 (*0-915230-51-8*) Rue Morgue Pr.

Simmons, Dan. Fires of Eden. 1994. 400p. 22.95 o.p. (*0-399-13922-2*) Penguin Group (USA) Inc.

Slama, Carol D. Shroud of Silence. 1998. (Portraits Ser.). 256p. pap. 8.99 o.p. (*0-7642-2039-X*) Bethany Hse. Pubs.

—Shroud of Silence. l.t. ed. 1999. (Christian Fiction Ser.). 271p. 22.95 (*0-7862-1743-X*, Five Star) Gale Group.

Smolinski, Jill. Flip-Flopped. 2003. 304p. pap. 12.95 (*0-312-31611-9*, Saint Martin's Griffin); 2002. 320p. 23.95 (*0-312-28514-0*) St. Martin's Pr.

Snelling, Lauraine. Hawaiian Sunrise. l.t. ed. 2001. (Thorndike Press Large Print Christian Romance Ser.). 429p. 24.95 (*0-7862-3284-6*) Thorndike Pr.

—Hawaiian Sunrise: A Novel. 1999. 288p. pap. 9.99 (*1-55661-991-X*) Bethany Hse. Pubs.

Stevenson, Robert Louis. The Bottle Imp. 2002. 60p. reprint ed. 17.00 (*0-7567-5801-7*) DIANE Publishing Co.

—The Bottle Imp. 1984. reprint ed. pap. 4.95 o.p. (*0-916411-88-5*) Holmes Publishing Group, LLC.

—The Bottle Imp. 1994. (Illus.). 77p. 29.95 (*0-9642169-0-6*) Tree Garden Workshop.

Stewart, Constance H. Lost in Paradise: Stories. 1997. 144p. (Orig.). pap. 11.00 (*1-56474-203-2*) Fithian Pr.

Stewart, Frank, ed. Passages to the Dream Shore: Short Stories of Contemporary Hawaii. 1987. 224p. pap. 12.95 o.p. (*0-8248-1122-4*, Kolowalu Bk.) Univ. of Hawaii Pr.

Streshinsky, Shirley. The Shores of Paradise. 1991. 416p. 22.95 o.p. (*0-399-13568-5*, G. P. Putnam's Sons) Penguin Group (USA) Inc.

Swanson, Helen M. Angel & Tutu, Vol. 3. 1997. (Intermediate Reader Ser.). 112p. (J). (gr. 4-7). pap. 5.21 (*1-57306-066-6*) Bess Pr., Inc.

Swigart, Rob. Venom. 1991. 17.95 o.p. (*0-312-05986-8*, Saint Martin's Minotaur) St. Martin's Pr.

Tabrah, Ruth M. The Red Shark. 2nd ed. 1991. (Illus.). 224p. (J). (gr. 5-10). reprint ed. pap. 8.95 (*0-916630-67-6*) Press Pacifica, Ltd.

Theroux, Paul. Hotel Honolulu: A Novel. 2001. 432p. 26.00 (*0-618-09501-2*) Houghton Mifflin Co.

—Hotel Honolulu: A Novel. 2002. 432p. pap. 14.00 (*0-618-21915-3*, Mariner Bks.) Houghton Mifflin Co. Trade & Reference Div.

Tyau, Kathleen. A Little Too Much Is Enough. 1995. 228p. 18.00 o.p. (*0-374-18950-1*) Farrar, Straus & Giroux.

—A Little Too Much Is Enough. 1996. 240p. pap. 12.00 (*0-393-31559-2*) Norton, W. W. & Co., Inc.

—Makai. 2000. (Bluestreak Ser.). 296p. pap. 14.00 (*0-8070-8345-3*) Beacon Pr.

—Makai. 1999. 256p. 24.00 o.p. (*0-374-20000-9*) Farrar, Straus & Giroux.

Tyler, Lee. The Teed-Off Ghost: A Hawai'ian Golf Mystery. 2002. 192p. pap. 12.95 (*1-56474-389-6*) Fithian Pr.

Von Tempski, Armine. Bright Spurs. 1992. (Illus.). x, 284p. (YA). reprint ed. pap. 14.95 (*0-918024-95-1*) Ox Bow Pr.

—Fire: A Novel of Hawaii. 1993. 352p. reprint ed. pap. 14.95 (*0-918024-99-4*) Ox Bow Pr.

—Pam's Paradise Ranch: A Story of Hawaii. 1992. (Illus.). viii, 334p. (YA). reprint ed. pap. 14.95 (*0-918024-96-X*) Ox Bow Pr.

—Ripe Breadfruit. 1993. 384p. reprint ed. pap. 14.95 (*0-918024-98-6*) Ox Bow Pr.

Walker, Alice. Now Is the Time to Open Your Heart: A Novel. 2004. 240p. 24.95 (*1-4000-6173-3*) Random Hse., Inc.

Watanabe, Sylvia. Talking to the Dead. 1992. 144p. 20.00 o.s.i (*0-385-41887-6*) Doubleday Publishing.

—Talking to the Dead & Other Stories. 1993. 144p. pap. 15.00 (*0-385-41888-4*) Doubleday Publishing.

Weber, Joe. Honorable Enemies. 1994. 336p. mass mkt. 5.99 o.s.i (*0-515-11522-3*, Jove) Berkley Publishing Group.

—Honorable Enemies. abr. ed. 1994. audio 17.00 o.p. (*1-56100-369-7*, 902, Nova Audio Bks.); audio 73.25 o.p. (*1-56100-188-0*, 1241, Unabridged Library Editions); audio 23.95 o.p. (*1-56100-562-2*, 139, Bookcassette) Brilliance Audio.

—Honorable Enemies. abr. ed. 2000. audio 7.95 (*1-57815-013-2*, 1039, Media Bks. Audio Publishing) Media Bks., L. L. C.

—Honorable Enemies. 1994. 384p. 22.95 o.s.i (*0-399-13939-7*, G. P. Putnam's Sons) Penguin Group (USA) Inc.

Wick, Lori. Bamboo & Lace. l.t. ed. 2003. 637p. pap. 16.95 (*1-4104-0100-6*, Walker Large Print) Gale Group.

—Bamboo & Lace. 2001. 456p. pap. 11.99 (*0-7369-0328-3*) Harvest Hse. Pubs.

—Bamboo & Lace. 2003. (Christian Romance Ser.). 27.95 (*0-7862-4639-1*) Thorndike Pr.

Wong, Norman. Cultural Revolution. 1995. 192p. pap. 15.00 (*0-345-39648-0*) Ballantine Bks.

—Cultural Revolution. 1994. 192p. 21.00 (*0-89255-197-6*) Persea Bks., Inc.

Wythe, M. William. One Hand Clapping. 1999. 181p. pap. 11.95 o.p. (*1-58348-322-5*) iUniverse, Inc.

Yamanaka, Cedric. In Good Company. 2002. 128p. (C). pap. 14.95 (*0-8248-2498-9*, Latitude 20 Bks.) Univ. of Hawaii Pr.

Yamanaka, Lois A. Wild Meat & the Bully Burgers. 1997. (Harvest American Writing Ser.). 288p. pap. 12.00 (*0-15-600483-6*, Harvest Bks.) Harcourt Trade Pubs.

Yamanaka, Lois-Ann. Father of the Four Passages. 2001. 288p. 23.00 (*0-374-15387-6*) Farrar, Straus & Giroux.

—Heads by Harry. 1999. 336p. 24.00 o.p. (*0-374-16850-4*) Farrar, Straus & Giroux.

—Heads by Harry. 2000. 320p. pap. 13.00 (*0-380-73316-1*) Morrow/Avon.

—Wild Meat & the Bully Burgers. 1996. 240p. 20.00 o.p. (*0-374-29020-2*) Farrar, Straus & Giroux.

Yardley, Maili. Letters from the Lanai. 2002. 200p. pap. 19.00 (*0-915013-22-3*) Editions, Ltd.

**HELLICONIA (IMAGINARY PLACE)—FICTION**

Aldiss, Brian W. Helliconia Spring. 1987. mass mkt. 4.50 o.s.i (*0-441-32626-9*) Ace Bks.

—Helliconia Spring. 1985. 480p. 3.95 o.s.i (*0-425-08895-2*); 1984. 3.50 o.s.i (*0-425-07328-9*); 1983. pap. 6.95 o.p. (*0-425-06186-8*) Berkley Publishing Group.

—Helliconia Spring. 1982. 15.95 o.s.i (*0-689-11196-7*, Scribner) Simon & Schuster.

—Helliconia Summer. 1986. 496p. mass mkt. 4.50 o.s.i (*0-441-32632-3*) Ace Bks.

—Helliconia Summer. 1983. 384p. 16.95 o.p. (*0-689-11388-9*, Scribner) Simon & Schuster.

—The Helliconia Trilogy, 3 vols. 1985. 1184p. 55.00 o.s.i (*0-689-11566-0*, Scribner) Simon & Schuster.

—Helliconia Winter. 1987. mass mkt. 3.95 o.s.i (*0-441-32629-3*) Ace Bks.

—Helliconia Winter. 1987. 3.95 o.s.i (*0-425-09704-8*); 1986. 304p. pap. 6.95 o.p. (*0-425-08994-0*) Berkley Publishing Group.

—Helliconia Winter. 1985. 384p. 17.95 o.p. (*0-689-11541-5*, Scribner) Simon & Schuster.

—Helliconia Winter. 2002. (Helliconia Trilogy Ser.: Bk. 3). 304p. pap. 14.00 (*0-7434-4516-3*) ibooks, Inc.

**HEMLOCK FALLS (N.Y.: IMAGINARY PLACE)—FICTION**

Bishop, Claudia. A Dash of Death. 1995. 240p. (Orig.). mass mkt. 5.99 (*0-425-14638-3*, Prime Crime) Berkley Publishing Group.

—Death Dines Out. 1997. (Hemlock Falls Mysteries Ser.). 256p. mass mkt. 5.99 (*0-425-16111-0*, Prime Crime) Berkley Publishing Group.

—Marinade for Murder. 2000. (Hemlock Falls Mysteries Ser.). 256p. mass mkt. 5.99 (*0-425-17611-8*, Prime Crime) Berkley Publishing Group.

—Murder Well-Done. 1996. (Hemlock Falls Mysteries Ser.). 272p. mass mkt. 5.99 o.s.i (*0-425-15336-3*) Berkley Publishing Group.

—A Pinch of Poison. 1995. (Hemlock Falls Mysteries Ser.). 256p. mass mkt. 5.99 (*0-425-15104-2*) Berkley Publishing Group.

—A Steak in Murder. 1999. (Hemlock Falls Mysteries Ser.). 272p. mass mkt. 5.99 o.s.i (*0-425-16966-9*, Prime Crime) Berkley Publishing Group.

—A Taste for Murder. 1994. 240p. mass mkt. 5.99 (*0-425-14350-3*, Prime Crime) Berkley Publishing Group.

—A Touch of the Grape. 1998. (Hemlock Falls Mysteries Ser.). 256p. mass mkt. 5.99 (*0-425-16397-0*, Prime Crime) Berkley Publishing Group.

**HOLLYWOOD (LOS ANGELES, CALIF.)—FICTION**

Appelman, William. Claim to Fame. 1993. 256p. 19.95 o.p. (*0-88184-935-9*, Carroll & Graf Pubs.) Avalon Publishing Group.

Bagshawe, Loiuse. Triple Feature. 1997. 336p. 22.50 (*0-684-83069-8*, Simon & Schuster) Simon & Schuster.

Baker, James Robert. Adrenaline. 2000. 302p. reprint ed. pap. 11.95 o.p. (*1-55583-565-1*, Alyson Bks.) Alyson Pubns.

Baker, Kage. Mendoza in Hollywood. 2001. 384p. mass mkt. 6.99 o.s.i (*0-380-81900-7*) Morrow/Avon.

Barker, Clive. Coldheart Canyon: A Hollywood Ghost Story. 2002. E-Book 19.95 (*0-06-001035-5*); 2001. ix, 606p. (*0-00-255864-5*) HarperCollins Pubs.

—Coldheart Canyon: A Hollywood Ghost Story. 2001. 688p. 27.95 (*0-06-018297-0*, HarperCollins); audio 49.95 (*0-694-52401-8*, HarperAudio); audio compact disk 75.00 (*0-694-52663-0*, HarperAudio) HarperTrade.

—Coldheart Canyon: A Hollywood Ghost Story. 2002. 704p. mass mkt. 7.99 (*0-06-103018-X*) Morrow/Avon.

—Coldheart Canyon: A Hollywood Ghost Story. aut. ltd. collector's ed. 2001. 688p. 150.00 (*1-890885-12-6*) Trice, B.E. Publishing.

Barnes, Joanna. The Deceivers. 1970. 6.95 o.p. (*0-87795-007-5*, Morrow, William & Co.) Morrow/Avon.

Barton, Dan. Dead Crowd. E-Book 23.95 (*0-312-70622-7*); 2002. 272p. 23.95 (*0-312-29034-9*, Saint Martin's Minotaur) St. Martin's Pr.

—Killer Material. 2000. vii, 293p. 24.95 (*0-312-25222-6*, Saint Martin's Minotaur) St. Martin's Pr.

—Killer Material: A Mystery. E-Book 24.95 (*0-312-27386-X*) St. Martin's Pr.

Bauer, Tricia. Hollywood & Hardwood. 2000. 192p. pap. 11.95 (*0-312-26337-6*, Saint Martin's Griffin) St. Martin's Pr.

Baxt, George. The Clark Gable & Carole Lombard Murder Case. 1997. 208p. 20.95 o.p. (*0-312-16799-7*, Saint Martin's Minotaur) St. Martin's Pr.

—Fred Astaire & Ginger Rogers Murder Case. 1996. 208p. text 20.95 o.p. (*0-312-15129-2*, Saint Martin's Minotaur) St. Martin's Pr.

—The Talking Pictures Murder Case. 1990. 208p. 15.95 o.p. (*0-312-05043-7*, Saint Martin's Minotaur) St. Martin's Pr.

—The Tallulah Bankhead Murder Case. 1987. 240p. 15.95 o.p. (*0-312-01098-2*, Saint Martin's Minotaur) St. Martin's Pr.

—The William Powell & Myrna Loy Murder Case. 1996. 208p. 20.95 o.p. (*0-312-14071-1*, Saint Martin's Minotaur) St. Martin's Pr.

Beck, K. K. The Revenge of Kali-Ra. 1999. 229p. 22.00 (*0-89296-670-X*) Mysterious Pr.

Blatty, William P. Demons Five, Exorcists Nothing: A Fable. 1996. 188p. 18.95 o.p. (*1-55611-501-6*) Fine, Donald I. Bks.

Bloch, Jon P. Best Murder of the Year. E-Book 23.95 (*0-312-70437-2*); 2004. 288p. pap. 13.95 (*0-312-30111-1*, Saint Martin's Griffin); 2002. 256p. 23.95 (*0-312-28090-4*, Saint Martin's Minotaur) St. Martin's Pr.

Blumenthal, John. What's Wrong with Dorfman? A Novel. 2003. 240p. pap. 12.95 (*0-312-31188-5*, Saint Martin's Griffin) St. Martin's Pr.

Bochco, Steven. Death by Hollywood. 2004. 256p. mass mkt. 7.99 (*0-345-46687-X*, Fawcett) Ballantine Bks.

—Death by Hollywood. l.t. ed. 2003. 352p. 26.95 (*0-375-43298-1*) Random Hse. Large Print.

—Death by Hollywood: A Novel. 2003. 288p. 24.95 (*1-4000-6156-3*) Random Hse., Inc.

Bogart, Stephen Humphrey. Play It Again. 1996. 246p. pap. text 5.99 (*0-8125-5162-1*); 1995. 240p. 19.95 o.p. (*0-312-85665-2*) Doherty, Tom Assocs., LLC. (Forge Bks.).

—The Remake: As Time Goes By. 288p. 1997. 22.95 o.p. (*0-312-85666-0*); Vol. 1. 1998. (Remake Ser.: Vol. 1). mass mkt. 6.99 (*0-8125-5164-8*) Doherty, Tom Assocs., LLC. (Forge Bks.).

Borton, Della. Fade to Black. 1999. (Movie Lover's Mysteries Ser.). 288p. mass mkt. 5.99 o.s.i (*0-449-00407-4*, Fawcett) Ballantine Bks.

—Slow Dissolve. 2001. 288p. mass mkt. 6.50 (*0-449-00705-7*, Fawcett) Ballantine Bks.

Boyd, William. The New Confessions. 1989. 480p. pap. 8.95 o.p. (*0-14-010699-5*, Penguin Bks.) Viking Penguin.

Bradbury, Ray. A Graveyard for Lunatics. 1991. 304p. mass mkt. 5.99 o.s.i (*0-553-18046-0*) Bantam Bks.

—A Graveyard for Lunatics. 2001. 320p. pap. 13.00 (*0-380-81200-2*, Perennial) HarperTrade.

—A Graveyard for Lunatics. 1994. 3.99 o.p. (*0-517-11536-0*); 1992. 4.99 o.p. (*0-517-08571-2*) Random Hse. Value Publishing.

—Let's All Kill Constance. 2003. pap. 13.95 (*0-06-051585-6*); 224p. 23.95 (*0-06-051584-8*) HarperCollins Pubs.

—Let's All Kill Constance. 2004. 256p. mass mkt. 7.50 (*0-06-056178-5*, Avon Bks.) Morrow/Avon.

—Let's All Kill Constance. l.t. ed. 2003. (Core Ser.). 28.95 (*0-7862-5523-4*) Thorndike Pr.

Brockmann, Suzanne. Heartthrob. 2004. 368p. mass mkt. 3.99 (*0-345-46608-X*); 2004. 368p. mass mkt. (*0-345-47128-8*); 1999. 352p. mass mkt. 6.99 (*0-449-00255-1*, Fawcett) Ballantine Bks.

Bukowski, Charles. Hollywood. 1989. 35.00 o.p. (*0-87685-765-9*, Black Sparrow Pr.) Godine, David R. Pub.

—Hollywood. 1998. reprint ed. 244p. 25.00 (*0-87685-764-0*); 248p. pap. 16.00 (*0-87685-763-2*) HarperCollins Pubs.

Buschlen, Jack P. Heil Hollywood. Kupelnick, Bruce S., ed. 1978. (Classics of Film Literature Ser.). lib. bdg. 11.00 o.p. (*0-8240-2869-4*) Garland Publishing, Inc.

Cameron, Julia. Popcorn: Hollywood Stories. 2000. 233p. pap. 14.95 (*1-893329-12-7*) Really Great Bks.

Cannell, Stephen J. Hollywood Tough: A Shane Scully Novel. l.t. ed. 2003. 30.95 (*1-58724-416-0*, Wheeler Publishing, Inc.) Gale Group.

—Hollywood Tough: A Shane Scully Novel. 2003. 352p. 24.95 (*0-312-29102-7*) St. Martin's Pr.

Carter, Dori. Beautiful Wasps Having Sex. 2000. 320p. 24.00 (*0-688-17464-7*, Morrow, William & Co.) Morrow/Avon.

—Beautiful Wasps Having Sex: A Hollywood Novel. 2001. 336p. pap. 14.00 (*0-06-093500-6*, Perennial) HarperTrade.

Caspery, Vera. Laura: An Otto Penzler Hollywood Mystery. 2000. (Illus.). 240p. pap. 14.00 (*0-7434-0010-0*) ibooks, Inc.

Chadwick, Cydney. Interims. 1997. 26p. pap. 5.00 (*0-9646017-4-5*) 3300 Pr.

Childress, Mark. Crazy in Alabama. 1999. 448p. mass mkt. 6.99 (*0-345-43247-9*); 1994. 384p. reprint ed. pap. 12.00 (*0-345-38924-7*) Ballantine Bks.

—Crazy in Alabama, Set. abr. ed. 1999. audio 18.00 Highsmith Inc.

—Crazy in Alabama. 1993. 384p. 22.95 o.p. (*0-399-13855-2*) Penguin Group (USA) Inc.

Collins, Jackie. Chances. abr. ed. 1991. audio 15.95 (*0-671-73807-0*); Pt. 2. 1995. audio 15.95 (*0-671-75510-2*) Simon & Schuster Audio. (Simon & Schuster Audioworks).

—Chances. 816p. 1981. 14.95 o.s.i (*0-446-51237-0*); 1991. reprint ed. mass mkt. 7.99 (*0-446-35717-0*) Warner Bks., Inc.

—Dangerous Kiss: A Lucky Santangelo Novel. l.t. ed. 2000. (Thorndike/G. K. Hall Paperback Bestsellers Ser.). 620p. pap. 28.95 (*0-7838-8748-5*, Macmillan Reference USA) Gale Group.

—Dangerous Kiss: A Lucky Santangelo Novel, Set. abr. ed. 1999. audio 25.00 Highsmith Inc.

—Dangerous Kiss: A Lucky Santangelo Novel. abr. ed. 2001. audio (*0-333-78160-0*) Macmillan U.K. GBR. *Dist:* Macmillan Publishing Co., Inc.

—Dangerous Kiss: A Lucky Santangelo Novel. unabr. ed. 2001. audio 94.00 (*0-7887-4979-X*, 96486L8) Recorded Bks., LLC.

—Dangerous Kiss: A Lucky Santangelo Novel. 2000. E-Book 25.00 (*0-684-87371-0*, Simon & Schuster); 1999. 528p. 25.00 (*0-684-85030-3*, Simon & Schuster); 2000. (Illus.). 592p. reprint ed. pap. 7.99 (*0-671-02095-1*, Pocket) Simon & Schuster.

—Dangerous Kiss: A Lucky Santangelo Novel. abr. ed. 1999. audio 25.00 (*0-671-58199-6*, Simon & Schuster Audioworks) Simon & Schuster Audio.

—Dangerous Kiss: A Lucky Santangelo Novel. l.t. ed. 1999. (Core Ser.). 620p. 31.95 (*0-7838-8747-7*) Thorndike Pr.

—Hollywood Divorces. 2004. mass mkt. (*0-7434-2411-5*, Pocket); 2003. 768p. 26.00 (*0-7432-5404-X*, Simon & Schuster); 2003. 480p. 26.00 (*0-7432-1649-0*, Simon & Schuster) Simon & Schuster.

—Hollywood Husbands. 1986. 512p. 18.45 o.p. (*0-671-52500-X*, Simon & Schuster) Simon & Schuster.

—Hollywood Kids. l.t. ed. 1995. (G. K. Hall Core Ser.). 850p. 25.95 (*0-7838-1211-6*); 733p. 20.95 o.p. (*0-7838-1212-4*) Gale Group. (Macmillan Reference USA).

—Hollywood Kids. 1999. per. 7.99 (*0-671-02356-X*, Pocket); 1995. pap. 6.50 (*0-671-89856-6*, Pocket); 1994. 624p. 23.50 (*0-671-66627-4*, Simon & Schuster); 1995. 624p. reprint ed. mass mkt. 7.99 (*0-671-89849-3*, Pocket) Simon & Schuster.

—Hollywood Kids. abr. ed. 1999. 5p. audio 23.00 (*0-671-88859-5*, 492040, Simon & Schuster Audioworks) Simon & Schuster Audio.

—Hollywood Wives: The New Generation. 2003. 10p. pap. 84.95 incl. audio (*0-7927-2912-9*); pap. 94.95 incl. audio compact disk (*0-7927-2913-7*) BBC Audiobooks America.

—Hollywood Wives: The New Generation. 1994. pap. 16.95 o.p. (*0-7871-0156-7*, NewStar Pr.) NewStar Media, Inc.

—Hollywood Wives: The New Generation. 2003. 560p. mass mkt. 5.99 (*0-7434-6735-3*, Pocket); 2001. 528p. 26.00 (*0-7432-1634-2*, Simon & Schuster); 1999. per. 7.99 (*0-671-02355-1*, Pocket); 1986. 560p. mass mkt. 4.95 o.s.i (*0-671-62425-3*, Pocket); 1985. mass mkt. 4.50 o.s.i (*0-671-54764-X*, Pocket); 1984. mass mkt. 4.50 o.s.i (*0-671-49227-6*, Pocket); 1983. 512p. 16.50 o.p. (*0-671-47406-5*, Simon & Schuster); 2002. 704p. pap. 26.00 (*0-7432-3646-7*, Simon & Schuster); 2001. 704p. 26.00 (*0-7432-1744-6*, Simon & Schuster); 2002. 560p. reprint ed. mass mkt. 7.99 (*0-7434-2368-2*, Pocket); 1987. 560p. reprint ed. mass mkt. 7.99 (*0-671-70459-1*, Pocket) Simon & Schuster.

—Lady Boss. l.t. ed. 1991. (General Ser.). 760p. 16.95 o.p. (*0-8161-5189-X*); lib. bdg. 22.95 o.p. (*0-8161-5193-8*) Gale Group. (Macmillan Reference USA).

—Lady Boss. Peters, Sally, ed. 1992. mass mkt. 5.99 (*0-671-79571-6*, Pocket) Simon & Schuster.

—Lady Boss. 1990. 21.95 o.p. (*0-671-61937-3*); 21.95 (*0-671-94826-1*) Simon & Schuster. (Simon & Schuster).

—Lady Boss. Grose, Bill, ed. 1991. 640p. reprint ed. mass mkt. 7.99 (*0-671-74418-6*, Pocket) Simon & Schuster.

—Lady Boss. rev. ed. 1998. 640p. mass mkt. 7.99 (*0-671-02347-0*, Pocket) Simon & Schuster.

—Lady Boss. abr. ed. 1990. audio 15.95 (*0-671-73710-4*, Simon & Schuster Audioworks) Simon & Schuster Audio.

—Lucky. 1990. 608p. mass mkt. 5.95 o.s.i (*0-671-63845-9*); 1987. mass mkt. 6.99 (*0-671-70419-2*); 1986. 608p. mass mkt. 4.95 o.s.i (*0-671-52496-8*); 1998. 624p. mass mkt. 7.99 (*0-671-02348-9*) Simon & Schuster. (Pocket).

—Lucky. abr. ed. 1991. audio 15.95 (*0-671-73808-9*, Simon & Schuster Audioworks) Simon & Schuster Audio.

—Vendetta: Lucky's Revenge. l.t. ed. 1997. (Large Print Book Ser.). 28.95 (*1-56895-435-2*, Wheeler Publishing, Inc.) Gale Group.

—Vendetta: Lucky's Revenge. 1997. 544p. 25.00 o.p. (*0-06-039209-6*, ReganBooks); audio 25.00 o.p. (*0-694-51809-3*, CPN 4048, HarperAudio) HarperTrade.

—Vendetta: Lucky's Revenge. 1998. 5.98 o.p. (*0-7651-0824-0*) Smithmark Pubs., Inc.

Collins, Joan. Star Quality. 2003. 368p. mass mkt. 6.99 (*0-7868-9048-7*) Hyperion Pr.

—Star Quality: A Novel. 2003. mass mkt. 7.99 (*0-7868-9060-6*); 2002. 368p. 23.95 (*1-4013-0000-6*); 2002. mass mkt. 7.99 (*0-7868-9064-9*) Hyperion Pr.

—Star Quality: A Novel. 2003. (Core Ser.). 32.95 (*0-7862-4694-4*) Thorndike Pr.

Cort, Robert. Action! A Novel. 2004. 400p. pap. 13.95 (*0-8129-7216-3*, Random Hse. Trade Paperbacks) Random House Adult Trade Publishing Group.

—Action! A Novel. 2003. 400p. 24.95 (*0-679-45232-X*); E-Book 17.50 (*1-58836-293-0*) Random Hse., Inc.

Coscarelli, Kate. Leading Lady. 1991. 19.95 o.p. (*0-312-05889-6*) St. Martin's Pr.

Covino, Michael. The Negative. 1993. 368p. 21.00 o.p. (*0-670-85078-0*, Viking) Viking Penguin.

Crace, Jim. Genesis. 2003. 256p. 23.00 (*0-374-22730-6*) Farrar, Straus & Giroux.

Craig, Michael D. The Ice Sculptures: A Novel of Hollywood. 2004. pap. (*1-56023-481-4*, Southern Tier Editions) Haworth Pr., Inc., The.

Craig, Peter. The Martini Shot: A Hollywood Novel. 2000. 288p. pap. 13.00 (*0-688-17581-3*, Quill) HarperTrade.

—The Martini Shot: A Hollywood Novel. 1998. 256p. 22.00 (*0-688-15658-4*, Morrow, William & Co.) Morrow/Avon.

Dart, Iris Rainer. The Stork Club. l.t. ed. 1993. 22.95 o.p. (*0-7927-1670-1*); pap. 20.95 o.p. (*0-7927-1669-8*) BBC Audiobooks America.

—The Stork Club. 1992. 400p. 21.95 o.p. (*0-316-17332-0*) Little Brown & Co.

De Vries, Hilary. So 5 Minutes Ago: A Novel. 2004. 304p. 21.95 (*1-4000-6138-5*, Villard Bks.) Random House Adult Trade Publishing Group.

Dell, Pamela. Gavilan: A Story of Hollywood During the McCarthy ERA. 2003. (*1-59187-041-0*) Tradition Publishing Co.

Douglas, Kirk. Dance with the Devil. l.t. ed. 1994. 554p. lib. bdg. 23.95 o.p. (*0-8161-7464-4*, Macmillan Reference USA) Gale Group.

—Dance with the Devil. abr. ed. 1993. 15.95 o.p. (*1-55800-406-8*) NewStar Media, Inc.

—Dance with the Devil. 1992. 3.99 o.p. (*0-517-08346-9*) Random Hse. Value Publishing.

—Dance with the Devil. 1991. 384p. mass mkt. 5.99 o.s.i (*0-446-36191-7*) Warner Bks., Inc.

Dunbar, Sophie. Fashion Victims. 2001. 329p. (*1-890768-29-4*, Intrigue Pr.) Corvus Publishing.

Ellroy, James. Hollywood Nocturnes. unabr. collector's ed. 1996. audio 48.00 (*0-7366-3255-7*, 3912) Books on Tape, Inc.

—Hollywood Nocturnes. 1995. 368p. mass mkt. 5.99 o.s.i (*0-440-22098-X*) Dell Publishing.

—Hollywood Nocturnes. 1994. (Illus.). 272p. bds. 20.00 o.s.i (*1-883402-54-9*, Scribner) Simon & Schuster.

Ellroy, James, et al. Hollywood Nocturnes. 1998. 304p. pap. 13.95 (*0-385-33328-5*) Dell Publishing.

Epstein, Leslie. Pandaemonium. 1998. 416p. pap. 14.95 (*0-312-18752-1*, Saint Martin's Griffin); 1997. 384p. 24.95 o.p. (*0-312-15622-7*) St. Martin's Pr.

—San Remo Drive: A Novel from Memory. 2003. (Illus.). 300p. 24.00 (*1-59051-066-6*) Other Pr., LLC.

Faherty, Terence. Come Back Dead. 1997. 336p. 22.00 o.p. (*0-684-83084-1*, Simon & Schuster) Simon & Schuster.

—Kill Me Again: A Scott Elliott Mystery. 1996. 304p. 22.00 o.p. (*0-684-82688-7*, Simon & Schuster) Simon & Schuster.

—Raise the Devil. 2000. (Scott Elliott Mysteries Ser.). 264p. 23.95 (*0-312-26640-5*, Saint Martin's Minotaur) St. Martin's Pr.

Farmer, Jerrilyn. Immaculate Reception. l.t. ed. 2002. (Mystery Ser.). 396p. 28.95 (*0-7862-4755-X*) Gale Group.

—Immaculate Reception. 1999. (Madeline Bean Catering Mysteries Ser.). 256p. mass mkt. 6.50 (*0-380-79597-3*, Avon Bks.) Morrow/Avon.

—Killer Wedding. 2000. (Madeline Bean Catering Mysteries Ser.). 256p. mass mkt. 6.50 (*0-380-79598-1*, Avon Bks.) Morrow/Avon.

—Sympathy for the Devil. 1998. (Madeline Bean Mystery Ser.). 256p. mass mkt. 5.99 (*0-380-79596-5*, Avon Bks.) Morrow/Avon.

—Sympathy for the Devil. l.t. ed. 2002. (Mystery Ser.). 404p. 28.95 (*0-7862-4743-6*) Thorndike Pr.

Felske, Coerte V. W. Word: The Talk of L. A. 2000. 416p. pap. 13.99 (*0-446-67540-7*); 1998. 399p. 24.00 o.p. (*0-446-52331-3*) Warner Bks., Inc.

Ferrigno, Robert. Scavenger Hunt. 336p. 2004. pap. 13.00 (*1-4000-3254-7*, Vintage); 2003. 24.95 (*0-375-42173-4*, Pantheon) Knopf Publishing Group.

Files, Lolita. Blind Ambitions. 288p. 2000. 23.00 o.s.i (*0-684-87144-0*); 2001. reprint ed. pap. 13.00 (*0-684-87145-9*) Simon & Schuster. (Simon & Schuster).

Fitzgerald, F. Scott. The Last Tycoon. 1977. (Hudson River Editions Ser.). 176p. 35.00 (*0-684-15311-4*, Macmillan Reference USA) Gale Group.

Foglia, Leonard & Richards, David. Face down in the Park. 1999. 320p. 23.00 (*0-671-02728-X*, Atria) Simon & Schuster.

Fottrell, M. K. The Color of Blood. 2002. 351p. pap. 14.95 (*1-58124-699-4*) Fiction Works, The.

Freeman, David. A Hollywood Education: Tales of Movie Dreams & Easy Money. 1992. 288p. pap. 10.95 (*0-88184-870-0*, Carroll & Graf Pubs.) Avalon Publishing Group.

—A Hollywood Education: Tales of Movie Dreams & Easy Money. 1987. pap. 6.95 o.s.i (0-440-53738-X, Laurel) Dell Publishing.
—A Hollywood Education: Tales of Movie Dreams & Easy Money. 1986. 256p. 17.95 o.p. (0-399-13044-6) Putnam Publishing Group, The.
—A Hollywood Life. 1991. 19.95 o.p. (0-671-72738-9, Simon & Schuster) Simon & Schuster.
—It's All True: A Story of Hollywood. 2004. 288p. 23.00 (0-7432-4975-5, Simon & Schuster) Simon & Schuster.
Gage, Elizabeth. Taboo. l.t. ed. 1994. pap. 23.95 o.p. (0-7927-1731-7); 1993. 25.95 o.p. (0-7927-1732-5) BBC Audiobooks America.
—Taboo. abr. ed. 1993. 16.95 o.p. (1-55800-698-2); audio 8.99 o.p. (1-55800-905-1, Dove Audio) NewStar Media, Inc.
—Taboo. Zion, Claire, ed. 1993. 480p. 22.00 (0-671-78641-5, Atria); 576p. reprint ed. mass mkt. 5.99 (0-671-78644-X, Pocket) Simon & Schuster.
Gardner, J. J. Cat's Don't Dance: Digest. 1997. (J). mass mkt. 2.99 (0-590-30844-0) Scholastic, Inc.
Garrison, Zoe. Golden Triple Time. 1986. mass mkt. 2.95 o.p. (0-451-15163-1, Signet Bks.); 1986. mass mkt. 3.95 o.p. (0-451-14150-4, Signet Bks.); 1985. 448p. 15.95 o.p. (0-453-00478-4) NAL.
Garton, Ray. Sex & Violence in Hollywood. 2001. 505p. 40.00 (1-931081-44-1) Subterranean Pr.
Goldemberg, Rose Leiman. Adios, Hollywood: My Story by Dick, Dog of Oaxaca As Told to Rose Leiman Goldemberg. 2000. 180p. pap. 16.95 (0-595-08907-0) iUniverse, Inc.
Goldemberg, Rose Leiman, told to. Adios, Hollywood: My Story by Dick, Dog of Oaxaca As Told to Rose Leiman Goldemberg. 1994. 176p. 18.95 o.p. (0-312-10455-3) St. Martin's Pr.
Goldman, William. Tinsel. 1980. mass mkt. 2.75 o.s.i (0-440-18735-4); 1979. pap. 10.95 o.s.i (0-385-29031-4, Delacorte Pr.) Dell Publishing.
Goldsmith, Olivia. Flavor of the Month. 1993. 704p. 23.00 o.p. (0-671-79449-3, Simon & Schuster) Simon & Schuster.
Goulart, Ron. Elementary My Dear Groucho. 1999. 261p. (J). 23.95 (0-312-20892-8, Saint Martin's Minotaur) St. Martin's Pr.
—Groucho Marx: Master Detective. 1998. 262p. (YA). 22.95 o.p. (0-312-18106-X, Saint Martin's Minotaur) St. Martin's Pr.
—Groucho Marx, Private Eye. 1999. 263p. 23.95 (0-312-19895-7, Saint Martin's Minotaur) St. Martin's Pr.
Graham, Carroll & Graham, Garrett. Queer People: A Novel. 1976. (Lost American Fiction Ser.). 285p. reprint ed. 16.95 (0-8093-0784-7) Southern Illinois Univ. Pr.
Grazer, Gigi Levangie. Maneater. 320p. 2004. pap. 13.00 (0-7434-6400-1, Downtown Pr.); 2003. 21.95 (0-7432-2685-2, Simon & Schuster) Simon & Schuster.
Greenberg, Martin H. & Waugh, Charles, eds. Hollywood Unreel: Fantasies About Hollywood & the Movies. 1982. 304p. 14.95 o.s.i (0-8008-3197-7) Taplinger Publishing Co., Inc.
Grimson, Todd. Brand New Cherry Flavor. 1996. 368p. mass mkt. 20.00 o.p. (0-06-105233-7) HarperCollins Pubs.
—Brand New Cherry Flavor. 1997. mass mkt. 13.00 o.s.i (0-06-105320-1, Eos) Morrow/Avon.
Gross, Shelly. Stardust. 1985. 448p. 18.95 o.p. (0-312-75588-0) St. Martin's Pr.
Guinan, Doug. California Screaming: A Novel. 1999. 208p. reprint ed. pap. 12.95 (1-55583-539-2) Alyson Pubns.
—California Screaming: A Novel. 1998. 304p. 24.00 (0-684-84936-4, Simon & Schuster) Simon & Schuster.
Hall, Jennifer. Star Quality: A Novel. 1993. 21.00 o.p. (1-55611-346-3) Fine, Donald I. Bks.
Hallinan, Timothy. The Bone Polisher. 1996. (Simeon Grist Mystery Ser.). 304p. mass mkt. 5.99 o.p. (0-380-71372-1, Avon Bks.) Morrow/Avon.
Hare, Mimi & Naylor, Clare. The Second Assistant. 2004. 336p. 21.95 (0-670-03307-3) Viking Penguin.
Harrington, William. Columbo: The Glitter Murder. (Columbo Ser.). 1997. 240p. 21.95 o.p. (0-312-86161-3); Vol. 5. 1998. 192p. mass mkt. 5.99 (0-8125-6273-9) Doherty, Tom Assocs., LLC. (Forge Bks.).
—Columbo: The Glitter Murder. l.t. ed. 1998. (Nightingale Ser.). 256p. pap. 21.95 (0-7838-0134-3) Thorndike Pr.
Harris, G. N. Highlights from a Lowlife. 2001. 189p. pap. 20.99 (0-7388-6282-7) Xlibris Corp.
Hauck, Charlie. Artistic Differences. 1993. 238p. 21.00 o.p. (0-688-12152-7, Morrow, William & Co.) Morrow/Avon.
Hayes, Helen & Chastain, Thomas. Where the Truth Lies. 1988. 288p. 16.95 o.p. (0-688-06933-9, Morrow, William & Co.) Morrow/Avon.
Haynes, Betsy. Taffy Sinclair Goes to Hollywood. 1990. 144p. (J). (gr. 4 up). pap. 2.95 o.s.i (0-553-15819-8) Bantam Bks.
Heller, Jane. Lucky Stars. E-Book 24.95 (0-312-70995-1); 2004. 352p. mass mkt. 6.99 (0-312-99006-5, St. Martin's Paperbacks); 2003. 352p. 24.95 (0-312-28848-4) St. Martin's Pr.
Hensley, Dennis. Misadventures in the (213) 1999. 304p. pap. 15.00 (0-688-17128-1, Perennial) HarperTrade.
—Misadventures in the (213) 1998. 304p. 24.00 (0-688-15452-2, Morrow, William & Co.) Morrow/Avon.
—Screening Party. 2002. 256p. pap. 16.95 (1-55583-733-6) Alyson Pubns.
Holland, Cecelia. The Bear Flag. 1990. 448p. 19.95 o.p. (0-395-48886-9) Houghton Mifflin Co.
Hollywood's Silent Closet. 2001. 745p. mass mkt. 24.95 (0-9668030-2-7) Georgia Literary Assn.
Huneven, Michelle. Jamesland: A Novel. 2003. 400p. 24.00 (0-375-41382-0) Knopf, Alfred A. Inc.
Huxley, Aldous. After Many a Summer Dies the Swan. 1977. reprint ed. lib. bdg. 25.95 (0-89190-395-X, Queens Hse., Inc.) Amereon, Ltd.
—After Many a Summer Dies the Swan. 1993. 95p. reprint ed. pap. 14.95 (1-56663-018-5, Elephant Paperbacks) Dee, Ivan R. Pub.
—After Many a Summer Dies the Swan. 1965. pap. 2.25 o.p. (0-06-083046-8, P3046) HarperCollins Pubs.
—After Many a Summer Dies the Swan. 1983. 256p. mass mkt. 5.95 o.p. (0-06-091063-1, CN1063, Perennial) HarperTrade.
Isenberg, Lynn. My Life Uncovered. 2003. 336p. pap. (0-373-25043-6, Red Dress Ink) Harlequin Enterprises, Ltd.
Jacobs, Nancy Baker. Star Struck: A Quinn Collins Mystery. 2002. (Five Star First Edition Mystery Ser.). 327p. 25.95 (0-7862-4171-3, Five Star) Gale Group.
Jones, Adrienne. A Matter of Spunk. 1983. (Charlotte Zolotow Bk.). 320p. (YA). (gr. 7 up). lib. bdg. 13.89 o.p. (0-06-023054-1) HarperCollins Children's Bk. Group.
Jong, Erica. How to Save Your Own Life. 1995. 320p. pap. 11.95 o.p. (0-452-27454-0, Plume) Dutton/Plume.
Kalman, Maira. Max in Hollywood, Baby. 1992. (Illus.). 400p. (J). (gr. 2 up). 17.99 (0-670-84479-9, Viking Children's Bks.) Penguin Putnam Bks. for Young Readers.
Kaminsky, Stuart M. Bullet for a Star. unabr. ed. 1994. audio 23.95 (0-7861-0731-6, 1482) Blackstone Audio Bks., Inc.
—Bullet for a Star. 1985. (Toby Peters Mystery Ser.). pap. 3.95 o.p. (0-89296-147-3) Mysterious Pr.
—Bullet for a Star. 1977. (Toby Peters Mystery Ser.). 188p. 7.95 o.p. (0-312-10797-8) St. Martin's Pr.
—Bullet for a Star. 1991. (Toby Peters Mystery Ser.). 192p. mass mkt. 4.99 (0-446-40061-0, Mysterious Pr. Paperback Bks.) Warner Bks., Inc.
—Buried Caesars. l.t. ed. 1991. (Toby Peters Mystery Ser.). 281p. 18.95 o.p. (0-7927-0490-8); pap. 16.95 o.p. (0-7927-0491-6, C0783) BBC Audiobooks America.
—Buried Caesars. 1989. (Toby Peters Mystery Ser.). 192p. 15.45 o.p. (0-89296-374-3) Mysterious Pr.
—Buried Caesars. unabr. ed. 1997. (Toby Peters Mystery Ser.: Vol. 14). audio 44.00 (0-7887-0401-X, 94593E7) Recorded Bks., LLC.
—Buried Caesars. 1990. (Toby Peters Mystery Ser.). 192p. mass mkt. 4.50 (0-445-40878-2, Mysterious Pr. Paperback Bks.) Warner Bks., Inc.
—Catch a Falling Clown. 1981. (Toby Peters Mystery Ser.). 182p. 10.95 o.p. (0-312-12377-9) St. Martin's Pr.
—Catch a Falling Clown. 1984. (Toby Peters Mystery Ser.). 182p. reprint ed. pap. 3.95 o.p. (0-14-007022-2, Penguin Bks.) Viking Penguin.
—Dancing in the Dark. unabr. ed. 1996. (Toby Peters Mystery Ser.). 30p. audio 39.95 (0-7861-0961-0, 754074) Blackstone Audio Bks., Inc.
—Dancing in the Dark. 1996. (Toby Peters Mystery Ser.). 228p. 19.95 o.s.i (0-89296-528-2) Mysterious Pr.
—Dancing in the Dark. unabr. ed. audio. 1996. (Toby Peters Mystery Ser.: Vol. 19). audio 44.00 (0-7887-0621-7, 94795E7) Recorded Bks., LLC.
—Dancing in the Dark. 1997. (Toby Peters Mystery Ser.). 224p. mass mkt. 5.99 o.p. (0-446-40337-7) Warner Bks., Inc.
—The Devil Met a Lady. unabr. ed. 1995. audio 39.95 (0-7861-0881-9, 1536) Blackstone Audio Bks., Inc.
—The Devil Met a Lady. 1993. (Toby Peters Mystery Ser.). 208p. 18.95 (0-89296-436-7) Mysterious Pr.
—The Devil Met a Lady. 1995. (Toby Peters Mystery Ser.). 208p. mass mkt. 5.50 (0-446-40423-3, Mysterious Pr. Paperback Bks.) Warner Bks., Inc.
—The Devil Met a Lady. 2000. (Toby Peters Mysteries Ser.). 240p. pap. 12.00 (0-7434-0004-6) ibooks, Inc.
—Down for the Count. l.t. ed. 1986. (Toby Peters Mystery Ser.). 307p. 11.95 o.p. (0-8161-4000-6, Macmillan Reference USA) Gale Group.
—Down for the Count. 1985. (Toby Peters Mystery Ser.). 192p. 12.95 o.p. (0-312-21862-1) St. Martin's Pr.
—Down for the Count. 1990. (Toby Peters Mystery Ser.). mass mkt. 4.50 o.s.i (0-445-40908-8, Mysterious Pr. Paperback Bks.) Warner Bks., Inc.
—The Fala Factor. 1985. (Toby Peters Mystery Ser.). pap. 3.95 o.p. (0-89296-148-1) Mysterious Pr.
—The Fala Factor. 1984. (Toby Peters Mystery Ser.). 174p. 11.95 o.p. (0-312-27967-1) St. Martin's Pr.
—The Fala Factor. 1993. (Toby Peters Mystery Ser.). 224p. mass mkt. 4.99 (0-446-40065-3, Mysterious Pr. Paperback Bks.) Warner Bks., Inc.
—A Fatal Glass of Beer. unabr. ed. 1998. (Toby Peters Mystery Ser.). audio 29.95 (0-7861-1465-7); audio 44.95 (0-7861-1346-4, 1766) Blackstone Audio Bks., Inc.
—A Fatal Glass of Beer, Set. unabr. ed. 1999. audio 44.95 Highsmith Inc.
—A Fatal Glass of Beer. 1997. (Toby Peters Mystery Ser.). (ACE.). 256p. 21.50 o.p. (0-89296-630-0) Mysterious Pr.
—A Fatal Glass of Beer. unabr. ed. 1997. (Toby Peters Mystery Ser.: Vol. 20). audio 51.00 (0-7887-0650-0, 94827E7) Recorded Bks., LLC.
—A Few Minutes Past Midnight. 2001. 240p. 24.00 (0-7867-0862-X, Carroll & Graf Pubs.) Avalon Publishing Group.
—A Few Minutes Past Midnight. l.t. ed. 2002. 347p. 29.95 (0-7862-4118-7) Gale Group.
—He Done Her Wrong. unabr. ed. 1998. audio 39.95 (0-7861-1280-8, 2175) Blackstone Audio Bks., Inc.
—He Done Her Wrong. 1984. (Toby Peters Mystery Ser.). reprint ed. pap. 3.95 o.p. (0-89296-095-7) Mysterious Pr.
—He Done Her Wrong. 1983. (Toby Peters Mystery Ser.). 168p. 10.95 o.p. (0-312-36491-1) St. Martin's Pr.
—He Done Her Wrong. 1995. (Toby Peters Mystery Ser.). 208p. mass mkt. 5.50 (0-446-40191-9, Mysterious Pr. Paperback Bks.) Warner Bks., Inc.
—High Midnight. unabr. ed. 1995. audio 32.95 (0-7861-0765-0, 1614) Blackstone Audio Bks., Inc.
—High Midnight. 1984. (Toby Peters Mystery Ser.). reprint ed. pap. 3.95 o.p. (0-89296-091-4) Mysterious Pr.
—High Midnight. 1981. (Toby Peters Mystery Ser.). 188p. 9.95 o.p. (0-312-37234-5) St. Martin's Pr.
—The Howard Hughes Affair. 1980. (Toby Peters Mystery Ser.). 192p. 2.25 o.s.i (0-441-34462-3) Ace Bks.
—The Howard Hughes Affair. unabr. ed. 1999. audio 32.95 (0-7861-1397-9, 1570); 1995. audio 32.95 (0-7861-0668-9, 1570) Blackstone Audio Bks., Inc.
—The Howard Hughes Affair. 1979. (Toby Peters Mystery Ser.). 207p. 8.95 o.p. (0-312-39617-1) St. Martin's Pr.
—The Howard Hughes Affair. 1990. (Toby Peters Mystery Ser.). 224p. mass mkt. 4.95 o.s.i (0-445-40905-3, Mysterious Pr. Paperback Bks.) Warner Bks., Inc.
—The Man Who Shot Lewis Vance. unabr. ed. 1998. audio 5.99 (0-88646-963-5, PAC-7963) Durkin Hayes Publishing Ltd.
—The Man Who Shot Lewis Vance. 1986. (Toby Peters Mystery Ser.). 224p. 14.95 o.p. (0-312-51394-1) St. Martin's Pr.
—The Man Who Shot Lewis Vance. 1990. (Toby Peters Mystery Ser.). 208p. mass mkt. 4.50 o.s.i (0-445-40909-6, Mysterious Pr. Paperback Bks.) Warner Bks., Inc.
—The Melting Clock. l.t. ed. 1992. (Toby Peters Mystery Ser.). 260p. 19.95 o.p. (0-7927-1280-3); pap. 17.95 o.p. (0-7927-1281-1) BBC Audiobooks America.
—The Melting Clock. unabr. ed. 1998. (Toby Peters Mystery Ser.). audio 32.95 (0-7861-1468-1, 2227) Blackstone Audio Bks., Inc.
—The Melting Clock. 1991. (Toby Peters Mystery Ser.). 192p. 17.45 o.p. (0-89296-435-9) Mysterious Pr.
—The Melting Clock. 1993. (Toby Peters Mystery Ser.). 208p. mass mkt. 4.99 (0-446-40304-0, Mysterious Pr. Paperback Bks.) Warner Bks., Inc.
—Mildred Pierced. 2003. (Otto Penzler Book Ser.). 224p. 24.00 (0-7867-1182-5, Carroll & Graf Pubs.) Avalon Publishing Group.
—Murder on the Yellow Brick Road. unabr. ed. 1994. audio 23.95 (0-7861-0785-5, 1511) Blackstone Audio Bks., Inc.
—Murder on the Yellow Brick Road. 1978. (Toby Peters Mystery Ser.). 197p. 7.95 o.p. (0-312-55318-8) St. Martin's Pr.
—Murder on the Yellow Brick Road. 1979. (Toby Peters Mystery Ser.). 208p. pap. 3.95 o.p. (0-14-005124-4, Penguin Bks.) Viking Penguin.
—Murder on the Yellow Brick Road. 2000. (Toby Peters Mysteries Ser.). 192p. pap. 12.00 (0-7434-0000-3) ibooks, Inc.
—Never Cross a Vampire. unabr. ed. 2000. audio compact disk 48.00 (0-7861-9943-1, z2256); 1999. audio compact disk 24.95 (0-7861-1461-4); 1998. audio 32.95 (0-7861-1353-7, 2256) Blackstone Audio Bks., Inc.
—Never Cross a Vampire. unabr. ed. 1999. audio 32.95 Highsmith Inc.
—Never Cross a Vampire. 1984. (Toby Peters Mystery Ser.). reprint ed. pap. 3.95 o.s.i (0-89296-087-6) Mysterious Pr.
—Never Cross a Vampire. 1980. (Toby Peters Mystery Ser.). 182p. 8.95 o.p. (0-312-56471-6) St. Martin's Pr.
—Never Cross a Vampire. 1995. (Toby Peters Mystery Ser.). 192p. mass mkt. 5.50 (0-446-40190-0, Mysterious Pr. Paperback Bks.) Warner Bks., Inc.
—Never Cross a Vampire. 2000. 224p. pap. 12.00 (0-7434-0713-X) ibooks, Inc.
—Poor Butterfly. unabr. ed. 1996. audio 32.95 (0-7861-1018-X, 1796) Blackstone Audio Bks., Inc.
—Poor Butterfly. 1990. (Toby Peters Mystery Ser.). 179p. 17.95 o.p. (0-89296-411-1) Mysterious Pr.
—Poor Butterfly. unabr. ed. 1997. (Toby Peters Mystery Ser.: Vol. 15). audio 35.00 (0-7887-0833-3, 94978E7) Recorded Bks., LLC.
—Poor Butterfly. 1991. (Toby Peters Mystery Ser.). mass mkt. 4.95 o.s.i (0-446-40011-4) Warner Bks., Inc.
—Smart Moves. unabr. ed. 1997. audio 39.95 (0-7861-1167-4, 1934) Blackstone Audio Bks., Inc.
—Smart Moves. 1987. (Toby Peters Mystery Ser.). 272p. 15.95 o.p. (0-312-00190-8) St. Martin's Pr.
—Smart Moves. 1996. (Toby Peters Mystery Ser.). 224p. reprint ed. mass mkt. 5.99 o.p. (0-446-40438-1, Mysterious Pr. Paperback Bks.) Warner Bks., Inc.
—Think Fast, Mr. Peters. 1996. (Toby Peters Mystery Ser.). 224p. mass mkt. 5.99 (0-446-40440-3, Mysterious Pr. Paperback Bks.) Warner Bks., Inc.
—To Catch a Spy. 2002. 240p. 24.00 (0-7867-1023-3, Carroll & Graf Pubs.) Avalon Publishing Group.
—Tomorrow Is Another Day. 1995. (Toby Peters Mystery Ser.). 208p. 18.95 o.s.i (0-89296-527-4) Mysterious Pr.
—Tomorrow Is Another Day. unabr. ed. 1995. (Toby Peters Mystery Ser.: Vol. 18). audio 51.00 (0-7887-0354-4, 94546E7) Recorded Bks., LLC.
—Tomorrow Is Another Day. 1996. (Toby Peters Mystery Ser.). 224p. mass mkt. 5.99 (0-446-40336-9, Mysterious Pr. Paperback Bks.) Warner Bks., Inc.
—You Bet Your Life. 1979. (Toby Peters Mystery Ser.). 215p. 8.95 o.p. (0-312-89662-X) St. Martin's Pr.
—You Bet Your Life. 1990. (Toby Peters Mystery Ser.). 224p. mass mkt. 4.95 o.s.i (0-445-40906-1, Mysterious Pr. Paperback Bks.) Warner Bks., Inc.
Kane, John. Best Actress. 1998. 288p. pap. 10.95 o.s.i (0-345-42071-3) Ballantine Bks.
Kanin, Garson. Moviola. 1979. 12.95 o.s.i (0-671-24822-7, Simon & Schuster) Simon & Schuster.
Karbo, Karen. The Diamond Lane. 1991. 320p. 21.95 o.p. (0-399-13597-9, G. P. Putnam's Sons) Penguin Group (USA) Inc.
Keene, Carolyn. Dangerous Loves. 1997. (Nancy Drew Files: No. 120). 160p. (YA). (gr. 6 up). per. 3.99 (0-671-56878-7, Simon Pulse) Simon & Schuster Children's Publishing.
—Hollywood Horror. Greenberg, Anne, ed. 1994. (Nancy Drew & Hardy Boys Super Mystery Ser.: No. 21). 224p. (Orig.). (YA). (gr. 6 up). mass mkt. 3.99 (0-671-78181-2, Simon Pulse) Simon & Schuster Children's Publishing.
Kendall, Jane, et al. Miranda Goes to Hollywood. 1999. 256p. (YA). (gr. 5-9). 16.00 o.s.i (0-15-202059-4) Harcourt Children's Bks.
Kihn, Greg. The Horror Show. 1997. 274p. pap. text 5.99 (0-8125-5108-7); 1996. 352p. 23.95 (0-312-86045-5) Doherty, Tom Assocs., LLC. (Tor Bks.).
Kincaid, Tim. Today, Tomorrow & Always. 1997. 480p. mass mkt. 5.99 o.s.i (1-57566-187-X); 1996. 432p. 22.00 o.p. (1-57566-077-6, Kensington Bks.) Kensington Publishing Corp.
Knode, Helen. The Ticket Out. 352p. 2004. pap. 13.00 (0-15-602905-7, Harvest Bks.); 2003. 24.00 (0-15-100184-7) Harcourt Trade Pubs.
Koontz, Dean. The Face. 2004. 672p. mass mkt. 7.99 (0-553-58448-0); 2003. 624p. 26.95 (0-553-80248-8) Bantam Bks.
—The Face. unabr. ed. 2003. audio 49.95 (0-7393-0174-8, RH Audio); audio compact disk 59.95 (0-7393-0745-2, Listening Library) Random Hse. Audio Publishing Group.
Lehman, Ernest. Sweet Smell of Success: Short Fiction of Ernest Lehman. 2000. 272p. 15.95 (1-58567-047-2) Overlook Pr., The.
Leigh, Janet. The Dream Factory. 2003. 400p. mass mkt. (1-55166-650-2); 2002. 384p. (1-55166-874-2, 1-66874-8) Harlequin Enterprises, Ltd. (Mira Bks.).
—House of Destiny. 1996. 507p. mass mkt. (1-55166-159-4, 1-66159-4); 1995. 512p. (1-55166-125-X) Harlequin Enterprises, Ltd. (Mira Bks.).

Levien, D. J. Wormwood. 1999. 247p. 22.95 (0-7868-6506-7) Hyperion Pr.

—Wormwood: A Novel. 2000. 256p. pap. 14.00 (0-7868-8436-3) Hyperion Pr.

Levinson, Robert S. The James Dean Affair. 2000. (Neil Gulliver & Steve Marriner Novels Ser.). 320p. 24.95 o.p. (0-312-87268-2, Forge Bks.) Doherty, Tom Assocs., LLC.

Lilly, Mike. West Virginia Jew. 2001. 128p. pap. 12.95 (1-57197-245-5) Pentland Pr., Inc.

Lynch, Patrick. Figure of Eight. 2000. (Illus.). 320p. 24.95 o.s.i (0-525-94510-5, Dutton) Dutton/Plume.

Mailer, Norman. The Deer Park. 1976. 2.95 o.s.i (0-425-03264-7) Berkley Publishing Group.

—The Deer Park. 1980. 375p. reprint ed. 35.00 o.p. (0-86527-235-2) Fertig, Howard Inc.

—The Deer Park. 1997. 384p. pap. 14.00 (0-375-70040-4, Vintage) Knopf Publishing Group.

—The Deer Park. 1981. 384p. pap. 8.95 o.p. (0-399-50531-8) Putnam Publishing Group, The.

Mallory, Carole. Flash. 1991. 2.99 o.p. (0-517-07575-X) Random Hse. Value Publishing.

—Flash. 1989. mass mkt. 4.50 o.s.i (0-671-64465-3, Pocket); 1988. 16.95 o.p. (0-671-64464-5, Simon & Schuster) Simon & Schuster.

Manaster, Benjamin. Skyla. Caso, Adolph, ed. 1995. 246p. 21.95 (0-8283-2002-0) Branden Bks.

Maracotta, Lindsay. The Dead Celeb. 1998. mass mkt. 5.99 (0-380-72689-0, Avon Bks.); 1997. 288p. 24.00 o.p. (0-688-14499-3, Morrow, William & Co.) Morrow/Avon.

—The Dead Hollywood Moms Society. 320p. 1997. mass mkt. 5.99 (0-380-72688-2, Avon Bks.); 1996. 24.00 o.p. (0-688-14498-5, Morrow, William & Co.) Morrow/Avon.

—Playing Dead: A Hollywood Mystery. 1999. 288p. 24.00 (0-688-15867-6, Morrow, William & Co.) Morrow/Avon.

Marton, Sandra. Mariage a Hollywood. 1997. (Harlequin Azur Ser.). (FRE.). pap. (0-373-34655-7, 1-34655-0, Harlequin Bks.) Harlequin Enterprises, Ltd.

Marx, Pat. Blockbuster. 1988. 224p. pap. 15.00 (0-553-34498-6) Bantam Bks.

McCarthy, Kevin. Into the Darkness Bk. 2, Vol. 2. 2002. 464p. mass mkt. 6.99 o.s.i (0-7564-0021-X) DAW Bks., Inc.

McCoy, Horace. I Should Have Stayed Home. Kupelnick, Bruce S., ed. 1978. (Classics of Film Literature Ser.). lib. bdg. 21.00 o.p. (0-8240-2883-X) Garland Publishing, Inc.

McLaughlin, Christian. Glamourpuss. 1994. 256p. 19.95 o.p. (0-525-93866-4) Dutton/Plume.

Miles, Cassie. Critic's Choice. l.t. ed. 2002. 217p. 27.95 (0-7862-4262-0) Gale Group.

Monette, Paul. The Long Shot. 2001. 336p. pap. 15.00 (0-7582-0058-7) Kensington Publishing Corp.

—The Long Shot. 1981. mass mkt. 5.95 o.p. (0-380-76828-3, 76828-3, Avon Bks.) Morrow/Avon.

Monteilh, Marissa. May December Souls. Jones, Nicole, ed. 2000. 287p. pap. 13.95 (0-9704141-0-2) 4D Publishing.

—May December Souls: A Novel. 2002. 288p. pap. 13.95 (0-06-000732-X, Avon Bks.) Morrow/Avon.

Morris, Wright. Love among the Cannibals. 1977. 253p. reprint ed. pap. 8.95 o.p. (0-8032-5842-9, Bison Bks.) Univ. of Nebraska Pr.

Mosiman, Billie Sue. Final Cut. 2003. 285p. pap. 13.95 (1-4104-0112-X, Five Star Trade); 2002. 300p. 24.95 (0-7862-4175-6, Five Star) Gale Group.

Nagy, Gloria. Marriage: A Novel. 1995. 448p. 22.95 o.p. (0-316-59675-2) Little Brown & Co.

Naylor, Clare. Catching Alice. 2000. 336p. pap. 14.00 (0-449-00557-7, Ballantine Bks.) Ballantine Bks.

Neri, Kris. Dem Bones' Revenge. 2003. (WWL Mystery Ser.: No. 466). 272p. mass mkt. (0-373-26466-6, Worldwide Library) Harlequin Enterprises, Ltd.

Nicholson, Geoff. The Hollywood Dodo: A Novel. 2004. 304p. 23.00 (0-7432-5779-0, Simon & Schuster) Simon & Schuster.

Nixon, Joan Lowery. Encore, 1992. (Hollywood Daughters Ser.: Bk. 3). 208p. (YA). mass mkt. 3.50 o.s.i (0-553-29287-0) Bantam Bks.

—Encore. 1990. (Hollywood Daughters Ser.: Bk. 3). 208p. (YA). (gr. 7 up). 14.95 o.s.i (0-553-07024-X, Starfire) Random Hse. Children's Bks.

—Overnight Sensation. 1991. (Hollywood Daughters Ser.: No. 2). 192p. (YA). mass mkt. 3.50 o.s.i (0-553-29019-3) Bantam Bks.

—An Overnight Sensation. 1990. (Hollywood Daughters Ser.: No. 2). 192p. (YA). 14.95 o.s.i (0-553-05865-7) Bantam Bks.

—Star Baby. (Hollywood Daughters Ser.: Bk. 1). 192p. (YA). 1991. mass mkt. 3.50 o.s.i (0-553-28957-8); 1989. (gr. 7 up). 14.95 o.s.i (0-553-05838-X) Bantam Bks.

Oates, Joyce Carol. Blonde. 2001. 752p. pap. 15.00 (0-06-093493-X, Ecco); 2000. 752p. 27.50 (0-06-019607-6, Ecco); 2000. 9p. audio 29.95 (0-694-52312-7, HarperAudio) HarperTrade.

—Blonde. 2000. (SPA.). 942p. pap. (84-01-01400-X) Plaza & Janés Editories, S.A. ESP. *Dist:* Libros Sin Fronteras.

—Blonde. 2002. (SPA.). 944p. pap. 23.95 (1-4000-0146-3) Random Hse., Inc.

O'Brien, Darcy. Margaret in Hollywood. 1991. 320p. 20.95 o.p. (0-688-09169-5, Morrow, William & Co.) Morrow/Avon.

—A Way of Life, Like Any Other. 2001. (New York Review Books Classics Ser.). 153p. pap. 12.95 (0-940322-79-X) New York Review of Bks., Inc., The.

—A Way of Life, Like Any Other. 1978. 7.95 o.p. (0-393-08798-0) Norton, W. W. & Co., Inc.

Oldfield, Jenny. Hollywood Princess. 2001. (Illus.). 158p. pap. 7.95 (0-340-75728-0) Hodder & Stoughton, Ltd. GBR. *Dist:* Trafalgar Square.

Pella, Judith. Written on the Wind. 2001. (Daughters of Fortune Ser.). 464p. pap. 13.99 (0-7642-2421-2); 464p. text 18.99 o.s.i (0-7642-2608-8); 720p. pap. 18.99 (0-7642-2609-6) Bethany Hse. Pubs.

Platt, Randall Beth. The Royalscope Fe-As-Ko. 1997. 288p. 21.95 (0-945774-35-4, PS3566.L293R68) Catbird Pr.

Puzo, Mario. The Last Don. 1997. mass mkt. 7.99 (0-345-91220-9); 512p. mass mkt. 7.99 (0-345-41221-4) Ballantine Bks.

—The Last Don, Set. abr. ed. 1996. audio 24.00 o.s.i (0-679-45270-2, RH Audio) Random Hse. Audio Publishing Group.

—The Last Don. l.t. ed. 1996. 720p. 25.95 o.p. (0-7838-1916-1) Random Hse. Large Print.

Queen, Ellery. The Four of Hearts: An Ellery Queen Mystery. 1994. 224p. reprint ed. pap. 8.00 o.p. (0-06-097604-7, Perennial) HarperTrade.

—The Hollywood Murders. 2000. 468p. pap. 17.00 (1-56858-173-4) Four Walls Eight Windows.

Rechy, John. The Miraculous Day of Amalia Gomez: A Novel. 2001. 224p. pap. 13.00 (0-8021-3847-0, Grove Pr.) Grove/Atlantic, Inc.

Ridley, John. Love Is a Racket. 352p. 2003. pap. 13.95 (0-345-42146-9); 1999. mass mkt. 6.99 (0-345-43409-9) Ballantine Bks.

—Love Is a Racket. aut. ed. 1998. 24.00 o.s.i (0-676-54304-9) Random Hse., Inc.

Robbins, Harold. The Storyteller. l.t. ed. 1987. 8.95 o.p. (1-55504-244-9); pap. 18.95 o.p. (1-55504-359-3) BBC Audiobooks America.

—The Storyteller. 1985. 17.45 o.p. (0-671-55749-1, Simon & Schuster) Simon & Schuster.

Roberts, Nora. Genuine Lies. 1991. 528p. reprint ed. mass mkt. 7.99 (0-553-29078-9) Bantam Bks.

—Genuine Lies. l.t. ed. 1998. (Large Print Book Ser.). 27.95 (1-56895-678-9, Wheeler Publishing, Inc.) Gale Group.

—River's End. 2000. 480p. mass mkt. 7.99 (0-515-12783-3, Jove) Berkley Publishing Group.

—River's End. abr. ed. 2000. audio 7.99 (1-56740-986-5, 2156, Paperback Nova Audio Bks.); 1999. audio 17.95 o.p. (1-56740-828-1, 1622, Nova Audio Bks.); 1999. audio 39.95 (1-56740-412-X, 1621, Brilliance Audio Unabridged); 1999. 14p. audio 73.25 (1-56740-640-8, 1635, Unabridged Library Editions) Brilliance Audio.

—River's End. abr. ed. 1999. audio 17.95. audio 39.95 Highsmith Inc.

—River's End. 2001. (0-399-15029-3); 1999. 420p. 23.95 o.s.i (0-399-14470-6) Penguin Group (USA) Inc.

—River's End. l.t. ed. (Paperback Bestsellers Ser.). 2000. 664p. 28.95 (0-7862-1862-2); 1999. 714p. pap. 31.95 (0-7862-1861-4) Thorndike Pr.

Robinson, Jill. Star Country. 9999. mass mkt. o.p. (0-449-22257-8, Fawcett); 1997. mass mkt. 6.50 o.s.i (0-8041-1551-6, Ivy Bks.) Ballantine Bks.

Rodi, Robert. Bitch Goddess: A Novel. 2002. 320p. pap. 13.00 (0-452-28310-8, Plume) Dutton/Plume.

Rogers, Mark E. Samurai Cat Goes to the Movies. 1994. 288p. pap. 10.95 o.p. (0-312-85744-6, Tor Bks.) Doherty, Tom Assocs., LLC.

Ross, JoAnn. Legacy of Lies. 2001. 384p. mass mkt. (1-55166-821-1, Harlequin Bks.) Harlequin Enterprises, Ltd.

Rubin, Charles. 4-F Blues: A Novel of WWII Hollywood. 2002. 308p. pap. 14.00 (0-9679790-0-5) NewCentury Pubs.

Rudner, Rita. Tickled Pink. abr. ed. 2004. audio compact disk 14.99 (1-59355-666-7, 5285) Brilliance Audio.

—Tickled Pink. 2001. 320p. 25.00 (0-7434-4261-X); E-Book 25.00 (0-7434-5135-X) Simon & Schuster. (Atria).

—Tickled Pink: A Comic Novel. l.t. ed. 2002. 486p. 29.95 (0-7862-4074-1) Gale Group.

—Tickled Pink: A Comic Novel. 2002. 320p. reprint ed. pap. 14.00 (0-7434-4262-8, Washington Square Pr.) Simon & Schuster.

Rushfield, Richard. On Spec: A Novel of Young Hollywood. 2001. 192p. pap. 12.95 (0-312-28053-X, Saint Martin's Griffin) St. Martin's Pr.

Sahgal, Ajay. Pool: A Novel. 224p. 1995. pap. 10.00 (0-8021-3343-6, Grove Pr.); 1994. 20.00 o.p. (0-87113-559-0, Atlantic Monthly Pr.) Grove/Atlantic, Inc.

Sanders, Lawrence. The Dream Lover. 1987. 320p. mass mkt. 7.50 (0-425-09473-1) Berkley Publishing Group.

—Stolen Blessings. l.t. ed. 1992. pap. 14.95 o.p. (0-7927-0558-0) BBC Audiobooks America.

Schulberg, Budd. The Disenchanted. 1975. 416p. pap. 3.95 o.p. (0-670-00584-3, Penguin Bks.) Viking Penguin.

—What Makes Sammy Run? 1979. reprint ed. lib. bdg. 16.00 (0-8376-0435-4) Bentley Pubs.

—What Makes Sammy Run? 1994. reprint ed. lib. bdg. 32.95 (1-56849-333-9) Buccaneer Bks., Inc.

—What Makes Sammy Run? 1993. 352p. pap. 14.00 (0-679-73422-8, Vintage) Knopf Publishing Group.

—What Makes Sammy Run? 1990. 19.95 o.s.i (0-394-57618-7) Random Hse., Inc.

—What Makes Sammy Run? 1978. pap. 3.95 o.p. (0-14-004795-6, Penguin Bks.) Viking Penguin.

—What Makes Sammy Run? A Novel. 2002. 320p. 22.00 (0-375-50831-7) Random Hse., Inc.

Schultz, Marion. Going Hollywood. 1989. (J). (gr. 6 up). mass mkt. 2.95 o.s.i (0-449-70281-2, Fawcett) Ballantine Bks.

Shagan, Steve. A Cast of Thousands. l.t. ed. 1993. 22.95 o.p. (1-56895-021-7, Wheeler Publishing, Inc.) Gale Group.

—A Cast of Thousands. Grose, Bill, ed. 1993. 368p. 22.00 (0-671-74132-2, Atria); 1994. 384p. reprint ed. mass mkt. 5.99 (0-671-74133-0, Pocket) Simon & Schuster.

Shah, Diane K. Dying Cheek to Cheek. 1992. 464p. 18.50 o.s.i (0-385-42250-4) Doubleday Publishing.

Shaw, Diana. Gone Hollywood: A Carter Colborn Mystery. 1988. (YA). (gr. 7 up). 12.95 o.p. (0-316-78343-9, Joy Street Bks.) Little Brown & Co.

Sheldon, Sidney. A Stranger in the Mirror. 1976. 21.50 o.p. (0-688-03002-5, Morrow, William & Co.) Morrow/Avon.

—A Stranger in the Mirror. l.t. ed. 1983. (Charnwood Large Print Ser.). 400p. o.p. (0-7089-8111-9, Charnwood) Thorpe, F. A. Pubs. GBR. *Dist:* Ulverscroft Large Print Canada, Ltd.

—A Stranger in the Mirror. 1988. 320p. reprint ed. mass mkt. 7.99 (0-446-35657-3) Warner Bks., Inc.

Sherrill, Martha. My Last Movie Star: A Novel of Hollywood. 2004. 384p. pap. 13.95 (0-375-75949-2, Random Hse. Trade Paperbacks) Random House Adult Trade Publishing Group.

—My Last Movie Star: A Novel of Hollywood. 2003. 368p. 23.95 (0-375-50769-8) Random Hse., Inc.

Sinykin, Sheri Cooper. Heather Goes to Hollywood. 1997. (Magic Attic Club Ser.). (Illus.). 80p. (J). (gr. 2-6). 18.90 (1-57513-180-3); pap. 5.95 (1-57513-088-2) Millbrook Pr., Inc. (Magic Attic Pr.).

—Heather Goes to Hollywood. 1997. (Magic Attic Club Ser.). (J). (gr. 2-6). 12.10 (0-606-19138-0) Turtleback Bks.

Smith, Charlie. Chimney Rock: A Novel. 1997. 352p. pap. 14.00 o.p. (0-8050-5592-4, Owl Bks.); 1993. 400p. 22.50 o.p. (0-8050-2244-9) Holt, Henry & Co.

Steel, Danielle. The Cottage. 2003. 400p. mass mkt. 7.99 (0-440-23681-9, Dell Bks.); 2002. 312p. 200.00 (0-385-33622-5, Delacorte Pr.); 2002. 312p. 26.95 (0-385-33552-0, Delacorte Pr.) Dell Publishing.

—The Cottage. abr. ed. 2002. audio 26.95 (0-553-52893-9); audio compact disk 31.95 (0-553-71465-1); audio 39.95 (0-553-52899-8) Random Hse. Audio Publishing Group. (RH Audio).

—The Cottage. l.t. ed. 496p. 2003. pap. 15.95 (0-375-43198-5); 2002. 26.95 (0-375-43150-0) Random Hse. Large Print.

—Heartbeat. l.t. ed. 1991. 608p. 24.95 o.s.i (0-385-30320-3, Delacorte Large Type) Bantam Doubleday Dell Large Print Group, Inc.

—Heartbeat. 1992. 416p. mass mkt. 7.50 (0-440-21189-1); 1991. 368p. 23.95 o.s.i (0-385-29908-7, Delacorte Pr.) Dell Publishing.

—Heartbeat. l.t. ed. 1994. 428p. pap. 20.95 o.p. (0-8161-5789-8, Macmillan Reference USA) Gale Group.

—Heartbeat. l.t. ed. 2004. 592p. 24.95 (0-375-43324-4) Random Hse. Large Print.

—Heartbeat. 1991. 13.04 (0-606-05346-8) Turtleback Bks.

—Secrets. 1985. 336p. 19.95 o.s.i (0-385-29418-2, Delacorte Pr.) Dell Publishing.

—Secrets. l.t. ed. 1986. (Special Editions Ser.). 18.95 o.p. (0-8161-4013-8, Macmillan Reference USA) Gale Group.

Stern, Richard. Pacific Tremors. 2002. 200p. 26.95 (0-8101-5131-6) Northwestern Univ. Pr.

Stevens, Stella & Hegner, William. Razzle Dazzle. 1999. 352p. 24.95 (0-312-85379-3, Forge Bks.) Doherty, Tom Assocs., LLC.

Stokoe, Matthew. High Life. 2002. 326p. pap. 16.95 (1-888451-32-7) Akashic Bks.

Stone, Robert. Children of Light. 1992. 272p. pap. 13.00 (0-679-73593-3, Vintage) Knopf Publishing Group.

Stratton, Bradford D. Colored Waters. 2001. 286p. pap. 21.99 (0-7388-6976-7) Xlibris Corp.

Susann, Jacqueline. Valley of the Dolls. unabr. ed. 2000. audio 29.95 (0-929071-50-6) B&B Audio, Inc.

—Valley of the Dolls. 1981. 512p. pap. 3.95 o.p. (0-553-24286-5) Bantam Bks.

—Valley of the Dolls. 1997. 448p. reprint ed. pap. 12.00 (0-8021-3519-6, Grove Pr.) Grove/Atlantic, Inc.

—Valley of the Dolls. abr. ed. 1993. pap. 15.95 o.p. incl. audio (1-55800-059-3, 40190) NewStar Media, Inc.

—Valley of the Dolls. 1991. (Newmarket Home Library). 448p. reprint ed. 5.95 o.p. (0-937858-02-1) Newmarket Pr.

Tolkin, Michael. The Player. 1997. 208p. pap. 12.00 (0-8021-3513-7, Grove Pr.); 1988. 204p. 17.95 o.p. (0-87113-228-1) Grove/Atlantic, Inc.

—The Player. 1992. pap. 10.00 (0-394-23924-5); 1989. pap. 10.00 o.s.i (0-679-72254-8) Knopf Publishing Group. (Vintage).

—The Player. 1992. audio 16.00 o.p. (0-679-41849-0, RH Audio) Random Hse. Audio Publishing Group.

—The Player. 1993. 3.99 o.p. (0-517-10912-3) Random Hse. Value Publishing.

Tolnay, Tom. The Big House. 1992. 188p. 19.95 o.p. (0-8027-3218-6) Walker & Co.

Toops, Laura Mazzuca. Slapstick: A Novel of 1920s Hollywood. 2001. 309p. pap. 22.99 o.p. (0-7388-6095-6) Xlibris Corp.

Townsend, Larry. The Case of the Severed Head. 1994. 239p. (Orig.). pap. 8.95 (1-881684-04-0) L.T. Pubns.

Tyler, Ben. Tricks of the Trade. 2002. 256p. pap. 14.00 (1-57566-814-9); 2001. 288p. 23.00 (1-57566-813-0) Kensington Publishing Corp.

Vanderhaeghe, Guy. The Englishman's Boy. 1998. 352p. pap. 14.00 (0-312-19544-3); 1997. 336p. 24.00 o.p. (0-312-16823-3) Picador.

Vidal, Gore. Hollywood: A Novel of America in the 1920's. 1991. (American Chronicle Ser.). 432p. mass mkt. 7.99 o.s.i (0-345-37013-9, Ballantine Bks.) Ballantine Bks.

—Hollywood: A Novel of America in the 1920's. unabr. ed. 1993. (American Chronicles Ser.). audio 104.00 (0-7366-2529-1, 3281) Books on Tape, Inc.

—Hollywood: A Novel of America in the 1920's. 2000. (International Ser.). 448p. pap. 15.00 (0-375-70875-8, Vintage) Knopf Publishing Group.

—Hollywood: A Novel of America in the 1920's. aut. ed. 1999. 24.95 (0-676-58932-4, Modern Library) Random House Adult Trade Publishing Group.

—Hollywood: A Novel of America in the 1920's. 1993. 4.99 o.p. (0-517-10710-4); 1992. 5.99 o.p. (0-517-08085-0) Random Hse. Value Publishing.

—Hollywood: A Novel of America in the 1920's. (Modern Library Ser.). 1999. 640p. 24.95 o.s.i (0-679-60292-5); 1990. 100.00 o.p. (0-394-57660-8) Random Hse., Inc.

—Myron. 1975. mass mkt. 1.75 o.s.i (0-345-24625-X, Ballantine Bks.) Ballantine Bks.

Wagner, Bruce. I'm Losing You. 1997. 336p. pap. 12.95 (0-452-27868-6, Signet Bks.) Dutton/Plume.

Walker, Mike. Malicious Intent: A Hollywood Fable. 1999. 400p. 24.00 (1-890862-05-3) Bancroft Pr.

Walter, Richard. Escape from Film School. 2nd ed. 1999. 243p. 22.95 (0-312-20537-6) St. Martin's Pr.

Ward, Donald. Death Takes the Stage. 1988. 15.95 o.p. (0-312-02128-3, Saint Martin's Minotaur) St. Martin's Pr.

Washburn, L. J. Dead-Stick. l.t. ed. 1992. pap. 20.95 o.p. (0-7927-1177-7); 22.95 o.p. (0-7927-1176-9, CH0242) BBC Audiobooks America.

—Dead-Stick, Vol. 1. 1989. 16.95 o.p. (0-312-93133-6, Tor Bks.) Doherty, Tom Assocs., LLC.

—Dog Heavies: A Lucas Hallam Mystery. 1990. 288p. 17.95 o.p. (0-312-93160-3, Tor Bks.) Doherty, Tom Assocs., LLC.

—Wild Night. l.t. ed. 1991. 12.95 o.p. (0-7927-0188-7, 4718); pap. 10.95 o.p. (0-7927-0189-5, C0086) BBC Audiobooks America.

—Wild Night. 1987. 320p. pap. 3.95 o.p. (0-8125-1041-0, Tor Bks.) Doherty, Tom Assocs., LLC.

—Wild Night. 1998. (Mystery Ser.). 253p. 20.95 (0-7862-1658-1, Five Star) Gale Group.

Waugh, Evelyn. The Loved One. unabr. collector's ed. 1992. audio 24.00 (0-7366-2108-3, 2912) Books on Tape, Inc.

—The Loved One. 1994. reprint ed. lib. bdg. 27.95 (1-56849-358-4) Buccaneer Bks., Inc.

—The Loved One. rev. ed. 1977. 13.95 o.s.i (0-316-92618-3) Little Brown & Co.

—The Loved One. l.t. ed. 1999. (Perennial Bestsellers Ser.). 131p. 27.95 (0-7838-8787-6) Thorndike Pr.

—The Loved One. lib. bdg. 20.95 (1-56723-177-2) Yestermorrow, Inc.

—The Loved One: A Novel. rev. ed. 1977. (Illus.). 176p. pap. 13.95 (*0-316-92608-6*, Back Bay) Little Brown & Co.

Weaver, Lydia. Child Star: When Talkies Came to Hollywood. 1992. (Once upon America Ser.). (Illus.). 64p. (J). (gr. 2-6). 12.00 o.p. (*0-670-84039-4*, Viking Children's Bks.) Penguin Putnam Bks. for Young Readers.

West, Cameron. The Medici Dagger. 2002. 320p. reprint ed. mass mkt. 6.99 (*0-7434-2036-5*, Pocket Star) Simon & Schuster.

Whitfield, Raoul. Death in a Bowl. 1986. (Quill Mysterious Classic Ser.). 288p. pap. 3.95 o.p. (*0-688-02864-0*, Quill) HarperTrade.

—Death in a Bowl. 1989. (C). 35.00 (*0-948353-23-6*) Oldcastle Bks., Ltd. GBR. *Dist:* State Mutual Bk. & Periodical Service, Ltd.

Wilkins, Barbara. In Name Only: A Novel. 1992. 432p. 20.00 o.p. (*0-06-017957-0*) HarperTrade.

Willis, Connie. Remake. 1996. 176p. mass mkt. 5.99 (*0-553-57441-8*) Bantam Bks.

—Remake. ltd. ed. 1994. 45.00 (*0-929480-48-1*) Ziesing, Mark V.

Wodehouse, P. G. Laughing Gas. 2002. 286p. 16.95 (*1-58567-232-7*) Overlook Pr., The.

Wojciechowska, Maia. The Hollywood Kid. 1966. (YA). (gr. 7 up). lib. bdg. 11.89 o.p. (*0-06-026573-6*) HarperCollins Children's Bk. Group.

Wolfe, Elle. Palm Beach Prep No. 4: Screen Test. 1990. (J). (gr. 4-7). mass mkt. 2.95 (*0-8125-1062-3*, Tor Bks.) Doherty, Tom Assocs., LLC.

Wolper, Carol. The Cigarette Girl. 1999. 208p. 22.95 o.p. (*1-57322-137-6*, Riverhead Bks. (Hardcovers)) Putnam Publishing Group, The.

—The Cigarette Girl: A Novel. 2000. 288p. pap. 12.95 (*1-57322-818-4*, Riverhead Trade (Paperbacks)) Berkley Publishing Group.

—Secret Celebrity. 2002. 336p. 24.95 o.s.i (*1-57322-214-3*, Riverhead Bks. (Hardcovers)) Putnam Publishing Group, The.

—The Secret Celebrity. 2003. 304p. pap. 13.00 (*1-57322-991-1*, Riverhead Trade (Paperbacks)) Berkley Publishing Group.

Woods, Stuart. L. A. Times. 1994. 400p. mass mkt. 7.99 (*0-06-109156-1*) HarperCollins Pubs.

—L. A. Times. 1993. 320p. 21.00 o.p. (*0-06-017714-4*) HarperTrade.

—L. A. Times. l.t. ed. 1995. 79p. mass mkt. 3.99 o.p. (*0-06-109479-X*, HarperTorch) Morrow/Avon.

—L. A. Times, unabr. ed. 1993. audio 60.00 (*1-55690-905-5*, 93401E7) Recorded Bks., LLC.

—L. A. Times. pap. 5.98 o.p. (*0-8317-0036-X*) Smithmark Pubs., Inc.

Wurlitzer, Rudolph. Slow Fade. 1984. 209p. (Orig.). 13.95 o.p. (*0-394-53610-X*) Knopf, Alfred A. Inc.

Zindel, Bonnie. Hollywood Dream Machine. 1985. 192p. (YA). (gr. 7-12). mass mkt. 2.50 o.s.i (*0-553-25240-2*, Starfire) Random Hse. Children's Bks.

—Hollywood Dream Machine. 1984. (J). 12.95 o.p. (*0-670-23220-3*) Viking Penguin.

**HONDURAS—FICTION**

Fast, Howard. The Confession of Joe Cullen. 1990. 400p. reprint ed. mass mkt. 5.95 o.s.i (*0-440-20669-3*) Dell Publishing.

—The Confession of Joe Cullen. l.t. ed. 1990. (Large Print Bks.). 398p. lib. bdg. 19.95 o.p. (*0-8161-4954-2*, Macmillan Reference USA) Gale Group.

—The Confession of Joe Cullen. 1989. 256p. 18.95 o.p. (*0-395-50936-X*) Houghton Mifflin Co.

—The Confession of Joe Cullen. 1992. 3.99 o.p. (*0-517-07943-7*) Random Hse. Value Publishing.

Jacobs, Mark. The Liberation of Little Heaven: And Other Stories. 1999. 254p. 23.00 (*1-56947-135-5*) Soho Pr., Inc.

Montoya, Tracy. Isabela's Dreams. 2000. (Encanto Ser.). 28p. mass mkt. 3.99 o.s.i (*0-7860-1154-8*); mass mkt. 3.99 o.s.i (*0-7860-1158-0*) Kensington Publishing Corp. (Pinnacle Bks.).

Quesada, Roberto. Never Through Miami. Duncan, Patricia J., tr. from SPA. 2002. 192p. pap. 12.95 (*1-55885-366-9*) Arte Publico Pr.

Shevin, Elaine. Green Passions. 2003. 220p. 21.95 (*1-931741-27-1*) Reed, Robert D. Pubs.

Theroux, Paul. The Mosquito Coast. l.t. ed. 1982. (Charnwood Large Print Ser.). 575p. 29.99 o.p. (*0-7089-8064-3*, Charnwood) Thorpe, F. A. Pubs. GBR. *Dist:* Ulverscroft Large Print Bks., Ltd., Ulverscroft Large Print Canada, Ltd.

Tolliver, Ruby C. Sarita, Be Brave. 1999. 128p. (J). (gr. 3-6). 14.95 (*1-57168-184-1*) Eakin Pr.

—Sarita, Be Brave. 1999. E-Book 14.95 (*0-585-23975-4*) netLibrary, Inc.

**HONG KONG (CHINA)—FICTION**

Arnote, Ralph. Hong Kong, China. 1997. 369p. pap. text 6.99 (*0-8125-4289-4*, Tor Bks.); 1996. 304p. 23.95 o.p. (*0-312-86097-8*, Forge Bks.) Doherty, Tom Assocs., LLC.

Benson, Raymond. Zero Minus Ten. 1997. 288p. 22.95 o.p. (*0-399-14257-6*, G. P. Putnam's Sons) Penguin Group (USA) Inc.

Clavell, James. Noble House. 1984. 1376p. mass mkt. 7.99 (*0-440-16484-2*); 1981. 1216p. 29.95 o.s.i (*0-385-28737-2*, Delacorte Pr.) Dell Publishing.

Coonts, Stephen. Hong Kong: A Jake Grafton Novel. l.t. ed. 2000. (Wheeler Hardcover Ser.). 522p. 27.95 (*1-56895-985-0*, Wheeler Publishing, Inc.) Gale Group.

—Hong Kong: A Jake Grafton Novel. 2001. 416p. mass mkt. 7.99 (*0-312-97837-5*, St. Martin's Paperbacks); 2000. 350p. 25.95 (*0-312-25339-7*) St. Martin's Pr.

Diehl, William. Thai Horse. 1996. mass mkt. 5.99 (*0-345-90985-2*); 1989. 416p. mass mkt. 7.99 (*0-345-32745-4*); 1988. mass mkt. 4.95 o.s.i (*0-345-35782-5*) Ballantine Bks.

Elegant, Robert S. Last Year in Hong Kong: A Love Story. 1997. 256p. 23.00 (*0-688-14890-5*, Morrow, William & Co.) Morrow/Avon.

Gilman, Dorothy. Mrs. Pollifax & the Hong Kong Buddha. 1986. pap. 94.50 o.p. (*0-449-28189-2*); 224p. mass mkt. 6.99 (*0-449-20983-0*) Ballantine Bks. (Fawcett).

—Mrs. Pollifax & the Hong Kong Buddha. 1985. 192p. 14.95 o.p. (*0-385-19959-7*) Doubleday Publishing.

Harrison, Colin. Afterburn. pap. (*0-374-90064-7*); 2000. E-Book 9.00 (*0-374-70019-2*); 2000. E-Book 9.00 o.p. (*0-374-70013-3*); 2000. E-Book 9.00 (*0-374-70027-3*); 2000. (Illus.). 416p. 25.00 o.s.i (*0-374-10205-8*) Farrar, Straus & Giroux.

—Afterburn. l.t. ed. 2001. (Softcover Ser.). 670p. pap. 23.95 (*1-58724-055-6*, Wheeler Publishing, Inc.) Gale Group.

—Afterburn. 2001. reprint ed. mass mkt. 6.99 (*0-312-97870-7*, St. Martin's Paperbacks) St. Martin's Pr.

Herschensohn, Bruce. Passport. 2003. 896p. 27.95 (*0-7434-7984-X*) ibooks, Inc.

Hicks, Barbara Jean. China Doll. l.t. ed. 1999. (Christian Fiction Ser.). 332p. 23.95 o.p. (*0-7862-2155-0*) Thorndike Pr.

Hicks, Barbara Jean, et al. China Doll. 1998. (Palisades Pure Romance Ser.). 266p. pap. 9.99 o.p. (*1-57673-262-2*, Palisades) Multnomah Pubs., Inc.

Holt, Victoria. The House of a Thousand Lanterns. 1974. 336p. 9.95 o.s.i (*0-385-00817-1*) Doubleday Publishing.

Iles, Greg. Dead Sleep. 2002. 480p. reprint ed. mass mkt. 7.99 (*0-451-20652-5*, Signet Bks.) NAL.

—Dead Sleep. 2001. 352p. 19.95 o.p. (*0-399-14735-7*) Penguin Group (USA) Inc.

—Dead Sleep. l.t. ed. 12.95 (*1-4104-0053-0*, Large Print Pr.); 2003. 703p. pap. 12.95 (*0-7862-3681-7*); 2001. 681p. 30.95 (*0-7862-3682-5*) Thorndike Pr.

Kenrick, Tony. Neon Tough. 1989. mass mkt. 4.50 o.s.i (*0-440-20475-5*) Dell Publishing.

—Neon Tough. 1988. 320p. 19.95 o.p. (*0-399-13392-5*, G. P. Putnam's Sons) Penguin Putnam Bks. for Young Readers.

Kershaw, Melanie. Water Music. 2002. 285p. 12.92 (*0-9705049-7-7*) Avocet Pr., Inc.

Kok, Marilyn. Stillpoint. 1996. (Portraits Ser.: No. 2). 256p. pap. 8.99 o.p. (*1-55661-821-2*) Bethany Hse. Pubs.

—Stillpoint. l.t. ed. 2000. (Christian Mystery Ser.). 398p. 23.95 (*0-7862-2698-6*) Thorndike Pr.

Kung, Dinah L. Left in the Care of: A Novel of Suspense. 1997. 272p. 23.00 o.p. (*0-7867-0494-2*, Carroll & Graf Pubs.) Avalon Publishing Group.

—Left in the Care Of: A Novel of Suspense. 1999. 270p. lib. bdg. 29.95 (*0-7351-0224-4*) Replica Bks.

Lachs, Lorraine. Flowers for Mei-Ling. 1997. 416p. 24.00 o.p. (*0-7867-0414-4*, Carroll & Graf Pubs.) Avalon Publishing Group.

Lanchester, John. Fragrant Harbor. 2003. 352p. pap. 14.00 (*0-14-200337-9*) Penguin Group (USA) Inc.

—Fragrant Harbour. 2002. (Illus.). 352p. 25.95 o.s.i (*0-399-14866-3*) Penguin Group (USA) Inc.

Leib, Franklin A. Sea Lion. 1991. 416p. mass mkt. 5.99 o.p. (*0-451-16968-9*, Signet Bks.); 1990. 355p. 19.95 o.p. (*0-453-00729-5*) NAL.

Lowell, Elizabeth. Jade Island. l.t. ed. 1998. 26.95 o.p. (*1-56895-691-6*, Wheeler Publishing, Inc.) Gale Group.

—Jade Island. 2002. E-Book 7.50 (*0-06-050379-3*); E-Book 7.50 (*0-06-050381-5*); E-Book 7.50 (*0-06-050380-7*); E-Book 7.50 (*0-06-050378-5*) HarperCollins General Bks. Group. (PerfectBound).

—Jade Island. 1999. 372p. mass mkt. 7.50 (*0-380-78987-6*); 1998. 375p. 23.00 (*0-380-97403-7*) Morrow/Avon. (Avon Bks.).

Maas, Peter. China White. l.t. ed. 1995. (Large Print Bks.). pap. 23.95 (*1-56895-096-9*, Wheeler Publishing, Inc.) Gale Group.

—China White. 1994. 272p. 23.00 o.s.i (*0-671-69417-0*, Simon & Schuster) Simon & Schuster.

Marshall, William. The Far-Away Man: A Yellowthread Street Mystery. 1985. o.p. (*0-03-070527-4*) Holt, Henry & Co.

—The Far-Away Man: A Yellowthread Street Mystery. 1988. 208p. mass mkt. 3.95 o.s.i (*0-445-40662-3*, Mysterious Pr. Paperback Bks.) Warner Bks., Inc.

—Frogmouth. 1987. 192p. 15.45 o.p. (*0-89296-197-X*) Mysterious Pr.

—Frogmouth. 1988. mass mkt. 3.50 o.s.i (*0-445-40705-0*, Mysterious Pr. Paperback Bks.) Warner Bks., Inc.

—Gelignite. l.t. ed. 1911. 12.95 o.p. (*1-55504-976-1*, 31); pap. 10.95 o.p. (*1-55504-975-3*, 448) BBC Audiobooks America.

—Gelignite. 1977. o.p. (*0-03-016906-2*) Holt, Henry & Co.

—Gelignite. 1988. (Yellowthread Street Mystery Ser.). 208p. pap. 3.50 o.s.i (*0-445-40660-7*, Mysterious Pr. Paperback Bks.) Warner Bks., Inc.

—The Hatchet Man: A Yellowthread Street Mystery. l.t. ed. 1989. 8.95 o.p. (*1-55504-887-0*, 549); pap. 8.95 o.p. (*1-55504-888-9*) BBC Audiobooks America.

—The Hatchet Man: A Yellowthread Street Mystery. 1977. o.p. (*0-03-016901-1*) Holt, Henry & Co.

—The Hatchet Man: A Yellowthread Street Mystery. 1988. (Yellowthread Street Mystery Ser.). 208p. 3.50 o.s.i (*0-445-40659-3*, Mysterious Pr. Paperback Bks.) Warner Bks., Inc.

—Head First: A Yellowthread Street Mystery. l.t. ed. 1988. (Yellowthread Street Mystery Ser.). 18.95 o.p. (*1-55504-348-8*); pap. 16.95 o.p. (*1-55504-473-5*) BBC Audiobooks America.

—Head First: A Yellowthread Street Mystery. 1986. (Rinehart Suspense Novel Ser.). 192p. 14.95 o.p. (*0-8050-0061-5*) Holt, Henry & Co.

—Head First: A Yellowthread Street Mystery. 1988. 208p. pap. 3.50 o.s.i (*0-445-40665-8*, Mysterious Pr. Paperback Bks.) Warner Bks., Inc.

—Inches. 1994. 304p. 19.95 o.s.i (*0-89296-368-9*) Mysterious Pr.

—Inches. 1995. 256p. mass mkt. 5.99 (*0-446-40455-1*, Mysterious Pr. Paperback Bks.) Warner Bks., Inc.

—Nightmare Syndrome. 1997. 256p. 21.50 o.p. (*0-89296-574-6*) Warner Bks., Inc.

—Out of Nowhere. 1988. 224p. 15.45 o.p. (*0-89296-199-6*) Mysterious Pr.

—Out of Nowhere. 1989. mass mkt. 3.95 (*0-445-40842-1*, Mysterious Pr. Paperback Bks.) Warner Bks., Inc.

—Perfect End. 1984. pap. o.p. (*0-03-071062-6*, Owl Bks.); 1983. 204p. 13.00 o.p. (*0-03-047481-7*) Holt, Henry & Co.

—Roadshow. l.t. ed. 1987. (Yellowthread Street Mystery Ser.). 19.95 o.p. (*1-55504-326-7*); pap. 17.95 o.p. (*1-55504-467-0*) BBC Audiobooks America.

—Roadshow. 1985. 192p. 14.95 o.p. (*0-03-001744-0*) Holt, Henry & Co.

—Sci-Fi. 1984. pap. o.p. (*0-03-071063-4*, Owl Bks.); 1981. 192p. o.p. (*0-03-047486-8*) Holt, Henry & Co.

—Skulduggery. 1984. pap. o.p. (*0-03-071064-2*, Owl Bks.); 1980. 192p. o.p. (*0-03-047491-4*) Holt, Henry & Co.

—Thin Air: A Yellowthread Street Mystery. 1978. o.p. (*0-03-021071-2*) Holt, Henry & Co.

—Thin Air: A Yellowthread Street Mystery. 1982. (Crime Monthly Ser.). 192p. pap. 2.95 o.p. (*0-14-006137-1*, Penguin Bks.) Viking Penguin.

—To the End. 1998. (Yellowthread Street Mysteries Ser.). 240p. 23.00 (*0-89296-575-4*) Mysterious Pr.

—War Machine. 1988. 15.45 o.p. (*0-89296-198-8*) Mysterious Pr.

—War Machine. 1989. (Yellowthread Street Mystery Ser.). mass mkt. 3.95 (*0-445-40595-3*, Mysterious Pr. Paperback Bks.) Warner Bks., Inc.

—Yellowthread Street. 1976. o.p. (*0-03-016836-8*) Holt, Henry & Co.

—Yellowthread Street. 1988. 144p. pap. 3.50 o.s.i (*0-445-40548-1*, Mysterious Pr. Paperback Bks.) Warner Bks., Inc.

McBride, Laura. Fragrant Harbor. 2003. 264p. pap. 21.99 (*1-4010-9543-7*); text 31.99 (*1-4010-9544-5*); E-Book 8.00 (*1-4010-9545-3*) Xlibris Corp.

Nadelson, Reggie. Hot Poppies. l.t. ed. 1999. (Ulverscroft Large Print Ser.). 384p. 31.99 (*0-7089-4077-3*, Ulverscroft) Thorpe, F. A. Pubs. GBR. *Dist:* Ulverscroft Large Print Bks., Ltd., Ulverscroft Large Print Canada, Ltd.

—Hot Poppies: An Artie Cohen Mystery. 1998. 256p. 22.95 o.p. (*0-312-19986-4*, Saint Martin's Minotaur) St. Martin's Pr.

Piot, Joseph L. Concentric Circles. 1999. 350p. pap. 22.99 (*0-7388-0585-8*); text 32.99 (*0-7388-0584-X*) Xlibris Corp.

Reboy, Kelley, et al. Breakfast in Singapore: How to Write a Novel in a Writers Class. Smith, Helene, ed. 2000. 19.95 (*0-945437-43-9*) MacDonald Sward Publishing Co.

Roberts, Les. The Chinese Fire Drill. 2003. 192p. pap. 13.95 (*1-4104-0114-6*, Five Star Trade); 2001. 188p. 23.95 (*0-7862-3760-0*, Five Star) Gale Group.

Stuart, Dee. Deadly Legacy. 1996. 352p. mass mkt. 4.99 o.s.i (*0-8217-5316-9*) Kensington Publishing Corp.

Tallman, Shirley B. Fragrant Harbor. 1983. mass mkt. (*0-373-49573-0*, Harlequin Bks.) Harlequin Enterprises, Ltd.

Tarrant, John. China Gold. 1991. 252p. 19.95 (*0-8128-4020-8*, Scarborough Hse.) Madison Bks., Inc.

Taylor, Charles D. Sightings. McCarthy, Paul, ed. 1993. 416p. (Orig.). mass mkt. 5.50 (*0-671-73632-9*, Pocket) Simon & Schuster.

Thayer, James. The Gold Swan: A Novel. 2003. 448p. mass mkt. 7.99 (*0-671-03433-2*, Pocket Star) Simon & Schuster.

Theroux, Paul. Kowloon Tong: A Novel. l.t. ed. 1997. (G. K. Hall Core Ser.). 281p. lib. bdg. 25.95 (*0-7838-8275-0*, Macmillan Reference USA) Gale Group.

—Kowloon Tong: A Novel. 1997. 256p. 23.00 o.p. (*0-395-86029-6*) Houghton Mifflin Co.

—Kowloon Tong: A Novel. 1998. 248p. pap. 12.00 (*0-395-90141-3*, Mariner Bks.) Houghton Mifflin Co. Trade & Reference Div.

—Kowloon Tong: A Novel. 1997. 256p. 29.99 (*0-7710-8576-1*) McClelland & Stewart/Tundra Bks.

—Kowloon Tong: A Novel. unabr. ed. 1997. 25.00 o.p. (*0-7871-1465-0*) NewStar Media, Inc.

Tsukiyama, Gail. The Language of Threads. 1999. 276p. 23.95 o.p. (*0-312-20376-4*); 2000. (Illus.). 288p. reprint ed. pap. 12.95 (*0-312-26756-8*, Saint Martin's Griffin) St. Martin's Pr.

—Night of Many Dreams. unabr. ed. 1999. audio 29.95 (*0-7861-1546-7*); pap. 44.95 incl. audio (*0-7861-1335-9*, 2229) Blackstone Audio Bks., Inc.

—Night of Many Dreams. 1999. E-Book 12.95 o.s.i (*0-312-20733-6*); 1998. 288p. 22.95 o.p. (*0-312-17194-3*); 1998. 288p. reprint ed. pap. 12.95 (*0-312-19940-6*, NPB 0230, Saint Martin's Griffin) St. Martin's Pr.

Whitnell, Barbara. Fragrant Harbor. 1999. 176p. 24.00 (*0-7278-5419-4*) Severn Hse. Pubs., Ltd.

—Fragrant Harbor. l.t. ed. 2000. (Ulverscroft Large Print Ser.). 256p. 31.99 (*0-7089-4325-X*, Ulverscroft) Thorpe, F. A. Pubs. GBR. *Dist:* Ulverscroft Large Print Bks., Ltd., Ulverscroft Large Print Canada, Ltd.

Xi, Xu. Hong Kong Rose. 1999. 288p. pap. 14.00 (*962-7160-55-5*) Weatherhill, Inc.

**HOUSTON (TEX.)—FICTION**

Alter, Judy. Sam Houston Is My Hero. 2003. (Chaparral Book for Young Readers Ser.). 140p. (J). pap. 15.95 (*0-87565-277-8*) Texas Christian Univ. Pr.

Baisden, Michael. God's Gift to Women: A Novel. 2003. 304p. pap. 13.00 (*0-7432-4997-6*, Touchstone) Simon & Schuster.

—God's Gift to Women: A Novel. 2003. (African American Ser.). 29.95 (*0-7862-5147-6*) Thorndike Pr.

Barthelme, Frederick. Natural Selection. 2001. 224p. pap. text 14.00 (*1-58243-131-0*, Counterpoint Pr.) Basic Bks.

Berry, Venise. Colored Sugar Water. 2002. 256p. 23.95 o.s.i (*0-525-94471-0*, Dutton) Dutton/Plume.

—Colored Sugar Water. 2003. 272p. reprint ed. pap. 13.95 (*0-451-20775-0*) NAL.

Bickmore, Barbara. Deep in the Heart. l.t. ed. 1996. lib. bdg. 24.95 (*1-57490-067-6*, Beeler Large Print Bks.) Beeler, Thomas T. Publisher.

—Deep in the Heart. 1997. 448p. mass mkt. 5.99 o.s.i (*1-57566-225-6*); 1996. 358p. 22.95 o.s.i (*1-57566-039-3*) Kensington Publishing Corp.

Bingham, Linda S. All Roads Lead Home. 2003. 24.95 (*1-57168-774-2*, Eakin Pr.) Eakin Pr.

Blish, Nelson Adrian. Ishmael's Son. 2003. (Illus.). 288p. per. 19.95 (*1-889901-29-6*, Palo Alto Bks.) Glencannon Pr.

Bradley, Lynn. Stand-In for Murder. 1996. (WWL Mystery Ser.). per. (*0-373-26199-3*, 1-26199-9, Worldwide Library) Harlequin Enterprises, Ltd.

—Stand-In for Murder: A Cole January Mystery. 1994. 214p. 19.95 o.p. (*0-8027-3189-9*) Walker & Co.

Brandon, Jay. Predator's Waltz. Isaacson, Dana, ed. 1992. 304p. reprint ed. mass mkt. 4.99 (*0-671-70889-9*, Pocket) Simon & Schuster.

—Predator's Waltz. 1989. 288p. 17.95 o.p. (*0-312-03413-X*, Saint Martin's Minotaur) St. Martin's Pr.

Brown, Rosellen. Half a Heart. 2000. (*0-374-93384-7*); 2000. 368p. 24.00 o.p. (*0-374-29987-0*); 2000. 402p. (*0-374-44013-1*); 1999. o.p. (*0-374-16772-9*) Farrar, Straus & Giroux.

—Half a Heart. l.t. ed. 2001. (Large Print Book Ser.). 575p. 29.95 (*1-58724-017-3*, Wheeler Publishing, Inc.) Gale Group.

—Half a Heart. 2001. 416p. pap. 14.00 (*0-312-27830-6*) Picador.

—Half a Heart. abr. ed. 2000. audio 25.00 (*0-7435-0579-4*, Simon & Schuster Audioworks) Simon & Schuster Audio.

Bullard, Linda M. Shades of Justice. 1999. 352p. reprint ed. mass mkt. 6.99 o.s.i (*0-451-19768-2*, Signet Bks.) NAL.

Cullin, Mitch. The Cosmology of Bing. 2001. (Illus.). 192p. 24.00 (*1-57962-030-2*) Permanent Pr., The.

Daugherty, Tracy. Axeman's Jazz: A Novel. 2003. 240p. 22.50 (*0-87074-481-X*) Southern Methodist Univ. Pr.

—It Takes a Worried Man: Stories. 2002. 22.50 (*0-87074-469-0*) Southern Methodist Univ. Pr.

Hemlin, Tim. A Catered Christmas. 1998. (Culinary Mysteries Ser.). 272p. mass mkt. 5.99 o.s.i (*0-345-42001-2*) Ballantine Bks.
—Dead Man's Broth. 1999. (Culinary Mysteries Ser.). 304p. mass mkt. 5.99 o.s.i (*0-345-42002-0*) Ballantine Bks.
—If Wishes Were Horses. 1996. mass mkt. 5.50 o.s.i (*0-345-40318-5*) Ballantine Bks.
—People in Glass Houses. 1997. (Culinary Mysteries Ser.). 230p. mass mkt. 5.50 o.s.i (*0-345-40902-7*) Ballantine Bks.
—A Whisper of Rage. 1997. (Culinary Mysteries Ser.). mass mkt. 5.50 o.s.i (*0-345-40319-3*) Ballantine Bks.
Irving, Clifford. Trial. 1990. 19.95 o.p. (*0-671-66422-0*) Summit Bks.
Jarrett, Norma L. Sunday Brunch. 1999. 238p. pap. 15.95 (*0-9671923-5-8*) Jarrett, Norma L.
Kiecolt-Glaser, Janice K. Detecting Lies. 1997. 256p. (Orig.). mass mkt. 5.50 (*0-380-78991-4*, Avon Bks.) Morrow/Avon.
—Unconscious Truths. 1998. mass mkt. 5.99 (*0-380-78992-2*, Avon Bks.) Morrow/Avon.
Lindsey, David L. An Absence of Light. 1995. 576p. mass mkt. 6.99 (*0-553-56941-4*) Bantam Bks.
—An Absence of Light. unabr. ed. 1994. audio 105.25 (*1-56100-195-3*, 785, Unabridged Library Editions) Brilliance Audio.
—Body of Truth. 1993. 480p. mass mkt. 6.99 (*0-553-28964-0*) Bantam Bks.
—A Cold Mind. 1994. 368p. mass mkt. 6.99 (*0-553-56081-6*) Bantam Bks.
—A Cold Mind. 1996. pap. o.s.i (*0-385-48406-2*) Doubleday Publishing.
—A Cold Mind. 1990. 352p. mass mkt. 5.99 (*0-671-73338-9*); 1984. mass mkt. 3.95 (*0-671-49933-5*) Simon & Schuster. (Pocket).
—The Color of Night. l.t. ed. 1999. (Americana Ser.). 629p. 28.95 (*0-7862-1995-5*) Thorndike Pr.
—The Color of Night. 1999. 496p. 25.00 (*0-446-52361-5*); 2001. 480p. reprint ed. mass mkt. 7.99 (*0-446-60803-3*) Warner Bks., Inc.
—Heat from Another Sun. 1996. 384p. mass mkt. 6.99 (*0-553-56790-X*) Bantam Bks.
—Heat from Another Sun. 1984. 256p. 14.95 o.p. (*0-06-015346-6*) HarperTrade.
—Heat from Another Sun. 1985. mass mkt. 5.95 (*0-671-54632-5*, Pocket) Simon & Schuster.
—In the Lake of the Moon. 1990. 400p. mass mkt. 6.50 o.s.i (*0-553-28344-8*) Bantam Bks.
—In the Lake of the Moon. 1988. 320p. 17.95 o.s.i (*0-689-11626-8*, Scribner) Simon & Schuster.
—Mercy. 1991. 608p. mass mkt. 7.50 (*0-553-28972-1*) Bantam Bks.
—Mercy. 1992. audio 12.79 o.s.i (*0-553-70055-3*); 1999. audio 9.99 o.s.i (*0-553-70205-X*) Random Hse. Audio Publishing Group. (RH Audio).
—Requiem for a Glass Heart. 1997. 448p. mass mkt. 6.99 (*0-553-57594-5*) Bantam Bks.
—Requiem for a Glass Heart. l.t. ed. 1996. (Core Collection). 681p. lib. bdg. 28.95 (*0-7838-1885-8*) Thorndike Pr.
—Spiral. (Orig.). 1990. mass mkt. 5.99 (*0-671-73337-0*, Pocket); 1988. 416p. mass mkt. 4.50 (*0-671-64666-4*, Pocket); 1986. 320p. pap. 16.95 o.p. (*0-689-11625-X*, Scribner) Simon & Schuster.
McGhee, George C. Dance of the Billions: Texas Oil Creed. Seidl, Tony, ed. 1989. 288p. 17.95 o.p. (*0-89015-692-1*) Eakin Pr.
Miller, J. P. Surviving Joy. 1995. 256p. 21.50 o.s.i (*1-55611-448-6*) Fine, Donald I. Bks.
Nighbert, David F. Squeezeplay: A Mystery. 1992. 272p. 18.95 o.p. (*0-312-07847-1*, Saint Martin's Minotaur) St. Martin's Pr.
Page, Patricia. Hope's Cadillac: A Novel. 1996. 264p. 25.00 o.p. (*0-393-03974-9*) Norton, W. W. & Co., Inc.
Pendleton, Don. Vendetta Force. 2002. (Executioner Ser.: No. 289). 224p. mass mkt. (*0-373-64289-X*, Gold Eagle) Harlequin Enterprises, Ltd.
Pete, Eric E. Someone's in the Kitchen. 2002. 243p. pap. 15.00 (*0-9704995-1-5*) E-fect Publishing.
Rogers, Chris. Bitch Factor. 1998. 336p. mass mkt. 5.99 (*0-553-58001-9*) Bantam Bks.
—The Rage Factor. 2000. 400p. mass mkt. 5.99 (*0-553-58070-1*) Bantam Bks.
Storey, Gail D. God's Country Club. 1999. 238p. reprint ed. pap. 12.95 (*0-89255-242-5*) Persea Bks., Inc.
—God's Country Club: A Novel. 1996. 224p. 22.95 (*0-89255-219-0*) Persea Bks., Inc.
—The Lord's Motel. 1993. reprint ed. pap. 12.95 (*0-89255-194-1*) Persea Bks., Inc.
—The Lord's Motel: A Novel. 1992. 224p. 19.95 o.p. (*0-89255-178-X*) Persea Bks., Inc.
Webb, Paula. Domestic Life. 1992. 224p. 20.00 o.s.i (*0-671-74433-X*, Simon & Schuster) Simon & Schuster.
Williams, Lori Aurelia. When Kambia Elaine Flew in from Neptune. l.t. ed. 2001. 369p. 22.95 (*0-7862-3657-4*) Thorndike Pr.

## HUNGARY—FICTION

Andrews, Val. Sherlock Holmes & the Houdini Birthright. l.t. ed. 1998. (Linford Mystery Large Print Ser.). 320p. pap. 17.99 (*0-7089-5292-5*, Linford) Thorpe, F. A. Pubs. GBR. *Dist:* Ulverscroft Large Print Bks., Ltd., Ulverscroft Large Print Canada, Ltd.
Bart, Istvan. The Kiss: 20th Century Hungarian Short Stories. 1999. pap. 23.00 (*963-13-4250-6*); 1989. 428p. pap. 60.00 (*963-13-4099-6*) Corvina Books HUN. *Dist:* State Mutual Bk. & Periodical Service, Ltd.
Blackburn, Alexander. Suddenly, a Mortal Splendor. 1995. 309p. 20.00 (*1-880909-23-5*) Baskerville Pubs., Inc.
Bozai, Agota. To Err Is Divine. 2004. 256p. text 23.00 (*1-58243-277-5*, Counterpoint Pr.) Basic Bks.
Codrescu, Andrei. The Blood Countess: A Novel. 1996. 432p. mass mkt. 6.99 o.s.i (*0-440-22191-9*) Dell Publishing.
—The Blood Countess: A Novel. 1995. 347p. 23.00 o.p. (*0-684-80244-9*, Simon & Schuster) Simon & Schuster.
—The Blood Countess: A Novel. abr. ed. 1995. audio 23.00 o.p. (*0-671-52924-2*, Simon & Schuster Audioworks) Simon & Schuster Audio.
Esterhazy, Peter. Helping Verbs of the Heart. Heim, Michael H., tr. from HUN. 1990. 80p. 14.95 o.p. (*0-8021-1123-8*) Grove/Atlantic, Inc.
—A Little Hungarian Pornography. Sollosy, Judith, tr. 1997. 216p. pap. 19.00 (*0-8101-1577-8*); 1995. 224p. (C). 30.00 (*0-8101-1340-6*) Northwestern Univ. Pr. (Hydra Bks.).
Eversz, Robert M. Gypsy Hearts. 1997. 272p. 23.00 o.p. (*0-8021-1609-4*, Grove Pr.) Grove/Atlantic, Inc.
Fischer, Tibor. Under the Frog. 1997. 256p. pap. 13.00 o.s.i (*0-8050-5245-3*, Owl Bks.) Holt, Henry & Co.
—Under the Frog. 2001. 256p. pap. 13.00 (*0-312-27871-3*) Picador.
—Under the Frog. 1992. 18.00 (*0-7486-6133-6*) Polygon GBR. *Dist:* Subterranean Co.
—Under the Frog: A Black Comedy. 1995. 302p. pap. 11.00 o.p. (*1-56584-149-2*); 1994. 256p. 17.00 o.p. (*1-56584-148-4*) New Pr., The.
Fishtein, Oscar. I'll Sell You a Million Jews. 1995. 272p. 19.95 (*0-8158-0517-9*) Christopher Publishing Hse.
Frame, Veronica F. On Whom I Have Mercy. 1993. (Illus.). 271p. 19.00 (*0-9635160-0-0*); pap. 10.00 (*0-9635160-1-9*) Riverview Publishing.
Furst, Alan. Kingdom of Shadows: A Novel. E-Book 19.95 (*1-58945-591-6*) Adobe Systems, Inc.
—Kingdom of Shadows: A Novel. l.t. ed. 2001. (Illus.). 359p. 28.95 (*0-7838-9427-9*); (*0-7540-1587-4*); pap. (*0-7540-2448-2*) Gale Group. (Macmillan Reference USA).
—Kingdom of Shadows: A Novel. 2001. 272p. pap. 11.95 (*0-375-75826-7*) Random House Adult Trade Publishing Group.
Fust, Milan. The Story of My Wife. Sanders, Ivan, tr. 1989. (International Ser.). pap. 8.95 o.s.i (*0-679-72217-3*, Vintage) Knopf Publishing Group.
—The Story of My Wife. Sanders, Ivan, tr. 1987. 250p. 18.95 o.p. (*1-55554-018-X*) PAJ Pubns.
Galgoczi, Erzsebet. Another Love. Rieder, Ines & Newman, Felice, trs. from GER. 1991. 160p. 24.95 o.p. (*0-939416-52-2*); pap. 8.95 o.p. (*0-939416-51-4*) Cleis Pr.
Kaffka, Margitt. The Ant Heap. Franklin, Charlotte, tr. from HUN. 1995. 176p. pap. 16.95 o.p. (*0-7145-2989-3*) Boyars, Marion Pubs., Inc.
Kertesz, Imre. Fateless. 1996. pap. 14.95 o.p. (*0-8101-1465-8*) Northwestern Univ. Pr.
—Fateless. Wilson, Christopher & Wilson, Katharina, trs. from HUN. 1996. 191p. pap. 19.95 (*0-8101-1049-0*, Hydra Bks.); 1992. 200p. 68.00 (*0-8101-1024-5*) Northwestern Univ. Pr.
—Kaddish for a Child Not Born. Wilson, Christopher C. & Wilson, Katharina M., trs. from HUN. 1999. 95p. pap. 14.95 (*0-8101-1161-6*, Hydra Bks.) Northwestern Univ. Pr.
—Kaddish for a Child Not Born. Wilson, Christopher C. & Wilson, Katharine M., trs. 1997. 95p. 24.95 (*0-8101-1176-4*, Hydra Bks.) Northwestern Univ. Pr.
Kevey, Andrew. Bela Keredy: A Hungarian Odyssey. 1991. (Illus.). 384p. (Orig.). pap. 11.95 (*0-931832-83-7*) Fithian Pr.
Konrad, George. The Case Worker. 1974. (Helen & Kurt Wolff Bk.). 6.95 o.p. (*0-15-115790-1*) Harcourt Trade Pubs.
—The Case Worker. Aston, Paul, tr. 1978. 176p. reprint ed. pap. 4.95 o.p. (*0-15-615412-9*, Harvest Bks.) Harcourt Trade Pubs.
—The Case Worker. Roth, Philip, ed. Aston, Paul, tr. 1987. 192p. pap. 6.95 o.p. (*0-14-009946-8*, Penguin Bks.) Viking Penguin.
—A Feast in the Garden. 1992. 23.95 o.s.i (*0-15-130548-X*) Harcourt Trade Pubs.
—Feast in the Garden. 1993. 408p. pap. 14.95 o.s.i (*0-15-630454-6*) Harcourt Trade Pubs.
—The Loser. Sanders, Ivan, tr. from HUN. 1982. (Helen & Kurt Wolff Bk.). 320p. 14.95 o.p. (*0-15-153442-X*); pap. 17.00 (*0-15-653584-X*, Harvest Bks.) Harcourt Trade Pubs.
Kosztolanyi, Dezso. Anna Edes. Szirtes, George, tr. from HUN. & intro. by. 1993. (Revived Modern Classic Ser.). 240p. pap. 10.95 (*0-8112-1255-6*, NDP772) New Directions Publishing Corp.
Krasznahorkai, Laszlo. The Melancholy of Resistance. Szirtes, tr. 2002. 320p. reprint ed. pap. 15.95 (*0-8112-1504-0*) New Directions Publishing Corp.
Krasznahorkai, Laszlo. The Melancholy of Resistance. Szirtes, George, tr. 2000. pap. 13.95 (*0-7043-8009-9*) Quartet Bks., Ltd. GBR. *Dist:* Interlink Publishing Group, Inc.
Ling, Gyula. Guiding Stars. 2001. 418p. pap. (*1-55212-680-3*) Trafford Publishing.
Nadas, Peter. The End of a Family Story. 1998. 224p. 23.00 o.p. (*0-374-14832-5*) Farrar, Straus & Giroux.
—End of a Family Story. 2000. 256p. pap. 12.95 o.s.i (*0-14-029179-2*) Penguin Group (USA) Inc.
Nyiri, Janos. Battlefields & Playgrounds. Nyiri, Janos & Brandon, William, trs. from HUN. 1995. 536p. 25.00 o.p. (*0-374-10918-4*) Farrar, Straus & Giroux.
—Battlefields & Playgrounds. Brandon, William, tr. from HUN. 1997. (Tauber Institute Ser.: No. 23). 544p. reprint ed. per. 19.95 (*0-87451-801-6*) Univ. Pr. of New England.
Pap, Karoly. Azarel: A Novel. Olchvary, Paul, tr. from HUN. 2001. 224p. pap. 14.00 (*1-58642-019-4*) Steerforth Pr.
Pearson, Diane. Csardas. 1984. 608p. mass mkt. 3.50 o.s.i (*0-449-20615-7*, Fawcett) Ballantine Bks.
Petrovics, Ofner L. Broken Places. 1990. 19.95 o.p. (*0-87113-359-8*) Grove/Atlantic, Inc.
Phillips, Arthur. Prague: A Novel. 2003. 400p. pap. 13.95 (*0-375-75977-8*) Random House Adult Trade Publishing Group.
—Prague: A Novel. 2002. 384p. 24.95 (*0-375-50787-6*) Random Hse., Inc.
Pressburger, Giorgio & Pressburger, Nicola. Homage to the Eighth District: Tales from Budapest. Moore, Gerald, tr. from ITA. 1990. 200p. (Orig.). pap. 17.95 (*0-930523-75-X*); pap. 9.95 (*0-930523-76-8*) Readers International.
Rothsteis, Shmuel. Heir to the Throne. 1990. (Illus.). 224p. (J). (gr. 5-8). pap. 13.95 (*1-56062-044-7*, CFR106S) CIS Communications, Inc.
Sennett, Richard. The Frog Who Dared to Croak. 1982. 182p. 11.95 o.p. (*0-374-15884-3*) Farrar, Straus & Giroux.
Seredy, Kate. The Good Master. 1935. (Illus.). (J). (gr. 4-6). 13.95 o.s.i (*0-670-34592-X*, Viking Children's Bks.) Penguin Putnam Bks. for Young Readers.
Sinclair, Jo. Anna Teller. 1992. 624p. 35.00 (*1-55861-066-9*); pap. 16.95 (*1-55861-055-3*) Feminist Pr. at The City Univ. of New York.
Szablya, Helen M. & Anderson, Peggy King. The Fall of the Red Star. 1996. (HUN.). 168p. (J). 15.95 (*1-56397-897-0*) Boyds Mills Pr.
Zelitch, Simone. Louisa. 2001. 400p. reprint ed. pap. 14.00 (*0-425-18195-2*) Berkley Publishing Group.
—Louisa. 2000. 384p. 24.95 o.s.i (*0-399-14659-8*) Penguin Group (USA) Inc.
Zilahy, Lajos. The Dukays: Lost Treasures. 2001. 800p. pap. 19.95 (*1-85375-422-6*) Prion GBR. *Dist:* Trafalgar Square.

# I

## ICELAND—FICTION

Bachman, W. Bryant, Jr. Forty Old Icelandic Tales. 1992. 106p. 43.50 (*0-8191-8500-0*); 322p. pap. 75.00 (*0-8191-8499-3*) Univ. Pr. of America.
Bagley, Desmond. Running Blind. l.t. ed. 1993. 21.95 o.p. (*0-7927-1684-1*); pap. 19.95 o.p. (*0-7927-1683-3*) BBC Audiobooks America.
—Running Blind. 1984. 224p. pap. 2.95 o.p. (*0-06-080693-1*, P 693, Perennial) HarperTrade.
—Running Blind. l.t. ed. 1976. (Ulverscroft Large Print Ser.). 441p. 12.50 o.p. (*0-85456-418-7*, Ulverscroft) Thorpe, F. A. Pubs. GBR. *Dist:* Ulverscroft Large Print Bks., Ltd., Ulverscroft Large Print Canada, Ltd.
Cooper, Dominic. Men at Axlir. 1980. 10.95 o.p. (*0-312-52873-6*) St. Martin's Pr.
Crowell, Jenn. Letting the Body Lead. 2002. 288p. 23.95 o.s.i (*0-399-14859-0*, Putnam & Grosset) Penguin Group (USA) Inc.
French, Allen. The Story of Rolf & the Viking Bow. 1994. (Adventure Library). 240p. (YA). (gr. 5 up). reprint ed. pap. 13.95 (*1-883937-01-9*, 01-9) Bethlehem Bks.
Gudmundsson, Einar M. Angels of the Universe. 1997. 176p. 19.95 o.p. (*0-312-15053-9*) St. Martin's Pr.
Gunnarsson, Olafur & McDuff, David. Trolls' Cathedral. 1997. 294p. pap. 14.95 (*1-899197-30-3*) Dufour Editions, Inc.
Helgason, Hallgrimur. 101 Reykjavik: A Novel. Fitzgibbons, Brian M., tr. from ICE. 2003. 352p. 23.00 (*0-7432-2514-7*, Scribner) Simon & Schuster.
Knox, Bill. An Incident in Iceland. l.t. ed. 1996. (Linford Mystery Library). 320p. pap. 17.99 (*0-7089-7936-X*, Ulverscroft) Thorpe, F. A. Pubs. GBR. *Dist:* Ulverscroft Large Print Bks., Ltd., Ulverscroft Large Print Canada, Ltd.
Laker, Rosalind, pseud. The Fragile Hour. 1996. 320p. 24.00 o.p. (*0-7278-5181-0*) Severn Hse. Pubs., Ltd.
Laxness, Halldor Kiljan. The Atom Station. 1976. 20.95 (*0-8488-0177-6*) Amereon, Ltd.
—The Atom Station. 1982. 16.95 o.p. (*0-531-07338-6*, Watts, Franklin) Scholastic Library Publishing.
—The Atom Station. 1982. (C). reprint ed. 206p. 21.95 o.p. (*0-933256-30-2*); 202p. pap. 16.95 (*0-933256-31-0*) Second Chance Pr.
—Iceland's Bell. 2003. 448p. pap. 15.00 (*1-4000-3425-6*, Vintage) Knopf Publishing Group.
—Independent People: An Epic. Thompson, J. A., tr. from ICE. 1976. reprint ed. lib. bdg. 37.50 o.p. (*0-8371-8872-5*, LAIP, Greenwood Pr.) Greenwood Publishing Group, Inc.
—Independent People: An Epic. Thompson, J. A., tr. 1997. 512p. pap. 15.00 (*0-679-76792-4*, Vintage) Knopf Publishing Group.
—Independent People: An Epic. Thompson, J. A., tr. 2001. 475p. im. lthr. 39.95 (*1-57179-100-0*) Library of New Atlantis, Inc.
—Independent People: An Epic. 1998. 27.75 (*0-8446-6949-0*) Smith, Peter Pub., Inc.
—Paradise Reclaimed. 2002. 320p. pap. 13.00 (*0-375-72758-2*, Vintage) Knopf Publishing Group.
—World Light. Magnusson, Magnus, tr. from ICE. 2002. 624p. pap. 16.00 (*0-375-72757-4*) Random Hse., Inc.
Sigurdsson, Olafur J. Pastor Bodvar's Letter. Johnston, George, tr. 1985. 63p. 6.95 (*0-920806-72-4*) Penumbra Pr. CAN. *Dist:* Univ. of Toronto Pr.
—Stars of Constantinople. Stories. Boucher, Alan, tr. from ICE. 1992. 256p. (C). 24.95 o.p. (*0-8071-1778-1*) Louisiana State Univ. Pr.
Thordarson, Agnar. Called Home. Kellogg, Robert, tr. from ICE. 1996. 208p. pap. 24.00 (*1-870041-28-3*) Norvik Pr. GBR. *Dist:* Dufour Editions, Inc.
—Medal of Distinction. Cook, Robert, tr. from ICE. 1984. 196p. 12.95 o.p. (*0-88254-936-7*) Hippocrene Bks., Inc.
Webster, Noah. An Incident in Iceland. 1979. (Crime Club Ser.). 7.95 o.p. (*0-385-15478-X*) Doubleday Publishing.
Yates, Elizabeth. Iceland Adventures. 1997. 144p. (J). (gr. 4-6). pap. 6.49 (*0-89084-935-8*, 110031) Jones, Bob Univ. Pr.

## IDAHO—FICTION

Adam, Christina. Love & Country. 2003. (Illus.). 288p. 23.95 (*0-316-73500-0*) Little Brown & Co.
Baldwin, Faith. White Magic. 1976. reprint ed. lib. bdg. 24.95 (*0-88411-615-8*) Amereon, Ltd.
—White Magic. l.t. ed. 2000. (Romance Ser.). 373p. 26.95 (*0-7862-2874-1*) Thorndike Pr.
Barkdull, Larry. The Mourning Dove: A Story of Love. abr. ed. 1997. audio 11.95 o.p. (*1-55927-481-6*) Audio Renaissance.
—The Mourning Dove: A Story of Love. 1996. 96p. pap. (*1-889025-00-3*, KenningHouse) Maasai, Inc.
—The Mourning Dove: A Story of Love. unabr. ed. 1997. 96p. (J). 9.95 o.s.i (*0-307-44011-7*, Golden Bks. Adult Publishing Group) St. Martin's Pr.
Barnes, Kim. Finding Caruso. 2004. 320p. pap. 14.00 (*0-425-19393-4*) Berkley Publishing Group.
—Finding Caruso. 2003. 320p. 23.95 (*0-399-14967-8*) Putnam Publishing Group, The.
—Hungry for the World: A Memoir. 2001. 256p. pap. 13.00 (*0-385-72044-0*, Knopf Bks. for Young Readers) Random Hse. Children's Bks.
Bergera, Janet. Vital Signs: A Mission of the Heart. 1995. (J). pap. 9.95 (*1-55503-773-9*, 01111817) Covenant Communications, Inc.
Bloom, Rebecca. Tangled up in Daydreams. 2003. 288p. 24.95 (*0-06-621258-8*, Morrow, William & Co.) Morrow/Avon.
Boyer, Glenn G. Morgette & the Shadow Bomber: A Western Story. 2003. 296p. 25.95 (*0-7862-3791-0*, Five Star) Gale Group.
Brink, Carol Ryrie. Buffalo Coat. E-Book 17.95 (*0-87422-199-4*); 1993. (Illus.). 421p. reprint ed. pap. 19.95 (*0-87422-095-5*) Washington State Univ. Pr.
—Strangers in the Forest. 1993. (Reprint Ser.). 314p. reprint ed. pap. 19.95 (*0-87422-096-3*) Washington State Univ. Pr.
Combe, Louis. Watching the Watcher. 2000. (Illus.). 174p. pap. 12.95 (*1-880849-24-0*) Chapel Hill Pr.
Cook, Marion H. Reflections of a Farm Boy. 2001. 208p. 16.50 (*0-9727079-1-3*, 1) Bard Pubns.
Cooke, John Peyton. Haven: A Novel of Anxiety. 1996. 480p. 22.95 o.s.i (*0-89296-610-6*) Mysterious Pr.
—Haven: A Novel of Anxiety. 1998. mass mkt. (*0-446-40465-9*, Mysterious Pr. Paperback Bks.) Warner Bks., Inc.

Coyle, Harold. Against All Enemies. E-Book 25.95 (*0-312-70612-X*, Tor Bks.); 2002. 416p. 25.95 (*0-7653-0239-X*, Forge Bks.); 2003. 432p. reprint ed. mass mkt. 7.99 (*0-7653-4169-7*, Forge Bks.) Doherty, Tom Assocs., LLC.

Crane, Cheri J. The Girls Next Door: A Novel. 2002. (Illus.). 325p. (*1-59156-072-1*) Covenant Communications.

Crow, Donna Fletcher. Kathryn: Days of Struggle & Triumph. 1992. (Daughters of Courage Ser.). pap. 8.99 o.p. (*0-8024-4527-6*) Moody Pr.

Cummings, Jack. The Indian Fighter's Return. l.t. ed. 1994. 268p. lib. bdg. 16.95 (*0-8161-5991-2*, Macmillan Reference USA) Gale Group.

—The Indian Fighter's Return. 1993. 182p. 19.95 (*0-8027-1268-1*) Walker & Co.

Dennett, Nolan. Place of Shelter. 1994. (New American Fiction Ser.: No. 30). 224p. 19.95 o.p. (*1-55713-130-9*) Sun & Moon Pr.

Duncombe, Sydney. Blizzard in August. 2001. 320p. pap. 24.95 (*1-58851-126-X*) PublishAmerica, Inc.

—Enduring Faith. 2001. 291p. pap. 24.95 (*1-58851-111-1*) PublishAmerica, Inc.

Freeman, Judith. Set for Life. 1993. mass mkt. 4.99 o.s.i (*0-345-37947-0*) Ballantine Bks.

—Set for Life. 1994. 3.99 o.p. (*0-517-12511-0*) Random Hse. Value Publishing.

—Set for Life: A Novel. 1991. 352p. 19.95 o.p. (*0-393-03027-X*) Norton, W. W. & Co., Inc.

Garrison, Joan. Come Walk with Love. l.t. ed. 1991. 16.95 o.p. (*0-7927-0898-9*, CH0140); pap. 14.95 o.p. (*0-7927-0899-7*, CS0237) BBC Audiobooks America.

Gibson, Rachel. True Confessions. 2001. 384p. mass mkt. 6.99 (*0-380-81438-2*, Avon Bks.) Morrow/Avon.

Glad, Judith B. The Duchess of Ophir Creek. 2001. (Behind the Ranges Ser.). E-Book 4.75 incl. disk (*1-58749-038-2*); E-Book 4.75 (*1-58749-039-0*) Awe-Struck E-Bks.

Hansen, Jennie L. Beyond Summer Dreams. 2001. 282p. 14.95 (*1-57734-889-3*) Covenant Communications.

Hart, Griffin. Wyakin. 2000. 314p. 24.95 (*1-929897-05-7*) Holdfast Bks.

Hatcher, Robin Lee. Catching Katie. 2004. (HeartQuest Ser.). pap. 9.99 (*0-8423-6099-9*) Tyndale Hse. Pubs.

—In His Arms. l.t. ed. 2000. 312p. 26.95 (*1-57490-279-2*, Beeler Large Print Bks.) Beeler, Thomas T. Publisher.

—In His Arms. 1998. 432p. mass mkt. 6.99 o.s.i (*0-06-108689-4*) HarperCollins Pubs.

—In His Arms. 2001. (Coming to America Bk.). 304p. pap. 10.99 (*0-310-23120-5*) Zondervan.

—The Shepherd's Voice. 2000. 384p. pap. 11.95 (*1-57856-152-3*) WaterBrook Pr.

—The Shepherd's Voice: A Novel. 2003. 289p. 25.95 (*0-7862-4936-6*, Five Star) Gale Group.

Hayes, Penny. Grassy Flats. 1992. 256p. pap. 9.95 (*1-56280-010-8*) Naiad Pr., Inc.

Hendricksen, Louise. Grave Secrets. 1994. (Dr. Amy Prescott Mystery Ser.). 288p. mass mkt. 3.99 o.s.i (*0-8217-4737-1*, Zebra Bks.) Kensington Publishing Corp.

Henry, Will. Winter Shadows: A Western Duo. 2003. 205p. 25.95 (*0-7862-3770-8*, Five Star) Gale Group.

—Winter Shadows: A Western Duo. l.t. ed. 2004. 277p. 25.95 (*0-7862-6213-3*) Thorndike Pr.

Hogan, Chuck. The Standoff. 1996. 368p. mass mkt. 6.50 o.s.i (*0-553-57446-9*) Bantam Bks.

—The Standoff. l.t. ed. 1995. 25.95 o.p. (*1-56895-231-7*, Wheeler Publishing, Inc.) Gale Group.

Hunter, Stephen. Time to Hunt. 1999. 608p. mass mkt. 7.99 (*0-440-22645-7*) Dell Publishing.

Irvine, Robert. Barking Dogs. 1994. 224p. 19.95 o.p. (*0-312-10419-7*, Saint Martin's Minotaur) St. Martin's Pr.

Johnston, Terry C. Lay the Mountains Low, No. 2. 2000. (Plainsmen Ser.: Vol. 15). (Illus.). xxii, 495p. 24.95 (*0-312-26189-6*) St. Martin's Pr.

—Lay the Mountains Low: The Flight of the Nez Perce from Idaho & the Battle of the Big Hole, August 9-10, 1877. mass mkt. o.p. (*0-312-97547-3*, St. Martin's Paperbacks) St. Martin's Pr.

Johnstone, William W. Law of the Mountain Man. l.t. ed. 1999. (Western Ser.). 319p. 24.95 o.p. (*0-7838-8730-2*, Macmillan Reference USA) Gale Group.

—Law of the Mountain Man. 1998. 256p. mass mkt. 4.99 o.s.i (*0-8217-5854-3*, Zebra Bks.); 1995. mass mkt. 4.50 o.s.i (*0-8217-5117-4*); 1989. mass mkt. 3.50 o.s.i (*0-8217-4085-7*, Zebra Bks.); 1995. 256p. mass mkt. 4.99 o.s.i (*0-8217-5367-3*) Kensington Publishing Corp.

—Return of the Mountain Man. 2000. 192p. mass mkt. 5.99 (*0-7860-1296-X*); 1996. mass mkt. 4.99 o.s.i (*0-8217-5298-7*, Zebra Bks.); 1989. mass mkt. 2.95 o.p. (*0-8217-2940-3*); 1989. mass mkt. 3.50 o.s.i (*0-8217-4018-0*, Zebra Bks.) Kensington Publishing Corp.

—Return of the Mountain Man. l.t. ed. 1998. (Western Ser.). 223p. 24.95 (*0-7838-0334-6*) Thorndike Pr.

Kulchak, Craig. The Creeks: An Upland Adventure. Brunson, Laura, ed. 1996. (Illus.). 125p. 29.00 (*0-9655833-0-9*) Walkabout Pr.

Lacey, Al & Lacey, JoAnna. A Measure of Grace. 2003. (Mail Order Bride Ser.: Bk. 8). 320p. pap. 10.99 (*1-57673-808-6*) Multnomah Pubs., Inc.

Lacey, Al & Lacy, JoAnna. A Measure of Grace. l.t. ed. 2003. (Mail Order Bride Series Book Ser.). 530p. 28.95 (*0-7862-5362-2*) Thorndike Pr.

McCall, Wendell. Dead Aim. l.t. ed. 2001. 400p. lib. bdg. 28.95 (*1-58547-141-0*); 319p. (*1-74030-542-6*) Ctr. Point Large Print.

—Dead Aim. 1990. 272p. reprint ed. mass mkt. 3.95 o.s.i (*0-440-20510-7*) Dell Publishing.

—Dead Aim. 1999. (Chris Klick Mysteries Ser.: Vol. 11). 250p. pap. 14.95 (*1-890208-20-5*) Poisoned Pen Pr.

—Dead Aim. 1991. 2.99 o.p. (*0-517-07670-5*) Random Hse. Value Publishing.

—Dead Aim. 1988. 272p. 16.95 o.p. (*0-312-02184-4*, Saint Martin's Minotaur) St. Martin's Pr.

McLeod, Adelaide. Out of Innocence. 2000. 260p. pap. 14.95 (*0-9666002-1-5*) Coffee Table Bks.

Morris, Keith Lee. The Greyhound God. 2003. (Western Literature Ser.). 328p. 23.00 (*0-87417-555-0*) Univ. of Nevada Pr.

Muller, Marcia. Listen to the Silence. l.t. ed. 2000. (Wheeler Large Print Book Ser.). 328p. 28.95 o.p. (*1-56895-908-7*, Wheeler Publishing, Inc.) Gale Group.

—Listen to the Silence. 2000. 304p. 23.95 (*0-89296-689-0*) Mysterious Pr.

Ozeki, Ruth L. All over Creation: A Novel. 2004. 432p. pap. 14.00 (*0-14-200389-1*) Penguin Group (USA) Inc.

—All over Creation: A Novel. 2003. 432p. 24.95 (*0-670-03091-0*, Viking) Viking Penguin.

Parkinson, Heather. Across Open Ground: A Novel. 2003. (Illus.). 256p. pap. 14.95 (*1-58234-289-X*); 2002. 288p. 23.95 (*1-58234-243-1*) Bloomsbury Publishing.

Pearson, Carol Lynn. A Stranger for Christmas: A Novel. 2003. 14.95 (*0-8294-1762-1*) Loyola Pr.

Roberts, Ronald R. The Ditches of Edison County. 1993. (*0-525-27256-9*); 96p. pap. 7.00 o.s.i (*0-452-27256-4*) Dutton/Plume. (Plume).

—The Ditches of Edison County. 1999. pap. (*0-451-18266-9*, Signet Bks.) NAL.

Ross, Dana Fuller, pseud. Idaho! l.t. ed. 1985. lib. bdg. 15.95 o.p. (*0-8161-3791-9*, Macmillan Reference USA) Gale Group.

Saul, John. Guardian. 1994. 384p. mass mkt. 7.99 (*0-449-22304-3*, Fawcett) Ballantine Bks.

—Guardian. unabr. ed. 1993. audio 23.95 o.p. (*1-56100-532-0*, 130, Bookcassette); audio 73.25 o.p. (*1-56100-160-0*, 886, Unabridged Library Editions) Brilliance Audio.

—Guardian. abr. ed. 1994. audio 8.99 o.s.i (*0-679-43791-6*, RH Audio) Random Hse. Audio Publishing Group.

Sharpe, Jon. Idaho Ghost Town. 2000. (Trailsman Ser.: Vol. 223). 176p. mass mkt. 4.99 o.s.i (*0-451-20024-1*, Signet Bks.) NAL.

Thon, Melanie Rae. Iona Moon. 1994. 320p. pap. 11.95 o.p. (*0-452-27280-7*, Plume) Dutton/Plume.

—Iona Moon. 1993. 320p. 21.00 o.p. (*0-671-79687-9*, Simon & Schuster) Simon & Schuster.

Transtrum, Kenya. Love Springs a Leak. 2004. pap. 9.95 (*0-9728071-1-X*) Mapletree Publishing Co.

Wassom, Warren. Pure Gold. 2002. (Illus.). 270p. pap. 15.95 (*1-55517-607-0*, Bonneville Bks.) Cedar Fort, Inc./CFI Distribution.

Woods, Stuart. Heat. 1994. 320p. 138.00 o.p. (*0-06-017623-7*, HarperCollins); 23.00 o.p. (*0-06-017776-4*) HarperTrade.

—Heat. 1995. 384p. mass mkt. 7.99 (*0-06-109358-0*, HarperTorch) Morrow/Avon.

## ILLINOIS—FICTION

Algren, Nelson. The Neon Wilderness: 24 Short Stories. 1988. 23.95 (*0-8488-0415-5*) Amereon, Ltd.

—The Neon Wilderness: 24 Short Stories. Simon, Dan, ed. 1997. 304p. reprint ed. pap. 10.95 (*1-888363-21-5*) Seven Stories Pr.

Amberg, Jay. Blackbird Singing. 2000. mass mkt. 6.99 (*0-8125-9006-6*); 1998. 302p. 23.95 (*0-312-86554-6*) Doherty, Tom Assocs., LLC. (Forge Bks.).

Baker, Nikki. In the Game. 1991. (Virginia Kelly Mystery Ser.). 224p. (Orig.). pap. 9.95 (*1-56280-004-3*) Naiad Pr., Inc.

—The Lavender House Murder. 1992. (Virginia Kelly Mystery Ser.). 224p. pap. 9.95 o.p. (*1-56280-012-4*) Naiad Pr., Inc.

—The Long Goodbyes. 1993. (Virginia Kelly Mystery Ser.: No. 3). 208p. pap. 9.95 o.p. (*1-56280-042-6*) Naiad Pr., Inc.

Baker, Scott. Ancestral Hungers. 320p. 1996. pap. 14.95 (*0-312-86305-5*); 1996. mass mkt. 5.99 (*0-8125-0259-0*); 1995. 21.95 o.p. (*0-312-85868-X*) Doherty, Tom Assocs., LLC. (Tor Bks.).

Barrett, Neal, Jr. Pink Vodka Blues. 1997. 304p. mass mkt. 5.99 o.s.i (*1-57566-237-X*) Kensington Publishing Corp.

—Pink Vodka Blues. 1992. 320p. 18.95 (*0-312-07766-1*, Saint Martin's Minotaur) St. Martin's Pr.

Baumbich, Charlene. Dearest Dorothy, Slow down, You're Wearing Us Out! 2004. 256p. pap. 10.95 (*0-14-200418-9*) Penguin Group (USA) Inc.

Baumbich, Charlene Ann. Dearest Dorothy, Are We There Yet? 2004. 224p. pap. 10.95 (*0-14-200379-4*) Penguin Group (USA) Inc.

—Dearest Dorothy, Slow down, You're Wearing Us Out! l.t. ed. 2003. 383p. 26.95 (*0-7862-5559-5*) Thorndike Pr.

Bellow, Saul. The Dean's December. 1982. (General Ser.). lib. bdg. 16.95 o.p. (*0-8161-3404-9*, Macmillan Reference USA) Gale Group.

—The Dean's December. 1982. 320p. 14.95 o.p. (*0-06-014849-7*) HarperTrade.

—The Dean's December. 1985. 346p. mass mkt. 4.50 (*0-671-60254-3*); 1983. mass mkt. 3.95 o.s.i (*0-671-46476-0*) Simon & Schuster. (Pocket).

—The Dean's December. 1998. (Great Books of the 20th Century Ser.). 320p. 13.95 (*0-14-018913-0*, Penguin Classics) Viking Penguin.

Blagg, Kim D. Gambler's Nook. l.t. ed. 1999. (Illus.). E-Book 14.99 incl. cd-rom (*1-929077-00-9*, Books OnScreen) PageFree Publishing, Inc.

Bland, Eleanor Taylor. Dead Time. 1993. 304p. mass mkt. 4.99 o.s.i (*0-451-40427-0*, Signet Bks.) NAL.

—Dead Time: A Marti MacAlister Mystery. 1992. 224p. 17.95 o.p. (*0-312-07053-5*, Saint Martin's Minotaur) St. Martin's Pr.

—Done Wrong. 1996. mass mkt. 5.99 (*0-312-95794-7*, St. Martin's Paperbacks); 1995. 216p. 20.95 o.p. (*0-312-13053-8*, Saint Martin's Minotaur) St. Martin's Pr.

—Gone Quiet. 1995. 336p. mass mkt. 4.99 o.s.i (*0-451-18267-7*, Signet Bks.) NAL.

—Gone Quiet: A Marti MacAlister Mystery. 1994. 224p. 19.95 o.p. (*0-312-11018-9*, Saint Martin's Minotaur) St. Martin's Pr.

—Keep Still. l.t. ed. 1996. (G. K. Hall Mystery Ser.). 316p. 21.95 o.p. (*0-7838-1931-5*, Macmillan Reference USA) Gale Group.

—Keep Still. 1996. 224p. 20.95 o.p. (*0-312-14318-4*, Saint Martin's Minotaur); Vol. 1. 1998. 240p. mass mkt. 5.99 (*0-312-96172-3*, St. Martin's Paperbacks) St. Martin's Pr.

—Scream in Silence. 2001. 320p. reprint ed. mass mkt. 6.50 (*0-312-97494-9*, 20-3259, St. Martin's Paperbacks) St. Martin's Pr.

—Scream in Silence: A Marti MacAlister Mystery. 2000. 290p. 23.95 (*0-312-20378-0*, Saint Martin's Minotaur) St. Martin's Pr.

—See No Evil. (Marti MacAlister Ser.). 288p. 1999. mass mkt. 5.99 (*0-312-96818-3*, St. Martin's Paperbacks); 1998. 22.95 o.p. (*0-312-16910-8*, Saint Martin's Minotaur) St. Martin's Pr.

—See No Evil. l.t. ed. 1998. (Core Ser.). 392p. 29.95 (*0-7838-0112-2*) Thorndike Pr.

—Slow Burn. 1994. 320p. mass mkt. 4.99 o.s.i (*0-451-17944-7*, Signet Bks.) NAL.

—Slow Burn: A Marti MacAlister Mystery. 1993. 224p. 17.95 o.p. (*0-312-09237-7*, Saint Martin's Minotaur) St. Martin's Pr.

—Tell No Tales: A Marti MacAlister Mystery. l.t. ed. 1999. (Wheeler Large Print Book Ser.). 352p. pap. 23.95 (*1-56895-756-4*, Wheeler Publishing, Inc.) Gale Group.

—Tell No Tales: A Marti MacAlister Mystery. (Marti MacAlister Ser.). 2000. 288p. mass mkt. 5.99 (*0-312-97113-3*, St. Martin's Paperbacks); 1999. vii, 264p. 22.95 o.p. (*0-312-20067-6*, Saint Martin's Minotaur) St. Martin's Pr.

Bonansinga, Jay. Head Case. 1998. 318p. 23.00 (*0-684-82514-7*); 23.00 (*0-684-84931-3*) Simon & Schuster. (Simon & Schuster).

—Head Case. l.t. ed. 1998. (Core Ser.). 480p. 28.95 (*0-7838-0168-8*) Thorndike Pr.

—The Killer's Game, Set. abr. ed. 1997. 24.95 o.p. (*0-7871-1428-6*, 694908) NewStar Media, Inc.

Bonansinga, Jay R. The Killer's Game. 1997. 300p. 22.50 o.p. (*0-684-82513-9*, Simon & Schuster) Simon & Schuster.

Bradburg, Ray. Dandelion Wine. 9999. pap. 2.25 o.s.i (*0-590-03100-7*) Scholastic, Inc.

Bradbury, Ray. Dandelion Wine. 1985. mass mkt. 3.50 o.s.i (*0-553-27051-6*); mass mkt. 2.95 o.s.i (*0-553-25236-4*); 256p. (gr. 6 up). mass mkt. 7.50 (*0-553-27753-7*) Bantam Bks.

—Dandelion Wine. unabr. collector's ed. 1987. audio 48.00 (*0-7366-0500-2*, 1474) Books on Tape, Inc.

—Dandelion Wine. 1994. (YA). lib. bdg. 24.95 o.p. (*1-56849-448-3*) Buccaneer Bks., Inc.

—Dandelion Wine. 1975. (YA). 24.95 o.p. (*0-394-49605-1*) Knopf, Alfred A. Inc.

—Dandelion Wine. 1999. 288p. 15.95 (*0-380-97726-5*, Avon Bks.) Morrow/Avon.

—Dandelion Wine. l.t. ed. 1999. (Science Fiction Ser.). 334p. 25.95 (*0-7838-8817-1*) Thorndike Pr.

—Dandelion Wine. 1976. (Grand Master Editions Ser.). 12.55 (*0-606-00520-X*) Turtleback Bks.

—From the Dust Returned. l.t. ed. 2002. 203p. 29.95 (*0-7862-4043-1*) Gale Group.

—From the Dust Returned. 2002. 288p. mass mkt. 6.99 (*0-380-78961-2*); 2001. (Illus.). 224p. 23.00 (*0-380-97382-0*, Morrow, William & Co.) Morrow/Avon.

Branton, Matthew. The House of Whacks. 1999. 256p. pap. 13.95 (*1-58234-024-2*) Bloomsbury Publishing.

Brod, D. C. Brothers in Blood: A Quint McCauley Mystery. 1993. 288p. 21.95 (*0-8027-3239-9*) Walker & Co.

—Masquerade in Blue. 1991. 208p. 19.95 (*0-8027-5792-8*) Walker & Co.

Brooks, Terry. Angel Fire East. 2000. 384p. mass mkt. 7.99 (*0-345-43525-7*, Del Rey) Ballantine Bks.

—Angel Fire East. unabr. ed. 1999. audio 80.00 (*0-7887-4052-0*, 96159E7, Clipper Audio) Recorded Bks., LLC.

—Running with the Demon. 1998. (Trolltown Ser.: Vol. 1). 448p. mass mkt. 7.99 (*0-345-42258-9*); 1997. 432p. 5.99 o.s.i (*0-345-37962-4*) Ballantine Bks. (Del Rey).

—Running with the Demon. unabr. ed. 1998. audio 97.00 (*0-7887-2168-2*, 95464E7) Recorded Bks., LLC.

Browne, Howard. Pork City. 1988. 272p. 16.95 o.p. (*0-312-01493-7*) St. Martin's Pr.

Buckman, Daniel. Morning Dark. 2003. 224p. 22.95 (*0-312-31462-0*) St. Martin's Pr.

Burgin, Richard. Private Fame. 1991. (Illinois Short Fiction Ser.). 168p. 16.95 (*0-252-01843-5*) Univ. of Illinois Pr.

Butler, Robert Olen. Wabash: A Novel. 1988. mass mkt. 3.95 o.s.i (*0-345-35211-4*) Ballantine Bks.

—Wabash: A Novel. 1994. 25.00 o.p. (*0-8050-3200-2*); 207p. pap. 11.00 o.s.i (*0-8050-3138-3*, Owl Bks.) Holt, Henry & Co.

Cameron, Julia. The Dark Room. 1998. 448p. 25.00 o.p. (*0-7867-0564-7*, Carroll & Graf Pubs.) Avalon Publishing Group.

Campbell, Robert. Boneyards. Chelius, Jane, ed. 304p. 1992. 21.00 o.p. (*0-671-70319-6*, Atria); 1993. reprint ed. mass mkt. 5.50 (*0-671-70320-X*, Pocket) Simon & Schuster.

—The Cat's Meow. (Jimmy Flannery Mystery Ser.). 1990. 208p. mass mkt. 4.50 o.p. (*0-451-16431-8*, Signet Bks.); 1988. 240p. 16.95 o.p. (*0-453-00615-9*) NAL.

—A Flannery Trilogy: Featuring The Junkyard Dog, 600-Pound Gorilla & Hip-Deep in Alligators. rev. ed. 1999. (Flannery Trilogies Ser.: Vol. 1). 384p. pap. 24.95 (*1-58444-073-2*) Disc-Us Bks., Inc.

—A Flannery Trilogy: Featuring the Junkyard Dog, 600-Pound Gorilla & Hip-Deep in Alligators, I. 2003. (Jimmy Flannery Mystery Ser.). E-Book 16.95 incl. cd-rom (*1-58444-084-8*) Disc-Us Bks., Inc.

—The Gift Horse's Mouth. Chelius, Jane, ed. 208p. 1990. 17.95 o.p. (*0-671-67586-9*, Atria); 1991. reprint ed. mass mkt. 4.99 (*0-671-74340-6*, Pocket) Simon & Schuster.

—Hip Deep in Alligators. 1988. 208p. mass mkt. 3.95 o.p. (*0-451-40096-8*, Onyx); 1987. 16.95 o.p. (*0-453-00577-2*) NAL.

—In a Pig's Eye. Chelius, Jane, ed. 224p. 1991. 19.00 (*0-671-70327-7*, Atria); 1992. reprint ed. mass mkt. 4.99 (*0-671-70328-5*, Pocket) Simon & Schuster.

—The Junkyard Dog. 2000. E-Book 14.50 o.p. incl. cd-rom (*1-58444-047-3*) Disc-Us Bks., Inc.

—The Junkyard Dog. 1986. mass mkt. 2.95 o.p. (*0-451-14396-5*); 192p. mass mkt. 3.99 o.s.i (*0-451-15899-7*) NAL. (Signet Bks.).

—The Junkyard Dog. unabr. ed. 1991. (Jimmy Flannery Mystery Ser.: Vol. 1). audio 35.00 (*1-55690-277-8*, 91231E7) Recorded Bks., LLC.

—The Lion's Share. 1996. 82p. 21.95 o.s.i (*0-89296-609-2*) Mysterious Pr.

—The Lion's Share. 1997. 224p. mass mkt. 5.99 o.s.i (*0-446-40464-0*) Warner Bks., Inc.

—Nibbled to Death by Ducks. unabr. ed. 1992. (Jimmy Flannery Mystery Ser.: Vol. 6). audio 44.00 (*1-55690-703-6*, 92105E7) Recorded Bks., LLC.

—Nibbled to Death by Ducks. 1989. 208p. 17.95 o.p. (*0-671-67585-0*, Atria) Simon & Schuster.

—Nibbled to Death by Ducks. Chelius, Jane, ed. 1990. 288p. reprint ed. mass mkt. 4.99 (*0-671-67583-4*, Pocket) Simon & Schuster.

—Pigeon Pie. 1998. (Jimmy Flannery Mystery Ser.: Vol. 27). 240p. 22.00 o.s.i (*0-89296-665-3*) Mysterious Pr.

—Sauce for the Goose. 1995. 240p. 18.95 o.s.i (*0-89296-608-4*) Mysterious Pr.

—Sauce for the Goose. 1996. 208p. mass mkt. 5.99 o.p. (*0-446-40463-2*) Warner Bks., Inc.

—Thinning the Turkey Herd. 1989. mass mkt. 3.50 o.p. (*0-451-15920-9*, Signet Bks.); 1988. 16.95 o.p. (*0-453-00583-7*) NAL.

—600-Pound Gorilla. 1987. 240p. mass mkt. 3.95 o.p. (*0-451-15390-1*, Signet Bks.) NAL.

—The 600-Pound Gorilla. unabr. ed. 1991. (Jimmy Flannery Mystery Ser.: Vol. 2). audio 35.00 (*1-55690-582-3*, 91307E7) Recorded Bks., LLC.

Cannell, Dorothy. Mum's the Word. 1991. 272p. mass mkt. 6.50 o.s.i (*0-553-28686-2*) Bantam Bks.

—Mum's the Word. l.t. ed. 2001. (Beeler Large Print Mystery Ser.). 324p. 26.95 (*1-57490-352-7*, Beeler Large Print Bks.) Beeler, Thomas T. Publisher.

Cappetta, Gary Michael. Fall for the Dream: A Script of Wrestling Fiction. 2000. 168p. (Orig.). pap. 14.95 (*0-9703991-5-4*) Little Bro' Ltd.

Carter, Betty Smartt. The Tower, the Mask, & the Grave: A Mystery. 2000. 304p. pap. 12.99 (*0-87788-559-1*, Shaw) WaterBrook Pr.

Casey, Maud. The Shape of Things to Come: A Novel. 2002. 272p. pap. 12.95 (*0-06-008441-3*, Perennial) HarperTrade.

—The Shape of Things to Come: A Novel. 2001. 272p. 24.00 (*0-688-17695-X*, Morrow, William & Co.) Morrow/Avon.

Castillo, Ana. Peel My Love Like an Onion. 1999. 240p. 23.95 o.s.i (*0-385-49676-1*) Doubleday Publishing.

—Peel My Love Like an Onion: A Novel. 2000. 240p. reprint ed. pap. 12.00 (*0-385-49677-X*) Doubleday Publishing.

Champlin, Tim. Lincoln's Ransom. 1999. (Western Ser.). 280p. 19.95 (*0-7862-1574-7*, Five Star) Gale Group.

—Lincoln's Ransom. l.t. ed. 2000. (G. K. Hall Western Ser.). 352p. 24.95 (*0-7838-0313-3*) Thorndike Pr.

Chernoff, Maxine. A Boy in Winter. 1999. 256p. 22.00 o.s.i (*0-609-60522-4*) Crown Publishing Group.

Child, Lee. Die Trying. 1999. 448p. reprint ed. mass mkt. 7.99 (*0-515-12502-4*, Jove) Berkley Publishing Group.

—Die Trying. abr. ed. 1999. audio 7.99 (*1-56740-296-8*, 1855, Paperback Nova Audio Bks.); 1998. audio 28.95 (*1-56100-791-9*, 14, Bookcassette); 1998. audio 89.25 (*1-56740-570-3*, 864, Unabridged Library Editions); Set. 1998. audio 17.95 o.p. (*1-56740-766-8*, 445, Nova Audio Bks.) Brilliance Audio.

—Die Trying. 1998. 384p. 23.95 o.s.i (*0-399-14379-3*, G. P. Putnam's Sons) Penguin Group (USA) Inc.

Churchill, Jill. Class Menagerie. 1999. (Jane Jeffry Mystery Ser.). 224p. mass mkt. 6.99 (*0-380-77380-5*, Avon Bks.) Morrow/Avon.

—Farewell to Yarns. 1991. (Jane Jeffry Mystery Ser.). 256p. mass mkt. 6.99 (*0-380-76399-0*, Avon Bks.) Morrow/Avon.

—Fear of Frying. (Jane Jeffry Mystery Ser.). 1998. 256p. mass mkt. 6.99 (*0-380-78707-5*); 1997. 224p. pap. 22.00 (*0-380-97324-3*) Morrow/Avon. (Avon Bks.).

—From Here to Paternity. 1995. (Jane Jeffry Mystery Ser.). 256p. (Orig.). mass mkt. 6.99 (*0-380-77715-0*, Avon Bks.) Morrow/Avon.

—Grime & Punishment. 1989. 208p. (Orig.). mass mkt. 3.50 o.s.i (*0-553-27646-8*) Bantam Bks.

—Grime & Punishment. 1992. (Jane Jeffry Mystery Ser.). 256p. (Orig.). mass mkt. 6.99 (*0-380-76400-8*, Avon Bks.) Morrow/Avon.

—A Groom with a View: A Jane Jeffry Mystery. (Jane Jeffry Mystery Ser.). 2000. 288p. mass mkt. 6.50 (*0-380-79450-0*); Bk. C. 1999. 224p. 22.00 (*0-380-97570-X*) Morrow/Avon. (Avon Bks.).

—A Groom with a View: A Jane Jeffry Mystery. l.t. ed. 2000. (Americana Ser.). 293p. 27.95 (*0-7862-2454-1*) Thorndike Pr.

—The House of Seven Mabels: A Jane Jeffry Mystery. 2002. 240p. 23.95 (*0-380-97736-2*, Morrow, William & Co.) Morrow/Avon.

—A Knife to Remember. 1999. (Jane Jeffry Mystery Ser.). 224p. mass mkt. 6.99 (*0-380-77381-3*, Avon Bks.) Morrow/Avon.

—The Merchant of Menace: A Jane Jeffry Mystery. 1998. 224p. 21.00 (*0-380-97569-6*, Avon Bks.) Morrow/Avon.

—Mulch Ado about Nothing: A Jane Jeffry Mystery. 2000. 216p. 23.00 (*0-380-97735-4*, Morrow, William & Co.) Morrow/Avon.

—Quiche Before Dying. 1993. (Jane Jeffry Mystery Ser.). 192p. mass mkt. 6.99 (*0-380-76932-8*, Avon Bks.) Morrow/Avon.

—Silence of the Hams. 1996. (Jane Jeffry Mystery Ser.). 288p. mass mkt. 6.99 (*0-380-77716-9*, Avon Bks.) Morrow/Avon.

—War & Peas. (Jane Jeffry Mystery Ser.). 1997. 288p. mass mkt. 6.99 (*0-380-78706-7*); 1996. 224p. mass mkt. 20.00 (*0-380-97323-5*) Morrow/Avon. (Avon Bks.).

Cisneros, Sandra. The House on Mango Street. 1989. 80p. 7.50 o.p. (*0-934770-20-4*) Arte Publico Pr.

—The House on Mango Street. 1991. (Contemporaries Ser.). 128p. pap. 9.95 (*0-679-73477-5*, RH4775, Vintage) Knopf Publishing Group.

—The House on Mango Street. 1994. 160p. 24.00 (*0-679-43335-X*) Random Hse., Inc.

—The House on Mango Street. 1991. (Vintage Contemporaries Ser.). 16.00 (*0-606-05352-2*) Turtleback Bks.

Clark, Mary Higgins, et al. Great Mysteries, Great Writers. abr. ed. 1994. audio 24.95 o.p. (*0-7871-0047-1*, 692220, Dove Audio) NewStar Media, Inc.

Clason, Clyde B. The Man from Tibet. 1998. 224p. pap. 14.00 (*0-915230-17-8*) Rue Morgue Pr.

Clement, Alison. Pretty Is As Pretty Does: A Novel. 2001. 268p. 25.00 (*0-9673701-9-1*) MacAdam/Cage Publishing, Inc.

Collins, Max Allan. Road to Perdition. Heifer, Andrew, ed. 1998. (Illus.). 304p. pap. 13.95 (*1-56389-449-1*) DC Comics.

—Road to Perdition. (Illus.). 304p. 2002. pap. 14.00 (*0-7434-4224-5*); 1998. per. 14.00 (*0-671-00921-4*) Simon & Schuster. (Pocket).

Conrad, James. Making Love to the Minor Poets of Chicago. E-Book 14.95 (*0-312-27372-X*); 2001. 432p. pap. 14.95 (*0-312-27073-9*, Saint Martin's Griffin); 2000. 436p. 25.95 (*0-312-20472-8*) St. Martin's Pr.

Cooper, Susan Rogers. Funny As a Dead Comic. 1993. 224p. 18.95 o.p. (*0-312-09815-4*, Saint Martin's Minotaur) St. Martin's Pr.

Cormany, Michael. Lost Daughter. 1991. 224p. reprint ed. pap. 3.50 (*0-8439-3063-2*) Dorchester Publishing Co., Inc.

—Polaroid Man. 1993. 240p. reprint ed. pap. 3.99 (*0-8439-3542-1*) Dorchester Publishing Co., Inc.

—Red Winter. 1991. 224p. (Orig.). reprint ed. pap. 3.50 (*0-8439-3142-6*) Dorchester Publishing Co., Inc.

—Red Winter. 1991. (Orig.). 2.99 o.p. (*0-517-06332-8*) Random Hse. Value Publishing.

—Rich or Dead. 1991. 208p. reprint ed. pap. 3.50 (*0-8439-3186-8*) Dorchester Publishing Co., Inc.

Craft, Michael. Eye Contact. 1998. 352p. 21.95 o.s.i (*1-57566-292-2*, Kensington Bks.) Kensington Publishing Corp.

—Flight Dreams. 1998. 256p. pap. 10.95 o.s.i (*1-57566-294-9*); 1997. (Mark Manning Mystery Ser.: Vol. 1). 224p. 19.95 o.s.i (*1-57566-174-8*) Kensington Publishing Corp. (Kensington Bks.).

Cresswell, Jasmine. The Inheritance. 2000. 408p. mass mkt. (*1-55166-511-5*, 1-66511-6, Mira Bks.) Harlequin Enterprises, Ltd.

D'Amato, Barbara. Authorized Personnel Only. 2000. 352p. 24.95 (*0-312-86564-3*, Forge Bks.) Doherty, Tom Assocs., LLC.

—Good Cop, Bad Cop. 1999. 304p. mass mkt. 6.99 (*0-8125-9014-7*); 1998. 320p. 22.95 o.p. (*0-312-86562-7*) Doherty, Tom Assocs., LLC. (Forge Bks.).

—Hard Bargain: A Cat Marsala Mystery. 1999. (Cat Marsala Ser.). 288p. mass mkt. 5.99 o.s.i (*0-425-16898-0*) Berkley Publishing Group.

—Hard Bargain: A Cat Marsala Mystery. 1997. (Illus.). 288p. 21.00 o.s.i (*0-684-83353-0*, Scribner) Simon & Schuster.

—Hard Case: A Cat Marsala Mystery. 1995. 240p. mass mkt. 4.99 o.s.i (*0-425-15009-7*, Prime Crime) Berkley Publishing Group.

—Hard Case: A Cat Marsala Mystery. 1994. 288p. 20.00 o.p. (*0-684-19686-7*, Macmillan Reference USA) Gale Group.

—Hard Christmas: A Cat Marsala Mystery. 1996. 288p. mass mkt. 5.99 o.s.i (*0-425-15465-3*, Prime Crime) Berkley Publishing Group.

—Hard Christmas: A Cat Marsala Mystery. 1995. 288p. 20.00 (*0-684-19687-5*, Scribner) Simon & Schuster.

—Hard Evidence: A Cat Marsala Mystery. 2000. (Cat Marsala Mysteries Ser.). (Illus.). 255p. mass mkt. 6.50 o.s.i (*0-425-17412-3*, Prime Crime) Berkley Publishing Group.

—Hard Evidence: A Cat Marsala Mystery. l.t. ed. 2000. (Wheeler Large Print Bks.). (Illus.). 247p. pap. 23.95 (*1-56895-861-7*, Wheeler Publishing, Inc.) Gale Group.

—Hard Evidence: A Cat Marsala Mystery. 1999. (Cat Marsala Mysteries Ser.). 256p. 22.00 (*0-684-83354-9*, Scribner) Simon & Schuster.

—Hard Luck: A Cat Marsala Mystery. 1992. 224p. text 20.00 (*0-684-19408-2*, Macmillan Reference USA) Gale Group.

—Hard Luck: A Cat Marsala Mystery. 1993. (Mystery Ser.). per. (*0-373-26124-1*, 1-26124-7, Harlequin Bks.) Harlequin Enterprises, Ltd.

—Hard Tack: A Cat Marsala Mystery. 1991. 224p. 18.95 o.s.i (*0-684-19299-3*, Macmillan Reference USA) Gale Group.

—Hard Tack: A Cat Marsala Mystery. 1992. (WWL Mystery Ser.: No. 97). per. (*0-373-26097-0*, 1-26097-5, Harlequin Bks.) Harlequin Enterprises, Ltd.

—Hard Women: A Cat Marsala Mystery. 1993. 256p. 20.00 o.p. (*0-684-19564-X*, Macmillan Reference USA) Gale Group.

—Hard Women: A Cat Marsala Mystery. 1994. per. (*0-373-26150-0*, 1-26150-2, Harlequin Bks.) Harlequin Enterprises, Ltd.

—Hardball. 2003. 224p. pap. 13.00 (*1-932325-01-8*) Crum Creek Pr.

—Hardball. 1990. 224p. 17.95 o.s.i (*0-684-19140-7*, Macmillan Reference USA) Gale Group.

—Hardball. 1993. (Illus.). per. (*0-373-83302-4*, 1-83302-9); 1991. mass mkt. (*0-373-26066-0*) Harlequin Enterprises, Ltd. (Harlequin Bks.).

—Help Me, Please! 2nd ed. 1999. 336p. 23.95 (*0-312-86563-5*, Forge Bks.) Doherty, Tom Assocs., LLC.

—Killer.app. 350p. 1997. mass mkt. 5.99 (*0-8125-5391-8*); 1996. 22.95 o.p. (*0-312-85991-0*) Doherty, Tom Assocs., LLC. (Forge Bks.).

Davis-Gardner, Angela. Forms of Shelter. l.t. ed. 1993. (General Ser.). 346p. 16.95 o.p. (*0-8161-5423-6*, Macmillan Reference USA) Gale Group.

—Forms of Shelter. 1991. 256p. 19.95 o.p. (*0-395-59312-3*) Houghton Mifflin Co.

Diehl, William. Reign in Hell. 1998. 480p. mass mkt. 7.99 (*0-345-39506-9*, Ballantine Bks.) Ballantine Bks.

—Show of Evil. 1998. pap. 6.99 (*0-345-91453-8*); 1996. 416p. mass mkt. 7.99 (*0-345-37536-X*, Ballantine Bks.); 1995. mass mkt. 6.99 (*0-345-40133-6*) Ballantine Bks.

—Show of Evil. abr. ed. 1995. audio 17.00 o.s.i (*0-679-44304-5*, RH Audio) Random Hse. Audio Publishing Group.

Dunlop, Susan, et al. Crime's Leading Ladies. unabr. ed. 1995. 3p. audio 16.99 (*0-88646-376-9*, 390575) Durkin Hayes Publishing Ltd.

Dybek, Stuart. The Coast of Chicago. 2003. 192p. pap. 13.00 (*0-312-42282-2*) Picador.

Dymmoch, Michael A. Incendiary Designs. 1998. 304p. 15.95 (*0-312-19245-2*, Saint Martin's Minotaur) St. Martin's Pr.

Eberhart, Mignon G. The House on the Roof. 1976. reprint ed. lib. bdg. 23.95 (*0-88411-762-6*) Amereon, Ltd.

—The House on the Roof. 1996. 304p. pap. 13.00 (*0-8032-6734-7*, Bison Bks.) Univ. of Nebraska Pr.

—Postmark Murder. 1983. 208p. mass mkt. 5.50 (*0-446-31181-2*) Warner Bks., Inc.

Elliott, Ray. Wild Hands Toward the Sky: A Novel. 2002. (Illus.). 431p. 28.00 (*0-9641423-7-6*) Tales Pr.

Ellis, David. Life Sentence. 2004. 416p. mass mkt. 7.99 (*0-425-19480-9*) Berkley Publishing Group.

—Life Sentence. 2003. 448p. 24.95 (*0-399-14979-1*, Putnam & Grosset) Putnam Publishing Group, The.

—Life Sentence. l.t. ed. 2003. 28.95 (*0-7862-5483-1*) Thorndike Pr.

Elrod, P. N. A Chill in the Blood. (Vampire Files Ser.: Vol. 7). 336p. 1998. 20.95 o.s.i (*0-441-00501-2*); 1999. reprint ed. mass mkt. 6.50 o.s.i (*0-441-00627-2*) Ace Bks.

—Dark Sleep. (Vampire Files Ser.: Vol. 8). 368p. 2000. mass mkt. 6.99 (*0-441-00723-6*); 1999. 21.95 o.s.i (*0-441-00591-8*) Ace Bks.

—Lady Crymsyn: A Novel of the Vampire Files. 2000. (Vampire Files Ser.: Vol. 9). (Illus.). 416p. 22.95 o.s.i (*0-441-00724-4*) Ace Bks.

—Vampire Files: Blood Art. 1991. (Vampire Files Ser.: Vol. 4). 208p. mass mkt. 5.99 o.s.i (*0-441-85945-3*) Ace Bks.

—Vampire Files: Blood on the Water. 1992. (Vampire Files Ser.: Vol. 6). 208p. mass mkt. 5.99 o.s.i (*0-441-85947-X*) Ace Bks.

—Vampire Files: Fire in the Blood. 1991. (Vampire Files Ser.: Vol. 5). mass mkt. 5.99 o.s.i (*0-441-85946-1*) Ace Bks.

—Vampire Files No. 01: Bloodlist. 1990. (Vampire Files Ser.). 208p. mass mkt. 6.50 o.s.i (*0-441-06795-6*) Ace Bks.

—Vampire Files No. 2: Lifeblood. 1990. (Vampire Files Ser.: Vol. 2). 208p. mass mkt. 5.99 o.s.i (*0-441-84776-5*) Ace Bks.

—Vampire Files No. 3: Bloodcircle. 1990. (Vampire Files Ser.: Vol. 3). mass mkt. 5.99 o.s.i (*0-441-06717-4*) Ace Bks.

Engleman, Paul. The Man with My Cat. 2000. 228p. 23.95 o.p. (*0-312-24651-X*, Saint Martin's Minotaur) St. Martin's Pr.

Eno, Thomas D. Deep Waters: A Novel. 2002. (Illus.). 170p. 14.95 (*1-57734-996-2*) Covenant Communications.

Farmer, Philip Jose. Nothing Burns in Hell. 1999. 287p. mass mkt. 6.99 (*0-8125-6495-2*, Tor Bks.); 1998. 288p. 22.95 o.p. (*0-312-86470-1*, Forge Bks.) Doherty, Tom Assocs., LLC.

Farmer, Philip Jose, et al. Naked Came the Farmer: A Round-Robin Rural Romance & Murder Mystery. 1998. pap. 12.95 (*0-9624613-7-7*) Mayfly Productions.

Faust, Ron. Split Image. 2000. 224p. pap. 12.95 (*0-312-87719-6*, Forge Bks.); 1999. mass mkt. (*0-8125-4924-4*, Tor Bks.); 1997. 224p. 20.95 o.p. (*0-312-86011-0*, Forge Bks.) Doherty, Tom Assocs., LLC.

Fielding, Joy. The First Time. l.t. ed. 2001. (Wheeler Large Print Book Ser.). 510p. 29.95 o.p. (*1-58724-057-2*, Wheeler Publishing, Inc.) Gale Group.

—The First Time. 2003. (Illus.). 512p. mass mkt. 5.99 (*0-7434-6714-0*, Pocket Star); 2000. (Illus.). 400p. 24.95 (*0-7434-0705-9*, Atria); 1999. (*0-7434-2268-6*, Atria); 1999. 512p. mass mkt. 7.99 (*0-7434-4636-4*, Pocket); 2001. (Illus.). 512p. reprint ed. mass mkt. 7.99 (*0-7434-0706-7*, Pocket Star); 2001. 400p. reprint ed. mass mkt. 7.99 (*0-7434-1724-0*, Pocket) Simon & Schuster.

Fiffer, Sharon Sloan. Dead Guy's Stuff. 2002. (Jane Wheel Mystery Ser.). 320p. 24.95 (*0-312-27822-5*, Saint Martin's Minotaur) St. Martin's Pr.

Fleming, Kathleen Anne. The Jazz Age Murders. 1999. 180p. pap. 14.50 (*0-88739-203-2*) Creative Arts Bk. Co.

Flynn, Joseph. Digger. 1998. 512p. mass mkt. 6.50 (*0-553-57809-X*) Bantam Bks.

Forrest, Leon. The Bloodworth Orphans. 2001. 383p. pap. 18.00 (*0-226-25722-3*) Univ. of Chicago Pr.

Frasier, Anne. Hush. 2002. (Illus.). 384p. mass mkt. 6.99 (*0-451-41031-9*, Onyx) NAL.

Frommer, Sara H. Witness in Bishop Hill: A Joan Spencer Mystery. 2002. 256p. 23.95 (*0-312-30243-6*, Saint Martin's Minotaur) St. Martin's Pr.

Gagliano, Peter. The Rosary Roulette. 1999. 139p. 15.95 o.p. (*1-58141-008-5*) Rivercross Publishing, Inc.

Garland, Ardella. Details at Ten. E-Book 21.00 (*1-58945-169-4*) Adobe Systems, Inc.

—Details at Ten: A Georgia Barnett Mystery. 2000. 208p. 21.00 o.s.i (*0-684-87375-3*, Simon & Schuster) Simon & Schuster.

Garlock, Dorothy. Lonesome River. 1991. 20.00 o.p. (*0-7278-4142-4*) Severn Hse. Pubs., Ltd.

Glass, Joseph. Blood: A Susan Shader Novel. 2000. (Susan Shader Novels Ser.). 400p. 24.00 (*0-684-85963-7*, Simon & Schuster) Simon & Schuster.

—Eyes. 1999. mass mkt. 6.99 o.s.i (*0-449-00512-7*, Fawcett) Ballantine Bks.

Gleiter, Jan. Lie down with Dogs. (Dead Letter Mysteries Ser.). 240p. 1997. mass mkt. 5.99 o.p. (*0-312-96175-8*, St. Martin's Paperbacks); 1996. 21.95 o.p. (*0-312-14003-7*, Saint Martin's Minotaur) St. Martin's Pr.

Granger, Bill. Drover & the Zebras. 1993. 240p. mass mkt. 4.99 (*0-380-71211-3*, Avon Bks.); 1992. 20.00 o.p. (*0-688-09857-6*, Morrow, William & Co.) Morrow/Avon.

Greeley, Andrew M. The Bishop at Sea: A Blackie Ryan Mystery. 1997. (Blackie Ryan Novels Ser.). 304p. mass mkt. 6.99 (*0-425-16080-7*) Berkley Publishing Group.

—The Bishop at Sea: A Blackie Ryan Mystery. l.t. ed. 2000. (Americana Ser.). 407p. 27.95 (*0-7862-2322-7*) Thorndike Pr.

—Contract with an Angel: A Novel of Angelic Intervention. abr. ed. 1999. audio 7.99 o.s.i (*1-56740-300-X*, 1862, Paperback Nova Audio Bks.); 1998. audio 26.95 (*1-56740-068-X*, 13, Bookcassette); 1998. 10p. audio 73.25 (*1-56740-597-5*, 830, Unabridged Library Editions); Set. 1998. audio 17.95 o.p. (*1-56740-793-5*, 444, Nova Audio Bks.) Brilliance Audio.

—Contract with an Angel: A Novel of Angelic Intervention. 1999. 384p. mass mkt. 6.99 (*0-8125-4443-9*); 1998. 304p. 23.95 o.p. (*0-312-86081-1*) Doherty, Tom Assocs., LLC. (Tor Bks.).

—Happy Are the Clean of Heart: A Blackie Ryan Novel. l.t. ed. 1987. 412p. 18.95 o.p. (*0-8161-4278-5*, Macmillan Reference USA) Gale Group.

—Happy Are the Clean of Heart: A Blackie Ryan Novel. 1988. mass mkt. 4.95 (*0-446-35722-7*) Warner Bks., Inc.

—Happy Are the Meek: A Blackie Ryan Novel. l.t. ed. 1986. (General Ser.). 373p. 16.95 o.p. (*0-8161-4029-4*, Macmillan Reference USA) Gale Group.

—Happy Are the Meek: A Blackie Ryan Novel. 1985. 288p. mass mkt. 3.95 (*0-446-32706-9*) Warner Bks., Inc.

—Happy Are the Merciful: A Blackie Ryan Novel. 1992. 336p. mass mkt. 6.99 o.s.i (*0-515-10726-3*, Jove) Berkley Publishing Group.

—Happy Are the Oppressed: A Blackie Ryan Novel. l.t. ed. 1997. lib. bdg. 24.95 (*1-57490-083-8*, Beeler Large Print Bks.) Beeler, Thomas T. Publisher.

—Happy Are the Oppressed: A Blackie Ryan Novel. 1996. (Illus.). 320p. mass mkt. 7.50 (*0-515-11921-0*, Jove) Berkley Publishing Group.

—Happy Are the Peace Makers: A Blackie Ryan Novel. l.t. ed. 1993. 24.95 o.p. (*0-7927-1680-9*); 22.95 o.p. (*0-7927-1679-5*) BBC Audiobooks America.

—Happy Are the Peace Makers: A Blackie Ryan Novel. 1993. 320p. mass mkt. 6.99 o.s.i (*0-515-11075-2*, Jove) Berkley Publishing Group.

—Happy Are the Poor in Spirit: A Blackie Ryan Novel. 1994. (Blackie Ryan Novels Ser.). (Illus.). 304p. mass mkt. 6.99 o.s.i (*0-515-11502-9*, Jove) Berkley Publishing Group.

—Happy Are Those Who Mourn: A Blackie Ryan Novel. l.t. ed. 1996. (Large Print Ser.). 352p. lib. bdg. 23.95 (*1-57490-038-2*, Beeler Large Print Bks.) Beeler, Thomas T. Publisher.

—Happy Are Those Who Mourn: A Blackie Ryan Novel. 1995. (Illus.). 304p. mass mkt. 6.99 o.s.i (*0-515-11761-7*, Jove) Berkley Publishing Group.

—Happy Are Those Who Thirst for Justice: A Blackie Ryan Novel. l.t. ed. 1988. (General Ser.). 440p. 18.95 o.p. (*0-8161-4488-5*, Macmillan Reference USA) Gale Group.

—Happy Are Those Who Thirst for Justice: A Blackie Ryan Novel. 1987. 320p. 16.95 (*0-89296-180-5*) Mysterious Pr.

—Happy Are Those Who Thirst for Justice: A Blackie Ryan Novel. 1988. mass mkt. 4.50 (*0-446-34946-1*) Warner Bks., Inc.

—Irish Eyes: A Nuala Anne McGrail Novel. 2000. 320p. 24.95 (*0-312-86570-8*); 2001. 352p. reprint ed. mass mkt. 6.99 (*0-8125-9024-4*) Doherty, Tom Assocs., LLC. (Forge Bks.).

—Irish Eyes: A Nuala Anne McGrail Novel. l.t. ed. 2001. 525p. 29.95 (*0-7862-3091-6*); (*0-7540-1621-8*) Thorndike Pr.

—Irish Lace: A Nuala Anne McGrail Novel. (Nuala Anne McGrail Novel Ser.). 1997. 345p. pap. 6.99 (*0-8125-5077-3*, Tor Bks.); 1996. 304p. 23.95 o.p. (*0-312-86234-2*, Forge Bks.) Doherty, Tom Assocs., LLC.

—Irish Lace: A Nuala Anne McGrail Novel. abr. ed. 1996. 17.95 o.p. (*0-7871-1022-1*, 394462) NewStar Media, Inc.

—Irish Lace: A Nuala Anne McGrail Novel. 1998. 4.98 o.p. (*0-7651-1156-X*) Smithmark Pubs., Inc.

—Irish Whiskey: A Nuala Anne McGrail Novel. 1998. (Nuala Anne McGrail Novel Ser.). 309p. pap. 6.99 (*0-8125-7770-1*, Tor Bks.); 304p. 23.95 o.p. (*0-312-85596-6*, Forge Bks.) Doherty, Tom Assocs., LLC.

—Irish Whiskey: A Nuala Anne McGrail Novel. l.t. ed. 2000. (Basic Ser.). 549p. 28.95 (*0-7862-2930-6*) Thorndike Pr.

—A Midwinter's Tale. 1999. 448p. mass mkt. 6.99 (*0-8125-9025-2*); No. 1. 1998. (Midwinter's Tale Ser.: Vol. 1). 383p. 24.95 (*0-312-86571-6*) Doherty, Tom Assocs., LLC. (Forge Bks.).

—A Midwinter's Tale. l.t. ed. 2000. 542p. 26.95 (*1-56895-949-4*, Wheeler Publishing, Inc.) Gale Group.

—Rite of Spring. 1988. 416p. mass mkt. 4.95 o.s.i (*0-446-34341-2*) Warner Bks., Inc.

—Star Bright! A Christmas Story. l.t. ed. 1998. 19.95 (*1-57490-166-4*) Beeler, Thomas T. Publisher.

—Star Bright! A Christmas Story. 1997. 127p. 13.95 (*0-312-86387-X*); 128p. 111.60 o.s.i (*0-312-86500-7*) Doherty, Tom Assocs., LLC. (Forge Bks.).

—Star Bright! A Christmas Story. 1999. 13.95 (*0-312-87116-3*) St. Martin's Pr.

—Wages of Sin. 1993. mass mkt. 6.99 o.s.i (*0-515-11222-4*, Jove) Berkley Publishing Group.

—Wages of Sin. 1992. 352p. 21.95 o.p. (*0-399-13752-1*, G. P. Putnam's Sons) Penguin Group (USA) Inc.

—Younger Than Springtime, collector's ed. 1999. audio 72.00 (*0-7366-4654-X*, 5036) Books on Tape, Inc.

—Younger Than Springtime. 1999. 348p. 24.95 (*0-312-86572-4*); 2000. 469p. reprint ed. mass mkt. 6.99 (*0-8125-9026-0*) Doherty, Tom Assocs., LLC. (Forge Bks.).

Grimm, Jo. Putting on Her Face. 2001. 392p. pap. 25.50 (*0-7596-4366-0*) 1stBooks Library.

Haddad, C. A. Caught in the Shadows: A Mystery. 1994. (WWL Mystery Ser.). per. (*0-373-26138-1*, 1-26138-7, Harlequin Bks.) Harlequin Enterprises, Ltd.

—Caught in the Shadows: A Mystery. 1992. 272p. 17.95 o.p. (*0-312-07666-5*, Saint Martin's Minotaur) St. Martin's Pr.

Hamilton, Jane. Disobedience: A Novel. 2001. 288p. pap. 13.00 (*0-385-72046-7*, Knopf Bks. for Young Readers) Random Hse. Children's Bks.

—Disobedience: A Novel. l.t. ed. 2001. (Thorndike Basic Ser.). 463p. 31.95 (*0-7862-3159-9*); pap. 29.95 (*0-7862-3158-0*) Thorndike Pr.

Handeland, Lori. The Farmer's Wife. 2002. (Harlequin Superromance Ser.: No. 1099). 304p. mass mkt. (*0-373-71099-2*, Harlequin Bks.) Harlequin Enterprises, Ltd.

Hartzmark, Gini. A Bitter Business. (Kate Millholland Novel Ser.). 1997. 340p. mass mkt. 5.99 o.s.i (*0-8041-1241-X*, Ivy Bks.); 1995. 320p. 4.99 o.s.i (*0-449-90989-1*, Fawcett) Ballantine Bks.

—Dead Certain. 2000. (Kate Millholland Novel Ser.). 320p. mass mkt. 6.50 o.s.i (*0-8041-1900-7*, Ivy Bks.) Ballantine Bks.

—Fatal Reaction. 1998. (Kate Millholland Novel Ser.). 352p. mass mkt. 6.50 o.s.i (*0-8041-1743-8*, Ivy Bks.) Ballantine Bks.

—Final Option. 1994. (Midwest Mysteries Ser.). (Orig.). mass mkt. 5.99 o.s.i (*0-8041-1227-4*, Ivy Bks.) Ballantine Bks.

—Principal Defense. 1992. (Midwest Mysteries Ser.). mass mkt. 5.99 o.s.i (*0-8041-1074-3*, Ivy Bks.) Ballantine Bks.

—Rough Trade. 1999. 293p. mass mkt. 6.50 (*0-8041-1829-9*, Ivy Bks.) Ballantine Bks.

Hecht, Ben. A Thousand & One Afternoons in Chicago. 1992. (Illus.). 290p. pap. text 27.00 (*0-226-32279-3*) Univ. of Chicago Pr.

Hemon, Aleksandar. The Question of Bruno. 2000. E-Book 18.50 (*1-58945-546-0*) Adobe Systems, Inc.

—The Question of Bruno. 2000. E-Book 2.99 (*0-385-50223-0*, Talese, Nan A.) Doubleday Publishing.

—The Question of Bruno. 2001. (Illus.). 240p. reprint ed. pap. 12.00 (*0-375-72700-0*, Vintage) Knopf Publishing Group.

Hoffman, Eva. The Secret. 2004. 272p. pap. 12.95 (*0-345-46536-9*) Ballantine Bks.

—The Secret. 2002. 272p. text 25.00 (*1-58648-150-9*) PublicAffairs.

Holton, Hugh. Chicago Blues. 1997. 373p. mass mkt. 5.99 (*0-8125-4464-1*); 1996. 384p. 23.95 o.p. (*0-312-85984-8*) Doherty, Tom Assocs., LLC. (Forge Bks.).

—The Left Hand of God. 2000. 416p. mass mkt. 6.99 (*0-8125-7084-7*); 1998. (Illus.). 384p. 24.95 (*0-312-86763-8*) Doherty, Tom Assocs., LLC. (Forge Bks.).

—Presumed Dead. 1995. 351p. pap. 5.99 (*0-8125-4813-2*); 1994. 320p. 21.95 o.p. (*0-312-85710-1*) Doherty, Tom Assocs., LLC. (Forge Bks.).

—Presumed Dead. 318p. 3.98 o.p. (*0-8317-5214-9*) Smithmark Pubs., Inc.

—Red Lightning. 320p. 1999. mass mkt. 6.99 (*0-8125-8912-2*); 1998. 23.95 o.p. (*0-312-86687-9*) Doherty, Tom Assocs., LLC. (Forge Bks.).

—Red Lightning. 1998. 6.99 (*0-312-87125-2*) St. Martin's Pr.

—Time of the Assassins. 2000. 383p. 24.95 (*0-312-87333-6*, Forge Bks.) Doherty, Tom Assocs., LLC.

—Violent Crimes. 1998. (Illus.). 512p. mass mkt. 6.99 (*0-8125-7187-8*); 1996. 384p. text 23.95 o.p. (*0-312-86281-4*) Doherty, Tom Assocs., LLC. (Forge Bks.).

—Violent Crimes. 1999. 6.99 (*0-312-87126-0*) St. Martin's Pr.

—Windy City. 1996. 310p. mass mkt. 5.99 (*0-8125-6714-5*, Tor Bks.); 1996. mass mkt. 5.99 (*0-8125-3695-9*, Forge Bks.); 1995. 352p. 22.95 o.p. (*0-312-85711-X*, Forge Bks.) Doherty, Tom Assocs., LLC.

Homburg, Michael. Downers Grove. 2001. 231p. reprint ed. pap. 12.00 (*0-8021-3793-8*, Grove Pr.) Grove/Atlantic, Inc.

—Downers Grove: A Novel. 1999. 231p. 23.00 o.p. (*0-688-16528-1*, Morrow, William & Co.) Morrow/Avon.

Howard, Clark. City Blood: A Novel of Revenge. 1994. 320p. 23.00 (*1-883402-39-5*, Scribner) Simon & Schuster.

Hunter, Fred. Capital Queers. (Alex Reynolds Mysteries Ser.). 2000. 232p. pap. 12.95 (*0-312-26301-5*, Saint Martin's Griffin); 1999. 224p. 23.95 o.p. (*0-312-20463-9*, Saint Martin's Minotaur) St. Martin's Pr.

—The Chicken Asylum. 2002. 256p. pap. 12.95 (*0-312-28710-0*, Saint Martin's Griffin) St. Martin's Pr.

—Federal Fag. (Alex Reynolds Mysteries Ser.). 272p. 1999. pap. 11.95 (*0-312-20649-6*, Saint Martin's Griffin); 1998. 22.95 o.p. (*0-312-18580-4*, Saint Martin's Minotaur) St. Martin's Pr.

—Government Gay. (Alex Reynolds Mysteries Ser.). 1998. 224p. pap. 11.95 (*0-312-18721-1*, Saint Martin's Griffin); 1997. 215p. text 21.95 o.p. (*0-312-15536-0*, Saint Martin's Minotaur) St. Martin's Pr.

—National Nancys. 2000. (Alex Reynolds Mysteries Ser.). 240p. 22.95 (*0-312-25233-1*, Saint Martin's Minotaur) St. Martin's Pr.

—Presence of Mind. 1998. (WWL Mystery Ser.). per. (*0-373-26282-5*, 1-26282-3, Worldwide Library) Harlequin Enterprises, Ltd.

—Presence of Mind. 1994. 19.95 (*0-8027-3245-3*) Walker & Co.

—Ransom for a Holiday. 1997. (Jeremy Ransom/Emily Charters Mysteries Ser.). 240p. 20.95 (*0-312-16976-0*, Saint Martin's Minotaur) St. Martin's Pr.

—Ransom for a Killing, 329. 1999. (WWL Mystery Ser.: Vol. 329). mass mkt. (*0-373-26329-5*, Worldwide Library) Harlequin Enterprises, Ltd.

—Ransom for a Killing. 1998. (Jeremy Ransom/Emily Charters Mysteries Ser.). 240p. 21.95 o.p. (*0-312-19323-8*, Saint Martin's Minotaur) St. Martin's Pr.

—Ransom for an Angel. 1996. mass mkt. (*0-373-26224-8*, 1-26224-5, Worldwide Library) Harlequin Enterprises, Ltd.

—Ransom for an Angel. 1995. 246p. 19.95 (*0-8027-3253-4*) Walker & Co.

—Ransom for Our Sins. 1997. per. (*0-373-26249-3*, 1-26249-2, Worldwide Library) Harlequin Enterprises, Ltd.

—Ransom for Our Sins. 1996. 238p. 22.95 (*0-8027-3284-4*) Walker & Co.

—Ransom Unpaid. 2000. (WWL Mystery Ser.: Vol. 365). mass mkt. (*0-373-26365-1*, 1-26365-6, Worldwide Library) Harlequin Enterprises, Ltd.

—Ransom Unpaid. 1999. 216p. 22.95 (*0-312-24233-6*, Saint Martin's Minotaur) St. Martin's Pr.

Izzi, Eugene. A Matter of Honor. 1998. pap. 6.99 (*0-380-78842-X*); 1997. 432p. 24.00 (*0-380-97342-1*) Morrow/Avon. (Avon Bks.).

—The Take. 1988. mass mkt. 3.50 (*0-312-91120-3*, St. Martin's Paperbacks); 1987. 256p. 16.95 o.p. (*0-312-01038-9*) St. Martin's Pr.

Jackson, Neta. The Yada Yada Prayer Group. 2003. 400p. 13.99 (*1-59145-074-8*) Integrity Pubs.

Jakes, John. American Dreams. unabr. collector's ed. 1999. audio 112.00 (*0-7366-4355-9*, 4812) Books on Tape, Inc.

—American Dreams. 1998. 464p. 24.95 o.p. (*0-525-94437-0*, Dutton) Dutton/Plume.

—American Dreams. l.t. ed. 1998. (G. K. Hall Core Ser.). 802p. 28.95 o.p. (*0-7838-0379-6*, Macmillan Reference USA) Gale Group.

—American Dreams. 1999. 560p. reprint ed. mass mkt. 7.99 (*0-451-19701-1*, Signet Bks.) NAL.

—American Dreams. abr. ed. 1998. audio 30.00 (*0-7871-1733-1*, 896030, Dove Audio) NewStar Media, Inc.

Johnson. Belief. Date not set. pap. (*0-312-29112-4*, Saint Martin's Griffin) St. Martin's Pr.

Johnson, Charles. Dreamer: A Novel. 240p. 1999. pap. 12.00 (*0-684-85443-0*); 1998. 23.00 (*0-684-81224-X*) Simon & Schuster. (Scribner).

—Dreamer: A Novel. abr. ed. 1998. audio 25.00 (*0-671-58240-2*, Simon & Schuster Audioworks) Simon & Schuster Audio.

Johnson, R. M. The Harris Men. 336p. 1999. 23.00 o.s.i (*0-684-84470-2*); 2000. reprint ed. pap. 12.95 (*0-7434-0059-3*) Simon & Schuster. (Simon & Schuster).

Johnson, Stephanie. Belief. 2002. 496p. 26.95 (*0-312-29110-8*) St. Martin's Pr.

Kahn, Michael A. Death Benefits: A Rachel Gold Mystery. 1992. (Rachel Gold Mystery Ser.). 320p. 19.00 o.p. (*0-525-93456-1*, Dutton) Dutton/Plume.

—Death Benefits: A Rachel Gold Mystery. 1994. (Rachel Gold Mystery Ser.). 320p. mass mkt. 4.99 o.s.i (*0-451-17687-1*, Signet Bks.) NAL.

—Grave Designs: A Rachel Gold Mystery. 1992. (Rachel Gold Mystery Ser.). 352p. mass mkt. 5.50 o.s.i (*0-451-40293-6*, Signet Bks.) NAL.

Kaminsky, Stuart M. The Big Silence. 2000. 288p. 23.95 (*0-312-86926-6*, Forge Bks.) Doherty, Tom Assocs., LLC.

—The Big Silence. l.t. ed. 2001. (Thorndike Basic Ser.). 411p. 29.95 (*0-7862-3148-3*) Thorndike Pr.

—Lieberman's Choice. l.t. ed. 1994. 222p. 24.95 o.p. (*0-7927-2109-8*); pap. 23.95 o.p. (*0-7927-2108-X*) BBC Audiobooks America.

—Lieberman's Choice. 1994. (Midwest Mysteries Ser.). mass mkt. 4.99 o.s.i (*0-8041-1176-6*, Ivy Bks.) Ballantine Bks.

—Lieberman's Choice. abr. ed. 1995. (Abe Lieberman Mystery Ser.). audio 16.99 (*0-88646-384-X*, 391066) Durkin Hayes Publishing Ltd.

—Lieberman's Choice. 1993. 216p. 18.95 o.p. (*0-312-08836-1*, Saint Martin's Minotaur) St. Martin's Pr.

—Lieberman's Day. 1994. mass mkt. 4.99 o.s.i (*0-8041-1286-X*, Ivy Bks.) Ballantine Bks.

—Lieberman's Day. abr. ed. 1994. (Abe Lieberman Mystery Ser.). audio 16.99 (*0-88646-346-7*, 391067) Durkin Hayes Publishing Ltd.

—Lieberman's Day. l.t. ed. 1994. 286p. 23.95 o.p. (*1-56895-115-9*, Wheeler Publishing, Inc.) Gale Group.

—Lieberman's Day. 1994. (Henry Holt Mystery Ser.). 260p. 19.95 o.p. (*0-8050-2575-8*) Holt, Henry & Co.

—Lieberman's Day. unabr. ed. 2000. (Abe Lieberman Mystery Ser.). audio 51.00 (*0-7887-0418-4*, 94610E7) Recorded Bks., LLC.

—Lieberman's Folly. l.t. ed. 1994. 290p. 20.95 o.p. (*0-7927-1979-4*); pap. 19.95 o.p. (*0-7927-1978-6*) BBC Audiobooks America.

—Lieberman's Folly. 1992. (Midwest Mysteries Ser.). mass mkt. 4.99 o.s.i (*0-8041-0924-9*, Ivy Bks.) Ballantine Bks.

—Lieberman's Folly. 1991. 216p. 15.95 o.p. (*0-312-05398-3*, Saint Martin's Minotaur) St. Martin's Pr.

—Lieberman's Law. unabr. ed. 1999. audio 49.95 Blackstone Audio Bks., Inc.

—Lieberman's Law. 1996. (Henry Holt Mystery Ser.). 309p. 22.50 o.p. (*0-8050-3749-7*) Holt, Henry & Co.

—Lieberman's Law. unabr. ed. 1996. (Abe Lieberman Mystery Ser.). audio 60.00 (*0-7887-0586-5*, 94705E7) Recorded Bks., LLC.

—Lieberman's Thief. 1996. mass mkt. 5.50 o.s.i (*0-8041-1287-8*, Ivy Bks.) Ballantine Bks.

—Lieberman's Thief. abr. ed. 1996. audio 7.99 o.p. (*1-56740-112-0*, 1321, Paperback Nova Audio Bks.); 1995. (Abe Lieberman Mystery Ser.: Bk. 4). audio 16.95 o.p. (*1-56100-430-8*, 1320, Nova Audio Bks.); 1995. (Abe Lieberman Mystery Ser.: Vol. 4). audio 57.25 o.p. (*1-56100-263-1*, 1266, Unabridged Library Editions); 1995. (Abe Lieberman Mystery Ser.: Vol. Bk. 4). audio 23.95 o.p. (*1-56100-638-6*, 162, Bookcassette) Brilliance Audio.

—Lieberman's Thief. 1995. (Henry Holt Mystery Ser.). 238p. 22.50 o.p. (*0-8050-2576-6*) Holt, Henry & Co.

Karaim, Reed. If Men Were Angels. abr. ed. 2000. audio 7.99 o.s.i (*1-56740-983-0*, 2106, Paperback Nova Audio Bks.); 1999. audio 26.95 (*1-56740-433-2*, 1725, Bookcassette); 1999. audio 73.25 (*1-56740-658-0*, 1726, Unabridged Library Editions) Brilliance Audio.

—If Men Were Angels. 1999. 320p. 24.95 o.p. (*0-393-04780-6*) Norton, W. W. & Co., Inc.

Katz, Michael J. The Big Freeze. 1991. 256p. 21.95 o.p. (*0-399-13558-8*, G. P. Putnam's Sons) Penguin Group (USA) Inc.

—Last Dance in Redondo Beach. 1989. 256p. 17.95 o.p. (*0-399-13445-X*, G. P. Putnam's Sons) Penguin Putnam Bks. for Young Readers.

—Last Dance in Redondo Beach. 1990. 288p. bds. 3.95 (*0-671-67913-9*, Pocket) Simon & Schuster.

—Murder off the Glass. 1987. 16.95 o.p. (*0-8027-5667-0*) Walker & Co.

Kelly, Mary P. Special Intentions. 1998. 380p. pap. 13.95 (*1-874597-71-5*) New Island Bks. IRL. *Dist:* Irish Bks. & Media, Inc.

LaHaye, Tim. Tribulation Force: The Continuing Drama of Those Left Behind. 2002. No. 2. E-Book 14.99 (*0-8423-6157-X*) Tyndale Hse. Pubs.

LaHaye, Tim & Jenkins, Jerry B. El Comando Tribulacion. 2000. (Left Behind Ser.: Bk. 2). Tr. of Tribulation Force. (SPA.). pap. 9.99 (*0-7899-0374-1*, 497476) Editorial Unilit.

—El Comando Tribulacion. l.t. ed. 2003. (Left Behind Ser.).Tr. of Tribulation Force. 28.95 (*0-7862-5030-5*) Thorndike Pr.

—Left Behind: A Novel of the Earth's Last Days. unabr. ed. 2000. (Left Behind Ser.: Bk. 1). audio 34.95 (*0-7887-4972-2*) Recorded Bks., LLC.

—Left Behind: A Novel of the Earth's Last Days. l.t. ed. 2000. (Left Behind Ser.: Bk. 1). 575p. 29.95 (*0-7862-2468-1*) Thorndike Pr.

—Left Behind: A Novel of the Earth's Last Days. (Left Behind Ser.: Bk. 1). 2000. 352p. mass mkt. 7.99 o.p. (*0-8423-4270-2*); 1996. 320p. pap. 14.99 (*0-8423-2912-9*); 1995. 320p. 22.99 (*0-8423-2911-0*); 2001. 560p. pap. 19.99 (*0-8423-5420-4*) Tyndale Hse. Pubs.

—Left Behind Vol. 1: Graphic Novel, 5 vols. 2001. (Left Behind Ser.: Bk. 1). (Illus.). 48p. pap. 5.99 (*0-8423-5502-2*) Tyndale Hse. Pubs.

—Left Behind Vol. 2: Graphic Novel, 5 vols. 2001. (Left Behind Ser.: Bk. 1). (Illus.). 48p. pap. 5.99 (*0-8423-5503-0*) Tyndale Hse. Pubs.

—Left Behind Vol. 3: Graphic Novel, 5 vols. 2002. (Left Behind Ser.: Bk. 1). (Illus.). 48p. pap. 5.99 (*0-8423-5504-9*) Tyndale Hse. Pubs.

—Left Behind Vol. 4: Graphic Novel, 5 vols. 2002. (Left Behind Ser.: Bk. 1). (Illus.). 48p. pap. 5.99 (*0-8423-5505-7*) Tyndale Hse. Pubs.

—Tribulation Force: The Continuing Drama of Those Left Behind. l.t. ed. 2000. (Left Behind Ser.: Bk. 2). 552p. 29.95 (*0-7862-2471-1*) Thorndike Pr.

—Tribulation Force: The Continuing Drama of Those Left Behind. (Left Behind Ser.: Bk. 2). 1996. 450p. pap. 14.99 (*0-8423-2921-8*); 1996. 450p. 22.99 (*0-8423-2913-7*); 2002. 528p. pap. 19.99 (*0-8423-6551-6*) Tyndale Hse. Pubs.

—Tribulation Force Vol. 1: Graphic Novel. 2002. (Left Behind Ser.: Bk. 2). (Illus.). 48p. pap. 5.99 (*0-8423-5759-9*) Tyndale Hse. Pubs.

—Tribulation Force Vol. 2: Graphic Novel. 2002. (Left Behind Ser.: Bk. 2). (Illus.). 48p. pap. 5.99 (*0-8423-5760-2*) Tyndale Hse. Pubs.

Lanigan, Catherine. In Love's Shadow. 1998. 384p. mass mkt. (*1-55166-435-6*, 1-66435-8, Mira Bks.) Harlequin Enterprises, Ltd.

Lindsay, Vachel. The Golden Book of Springfield. (Collected Works of Vachel Lindsay). 329p. 2001. (Illus.). pap. text 28.00 (*0-7426-5696-9*); 1998. reprint ed. lib. bdg. 98.00 (*1-58201-696-8*) Classic Bks.

—The Golden Book of Springfield. 2nd ed. 1999. (Illus.). reprint ed. 38.00 (*0-88286-243-X*); 329p. pap. 22.00 (*0-88286-242-1*) Kerr, Charles H. Publishing Co.

Linz, Cathie. Private Account. 1984. (Candlelight Regency Romance Ser.: No. 242). 192p. pap. 1.95 o.p. (*0-440-17072-9*) Dell Publishing.

—Private Account. l.t. ed. 2001. 217p. 28.95 (*0-7838-9599-2*, Macmillan Reference USA) Gale Group.

Manderino, John. The Man Who Once Played Catch with Nellie Fox. 1998. 280p. 22.50 (*0-89733-448-5*) Academy Chicago Pubs., Ltd.

Martin, Gail Gaymer. Upon a Midnight Clear. 2000. (Steeple Hill Love Inspired Ser.: Bk. 117). 256p. mass mkt. (*0-373-87123-6*, 1-87123-5, Steeple Hill) Harlequin Enterprises, Ltd.

Martin, Lee. Turning Bones. 2003. (American Lives Ser.). (Illus.). 194p. 28.95 (*0-8032-3231-4*) Univ. of Nebraska Pr.

Matthews, Alex. Cat's Claw. 2000. (Cassidy McCabe Mysteries Ser.: No. 5). 272p. 22.95 (*1-890768-22-7*, Intrigue Pr.) Corvus Publishing.

—Satan's Silence. 1998. (Cassidy McCabe Mysteries Ser.: No. 2). 368p. mass mkt. 5.50 (*1-890768-04-9*, Intrigue Pr.) Corvus Publishing.

—Satan's Silence. Ellison, Lee, ed. 1997. (Cassidy McCabe Mystery Ser.: No. 2). 304p. 22.50 o.p. (*0-9643161-5-3*, Intrigue Pr.) Corvus Publishing.

—Secret's Shadow. unabr. ed. 1998. (Cassidy McCabe Mystery Ser.). audio 49.95 (*1-55686-745-X*) Books in Motion.

—Secret's Shadow: The First Cassidy McCabe Mystery. 1998. (Cassidy McCabe Mysteries Ser.: Vol. 1). 352p. mass mkt. 5.50 (*1-890768-03-0*, Intrigue Pr.) Corvus Publishing.

—Secret's Shadow: The First Cassidy McCabe Mystery. Ellison, Lee, ed. 1996. 296p. 22.50 o.p. (*0-9643161-3-7*, Intrigue Pr.) Corvus Publishing.

—Vendetta's Victim: The Third Cassidy McCabe Mystery. (Cassidy McCabe Mysteries Ser.). 1999. 256p. mass mkt. 5.95 (*1-890768-14-6*); 1998. 222p. 22.95 o.p. (*0-9643161-9-6*) Corvus Publishing. (Intrigue Pr.).

—Wanton's Web. 1999. (Cassidy McCabe Mysteries Ser.). 316p. 22.95 (*1-890768-12-X*, Intrigue Pr.) Corvus Publishing.

Maxwell, William. All the Days & Nights: The Collected Stories of William Maxwell. 1995. 432p. pap. 15.00 (*0-679-76102-0*, Vintage) Knopf Publishing Group.

McConnell, Frank. Blood Lake: A Harry Garnish/Bridget O'Toole Mystery. l.t. ed. 1988. 19.95 o.p. (*1-55504-590-1*); pap. 17.95 o.p. (*1-55504-573-1*) BBC Audiobooks America.

—Blood Lake: A Harry Garnish/Bridget O'Toole Mystery. 1988. (Crime Ser.). 256p. pap. 3.95 o.p. (*0-14-010755-X*, Penguin Bks.); 39.50 o.p. (*0-14-778359-3*) Viking Penguin.

—Blood Lake: A Harry Garnish/Bridget O'Toole Mystery. 1987. 256p. 16.95 o.s.i (*0-8027-5673-5*) Walker & Co.

—Liar's Poker: A Harry Garnish/Bridget O'Toole Mystery. 1993. 234p. 19.95 (*0-8027-3229-1*) Walker & Co.

—Murder among Friends: A Harry Garnish/Bridget O'Toole Mystery. l.t. ed. 1986. pap. 13.95 o.p. (*0-7451-9149-5*) BBC Audiobooks America.

—Murder among Friends: A Harry Garnish/Bridget O'Toole Mystery. 1988. pap. 39.50 o.p. (*0-14-778313-5*); 192p. mass mkt. 3.95 o.p. (*0-451-82189-0*, Penguin Bks.) Viking Penguin.

—Murder among Friends: A Harry Garnish/Bridget O'Toole Mystery. 1983. 192p. 12.95 o.s.i (*0-8027-5567-4*) Walker & Co.

McInerny, Ralph. Abracadaver. l.t. ed. 1990. (Nightingale Ser.). pap. 12.95 o.p. (*0-8161-4904-6*, Macmillan Reference USA) Gale Group.

—Abracadaver. 1994. (WWL Mystery Ser.). per. (*0-373-26152-7*, 1-26152-8, Harlequin Bks.) Harlequin Enterprises, Ltd.

—Abracadaver. 1989. 176p. 14.95 o.p. (*0-312-02533-5*, Saint Martin's Minotaur) St. Martin's Pr.

—The Basket Case. l.t. ed. 1992. (Nightingale Ser.). 280p. pap. 14.95 o.p. (*0-8161-5569-0*, Macmillan Reference USA) Gale Group.

—The Basket Case. 1988. mass mkt. 3.50 (*0-312-91157-2*, St. Martin's Paperbacks); 1987. 208p. 14.95 o.p. (*0-312-00997-6*, Saint Martin's Minotaur) St. Martin's Pr.

—A Cardinal Offense. 1994. 384p. 21.95 o.p. (*0-312-11283-1*, Saint Martin's Minotaur) St. Martin's Pr.

—Desert Sinner. 1994. (WWL Mystery Ser.). per. (*0-373-26158-6*, 1-26158-5, Harlequin Bks.) Harlequin Enterprises, Ltd.

—Desert Sinner. 1992. (Father Dowling Mysteries Ser.). 192p. 16.95 o.p. (*0-312-08177-4*, Saint Martin's Minotaur) St. Martin's Pr.

—Easeful Death. 1994. 3.99 o.p. (*0-517-11437-2*) Random Hse. Value Publishing.

—Easeful Death. 1991. 256p. 19.95 o.s.i (*0-689-12131-8*, Scribner) Simon & Schuster.

—Four on the Floor. 1994. pap. (*0-373-26154-3*, Harlequin Bks.) Harlequin Enterprises, Ltd.

—Four on the Floor. 1989. 192p. 15.95 o.p. (*0-312-03345-1*, Saint Martin's Minotaur) St. Martin's Pr.

—Getting a Way with Murder. l.t. ed. 1985. (Nightingale Ser.). 256p. 9.95 o.p. (*0-8161-3924-5*, Macmillan Reference USA) Gale Group.

—Grave Undertakings: A Father Dowling Mystery. 2000. (Father Dowling Mysteries Ser.). 374p. 24.95 (*0-312-20309-8*, Saint Martin's Minotaur) St. Martin's Pr.

—Grave Undertakings: A Father Dowling Mystery. l.t. ed. 2000. (Basic Ser.). 448p. 29.95 (*0-7862-2925-X*) Thorndike Pr.

—Her Death of Cold. 1979. (Father Dowling Mysteries Ser.). 224p. 1.95 o.s.i (*0-441-32780-X*) Ace Bks.

—Infra Dig. l.t. ed. 1993. 21.95 o.p. (*0-7927-1461-X*); pap. 19.95 o.p. (*0-7927-1460-1*) BBC Audiobooks America.

—Infra Dig. 1992. 218p. 19.00 o.s.i (*0-689-12132-6*) Central Bureau voor Schimmelcultures NLD. *Dist:* Lubrecht & Cramer, Ltd.

—Judas Priest: A Father Dowling Mystery. 1994. per. (*0-373-26156-X*, 1-26156-9, Harlequin Bks.) Harlequin Enterprises, Ltd.

—Judas Priest: A Father Dowling Mystery. 1991. 208p. 17.95 o.p. (*0-312-06375-X*, Saint Martin's Minotaur) St. Martin's Pr.

—Last Things. Date not set. pap. (*0-312-30900-7*, Saint Martin's Griffin); mass mkt. (*0-312-98690-4*, St. Martin's Paperbacks); 2003. 352p. 24.95 (*0-312-30899-X*, Saint Martin's Minotaur) St. Martin's Pr.

—Last Things. l.t. ed. 2003. (Father Dowling Mystery Ser.). 460p. 29.95 (*0-7862-5735-0*) Thorndike Pr.

—Lying Three. 1980. 256p. 2.25 o.s.i (*0-441-50515-5*) Ace Bks.

—Lying Three. l.t. ed. 1981. 374p. reprint ed. 11.95 o.p. (*0-89621-304-8*) Thorndike Pr.

—Prodigal Father. l.t. ed. 2003. (Mystery Ser.). 28.95 (*1-57490-487-6*, Beeler Large Print Bks.) Beeler, Thomas T. Publisher.

—Prodigal Father. E-Book 24.95 (*0-312-70741-X*); 2002. 384p. 24.95 (*0-312-29129-9*, Saint Martin's Minotaur) St. Martin's Pr.

—Rest in Pieces. l.t. ed. 1991. (Nightingale Ser.). 280p. lib. bdg. 13.95 o.p. (*0-8161-5107-5*, Macmillan Reference USA) Gale Group.

—Second Vespers. 1981. (Father Dowling Mysteries Ser.). 2.50 o.s.i (*0-441-75724-3*) Ace Bks.

—Second Vespers. l.t. ed. 1981. reprint ed. 10.95 o.p. (*0-89621-272-6*) Thorndike Pr.

—Seed of Doubt. 1993. 352p. 19.95 o.p. (*0-312-09381-0*) St. Martin's Pr.

—The Seventh Station. 1979. (Father McDowling Ser.). 224p. 1.95 o.s.i (*0-441-75947-5*) Ace Bks.

—The Tears of Things. 1996. o.p. (*0-03-214746-5*); 368p. text 24.95 o.p. (*0-312-14746-5*, Saint Martin's Minotaur) St. Martin's Pr.

—Triple Pursuit: A Father Dowling Mystery. 2002. E-Book 24.95 (*1-59061-754-1*) Adobe Systems, Inc.

—Triple Pursuit: A Father Dowling Mystery. 2001. (Father Dowling Mysteries Ser.). 371p. 24.95 (*0-312-26948-X*, Saint Martin's Minotaur) St. Martin's Pr.

—Triple Pursuit: A Father Dowling Mystery. l.t. ed. 2001. 547p. (*0-7862-3295-1*) Thorndike Pr.

Miles, Keith. Saint's Rest. 1999. (Merlin Richards Mystery Ser.). 312p. 23.95 (*0-8027-3332-8*) Walker & Co.

Monroe, Mary Alice. The Four Seasons. 2004. 368p. pap. (*0-7783-2018-9*); 2001. 408p. mass mkt. (*1-55166-789-4*, 1-66789-8) Harlequin Enterprises, Ltd. (Mira Bks.).

Moquist, Richard. Eye of the Agency, Vol. 1. 1997. ix, 207p. text 22.95 o.p. (*0-312-15526-3*, Saint Martin's Minotaur) St. Martin's Pr.

Mouritsen, Laurel. The Turning Point: A Novel. 2002. 241p. 14.95 (*1-59156-015-2*) Covenant Communications.

Navarro, Yvonne. That's Not My Name. 2000. 432p. mass mkt. 6.50 o.s.i (*0-553-57750-6*) Bantam Bks.

Nowlan, James D. The Itinerant: A Heartland Story. 2000. (Illus.). 256p. pap. 15.95 (*0-9634395-6-1*) Conversation Pr., Inc.

O'Brien, Patricia. Good Intentions. l.t. ed. 1998. 357 p. 25.95 (*1-57490-163-X*, Beeler Large Print Bks.) Beeler, Thomas T. Publisher.

—Good Intentions. 1998. 352p. mass mkt. 5.99 o.s.i (*1-57566-311-2*) Kensington Publishing Corp.

—Good Intentions. 1997. 384p. 23.00 (*0-684-81355-6*, Simon & Schuster) Simon & Schuster.

Paretsky, Sara. Bitter Medicine. 1988. 272p. mass mkt. 6.99 o.s.i (*0-345-34722-6*) Ballantine Bks.

—Bitter Medicine. 1993. audio compact disk 56.00 (*0-7366-7125-0*); audio 48.00 (*0-7366-2417-1*, 3184) Books on Tape, Inc.

—Bitter Medicine. 1999. 352p. mass mkt. 7.50 (*0-440-23476-X*) Dell Publishing.

—Bitter Medicine. l.t. ed. 1989. 352p. 19.95 o.p. (*0-8161-4467-2*, Macmillan Reference USA) Gale Group.

—Bitter Medicine. 1987. 320p. 17.95 o.p. (*0-688-06448-5*, Morrow, William & Co.) Morrow/Avon.

—Blood Shot. unabr. ed. 1993. (V. I. Warshawski Ser.). audio 56.00 (*0-7366-2328-0*, 3108) Books on Tape, Inc.

—Blood Shot. 1989. (V.I. Warshawski Novels Ser.). 384p. mass mkt. 7.99 (*0-440-20420-8*) Dell Publishing.

—Blood Shot. l.t. ed. 1989. (General Ser.). 20.95 o.p. (*0-8161-4775-2*, Macmillan Reference USA) Gale Group.

—Blood Shot. abr. ed. 1990. audio 14.95 o.s.i (*0-553-45215-0*, RH Audio) Random Hse. Audio Publishing Group.

—Blood Shot. unabr. ed. 1993. (V. I. Warshawski Mystery Ser.: Vol. 1). audio 70.00 (*1-55690-899-7*, 93341E7) Recorded Bks., LLC.

—Burn Marks. unabr. ed. 1992. (V. I. Warshawski Ser.). audio 64.00 (*0-7366-2168-7*, 2967) Books on Tape, Inc.

—Burn Marks. 1991. (V.I. Warshawski Novels Ser.). 416p. mass mkt. 7.99 (*0-440-20845-9*) Dell Publishing.

—Burn Marks. l.t. ed. 1990. (Large Print Bks.). 533p. lib. bdg. 21.95 o.p. (*0-8161-5004-4*, Macmillan Reference USA) Gale Group.

—Burn Marks. abr. ed. 1990. audio 14.95 o.s.i (*0-553-45208-8*, RH Audio) Random Hse. Audio Publishing Group.

—Deadlock. l.t. ed. 1985. lib. bdg. 13.95 o.p. (*0-89340-898-0*, 842) BBC Audiobooks America.

—Deadlock. 1984. 272p. mass mkt. 5.95 o.s.i (*0-345-31954-0*) Ballantine Bks.

—Deadlock. unabr. collector's ed. 1993. (V. I. Warshawski Ser.). audio 48.00 (*0-7366-2382-5*, 3153) Books on Tape, Inc.

—Deadlock. unabr. ed. 1985. audio 14.95 o.p. (*0-930435-02-8*, 364); audio 57.25 o.p. (*1-56100-001-9*, 549, Unabridged Library Editions) Brilliance Audio.

—Deadlock. 1992. (V.I. Warshawski Novels Ser.). 320p. mass mkt. 6.99 (*0-440-21332-0*) Dell Publishing.

—Deadlock. 1984. 264p. 14.95 o.p. (*0-385-27933-7*) Doubleday Publishing.

—Deadlock. l.t. ed. 1993. (General Ser.). 271p. pap. 18.95 o.p. (*0-8161-5562-3*); lib. bdg. 20.95 o.p. (*0-8161-5561-5*) Gale Group. (Macmillan Reference USA).

—Ghost Country. 1999. 416p. pap. 14.95 (*0-385-33336-6*, Delta) Dell Publishing.

—Ghost Country. l.t. ed. 1998. 26.95 o.p. (*1-56895-682-7*, Wheeler Publishing, Inc.) Gale Group.

—Guardian Angel. unabr. ed. 1992. (V. I. Warshawski Ser.). audio 72.00 (*0-7366-2203-9*, 2998) Books on Tape, Inc.

—Guardian Angel. 1993. 432p. mass mkt. 7.99 (*0-440-21399-1*) Dell Publishing.

—Guardian Angel. l.t. ed. 1992. (General Ser.). 544p. 18.95 o.p. (*0-8161-5542-9*); lib. bdg. 21.95 o.p. (*0-8161-5541-0*) Gale Group. (Macmillan Reference USA).

—Guardian Angel. 1992. audio 15.95 o.s.i (*0-553-74558-1*); audio 16.99 o.s.i (*0-553-47035-3*) Random Hse. Audio Publishing Group. (RH Audio).

—Guardian Angel. 1993. 5.99 o.p. (*0-517-10926-3*) Random Hse. Value Publishing.

—Guardian Angel. unabr. ed. 1992. (V. I. Warshawski Mystery Ser.: Vol. 7). audio 85.00 (*1-55690-669-2*, 92233E7) Recorded Bks., LLC.

—Guardian Angel. 1992. (Audio Books Ser.). 69.95 o.p. incl. audio (*0-7838-8000-6*) Thorndike Pr.

—Guardian Angel: International Edition. 1992. 432p. mass mkt. 5.50 o.s.i (*0-440-29522-X*) Dell Publishing.

—Hard Time. (V.I. Warshawski Novels Ser.). 2000. 512p. mass mkt. 7.99 (*0-440-22470-5*, Delta); 1999. 400p. 24.95 (*0-385-31363-2*, Delacorte Pr.) Dell Publishing.

—Hard Time. l.t. ed. 1999. pap. 24.95 o.p. (*0-7838-8696-9*, Macmillan Reference USA) Gale Group.

—Hard Time, Set. abr. ed. 1999. audio 25.00 Highsmith Inc.

—Hard Time. abr. ed. 1999. audio 25.00 (*0-7871-2013-8*); audio compact disk 50.00 (*0-7871-2371-4*); audio 36.00 (*0-7871-2012-X*) NewStar Media, Inc. (Dove Audio).

—Hard Time. l.t. ed. 2000. 656p. pap. 13.95 (*0-375-70780-8*) Random Hse. Large Print.

—Hard Time. 2000. 13.04 (*0-606-18985-8*) Turtleback Bks.

—Indemnity Only. 1985. 224p. mass mkt. 4.95 o.s.i (*0-345-33634-8*); 1983. mass mkt. 2.50 o.s.i (*0-345-30684-8*) Ballantine Bks.

—Indemnity Only. unabr. ed. 1992. (V. I. Warshawski Ser.). audio 48.00 (*0-7366-2282-9*, 3069) Books on Tape, Inc.

—Indemnity Only. 1991. (V.I. Warshawski Novels Ser.). 336p. mass mkt. 6.99 (*0-440-21069-0*) Dell Publishing.

—Indemnity Only. 1982. 14.95 o.p. (*0-385-27213-8*) Doubleday Publishing.

—Indemnity Only. (Nightingale Ser.). 1982. pap. 9.95 o.p. (*0-8161-3439-1*); 1992. 381p. lib. bdg. 20.95 (*0-8161-5455-4*) Gale Group. (Macmillan Reference USA).

—Indemnity Only. abr. ed. 1991. audio 15.99 o.s.i (*0-553-45271-1*, RH Audio) Random Hse. Audio Publishing Group.

—Indemnity Only. l.t. ed. 1992. (Novels Ser.). 381p. pap. 20.95 (*0-8161-5456-2*) Thorndike Pr.

—Killing Orders. l.t. ed. 1986. lib. bdg. 17.95 o.p. (*1-55504-024-1*) BBC Audiobooks America.

—Killing Orders. 1988. pap. o.p. (*0-345-00730-1*); 1986. 288p. mass mkt. 5.95 o.s.i (*0-345-32777-2*) Ballantine Bks.

—Killing Orders. unabr. collector's ed. 1993. (V. I. Warshawski Ser.). audio 48.00 (*0-7366-2391-4*, 3162) Books on Tape, Inc.

—Killing Orders. 1993. 352p. mass mkt. 7.99 (*0-440-21528-5*, Dell Bks.) Dell Publishing.

—Sara Paretsky, 3 vols., Set. 1992. pap. 14.85 o.s.i (*0-440-36046-3*) Dell Publishing.

—Sara Paretsky: Three Complete Novels. 1995. 704p. 13.99 o.s.i (*0-517-14801-3*) Random Hse., Inc.

—Settled Score. abr. ed. 1998. audio 4.99 (*0-88646-964-3*, 7964) Durkin Hayes Publishing Ltd.

—Skin Deep & Other Stories. unabr. ed. 1994. (V. I. Warshawski Mystery Ser.). audio 16.99 (*0-88646-373-4*, 391592) Durkin Hayes Publishing Ltd.

—Strung Out. unabr. ed. 1997. audio 4.99 (*0-88646-940-6*, 7940) Durkin Hayes Publishing Ltd.

—Three-Dot Po. unabr. ed. 1994. audio 8.95 o.p. (*1-879371-80-4*, 30030) Publishing Mills, Inc., The.

—Total Recall. l.t. ed. 2001. 25.95 (*0-375-43136-5*) Random Hse. Large Print.

—Tunnel Vision. unabr. ed. 1994. (V. I. Warshawski Ser.). audio 80.00 (*0-7366-2842-8*, 3550) Books on Tape, Inc.

—Tunnel Vision. (V.I. Warshawski Novels Ser.). 1995. 480p. mass mkt. 7.50 (*0-440-21752-0*); 1995. E-Book 6.99 (*0-440-33393-8*); 1994. 736p. 26.95 o.s.i (*0-385-31307-1*, Delacorte Pr.) Dell Publishing.

—Tunnel Vision. l.t. ed. 1994. (Large Print Bks.). pap. 22.95 o.p. (*1-56895-084-5*, Wheeler Publishing, Inc.) Gale Group.

—Tunnel Vision. abr. ed. 1993. (V.I. Warshawski Novels Ser.). audio 24.95 o.p. (*1-55800-975-2*, 692333) NewStar Media, Inc.

—Windy City Blues. unabr. ed. 1996. (V. I. Warshawski Ser.). audio 48.00 (*0-7366-3243-3*, 3902) Books on Tape, Inc.

—Windy City Blues. 1996. (V.I. Warshawski Novels Ser.). 352p. mass mkt. 7.99 (*0-440-21873-X*) Dell Publishing.

—Windy City Blues. 1996. pap. 6.99 (*0-440-29546-7*) Doubleday Publishing.

—Windy City Blues. unabr. ed. 1995. (V. I. Warshawski Mystery Ser.). 24.95 o.p. (*0-7871-0478-7*, 693248) NewStar Media, Inc.

—Windy City Blues. l.t. ed. 1996. (Paperback Bestsellers Ser.). 336p. pap. 24.95 (*0-7838-1562-X*); 26.95 (*0-7838-1561-1*) Thorndike Pr.

—A Woman's Eye. 1992. 464p. reprint ed. mass mkt. 6.99 (*0-440-21335-5*) Dell Publishing.

—A Woman's Eye. 1993. 5.99 o.p. (*0-517-11187-X*) Random Hse. Value Publishing.

—Women on the Case: 26 Original Stories by the Best Women Crime Writers of Our Times. 1997. 464p. mass mkt. 7.50 (*0-440-22325-3*) Dell Publishing.

Paretsky, Sara, ed. Beastly Tales. 1995. (Select Sound, Dove Ser.). 4.99 o.p. (*0-7871-0326-8*); 4.99 o.p. (*0-7871-0311-X*) Penguin Group (USA) Inc.

—Beastly Tales. 1989. 17.95 o.p. (*0-922066-14-0*) Wynwood.

Paretsky, Sara, intro. A Woman's Eye. l.t. ed. 1992. (General Ser.). 569p. lib. bdg. 21.95 o.p. (*0-8161-5457-0*, Macmillan Reference USA) Gale Group.

Paretsky, Sara & McCrumb, Sharyn. Lily & the Sockeyes & Happiness Is a Dead Poet. unabr. ed. 1994. audio 4.99 (*0-88646-725-X*) Durkin Hayes Publishing Ltd.

Patterson, James & de Jonge, Peter. Miracle on the 17th Green. l.t. ed. 2001. (Thorndike Famous Authors Ser.). 176p. 28.95 (*0-7862-3315-X*) Thorndike Pr.

Pemberton, S. C. Murder in Winnetka. 2000. 192p. pap. 11.95 (*1-56315-251-7*) SterlingHouse Pubs., Inc.

Powers, Richard. Gain. 1998. 356p. 25.00 o.p. (*0-374-15996-3*) Farrar, Straus & Giroux.

—Gain. 1999. 368p. pap. 14.00 (*0-312-20409-4*) Picador.

Purdy, James. Gertrude of Stony Island Avenue. 1999. 192p. pap. 13.00 o.s.i (*0-688-17226-1*, Quill) HarperTrade.

—Gertrude of Stony Island Avenue. 1998. 144p. 19.95 (*0-688-15901-X*, Morrow, William & Co.) Morrow/Avon.

—Gertrude of Stony Island Avenue. 1996. 256p. 27.95 (*0-7206-1011-7*) Owen, Peter Ltd. GBR. *Dist:* Dufour Editions, Inc.

Quill, Monica. Sister Hood: A Sister Mary Teresa Mystery. 1991. 16.95 o.p. (*0-312-04602-2*, Saint Martin's Minotaur) St. Martin's Pr.

—The Veil of Ignorance: A Sister Mary Teresa Mystery. 1988. 208p. 15.95 o.p. (*0-312-02308-1*, Saint Martin's Minotaur) St. Martin's Pr.

Raleigh, Michael. A Body in Belmont Harbor. 1993. 277p. 17.95 o.p. (*0-312-08707-1*, Saint Martin's Minotaur) St. Martin's Pr.

—A Body in Belmont Harbor. 2000. (Paul Whelan Mystery Ser.). 292p. pap. 15.95 (*0-595-09340-X*) iUniverse, Inc.

—Death in Uptown. 2000. (Paul Whelan Mystery Ser.). 256p. pap. 14.95 (*0-595-09341-8*) iUniverse, Inc.

—Death in Uptown: A Paul Whelan Mystery. 1991. 17.95 o.p. (*0-312-05849-7*, Saint Martin's Minotaur) St. Martin's Pr.
—Killer on Argyle Street. 2000. (Paul Whelan Mystery Ser.). 256p. pap. 14.95 (*0-595-09343-4*) iUniverse, Inc.
—Killer on Argyle Street: A Chicago Mystery Featuring Paul Whelan. 1995. 298p. 21.95 o.p. (*0-312-13532-7*, Saint Martin's Minotaur) St. Martin's Pr.
—The Maxwell Street Blues. 1994. 280p. 20.95 o.p. (*0-312-11394-3*, Saint Martin's Minotaur) St. Martin's Pr.
—The Maxwell Street Blues. 2000. (Paul Whelan Mystery Ser.). 288p. pap. 15.95 (*0-595-09342-6*) iUniverse, Inc.
—The Riverview Murders. 1997. 213p. 21.95 o.p. (*0-312-15641-3*, Saint Martin's Minotaur) St. Martin's Pr.
Randisi, Robert J. East of the Arch: A Joe Keough Mystery. 2002. 336p. 24.95 (*0-312-28398-9*, Saint Martin's Minotaur) St. Martin's Pr.
Reaves, Sam. A Long Cold Fall. 1992. 304p. pap. 4.50 (*0-380-71641-0*, Avon Bks.) Morrow/Avon.
Reed, Myrtle. The Shadow of Victory. 2000. 252p. E-Book 9.95 (*0-594-02741-1*) 1873 Pr.
Roby, Kimberla Lawson. Behind Closed Doors. 1997. 244p. reprint ed. pap. 12.00 (*1-57478-005-0*) Black Classic Pr.
—Behind Closed Doors. 1997. x, 250p. pap. 12.00 (*0-9653470-4-4*) Lenox Pr.
—Here & Now. 288p. 2000. pap. 13.00 o.s.i (*1-57566-494-1*, Dafina); 1998. 22.00 o.s.i (*1-57566-336-8*) Kensington Publishing Corp.
Rodi, Robert. Drag Queen. 272p. 1996. pap. 12.95 o.s.i (*0-452-27344-7*, Plume); 1995. 21.95 o.p. (*0-525-93925-3*, Dutton) Dutton/Plume.
Rogers, Kenny. The Gift. 1996. (Illus.). 64p. 10.99 o.p. (*0-7852-7174-0*) Nelson, Thomas Inc.
Rolens, Sharon. What Else but Home: A Novel. 2003. 336p. 23.95 (*1-882593-75-8*) Bridge Works Publishing Co., Inc.
—Worthy's Town: A Novel. 2000. 230p. 22.95 (*1-882593-35-9*); 2002. 288p. reprint ed. pap. 13.95 (*1-882593-57-X*) Bridge Works Publishing Co., Inc.
—Worthy's Town: A Novel. l.t. ed. 2001. 343p. 28.95 (*0-7862-3376-1*) Thorndike Pr.
Rubino, Jane, et al. Homicide for the Holidays: Fruitcake; Milwaukee Winters Can Be Murder; A Perfect Time for Murder. 2000. (WWL Mystery Ser.: Vol. 362). 512p. mass mkt. (*0-373-26362-7*, 1-26362-3, Worldwide Library) Harlequin Enterprises, Ltd.
Russell, Charlotte M. Cook up a Crime. Schantz, Tom & Schantz, Enid, eds. 1998. 160p. reprint ed. pap. 13.00 (*0-915230-18-6*) Rue Morgue Pr.
Saberhagen, Fred. A Matter of Taste. 1992. 288p. mass mkt. 3.99 (*0-8125-2575-2*); 1990. 16.95 o.p. (*0-312-85046-8*) Doherty, Tom Assocs., LLC. (Tor Bks.).
Saenz, Benjamin Alire. The House of Forgetting. 1998. mass mkt. 6.99 o.s.i (*0-8041-1831-0*, Ivy Bks.) Ballantine Bks.
Saenz, Benjamin Alire, ed. The House of Forgetting. 1998. pap. (*0-449-00308-6*, Fawcett) Ballantine Bks.
—The House of Forgetting. 1997. 352p. 24.00 o.s.i (*0-06-018738-7*) HarperCollins Pubs.
Sharpe, Jon. Chicago Six-Guns. 1993. (Canyon O'Grady Ser.: No. 24). 176p. (Orig.). mass mkt. 3.50 o.p. (*0-451-17529-8*, Signet Bks.) NAL.
Shields, Carol. Happenstance. 1980. 224p. 12.95 o.p. (*0-07-092377-9*) McGraw-Hill Cos., The.
—Happenstance. 1994. pap. 10.95 (*0-14-771022-7*) NAL.
—Happenstance. 1994. 416p. pap. 14.00 (*0-14-017951-8*, Penguin Bks.) Penguin Group (USA) Inc.
Simmons, Dan. Summer of Night. 1992. 608p. reprint ed. mass mkt. 7.99 (*0-446-36266-2*, Aspect) Warner Bks., Inc.
—A Winter Haunting. 2002. 320p. 25.95 (*0-380-97886-5*, Morrow, William & Co.) Morrow/Avon.
Sinclair, April. I Left My Back Door Open. 1999. 290p. 22.95 (*0-7868-6229-7*) Hyperion Pr.
—I Left My Back Door Open: A Novel. 2000. 304p. pap. 13.00 (*0-380-73280-7*) Morrow/Avon.
Sinclair, Upton. The Jungle. 1997. (C). pap. text (*0-321-02602-0*) Addison-Wesley Educational Pubs., Inc.
—The Jungle. 26.95 (*0-8488-0630-1*) Amereon, Ltd.
—The Jungle, Set. unabr. ed. 1997. audio 59.95 (*1-55685-473-0*, 473-0) Audio Bk. Contractors, Inc.
—The Jungle. 1981. (Bantam Classics Ser.). 400p. reprint ed. mass mkt. 5.95 (*0-553-21245-1*) Bantam Dell Publishing Group.
—The Jungle. 1971. 342p. reprint ed. lib. bdg. 20.00 (*0-8376-0400-1*) Bentley Pubs.
—The Jungle. 1991. 3.95 (*0-425-12527-0*) Berkley Publishing Group.
—The Jungle. unabr. ed. 1994. audio 76.95 (*0-7861-0789-8*, 132758) Blackstone Audio Bks., Inc.
—The Jungle. 1981. reprint ed. lib. bdg. 27.95 (*0-89966-415-6*) Buccaneer Bks., Inc.
—The Jungle. (Best Sellers of 1906 Ser.). reprint ed. lib. bdg. 48.00 (*0-7426-1156-6*); 1999. 413p. lib. bdg. 118.00 (*1-58201-821-9*) Classic Bks.
—The Jungle. 1999. 410p. pap. 9.95 o.p. (*1-930128-07-X*, JNMedia Bks.) JNMedia, Inc.
—The Jungle. E-Book 1.95 (*1-57799-892-8*) Logos Research Systems, Inc.
—The Jungle. 2001. 352p. mass mkt. 5.95 (*0-451-52804-2*, Signet Classics); 1960. mass mkt. 2.25 o.p. (*0-451-52210-9*); 1960. 352p. mass mkt. 5.95 o.s.i (*0-451-52420-9*, Signet Bks.) NAL.
—The Jungle, unabr. ed. 1994. audio 91.00 (*1-55690-977-2*, 94116E7) Recorded Bks., LLC.
—The Jungle. 1999. 424p. reprint ed. lib. bdg. 29.95 (*0-7351-0120-5*) Replica Bks.
—The Jungle. 1990. 12.00 (*0-606-00909-4*) Turtleback Bks.
—The Jungle. 1988. (Prairie State Bks.). 388p. pap. text 16.95 (*0-252-01480-4*); 34.95 o.p. (*0-252-01494-4*) Univ. of Illinois Pr.
—The Jungle. 1985. (American Library). 448p. pap. 9.95 (*0-14-039031-6*, Penguin Classics) Viking Penguin.
Skom, Edith. The Charles Dickens Murders: A Beth Austin Mystery. (Beth Austin Mysteries Ser.). 304p. 1999. mass mkt. 5.99 (*0-440-21776-8*); 1998. 21.95 o.s.i (*0-385-31230-X*) Dell Publishing.
—The George Eliot Murders: A Beth Austin Mystery. (Beth Austin Mysteries Ser.). 1996. 288p. mass mkt. 5.99 o.s.i (*0-440-21775-X*); 1995. 243p. 19.95 o.s.i (*0-385-31228-8*, Delacorte Pr.) Dell Publishing.
—The Mark Twain Murders: A Beth Austin Mystery. 1989. (Brown Bag Mystery Line Ser.). 277p. 12.95 o.p. (*0-933031-17-3*) Council Oak Bks.
—The Mark Twain Murders: A Beth Austin Mystery. 1990. (Beth Austin Mysteries Ser.). 304p. mass mkt. 5.99 o.s.i (*0-440-20608-1*) Dell Publishing.
Smiley, Jane. Barn Blind. 1993. 224p. pap. 14.00 (*0-449-90874-7*, Fawcett) Ballantine Bks.
—Barn Blind. 1998. reprint ed. 35.95 (*1-56849-700-8*) Buccaneer Bks., Inc.
Smith, Craig. The Whisper of Leaves. 2002. 336p. pap. 14.00 (*0-8093-2480-6*) Southern Illinois Univ. Pr.
Soos, Troy. Murder at Wrigley Field. (Mickey Rawlings Baseball Mystery Ser.). 304p. 1997. mass mkt. 5.50 o.s.i (*1-57566-155-1*); 1996. pap. 18.95 o.p. (*1-57566-023-7*) Kensington Publishing Corp.
—Murder at Wrigley Field, unabr. ed. 1998. (Mickey Rawlings Baseball Ser.: Vol. 3). audio 53.00 (*0-7887-2282-4*, 95533E7) Recorded Bks., LLC.
Sprinkle, Patricia H. Murder at Markham. 1992. (Sheila Travis Mystery Ser.). reprint ed. per. (*0-373-26108-X*, Harlequin Bks.) Harlequin Enterprises, Ltd.
Straub, Peter. The Throat. 1993. 688p. 24.00 o.p. (*0-525-93503-7*) Dutton/Plume.
—The Throat. 1994. 704p. mass mkt. 7.99 (*0-451-17918-8*, Signet Bks.) NAL.
—The Throat. abr. ed. 1993. audio 25.00 (*0-671-72591-2*, 692323, Simon & Schuster Audioworks) Simon & Schuster Audio.
Sussman, Susan. Audition for Murder. 2000. (Morgan Taylor Mysteries Ser.: Bk. 351). per. (*0-373-26351-1*, 1-26351-6, Worldwide Library) Harlequin Enterprises, Ltd.
Sussman, Susan & Avidon, Sarajane. Audition for Murder. 1999. vii, 279p. 23.95 (*0-312-19968-6*, Saint Martin's Minotaur) St. Martin's Pr.
Thompson, Jean. Wide Blue Yonder. 368p. 2003. pap. 13.00 (*0-7432-2958-4*); 2002. (Illus.). 24.00 (*0-7432-0512-X*) Simon & Schuster. (Simon & Schuster).
Tooley, S. D. Nothing Else Matters. 2000. (Sam Casey Mystery Ser.). 288p. 22.95 (*0-9666021-2-9*) Full Moon Publishing.
—When the Dead Speak. 2000. (Sam Casey Mystery Ser.). 304p. pap. 6.50 (*0-9666021-3-7*) Full Moon Publishing.
—When the Dead Speak. Roerden, Chris, ed. 1999. (Sam Casey Mystery Ser.). 304p. 21.95 (*0-9666021-0-2*) Full Moon Publishing.
Turow, Scott. Personal Injuries. stu. ed. (*0-374-96409-2*); 1999. E-Book 27.00 (*0-374-70194-6*); 1999. E-Book 9.00 (*0-374-70018-4*); 1999. E-Book 9.00 o.p. incl. cd-rom (*0-374-70007-9*) Farrar, Straus & Giroux.
—Personal Injuries. 2000. 528p. reprint ed. mass mkt. 7.99 (*0-446-60860-2*) Warner Bks., Inc.
Vachss, Andrew. Shella. 2001. E-Book 11.00 (*1-59061-227-2*) Adobe Systems, Inc.
—Shella. 1994. 240p. pap. 12.00 (*0-679-75681-7*, Vintage) Knopf Publishing Group.
Walker, David J. Applaud the Hollow Ghost. 1997. 288p. 23.95 (*0-312-18041-1*, Saint Martin's Minotaur) St. Martin's Pr.
—A Beer at a Bawdy House. E-Book 23.95 o.p. (*0-312-27340-1*); 2000. 307p. 23.95 (*0-312-25242-0*, Saint Martin's Minotaur) St. Martin's Pr.
—End of Emerald Woods: A Wild Onion. 2000. (Wild Onion Ltd. Mysteries Ser.). 310p. 23.95 (*0-312-25215-3*, Saint Martin's Minotaur) St. Martin's Pr.
—Fixed in His Folly. 1999. (WWL Mystery Ser.: Bk. 315). 256p. per. (*0-373-26315-5*, 1-26315-1, Worldwide Library) Harlequin Enterprises, Ltd.
—Fixed in His Folly: A Malachy Foley Mystery. 1995. 262p. 21.95 o.p. (*0-312-13074-0*, Saint Martin's Minotaur) St. Martin's Pr.
—Half the Truth. 1996. 288p. 22.95 (*0-312-14611-6*, Saint Martin's Minotaur) St. Martin's Pr.
—Ticket to Die For. 1998. (Wild Onion Ltd. Mysteries Ser.). 272p. 22.95 (*0-312-19345-9*, Saint Martin's Minotaur) St. Martin's Pr.
Weis, Margaret & Baldwin, David. Dark Heart. 1998. (Dragon's Disciples Ser.: Vol. 1). 352p. 23.00 o.s.i (*0-06-105298-1*) HarperCollins Pubs.
—Dark Heart. 1999. (Dragon's Disciples Ser.: Vol. 1). 448p. mass mkt. 5.99 (*0-06-105791-6*, Eos) Morrow/Avon.
Welk, Mary V. A Deadly Little Christmas: A Caroline Rhodes Mystery. 1998. 262p. pap. 10.00 (*0-9665157-0-6*) Kleworks Publishing Co.
—Something Wicked in the Air: A Caroline Rhodes Mystery. 1999. 225p. pap. 10.00 (*0-9665157-1-4*) Kleworks Publishing Co.
Wessel, John. Kiss It Goodbye: A Novel. 2002. 336p. E-Book 24.00 (*0-7432-2605-4*, Simon & Schuster) Simon & Schuster.
—Pretty Ballerina. 1998. 240p. 23.50 (*0-684-81464-1*, Simon & Schuster) Simon & Schuster.
—This Far, No Further. 1997. 384p. mass mkt. 6.99 o.s.i (*0-440-22490-X*) Dell Publishing.
—This Far, No Further. l.t. ed. 1997. (Large Print Book Ser.). 25.95 (*1-56895-418-2*, Wheeler Publishing, Inc.) Gale Group.
—This Far, No Further, unabr. ed. 1997. audio 75.00 (*0-7887-0803-1*, 94952E7) Recorded Bks., LLC.
—This Far, No Further. 1996. 336p. 23.00 (*0-684-81463-3*, Simon & Schuster) Simon & Schuster.
—This Far, No Further. 1999. pap. 9.98 (*0-671-04467-2*); Set. 1988. audio 18.00 (*0-671-57433-7*, 394372) Simon & Schuster Audio. (Simon & Schuster Audioworks).
Whack, Rita Coburn. Meant to Be: A Novel. 2002. 320p. pap. 11.95 (*0-375-75809-7*, Villard Bks.) Random House Adult Trade Publishing Group.
Whittingham, Richard. Their Kind of Town. 1994. 384p. 22.50 o.p. (*1-55611-358-7*) Fine, Donald I. Bks.
—Their Kind of Town. 1996. mass mkt. 5.99 (*0-380-72502-9*, Avon Bks.) Morrow/Avon.
Wiggs, Susan. The Mistress. 2000. 408p. mass mkt. (*1-55166-610-3*, 1-66610-6, Mira Bks.) Harlequin Enterprises, Ltd.
Wilson, Pamela J. & Dorman, Ruth E. R. Don't Forget I Love You. 2001. pap. 15.54 (*0-7596-2669-3*) 1stBooks Library.
Wright, Richard A. Native Son. Date not set. 371p. 26.95 (*0-8488-2577-2*) Amereon, Ltd.
—Native Son. 1997. 594p. 49.95 (*1-56849-694-X*) Buccaneer Bks., Inc.
—Native Son. audio 19.95 Filmic Archives.
—Native Son. abr. ed. 1989. 432p. pap. 7.95 (*0-06-080977-9*) HarperCollins Pubs.
—Native Son. (Perennial Classics Ser.). 2004. 528p. pap. 13.00 (*0-06-092980-4*, Perennial); 1986. 398p. mass mkt. 4.95 o.p. (*0-06-080855-1*, P 855, Perennial); 1942. mass mkt. 3.95 o.p. (*0-06-083055-7*, P 3055, Perennial); 1998. audio 18.00 (*0-89845-916-8*, 393493, HarperAudio); 1993. 624p. reprint ed. pap. 7.00 o.p. (*0-06-081249-4*, P 977, Perennial); 1969. reprint ed. 24.95 o.p. (*0-06-014762-8*) HarperTrade.
—Native Son. unabr. ed. 1998. audio 102.00 audio 102.00 (*0-7887-2112-7*, 95437E7) Recorded Bks., LLC.
—Native Son. l.t. ed. 1993. 619p. lib. bdg. 22.95 (*0-8161-5787-1*) Thorndike Pr.
Wubbels, Lance. In the Shadow of a Secret. 1999. 288p. pap. 10.99 o.p. (*0-7642-2183-3*) Bethany Hse. Pubs.
Young, Margaret Blair & Gray, Darius. The Last Mile of the Way, 3. 2003. (Standing on the Promises Ser.: 3). xvi, 448p. 21.95 (*1-57008-904-3*, 5730) Deseret Bk. Co.
Zagel, James. Money to Burn. 2002. 384p. 24.95 o.s.i (*0-399-14891-4*, Putnam & Grosset) Penguin Group (USA) Inc.
Zubro, Mark Richard. Another Dead Teenager. 1995. 194p. 19.95 o.p. (*0-312-13024-4*, Saint Martin's Minotaur) St. Martin's Pr.
—Are You Nuts? (Tom & Scott Mystery Ser.). 256p. 1999. pap. 12.95 (*0-312-20634-8*, Saint Martin's Griffin); 1998. 21.95 (*0-312-18528-6*, Saint Martin's Minotaur) St. Martin's Pr.
—Drop Dead. (Paul Turner Mystery Ser.). 2000. 256p. pap. 12.95 (*0-312-26314-7*, Saint Martin's Griffin); 1999. 245p. 22.95 (*0-312-20532-5*, Saint Martin's Minotaur) St. Martin's Pr.
—An Echo of Death: A Tom & Scott Mystery. (Tom & Scott Mystery Ser.). 1995. 208p. pap. 11.95 (*0-312-13480-0*, Saint Martin's Griffin); 1994. 192p. 18.95 o.p. (*0-312-11268-8*, Saint Martin's Minotaur) St. Martin's Pr.
—One Dead Drag Queen. E-Book 22.95 (*0-312-27586-2*); 2001. 256p. pap. 12.95 (*0-312-27702-4*, Saint Martin's Griffin); 2000. 256p. 22.95 o.s.i (*0-312-20937-1*, Saint Martin's Minotaur) St. Martin's Pr.
—The Only Good Priest. (Tom & Scott Mystery Ser.). 1992. 192p. pap. 10.95 (*0-312-07054-3*, Saint Martin's Griffin); 1991. 8.99 o.p. (*0-312-05486-6*, Saint Martin's Minotaur) St. Martin's Pr.
—Political Poison: A Paul Turner Mystery. (Paul Turner Mystery Ser.). 1994. 208p. pap. 11.95 (*0-312-11044-8*, Saint Martin's Griffin); 1993. 192p. 10.99 o.p. (*0-312-09364-0*, Saint Martin's Minotaur) St. Martin's Pr.
—The Principal Cause of Death. (Tom & Scott Mystery Ser.). 1993. 192p. pap. 11.95 (*0-312-09896-0*, Saint Martin's Griffin); 1992. 208p. 11.99 o.p. (*0-312-07767-X*, Saint Martin's Minotaur) St. Martin's Pr.
—A Simple Suburban Murder. (Stonewall Inn Editions Ser.). 1990. 6.50 o.p. (*0-312-03887-9*, Saint Martin's Minotaur); 1990. 224p. pap. 8.95 (*0-312-03933-6*, Saint Martin's Griffin); 1989. 224p. 15.95 o.p. (*0-312-02640-4*, Saint Martin's Minotaur) St. Martin's Pr.
—Sorry Now? 1991. 208p. 11.99 o.p. (*0-312-06470-5*, Saint Martin's Minotaur); 3rd ed. 1992. 192p. pap. 10.95 (*0-312-08299-1*, Saint Martin's Griffin) St. Martin's Pr.
—The Truth Can Get You Killed. (Stonewall Inn Editions Ser.). 224p. 1998. pap. 11.95 (*0-312-18765-3*, Saint Martin's Griffin); 1997. 21.95 (*0-312-15679-0*, Saint Martin's Minotaur) St. Martin's Pr.
—Why Isn't Becky Twitchell Dead? 1970. 208p. 15.00 o.p. (*0-312-03955-7*) Palgrave Macmillan.
—Why Isn't Becky Twitchell Dead? 1991. (Stonewall Inn Editions Ser.). 189p. pap. 12.95 (*0-312-05996-5*, Saint Martin's Griffin) St. Martin's Pr.

**IMAGINARY PLACES—FICTION**

Brown, Calef. Tippintown: A Guided Tour. 2003. (Illus.). 32p. (J). (ps-3). lib. bdg., tchr. ed. 16.00 (*0-618-14972-4*) Houghton Mifflin Co.
Crimmins, G. Garfield. The Republic of Dreams: A Reverie. 1998. (Illus.). 96p. 21.95 (*0-393-04633-8*) Norton, W. W. & Co., Inc.
Douglass, Sara. Enchanter. pap. (*0-312-87889-3*); 2002. mass mkt. 7.99 (*0-7653-4196-4*) Doherty, Tom Assocs., LLC. (Tor Bks.).
Ice, Kathy, ed. Tapestries: An Anthology. 1999. (Magic, the Gathering Ser.). 289p. (C). reprint ed. pap. text 12.00 (*0-7881-6474-0*) DIANE Publishing Co.
—Tapestries: An Anthology. 1995. (Magic - The Gathering Ser.). 304p. mass mkt. 12.00 o.p. (*0-06-105308-2*) HarperCollins Pubs.
—Tapestries: An Anthology. 1996. (Magic the Gathering Ser.). 384p. mass mkt. 5.99 o.p. (*0-06-105428-3*, HarperTorch) Morrow/Avon.
Leithauser, Brad. The Friends of Freeland. unabr. collector's ed. 1997. Pt. 1. audio 72.00 (*0-7366-4003-7*, 4502-A); Pt. 2. audio 56.00 (*0-7366-4004-5*, 4502-B) Books on Tape, Inc.
—The Friends of Freeland. 1998. 528p. pap. 14.00 (*0-679-77270-7*, Vintage) Knopf Publishing Group.
Watt-Evans, Lawrence. Night of Madness. 2000. 384p. 24.95 o.p. (*0-312-87368-9*); 2002. reprint ed. mass mkt. 6.99 (*0-8125-7794-9*) Doherty, Tom Assocs., LLC. (Tor Bks.).

**INDIA—FICTION**

Abbas, Khwaja A. Bombay My Bombay. 1987. 167p. 12.50 o.p. (*81-202-0174-4*) Ajanta Pubns/Ajanta Bks. International IND. *Dist:* South Asia Bks.
Aikath-Gyaltsen, Indrani. Crane's Morning. 1994. 256p. 20.00 o.s.i (*0-345-38366-4*, One World/Ballantine) Ballantine Bks.
—Daughters of the House. 1994. 208p. pap. 15.00 (*0-345-38655-8*); 1993. 18.00 o.p. (*0-345-38073-8*, One World/Ballantine) Ballantine Bks.
Ali, Ahmed. Twilight in Dehli. 1994. (Paperbook Ser.: Vol. 782). 224p. (Orig.). pap. 12.95 (*0-8112-1267-X*, NDP782) New Directions Publishing Corp.
Ali, Thalassa. A Singular Hostage. 2003. (*0-553-80234-8*); 2002. (Illus.). 368p. pap. 13.95 (*0-553-38176-8*, Spectra) Bantam Bks.
Allington, Maynard. The Fox in the Field: A WWII Novel of India. 1994. (World War II Commemorative Ser.). 224p. 19.95 (*0-02-881085-6*) Brassey's, Inc.
Alter, Stephen. Neglected Lives. 1978. 192p. 8.95 o.s.i (*0-374-22024-7*) Farrar, Straus & Giroux.
—Silk & Steel. 1980. 327p. 11.95 o.p. (*0-374-26411-2*) Farrar, Straus & Giroux.
Anand, Mulk Raj. Sword & the Sickle. 1984. (C). 11.00 (*0-8364-2793-9*) Arnold Pubs. IND. *Dist:* South Asia Bks.
Anand, Valerie. To a Native Shore. 1983. 304p. 15.95 o.p. (*0-684-18007-3*, Scribner) Simon & Schuster.

Appachana, Anjana. Incantations & Other Stories. 1992. o.s.i (1-85381-261-7) Random Hse., Inc.
—Incantations & Other Stories. 1992. 180p. pap. 12.95 (0-8135-1828-8); text 32.00 (0-8135-1827-X) Rutgers Univ. Pr.
Awasthy, Rajendra, ed. Hindi Short Stories-an Anthology. 1981. (Vikas Library of Modern Indian Writing: No. 16). 175p. text 15.95 o.p. (0-7069-1312-4) Vikas Publishing Hse. Private, Ltd. IND. *Dist:* South Asia Bks.
Bacon, Charlotte. There Is Room for You. 2004. 288p. 23.00 (0-374-28185-8) Farrar, Straus & Giroux.
Badami, Anita Rau. The Hero's Walk. 2001. 359p. 23.95 (1-56512-312-3) Algonquin Bks. of Chapel Hill.
—Tamarind Woman. 2002. 272p. 23.95 (1-56512-335-2) Algonquin Bks. of Chapel Hill.
—Tamarind Woman. 2004. 304p. pap. 13.95 (0-345-46494-X) Ballantine Bks.
Bahal, Aniruddha. Bunker 13. 2003. E-Book 15.00 (0-374-70441-4); 2003. E-Book 15.00 (0-374-70442-2); 2002. pap. (0-374-91095-2); 2002. E-Book (0-374-70444-9); 2002. E-Book (0-374-70445-7) Farrar, Straus & Giroux.
Balasubramanyam, Rajeev. In Beautiful Disguises. 2001. 246p. pap. 14.95 (1-58234-127-3) Bloomsbury Publishing.
Baldwin, Shauna Singh. What the Body Remembers. 2000. 528p. pap. 19.95 (0-676-97318-3, Vintage) Random Hse. of Canada, Ltd. CAN. *Dist:* Random Hse., Inc.
—What the Body Remembers: A Novel. (Illus.). 496p. 1999. 25.95 o.s.i (0-385-49604-4, Talese, Nan A.); 2001. reprint ed. pap. 15.00 (0-385-49605-2) Doubleday Publishing.
Banker, Ashok. Prince of Ayodhya. (Ramayana Ser.: Bk. I). 2004. mass mkt. (0-446-61199-9); 2003. 350p. 24.95 (0-446-53092-1) Warner Bks., Inc. (Aspect).
Barrett, Maria. Dishonored. 1998. 416p. mass mkt. 6.50 (0-446-60628-6); 1996. 432p. 23.00 o.p. (0-446-52035-7) Warner Bks., Inc.
Bates, H. E. The Scarlett Sword. l.t. ed. 1993. 22.95 o.p. (0-7927-1416-4); pap. 20.95 o.p. (0-7927-1415-6) BBC Audiobooks America.
Bhattacharya, Keron. The Pearls of Coromandel. 1996. 256p. 21.95 o.p. (0-312-14389-3) St. Martin's Pr.
—The Pearls of Coromandel. l.t. ed. 1997. (Ulverscroft Large Print Ser.). 576p. 29.99 o.p. (0-7089-3679-2, Ulverscroft) Thorpe, F. A. Pubs. GBR. *Dist:* Ulverscroft Large Print Bks., Ltd., Ulverscroft Large Print Canada, Ltd.
Bibhutibhushan Bandyopadhyay. A Strange Attachment & Other Stories. Granoff, Phyllis, tr. 1995. 277p. pap. 12.95 (0-88962-222-1) Mosaic Pr.
Billington, Rachel. The Garish Day. 1986. 304p. 17.95 o.p. (0-688-06167-2, Morrow, William & Co.) Morrow/Avon.
—The Garish Day. l.t. ed. 1986. (Charnwood Large Print Ser.). 560p. 29.99 o.p. (0-7089-8361-8, Ulverscroft) Thorpe, F. A. Pubs. GBR. *Dist:* Ulverscroft Large Print Bks., Ltd., Ulverscroft Large Print Canada, Ltd.
Bonnici, Peter. The First Rains. 1985. (Arjuna Bks.). (Illus.). 24p. (J). (ps-3). lib. bdg. 9.95 o.p. (0-87614-228-5, Carolrhoda Bks.) Lerner Publishing Group.
Bradley, Don. Angels in a Harsh World. 1997. pap. text 17.95 (1-888298-02-2) Native Planet Publishing.
—Angels in a Harsh World. 1998. 19.95 o.p. (0-399-14359-9, G. P. Putnam's Sons) Penguin Group (USA) Inc.
Bradley, Don & Olsten, Haley. Angels in a Harsh World: A Novel. 1999. 320p. reprint ed. pap. 13.00 o.s.i (0-425-16690-2) Berkley Publishing Group.
Bromfield, Louis. The Rains Came. 1976. reprint ed. lib. bdg. 34.95 (0-88411-505-4) Amereon, Ltd.
—The Rains Came. 1996. reprint ed. lib. bdg. 45.95 (1-56849-190-5) Buccaneer Bks., Inc.
Buck, Pearl S. Mandala. 1995. 384p. pap. 9.95 (1-55921-037-0) Moyer Bell.
Campion, Anna & Campion, Jane. Holy Smoke: A Novel. 1999. (Illus.). 272p. pap. 14.00 (0-7868-8563-7); 259p. 22.95 (0-7868-6349-8) Hyperion Pr.
Carnac, Nicholas. Indigo. 1982. 448p. 14.95 o.p. (0-312-41413-7) St. Martin's Pr.
Chaikin, Linda L. Kingscote. 1994. (Heart of India Ser.: No. 3). 400p. pap. 10.99 o.p. (1-55661-378-4) Bethany Hse. Pubs.
—Silk. 1993. (Heart of India Ser.: Bk. 1). 352p. (Orig.). pap. 10.99 o.p. (1-55661-248-6) Bethany Hse. Pubs.
—Under the Eastern Stars. 1993. (Heart of India Ser.: Bk. 2). 384p. pap. 10.99 o.p. (1-55661-366-0) Bethany Hse. Pubs.
Champagne, Maurice. The Mysterious Valley. Bucko, Bill, tr. from FRE. 1994. (Illus.). 256p. (J). pap. 19.95 (0-9626854-9-6); (gr. 3 up). 29.95 (0-9626854-6-1) Atlantean Pr.
Chandra, Vikram. Love & Longing in Bombay. 1998. pap. 13.00 (0-316-18970-7, Back Bay); 1998. 272p. pap. 13.95 (0-316-13677-8); 1997. 288p. (gr. 8). 22.95 o.p. (0-316-13307-8) Little Brown & Co.
Chatterjee, Amal. Across the Lakes. 1998. 246p. pap. 27.00 o.p. (1-86159-052-0) Orion Publishing Group, Ltd. GBR. *Dist:* Trafalgar Square.
—Across the Lakes. 1998. 246p. pap. 17.95 (1-86159-053-9) Phoenix Hse. GBR. *Dist:* Trafalgar Square.
—Across the Lakes. 1998. 246 p. (0-14-027706-4) Viking Penguin.
Chatterji, Bankim C. Anandamath: A Novel. 1991. (C). 14.00 (81-7094-091-5) Vision IND. *Dist:* South Asia Bks.
Chaudhuri, Amit. Freedom Song: Three Novels. 2000. 448p. pap. 14.00 (0-375-70400-0); 1999. 480p. 24.00 (0-375-40427-9) Knopf, Alfred A. Inc.
—Real Time: Stories & a Reminiscence. 2002. 192p. 21.00 o.p. (0-374-28169-6) Farrar, Straus & Giroux.
—Real Time: Stories & a Reminiscence. 2003. 192p. pap. 12.00 (0-312-42114-1) Picador.
Chopra, Gautama. Child of the Dawn: A Magical Journey of Awakening. 208p. 1998. pap. 10.95 (1-878424-38-6); 1996. 16.00 o.p. (1-878424-24-6) Amber-Allen Publishing.
—Child of the Dawn: A Magical Journey of Awakening. 1998. 180p. text 16.00 (0-7881-5798-1) DIANE Publishing Co.
Cleverly, Barbara. The Last Kashmiri Rose: Murder & Mystery in the Final Days of the Raj. 2002. 288p. 24.00 (0-7867-1059-4, Carroll & Graf Pubs.) Avalon Publishing Group.
—The Last Kashmiri Rose: Murder & Mystery in the Final Days of the Raj. 2003. 320p. mass mkt. 6.99 (0-440-24156-1, Dell Bks.) Dell Publishing.
—The Last Kashmiri Rose: Murder & Mystery in the Final Days of the Raj. unabr. ed. 2002. audio 69.95 (1-84283-243-3) Soundings, Ltd. GBR. *Dist:* Ulverscroft Large Print Bks., Ltd.
—The Last Kashmiri Rose: Murder & Mystery in the Final Days of the Raj. l.t. ed. 2003. (Ulverscroft Large Print Ser.). 432p. 32.50 (0-7089-4935-5) Thorpe, F. A. Pubs. GBR. *Dist:* Ulverscroft Large Print Bks., Ltd.
—Ragtime in Simla. 2003. 288p. 24.00 (0-7867-1246-5, Carroll & Graf Pubs.) Avalon Publishing Group.
—Ragtime in Simla. unabr. ed. 2003. audio 69.95 (1-84283-461-4) Soundings, Ltd. GBR. *Dist:* Ulverscroft Large Print Bks., Ltd.
Clough, E. The Princess' Lover. 1993. 640p. 14.95 (1-877978-49-3, FLF Pr.) Florida Literary Foundation.
Coovadia, Imraan. The Wedding. 2001. 320p. 23.00 (0-312-27219-7) Picador.
—The Wedding. E-Book 10.00 (0-312-70343-0) St. Martin's Pr.
Cornwell, Bernard. Sharpe's Fortress: Richard Sharpe & the Siege of Gawilghur, December 1803. 2002. 320p. pap. 12.95 (0-06-109863-9, Perennial) HarperTrade.
—Sharpe's Tiger: Richard Sharpe & the Siege of Seringapatam, 1799. 1997. (Richard Sharpe Adventure Ser.: No. 1). (Illus.). 303p. o.p. (0-00-225010-1) HarperSanFrancisco.
—Sharpe's Tiger: Richard Sharpe & the Siege of Seringapatam, 1799. 1999. (Richard Sharpe Adventure Ser.: No. 1). 400p. pap. 13.00 (0-06-093230-9, Perennial) HarperTrade.
—Sharpe's Tiger: Richard Sharpe & the Siege of Seringapatam, 1799. 1997. (Richard Sharpe Adventure Ser.: No. 1). 496p. mass mkt. 6.50 o.s.i (0-06-101269-6, HarperTorch) Morrow/Avon.
—Sharpe's Tiger: Richard Sharpe & the Siege of Seringapatam, 1799. 1999. (Richard Sharpe Adventures Ser.). (Illus.). 19.05 (0-606-21714-2) Turtleback Bks.
—Sharpe's Triumph: Richard Sharpe & the Battle of Assaye, September 1803. 1999. (Richard Sharpe Adventure Ser.: No. 2). 304p. 24.00 (0-06-101270-X) HarperCollins Pubs.
—Sharpe's Triumph: Richard Sharpe & the Battle of Assaye, September 1803. 2000. (Richard Sharpe Adventure Ser.: No. 2). 304p. pap. 13.00 (0-06-095197-4, Perennial) HarperTrade.
—Sharpe's Triumph: Richard Sharpe & the Battle of Assaye, September 1803. 2000. (Richard Sharpe Adventures Ser.). (Illus.). (J). 19.05 (0-606-21715-0) Turtleback Bks.
Crasta, Richard. Beauty Queens, Children, & the Death of Sex. 1997. (81-7223-281-0) HarperCollins Pubs. India.
Crawford, F. Marion. Mr. Isaacs: A Tale of India. 2000. 252p. E-Book 3.95 (0-594-06489-9) 1873 Pr.
—Mr. Isaacs: A Tale of India. 1969. (BCL Ser. I). reprint ed. 37.50 (0-404-01835-1) AMS Pr., Inc.
—Mr. Isaacs: A Tale of India. collector's ed. 2002. (Illus.). im. lthr. 38.85 (1-4115-1202-2); pap. 19.95 (1-4115-0502-6); 25.95 (1-4115-0852-1); pap. 17.95 (1-4115-0242-6) Polyglot Pr., Inc.
—Mr. Isaacs: A Tale of India. 1882. 9.00 (0-403-00015-7) Scholarly Pr., Inc.
Croskery, Beverly F. Shamir, the White Elephant: A Rain Forest Adventure. 1997. (Illus.). 128p. (J). (gr. 3-6). 14.95 (0-9657619-4-0) Bell-Forsythe Publishing Co.
Dalkey, Kara. Blood of the Goddess: Goa, Vol. 1. 1996. 256p. 21.95 o.p. (0-312-86000-5, Tor Bks.) Doherty, Tom Assocs., LLC.
Damle, Veena. I Am Om. 2001. (Illus.). 165p. 25.00 (0-942979-80-X); pap. 12.00 (0-942979-79-6) Livingston Pr.
Danner, Craig Joseph. Himalayan Dhaba: A Novel. 2001. 256p. 24.00 (0-9706405-9-5, HD134) Crispin/Hammer Pr.
—Himalayan Dhaba: A Novel. 2002. 23.95 o.s.i (0-525-94690-X); 2003. 320p. reprint ed. pap. 13.00 (0-452-28387-6, Plume) Dutton/Plume.
Darmstaedter, Eric. The Emerald Pendant. 1995. (Illus.). 220p. (Orig.). pap. 10.00 o.p. (1-879418-99-1) Audenreed Pr.
Daswani, Kavita. For Matrimonial Purposes. 2003. 288p. 23.95 (0-399-15070-6) Putnam Publishing Group, The.
David, Esther. Book of Esther. 2003. 416p. 9.99 (0-670-04909-3, Viking) Viking Penguin.
Davidar, David. The House of Blue Mangoes: A Novel. 2003. 432p. pap. 14.95 (0-06-093678-9, Perennial) HarperTrade.
—The House of Blue Mangoes: A Novel. 2002. 421p. (0-670-04918-2) Viking Penguin.
Davidar, David J. The House of Blue Mangoes: A Novel. 2002. 432p. 26.95 (0-06-621254-5) HarperCollins Pubs.
Deane, Alyssa. Once & Always. 2000. 352p. mass mkt. 5.99 o.s.i (0-8217-6615-5) Kensington Publishing Corp.
Deaner, Janice. Notes on Extinction. 256p. 2001. 25.95 o.s.i (0-525-94415-X); 2003. reprint ed. pap. 14.00 (0-452-27974-7, Plume) Dutton/Plume.
Deb, Siddartha. The Point of Return: A Novel. 2003. 320p. 24.95 (0-06-050151-0, Ecco) HarperTrade.
Deb, Siddhartha. The Point of Return. 2004. 320p. pap. 13.95 (0-06-050153-7) HarperTrade.
Debi, Swarnakumari. The Uprooted Vine. Sogani, Rajul & Gupta, Indira, trs. 2004. 250p. text 19.95 (0-19-566502-3) Oxford Univ. Pr., Inc.
DeFelice, Jim. War Breaker. 1999. 448p. reprint ed. mass mkt. 6.99 (0-8439-4601-6, Leisure Bks.) Dorchester Publishing Co., Inc.
—War Breaker. 1993. 320p. 19.95 o.p. (0-312-09404-3) St. Martin's Pr.
—The War Breaker. 1996. 400p. reprint ed. pap. 6.99 (0-8439-4043-3, Leisure Bks.) Dorchester Publishing Co., Inc.
Delderfield, R. F. God Is an Englishman. 1998. 704p. pap. 15.95 (0-7867-0528-0, Carroll & Graf Pubs.) Avalon Publishing Group.
—God Is an Englishman. unabr. collector's ed. 1983. Pt. 1. audio 104.00 (0-7366-0487-1, 1462-A); Pt. 2. audio 72.00 (0-7366-0488-X, 1462-B) Books on Tape, Inc.
—God Is an Englishman. 1986. 832p. mass mkt. 4.95 o.s.i (0-671-62722-8, Pocket) Simon & Schuster.
Desai, Anita. Baumgartner's Bombay. 2000. (Illus.). 240p. pap. 13.00 (0-618-05680-7) Houghton Mifflin Co.
—Baumgartner's Bombay. 1989. 18.95 o.s.i (0-394-57229-7) Knopf, Alfred A. Inc.
—Baumgartner's Bombay. 1990. 240p. pap. 9.00 o.p. (0-14-013176-0, Penguin Bks.); pap. 11.95 o.p. (0-14-011474-2, Viking) Viking Penguin.
—Clear Light of Day. 1980. 183p. o.p. (0-06-010984-X) HarperCollins Pubs.
—Clear Light of Day. 2000. 192p. pap. 12.00 (0-618-07451-1, Mariner Bks.) Houghton Mifflin Co. Trade & Reference Div.
—Clear Light of Day. 1982. pap. 5.95 o.p. (0-14-005860-5) Penguin Group (USA) Inc.
—Clear Light of Day. 192p. 1989. pap. 12.95 o.p. (0-14-010859-9); 1986. pap. 6.95 o.p. (0-14-008670-6) Viking Penguin. (Penguin Bks.).
—Fasting, Feasting. 2000. 240p. pap. 13.00 (0-618-06582-2, Mariner Bks.) Houghton Mifflin Co. Trade & Reference Div.
—Fasting, Feasting. 1999. 227p. (0-7011-6894-3) Random Hse. of Canada, Ltd. CAN. *Dist:* Random Hse., Inc.
—Fasting, Feasting. l.t. ed. 2000. (Basic Ser.). 323p. 27.95 (0-7862-2638-2); (0-7540-4239-1); (0-7540-4240-5) Thorndike Pr.
—Fire on the Mountain. 1977. 12.95 o.p. (0-06-011066-X) HarperTrade.
—In Custody. 1985. 204p. 16.95 o.p. (0-06-039038-7) HarperCollins Pubs.
—In Custody. unabr. ed. 2001. audio 54.95 (1-85089-717-4, 90024) ISIS Audio Bks. GBR. *Dist:* Ulverscroft Large Print Bks., Ltd.
—In Custody. 1994. 208p. pap. 9.95 o.p. (0-14-023932-4, Penguin Bks.) Penguin Group (USA) Inc.
—In Custody. (Fiction Ser.). 208p. 1989. pap. 10.00 o.p. (0-14-010868-8); 1986. pap. 4.95 o.p. (0-14-007752-9) Viking Penguin. (Penguin Bks.).
—Journey to Ithaca. 1995. 320p. 23.00 o.s.i (0-679-43900-5) Knopf, Alfred A. Inc.
—Journey to Ithaca. 1996. 336p. pap. 15.00 o.s.i (0-14-025818-3) Penguin Group (USA) Inc.
Desai, Kiran. Hullabaloo in the Guava Orchard. 1999. 224p. pap. 12.95 (0-385-49370-3) Doubleday Publishing.
—Hullabaloo in the Guava Orchard. 1998. 224p. (YA). (gr. 8 up). 22.00 o.p. (0-87113-711-9, Atlantic Monthly Pr.) Grove/Atlantic, Inc.
—Hullabaloo in the Guava Orchard. l.t. unabr. ed. 1998. (Isis Large Print Bks.). 232p. (0-7531-5949-X, 15949X) ISIS Large Print Bks. GBR. *Dist:* Ulverscroft Large Print Canada, Ltd.
Desani, G. V. Hali, & Collected Stories. 1991. 224p. 20.00 (0-929701-12-7) McPherson & Co.
Deshpande, Shashi. Binding Vine. 2001. 256p. 23.95 (1-55861-267-X) Feminist Pr. at The City Univ. of New York.
—A Matter of Time. 1999. 272p. 21.95 (1-55861-214-9) Feminist Pr. at The City Univ. of New York.
—Small Remedies. 2000. xx, 324p. (0-670-89251-3) Viking.
Devi, Mahasweta. Chotti Munda & His Arrow. Spivak, Gayatri Chakravorty, tr. from BEN. 2003. 256p. 54.95 (1-4051-0704-9); pap. 19.95 (1-4051-0705-7) Blackwell Publishing.
Dhondy, Farrukh. Poona Company. 1985. 160p. (J). (gr. 6-8). 16.95 o.p. (0-575-03555-2) Gollancz, Victor GBR. *Dist:* Trafalgar Square.
Divakaruni, Chitra Banerjee. Arranged Marriage. 1996. 320p. pap. 13.95 (0-385-48350-3, Knopf Bks. for Young Readers) Random Hse. Children's Bks.
—Arranged Marriage: Stories. 1995. 307p. 22.00 o.s.i (0-385-47558-6) Doubleday Publishing.
—Sister of My Heart. 2000. 336p. pap. 13.00 (0-385-48951-X, Knopf Bks. for Young Readers) Random Hse. Children's Bks.
Dockendorf, Margo. The Mahdi: A Millennium Thriller. 1999. 440p. 24.95 (1-879384-35-3) Cypress Hse.
Drummond, Emma. Forget the Glory. 1987. pap. 3.95 o.p. (0-312-90678-1, St. Martin's Paperbacks); 1985. 480p. 15.95 o.p. (0-312-29892-7) St. Martin's Pr.
—Forget the Glory. l.t. ed. 1986. (Charnwood Large Print Ser.). 640p. 29.99 o.p. (0-7089-8336-7, Charnwood) Thorpe, F. A. Pubs. GBR. *Dist:* Ulverscroft Large Print Bks., Ltd., Ulverscroft Large Print Canada, Ltd.
—That Sweet & Savage Land. 1991. 288p. 17.95 o.p. (0-312-05973-6) St. Martin's Pr.
Duggal, Kartar S. Night of the Full Moon & Other Stories. 1992. (C). text 8.00 (81-7201-228-4) National Sahitya Akademi IND. *Dist:* South Asia Bks.
Edwards, Jonathan. Tales in the Key of Sea. 2001. 185p. pap. 13.95 (0-595-16841-8) iUniverse, Inc.
Endo, Shusaku. Deep River. Gessel, Van C., tr. from JPN. 1996. 224p. pap. 11.95 (0-8112-1320-X, NDP820); 1995. 216p. 19.95 o.p. (0-8112-1289-0) New Directions Publishing Corp.
—Deep River. 1994. 216p. 11.95 (1-55082-111-3) Quarry Pr. CAN. *Dist:* LPC/InBook.
Etteth, Ravi Shankar. The Tiger by the River. 2002. 270p. (0-385-60363-0) Doubleday Publishing.
Farrell, J. G. The Siege of Krishnapur. 1997. 368p. pap. 12.95 (0-7867-0484-5); 1985. 344p. mass mkt. 4.95 o.p. (0-88184-195-1) Avalon Publishing Group. (Carroll & Graf Pubs.).
—The Siege of Krishnapur. unabr. ed. 2000. audio 69.95 (0-7451-2743-6, SAB 109) Chivers Audio Bks. GBR. *Dist:* BBC Audiobooks America.
—The Siege of Krishnapur. 1974. 352p. 7.95 o.p. (0-15-182323-5) Harcourt Trade Pubs.
—The Siege of Krishnapur. 2004. 352p. pap. 14.95 (1-59017-092-X) New York Review of Bks., Inc., The.
Fast, Jonathan. Golden Fire. 1987. 418p. reprint ed. mass mkt. 4.50 o.s.i (0-553-26850-3) Bantam Bks.
—Golden Fire: A Novel of Ancient India. 1986. 18.95 o.p. (0-87795-764-9, Morrow, William & Co.) Morrow/Avon.
Fatima, Altaf. The One Who Did Not Ask. 1994. (Asian Writers Ser.). 335p. pap. 10.95 (0-435-95084-3, 95084) Heinemann.
Forbes, Leslie. Bombay Ice. 1999. 416p. reprint ed. pap. 13.95 (0-553-38047-8) Bantam Bks.
—Bombay Ice. unabr. ed. 1998. audio 76.95 (0-7861-1430-4, 2316) Blackstone Audio Bks., Inc.
—Bombay Ice. 1998. (0-374-90777-3); 400p. 24.00 o.p. (0-374-11530-3) Farrar, Straus & Giroux.
—Bombay Ice. abr. ed. 1998. 3p. audio 17.95 (1-55935-277-9) Soundelux Audio Publishing.
—Bombay Ice. (GER.). pap. (3-548-24703-2) Ullstein-Taschenbuch-Verlag DEU. *Dist:* International Bk. Import Service, Inc.
—Fish, Blood & Bone. 2002. 448p. pap. 13.95 (0-553-38163-6) Bantam Bks.
—Fish, Blood & Bone. 2001. (Illus.). 436p. 25.00 o.p. (0-374-15506-2); 2000. (0-374-92746-4) Farrar, Straus & Giroux.

Forster, E. M. A Passage to India. unabr. ed. 1998. audio 47.95 (*1-55685-562-1*) Audio Bk. Contractors, Inc.
—A Passage to India. unabr. ed. 2003. audio 34.95 (*1-57270-329-6*, Cover to Cover Classics) Audio Partners Publishing Corp.
—A Passage to India. unabr. ed. 1992. audio 56.95 (*0-7861-0350-7*, 102645) Blackstone Audio Bks., Inc.
—A Passage to India. 1995. audio compact disk 80.00 (*0-7366-6218-9*); (J). audio 64.00 (*0-7366-2952-1*, 3646) Books on Tape, Inc.
—A Passage to India. 1981. reprint ed. 429p. lib. bdg. 25.95 (*0-89966-300-1*); 450p. lib. bdg. 25.95 o.p. (*0-89968-223-5*, Lightyear Pr.) Buccaneer Bks., Inc.
—A Passage to India. unabr. ed. 2000. audio 69.95 (*0-7451-2701-0*, SAB 074) Chivers Audio Bks. GBR. *Dist:* BBC Audiobooks America.
—A Passage to India. (HBJ Book Ser.). 1989. 372p. 18.00 (*0-15-171141-0*); 1965. 368p. reprint ed. pap. 13.00 (*0-15-671142-7*, Harvest Bks.) Harcourt Trade Pubs.
—A Passage to India. 1978. (Abinger Edition Ser.). xxviii, 371p. (*0-7131-6107-8*) Hodder Arnold GBR. *Dist:* Routledge.
—A Passage to India. Stallybrass, Oliver, ed. 1979. (Abinger Edition of E. M. Forster Ser.: Vol. 6). 671p. 64.50 o.p. (*0-8419-0469-3*) Holmes & Meier Pubs., Inc.
—A Passage to India. mass mkt. 0.25 o.p. (*0-451-00574-0*, Signet Bks.) NAL.
—A Passage to India. (SparkNotes Literature Study Guides). 64-96p. pap., stu. ed. 4.95 (*1-58663-819-X*) Spark Publishing Group.
—A Passage to India. l.t. ed. 1981. (Classics Ser.). 436p. 13.00 o.p. (*0-7089-8000-7*, Charnwood) Thorpe, F. A. Pubs. GBR. *Dist:* Ulverscroft Large Print Bks., Ltd., Ulverscroft Large Print Canada, Ltd.
—A Passage to India. l.t. ed. 1998. 377p. pap. text 29.95 (*1-56000-507-6*) Transaction Pubs.
—A Passage to India. 1952. 19.05 (*0-606-01711-9*) Turtleback Bks.
—A Passage to India. abr. ed. 1997. (Classic Ser.). audio 23.95 (*0-14-086292-7*, Penguin AudioBooks) Viking Penguin.
Forster, E. M. & Everyman's Library Staff. A Passage to India. 1992. (Everyman's Library). 336p. 18.00 (*0-679-40549-6*) Knopf, Alfred A. Inc.
Fraser, George MacDonald. Flashman in the Great Game. unabr. collector's ed. 1995. (Flashman Ser.). audio 72.00 (*0-7366-2908-4*, 3605) Books on Tape, Inc.
—Flashman in the Great Game. 1989. (Flashman Ser.). 336p. pap. 13.95 (*0-452-26303-4*, Plume) Dutton/Plume.
—Flashman in the Great Game. 1977. (Flashman Ser.). mass mkt. 2.50 o.p. (*0-451-09688-6*, E9688); mass mkt. 1.95 o.p. (*0-451-07429-7*) NAL. (Signet Bks.).
—Flashman in the Great Game. 1975. 8.95 o.p. (*0-394-49893-3*, Knopf Bks. for Young Readers) Random Hse. Children's Bks.
—Flashman in the Great Game. l.t. ed. 1985. (Charnwood Large Print Ser.). 512p. 29.99 o.p. (*0-7089-8264-6*, Ulverscroft) Thorpe, F. A. Pubs. GBR. *Dist:* Ulverscroft Large Print Bks., Ltd., Ulverscroft Large Print Canada, Ltd.
Gajjar, Irina N. The Pokhraj. 2003. 502p. pap. 16.95 (*1-885373-44-9*) Emerald Ink Publishing.
Galdone, Paul. The Monkey & The Crocodile: A Jataka Tale from India. 1987. (Illus.). 32p. (J). (ps-3). pap. 6.95 (*0-89919-524-5*, Clarion Bks.) Houghton Mifflin Co. Trade & Reference Div.
Ganesan, Indira. Inheritance. 1999. (Bluestreak Ser.). 208p. pap. 14.00 (*0-8070-6227-8*) Beacon Pr.
—Inheritance. 1998. 208p. (gr. 5-12). 22.00 o.s.i (*0-679-43442-9*) Knopf, Alfred A. Inc.
Gardner, Katy. Losing Gemma: A Novel. 2002. 368p. pap. 13.00 (*1-57322-933-4*, Riverhead Bks. (Hardcovers)) Putnam Publishing Group, The.
Ghosh, Amitav. The Calcutta Chromosome: A Novel of Fevers, Delirium & Discovery. 1996. 18.00 (*81-7530-005-1*) Dayal, Ravi Pub. IND. *Dist:* South Asia Bks.
—The Calcutta Chromosome: A Novel of Fevers, Delirium & Discovery. 1998. 320p. mass mkt. 6.99 o.s.i (*0-380-79493-4*, Avon Bks.); 1997. 320p. mass mkt. 23.00 (*0-380-97585-8*, Avon Bks.); 1924. o.s.i (*0-688-15214-7*, Morrow, William & Co.) Morrow/Avon.
—The Calcutta Chromosome: A Novel of Fevers, Delirium, & Discovery. 2001. 320p. pap. 14.00 (*0-380-81394-7*, Perennial) HarperTrade.
—Circle of Reason. 2000. 423p. 19.95 (*81-7530-039-6*) Dayal, Ravi Pub. IND. *Dist:* South Asia Bks.
—Circle of Reason. 1986. 432p. 17.95 o.p. (*0-670-80984-5*) Viking Penguin.
—The Circle of Reason. 1990. 432p. pap. 8.95 o.p. (*0-14-013368-2*, Penguin Bks.) Viking Penguin.
—The Shadow Lines. 1988. (C). 16.50 (*0-02-516001-X*) South Asia Bks.
—The Shadow Lines. 1990. 256p. pap. 7.95 o.p. (*0-14-011835-7*, Penguin Bks.) Viking Penguin.
Gibson, Tom. A Soldier of India. 1982. 288p. 11.95 o.p. (*0-312-74245-2*) St. Martin's Pr.
Godden, Rumer. Coromandel Sea Change. Set. unabr. ed. 1995. audio 54.95 (*1-56054-915-7*, SAB 027, Sterling Audio Bks.) BBC Audiobooks America.
—Coromandel Sea Change. 1993. pap. 9.00 o.p. (*0-688-12572-7*, Quill) HarperTrade.
—Coromandel Sea Change. 1991. 224p. 18.00 o.p. (*0-688-10397-9*, Morrow, William & Co.) Morrow/Avon.
—Cromartie vs. the God Shiva: Acting Through the Government of India. 1998. 176p. pap. 13.00 o.s.i (*0-688-16343-2*, Quill) HarperTrade.
—Cromartie vs. the God Shiva: Acting Through the Government of India. l.t. ed. 1997. 208p. 22.00 o.p. (*0-688-15550-2*, Morrow, William & Co.) Morrow/Avon.
—Cromartie vs. the God Shiva: Acting Through the Government of India. l.t. ed. 1998. (Basic Ser.). 200p. 29.95 (*0-7862-1347-7*) Thorndike Pr.
—Kingfishers Catch Fire. 1994. 244p. reprint ed. pap. 12.95 o.s.i (*0-915943-81-6*) Milkweed Editions.
—Kingfishers Catch Fire. 1975. pap. 1.50 o.p. (*0-380-00512-3*, 25064, Avon Bks.) Morrow/Avon.
—Kingfishers Catch Fire. unabr. ed. 1981. (J). audio 51.00 (*1-55690-288-3*, 81080E7) Recorded Bks., LLC.
—Kingfishers Catch Fire. lib. bdg. 23.95 (*1-56723-182-9*) Yestermorrow, Inc.
—The Peacock Spring. 1976. 286p. (YA). 10.95 o.p. (*0-670-54558-9*) Viking Penguin.
Gour, Neelum Saran. Winter Companions & Other Stories. 1997. (*0-14-024989-3*) Penguin Bks. Canada, Ltd.
Graham, Winston. Stephanie. 1993. 304p. 19.95 o.p. (*0-88184-939-1*, Carroll & Graf Pubs.) Avalon Publishing Group.
—Stephanie. 2002. 304p. mass mkt. 8.95 (*0-330-32689-9*) Pan Bks. Ltd. GBR. *Dist:* Trafalgar Square.
—Stephanie. l.t. ed. 1993. (Charnwood Library). 416p. 29.99 o.p. (*0-7089-8731-1*, Ulverscroft) Thorpe, F. A. Pubs. GBR. *Dist:* Ulverscroft Large Print Bks., Ltd., Ulverscroft Large Print Canada, Ltd.
Gupta, Sunetra. Memories of Rain: A Novel. 1992. 17.95 o.p. (*0-8021-1448-2*) Grove/Atlantic, Inc.
—A Sin of Color: A Novel of Obsession. 2001. 288p. pap. 15.00 (*1-57071-856-3*, Sourcebooks Landmark) Sourcebooks, Inc.
Hagberg, David. By Dawn's Early Light. E-Book (*0-312-71083-6*, Tor Bks.);Vol. 1. 2003. 336p. 25.95 (*0-7653-0454-6*, Forge Bks.) Doherty, Tom Assocs., LLC.
Hariharan, Githa. In Times of Siege: A Novel. 2004. 224p. pap. 13.00 (*1-4000-3337-3*, Vintage) Knopf Publishing Group.
—In Times of Siege: A Novel. 2003. 224p. 22.00 (*0-375-42239-0*) Knopf, Alfred A. Inc.
Harris, Sarah, adapted by. The Jungle Book: U. K. English. 1995. (Comes to Life Bks.). 16p. (J). (ps-2). (*1-57234-027-4*) YES! Entertainment Corp.
—Le Livre de la Jungle (Jungle Book) 1995. (Comes to Life Bks.). (ENG & FRE.). 16p. (J). (ps-2). (*1-57234-039-8*) YES! Entertainment Corp.
Hesse, Hermann. Siddhartha. 2002. (Shambhala Library). (Illus.). 192p. 14.95 (*1-57062-970-6*) Shambhala Pubns., Inc.
Highwater, Jamake. Rama: A Legend, ERS. 1994. (J). 15.95 o.p. (*0-8050-3052-2*, Holt, Henry & Co. Bks. For Young Readers) Holt, Henry & Co.
Hill, Dorothea. Risa. 2000. 256p. pap. 14.95 (*0-88739-269-5*) Creative Arts Bk. Co.
Hill, Porter. The Bombay Marines. 2000. 288p. mass mkt. 5.99 o.s.i (*0-425-17786-6*) Berkley Publishing Group.
—The Bombay Marines. 1988. (Adam Horne Adventure Ser.). 228p. 17.95 (*0-8027-1048-4*) Walker & Co.
Hirshkowith, Sandra. Premlata & the Festival of Lights. 1999. (Chapter Bks.). (Illus.). 96p. (J). (gr. 2-5). pap. 4.25 (*0-06-442091-4*, Harper Trophy) HarperCollins Children's Bk. Group.
Hosain, Attia. Phoenix Fled. 1989. 22p. pap. 7.95 o.p. (*0-14-016192-9*, Penguin Bks.) Viking Penguin.
Hower, Edward. Shadows & Elephants. 2002. 317p. pap. 14.95 (*0-9679520-3-4*) Leapfrog Pr.
Hughes, Susan. Anything Can Happen. 1992. 176p. 13.50 o.s.i (*0-385-25352-4*) Doubleday Publishing.
Hume, Bem Le. The Seduction of Silence. 2003. (Illus.). 416p. 25.95 (*0-06-052197-X*) HarperSan-Francisco.
Hylton, Sara. Footsteps in the Rain. l.t. ed. 1999. (Magna Large Print Ser.). 512p. (*0-7505-1313-6*) Magna Large Print Bks. GBR. *Dist:* Ulverscroft Large Print Canada, Ltd.
—Footsteps in the Rain. 1998. 368p. 23.95 o.p. (*0-312-19413-7*) St. Martin's Pr.
Iglehart, David. An Atmosphere of Eternity: Stories of India. 2002. (Illus.). 157p. pap. 16.95 (*0-9647783-1-9*) Sunflower Pr.
Irving, John. A Son of the Circus. 1999. 7.99 (*0-345-91561-5*); 1999. pap. 12.95 (*0-345-91562-3*); 1997. 672p. pap. 14.95 (*0-345-41799-2*); 1995. 704p. mass mkt. 7.99 (*0-345-38996-4*); 1995. mass mkt. 7.99 o.s.i (*0-345-39475-5*) Ballantine Bks.
Isherwood, Christopher. A Meeting by the River. 1988. (Michael di Capua Bks.). 192p. pap. 9.95 o.s.i (*0-374-52076-3*) Farrar, Straus & Giroux.
Jaffrey, Madhur. Robi Dobi: The Marvellous Adventures of an Indian Elephant. 1997. (Illus.). 80p. (J). 14.99 o.s.i (*0-8037-2193-5*, Dial Bks. for Young Readers) Penguin Putnam Bks. for Young Readers.
Jekel, Pamela. The Third Jungle Book. 1992. (Illus.). 220p. (J). (ps-12). 19.95 (*1-879373-22-X*) Rinehart, Roberts Pubs.
Jha, Raj Kamal. The Blue Bedspread. 2001. (Harvest Book Ser.). 240p. reprint ed. pap. 13.00 (*0-15-601088-7*, Harvest Bks.) Harcourt Trade Pubs.
—The Blue Bedspread: A Novel. 1999. 228p. 16.95 (*0-330-37385-4*) Picador GBR. *Dist:* Trans-Atlantic Pubns., Inc.
Jhabvala, Ruth Prawer. Amrita or, To Whom She Will. 1989. 237p. pap. 8.95 o.s.i (*0-671-67979-1*, Fireside) Simon & Schuster.
—A Backward Place. 1990. pap. 7.95 o.p. (*0-671-68341-1*, Fireside) Simon & Schuster.
—Esmond in India. 1990. 205p. pap. 7.95 o.s.i (*0-671-68339-X*, Fireside) Simon & Schuster.
—Get Ready for Battle. 1989. pap. 7.95 o.p. (*0-671-68340-3*, Fireside) Simon & Schuster.
—Heat & Dust. 1995. (Longman Literature Ser.). pap. text 50.95 (*0-582-25398-5*) Addison-Wesley Longman, Ltd. GBR. *Dist:* Trans-Atlantic Pubns., Inc.
—Heat & Dust. 1999. 190p. pap. text 14.50 (*1-58243-015-2*, Counterpoint Pr.) Basic Bks.
—Heat & Dust. unabr. ed. 2000. audio 49.95 (*0-7451-2715-0*, SAB 081) Chivers Audio Bks. GBR. *Dist:* BBC Audiobooks America.
—Heat & Dust. 1975. 181 p. (*0-7195-3401-1*) Murray, John Pubs., Ltd.
—Heat & Dust. 1987. 192p. pap. 13.00 (*0-671-64657-5*, Touchstone) Simon & Schuster.
—Heat & Dust. 1988. 26.50 (*0-8446-6335-2*) Smith, Peter Pub., Inc.
—Heat & Dust: Movie Tie in Edition. 1983. 181p. reprint ed. pap. o.p. (*0-06-080641-9*, P641) HarperCollins Pubs.
—The Householder. 2001. (Norton Library). 192p. reprint ed. pap. 13.00 (*0-393-00851-7*) Norton, W. W. & Co., Inc.
—In Search of Love & Beauty. 1983. 256p. 12.95 o.p. (*0-688-02035-6*, Morrow, William & Co.) Morrow/Avon.
—The Nature of Passion. 1990. 191p. pap. 7.95 o.p. (*0-671-68338-1*, Fireside) Simon & Schuster.
—Out of India: Selected Stories. 1999. 288p. pap. text 14.00 (*1-58243-052-7*, Counterpoint Pr.) Basic Bks.
—Out of India: Selected Stories. 1986. 384p. 16.95 o.p. (*0-688-06382-9*, Morrow, William & Co.) Morrow/Avon.
—Out of India: Selected Stories. 1987. 288p. pap. 9.00 o.s.i (*0-671-64221-9*, Touchstone) Simon & Schuster.
—Shards of Memory. 224p. 1996. pap. 11.00 (*0-385-47723-6*); 1995. 22.95 o.s.i (*0-385-47722-8*) Doubleday Publishing.
—Three Continents. 1987. 416p. 18.95 o.p. (*0-688-07184-8*, Morrow, William & Co.) Morrow/Avon.
—Three Continents. 1988. 384p. pap. 7.95 o.p. (*0-671-66362-3*, Fireside) Simon & Schuster.
—Travelers. 1987. 256p. pap. 7.95 o.p. (*0-671-64378-9*, Fireside) Simon & Schuster.
John, Aviott. Sudarshan's Gift. E-Book (*1-84045-040-1*) Online Originals.
Joshi, Ruchir. The Last Jet-Engine Laugh. 2003. (Illus.). 384p. 29.95 o.p. (*0-00-257089-0*) Harper-Collins Pubs. Ltd. GBR. *Dist:* Trafalgar Square.
Kakar, Sudhir. The Ascetic of Desire. 2000. 256p. 25.95 (*1-58567-007-3*) Overlook Pr., The.
—The Ascetic of Desire: A Novel of the Kama Sutra. 2002. 304p. 14.95 (*1-58567-280-7*) Overlook Pr., The.
—Ecstasy. 251p. 2003. pap. 14.95 (*1-58567-458-3*); 2002. 26.95 (*1-58567-210-6*) Overlook Pr., The.
Kamani, Ginu. Junglee Girl. 1995. 208p. 19.95 (*1-879960-41-9*); pap. 11.95 (*1-879960-40-0*) Aunt Lute Bks.
Kanwal, Jaswant S. Dawn of the Blood. 1989. (C). 34.00 (*81-202-0237-6*) Ajanta Pubns/Ajanta Bks. International IND. *Dist:* South Asia Bks.
Kapur, Manju. Difficult Daughters. 1998. 262 p. (*0-14-027862-1*) Viking Penguin.
Kaye, M. M. The Far Pavilions. 1978. 12.95 o.p. (*0-312-28259-1*) St. Martin's Pr.
—The Shadow of the Moon. 1979. 12.95 o.p. (*0-312-71410-6*) St. Martin's Pr.
Keating, H. R. F. Asking Questions. unabr. ed. 1997. audio 54.95 ISIS Audio Bks. GBR. *Dist:* Ulverscroft Large Print Bks., Ltd.
—Asking Questions. 1997. 282p. text 20.95 o.p. (*0-312-15057-1*, Saint Martin's Minotaur) St. Martin's Pr.
—Bats Fly up for Inspector Ghote. 1984. (Inspector Ghote Mystery Ser.). 190p. pap. 7.95 (*0-89733-120-6*) Academy Chicago Pubs., Ltd.
—The Body in the Billiard Room. 1987. 224p. 15.95 o.p. (*0-670-81744-9*) Viking Penguin.
—Body in the Billiard Room. l.t. ed. 1988. (Mainstream Ser.). 19.95 o.p. (*1-85089-133-8*) ISIS Large Print Bks. GBR. *Dist:* Transaction Pubs.
—The Body in the Billiard Room. unabr. ed. 1988. audio 49.00 (*1-55690-064-3*, 88990) Recorded Bks., LLC.
—Breaking & Entering. unabr. ed. 2001. (Inspector Ghote Mystery Ser.). audio 54.95 (*0-7531-0991-3*, 010306) ISIS Audio Bks. GBR. *Dist:* ISIS Publishing.
—Breaking & Entering: An Inspector Ghote Mystery. 2001. 272p. 23.95 (*0-312-26952-8*, Saint Martin's Minotaur) St. Martin's Pr.
—Bribery, Corruption Also. 1999. 256p. 23.95 o.p. (*0-312-20502-3*, Saint Martin's Minotaur) St. Martin's Pr.
—Bribery, Corruption Also. l.t. ed. 1999. (Ulverscroft Large Print Ser.). 368p. 31.99 o.p. (*0-7089-4149-4*, Ulverscroft) Thorpe, F. A. Pubs. GBR. *Dist:* Ulverscroft Large Print Bks., Ltd., Ulverscroft Large Print Canada, Ltd.
—Cheating Death. unabr. ed. 2001. audio 49.95 (*1-85695-835-3*, 940810) ISIS Audio Bks. GBR. *Dist:* Ulverscroft Large Print Bks., Ltd.
—Cheating Death. l.t. ed. 1993. (Magna Large Print Ser.). 352p. o.p. (*0-7505-0480-3*) Magna Large Print Bks. GBR. *Dist:* Ulverscroft Large Print Canada, Ltd.
—Cheating Death. 1994. 176p. 18.95 o.s.i (*0-89296-512-6*) Mysterious Pr.
—Dead on Time. l.t. ed. 1990. 16.95 o.p. (*0-7451-9762-0*, C0078); pap. 15.95 o.p. (*0-7927-0218-2*) BBC Audiobooks America.
—Dead on Time. l.t. ed. 1989. 288p. reprint ed. 19.95 o.p. (*1-85089-283-0*) ISIS Large Print Bks. GBR. *Dist:* Transaction Pubs.
—Dead on Time. 1990. 208p. mass mkt. 4.95 (*0-445-40800-6*, Mysterious Pr. Paperback Bks.) Warner Bks., Inc.
—Dead on Time: An Inspector Ghote Mystery. 1989. 208p. 16.45 o.p. (*0-89296-386-7*) Mysterious Pr.
—Doing Wrong. 1995. 218p. 44.00 o.p. (*0-333-60413-X*); pap. 24.00 (*0-330-34004-2*) Pan Bks. Ltd. GBR. *Dist:* Trans-Atlantic Pubns., Inc.
—Doing Wrong: An Inspector Ghote Novel. 1994. 192p. 20.00 o.s.i (*1-883402-80-8*, Scribner) Simon & Schuster.
—Filmi, Filmi, Inspector Ghote. 1985. (Inspector Ghote Mystery Ser.). 192p. pap. 7.95 (*0-89733-138-9*) Academy Chicago Pubs., Ltd.
—Go West, Inspector Ghote. 1982. pap. 3.95 o.p. (*0-14-006319-6*, Penguin Bks.) Viking Penguin.
—Go West Inspector Ghote. 1981. (Crime Club Ser.). 192p. 10.95 o.p. (*0-385-17683-X*) Doubleday Publishing.
—The Iciest Sin. l.t. ed. 1992. (Magna Large Print Ser.). 323p. 29.99 o.p. (*0-7505-0421-8*) Magna Large Print Bks. GBR. *Dist:* Ulverscroft Large Print Bks., Ltd., Ulverscroft Large Print Canada, Ltd.
—The Iciest Sin. 1990. 176p. 18.45 o.p. (*0-89296-427-8*) Mysterious Pr.
—The Iciest Sin. unabr. ed. 1993. audio 42.00 (*1-55690-891-1*, 93333) Recorded Bks., LLC.
—The Iciest Sin. 1991. 192p. mass mkt. 4.99 o.s.i (*0-446-40062-9*, Mysterious Pr. Paperback Bks.) Warner Bks., Inc.
—Inspector Ghote Breaks an Egg. 1985. (Inspector Ghote Mystery Ser.). 192p. reprint ed. pap. 7.95 (*0-89733-177-X*) Academy Chicago Pubs., Ltd.
—Inspector Ghote Breaks an Egg. 1997. pap. text o.p. (*0-17-556422-1*) Addison-Wesley Longman, Inc.
—Inspector Ghote Breaks an Egg. 1974. pap. 1.25 o.p. (*0-14-003839-6*) Penguin Group (USA) Inc.
—Inspector Ghote Caught in Meshes. 1985. (Inspector Ghote Mystery Ser.). 224p. reprint ed. pap. 7.95 (*0-89733-178-8*) Academy Chicago Pubs., Ltd.
—Inspector Ghote Draws a Line. 1985. (Inspector Ghote Mystery Ser.). 195p. pap. 7.95 (*0-89733-139-7*) Academy Chicago Pubs., Ltd.
—Inspector Ghote Draws a Line. 2002. 192p. (*0-7540-8613-5*, Black Dagger) BBC Audiobooks America.
—Inspector Ghote Draws a Line. 1979. 7.95 o.p. (*0-385-14873-9*) Doubleday Publishing.
—Inspector Ghote Hunts the Peacock. 1985. (Inspector Ghote Mystery Ser.). 192p. reprint ed. pap. 7.95 (*0-89733-179-6*) Academy Chicago Pubs., Ltd.
—Inspector Ghote Hunts the Peacock. l.t. ed. 1992. pap. 20.95 o.p. (*0-7927-1136-X*, CS0303); 1991. 22.95 o.p. (*0-7927-1135-1*, CH0232) BBC Audiobooks America.
—Inspector Ghote Plays a Joker. 1984. (Inspector Ghote Mystery Ser.). 189p. reprint ed. pap. 5.95 o.s.i (*0-89733-096-X*) Academy Chicago Pubs., Ltd.

—Inspector Ghote Trusts the Heart. 1983. (Inspector Ghote Mystery Ser.). 250p. reprint ed. pap. 5.95 o.s.i (*0-89733-083-8*) Academy Chicago Pubs., Ltd.

—The Perfect Murder. 1997. (Inspector Ghote Mystery Ser.). 256p. pap. 10.95 (*0-89733-078-1*) Academy Chicago Pubs., Ltd.

—The Perfect Murder. 2003. 224p. 21.95 (*0-7540-8635-6*, Black Dagger); 1991. 22.95 o.p. (*0-7927-0980-2*, CH0156); 1991. pap. 20.95 o.p. (*0-7927-0981-0*, CS0255) BBC Audiobooks America.

—The Perfect Murder. unabr. ed. 1995. audio 44.95 (*0-7861-0813-4*, 1636) Blackstone Audio Bks., Inc.

—The Sheriff of Bombay. 1984. (Crime Club Ser.). 192p. 11.95 o.p. (*0-385-19461-7*) Doubleday Publishing.

—Under a Monsoon Cloud. l.t. ed. 1988. (Mainstream Ser.). 283p. reprint ed. lib. bdg. 18.95 o.p. (*1-85089-233-4*) ISIS Large Print Bks. GBR. *Dist:* Transaction Pubs.

—Under a Monsoon Cloud. unabr. ed. 1990. audio 42.00 (*1-55690-536-X*, 90040) Recorded Bks., LLC.

—Under a Monsoon Cloud. 224p. 1987. pap. 3.95 o.p. (*0-14-009209-9*, Penguin Bks.); 1986. 15.95 o.p. (*0-670-80367-7*) Viking Penguin.

Kerstan, Lynn. The Golden Leopard. 2002. 384p. mass mkt. 6.50 (*0-451-41057-2*, Onyx) NAL.

Kesavan, Mukul. Looking Through Glass. 1995. (C). 19.50 (*0-02-516006-0*) Dayal, Ravi Pub. IND. *Dist:* South Asia Bks.

—Looking Through Glass. 1995. 375p. 25.00 o.p. (*0-374-19085-2*) Farrar, Straus & Giroux.

King, Laurie R. The Game. 2004. 384p. 23.95 (*0-553-80194-5*) Bantam Bks.

Kipling, Rudyard. Kim. 1998. pap. 4.99 o.p. (*1-57840-185-2*) Acclaim Bks.

—Kim. 23.95 (*0-89190-271-6*) Amereon, Ltd.

—Kim. 1997. 460 p. (*81-206-1148-9*) Asian Educational Services.

—Kim, Set. 1995. audio 47.95 (*1-55685-371-8*) Audio Bk. Contractors, Inc.

—Kim. unabr. ed. 1999. audio 34.95 (*1-57270-112-9*, F81112u, Cover to Cover Classics) Audio Partners Publishing Corp.

—Kim. 1997. (Bantam Classics Ser.). 288p. mass mkt. 4.95 (*0-553-21332-6*, Bantam Classics) Bantam Bks.

—Kim. unabr. ed. 1982. audio 56.95 (*0-7861-0533-X*, 2030) Blackstone Audio Bks., Inc.

—Kim. unabr. collector's ed. 1998. (J). audio 64.00 (*0-7366-4153-X*, 4656) Books on Tape, Inc.

—Kim. reprint ed. lib. bdg. 98.00 (*0-7426-2848-5*) Classic Bks.

—Kim. 1999. 320p. pap. text 2.99 (*0-8125-6575-4*, Tor Classics) Doherty, Tom Assocs., LLC.

—Kim. abr. ed. 1986. (YA). (gr. 7-9). audio 29.95 o.p. (*0-88646-819-1*, R 7139); Set. 1990. audio 9.99 (*1-55204-003-8*, 393857) Durkin Hayes Publishing Ltd.

—Kim. l.t. ed. 1995. (*0-7838-1353-8*, Macmillan Reference USA) Gale Group.

—Kim. 1989. audio 48.00 Jimcin Recordings.

—Kim. 1995. 17.00 (*0-679-44360-6*) Knopf, Alfred A. Inc.

—Kim. 1984. mass mkt. 2.50 o.p. (*0-451-52144-7*); 288p. mass mkt. 3.95 o.s.i (*0-451-52549-3*) NAL. (Signet Classics).

—Kim. abr. ed. 1994. audio 13.98 (*962-634-518-7*, NA201814, Naxos AudioBooks) Naxos of America, Inc.

—Kim. 1998. (Twelve-Point Ser.). 330p. reprint ed. lib. bdg. 25.00 (*1-58287-043-8*) North Bks.

—Kim. 2002. (Critical Editions Ser.). (Illus.). x, 458p. (C). pap. text 11.40 (*0-393-96650-X*, Norton Paperbacks) Norton, W. W. & Co., Inc.

—Kim. Sandison, Alan, ed. & intro. by. (Oxford World's Classics Ser.). 1998. 352p. pap. 5.95 (*0-19-283513-0*); 1987. 344p. pap. 3.95 o.p. (*0-19-281651-9*) Oxford Univ. Pr., Inc.

—Kim. 1979. 288p. (gr. 5-9). mass mkt. 2.95 o.s.i (*0-440-94500-3*, Laurel Leaf) Random Hse. Children's Bks.

—Kim. 1992. (BCL1-PR English Literature Ser.). 345p. reprint ed. lib. bdg. 89.00 (*0-7812-7581-4*) Reprint Services Corp.

—Kim. audio 10.95 (*0-8045-1065-2*, SAC 1065) Spoken Arts, Inc.

—Kim. l.t. ed. 1983. (Charnwood Large Print Ser.). 448p. 29.99 (*0-7089-8152-6*, Ulverscroft) Thorpe, F. A. Pubs. GBR. *Dist:* Ulverscroft Large Print Bks., Ltd., Ulverscroft Large Print Canada, Ltd.

—Kim. 1999. (Illus.). 9.04 (*0-606-18645-X*); 1983. 10.00 (*0-606-02458-1*) Turtleback Bks.

—Kim. Royle, Trevor, ed. 1994. pap. 4.95 (*0-460-87408-X*, Everyman's Classic Library in Paperback) Tuttle Publishing.

—Kim. 1983. (Madhuban Abridged Classics Ser.). 178p. text 6.95 o.p. (*0-7069-1838-X*); pap. text 3.95 o.p. (*0-7069-5151-4*) Vikas Publishing Hse. Private, Ltd. IND. *Dist:* South Asia Bks.

—Kim. 1987. pap. 2.95 o.p. (*0-14-043281-7*, Penguin Bks.) Viking Penguin.

—Kim. Said, Edward W., ed. & intro. by. 1987. (Twentieth Century Classics Ser.). 320p. 7.00 (*0-14-018352-3*, 433, Penguin Classics) Viking Penguin.

—Kim. (Classics Library). pap. 3.95 (*1-85326-099-1*, 0991WW) Wordsworth Editions, Ltd. GBR. *Dist:* Combined Publishing.

—Kipling: Short Stories, Vol. 1. Rutherford, Andrew, ed. 1977. pap. 5.95 o.p. (*0-14-003281-9*, Penguin Bks.) Viking Penguin.

—Kipling's Kingdom: Twenty-Five of Rudyard Kipling's Best Indian Stories — Known & Unknown. 1987. (Illus.). 288p. 25.00 o.p. (*0-7181-2570-3*) Viking Penguin.

—Life's Handicap. 2001. (Collected Works of Rudyard Kipling). (Illus.). 351p. reprint ed. pap. text 28.00 (*0-7426-5492-3*) Classic Bks.

—Life's Handicap. 2001. 372p. per. 24.95 (*1-58963-494-2*) Fredonia Bks.

—The Maltese Cat. 1991. (Short Story Library). (Illus.). 48p. (YA). (gr. 4 up). lib. bdg. 13.95 o.p. (*0-88682-475-3*, Creative Education) Creative Co., The.

—The Mark of the Beast & Other Horror Tales. Joshi, S. T., ed. 2000. (Horror Classics Ser.). 192p. pap. 8.95 (*0-486-41429-9*) Dover Pubns., Inc.

—Mulvaney Stories. 1977. (Short Story Index Reprint Ser.). reprint ed. 19.95 (*0-8369-4045-8*) Ayer Co. Pubs., Inc.

—Mulvaney Stories. 2001. 236p. per. 24.95 (*1-58963-139-0*) International Law & Taxation Pubs.

—Picking up Gold & Silver: Stories. 1990. 281p. 18.95 o.p. (*0-312-04686-3*) St. Martin's Pr.

—Plain Tales from the Hills. Rutherford, Andrew, ed. & intro. by. 1987. (Oxford World's Classics Ser.). 314p. pap. 7.95 o.p. (*0-19-281652-7*) Oxford Univ. Pr., Inc.

—The Second Jungle Book. reprint ed. lib. bdg. 98.00 (*0-7426-2836-1*); 2001. (Illus.). pap. text 28.00 (*0-7426-7836-9*) Classic Bks.

—The Second Jungle Book. Robson, Wallace, ed. & intro. by. 1987. (Oxford World's Classics Ser.). xxxviii, 215p. pap. 4.95 o.p. (*0-19-281655-1*) Oxford Univ. Pr., Inc.

—The Two Jungle Books, 2 Vols. 1977. (Short Story Index Reprint Ser.). (J). reprint ed. 32.95 (*0-8369-3818-6*) Ayer Co. Pubs., Inc.

—The Works of Rudyard Kipling. 2002. Vol. I. 452p. per. 23.99 (*1-58827-815-8*); Vol. I. 452p. 28.99 (*1-58827-814-X*); Vol. II. 548p. per. 25.99 (*1-58827-817-4*); Vol. II. 548p. 29.99 (*1-58827-816-6*) IndyPublish.com.

—The Works of Rudyard Kipling. 2001. (Poetry Library). 880p. pap. 6.95 (*1-85326-405-9*) Wordsworth Editions, Ltd. GBR. *Dist:* Advanced Global Distribution Services.

—The Works of Rudyard Kipling: Jungle Book, Second Jungle Book Kim, Just So Stories. 1995. (Classic Bonded Leather Ser.). 800p. (YA). 24.95 o.p. (*0-681-10374-4*) Borders Pr.

Kirchner, Bharti. Darjeeling. E-Book 24.95 (*0-312-70733-9*); 2002. 320p. 24.95 (*0-312-28642-2*) St. Martin's Pr.

—Sharmila's Book. 1999. 352p. 24.95 o.p. (*0-525-94368-4*) Dutton/Plume.

—Sharmila's Book: A Novel. 2000. 400p. pap. 12.95 o.s.i (*0-452-27884-8*, Plume) Dutton/Plume.

—Shiva Dancing. 336p. 1999. pap. 12.95 o.s.i (*0-452-27882-1*, Plume); 1998. 23.95 o.p. (*0-525-94367-6*) Dutton/Plume.

Kohli, Narendra. Initiation. 1997. (Illus.). (*81-86798-02-1*) Creative Bk. Co. IND. *Dist:* South Asia Bks.

Kumar, Shiv. Contemporary Indian Short Stories in English. 1991. 16.00 (*81-7201-059-1*) National Sahitya Akademi IND. *Dist:* South Asia Bks.

Kumar, Shiv K. River with Three Banks: The Partition of India: Agony & Ecstasy. 1998. 214p. pap. 14.00 (*81-7476-219-1*) UBS Pubs. Distributions, Ltd. IND. *Dist:* South Asia Bks.

Kunzru, Hari. The Impressionist. 2002. 416p. 24.95 o.s.i (*0-525-94642-X*, Dutton); 2003. 480p. reprint ed. pap. 14.00 (*0-452-28397-3*) Dutton/Plume.

Laity, Sally & Crawford, Dianna. Torch of Triumph. 1997. (Freedom's Holy Light Ser.: Vol. 6). 415p. pap. 10.99 o.p. (*0-8423-1417-2*) Tyndale Hse. Pubs.

Lasky, Kathryn. Jahanara: Princess of Princesses. 2002. (Royal Diaries Ser.). 192p. (J). (gr. 4-8). 10.95 (*0-439-22350-4*, Scholastic Pr.) Scholastic, Inc.

Le Hunte, Bem. The Seduction of Silence. 2004. 416p. pap. 14.95 (*0-06-057368-6*) HarperSanFrancisco.

—The Seduction of Silence. 2001. 433p. (*0-14-100715-X*) Penguin Group (USA) Inc.

Liu, Aimee E. Flash House. 2004. 472p. pap. 13.95 (*0-446-69121-6*); 2003. (Illus.). 464p. 24.95 (*0-446-53097-2*) Warner Bks., Inc.

Lucas, Russell. Evenings at Mongini's: And Other Stories. 1991. 264p. 18.95 o.p. (*0-671-72746-X*) Summit Bks.

MacNeil, Duncan. By Command of the Viceroy. 1975. 224p. 8.95 o.p. (*0-312-11060-X*) St. Martin's Pr.

—By Command of the Viceroy. l.t. ed. 1979. (Ulverscroft Large Print Ser.). 29.99 o.p. (*0-7089-0341-X*, Ulverscroft) Thorpe, F. A. Pubs. GBR. *Dist:* Ulverscroft Large Print Bks., Ltd., Ulverscroft Large Print Canada, Ltd.

—Charge of Cowardice. 1978. 8.95 o.p. (*0-312-13006-6*) St. Martin's Pr.

—Cunningham's Revenge. l.t. ed. 1986. lib. bdg. 17.95 o.p. (*0-89340-949-9*, 113) BBC Audiobooks America.

—Cunningham's Revenge. 1985. 192p. 13.95 o.s.i (*0-8027-0847-1*) Walker & Co.

—The Red Daniel. 1977. reprint ed. pap. 1.50 o.s.i (*0-8439-0477-1*) Dorchester Publishing Co., Inc.

—The Restless Frontier. 1980. 8.95 o.p. (*0-312-67782-0*) St. Martin's Pr.

—The Train at Bundarbar. 1986. 192p. 15.95 o.s.i (*0-8027-0895-1*) Walker & Co.

—Wolf in the Fold. 1977. 8.95 o.p. (*0-312-88637-3*) St. Martin's Pr.

Macwan, Joseph. The Stepchild: Angaliyat. Kothari, Rita, tr. 2004. 288p. 18.95 (*0-19-566624-0*) Oxford Univ. Pr., Inc.

Mahindra, Indira. The End Play. 1994. (Emerging Voices Ser.). 192p. 24.95 (*1-56656-175-2*); pap. 11.95 (*1-56656-166-3*) Interlink Publishing Group, Inc.

Mallabarman, Adwaita. A River Called Titash. Bardhan, Kalpana, tr. & afterword by by. 1993. (Voices from Asia Ser.: Vol. 7). 280p. pap. text 25.00 (*0-520-08050-5*) Univ. of California Pr.

Mallinson, Allan. Honorable Company: A Novel of India Before the Raj. 2001. 320p. pap. 13.95 (*0-553-38044-3*) Bantam Bks.

Mandava, Bhargavi C. Where the Oceans Meet. 1996. 272p. (Orig.). 22.95 o.p. (*1-878067-86-9*, Seal Pr.) Avalon Publishing Group.

Mann, Paul. The Burning Ghats. (George Sansi Mystery Ser.). 1997. 336p. mass mkt. 5.99 o.s.i (*0-8041-1550-8*, Ivy Bks.); 1996. 368p. 23.00 o.s.i (*0-449-90770-8*, Fawcett) Ballantine Bks.

—The Ganja Coast. 1995. (George Sansi Mystery Ser.). mass mkt. 5.99 o.s.i (*0-8041-1419-6*, Ivy Bks.); 336p. 22.50 o.s.i (*0-449-90769-4*, Fawcett) Ballantine Bks.

—Season of the Monsoon. (George Sansi Mystery Ser.). 1994. mass mkt. 5.99 o.s.i (*0-8041-1259-2*, Ivy Bks.); 1993. 352p. 20.00 o.s.i (*0-449-90768-6*, Fawcett) Ballantine Bks.

Markandaya, Kamala. Nectar in a Sieve. 2002. (EMC Masterpiece Series Access Editions). (Illus.). xix, 219p. (YA). 10.95 (*0-8219-2410-9*, 35366) EMC/Paradigm Publishing.

—Nectar in a Sieve. 2002. 208p. mass mkt. 6.95 (*0-451-52823-9*, Signet Classics); 1996. pap., tchr.'s training gde. ed. (*0-451-52631-7*, Signet Bks.); 1970. mass mkt. 0.95 o.p. (*0-451-04510-6*, Signet Bks.); 1968. mass mkt. 0.75 o.p. (*0-451-03566-6*, Signet Bks.); 1956. mass mkt. 1.25 o.p. (*0-451-05955-7*, Signet Bks.); 1956. mass mkt. 0.50 o.p. (*0-451-01899-0*, Signet Bks.); 1956. mass mkt. 0.35 o.p. (*0-451-01336-0*, Signet Bks.); 1956. mass mkt. 0.60 o.p. (*0-451-02359-5*, Signet Bks.); 1956. 192p. (C). mass mkt. 5.99 o.s.i (*0-451-16836-4*, AE2291); 1956. mass mkt. 1.75 o.p. (*0-451-08990-1*, Signet Bks.); 1956. mass mkt. 1.95 o.p. (*0-451-09646-0*, Signet Bks.); 1956. mass mkt. 1.50 o.p. (*0-451-07482-3*, Signet Bks.); 1956. mass mkt. 2.50 o.p. (*0-451-12291-7*, Signet Bks.); 1956. mass mkt. 2.95 o.p. (*0-451-13460-5*, Signet Bks.); 1956. mass mkt. 3.50 o.p. (*0-451-15347-2*, Signet Bks.); 1956. mass mkt. 4.50 o.p. (*0-451-16318-4*, Signet Bks.); 1956. mass mkt. 3.95 o.p. (*0-451-15647-1*, Signet Bks.) NAL.

—Nectar in a Sieve. 1982. 12.04 (*0-606-01922-7*) Turtleback Bks.

Mason, Philip. The Wild Sweet Witch. 1990. 240p. pap. 7.95 o.p. (*0-14-011464-5*, Penguin Bks.) Viking Penguin.

Masters, John. Bhowani Junction. 1987. 450p. pap. 4.50 o.p. (*0-88184-310-5*, Carroll & Graf Pubs.) Avalon Publishing Group.

—Nightrunners of Bengal. 1988. 350p. pap. 4.95 o.p. (*0-88184-355-5*, Carroll & Graf Pubs.) Avalon Publishing Group.

—Nightrunners of Bengal. 1969. mass mkt. 0.95 o.s.i (*0-345-21587-7*) Ballantine Bks.

—Nightrunners of Bengal. l.t. ed. 1980. (Ulverscroft Large Print Ser.). 29.99 o.p. (*0-7089-0419-X*, Ulverscroft) Thorpe, F. A. Pubs. GBR. *Dist:* Ulverscroft Large Print Bks., Ltd., Ulverscroft Large Print Canada, Ltd.

McCallum, Dawood Ali. The Lords of Alijah. 1997. (*0-670-87657-7*, Viking) Viking Penguin.

McCutchan, Philip. The First Command. 1999. 315p. (*0-7540-3471-2*); pap. (*0-7540-3472-0*) BBC Audiobooks America.

—The First Command. 1998. 192p. 22.00 o.p. (*0-7278-5290-6*) Severn Hse. Pubs., Ltd.

—The First Command. l.t. ed. 1999. (General Ser.). 315p. pap. 23.95 (*0-7862-1589-5*) Thorndike Pr.

—Honour & Empire. 1999. 224p. 25.00 (*0-7278-2293-4*) Severn Hse. Pubs., Ltd.

—Honour & Empire. l.t. ed. 2000. (General Ser.). 324p. pap. 23.95 (*0-7862-2303-0*); (*0-7540-3987-0*); (*0-7540-3988-9*) Thorndike Pr.

—Ogilvie & the Mem'Sahib. 2002. 224p. 25.99 (*0-7278-5827-0*) Severn Hse. Pubs., Ltd.

—Soldier of the Queen. 1998. 224p. 24.00 o.p. (*0-7278-5345-7*) Severn Hse. Pubs., Ltd.

McIlwraith, Hiro. Shahnaz. 2000. 365p. pap. (*0-88982-188-7*) Oolichan Bks.

McNeill, Elisabeth. Unforgettable. 288p. 25.99 (*0-7278-5761-4*); 29.99 (*0-7278-7209-5*) Severn Hse. Pubs., Ltd.

Meer, Ameena. Bombay Talkie. 1999. 280p. pap. (*1-85242-707-8*) Serpent's Tail Ltd.

—Bombay Talkie. Silverberg, Ira, ed. 1999. 280p. pap. o.p. (*1-85242-325-0*) Serpent's Tail Ltd.

Mehta, Gita. Raj. unabr. ed. 1999. audio 83.95 (*0-7861-1608-0*, 2436) Blackstone Audio Bks., Inc.

—Raj. 1991. 4.99 o.p. (*0-517-07188-6*) Random Hse. Value Publishing.

—Raj. 1989. 19.95 o.p. (*0-671-43248-6*, Simon & Schuster) Simon & Schuster.

—Raj: A Novel. 1991. 480p. pap. 15.95 (*0-449-90566-7*, Fawcett) Ballantine Bks.

—A River Sutra. 1994. 304p. pap. 13.00 (*0-679-75247-1*, Vintage) Knopf Publishing Group.

—A River Sutra. abr. ed. 1994. audio 17.00 o.s.i (*0-679-43200-0*, 391481, RH Audio) Random Hse. Audio Publishing Group.

Mehta, Ved. Three Stories of the Raj. 1986. (Illus.). 64p. 85.00 o.p. (*0-85967-722-2*) Ashgate Publishing, Ltd. GBR. *Dist:* Ashgate Publishing Co.

Metzer, Patty. Lights of the Veil. 2003. (Palisades Pure Romance Ser.). 368p. pap. 11.99 (*1-57673-627-X*) Multnomah Pubs., Inc.

Meyers, Jeffrey, intro. Best Short Stories of Rudyard Kipling. 1987. 400p. mass mkt. 4.50 o.p. (*0-451-52140-4*, Signet Classics) NAL.

Mishra, Pankaj. The Romantics. 2001. 288p. reprint ed. pap. 13.00 (*0-385-72080-7*, Knopf Bks. for Young Readers) Random Hse. Children's Bks.

—The Romantics. l.t. ed. 2000. (Basic Ser.). 368p. 27.95 (*0-7862-3001-0*) Thorndike Pr.

—The Romantics: A Novel. 2000. 277p. (*81-86939-05-9*) RST Indiaink Publishing.

Mistry, Rohinton. Family Matters: A Novel. 2001. 352p. (*0-571-19427-3*); pap. (*0-571-20421-X*) Faber & Faber, Inc.

—Family Matters: A Novel. 2003. 448p. pap. 14.95 (*0-375-70342-X*, Vintage) Knopf Publishing Group.

—Family Matters: A Novel. 2002. 448p. 26.00 (*0-375-40373-6*) Knopf, Alfred A. Inc.

—A Fine Balance: A Novel, 2 pts. unabr. ed. 2001. Pt. 1 & 2. audio 160.00 (*0-7366-8442-5*); Pt. 2. audio 56.00 (*0-7366-8453-0*) Books on Tape, Inc.

—A Fine Balance: A Novel. l.t. ed. 2002. 32.95 (*0-7862-4196-9*) Gale Group.

—A Fine Balance: A Novel. 2001. 624p. pap. 15.00 (*1-4000-3065-X*, Vintage) Knopf Publishing Group.

—A Fine Balance: A Novel. 1997. 624p. pap. 15.00 (*0-679-77645-1*) Knopf, Alfred A. Inc.

—A Fine Balance: A Novel. 2001. 624p. 26.95 (*0-375-41481-9*, Knopf Bks. for Young Readers) Random Hse. Children's Bks.

—A Fine Balance: A Novel. 1996. 640p. 26.00 o.s.i (*0-679-44608-7*) Random Hse., Inc.

—A Fine Balance: A Novel. l.t. ed. 2002. pap. 13.95 (*0-7862-4197-7*) Thorndike Pr.

—Such a Long Journey. 1992. 352p. pap. 14.00 (*0-679-73871-1*, Vintage) Knopf Publishing Group.

—Such a Long Journey. 1993. 424p. mass mkt. (*0-7710-9897-9*) McClelland & Stewart.

—Swimming Lessons: And Other Stories from Firozsha Baag. 1989. 16.95 o.p. (*0-395-49862-7*) Houghton Mifflin Co.

—Swimming Lessons: And Other Stories from Firozsha Baag. 1997. 256p. pap. 13.00 (*0-679-77632-X*) Random Hse., Inc.

—Swimming Lessons: And Other Stories from Firozsha Baag. 1990. 256p. pap. 7.95 o.p. (*0-14-012807-7*, Penguin Bks.) Viking Penguin.

Mohanty, Prafulla K. Stories from Sarala's Mahabharat. 1990. 205p. text 27.50 (*0-7069-4589-1*) Vikas Publishing Hse. Private, Ltd. IND. *Dist:* South Asia Bks.

Mouse Works Staff. El Libro de la Selva. 1996. (Spanish Classics Ser.).Tr. of Jungle Book. (SPA.). 96p. (J). 7.98 o.p. (*1-57082-511-4*) Mouse Works.

Moynihan, Maura. Yoga Hotel: Stories. 2003. 304p. pap. 13.95 (*0-06-055932-2*, ReganBooks) HarperTrade.

Mukherjee, Bharati. Desirable Daughters: A Novel. 2003. mass mkt. (*0-7868-8976-4*) Disney Pr.

—Desirable Daughters: A Novel. 2003. pap. 13.95 (*0-7868-8515-7*); 2002. 320p. 24.95 (*0-7868-6598-9*) Hyperion Pr.

—The Holder of the World. 1994. 304p. reprint ed. pap. 13.95 (*0-449-90966-2*, Fawcett) Ballantine Bks.

—Jasmine. audio 8.95 American Audio Prose Library, Inc.

—Jasmine. 1990. 244p. mass mkt. 6.99 o.s.i (*0-449-21923-2*, Fawcett) Ballantine Bks.
—Jasmine. 1989. 228p. 17.95 o.p. (*0-8021-1032-0*); 1999. 256p. reprint ed. pap. 12.00 (*0-8021-3630-3*, Grove Pr.) Grove/Atlantic, Inc.
—The Middleman & Other Stories. 1988. 206p. 16.95 o.p. (*0-8021-1031-2*) Grove/Atlantic, Inc.
—The Tiger's Daughter. 1996. 248p. pap. 11.00 o.s.i (*0-449-91270-1*); 1991. mass mkt. 5.99 o.s.i (*0-449-22100-8*) Ballantine Bks. (Fawcett).
—The Tiger's Daughter. 1987. 224p. pap. 6.95 o.p. (*0-14-009301-X*, Penguin Bks.) Viking Penguin.
Mundy, Talbot. King of the Khyber Rifles. 1976. 27.95 (*0-8488-0837-1*) Amereon, Ltd.
—King of the Khyber Rifles. 1985. 256p. pap. 3.95 o.p. (*0-88184-169-2*, Carroll & Graf Pubs.) Avalon Publishing Group.
—King of the Khyber Rifles. 1983. 461p. reprint ed. lib. bdg. 17.95 o.p. (*0-89966-458-X*) Buccaneer Bks., Inc.
Murali, Janaki. The Colour of Dawn. 2002. xiv, 198p. (*81-7223-439-2*) HarperCollins Pubs. India.
Murari, T. N. The Imperial Agent. 1989. 19.95 o.p. (*0-312-02933-0*) St. Martin's Pr.
—The Last Victory. 1991. 4.99 o.p. (*0-517-07812-0*) Random Hse. Value Publishing.
—The Last Victory. 1990. 336p. 19.95 o.p. (*0-312-03857-7*) St. Martin's Pr.
Myers, L. H. The Root & the Flower. 2001. (New York Review Books Classics Ser.). 153p. pap. 16.95 (*0-940322-60-9*) New York Review of Bks., Inc., The.
—The Root & the Flower. 1986. (Twentieth Century Classics Ser.). 583p. pap. 7.95 o.p. (*0-19-281911-9*) Oxford Univ. Pr., Inc.
Myers, Lucas. Dolma Ling: A Pilgrim's Progress Across the Himalayas. 1997. (Illus.). (*81-86230-07-6*) Paljor Pubns. IND. *Dist:* South Asia Bks.
Naik, Pundalik N. The Upheaval. Pai, Vidya, tr. 2002. 276p. text 19.95 (*0-19-566039-0*) Oxford Univ. Pr., Inc.
Naipaul, V. S. A Bend in the River. 1989. (International Ser.). 288p. pap. 13.00 (*0-679-72202-5*, Vintage) Knopf Publishing Group.
—A Bend in the River. 1979. 13.95 o.s.i (*0-394-50573-5*) Knopf, Alfred A. Inc.
—A Bend in the River. 1980. pap. 5.95 o.p. (*0-394-74314-8*) Random Hse., Inc.
—A Bend in the River. 1992. 26.75 (*0-8446-6631-9*) Smith, Peter Pub., Inc.
—A Bend in the River. l.t. ed. 1999. (Perennial Bestsellers Ser.). 439p. 27.95 (*0-7838-8616-0*) Thorndike Pr.
Naipaul, V. S. & Hardwick, Elizabeth. A Bend in the River. 1997. (Modern Library Ser.). 448p. 17.95 o.s.i (*0-679-60267-4*) Random Hse., Inc.
Nair, Anita. The Better Man. 2000. 288p. 24.00 (*0-312-25311-7*) Picador.
Nair, Meera. Video: Stories. 2003. 208p. reprint ed. pap. 12.00 (*0-385-72103-X*) Doubleday Publishing.
Namjoshi, Suniti. Goja: An Autobiographical Myth. 2001. 160p. pap. 13.95 (*1-875559-97-3*) Spinifex Pr. AUS. *Dist:* Stackpole Bks.
Narang, Saloni. The Coloured Bangles & Other Stories. 1984. 78p. (C). 17.00 (*0-89410-403-9*, Three Continents) Rienner, Lynne Pubs., Inc.
Narayan, R. K. The Bachelor of Arts. 1980. 268p. pap. 15.00 (*0-226-56833-4*); lib. bdg. 13.00 o.s.i (*0-226-56832-6*) Univ. of Chicago Pr.
—The English Teacher. 1980. 184p. pap. 15.00 (*0-226-56835-0*); lib. bdg. 9.95 o.p. (*0-226-56834-2*) Univ. of Chicago Pr.
—The Grandmother's Tale & Selected Stories. 1994. 320p. 24.95 o.p. (*0-670-85220-1*, Viking) Viking Penguin.
—Malgudi Days. 1989. 256p. pap. 7.95 o.p. (*0-14-011792-X*) Penguin Group (USA) Inc.
—Malgudi Days. (Twentieth Century Classics Ser.). 1995. 256p. pap. 12.95 (*0-14-018543-7*, Penguin Classics); 1985. 240p. pap. 6.95 o.p. (*0-14-006910-0*, Penguin Bks.); 1982. (Illus.). 224p. 14.95 o.p. (*0-670-45178-9*) Viking Penguin.
—Malgudi Days II. 1999. pap. (*0-670-80632-3*) Viking Penguin.
—Mr. Sampath: The Printer of Malgudi. 1957. 276p. 6.00 o.p. (*0-87013-025-0*) Michigan State Univ. Pr.
—Mr. Sampath: The Printer of Malgudi. 1981. 220p. (C). pap. 12.00 (*0-226-56839-3*); lib. bdg. 15.00 o.s.i (*0-226-56838-5*) Univ. of Chicago Pr.
—The Painter of Signs. 1990. 144p. pap. 7.95 o.p. (*0-14-011864-0*) Penguin Group (USA) Inc.
—The Painter of Signs. (Twentieth Century Classics Ser.). 1993. 144p. 14.00 (*0-14-018549-6*, Penguin Classics); 1983. pap. 5.95 o.p. (*0-14-006259-9*, Penguin Bks.); 1976. 192p. 11.95 o.p. (*0-670-53567-2*) Viking Penguin.
—Swami & Friends. 192p. 1994. lib. bdg. 13.00 o.s.i (*0-226-56829-6*); 1980. pap. 14.00 (*0-226-56831-8*) Univ. of Chicago Pr.
—Talkative Man. (Penguin Twentieth-Century Classics Ser.). 128p. 1994. pap. 9.95 o.s.i (*0-14-018546-1*, Penguin Classics); 1987. 15.95 o.p. (*0-670-81341-9*) Viking Penguin.
—A Tiger for Malgudi. 1983. 176p. 14.75 o.p. (*0-670-71260-4*) Viking Penguin.
—Under the Banyan Tree & Other Stories. 1985. 224p. 16.95 o.p. (*0-670-80452-5*) Viking Penguin.
—The World of Nagaraj. 1990. 256p. 18.95 o.p. (*0-670-83132-8*) Viking Penguin.
Norbu, Jamyang. Sherlock Holmes - The Missing Years: The Adventures of the Great Detective in India & Tibet. 2001. 288p. 23.95 (*1-58234-132-X*) Bloomsbury Publishing.
O'Brian, Patrick. Hussein: An Entertainment, 2 vols. 2nd ed. 1999. 239p. (*0-7123-1109-2*); (*0-7123-1115-7*) British Library Document Supply Ctr.
—Hussein: An Entertainment. 2001. 288p. pap. 13.00 (*0-393-32181-9*, Norton Paperbacks); 2000. 239p. 23.95 (*0-393-04919-1*) Norton, W. W. & Co., Inc.
Osman, Shaukat. Janani. 1994. (Asian Writers Ser.). 213p. pap. 9.95 (*0-435-95083-5*, 95083) Heinemann.
Owenson, Sydney. The Missionary: An Indian Tale. Wright, Julia M., ed. 2002. (Broadview Literary Texts Ser.). 337p. (*1-55111-263-9*) Broadview Pr.
Paniker, K. Ayyappa, ed. Malayalam Short Stories: An Anthology. 1982. 175p. text 17.95 o.p. (*0-7069-1297-7*) Vikas Publishing Hse. Private, Ltd. IND. *Dist:* South Asia Bks.
Parekh, Sameer. Stealing the Ambassador. 288p. 2002. 23.00 (*0-7432-1429-3*); 2003. reprint ed. pap. 13.00 (*0-7432-1430-7*) Simon & Schuster. (Free Pr.).
Payne, Peggy. Sister India. 2002. 320p. reprint ed. pap. 14.00 (*1-57322-910-5*, Riverhead Trade (Paperbacks)) Berkley Publishing Group.
—Sister India. 2001. 288p. 24.95 o.p. (*1-57322-176-7*, Riverhead Bks. (Hardcovers)) Putnam Publishing Group, The.
Pittalwala, Iqbal. Dear Paramount Pictures: Stories. 2002. 184p. 19.95 (*0-87074-475-5*) Southern Methodist Univ. Pr.
Prabhakar, Eric. Madiera at Sundown: A Raj Trilogy. 1990. (C). 23.00 (*81-7001-071-3*) Chanakya Publications IND. *Dist:* South Asia Bks.
Prabhu, Avatar. The Revised Kama Sutra: A Novel. 1998. 480p. 22.95 (*1-887472-41-X*) Sunstar Publishing, Ltd.
Premchand. The Gift of a Cow: A Translation of the Hindi Novel, Godaan. Roadarmel, Gordon C., tr. from HIN. 2002. 480p. pap. 21.95 (*0-253-21567-6*) Indiana Univ. Pr.
—Nirmala. Rai, Alok, tr. from HIN. 2001. 218p. pap. 15.95 (*0-19-565826-4*) Oxford Univ. Pr., Inc.
Premchand, Munshi. Courtesan's Quarter. Azfar, Amina, tr. 2004. 280p. (Orig.). pap. 19.95 (*0-19-597710-6*) Oxford Univ. Pr., Inc.
Putney, Jo Mary. Veils of Silk. 2002. 400p. mass mkt. 7.50 (*0-451-20455-7*) NAL.
Ramaya, Shona. Flute. 1989. 272p. 17.95 o.p. (*0-670-82914-5*) Viking Penguin.
—Operation Monsoon. 2003. 272p. pap. 15.00 o.s.i (*1-55597-387-6*) Graywolf Pr.
Rangel-Ribeiro, Victor. Tivolem. 1998. 400p. 24.00 (*1-57131-019-3*) Milkweed Editions.
Rao, Narasimha, contrib. by. The Insider. 1998. (*0-670-87850-2*) Viking Penguin.
Rath, Chandrasekhar. Astride the Wheel. Nayak, Jatindra Kumar, tr. from ORI. 2003. 208p. 17.95 (*0-19-566477-9*) Oxford Univ. Pr., Inc.
Raven, Simon. Sound the Retreat. 1986. 224p. 14.95 o.p. (*0-8253-0343-5*) Beaufort Bks., Inc.
Ray, Satyajit. The Unicorn Expedition: And Other Fantastic Tales of India. 1987. (Illus.). 208p. 16.95 o.p. (*0-525-24544-8*, Dutton) Dutton/Plume.
Rayudu, A. V. Chaman Nahal's The Ghandi Quartet: Gandhian Ideology & the Indian Novel. 2000. 29.50 (*81-7551-075-7*) Prestige Bks. IND. *Dist:* South Asia Bks.
Rhode, William. Paperback Orginal: When the Travelling Ends, & the Drugs Wear Off, the Writing Must Begin. 2003. 464p. pap. 14.00 o.p. (*1-57322-980-6*, Riverhead Trade (Paperbacks)) Berkley Publishing Group.
Roadarmel, Gordon, ed. & tr. A Death in Delhi: Modern Hindi Short Stories. 1973. (Center for South & Southeast Asia Studies, UC Berkeley). 27.50 o.p. (*0-520-02220-3*) Univ. of California Pr.
Rockland, Michael A. A Bliss Case. 1989. 176p. (Orig.). (C). pap. 9.95 (*0-918273-55-2*) Coffee Hse. Pr.
Rovin, Jeff. Line of Control, Vol. 8. 2001. (Tom Clancy's Op Center Ser.: Vol. 8). 384p. mass mkt. 7.99 (*0-425-18005-0*) Berkley Publishing Group.
Roy, Arundhati. The God of Small Things. 1998. audio compact disk 64.00 (*0-7366-8536-7*); audio 64.00 (*0-7366-4162-9*, 4665) Books on Tape, Inc.
—The God of Small Things. 1998. 336p. pap. 14.00 (*0-06-097749-3*, Perennial); 1997. 6p. audio 25.00 (*0-694-51960-X*, Caedmon) HarperTrade.
—The God of Small Things. l.t. ed. 1997. (G. K. Hall Core Ser.). 471p. 26.95 (*0-7838-8296-3*) Thorndike Pr.
Roy, Arundhati, contrib. by. The God of Small Things. 1997. (*81-86939-00-8*) RST Indiaink Publishing.
Rushdie, Salman. The Ground Beneath Her Feet: A Novel. l.t. ed. 2000. (Thorndike/G. K. Hall Paperback Bestsellers Ser.). 816p. pap. 30.95 (*0-7838-8712-4*, Macmillan Reference USA) Gale Group.
—The Ground Beneath Her Feet: A Novel. 1999. 592p. 27.50 o.s.i (*0-8050-5308-5*) Holt, Henry & Co.
—The Ground Beneath Her Feet: A Novel. abr. ed. 1999. audio 25.00 (*0-7871-1917-2*, Dove Audio) NewStar Media, Inc.
—The Ground Beneath Her Feet: A Novel. 2000. 592p. pap. 16.00 (*0-312-25499-7*) Picador.
—The Ground Beneath Her Feet: A Novel. unabr. ed. 1999. audio 104.00 (*0-7887-3747-3*, 95939E5); audio 163.00 (*0-7887-4350-3*, 95939E7) Recorded Bks., LLC.
—The Ground Beneath Her Feet: A Novel. l.t. ed. 1999. (G. K. Hall Core Ser.). 816p. 31.95 (*0-7838-8713-2*) Thorndike Pr.
—Midnight's Children. 1995. 624p. 22.00 (*0-679-44462-9*) Knopf, Alfred A. Inc.
—Midnight's Children. 1982. 560p. mass mkt. 5.95 o.p. (*0-380-58099-3*, Avon Bks.) Morrow/Avon.
—Midnight's Children. Smale, David, ed. 2002. (Readers' Guides to Essential Criticism Ser.). 208p. pap. 14.99 (*1-84046-253-1*) Palgrave Macmillan.
—Midnight's Children. 2000. (Penguin Great Books of the 20th Century Ser.). (Illus.). 544p. pap. 15.95 o.s.i (*0-14-028339-0*) Penguin Group (USA) Inc.
—Midnight's Children. 1991. 21.05 (*0-606-22205-7*) Turtleback Bks.
—Midnight's Children. 1991. 448p. (C). 15.00 (*0-14-013270-8*) Viking Penguin.
—The Moor's Last Sigh. l.t. ed. 1996. 625p. 26.95 o.p. (*0-7838-1664-2*, Macmillan Reference USA) Gale Group.
—The Moor's Last Sigh. 448p. 1997. pap. 14.95 (*0-679-74466-5*); 1996. 25.00 o.s.i (*0-679-42049-5*) Knopf Publishing Group. (Pantheon).
—The Satanic Verses. 1992. 546p. pap. 14.00 (*0-9632707-0-2*) Consortium, Inc.
—The Satanic Verses. 1997. 576p. pap. 16.00 o.s.i (*0-8050-5309-3*, Owl Bks.) Holt, Henry & Co.
—The Satanic Verses. 2000. 576p. pap. 16.00 (*0-312-27082-8*) Picador.
—The Satanic Verses. 1989. 496p. 27.95 (*0-670-82537-9*) Viking Penguin.
Ryman, Rebecca. Olivia & Jai. 1990. 19.95 o.p. (*0-312-04146-2*) St. Martin's Pr.
—The Veil of Illusion. 1995. 640p. 24.95 o.p. (*0-312-13200-X*) St. Martin's Pr.
Satthianadhan, Krupabai. Kamala: The Story of a Hindu Child-Wife. 2002. 182p. (Orig.). pap. 13.95 (*0-19-565830-2*) Oxford Univ. Pr., Inc.
Satthianadhan, Krupabai & Lokuge, Chandani, contrib. by. Kamala: The Story of a Hindu Life. 1998. 208p. (*0-19-564453-0*) Oxford Univ. Pr., Inc.
Schartz, Vijaya. Ashes for the Elephant God. 2000. 328p. pap. 17.95 (*1-930501-00-5*) Blue Planet Bks., Inc.
Scott, Paul. The Birds of Paradise. 1986. 280p. mass mkt. 4.50 o.p. (*0-88184-232-X*, Carroll & Graf Pubs.) Avalon Publishing Group.
—The Day of the Scorpion. unabr. collector's ed. 1992. (Raj Quartet Ser.). Pt. 1. audio 64.00 (*0-7366-2099-0*, 2905A); Pt. 2. audio 72.00 (*0-7366-2100-8*, 2905B) Books on Tape, Inc.
—The Day of the Scorpion. l.t. ed. 1985. (Raj Quartet Ser.: Bk. 2). 17.95 o.p. (*0-8161-3845-1*, Macmillan Reference USA) Gale Group.
—The Day of the Scorpion. unabr. ed. 1999. audio 104.95 (*0-7531-0340-0*, 980505) ISIS Audio Bks. GBR. *Dist:* Ulverscroft Large Print Bks., Ltd.
—The Day of the Scorpion. (Raj Quartet Ser.). 512p. 1992. pap. 11.00 (*0-380-71809-X*); 1979. mass mkt. 4.95 (*0-380-40923-2*) Morrow/Avon. (Avon Bks.).
—The Day of the Scorpion. 1998. (Raj Quartet Ser.: Vol. 2). 483p. pap. 17.00 (*0-226-74341-1*) Univ. of Chicago Pr.
—A Division of the Spoils. l.t. ed. 1985. (Raj Quartet Ser.: Bk. 4). 19.95 o.p. (*0-8161-3847-8*, Macmillan Reference USA) Gale Group.
—A Division of the Spoils. 1998. (Raj Quartet Ser.: Vol. 4). 597p. pap. 18.00 (*0-226-74344-6*) Univ. of Chicago Pr.
—The Jewel in the Crown. unabr. collector's ed. 1991. (Raj Quartet Ser.: Vol. 1). Pt. 1. audio 64.00 (*0-7366-2062-1*, 2871-A ); Pt. 2. audio 64.00 (*0-7366-2063-X*, 2871-B) Books on Tape, Inc.
—The Jewel in the Crown. unabr. ed. 1995. audio 124.95 (*0-7451-6577-X*, CAB 1193) Chivers Audio Bks. GBR. *Dist:* BBC Audiobooks America.
—The Jewel in the Crown. l.t. ed. 1985. (Raj Quartet Ser.: Bk. 1). 17.95 o.p. (*0-8161-3844-3*, Macmillan Reference USA) Gale Group.
—The Jewel in the Crown. (Raj Quartet Ser.). 480p. 1992. pap. 11.00 (*0-380-71808-1*); 1979. mass mkt. 4.50 (*0-380-40410-9*) Morrow/Avon. (Avon Bks.).
—The Jewel in the Crown. 1998. (Raj Quartet Ser.: Vol. 1). 462p. pap. 17.50 (*0-226-74340-3*) Univ. of Chicago Pr.
—The Raj Quartet. 1984. 1950p. 27.50 o.p. (*0-688-04212-0*, Morrow, William & Co.); pap. 18.00 o.p. (*0-380-46698-8*, Avon Bks.) Morrow/Avon.
—Staying On. Date not set. pap. text 57.50 (*0-582-07718-4*) Addison-Wesley Longman, Ltd. GBR. *Dist:* Trans-Atlantic Pubns., Inc.
—Staying On. unabr. ed. 1992. 69.95 incl. audio (*0-7451-4029-7*, CAB 726) BBC Audiobooks America.
—Staying On. unabr. collector's ed. 1992. audio 56.00 (*0-7366-2159-8*, 2958) Books on Tape, Inc.
—Staying On, Set. abr. ed. 1986. audio 16.99 (*0-88646-154-5*, 391679) Durkin Hayes Publishing Ltd.
—Staying On. 1979. 240p. pap. 3.50 (*0-380-46045-9*, Avon Bks.); 1977. 15.95 o.p. (*0-688-03205-2*, Morrow, William & Co.) Morrow/Avon.
—Staying On. 1998. 222p. pap. 15.00 (*0-226-74349-7*) Univ. of Chicago Pr.
—The Towers of Silence. unabr. collector's ed. 1992. (Raj Quartet Ser.). audio 104.00 (*0-7366-2125-3*, 2927) Books on Tape, Inc.
—The Towers of Silence. l.t. ed. 1985. (Raj Quartet Ser.: Bk. 3). 16.95 o.p. (*0-8161-3846-X*, Macmillan Reference USA) Gale Group.
—The Towers of Silence. unabr. ed. 1999. audio 94.95 (*0-7531-0341-9*, 980806) ISIS Audio Bks. GBR. *Dist:* Ulverscroft Large Print Bks., Ltd.
—The Towers of Silence. (Raj Quartet Ser.). 400p. 1992. pap. 11.00 (*0-380-71810-3*); 1979. mass mkt. 4.95 (*0-380-44198-5*) Morrow/Avon. (Avon Bks.).
—The Towers of Silence. 1998. (Raj Quartet Ser.: Vol. 3). 400p. pap. 16.00 (*0-226-74343-8*) Univ. of Chicago Pr.
Sealy, I. Allan. The Brainfever Bird. 2003. 200p. (*0-330-41205-1*) Picador.
Seth, Vikram. A Suitable Boy: A Novel. 1993. 1376p. pap. o.p. (*0-06-017029-8*) HarperCollins Pubs.
—A Suitable Boy: A Novel. 1993. 1376p. 30.00 o.p. (*0-06-017012-3*); 1994. 1488p. reprint ed. pap. 21.00 (*0-06-092500-0*, Perennial) HarperTrade.
Sethi, Robbie Clipper. Fifty-Fifty: A Novel in Many Voices. 2003. (Illus.). 217p. 24.95 (*0-929306-24-4*) Silicon Pr.
Shah, Hasan. The Dancing Girl. Hyder, Qurratulain, tr. from URD. 1993. 112p. (Orig.). pap. 9.95 (*0-8112-1256-4*, NDP777) New Directions Publishing Corp.
Shamsie, Kamila. In the City by the Sea. 1998. 213 p. (*0-14-028181-9*, Penguin Classics) Viking Penguin.
Shankar, S. A Map of Where I Live. 1997. (Asian Writers Ser.). 176p. pap. 14.95 (*0-435-08143-8*, 08143) Heinemann.
Sharma, Akhil. An Obedient Father. 2000. 282p. 23.00 o.p. (*0-374-10501-4*) Farrar, Straus & Giroux.
—An Obedient Father. 2001. 300p. pap. 13.00 (*0-15-601203-0*, Harvest Bks.) Harcourt Trade Pubs.
Sharma, Damodar. RAJ Legends of Lady Edna. 1990. 16.95 o.p. (*0-533-08650-7*) Vantage Pr., Inc.
Sharma, Prem. Mandalay's Child: A Novel. 1999. 392p. pap. 12.00 (*1-880404-20-6*) Bookwrights Pr.
Shivanath, tr. Echoes & Shadows: A Selection of Dogri Short Stories. 1992. (C). text 8.00 (*81-7201-232-2*) National Sahitya Akademi IND. *Dist:* South Asia Bks.
Sidhwa, Bapsi. Cracking India: A Novel. (Illus.). 296p. reprint ed. 1992. (gr. 4-7). pap. 14.95 (*0-915943-56-5*); 1991. 18.95 o.p. (*0-915943-51-4*) Milkweed Editions.
Siegel, Lee. Love in a Dead Language. 1999. (Illus.). 312p. 25.00 (*0-226-75697-1*) Univ. of Chicago Pr.
Singh, Jacquelin. Home to India. 1997. 217p. 24.00 (*1-877946-85-0*) Permanent Pr., The.
Singh, Jasprit. Gursharan Kaur's Journey. Singh, Teresa, ed. & illus. by. 2001. 44p. 15.00 (*0-9660942-3-9*) Akal Pubns.
Singh, Khushwant. The Collected Short Stories of Khushwant Singh. 1989. (C). 12.50 o.p. (*0-86311-063-0*) Dayal, Ravi Pub. IND. *Dist:* South Asia Bks.
—Train to Pakistan. 1975. Orig. Title: Mano Majra. 181p. reprint ed. 62.95 (*0-8371-8226-3*, SIMM, Greenwood Pr.) Greenwood Publishing Group, Inc.
—Train to Pakistan. Orig. Title: Mano Majra. 192p. 1990. pap. 13.00 (*0-8021-3221-9*, Grove Pr.); 1988. (YA). (gr. 9 up). pap. 5.95 o.p. (*0-394-17887-4*) Grove/Atlantic, Inc.
—Train to Pakistan. 1988. Orig. Title: Mano Majra. (C). 8.50 (*0-86131-985-0*) South Asia Bks.
Smith, Rita P. In the Forest at Midnight. 1989. 320p. 18.95 o.p. (*1-55611-131-2*) Fine, Donald I. Bks.
Sparling, Joyce B. North of Delhi, East of Heaven. 1988. 192p. 18.95 (*0-8027-5719-7*) Walker & Co.
Sreenivasan, Jyotsna. Aruna's Journeys. 1997. (Illus.). 136p. (Orig.). (J). (gr. 1-4). pap. 6.95 (*0-9619401-7-4*) Smooth Stone Pr.
Stirling, S. M. The Peshawar Lancers. 2002. 448p. 23.95 (*0-451-45848-6*); 2003. 496p. reprint ed. mass mkt. 6.99 (*0-451-45873-7*) NAL. (ROC).
Stuart, V. A. The Heroic Garrison. 2003. (Alexander Sheridan Novels: No. 5). 256p. pap. 13.95 (*1-59013-030-8*) McBooks Pr., Inc.

Suri, Manil. The Death of Vishnu. 2001. 256p. 24.95 (*0-393-05042-4*) Norton, W. W. & Co., Inc.

Sutcliffe, Katherine. Notorious. 2000. 368p. mass mkt. 7.50 o.s.i (*0-515-12948-8*, Jove) Berkley Publishing Group.

Taylor, Phillip Meadows. Confessions of a Thug. 1988. reprint ed. 17.50 (*81-206-0330-3*) Asian Educational Services IND. *Dist:* South Asia Bks.

—Confessions of a Thug. 1986. 22.00 o.p. (*0-8364-1737-2*) Manohar Pubns. IND. *Dist:* South Asia Bks.

—Confessions of a Thug. Brantlinger, Patrick, ed. & intro. by. 1998. (Oxford World's Classics Ser.). (Illus.). 578p. pap. 11.95 o.p. (*0-19-288021-7*) Oxford Univ. Pr., Inc.

Tharoor, Shashi. The Five Dollar Smile: And Other Stories. 1993. 192p. 18.95 (*1-55970-225-7*) Arcade Publishing, Inc.

—The Great Indian Novel. 432p. 1991. lib. bdg. 19.95 o.p. (*1-55970-116-1*); 2001. reprint ed. pap. 14.45 (*1-55970-194-3*) Arcade Publishing, Inc.

—Riot: A Love Story. 2001. 304p. 24.95 (*1-55970-605-8*); 2002. 288p. reprint ed. pap. 13.95 (*1-55970-645-7*) Arcade Publishing, Inc.

—Show Business. 1992. 352p. 19.95 (*1-55970-181-1*); 2001. 312p. reprint ed. pap. 12.95 (*1-55970-227-3*) Arcade Publishing, Inc.

Thomas, Craig. Playing with Cobras. unabr. ed. 1995. (ACE.). audio 79.95 (*0-7451-4365-2*, CAB 1048) Chivers Audio Bks. GBR. *Dist:* BBC Audiobooks America.

—Playing with Cobras. 1994. 432p. mass mkt. 5.99 o.p. (*0-06-109168-5*, HarperTorch) Morrow/Avon.

—Playing with Cobras. pap. 5.98 o.p. (*0-8317-3494-9*) Smithmark Pubs., Inc.

—Playing with Cobras, Set. 1994. (Studio Ser.). audio 89.95 o.p. (*0-7862-9983-5*) Thorndike Pr.

—Playing with Cobras: A Novel. 1993. 416p. 18.00 o.p. (*0-06-017955-4*) HarperTrade.

Thurley, Jon. Household Gods. Golbitz, Pat & Hamilton, Jill, eds. 1988. 288p. 18.95 o.p. (*0-688-07939-3*, Morrow, William & Co.) Morrow/Avon.

Umrigar, Thrity. Bombay Time. 2002. 288p. pap. 13.00 (*0-312-28623-6*); 2001. 256p. 24.00 (*0-312-27716-4*) Picador.

Upadhyay, Samrat. The Guru of Love. 2003. 304p. tchr. ed. 23.00 (*0-618-24727-0*) Houghton Mifflin Co. Trade & Reference Div.

Vaswani, Neela. Where the Long Grass Bends: Stories. 2004. 192p. pap. 13.95 (*1-889330-96-5*) Sarabande Bks., Inc.

Vatsyayan, S. H. Islands in the Stream. 1980. (Vikas Library of Modern Moian Writing: No. 2). 384p. text 25.00 o.p. (*0-7069-1089-3*) Vikas Publishing Hse. Private, Ltd. IND. *Dist:* South Asia Bks.

Vernede, R. V. The Collector's Bag: Traveller's Tales from India & Elsewhere. 1993. (Illus.). 267p. 30.00 (*0-86140-352-5*) Smythe, Colin Ltd. GBR. *Dist:* Dufour Editions, Inc.

—The Enchanted Loom. 1995. 172p. 24.95 (*0-86140-381-9*) Smythe, Colin Ltd. GBR. *Dist:* Dufour Editions, Inc.

Vijayaraghavan, Vineeta. Motherland. 2002. 232p. pap. 12.00 (*1-56947-283-1*); 2001. 231p. trans. 23.00 (*1-56947-217-3*) Soho Pr., Inc.

Waller, Robert James. Slow Waltz in Cedar Bend. unabr. ed. 1994. audio 30.00 o.p. Books on Tape, Inc.

—Slow Waltz in Cedar Bend. unabr. ed. 1993. audio 22.95 o.p. (*1-55800-876-4*, 592099); audio compact disk 59.95 o.p. (*1-55800-880-2*) NewStar Media, Inc.

—Slow Waltz in Cedar Bend. 1994. 227p. mass mkt. 4.99 o.s.i (*0-446-60164-0*); 1993. 200p. 25.00 (*0-446-51653-8*) Warner Bks., Inc.

—Slow Waltz in Cedar Bend & the Bridges of Madison County. 1993. audio 19.88 o.p. (*1-55800-927-2*, Dove Audio) NewStar Media, Inc.

Ward, Andrew. The Blood Seed: A Novel of India. 1985. 592p. 17.95 o.p. (*0-670-58934-9*) Viking Penguin.

Weston, Christine, et al. Four Raj Novels: Indigo, Siri Ram Revolutionist, on the Face of the Waters, the Wild Sweet Witch. Cowasjee, Saros, ed. 2004. 1200p. 29.95 (*0-19-566500-7*) Oxford Univ. Pr., Inc.

Wiloch, Thomas. Tales of Lord Shantih. 1990. (Illus.). 52p. 25.00 (*0-87775-225-7*); pap. 12.95 (*0-87775-226-5*) Unicorn Pr., Inc.

Woodward, Lilian. Nurse to the Maharajah. l.t. ed. 1994. 19.95 o.p. (*0-7927-1817-8*); pap. 17.95 o.p. (*0-7927-1816-X*) BBC Audiobooks America.

Worthington, Gary, Sr. India Fortunes: A Novel of Rajasthan & Northern India Through Past Centuries. 2003. (Illus.). 592p. 26.95 (*0-9707662-1-1*); pap. 15.95 (*0-9707662-3-8*) TimeBridges Pubs. LLC.

Worthington, Gary. India Treasures: An Epic Novel of Rajasthan & Northern India Through the Ages. 2001. (Illus.). 640p. pap. 15.95 (*0-9707662-0-3*) TimeBridges Pubs. LLC.

Yolen, Jane. Children of the Wolf. 1994. (J). 17.55 o.p. (*0-8446-6764-1*) Smith, Peter Pub., Inc.

—Children of the Wolf. 1993. 10.09 o.p. (*0-606-05202-X*) Turtleback Bks.

## INDIANA—FICTION

Allen, Shirley S. Roxanna Britton. 2001. 388p. per. 16.00 (*1-884162-08-8*) Criterion Hse.

Baxter, Nancy N. Charmed Circle-Indianapolis, 1895: A Mystery. 1994. 350p. pap. 18.95 (*1-878208-52-7*) Emmis Bks.

Carlson, Pat M. Bloodstream. 1996. 336p. mass mkt. 5.99 (*0-671-76978-2*, Pocket) Simon & Schuster.

—Bloodstream. Chelius, Jane, ed. 1995. 336p. 20.00 o.p. (*0-671-76977-4*, Atria) Simon & Schuster.

—Gravestone. Chelius, Jane, ed. 336p. 1993. 20.00 (*0-671-76974-X*, Atria); 1994. reprint ed. mass mkt. 5.50 (*0-671-76975-8*, Pocket) Simon & Schuster.

Dams, Jeanne M. Death in Lacquer Red: A Hilda Johansson Mystery. l.t. ed. 1999. (Beeler Large Print Mystery Ser.). 225p. 25.95 (*1-57490-240-7*, Beeler Large Print Bks.) Beeler, Thomas T. Publisher.

—Death in Lacquer Red: A Hilda Johansson Mystery. 1999. (Hilda Johansson Mysteries Ser.). vii, 225p. 22.95 (*0-8027-3329-8*) Walker & Co.

—Green Grow the Victims: A Hilda Johansson Mystery. l.t. ed. 2001. (Beeler Large Print Mystery Ser.). x, 236p. 25.95 (*1-57490-369-1*, Beeler Large Print Bks.) Beeler, Thomas T. Publisher.

—Killing Cassidy: A Dorothy Martin Mystery. l.t. ed. 2001. 344p. 28.95 (*0-7862-3332-X*) Thorndike Pr.

—Killing Cassidy: A Dorothy Martin Mystery. 2000. (Dorothy Martin Mystery Ser.). 210p. 23.95 (*0-8027-3347-6*) Walker & Co.

—Red, White & Blue Murder: A Hilda Johansson Mystery. 2002. reprint ed. pap. 8.95 (*0-8027-7630-2*) Walker & Co.

—Red, White & Blue Murders: A Hilda Johansson Mystery. 2000. (Hilda Johansson Mysteries Ser.). 189p. 23.95 (*0-8027-3341-7*) Walker & Co.

—Silence Is Golden: A Hilda Johansson Mystery. 2002. 240p. 23.95 (*0-8027-3373-5*) Walker & Co.

Day, Marlis. Death of a Hoosier Schoolmaster. 2002. 192p. pap. 11.95 (*1-56315-288-6*) SterlingHouse Pubs., Inc.

Driver, Lee. The Good Die Twice. (Chase Dagger Mystery Ser.). 2000. 304p. pap. 6.50 (*0-9666021-5-3*); 1999. 315p. 21.95 o.p. (*0-9666021-1-0*) Full Moon Publishing.

Dye, Kitty. Meet George Winter: Pioneer Artist, Journalist, Entrepreneur. 2001. (Illus.). 232p. pap. 17.95 (*0-9702501-1-8*) LeClere Publishing Co.

Eggleston, Edward. The Hoosier School Master. 1984. (Library of Indiana Classics). (Illus.). 232p. reprint ed. 20.00 o.p. (*0-253-32850-0*) Indiana Univ. Pr.

—The Hoosier School Master. 1988. (Collected Works of Edward Eggleston). reprint ed. lib. bdg. 79.00 (*0-7812-1172-7*) Reprint Services Corp.

—The Hoosier School Master. 1871. reprint ed. 69.00 Somerset Pubs., Inc.

Faherty, Terence. Die Dreaming: An Owen Keane Mystery. 1996. pap. (*0-373-28207-9*, Harlequin Bks.); per. (*0-373-26207-8*, 1-26207-0, Worldwide Library) Harlequin Enterprises, Ltd.

—Die Dreaming: An Owen Keane Mystery. 1994. 272p. 20.95 o.p. (*0-312-11045-6*, Saint Martin's Minotaur) St. Martin's Pr.

—The Lost Keats: An Owen Keane Mystery. 1996. (Mystery Ser.). 250p. per. (*0-373-26192-6*, 1-26192-4, Worldwide Library) Harlequin Enterprises, Ltd.

—The Lost Keats: An Owen Keane Mystery. 1993. 272p. 18.95 o.p. (*0-312-09329-2*, Saint Martin's Minotaur) St. Martin's Pr.

—The Ordained: An Owen Keane Mystery. 1998. per. (*0-373-26296-5*, 1-26296-3, Mira Bks.) Harlequin Enterprises, Ltd.

—The Ordained: An Owen Keane Mystery. 1997. (Owen Keane Mysteries Ser.). 240p. 21.95 o.p. (*0-312-16958-2*, Saint Martin's Minotaur) St. Martin's Pr.

Frommer, Sara H. Buried in Quilts. 1996. (WWL Mystery Ser.). per. (*0-373-26204-3*, 1-26204-7, Worldwide Library) Harlequin Enterprises, Ltd.

—Buried in Quilts. 1994. (Joan Spencer Mystery Ser.). 224p. 19.95 o.p. (*0-312-11472-9*, Saint Martin's Minotaur) St. Martin's Pr.

—Murder & Sullivan: A Joan Spencer Mystery. 1998. (WWL Mystery Ser.). per. (*0-373-26285-X*, 1-26285-6, Worldwide Library) Harlequin Enterprises, Ltd.

—Murder & Sullivan: A Joan Spencer Mystery. 1997. 256p. 21.95 o.p. (*0-312-15595-6*, Saint Martin's Minotaur) St. Martin's Pr.

—Murder in C Major. 1988. 224p. reprint ed. spiral bd. (*0-373-26017-2*, Harlequin Bks.) Harlequin Enterprises, Ltd.

—Murder in C Major. 2000. (Missing Mysteries Ser.: Vol. 17). 183p. pap. 14.95 (*1-890208-31-0*) Poisoned Pen Pr.

—Murder in C Major. 1986. 240p. 14.95 o.p. (*0-312-55299-8*) St. Martin's Pr.

—Murder in C Major. l.t. ed. 2003. 331p. 24.95 (*0-7862-5987-6*) Thorndike Pr.

—The Vanishing Violinist. 2000. (WWL Mystery Ser.: No. 359). 256p. mass mkt. (*0-373-26359-7*, 1-26359-9, Worldwide Library) Harlequin Enterprises, Ltd.

—The Vanishing Violinist: A Joan Spencer Mystery. 2nd ed. 1999. 272p. 23.95 (*0-312-24104-6*, Saint Martin's Minotaur) St. Martin's Pr.

Gaskill, Cathy. Ruth's Gift: A Family Legend. exp. ed. 1998. (Illus.). 160p. per. 15.00 (*1-887774-03-3*) Canmore Pr.

Gould, Sandra. Faradays Popcorn Factory. 2000. 2888p. pap. 13.95 (*0-312-25385-0*, Saint Martin's Griffin) St. Martin's Pr.

Gould, Sandra Lee. Faraday's Popcorn Factory. 1999. 23.95 o.s.i (*0-312-20780-8*); 1998. 288p. 23.95 o.p. (*0-312-18578-2*) St. Martin's Pr.

Gulley, Philip. Home to Harmony. 2004. 240p. pap. 12.95 (*0-06-072766-7*) HarperSanFrancisco.

—Signs & Wonders. 2004. 224p. pap. 12.95 (*0-06-072707-1*) HarperSanFrancisco.

—Signs & Wonders: A Harmony Novel. 2003. (Illus.). 224p. 17.95 (*0-06-000633-1*) HarperSanFrancisco.

—Signs & Wonders: A Harmony Novel. l.t. ed. 2003. 285p. 28.95 (*0-7862-5639-7*) Thorndike Pr.

Gutteridge, Rene. Boo. 2003. 256p. pap. 11.99 (*1-57856-573-1*) WaterBrook Pr.

Hamilton, Dorothy. Rosalie at Eleven. 1980. (Illus.). 112p. (J). (gr. 3-8). pap. 3.95 o.p. (*0-8361-1931-2*) Herald Pr.

Harper, Karen. The Stone Forest. 2002. 400p. mass mkt. (*1-55166-909-9*, 1-66909-2, Mira Bks.) Harlequin Enterprises, Ltd.

Hemley, Robin. The Last Studebaker. 256p. 1993. pap. 12.00 (*1-55597-200-4*); 1992. 20.00 o.s.i (*1-55597-167-9*) Graywolf Pr.

Henley, Patricia. In the River Sweet: A Novel. 2002. 304p. 24.00 (*0-375-42127-0*, Pantheon) Knopf Publishing Group.

Hensley, Joe L. Robak in Black: A Don Robak Mystery. 2001. 256p. 23.95 (*0-312-24109-7*) St. Martin's Pr.

—Robak's Witch: A Dan Robak Mystery. 1997. 256p. 21.95 o.p. (*0-312-15642-1*, Saint Martin's Minotaur) St. Martin's Pr.

Hunnicut, Ellen. Suite for Calliope: A Novel of Music & the Circus. 1987. 272p. 17.95 o.p. (*0-8027-0965-6*) Walker & Co.

Hunt, Laird. Indiana, Indiana. 2003. 200p. 20.00 (*1-56689-144-2*) Coffee Hse. Pr.

Kimmel, Haven. The Solace of Leaving Early. 2003. 288p. reprint ed. pap. 13.00 (*1-4000-3334-9*, Anchor) Knopf Publishing Group.

—The Solace of Leaving Early: A Novel. 2002. 272p. 23.95 (*0-385-49983-3*) Doubleday Publishing.

King, Kathleen W. The True Life Story of Isabel Roundtree. Rugenstein, Julie, ed. 1995. 176p. pap. 13.95 (*0-671-89185-5*, Pocket) Simon & Schuster.

Kingsbury, Karen & Smalley, Gary. Remember. 2003. (Redemption Ser.). 432p. pap. 12.99 (*0-8423-5629-0*) Tyndale Hse. Pubs.

—Return. 2003. (Redemption Ser.). 250p. pap. 12.99 (*0-8423-8289-5*) Tyndale Hse. Pubs.

Kurtz, Donald. South of the Big Four. 1995. (Illus.). 288p. 19.95 o.p. (*0-8118-0908-0*) Chronicle Bks. LLC.

—South of the Big Four. 1996. 384p. pap. 12.00 o.p. (*0-380-72765-X*, Avon Bks.) Morrow/Avon.

Lewin, Michael Z. And Baby Will Fall. l.t. ed. 1989. 304 p. pap. (*1-55504-755-6*) BBC Audiobooks America.

—And Baby Will Fall. 1990. mass mkt. (*0-373-26042-3*, Harlequin Bks.) Harlequin Enterprises, Ltd.

—And Baby Will Fall. 1988. 224p. 16.95 o.p. (*0-688-06880-4*, Morrow, William & Co.) Morrow/Avon.

—Ask the Right Question. 1979. 1.75 o.p. (*0-425-04027-5*) Berkley Publishing Group.

—Ask the Right Question. 1984. 192p. reprint ed. mass mkt. 3.50 o.p. (*0-06-080711-3*, P 711) HarperCollins Pubs.

—Ask the Right Question. 1991. mass mkt. 4.95 o.s.i (*0-446-40021-1*, Mysterious Pr. Paperback Bks.) Warner Bks., Inc.

—Called by a Panther. 1991. 17.95 o.p. (*0-89296-439-1*) Mysterious Pr.

—Called by a Panther. 1992. 272p. mass mkt. 4.99 o.s.i (*0-446-40159-5*) Warner Bks., Inc.

—The Enemies Within. 1979. mass mkt. 1.75 o.p. (*0-425-04029-1*) Berkley Publishing Group.

—Enemies Within. 1991. mass mkt. 4.95 o.s.i (*0-446-40024-6*, Mysterious Pr. Paperback Bks.) Warner Bks., Inc.

—The Enemies Within. 1984. 240p. reprint ed. mass mkt. 3.50 o.p. (*0-06-080712-1*, P 712, Perennial) HarperTrade.

—Hard Line. 1984. 256p. mass mkt. 3.50 o.p. (*0-06-080720-2*, P 720) HarperCollins Pubs.

—Hard Line: A Lt. Leroy Powder Novel. 1996. (Lt. Leroy Powder Novel Ser.). 256p. reprint ed. pap. 10.00 (*0-88150-346-0*, Foul Play) Norton, W. W. & Co., Inc.

—Late Payments. 1986. 224p. 13.95 o.p. (*0-688-04342-9*, Morrow, William & Co.) Morrow/Avon.

—Late Payments. 1987. 224p. pap. 3.50 o.p. (*0-14-009875-5*, Penguin Bks.) Viking Penguin.

—Late Payments: A Lt. Leroy Powder Novel. 1996. (Lt. Leroy Powder Novel Ser.). 216p. reprint ed. pap. 10.00 (*0-88150-347-9*, Foul Play) Norton, W. W. & Co., Inc.

—Missing Woman. 1982. mass mkt. 2.25 o.p. (*0-425-05391-1*) Berkley Publishing Group.

—Missing Woman. 1985. 224p. reprint ed. mass mkt. 3.50 o.p. (*0-06-080709-1*, P 709, Perennial) HarperTrade.

—Missing Woman. 1981. 224p. 10.95 o.p. (*0-394-50007-5*, Knopf Bks. for Young Readers) Random Hse. Children's Bks.

—Missing Woman. 1991. mass mkt. 4.99 (*0-446-40026-2*, Mysterious Pr. Paperback Bks.) Warner Bks., Inc.

—Night Cover. 1995. (Lt. Leroy Powder Novel Ser.). 256p. reprint ed. pap. 10.00 o.p. (*0-88150-345-2*, Foul Play) Norton, W. W. & Co., Inc.

—Night Cover. 1976. 7.95 o.p. (*0-394-49644-2*, Knopf Bks. for Young Readers) Random Hse. Children's Bks.

—Out of Season. 1985. (Albert Samson Novel Ser.). 256p. reprint ed. mass mkt. 3.50 o.p. (*0-06-080774-1*, P 774, Perennial) HarperTrade.

—Out of Season. 1984. (Albert Samson, Private Eye Ser.). 256p. 12.95 o.p. (*0-688-03903-0*, Morrow, William & Co.) Morrow/Avon.

—Out of Season. 1991. mass mkt. 4.99 o.s.i (*0-446-40027-0*, Mysterious Pr. Paperback Bks.) Warner Bks., Inc.

—The Silent Salesman. 1981. mass mkt. 2.25 o.p. (*0-425-04031-3*) Berkley Publishing Group.

—The Silent Salesman. 1985. 272p. mass mkt. 3.50 o.p. (*0-06-080736-9*, P 736, Perennial) HarperTrade.

—The Silent Salesman. 1978. 7.95 o.p. (*0-394-40433-5*, Knopf Bks. for Young Readers) Random Hse. Children's Bks.

—The Silent Salesman. 1991. mass mkt. 4.99 o.s.i (*0-446-40025-4*, Mysterious Pr. Paperback Bks.) Warner Bks., Inc.

—Underdog. 1993. 272p. 18.95 (*0-89296-440-5*) Mysterious Pr.

—Underdog. 1995. 256p. mass mkt. 5.50 (*0-446-40436-5*, Mysterious Pr. Paperback Bks.) Warner Bks., Inc.

—Way We Die Now. 1991. mass mkt. 4.95 o.s.i (*0-446-40023-8*, Mysterious Pr. Paperback Bks.) Warner Bks., Inc.

—The Way We Die Now. 1979. 1.75 o.p. (*0-425-04028-3*) Berkley Publishing Group.

—The Way We Die Now. 1984. 224p. reprint ed. mass mkt. 3.50 o.p. (*0-06-080710-5*, P 710) HarperCollins Pubs.

Lockridge, Ross, Jr. Raintree County. 1991. 1066p. reprint ed. lib. bdg. 49.95 (*0-89966-865-8*) Buccaneer Bks., Inc.

—Raintree County, 001. 9999. 15.50 o.p. (*0-395-07919-5*) Houghton Mifflin Co.

—Raintree County. 1984. 1066p. pap. 12.95 o.p. (*0-87795-606-5*, Morrow, William & Co.) Morrow/Avon.

Loveall, Jaquelyn. Phila Campbell: A Story of 1909. 1994. 120p. 14.95 (*1-878208-39-X*) Emmis Bks.

Maher, Jan. Heaven, Indiana. unabr. ed. 2000. 169p. pap. 14.00 (*0-9703993-0-8*) Dog Hollow Pr.

Major, Charles. The Bears of Blue River. 1984. (Library of Indiana Classics). (Illus.). 288p. (gr. 4-7). 20.00 (*0-253-10590-0*); pap. 10.95 (*0-253-20330-9*, MB-330) Indiana Univ. Pr.

—Bears of Blue River. reprint ed. lib. bdg. 23.95 (*0-88411-094-X*) Amereon, Ltd.

—Bears of Blue River. 1983. (Illus.). 277p. (J). (gr. 3 up). reprint ed. pap. 5.95 o.p. (*0-913428-37-X*) Landfall Pr., Inc.

—The Bears of Blue River. 1998. (gr. 4-7). reprint ed. 35.95 (*1-56849-716-4*) Buccaneer Bks., Inc.

—Uncle Tom Andy Bill. 1992. 350p. reprint ed. lib. bdg. 26.95 (*0-89966-914-X*) Buccaneer Bks., Inc.

—Uncle Tom Andy Bill: A Story of Bears & Indian Treasure. 1993. (Library of Indiana Classics). (C). 352p. 17.95 (*0-253-33653-8*); pap. 10.95 (*0-253-33654-6*) Indiana Univ. Pr.

Marshall, Kirk. Fast Breaks. 1989. (Hoops Ser.: No. 1). 144p. (J). (gr. 4 up). mass mkt. 4.50 o.s.i (*0-345-35908-9*) Ballantine Bks.

—Pressure Play. 1989. (Hoops Ser.: No. 6). (J). (gr. 6-10). mass mkt. 3.99 o.s.i (*0-345-35913-5*) Ballantine Bks.

Martone, Michael. Fort Wayne Is Seventh on Hitler's List: Indiana Stories. 1990. 144p. 20.00 o.p. (*0-253-33679-1*); 1993. 160p. 24.95 (*0-253-33687-2*); 1993. 160p. pap. 14.95 (*0-253-20851-3*) Indiana Univ. Pr.

McInerny, Ralph. As Good As Dead. 2003. 208p. pap. 13.95 (1-4104-0104-9, Five Star Trade); 2002. 300p. 25.95 (0-7862-4179-9, Five Star) Gale Group.
—Body & Soil: An Andrew Broom Mystery. 1990. mass mkt. (0-373-26063-6, Harlequin Bks.) Harlequin Enterprises, Ltd.
—Body & Soil: An Andrew Broom Mystery. 1989. 224p. 17.95 o.p. (0-689-12036-2, Scribner) Simon & Schuster.
—The Book of Kills: A Mystery Set at the University of Notre Dame. E-Book 23.95 (0-312-27604-4); 2000. 275p. 23.95 o.p. (0-312-20346-2, Saint Martin's Minotaur); 2001. 288p. reprint ed. mass mkt. 6.50 o.s.i (0-312-97922-3, St. Martin's Paperbacks) St. Martin's Pr.
—The Book of Kills: A Mystery Set at the University of Notre Dame. 2001. (Basic Ser.). 375p. 28.95 o.p. (0-7862-3642-6) Thorndike Pr.
—Cause & Effect: An Andrew Broom Mystery. 1990. mass mkt. (0-373-26046-6, Harlequin Bks.) Harlequin Enterprises, Ltd.
—Cause & Effect: An Andrew Broom Mystery. 1987. 224p. 15.95 o.p. (0-689-11894-5, Scribner) Simon & Schuster.
—Celt & Pepper: A Mystery Set at the University of Notre Dame. 2002. 240p. 22.95 (0-312-29117-5, Saint Martin's Minotaur) St. Martin's Pr.
—Celt & Pepper: A Mystery Set at the University of Notre Dame. 2003. 28.95 (0-7862-5179-4) Thorndike Pr.
—Emerald Aisle: A Mystery Set at the University of Notre Dame. 2002. E-Book 23.95 (1-59061-743-6) Adobe Systems, Inc.
—Emerald Aisle: A Mystery Set at the University of Notre Dame. l.t. ed. 2002. 344p. 28.95 (0-7862-4345-7) Gale Group.
—Emerald Aisle: A Mystery Set at the University of Notre Dame. mass mkt. (0-312-98277-1, St. Martin's Paperbacks); E-Book 23.95 (0-312-70326-0); 2001. 288p. 22.95 (0-312-26938-2, Saint Martin's Minotaur) St. Martin's Pr.
—Frigor Mortis. l.t. ed. 1991. 19.95 o.p. (0-7927-0733-8, CH017); pap. 17.95 o.p. (0-7927-0734-6, CS0121) BBC Audiobooks America.
—Frigor Mortis. 1991. reprint ed. mass mkt. (0-373-26080-6, Harlequin Bks.) Harlequin Enterprises, Ltd.
—Frigor Mortis. 1989. 288p. 18.95 o.s.i (0-689-12081-8, Scribner) Simon & Schuster.
—Heirs & Parents: An Andrew Broom Mystery. 2000. (Andrew Broom Mysteries Ser.). 240p. 23.95 (0-312-20311-X, Saint Martin's Minotaur) St. Martin's Pr.
—Irish Coffee. Date not set. pap. (0-312-30902-3, Saint Martin's Griffin); mass mkt. (0-312-98691-2, St. Martin's Paperbacks); 2003. 288p. 23.95 (0-312-30901-5, Saint Martin's Minotaur) St. Martin's Pr.
—Irish Tenure: A Mystery Set at the University of Notre Dame. 2000. 263p. mass mkt. 5.99 (0-312-97320-9, St. Martin's Paperbacks); 1999. 246p. 22.95 o.p. (0-312-20345-4, Saint Martin's Minotaur) St. Martin's Pr.
—Irish Tenure: A Mystery Set at the University of Notre Dame. l.t. ed. 2000. (Basic Ser.). 336p. 28.95 (0-7862-2667-6) Thorndike Pr.
—Lack of the Irish: A Mystery Set at the University of Notre Dame. (Notre Dame Mystery Ser.). 1999. 240p. mass mkt. 5.99 (0-312-96927-9, St. Martin's Paperbacks); 1998. 224p. 21.95 o.p. (0-312-19294-0, Saint Martin's Minotaur) St. Martin's Pr.
—Law & Ardor: An Andrew Broom Mystery. l.t. ed. 2001. (Beeler Large Print Mystery Ser.). 202p. 25.95 (1-57490-410-8, Beeler Large Print Bks.) Beeler, Thomas T. Publisher.
—Law & Ardor: An Andrew Broom Mystery. 1995. 256p. 21.00 (0-684-80462-X, Scribner) Simon & Schuster.
—Mom & Dead: An Andrew Broom Mystery. 1994. 256p. 20.00 o.p. (0-689-12181-4, Scribner) Simon & Schuster.
—On This Rockne: A Notre Dame Mystery. (Notre Dame Mystery Ser.). 1998. 320p. pap. 5.99 (0-312-96738-1, St. Martin's Paperbacks); 1997. 224p. 20.95 o.p. (0-312-17054-8, 749186, Saint Martin's Minotaur) St. Martin's Pr.
—Savings & Loam: An Andrew Broom Mystery. 1992. (WWL Mystery Ser.: No. 91). mass mkt. (0-373-26091-1, 1-26091-8, Harlequin Bks.) Harlequin Enterprises, Ltd.
—Savings & Loam: An Andrew Broom Mystery. 1993. 2.99 o.p. (0-517-09633-1) Random Hse. Value Publishing.
—Savings & Loam: An Andrew Broom Mystery. 1990. 224p. 17.95 o.s.i (0-689-12037-0, Scribner) Simon & Schuster.
McNaught, Judith. Paradise/Perfect Omnibus. 2001. 752p. reprint ed. pap. 12.95 (0-7434-2833-1, Pocket) Simon & Schuster.
Nicholson, Meredith. The House of a Thousand Candles. 1975. lib. bdg. 16.70 o.s.i (0-89966-142-4) Buccaneer Bks., Inc.
—The House of a Thousand Candles. reprint ed. lib. bdg. 48.00 (0-7426-1155-8); 2001. pap. text 28.00 (0-7426-6155-5) Classic Bks.
—The House of a Thousand Candles. 1986. (Library of Indiana Classics). (Illus.). 392p. 20.00 (0-253-32852-7); pap. 3.25 (0-253-20381-3, MB-381) Indiana Univ. Pr.
O'Brien, Linda. His Forbidden Touch. 2000. 384p. mass mkt. 5.99 (0-380-81343-2, Avon Bks.) Morrow/Avon.
Outlet Book Company Staff. Murder in C Major. 1987. 1.99 o.p. (0-517-65735-X) Random Hse. Value Publishing.
Page, Carole Gift. A Locket for Maggie: A Novel. 2000. (Heartland Memories Ser.: Vol. 6). 252p. pap. 10.99 (0-7852-7673-4) Nelson, Thomas Pubs.
Perona, Tony. Second Advent: A Novel. 2002. (Five Star First Edition Mystery Ser.). 285p. 24.95 (0-7862-4327-9, Five Star) Gale Group.
Reynolds, Marjorie. The Starlite Drive-In. 1998. 304p. pap. 6.99 o.s.i (0-425-16572-8) Berkley Publishing Group.
—The Starlite Drive-In. 1997. 224p. 23.00 (0-688-15389-5, Morrow, William & Co.) Morrow/Avon.
—Starlite Drive-in. 1999. 356p. pap. 13.95 o.s.i (0-425-17264-3) Berkley Publishing Group.
Schanker, D. R. A Criminal Appeal. 2000. 352p. mass mkt. 5.99 o.s.i (0-440-23581-2) Dell Publishing.
—A Criminal Appeal. 1998. 288p. 23.95 (0-312-19253-3, Saint Martin's Minotaur) St. Martin's Pr.
—Natural Law. 2001. 242p. 22.95 (0-312-26684-7, Saint Martin's Minotaur) St. Martin's Pr.
Schulze, Dallas. Sleeping Beauty. 1999. 384p. mass mkt. (1-55166-553-0, 1-66553-8, Mira Bks.) Harlequin Enterprises, Ltd.
Scifres, Bill. Bayou Bill's Best Stories: Most of Them True. 1990. (Illus.). 216p. 19.95 o.p. (0-253-35059-X); pap. 4.95 (0-253-20596-4, MB-596) Indiana Univ. Pr.
Soule, Maris. Lyon's Pride. 1993. (Harlequin Romance Ser.). pap. (0-373-08930-9, 5-08930-5, Silhouette) Harlequin Enterprises, Ltd.
Stratton-Porter, Gene. The Harvester. reprint ed. lib. bdg. 31.95 (0-89190-932-X, Rivercity Pr.) Amereon, Ltd.
—The Harvester. unabr. ed. 1989. audio 64.95 (1-55686-295-4, 112674) Books in Motion.
—The Harvester. 1977. 24.95 o.s.i (0-89967-004-0, Harmony Raine & Co.) Buccaneer Bks., Inc.
—The Harvester. reprint ed. lib. bdg. 48.00 (0-7426-1212-0); 2001. 564p. pap. text 28.00 (0-7426-6212-8) Classic Bks.
—The Harvester. E-Book 2.49 (1-58627-574-7) Electric Umbrella Publishing.
—The Harvester. 1987. (Library of Indiana Classics). 528p. 25.00 (0-253-32746-6); pap. 12.95 (0-253-20457-7, MB-457) Indiana Univ. Pr.
—The Harvester. 2002. 388p. 27.99 (1-4043-0666-8); per. 22.99 (1-4043-0667-6) IndyPublish.com.
—The Harvester. E-Book 2.95 (1-57799-877-4) Logos Research Systems, Inc.
—The Harvester, Vol. 2. 2000. 23.99 (1-930142-27-7) Write Together Publishing.
—The Keeper of the Bees. 29.95 (0-89190-946-X) Amereon, Ltd.
—The Keeper of the Bees. 1991. (Library of Indiana Classics). 528p. 25.95 (0-253-35496-X); pap. 14.95 (0-253-20691-X, MB-691) Indiana Univ. Pr.
—Michael O'Halloran. reprint ed. lib. bdg. 33.95 (0-89190-934-6, Rivercity Pr.) Amereon, Ltd.
—Michael O'Halloran. reprint ed. lib. bdg. 48.00 (0-7426-1264-3); 2001. (Illus.). 560 P.p. pap. text 28.00 (0-7426-6264-0) Classic Bks.
—Michael O'Halloran. 1996. (Library of Indiana Classics). 576p. 27.95 (0-253-33021-1); pap. 14.95 (0-253-21045-3) Indiana Univ. Pr.
—Strike at Shane's: A Prize Story of Indiana. 1999. 91p. (J). reprint ed. pap. 9.95 (1-55709-308-3) Applewood Bks.
Tarkington, Booth. Alice Adams. 2003. (Library of Indiana Classics). (Illus.). xix, 434p. 32.95 (0-253-34227-9) Indiana Univ. Pr.
—Beauty & the Jacobin: An Interlude of the French Revolution. (Works of Booth Tarkington). 99p. 2001. pap. text 28.00 (0-7426-5845-7); 1999. reprint ed. lib. bdg. 88.00 (1-58201-845-6) Classic Bks.
—The Magnificent Ambersons. 24.95 (0-88411-700-6) Amereon, Ltd.
—The Magnificent Ambersons. unabr. ed. 1993. audio 47.95 (1-55685-258-4) Audio Bk. Contractors, Inc.
—The Magnificent Ambersons. 1994. 352p. mass mkt. 4.95 o.s.i (0-553-21430-6) Bantam Bks.
—The Magnificent Ambersons. 1918. E-Book (1-58734-061-5) Bartleby.com.
—The Magnificent Ambersons. 1999. (Works of Booth Tarkington). 516p. reprint ed. lib. bdg. 128.00 (1-58201-861-8) Classic Bks.
—The Magnificent Ambersons. 1967. pap. 2.45 o.p. (0-8090-0002-4, Hill & Wang) Farrar, Straus & Giroux.
—The Magnificent Ambersons. 1989. (Library of Indiana Classics). (Illus.). 536p. pap. 14.95 (0-253-20546-8, MB-546) Indiana Univ. Pr.
—The Magnificent Ambersons. 1986. pap. 6.95 o.p. (0-87795-795-9, Morrow, William & Co.); 1982. pap. 1.50 o.p. (0-380-01406-8, 17236, Avon Bks.) Morrow/Avon.
—The Magnificent Ambersons. 1987. (Radiobook Ser.). audio 4.98 (0-929541-15-4) Radiola Co.
—The Magnificent Ambersons. 2000. (Modern Library Ser.). E-Book 4.95 (0-679-64200-5, Modern Library) Random House Adult Trade Publishing Group.
—The Magnificent Ambersons. annuals 98th ed. 1998. (Modern Library Ser.). 288p. pap. 12.95 (0-375-75250-1) Random Hse., Inc.
—The Magnificent Ambersons. 1960. 14.50 o.p. (0-8446-1443-2) Smith, Peter Pub., Inc.
—The Magnificent Ambersons. l.t. ed. 1995. 446p. 21.95 (0-7838-1223-X) Thorndike Pr.
—Penrod. reprint ed. lib. bdg. 25.95 (0-88411-701-4) Amereon, Ltd.
—Penrod, Set. 1990. (J). audio 35.95 (1-55685-172-3) Audio Bk. Contractors, Inc.
—Penrod. 1983. 321p. reprint ed. lib. bdg. 27.95 (0-89966-178-5) Buccaneer Bks., Inc.
—Penrod. 1999. (Works of Booth Tarkington). 345p. reprint ed. lib. bdg. 108.00 (1-58201-864-2) Classic Bks.
—Penrod. 1985. (Library of Indiana Classics). (Illus.). 320p. 25.00 (0-253-34311-9); pap. 11.95 (0-253-20361-9, MB-361) Indiana Univ. Pr.
Thom, James A. The Red Heart. 1997. 448p. 25.00 o.p. (0-345-39004-0) Ballantine Bks.
Thom, James Alexander. The Red Heart. 1998. 544p. mass mkt. 7.50 (0-345-36471-6, Ballantine Bks.) Ballantine Bks.
Thomas, Mary A. Jump with Jeremy: What Hoosiers Do on the Way to the Zoo. Hodge, Ellen & Poore, Luz, eds. Still, James & Escabar, Urias, trs. from ENG. 1988. (SPA., Illus.). 47p. (Orig.). (J). pap. 9.95 (0-944326-00-5) Children's Corner Pr.
Thompson, Maurice. Alice of Old Vincennes. reprint ed. lib. bdg. 48.00 (0-7426-1113-2); 2001. pap. text 28.00 (0-7426-6113-X) Classic Bks.
—Alice of Old Vincennes. 2003. 280p. 26.95 (1-59408-485-8); pap. 18.00 (1-59408-269-3) Cork Hill Pr.
—Alice of Old Vincennes. 1996. (Illus.). 24p. pap. 9.95 (0-915992-99-X) Eastern National.
—Alice of Old Vincennes. 1985. (Library of Indiana Classics). (Illus.). 438p. 20.00 o.p. (0-253-30402-4); pap. 8.95 o.p. (0-253-20362-7, MB-362) Indiana Univ. Pr.
—Alice of Old Vincennes. 1985. (Illus.). reprint ed. lib. bdg. 15.50 o.p. (0-8398-1955-2) Irvington Pubs.
—Stories of the Cherokee Hills. 1977. (Short Story Index Reprint Ser.). 23.95 (0-8369-3415-6) Ayer Co. Pubs., Inc.
Thrasher, Crystal. End of a Dark Road. 1982. 228p. (J). (gr. 3-7). 12.95 o.p. (0-689-50250-8, McElderry, Margaret K.) Simon & Schuster Children's Publishing.
Tierney, Ronald. The Concrete Pillow. 1997. (Mystery Ser.). 256p. per. (0-373-26230-2, 1-26230-2, Worldwide Library) Harlequin Enterprises, Ltd.
—The Concrete Pillow. 1995. 230p. 21.00 o.p. (0-312-11762-0, Saint Martin's Minotaur) St. Martin's Pr.
—The Iron Glove. 1992. 224p. 17.95 o.p. (0-312-08226-6, Saint Martin's Minotaur) St. Martin's Pr.
—The Steel Web. l.t. ed. 1993. (General Ser.). 321p. pap. 17.95 (0-8161-5458-9, Macmillan Reference USA) Gale Group.
—The Steel Web. 1991. 240p. 17.95 o.p. (0-312-06473-X, Saint Martin's Minotaur) St. Martin's Pr.
—The Stone Veil. 1990. 208p. 15.95 o.p. (0-312-03940-9, Saint Martin's Minotaur) St. Martin's Pr.
Vice, Lisa. Reckless Driver. 288p. 1996. pap. 10.95 o.p. (0-452-27261-0, Plume); 1995. 21.95 o.s.i (0-525-93863-X, Dutton) Dutton/Plume.
Wallace, Kathleen. The True Life Story of Isobel Roundtree: A Novel. 1993. 178p. 19.00 o.p. (0-87483-263-2) August Hse. Pubs., Inc.
West, Jessamyn. The Friendly Persuasion. 2003. 228p. pap. 13.00 (0-15-602909-X, Harvest Bks.); 1991. 228p. pap. 12.00 o.s.i (0-15-633606-5, Harvest Bks.); 1945. 216p. 10.95 o.s.i (0-15-133605-9) Harcourt Trade Pubs.
—The Friendly Persuasion. 1981. pap. 5.95 o.p. (0-14-005706-4, Penguin Bks.) Viking Penguin.
—Friendly Persuasion. 22.95 (0-8488-0663-8) Amereon, Ltd.
—Friendly Persuasion. 1982. reprint ed. lib. bdg. 27.95 (0-89966-395-8) Buccaneer Bks., Inc.
—The Friendly Persuasion. unabr. ed. 1979. audio 48.00 (0-7366-0166-X, 1168) Books on Tape, Inc.
—The Massacre at Fall Creek. 1976. 320p. mass mkt. 1.95 o.s.i (0-449-22771-5, C2771, Fawcett) Ballantine Bks.
—The Massacre at Fall Creek. unabr. ed. 1980. audio 72.00 (0-7366-0255-0, 1250) Books on Tape, Inc.
—The Massacre at Fall Creek. 1986. 384p. pap. 12.00 (0-15-657681-3, Harvest Bks.); 1975. 14.95 o.s.i (0-15-157820-6) Harcourt Trade Pubs.
—The Massacre at Fall Creek. 1987. 18.50 o.p. (0-8446-6274-7) Smith, Peter Pub., Inc.
Wilkerson, Michael & Galyan, Deborah, eds. New Territory: Contemporary Indiana Fiction. 1990. 176p. 23.95 (0-253-36544-9); pap. 5.95 (0-253-20595-6, MB-595) Indiana Univ. Pr.

**INDIANAPOLIS (IND.)—FICTION**

Baxter, Nancy N. Charmed Circle-Indianapolis, 1895: A Mystery. 1994. 350p. pap. 18.95 (1-878208-52-7) Emmis Bks.
Lewin, Michael Z. And Baby Will Fall. l.t. ed. 1989. 304 p. pap. (1-55504-755-6) BBC Audiobooks America.
—And Baby Will Fall. 1990. mass mkt. (0-373-26042-3, Harlequin Bks.) Harlequin Enterprises, Ltd.
—And Baby Will Fall. 1988. 224p. 16.95 o.p. (0-688-06880-4, Morrow, William & Co.) Morrow/Avon.
—Ask the Right Question. 1979. 1.75 o.p. (0-425-04027-5) Berkley Publishing Group.
—Ask the Right Question. 1984. 192p. reprint ed. mass mkt. 3.50 o.p. (0-06-080711-3, P 711) HarperCollins Pubs.
—Ask the Right Question. 1991. mass mkt. 4.95 o.s.i (0-446-40021-1, Mysterious Pr. Paperback Bks.) Warner Bks., Inc.
—Called by a Panther. 1991. 17.95 o.p. (0-89296-439-1) Mysterious Pr.
—Called by a Panther. 1992. 272p. mass mkt. 4.99 o.s.i (0-446-40159-5) Warner Bks., Inc.
—The Enemies Within. 1979. mass mkt. 1.75 o.p. (0-425-04029-1) Berkley Publishing Group.
—Enemies Within. 1991. mass mkt. 4.95 o.s.i (0-446-40024-6, Mysterious Pr. Paperback Bks.) Warner Bks., Inc.
—The Enemies Within. 1984. 240p. reprint ed. mass mkt. 3.50 o.p. (0-06-080712-1, P 712, Perennial) HarperTrade.
—Hard Line. 1984. 256p. mass mkt. 3.50 o.p. (0-06-080720-2, P 720) HarperCollins Pubs.
—Hard Line: A Lt. Leroy Powder Novel. 1996. (Lt. Leroy Powder Novel Ser.). 256p. reprint ed. pap. 10.00 (0-88150-346-0, Foul Play) Norton, W. W. & Co., Inc.
—Late Payments. 1986. 224p. 13.95 o.p. (0-688-04342-9, Morrow, William & Co.) Morrow/Avon.
—Late Payments. 1987. 224p. pap. 3.50 o.p. (0-14-009875-5, Penguin Bks.) Viking Penguin.
—Late Payments: A Lt. Leroy Powder Novel. 1996. (Lt. Leroy Powder Novel Ser.). 216p. reprint ed. pap. 10.00 (0-88150-347-9, Foul Play) Norton, W. W. & Co., Inc.
—Missing Woman. 1982. mass mkt. 2.25 o.p. (0-425-05391-1) Berkley Publishing Group.
—Missing Woman. 1985. 224p. reprint ed. mass mkt. 3.50 o.p. (0-06-080709-1, P 709, Perennial) HarperTrade.
—Missing Woman. 1981. 224p. 10.95 o.p. (0-394-50007-5, Knopf Bks. for Young Readers) Random Hse. Children's Bks.
—Missing Woman. 1991. mass mkt. 4.99 (0-446-40026-2, Mysterious Pr. Paperback Bks.) Warner Bks., Inc.
—Night Cover. 1995. (Lt. Leroy Powder Novel Ser.). 256p. reprint ed. pap. 10.00 o.p. (0-88150-345-2, Foul Play) Norton, W. W. & Co., Inc.
—Night Cover. 1976. 7.95 o.p. (0-394-49644-2, Knopf Bks. for Young Readers) Random Hse. Children's Bks.
—Out of Season. 1985. (Albert Samson Novel Ser.). 256p. reprint ed. mass mkt. 3.50 o.p. (0-06-080774-1, P 774, Perennial) HarperTrade.
—Out of Season. 1984. (Albert Samson, Private Eye Ser.). 256p. 12.95 o.p. (0-688-03903-0, Morrow, William & Co.) Morrow/Avon.
—Out of Season. 1991. mass mkt. 4.99 o.s.i (0-446-40027-0, Mysterious Pr. Paperback Bks.) Warner Bks., Inc.
—The Silent Salesman. 1981. mass mkt. 2.25 o.p. (0-425-04031-3) Berkley Publishing Group.
—The Silent Salesman. 1985. 272p. mass mkt. 3.50 o.p. (0-06-080736-9, P 736, Perennial) HarperTrade.
—The Silent Salesman. 1978. 7.95 o.p. (0-394-40433-5, Knopf Bks. for Young Readers) Random Hse. Children's Bks.
—The Silent Salesman. 1991. mass mkt. 4.99 o.s.i (0-446-40025-4, Mysterious Pr. Paperback Bks.) Warner Bks., Inc.
—Underdog. 1993. 272p. 18.95 (0-89296-440-5) Mysterious Pr.
—Underdog. 1995. 256p. mass mkt. 5.50 (0-446-40436-5, Mysterious Pr. Paperback Bks.) Warner Bks., Inc.
—Way We Die Now. 1991. mass mkt. 4.95 o.s.i (0-446-40023-8, Mysterious Pr. Paperback Bks.) Warner Bks., Inc.
—The Way We Die Now. 1979. 1.75 o.p. (0-425-04028-3) Berkley Publishing Group.

—The Way We Die Now. 1984. 224p. reprint ed. mass mkt. 3.50 o.p. (*0-06-080710-5*, P 710) HarperCollins Pubs.

Schanker, D. R. A Criminal Appeal. 2000. 352p. mass mkt. 5.99 o.s.i (*0-440-23581-2*) Dell Publishing.

—A Criminal Appeal. 1998. 288p. 23.95 (*0-312-19253-3*, Saint Martin's Minotaur) St. Martin's Pr.

—Natural Law. 2001. 242p. 22.95 (*0-312-26684-7*, Saint Martin's Minotaur) St. Martin's Pr.

Thomas, Mary A. Jump with Jeremy: What Hoosiers Do on the Way to the Zoo. Hodge, Ellen & Poore, Luz, eds. Still, James & Escabar, Urias, trs. from ENG. 1988. (SPA., Illus.). 47p. (Orig.). (J). pap. 9.95 (*0-944326-00-5*) Children's Corner Pr.

Tierney, Ronald. The Concrete Pillow. 1997. (Mystery Ser.). 256p. per. (*0-373-26230-2*, 1-26230-2, Worldwide Library) Harlequin Enterprises, Ltd.

—The Concrete Pillow. 1995. 230p. 21.00 o.p. (*0-312-11762-0*, Saint Martin's Minotaur) St. Martin's Pr.

—The Iron Glove. 1992. 224p. 17.95 o.p. (*0-312-08226-6*, Saint Martin's Minotaur) St. Martin's Pr.

—The Steel Web. l.t. ed. 1993. (General Ser.). 321p. pap. 17.95 (*0-8161-5458-9*, Macmillan Reference USA) Gale Group.

—The Steel Web. 1991. 240p. 17.95 o.p. (*0-312-06473-X*, Saint Martin's Minotaur) St. Martin's Pr.

—The Stone Veil. 1990. 208p. 15.95 o.p. (*0-312-03940-9*, Saint Martin's Minotaur) St. Martin's Pr.

## INDONESIA—FICTION

Alberts, A. The Islands. Beekman, E. M., ed. Koning, Hans, tr. from DUT. 1983. (Library of the Indies). Orig. Title: De Eilanden. (Illus.). 160p. text 30.00 (*0-87023-385-8*) Univ. of Massachusetts Pr.

Baum, Vicki. A Tale from Bali. 2000. 512p. pap. 19.95 (*962-593-502-9*) Periplus Editions (HK), Ltd. HKG. *Dist:* Tuttle Publishing.

Bloem, Marion. Cockatoo's Lie. Boeke, Wanda, tr. 1996. 250p. pap. text 11.95 o.p. (*1-879679-08-6*) Women In Translation.

Bosse, Malcolm. Stranger at the Gate. 1991. 4.99 o.p. (*0-517-07520-2*) Random Hse. Value Publishing.

—Stranger at the Gate. 1989. 19.95 o.p. (*0-671-66785-8*, Simon & Schuster) Simon & Schuster.

Conrad, Joseph. Almayer's Folly: A Story of an Eastern River. Higdon, David L. et al, eds. 1994. (Cambridge Edition of the Works of Joseph Conrad). (Illus.). 324p. 95.00 (*0-521-43205-7*) Cambridge Univ. Pr.

—Lord Jim. 2000. 252p. E-Book 9.95 (*0-594-06669-7*) 1873 Pr.

—Lord Jim. 8.97 (*0-673-58342-2*) Addison-Wesley Longman, Inc.

—Lord Jim. Date not set. lib. bdg. 24.95 (*0-8488-1272-7*) Amereon, Ltd.

—Lord Jim. l.t. ed. 1999. 509p. pap. 22.95 (*1-55701-275-X*) BNI Pubns., Inc.

—Lord Jim. 1981. 288p. mass mkt. 4.95 (*0-553-21361-X*); mass mkt. 1.95 o.s.i (*0-553-21027-0*) Bantam Bks. (Bantam Classics).

—Lord Jim. 1971. 320p. reprint ed. lib. bdg. 14.00 (*0-8376-0409-5*) Bentley Pubs.

—Lord Jim. 2001. per. 9.90 (*1-891355-07-4*) Blue Unicorn Editions.

—Lord Jim. 1988. lib. bdg. 25.95 (*0-89966-057-6*) Buccaneer Bks., Inc.

—Lord Jim. (Collected Works of Joseph Conrad). 2001. pap. text 28.00 (*0-7426-7652-8*); reprint ed. lib. bdg. 98.00 (*0-7426-2652-0*) Classic Bks.

—Lord Jim. l.t. ed. 1999. 509p. pap. 22.95 (*1-58855-017-6*) Cyber Classics, Inc.

—Lord Jim. 1927. 12.95 o.p. (*0-385-04265-5*) Doubleday Publishing.

—Lord Jim. 1999. (Dover Thrift Editions Ser.). 256p. pap. 2.00 (*0-486-40650-4*) Dover Pubns., Inc.

—Lord Jim. 1978. 1.95 o.p. (*0-460-01925-2*, Dutton) Dutton/Plume.

—Lord Jim. 1982. (FRE.). 512p. pap. 13.95 (*0-7859-1962-7*, 2070374033) French & European Pubns., Inc.

—Lord Jim. l.t. ed. 2001. 310p. 27.95 (*0-7838-9524-0*, Macmillan Reference USA) Gale Group.

—Lord Jim. 1998. (SPA.). 416p. (*84-320-3974-8*) GeoPlaneta, Editorial, S. A.

—Lord Jim. Zabel, Morton D., ed. 1958. pap. 16.36 (*0-395-05121-5*, Riverside Editions) Houghton Mifflin Co.

—Lord Jim. l.t. ed. 1680p. pap. 113.00 (*0-7583-1423-X*); 1177p. pap. 81.00 (*0-7583-1421-3*); 957p. pap. 70.00 (*0-7583-1420-5*); 748p. pap. 50.00 (*0-7583-1419-1*); 584p. pap. 41.00 (*0-7583-1418-3*); 426p. pap. 33.00 (*0-7583-1417-5*); 328p. pap. 28.00 (*0-7583-1416-7*); 1448p. pap. 93.00 (*0-7583-1422-1*); 328p. lib. bdg. 34.00 (*0-7583-1408-6*); 957p. lib. bdg. 82.00 (*0-7583-1412-4*); 1680p. lib. bdg. 131.00 (*0-7583-1415-9*); 1448p. lib. bdg. 105.00 (*0-7583-1414-0*); 1177p. lib. bdg. 93.00 (*0-7583-1413-2*); 748p. lib. bdg. 56.00 (*0-7583-1411-6*); 584p. lib. bdg. 47.00 (*0-7583-1410-8*); 426p. lib. bdg. 39.00 (*0-7583-1409-4*) Huge Print Pr.

—Lord Jim. unabr. ed. 1998. (Wordsworth Classics Ser.). (J). (gr. 6-12). 5.27 (*0-89061-037-1*, R0371WW) Jamestown.

—Lord Jim. Stemach, Jerry, ed. l.t. ed. (Illus.). 2002. text 150.00 (*1-58702-045-9*); 2001. text 50.00 (*1-58702-755-0*) Johnston, Don Inc.

—Lord Jim. 1992. (Everyman's Library). 400p. 17.00 (*0-679-40544-5*) Knopf, Alfred A. Inc.

—Lord Jim. 1999. (Cloth Bound Pocket Ser.). (Illus.). 7.95 (*3-8290-2842-3*, 521119) Konemann.

—Lord Jim. 1981. (English As a Second Language Bk.). pap. text 5.95 o.p. (*0-582-53420-8*, 74062) Longman Publishing Group.

—Lord Jim. mass mkt. 0.50 o.p. (*0-451-02641-1*, Signet Bks.); 1961. mass mkt. 0.50 o.p. (*0-451-50051-2*, Signet Classics); 1961. mass mkt. 1.25 o.p. (*0-451-50922-6*, Signet Classics); 1961. mass mkt. 1.50 o.p. (*0-451-51057-7*, Signet Classics); 1961. mass mkt. 1.95 o.p. (*0-451-51195-6*, Signet Classics); 1961. 320p. mass mkt. 4.95 o.s.i (*0-451-52234-6*, CJ1195, Signet Classics); 1961. mass mkt. 0.75 o.p. (*0-451-50757-6*, Signet Classics); 100th anniv. ed. 2000. 352p. mass mkt. 4.95 (*0-451-52767-4*, Signet Bks.) NAL.

—Lord Jim. 1968. pap. text o.p. (*0-393-09656-4*) Norton, W. W. & Co., Inc.

—Lord Jim. 2000. (Oxford World's Classics Ser.). 368p. 15.00 o.p. (*0-19-210044-0*) Oxford Univ. Pr., Inc.

—Lord Jim. Batchelor, John, ed. & intro. by. (Oxford World's Classics Ser.). 2000. 352p. pap. 4.95 (*0-19-283512-2*); 1983. 460p. pap. 4.95 o.p. (*0-19-281625-X*) Oxford Univ. Pr., Inc.

—Lord Jim. Berthoud, Jacques, ed. 2nd ed. 2003. (Oxford World's Classics). (Illus.). 400p. pap. 5.95 (*0-19-284067-3*) Oxford Univ. Pr., Inc.

—Lord Jim. 1971. pap. 1.95 o.p. (*0-14-000529-3*) Penguin Group (USA) Inc.

—Lord Jim. l.t. ed. 1981. (Charnwood Large Print Ser.). 493p. 29.99 (*0-7089-8014-7*, Charnwood) Thorpe, F. A. Pubs. GBR. *Dist:* Ulverscroft Large Print Bks., Ltd., Ulverscroft Large Print Canada, Ltd.

—Lord Jim. 1961. (Signet Classics Ser.). 11.00 (*0-606-02758-0*) Turtleback Bks.

—Lord Jim. 2000. (Illus.). 320p. pap. 7.95 (*0-460-87665-1*, Everyman's Classic Library in Paperback) Tuttle Publishing.

—Lord Jim. Hampson, Robert, ed. 1989. (Penguin Great Books of the 20th Century). 384p. 5.95 (*0-14-018092-3*, Penguin Classics) Viking Penguin.

—Lord Jim. Hampton, Robert, ed. 1986. (Penguin Twentieth-Century Classics Ser.). 384p. pap. 1.95 o.p. (*0-14-043169-1*, Penguin Classics) Viking Penguin.

—Lord Jim. 1998. (Classics Library). 272p. pap. 3.95 (*1-85326-037-1*, 0371WW) Wordsworth Editions, Ltd. GBR. *Dist:* Casemate Pubs. & Bk. Distributors, LLC.

—Lord Jim: An Authoritative Text, Backgrounds, Essays in Criticism. Moser, Thomas C. & Sherry, Norman, eds. 2nd ed. 1996. (Critical Editions Ser.). (C). pap. text 10.50 (*0-393-96335-7*) Norton, W. W. & Co., Inc.

—Lord Jim & Nostromo. 2000. (Modern Library Ser.). 816p. pap. 12.95 (*0-375-75489-X*, Modern Library) Random House Adult Trade Publishing Group.

—Nostromo & Lord Jim. 2000. E-Book 4.95 (*0-679-64125-4*, Modern Library) Random House Adult Trade Publishing Group.

Conrad, Joseph & Batchelor, John. Lord Jim. 2000. E-Book 5.20 (*0-585-36167-3*) netLibrary, Inc.

Conrad, Joseph & Watts, Cedric. Lord Jim. 2000. (Literary Texts Ser.). (Illus.). 455p. (C). pap. (*1-55111-172-1*) Broadview Pr.

Darling, Diana. The Painted Alphabet. 1994. 224p. reprint ed. pap. 12.00 o.p. (*1-55597-214-4*) Graywolf Pr.

Duncan, Robert L. In the Enemy Camp. 1985. 312p. 15.95 o.s.i (*0-385-29388-7*, Delacorte Pr.) Dell Publishing.

Highland, Frederick. Ghost Eater. 2003. 320p. 24.95 (*0-312-30671-7*) St. Martin's Pr.

Koch, C. J. The Year of Living Dangerously. 1983. 304p. pap. 14.00 (*0-14-006535-0*, Penguin Bks.) Penguin Group (USA) Inc.

Lynch, Patrick. Carriers. 1996. 448p. mass mkt. 6.99 o.s.i (*0-425-15488-2*) Berkley Publishing Group.

McKinna, John. Tiger Reef. 2000. 400p. mass mkt. 6.99 o.s.i (*0-451-40919-1*, Onyx) NAL.

Schulman, Audrey. Swimming with Jonah: A Novel. 1999. 261p. 22.00 (*0-380-97686-2*, Avon Bks.) Morrow/Avon.

Starrenburg, Johan W. Papuan Adventure. Starrenburg, Hasko, tr. from DUT. 1991. 10.95 o.p. (*0-533-09096-2*) Vantage Pr., Inc.

Toer, Pramoedya Ananta. Child of All Nations. Lane, Max, tr. from IND. 1993. 352p. 22.00 o.p. (*0-688-12726-6*, Morrow, William & Co.) Morrow/Avon.

—Fugitive. 2000. 176p. pap. 12.00 (*0-14-029652-2*) Penguin Group (USA) Inc.

—House of Glass: A Novel. Lane, Max, tr. & intro. by. 1996. 352p. 26.00 o.p. (*0-688-14594-9*, Morrow, William & Co.) Morrow/Avon.

Van Dis, Adriaan. My Father's War: A Novel. White, Claire N., tr. from DUT. 1996. (International Fiction Ser.). 272p. text 23.00 (*1-56584-033-X*) New Pr., The.

Vogelaar-Van Amersfoort, Alie. Tekko & the White Man. Ekema, Alice, tr. from DUT. 1993. (Tekko Ser.: No. 1). (Illus.). 106p. (Orig.). pap. 6.90 (*0-921100-47-7*) Inheritance Pubns.

—Tekko Returns. 1997. (Tekko Ser.). (Illus.). (J). pap. 6.90 (*0-921100-75-2*) Inheritance Pubns.

—Tekko the Fugitive. Van Brugge, Jean, tr. from DUT. 1995. (Tekko Ser.: No. 2). (Illus.). 93p. (Orig.). pap. 6.90 (*0-921100-74-4*) Inheritance Pubns.

Wiese, Michael. On the Edge of a Dream: Magic & Madness in Bali. 1994. (Illus.). 326p. pap. 16.95 (*0-941188-19-1*, BALI) Wiese, Michael Productions.

Wilson, Greta. The Ripening Corn. 1998. 320p. pap. 15.00 (*0-9666160-0-6*) Matahari Pr.

## IOWA—FICTION

Agee, Jonis. Sweet Eyes. 2003. vi, 405p. pap. 15.95 (*0-8032-5948-4*, Bison Bks.) Univ. of Nebraska Pr.

—Sweet Eyes: A Novel. 1992. 416p. reprint ed. pap. 13.00 o.p. (*0-06-097450-8*, Perennial) HarperTrade.

Bauer, Douglas. The Book of Famous Iowans: A Novel. 256p. 1998. pap. 12.00 o.s.i (*0-8050-6002-2*, Owl Bks.); 1997. 25.00 o.s.i (*0-8050-4300-4*) Holt, Henry & Co.

Bingham, Doris. Jim McKay. 2001. 125p. pap. 20.99 (*1-4010-0357-5*) Xlibris Corp.

Bly, Stephen A. The Senator's Other Daughter. 2001. (Belles of Lordsburg Ser.: Vol. 1). 236p. pap. 10.99 (*1-58134-236-5*) Crossway Bks.

—The Senator's Other Daughter. l.t. ed. 2002. 420p. (Belles of Lordsburg Ser.: No. 1). pap. 16.95 (*1-4104-0035-2*, Walker Large Print); 26.95 (*0-7862-4026-1*) Gale Group.

Bullard, Lucy & Sollitt, Kenneth. A Family History. 1992. (Ann of the Prairie Ser.: Vol. 5). 233p. pap. 7.95 (*0-940652-10-2*) Inheritance Pubns.

Bury, Stephen. The Cobweb. 1997. 448p. mass mkt. 6.50 o.s.i (*0-553-57545-7*) Bantam Bks.

Calia, Charles L. The Unspeakable. 1924. pap. (*0-688-16642-3*, Quill) HarperTrade.

—The Unspeakable. 1998. 224p. 23.00 (*0-688-15119-1*, Morrow, William & Co.) Morrow/Avon.

—The Unspeakable: A Novel. 1999. 224p. reprint ed. pap. 12.00 o.s.i (*0-688-16710-1*, Quill) HarperTrade.

Chlehak, Susan T. Harmony. 1990. 256p. 18.95 o.p. (*0-89919-941-0*) Houghton Mifflin Co.

Collins, Max Allan. The Baby Blue Rip-Off. 1987. 224p. pap. 2.95 o.p. (*0-8125-0154-3*, Tor Bks.) Doherty, Tom Assocs., LLC.

—The Baby Blue Rip-Off. 1983. 11.95 o.s.i (*0-8027-5475-9*) Walker & Co.

—Bait Money, No. 1. 1981. 192p. pap. 1.95 o.p. (*0-523-41159-6*, Pinnacle Bks.) Kensington Publishing Corp.

—Blood Money. rev. ed. 1981. 192p. pap. 1.95 o.p. (*0-523-41160-X*, Pinnacle Bks.) Kensington Publishing Corp.

—The Broker's Wife. 1976. (Quarry Ser.). 1.50 o.p. (*0-425-03187-X*) Berkley Publishing Group.

—Fly Paper. 1981. 192p. pap. 1.95 o.p. (*0-523-41161-8*, Pinnacle Bks.) Kensington Publishing Corp.

—Hush Money. 1981. (Nolan Ser.: No.4). 192p. pap. 1.95 o.p. (*0-523-41162-6*, Pinnacle Bks.) Kensington Publishing Corp.

—Kill Your Darlings. 1988. 224p. pap. 3.95 o.p. (*0-8125-0161-6*, Tor Bks.) Doherty, Tom Assocs., LLC.

—Kill Your Darlings. 1984. 192p. 13.95 o.s.i (*0-8027-5594-1*) Walker & Co.

—Nice Weekend for a Murder. 1986. 192p. 15.95 o.s.i (*0-8027-5656-5*) Walker & Co.

—A Nice Weekend for a Murder. 1994. 208p. mass mkt. 3.99 (*0-8125-0138-1*, Tor Bks.) Doherty, Tom Assocs., LLC.

—No Cure for Death. 1987. 288p. reprint ed. pap. 3.50 o.p. (*0-8125-0157-8*, Tor Bks.) Doherty, Tom Assocs., LLC.

—No Cure for Death. 1983. 192p. 12.95 o.p. (*0-8027-5488-0*) Walker & Co.

—Primary Target. 1987. (Quarry Novel Ser.). 208p. 14.95 o.p. (*0-88150-098-4*) Countryman Pr.

—Quarry. 1985. (Quarry Ser.). 224p. pap. 4.95 o.p. (*0-88150-057-7*) Countryman Pr.

—Quarry's Cut. 1986. (Quarry Ser.). 224p. reprint ed. pap. 4.95 o.p. (*0-88150-069-0*) Countryman Pr.

—Quarry's Deal. 1986. (Quarry Ser.). 192p. reprint ed. pap. 4.95 o.p. (*0-88150-068-2*) Countryman Pr.

—Quarry's List. 1985. (Quarry Ser.). 192p. pap. 4.95 o.p. (*0-88150-058-5*) Countryman Pr.

—Scratch Fever. 1982. 192p. pap. 1.95 o.p. (*0-523-41164-2*, Pinnacle Bks.) Kensington Publishing Corp.

—A Shroud for Aquarius. 1988. 256p. pap. 3.95 o.p. (*0-8125-0163-2*, Tor Bks.) Doherty, Tom Assocs., LLC.

—A Shroud for Aquarius. 1985. (Mallory Mystery Ser.). 175p. 14.95 o.p. (*0-8027-5629-8*) Walker & Co.

—Spree. 320p. 1988. pap. 3.95 o.p. (*0-8125-0165-9*); 1987. 15.95 o.p. (*0-312-93029-1*) Doherty, Tom Assocs., LLC. (Tor Bks.).

Creighton, Kathleen. The Black Sheep's Baby. 2002. (Silhouette Intimate Moments Ser.). 256p. mass mkt. (*0-373-27231-6*, Silhouette) Harlequin Enterprises, Ltd.

Curtis, Robert. The Baseball Patch. 2001. pap. 12.95 (*0-595-18893-1*) iUniverse, Inc.

Dallas, Sandra. Alice's Tulips. 2001. 256p. pap. 12.95 (*0-312-28378-4*, Saint Martin's Griffin); 2000. 246p. 22.95 (*0-312-20359-4*) St. Martin's Pr.

—Alice's Tulips. l.t. ed. 2001. (Thorndike Press Large Print Americana Ser.). 413p. 28.95 (*0-7862-3224-2*) Thorndike Pr.

Denhart, Jeffrey. Just Bones. 1997. mass mkt. 5.95 (*1-885173-45-8*); 1996. 225p. text 20.95 o.p. (*1-885173-15-6*) Write Way Publishing.

Dick, Philip K. Ubik. 1983. 176p. mass mkt. 2.50 o.p. (*0-87997-859-7*) DAW Bks., Inc.

—Ubik. (Science Fiction Ser.). 1979. lib. bdg. 10.95 o.p. (*0-8398-2478-5*, Macmillan Reference USA); 2001. 279p. 26.95 (*0-7838-9585-2*, Hall, G. K. & Co.) Gale Group.

—Ubik. 1991. 224p. pap. 12.00 (*0-679-73664-6*, Vintage) Knopf Publishing Group.

Disch, Thomas M. On Wings of Song. 1988. 359p. mass mkt. 3.95 (*0-88184-443-8*, Carroll & Graf Pubs.) Avalon Publishing Group.

—On Wings of Song. 1985. 368p. pap. 3.50 o.p. (*0-553-25076-0*) Bantam Bks.

—On Wings of Song. 2002. pap. (*0-375-71364-6*, Vintage) Knopf Publishing Group.

—On Wings of Song. 1979. 10.95 o.p. (*0-312-58466-0*) St. Martin's Pr.

Evanick, Marcia. Wild Rose: Hand in Hand. 2000. (Zebra Bouquet Ser.: Vol. 61). 256p. mass mkt. 4.99 o.s.i (*0-8217-6684-8*, Zebra Bks.) Kensington Publishing Corp.

—Wild Rose: Wife in Name Only. 2000. (Zebra Bouquet Ser.: No. 45). 256p. mass mkt. 3.99 o.s.i (*0-8217-6603-1*) Kensington Publishing Corp.

Garlock, Dorothy. More Than Memory. l.t. ed. 2001. (Wheeler Large Print Book Ser.). 386p. 26.95 (*1-58724-009-2*, Wheeler Publishing, Inc.) Gale Group.

—More Than Memory. 2001. 416p. reprint ed. mass mkt. 6.99 (*0-446-60814-9*) Warner Bks., Inc.

Garwood, Julie. Heartbreaker. 2001. E-Book 9.99 (*1-58945-199-6*) Adobe Systems, Inc.

—Heartbreaker. l.t. ed. 2000. (Large Print Book Ser.). 556p. 30.95 (*1-56895-918-4*, Wheeler Publishing, Inc.) Gale Group.

—Heartbreaker. 544p. 2003. pap. 10.00 (*0-7434-7419-8*); 2001. mass mkt. 7.99 (*0-671-03400-6*) Simon & Schuster. (Pocket).

Gorman, Ed. Blood Moon. 1996. 308p. mass mkt. 5.99 o.p. (*0-312-95760-2*, St. Martin's Paperbacks) St. Martin's Pr.

—The Day the Music Died. 1999. 212p. 22.95 (*0-7867-0569-8*, Carroll & Graf Pubs.) Avalon Publishing Group.

—The Day the Music Died. 2000. (Sam McCain Mystery Ser.). 258p. mass mkt. 5.99 o.s.i (*0-425-17411-5*) Berkley Publishing Group.

—The Day the Music Died. l.t. ed. 1999. (Mystery Ser.). 323p. 27.95 (*0-7862-2032-5*) Thorndike Pr.

—The Day the Music Died. 2000. (Illus.). 12.04 (*0-606-18007-9*) Turtleback Bks.

—Harlot's Moon. 256p. 1999. mass mkt. 5.99 (*0-312-96771-3*, St. Martin's Paperbacks); 1998. 21.95 o.p. (*0-312-18108-6*, Saint Martin's Minotaur) St. Martin's Pr.

—Hawk Moon. 1996. 256p. 21.95 o.p. (*0-312-13980-2*, Saint Martin's Minotaur) St. Martin's Pr.

—Save the Last Dance for Me. 2001. 224p. 24.00 (*0-7867-0968-5*, Carroll & Graf Pubs.) Avalon Publishing Group.

—Save the Last Dance for Me. 2003. (WWL Mystery Ser.: No. 461). 256p. mass mkt. (*0-373-26461-5*, Worldwide Library) Harlequin Enterprises, Ltd.

—Save the Last Dance for Me. l.t. ed. 2002. (Mystery Ser.). 335p. 29.95 (*0-7862-4398-8*) Thorndike Pr.

—Wake up Little Susie: A Sam McCain Mystery. 2000. 225p. 22.95 (*0-7867-0665-1*, Carroll & Graf Pubs.) Avalon Publishing Group.

—Wake up Little Susie: A Sam McCain Mystery. 2001. 240p. mass mkt. 5.99 o.s.i (*0-425-17855-2*) Berkley Publishing Group.

—Wake up Little Susie: A Sam McCain Mystery. l.t. ed. 2000. (Mystery Ser.). 337p. 29.95 (*0-7862-2464-9*) Thorndike Pr.

—Will You Still Love Me Tomorrow? 2001. 256p. 22.95 (*0-7867-0775-5*, Carroll & Graf Pubs.) Avalon Publishing Group.

—Will You Still Love Me Tomorrow? 2002. 208p. reprint ed. mass mkt. 5.99 (*0-425-18716-0*, Prime Crime) Berkley Publishing Group.

—Will You Still Love Me Tomorrow? l.t. ed. 2001. 301p. 29.95 (*0-7862-3672-8*); 280p. (*0-7540-4738-5*); 280p. (*0-7540-4739-3*) Thorndike Pr.

Hall, Lynn. Dagmar Schultz & the Angel Edna. 1989. (Dagmar Schultz Ser.). 96p. (J). (gr. 5-8). lib. bdg. 13.95 o.s.i (*0-684-19097-4*, Atheneum) Simon & Schuster Children's Publishing.

Harrison, Nick. While Yet We Live. 1991. (Ann of the Prairie Ser.: Vol. 4). 224p. (YA). pap. 6.95 o.p. (*0-940652-08-0*) Sunrise Bks.

Harrison, Nick & Sollitt, Kenneth. These Years of Promise. 1988. (Ann of the Prairie Ser.: Vol. 3). 203p. pap. 6.95 (*0-940652-05-6*) Inheritance Pubns.

Harstad, Donald. Code Sixty-One. 2002. 384p. 23.95 (*0-385-50118-8*) Doubleday Publishing.

—Code 61. 2003. 480p. mass mkt. 6.99 (*0-553-58098-1*) Bantam Bks.

—Eleven Days in Nation County. 1998. 304p. 22.95 o.s.i (*0-385-48894-7*) Doubleday Publishing.

—The Heartland Experiment: A Novel. 2003. 320p. 23.95 (*0-385-50119-6*) Doubleday Publishing.

—Known Dead. 1999. 336p. 23.95 o.s.i (*0-385-48895-5*) Doubleday Publishing.

Hatcher, Robin Lee. Patterns of Love. l.t. ed. 1998. 320p. 25.95 (*1-57490-143-5*, Beeler Large Print Bks.) Beeler, Thomas T. Publisher.

—Patterns of Love. 1998. 416p. mass mkt. 6.50 o.s.i (*0-06-108688-6*) HarperCollins Pubs.

—Patterns of Love. 2001. 320p. pap. 10.99 (*0-310-23105-1*) Zondervan.

Hedges, Peter. An Ocean in Iowa: A Novel. 1998. 248p. (J). 22.95 (*0-7868-6404-4*) Hyperion Pr.

—An Ocean in Iowa: A Novel. 1999. 256p. pap. 11.00 (*0-684-85970-X*, Touchstone) Simon & Schuster.

Herbst, Josephine. Pity Is Not Enough. 1998. (Radical Novel Reconsidered Ser.). 400p. pap. text 18.95 (*0-252-06652-9*) Univ. of Illinois Pr.

Heynen, Jim. The Boys' House: New & Selected Stories. 2002. 208p. pap. 11.95 (*0-87351-438-6*) Minnesota Historical Society Pr.

Howard, Mary. Discovering the Body: A Novel. 2001. 304p. pap. 13.00 (*0-06-093717-3*, Perennial) HarperTrade.

—Discovering the Body: A Novel. 2000. 304p. 24.00 (*0-688-17156-7*, Morrow, William & Co.) Morrow/Avon.

Huffey, Rhoda. The Hallelujah Side. 1999. 262p. 23.00 (*1-883285-17-8*) Delphinium Bks., Inc.

—The Hallelujah Side. 2000. (Illus.). 272p. pap. 13.00 (*0-618-07471-6*, Mariner Bks.) Houghton Mifflin Co. Trade & Reference Div.

Hughes, Kathleen. Dear Mrs. Lindbergh. 2003. 320p. text 24.95 (*0-393-05785-2*) Norton, W. W. & Co., Inc.

King, Stephen. The Library Policeman. abr. unabr. ed. 1991. (Four Past Midnight Ser.). audio 30.95 (*0-453-00748-1*, 892527) Penguin/HighBridge.

Kinsella, W. P. Magic Time. 1999. 240p. pap. (*0-385-25767-8*) Doubleday Canada, Ltd. CAN. *Dist:* Random Hse., Inc.

—Magic Time. 2001. 224p. 19.95 (*0-89658-575-1*) Voyageur Pr., Inc.

—Shoeless Joe. 1996. pap. 11.00 o.s.i (*0-345-41007-6*); 1987. 256p. mass mkt. 6.99 o.s.i (*0-345-34256-9*, Del Rey); 1986. mass mkt. 3.50 o.s.i (*0-345-34226-7*); 1983. mass mkt. 2.95 o.s.i (*0-345-30921-9*) Ballantine Bks.

—Shoeless Joe. 265p. 1999. pap. 12.00 (*0-395-95773-7*); 1982. 12.20 o.p. (*0-395-32047-X*) Houghton Mifflin Co.

—Shoeless Joe. 2002. E-Book 5.99 (*0-7953-0532-X*) RosettaBooks.

Knapp, Susan. Bells Goes to the Fair. l.t. ed. 2002. (Illus.). 44p. (J). 12.95 (*1-888223-34-0*) McMillen Publishing.

Larimer, Jack H. Tulips: A Love Story Etched on the Higher Road of Life. 196p. 2002. 23.35 (*0-7596-2147-0*); 2001. pap. 15.54 (*0-7596-2017-2*) 1stBooks Library.

Manfred, Frederick. Of Lizards & Angels: A Saga of Siouxland. 1992. 624p. 24.95 o.p. (*0-8061-2417-2*) Univ. of Oklahoma Pr.

McCracken, Susan. For the Call of a Friend. 1997. 313p. 12.50 (*0-944350-41-0*) Friends United Pr.

—For the Gift of a Friend. 1995. 192p. pap. 11.00 (*0-944350-35-6*) Friends United Pr.

—For the Love of a Friend. 1994. 168p. 10.00 (*0-944350-29-1*) Friends United Pr.

McDonald, Julie. Petra. 1978. (Illus.). text 12.95 o.p. (*0-8138-1260-7*) Iowa State Pr.

Millhiser, Marlys. The Rampant Reaper: A Charlie Greene Mystery. 2002. 288p. 23.95 (*0-312-29096-9*, Saint Martin's Minotaur) St. Martin's Pr.

Moore, Patrick. Iowa. (Orig.). 1996. mass mkt. 6.95 o.s.i (*1-56333-423-2*); 2nd ed. 1998. reprint ed. mass mkt. 7.95 (*1-56333-702-9*) Masquerade Bks., Inc. (Hard Candy).

Mossman, Dow. The Stones of Summer. 2003. 576p. 19.95 (*0-7607-4884-5*); audio compact disk 29.95 (*0-7607-5215-X*) Barnes & Noble, Inc.

—The Stones of Summer. 2004. 576p. pap. 13.95 (*1-58567-517-2*) Overlook Pr., The.

Mukherjee, Bharati. Jasmine. audio 8.95 American Audio Prose Library, Inc.

—Jasmine. 1990. 244p. mass mkt. 6.99 o.s.i (*0-449-21923-2*, Fawcett) Ballantine Bks.

—Jasmine. 1989. 228p. 17.95 o.p. (*0-8021-1032-0*); 1999. 256p. reprint ed. pap. 12.00 (*0-8021-3630-3*, Grove Pr.) Grove/Atlantic, Inc.

Phillips, Susan Elizabeth. Wer Will Schon Einen Traummann: Roman. 2003. (GER.). 416p. pap. 23.00 (*1-4000-3999-1*) Random Hse. Information Group.

Rich, Virginia. The Cooking School Murders. 1982. 168p. 11.95 o.p. (*0-525-24110-8*, 01160-350, Dutton) Dutton/Plume.

—The Cooking School Murders. l.t. ed. 1982. 384p. reprint ed. 10.95 o.p. (*0-89621-399-4*) Thorndike Pr.

Roberts, James P. Bourland. 1999. (Other Door - Science Fiction - Macabre Ser.). 268p. 30.00 (*1-55246-162-9*); pap. 18.00 (*1-55246-163-7*) Battered Silicon Dispatch Box, The.

Schaap, James Calvin. In the Silence There Are Ghosts: A Novel. 1995. (Literary Fiction Ser.). 232p. (Orig.). (gr. 10). pap. 11.99 o.p. (*0-8010-8381-8*) Baker Bks.

Schultz, Robert. Madhouse Nudes. 1997. 287p. 21.50 (*0-684-83262-3*, Simon & Schuster) Simon & Schuster.

Smiley, Jane. At Paradise Gate. 16th l.t. ed. 2001. 271p. lib. bdg. 27.95 (*1-58547-073-2*) Ctr. Point Large Print.

—At Paradise Gate. 224p. 1998. pap. 12.00 (*0-684-85223-3*); 1993. pap. 11.00 (*0-671-88533-2*) Simon & Schuster. (Touchstone).

—A Thousand Acres. 1997. mass mkt. 9.50 (*0-8041-9717-2*); 1996. 416p. mass mkt. 7.99 o.s.i (*0-8041-1576-1*) Ballantine Bks. (Ivy Bks.).

—A Thousand Acres. 1991. 371p. 25.00 o.s.i (*0-394-57773-6*) Knopf, Alfred A. Inc.

—A Thousand Acres. 1992. 18.05 (*0-606-20075-4*) Turtleback Bks.

Sollitt, Kenneth. Our Changing Lives. 1986. (Ann of the Prairie Ser.: Pt. II). 182p. (J). reprint ed. pap. 6.95 (*0-940652-04-8*) Inheritance Pubns.

Steel, Danielle. Leap of Faith. 2001. 216p. 19.95 (*0-385-33296-3*, Delacorte Pr.) Dell Publishing.

—Leap of Faith. l.t. ed. 2001. 256p. 19.95 (*0-375-43109-8*) Random Hse. Large Print.

Steinbach, Meredith. Zara. 1996. 277p. pap. 15.95 (*0-8101-5059-X*, TriQuarterly Bks.) Northwestern Univ. Pr.

Suckow, Ruth. The Folks. 1992. E-Book 35.95 (*1-58729-233-5*); (Illus.). 740p. reprint ed. pap. text 17.95 (*0-87745-374-8*) Univ. of Iowa Pr.

—Iowa Interiors. Hardwick, Elizabeth, ed. 1977. (Rediscovered Fiction by American Women Ser.). reprint ed. lib. bdg. 29.95 (*0-405-10057-4*) Ayer Co. Pubs., Inc.

Taylor, John. Mysteries of the Body & the Mind. 1998. 130p. pap. text 12.95 (*1-885266-53-7*) Story Line Pr.

Taylor, Valerie. The Girls in 3-B. 2003. (Femmes Fatales Ser.). 208p. pap. 13.95 (*1-55861-456-7*); lib. bdg. 14.95 (*1-55861-462-1*) Feminist Pr. at The City Univ. of New York.

Waller, Robert James. The Bridges of Madison County. (Illus.). 1992. 192p. 12.95 (*0-446-51652-X*); 1995. 224p. reprint ed. mass mkt. 6.99 (*0-446-36449-5*) Warner Bks., Inc.

—Slow Waltz in Cedar Bend. unabr. ed. 1994. audio 30.00 o.p. Books on Tape, Inc.

—Slow Waltz in Cedar Bend. unabr. ed. 1993. audio 22.95 o.p. (*1-55800-876-4*, 592099); audio compact disk 59.95 o.p. (*1-55800-880-2*) NewStar Media, Inc.

—Slow Waltz in Cedar Bend. 1994. 227p. mass mkt. 4.99 o.s.i (*0-446-60164-0*); 1993. 200p. 25.00 (*0-446-51653-8*) Warner Bks., Inc.

—Slow Waltz in Cedar Bend & the Bridges of Madison County. 1993. audio 19.88 o.p. (*1-55800-927-2*, Dove Audio) NewStar Media, Inc.

Yepsen, David, et al. Politics is Murder: An Iowa Mystery. 2000. 224p. pap. 10.95 (*0-9662041-3-1*) KUNI/KHKE.

Young Bear, Ray A. Black Eagle Child: The Facepaint Narratives. 1992. (Singular Lives Ser.). (Illus.). 281p. 25.95 (*0-87745-356-X*) Univ. of Iowa Pr.

—Remnants of the First Earth. 320p. 1996. 23.00 o.p. (*0-8021-1581-0*); 1998. reprint ed. pap. 12.00 (*0-8021-3552-8*) Grove/Atlantic, Inc. (Grove Pr.).

## IRAN—FICTION

Barkhordar-Nahai, Gina. Cry of the Peacock, an Excerpt. 1991. o.s.i (*0-517-58475-1*) Crown Publishing Group.

Behrangi, Samad. The Little Black Fish & Other Modern Persian Stories. 1986. pap. 7.00 o.p. (*0-914478-22-2*, Three Continents) Rienner, Lynne Pubs., Inc.

—The Little Black Fish & Other Modern Persian Stories. Hegland, Mary & Hooglund, Eric, trs. from PER. 2nd ed. 1987. 106p. reprint ed. pap. 10.00 (*0-89410-621-X*, Three Continents) Rienner, Lynne Pubs., Inc.

Buchan, James. The Persian Bride: A Novel. 2002. 344p. pap. 13.00 (*0-618-21923-4*); 2000. (Illus.). 352p. 23.00 (*0-618-06740-X*) Houghton Mifflin Co. Trade & Reference Div. (Mariner Bks.).

Chubak, Sadeq. The Patient Stone. Ghanoonparvar, Mohammad R., tr. from PER. & intro. by. 1989. (Persian Literature in Translation: No. 1). 290p. 12.95 (*0-939214-62-8*) Mazda Pubs., Inc.

Cook, Jennifer. An Iranian Mosaic. 2003. 204p. pap. (*1-4120-0130-7*) Trafford Publishing.

Coyle, Harold. Sword Point. 1990. 416p. mass mkt. 6.99 (*0-671-73712-0*, Pocket); 1988. 388p. 18.95 o.p. (*0-671-66553-7*, Simon & Schuster) Simon & Schuster.

Danishvar, Simin. A Persian Requiem. Zand, Roxane, tr. from PER. 1992. 288p. 22.50 (*0-8076-1273-1*); pap. 12.50 (*0-8076-1274-X*) Braziller, George Inc.

Firouz, Anahita. In the Walled Gardens. 2003. 432p. (gr. 8 up). mass mkt. 7.99 (*0-316-71159-4*); 368p. reprint ed. pap. 13.95 (*0-316-16901-3*, Back Bay) Little Brown & Co.

—In the Walled Gardens: A Novel. 2002. 352p. 24.95 (*0-316-60854-8*); pap. (*0-316-09105-7*) Little Brown & Co.

Graham, Mark. The Fire Theft. l.t. ed. 1994. 607p. lib. bdg. 23.95 o.p. (*0-8161-5950-5*, Macmillan Reference USA) Gale Group.

—The Fire Theft. 406p. 4.98 o.p. (*0-8317-9315-5*) Smithmark Pubs., Inc.

—The Fire Theft. 1993. 400p. 21.00 o.p. (*0-670-84870-0*, Viking) Viking Penguin.

MarElia, Beatrice. The Great Mirage. 1986. pap. 13.95 (*0-87949-249-X*) Ashley Bks., Inc.

Morier, James. Sargozasht-e Haji Baba-Ye Isfahani Haji Baba-Ye Isfahani. Isfahani, Mirza H., tr. 1996. (Bibliotheca Iranica Ser.: No. 9). Orig. Title: The Adventures of Haji Baba of Isphahan. (PER., Illus.). 432p. (Orig.). pap. text 24.95 (*1-56859-042-3*) Mazda Pubs., Inc.

Mossanen, Dora Levy. Harem: A Novel. 2002. 384p. pap. 14.00 (*0-7432-3021-3*, Touchstone) Simon & Schuster.

Nahai, Gina B. Cry of the Peacock. 2000. 352p. reprint ed. pap. 13.95 (*0-7434-0337-1*, Washington Square Pr.) Simon & Schuster.

Noori, Naveed. Dakhmeh. 2003. 200p. pap. 14.95 (*1-902881-77-X*) Toby Pr.

Parsipur, Shahrnush. Women Without Men: A Novel of Modern Iran. Talattof, Kamran & Sharlet, Jocelyn, trs. 2004. 192p. pap. 13.95 (*1-55861-452-4*) Feminist Pr. at The City Univ. of New York.

—Women Without Men: A Novella. Talattof, Kamran & Sharlet, Jocelyn, trs. from PER. 1998. (Middle East Literature in Translation Ser.). 150p. 22.95 (*0-8156-0552-8*) Syracuse Univ. Pr.

Rabinyan, Dorit. Persian Brides. 2000. 236p. pap. 15.95 (*0-8076-1461-0*) Braziller, George Inc.

—Persian Brides. Lotan, Yael, tr. from HEB. 1998. 240p. 22.50 (*0-8076-1430-0*) Braziller, George Inc.

Rachlin, Nahid. Married to a Stranger. 1993. 232p. pap. 12.95 (*0-87286-276-3*) City Lights Bks.

Rizzi, Timothy. The Phalanx Dragon. 2000. 480p. reprint ed. pap. 6.99 (*0-8439-3885-4*, Leisure Bks.) Dorchester Publishing Co., Inc.

—The Phalanx Dragon. 1994. (Illus.). 432p. 21.95 o.p. (*1-55611-391-9*) Fine, Donald I. Bks.

Rufin, Jean C. The Siege of Isfahan. Wood, Willard, tr. from FRE. 2001. 416p. 26.95 (*0-393-04988-4*) Norton, W. W. & Co., Inc.

Rufin, Jean-Christophe. The Siege of Isfahan. 2002. 384p. pap. 14.95 (*0-393-32339-0*) Norton, W. W. & Co., Inc.

Seymour, Gerald. A Line in the Sand. 2000. (Illus.). 469p. mass mkt. (*0-552-14682-X*, Corgi) Bantam Bks.

—A Line in the Sand. 2000. (Illus.). 400p. 25.00 (*0-684-85477-5*, Simon & Schuster); 2001. 464p. reprint ed. mass mkt. 7.99 (*0-671-02530-9*, Pocket) Simon & Schuster.

—A Line in the Sand. l.t. ed. 2000. (Charnwood Large Print Ser.). 480p. o.p. (*0-7089-9131-9*, Ulverscroft) Thorpe, F. A. Pubs. GBR. *Dist:* Ulverscroft Large Print Bks., Ltd., Ulverscroft Large Print Canada, Ltd.

Xenophon. The Education of Cyrus. Ambler, Wayne, tr. from GEC. & anno. by. 2001. (Agora Editions Ser.). (Illus.). 336p. 45.00 (*0-8014-3818-7*); pap. 19.95 (*0-8014-8750-1*) Cornell Univ. Pr.

## IRELAND—FICTION

Aakhus, Patricia. The Voyage of Mael Duin's Curragh. 2nd ed. 1989. (Irish Literature Ser.). 236p. pap. 12.95 (*0-934257-31-0*) Story Line Pr.

Adler, Elizabeth A. Legacy of Secrets. 1994. 624p. mass mkt. 6.99 (*0-440-21657-5*) Dell Publishing.

Allison, Alcott. The White Stone: A Mystical Novel from Early Ireland. 1992. 155p. (Orig.). pap. 8.95 (*0-9620507-2-5*) Cosmic Concepts Pr.

Allison, Linda. The Journey of the Emerald Bottle. 2003. 189p. pap. 19.95 (*1-59129-774-5*) PublishAmerica, Inc.

Andrews, J. S. Cargo for a King. 1973. 176p. (J). (gr. 4-7). 6.95 o.p. (*0-525-27460-X*, Dutton) Dutton/Plume.

Andrews, Lyn. The Sisters O'Donnell. 2000. pap. 11.95 (*0-552-13600-X*) Transworld Publishers Ltd. GBR. *Dist:* Trafalgar Square.

—When Tomorrow Dawns. l.t. ed. 1999. (Magna Large Print Ser.). 464p. (*0-7505-1404-3*) Magna Large Print Bks. GBR. *Dist:* Ulverscroft Large Print Canada, Ltd.

Armstrong, Campbell. Jig. Congdon, Thomas, ed. 1987. 512p. 18.95 o.p. (*0-688-06879-0*, Morrow, William & Co.) Morrow/Avon.

—Jig. 1989. bds. 4.95 (*0-671-66524-3*, Pocket) Simon & Schuster.

Baker, Jeanette. Irish Fire. E-Book 6.50 (*1-58945-205-4*) Adobe Systems, Inc.

—Irish Fire. 2000. (Illus.). 384p. pap. 6.50 (*0-671-03407-3*, Pocket) Simon & Schuster.

—Nell. 1999. 418p. pap. 6.50 (*0-671-01735-7*, Pocket) Simon & Schuster.

—Spellbound. 2001. 368p. pap. 6.99 (*0-671-03458-8*); reprint ed. E-Book 6.99 (*0-7434-1807-7*) Simon & Schuster. (Pocket).

Ball, H. A. The Side Door: A Story of Action, Tension, Suspense. 1999. 244p. pap. 18.95 o.p. (*1-85756-309-3*) Janus Publishing Co. GBR. *Dist:* Paul & Co. Pubs. Consortium, Inc.

Banim, John. The Anglo-Irish of the Nineteenth Century 1828. 2003. (Hibernia Ser.). 248p. (*1-85477-221-X*) Woodstock Books.

Banim, John & Banim, Michael. The Anglo-Irish of the Nineteenth Century. Wolff, Robert L., ed. 1978. (Ireland Nineteenth Century Fiction Ser.: Vol. 20). 934p. lib. bdg. 152.00 o.p. (*0-8240-3469-4*) Garland Publishing, Inc.

Banville, John. Birchwood. 1973. 176p. 5.95 o.p. (*0-393-08572-4*) Norton, W. W. & Co., Inc.

Barlow, Jane. Irish Idylls. 1977. (Short Story Index Reprint Ser.). 23.95 (*0-8369-3082-7*) Ayer Co. Pubs., Inc.

—Irish Ways. 1977. (Short Story Index Reprint Ser.). (Illus.). 26.95 (*0-8369-3477-6*) Ayer Co. Pubs., Inc.

—Strangers at Lisconnel: A Second Series of Irish Idylls. 1977. (Short Story Index Reprint Ser.). reprint ed. 19.95 (*0-8369-3832-1*) Ayer Co. Pubs., Inc.

Barrett, Suzanne. Wild Irish Rogue. 2001. (Five Star Romance Ser.). 199p. 26.95 (*0-7862-3500-4*, Five Star) Gale Group.

—Wild Irish Rogue. 2000. (Zebra Bouquet Ser.: Vol. 53). 256p. mass mkt. 3.99 o.s.i (*0-8217-6649-X*, Zebra Bks.) Kensington Publishing Corp.

Barry, Sebastian. Annie Dunne. 2002. 224p. pap. (*0-571-20304-3*) Faber & Faber, Inc.

—Annie Dunne. l.t. ed. 2002. (Basic Ser.). 27.95 o.p. (*0-7862-4592-1*) Thorndike Pr.

—Annie Dunne. 2003. 256p. pap. 14.00 (*0-14-200287-9*); 2002. 320p. 24.95 (*0-670-03112-7*, Viking) Viking Penguin.

—The Whereabouts of Eneas McNulty. 1998. 308p. pap. 34.00 (*0-330-35196-6*) Picador GBR. *Dist:* Trans-Atlantic Pubns., Inc.

—The Whereabouts of Eneas McNulty. l.t. ed. 1998. (Basic Ser.). 429p. 28.95 (*0-7862-1709-X*) Thorndike Pr.

—The Whereabouts of Eneas McNulty. 320p. 1999. 12.95 (*0-14-028018-9*); 1998. 23.95 o.p. (*0-670-87828-6*) Viking Penguin.

Bateman, Colin. Cycle of Violence. 1997. pap. 12.95 (*1-55970-378-4*); 1996. 256p. 21.95 (*1-55970-349-0*) Arcade Publishing, Inc.

—Divorcing Jack. 1996. 288p. pap. 11.95 (*1-55970-359-8*); 1995. 272p. 19.95 (*1-55970-310-5*) Arcade Publishing, Inc.

—Mohammed Maguire. 2001. (*0-00-226118-9*) HarperCollins Pubs.

—Of Wee Sweetie Mice & Men. 1997. 326p. 23.95 (*1-55970-376-8*) Arcade Publishing, Inc.

Beckett, Samuel. Dream of Fair to Middling Women. Date not set. (*0-7145-4212-1*); 1996. 252p. pap. 15.95 (*0-7145-4213-X*) Riverrun Pr., Inc.

—Endgame. 1993. 264p. 21.95 (*1-55970-217-6*) Arcade Publishing, Inc.

—Endgame. Beckett, Samuel, tr. from FRE. 1958. pap. 3.95 o.p. (*0-394-17208-6*, E96) Grove/Atlantic, Inc.

—Endgame: Production Notebook. rev. ed. 1993. (Theatrical Notebooks of Samuel Beckett Ser.: Vol. 2). Tr. of Fin de Partie. (ENG & FRE.). 256p. 75.00 (*0-8021-1089-4*, Grove Pr.) Grove/Atlantic, Inc.

Behan, Beatrice. The Dubbalin Man - Brendan Behan: A New Selection from Brendan Behan's Irish Press Column. 1998. (Illus.). 134p. pap. 15.95 (*1-899047-15-8*) Farmar, A. & A. IRL. *Dist:* Irish Bks. & Media, Inc.

Beirne, Gerard. The Eskimo in the Net: A Novel. 2003. 388p. pap. 14.95 (*0-7145-3093-X*) Boyars, Marion Pubs., Inc.

Bellacera, Carole. Border Crossing. 2000. 448p. mass mkt. 6.99 (*0-8125-7573-3*, Forge Bks.) Doherty, Tom Assocs., LLC.

—Border Crossings. 1999. 381p. 25.95 (*0-312-86858-8*, Forge Bks.) Doherty, Tom Assocs., LLC.

Bernen, Robert. The Hills: More Tales from the Blue Stacks; Stories of Ireland. 1983. 160p. 12.95 o.p. (*0-684-18005-7*, Macmillan Reference USA) Gale Group.

—Tales from the Blue Stacks. 1978. 8.95 o.p. (*0-684-15540-0*, Scribner) Simon & Schuster.

Binchy, Dan. Fireballs. 1994. 320p. 19.95 o.p. (*0-312-10984-9*) St. Martin's Pr.

—The Last Resort. 1993. 266p. 18.95 o.p. (*0-312-08834-5*) St. Martin's Pr.

Binchy, Maeve. Circle of Friends. 1991. 608p. mass mkt. 5.99 o.s.i (*0-440-20996-X*); 1991. 608p. mass mkt. 7.99 (*0-440-21126-3*, 2766354); 1990. 576p. 19.95 o.s.i (*0-440-29400-2*) Dell Publishing.

—Circle of Friends. l.t. ed. 1991. (General Ser.). 755p. 22.95 o.p. (*0-8161-5207-1*, Macmillan Reference USA) Gale Group.

—Circle of Friends. abr. ed. 2000. audio 9.99 (*0-553-52729-0*); 1991. 180p. audio 16.99 o.s.i (*0-553-45270-3*) Random Hse. Audio Publishing Group. (RH Audio).

—Circle of Friends. 1999. (*0-7621-0252-7*) Reader's Digest Assn., Inc., The.

—The Copper Beech. 1993. 400p. mass mkt. 7.99 (*0-440-21329-0*, 2766520) Bantam Dell Publishing Group.

—The Copper Beech. unabr. ed. 2000. audio 69.95 (*0-7451-4222-2*, CAB 905) Chivers Audio Bks. GBR. *Dist:* BBC Audiobooks America.

—The Copper Beech. l.t. ed. 1994. 495p. pap. 19.95 o.p. (*0-8161-5810-X*, Macmillan Reference USA) Gale Group.

—The Copper Beech. abr. ed. 2001. audio 9.99 o.s.i (*0-553-52773-8*); 1992. audio 15.95 o.s.i (*0-553-74501-8*); 1992. audio 16.99 o.s.i (*0-553-47093-0*, 390561) Random Hse. Audio Publishing Group. (RH Audio).

—The Copper Beech. unabr. ed. 2000. audio 78.00 (*1-55690-865-2*, 93307K8) Recorded Bks., LLC.

—The Copper Beech: International Edition. 1993. 400p. mass mkt. 5.99 o.s.i (*0-440-29525-4*) Dell Publishing.

—Echoes. unabr. ed. 2001. audio 89.95 (*0-7451-4347-4*, CAB 1030); Set. audio 110.95 Chivers Audio Bks. GBR. *Dist:* BBC Audiobooks America.

—Echoes. 1997. 496p. mass mkt. 7.99 (*0-440-12209-0*); mass mkt. 6.99 o.s.i (*0-440-21388-6*) Dell Publishing.

—Echoes. l.t. ed. 1992. (General Ser.). 767p. 17.95 o.p. (*0-8161-5330-2*); 17.95 o.p. (*0-8161-5331-0*) Gale Group. (Macmillan Reference USA).

—Echoes. 1986. 477p. 17.95 o.p. (*0-670-80938-1*) Viking Penguin.

—Evening Class. 2001. E-Book 7.99 (*1-58945-902-4*) Adobe Systems, Inc.

—Evening Class. unabr. ed. 1998. audio 96.95 o.p. (*0-7540-0000-1*, CAB 1423) BBC Audiobooks America.

—Evening Class. 1998. 544p. mass mkt. 7.99 (*0-440-22320-2*, 25456916, Dell Bks.); 1997. pap. 6.99 (*0-440-29550-5*) Dell Publishing.

—Evening Class. abr. ed. 1997. audio 24.95 (*0-553-47765-X*, 695019); audio compact disk 29.95 o.s.i (*0-553-45554-0*) Random Hse. Audio Publishing Group. (RH Audio).

—Evening Class. 1999. E-Book 7.50 (*0-440-33414-4*) Random Hse., Inc.

—Evening Class. unabr. ed. 2000. audio 95.00 (*0-7887-3999-9*, H1076K8, Clipper Audio) Recorded Bks., LLC.

—Evening Class. l.t. ed. (Paperback Bestsellers Ser.). 661p. 1998. pap. 27.95 (*0-7838-8113-4*); 1997. 29.95 (*0-7838-8112-6*) Thorndike Pr.

—Firefly Summer. 1989. 672p. mass mkt. 7.99 (*0-440-20419-4*, 2765753); 1988. 608p. 19.95 o.s.i (*0-440-50017-6*, Delacorte Pr.) Dell Publishing.

—Firefly Summer. l.t. ed. 1989. (General Ser.). 1056p. 21.95 o.p. (*0-8161-4750-7*, Macmillan Reference USA) Gale Group.

—The Glass Lake. 1996. 768p. mass mkt. 7.99 (*0-440-22159-5*); 1995. 592p. 23.95 o.s.i (*0-385-31354-3*, Delacorte Pr.) Dell Publishing.

—The Glass Lake. abr. ed. 1995. audio 23.98 o.s.i (*0-553-74616-2*); 360p. pap. 25.00 incl. audio (*0-553-47315-8*) Random Hse. Audio Publishing Group. (RH Audio).

—The Glass Lake. unabr. ed. 1995. audio audio 144.00 (*0-7887-0269-6*, 94478K8) Recorded Bks., LLC.

—The Glass Lake. l.t. ed. (Paperback Bestsellers Ser.). 911p. 1996. pap. 24.95 (*0-7838-1119-5*); 1995. lib. bdg. 28.95 (*0-7838-1118-7*) Thorndike Pr.

—Light a Penny Candle. 1992. 600p. mass mkt. (*0-09-919651-4*) Arrow Bks., Ltd. GBR. *Dist:* Random Hse. of Canada, Ltd.

—Light a Penny Candle. unabr. ed. 2000. audio 124.95 (*0-7540-0405-8*, CAB 1828) Chivers Audio Bks. GBR. *Dist:* BBC Audiobooks America.

—Light a Penny Candle. l.t. ed. 1991. (General Ser.). 772p. 16.95 o.p. (*0-8161-5067-2*); lib. bdg. 16.95 o.p. (*0-8161-5066-4*) Gale Group. (Macmillan Reference USA).

—Light a Penny Candle. 2003. 592p. pap. 10.00 (*0-451-21143-X*); 2001. 608p. mass mkt. 7.99 (*0-451-20304-6*, 51993365, Signet Bks.); 1997. 592p. mass mkt. 7.50 o.s.i (*0-451-19202-8*, Signet Bks.) NAL.

—Light a Penny Candle. abr. ed. 1996. audio 18.00 o.s.i (*0-553-47699-8*, 393455, RH Audio) Random Hse. Audio Publishing Group.

—Light a Penny Candle. 1983. 540p. 17.75 o.p. (*0-670-42827-2*) Viking Penguin.

—The Lilac Bus. unabr. ed. 1993. audio 54.95 (*0-7451-5789-0*, CAB 198) BBC Audiobooks America.

—The Lilac Bus. 1992. 400p. mass mkt. 7.50 (*0-440-21302-9*) Dell Publishing.

—The Lilac Bus. l.t. ed. 1992. (General Ser.). 480p. 18.95 o.p. (*0-8161-5384-1*); lib. bdg. 21.95 o.p. (*0-8161-5383-3*) Gale Group. (Macmillan Reference USA).

—The Lilac Bus. 1984. 200p. pap. 7.95 o.p. (*0-907085-79-2*) Irish Bks. & Media, Inc.

—Quentins. 2002. 368p. 25.95 (*0-525-94682-9*) Dutton/Plume.

—Quentins. l.t. ed. 2003. 608p. pap. 13.95 (*1-4104-0162-6*, Wheeler Publishing, Inc.) Gale Group.

—Quentins. 2003. 488p. mass mkt. 7.99 (*0-451-20990-7*, Signet Bks.) NAL.

—Quentins. 2003. (Basic Ser.). 33.95 (*0-7862-4862-9*) Thorndike Pr.

—Quentins. abr. ed. 2002. audio 24.95 (*0-14-280012-0*); audio compact disk 29.95 (*0-14-280013-9*, Penguin AudioBooks); audio 39.95 (*0-14-280014-7*) Viking Penguin.

—The Return Journey. 1999. 240p. mass mkt. 6.99 (*0-440-22459-4*) Broadway Bks.

—Tara Road. l.t. ed. 1999. 743p. (*0-7540-2212-9*) BBC Audiobooks America.

—Tara Road. 2000. 656p. mass mkt. 7.99 (*0-440-23559-6*); 1999. 512p. 24.95 o.s.i (*0-385-33395-1*, Delacorte Pr.) Dell Publishing.

—Tara Road. l.t. ed. (Paperback Bestsellers Ser.). 743p. 2000. pap. 28.95 (*0-7862-1837-1*); 1999. 31.95 (*0-7862-1836-3*) Thorndike Pr.

—Tara Road. 2000. 14.04 (*0-606-18987-4*) Turtleback Bks.

—Three Complete Novels: The Lilac Bus; Firefly Summer; Silver Wedding. 1995. 864p. 13.99 (*0-517-14864-1*) Random Hse., Inc.

Binchy, Maeve, contrib. by. Tara Road. (*0-7540-1282-4*) BBC Audiobooks America.

Binchy, Maeve & et al. Irish Girls about Town: An Anthology of Short Stories. l.t. ed. 2003. 396p. pap. 25.95 (*1-58724-478-0*, Wheeler Publishing, Inc.) Gale Group.

Binchy, Maeve, et al. Irish Girls about Town: An Anthology of Short Stories. 2003. 320p. reprint ed. pap. 13.00 (*0-7434-5746-3*, Pocket) Simon & Schuster.

—Ladies' Night at Finbar's Hotel. Bolger, Dermot, ed. 2000. (Harvest Original Ser.). 276p. pap. 14.00 (*0-15-600866-1*, Harvest Bks.) Harcourt Trade Pubs.

Birdsall, Ben. Blue Charm. 1996. 200p. pap. 16.95 (*0-85640-544-2*) Blackstaff Pr., The IRL. *Dist:* Dufour Editions, Inc.

Boland, Bridget. The Wild Geese. 1991. (Virago Modern Classics Ser.). 272p. (Orig.). pap. 8.95 o.p. (*0-14-016220-8*) Penguin Group (USA) Inc.

Bolger, Dermot. Finbar's Hotel. 273p. 19.95 (*0-330-36878-8*) Picador GBR. *Dist:* Trans-Atlantic Pubns., Inc.

—Temptation. 2000. 222p. (*0-00-226152-9*) HarperCollins Pubs.

—The Vintage Book of Contemporary Irish Fiction. 1995. 592p. pap. 16.00 (*0-679-76546-8*, Vintage) Knopf Publishing Group.

Bolger, Dermot, ed. Ladies' Night at Finbars Hotel. 2000. (*0-15-100608-3*) Harcourt Trade Pubs.

Bowen, Elizabeth. Ann Lee's & Other Stories. 1977. (Short Story Index Reprint Ser.). 19.95 (*0-8369-3239-0*) Ayer Co. Pubs., Inc.

—The Collected Stories of Elizabeth Bowen. 1989. 784p. reprint ed. pap. o.p. (*0-88001-224-2*, Ecco) HarperTrade.

—The Last September. 2000. 320p. pap. 13.00 (*0-385-72014-9*, Knopf Bks. for Young Readers) Random Hse. Children's Bks.

—The Last September. (Penguin Twentieth-Century Classics Ser.). 208p. 1990. pap. 11.95 o.p. (*0-14-018304-3*, 83, Penguin Classics); 1987. pap. 5.95 o.p. (*0-14-000372-X*, Penguin Bks.) Viking Penguin.

Bowen, Elizabeth & Wilson, Angus. The Collected Stories of Elizabeth Bowen. 1982. 784p. pap. 8.95 o.p. (*0-394-75296-1*, Vintage) Knopf Publishing Group.

Bowler, Michael. Destiny of Dreams. 1990. 200p. (Orig.). pap. 14.95 (*1-85371-065-2*) Poolbeg Pr. IRL. *Dist:* Dufour Editions, Inc.

Boylan, Claire. Holy Pictures. 1983. 208p. 13.50 o.p. (*0-671-46750-6*) Summit Bks.

—Holy Pictures. 1984. 224p. pap. 3.95 o.p. (*0-14-006811-2*, Penguin Bks.) Viking Penguin.

Boylan, Clare. Another Family Christmas: A Collection of Short Stories. 1997. 195p. (*1-85371-785-1*) Poolbeg Pr.

—The Collected Stories. 2002. 416p. pap. text 16.50 (*1-58243-261-9*, Counterpoint Pr.) Basic Bks.

Boylan, Roger. The Great Pint-Pulling Olympiad: A Mostly Irish Farce. 2003. 445p. 14.00 (*0-8021-4032-7*, Grove Pr.) Grove/Atlantic, Inc.

—Killoyle: An Irish Farce. 1997. (American Literature Ser.). 248p. (Orig.). pap. 13.95 (*1-56478-145-3*) Dalkey Archive Pr.

Brady, John. All Souls. 1993. 304p. 20.95 o.p. (*0-312-09735-2*, Saint Martin's Minotaur) St. Martin's Pr.

—All Souls. 2002. (Matt Minogue Mystery Ser.). 306p. pap. 14.95 (*1-58642-043-7*) Steerforth Pr.

—The Good Life. 1995. 352p. 22.95 o.p. (*0-312-13083-X*, Saint Martin's Minotaur) St. Martin's Pr.

—The Good Life: An Inspector Matt Minogue Mystery. 2002. (Matt Minogue Mystery Ser.). reprint ed. pap. 14.95 (*1-58642-049-6*) Steerforth Pr.

—Kaddish in Dublin. 1992. 288p. 18.95 o.p. (*0-312-08229-0*, Saint Martin's Minotaur) St. Martin's Pr.

—Kaddish in Dublin. 2002. (Matt Minogue Mystery Ser.). 253p. pap. 14.95 (*1-58642-042-9*) Steerforth Pr.

—A Stone of the Heart. 1988. 256p. 16.95 o.p. (*0-312-01829-0*, Saint Martin's Minotaur) St. Martin's Pr.

—A Stone of the Heart. 2001. (Matt Minogue Mystery Ser.). (Illus.). xxiii, 247p. pap. 14.95 (*1-58642-029-1*) Steerforth Pr.

—A Stone of the Heart. 1990. 256p. pap. 3.95 o.p. (*0-14-013847-1*, Penguin Bks.) Viking Penguin.

—Unholy Ground. 1991. 288p. 18.95 o.p. (*0-312-07109-4*, Saint Martin's Minotaur) St. Martin's Pr.

—Unholy Ground. 2002. (Matt Minogue Mystery Ser.). 208p. reprint ed. pap. 14.95 (*1-58642-037-2*) Steerforth Pr.

Breasted, Mary. Why Should You Doubt Me Now? 2003. 292p. pap. 21.00 (*0-374-52823-3*); 1993. 279p. 23.00 o.p. (*0-374-29007-5*) Farrar, Straus & Giroux.

Breathnach, Padraic. The March Hare. Rosenstock, Gabriel, tr. from IRI. 154p. pap. 14.95 (*1-874700-03-6*) Clo Iar-Chonnachta Teo IRL. *Dist:* Dufour Editions, Inc.

Brennan, Maeve. The Rose Garden: Short Stories. 1999. 320p. text 23.00 o.p. (*1-58243-050-0*, Counterpoint Pr.) Basic Bks.

—Rose Garden: Short Stories. 2001. 320p. pap. text 14.50 (*1-58243-119-1*, Counterpoint Pr.) Basic Bks.

—The Springs of Affection: Stories of Dublin. 1998. 368p. pap. 13.00 (*0-395-93759-0*); 1997. 358p. tchr. ed. 24.00 o.p. (*0-395-87046-1*) Houghton Mifflin Co.

Brown, Christy. My Left Foot. 1997. 192p. (C). reprint ed. pap. (*0-7493-9177-4*, A0571) Random Hse. of Canada, Ltd. CAN. *Dist:* Random Hse., Inc.

—My Left Foot. l.t. ed. 2003. (General Ser.). lib. bdg. 24.95 (*0-7862-5664-8*) Thorndike Pr.

Browne, Gretta Curran. Tread Softly on my Dreams: Robert Emmet's Story. 1998. 704p. pap. 11.95 (*0-86327-648-2*) Wolfhound Pr. IRL. *Dist:* Irish American Bk. Co.

Bruen, Ken. The Guards: A Novel. 304p. 2004. pap. 12.95 (*0-312-32027-2*, Saint Martin's Griffin); 2003. 23.95 (*0-312-30355-6*, Saint Martin's Minotaur) St. Martin's Pr.

—The Killing of the Tinkers. Date not set. (*0-312-30357-2*); 2004. 256p. 22.95 (*0-312-30411-0*) St. Martin's Pr. (Saint Martin's Minotaur).

Burns, Anna. No Bones. 2002. 272p. pap. 13.95 (*0-393-32303-X*) Norton, W. W. & Co., Inc.

Butler, Pierce. A Riddle of Stars. 1999. 287p. pap. o.p. (*1-58195-007-1*, Zoland Bks., Inc.) Steerforth Pr.

Callaghan, Mary Rose. The Last Summer. 1997. (*1-85371-607-3*) Poolbeg Pr.

Canter, John. Aran Song. 88p. pap. 8.95 (*1-874700-88-5*) Clo Iar-Chonnachta Teo IRL. *Dist:* Dufour Editions, Inc.

Carey, Lisa. The Mermaids Singing. 2001. 288p. pap. 13.00 (*0-380-81559-1*, Perennial) HarperTrade.

—The Mermaids Singing. 1998. 257p. (YA). 22.00 (*0-380-97674-9*, Avon Bks.) Morrow/Avon.

—Mermaids Singing. 1999. 352p. (gr. 8 up). mass mkt. 6.99 (*0-380-79960-X*, Avon Bks.) Morrow/Avon.

—The Mermaids Singing. abr. ed. 1998. audio 18.00 (*0-671-58124-4*, Simon & Schuster Audioworks) Simon & Schuster Audio.

Carleton, William. The Black Prophet. Wolff, Robert L., ed. 1979. (Ireland Nineteenth Century Fiction Ser.: Vol. 41). 324p. lib. bdg. 51.00 o.p. (*0-8240-3490-2*) Garland Publishing, Inc.

—The Black Prophet, 1847. 2003. (Hibernia Ser.). (Illus.). 492p. (*1-85477-216-3*) Woodstock Books.

—Traits & Stories of the Irish Peasantry. 1990. (Illus.). (C). pap. text 22.00 (*0-389-20941-4*);I. 72.00 (*0-389-20908-2*);II. 208p. 72.00 (*0-389-20909-0*);Vol. 2. pap. text 22.00 (*0-389-20942-2*) Barnes & Noble Bks.-Imports.

—Traits & Stories of the Irish Peasantry. 1979. (Nineteenth Century Fiction Ser.: Ireland: Vol. 34). 596p. lib. bdg. 92.00 o.p. (*0-8240-3483-X*) Garland Publishing, Inc.

—Traits & Stories of the Irish Peasantry: Second Series. Wolff, Robert L., ed. 1979. (Ireland Nineteenth Century Fiction Ser.: Vol. 35). 1412p. lib. bdg. 138.00 o.p. (*0-8240-3484-8*) Garland Publishing, Inc.

—Traits & Stories of the Irish Peasantry: With Illustrations by Phiz, Wrightson Lee & Others, 4 Vols. 1977. (Short Story Index Reprint Ser.). (Illus.). reprint ed. 88.95 (*0-8369-3936-0*) Ayer Co. Pubs., Inc.

Carroll, James. Supply of Heroes. 1987. 432p. mass mkt. 4.95 o.p. (*0-451-14875-4*, Signet Bks.) NAL.

Carroll, James. Supply of Heroes. 1986. 17.95 o.p. (*0-525-24450-6*, Dutton) Dutton/Plume.

—Supply of Heroes. l.t. ed. 1987. 614p. 19.95 o.p. (*0-8161-4264-5*, Macmillan Reference USA) Gale Group.

Carson, Michael. Dying in Style. 1998. 256p. (*1-85371-817-3*) Poolbeg Pr. IRL. *Dist:* Dufour Editions, Inc.

Castro, Fidel. The World Crisis: Its Economic & Social Impact on the Underdeveloped Countries. 1983. (Illus.). 224p. (C). text 21.75 o.p. (*0-86232-250-2*) Zed Bks., Ltd. GBR. *Dist:* St. Martin's Pr.

Cates, Kimberly. Briar Rose. 1999. (Illus.). 400p. pap. 6.50 (*0-671-01495-1*, Pocket) Simon & Schuster.

Center for Learning Network Staff. Tara Road/the Return Journey: Curriculum Unit —Novel Series— Grades 9-12. 1999. (Novel Ser.). 65p. (YA). (gr. 9-12). tchr. ed., spiral bd. 18.95 (*1-56077-636-6*) Ctr. for Learning, The.

Charbonneau, Eileen. Rachel Lemoyne. (Women of the West Novels Ser.). 320p. 1999. pap. 5.99 (*0-8125-7114-2*); 1998. (YA). (gr. 8 up). 22.95 o.p. (*0-312-86448-5*) Doherty, Tom Assocs., LLC. (Forge Bks.).

Claremont, Chris. Dragon Moon. 1994. 128p. 14.95 o.s.i (*0-553-37434-6*); (Illus.). pap. 14.95 o.s.i (*0-553-37448-6*) Bantam Bks.

Clark, Carol Higgins. Twanged. abr. ed. 1997. audio 18.00 (*0-7871-1555-X*); audio 30.00 (*0-7871-1556-8*) NewStar Media, Inc. (Dove Audio).

—Twanged. l.t. ed. 1998. (Basic Ser.). 389p. 29.95 (*0-7862-1417-1*) Thorndike Pr.

—Twanged. abr. ed. 1998. (Regan Reilly Mysteries Ser.). audio 17.98 (*1-57042-612-0*, 395934 ) Time Warner AudioBooks.

—Twanged. 1999. 336p. mass mkt. 7.50 (*0-446-60536-0*); 1998. 272p. 28.00 (*0-446-51763-1*) Warner Bks., Inc.

Conaola, Dara O. Night Ructions. Rosenstock, Gabriel, tr. from IRI. 1990. (Illus.). 58p. (Orig.). pap. 9.95 (*0-948259-93-0*) Forest Bks. GBR. *Dist:* Dufour Editions, Inc.

Conlon, Evelyn. A Glassful of Letters. 1998. 208p. pap. 16.95 (*0-85640-618-X*) Blackstaff Pr., The IRL. *Dist:* Dufour Editions, Inc.

—Taking Scarlet As a Real Colour. 1993. 176p. pap. 13.95 (*0-85640-501-9*) Blackstaff Pr., The IRL. *Dist:* Dufour Editions, Inc.

Conlon, Evelyn & Oesr, Hans-Christian, eds. Cutting the Night in Two: Short Stories by Irish Women Writers. 2001. 320p. pap. 16.95 (*1-902602-52-8*) New Island Bks. IRL. *Dist:* Dufour Editions, Inc.

Conlon-McKenna, Marita. The Magdalen. l.t. ed. 2001. (Magna Large Print Ser.). 384p. (*0-7505-1733-6*) Magna Large Print Bks. GBR. *Dist:* Ulverscroft Large Print Canada, Ltd.

Connaughton, Shane. A Border Station. 1990. 176p. 14.95 o.p. (*0-312-03799-6*) St. Martin's Pr.

—A Border Station. 1991. 176p. reprint ed. mass mkt. 8.99 (*0-446-39302-9*) Warner Bks., Inc.

—The Run of the Country. 1993. pap. 10.95 o.p. (*0-312-08883-3*, Saint Martin's Griffin); 1992. 224p. 17.95 o.p. (*0-312-07077-2*) St. Martin's Pr.

—The Run of the Country: A Novel. 1995. pap. 12.00 o.p. (*0-312-13599-8*) Picador.

Conway, Simon. Damaged. 2000. 377p. pap. (*0-86241-895-X*) Canongate Bks.

—Damaged. 2000. 377p. pap. 15.00 (*0-86241-760-0*) Canongate Bks. GBR. *Dist:* Interlink Publishing Group, Inc.

Coogan, Beatrice. The Big Wind: A Novel of Ireland. rev. ed. 1995. 684p. pap. 14.95 (*1-57098-031-4*) Rinehart, Roberts Pubs.

Cookson, Catherine. The Desert Crop. unabr. ed. 1998. audio 69.95 (*0-7540-0151-2*, CAB 1574) BBC Audiobooks America.

—The Desert Crop. 2000. 384p. mass mkt. (*1-55166-583-2*, Harlequin Bks.) Harlequin Enterprises, Ltd.

—The Desert Crop. 1999. 320p. 23.00 (*0-684-85683-2*, Simon & Schuster) Simon & Schuster.

—The Desert Crop. 16th l.t. ed. 1999. (Basic Ser.). 483p. 29.95 (*0-7862-1830-4*) Thorndike Pr.

—The Desert Crop. 2000. 320p. 29.95 (*0-593-03476-7*); 1998. (Illus.). 512p. mass mkt. 10.95 (*0-552-14156-9*) Transworld Publishers Ltd. GBR. *Dist:* Trafalgar Square.
Cordell, Alexander. White Cockade. 1970. 4.95 o.p. (*0-670-76248-2*) Viking Penguin.
—Witches Sabbath. 1970. 4.95 o.p. (*0-670-77617-3*) Viking Penguin.
Corkery, Daniel. Nightfall & Other Stories. 1988. 204p. pap. 12.95 (*0-85640-414-4*) Blackstaff Pr., The IRL. *Dist:* Dufour Editions, Inc.
Cornell, Jennifer C. Departures. 176p. (C). 1996. pap. 14.95 (*0-8229-5604-7*); 1995. (gr. 9-12). text 22.50 o.p. (*0-8229-3855-3*) Univ. of Pittsburgh Pr.
Costello, Mary. Titanic Town. 2000. 340p. pap. 10.95 (*0-413-77210-1*, Methuen Drama) Methuen Publishing Ltd. GBR. *Dist:* Consortium Bk. Sales & Distribution.
Costello, Peter. The Life of Leopold Bloom: A Novel. 1993. 197p. (Orig.). pap. 9.95 (*1-879373-34-3*) Rinehart, Roberts Pubs.
Cremins, Robert. A Sort of Homecoming: A Novel. 2000. 304p. pap. 13.95 (*0-393-32023-5*, Norton Paperbacks) Norton, W. W. & Co., Inc.
Crowley, Elaine. A Family Cursed. 1996. 309p. 27.00 o.p. (*1-85797-767-X*) Orion Publishing Group, Ltd. GBR. *Dist:* Trafalgar Square.
Cullen, Leo. Clocking Ninety on the Rd. to Cloughjordan & Other: Stories. 1995. 240p. pap. 14.95 (*0-85640-537-X*) Blackstaff Pr., The IRL. *Dist:* Dufour Editions, Inc.
Cunningham, Peter. Tapes of the River Delta. 1996. 352p. text 23.95 o.p. (*0-312-14051-7*) St. Martin's Pr.
Daniel, Mark. The Bold Thing. 1994. 279p. 19.95 o.p. (*0-316-17266-9*) Little Brown & Co.
Davis-Goff, Annabel. The Dower House. 1999. 288p. pap. 13.95 (*0-312-20645-3*, Saint Martin's Griffin); 1998. 274p. 22.95 (*0-312-17028-9*) St. Martin's Pr.
—The Fox's Walk. 2003. 336p. 25.00 (*0-15-101020-X*, 53597467) Harcourt Trade Pubs.
—This Cold Country. 368p. 2003. pap. 14.00 (*0-15-602738-0*, Harvest Bks.); 2002. (Illus.). 25.00 (*0-15-100847-7*) Harcourt Trade Pubs.
—This Cold Country. Date not set. (*0-312-28448-9*) St. Martin's Pr.
De Rosa, Peter. Pope Patrick. 1997. 352p. 23.95 o.s.i (*0-385-48548-4*) Doubleday Publishing.
—Rebels: The Irish Rising of 1916. 1992. 560p. pap. 15.95 (*0-449-90682-5*, Fawcett) Ballantine Bks.
—Rebels: The Irish Rising of 1916. 1991. 560p. 25.00 o.s.i (*0-385-26752-5*) Doubleday Publishing.
—Rebels: The Irish Uprising of 1916. 1996. pap. 14.00 o.s.i (*0-449-45660-9*) Ballantine Bks.
Deane, John F. In the Name of the Wolf. 2000. 172p. (Orig.). pap. 17.95 (*0-85640-640-6*) Blackstaff Pr., The IRL. *Dist:* Dufour Editions, Inc.
Deere, Dicey. The Irish Cairn Murder. 2002. 256p. 23.95 (*0-312-27519-6*, Saint Martin's Minotaur) St. Martin's Pr.
—The Irish Cottage Murder. (Torrey Tunet Mysteries Ser.). 2000. 295p. mass mkt. 6.50 (*0-312-97131-1*, St. Martin's Paperbacks); 1999. 240p. 22.95 (*0-312-20552-X*, Saint Martin's Minotaur) St. Martin's Pr.
—The Irish Manor House Murder. l.t. ed. 2000. (G. K. Hall Core Ser.). 296p. 27.95 (*0-7838-9283-7*, Macmillan Reference USA) Gale Group.
—The Irish Manor House Murder. 2001. 288p. mass mkt. 6.99 (*0-312-97645-3*, St. Martin's Paperbacks) St. Martin's Pr.
—The Irish Manor House Murder: A Torrey Tunet Mystery. 2000. 260p. 23.95 (*0-312-20606-2*, Saint Martin's Minotaur) St. Martin's Pr.
—The Irish Village Murder. 2004. 304p. 23.95 (*0-312-27522-6*, Saint Martin's Minotaur) St. Martin's Pr.
Dengler, Sandy. Dublin Crossing: Romance & Adventure in the Viking Era. 1993. (Heroes of Misty Isle Ser.). 348p. pap. 9.99 o.p. (*0-8024-2293-4*) Moody Pr.
—The Shamrock Shore: In the Footsteps of Patrick Through the Hills of Erin. 1994. (Heroes of Misty Isle Ser.). pap. 9.99 o.p. (*0-8024-2294-2*) Moody Pr.
DeSalvo, Louise A. Territories of the Voice. 1989. 19.95 o.p. (*0-8070-8320-8*) Beacon Pr.
DeSalvo, Louise A., et al, eds. Short Fiction by Irish Women Writers. rev. ed. 1999. (Illus.). xxii, 270p. reprint ed. pap. 15.00 o.p. (*0-8070-8341-0*) Beacon Pr.
Desjarlais, John. The Throne of Tara. 1990. 256p. pap. 10.99 o.p. (*0-89107-574-7*) Crossway Bks.
—The Throne of Tara. 2000. 249p. pap. 14.95 (*0-595-15597-9*) iUniverse, Inc.
Deveraux, Jude. The Black Lyon. (Star-Romance Ser.). 1997. 339p. 23.95 o.p. (*0-7862-0951-8*, Five Star); 1987. 429p. 19.95 o.p. (*0-8161-4177-0*, Macmillan Reference USA) Gale Group.
—The Black Lyon. 2000. 352p. pap. 12.50 (*0-380-81206-1*); 1980. 288p. mass mkt. 7.99 (*0-380-75911-X*) Morrow/Avon. (Avon Bks.).
—The Black Lyon. 1991. reprint ed. 18.95 o.p. (*0-7278-4049-5*) Severn Hse. Pubs., Ltd.
Dillon, Charles R. Eaten by the Gods. 424p. mass mkt. (*1-55197-083-X*) Picasso Pubns., Inc.
Dillon, Eilis, et al. The Sea Wall. 1994. 119p. (J). (gr. 4-10). reprint ed. pap. 8.95 (*1-85371-304-X*) Poolbeg Pr. IRL. *Dist:* Dufour Editions, Inc.
Donleavy, J. P. Destinies of Darcy Dancer, Gentleman. 1978. pap. 8.95 o.s.i (*0-385-28216-8*, Delta); 1977. 9.95 o.s.i (*0-440-01903-6*, Delacorte Pr.) Dell Publishing.
—Destinies of Darcy Dancer, Gentleman. 1990. 416p. pap. 9.95 (*0-87113-289-3*, Atlantic Monthly Pr.) Grove/Atlantic, Inc.
—Leila: Further in the Life & Destinies of Darcy Dancer, Gentleman. 1983. 440p. 17.50 o.s.i (*0-385-29260-0*, Delacorte Pr.) Dell Publishing.
—Leila: Further in the Life & Destinies of Darcy Dancer, Gentleman. 1990. 432p. pap. 12.00 (*0-87113-288-5*, Atlantic Monthly Pr.) Grove/ Atlantic, Inc.
—That Darcy, That Dancer, That Gentleman. 1991. 22.95 o.p. (*0-87113-449-7*) Grove/Atlantic, Inc.
Dorcey, Mary. Biography of Desire. 1997. 375p. (*1-85371-707-X*) Poolbeg Pr.
Doughty, Anne. On a Clear Day. 2002. 374p. 26.99 (*0-7278-5750-9*); 29.99 (*0-7278-7128-5*) Severn Hse. Pubs., Ltd.
Doyle, Mogue. Dancing with Minnie the Twig. 2002. 253p. 17.95 (*0-593-04923-3*) Bantam Bks.
Doyle, Roddy. The Barrytown Trilogy: The Commitments, the Snapper, the Van. 1995. 640p. 18.00 (*0-14-025262-2*) Viking Penguin.
—The Commitments. 1989. (Vintage Contemporaries Ser.). 176p. pap. 12.00 (*0-679-72174-6*, Vintage) Knopf Publishing Group.
—Paddy Clarke Ha Ha Ha. 288p. 1995. 14.00 (*0-14-023390-3*); 1994. 20.95 o.p. (*0-670-85345-3*, Viking) Viking Penguin.
—Paddy Clarke Ha, Ha, Ha. abr. ed. 1995. (Classics on Cassette). (J). audio 16.95 (*0-453-00953-0*) Penguin/HighBridge.
—Paddy Clarke Ha Ha Ha. l.t. ed. 1994. 23.95 o.p. (*1-56895-070-5*, Wheeler Publishing, Inc.) Gale Group.
—Paddy Clarke Ha, Ha, Ha!, unabr. ed. 1995. (J). audio 59.95 (*0-7451-4384-9*, CAB 1068) Chivers Audio Bks. GBR. *Dist:* BBC Audiobooks America.
—The Snapper. 1992. 224p. 12.00 (*0-14-017167-3*) Viking Penguin.
—A Star Called Henry. l.t. ed. 2000. (Illus.). 487p. 26.95 (*1-56895-818-8*, Wheeler Publishing, Inc.) Gale Group.
—A Star Called Henry. 2000. (Last Roundup Ser.: Vol. 1). (Illus.). 384p. pap. 14.00 (*0-14-029613-1*) Penguin Group (USA) Inc.
—A Star Called Henry. 2000. 20.05 (*0-606-19864-4*) Turtleback Bks.
—A Star Called Henry. 1999. (Last Roundup Ser.). 343p. 24.95 o.s.i (*0-670-88757-9*) Viking Penguin.
—The Van. 1997. 320p. pap. 11.95 o.s.i (*0-14-026002-1*) Penguin Group (USA) Inc.
—The Van. 1993. 320p. 13.00 (*0-14-017191-6*); 1992. 320p. 21.00 o.p. (*0-670-84587-6*, Viking); 1997. audio 16.95 o.s.i (*0-14-086426-1*, Penguin AudioBooks) Viking Penguin.
—The Woman Who Walked into Doors. unabr. ed. 1996. audio 51.00 (*0-7887-0612-8*, 94793E7) Recorded Bks., LLC.
—The Woman Who Walked into Doors. l.t. ed. 1996. pap. 22.95 o.p. (*0-7862-0831-7*) Thorndike Pr.
—The Woman Who Walked into Doors. 1997. 240p. 14.00 (*0-14-025512-5*); 1996. 240p. 22.95 o.s.i (*0-670-86775-6*, Viking); 1996. audio 16.95 o.p. (*0-14-086288-9*, Penguin AudioBooks) Viking Penguin.
Dwyer-Joyce, Alice. The Unwinding Corner. 1983. 205p. 10.95 o.p. (*0-312-83377-6*) St. Martin's Pr.
Easterman, Daniel. Brotherhood of the Tomb. 1991. 480p. mass mkt. 5.50 o.p. (*0-06-100206-2*, HarperTorch) Morrow/Avon.
—Night of the Apocalypse. 1995. 430p. 24.00 o.p. (*0-06-017742-X*) HarperTrade.
—Night of the Apocalypse. 1996. 448p. mass mkt. 5.99 o.p. (*0-06-109205-3*, HarperTorch) Morrow/ Avon.
Edgeworth, Maria. The Absentee. 2000. 252p. E-Book 3.95 (*0-594-03453-1*) 1873 Pr.
—The Absentee. 2001. (Tales & Novels Ser.). reprint ed. pap. text 28.00 (*0-7426-8386-9*) Classic Bks.
—The Absentee. E-Book 2.49 (*1-58744-109-8*) Electric Umbrella Publishing.
—The Absentee. 268p. 2002. 25.99 (*1-58827-696-1*); 2001. per. 20.99 (*1-58827-697-X*) IndyPublish-.com.
—The Absentee. (Ebook Classic Ser.). E-Book 5.00 (*0-7410-1397-5*) SoftBook Pr.
—Ormond. 1972. reprint ed. 13.00 o.p. (*0-7165-1799-X*) Biblio Distribution.
—Ormond. 2001. (Tales & Novels Ser.). reprint ed. pap. text 28.00 (*0-7426-8398-2*) Classic Bks.
—Ormond. 2001. (Penguin Classics Ser.). 352p. 12.00 (*0-14-043644-8*) Viking Penguin.
Edwards, Jane. The Ghost of Castle Kilgarrom. l.t. ed. 1997. (Paperback Ser.). 201p. lib. bdg. 22.95 (*0-7838-8328-5*) Thorndike Pr.
Edwards, Ruth Dudley. The Anglo-Irish Murders. l.t. ed. 2001. 288p. pap. 24.95 (*0-7862-3322-2*) Thorndike Pr.
Eickhoff, Randy Lee. The Destruction of the Inn. (Ulster Cycle Ser.). 2001. 288p. 23.95 (*0-312-87026-4*); 2002. 240p. reprint ed. pap. 13.95 (*0-312-87022-1*) Doherty, Tom Assocs., LLC. (Forge Bks.).
—The Feast. 2001. E-Book 13.95 (*1-58945-724-2*) Adobe Systems, Inc.
—The Feast. 1999. (Illus.). 254p. 23.95 (*0-312-86647-X*); Bk. 2. 2001. 256p. pap. 13.95 (*0-312-87299-2*) Doherty, Tom Assocs., LLC. (Forge Bks.).
—He Stands Alone: The Story of Irish National Hero Cuchulainn. 2003. (Ulster Cycle Ser.: Bk. 5). 224p. reprint ed. pap. 13.95 (*0-312-87020-5*, Forge Bks.) Doherty, Tom Assocs., LLC.
—The Raid. 2000. 283p. pap. 13.95 (*0-312-85192-8*, Forge Bks.); 1999. mass mkt. (*0-8125-7188-6*, Tor Bks.); 1997. 320p. 22.95 o.p. (*0-312-86238-5*, Forge Bks.) Doherty, Tom Assocs., LLC.
—The Sorrows. 2000. (Illus.). 284p. 23.95 (*0-312-87028-0*); 2001. 288p. reprint ed. pap. 14.95 (*0-312-87027-2*) Doherty, Tom Assocs., LLC. (Forge Bks.).
Fallon, Ann C. Blood Is Thicker. 1990. 256p. (Orig.). mass mkt. 3.95 (*0-671-70623-3*, Pocket) Simon & Schuster.
—Dead Ends. Isaacson, Dana, ed. 1992. 256p. (Orig.). mass mkt. 4.99 (*0-671-75134-4*, Pocket) Simon & Schuster.
—Hour of Our Death. Chelius, Jane, ed. 1995. 256p. (Orig.). mass mkt. 5.50 (*0-671-88515-4*, Pocket) Simon & Schuster.
—Potter's Field. Isaacson, Dana, ed. 1993. 256p. (Orig.). mass mkt. 4.99 (*0-671-75136-0*, Pocket) Simon & Schuster.
—Where Death Lies. Isaacson, Dana, ed. 1991. 256p. mass mkt. 4.99 (*0-671-70624-1*, Pocket) Simon & Schuster.
Farrell, J. G. Troubles. 1986. 448p. mass mkt. 4.95 o.p. (*0-88184-269-9*, Carroll & Graf Pubs.) Avalon Publishing Group.
—Troubles. 2002. (New York Review Books Classics Ser.). 512p. pap. 16.95 (*1-59017-018-0*) New York Review of Bks., Inc., The.
Fetzer, Amy J. The Irish Knight. 2002. (Zebra Historical Romance Ser.). 384p. mass mkt. 5.99 o.s.i (*0-8217-7218-X*) Kensington Publishing Corp.
Finlay, Lilian R. A Bona Fide Husband: And Other Stories. 1991. 220p. reprint ed. pap. 13.95 (*1-85371-210-8*) Poolbeg Pr. IRL. *Dist:* Dufour Editions, Inc.
—A Bona Fide Husband & Other Stories. 1991. 265p. (Orig.). pap. 12.95 (*1-85371-107-1*) Poolbeg Pr. IRL. *Dist:* Dufour Editions, Inc.
Fitzpatrick, Nina. Daimons. 2003. 312p. 24.95 (*1-932112-14-6*) Justin, Charles & Co. Pubs.
—Fables of the Irish Intelligentsia. 1993. 176p. (Orig.). pap. 13.00 o.s.i (*0-14-017324-2*, Penguin Bks.) Penguin Group (USA) Inc.
Flanagan, Thomas. The End of the Hunt. 1994. 640p. 24.95 o.p. (*0-525-93681-5*, Dutton) Dutton/Plume.
—The Tenants of Time. 1988. 656p. 22.95 o.p. (*0-525-24619-3*, Abrahams, William Bks.) Dutton/Plume.
—The Year of the French. 1989. 528p. pap. 15.95 o.s.i (*0-8050-1020-3*, Owl Bks.) Holt, Henry & Co.
—The Year of the French. 1980. mass mkt. 3.75 o.s.i (*0-671-83301-4*, Pocket) Simon & Schuster.
—The Year of the French: A Novel. 1979. 516 p. (J). o.p. (*0-03-044591-4*) Holt, Henry & Co.
Fleck, Richard. The Clearing of the Mist. 2nd ed. 2001. 176p. 19.95 (*1-58345-937-5*); pap. 13.95 (*1-58345-938-3*) Domhan Bks.
Fletcher, Donna. Irish Hope. 2001. (Irish Eyes Ser.). 384p. mass mkt. 5.99 o.s.i (*0-515-13043-5*, Jove) Berkley Publishing Group.
Florde, Katie. Dot to Dot. 2002. 320p. 24.95 (*0-312-27571-4*) St. Martin's Pr.
Foote, Tom. The Undertow. 1998. 352p. pap. 14.95 (*0-8023-1320-5*) Dufour Editions, Inc.
—The Undertow. 1998. 352p. pap. 14.95 (*1-897648-93-6*) Salmon Publishing IRL. *Dist:* Dufour Editions, Inc.
Forkner, Ben, ed. & intro. Modern Irish Short Stories. rev. ed. 1980. 560p. 15.00 (*0-14-024699-1*) Viking Penguin.
Forkner, Benjamin, ed. Modern Irish Short Stories. 1980. 512p. 15.95 o.p. (*0-670-48324-9*) Viking Penguin.
Fraser, Christine M. Noble Beginnings. unabr. ed. 1995. audio 69.95 (*0-7451-6499-4*, CAB 1115) BBC Audiobooks America.
—Noble Seed. unabr. ed. 1998. (Noble Ser. : Vol. 3). audio 69.95 (*0-7540-0138-5*, CAB1561) BBC Audiobooks America.
Freiman, Kate. Irish Moonlight. 2000. (Irish Eyes Ser.). 352p. mass mkt. 5.99 o.s.i (*0-515-12927-5*, Jove) Berkley Publishing Group.
French, Judith E. The Irish Rogue. 2000. 352p. mass mkt. 6.50 o.s.i (*0-345-43759-4*, Ivy Bks.) Ballantine Bks.
Gable, Hans W., ed. Ulysses: A Critical & Synoptic Edition, 3 vols. 1990. (James Joyce Ser.). 1930p. pap. text 58.00 o.p. (*0-8240-4748-6*) Garland Publishing, Inc.
Gallagher, Francis. Leaving Ireland. Asbury, Martha, ed. 1995. (Illus.). 200p. (Orig.). pap. 11.95 (*0-9647147-0-1*) Plimsoll Pr.
Geaney, Ray. The Honest Liar. 2001. 229p. pap. (*1-55212-831-8*) Trafford Publishing.
Gebler, Carlo. How to Murder a Man. 1999. 373p. 24.95 (*0-7145-3058-1*) Boyars, Marion Pubs., Inc.
Gherasim, Louise. Magheen. 2002. (Orig.). pap. 22.95 (*1-4033-3841-8*) 1stBooks Library.
—Magheen. 1997. 347p. (Orig.). pap. 26.95 (*1-880664-24-0*) E. M. Productions.
Gieseking, Hal E. Morgan's Justice: Murder & Madness on Ireland's Cliffs of Moher. 2002. 197p. pap. 19.95 (*1-58851-449-8*) PublishAmerica, Inc.
Gill, Bartholomew. The Death of a Joyce Scholar. 1990. (Peter McGarr Mystery Ser.). 336p. reprint ed. mass mkt. 6.99 (*0-380-71129-X*, Avon Bks.) Morrow/Avon.
—The Death of a Joyce Scholar: A Peter McGarr Mystery. 1989. 310p. 18.95 o.p. (*0-688-08713-2*, Morrow, William & Co.) Morrow/Avon.
—The Death of an Ardent Bibliophile: A Peter McGarr Mystery. 1996. 256p. mass mkt. 5.50 (*0-380-72206-2*, Avon Bks.); 1995. 288p. 20.00 o.p. (*0-688-12909-9*, Morrow, William & Co.) Morrow/ Avon.
—The Death of An Irish Consul. 2003. 320p. mass mkt. 6.99 (*0-06-052257-7*, Avon Bks.) Morrow/ Avon.
—The Death of an Irish Lover: A Peter McGarr Mystery. 2001. 320p. mass mkt. 6.50 (*0-380-80863-3*, Avon Bks.) Morrow/Avon.
—The Death of an Irish Politician. 2000. (Inspector Peter McGarr Mysteries Ser.). 240p. mass mkt. 6.99 (*0-380-73273-4*, Avon Bks.) Morrow/Avon.
—The Death of an Irish Sea Wolf. 1997. (Peter McGarr Mystery Ser.). 304p. mass mkt. 6.50 (*0-380-72578-9*, Avon Bks.) Morrow/Avon.
—The Death of an Irish Sea Wolf: A Peter McGarr Mystery. 1996. 288p. 23.00 o.p. (*0-688-14183-8*, Morrow, William & Co.) Morrow/Avon.
—The Death of an Irish Sinner. 2001. (Inspector Peter McGarr Mysteries Ser.). 288p. 24.00 (*0-380-97798-2*, Morrow, William & Co.) Morrow/Avon.
—The Death of an Irish Tinker. 1998. (Inspector Peter McGarr Mysteries Ser.). 256p. mass mkt. 6.99 (*0-380-72579-7*, Avon Bks.) Morrow/Avon.
—The Death of an Irish Tinker: A Peter McGarr Mystery. 1997. 288p. 23.00 (*0-688-14184-6*, Morrow, William & Co.) Morrow/Avon.
—The Death of Love: A Peter McGarr Mystery. 1993. 352p. mass mkt. 4.99 (*0-380-71982-7*, Avon Bks.); 1992. 356p. 20.00 o.p. (*0-688-08715-9*, Morrow, William & Co.) Morrow/Avon.
—Death on a Cold, Wild River: A Peter McGarr Mystery. Date not set. 256p. mass mkt. 4.99 (*0-380-72205-4*, Avon Bks.); 1993. 251p. 20.00 o.p. (*0-688-12881-5*, Morrow, William & Co.) Morrow/Avon.
—McGarr & the Legacy of a Woman Scorned. 224p. 1987. mass mkt. 3.50 o.p. (*0-14-009609-4*, Penguin Bks.); 1986. 14.95 o.p. (*0-670-80673-0*) Viking Penguin.
—McGarr & the Method of Descartes. (Crime Monthly Ser.). 1985. 304p. pap. 3.95 o.p. (*0-14-008405-3*, Penguin Bks.); 1984. 288p. 14.95 o.p. (*0-670-46432-5*) Viking Penguin.
—McGarr & the P. M. of Belgrave Square. (Crime Monthly Ser.). 1984. 256p. pap. 3.95 o.p. (*0-14-007323-X*, Penguin Bks.); 1983. 240p. 13.95 o.p. (*0-670-46430-9*) Viking Penguin.
—McGarr & the Politician's Wife. 1982. (Crime Monthly Ser.). pap. 3.95 o.p. (*0-14-005984-9*, Penguin Bks.) Viking Penguin.
—McGarr & the Sienese Conspiracy. 1980. pap. 2.25 o.p. (*0-440-15784-6*) Dell Publishing.
—McGarr & the Sienese Conspiracy. 1977. 7.95 o.s.i (*0-684-15185-5*, Macmillan Reference USA) Gale Group.
—McGarr & the Sienese Conspiracy. 1986. (Crime Ser.). 224p. pap. 3.95 o.p. (*0-14-008580-7*, Penguin Bks.) Viking Penguin.
—McGarr at the Dublin Horse Show. 1981. pap. 2.25 o.p. (*0-440-15379-4*) Dell Publishing.
—McGarr on the Cliffs of Moher. 1982. (Crime Monthly Ser.). 252p. pap. 3.50 o.p. (*0-14-006197-5*, Penguin Bks.) Viking Penguin.
Gordon, Mary. The Other Side. audio 8.95 American Audio Prose Library, Inc.
—The Other Side. l.t. ed. 1994. 24.95 o.p. (*1-56895-072-1*, Wheeler Publishing, Inc.) Gale Group.
—The Other Side. 1990. (Contemporary American Fiction Ser.). 400p. pap. 15.00 (*0-14-014408-0*, Penguin Bks.) Penguin Group (USA) Inc.
—The Other Side. 1992. 4.99 o.p. (*0-517-08006-0*) Random Hse. Value Publishing.

Settings

—The Other Side. 1989. 400p. 19.95 o.p. (*0-670-82566-2*) Viking Penguin.

Graham, Heather. Lord of the Wolves. 1993. 416p. mass mkt. 6.99 (*0-440-21149-2*) Dell Publishing.

Greacen, Robert. The Sash My Father Wore. 1997. 192p. 35.00 (*1-85158-923-6*) Mainstream Publishing Co., Ltd. GBR. *Dist:* Trafalgar Square.

Greeley, Andrew M. Irish Love: A Nuala Anne McGrail Novel. 2001. 304p. 24.95 (*0-312-87187-2*); 2002. 368p. reprint ed. mass mkt. 6.99 (*0-8125-7606-3*) Doherty, Tom Assocs., LLC. (Forge Bks.).

—Irish Love: A Nuala Anne McGrail Novel. l.t. ed. 2001. (Wheeler Large Print Book Ser.). 386p. 29.95 o.p. (*1-58724-058-0*, Wheeler Publishing, Inc.) Gale Group.

—Irish Mist: A Nuala Anne McGrail Novel. (Nuala Anne McGrail Novel Ser.). 2000. 384p. mass mkt. 6.99 (*0-8125-9023-6*); 1999. (Illus.). 319p. 23.95 (*0-312-86569-4*) Doherty, Tom Assocs., LLC. (Forge Bks.).

—Irish Mist: A Nuala Anne McGrail Novel. l.t. ed. 2001. (Basic Ser.). 517p. 28.95 (*0-7862-3085-1*) Thorndike Pr.

Green, Terence M. St. Patrick's Bed. (Illus.). 224p. 2001. 21.95 (*0-7653-0043-5*); 2002. reprint ed. pap. 12.95 (*0-7653-0044-3*) Doherty, Tom Assocs., LLC. (Forge Bks.).

Greenberg, Martin Harry, ed. Murder Most Celtic: Tall Tales of Irish Mayhem. 2003. 304p. 9.99 (*0-517-22155-1*) Gramercy Bks.

Haining, Peter. Irish Tales of Terror. 1994. (Illus.). 320p. 9.99 o.s.i (*0-517-12245-6*) Random Hse. Value Publishing.

—Irish Tales of Terror: Twenty-Two Bewitching Tales of Irish Mystery & Magic. 1988. 9.99 o.p. (*0-517-65499-7*) Random Hse. Value Publishing.

Haining, Peter, ed. Great Irish Humorous Stories: An Anthology of Laughter & Wit. 1998. (Illus.). (*0-285-63250-7*) Souvenir Pr. Ltd.

Hall, Anna M. Tales of Irish Life & Character. 1977. (Short Story Index Reprint Ser.). 25.95 (*0-8369-3694-9*) Ayer Co. Pubs., Inc.

—Tales of Irish Life & Character. 1972. 323p. reprint ed. 29.95 (*0-405-08592-3*) Blom Pubns. GBR. *Dist:* Ayer Co. Pubs., Inc.

Hamilton, Joan L. The Lion & the Cross. 1979. 10.00 o.p. (*0-385-14480-6*) Doubleday Publishing.

Hamilton, Lyn. The Celtic Riddle. 2000. 304p. mass mkt. 6.50 (*0-425-17775-0*, Prime Crime) Berkley Publishing Group.

—The Celtic Riddle: An Archaeological Mystery. 2000. 296p. 21.95 o.s.i (*0-425-17235-X*, Prime Crime) Berkley Publishing Group.

Hanley, James. The Furys. 1993. 400p. pap. 11.95 o.p. (*0-14-018507-0*, Penguin Classics) Viking Penguin.

Hannon, Irene. A Rainbow in the Glen. 1993. 18.95 o.s.i (*0-8034-9012-7*, Avalon Bks.) Bouregy, Thomas & Co., Inc.

—A Rainbow in the Glen. l.t. ed. 1995. (Large Print Romance Ser.). 250p. 17.95 o.p. (*0-7838-1440-2*, Macmillan Reference USA) Gale Group.

Hardie, Kerry. A Winter Marriage. 2002. 400p. 24.95 (*0-316-07622-8*) Little Brown & Co.

Harrington, Jonathan. The Death of Cousin Rose. 2000. mass mkt. (*0-373-26347-3*, Worldwide Library) Harlequin Enterprises, Ltd.

—The Death of Cousin Rose. 1996. (Danny O'Flaherty Mysteries Ser.). 215p. 19.95 o.p. (*1-885173-06-7*) Write Way Publishing.

—The Second Sorrowful Mystery. 2000. (Danny O'Flaherty Mysteries Ser.). 256p. mass mkt. (*0-373-26358-9*, 1-26358-1, Worldwide Library) Harlequin Enterprises, Ltd.

—The Second Sorrowful Mystery. 1999. 240p. 21.95 (*1-885173-37-7*) Write Way Publishing.

Harris, Cindy. Lover's Knot. 2002. 352p. mass mkt. 5.99 o.s.i (*0-8217-7072-1*) Kensington Publishing Corp.

Hart, Erin. Haunted Ground: A Crime Novel. 2003. (Illus.). 352p. 24.00 (*0-7432-3505-3*, Scribner) Simon & Schuster.

Hart, Josephine. The Reconstructionist. l.t. ed. 2002. 256p. pap. 24.95 (*0-7862-3726-0*) Gale Group.

—The Reconstructionist. 2001. 288p. 26.95 (*1-58567-170-3*) Overlook Pr., The.

Hatcher, Robin Lee. In His Arms. l.t. ed. 2000. 312p. 26.95 (*1-57490-279-2*, Beeler Large Print Bks.) Beeler, Thomas T. Publisher.

—In His Arms. 1998. 432p. mass mkt. 6.99 o.s.i (*0-06-108689-4*) HarperCollins Pubs.

—In His Arms. 2001. (Coming to America Bk.). 304p. pap. 10.99 (*0-310-23120-5*) Zondervan.

Haverty, Anne M. One Day as a Tiger. 1999. 264p. pap. o.p. (*0-88001-667-1*); 1998. 224p. 22.00 o.s.i (*0-88001-558-6*) HarperTrade. (Ecco).

Hawkes, John. An Irish Eye. l.t. ed. 1997. (G. K. Hall Core Ser.). 143p. 25.95 (*0-7838-8380-3*, Macmillan Reference USA) Gale Group.

—An Irish Eye. 1998. 256p. pap. 11.95 o.p. (*0-14-026758-1*) Penguin Group (USA) Inc.

—An Irish Eye. 1997. 176p. 22.95 o.s.i (*0-670-87591-0*) Viking Penguin.

Hayes, Katy. Gossip. 2002. 272p. 28.00 (*1-86159-042-3*); pap. 16.95 (*1-86159-153-5*) Orion Publishing Group, Ltd. GBR. *Dist:* Trafalgar Square.

Healy, Dermot. A Goat's Song. 1998. (Harvest Book Ser.). 420p. pap. 14.00 (*0-15-600582-4*, Harvest Bks.) Harcourt Trade Pubs.

—A Goat's Song. 1999. pap. 11.95 (*0-14-024695-9*); 1995. (Illus.). 416p. 24.95 o.p. (*0-670-86156-1*, Viking) Viking Penguin.

—Sudden Times. 2000. 352p. 23.00 o.s.i (*0-15-100578-8*) Harcourt Trade Pubs.

Hendrix, Lisa. To Marry an Irish Rogue. 2000. (Irish Eyes Ser.). 336p. mass mkt. 5.99 o.s.i (*0-515-12786-8*, Jove) Berkley Publishing Group.

Higgins, Aidan. Flotsam & Jetsam. 2002. (Irish Literature Ser.). 470p. pap. 13.95 (*1-56478-316-2*) Dalkey Archive Pr.

Higgins, Jack. Drink with the Devil. 1997. 336p. mass mkt. 7.99 (*0-425-15754-7*); mass mkt. 6.99 o.s.i (*0-425-16049-1*) Berkley Publishing Group.

—Drink with the Devil, Set. unabr. ed. 1999. audio 29.95 Highsmith Inc.

—Drink with the Devil. abr. ed. 1996. 2 cass. audio 17.95 o.p. (*0-7871-0966-5*); Set. 29.95 o.p. (*0-7871-0872-3*, 893923) NewStar Media, Inc.

—Drink with the Devil. 1996. 320p. 24.95 o.p. (*0-399-14154-5*, G. P. Putnam's Sons) Penguin Group (USA) Inc.

—Drink with the Devil. 1998. 5.98 o.p. (*0-7651-0898-4*) Smithmark Pubs., Inc.

—Drink with the Devil. l.t. ed. 1999. 430p. pap. 26.95 (*0-7862-0797-3*) Thorndike Pr.

—Pay the Devil. 1999. 304p. mass mkt. 7.99 (*0-425-17189-2*) Berkley Publishing Group.

—Pay the Devil. l.t. ed. 2001. (Large Print Book Ser.). 244p. 28.95 (*1-58724-015-7*, Wheeler Publishing, Inc.) Gale Group.

Hing, Robert J. Ulysses: His Story. 1996. (Illus.). 176p. (Orig.). pap. 12.95 o.p. (*0-9631460-1-7*) Anchor Watch Pr.

Hoff, B. J. Dawn of the Golden Promise. 1994. (Emerald Ballad Ser.: Bk. 5). 400p. pap. 11.99 o.p. (*1-55661-114-5*) Bethany Hse. Pubs.

—Dawn of the Golden Promise. l.t. ed. 2002. 707p. 28.95 (*0-7862-3578-0*) Gale Group.

—An Emerald Ballad, Bks. 1-5. 1994. (Emerald Ballad Ser.). 59.99 o.p. (*1-55661-794-1*, 252794) Bethany Hse. Pubs.

—An Emerald Ballad 1-3 Giftset. 1992. (Emerald Ballad Ser.). (YA). 29.99 o.p. (*1-55661-771-2*) Bethany Hse. Pubs.

—Heart of the Lonely Exile. 1991. (Emerald Ballad Ser.: Bk. 2). 384p. pap. 11.99 o.p. (*1-55661-111-0*) Bethany Hse. Pubs.

—Heart of the Lonely Exile. l.t. ed. 2002. (Emerald Ballad Ser.: No. 2). 715p. pap. 17.95 (*1-4104-0020-4*, Walker Large Print) Gale Group.

—Heart of the Lonely Exile. l.t. ed. 2001. (Christian Fiction Ser.). 716p. 27.95 (*0-7862-3577-2*) Thorndike Pr.

—Land of a Thousand Dreams. 1992. (Emerald Ballad Ser.: Bk. 3). 400p. pap. 11.99 o.p. (*1-55661-112-9*) Bethany Hse. Pubs.

—Land of a Thousand Dreams. l.t. ed. 2002. (Emerald Ballad Ser.: No. 3). 672p. pap. 17.95 (*1-4104-0024-7*, Walker Large Print) Gale Group.

—Land of a Thousand Dreams. l.t. ed. 2001. 672p. 27.95 (*0-7862-3576-4*) Thorndike Pr.

—Song of the Silent Harp. 1991. (Emerald Ballad Ser.: Vol. 1). 416p. (ps-3). pap. 11.99 o.p. (*1-55661-110-2*) Bethany Hse. Pubs.

—Song of the Silent Harp. l.t. ed. 2002. (Emerald Ballad Ser.: No. 1). 715p. pap. 17.95 (*1-4104-0030-1*, Walker Large Print) Gale Group.

—Song of the Silent Harp. l.t. ed. 2000. (Christian Fiction Ser.). 709p. 26.95 (*0-7862-2880-6*) Thorndike Pr.

—Sons of an Ancient Glory. 1993. (Emerald Ballad Ser.: Vol. 4). 400p. pap. 11.99 o.p. (*1-55661-113-7*) Bethany Hse. Pubs.

—Sons of an Ancient Glory. l.t. ed. 2002. 698p. 28.95 (*0-7862-3575-6*) Gale Group.

Hogan, Desmond. A Curious Street. 1984. 194p. 12.95 o.p. (*0-8076-1099-2*) Braziller, George Inc.

—A Link with the River. 1989. 326p. 17.95 o.s.i (*0-374-18461-5*) Farrar, Straus & Giroux.

Holland, Cecelia. The Kings in Winter. 2000. 205p. pap. 12.95 (*0-312-86888-X*, Forge Bks.) Doherty, Tom Assocs., LLC.

—The Soul Thief. E-Book 24.95 (*0-312-70605-7*, Tor Bks.); 2004. 304p. pap. 14.95 (*0-312-86997-5*, Forge Bks.); 2002. 304p. 24.95 o.s.i (*0-312-84885-4*, Forge Bks.) Doherty, Tom Assocs., LLC.

Holt, Cheryl. My True Love. 2001. 352p. mass mkt. 5.99 (*0-8217-7079-9*, Zebra Bks.) Kensington Publishing Corp.

Horsley, Kate. The Changeling of Finnistuath: A Novel. 2003. 304p. 22.95 (*1-59030-048-3*) Shambhala Pubns., Inc.

—Confessions of a Pagan Nun: A Novel. 2002. 208p. reprint ed. pap. 10.95 (*1-57062-913-7*) Shambhala Pubns., Inc.

How to Murder a Man. 2002. pap. 14.95 (*0-7145-3065-4*) Boyars, Marion Pubs., Inc.

Howe, Fanny. Nod. 1997. (Sun & Moon Classics Ser.: No. 124). 218p. 18.95 o.p. (*1-55713-307-7*) Sun & Moon Pr.

Hughes, Sean. The Detainees. 1997. 322p. o.p. (*0-684-82081-1*) Simon & Schuster.

Hunt, Angela Elwell. Ingram of the Irish. 1994. (Theyn Chronicles Ser.: Vol.3). 480p. pap. 9.99 o.p. (*0-8423-1623-X*) Tyndale Hse. Pubs.

—Ingram of the Irish. 2000. 432p. pap. 24.95 (*0-595-14330-X*, Backinprint.com) iUniverse, Inc.

—The Secret of Cravenhill Castle. 1994. (Nicki Holland Mystery Ser.: Vol. 8). (J). pap. 4.99 o.p. (*0-8407-6305-0*) Nelson, Thomas Inc.

Hunter, Aislinn. Stay. 2002. (Illus.). 224p. pap. (*1-55192-568-0*) Raincoast Bk. Distribution.

Hutchinson, Meg. The Deverell Woman. 432p. mass mkt. 9.95 (*0-340-81820-4*) Coronet GBR. *Dist:* Trafalgar Square.

—The Deverell Woman. 2002. 380p. 29.95 (*0-340-81819-0*) Hodder & Stoughton, Ltd. GBR. *Dist:* Trafalgar Square.

—The Deverell Woman. l.t. ed. 2003. (Magna Large Print Ser.). 528p. (*0-7505-2040-X*) Magna Large Print Bks. GBR. *Dist:* Ulverscroft Large Print Canada, Ltd.

Irish Girls about Town. 2002. 400p. pap. (*1-903650-26-7*) Pocket Bks.

Isidore, Sarah. Shrine of Light. Gill, D. C. G., ed. 2000. (Daughters of Bast Ser.: Vol. 2). 352p. mass mkt. 6.50 (*0-380-80319-4*, Eos) Morrow/Avon.

Jewett, Sarah Orne. The Irish Short Stories of Sarah Orne Jewett. Morgan, Jack & Renza, Louis A., eds. 1996. (Illus.). 192p. (C). 24.95 (*0-8093-2039-8*) Southern Illinois Univ. Pr.

Johnson, Mary. The Judge & the Barfly. 2003. 216p. pap. 19.95 (*1-59286-479-1*) PublishAmerica, Inc.

Johnston, Jennifer. The Invisible Worm. 1993. 192p. 19.95 o.p. (*0-88184-950-2*, Carroll & Graf Pubs.) Avalon Publishing Group.

—The Invisible Worm. 1998. 192p. o.p. (*1-85619-041-2*) Random Hse. of Canada, Ltd. CAN. *Dist:* Random Hse., Inc.

Jones, Ann T. A Country Divorce. 1992. 310p. 20.00 (*1-883285-11-9*) Delphinium Bks., Inc.

Jones, Shelagh. Save the Unicorns. 1989. (Illus.). 140p. (J). (gr. 4-7). 11.95 o.p. (*0-947962-48-4*) Children's Pr., Ltd. IRL. *Dist:* Irish Bks. & Media, Inc.

Jordan, John. Collected Stories. McFadden, Hugh, ed. 1991. 206p. pap. 16.95 (*1-85371-105-5*) Poolbeg Pr. IRL. *Dist:* Dufour Editions, Inc.

Jordan, Neil. Collected Fiction. 1997. 394p. (*0-09-975361-8*) Trafalgar Square.

—Nightlines. 1995. 192p. 21.00 (*0-679-44438-6*) Random Hse., Inc.

—The Past. 1980. 8.95 o.p. (*0-8076-0982-X*) Braziller, George Inc.

Joyce, James. Dubliners. 1993. (Modern Library Ser.). E-Book 4.95 (*1-931208-61-1*) Adobe Systems, Inc.

—Dubliners. 1976. 24.95 (*0-8488-1064-3*) Amereon, Ltd.

—Dubliners. 1990. 208p. mass mkt. 4.95 (*0-553-21380-6*) Bantam Bks.

—Dubliners. 1992. reprint ed. lib. bdg. 27.95 (*0-89968-285-5*, Lightyear Pr.) Buccaneer Bks., Inc.

—Dubliners. Goodwyn, Andrew, ed. 1995. (Literature Ser.). (Illus.). 240p. pap. text 9.50 (*0-521-48544-4*) Cambridge Univ. Pr.

—Dubliners. (Collected Works of James Joyce). reprint ed. lib. bdg. 98.00 (*0-7426-3126-5*); 2001. pap. text 28.00 (*0-7426-8126-2*) Classic Bks.

—Dubliners. 1991. (Thrift Editions Ser.). 160p. reprint ed. pap. 1.50 (*0-486-26870-5*) Dover Pubns., Inc.

—Dubliners. Gabler, Hans W. & Hettche, Wettche, eds. 1993. 462p. 55.00 o.p. (*0-8153-1277-6*) Garland Publishing, Inc.

—Dubliners. 1992. 33.00 o.p. (*0-7171-1901-7*) Gill & MacMillan, Ltd. IRL. *Dist:* Irish Bks. & Media, Inc.

—Dubliners. 1993. 304p. pap. 10.00 (*0-679-73990-4*, Vintage) Knopf Publishing Group.

—Dubliners. pap., tchr. ed. (*0-451-52617-1*); 1991. 256p. mass mkt. 4.95 (*0-451-52543-4*) NAL. (Signet Classics).

—Dubliners. 1969. pap. 2.95 o.p. (*0-670-01805-8*); 1968. pap. 1.45 o.p. (*0-670-00041-8*) Penguin Group (USA) Inc.

—Dubliners. 8th abr. unabr. ed. 1993. (Classics on Cassette). 16.00 incl. audio (*0-453-00845-3*, 390003) Penguin/HighBridge.

—Dubliners. 2000. E-Book 4.95 (*0-679-64160-2*, Modern Library) Random House Adult Trade Publishing Group.

—Dubliners. 1993. (Modern Library Ser.). 304p. 14.95 (*0-679-60049-3*); 1991. (Everyman's Library: Vol. 49). 352p. 18.00 (*0-679-40574-7*); 1978. 9.95 o.s.i (*0-394-60464-4*); 1926. 3.95 o.s.i (*0-394-60124-6*) Random Hse., Inc.

—Dubliners. 1998. (Enriched Classics Ser.). (Illus.). 256p. reprint ed. mass mkt. 4.99 (*0-671-01537-0*, Pocket) Simon & Schuster.

—Dubliners. annot. ed. 1995. (Illus.). pap. 19.95 (*0-312-11779-5*, Saint Martin's Griffin) St. Martin's Pr.

—Dubliners. 1992. (Illus.). 192p. (C). reprint ed. 30.00 o.p. (*0-7509-0015-6*) Sutton Publishing, Ltd. GBR. *Dist:* International Publishers Marketing.

—Dubliners. 1998. (Washington Square Press Enriched Classic Ser.). (Illus.). (J). 11.04 (*0-606-20641-8*) Turtleback Bks.

—Dubliners. (Twentieth Century Classics Ser.). 1993. 368p. pap. 9.95 (*0-14-018647-6*, Penguin Classics); 1982. 17.50 o.p. (*0-670-28586-2*); 1982. pap. 6.95 o.p. (*0-14-006285-8*, Penguin Bks.); 1976. 512p. pap. 14.95 o.p. (*0-14-015505-8*); 1976. 224p. pap. 7.95 o.p. (*0-14-004222-9*, Viking); 1969. pap. 5.95 o.p. (*0-670-28585-4*); 1968. 4.50 o.p. (*0-670-28584-6*); 1916. 3.50 o.p. (*0-670-28583-8*) Viking Penguin.

—Dubliners. 1998. (Classics Library). 176p. pap. 3.95 (*1-85326-048-7*, 0487WW) Wordsworth Editions, Ltd. GBR. *Dist:* Casemate Pubs. & Bk. Distributors, LLC.

—Listen & Read James Joyce's Dubliners. 1996. (Thrift Editions Ser.). (Illus.). 160p. (Orig.). pap. 6.95 incl. audio (*0-486-29121-9*) Dover Pubns., Inc.

—A Portrait of an Artist As a Young Man. 1992. 256p. mass mkt. 4.95 (*0-553-21404-7*, Bantam Classics) Bantam Bks.

—A Portrait of the Artist As a Young Man. 22.95 (*0-89190-725-4*) Amereon, Ltd.

—A Portrait of the Artist As a Young Man. abr. ed. 1993. audio 16.99 (*0-88646-343-2*) Durkin Hayes Publishing Ltd.

—A Portrait of the Artist As a Young Man. Gabler, Hans W. & Hettche, Walter, eds. 1993. 366p. text 61.00 (*0-8153-1278-4*) Garland Publishing, Inc.

—A Portrait of the Artist As a Young Man. abr. ed. audio 12.95 o.p. (*0-694-50084-4*, SWC 1110, Caedmon) HarperTrade.

—A Portrait of the Artist As a Young Man. 1993. 288p. pap. 10.00 (*0-679-73989-0*, Vintage) Knopf Publishing Group.

—A Portrait of the Artist As a Young Man. 1991. (Everyman's Library: Vol. 9). 368p. 17.00 (*0-679-40575-5*) Knopf, Alfred A. Inc.

—A Portrait of the Artist As a Young Man. 1991. 256p. mass mkt. 4.95 (*0-451-52544-2*, Signet Classics) NAL.

—A Portrait of the Artist As a Young Man. abr. ed. 1996. (Works of James Joyce). audio 17.98 (*962-634-570-5*, NA307014, Naxos AudioBooks) Naxos of America, Inc.

—A Portrait of the Artist As a Young Man. Kershner, R. B., ed. 1993. (Case Studies in Contemporary Criticism). 416p. (C). text 35.00 o.p. (*0-312-08987-2*) Palgrave Macmillan.

—A Portrait of the Artist As a Young Man. 1999. (Penguin Great Books of the 20th Century Ser.). 240p. pap. 10.95 (*0-14-028328-5*) Penguin Group (USA) Inc.

—A Portrait of the Artist As a Young Man. 1996. (Modern Library Ser.). 368p. 17.95 (*0-679-60232-1*) Random Hse., Inc.

—A Portrait of the Artist As a Young Man. 1995. pap. 13.95 o.p. (*0-312-13845-8*) St. Martin's Pr.

—A Portrait of the Artist As a Young Man. 1916. 15.00 (*0-606-02826-9*) Turtleback Bks.

—A Portrait of the Artist As a Young Man. 1993. (Penguin Twentieth-Century Classics Ser.). 384p. pap. 8.95 o.s.i (*0-14-018683-2*, Penguin Classics) Viking Penguin.

—A Portrait of the Artist As a Young Man. Ellmann, Richard, ed. 1982. 17.50 o.p. (*0-670-56683-7*) Viking Penguin.

—A Portrait of the Artist As a Young Man. 1964. 256p. pap. 7.00 o.p. (*0-14-004221-0*, Penguin Bks.) Viking Penguin.

—A Portrait of the Artist As a Young Man. 1997. (Classics Ser.). 208p. pap. 3.95 (*1-85326-006-1*, 0061WW) Wordsworth Editions, Ltd. GBR. *Dist:* Casemate Pubs. & Bk. Distributors, LLC.

—A Portrait of the Artist As a Young Man. abr. ed. 1995. (Works of James Joyce). audio compact disk 19.98 (*962-634-070-3*, NA307012, Naxos AudioBooks) Naxos of America, Inc.

—A Portrait of the Artist As a Young Man, Set. unabr. ed. 1994. audio 41.95 (*1-55685-317-3*) Audio Bk. Contractors, Inc.

—A Portrait of the Artist As a Young Man. unabr. ed. 1995. audio 49.95 (*0-7861-0655-7*, 1559) Blackstone Audio Bks., Inc.

—A Portrait of the Artist As a Young Man. unabr. collector's ed. 1992. (J). audio 56.00 (*0-7366-2301-9*, 3085) Books on Tape, Inc.

—A Portrait of the Artist As a Young Man. 1992. 350p. reprint ed. lib. bdg. 26.95 (*0-89966-899-2*) Buccaneer Bks., Inc.

—A Portrait of the Artist As a Young Man. reprint ed. lib. bdg. 98.00 (*0-7426-3127-3*) Classic Bks.

—A Portrait of the Artist As a Young Man. 1994. (Thrift Editions Ser.). 192p. reprint ed. pap. 2.00 (*0-486-28050-0*) Dover Pubns., Inc.
—A Portrait of the Artist As a Young Man. unabr. ed. 1993. (YA). (gr. 11-12). audio 28.00 Jimcin Recordings.
—A Portrait of the Artist As a Young Man. l.t. ed. 1995. 410p. lib. bdg. 26.00 (*0-939495-86-4*); 1998. 255p. reprint ed. lib. bdg. 25.00 (*1-58287-057-8*) North Bks.
—A Portrait of the Artist As a Young Man. unabr. ed. 1999. audio 70.00 (*1-55690-421-5*, 91106E7) Recorded Bks., LLC.
—A Portrait of the Artist As a Young Man. 1998. (Enriched Classics Ser.). (Illus.). 288p. reprint ed. mass mkt. 5.99 (*0-671-01538-9*, Pocket) Simon & Schuster.
—A Portrait of the Artist As a Young Man: Text & Criticism. Anderson, Chester G., ed. (Critical Studies). 1977. 576p. 15.95 (*0-14-015503-1*); 1964. (J). (gr. 9 up). pap. 8.95 o.p. (*0-670-56648-9*) Viking Penguin.
—Shorter Finnegans Wake. 1967. 6.00 o.p. (*0-670-64270-3*) Viking Penguin.
—Stephen Hero. rev. ed. 1963. (Illus.). pap. 11.95 (*0-8112-0074-4*, NDP133) New Directions Publishing Corp.
—Ulysses. 799p. 38.95 (*0-8488-2569-1*) Amereon, Ltd.
—Ulysses. 1992. reprint ed. lib. bdg. 27.95 (*0-89968-284-7*, Lightyear Pr.) Buccaneer Bks., Inc.
—Ulysses, 3 vols. Gabler, Hans W. & Melchior, Claus, eds. 1984. 1954p. text 202.00 o.p. (*0-8240-4375-8*) Garland Publishing, Inc.
—Ulysses. abr. ed. 1972. audio 12.95 o.s.i (*0-694-50050-X*, SWC 1063, Caedmon); Set. 1984. audio 19.95 (*0-694-50866-7*, SWC 328, Caedmon); Set. 1992. audio 18.00 o.s.i (*1-55994-633-4*, DCN 328, HarperAudio) HarperTrade.
—Ulysses. 1990. 816p. pap. 17.00 (*0-679-72276-9*, Vintage) Knopf Publishing Group.
—Ulysses. 1997. 1136p. 25.00 (*0-679-45513-2*) Knopf, Alfred A. Inc.
—Ulysses. 2015. 880p. mass mkt. 7.95 o.s.i (*0-451-52674-0*, Signet Classics) NAL.
—Ulysses. abr. ed. (Works of James Joyce). 1996. audio 22.98 (*962-634-511-X*, NA401114); 1994. audio compact disk 26.98 (*962-634-011-8*, NA401112) Naxos of America, Inc. (Naxos AudioBooks).
—Ulysses. Date not set. 35.00 (*0-393-03390-2*) Norton, W. W. & Co., Inc.
—Ulysses. 1998. 732p. 75.00 (*0-914061-70-4*) Orchises Pr.
—Ulysses. Johnson, Jeri, ed. & intro. by. unexpurg. ed. 1993. (Oxford World's Classics Ser.). (Illus.). 1056p. pap. 15.95 o.p. (*0-19-282866-5*) Oxford Univ. Pr., Inc.
—Ulysses. 1993. audio 22.00 o.s.i (*0-553-47163-5*, RH Audio) Random Hse. Audio Publishing Group.
—Ulysses. (Modern Library of the World's Best Bks.). 1992. 816p. 22.95 (*0-679-60011-6*); 1967. 20.00 o.p. (*0-394-45005-1*); 1967. pap. 10.95 o.p. (*0-394-70380-4*); 1940. 5.95 o.s.i (*0-394-60752-X*) Random Hse., Inc.
—Ulysses. 2004. audio compact disk 79.99 (*1-4025-7203-4*); Pt. 2, set. audio o.s.i; Set. 1999. audio 186.00 (*0-7887-0225-4*, 94502); Vols. 1 & 2. 1996. audio 186.00 (*0-7887-0309-9*, 94502E7) Recorded Bks., LLC.
—Ulysses. 1040p. 1999. pap. 14.95 (*0-14-118086-2*); 1998. pap. 14.95 (*0-14-018558-5*, Penguin Classics) Viking Penguin.
—Ulysses: A Facsimile of the Manuscript, 3 vols. ltd. ed. 1976. (Octagon Bk.). 1066p. 200.00 o.p. (*0-374-28033-9*) Farrar, Straus & Giroux.
—Ulysses: A Facsimile of the Manuscript & the Manuscript & First Printings Compared, 3 vols. 1975. 100.00 o.p. (*0-374-94440-7*) Univ. Pr. of Virginia.
—Ulysses: A Reader's Edition. Rose, Danis, ed. 1998. 826p. pap. 19.95 (*0-330-35230-X*); 1997. 824p. 47.50 o.p. (*0-330-35229-6*) Picador GBR. *Dist:* Trans-Atlantic Pubns., Inc.
—Ulysses: The Corrected Text. 1986. 608p. 29.95 o.s.i (*0-394-55373-X*); 680p. pap. 19.00 (*0-394-74312-1*) Knopf Publishing Group. (Vintage).
—Ulysses: The Corrected Text. rev. ed. 1986. 16.95 (*0-07-544944-7*) McGraw-Hill Cos., The.
Joyce, James, contrib. by. Ulysses. 1997. (*1-874675-98-8*); (*1-874675-99-6*) Dufour Editions, Inc.
Joyce, James, et al. Dubliners. Jackson, John W. & MCGinley, Bernard, eds. 1993. 35.00 (*0-312-09790-5*) St. Martin's Pr.
—A Portrait of the Artist As a Young Man. 1999. (Literature Made Easy Ser.). 85p. pap. 4.95 (*0-7641-0825-5*) Barron's Educational Series, Inc.
Joyce, Joe. Trigger Man: A Novel. 1991. 18.95 o.p. (*0-393-02980-8*) Norton, W. W. & Co., Inc.
Kavanagh, Herminie T. Ashes of Old Wishes, & Other Darby O'Gill Tales. 1977. (Short Story Index Reprint Ser.). reprint ed. 33.98 (*0-8369-4018-0*) Ayer Co. Pubs., Inc.
—Darby O'Gill & the Good People. rev. ed. 1998. 182p. pap. 13.95 (*0-9666701-0-8*) One Faithful Harp Publishing Co.
Keady, Walter. The Altruist: A Novel. 2003. 283p. pap. 13.50 (*1-931561-39-7*) MacAdam/Cage Publishing, Inc.
—Celibates & Other Lovers. 1998. (Harvest Book Ser.). 240p. pap. 13.00 o.s.i (*0-15-600571-9*, Harvest Bks.) Harcourt Trade Pubs.
—Celibates & Other Lovers. 1997. 225p. 20.00 (*1-878448-77-3*) MacMurray & Beck, Inc.
Keane, John B. The Bodhran Makers. 1992. 256p. reprint ed. 18.95 (*0-941423-80-8*) Four Walls Eight Windows.
—The Bodhran Makers. 2001. 354p. 14.95 (*1-56833-186-X*) Madison Bks., Inc.
—The Bodhran Makers. 1996. 354p. pap. 14.95 (*1-57098-063-2*) Rinehart, Roberts Pubs.
—Durango. 1995. 300p. 22.95 (*1-57098-038-1*) Rinehart, Roberts Pubs.
—An Irish Christmas: Stories. 2002. 224p. pap. 12.00 (*0-7867-1055-1*, Carroll & Graf Pubs.) Avalon Publishing Group.
—An Irish Christmas Feast: The Best of John B. Keane. 2002. 416p. 23.00 (*0-7867-1054-3*, Carroll & Graf Pubs.) Avalon Publishing Group.
—Irish Stories. 1998. audio 11.95 (*1-57098-239-2*); 192p. 24.95 (*1-57098-070-5*, Rinehart, Roberts International); 192p. pap. 14.95 (*1-57098-242-2*, Rinehart, Roberts International) Rinehart, Roberts Pubs.
—Irish Stories for Christmas. audio 9.95 o.p. (*1-57098-051-9*) Dragonhawk Publishing.
—Irish Stories for Christmas. 160p. 1995. pap. 10.95 (*1-57098-050-0*); 1994. 19.95 (*1-879373-97-1*) Rinehart, Roberts Pubs.
—Letters of a Love-Hungry Farmer. 1993. 96p. 10.95 o.p. (*0-312-09862-6*) St. Martin's Pr.
—Letters of a Successful T. D. 1990. pap. 10.95 (*0-85342-824-7*) Dufour Editions, Inc.
—More Irish Stories for Christmas. 1996. 160p. 19.95 (*1-57098-069-1*); audio 11.95 (*1-57098-108-6*) Rinehart, Roberts Pubs.
—Under the Sycamore Tree, & Other Tales. 1997. (*1-85635-170-X*) Mercier Pr., Ltd., The IRL. *Dist:* Irish Bks. & Media, Inc.
—A Warm Bed on a Cold Night, & Other Stories. 1997. (*1-85635-184-X*) Mercier Pr., Ltd., The IRL. *Dist:* Irish Bks. & Media, Inc.
Keane, Molly. Treasure Hunt. l.t. ed. 1992. 272p. 24.95 (*1-85089-554-6*) ISIS Large Print Bks. GBR. *Dist:* Transaction Pubs.
Keegan, Claire. Antarctica. 2001. 207p. 23.00 o.p. (*0-87113-779-8*, Atlantic Monthly Pr.); 2002. 224p. reprint ed. pap. 12.00 (*0-8021-3901-9*, Grove Pr.) Grove/Atlantic, Inc.
Kelleher, Lawrence. Seanachie: A Story of the Irish. 2001. pap. 26.95 (*0-595-19758-2*) iUniverse, Inc.
Kelly, Cathy. Someone Like You: A Novel. 2001. 480p. 24.95 o.p. (*0-525-94605-5*) Dutton/Plume.
—Someone Like You: A Novel. 2000. viii, 581p. (*1-85371-904-8*) Poolbeg Pr.
Kelly, Eamon. Bless Me Father. 1977. (Illus.). 90 p. (*0-85342-489-6*) Irish American Bk. Co.
Kenny, Sean. The Hungry Earth. 1997. 262p. 19.95 (*1-57098-136-1*) Rinehart, Roberts Pubs.
Kenyon, Michael. May You Die in Ireland. 2002. (Black Dagger Crime Ser.). 224p. 21.95 (*0-7540-8608-9*, Black Dagger) BBC Audiobooks America.
Kerr, Simon. The Rainbow Singer: A Novel. 2003. pap. (*0-7868-8682-X*); 2002. 304p. 23.95 (*0-7868-6798-1*) Hyperion Pr.
—Reappeared. 2004. pap. 13.95 (*0-7868-8683-8*); 2003. 23.95 (*0-7868-6799-X*) Hyperion Pr.
Kerr, William. The Red Hand. 200p. 2002. 23.35 (*0-7596-4748-8*); 2001. pap. 15.54 (*0-7596-3378-9*) 1stBooks Library.
Keyes, Marian. Watermelon. 2002. 432p. pap. 13.95 (*0-06-009036-7*, Perennial) HarperTrade.
—Watermelon. 1999. 448p. mass mkt. 6.99 (*0-380-79609-0*); 1998. 432p. mass mkt. 15.95 (*0-380-97617-X*) Morrow/Avon. (Avon Bks.).
—Watermelon. 1995. 612p. pap. 11.95 (*1-85371-508-5*) Poolbeg Pr. IRL. *Dist:* Dufour Editions, Inc.
Kiely, Benedict. The Cards of The Gambler. 1997. 240p. pap. 12.95 (*0-86327-477-3*) Wolfhound Pr. IRL. *Dist:* Irish American Bk. Co.
—A Letter to Peachtree & Nine Other Stories. 1988. 17.95 o.p. (*0-87923-727-9*) Godine, David R. Pub.
—The State of Ireland: A Novella & Seventeen Short Stories. 1980. (Illus.). 400p. 16.95 o.p. (*0-87923-320-6*) Godine, David R. Pub.
Kiely, David M. The Angel Tapes: A Blade Macken Mystery. 1997. (Blade Macken Mystery Ser.). 304p. text 23.95 o.p. (*0-312-16772-5*) St. Martin's Pr.
King, Peter. Terrible Beauty. 1999. 264p. 22.95 (*1-57098-262-7*) Rinehart, Roberts Pubs.
Koch, C. J. Out of Ireland. 1999. (Illus.). x, 706p. (*1-86471-038-1*) Doubleday Publishing.
Kurtz, Katherine. St. Patrick's Gargoyle. 2001. 240p. 21.95 o.s.i (*0-441-00725-2*); 2002. 304p. reprint ed. mass mkt. 7.50 (*0-441-00905-0*) Ace Bks.
Kurtz, Katherine & Harris, Deborah T. Dagger Magic. (Adept Ser.: No. 4). 1996. 384p. mass mkt. 6.99 (*0-441-00304-4*); 1995. 375p. 19.95 o.p. (*0-441-00149-1*) Ace Bks.
Labiner, Norah. Miniatures: A Novel. 2003. 400p. pap. 16.00 (*1-56689-151-5*); 2002. 381p. 23.00 (*1-56689-136-1*); 2002. pap. (*1-56689-132-9*) Coffee Hse. Pr.
Lady Morgan. The Wild Irish Girl, 1807. 2003. (Revolution & Romanticism, 1789-1834 Ser.). (*1-85477-189-2*) Woodstock Books.
Laverty, Maura. Never No More. 1960. 285p. 6.95 o.p. (*0-87243-013-8*) Templegate Pubs.
Lavin, Mary. The House in Clewe Street. 1988. 476p. pap. 7.95 o.p. (*0-14-016184-8*, Penguin Bks.) Viking Penguin.
—Mary O'Grady. 1986. 392p. pap. 6.95 o.p. (*0-14-016133-3*, Penguin Bks.) Viking Penguin.
—Selected Stories. 1984. 272p. pap. 6.95 o.p. (*0-14-005602-5*, Penguin Bks.) Viking Penguin.
—The Shrine & Other Stories. 1977. 6.95 o.p. (*0-395-25773-5*) Houghton Mifflin Co.
Lawrence, Anthony. In the Half Light. 384p. 2003. pap. 14.00 (*0-7867-1230-9*); 2002. 26.00 (*0-7867-0999-5*, Carroll & Graf Pubs.) Avalon Publishing Group.
—In the Half Light. 2000. 384p. (*0-330-36235-6*) Picador.
Le Fanu, J. Sheridan. Green Tea & Other Ghost Stories, Vol. 100. 1998. (Thrift Editions Ser.). 96p. pap. 1.00 (*0-486-27795-X*) Dover Pubns., Inc.
—In a Glass Darkly, 3 vols., Set. 1977. (Collected Works). reprint ed. 80.95 (*0-405-09216-4*) Ayer Co. Pubs., Inc.
—In a Glass Darkly, 3 vols. Varma, Devendra P., ed. 1977. (Collected Works). reprint ed. Vol. 1. 26.95 (*0-405-09217-2*); Vol. 2. 26.95 (*0-405-09218-0*); Vol. 3. 26.95 (*0-405-09219-9*) Ayer Co. Pubs., Inc.
—In a Glass Darkly. Tracy, Robert, ed. 1999. (Oxford World's Classics Ser.). 384p. pap. 12.95 (*0-19-283947-0*) Oxford Univ. Pr., Inc.
—In a Glass Darkly. 1993. (Oxford World's Classics Ser.). 380p. pap. 10.95 o.p. (*0-19-282805-3*) Oxford Univ. Pr., Inc.
—In a Glass Darkly. 1998. (Classics Library). 320p. pap. 3.95 (*1-85326-265-X*, 265XWW) Wordsworth Editions, Ltd. GBR. *Dist:* Casemate Pubs. & Bk. Distributors, LLC.
—Madame Crowl's Ghost & Other Tales of Mystery. James, M. R., ed. 1977. (Short Story Index Reprint Ser.). reprint ed. 19.95 (*0-8369-3985-9*) Ayer Co. Pubs., Inc.
Leitch, Maurice. Eggman's Apprentice. 2001. 276p. pap. (*0-436-40403-6*) Random Hse. of Canada, Ltd. CAN. *Dist:* Random Hse., Inc.
Leland, Mary. Approaching Priests. 1992. 224p. 23.95 o.p. (*1-85619-065-X*) Trafalgar Square.
Lennon, Tom. Crazy Love. 1999. 240p. (*0-86278-560-X*) O'Brien Pr., Ltd., The.
Lentin, Ronit. Songs on the Death of Children. 1997. 220p. pap. 13.95 (*1-85371-625-1*) Poolbeg Pr. IRL. *Dist:* Dufour Editions, Inc.
Leonard, Hugh. Parnell & the Englishwoman. 1991. 256p. 19.95 o.s.i (*0-689-12127-X*, Scribner) Simon & Schuster.
Levesque, John. Sometime Soon: A Novel. 2001. 251p. pap. 15.00 (*0-88962-753-3*) Mosaic Pr.
Liam, Cathal. Consumed in Freedom's Flame: A Novel of Ireland's Struggle for Freedom 1916-1921. (Illus.). 2004. 400p. 16.00 (*0-9704155-2-4*); 2001. 448p. 24.00 (*0-9704155-0-8*) St. Padraic Pr.
Llywelyn, Morgan. Bard: The Odyssey of the Irish. 1987. 480p. mass mkt. 6.99 (*0-8125-8515-1*, Tor Bks.) Doherty, Tom Assocs., LLC.
—Bard: The Odyssey of the Irish, 001. 1984. 463p. 16.95 o.p. (*0-395-35352-1*) Houghton Mifflin Co.
—Finn Mac Cool. 1994. 432p. 23.95 o.p. (*0-312-85476-5*, Tor Bks.) Doherty, Tom Assocs., LLC.
—Grania: She-King of the Irish Seas. 1987. 480p. mass mkt. 4.50 o.s.i (*0-8041-0116-7*, Ivy Bks.) Ballantine Bks.
—Grania: She-King of the Irish Seas. 2003. 416p. pap. 15.95 (*0-7653-0838-X*, Forge Bks.) Doherty, Tom Assocs., LLC.
—Grania: She-King of the Irish Seas. 1986. 422p. 3.99 o.s.i (*0-517-55951-X*) Random Hse. Value Publishing.
—The Last Prince of Ireland. 1992. 22.00 o.p. (*0-688-10794-X*, Morrow, William & Co.) Morrow/Avon.
—Lion of Ireland. 1985. 560p. mass mkt. 4.95 o.p. (*0-425-08846-4*); 1984. mass mkt. 3.95 o.s.i (*0-425-07478-1*); 1983. mass mkt. 3.95 o.s.i (*0-425-06162-0*) Berkley Publishing Group.
—Lion of Ireland. 1996. 560p. mass mkt. 6.99 (*0-8125-5399-3*); 2002. 400p. reprint ed. pap. 15.95 (*0-7653-0257-8*) Doherty, Tom Assocs., LLC. (Tor Bks.).
—Lion of Ireland: The Legend of Brian Boru, 001. 1980. 17.95 o.p. (*0-395-28588-7*) Houghton Mifflin Co.
—The Pride of Lions. 1997. 399p. mass mkt. 6.99 (*0-8125-3650-9*, Tor Bks.); 1996. 352p. 23.95 o.p. (*0-312-85700-4*, Forge Bks.) Doherty, Tom Assocs., LLC.
—Strongbow. 1996. 160p. 15.95 o.p. (*0-312-86150-8*, Tor Bks.) Doherty, Tom Assocs., LLC.
—Strongbow: The Story of Richard & Aoife. 1997. 156p. (gr. 7-12). mass mkt. 4.99 (*0-8125-4462-5*, Tor Bks.) Doherty, Tom Assocs., LLC.
—1921. 2002. E-Book 25.95 (*1-59061-720-7*) Adobe Systems, Inc.
—1921. 2001. 432p. 25.95 (*0-312-86754-9*); 2002. 560p. reprint ed. mass mkt. 7.99 (*0-8125-7079-0*) Doherty, Tom Assocs., LLC. (Forge Bks.).
—1949. 512p. mass mkt. 7.99 (*0-8125-7080-4*, Forge Bks.); E-Book 25.95 (*0-312-70984-6*, Tor Bks.) Doherty, Tom Assocs., LLC.
—1949: A Novel of the Irish Free State. 2003. 416p. 25.95 (*0-312-86753-0*, Forge Bks.) Doherty, Tom Assocs., LLC.
Lofts, Norah. A Wayside Tavern. 1983. 368p. mass mkt. 3.50 o.s.i (*0-449-20140-6*, Fawcett) Ballantine Bks.
Lordan, Beth. But Come Ye Back: A Novel. 2004. 288p. 23.95 (*0-06-053036-7*, Morrow, William & Co.) Morrow/Avon.
Lusby, Jim. Making the Cut. 2003. 254p. pap. 7.95 (*0-7528-4375-3*) Orion Publishing Group, Ltd. GBR. *Dist:* Trafalgar Square.
Lynch, Sarah-Kate. Blessed Are the Cheesemakers. 2003. 336p. 22.95 (*0-446-53128-6*) Warner Bks., Inc.
MacDonald, Janice. The Man on the Cliff. 2002. (Harlequin Superromance Ser.: No. 1077). mass mkt. (*0-373-71077-1*, Harlequin Bks.) Harlequin Enterprises, Ltd.
MacDonald, John F. Tribe. 2002. 279p. 22.00 (*1-931561-06-0*) MacAdam/Cage Publishing, Inc.
MacDonald, Malcolm. For I Have Sinned. 1995. 384p. 22.95 o.p. (*0-312-13078-3*) St. Martin's Pr.
Macdonald, Malcolm. Hell Hath No Fury. 1992. 384p. 21.95 o.p. (*0-312-06994-4*) St. Martin's Pr.
—A Woman Scorned. 1992. 432p. 22.95 o.p. (*0-312-08341-6*) St. Martin's Pr.
MacDonogh, Steve. The Brandon Book of Irish Short Stories. 1998. 284p. (*0-86322-237-4*) Brandon Bk. Pubs., Ltd.
Macken, Walter. The Bogman. 1998. 288p. reprint ed. pap. 13.95 (*0-86322-184-X*) Brandon Bk. Pubs., Ltd. IRL. *Dist:* Irish Bks. & Media, Inc.
—God Made Sunday: And Other Stories. 1996. 222p. reprint ed. pap. 11.95 (*0-86322-217-X*) Brandon Bk. Pubs., Ltd. IRL. *Dist:* Irish Bks. & Media, Inc.
—The Green Hills, & Other Stories. 1996. 220p. reprint ed. pap. 11.95 (*0-86322-216-1*) Brandon Bk. Pubs., Ltd. IRL. *Dist:* Irish Bks. & Media, Inc.
—Quench the Moon. 1995. 412p. pap. 11.95 (*0-86322-202-1*) Brandon Bk. Pubs., Ltd. IRL. *Dist:* Irish Bks. & Media, Inc.
MacKenna, John. The Fallen & Other Stories. 1993. 169p. pap. 15.95 (*0-85640-495-0*) Blackstaff Pr., The IRL. *Dist:* Dufour Editions, Inc.
MacLaverty, Bernard. Cal. 1983. 170p. 12.95 o.p. (*0-8076-1070-4*) Braziller, George Inc.
—Cal. l.t. unabr. ed. 1998. 24.95 (*1-85089-288-1*, 892281) ISIS Large Print Bks. GBR. *Dist:* ISIS Publishing.
—Grace Notes. unabr. ed. 2000. audio 59.95 (*0-7540-0186-5*, CAB 1609) Chivers Audio Bks. GBR. *Dist:* BBC Audiobooks America.
—Grace Notes: A Novel. 1998. 288p. pap. 13.00 (*0-393-31841-9*, Norton Paperbacks); 1997. 224p. 23.00 (*0-393-04542-0*) Norton, W. W. & Co., Inc.
—Grace Notes: A Novel. 1997. 277p. o.p. (*0-224-04429-X*) Random Hse. UK, Ltd.
—Lamb. l.t. ed. 1999. (*0-7540-3475-5*); 200p. pap. (*0-7540-3476-3*) BBC Audiobooks America.
—Lamb. 1997. 160p. pap. 11.00 (*0-393-31701-3*) Norton, W. W. & Co., Inc.
—Lamb. l.t. ed. 1998. (General Ser.). 208p. pap. 23.95 (*0-7862-1609-3*) Thorndike Pr.
—Lamb. 1981. 160p. pap. 5.95 o.p. (*0-14-005769-2*, Penguin Bks.) Viking Penguin.
MacManus, Seumas. Through the Turf Smoke. 1977. (Short Story Index Reprint Ser.). 22.95 (*0-8369-3025-8*) Ayer Co. Pubs., Inc.
MacMurrough, Sorcha. The Hart & the Harp. 2001. 19.95 (*1-58345-943-X*) Domhan Bks.
—The Sea of Love. 2001. 19.95 (*1-58345-788-7*); 155p. pap. 13.95 (*1-58345-789-5*) Domhan Bks.
MacNamara, Brinsley. The Various Lives of Marcus Igoe. 1996. 237p. pap. 13.95 (*0-8023-1304-3*) Dufour Editions, Inc.
MacNamara, Desmond. The Book of Intrusions. 1994. 214p. 19.95 (*1-56478-041-4*) Dalkey Archive Pr.
Madden, Deirdre. Authenticity. 2002. 300p. pap. (*0-571-21446-0*) Faber & Faber, Inc.
Madden, Sandra. Prince's Heart. 2002. 352p. mass mkt. 5.99 o.s.i (*0-8217-7251-1*) Kensington Publishing Corp.

Mallace, M. As for Ireland. 2001. (Illus.). 288p. pap. 29.95 (0-9709333-0-4) SakonnetPr., Inc.
Mallon, James. Magazine. 2000. 278p. 22.95 o.p. (1-57197-181-5) Pentland Pr., Inc.
Manning, Olivia. The Wind Changes. 1991. (Modern Classics Ser.). 336p. (Orig.). pap. 8.95 o.p. (0-14-016219-4) Penguin Group (USA) Inc.
Mantel, Hilary. The Giant, O'Brien. 1998. 208p. o.s.i (0-385-25832-1) Doubleday Canada, Ltd. CAN. Dist: Random Hse., Inc.
—The Giant O'Brien. 1999. (Illus.). 208p. (gr. 9). pap. (0-385-25895-X) Doubleday Canada, Ltd. CAN. Dist: Random Hse., Inc.
—The Giant, O'Brien: A Novel. 1999. 208p. pap. 13.00 (0-8050-6295-5, Owl Bks.); 1998. 192p. 22.00 o.s.i (0-8050-4428-0) Holt, Henry & Co.
—The Giant, O'Brien: A Novel. l.t. ed. 1999. (Basic Ser.). 296p. 29.95 (0-7862-1797-9) Thorndike Pr.
Martin, David. The Road to Ballyshannon. 1983. 160p. 10.95 o.p. (0-312-68514-9) St. Martin's Pr.
Martin, Emer. More Bread or I'll Appear. 2000. 288p. pap. 12.00 (0-385-72009-2) Doubleday Publishing.
—More Bread or I'll Appear. 1999. 268p. tchr. ed. 23.00 (0-395-91871-5) Houghton Mifflin Co.
Martin, William. The Rising of the Moon. 1987. mass mkt. 4.95 o.s.i (0-8041-0211-2, Ivy Bks.) Ballantine Bks.
—The Rising of the Moon. 1995. 544p. mass mkt. 5.99 o.s.i (0-446-36418-5) Warner Bks., Inc.
Massie, Sonja. Daughter of Ireland. 2000. (Irish Eyes Ser.). 304p. mass mkt. 5.99 o.s.i (0-515-12835-X, Jove) Berkley Publishing Group.
Matthews, John, intro. Within the Hollow Hills: An Anthology of New Celtic Writing. 1995. 336p. (Orig.). pap. 17.95 (0-940262-70-3, Lindisfarne Bks.) SteinerBooks, Inc.
Maturin, Charles R. The Wild Irish Boy. Varma, Devendra P., ed. 1977. (Gothic Novels Ser.: No. III). lib. bdg. 72.95 (0-405-10141-4) Ayer Co. Pubs., Inc.
—The Wild Irish Boy. Wolff, Robert L., ed. 1979. (Ireland Nineteenth Century Fiction Ser.: Vol. 11). lib. bdg. 138.00 o.p. (0-8240-3460-0) Garland Publishing, Inc.
Maxwell, Robin. The Wild Irish: A Novel. 2003. 400p. 24.95 (0-06-009142-8, Morrow, William & Co.) Morrow/Avon.
May, Ena. Close Shave with the Devil. 1999. 159p. pap. text 15.95 (1-901866-17-3, Liplop Pr.) Goodfellow Catalog Pr., Inc.
McBride, Regina. The Land of Women. 2003. 256p. pap. 13.00 (0-7432-2888-X, Touchstone) Simon & Schuster.
—The Nature of Water & Air, 7 cass. 2002. audio 29.99 (1-4025-0863-8, 00994) Recorded Bks., LLC.
—The Nature of Water & Air: A Novel. 2001. 320p. pap. 13.00 (0-7432-0323-2, Touchstone) Simon & Schuster.
McCabe, Eugene. Tales from the Poorhouse. 2000. 126p. 27.95 (1-85235-249-3); pap. 18.95 (1-85235-248-5) Gallery Pr., The IRL. Dist: Dufour Editions, Inc.
McCabe, Patrick. The Butcher Boy. 1994. 240p. pap. 12.95 (0-385-31237-7) Doubleday Publishing.
—The Butcher Boy. abr. ed. 1994. audio 17.00 (0-671-88759-9, Simon & Schuster Audioworks) Simon & Schuster Audio.
—Emerald Germs of Ireland. 2001. 320p. 25.00 (0-06-019678-5) HarperCollins Pubs.
—Emerald Germs of Ireland. 2002. 336p. pap. 13.95 (0-06-095678-X, Perennial) HarperTrade.
—Mondo Desperado. 2000. xii, 240p. 24.00 (0-06-019461-8) HarperCollins Pubs.
—Mondo Desperado. 2001. 256p. pap. 13.00 (0-06-093258-9, Perennial) HarperTrade.
McCafferty, Maureen. Let Go the Glass Voice: A Novel. unabr. ed. 1997. (Illus.). 128p. 19.95 (0-942979-27-3, 942979); pap. 9.95 (0-942979-28-1, 942979) Livingston Pr.
McCann, Colum. Fishing the Sloe-Black River: Stories. 1997. 208p. pap. 12.00 o.s.i (0-8050-4107-9, Owl Bks.); 1996. 196p. 22.00 o.s.i (0-8050-4106-0, Metropolitan Bks.) Holt, Henry & Co.
—Fishing the Sloe-Black River: Stories. 2004. 208p. pap. 12.00 (0-312-42338-1) Picador.
—Songdogs. 1996. 224p. pap. 12.00 (0-312-14741-4) Picador.
—Songdogs: A Novel. 1995. 89p. 22.50 o.p. (0-8050-4104-4, Metropolitan Bks.) Holt, Henry & Co.
McCarthy, Thomas. Asya & Christine. 1993. 217p. pap. 14.95 (1-85371-175-6) Poolbeg Pr. IRL. Dist: Dufour Editions, Inc.
McCormack, Mike. Crowe's Requiem: A Novel. 1999. 240p. 23.00 o.s.i (0-8050-5370-0) Holt, Henry & Co.
McEldowney, Eugene. A Kind of Homecoming. 1994. 256p. 20.95 o.p. (0-312-11016-2, Saint Martin's Minotaur) St. Martin's Pr.
McGahern, John. Amongst Women. 1991. 192p. reprint ed. pap. 13.00 (0-14-009255-2, Penguin Bks.) Penguin Group (USA) Inc.
—Amongst Women. 1990. 192p. 17.95 o.p. (0-670-81182-3, Viking) Viking Penguin.
—By the Lake: A Novel. 2003. 352p. reprint ed. pap. 14.00 (0-679-74402-9, Vintage) Knopf Publishing Group.
—By the Lake: A Novel. 2002. 352p. 24.00 (0-679-41914-4) Knopf, Alfred A. Inc.
—The Collected Stories. 1994. 416p. pap. 15.00 (0-679-74401-0, Vintage) Knopf Publishing Group.
—The Collected Stories. 1993. 408p. 24.00 o.s.i (0-679-41913-6) Knopf, Alfred A. Inc.
—The Dark. 1983. 192p. pap. 4.95 o.p. (0-14-006237-8, Penguin Bks.) Viking Penguin.
—High Ground. 1987. 160p. 15.95 o.p. (0-670-81181-5) Viking Penguin.
—The Pornographer. 1979. 11.45 o.p. (0-06-013021-0) HarperCollins Pubs.
—The Pornographer. 1983. 256p. pap. 6.95 o.p. (0-14-006489-3, Penguin Bks.) Viking Penguin.
—That They May Face the Rising Sun. 2002. 304p. (0-571-21216-6) Faber & Faber, Inc.
McGinley, Patrick. The Devil's Diary. 1988. 256p. 16.95 o.p. (0-312-02193-3) St. Martin's Pr.
—Goosefoot: A Novel with Murder. 1982. 280p. 13.95 o.p. (0-525-24142-6, 01354-410, Dutton) Dutton/Plume.
McGoldrick, May. The Rebel. 2002. (Signet Historical Romance Ser.). 384p. mass mkt. 6.99 (0-451-20654-1) NAL.
McKinney, Meagan. The Ground She Walks Upon. 1995. 448p. mass mkt. 5.99 o.s.i (0-440-21579-X) Dell Publishing.
—The Ground She Walks Upon. l.t. ed. 1994. (G. K. Hall Core Ser.). 620p. lib. bdg. 24.95 o.p. (0-8161-7442-3, Macmillan Reference USA) Gale Group.
McKnight, Juilene Osborne. Bright Sword of Ireland. 2004. 288p. 24.95 (0-7653-0698-0, Forge Bks.) Doherty, Tom Assocs., LLC.
—Bright Sword of Irelaunde. Date not set. pap. (0-7653-0699-9, Forge Bks.) Doherty, Tom Assocs., LLC.
—Daughter of Ireland. 2003. 304p. mass mkt. 6.99 (0-7653-4642-7, Tor Bks.) Doherty, Tom Assocs., LLC.
—I Am of Irelaunde. 2001. 304p. pap. 14.95 (0-312-87567-3, Forge Bks.) Doherty, Tom Assocs., LLC.
McManus, Liz. Acts of Subversion. 1991. 236p. pap. 14.95 (1-85371-124-1) Poolbeg Pr. IRL. Dist: Dufour Editions, Inc.
McNamee, Eoin. The Blue Tango. l.t. ed. 2003. (Ulverscroft Large Print Ser.). 416p. 32.50 (0-7089-4709-3) Thorpe, F. A. Pubs. GBR. Dist: Ulverscroft Large Print Bks., Ltd., Ulverscroft Large Print Canada, Ltd.
—The Last of Deeds & Love in History. 192p. 1997. pap. 11.00 o.s.i (0-312-16879-9); 1996. 21.00 o.p. (0-312-14641-8) Picador.
Meredith, Albert. The Fields of Innishannon. 2001. 264p. 21.00 o.p. (0-8059-5106-7) Dorrance Publishing Co., Inc.
Miles, Rosalind. Isolde: Queen of the Western Isle. 2003. (Tristan & Isolde Trilogy: Bk. 1). (Illus.). 368p. pap. 12.95 (1-4000-4786-2) Crown Publishing Group.
Montague, John. The Death of a Chieftain: And Other Stories. 1999. 168p. pap. 15.95 (0-86327-673-3) Irish American Bk. Co.
—A Love Present & Other Stories. 176p. (0-86327-608-3) Wolfhound Pr.
Moore, Ann. Gracelin O'Malley. 2004. 432p. mass mkt. 7.99 (0-451-21241-X, Signet Bks.); 2001. (Illus.). 416p. pap. 13.95 (0-451-20299-6) NAL.
—Gracelin O'Malley. l.t. ed. 2001. (Large Print Women's Fiction Ser.). (Illus.). 696p. 28.95 o.p. (0-7862-3671-X) Thorndike Pr.
Moore, Brian. Lies of Silence. Date not set. pap. 5.51 (0-582-08170-X) Addison-Wesley Longman, Ltd. GBR. Dist: Trans-Atlantic Pubns., Inc.
—Lies of Silence. unabr. ed. 1993. 54.95 incl. audio (0-7451-6171-5, CAB 532) BBC Audiobooks America.
—Lies of Silence. 1991. 208p. pap. 9.00 (0-380-71547-3, Avon Bks.) Morrow/Avon.
—Lies of Silence. 1993. 3.99 o.p. (0-517-09878-4) Random Hse. Value Publishing.
—Lies of Silence. unabr. ed. 1997. audio 44.00 (0-7887-1304-3, 95141E7) Recorded Bks., LLC.
—Lies of Silence. 1991. audio 53.95 o.p. (0-8161-9563-3) Thorndike Pr.
—Lies of Silence. l.t. ed. 1991. (Charnwood Large Print Ser.). 29.99 o.p. (0-7089-8611-0, Charnwood) Thorpe, F. A. Pubs. GBR. Dist: Ulverscroft Large Print Bks., Ltd.
Moore, F. Frankfort. Castle Omeragh. 2000. 252p. E-Book 9.95 (0-594-02665-2) 1873 Pr.
Moore, George. In Minor Keys: The Uncollected Short Stories of George Moore. Eakin, David B. & Gerber, Helmut E., eds. (Irish Studies). 180p. 1987. pap. text 19.95 (0-8156-0212-X); 1985. (Illus.). text 44.95 (0-8156-2338-0) Syracuse Univ. Pr.
—The Untilled Field. 1977. (Short Story Index Reprint Ser.). 32.95 (0-8369-3600-0) Ayer Co. Pubs., Inc.
—The Untilled Field. 1976. text 12.95 o.p. (0-7705-1378-6) Brill Academic Pubs., Inc.
—The Untilled Field. 2001. (Collected Works of George Moore). reprint ed. pap. text 28.00 (0-7426-8704-X) Classic Bks.
—The Untilled Field. 2000. 260p. pap. 15.95 (0-86140-199-9); 1976. 21.00 o.p. (0-900675-63-2) Smythe, Colin Ltd. GBR. Dist: Dufour Editions, Inc.
Moorhouse, Geoffrey. Sun Dancing. 1999. 304p. pap. 13.00 (0-15-600602-2, Harvest Bks.) Harcourt Trade Pubs.
—Sun Dancing: A Vision of Medieval Ireland. 1997. 304p. 27.00 o.s.i (0-15-100277-0) Harcourt Trade Pubs.
Moran, Thomas. Water, Carry Me. abr. ed. 2000. audio 17.95 o.p. (1-56740-814-1, 1520, Nova Audio Bks.); audio 27.95 (1-56740-092-2, 1518, Brilliance Audio Unabridged); audio 57.25 (1-56740-621-1, 1519, Unabridged Library Editions) Brilliance Audio.
—Water, Carry Me. 2000. 288p. 24.95 o.s.i (1-57322-138-4, Riverhead Bks. (Hardcovers)) Putnam Publishing Group, The.
—Water, Carry Me. l.t. ed. 2000. (Basic Ser.). 409p. 28.95 (0-7862-2510-6) Thorndike Pr.
—Water, Carry Me: A Love Story. 2001. 336p. reprint ed. pap. 13.00 (1-57322-854-0, Riverhead Bks. (Hardcovers)) Putnam Publishing Group, The.
Moreton, Cole. Hungry for Home: Leaving the Blaskets: A Journey from the Edge of Ireland. 2000. 288p. reprint ed. pap. 24.00 (0-7567-5614-6) DIANE Publishing Co.
—Hungry for Home: Leaving the Blaskets: A Journey from the Edge of Ireland. 2000. (Illus.). 288p. 23.95 o.s.i (0-670-89207-6, Viking) Viking Penguin.
Morgan, Llywelyn. Brendan. mass mkt. (0-8125-5111-7, Forge Bks.) Doherty, Tom Assocs., LLC.
Morgan, Sydney O. The Wild Irish Girl: A National Tale. reprint ed. 44.50 (0-404-62064-7) AMS Pr., Inc.
Morrissy, Mary. Mother of Pearl: A Novel. 1995. 281p. 22.00 o.p. (0-684-19667-0, Scribner) Simon & Schuster.
Moyes, Jojo. Sheltering Rain. 2003. 448p. mass mkt. 7.50 (0-06-001289-7) HarperCollins Pubs.
—Sheltering Rain. l.t. ed. 2002. (Magna Large Print Ser.). 512p. (0-7505-1938-X) Magna Large Print Bks. GBR. Dist: Ulverscroft Large Print Canada, Ltd.
—Sheltering Rain. 2002. 368p. 24.95 (0-06-001288-9, Morrow, William & Co.) Morrow/Avon.
Mulrooney, Gretta. Araby. 1998. 182p. pap. (0-00-225688-6, HarperCollins) HarperTrade.
Murchison, Shanna. The Wizard Woman. 2001. 204p. 19.95 (1-58345-018-1) Domhan Bks.
Murdoch, Iris. The Red & the Green. l.t. ed. 2000. (Perennial Bestsellers Ser.). (Illus.). 432p. pap. 28.95 (0-7838-9085-0) Thorndike Pr.
—The Red & the Green. 1988. 288p. pap. 10.95 o.s.i (0-14-002756-4, Penguin Bks.); 1965. 5.00 o.p. (0-670-59100-9) Viking Penguin.
—Something Special: A Story. 2000. (Illus.). 55p. 15.95 (0-393-05007-6) Norton, W. W. & Co., Inc.
—Something Special: A Story. 1999. (Illus.). 48p. o.p. (0-7011-6918-4) Random Hse. of Canada, Ltd. CAN. Dist: Random Hse., Inc.
Murphy, Henry. Brief Cases. 1999. (1-901658-23-6) Ashfield Pr., Dublin.
—An Eye on the Whiplash & Other Stories. 1997. 140p. (1-901658-11-2); (1-901658-10-4) Ashfield Pr., Dublin.
Murphy, James H., ed. & intro. Rosa Mulholland's Marcella Grace. 2001. (Irish Research Ser.: No. 5). 74.95 (1-930901-04-6) Academica Pr., LLC.
Nestor, Tom. The Blue Pool. 2002. 332p. pap. 12.95 (1-903464-17-X) Collins Pr., The IRL. Dist: Dufour Editions, Inc.
—The Blue Pool. l.t. ed. 2003. (Ulverscroft Large Print Ser.). 480p. 32.50 (0-7089-4817-0) Thorpe, F. A. Pubs. GBR. Dist: Ulverscroft Large Print Bks., Ltd., Ulverscroft Large Print Canada, Ltd.
Ni Dhuibhne, Eilis. The Bray House. 1989. (Orig.). (C). pap. (0-946211-96-5) Attic Pr.
Ni Dhuibhne, Eilis, et al. Blackstaff Book of Short Stories. 1989. 160p. pap. 14.95 (0-85640-399-7) Blackstaff Pr., The IRL. Dist: Dufour Editions, Inc.
Ni Dhuibhne, Ellis. The Inland Ice & Other Stories. 1997. 208p. pap. 16.95 (0-85640-596-5) Blackstaff Pr., The IRL. Dist: Dufour Editions, Inc.
Nielsen, Elizabeth. Soda Bread on Sunday. 1997. 18.95 o.p. (0-944957-69-2) Rivercross Publishing, Inc.
Nolan, Christopher. The Banyan Tree: A Novel. 2000. 374p. 25.95 (1-55970-511-6); 2001. 384p. reprint ed. pap. 13.95 (1-55970-574-4) Arcade Publishing, Inc.
—The Banyan Tree: A Novel. l.t. unabr. ed. 2000. 512p. 32.50 o.p. (0-7531-6104-4, 161044) ISIS Large Print Bks. GBR. Dist: Ulverscroft Large Print Bks., Ltd.
—The Banyan Tree: A Novel. 2002. 384p. reprint ed. pap. 13.00 (0-385-72068-8, Knopf Bks. for Young Readers) Random Hse. Children's Bks.
O'Brein, FLann. Poor Mouth. 1988. 4.95 o.p. (0-8050-0183-2) Holt, Henry & Co.
O'Brien, Edna. The Country Girls Trilogy: Second Epilogue. 1987. pap. 8.95 o.p. (0-452-25926-6) NAL.
—The Country Girls Trilogy: Second Epilogue. 1992. o.p. (0-224-02421-3) Random Hse., Inc.
—The Country Girls Trilogy & Epilogue. 1987. 544p. pap. 9.95 o.p. (0-452-26182-1, Plume) Dutton/Plume.
—The Country Girls Trilogy & Epilogue. 1986. 531p. 18.95 o.s.i (0-374-13027-2) Farrar, Straus & Giroux.
—Down by the River. 1998. 272p. pap. 12.95 (0-452-27877-5, Plume) Dutton/Plume.
—Down by the River. 1997. 256p. 23.00 o.p. (0-374-14327-7) Farrar, Straus & Giroux.
—A Fanatic Heart: Selected Stories of Edna O'Brien. 1984. 461p. 17.95 o.p. (0-374-15342-6) Farrar, Straus & Giroux.
—House of Splendid Isolation. unabr. ed. 2000. audio 59.95 (0-7451-2733-9, SAB 099) Chivers Audio Bks. GBR. Dist: BBC Audiobooks America.
—House of Splendid Isolation. 1995. 240p. pap. 14.00 (0-452-27452-4, Plume) Dutton/Plume.
—House of Splendid Isolation. 1994. 224p. 21.00 o.p. (0-374-17309-5) Farrar, Straus & Giroux.
—House of Splendid Isolation. l.t. ed. 1994. 314p. lib. bdg. 23.95 o.p. (0-8161-7485-7, Macmillan Reference USA) Gale Group.
—In the Forest. 2002. 264p. tchr. ed. 24.00 (0-618-19730-3) Houghton Mifflin Co.
—In the Forest. 2003. 272p. pap. 13.00 (0-618-33965-5, Mariner Bks.) Houghton Mifflin Co. Trade & Reference Div.
—In the Forest. l.t. ed. 2003. 314p. 28.95 (0-7862-5728-8) Thorndike Pr.
—Nights. 1987. 15.95 o.p. (0-374-22198-7); pap. 12.00 o.s.i (0-374-52051-8) Farrar, Straus & Giroux.
—Nights. 2001. 120p. pap. 11.00 (0-618-12689-9, Mariner Bks.) Houghton Mifflin Co. Trade & Reference Div.
—A Pagan Place: A Play. 1973. 64p. o.p. (0-571-10336-7); pap. o.p. (0-571-10316-2) Faber & Faber Ltd.
—A Pagan Place: A Play. 1984. 234p. pap. 8.00 o.p. (0-915308-59-2) Graywolf Pr.
—A Pagan Place: A Play. 2001. 240p. pap. 13.00 (0-618-12690-2, Mariner Bks.) Houghton Mifflin Co. Trade & Reference Div.
—A Pagan Place: A Play. l.t. ed. 1985. (Mainstream Ser.). 238p. 14.95 o.p. (1-85089-055-2) ISIS Large Print Bks. GBR. Dist: Transaction Pubs.
—Wild Decembers: A Novel. 2000. 256p. 24.00 (0-618-04567-8) Houghton Mifflin Co.
—Wild Decembers: A Novel. 2001. 272p. pap. 13.00 (0-618-12691-0, Mariner Bks.) Houghton Mifflin Co. Trade & Reference Div.
—Wild Decembers: A Novel. l.t. ed. 2000. (Core Ser.). 358p. pap. 27.95 (0-7838-9072-9) Thorndike Pr.
O'Brien, Flann. At Swim, Two Birds. 1998. (Irish Literature Ser.). 316p. reprint ed. pap. 13.95 (1-56478-181-X) Dalkey Archive Pr.
—At Swim, Two Birds. 1976. pap. 5.95 o.p. (0-452-25262-8); 320p. pap. 13.95 o.p. (0-452-25913-4) Dutton/Plume. (Plume).
—At Swim, Two Birds. 1976. 316p. (0-246-10890-8) Grafton, HarperCollins Pubs., Ltd.
—The Dalkey Archive. 1977. pap. 3.95 o.p. (0-14-004516-3, Penguin Bks.) Viking Penguin.
—The Hard Life. 2nd ed. 179p. reprint ed. 1996. pap. 11.95 (1-56478-141-0); 1994. pap. 9.95 o.p. (1-56478-042-2) Dalkey Archive Pr.
—The Hard Life. 1977. pap. 3.50 o.p. (0-14-004517-1, Penguin Bks.) Viking Penguin.
—The Poor Mouth: A Bad Story about the Hard Life. 1996. (Illus.). 128p. reprint ed. pap. 10.95 (1-56478-091-0) Dalkey Archive Pr.
—The Third Policeman. 1999. (John F. Byrne Irish Literature Ser.). 200p. reprint ed. pap. 12.95 (1-56478-214-X) Dalkey Archive Pr.
—The Third Policeman. 1976. pap. 4.95 o.p. (0-452-25350-0); pap. 5.95 o.p. (0-452-25636-4); 208p. pap. 12.95 o.p. (0-452-25912-6); pap. 3.95 o.p. (0-452-25134-6) Dutton/Plume. (Plume).
O'Brien, Judith. Enter the Hero. 2003. 384p. mass mkt. 6.99 (0-7434-2798-X, Pocket) Simon & Schuster.
O'Brien, Kate Cruise & Maher, Mary. If Only. 1997. 314p. (1-85371-751-7) Poolbeg Pr.
O'Brien, Linda. Ballyrourke. 2002. 272p. mass mkt. 5.99 o.s.i (0-515-13409-0) Penguin Group (USA) Inc.
O'Cadhain, Mairtin. The Road to Brightcity. 1981. 112p. pap. 10.95 (0-905169-47-6) Poolbeg Pr. IRL. Dist: Dufour Editions, Inc.
O'Carroll, Brendan. Agnes Browne - The Mammy: MTV. 2000. 176p. pap. 10.95 o.s.i (0-452-28169-5, Plume) Dutton/Plume.

—The Chisellers. 2000. 192p. pap. 11.95 (*0-452-28122-9*, Plume) Dutton/Plume.
—The Chisellers. l.t. ed. 2000. (G. K. Hall Core Ser.). 230p. 28.95 (*0-7838-9259-4*, Macmillan Reference USA) Gale Group.
—The Granny. l.t. ed. 2000. (G. K. Hall Core Ser.). 229p. 29.95 (*0-7838-9260-8*, Macmillan Reference USA) Gale Group.
—The Granny: A Novel. 2000. 192p. pap. 11.95 (*0-452-28184-9*, Plume) Dutton/Plume.
—The Mammy. 2000. audio 24.95 (*0-7366-4691-4*); audio 29.95 (*0-7366-4696-5*) Books on Tape, Inc.
—The Mammy. l.t. ed. 2000. 262p. lib. bdg. 26.95 (*1-58547-037-6*) Ctr. Point Large Print.
—The Mammy. 1999. 176p. pap. 11.95 (*0-452-28103-2*, Plume) Dutton/Plume.
—The Mammy. 1994. 174 p. (*0-86278-372-0*) O'Brien Pr., Ltd., The.
—The Mammy. abr. ed. 1999. audio 18.95 (*0-14-180079-8*, Penguin AudioBooks) Viking Penguin.
O'Conaola, Dara. Night Ructions: Selected Short Stories. 2000. (Illus.). 58p. (gr. 3-7). pap. 7.95 (*1-900693-15-1*) Clo Iar-Chonnachta Teo IRL. *Dist:* Dufour Editions, Inc.
O'Connor, Frank. Bones of Contention & Other Stories. 1978. (Short Story Index in Reprint Ser.). reprint ed. 19.50 o.p. (*0-8486-5004-2*) Roth Publishing, Inc.
—Collected Stories. 1982. 720p. pap. 20.00 (*0-394-71048-7*, Vintage) Knopf Publishing Group.
O'Connor, Frank, ed. Classic Irish Short Stories. 1990. 352p. pap. 12.95 (*0-19-281918-6*) Oxford Univ. Pr., Inc.
O'Connor, Gemma. Farewell to the Flesh. 2000. 444p. pap. 10.95 (*0-553-50586-6*) Transworld Publishers Ltd. GBR. *Dist:* Trafalgar Square.
—Walking on Water. 2003. 352p. mass mkt. 7.50 (*0-515-13597-6*, Jove) Berkley Publishing Group.
O'Connor, Joseph. The Salesman. 400p. 2000. pap. 14.00 (*0-312-20431-0*); 1999. (Illus.). 24.00 o.p. (*0-312-19998-8*) Picador.
—Star of the Sea. 2004. 432p. pap. 14.00 (*0-15-602966-9*, Harvest Bks.); 2003. (Illus.). 416p. 25.00 (*0-15-100908-2*) Harcourt Trade Pubs.
—True Believers. 1993. 224p. 23.95 o.p. (*1-85619-074-9*) Trafalgar Square.
O'Connor, Kathleen Sheehan. By Shannon's Way. 1999. 384p. (*1-902011-11-2*) Mount Eagle Pubns., Ltd.
—Different Kinds of Loving. 2000. 346p. (*1-902011-14-7*) Mount Eagle Pubns., Ltd.
O'Doherty, Brian. The Deposition of Father McGreevy. 2001. 313p. pap. 14.95 (*1-900850-48-6*) Arcadia Bks. GBR. *Dist:* Consortium Bk. Sales & Distribution.
—The Deposition of Father McGreevy. 1999. 417p. 25.00 (*1-885983-39-5*) Turtle Point Pr.
O'Donnell, Mary. Strong Pagans & Other Stories. 1991. 258p. pap. 14.95 (*1-85371-123-3*) Poolbeg Pr. IRL. *Dist:* Dufour Editions, Inc.
O'Donoghue, Maureen. Winner. 1990. 3.99 o.p. (*0-517-05547-3*) Random Hse. Value Publishing.
—Winner. 1988. 19.95 o.p. (*0-671-53198-0*, Simon & Schuster) Simon & Schuster.
O'Donovan, Siofra. Malinski. 2002. 214p. pap. 16.95 (*1-901866-51-3*); pap. 16.95 (*1-901866-69-6*) Lilliput Pr., Ltd., The IRL. *Dist:* Dufour Editions, Inc.
O'Faolain, Julia. The Irish Signorina: Divertimento. 1986. 187p. 15.95 o.p. (*0-917561-12-0*) Adler & Adler Pubs., Inc.
—No Country for Young Men. 1986. 416p. pap. 8.95 o.p. (*0-88184-354-7*, Carroll & Graf Pubs.) Avalon Publishing Group.
O'Faolain, Nuala. My Dream of You. 2002. 544p. reprint ed. pap. 14.00 (*1-57322-908-3*, Riverhead Trade (Paperbacks)) Berkley Publishing Group.
—My Dream of You. 2001. 480p. 25.95 o.s.i (*1-57322-177-5*, Riverhead Bks. (Hardcovers)) Putnam Publishing Group, The.
—My Dream of You. l.t. ed. 2001. 751p. 29.95 (*0-7862-3386-9*); (*0-7540-1632-3*); pap. (*0-7540-2487-3*) Thorndike Pr.
O'Faoláin, Seán. The Collected Stories of Sean O'Faolain. 1983. (Illus.). 1312p. 29.95 o.s.i (*0-316-63294-5*) Little Brown & Co.
—Selected Stories of Sean O'Faolain. 1978. 14.95 o.p. (*0-316-63285-6*) Little Brown & Co.
O'Flaherty, Liam. The Black Soul. 1997. 192p. pap. 11.95 (*0-86327-478-1*) Wolfhound Pr. IRL. *Dist:* Irish American Bk. Co.
—Famine. 1982. reprint ed. 480p. pap. 18.95 o.p. (*0-87923-412-1*); 458p. pap. 15.95 o.p. (*0-87923-434-2*) Godine, David R. Pub.
—Famine. 2002. 448p. reprint ed. pap. 15.00 (*0-86327-043-3*) Wolfhound Pr. IRL. *Dist:* Interlink Publishing Group, Inc.
—Informer. 1961. mass mkt. 1.25 o.p. (*0-451-50949-8*, CY949, Signet Classics) NAL.
—The Informer. 1980. (Harvest Book Ser.). 192p. reprint ed. pap. 10.00 (*0-15-644356-2*, Harvest Bks.) Harcourt Trade Pubs.
—The Informer. 1968. mass mkt. 0.75 o.p. (*0-451-50351-1*); mass mkt. 0.95 o.p. (*0-451-50407-0*); mass mkt. 0.60 o.p. (*0-451-50080-6*) NAL. (Signet Classics).
—The Informer. 1999. 160p. pap. 13.95 (*0-86327-677-6*) Wolfhound Pr. IRL. *Dist:* Interlink Publishing Group, Inc.
—Mountain Tavern, & Other Stories. 1980. (Short Story Index Reprint Ser.). reprint ed. 19.95 (*0-8369-4054-7*) Ayer Co. Pubs., Inc.
—Mr. Gilhooley. 1997. 288p. (Orig.). pap. 11.95 (*0-86327-289-4*); pap. 11.95 (*0-86327-641-5*) Wolfhound Pr. IRL. *Dist:* Irish American Bk. Co.
—Spring Sowing. 1977. (Short Story Index Reprint Ser.). reprint ed. 25.95 (*0-8369-4221-3*) Ayer Co. Pubs., Inc.
O'Flaherty, Liam & Kelly, A. A. Liam O'Flaherty Vol. 1: The Collected Stories. 2000. 396p. 45.00 (*0-312-22903-8*) Palgrave Macmillan.
—Liam O'Flaherty Vol. 2: The Collected Stories. 2000. 397p. 45.00 (*0-312-22904-6*) Palgrave Macmillan.
—Liam O'Flaherty Vol. 3: The Collected Stories. 2000. 224p. 45.00 (*0-312-22905-4*) Palgrave Macmillan.
O'Grady, Timothy. Motherland. 1990. 240p. 19.95 o.p. (*0-8050-1230-3*) Holt, Henry & Co.
O'Griofa, Mairtin. Irish Scalawags & Scoundrels. 1996. (Illus.). 128p. (J). pap. 6.95 o.p. (*0-8069-5963-0*) Sterling Publishing Co., Inc.
O'Griofa, Mairtin, ed. Celtic Tales of Terror. 1994. (Illus.). 144p. pap. 6.95 o.p. (*0-8069-0868-8*, Sterling/Main St.) Sterling Publishing Co., Inc.
—The Leprechaun Book. 1994. (Illus.). 128p. pap. 6.95 o.p. (*0-8069-0829-7*) Sterling Publishing Co., Inc.
O'Hanlon, Ardal. Knick Knack Paddy Whack. 2001. 256p. reprint ed. pap. 13.00 (*0-15-601353-3*, Harvest Bks.) Harcourt Trade Pubs.
—Knick Knack Paddy Whack: A Novel. 2000. (Illus.). 244p. 23.00 o.s.i (*0-8050-6330-7*) Holt, Henry & Co.
O'Kelly, Seumas. Waysiders: Stories of Connacht. 1977. (Short Story Index Reprint Ser.). reprint ed. 17.00 (*0-8369-3821-6*) Ayer Co. Pubs., Inc.
O'Reilly, Victor. Games of the Hangman. 1992. 512p. mass mkt. 7.50 o.s.i (*0-425-13456-3*) Berkley Publishing Group.
—Games of the Hangman. 1991. 512p. 19.95 o.p. (*0-8021-1431-8*) Grove/Atlantic, Inc.
O'Riordan, Kate. Angel in the House. 2000. 336p. pap. (*0-00-225880-3*) HarperCollins Pubs.
Osborne, Mary Pope. Viking Ships at Sunrise. 1998. (Magic Tree House Ser.: No. 15). (Illus.). 96p. (J). (gr. k-3). pap. 3.99 (*0-679-89061-0*); lib. bdg. 11.99 (*0-679-99061-5*) Random Hse., Inc.
Osborne-McKnight, Juilene. Daughter of Ireland. 2003. pap. (*0-7653-0128-8*); 2002. 300p. 24.95 (*0-7653-0127-X*) Doherty, Tom Assocs., LLC. (Forge Bks.).
—I Am of Irelaunde: A Novel of Patrick & Osian. 2000. (Tom Doherty Associates Book Ser.). 301p. 24.95 (*0-312-87320-4*, Forge Bks.) Doherty, Tom Assocs., LLC.
O'Sullivan, Mark. Silent Stones. 1999. 192p. (YA). (gr. 7 up). (*0-86327-722-5*) Wolfhound Pr.
Owenson, Sydney. The Wild Irish Girl, 1807: A National Tale. Kirkpatrick, Kathryn, ed. 1999. (Oxford World's Classics Ser.). 304p. pap. 11.95 (*0-19-283283-2*) Oxford Univ. Pr., Inc.
Parker, Dorothy D. Liam's Catch. 1972. (Illus.). (J). (gr. k-3). 8.95 o.p. (*0-670-42744-6*) Viking Penguin.
Parker, Gary E. Rumors of Peace. l.t. ed. 2002. 691p. pap. 17.95 (*1-4104-0027-1*, Walker Large Print); 25.95 (*0-7862-4270-1*) Gale Group.
Parker, Robert B. All Our Yesterdays. 1995. 480p. mass mkt. 7.50 (*0-440-22146-3*); 1994. 528p. 27.95 o.s.i (*0-385-31374-8*, Delacorte Pr.) Dell Publishing.
Parkinson, Siobhan. The Moon King. 1998. 176p. (*0-86278-573-1*) O'Brien Pr., Ltd., The.
Parsons, Julie. The Courtship Gift. 2000. 320p. 24.00 (*0-684-86982-9*, Simon & Schuster); 2001. (Illus.). 400p. reprint ed. mass mkt. 6.99 (*0-7434-2665-7*, Pocket) Simon & Schuster.
—The Courtship Gift. 1999. 390p. (*1-86059-102-7*) Town Hse. IRL. *Dist:* Rinehart, Roberts Pubs.
—Mary, Mary. 1998. viii, 376p. (*1-86059-080-2*) Town Hse. IRL. *Dist:* Rinehart, Roberts Pubs.
—Mary, Mary: A Novel. 1999. 304p. 23.00 (*0-684-85324-8*, Simon & Schuster) Simon & Schuster.
Parsons, Julie & Simon and Schuster Staff. Mary, Mary. 2000. 336p. mass mkt. 6.99 (*0-06-103049-X*) HarperCollins Pubs.
Paxson, Diana & Martine-Barnes, Adrienne. Master of Earth & Water. 1993. (Legends of Fionn MacCumhall Ser.: Vol. 1). 22.00 o.s.i (*0-688-12505-0*, Morrow, William & Co.) Morrow/Avon.
Paxson, Diana L. The Shield Between the Worlds. 1994. xv, 317p. 22.00 o.p. (*0-688-13176-X*, Morrow, William & Co.) Morrow/Avon.
Paxson, Diana L. & Martin-Barnes, Adrienne. Sword of Fire & Shadow. 1995. xviii, 426p. 22.00 (*0-688-14156-0*, Avon Bks.) Morrow/Avon.
Paxson, Diana L. & Martine-Barnes, Adrienne. Master of Earth & Water. 2000. 22.00 (*0-380-97219-0*); 1994. 416p. mass mkt. 4.99 (*0-380-75801-6*) Morrow/Avon. (Avon Bks.).
—Sword of Fire & Shadow. 2000. 22.00 (*0-380-97255-7*) Morrow/Avon.
Peart, Jane. A Perilous Bargain. 1997. (Edgecliffe Manor Mysteries Ser.). 240p. (gr. 12). pap. 10.99 o.p. (*0-8007-5626-6*) Revell, Fleming H. Co.
—A Perilous Bargain. l.t. ed. 2000. (Christian Mystery Ser.). 360p. 24.95 (*0-7862-2380-4*) Thorndike Pr.
Perrin, Robert. Jewels. 1979. 9.95 o.s.i (*0-8128-2592-6*, Scarborough Hse.) Madison Bks., Inc.
Petit, Chris. The Psalm Killer. 1998. mass mkt. 6.99 (*0-345-42090-X*); 512p. mass mkt. 6.99 o.s.i (*0-449-00289-6*, Fawcett) Ballantine Bks.
Phelan, Tom. Derrycloney. 1999. 273p. pap. 17.95 (*0-86322-253-6*) Brandon Bk. Pubs., Ltd. IRL. *Dist:* Irish Bks. & Media, Inc.
—In the Season of the Daisies. 1996. 230p. 22.00 (*1-56858-074-6*); 2nd ed. 1998. 238p. reprint ed. pap. 12.95 (*1-56858-108-4*) Four Walls Eight Windows.
—In the Season of the Daisies. 1993. 240p. pap. 17.95 o.p. (*0-946640-97-1*) Lilliput Pr., Ltd., The IRL. *Dist:* Irish Bks. & Media, Inc.
Philipott, Anthony. The Files of Flynn de Courcy: An Eroto-Comedic Romp Through the Correspondence of Ireland's Finest Legal Mind. 1999. (*1-901658-22-8*) Ashfield Pr., Dublin.
Porter, Margaret E. Irish Autumn. 1993. 2.99 o.p. (*0-517-09668-4*) Random Hse. Value Publishing.
—Irish Autumn. 1990. 216p. 19.95 (*0-8027-1115-4*) Walker & Co.
Power, Una. The Spellbinder. 1993. 480p. o.p. (*0-7126-5636-7*) Random Hse. of Canada, Ltd. CAN. *Dist:* Random Hse., Inc.
Powers, Anne. The Gallant Years. l.t. ed. 1998. (Romance Ser.). 493p. 26.95 (*0-7862-1440-6*) Thorndike Pr.
Prunty, Morag. Wild Cats & Colleens: A Novel. 2001. pap. 13.95 (*0-06-095979-7*); 304p. 25.00 (*0-06-018508-2*) HarperCollins Pubs.
Queneau, Raymond. On Est Toujours Trop Bon avec les Femmes: Un Roman Irlandais De Sally Mara. 1971. (Folio Ser.: No. 1312). (FRE.). 200p. pap. 8.95 (*2-07-037312-6*) Schoenhof's Foreign Bks., Inc.
Rawlings, Wendy Mai. Come Back Irish. 2001. 234p. 44.95 (*0-8142-0887-8*); pap. 21.95 (*0-8142-5085-8*) Ohio State Univ. Pr. (Sandstone Bks.).
Raymo, Chet. The Dork of Cork. (Fresh Voices Ser.). 1994. 354p. pap. 12.95 (*0-446-67000-6*); 1993. 368p. 18.95 o.s.i (*0-446-51706-2*) Warner Bks., Inc.
Rhodes, Elvi. The Bright One. 2000. 476p. pap. 9.95 (*0-552-14057-0*) Transworld Publishers Ltd. GBR. *Dist:* Trafalgar Square.
Richards, Emilie. The Parting Glass. 2003. 464p. (*1-55166-709-6*, Mira Bks.) Harlequin Enterprises, Ltd.
Ridgway, Keith. The Long Falling. 1999. 306p. pap. 13.00 (*0-395-95782-6*); 1998. 320p. 22.00 o.p. (*0-395-90530-3*) Houghton Mifflin Co.
Ripley, Alexandra. Scarlett: The Sequel to Margaret Mitchell's Gone with the Wind. 1991. (SPA.). (*84-406-2275-9*) B Ediciones S.A.
—Scarlett: The Sequel to Margaret Mitchell's Gone with the Wind. 1992. audio 80.00 (*0-7366-2309-4*);Pt. A. audio 88.00 (*0-7366-2308-6*, 3091A);Pt. B. audio 80.00 Books on Tape, Inc.
—Scarlett: The Sequel to Margaret Mitchell's Gone with the Wind. l.t. ed. 1992. (General Ser.). 1184p. pap. 21.95 (*0-8161-5528-3*); 1184p. lib. bdg. 28.95 o.p. (*0-8161-5527-5*); lib. bdg. 11.97 (*0-8161-5535-6*); lib. bdg. 11.97 (*0-8161-5536-4*) Gale Group. (Macmillan Reference USA).
—Scarlett: The Sequel to Margaret Mitchell's Gone with the Wind. abr. ed. 1992. audio 25.00 (*0-671-77966-4*, 692301, Simon & Schuster Audioworks) Simon & Schuster Audio.
—Scarlett: The Sequel to Margaret Mitchell's Gone with the Wind. 1991. 13.04 (*0-606-02212-0*) Turtleback Bks.
—Scarlett: The Sequel to Margaret Mitchell's Gone with the Wind. 1992. 896p. mass mkt. 7.99 (*0-446-36325-1*); 1991. 823p. 24.45 o.p. (*0-446-51507-8*); 1992. 100.00 (*0-446-51718-6*) Warner Bks., Inc.
—Scarlett Home Companion. abr. ed. 1993. audio 29.95 (*1-55800-763-6*, Dove Audio) NewStar Media, Inc.
Robards, Karen. Dark of the Moon. 1988. 416p. mass mkt. 7.99 (*0-380-75437-1*, Avon Bks.) Morrow/Avon.
—Forbidden Love. 1997. 384p. mass mkt. 7.50 (*0-440-22106-4*) Dell Publishing.
—Forbidden Love. 384p. 1994. pap. 4.99 (*0-8439-3592-8*); 1983. pap. 3.50 o.s.i (*0-8439-2024-6*); 1990. reprint ed. pap. 4.50 (*0-8439-2920-0*); 1987. reprint ed. pap. 3.95 o.p. (*0-8439-2459-4*) Dorchester Publishing Co., Inc.
—Forbidden Love. l.t. ed. 2001. (Large Print Book Ser.). 28.95 (*1-58724-035-1*, Wheeler Publishing, Inc.) Gale Group.
Roberts, Nora. Heart of the Sea. 2000. 384p. mass mkt. 7.99 (*0-515-12855-4*, Jove) Berkley Publishing Group.
—Heart of the Sea. abr. ed. 2001. (Irish Ser.: Vol. 3). audio 12.99 (*1-58788-341-4*, 2953, Paperback Nova Audio Bks.); 2000. (Irish Jewels Trilogy Ser.). audio 24.95 o.s.i (*1-56740-871-0*, 1916, Nova Audio Bks.); 2000. (Irish Jewels Trilogy Ser.). audio 32.95 (*1-56740-470-7*, 1914, Brilliance Audio Unabridged); 2000. (Irish Jewels Trilogy Ser.). audio 73.25 (*1-56740-693-9*, 1915, Unabridged Library Editions) Brilliance Audio.
—Heart of the Sea. l.t. ed. 2001. (G. K. Hall Core Ser.). 429p. 32.95 (*0-7838-8987-9*, Macmillan Reference USA) Gale Group.
—Heart of the Sea. l.t. ed. 2002. 429p. pap. 0.95 (*0-7838-8988-7*) Thorndike Pr.
—Irish Born. 2003. 768p. pap. 14.00 (*0-425-19589-9*, 53840071) Berkley Publishing Group.
—Irish Rose. l.t. ed. pap. 14.95 o.p. (*0-373-58456-3*, C0463) BBC Audiobooks America.
—Irish Rose. 1992. (NR Flowers Ser.: No. 3). mass mkt. (*0-373-51003-9*, 5-51003-7); 1988. mass mkt. (*0-373-07232-5*) Harlequin Enterprises, Ltd. (Harlequin Bks.).
—Irish Thoroughbred. l.t. ed. 1985. (Nightingale Ser.). 240p. pap. 9.95 o.p. (*0-8161-3828-1*, Macmillan Reference USA) Gale Group.
—Irish Thoroughbred. 1992. (NR Flowers Ser.: No. 1). per. (*0-373-51001-2*, 5-51001-1, Harlequin Bks.) Harlequin Enterprises, Ltd.
—Jewels of the Sun. 1999. 384p. mass mkt. 7.99 (*0-515-12677-2*, Jove) Berkley Publishing Group.
—Jewels of the Sun. abr. ed. 1999. (Irish Ser.). audio 17.95 o.p. (*1-56740-869-9*, 1908, Nova Audio Bks.); 10p. audio 73.25 (*1-56740-691-2*, 1907, Unabridged Library Editions); audio 26.95 (*1-56740-468-5*, 1906, Bookcassette) Brilliance Audio.
—Jewels of the Sun. abr. ed. 1999. audio 17.95. audio 73.25 Highsmith Inc.
—Jewels of the Sun. l.t. ed. (Paperback Bestsellers Ser.). 445p. 2001. 28.95 (*0-7838-8990-9*); 2000. 30.95 (*0-7838-8989-5*) Thorndike Pr.
—A Little Magic. 2001. 304p. pap. 13.95 (*0-425-18318-1*) Berkley Publishing Group.
—Tears of the Moon. 2000. 384p. mass mkt. 7.99 (*0-515-12854-6*, Jove) Berkley Publishing Group.
—Tears of the Moon. abr. ed. 2000. (Irish Jewels Trilogy Ser.). audio 24.95 o.p. (*1-56740-870-2*, 1913, Nova Audio Bks.); 10p. audio 73.25 (*1-56740-692-0*, 1911, Unabridged Library Editions); audio 32.95 (*1-56740-469-3*, 1910, Brilliance Audio Unabridged) Brilliance Audio.
—Tears of the Moon. l.t. ed. 2000. (Core Ser.). 400p. 31.95 (*0-7838-8991-7*); (Illus.). pap. 29.95 (*0-7838-8992-5*) Thorndike Pr.
Roberts, Paul A. The Rasherhouse. 1997. 178p. pap. 14.95 (*1-898256-21-7*) Dufour Editions, Inc.
Rogers, Evelyn. Angel. 1995. mass mkt. 4.99 o.s.i (*0-8217-5163-8*) Kensington Publishing Corp.
Roper, Martin. Gone: A Novel. 2002. 256p. 23.00 o.s.i (*0-8050-6775-2*) Holt, Henry & Co.
—Gone: A Novel. 2003. 240p. pap. 13.00 (*0-312-42125-7*) Picador.
Ros, Amanda M. Thine in Storm & Calm: An Amanda McKittrick Ros Reader. 1989. 166p. pap. 12.95 (*0-85640-408-X*) Blackstaff Pr., The IRL. *Dist:* Dufour Editions, Inc.
Ross, JoAnn. Fair Haven. 2000. 432p. pap. 6.99 (*0-671-78611-3*, Pocket) Simon & Schuster.
—Legends Lake. (Illus.). 416p. 2003. mass mkt. 5.99 (*0-7434-6722-1*); 2001. mass mkt. 6.99 (*0-671-78617-2*) Simon & Schuster. (Pocket).
—A Woman's Heart. l.t. ed. 2003. (Thorndike Romance Ser.). 537p. 29.95 (*0-7862-4983-8*) Gale Group.
—A Woman's Heart. 2002. 384p. mass mkt. (*1-55166-849-1*); 1998. 475p. mass mkt. (*1-55166-461-5*) Harlequin Enterprises, Ltd. (Mira Bks.).
Rossi, Agnes. The Houseguest. 2000. 304p. reprint ed. 13.00 o.s.i (*0-452-28197-0*, Plume) Dutton/Plume.
—The Houseguest: A Novel. l.t. ed. 2000. (Americana Ser.). 504p. 28.95 (*0-7862-2547-5*) Thorndike Pr.
Royce, Kenneth. Patriots. 1989. 272p. mass mkt. 4.95 o.s.i (*0-446-35579-8*) Warner Bks., Inc.
—The President Is Dead. l.t. ed. 1989. (Ulverscroft Large Print Ser.). 518p. 29.99 o.p. (*0-7089-1967-7*, Ulverscroft) Thorpe, F. A. Pubs. GBR. *Dist:* Ulverscroft Large Print Bks., Ltd., Ulverscroft Large Print Canada, Ltd.
Ruell, Patrick. The Only Game: A Novel of Suspense. 1993. 288p. 20.00 o.p. (*0-88150-253-7*) Countryman Pr.
Ryan, James. Seeds of Doubt. 2002. 295p. 22.95 (*1-86159-106-3*) Orion Publishing Group, Ltd. GBR. *Dist:* Trafalgar Square.
Ryan, Liz. Bloodlines. 1995. 400p. 24.95 o.p. (*0-312-13933-0*) St. Martin's Pr.

Ryan, Mary. Glenallen. 1993. 24.95 o.p. (0-312-08797-7) St. Martin's Pr.
—Mask of the Night. 1997. 320p. 22.95 o.p. (0-312-16925-6) St. Martin's Pr.
—Mask of the Night. l.t. ed. 1998. (G. K. Hall Romance Ser.). 531p. 28.95 (0-7838-0380-X) Thorndike Pr.
—Shadows from the Fire. 1995. 288p. 21.95 o.p. (0-312-13168-2) St. Martin's Pr.
—The Song of the Tide. 2000. 352p. 24.95 (0-312-26648-0) St. Martin's Pr.
—The Song of the Tide. l.t. ed. 1999. (Ulverscroft Large Print Ser.). 472p. 31.99 o.p. (0-7089-4163-X, Ulverscroft) Thorpe, F. A. Pubs. GBR. Dist: Ulverscroft Large Print Bks., Ltd., Ulverscroft Large Print Canada, Ltd.
—Summer's End. 1996. 352p. 23.95 o.p. (0-312-14427-X) St. Martin's Pr.
Seymour, Ana. Maid of Killarney. 2002. 272p. mass mkt. 5.99 (0-515-13415-5, Jove) Berkley Publishing Group.
Seymour, Gerald. The Journeyman Tailor. l.t. ed. 1994. pap. 20.95 o.p. (0-7927-1602-7); 1993. 22.95 o.p. (0-7927-1603-5) BBC Audiobooks America.
—The Journeyman Tailor. 1993. 384p. 20.00 o.p. (0-06-017998-8) HarperTrade.
—The Journeyman Tailor. 1994. 432p. mass mkt. 5.99 o.p. (0-06-109987-2, HarperTorch) Morrow/Avon.
Shea, Christina. Moira's Crossing. 2001. (Illus.). 256p. pap. 12.95 (0-7434-1057-2, Pocket) Simon & Schuster.
—Moira's Crossing. 2000. 248p. 22.95 (0-312-20347-0); E-Book 12.95 (0-312-27345-2) St. Martin's Pr.
Shriver, Lionel. Bleeding Heart. 1990. 22.95 o.p. (0-374-11432-3) Farrar, Straus & Giroux.
Silva, Daniel. The Marching Season. 2000. 384p. mass mkt. 7.50 o.s.i (0-449-00211-X) Ballantine Bks.
—The Marching Season. l.t. ed. 1999. pap. 25.95 o.p. (0-7838-8510-5, Macmillan Reference USA) Gale Group.
—The Marching Season. 2004. 384p. mass mkt. 7.99 (0-451-20932-X, Signet Bks.) NAL.
—The Marching Season. abr. ed. 1999. audio compact disk 29.95 o.s.i (0-553-45638-5, RH Audio) Random Hse. Audio Publishing Group.
—The Marching Season. unabr. ed. 2000. audio compact disk 90.00 (0-7887-3972-7, C1009E7); 1999. audio 75.00 (0-7887-3097-5, 95808E7) Recorded Bks., LLC.
Simonson, Sheila. Malarkey. 1998. (WWL Mystery Ser.). per. (0-373-26275-2, 1-26275-7, Worldwide Library) Harlequin Enterprises, Ltd.
—Malarkey. 1996. 288p. 23.95 o.p. (0-312-15168-3, Saint Martin's Minotaur) St. Martin's Pr.
Skilton. Castle Richmond: (trollope 1994) 1994. 43.00 (1-870587-35-9) Ashgate Publishing Co.
Snell, Gordon, ed. Thicker Than Water: Coming-of-Age Stories by Irish & Irish American Writers. 2001. 256p. (YA). (gr. 7 up). 17.95 o.s.i (0-385-32571-1, Random Hse. Bks. for Young Readers) Random Hse. Children's Bks.
Somerville, Edith A. & Martin, Violet F. All on the Irish Shore. 1977. (Short Story Index Reprint Ser.). 22.95 (0-8369-3027-4) Ayer Co. Pubs., Inc.
Somerville, Edith O. & Ross, Martin. The Real Charlotte. Beards, Virginia, ed. 1986. 350p. text 35.00 o.p. (0-8135-1133-X); pap. text 14.00 o.p. (0-8135-1134-8) Rutgers Univ. Pr.
Spaight, Breda. God on the Wall. 1997. 164p. pap. 14.95 (1-898256-23-3) Dufour Editions, Inc.
Standun, Padraig. A Woman's Love. 1994. 238p. pap. 10.95 (1-85371-346-5) Poolbeg Pr. IRL. Dist: Dufour Editions, Inc.
Sternlicht, Sanford, ed. Selected Short Stories of Padraic Colum. 1986. (Irish Studies). (Illus.). 160p. pap. 19.95 (0-8156-0202-2) Syracuse Univ. Pr.
Stuart, Francis. Black List, Section H. 1997. (Penguin Twentieth-Century Classics Ser.). 416p. pap. 13.95 o.p. (0-14-018926-2) Viking Penguin.
Sweeney, Eamonn. Waiting for the Healer. 1999. 320p. pap. 13.00 (0-312-20046-3); 1998. 308p. 23.00 (0-312-18206-6) Picador.
Swift, Carolyn. Bugsy Goes to Cork. 1990. 190p. (J). (gr. 3-7). pap. 7.95 (1-85371-071-7) Poolbeg Pr. IRL. Dist: Dufour Editions, Inc.
Talbott, Hudson. O'Sullivan Stew. 1999. (Illus.). 48p. (YA). (gr. k-3). 15.99 (0-399-23162-5, G. P. Putnam's Sons) Penguin Group (USA) Inc.
Taylor, Alice. Across the River. 2000. 283p. (1-902011-13-9) Mount Eagle Pubns., Ltd.
—Across the River. 2001. 288p. 23.95 (0-312-27843-8) St. Martin's Pr.
—The Woman of the House. 1997. 315p. (1-902011-00-7) Mount Eagle Pubns., Ltd.
—The Woman of the House. 1999. 315p. 23.95 o.p. (0-312-20065-X) St. Martin's Pr.
Taylor, Patrick. Pray for Us Sinners. 2000. 305p. pap. 15.95 (1-895837-61-8) Insomniac Pr. CAN. Dist: 7 Hills Bk. Distributors.
Thoene, Bodie. Only the River Runs Free: A Novel. 1998. (Galway Chronicles Ser.). pap. 12.99 (0-7852-7016-7) Nelson, Thomas Pubs.
Thoene, Bodie & Brock. Only the River Runs Free: A Novel. 2003. pap. 12.99 (0-7852-6378-0) Nelson, Thomas Inc.
Thoene, Bodie & Thoene, Brock. All Rivers to the Sea: A Novel. 2001. 320p. pap. 12.99 (0-7852-6622-4) Nelson, Thomas Inc.
—All Rivers to the Sea: A Novel. 2000. (Galway Chronicles Ser.: Bk. 4). xv, 304p. 22.99 (0-7852-8076-6) Nelson, Thomas Pubs.
—Only the River Runs Free: A Novel. (Galway Chronicles Ser.). 320p. 1999. pap. 9.99 (0-7852-6925-8); 1997. 19.99 (0-7852-8067-7) Nelson, Thomas Pubs.
Thoene, Bodie, et al. All Rivers to the Sea: A Novel. 1999. 16.97 o.p. (0-7852-6800-6) Nelson, Tommy.
Thoene, Brock. Only the River Runs Free. abr. ed. 1997. (Galway Chronicles Ser.). audio 16.99 (0-7852-7128-7, 71287) Nelson, Thomas Pubs.
Thomas, David M. Angers Violin. 1998. 288p. (1-902011-04-X) Mount Eagle Pubns., Ltd.
Thompson, Kate. Switchers. 1998. 224p. (J). (gr. 7-12). 14.95 (0-7868-0380-0) Hyperion Bks. for Children.
Toibin, Colm. The Blackwater Lightship. 1999. 272p. 16.95 o.p. (0-330-38985-8) Picador GBR. Dist: Trans-Atlantic Pubns., Inc.
—The Blackwater Lightship. 288p. 2000. 24.00 o.s.i (0-684-87389-3); 2001. reprint ed. pap. 13.00 (0-7432-0331-3) Simon & Schuster. (Scribner).
—The Heather Blazing. 1993. 256p. 20.00 o.p. (0-670-84789-5, Viking) Viking Penguin.
—Penguin Anthology of Irish Fiction. 2000. 1184p. text (0-670-85497-2, Viking) Viking Penguin.
Toibin, Colm, ed. Book of Irish Fiction. 2001. 1122p. 20.00 (0-14-029849-5) Viking Penguin.
Toibin, Colm & Doyle, Roddy. Finbar's Hotel. Bolger, Dermot, ed. 1999. (Harvest Original Ser.). 288p. pap. 13.00 (0-15-600633-2, Harvest Bks.) Harcourt Trade Pubs.
Tracey, Monica. Unweaving the Thread. 2001. 318p. pap. 12.95 (1-86023-140-3, Marino Pr.) Mercier Pr., Ltd., The IRL. Dist: Irish Bks. & Media, Inc.
Tremayne, Peter. Absolution by Murder: A Sister Fidelma Mystery. l.t. ed. 1996. (Magna Large Print Ser.). 351p. 29.99 o.p. (0-7505-0929-5) Magna Large Print Bks. GBR. Dist: Ulverscroft Large Print Bks., Ltd., Ulverscroft Large Print Canada, Ltd.
—Absolution by Murder: A Sister Fidelma Mystery. 1997. (Sister Fidelma Mysteries Ser.). 272p. mass mkt. 6.50 (0-451-19299-0, Signet Bks.) NAL.
—Absolution by Murder: A Sister Fidelma Mystery. 1995. 288p. 21.95 o.p. (0-312-13918-7, Saint Martin's Minotaur) St. Martin's Pr.
—Hemlock at Vespers: Fifteen Sister Fidelma Mysteries. 2000. xiii, 398p. pap. 15.95 (0-312-25288-9, Saint Martin's Griffin) St. Martin's Pr.
—The Monk Who Vanished. 2001. 288p. 23.95 (0-312-24219-0, Saint Martin's Minotaur) St. Martin's Pr.
—Shroud for the Archbishop: A Sister Fidelma Mystery. l.t. ed. 1996. (Magna Large Print Ser.). (Illus.). 436p. 29.99 (0-7505-0930-9) Magna Large Print Bks. GBR. Dist: Ulverscroft Large Print Bks., Ltd.
—Shroud for the Archbishop: A Sister Fidelma Mystery. 1998. (Sister Fidelma Mysteries Ser.). 304p. mass mkt. 6.99 (0-451-19300-8, Signet Bks.) NAL.
—Shroud for the Archbishop: A Sister Fidelma Mystery. 1996. (Sister Fidelma Mysteries Ser.). 352p. 23.95 (0-312-14734-1, Saint Martin's Minotaur) St. Martin's Pr.
—Smoke in the Wind: A Mystery of Ancient Ireland. 2002. xxvi, 358p. mass mkt. 9.95 (0-7472-6434-1) Headline Bk. Publishing, Ltd. GBR. Dist: Trafalgar Square.
—The Spider's Web: A Celtic Mystery. l.t. ed. 1998. (Magna Large Print Ser.). 512p. (0-7505-1245-8) Magna Large Print Bks. GBR. Dist: Ulverscroft Large Print Canada, Ltd.
—The Spider's Web: A Celtic Mystery. 1999. (Celtic Mysteries Ser.). (Illus.). 352p. 23.95 (0-312-20589-9, Saint Martin's Minotaur) St. Martin's Pr.
—The Subtle Serpent. l.t. ed. 1998. (Magna Large Print Ser.). 488p. o.p. (0-7505-1244-X) Magna Large Print Bks. GBR. Dist: Ulverscroft Large Print Canada, Ltd.
—The Subtle Serpent: A Celtic Mystery. 1998. (Sister Fidelma Mysteries Ser.). 352p. 23.95 (0-312-18670-3, Saint Martin's Minotaur) St. Martin's Pr.
—The Subtle Serpent: A Mystery of Ancient Ireland, 1, 4. 1999. (Sister Fidelma Mysteries Ser.). 320p. mass mkt. 6.99 (0-451-19558-2, Signet Bks.) NAL.
—Suffer Little Children: A Sister Fidelma Mystery, 1 vol. 1999. (Sister Fidelma Mysteries Ser.). 320p. mass mkt. 6.50 (0-451-19557-4) NAL.
—Suffer Little Children: A Sister Fidelma Mystery. 1997. (Sister Fidelma Mysteries Ser.). 352p. 23.95 (0-312-15665-0, Saint Martin's Minotaur) St. Martin's Pr.
—Valley of the Shadow. 1999. reprint ed. pap. 5.99 (0-451-26330-8, Signet Bks.) NAL.
Trevor, William. After Rain. unabr. collector's ed. 1997. audio 42.00 (0-7366-3654-4, 4321) Books on Tape, Inc.
—After Rain. l.t. ed. 1997. (Core Ser.). 314p. lib. bdg. 26.95 (0-7838-8052-9, Macmillan Reference USA) Gale Group.
—After Rain. 1997. 224p. pap. 13.00 (0-14-025834-5, Viking) Penguin Group (USA) Inc.
—After Rain. 1996. 224p. 22.95 o.p. (0-670-87007-2) Viking Penguin.
—Fools of Fortune. 1983. 239p. 13.95 o.p. (0-670-32355-1) Viking Penguin.
—Ireland: Selected Stories. 1998. 384p. (gr. 1). pap. 14.00 (0-14-027759-5) Penguin Group (USA) Inc.
—Ireland: Selected Stories. 2000. (Classics Ser.). 272p. pap. 12.95 (0-14-024263-5) Viking Penguin.
—Nights at the Alexandra. 1987. (Harper Short Novel Ser.). (Illus.). 80p. 10.95 o.p. (0-06-015848-4) HarperTrade.
—Nights at the Alexandra. 2001. 112p. 14.95 o.s.i (0-375-50471-0, Modern Library) Random House Adult Trade Publishing Group.
—The Silence in the Garden. 1988. 208p. 17.95 o.p. (0-670-82404-6) Viking Penguin.
—The Story of Lucy Gault. l.t. ed. 2003. 31.95 (1-58724-381-4, Wheeler Publishing, Inc.) Gale Group.
—The Story of Lucy Gault. 2003. 240p. pap. 14.00 (0-14-200331-X) Penguin Group (USA) Inc.
—The Story of Lucy Gault. 2002. 288p. 24.95 (0-670-03154-2, Viking) Viking Penguin.
—Three Early Novels. 2000. 640p. 18.00 (0-14-028418-4) Viking Penguin.
Trollope, Anthony. Castle Richmond, unabr. ed. 1997. audio 77.95 (1-55685-489-7, 489-7) Audio Bk. Contractors, Inc.
—Castle Richmond, 3 vols. Hall, N. John, ed. 1981. (Selected Works of Anthony Trollope). reprint ed. lib. bdg. 115.95 (0-405-14134-3) Ayer Co. Pubs., Inc.
—Castle Richmond, 3. (Collected Works of Anthony Trollope). reprint ed. lib. bdg. 294.00 (0-7426-2440-4); 2001. pap. text 84.00 (0-7426-7440-1) Classic Bks.
—Castle Richmond. 1984. 440p. reprint ed. pap. 8.50 (0-486-24760-0) Dover Pubns., Inc.
—Castle Richmond. Wolff, Robert L., ed. 1979. (Ireland Nineteenth Century Fiction Ser.: Vol. 55). 912p. lib. bdg. 152.00 o.p. (0-8240-3504-6) Garland Publishing, Inc.
—Castle Richmond. Hamer, Mary, ed. 1989. (Oxford World's Classics Ser.). (Illus.). 530p. pap. 10.95 o.p. (0-19-282173-3) Oxford Univ. Pr., Inc.
—Castle Richmond, 1860. 1993. (Trollope Ser.). 912p. pap. 9.95 o.p. (0-14-043808-4, Penguin Classics) Viking Penguin.
—An Eye for an Eye, 2 vols. Hall, N. John, ed. 1981. (Selected Works of Anthony Trollope). reprint ed. lib. bdg. 49.95 (0-405-14169-6) Ayer Co. Pubs., Inc.
—An Eye for an Eye, 2. reprint ed. lib. bdg. 196.00 (0-7426-2481-1) Classic Bks.
—An Eye for an Eye. Wolff, Robert L., ed. 1979. (Ireland Nineteenth Century Fiction Ser.: Vol. 56). 440p. lib. bdg. 101.00 o.p. (0-8240-3505-4) Garland Publishing, Inc.
—An Eye for an Eye. Sutherland, John, ed. 1992. (Oxford World's Classics Ser.). 250p. pap. 8.95 o.p. (0-19-282910-6) Oxford Univ. Pr., Inc.
—An Eye for an Eye. 1994. (Trollope Ser.). 448p. pap. 8.95 o.p. (0-14-043840-8, Penguin Classics) Viking Penguin.
—The Kellys & the O'Kellys. Wolff, Robert L., ed. 1979. (Ireland Nineteenth Century Fiction Ser.: Vol. 54). 888p. lib. bdg. 152.00 o.p. (0-8240-3503-8) Garland Publishing, Inc.
—The Kellys & the O'Kellys. 2003. (Twelve-Point Ser.). lib. bdg. 25.00 (1-58287-264-3); lib. bdg. 26.00 (1-58287-748-3) North Bks.
—The Kellys & the O'Kellys: Or Landlords & Tenants. McCormack, W. J., ed. 1982. (Oxford World's Classics Ser.). 560p. pap. 8.95 o.p. (0-19-281577-6) Oxford Univ. Pr., Inc.
—The Landleaguers, 3 vols. Hall, N. John, ed. 1981. (Selected Works of Anthony Trollope). reprint ed. lib. bdg. 115.95 (0-405-14198-X) Ayer Co. Pubs., Inc.
—The Landleaguers, 3. reprint ed. lib. bdg. 294.00 (0-7426-2497-8); 2001. pap. text 84.00 (0-7426-7497-5) Classic Bks.
—The Landleaguers. 1993. (Oxford World's Classics Ser.). 476p. pap. 10.95 o.p. (0-19-282891-6) Oxford Univ. Pr., Inc.
—The Landleaguers. Super, R. H., ed. 1992. (Illus.). 360p. (C). text 44.50 o.p. (0-472-09485-8, 09485); pap. text 18.95 o.p. (0-472-06485-1, 06485) Univ. of Michigan Pr.
—The Landleaguers, 1883. 1994. (Penguin Trollope Ser.). 320p. pap. 6.95 o.p. (0-14-043851-3, Penguin Classics) Viking Penguin.
—The Macdermots of Ballycloran, 3 vols. Hall, N. John, ed. 1981. (Selected Works of Anthony Trollope). reprint ed. lib. bdg. 115.95 (0-405-14118-1) Ayer Co. Pubs., Inc.
—The Macdermots of Ballycloran, 3. reprint ed. lib. bdg. 294.00 (0-7426-2506-0); 2001. pap. text 84.00 (0-7426-7506-8) Classic Bks.
—The Macdermots of Ballycloran. 1988. 384p. reprint ed. pap. 9.95 o.p. (0-486-25572-7) Dover Pubns., Inc.
—The Macdermots of Ballycloran. Wolff, Robert L., ed. 1979. (Ireland Nineteenth Century Fiction Ser.: Vol. 53). 1372p. lib. bdg. 152.00 o.p. (0-8240-3502-X) Garland Publishing, Inc.
—The Macdermots of Ballycloran. Tracy, Robert, ed. 1989. (Oxford World's Classics Ser.). (Illus.). 736p. pap. 10.95 o.p. (0-19-282181-4) Oxford Univ. Pr., Inc.
—The Macdermots of Ballycloran, 1847. 1993. (Trollope Ser.). 384p. pap. 7.95 o.p. (0-14-043800-9, Penguin Classics) Viking Penguin.
—Phineas Finn, unabr. ed. 1993. audio 101.95 (1-55685-267-3) Audio Bk. Contractors, Inc.
—Phineas Finn. unabr. ed. audio 114.95 o.p. (1-85549-937-1, CTC 102) BBC Audiobooks America.
—Phineas Finn. unabr. ed. 2000. audio 99.95 (0-7861-1782-6, 2581) Blackstone Audio Bks., Inc.
—Phineas Finn, Pt. 1. unabr. collector's ed. 1994. audio 72.00 (0-7366-2618-2, 3359-A) Books on Tape, Inc.
—Phineas Finn. 1973. pap. 5.95 o.p. (0-19-281144-4); 1968. 17.95 o.p. (0-19-250447-9) Oxford Univ. Pr., Inc.
—Phineas Finn. MacCormack, Bill, ed. 1997. (Everyman Paperback Classics Ser.). (Illus.). 432p. pap. 6.95 (0-460-87497-7, Everyman's Classic Library in Paperback) Tuttle Publishing.
—Phineas Finn. Sutherland, John, ed. 1975. (Penguin Classics Ser.). 752p. pap. 8.95 o.p. (0-14-043085-7, Penguin Classics) Viking Penguin.
—Phineas Finn: The Irish Member, 2. reprint ed. lib. bdg. 98.00 (0-7426-2460-9); 2001. pap. text 28.00 (0-7426-7460-6) Classic Bks.
—Phineas Finn: The Irish Member. 1991. (Palliser Novels Ser.). (Illus.). 323p. 21.00 o.p. (0-19-520896-X) Oxford Univ. Pr., Inc.
—Phineas Finn: The Irish Member. Berthoud, Jacques, ed. 1984. (Oxford World's Classics Ser.). (Illus.). 776p. pap. 6.95 o.p. (0-19-281587-3) Oxford Univ. Pr., Inc.
—Phineas Finn: The Irish Member. Berthoud, Jacques, ed. & intro. by. 1999. (Oxford World's Classics Ser.). (Illus.). 776p. reprint ed. pap. 7.95 (0-19-283533-5) Oxford Univ. Pr., Inc.
—Phineas Finn: The Irish Member. 1994. (Trollope Ser.). 688p. pap. 8.95 o.p. (0-14-043825-4, Penguin Classics) Viking Penguin.
—Phineas Redux. unabr. ed. Pt. 1. 1994. audio 59.95 (1-55685-312-2); Pt. 2. 1999. audio 59.95 Audio Bk. Contractors, Inc.
—Phineas Redux. unabr. ed. (Palliser Novels: Vol. 4). audio 114.95 o.p. (1-85549-939-8, CTC 130) BBC Audiobooks America.
—Phineas Redux, Pt. 1. unabr. collector's ed. 1994. audio 72.00 (0-7366-2790-1, 3506-A) Books on Tape, Inc.
—Phineas Redux, 2. reprint ed. lib. bdg. 196.00 (0-7426-2471-4); 2001. pap. text 56.00 (0-7426-7471-1) Classic Bks.
—Phineas Redux. 2002. (Oxford World's Classics Ser.). (Illus.). 768p. pap. 8.95 (0-19-283559-9) Oxford Univ. Pr., Inc.
—Phineas Redux. Whale, John C., ed. (Palliser Novels Ser.). (Illus.). 1991. 784p. 21.00 o.p. (0-19-520898-6); 1984. 768p. pap. 7.95 o.p. (0-19-281589-X) Oxford Univ. Pr., Inc.
—Phineas Redux. 1968. (Oxford World's Classics Ser.: No. 450). 14.95 o.p. (0-19-250450-9) Oxford Univ. Pr., Inc.
—Phineas Redux. 1994. (Trollope Ser.). 896p. pap. 8.95 o.s.i (0-14-043833-5) Penguin Group (USA) Inc.
—Phineas Redux. 2003. (Illus.). 688p. pap. 11.00 (0-14-043762-2, Penguin Classics) Viking Penguin.
Trollope, Anthony & Sutherland, John. An Eye for an Eye. l.t. ed. 1998. (Perennial Bestsellers Ser.). 291p. 25.95 (0-7838-8454-0) Thorndike Pr.
Tuomey, Nesta. Like One of the Family. 1999. 456p. pap. (1-902011-12-0) Mount Eagle Pubns., Ltd.
Uris, Leon. Redemption, Pt. 1. unabr. ed. 1996. audio 88.00 (0-7366-3427-4, 4072-A) Books on Tape, Inc.
—Redemption. 1999. 896p. reprint ed. pap. 4.99 o.s.i (0-06-109844-2) HarperCollins Pubs.
—Redemption. 1995. 480p. 300.00 o.p. (0-06-018356-X, HarperCollins); 827p. 25.00 o.p. (0-06-018333-0) HarperTrade.
—Redemption. 1996. 896p. mass mkt. 7.99 (0-06-109174-X, HarperTorch) Morrow/Avon.
—Redemption. l.t. ed. 1995. (Core Collection). 1054p. 28.95 (0-7838-1453-4) Thorndike Pr.
—Trinity. 1983. 832p. mass mkt. 7.99 (0-553-25846-X) Bantam Bks.

—Trinity. 1976. 751p. 21.95 o.s.i (*0-385-03458-X*) Doubleday Publishing.

Urquhart, Jane. Away. 1998. (BTC Audiobooks). audio (*0-86492-211-6*); incl. audio compact disk (*0-86492-209-4*) Goose Lane Editions.

—Away. 1995. 368p. pap. 14.00 (*0-14-024926-5*, Penguin Bks.) Penguin Group (USA) Inc.

—Away. 1994. 304p. 21.95 o.s.i (*0-670-85504-9*, Viking) Viking Penguin.

Van Stockum, Hilda. The Cottage at Bantry Bay. 1995. (Bantry Bay Ser.). (Illus.). 256p. (J). (gr. 4-7). pap. 11.95 (*1-883937-06-X*, 06-X) Bethlehem Bks.

—Francie on the Run. 1996. (Bantry Bay Ser.). (Illus.). 312p. (J). (gr. 4 up). reprint ed. pap. 12.95 (*1-883937-13-2*, 13-2) Bethlehem Bks.

Waldon, Clarence. The Old Man. 2003. 115p. pap. 13.95 (*1-59286-466-X*) PublishAmerica, Inc.

Wall, William. Alice Falling. 2000. 208p. 23.95 (*0-393-05001-7*) Norton, W. W. & Co., Inc.

Wallace, Brian. Labyrinth of Chaos. 2000. 288p. pap. 16.95 (*1-56184-148-X*) New Falcon Pubns.

Walsh, Maurice. The Quiet Man & Other Stories. 2002. Orig. Title: Green Rushes. 240p. reprint ed. pap. 12.95 (*0-86281-307-7*) Appletree Pr., Ltd. IRL. *Dist:* Independent Pubs. Group.

Watkins, Paul. The Promise of Light, Set. l.t. ed. 1993. (Studio Ser.). 64.95 o.p. incl. audio (*0-7862-9998-3*, Macmillan Reference USA) Gale Group.

Webb, Sarah. Always the Bridesmaid. 2004. 352p. pap. 13.95 (*0-06-057166-7*, Avon Bks.) Morrow/Avon.

Weber, Katharine. The Music Lesson. 2000. 192p. pap. 12.00 (*0-312-25285-4*) Picador.

—The Music Lesson: A Novel. 1998. 178p. 21.00 o.s.i (*0-609-60317-5*) Crown Publishing Group.

West, Anthony C. The Ferret Fancier. 1984. (Classic Irish Fiction Ser.). 256p. 15.95 (*0-8159-5522-7*) Devin-Adair Pubs., Inc.

West, Gabrielle. Time of Grace. 2002. 272p. pap. 13.95 (*0-86327-863-9*) Wolfhound Pr. IRL. *Dist:* Inter-link Publishing Group, Inc.

White, James. Silent Stars Go By. 1991. mass mkt. 5.99 o.s.i (*0-345-37110-0*, Ballantine Bks.) Ballantine Bks.

Williams, Niall. As It Is in Heaven. l.t. ed. 1999. (Basic Ser.). 488p. 29.95 (*0-7862-2282-4*) Thorndike Pr.

—As It Is in Heaven. abr. ed. 1999. audio 17.98 (*1-57042-703-8*) Time Warner AudioBooks.

—As It Is in Heaven. 1999. E-Book 9.95 (*0-446-91304-9*); 1999. 320p. 23.00 (*0-446-52548-0*); 2000. 336p. reprint ed. pap. 13.95 (*0-446-67601-2*) Warner Bks., Inc.

—The Fall of Light. l.t. ed. 2002. 509p. 27.95 (*0-7862-3945-X*) Gale Group.

—The Fall of Light. 2003. (Illus.). 384p. pap. 13.95 (*0-446-67987-9*); 2002. 320p. 24.95 o.p. (*0-446-52840-4*) Warner Bks., Inc.

—Four Letters of Love. unabr. ed. 1998. audio 48.00 (*0-7366-4148-3*, 4651) Books on Tape, Inc.

—Four Letters of Love. 1997. 352p. 23.00 o.p. (*0-374-15817-7*) Farrar, Straus & Giroux.

—Four Letters of Love. l.t. ed. 1997. (G. K. Hall Core Ser.). 371p. 26.95 (*0-7838-8297-1*) Thorndike Pr.

—Four Letters of Love. 1998. 288p. reprint ed. pap. 13.99 (*0-446-67493-1*) Warner Bks., Inc.

Williams, Paul. The General. mass mkt. (*0-7653-4542-0*, Forge Bks.); 2004. (Illus.). 288p. pap. 14.95 (*0-7653-0878-9*, Tor Bks.) Doherty, Tom Assocs., LLC.

Wilson, Rachel. My Wild Irish Rose. 2000. (Irish Eyes Ser.). 304p. 5.99 o.s.i (*0-515-12972-0*, Jove) Berkley Publishing Group.

Wilson, Robert McLiam. Eureka Street: A Novel of Ireland Like No Other. Date not set. pap. 12.95 (*0-345-91746-4*) Ballantine Bks.

Wimmer, Dick. The Irish Wine Trilogy. 2001. 320p. 13.00 (*0-14-100059-7*) Viking Penguin.

Windsor, Linda. Deirdre. 2003. (Fires of Gleannmara Ser.: Bk. 3). 352p. pap. 11.99 (*1-57673-891-4*) Multnomah Pubs., Inc.

Winton, Tim. The Riders. l.t. ed. 1996. 392p. lib. bdg. 24.95 (*1-57490-036-6*) Beeler, Thomas T. Publisher.

—The Riders. unabr. ed. 1998. audio (*1-86340-607-7*, 551206) Bolinda Publishing Pty, Ltd.

—The Riders. 384p. 1996. pap. 12.00 (*0-684-82277-6*); 1995. 22.50 (*0-684-80296-1*) Simon & Schuster. (Scribner).

Wykham, Helen. Ribstone Pippins. 1996. 226p. (Orig.). pap. 14.95 (*0-7145-3017-4*) Boyars, Marion Pubs., Inc.

Yeats, W. B. The Secret Rose. Marcus, Phillip L. et al, eds. 1981. (Cornell Yeats Ser). 312p. 39.50 o.p. (*0-8014-1194-7*) Cornell Univ. Pr.

Yeats, W. B. & Thuente, M. H., eds. Representative Irish Tales. 3rd ed. 1979. 364p. (C). text 25.00 o.p. (*0-391-00988-5*) Brill Academic Pubs., Inc.

Yeats, W. B., et al. The Secret Rose. 2nd ed. 1992. xlvii, 297p. 26.50 o.p. (*0-333-49257-9*) Macmillan U.K. GBR. *Dist:* Trans-Atlantic Pubns., Inc.

Zaczek, Iain. Irish Legends. 1998. (Illus.). 128p. 24.95 (*0-8092-2809-2*, 280920, Contemporary Bks.) McGraw-Hill Trade.

Zaczek, Iain, contrib. by. Irish Legends. 1998. (Illus.). (*0-7171-2751-6*) Gill & MacMillan, Ltd.

**IRIS HOUSE (VICTORIA SPRINGS, MO.: IMAGINARY PLACE)—FICTION**

Hager, Jean. Blooming Murder. 1994. (Iris House Mystery Ser.). pap. 5.50 (*0-380-77209-4*, Avon Bks.) Morrow/Avon.

—Blooming Murder. l.t. ed. 2001. (Illus.). 339p. (*0-7862-3215-3*) Thorndike Pr.

—Bride & Doom. l.t. ed. 2001. (Beeler Large Print Mystery Ser.). 230p. 25.95 (*1-57490-408-6*, Beeler Large Print Bks.) Beeler, Thomas T. Publisher.

—Bride & Doom. 2000. (Iris House Mystery Ser.: No. 2). 224p. mass mkt. 5.99 (*0-380-80376-3*, Avon Bks.) Morrow/Avon.

—Dead & Buried. 1995. (Iris House Mystery Ser.). mass mkt. 5.50 (*0-380-77210-8*, Avon Bks.) Morrow/Avon.

—Dead & Buried. l.t. ed. 2000. (Mystery Ser.). (Illus.). 339p. 27.95 (*0-7862-2928-4*) Thorndike Pr.

—Death on the Drunkard's Path. 1996. (Iris House Mystery Ser.: No. 3). pap. 5.50 (*0-380-77211-6*, Avon Bks.) Morrow/Avon.

—Death on the Drunkard's Path. l.t. ed. 2000. (Mystery Ser.). 328p. 26.95 (*0-7862-2353-7*) Thorndike Pr.

—The Last Noel. 1997. (Iris House Mystery Ser.). 224p. mass mkt. 5.99 (*0-380-78637-0*, Avon Bks.) Morrow/Avon.

—Sew Deadly. l.t. ed. 2001. 303p. (*0-7838-9498-8*); (*0-7540-4587-0*); (*0-7540-4588-9*) Gale Group. (Macmillan Reference USA).

—Sew Deadly. 1998. (Iris House Mystery Ser.). 224p. mass mkt. 5.99 (*0-380-78638-9*, Avon Bks.) Morrow/Avon.

—Weigh Dead. 2003. (Mystery Ser.). 27.95 (*1-57490-468-X*) Beeler, Thomas T. Publisher.

—Weigh Dead. 1999. (Iris House Mystery Ser.: Vol. 6). 224p. mass mkt. 5.99 (*0-380-80375-5*, Avon Bks.) Morrow/Avon.

**ISLANDS OF THE INDIAN OCEAN—FICTION**

Blackburn, Julia. The Book of Color. 1996. 192p. pap. 15.00 (*0-679-75837-2*) Random Hse., Inc.

**ISOLA (N.Y.: IMAGINARY PLACE)—FICTION**

McBain, Ed, pseud. And All Through the House. 1994. 48p. 12.45 o.p. (*0-446-51845-X*) Warner Bks., Inc.

—Ax. unabr. ed. 1996. (Eighty-Seventh Precinct Ser.). audio 30.00 (*0-7366-3506-8*, 4145) Books on Tape, Inc.

—Ax. 1977. (87th Precinct Mystery Ser.). mass mkt. 2.95 o.p. (*0-451-14599-2*); mass mkt. 1.25 o.p. (*0-451-07654-0*, Signet Bks.); 160p. mass mkt. 4.50 o.s.i (*0-451-16407-5*, Signet Bks.) NAL.

—Ax. 1964. 3.50 o.p. (*0-671-06283-2*) Simon & Schuster.

—The Big Bad City. abr. ed. 1998. (Eighty Seventh Precinct Ser.). audio 24.95 (*1-55927-536-7*, 696064) Audio Renaissance.

—The Big Bad City. unabr. ed. 1999. (Eighty-Seventh Precinct Ser.). audio 40.00 (*0-7366-4460-1*, 4905) Books on Tape, Inc.

—The Big Bad City. l.t. ed. 1999. 27.95 (*1-56895-714-9*, Wheeler Publishing, Inc.) Gale Group.

—The Big Bad City. 1999. 272p. mass mkt. 7.99 (*0-671-03473-1*, Pocket); 25.00 (*0-684-85512-7*, Simon & Schuster) Simon & Schuster.

—Blood Relatives. 1977. pap. 1.50 o.p. (*0-394-25462-7*) Ballantine Bks.

—Blood Relatives. 1978. (Eighty-Seventh Precinct Ser). pap. 1.75 o.p. (*0-553-11759-9*) Bantam Bks.

—Blood Relatives. unabr. ed. 1987. (Eighty-Seventh Precinct Ser.). audio 36.00 (*0-7366-1147-9*, 2071) Books on Tape, Inc.

—Blood Relatives. 1987. mass mkt. 3.50 o.p. (*0-451-15084-8*, Signet Bks.) NAL.

—Bread. unabr. ed. 1987. (Eighty-Seventh Precinct Ser.). audio 42.00 (*0-7366-1198-3*, 2116) Books on Tape, Inc.

—Bread. 1987. 176p. mass mkt. 4.50 (*0-380-70368-8*, Avon Bks.) Morrow/Avon.

—Bread. 1982. mass mkt. 2.25 o.p. (*0-451-11279-2*, AE1279); 1975. mass mkt. 1.25 o.p. (*0-451-06754-1*) NAL. (Signet Bks.).

—Bread. 1974. 213p. (J). o.p. (*0-394-48580-7*) Random Hse., Inc.

—Bread. 1997. (Eighty Seventh Precinct Ser.). 224p. reprint ed. mass mkt. 6.50 (*0-446-60425-9*) Warner Bks., Inc.

—Calypso. 1980. 208p. pap. 1.95 o.s.i (*0-553-13399-3*) Bantam Bks.

—Calypso. unabr. ed. 1998. (Eighty-Seventh Precinct Ser.). audio 42.00 (*0-7366-3775-3*, 4448) Books on Tape, Inc.

—Calypso. 1988. 208p. mass mkt. 4.99 (*0-380-70591-5*, Avon Bks.) Morrow/Avon.

—Calypso. 1979. 10.95 o.p. (*0-670-20030-1*) Viking Penguin.

—The Con Man. unabr. ed. 1993. audio 54.95 (*0-7451-4157-9*, CAB 840) BBC Audiobooks America.

—The Con Man. unabr. ed. 1990. (Eighty-Seventh Precinct Ser.). audio 36.00 (*0-7366-1787-6*, 2624) Books on Tape, Inc.

—The Con Man. l.t. ed. 1986. (Nightingale Ser.). 296p. 10.95 o.p. (*0-8161-3982-2*, Macmillan Reference USA) Gale Group.

—The Con Man. (Eighty-Seventh Precinct Mysteries Ser.). 1987. 160p. mass mkt. 3.99 o.s.i (*0-451-15085-6*); 1980. mass mkt. 1.75 o.p. (*0-451-09351-8*); 1974. mass mkt. 0.95 o.p. (*0-451-05863-1*) NAL. (Signet Bks.).

—Cop Hater. unabr. ed. 1992. (Eighty-Seventh Precinct Novels Ser.). audio 54.95 (*0-7451-6153-7*, CAB 674) BBC Audiobooks America.

—Cop Hater. unabr. ed. 1990. (Eighty-Seventh Precinct Ser.). audio 36.00 (*0-7366-1710-8*, 2552) Books on Tape, Inc.

—Cop Hater. l.t. ed. 1989. (Nightingale Ser.). 316p. 13.95 o.p. (*0-8161-4517-2*, Macmillan Reference USA) Gale Group.

—Cop Hater. (Eighty-Seventh Precinct Mysteries Ser.). 9999. 160p. mass mkt. 3.95 o.p. (*0-451-16441-5*); 1987. 160p. mass mkt. 3.99 o.p. (*0-451-15079-1*); 1980. mass mkt. 1.75 o.p. (*0-451-09170-1*); 1973. mass mkt. 0.95 o.p. (*0-451-05617-5*) NAL. (Signet Bks.).

—Cop Hater. 1999. (Eighty-Seventh Precinct Ser.). (Illus.). 272p. pap. 7.99 (*0-671-77547-2*, Pocket) Simon & Schuster.

—Doll. 1981. mass mkt. 2.25 o.s.i (*0-345-29289-8*) Ballantine Bks.

—Doll. unabr. ed. 1996. (Eighty-Seventh Precinct Ser.). audio 30.00 (*0-7366-3512-2*, 4151) Books on Tape, Inc.

—Doll. 1986. (Eighty-Seventh Precinct Novel Ser.). 160p. mass mkt. 4.50 (*0-380-70082-4*, Avon Bks.) Morrow/Avon.

—Doll. 1997. (Eighty Seventh Precinct Ser.). 208p. reprint ed. mass mkt. 5.99 (*0-446-60146-2*) Warner Bks., Inc.

—Ed McBain: Three Complete Novels: Wings Suspense. 1992. (Illus.). 528p. 13.99 o.s.i (*0-517-06499-5*) Random Hse. Value Publishing.

—Eight Black Horses. l.t. ed. 1986. (General Ser.). 350p. 15.95 o.p. (*0-8161-4022-7*, Macmillan Reference USA) Gale Group.

—Eight Black Horses. (Eighty-Seventh Precinct Novel Ser.). 1986. 256p. mass mkt. 4.99 (*0-380-70029-8*, Avon Bks.); 1985. 15.95 o.p. (*0-87795-681-2*, Morrow, William & Co.) Morrow/Avon.

—Eight Black Horses. 2003. (Illus.). 336p. pap. 7.99 (*0-7434-6308-0*, Pocket) Simon & Schuster.

—Eighty Million Eyes. 1983. 192p. mass mkt. 2.25 o.s.i (*0-345-29292-8*); 1975. mass mkt. 1.25 o.s.i (*0-345-24604-7*) Ballantine Bks.

—Eighty Million Eyes. unabr. ed. 1997. (Eighty-Seventh Precinct Ser.). audio 30.00 (*0-7366-3565-3*, 4209) Books on Tape, Inc.

—Eighty Million Eyes. l.t. ed. 2000. 229p. lib. bdg. 25.95 (*1-58547-011-2*) Ctr. Point Large Print.

—Eighty Million Eyes. 1987. 176p. mass mkt. 4.50 (*0-380-70367-X*, Avon Bks.) Morrow/Avon.

—Eighty Million Eyes. 1997. (Eighty Seventh Precinct Ser.). 208p. reprint ed. mass mkt. 5.99 (*0-446-60386-4*) Warner Bks., Inc.

—The Eighty-Seventh Precinct Companion. 1995. (Orig.). pap. (*0-89296-989-X*, Mysterious Pr. Paperback Bks.) Warner Bks., Inc.

—The Empty Hours. unabr. ed. 1996. (Eighty-Seventh Precinct Ser.). audio 36.00 (*0-7366-3409-6*, 4056) Books on Tape, Inc.

—The Empty Hours. (87th Precinct Mystery Ser.). 1982. mass mkt. 2.25 o.p. (*0-451-11835-9*); 1982. 256p. mass mkt. 4.50 o.p. (*0-451-14601-8*); 1977. mass mkt. 1.25 o.p. (*0-451-07287-1*) NAL. (Signet Bks.).

—Fuzz. unabr. ed. 1995. (87th Precinct Mystery Ser.). audio 54.95 (*0-7451-6157-X*, CAB 133) BBC Audiobooks America.

—Fuzz. unabr. ed. 1997. (Eighty-Seventh Precinct Ser.). audio 42.00 (*0-7366-3637-4*, 4298) Books on Tape, Inc.

—Fuzz. 1978. mass mkt. 1.75 o.p. (*0-451-08399-7*); 1978. 192p. mass mkt. 3.99 o.p. (*0-451-15554-8*, E8399); 1972. mass mkt. 0.75 o.p. (*0-451-05151-3*); 1969. mass mkt. 0.60 o.p. (*0-451-04001-5*) NAL. (Signet Bks.).

—Fuzz. E-Book 6.99 (*0-7953-0320-3*); E-Book 6.99 (*0-7953-0322-X*) RosettaBooks.

—Fuzz. 2000. (Eighty Seventh Precinct Ser.). 288p. mass mkt. 6.50 o.s.i (*0-446-60971-4*) Warner Bks., Inc.

—Ghosts. 1981. 176p. pap. 2.50 o.p. (*0-553-23240-1*) Bantam Bks.

—Ghosts. unabr. ed. 1998. (Eighty-Seventh Precinct Ser.). audio 36.00 (*0-7366-4109-2*, 4614) Books on Tape, Inc.

—Ghosts. 1980. 212p. 9.95 o.p. (*0-670-33806-0*) Viking Penguin.

—Give the Boys a Great Big Hand. unabr. ed. 1992. (Eighty-Seventh Precinct Ser.). audio 36.00 (*0-7366-2251-9*, 3040) Books on Tape, Inc.

—Give the Boys a Great Big Hand. l.t. ed. 1988. (Nightingale Ser.). 307p. 12.95 o.p. (*0-8161-4516-4*, Macmillan Reference USA) Gale Group.

—Give the Boys a Great Big Hand. (87th Precinct Mystery Ser.). 1981. mass mkt. 2.25 o.p. (*0-451-11081-1*); 1981. 240p. mass mkt. 4.50 o.p. (*0-451-15921-7*); 1981. mass mkt. 2.95 o.p. (*0-451-13900-3*); 1975. mass mkt. 1.25 o.p. (*0-451-06683-9*) NAL. (Signet Bks.).

—Hail, Hail, the Gang's All Here. unabr. ed. 1997. (Eighty-Seventh Precinct Ser.). audio 36.00 (*0-7366-3752-4*, 4427) Books on Tape, Inc.

—Hail, Hail, the Gang's All Here. 1972. 307p. (J). (*0-8161-6025-2*, Macmillan Reference USA) Gale Group.

—Hail, Hail, the Gang's All Here. 1972. 160p. mass mkt. 3.99 o.s.i (*0-451-15609-9*, Signet Bks.) NAL.

—Hail to the Chief. unabr. ed. 1995. audio 36.00 o.p. audio o.p. audio 30.00 (*0-7366-3199-2*, 3863) Books on Tape, Inc.

—Hail to the Chief. l.t. ed. 2003. lib. bdg. 28.95 (*1-58547-307-3*, Premier) Ctr. Point Large Print.

—Hail to the Chief. 1987. (Eighty-Seventh Precinct Novel Ser.). 160p. mass mkt. 4.50 o.p. (*0-380-70370-X*, Avon Bks.) Morrow/Avon.

—Hail to the Chief. 1981. mass mkt. 2.25 o.p. (*0-451-11214-8*); 1975. mass mkt. 1.25 o.p. (*0-451-06548-4*) NAL. (Signet Bks.).

—Hail to the Chief. 1973. 182p. o.p. (*0-394-48581-5*) Random Hse., Inc.

—Hail to the Chief. 1997. 192p. reprint ed. mass mkt. 5.99 (*0-446-60405-4*) Warner Bks., Inc.

—He Who Hesitates. 1981. 160p. mass mkt. 2.25 o.s.i (*0-345-29291-X*); 1975. mass mkt. 1.25 o.s.i (*0-345-24757-4*) Ballantine Bks.

—He Who Hesitates. l.t. ed. 1990. (Nightingale Ser.). 248p. 13.95 o.p. (*0-8161-4769-8*, Macmillan Reference USA) Gale Group.

—He Who Hesitates. 2000. mass mkt. 3.50 (*0-380-64198-4*); 1986. 160p. mass mkt. 4.50 (*0-380-70084-0*, Avon Bks.) Morrow/Avon.

—He Who Hesitates. 1996. 160p. reprint ed. mass mkt. 5.99 (*0-446-60147-0*) Warner Bks., Inc.

—Heat. 1987. 208p. mass mkt. 3.95 o.s.i (*0-345-34597-5*); 1983. mass mkt. 2.95 o.s.i (*0-345-30673-2*) Ballantine Bks.

—Heat. unabr. ed. 1998. (Eighty-Seventh Precinct Ser.). audio 42.00 (*0-7366-4110-6*, 4615) Books on Tape, Inc.

—Heat. 1992. (Eighty-Seventh Precinct Mysteries Ser.). 208p. mass mkt. 4.99 o.s.i (*0-451-17078-4*, Signet Bks.) NAL.

—Heat. 1981. 288p. 12.95 o.p. (*0-670-36479-7*) Viking Penguin.

—The Heckler. unabr. ed. 1996. (Eighty-Seventh Precinct Ser.). audio 36.00 (*0-7366-3254-9*, 3911) Books on Tape, Inc.

—The Heckler. 1982. mass mkt. 2.25 o.p. (*0-451-11421-3*); 1982. 176p. mass mkt. 4.50 o.p. (*0-451-15970-5*); 1982. mass mkt. 2.95 o.p. (*0-451-13901-1*); 1976. mass mkt. 1.25 o.p. (*0-451-06839-4*) NAL. (Signet Bks.).

—The Heckler. 2003. (Illus.). 288p. pap. 7.99 (*0-7434-6307-2*, Pocket) Simon & Schuster.

—Ice. unabr. ed. 1995. (Eighty-Seventh Precinct Ser.). audio 56.00 (*0-7366-3180-1*, 3849) Books on Tape, Inc.

—Ice. l.t. ed. 1983. 510p. lib. bdg. 17.95 o.p. (*0-8161-3568-1*, Macmillan Reference USA) Gale Group.

—Ice. 1984. 320p. pap. 5.99 (*0-380-67108-5*, Avon Bks.); 1983. 305p. 15.50 o.p. (*0-87795-468-2*, Morrow, William & Co.) Morrow/Avon.

—Ice. 2003. (Best Mysteries of All Time Ser.). 360p. (*0-7621-8889-8*, Impress) Scriptorium Pr., The.

—Ice. 1996. 336p. reprint ed. mass mkt. 5.99 o.p. (*0-446-60390-2*) Warner Bks., Inc.

—Jigsaw. unabr. ed. 1997. (Eighty-Seventh Precinct Ser.). audio 30.00 (*0-7366-3641-2*, 4303) Books on Tape, Inc.

—Jigsaw. 1970. (Eighty-Seventh Precinct Mysteries Ser.). 160p. mass mkt. 4.50 o.p. (*0-451-15480-0*, Signet Bks.) NAL.

—Killer's Choice. 1981. mass mkt. 2.25 o.s.i (*0-345-29288-X*) Ballantine Bks.

—Killer's Choice. unabr. ed. 1991. (Eighty-Seventh Precinct Ser.). audio 36.00 (*0-7366-2064-8*, 2872) Books on Tape, Inc.

—Killer's Choice. 1986. (Eighty-Seventh Precinct Novel Ser.). pap. 4.50 (*0-380-70083-2*, Avon Bks.) Morrow/Avon.

—Killer's Choice. 1996. 160p. mass mkt. 5.99 o.s.i (*0-446-60144-6*) Warner Bks., Inc.

—Killer's Payoff. unabr. ed. 1991. (Eighty-Seventh Precinct Ser.). audio 36.00 (*0-7366-2065-6*, 2873) Books on Tape, Inc.

—Killer's Payoff. l.t. ed. 1987. (Nightingale Ser.). 295p. 11.95 o.p. (*0-8161-4257-2*, Macmillan Reference USA) Gale Group.

Settings

—Killer's Payoff. (Eighty-Seventh Precinct Mysteries Ser.). 1987. 160p. mass mkt. 3.99 o.p. (*0-451-15081-3*); 1980. mass mkt. 1.75 o.p. (*0-451-09464-6*); 1974. mass mkt. 0.95 o.p. (*0-451-05939-5*) NAL. (Signet Bks.).

—Killer's Payoff. 2003. (Illus.). 272p. pap. 6.99 (*0-7434-6306-4*, Pocket) Simon & Schuster.

—Killer's Wedge. unabr. ed. 1992. (Eighty-Seventh Precinct Ser.). audio 36.00 (*0-7366-2105-9*, 2909) Books on Tape, Inc.

—Killer's Wedge. l.t. ed. 2000. 198p. lib. bdg. 27.95 o.p. (*1-58547-032-5*) Ctr. Point Large Print.

—Killer's Wedge. 1981. mass mkt. 1.75 o.p. (*0-451-09614-2*); 1981. 160p. mass mkt. 3.99 o.p. (*0-451-16336-2*); 1981. mass mkt. 2.95 o.p. (*0-451-14597-6*); 1974. mass mkt. 0.95 o.p. (*0-451-06219-1*) NAL. (Signet Bks.).

—King's Ransom. unabr. ed. 1991. (Eighty-Seventh Precinct Ser.). audio 42.00 (*0-7366-1894-5*, 2721) Books on Tape, Inc.

—King's Ransom. l.t. ed. 1986. (Nightingale Ser.). 327p. 11.95 o.p. (*0-8161-4127-4*, Macmillan Reference USA) Gale Group.

—King's Ransom. (87th Precinct Mystery Ser.). 1981. mass mkt. 2.25 o.p. (*0-451-09815-3*, Signet Bks.); 1981. 176p. mass mkt. 4.50 o.p. (*0-451-15933-0*); 1981. mass mkt. 2.95 o.p. (*0-451-13898-8*, Signet Bks.); 1975. mass mkt. 1.25 o.p. (*0-451-06467-4*, Signet Bks.) NAL.

—Kiss. unabr. ed. 1992. (Eighty-Seventh Precinct Ser.). audio 64.00 (*0-7366-2286-1*, 3072) Books on Tape, Inc.

—Kiss. unabr. ed. 1992. audio 22.95 o.p. (*1-56100-461-8*, 155, Bookcassette); audio 57.25 o.p. (*1-56100-095-7*, 543, Unabridged Library Editions) Brilliance Audio.

—Kiss. l.t. ed. 1993. (General Ser.). 458p. 16.95 o.p. (*0-8161-5589-5*); 21.95 o.p. (*0-8161-5588-7*) Gale Group. (Macmillan Reference USA).

—Kiss. 2002. 400p. audio 9.99 (*0-06-008392-1*); 1992. audio 16.00 o.p. (*1-55994-461-7*) HarperTrade. (HarperAudio).

—Kiss. abr. ed. 2000. (Eighty Seventh Precinct Novels Ser.). audio 7.95 (*1-57815-052-3*, 1013, Media Bks. Audio Publishing) Media Bks., L. L. C.

—Kiss. 1992. 384p. pap. 5.99 (*0-380-71382-9*, Avon Bks.); 330p. 17.00 o.p. (*0-688-10220-4*, Morrow, William & Co.) Morrow/Avon.

—Kiss. 1993. 4.99 o.p. (*0-517-11033-4*) Random Hse. Value Publishing.

—Lady Killer. unabr. ed. 1995. (Eighty-Seventh Precinct Novels Ser.). audio 39.95 BBC Audiobooks America.

—Lady Killer. unabr. ed. 1996. (Eighty-Seventh Precinct Ser.). audio 30.00 (*0-7366-3219-0*, 3882) Books on Tape, Inc.

—Lady Killer. l.t. ed. 1984. (General Ser.). lib. bdg. 12.95 o.p. (*0-8161-3665-3*, Macmillan Reference USA) Gale Group.

—Lady Killer. (Eighty-Seventh Precinct Mysteries Ser.). 1987. 160p. mass mkt. 4.50 o.s.i (*0-451-15082-1*); 1980. mass mkt. 1.75 o.p. (*0-451-09532-4*); 1974. mass mkt. 0.95 o.p. (*0-451-06067-9*) NAL. (Signet Bks.).

—Lady, Lady, I Did It! unabr. ed. 1996. (Eighty-Seventh Precinct Ser.). audio 30.00 (*0-7366-3495-9*, 4135) Books on Tape, Inc.

—Lady, Lady, I Did It! (87th Precinct Mystery Ser.). 1982. mass mkt. 2.25 o.p. (*0-451-11779-4*); 1982. 256p. mass mkt. 4.50 o.p. (*0-451-15841-5*); 1982. mass mkt. 2.95 o.p. (*0-451-13899-6*); 1976. mass mkt. 1.25 o.p. (*0-451-07151-4*) NAL. (Signet Bks.).

—Lady, Lady, I Did It! 1961. 3.50 o.p. (*0-671-40555-1*) Simon & Schuster.

—The Last Dance. l.t. ed. 2000. (Wheeler Large Print Book Ser.). 27.95 (*1-56895-814-5*, Wheeler Publishing, Inc.) Gale Group.

—The Last Dance. 2000. (Illus.). 272p. 25.00 o.s.i (*0-684-85513-5*, Simon & Schuster); 1999. E-Book 25.00 (*0-7432-0047-0*, Simon & Schuster); 2000. (Illus.). 336p. reprint ed. mass mkt. 7.99 (*0-671-02570-8*, Pocket) Simon & Schuster.

—Let's Hear It for the Deaf Man. unabr. ed. 1998. (Eighty-Seventh Precinct Ser.). audio 36.00 (*0-7366-3776-1*, 4449) Books on Tape, Inc.

—Let's Hear It for the Deaf Man. 1973. 231p. (J). o.p. (*0-385-01600-X*) Doubleday Publishing.

—Let's Hear It for the Deaf Man. 1974. (87th Precinct Mystery Ser.). 160p. mass mkt. 3.99 o.p. (*0-451-15403-7*, Signet Bks.) NAL.

—Lightning. 1999. (Eighty-Seventh Precinct Ser.). audio 56.00 (*0-7366-4624-8*, 5009) Books on Tape, Inc.

—Lightning. abr. ed. audio 17.00 o.p. (*0-694-51547-7*, CPN 2489, HarperAudio) HarperTrade.

—Lightning. (Eighty-Seventh Precinct Novel Ser.). 1985. 304p. mass mkt. 4.95 (*0-380-69974-5*, Avon Bks.); 1984. 15.95 o.p. (*0-87795-581-6*, Morrow, William & Co.) Morrow/Avon.

—Like Love. unabr. ed. 1996. (Eighty-Seventh Precinct Ser.). audio 36.00 (*0-7366-3496-7*, 4136) Books on Tape, Inc.

—Like Love. l.t. ed. 1993. (Nightingale Ser.). 304p. lib. bdg. 15.95 o.p. (*0-8161-5705-7*, Macmillan Reference USA) Gale Group.

—Like Love. (87th Precinct Mystery Ser.). 1982. mass mkt. 2.25 o.p. (*0-451-11628-3*); 1982. 176p. mass mkt. 2.95 o.p. (*0-451-13903-8*); 1982. 160p. mass mkt. 4.50 o.s.i (*0-451-16383-4*); 1976. mass mkt. 1.25 o.p. (*0-451-07221-9*) NAL. (Signet Bks.).

—Long Time No See. 1982. pap. 2.50 o.p. (*0-553-23130-8*) Bantam Bks.

—Long Time No See. unabr. ed. 1986. (Eighty-Seventh Precinct Ser.). audio 40.00 (*0-7366-0823-0*, 1773) Books on Tape, Inc.

—Long Time No See. abr. ed. audio 17.00 o.p. (*0-694-51546-9*, CPN 2488, HarperAudio) HarperTrade.

—Long Time No See. 1987. 272p. mass mkt. 4.99 (*0-380-70369-6*, Avon Bks.) Morrow/Avon.

—Long Time No See. 1997. 304p. mass mkt. 5.99 (*0-446-60449-6*) Warner Bks., Inc.

—Lullaby. unabr. ed. 1992. (Audio Bks.). audio 69.95 (*0-7451-6154-5*, CAB 549) BBC Audiobooks America.

—Lullaby. 1999. audio 48.00 (*0-7366-4872-0*); 1989. audio 48.00 Books on Tape, Inc.

—Lullaby. l.t. ed. 1990. (General Ser.). 437p. 20.95 o.p. (*0-8161-4923-2*, Macmillan Reference USA) Gale Group.

—Lullaby. abr. ed. audio 16.00 o.p. (*1-55994-819-1*, CPN 2392, HarperAudio) HarperTrade.

—Lullaby. abr. ed. 2000. (Eighty Seventh Precinct Novels Ser.). audio 7.95 (*1-57815-050-7*, 1014, Media Bks. Audio Publishing) Media Bks., L. L. C.

—Lullaby. 1990. 352p. mass mkt. 5.99 (*0-380-70384-X*, Avon Bks.); 1989. 17.95 o.p. (*0-87795-994-3*, Morrow, William & Co.) Morrow/Avon.

—McBain's Ladies: The Women of the 87th Precinct. 1988. 320p. 16.95 o.s.i (*0-89296-284-4*) Mysterious Pr.

—McBain's Ladies: The Women of the 87th Precinct. 1989. mass mkt. 4.95 (*0-445-40334-9*, Mysterious Pr. Paperback Bks.) Warner Bks., Inc.

—McBain's Ladies Too. 1989. 272p. 17.95 o.p. (*0-89296-285-2*) Mysterious Pr.

—McBain's Ladies Too. 1990. mass mkt. 4.95 o.s.i (*0-445-40893-6*, Mysterious Pr. Paperback Bks.) Warner Bks., Inc.

—Mischief. l.t. ed. 1995. pap. 23.95 o.p. (*0-7927-2014-8*); 1994. 25.95 o.p. (*0-7927-2015-6*) BBC Audiobooks America.

—Mischief. unabr. ed. 1993. (Eighty-Seventh Precinct Ser.). audio 64.00 (*0-7366-2591-7*, 3336) Books on Tape, Inc.

—Mischief. unabr. ed. 1993. 57.25 o.p. incl. audio (*1-56100-147-3*, 942, Unabridged Library Editions); audio 21.95 o.p. (*1-56100-514-2*, 176, Bookcassette) Brilliance Audio.

—Mischief. abr. ed. 2000. audio 9.99 (*0-694-52329-1*, HarperAudio) HarperTrade.

—Mischief. abr. ed. 2000. (Eighty Seventh Precinct Novels Ser.). audio 7.95 (*1-57815-051-5*, 1043, Media Bks. Audio Publishing) Media Bks., L. L. C.

—Mischief. 1994. 352p. pap. 5.99 (*0-380-71384-5*, Avon Bks.); 1993. 346p. 20.00 o.p. (*0-688-10221-2*, Morrow, William & Co.) Morrow/Avon.

—The Mugger. unabr. ed. 1995. (Eighty-Seventh Precinct Novels Ser.). audio 39.95 (*0-7451-6855-8*, CAB 321) BBC Audiobooks America.

—The Mugger. 1981. 160p. mass mkt. 2.25 o.s.i (*0-345-29290-1*) Ballantine Bks.

—The Mugger. unabr. ed. 1990. (Eighty-Seventh Precinct Ser.). audio 36.00 (*0-7366-1721-3*, 2562) Books on Tape, Inc.

—The Mugger. 1986. (Eighty-Seventh Precinct Novel Ser.). 160p. mass mkt. 3.50 (*0-380-70081-6*, Avon Bks.) Morrow/Avon.

—The Mugger. 1996. 192p. mass mkt. 5.99 (*0-446-60143-8*) Warner Bks., Inc.

—Nocturne. abr. ed. 1997. (Eighty Seventh Precinct Ser.). audio 24.95 (*1-55927-439-5*, 695087) Audio Renaissance.

—Nocturne. unabr. ed. 1997. (Eighty-Seventh Precinct Ser.). audio 48.00 (*0-7366-3777-X*, 4450) Books on Tape, Inc.

—Nocturne. (Eighty Seventh Precinct Ser.). 1998. mass mkt. 188.73 (*0-446-16558-1*); 1997. 320p. 23.50 o.p. (*0-446-51805-0*); 1998. 352p. reprint ed. mass mkt. 6.99 (*0-446-60538-7*) Warner Bks., Inc.

—Poison. 2001. audio 64.00 (*0-7366-5935-8*) Books on Tape, Inc.

—Poison. l.t. ed. 1988. 352p. 19.95 o.p. (*0-8161-4299-8*, Macmillan Reference USA) Gale Group.

—Poison. 1988. 256p. mass mkt. 4.99 (*0-380-70030-1*, Avon Bks.); 1987. 242p. 16.95 o.p. (*0-87795-787-8*, Morrow, William & Co.) Morrow/Avon.

—Poison. abr. ed. 1987. audio 14.95 (*0-671-64160-3*, Simon & Schuster Audioworks) Simon & Schuster Audio.

—The Pusher. unabr. ed. 1994. (Eighty-Seventh Precinct Novels Ser.). audio 54.95 (*0-7451-4228-1*, CAB 911) BBC Audiobooks America.

—The Pusher. unabr. ed. 1992. (Eighty-Seventh Precinct Ser.). audio 36.00 (*0-7366-2155-5*, 2954) Books on Tape, Inc.

—The Pusher. l.t. ed. 1987. (Large Print Books, Nightingale Ser.). 266p. 11.95 o.p. (*0-8161-4258-0*, Macmillan Reference USA) Gale Group.

—The Pusher. 9999. pap. 3.95 o.p. (*0-451-16480-6*); 1987. 160p. mass mkt. 3.99 o.p. (*0-451-15080-5*, Signet Bks.); 1980. mass mkt. 1.75 o.p. (*0-451-09256-2*, Signet Bks.); 1973. mass mkt. 0.95 o.p. (*0-451-05705-8*, Signet Bks.) NAL.

—The Pusher. 2002. 256p. pap. 6.99 (*0-7434-6305-6*, Pocket) Simon & Schuster.

—Romance. unabr. ed. 1995. (Eighty-Seventh Precinct Ser.). audio 48.00 (*0-7366-3122-4*, 3798) Books on Tape, Inc.

—Romance. abr. ed. audio 17.00 o.p. (*1-55994-995-3*, CPN 2484, HarperAudio) HarperTrade.

—Romance. 338p. pap. 5.98 o.p. (*0-7651-0365-6*) Smithmark Pubs., Inc.

—Romance. 1995. 336p. 22.95 o.s.i (*0-446-51804-2*); 1996. 352p. reprint ed. mass mkt. 6.50 o.s.i (*0-446-60280-9*) Warner Bks., Inc.

—Sadie When She Died. unabr. ed. 1998. (Eighty-Seventh Precinct Ser.). audio 30.00 (*0-7366-3993-4*, 4356) Books on Tape, Inc.

—Sadie When She Died. 1973. (87th Precinct Mystery Ser.). 160p. mass mkt. 3.99 o.s.i (*0-451-15366-9*, Signet Bks.) NAL.

—See Them Die. unabr. ed. 1996. (Eighty-Seventh Precinct Ser.). audio 36.00 (*0-7366-3359-6*, 4009) Books on Tape, Inc.

—See Them Die. (87th Precinct Mystery Ser.). 1982. mass mkt. 2.25 o.p. (*0-451-11561-9*, Signet Bks.); 1982. mass mkt. 2.95 o.p. (*0-451-14596-8*); 1976. mass mkt. 1.25 o.p. (*0-451-07030-5*, Signet Bks.); 1982. 160p. reprint ed. mass mkt. 4.50 o.p. (*0-451-16426-1*, Signet Bks.) NAL.

—Shotgun. unabr. ed. 1997. (Eighty-Seventh Precinct Ser.). audio 30.00 (*0-7366-3578-5*, 4230) Books on Tape, Inc.

—Shotgun. 1970. (87th Precinct Mystery Ser.). 176p. mass mkt. 4.50 o.p. (*0-451-15674-9*); mass mkt. 2.50 o.p. (*0-451-11971-1*) NAL. (Signet Bks.).

—So Long As You Both Shall Live. unabr. ed. 1998. (Eighty-Seventh Precinct Ser.). audio 30.00 (*0-7366-3778-8*, 4451) Books on Tape, Inc.

—So Long As You Both Shall Live. 1977. mass mkt. 3.50 o.p. (*0-451-15718-4*); mass mkt. 1.50 o.p. (*0-451-07749-0*) NAL. (Signet Bks.).

—Ten Plus One. unabr. ed. 1997. (Eighty-Seventh Precinct Ser.). audio 36.00 (*0-7366-3532-7*, 4171) Books on Tape, Inc.

—Ten Plus One. (87th Precinct Mystery Ser.). 1982. mass mkt. 2.25 o.p. (*0-451-11923-1*, Signet Bks.); 1982. 176p. mass mkt. 4.50 o.s.i (*0-451-16367-2*, Signet Bks.); 1982. mass mkt. 2.95 o.p. (*0-451-14598-4*); 1977. mass mkt. 1.25 o.p. (*0-451-07463-7*, Signet Bks.) NAL.

—'Til Death. unabr. ed. 1992. (Eighty-Seventh Precinct Ser.). audio 36.00 (*0-7366-2123-7*, 2925) Books on Tape, Inc.

—'Til Death. (Eighty-Seventh Precinct Mysteries Ser.). 1989. 176p. mass mkt. 4.50 o.s.i (*0-451-15891-1*); 1981. mass mkt. 2.25 o.p. (*0-451-09734-3*); 1981. mass mkt. 2.95 o.p. (*0-451-13896-1*) NAL. (Signet Bks.).

—Till Death Us Do Part. 1975. mass mkt. 1.25 o.p. (*0-451-06320-1*, Signet Bks.) NAL.

—Tricks. unabr. ed. 1992. (Eighty-Seventh Precinct Novels Ser.). audio 54.95 (*0-7451-6156-1*, CAB 616) BBC Audiobooks America.

—Tricks. 2001. audio 56.00 (*0-7366-6021-6*) Books on Tape, Inc.

—Tricks. 256p. 1987. 16.95 o.p. (*0-87795-927-7*, Morrow, William & Co.); 1989. reprint ed. mass mkt. 5.99 (*0-380-70383-1*, Avon Bks.) Morrow/Avon.

—Tricks. 1989. 3.99 o.p. (*0-517-69431-X*) Random Hse. Value Publishing.

—Tricks. abr. ed. 1988. audio 14.95 Simon & Schuster Audio.

—Vespers. unabr. ed. 1990. (Eighty-Seventh Precinct Ser.). audio 64.00 (*0-7366-1807-4*, 2644) Books on Tape, Inc.

—Vespers. l.t. ed. 1991. 470p. 24.95 o.p. (*1-85089-498-1*) ISIS Large Print Bks. GBR. *Dist:* Transaction Pubs.

—Vespers. 1991. 352p. mass mkt. 5.99 (*0-380-70385-8*, Avon Bks.); 1990. 350p. 18.95 o.p. (*0-87795-987-0*, Morrow, William & Co.) Morrow/Avon.

—Widows. unabr. ed. 1991. (Eighty-Seventh Precinct Ser.). audio 64.00 (*0-7366-1965-8*, 2786) Books on Tape, Inc.

—Widows. l.t. ed. 1992. (General Ser.). 454p. lib. bdg. 21.95 o.p. (*0-8161-5311-6*, Macmillan Reference USA) Gale Group.

—Widows. abr. ed. 2000. (Eighty Seventh Precinct Novels Ser.). audio 7.95 (*1-57815-056-6*, 1054, Media Bks. Audio Publishing) Media Bks., L. L. C.

—Widows. 1991. 330p. 19.00 o.p. (*0-688-10219-0*, Morrow, William & Co.); 1992. 336p. reprint ed. mass mkt. 6.50 (*0-380-71383-7*, Avon Bks.) Morrow/Avon.

**ISRAEL—FICTION**

Agnon, Shmuel Yosef. Only Yesterday. Harshav, Barbara, tr. from HEB. 2002. 688p. (C). pap. 24.95 (*0-691-09544-2*) Princeton Univ. Pr.

Almagor, Gila. Under the Domim Tree. Schenker, Hillel, tr. 1995. 176p. (J). (gr. 7 up). 15.00 (*0-671-89020-4*, Simon & Schuster Children's Publishing) Simon & Schuster Children's Publishing.

Arnold, Margot, pseud. Zadok's Treasure. 1982. 192p. 2.50 (*0-86721-228-4*, Jove) Berkley Publishing Group.

—Zadok's Treasure. 1989. (Penny Spring & Sir Toby Glendower Mystery Ser.). 192p. reprint ed. pap. 7.95 (*0-88150-133-6*, Foul Play) Norton, W. W. & Co., Inc.

Austin, Lynn. Wings of Refuge. 2000. 400p. pap. 11.99 (*0-7642-2196-5*) Bethany Hse. Pubs.

Aved, Joe. Ami. 1981. 192p. 16.95 o.p. (*0-88400-077-X*, Shengold Bks.) Schreiber Publishing, Inc.

Bayer, William. Pattern Crimes. 1988. mass mkt. 4.95 o.p. (*0-451-15281-6*, Signet Bks.) NAL.

—Pattern Crimes. 1988. 3.99 o.p. (*0-517-65459-8*) Random Hse. Value Publishing.

—Pattern Crimes. 1980. pap. o.s.i (*0-394-75357-7*) Random Hse., Inc.

Be'er, Haim. The Pure Element of Time. Harshav, Barbara, tr. from HEB. 2003. (Tauber Institute for the Study of European Jewry Ser.). 304p. text 26.00 (*1-58465-277-2*) Univ. Pr. of New England.

Boland, John. Death in Jerusalem. 1994. 224p. 19.95 o.p. (*0-312-10965-2*, Saint Martin's Minotaur) St. Martin's Pr.

Bowen, Kevin. Wil's Bones. 2000. 256p. pap. 12.95 (*1-930892-12-8*) Engage Publishing.

Chafets, Zev, Jr. Hang Time. 1996. 82p. 21.95 o.s.i (*0-446-52047-0*) Warner Bks., Inc.

Chafets, Zev. The Project. l.t. ed. 1997. (Core Ser.). 286p. lib. bdg. 25.95 (*0-7838-8207-6*, Macmillan Reference USA) Gale Group.

—The Project. 272p. 1998. mass mkt. 6.50 (*0-446-60542-5*); 1997. 24.00 o.p. (*0-446-51886-7*) Warner Bks., Inc.

Christie, Agatha. Appointment with Death. 1987. 9.95 o.p. (*0-553-35062-5*) Bantam Bks.

—Appointment with Death. Pliner, Jayne, ed. 1988. (Hercule Poirot Mystery Ser.). 224p. mass mkt. 5.99 (*0-425-10858-9*) Berkley Publishing Group.

—Appointment with Death. 1986. mass mkt. 2.95 o.s.i (*0-425-09356-5*); 1984. mass mkt. 2.95 o.s.i (*0-425-06775-0*) Berkley Publishing Group.

—Appointment with Death. 1981. 192p. pap. 2.95 o.p. (*0-440-10246-4*) Dell Publishing.

—Appointment with Death. l.t. ed. 1993. 336p. pap. 12.95 o.p. (*0-8161-4530-X*); 1992. 296p. lib. bdg. 19.95 o.p. (*0-8161-4529-6*) Gale Group. (Macmillan Reference USA).

—Appointment with Death. 1996. 240p. 24.95 (*0-399-14136-7*); 1988. (YA). 14.95 (*0-396-09298-5*) Penguin Group (USA) Inc. (G. P. Putnam's Sons).

—Appointment with Death. l.t. ed. 1975. (Ulverscroft Large Print Ser.). 334p. 12.00 o.p. (*0-85456-366-0*, Ulverscroft) Thorpe, F. A. Pubs. GBR. *Dist:* Ulverscroft Large Print Bks., Ltd., Ulverscroft Large Print Canada, Ltd.

—Appointment with Death. 1988. 12.04 (*0-606-12169-2*) Turtleback Bks.

Clifford, Alan N. The Fatherland Files. 1994. 288p. 22.00 (*1-56881-034-2*) AK Peters, Ltd.

Dolan, David. The End of Days. l.t. ed. 2003. 336p. per. 12.99 (*0-9725719-3-0*) 21st Century Pr.

—The End of Days. 1997. (Illus.). 336p. (gr. 13 up). pap. 10.99 (*0-8007-5630-4*, The End of the) Revell, Fleming H. Co.

Edghill, India. Queenmaker: A Novel of King David's Queen. 2003. 384p. pap. 14.00 (*0-312-28919-7*) Picador.

—Queenmaker: A Novel of King David's Queen. 2002. 384p. 24.95 (*0-312-28918-9*) St. Martin's Pr.

—Queenmaker: A Novel of King David's Queen. l.t. ed. 2001. (Christian Fiction Ser.). 584p. 26.95 (*0-7862-2922-5*) Thorndike Pr.

—Queenmaker: A Novel of King David's Queen. 2000. 377p. pap. 16.00 o.p. (*0-7388-0733-8*); text 25.00 o.p. (*0-7388-0732-X*); E-Book 8.00 (*0-7388-8260-7*) Xlibris Corp.

Esrati, Stephen G. The Tenth Prayer: A Novel of Israel. 2000. 352p. pap. 22.99 (*0-7388-2154-3*); E-Book 8.00 (*0-7388-7115-X*) Xlibris Corp.

Eve, Nomi. The Family Orchard: A Novel. 2001. (Illus.). 336p. reprint ed. pap. 13.00 (*0-375-72457-5*, Vintage) Knopf Publishing Group.

—The Family Orchard: A Novel. l.t. ed. 2001. (Women's Fiction Ser.). (Illus.). 499p. 28.95 (*0-7862-3303-6*) Thorndike Pr.

Farnsworth, Clyde. Shadow Wars. 1998. 352p. 24.95 o.p. (*1-55611-518-0*) Fine, Donald I. Bks.

Feldman, Ian. Har Megiddon. l.t. ed. 2004. 559p. 29.95 (*1-932623-02-7*) SSI, Inc. Publishing.

Fish, Robert L. Pursuit: A Novel. 1978. 10.00 o.p. (0-385-13398-7) Doubleday Publishing.
Follett, Ken. Triple. l.t. ed. 1994. pap. 20.95 o.p. (0-7927-1600-0); 1993. 22.95 o.p. (0-7927-1601-9); 1993. 84.95 incl. audio (0-7451-5939-7, CAB 493) BBC Audiobooks America.
—Triple. 1980. pap. 9.95 o.p. (0-8161-3099-X); 1979. lib. bdg. 15.95 o.p. (0-8161-3005-1) Gale Group. (Macmillan Reference USA).
—Triple. 1979. 18.95 o.p. (0-87795-223-X, Morrow, William & Co.) Morrow/Avon.
—Triple. 2004. 320p. pap. 14.00 (0-451-21208-8); 1980. mass mkt. 3.95 o.p. (0-451-12790-0, Signet Bks.); 1980. mass mkt. 3.95 o.p. (0-451-12429-4, Signet Bks.); 1980. 352p. mass mkt. 4.50 o.p. (0-451-13988-7, Signet Bks.); 1980. 352p. mass mkt. 7.99 (0-451-16354-0); 1980. mass mkt. 3.95 o.p. (0-451-12160-0, Signet Bks.); 1980. mass mkt. 3.50 o.p. (0-451-09447-6, Signet Bks.) NAL.
—Triple. 11th ed. (SPA., Illus.). 368p. (84-01-49955-0) Plaza & Janés Editories, S.A.
—Triple. 1999. (SPA.). 472p. 9.95 (84-01-49963-1) Plaza & Janés Editories, S.A. ESP. *Dist:* Libros Sin Fronteras.
Gabay, Taity. Bonjour Bijoux. 1992. 350p. pap. text (0-9632052-0-X) Cliffrose Pubns.
Girzone, Joseph F. Joshua in the Holy Land. l.t. ed. 1995. 17.95 (0-8161-5743-X); 1994. 271p. lib. bdg. 23.95 (0-8161-5742-1) Gale Group. (Macmillan Reference USA).
—Joshua in the Holy Land. abr. ed. 1992. audio 15.99 o.s.i (0-553-47117-1, RH Audio) Random Hse. Audio Publishing Group.
—Joshua in the Holy Land. 1995. 224p. pap. 11.00 (0-684-81344-0, Touchstone); 1992. 16.00 o.s.i (0-02-543445-4, Scribner) Simon & Schuster.
Gluzman, Michael & Seidman, Naomi, eds. Israel Vol. 4: A Traveler's Literary Companion. 1996. (Travelers' Literary Companions Ser.: Vol. 4). (Illus.). 256p. (Orig.). pap. 12.95 (1-883513-03-0) Whereabouts.
Gordon, Neil. The Sacrifice of Isaac. 1996. 352p. mass mkt. 6.50 o.s.i (0-553-57635-6) Bantam Bks.
—The Sacrifice of Isaac. 2003. 320p. pap. 14.00 (0-14-200185-6) Penguin Group (USA) Inc.
—Sacrifice of Isaac. 1999. pap. 12.98 (0-671-04427-3); audio 21.00 (0-671-52827-0, 593063) Simon & Schuster Audio. (Simon & Schuster Audioworks).
Grant, Linda. When I Lived in Modern Times. 2001. (Illus.). 288p. 23.95 o.s.i (0-525-94594-6) Dutton/Plume.
—When I Lived in Modern Times. l.t. ed. 2001. (Women's Fiction Ser.). 399p. 28.95 (0-7862-3396-6) Thorndike Pr.
Grossman, David. Be My Knife: A Novel. Almog, Vered & Gurantz, Maya, trs. from HEB. 2002. 324p. 25.00 o.p. (0-374-29977-3) Farrar, Straus & Giroux.
—Be My Knife: A Novel. Gurantz, Maya & Almog, Vered, trs. 2003. 320p. pap. 14.00 (0-312-42147-8) Picador.
—See Under: Love. Rosenberg, Betsy, tr. 2002. 464p. pap. 15.00 (0-312-42069-2) Picador.
—Someone to Run With. Almog, Vered & Gurantz, Maya, trs. from HEB. 2004. 352p. 25.00 (0-374-26657-3) Farrar, Straus & Giroux.
—Words into Flesh. 2002. o.p. (0-374-29284-1) Farrar, Straus & Giroux.
—The Zigzag Kid. Rosenberg, Betsy, tr. from HEB. 1997. 384p. 24.00 o.p. (0-374-29692-8) Farrar, Straus & Giroux.
Gur, Batya. Murder on a Kibbutz: A Communal Case. 1995. 368p. pap. 13.95 (0-06-092654-6, Perennial) HarperTrade.
—Murder on the Kibbutz. 1994. 368p. 20.00 o.p. (0-06-019026-4) HarperTrade.
—The Saturday Morning Murder: A Psychoanalytic Case. Bilu, Dalya, tr. from ENG. 1992. 320p. 20.00 o.p. (0-06-019024-8); 1993. 304p. reprint ed. pap. 11.00 (0-06-099508-4, Perennial) HarperTrade.
Haddad, Carolyn. A Mother's Secret. 1988. 512p. 19.95 (0-15-162666-9) Harcourt Trade Pubs.
Hannah, Janet. The Wish to Kill. 1999. 224p. 21.00 (1-56947-177-0) Soho Pr., Inc.
Hardie, Sean. Table for Six. 1991. 19.95 o.p. (0-671-72329-4, Simon & Schuster) Simon & Schuster.
Hartov, Steven. The Nylon Hand of God. 1996. 512p. 23.00 o.p. (0-688-14120-X, Morrow, William & Co.) Morrow/Avon.
Hedaya, Yael. Accidents. 2004. (0-8050-7348-5, Metropolitan Bks.) Holt, Henry & Co.
Hoffmann, Yoel. The Heart Is Katmandu: Novel. Cole, Peter, tr. from HEB. 2001. 144p. 22.95 (0-8112-1465-6) New Directions Publishing Corp.
Horn, Shifra. The Fairest among Women. Sacks, Hebrew H., tr. from HEB. 2001. 288p. 23.95 (0-312-26590-5) St. Martin's Pr.
—Four Mothers. 2000. 288p. pap. 14.00 (0-312-26323-6) Picador.
—Four Mothers, Set. 1999. o.s.i (0-312-20871-5) St. Martin's Pr.
Horn, Shifra & Bilu, Dalya. Four Mothers. 1999. 288p. 23.95 o.p. (0-312-20547-3) St. Martin's Pr.
Israel, Alec. The Kabbalists. 2001. 104p. pap. 12.95 (965-229-265-6) Gefen Publishing Hse., Ltd ISR. *Dist:* Gefen Bks.
Kalechofsky, Roberta. A Boy, a Chicken & the Lion of Judah: How Ari Became a Vegetarian. 1995. (Illus.). 45p. (J). (gr. 2-5). pap. 8.00 (0-916288-39-0) Micah Pubns.
Kaniuk, Yoram. Adam Resurrected. Simckes, Seymour, tr. from HEB. 2001. 384p. pap. 14.00 (0-8021-3689-3) Grove/Atlantic, Inc.
—Adam Resurrected. 1978. reprint ed. mass mkt. 4.95 o.p. (0-06-090620-0, CN 620) HarperCollins Pubs.
—His Daughter. Simckes, Seymour, tr. from HEB. 1989. 293p. (C). text 17.50 (0-8076-1215-4) Braziller, George Inc.
Katzier, Yehudit. Closing the Sea. 1992. 18.95 o.s.i (0-15-118200-0) Harcourt Trade Pubs.
Kellerman, Jonathan. The Butcher's Theater. 2003. 640p. mass mkt. 7.99 (0-345-46067-7, Ballantine Bks.) Ballantine Bks.
—The Butcher's Theater. 1989. 640p. mass mkt. 7.99 o.s.i (0-553-27510-0); audio 16.99 (0-553-45156-1) Bantam Bks.
—The Butcher's Theater. l.t. ed. 1996. (Large Print Bks.). 888p. pap. 22.95 o.p. (1-56895-342-9, Wheeler Publishing, Inc.) Gale Group.
Kemelman, Harry. One Fine Day the Rabbi Bought a Cross. 1988. (Boston Mysteries Ser.). mass mkt. 5.99 o.s.i (0-449-20687-4, Fawcett) Ballantine Bks.
—One Fine Day the Rabbi Bought a Cross. l.t. ed. 1988. (Large Print Bks.). 353p. 18.95 o.p. (0-8161-4347-1, Macmillan Reference USA) Gale Group.
—One Fine Day the Rabbi Bought a Cross. 1987. 234p. 15.95 o.p. (0-688-05631-8, Morrow, William & Co.) Morrow/Avon.
—One Fine Day the Rabbi Bought a Cross. 1990. 3.99 o.p. (0-517-05752-2) Random Hse. Value Publishing.
—One Fine Day the Rabbi Bought a Cross. 2003. 320p. pap. 6.99 (0-7434-7478-3) ibooks, Inc.
Klein, A. M. The Second Scroll. Popham, Elizabeth A. & Pollock, Zailig, eds. 1999. (Illus.). 594p. text (0-8020-4478-6) Univ. of Toronto Pr.
Klein, Zachary. Still among the Living. 1990. 288p. 18.95 o.p. (0-06-016411-5) HarperTrade.
—Two Way Toll: A Novel of Suspense. 1991. 275p. 20.00 o.p. (0-06-016420-4) HarperTrade.
Koperwas, Sam. The Flash Effect. 1994. 256p. 22.00 o.p. (0-688-10944-6, Morrow, William & Co.) Morrow/Avon.
Koren, Yeshayahu. Funeral at Noon: A Novel. Bilu, Dalya, tr. 1996. 224p. 23.00 o.p. (1-883642-03-5) Steerforth Pr.
LaHaye, Tim & Jenkins, Jerry B. Desecration: Antichrist Takes the Throne. l.t. ed. 2002. 535p. 30.95 (0-7862-3861-5) Gale Group.
—Desecration: Antichrist Takes the Throne. 2001. (Left Behind Ser.: Bk. 9). 432p. 24.99 (0-8423-3226-X); E-Book 24.99 (0-8423-7067-6) Tyndale Hse. Pubs.
—El Sacrilegio: El Anticristo Toma el Trono. (Left Behind Ser.: No. 9). Tr. of Desecration: Antichrist Takes the Throne. (SPA.). pap. (0-7899-0985-5) Editorial Unilit.
Land, Jon. The Blue Widows. Date not set. mass mkt. (0-7653-4526-9); 2003. 384p. 24.95 (0-7653-0599-2) Doherty, Tom Assocs., LLC. (Forge Bks.).
—Keepers of the Gate. Date not set. (0-312-87830-3); 2001. 320p. 25.95 (0-312-85655-5) Doherty, Tom Assocs., LLC. (Forge Bks.).
—A Walk in the Darkness. 2000. 352p. 25.95 (0-312-87265-8, Forge Bks.) Doherty, Tom Assocs., LLC.
Leonard, Elmore. The Hunted. unabr. collector's ed. 1995. audio 42.00 (0-7366-3161-5, 3832) Books on Tape, Inc.
—The Hunted. 2000. 288p. mass mkt. 7.50 o.s.i (0-440-13425-0) Dell Publishing.
—The Hunted. l.t. ed. 1989. (General Ser.). 280p. 20.95 o.p. (0-8161-4713-2, Macmillan Reference USA) Gale Group.
—The Hunted. 2003. 336p. mass mkt. 7.50 (0-06-008406-5, HarperTorch) Morrow/Avon.
—The Hunted. unabr. ed. 2000. audio 53.00 (0-7887-0838-4, 94983E7); 1999. audio compact disk 65.00 (0-7887-3729-5, C1086E7) Recorded Bks., LLC.
—The Hunted. 1986. 240p. mass mkt. 3.95 o.s.i (0-445-40204-0, Mysterious Pr. Paperback Bks.) Warner Bks., Inc.
Liebrecht, Savyon. Apples from the Desert: Selected Stories. Institute for the Translation of Hebrew Staff, tr. from HEB. 1998. (Helen Rose Schever Jewish Women Ser.). 240p. 19.95 (1-55861-190-8) Feminist Pr. at The City Univ. of New York.
—Apples from the Desert: Selected Stories. unabr. ed. 2000. (Helen Rose Schever Jewish Women Ser.). 240p. pap. 13.95 (1-55861-235-1) Feminist Pr. at The City Univ. of New York.
—A Man & a Woman & a Man. Pomerantz, Marsha, tr. from HEB. 2001. 224p. 24.95 (0-89255-266-2) Persea Bks., Inc.
—A Man & a Woman & a Man: A Novel. Pomerantz, Marsha, tr. 2003. 256p. pap. 14.00 (0-89255-297-2) Persea Bks., Inc.
Lindgren, Torgny. Bathsheba. Geddes, Tom, tr. from SWE. 1989. 256p. 17.95 o.p. (0-06-015963-4) HarperTrade.
—Bathsheba. 1990. 3.99 o.p. (0-517-05336-5) Random Hse. Value Publishing.
Magun, Carol. Circling Eden: A Novel of Israel in Stories. 1995. 200p. 19.95 (0-89733-412-4) Academy Chicago Pubs., Ltd.
Maier, Paul L. Pontius Pilate: A Biographical Novel. 384p. 1995. pap. 13.99 (0-8254-3296-0); 1990. 19.99 (0-8254-3261-8) Kregel Pubns.
—Pontius Pilate: A Biographical Novel. 1981. pap. 4.95 o.p. (0-8423-4852-2) Tyndale Hse. Pubs.
—A Skeleton in God Closet. 1996. 360p. mass mkt. 5.99 (0-7852-7537-1) Nelson, Thomas Inc.
Marcum, Robert. The Return: A Novel. 2002. 437p. 22.95 (1-59156-067-5) Covenant Communications.
Matalon, Ronit. Bliss: A Novel. Cohen, Jessica, tr. from HEB. 2003. 272p. 23.00 (0-8050-6602-0, Metropolitan Bks.) Holt, Henry & Co.
Megged, Aharon. Foigelman. 2003. 250p. 19.95 (1-59264-032-X) Toby Pr.
Meier, Paul & Wise, Robert L. The Fourth Millennium. 1996. 324p. pap. 12.99 (0-7852-8149-5) Nelson, Thomas Inc.
Mendes, Bob. Vengeance: Prelude to Saddam's War. Smittenaar, H. S., tr. from DUT. 1996. 303p. pap. 9.95 (1-881164-71-3) Intercontinental Publishing, Inc.
Michael, Sami. Refuge. Grossman, Edward, tr. from HEB. 1988. 376p. 22.50 o.p. (0-8276-0308-8) Jewish Pubn. Society.
Miklowitz, Gloria D. Masada: The Last Fortress. 1999. 198p. (J). (gr. 4-7). 16.00 (0-8028-5165-7, Eerdmans Bks For Young Readers) Eerdmans, William B. Publishing Co.
Mosely, Nicholas. Serpent. 2000. 192p. pap. 11.95 (1-56478-244-1) Dalkey Archive Pr.
Mosley, Nicholas. Serpent. rev. ed. 1990. 190p. 19.95 (0-916583-49-X) Dalkey Archive Pr.
Nord, Myrtle. The King & the Apostle. 2002. (Illus.). 140p. pap. 14.95 (1-58736-104-3, Iceni Bks.) Wheatmark, Inc.
Osina, Lisa. Moving. 2000. E-Book (1-930739-00-1) Internet Book Co., Inc.
Ostrovsky, Victor. Lion of Judah. 1993. 320p. 21.95 o.p. (0-312-10016-7) St. Martin's Pr.
Oxley, A. T. Nathan the Littlest Disciple. 2000. (Illus.). pap. 12.00 o.p. (0-8059-5044-3) Dorrance Publishing Co., Inc.
Oz, Amos. A Perfect Peace. 1993. (Harvest in Translation Ser.). 384p. pap. 13.00 (0-15-671683-6, Harvest Bks.) Harcourt Trade Pubs.
—A Perfect Peace. Halkin, Hillel, tr. from HEB. 1985. (Helen & Kurt Wolff Bk.). 400p. 16.95 (0-15-171696-X) Harcourt Trade Pubs.
—A Perfect Peace. Halkin, Hillel, tr. 1986. 384p. pap. 6.95 o.p. (0-14-008885-7, Penguin Bks.) Viking Penguin.
—To Know a Woman. 1992. 272p. pap. 13.00 (0-15-690680-5, Harvest Bks.); 1991. 262p. 13.00 o.s.i (0-15-190499-5) Harcourt Trade Pubs.
—To Know a Woman. 262p. 4.98 o.p. (0-8317-7448-7) Smithmark Pubs., Inc.
Paul, Carolyn K. T'shuva. 1996. 240p. (Orig.). pap. 10.95 (0-89407-115-7) Strawberry Hill Pr.
Phillips, Caryl. The Nature of Blood. 1997. 224p. 23.00 o.s.i (0-679-45470-5) Knopf, Alfred A. Inc.
—The Nature of Blood. 1998. pap. o.s.i (0-676-97104-0, Vintage) Random Hse. of Canada, Ltd. CAN. *Dist:* Random Hse., Inc.
—The Nature of Blood. 1998. 224p. pap. 13.00 (0-679-77675-3) Random Hse., Inc.
Rabinyan, Dorit. Our Weddings. 2001. 245p. (0-7475-5275-4) Bloomsbury Pr.
Ramras-Rauch, Gila & Michman-Melkman, Joseph, eds. Facing the Holocaust: Selected Israeli Fiction. 1986. 292p. 24.95 (0-8276-0253-7) Jewish Pubn. Society.
Reich, Tova. The Jewish War: A Novel. 1995. 272p. 22.00 (0-679-43987-0, Pantheon) Knopf Publishing Group.
—The Jewish War: A Novel. 1997. (Library of Modern Jewish Literature). 288p. pap. 17.95 (0-8156-0452-1) Syracuse Univ. Pr.
Rogan, Barbara. Cafe Nevo. 1988. 324p. pap. 7.95 o.p. (0-452-26141-4, Plume) Dutton/Plume.
—Cafe Nevo. 1987. 320p. 19.95 o.s.i (0-689-11840-6, Scribner) Simon & Schuster.
Rosenberg, Robert. An Accidental Murder. 1999. (Avram Cohen Mysteries Ser.). 288p. 22.00 o.s.i (0-684-85032-X, Scribner) Simon & Schuster.
—Crimes of the City. 1992. (Crime Ser.). 288p. pap. 5.95 o.p. (0-14-016686-6, Penguin Bks.) Penguin Group (USA) Inc.
—Crimes of the City. 1997. (Missing Mysteries Ser.: Vol. 3). mass mkt. 7.95 (1-890208-03-5) Poisoned Pen Pr.
—Crimes of the City. 1991. 272p. 18.95 o.p. (0-671-70222-X, Simon & Schuster) Simon & Schuster.
—The Cutting Room: An Avram Cohen Mystery. 1993. (Crime Ser.). 304p. reprint ed. pap. 5.95 o.p. (0-14-023112-9, Penguin Bks.) Penguin Group (USA) Inc.
—The Cutting Room: An Avram Cohen Mystery. 1993. 320p. 20.00 (0-671-74344-9, Simon & Schuster) Simon & Schuster.
—House of Guilt: An Avram Cohen Mystery. 1996. 368p. 21.50 o.p. (0-684-82654-2, Scribner) Simon & Schuster.
Roth, Philip. Operation Shylock: A Confession. 1994. 400p. pap. 14.00 (0-679-75029-0, Vintage) Knopf Publishing Group.
—Operation Shylock: A Confession. 1993. 400p. 23.00 o.p. (0-671-70376-5, Simon & Schuster) Simon & Schuster.
Sabato, Haim. Adjusting Sights. Halkin, Hillel, tr. from HEB. 2003. Tr. of Tiyum Kavanot. 168p. 19.95 (1-902881-70-2) Toby Pr.
Salmon, Elon. When There Were Heroes. 2003. 256p. pap. 13.95 (1-899235-59-0) Lewis, Dewi Publishing GBR. *Dist:* Consortium Bk. Sales & Distribution.
Segal, Sheila F. Joshua's Dream. 1985. (Illus.). 32p. (J). (gr. 1-3). pap. 6.95 o.p. (0-8074-0272-9, 101060) UAHC Pr.
Shabtai, Yaakov. Past Continuous. Bilu, Dalya, tr. from HEB. 1985. 389p. 16.95 o.p. (0-8276-0239-1) Jewish Pubn. Society.
—Past Continuous. 2002. 389p. pap. 16.95 (1-58567-339-0) Overlook Pr., The.
—Past Perfect. Bilu, Dalya, tr. 1987. 18.95 o.p. (0-670-81308-7) Viking Penguin.
Shalev, Meir. The Blue Mountain. Halkin, Hillel, tr. from HEB. 2002. 376p. pap. 14.00 (1-84195-242-7); pap. 14.00 (1-84195-115-3) Canongate Bks. GBR. *Dist:* Publishers Group West, Grove/Atlantic, Inc.
—Esau: A Novel. 1994. 384p. 25.00 o.p. (0-06-019040-X, HarperCollins) HarperTrade.
Shamir, Moshe. The Fifth Wheel. Hodes, Aubrey, tr. from HEB. rev. ed. 1986. (Illus.). 115p. (YA). (gr. 8 up). reprint ed. pap. 8.95 o.p. (0-917883-02-0) Benmir Bks.
Shelach, Oz. Picnic Grounds: A Novel in Fragments. 2003. 116p. pap. 10.95 (0-87286-419-7) City Lights Bks.
Simon, Roger L. Raising the Dead: A Moses Wine Mystery. 1989. 240p. mass mkt. 4.95 (0-446-34822-8) Warner Bks., Inc.
Singer, Isaac Bashevis. The Penitent. 1983. 169p. 13.95 o.s.i (0-374-23064-1) Farrar, Straus & Giroux.
—The Penitent. l.t. ed. 1984. (General Ser.). 13.95 o.p. (0-8161-3641-6, Macmillan Reference USA) Gale Group.
Sofer, Barbara. The Thirteenth Hour. 1996. 352p. 24.95 o.s.i (0-525-94181-9) Dutton/Plume.
—The Thirteenth Hour. 1997. 416p. mass mkt. 5.99 o.s.i (0-451-19106-4, Signet Bks.) NAL.
—The Thirteenth Hour, unabr. ed. 1997. audio 91.00 (0-7887-0921-6, 95061E7) Recorded Bks., LLC.
Spencer, Jon M. Tribes of Benjamin: A Novel. 1999. 199 p. (1-893562-01-8) Tubman, Harriet Pr.
Steinberg, Janice. Death in a City of Mystics. 1998. (Prime Crime Mysteries Ser.). 288p. mass mkt. 5.99 o.s.i (0-425-16615-5, Prime Crime) Berkley Publishing Group.
Stevens, Serita & Moore, Rayanne. Red Sea, Dead Sea. l.t. ed. 1993. (General Ser.). 348p. lib. bdg. 19.95 o.p. (0-8161-5442-2, Macmillan Reference USA) Gale Group.
—Red Sea, Dead Sea. 2002. 176p. pap. 10.95 (0-7599-0373-5); 2000. (Fanny Zendel Mystery Ser.: Vol. 1). 235p. E-Book 5.50 (1-58200-505-2); 2000. (Fanny Zendel Mystery Ser.: Vol.1). E-Book 5.50 (1-58200-327-0) Hard Shell Word Factory.
—Red Sea, Dead Sea. 1991. 224p. 17.95 o.p. (0-312-06451-9, Saint Martin's Minotaur) St. Martin's Pr.
Stone, Robert. Damascus Gate. l.t. ed. 1998. (Americana Ser.). 751p. 29.95 (0-7862-1632-8) Thorndike Pr.
Stuart, Francis. King David Dances. 1997. 62p. pap. 12.95 (1-874597-44-8) Dufour Editions, Inc.
Thoene, Bodie. A Daughter of Zion. (Zion Chronicles Ser.: Bk. 2). 336p. 1998. mass mkt. 6.99 o.p. (0-7642-2108-6, 202108); 1987. pap. 11.99 (0-87123-940-X) Bethany Hse. Pubs.
—Jerusalem's Heart, Vol. 3. abr. ed. 2001. (Zion Legacy Ser.: No. 3). 4p. 25.95 o.p. incl. audio (0-14-180275-8) Viking Penguin.
—The Key to Zion. 1988. (Zion Chronicles Ser.: Vol. 5). 352p. pap. 11.99 (1-55661-034-3) Bethany Hse. Pubs.
—Light in Zion. (Zion Chronicles Ser.: Bk. 4). 1998. 368p. pap. 6.99 (0-7642-2110-8, 202110); 1988. 352p. pap. 11.99 (0-87123-990-6) Bethany Hse. Pubs.
—The Silver Branch. 1987. (Zion Chronicles Ser.: Vol. 3). 352p. pap. 11.99 (0-87123-939-6) Bethany Hse. Pubs.

Thoene, Bodie & Thoene, Brock. A Daughter of Zion. l.t. ed. 1998. (Five Star Christian Fiction Ser.). 357p. 24.95 (*0-7862-1439-2*, Five Star) Gale Group.

—Jerusalem's Heart. 2002. (Zion Legacy Ser.: No. 3). 336p. pap. 13.00 (*0-14-200038-8*) Penguin Group (USA) Inc.

—Jerusalem's Hope, Vol. 6. 2002. (Illus.). 272p. 24.95 (*0-670-03084-8*, Viking) Viking Penguin.

Thoene, Brock & Thoene, Bodie. Jerusalem's Heart. l.t. ed. 2002. lib. bdg. 27.95 (*1-58547-134-8*, Premier) Ctr. Point Large Print.

—Jerusalem's Heart. 2001. (Zion Legacy Ser.: No. 3). 304p. 23.95 o.s.i (*0-670-89487-7*, Viking) Viking Penguin.

—Jerusalem's Hope. 2003. 272p. pap. 14.00 (*0-14-200357-3*) Penguin Group (USA) Inc.

Townsend, Sue. Ghost Children. 192p. 1999. pap. 12.00 (*1-56947-151-7*); 1998. 22.00 (*1-56947-117-7*) Soho Pr., Inc.

Tyberg, Sarah. El Al Hold That Flight. 1992. 10.95 o.p. (*0-87306-591-3*) Feldheim, Philipp Inc.

Uris, Leon. Mitla Pass. l.t. ed. 1990. (General Ser.). 615p. lib. bdg. 21.95 o.p. (*0-8161-4847-3*); 620p. pap. 13.95 o.p. (*0-8161-4871-6*) Gale Group. (Macmillan Reference USA).

Weisman, John. Blood Cries. 1987. 17.95 o.p. (*0-670-81381-8*) Viking Penguin.

West, Laurel. Beloved Dissident. 1999. 256p. pap. 12.99 (*1-880226-76-6*) Messianic Jewish Pubs.

Windsor, Mary L. & Windsor, Rudolph R. Deborah & Barak: A Historical Novel about Love, War & Spirituality in Ancient Israel. Windsor, Mary L., ed. 2001. (Illus.). 272p. (Orig.). pap. 12.95 (*0-9620881-4-5*) Windsor's Golden Series.

Wise, Robert L. All That Remains. 1995. 12.99 o.p. (*0-8407-6783-8*) Nelson, Thomas Inc.

Wouk, Herman. The Glory. 1995. 704p. mass mkt. 6.99 o.s.i (*0-316-95528-0*); 1995. pap. (*0-316-95530-2*); 1994. 704p. (gr. 8). 40.00 (*0-316-95525-6*); 1994. 685p. 125.00 o.p. (*0-316-95527-2*); 2002. 688p. reprint ed. pap. 15.95 (*0-316-95319-9*, Back Bay) Little Brown & Co.

—The Hope. unabr. ed. 1994. audio 74.95 (*1-55927-275-9*);Vol. 2. audio 74.95 (*1-55927-278-3*) Audio Renaissance.

—The Hope. 1995. mass mkt. (*0-316-99978-4*); 1994. 704p. mass mkt. 6.99 (*0-316-85257-0*); 1993. 693p. 24.95 o.s.i (*0-316-95519-1*); 1993. 693p. 125.00 o.p. (*0-316-95521-3*) Little Brown & Co.

Yakhlif, Yahya. A Lake Beyond the Wind. Jayyusi, M. & Tingley, C., trs. 1998. (Emerging Voices Ser.). 160p. pap. 12.95 (*1-56656-301-1*) Interlink Publishing Group, Inc.

Yehoshua, A. B. The Lover. Simpson, Philip, tr. 1978. 352p. 10.00 o.p. (*0-385-12134-2*) Doubleday Publishing.

—The Lover. Simpson, Philip, tr. 1993. (Harvest in Translation Ser.). 368p. pap. 14.00 (*0-15-653912-8*, Harvest Bks.) Harcourt Trade Pubs.

—The Lover. 1985. pap. 10.95 o.p. (*0-525-48400-0*); reprint ed. pap. 9.95 o.p. (*0-525-48163-X*) NAL. (Obelisk).

Zakon, Miriam S. The Cohens of Tzefat. 1985. (ArtScroll Youth Ser.). (Illus.). 128p. (YA). (gr. 6-12). 14.99 (*0-89906-783-2*) Mesorah Pubns., Ltd.

## ISTANBUL (TURKEY)—FICTION

Ali, Tariq. The Stone Woman. 2001. 288p. pap. 12.00 (*1-85984-364-6*) Verso.

—The Stone Woman: A Novel. 2000. (Islamic Quartet Ser.). 274p. 23.00 (*1-85984-764-1*) Verso.

Eco, Umberto. Baudolino. Weaver, William, tr. 2003. (Illus.). 544p. pap. 15.00 (*0-15-602906-5*, Harvest Bks.); 2002. 528p. 27.00 (*0-15-100690-3*) Harcourt Trade Pubs.

Falconer, Colin. The Sultan's Harem. 2004. 480p. 22.95 (*0-609-61030-9*) Crown Publishing Group.

Hill, Tobias. The Love of Stones. 2001. 400p. pap. (*0-571-19454-0*) Faber & Faber, Inc.

—The Love of Stones. 2002. 416p. 25.00 (*0-312-28773-9*) Picador.

—The Love of Stones: A Novel. 2003. 400p. pap. 14.00 (*0-312-31131-1*) Picador.

Ignatius, David. Siro. 1991. 448p. 19.95 o.p. (*0-374-26506-2*) Farrar, Straus & Giroux.

—Siro. 1993. 464p. pap. 4.99 (*0-380-71820-0*, Avon Bks.) Morrow/Avon.

—Siro, unabr. ed. 1991. audio 97.00 (*1-55690-479-7*, 91303E7) Recorded Bks., LLC.

Irwin, Robert. Prayer - Cushions of the Flesh. 1999. (Original Fiction in Paperback Ser.). 140p. pap. 11.99 (*1-873982-63-1*) Dedalus, Ltd.

Moody, Susan. Mosaic. 1992. 432p. mass mkt. 4.99 o.s.i (*0-440-21260-X*) Dell Publishing.

—Mosaic. l.t. ed. 1992. (General Ser.). 563p. lib. bdg. 21.95 o.p. (*0-8161-5367-1*, Macmillan Reference USA) Gale Group.

Pamuk, Orhan. The Black Book. Gun, Guneli, tr. 1994. 356p. 25.00 o.p. (*0-374-11394-7*) Farrar, Straus & Giroux.

—The Black Book. Gun, Guneli, tr. 1996. (Harvest in Translation Ser.). 408p. pap. 17.00 (*0-15-600329-5*, Harvest Bks.) Harcourt Trade Pubs.

—My Name Is Red. 2002. (Illus.). 432p. pap. 14.95 (*0-375-70685-2*, Vintage) Knopf Publishing Group.

—My Name Is Red. Goknar, Erdag, tr. from TUR. 2001. (Illus.). 448p. 26.95 (*0-375-40695-6*) Knopf, Alfred A. Inc.

Reed, Mary & Mayer, Eric. Four for a Boy: A John the Eunuch Mystery. 2003. (Illus.). 292p. 24.95 o.s.i (*1-59058-031-1*) Poisoned Pen Pr.

—Two for Joy. 2000. (Illus.). 345p. 24.95 (*1-890208-37-X*) Poisoned Pen Pr.

Sobin, Gustaf. In Pursuit of Vanishing a Star: A Novel. 2002. 192p. 23.95 (*0-393-04204-9*) Norton, W. W. & Co., Inc.

## ITALY—FICTION

Adler, Elizabeth A. Summer in Tuscany. l.t. ed. 2002. 425p. 30.95 (*1-58724-256-7*, Wheeler Publishing, Inc.) Gale Group.

—Summer in Tuscany. E-Book 23.95 (*0-312-70707-X*) St. Martin's Pr.

Alder, Elizabeth. A Summer in Tuscany. 2002. (Illus.). 304p. 23.95 o.s.i (*0-312-26996-X*) St. Martin's Pr.

Alexander, Alfred, ed. & intro. Stories of Sicily. 1975. 208p. 10.95 o.p. (*0-8052-3592-2*, Schocken) Knopf Publishing Group.

Alexander, Sidney. The Hand of Michelangelo. 1966. 693p. reprint ed. pap. 15.95 o.p. (*0-8214-0235-8*) Ohio Univ. Pr.

—Michelangelo the Florentine. 1985. 464p. pap. 17.95 o.p. (*0-8214-0236-6*) Ohio Univ. Pr.

Alhadeff, Gini. Diary of a Djinn: A Novel. 2004. 224p. pap. 13.00 (*1-4000-3461-2*, Anchor) Knopf Publishing Group.

—Diary of a Djinn: Novel. 2003. 224p. 22.00 (*0-375-40234-9*, Pantheon) Knopf Publishing Group.

Allen, Nancy Campbell. Echoes. 2001. 262p. 14.95 (*1-57734-813-3*) Covenant Communications.

Alvarez, Corwyn. The Conversion. 2000. 107p. 15.95 (*1-56167-567-9*) Noble Hse.

Ammaniti, NiccolÓ. I'm Not Scared. Hunt, Jonathan, tr. from ITA. 2003. Tr. of Io non ho paura. 144p. pap. 23.00 (*1-84195-297-4*) Canongate Bks. GBR. *Dist:* Publishers Group West.

—I'm Not Scared. Hunt, Jonathan, tr. from ITA. 2004. Tr. of Io non ho paura. 208p. pap. 10.00 (*1-4000-7563-7*, Anchor) Knopf Publishing Group.

Antonioni, Michelangelo. That Bowling Alley on the Tiber: Tales of a Director. Arrowsmith, William, tr. from ITA. & intro. by. 208p. 1987. pap. 8.95 o.p. (*0-19-504224-7*); 1986. 22.95 o.p. (*0-19-503676-X*) Oxford Univ. Pr., Inc.

Ardizzone, Tony. In the Garden of Papa Santuzzu. 2000. 352p. pap. 14.00 (*0-312-26341-4*); 1999. 368p. 24.00 o.p. (*0-312-20307-1*) Picador.

Armanno, Venero. The Volcano. 2001. (Illus.). 677p. (*1-74051-053-4*) Knopf, Alfred A. Inc.

Astor, William Waldorf. Valentino. 2000. 252p. E-Book 3.95 (*0-594-01839-0*) 1873 Pr.

Atzeni, Sergio. Bakunin's Son. Rugman, John H., tr. from ITA. 1996. 100p. (Orig.). pap. 11.00 (*0-934977-44-5*) Italica Pr.

Balestrini, Nanni. The Unseen. Heron, Liz, tr. from ITA. 1989. 272p. 18.95 o.p. (*0-86091-242-6*, A3312) Verso.

Banti, Anna. Artemisia. Caracciolo, Shirley D., tr. 1988. (European Women Writers Ser.). viii, 219p. text 30.00 o.p. (*0-8032-1203-8*) Univ. of Nebraska Pr.

Banville, John. Shroud. 2004. 272p. pap. 13.00 (*0-375-72530-X*, Vintage) Knopf Publishing Group.

—Shroud. 2003. 272p. 25.00 (*0-375-41130-5*) Knopf, Alfred A. Inc.

—Shroud. l.t. ed. 2003. 408p. 28.95 (*0-7862-5748-2*) Thorndike Pr.

Barolini, Helen. More Italian Hours & Other Stories. 2001. (VIA Folios Ser.: Vol. 28). 176p. (C). per. (*1-884419-48-8*, VIA Folios) Bordighera, Inc.

—Umbertina. 1983. audio 13.95 (*1-55644-064-2*, 3021) American Audio Prose Library, Inc.

—Umbertina. 1989. 432p. (C). reprint ed. pap. 12.95 (*0-88143-107-9*) Ayer Co. Pubs., Inc.

—Umbertina. 1985. 448p. pap. 2.75 o.p. (*0-553-13817-0*) Bantam Bks.

Barolini, Helena. Umbertina. 1998. 464p. 35.00 (*1-55861-204-1*); pap. 18.95 (*1-55861-205-X*) Feminist Pr. at The City Univ. of New York.

Bassani, Giorgio. Five Stories of Ferrara. 1971. (Helen & Kurt Wolff Bk.). 216p. 5.95 o.p. (*0-15-131400-4*) Harcourt Trade Pubs.

Bayer, William. Wallflower. 1992. mass mkt. 5.99 o.s.i (*0-515-10843-X*, Jove) Berkley Publishing Group.

—Wallflower. 1993. 3.99 o.p. (*0-517-10959-X*) Random Hse. Value Publishing.

Bellorci, Maria. Private Renaissance: A Novel. Weaver, William, ed. 1989. 400p. 24.95 o.p. (*0-688-08188-6*, Morrow, William & Co.) Morrow/Avon.

Berger, John. G. 1992. (Vintage International Ser.). 336p. pap. 15.00 (*0-679-73654-9*, Vintage) Knopf Publishing Group.

—G. A Novel. 1991. pap. 11.00 o.p. (*0-394-73654-0*, Pantheon) Knopf Publishing Group.

Bernardi, Adria. The Day Laid on the Altar. 2000. (Middlebury/Bread Loaf Book Ser.). (Illus.). 220p. 29.95 (*1-58465-044-3*) Univ. Pr. of New England.

—The Day Laid on the Altar: A Novel. 2001. 224p. pap. 13.00 (*0-452-28257-8*, Plume) Dutton/Plume.

Bernhard, Thomas. Extinction. McClintock, David, tr. 1996. (Phoenix Fiction Ser.). 336p. pap. 15.00 (*0-226-04383-5*) Univ. of Chicago Pr.

—Voice Imitator. 1998. 104p. pap. 10.00 (*0-226-04402-5*) Univ. of Chicago Pr.

Berry, R. M. Leonardo's Horse. 1997. (Illus.). 317p. (Orig.). pap. 13.95 (*1-57366-031-0*) Fiction Collective Two, Inc.

Berto, Giuseppe. Sky Is Red. Davidson, Angus, tr. from ITA. 1971. 397p. reprint ed. 89.95 (*0-8371-5774-9*, BESR, Greenwood Pr.) Greenwood Publishing Group, Inc.

Bevilacqua, Alberto. Califfe. 2001. 240p. 18.00 (*88-7301-436-4*) Gremese International ITA. *Dist:* National Bk. Network.

Bhabra, Hargurchet S. Gestures. 288p. 1987. pap. 6.95 o.p. (*0-14-009265-X*, Penguin Bks.); 1986. 16.95 o.p. (*0-670-80980-2*) Viking Penguin.

Bianchini, Angela. The Edge of Europe. Jeannet, Angela M. & Castronuovo, David, trs. from ITA. 2000. (European Women Writers Ser.). 145p. pap. 15.00 (*0-8032-6171-3*, Bison Bks.); text 50.00 (*0-8032-1308-5*) Univ. of Nebraska Pr.

Biggins, John. Two-Headed Eagle. 1996. 368p. 24.95 o.p. (*0-312-14751-1*) St. Martin's Pr.

Bocelli, Andrea. The Music of Silence. l.t. ed. 2002. (Thorndike Press Large Print Biography Ser.). 400p. 29.45 (*0-7862-3900-X*) Gale Group.

—The Music of Silence. 2000. pap. 13.00 (*0-06-093749-1*) HarperCollins Pubs.

—The Music of Silence. 2001. (Illus.). 256p. 25.00 (*0-06-621286-3*, HarperEntertainment) Morrow/Avon.

Bortolussi, Stefano. Head above Water. 2003. (City Lights Italian Voices Ser.). 128p. (Orig.). pap. 11.95 (*0-87286-426-X*) City Lights Bks.

Bowen, Elizabeth. The Hotel. 1972. 294p. reprint ed. lib. bdg. 15.50 o.p. (*0-8371-4685-2*, BOHO) Greenwood Publishing Group, Inc.

—The Hotel. 1996. (Penguin Twentieth-Century Classics Ser.). 176p. pap. 11.95 o.p. (*0-14-018302-7*, Penguin Classics) Viking Penguin.

Bowen, Marjorie. The Viper of Milan. 2000. 252p. E-Book 3.95 (*0-594-01895-1*) 1873 Pr.

—The Viper of Milan. 1963. pap. 1.25 o.p. (*0-14-047018-2*, Puffin Bks.) Penguin Putnam Bks. for Young Readers.

Bradberry, James. The Seventh Sacrament. 1994. 208p. 19.95 o.p. (*0-312-11059-6*, Saint Martin's Minotaur); Vol. 1. 1995. (Seventh Sacrament Ser.: Vol. 1). 209p. mass mkt. 4.99 (*0-312-95636-3*, St. Martin's Paperbacks) St. Martin's Pr.

Brodkey, Harold. Profane Friendship. 1994. 387p. 23.00 o.p. (*0-374-23544-9*) Farrar, Straus & Giroux.

—Profane Friendship. 1995. 400p. reprint ed. pap. 14.00 o.p. (*1-56279-071-4*) Mercury Hse.

Brooke, Gabriella. The Words of Bernfrieda: A Chronicle of Hauteville. 2002. 258p. reprint ed. per. 18.95 (*0-9719988-0-9*, Malgari Pr.) Brooke, Gabriella.

—The Words of Bernfrieda: A Chronicle of Hauteville. 1998. (Illus.). 258p. (*0-910055-50-5*); 304p. pap. 18.95 (*0-910055-49-1*) Eastern Washington Univ. Pr.

Broughton, T. Alan. Suicidal Tendencies: Stories. 2003. (Series in Contemporary Fiction). 311p. 23.95 (*1-885635-05-2*) Ctr. for Literary Publishing, Colorado State Univ.

—Winter Journey. 1985. 10.95 o.p. (*0-525-23515-9*, Dutton) Dutton/Plume.

Browne, Marshall. Inspector Anders & the Ship of Fools. 2002. 272p. 23.95 (*0-312-27821-7*, Saint Martin's Minotaur) St. Martin's Pr.

—The Wooden Leg of Inspector Anders. 2002. 240p. pap. 12.95 (*0-312-29149-3*, Saint Martin's Griffin); 2001. 256p. 23.95 (*0-312-27838-1*, Saint Martin's Minotaur) St. Martin's Pr.

Buchan, James. Davy Chadwick. 1988. 16.95 o.s.i (*0-689-11995-X*, Scribner) Simon & Schuster.

—Davy Chadwick. l.t. ed. 1990. (Ulverscroft Large Print Ser.). 29.99 o.p. (*0-7089-2150-7*, Ulverscroft) Thorpe, F. A. Pubs. GBR. *Dist:* Ulverscroft Large Print Bks., Ltd., Ulverscroft Large Print Canada, Ltd.

Bufalino, Gesualdo. The Plague-Sower. Sartarelli, Stephen, tr. from ITA. 1988. 186p. 22.00 o.p. (*0-941419-12-6*); pap. 13.00 (*0-941419-13-4*) Marsilio Pubs. (Eridanos Library).

Burns, John Horne. The Gallery. 1985. pap. 6.95 o.p. (*0-87795-709-6*, Morrow, William & Co.); 1984. pap. 2.25 o.p. (*0-380-01667-2*, 33357-0, Avon Bks.) Morrow/Avon.

—The Gallery. 2004. (New York Review Books Classics Ser.). 392p. pap. 14.95 (*1-59017-080-6*) New York Review of Bks., Inc., The.

Caldwell, Joseph. The Uncle from Rome. 1992. 304p. 22.00 o.p. (*0-670-84058-0*, Viking) Viking Penguin.

Calvino, Italo. The Castle of Crossed Destinies. Weaver, William, tr. 1979. (Harvest Book Ser.). 144p. pap. 14.00 (*0-15-615455-2*, Harvest Bks.) Harcourt Trade Pubs.

—The Castle of Crossed Destinies. 1979. (Helen & Kurt Wolff Bk.). (Illus.). reprint ed. 10.00 o.p. (*0-15-115998-X*) Harcourt Trade Pubs.

—Marcovaldo: Or the Seasons in the City, Level B. (ITA.). pap. 8.95 (*0-88436-993-5*, 55264) EMC/Paradigm Publishing.

—Marcovaldo: Or the Seasons in the City. Weaver, William, tr. from ITA. 1983. (Helen & Kurt Wolff Bk.). 128p. pap. 12.00 (*0-15-657204-4*, Harvest Bks.); 121p. reprint ed. 9.95 o.p. (*0-15-157081-7*) Harcourt Trade Pubs.

—The Path to the Spiders' Nests. rev. ed. 2000. Orig. Title: The Path to the Nest of Spiders. 192p. pap. 12.00 (*0-06-095658-5*, Ecco) HarperTrade.

—The Path to the Spiders' Nests. McLaughlin, Martin, ed. Colquhoun, Archibald, tr. from ITA. rev. ed. 1998. Orig. Title: The Path to the Nest of Spiders. 192p. o.p. (*0-88001-621-3*, Ecco) HarperTrade.

—T-Zero. Weaver, William, tr. 1976. (Harbrace Paperbound Library: Vol. 70). 168p. pap. 10.00 (*0-15-692400-5*, Harvest Bks.) Harcourt Trade Pubs.

—Under the Jaguar Sun. Weaver, William, tr. 96p. 1990. pap. 12.00 (*0-15-692794-2*, Harvest Bks.); 1988. 12.95 (*0-15-192820-7*) Harcourt Trade Pubs.

—The Watcher & Other Stories. Weaver, William & Colquhoun, Archibald, trs. from ITA. 1975. (Harbrace Paperbound Library). 192p. pap. 10.00 (*0-15-694952-0*, Harvest Bks.) Harcourt Trade Pubs.

Camilleri, Andrea. The Shape of Water: A Salvo Montalbano Mystery. Sartarelli, Stephen, tr. 2002. 208p. 5.99 (*0-14-200239-9*); (Illus.). 176p. text 19.95 o.s.i (*0-670-03092-9*, Viking) Viking Penguin.

—Terra Cotta Dog: An Inspector Montalbano Mystery. 2003. 208p. mass mkt. 5.99 (*0-14-200263-1*) Penguin Group (USA) Inc.

Camon, Ferdinando. Life Everlasting. Shepley, John, tr. from ITA. 1987. 192p. 29.95 (*0-910395-31-4*); pap. 10.95 (*0-910395-32-2*) Marlboro Pr., Inc., The.

Caponegro, Mary. 5 Doubts. 1998. 152p. 19.95 (*1-56886-059-5*) Marsilio Pubs.

Carcaterra, Lorenzo. Street Boys. 2003. 352p. mass mkt. 7.99 (*0-345-41099-8*); 2002. 336p. 25.95 (*0-345-41096-3*, Ballantine Bks.); 2002. E-Book 20.95 (*0-345-46180-0*, Ballantine Bks.) Ballantine Bks.

—Street Boys. 2002. (Basic Ser.). 30.95 (*0-7862-4863-7*) Thorndike Pr.

Cardella, Lara. Good Girls Don't Wear Trousers. Di Carcaci, Diana, tr. from ITA. 1994. 128p. 16.95 (*1-55970-263-X*) Arcade Publishing, Inc.

Caroselli, Marlene. The Boy Who Braved the Mountains. 2003. 128p. pap. 17.95 (*1-59129-951-9*) PublishAmerica, Inc.

Cartland, Barbara. A Kiss in Rome. l.t. ed. 2001. (G. K. Hall Paperback Ser.). 163p. pap. 23.95 (*0-7838-9442-2*, Macmillan Reference USA) Gale Group.

Case, John. The Genesis Code. 1998. 480p. mass mkt. 7.99 (*0-345-42231-7*) Ballantine Bks.

—The Genesis Code. abr. ed. 1998. 3p. audio 7.99 o.p. (*1-56740-241-0*, 655, Paperback Nova Audio Bks.); 1997. audio 27.95 o.p. (*1-56100-753-6*, 121, Bookcassette); 1997. audio 105.25 o.p. (*1-56100-828-1*, 880, Unabridged Library Editions) Brilliance Audio.

—The Genesis Code. l.t. ed. 1997. (Basic Ser.). 761p. 26.95 o.p. (*0-7862-1205-5*) Thorndike Pr.

Caso, Adolph. The Straw Obelisk. 1995. (Illus.). 390p. 24.95 (*0-8283-2005-5*) Branden Bks.

—Straw Obelisk. 1972. 6.95 o.s.i (*0-8283-1293-1*) Branden Bks.

Castellani, Christopher. A Kiss from Maddalena. 2003. 352p. tchr. ed. 23.95 (*1-56512-389-1*, 72389) Algonquin Bks. of Chapel Hill.

—A Kiss from Maddalena. 2004. 352p. pap. 13.00 (*0-425-19642-9*) Berkley Publishing Group.

Cate, Nathan. Sanctuary of the Gods. 2000. 388p. pap. (*1-55212-447-9*) Trafford Publishing.

Cherne, Barbara. Bella Donna: A Renaissance Mystery Novel. 2001. 160p. pap. 10.95 (*1-56474-362-4*) Fithian Pr.

Chiarella, Peter. Calabrian Tales: A Memoir of 19th Century Southern Italy. 2002. (Illus.). 380p. pap. 20.00 (*1-58790-030-0*) Regent Pr.

Christmas, Joyce. Forged in Blood: A Lady Margaret Priam/Betty Trenka Mystery. 2002. 277p. (*0-7540-8849-9*) Thorndike Pr.

Cipriani, Harry. Heloise & Bellinis. 1991. 160p. 17.95 o.s.i (*1-55970-144-7*) Arcade Publishing, Inc.

Coffman, Elaine. The Italian. 2002. 448p. mass mkt. (*1-55166-946-3*, Mira Bks.) Harlequin Enterprises, Ltd.

Coleman, Jane Candia. The Italian Quartet. 2001. (Five Star First Edition Women's Fiction Ser.). 197p. 25.95 (*0-7862-3379-6*, Five Star) Gale Group.

Collin, Richard O. Contessa. 1994. 496p. 25.95 o.p. (*0-312-09773-5*) St. Martin's Pr.

Collins, Wilkie. The Haunted Hotel, Set. 1990. audio 29.95 (*1-55685-174-X*) Audio Bk. Contractors, Inc.

—The Haunted Hotel. unabr. collector's ed. 1984. (J). audio 42.00 (*0-7366-3899-7*, 9131) Books on Tape, Inc.

—The Haunted Hotel. 1982. (Mystery Ser.). 127p. reprint ed. pap. 6.95 (*0-486-24333-8*) Dover Pubns., Inc.

—The Haunted Hotel. 2002. 192p. 94.99 (*1-4043-0806-7*); per. 89.99 (*1-4043-0807-5*) IndyPublish-.com.

—The Haunted Hotel. unabr. ed. 1984. (J). audio 28.00 Jimcin Recordings.

—The Haunted Hotel. (Ebook Classic Ser.). E-Book 5.00 (*0-7410-0799-1*) SoftBook Pr.

—The Haunted Hotel. 2002. 228p. pap. 19.95 (*1-58715-690-3*); lib. bdg. 29.95 (*1-58715-691-1*) Wildside Pr.

—The Haunted Hotel: And My Lady's Money. (Works of Wilkie Collins: Vol. 22). 477p. reprint ed. 2001. pap. text 28.00 (*0-7426-5043-X*); 1999. lib. bdg. 98.00 (*1-58201-043-9*) Classic Bks.

Conroy, Pat. Beach Music. 1996. (Illus.). 816p. reprint ed. mass mkt. 7.99 (*0-553-57457-4*) Bantam Bks.

—Beach Music, 2 Pts. unabr. ed. 1995. audio 152.00 (*0-7366-3080-5*, 3761A/B); audio 72.00. audio 80.00 Books on Tape, Inc.

—Beach Music. 1995. 640p. 32.50 (*0-385-41304-1*, Talese, Nan A.); 628p. 200.00 o.s.i (*0-385-47590-X*) Doubleday Publishing.

—Beach Music. abr. ed. 1995. audio 29.95 (*0-553-47270-4*, 892989); audio 27.50 o.s.i (*0-553-74619-7*) Random Hse. Audio Publishing Group. (RH Audio).

—Beach Music. unabr. ed. audio 158.00 (*0-7887-0335-8*, 94527E7) Recorded Bks., LLC.

—Beach Music. 628p. pap. 8.98 o.p. (*0-7651-0633-7*) Smithmark Pubs., Inc.

—Beach Music. 1996. 14.04 (*0-606-11096-8*) Turtle-back Bks.

Cooney, John. Acts of Contrition. 1994. 416p. mass mkt. 5.99 (*0-671-78316-5*, Pocket) Simon & Schuster.

Coover, Robert. Pinocchio in Venice. 1997. 336p. reprint ed. pap. 13.50 (*0-8021-3485-8*, Grove Pr.) Grove/Atlantic, Inc.

—Pinocchio in Venice. 1991. 336p. 19.95 o.p. (*0-671-64471-8*, Simon & Schuster) Simon & Schuster.

Corti, Maria. Otranto. Bright, Jessie, tr. from ITA. 1993. 288p. (Orig.). pap. 12.50 (*0-934977-29-1*) Italica Pr.

Corvo, Baron, pseud. The Desire & Pursuit of the Whole: A Romance of Modern Venice. 1986. (Quality Paperbacks Ser.). 316p. reprint ed. pap. text 10.00 o.p. (*0-306-80258-9*) Da Capo Pr., Inc.

Costantini, Costanzo. Bird of Paradise: A Novel. 2000. 160p. 18.00 (*88-7301-403-8*) Gremese International ITA. *Dist:* National Bk. Network.

Coulter, Catherine. Devil's Embrace. l.t. ed. 2000. (Romance Ser.). 542p. 27.95 (*1-56895-145-0*, Wheeler Publishing, Inc.) Gale Group.

—Devil's Embrace. 2000. 416p. mass mkt. 7.99 (*0-451-20026-8*, Signet Bks.); 1985. 384p. mass mkt. 7.50 o.s.i (*0-451-14198-9*, Onyx); 1982. mass mkt. 3.50 o.p. (*0-451-11853-7*, Signet Bks.) NAL.

Cowan, James. A Mapmaker's Dream: The Meditations of Fra Mauro, Cartographer to the Court of Venice. 1996. 208p. 18.00 o.p. (*1-57062-196-9*) Shambhala Pubns., Inc.

—A Mapmaker's Dream: The Meditations of Fra Mauro, Cartographer to the Court of Venice. 1997. 176p. pap. 10.99 o.s.i (*0-446-67338-2*) Warner Bks., Inc.

Craig, Amanda. Love in Idleness. novel ed. 2003. 352p. 23.95 (*0-385-50776-3*) Doubleday Publishing.

—Love in Idleness. 2004. 352p. pap. 14.00 (*1-4000-3107-9*, Anchor) Knopf Publishing Group.

Crane, Teresa. Italian House. 1996. 304p. 21.95 o.p. (*0-312-13992-6*) St. Martin's Pr.

—The Italian House. unabr. ed. 1996. audio 54.95 (*0-7451-6634-2*, CAB 1250) BBC Audiobooks America.

Crawford, F. Marion. Marietta: A Maid of Venice. rev. ed. 2000. 376p. E-Book 3.95 (*0-594-02055-7*) 1873 Pr.

—Marietta: A Maid of Venice. collector's ed. 2002. (Illus.). im. lthr. 38.85 (*1-4115-1226-X*); pap. 19.95 (*1-4115-0483-6*); 25.95 (*1-4115-0848-3*); pap. 17.95 (*1-4115-0261-2*) Polyglot Pr., Inc.

—Marietta: A Maid of Venice. 1990. (Works of Francis Marion Crawford). reprint ed. lib. bdg. 79.00 (*0-7812-2552-3*) Reprint Services Corp.

—Pietro Ghisleri. 2000. 252p. E-Book 3.95 (*0-594-06353-1*) 1873 Pr.

Crespi, Camilla T. The Trouble with Going Home. 1996. 224p. mass mkt. 4.99 o.s.i (*0-06-109153-7*) HarperCollins Pubs.

—The Trouble with Going Home. 1994. 288p. 20.00 o.p. (*0-06-017725-X*) HarperTrade.

Cusumano, Camille. The Last Cannoli: A Novel: A Sicilian American Family Comes of Age Through the Ancient Power of Storytelling. 1999. (Illus.). 237p. per. (*1-881901-20-3*) LEGAS.

Damioli, Carol. Rogue Angel - A Novel of Fra Pilippo Lippi. Caso, Adolph, ed. 1994. (Illus.). 248p. reprint ed. text 21.95 (*0-937832-33-2*) Branden Bks.

Dann, Jack. The Memory Cathedral: A Secret History of Leonardo da Vinci. 1995. 512p. 22.95 o.s.i (*0-553-09637-0*); 1996. 508p. reprint ed. pap. 27.00 (*0-553-37857-0*) Bantam Bks.

D'Annunzio, Gabriele. Nocturne & Five Tales of Love & Death. Rosenthal, Raymond, tr. from ITA. 1988. 29.95 (*0-910395-40-3*); pap. 13.00 (*0-910395-41-1*) Marlboro Pr., Inc., The.

Davis, Genevieve. A Passion in the Blood. 1980. pap. 1.95 o.p. (*0-523-40255-4*, Pinnacle Bks.) Kensington Publishing Corp.

—A Passion in the Blood. 1977. 9.95 o.s.i (*0-671-02249-0*) Simon & Schuster.

De Amicis, Edmondo. Coure: The Heart of a Boy. 1986. 253p. 30.00 o.p. (*0-7206-0657-8*) Owen, Peter Ltd. GBR. *Dist:* Dufour Editions, Inc.

De Prada, Juan Manuel. Tempest. 2003. 341p. 24.95 (*1-58567-387-0*) Overlook Pr., The.

De Wohl, Louis. Citadel of God: A Novel about Saint Benedict. 1987. 345p. pap. 14.95 (*0-89870-404-9*) Ignatius Pr.

Defirenze, Rina. Mystery of the Mona Lisa: Leonardo Da Vinci's Greatest Painting. 1996. 354p. 22.95 o.p. (*0-8038-9381-7*) Hastings Hse. Daytrips Pubs.

Deledda, Grazia. Cosima. 1988. 153p. (Orig.). pap. 12.50 (*0-934977-06-2*) Italica Pr.

Dessaix, Robert. Night Letters: A Journey Through Switzerland & Italy. 1999. 276p. pap. 13.00 o.s.i (*0-312-19939-2*) Picador.

—Night Letters: A Journey Through Switzerland & Italy. 1997. 276p. 22.95 (*0-312-16950-7*) St. Martin's Pr.

Dibdin, Michael. Blood Rain: An Aurelio Zen Mystery. 2000. (Aurelio Zen Mystery Ser.: Vol. 7). 288p. 23.00 o.s.i (*0-375-40915-7*, Pantheon) Knopf Publishing Group.

—Cabal. 2000. (Aurelio Zen Mystery Ser.). 256p. pap. 12.00 (*0-375-70770-0*, Vintage) Knopf Publishing Group.

—Cosi Fan Tutti. 1996. 332p. o.p. (*0-571-17920-7*) Faber & Faber Ltd.

—Cosi Fan Tutti: An Aurelio Zen Mystery. 1998. 256p. pap. 12.00 (*0-679-77911-6*, Vintage) Knopf Publishing Group.

—Cosi Fan Tutti: An Aurelio Zen Mystery. l.t. ed. 1997. (Cloak & Dagger Ser.). 423p. 25.95 (*0-7862-1244-6*) Thorndike Pr.

—Dead Lagoon: An Aurelio Zen Mystery. 1996. 320p. pap. 13.00 (*0-679-75311-7*) Random Hse., Inc.

—A Long Finish: An Aurelio Zen Mystery. 2000. (Aurelio Zen Mystery Ser.). 272p. pap. 12.00 (*0-375-70401-9*, Vintage) Knopf Publishing Group.

—A Long Finish: An Aurelio Zen Mystery. l.t. ed. 1999. (Mystery Ser.). 408p. 27.95 (*0-7862-1762-6*) Thorndike Pr.

—Medusa: An Aurelio Zen Mystery. 2004. 288p. (*0-385-66035-9*) Doubleday Canada, Ltd. CAN. *Dist:* Random Hse., Inc.

—Medusa: An Aurelio Zen Mystery. 2004. 272p. 23.00 (*0-375-42269-2*, Pantheon) Knopf Publishing Group.

—Ratking. 1997. 272p. pap. 12.00 (*0-679-76854-8*, Vintage) Knopf Publishing Group.

—A Rich Full Death. 1999. 208p. pap. 12.00 (*0-375-70614-3*, Vintage) Knopf Publishing Group.

—Vendetta. 1993. 304p. mass mkt. 4.99 o.s.i (*0-553-29639-6*) Bantam Bks.

—Vendetta: An Aurelio Zen Mystery. 1998. (Aurelio Zen Mystery Ser.). 272p. pap. 12.00 (*0-679-76853-X*, Vintage) Knopf Publishing Group.

DiFonte, Ugo. The Foodtaster. Elbling, Peter, tr. from ITA. 2002. 284p. 28.00 (*1-57962-047-7*) Permanent Pr., The.

Donachie, David. The Dying Trade Book #2: Privateersman Mysteries. 2001. (Privateersman Mysteries Ser.: Vol. 2). 384p. pap. 16.95 (*1-59013-006-5*) McBooks Pr., Inc.

—Tested by Fate. 2004. (Nelson & Emma Trilogy Ser.: Vol. 2). 416p. pap. 17.95 (*1-59013-042-1*) McBooks Pr., Inc.

Dowling, Gregory. Every Picture Tells a Story. 1991. 22.95 o.p. (*0-312-05815-2*, Saint Martin's Minotaur) St. Martin's Pr.

—A Nice Steady Job. 1994. 296p. 20.95 o.p. (*0-312-11035-9*, Saint Martin's Minotaur) St. Martin's Pr.

—See Naples & Kill. 1988. 256p. 15.95 o.p. (*0-312-02277-8*, Saint Martin's Minotaur) St. Martin's Pr.

Drake, Shannon. Deep Midnight. l.t. ed. 2002. (Thorndike Romance Ser.). 616p. 29.95 (*0-7862-3908-5*) Gale Group.

—Deep Midnight. 2001. 480p. mass mkt. 3.99 (*0-8217-7739-4*, Zebra Bks.); mass mkt. 6.99 (*0-8217-6837-9*) Kensington Publishing Corp.

Dunant, Sarah. The Birth of Venus: A Novel. 2003. 412p. (*0-316-72549-8*) Little Brown & Co.

—The Birth of Venus: A Novel. 2004. 416p. 21.95 (*1-4000-6073-7*) Random Hse., Inc.

—Mapping the Edge: A Novel. 2002. 320p. pap. 12.95 (*0-375-75861-5*) Random House Adult Trade Publishing Group.

Dunham, Mikel. Casting for Murder. 1992. 320p. 18.95 o.p. (*0-312-06924-3*, Saint Martin's Minotaur) St. Martin's Pr.

Dunnett, Dorothy. Race of Scorpions: Third Book of the House of Niccolo. 1999. (House of Niccolo Ser.: Vol. III). (Illus.). 560p. pap. 15.00 (*0-375-70479-5*, Vintage) Knopf Publishing Group.

Duranti, Francesca. Happy Ending. 1992. 3.99 o.p. (*0-517-09105-4*) Random Hse. Value Publishing.

Eco, Umberto. The Name of the Rose. abr. ed. 1995. audio 24.95 (*1-55927-361-5*, 693211) Audio Renaissance.

—The Name of the Rose. unabr. ed. 1996. audio 112.00 (*0-7366-3259-X*, 3916) Books on Tape, Inc.

—The Name of the Rose. 1994. reprint ed. lib. bdg. 29.95 (*1-56849-544-7*) Buccaneer Bks., Inc.

—The Name of the Rose. l.t. ed. 1984. 9.95 o.p. (*0-8161-3695-5*, Macmillan Reference USA) Gale Group.

—The Name of the Rose. Weaver, William, tr. l.t. ed. 1984. (General Ser.). 16.95 o.p. (*0-8161-3663-7*, Macmillan Reference USA) Gale Group.

—The Name of the Rose. 1995. pap. 10.95 (*0-15-600370-8*) Harcourt Trade Pubs.

—The Name of the Rose. Weaver, William, tr. 1995. 29.95 (*0-15-100213-4*); 1994. (Illus.). 552p. pap. 15.00 (*0-15-600131-4*, Harvest Bks.); 1983. 512p. 35.00 (*0-15-144647-4*) Harcourt Trade Pubs.

—The Name of the Rose. 640p. 1988. mass mkt. 6.99 (*0-446-35720-0*); 4th ed. 1986. mass mkt. 4.95 (*0-446-34410-9*) Warner Bks., Inc.

Elbling, Peter. The Food Taster: A Novel. 2003. 272p. reprint ed. pap. 13.00 (*0-452-28434-1*, Plume) Dutton/Plume.

Eliot, George. Romola. unabr. ed. 1997. audio 95.95 (*1-55685-453-6*, 453-6) Audio Bk. Contractors, Inc.

—Romola. unabr. ed. 1999. audio 99.95 (*0-7861-1287-5*, 2186) Blackstone Audio Bks., Inc.

—Romola. (Writings of George Eliot Ser.: Vol. 8). 400p. reprint ed. Pt. 1. 2001. pap. text 28.00 (*0-7426-5075-8*); Pt. 1. 1999. lib. bdg. 88.00 (*1-58201-075-7*); Pt. 2. 2001. pap. text 28.00 (*0-7426-5076-6*); Pt. 2. 1999. lib. bdg. 88.00 (*1-58201-076-5*) Classic Bks.

—Romola, 2 vols. 2000. (Cloth Bound Pocket Ser.). 14.95 (*3-8290-5386-X*, 522079) Konemann.

—Romola. Brown, Andrew, ed. & intro. by. 1998. (Oxford World's Classics Ser.). 656p. pap. 11.95 (*0-19-283568-8*) Oxford Univ. Pr., Inc.

—Romola. 1994. (Oxford World's Classics Ser.). 652p. pap. 7.95 o.p. (*0-19-282964-5*) Oxford Univ. Pr., Inc.

—Romola. Brown, Andrew, ed. 1993. 774p. 160.00 o.p. (*0-19-812594-1*, Clarendon Press) Oxford Univ. Pr., Inc.

—Romola. 1968. (Oxford World's Classics Ser.: No. 178). 16.95 o.p. (*0-19-250178-X*) Oxford Univ. Pr., Inc.

—Romola. 2003. 656p. pap. 11.95 (*0-375-76121-7*, Modern Library) Random House Adult Trade Publishing Group.

—Romola. 1999. (Everyman Paperback Classics Ser.). 720p. mass mkt. 8.95 o.p. (*0-460-87563-9*) Tuttle Publishing.

—Romola. Barrett, Dorothea, ed. & intro. by. 1997. (Classics Ser.). 688p. 12.00 (*0-14-043470-4*, Penguin Classics) Viking Penguin.

—Romola. Sanders, Andrew, ed. 1980. (English Library). 736p. pap. 8.95 o.p. (*0-14-043139-X*, Penguin Classics) Viking Penguin.

Elkann, Alain. Misguided Lives. 1989. 18.95 o.p. (*0-87113-295-8*) Grove/Atlantic, Inc.

Ellis, Julie. The Italian Affair, Set. unabr. ed. 1999. audio 54.95 (*0-7927-2308-2*, CSL197, Chivers Sound Library) BBC Audiobooks America.

—The Italian Affair. l.t. ed. 1998. 25.95 o.p. (*0-7838-0388-5*, Macmillan Reference USA) Gale Group.

—The Italian Affair. 1998. 192p. 24.00 (*0-7278-5348-1*) Severn Hse. Pubs., Ltd.

Ennis, Michael. Duchess of Milan. 1993. 576p. reprint ed. mass mkt. 5.99 o.s.i (*0-451-40428-9*, Signet Bks.) NAL.

—Duchess of Milan. 1999. pap. 9.00 (*0-14-014799-3*); 1992. (Illus.). 592p. 22.50 o.p. (*0-670-83783-0*) Viking Penguin. (Viking).

Enright, Rosemary. Isobel. 1995. mass mkt. 5.99 o.s.i (*0-8041-1314-9*, Ivy Bks.) Ballantine Bks.

—Isobel. 1994. 464p. 23.95 o.p. (*0-312-11063-4*) St. Martin's Pr.

Evans, Richard Paul. The Last Promise. 2002. 304p. 22.95 (*0-525-94696-9*) Dutton/Plume.

—The Last Promise. l.t. ed. 2003. (Wheeler Romance Ser.). 32.95 (*1-58724-375-X*, Wheeler Publishing, Inc.) Gale Group.

—The Last Promise. 2003. mass mkt. 6.99 (*0-451-41092-0*); 320p. mass mkt. 6.99 (*0-451-21101-4*) NAL. (Signet Bks.).

Eyre, Elizabeth. Axe for an Abbot: An Italian Renaissance Whodunnit. 1996. 320p. 23.95 o.p. (*0-312-13925-X*, Saint Martin's Minotaur) St. Martin's Pr.

—Bravo for the Bride. 1995. 192p. 21.95 o.p. (*0-312-11756-6*, Saint Martin's Minotaur) St. Martin's Pr.

—Curtains for the Cardinal. 1994. 256p. mass mkt. 4.99 o.p. (*0-425-14126-8*) Berkley Publishing Group.

—Curtains for the Cardinal. 1993. vi, 260p. 19.95 (*0-15-123682-8*) Harcourt Trade Pubs.

—Curtains for the Cardinal. 26p. 3.98 o.p. (*0-8317-7438-X*) Smithmark Pubs., Inc.

—Death of the Duchess. 1993. 256p. mass mkt. 4.50 o.p. (*0-425-13902-6*) Berkley Publishing Group.

—Death of the Duchess. 1992. 19.95 (*0-15-124102-3*) Harcourt Trade Pubs.

—Dirge for a Doge. 1997. 320p. 23.95 o.p. (*0-312-15109-8*, Saint Martin's Minotaur) St. Martin's Pr.

—Poison for the Prince. 1994. viii, 309p. 19.95 (*0-15-172540-3*) Harcourt Trade Pubs.

Faunce, John. Lucrezia Borgia: A Novel. 2004. 352p. pap. 13.95 (*1-4000-5122-3*, Three Rivers Pr.); 2003. 288p. 22.95 (*0-609-60974-2*) Crown Publishing Group.

Feehan, Christine. Dark Symphony. 2003. 352p. mass mkt. 6.99 (*0-515-13521-6*, Jove) Berkley Publishing Group.

—Dark Symphony. l.t. ed. 2003. (Romance Ser.). 28.95 (*0-7862-5587-0*) Thorndike Pr.

Fitzgerald, Penelope. Innocence. 1987. 16.95 o.p. (*0-8050-0373-8*) Holt, Henry & Co.

Fletcher, David. Confetti for Cortorelli. 1957. 2.75 o.s.i (*0-394-81045-7*) Random Hse., Inc.

Fogazzaro, Antonio. The Patriot. E-Book 3.95 (*0-594-02207-X*) 1873 Pr.

—The Saint. 2000. 252p. E-Book 3.95 (*0-594-02209-6*) 1873 Pr.

Forster, E. M. A Room with a View. unabr. ed. 2000. audio compact disk 56.00 (*0-7861-9926-1*, z1285) Blackstone Audio Bks., Inc.

—A Room with a View. Stallybrass, Oliver, ed. 1978. (Abinger Edition of E. M. Forster Ser.). text 29.50 o.p. (*0-8419-5804-1*) Holmes & Meier Pubs., Inc.

Froio, Salvatore Robert. I Venti Corni: The Twenty Horns. 2001. 150p. vinyl bd. 8.99 (*0-9706544-0-5*) Brighton Publishing.

Frutkin, Mark. The Lion of Venice. 2000. (Porc Epic Book Ser.). 213p. pap. 12.95 (*0-88878-378-7*, Porcepic Bks.) Beach Holme Pubs., Ltd. CAN. *Dist:* Strauss Consultants.

Fruttero, Carl & Lucentini, Franco. The D. Case: The Truth about the Mystery of Edwin Drood. Dowling, Gregory, tr. 1992. 587p. 23.95 (*0-15-113732-3*) Harcourt Trade Pubs.

Fruttero, Carlo, et al. The D. Case: The Truth about the Mystery of Edwin Drood. Dowling, Gregory, tr. from ITA. 1993. 608p. pap. 12.95 o.s.i (*0-15-623600-1*, Harvest Bks.) Harcourt Trade Pubs.

Gadda, Carlo Emilio. That Awful Mess on Via Merulana. Weaver, William, tr. 1984. 392p. pap. 8.95 (*0-8076-1093-3*) Braziller, George Inc.

—That Awful Mess on Via Merulana: A Novel. Weaver, W., tr. 1965. 5.95 o.p. (*0-8076-0305-8*) Braziller, George Inc.

Gallizier, Nathan. Castel del Monte. 2000. 252p. E-Book 9.95 (*0-594-02229-0*) 1873 Pr.

—The Court of Lucifer. 2000. 252p. E-Book 3.95 (*0-594-02231-2*) 1873 Pr.

—The Leopard Prince. 2000. 252p. pap. 9.95 (*0-594-00327-X*); E-Book 3.95 (*0-594-02235-5*) 1873 Pr.

—The Sorceress of Rome. 2000. 252p. E-Book 3.95 (*0-594-02237-1*) 1873 Pr.

Gaye, Carol. Long Shadows. l.t. ed. 1985. 12.50 o.p. (*0-8166-6646-6*, Macmillan Reference USA) Gale Group.

Gilman, Dorothy. Mrs. Pollifax & the Second Thief. 1995. 208p. mass mkt. 6.99 (*0-449-14905-6*, Fawcett) Ballantine Bks.

—Mrs. Pollifax & the Second Thief. abr. ed. 1993. audio 16.95 o.p. (*1-56100-351-4*, 1328); audio 57.25 o.p. (*1-56100-161-9*, 954, Unabridged Library Editions); audio 21.95 o.p. (*1-56100-533-9*, 354, Bookcassette) Brilliance Audio.

—Mrs. Pollifax & the Second Thief. 1993. 208p. 20.00 o.s.i (*0-385-47109-2*) Doubleday Publishing.

—Mrs. Pollifax & the Second Thief. l.t. ed. 1994. 228p. lib. bdg. 16.95 o.p. (*0-8161-5918-1*); lib. bdg. 21.95 (*0-8161-5917-3*) Gale Group. (Macmillan Reference USA).

—Mrs. Pollifax & the Second Thief. abr. ed. 2000. audio 7.95 (*1-57815-020-5*, 1005, Media Bks. Audio Publishing) Media Bks., L. L. C.

—Mrs. Pollifax & the Second Thief. unabr. ed. 1993. (Mrs. Pollifax Mystery Ser.: Vol. 10). audio 44.00 (*1-55690-911-X*, 93407E7) Recorded Bks., LLC.

Giono, Jean. The Straw Man. Johnson, Phyllis, tr. 1982. (Giono Novels Ser.). 472p. pap. 14.00 o.p. (*0-86547-071-5*, North Point Pr.) Farrar, Straus & Giroux.

Glanville, Brian. The Catacomb. 1988. 352p. 22.95 (*0-340-42327-7*) Hodder & Stoughton, Ltd. GBR. *Dist:* Lubrecht & Cramer, Ltd., Trafalgar Square.

Godden, Rumer. Pippa Passes. unabr. ed. 2001. audio 44.95 (*1-85695-933-3*, 950412) ISIS Audio Bks. GBR. *Dist:* Ulverscroft Large Print Bks., Ltd.

—Pippa Passes. 1994. 22.00 o.p. (*0-688-13397-5*, Morrow, William & Co.) Morrow/Avon.

Golding, Michael. Simple Prayers. abr. ed. 1994. audio 17.00 o.s.i (*1-57042-028-9*, 4-520289) Time Warner AudioBooks.

—Simple Prayers. 320p. 1994. 25.00 (*0-446-51790-9*); 1996. reprint ed. pap. 11.99 (*0-446-67086-3*) Warner Bks., Inc.

Goold, G. P., ed. Callirhoe: Love Story in Syracuse. 1995. (Loeb Classical Library: Vol. 481). 400p. text 21.50 (*0-674-99530-9*, L481) Harvard Univ. Pr.

Gordon, Alan. Thirteenth Night. 2000. (Illus.). 256p. mass mkt. 5.99 (*0-312-97684-4*, St. Martin's Paperbacks) St. Martin's Pr.

Gordon, Lucy. La Esposa del Magnate. 2004. (Harlequin Jazmin Ser.: No. 153). (SPA.). 160p. mass mkt. (*0-373-68203-4*, Harlequin Spanish) Harlequin Enterprises, Ltd.

—Rico's Secret Child. 2000. (Harlequin Romance Ser.: Vol. 359). per. (*0-373-03596-9*); 250p. per. (*0-373-15842-4*) Harlequin Enterprises, Ltd. (Harlequin Bks.).

Graves, Robert. Homer's Daughter. 283p. 1987. reprint ed. 14.95 o.p. (*0-89733-058-7*); 1998. pap. 16.00 (*0-89733-059-5*) Academy Chicago Pubs., Ltd.

—Homer's Daughter. unabr. collector's ed. 1986. audio 48.00 (*0-7366-1051-0*, 1979) Books on Tape, Inc.

Greenfield, David. Come Back to Sorrento. 1999. (Illus.). 88p. pap. 9.00 (*0-8059-4821-X*) Dorrance Publishing Co., Inc.

Haasse, Hella S. The Scarlet City: A Novel of Sixteenth-Century Italy. Miller, Anita, tr. from DUT. & intro. by. 1990. 594p. 22.95 o.p. (*0-89733-349-7*) Academy Chicago Pubs., Ltd.

—The Scarlet City: A Novel of Sixteenth-Century Italy. Miller, Anita, tr. from DUT. 2nd ed. 1997. 368p. reprint ed. pap. 18.95 (*0-89733-372-1*) Academy Chicago Pubs., Ltd.

Hall, Robert A., Jr. Italian Stories: Novelle Italiane. 1990. 364p. pap. 8.95 (*0-486-26180-8*, 26180-8) Dover Pubns., Inc.

Harris, Robert. Pompeii: A Novel. 2003. (Illus.). 432p. 39.95 (*0-09-177925-1*) Hutchinson GBR. *Dist:* Trafalgar Square.

—Pompeii: A Novel. l.t. ed. 2003. 460p. 26.95 (*0-375-43281-7*) Random Hse. Large Print.

—Pompeii: A Novel. 2003. (Illus.). 304p. 24.95 (*0-679-42889-5*) Random Hse., Inc.

Harris, Thomas. Hannibal. 1999. 496p. 27.95 (*0-385-29929-X*) Broadway Bks.

—Hannibal. 2000. 560p. mass mkt. 7.99 (*0-440-22467-5*) Dell Publishing.

Hassel, Sven. Monte Cassino. 2003. (Cassell Military Paperbacks Ser.). 256p. pap. 7.95 (*0-304-36632-3*) Cassell P L C GBR. *Dist:* Sterling Publishing Co., Inc.

Haythe, Justin. The Honeymoon. 2004. 224p. 22.00 (*0-87113-914-6*, Atlantic Monthly Pr.) Grove/Atlantic, Inc.

Hazzard, Shirley. The Bay of Noon. 1988. 160p. pap. 8.95 o.p. (*0-14-010450-X*, Penguin Bks.) Viking Penguin.

—The Evening of the Holiday. 1988. 144p. pap. 6.95 o.p. (*0-14-010451-8*, Penguin Bks.) Viking Penguin.

—Evening of the Holiday. 2004. pap. (*0-312-42326-8*) Picador.

Hellenga, Robert R. The Fall of a Sparrow, Set. abr. ed. 1999. audio 26.95 (*0-7871-1752-8*, 696024, Dove Audio) NewStar Media, Inc.

—The Fall of a Sparrow. 1998. 464p. 25.00 o.s.i (*0-684-85026-5*, Scribner) Simon & Schuster.

—The Fall of the Sparrow: A Novel. 1999. 464p. pap. 14.00 (*0-684-85027-3*, Scribner) Simon & Schuster.

—The Sixteen Pleasures. 1995. 384p. pap. 13.95 (*0-385-31469-8*, Delta) Dell Publishing.

—The Sixteen Pleasures. audio o.p. National Humanities Ctr.

—The Sixteen Pleasures. 1994. 327p. 22.00 o.p. (*1-56947-006-5*) Soho Pr., Inc.

Helprin, Mark. A Soldier of the Great War. 1991. 800p. 32.00 (*0-15-183600-0*); 100.00 (*0-15-183601-9*) Harcourt Trade Pubs.

—A Soldier of the Great War. 1992. 736p. mass mkt. 7.99 (*0-380-71589-9*); 1996. 800p. reprint ed. pap. 15.00 o.s.i (*0-380-72736-6*) Morrow/Avon. (Avon Bks.).

Hemingway, Ernest. Across the River & into the Trees. unabr. collector's ed. 1990. audio 48.00 (*0-7366-1731-0*, 2571) Books on Tape, Inc.

—Across the River & into the Trees. 320p. 1985. pap. 5.95 o.s.i (*0-684-18496-6*); 1977. 40.00 (*0-684-15313-0*); 1950. pap. 9.95 o.s.i (*0-684-71795-6*, SL 202) Gale Group. (Macmillan Reference USA).

—Across the River & into the Trees. (Classic Ser.). 1998. 272p. 26.00 (*0-684-84464-8*, Scribner); 1996. 288p. pap. 13.00 (*0-684-82553-8*, Scribner); 1988. 308p. pap. 7.00 o.s.i (*0-02-051920-6*, Scribner Paper Fiction) Simon & Schuster.

—A Farewell to Arms. Bloom, Harold, ed. 1999. (Bloom's Reviews Comprehensive Research & Study Guides). 79p. (J). (gr. 4-7). pap. 4.95 (*0-7910-4120-4*) Chelsea Hse. Pubs.

—A Farewell to Arms. 1982. 336p. pap. 4.95 o.s.i (*0-684-17469-3*); 1978. 334p. 35.00 (*0-684-15562-1*); 1929. 332p. pap. 11.95 o.s.i (*0-684-71797-2*); 1920. 336p. 14.95 o.s.i (*0-684-10236-6*) Gale Group. (Macmillan Reference USA).

—A Farewell to Arms. 1929. (Illus.). 358p. (C). pap. text 24.20 o.p. (*0-02-352980-6*, Macmillan College) Prentice Hall PTR.

Henry, Marguerite. Gaudenzia Pride of the Palio. 1989. (J). 12.95 o.s.i (*0-02-689416-5*, Simon & Schuster Children's Publishing) Simon & Schuster Children's Publishing.

Herman, George. A Comedy of Murders. 1994. 448p. 23.95 o.p. (*0-7867-0064-5*, Carroll & Graf Pubs.) Avalon Publishing Group.

—The Tears of the Madonna. 1996. 288p. 22.95 o.p. (*0-7867-0243-5*, Carroll & Graf Pubs.) Avalon Publishing Group.

Herman, George A. Carnival of Saints. 1994. 432p. 22.00 o.s.i (*0-345-38150-5*) Ballantine Bks.

Hersey, John. A Bell for Adano. unabr. collector's ed. 1981. audio 48.00 (*0-7366-0316-6*, 1304) Books on Tape, Inc.

—A Bell for Adano. 1991. 300p. reprint ed. lib. bdg. 22.95 o.p. (*0-89966-845-3*) Buccaneer Bks., Inc.

—A Bell for Adano. abr. ed. audio 19.98 o.p. HarperTrade.

—A Bell for Adano. 1988. 288p. reprint ed. pap. 13.00 (*0-394-75695-9*, Vintage) Knopf Publishing Group.

—A Bell for Adano. 1944. 22.95 o.s.i (*0-394-41660-0*) Knopf, Alfred A. Inc.

—A Bell for Adano, unabr. ed. 1999. audio 51.00 (*1-55690-042-2*, 89550E7) Recorded Bks., LLC.

—A Bell for Adano. 1988. (J). 19.05 (*0-606-03728-4*) Turtleback Bks.

Hewlett, Maurice Henry. Little Novels of Italy. rev. ed. 2000. 314p. E-Book 3.95 (*0-594-04354-9*) 1873 Pr.

Higgins, Jack. In the Hour Before Midnight. 1984. mass mkt. 2.95 o.s.i (*0-449-12807-5*); 1980. mass mkt. 2.25 o.s.i (*0-449-13954-9*) Ballantine Bks. (Fawcett).

—In the Hour Before Midnight. 2000. 304p. reprint ed. mass mkt. 7.50 (*0-425-17631-2*) Berkley Publishing Group.

—In the Hour Before Midnight. unabr. collector's ed. 1984. audio 36.00 (*0-7366-0481-2*, 1456) Books on Tape, Inc.

—In the Hour Before Midnight. unabr. ed. 2000. audio 34.95 (*0-7451-6021-2*, CAB 337) Chivers Audio Bks. GBR. *Dist:* BBC Audiobooks America.

—In the Hour Before Midnight. 1982. 192p. mass mkt. 2.95 o.s.i (*0-440-14350-0*) Dell Publishing.

—In the Hour Before Midnight. l.t. ed. 1978. o.p. (*0-7089-0113-1*, Ulverscroft) Thorpe, F. A. Pubs.

Highsmith, Patricia. The Talented Mr. Ripley. unabr. ed. 2001. (Mr. Ripley Series). audio 69.95 (*1-85089-775-1*, 89102) ISIS Audio Bks. GBR. *Dist:* Ulverscroft Large Print Bks., Ltd.

—The Talented Mr. Ripley. l.t. ed. 1988. (Mr. Ripley Ser.). 392p. reprint ed. lib. bdg. 18.95 o.p. (*1-85089-184-2*) ISIS Large Print Bks. GBR. *Dist:* Transaction Pubs.

—The Talented Mr. Ripley. (Mr. Ripley Ser.). 304p. 1999. pap. 13.00 (*0-676-58972-3*); 1992. pap. 13.00 (*0-679-74229-8*) Knopf Publishing Group. (Vintage).

—The Talented Mr. Ripley, Set. unabr. ed. 1999. (Mr. Ripley Ser.). audio 39.95 (*0-375-40511-9*, RH Audio) Random Hse. Audio Publishing Group.

—The Talented Mr. Ripley. 2000. (Mr. Ripley Ser.). 287p. (*0-7621-8856-1*) Reader's Digest Assn., Inc., The.

—The Talented Mr. Ripley. 1982. (Mr. Ripley Ser.). 256p. pap. 4.95 o.p. (*0-14-004020-X*, Penguin Bks.) Viking Penguin.

Hill, John Spencer. Ghirlandaio's Daughter. 1998. (WWL Mystery Ser.). per. (*0-373-26279-5*, 1-26279-9, Worldwide Library) Harlequin Enterprises, Ltd.

—Ghirlandaio's Daughter. 1998. 304p. mass mkt. 8.99 (*0-7710-4114-4*); 1997. 320p. 26.99 (*0-7710-4113-6*) McClelland & Stewart/Tundra Bks.

—Ghirlandaio's Daughter: A Detective Carlo Arbati Mystery. 1997. 320p. 22.95 (*0-312-15133-0*, Saint Martin's Minotaur) St. Martin's Pr.

—The Last Castrato. 1997. (WWL Mystery Ser.). per. (*0-373-26229-9*, 1-26229-4, Worldwide Library) Harlequin Enterprises, Ltd.

—The Last Castrato. 1995. 224p. 20.95 (*0-312-13107-0*, Saint Martin's Minotaur) St. Martin's Pr.

Hodge, Jane Aiken. Escapade. 1993. 240p. 18.95 o.p. (*0-312-09799-9*) St. Martin's Pr.

Holland, Cecelia. Great Maria. 1987. 528p. pap. 8.95 o.s.i (*0-345-34110-4*) Ballantine Bks.

—Great Maria. 1974. 8.95 o.p. (*0-394-48509-2*, Knopf Bks. for Young Readers) Random Hse. Children's Bks.

—Great Maria. 1993. (Hera Ser.). 519p. pap. 17.00 (*0-939149-84-2*) Soho Pr., Inc.

—Great Maria. 1979. pap. 2.75 o.p. (*0-446-95203-6*) Warner Bks., Inc.

Holman, S. R. Domitian the Younger: A Novel. 1999. 225p. pap. 16.95 o.p. (*1-889298-96-4*) Rhwymbooks.

Horby, Simonetta Agnello. La Mennulara (The Almond Picker) 2005. (*0-374-18234-5*) Farrar, Straus & Giroux.

Howlett, John. Murder of a Moderate Man. 1988. 352p. reprint ed. pap. (*0-373-97083-8*, Harlequin Bks.) Harlequin Enterprises, Ltd.

—Murder of a Moderate Man. 1986. 272p. 15.95 o.p. (*0-312-00055-3*) St. Martin's Pr.

Humphreys, Emyr. The Gift of a Daughter. 2000. 240p. 22.00 (*1-85411-222-8*) Seren Bks. GBR. *Dist:* Dufour Editions, Inc.

Huxley, Aldous. Those Barren Leaves. 1998. 320p. reprint ed. pap. 13.95 (*1-56478-169-0*) Dalkey Archive Pr.

Jaffe, Michele. The Stargazer. l.t. ed. 2000. (G. K. Hall Core Ser.). 567p. 28.95 (*0-7838-8931-3*, Macmillan Reference USA) Gale Group.

—The Stargazer. 1999. 400p. 18.00 o.s.i (*0-671-02739-5*, Atria); 2000. (Illus.). 480p. reprint ed. pap. 6.99 (*0-671-02740-9*, Pocket) Simon & Schuster.

James, Henry. The Portrait of a Lady: Complete Text with Introduction, Historical Contexts. Cohn, Jan, ed. 2001. (New Riverside Editions Ser.). viii, 619p. 12.36 (*0-618-10735-5*) Houghton Mifflin Co.

—The Wings of the Dove. abr. ed. 1992. audio 15.95 o.p. (*0-88646-333-5*, 7333) Durkin Hayes Publishing Ltd.

—The Wings of the Dove. 1997. (Illus.). 528p. (J). pap. 12.95 (*0-7868-8251-4*) Hyperion Pr.

—The Wings of the Dove. 2000. (Cloth Bound Pocket Ser.). 7.95 (*3-8290-5387-8*, 522085) Konemann.

—The Wings of the Dove. (Signet Classics). 1999. 512p. mass mkt. 6.95 (*0-451-52728-3*, Signet Classics); 1964. pap. 4.50 o.p. (*0-452-00858-1*, Meridian Bks.); 1964. mass mkt. 3.95 o.p. (*0-451-51872-1*, CE1872, Signet Classics) NAL.

—The Wings of the Dove. Crowley, Joseph Donald & Hocks, Richard A., eds. 1978. (Critical Editions Ser.). (C). o.p. (*0-393-04478-5*); 583p. pap. text 12.00 (*0-393-09088-4*) Norton, W. W. & Co., Inc.

—The Wings of the Dove. Brooks, Peter, ed. & intro. by. 1998. (Oxford World's Classics Ser.). 592p. pap. 8.95 (*0-19-283861-X*) Oxford Univ. Pr., Inc.

—The Wings of the Dove. Brooks, Peter, ed. 1985. (Oxford World's Classics Ser.). 584p. pap. 6.95 o.p. (*0-19-281631-4*) Oxford Univ. Pr., Inc.

—The Wings of the Dove. 1974. pap. 3.95 o.p. (*0-14-002320-8*) Penguin Group (USA) Inc.

—The Wings of the Dove. 2000. E-Book 4.95 (*0-679-64156-4*, Modern Library) Random House Adult Trade Publishing Group.

—The Wings of the Dove. 1993. (Modern Library Ser.). 712p. 19.00 o.s.i (*0-679-60067-1*) Random Hse., Inc.

—The Wings of the Dove. 1997. (Everyman Paperback Classics Ser.). 464p. pap. 5.95 (*0-460-87617-1*, Everyman's Classic Library in Paperback) Tuttle Publishing.

—The Wings of the Dove. Bayley, John, ed. & intro. by. 1986. (Penguin Classics Ser.). 528p. pap. 9.95 (*0-14-043263-9*, Penguin Classics) Viking Penguin.

—The Wings of the Dove. abr. ed. 1997. (Classic Fiction Ser.). audio 17.98 o.p. (*962-634-612-4*, NA311214); audio compact disk 19.98 o.p. (*962-634-112-2*, NA311212) Naxos of America, Inc. (Naxos AudioBooks).

—The Wings of the Dove, Set. unabr. ed. 1993. audio 77.95 (*1-55685-286-X*) Audio Bk. Contractors, Inc.

—The Wings of the Dove. unabr. ed. 1999. audio 89.95 (*0-7861-1525-4*, 2375) Blackstone Audio Bks., Inc.

—The Wings of the Dove. 1977. (Novels & Tales of Henry James Ser.: Vol. 19). reprint ed. xxii, 301p. lib. bdg. 37.50 o.p. (*0-678-02819-2*);Vol. 2. 404p. lib. bdg. 37.50 (*0-678-02820-6*) Kelley, Augustus M. Pubs.

—The Wings of the Dove. (BCL1-PS American Literature Ser.). reprint ed. 1993. 329p. lib. bdg. 89.00 (*0-7812-6978-4*); 1992. lib. bdg. 75.00 (*0-7812-3429-8*) Reprint Services Corp.

Johns, Deborah. The Lion of Venice. 2001. 384p. mass mkt. 5.99 o.s.i (*0-8217-7084-5*) Kensington Publishing Corp.

Johnston, Tony. Pages of Music. 1988. (Illus.). 32p. (J). (gr. k-3). 13.95 o.s.i (*0-399-21436-4*, G. P. Putnam's Sons) Penguin Putnam Bks. for Young Readers.

Johnston, Velda. The Etruscan Smile. 1980. mass mkt. 2.25 o.p. (*0-451-09020-9*, E9020, Signet Bks.) NAL.

—The Etruscan Smile: A Novel of Suspense. l.t. ed. 2000. (Candlelight Romance Ser.). 271p. 22.95 (*0-7862-2449-5*) Thorndike Pr.

—Masquerade in Venice. l.t. ed. 1987. (Nightingale Ser.). 299p. 12.95 o.p. (*0-8161-4339-0*, Macmillan Reference USA) Gale Group.

Judd, Bob. Monza. l.t. ed. 1993. (Magna Large Print Ser.). 400p. 29.99 (*0-7505-0533-8*) Magna Large Print Bks. GBR. *Dist:* Ulverscroft Large Print Bks., Ltd.

—Monza. 1992. 20.00 o.p. (*0-688-11320-6*, Morrow, William & Co.) Morrow/Avon.

Keates, Jonathan. Allegro Postillions. 1985. 120p. 12.95 o.s.i (*0-8076-1110-7*); pap. 6.95 o.s.i (*0-8076-1121-2*) Braziller, George Inc.

Kennedy, William P. Toy Soldiers. 1988. 448p. 19.95 o.p. (*0-312-01478-3*) St. Martin's Pr.

—Toy Soldiers: The Sins of Their Fathers Fell upon Their Sons. 1991. mass mkt. 4.95 (*0-312-92610-3*, St. Martin's Paperbacks) St. Martin's Pr.

Kent, Stella. Trust in Your Heart. l.t. ed. 1992. 18.95 o.p. (*0-7451-8299-2*, AH0278) BBC Audiobooks America.

Kenyon, F. W. The Naked Sword. 1979. reprint ed. pap. 1.95 o.s.i (*0-505-51341-2*) Dorchester Publishing Co., Inc.

Ker, Madeleine. Fire of the Gods. l.t. ed. 1995. (Nightingale Ser.). 232p. pap. 17.95 (*0-7838-1221-3*, Macmillan Reference USA) Gale Group.

—Fire of the Gods. 1985. mass mkt. (*0-373-10795-1*, Harlequin Bks.) Harlequin Enterprises, Ltd.

King, Peter. Death Al Dente: A Gourmet Detective Mystery. 2000. (Culinary Mysteries Ser.). 256p. mass mkt. 5.99 (*0-312-97038-2*, St. Martin's Paperbacks); 1999. (Gourmet Detective Mystery Ser.: Vol. 4). 240p. 22.95 o.p. (*0-312-19891-4*, Saint Martin's Minotaur) St. Martin's Pr.

Koeppen, Wolfgang. Death in Rome. Hofmann, Michael, tr. 2001. 224p. pap. 12.95 (*0-393-32194-0*) Norton, W. W. & Co., Inc.

—Death in Rome. Hoffman, Michael, tr. & intro. by. 1994. (Penguin Twentieth-Century Classics Ser.). 224p. pap. 10.95 o.s.i (*0-14-018790-1*, Penguin Classics) Viking Penguin.

La Tourrette, Jacqueline. The Pompeii Scroll. 1975. 256p. pap. 7.95 o.p. (*0-440-06091-5*, Delacorte Pr.) Dell Publishing.

—Shadows in Umbria. 1979. 9.95 o.p. (*0-399-12182-X*) Putnam Publishing Group, The.

Langton, Jane. The Dante Game: A Homer Kelly Mystery. 1992. (Homer Kelly Mystery Ser.). (Illus.). 336p. pap. 6.99 o.s.i (*0-14-013887-0*, Penguin Bks.) Penguin Group (USA) Inc.

—The Dante Game: A Homer Kelly Mystery. 1991. (Homer Kelly Mystery Ser.). (Illus.). 336p. 18.95 o.p. (*0-670-83439-4*) Viking Penguin.

—The Thief of Venice: A Homer Kelly Mystery. 2000. (Homer Kelly Mystery Ser.). (Illus.). 256p. pap. 5.99 (*0-14-029189-X*) Penguin Group (USA) Inc.

—The Thief of Venice: A Homer Kelly Mystery. 1999. (Homer Kelly Mystery Ser.). 256p. 22.95 o.p. (*0-670-88210-0*, Viking) Viking Penguin.

Lawrence, D. H. D. H. Lawrence: The Lost Girl. Worthen, John, ed. 1981. (Cambridge Edition of the Works of D. H. Lawrence). (Illus.). 483p. 99.95 o.p. (*0-521-22263-X*) Cambridge Univ. Pr.

—The Lost Girl. 26.95 (*0-89190-611-8*) Amereon, Ltd.

—The Lost Girl. 1996. 416p. mass mkt. 5.95 o.s.i (*0-553-21448-9*, Bantam Classics) Bantam Bks.

—The Lost Girl. Worthen, John, ed. 1981. (Cambridge Edition of the Works of D. H. Lawrence). (Illus.). 484p. pap. 45.00 (*0-521-29423-1*) Cambridge Univ. Pr.

—The Lost Girl. reprint ed. lib. bdg. 98.00 (*0-7426-3143-5*); 2001. pap. text 28.00 (*0-7426-8143-2*) Classic Bks.

—The Lost Girl. 1968. pap. 2.75 o.p. (*0-670-00226-7*) Penguin Group (USA) Inc.

—The Lost Girl. 2003. (Modern Library Classics). 400p. pap. 13.95 (*0-8129-6997-9*, Modern Library) Random House Adult Trade Publishing Group.

—The Lost Girl. Worthen, John, ed. 1996. (Penguin Twentieth-Century Classics Ser.). 416p. pap. 11.95 o.s.i (*0-14-018808-8*) Viking Penguin.

—The Lost Girl. 1990. 400p. pap. 7.95 o.p. (*0-14-018206-3*, Penguin Classics) Viking Penguin.

—The Lost Girl. Worthen, John, ed. 1982. 432p. 22.95 o.p. (*0-670-44101-5*) Viking Penguin.

—The Lost Girl. 1978. 400p. pap. 5.95 o.p. (*0-14-000752-0*, Penguin Bks.) Viking Penguin.

Lee, Vernon. Supernatural Tales: Excursions into Fantasy. 1987. 222p. 27.00 (*0-7206-0680-2*) Owen, Peter Ltd. GBR. *Dist:* Dufour Editions, Inc.

Lennox, Judith. The Italian Garden. 1993. 480p. 24.95 o.p. (*0-312-09810-3*) St. Martin's Pr.

Leon, Donna. Acqua Alta. unabr. collector's ed. 1998. audio 48.00 (*0-7366-4294-3*, 4787) Books on Tape, Inc.

—Acqua Alta. 1996. 288p. 22.50 o.p. (*0-06-018651-8*) HarperCollins Pubs.

—Death & Judgement. unabr. ed. 1998. audio 44.95 Blackstone Audio Bks., Inc.

—Death & Judgement. 1995. 304p. 20.00 o.p. (0-06-017796-9) HarperCollins Pubs.
—Death & Judgement: A Question of Motive. unabr. ed. 2000. audio 29.95 (0-7861-1549-1) Blackstone Audio Bks., Inc.
—Death & Judgment. 1996. 304p. mass mkt. 4.99 o.p. (0-06-109523-0, HarperTorch) Morrow/Avon.
—Death at la Fenice. 1995. 288p. mass mkt. 6.99 (0-06-104337-0, HarperTorch) Morrow/Avon.
—Death at la Fenice. l.t. ed. 2003. (General Ser.). (FRE.). lib. bdg. 24.95 (0-7862-5107-7) Thorndike Pr.
—Death at La Fenice. unabr. ed. 1999. audio 27.95 (0-7861-1538-6); 1997. audio 44.95 (0-7861-1193-3, 1951) Blackstone Audio Bks., Inc.
—Death at La Fenice. unabr. collector's ed. 1998. (Guido Brunetti Mystery Ser.). audio 48.00 (0-7366-4217-X, 4715) Books on Tape, Inc.
—Death at La Fenice: A Novel of Suspense. 1992. 224p. 19.00 o.p. (0-06-016871-4) HarperTrade.
—Death in a Strange Country: A Guido Brunetti Mystery. unabr. ed. 1997. audio 44.95 (0-7861-1228-X, 1971) Blackstone Audio Bks., Inc.
—Death in a Strange Country: A Guido Brunetti Mystery. unabr. collector's ed. 1998. (Guido Brunetti Mystery Ser.). audio 48.00 (0-7366-4218-8, 4716) Books on Tape, Inc.
—Death in a Strange Country: A Guido Brunetti Mystery. 1993. 304p. 20.00 o.p. (0-06-017008-5) HarperTrade.
—Death in a Strange Country: A Guido Brunetti Mystery. 1995. 288p. mass mkt. 4.50 o.p. (0-06-109406-4, HarperTorch) Morrow/Avon.
—Dressed for Death. unabr. ed. 1997. audio 44.95 (0-7861-1194-1, 1953) Blackstone Audio Bks., Inc.
—Dressed for Death, , unabr. collector's ed. 1999. (Guido Brunetti Mystery Ser.). audio 48.00 (0-7366-4317-6, 4785) Books on Tape, Inc.
—Dressed for Death. 1994. 288p. 20.00 o.p. (0-06-017795-0) HarperTrade.
—Dressed for Death. 1995. 304p. mass mkt. 4.99 o.p. (0-06-109418-8, HarperTorch) Morrow/Avon.
Leonard, Elmore. Riding the Rap. 1998. 304p. pap. 10.95 o.s.i (0-385-32417-0, Delta); 1996. 352p. mass mkt. 6.50 o.s.i (0-440-21441-6); 1995. 336p. mass mkt. 6.50 (0-440-29539-4) Dell Publishing.
—Riding the Rap. l.t. ed. 1995. (Large Print Bks.). 27.95 (1-56895-224-4, Wheeler Publishing, Inc.) Gale Group.
—Riding the Rap. 2002. 352p. mass mkt. 7.50 (0-06-008218-6) HarperCollins Pubs.
Levi, Primo. The Mirror Maker: Stories & Essays. 1990. 192p. pap. 15.00 (0-8052-0989-1, Schocken) Knopf Publishing Group.
—The Mirror Maker: Stories & Essays. 1998. x, 214p. pap. o.s.i (0-349-11047-6) Little Brown & Co.
—The Mirror Maker: Stories & Essays. 1992. 3.99 o.p. (0-517-08845-2) Random Hse. Value Publishing.
—The Sixth Day & Other Stories. Rosenthal, Raymond, tr. 1990. 18.95 o.p. (0-671-62617-5) Summit Bks.
Lewitt, Shariann. Interface Masque. 2002. mass mkt. 6.99 (0-7653-4459-9); 1997. 350p. text 23.95 o.p. (0-312-85627-X) Doherty, Tom Assocs., LLC. (Tor Bks.).
—Interface Masque. 1999. 23.95 (0-312-87139-2) St. Martin's Pr.
Lindsay, Andrew. The Breadmaker's Carnival. 2000. 336p. 25.00 (0-06-019842-7); 1999. (0-88001-700-7) HarperTrade. (Ecco).
Long, Joanna. An Artist Now Unknown. 2000. (Illus.). xiv, 210p. pap. 19.95 (1-57736-201-2, Hillsboro Pr.) Providence Hse. Pubs.
Lucarelli, Carlo. Almost Blue. Stransky, Oonagh, tr. from ITA. 2001. 184p. pap. 11.95 (0-87286-389-1) City Lights Bks.
Lucas, Frank L. Woman Clothed with the Sun, & Other Stories. 1977. (Short Story Index Reprint Ser.). 22.95 (0-8369-3564-0) Ayer Co. Pubs., Inc.
Luck, Geoffrey. Villa Fortuna: An Italian Interlude. 2001. 303p. pap. 15.95 (1-86436-604-4) New Holland Pubs. NZL. Dist: BHB International, Inc.
MacAvoy, R. A. Damiano. 1984. 243p. mass mkt. 2.95 o.s.i (0-553-25347-6, Spectra) Bantam Bks.
—Damiano's Lute. 1984. mass mkt. 2.75 o.s.i (0-553-24102-8); 272p. mass mkt. 2.95 o.s.i (0-553-25977-6, Spectra) Bantam Bks.
—Raphael. 1984. 240p. mass mkt. 2.95 o.s.i (0-553-25978-4) Bantam Bks.
—Trio for Lute. 1988. mass mkt. 4.95 o.s.i (0-553-27480-5, Spectra) Bantam Bks.
Maddox, Muriel. Captain from Corfu: A Novel. 1999. 256p. 22.95 (0-86534-287-3) Sunstone Pr.
Maguire, Gregory. Mirror Mirror. 2003. E-Book 19.95 (0-06-057568-9); E-Book 19.95 (0-06-057569-7); E-Book 19.95 (0-06-057570-0); E-Book 19.95 (0-06-057567-0) HarperCollins Pubs.
—Mirror Mirror. 2003. 304p. pap. 16.00 (0-06-059453-5); 304p. 24.95 (0-06-039384-X); 224.55 (0-06-057926-9); 304.45 (0-06-058011-9); audio 34.95 (0-06-056767-8) HarperTrade. (ReganBooks).
Malaparte, Curzio. The Skin. 1988. pap. 12.95 o.p. (0-910395-37-3) Marlboro Pr., Inc., The.
—The Skin. Moore, David, tr. 1997. (European Classics Ser.). 274p. pap. 21.00 (0-8101-1572-7) Northwestern Univ. Pr.
The Man Who Moved the World. 1990. (Illus.). pap. 7.95 o.p. (0-8423-4003-3, 754003-3) Tyndale Hse. Pubs.
Manetti, Antonio. The Fat Woodworker. Martone, Valerie, tr. from ITA. 1991. (Illus.). 88p. (Orig.). pap. 10.00 (0-934977-23-2) Italica Pr.
Mann, Thomas. Death in Venice. Appelbaum, Stanley, tr. & comment by. annot. ed. 1995. (Thrift Editions Ser.). 96p. pap. 1.50 (0-486-28714-9) Dover Pubns., Inc.
—Death in Venice. 2004. 128p. 19.95 (0-06-057605-7, Ecco) HarperTrade.
—Death in Venice. Lowe-Porter, H. T., tr. abr. ed. pap. 15.95 o.p. incl. audio (0-89845-427-1, CDL5 2090, Caedmon) HarperTrade.
—Death in Venice. Heller, Erich, tr. 1970. (Modern Library College Editions Ser.). 436p. (C). 11.25 (0-07-553669-2, T99, McGraw-Hill Humanities, Social Sciences & World Languages) McGraw-Hill Higher Education.
—Death in Venice. 1954. pap. 4.95 o.p. (0-394-70003-1) Random Hse., Inc.
—Death in Venice: A Case Study in Contemporary Criticism, Vol. 1. Ritter, Naomi, ed. 1998. (Death in Venice Ser.: Vol. 1). 288p. pap. text 13.50 (0-312-12002-8) Bedford/Saint Martin's.
—Death in Venice: And Seven Other Stories. Lowe-Porter, Helen T., tr. 1989. (Vintage International Ser.). 416p. (Orig.). pap. 10.95 (0-679-72206-8, Vintage) Knopf Publishing Group.
—Death in Venice: And Seven Other Stories. Lowe-Porter, Helen T., tr. from GER. 1992. 462p. (Orig.). 15.50 o.s.i (0-679-60040-X) Random Hse., Inc.
—Death in Venice & Other Stories. Luke, David, tr. & intro. by. 1988. 320p. mass mkt. 5.95 (0-553-21333-4) Bantam Bks.
—Death in Venice & Other Stories. 1991. 400p. 17.00 o.s.i (0-679-40666-2) Random Hse., Inc.
—Death in Venice & Other Tales. 1976. 13.95 (0-8488-0574-7) Amereon, Ltd.
—Death in Venice & Other Tales. 1983. 451p. reprint ed. lib. bdg. 16.95 (0-89966-455-5) Buccaneer Bks., Inc.
—Death in Venice & Other Tales. Chase, Jefferson S., tr. from GER. 1999. (Signet Classics). 256p. mass mkt. 5.95 (0-451-52609-0, Signet Classics) NAL.
—Death in Venice & Other Tales. Kolb, Clayton, ed. & tr. by. 1994. (Critical Editions Ser.). (C). pap. 13.50 (0-393-96013-7) Norton, W. W. & Co., Inc.
—Death in Venice & Other Tales. 1998. (Case Studies in Contemporary Criticism). 314p. 35.00 o.p. (0-312-21064-7) Palgrave Macmillan.
—Death in Venice & Other Tales. Neugroschel, Joachim, tr. unabr. ed. 2000. audio 85.00 (0-7887-2482-7, 95557E7) Recorded Bks., LLC.
—Death in Venice & Other Tales. 1999. 384p. pap. 11.00 (0-14-118173-7, Penguin Classics) Viking Penguin.
—Death in Venice & Other Tales. Neugroschel, Joachim, tr. from GER. 1998. 400p. 25.95 o.p. (0-670-87424-8) Viking Penguin.
Manning, Liza. The Glass Madonna. l.t. ed. 2000. (G. K. Hall Nightingale Ser.). 242p. pap. 20.95 (0-7838-9193-8); (0-7540-4291-X); (0-7540-4292-8) Gale Group. (Macmillan Reference USA).
—The Glass Madonna. 1987. per. (0-373-02818-0, Harlequin Bks.) Harlequin Enterprises, Ltd.
Maraini, Dacia. The Silent Dutchess. Kitto, Dick & Spottiswoode, Elspeth, trs. from ITA. 1992. 235p. 30.00 (0-7206-0859-7) Owen, Peter Ltd. GBR. Dist: Dufour Editions, Inc.
—Woman at War. Benetti, Mara & Spottiswood, Elspeth, trs. from ITA. 1989. Orig. Title: Donna in Guerra. 282p. (Orig.). pap. 14.50 (0-934977-12-7) Italica Pr.
Maraini, Dacia, et al. The Silent Dutchess. Kitto, Dick & Spottiswood, Elspeth, trs. from ENG. 1998. 264p. 19.95 (1-55861-194-0) Feminist Pr. at The City Univ. of New York.
Marciano, Francesca. Casa Rossa. 352p. 2003. pap. 14.00 (0-375-72637-3, Vintage); 2002. 25.00 (0-375-42123-8, Pantheon) Knopf Publishing Group.
Marinello, Edward A. Lorenzo. 2002. 151p. lib. bdg. 17.50 (1-59033-183-4) Nova Science Pubs., Inc.
Marshall-Andrews, Bob. The Palace of Wisdom. 1990. 336p. 18.95 o.p. (0-525-24810-2, Dutton) Dutton/Plume.
Martin, Gail Gaymer. From Italy with Love: Motivated by Letters, Four Women Travel to Italian Cities & Find Love. 2004. 352p. pap. 6.97 (1-59310-081-7) Barbour Publishing, Inc.
Martin, Malachi. Windswept House: A Vatican Novel. 656p. 1998. pap. 18.95 (0-385-49231-6); 1996. 24.95 o.s.i (0-385-48408-9) Doubleday Publishing.
Martin, Valerie. Italian Fever. l.t. ed. 2000. (G. K. Hall Core Ser.). 323p. 29.95 (0-7838-8840-6, Macmillan Reference USA) Gale Group.
—Italian Fever. 2000. (Contemporaries Ser.). 272p. pap. 12.00 (0-375-70522-8) Knopf, Alfred A. Inc.
—Redencion: Escenas de la Vida de San Francisco de Asis. 2002. (SPA.). 288p. pap. 16.95 (1-4000-0000-9) Random Hse., Inc.
Maugham, W. Somerset. The Making of a Saint. 1977. (Works of W. Somerset Maugham). reprint ed. 26.95 (0-405-07815-3) Ayer Co. Pubs., Inc.
—The Making of a Saint. reprint ed. lib. bdg. 98.00 (0-7426-3204-0); 2001. pap. text 28.00 (0-7426-8204-8) Classic Bks.
Mawer, Simon. The Gospel of Judas. 2002. 368p. reprint ed. pap. 13.95 (0-316-97374-2, Back Bay) Little Brown & Co.
Mayes, Frances. Frances Mayes: Balla Tuscany/Under the Tuscan Sky, 2 vol., set. 2000. 30.00 (0-7679-9905-3) Broadway Bks.
McAuley, Paul J. Pasquale's Angel. 2000. 22.00 (0-380-97253-0) Morrow/Avon.
McAuley, Paul J. Pasquale's Angel. 1997. mass mkt. 5.99 (0-380-77820-3, Avon Bks.); 1995. 384p. 22.00 o.p. (0-688-14154-4, Morrow, William & Co.) Morrow/Avon.
McBride, James. Miracle at St. Anna. l.t. ed. 2003. 345p. 29.95 (1-58724-473-X, Wheeler Publishing, Inc.) Gale Group.
—Miracle at St. Anna: A Novel. 2002. 64p. audio 25.95 (0-06-009318-8); 64p. audio compact disk 29.95 (0-06-009319-6); 128p. audio 34.95 (0-06-009320-X) HarperTrade. (Caedmon).
—Miracle at St. Anna: A Novel. 2002. 228p. 24.95 o.s.i (1-57322-212-7, Riverhead Bks. (Hardcovers)) Putnam Publishing Group, The.
McEwan, Ian. The Comfort of Strangers. l.t. ed. 2002. 155p. pap. 24.95 (0-7862-4040-7) Gale Group.
—The Comfort of Strangers. 1994. 128p. pap. 11.00 (0-679-74984-5, Vintage) Knopf Publishing Group.
—The Comfort of Strangers. 1981. 9.95 o.p. (0-671-42850-0, Simon & Schuster); 1982. reprint ed. mass mkt. 3.95 o.s.i (0-671-44956-7, Pocket) Simon & Schuster.
—The Comfort of Strangers. 1989. 144p. pap. 9.00 o.p. (0-14-011283-9, Penguin Bks.) Viking Penguin.
Mele, Michael. A Gift for the Contessa. 1997. (Illus.). 40p. (J). 15.95 (1-56554-216-9) Pelican Publishing Co., Inc.
Michaels, Barbara, pseud. The Grey Beginning. unabr. ed. 1992. audio 69.95 (0-7451-4079-3, CAB 776) BBC Audiobooks America.
—The Grey Beginning. 1992. mass mkt. 4.50 (0-8125-3031-4); 1988. 288p. pap. 3.95 o.s.i (0-8125-0681-2); 1985. 288p. reprint ed. pap. 3.50 o.s.i (0-8125-2252-4) Doherty, Tom Assocs., LLC. (Tor Bks.).
—The Grey Beginning. l.t. ed. 1985. (General Ser.). 15.95 o.p. (0-8161-3787-0, Macmillan Reference USA) Gale Group.
—The Grey Beginning. 1999. 304p. mass mkt. 6.99 (0-06-104471-7); 1995. 800p. mass mkt. 5.50 (0-06-100725-0) HarperCollins Pubs.
—The Grey Beginning. 1994. 288p. reprint ed. 20.00 (0-7278-4538-1) Severn Hse. Pubs., Ltd.
—The Grey Beginning. l.t. ed. 1995. (Charnwood Large Print Ser.). 352p. 29.99 o.p. (0-7089-8842-3, Charnwood) Thorpe, F. A. Pubs. GBR. Dist: Ulverscroft Large Print Bks., Ltd.
Montalbano, William D. Basilica. 2000. 368p. reprint ed. mass mkt. 6.99 o.s.i (0-515-12723-X, Jove) Berkley Publishing Group.
—Basilica. 1998. 304p. 23.95 o.p. (0-399-14418-8) Penguin Group (USA) Inc.
Monteleone, Thomas F. Blood of the Lamb. 1993. 448p. mass mkt. 5.99 (0-8125-2222-2); 1992. 416p. 21.95 o.p. (0-312-85031-X) Doherty, Tom Assocs., LLC. (Tor Bks.).
Montrucchio, Alessandra. Cardiofitness. 192p. 2000. pap. 12.95 (1-902881-19-2); 1999. 19.95 (1-902881-03-6) Toby Pr.
Moon, Lawrence D. God's Fool. 1981. 12.95 o.p. (0-531-09946-6, Watts, Franklin) Scholastic Library Publishing.
Moore, Christine P. The Virgin Knows. 1995. 320p. 22.95 o.p. (0-312-13203-4) St. Martin's Pr.
Moran, Thomas. Anja the Liar. 2003. 336p. 25.95 (1-57322-260-7, Riverhead Bks. (Hardcovers)) Putnam Publishing Group, The.
Morante, Elsa. History: A Novel. 1984. pap. 10.95 o.p. (0-394-72496-8, Vintage) Knopf Publishing Group.
Moravia, Alberto. Erotic Tales. Parks, Tim, tr. from ITA. 1986. 256p. 15.95 o.p. (0-374-14868-6) Farrar, Straus & Giroux.
—The Voyeur. Parks, Tim, tr. from ITA. 1987. 280p. 18.95 o.s.i (0-374-28544-6) Farrar, Straus & Giroux.
Mordden, Ethan. Venice Adriana. 1998. 304p. 23.95 o.p. (0-312-18202-3) St. Martin's Pr.
Mortimer, John. Summer's Lease. 1989. 288p. pap. 7.95 o.p. (0-14-010573-5) Penguin Group (USA) Inc.
—Summer's Lease. 1988. 288p. 19.95 o.p. (0-670-81984-0) Viking Penguin.
Murphy, Haughton. A Very Venetian Murder. 1993. mass mkt. 4.50 o.s.i (0-449-22066-4, Fawcett) Ballantine Bks.
—A Very Venetian Murder. 1992. 256p. 19.00 o.p. (0-671-70664-0, Simon & Schuster) Simon & Schuster.
Murray, William. A Fine Italian Hand: A Shifty Lou Anderson Mystery. 1996. 256p. 21.00 o.p. (0-87131-797-4) Evans, M. & Co., Inc.
Nabb, Magdalen. Death in Autumn. l.t. ed. 1986. 13.95 o.p. (0-89340-954-5, 291) BBC Audiobooks America.
—Death in Autumn. 2002. 158p. pap. 11.00 (1-56947-296-3) Soho Pr., Inc.
—Death in Autumn. 1987. (Crime Ser.). 160p. pap. 3.50 o.p. (0-14-009480-6, Penguin Bks.) Viking Penguin.
—Death in Autumn: A Florentine Mystery. 1985. (Marshall Guarnacci Mystery Ser.). 160p. 12.95 o.s.i (0-684-18337-4, Macmillan Reference USA) Gale Group.
—Death in Springtime. l.t. ed. 1985. 13.95 o.p. (0-89340-816-6, 932) BBC Audiobooks America.
—Death in Springtime. 1985. (Crime Ser.). 160p. pap. 3.95 o.p. (0-14-007770-7, Penguin Bks.) Viking Penguin.
—Death in Springtime: A Florentine Mystery. 1984. 168p. 11.95 o.s.i (0-684-18133-9, Macmillan Reference USA) Gale Group.
—Death of a Dutchman. 1984. (Crime Monthly Ser.). 224p. pap. 4.95 o.p. (0-14-006935-6, Penguin Bks.) Viking Penguin.
—Death of a Dutchman: A Novel of Murder in Florence. 1983. 176p. 11.95 o.p. (0-684-17847-8, Macmillan Reference USA) Gale Group.
—Death of an Englishman. 1982. 176p. 10.95 o.s.i (0-684-17757-9, Macmillan Reference USA) Gale Group.
—Death of an Englishman. 1984. (Crime Monthly Ser.). 176p. pap. 3.95 o.p. (0-14-006893-7, Penguin Bks.) Viking Penguin.
—Death of an Englishman: A Marshal Guarnaccia Investigation. 2001. (Marshal Guarnaccia Investigaion Ser.). 203p. reprint ed. pap. 12.00 o.s.i (1-56947-254-8) Soho Pr., Inc.
—The Marshal & the Madwoman. l.t. ed. 1989. (Atlantic Mystery Ser.). pap. 14.95 o.p. (1-55504-663-0, 824) BBC Audiobooks America.
—The Marshal & the Madwoman. 1988. 224p. 16.95 o.s.i (0-684-18984-4, Macmillan Reference USA) Gale Group.
—The Marshal & the Madwoman. 2003. 224p. pap. 12.00 (1-56947-340-4) Soho Pr., Inc.
—The Marshal & the Madwoman. 1989. (Crime Ser.). 224p. pap. 3.95 o.p. (0-14-011881-0, Penguin Bks.) Viking Penguin.
—The Marshal & the Murderer. 1987. (Marshall Guarnacci Mystery Ser.). 160p. 14.95 o.s.i (0-684-18884-8, Macmillan Reference USA) Gale Group.
—The Marshal & the Murderer. 1988. (Crime Ser.). 208p. pap. 3.95 o.p. (0-14-010678-2, Penguin Bks.) Viking Penguin.
—The Marshal at the Villa Torrini. 1994. 192p. 20.00 o.p. (0-06-016915-X) HarperCollins Pubs.
—Marshal Makes His Report: A Marshal Guarnaccia Mystery. 1992. 240p. 19.00 o.p. (0-06-016914-1) HarperTrade.
—The Marshall & the Murderer. 2002. 196p. pap. 12.00 (1-56947-297-1) Soho Pr., Inc.
—The Marshal's Own Case. l.t. ed. 1990. 17.95 o.p. (0-7451-9921-6, C0640); pap. 15.95 o.p. (0-7927-0372-3, C0834) BBC Audiobooks America.
—The Marshal's Own Case. 1991. (Crime Monthly Ser.). 176p. pap. 4.95 o.p. (0-14-014323-8, Penguin Bks.) Penguin Group (USA) Inc.
—The Marshal's Own Case: A Marshal Guarnaccia Mystery. 1990. 224p. 17.95 o.s.i (0-684-19201-2, Macmillan Reference USA) Gale Group.
—The Property of Blood. 2001. (Marshal Guarnaccia Investigaion Ser.). 224p. 23.00 o.s.i (1-56947-251-3) Soho Pr., Inc.
—Some Bitter Taste. 2003. pap. 12.00 (1-56947-339-0) Soho Pr., Inc.
—Some Bitter Taste. l.t. ed. 2003. 289p. pap. 24.95 (0-7862-5418-1) Thorndike Pr.
—Some Bitter Taste: A Marshal Guarnaccia Investigation. 2002. 272p. 24.00 (1-56947-317-X) Soho Pr., Inc.
Naess, Atle. Doubting Thomas: A Novel about Caravaggio. 160p. 19.95 (0-7206-1151-2) Dufour Editions, Inc.
—Doubting Thomas: A Novel about Caravaggio. Born, Anne, tr. from NOR. 2000. 159p. 29.95 (0-7206-1082-6) Owen, Peter Ltd. GBR. Dist: Dufour Editions, Inc.
Newman, Kim. Judgement of Tears: Anno Dracula 1959. 1998. 240p. 22.95 o.p. (0-7867-0558-2, Carroll & Graf Pubs.) Avalon Publishing Group.
Nugent, Madeline Pecora. Clare & Her Sisters: Lovers of the Poor Christ. 2003. (Illus.). xxxiv, 299p. pap. (0-8198-1561-6) Pauline Bks. & Media.
O'Hagan, Joan. Death & a Madonna. 1987. (Crime Club Ser.). 192p. o.s.i (0-385-24306-5) Doubleday Publishing.
Olschki, Marcella. Sixth Form 1939. 2002. 72p. pap. 12.95 (1-902881-63-X) Toby Pr.

Ondaatje, Michael. The English Patient. 1993. 320p. pap. 13.00 (*0-679-74520-3*); 1996. reprint ed. pap. 12.00 (*0-676-51420-0*) Knopf Publishing Group. (Vintage).

—The English Patient. 1993. 320p. pap. 10.50 (*0-394-28013-X*); 1993. pap. 7.00 o.p. (*0-679-74706-0*); 1992. 320p. 27.50 (*0-679-41678-1*) Knopf, Alfred A. Inc.

—The English Patient. abr. ed. 1993. audio 18.00 o.s.i (*0-679-42924-7*, 390725, RH Audio) Random Hse. Audio Publishing Group.

Ondaatje, Michael & Minghella, Anthony. The English Patient: A Screenplay. 1996. (Illus.). 208p. (J). pap. 10.95 (*0-7868-8245-X*) Hyperion Pr.

Otto, Whitney. The Passion Dream Book. 1998. 288p. pap. 13.00 (*0-06-109623-7*, Perennial); 1997. audio 18.00 o.p. (*0-694-51779-8*, CPN 2621, HarperAudio) HarperTrade.

—Passion Dream Book: A Novel. 1997. 288p. 22.00 o.s.i (*0-06-017824-8*) HarperCollins Pubs.

—The Passion Dream Book: A Novel. l.t. ed. 1997. (Americana Ser.). 432p. lib. bdg. 25.95 (*0-7862-1247-0*) Thorndike Pr.

Parini, Jay. Apprentice Lover: A Novel. 320p. 2003. pap. 12.95 (*0-06-093556-1*); 2002. 24.95 (*0-06-621071-2*) HarperCollins Pubs.

Park, Jacqueline. The Secret Book of Grazia Dei Rossi. 576p. 1998. pap. 14.00 (*0-684-84840-6*); 1997. 25.50 (*0-684-81603-2*) Simon & Schuster. (Simon & Schuster).

Parks, Tim. Destiny. 2000. 248p. 24.95 (*1-55970-517-5*); 2001. 256p. reprint ed. pap. 12.95 (*1-55970-575-2*) Arcade Publishing, Inc.

—Destiny. 1999. 248p. (*0-436-22088-1*) Secker, Martin & Warburg, Ltd.

—Europa. 1999. 272p. pap. 12.95 (*1-55970-506-X*) Arcade Publishing, Inc.

—Europa. 1997. 261p. (*0-436-20213-1*) Secker, Martin & Warburg, Ltd.

—Europa: A Novel. 1998. 272p. 23.95 (*1-55970-444-6*) Arcade Publishing, Inc.

—Home Thoughts. 1988. 208p. 16.95 o.p. (*0-8021-1035-5*) Grove/Atlantic, Inc.

—Juggling the Stars. 2001. 224p. pap. 12.95 (*1-55970-551-5*) Arcade Publishing, Inc.

—Juggling the Stars. l.t. ed. 1993. 21.95 o.p. (*0-7927-1642-6*); pap. 19.95 o.p. (*0-7927-1641-8*) BBC Audiobooks America.

—Juggling the Stars. 1993. 218p. 19.95 o.p. (*0-8021-1501-2*) Grove/Atlantic, Inc.

—Mimi's Ghost: A Novel. 2001. (Illus.). 313p. 24.95 (*1-55970-556-6*) Arcade Publishing, Inc.

Pasolini, Pier Paolo. A Violent Life. Weaver, William, tr. from ITA. 1992. 320p. reprint ed. pap. 13.00 o.s.i (*0-679-73505-4*, Pantheon) Knopf Publishing Group.

Pasqualino, Fortunato. The Little Jesus of Sicily. Rozier, Louise, tr. from ITA. 1999. (Illus.). xiv, 90p. 22.00 (*1-55728-572-1*); pap. 16.95 (*1-55728-573-X*) Univ. of Arkansas Pr.

Pastor, Ben. Liar Moon. 2001. 207p. pap. 18.00 (*1-929871-01-5*) Van Neste Bks.

Paul, Barbara. A Cadenza for Caruso: An Operatic Mystery. l.t. ed. 1986. (Nightingale Ser.). 227p. 10.95 o.p. (*0-8161-3781-1*, Macmillan Reference USA) Gale Group.

—A Cadenza for Caruso: An Operatic Mystery. 1986. mass mkt. 2.95 o.p. (*0-451-14523-2*, Signet Bks.) NAL.

—A Cadenza for Caruso: An Operatic Mystery. 1984. 175p. 11.95 o.p. (*0-312-11328-5*) St. Martin's Pr.

—Chorus of Detectives. 1987. 288p. 16.95 o.p. (*0-312-00576-8*) St. Martin's Pr.

—Prima Donna at Large. 1985. 304p. 15.95 o.p. (*0-312-64414-0*) St. Martin's Pr.

Pavese, Cesare. Among Women Only. Paige, D. D., tr. from ITA. 1979. 168p. 24.00 (*0-7206-0350-1*) Dufour Editions, Inc.

—Among Women Only. Paige, D. D., tr. from ITA. 1997. 198p. pap. 14.95 (*0-7206-1030-3*) Owen, Peter Ltd. GBR. *Dist:* Dufour Editions, Inc.

—Among Women Only. 1996. 168p. pap. 14.95 (*0-7206-1005-2*) Owen, Peter Ltd. GBR. *Dist:* Dufour Editions, Inc.

—The Moon & the Bonfire. Sinclair, Louis, tr. 1974. 15.95 o.p. (*0-7206-0383-8*) Dufour Editions, Inc.

—The Moon & the Bonfires. Flint, R. W., tr. from ITA. 2002. (New York Review Books Classics Ser.). 176p. pap. 12.95 (*1-59017-021-0*) New York Review of Bks., Inc., The.

—The Moon & the Bonfires. Sinclair, Louise, tr. from ITA. 2002. (Peter Owen Modern Classics Ser.). 189p. reprint ed. pap. 18.95 (*0-7206-1119-9*) Owen, Peter Ltd. GBR. *Dist:* Dufour Editions, Inc.

—Stories of Pavese. Murch, A. E., tr. from ITA. & intro. by. 1987. 415p. pap. o.p. (*0-88001-124-6*, Ecco) HarperTrade.

—Told in Confidence. Murch, A. E., tr. from ITA. 1971. 25.00 o.p. (*0-7206-0390-0*) Dufour Editions, Inc.

Peachment, Christopher. Caravaggio. Date not set. pap. (*0-312-31449-3*, St. Martin's Paperbacks) St. Martin's Pr.

—Caravaggio: A Novel. 2003. 240p. pap. (*0-330-48732-9*) Picador.

—Caravaggio: A Novel. 2003. 304p. 23.95 (*0-312-31448-5*) St. Martin's Pr.

Pears, Iain. The Bernini Bust. 1994. 192p. 19.95 o.s.i (*0-15-111830-2*) Harcourt Trade Pubs.

—Death & Restoration: A Jonathan Argyll Mystery. (Art History Mysteries Ser.). 2000. 288p. mass mkt. 6.50 (*0-425-17742-4*, Prime Crime); 2000. 223p. mass mkt. 6.50 (*0-00-649875-2*); 2003. 320p. reprint ed. pap. 13.00 (*0-425-19042-0*, Prime Crime) Berkley Publishing Group.

—Death & Restoration: A Jonathan Argyll Mystery. 1998. (Jonathan Argyll Mysteries Ser.: Vol. 6). 224p. 22.00 o.s.i (*0-684-81461-7*, Scribner) Simon & Schuster.

—Giotto's Hand. 2000. (Art History Mysteries Ser.). 288p. mass mkt. 6.50 (*0-425-17358-5*, Prime Crime) Berkley Publishing Group.

—Giotto's Hand. l.t. ed. 1997. (G. K. Hall Mystery Ser.). 305p. 25.95 o.p. (*0-7838-8362-5*, Macmillan Reference USA) Gale Group.

—Giotto's Hand. 1997. 224p. 20.50 (*0-684-81460-9*, Scribner) Simon & Schuster.

—The Last Judgement: A Jonathan Argyll Mystery. 1999. (Art History Mysteries Ser.). 288p. mass mkt. 6.50 (*0-425-17148-5*, Prime Crime) Berkley Publishing Group.

—The Last Judgement: A Jonathan Argyll Mystery. 1996. 224p. 20.50 (*0-684-81459-5*); 1995. 21.00 (*1-57283-001-8*) Simon & Schuster. (Scribner).

—The Raphael Affair. 1998. (Prime Crime Mysteries Ser.: Bk. 1). 240p. reprint ed. mass mkt. 6.50 (*0-425-16613-9*, Prime Crime) Berkley Publishing Group.

—The Raphael Affair. 1992. 191p. 18.95 (*0-15-178912-6*) Harcourt Trade Pubs.

—The Raphael Affair. l.t. ed. 1991. (Linford Mystery Library). pap. 17.99 o.p. (*0-7089-7155-5*, Ulverscroft) Thorpe, F. A. Pubs. GBR. *Dist:* Ulverscroft Large Print Bks., Ltd., Ulverscroft Large Print Canada, Ltd.

—The Titian Committee. 2002. 272p. pap. 12.00 (*0-425-18500-1*); 1999. 240p. reprint ed. pap. 6.50 (*0-425-16895-6*, Prime Crime) Berkley Publishing Group.

—The Titian Committee. 1993. 189p. 19.95 (*0-15-190472-3*) Harcourt Trade Pubs.

Pekarkova, Iva. The World Is Round. Powelstock, David, tr. 1994. Tr. of Kulaty Svet. (RUS.). 224p. 22.00 o.p. (*0-374-29287-6*) Farrar, Straus & Giroux.

Pemberton, Max. Signors of the Night. 1977. (Short Story Index Reprint Ser.). 22.95 (*0-8369-3680-9*) Ayer Co. Pubs., Inc.

Peters, Elizabeth, pseud. The Seventh Sinner. unabr. ed. 2001. audio compact disk 19.95; 2000. audio compact disk 40.00 (*0-7861-9942-3*, z2249); 1998. audio 32.95 (*0-7861-1467-3*, 2249); 1998. audio 32.95 (*0-7861-1324-3*, 696025) Blackstone Audio Bks., Inc.

—The Seventh Sinner. l.t. ed. 2002. lib. bdg. 27.95 (*1-58547-188-7*, Premier) Ctr. Point Large Print.

—The Seventh Sinner. 1991. reprint ed. 18.95 o.p. (*0-7278-4195-5*) Severn Hse. Pubs., Ltd.

—The Seventh Sinner. 1990. mass mkt. 3.95 (*0-445-77323-5*); 1989. 256p. mass mkt. 6.99 (*0-445-40778-6*); 1986. mass mkt. 3.95 o.s.i (*0-445-40225-3*) Warner Bks., Inc.

Petri, Romana. An Umbrian War. 2000. 266p. pap. 15.95 (*1-902881-14-1*); (*1-902881-09-5*) Toby Pr.

Phillips, Pat, contrib. by. Mediterranean Adventure. 22.95 (*0-7540-3629-4*) BBC Audiobooks America.

Phillips, Susan Elizabeth. Breathing Room. 2002. E-Book 19.95 (*0-06-009851-1*); E-Book 19.95 (*0-06-009850-3*); E-Book 7.99 (*0-06-009849-X*) HarperCollins General Bks. Group. (Perfect-Bound).

—Breathing Room. 2002. E-Book 7.99 (*0-06-009848-1*) HarperCollins Pubs.

—Breathing Room. 2003. 400p. mass mkt. 7.99 (*0-06-103209-3*, Avon Bks.); 2002. 528p. pap. 24.95 (*0-06-009391-9*) Morrow/Avon.

—Breathing Room: A Novel. 2002. 384p. 24.95 (*0-06-621122-0*, Morrow, William & Co.) Morrow/Avon.

Pippa Passes. audio HarperTrade.

Pirandello, Luigi. Tales of Madness: A Selection from Luigi Pirandello's Short Stories for a Year. Bussino, Giovanni R., tr. 1984. (ITA.). 17.95 (*0-937832-26-X*) Dante Univ. of America Pr., Inc.

—Tales of Suicide: A Selection from Luigi Pirandello's Short Stories for a Year. Bussino, Giovanni R., tr. & intro. by. 1988. 14.95 (*0-937832-31-6*) Dante Univ. of America Pr., Inc.

Plaidy, Jean. Light on Lucrezia. 1977. 240p. mass mkt. 1.75 o.s.i (*0-449-23108-9*, Fawcett) Ballantine Bks.

—Light on Lucrezia. 1976. 8.95 o.p. (*0-399-11723-7*) Putnam Publishing Group, The.

—Madonna of the Seven Hills. 1976. 288p. mass mkt. 1.75 o.s.i (*0-449-23026-0*, Fawcett) Ballantine Bks.

Pozzessere, Heather G. The Di Medici Bride. 1999. mass mkt. (*1-55166-469-0*, Mira Bks.) Harlequin Enterprises, Ltd.

—The Di Medici Bride. l.t. ed. 2000. (Americana Ser.). 427p. 28.95 (*0-7862-2610-2*) Thorndike Pr.

Prantera, Amanda. Don Giovanna. 2002. 241p. pap. 12.00 (*0-7475-5336-X*); 2000. 240p. 24.95 (*0-7475-4927-3*) Bloomsbury Publishing, Ltd. GBR. *Dist:* Trafalgar Square.

—Letter to Lorenzo. 2000. 224p. pap. 13.00 (*0-7475-4509-X*) Bloomsbury Publishing, Ltd. GBR. *Dist:* Trafalgar Square.

Pratolini, Vasco. A Tale of Poor Lovers. 1988. (Voices of Resistance Ser.). 368p. reprint ed. pap. 13.00 (*0-85345-723-9*) Monthly Review Pr.

Prior, Lily. Ardor: A Novel of Enchantment. 2004. (*0-06-052786-2*, Ecco) HarperTrade.

—Nectar: A Novel of Temptation. 272p. 2003. pap. 12.95 (*0-06-093682-7*); 2002. 23.95 (*0-06-621259-6*) HarperTrade. (Ecco).

Puzo, Mario. The Family. abr. ed. 2001. audio 25.95 (*0-694-52644-4*); audio compact disk 29.95 (*0-694-52643-6*); audio 39.95 (*0-694-52642-8*) HarperTrade. (HarperAudio).

—The Family. 2002. 432p. mass mkt. 7.99 (*0-06-103242-5*) Morrow/Avon.

—The Godfather. abr. ed. 1998. audio 24.95 (*1-882071-84-0*) B&B Audio, Inc.

—The Godfather. unabr. collector's ed. 1993. audio 88.00 (*0-7366-2386-8*, 3157) Books on Tape, Inc.

—The Godfather. unabr. ed. 1986. audio 23.95 o.p. (*0-930435-21-4*, 122, Bookcassette); audio 89.25 (*1-56100-016-7*, 1220, Unabridged Library Editions) Brilliance Audio.

—The Godfather. l.t. ed. 1985. (Special Editions Ser.). 688p. 19.95 o.p. (*0-8161-3875-3*, Macmillan Reference USA) Gale Group.

—The Godfather. 1983. 448p. mass mkt. 7.99 (*0-451-16771-6*); mass mkt. 4.95 o.p. (*0-451-15736-2*) NAL. (Signet Bks.).

—The Godfather. 1969. 448p. 24.95 (*0-399-10342-2*, G. P. Putnam's Sons) Penguin Group (USA) Inc.

—The Godfather. l.t. ed. 1986. (Charnwood Large Print Ser.). 752p. 29.99 o.p. (*0-7089-8351-0*, Charnwood) Thorpe, F. A. Pubs. GBR. *Dist:* Ulverscroft Large Print Bks., Ltd., Ulverscroft Large Print Canada, Ltd.

—The Godfather Papers & Other Confessions. 1972. 224p. 6.95 o.p. (*0-399-10935-8*) Putnam Publishing Group, The.

—The Sicilian. 1985. 416p. mass mkt. 6.99 o.s.i (*0-553-25282-8*) Bantam Bks.

—The Sicilian. unabr. ed. 1985. audio 19.95 (*0-930435-13-3*, 357, Bookcassette); audio 73.25 o.p. (*1-56100-008-6*, 1042, Unabridged Library Editions) Brilliance Audio.

—The Sicilian. l.t. ed. 1985. (Special Editions Ser.). 560p. 19.95 o.p. (*0-8161-3837-0*, Macmillan Reference USA) Gale Group.

—The Sicilian. unabr. ed. 1992. audio 91.00 (*1-55690-730-3*, 92230E7) Recorded Bks., LLC.

—The Sicilian. 1984. 448p. 17.45 o.p. (*0-671-43564-7*, Simon & Schuster) Simon & Schuster.

—The Sicilian. l.t. ed. 1986. (Charnwood Large Print Ser.). 574p. 29.99 o.p. (*0-7089-8317-0*, Charnwood) Thorpe, F. A. Pubs. GBR. *Dist:* Ulverscroft Large Print Bks., Ltd., Ulverscroft Large Print Canada, Ltd.

Puzo, Mario & Gino, Carol. The Family. l.t. ed. 2001. 608p. pap. 27.00 (*0-06-621398-3*) HarperCollins Pubs.

—The Family. 2001. (Illus.). 384p. 27.00 (*0-06-039445-5*, ReganBooks) HarperTrade.

Puzo, Mario & Sinatra, Nancy. The Godfather Pack: The Godfather & Frank Sinatra: An American Legend. abr. unabr. ed. 2001. audio 34.95 (*0-929071-26-3*) B&B Audio, Inc.

Quick, Amanda, pseud. Slightly Shady. l.t. ed. 2001. (Large Print Book Ser.). 391p. 31.95 (*1-58724-026-2*, Wheeler Publishing, Inc.) Gale Group.

Radcliffe, Ann. A Sicilian Romance. 1972. (Gothic Novels Ser.). reprint ed. 46.95 (*0-405-00809-0*) Ayer Co. Pubs., Inc.

—A Sicilian Romance. Milbank, Alison, ed. (Oxford World's Classics Ser.). 1999. 256p. pap. 10.95 (*0-19-283666-8*); 1993. 244p. (C). pap. 8.95 o.p. (*0-19-282212-8*) Oxford Univ. Pr., Inc.

—A Sicilian Romance, 1792, 2 vols. in 1. 2003. (Revolution & Romanticism Ser.). 498p. (*1-85477-190-6*) Woodstock Books.

Reeve, Clara, et al. The Old English Baron/the Castle of Otranto. 2001. (Eighteenth Century Literature Ser.: Vol. 1). (Illus.). 273p. per. 11.20 net. (*0-9679121-2-1*) College Publishing.

Remmert, Enrico. The Ballad of the Low Lives. Botsford, Aubrey, tr. from ITA. 2004. 250p. 19.95 (*1-59264-054-0*) Toby Pr.

Revely, Edith. In Good Faith. 1985. 272p. 22.95 (*0-87951-992-4*) Overlook Pr., The.

Ricci, Nino. Lives of the Saints. 1995. pap. 12.00 o.s.i (*0-312-13441-X*) Picador.

Rice, Anne. Cry to Heaven. 1995. 576p. mass mkt. 7.99 (*0-345-39693-6*); 1991. 544p. pap. 15.95 (*0-345-37370-7*); Set. 1994. 28.00 o.s.i (*0-345-38541-1*) Ballantine Bks.

—Cry to Heaven. 1988. 536p. mass mkt. 4.95 o.p. (*1-55817-105-3*); 1983. 544p. pap. 3.95 o.p. (*0-523-42063-3*) Kensington Publishing Corp. (Pinnacle Bks.).

—Cry to Heaven. 1982. 544p. 29.95 (*0-394-52351-2*) Knopf, Alfred A. Inc.

—Cry to Heaven. abr. ed. 1991. audio 16.00 o.p. (*0-394-58813-4*); Set. 1995. audio 8.99 o.s.i (*0-679-44349-5*, 390586) Random Hse. Audio Publishing Group. (RH Audio).

—Interview with the Vampire. 1997. (Vampire Chronicles: Bk. 1). pap. 14.00 o.s.i (*0-345-91272-1*); 1994. (Vampire Chronicles: Bk. 1). pap. 6.99 o.p. (*0-345-90444-3*); 1994. (Vampire Chronicles: Bk. 1). mass mkt. 6.99 o.p. (*0-345-90333-1*); 1991. (Vampire Chronicles: Bk. 1). 352p. mass mkt. 7.99 (*0-345-33766-2*); 1985. mass mkt. 3.50 o.p. (*0-345-32899-X*); 1982. mass mkt. 2.95 o.p. (*0-345-31059-4*); 1981. mass mkt. 2.75 o.p. (*0-345-29882-9*); 1979. mass mkt. 2.25 o.p. (*0-345-28126-8*); 20th ed. 1997. (Vampire Chronicles: Bk. 1). 352p. pap. 14.95 (*0-345-40964-7*) Ballantine Bks.

—Interview with the Vampire. 1991. (Vampire Chronicles: Bk. 1). 320p. reprint ed. lib. bdg. 35.95 (*0-89966-781-3*) Buccaneer Bks., Inc.

—Interview with the Vampire. (Vampire Chronicles: Bk. 1). 1994. 23.00 o.s.i (*0-394-26725-7*); 1993. o.s.i (*0-394-25662-X*); 1976. 352p. 27.95 (*0-394-49821-6*); 1996. 384p. 35.00 o.s.i (*0-679-45084-X*) Knopf, Alfred A. Inc.

—Interview with the Vampire. 1987. audio 14.95 o.p. (*0-394-55747-6*); Set. 1995. audio compact disk 25.00 (*0-679-44764-4*); Set. 1986. audio 17.00 (*0-394-55617-8*, 390985) Random Hse. Audio Publishing Group. (RH Audio).

—Interview with the Vampire. unabr. ed. (Vampire Chronicles: Bk. 1). 1999. audio compact disk 114.00 (*0-7887-3442-3*, C1048E7); 1994. audio 85.00 (*0-7887-0065-0*, 94321E7) Recorded Bks., LLC.

—The Vampire Armand. (New Tales of the Vampires Ser.: Bk. 2). mass mkt. 7.50 o.s.i (*0-345-42930-3*); 2002. (Vampire Chronicles). E-Book 7.99 (*0-345-46453-2*, Ballantine Bks.); 2000. (Vampire Chronicles). 480p. mass mkt. 7.99 (*0-345-43480-3*, Ballantine Bks.); 1999. (Vampire Chronicles: Bk. 2). 400p. pap. 14.95 (*0-345-40927-2*) Ballantine Bks.

—The Vampire Armand. unabr. ed. 1998. (New Tales of the Vampires Ser.: Bk. 2). audio 88.00 (*0-7366-4225-0*, 4726) Books on Tape, Inc.

—The Vampire Armand. l.t. ed. 1999. (New Tales of the Vampires Ser.: Bk. 2). pap. 26.95 o.p. (*0-7838-0263-3*, Macmillan Reference USA) Gale Group.

—The Vampire Armand. abr. ed. 1999. audio 24.00. audio 44.95 Highsmith Inc.

—The Vampire Armand. 1998. (Vampire Chronicles: Bk. 2). 384p. 26.95 (*0-679-45447-0*) Knopf, Alfred A. Inc.

—The Vampire Armand. abr. ed. 1998. audio 24.00 (*0-375-40181-4*, 493414); audio compact disk 27.50 (*0-375-40433-3*); audio 44.95 (*0-375-40434-1*, 134535) Random Hse. Audio Publishing Group. (RH Audio).

—The Vampire Armand. l.t. ed. 1998. (Vampire Chronicles). 576p. pap. 26.95 (*0-375-70415-9*) Random Hse. Large Print.

—The Vampire Armand. ltd. ed. 1998. (Vampire Chronicles: Bk. 6). 150.00 (*1-890885-06-1*) Trice, B.E. Publishing.

—The Vampire Chronicles, 4 vols. (Vampire Chronicles). 1993. 31.96 (*0-345-38540-3*); Set. 1989. 20.97 (*0-345-36422-8*) Ballantine Bks.

—The Vampire Chronicles, 3 vols. 1990. (Vampire Chronicles). 99.50 o.s.i (*0-394-58186-5*) Random Hse., Inc.

—The Vampire Lestat. (Vampire Chronicles: Bk. 2). 1997. 496p. pap. 15.95 (*0-345-41964-2*); 1994. mass mkt. 6.99 o.p. (*0-345-90334-X*); 1986. 560p. mass mkt. 7.99 (*0-345-31386-0*) Ballantine Bks.

—The Vampire Lestat. (Vampire Chronicles: Bk. 2). 1993. o.s.i (*0-394-25661-1*); 1985. 496p. 27.95 (*0-394-53443-3*) Knopf, Alfred A. Inc.

—The Vampire Lestat, Set. abr. ed. 1989. (Vampire Chronicles). audio 18.00 (*0-394-57705-1*, 391846, RH Audio) Random Hse. Audio Publishing Group.

—The Vampire Lestat. unabr. ed. 1994. (Vampire Chronicles: Bk. 2). audio 128.00 (*0-7887-0098-7*, 94339E7) Recorded Bks., LLC.

—Vittorio, the Vampire: New Tales of the Vampires. 2001. (New Tales of the Vampires Ser.: Bk. 3). 304p. mass mkt. 7.99 (*0-345-42239-2*, Ballantine Bks.) Ballantine Bks.

—Vittorio, the Vampire: New Tales of the Vampires. l.t. ed. 1999. (New Tales of the Vampires Ser.: Bk. 3). pap. 30.00 o.p. (*0-7838-8486-9*, Macmillan Reference USA) Gale Group.

—Vittorio, the Vampire: New Tales of the Vampires. abr. ed. 1999. audio 18.00 Highsmith Inc.

—Vittorio, the Vampire: New Tales of the Vampires. 1999. (New Tales of the Vampires Ser.: Bk. 3). o.s.i (0-676-58668-6); (Illus.). 304p. 19.95 (0-375-40160-1) Knopf, Alfred A. Inc.
—Vittorio, the Vampire: New Tales of the Vampires. abr. unabr. ed. 1999. (New Tales of the Vampires Ser.). audio 29.95 (0-375-40569-0, 895874, RH Audio) Random Hse. Audio Publishing Group.
—Vittorio, the Vampire: New Tales of the Vampires. l.t. ed. 1999. (New Tales of the Vampires Ser.: Bk. 3). 352p. pap. 19.95 (0-375-70572-4) Random Hse. Large Print.
—Vittorio, the Vampire: New Tales of the Vampires. ltd. ed. 1999. (New Tales of the Vampires Ser.: Bk. 3). 292p. 150.00 (1-890885-07-X) Trice, B.E. Publishing.
Ringo, James. Uncle Theodor. 1997. 80p. 16.95 o.p. (1-57197-058-4) Pentland Pr., Inc.
Riotta, Gianni. Prince of the Clouds. Sartarelli, Stephen, tr. from ITA. 2000. (Illus.). 287p. 24.00 o.p. (0-374-23725-5) Farrar, Straus & Giroux.
—Prince of the Clouds. Sartarelli, Stephen, tr. from ITA. 2001. 304p. pap. 13.00 o.p. (0-312-42015-3) Picador.
Ripley, Alexandra. The Time Returns. 1985. 360p. 16.95 o.p. (0-385-19408-0) Doubleday Publishing.
—The Time Returns. 1987. 432p. mass mkt. 4.50 o.p. (0-380-70162-6, Avon Bks.) Morrow/Avon.
Riviere, William. Kate Caterina. 2002. 384p. 25.00 (0-87113-839-5, Atlantic Monthly Pr.) Grove/ Atlantic, Inc.
Roberts, John Maddox. The Catiline Conspiracy. 1991. (SPQR Ser. : No. 2). 224p. mass mkt. 3.50 (0-380-75995-0, Avon Bks.) Morrow/Avon.
Roberts, Nora. Homeport. 1999. 496p. reprint ed. mass mkt. 7.99 (0-515-12489-3, Jove) Berkley Publishing Group.
—Homeport. abr. ed. 1999. audio 7.99 (1-56740-283-6, 1751, Paperback Nova Audio Bks.); 1998. audio 17.95 o.p. (1-56740-761-7, 477, Nova Audio Bks.); 1998. audio 25.95 (1-56100-786-2, 136, Bookcassette); 1998. audio 89.25 (1-56740-565-7, 899, Unabridged Library Editions) Brilliance Audio.
—Homeport. 1998. 448p. 23.95 o.s.i (0-399-14387-4, Grosset & Dunlap) Penguin Group (USA) Inc.
—Homeport. l.t. ed. (Paperback Bestsellers Ser.). 717p. 1999. pap. 26.95 (0-7862-1427-9); 1998. 29.95 (0-7862-1426-0) Thorndike Pr.
Robinson, Mary. Poems, 1791. 2003. (Revolution & Romanticism Ser.). 262p. (1-85477-191-4) Woodstock Books.
Roeske, Paulette. Bridge of Sighs: A Novella & Stories. 2002. 200p. 15.00 (1-58654-019-X) Story Line Pr.
Rolfe, Frederick W. The Desire & Pursuit of the Whole. 1986. (Twentieth Century Classics Ser.). 320p. pap. 6.95 o.p. (0-19-281941-0) Oxford Univ. Pr., Inc.
—Desire & Pursuit of the Whole: A Romance of Modern Venice. Eburne, Andrew, ed. 1994. 300p. 20.00 (0-8076-1331-2) Braziller, George Inc.
—The Desire & Pursuit of the Whole: A Romance of Modern Venice. (Gay Experience Ser.). reprint ed. 25.50 (0-404-61536-8) AMS Pr., Inc.
—The Desire & Pursuit of the Whole: A Romance of Modern Venice. 1977. 299p. reprint ed. 35.00 o.s.i (0-8371-9808-9, RODP, Greenwood Pr.) Greenwood Publishing Group, Inc.
Romano, Lalla. The Penumbra. Williams, Sian, tr. 1999. pap. 12.95 (0-7043-8071-4) Interlink Publishing Group, Inc.
Rossi, Hozy. Appointment with il Duce. 2003. 256p. pap. 15.00 (1-56649-254-8); 2001. 224p. 25.00 (1-56649-201-7) Welcome Rain Pubs.
Rotundi, Cesar. The Garden of Persephone. 1982. 340p. 19.95 o.p. (0-312-31682-8) St. Martin's Pr.
Ryan, Mary. The Promise. 1999. 288p. 22.95 o.p. (0-312-20571-6) St. Martin's Pr.
Sand, George. Consuelo: A Romance of Venice. 1979. (Quality Paperbacks Ser.). 225p. pap. text 9.00 o.p. (0-306-80102-7) Da Capo Pr., Inc.
Saylor, Steven. Arms of Nemesis. 1993. 336p. reprint ed. mass mkt. 5.99 o.s.i (0-8041-1127-8, Ivy Bks.) Ballantine Bks.
—Arms of Nemesis. unabr. ed. 1997. audio 56.95 Blackstone Audio Bks., Inc.
—Arms of Nemesis. 1992. 320p. 19.95 o.p. (0-312-08135-9, Saint Martin's Minotaur) St. Martin's Pr.
—Catilina's Riddle. unabr. ed. 1997. audio 85.95 (0-7861-1177-1, 1920) Blackstone Audio Bks., Inc.
—Catilina's Riddle. 1993. 22.95 o.p. (0-312-09763-8) St. Martin's Pr.
—The House of the Vestals: The Investigations of Gordianus the Finder. 1998. mass mkt. (0-312-96628-8, St. Martin's Paperbacks); 1998. (House of Vestals Ser.: Vol. 1). 272p. mass mkt. 6.99 (0-312-96452-8, St. Martin's Paperbacks); 1997. 288p. 22.95 (0-312-15444-5, Saint Martin's Minotaur) St. Martin's Pr.
—A Murder on the Appian Way. unabr. ed. 1996. audio 83.95 (0-7861-0983-1, 1760) Blackstone Audio Bks., Inc.
—A Murder on the Appian Way. 1996. 384p. 23.95 o.p. (0-312-14377-X, Saint Martin's Minotaur); 1997. 432p. reprint ed. mass mkt. 6.99 (0-312-96173-1, St. Martin's Paperbacks) St. Martin's Pr.
—Roman Blood. 1992. 416p. mass mkt. 6.50 o.s.i (0-8041-1039-5, Ivy Bks.) Ballantine Bks.
—Roman Blood. unabr. ed. 1996. audio 76.95 (0-7861-1058-9, 1829) Blackstone Audio Bks., Inc.
—Roman Blood. (St. Martin's Minotaur Mysteries Ser.). 2000. 416p. mass mkt. 6.99 (0-312-97296-2, St. Martin's Paperbacks); 1991. 288p. 19.95 (0-312-06454-3, Saint Martin's Minotaur) St. Martin's Pr.
—Rubicon. 2000. 301p. mass mkt. 6.50 (0-312-97118-4, St. Martin's Paperbacks); 1999. 288p. 23.95 o.p. (0-312-20576-7, Saint Martin's Minotaur) St. Martin's Pr.
—The Venus Throw. unabr. ed. 1997. audio 62.95 (0-7861-1218-2, 1998) Blackstone Audio Bks., Inc.
—The Venus Throw. l.t. ed. 1995. 587p. 25.95 o.p. (0-7838-1443-7, Macmillan Reference USA) Gale Group.
—The Venus Throw. 1995. x, 308p. 22.95 o.p. (0-312-11912-7, Saint Martin's Minotaur); 1996. 400p. reprint ed. pap. text 6.99 (0-312-95778-5, St. Martin's Paperbacks) St. Martin's Pr.
Schaeffer, Frank. Portofino. 304p. 1999. pap. 14.00 o.s.i (0-425-16694-5); 1996. mass mkt. 6.99 o.s.i (0-425-14981-1) Berkley Publishing Group.
—Portofino. unabr. ed. 1994. audio 39.95 (0-7861-0474-0, 1426) Blackstone Audio Bks., Inc.
—Portofino. 2002. 256p. pap. 17.95 (0-7432-4687-X, Scribner) Simon & Schuster.
Sciascia, Leonardo. Candido or, Dream Dreamed in Sicily. Wolff, Helen, ed. Foulke, Adrienne, tr. 1979. (Helen & Kurt Wolff Bk.). 7.95 o.p. (0-15-115380-9) Harcourt Trade Pubs.
Scott, Joanna. Tourmaline: A Novel. 288p. 2002. 23.95 (0-316-77618-1); 2003. reprint ed. pap. 13.95 (0-316-60848-3, Back Bay) Little Brown & Co.
—Tourmaline: A Novel. 2002. (Basic Ser.). 27.95 o.p. (0-7862-4893-9) Thorndike Pr.
Scragg, Leah, ed. John Lyly Euphues: Anatomy of Wit & 'Euphues & His England' 2003. (Revels Plays Companions Library). (Illus.). 400p. 74.95 o.s.i (0-7190-6458-9) Manchester Univ. Pr. GBR. *Dist:* Holtzbrinck Pubs.
Serao, Mathilde. The Conquest of Rome. Caesar, Ann, ed. (Women's Classics Ser.). 250p. (C). 1993. pap. text 20.00 (0-8147-7964-6); 1992. text 55.00 (0-8147-7955-7) New York Univ. Pr.
Seymour, Gerald. The Killing Ground. 1998. 576p. mass mkt. 16.95 (0-552-54535-X) Bantam Bks.
—The Killing Ground. l.t. ed. 1997. (G. K. Hall Mystery Ser.). 724p. lib. bdg. 25.95 o.p. (0-7838-8139-8, Macmillan Reference USA) Gale Group.
—The Killing Ground. 1997. 400p. 23.00 o.p. (0-06-101195-9) HarperCollins Pubs.
—The Killing Ground. l.t. ed. 1998. 576p. mass mkt. 6.99 (0-06-101196-7, Eos) Morrow/Avon.
Seymour, Miranda. Daughter of Shadows. 1977. 8.95 o.p. (0-698-10784-5) Putnam Publishing Group, The.
Sgorlon, Carlo. Army of Lost Rivers. Bright, Jessie, tr. from ITA. 1998. (Italian Fiction in Translation Ser.). 288p. pap. 17.50 (0-934977-62-3) Italica Pr.
Sharp, Alan. Unsolved Case of Sherlock Holmes. 1984. (Storytrails Ser.). 91p. pap. text 9.95 o.p. (0-521-27708-6) Cambridge Univ. Pr.
Shellabarger, Samuel. Prince of Foxes: The Best-Selling Historical Epic. 2002. reprint ed. 433p. 18.95 (1-882593-64-2); 226p. 32.50 (1-882593-65-0) Bridge Works Publishing Co., Inc.
Sherwood, John. Menacing Groves. 1990. (Garden Mystery Ser.: No. 5). 208p. mass mkt. 3.95 o.s.i (0-345-35975-5) Ballantine Bks.
—Menacing Groves. 1989. 192p. 15.95 o.s.i (0-684-18967-4, Macmillan Reference USA) Gale Group.
—Menacing Groves. l.t. ed. 1990. (Magna Large Print Ser.). 320p. o.p. (1-85057-661-0) Magna Large Print Bks. GBR. *Dist:* Ulverscroft Large Print Canada, Ltd.
Shimony, Abner. Tibaldo & the Hole in the Calendar. 1997. (Copernicus Ser.). (Illus.). 165p. (gr. 4-7). text 21.00 (0-387-94935-6) Springer-Verlag New York, Inc.
Siddons, Anne Rivers. Hill Towns. unabr. ed. 1994. audio 80.00 (0-7366-2574-7, 3323) Books on Tape, Inc.
—Hill Towns. l.t. ed. 501p. 1994. pap. 17.95 (0-8161-5849-5); 1993. lib. bdg. 23.95 (0-8161-5848-7) Gale Group. (Macmillan Reference USA).
—Hill Towns. 1993. 464p. 22.00 o.p. (0-06-017935-X); 264.00 o.p. (0-06-017746-2) HarperCollins Pubs.
—Hill Towns. abr. ed. 1993. audio 16.00 (1-55994-718-7, Caedmon) HarperTrade.
—Hill Towns. 1994. 432p. mass mkt. 7.99 (0-06-109969-4, HarperTorch) Morrow/Avon.
—Hill Towns. pap. 6.98 o.p. (0-8317-7904-7) Smithmark Pubs., Inc.
Silone, Ignazio. The Abruzzo Trilogy: Fontamara, Bread & Wine, The Seed Beneath the Snow. Mosbacher, Eric, tr. from ITA. 2000. (Steerforth Italia Ser.). xxiv, 927p. pap. 27.00 (1-58642-006-2, Steerforth Italia) Steerforth Pr.
Skimin, Robert & Pacheco, Ferdie. Renegade Lightning: A Novel. 1992. 304p. 19.95 o.p. (0-89141-437-1, Presidio Pr.) Ballantine Bks.
Sklepowich, Edward. Black Bridge: A Mystery of Venice. 1995. 224p. 20.50 (0-684-81520-6); o.s.i (1-883402-84-0) Simon & Schuster. (Scribner).
—Death in a Serene City. 1992. 304p. pap. 4.50 (0-380-71636-4, Avon Bks.); 1990. 18.95 o.p. (0-688-09180-6, Morrow, William & Co.) Morrow/ Avon.
—Death in the Palazzo: A Venetian Mystery. 1997. 250p. 21.50 o.p. (0-684-83031-0, Scribner) Simon & Schuster.
—Farewell to the Flesh: An Urbino Macintyre Mystery. 1993. 288p. pap. 4.99 (0-380-71814-6, Avon Bks.); 1991. 352p. 19.00 o.p. (0-688-11006-1, Morrow, William & Co.) Morrow/Avon.
—Liquid Desires: An Urbino Macintyre Mystery. 1993. 315p. 22.00 o.p. (0-688-11165-3, Morrow, William & Co.); 1994. 320p. reprint ed. mass mkt. 4.99 (0-380-72150-3, Avon Bks.) Morrow/Avon.
—Liquid Desires: An Urbino Macintyre Mystery. 316p. 4.98 o.p. (0-7651-0268-4) Smithmark Pubs., Inc.
Slavitt, David R. Cliff. Novel. abr. ed. 1994. 154p. 21.95 (0-8071-1781-1) Louisiana State Univ. Pr.
Smith, D. L. The Miracles of Santo Fico. 2003. 28.95 (0-7862-5243-X) Thorndike Pr.
—The Miracles of Santo Fico. 368p. 2004. pap. 16.00 (0-446-69036-8); 2003. 22.95 (0-446-53103-0) Warner Bks., Inc.
Smith, Noble. Stolen from Gypsies. 2000. (Illus.). 279p. 23.95 (0-9675448-0-7) Aubrey Hse.
—Stolen from Gypsies. 2002. (Illus.). 282p. pap. 15.95 (1-883991-82-X) White Cloud Pr.
Smith, Wilbur. Cry Wolf. unabr. ed. 1991. (Audio Bks.). audio 96.95 (0-7451-6290-8, CAB 560) BBC Audiobooks America.
—Cry Wolf. unabr. collector's ed. 1988. (Ballantyne Novels Ser.). audio 88.00 (0-7366-1396-X, 2285) Books on Tape, Inc.
—Cry Wolf. 1978. pap. 2.25 o.p. (0-440-11495-0) Dell Publishing.
—Cry Wolf. 1977. 15.95 o.p. (0-385-12449-X) Doubleday Publishing.
—Cry Wolf. 1996. 450p. pap. 6.99 (0-7493-2421-X, Butterworth-Heinemann) Elsevier Science & Technology Bks.
Sollers, Philippe. Watteau in Venice. 1994. Orig. Title: Fete a Venise. 288p. text 22.00 (0-684-19451-1, Scribner) Simon & Schuster.
Spark, Muriel. The Driver's Seat. 1994. (Bibelots Ser.). 112p. pap. 7.00 (0-8112-1271-8, NDP786) New Directions Publishing Corp.
—The Driver's Seat. 1984. 128p. pap. 6.95 o.p. (0-399-50928-3) Putnam Publishing Group, The.
—Territorial Rights. 1984. 248p. pap. 6.95 o.p. (0-399-50930-5) Putnam Publishing Group, The.
Spencer, Elizabeth. The Light in the Piazza. 1986. 256p. pap. 7.95 o.p. (0-14-008712-5, Penguin Bks.) Viking Penguin.
—Light in the Piazza. 1960. pap. o.p. (0-07-060190-9) McGraw-Hill Cos., The.
—The Light in the Piazza & Other Italian Tales. 1995. (Banner Bks.). 304p. reprint ed. pap. 16.95 (0-87805-837-0); lib. bdg. 48.00 (0-87805-836-2) Univ. Pr. of Mississippi.
St. Aubin De Teran, Lisa. Nocturne. 1993. 224p. 19.95 o.p. (0-312-09888-X) St. Martin's Pr.
Stark, Jerry. Foreign Exchange. 2004. 220p. pap. (1-932162-22-4) Benoy Publishing.
Stein, Gertrude. The World Is Round. 1985. (Illus.). (J). (gr. 3 up). 200.00 o.p. (0-910457-16-6) Arion Pr.
—The World Is Round. 1988. (Illus.). 176p. reprint ed. 19.95 o.p. (0-86547-326-9, North Point Pr.) Farrar, Straus & Giroux.
—The World Is Round. 1965. (Illus.). 59p. (C). lib. bdg. 75.00 (0-8383-0629-2) M.S.G. Haskell Hse.
—The World Is Round. 1973. (Illus.). 96p. (J). (gr. 3-5). pap. 0.95 o.p. (0-380-01475-0, 08169, Avon Bks.) Morrow/Avon.
Stendhal. The Charterhouse of Parma. lib. bdg. 30.95 (0-8488-1883-0) Amereon, Ltd.
—The Charterhouse of Parma. 1990. 480p. mass mkt. 4.95 o.s.i (0-553-21389-X) Bantam Bks.
—The Charterhouse of Parma. Scott-Moncrieff, C. K., tr. from FRE. 1992. (Everyman's Library). 560p. 20.00 (0-679-41743-5) Knopf, Alfred A. Inc.
—The Charterhouse of Parma. 1982. mass mkt. 0.75 o.p. (0-451-50144-6, Signet Classics); 1982. mass mkt. 3.95 o.p. (0-451-51731-8, Signet Classics); 1962. pap. 4.95 o.p. (0-452-00891-3, Meridian Bks.) NAL.
—The Charterhouse of Parma. Scott-Moncrieff, C. K., tr. 1962. mass mkt. 4.95 o.p. (0-451-51858-6, C1858, Signet Classics) NAL.
—The Charterhouse of Parma. Pearson, Roger, ed. Mauldon, Margaret, tr. from FRE. (Oxford World's Classics Ser.). (Illus.). 1999. 560p. pap. 10.95 (0-19-283957-8); 1997. 546p. pap. 9.95 o.p. (0-19-283183-6) Oxford Univ. Pr., Inc.
—The Charterhouse of Parma. 2000. (Classics Ser.). (Illus.). 560p. pap. 11.95 (0-679-78318-0, Modern Library) Random House Adult Trade Publishing Group.
—The Charterhouse of Parma. Howard, Richard, tr. from FRE. 1999. (Modern Library Ser.). (Illus.). 528p. 24.95 (0-679-60245-3, Modern Library) Random House Adult Trade Publishing Group.
—The Charterhouse of Parma. Scott-Moncrieff, C. K. & Shaw, Margaret R., trs. 1958. (Classics Ser.). 496p. pap. 11.95 (0-14-044061-5, Penguin Classics) Viking Penguin.
—La Chartreuse de Parme. (FRE.). pap. 9.25 (2-08-070026-X) Flammarion et Cie FRA. *Dist:* Continental Bk. Co., Inc.
—La Chartreuse de Parme. 1999. (FRE.). pap. 10.95 (2-266-08269-8) Presses Pocket FRA. *Dist:* Distribooks, Inc.
—Three Italian Chronicles. Scott-Moncrieff, C. K., tr. from FRE. 1991. (Revived Modern Classic Ser.: Vol. 704). 208p. pap. 11.95 (0-8112-1150-9, NDP704) New Directions Publishing Corp.
Stern, Richard. Stitch. 1986. 205p. pap. 5.95 o.p. (0-87795-837-8, Morrow, William & Co.) Morrow/ Avon.
Sterne, Laurence. A Sentimental Journey. 2000. per. 9.90 (1-891355-67-8); per. 15.50 (1-58396-233-6) Blue Unicorn Editions.
—A Sentimental Journey. 2004. 112p. pap. 2.50 (0-486-43473-7) Dover Pubns., Inc.
—A Sentimental Journey. E-Book 2.49 (1-58627-640-9) Electric Umbrella Publishing.
—A Sentimental Journey. mass mkt. 0.60 o.p. (0-451-50254-X, Signet Classics) NAL.
—A Sentimental Journey. (Ebook Classic Ser.). E-Book 5.00 (0-7410-1326-6) SoftBook Pr.
—A Sentimental Journey. 1995. 282p. 5.50 (0-460-87336-9, Everyman's Classic Library in Paperback) Tuttle Publishing.
—A Sentimental Journey. Goring, Paul, ed. & intro. by. 2002. (Classics Ser.). 160p. pap. 7.00 (0-14-043779-7) Viking Penguin.
—A Sentimental Journey. Alvarez, A. & Petrie, Graham, eds. 1967. (Penguin Classics Ser.). 160p. pap. 5.95 o.s.i (0-14-043026-1, Penguin Classics) Viking Penguin.
—A Sentimental Journey Through France & Italy. 2002. E-Book 3.95 (0-594-08623-X) 1873 Pr.
—A Sentimental Journey Through France & Italy. 1983. 19.50 o.p. (0-913720-29-1); ring bd. 37.50 o.p. (0-913720-28-3) Beil, Frederic C. Pub., Inc.
—A Sentimental Journey Through France & Italy. 1975. reprint ed. 11.95 o.p. (0-460-00796-3); 2.50 o.p. (0-460-01796-9) Biblio Distribution.
—A Sentimental Journey Through France & Italy. reprint ed. lib. bdg. 196.00 (0-7426-2068-9); 2001. (Collected Works of Laurence Sterne: Vol. 4). pap. text 56.00 (0-7426-7068-6) Classic Bks.
—A Sentimental Journey Through France & Italy. 1968. (Oxford World's Classics Ser.). 8.95 o.p. (0-19-250333-2) Oxford Univ. Pr., Inc.
—A Sentimental Journey Through France & Italy by Mr. Yorick. Stout, Gardner D., ed. rev. ed. 1967. (Illus.). 42.00 o.p. (0-520-01228-3) Univ. of California Pr.
—A Sentimental Journey Through France & Italy by Mr. Yorick: With the Journal to Eliza & a Political Romance. Jack, Ian, ed. & intro. by. 1998. (Oxford World's Classics Ser.). 272p. pap. 6.95 (0-19-283522-X) Oxford Univ. Pr., Inc.
—A Sentimental Journey Through France & Italy by Mr. Yorick: With the Journal to Eliza & a Political Romance. Jack, Ian, ed. 1984. (Oxford World's Classics Ser.). 270p. pap. 4.95 o.p. (0-19-281685-3) Oxford Univ. Pr., Inc.
Stewart, Sally A. A Rose for Every Month. l.t. ed. 1993. (Magna Large Print Ser.). 648p. 29.99 o.p. (0-7505-0541-9) Magna Large Print Bks. GBR. *Dist:* Ulverscroft Large Print Bks., Ltd., Ulverscroft Large Print Canada, Ltd.
—A Rose for Every Month. 1994. 432p. 23.95 o.p. (0-312-10498-7) St. Martin's Pr.
Stone, Irving. Agony & the Ecstasy. 1987. 776p. mass mkt. 5.95 o.p. (0-451-15947-0, AE2643); mass mkt. 4.95 o.p. (0-451-14692-1) NAL. (Signet Bks.).
—Agony & the Ecstasy. 1995. 15.04 (0-606-04125-7) Turtleback Bks.
—The Agony & the Ecstasy. Date not set. 774p. 38.95 (0-8488-2402-4) Amereon, Ltd.
—The Agony & the Ecstasy. unabr. ed. 1977. Pt. 1. audio 80.00; Pt. 2. audio 88.00 Books on Tape, Inc.
—The Agony & the Ecstasy. 1994. reprint ed. lib. bdg. 39.95 (1-56849-340-1) Buccaneer Bks., Inc.
—The Agony & the Ecstasy. 1976. mass mkt. 2.25 o.p. (0-451-07444-0); 1971. mass mkt. 1.75 o.p. (0-451-05189-0); 1969. mass mkt. 1.50 o.p.

(*0-451-04050-3*); 1963. mass mkt. 4.50 o.p. (*0-451-14083-4*); 1963. mass mkt. 2.75 o.p. (*0-451-08276-1*); 1963. mass mkt. 3.50 o.p. (*0-451-09284-8*); 1963. mass mkt. 1.95 o.p. (*0-451-06378-3*); 1963. mass mkt. 0.95 o.p. (*0-451-02246-7*); 1963. mass mkt. 3.95 o.p. (*0-451-12643-2*); 1963. mass mkt. 1.75 o.p. (*0-451-04648-X*); 1963. mass mkt. 3.95 o.p. (*0-451-11010-2*); 1963. mass mkt. 1.25 o.p. (*0-451-02800-7*) NAL. (Signet Bks.).

—The Agony & the Ecstasy. abr. l.t. ed. 1976. (Ulverscroft Large Print Ser.). 12.00 o.p. (*0-85456-561-2*, Ulverscroft) Thorpe, F. A. Pubs. GBR. *Dist:* Ulverscroft Large Print Bks., Ltd., Ulverscroft Large Print Canada, Ltd.

—The Agony & the Ecstasy, Pts. 1 & 2. unabr. ed. Incl. Pt. 1. audio 80.00 Pt. 2. audio 88.00 1977. Set audio 168.00 (*0-7366-0048-5*, 1061-A/B) Books on Tape, Inc.

—The Agony & the Ecstasy: A Biographical Novel of Michelangelo. 1987. 776p. mass mkt. 8.99 (*0-451-17135-7*, Signet Classics) NAL.

—The Agony & the Ecstasy: A Novel of Michelangelo. 1961. 19.95 o.s.i (*0-385-01092-3*) Doubleday Publishing.

Stone, Ralph O. Passion & Death in Tuscany: At the Edge of Time. 2001. 401p. pap. 24.99 (*0-7388-2814-9*); (Illus.). text 34.99 (*0-7388-2813-0*) Xlibris Corp.

Strong, Susan. Romantic Assignment. l.t. ed. 1991. 17.95 o.p. (*0-7451-8039-6*, AH089); pap. 15.95 o.p. (*0-7927-0510-6*, AS0125) BBC Audiobooks America.

Stuart, Anne. The Widow. 2001. 384p. mass mkt. (*1-55166-813-0*, Mira Bks.) Harlequin Enterprises, Ltd.

Sturz, James. Sasso. 2002. 306p. 25.95 (*0-8027-3372-7*) Walker & Co.

Styron, William. Set This House on Fire. 1981. 528p. pap. 3.95 o.p. (*0-553-14666-1*) Bantam Bks.

—Set This House on Fire. unabr. collector's ed. 1986. Pt. 1. audio 72.00 (*0-7366-0557-6*, 1530-A); Pt. 2. audio 72.00 (*0-7366-0558-4*, 1530-B) Books on Tape, Inc.

—Set This House on Fire. 1977. mass mkt. 0.95 o.p. (*0-451-01944-X*, Signet Bks.) NAL.

—Set This House on Fire. 1993. 528p. pap. 15.00 (*0-679-73674-3*) Random Hse., Inc.

Tabucchi, Antonio. Letter from Casablanca. Thresher, Janice M., tr. from ITA. 1986. Tr. of Gioco del Rovescio. 128p. 17.95 (*0-8112-0985-7*); pap. 7.95 o.s.i (*0-8112-0986-5*, NDP620) New Directions Publishing Corp.

Tamaro, Susanna. Answer Me. 2003. 224p. pap. 12.95 (*0-385-72190-0*, Anchor Canada) Doubleday Canada, Ltd. CAN. *Dist:* Random Hse., Inc.

—Follow Your Heart. 1996. 208p. pap. 11.95 (*0-385-31657-7*, Delta); mass mkt. 6.50 (*0-440-29549-1*) Dell Publishing.

—Follow Your Heart. Cullen, John, tr. from ITA. l.t. ed. 1996. 23.95 o.p. (*1-56895-310-0*, Wheeler Publishing, Inc.) Gale Group.

—Follow Your Heart. unabr. ed. 1999. audio 35.00 (*0-7887-0616-0*, 94787E7) Recorded Bks., LLC.

Tarchetti, Igino U. Fantastic Tales. Venuti, Lawrence, tr. 1992. (Illus.). 200p. 25.00 (*1-56279-020-X*) Mercury Hse.

Terpening, Ron. Storm Track. 1989. 360p. 22.95 (*0-8027-1069-7*) Walker & Co.

Tessier, Thomas. Father Panic's Opera Macabre. 2001. 170p. 40.00 (*1-931081-12-3*) Subterranean Pr.

Timpanelli, Gioia. Sometimes the Soul: Two Novellas of Sicily. 1999. 192p. pap. 11.95 (*0-375-70722-0*) Knopf, Alfred A. Inc.

—Sometimes the Soul: Two Novellas of Sicily. 1998. 192p. 23.00 (*0-393-02744-9*) Norton, W. W. & Co., Inc.

Tine, Robert. Black Market. 1992. 320p. 21.95 o.p. (*0-312-06907-3*) St. Martin's Pr.

Todd, Marilyn. Man Eater. 2002. 384p. mass mkt. 11.95 (*0-330-35407-8*) Pan Bks. Ltd. GBR. *Dist:* Trafalgar Square.

—Virgin Territory. l.t. unabr. ed. 1997. 351p. 32.50 o.p. (*0-7531-5529-X*, 15529X) ISIS Large Print Bks. GBR. *Dist:* Ulverscroft Large Print Bks., Ltd., Ulverscroft Large Print Canada, Ltd.

—Wolf Whistle. 2002. 356p. mass mkt. 11.95 (*0-330-37199-1*) Pan Bks. Ltd. GBR. *Dist:* Trafalgar Square.

Tomasi Di Lampedusa, Giuseppe. The Leopard. 1976. 23.95 (*0-8488-0985-8*) Amereon, Ltd.

—The Leopard. Calquhoun, Archibald, tr. 1983. audio 12.95 o.p. (*0-694-50363-0*, SWC 1720, Caedmon) HarperTrade.

—The Leopard. 1991. (Everyman's Library). 240p. 18.00 (*0-679-40757-X*, Everyman's Library) Knopf Publishing Group.

—The Leopard. Colquhoun, Archibald, tr. from ITA. 1991. 320p. pap. 13.00 (*0-679-73121-0*, Pantheon) Knopf Publishing Group.

—The Leopard. 1987. (Modern Writers Ser.). pap. 9.95 o.s.i (*0-394-75668-1*, Pantheon) Knopf Publishing Group.

—The Leopard. Colquhoun, A., tr. 1960. 14.00 o.p. (*0-394-43291-6*, Pantheon) Knopf Publishing Group.

—The Leopard. 1992. 22.00 o.p. (*0-8446-6617-3*) Smith, Peter Pub., Inc.

Tomasi di Lampedusa, Giuseppe. Der Leopard. audio 42.95 o.p. Olivia & Hill Pr., The.

Tomasi di Lampedusa, Giuseppe. The Leopard. rev. ed. 1982. (Modern Classics Ser.). 320p. pap. 6.95 o.s.i (*0-394-74949-9*, Pantheon) Knopf Publishing Group.

Townsend, Lindsay. Voices in the Dark. l.t. ed. 1999. (Magna Large Print Ser.). 560p. 31.99 (*0-7505-1372-1*) Magna Large Print Bks. GBR. *Dist:* Ulverscroft Large Print Bks., Ltd., Ulverscroft Large Print Canada, Ltd.

Tozzi, Federigo. Ghisola. Wilhelm, James J., ed. Klopp, Charles, tr. from ITA. 1990. (Library of World Literature in Translation: Vol. 18). 160p. reprint ed. text 15.00 (*0-8240-3313-2*) Garland Publishing, Inc.

Trevor, William. My House in Umbria: Movie Tie Edition. 2003. 160p. pap. 10.00 (*0-14-200365-4*) Penguin Group (USA) Inc.

Unsworth, Barry. After Hannibal. 1998. (Illus.). 264p. pap. 13.00 (*0-393-31770-6*) Norton, W. W. & Co., Inc.

Valens, Amy. Danilo the Fruit Man. (Illus.). 16p. (J). 3.98 o.p. (*0-8317-9395-3*) Smithmark Pubs., Inc.

Vansittart, Peter. Choice of Murder. 1993. 216p. 30.00 (*0-7206-0832-5*) Dufour Editions, Inc.

—A Choice of Murder. 1992. 216p. pap. 29.95 (*0-7206-0851-1*) Owen, Peter Ltd. GBR. *Dist:* Dufour Editions, Inc.

Vassalli, Sebastiano. The Chimera. Creagh, Patrick, tr. from ITA. 320p. 1995. 24.00 (*0-684-80260-0*); 1994. 21.00 (*0-689-12202-0*) Simon & Schuster. (Scribner).

Verga, Giovanni. Cavalleria Rusticana: And Other Stories. Lawrence, D. H., tr. from ITA. 1975. 301p. reprint ed. lib. bdg. 22.50 o.p. (*0-8371-8105-4*, VECR, Greenwood Pr.) Greenwood Publishing Group, Inc.

—The House by the Medlar Tree. Mosbacher, Eric, tr. from ITA. 1975. 247p. reprint ed. o.p. (*0-8371-8205-0*, VEMT, Greenwood Pr.) Greenwood Publishing Group, Inc.

—Little Novels of Sicily. Lawrence, D. H., tr. 1975. 226p. reprint ed. lib. bdg. 22.50 o.p. (*0-8371-8199-2*, VENS, Greenwood Pr.) Greenwood Publishing Group, Inc.

—Little Novels of Sicily. Lawrence, D. H., tr. from ITA. 3rd ed. 2000. (Steerforth Italia Ser.). 200p. pap. 12.00 (*1-883642-54-X*) Steerforth Pr.

—Short Sicilian Novels. Lawrence, D. H., tr. from ITA. 1985. (Dedalus European Classcis Ser.). 171p. pap. 4.95 o.p. (*0-946626-04-9*) Dedalus, Ltd.

—Short Sicilian Novels. Lane, Eric, ed. Lawrence, D. H., tr. from ITA. 3rd ed. 1999. (European Classics Ser.). 173p. reprint ed. pap. 11.95 (*1-873982-40-2*) Dedalus, Ltd.

Vickers, Salley. Miss Garnet's Angel. l.t. ed. 2001. (Illus.). 352p. 25.00 (*0-7867-0823-9*, Carroll & Graf Pubs.) Avalon Publishing Group.

—Miss Garnet's Angel. 2002. 352p. pap. 13.00 (*0-452-28297-7*) Dutton/Plume.

—Miss Garnet's Angel. l.t. ed. 2002. 320p. pap. 24.95 (*0-7862-3690-6*) Gale Group.

Vinci, Simona. What We Don't Know about Children. Proctor, Minna, tr. from ITA. 2000. 176p. 21.00 o.s.i (*0-375-40411-2*) Knopf, Alfred A. Inc.

Vittorini, Elio. Women of Messina. Frenaye, Frances & Keene, Frances, trs. from ITA. 1973. 320p. 9.50 o.p. (*0-8112-0496-0*); pap. 3.75 o.p. (*0-8112-0497-9*, NDP365) New Directions Publishing Corp.

Volponi, Paolo. Last Act in Urbino (Il Sipario Ducale) Pedroni, Peter N., tr. from ITA. & intro. by. 1995. 320p. (Orig.). pap. 15.00 (*0-934977-33-X*) Italica Pr.

Von Arnim, Elizabeth. Enchanted April. lib. bdg. 24.95 (*0-8488-1888-1*) Amereon, Ltd.

—Enchanted April. abr. ed. 1994. (Read-Along Ser.). pap. 29.99 incl. audio (*0-88646-836-1*, LSR 7347) Durkin Hayes Publishing Ltd.

—Enchanted April. 1993. 320p. mass mkt. 5.99 (*0-671-86864-0*, Pocket) Simon & Schuster.

—The Enchanted April, Set. unabr. ed. 1998. 35.95 incl. audio (*1-55685-519-2*) Audio Bk. Contractors, Inc.

—The Enchanted April. unabr. ed. 2000. audio compact disk 56.00 (*0-7861-9927-X*, z1428); 1994. audio 44.95 (*0-7861-0476-7*, 1428) Blackstone Audio Bks., Inc.

—The Enchanted April. unabr. ed. 2000. audio 49.95 (*0-7451-2757-6*, SAB 123) Chivers Audio Bks. GBR. *Dist:* BBC Audiobooks America.

—The Enchanted April, Set. unabr. ed. 1999. audio 44.95 Highsmith Inc.

—The Enchanted April. Ng, Donna, ed. 1995. 192p. reprint ed. pap. (*0-671-53614-1*, Washington Square Pr.) Simon & Schuster.

—The Enchanted April. 2001. (Modern Classics). 361p. reprint ed. 13.95 (*0-86068-517-9*) Virago Pr., Ltd. GBR. *Dist:* Trafalgar Square.

Von Hofmannsthal, Hugo. Andreas. Hottinger, Marie D., tr. 2001. 192p. pap. 14.00 (*1-901285-01-4*) Pushkin Pr., Ltd. GBR. *Dist:* Consortium Bk. Sales & Distribution.

—Andreas. Hottinger, Marie D., tr. from GER. 2000. 192p. pap. 12.95 (*1-885586-03-5*) Turtle Point Pr.

Vreeland, Susan. The Passion of Artemesia. l.t. ed. 2002. 497p. 29.95 (*0-7862-3856-9*) Gale Group.

—The Passion of Artemesia. abr. unabr. ed. 2002. audio 34.95 (*1-56511-525-2*) HighBridge Co.

—The Passion of Artemesia. 2002. 352p. pap. 13.00 (*0-14-200182-1*) Penguin Group (USA) Inc.

—The Passion of Artemesia. 2002. 320p. 24.95 o.s.i (*0-670-89449-4*, Viking) Viking Penguin.

Wagner, Geoffrey. A Singular Passion. 1994. 303p. 20.00 (*1-880909-22-7*) Baskerville Pubs., Inc.

Wall, Michael. The Cassino Legacy. 1999. 379p. (*0-14-028836-8*) Viking Penguin.

Warner, Marina. The Lost Father. 1989. 18.95 o.p. (*0-671-67455-2*, Simon & Schuster) Simon & Schuster.

Weale, Anne. Retrouvailles a Venise. 1997. (Harlequin Azur Ser.). (FRE.). pap. (*0-373-34650-6*, 1-34650-1, Harlequin Bks.) Harlequin Enterprises, Ltd.

Weaver, William F. A Tent in This World. 1999. 160p. 20.00 (*0-929701-58-5*) McPherson & Co.

West, Cameron. The Medici Dagger. 2002. E-Book 5.99 (*0-7434-2451-4*); 2001. (Illus.). 256p. 25.00 (*0-7434-2035-7*) Simon & Schuster. (Atria).

West, Morris. The Devil's Advocate. 1959. 17.95 o.p. (*0-688-01453-4*, Morrow, William & Co.) Morrow/Avon.

—Eminence. l.t. ed. 2000. 424p. lib. bdg. 27.95 (*1-58547-044-9*) Ctr. Point Large Print.

—Eminence. 1998. 336p. 25.00 o.s.i (*0-15-100439-0*) Harcourt Trade Pubs.

—Eminence. 1998. (*0-7322-6704-8*) HarperCollins Pubs.

—Eminence. unabr. ed. 1999. audio 71.00 (*1-84197-007-7*, H1007E7, Clipper Audio) Recorded Bks., LLC.

—Eminence. 2003. 328p. pap. 14.95 (*1-902881-69-9*) Toby Pr.

—The Last Confession. l.t. ed. 2001. 217p. lib. bdg. 25.95 (*1-58547-131-3*); 248p. (*0-7531-6545-7*) Ctr. Point Large Print.

—The Last Confession. 2000. (Illus.). xxi, 214p. pap. (*0-7322-6595-9*) HarperCollins Pubs.

—The Last Confession. 2003. 192p. pap. 12.95 (*1-902881-44-3*) Toby Pr.

Weston, Carol. The Diary of Melanie Martin: Or How I Survived Matt the Brat, Michelangelo & the Leaning Tower of Pizza. 2001. (Illus.). 160p. (gr. 3-7). pap. text 4.99 (*0-440-41667-1*, Yearling) Random Hse. Children's Bks.

Wheatcroft, John. The Education of Malcolm Palmer. 1997. 160p. 18.95 (*0-8453-4863-9*, Cornwall Bks.) Associated Univ. Presses.

Williams, Niall. As It Is in Heaven. abr. ed. 2001. audio (*0-333-78257-7*) Macmillan U.K. GBR. *Dist:* Macmillan Publishing Co., Inc.

—As It Is in Heaven. l.t. ed. 1999. (Basic Ser.). 488p. 29.95 (*0-7862-2282-4*) Thorndike Pr.

—As It Is in Heaven. abr. ed. 1999. audio 17.98 (*1-57042-703-8*) Time Warner AudioBooks.

—As It Is in Heaven. 2000. 310p. E-Book 9.95 (*0-446-92334-6*); 1999. E-Book 9.95 (*0-446-96005-5*) Time Warner Bk. Group.

—As It Is in Heaven. 1999. E-Book 9.95 (*0-446-91304-9*); 1999. 320p. 23.00 (*0-446-52548-0*); 2000. 336p. reprint ed. pap. 13.95 (*0-446-67601-2*) Warner Bks., Inc.

Winterson, Jeanette. The Passion. 1997. 176p. pap. 12.00 (*0-8021-3522-6*, Grove Pr.); 1988. 180p. 16.95 o.p. (*0-87113-183-8*) Grove/Atlantic, Inc.

—The Passion. 1990. (Vintage International Ser.). pap. 10.00 o.s.i (*0-679-72437-0*, Vintage) Knopf Publishing Group.

Woodhouse, Sarah. Meeting Lily. (Rosamunde Pilcher's Bookshelf Ser.). 1998. 320p. pap. 5.99 (*0-312-96583-4*, St. Martin's Paperbacks); 1995. 224p. 20.95 o.p. (*0-312-13563-7*) St. Martin's Pr.

—Meeting Lily. l.t. ed. 1996. (Ulverscroft Large Print Ser.). 368p. 29.99 o.p. (*0-7089-3475-7*, Ulverscroft) Thorpe, F. A. Pubs. GBR. *Dist:* Ulverscroft Large Print Bks., Ltd., Ulverscroft Large Print Canada, Ltd.

Woodruff, William. Vessel of Sadness. 1996. 202p. reprint ed. pap. 16.95 (*1-57488-054-3*) Brassey's, Inc.

—Vessel of Sadness. 1987. 192p. 15.95 o.p. (*0-06-015709-7*) HarperTrade.

—Vessel of Sadness. 1969. 14.95 o.p. (*0-910824-12-6*); pap. text 5.95 o.p. (*0-910824-13-4*) Kallman Publishing Co.

—Vessel of Sadness. 1978. 200p. 8.95 o.p. (*0-8093-0875-4*) Southern Illinois Univ. Pr.

Woolson, Constance F. Front Yard & Other Italian Stories. 1977. (Short Story Index Reprint Ser.). 22.95 (*0-8369-3214-5*) Ayer Co. Pubs., Inc.

# J

## JACKSON HOLE (WYO.)—FICTION

Horton, J. Royal. Murder in Jackson Hole. 2nd ed. 1996. 290p. (Orig.). pap. 12.95 (*0-9643978-0-3*) Sunlight Publishing, Inc.

McClendon, Lise. Nordic Nights. 1999. (Alix Thorssen Mysteries Ser.). 292p. 23.95 (*0-8027-3340-9*) Walker & Co.

—Painted Truth: An Alix Thorssen Mystery. 1996. per. (*0-373-26222-1*, 1-26222-9, Worldwide Library) Harlequin Enterprises, Ltd.

—Painted Truth: An Alix Thorssen Mystery. 1995. 252p. 22.95 (*0-8027-3271-2*) Walker & Co.

## JALNA (CANADA: IMAGINARY PLACE)—FICTION

De La Roche, Mazo. The Building of Jalna. unabr. ed. 1993. 69.95 incl. audio (*0-7451-6246-0*); 1990. audio 64.95 o.s.i (*0-8161-9513-7*) BBC Audiobooks America.

—The Building of Jalna. 1976. 288p. mass mkt. 1.50 o.s.i (*0-449-23071-6*, Fawcett) Ballantine Bks.

—The Building of Jalna. 1944. (Jalna Ser.). 8.95 o.p. (*0-316-17996-5*) Little Brown & Co.

—The Building of Jalna. l.t. ed. 1972. (Whiteoak Chronicles Ser.). 16.95 o.p. (*0-85456-673-2*, Ulverscroft) Thorpe, F. A. Pubs. GBR. *Dist:* Ulverscroft Large Print Bks., Ltd.

—Centenary at Jalna. l.t. ed. 1973. (Whiteoak Chronicles Ser.). 12.00 o.p. (*0-85456-688-0*, Ulverscroft) Thorpe, F. A. Pubs. GBR. *Dist:* Ulverscroft Large Print Bks., Ltd.

—Finch's Fortune. 1976. mass mkt. 1.50 o.s.i (*0-449-23053-8*, Fawcett) Ballantine Bks.

—Finch's Fortune. l.t. ed. 1973. (Whiteoak Chronicles Ser.). 12.00 o.p. (*0-85456-681-3*, Ulverscroft) Thorpe, F. A. Pubs. GBR. *Dist:* Ulverscroft Large Print Bks., Ltd.

—Jalna. 1979. mass mkt. 1.95 o.s.i (*0-449-24118-1*, Fawcett); 1976. mass mkt. 1.50 o.s.i (*0-449-23138-0*) Ballantine Bks.

—Jalna. l.t. ed. 2002. 400p. pap. 21.99 (*0-7531-6462-0*) ISIS Large Print Bks. GBR. *Dist:* Ulverscroft Large Print Bks., Ltd., Ulverscroft Large Print Canada, Ltd.

—Jalna. l.t. ed. 2001. 400p. 32.50 (*0-7531-6461-2*); 1973. 29.99 o.p. (*0-85456-679-1*, Ulverscroft) Thorpe, F. A. Pubs. GBR. *Dist:* Ulverscroft Large Print Bks., Ltd., Ulverscroft Large Print Canada, Ltd.

—Mary Wakefield. unabr. ed. 1991. (Audio Bks.). audio 69.95 (*0-7451-6244-4*) BBC Audiobooks America.

—Mary Wakefield. 1976. mass mkt. 1.50 o.s.i (*0-449-23057-0*, Fawcett) Ballantine Bks.

—Mary Wakefield. l.t. ed. 1973. (Whiteoak Chronicles Ser.). 12.00 o.p. (*0-85456-675-9*, Ulverscroft) Thorpe, F. A. Pubs. GBR. *Dist:* Ulverscroft Large Print Bks., Ltd., Ulverscroft Large Print Canada, Ltd.

—The Master of Jalna. (Jalna Ser.). 1979. mass mkt. 1.95 o.s.i (*0-449-23932-2*, Fawcett); 1975. mass mkt. 1.50 o.s.i (*0-449-22797-9*) Ballantine Bks.

—The Master of Jalna. l.t. ed. 1973. (Whiteoak Chronicles Ser.). 29.99 o.p. (*0-85456-682-1*, Ulverscroft) Thorpe, F. A. Pubs. GBR. *Dist:* Ulverscroft Large Print Bks., Ltd., Ulverscroft Large Print Canada, Ltd.

—Morning at Jalna. unabr. ed. 1991. (Audio Bks.). audio 69.95 (*0-7451-6245-2*) BBC Audiobooks America.

—Morning at Jalna. (Jalna Ser.). 1978. mass mkt. 1.75 o.s.i (*0-449-23712-5*, Fawcett); 1975. mass mkt. 1.25 o.s.i (*0-449-22411-2*) Ballantine Bks.

—Morning at Jalna. 1960. (Jalna Ser.). 8.95 o.p. (*0-316-18003-3*) Little Brown & Co.

—Morning at Jalna. l.t. ed. 1972. (Whiteoak Chronicles Ser.). 29.99 o.p. (*0-85456-674-0*, Ulverscroft) Thorpe, F. A. Pubs. GBR. *Dist:* Ulverscroft Large Print Bks., Ltd., Ulverscroft Large Print Canada, Ltd.

—Renny's Daughter. 1975. 304p. mass mkt. 1.50 o.s.i (*0-449-22550-X*, Q2550, Fawcett) Ballantine Bks.

—Renny's Daughter. l.t. ed. 1973. (Whiteoak Chronicles Ser.). 29.99 o.p. (*0-85456-686-4*, Ulverscroft) Thorpe, F. A. Pubs. GBR. *Dist:* Ulverscroft Large Print Bks., Ltd., Ulverscroft Large Print Canada, Ltd.

—Return to Jalna. 1977. (Jalna Ser.). mass mkt. 1.75 o.s.i (*0-449-23386-3*, Fawcett) Ballantine Bks.

—Return to Jalna. l.t. ed. 1973. (Whiteoak Chronicles Ser.). 12.00 o.p. (*0-85456-685-6*, Ulverscroft) Thorpe, F. A. Pubs. GBR. *Dist:* Ulverscroft Large Print Bks., Ltd.

—Variable Winds at Jalna. l.t. ed. 1973. (Whiteoak Chronicles Ser.). 12.00 o.p. (*0-85456-687-2*, Ulverscroft) Thorpe, F. A. Pubs. GBR. *Dist:* Ulverscroft Large Print Bks., Ltd.
—Wakefield's Course. 1977. (Jalna Ser.). mass mkt. 1.95 o.s.i (*0-449-23431-2*, Fawcett) Ballantine Bks.
—Wakefield's Course. l.t. ed. 1973. (Whiteoak Chronicles Ser.). o.p. (*0-85456-684-8*, Ulverscroft) Thorpe, F. A. Pubs.
—Whiteoak Brothers. 1978. (Jalna Ser.). mass mkt. 1.75 o.s.i (*0-449-23643-9*, Fawcett) Ballantine Bks.
—The Whiteoak Brothers. l.t. ed. 1973. (Whiteoak Chronicles Ser.). 29.99 o.p. (*0-85456-678-3*, Ulverscroft) Thorpe, F. A. Pubs. GBR. *Dist:* Ulverscroft Large Print Bks., Ltd., Ulverscroft Large Print Canada, Ltd.
—Whiteoak Harvest. 1978. (Jalna Ser.). mass mkt. 1.75 o.s.i (*0-449-23521-1*, Fawcett) Ballantine Bks.
—Whiteoak Harvest. 1936. (Jalna Ser.). 7.95 o.p. (*0-316-18013-0*) Little Brown & Co.
—Whiteoak Harvest. l.t. ed. 1973. (Whiteoak Chronicles Ser.). 12.00 o.p. (*0-85456-683-X*, Ulverscroft) Thorpe, F. A. Pubs. GBR. *Dist:* Ulverscroft Large Print Bks., Ltd.
—Whiteoak Heritage. 1979. mass mkt. 1.95 o.s.i (*0-449-22214-4*, Fawcett) Ballantine Bks.
—Whiteoak Heritage. 1940. (Jalna Ser.). 8.95 o.p. (*0-316-18012-2*) Little Brown & Co.
—Whiteoak Heritage. l.t. ed. 1973. (Whiteoak Chronicles Ser.). o.p. (*0-85456-677-5*, Ulverscroft) Thorpe, F. A. Pubs.
—Whiteoaks of Jalna. (Jalna Ser.). 1980. mass mkt. 2.25 o.s.i (*0-449-23510-6*, Fawcett); 1975. mass mkt. 1.50 o.s.i (*0-449-22764-2*) Ballantine Bks.

**JAMAICA—FICTION**

Adisa, Opal Palmer, et al. Bake - Face & Other Guava Stories. Lisanevich, Xenia, ed. 2nd ed. 1987. (Illus.). 136p. (Orig.). pap. 7.50 o.p. (*0-932716-20-2*) Kelsey Street Pr.
Banks, Russell. The Book of Jamaica. 1986. 320p. mass mkt. 5.95 o.s.i (*0-345-33074-9*) Ballantine Bks.
—The Book of Jamaica. 1996. 352p. pap. 13.00 (*0-06-097707-8*, Perennial) HarperTrade.
—The Book of Jamaica. 1980. 10.95 o.p. (*0-395-29085-6*) Houghton Mifflin Co.
—The Book of Jamaica. 1996. 288p. 33.00 o.p. (*0-8095-9199-5*) Millefleurs.
—Gangsta Bone. 2003. (GER.). 384p. pap. 19.00 (*1-4000-3993-2*) Random Hse. Information Group.
—Rule of the Bone: A Novel. 1996. 400p. pap. 60.00 o.p. (*0-06-092743-7*); 1995. 390p. 22.00 o.p. (*0-06-017275-4*) HarperCollins Pubs.
Brown, Sandra. Tiger Prince. l.t. ed. 29.95 (*1-58724-251-6*, Wheeler Publishing, Inc.) Gale Group.
—Tiger Prince. 1999. 298p. mass mkt. (*1-55166-531-X*, 1-66531-4, Mira Bks.); 1994. 251p. per. (*1-55166-023-7*, 1-66023-2, Mira Bks.); 1994. mass mkt. (*0-373-48295-7*, 5-48295-5, Silhouette) Harlequin Enterprises, Ltd.
Bruns, Donn. Jamaica Blue. Date not set. pap. (*0-312-30491-9*, Saint Martin's Griffin); E-Book 24.95 (*0-312-70486-0*); E-Book 18.95 (*0-312-70853-X*); 2003. 336p. mass mkt. 6.99 (*0-312-98506-1*, St. Martin's Paperbacks); 2002. 320p. 24.95 (*0-312-30490-0*, Saint Martin's Minotaur) St. Martin's Pr.
Bruns, Jana. Jamaica Blue. 2003. mass mkt. (*0-312-99221-1*, St. Martin's Paperbacks) St. Martin's Pr.
Cezair-Thompson, Margaret. The True History of Paradise: A Novel. 2000. 352p. pap. 13.95 (*0-452-28075-3*, Plume); 1999. (Illus.). 334p. 24.95 o.s.i (*0-525-94490-7*) Dutton/Plume.
Chaikin, Linda L. Jamaican Sunset. 1997. (Buccaneers Ser.: No. 3). pap. 10.99 (*0-8024-1073-1*, 6) Moody Pr.
Channer, Colin. Satisfy My Soul. 256p. 2003. pap. 12.95 (*0-345-43790-X*, Ballantine Bks.); 2002. 19.95 (*0-345-43789-6*, One World/Ballantine) Ballantine Bks.
—Satisfy My Soul. l.t. ed. 2003. 367p. 29.95 (*0-7862-5906-X*) Thorndike Pr.
Cliff, Michelle. No Telephone to Heaven. 1987. 288p. 17.95 o.p. (*0-525-24508-1*, 01646-490, Dutton) Dutton/Plume.
—No Telephone to Heaven. 1989. (International Ser.). pap. 11.00 o.s.i (*0-679-73942-4*, Vintage) Knopf Publishing Group.
Coulter, Catherine. The Hellion Bride. 1992. (Bride Trilogy Ser.: Vol. 2). 384p. mass mkt. 7.99 (*0-515-10974-6*, Jove) Berkley Publishing Group.
—The Hellion Bride. l.t. ed. 1996. 456p. 25.95 o.p. (*0-7838-1294-9*, Macmillan Reference USA) Gale Group.
—The Hellion Bride. l.t. ed. 1995. (Magna Large Print Ser.). 500p. o.p. (*0-7505-0764-0*) Magna Large Print Bks. GBR. *Dist:* Ulverscroft Large Print Canada, Ltd.
—The Hellion Bride. abr. ed. 1992. (Bride Trilogy Ser.: Bk. 2). 3p. audio 15.95 (*1-879371-22-7*, 40090) Publishing Mills, Inc., The.
Craig, Christine. Mint Tea & Other Stories. 1993. (Caribbean Writers Ser.). 150p. pap. 11.95 (*0-435-98932-4*, 98932) Heinemann.
Crooks, Paul. Ancestors. 2002. (Illus.). 296p. pap. 12.95 (*1-901969-07-X*) BlackAmber Bks. GBR. *Dist:* SPD-Small Pr. Distribution.
—Ancestors. l.t. ed. 2003. (Ulverscroft Large Print Ser.). 456p. 32.50 (*0-7089-4791-3*) Thorpe, F. A. Pubs. GBR. *Dist:* Ulverscroft Large Print Bks., Ltd., Ulverscroft Large Print Canada, Ltd.
Dawes, Kwame. A Place to Hide. 2002. 256p. pap. 14.95 (*1-900715-48-1*) Peepal Tree Pr., Ltd. GBR. *Dist:* Independent Pubs. Group, Paul & Co. Pubs. Consortium, Inc.
Dold, Gaylord. Rude Boys. 1992. 256p. 18.95 o.p. (*0-312-08286-X*, Saint Martin's Minotaur) St. Martin's Pr.
Douglas, Marcia. Madam Fate. 1998. 258p. 24.00 (*1-56947-134-7*) Soho Pr., Inc.
Dyer, Bernadette. Villa Fair. 2000. (Illus.). ix, 174p. pap. 14.95 (*0-88878-410-4*) Beach Holme Pubs., Ltd. CAN. *Dist:* Stackpole Bks.
Faith, Barbara. Kill Me Gently, Darling. 2000. (Five Star Romance Ser.). 191p. pap. 25.95 (*0-7862-2637-4*, Five Star) Gale Group.
Fleming, Ian. Octopussy & the Living Daylights. 2004. 128p. pap. 13.00 (*0-14-200329-8*) Penguin Group (USA) Inc.
Foster, B. J. Bayou Shadows. 2000. 267p. 21.95 (*0-9675884-5-6*) Cresent Hse. Publishing.
Fuller, Vernella. Unlike Normal Women. 1997. 330p. pap. 14.95 (*0-7043-4431-9*) Women's Pr., Ltd., The GBR. *Dist:* Trafalgar Square.
Goodison, Lorna. Baby Mother & the King of Swords. 1995. (Longman Caribbean Writers Ser.). 84p. (C). pap. 18.20 (*0-582-05492-3*, TG7547) Longman Publishing Group.
Henzell, Perry. Power Game. 1997. 27.95 o.p. (*0-8038-9402-3*); pap. text 14.95 o.p. (*0-8038-9400-7*) Hastings Hse. Daytrips Pubs.
Holiday, Magnolia. Me Com' Back. 1999. 69p. pap. 6.95 (*0-9611952-8-2*, 122P) Magnolia Productions.
Hughes, Richard Arthur Warren. A High Wind in Jamaica. 1995. reprint ed. lib. bdg. 21.95 (*1-56849-582-X*) Buccaneer Bks., Inc.
—A High Wind in Jamaica. 1972. pap. 2.95 o.p. (*0-06-083099-9*, P3099, Perennial); audio 19.95 o.p. (*1-55994-089-1*, CPN 1563, Caedmon); 1989. 224p. reprint ed. pap. 11.00 o.p. (*0-06-091627-3*, Perennial) HarperTrade.
—A High Wind in Jamaica. 1991. 220p. reprint ed. lib. bdg. 29.00 o.p. (*0-8095-9099-9*) Millefleurs.
—A High Wind in Jamaica. 1999. 290p. reprint ed. pap. 12.95 (*0-940322-15-3*) New York Review of Bks., Inc., The.
—A High Wind in Jamaica or the Innocent Voyage. 1972. 20.95 (*0-88411-128-8*) Amereon, Ltd.
James, Osmund. Tough Girls Don't Dance. 1996. 187p. (*976-625-083-9*) Kingston Publishing, Ltd.
Kennaway, Guy. One People. 2nd ed. 2001. 256p. pap. 13.00 (*0-86241-829-1*) Canongate Bks. GBR. *Dist:* Publishers Group West.
Ludlum, Robert. The Cry of the Halidon. 1996. 448p. mass mkt. 7.99 (*0-553-57614-3*) Bantam Bks.
—The Cry of the Halidon. l.t. ed. 1997. (Wheeler Large Print Book Ser.). 26.95 o.p. (*1-56895-445-X*, Wheeler Publishing, Inc.) Gale Group.
—The Cry of the Halidon, Set. abr. ed. 1996. 24.95 o.p. (*0-7871-1264-X*, 694324) NewStar Media, Inc.
Manley, Rachel. Drumblair: Memories of a Jamaican Childhood. 1996. 324p. o.s.i (*0-394-28195-0*) Knopf, Alfred A. Inc.
McMillan, Terry. How Stella Got Her Groove Back. l.t. ed. 1996. (Large Print Bks.). 28.95 (*1-56895-355-0*, Wheeler Publishing, Inc.) Gale Group.
—How Stella Got Her Groove Back. 448p. 2004. pap. 14.00 (*0-451-20914-1*); 1998. mass mkt. 7.99 o.s.i (*0-451-19741-0*, Signet Bks.); 1997. mass mkt. 7.99 (*0-451-19200-1*, Signet Bks.) NAL.
—How Stella Got Her Groove Back. 1996. 384p. 23.95 (*0-670-86990-2*, Viking) Viking Penguin.
Mullings, Pal. The Final Draw. 1996. 275p. 18.95 o.p. (*0-944957-57-9*) Rivercross Publishing, Inc.
Neita-Chen, Denise. Journey. 2000. 128p. 16.95 (*1-56167-624-1*) American Literary Pr., Inc.
Palmer, Joyce. Greenwichtown. 2001. 272p. 23.95 (*0-312-26597-2*) St. Martin's Pr.
—Greenwichtown: A Novel. 2002. 272p. pap. 14.95 (*0-312-28321-0*, Saint Martin's Griffin) St. Martin's Pr.
Paver, Michelle. The Shadow Catcher. 2003. 416p. mass mkt. (*0-552-15041-X*, Corgi) Bantam Bks.
—The Shadow Catcher. l.t. ed. 2003. 544p. 32.50 (*0-7531-6815-4*) ISIS Large Print Bks. GBR. *Dist:* Ulverscroft Large Print Bks., Ltd., Ulverscroft Large Print Canada, Ltd.
—The Shadow Catcher. 2003. (Illus.). 579p. pap. 9.95 (*0-552-14872-5*) Transworld Publishers Ltd. GBR. *Dist:* Trafalgar Square.
Perkins, Cyrus F. Busha's Mistress: A Stirring Romance of the Days of Slavery in Jamaica. Lovejoy, Paul E. et al, eds. (Illus.). 2003. 172p. 59.95 (*1-55876-286-8*); 2002. 160p. pap. 18.95 (*1-55876-287-6*) Wiener, Markus Pubs., Inc.
Philp, Geoffrey. Benjamin, My Son. 2003. 200p. pap. 14.95 (*1-900715-78-3*) Peepal Tree Pr., Ltd. GBR. *Dist:* Independent Pubs. Group.
Powell, Patricia. The Pagoda. 1999. 256p. pap. 13.00 (*0-15-600829-7*, Harvest Bks.) Harcourt Trade Pubs.
—The Pagoda. 1998. 256p. 23.00 o.s.i (*0-679-45489-6*) Knopf, Alfred A. Inc.
—A Small Gathering of Bones. 2003. 144p. pap. 13.00 (*0-8070-8367-4*) Beacon Pr.
Reid, Desmond A. Dana Meets the Cow Who Lost Its Moo. 1985. 32p. 5.95 (*0-912444-29-0*) DARE Bks.
Senior, Olive. Discerner of Hearts: And Other Stories. 1995. 232p. (Orig.). pap. 13.95 o.p. (*0-7710-8053-0*) McClelland & Stewart/Tundra Bks.
Silvera, Makeda. The Heart Does Not Bend. 2003. 272p. pap. 12.95 (*0-679-31187-4*) Knopf, Alfred A. Inc.
Smith, Horane. Port Royal. 2001. 176p. pap. 16.95 (*1-894498-01-1*) Boheme Pr. CAN. *Dist:* Independent Pubs. Group, Univ. of Toronto Pr.
Tolkin, Michael. Under Radar. 2003. 224p. pap. 12.00 (*0-8021-3990-6*); 2002. 256p. 24.00 (*0-87113-848-4*, Atlantic Monthly Pr.) Grove/Atlantic, Inc.
York, Rebecca & Roberts, Kelsey. Secret Vows: Till Death Do Us Part; Unlawfully Wedded, 2 bks. in 1. 2000. 480p. mass mkt. o.s.i (*0-373-21702-1*, 1-21702-5, Harlequin Bks.) Harlequin Enterprises, Ltd.

**JAMES RIVER (VA.)—FICTION**

Deveraux, Jude. Counterfeit Lady. l.t. ed. 1985. (General Ser.). 496p. 17.95 o.p. (*0-8161-3826-5*, Macmillan Reference USA) Gale Group.
—Counterfeit Lady. 1998. (Illus.). 400p. mass mkt. 3.99 (*0-671-02011-0*, Pocket) Simon & Schuster.
—Counterfeit Lady. Marrow, Linda, ed. 1991. 384p. mass mkt. 7.99 (*0-671-73976-X*, Pocket) Simon & Schuster.
—Counterfeit Lady. 1990. mass mkt. 4.95 (*0-671-70674-8*, Pocket) Simon & Schuster.
—Counterfeit Lady. Marrow, Linda, ed. 1988. mass mkt. 4.50 (*0-671-67519-2*, Pocket) Simon & Schuster.
—Lost Lady. l.t. ed. 1985. (General Ser.). 371p. 14.95 o.p. (*0-8161-3950-4*, Macmillan Reference USA) Gale Group.
—Lost Lady. Marrow, Linda, ed. 1991. 352p. mass mkt. 7.99 (*0-671-73977-8*, Pocket) Simon & Schuster.
—Lost Lady. 1990. mass mkt. 4.95 (*0-671-70675-6*, Pocket) Simon & Schuster.
—Lost Lady. Marrow, Linda, ed. 1988. mass mkt. 4.50 (*0-671-67430-7*, Pocket) Simon & Schuster.
—River Lady. l.t. ed. 1986. (General Ser.). 431p. 17.95 o.p. (*0-8161-4138-X*, Macmillan Reference USA) Gale Group.
—River Lady. Marrow, Linda, ed. 1991. 320p. mass mkt. 7.99 (*0-671-73978-6*); 1988. mass mkt. 4.50 (*0-671-67297-5*) Simon & Schuster. (Pocket).
—Sweetbriar. 1990. mass mkt. 4.95 (*0-671-72402-9*); 1991. 352p. reprint ed. mass mkt. 7.99 (*0-671-74382-1*) Simon & Schuster. (Pocket).

**JAPAN—FICTION**

Abe, Kobo. Woman in the Dunes. Saunders, E. Dale, tr. from JPN. Orig. Title: Suna no onna. 1991. 256p. pap. 13.00 (*0-679-73378-7*); 1972. pap. 7.95 o.p. (*0-394-71814-3*, V814) Knopf Publishing Group. (Vintage).
Adamson, Isaac. Hokkaido Popsicle. 2002. 336p. pap. 12.95 (*0-380-81292-4*, Perennial) HarperTrade.
—Osaka Nocturne. 2004. pap. (*0-06-051624-0*, Perennial) HarperTrade.
Agawa, Hiroyuki. The Citadel in Spring. Rogers, Lawrence, tr. from JPN. 1991. 256p. 18.95 (*0-87011-960-5*) Kodansha America, Inc.
Akutagawa, Ryunosuke. Rashomon & Other Stories. Takashi, Kojima, tr. from JPN. 2nd ed. 1989. (Illus.). 102p. pap. 12.95 (*0-8048-1457-0*) Tuttle Publishing.
Albery, Nobuko. The House of Kanze. 1987. pap. 8.95 o.p. (*0-671-64002-X*, Touchstone); 1986. 320p. 17.45 o.p. (*0-671-60520-8*, Simon & Schuster) Simon & Schuster.
Alexander, Victoria N. Smoking Hopes. 1996. 208p. 24.00 (*1-877946-69-9*) Permanent Pr., The.
Anderson, Jack. The Japan Conspiracy. 1993. 352p. mass mkt. 20.00 o.s.i (*0-8217-4212-4*, Zebra Bks.) Kensington Publishing Corp.
Apostolou, John L. & Greenberg, Martin H., eds. The Best Japanese Science Fiction Stories. 1989. 16.95 o.p. (*0-942637-06-2*, Dembner Bks.) Barricade Bks., Inc.
—Murder in Japan: Japanese Stories of Crime & Detection. 1987. 15.95 o.p. (*0-934878-87-0*, Dembner Bks.) Barricade Bks., Inc.
Ariyoshi, Sawako. Kabuki Dancer. 2001. 352p. pap. 16.95 (*4-7700-2735-4*) Kodansha International JPN. *Dist:* Kodansha America, Inc.
Asada, Teruhiko. The Night of a Thousand Suicides: The Japanese Outbreak at Cowra. 1970. 125p. (*0-207-12052-8*) Consortium Bk. Sales & Distribution.
Atoda, Takashi. The Square Persimmon & Other Stories. Horton, Millicent, tr. 1991. 208p. 12.95 (*0-8048-1678-6*) Tuttle Publishing.
Backer, Sara. American Fuji. 2002. 416p. pap. 14.00 (*0-425-18336-X*) Berkley Publishing Group.
—American Fuji. 2001. 320p. 24.95 o.s.i (*0-399-14691-1*, Wood, Marian Bks.) Penguin Group (USA) Inc.
Backus, Robert L., tr. from JPN. The Riverside Counselor's Stories: Vernacular Fiction of Late Heian Japan. 1985. 272p. 49.50 (*0-8047-1260-3*) Stanford Univ. Pr.
Barkan, Joshua. Before Hiroshima: The Confession of Murayama Kazuo & Other Stories. 2000. 148p. pap. 12.95 (*1-902881-13-3*); (*1-902881-08-7*) Toby Pr.
Benson, Raymond. The Man with the Red Tattoo. 2003. (James Bond Ser.). 320p. mass mkt. 7.99 (*0-515-13563-1*, Jove) Berkley Publishing Group.
—The Man with the Red Tattoo. unabr. ed. 2002. audio compact disk 19.95 (*0-7861-9111-2*) Blackstone Audio Bks., Inc.
—The Man with the Red Tattoo. 2002. 272p. 23.95 o.s.i (*0-399-14884-1*) Penguin Group (USA) Inc.
Blaker, Richard. The Needle-Watcher: The Will Adams Story, British Samurai. 1973. 512p. pap. 16.95 (*0-8048-1094-X*) Tuttle Publishing.
Bock, Dennis. The Ash Garden. 2001. E-Book 18.50 (*1-59061-597-2*) Adobe Systems, Inc.
—The Ash Garden. 2003. 304p. pap. 13.00 (*0-375-72749-3*, Vintage) Knopf Publishing Group.
Brown, Alan. Audrey Hepburn's Neck. 1997. 304p. pap. 12.95 (*0-671-52672-3*, Pocket) Simon & Schuster.
—Audrey Hepburn's Neck. Ng, Donna, ed. 1996. 304p. 21.00 o.p. (*0-671-52671-5*, Atria) Simon & Schuster.
Buck, Pearl S. The Big Wave. (Trophy Bk.). (Illus.). (J). 1986. 64p. (gr. 3-7). pap. 4.99 (*0-06-440171-5*, Harper Trophy); 1973. 80p. (gr. 2-6). lib. bdg. 16.89 (*0-381-99923-8*) HarperCollins Children's Bk. Group.
Card, Orson Scott & Ferrell, Keith, eds. Black Mist: And Other Japanese Futurers. 1997. 304p. mass mkt. 5.99 o.s.i (*0-88677-767-4*) DAW Bks., Inc.
Castro, Brian. Stepper. 1997. (*0-09-183502-X*) Trafalgar Square.
Chand, Meira. The Bonsai Tree. 1983. 240p. 12.45 o.p. (*0-89919-166-5*) Houghton Mifflin Co.
Chiyo, Uno. The Story of a Single Woman. Copeland, Rebecca, tr. from JPN. & intro. by. 1993. 132p. pap. 19.95 (*0-7206-0878-3*) Owen, Peter Ltd. GBR. *Dist:* Dufour Editions, Inc.
Clavell, James. Gai-Jin: A Novel of Japan, 2 vols. l.t. ed. 1994. pap. 35.95 o.p. (*0-7927-1887-9*);Set. 38.95 o.p. (*0-7927-1888-7*) BBC Audiobooks America.
—Gai-Jin: A Novel of Japan. 1994. 1248p. mass mkt. 7.99 (*0-440-21680-X*); 1993. 1056p. 300.00 o.s.i (*0-385-31022-6*, Delacorte Pr.) Dell Publishing.
—Shogun. 1986. pap.; 1983. 816p. 21.95 o.s.i (*0-385-29224-4*, Delacorte Pr.); 1983. 21.95 o.s.i (*0-440-08721-X*) Dell Publishing.
—Shogun. 1910. mass mkt. o.s.i (*0-385-31988-6*) Doubleday Publishing.
—Shogun. 1990. (SPA.). 984p. 17.95 (*84-01-46441-2*) Plaza & Janés Editories, S.A. ESP. *Dist:* Distribooks, Inc.
—Shogun. 1975. (C). 19.95 o.p. (*0-689-10565-7*, Scribner) Simon & Schuster.
Collins, Clive. The Foreign Husband. 1989. 19.95 o.p. (*0-7145-2893-5*) Boyars, Marion Pubs., Inc.
Coonts, Stephen. Fortunes of War. 1998. audio compact disk 112.00 (*0-7366-8040-3*); audio 96.00 (*0-7366-4207-2*, 4704) Books on Tape, Inc.
—Fortunes of War, Set. abr. ed. 1999. audio 25.00 Highsmith Inc.
—Fortunes of War, Set. abr. ed. 1998. audio 25.00 (*0-7871-1731-5*, 695766, Dove Audio) NewStar Media, Inc.
—Fortunes of War. 1999. 436p. mass mkt. 7.99 (*0-312-96941-4*, St. Martin's Paperbacks); 1998. 368p. 24.95 (*0-312-18583-9*) St. Martin's Pr.
—Fortunes of War. l.t. ed. 1998. (Americana Ser.). 664p. 29.95 (*0-7862-1463-5*) Thorndike Pr.
Dalby, Liza. The Tale of Murasaki. pap. (*0-385-72851-4*) Knopf Publishing Group.
—The Tale of Murasaki: A Novel. 2003. 426p. reprint ed. 25.00 (*0-7567-6903-5*) DIANE Publishing Co.
—The Tale of Murasaki: A Novel. 2001. (Illus.). 448p. reprint ed. pap. 14.00 (*0-385-49795-4*, Knopf Bks. for Young Readers) Random Hse. Children's Bks.
Dalkey, Kara. Genpei. Date not set. pap. 13.95 (*0-312-89070-2*); 2001. (Illus.). 448p. 25.95 (*0-312-89071-0*) Doherty, Tom Assocs., LLC. (Tor Bks.).

Settings

De Benneville, James S. Tales of the Samurai. 1987. 480p. pap. 19.95 o.p. (*0-7103-0233-9*, 02339) Routledge.
—Tales of the Samurai. 2003. (Illus.). pap. 29.95 (*1-4102-0491-X*) Univ. Pr. of the Pacific.
de la Trobe, Henry. War & Cherry Blossoms: Secret Mission in Japan. 2001. 292p. E-Book 8.00 (*0-7388-7834-0*) Xlibris Corp.
Deford, Frank. Love & Infamy. 1995. 576p. mass mkt. 5.99 (*0-8217-0122-3*, Zebra Bks.); mass mkt. 5.99 o.s.i (*0-7860-0122-4*, Pinnacle Bks.) Kensington Publishing Corp.
—Love & Infamy. 1993. 576p. 24.00 o.p. (*0-670-82995-1*) Viking Penguin.
Dempsey, Al. Pika Don. 1993. 384p. (Orig.). mass mkt. 4.99 o.p. (*0-8125-0939-0*, Tor Bks.) Doherty, Tom Assocs., LLC.
Dunlop, Lane, tr. A Late Chrysanthemum: 21 Stories from the Japanese. 1986. (Illus.). 192p. 16.50 o.p. (*0-86547-229-7*, North Point Pr.) Farrar, Straus & Giroux.
Eisler, Barry. Hard Rain. abr. ed. (John Rain Ser.). 2004. audio 12.99 (*1-59086-957-5*, 4559, Brilliance Audio Paperback Audiobooks); 2003. audio 24.95 (*1-59086-956-7*, 4558, Brilliance Audio); 2003. audio 32.95 (*1-59086-954-0*, 4556, Brilliance Audio Unabridged); 2003. audio 82.25 (*1-59086-955-9*, 4557, Unabridged Library Editions) Brilliance Audio.
—Hard Rain. 2003. 320p. text 24.95 (*0-399-15052-8*, Putnam & Grosset) Putnam Publishing Group, The.
—Rain Fall. 2003. 384p. reprint ed. mass mkt. 6.99 (*0-451-20915-X*, Signet Bks.) NAL.
—Rain Fall. 2002. 336p. 24.95 o.s.i (*0-399-14910-4*) Penguin Group (USA) Inc.
Enchi, Fumiko. Masks. 1983. 160p. pap. 11.95 (*0-394-72218-3*, Vintage) Knopf Publishing Group.
Endo, Shusaku. The Samurai. Gessel, Van C., tr. from JPN. 2000. 272p. 12.95 (*0-06-859852-1*) HarperTrade.
—The Samurai. 1984. 272p. pap. 12.00 o.s.i (*0-394-72726-6*, Vintage) Knopf Publishing Group.
—The Samurai. Gessel, Van C., tr. from JPN. 1997. (Classics Ser.). 196p. pap. 12.95 (*0-8112-1346-3*, 839) New Directions Publishing Corp.
—Scandal. Gessel, Van C., tr. 1989. (Vintage International Ser.). pap. 10.00 o.s.i (*0-679-72355-2*, Vintage) Knopf Publishing Group.
—Scandal. 1988. 238p. 30.00 (*0-7206-0682-9*) Owen, Peter Ltd. GBR. *Dist:* Dufour Editions, Inc.
—Silence. Johnston, William, tr. from JPN. 1996. 312p. pap. (*0-7206-1007-9*) Owen, Peter Ltd. GBR. *Dist:* Dufour Editions, Inc.
—Silence. Johnston, William, tr. from JPN. 1997. (Illus.). 201p. pap. 11.95 (*0-8008-7186-3*); 1979. 9.95 o.p. (*0-8008-7183-9*) Taplinger Publishing Co., Inc.
—Silence. Johnston, William, tr. 1969. 15.00 o.p. (*0-8048-0720-5*) Tuttle Publishing.
—Wonderful Fool. Mathy, Francis, tr. from JPN. 1983. 224p. 13.95 (*0-06-859853-X*) HarperTrade.
—Wonderful Fool. Mathy, Francis, tr. from JPN. 1995. 240p. pap. 28.00 (*0-7206-0979-8*) Owen, Peter Ltd. GBR. *Dist:* Dufour Editions, Inc.
Endo, Shusaku & Shusako. Silence. 1977. 8.95 o.p. (*0-316-23860-0*) Little Brown & Co.
Fell, Alison. The Pillow Boy of the Lady Onogoro. Blower, Arye, tr. 1997. 256p. pap. 12.00 (*0-15-600468-2*, Harvest Bks.) Harcourt Trade Pubs.
Fell, Alison, ed. The Pillow Boy of the Lady Onogoro. Blower, Arye, tr. 1996. 256p. 22.00 o.s.i (*0-15-100186-3*) Harcourt Trade Pubs.
Fleming, Ian. You Only Live Twice. 1995. (James Bond Ser.). 256p. 9.98 (*1-56731-080-X*, MJF Bks.) Fine Communications.
—You Only Live Twice. 1965. (James Bond Ser.). mass mkt. 2.95 o.p. (*0-451-13708-6*, AE2108, Signet Bks.) NAL.
Foss, Patrick. The Bang Devils. 2003. (Dark Alley Ser.). 320p. pap. 13.95 (*0-06-055477-0*, Avon Bks.) Morrow/Avon.
Freedman, Nancy. The Seventh Stone. 1992. 384p. 20.00 o.p. (*0-525-93424-3*, Dutton) Dutton/Plume.
—The Seventh Stone. 1993. 448p. mass mkt. 5.99 o.p. (*0-451-17520-4*, Signet Bks.) NAL.
Furutani, Dale. Death at the Crossroads: A Samurai Mystery. 1999. audio 24.95 (*0-7366-4703-1*) Books on Tape, Inc.
—Death at the Crossroads: A Samurai Mystery. 1998. 256p. 22.00 (*0-688-15817-X*, Morrow, William & Co.) Morrow/Avon.
—Jade Palace Vendetta: A Samurai Mystery. 1999. (Samurai Mysteries Ser.). 222p. 23.00 (*0-688-15818-8*, Morrow, William & Co.) Morrow/Avon.
—Kill the Shogun. 2000. (Samurai Mysteries Ser.). 240p. 23.00 o.s.i (*0-688-15819-6*, Morrow, William & Co.) Morrow/Avon.
—Kill the Shogun: A Samurai Mystery. l.t. ed. 2001. (Thorndike Mystery Ser.). 327p. 27.95 (*0-7862-3190-4*) Thorndike Pr.
Glaister, Lesley. Easy Peasy. 1997. 224p. 20.95 o.p. (*0-312-16822-5*) St. Martin's Pr.
Golden, Arthur. Memoirs of a Geisha. E-Book 12.50 (*1-58945-822-2*) Adobe Systems, Inc.
—Memoirs of a Geisha. 1999. 448p. pap. 14.95 (*0-679-78158-7*, Vintage) Knopf Publishing Group.
—Memoirs of a Geisha. 1997. 448p. 27.50 (*0-375-40011-7*) Knopf, Alfred A. Inc.
—Memoirs of a Geisha. 1999. E-Book 12.50 (*0-375-40678-6*) Random Hse., Inc.
—Memoirs of a Geisha. l.t. ed. (Paperback Bestsellers Ser.). 701p. 1999. pap. 27.95 (*0-7838-0146-7*); 1998. 30.95 (*0-7838-0145-9*) Thorndike Pr.
—Memoirs of a Geisha. 1999. 20.05 (*0-606-22204-9*) Turtleback Bks.
Gralla, Cynthia. The Floating World. 2003. 304p. 21.95 (*0-345-45291-7*, Ballantine Bks.) Ballantine Bks.
Guest, Lynn. The Sword of Hachiman. 1982. 416p. mass mkt. 3.50 o.p. (*0-8217-1104-0*, Zebra Bks.) Kensington Publishing Corp.
—The Sword of Hachiman. 1981. text 12.95 o.p. (*0-07-025108-8*) McGraw-Hill Cos., The.
—Yedo. 1985. 14.95 o.p. (*0-312-89632-8*) St. Martin's Pr.
Hagberg, David. High Flight. 1996. 879p. mass mkt. 7.99 (*0-8125-1012-7*, Tor Bks.); 1995. 640p. 24.95 o.p. (*0-312-85092-1*, Forge Bks.) Doherty, Tom Assocs., LLC.
Hall, Charlotte. The Barbarian Geisha. 1998. (Black Lace Ser.). 252p. mass mkt. 6.95 (*0-352-33267-0*) Black Lace GBR. *Dist:* London Bridge.
Hamill, Pete. Tokyo Sketches. Shaw, S., ed. 1995. 168p. pap. 10.00 (*4-7700-1950-5*) Kodansha America, Inc.
—Tokyo Sketches. 1993. 224p. 20.00 o.s.i (*4-7700-1697-2*) Kodansha America, Inc.
Haylock, John. Uneasy Relations. 1993. 223p. 30.00 (*0-7206-0880-5*) Owen, Peter Ltd. GBR. *Dist:* Dufour Editions, Inc.
Hearn, Lafcadio. Kwaidan. 1968. (Illus.). pap. 3.95 o.p. (*0-486-21901-1*) Dover Pubns., Inc.
—Kwaidan. l.t. ed. 1998. (Large Print Ser.). reprint ed. 135p. lib. bdg. 25.00 (*0-939495-71-6*); 95p. lib. bdg. 24.00 (*1-58287-093-4*) North Bks.
—Kwaidan: Stories & Studies of Strange Things. 2000. E-Book 2.49 (*1-58744-189-6*) Electric Umbrella Publishing.
—Kwaidan: Stories & Studies of Strange Things. 2002. 140p. 93.99 (*1-4043-1230-7*); per. 88.99 (*1-4043-1231-5*) IndyPublish.com.
—Kwaidan: Stories & Studies of Strange Things. 1983. (Illus.). 4.50 o.p. (*0-8446-2228-1*) Smith, Peter Pub., Inc.
—Kwaidan: Stories & Studies of Strange Things. 1971. (Illus.). 256p. reprint ed. pap. 12.95 (*0-8048-0954-2*) Tuttle Publishing.
Hearn, Lian. Across the Nightingale Floor. 2003. (Tales of the Otori Trilogy: Bk. 1). 320p. pap. 14.00 (*1-57322-332-8*, Riverhead Trade (Paperbacks)) Berkley Publishing Group.
—Across the Nightingale Floor. 2002. (Tales of the Otori Trilogy: Bk. 1). 288p. 24.95 o.s.i (*1-57322-225-9*, Riverhead Bks. (Hardcovers)) Putnam Publishing Group, The.
—Grass for His Pillow. 2004. 368p. pap. 14.00 (*1-59448-003-6*, Riverhead Trade (Paperbacks)) Berkley Publishing Group.
—Grass for His Pillow. unabr. ed. 2003. (Tales of the Otori Trilogy: Bk. 2). audio compact disk 34.95 (*1-56511-799-9*); audio 34.95 (*1-56511-798-0*) HighBridge Co.
—Grass for His Pillow. 2003. (Tales of the Otori Trilogy: Bk. 2). (Illus.). 320p. 24.95 (*1-57322-251-8*, Riverhead Bks. (Hardcovers)) Putnam Publishing Group, The.
Highbridge, Dianne. In the Empire of Dreams. 2000. 248p. pap. 12.00 (*1-56947-190-8*); 1999. 288p. 24.00 (*1-56947-146-0*) Soho Pr., Inc.
Holt, Tate. Yamashita's Gold: A Novel. 1998. (Illus.). 428p. 23.95 (*0-9653774-6-6*) Berkeley Hills Bks.
Hoobler, Dorothy & Hoobler, Thomas. The Demon in the Teahouse. (J). 2002. 192p. pap. 5.99 (*0-698-11971-1*, PaperStar); 2001. 181p. (gr. 5-8). 17.99 (*0-399-23499-3*, G. P. Putnam's Sons) Penguin Putnam Bks. for Young Readers.
—The Ghost in the Tokaido Inn. 1999. 214p. (J). (gr. 5-9). 17.99 (*0-399-23330-X*, G. P. Putnam's Sons) Penguin Putnam Bks. for Young Readers.
Houston, Jeanne Wakatsuki. The Legend of Fire Horse Woman. 2003. 336p. 23.00 (*0-7582-0455-8*) Kensington Publishing Corp.
Hoyt, Richard. Japanese Game. 1996. 308p. mass mkt. 5.99 (*0-8125-3107-8*); 1995. 288p. 13.99 o.p. (*0-312-85553-2*) Doherty, Tom Assocs., LLC. (Forge Bks.).
—Old Soldiers Sometimes Lie. E-Book 19.95 (*0-312-70863-7*, Tor Bks.); 2002. 432p. 25.95 (*0-7653-0331-0*, Forge Bks.) Doherty, Tom Assocs., LLC.
Ibuse, Masuji. Black Rain. 1985. 304p. mass mkt. 3.95 o.s.i (*0-553-24988-6*) Bantam Bks.
—Black Rain. Shaw, ed. Bester, John, tr. from JPN. 1988. 304p. pap. 12.00 (*0-87011-364-X*) Kodansha America, Inc.
—Black Rain. 1988. 18.05 (*0-606-20070-3*) Turtleback Bks.
Ihara, Saikaku. The Life of an Amorous Man. 2001. 223p. pap. 14.95 (*0-8048-1069-9*) Tuttle Publishing.
Ikeda, Daisaku. The Human Revolution, Vol. 1. 1973. 272p. 25.00 (*0-8348-0074-8*) Weatherhill, Inc.
—The Human Revolution. Gage, Richard L., tr. from JPN. Vol. 2. 1974. (Illus.). 288p. 25.00 (*0-8348-0087-X*); Vol. 3. 1976. 152p. 25.00 (*0-8348-0118-3*) Weatherhill, Inc.
—The Human Revolution. (Illus.). Vol. 4. 1982. (JPN.). 256p. 25.00 (*0-8348-0175-2*); Vol. 5. 1984. 216p. 25.00 (*0-8348-0198-1*); Vol. 6. 1997. 224p. 30.00 (*0-8348-0361-5*) Weatherhill, Inc.
Ikenami, Shotaro. The Master Assassin: Tales of Murder from the Shogun's City. Frew, Gavin, tr. from JPN. 1992. 224p. 19.95 (*4-7700-1534-8*) Kodansha America, Inc.
Inoue, Yasushi. The Dancing Girl of Izu & Other Stories. Picon, Leon, tr. from JPN. Incl. Counterfeiter, Obasute & the Full Moon. 1974. pap. (Tut Books. L). 144p. 1989. Set pap. 14.95 (*0-8048-1141-5*) Tuttle Publishing.
—The Hunting Gun. Goldstein, Sanford, tr. from JPN. 1989. 74p. pap. 12.95 (*0-8048-0257-2*) Tuttle Publishing.
—Lou-Lan & Other Stories. Araki, J. & Seidensticker, Edward G., trs. from JPN. 1994. 164p. reprint ed. pap. 10.00 (*0-87011-472-7*) Kodansha America, Inc.
—Shirobamba: A Childhood in Old Japan. 1991. 200p. 30.00 (*0-7206-0837-6*) Dufour Editions, Inc.
—Shirobamba: A Childhood in Old Japan. Moy, Jean O., tr. from JPN. & intro. by. 1993. (Illus.). 200p. pap. 12.95 (*0-8348-0269-4*) Weatherhill, Inc.
Ishiguro, Kazuo. A Pale View of Hills. l.t. ed. 1999. (*0-7540-3914-5*); (*0-7540-3913-7*) Thorndike Pr.
Itaya, Kikuo. Tengu Child. Gardner, John, tr. 1983. (Illus.). 243p. 17.95 (*0-8093-1081-3*) Southern Illinois Univ. Pr.
Jackson, Marjorie. Shintaro's Umbrellas. 1996. (Books for Young Learners). (Illus.). 16p. (J). (gr. k-2). pap. text 5.00 (*1-57274-025-6*, A2770) Owen, Richard C. Pubs., Inc.
Johnson, K. & Rasche, John. Hiroshima: Chronicles of a Survivor. Caso, A., ed. 1994. (Illus.). 208p. text 22.95 (*0-8283-2001-2*) Branden Bks.
Joji Tsubota. Children in the Wind. Epp, Robert, tr. 1991. 180p. 22.50 (*0-7103-0393-9*, A5365) Routledge.
Kadohata, Cynthia. The Floating World. 1997. 196p. reprint ed. text 15.00 (*0-7881-5046-4*) DIANE Publishing Co.
Kaga, Otohiko. Riding the East Wind: A Novel. 2002. 518p. pap. 19.00 (*4-7700-2775-3*); 520p. pap. 19.00 (*4-7700-2856-3*) Kodansha International JPN. *Dist:* Kodansha America, Inc.
Kamata, Suzanne, ed. The Broken Bridge: Fiction from Expatriates in Literary Japan. 1997. 0360p. (Orig.). pap. 18.95 (*1-880656-31-0*) Stone Bridge Pr.
Kamo, Chomei. Ten Foot Square Hut & Tales of the Heike. Sadler, Arthur L., ed. 1970. 271p. reprint ed. 69.95 (*0-8371-3114-6*, KATF, Greenwood Pr.) Greenwood Publishing Group, Inc.
Kanzaki, Masami. Xenon: Heavy Metal Warrior. 1992. (Xenon Ser.: Vol. 3). (Illus.). Vol. 3. 194p. pap. 14.95 (*0-929279-43-3*); Vol. 4. 176p. pap. 14.95 (*0-929279-47-6*) Viz Communications, Inc.
—Xenon, Vol. 2: Heavy Metal Warrior, Vol. 2. 1992. (Xenon Ser.: Vol. 2). (Illus.). 192p. pap. 14.95 (*0-929279-42-5*) Viz Communications, Inc.
Kawabata, Yasunari. Beauty & Sadness. Hibbett, Howard S., Jr., tr. from JPN. 1981. (Perigee Japanese Library). Orig. Title: Utsukushisa to Kanashimi to. 224p. pap. 9.95 o.p. (*0-399-50529-6*, Perigee Bks.) Berkley Publishing Group.
—The Master of Go. Seidensticker, Edward G., tr. from JPN. 1981. (Perigee Japanese Library). Orig. Title: Meijin. 196p. pap. 8.95 o.p. (*0-399-50528-8*, Perigee Bks.) Berkley Publishing Group.
—The Master of Go. 1996. Orig. Title: Meijin. 208p. pap. 12.00 (*0-679-76106-3*) Random Hse. Value Publishing.
—Snow Country. Seidensticker, Edward G., tr. from JPN. 1981. (Perigee Japanese Library). Orig. Title: Yukiguni. 192p. pap. 9.50 o.p. (*0-399-50525-3*, Perigee Bks.) Berkley Publishing Group.
—The Sound of the Mountain. Seidensticker, Edward G., tr. from JPN. 1981. (Perigee Japanese Library). Orig. Title: Yama no Oto. 288p. pap. 9.95 o.p. (*0-399-50527-X*, Perigee Bks.) Berkley Publishing Group.
—The Sound of the Mountain. Seidensticker, Edward G., tr. from JPN. 1996. Orig. Title: Yama no Oto. 288p. pap. 13.00 (*0-679-76264-7*) Knopf, Alfred A. Inc.
—Thousand Cranes. Seidensticker, Edward G., tr. from JPN. 1981. (Perigee Japanese Library). Orig. Title: Senbazuru. (Illus.). 160p. pap. 7.95 o.p. (*0-399-50526-1*, Perigee Bks.) Berkley Publishing Group.
Keene, Carolyn. The Runaway Bride. Ashby, Rush, ed. 1994. (Nancy Drew Files: No. 96). 160p. (YA). (gr. 6 up). mass mkt. 3.99 (*0-671-79488-4*, Simon Pulse) Simon & Schuster Children's Publishing.
Kikuchi, Kan, et al. Beyond the Pale of Vengeance. Perry, Jisho & Vago, Kimiko, trs. from JPN. 1998. (Illus.). 78p. per. 5.95 (*0-930066-19-7*) Shasta Abbey Pr.
Kita, Morio. The House of Nire. Keene, Dennis, tr. 1984. 816p. (C). 17.95 o.p. (*0-87011-592-8*); 1991. 772p. reprint ed. pap. 7.95 o.s.i (*0-87011-859-5*) Kodansha America, Inc.
—The House of Nire. 1999. 782p. pap. 14.00 (*4-7700-2393-6*) Kodansha International JPN. *Dist:* Kodansha America, Inc.
Kobayashi, Takiji. The Cannery Boat & Other Japanese Short Stories. reprint ed. 12.50 (*0-404-03736-4*) AMS Pr., Inc.
—The Cannery Boat & Other Japanese Short Stories. 1969. (Illus.). 271p. reprint ed. 35.00 o.s.i (*0-8371-0133-6*, KOCB, Greenwood Pr.) Greenwood Publishing Group, Inc.
Koike, Kazuo. Shades of Death: Crying Freeman. 1996. (Illus.). 292p. pap. 19.95 o.p. (*1-56931-061-0*) Viz Communications, Inc.
—Shades of Death: Crying Freeman Graphic Novel. Horibuchi, Seiji, ed. Fujii, Satoru, tr. from JPN. (Illus.). 212p. (gr. 12 up). Pt. 1. 1991. pap. 14.95 (*0-929279-75-1*); Pt. 2. 1992. pap. 14.95 (*0-929279-76-X*); Pt. 3. 1992. pap. 14.95 (*0-929279-77-8*) Viz Communications, Inc.
Koontz, Dean. The Key to Midnight. 1995. 432p. mass mkt. 7.99 (*0-425-14751-7*); 1990. 315p. 19.95 o.p. (*0-913165-51-4*) Berkley Publishing Group.
—The Key to Midnight. 1995. 14.04 (*0-606-15883-9*) Turtleback Bks.
Koto, Doreen. Sashimi. 1997. 668p. 29.95 o.p. (*0-533-12054-3*) Vantage Pr., Inc.
Lee, Javanne. Sake, Karaoke & Love. 2001. 166p. pap. 20.99 (*0-7388-6326-2*) Xlibris Corp.
Loewen, Paul. Butterfly. 1996. 288p. pap. 10.95 o.p. (*0-452-27583-0*, Plume) Dutton/Plume.
—Butterfly. 1988. 272p. 16.95 o.p. (*0-312-01395-7*) St. Martin's Pr.
Lolling, Atsuko G. Aki & the Banner of Names: And Other Stories from Japan. 1991. (Orig.). (J). (gr. 1-6). pap. 4.95 (*0-377-00218-6*) Friendship Pr.
London, Jonathan. Moshi Moshi. 1998. (Around the World Ser.). (Illus.). 32p. (gr. k-4). lib. bdg. 23.90 o.p. (*0-7613-0110-0*) Millbrook Pr., Inc.
Long, John L. Madame Butterfly. 1972. reprint ed. lib. bdg. 27.00 (*0-8422-8092-8*) Irvington Pubs.
—Madame Butterfly. 1997. 14.95 o.s.i (*0-9666591-0-4*) Seconda Donna, Inc.
Long, John Luther. Madame Butterfly. 2003. per. 14.95 (*0-9666591-2-0*) Seconda Donna, Inc.
Long, John Luther, et al, eds. Madame Butterfly. 2002. (Illus.). 192p. (C). pap. text 59.00 (*0-8135-3062-8*); pap. 19.00 (*0-8135-3063-6*) Rutgers Univ. Pr.
Loti, Pierre. Japan: Madame Chrysanthemum. 2002. (Kegan Paul Asia Library). 200p. 76.50 (*0-7103-0820-5*) Kegan Paul International Ltd. GBR. *Dist:* Columbia Univ. Pr.
Lovesey, Peter. Diamond Solitaire. 2002. 327p. pap. 13.00 (*1-56947-292-0*) Soho Pr., Inc.
Lovitt, Chip. Batman & the Ninja. 1995. (Illus.). 24p. (J). (ps-3). pap. 3.29 o.s.i (*0-307-12837-7*, Golden Bks.) Random Hse. Children's Bks.
MacKinnon, Robert F. Samurai Bridge: A Tale of Old Japan. 2001. (Illus.). 256p. pap. (*1-894154-29-0*) Master Point Pr.
Marcinko, Richard & Weisman, John. Red Cell. 1998. (Rogue Warrior Ser.: Vol. 2). 400p. mass mkt. 3.99 (*0-671-01977-5*, Pocket) Simon & Schuster.
Marquand, John P. Last Laugh, Mr. Moto. Date not set. 192p. 20.95 (*0-8488-2363-X*) Amereon, Ltd.
—Last Laugh, Mr. Moto. 1986. mass mkt. 4.95 o.p. (*0-316-54705-0*) Little Brown & Co.
—Mr. Moto Is So Sorry. 1976. 17.95 (*0-89387-016-1*) Amereon, Ltd.
—Mr. Moto Is So Sorry. 1986. mass mkt. 3.95 o.p. (*0-316-54702-6*) Little Brown & Co.
—Right You Are, Mr. Moto. Date not set. 256p. 22.95 (*0-8488-2362-1*) Amereon, Ltd.
—Right You Are, Mr. Moto. 1986. mass mkt. 4.95 o.p. (*0-316-54706-9*) Little Brown & Co.
—Thank You, Mr. Moto. reprint ed. lib. bdg. 23.95 (*0-88411-142-3*) Amereon, Ltd.
—Thank You, Mr. Moto. 1985. 288p. reprint ed. mass mkt. 3.95 o.p. (*0-316-54698-4*) Little Brown & Co.
—Think Fast, Mr. Moto. 150p. 18.95 (*0-8488-2670-1*) Amereon, Ltd.
—Think Fast, Mr. Moto. 1986. mass mkt. 3.95 o.p. (*0-316-54703-4*) Little Brown & Co.
—Your Turn, Mr. Moto. 128p. 17.95 (*0-8488-2669-8*) Amereon, Ltd.
—Your Turn, Mr. Moto. 1985. 288p. reprint ed. mass mkt. 3.95 o.p. (*0-316-54697-6*) Little Brown & Co.
Maruya, Saiichi. Rain in the Wind: Four Stories. Keene, Dennis, tr. from JPN. 1990. 240p. (YA). 18.95 (*0-87011-940-0*) Kodansha America, Inc.
Massey, Sujata. The Flower Master. 1999. 304p. 24.00 (*0-06-019228-3*) HarperCollins Pubs.

—The Flower Master. 2000. 400p. mass mkt. 6.99 (0-06-109734-9, HarperTorch) Morrow/Avon.
—The Flower Master. 2000. 13.04 (0-606-21840-8) Turtleback Bks.
—The Salaryman's Wife. 1997. 432p. mass mkt. 7.50 (0-06-104443-1, HarperTorch) Morrow/Avon.
—Salarymans Wife Arc. 2000. 368p. pap. 5.99 (0-06-104384-2) HarperCollins Pubs.
—Zen Attitude. 1998. 320p. mass mkt. 6.99 (0-06-104444-X, HarperTorch) Morrow/Avon.
Matsumoto, Seicho. Inspector Imanishi Investigates. 310p. 1994. pap. 13.00 (1-56947-019-7); 1990. pap. 9.95 o.p. (0-939149-43-5); 1989. 18.95 o.p. (0-939149-28-1) Soho Pr., Inc.
Matsuoka, Takashi. Autumn Bridge. 2003. 416p. 24.95 (0-385-33641-1, Delacorte Pr.) Dell Publishing.
—Cloud of Sparrows. 2003. 592p. mass mkt. 7.50 (0-440-24085-9, 53628844); 2002. E-Book 19.95 (0-440-33397-0); 2002. (Illus.). 416p. 24.95 (0-385-33640-3) Dell Publishing. (Delacorte Pr.).
Maurakami, Ryu & McCarthy, Ralph F. 69. 1993. 184p. 20.00 (4-7700-1736-7) Kodansha America, Inc.
McCullough, Helen C., tr. The Taiheiki: A Chronicle of Medieval Japan. 1976. (Illus.). reprint ed. lib. bdg. 37.50 o.p. (0-8371-8510-6, TATA, Greenwood Pr.) Greenwood Publishing Group, Inc.
—The Taiheiki: A Chronicle of Medieval Japan. 1979. (Illus.). pap. 12.95 o.p. (0-8048-1322-1) Tuttle Publishing.
—The Tale of the Heike. 1988. (Illus.). 504p. 69.50 o.p. (0-8047-1418-5) Stanford Univ. Pr.
McFall, Patricia. Night Butterfly. 1992. 304p. 18.95 o.p. (0-312-07750-5, Saint Martin's Minotaur) St. Martin's Pr.
McFerrin, Linda W. Namako: Sea Cucumber. 1998. 256p. (YA). pap. 14.95 (1-56689-075-6) Coffee Hse. Pr.
McKee, David. The Magician & the Petnapping, 001. 1977. (Illus.). (J). (gr. k-3). 5.95 o.p. (0-395-24916-3) Houghton Mifflin Co.
Meigs, Henry. Gate of the Tigers. 1992. 416p. 21.00 o.p. (0-670-83620-6, Viking) Viking Penguin.
Melville, James. The Body Wore Brocade: A Superintendent Otani Mystery. 1994. mass mkt. 4.99 o.s.i (0-449-22189-X, Fawcett) Ballantine Bks.
—The Body Wore Brocade: A Superintendent Otani Mystery. 1992. 224p. text 20.00 (0-684-19413-9, Macmillan Reference USA) Gale Group.
—The Body Wore Brocade: A Superintendent Otani Mystery. l.t. ed. 1994. (Ulverscroft Ser.). 304p. 29.99 o.p. (0-7089-3064-6, Ulverscroft) Thorpe, F. A. Pubs. GBR. Dist: Ulverscroft Large Print Bks., Ltd., Ulverscroft Large Print Canada, Ltd.
—The Bogus Buddha. 1991. mass mkt. 3.99 o.s.i (0-449-21971-2, Fawcett) Ballantine Bks.
—The Bogus Buddha. 1991. (Superintendent Otani Mystery Ser.). 224p. 17.95 o.s.i (0-684-19247-0, Macmillan Reference USA) Gale Group.
—The Bogus Buddha. l.t. ed. 1992. (Keating's Choice Ser.). 249p. 21.95 o.p. (1-85089-569-4) ISIS Large Print Bks. GBR. Dist: Transaction Pubs.
—The Chrysanthemum Chain. 1986. mass mkt. 2.95 o.s.i (0-449-20822-2, Fawcett) Ballantine Bks.
—The Chrysanthemum Chain. 1982. 182p. 9.95 o.p. (0-312-13463-0) St. Martin's Pr.
—The Chrysanthemum Chain. l.t. ed. 1982. (Ulverscroft Large Print Ser.). 370p. 29.99 o.p. (0-7089-0758-X, Ulverscroft) Thorpe, F. A. Pubs. GBR. Dist: Ulverscroft Large Print Bks., Ltd., Ulverscroft Large Print Canada, Ltd.
—The Death Ceremony. 1987. 208p. mass mkt. 2.95 o.s.i (0-449-21131-2, Fawcett) Ballantine Bks.
—The Death Ceremony. 1985. 192p. 12.95 o.p. (0-312-18549-9) St. Martin's Pr.
—Death of a Daimyo. 1986. mass mkt. 2.95 o.s.i (0-449-20824-9, Fawcett) Ballantine Bks.
—Death of a Daimyo. 1984. 152p. 10.95 o.p. (0-312-18635-5) St. Martin's Pr.
—Death of a Daimyo. l.t. ed. 1986. (Ulverscroft Large Print Ser.). 288p. 29.99 o.p. (0-7089-1462-4, Ulverscroft) Thorpe, F. A. Pubs. GBR. Dist: Ulverscroft Large Print Bks., Ltd., Ulverscroft Large Print Canada, Ltd.
—Diplomatic Baggage. 1996. 224p. 20.00 o.p. (0-7278-4717-1) Severn Hse. Pubs., Ltd.
—Go Gently, Gaijin. l.t. ed. 1991. pap. 8.95 o.p. (1-55504-847-1, 163); 1989. 19.95 o.p. (1-55504-846-3, 130) BBC Audiobooks America.
—Go Gently, Gaijin. 1988. (Superintendent Otani Mystery Ser.). 192p. mass mkt. 2.95 o.s.i (0-449-21413-3, Fawcett) Ballantine Bks.
—Go Gently, Gaijin. 1986. 192p. 12.95 o.p. (0-312-32989-X, Saint Martin's Minotaur) St. Martin's Pr.
—A Haiku for Hanae. 1990. 176p. mass mkt. 3.95 o.s.i (0-449-21835-X, Fawcett) Ballantine Bks.
—A Haiku for Hanae. 1989. 288p. 16.95 o.s.i (0-684-19131-8, Macmillan Reference USA) Gale Group.
—A Haiku for Hanae. l.t. ed. 1991. (Magna Large Print Ser.). 268p. o.p. (1-85057-897-4) Magna Large Print Bks. GBR. Dist: Ulverscroft Large Print Canada, Ltd.
—The Imperial Way. 1987. 240p. 18.95 o.p. (0-233-97819-4) Andre Deutsch GBR. Dist: Trafalgar Square, Trans-Atlantic Pubns., Inc.
—The Imperial Way. 1987. 304p. reprint ed. mass mkt. 3.95 o.s.i (0-449-21374-9, Fawcett) Ballantine Bks.
—Kimono for a Corpse. 1989. mass mkt. 3.50 o.s.i (0-449-21644-6, Fawcett) Ballantine Bks.
—Kimono for a Corpse. 1988. 208p. 14.95 o.p. (0-312-01454-6, Saint Martin's Minotaur) St. Martin's Pr.
—The Ninth Netsuke. 1986. mass mkt. 2.95 o.s.i (0-449-20823-0, Fawcett) Ballantine Bks.
—The Ninth Netsuke. 1982. 160p. 9.95 o.p. (0-312-57476-2) St. Martin's Pr.
—The Ninth Netsuke. l.t. ed. 1986. (Ulverscroft Large Print Ser.). 320p. 29.99 o.p. (0-7089-1404-7, Ulverscroft) Thorpe, F. A. Pubs. GBR. Dist: Ulverscroft Large Print Bks., Ltd., Ulverscroft Large Print Canada, Ltd.
—The Reluctant Ronin: A Superintendent Otani Mystery. 1989. 224p. mass mkt. 3.50 o.s.i (0-449-21619-5, Fawcett) Ballantine Bks.
—The Reluctant Ronin: A Superintendent Otani Mystery. l.t. ed. 1989. 304p. lib. bdg. 23.95 o.p. (0-7451-0950-0, Macmillan Reference USA) Gale Group.
—The Reluctant Ronin: A Superintendent Otani Mystery. 1988. 192p. 15.95 o.s.i (0-684-18947-X, Scribner) Simon & Schuster.
—Sayonara, Sweet Amaryllis. 1987. 208p. mass mkt. 2.95 o.s.i (0-449-20825-7, Fawcett) Ballantine Bks.
—Sayonara, Sweet Amaryllis. 1985. 160p. 10.95 o.p. (0-312-69995-6) St. Martin's Pr.
—Sayonara, Sweet Amaryllis. l.t. ed. 1986. (Ulverscroft Large Print Ser.). 320p. 29.99 o.p. (0-7089-1433-0, Ulverscroft) Thorpe, F. A. Pubs. GBR. Dist: Ulverscroft Large Print Bks., Ltd., Ulverscroft Large Print Canada, Ltd.
—A Sort of Samurai. 1985. 208p. mass mkt. 2.95 o.s.i (0-449-20821-4, Fawcett) Ballantine Bks.
—A Sort of Samurai. 1983. 176p. pap. 5.95 o.p. (0-312-74559-1, Saint Martin's Griffin); 1982. 168p. 9.95 o.p. (0-312-74558-3) St. Martin's Pr.
—A Tarnished Phoenix. l.t. ed. 1992. (Adventure Suspense Ser.). 432p. 29.99 o.p. (0-7089-2666-5, Ulverscroft) Thorpe, F. A. Pubs. GBR. Dist: Ulverscroft Large Print Bks., Ltd., Ulverscroft Large Print Canada, Ltd.
—The Wages of Zen. 1985. 224p. mass mkt. 3.50 o.s.i (0-449-20838-9, Fawcett) Ballantine Bks.
Minatoya, Lydia Y. The Strangeness of Beauty. 1999. (Illus.). 384p. 23.00 (0-684-85362-0, Simon & Schuster) Simon & Schuster.
Mishima, Yukio. After the Banquet. Keene, Donald, tr. 1981. (Perigee Japanese Library). 288p. pap. 10.50 o.p. (0-399-50486-9, Perigee Bks.) Berkley Publishing Group.
—After the Banquet. 1999. 288p. pap. 14.00 (0-375-70515-5) Knopf, Alfred A. Inc.
—After the Banquet. 1963. 7.95 o.p. (0-394-41429-2, Knopf Bks. for Young Readers) Random Hse. Children's Bks.
—Death in Midsummer & Other Stories. 1966. (Orig.). pap. 10.95 (0-8112-0117-1, NDP215) New Directions Publishing Corp.
—The Decay of the Angel. Seidensticker, Edward G., tr. from JPN. 1990. (Sea of Fertility Ser.: Vol. 4). 256p. pap. 13.00 (0-679-72243-2, Vintage) Knopf Publishing Group.
—The Decay of the Angel. 1974. 11.95 o.p. (0-394-46613-6, Knopf Bks. for Young Readers) Random Hse. Children's Bks.
—Forbidden Colors. Marks, Alfred H., tr. 1981. (Perigee Japanese Library). 416p. pap. 10.95 o.p. (0-399-50490-7, Perigee Bks.) Berkley Publishing Group.
—Forbidden Colors. Marks, Alfred H., tr. from JPN. 1999. 416p. pap. 15.00 (0-375-70516-3) Knopf, Alfred A. Inc.
—Runaway Horses. Gallagher, Michael, tr. from JPN. 1990. (Sea of Fertility Ser.). 432p. pap. 14.95 (0-679-72240-8, Vintage) Knopf Publishing Group.
—Spring Snow. Gallagher, Michael, tr. from JPN. 1990. (Sea of Fertility Ser.: Vol. 1). 400p. pap. 14.00 (0-679-72241-6, Vintage) Knopf Publishing Group.
—Spring Snow. Gallagher, Michael, tr. from JPN. 1972. 13.95 o.s.i (0-394-44239-3) Knopf, Alfred A. Inc.
—The Temple of Dawn. Saunders, E. Dale & Seigle, Cecilia S., trs. 1990. (Sea of Fertility Ser.: Vol. 3). 352p. pap. 14.00 (0-679-72242-4, Vintage) Knopf Publishing Group.
—The Temple of the Golden Pavilion. Morris, Ivan, tr. 1981. (Perigee Japanese Library). (Illus.). 288p. pap. 9.95 o.p. (0-399-50488-5, Perigee Bks.) Berkley Publishing Group.
—The Temple of the Golden Pavilion. 1959. 8.95 o.p. (0-394-44810-3, Knopf Bks. for Young Readers) Random Hse. Children's Bks.
—The Temple of the Golden Pavilion. Morris, Ivan, tr. (Everyman's Library). 1995. 304p. 17.00 (0-679-43315-5); 1994. (Illus.). 288p. pap. 13.00 (0-679-75270-6) Random Hse., Inc.
—Thirst for Love. Marks, Alfred H., tr. 1981. (Perigee Japanese Library). 224p. pap. 8.95 o.p. (0-399-50494-X, Perigee Bks.) Berkley Publishing Group.
—Thirst for Love. Marks, Alfred H., tr. from JPN. 1999. 208p. pap. 12.00 (0-375-70507-4, Vintage) Knopf Publishing Group.
—Thirst for Love. 1969. 10.95 o.p. (0-394-44844-8, Knopf Bks. for Young Readers) Random Hse. Children's Bks.
Miyabe, Miyuki. All She Was Worth. Birnbaum, Alfred, tr. from JPN. 1999. 296p. pap. 12.00 (0-395-96658-2, Mariner Bks.) Houghton Mifflin Co. Trade & Reference Div.
—All She Was Worth. Floyd, E., ed. Birnbaum, Alfred T., tr. from JPN. 1997. 264p. 22.00 o.p. (4-7700-1922-X) Kodansha America, Inc.
Mori Ogai. The Wild Goose (Gan) 1995. (Michigan Monograph Series in Japanese Studies: No. 14). 166p. 28.95 (0-939512-70-X) Univ. of Michigan, Ctr. for Japanese Studies.
—The Wild Goose (Gan) Watson, Burton, tr. 1995. (Michigan Monograph Series in Japanese Studies: No. 14). 166p. pap. 14.95 (0-939512-71-8) Univ. of Michigan, Ctr. for Japanese Studies.
Murakami, Haruki. Dance Dance Dance. 1995. Tr. of Dansu Dansu Dansu. 416p. pap. 14.00 (0-679-75379-6, Vintage) Knopf Publishing Group.
—Dance Dance Dance. Luke, Elmer, ed. Birnbaum, Alfred T., tr. from JPN. 1994. Tr. of Dansu Dansu Dansu. 352p. 22.00 (4-7700-1683-2) Kodansha America, Inc.
—The Elephant Vanishes. 1993. 327p. 21.00 o.s.i (0-679-42057-6) Knopf, Alfred A. Inc.
—Norwegian Wood. Rubin, Jay, tr. from JPN. 2000. (Vintage International Ser.). 304p. pap. 13.00 (0-375-70402-7, Vintage) Knopf Publishing Group.
—South of the Border, West of the Sun: A Novel. 2000. 224p. pap. 12.00 (0-679-76739-8, Vintage) Knopf Publishing Group.
—South of the Border, West of the Sun: A Novel. Gabriel, Philip, tr. 1999. 224p. 22.00 (0-375-40251-9) Knopf, Alfred A. Inc.
—Sputnik Sweetheart. 2000. E-Book 11.00 (1-58945-762-5) Adobe Systems, Inc.
—Sputnik Sweetheart: A Novel. 2002. (Vintage International Ser.). 224p. pap. 12.00 (0-375-72605-5, Vintage) Knopf Publishing Group.
—Sputnik Sweetheart: A Novel. Gabriel, Philip, tr. from JPN. 2001. 224p. 23.00 (0-375-41169-0) Knopf, Alfred A. Inc.
—The Wind-Up Bird Chronicle. Rubin, Jay, tr. 1997. 640p. 25.95 o.s.i (0-679-44669-9) Knopf, Alfred A. Inc.
—The Wind-Up Bird Chronicle: A Novel. 1998. 624p. pap. 15.00 (0-679-77543-9, Vintage) Knopf Publishing Group.
Murakami, Ryu. Coin Locker Babies. Snyder, Stephen, tr. from JPN. 1995. 400p. 23.00 (4-7700-1590-9) Kodansha America, Inc.
—Coin Locker Babies. Snyder, Stephen, tr. 1998. 400p. pap. 13.00 (4-7700-2308-1) Kodansha International JPN. Dist: Kodansha America, Inc.
—Coin Locker Babies. 2002. 400p. reprint ed. pap. 18.00 (4-7700-2896-2) Kodansha International JPN. Dist: Kodansha America, Inc.
Murasaki Shikibu. Genji Monogatari. Suematsu, Kencho, tr. 1973. 232p. reprint ed. pap. 12.95 (0-8048-1045-1) Tuttle Publishing.
Murasaki, Shikibu. The Tale of Genji. 1953. mass mkt. 4.95 o.p. (0-385-09275-X) Doubleday Publishing.
—The Tale of Genji. Waley, Arthur, tr. from JPN. & intro. by. 2000. (Thrift Editions Ser.). 256p. pap. 2.50 (0-486-41415-9) Dover Pubns., Inc.
—The Tale of Genji. Seidensticker, Edward G., tr. abr. ed. 1990. (Vintage Bks.). (Illus.). 384p. pap. 14.00 (0-679-72953-4, Vintage) Knopf Publishing Group.
—The Tale of Genji. abr. ed. 1993. (Everyman's Library). 1216p. 25.00 (0-679-41738-9) Knopf, Alfred A. Inc.
—The Tale of Genji. Seidensticker, Edward G., tr. from JPN. abr. ed. 1978. 1120p. pap. 29.95 (0-394-73530-7) Knopf, Alfred A. Inc.
—The Tale of Genji. Waley, Arthur, tr. 1993. 1354p. 22.00 o.s.i (0-679-42467-9); 1977. 16.95 o.s.i (0-394-60405-9) Random Hse., Inc.
—The Tale of Genji. Suematsu, Kendo, tr. 2000. 232p. pap. 12.95 (0-8048-3256-0) Tuttle Publishing.
—The Tale of Genji, 2 vols. Tyler, Royall, tr. from JPN. 2001. (Illus.). 1200p. 60.00 (0-670-03020-1, Viking) Viking Penguin.
Nakagami, Kenji. The Cape: And Other Stories from the Japanese Ghetto. Zimmerman, Eve, tr. from JPN. 1999. (Illus.). 0192p. pap. 14.95 (1-880656-39-6) Stone Bridge Pr.
Nakazawa, Keiji. Barefoot Gen: Life after the Bomb. 1988. (Barefoot Gen Ser.: Vol. 3). (Illus.). 180p. (Orig.). pap. o.p. (0-86571-148-8); lib. bdg. o.p. (0-86571-147-X) New Society Pubs., Ltd.
Natsuki, Shizuko. Murder at Mount Fuji. 1984. 224p. 12.95 o.p. (0-312-55287-4) St. Martin's Pr.
Natsume Soseki. And Then. Field, Norma, tr. from JPN. 1982. (Perigee Japanese Library). 6.95 o.p. (0-399-50611-X) Putnam Publishing Group, The.
—And Then: A Novel. Field, Norma, tr. 1978. 25.00 o.p. (0-8071-0387-X) Louisiana State Univ. Pr.
—Grass on the Wayside. McClellan, Edwin, tr. & intro. by. 1990. (Michigan Classics in Japanese Studies: No. 2). xii, 169p. reprint ed. pap. text 8.95 (0-939512-45-9) Univ. of Michigan, Ctr. for Japanese Studies.
—I Am a Cat. Shibata, Katsue & Kai, Motonari, trs. from JPN. 1982. (UNESCO Collection of Representative Works of Translations from the Literature of the Union of Soviet Socialist Republics). 431p. pap. 8.95 o.p. (0-399-50609-8) Putnam Publishing Group, The.
—Light & Darkness. 1971. 397p. 33.00 (0-7206-0400-1) Owen, Peter Ltd. GBR. Dist: Dufour Editions, Inc.
—The Wayfarer. Yu, Beongcheon, tr. from JPN. 1982. (Perigee Japanese Library). 324p. pap. 6.95 o.p. (0-399-50612-8) Putnam Publishing Group, The.
Nicol, C. W. Harpoon: A Novel. 1987. 512p. 22.95 o.p. (0-399-13177-9, G. P. Putnam's Sons) Penguin Putnam Bks. for Young Readers.
Nitta, Jiro. Death March on Mount Hakkoda. Westerhoven, James, tr. from JPN. 1992. (Rock Spring Collection). 0204p. (Orig.). pap. 10.95 (0-9628137-2-9, Rock Spring Collection) Stone Bridge Pr.
Nothomb, Amelie. Fear & Trembling. 2001. E-Book 19.95 (1-58945-722-6) Adobe Systems, Inc.
—Fear & Trembling. Hunter, Adriana, tr. from FRE. 2001. 132p. 19.95 (0-312-27218-9) St. Martin's Pr.
Oe, Kenzaburo. Nip the Buds, Shoot the Kids: A Novel. Mackintosh, Paul S. & Sugiyama, Maki, trs. from JPN. 1995. 189p. 22.95 (0-7145-2997-4) Boyars, Marion Pubs., Inc.
—Nip the Buds, Shoot the Kids: A Novel. Mackintosh, Paul S. & Sugiyama, Maki, trs. from JPN. 1996. 192p. reprint ed. pap. 11.00 (0-8021-3463-7, Grove Pr.) Grove/Atlantic, Inc.
—The Pinch Runner Memorandum. Wilson, Michiko N. & Wilson, Michael K., trs. from JPN. 1994. 265p. (C). (gr. 13). 62.95 (1-56324-183-8); pap. 22.95 (1-56324-184-6) Sharpe, M.E. Inc. (East Gate Bk.).
—A Quiet Life. Yanagishita, Kunioki & Wetherall, William, trs. from JPN. 1996. 256p. 22.00 o.p. (0-8021-1597-7, Grove Pr.) Grove/Atlantic, Inc.
Ogai, Mori. Vita Sexualis. Goldstein, Sanford & Ninomiya, Kazuji, trs. from JPN. 1989. 153p. pap. 12.95 (0-8048-1048-6) Tuttle Publishing.
Okuizumi, Hikaru. Stones Cry Out. 2000. 144p. pap. 12.00 (0-15-601183-2, Harvest Bks.) Harcourt Trade Pubs.
Okuizumi, Hiraku. The Stones Cry Out. Westerhoven, James, tr. from JPN. 1999. 144p. 20.00 o.s.i (0-15-100365-3) Harcourt Trade Pubs.
Ooka, Shohei. Fires on the Plain. Morris, Ivan, tr. from JPN. 1978. Tr. of Nobi. 246p. reprint ed. 38.50 o.s.i (0-313-20567-1, OOFP, Greenwood Pr.) Greenwood Publishing Group, Inc.
—Fires on the Plain. Morris, Ivan, tr. from JPN. 1989. Tr. of Nobi. 248p. pap. 14.95 (0-8048-1379-5) Tuttle Publishing.
O'Reilly, Victor. Rules of the Hunt. 1995. 512p. mass mkt. 6.99 o.s.i (0-425-15097-6) Berkley Publishing Group.
—Rules of the Hunt. abr. ed. 1996. audio 7.99 o.p. (1-56740-104-X, 694, Paperback Nova Audio Bks.); 1995. audio 16.95 o.p. (1-56100-413-8, 1358, Nova Audio Bks.); 1995. audio 89.25 o.p. (1-56100-244-5, 1020, Unabridged Library Editions); 1995. audio 25.95 o.p. (1-56100-619-X, 242, Bookcassette) Brilliance Audio.
—Rules of the Hunt. 1995. 416p. 23.95 o.p. (0-399-13869-2, G. P. Putnam's Sons) Penguin Group (USA) Inc.
—Rules of the Hunt. 402p. pap. 4.98 o.p. (0-7651-0430-X) Smithmark Pubs., Inc.
Osaragi, Jiro. Homecoming. Horwitz, Brewster, tr. from JPN. 1977. Tr. of Kikyo. 303p. reprint ed. lib. bdg. o.p. (0-8371-9369-9, OSHO, Greenwood Pr.) Greenwood Publishing Group, Inc.
Parker, I. J. Roshomon Gate: A Mystery of Ancient Japan. 2002. (Illus.). 352p. 24.95 (0-312-28798-4, Saint Martin's Minotaur) St. Martin's Pr.
Parker, Ingrid J. The Hell Screen: A Mystery of Ancient Japan. 2003. (Illus.). 352p. 24.95 (0-312-28795-X, Saint Martin's Minotaur) St. Martin's Pr.
Pendleton, Don. Stranglehold. 1998. (StonyMan Ser.: Vol. 36). per. (0-373-61920-0, 1-61920-4, Worldwide Library) Harlequin Enterprises, Ltd.
Perdue, Lewis. Slatewiper. 2003. 368p. 24.95 (0-7653-0111-3, Forge Bks.) Doherty, Tom Assocs., LLC.
Prindle, Tamae K., tr. from JPN. Made in Japan & Other Japanese 'Business Novels' 1990. 200p. (C). (gr. 13). 56.95 (0-87332-529-X); pap. 27.50 (0-87332-772-1) Sharpe, M.E. Inc. (East Gate Bk.).
Pywell, Sharon L. What Happened to Henry. 2004. 272p. 19.95 (0-399-15168-0, Putnam & Grosset) Putnam Publishing Group, The.

Richie, Donald. Memoirs of a Warrior Kumagai: A Historical Novel. 1999. 176p. 18.95 (*0-8048-2126-7*) Tuttle Publishing.

—Where Are the Victors? 1986. (Illus.). 317p. pap. 7.25 o.p. (*0-8048-1512-7*) Tuttle Publishing.

Richman, Alyson. The Mask Carver's Son. 384p. 2001. pap. 14.95 (*1-58234-129-X*); 2000. 23.95 (*1-58234-063-3*) Bloomsbury Publishing.

Robson, Lucia St Clair. The Tokaido Road: A Novel of Feudal Japan. 1992. mass mkt. 5.99 o.s.i (*0-345-35639-X*) Ballantine Bks.

Roe, JoAnn. Samurai Cat. 1992. (Illus.). 64p. pap. 6.95 (*0-931551-07-2*); lib. bdg. 11.95 (*0-931551-08-0*) Montevista Pr.

Rogers, Lawrence, tr. from JPN. & intro. Tokyo Stories: A Literary Stroll. 2002. (Voices from Asia Ser.: Vol. 12). (Illus.). 368p. text 50.00 (*0-520-21786-1*); pap. text 19.95 (*0-520-21788-8*) Univ. of California Pr.

Rowland, Laura J. Black Lotus. 2001. 341p. 24.95 (*0-312-26872-6*, Saint Martin's Minotaur) St. Martin's Pr.

Rowland, Laura Joh. Bundori. 1997. 432p. mass mkt. 6.99 (*0-06-101197-5*, HarperTorch) Morrow/Avon.

—The Concubine's Tattoo. 2000. 384p. mass mkt. 6.99 (*0-312-96922-8*, St. Martin's Paperbacks); 1999. E-Book 6.50 (*0-312-24607-2*); 1998. 336p. 23.95 o.p. (*0-312-19252-5*, Saint Martin's Minotaur) St. Martin's Pr.

—The Dragon King's Palace. 2004. mass mkt. 6.99 (*0-312-99003-0*, St. Martin's Paperbacks) St. Martin's Pr.

—The Samurai's Wife. 2000. 203p. 23.95 (*0-312-20325-X*, Saint Martin's Minotaur) St. Martin's Pr.

—Shinju. Date not set. 384p. mass mkt. (*0-06-101035-9*); 1996. 448p. mass mkt. 6.99 (*0-06-100950-4*) Morrow/Avon. (HarperTorch).

—The Way of the Traitor. 1998. 384p. mass mkt. 6.99 (*0-06-101090-1*) HarperCollins Pubs.

Ryan, Marleigh G. Japan's First Modern Novel: "Ukigumo" of Futabatei Shimei. 1983. 381p. reprint ed. 65.00 o.s.i (*0-313-24128-7*, RYJA, Greenwood Pr.) Greenwood Publishing Group, Inc.

Ryan, Marleigh G., tr. from JPN. & comment. Japan's First Modern Novel: "Ukigumo" of Futabatei Shimei. 1990. (Michigan Classics in Japanese Studies: No. 1). xiv, 381p. reprint ed. pap. text 15.95 (*0-939512-44-0*) Univ. of Michigan, Ctr. for Japanese Studies.

Ryuji, Tsugihara & Yoshiki, Hidaka. The First President of Japan, Vol. 1. 2003. (Illus.). 190p. pap. 9.95 (*0-9725037-7-3*, Raijin Comics Collection) Gutsoon! Entertainment, Inc.

Sadler, A. L., tr. The Ten Foot Square Hut & Tales of the Heike. 1989. (Tut Books. L). (Illus.). 304p. reprint ed. pap. 14.95 (*0-8048-0879-1*) Tuttle Publishing.

Sakabe, Yoshio. Night Autopsy Room: Seven Tales of Life, Death & Hope. 1994. 350p. 39.95 (*0-940121-20-4*, H207, Cross Roads Books) Cross Cultural Pubns., Inc.

Sarashina, Lady. As I Crossed a Bridge of Dreams: Recollections of a Woman in Eleventh Century Japan. Morris, Ivan, tr. lib. bdg. 19.95 (*0-8488-2007-X*) Amereon, Ltd.

—As I Crossed a Bridge of Dreams: Recollections of a Woman in Eleventh Century Japan. Morris, Ivan, tr. & intro. by. 1989. (Classics Ser.). 176p. 13.00 (*0-14-044282-0*, Penguin Classics) Viking Penguin.

Say, Allen. The Feast of Lanterns. 1976. (Illus.). (J). (gr. k-4). 9.95 (*0-06-025213-8*) HarperCollins Children's Bk. Group.

—Grandfather's Journey. 1993. (Illus.). 32p. (J). (ps-3). lib. bdg., tchr. ed. 16.95 (*0-395-57035-2*) Houghton Mifflin Co.

Schaeffer, Susan Fromberg. Snow Fox. 2004. 448p. text 24.95 (*0-393-05814-X*) Norton, W. W. & Co., Inc.

Schroder, Russell. Mulan Special Collector's Edition. deluxe ed. 1998. (Illus.). 72p. (J). (gr. 4-7). 16.95 (*0-7868-3173-1*) Disney Pr.

Schwartz, John B. Bicycle Days. 1990. 256p. pap. 8.95 o.p. (*0-452-26421-9*, Plume) Dutton/Plume.

—Bicycle Days. 1989. 256p. 18.95 o.p. (*0-671-66600-2*) Summit Bks.

Setlowe, Richard. Sexual Occupation of Japan: A Novel. 1999. 320p. 24.00 (*0-06-018393-4*) HarperCollins Pubs.

Shea, Robert. Shike: Time of the Dragons Last of the Zinja. 1992. 784p. pap. 14.00 o.s.i (*0-345-36046-X*) Ballantine Bks.

Sherwin, Hiroko. Eight Million Gods & Demons. 2003. 336p. pap. 14.00 (*0-452-28451-1*); (*0-452-15990-3*) Dutton/Plume. (Plume).

Shikibu, Murasaki. The Tale Of Genji. 2002. (Illus.). 1216p. pap. 28.00 (*0-14-243714-X*, Penguin Classics) Viking Penguin.

Shimada, Masahiko. Dream Messenger. Luke, Elmer, ed. Gabriel, Philip, tr. from JPN. 1992. 304p. 22.00 (*4-7700-1535-6*) Kodansha America, Inc.

—Dream Messenger. 1994. pap. (*0-446-60062-8*); 293p. pap. 10.99 o.s.i (*0-446-67010-3*) Warner Bks., Inc.

Shimoda, Todd A. The Fourth Treasure. 2002. (Illus.). 368p. 24.95 (*0-385-50352-0*, Talese, Nan A.) Doubleday Publishing.

Shimoda, Todd A. & Shimoda, L. J. C. The Fourth Treasure. 2002. (Illus.). 349p. E-Book 22.50 (*0-385-50561-2*, Talese, Nan A.) Doubleday Publishing.

Shono, Junzo. Evening Clouds: A Novel. Lammers, Wayne P., tr. from JPN. 2000. (Rock Spring Collection of Japanese Literature). 0222p. pap. 12.95 (*1-880656-48-5*) Stone Bridge Pr.

Shorey, Wayne. The Little Yokozuna. 2003. 160p. pap. 7.95 (*0-8048-3479-2*) Tuttle Publishing.

Skimin, Robert. Chikara! A Sweeping Novel of Japan & America. 1984. 544p. 16.95 o.p. (*0-312-13182-8*) St. Martin's Pr.

Smith, Martin Cruz. December 6: A Novel. 2003. 400p. mass mkt. 7.99 (*0-671-77592-8*, Pocket Star) Simon & Schuster.

Stroup, Dorothy. In the Autumn Wind. 1987. 448p. 19.95 o.p. (*0-684-18642-X*, Macmillan Reference USA) Gale Group.

Suzuki, Toshimichi. Ad Police. 1994. (Advances in Organization Studies,). (Illus.). 144p. (Orig.). pap. 14.95 (*1-56931-005-X*) Viz Communications, Inc.

Tabrah, Ruth M. The Monk Who Dared: A Novel about Shinran. 1995. 15.95 (*0-916630-75-7*) Press Pacifica, Ltd.

Tachihara, Masaaki. Wind & Stone: A Novel. Kohl, Stephen W., tr. from JPN. 1992. (Rock Spring Collection). (Illus.). 0159p. pap. 10.95 (*0-9628137-7-X*) Stone Bridge Pr.

Taguchi, Randy. Outlet. 2003. 272p. pap. 15.95 (*1-932234-04-7*) Vertical, Inc.

Takagi, Akimitsu. Honeymoon to Nowhere. Mizuguchi, Sadako, tr. from JPN. 1999. 288p. pap. 12.00 (*1-56947-154-1*) Soho Pr., Inc.

Takagi, Akimitsu. The Tattoo Murder Case. Boehm, Deborah, tr. 1997. 240p. 23.00 (*1-56947-108-8*) Soho Pr., Inc.

Takashi, Nagatsuka. The Soil: A Portrait of Rural Life in Meiji Japan. Waswo, Anne, tr. 1990. (Nissan Institute/Routledge Japanese Studies). 272p. (C). (gr. 13). text 29.95 o.p. (*0-415-03074-9*, A6761) Routledge.

Talarigo, Jeff. The Pearl Diver: A Novel. 2004. 200p. 18.95 (*0-385-51051-9*, Talese, Nan A.) Doubleday Publishing.

Tanizaki, Jun'ichiro. Ashikari & the Story of Shunkin: Modern Japanese Novels. 1970. reprint ed. o.p. (*0-8371-3150-2*, TAJN, Greenwood Pr.) Greenwood Publishing Group, Inc.

—A Cat, a Man & Two Women. McCarthy, Paul, tr. from JPN. 1990. 192p. 18.95 o.s.i (*0-87011-755-6*) Kodansha America, Inc.

—A Cat, a Man & Two Women. McCarthy, Paul, tr. from JPN. 1992. 180p. reprint ed. pap. (*4-7700-1605-0*) Kodansha International.

—Diary of a Mad Old Man. Hibbett, Howard S., Jr., tr. 1991. (Vintage International Ser.). 192p. pap. 12.00 (*0-679-73024-9*, Vintage) Knopf Publishing Group.

—The Gourmet Club. 2003. 204p. pap. 15.00 (*4-7700-2972-1*) Kodansha International JPN. *Dist:* Kodansha America, Inc.

—The Gourmet Club. Chambers, Anthony H. & McCarthy, Paul, trs. from JPN. 2001. 240p. 24.00 (*4-7700-2690-0*) Kodansha International JPN. *Dist:* Kodansha America, Inc.

—The Key. Hibbett, Howard S., Jr., tr. 1991. (Vintage International Ser.). 192p. pap. 12.00 (*0-679-73023-0*, Vintage) Knopf Publishing Group.

—The Key. mass mkt. 0.50 o.p. (*0-451-02073-1*, Signet Bks.) NAL.

—The Makioka Sisters. Seidensticker, Edward G., tr. from JPN. 1981. (Perigee Japanese Library). 538p. pap. 13.95 o.p. (*0-399-50520-2*, Perigee Bks.) Berkley Publishing Group.

—Quicksand. Hibbett, Howard S., Jr., tr. from JPN. 1994. (ENG.). 224p. 22.00 o.s.i (*0-394-58547-X*) Knopf, Alfred A. Inc.

—Quicksand. 1995. 240p. pap. 13.00 (*0-679-76022-9*) Random Hse., Inc.

—Some Prefer Nettles. Seidensticker, Edward G., tr. from JPN. 1981. (Perigee Japanese Library). 224p. pap. 8.95 o.p. (*0-399-50521-0*, Perigee Bks.) Berkley Publishing Group.

Tasker, Peter. Silent Thunder: A Novel. 1992. 288p. 20.00 o.s.i (*4-7700-1685-9*) Kodansha America, Inc.

Tatematsu, Wahei. Distant Thunder: A Novel of Contemporary Japan. Howell, Lawrence J. & Morimoto, Hikaru, trs. 1999. 272p. pap. 14.95 (*0-8048-2120-8*) Tuttle Publishing.

Tejima, Keizaburo. The Bears' Autumn. Matsui, Susan, tr. from JPN. 1991. (Illus.). 42p. (J). (gr. 1-4). 12.95 (*0-671-74981-1*, Simon & Schuster Children's Publishing) Simon & Schuster Children's Publishing.

Thompson, Holly. Ash: A Novel. 2001. 292p. pap. 16.95 (*1-880656-65-5*) Stone Bridge Pr.

Thomson, Maynard F. Dreams of Gold. 2001. 464p. E-Book 4.95 (*0-7595-0628-0*); 2001. 464p. E-Book 4.95 (*0-7595-6629-1*); 2001. 464p. E-Book 4.95 (*0-7595-8638-1*); 2001. 464p. E-Book 4.95 (*0-7595-9699-9*); 2001. 464p. E-Book 4.95 (*0-7595-4631-2*); 2000. 464p. mass mkt. 6.99 (*0-446-60775-4*); 1999. 452p. 22.00 o.p. (*0-446-52445-X*) Warner Bks., Inc.

Toland, John. Occupation. 1988. 512p. mass mkt. 4.95 o.p. (*0-8125-8902-5*, Tor Bks.) Doherty, Tom Assocs., LLC.

Tsuji, Kunio. The Signore: Shogun of the Warring States. Snyder, Stephen, tr. from JPN. & intro. by. 210p. 1996. pap. 12.00 (*4-7700-2066-X*); 1990. 17.95 o.s.i (*0-87011-939-7*) Kodansha America, Inc.

Tsujii, Takashi. A Spring Like Any Other: A Novel. Cary, Beth, tr. from JPN. 1992. 272p. 19.95 (*4-7700-1550-X*) Kodansha America, Inc.

Tsukiyama, Gail. The Samurai's Garden. 1995. text 18.95 o.p. (*0-312-11813-9*); 1996. 224p. reprint ed. pap. 12.95 (*0-312-14407-5*, NPB 0231, Saint Martin's Griffin) St. Martin's Pr.

Tsushima, Yuko. The Shooting Gallery. Harcourt, Geraldine, tr. 1988. 160p. 11.95 o.p. (*0-394-56559-2*, Pantheon) Knopf Publishing Group.

—The Shooting Gallery. Harcourt, Geraldine, tr. 1997. (Classics Ser.). 144p. pap. 11.95 (*0-8112-1356-0*, NDP846) New Directions Publishing Corp.

Tsutsui, Yasutaka. What the Maid Saw. Kabat, Adam, tr. from JPN. 1990. 192p. 18.95 o.s.i (*0-87011-992-3*) Kodansha America, Inc.

Tyler, William J., tr. Ishikawa Jun: The Bodhisattva. 1990. (Modern Asian Literature Ser.). 248p. text 52.50 (*0-231-06962-6*) Columbia Univ. Pr.

Uchida, Yasuo. Togakushi Legend Murders. 1994. 352p. pap. 12.95 (*0-8048-1928-9*) Tuttle Publishing.

Umehara, Takeshi. Lotus & Other Tales of Medieval Japan. McCarthy, Paul, tr. 1997. 200p. 16.95 (*0-8048-2062-7*) Tuttle Publishing.

Uno-Chiyo. Confessions of Love: A Novel. Birnbaum, Phyllis, tr. from JPN. 1989. 176p. text 27.00 o.p. (*0-8248-1170-4*); pap. 14.95 (*0-8248-1176-3*) Univ. of Hawaii Pr.

Van Lustbader, Eric. Black Blade. 1995. 558p. pap. 27.00 (*0-345-46684-5*, Fawcett) Ballantine Bks.

—Black Blade. abr. ed. 1993. 16.95 o.p. (*1-55800-643-5*) NewStar Media, Inc.

—The Kaisho. abr. ed. 1993. audio 16.95 o.p. (*1-55800-889-6*) NewStar Media, Inc.

—The Kaisho. 1998. 3.99 (*0-671-02329-2*, Pocket) Simon & Schuster.

—White Ninja. 1995. 512p. pap. 27.00 (*0-345-46677-2*, Fawcett); 1993. mass mkt. 3.99 o.p. (*0-449-22265-9*); 1991. 512p. mass mkt. 6.99 (*0-449-21851-1*, Fawcett); 1990. mass mkt. 5.95 o.s.i (*0-449-21972-0*) Ballantine Bks.

—White Ninja. abr. ed. 1993. audio 15.95 o.p. (*1-55800-249-9*, 40990); audio 8.99 o.p. (*1-55800-903-5*) NewStar Media, Inc. (Dove Audio).

—White Ninja. 1991. 4.99 o.p. (*0-517-07909-7*) Random Hse. Value Publishing.

Vizenor, Gerald, contrib. by. Hiroshima Bugi: Atomu 57. 2003. (Native Storiers Ser.). 224p. 26.95 (*0-8032-4673-0*) Univ. of Nebraska Pr.

Watanabe, Kazuo. Labor Relations: Japanese Business Novel. Prindle, Tamae, ed. 1993. 136p. 40.50 (*0-8191-9304-6*) Univ. Pr. of America.

Watanna, Onoto. The Heart of Hyacinth. 2000. xlvi, 250p. pap. 18.95 (*0-295-97916-X*) Univ. of Washington Pr.

Waters, Mary Yukari. The Laws of Evening. 2003. 192p. 21.00 (*0-7432-4748-5*, Scribner) Simon & Schuster.

—The Laws of Evening: Stories. 192p. 2004. pap. 12.00 (*0-7432-4333-1*); 2003. 21.00 (*0-7432-4332-3*) Simon & Schuster. (Scribner).

White, Robin A. The Last High Ground. 1996. mass mkt. 5.99 o.s.i (*0-449-18319-X*, Fawcett) Ballantine Bks.

—The Last High Ground. 1995. 307p. 23.00 o.s.i (*0-517-59694-6*) Crown Publishing Group.

Wilde, Kelley. Angel Kiss. 1993. 384p. mass mkt. 4.99 o.s.i (*0-440-20728-2*) Dell Publishing.

Willig, Rosette F., tr. from JPN. & intro. The Changelings: A Classical Japanese Court Tale. 1983. xii, 248p. 49.50 (*0-8047-1124-0*) Stanford Univ. Pr.

Wisniewski, David. The Warrior & the Wise Man. (Illus.). 32p. (J). (ps-3). 1998. pap. 6.99 (*0-688-16159-6*, Harper Trophy); 1989. 16.00 o.p. (*0-688-07889-3*); 1989. lib. bdg. 15.93 (*0-688-07890-7*) HarperCollins Children's Bk. Group.

—The Warrior & the Wise Man. 1998. 12.10 (*0-606-15758-1*) Turtleback Bks.

Witham, Larry. Dark Blossom. 1997. 260p. pap. 10.95 (*0-9640428-2-7*) Meridian Bks. of Maryland.

—Dark Blossom: A Novel of East & West. 1997. 260p. (Orig.). pap. text 17.95 (*0-9640428-1-9*) Meridian Bks. of Maryland.

Wojciechowska, Maia. Dreams of Golf. 1993. (Dreams of...Ser.). (Illus.). 52p. (J). 14.50 (*1-883740-01-0*) Pebble Beach Pr., Ltd.

Wolbers, Marian. Rider. 1996. 192p. 21.95 o.p. (*0-312-14718-X*) St. Martin's Pr.

Wynd, Oswald. The Ginger Tree. 1978. mass mkt. 2.25 o.s.i (*0-345-27558-6*) Ballantine Bks.

—The Ginger Tree. 1977. 10.95 o.p. (*0-06-014729-6*) HarperCollins Pubs.

—The Ginger Tree. (Perennial Classics Ser.). 2002. 336p. pap. 12.95 (*0-06-095967-3*); 1990. 304p. reprint ed. pap. 13.00 (*0-06-097332-3*) Harper-Trade. (Perennial).

—The Ginger Tree. 1989. (Eland Travel Fiction Ser.). 294p. pap. 9.95 o.p. (*0-87052-725-8*) Hippocrene Bks., Inc.

—The Ginger Tree. 1991. 304p. (C). reprint ed. lib. bdg. 27.00 o.p. (*0-8095-9037-9*) Millefleurs.

—The Ginger Tree. l.t. ed. 1981. 563p. 12.00 o.p. (*0-7089-0614-1*, Ulverscroft) Thorpe, F. A. Pubs. GBR. *Dist:* Ulverscroft Large Print Bks., Ltd.

Yagawa, Sumiko. The Crane Wife. Paterson, Katherine, tr. from JPN. 1987. Orig. Title: Tsuru-Nyobo. (Illus.). 32p. (J). (gr. k up). pap. 4.95 o.p. (*0-688-07048-5*, Morrow, William & Co.) Morrow/Avon.

—The Crane Wife. 1992. Orig. Title: Tsuru-Nyobo. (J). (ps-3). 18.75 o.p. (*0-8446-6589-4*) Smith, Peter Pub., Inc.

Yamashita, Karen Tei. Circle K Cycles. 2001. (Illus.). 220p. pap. 16.95 (*1-56689-108-6*) Coffee Hse. Pr.

Yoshikawa, Eiji. Musashi: An Epic Novel of the Samurai Era. Terry, Charles S., tr. from JPN. 1981. (Illus.). 992p. 23.45 o.s.i (*0-06-859851-3*) Harper-Trade.

—Musashi: An Epic Novel of the Samurai Era. Terry, Charles S., tr. from JPN. 1995. 984p. (*4-7700-1957-2*) Kodansha International.

—Taiko: A Novel. Moriyasu & Chaline, Eric, eds. Wilson, William S., tr. from JPN. 1992. 940p. 38.00 (*4-7700-1570-4*) Kodansha America, Inc.

—Taiko: An Epic Novel of War & Glory in Feudal Japan. 2001. 944p. (*4-7700-2609-9*) Kodansha International.

Yoshikawa, Mako. One Hundred & One Ways. 2000. 288p. pap. 12.95 (*0-553-37969-0*, Spectra) Bantam Bks.

Yoshimoto, Banana. Amrita. Wasden, Russel F., tr. from JPN. 1996. Tr. of Amurita. 366p. 22.00 o.p. (*0-8021-1590-X*, Grove Pr.) Grove/Atlantic, Inc.

—Amrita. 1998. Tr. of Amurita. mass mkt. 6.99 (*0-671-02577-5*, Pocket) Simon & Schuster.

—Goodbye Tsugumi. Emmerich, Michael, tr. 192p. 2003. pap. 12.00 (*0-8021-3991-4*); 2002. 22.00 (*0-8021-1638-8*) Grove/Atlantic, Inc. (Grove Pr.).

—Kitchen. Backus, Megan, tr. from JPN. 1993. Tr. of Kitchin. 152p. 14.95 o.p. (*0-8021-1516-0*) Grove/Atlantic, Inc.

—Kitchen. Backus, Megan, tr. from JPN. 1994. Tr. of Kitchin. 160p. pap. 12.00 (*0-671-88018-7*, Washington Square Pr.) Simon & Schuster.

—N. P. Sherif, Ann, tr. from JPN. 1994. 194p. 18.00 o.p. (*0-8021-1545-4*, Grove Pr.) Grove/Atlantic, Inc.

—N. P. Rosenman, Jane, ed. 1995. 208p. pap. 10.00 (*0-671-89826-4*, Washington Square Pr.) Simon & Schuster.

Yoshimura, Akira. On Parole. 2000. 256p. pap. 13.00 (*0-15-601147-6*, Harvest Bks.) Harcourt Trade Pubs.

—On Parole: A Novel. Snyder, Stephen, tr. from JPN. 2000. 256p. 23.00 o.s.i (*0-15-100270-3*, Harvest Bks.) Harcourt Trade Pubs.

—One Man's Justice. Ealey, Mark & Hopkinson, Amanda, trs. 2002. 288p. reprint ed. pap. 14.00 (*0-15-600725-8*, Harvest Bks.) Harcourt Trade Pubs.

—One Man's Justice: Novel. Ealey, Mark, tr. from JPN. 2001. 288p. 23.00 (*0-15-100639-3*) Harcourt Trade Pubs.

—Shipwrecks. 2000. 192p. pap. 12.00 (*0-15-600835-1*, Harvest Bks.) Harcourt Trade Pubs.

—Shipwrecks. Ealey, Mark, tr. from JPN. 1996. 174p. 22.00 (*0-15-100194-4*) Harcourt Trade Pubs.

—Shipwrecks: A Novel. Ealey, Mark, tr. from JPN. 1996. 192p. 21.00 o.s.i (*0-15-100211-8*, Harvest Bks.) Harcourt Trade Pubs.

## JERUSALEM—FICTION

Baron, Aileen. A Fly Has a Hundred Eyes. 2002. 272p. text 24.00 (*0-89733-509-0*) Academy Chicago Pubs., Ltd.

Benig, Irving. The Messiah Stones: A Tale of Our Times. l.t. ed. 1996. 25.95 (*1-56895-318-6*, Wheeler Publishing, Inc.) Gale Group.

Christie, Agatha. Appointment with Death. 1987. 9.95 o.p. (*0-553-35062-5*) Bantam Bks.

—Appointment with Death. Pliner, Jayne, ed. 1988. (Hercule Poirot Mystery Ser.). 224p. mass mkt. 5.99 (*0-425-10858-9*) Berkley Publishing Group.

—Appointment with Death. 1986. mass mkt. 2.95 o.s.i (*0-425-09356-5*); 1984. mass mkt. 2.95 o.s.i (*0-425-06775-0*) Berkley Publishing Group.

—Appointment with Death. 1981. 192p. pap. 2.95 o.p. (*0-440-10246-4*) Dell Publishing.

—Appointment with Death. l.t. ed. 1993. 336p. pap. 12.95 o.p. (0-8161-4530-X); 1992. 296p. lib. bdg. 19.95 o.p. (0-8161-4529-6) Gale Group. (Macmillan Reference USA).
—Appointment with Death. 1996. 240p. 24.95 (0-399-14136-7); 1988. (YA). 14.95 (0-396-09298-5) Penguin Group (USA) Inc. (G. P. Putnam's Sons).
—Appointment with Death. l.t. ed. 1975. (Ulverscroft Large Print Ser.). 334p. 12.00 o.p. (0-85456-366-0, Ulverscroft) Thorpe, F. A. Pubs. GBR. Dist: Ulverscroft Large Print Bks., Ltd., Ulverscroft Large Print Canada, Ltd.
—Appointment with Death. 1988. 12.04 (0-606-12169-2) Turtleback Bks.
Cohen, Gary. Weep Not for Me. 1995. 179p. pap. 6.99 o.p. (0-89957-099-2) AMG Pubs.
Elliott, Janice. City of Gates. 1993. 190p. 24.95 o.p. (0-340-57115-2) Hodder & Stoughton, Ltd. GBR. Dist: Lubrecht & Cramer, Ltd., Trafalgar Square.
Eve, Nomi. The Family Orchard: A Novel. 2001. (Illus.). 336p. reprint ed. pap. 13.00 (0-375-72457-5, Vintage) Knopf Publishing Group.
—The Family Orchard: A Novel. l.t. ed. 2001. (Women's Fiction Ser.). (Illus.). 499p. 28.95 (0-7862-3303-6) Thorndike Pr.
Ganz, Yaffa. Savta Simcha & the Cinnamon Tree. 1983. (Illus.). (J). (gr. 6-10). 14.95 (0-87306-354-6) Feldheim, Philipp Inc.
Grossman, David. The Book of Intimate Grammar. 1995. 464p. 13.00 o.s.i (1-57322-515-0, Riverhead Trade (Paperbacks)) Berkley Publishing Group.
—The Book of Intimate Grammar. Rosenberg, Betsy, tr. from HEB. 1994. 480p. 22.00 o.p. (0-374-11547-8) Farrar, Straus & Giroux.
—The Book of Intimate Grammar: A Novel. Rosenberg, Betsy, tr. from HEB. 2002. 352p. pap. 14.00 (0-312-42095-1) Picador.
Gur, Batya. Literary Murder: A Critical Case. 1994. Tr. of Mavet Ba-Hug Le-Sifrut. 368p. pap. 12.95 (0-06-092548-5, Perennial) HarperTrade.
—Literary Murder: A Critical Case. Bilu, Dalya, tr. from ENG. 1993. Tr. of Mavet Ba-Hug Le-Sifrut. 384p. 20.00 o.p. (0-06-019023-X, HarperCollins) HarperTrade.
—Murder Duet: A Musical Case. 1999. (Michael Ohayon Mysteries Ser.). 448p. 25.00 (0-06-017268-1) HarperCollins Pubs.
—Murder on a Kibbutz: A Communal Case. 1995. 368p. pap. 13.95 (0-06-092654-6, Perennial) HarperTrade.
Hareven, Shulamith. City of Many Days: A Novel. Halkin, Hillel, tr. from HEB. rev. ed. 1993. 224p. reprint ed. pap. 11.95 (1-56279-050-1) Mercury Hse.
Heimerdinger, Chris. Tennis Shoes & the Seven Churches. 1997. (J). pap. 6.95 (1-57734-217-8, 01113275) Covenant Communications, Inc.
Henty, G. A. For the Temple: A Tale of the Fall of Jerusalem. 2000. 252p. pap. 9.95 (0-594-01651-7) 1873 Pr.
—For the Temple: A Tale of the Fall of Jerusalem. 2002. 404p. 29.95 (1-59087-059-X, GAH059); per. 19.95 (1-59087-058-1, GAH058) Althouse Pr.
—For the Temple: A Tale of the Fall of Jerusalem. collector's ed. 2002. (Illus.). im. lthr. 38.85 (1-4115-1273-1); pap. 19.95 (1-4115-0648-0); 25.95 (1-4115-0934-X); pap. 17.95 (1-4115-0095-4) Polyglot Pr., Inc.
—For the Temple: A Tale of the Fall of Jerusalem. (Illus.). 1998. 336p. (YA). pap. 14.99 (1-887159-19-3); 1995. 338p. (J). 20.99 (1-887159-00-2) Preston-Speed Pubns.
Herold, Ann B. The Mysterious Passover Visitors. 1989. (Illus.). 112p. (Orig.). (J). (gr. 4-7). pap. 5.99 (0-8361-3494-X) Herald Pr.
Holland, Cecelia. Jerusalem. 1997. 405p. pap. text 6.99 (0-8125-5397-7); 1995. 320p. 23.95 o.p. (0-312-85956-2) Doherty, Tom Assocs., LLC. (Forge Bks.).
Honsa, Vladimir. An Old Spanish Reader: Episodes from 'La Gran Conquista de Ultramar' with Introduction, English Summary of the Chronicle, & Etymological Vocabulary. 1986. (American University Studies: Ser. II, Vol. 32). 77p. (C). text 15.00 o.p. (0-8204-0265-6) Lang, Peter Publishing, Inc.
Horn, Shifra. Four Mothers. 2000. 288p. pap. 14.00 (0-312-26323-6) Picador.
—Four Mothers, Set. 1999. o.s.i (0-312-20871-5) St. Martin's Pr.
Horn, Shifra & Bilu, Dalya. Four Mothers. 1999. 288p. 23.95 o.p. (0-312-20547-3) St. Martin's Pr.
Joyce, Graham. Requiem. 288p. 1998. pap. 13.95 (0-312-86452-3); 1996. 22.95 o.p. (0-312-86088-9) Doherty, Tom Assocs., LLC. (Tor Bks.).
Kadish, Rachel. From a Sealed Room. 2000. 368p. pap. 13.95 (0-425-17641-X) Berkley Publishing Group.
—From a Sealed Room. 1998. 320p. 25.95 o.s.i (0-399-14300-9, G. P. Putnam's Sons) Penguin Group (USA) Inc.
Kellerman, Jonathan. The Butcher's Theater. 2003. 640p. mass mkt. 7.99 (0-345-46067-7, Ballantine Bks.) Ballantine Bks.
—The Butcher's Theater. 1989. 640p. mass mkt. 7.99 o.s.i (0-553-27510-0); audio 16.99 (0-553-45156-1) Bantam Bks.
—The Butcher's Theater. l.t. ed. 1996. (Large Print Bks.). 888p. pap. 22.95 o.p. (1-56895-342-9, Wheeler Publishing, Inc.) Gale Group.
King, Laurie R. O Jerusalem. 1999. (Mary Russell Novels Ser.). (Illus.). 384p. 23.95 o.s.i (0-553-11093-4) Broadway Bks.
King, Ruchama. Seven Blessings: A Novel. 2003. 256p. 23.95 (0-312-30915-5) St. Martin's Pr.
Lapid, Haim. Breznitz. 2000. 244p. pap. 15.95 (1-902881-15-X); (1-902881-10-9) Toby Pr.
Lawhead, Stephen R. The Black Rood. 2001. (Illus.). 448p. pap. 16.99 (0-310-21783-0) Zondervan.
Lipshitz, Arye. We Built Jerusalem: Tales of Pioneering Days. Louvish, Misha, tr. 1985. 176p. 14.95 (0-8453-4787-X, Cornwall Bks.) Associated Univ. Presses.
Makiya, Kanan. The Rock: A Tale of Seventh-Century Jerusalem. 2001. (Illus.). 368p. 26.00 (0-375-40087-7, Pantheon) Knopf Publishing Group.
Mitgutsch, Anna. Lover, Traitor: A Jerusalem Story. Theobald, Roslyn, tr. 1997. 211p. 23.00 o.p. (0-8050-4174-5, Metropolitan Bks.) Holt, Henry & Co.
Oz, Amos. Fima. 1994. 336p. (C). pap. 13.00 (0-15-600143-8, Harvest Bks.); 1993. 322p. 22.95 (0-15-189851-0) Harcourt Trade Pubs.
—Fima. 322p. 4.98 o.p. (0-8317-3599-6) Smithmark Pubs., Inc.
—Soumchi. Oz, Amos & Farmer, Penelope, trs. from HEB. 1995. (Harvest Book Ser.). (Illus.). 96p. (J). (gr. 4 up). pap. 10.00 o.s.i (0-15-600193-4, Harvest Bks.) Harcourt Trade Pubs.
Popkin, Zelda. Quiet Street. 2001. 382p. 27.95 (0-7351-0535-9) Replica Bks.
—Quiet Street. 2002. 382p. pap. 18.95 (0-8032-8770-4, Bison Bks.) Univ. of Nebraska Pr.
Ragen, Naomi. Sotah. 1993. 496p. mass mkt. 5.99 o.p. (0-06-100707-2, HarperTorch) Morrow/Avon.
—Sotah. l.t. ed. 2003. 754p. 24.95 (1-902881-73-7) Toby Pr.
Reich, Tova. Master of the Return. 1988. 300p. 19.95 o.s.i (0-15-157880-X) Harcourt Trade Pubs.
—Master of the Return. 1999. (Library of Modern Jewish Literature). 256p. pap. text 17.95 (0-8156-0620-6) Syracuse Univ. Pr.
Rivele, Stephen J. A Booke of Days: A Journal of the Crusades. 1997. 448p. 24.00 o.p. (0-7867-0348-2, Carroll & Graf Pubs.) Avalon Publishing Group.
—A Booke of Days: A Novel of the Crusades. 1998. 448p. pap. 13.95 (0-7867-0462-4, Carroll & Graf Pubs.) Avalon Publishing Group.
Rosenberg, Joel C. The Last Days. Date not set. mass mkt. (0-7653-4820-9); 2003. 352p. 24.95 (0-7653-0928-9) Doherty, Tom Assocs., LLC. (Forge Bks.).
Rosenberg, Robert. An Accidental Murder. 1999. (Avram Cohen Mysteries Ser.). 288p. 22.00 o.s.i (0-684-85032-X, Scribner) Simon & Schuster.
—Crimes of the City. 1992. (Crime Ser.). 288p. pap. 5.95 o.p. (0-14-016686-6, Penguin Bks.) Penguin Group (USA) Inc.
—Crimes of the City. 1997. (Missing Mysteries Ser.: Vol. 3). mass mkt. 7.95 (1-890208-03-5) Poisoned Pen Pr.
—Crimes of the City. 1991. 272p. 18.95 o.p. (0-671-70222-X, Simon & Schuster) Simon & Schuster.
—Crimes of the City. 2001. 200p. pap. 13.95 (1-890208-81-7) Poisoned Pen Pr.
—The Cutting Room: An Avram Cohen Mystery. 1993. (Crime Ser.). 304p. reprint ed. pap. 5.95 o.p. (0-14-023112-9, Penguin Bks.) Penguin Group (USA) Inc.
—The Cutting Room: An Avram Cohen Mystery. 1993. 320p. 20.00 (0-671-74344-9, Simon & Schuster) Simon & Schuster.
—House of Guilt: An Avram Cohen Mystery. 1996. 368p. 21.50 o.p. (0-684-82654-2, Scribner) Simon & Schuster.
Shames, Germaine W. Between Two Deserts. 2002. 155p. 24.00 (1-931561-13-3) MacAdam/Cage Publishing, Inc.
Simon, Frank. Veiled Threats. 1996. 356p. pap. 12.99 o.p. (0-89107-880-0) Crossway Bks.
Stone, Robert. Damascus Gate. 1998. 512p. tchr. ed. 26.00 (0-395-66569-8) Houghton Mifflin Co.
—Damascus Gate, Set. abr. ed. 1999. audio 29.95 (1-57511-058-X) Publishing Mills, Inc., The.
—Damascus Gate. unabr. ed. 1998. audio 117.00 (0-7887-2208-5, 95451E7) Recorded Bks., LLC.
—Damascus Gate. 1999. (Illus.). 528p. pap. 14.00 (0-684-85911-4, Touchstone) Simon & Schuster.
—Damascus Gate. l.t. ed. 1998. (Americana Ser.). 751p. 29.95 (0-7862-1632-8) Thorndike Pr.
Tarr, Judith. The Queen of Swords. 2000. 464p. pap. 17.95 (0-312-86805-7, Forge Bks.); 1998. mass mkt. 6.99 (0-8125-5085-4, Tor Bks.); 1997. 464p. 25.95 (0-312-85821-3, Forge Bks.) Doherty, Tom Assocs., LLC.
Tel, Jonathan. Arafat's Elephant. 2002. 208p. pap. text 14.00 (1-58243-183-3, Counterpoint Pr.) Basic Bks.
Thoene, Bodie & Thoene, Brock. First Light. 2003. (A. D. Chronicles Ser.). (Illus.). 416p. 24.99 (0-8423-7506-6); xix, 395p. pap. (0-8423-7507-4) Tyndale Hse. Pubs.
—Jerusalem Vigil. 2000. (Zion Legacy Ser.: No. 1). (Illus.). 352p. 19.95 o.p. (0-670-88911-3) Viking Penguin.
—Jerusalem's Hope, Vol. 6. 2002. (Illus.). 272p. 24.95 (0-670-03084-8, Viking) Viking Penguin.
—Thunder from Jerusalem. 2000. (Zion Legacy Ser.: No. 2). (Illus.). 352p. 19.95 o.s.i (0-670-89206-8, Viking); 4p. 25.95 o.s.i (0-14-180237-5, Penguin AudioBooks) Viking Penguin.
Thoene, Brock & Thoene, Bodie. Jerusalem's Heart. l.t. ed. 2002. lib. bdg. 27.95 (1-58547-134-8, Premier) Ctr. Point Large Print.
Traylor, Ellen G. Jerusalem - The City of God: A Novel. 1995. pap. 14.99 o.p. (0-89081-985-8) Harvest Hse. Pubs.
—The Priest. 1998. 370 p. pap. 12.99 o.s.i (0-8499-4099-0) W Publishing Group.
Waysman, Dvora. Esther: A Jerusalem Love Story. 2000. 150p. pap. 9.95 (1-55874-822-9, Simcha Pr.) Health Communications, Inc.
Weinberg, Norbert. Beyond the Wall. 1978. 7.95 (0-8197-0462-8) Bloch Publishing Co.
Wheeler, Gerald, ed. Return to Jerusalem. 1988. 160p. (Orig.). (J). pap. 6.95 o.p. (0-8280-0426-9) Review & Herald Publishing Assn.
Wilentz, Amy. Martyrs' Crossing. 2001. 320p. 24.00 (0-684-85436-8, Simon & Schuster) Simon & Schuster.
Yehoshua, A. B. Mr. Mani. Halkin, Hillel, tr. 1992. 369p. 22.50 o.s.i (0-385-26792-4) Doubleday Publishing.
—Mr. Mani. Halkin, Hillel, tr. 1993. 384p. pap. 14.00 (0-15-662769-8, Harvest Bks.) Harcourt Trade Pubs.
Zager, Muriel K. Bystander. 1993. (Illus.). 192p. (Orig.). pap. 9.95 (0-89407-109-2) Strawberry Hill Pr.

**JESUS CREEK (TENN.: IMAGINARY PLACE)—FICTION**

Adams, Deborah. All the Blood Relations. 1996. mass mkt. 5.50 o.s.i (0-345-40378-9) Ballantine Bks.
—All the Crazy Winters. 1992. (Holiday Mysteries Ser.). mass mkt. 5.50 o.s.i (0-345-37076-7, Ballantine Bks.) Ballantine Bks.
—All the Dark Disguises. 1993. mass mkt. 4.99 o.s.i (0-345-37765-6) Ballantine Bks.
—All the Deadly Beloved. 1995. mass mkt. 5.99 (0-345-39222-1); 240p. pap. 15.00 (0-345-47170-9) Ballantine Bks.
—All the Great Pretenders. 1991. (Orig.). mass mkt. 5.99 o.s.i (0-345-37075-9, Ballantine Bks.) Ballantine Bks.
—All the Hungry Mothers. 1994. (Southern Mysteries Ser.). mass mkt. 4.99 o.s.i (0-345-38552-7) Ballantine Bks.
—All the Hungry Mothers. 1999. 192p. pap. 14.95 (1-57072-122-X); reprint ed. 24.95 (1-57072-106-8) Overmountain Pr. (Silver Dagger Mysteries).

**JOHANNESBURG (SOUTH AFRICA)—FICTION**

Brown, James A. The Ridge of Gold. 1986. 336p. 17.95 o.p. (0-312-68231-X) St. Martin's Pr.
Essop, Ahmed. Hajji Musa & the Hindu Fire-Walker. 1988. (Readers International Ser.). 280p. (Orig.). 16.95 (0-930523-51-2); pap. 8.95 (0-930523-52-0) Readers International.

**JOLIET (ILL.)—FICTION**

Bonansinga, Jay. Head Case. 1998. 318p. 23.00 (0-684-82514-7); 23.00 (0-684-84931-3) Simon & Schuster. (Simon & Schuster).
—Head Case. l.t. ed. 1998. (Core Ser.). 480p. 28.95 (0-7838-0168-8) Thorndike Pr.

**JURASSIC PARK (IMAGINARY PLACE)—FICTION**

Crichton, Michael. Jurassic Park. 1997. pap. 12.00 o.s.i (0-345-41895-6); 1995. pap. 6.99 o.p. (0-345-90878-3); 1993. (YA). mass mkt. 6.99 o.p. (0-345-90231-9); 1991. (YA). mass mkt. 6.99 (0-345-01954-7); 1991. (Illus.). 416p. mass mkt. 7.99 (0-345-37077-5, Ballantine Bks.); 1991. mass mkt. 5.99 o.s.i (0-345-37473-8) Ballantine Bks.
—Jurassic Park. l.t. ed. 1991. 592p. (YA). lib. bdg. 22.95 o.p. (0-8161-5252-7, Macmillan Reference USA) Gale Group.
—Jurassic Park. 1990. 416p. 27.95 (0-394-58816-9) Knopf, Alfred A. Inc.
—Jurassic Park. 2002. pap. 7.67 (0-582-50382-5) Longman Publishing Group.
—Jurassic Park. (FRE.). pap. 14.95 (2-266-00566-9) Presses Pocket FRA. Dist: Distribooks, Inc.
—Jurassic Park. 1992. 5.99 o.p. (0-517-08349-3) Random Hse. Value Publishing.
—Jurassic Park. 1991. (YA). 14.04 (0-606-01181-1) Turtleback Bks.
—Jurassic Park, Set. abr. ed. 1990. audio 17.00 (0-394-58830-4, 391009, RH Audio) Random Hse. Audio Publishing Group.
—The Lost World: A Novel. 1997. pap. 12.00 (0-345-41900-6); 1997. (YA). mass mkt. 7.99 (0-345-91166-0); 1996. (Illus.). 448p. mass mkt. 7.99 (0-345-40288-X, Ballantine Bks.); 1996. mass mkt. 7.50 o.s.i (0-345-40507-2) Ballantine Bks.
—The Lost World: A Novel. l.t. ed. 1995. 640p. (YA). 25.95 (0-7838-1589-1, Macmillan Reference USA) Gale Group.
—The Lost World: A Novel. 1995. 416p. 29.95 (0-679-41946-2); 1997. (YA). 14.95 o.s.i (0-679-45540-X) Knopf, Alfred A. Inc.
—The Lost World: A Novel. abr. ed. 1995. audio 24.00 (0-679-44548-X, 493139); audio compact disk 27.50 (0-679-44763-6) Random Hse. Audio Publishing Group. (RH Audio).
—The Lost World: A Novel. unabr. ed. 1999. audio compact disk 104.00 (0-7887-3725-2, C1082E7); audio 80.00 (0-7887-3093-2, 95804E7) Recorded Bks., LLC.
—The Lost World: A Novel. l.t. ed. 1996. (Charnwood Large Print Ser.). 608p. 29.99 (0-7089-8922-5, Charnwood) Thorpe, F. A. Pubs. GBR. Dist: Ulverscroft Large Print Bks., Ltd., Ulverscroft Large Print Canada, Ltd.



## K

**KANSAS—FICTION**

Adams, Andy. The Ranch on the Beaver. 1997. (Illus.). 313p. pap. 12.95 (0-8032-5930-1, Bison Bks.) Univ. of Nebraska Pr.
Angers, Renee. Wasted Land. 2000. E-Book 7.99 (1-929429-43-6); E-Book 9.97 (1-929429-46-0) Dead End Street, LLC.
Ascher, Carol. The Flood. 1987. 22.95 o.p. (0-89594-227-5); pap. 8.95 o.p. (0-89594-256-9) Crossing Pr., Inc., The.
—The Flood: A Novel. 1996. 184p. reprint ed. pap. 11.95 (1-880684-43-8) Curbstone Pr.
Averill, Thomas F. Seeing Mona Naked. 1989. 172p. pap. 9.75 (0-922820-01-5) Watermark Pr., Inc.
Averill, Thomas Fox. The Slow Air of Ewan MacPherson. 2003. 272p. pap. 13.00 (0-425-19081-1, BlueHen Bks.) Putnam Publishing Group, The.
Babb, Sanora. The Lost Traveler. 1995. 314p. pap. 10.95 (0-8263-1568-2) Univ. of New Mexico Pr.
—The Lost Traveler. 1995. E-Book 10.95 (0-585-24077-9) netLibrary, Inc.
Bakst, Harold. Prairie Widow. 1992. 16.95 o.p. (0-87131-694-3) Evans, M. & Co., Inc.
Ballard, Todhunter. West of Quarantine. l.t. ed. 1996. (G. K. Hall Nightingale Ser.). 236p. pap. 17.95 o.p. (0-7838-1849-1, Macmillan Reference USA) Gale Group.
Bassett, Marjory. Never Say Stark Naked. 2002. 320p. 25.00 (1-56649-246-7) Welcome Rain Pubs.
Bennett-Brown, Irene. Before the Lark. l.t. ed. 2002. (Juvenile Ser.). 205p. (J). 21.95 (0-7862-4127-6) Gale Group.
Black, Michelle. Lightning in a Drought Year. 1999. 337p. E-Book 6.00 (1-58200-542-7) Hard Shell Word Factory.
—Lightning in a Drought Year: A Novel of the Heartland. 260p. 2000. pap. 13.95 (1-929705-00-X); 1999. (Illus.). 22.95 (0-9658014-2-X) WinterSun Pr.
—Solomon Spring. 2002. (Eden Murdoch Ser.). 304p. 24.95 (0-7653-0465-1, Forge Bks.) Doherty, Tom Assocs., LLC.
Blake, James Carlos. Wildwood Boys: A Novel. 2001. 384p. pap. 13.00 (0-380-80593-6, Perennial) HarperTrade.
Bowers, Terrell L. Ride Against the Wind. l.t. ed. Date not set. 30.00 (0-7838-0433-4, Macmillan Reference USA) Gale Group.
—Ride Against the Wind. l.t. ed. 1997. (Western Ser.). 288p. 22.95 (0-7862-1076-1) Thorndike Pr.
—Ride Against the Wind. 1996. 200p. 21.95 (0-8027-4156-8) Walker & Co.
Brady, Taylor. Mountain Fury. 2000. (Kincaids Ser.). 291p. 26.95 (0-7862-2336-7, Five Star) Gale Group.
—Westward Winds. 2000. (Kincaids Ser.: Vol. 4). 280p. 26.95 (0-7862-2727-3, Five Star) Gale Group.
Brown, Irene Bennett. Blue Horizons. 2001. (Five Star First Edition Romance Ser.). 311p. 25.95 (0-7862-2815-6, Five Star) Gale Group.
—Long Road Turning. 238p. 2004. pap. 13.95 (1-4104-0179-0, Five Star Trade); 2000. 25.95 (0-7862-2813-X, Five Star) Gale Group.
—No Other Place, Vol. 3. 2002. (Five Star First Edition Romance Ser.). 323p. 26.95 (0-7862-2816-4, Five Star) Gale Group.
—The Plainswoman. 1994. mass mkt. 4.99 o.s.i (0-345-38305-2) Ballantine Bks.
—The Plainswoman. 2000. 412p. 27.95 (0-7862-2775-3, Five Star); 1996. 508p. 21.95 (0-7838-1599-9, Macmillan Reference USA) Gale Group.

—Reap the South Wind. 2002. (Five Star First Edition Romance Ser.). 215p. 27.95 (0-7862-2817-2, Five Star) Gale Group.

Cameron, Kate. Under the Wolf's Head: The First Callista Bagley Gardening Mystery. 1999. 274p. 24.95 (0-9661879-3-8, SKP98-44) St Kitts Pr.

Cameron, Peter. The City of Your Final Destination. 2003. 320p. reprint ed. pap. 14.00 (0-452-28430-9, Plume) Dutton/Plume.

—The City of Your Final Destination. 2002. 320p. 24.00 (0-374-28197-1) Farrar, Straus & Giroux.

Carlson, Nolan. Summer & Shiner. 1992. (Illus.). 158p. (YA). (gr. 4-8). pap. 6.95 (0-9627947-4-0) Hearth Publishing.

Carter, Vincent O. Such Sweet Thunder: A Novel. 2003. (Illus.). 560p. 25.95 (1-58642-058-5) Steerforth Pr.

Chalmers, Robert. Who's Who in Hell. 2002. 368p. pap. 13.00 (0-8021-3924-8, Grove Pr.) Grove/Atlantic, Inc.

Clair, Maxine. Rattlebone. 1994. 224p. 19.00 o.p. (0-374-24716-1) Farrar, Straus & Giroux.

—Rattlebone. 1995. 224p. 10.95 (0-14-024825-0) Viking Penguin.

Coates, Grace Stone. Black Cherries. 2003. 99p. pap. 14.95 (0-8032-6429-1, Bison Bks.) Univ. of Nebraska Pr.

Connell, Evan S. Mr. Bridge. unabr. collector's ed. 1989. audio 56.00 (0-7366-1506-7, 2378) Books on Tape, Inc.

—Mr. Bridge. reprint ed. 1990. 367p. pap. 9.95 o.s.i (0-86547-054-5); 1982. 384p. 35.00 o.p. (0-86547-057-X) Farrar, Straus & Giroux. (North Point Pr.).

—Mr. Bridge. l.t. ed. 1991. (Paperback Ser.). 436p. pap. 15.95 o.p. (0-8161-5205-5, Macmillan Reference USA) Gale Group.

—Mr. Bridge. unabr. ed. 1991. audio 78.00 (1-55690-353-7, 91214E7) Recorded Bks., LLC.

—Mr. Bridge. 1977. pap. 2.50 o.p. (0-671-82937-8, Pocket) Simon & Schuster.

—Mrs. Bridge. unabr. collector's ed. 1989. audio 40.00 (0-7366-1485-0, 2361) Books on Tape, Inc.

—Mrs. Bridge. 1990. 246p. reprint ed. pap. 9.95 (0-86547-056-1, North Point Pr.) Farrar, Straus & Giroux.

—Mrs. Bridge. l.t. ed. 1991. pap. 15.95 o.p. (0-8161-5206-3, Macmillan Reference USA) Gale Group.

—Mrs. Bridge. 1963. pap. 1.65 o.p. (0-670-00122-8) Penguin Group (USA) Inc.

—Mrs. Bridge. unabr. ed. 1991. audio 60.00 (1-55690-356-1, 91201E7) Recorded Bks., LLC.

—Mrs. Bridge. 1979. pap. 2.50 o.p. (0-671-83029-5, Pocket) Simon & Schuster.

—Mrs. Bridge. 1959. 3.75 o.p. (0-670-49448-8) Viking Penguin.

Copeland, Lori. Courtship of Cade Kolby. l.t. ed. 1999. pap. 23.95 (1-56895-627-4, Wheeler Publishing, Inc.) Gale Group.

—Courtship of Cade Kolby. 1997. mass mkt. 5.99 o.s.i (0-380-79156-0, Avon Bks.) Morrow/Avon.

Coplin, Keith. Croftons Fire. 2004. 288p. 21.95 (0-399-15112-5, G. P. Putnam's Sons) Penguin Putnam Bks. for Young Readers.

Curtis, Jack. The Sheriff Kill. Grad, Doug, ed. 1991. 192p. (Orig.). bds. 2.95 (0-671-67275-4, Pocket) Simon & Schuster.

—The Sheriff Kill. l.t. ed. 2001. (Thorndike Western Ser.). 232p. 24.95 (0-7862-3122-X) Thorndike Pr.

Dallas, Sandra. The Persian Pickle Club. Set. abr. ed. 1995. audio 22.95 (1-56876-047-7, 693294) Soundlines Entertainment, Inc.

—The Persian Pickle Club. 208p. 1995. 20.95 o.p. (0-312-13586-6); 1996. reprint ed. pap. 12.95 (0-312-14701-5, NPB 0319, Saint Martin's Griffin) St. Martin's Pr.

—The Persian Pickle Club. l.t. ed. 1998. (Niagara Large Print Ser.). 270p. 29.50 o.p. (0-7089-5856-7, Linford) Thorpe, F. A. Pubs. GBR. *Dist:* Ulverscroft Large Print Bks., Ltd., Ulverscroft Large Print Canada, Ltd.

Dawkins, Cecil. Charleyhorse. 1995. 224p. reprint ed. pap. 9.95 o.p. (1-55583-289-X) Alyson Pubns.

—Charleyhorse. 1986. 288p. pap. 6.95 o.p. (0-14-008010-4, Penguin Bks.); 1985. 256p. 15.95 o.p. (0-670-80631-5) Viking Penguin.

Deaver, Jeffery. A Maiden's Grave. l.t. ed. 1996. 608p. lib. bdg. 25.95 o.p. (0-7838-1621-9, Macmillan Reference USA) Gale Group.

—A Maiden's Grave. 432p. 2001. mass mkt. 7.99 (0-451-20429-8); 1996. mass mkt. 7.99 o.s.i (0-451-18848-9); 1996. mass mkt. 6.99 o.s.i (0-451-19337-7) NAL. (Signet Bks.).

—A Maiden's Grave. 1995. 432p. 22.95 o.p. (0-670-86622-9, Viking); audio 16.95 o.p. (0-14-086210-2, Penguin AudioBooks) Viking Penguin.

Donnelly, Ignatius. The Golden Bottle. (Muckrakers Ser.). reprint ed. lib. bdg. 27.00 (0-8398-0368-0) Irvington Pubs.

Eidson, Thomas. All God's Children. 1997. 320p. 23.95 o.p. (0-525-94235-1) Dutton/Plume.

—All God's Children. 1998. 400p. mass mkt. 5.99 o.s.i (0-451-19081-5, Signet Bks.) NAL.

Eight Kansas Short Story Writers. Kansas Stories, 1989. Girard, James P., ed. 1989. 160p. (Orig.). pap. 5.00 (0-939391-12-0) Woodley, Bob Memorial Pr., The.

Epperson, S. K. Borderland. 1992. 288p. 19.95 o.p. (1-55611-317-X) Fine, Donald I. Bks.

—Dumford Blood. 1991. 304p. 18.95 o.p. (0-312-06342-3, Saint Martin's Minotaur) St. Martin's Pr.

—The Neighborhood. 1995. 288p. 21.95 o.p. (1-55611-466-4) Fine, Donald I. Bks.

—Nightmare. 1992. 288p. 20.00 o.p. (1-55611-338-2) Fine, Donald I. Bks.

Fitzwater, Marlin. Esther's Pillow: A Novel. 2001. 256p. text 25.00 (1-58648-035-9) PublicAffairs.

Fowler, Earlene. Kansas Troubles. l.t. ed. 2000. (Beeler Large Print Mystery Ser.). 329p. 25.95 (1-57490-293-8, Beeler Large Print Bks.) Beeler, Thomas T. Publisher.

—Kansas Troubles. 320p. 1996. 19.95 o.p. (0-425-15148-4); 1997. reprint ed. mass mkt. 6.99 (0-425-15696-6, Prime Crime) Berkley Publishing Group.

Gallagher, Diana G. Shadows. 2003. (Smallville Ser.: No. 6). 272p. mass mkt. 5.99 (0-446-61360-6, Aspect) Warner Bks., Inc.

Garlock, Dorothy. With Song. unabr. ed. 2000. (Tumultuous 1930's Trilogy Ser.: Vol. 2). audio 69.95 (0-7927-2333-3, CSL 222, Chivers Sound Library) BBC Audiobooks America.

—With Song. l.t. ed. 1999. (Basic Ser.). 552p. 29.95 (0-7862-1918-1) Thorndike Pr.

—With Song. 1999. 480p. reprint ed. mass mkt. 6.99 (0-446-60588-3) Warner Bks., Inc.

Girard, James P. The Late Man. unabr. collector's ed. 1995. audio 56.00 (0-7366-3177-1, 3846) Books on Tape, Inc.

—The Late Man. 1994. 384p. mass mkt. 5.99 o.s.i (0-451-40588-9, Onyx) NAL.

—The Late Man. Goerner, Lee, ed. 1993. 288p. text 20.00 (0-689-12183-0, Scribner) Simon & Schuster.

Graham, Janice. Firebird. 1999. 352p. reprint ed. mass mkt. 6.99 o.s.i (0-425-16987-1) Berkley Publishing Group.

—Firebird. l.t. ed. 1998. (Large Print Book Ser.). 27.95 (1-56895-665-7, Wheeler Publishing, Inc.) Gale Group.

—Firebird, Set. abr. ed. 1998. audio 25.00 o.s.i (0-694-51989-8, 696026, HarperAudio) HarperTrade.

—Firebird. abr. ed. 1999. audio 25.00 Highsmith Inc.

—Firebird. unabr. ed. 1999. audio 56.00 (0-7887-2912-8, 95705E7) Recorded Bks., LLC.

—Firebird: A Novel. 1998. 288p. 19.95 o.s.i (0-399-14404-8, G. P. Putnam's Sons) Penguin Group (USA) Inc.

—Sarah's Window. 2002. 320p. reprint ed. mass mkt. 6.99 (0-515-13412-0, Jove) Berkley Publishing Group.

—Sarah's Window. l.t. ed. 2002. 458p. 29.95 (0-7862-3891-7) Gale Group.

—Sarah's Window. 2001. 304p. 23.95 o.s.i (0-399-14629-6) Penguin Group (USA) Inc.

Grant, Alan. Dragon. 2002. (Smallville Ser.). 256p. reprint ed. mass mkt. 5.99 (0-446-61214-6, Aspect) Warner Bks., Inc.

Grimes, Janice Brown. A Different World: Almena, Kansas, 1930-1939. 1998. (Illus.). 328p. pap. 14.95 (1-883911-24-9) Brandylane Pubs., Inc.

Hanson, Jacquelyn. Matilda's Story: A Biographical Novel. 1997. (Illus.). 672p. 24.95 (0-9637265-3-6, 9704); pap. 12.95 (0-9637265-4-4, 9704) Glenhaven Pr.

Harson, Dylan. Kansas Blue. 1993. 288p. 21.50 o.p. (1-55611-375-7) Fine, Donald I. Bks.

Hayes, J. M. Mad Dog & Englishman. 2001. 190p. pap. 13.95 (1-890208-74-4) Poisoned Pen Pr.

—Prairie Gothic. 2003. 250p. 24.95 o.s.i (1-59058-050-8) Poisoned Pen Pr.

—Prairie Gothic. 2004. 272p. mass mkt. 6.99 (0-7434-7907-6) ibooks, Inc.

Heim, Scott. In Awe: A Novel. 1997. 291p. 24.00 o.p. (0-06-018687-9) HarperCollins Pubs.

—Mysterious Skin. abr. ed. 1996. audio 17.95 (1-57453-009-7, 330045) Audio Literature.

—Mysterious Skin: A Novel. 1995. 292p. 20.00 o.p. (0-06-017175-8) HarperCollins Pubs.

—Mysterious Skin: A Novel. 1996. 304p. pap. 13.00 (0-06-092686-4, Perennial) HarperTrade.

Holder, Nancy. Hauntings. 2003. (Smallville Ser.). 288p. reprint ed. mass mkt. 5.99 (0-446-61215-4, Aspect) Warner Bks., Inc.

—Silence. 2003. (Smallville Ser.). 320p. mass mkt. 5.99 (0-446-61359-2, Aspect) Warner Bks., Inc.

Hubalek, Linda K. Looking Back: The Final Tale of Life on the Prairie. 1995. (Butter in the Well Ser.: Bk. 4). (Illus.). 140p. (J). (gr. 4-12). reprint ed. pap. 9.95 (1-886652-03-1) Butterfield Bks., Inc.

—Planting Dreams: A Swedish Immigrant's Journey to America. 1997. (Illus.). 128p. (Orig.). pap. 9.95 (1-886652-11-2) Butterfield Bks., Inc.

—Thimble of Soil: A Woman's Quest for Land. 1996. (Trail of Thread Ser.: Bk. 2). (Illus.). 120p. (Orig.). pap. 9.95 (1-886652-07-4) Butterfield Bks., Inc.

Hughes, Langston. Not Without Laughter. 1976. 23.95 (0-8488-1055-4) Amereon, Ltd.

—Not Without Laughter. xiv, 224p. pap. 12.95 (0-86241-768-6) Payback Pr. GBR. *Dist:* AK Pr. Distribution.

—Not Without Laughter. 1995. 17.05 (0-606-16259-3) Turtleback Bks.

Jaffe, Michael Grant. Dance Real Slow. abr. ed. 1996. audio 16.95 (1-55927-385-2, 393544) Audio Renaissance.

—Dance Real Slow. unabr. ed. 1996. audio 36.00 (0-913369-61-6, 4293) Books on Tape, Inc.

—Dance Real Slow. 2001. 242p. pap. 20.00 (0-374-52829-2); 1996. o.s.i (0-374-92050-8) Farrar, Straus & Giroux.

—Dance Real Slow: A Novel. 1996. 272p. 20.00 o.p. (0-374-13466-9) Farrar, Straus & Giroux.

Jenkins, Beverly. Always & Forever. 2000. 384p. mass mkt. 5.99 (0-380-81374-2, Avon Bks.) Morrow/Avon.

Jones, Annie. Cupid's Corner. l.t. ed. 2001. 239p. 23.95 (0-7862-3093-2, Five Star) Gale Group.

Judd, Cameron. Mr. Littlejohn. l.t. ed. 1992. (General Ser.). 288p. lib. bdg. 19.95 o.p. (0-8161-5565-8, Macmillan Reference USA) Gale Group.

Ladd, Justin. Abilene: The Peacemaker. l.t. ed. 1995. (Nightingale Ser.: Bk. 1). 313p. pap. 17.95 (0-7838-1137-3, Macmillan Reference USA) Gale Group.

—Abilene Book I: The Peacemaker. 1988. 224p. (Orig.). bds. 2.95 o.s.i (0-671-64897-7, Pocket) Simon & Schuster.

—The Barlow Brides. l.t. ed. 1993. 304p. lib. bdg. 15.95 o.p. (0-8161-5723-5, Macmillan Reference USA) Gale Group.

Law, Susan Kay. The Bad Man's Bride: Marrying Miss Bright. 2001. 384p. mass mkt. 5.99 (0-380-81906-6, Avon Bks.) Morrow/Avon.

Lehrer, Kate. Out of Eden. l.t. ed. 1997. (Niagara Large Print Ser.). 548p. 29.50 o.p. (0-7089-5869-9, Ulverscroft) Thorpe, F. A. Pubs. GBR. *Dist:* Ulverscroft Large Print Bks., Ltd.

—Out of Eden: A Novel. 2003. ix, 342p. pap. 16.95 (1-931868-33-6) Capital Bks., Inc.

Lerman, Rhoda. God's Ear: A Novel. 1988. 320p. 19.95 o.s.i (0-8050-0413-0) Holt, Henry & Co.

—God's Ear: A Novel. 1996. (Library of Modern Jewish Literature). 309p. reprint ed. pap. 17.95 (0-8156-0427-0, LEGEP) Syracuse Univ. Pr.

McCracken, Susan Nyswonger. For the Blessings of a Friend. 2001. 284p. pap. 15.00 (0-944350-55-0) Friends United Pr.

McMahon, Thomas. McKay's Bees. 1979. 10.95 o.p. (0-06-012974-3); 1986. 208p. reprint ed. pap. 5.95 o.p. (0-06-091368-1, PL1368, Perennial) HarperTrade.

McMahon, Thomas A. McKay's Bees: A Novel. 2003. (Phoenix Fiction Ser.). 288p. pap. 14.00 (0-226-56111-9) Univ. of Chicago Pr.

Moriarty, Laura. The Center of Everything: A Novel. 2003. 304p. 22.95 (1-4013-0031-6) Hyperion Pr.

—The Center of Everything: A Novel. l.t. ed. 2003. 610p. 30.95 (0-7862-5563-3) Thorndike Pr.

—People in General. 2004. pap. 14.00 (0-7868-8845-8) Hyperion Pr.

Moser, Nancy. A Steadfast Surrender. 2003. 350p. pap. 11.99 (1-59052-143-9) Multnomah Pubs., Inc.

Murray, Nancy. An Inner Voice for Public Administration. 1997. 208p. 64.95 (0-275-95250-9, Praeger Pubs.) Greenwood Publishing Group, Inc.

Nelson, Antonya. Living to Tell: A Novel. l.t. ed. 2000. (G. K. Hall Core Ser.). 512p. 29.95 (0-7838-9188-1, Macmillan Reference USA) Gale Group.

—Living to Tell: A Novel. 2000. 320p. 24.00 o.s.i (0-684-83933-4); 2000. E-Book 24.00 (0-7432-1088-3); 2001. 320p. reprint ed. pap. 13.00 (0-7432-0060-8) Simon & Schuster. (Scribner).

Palmer, Catherine. Prairie Fire. l.t. ed. 2002. 368p. 25.95 (0-7862-3822-4) Gale Group.

—Prairie Fire. 1998. (Town Called Hope Ser.: No. 2). 288p. pap. 7.99 (0-8423-7057-9) Tyndale Hse. Pubs.

—Prairie Rose. l.t. ed. 2002. (Christian Romance Ser.). 416p. 25.95 (0-7862-3821-6) Gale Group.

—Prairie Rose. 1997. (Town Called Hope Ser.: Vol. 1). 262p. pap. 7.99 (0-8423-7056-0) Tyndale Hse. Pubs.

—Prairie Storm. l.t. ed. 2002. (Christian Romance Ser.). 358p. 25.95 o.p. (0-7862-3820-8) Thorndike Pr.

—Prairie Storm, Vol. 3. 1999. (Town Called Hope Ser.). 272p. pap. 7.99 (0-8423-7058-7) Tyndale Hse. Pubs.

Parker, Robert B. Gunman's Rhapsody. l.t. ed. 2001. (Hardcover Ser.). 247p. 31.95 (1-58724-061-0, Wheeler Publishing, Inc.) Gale Group.

—Gunman's Rhapsody. 2001. 320p. 22.95 o.p. (0-399-14762-4) Penguin Group (USA) Inc.

Peck, Dale. Now It's Time to Say Goodbye: A Novel. 1998. 480p. 25.00 o.p. (0-374-22271-1) Farrar, Straus & Giroux.

—Now It's Time to Say Goodbye: A Novel. 1999. 464p. pap. 15.95 (0-688-16841-8, Quill) HarperTrade.

—Now It's Time to Say Goodbye Readers Guide. stu. ed. (0-374-96122-0) Farrar, Straus & Giroux.

Peterson, Tracie. Entangled. 1997. (Portraits Ser.). 256p. pap. 8.99 o.p. (1-55661-936-7) Bethany Hse. Pubs.

—Entangled. 2000. (Christian Fiction Ser.). 290p. 23.95 (0-7862-2228-X, Five Star) Gale Group.

—A Slender Thread. 2000. 384p. pap. 12.99 (0-7642-2251-1) Bethany Hse. Pubs.

Phillips, Michael R. A Dangerous Love. 1997. (Mercy & Eagleflight Ser.). pap. 10.99 o.p. (0-8423-3921-3) Tyndale Hse. Pubs.

—Mercy & Eagleflight. 1996. 335p. pap. 10.99 o.p. (0-8423-3920-5) Tyndale Hse. Pubs.

Phillips, Scott. The Ice Harvest. 2000. 224p. 19.95 (0-345-44018-8, Ballantine Bks.) Ballantine Bks.

Pickard, Nancy. Bum Steer. unabr. ed. 2000. (Jenny Cain Mystery Ser.). audio 49.95 (0-7927-2238-8, CSL 127) Chivers Audio Bks. GBR. *Dist:* BBC Audiobooks America.

—Bum Steer. 1990. (Jenny Cain Mystery Ser.). 256p. 16.95 o.p. (0-671-68040-4, Atria) Simon & Schuster.

—Bum Steer. Marrow, Linda, ed. 1991. (Jenny Cain Mystery Ser.). 288p. reprint ed. mass mkt. 5.99 (0-671-68042-0, Pocket) Simon & Schuster.

Preston, Douglas & Child, Lincoln. Still Life with Crows. l.t. ed. 2003. 741p. 31.95 (0-7862-5942-6) Thorndike Pr.

Preston, Douglas J. & Child, Lincoln. Still Life with Crows. 2004. mass mkt. (0-446-61276-6); 2003. 448p. 25.95 (0-446-53142-1) Warner Bks., Inc.

Roderus, Frank. His Royal Highness: J. Aubrey Whitford. 1992. 192p. 15.00 o.s.i (0-385-26691-X) Doubleday Publishing.

Ross, David W. Savage Plains. 1996. 480p. (Orig.). mass mkt. 5.99 (0-380-78324-X, Avon Bks.) Morrow/Avon.

Schenk, Martin. A Small Dark Place. 1999. 404p. mass mkt. 6.99 o.s.i (0-345-43047-6) Ballantine Bks.

Segerhammar, Robert E. Dugouts & Daisies: A Novel about Early Lindsborg, Kansas, & the Smoky Valley. 1993. (Illus.). 278p. 17.00 (0-918331-03-X) Smoky Valley Historical Pubns.

—Still Pioneers: A Novel about Lindsborg, Kansas, & the Smoky Valley in Modern Times. 1995. (Saga of Smoky Hill Ser.: Vol. 3). (Illus.). (0-918331-05-6) Smoky Valley Historical Pubns.

Segerhammer, Robert E. Swedish Mecca of the Plains: A Novel about Lindsborg, Kansas, & the Smoky Valley During the Middle Years. 1993. (Saga of Smoky Hill Ser.: Vol. 2). (Illus.). 15.00 (0-918331-04-8) Smoky Valley Historical Pubns.

Sharpe, Jon. Bleeding Kansas. 1990. (Canyon O'Grady Ser.: No. 8). 176p. mass mkt. 3.50 o.p. (0-451-16610-8, Signet Bks.) NAL.

—Kansas Carnage. 1998. (Trailsman Ser.: Vol. 196). 176p. mass mkt. 4.99 o.s.i (0-451-19385-7, Signet Bks.) NAL.

Shelley, Deborah. Talk about Love. 1999. 171p. pap. 1.96 (0-8217-6328-8) Kensington Publishing Corp.

Short, Luke, Jr. The Some-Day Country. 1990. 144p. (Orig.). mass mkt. 2.95 o.s.i (0-440-20673-1) Dell Publishing.

Short, Luke. The Some-Day Country. 1979. pap. 2.25 o.p. (0-553-23859-0) Bantam Bks.

Simons, Paullina. Tully. 1994. 594p. 23.95 o.p. (0-312-11083-9) St. Martin's Pr.

Smith, Florence B. Labette County's Ultimate Deception. l.t. ed. 2001. (G. K. Hall Romance Ser.). 303p. 27.95 (0-7838-9375-2, Macmillan Reference USA) Gale Group.

Snodgrass, Steven L. Lethal Dose. 1996. 350p. 22.95 (0-9642463-1-7) ICAM Publishing Co.

Stern, Roger. Strange Visitors. Levine, Jaime, ed. 2002. (Smallville Ser.). 304p. reprint ed. mass mkt. 5.99 (0-446-61213-8, Aspect) Warner Bks., Inc.

Stevenson, Melody. The Life Stone of Singing Bird: A Novel. 1996. 176p. 19.95 o.p. (0-571-19886-4) Faber & Faber, Inc.

Stutzman, Ervin R. Tobias of the Amish: A True Story of Tangled Strands in Faith, Family & Community. 2001. 352p. (Illus.). pap. 15.99 (0-8361-9170-6); 22.99 (0-8361-9190-0) Herald Pr.

Swearingen, Ida. Owl of the Desert: A Mystery. 2003. 220p. 12.95 (1-892281-19-8) New Victoria Pubs., Inc.

Thompson, Earl. A Garden of Sand. 2001. 544p. pap. 14.00 (0-7867-0946-4); 1990. 500p. mass mkt. 5.95 (0-88184-653-8) Avalon Publishing Group. (Carroll & Graf Pubs.).

—A Garden of Sand. 1981. mass mkt. 3.95 o.p. (0-451-11156-7, Signet Bks.) NAL.

Thompson, Thomas. Forbidden Valley. l.t. ed. 1992. (Nightingale Ser.). 316p. pap. 14.95 o.p. (0-8161-5479-1, Macmillan Reference USA) Gale Group.

—King of Abilene. l.t. ed. 1992. (General Ser.). 280p. lib. bdg. 19.95 o.p. (0-8161-5439-2, Macmillan Reference USA) Gale Group.

Troy, Judy. West of Venus. 1997. 237p. 23.00 o.s.i (*0-679-45153-6*) Random Hse., Inc.

Vaughan, Robert. Adobe Walls. 1998. (Adobe Walls Ser.: Vol. 1). 272p. mass mkt. 5.99 (*0-312-96737-3*, St. Martin's Paperbacks) St. Martin's Pr.

Vogt, Esther Loewen. Edge of Dawn. 1990. 176p. pap. 7.99 (*0-8361-3520-2*) Herald Pr.

—Edge of Dawn. l.t. ed. 1999. (Christian Mystery Ser.). 256p. 23.95 (*0-7862-1800-2*) Thorndike Pr.

—Edge of Dawn. 1990. E-Book 7.99 (*0-585-26283-7*) netLibrary, Inc.

—The Flame & the Fury. 1998. 173p. pap. 9.99 (*0-88965-143-4*, Horizon Bks.) Christian Pubns., Inc.

—The Flame & the Fury. l.t. ed. 2000. (Candlelight Romance Ser.). 192p. 20.95 (*0-7862-2796-6*) Thorndike Pr.

—The Lonely Plains. 1993. (Heart for the Prairie Ser.: Bk. 2). 125p. (gr. 11-12). pap. 9.99 (*0-88965-100-0*, 0021000, Horizon Bks.) Christian Pubns., Inc.

—Song of the Prairie. 1995. 182p. (gr. 11-12). pap. 9.99 (*0-88965-109-4*, 0021094, Horizon Bks.) Christian Pubns., Inc.

—Song of the Prairie. l.t. ed. 1998. (Christian Fiction Ser.). 240p. 23.95 (*0-7862-1490-2*) Thorndike Pr.

Weddle, Virginia B. The Moon of the Falling Leaves. 1994. 125p. per. (*0-9640352-0-0*) Weddle, Virginia B.

Weir, Charlene. A Cold Christmas. 2002. (WWL Mystery Ser.: No. 439). 256p. mass mkt. (*0-373-26439-9*, Worldwide Library) Harlequin Enterprises, Ltd.

—A Cold Christmas. 2001. 272p. 23.95 (*0-312-26931-5*, Saint Martin's Minotaur) St. Martin's Pr.

—Consider the Crows. 1995. (WWL Mystery Ser.). 251p. per. (*0-373-26172-1*, 1-26172-6, Harlequin Bks.) Harlequin Enterprises, Ltd.

—Consider the Crows. 1993. 272p. 19.95 o.p. (*0-312-09772-7*, Saint Martin's Minotaur) St. Martin's Pr.

—Family Practice. 1997. (Susan Wren Mystery Ser.). 301p. per. (*0-373-26236-1*, 0-26236-0, Worldwide Library) Harlequin Enterprises, Ltd.

—Family Practice. 1995. 320p. 22.95 (*0-312-13492-4*, Saint Martin's Minotaur) St. Martin's Pr.

—Murder Take Two. pap. 15.95 (*0-312-29193-0*, Saint Martin's Griffin); pap. 16.95 o.p. (*0-312-30029-8*, Saint Martin's Griffin); 1998. 336p. 23.95 (*0-312-18136-1*, Saint Martin's Minotaur) St. Martin's Pr.

—The Winter Widow. 1993. per. (*0-373-26128-4*, 1-26128-8, Harlequin Bks.) Harlequin Enterprises, Ltd.

—The Winter Widow. 1992. 256p. 18.95 o.p. (*0-312-07009-8*, Saint Martin's Minotaur) St. Martin's Pr.

Wheeler, Richard S. Drum's Ring. 2001. 304p. mass mkt. 5.99 o.s.i (*0-451-20363-1*) NAL.

White, William A. Real Issue. 1977. (Short Story Index Reprint Ser.). 19.95 (*0-8369-3177-7*) Ayer Co. Pubs., Inc.

Wilks, Eileen. Proposition: Marriage. 1999. (Silhouette Desire Ser.: No. 1239). 185p. per. (*0-373-76239-9*, 1-76239-2, Silhouette) Harlequin Enterprises, Ltd.

Williams, Jeanne. The Longest Road. 1994. mass mkt. 4.99 o.p. (*0-312-95239-2*, St. Martin's Paperbacks); 1993. 416p. 21.95 o.p. (*0-312-08838-8*) St. Martin's Pr.

—The Longest Road. 2000. 389p. pap. 23.95 (*0-595-16101-4*) iUniverse, Inc.

—The Unplowed Sky. 1994. 368p. 21.95 o.p. (*0-312-11361-7*) St. Martin's Pr.

Wright, Vinita H. Grace at Bender Springs. 1999. 400p. pap. 12.99 (*0-8054-2127-0*) Broadman & Holman Pubs.

Wright, Vinita Hampton. Velma Still Cooks in Leeway: A Novel. 2000. viii, 294p. pap. 12.99 (*0-8054-2128-9*) Broadman & Holman Pubs.

Yoho, Max. The Revival. 2001. 208p. pap. 12.95 (*0-9708160-0-6*) Dancing Goat Pr.

**KANSAS CITY (MO.)—FICTION**

Bowen, Lindsey M. Cicada Grove. 1992. 96p. (Orig.). pap. 7.50 (*1-881048-01-2*) Paladin Contemporaries.

Boyle, Christine A. Death by Choice. 1996. 164p. E-Book 6.00 (*1-58200-002-6*); E-Book 6.00 (*1-58200-157-X*) Hard Shell Word Factory.

Clair, Maxine. October Suite: A Novel. 2002. E-Book 19.00 (*1-59061-867-X*) Adobe Systems, Inc.

—October Suite: A Novel. 2002. 352p. pap. 12.95 (*0-375-76095-4*) Random House Adult Trade Publishing Group.

Deyo, Elaine E. The Kansas City Marvels: The FBI Briefcase. 2002. 108p. per. 11.45 (*1-4033-0171-9*) 1stBooks Library.

Kagan, Elaine. The Girls. 1995. mass mkt. 6.99 o.s.i (*0-345-39351-1*) Ballantine Bks.

—The Girls: A Novel. 1994. 307p. 23.00 o.s.i (*0-679-43395-3*) Knopf, Alfred A. Inc.

McCledon, Lise. One O'Clock Jump: A Dorie Lennox Mystery. 2001. 276p. 23.95 (*0-312-25195-5*, Saint Martin's Minotaur) St. Martin's Pr.

McClendon, Lise. Sweet & Lowdown: A Dorie Lennox Mystery. 2002. 288p. 23.95 (*0-312-28689-9*, Saint Martin's Minotaur) St. Martin's Pr.

Nida, Jackie. Render Safe. 2002. 336p. mass mkt. 6.99 (*0-425-18720-9*) Berkley Publishing Group.

Temple, Lou Jane. Bread on Arrival. l.t. ed. 2003. (Mystery Ser.). 27.95 (*1-57490-486-8*, Beeler Large Print Bks.) Beeler, Thomas T. Publisher.

—Bread on Arrival. (St. Martin's Minotaur Mysteries Ser.). 1999. 288p. mass mkt. 6.50 (*0-312-96942-2*, St. Martin's Paperbacks); 1998. 272p. 22.95 o.p. (*0-312-19244-4*, Saint Martin's Minotaur) St. Martin's Pr.

—The Cornbread Killer. 2000. 272p. mass mkt. 5.99 (*0-312-97427-2*, St. Martin's Paperbacks); 1999. 242p. 22.95 o.p. (*0-312-20605-4*, Saint Martin's Minotaur) St. Martin's Pr.

—The Cornbread Killer: A Heaven Lee Mystery. l.t. ed. 2001. (Beeler Large Print Mystery Ser.). 245p. 25.95 (*1-57490-336-5*, Beeler Large Print Bks.) Beeler, Thomas T. Publisher.

—Death of Rhubarb. 1996. 220p. mass mkt. 6.50 (*0-312-95891-9*, St. Martin's Paperbacks) St. Martin's Pr.

—Revenge of the Barbeque Queens. 1997. (Dead Letter Mysteries Ser.). 217p. mass mkt. 6.50 (*0-312-96074-3*, St. Martin's Paperbacks) St. Martin's Pr.

—Stiff Risotto. 1997. 224p. mass mkt. 6.50 (*0-312-96321-1*, St. Martin's Paperbacks) St. Martin's Pr.

Terrell, Whitney. The Huntsman. 2001. 384p. 25.95 o.s.i (*0-670-89465-6*, Viking); 2002. 368p. reprint ed. 14.00 (*0-14-200131-7*) Viking Penguin.

**KENTUCKY—FICTION**

Allen, James L. Flute & Violin & Other Kentucky Tales & Romances. 1977. (Short Story Index Reprint Ser.). 19.95 (*0-8369-3129-7*) Ayer Co. Pubs., Inc.

—A Kentucky Cardinal, Aftermath, & Other Selected Works. Bottorff, William K., ed. 1967. 192p. 24.95 (*0-8084-0200-5*) Rowman & Littlefield Pubs., Inc.

—Landmark. 1977. (Short Story Index Reprint Ser.). 19.95 (*0-8369-3328-1*) Ayer Co. Pubs., Inc.

—The Reign of Law: A Tale of the Kentucky Hemp Fields. 1977. (American Fiction Reprint Ser.). reprint ed. 36.95 (*0-8369-7032-2*) Ayer Co. Pubs., Inc.

—The Reign of Law: A Tale of the Kentucky Hemp Fields. 1989. (Principle Works of James Lane Allen). reprint ed. lib. bdg. 79.00 (*0-7812-1734-2*) Reprint Services Corp.

Allen, James Lane. The Choir Invisible. 2000. 252p. pap. 9.95 (*0-594-00261-3*); E-Book 3.95 (*0-594-01817-X*) 1873 Pr.

—The Choir Invisible. reprint ed. 22.50 (*0-404-00327-3*) AMS Pr., Inc.

—The Choir Invisible. reprint ed. lib. bdg. 48.00 (*0-7426-1078-0*); 2001. 361p. pap. text 28.00 (*0-7426-6078-8*) Classic Bks.

—The Choir Invisible. E-Book 2.49 (*0-7574-2855-X*) Electric Umbrella Publishing.

—The Choir Invisible. 1974. pap. 0.95 o.p. (*0-380-00035-0*, 19570, Avon Bks.) Morrow/Avon.

—The Choir Invisible. 1989. (Principle Works of James Lane Allen). reprint ed. lib. bdg. 79.00 (*0-7812-1732-6*) Reprint Services Corp.

—The Choir Invisible. 1897. 7.00 (*0-403-00000-9*) Scholarly Pr., Inc.

—A Kentucky Cardinal. E-Book 39.95 (*0-594-06257-8*); 2000. 252p. pap. 9.95 (*0-594-00486-1*); 2000. 252p. E-Book 3.95 (*0-594-01818-8*) 1873 Pr.

—The Kentucky Warbler. 2000. 252p. E-Book 3.95 (*0-594-04383-2*) 1873 Pr.

—The Mettle of the Pasture. 2000. 252p. E-Book 3.95 (*0-594-04193-7*) 1873 Pr.

Arnold, Madelyn. Year of Full Moons. 2000. 498p. 25.95 (*0-312-19965-1*) St. Martin's Pr.

—A Year of Full Moons. 2002. 512p. pap. 16.95 (*0-312-28724-0*, Saint Martin's Griffin) St. Martin's Pr.

Arnow, Harriette Louisa Simpson. Between the Flowers. 1999. 448p. 34.95 (*0-87013-535-X*) Michigan State Univ. Pr.

—Hunter's Horn. rev. ed. 1997. 375p. pap. 18.95 (*0-87013-437-X*) Michigan State Univ. Pr.

—Hunter's Horn. 1979. (YA). (gr. 7 up). pap. 2.50 o.p. (*0-380-42283-2*, 42283-2, Avon Bks.) Morrow/Avon.

—Hunter's Horn. 1986. 416p. 24.00 o.p. (*0-8131-1600-7*) Univ. Pr. of Kentucky.

Babcock, Bernie. The Soul of Ann Rutledge. E-Book 3.95 (*0-594-01175-2*) 1873 Pr.

Berry, Wendell. Fidelity: Five Stories. 1992. 208p. 20.00 o.s.i (*0-679-41633-1*, Pantheon) Knopf Publishing Group.

—Jayber Crow: The Life Story of Jayber Crow, Barber, of the Port William Membership, as Written by Himself. 384p. 2001. pap. text 15.00 (*1-58243-160-4*); 2000. text 25.00 o.p. (*1-58243-029-2*) Basic Bks. (Counterpoint Pr.).

—A Place on Earth. 1982. pap. 12.95 o.p. (*0-86547-083-9*); 352p. reprint ed. pap. 13.00 o.p. (*0-86547-044-8*) Farrar, Straus & Giroux. (North Point Pr.).

—Place on Earth. rev. ed. 2001. 336p. pap. text 15.00 (*1-58243-124-8*, Counterpoint Pr.) Basic Bks.

—Remembering. 1990. 124p. pap. 11.00 o.p. (*0-86547-331-5*); 1988. 144p. 14.95 o.p. (*0-86547-330-7*) Farrar, Straus & Giroux. (North Point Pr.).

—Two More Stories of the Port William Membership. 1997. (Chapbook Ser.: Vol. 4). 64p. 15.00 o.p. (*0-917788-64-8*); 1997. (Chapbook Ser.: Vol. 4). 64p. 35.00 o.p. (*0-917788-67-2*); 1999. 62p. reprint ed. pap. 10.50 (*0-917788-71-0*) Gnomon Pr.

—The Wild Birds: Six Stories of the Port William Membership. 160p. 1989. pap. 11.00 o.p. (*0-86547-217-3*); 1986. 13.95 o.p. (*0-86547-216-5*) Farrar, Straus & Giroux. (North Point Pr.).

—A World Lost. 160p. 1997. pap. text 12.50 (*1-887178-54-6*); 1996. text 20.00 o.p. (*1-887178-22-8*) Basic Bks. (Counterpoint Pr.).

Berry, Wendell, ed. Jayber Crow: The Life Story of Jayber Crow, Barber, of the Port William Membership, as Written by Himself. l.t. ed. 2001. (Thorndike Press Large Print Americana Ser.). 687p. 28.95 o.p. (*0-7862-3222-6*) Thorndike Pr.

Bird, Robert M. Nick of the Woods. 1989. (Works of Robert Montgomery Bird). reprint ed. lib. bdg. 79.00 (*0-7812-1992-2*) Reprint Services Corp.

—Nick of the Woods. Dahl, Curtis, ed. 1967. pap. 37.95 o.p. (*0-8084-0235-8*) Rowman & Littlefield Pubs., Inc.

Birkett, John. The Queen's Mare. 1990. 240p. pap. 3.50 (*0-380-75683-8*, Avon Bks.) Morrow/Avon.

Blaise, Clark. Southern Stories: Selected Stories. 2000. 192p. pap. 17.95 (*0-88984-219-1*) Porcupine's Quill, Inc. CAN. *Dist:* General Distribution Services, Inc.

Blank, Grace W. Jennie & Sue Visit a Kentucky Farm: Grace Delight's Second Book. 1994. (Illus.). 70p. (J). (gr. 3-6). 8.95 (*0-9634122-5-6*) Feather Fables Publishing Company.

Blythe, Hal & Sweet, Charlie. Bloody Ground: Stories of Mystery & Intrigue from Kentucky. 2001. 300p. 15.00 (*1-931672-01-6*) Stuart, Jesse Foundation, The.

Brown, David E. Home to Kentucky. 1999. (Legend of the Golden Feather Ser.: Vol. 3). 300p. pap. 14.95 (*1-878406-22-1*) Parker Distributing.

Browne, Martha G. Autobiography of a Female Slave. 1970. 401p. reprint ed. 45.00 o.s.i (*0-8371-2194-9*, GRS&) Greenwood Publishing Group, Inc.

—Autobiography of a Female Slave. 1991. (American Biography Ser.). 401p. reprint ed. lib. bdg. 89.00 (*0-7812-8046-X*) Reprint Services Corp.

Bruckheimer, Linda. The Southern Belles of Honeysuckle Way. 2004. 336p. 24.95 (*0-525-94454-0*, Dutton) Dutton/Plume.

Burns, Ron. Enslaved: A Mystery. 1994. 288p. 20.95 o.p. (*0-312-10977-6*, Saint Martin's Minotaur) St. Martin's Pr.

Butler, Luther. Tuck. 2001. 328p. pap. 22.99 (*0-7388-9933-X*) Xlibris Corp.

Caudill, Harry M. Dark Hills to Westward: The Saga of Jenny Wiley. 1994. 256p. reprint ed. 22.00 (*0-945084-45-5*) Stuart, Jesse Foundation, The.

Caudill, Rebecca. Saturday Cousins. 1989. 128p. (J). (gr. k-6). pap. 2.75 o.s.i (*0-440-40208-5*, Yearling) Random Hse. Children's Bks.

Clark, Billy C. Miss America Kissed Caleb. 2003. (Kentucky Voices Ser.). 160p. 24.95 (*0-8131-2296-1*) Univ. Pr. of Kentucky.

—Mooneyed Hound. Gifford, James M. & Hall, Patricia A., eds. 2nd ed. 1995. (Illus.). 128p. (J). (gr. 4 up). pap. 8.50 (*0-945084-49-8*) Stuart, Jesse Foundation, The.

—Song of the River. Gifford, James M. et al, eds. rev. ed. 1993. (Illus.). 176p. (YA). (gr. 7 up). reprint ed. 15.00 o.p. (*0-945084-35-8*) Stuart, Jesse Foundation, The.

—Sourwood Tales: Stories. 2001. (Illus.). 256p. (*0-945084-96-X*) Stuart, Jesse Foundation, The.

Collins, Brandilyn. Capture the Wind for Me. 2003. (Bradleyville Ser.). 352p. pap. 12.99 (*0-310-24243-6*) Zon Bks.

—Cast a Road Before Me. 2003. 288p. pap. 12.99 (*0-310-25327-6*) Zondervan.

—Color the Sidewalk for Me. 2002. 384p. pap. 12.99 (*0-310-24242-8*) Zondervan.

Collins, Tess. The Law of Revenge. 9999. mass mkt. o.p. (*0-345-41484-5*); 1997. (*0-449-91075-X*, Fawcett); 1997. mass mkt. 6.99 (*0-449-22534-8*, Fawcett); 1997. mass mkt. 5.99 o.s.i (*0-8041-1684-9*, Ivy Bks.) Ballantine Bks.

—The Law of Revenge. l.t. ed. 1997. (Niagara Large Print Ser.). 416p. 29.50 o.p. (*0-7089-5888-5*, Ulverscroft) Thorpe, F. A. Pubs. GBR. *Dist:* Ulverscroft Large Print Bks., Ltd.

—The Law of the Dead. 1999. mass mkt. 6.99 o.s.i (*0-8041-1795-0*, Ivy Bks.) Ballantine Bks.

Crusie, Jennifer. Manhunting. 2000. 256p. mass mkt. (*1-55166-618-9*, 1-66618-9, Mira Bks.); 2000. mass mkt. (*0-373-82215-4*, 1-82215-4, Harlequin Bks.); 1993. per. (*0-373-25563-2*, 1-25563-7, Harlequin Bks.) Harlequin Enterprises, Ltd.

—Strange Bedpersons. 2003. 256p. mass mkt. (*1-55166-743-6*, Mira Bks.) Harlequin Enterprises, Ltd.

Dale, Madeline M. Southern Cross. 1998. 256p. 24.95 (*1-880090-61-9*) Galde Pr., Inc.

Davis, Jenny. Good-Bye & Keep Cold. 1989. 224p. (J). mass mkt. 2.95 o.s.i (*0-440-20481-X*, Laurel Leaf) Random Hse. Children's Bks.

Deveraux, Jude. The Blessing. l.t. ed. 1999. 27.95 (*1-56895-629-0*, Wheeler Publishing, Inc.) Gale Group.

—The Blessing. 1999. 336p. pap. 7.99 (*0-671-89109-X*, Pocket Star); 1998. 320p. 20.00 o.s.i (*0-671-89108-1*, Atria) Simon & Schuster.

—Sweetbriar. 16th l.t. ed. 2002. 256p. lib. bdg. 29.95 (*1-58547-162-3*) Ctr. Point Large Print.

—Sweetbriar. 1985. mass mkt. 3.95 o.s.i (*0-671-60074-5*, Pocket) Simon & Schuster.

Dew, Lee A. Kentucky Home Place. 1999. (New Books for New Readers). (Illus.). 80p. (YA). (gr. 4 up). pap. 5.95 (*0-8131-0911-6*) Univ. Pr. of Kentucky.

Dewolfe, Adrienne. Always Her Hero. 2000. 384p. mass mkt. 5.99 (*0-380-80528-6*, Avon Bks.) Morrow/Avon.

Dorris, Michael. Cloud Chamber: A Novel. 1998. 320p. pap. 13.00 (*0-684-83535-5*, Scribner); 1998. pap. (*0-684-00606-5*, Scribner Paper Fiction); 1997. 320p. 23.50 (*0-684-81567-2*, Scribner) Simon & Schuster.

—Cloud Chamber: A Novel. 1998. 18.05 (*0-606-12660-0*) Turtleback Bks.

Ellis, Ron. Cogan's Woods. 2001. 166p. 19.95 (*0-87108-915-7*) Pruett Publishing Co.

Ellis, William E. River Bends & Meanders: Stories, Sketches, & Tales of the Kentucky River Region. 1993. (Illus.). 160p. pap. text 11.95 o.p. (*0-923687-25-4*) Celo Valley Bks.

Feldmeyer, Dean. Pitchfork Hollow. Chelius, Jane, ed. 1995. 256p. (Orig.). mass mkt. 5.50 (*0-671-76983-9*, Pocket) Simon & Schuster.

—Viper Quarry. 1994. 256p. mass mkt. 4.99 (*0-671-76982-0*, Pocket) Simon & Schuster.

Finney, Nikky. Heartwood. 1997. (New Books for New Readers: Vol. 10). 80p. pap. text 5.95 (*0-8131-0910-8*) Univ. Pr. of Kentucky.

Floyd, Marguerite, et al, eds. Groundwater: A Collection of Contemporary Kentucky Fiction. 1992. 157p. (Orig.). pap. 10.50 (*0-9628089-1-1*) Lexington Pr., Inc.

Fox, John. Crittenden: A Kentucky Story of Love & War. 1976. lib. bdg. 12.95 (*0-89968-035-6*, Lightyear Pr.) Buccaneer Bks., Inc.

Fox, John, Jr. Crittenden: A Kentucky Story of Love & War. E-Book 3.95 (*0-594-02217-7*) 1873 Pr.

—Heart of the Hills. 1996. 432p. 32.00 (*0-8131-1981-2*); pap. 18.00 (*0-8131-0882-9*) Univ. Pr. of Kentucky.

Fox, John. The Kentuckians. 2000. 252p. pap. 9.95 (*0-594-06039-7*); E-Book 3.95 (*0-594-06042-7*) 1873 Pr.

—The Kentuckians. 1977. (American Fiction Reprint Ser.). reprint ed. 25.95 (*0-8369-7037-3*) Ayer Co. Pubs., Inc.

—The Kentuckians. 1976. lib. bdg. 13.50 o.s.i (*0-89968-038-0*, Lightyear Pr.) Buccaneer Bks., Inc.

Fox, John, Jr. The Little Shepherd of Kingdom Come. 1973. pap. 1.25 o.p. (*0-380-01330-4*, 17707, Avon Bks.) Morrow/Avon.

Garlock, Dorothy. Love & Cherish. l.t. ed. 2001. 302p. lib. bdg. 27.95 (*1-58547-054-6*) Ctr. Point Large Print.

—Love & Cherish. l.t. ed. 1998. (Romance Ser.). 26.95 o.p. (*0-7862-1493-7*, Five Star) Gale Group.

—Love & Cherish. 1982. mass mkt. 2.50 o.p. (*0-89083-897-6*, Zebra Bks.); mass mkt. 2.50 o.p. (*0-8217-1119-9*) Kensington Publishing Corp.

—Love & Cherish. 352p. reprint ed. 1998. mass mkt. 3.99 (*0-446-60648-0*); 1995. mass mkt. 5.99 (*0-446-36524-6*) Warner Bks., Inc.

Giles, Janice H. The Enduring Hills. 1988. 256p. 30.00 (*0-8131-1673-2*); pap. 17.00 (*0-8131-0185-9*) Univ. Pr. of Kentucky.

—Enduring Hills. l.t. ed. 1984. (General Ser.). lib. bdg. 17.50 o.p. (*0-8161-3648-3*, Macmillan Reference USA) Gale Group.

—Enduring Hills, 001. 2nd ed. 1971. 7.95 o.p. (*0-395-12042-X*) Houghton Mifflin Co.

—Hannah Fowler. 1980. (Reader's Request Ser.). lib. bdg. 16.95 o.p. (*0-8161-3051-5*, Macmillan Reference USA) Gale Group.

—Hannah Fowler. 1992. 232p. (C). reprint ed. 30.00 o.p. (*0-8131-1793-3*); pap. 17.00 (*0-8131-0810-1*) Univ. Pr. of Kentucky.

—The Kentuckians. 1980. (Reader's Request Ser.). lib. bdg. 15.95 o.p. (*0-8161-3050-7*, Macmillan Reference USA) Gale Group.

—The Kentuckians, 001. 1953. 7.95 o.p. (*0-395-07737-0*) Houghton Mifflin Co.

—The Kentuckians. 1987. 256p. 28.00 o.p. (*0-8131-1639-2*); pap. 17.00 (*0-8131-0177-8*) Univ. Pr. of Kentucky.

—The Land Beyond the Mountains. 1976. 24.95 (*0-88411-644-1*) Amereon, Ltd.

—The Land Beyond the Mountains. 1990. 316p. reprint ed. 36.00 (*0-87797-186-2*) Cherokee Publishing Co.
—The Land Beyond the Mountains. 1995. 320p. 30.00 (*0-8131-1936-7*); pap. 17.00 (*0-8131-0848-9*) Univ. Pr. of Kentucky.
—Miss Willie. 1976. 22.95 (*0-8488-1012-0*) Amereon, Ltd.
—Miss Willie. 1984. (General Ser.). lib. bdg. 15.95 o.p. (*0-8161-3649-1*, Macmillan Reference USA) Gale Group.
—Miss Willie. 1994. 272p. 30.00 (*0-8131-1885-9*); pap. 19.00 (*0-8131-0831-4*) Univ. Pr. of Kentucky.
—Six-Horse Hitch. 1976. 29.95 (*0-8488-1011-2*) Amereon, Ltd.
—Six-Horse Hitch. 1982. 408p. pap. 2.75 o.p. (*0-380-51532-6*, 51532-6, Avon Bks.) Morrow/Avon.
—Tara's Healing. 1976. 22.95 (*0-8488-0503-8*) Amereon, Ltd.
—Tara's Healing. l.t. ed. 1986. (General Ser.). 313p. 16.95 o.p. (*0-8161-4050-2*, Macmillan Reference USA) Gale Group.
—Tara's Healing. 1994. 256p. 28.00 o.p. (*0-8131-1886-7*); pap. 17.00 (*0-8131-0832-2*) Univ. Pr. of Kentucky.
—Wellspring, 001. 1975. 272p. 8.95 o.p. (*0-395-20731-2*) Houghton Mifflin Co.
Giles, Janice Holt. Hill Man. 2000. 160p. reprint ed. 20.00 (*0-8131-2165-5*) Univ. Pr. of Kentucky.
—Wellspring. 2003. (*1-57490-533-3*, Beeler Large Print Bks.) Beeler, Thomas T. Publisher.
—Wellspring. 2002. 288p. reprint ed. 32.00 (*0-8131-2239-2*); pap. 19.00 (*0-8131-9025-8*) Univ. Pr. of Kentucky.
Goebel, Joey. The Anomalies. 2003. 205p. 22.00 (*1-931561-29-X*) MacAdam/Cage Publishing, Inc.
Green, Terence M. Shadow of Ashland. 2000. 223p. pap. 13.95 (*0-312-87301-8*, Forge Bks.); 1997. 223p. mass mkt. 5.99 (*0-8125-5526-0*, Tor Bks.); 1996. 224p. 17.95 o.p. (*0-312-85958-9*, Forge Bks.) Doherty, Tom Assocs., LLC.
—St. Patrick's Bed. (Illus.). 224p. 2001. 21.95 (*0-7653-0043-5*); 2002. reprint ed. pap. 12.95 (*0-7653-0044-3*) Doherty, Tom Assocs., LLC. (Forge Bks.).
Griffith, Mattie. Autobiography of a Female Slave. 1998. 408p. 48.00 (*1-57806-046-X*); pap. 18.00 (*1-57806-047-8*) Univ. Pr. of Mississippi. (A Banner Bk.).
Grubbs, Morris A. & Young, Grant. Home & Beyond: An Anthology of Kentucky Short Stories. 2001. xxiv, 400p. 38.00 (*0-8131-2192-2*) Univ. Pr. of Kentucky.
Hall, Eliza C. Aunt Jane of Kentucky. 1994. (Illus.). 283p. reprint ed. 17.95 (*0-936810-05-X*) Miles & Miles.
—Aunt Jane of Kentucky. Graulich, Melody, ed. 1991. 150p. pap. 24.95 (*0-8084-0432-6*) Rowman & Littlefield Pubs., Inc.
—Aunt Jane of Kentucky. 1995. (Illus.). 304p. pap. 18.00 (*0-8131-0838-1*); text 34.95 (*0-8131-1915-4*) Univ. Pr. of Kentucky.
—A Quilter's Wisdom: Conversations with Aunt Jane. 1994. (Illus.). 84p. 14.95 o.p. (*0-8118-0333-3*) Chronicle Bks. LLC.
Harper, Karen. The Baby Farm. 2004. mass mkt. (*0-7783-2116-9*); 1999. mass mkt. (*1-55166-520-4*, 1-66520-7) Harlequin Enterprises, Ltd. (Mira Bks.).
—Circle of Gold. l.t. ed. 1997. lib. bdg. 25.95 (*1-57490-081-1*, Beeler Large Print Bks.) Beeler, Thomas T. Publisher.
—Circle of Gold. 1992. 400p. 20.00 o.p. (*0-525-93453-7*, Dutton) Dutton/Plume.
—Circle of Gold. 1993. 456p. reprint ed. mass mkt. 5.99 o.s.i (*0-451-40381-9*, Signet Bks.) NAL.
Hart, Catherine. Temptation. l.t. ed. 1993. (General Ser.). 514p. lib. bdg. 22.95 (*0-8161-5463-5*, Macmillan Reference USA) Gale Group.
—Temptation. 1992. 400p. mass mkt. 4.99 (*0-380-76006-1*, Avon Bks.) Morrow/Avon.
Hensley, Joe L. Grim City. 1994. 240p. 19.95 o.p. (*0-312-11429-X*, Saint Martin's Minotaur) St. Martin's Pr.
High, Ellesa C. Past Titan Rock: Journeys into an Appalachian Valley. 1984. 192p. 16.00 o.p. (*0-8131-1505-1*) Univ. Pr. of Kentucky.
Hightower, Lynn S. Satan's Lambs. 1995. 256p. mass mkt. 4.99 o.p. (*0-425-14557-3*, Prime Crime) Berkley Publishing Group.
—Satan's Lambs, Set. l.t. ed. 1994. (Studio Ser.). 64.95 o.p. incl. audio (*0-7862-9993-2*, Macmillan Reference USA) Gale Group.
—Satan's Lambs. 1993. 256p. 19.95 o.p. (*0-8027-1229-0*) Walker & Co.
Hill, Teresa. Unbreak My Heart. 2001. 368p. mass mkt. 6.99 o.s.i (*0-451-40931-0*, Onyx) NAL.
Hirschfield, Corson. Too High. 2001. 464p. 25.95 (*0-7653-0011-7*, Forge Bks.) Doherty, Tom Assocs., LLC.
Hoff, B. J. Dark River Legacy. unabr. ed. 1999. (Daybreak Mystery Ser.: Bk. 5). audio 39.95 (*1-55686-859-6*) Books in Motion.
—Dark River Legacy. 1992. 208p. pap. 6.99 o.p. (*0-7814-0479-7*); (Daybreak Mystery Ser.: No. 5). 192p. pap. 6.95 o.p. (*0-89636-248-5*) Cook Communications Ministries.
—Dark River Legacy. l.t. ed. 1999. (Christian Mystery Ser.). 272p. 24.95 (*0-7862-1677-8*) Thorndike Pr.
—Dark River Legacy. 1997. (Daybreak Mysteries Ser.). 179p. pap. 8.99 o.p. (*0-8423-7196-6*) Tyndale Hse. Pubs.
—The Penny Whistle: A Gift of Hope for the Beloved Teacher Who Had Given Them So Much. l.t. ed. 1996. (Gift Size Ser.). 160p. text 11.99 o.p. (*1-55661-877-8*) Bethany Hse. Pubs.
House, Silas. Clay's Quilt. 2001. 292p. tchr. ed. 22.95 (*1-56512-307-7*) Algonquin Bks. of Chapel Hill.
—Clay's Quilt. 2002. 320p. pap. 14.00 (*0-345-45069-8*, Ballantine Bks.) Ballantine Bks.
—Clay's Quilt. l.t. ed. 2001. (Wheeler Large Print Book Ser.). 24.95 (*1-58724-143-9*, Wheeler Publishing, Inc.) Gale Group.
—A Parchment of Leaves: A Novel. 2002. 288p. tchr. ed. 23.95 (*1-56512-367-0*, 72367) Algonquin Bks. of Chapel Hill.
—A Parchment of Leaves: A Novel. 2003. 304p. pap. 13.95 (*0-345-46497-4*) Ballantine Bks.
—A Parchment of Leaves: A Novel. l.t. ed. 2003. (Core Ser.). 444p. 28.95 (*0-7862-4997-8*) Thorndike Pr.
Jackson, Carlton, et al. Kentucky Outlaw Man: A Novel Based on the Life of George Al Edwards. 1994. o.p. (*0-916078-36-1*) Bell Buckle Pr.
Johnson, Fenton. Scissors, Paper, Rock. 1993. 240p. 20.00 (*0-671-79541-4*, Atria) Simon & Schuster.
Kelsay, Michael. Too Close to Call. 2001. 232p. 26.00 (*1-57806-369-8*) Univ. Pr. of Mississippi.
Luttrell, Wanda. The Legacy of Drennan's Crossing. 1985. 400p. 4.50 o.p. (*0-8423-2112-8*) Tyndale Hse. Pubs.
Madden, David. Cassandra Singing. 1999. 288p. pap. 18.95 (*1-57233-035-X*) Univ. of Tennessee Pr.
Mason, Bobbie Ann. Feather Crowns. 1993. 400p. 23.00 o.p. (*0-06-016780-7*) HarperTrade.
—Shiloh & Other Stories. 1983. 248p. reprint ed. pap. 10.00 o.p. (*0-06-091068-2*) HarperCollins Pubs.
—Shiloh & Other Stories. 1982. 288p. 12.95 o.p. (*0-06-015062-9*); 1990. 256p. reprint ed. pap. 12.00 o.p. (*0-06-091330-4*, PL1330, Perennial) HarperTrade.
—Shiloh & Other Stories. 2001. 256p. pap. 12.95 (*0-375-75843-7*, Modern Library) Random House Adult Trade Publishing Group.
—Shiloh & Other Stories. 1995. 264p. 18.00 (*0-8131-1948-0*) Univ. Pr. of Kentucky.
McCafferty, Barbara Taylor. Double Cross. (Bert & Nan Tatum Mystery Ser.). 2000. 256p. mass mkt. 5.99 o.s.i (*1-57566-511-5*); 1998. 240p. 20.00 o.s.i (*1-57566-338-4*) Kensington Publishing Corp.
—Double Dealer. 2000. (Bert & Nan Tatum Mystery Ser.). 250p. 20.00 o.s.i (*1-57566-507-7*, Kensington Bks.) Kensington Publishing Corp.
—Double Murder. 1996. 288p. 18.95 o.s.i (*1-57566-084-9*, Kensington Bks.) Kensington Publishing Corp.
McCafferty, Barbara Taylor & Herald, Beverly Taylor. Double Date. (Partners in Crime Ser.). 2002. 288p. mass mkt. 5.99 (*1-57566-732-0*); 2001. 256p. 22.00 o.s.i (*1-57566-639-1*) Kensington Publishing Corp.
—Double Date. l.t. ed. 2001. 336p. 28.95 (*0-7862-3326-5*) Thorndike Pr.
—Double Dealer. 2000. 272p. mass mkt. 5.99 o.s.i (*1-57566-642-1*) Kensington Publishing Corp.
—Double Exposure. annuals 1997. (Bert & Nan Tatum Mystery Ser.). 288p. 18.95 o.s.i (*1-57566-207-8*) Kensington Publishing Corp.
—Double Murder. 1997. (Bert & Nan Tatum Mystery Ser.). 288p. mass mkt. 5.50 (*1-57566-212-4*) Kensington Publishing Corp.
McCafferty, Taylor. Bed Bugs. Chelius, Jane, ed. 1993. 256p. (Orig.). mass mkt. 5.50 (*0-671-75468-8*, Pocket) Simon & Schuster.
—Hanky Panky. 1995. 256p. mass mkt. 5.50 (*0-671-51049-5*, Pocket) Simon & Schuster.
—Pet Peeves. Chelius, Jane, ed. 1990. 224p. (Orig.). mass mkt. 4.99 (*0-671-72802-4*, Pocket) Simon & Schuster.
—Ruffled Feathers. Chelius, Jane, ed. 1992. 224p. (Orig.). mass mkt. 4.50 (*0-671-72803-2*, Pocket) Simon & Schuster.
—Thin Skins. 1994. 256p. mass mkt. 4.99 (*0-671-79977-0*, Pocket) Simon & Schuster.
McCall, Dinah. Chase the Moon, 1. 1999. (Romance Ser.). 263p. 26.95 (*0-7862-1784-7*, Five Star); pap. 24.95 (*1-56895-705-X*, Wheeler Publishing, Inc.) Gale Group.
—The Return. abr. ed. 2000. (Mira Ser.). audio 9.99 (*1-55204-218-9*, MIR-1218) Durkin Hayes Publishing Ltd.
—The Return. 2000. 384p. mass mkt. (*1-55166-584-0*, Mira Bks.) Harlequin Enterprises, Ltd.
McCampbell, Debbie L. Natural Bridges. 1997. 238p. 26.00 (*1-877946-79-6*) Permanent Pr., The.
McClellan, Tierney. Closing Statement: A Schuyler Ridgway Mystery. 1995. 304p. (Orig.). mass mkt. 4.99 o.s.i (*0-451-18464-5*, Signet Bks.) NAL.
—Heir Condition. 1995. 256p. (Orig.). mass mkt. 5.50 o.s.i (*0-451-18144-1*, Signet Bks.) NAL.
—Killing in Real Estate. 1996. (Schuyler Ridgway Mystery Ser.). 256p. mass mkt. 5.50 o.s.i (*0-451-18765-2*) NAL.
—Two-Story Frame. 1997. (Schuyler Ridgway Mystery Ser.). 256p. mass mkt. 5.99 o.s.i (*0-451-19197-8*, Signet Bks.) NAL.
McElmurray, Karen Salyer. Strange Birds in the Tree of Heaven: A Novel. 1999. 320p. 25.00 o.p. (*1-892514-24-9*) Hill Street Pr., LLC.
Michaels, Fern. Kentucky Heat. l.t. ed. 2002. 30.95 (*1-58724-226-5*, Wheeler Publishing, Inc.) Gale Group.
—Kentucky Heat. 2002. 384p. mass mkt. 7.99 (*0-8217-7368-2*); 336p. 24.00 (*1-57566-762-2*, Kensington Bks.) Kensington Publishing Corp.
—Kentucky Heat. l.t. ed. 2002. 13.95 (*1-4104-0047-6*, Large Print Pr.) Thorndike Pr.
—Kentucky Rich. abr. ed. 2001. (Kentucky Ser.). audio 19.95 o.p. (*1-58788-238-8*, 2499, Nova Audio Bks.); audio 32.95 (*1-58788-236-1*, 2497, Brilliance Audio Unabridged) Brilliance Audio.
—Kentucky Rich. l.t. ed. 2002. 13.95 (*1-56895-195-7*); 2001. 425p. 31.95 (*1-58724-105-6*) Gale Group. (Wheeler Publishing, Inc.).
—Kentucky Rich. 2002. 48p. mass mkt. 7.99 (*0-8217-7234-1*); 2001. 336p. 24.00 o.s.i (*1-57566-761-4*, Kensington Bks.) Kensington Publishing Corp.
—Kentucky Sunrise. l.t. ed. 2003. 451p. 13.95 (*1-4104-0165-0*); 2002. 466p. 32.95 (*1-58724-361-X*) Gale Group. (Wheeler Publishing, Inc.).
—Kentucky Sunrise. 2003. 359p. mass mkt. 7.99 (*0-8217-7462-X*); 2002. 304p. 24.00 (*1-57566-763-0*); 2002. 304p. pap. 16.00 (*0-7582-0457-4*) Kensington Publishing Corp.
Moffett, Judith. Time, Like an Ever-Rolling Stream. 1992. 352p. 21.95 o.p. (*0-312-08323-8*) St. Martin's Pr.
Offutt, Chris. The Good Brother: A Novel. 1998. 320p. pap. 13.00 (*0-684-84619-5*); 1997. 317p. 23.00 o.s.i (*0-684-80983-4*) Simon & Schuster. (Simon & Schuster).
—Kentucky Straight. 1992. (Vintage Contemporaries Ser.). 192p. pap. 12.00 (*0-679-73886-X*, Vintage) Knopf Publishing Group.
Palencia, Elaine F. Small Caucasian Woman: Stories. 1993. 176p. (C). 19.95 o.s.i (*0-8262-0906-8*) Univ. of Missouri Pr.
Patchett, Ann. The Patron Saint of Liars. 1996. 352p. pap. 13.95 o.s.i (*0-449-91205-1*, Fawcett); 1993. 320p. mass mkt. 5.99 o.s.i (*0-8041-1151-0*, Ivy Bks.) Ballantine Bks.
—The Patron Saint of Liars. 2003. 352p. pap. 13.95 (*0-06-054075-3*, Perennial) HarperTrade.
—The Patron Saint of Liars. 1992. 368p. 21.00 o.p. (*0-395-61306-X*) Houghton Mifflin Co. Trade & Reference Div.
Payne, Johnny. Chalk Lake: A Novel. 1996. 176p. (Orig.). 18.95 (*0-9647515-2-6*); pap. 12.95 (*0-9647515-1-8*) Limited Editions.
—Kentuckiana. 1999. 272p. pap. 14.95 (*0-8101-5090-5*); 1997. 255p. 30.00 o.p. (*0-8101-5075-1*) Northwestern Univ. Pr. (TriQuarterly Bks.).
Perkins, James Ashbrook. Snakes, Butterbeans & the Discovery of Electricity: Stories. 2003. (Illus.). xiv, 189p. 25.00 (*0-86554-814-5*); pap. (*0-86554-815-3*) Mercer Univ. Pr.
Perry, Thomas. Pursuit. 2003. 416p. mass mkt. 7.50 (*0-8041-1543-5*, Ballantine Bks.) Ballantine Bks.
—Pursuit. l.t. ed. 2002. 715p. 28.95 (*0-7862-4209-4*) Gale Group.
Porter, Joe A. The Kentucky Stories. 1990. (Johns Hopkins: Poetry & Fiction Ser.). 144p. 17.95 o.p. (*0-8018-3008-7*) Johns Hopkins Univ. Pr.
Pryor, Bonnie. Joseph's Choice, 1861. 2000. (American Adventures Ser.). (Illus.). 176p. (J). (gr. 3 up). 14.89 (*0-06-029226-1*); 15.99 (*0-688-17633-X*) HarperCollins Children's Bk. Group.
Rice, Patricia. Garden of Dreams. 1997. mass mkt. 5.99 o.s.i (*0-449-15062-3*, Fawcett) Ballantine Bks.
Robards, Karen. Hunter's Moon. 1996. 448p. mass mkt. 7.99 (*0-440-21593-5*) Dell Publishing.
—Hunter's Moon. l.t. ed. 1996. 25.95 o.p. (*1-56895-296-1*, Wheeler Publishing, Inc.) Gale Group.
—One Summer. l.t. ed. 1994. pap. 21.95 o.p. (*0-7927-1608-6*); 1993. 23.95 o.p. (*0-7927-1609-4*) BBC Audiobooks America.
—Paradise County. 2001. E-Book 24.95 (*1-58945-232-1*) Adobe Systems, Inc.
—Paradise County. unabr. ed. 2001. audio 96.95 (*0-7927-2462-3*, CSL 351); audio compact disk 119.95 (*0-7927-9903-8*, SLD 054) BBC Audiobooks America. (Chivers Sound Library).
—Paradise County. l.t. ed. 2002. 551p. pap. 29.95 (*0-7838-9388-4*, Macmillan Reference USA) Gale Group.
—Paradise County. 2003. (Illus.). 464p. mass mkt. 5.99 (*0-7434-6723-X*, Pocket); 2000. 384p. 24.95 (*0-671-78645-8*, Atria); 2001. (Illus.). 464p. reprint ed. mass mkt. 7.99 (*0-671-78646-6*, Pocket) Simon & Schuster.
—Paradise County. abr. ed. 2000. 50p. audio 25.00 (*0-7435-0678-2*, Simon & Schuster Audioworks) Simon & Schuster Audio.
—Paradise County. l.t. ed. 2001. (G. K. Hall Core Ser.). 551p. 32.95 (*0-7838-9387-6*) Thorndike Pr.
Roberts, Elizabeth Maddox. The Great Meadow. 1980. reprint ed. 27.50 o.p. (*0-404-15235-X*) AMS Pr., Inc.
Roberts, Elizabeth Madox. The Time of Man. Date not set. 288p. 23.95 (*0-8488-2630-2*) Amereon, Ltd.
—The Time of Man. l.t. ed. reprint ed. 2000. 304p. pap. 18.00 (*0-8131-0981-7*); 1982. (Illus.). 424p. 23.00 o.p. (*0-8131-1467-5*); 1982. (Illus.). 424p. pap. 12.00 o.p. (*0-8131-0152-2*) Univ. Pr. of Kentucky.
Robinson, Derek. Kentucky Blues. 2003. 544p. pap. 8.95 (*0-304-36566-1*); 2002. 520p. 27.50 (*0-304-36182-8*) Cassell P L C GBR. *Dist:* Trafalgar Square.
Rold, Jim. First Degree Love: A Novel of Euthanasia. 1992. 208p. (Orig.). pap. 9.95 (*0-89407-106-8*) Strawberry Hill Pr.
Rubio, Gwyn Hyman. Icy Sparks. 1999. 320p. pap. 12.95 o.s.i (*0-14-028014-6*) Penguin Group (USA) Inc.
—Icy Sparks. l.t. ed. 2001. (G.K. Hall Large Print Core Ser.). 505p. 32.95 o.p. (*0-7838-9509-7*) Thorndike Pr.
—Icy Sparks. 2001. 24.95 o.s.i (*0-670-03049-X*); 2001. 320p. 13.95 (*0-14-200020-5*); 1998. 320p. 24.95 o.s.i (*0-670-87311-X*, Viking) Viking Penguin.
Sala, Sharon. Chase the Moon. 1997. 352p. mass mkt. 6.99 (*0-06-108445-X*, 15477440, HarperTorch) Morrow/Avon.
Scarbrough, Jan. Reunited. 2003. 146p. 25.95 (*0-7862-5228-6*, Five Star) Gale Group.
Sharpe, Jon. Kentucky Colts. 1992. (Trailsman Ser.: No. 132). 176p. (Orig.). mass mkt. 3.50 o.p. (*0-451-17374-0*, Signet Bks.) NAL.
Sheldon, Sidney. The Best Laid Plans. 1997. 375p. 25.00 (*0-688-14911-1*); 1997. 400.00 (*0-688-15642-8*); 1997. 464p. 28.00 (*0-688-15624-X*); 1924. o.s.i (*0-688-15923-0*) Morrow/Avon. (Morrow, William & Co.).
—The Best Laid Plans. unabr. ed. 1997. 35.00 o.p. (*0-7871-1472-3*, 895983);Set. 18.00 o.p. (*0-7871-1471-5*, 395982) NewStar Media, Inc.
—The Best Laid Plans. 1998. 384p. mass mkt. 7.99 (*0-446-60408-9*) Warner Bks., Inc.
Shoemaker, Bill. Dark Horse. 1997. 312p. mass mkt. 6.99 (*0-449-15003-8*); 1996. 304p. 22.00 o.p. (*0-449-90597-7*) Ballantine Bks. (Fawcett).
Simms, William Gilmore. Beauchampe: or The Kentucky Tragedy. rev. ed. reprint ed. 21.50 (*0-404-06006-4*) AMS Pr., Inc.
—Charlemont: or the Pride of the Village: A Tale of Kentucky. rev. ed. reprint ed. 29.50 (*0-404-06008-0*) AMS Pr., Inc.
Slone, Verna M. Rennie's Way. 1994. (Illus.). 232p. 20.00 (*0-8131-1855-7*) Univ. Pr. of Kentucky.
Snelling, Lauraine. Daughter of Twin Oaks. 2000. (Secret Refuge Ser.: Vol. 1). 288p. pap. 11.99 (*1-55661-839-5*) Bethany Hse. Pubs.
—Daughter of Twin Oaks. 2001. 350p. 24.95 o.p. (*0-7862-3684-1*, Five Star) Gale Group.
Spitz, Marc. How Soon Is Never? 2003. 368p. pap. 13.00 (*0-609-81040-5*, Three Rivers Pr.) Crown Publishing Group.
Stewart, Jesse. Best Loved Short Stories of Jesse Stewart. 1982. 448p. text 14.95 o.p. (*0-07-062305-8*) McGraw-Hill Cos., The.
Still, James. The Run for the Elbertas. 1980. 160p. 22.00 (*0-8131-1414-4*); pap. 14.00 (*0-8131-0151-4*) Univ. Pr. of Kentucky.
Struck, Frank C. Jordon's Showdown: A Berkley Jordan Mystery. 1993. 224p. 19.95 (*0-8027-3222-4*) Walker & Co.
Strunk, Frank C. Throwback. 1997. 448p. mass mkt. 6.50 o.s.i (*0-06-101058-8*, HarperTorch) Morrow/Avon.
Stuart, Jesse. Clearing in the Sky & Other Stories. 1984. (Illus.). 280p. 28.00 (*0-8131-1510-8*); pap. 17.00 (*0-8131-0157-3*) Univ. Pr. of Kentucky.
—Come Back to the Farm. 2001. (Illus.). xix, 246p. 22.00 (*0-945084-94-3*) Stuart, Jesse Foundation, The.
—Head O' W-Hollow. 1979. 352p. reprint ed. pap. 18.00 (*0-8131-0142-5*) Univ. Pr. of Kentucky.
—Head O'w-Hollow. 1980. (Short Story Index Reprint Ser.). reprint ed. 22.95 (*0-8369-4065-2*) Ayer Co. Pubs., Inc.
—Men of the Mountains. 1979. 352p. reprint ed. pap. 18.00 (*0-8131-0143-3*) Univ. Pr. of Kentucky.
—New Harvest. Palmore, David R., ed. 2003. 288p. 24.00 (*1-931672-17-2*) Stuart, Jesse Foundation, The.

Settings

Stuart, Jesse H. Andy Finds a Way. Herndon, Jerry A., ed. & afterword by by. rev. ed. 1992. (Jesse Stuart Foundation Juvenile Ser.). (Illus.). 96p. (J). (gr. 3-6). reprint ed. 12.00 (*0-945084-25-0*); pap. 6.00 (*0-945084-26-9*) Stuart, Jesse Foundation, The.

—A Penny's Worth of Character. Herndon, Jerry A. et al, eds. 3rd ed. 1993. (Jesse Stuart Foundation Juvenile Ser.). (Illus.). 62p. (J). (gr. 3-6). reprint ed. pap. 4.00 (*0-945084-32-3*) Stuart, Jesse Foundation, The.

—Plowshare in Heaven. Herndon, Jerry A. et al, eds. 2nd ed. 1991. (Illus.). 268p. (YA). (gr. 7 up). reprint ed. 22.00 (*0-945084-21-8*) Stuart, Jesse Foundation, The.

—Tales from the Plum Grove Hills. Daughaday, Charles H., ed. & intro. by. 1997. (Illus.). 288p. (J). reprint ed. 22.00 (*0-945084-62-5*) Stuart, Jesse Foundation, The.

—Taps for Private Tussie. 1992. (Illus.). 255p. reprint ed. 22.00 (*0-945084-24-2*) Stuart, Jesse Foundation, The.

Taylor-Hall, Mary A. Come & Go, Molly Snow. 1996. 272p. pap. 11.00 o.p. (*0-380-72702-1*, Avon Bks.) Morrow/Avon.

—Come & Go, Molly Snow: A Novel. 1995. 256p. 21.00 (*0-393-03735-5*) Norton, W. W. & Co., Inc.

Thirty-Two Votes Before Breakfast. 1974. 350p. 20.00 (*0-07-062299-X*) McGraw-Hill Cos., The.

Wall, Jack. Prime Leaf: A Novel of the Kentucky Tobacco Wars. 2000. (Illus.). 320p. 25.00 o.p. (*1-892514-82-6*) Hill Street Pr., LLC.

Wiggin, Kate Douglas. A Cathedral Courtship. 2000. 252p. E-Book 3.95 (*0-594-01824-2*) 1873 Pr.

Wilkinson, Crystal E. Water Street. 2002. 192p. 24.95 (*1-902881-59-1*) Toby Pr.

Williams, Philip Lee. Blue Crystal. 1993. 277p. 19.95 o.p. (*0-8021-1499-7*) Grove/Atlantic, Inc.

Williamson, Jack. The Silicon Dagger. 2000. 352p. mass mkt. 6.99 o.s.i (*0-8125-4042-5*); 1999. 304p. 23.95 o.p. (*0-312-86540-6*) Doherty, Tom Assocs., LLC. (Tor Bks.).

Witt, Lana. The Heart of a Thirsty Woman. 368p. 2000. pap. 13.95 o.s.i (*0-671-01146-4*); 1999. 23.00 o.s.i (*0-684-84152-5*) Simon & Schuster. (Scribner).

—Slow Dancing on Dinosaur Bones. 416p. 1997. pap. 12.00 (*0-671-89122-7*); 1996. 22.00 (*0-684-81535-4*) Simon & Schuster. (Scribner).

Woodworth, Deborah. Deadly Shaker Spring. 1998. (Sister Rose Callahan Mystery Ser.). 304p. mass mkt. 5.99 (*0-380-79203-6*, Avon Bks.) Morrow/Avon.

—The Death of a Winter Shaker. 1997. (Sister Rose Callahan Mystery Ser.). 224p. mass mkt. 5.50 (*0-380-79201-X*, Avon Bks.) Morrow/Avon.

—Killing Gifts. 2001. (Shaker Mysteries Ser.). 272p. mass mkt. 5.99 (*0-380-80426-3*, Avon Bks.) Morrow/Avon.

—A Simple Shaker Murder. 2000. (Sister Rose Callahan Mystery Ser.). 256p. mass mkt. 5.99 (*0-380-80425-5*, Avon Bks.) Morrow/Avon.

—The Sins of a Shaker Summer: A Sister Rose Callahan Mystery. 1999. 272p. mass mkt. 5.99 (*0-380-79204-4*, Avon Bks.) Morrow/Avon.

Wright, Don. The Devil's Harvest. 2000. 225p. 21.00 (*0-9702567-0-1*) New Way Publishing.

Wright, Zara. Black & White Tangled Threads. reprint ed. 45.00 (*0-404-11378-8*) AMS Pr., Inc.

Wright, Zara & Sale, Maggie. Black & White Tangled Threads: Band, Kenneth. 1995. xxxiv, 340p. 25.00 (*0-8161-1626-1*, Macmillan Reference USA) Gale Group.

Yount, John. Hardcastle. 1986. audio 13.95 (*1-55644-169-X*, 6121) American Audio Prose Library, Inc.

—Hardcastle. 1980. 10.95 o.p. (*0-399-90061-6*) Putnam Publishing Group, The.

—Hardcastle. 1984. 288p. pap. 6.95 o.p. (*0-312-36207-2*, Saint Martin's Griffin) St. Martin's Pr.

—Hardcastle: A Novel. 1992. 288p. reprint ed. pap. 10.95 (*0-87074-341-4*) Southern Methodist Univ. Pr.

**KENYA—FICTION**

Brien, Nell. Lioness. 2000. 408p. mass mkt. (*1-55166-598-0*, 1-66598-3, Mira Bks.) Harlequin Enterprises, Ltd.

Bull, Bartle. The White Rhino Hotel. 2000. (Illus.). 416p. reprint ed. pap. 14.00 (*0-7867-0798-4*, Carroll & Graf Pubs.) Avalon Publishing Group.

—The White Rhino Hotel. 1993. 448p. mass mkt. 5.99 o.p. (*0-451-17583-2*, Signet Bks.) NAL.

—The White Rhino Hotel. 1992. (Illus.). 464p. 24.00 o.p. (*0-670-83998-1*, Viking) Viking Penguin.

Chaikin, Linda L. Endangered. l.t. ed. 1999. (Christian Mystery Ser.). 421p. 24.95 o.p. (*0-7862-2059-7*) Thorndike Pr.

Douglass, Keith. Battleground: Seal Team Seven. l.t. ed. 1998. (Paperback Ser.). 391p. pap. 23.95 (*0-7838-0416-4*) Thorndike Pr.

Haulsey, Kuwana. The Red Moon: A Novel. 2001. (Illus.). 288p. 22.95 o.s.i (*0-375-50557-1*, Villard Bks.) Random House Adult Trade Publishing Group.

Huxley, Elspeth. Red Strangers. 2000. (Penguin Classics Ser.). 432p. pap. 15.00 o.s.i (*0-14-118205-9*, Penguin Bks.) Viking Penguin.

Kaye, M. M. Death in Kenya. unabr. ed. 1993. 54.95 incl. audio (*0-7451-6083-2*, CAB 088) BBC Audiobooks America.

—Death in Kenya. 1999. 208p. pap. 12.95 (*0-312-24561-0*, Saint Martin's Griffin); 1984. pap. 3.95 o.p. (*0-312-90117-8*, St. Martin's Paperbacks); 1983. 208p. 12.95 o.p. (*0-312-18611-8*) St. Martin's Pr.

Lambkin, David. The Hanging Tree. 400p. 1998. pap. text 18.00 (*1-887178-71-6*); 1996. text 23.00 o.p. (*1-887178-19-8*) Basic Bks. (Counterpoint Pr.).

Le Carré, John. The Constant Gardener. E-Book 9.99 (*1-58945-504-5*) Adobe Systems, Inc.

—The Constant Gardener. 2001. 496p. 7.99 (*0-7434-2855-2*, Pocket); 2000. 496p. 28.00 o.s.i (*0-7432-1505-2*, Scribner); 2001. 576p. reprint ed. mass mkt. 7.99 (*0-7434-2291-0*, Pocket) Simon & Schuster.

—The Constant Gardener. E-Book 9.99 (*0-7410-0341-4*) SoftBook Pr.

—The Constant Gardener. l.t. ed. 2001. 704p. 32.50 o.p. (*0-7432-1556-7*) Thorpe, F. A. Pubs. GBR. *Dist:* Ulverscroft Large Print Bks., Ltd.

Macgoye, Marjorie. Coming to Birth. 2000. (Women Writing Africa Ser.). 192p. 30.00 (*1-55861-253-X*) Feminist Pr. at The City Univ. of New York.

—The Present Moment. 2000. (Women Writing Africa Ser.). 192p. 30.00 (*1-55861-254-8*); pap. 11.95 (*1-55861-248-3*) Feminist Pr. at The City Univ. of New York.

Macgoye, Marjorie Oludhe. Coming to Birth. 2000. (Women Writing Africa Ser.). 192p. pap. 11.95 (*1-55861-249-1*) Feminist Pr. at The City Univ. of New York.

Marciano, Francesca. Rules of the Wild. 1999. pap. text 144.00 (*0-679-78718-6*) Random Hse., Inc.

—Rules of the Wild: A Novel of Africa. 1999. 304p. pap. 13.00 (*0-375-70343-8*) Knopf, Alfred A. Inc.

McQuillan, Karin. The Cheetah Chase. 1995. mass mkt. 5.99 o.s.i (*0-345-39780-0*); 1994. 304p. 20.00 o.s.i (*0-345-38183-1*) Ballantine Bks.

—Deadly Safari. 1991. (Boston Mysteries Ser.). 272p. mass mkt. 4.99 o.s.i (*0-345-37057-0*, Ballantine Bks.) Ballantine Bks.

—Deadly Safari. 1990. 304p. 17.95 o.p. (*0-312-03808-9*, Saint Martin's Minotaur) St. Martin's Pr.

—Deadly Safari. l.t. ed. 1994. (Ulverscroft Large Print Ser.). 512p. 29.99 o.p. (*0-7089-3189-8*, Ulverscroft) Thorpe, F. A. Pubs. GBR. *Dist:* Ulverscroft Large Print Bks., Ltd., Ulverscroft Large Print Canada, Ltd.

—Elephants' Graveyard. 1994. (Boston Mysteries Ser.). 272p. mass mkt. 4.99 o.s.i (*0-345-38862-3*) Ballantine Bks.

Ngugi wa Thiong'o. The River Between. 1965. (African Writers Ser.). pap. text 6.50 o.p. (*0-435-90017-X*); 152p. (C). pap. 10.95 (*0-435-90548-1*, 90548, African Writers Series) Heinemann.

Palmer, Catherine. Sunrise Song. 2003. (HeartQuest Ser.). 352p. pap. 9.99 (*0-8423-7230-X*) Tyndale Hse. Pubs.

Shreve, Anita. The Last Time They Met. 2001. 320p. E-Book 14.95 (*0-7595-4308-9*); E-Book 14.95 (*0-7595-9338-8*); E-Book 14.95 (*0-7595-6305-5*); E-Book 14.95 (*0-7595-8311-0*); E-Book 14.95 (*0-7595-0305-2*) Little Brown & Co.

—The Last Time They Met. Pietsch, Michael, ed. 2001. 320p. 24.95 o.p. (*0-316-78114-2*) Little Brown & Co.

—The Last Time They Met. 2002. 352p. reprint ed. pap. 13.95 (*0-316-78126-6*, Back Bay) Little Brown & Co.

—The Last Time They Met. l.t. ed. (Paperback Bestsellers Ser.). 2002. 475p. pap. 13.95 (*0-7862-3311-7*); 2001. 496p. 31.95 (*0-7862-3310-9*); 2001. 475p. (*0-7540-1660-9*); 2001. 475p. (*0-7540-9074-4*) Thorndike Pr.

**KEY LARGO (FLA.)—FICTION**

Hall, James W. Buzz Cut. 1997. 464p. mass mkt. 7.50 (*0-440-21782-2*) Dell Publishing.

—Buzz Cut. abr. ed. 1999. audio 9.99 o.s.i (*0-553-70207-6*, RH Audio) Random Hse. Audio Publishing Group.

—Buzz Cut. unabr. ed. 1999. audio compact disk 99.00 (*0-7887-3413-X*, C1019E7); 1996. audio 85.00 (*0-7887-0628-4*, 94802E7) Recorded Bks., LLC.

—Gone Wild. 1996. 464p. mass mkt. 7.50 (*0-440-21781-4*) Dell Publishing.

—Gone Wild. l.t. ed. 1995. 607p. 25.95 o.p. (*0-7838-1368-6*, Macmillan Reference USA) Gale Group.

—Gone Wild. unabr. ed. 1995. audio 85.00 (*0-7887-0264-5*, 94473E7) Recorded Bks., LLC.

—Hard Aground. 1994. 464p. mass mkt. 7.50 (*0-440-21357-6*) Dell Publishing.

—Hard Aground. l.t. ed. 1993. 89.95 o.p. incl. audio (*0-7838-1113-6*, Macmillan Reference USA) Gale Group.

—Mean High Tide. 1995. 448p. mass mkt. 7.50 (*0-440-21355-X*) Dell Publishing.

—Mean High Tide. l.t. ed. 1994. 545p. lib. bdg. 23.95 (*0-8161-7441-5*, Macmillan Reference USA) Gale Group.

—Mean High Tide. abr. ed. 1999. audio 9.99 o.s.i (*0-553-70191-6*, RH Audio) Random Hse. Audio Publishing Group.

—Mean High Tide, unabr. ed. 1994. audio 78.00 (*0-7887-0026-X*, 94225E7) Recorded Bks., LLC.

—Mean High Tide. 372p. 4.98 o.p. (*0-8317-5431-1*) Smithmark Pubs., Inc.

—Red Sky at Night. l.t. ed. 2001. 384p. lib. bdg. 28.95 (*1-58547-117-8*) Ctr. Point Large Print.

—Red Sky at Night. 1998. 400p. reprint ed. mass mkt. 6.99 (*0-440-22574-4*) Doubleday Publishing.

—Red Sky at Night, unabr. ed. 1997. audio 75.00 (*0-7887-1294-2*, 95128E7) Recorded Bks., LLC.

—Tropical Freeze. l.t. ed. 2003. lib. bdg. 28.95 (*1-58547-288-3*, Premier) Ctr. Point Large Print.

—Tropical Freeze. 1999. 446p. pap. 9.00 (*0-393-31895-8*); 1989. 18.95 o.p. (*0-393-02694-9*) Norton, W. W. & Co., Inc.

—Tropical Freeze. 1991. 320p. mass mkt. 6.50 o.p. (*0-446-36062-7*) Warner Bks., Inc.

—Under Cover of Daylight. 1997. 352p. pap. 9.95 o.s.i (*0-385-31867-7*, Delta) Dell Publishing.

—Under Cover of Daylight. l.t. ed. 2001. (Large Print Book Ser.). 358p. 26.95 (*1-58724-028-9*, Wheeler Publishing, Inc.) Gale Group.

—Under Cover of Daylight. 2001. 272p. pap. 10.00 (*0-393-32125-8*); 1987. 16.95 o.p. (*0-393-02484-9*) Norton, W. W. & Co., Inc.

—Under Cover of Daylight. 1988. 384p. mass mkt. 6.50 o.s.i (*0-446-35231-4*) Warner Bks., Inc.

**KEY WEST (FLA.)—FICTION**

Amberg, Jay. Doubloon. mass mkt. (*0-7653-4036-4*); 2003. 320p. 24.95 (*0-7653-0100-8*) Doherty, Tom Assocs., LLC. (Tor Bks.).

—Doubloon. 2003. (Adventure Ser.). 307p. 28.95 (*0-7862-5399-1*) Thorndike Pr.

Brackenbury, Rosalind. Seas Outside the Reef: A Novel. 2000. 222p. pap. 14.95 (*1-880284-41-3*) Daniel, John & Co., Pubs.

Cameron, Stella. Key West. l.t. ed. 2000. 27.95 (*1-56895-851-X*, Wheeler Publishing, Inc.) Gale Group.

—Key West. 2000. 48p. mass mkt. 6.99 (*0-8217-6595-7*); 1999. 392p. 23.00 o.s.i (*1-57566-454-2*) Kensington Publishing Corp.

Child, Lee. Tripwire. 2000. 432p. mass mkt. 7.99 (*0-515-12863-5*, Jove) Berkley Publishing Group.

—Tripwire. l.t. ed. 2000. (Wheeler Softcover Ser.). pap. 25.95 (*1-56895-912-5*, Wheeler Publishing, Inc.) Gale Group.

—Tripwire. 1999. 343p. 23.95 o.p. (*0-399-14467-6*, G. P. Putnam's Sons) Penguin Group (USA) Inc.

—Tripwire, unabr. ed. 2000. 12p. audio 94.95 (*1-86042-691-3*, 26913) Soundings, Ltd. GBR. *Dist:* Ulverscroft Large Print Bks., Ltd.

Corcoran, Tom. Bone Island Mambo. 2002. 352p. mass mkt. 6.99 (*0-312-98008-6*, St. Martin's Paperbacks) St. Martin's Pr.

—Bone Island Mambo: An Alex Rutledge Mystery. 2001. E-Book 23.95 (*1-58945-795-1*) Adobe Systems, Inc.

—Bone Island Mambo: An Alex Rutledge Mystery. 2001. 278p. 23.95 (*0-312-24281-6*, Saint Martin's Minotaur) St. Martin's Pr.

—Gumbo Limbo. 1999. 293p. 23.95 (*0-312-24194-1*, Saint Martin's Minotaur) St. Martin's Pr.

—Gumbo Limbo: An Alex Rutledge Mystery. 2000. 304p. mass mkt. 6.50 (*0-312-97570-8*, St. Martin's Paperbacks) St. Martin's Pr.

—The Mango Opera. 304p. 1999. mass mkt. 6.99 (*0-312-96988-0*, St. Martin's Paperbacks); Vol. 1. 1998. (Mango Opera Ser.: Vol. 1). 22.95 (*0-312-18628-2*, Saint Martin's Minotaur) St. Martin's Pr.

—Octopus Alibi: An Alex Rutledge Mystery. 2003. (Alex Rutledge Mystery Ser.). 304p. 24.95 (*0-312-29127-2*, Saint Martin's Minotaur) St. Martin's Pr.

Francis, Dorothy Brenner. Conch Shell Murder. 2003. (Five Star First Edition Mystery Ser.). 244p. 25.95 (*0-7862-5029-1*, Five Star) Gale Group.

—Keys to Love. l.t. ed. 2002. 185p. 26.95 (*0-7862-4036-9*) Gale Group.

Gallo, Gina. Crime Scenes. 2000. (Illus.). 233p. pap. 14.95 (*0-9678809-1-2*) Blue Murder Pr.

Grey, Harper. Fast Ride with the Top Down. 160p. 1997. pap. text 9.95 o.p. (*1-55583-416-7*); 2nd ed. 1996. reprint ed. 19.95 o.p. (*1-55583-370-5*) Alyson Pubns.

Hanlon, Julia. The Wedding Wager. 2000. 352p. mass mkt. 5.99 o.s.i (*0-8217-6524-8*, Zebra Bks.) Kensington Publishing Corp.

Harrison, Ben. Undying Love: The Shocking Story of a Passion That Defied Death. 2001. (St. Martin's Paperbacks True Crime Library). 256p. reprint ed. mass mkt. 6.50 (*0-312-97802-2*, 20-3284, St. Martin's Paperbacks) St. Martin's Pr.

Jackson, Hialeah. Farewell, Conch Republic. 1999. 368p. mass mkt. 5.99 o.s.i (*0-440-22663-5*) Dell Publishing.

Key West Author's Co-Op Staff, contrib. by. Mango Summers: Short Stories from the Key West Authors' Coop. 2002. 175p. (*0-9668854-2-2*) Perky Pr.

Lee, Rachel. After I Dream. l.t. ed. 2000. 377p. 27.95 (*1-57490-278-4*, Beeler Large Print Bks.) Beeler, Thomas T. Publisher.

—After I Dream. 2000. 400p. reprint ed. mass mkt. 6.50 (*0-446-60654-5*, Warner Romance) Warner Bks., Inc.

Lennon, Patrick. Key West Gun Runner. 1999. E-Book 7.18 (*1-929429-26-6*) Dead End Street, LLC.

Lennon, Patrick A. The Key West Gun Runner. E-Book 8.97 (*1-929429-20-7*) Dead End Street, LLC.

Lurie, Alison. The Last Resort. l.t. ed. 1998. (Thorndike Americana Ser.). 381p. 26.95 (*0-7862-1642-5*, Macmillan Reference USA) Gale Group.

—The Last Resort. 336p. 1999. pap. 13.00 (*0-8050-6174-6*, Owl Bks.); 1998. 22.00 o.s.i (*0-8050-5866-4*) Holt, Henry & Co.

Lurie, Alison, contrib. by. The Last Resort. 1998. 254p. (*0-7011-6713-0*) Chatto & Windus.

Parker, Barbara. Suspicion of Madness. 2003. (Illus.). 368p. 24.95 (*0-525-94681-0*) Dutton/Plume.

—Suspicion of Madness. 2003. 416p. mass mkt. 7.99 (*0-451-21089-1*, Signet Bks.) NAL.

—Suspicion of Madness. 2003. (Gail Connor & Anthony Quintana Novel Ser.). 597p. 30.95 (*0-7862-5422-X*) Thorndike Pr.

Robbins, David L. Souls to Keep: A Novel. 1999. 272p. mass mkt. 6.50 o.s.i (*0-06-109791-8*); 1998. 320p. 23.00 o.s.i (*0-06-101300-5*) HarperCollins Pubs.

Rutledge, Leigh W. The Lighthouse, the Cat & the Sea: A Tropical Tale. 1999. (Illus.). 128p. 17.95 o.p. (*0-525-94349-8*, Dutton Children's Bks.) Dutton/Plume.

—The Lighthouse, the Cat, & the Sea: A Tropical Tale. l.t. ed. 2000. (Americana Ser.). 175p. 26.95 (*0-7862-2528-9*) Thorndike Pr.

Sawyer, Meryl. Half Moon Bay. 2002. 9.95 o.p. (*0-7582-0476-0*, Kensington Bks.); 1999. 432p. mass mkt. 6.50 (*0-8217-6144-7*) Kensington Publishing Corp.

Shames, Laurence. Florida Straits. unabr. collector's ed. 1998. audio 48.00 (*0-7366-4079-7*, 4588) Books on Tape, Inc.

—Florida Straits. 1993. 368p. mass mkt. 6.50 (*0-440-21511-0*) Dell Publishing.

—Florida Straits, unabr. ed. 1997. audio 60.00 (*0-7887-1751-0*, 95229E7) Recorded Bks., LLC.

—Florida Straits. 1992. 256p. 20.00 o.p. (*0-671-74933-1*, Simon & Schuster) Simon & Schuster.

—Mangrove Squeeze. abr. ed. 1998. audio 16.95 (*1-55927-485-9*) Audio Renaissance.

—Mangrove Squeeze. 1999. 352p. mass mkt. 6.99 (*0-345-43306-8*) Ballantine Bks.

—Mangrove Squeeze. unabr. collector's ed. 1998. audio 56.00 (*0-7366-4261-7*, 4760) Books on Tape, Inc.

—Mangrove Squeeze. 1998. 320p. 22.95 o.p. (*0-7868-6301-3*); mass mkt. 5.99 (*0-7868-8945-4*) Hyperion Pr.

—Mangrove Squeeze, unabr. ed. 1998. audio 60.00 (*0-7887-2037-6*, 95401E7) Recorded Bks., LLC.

—Scavenger Reef. unabr. collector's ed. 1998. audio 48.00 (*0-7366-4080-0*, 4589) Books on Tape, Inc.

—Scavenger Reef. 1995. 336p. mass mkt. 6.99 (*0-440-21797-0*) Dell Publishing.

—Scavenger Reef. unabr. ed. 1999. audio compact disk 73.00 (*0-7887-3443-1*, C1049E7); 1998. audio 60.00 (*0-7887-1982-3*, 95369E7) Recorded Bks., LLC.

—Scavenger Reef. 1994. 254p. 21.00 o.s.i (*0-671-86493-9*, Simon & Schuster) Simon & Schuster.

—Sunburn. unabr. collector's ed. 1998. audio 48.00 (*0-7366-4167-X*, 4669) Books on Tape, Inc.

—Sunburn. 1996. 384p. mass mkt. 4.99 (*0-7868-8903-9*); 1995. 288p. 21.95 (*0-7868-6068-5*) Hyperion Pr.

—Sunburn, unabr. ed. 1998. audio 60.00 (*0-7887-1882-7*, 95304E7) Recorded Bks., LLC.

—Tropical Depression. abr. ed. 1996. audio 16.95 (*1-55927-372-0*) Audio Renaissance.

—Tropical Depression. unabr. ed. 1996. audio 48.00 (*0-7366-3375-8*, 4025) Books on Tape, Inc.

—Tropical Depression. 1997. 368p. mass mkt. 5.99 (*0-7868-8909-8*); 1996. 304p. 21.95 (*0-7868-6109-6*) Hyperion Pr.

—Tropical Depression. 2000. 360p. pap. 20.95 (*0-595-00639-6*, Backinprint.com) iUniverse, Inc.

—Virgin Heat. abr. ed. 1997. audio 16.95 (*1-55927-415-8*) Audio Renaissance.

—Virgin Heat. l.t. ed. 1997. lib. bdg. 24.95 (*1-57490-084-6*, Beeler Large Print Bks.) Beeler, Thomas T. Publisher.

—Virgin Heat. unabr. ed. 1997. audio 48.00 (*0-7366-4056-8*, 4567) Books on Tape, Inc.

—Virgin Heat. 1998. (J). mass mkt. 5.99 (*0-7868-8927-6*); 1997. 320p. 21.95 (*0-7868-6203-3*) Hyperion Pr.

—Welcome to Paradise. 2000. 256p. mass mkt. 6.99 o.s.i (*0-345-43218-5*, Ballantine Bks.) Ballantine Bks.

—Welcome to Paradise. unabr. ed. 2000. audio compact disk 58.00 (*0-7887-4633-2*, C1208E7); 1999. audio 44.00 (*0-7887-3475-X*, 95763E7) Recorded Bks., LLC.

—Welcome to Paradise: A Novel. aut. ed. 1999. 22.95 o.s.i (*0-676-58659-7*) Random Hse., Inc.

**KINDLE COUNTY (IMAGINARY PLACE)—FICTION**

Turow, Scott. The Burden of Proof. 1990. audio 8.95 American Audio Prose Library, Inc.

—The Burden of Proof. unabr. collector's ed. 1990. audio 96.00 (*0-7366-1786-8*, 2623) Books on Tape, Inc.

—The Burden of Proof. 1990. 367.20 o.p. (*0-374-11735-7*); 640p. 30.00 (*0-374-11734-9*); E-Book 22.92 (*0-374-70092-3*); 640p. E-Book 9.95 o.p. (*0-374-70091-5*); E-Book 22.95 (*0-374-70093-1*) Farrar, Straus & Giroux.

—The Burden of Proof. l.t. ed. 1991. (General Ser.). 690p. 14.95 o.p. (*0-8161-5125-3*); 14.95 o.p. (*0-8161-5132-6*) Gale Group. (Macmillan Reference USA).

—The Burden of Proof. abr. ed. 1990. audio 17.00 (*0-671-70743-4*, Simon & Schuster Audioworks) Simon & Schuster Audio.

—The Burden of Proof. reprint ed. 2000. 608p. pap. 14.95 (*0-446-67712-4*); 1991. 576p. mass mkt. 7.99 (*0-446-36058-9*) Warner Bks., Inc.

—The Laws of Our Fathers. unabr. ed. 1997. Pt. 1. audio 64.00 (*0-7366-3642-0*, 4304-A); Pt. 2. (Illus.). audio 64.00 (*0-7366-3643-9*, 4304-B) Books on Tape, Inc.

—The Laws of Our Fathers. 1996. 817p. 26.95 (*0-374-18423-2*) Farrar, Straus & Giroux.

—The Laws of Our Fathers. abr. ed. 1996. audio 26.00 (*0-671-57432-9*); audio 20.80 (*0-671-57741-7*, 908770) Simon & Schuster Audio. (Simon & Schuster Audioworks).

—The Laws of Our Fathers. l.t. ed. (Paperback Bestsellers Ser.). 931p. 1997. pap. 26.95 (*0-7838-1946-3*); 1996. 29.95 (*0-7838-1945-5*) Thorndike Pr.

—The Laws of Our Fathers. 1997. 832p. reprint ed. mass mkt. 7.99 (*0-446-60440-2*) Warner Bks., Inc.

—Personal Injuries. stu. ed. (*0-374-96409-2*); 1999. 384p. 27.00 (*0-374-28194-7*); 1999. E-Book 27.00 (*0-374-70194-6*); 1999. E-Book 9.00 (*0-374-70018-4*); 1999. E-Book 9.00 o.p. incl. cd-rom (*0-374-70007-9*) Farrar, Straus & Giroux.

—Personal Injuries. l.t. ed. 1999. (Basic Ser.). 731p. 31.95 (*0-7862-2014-7*) Thorndike Pr.

—Personal Injuries. 2000. 528p. reprint ed. mass mkt. 7.99 (*0-446-60860-2*) Warner Bks., Inc.

—Personal Injuries: Special Edition. E-Book 6.00 (*1-58945-505-3*) Adobe Systems, Inc.

—Pleading Guilty. unabr. ed. 1993. audio 64.00 (*0-7366-2605-0*, 3348) Books on Tape, Inc.

—Pleading Guilty. E-Book 4.95 (*0-374-70105-9*); E-Book 4.95 (*0-374-70118-0*); 2001. E-Book 4.95 o.p. (*0-374-70104-0*); 1993. 400p. 24.00 (*0-374-23457-4*); 1993. E-Book 24.00 (*0-374-70106-7*) Farrar, Straus & Giroux.

—Pleading Guilty. l.t. ed. 1993. 495p. pap. 19.95 o.p. (*0-8161-5747-2*); lib. bdg. 25.95 (*0-8161-5746-4*) Gale Group. (Macmillan Reference USA).

—Pleading Guilty. abr. ed. 1993. audio 24.00 (*0-671-87043-2*, Simon & Schuster Audioworks) Simon & Schuster Audio.

—Pleading Guilty. 1994. 480p. reprint ed. mass mkt. 7.99 (*0-446-36550-5*) Warner Bks., Inc.

—Presumed Innocent. 1989. audio 13.95 (*1-55644-337-4*, 9061) American Audio Prose Library, Inc.

—Presumed Innocent. unabr. collector's ed. 1988. audio 80.00 (*0-7366-1336-6*, 2239) Books on Tape, Inc.

—Presumed Innocent. 1987. 480p. 30.00 (*0-374-23713-1*); E-Book 4.95 (*0-374-70109-1*); E-Book 4.95 o.p. (*0-374-70108-3*); E-Book 4.95 (*0-374-70117-2*); E-Book 4.95 (*0-374-70111-3*) Farrar, Straus & Giroux.

—Presumed Innocent. l.t. ed. 1988. (General Ser.). 606p. 13.95 o.p. (*0-8161-4470-2*, Macmillan Reference USA) Gale Group.

—Presumed Innocent. 1999. (*0-7621-0254-3*) Reader's Digest Assn., Inc., The.

—Presumed Innocent. abr. ed. 1988. 17.00 incl. audio (*0-671-65218-4*, Simon & Schuster Audioworks) Simon & Schuster Audio.

—Presumed Innocent. reprint ed. 2000. 512p. pap. 14.95 (*0-446-67644-6*); 1989. 432p. mass mkt. 7.99 (*0-446-35986-6*) Warner Bks., Inc.

—Reversible Errors: A Novel. 2002. E-Book 15.00 (*0-374-70394-9*); E-Book 15.00 (*0-374-70393-0*); E-Book 15.00 o.p. (*0-374-70395-7*); E-Book 15.00 (*0-374-70396-5*); (Illus.). 448p. 28.00 (*0-374-28160-2*); E-Book 28.00 (*0-374-70397-3*); pap. (*0-374-96781-4*) Farrar, Straus & Giroux.

—Reversible Errors: A Novel. l.t. ed. 2003. 720p. pap. 13.95 (*1-4104-0161-8*, Wheeler Publishing, Inc.) Gale Group.

—Reversible Errors: A Novel. pap. o.p. (*0-7862-4269-8*); 2002. 32.95 (*0-7862-4268-X*) Thorndike Pr.

—Reversible Errors: A Novel. 2003. 576p. mass mkt. 7.99 (*0-446-61262-6*, Warner Vision) Warner Bks., Inc.

**KOREA—FICTION**

Ahn, Junghyo. White Badge: A Novel of Korea. 1989. 270p. 19.95 o.s.i (*0-939149-16-8*) Soho Pr., Inc.

Antal, John F. Proud Legions. 1999. (Illus.). 368p. 24.95 o.p. (*0-89141-667-6*, Presidio Pr.) Ballantine Bks.

—Proud Legions. 2000. (Illus.). 416p. mass mkt. 6.99 o.s.i (*0-515-12784-1*, Jove) Berkley Publishing Group.

Chang-sop, Son, et al. A Respite & Other Korean Short Stories. Korean National Commission for UNESCO, ed. Chong-un, Kim et al, trs. from KOR. 1983. (Modern Korean Short Stories Ser.: No. 6). vii, 169p. 20.00 (*0-89209-207-6*) Pace Group International.

Davis, Patrick A. The Commander. 2002. 352p. 24.95 o.s.i (*0-399-14882-5*) Penguin Group (USA) Inc.

—The Commander. 2004. 400p. mass mkt. 6.99 (*0-7434-7572-0*, Pocket Star) Simon & Schuster.

Fenkl, Heinz I. Memories of My Ghost Brother: A Novel. 1996. 288p. 23.95 o.s.i (*0-525-94175-4*) Dutton/Plume.

Griffin, W. E. B. Under Fire. 2002. (Corps Ser.). 544p. 26.95 o.s.i (*0-399-14788-8*); audio 49.95 (*0-399-14826-4*) Penguin Group (USA) Inc.

—Under Fire. abr. ed. 2002. (Corps Ser.). 4p. audio 24.95 o.s.i (*0-399-14821-3*); 5p. audio compact disk 29.95 (*0-399-14830-2*) Putnam Publishing Group, The. (Putnam Berkley Audio).

Haig, Brian. Mortal Allies. (Wheeler Hardcover Ser.). 28.95 (*1-58724-294-X*, Wheeler Publishing, Inc.) Gale Group.

—Mortal Allies. 2002. 496p. 24.95 (*0-446-53026-3*); 2003. 608p. reprint ed. mass mkt. 6.99 (*0-446-61258-8*) Warner Bks., Inc.

Holinger, William. The Fence-Walker. 1985. 290p. (C). text 19.50 (*0-88706-024-2*) State Univ. of New York Pr.

Hooker, Richard. M*A*S*H: A Novel about Three Army Doctors. 188p. reprint ed. lib. bdg. 20.95 (*0-88411-198-9*) Amereon, Ltd.

—M*A*S*H: A Novel about Three Army Doctors. 1997. (Illus.). 224p. (ps-3). reprint ed. pap. 13.00 (*0-688-14955-3*, Quill) HarperTrade.

Hwi, Sonu & In-hun, Choe. One Way & Other Korean Short Stories. Korean National Commission for UNESCO et al, eds. Chong-un, Kim et al, trs. from KOR. 1983. (Modern Korean Short Stories Ser.: No. 5). viii, 204p. 20.00 (*0-89209-206-8*) Pace Group International.

Hyun, Peter, ed. Korean Children's Stories & Songs. 1996. (Illus.). 62p. (J). (gr. 1-7). 16.95 (*1-56591-065-6*) Hollym International Corp.

Inoue, Yasushi. Wind & Waves. Araki, James T., tr. from JPN. 1989. 214p. text 20.00 o.p. (*0-8248-1178-X*) Univ. of Hawaii Pr.

Ji-Moon, Suh, ed. & tr. The Rainy Spell & Other Korean Stories. exp. rev. ed. 1997. (C). (gr. 13). 304p. pap. 22.50 (*0-7656-0139-7*); 290p. 70.95 (*0-7656-0138-9*) Sharpe, M.E. Inc. (East Gate Bk.).

Junghyo, Ahn. White Badge: A Novel of Korea. 1993. 337p. pap. 13.00 (*1-56947-004-9*) Soho Pr., Inc.

Kajiyama, Toshiyuki. The Clan Records: Five Stories of Korea. Dykstra, Yoshiko, tr. from JPN. 1995. 192p. 18.00 (*0-8248-1532-7*) Univ. of Hawaii Pr.

Kajiyama, Toshiyuki & Dykstra, Yoshiko Kurata. The Clan Records: Five Stories of Korea. 1995. E-Book 18.00 (*0-585-33048-4*) netLibrary, Inc.

Kang, Youngkill. East Goes West. 2015. 416p. mass mkt. 5.95 o.s.i (*0-451-52654-6*) NAL.

Kang, Younghill. East Goes West: The Making of an Oriental Yankee. 1998. 425p. pap. text 16.95 (*1-885030-11-8*) Kaya Production.

Keller, Nora Okja. Fox Girl. 2003. 304p. 14.00 (*0-14-200196-1*); 2002. 256p. 24.95 o.s.i (*0-670-03073-2*, Viking) Viking Penguin.

Ki-won, So, et al. Two Travellers & Other Korean Short Stories. Korean National Commission for UNESCO, ed. Sang-Duk, Mun et al, trs. from KOR. 1983. (Modern Korean Short Stories Ser.: No. 7). viii, 144p. 20.00 (*0-89209-208-4*) Pace Group International.

Kyong-ni, Park. Land. Tennant, Agnita, tr. from KOR. 1995. Tr. of Toji. 512p. 34.00 (*0-7103-0508-7*) Routledge.

Lee, Peter H., ed. Flowers of Fire: Twentieth-Century Korean Stories. rev. ed. 1986. 512p. pap. 13.50 o.p. (*0-8248-1036-8*) Univ. of Hawaii Pr.

Lee, Veronica. Princess June: A Novel. 2001. 271p. pap. 14.95 (*1-56474-346-2*) Fithian Pr.

Limon, Martin. Buddha's Money. 1999. 416p. mass mkt. 5.99 o.s.i (*0-553-57610-0*) Bantam Bks.

—Jade Lady Burning. 1994. 224p. pap. 13.00 (*1-56947-020-0*); 1992. 226p. 19.95 (*0-939149-71-0*) Soho Pr., Inc.

—Slicky Boys. 1998. 416p. reprint ed. mass mkt. 5.99 o.s.i (*0-553-57609-7*) Bantam Bks.

—Slicky Boys. abr. ed. 1997. audio 23.00 (*1-56876-067-1*) Soundlines Entertainment, Inc.

Luchessa, Paul. Women of Uneasy Virtue: Tales of Korea in the Modern Warlord Era. 2000. 144p. pap. 20.99 (*0-7388-2273-6*); E-Book 8.00 (*0-7388-9706-X*) Xlibris Corp.

Lyon, Larry B., Jr. Before the Morning Calm: A Novel of Korea. Lyon, Larry B., Jr., ed. 1997. (Illus.). 140p. pap. 4.95 (*0-9656601-0-9*) Lyon, Jr., Lawrence B.

Meador, Daniel J. Unforgotten. 1999. 400p. 25.00 (*1-56554-349-1*) Pelican Publishing Co., Inc.

Paik, Beverly. Last Hill of Arirang: A Story of Korea. 2002. 474p. pap. 26.95 (*0-595-24098-4*, Writer's Showcase Pr.) iUniverse, Inc.

Park, Frances. To Swim Across the World. 2002. (Illus.). 304p. pap. 12.95 (*0-7868-8631-5*) Hyperion Pr.

Park, Frances & Park, Ginger. To Swim Across the World. 2001. 280p. 21.95 (*0-7868-6733-7*) Talk Miramax Bks.

Park, Therese. A Gift of the Emperor. 1997. 360p. pap. 10.95 (*1-883523-21-4*) Spinsters Ink Bks.

Park, Yongsoo. Boy Genius. 2002. 228p. pap. 14.95 (*1-888451-24-6*) Akashic Bks.

Scott, Joanna C. The Lucky Gourd Shop. 2000. 220p. 25.00 (*1-878448-01-3*) MacMurray & Beck, Inc.

Se-Hui, Cho, et al. The Road to Sampo & Other Korean Short Stories. UNESCO, Korean National Commission Staff, ed. McHale, B. & Ji-mun, Sol, trs. from KOR. 1983. (Modern Korean Short Stories Ser.: No. 9). viii, 237p. 20.00 o.s.i (*0-89209-210-6*) Pace Group International.

Stout, Mira. One Thousand Chestnut Trees: A Novel of Korea. 1999. 368p. reprint ed. 14.00 o.s.i (*1-57322-738-2*, Riverhead Trade (Paperbacks)) Berkley Publishing Group.

—One Thousand Chestnut Trees: A Novel of Korea. 1998. 336p. 23.95 o.p. (*1-57322-073-6*, Riverhead Bks. (Hardcovers)) Putnam Publishing Group, The.

Sun-won, Hwang. The Descendants of Cain. Ji-Moon, Suh & Pickering, Julie, trs. 1997. (UNESCO Collection of Representative Works). 192p. (gr. 13). (YA). pap. text 22.95 (*0-7656-0137-0*); (C). text 58.95 (*0-7656-0136-2*) Sharpe, M.E. Inc. (East Gate Bk.).

Sun-won, Hwang & Pom-son, Yi. The Drizzle & Other Korean Short Stories. Chong-un, Kim et al, trs. from KOR. 1983. (Modern Korean Short Stories Ser.: No. 2). viii, 191p. 20.00 o.s.i (*0-89209-203-3*) Pace Group International.

Sung-won, Han. Father & Son: A Novel. Young-nan, Yu & Pickering, Julie, trs. 2002. 285p. pap. 17.95 (*1-931907-04-8*) Homa & Sekey Bks.

Wehry, Whalen M. The Yobo: A Novel of Korea. 1984. 458p. 19.50 (*0-930878-38-8*) Hollym International Corp.

Won-il, Kim, et al. Early Spring, Mid-Summer, & Other Korean Short Stories. Korean National Commission for UNESCO, ed. Sun-bong, Sol et al, trs. 1983. (Modern Korean Short Stories Ser.: No. 10). viii, 191p. 20.00 o.s.i (*0-89209-211-4*) Pace Group International.

Wong, Janet S. The Trip Back Home. 2000. (Illus.). 32p. (J). (ps-2). 16.00 (*0-15-200784-9*) Harcourt Children's Bks.

Yun, Mia. House of the Winds. 1998. (Emerging Voices Ser.). 256p. 22.95 (*1-56656-305-4*) Interlink Publishing Group, Inc.

—House of the Winds. 2000. 240p. pap. 12.95 (*0-14-029194-6*) Penguin Group (USA) Inc.

**KRONDOR (MIKDEMIA: IMAGINARY PLACE)—FICTION**

Feist, Raymond E. Krondor: Tear of the Gods. 2001. (Riftwar Legacy Ser.: Bk. 3). 384p. mass mkt. 7.99 (*0-06-101500-8*) HarperCollins Pubs.

—Krondor: Tear of the Gods. 2001. (Riftwar Legacy Ser.: Bk. 3). (Illus.). 384p. 25.00 (*0-380-97800-8*, Eos) Morrow/Avon.

—Krondor: The Assassins. (Riftwar Legacy Ser.: Bk. 2). 2000. 416p. mass mkt. 7.99 (*0-380-80323-2*, HarperTorch); 1999. 374p. 25.00 (*0-380-97707-9*, Avon Bks.) Morrow/Avon.

—Krondor: The Betrayal. (Riftwar Legacy Ser.: Bk. 1). 1999. 432p. mass mkt. 7.50 (*0-380-79527-2*, Eos); 1998. 384p. 24.00 (*0-380-97715-X*, Avon Bks.) Morrow/Avon.

**KRYNN (IMAGINARY PLACE)—FICTION**

Crook, Jeff. The Thieves' Guild, Vol. 2. 2000. (Dragonlance: Crossroads Ser.: Vol. 2). (Illus.). 320p. mass mkt. 6.99 (*0-7869-1681-8*) Wizards of the Coast.

Dragonlance Saga Graphic Novel. 1990. No. 4. 9.95 o.p. (*0-88038-973-7*); No. 5. pap. 9.95 o.p. (*0-88038-974-5*) TSR, Inc.

Dungeons & Dragons D115: Mists of Krynn. 1988. pap. 9.95 o.p. (*0-88038-574-X*) TSR, Inc.

Fahlgren, Greg & Fahlgren, Nancy. Dragonwand of Krynn: A Dragonlance Adventure, 2 bks. 1987. (One-on-One Advanced Dungeons & Dragons Adventure Gamebook Ser.). 320p. (Orig.). pap. 5.95 o.p. (*0-88038-460-3*) TSR, Inc.

Herbert, Mary H. The Clandestine Circle. 2000. (Dragonlance Ser.: Vol. 1). (Illus.). 312p. mass mkt. 6.99 (*0-7869-1610-9*) Wizards of the Coast.

Hickman, Tracy, ed. The Magic of Krynn. 2000. (DragonLance Tales Ser.: Vol. 1). (Illus.). 350p. (Orig.). pap. 6.99 (*0-88038-454-9*) Wizards of the Coast.

Hickman, Tracy & Weis, Margaret. Dragonlance Adventures. 1987. 15.00 o.p. (*0-88038-452-2*) TSR, Inc.

Knaak, Richard A. The Citadel. 2000. (Dragonlance Classics Ser.). 312p. mass mkt. 6.99 (*0-7869-1683-4*) Wizards of the Coast.

—Land of the Minotaurs. 1996. (DragonLance Lost Histories Ser.: Vol. 4). 314p. pap. 5.99 (*0-7869-0472-0*) Wizards of the Coast.

—Legend of Huma. 1988. (DragonLance Heroes Trilogy: Vol. 1). (Illus.). 379p. (Orig.). pap. 6.99 (*0-88038-548-0*) Wizards of the Coast.

The Land Reborn. 1993. (DragonLance New Tales Ser.: Bk. 1). 10.95 o.p. (*1-56076-607-7*) TSR, Inc.

Niles, Douglas. Dwarven Kingdoms of Krynn. 1993. 20.00 o.p. (*1-56076-669-7*) TSR, Inc.

Rabe, Jean. Downfall Bk. 1: The Dhamon Saga. 2000. (Dragonlance Ser.). (Illus.). 378p. 21.95 (*0-7869-1572-2*) Wizards of the Coast.

Stein, Kevin. Brothers Majere. (Illus.). 2003. 352p. mass mkt. 6.99 (*0-7869-2971-5*); 1989. (DragonLance Preludes Trilogy Ser.: Vol. 3). 349p. mass mkt. 5.99 (*0-88038-776-9*) Wizards of the Coast.

Thomas, Roy. The Dragonlance Saga, No. 5. Maggin, Elliot S., ed. 1991. (Illus.). 80p. (Orig.). (YA). pap. 12.95 o.p. (*0-930289-93-5*) DC Comics.

—The Dragonlance Saga, Vol. 3. 1989. (Dragonlance Graphic Novel Ser.). (Illus.). 80p. (Orig.). (J). (gr. 5 up). pap. 9.95 o.p. (*0-88038-611-8*) TSR, Inc.

Thomas, Roy, ed. The Dragonlance Saga. (Dragonlance Graphic Novel Ser.). 80p. (Orig.). Vol. 1. 1987. (Illus.). pap. 9.95 o.p. (*0-88038-528-6*); Vol. 2. 1988. pap. 9.95 o.p. (*0-88038-571-5*) TSR, Inc.

Thompson, Paul B. & Cook, Tonya C. Children of the Plains. 2000. (Barbarians Ser.: No. 1). (Illus.). 320p. mass mkt. 6.99 (*0-7869-1391-6*) Wizards of the Coast.

TSR Inc. Staff. The Corrupted: Ogres of Krynn. 2000. (Dragonlance Ser.). (Illus.). 96p. pap. 17.95 (*0-7869-1396-7*) Wizards of the Coast.

—The Puppet King. 1999. (DragonLance Chaos War Ser.). 316p. pap. 6.99 (*0-7869-1324-X*) Wizards of the Coast.

—The Silver Stair, Vol. 3. 1999. (DragonLance Bridges of Time Ser.). 314p. mass mkt. 5.99 (*0-7869-1315-0*) Wizards of the Coast.

—The Soulforge. 1999. (Dragonlance Chronicles : Vol. 1). 405p. mass mkt. 7.99 (*0-7869-1314-2*) Wizards of the Coast.

—The Sylvan Veil: The Elves of Krynn. 1999. (DragonLance the Fifth Age Ser.). 112p. 18.95 o.p. (*0-7869-1329-0*) Wizards of the Coast.

Weis, Margaret. Dragonlance Chronicles Collector's Edition. 1988. (Dragonlance Chronicles ). pap. 16.99 o.p. (*0-88038-652-5*) Wizards of the Coast.

—Dragonlance Legends Trilogy. 1986. (DragonLance Legends Ser.). pap. 14.85 o.p. (*0-88038-303-8*) TSR, Inc.

—Dragons of Autumn Twilight. 2000. (Dragonlance Ser.). (Illus.). 444p. mass mkt. 7.99 (*0-7869-1574-9*) Wizards of the Coast.

—Dragons of Summer Flame. abr. ed. 2001. audio 21.95 (*1-56511-585-6*) HighBridge Co.

—Dragons of Winter Night. (Illus.). 2003. (Dragonlance Chronicles : Vol. 2). 368p. 27.95 (*0-7869-3067-5*); Vol. 2. 2000. 395p. mass mkt. 7.99 (*0-7869-1609-5*) Wizards of the Coast.

—The Soul Forge. 1998. (Dragonlance Saga Ser.). 347p. 23.95 (*0-7869-0645-6*) Wizards of the Coast.

—Test of the Twins, Vol. 3. 1993. 3.99 o.p. (*0-517-10712-0*) Random Hse. Value Publishing.

Weis, Margaret & Hickman, Tracy. Dragonlance Chronicles. 1988. (Dragonlance Chronicles ). 16.95 o.p. (*0-88038-543-X*) TSR, Inc.

—Dragonlance Chronicles Gift Set, 3 vols. Incl. Dragons of Autumn Twilight. 448p. 1984. pap. 2.95 o.p. (*0-394-72792-4*); . Dragons of Spring Dawning. 400p. 1985. pap. 3.50 o.p. (*0-394-74183-8*); . Dragons of Winter Night. 400p. 1985. pap. 3.50 o.p. (*0-394-73975-2*); (Illus.). 1985. Set pap. 9.95 o.p. (*0-394-74182-X*, Random Hse. Bks. for Young Readers) Random Hse. Children's Bks.

—The Dragonlance Legends. 1988. (Dragonlance Collector's Edition Ser.). 912p. 16.95 o.p. (*0-88038-610-X*) TSR, Inc.

—The Dragonlance Legends. 1988. (Dragonlance Collector's Edition Ser.). 912p. pap. 12.95 o.p. (*0-88038-653-3*) Wizards of the Coast.

—Dragons of a Fallen Sun. (Dragonlance Legends Ser.: Vol. 1). (Illus.). 2003. 624p. mass mkt. 7.99 (*0-7869-1807-1*); 2000. 548p. 27.95 (*0-7869-1564-1*) Wizards of the Coast.
—Dragons of a Vanished Moon. (Dragonlance Ser.: Vol. III). 2003. 624p. mass mkt. 7.99 (*0-7869-2950-2*); 2002. (Illus.). 560p. 27.95 (*0-7869-2740-2*) Wizards of the Coast.
—Dragons of Autumn Twilight. 1984. (Dragonlance Chronicles : Vol. 1). 448p. pap. 2.95 o.p. (*0-394-72792-4*, Random Hse. Bks. for Young Readers) Random Hse. Children's Bks.
—Dragons of Autumn Twilight. 2003. (Dragonlance Chronicles : Vol. 1). 416p. 27.95 (*0-7869-3064-0*) Wizards of the Coast.
—Dragons of Spring Dawning. 1985. (Dragonlance Chronicles : Vol. 3). 400p. pap. 3.50 o.p. (*0-394-74183-8*, Random Hse. Bks. for Young Readers) Random Hse. Children's Bks.
—Dragons of Spring Dawning. (Illus.). 2003. 352p. 27.95 (*0-7869-3070-5*); 2000. (Dragonlance Chronicles : Vol. 3). 379p. pap. 6.99 o.p. (*0-88038-175-2*); 2000. (Dragonlance Chronicles : Vol. 3). 380p. mass mkt. 7.99 (*0-7869-1589-7*, TSR21589) Wizards of the Coast.
—Dragons of Summer Flame. (Dragonlance Chronicles ). 1996. (Illus.). 585p. pap. 7.99 (*0-7869-0523-9*); 1995. (Illus.). 560p. 23.95 o.p. (*0-7869-0189-6*); 2002. 608p. reprint ed. pap. 7.99 (*0-7869-2708-9*) Wizards of the Coast.
—Dragons of Winter Night. 1985. (Dragonlance Chronicles : Vol. 2). 400p. pap. 3.50 o.p. (*0-394-73975-2*, Random Hse. Bks. for Young Readers) Random Hse. Children's Bks.
—Dragons of Winter Night. 1995. (Dragonlance Chronicles : Vol. 2). (Illus.). 399p. pap. 6.99 (*0-88038-174-4*) Wizards of the Coast.
—The Second Generation. (Dragonlance Saga Ser.). 1995. (Illus.). 440p. pap. 5.99 (*0-7869-0260-4*); 1994. 320p. 19.95 o.p. (*1-56076-822-3*); 2002. 448p. reprint ed. pap. 7.99 (*0-7869-2694-5*) Wizards of the Coast.
—Test of the Twins. (Dragonlance Legends Ser.: Vol. 3). 2001. 400p. pap. 7.99 (*0-7869-1806-3*); 1995. 343p. pap. 6.99 o.p. (*0-7869-0264-7*) Wizards of the Coast.
—Time of the Twins. 1996. (Dragonlance Legends Ser.: Vol. 1). 398p. mass mkt. 6.99 o.s.i (*0-7869-0262-0*) Wizards of the Coast.
—War of the Twins. 1995. (Dragonlance Legends Ser.: Vol. 2). 387p. mass mkt. 6.99 o.p. (*0-7869-0263-9*) Wizards of the Coast.
Weis, Margaret & Hickman, Tracy, eds. The Dragons of Krynn. 1994. (Dragonlance Ser.). 390p. (Orig.). pap. 5.99 (*1-56076-830-4*) Wizards of the Coast.
—Love & War. 1987. (DragonLance Tales Ser.: Vol. 3). (Illus.). 364p. mass mkt. 5.99 (*0-88038-519-7*) Wizards of the Coast.
Weis, Margaret & Perrin, Don. The Doom Brigade. 1996. 309p. 23.99 o.p. (*0-7869-0526-3*) TSR, Inc.
—The Doom Brigade. 1998. (DragonLance Chaos War Ser.). 344p. mass mkt. 7.99 (*0-7869-0785-1*) Wizards of the Coast.
Weis, Margaret, et al. Dragons of Autumn Twilight. 1994. (Dragonlance Chronicles : Vol. 1). (Illus.). 447p. pap. 6.99 (*0-88038-173-6*) Wizards of the Coast.

**KZIN (IMAGINARY PLACE)—FICTION**

Anderson, Poul. Inconstant Star: Man-Kzin Wars. 1991. 320p. mass mkt. 4.95 o.s.i (*0-671-72031-7*) Baen Bks.
Ing, Dean. Cathouse: Man-Kzin Wars. 1990. pap. 3.95 o.s.i (*0-671-69872-9*) Baen Bks.
Martin, Mark O. & Benford, Gregory. A Darker Geometry: A Man-Kzin Novel. 1996. 432p. pap. 5.99 (*0-671-87740-2*) Baen Bks.
Niven, Larry. The Best of All Possible Wars: The Best of the Man-Kzin Wars. 1998. pap. 62.91 (*0-671-71327-2*) Baen Bks.
—The Man-Kzin Wars. 1990. mass mkt. 4.50 o.s.i (*0-671-72035-X*) Baen Bks.
—The Man-Kzin Wars IV. 1991. 320p. mass mkt. 4.95 o.s.i (*0-671-72079-1*) Baen Bks.
Niven, Larry, creator. The Best of All Possible Wars. 1998. (Man-Kzin Wars Ser.). 352p. pap. 6.99 (*0-671-87879-4*) Baen Bks.
—Choosing Names. 2002. (Man-Kzin Wars Ser.: Vol. 8). 288p. pap. 6.99 (*0-671-87888-3*) Baen Bks.
—The Man-Kzin Wars. (Man-Kzin Wars Ser.). 1991. 304p. reprint ed. pap. 6.99 (*0-671-72076-7*); Vol. 6. 1994. 320p. pap. 5.99 (*0-671-87607-4*); Vol. IX. 2002. 352p. 22.00 (*0-671-31838-1*) Baen Bks.
—The Man-Kzin Wars V. 2002. (Man-Kzin Wars Ser.: Vol. 5). 336p. pap. 5.99 (*0-671-72137-2*) Baen Bks.
—The Man-Kzin Wars VII. 1995. 352p. pap. 5.99 (*0-671-87670-8*) Baen Bks.
—The Wunder War: Man-Kzin Wars X. 2003. 352p. 21.00 (*0-7434-3619-9*) Baen Bks.
Niven, Larry, et al. The Man-Kzin Wars II. 1990. 320p. mass mkt. 5.99 (*0-671-72036-8*) Baen Bks.
—The Man-Kzin Wars III. 1990. 320p. mass mkt. 5.99 (*0-671-72008-2*) Baen Bks.

## L

**LABORNOK (IMAGINARY PLACE)—FICTION**

Bradley, Marion Zimmer. Lady of the Trillium. 1996. 320p. mass mkt. 5.99 o.s.i (*0-553-57263-6*, Spectra); 1995. 304p. 22.95 o.s.i (*0-553-09299-5*) Bantam Bks.

**LAKE WOBEGON (MINN.: IMAGINARY PLACE)—FICTION**

Boyd, Frances & Quinn, David. Stories from Lake Wobegon: Advanced Listening & Conversation Skills. 1990. (Illus.). 184p. (YA). pap. text 23.45 (*0-8013-0312-5*, 78017) Longman Publishing Group.
Keillor, Garrison. The Garrison Keillor Box: Lake Wobegon Days, Leaving Home, Happy to Be Here, & We Are Still Married, 4 bks., Set. 1992. reprint ed. 37.50 o.p. (*0-14-095358-2*, Penguin Bks.) Penguin Group (USA) Inc.
—Gospel Birds & Other Stories of Lake Wobegon. audio 14.38. audio compact disk 23.98 NewSound, LLC.
—Lake Wobegon Days. abr. ed. 1999. audio compact disk 36.95 (*1-56511-314-4*); 1991. audio 34.95 (*0-942110-08-0*) HighBridge Co.
—Lake Wobegon Days. 1990. (Illus.). 352p. pap. 14.00 (*0-14-013161-2*, Penguin Bks.); 1989. 432p. pap. 4.95 o.p. (*0-14-012918-9*) Penguin Group (USA) Inc.
—Lake Wobegon Days. 1986. 420p. pap. 3.95 o.p. (*0-14-009232-3*, Penguin Bks.); 1986. 432p. pap. 4.95 o.p. (*0-14-009983-2*, Penguin Bks.); 1985. 384p. 17.95 o.p. (*0-670-80514-9*) Viking Penguin.
—Lake Wobegon Loyalty Days. abr. ed. 1991. (Lake Wobegon Ser.). audio 11.00 (*0-942110-33-1*); audio compact disk 13.95 (*0-942110-34-X*) HighBridge Co.
—Lake Wobegon Sampler. 1986. audio 5.95 (*0-440-85047-9*, RH Audio) Random Hse. Audio Publishing Group.
—Lake Wobegon Summer 1956. l.t. ed. 2001. 341p. pap. 14.00 (*0-7838-9569-0*, Wheeler Publishing, Inc.) Gale Group.
—Lake Wobegon Summer 1956. 2002. 304p. pap. 14.00 (*0-14-200093-0*) Penguin Group (USA) Inc.
—Lake Wobegon Summer 1956. l.t. ed. 2001. 350p. 31.95 (*0-7838-9564-X*) Thorndike Pr.
—Lake Wobegon Summer 1956. 2001. (Illus.). 336p. 24.95 o.s.i (*0-670-03003-1*, Viking) Viking Penguin.
—Lake Wobegon U. S. A. abr. unabr. ed. 1993. (Lake Wobegon Ser.). 23p. audio compact disk 34.95 (*1-56511-001-3*); audio compact disk 36.95 (*1-56511-008-0*) HighBridge Co.
—Lake Wobegon U. S. A. Fertility. abr. unabr. ed. 1995. (Lake Wobegon Ser.). audio 11.00 (*1-56511-110-9*) HighBridge Co.
—Lake Wobegon U. S. A. Patience. abr. unabr. ed. 1995. (Lake Wobegon Ser.). audio 11.00 (*1-56511-109-5*) HighBridge Co.
—Lake Wobegon U. S. A. Rhubarb. abr. unabr. ed. 1995. (Lake Wobegon Ser.). audio 11.00 (*1-56511-112-5*) HighBridge Co.
—Lake Wobegon U. S. A. Youth. abr. unabr. ed. 1995. (Lake Wobegon Ser.). pap. 11.00 incl. audio (*1-56511-111-7*) HighBridge Co.
—Leaving Home. 1989. 288p. mass mkt. 4.95 o.p. (*0-451-82197-1*) NAL.
—Leaving Home. 1990. 288p. pap. 14.00 (*0-14-013160-4*); 1989. (*0-14-770045-0*) Penguin Group (USA) Inc. (Penguin Bks.).
—Leaving Home. 1987. 288p. 18.95 o.p. (*0-670-81976-X*, Viking) Viking Penguin.
—Life These Days: Stories from Lake Wobegon. abr. unabr. ed. 1998. 3p. audio 18.95 (*1-56511-293-8*); audio 30.00 (*1-56511-307-1*) HighBridge Co.
—More News from Lake Wobegon. abr. ed. 1991. (Lake Wobegon Ser.). audio compact disk 36.95 (*0-942110-37-4*); audio 34.95 (*0-942110-30-7*) HighBridge Co.
—More News from Lake Wobegon: Faith. abr. ed. 1991. (More News from Lake Wobegon Ser.). audio 11.00 (*0-942110-75-7*) HighBridge Co.
—More News from Lake Wobegon: Hope. abr. ed. 1991. (More News from Lake Wobegon Ser.). audio 11.00 (*0-942110-76-5*) HighBridge Co.
—More News from Lake Wobegon: Humor. abr. ed. 1991. (More News from Lake Wobegon Ser.). audio 12.95 (*0-942110-78-1*) HighBridge Co.
—More News from Lake Wobegon: Love. abr. ed. 1991. (Lake Wobegon Ser.). audio 11.00 (*0-942110-77-3*) HighBridge Co.
—News from Lake Wobegon: Fall. abr. ed. (News from Lake Wobegon Ser.). 1997. audio compact disk 13.95 (*1-56511-214-8*); 1991. audio 11.00 (*0-942110-22-6*) HighBridge Co.
—News from Lake Wobegon: Spring. abr. ed. 1991. (News from Lake Wobegon Ser.). audio 11.00 (*0-942110-19-6*) HighBridge Co.
—News from Lake Wobegon: Summer. abr. ed. (News from Lake Wobegon Ser.). 1997. audio compact disk 13.95 (*1-56511-209-1*); 1991. audio 11.00 (*0-942110-20-X*) HighBridge Co.
—News from Lake Wobegon: Winter. abr. ed. (News from Lake Wobegon Ser.). 1997. audio compact disk 13.95 (*1-56511-215-6*); 1991. audio 11.00 (*0-942110-21-8*, 25024-10749) HighBridge Co.
—News from Lake Wobegon 1974-1994. 20th abr. ed. 1994. (Prairie Home Companion Ser.). audio 34.95 (*1-56511-105-2*) HighBridge Co.
—Wobegon Boy. l.t. ed. 1998. 426p. 27.95 (*1-56895-560-X*, Wheeler Publishing, Inc.) Gale Group.
—Wobegon Boy. 1998. 288p. pap. 14.00 (*0-14-027478-2*) Penguin Group (USA) Inc.
—Wobegon Boy. abr. ed. 1997. (Lake Wobegon Ser.). audio 29.95 (*0-453-00965-4*, 695573) Penguin/HighBridge.
—Wobegon Boy. 1997. 320p. 24.95 (*0-670-87807-3*) Viking Penguin.
Lindvall, Michael L. Leaving North Haven: The Further Adventures of a Small Town Pastor: A Novel. 2002. 224p. pap. 16.95 (*0-8245-2013-0*) Crossroad Publishing Co.
Winter Lake Wobegon. 1986. audio 5.95 (*0-440-85037-1*, RH Audio) Random Hse. Audio Publishing Group.

**LAND OF TRUE GAME (IMAGINARY PLACE)—FICTION**

Tepper, Sheri S. Dervish Daughter. 1986. 224p. (Orig.). mass mkt. 2.95 (*0-8125-5612-7*, Tor Bks.) Doherty, Tom Assocs., LLC.
—The Flight of Mavin Manyshaped. 1985. 192p. mass mkt. 2.75 o.s.i (*0-441-24092-5*) Ace Bks.
—Jinian Footseer. 1985. 288p. mass mkt. 2.95 (*0-8125-5610-0*, Tor Bks.) Doherty, Tom Assocs., LLC.
—Jinian Star Eye. 1986. (Illus.). 256p. (Orig.). mass mkt. 2.95 (*0-8125-5614-3*, Tor Bks.) Doherty, Tom Assocs., LLC.
—King's Blood Four. 1985. 208p. mass mkt. 3.50 o.s.i (*0-441-44526-8*); 1984. mass mkt. 2.75 o.s.i (*0-441-44525-X*); 1983. mass mkt. 2.50 o.s.i (*0-441-44524-1*) Ace Bks.
—Necromancer Nine. 1984. 192p. mass mkt. 3.50 o.s.i (*0-441-56857-2*); 1983. mass mkt. 2.50 o.s.i (*0-441-56853-X*) Ace Bks.
—The Search of Mavin Manyshaped. 1985. 176p. mass mkt. 2.95 o.s.i (*0-441-75712-X*) Ace Bks.
—The Song of Mavin Manyshaped. 1985. 192p. mass mkt. 2.75 o.s.i (*0-441-77523-3*) Ace Bks.
—Wizard's Eleven. 1984. 208p. mass mkt. 3.50 o.s.i (*0-441-90209-X*); mass mkt. 2.50 o.s.i (*0-441-90208-1*) Ace Bks.

**LANDOVER (IMAGINARY PLACE)—FICTION**

*see Magic Kingdom of Landover (Imaginary Place)—Fiction*

**LANKHMAR (IMAGINARY PLACE)—FICTION**

Leiber, Fritz. The Knight & Knave of Swords. 1990. mass mkt. 3.95 o.s.i (*0-441-45125-X*) Ace Bks.
—Swords Against Death. (Fafhrd & Grey Mouser Ser.). 1986. mass mkt. 3.95 o.p. (*0-441-79193-X*); 1984. mass mkt. 2.75 o.s.i (*0-441-79190-5*); 1983. mass mkt. 2.75 o.s.i (*0-441-79158-1*); 1982. mass mkt. 2.50 o.s.i (*0-441-79157-3*); 1981. mass mkt. 2.25 o.s.i (*0-441-79156-5*) Ace Bks.
—Swords Against Death. 1977. (Science Fiction Ser.). lib. bdg. 9.95 o.p. (*0-8398-2399-1*, Macmillan Reference USA) Gale Group.
—Swords Against Death. 2003. 304p. mass mkt. 6.99 (*0-7434-5828-1*) ibooks, Inc.
—Swords Against Wizardry. 1986. (Fafhrd & Grey Mouser Ser.). mass mkt. 3.95 o.s.i (*0-441-79194-8*) Ace Bks.
—Swords Against Wizardry. 1977. (Science Fiction Ser.). lib. bdg. 9.95 o.p. (*0-8398-2401-7*, Macmillan Reference USA) Gale Group.
—Swords Against Wizardry. E-Book 6.99 (*1-58586-363-7*); 2001. E-Book 6.99 (*0-7592-0913-8*) ereads.com.
—Swords Against Wizardry. 2003. 240p. mass mkt. 6.99 (*0-7434-7537-2*) ibooks, Inc.
—Swords & Deviltry. 1986. (Fafhrd & Grey Mouser Ser.: No. 1). 256p. mass mkt. 2.95 o.s.i (*0-441-79198-0*); 1985. mass mkt. 2.95 o.s.i (*0-441-79197-2*); 1985. mass mkt. 2.95 o.s.i (*0-441-79191-3*); 1983. mass mkt. 2.75 o.s.i (*0-441-79179-4*); 1982. mass mkt. 2.50 o.s.i (*0-441-79177-8*); 1981. mass mkt. 2.25 o.s.i (*0-441-79176-X*) Ace Bks.
—Swords & Deviltry. 1977. (Fafhrd & Grey Mouser Ser.). lib. bdg. 9.95 o.p. (*0-8398-2398-3*, Macmillan Reference USA) Gale Group.
—Swords & Deviltry. 2003. 224p. mass mkt. 6.99 (*0-7434-4558-9*) ibooks, Inc.
—Swords & Ice Magic. 1986. mass mkt. 3.95 o.s.i (*0-441-79196-4*); 1984. mass mkt. 2.75 o.s.i (*0-441-79189-1*); 1983. mass mkt. 2.50 o.s.i (*0-441-79178-6*); 1981. mass mkt. 2.25 o.s.i (*0-441-79169-7*) Ace Bks.
—Swords & Ice Magic. 1977. lib. bdg. 9.95 o.p. (*0-8398-2403-3*, Macmillan Reference USA) Gale Group.
—Swords in the Mist. mass mkt. 3.95 o.s.i (*0-441-79129-8*); 1985. mass mkt. 3.95 o.s.i (*0-441-79192-1*); 1983. mass mkt. 2.50 o.s.i (*0-441-79186-7*); 1981. mass mkt. 2.25 o.s.i (*0-441-79185-9*) Ace Bks.
—Swords in the Mist. 1977. (Science Fiction Ser.). lib. bdg. 9.95 o.p. (*0-8398-2400-9*, Macmillan Reference USA) Gale Group.
—Swords in the Mist. E-Book 6.99 (*1-58586-366-1*); E-Book 6.99 (*0-7592-0914-6*) ereads.com.
—Swords in the Mist. 2003. pap. 6.99 (*0-7434-7465-1*) ibooks, Inc.
—The Swords of Lankhmar. 1986. (Fafhrd & Grey Mouser Ser.: No. 4). 320p. mass mkt. 3.95 o.s.i (*0-441-79195-6*) Ace Bks.
—The Swords of Lankhmar. Date not set. 224p. 21.95 (*0-8488-2352-4*) Amereon, Ltd.

Settings

**LAS VEGAS (NEV.)—FICTION**

Baker, Elliott. Klynts Law. 1976. 312p. 8.95 o.p. (*0-15-147283-1*) Harcourt Trade Pubs.
Barton, Dan. Heckler. 2001. 365p. 22.95 (*0-312-27183-2*, Saint Martin's Minotaur) St. Martin's Pr.
Berlin, Adam. Headlock. 2000. 265p. tchr. ed. 21.95 (*1-56512-266-6*, 72266) Algonquin Bks. of Chapel Hill.
Berman, Susan. Lady Las Vegas. 2001. pap. 16.00 (*1-57500-174-8*) TV Bks., L.L.C.
Collins, Jackie. Lethal Seduction. 2003. E-Book 26.00 (*0-7432-1112-X*); 2000. 480p. 26.00 (*0-684-85031-1*) Simon & Schuster. (Simon & Schuster).
—Lethal Seduction. l.t. ed. 2001. 720p. 32.50 o.p. (*0-7432-0425-5*) Thorpe, F. A. Pubs. GBR. *Dist:* Ulverscroft Large Print Bks., Ltd.
Connelly, Michael. Angels Flight. 1999. (Detective Harry Bosch Mysteries Ser.). 400p. (YA). (gr. 8 up). 25.00 o.p. (*0-316-15219-6*) Little Brown & Co.
—Angels Flight. l.t. ed. (Thorndike/G. K. Hall Paperback Bestsellers Ser.). 595p. 2000. pap. 27.95 (*0-7862-1865-7*); 1999. 30.95 (*0-7862-1864-9*) Thorndike Pr.
—Void Moon. 1999. 400p. 24.95 (*0-316-15406-7*); pap. (*0-316-15232-3*) Little Brown & Co.
—Void Moon. l.t. ed. 2000. 592p. 25.00 (*0-375-40862-2*) Random Hse. Large Print.
—Void Moon. abr. ed. 2000. audio 24.98 (*1-57042-711-9*); audio 39.98 (*1-57042-712-7*) Time Warner AudioBooks.
—Void Moon. 2001. 480p. reprint ed. mass mkt. 7.99 (*0-446-60914-5*) Warner Bks., Inc.
Connelly, Michael, contrib. by. Angels Flight. 1999. (*0-7540-1281-6*) BBC Audiobooks America.
Danks, Denise. Wink a Hopeful Eye. 2003. 224p. mass mkt. 7.95 (*0-7528-4397-4*) Orion Publishing Group, Ltd. GBR. *Dist:* Trafalgar Square.
—Wink a Hopeful Eye. 1994. 224p. 19.95 o.p. (*0-312-11355-2*, Saint Martin's Minotaur) St. Martin's Pr.
Dorantes, Jorge. Nada que Ver. 2001. Tr. of Nothing to See. (SPA.). 125p. pap. 13.10 (*968-411-513-X*) Ediciones Era MEX. *Dist:* Continental Bk. Co., Inc.
Douglas, Carole Nelson. The Cat & the Jill of Diamonds. 2000. (Five Star Mystery Ser.). 199p. 22.95 o.p. (*0-7862-2540-8*, Five Star) Gale Group.
—The Cat & the King of Clubs. 1999. (Mystery Ser.). 227p. 20.95 (*0-7862-1920-3*, Five Star) Gale Group.
—The Cat & the Queen of Hearts. 1999. (Mystery Ser.). 223p. 21.95 (*0-7862-2173-9*, Five Star) Gale Group.
—Cat in a Crimson Haze: A Midnight Louie Mystery. 1996. mass mkt. 219.68 (*0-8125-6330-1*); 1996. 408p. mass mkt. 6.99 (*0-8125-4414-5*, Forge Bks.); 1995. 352p. 22.95 o.p. (*0-312-85901-5*, Forge Bks.) Doherty, Tom Assocs., LLC.
—Cat in a Crimson Haze: A Midnight Louie Mystery. l.t. ed. 1995. (Midnight Louie Mystery Ser.). 604p. 24.95 o.p. (*0-7838-1390-2*, Macmillan Reference USA) Gale Group.
—Cat in a Crimson Haze: A Midnight Louie Mystery. 1996. mass mkt. 223.68 (*0-8125-6329-8*) Holtzbrinck Pubs.
—Cat in a Diamond Dazzle: A Midnight Louie Mystery. (Midnight Louie Mystery Ser.). 1997. 411p. mass mkt. 6.99 (*0-8125-5506-6*); 1996. 416p. 24.95 o.p. (*0-312-86085-4*) Doherty, Tom Assocs., LLC. (Forge Bks.).
—Cat in a Flamingo Fedora: A Midnight Louie Mystery. (Midnight Louie Mystery Ser.). 1998. 373p. mass mkt. 6.99 (*0-8125-6535-5*); 1997. 384p. 24.95 o.p. (*0-312-86329-2*) Doherty, Tom Assocs., LLC. (Forge Bks.).
—Cat in a Golden Garland: A Midnight Louie Mystery. (Midnight Louie Mystery Ser.). 1998. 406p. mass mkt. 6.99 (*0-8125-3036-5*); 1997. 352p. 23.95 (*0-312-86386-1*) Doherty, Tom Assocs., LLC. (Forge Bks.).

—Cat in a Golden Garland: A Midnight Louie Mystery. l.t. ed. 1998. (G. K. Hall Core Ser.). 576p. 25.95 o.p. (*0-7838-8419-2*, Macmillan Reference USA) Gale Group.

—Cat in a Jeweled Jumpsuit: A Midnight Louie Mystery. 2000. 432p. mass mkt. 6.99 (*0-8125-6674-2*); 1999. 384p. 24.95 (*0-312-86817-0*) Doherty, Tom Assocs., LLC. (Forge Bks.).

—Cat in a Jeweled Jumpsuit: A Midnight Louie Mystery. l.t. ed. 2000. (Americana Ser.). 599p. 29.95 (*0-7862-2455-X*) Thorndike Pr.

—Cat in a Kiwi Con: A Midnight Louie Mystery. (Midnight Louie Mystery Ser.). 2001. 432p. mass mkt. 6.99 (*0-8125-8425-2*); 2000. 384p. 24.95 o.p. (*0-312-86955-X*) Doherty, Tom Assocs., LLC. (Forge Bks.).

—Cat in a Leopard Spot: A Midnight Louie Mystery. E-Book 24.95 (*0-312-70128-4*, Tor Bks.); 2002. 416p. pap. 6.99 (*0-8125-7022-7*, Forge Bks.); 2001. 384p. 24.95 (*0-312-85370-X*, Forge Bks.) Doherty, Tom Assocs., LLC.

—Cat in a Midnight Choir: A Midnight Louie Mystery. E-Book 24.95 (*0-312-70619-7*, Tor Bks.); 2003. 416p. mass mkt. 24.95 (*0-8125-7021-9*, Forge Bks.); 2002. 336p. 24.95 (*0-312-85797-7*, Forge Bks.) Doherty, Tom Assocs., LLC.

—Cat in a Neon Nightmare. Date not set. mass mkt. (*0-7653-4592-7*, Forge Bks.) Doherty, Tom Assocs., LLC.

—Cat in a Neon Nightmare. l.t. ed. 2003. 582p. 29.95 (*0-7862-5755-5*) Thorndike Pr.

—Cat in a Neon Nightmare: A Midnight Louie Mystery. 2003. (Midnight Louie Mystery Ser.). 384p. 24.95 (*0-7653-0680-8*, Forge Bks.) Doherty, Tom Assocs., LLC.

—Cat in an Indigo Mood: A Midnight Louie Mystery. l.t. ed. 2003. (Large Print Ser.). 29.95 (*1-57490-473-6*, Beeler Large Print Bks.) Beeler, Thomas T. Publisher.

—Cat in an Indigo Mood: A Midnight Louie Mystery. 1999. 384p. mass mkt. 6.99 (*0-8125-6187-2*); (Illus.). 381p. 24.95 (*0-312-86635-6*) Doherty, Tom Assocs., LLC. (Forge Bks.).

—Cat on a Blue Monday: A Midnight Louie Mystery. l.t. ed. 1994. o.p. (*0-7927-2111-X*); pap. o.p. (*0-7927-2110-1*) BBC Audiobooks America.

—Cat on a Blue Monday: A Midnight Louie Mystery. 1994. (Midnight Louie Mystery Ser.). 374p. mass mkt. 6.99 (*0-8125-3441-7*); 384p. 21.95 o.p. (*0-312-85607-5*) Doherty, Tom Assocs., LLC. (Forge Bks.).

—Cat on a Blue Monday: A Midnight Louie Mystery. l.t. ed. 1994. 540p. pap. 17.95 o.p. (*0-8161-7456-3*, Macmillan Reference USA) Gale Group.

—Cat on a Hyacinth Hunt: A Midnight Louie Mystery. (Midnight Louie Mystery Ser.). 384p. 1999. mass mkt. 6.99 (*0-8125-6186-4*); 1998. 23.95 (*0-312-86634-8*) Doherty, Tom Assocs., LLC. (Forge Bks.).

—Cat on a Hyacinth Hunt: A Midnight Louie Mystery. l.t. ed. 2000. pap. 23.95 (*1-56895-872-2*, Wheeler Publishing, Inc.) Gale Group.

—Cat with an Emerald Eye: A Midnight Louie Mystery. (Midnight Louie Mystery Ser.). 384p. 1997. mass mkt. 6.99 (*0-8125-4012-3*); 1996. 24.95 o.p. (*0-312-86228-8*) Doherty, Tom Assocs., LLC. (Forge Bks.).

—Catnap: A Midnight Louie Mystery. l.t. ed. 1993. (Midnight Louie Mystery Ser.). 23.95 o.p. (*0-7927-1644-2*); pap. 21.95 o.p. (*0-7927-1643-4*) BBC Audiobooks America.

—Catnap: A Midnight Louie Mystery. (Midnight Louie Mystery Ser.). 1993. 241p. mass mkt. 6.99 (*0-8125-1682-6*, Forge Bks.); 1992. 256p. 17.95 o.p. (*0-312-85217-7*, Tor Bks.) Doherty, Tom Assocs., LLC.

—Pussyfoot: A Midnight Louie Mystery. l.t. ed. 1994. (Midnight Louie Mystery Ser.). 24.95 o.p. (*0-7927-1846-1*); pap. 22.95 o.p. (*0-7927-1845-3*) BBC Audiobooks America.

—Pussyfoot: A Midnight Louie Mystery. (Midnight Louie Mystery Ser.). 1994. 304p. mass mkt. 5.99 (*0-8125-1683-4*); 1993. 256p. 19.95 o.p. (*0-312-85218-5*) Doherty, Tom Assocs., LLC. (Tor Bks.).

Ellroy, James. The Cold Six Thousand. 2002. 688p. pap. 15.95 (*0-375-72740-X*) Knopf, Alfred A. Inc.

Erdman, Paul E. The Palace. 1988. 320p. mass mkt. 4.95 o.s.i (*0-553-27538-0*) Bantam Bks.

Faherty, Terence. Raise the Devil. 2000. (Scott Elliott Mysteries Ser.). 264p. 23.95 (*0-312-26640-5*, Saint Martin's Minotaur) St. Martin's Pr.

Fleming, Charles. The Ivory Coast: A Novel. 2004. 352p. pap. 14.00 (*0-312-42214-8*) Picador.

—The Ivory Coast: A Novel. 2002. (Illus.). 304p. 24.95 (*0-312-27464-5*, Saint Martin's Minotaur) St. Martin's Pr.

Fletcher, Jessica. You Bet Your Life. 2002. (Murder She Wrote Ser.). 272p. mass mkt. 6.50 (*0-451-20721-1*, Signet Bks.) NAL.

Freeman, Judith. A Desert of Pure Feeling. 1997. 288p. pap. 19.00 (*0-679-75271-4*) Random Hse., Inc.

—A Desert of Pure Feeling: A Novel. 1996. 288p. 24.00 o.s.i (*0-679-43290-6*, Pantheon) Knopf Publishing Group.

Goldman, Ivan G. Where the Money Is: A Novel of Las Vegas. 1995. 192p. 22.00 (*1-56980-052-9*) Barricade Bks., Inc.

Granger, Bill. Drover. 1992. 272p. mass mkt. 4.99 (*0-380-71210-5*, Avon Bks.) Morrow/Avon.

—Drover & the Designated Hitter. 1995. 240p. mass mkt. 4.99 o.p. (*0-380-71909-6*, Avon Bks.); 1994. 223p. 20.00 o.p. (*0-688-11884-4*, Morrow, William & Co.) Morrow/Avon.

—Drover & the Zebras. 1993. 240p. mass mkt. 4.99 (*0-380-71211-3*, Avon Bks.); 1992. 20.00 o.p. (*0-688-09857-6*, Morrow, William & Co.) Morrow/Avon.

Griffin, Dennis N. Killer in Pair a Dice. 2002. 24.91 (*0-7596-2191-8*); 2001. pap. 17.10 (*0-7596-2190-X*) 1stBooks Library.

Hammond, George. Bob & Charlie. 2000. 268p. pap. 21.99 (*0-7388-0593-9*); text 31.99 (*0-7388-0592-0*) Xlibris Corp.

Havens, Dennis. Lucinda. 2001. 216p. pap. 21.99 (*0-7388-6251-7*) Xlibris Corp.

Hodge, Brian. Wild Horses. 2001. 320p. reprint ed. mass mkt. 6.99 (*0-345-43810-8*, Ballantine Bks.) Ballantine Bks.

Kakonis, Tom. Shadow Counter. 1993. 336p. 21.00 o.p. (*0-525-93633-5*, Dutton) Dutton/Plume.

Kellerman, Faye. Moon Music. l.t. ed. 1998. (Large Print Bks.). 621p. 27.95 (*1-56895-672-X*, Wheeler Publishing, Inc.) Gale Group.

—Moon Music, abr. ed. 1999. audio 25.00 Highsmith Inc.

—Moon Music. 1999. 512p. pap. 7.50 (*0-380-72626-2*); 1998. 424p. 25.50 (*0-688-14369-5*, Morrow, William & Co.) Morrow/Avon.

—Moon Music. abr. ed. 1998. audio 25.00 (*0-671-57758-1*, 496018, Simon & Schuster Audioworks) Simon & Schuster Audio.

King, Gary C. An Early Grave. 2001. (True Crime Library). 320p. mass mkt. 6.50 (*0-312-97926-6*, St. Martin's Paperbacks) St. Martin's Pr.

Klein, Daniel. Viva las Vengeance: A Murder Mystery Featuring Elvis Presley. 2003. 288p. 23.95 (*0-312-28806-9*, Saint Martin's Minotaur) St. Martin's Pr.

Kranes, David. Keno Runner: A Dark Romance. 1995. (Western Literature Ser.). 288p. reprint ed. pap. 15.00 (*0-87417-276-4*) Univ. of Nevada Pr.

—Keno Runner: A Romance. 1989. (Fiction Ser.). 17.95 o.p. (*0-87480-320-9*) Univ. of Utah Pr.

Lane, Connie. Guilty Little Secrets. 2003. 352p. mass mkt. 5.99 (*0-440-23746-7*) Dell Publishing.

Lewis, Jim. Real Gone. 1994. (Illus.). 56p. 15.00 (*0-9631095-2-9*) Artspace Bks.

Logsdon, Richard, et al, eds. In the Shadow of the Strip: Las Vegas Stories. 2003. (Western Literature Ser.). 160p. pap. 16.00 (*0-87417-549-6*) Univ. of Nevada Pr.

Lowell, Elizabeth. Running Scared: A Novel of Suspense. 2002. 400p. 24.95 (*0-06-019876-1*, Morrow, William & Co.) Morrow/Avon.

Luke, John. MooMoo's Lottery: Las Vegas. 2001. 266p. pap. 21.99 (*0-7388-6235-5*); text 31.99 (*0-7388-6238-X*); E-Book 8.00 (*0-7388-6236-3*) Xlibris Corp.

Marton, Sandra. Raising the Stakes. 2002. 304p. mass mkt. (*0-373-83511-6*, Harlequin Bks.) Harlequin Enterprises, Ltd.

McMillan, Terry. A Day Late & a Dollar Short. l.t. ed. 661p. 2002. 29.95 (*0-7862-3350-8*); 2001. 32.95 (*0-7862-3349-4*) Thorndike Pr.

—A Day Late & a Dollar Short. Date not set. (*0-670-78287-4*, Viking); 2001. (Illus.). 448p. 25.95 o.s.i (*0-670-89676-4*); 2000. 23.95 (*0-670-86042-5*, Viking) Viking Penguin.

McMurtry, Larry. The Desert Rose. 1976. 22.95 (*0-8488-0371-X*) Amereon, Ltd.

—The Desert Rose. unabr. collector's ed. 1985. audio 48.00 (*0-7366-1007-3*, 1940) Books on Tape, Inc.

—The Desert Rose. Grose, Bill, ed. 1990. 288p. mass mkt. 7.50 (*0-671-72763-X*, Pocket) Simon & Schuster.

—The Desert Rose. 1988. mass mkt. 4.50 (*0-671-66016-0*, Pocket); 1987. 256p. pap. 12.00 (*0-671-63721-5*, Simon & Schuster); 1985. pap. 7.95 o.s.i (*0-671-55537-5*, Touchstone); 1983. 254p. 14.50 o.p. (*0-671-46143-5*, Simon & Schuster); 1983. 254p. 75.00 o.p. (*0-671-49423-6*, Simon & Schuster); 2002. 256p. reprint ed. pap. 12.00 (*0-684-85384-1*, Simon & Schuster) Simon & Schuster.

Michaels, Fern. Vegas Heat. abr. ed. 1997. (Vegas Ser.). audio 7.99 o.p. (*1-56740-236-4*, 715, Paperback Nova Audio Bks.); audio 16.95 o.p. (*1-56100-973-3*, 1399, Nova Audio Bks.); 15p. audio 89.25 o.p. (*1-56100-810-9*, 1086, Unabridged Library Editions); audio 29.95 o.p. (*1-56100-735-8*, 308, Bookcassette) Brilliance Audio.

—Vegas Heat. 1997. 480p. mass mkt. 6.99 o.s.i (*0-8217-5758-X*); 400p. 25.00 o.s.i (*1-57566-138-1*) Kensington Publishing Corp.

—Vegas Rich. abr. ed. (Vegas Ser.). 1997. audio 7.99 o.p. (*1-56740-183-X*, 714, Paperback Nova Audio Bks.); 1996. audio 16.95 o.p. (*1-56100-914-8*, 1400, Nova Audio Bks.); 1996. audio 29.95 o.p. (*1-56100-706-4*, 307, Bookcassette); 1996. audio 121.25 o.p. (*1-56100-331-X*, 1087, Unabridged Library Editions) Brilliance Audio.

—Vegas Rich, Vol. 1. l.t. ed. 1996. 26.95 o.p. (*1-56895-370-4*, Wheeler Publishing, Inc.) Gale Group.

—Vegas Rich. 2001. 54p. mass mkt. 7.50 (*0-8217-7206-6*); 1997. 544p. mass mkt. 6.99 o.s.i (*0-8217-5594-3*); 1996. 512p. 25.00 o.s.i (*1-57566-057-1*) Kensington Publishing Corp.

—Vegas Sunrise. abr. ed. (Vegas Ser.). 1998. audio 7.99 o.s.i (*1-56740-259-3*, 1402, Paperback Nova Audio Bks.); 1997. audio 16.95 o.p. (*1-56100-995-4*, 514, Nova Audio Bks.); 1999. audio 17.95 o.p. (*1-56740-844-3*, 1727, Bookcassette); 1997. audio 89.25 (*1-56100-844-3*, 1088, Unabridged Library Editions); 1997. audio 25.95 (*1-56100-769-2*, 309, Bookcassette) Brilliance Audio.

—Vegas Sunrise. l.t. ed. 1998. 28.95 (*1-56895-571-5*, Wheeler Publishing, Inc.) Gale Group.

—Vegas Sunrise. 1998. 48p. mass mkt. 7.50 o.s.i (*0-8217-7208-2*); 1998. 480p. mass mkt. 6.99 o.s.i (*0-8217-5983-3*); 1997. 384p. 25.00 o.s.i (*1-57566-214-0*) Kensington Publishing Corp.

Moody, Bill. Death of A Tenor Man: An Evan Horne Mystery. 1995. 240p. 21.95 (*0-8027-3269-0*) Walker & Co.

—Death of a Tenor Man: An Evan Horne Mystery. 1997. 288p. mass mkt. 5.50 o.s.i (*0-440-22324-5*) Dell Publishing.

—The Sound of the Trumpet: An Evan Horne Mystery. 1998. (Evan Horne Mysteries Ser.: Vol. 3). 304p. mass mkt. 5.99 o.s.i (*0-440-22194-3*) Dell Publishing.

—The Sound of the Trumpet: An Evan Horne Mystery. 1997. (Evan Horne Mysteries Ser.). 240p. 21.95 (*0-8027-3291-7*) Walker & Co.

Murray, Yxta Maya. What It Takes to Get to Vegas. 2000. 320p. reprint ed. pap. 12.00 (*0-8021-3737-7*, Grove Pr.) Grove/Atlantic, Inc.

Myers, Helen R. Final Stand. 2002. 384p. mass mkt. (*1-55166-878-5*, 1-66878-9, Mira Bks.) Harlequin Enterprises, Ltd.

O'Brien, John. Leaving Las Vegas. 1996. 200p. reprint ed. pap. 11.00 (*0-8021-3445-9*, Grove Pr.) Grove/Atlantic, Inc.

—Leaving Las Vegas. 1991. 206p. 19.50 (*0-922820-12-0*) Watermark Pr., Inc.

Phillips, Gary. High Hand. 2000. 32p. reprint ed. 22.00 o.s.i (*1-57566-616-2*, Dafina) Kensington Publishing Corp.

—High Hand: A Martha Chainey Mystery. 2001. 34p. mass mkt. 5.99 o.s.i (*1-57566-684-7*) Kensington Publishing Corp.

—Shooter's Point. 2002. 34p. mass mkt. 5.99 (*1-57566-745-2*); 2001. 24p. 22.00 (*1-57566-682-0*) Kensington Publishing Corp.

Powers, Tim. Last Call. 1992. (Illus.). 576p. 150.00 (*0-927389-05-3*); tchr. ed. 650.00 (*0-927389-04-5*) Charnel Hse.

—Last Call. 1996. 544p. pap. 15.00 (*0-380-72846-X*, Avon Bks.); 1993. 544p. mass mkt. 4.99 (*0-380-71557-0*, Avon Bks.); 1992. 420p. 23.00 o.p. (*0-688-10732-X*, Morrow, William & Co.) Morrow/Avon.

Puzo, Mario. The Godfather, abr. ed. 1998. audio 24.95 (*1-882071-84-0*) B&B Audio, Inc.

—The Godfather. unabr. collector's ed. 1993. audio 88.00 (*0-7366-2386-8*, 3157) Books on Tape, Inc.

—The Godfather. unabr. ed. 1986. audio 23.95 o.p. (*0-930435-21-4*, 122, Bookcassette); audio 89.25 (*1-56100-016-7*, 1220, Unabridged Library Editions) Brilliance Audio.

—The Godfather. l.t. ed. 1985. (Special Editions Ser.). 688p. 19.95 o.p. (*0-8161-3875-3*, Macmillan Reference USA) Gale Group.

—The Godfather. 1983. 448p. mass mkt. 7.99 (*0-451-16771-6*); mass mkt. 4.95 o.p. (*0-451-15736-2*) NAL. (Signet Bks.).

—The Godfather. 1969. 448p. 24.95 (*0-399-10342-2*, G. P. Putnam's Sons) Penguin Group (USA) Inc.

—The Godfather. l.t. ed. 1986. (Charnwood Large Print Ser.). 752p. 29.99 o.p. (*0-7089-8351-0*, Charnwood) Thorpe, F. A. Pubs. GBR. *Dist:* Ulverscroft Large Print Bks., Ltd., Ulverscroft Large Print Canada, Ltd.

—The Godfather Papers & Other Confessions. 1972. 224p. 6.95 o.p. (*0-399-10935-8*) Putnam Publishing Group, The.

Puzo, Mario & Sinatra, Nancy. The Godfather Pack: The Godfather & Frank Sinatra: An American Legend. abr. unabr. ed. 2001. audio 34.95 (*0-929071-26-3*) B&B Audio, Inc.

Robbins, Harold. The Raiders. unabr. ed. 1996. audio 80.00 (*0-7366-3232-8*, 3893) Books on Tape, Inc.

—The Raiders. l.t. ed. 1995. 24.95 o.p. (*1-56895-262-7*, Wheeler Publishing, Inc.) Gale Group.

—The Raiders. 1995. 496p. mass mkt. 6.99 o.p. (*0-671-87293-1*, Pocket); 363p. 23.00 (*0-671-87289-3*, Simon & Schuster) Simon & Schuster.

—The Raiders. abr. ed. 1995. audio 17.00 (*0-671-52033-4*, Simon & Schuster Audioworks) Simon & Schuster Audio.

Robbins, Harold S. Sin City. 2002. 448p. 25.95 (*0-7653-0001-X*); 2003. 432p. reprint ed. mass mkt. 7.99 (*0-7653-4051-8*) Doherty, Tom Assocs., LLC. (Forge Bks.).

Roman, Hebby. The Best Bet. 2000. 28p. mass mkt. 3.99 o.s.i (*0-7860-1168-8*) Kensington Publishing Corp.

Ruth, Jenifer. The Protector. 2003. 258p. 26.95 (*1-59414-027-8*, Five Star) Gale Group.

Schorr, Mark. Ace of Diamonds. 1984. 224p. 13.95 o.p. (*0-312-00260-2*) St. Martin's Pr.

Shannon, Ray. Firecracker. 2004. 320p. 23.95 (*0-399-15146-X*) Putnam Publishing Group, The.

Sizemore, Susan. Heroes. 2003. (Laws of the Blood Ser.: No. 5). 288p. mass mkt. 6.50 (*0-441-01108-X*) Ace Bks.

Stella, Charlie. Charlie Opera. 2003. 352p. 25.00 (*0-7867-1213-9*) Avalon Publishing Group.

Swain, James. Grift Sense. 2003. 336p. mass mkt. 6.99 (*0-345-46383-8*, Ballantine Bks.) Ballantine Bks.

—Grift Sense. 2001. 320p. 23.95 o.s.i (*0-7434-0622-2*, Atria); 2002. (Illus.). 416p. reprint ed. pap. 6.99 (*0-7434-0623-0*, Pocket) Simon & Schuster.

Tarcher, Mallory. Starring Mom. 1994. (Voices Romance Ser.: No. 3). 224p. mass mkt. 15.00 o.s.i (*0-8217-4675-8*) Kensington Publishing Corp.

Taylor, Theodore. Monocolo. 1989. 18.95 o.p. (*1-55611-165-7*) Fine, Donald I. Bks.

—Monocolo. 1991. 2.99 o.p. (*0-517-06895-8*) Random Hse. Value Publishing.

Ventura, Michael. The Death of Frank Sinatra: A Novel. 1996. 320p. 22.50 o.p. (*0-8050-3738-1*) Holt, Henry & Co.

—The Death of Frank Sinatra: A Novel. 1997. (Dead Letter Mysteries Ser.). 320p. mass mkt. 5.99 (*0-312-96474-9*, St. Martin's Paperbacks) St. Martin's Pr.

Wegner, Hart. Off Paradise. 2001. (Western Literature Ser.). 224p. pap. 17.00 (*0-87417-486-4*) Univ. of Nevada Pr.

Wieland, Liza. Bombshell. 2001. 272p. 19.95 (*0-87074-462-3*) Southern Methodist Univ. Pr.

Winslow, Don. While Drowning in the Desert. 1998. (Neal Carey Mysteries Ser.). 224p. mass mkt. 5.99 (*0-312-96118-9*, St. Martin's Paperbacks) St. Martin's Pr.

—While Drowning in the Desert: A Neal Carey Mystery. 1996. 192p. 20.95 o.p. (*0-312-14446-6*, Saint Martin's Minotaur) St. Martin's Pr.

Yamanaka, Lois-Ann. Father of the Four Passages. 2001. 288p. 23.00 (*0-374-15387-6*) Farrar, Straus & Giroux.

### LATIN AMERICA—FICTION

Argueta, Manlio. A Place Called Milagro de la Paz. Miller, Michael B., tr. 2000. 160p. pap. 14.95 (*1-880684-68-3*) Curbstone Pr.

Buckley, William F., Jr. See You Later, Alligator. 1997. (Blackford Oakes Novel Ser.). 320p. reprint ed. pap. 10.95 (*1-888952-51-2*) Cumberland Hse. Publishing.

—See You Later, Alligator. 1986. mass mkt. 3.95 o.s.i (*0-440-17682-4*) Dell Publishing.

—See You Later, Alligator. 1985. 312p. 16.95 o.p. (*0-385-19442-0*) Doubleday Publishing.

Cabrera, Vicente. La Sombra del Espia. 2002. (SPA.). 297p. pap. 8.00 (*9978-42-083-5*) Editorial Gutenberg.

Conrad, Joseph. Lord Jim & Nostromo. 2000. (Modern Library Ser.). 816p. pap. 12.95 (*0-375-75489-X*, Modern Library) Random House Adult Trade Publishing Group.

—Nostromo & Lord Jim. 2000. E-Book 4.95 (*0-679-64125-4*, Modern Library) Random House Adult Trade Publishing Group.

Freeman, Castle, Jr. My Life & Adventures: A Novel. 2002. 416p. 25.95 (*0-312-28261-3*) St. Martin's Pr.

Garcia Márquez, Gabriel. Cien Anos de Soledad. Joset, Jacques, ed. 8th ed. 1989. (Letras Hispanicas Ser.: Vol. 215). (SPA., Illus.). 559p. pap. 16.95 (*84-376-0494-X*) Ediciones Cátedra ESP. *Dist:* Continental Bk. Co., Inc., Distribooks, Inc., Lectorum Pubns., Inc.

—Cien Anos de Soledad. annot. ed. (Coleccion Centro Literario). (SPA.). pap., stu. ed. 7.95 (*958-02-0503-5*, CAR034) Editorial Voluntad S.A. COL. *Dist:* Continental Bk. Co., Inc.

—Cien Anos de Soledad. 18th ed. 2000. (Nueva Austral Ser.: Vol. 100). (SPA., Illus.). 456p. 14.95 (*84-239-1900-5*) Elliot's Bks.

—Cien Anos de Soledad. (SPA.). 1986. 12.50 o.p. (*0-8288-2516-5*); 11th ed. 1990. 448p. 15.95 o.p. (*0-8288-2567-X*, S7542); 11th ed. 1990. 448p. pap. 19.95 (*0-7859-5010-9*) French & European Pubns., Inc.

—Cien Anos de Soledad. 1997. (SPA.). pap. text 25.98 o.s.i (*968-13-1574-X*) Libros Sin Fronteras.

—Cien Anos de Soledad. (SPA.). 14.00 (*958-04-3952-4*) Norma S.A. COL. *Dist:* Distribuidora Norma, Inc.

—Cien Anos de Soledad. 7th ed. (SPA., Illus.). 496p. 16.95 (*84-01-24226-6*, PJ2266) Plaza & Janés Editories, S.A. ESP. *Dist:* Continental Bk. Co., Inc., Lectorum Pubns., Inc.

—One Hundred Years of Solitude. 1997. Tr. of Cien Anos de Soledad. (C). text 9.38 o.p. (*0-06-502396-X*) Addison-Wesley Longman, Inc.

—One Hundred Years of Solitude. 1976. Tr. of Cien Anos de Soledad. 25.95 (*0-8488-1429-0*) Amereon, Ltd.

—One Hundred Years of Solitude. 1990. Tr. of Cien Anos de Soledad. reprint ed. lib. bdg. 24.95 (*0-89966-703-1*) Buccaneer Bks., Inc.

—One Hundred Years of Solitude. Rabassa, Gregory, tr. from SPA. l.t. ed. 1993. (General Ser.).Tr. of Cien Anos de Soledad. 533p. lib. bdg. 21.95 o.p. (*0-8161-5483-X*, Macmillan Reference USA) Gale Group.

—One Hundred Years of Solitude.Tr. of Cien Anos de Soledad. 2003. 432p. 24.95 (*0-06-053104-5*, HarperCollins); 1998. 464p. pap. 14.00 (*0-06-092979-0*, Perennial) HarperTrade.

—One Hundred Years of Solitude. Rabassa, Gregory, tr. Tr. of Cien Anos de Soledad. 432p. 1970. 30.00 (*0-06-011418-5*); 1991. reprint ed. pap. 13.50 o.p. (*0-06-091965-5*, Perennial) HarperTrade.

—One Hundred Years of Solitude. 1995. Tr. of Cien Anos de Soledad. 480p. 20.00 (*0-679-44465-3*, RH4653) Knopf, Alfred A. Inc.

—One Hundred Years of Solitude. 1976. Tr. of Cien Anos de Soledad. mass mkt. 5.95 o.p. (*0-380-01503-X*, Avon Bks.) Morrow/Avon.

—One Hundred Years of Solitude. 1988. (Monarch Ser.).Tr. of Cien Anos de Soledad. pap. 3.95 o.p. (*0-671-64756-3*) Simon & Schuster.

—One Hundred Years of Solitude. 1998. Tr. of Cien Anos de Soledad. 19.55 (*0-606-20288-9*) Turtleback Bks.

Knox, Elizabeth. Black Oxen. 2001. 448p. 25.00 o.p. (*0-374-11405-6*) Farrar, Straus & Giroux.

—Black Oxen. 2002. 448p. pap. 14.00 (*0-312-42049-8*) Picador.

Lascurain, Randolph E. The Aztec Knight. 2000. 142p. pap. 9.95 (*0-595-00310-9*) F&W Pubns., Inc.

Poniatowska, Elena. The Skin of the Sky. 2004. (*0-374-26575-5*) Farrar, Straus & Giroux.

Restrepo, Laura. A Tale of the Dispossessed. 2004. 176p. pap. 13.95 (*0-06-072370-X*, Ecco) HarperTrade.

**LEBANON—FICTION**

Caputo, Philip. Delcorso's Gallery. 1983. 374p. o.p. (*0-03-058277-6*) Holt, Henry & Co.

—DelCorso's Gallery. 2001. 368p. pap. 14.00 (*0-375-72509-1*, Vintage) Knopf Publishing Group.

—Delcorso's Gallery. 1991. 368p. reprint ed. pap. 11.00 (*0-06-098606-9*, Perennial) HarperTrade.

Chedid, Andree. The Return to Beirut. Schwartss, Ros, tr. from FRE. 1990. Orig. Title: Maison sans racines. 176p. (Orig.). pap. (*1-85242-149-5*) Serpent's Tail Ltd.

Gordon, Alan. Widow of Jerusalem: A Medieval Mystery. 2003. 288p. 23.95 (*0-312-30089-1*, Saint Martin's Minotaur) St. Martin's Pr.

Land, Jon. The Ninth Dominion. 1991. (Orig.). mass mkt. 5.99 o.s.i (*0-449-14775-4*, Fawcett) Ballantine Bks.

Marcom, Micheline Aharonian. Daydreaming Boy. 2004. 208p. 23.95 (*1-57322-264-X*, Riverhead Bks. (Hardcovers)) Putnam Publishing Group, The.

Mattar, Farid. Columns of Stars. 1996. (Orig.). pap. 12.95 (*0-533-11629-5*) Vantage Pr., Inc.

Moreau, C. X. Distant Valor. 1999. 351p. reprint ed. text 24.00 (*0-7881-6623-9*) DIANE Publishing Co.

—Distant Valor. 1998. (Illus.). 416p. mass mkt. 6.99 (*0-8125-5389-6*); 1996. 352p. 23.95 o.p. (*0-312-85941-4*) Doherty, Tom Assocs., LLC. (Forge Bks.).

Peters, Elizabeth, pseud. The Dead Sea Cipher. unabr. ed. 1998. audio compact disk 29.95 (*0-7861-1458-4*); audio 44.95 (*0-7861-1357-X*, 2266) Blackstone Audio Bks., Inc.

—The Dead Sea Cipher. l.t. ed. 2000. 303p. lib. bdg. 25.95 (*1-58547-039-2*) Ctr. Point Large Print.

—The Dead Sea Cipher. 1988. 216p. mass mkt. 4.99 (*0-8125-0756-8*, Tor Bks.) Doherty, Tom Assocs., LLC.

—The Dead Sea Cipher, Set. unabr. ed. 1999. audio 44.95 Highsmith Inc.

—The Dead Sea Cipher. 2001. 384p. mass mkt. 6.99 (*0-380-73114-2*, Avon Bks.) Morrow/Avon.

Pope, Liston, Jr. Redemption: A Novel of War in Lebanon. 294p. 1994. (Works Ser.: Vol. I). 24.95 (*0-9638900-0-X*); 2nd ed. 1997. reprint ed. pap. 15.00 (*0-9638900-2-6*) Mantis Pr.

Saleh, Nabil. Open House. 2001. 208p. pap. 13.95 (*0-7043-8145-1*) Quartet Bks., Ltd. GBR. *Dist:* Interlink Publishing Group, Inc.

**LEMURIA (IMAGINARY PLACE)—FICTION**

Carter, Lin. Thongor Against the Gods. 1967. pap. 1.75 o.s.i (*0-446-94178-6*) Warner Bks., Inc.

—Thongor & the Wizard of Lemuria. 1976. 1.25 o.s.i (*0-425-03435-6*) Berkley Publishing Group.

—Thongor at the End of Time. 1968. pap. 1.75 o.s.i (*0-446-94332-0*) Warner Bks., Inc.

—Thongor Fights the Pirates of Takakus. 1976. 1.25 o.s.i (*0-425-03147-0*) Berkley Publishing Group.

—Thongor in the City of Magicians. 1968. pap. 1.75 o.s.i (*0-446-94208-1*) Warner Bks., Inc.

**LENFELL (IMAGINARY PLACE)—FICTION**

Rawn, Melanie. The Mageborn Traitor. (Exiles Ser.: Vol. 2). 1998. 784p. mass mkt. 7.99 (*0-88677-731-3*); 1997. 626p. 23.95 o.s.i (*0-88677-730-5*) DAW Bks., Inc.

—The Ruins of Ambrai. 1995. (Exiles Ser.: Vol. 1). 848p. mass mkt. 7.99 (*0-88677-668-6*) DAW Bks., Inc.

**LEXINGTON (KY.)—FICTION**

Shoemaker, Bill. Dark Horse. 1997. 312p. mass mkt. 6.99 (*0-449-15003-8*); 1996. 304p. 22.00 o.p. (*0-449-90597-7*) Ballantine Bks. (Fawcett).

**LIADEN UNIVERSE (IMAGINARY PLACE)—FICTION**

Lee, Sharon & Miller, Steve. Partners in Necessity: A Liaden Adventure, 4 vols. 2000. 648p. reprint ed. pap. 18.00 (*1-892065-01-0*) Meisha Merlin Publishing, Inc.

—Plan B Set: A Liaden Adventure, 4 vols. 1999. 335p. pap. 14.00 (*1-892065-00-2*) Meisha Merlin Publishing, Inc.

Miller, Steve & Lee, Sharon. Carpe Diem. 1989. 288p. mass mkt. 3.95 o.s.i (*0-345-36310-8*, Del Rey) Ballantine Bks.

—Conflict of Honors. 1988. 336p. mass mkt. 3.50 o.s.i (*0-345-35353-6*, Del Rey) Ballantine Bks.

—Conflict of Honors. 2000. E-Book 5.00 (*1-58787-002-9*) Embiid Publishing.

Miller, Steve & Lee, Shawn. Agent of Change. 1988. 256p. mass mkt. 3.95 o.s.i (*0-345-34828-1*, Del Rey) Ballantine Bks.

**LICKIN CREEK (PA.: IMAGINARY PLACE)—FICTION**

Malmont, Valerie S. Death, Guns & Sticky Buns. 2000. (Tori Miracle Mysteries Ser.). 320p. mass mkt. 6.50 (*0-440-23598-7*) Bantam Dell Publishing Group.

—Death, Lies & Apple Pies. 1998. (Tori Miracle Mysteries Ser.). 288p. mass mkt. 5.99 (*0-440-22634-1*) Dell Publishing.

—Death, Lies & Apple Pies. l.t. ed. 1997. (Core Ser.). 326p. lib. bdg. 25.95 o.p. (*0-7838-8333-1*, Macmillan Reference USA) Gale Group.

—Death, Lies & Apple Pies. 1997. (Illus.). 224p. 22.00 o.s.i (*0-684-80189-2*, Simon & Schuster) Simon & Schuster.

—Death Pays the Rose Rent: A Tori Miracle Mystery. (Tori Miracle Mysteries Ser.). 1999. 304p. mass mkt. 6.50 (*0-440-22633-3*); 1998. 352p. mass mkt. 5.99 o.s.i (*0-440-22628-7*) Dell Publishing.

—Death Pays the Rose Rent: A Tori Miracle Mystery. 1994. 286p. 20.00 (*0-671-86967-1*, Simon & Schuster) Simon & Schuster.

—Death, Snow & Mistletoe. 2000. (Tori Miracle Mysteries Ser.). 320p. mass mkt. 5.99 (*0-440-23601-0*) Dell Publishing.

**LINCOLN PRAIRIE (ILLINOIS: IMAGINARY PLACE)—FICTION**

Bland, Eleanor Taylor. Dead Time. 1993. 304p. mass mkt. 4.99 o.s.i (*0-451-40427-0*, Signet Bks.) NAL.

—Dead Time: A Marti MacAlister Mystery. 1992. 224p. 17.95 o.p. (*0-312-07053-5*, Saint Martin's Minotaur) St. Martin's Pr.

—Done Wrong. 1996. mass mkt. 5.99 (*0-312-95794-7*, St. Martin's Paperbacks); 1995. 216p. 20.95 o.p. (*0-312-13053-8*, Saint Martin's Minotaur) St. Martin's Pr.

—Gone Quiet. 1995. 336p. mass mkt. 4.99 o.s.i (*0-451-18267-7*, Signet Bks.) NAL.

—Gone Quiet: A Marti MacAlister Mystery. 1994. 224p. 19.95 o.p. (*0-312-11018-9*, Saint Martin's Minotaur) St. Martin's Pr.

—Keep Still. l.t. ed. 1996. (G. K. Hall Mystery Ser.). 316p. 21.95 o.p. (*0-7838-1931-5*, Macmillan Reference USA) Gale Group.

—Keep Still. 1996. 224p. 20.95 o.p. (*0-312-14318-4*, Saint Martin's Minotaur); Vol. 1. 1998. 240p. mass mkt. 5.99 (*0-312-96172-3*, St. Martin's Paperbacks) St. Martin's Pr.

—Scream in Silence: A Marti MacAlister Mystery. 2000. 290p. 23.95 (*0-312-20378-0*, Saint Martin's Minotaur) St. Martin's Pr.

—See No Evil. (Marti MacAlister Ser.). 288p. 1999. mass mkt. 5.99 (*0-312-96818-3*, St. Martin's Paperbacks); 1998. 22.95 o.p. (*0-312-16910-8*, Saint Martin's Minotaur) St. Martin's Pr.

—Slow Burn. 1994. 320p. mass mkt. 4.99 o.s.i (*0-451-17944-7*, Signet Bks.) NAL.

—Slow Burn: A Marti MacAlister Mystery. 1993. 224p. 17.95 o.p. (*0-312-09237-7*, Saint Martin's Minotaur) St. Martin's Pr.

—Tell No Tales: A Marti MacAlister Mystery. l.t. ed. 1999. (Wheeler Large Print Book Ser.). 352p. pap. 23.95 (*1-56895-756-4*, Wheeler Publishing, Inc.) Gale Group.

—Tell No Tales: A Marti MacAlister Mystery. (Marti MacAlister Ser.). 2000. 288p. mass mkt. 5.99 (*0-312-97113-3*, St. Martin's Paperbacks); 1999. vii, 264p. 22.95 o.p. (*0-312-20067-6*, Saint Martin's Minotaur) St. Martin's Pr.

**LISBON (PORTUGAL)—FICTION**

Bianchini, Angela. The Edge of Europe. Jeannet, Angela M. & Castronuovo, David, trs. from ITA. 2000. (European Women Writers Ser.). 145p. pap. 15.00 (*0-8032-6171-3*, Bison Bks.); text 50.00 (*0-8032-1308-5*) Univ. of Nebraska Pr.

Cartland, Barbara. Lovers in Lisbon. 1988. (Camfield Romance Ser.: No. 57). mass mkt. 2.75 o.s.i (*0-515-09545-1*, Jove) Berkley Publishing Group.

—Lovers in Lisbon. l.t. ed. 2000. (G. K. Hall Paperback Ser.). 183p. pap. 23.95 (*0-7838-8929-1*, Macmillan Reference USA) Gale Group.

Nooteboom, Cees. Following Story. 1994. 128p. 14.95 (*0-15-100098-0*) Harcourt Trade Pubs.

—The Following Story. Rilke, Ina, tr. from DUT. 1996. (Harvest Book Ser.). 128p. reprint ed. pap. 11.00 (*0-15-600254-X*, Harvest Bks.) Harcourt Trade Pubs.

Saramago, José. The History of the Siege of Lisbon: A Novel. Pontiero, Giovanni, tr. from POR. & afterword by by. 1998. 324p. pap. 14.00 (*0-15-600624-3*, Harvest Bks.) Harcourt Trade Pubs.

—The History of the Siege of Lisbon: A Novel. Pontiero, Giovanni, tr. from POR. 1997. 320p. 24.00 (*0-15-100238-X*) Harcourt Trade Pubs.

Tabucchi, Antonio. Requiem: A Hallucination. Costa, Jull, tr. 2002. 112p. pap. 12.95 (*0-8112-1517-2*, NDP944) New Directions Publishing Corp.

—Requiem: A Hallucination. Costa, Margaret Jull, tr. from POR. 1994. 128p. 15.95 (*0-8112-1270-X*) New Directions Publishing Corp.

Wilson, Robert. The Company of Strangers. 2002. 496p. pap. 14.00 (*0-15-602710-0*, Harvest Bks.); 2001. 480p. 25.00 o.s.i (*0-15-100846-9*); 2001. 480p. 25.00 (*0-15-100745-4*) Harcourt Trade Pubs.

—A Small Death in Lisbon. 2002. 464p. reprint ed. mass mkt. 7.99 (*0-425-18423-4*) Berkley Publishing Group.

—A Small Death in Lisbon. 2000. (Illus.). 448p. 25.00 (*0-15-100609-1*) Harcourt Trade Pubs.

**LITHUANIA—FICTION**

Brown, Dale. Night of the Hawk. 1993. 576p. mass mkt. 7.99 (*0-425-13661-2*) Berkley Publishing Group.

—Night of the Hawk. 1992. 400p. 22.95 o.p. (*0-399-13739-4*, G. P. Putnam's Sons) Penguin Group (USA) Inc.

—Night of the Hawk. 22.95 o.s.i (*0-399-13904-4*) Putnam Publishing Group, The.

Collishaw, Stephan. The Last Girl: A Novel. Date not set. mass mkt. (*0-312-98903-2*, St. Martin's Paperbacks); 2003. 320p. 24.95 (*0-312-31298-9*) St. Martin's Pr.

Milosz, Czeslaw. The Issa Valley. Iribarne, Louis, tr. from POL. 304p. 2000. pap. 14.00 (*0-374-51695-2*); 1981. 13.95 o.p. (*0-374-17798-8*) Farrar, Straus & Giroux.

Porter, Joe A. Lithuania. (Poetry & Fiction Ser.). 160p. 1990. text 26.00 o.p. (*0-8018-4091-0*); 1967. pap. text 15.95 (*0-8018-4092-9*) Johns Hopkins Univ. Pr.

Schunk, Laurel. A Clear North Light: Book One of the Lithuanian Trilogy. 2001. (Lithuanian Trilogy Ser.). 332p. 24.95 (*0-9661879-6-2*) St Kitts Pr.

**LLANFAIR (WALES: IMAGINARY PLACE)—FICTION**

Bowen, Rhys. Evan & Elle. l.t. ed. 2000. (Beeler Large Print Mystery Ser.). 236p. 26.95 (*1-57490-319-5*, Beeler Large Print Bks.) Beeler, Thomas T. Publisher.

—Evan & Elle: A Constable Evans Mystery. 2001. 224p. reprint ed. mass mkt. 5.99 (*0-425-17888-9*, Prime Crime) Berkley Publishing Group.

—Evan & Elle: A Constable Evans Mystery. 2000. 274p. 22.95 (*0-312-25244-7*, Saint Martin's Minotaur) St. Martin's Pr.

—Evan Help Us. l.t. ed. 1999. (Beeler Large Print Mystery Ser.). 25.95 (*1-57490-213-X*, Beeler Large Print Bks.) Beeler, Thomas T. Publisher.

—Evan Help Us. 1999. (Constable Evan Evans Mysteries Ser.). 224p. reprint ed. mass mkt. 5.99 (*0-425-17261-9*, Prime Crime) Berkley Publishing Group.

—Evan Help Us. 1998. (Constable Evans Mysteries Ser.). 224p. 21.95 (*0-312-19411-0*, Saint Martin's Minotaur) St. Martin's Pr.

—Evanly Choirs. l.t. ed. 1999. (Beeler Large Print Mystery Ser.). 249p. 25.95 (*1-57490-241-5*, Beeler Large Print Bks.) Beeler, Thomas T. Publisher.

—Evanly Choirs. 2000. (Constable Evan Evans Mysteries Ser.). 256p. mass mkt. 5.99 (*0-425-17613-4*) Berkley Publishing Group.

—Evanly Choirs. 1999. (Constable Evans Mysteries Ser.). x, 256p. 22.95 (*0-312-20539-2*, Saint Martin's Minotaur) St. Martin's Pr.

—Evans Above. l.t. ed. 1999. (Beeler Large Print Mystery Ser.). 218p. 25.95 (*1-57490-208-3*, Beeler Large Print Bks.) Beeler, Thomas T. Publisher.

—Evans Above. 1998. (Constable Evan Evans Mysteries Ser.). 224p. reprint ed. mass mkt. 5.99 (*0-425-16642-2*, Prime Crime) Berkley Publishing Group.

Bowen, Rhys & Bowen, J. Evans Above. 1997. (Evan Evans Ser.). 236p. 21.95 (*0-312-16828-4*, Saint Martin's Minotaur) St. Martin's Pr.

**LOBELIA FALLS (ONT.: IMAGINARY PLACE)—FICTION**

Craig, Alisa, pseud. The Grub & Stakers House a Haunt. l.t. ed. 1994. 21.95 o.p. (*0-7927-1919-0*); pap. 19.95 o.p. (*0-7927-1918-2*) BBC Audiobooks America.

—The Grub & Stakers House a Haunt. 224p. 1994. pap. 4.99 (*0-380-71044-7*, Avon Bks.); 1993. 18.00 o.p. (*0-688-08644-6*, Morrow, William & Co.) Morrow/Avon.

—The Grub-&-Stakers Move a Mountain. 1981. (Crime Club Ser.). 192p. 10.95 o.p. (*0-385-17411-X*) Doubleday Publishing.

—The Grub-&-Stakers Move a Mountain. 1987. 192p. pap. 3.50 o.p. (*0-380-70331-9*, Avon Bks.) Morrow/Avon.

—The Grub-&-Stakers Move a Mountain. l.t. ed. 1981. 332p. reprint ed. 9.95 o.p. (*0-89621-288-2*) Thorndike Pr.

—The Grub-&-Stakers Pinch a Poke. 1988. (Illus.). 208p. (Orig.). pap. 3.50 (*0-380-75538-6*, Avon Bks.) Morrow/Avon.

—The Grub-&-Stakers Quilt a Bee. 1985. (Crime Club Ser.). 192p. 11.95 o.p. (*0-385-19767-5*) Doubleday Publishing.

—The Grub-&-Stakers Quilt a Bee. 1987. 192p. pap. 3.50 (*0-380-70337-8*, Avon Bks.) Morrow/Avon.

—The Grub-&-Stakers Spin a Yarn. 1990. 224p. pap. 3.50 (*0-380-75540-8*, Avon Bks.) Morrow/Avon.

**LOCHDUBH (SCOTLAND: IMAGINARY PLACE)—FICTION**

Beaton, M. C., pseud. Death of a Cad. 1988. mass mkt. 4.99 o.s.i (*0-8041-0225-2*, Ivy Bks.) Ballantine Bks.

—Death of a Cad. l.t. ed. 1995. 265p. pap. 17.95 (*0-7838-1457-7*, Macmillan Reference USA) Gale Group.

—Death of a Cad. unabr. ed. 1999. audio 46.00 (*0-7887-4080-6*, H1074E7, Clipper Audio) Recorded Bks., LLC.

—Death of a Cad. 1986. 208p. 13.95 o.p. (*0-312-00118-5*) St. Martin's Pr.

—Death of a Cad. 2000. 222p. pap. 6.95 o.p. (*0-553-40792-9*) Transworld Publishers Ltd. GBR. *Dist:* Trafalgar Square.

—Death of a Cad. 2004. mass mkt. (*0-446-60714-2*) Warner Bks., Inc.

—Death of a Charming Man. 2001. 208p. 18.95 (*0-89296-529-0*) Mysterious Pr.

—Death of a Charming Man. unabr. ed. 1997. (Hamish Macbeth Mystery Ser.). audio 44.00 (*0-7887-1084-2*, 95088E7) Recorded Bks., LLC.

—Death of a Charming Man. 1995. (Hamish Macbeth Mystery Ser.). 176p. reprint ed. mass mkt. 6.99 (*0-446-40338-5*) Warner Bks., Inc.

—Death of a Dentist. 2001. 256p. 22.00 (*0-89296-643-2*); E-Book 4.95 (*0-446-92301-X*); E-Book 4.95 (*0-446-91295-6*) Mysterious Pr.

—Death of a Dentist. unabr. ed. 1998. (Hamish Macbeth Mystery Ser.). audio 44.00 (*0-7887-2044-9*, 95408E7) Recorded Bks., LLC.

—Death of a Dentist. 1998. (Hamish Macbeth Mystery Ser.). 256p. mass mkt. 6.99 (*0-446-60601-4*); mass mkt. (*0-446-40494-2*, Mysterious Pr. Paperback Bks.) Warner Bks., Inc.

—Death of a Glutton. 1995. 176p. mass mkt. 6.50 (*0-8041-1212-6*, Ivy Bks.) Ballantine Bks.

—Death of a Glutton. l.t. ed. 1996. 17.95 o.p. (*0-7838-1484-4*, Macmillan Reference USA) Gale Group.

—Death of a Glutton. 1993. 152p. 16.95 o.p. (*0-312-08761-6*, Saint Martin's Minotaur) St. Martin's Pr.

—Death of a Glutton. 187p. pap. 6.95 o.p. (*0-553-40972-7*) Transworld Publishers Ltd. GBR. *Dist:* Trafalgar Square.

—Death of a Gossip. l.t. ed. 1986. 13.95 o.p. (*0-89340-955-3*, 254) BBC Audiobooks America.

—Death of a Gossip. 1988. 160p. reprint ed. mass mkt. 4.99 o.s.i (*0-8041-0226-0*, Ivy Bks.) Ballantine Bks.

—Death of a Gossip. l.t. ed. 1996. (Nightingale Ser.). 194p. pap. 17.95 o.p. (*0-7838-1472-0*, Macmillan Reference USA) Gale Group.

—Death of a Gossip. 1985. 192p. 12.95 o.p. (*0-312-18637-1*) St. Martin's Pr.

—Death of a Gossip. 1999. (Hamish Macbeth Mystery Ser.). 192p. reprint ed. mass mkt. 6.99 (*0-446-60713-4*) Warner Bks., Inc.

—Death of a Hussy. 1991. 160p. mass mkt. 6.99 (0-8041-0768-8, Ivy Bks.) Ballantine Bks.

—Death of a Hussy. 1990. 160p. 14.95 o.p. (0-312-05071-2, Saint Martin's Minotaur) St. Martin's Pr.

—Death of a Hussy. l.t. ed. 1999. (Nightingale Ser.). 208p. pap. 21.95 (0-7838-8664-0) Thorndike Pr.

—Death of a Hussy. 2000. pap. 6.95 (0-553-40967-0) Transworld Publishers Ltd. GBR. *Dist:* Trafalgar Square.

—Death of a Macho Man. 1996. (Hamish Macbeth Mystery Ser.). 224p. 4.95 o.p. (0-89296-531-2) Mysterious Pr.

—Death of a Macho Man. unabr. ed. 1997. (Hamish Macbeth Mystery Ser.: Vol. 12). audio 44.00 (0-7887-1749-9, 95227E7) Recorded Bks., LLC.

—Death of a Macho Man. 1997. (Hamish Macbeth Mystery Ser.). 240p. mass mkt. 6.99 (0-446-40340-7) Warner Bks., Inc.

—Death of a Nag. 2001. 192p. E-Book 4.95 (0-446-91296-4); 18.95 (0-89296-530-4); E-Book 4.95 (0-446-92302-8) Mysterious Pr.

—Death of a Nag. unabr. ed. 1997. (Hamish Macbeth Mystery Ser.). audio 44.00 (0-7887-1285-3, 95147E7) Recorded Bks., LLC.

—Death of a Nag. 1996. (Hamish Macbeth Mystery Ser.). 192p. mass mkt. 5.99 (0-446-40339-3) Warner Bks., Inc.

—Death of a Perfect Wife. 1990. mass mkt. 4.99 o.s.i (0-8041-0593-6, Ivy Bks.) Ballantine Bks.

—Death of a Perfect Wife. 1989. 224p. 15.95 o.p. (0-312-03322-2, Saint Martin's Minotaur) St. Martin's Pr.

—Death of a Perfect Wife. 2000. 202p. pap. 6.95 o.p. (0-553-40794-5) Transworld Publishers Ltd. GBR. *Dist:* Trafalgar Square.

—Death of a Prankster. 1993. (Hamish Macbeth Mystery Ser.: Vol. 7). 176p. mass mkt. 6.50 (0-8041-1102-2, Ivy Bks.) Ballantine Bks.

—Death of a Prankster. l.t. ed. 1998. (Hamish Macbeth Mystery Ser.). pap. 19.95 o.p. (0-7838-8417-6, Macmillan Reference USA) Gale Group.

—Death of a Prankster. 1992. 160p. 16.95 o.p. (0-312-07701-7, Saint Martin's Minotaur) St. Martin's Pr.

—Death of a Prankster. 187p. pap. 6.95 o.p. (0-553-40969-7) Transworld Publishers Ltd. GBR. *Dist:* Trafalgar Square.

—Death of a Scriptwriter. 224p. 2001. 22.00 (0-89296-644-0); 1999. E-Book 4.95 (0-446-91297-2) Mysterious Pr.

—Death of a Scriptwriter. unabr. ed. 1998. (Hamish Macbeth Mystery Ser.). audio 44.00 (0-7887-2175-5, 95471E7) Recorded Bks., LLC.

—Death of a Scriptwriter. 1999. (Hamish Macbeth Mystery Ser.). 224p. reprint ed. mass mkt. 6.99 (0-446-60698-7) Warner Bks., Inc.

—Death of a Snob. 1992. (Hamish Macbeth Mystery Ser.). 160p. mass mkt. 6.99 (0-8041-0912-5, Ivy Bks.) Ballantine Bks.

—Death of a Snob. l.t. ed. 2000. (G. K. Hall Nightingale Ser.). 210p. 30.00 (0-7838-8755-8, Macmillan Reference USA) Gale Group.

—Death of a Snob. 1991. 15.95 o.p. (0-312-05851-9, Saint Martin's Minotaur) St. Martin's Pr.

—Death of a Snob. 186p. pap. 6.95 o.p. (0-553-40968-9) Transworld Publishers Ltd. GBR. *Dist:* Trafalgar Square.

—Death of a Travelling Man. 1996. 176p. mass mkt. 6.99 (0-8041-1211-8, Ivy Bks.) Ballantine Bks.

—Death of a Travelling Man. 1993. (Hamish Macbeth Mystery Ser.). 208p. 17.95 o.p. (0-312-09783-2, Saint Martin's Minotaur) St. Martin's Pr.

—Death of an Addict. 2001. (Hamish Macbeth Mystery Ser.). 224p. 22.00 o.p. (0-89296-675-0) Mysterious Pr.

—Death of an Addict. unabr. ed. 1999. (Hamish Macbeth Mystery Ser.). audio 46.00 (0-7887-3486-5, 95690E7) Recorded Bks., LLC.

—Death of an Outsider. 1990. (Hamish Macbeth Mystery Ser.). 160p. mass mkt. 4.99 o.s.i (0-8041-0487-5, Ivy Bks.) Ballantine Bks.

—Death of an Outsider. l.t. ed. 1998. (Hamish Macbeth Mystery Ser.). pap. 19.95 o.p. (0-7838-8299-8); (0-7540-3136-5) Gale Group. (Macmillan Reference USA).

—Death of an Outsider. unabr. ed. 1999. (Hamish Macbeth Mystery Ser.). audio 38.00 (1-84197-009-3, H1009E7);Set. audio 38.00 Recorded Bks., LLC.

—Death of an Outsider. 1988. (Hamish Macbeth Mystery Ser.). 192p. 14.95 o.p. (0-312-02188-7, Saint Martin's Minotaur) St. Martin's Pr.

—Death of an Outsider. 2000. (Hamish Macbeth Mystery Ser.). 218p. pap. 6.95 o.p. (0-553-40793-7) Transworld Publishers Ltd. GBR. *Dist:* Trafalgar Square.

—Death of an Outsider: A Hamish Macbeth Mystery. 1991. (Hamish Macbeth Mystery Ser.). 3.99 o.p. (0-517-06864-8) Random Hse. Value Publishing.

**LONDON (ENGLAND)—FICTION**

Abe, Shana. A Kiss at Midnight. 2000. (Meet Me at Midnight Ser.). 368p. mass mkt. 5.99 o.s.i (0-553-58057-4) Bantam Bks.

Abse, Dannie. The Strange Case of Dr. Simmonds & Dr. Glas. 2003. 208p. 23.00 (0-7867-1201-5, Carroll & Graf Pubs.) Avalon Publishing Group.

Ackroyd, Peter. The Great Fire of London. 1982. 192p. o.p. (0-241-10704-0) David & Charles Pubs.

—The Great Fire of London. 1995. 176p. pap. 11.95 o.s.i (0-226-00264-0) Univ. of Chicago Pr.

—Hawksmoor. 1987. 288p. pap. 8.95 o.p. (0-06-091390-8, PL1390, Perennial); 1986. 217p. 16.95 o.p. (0-06-015503-5) HarperTrade.

—The Trial of Elizabeth Cree: A Novel of the Limehouse Murders. unabr. collector's ed. 1997. audio 48.00 (0-7366-3627-7, 4288) Books on Tape, Inc.

—The Trial of Elizabeth Cree: A Novel of the Limehouse Murders. 1995. 272p. 22.00 o.s.i (0-385-47707-4, Talese, Nan A.) Doubleday Publishing.

—The Trial of Elizabeth Cree: A Novel of the Limehouse Murders. unabr. ed. 2000. audio 51.00 (0-7887-0470-2, 94663E7) Recorded Bks., LLC.

Ackroyd, Peter, intro. Bleak House. 1991. (Complete Novels of Charles Dickens Ser.). (Illus.). 935p. (C). pap. 5.50 o.p. (0-7493-0765-X) Heinemann.

Adamoli, Vida. Sons, Lovers, Etcetera. 1997. 250p. pap. 13.95 o.p. (0-7472-5501-6) Headline Bk. Publishing, Ltd. GBR. *Dist:* Trafalgar Square.

Alexander, Bruce. Blind Justice. unabr. ed. 1998. (Sir John Fielding Mystery Ser.: Vol. 1). audio 56.00 (0-7366-4081-9, 4590) Books on Tape, Inc.

—Blind Justice: A Sir John Fielding Mystery. 1995. (Sir John Fielding Mystery Ser.). 336p. mass mkt. 6.50 (0-425-15007-0) Berkley Publishing Group.

—Blind Justice: A Sir John Fielding Mystery. 1994. (Sir John Fielding Ser.). 224p. 19.95 o.p. (0-399-13978-8, G. P. Putnam's Sons) Penguin Group (USA) Inc.

—Blind Justice: A Sir John Fielding Mystery. l.t. ed. 1996. (Large Print Ser.). 576p. 29.99 o.p. (0-7089-3606-7, Ulverscroft) Thorpe, F. A. Pubs. GBR. *Dist:* Ulverscroft Large Print Bks., Ltd., Ulverscroft Large Print Canada, Ltd.

—The Color of Death. 2001. 320p. reprint ed. mass mkt. 6.50 (0-425-18203-7, Prime Crime) Berkley Publishing Group.

—The Color of Death. l.t. ed. 2004. 416p. (0-06-072687-3, HarperLargePrint) HarperTrade.

—The Color of Death. 2004. (0-06-050413-7, Morrow, William & Co.) Morrow/Avon.

—The Color of Death: A Sir John Fielding Mystery. 2000. (Sir John Fielding Mystery Ser.). 288p. 24.95 o.s.i (0-399-14648-2) Penguin Group (USA) Inc.

—Death of a Colonial: A Sir John Fielding Mystery. 1999. (Sir John Fielding Mystery Ser.). 288p. 23.95 o.p. (0-399-14564-8, G. P. Putnam's Sons) Penguin Group (USA) Inc.

—The Death of a Colonial: A Sir John Fielding Mystery. 2000. (Sir John Fielding Ser.). 304p. mass mkt. 6.50 (0-425-17702-5) Berkley Publishing Group.

—Death of a Colonial: A Sir John Fielding Mystery. l.t. ed. 1999. (Core Ser.). 402p. 28.95 (0-7838-8823-6) Thorndike Pr.

—An Experiment in Treason. 2003. 336p. mass mkt. 6.99 (0-425-19281-4, Prime Crime) Berkley Publishing Group.

—An Experiment in Treason: A Sir John Fielding Mystery. 2002. 288p. 24.95 o.s.i (0-399-14923-6) Putnam Publishing Group, The.

—An Experiment in Treason: A Sir John Fielding Mystery. l.t. ed. 2003. (Core Ser.). 415p. 29.95 (0-7862-4992-7) Thorndike Pr.

—Jack, Knave & Fool. unabr. ed. 1999. (Sir John Fielding Mystery Ser.). audio 64.00 Books on Tape, Inc.

—Jack, Knave & Fool: A Sir John Fielding Mystery. 1999. (Sir John Fielding Ser.). 416p. reprint ed. mass mkt. 6.99 (0-425-17120-5, Prime Crime) Berkley Publishing Group.

—Jack, Knave & Fool: A Sir John Fielding Mystery. l.t. ed. 1999. (Basic Ser.). 631p. 28.95 (0-7862-1798-7) Thorndike Pr.

—Jack Knave the Fool. 1998. (Sir John Fielding Mystery Ser.). 288p. 22.95 o.p. (0-399-14419-6, G. P. Putnam's Sons) Penguin Group (USA) Inc.

—Murder in Grub Street. unabr. ed. 1998. (Sir John Fielding Mystery Ser.: Vol. 2). audio 56.00 (0-7366-3998-5, 4498) Books on Tape, Inc.

—Murder in Grub Street: A Sir John Fielding Mystery. 1996. (Sir John Fielding Mystery Ser.). 320p. reprint ed. mass mkt. 6.99 (0-425-15550-1, Prime Crime) Berkley Publishing Group.

—Murder in Grub Street: A Sir John Fielding Mystery. 1995. (Sir John Fielding Ser.). 256p. 21.95 o.p. (0-399-14085-9, G. P. Putnam's Sons) Penguin Group (USA) Inc.

—Murder in Grub Street: A Sir John Fielding Mystery. l.t. ed. 1997. (Ulverscroft Large Print Ser.). 608p. 29.99 (0-7089-3749-7, Ulverscroft) Thorpe, F. A. Pubs. GBR. *Dist:* Ulverscroft Large Print Bks., Ltd., Ulverscroft Large Print Canada, Ltd.

—Person or Persons Unknown, unabr. ed. 1999. (Sir John Fielding Mystery Ser.). audio 56.00 (0-7366-4337-0, 4826) Books on Tape, Inc.

—Person or Persons Unknown: A Sir John Fielding Mystery. 1998. (Sir John Fielding Mystery Ser.: Bk. 4). 336p. reprint ed. mass mkt. 6.99 (0-425-16566-3, Prime Crime) Berkley Publishing Group.

—Person or Persons Unknown: A Sir John Fielding Mystery. 1997. (Sir John Fielding Ser.). 256p. 22.95 o.s.i (0-399-14309-2, G. P. Putnam's Sons) Penguin Group (USA) Inc.

—The Price of Murder: A Sir John Fielding Mystery. 2003. 272p. 24.95 (0-399-15078-1) Putnam Publishing Group, The.

—Watery Grave. 1997. (Sir John Fielding Mystery Ser.). 320p. mass mkt. 6.99 (0-425-16036-X, Prime Crime) Berkley Publishing Group.

—Watery Grave. unabr. ed. 1998. (Sir John Fielding Mystery Ser.: Vol. 3). audio 56.00 (0-7366-3997-7, 4497) Books on Tape, Inc.

—Watery Grave. 1996. (Sir John Fielding Mystery Ser.). 272p. 22.95 o.p. (0-399-14155-3, G. P. Putnam's Sons) Penguin Group (USA) Inc.

—Watery Grave. l.t. ed. 1998. (Ulverscroft Large Print Ser.). 544p. 29.99 o.p. (0-7089-3984-8, Ulverscroft) Thorpe, F. A. Pubs. GBR. *Dist:* Ulverscroft Large Print Bks., Ltd., Ulverscroft Large Print Canada, Ltd.

Ali, Monica. Brick Lane: A Novel. l.t. ed. 2003. 676p. 30.95 (0-7862-6018-1) Gale Group.

—Brick Lane: A Novel. 2003. 384p. 25.00 (0-7432-4330-7); E-Book (0-7432-4971-2) Simon & Schuster. (Scribner).

—Seven Seas, Thirteen Rivers. 2004. 288p. pap. 13.00 (0-7432-4331-5, Scribner) Simon & Schuster.

Allbeury, Ted. The Stalking Angel. 208p. 1989. mass mkt. 3.95 o.s.i (0-445-40834-0); 1988. 17.95 (0-89296-184-8) Mysterious Pr.

Allingham, Margery. Flowers for the Judge. 1995. (Illus.). 248p. mass mkt. 4.50 (0-7867-0291-5, Carroll & Graf Pubs.) Avalon Publishing Group.

—Flowers for the Judge. 1984. 256p. mass mkt. 3.95 o.s.i (0-553-24190-7) Bantam Bks.

Alvarez, Alfred. Day of Atonement. 1993. 3.99 o.p. (0-517-09789-3) Random Hse. Value Publishing.

Ambrose, David. Coincidence. 2002. 320p. 23.95 o.p. (0-446-52797-1) Warner Bks., Inc.

Amis, Kingsley. The Folks That Live on the Hill. 1990. 18.95 o.p. (0-671-70816-3) Summit Bks.

Amis, Martin. London Fields. 1991. (Vintage International Ser.). 480p. pap. 14.00 (0-679-73034-6, Vintage) Knopf Publishing Group.

—Other People: A Mystery Story. 1994. 224p. pap. 13.00 (0-679-73589-5, Vintage) Knopf Publishing Group.

—Other People: A Mystery Story. 1981. 12.95 o.p. (0-670-52948-6) Viking Penguin.

Andersen, R. C. The Privateer. 1999. 192p. 19.95 (0-9666946-0-0) Spring Publishing.

Andrew, Sylvia. Serena. 2000. 256p. mass mkt. (0-373-51116-7, 1-51116-1, Harlequin Bks.) Harlequin Enterprises, Ltd.

Andrews, V. C. Lightning Strikes. 2001. 424p. (0-7540-2432-6); (0-7540-1570-X) Gale Group. (Macmillan Reference USA).

—Lightning Strikes. 2000. (Hudson Family Ser.: Vol. 2). 368p. 24.95 o.s.i (0-671-00768-8, Atria); 384p. pap. 7.99 (0-671-00769-6, Pocket) Simon & Schuster.

—Lightning Strikes. l.t. ed. 2001. (G. K. Hall Core Ser.). (Illus.). 352p. 31.95 (0-7838-9316-7) Thorndike Pr.

—Lightning Strikes. 2000. (Illus.). (J). 14.04 (0-606-18830-4) Turtleback Bks.

Argers, Helen. Noblesse Oblige. l.t. ed. 1995. 424p. reprint ed. lib. bdg. 22.95 (0-7838-1230-2, Macmillan Reference USA) Gale Group.

—Noblesse Oblige. 1994. 320p. 21.95 o.p. (0-312-11324-2) St. Martin's Pr.

Armstrong, Campbell. Jigsaw. 1996. 476p. mass mkt. 8.99 o.s.i (0-552-14168-2) Bantam Bks.

—Jigsaw. 1997. 352p. mass mkt. 5.99 o.s.i (0-7860-0412-6, Pinnacle Bks.) Kensington Publishing Corp.

—Jigsaw. 1995. 431p. 21.95 o.p. (0-316-04821-6) Little Brown & Co.

Arnott, Jake. He Kills Coppers: A Novel. 2002. 336p. pap. 13.00 (0-15-602693-7, Harvest Bks.) Harcourt Trade Pubs.

—He Kills Coppers: A Novel. 2002. 340p. 25.00 (1-56947-271-8) Soho Pr., Inc.

—The Long Firm. 2001. 343p. reprint ed. 25.00 (1-56947-169-X) Soho Pr., Inc.

Ashford, Jeffrey. Judgement Deferred. l.t. ed. 1995. (Nightingale Ser.). 252p. pap. 17.95 (0-8161-7470-9, Macmillan Reference USA) Gale Group.

—Judgment Deferred. 1994. 176p. 18.95 o.p. (0-312-11012-X, Saint Martin's Minotaur) St. Martin's Pr.

Aumonier, Stacy & Belcher, George F. Odd Fish. 1977. (Short Story Index Reprint Ser.). 19.95 (0-8369-3431-8) Ayer Co. Pubs., Inc.

Aycliffe, Jonathon. The Talisman. 2001. 210p. 24.99 (0-7278-5696-0) Severn Hse. Pubs., Ltd.

Babson, Marian. Break a Leg, Darlings. l.t. ed. 1997. (G. K. Hall Nightingale Ser.). 300p. lib. bdg. 18.95 o.p. (0-7838-8036-7, Macmillan Reference USA) Gale Group.

—Break a Leg, Darlings. 1997. 183p. 20.95 o.p. (0-312-15285-X, Saint Martin's Minotaur) St. Martin's Pr.

—The Cat Next Door. l.t. ed. 2002. (Mystery Ser.). 300p. 30.95 (0-7862-4552-2) Thorndike Pr.

—The Company of Cats. l.t. ed. 1999. (Beeler Large Print Mystery Ser.). 216p. 24.95 (1-57490-209-1, Beeler Large Print Bks.) Beeler, Thomas T. Publisher.

—The Company of Cats. 2000. 192p. mass mkt. 5.99 (0-312-97501-5, St. Martin's Paperbacks); 1999. 183p. 20.95 o.p. (0-312-19924-4, Saint Martin's Minotaur) St. Martin's Pr.

—Cover-up Story. 1991. 208p. mass mkt. 3.99 o.s.i (0-553-29330-3) Bantam Bks.

—Cover-up Story. l.t. ed. 1991. (Nightingale Ser.). 264p. pap. 14.95 o.p. (0-8161-4926-7, Macmillan Reference USA) Gale Group.

—Cover-up Story. 2003. 224p. mass mkt. 6.50 (0-312-98822-2, St. Martin's Paperbacks); 1988. 192p. 14.95 o.p. (0-312-02180-1, Saint Martin's Minotaur) St. Martin's Pr.

—Encore Murder. l.t. ed. 1991. (Nightingale Ser.). 275p. pap. 14.95 o.p. (0-8161-5139-3, Macmillan Reference USA) Gale Group.

—Encore Murder. 1990. 15.95 o.p. (0-312-04964-1, Saint Martin's Minotaur) St. Martin's Pr.

—In the Teeth of Adversity. 1992. 208p. mass mkt. 4.99 o.s.i (0-553-29131-9) Bantam Bks.

—In the Teeth of Adversity. l.t. ed. 1992. (Nightingale Ser.). 250p. 14.95 o.p. (0-8161-5259-4, Macmillan Reference USA) Gale Group.

—In the Teeth of Adversity. 2003. 176p. mass mkt. 6.50 (0-312-99103-7, St. Martin's Paperbacks); 1990. 14.95 o.p. (0-312-04332-5, Saint Martin's Minotaur) St. Martin's Pr.

—Murder at the Cat Show. 1990. 192p. reprint ed. mass mkt. 3.95 o.s.i (0-553-28590-4) Bantam Bks.

—Murder at the Cat Show. l.t. ed. 1992. (Nightingale Ser.). 264p. 14.95 o.p. (0-8161-5258-6, Macmillan Reference USA) Gale Group.

—Murder at the Cat Show. pap. 15.95 (0-312-31278-4, Saint Martin's Griffin); 2003. 192p. mass mkt. 5.99 (0-312-98974-1, St. Martin's Paperbacks); 1989. 14.95 o.p. (0-312-02954-3, Saint Martin's Minotaur) St. Martin's Pr.

—Past Regret. 1992. 192p. 16.95 o.p. (0-312-07763-7, Saint Martin's Minotaur) St. Martin's Pr.

—Reel Murder, unabr. ed. 1993. audio 39.95 (0-7451-5753-X, CAT 4025) BBC Audiobooks America.

—Reel Murder. 1988. mass mkt. 3.50 o.s.i (0-553-27361-2) Bantam Bks.

—Reel Murder. l.t. ed. 1988. (Nightingale Ser.). 307p. 12.95 o.p. (0-8161-4492-3, Macmillan Reference USA) Gale Group.

—Reel Murder. 1987. 192p. 12.95 o.p. (0-312-00227-0) St. Martin's Pr.

—Reel Murder. 1988. audio 35.95 o.p. (0-8161-7780-5) Thorndike Pr.

—Shadows in Their Blood. l.t. ed. 1994. 322p. lib. bdg. 16.95 (0-8161-5952-1, Macmillan Reference USA) Gale Group.

—Shadows in Their Blood. 1993. 192p. 16.95 o.p. (0-312-09383-7, Saint Martin's Minotaur) St. Martin's Pr.

—Tourists Are for Trapping. 1991. 192p. mass mkt. 3.99 o.s.i (0-553-29031-2) Bantam Bks.

—Tourists Are for Trapping. 1992. 2.99 o.p. (0-517-09060-0) Random Hse. Value Publishing.

—Tourists Are for Trapping. 2003. 208p. mass mkt. 5.99 (0-312-99099-5, St. Martin's Paperbacks); 1989. 192p. 14.95 o.p. (0-312-03444-X, Saint Martin's Minotaur) St. Martin's Pr.

—The Twelve Deaths of Christmas. 1981. 192p. mass mkt. 2.25 o.s.i (0-440-19183-1) Dell Publishing.

—The Twelve Deaths of Christmas. l.t. ed. 1993. 11.50 o.p. (0-8161-3183-X, Macmillan Reference USA) Gale Group.

—The Twelve Deaths of Christmas, Vol. 1. 1996. (Twelve Deaths of Christmas Ser.: Vol. 1). 170p. mass mkt. 4.99 (0-312-96039-5, St. Martin's Paperbacks) St. Martin's Pr.

—The Twelve Deaths of Christmas. 1980. 180p. 10.95 o.p. (0-8027-5426-0) Walker & Co.

Bagshawe, Louise. The Devil You Know: A Novel. 2003. 384p. 24.95 (0-312-27305-3) St. Martin's Pr.

Bailey, Eleanor. Idioglossia. 2003. 448p. pap. 13.00 (0-552-99860-5) Black Swan GBR. *Dist:* Trafalgar Square.

—Idioglossia. 2000. 381p. (0-385-60114-X) Doubleday Publishing.

Bainbridge, Beryl. According to Queeney. 224p. 2001. 22.00 (0-7867-0773-9); 2002. reprint ed. pap. 12.00 (0-7867-0982-0) Avalon Publishing Group. (Carroll & Graf Pubs.).

—According to Queeney. l.t. ed. 2002. 242p. pap. 23.95 (0-7862-3958-1) Gale Group.

—Sweet William. 1976. 192p. 7.95 o.s.i (0-8076-0816-5) Braziller, George Inc.

Baker, Donna. Fortune's Song. 2002. 256p. 25.99 (*0-7278-5648-0*); 28.99 (*0-7278-7134-X*) Severn Hse. Pubs., Ltd.

Ballard, J. G. Concrete Island. 176p. 1994. pap. 12.00 o.s.i (*0-374-52413-0*); 1974. 6.95 o.p. (*0-374-12807-3*) Farrar, Straus & Giroux.

—Concrete Island. 2001. 176p. pap. 13.00 (*0-312-42034-X*) Picador.

—Concrete Island. 1985. pap. 6.95 o.p. (*0-394-74107-2*) Random Hse., Inc.

Balogh, Mary. A Summer to Remember. l.t. ed. 2003. lib. bdg. 29.95 (*1-58547-269-7*, Platinum) Ctr. Point Large Print.

—A Summer to Remember. (Bedwyn Family Bks.). 2003. 384p. mass mkt. 5.99 (*0-440-23663-0*); 2002. 320p. 21.95 o.s.i (*0-385-33535-0*, Delacorte Pr.) Dell Publishing.

Bannister, Jo. The Lazarus Hotel. 1999. per. (*0-373-26307-4*, 1-26307-8, Worldwide Library) Harlequin Enterprises, Ltd.

—The Lazarus Hotel. 1997. 288p. 22.95 o.p. (*0-312-15565-4*, Saint Martin's Minotaur) St. Martin's Pr.

—The Lazarus Hotel. l.t. ed. 1997. (Ulverscroft Large Print Ser.). 432p. 29.99 o.p. (*0-7089-3858-2*, Ulverscroft) Thorpe, F. A. Pubs. GBR. *Dist:* Ulverscroft Large Print Bks., Ltd., Ulverscroft Large Print Canada, Ltd.

Bantock, Nick. The Golden Mean: In Which the Extraordinary Correspondence of Griffin & Sabine Concludes. 1993. (Illus.). 48p. 17.95 (*0-8118-0298-1*) Chronicle Bks. LLC.

—The Golden Mean: In Which the Extraordinary Correspondence of Griffin & Sabine Concludes. unabr. ed. 1993. (Griffin & Sabine Trilogy). 40p. audio 10.95 (*1-879371-49-9*) Publishing Mills, Inc., The.

—Griffin & Sabine: An Extraordinary Correspondence. (Illus.). 48p. 1991. 19.95 (*0-87701-788-3*); 10th anniv. ltd. ed. 2001. 19.95 o.p. (*0-8118-3200-7*) Chronicle Bks. LLC.

—Griffin & Sabine: An Extraordinary Correspondence. 1991. audio 10.95 (*1-879371-42-1*, 30000) Publishing Mills, Inc., The.

—The Griffin & Sabine Trilogy, 3 bks. 1994. (Illus.). 49.95 (*0-8118-0696-0*) Chronicle Bks. LLC.

—Sabine's Notebook: In Which the Extraordinary Correspondence of Griffin & Sabine Continues. 1992. (Illus.). 48p. 17.95 (*0-8118-0180-2*) Chronicle Bks. LLC.

—Sabine's Notebook: In Which the Extraordinary Correspondence of Griffin & Sabine Continues. 1992. audio 10.95 (*1-879371-41-3*, 30010) Publishing Mills, Inc., The.

Baratz-Logsted, Lauren. The Thin Pink Line. 2003. 304p. 21.95 (*0-373-25030-4*, Red Dress Ink) Harlequin Enterprises, Ltd. CAN. *Dist:* Simon & Schuster.

Barbour, Anne. Step in Time. 1996. 224p. mass mkt. 4.99 o.s.i (*0-451-18723-7*) NAL.

Barnacle, Hugo. Day One. 2000. 288p. 12.95 (*0-7043-8114-1*) Quartet Bks., Ltd. GBR. *Dist:* Interlink Publishing Group, Inc.

Barnacle, Hugo, contrib. by. Day One. 1998. (*0-7043-8085-4*) Quartet Bks., Ltd. GBR. *Dist:* Interlink Publishing Group, Inc.

Barnard, Robert. Bodies. unabr. ed. 2001. audio 34.95 (*0-7451-5775-0*, CAT 4026) Chivers Audio Bks. GBR. *Dist:* BBC Audiobooks America.

—Bodies. 1988. 224p. mass mkt. 3.50 o.s.i (*0-440-20007-5*) Dell Publishing.

—Bodies. 1986. 224p. 13.95 o.p. (*0-684-18729-9*, Macmillan Reference USA) Gale Group.

—Bodies. 1988. audio 35.95 o.s.i (*0-8161-7781-3*) Thorndike Pr.

—The Case of the Missing Bronte. 1983. 192p. 11.95 o.s.i (*0-684-17910-5*); 1984. 248p. 8.95 o.p. (*0-8161-3590-8*) Gale Group. (Macmillan Reference USA).

—The Cherry Blossom Corpse. 1988. 256p. mass mkt. 3.50 o.s.i (*0-440-20178-0*) Dell Publishing.

—The Cherry Blossom Corpse. 1996. (Crime Ser.). 256p. pap. 5.95 o.p. (*0-14-023789-5*, Penguin Bks.) Penguin Group (USA) Inc.

—The Cherry Blossom Corpse. 1987. 14.95 o.p. (*0-684-18825-2*, Scribner) Simon & Schuster.

—Death & the Princess, Vol. 66. 1983. 192p. mass mkt. 3.25 o.s.i (*0-440-12153-1*) Dell Publishing.

—Death & the Princess. 1982. 192p. 10.95 o.s.i (*0-684-17759-5*); 1985. (Nightingale Ser.: No. 2). pap. 9.95 o.p. (*0-8161-3520-7*) Gale Group. (Macmillan Reference USA).

—Death by Sheer Torture. 1982. 192p. 10.95 o.s.i (*0-684-17437-5*, Macmillan Reference USA) Gale Group.

—A Murder in Mayfair. l.t. ed. 2003. 260p. pap. 22.95 o.s.i (*1-59058-081-8*) Poisoned Pen Pr.

—A Murder in Mayfair. 2000. (Illus.). 272p. (YA). 23.00 o.s.i (*0-684-86445-2*, Scribner) Simon & Schuster.

—A Murder in Mayfair. l.t. ed. 2000. (Basic Ser.). 379p. 27.95 (*0-7862-2656-0*); (*0-7540-4229-4*); (*0-7540-4230-8*) Thorndike Pr.

—Sheer Torture. unabr. ed. 1998. audio 69.95 o.p. (*1-872672-22-1*) Magna Story Sound GBR. *Dist:* Ulverscroft Large Print Bks., Ltd.

—Touched by the Dead. 2000. 223p. mass mkt. (*0-00-651326-3*) HarperCollins Pubs.

—Touched by the Dead. unabr. ed. 2000. audio 69.95 (*1-86042-712-X*, 2712X) Soundings, Ltd. GBR. *Dist:* Ulverscroft Large Print Bks., Ltd.

Barnes, Julian. Love, Etc. 2002. 240p. pap. 12.00 (*0-375-72588-1*, Vintage) Knopf Publishing Group.

—Love, Etc. l.t. ed. 2001. 309p. pap. 25.95 (*0-7862-3335-4*); 268p. (*0-7540-4509-9*); 268p. (*0-7540-4510-2*) Thorndike Pr.

Barnes, Trevor. Midsummer Night's Killing: A Mystery Introducing Scotland Yard's Blanche Hampton. 1992. 18.00 o.p. (*0-688-11047-9*, Morrow, William & Co.) Morrow/Avon.

Barr, Robert. The Triumphs of Eugene Valmont. 1985. 192p. reprint ed. pap. 5.95 o.p. (*0-486-24894-1*) Dover Pubns., Inc.

—The Triumphs of Eugene Valmont. 1997. (Oxford Popular Fiction Ser.). 246p. pap. 9.95 o.p. (*0-19-283248-4*) Oxford Univ. Pr., Inc.

Barrowcliffe, Mark. Girlfriend 44. 2001. 371p. 24.95 (*0-312-26166-7*) St. Martin's Pr.

—Infidelity for First Time Fathers. 2002. 337p. 24.95 (*0-312-29146-9*) St. Martin's Pr.

—Infidelity for First-Time Fathers. 2003. 352p. pap. 13.95 (*0-312-31617-8*, Saint Martin's Griffin) St. Martin's Pr.

Basso, Eric. Bartholomew Fair. 1999. 134p. pap. 13.00 (*1-878580-24-8*) Asylum Arts.

—Bartholomew Fair. 1998. pap. 13.00 (*1-57650-099-3*) Hi Jinx Pr.

Baumbach, Jonathan. My Father More or Less. 1982. 152p. 15.95 (*0-914590-66-9*); pap. 10.95 (*0-914590-67-7*) Fiction Collective Two, Inc.

Bawden, Nina. A Little Love, a Little Learning. 21.95 (*0-88411-122-9*) Amereon, Ltd.

—A Little Love, a Little Learning. l.t. unabr. ed. 1998. 304p. pap. 21.99 (*0-7531-5863-9*, 158639); 32.50 (*0-7531-5584-2*, 155842) ISIS Large Print Bks. GBR. *Dist:* Ulverscroft Large Print Bks., Ltd., Ulverscroft Large Print Canada, Ltd.

Bayer, Valerie T. City of Childhood. 1992. 320p. 19.95 o.p. (*0-312-06926-X*) St. Martin's Pr.

—The Metaphysics of Sex. 1992. 384p. 21.95 o.p. (*0-312-08263-0*) St. Martin's Pr.

Beaumont, Matt. E: A Novel. 2000. 352p. 13.00 (*0-452-28188-1*, Plume) Dutton/Plume.

—In at the Shallow End. 2002. 320p. (*0-00-712767-7*) HarperCollins Pubs.

Beckett, Simon. Fine Lines: A Novel. 1994. 304p. 22.00 (*0-671-89206-1*, Simon & Schuster) Simon & Schuster.

Bedford, Martyn. Acts of Revision. 1998. 256p. pap. 19.95 o.s.i (*0-552-99674-2*) Bantam Bks.

Beechey, Alan. An Embarrassment of Corpses. 1997. 265p. 22.95 (*0-312-16936-1*, Saint Martin's Minotaur) St. Martin's Pr.

Bell, Madison Smartt. Doctor Sleep. 2003. (Illus.). 304p. pap. 13.00 (*0-8021-4016-5*) Grove/Atlantic, Inc.

—Doctor Sleep. 1991. 320p. 19.95 (*0-15-126100-8*) Harcourt Trade Pubs.

Benison, C. C. Death at Buckingham Palace: Her Majesty Investigates. 1996. (Her Majesty Investigates Ser.). 288p. mass mkt. 6.99 (*0-553-57476-0*, Crimeline) Bantam Bks.

Bennett, Alan. The Clothes They Stood up In. 2001. E-Book 11.95 (*1-58945-614-9*) Adobe Systems, Inc.

—The Clothes They Stood up In. 1998. 112p. pap. 8.00 (*1-86197-090-0*) Profile Bks. Ltd. GBR. *Dist:* Renouf Publishing Co., Ltd.

—The Clothes They Stood up In. 2001. E-Book 13.50 (*0-375-50689-6*) Random Hse., Inc.

—The Clothes They Stood up In: And the Lady in the Van. 2002. 240p. pap. 9.95 (*0-8129-6965-0*) Random House Adult Trade Publishing Group.

—The Clothes They Stood up in And the Lady in the Van. 2002. 240p. pap. 9.95 (*0-8129-6643-0*) Random House Adult Trade Publishing Group.

Bennett, Arnold. The Regent: A Five Town Story of Adventure. 1977. (Collected Works of Arnold Bennett: Vol. 70). reprint ed. 27.95 (*0-518-19151-6*) Ayer Co. Pubs., Inc.

—The Regent: A Five Town Story of Adventure. 2001. (Collected Works of Arnold Bennett). reprint ed. pap. text 28.00 (*0-7426-7579-3*) Classic Bks.

—The Regent: A Five Towns Story of Adventure. reprint ed. lib. bdg. 98.00 (*0-7426-2579-6*) Classic Bks.

Benson, Ann. The Plague Tales. 1998. 688p. mass mkt. 6.99 (*0-440-22510-8*) Dell Publishing.

Benson, E. F. Freaks of Mayfair. 2001. (Humour Classics Ser.). (Illus.). 224p. 14.95 (*1-85375-429-3*) Prion GBR. *Dist:* Trafalgar Square.

Berger, Arthur A. Durkheim Is Dead! Sherlock Holmes Is Introduced to Social Theory. 2003. 200p. pap. 24.95 (*0-7591-0298-8*) AltaMira Pr.

Berkeley, Anthony. The Piccadilly Murder. 1983. (Detective Stories Ser.). 352p. reprint ed. pap. 6.95 o.p. (*0-486-24518-7*) Dover Pubns., Inc.

Berry, Eleanor. O, Hitman, My Hitman! 1997. 176p. (*0-7223-3065-0*) Stockwell, Arthur H. Ltd.

Besant, Walter. All Sorts & Conditions of Men. 1997. (Oxford Popular Fiction Ser.). (Illus.). 464p. pap. 11.95 o.p. (*0-19-283258-1*) Oxford Univ. Pr., Inc.

—All Sorts & Conditions of Men: An Impossible Story. 1971. reprint ed. 39.00 o.p. (*0-403-00519-1*) Scholarly Pr., Inc.

Biderman, Bob. Judgement of Death. l.t. ed. 1992. 18.95 o.p. (*0-7451-8226-7*); pap. 16.95 o.p. (*0-7927-0774-5*) BBC Audiobooks America.

—Judgement of Death. 1992. 224p. 19.95 (*0-8027-3217-8*) Walker & Co.

Bidisha. Too Fast to Live: The Second Coming. 2001. (Duck Editions). 240p. pap. 15.95 (*0-7156-3008-3*) Duckworth, Gerald & Co., Ltd. GBR. *Dist:* International Publishers Marketing.

Billington, Rachel. Loving Attitudes. 1988. 224p. 15.95 o.p. (*0-688-07574-6*, Morrow, William & Co.) Morrow/Avon.

—Loving Attitudes. l.t. ed. 1989. (Ulverscroft Large Print Ser.). 473p. o.p. (*0-7089-1939-1*, Ulverscroft) Thorpe, F. A. Pubs. GBR. *Dist:* Ulverscroft Large Print Canada, Ltd.

Binchy, Maeve. London Transports. 1998. audio 29.95 (*0-7540-7513-3*) BBC Audiobooks America.

—London Transports. unabr. ed. 1993. audio 49.95 (*0-7451-5788-2*, CAB 247) Chivers Audio Bks. GBR. *Dist:* BBC Audiobooks America.

—London Transports. 1995. 384p. mass mkt. 7.50 (*0-440-21235-9*); 1986. mass mkt. 3.95 o.s.i (*0-440-14870-7*) Dell Publishing.

—London Transports. l.t. ed. 1995. (Large Print Bks.). pap. 22.95 o.p. (*1-56895-226-0*, Wheeler Publishing, Inc.) Gale Group.

—Silver Wedding. 1990. 432p. reprint ed. mass mkt. 7.99 (*0-440-20777-0*) Dell Publishing.

—Silver Wedding. l.t. ed. 2001. 382p. 29.95 (*0-7862-3583-7*); 453p. (*0-7540-1708-7*); 453p. (*0-7540-9107-4*) Thorndike Pr.

—Silver Wedding. l.t. ed. 1989. o.p. (*0-7089-8522-X*, Charnwood) Thorpe, F. A. Pubs.

Bingham, Charlotte. Belgravia. l.t. ed. 2000. (Magna Large Print Ser.). 416p. (*0-7505-1515-5*) Magna Large Print Bks. GBR. *Dist:* Ulverscroft Large Print Canada, Ltd.

—Belgravia. 2000. pap. 6.95 (*0-553-40427-X*) Transworld Publishers Ltd. GBR. *Dist:* Trafalgar Square.

Black, Veronica. A Vow of Fidelity: A Sister Joan Mystery. 1996. 208p. text 19.95 o.p. (*0-312-14064-9*, Saint Martin's Minotaur); Vol. 1. 1997. (Vow of Fidelity Ser.: Vol. 1). 192p. mass mkt. 5.50 (*0-312-96259-2*, St. Martin's Paperbacks) St. Martin's Pr.

—A Vow of Fidelity: A Sister Joan Mystery. l.t. ed. 1997. (Ulverscroft Large Print Ser.). 352p. 29.99 (*0-7089-3697-0*, Ulverscroft) Thorpe, F. A. Pubs. GBR. *Dist:* Ulverscroft Large Print Bks., Ltd., Ulverscroft Large Print Canada, Ltd.

Blackwell, Lawana. The Maiden of Mayfair. 2000. (Tales of London Ser.). 416p. pap. 12.99 (*0-7642-2258-9*) Bethany Hse. Pubs.

Blair, Emma. Moonlit Eyes. 2001. 416p. pap. (*0-316-85585-5*); lib. bdg. (*0-316-85578-2*) Little Brown & Co.

—Moonlit Eyes. l.t. ed. 2002. (Charnwood Large Print Ser.). 536p. 32.50 o.p. (*0-7089-9326-5*, Charnwood) Thorpe, F. A. Pubs. GBR. *Dist:* Ulverscroft Large Print Bks., Ltd., Ulverscroft Large Print Canada, Ltd.

Blair, Jessica. Portrait of Charlotte. l.t. ed. 2000. (Magna Large Print Ser.). 464p. 31.99 (*0-7505-1531-7*) Magna Large Print Bks. GBR. *Dist:* Ulverscroft Large Print Bks., Ltd., Ulverscroft Large Print Canada, Ltd.

Boast, Philip. Deus. 1998. (Illus.). 401p. pap. 8.95 (*0-7472-5380-3*) Headline Bk. Publishing, Ltd. GBR. *Dist:* Trafalgar Square.

—Resurrection. 1998. (Illus.). 480p. pap. 8.95 (*0-7472-5379-X*) Headline Bk. Publishing, Ltd. GBR. *Dist:* Trafalgar Square.

Bosse, Malcolm. A Vast Memory of Love. 1992. (Illus.). 448p. 22.95 o.p. (*0-395-62943-8*) Houghton Mifflin Co.

Boyle, Elizabeth. Brazen Angel. 1997. 400p. pap. 23.00 (*0-440-61370-1*, Delta); mass mkt. 5.50 o.s.i (*0-440-22412-8*) Dell Publishing.

Boyle, Josephine. Maiden's End. 1989. 272p. 17.95 o.p. (*0-312-03391-5*) St. Martin's Pr.

Boyt, Susie. The Characters of Love. 1997. 192p. 19.95 o.p. (*0-297-81766-3*) Weidenfeld & Nicolson, Ltd. GBR. *Dist:* Trafalgar Square.

Brayfield, Celia. Heartswap. l.t. ed. 2000. (General Ser.). 330p. 23.95 (*0-7862-2811-3*) Thorndike Pr.

Brett, Simon. An Amateur Corpse. l.t. ed. 1990. pap. 5.00 (*0-7451-1285-4*) BBC Audiobooks America.

—An Amateur Corpse. 1980. mass mkt. 1.95 o.p. (*0-425-04489-0*) Berkley Publishing Group.

—An Amateur Corpse. unabr. ed. 1994. audio 39.95 (*0-7861-0483-X*, 1435) Blackstone Audio Bks., Inc.

—An Amateur Corpse. 1986. mass mkt. 3.50 o.s.i (*0-440-10185-9*) Dell Publishing.

—An Amateur Corpse. l.t. ed. 1990. (Nightingale Ser.). 300p. pap. 13.95 (*0-8161-5040-0*, Macmillan Reference USA) Gale Group.

—An Amateur Corpse. unabr. ed. 2000. (Charles Paris Mystery Ser. : Vol. 4). audio 44.00 (*0-7887-1286-1*, 95146E7) Recorded Bks., LLC.

—An Amateur Corpse. 1991. mass mkt. 3.95 o.p. (*0-446-35960-2*) Warner Bks., Inc.

—An Amateur Corpse. 2000. 196p. pap. 12.95 (*0-595-00359-1*) iUniverse, Inc.

—Cast, in Order of Disappearance. unabr. ed. 1993. audio 39.95 (*0-7451-5803-X*, CSL 052) BBC Audiobooks America.

—Cast, in Order of Disappearance. 1981. mass mkt. 2.25 o.p. (*0-425-04934-5*) Berkley Publishing Group.

—Cast, in Order of Disappearance. l.t. ed. 1990. (Nightingale Ser.). 279p. pap. 13.95 o.p. (*0-8161-4917-8*, Macmillan Reference USA) Gale Group.

—Cast, in Order of Disappearance. unabr. ed. 1997. (Charles Paris Mystery Ser. : Vol. 1). audio 35.00 (*0-7887-0858-9*, 94984E7) Recorded Bks., LLC.

—A Comedian Dies. 1980. mass mkt. 2.25 o.p. (*0-425-04702-4*) Berkley Publishing Group.

—A Comedian Dies. unabr. ed. 1999. audio 39.95 Blackstone Audio Bks., Inc.

—A Comedian Dies. unabr. ed. 1998. (Charles Paris Mystery Ser. : Vol. 5). audio 44.00 (*0-7887-1886-X*, 95308E7) Recorded Bks., LLC.

—A Comedian Dies. 1990. mass mkt. 3.95 o.p. (*0-446-35958-0*) Warner Bks., Inc.

—A Comedian Dies. 2000. 164p. pap. 11.95 (*0-595-00358-3*) iUniverse, Inc.

—Corporate Bodies. l.t. ed. 1993. 22.95 o.p. (*0-7927-1418-0*); pap. 20.95 o.p. (*0-7927-1417-2*) BBC Audiobooks America.

—Corporate Bodies. unabr. ed. 1993. audio 39.95 (*0-7861-0394-9*, 752393) Blackstone Audio Bks., Inc.

—Corporate Bodies. unabr. ed. 2000. (Charles Paris Mystery Ser.: Bk. 14). audio 49.95 (*0-7451-4131-5*, CAB 814) Chivers Audio Bks. GBR. *Dist:* BBC Audiobooks America.

—Corporate Bodies. abr. ed. 1992. 2p. audio 16.99 (*0-88646-323-8*, 7323); Set. 1996. audio 9.99 (*1-55204-012-7*, 393577) Durkin Hayes Publishing Ltd.

—Corporate Bodies. 1992. 256p. 19.00 (*0-684-19397-3*, Macmillan Reference USA) Gale Group.

—Corporate Bodies. 1993. (Mystery Ser.). mass mkt. (*0-373-26130-6*, 1-26130-4, Harlequin Bks.) Harlequin Enterprises, Ltd.

—Corporate Bodies. unabr. ed. 2000. (Charles Paris Mystery Ser. : Vol. 15). audio 44.00 (*1-55690-654-4*, 92406E7) Recorded Bks., LLC.

—Dead Giveaway. 1987. 256p. mass mkt. 3.50 o.s.i (*0-440-11914-6*) Dell Publishing.

—Dead Giveaway. (Charles Paris Mystery Ser.). 1986. 169p. 13.95 o.p. (*0-684-18517-2*); 1987. 237p. 10.95 o.p. (*0-8161-4218-1*) Gale Group. (Macmillan Reference USA).

—Dead Giveaway. 2000. 180p. pap. 12.95 (*0-595-00357-5*) iUniverse, Inc.

—Dead Room Farce. unabr. ed. 1998. audio 54.95 (*0-7540-0150-4*, CAB 1573) BBC Audiobooks America.

—Dead Room Farce. unabr. ed. 1999. audio 39.95 (*0-7861-1642-0*, 2470) Blackstone Audio Bks., Inc.

—Dead Room Farce. 1998. 208p. 20.95 (*0-312-19251-7*, Saint Martin's Minotaur) St. Martin's Pr.

—Dead Room Farce. l.t. ed. 1998. (Mystery Ser.). 344p. 27.95 (*0-7862-1564-X*) Thorndike Pr.

—The Dead Side of the Mike. unabr. ed. 1997. audio 54.95 (*0-7451-6738-1*, CAB 1354) BBC Audiobooks America.

—The Dead Side of the Mike. unabr. ed. 1992. audio 39.95 (*0-7861-0340-X*, 1297) Blackstone Audio Bks., Inc.

—The Dead Side of the Mike. 1986. pap. 3.50 o.p. (*0-440-11763-1*) Dell Publishing.

—The Dead Side of the Mike. unabr. ed. 1998. (Charles Paris Mystery Ser. : No. 6). audio 44.00 (*0-7887-2520-3*, 95593E7) Recorded Bks., LLC.

—The Dead Side of the Mike. 1991. mass mkt. 3.95 o.p. (*0-446-35957-2*) Warner Bks., Inc.

—The Dead Side of the Mike. 2000. 180p. per. 11.95 (*0-595-00354-0*) iUniverse, Inc.

—Murder in the Title. 1986. pap. 3.50 o.p. (*0-440-16016-2*) Dell Publishing.

—Murder in the Title. 1983. 192p. 11.95 o.s.i (*0-684-17898-2*, Macmillan Reference USA) Gale Group.

—Murder in the Title. 1990. mass mkt. 3.95 o.p. (*0-446-35954-8*) Warner Bks., Inc.

—Murder in the Title. 2000. (Charles Paris Mystery Ser.). 196p. pap. 12.95 (*0-595-00353-2*) iUniverse, Inc.

Settings

Settings

—Murder Unprompted. unabr. ed. 1992. (Audio Bks.). audio 39.95 (0-7451-5804-8, CAB 686) BBC Audiobooks America.
—Murder Unprompted. unabr. ed. 1997. audio 32.95 (0-7861-1081-3, 1851) Blackstone Audio Bks., Inc.
—Murder Unprompted. 1986. (Murder Ink Mystery Ser.: No. 69). pap. 3.50 o.p. (0-440-16145-2) Dell Publishing.
—Murder Unprompted. (Nightingale Ser.). 1983. 290p. pap. 9.95 o.p. (0-8161-3540-1); 1982. 160p. 10.95 o.s.i (0-684-17659-9) Gale Group. (Macmillan Reference USA).
—Murder Unprompted. unabr. ed. 2001. audio compact disk 49.00 (0-7887-3982-4, C1145E7); 1999. audio 38.00 (0-7887-4081-4, H1075E7) Recorded Bks., LLC. (Clipper Audio).
—Murder Unprompted. 1990. mass mkt. 3.95 o.p. (0-446-35955-6) Warner Bks., Inc.
—Not Dead, Only Resting. l.t. ed. 1985. (Nightingale Ser.). 304p. 10.95 o.p. (0-8161-3831-1, Macmillan Reference USA) Gale Group.
—Not Dead, Only Resting. 1990. mass mkt. 3.95 o.p. (0-446-35952-1) Warner Bks., Inc.
—Not Dead, Only Resting. 2000. 180p. pap. 12.95 (0-595-00356-7) iUniverse, Inc.
—Not Dead, Only Resting: A Charles Paris Mystery. 1984. 176p. 11.95 o.s.i (0-684-18193-2, Macmillan Reference USA) Gale Group.
—A Reconstructed Corpse. unabr. ed. 2000. (Charles Paris Mystery Ser.: Bk. 15). audio (0-7451-4357-1, CAB 1040) Chivers Audio Bks. GBR. *Dist:* BBC Audiobooks America.
—A Reconstructed Corpse. l.t. ed. 1994. 234p. 24.95 (1-56895-117-5, Wheeler Publishing, Inc.) Gale Group.
—A Reconstructed Corpse. 1996. (WWL Mystery Ser.). per. (0-373-26194-2, 1-26194-0, Worldwide Library) Harlequin Enterprises, Ltd.
—A Reconstructed Corpse. l.t. ed. 1994. (Magna Large Print Ser.). 302p. o.p. (0-7505-0717-9) Magna Large Print Bks. GBR. *Dist:* Ulverscroft Large Print Canada, Ltd.
—A Reconstructed Corpse. unabr. ed. 1994. audio 44.00 (0-7887-0110-X, 94351E7) Recorded Bks., LLC.
—A Reconstructed Corpse. 1994. 192p. 20.00 (0-684-19700-6, Scribner) Simon & Schuster.
—A Series of Murders. unabr. ed. 1993. audio 39.95 (0-7451-5801-3, CAB 427) BBC Audiobooks America.
—A Series of Murders. 1989. 224p. 16.95 o.s.i (0-684-19096-6, Scribner) Simon & Schuster.
—A Series of Murders. 1990. mass mkt. 3.95 o.s.i (0-446-35949-1) Warner Bks., Inc.
—Sicken & So Die. unabr. ed. 1996. (Charles Paris Mystery Ser.). audio 54.95 (0-7451-6698-9, CAB1314) BBC Audiobooks America.
—Sicken & So Die. unabr. ed. (Charles Paris Mystery Ser.). 2000. audio compact disk 40.00 (0-7861-9896-6, z1874); 1997. audio 32.95 (0-7861-1108-9, 1874) Blackstone Audio Bks., Inc.
—Sicken & So Die. 1997. per. (0-373-26262-0, 1-26262-5, Worldwide Library) Harlequin Enterprises, Ltd.
—Sicken & So Die. 1997. 208p. 20.50 (0-684-82459-0, Scribner) Simon & Schuster.
—Situation Tragedy. unabr. ed. 1996. audio 32.95 (0-7861-0965-3, 1742) Blackstone Audio Bks., Inc.
—Situation Tragedy. 1986. pap. 3.50 o.p. (0-440-18792-3) Dell Publishing.
—Situation Tragedy. unabr. ed. 1998. audio 69.95 o.p. (1-872672-11-6) Magna Story Sound GBR. *Dist:* Ulverscroft Large Print Bks., Ltd.
—Situation Tragedy. 1981. (Charles Paris Mystery Ser. : Vol. 7). audio 44.00 (0-7887-3491-1, 95898E7) Recorded Bks., LLC.
—Situation Tragedy. 1981. 192p. 9.95 o.s.i (0-684-17268-2, Scribner) Simon & Schuster.
—Situation Tragedy. 1990. mass mkt. 3.95 o.s.i (0-446-35956-4) Warner Bks., Inc.
—So Much Blood. 1981. mass mkt. 2.25 o.s.i (0-425-04935-3); 1979. mass mkt. 1.75 o.s.i (0-425-04159-X) Berkley Publishing Group.
—So Much Blood. unabr. ed. 2000. (Charles Paris Mystery Ser.: Bk. 2). audio 49.95 (0-7451-4251-6, CAB 934) Chivers Audio Bks. GBR. *Dist:* BBC Audiobooks America.
—So Much Blood. 1986. mass mkt. 3.50 o.s.i (0-440-18069-4) Dell Publishing.
—So Much Blood. unabr. ed. 1997. (Charles Paris Mystery Ser. : Vol. 2). audio 44.00 (0-7887-0931-3, 95071E7) Recorded Bks., LLC.
—So Much Blood. 2000. 196p. pap. 12.95 (0-595-00360-5) iUniverse, Inc.
—Star Trap. unabr. ed. 1995. audio 54.95 (0-7451-6481-1, CAB 1097) BBC Audiobooks America.
—Star Trap. unabr. ed. 2000. audio 32.95 (0-7861-1750-8, 2554); audio compact disk 40.00 (0-7861-9901-6, z2554) Blackstone Audio Bks., Inc.
—Star Trap. 1986. mass mkt. 3.50 o.s.i (0-440-18300-6) Dell Publishing.
—Star Trap. l.t. ed. 1989. 315p. 13.95 o.p. (0-8161-4774-4, Macmillan Reference USA) Gale Group.
—Star Trap. unabr. ed. 1997. (Charles Paris Mystery Ser. : Vol. 3). audio 44.00 (0-7887-1146-6, 95084E7) Recorded Bks., LLC.
—Star Trap. 1990. mass mkt. 3.95 o.p. (0-446-35959-9) Warner Bks., Inc.
—What Bloody Man Is That? unabr. ed. 1993. 54.95 incl. audio (0-7451-5805-6, CAB 632) BBC Audiobooks America.
—What Bloody Man Is That? 1989. mass mkt. 3.50 o.s.i (0-440-20344-9) Dell Publishing.
—What Bloody Man Is That? l.t. ed. 1988. (Nightingale Ser.). 297p. 12.95 o.p. (0-8161-4398-6, Macmillan Reference USA) Gale Group.
—What Bloody Man Is That? unabr. ed. 2002. audio 40.00 (1-4025-1944-3, Clipper Audio) Recorded Bks., LLC.
—What Bloody Man Is That? 1987. 196p. 14.95 o.p. (0-684-18824-4, Scribner) Simon & Schuster.
—What Bloody Man Is That? 2000. 188p. pap. 12.95 (0-595-00349-4) iUniverse, Inc.
Brightwell, Emily. The Ghost & Mrs. Jeffries. 1993. (Victorian Mystery Ser.). mass mkt. 5.50 o.s.i (0-425-13949-2) Berkley Publishing Group.
—The Ghost & Mrs. Jeffries. l.t. ed. 1999. (Paperback Ser.). 279p. pap. 24.95 (0-7838-8602-0) Thorndike Pr.
—The Inspector & Mrs. Jeffries. 1993. (Victorian Mystery Ser.). 192p. mass mkt. 5.99 (0-425-13622-1) Berkley Publishing Group.
—The Inspector & Mrs. Jeffries. l.t. ed. 1999. (Paperback Ser.). 256p. pap. 23.95 (0-7838-0417-2) Thorndike Pr.
—Mrs. Jeffries & the Missing Alibi. 1996. (Victorian Mystery Ser.). 240p. mass mkt. 5.99 o.s.i (0-425-15256-1) Berkley Publishing Group.
—Mrs. Jeffries Dusts for Clues. 1993. (Victorian Mystery Ser.). 192p. mass mkt. 5.50 o.s.i (0-425-13704-X) Berkley Publishing Group.
—Mrs. Jeffries Dusts for Clues. 1999. (G. K. Hall Paperback Ser.). 253p. pap. 23.95 (0-7838-8721-3, Macmillan Reference USA) Gale Group.
—Mrs. Jeffries on the Ball. l.t. ed. 1995. (Nightingale Ser.). 282p. reprint ed. pap. 18.95 o.p. (0-7838-1284-1, Macmillan Reference USA) Gale Group.
—Mrs. Jeffries on the Ball: A Victorian Mystery. 1994. (Victorian Mystery Ser.). 208p. mass mkt. 5.99 o.s.i (0-425-14491-7, Prime Crime) Berkley Publishing Group.
—Mrs. Jeffries on the Trail. 1995. (Victorian Mystery Ser.). 240p. mass mkt. 5.50 o.s.i (0-425-14691-X, Prime Crime) Berkley Publishing Group.
—Mrs. Jeffries Pinches the Post. 2001. 208p. mass mkt. 5.99 (0-425-18004-2, Prime Crime) Berkley Publishing Group.
—Mrs. Jeffries Pinches the Post. 2002. (Paperback Ser.). lib. bdg. 24.95 (0-7862-4462-3) Thorndike Pr.
—Mrs. Jeffries Plays the Cook. 1995. (Victorian Mystery Ser.). 240p. mass mkt. 5.50 o.s.i (0-425-15053-4) Berkley Publishing Group.
—Mrs. Jeffries Questions the Answer. 1997. (Victorian Mystery Ser.). 240p. mass mkt. 5.99 o.s.i (0-425-16093-9, Prime Crime) Berkley Publishing Group.
—Mrs. Jeffries Questions the Answer. l.t. ed. 2000. (G. K. Hall Paperback Ser.). 287p. pap. 23.95 (0-7838-9266-7, Macmillan Reference USA) Gale Group.
—Mrs. Jeffries Rocks the Boat. 1999. (Victorian Mystery Ser.: Vol. 12). 208p. mass mkt. 5.99 o.s.i (0-425-16934-0) Berkley Publishing Group.
—Mrs. Jeffries Rocks the Boat. l.t. ed. 2002. pap. 24.95 (0-7862-4463-1) Thorndike Pr.
—Mrs. Jeffries Stands Corrected. 1996. (Victorian Mystery Ser.). 224p. mass mkt. 5.99 o.s.i (0-425-15580-3, Prime Crime) Berkley Publishing Group.
—Mrs. Jeffries Takes Stock. 1994. (Victorian Mystery Ser.). 208p. mass mkt. 4.99 o.s.i (0-425-14282-5, Prime Crime) Berkley Publishing Group.
—Mrs. Jeffries Takes Stock. l.t. ed. 2000. (Paperback Ser.). 261p. pap. 23.95 (0-7838-9157-1) Thorndike Pr.
—Mrs. Jeffries Takes the Cake. 1998. (Victorian Mystery Ser.). 240p. mass mkt. 5.99 o.s.i (0-425-16569-8, Prime Crime) Berkley Publishing Group.
—Mrs. Jeffries Takes the Cake. l.t. ed. 1999. (Paperback Ser.). 282p. pap. 24.95 (0-7838-8798-1, Macmillan Reference USA) Gale Group.
—Mrs. Jeffries Takes the Stage. 1997. (Victorian Mystery Ser.). 240p. mass mkt. 5.99 o.s.i (0-425-15724-5, Prime Crime) Berkley Publishing Group.
—Mrs. Jeffries Takes the Stage. l.t. ed. 2000. (G. K. Hall Paperback Ser.). 280p. pap. 23.95 (0-7838-9035-4, Macmillan Reference USA) Gale Group.
Broadbent, Tony. The Smoke: A Creeping Narrative. 2002. 320p. 23.95 (0-312-29027-6, Saint Martin's Minotaur) St. Martin's Pr.
Brodrick, William. The 6th Lamentation: A Novel. 2003. 400p. 24.95 (0-670-03191-7, Viking) Viking Penguin.
Brookfield, Amanda. Cast of Smiles. 1991. 15.95 o.p. (0-312-05399-1) St. Martin's Pr.
Brookner, Anita. The Bay of Angels. E-Book 9.95 (1-58945-826-5) Adobe Systems, Inc.
—The Bay of Angels. 2002. 208p. pap. 12.00 (0-375-72760-4) Knopf, Alfred A. Inc.
—The Bay of Angels. E-Book 19.00 (1-58836-006-7) Random Hse., Inc.
—The Bay of Angels. 2001. (Thorndike Press Large Print Women's Fiction Ser.). 335p. 29.95 (0-7862-3654-X) Thorndike Pr.
—Falling Slowly. l.t. ed. 1998. 26.95 (1-56895-700-9, Wheeler Publishing, Inc.) Gale Group.
—Family & Friends. l.t. ed. 1986. (General Ser.). 272p. 15.95 o.p. (0-8161-4061-8, Macmillan Reference USA) Gale Group.
—Family & Friends. 1998. 192p. pap. 12.00 (0-679-78164-1, Vintage) Knopf Publishing Group.
—Family & Friends. 1987. 1.99 o.p. (0-517-64896-2) Random Hse. Value Publishing.
—Family & Friends. 1986. pap. 6.95 o.s.i (0-671-62575-6, Pocket) Simon & Schuster.
—Fraud. (Vintage Contemporaries Ser.). 1994. 272p. pap. 13.00 (0-679-74308-1); 1994. mass mkt. o.s.i (0-394-22272-5); 1993. 262p. 21.00 o.s.i (0-679-41606-4) Random Hse., Inc.
—A Friend from England. l.t. ed. 1989. (General Ser.). 293p. lib. bdg. 19.95 o.p. (0-8161-4656-X, Macmillan Reference USA) Gale Group.
—A Friend from England. 1989. 208p. reprint ed. pap. 10.00 o.p. (0-06-097202-5, PL 7202, Perennial) HarperTrade.
—Look at Me. l.t. ed. 1991. 259p. 22.95 o.p. (1-85089-404-3) ISIS Large Print Bks. GBR. *Dist:* Transaction Pubs.
—Look at Me. 1997. 208p. pap. 12.00 (0-679-73813-4, Vintage) Knopf Publishing Group.
—Look at Me. 1985. pap. 7.95 o.p. (0-525-48156-7, Obelisk) NAL.
—Undue Influence. l.t. ed. 2000. (G. K. Hall Core Ser.). 306p. 29.95 (0-7838-9001-X, Macmillan Reference USA) Gale Group.
—Undue Influence. 2001. 240p. pap. 12.00 (0-375-70734-4, Vintage) Knopf Publishing Group.
Brooks, Roy. Brothel in Pimlico. 2001. (Illus.). 112p. 13.00 (0-7195-6028-4) Murray, John Pubs., Ltd. GBR. *Dist:* Trafalgar Square.
Brown, Carrie. Lamb in Love. 1999. 348p. tchr. ed. 21.95 (1-56512-203-8, 72203) Algonquin Bks. of Chapel Hill.
—Lamb in Love. unabr. ed. 1999. (Chivers Sound Library American Collections). audio 69.95 (0-7927-2318-X, CSL207, Chivers Sound Library) BBC Audiobooks America.
—Lamb in Love. 2000. 320p. reprint ed. pap. 12.95 (0-553-38085-0) Bantam Bks.
—Lamb in Love. l.t. ed. 1999. (Large Print Book Ser.). 26.95 (1-56895-732-7, Wheeler Publishing, Inc.) Gale Group.
Brown, Molly. Cracker: To Say I Love You. 1995. 256p. 21.95 o.p. (0-312-13951-9) St. Martin's Pr.
Browne, Douglas G. What Beckoning Ghost? 1986. 265p. reprint ed. pap. 5.95 o.p. (0-486-25055-5) Dover Pubns., Inc.
Browne, Gretta Curran. Ghosts in Sunlight. 1999. 437p. (0-86327-728-4) Wolfhound Pr.
Bruen, Ken. Rilke on Black. 1997. (Mask Noir Ser.). 144p. (Orig.). pap. text o.p. (1-85242-511-3) Serpent's Tail Ltd.
—Taming the Alien. 2000. 158p. pap. 15.95 (1-899344-49-7) Do-Not Pr., The GBR. *Dist:* Dufour Editions, Inc.
—The White Trilogy. 2003. 400p. pap. 14.99 (1-932112-02-2, Kate's Mystery Bks.) Justin, Charles & Co. Pubs.
Bunn, T. Davis. Florian's Gate. 1992. (Priceless Collection). 352p. (ps up). pap. 9.99 o.p. (1-55661-244-3) Bethany Hse. Pubs.
—Florian's Gate. l.t. ed. 2000. (Christian Mystery Ser.). 563p. 24.95 (0-7862-2877-6) Thorndike Pr.
—Winter Palace. 1993. (Priceless Collection: No. 3). 352p. pap. 9.99 o.p. (1-55661-324-5) Bethany Hse. Pubs.
—Winter Palace. l.t. ed. 2001. (Thorndike Christian Mystery Ser.). (Illus.). 512p. 24.95 (0-7862-3179-3) Thorndike Pr.
Bush, Catherine. The Rules of Engagement. 2002. pap. 24.00 (0-374-52870-5); 2000. 302p. 24.00 o.s.i (0-374-25280-7) Farrar, Straus & Giroux.
Butler, Gwendoline. Coffin & the Paper Man. 1993. (WWL Mystery Ser.). mass mkt. o.s.i (0-373-26133-0, 1-26133-8, Harlequin Bks.) Harlequin Enterprises, Ltd.
—Coffin & the Paper Man. pap. 15.95 (0-312-29192-2, Saint Martin's Griffin); 1991. 16.95 (0-312-05835-7, Saint Martin's Minotaur) St. Martin's Pr.
—Coffin for Baby. (Black Dagger Crime Ser.). 1993. 192p. 16.50 o.p. (0-7451-8606-8, Black Dagger); 1994. 18.95 o.p. (0-7451-6458-7) BBC Audiobooks America.
—A Coffin for Charley. 1996. (WWL Mystery Ser.). mass mkt. o.s.i (0-373-26200-0, 1-26200-5, Worldwide Library) Harlequin Enterprises, Ltd.
—A Coffin for Charley. l.t. ed. 1994. (Magna Large Print Ser.). 358p. o.p. (0-7505-0705-5) Magna Large Print Bks. GBR. *Dist:* Ulverscroft Large Print Canada, Ltd.
—A Coffin for Charley. 1994. 256p. 20.95 o.p. (0-312-11466-4, Saint Martin's Minotaur) St. Martin's Pr.
—A Coffin from the Past. l.t. ed. 1993. pap. 16.95 o.p. (0-7451-6419-6); 1992. 18.95 o.p. (0-7451-6413-7); 1993. audio 39.95 (0-7451-5814-5, CSL 075) BBC Audiobooks America.
—A Coffin from the Past. (Black Dagger Crime Ser.). 224p. 12.95 o.p. (0-86220-706-1) Chivers Pr. GBR. *Dist:* BBC Audiobooks America.
—Coffin in Fashion. 1992. mass mkt. o.s.i (0-373-26100-4, Harlequin Bks.) Harlequin Enterprises, Ltd.
—Coffin in Fashion. pap. 15.95 (0-312-29177-9, Saint Martin's Griffin); 1989. 176p. 16.95 (0-312-03802-X, Saint Martin's Minotaur) St. Martin's Pr.
—Coffin in Malta. unabr. ed. 1989. audio 39.95 (0-7451-5815-3, CAT 4038) BBC Audiobooks America.
—Coffin in Malta. 1989. (Black Dagger Crime Ser.). 224p. reprint ed. text 12.95 o.p. (0-86220-752-5) Chivers Pr. GBR. *Dist:* BBC Audiobooks America.
—Coffin in Malta. 1985. (Walker's British Paperback Mysteries Ser.). 192p. reprint ed. pap. 2.95 o.s.i (0-8027-3111-2) Walker & Co.
—Coffin in the Black Museum. unabr. ed. 1991. (Audio Ser.). audio 54.95 (0-7451-5816-1, CAT 4068) BBC Audiobooks America.
—Coffin in the Museum of Crime. 1993. (Mystery Ser.). mass mkt. o.s.i (0-373-26121-7, 1-26121-3, Harlequin Bks.) Harlequin Enterprises, Ltd.
—Coffin in the Museum of Crime. 1990. 16.95 (0-312-04282-5, Saint Martin's Minotaur) St. Martin's Pr.
—Coffin on Murder Street. 1994. (Mystery Ser.). mass mkt. o.s.i (0-373-26147-0, 1-26147-8, Harlequin Bks.) Harlequin Enterprises, Ltd.
—Coffin on Murder Street. 1992. 224p. 16.95 (0-312-07673-8, Saint Martin's Minotaur) St. Martin's Pr.
—Coffin on the Water. 1992. (WWL Mystery Ser.: No. 90). mass mkt. o.s.i (0-373-26090-3, 1-26090-0, Harlequin Bks.) Harlequin Enterprises, Ltd.
—Coffin on the Water. 1990. 2.99 o.p. (0-517-05811-1) Random Hse. Value Publishing.
—Coffin on the Water. 1989. 192p. 14.95 o.p. (0-312-02561-0, Saint Martin's Minotaur) St. Martin's Pr.
—The Coffin Tree. 1997. mass mkt. o.s.i (0-373-26250-7, 1-26250-0, Worldwide Library) Harlequin Enterprises, Ltd.
—The Coffin Tree. pap. 15.95 (0-312-29189-2, Saint Martin's Griffin); 1995. 240p. 21.95 (0-312-13946-2, Saint Martin's Minotaur) St. Martin's Pr.
—Coffin Underground. l.t. ed. 1989. 336p. lib. bdg. 11.95 o.p. (1-85057-722-6, Macmillan Reference USA) Gale Group.
—Coffin Underground. 1992. per. (0-373-26110-1, 1-26110-6, Harlequin Bks.) Harlequin Enterprises, Ltd.
—Coffin Underground. pap. 14.95 (0-312-31071-4, Saint Martin's Griffin); 1989. 16.95 (0-312-02886-5, Saint Martin's Minotaur) St. Martin's Pr.
—Coffin Waiting. unabr. ed. 1992. (Crimson Dagger Audio Bks.). audio 39.95 (0-7451-2406-2, CDA 007) BBC Audiobooks America.
—Coffin's Game. l.t. ed. 1999. (Thorndike General Ser.). 307p. pap. 22.95 o.p. (0-7862-1946-7, Macmillan Reference USA) Gale Group.
—Coffin's Game. 2000. (Commander John Coffin Mysteries Ser.: Bk. 353). 256p. mass mkt. o.s.i (0-373-26353-8, 1-26353-2, Worldwide Library) Harlequin Enterprises, Ltd.
—Coffin's Game. 1999. (Commander John Coffin Mysteries Ser.). 240p. 21.95 (0-312-20512-0, Saint Martin's Minotaur) St. Martin's Pr.
—Coffin's Ghost. 2001. 224p. 22.95 (0-312-27997-3, Saint Martin's Minotaur) St. Martin's Pr.
—Coffin's Ghost. l.t. ed. 2000. (General Ser.). 318p. 22.95 (0-7862-2803-2); (0-7540-4245-6); (0-7540-4246-4) Thorndike Pr.
—Cracking Open a Coffin. 1995. (WWL Mystery Ser.). 250p. mass mkt. o.s.i (0-373-26171-3, 1-29171-8, Harlequin Bks.) Harlequin Enterprises, Ltd.
—Cracking Open a Coffin. 1993. 240p. 16.95 (0-312-09777-8, Saint Martin's Minotaur) St. Martin's Pr.
—A Dark Coffin. 1998. (WWL Mystery Ser.). mass mkt. o.s.i (0-373-26265-5, 1-26265-8, Worldwide Library) Harlequin Enterprises, Ltd.
—A Dark Coffin. unabr. ed. 2001. audio 54.95 ISIS Audio Bks. GBR. *Dist:* Ulverscroft Large Print Bks., Ltd.
—A Dark Coffin. l.t. ed. 1996. (Magna Large Print Ser.). 325p. o.p. (0-7505-1049-8) Magna Large Print Bks. GBR. *Dist:* Ulverscroft Large Print Canada, Ltd.
—A Dark Coffin. 1996. 240p. 21.95 (0-312-14577-2, Saint Martin's Minotaur) St. Martin's Pr.
—Death Lives Next Door. 1992. (John Coffin Ser.). 192p. 16.95 o.p. (0-312-08175-8, Saint Martin's Minotaur) St. Martin's Pr.
—A Double Coffin. 1999. (WWL Mystery Ser.: No. 313). per. (0-373-26313-9, 1-26313-6, Worldwide Library) Harlequin Enterprises, Ltd.
—A Double Coffin. 1998. 240p. 21.95 o.p. (0-312-18569-3, Saint Martin's Minotaur) St. Martin's Pr.

—A Double Coffin. l.t. ed. 1998. (General Ser.). 336p. pap. 24.95 (*0-7862-1481-3*) Thorndike Pr.
—A Grave Coffin. 2000. 256p. 22.95 (*0-312-26167-5*, Saint Martin's Minotaur) St. Martin's Pr.
Butler, Gwendoline & Melling, John K. Coffin Waiting. 1990. (Black Dagger Crime Ser.). 200p. reprint ed. text 12.95 o.p. (*0-86220-767-3*) Chivers Pr. GBR. *Dist:* BBC Audiobooks America.
Byatt, A. S. Babel Tower. l.t. ed. 1996. 870p. 25.95 o.p. (*0-7838-1684-7*, Macmillan Reference USA) Gale Group.
—Babel Tower. 1997. 640p. pap. 15.00 (*0-679-73680-8*, Vintage) Knopf Publishing Group.
—A Whistling Woman. 2004. 448p. pap. 15.00 (*0-679-77690-7*, Vintage) Knopf Publishing Group.
—A Whistling Woman. 2002. 448p. 26.00 (*0-375-41534-3*) Knopf, Alfred A. Inc.
Byrne, Julia. Scandal & Miss Smith. 2000. 256p. mass mkt. (*0-373-51117-5*, 1-51117-9, Harlequin Bks.) Harlequin Enterprises, Ltd.
Callison, Brian R. The Stollenberg Legacy. l.t. ed. 2001. (Thorndike General Ser.). 380p. pap. 22.95 (*0-7862-3200-5*) Thorndike Pr.
Cameron, Stella. All Smiles. 2000. 448p. mass mkt. (*1-55166-615-4*, 1-66615-5, Mira Bks.) Harlequin Enterprises, Ltd.
Campbell, R. T. Bodies in a Bookshop. 1984. 192p. reprint ed. pap. 6.95 (*0-486-24720-1*) Dover Pubns., Inc.
—Unholy Dying. 1985. 128p. reprint ed. pap. 5.95 (*0-486-24977-8*) Dover Pubns., Inc.
Campbell, Ramsey. The Last Voice They Hear. 1999. 384p. pap. 6.99 (*0-8125-4194-4*, Tor Bks.) Doherty, Tom Assocs., LLC.
—The Last Voice They Hear. 1998. 6.99 (*0-312-87078-7*) St. Martin's Pr.
Campbell, Ramsey & Robbins, Harold. The Last Voice They Hear. 1998. 384p. 24.95 o.p. (*0-312-86611-9*, Forge Bks.) Doherty, Tom Assocs., LLC.
Campbell, Rebecca. Slave to Fashion: A Novel. 2002. Orig. Title: The Favours & Fortunes of Katie Castle. 240p. 22.95 (*0-375-50713-2*); 288p. pap. 11.95 (*0-375-76062-8*) Random House Adult Trade Publishing Group. (Villard Bks.).
Carey, Peter. Jack Maggs. 1999. 368p. pap. 13.00 (*0-679-76037-7*, Vintage) Knopf Publishing Group.
—Jack Maggs. 1998. 309p. 24.00 (*0-679-44008-9*) Knopf, Alfred A. Inc.
—Jack Maggs. l.t. ed. 1998. (Core Ser.). 535p. 28.95 (*0-7838-0285-4*) Thorndike Pr.
—Jack Maggs. 1998. 417p. pap. 16.95 (*0-7022-3049-9*) Univ. of Queensland Pr. AUS. *Dist:* International Specialized Bk. Services.
Carleton, Susannah. Marriage Campaign. 2003. (Signet Regency Romance Ser.). 240p. mass mkt. 4.99 (*0-451-20802-1*, Signet Bks.) NAL.
Carlson, Richard. Men & Other Mammals. 2002. 290p. pap. 13.00 (*0-7868-8861-X*) Hyperion Pr.
Carr, John Dickson. The Lost Gallows. 1986. 344p. pap. 3.50 o.p. (*0-88184-202-8*, Carroll & Graf Pubs.) Avalon Publishing Group.
Carter, Angela. Wise Children. 1992. 232p. 21.00 o.p. (*0-374-29133-0*) Farrar, Straus & Giroux.
—Wise Children. 1991. (*0-316-13053-2*) Little Brown & Co.
—Wise Children. 1993. 240p. pap. 12.95 (*0-14-017530-X*, Penguin Bks.) Penguin Group (USA) Inc.
Cartland, Barbara. Beyond the Stars. l.t. ed. 1997. (Nightingale Ser.). pap. 18.95 (*0-7838-1894-7*, Macmillan Reference USA) Gale Group.
—Beyond the Stars No. 145: Camfield. 1995. 176p. (Orig.). mass mkt. 4.50 o.s.i (*0-515-11706-4*, Jove) Berkley Publishing Group.
—The Glittering Lights. l.t. ed. 2001. (Thorndike Candlelight Romance Ser.). 320p. 23.95 (*0-7862-3136-X*, Macmillan Reference USA) Gale Group.
—Lights, Laughter, & a Lady. l.t. ed. 2001. (Candlelight Ser.). 238p. 24.95 o.p. (*0-7862-3624-8*) Thorndike Pr.
—Lucky Logan Finds Love. l.t. ed. 2000. (Candlelight Romance Ser.). 185p. 21.95 (*0-7862-2787-7*) Thorndike Pr.
—A Night of Gaiety, No. 142. 1981. pap. 1.95 o.p. (*0-553-14791-9*) Bantam Bks.
—A Night of Gaiety. l.t. ed. 2002. 27.95 (*0-7862-4033-4*) Gale Group.
Casey, Philip. The Water Star. 1999. 434p. pap. 34.00 (*0-330-37190-8*) Picador GBR. *Dist:* Trans-Atlantic Pubns., Inc.
Casey, Phillip. The Fisher Child. 2001. 300p. (*0-330-48301-3*) Picador.
Cather, Willa. Alexander's Bridge. 1977. reprint ed. lib. bdg. 19.95 (*0-89190-520-0*, Queens Hse., Inc.) Amereon, Ltd.
—Alexander's Bridge, Set. unabr. ed. 1993. audio 20.95 (*1-55685-287-8*) Audio Bk. Contractors, Inc.
—Alexander's Bridge. 2001. per. 12.50 (*1-58396-412-6*); per. 15.50 (*1-58396-413-4*) Blue Unicorn Editions.
—Alexander's Bridge. 1990. reprint ed. lib. bdg. 16.95 (*0-89968-491-2*) Buccaneer Bks., Inc.
—Alexander's Bridge. (Collected Works of Willa Cather). 174p. reprint ed. 2001. pap. 28.00 (*0-7426-5566-0*); 1998. lib. bdg. 88.00 (*1-58201-566-X*) Classic Bks.
—Alexander's Bridge. 2002. (Thrift Editions Ser.). 160p. pap. 2.00 (*0-486-42450-2*) Dover Pubns., Inc.
—Alexander's Bridge. 1999. E-Book 2.49 (*1-58627-088-5*) Electric Umbrella Publishing.
—Alexander's Bridge. l.t. ed. 79p. pap. 13.58 (*0-7583-0120-0*); 336p. pap. 35.67 (*0-7583-0126-X*); 390p. pap. 40.00 (*0-7583-0127-8*); 222p. pap. 26.47 (*0-7583-0124-3*); 99p. pap. 14.60 (*0-7583-0121-9*); 136p. pap. 18.72 (*0-7583-0122-7*); 174p. pap. 22.55 (*0-7583-0123-5*); 273p. pap. 30.60 (*0-7583-0125-1*); 99p. lib. bdg. 20.60 (*0-7583-0113-8*); 136p. lib. bdg. 24.72 (*0-7583-0114-6*); 174p. lib. bdg. 29.66 (*0-7583-0115-4*); 222p. lib. bdg. 34.47 (*0-7583-0116-2*); 273p. lib. bdg. 38.09 (*0-7583-0117-0*); 336p. lib. bdg. 42.54 (*0-7583-0118-9*); 390p. lib. bdg. 46.34 (*0-7583-0119-7*); 79p. lib. bdg. 19.58 (*0-7583-0112-X*) Huge Print Pr.
—Alexander's Bridge. 2001. 128p. 22.99 (*1-58827-482-9*); per. 18.99 (*1-58827-483-7*) IndyPublish-.com.
—Alexander's Bridge, l.t. ed. 2001. 135p. lib. bdg. 24.95 net. (*1-58118-080-2*) LRS.
—Alexander's Bridge. 2001. (Twelve-Point Ser.). 205p. lib. bdg. 25.00 (*1-58287-168-X*); 309p. lib. bdg. 26.00 (*1-58287-651-7*) North Bks.
—Alexander's Bridge. Lindemann, Marilee, ed. & intro. by. 1997. (Oxford World's Classics Ser.). 152p. pap. 8.95 o.p. (*0-19-283214-X*) Oxford Univ. Pr., Inc.
—Alexander's Bridge. 1998. 112p. 22.00 (*0-684-81907-4*, Simon & Schuster) Simon & Schuster.
—Alexander's Bridge. (Ebook Classic Ser.). E-Book 5.00 (*0-7410-1301-0*) SoftBook Pr.
—Alexander's Bridge. 1977. 140p. reprint ed. pap. 9.95 (*0-8032-5863-1*, Bison Bks.) Univ. of Nebraska Pr.
—Alexander's Bridge. 1990. xxiii, 176p. pap. 12.00 o.s.i (*1-85381-163-7*) Virago Pr., Ltd. GBR. *Dist:* Trafalgar Square.
—Alexander's Bridge. l.t. ed. 2000. 201p. 16.99 (*1-930142-29-3*); pap. 9.99 (*1-930142-28-5*) Write Together Publishing.
Cather, Willa & O'Brien, Sharon. Alexander's Bridge. 1988. 216p. pap. 6.00 o.p. (*0-452-00875-1*, Meridian Bks.) NAL.
Caxton, Tony. Bowker's Bonfire. 1996. 272p. 21.95 o.p. (*0-312-13936-5*, Saint Martin's Minotaur) St. Martin's Pr.
Celine, Louis-Ferdinand. London Bridge. Di Bernardi, Dominic, tr. from FRE. 1995. 449p. 23.95 (*1-56478-071-6*); 1999. 390p. reprint ed. pap. 14.50 (*1-56478-175-5*) Dalkey Archive Pr.
Chapman, Jean. The Soldier's Girl. l.t. ed. 1998. (Magna Large Print Ser.). 480p. 29.99 o.p. (*0-7505-1189-3*) Magna Large Print Bks. GBR. *Dist:* Ulverscroft Large Print Bks., Ltd., Ulverscroft Large Print Canada, Ltd.
Charles, Kate. Appointed to Die. 1994. 368p. 19.95 o.s.i (*0-89296-548-7*) Mysterious Pr.
—Appointed to Die. 1995. 352p. mass mkt. 5.99 o.s.i (*0-446-40361-X*) Warner Bks., Inc.
—A Dead Man Out of Mind. l.t. ed. 1996. (G. K. Hall Mystery Ser.). 429p. 22.95 o.p. (*0-7838-1706-1*, Macmillan Reference USA) Gale Group.
—A Dead Man Out of Mind. 1995. 82p. 19.95 o.p. (*0-89296-585-1*) Mysterious Pr.
—A Dead Man Out of Mind. 1996. 288p. mass mkt. 5.99 o.p. (*0-446-40432-2*) Warner Bks., Inc.
—A Drink of Deadly Wine. 1992. 336p. 17.95 (*0-89296-501-0*) Mysterious Pr.
—Evil Angels among Them. l.t. ed. 1997. (G. K. Hall Mystery Ser.). 371p. lib. bdg. 25.95 o.p. (*0-7838-2024-0*, Macmillan Reference USA) Gale Group.
—Evil Angels among Them. 352p. 1997. mass mkt. 6.50 (*0-446-40521-3*, Mysterious Pr. Paperback Bks.); 1996. 21.50 o.p. (*0-89296-639-4*) Warner Bks., Inc.
—The Snares of Death. 1993. 368p. 18.95 (*0-89296-498-7*) Mysterious Pr.
—The Snares of Death. 1994. 352p. mass mkt. 5.50 (*0-446-40195-1*) Warner Bks., Inc.
—Strange Children. 2001. 404p. pap. 8.95 (*0-7515-2542-1*) Warner Bks. GBR. *Dist:* Trafalgar Square.
—Unruly Passions. 2001. 440p. pap. 8.95 (*0-7515-2437-9*) Warner Bks. GBR. *Dist:* Trafalgar Square.
Charles, Paul. The Ballad of Sean & Wilko. 2000. (Inspector Christy Kennedy Mystery Ser.: No. 4). 284p. 31.00 (*1-899344-58-6*); 283p. pap. 15.95 (*1-899344-57-8*) Do-Not Pr., The GBR. *Dist:* Dufour Editions, Inc.
—The Ballad of Sean & Wilko. 2000. 283p. (*1-902602-02-1*) New Island Bks. IRL. *Dist:* Dufour Editions, Inc.
—Fountain of Sorrow. 1999. 230p. 31.00 (*1-899344-38-1*); pap. 14.95 (*1-899344-39-X*) Do-Not Pr., The GBR. *Dist:* Dufour Editions, Inc.
—The Hissing of the Silent Lonely Room. 2002. (Inspector Christy Kennedy Mystery Ser.: No. 5). 286p. 29.95 (*1-899344-70-5*); pap. 15.95 (*1-899344-71-3*) Do-Not Pr., The GBR. *Dist:* Dufour Editions, Inc.
—I Love the Sound of Breaking Glass: An Inspector Christy Kennedy Mystery. 1997. (Bloodlines Ser.). 232p. pap. 14.95 (*1-899344-16-0*) Do-Not Pr., The GBR. *Dist:* Dufour Editions, Inc.
—Last Boat to Camden Town: An Inspector Christy Kennedy Mystery. 1998. (Illus.). 168p. pap. 15.95 (*1-899344-30-6*); 34.95 (*1-899344-29-2*) Do-Not Pr., The GBR. *Dist:* Dufour Editions, Inc.
Chase, Loretta. The Last Hellion. 1999. 26.95 (*0-7862-1989-0*, Five Star) Gale Group.
—The Last Hellion. 1998. 384p. mass mkt. 6.99 (*0-380-77617-0*, Avon Bks.) Morrow/Avon.
Cheaney, Janie B. The Playmaker. Siscoe, Nancy, ed. 2000. 320p. (J). (gr. 5-7). lib. bdg. 17.99 (*0-375-90577-4*, Knopf Bks. for Young Readers) Random Hse. Children's Bks.
Cheek, Mavis. Parlor Games. 1989. 18.95 o.p. (*0-671-68309-8*, Simon & Schuster) Simon & Schuster.
—Parlour Games. 2003. (General Ser.). lib. bdg. 24.95 (*0-7862-4780-0*) Thorndike Pr.
Cheshire, Chloe. A Gypsy at Almack's. 1992. 18.95 o.p. (*0-312-08805-1*) St. Martin's Pr.
Chesney, Marion. Back in Society. l.t. ed. 1995. (G. K. Hall Nightingale Ser.: Vol. 6). pap. 18.95 o.p. (*0-7838-1454-2*, Macmillan Reference USA) Gale Group.
—Back in Society. (Poor Relation Ser.: Vol. 6). 1995. mass mkt. 4.50 (*0-312-95338-0*, St. Martin's Paperbacks); 1994. 160p. 12.99 o.p. (*0-312-10932-6*) St. Martin's Pr.
—Colonel Sandhurst to the Rescue. l.t. ed. 1995. (G. K. Hall Nightingale Ser.: Vol. 5). 208p. pap. 18.95 o.p. (*0-8161-7415-6*, Macmillan Reference USA) Gale Group.
—Colonel Sandhurst to the Rescue. (Poor Relation Ser.: Vol. 5). 1995. 152p. mass mkt. 4.50 (*0-312-95337-2*, St. Martin's Paperbacks); 1994. 160p. 17.95 o.p. (*0-312-10444-8*) St. Martin's Pr.
—Lady Fortescue Steps Out. l.t. ed. 1994. (Poor Relation Ser.: Vol. 1). 196p. lib. bdg. 15.95 o.p. (*0-8161-5836-3*, Macmillan Reference USA) Gale Group.
—Lady Fortescue Steps Out. (Poor Relation Ser.: Vol. 1). 1993. 152p. mass mkt. 3.99 (*0-312-95129-9*, St. Martin's Paperbacks); 1992. 160p. 17.95 o.p. (*0-312-08231-2*) St. Martin's Pr.
—Miss Tonks Takes a Risk. 1994. (Poor Relation Ser.: Vol. 2). 152p. mass mkt. 3.99 (*0-312-95219-8*, St. Martin's Paperbacks) St. Martin's Pr.
—Miss Tonks Turns to Crime. l.t. ed. 1994. (Poor Relation Ser.: Vol. 2). 251p. lib. bdg. 17.95 (*0-8161-5898-3*, Macmillan Reference USA) Gale Group.
—Miss Tonks Turns to Crime. 1993. (Poor Relation Ser.: Vol. 2). 16.95 o.p. (*0-312-08846-9*) St. Martin's Pr.
—Mrs. Budley Falls from Grace. l.t. ed. 1994. (Poor Relation Ser.: Vol. 3). 274p. lib. bdg. 15.95 o.p. (*0-8161-5980-7*, Macmillan Reference USA) Gale Group.
—Mrs. Budley Falls from Grace. (Poor Relation Ser.: Vol. 3). 160p. 1994. mass mkt. 3.99 (*0-312-95275-9*, St. Martin's Paperbacks); 1993. 16.95 o.p. (*0-312-09342-X*) St. Martin's Pr.
Chesterton, G. K. The Man Who Was Thursday. reprint ed. lib. bdg. 20.95 (*0-89190-577-4*, Rivercity Pr.) Amereon, Ltd.
—The Man Who Was Thursday. 1986. 196p. pap. 3.50 o.p. (*0-88184-225-7*, Carroll & Graf Pubs.) Avalon Publishing Group.
—The Man Who Was Thursday. 1908. E-Book (*1-58734-005-4*) Bartleby.com.
—The Man Who Was Thursday. 1990. reprint ed. lib. bdg. 16.95 (*0-89968-495-5*) Buccaneer Bks., Inc.
—The Man Who Was Thursday. l.t. unabr. ed. (Large Print Classics). 2002. vi, 249p. pap. 10.95 (*0-486-42250-X*); 1986. (Illus.). 128p. reprint ed. pap. 4.95 (*0-486-25121-7*) Dover Pubns., Inc.
—The Man Who Was Thursday. l.t. ed. 1987. (Nightingale Ser.). 296p. 11.95 o.p. (*0-8161-4322-6*, Macmillan Reference USA) Gale Group.
—The Man Who Was Thursday. 1960. pap. 5.95 o.p. (*0-399-50151-7*) Putnam Publishing Group, The.
—The Man Who Was Thursday. 2001. (Modern Library Classics). 224p. pap. 8.95 (*0-375-75791-0*, Modern Library) Random House Adult Trade Publishing Group.
—The Man Who Was Thursday. l.t. ed. 1999. 288p. text 24.95 (*1-56000-492-4*) Transaction Pubs.
—The Man Who Was Thursday. 1990. (Penguin Twentieth-Century Classics Ser.). 192p. 8.95 (*0-14-018388-4*, Penguin Classics) Viking Penguin.
—The Man Who Was Thursday. 1998. (Classics Library). 184p. pap. 3.95 (*1-85326-236-6*, 2366WW) Wordsworth Editions, Ltd. GBR. *Dist:* Casemate Pubs. & Bk. Distributors, LLC.
—The Man Who Was Thursday: And Related Pieces. Metcalf, Stephen, ed. 1996. (Oxford World's Classics Ser.). (Illus.). 238p. pap. 7.95 o.p. (*0-19-282359-0*) Oxford Univ. Pr., Inc.
—The Napoleon of Notting Hill. reprint ed. lib. bdg. 98.00 (*0-7426-3008-0*); 2001. 301p. pap. text 28.00 (*0-7426-8008-8*) Classic Bks.
—The Napoleon of Notting Hill. 1991. (Illus.). 160p. pap. 5.95 (*0-486-26551-X*) Dover Pubns., Inc.
Chevalier, Tracy. Falling Angels: A Novel. 2002. 336p. pap. 13.00 (*0-452-28320-5*, Plume); 2001. 324p. 24.95 o.s.i (*0-525-94581-4*, Dutton) Dutton/Plume.
Christie, Agatha. The Man in the Brown Suit. 2001. 288p. reprint ed. mass mkt. 5.99 (*0-312-97948-7*, St. Martin's Paperbacks) St. Martin's Pr.
—N or M? unabr. ed. 1997. (Tuppence & Tommy Beresford Mysteries Ser.). audio 54.95 o.p. (*0-7451-5832-3*, CAB 653) BBC Audiobooks America.
—N or M? (Agatha Christie Ser.). 1998. mass mkt. 3.99 o.s.i (*0-425-16929-4*); 1986. 240p. mass mkt. 5.99 o.s.i (*0-425-09845-1*); 1986. mass mkt. 2.95 o.s.i (*0-425-09329-8*); 1984. mass mkt. 2.95 o.s.i (*0-425-06796-3*) Berkley Publishing Group.
—N or M? 1974. 192p. pap. 2.50 o.s.i (*0-440-16254-8*) Dell Publishing.
—N or M? 2000. (Tommy & Tuppence Mysteries Ser.). 224p. mass mkt. 5.99 (*0-451-20113-2*, Signet Bks.) NAL.
—N or M? 1987. (Agatha Christie Ser.). 14.95 o.s.i (*0-396-09163-6*, G. P. Putnam's Sons) Penguin Putnam Bks. for Young Readers.
—N or M? l.t. ed. 1984. (Ulverscroft Large Print Ser.). 336p. 32.50 (*0-7089-1156-0*, Ulverscroft) Thorpe, F. A. Pubs. GBR. *Dist:* Ulverscroft Large Print Bks., Ltd., Ulverscroft Large Print Canada, Ltd.
—The Secret of Chimneys. 1984. 224p. mass mkt. 5.99 o.s.i (*0-425-06802-1*) Berkley Publishing Group.
—The Secret of Chimneys. 1981. 224p. pap. 2.95 o.p. (*0-440-17708-1*) Dell Publishing.
—The Secret of Chimneys. 1986. (Agatha Christie Ser.). 14.95 o.s.i (*0-396-08870-8*, G. P. Putnam's Sons) Penguin Putnam Bks. for Young Readers.
—The Secret of Chimneys. 2001. reprint ed. mass mkt. 5.99 (*0-312-97974-6*, St. Martin's Paperbacks) St. Martin's Pr.
—The Secret of Chimneys. l.t. ed. 1983. 452p. 12.50 o.p. (*0-7089-0983-3*, Ulverscroft) Thorpe, F. A. Pubs. GBR. *Dist:* Ulverscroft Large Print Bks., Ltd.
—Third Girl. 1991. (Agatha Christie Ser.). 400p. 12.95 o.p. (*0-8161-4608-X*, Macmillan Reference USA) Gale Group.
—Third Girl. 1990. (Hercule Poirot Ser.). 208p. 21.95 o.s.i (*0-399-13512-X*, G. P. Putnam's Sons) Penguin Putnam Bks. for Young Readers.
—Third Girl. 1984. mass mkt. 3.50 o.s.i (*0-671-54212-5*); 1982. mass mkt. 2.95 o.s.i (*0-671-46719-0*) Simon & Schuster. (Pocket).
—Third Girl. 1992. (Hercule Poirot Mystery Ser.). 12.04 (*0-606-12536-1*) Turtleback Bks.
—The Third Girl. 2000. (Hercule Poirot Mystery Ser.). 272p. mass mkt. 5.99 (*0-425-17471-9*) Berkley Publishing Group.
—Third Girl. l.t. ed. 1990. (Agatha Christie Ser.). 360p. lib. bdg. 13.95 o.p. (*0-8161-4607-1*, Macmillan Reference USA) Gale Group.
—Third Girl. l.t. ed. 1989. 406p. 12.00 o.p. (*0-85456-585-X*, Ulverscroft) Thorpe, F. A. Pubs. GBR. *Dist:* Ulverscroft Large Print Bks., Ltd.
—Third Girl: A Hercule Poirot Mystery. unabr. ed. 1997. audio 54.95 o.p. (*0-7451-5838-2*, CAB 105) BBC Audiobooks America.
—Three Blind Mice. abr. ed. 1990. audio 16.99 (*0-88646-172-3*, 7173) Durkin Hayes Publishing Ltd.
Clark, Douglas. The Big Grouse: A Masters & Green Mystery. 1987. 224p. 18.95 o.p. (*0-575-03909-4*) Gollancz, Victor GBR. *Dist:* Trafalgar Square.
—The Big Grouse: A Masters & Green Mystery. 1988. 272p. reprint ed. pap. 3.95 o.p. (*0-06-080918-3*, P-918, Perennial) HarperTrade.
—Bouquet Garni. l.t. ed. 1986. 368p. 12.50 o.p. (*0-7089-1415-2*, Ulverscroft) Thorpe, F. A. Pubs. GBR. *Dist:* Ulverscroft Large Print Bks., Ltd.
—Dead Letter: A Masters & Green Mystery. l.t. ed. 1989. (Ulverscroft Large Print Ser.). 379p. 29.99 o.p. (*0-7089-1972-3*, Ulverscroft) Thorpe, F. A. Pubs. GBR. *Dist:* Ulverscroft Large Print Bks., Ltd., Ulverscroft Large Print Canada, Ltd.
—Doone Walk. l.t. ed. 1987. (Linford Mystery Library). 336p. pap. 17.99 o.p. (*0-7089-6394-3*, Linford) Thorpe, F. A. Pubs. GBR. *Dist:* Ulverscroft Large Print Bks., Ltd., Ulverscroft Large Print Canada, Ltd.
—Dread & Water. l.t. ed. 1991. 17.95 o.p. (*0-7451-9999-2*, AH035); pap. 15.95 o.p. (*0-7927-0463-0*, AS071) BBC Audiobooks America.
—The Gimmel Flask. 1982. (Murder Ink Mystery Ser.: No. 41). pap. 2.25 o.p. (*0-440-13160-X*) Dell Publishing.

—Golden Rain. 1982. (Murder Ink Mystery Ser.: No. 47). 224p. pap. 2.50 o.p. (*0-440-12932-X*) Dell Publishing.

—Heberden's Seat. l.t. ed. 1991. 17.95 o.p. (*0-7451-8118-X*, AH0167); pap. 15.95 o.p. (*0-7927-0618-8*, AS0203) BBC Audiobooks America.

—Heberden's Seat. 1985. 192p. mass mkt. 3.50 o.p. (*0-06-080724-5*, P724, Perennial) HarperTrade.

—Jewelled Eye: A Masters & Green Mystery. l.t. ed. 1987. pap. 13.95 o.p. (*1-55504-251-1*) BBC Audiobooks America.

—Jewelled Eye: A Masters & Green Mystery. 1986. 189p. 17.95 o.p. (*0-575-03728-8*) Gollancz, Victor GBR. *Dist:* Trafalgar Square.

—Jewelled Eye: A Masters & Green Mystery. 1988. 272p. reprint ed. pap. 3.95 o.p. (*0-06-080919-1*, P-919, Perennial) HarperTrade.

—The Longest Pleasure. 1984. 192p. reprint ed. pap. 2.95 o.p. (*0-06-080689-3*, P689) HarperCollins Pubs.

—The Monday Theory. 1985. 208p. mass mkt. 3.50 o.p. (*0-06-080737-7*, P737, Perennial) HarperTrade.

—Nobody's Perfect. l.t. ed. (Atlantic Mystery Ser.). pap. 8.95 o.p. (*1-55504-561-8*, 844) BBC Audiobooks America.

—Nobody's Perfect. 1986. 192p. reprint ed. mass mkt. 3.50 o.p. (*0-06-080796-2*, P 796, Perennial) HarperTrade.

—Performance. 1986. 224p. reprint ed. mass mkt. 3.50 o.p. (*0-06-080810-1*, P 810, Perennial) HarperTrade.

—Plain Sailing: A Masters & Green Mystery. 1988. 272p. reprint ed. pap. 3.95 o.p. (*0-06-080917-5*, P-917, Perennial) HarperTrade.

—Plain Sailing: A Masters & Green Mystery. l.t. ed. 1989. (Ulverscroft Large Print Ser.). 384p. 29.99 o.p. (*0-7089-2008-X*, Ulverscroft) Thorpe, F. A. Pubs. GBR. *Dist:* Ulverscroft Large Print Bks., Ltd., Ulverscroft Large Print Canada, Ltd.

—Poacher's Bag. l.t. ed. 1989. (Atlantic Mystery Ser.). pap. 14.95 o.p. (*1-55504-716-5*, 149) BBC Audiobooks America.

—Poacher's Bag. 1983. 176p. pap. o.p. (*0-06-080643-5*, P 643) HarperCollins Pubs.

—Roast Eggs. 1983. 176p. pap. o.p. (*0-06-080644-3*, P 644) HarperCollins Pubs.

—Shelf Life. l.t. ed. 1992. 18.95 o.p. (*0-7451-8252-6*, AH0262); pap. 16.95 o.p. (*0-7927-0812-1*, AS0298) BBC Audiobooks America.

—Shelf Life. 1983. 176p. pap. o.p. (*0-06-080675-3*, P675) HarperCollins Pubs.

—Sick to Death. l.t. ed. 1990. 17.95 o.p. (*0-7451-9897-X*, C0628); pap. 15.95 o.p. (*0-7927-0360-X*, C0822) BBC Audiobooks America.

—Sick to Death. 1983. 176p. pap. o.p. (*0-06-080676-1*, P676) HarperCollins Pubs.

—Storm Centre. 1986. 18.95 o.p. (*0-575-03833-0*) Gollancz, Victor GBR. *Dist:* Trafalgar Square.

—Storm Centre. 1988. (Master & Green Mystery Ser.). 240p. reprint ed. pap. 3.95 o.p. (*0-06-080920-5*, P-920, Perennial) HarperTrade.

—Storm Centre. l.t. ed. 1987. (Linford Mystery Library). 368p. pap. 17.99 o.p. (*0-7089-6388-9*, Linford) Thorpe, F. A. Pubs. GBR. *Dist:* Ulverscroft Large Print Bks., Ltd., Ulverscroft Large Print Canada, Ltd.

—Table d'Hote. 1985. 208p. mass mkt. 3.50 o.p. (*0-06-080723-7*, P723, Perennial) HarperTrade.

—Table d'Hote. l.t. ed. 1981. (Ulverscroft Large Print Ser.). 315p. 29.99 o.p. (*0-7089-0603-6*, Ulverscroft) Thorpe, F. A. Pubs. GBR. *Dist:* Ulverscroft Large Print Bks., Ltd., Ulverscroft Large Print Canada, Ltd.

—Vicious Circle: A Masters & Green Mystery. l.t. ed. 1988. pap. 14.95 o.p. (*1-55504-629-0*, 313) BBC Audiobooks America.

—Vicious Circle: A Masters & Green Mystery. 1985. 208p. reprint ed. mass mkt. 3.50 o.p. (*0-06-080778-4*, P 778, Perennial) HarperTrade.

Clarke, Anna. Cabin Three Thousand Thirty-Three. 1989. 3.50 (*1-55773-251-5*, Diamond Bks.) Berkley Publishing Group.

—Cabin Three Thousand Thirty-Three. 1986. (Crime Club Ser.). 192p. 12.95 o.p. (*0-385-23264-0*) Doubleday Publishing.

—Cabin Three Thousand Thirty-Three. l.t. ed. 1988. (Nightingale Ser.). 285p. 12.95 o.p. (*0-8161-4387-0*, Macmillan Reference USA) Gale Group.

—The Case of the Anxious Aunt. 1996. 208p. mass mkt. 5.99 o.p. (*0-425-15311-8*) Berkley Publishing Group.

—The Case of the Ludicrous Letters. 1994. 208p. (Orig.). mass mkt. 4.50 o.p. (*0-425-14048-2*) Berkley Publishing Group.

—The Case of the Paranoid Patient. 1993. 192p. mass mkt. 3.99 o.p. (*0-425-13858-5*) Berkley Publishing Group.

—The Case of the Paranoid Patient. l.t. ed. 1993. (Nightingale Ser.). 300p. lib. bdg. 15.95 (*0-8161-5845-2*, Macmillan Reference USA) Gale Group.

—Last Judgment. 1985. (Crime Club Ser.). 192p. 11.95 o.p. (*0-385-19666-0*) Doubleday Publishing.

—Last Seen in London. 1987. (Crime Club Ser.). 192p. o.s.i (*0-385-23559-3*) Doubleday Publishing.

—Last Seen in London. l.t. ed. 1992. 340p. pap. 14.95 o.p. (*0-8161-5452-X*, Macmillan Reference USA) Gale Group.

—Murder in Writing. 1990. 3.50 (*1-55773-326-0*, Diamond Bks.) Berkley Publishing Group.

—Murder in Writing. 1988. (Crime Club Ser.). 192p. pap. 15.00 (*0-385-24325-1*) Doubleday Publishing.

—Mystery Lady. 1986. (Crime Club Ser.). 192p. 12.95 o.p. (*0-385-23546-1*) Doubleday Publishing.

—The Whitelands Affair. 1992. mass mkt. 3.99 o.p. (*0-425-13268-4*) Berkley Publishing Group.

Clynes, Michael, pseud. A Brood of Vipers: Being the Fourth Journal of Sir Roger Shallot Concerning Certain Wicked Conspiracies & Horrible Murders Perpetrated in the Reign of King Henry VIII. unabr. ed. 1998. audio 76.95 (*1-85903-164-1*) Magna Story Sound GBR. *Dist:* Ulverscroft Large Print Bks., Ltd.

—A Brood of Vipers: Being the Fourth Journal of Sir Roger Shallot Concerning Certain Wicked Conspiracies & Horrible Murders Perpetrated in the Reign of King Henry VIII. 1995. 256p. 21.95 o.p. (*0-312-13938-1*, Saint Martin's Minotaur) St. Martin's Pr.

—The Gallows Murders: Being the Fifth Journal of Sir Roger Shallot Concerning Certain Wicked Conspiracies & Horrible Murders Perpetrated in the Reign of King Henry VIII. 1996. 256p. text 21.95 o.p. (*0-312-14605-1*, Saint Martin's Minotaur) St. Martin's Pr.

—The Gallows Murders: Being the Fifth Journal of Sir Roger Shallot Concerning Certain Wicked Conspiracies & Horrible Murders Perpetrated in the Reign of King Henry VIII. l.t. ed. 1997. (Large Print Ser.). 448p. 29.99 (*0-7089-3789-6*, Ulverscroft) Thorpe, F. A. Pubs. GBR. *Dist:* Ulverscroft Large Print Bks., Ltd., Ulverscroft Large Print Canada, Ltd.

—The Grail Murders: Being the Third Journal of Sir Roger Shallot Concerning Certain Wicked Conspiracies & Horrible Murders Perpetrated in the Reign of King Henry the Eighth. unabr. ed. 1998. audio 76.95 (*1-85903-158-7*) Magna Story Sound GBR. *Dist:* Ulverscroft Large Print Bks., Ltd.

—The Grail Murders: Being the Third Journal of Sir Roger Shallot Concerning Certain Wicked Conspiracies & Horrible Murders Perpetrated in the Reign of King Henry the Eighth. 1994. 256p. reprint ed. 21.00 (*1-883402-49-2*, Scribner) Simon & Schuster.

—The Poisoned Chalice: Being the Second Journal of Sir Roger Shallot Concerning Wicked Conspiracies & Horrible Murders Perpetrated in the Reign of King Henry VIII. unabr. ed. 1998. audio 76.95 (*1-85903-137-4*) Magna Story Sound GBR. *Dist:* Ulverscroft Large Print Bks., Ltd.

—The Poisoned Chalice: Being the Second Journal of Sir Roger Shallot Concerning Wicked Conspiracies & Horrible Murders Perpetrated in the Reign of King Henry VIII. 1994. 288p. reprint ed. 20.00 (*1-883402-48-4*, Scribner) Simon & Schuster.

—The White Rose Murders: Being the First Journal of Sir Roger Shallot Concerning Wicked Conspiracies & Horrible Murders Perpetrated in the Reign of King Henry VIII. unabr. ed. 1998. audio 76.95 (*1-85903-113-7*) Magna Story Sound GBR. *Dist:* Ulverscroft Large Print Bks., Ltd.

—The White Rose Murders: Being the First Journal of Sir Roger Shallot Concerning Wicked Conspiracies & Horrible Murders Perpetrated in the Reign of King Henry VIII. l.t. ed. 1993. viii, 244p. 18.95 o.p. (*0-312-08920-1*, Saint Martin's Minotaur) St. Martin's Pr.

—The White Rose Murders: Being the First Journal of Sir Roger Shallot Concerning Wicked Conspiracies & Horrible Murders Perpetrated in the Reign of King Henry VIII. l.t. ed. 1995. (Ulverscroft Large Print Ser.). 464p. 29.99 o.p. (*0-7089-3218-5*, Ulverscroft) Thorpe, F. A. Pubs. GBR. *Dist:* Ulverscroft Large Print Bks., Ltd., Ulverscroft Large Print Canada, Ltd.

Cody, Liza. Backhand. 1992. 288p. mass mkt. 4.99 o.s.i (*0-553-29627-2*); mass mkt. 5.99 o.s.i (*0-7704-2531-3*) Bantam Bks.

—Backhand. unabr. ed. 1993. (Anna Lee Mystery Ser.: Vol. 6). audio 60.00 (*1-55690-808-3*, 93117E7) Recorded Bks., LLC.

—Backhand: An Anna Lee Mystery. 1992. 288p. 18.50 o.s.i (*0-385-42231-8*) Doubleday Publishing.

—Bad Company. 1983. 260p. 11.95 o.p. (*0-684-17760-9*, Macmillan Reference USA) Gale Group.

—Bad Company. 1992. pap. o.p. (*0-09-982120-6*) Hutchinson GBR. *Dist:* Random Hse. of Canada, Ltd.

—Bad Company. unabr. ed. 2000. audio compact disk 64.95 (*0-7531-0906-9*, 109069); 1997. audio 54.95 (*1-85695-740-3*, 940506) ISIS Audio Bks. GBR. *Dist:* Ulverscroft Large Print Bks., Ltd.

—Bad Company. 1984. 288p. mass mkt. 2.95 o.s.i (*0-446-30738-6*) Warner Bks., Inc.

—Bucket Nut. 1993. 240p. 18.50 o.s.i (*0-385-46776-1*) Doubleday Publishing.

—Bucket Nut. l.t. unabr. ed. 1998. 24.95 (*0-7531-5173-1*, 151731) ISIS Large Print Bks. GBR. *Dist:* ISIS Publishing.

—Bucket Nut. 1995. 224p. mass mkt. 5.50 o.p. (*0-446-40459-4*) Warner Bks., Inc.

—Dupe. 1992. mass mkt. 4.99 o.s.i (*0-7704-2439-2*); 256p. mass mkt. 4.99 o.s.i (*0-553-29641-8*) Bantam Bks.

—Dupe. 1981. 252p. 10.95 o.s.i (*0-684-17153-8*, Macmillan Reference USA) Gale Group.

—Dupe. 1992. pap. o.p. (*0-09-982110-9*) Hutchinson GBR. *Dist:* Random Hse. of Canada, Ltd.

—Dupe. 1984. mass mkt. 2.95 o.s.i (*0-446-30527-8*) Warner Bks., Inc.

—Head Case. l.t. ed. 1992. 18.95 o.p. (*0-7451-8282-8*, AH0274); pap. 16.95 o.p. (*0-7927-0951-9*, AS0310) BBC Audiobooks America.

—Head Case. 1989. 192p. reprint ed. mass mkt. 3.95 o.s.i (*0-553-27645-X*) Bantam Bks.

—Head Case. unabr. ed. 1997. audio 54.95 (*1-85695-745-4*, 940201) ISIS Audio Bks. GBR. *Dist:* Ulverscroft Large Print Bks., Ltd.

—Head Case: An Anna Lee Mystery. 1986. 196p. 13.95 o.s.i (*0-684-18586-5*, Macmillan Reference USA) Gale Group.

—Monkey Wrench. 1995. 256p. 18.95 o.s.i (*0-89296-600-9*) Mysterious Pr.

—Monkey Wrench. 1996. 240p. mass mkt. 5.99 o.p. (*0-446-40457-8*) Warner Bks., Inc.

—Muscle Bound. 1997. 288p. 22.00 o.p. (*0-89296-601-7*) Mysterious Pr.

—Stalker. 1986. 208p. mass mkt. 3.50 o.s.i (*0-446-32807-3*) Warner Bks., Inc.

—The Stalker. 1989. mass mkt. 1.95 o.s.i (*0-553-18503-9*) Bantam Bks.

—Stalker: A Mystery. 1985. 168p. 11.95 o.s.i (*0-684-18234-3*, Scribner) Simon & Schuster.

—Under Contract. 1990. 208p. mass mkt. 3.95 o.s.i (*0-553-28345-6*) Bantam Bks.

—Under Contract. unabr. ed. 1993. (Anna Lee Mystery Ser.: Vol. 5). audio 51.00 (*1-55690-929-2*, 93425E7) Recorded Bks., LLC.

—Under Contract: An Anna Lee Mystery. 1987. 16.95 o.p. (*0-684-18780-9*, Scribner) Simon & Schuster.

Coetzee, J. M. Youth: Scenes from Provincial Life II. 2002. 176p. 22.95 (*0-670-03102-X*, Viking) Viking Penguin.

Coleridge, Nicholas. Streetsmart. 2000. 387p. 26.95 o.p. (*0-312-19960-0*) St. Martin's Pr.

Colgan, Jenny. Amanda's Wedding. abr. ed. 2005. audio 7.99 (*1-58788-648-0*, 3013, Brilliance Audio Paperback Audiobooks); 2001. audio 29.95 (*1-58788-230-2*, 2491, Brilliance Audio Unabridged) Brilliance Audio.

—Amanda's Wedding. 288p. 2001. 23.95 o.p. (*0-446-52647-9*); 2002. reprint ed. pap. 13.95 (*0-446-67811-2*) Warner Bks., Inc.

Collins, Joan. Star Quality. 2003. 368p. mass mkt. 6.99 (*0-7868-9048-7*) Hyperion Pr.

—Star Quality: A Novel. 2003. mass mkt. 7.99 (*0-7868-9060-6*); 2002. 368p. 23.95 (*1-4013-0000-6*); 2002. mass mkt. 7.99 (*0-7868-9064-9*) Hyperion Pr.

—Star Quality: A Novel. 2003. (Core Ser.). 32.95 (*0-7862-4694-4*) Thorndike Pr.

Connolly, J. J. Layer Cake. 352p. mass mkt. 8.95 (*0-7156-3096-2*); 2001. 240p. pap. 15.95 (*0-7156-3018-0*) Duckworth, Gerald & Co., Ltd. GBR. *Dist:* International Publishers Marketing.

Conrad, Joseph. The Secret Agent. Harkness, Bruce & Reid, S. W., eds. 1990. (Cambridge Edition of the Works of Joseph Conrad). (Illus.). 469p. (Orig.). 110.00 (*0-521-34135-3*) Cambridge Univ. Pr.

—The Secret Agent. 1992. (Everyman's Library). 352p. (Orig.). 17.00 (*0-679-41723-0*) Knopf, Alfred A. Inc.

—The Secret Agent. Tennant, Roger, ed. 1996. (Oxford World's Classics Ser.). 356p. (Orig.). (C). pap. 6.95 o.p. (*0-19-281627-6*) Oxford Univ. Pr., Inc.

—The Secret Agent & Almayer's Folly. 1983. 240p. mass mkt. 3.50 o.s.i (*0-553-21134-X*, Bantam Classics) Bantam Bks.

Cook, David. Sunrising. 1990. 240p. pap. 9.95 o.s.i (*0-87951-261-X*); 1990. pap. 8.95 o.p. (*0-87951-338-1*); 1986. 248p. 16.95 o.p. (*0-87951-253-9*) Overlook Pr., The.

Cookson, Catherine. The Branded Man. l.t. ed. 2001. 400p. lib. bdg. 29.95 (*1-58547-067-8*) Ctr. Point Large Print.

—The Branded Man. 2000. 480p. mass mkt. 11.95 (*0-552-14348-0*) Transworld Publishers Ltd. GBR. *Dist:* Trafalgar Square.

—The Silent Lady. 2002. 352p. 25.00 (*0-7432-2761-1*, Simon & Schuster) Simon & Schuster.

—The Thursday Friend. 1999. 320p. (gr. 9). o.s.i (*0-593-03977-7*, Corgi) Bantam Bks.

Cooper, Katy. Lord Sebastian's Wife. 2002. (Harlequin Historicals Ser.: No. 638). 304p. mass mkt. (*0-373-29238-4*, Harlequin Bks.) Harlequin Enterprises, Ltd.

Cooper, Natasha. Creeping Ivy. 1999. 342p. 23.95 o.p. (*0-312-20520-1*, Saint Martin's Minotaur) St. Martin's Pr.

—Creeping Ivy. l.t. ed. 1999. (Ulverscroft Large Print Ser.). 376p. 31.99 o.p. (*0-7089-4144-3*, Ulverscroft) Thorpe, F. A. Pubs. GBR. *Dist:* Ulverscroft Large Print Bks., Ltd., Ulverscroft Large Print Canada, Ltd.

—Fault Lines. 2000. 346p. 23.95 (*0-312-25316-8*, Saint Martin's Minotaur) St. Martin's Pr.

—Fault Lines. l.t. ed. 2000. (Ulverscroft Large Print Ser.). 480p. 31.99 (*0-7089-4276-8*, Ulverscroft) Thorpe, F. A. Pubs. GBR. *Dist:* Ulverscroft Large Print Bks., Ltd., Ulverscroft Large Print Canada, Ltd.

—Prey to All. 2000. 304p. 23.95 (*0-312-26636-7*, Saint Martin's Minotaur) St. Martin's Pr.

—Prey to All. l.t. ed. 2001. (Ulverscroft Large Print Ser.). 464p. 32.50 (*0-7089-4428-0*) Ulverscroft Large Print Bks., Ltd.

Copper, Basil. The Further Adventures of Solar Pons. 1987. (Academy Book Ser.). 256p. pap. 7.95 (*0-89733-273-3*) Academy Chicago Pubs., Ltd.

—The Recollections of Solar Pons. 1995. 25.00 (*1-878252-20-8*); 75.00 (*1-878252-21-6*) Fedogan & Bremer.

Corelli, Marie. The Sorrows of Satan. 1980. (Illus.). pap. 6.95 o.p. (*0-910122-06-7*) Amherst Pr.

—The Sorrows of Satan. Keating, Peter, ed. 1999. (Oxford World's Classics Ser.). 426p. pap. 10.95 o.p. (*0-19-283324-3*) Oxford Univ. Pr., Inc.

—The Sorrows of Satan: Or the Strange Experience of One Geoffrey Tempest, Millionaire: A Romance. 1996. (Oxford Popular Fiction Ser.). 412p. pap. 10.95 o.p. (*0-19-283220-4*) Oxford Univ. Pr., Inc.

—The Sorrows of Satan (1896) 1998. 450p. reprint ed. pap. 27.00 (*0-7661-0146-0*) Kessinger Publishing Co.

Corn, Alfred Dewitt. Part of His Story. 1997. 264p. 24.00 (*0-922811-29-6*) Mid-List Pr.

Cornwell, Bernard. Gallows Thief. 2002. (Illus.). 304p. 24.95 (*0-06-008273-9*) HarperCollins Pubs.

—Gallows Thief. l.t. ed. 2002. 29.95 (*0-7862-4596-4*) Thorndike Pr.

Cottam, Francis. The Fire Fighter. 2001. 320p. o.p. (*0-7011-6981-8*) Random Hse. of Canada, Ltd. CAN. *Dist:* Random Hse., Inc.

—The Fire Fighter. 2002. 256p. 23.95 (*0-312-28679-1*) St. Martin's Pr.

Coulter, Catherine. Mad Jack. 1999. 352p. mass mkt. 7.99 (*0-515-12420-6*, Jove) Berkley Publishing Group.

—Mad Jack. l.t. ed. 1999. (Wheeler Large Print Book Ser.). 394p. 27.95 o.p. (*1-56895-784-X*, Wheeler Publishing, Inc.) Gale Group.

—Midsummer Magic. 1987. (J). mass mkt. 3.95 o.p. (*0-451-40057-7*); 1998. 416p. reprint ed. mass mkt. 7.99 o.s.i (*0-451-40870-5*, Topaz); 1987. 416p. reprint ed. mass mkt. 7.50 o.s.i (*0-451-40204-9*, Onyx) NAL.

—Midsummer Magic. 1999. 412p. 26.00 (*0-7278-5468-2*) Severn Hse. Pubs., Ltd.

Counts, Wilma. The Wagered Wife. 2001. (Zebra Regency Romance Ser.). 256p. mass mkt. 4.99 o.s.i (*0-8217-6806-9*, Zebra Bks.) Kensington Publishing Corp.

Coward, Mat. In & Out. l.t. ed. 2001. (Five Star First Edition Mystery Ser.). 184p. 23.95 (*0-7862-3017-7*) Thorndike Pr.

Cowell, Stephanie. Nicholas Cooke: Actor, Soldier, Physician, Priest. 1994. 448p. reprint ed. pap. 12.00 o.s.i (*0-345-39016-4*) Ballantine Bks.

—Nicholas Cooke: Actor, Soldier, Physician, Priest. 1993. 442p. 24.00 o.p. (*0-393-03543-3*) Norton, W. W. & Co., Inc.

Crichton, Michael. The Great Train Robbery. 1976. 320p. pap. 3.50 o.p. (*0-553-23112-X*) Bantam Bks.

—The Great Train Robbery. 1976. (Adult Ser.). reprint ed. lib. bdg. 13.50 o.p. (*0-8161-6228-X*, Macmillan Reference USA) Gale Group.

—The Great Train Robbery. 2002. 352p. mass mkt. 7.99 (*0-06-050230-4*, Avon Bks.) Morrow/Avon.

—The Great Train Robbery. abr. ed. 1996. audio 18.00 o.s.i (*0-679-44895-0*, 394068, RH Audio) Random Hse. Audio Publishing Group.

—The Great Train Robbery. l.t. ed. 1997. (Charnwood Large Print Ser.). 384p. 34.50 (*0-7089-8928-4*, Ulverscroft) Thorpe, F. A. Pubs. GBR. *Dist:* Ulverscroft Large Print Bks., Ltd., Ulverscroft Large Print Canada, Ltd.

Crombie, Deborah. All Shall Be Well. 1995. 272p. mass mkt. 6.99 (*0-425-14771-1*) Berkley Publishing Group.

—All Shall Be Well. 2004. 288p. mass mkt. 6.99 (*0-06-053439-7*, Avon Bks.) Morrow/Avon.

—All Shall Be Well: A Superintendent Duncan Kincaid - Sergeant Gemma James Mystery. 1994. 256p. text 20.00 (*0-684-19654-9*, Macmillan Reference USA) Gale Group.

—And Justice There is None. 2002. E-Book 19.50 (*0-553-89707-1*) Bantam Bks.

—And Justice There Is None. 2003. 416p. mass mkt. 6.99 (*0-553-57930-4*); 2002. 336p. 23.95 (*0-553-10973-1*) Bantam Bks.
—And Justice There Is None. l.t. ed. 2003. 29.95 (*1-58724-400-4*, Wheeler Publishing, Inc.) Gale Group.
—Dreaming of the Bones. 1998. 416p. mass mkt. 6.99 (*0-553-57931-2*) Bantam Bks.
—Dreaming of the Bones. l.t. ed. 2000. pap. 25.95 (*1-56895-899-4*, Wheeler Publishing, Inc.) Gale Group.
—Dreaming of the Bones. l.t. ed. 1998. (Magna Large Print Ser.). 480p. o.p. (*0-7505-1315-2*) Magna Large Print Bks. GBR. *Dist:* Ulverscroft Large Print Canada, Ltd.
—Dreaming of the Bones. 1997. 350p. 21.50 (*0-684-80141-8*); 21.50 (*0-684-84720-5*) Simon & Schuster. (Scribner).
—Kissed a Sad Goodbye. 1999. 336p. 23.95 o.s.i (*0-553-10943-X*) Bantam Bks.
—Kissed a Sad Goodbye. l.t. ed. 1999. (Large Print Book Ser.). pap. 24.95 (*1-56895-731-9*, Wheeler Publishing, Inc.) Gale Group.
—Kissed a Sad Goodbye. unabr. ed. 1999. audio 87.00 (*0-7887-3751-1*, 95869E7) Recorded Bks., LLC.
—Leave the Grave Green. 1996. 304p. mass mkt. 6.50 (*0-425-15308-8*) Berkley Publishing Group.
—Leave the Grave Green. l.t. ed. 2000. pap. 23.95 (*1-56895-846-3*, Wheeler Publishing, Inc.) Gale Group.
—Leave the Grave Green. l.t. ed. 1997. (Magna Large Print Ser.). 400p. (*0-7505-1114-1*) Magna Large Print Bks. GBR. *Dist:* Ulverscroft Large Print Canada, Ltd.
—Leave the Grave Green. 1995. 224p. 20.00 o.p. (*0-684-19770-7*, Scribner) Simon & Schuster.
—Mourn Not Your Dead. 1997. 304p. reprint ed. mass mkt. 6.99 (*0-425-15778-4*, Prime Crime) Berkley Publishing Group.
—Mourn Not Your Dead. l.t. ed. 1997. (Magna Large Print Ser.). 412p. (*0-7505-1175-3*) Magna Large Print Bks. GBR. *Dist:* Ulverscroft Large Print Canada, Ltd.
—Mourn Not Your Dead: A Duncan Kincaid/Gemma James Crime Novel. l.t. ed. 1996. 25.95 (*1-56895-367-4*, Wheeler Publishing, Inc.) Gale Group.
—Mourn Not Your Dead: A Duncan Kincaid/Gemma James Crime Novel. 1996. 288p. 21.00 o.p. (*0-684-80131-0*, Scribner) Simon & Schuster.
—A Share in Death: A Mystery Introducing Superintendent Duncan Kincaid & Sergeant Gemma James. 1994. 208p. reprint ed. mass mkt. 6.50 (*0-425-14197-7*, Prime Crime) Berkley Publishing Group.
—A Share in Death: A Mystery Introducing Superintendent Duncan Kincaid & Sergeant Gemma James. l.t. ed. 1995. (Magna Large Print Ser.). 259p. (*0-7505-0833-7*) Magna Large Print Bks. GBR. *Dist:* Ulverscroft Large Print Canada, Ltd.
—A Share in Death: A Mystery Introducing Superintendent Duncan Kincaid & Sergeant Gemma James. 1993. 256p. 20.00 o.p. (*0-684-19527-5*, Scribner) Simon & Schuster.
Cumming, Alan. Tommy's Tale: A Novel. 272p. 2003. pap. 12.95 (*0-06-098927-0*); 2002. 24.95 (*0-06-039444-7*) HarperTrade. (ReganBooks).
Currer-Briggs, Noel. Young Men at War. 1996. 240p. pap. 14.95 (*0-85449-236-4*) Millivres Prowler Group GBR. *Dist:* LPC Group.
Curtis, Jack. Glory. 1988. 352p. 18.95 o.p. (*0-525-24668-1*, Dutton) Dutton/Plume.
—Glory. 1989. mass mkt. 4.50 o.s.i (*0-451-40133-6*, Onyx) NAL.
Dahl, Sophie. The Man with the Dancing Eyes. 2003. (Illus.). 64p. 16.95 (*1-58234-342-X*) Bloomsbury Publishing.
D'Ancona, Matthew. Going East. 2004. 384p. 25.00 (*0-385-51049-7*, Talese, Nan A.) Doubleday Publishing.
Daniel, Mark. Unbridled. 1990. 224p. 17.95 o.p. (*0-89919-922-4*) Houghton Mifflin Co.
—Unbridled. 1992. 256p. mass mkt. 4.99 (*0-380-71443-4*, Avon Bks.) Morrow/Avon.
Daniels, Philip. Foolproof. 1995. 175p. 19.95 o.p. (*0-312-13077-5*, Saint Martin's Minotaur) St. Martin's Pr.
—Goldmine - London W. I. 1993. 160p. 17.95 o.p. (*0-312-09821-9*, Saint Martin's Minotaur) St. Martin's Pr.
Davidson, Alexander. Stock Market Rollercoaster - A Story of Risk, Greed, & Temptation. 2001. 286p. pap. 29.95 (*0-471-49933-1*) Wiley, John & Sons, Inc.
Davies, Andrew. B. Monkey. 1998. 224p. (J). pap. 11.95 (*0-7868-8249-2*) Hyperion Pr.
Davies, Linda. Nest of Vipers. 1995. 256p. mass mkt. 6.50 o.s.i (*0-440-22190-0*) Dell Publishing.
—Nest of Vipers. 1995. 416p. 23.00 o.s.i (*0-385-47596-9*) Doubleday Publishing.
—Nest of Vipers. l.t. ed. 1995. (Large Print Bks.). 25.95 o.p. (*1-56895-222-8*, Wheeler Publishing, Inc.) Gale Group.
Davis, Anna. Cheet. 2003. 304p. pap. 13.00 (*0-452-28429-5*, Plume) Dutton/Plume.
Davison, Philip. The Crooked Man. 1997. 214p. pap. o.p. (*0-224-04304-8*) Random Hse. UK, Ltd.
—The Crooked Man. 2002. 224p. 13.00 (*0-14-200208-9*) Viking Penguin.
Dawson, Jill. Fred & Edie. l.t. ed. 2002. 324p. pap. 25.95 (*0-7862-3956-5*) Gale Group.
—Fred & Edie. 2001. 288p. 25.00 (*1-56649-222-X*) Welcome Rain Pubs.
—Fred & Edie: A Novel. 2002. 288p. pap. 13.00 (*0-618-19728-1*) Houghton Mifflin Co.
De Botton, Alain. Kiss & Tell. 1997. 272p. pap. 13.00 (*0-312-15561-1*); 1996. 208p. 22.00 o.p. (*0-312-14282-X*) Picador.
DeAndrea, William L. Killed in the Fog. l.t. ed. 1997. (Large Print Book Ser.). pap. 23.95 (*1-56895-434-4*, Wheeler Publishing, Inc.) Gale Group.
—Killed in the Fog. 1996. 222p. 20.50 (*0-684-83054-X*, Simon & Schuster); 20.00 (*1-883402-30-1*, Scribner) Simon & Schuster.
Deans, Emily. The Scheming Spinster. 2001. E-Book 4.75 incl. disk (*1-58749-066-8*); E-Book 4.75 (*1-58749-067-6*) Awe-Struck E-Bks.
Defoe, Daniel. A Journal of the Plague Year. 2000. 252p. E-Book 9.95 (*0-594-02959-7*) 1873 Pr.
—A Journal of the Plague Year. (Illus.). reprint ed. (*0-404-07919-9*) AMS Pr., Inc.
—A Journal of the Plague Year. 1977. reprint ed. 11.95 o.p. (*0-460-00289-9*); 2.95 o.p. (*0-460-01289-4*) Biblio Distribution.
—A Journal of the Plague Year. 2001. per. 12.50 (*1-891355-77-5*); per. 15.50 (*1-58396-242-5*) Blue Unicorn Editions.
—A Journal of the Plague Year. (Shakespeare Head Edition of the Writings of Daniel Defoe Ser.: Vol. 6). 302p. 2001. pap. text 28.00 (*0-7426-5058-8*); 1999. reprint ed. lib. bdg. (*1-58201-058-7*) Classic Bks.
—A Journal of the Plague Year. 2001. (Dover Thrift Editions Ser.). 192p. pap. 2.50 (*0-486-41919-3*) Dover Pubns., Inc.
—A Journal of the Plague Year. 2002. 204p. 94.99 (*1-4043-1144-0*); per. 89.99 (*1-4043-1145-9*) IndyPublish.com.
—A Journal of the Plague Year. 1984. 240p. pap. 4.95 o.p. (*0-452-00689-9*, Meridian Bks.); 1984. pap. 5.95 o.p. (*0-452-01052-7*, Meridian Bks.); 1968. mass mkt. 0.75 o.p. (*0-451-50433-X*, Signet Classics); 1968. mass mkt. 0.50 o.p. (*0-451-50024-5*, Signet Classics); 1968. mass mkt. 0.60 o.p. (*0-451-50146-2*, Signet Classics); 1960. mass mkt. 0.95 o.p. (*0-451-50611-1*, Signet Classics); 1960. mass mkt. 1.25 o.p. (*0-451-50927-7*, Signet Classics); 1960. mass mkt. 1.50 o.p. (*0-451-51235-9*, CW1235, Signet Classics) NAL.
—A Journal of the Plague Year. Backsheider, Paula, ed. 1992. (Critical Editions Ser.). 361p. (C). pap. text 9.00 (*0-393-96188-5*) Norton, W. W. & Co., Inc.
—A Journal of the Plague Year. Landa, Louis, ed. (Oxford World's Classics Ser.). (Illus.). 1999. 336p. pap. 9.95 (*0-19-283618-8*); 1990. 330p. pap. 6.95 o.p. (*0-19-282682-4*) Oxford Univ. Pr., Inc.
—A Journal of the Plague Year. 2001. (Modern Library Classics). 272p. pap. 8.95 (*0-375-75789-9*, Modern Library) Random House Adult Trade Publishing Group.
—A Journal of the Plague Year. (Ebook Classic Ser.). E-Book 5.00 (*0-7410-1507-2*) SoftBook Pr.
—A Journal of the Plague Year. l.t. ed. 2000. (Perennial Bestsellers Ser.). 365p. 26.95 (*0-7838-9167-9*) Thorndike Pr.
—A Journal of the Plague Year. Man, John, ed. 1994. 336p. pap. 5.50 o.p. (*0-460-87462-4*, Everyman's Classic Library in Paperback) Tuttle Publishing.
—A Journal of the Plague Year. Burgess, Anthony & Bristow, Christopher, eds. 1966. (Penguin Classics Ser.). 256p. pap. 10.00 o.s.i (*0-14-043015-6*, Penguin Classics) Viking Penguin.
—A Journal of the Plague Year. Wall, Cynthia, ed. & intro. by. rev. ed. 2003. (Penguin Classics Ser.). (Illus.). 336p. pap. 10.00 (*0-14-043785-1*, Penguin Classics) Viking Penguin.
Deighton, Len. Ss-Gb. l.t. ed. 1992. 19.95 o.p. (*0-7927-1324-9*) BBC Audiobooks America.
Delacorte, Shawna. Falling for the Enemy. 2002. (Silhouette Desire Ser.: No. 1455). mass mkt. (*0-373-76455-3*, Silhouette) Harlequin Enterprises, Ltd.
Delafield, E. M. The Provincial Lady in London. 1999. (Provincial Lady Ser.). (Illus.). 302p. pap. 16.95 (*0-89733-085-4*) Academy Chicago Pubs., Ltd.
—The Provincial Lady in London. l.t. ed. 1991. pap. 19.95 o.p. (*0-7927-0940-3*, CS0245) BBC Audiobooks America.
Delaney, Frank. At Ruby's. 2001. 311p. (*0-00-226196-0*); pap. (*0-00-710195-3*) HarperCollins Pubs.
Delbanco, Nicholas. What Remains. 2001. 208p. pap. 13.95 (*0-446-67779-5*) Warner Bks., Inc.
Derleth, August. Solar Pons: The Chronicles of Solar Pons, No. 1. 1973. 8.95 o.p. (*0-87054-005-X*, Mycroft & Moran) Arkham Hse. Pubs.
—The Solar Pons Omnibus Edition, 2 Vols., Set. Copper, Basil, ed. 1982. (Illus.). 39.95 o.p. (*0-87054-006-8*, Mycroft & Moran) Arkham Hse. Pubs.
Deval, Jacqueline. Reckless Appetites: A Culinary Romance. 1993. 288p. text 21.00 o.p. (*0-88001-322-2*) HarperCollins Pubs.
Devon, Marian. Miss Kendal Sets Her Cap. 1996. mass mkt. 4.50 o.s.i (*0-449-22456-2*, Fawcett) Ballantine Bks.
Dewhurst, Eileen. Closing Stages. 192p. 25.99 (*0-7278-5698-7*); 27.00 (*0-7278-7078-5*) Severn Hse. Pubs., Ltd.
—Double Act. l.t. ed. 2001. (Magna Large Print Ser.). 320p. 31.99 (*0-7505-1601-1*) Magna Large Print Bks. GBR. *Dist:* Ulverscroft Large Print Bks., Ltd., Ulverscroft Large Print Canada, Ltd.
—Double Act. 2000. 218p. 26.00 (*0-7278-5533-6*) Severn Hse. Pubs., Ltd.
—No Love Lost. 2002. 256p. 25.99 (*0-7278-5816-5*) Severn Hse. Pubs., Ltd.
—The Sleeper. 1988. (Crime Club Ser.). 12.95 o.s.i (*0-385-24618-8*) Doubleday Publishing.
—The Sleeper. l.t. ed. 1990. (Ulverscroft Large Print Ser.). 29.99 o.p. (*0-7089-2188-4*, Ulverscroft) Thorpe, F. A. Pubs. GBR. *Dist:* Ulverscroft Large Print Bks., Ltd., Ulverscroft Large Print Canada, Ltd.
DeWitt, Helen. The Last Samurai: A Novel. 2002. 544p. pap. 14.95 (*0-7868-8700-1*); 2000. viii, 530p. 24.95 (*0-7868-6668-3*) Talk Miramax Bks.
Dibdin, Michael. The Tryst. 2003. (Vintage Crime/Black Lizard Ser.). 176p. pap. 12.00 (*0-375-70010-2*, Vintage) Knopf Publishing Group.
Dickens, Charles. The Annotated Christmas Carol. 1977. (Illus.). 15.00 o.s.i (*0-517-52741-3*) Crown Publishing Group.
—The Annotated Christmas Carol. 1984. (Illus.). mass mkt. 4.95 o.p. (*0-380-01722-9*, 34108-5, Avon Bks.) Morrow/Avon.
—The Annotated Christmas Carol. 2003. (Illus.). 288p. 29.95 (*0-393-05158-7*) Norton, W. W. & Co., Inc.
—The Annotated Christmas Carol. 1989. 5.99 o.s.i (*0-517-68780-1*) Random Hse. Value Publishing.
—Barnaby Rudge. Spence, G. W., ed. 1974. (Penguin English Library). (Illus.). 768p. 10.95 (*0-14-043090-3*, Penguin Classics) Viking Penguin.
—Bleak House. unabr. ed. Pt. 1. 1997. audio 65.95; Pt. 1, set. 1997. audio 77.95 (*1-55685-448-X*, 448-X); Pt. 2, set. 1999. audio 65.95; Pt. 2, set. 1997. audio 65.95 Audio Bk. Contractors, Inc.
—Bleak House. unabr. ed. audio 149.95 o.p. (*1-85549-961-4*, CTC 038) BBC Audiobooks America.
—Bleak House. abr. ed. 1999. audio 24.35 (*0-563-55836-9*) BBC Bk. Publishing GBR. *Dist:* Ulverscroft Large Print Bks., Ltd.
—Bleak House. 1992. (Bantam Classics Ser.). 848p. mass mkt. 6.95 (*0-553-21223-0*, Bantam Classics) Bantam Bks.
—Bleak House. E-Book 5.00 (*0-7607-1428-2*) Barnes & Noble, Inc.
—Bleak House. 1977. reprint ed. 10.95 o.p. (*0-460-00236-8*) Biblio Distribution.
—Bleak House. unabr. ed. 1999. Pt. 1. audio 89.95 (*0-7861-1478-9*, 2330-A); Pt. 2. audio 69.95 (*0-7861-1487-8*, 2330-B) Blackstone Audio Bks., Inc.
—Bleak House. 2000. per. 25.00 (*1-891355-95-3*) Blue Unicorn Editions.
—Bleak House. unabr. collector's ed. 1992. (J). Pt. A. audio 112.00 (*0-7366-2127-X*, 2929-A); Pt. B. audio 112.00 (*0-7366-2128-8*, 2929-B) Books on Tape, Inc.
—Bleak House. 1990. 880p. reprint ed. lib. bdg. 39.95 o.p. (*0-89966-679-5*) Buccaneer Bks., Inc.
—Bleak House. 2001. (Collected Works of Charles Dickens). (Illus.). reprint ed. pap. text 28.00 (*0-7426-7324-3*) Classic Bks.
—Bleak House. audio 220.00 Cover to Cover Cassettes, Ltd.
—Bleak House. Exams Unlimited, Inc. Staff, ed. 2001. 1128p. (C). reprint ed. cd-rom 9.25 (*1-885343-23-X*) Exams Unlimited, Inc.
—Bleak House. unabr. ed. 1999. Set, Pt. 1. audio 89.95; Set, Pt. 2. audio 69.95 Highsmith Inc.
—Bleak House, 001. Zabel, Morton D., ed. 1956. (YA). (gr. 9 up). pap. 16.36 (*0-395-05104-5*, Riverside Editions) Houghton Mifflin Co.
—Bleak House. 1987. audio 140.00 Jimcin Recordings.
—Bleak House. 1991. (Everyman's Library: Vol. 8). 1024p. 23.00 (*0-679-40568-2*, Everyman's Library) Knopf Publishing Group.
—Bleak House. 1964. 896p. mass mkt. 6.95 o.s.i (*0-451-52402-0*, CE1739, Signet Classics); mass mkt. 3.50 o.p. (*0-451-52001-7*) NAL.
—Bleak House. abr. ed. 1994. (Ultimate Classics Ser.). 16.95 o.p. (*1-55800-632-X*) NewStar Media, Inc.
—Bleak House. Ford, George & Monod, Sylvere, eds. (Critical Editions Ser.). (Illus.). 1978. 24.95 o.p. (*0-393-04374-6*); 1977. 986p. (C). pap. text 15.50 (*0-393-09332-8*) Norton, W. W. & Co., Inc.
—Bleak House. Gill, Stephen, ed. & intro. by. (Oxford World's Classics Ser.). (Illus.). 1998. 976p. pap. 10.95 (*0-19-283401-0*); 1996. 970p. pap. 7.95 o.p. (*0-19-282985-8*) Oxford Univ. Pr., Inc.
—Bleak House. 1987. (Illus.). 908p. 17.95 (*0-19-254503-5*) Oxford Univ. Pr., Inc.
—Bleak House. 1999. E-Book 3.99 incl. cd-rom (*1-57646-073-8*) Quiet Vision Publishing.
—Bleak House. Ford, George & Monod, Sylvere, eds. 1985. 840p. 10.95 o.s.i (*0-394-60520-9*) Random Hse., Inc.
—Bleak House. 1985. (Illus.). 13.00 (*0-606-20573-X*); 1983. 11.05 o.p. (*0-606-03733-0*) Turtleback Bks.
—Bleak House. 1994. (Everyman Paperback Classics Ser.). 512p. pap. 6.95 (*0-460-87423-3*, Everyman's Classic Library in Paperback) Tuttle Publishing.
—Bleak House. Bradbury, Nicola, ed. & intro. by. 1997. (Penguin Classics Ser.). (Illus.). 1088p. 10.95 o.s.i (*0-14-043496-8*, Penguin Classics) Viking Penguin.
—Bleak House. Page, Norma, ed. 1971. (English Library). 976p. pap. 8.95 o.p. (*0-14-043063-6*, Penguin Classics) Viking Penguin.
—Bleak House. abr. ed. 1997. 4p. audio 23.95 o.s.i (*0-14-086177-7*, Penguin AudioBooks) Viking Penguin.
—Bleak House. 1997. (Classics Ser.). 720p. pap. 3.95 (*1-85326-082-7*, 0827WW) Wordsworth Editions, Ltd. GBR. *Dist:* Casemate Pubs. & Bk. Distributors, LLC.
—A Christmas Carol. 1994. (Illustrated Classics Collection). 64p. pap. 3.60 o.p. (*1-56103-582-3*) American Guidance Service, Inc.
—A Christmas Carol. l.t. ed. 2001. per. 15.50 (*1-58396-135-6*) Blue Unicorn Editions.
—A Christmas Carol. 2002. 12.32 (*0-7587-7666-7*) Book Wholesalers, Inc.
—A Christmas Carol. l.t. unabr. ed. 2002. (Large Print Classics). 144p. pap. 8.95 (*0-486-42247-X*) Dover Pubns., Inc.
—A Christmas Carol. 1979. 15.50 o.p. (*0-460-00239-2*); 1972. 2.95 o.p. (*0-460-01239-8*) Dutton/Plume. (Dutton).
—A Christmas Carol. E-Book 2.49 (*1-58744-953-6*) Electric Umbrella Publishing.
—A Christmas Carol. Exams Unlimited, Inc. Staff, ed. 2002. (Illus.). 119p. (C). reprint ed. cd-rom 5.25 (*1-59132-047-X*) Exams Unlimited, Inc.
—A Christmas Carol. 2002. 166p. pap. 8.95 (*1-931243-18-2*) Green Integer.
—A Christmas Carol. 2003. audio 14.95 (*1-84032-776-6*) Hodder Headline Audiobooks GBR. *Dist:* Trafalgar Square.
—A Christmas Carol. Stemach, Jerry, ed. l.t. ed. (Illus.). 2002. text 150.00 (*1-58702-003-3*); 2000. text 50.00 (*1-58702-511-6*) Johnston, Don Inc.
—A Christmas Carol. 1984. mass mkt. 2.75 o.p. (*0-451-51869-1*, Signet Classics) NAL.
—A Christmas Carol. 2003. (Illus.). 176p. mass mkt. 3.95 (*0-7434-7737-5*, Pocket) Simon & Schuster.
—Cuento de Navidad. 2000. (Coleccion "Clasicos Juveniles" Ser.). (SPA.). 148p. (gr. 4-7). pap. 8.95 (*1-58348-825-1*) iUniverse, Inc.
—Dickens' Journalism Vol. 2: Sketches by Boz & Other Early Papers, 1833-39, 3 vols. Slater, Michael, ed. 1994. 580p. (C). text 50.00 (*0-8142-0629-8*) Ohio State Univ. Pr.
—Little Dorrit. 1992. (Everyman's Library: Vol. 111). 20.00 (*0-679-41725-7*) Knopf, Alfred A. Inc.
—Oliver Twist. 2002. (World Digital Library). E-Book 3.95 (*0-594-08303-6*) 1873 Pr.
—Oliver Twist. unabr. ed. 1963. (Classics Ser.). mass mkt. 3.50 (*0-8049-0009-4*, CL-9) Airmont Publishing Co., Inc.
—Oliver Twist. Date not set. 478p. 30.95 (*0-8488-2536-5*) Amereon, Ltd.
—Oliver Twist. l.t. ed. 1999. 657p. pap. 24.95 (*1-55701-274-1*) BNI Pubns., Inc.
—Oliver Twist. 1982. (Bantam Classics Ser.). 448p. mass mkt. 4.95 (*0-553-21102-1*, Bantam Classics) Bantam Bks.
—Oliver Twist. (J). E-Book 5.00 (*0-7607-1286-7*) Barnes & Noble, Inc.
—Oliver Twist. rev. ed. 2000. 500p. per. 14.00 (*1-58396-003-1*) Blue Unicorn Editions.
—Oliver Twist. 1982. reprint ed. lib. bdg. 28.95 (*0-89966-372-9*) Buccaneer Bks., Inc.
—Oliver Twist, 2. reprint ed. lib. bdg. 98.00 (*0-7426-2308-4*); lib. bdg. 48.00 (*0-7426-1017-9*); 2001. (Illus.). pap. text 28.00 (*0-7426-7308-1*); 2001. (Illus.). pap. text 28.00 (*0-7426-6017-6*) Classic Bks.
—Oliver Twist. l.t. ed. 1999. 657p. pap. 24.95 (*1-58855-016-8*) Cyber Classics, Inc.
—Oliver Twist. 1998. 496p. mass mkt. 4.99 (*0-8125-8003-6*, Tor Classics) Doherty, Tom Assocs., LLC.
—Oliver Twist. 2002. (Thrift Editions Ser.). 384p. pap. 3.00 (*0-486-42453-7*) Dover Pubns., Inc.
—Oliver Twist. 1972. 2.95 o.p. (*0-460-01233-9*); 1957. 12.95 o.p. (*0-460-00233-3*) Dutton/Plume. (Dutton).

—Oliver Twist. (SPA.). pap. (968-416-762-8, 884) Fernandez USA Publishing.

—Oliver Twist. 2003. (Barnes & Noble Classics Ser.). 560p. pap. 4.95 (1-59308-030-1) Fine Communications.

—Oliver Twist. l.t. ed. 2002. 637p. 28.95 (0-7862-4325-2) Gale Group.

—Oliver Twist. 1988. (SPA.). 448p. (84-320-3993-4) GeoPlaneta, Editorial, S. A.

—Oliver Twist. 1991. (Complete Novels of Charles Dickens Ser.). (Illus.). 472p. (C). pap. 3.95 o.p. (0-7493-0755-2, A0527) Heinemann.

—Oliver Twist. l.t. ed. 466p. pap. 35.36 (0-7583-1728-X); 582p. pap. 41.94 (0-7583-1729-8); 797p. pap. 59.53 (0-7583-1730-1); 2293p. pap. 143.93 (0-7583-1735-2); 1976p. pap. 121.94 (0-7583-1734-4); 1607p. pap. 107.34 (0-7583-1733-6); 1021p. pap. 71.03 (0-7583-1731-X); 1306p. pap. 84.84 (0-7583-1732-8); 466p. lib. bdg. 41.36 (0-7583-1720-4); 1607p. lib. bdg. 125.34 (0-7583-1725-5); 797p. lib. bdg. 71.53 (0-7583-1722-0); 2293p. lib. bdg. 172.68 (0-7583-1727-1); 582p. lib. bdg. 47.94 (0-7583-1721-2); 1021p. lib. bdg. 83.03 (0-7583-1723-9); 1976p. lib. bdg. 142.75 (0-7583-1726-3); 1306p. lib. bdg. 96.84 (0-7583-1724-7) Huge Print Pr.

—Oliver Twist. 2002. 448p. 98.99 (1-4043-2242-6); per. 93.99 (1-4043-2243-4) IndyPublish.com.

—Oliver Twist. Ba'Albaki, Munir, tr. 1982. (ARA.). 200p. pap. 14.95 (0-86685-138-0) International Bk. Ctr., Inc.

—Oliver Twist. 1992. (Everyman's Library). 528p. 20.00 (0-679-41724-9) Knopf, Alfred A. Inc.

—Oliver Twist. 1999. (Cloth Bound Pocket Ser.). (Illus.). 7.95 (3-8290-3004-5, 521121) Konemann.

—Oliver Twist. 1996. (Longman Fiction Ser.). pap. text 5.90 o.s.i (0-582-27519-9) Longman Publishing Group.

—Oliver Twist. Adams, Richard, ed. 1988. (Study Texts Ser.). pap. text 5.95 (0-582-33150-1, 72056) Longman Publishing Group.

—Oliver Twist. 1988. (English As a Second Language Bk.). pap. text 4.46 net. (0-582-53496-8, 74097) Longman Publishing Group.

—Oliver Twist. E-Book 1.95 (1-58515-055-X) MesaView, Inc.

—Oliver Twist. 1994. (Books of Wonder). (Illus.). 464p. 20.00 (0-688-12911-0, Morrow, William & Co.) Morrow/Avon.

—Oliver Twist. 1970. mass mkt. 0.60 o.p. (0-451-50102-0); 1970. mass mkt. 0.75 o.p. (0-451-50512-3); 1961. mass mkt. 2.25 o.p. (0-451-51334-7); 1961. mass mkt. 1.95 o.p. (0-451-51143-3); 1961. 496p. mass mkt. 4.95 (0-451-52351-2); 1961. mass mkt. 1.50 o.p. (0-451-50947-1); 1961. mass mkt. 0.95 o.p. (0-451-50804-1); 1961. 496p. mass mkt. 2.50 o.p. (0-451-51685-0); 1961. mass mkt. 2.50 o.p. (0-451-51516-1) NAL. (Signet Classics).

—Oliver Twist. l.t. ed. 1998. (Large Print Ser.). 560p. lib. bdg. 28.00 (0-939495-52-X); 482p. reprint ed. lib. bdg. 25.00 (1-58287-054-3) North Bks.

—Oliver Twist. Kaplan, Fred, ed. 1992. (Critical Editions Ser.). 611p. (C). pap. text 14.50 (0-393-96292-X) Norton, W. W. & Co., Inc.

—Oliver Twist. Tillotson, Kathleen, ed. & intro. by. 1998. (Oxford World's Classics Ser.). (Illus.). 392p. pap. 5.95 o.p. (0-19-283439-8) Oxford Univ. Pr., Inc.

—Oliver Twist. 1987. (Illus.). 446p. 17.95 (0-19-254505-1) Oxford Univ. Pr., Inc.

—Oliver Twist. Tillotson, Kathleen, ed. (Oxford World's Classics Ser.). 1982. (Illus.). 392p. pap. 5.95 o.p. (0-19-281591-1); 1967. 55.00 o.p. (0-19-811454-0); 2nd ed. 1999. (Illus.). 544p. pap. 5.95 (0-19-283339-1) Oxford Univ. Pr., Inc.

—Oliver Twist. 1999. E-Book 3.99 incl. cd-rom (1-57646-089-4) Quiet Vision Publishing.

—Oliver Twist. 2001. (Modern Library Classics). (Illus.). 480p. pap. 7.95 (0-375-75784-8, Modern Library) Random House Adult Trade Publishing Group.

—Oliver Twist. 1987. (Illus.). 416p. 12.95 o.p. (0-89577-258-2) Reader's Digest Assn., Inc., The.

—Oliver Twist. 1996. 480p. text 8.98 o.p. (1-56138-715-0, Courage Bks.) Running Pr. Bk. Pubs.

—Oliver Twist. Shefter, Harry, ed. 1981. (Enriched Classics Ser.). 512p. mass mkt. 3.50 o.s.i (0-671-44242-2, Pocket) Simon & Schuster.

—Oliver Twist. (SPA.). 104p. 5.95 (84-305-1317-5) Susaeta Ediciones, S.A. ESP. Dist: AIMS International Bks., Inc.

—Oliver Twist. l.t. ed. 1982. (Classics Ser.). 29.99 o.p. (0-7089-8019-8, Charnwood) Thorpe, F. A. Pubs. GBR. Dist: Ulverscroft Large Print Bks., Ltd., Ulverscroft Large Print Canada, Ltd.

—Oliver Twist. Daleski, H. M., ed. 2003. 560p. 9.95 (1-59264-007-9); pap. 7.95 (1-59264-006-0) Toby Pr.

—Oliver Twist. 1999. (Signature Classics Ser.). (Illus.). xiii, 438p. 24.95 (1-58279-037-X); 29.95 (1-58279-049-3) Trident Pr. International.

—Oliver Twist. (Saddleback Classics). 2001. (Illus.). 13.10 (0-606-21564-6); 1986. 11.00 (0-606-16029-9); 1961. 11.00 (0-606-00928-0) Turtleback Bks.

—Oliver Twist. 1994. (Everyman Paperback Classics Ser.). 432p. pap. 3.95 (0-460-87490-X, Everyman's Classic Library in Paperback) Tuttle Publishing.

—Oliver Twist. 1992. (Illus.). 373p. reprint ed. lib. bdg. 29.95 o.p. (1-877767-69-7) University Publishing Hse., Inc.

—Oliver Twist. 2003. (Classics Ser.). (Illus.). 608p. pap. 7.00 (0-14-143974-2, Penguin Classics) Viking Penguin.

—Oliver Twist. Horne, Philip, ed. & intro. by. 2002. (Classics Ser.). (Illus.). 464p. 7.00 (0-14-043522-0) Viking Penguin.

—Oliver Twist. Fairclough, Peter, ed. 1966. (Penguin Classics Ser.). 496p. pap. 6.95 (0-14-043017-2, Penguin Classics) Viking Penguin.

—Oliver Twist. 1997. (Wordsworth Collection). 400p. pap. 3.95 (1-85326-012-6, 0126WW) Wordsworth Editions, Ltd. GBR. Dist: Casemate Pubs. & Bk. Distributors, LLC.

—Oliver Twist: Digital Reprint of 1902 Harper & Brothers Edition. Exams Unlimited, Inc. Staff, ed. 2001. (Illus.). 589p. (C). reprint ed. cd-rom 8.25 (1-59132-017-8) Exams Unlimited, Inc.

—Our Mutual Friend. 1994. (Everyman's Library). 20.00 (0-679-42028-2) Knopf, Alfred A. Inc.

—Our Mutual Friend. Cotsell, Michael, ed. 1990. (Oxford World's Classics Ser.). (Illus.). 880p. pap. 6.95 o.p. (0-19-281795-7) Oxford Univ. Pr., Inc.

—Sketches by Boz: Illustrative of Everyday Life & Everyday People. 1968. 5.00 o.p. (0-460-00237-6) Biblio Distribution.

—Sketches by Boz: Illustrative of Everyday Life & Everyday People. 2. reprint ed. lib. bdg. 196.00 (0-7426-2350-5); 2001. pap. text 56.00 (0-7426-7350-2) Classic Bks.

—Sketches by Boz: Illustrative of Everyday Life & Everyday People. 1999. E-Book 3.99 incl. cd-rom (1-57646-092-4) Quiet Vision Publishing.

—Sketches by Boz: Illustrative of Everyday Life & Everyday People. Walder, Dennis, ed. & intro. by. 1996. (Classics Ser.). (Illus.). 688p. pap. 15.00 (0-14-043345-7, Penguin Classics) Viking Penguin.

—Sketches by Boz: Illustrative of Everyday Life & Everyday People. 2001. 496p. pap. 3.95 (1-84022-404-5) Wordsworth Editions, Ltd. GBR. Dist: Combined Publishing.

—A Tale of Two Cities. l.t. unabr. ed. 2001. (Large Print Classics Ser.). viii, 528p. 14.95 (0-486-41776-X) Dover Pubns., Inc.

—A Tale of Two Cities. 1993. (Everyman's Library). 480p. 20.00 (0-679-42073-8) Knopf, Alfred A. Inc.

—A Tale of Two Cities. 1996. (Modern Library Ser.). 512p. 19.95 (0-679-60208-9) Random Hse., Inc.

—A Tale of Two Cities. 1992. (Literary Classics Ser.). 272p. text 5.98 o.p. (1-56138-114-4, Courage Bks.) Running Pr. Bk. Pubs.

—A Tale of Two Cities. 2000. (Signature Classics Ser.). iv, 358p. 24.95 (1-58279-078-7); (1-58279-079-5) Trident Pr. International.

—A Tale of Two Cities. 2000. (Penguin Classics Ser.). (Illus.). 528p. 6.95 o.s.i (0-14-043730-4, Penguin Classics) Viking Penguin.

Dickens, Charles, et al. Oliver Twist. 1999. E-Book 6.25 (0-585-35371-9) netLibrary, Inc.

Dickinson, Barbara M. Small House, Large World. 1999. (Illus.). 239p. pap. 19.95 o.s.i (1-55618-182-5) Brunswick Publishing Corp.

Dickinson, David. Death of an Old Master. 2004. 272p. 24.00 (0-7867-1306-2, Carroll & Graf Pubs.) Avalon Publishing Group.

Disch, Thomas M. & Naylor, Charles. Neighboring Lives. 1992. 368p. reprint ed. pap. text 17.95 (0-8018-4219-0) Johns Hopkins Univ. Pr.

—Neighboring Lives. 1981. 351p. 25.00 (0-684-16644-5) Ultramarine Publishing Co., Inc.

Docx, Edward. The Calligrapher: A Novel. 2003. 368p. 24.00 (0-618-34397-0) Houghton Mifflin Co.

Dold, Gaylord. The World Beat. 1993. 288p. 19.95 o.p. (0-312-09945-2, Saint Martin's Minotaur) St. Martin's Pr.

Donachie, David. Tested by Fate. 2004. (Nelson & Emma Trilogy Ser.: Vol. 2). 416p. pap. 17.95 (1-59013-042-1) McBooks Pr., Inc.

Donald, Anabel. The Glass Ceiling. l.t. ed. 1995. pap. 20.95 o.p. (0-7838-1522-0, Macmillan Reference USA) Gale Group.

—The Glass Ceiling. 1995. 217p. 20.95 o.p. (0-312-13501-7, Saint Martin's Minotaur) St. Martin's Pr.

—An Uncommon Murder. 1993. 217p. 17.95 o.p. (0-312-08917-1, Saint Martin's Minotaur) St. Martin's Pr.

Donat, Peter C. & Gould, Barney. Sherlock Holmes & the Shakespeare Solution. 1997. 90p. 24.00 (1-55246-016-9); pap. 10.00 (1-55246-017-7) Battered Silicon Dispatch Box, The.

Donnelly, Jennifer. The Tea Rose. 2004. mass mkt. 7.99 (0-312-99356-0, St. Martin's Paperbacks) St. Martin's Pr.

—The Tea Rose: A Novel. 2002. 560p. 24.95 (0-312-28835-2) St. Martin's Pr.

Donoghue, Emma. Slammerkin. 2001. 352p. 24.00 (0-15-100672-5); 2002. 408p. reprint ed. pap. 14.00 (0-15-600747-9, Harvest Bks.) Harcourt Trade Pubs.

Douglas, Carole Nelson. Castle Rouge: A Novel of Suspense Featuring Sherlock Holmes, Irene Adler, & Jack the Ripper. 2002. (Irene Adler Novel Ser.). (Illus.). 544p. 25.95 (0-312-86941-X, Forge Bks.) Doherty, Tom Assocs., LLC.

Doyle, Arthur Conan. The White Company & Sir Nigel. 2000. (Common Reader Edition Ser.). 618p. pap. 24.95 (1-888173-90-4) Akadine Pr., The.

Drabble, Margaret. The Garrick Year. 1984. pap. 8.95 o.p. (0-452-26282-8); pap. 6.95 o.p. (0-452-25590-2) Dutton/Plume. (Plume).

—The Seven Sisters. 320p. 2003. pap. 14.00 (0-15-602875-1); 2002. 25.00 (0-15-100740-3) Harcourt Trade Pubs.

—The Seven Sisters. 2003. 320p. pap. (0-7710-2905-5) McClelland & Stewart.

Duane, Diane. To Visit the Queen. 1999. (Cat Novel Ser.: Vol. 2). 368p. pap. 18.99 (0-446-67318-8) Warner Bks., Inc.

Duffy, Maureen. Capital. 1976. 222p. 6.95 o.p. (0-8076-0817-3) Braziller, George Inc.

Duffy, Stella. Wavewalker. 1996. (Mask Noir Ser.). 272p. pap. o.p. (1-85242-508-3) Serpent's Tail Ltd.

Dunant, Sarah. Birth Marks. unabr. ed. 1993. (Hannah Wolfe Mysteries Ser.). audio 69.95 (0-7451-4034-3, CAB 731) BBC Audiobooks America.

—Birth Marks. 1992. 240p. 17.00 o.s.i (0-385-42318-7) Doubleday Publishing.

—Birth Marks. l.t. ed. 1992. (Magna Large Print Ser.). 373p. o.p. (0-7505-0270-3) Magna Large Print Bks. GBR. Dist: Ulverscroft Large Print Canada, Ltd.

—Fatlands. unabr. ed. 1994. (Hannah Wolfe Mysteries Ser.). audio 54.95 (0-7451-4297-4, CAB 980) BBC Audiobooks America.

—Fatlands: A Hannah Wolfe Mystery. 1994. 256p. reprint ed. pap. 21.00 (1-883402-82-4, Scribner) Simon & Schuster.

—Under My Skin: A Hannah Wolfe Novel. 1995. 288p. 20.00 (0-684-81521-4, Scribner) Simon & Schuster.

Duncan, Glen. I, Lucifer. 2003. 272p. pap. 13.00 (0-8021-4014-9, Grove Pr.) Grove/Atlantic, Inc.

Dunn, Carola. Die Laughing: A Daisy Dalrymple Mystery. 2003. 288p. 23.95 (0-312-30913-9, Saint Martin's Minotaur) St. Martin's Pr.

—Rattle His Bones: A Daisy Dalrymple Mystery. 2003. 256p. mass mkt. 5.99 (0-7582-0168-0) Kensington Publishing Corp.

—Rattle His Bones: A Daisy Dalrymple Mystery. 2000. (Daisy Dalrymple Mysteries Ser.). (Illus.). 243p. 22.95 (0-312-20572-4, Saint Martin's Minotaur) St. Martin's Pr.

—Rattle His Bones: A Daisy Dalrymple Mystery. l.t. ed. 2000. (Mystery Ser.). (Illus.). 355p. 26.95 (0-7862-2913-6) Thorndike Pr.

Dunn, Nell. Up the Junction. 2000. (Illus.). 128p. pap. text 13.00 (1-58243-066-7, Counterpoint Pr.) Basic Bks.

—Up the Junction. 1990. (Illus.). 112p. pap. 7.95 o.p. (0-14-016205-4, Penguin Bks.) Viking Penguin.

Eclair, J. Camberwell Beauty. 2000. 407p. (0-316-85318-6) Little Brown & Co.

Eden, Marc. The Spy. 1992. 19.95 o.p. (0-87131-703-6) Evans, M. & Co., Inc.

Edgar, Josephine. Bright Young Thing: A Novel of London in the Twenties. 1986. 320p. 15.95 o.p. (0-312-09627-5) St. Martin's Pr.

Edgeworth, Maria. Belinda. Kirkpatrick, Kathryn, ed. & intro. by. 1994. (Oxford World's Classics Ser.). 538p. pap. 12.95 o.p. (0-19-283123-2) Oxford Univ. Pr., Inc.

—The Works of Maria Edgeworth, 12 vols. Incl. Belinda. 91.66 (1-85196-176-3); 91.66 (1-85196-175-5); 91.66 (1-85196-178-X); 91.66 (1-85196-179-8); 91.66 (1-85196-180-1); 91.66 (1-85196-181-X); 91.66 (1-85196-182-8); 91.66 (1-85196-183-6); 91.66 (1-85196-184-4); 91.70 (1-85196-185-2); 91.70 (1-85196-187-9); 91.66 (1-85196-177-1); 1997. 4400p. 2003. 1100.00 (1-85196-186-0) Pickering & Chatto Pubs., Ltd. GBR. Dist: Ashgate Publishing Co.

Edwards, Ruth Dudley. Publish & Be Murdered. l.t. unabr. ed. 2000. 282p. 25.95 (0-7531-5975-9, 159759); 1999. 304p. pap. 21.99 (0-7531-5991-0, 159910) ISIS Large Print Bks. GBR. Dist: ISIS Publishing, Ulverscroft Large Print Bks., Ltd., Ulverscroft Large Print Canada, Ltd.

—Publish & Be Murdered. 1999. 217p. pap. 12.95 (1-890208-13-2) Poisoned Pen Pr.

Egleton, Clive. A Double Deception. 1992. 288p. 18.95 o.p. (0-312-07736-X, Saint Martin's Minotaur) St. Martin's Pr.

—A Double Deception. l.t. ed. 1994. (Charnwood Large Print Ser.). 496p. 29.99 o.p. (0-7089-8769-9, Ulverscroft) Thorpe, F. A. Pubs. GBR. Dist: Ulverscroft Large Print Bks., Ltd., Ulverscroft Large Print Canada, Ltd.

Elgin, Elizabeth. The House in Abercromby Square. l.t. ed. 1997. (Paperback Ser.). 234p. pap. 23.95 (0-7838-8262-9) Thorndike Pr.

Ellis, Alice Thomas. Pillars of Gold. 2003. 186p. pap. 15.95 (1-888173-54-8) Akadine Pr., The.

—Pillars of Gold. 2000. 181p. 22.95 (1-55921-284-5) Moyer Bell.

—Pillars of Gold. l.t. ed. 2000. (General Ser.). 236p. 24.95 (0-7862-2805-9); (0-7540-4247-2); (0-7540-4248-0) Thorndike Pr.

—The 27th Kingdom. 1999. 220p. 22.95 (1-55921-250-0) Moyer Bell.

—The 27th Kingdom. l.t. ed. 2000. (General Ser.). 206p. pap. 22.95 (0-7862-2628-5) Thorndike Pr.

Elrod, P. N., ed. Dracula in London. 2001. 272p. pap. 14.95 (0-441-00858-5) Ace Bks.

Elton, Ben. Inconceivable. 2000. mass mkt. (0-552-14819-9, Corgi); 1999. 271p. (0-593-04479-7) Bantam Bks.

Emecheta, Buchi. The Family. 1990. 240p. 17.95 o.s.i (0-8076-1245-6); pap. 10.95 (0-8076-1250-2) Braziller, George Inc.

—Kehinde. 1994. (African Writers Ser.). 160p. pap. 13.95 (0-435-90985-1, 90985) Heinemann.

Estleman, Loren D. Dr. Jekyll & Mr. Holmes. 2001. 224p. pap. 12.00 (0-7434-2392-5) ibooks, Inc.

—Dr. Jekyll & Mr. Holmes. E-Book 6.99 (1-59019-599-X) ipicturebooks, LLC.

Estleman, Loren D. & Watson, John H. Dr. Jekyll & Mr. Holmes. 1979. 8.95 o.p. (0-385-15257-4) Doubleday Publishing.

—Dr. Jekyll & Mr. Holmes. 1980. 256p. pap. 3.95 o.p. (0-14-005665-3, Penguin Bks.) Viking Penguin.

—Sherlock Holmes vs. Dracula or, The Adventure of the Sanguinary Count. 1978. 7.95 o.p. (0-385-14051-7) Doubleday Publishing.

—Sherlock Holmes vs. Dracula or, The Adventure of the Sanguinary Count. 1979. 224p. pap. 3.95 o.p. (0-14-005262-3, Penguin Bks.) Viking Penguin.

Evans, Pamela. Town Belles. 1997. 474p. mass mkt. 13.95 (0-7472-5166-5) Headline Bk. Publishing, Ltd. GBR. Dist: Trafalgar Square.

—Town Belles. l.t. ed. 1997. (General Ser.). 544p. pap. 22.95 (0-7862-1115-6) Thorndike Pr.

Evans, Penelope. Freezing. 288p. 2000. pap. 12.00 (1-56947-196-7); 1998. 22.00 (1-56947-121-5) Soho Pr., Inc.

—The Last Girl. 1997. (Last Girl Ser.: Vol. 1). 256p. mass mkt. 5.99 (0-312-96315-7, St. Martin's Paperbacks); 1995. 240p. text 21.95 o.p. (0-312-13998-5) St. Martin's Pr.

—The Last Girl. 2000. pap. 10.95 (0-552-99602-5) Transworld Publishers Ltd. GBR. Dist: Trafalgar Square.

Evaristo, Bernardine. The Emperor's Babe. 2004. 272p. pap. 14.00 (0-14-200171-6) Penguin Group (USA) Inc.

Ewing, Barbara. The Trespass: A Novel. 2003. 416p. 24.95 (0-312-31420-5) St. Martin's Pr.

Faber, Michel. The Crimson Petal & the White. 2003. 920p. pap. 15.00 (0-15-602877-8); 2002. 848p. 26.00 (0-15-100692-X) Harcourt Trade Pubs.

Falconer, Helen. Sky High. 2003. 224p. 24.95 (0-89255-301-4); pap. 12.95 (0-89255-304-9) Persea Bks., Inc.

Falconer, Helen L. Primrose Hill. 2001. 224p. 23.95 (0-89255-255-7) Persea Bks., Inc.

Farr, Diane. The Nobody. 1999. (Signet Regency Romance Ser.). 224p. mass mkt. 4.99 o.s.i (0-451-19771-2) NAL.

Fawcett, Quinn. Embassy Row. (Mycroft Holmes Novels Ser.). 384p. 1999. pap. 6.99 (0-8125-4522-2, Tor Bks.); 1998. 24.95 o.p. (0-312-86363-2, Forge Bks.) Doherty, Tom Assocs., LLC.

—The Flying Scotsman. 1999. (Mycroft Holmes Novels Ser.). (Illus.). 320p. 23.95 (0-312-86364-0, Forge Bks.) Doherty, Tom Assocs., LLC.

—The Flying Scotsman: A Mycroft Holmes Novel Authorized by Dame Jean Conan Coyle. 2000. (Mycroft Holmes Novels Ser.). 320p. pap. 14.95 (0-312-87689-0, Tor Bks.) Doherty, Tom Assocs., LLC.

—The Scottish Ploy. 2001. 352p. reprint ed. pap. 15.95 (0-312-87628-9, Forge Bks.) Doherty, Tom Assocs., LLC.

—The Scottish Ploy: The A. Mycroft Holmes Novel Authorized by Dame Jean Conan Doyle. 2000. (Mycroft Holmes Novels Ser.). 352p. 24.95 (0-312-87282-8, Forge Bks.) Doherty, Tom Assocs., LLC.

Ferguson, Jo Ann. Grave Intentions. 2003. 224p. mass mkt. 4.99 (0-8217-7520-0) Kensington Publishing Corp.

Fergusongedneyki. Murder at Almack's. 2003. 256p. mass mkt. 4.99 (0-8217-7481-6) Kensington Publishing Corp.

Ferrars, E. X. Beware of the Dog. l.t. ed. 1993. (Mystery Ser.). 304p. 29.99 o.p. (0-7505-0490-0) Magna Large Print Bks. GBR. Dist: Ulverscroft Large Print Bks., Ltd., Ulverscroft Large Print Canada, Ltd.

—Death of a Minor Character. 1983. (Crime Club Ser.). 192p. 11.95 o.p. (*0-385-18839-0*) Doubleday Publishing.
—Death of a Minor Character. l.t. ed. 1984. (Ulverscroft Large Print Ser.). 320p. 12.50 o.p. (*0-7089-1225-7*, Ulverscroft) Thorpe, F. A. Pubs. GBR. *Dist:* Ulverscroft Large Print Bks., Ltd., Ulverscroft Large Print Canada, Ltd.
—Frog in the Throat. 1981. 112p. pap. 1.95 o.p. (*0-553-20040-2*) Bantam Bks.
—Frog in the Throat. 1980. (Crime Club Ser.). 192p. 8.95 o.p. (*0-385-17207-9*) Doubleday Publishing.
—Frog in the Throat. unabr. ed. 1998. audio 54.95 (*0-7531-0239-0*, 980209) ISIS Audio Bks. GBR. *Dist:* Ulverscroft Large Print Bks., Ltd.
—Frog in the Throat. l.t. ed. 1986. (Ulverscroft Large Print Ser.). 304p. 12.50 o.p. (*0-7089-1430-6*, Ulverscroft) Thorpe, F. A. Pubs. GBR. *Dist:* Ulverscroft Large Print Bks., Ltd., Ulverscroft Large Print Canada, Ltd.
—I Met Murder. 1986. (Crime Club Ser.). 192p. 12.95 o.p. (*0-385-23367-1*) Doubleday Publishing.
—I Met Murder. unabr. ed. 1998. audio 49.95 (*0-7531-0408-3*, 970704) ISIS Audio Bks. GBR. *Dist:* Ulverscroft Large Print Bks., Ltd.
—I Met Murder. l.t. ed. 1987. (Ulverscroft Large Print Ser.). 320p. 14.50 o.p. (*0-7089-1586-8*, Ulverscroft) Thorpe, F. A. Pubs. GBR. *Dist:* Ulverscroft Large Print Bks., Ltd., Ulverscroft Large Print Canada, Ltd.
—In at the Kill. 1979. 9.95 o.p. (*0-385-14913-1*) Doubleday Publishing.
—In at the Kill. 1980. 192p. pap. 3.95 o.p. (*0-14-005644-0*, Penguin Bks.) Viking Penguin.
—Last Will & Testament. 1981. 160p. pap. 1.95 o.p. (*0-553-14795-1*) Bantam Bks.
—Last Will & Testament. 1978. 7.95 o.p. (*0-385-14455-5*) Doubleday Publishing.
—Last Will & Testament. unabr. ed. 2001. audio 39.95 (*1-85496-692-8*, 980704) Soundings, Ltd. GBR. *Dist:* Ulverscroft Large Print Bks., Ltd.
—Last Will & Testament. l.t. ed. 1980. 284p. 12.00 o.p. (*0-7089-0505-6*, Ulverscroft) Thorpe, F. A. Pubs. GBR. *Dist:* Ulverscroft Large Print Bks., Ltd.
—Thinner Than Water. unabr. ed. 1993. 39.95 incl. audio (*0-7451-5925-7*, CAT 4063) BBC Audiobooks America.
—Thinner Than Water. 1982. (Crime Club Ser.). 192p. 10.95 o.p. (*0-385-17946-4*) Doubleday Publishing.
—Woman Slaughter. unabr. ed. 2001. audio 49.95 (*1-85089-823-5*, 20891) ISIS Audio Bks. GBR. *Dist:* Ulverscroft Large Print Bks., Ltd.
Ferris, Paul. Infidelity. 1999. 266p. (*0-00-225350-X*) HarperCollins Pubs.
Fielding, Sarah. Adventures of David Simple. 2002. (Illus.). 336p. 15.00 (*0-14-043747-9*, Penguin Classics) Viking Penguin.
—The Adventures of David Simple & Volume the Last. Sabor, Peter, ed. 1998. (Eighteenth-Century Novels by Women Ser.). 416p. (C). reprint ed. 45.00 o.p. (*0-8131-2055-1*); (Illus.). pap. 17.95 (*0-8131-0945-0*) Univ. Pr. of Kentucky.
Fitzgerald, Ellen. The Damsels from Derbyshire. 1992. 224p. 19.95 o.s.i (*0-8027-1183-9*) Walker & Co.
Fitzgerald, Penelope. At Freddie's. 1985. 324p. 14.95 o.p. (*0-87923-439-3*) Godine, David R. Pub.
—At Freddie's. 1999. 160p. pap. 12.00 (*0-395-95618-8*, Mariner Bks.) Houghton Mifflin Co. Trade & Reference Div.
—At Freddie's. l.t. ed. 2000. 226p. (*0-7540-4074-7*); (*0-7540-4075-5*) Thorndike Pr.
—The Golden Child. 1999. 192p. pap. 12.00 (*0-395-95619-6*) Houghton Mifflin Co.
—The Golden Child. l.t. ed. 2000. (General Ser.). xix, 231p. 23.95 (*0-7862-2809-1*); (Illus.). 266p. pap. 23.95 (*0-7862-2808-3*) Thorndike Pr.
—The Golden Child. l.t. ed. 2000. 266p. (*0-7540-4257-X*); (*0-7540-4258-8*) Thorndike Pr.
—Offshore. 1989. 150p. pap. 7.95 o.p. (*0-88184-476-4*, Carroll & Graf Pubs.) Avalon Publishing Group.
—Offshore. l.t. ed. 1994. 18.95 o.p. (*0-7927-2028-8*); pap. 17.95 o.p. (*0-7927-2027-X*) BBC Audiobooks America.
—Offshore. 1987. 15.95 o.p. (*0-8050-0561-7*) Holt, Henry & Co.
—Offshore. 1998. 144p. pap. 11.00 (*0-395-47804-9*) Houghton Mifflin Co.
—Offshore, Human Voices: The Beginning of Spring. 2003. 480p. 23.00 (*1-4000-4125-2*, Everyman's Library) Knopf Publishing Group.
Fleming, Ian. Octopussy & the Living Daylights. 2004. 128p. pap. 13.00 (*0-14-200329-8*) Penguin Group (USA) Inc.
Flowers, R. Barri. In the Dark of Night. 2001. 252p. pap. 14.95 (*0-595-17650-X*) iUniverse, Inc.
Foley, Michael. Getting Used to Not Being Remarkable. 1998. 312p. pap. 18.95 (*0-85640-626-0*) Blackstaff Pr., The IRL. *Dist:* Dufour Editions, Inc.
Follett, Ken. Paper Money. 2nd ed. 1987. 216p. reprint ed. 15.95 o.p. (*0-688-05840-X*, Morrow, William & Co.) Morrow/Avon.
—Paper Money. 1987. mass mkt. 3.95 o.p. (*0-451-15002-3*); 256p. mass mkt. 4.50 o.p. (*0-451-15904-7*); 272p. mass mkt. 7.99 (*0-451-16730-9*) NAL. (Signet Bks.).
Forbes, Bryan. A Spy at Twilight. 1991. 432p. reprint ed. mass mkt. 5.99 o.s.i (*0-451-40263-4*, Onyx) NAL.
—A Spy at Twilight. 1993. 3.99 o.p. (*0-517-09107-0*) Random Hse. Value Publishing.
Forbes, Leslie. Fish, Blood & Bone. 2001. (Illus.). 436p. 25.00 o.p. (*0-374-15506-2*) Farrar, Straus & Giroux.
Forrester, Anouchka Grose. Ringing for You. l.t. ed. 2000. (Basic Ser.). 311p. 27.95 (*0-7862-2412-6*) Thorndike Pr.
—Ringing for You: A Love Story with Interruptions. 208p. 2000. pap. 15.95 (*0-671-03439-1*, Pocket); 1999. (Illus.). 22.00 o.s.i (*0-684-86292-1*, Scribner) Simon & Schuster.
Fowler, Christopher. Red Bride. 1994. 368p. mass mkt. 4.99 o.p. (*0-451-45293-3*); 1993. 320p. 20.00 o.p. (*0-451-45213-5*) NAL. (ROC).
Fraser, Anthea. Home Through the Dark. 2000. 21.95 (*0-7540-8575-9*, Black Dagger) BBC Audiobooks America.
—Home Through the Dark. l.t. ed. 2002. (Dales Large Print Ser.). 304p. pap. 21.99 o.p. (*1-84262-204-8*) Dales Large Print Bks. GBR. *Dist:* Ulverscroft Large Print Bks., Ltd., Ulverscroft Large Print Canada, Ltd.
—Home Through the Dark. 1977. (General Ser.). lib. bdg. 10.95 o.p. (*0-8161-6442-8*, Macmillan Reference USA) Gale Group.
Fraser, Antonia. The Cavalier Case. l.t. ed. 1992. (Jemima Shore Mystery Ser.). pap. 14.95 o.p. (*0-7927-0818-0*); 18.95 o.p. (*0-7927-0817-2*, E0014); audio 69.95 (*0-7451-5967-2*, CAB 673) BBC Audiobooks America.
—The Cavalier Case. 1992. 256p. mass mkt. 4.99 o.s.i (*0-553-29544-6*) Bantam Bks.
—Cool Repentance: A Jemima Shore Mystery. unabr. ed. 1993. audio 54.95 (*0-7451-5964-8*, CSL 064) BBC Audiobooks America.
—Cool Repentance: A Jemima Shore Mystery. 1991. 240p. mass mkt. 4.50 o.s.i (*0-553-28072-4*) Bantam Bks.
—Cool Repentance: A Jemima Shore Mystery. unabr. collector's ed. 1988. audio 40.00 (*0-7366-1303-X*, 2210) Books on Tape, Inc.
—Cool Repentance: A Jemima Shore Mystery. 1983. 12.95 o.p. (*0-393-01625-0*); 1985. 224p. reprint ed. pap. 3.95 o.p. (*0-393-30264-4*) Norton, W. W. & Co., Inc.
—Jemima Shore at the Sunny Grave. l.t. ed. 1993. pap. 16.95 o.p. (*0-7927-1348-6*); 1992. 18.95 o.p. (*0-7927-1349-4*) BBC Audiobooks America.
—Oxford Blood: A Jemima Shore Mystery. l.t. ed. 1986. pap. 13.95 o.p. (*1-55504-037-3*); 1993. 54.95 incl. audio (*0-7451-5966-4*, CAB 204) BBC Audiobooks America.
—Oxford Blood: A Jemima Shore Mystery. 1989. 224p. mass mkt. 3.95 o.s.i (*0-553-28070-8*) Bantam Bks.
—Oxford Blood: A Jemima Shore Mystery. (Jemima Shore Mystery Ser.). 1998. 224p. pap. 10.00 (*0-393-31824-9*, Norton Paperbacks); 1985. 13.95 o.p. (*0-393-02229-3*) Norton, W. W. & Co., Inc.
—Oxford Blood: A Jemima Shore Mystery. 1987. audio 49.95 o.s.i (*0-8161-9661-3*) Thorndike Pr.
—Political Death: A Jemima Shore Mystery. unabr. ed. 1996. audio 54.95 (*0-7451-6583-4*, CAB1199) BBC Audiobooks America.
—Political Death: A Jemima Shore Mystery. 1997. 240p. mass mkt. 5.99 (*0-553-57203-2*, Crimeline) Bantam Bks.
—Political Death: A Jemima Shore Mystery. unabr. ed. 1994. audio 40.00 Books on Tape, Inc.
—Quiet as a Nun. l.t. ed. 1993. (J). (gr. 5 up). pap. 18.95 o.p. (*0-7927-1689-2*); 1993. (YA). (gr. 5 up). 20.95 o.p. (*0-7927-1690-6*); audio 54.95 (*0-7451-5971-0*, CAB 397) BBC Audiobooks America.
—Quiet as a Nun. 1991. 192p. mass mkt. 4.50 o.s.i (*0-553-28311-1*) Bantam Bks.
—Quiet as a Nun. unabr. collector's ed. 1984. audio 42.00 (*0-7366-0884-2*, 1828) Books on Tape, Inc.
—Quiet as a Nun. unabr. ed. 2000. (Jemima Shore Mystery Ser.: Bk. 1). audio 49.95 Chivers Audio Bks. GBR. *Dist:* BBC Audiobooks America.
—Quiet as a Nun. (Jemima Shore Mystery Ser.). 1998. 192p. pap. 10.00 (*0-393-31822-2*, Norton Paperbacks); 1982. pap. 3.95 o.p. (*0-393-30120-6*) Norton, W. W. & Co., Inc.
—Quiet as a Nun. 1977. 8.95 o.p. (*0-670-58556-4*) Viking Penguin.
—A Splash of Red: A Jemina Shore Mystery. unabr. ed. 1993. 54.95 incl. audio (*0-7451-5963-X*, CAB 101) BBC Audiobooks America.
—A Splash of Red: A Jemina Shore Mystery. 1990. 224p. mass mkt. 3.95 o.s.i (*0-553-28071-6*) Bantam Bks.
—A Splash of Red: A Jemina Shore Mystery. 1984. pap. 3.50 o.p. (*0-393-30213-X*); 1982. 12.95 o.p. (*0-393-01511-4*); 1998. 240p. pap. 10.00 (*0-393-31687-4*) Norton, W. W. & Co., Inc.
—A Splash of Red: A Jemima Shore Mystery. unabr. ed. 1985. audio 53.95 o.s.i (*0-8161-9823-3*) Thorndike Pr.
—The Wild Island: A Jemima Shore Mystery. l.t. ed. 1993. 20.95 o.p. (*0-7927-1486-5*); 1993. pap. 18.95 o.p. (*0-7927-1485-7*); 1992. 54.95 incl. audio (*0-7451-5968-0*, CAB 522) BBC Audiobooks America.
—The Wild Island: A Jemima Shore Mystery. 1991. 224p. mass mkt. 4.50 o.s.i (*0-553-29324-9*) Bantam Bks.
—The Wild Island: A Jemima Shore Mystery. unabr. collector's ed. 1986. audio 42.00 (*0-7366-0885-0*, 1829) Books on Tape, Inc.
—The Wild Island: A Jemima Shore Mystery. 1978. 8.95 o.p. (*0-393-08831-6*) Norton, W. W. & Co., Inc.
—Your Royal Hostage. l.t. ed. 1988. 13.95 o.p. (*1-55504-394-1*); Set. 1993. 54.95 incl. audio (*0-7451-5969-9*, CAB 261) BBC Audiobooks America.
—Your Royal Hostage. 1989. 272p. mass mkt. 3.95 o.s.i (*0-553-28019-8*) Bantam Bks.
Fraser, George MacDonald. Mr. American. 1998. 585p. pap. 15.95 (*0-7867-0554-X*, Carroll & Graf Pubs.) Avalon Publishing Group.
—Mr. American. 1993. 585p. pap. 16.00 o.p. (*0-00-271235-0*) HarperCollins Pubs. Ltd. GBR. *Dist:* HarperCollins Pubs.
—Mr. American. 1981. 16.95 o.p. (*0-671-42571-4*, Simon & Schuster) Simon & Schuster.
Frayn, Michael. Headlong. 1999. (Illus.). 340p. 26.00 o.s.i (*0-8050-6285-8*, Metropolitan Bks.) Holt, Henry & Co.
—A Landing on the Sun: A Novel. 2003. 272p. pap. 14.00 (*0-312-42190-7*) Picador.
—Spies: A Novel. 2002. 288p. 23.00 o.s.i (*0-8050-7058-3*, Metropolitan Bks.) Holt, Henry & Co.
—Spies: A Novel. 2003. 272p. pap. 13.00 (*0-312-42117-6*) Picador.
—Spies: A Novel. l.t. ed. (General Ser.). 25.95 (*0-7862-4480-1*) Thorndike Pr.
Freeman, Austin R. For the Defence: Dr. Thorndyke. l.t. ed. 1992. pap. 14.95 o.p. (*0-7927-1062-2*) BBC Audiobooks America.
Freeman, Don. The Guard Mouse. 1974. (Seafarer Ser.). (Illus.). (J). (gr. k-2). pap. 1.50 o.p. (*0-670-05092-X*, Penguin Bks.) Viking Penguin.
Freeman, R. Austin. Mr. Pottermack's Oversight. 1985. (Detective Stories Ser.). 352p. reprint ed. pap. 5.95 o.p. (*0-486-24780-5*) Dover Pubns., Inc.
—The Red Thumb Mark. 1986. 305p. mass mkt. 3.95 o.p. (*0-88184-240-0*, Carroll & Graf Pubs.) Avalon Publishing Group.
—The Red Thumb Mark. 1986. 320p. reprint ed. pap. 6.95 (*0-486-25210-8*) Dover Pubns., Inc.
—The Red Thumb Mark. 2001. 230p. pap. 9.95 (*0-7551-0374-2*) House of Stratus, Inc. GBR. *Dist:* Midpoint Trade Bks., Inc.
—The Stoneware Monkey. 1987. (Mystery Classics Ser.). 224p. reprint ed. pap. 6.95 o.p. (*0-486-25471-2*) Dover Pubns., Inc.
French, Nicci. Beneath the Skin. l.t. ed. 2000. (Illus.). 495p. (*0-7540-1478-9*, Macmillan Reference USA) Gale Group.
—Beneath the Skin. 2000. 368p. 24.95 (*0-89296-726-9*) Mysterious Pr.
—Beneath the Skin. l.t. ed. 2000. (G. K. Hall Core Ser.). (Illus.). 495p. 30.95 (*0-7838-9006-0*) Thorndike Pr.
—Beneath the Skin. 2001. 448p. reprint ed. mass mkt. 7.99 (*0-446-60978-1*) Warner Bks., Inc.
—Killing Me Softly: A Novel of Obsession. 1999. (*0-07-862220-4*) McGraw-Hill Cos., The.
—Killing Me Softly: A Novel of Obsession. 1999. 320p. 24.00 (*0-89296-697-1*) Mysterious Pr.
—Killing Me Softly: A Novel of Obsession. l.t. ed. 1999. (Basic Ser.). 488p. 28.95 (*0-7862-2220-4*) Thorndike Pr.
—Killing Me Softly: A Novel of Obsession. movie tie-in ed. 2000. 400p. reprint ed. mass mkt. 7.50 (*0-446-60838-6*) Warner Bks., Inc.
—Land of the Living. l.t. ed. 2003. 562p. 30.95 (*0-7862-5655-9*) Thorndike Pr.
—Land of the Living. 2003. 352p. 23.95 (*0-446-53151-0*) Warner Bks., Inc.
Frewin, Anthony. Scorpian Rising: A Novel. 2001. 224p. pap. 12.95 (*1-56858-199-8*) Four Walls Eight Windows.
Frost, Mark. The List of Seven. 1993. 368p. 20.00 o.p. (*0-688-12245-0*, Morrow, William & Co.) Morrow/Avon.
—The List of Seven. abr. ed. 1993. audio 16.95 o.p. (*1-55800-840-3*) NewStar Media, Inc.
—The List of Seven. 1994. (Super Sound Buy, Dove Ser.). 8.99 o.p. (*0-7871-0238-5*) Penguin Group (USA) Inc.
—The List of 7. 1994. 416p. mass mkt. 5.99 (*0-380-72019-1*, Avon Bks.) Morrow/Avon.
Fyfield, Frances. Blind Date. l.t. ed. 1998. 384p. 32.50 (*0-7531-5923-6*) ISIS Large Print Bks. GBR. *Dist:* Ulverscroft Large Print Bks., Ltd., Ulverscroft Large Print Canada, Ltd.
—Blind Date. 2000. 304p. mass mkt. 5.99 (*0-14-028052-9*) Penguin Group (USA) Inc.
—Blind Date. l.t. ed. 1999. (Core Ser.). 421p. 27.95 o.p. (*0-7838-8559-8*) Thorndike Pr.
—Blind Date. 1998. 272p. 21.95 o.p. (*0-670-87889-8*, Viking) Viking Penguin.
—A Clear Conscience. unabr. ed. 1995. audio 69.95 (*0-7451-6547-8*, CAB 1163) BBC Audiobooks America.
—A Clear Conscience. 1996. (Helen West Mystery Ser.). mass mkt. 5.99 o.s.i (*0-345-38508-X*) Ballantine Bks.
—A Clear Conscience. unabr. ed. 2000. (West & Bailey Mystery Ser.). audio 59.95 Chivers Audio Bks. GBR. *Dist:* BBC Audiobooks America.
—A Clear Conscience. deluxe ed. 1995. 20.00 (*0-676-50224-5*, Pantheon) Knopf Publishing Group.
—A Clear Conscience. 2001. 272p. mass mkt. 6.99 (*0-14-028251-3*) Penguin Group (USA) Inc.
—A Clear Conscience. 1995. o.p. (*0-676-50194-X*) Random Hse., Inc.
—Deep Sleep. unabr. ed. 1996. (Prosecutor Helen West Mysteries Ser.). audio 54.95 (*0-7451-4144-7*, CAB827) BBC Audiobooks America.
—Deep Sleep. Chelius, Jane, ed. 240p. 1993. mass mkt. 4.99 o.p. (*0-671-73547-0*, Pocket); 1992. 18.00 o.p. (*0-671-73546-2*, Atria) Simon & Schuster.
—Not That Kind of Place. 1990. 224p. 17.95 o.p. (*0-671-67666-0*, Atria) Simon & Schuster.
—Not That Kind of Place. Chelius, Jane, ed. 1991. 256p. reprint ed. mass mkt. 5.50 (*0-671-73945-X*, Pocket) Simon & Schuster.
—Perfectly Pure & Good. unabr. ed. 1994. (Attorney Sarah Fortune Mysteries Ser.). audio 54.95 (*0-7451-4340-7*, CAB 1023) BBC Audiobooks America.
—Perfectly Pure & Good. 1995. (Mysteries Around the World Promotion Ser.). mass mkt. 5.99 o.s.i (*0-345-38279-X*, Ivy Bks.) Ballantine Bks.
—Perfectly Pure & Good. 1994. 224p. 20.00 o.s.i (*0-679-42665-5*, Pantheon) Knopf Publishing Group.
—Perfectly Pure & Good. l.t. ed. 1995. (Magna Large Print Ser.). 359p. o.p. (*0-7505-0797-7*) Magna Large Print Bks. GBR. *Dist:* Ulverscroft Large Print Canada, Ltd.
—Perfectly Pure & Good. 2000. 256p. pap. 5.99 (*0-14-029195-4*) Penguin Group (USA) Inc.
—A Question of Guilt. unabr. ed. 1993. (Prosecutor Helen West Mysteries Ser.). audio 69.95 (*0-7451-5972-9*, CAB 602) BBC Audiobooks America.
—A Question of Guilt. unabr. ed. 2000. (West & Bailey Mystery Ser.). audio 59.95 Chivers Audio Bks. GBR. *Dist:* BBC Audiobooks America.
—A Question of Guilt. 1990. 288p. mass mkt. 4.99 (*0-671-67665-2*, Pocket); 1989. 16.95 o.p. (*0-671-67664-4*, Atria) Simon & Schuster.
—A Question of Guilt. 1991. (Audio Books Ser.). audio 69.95 o.p. (*0-8161-9227-8*) Thorndike Pr.
—Shadow Play. l.t. ed. 1994. 22.95 o.p. (*0-7927-1828-3*); pap. 20.95 o.p. (*0-7927-1827-5*); audio 69.95 (*0-7451-4232-X*, CAB 915) BBC Audiobooks America.
—Shadow Play. 1994. mass mkt. 5.99 o.s.i (*0-345-38507-1*) Ballantine Bks.
—Shadow Play. unabr. ed. 2000. (West & Bailey Mystery Ser.). audio 59.95 Chivers Audio Bks. GBR. *Dist:* BBC Audiobooks America.
—Shadow Play. 1999. 288p. pap. 5.99 (*0-14-028683-7*, Penguin Bks.) Penguin Group (USA) Inc.
—Shadows on the Mirror. unabr. ed. 1994. audio 49.95 (*0-7451-4287-7*, CAB 970) Chivers Audio Bks. GBR. *Dist:* BBC Audiobooks America.
—Shadows on the Mirror. Chelius, Jane, ed. 1991. 17.95 o.p. (*0-671-70161-4*, Atria); 1992. 224p. reprint ed. mass mkt. 4.50 (*0-671-70162-2*, Pocket) Simon & Schuster.
—Staring at the Light. l.t. ed. 2000. (Basic Ser.). 511p. 27.95 (*0-7862-2514-9*) Thorndike Pr.
—Staring at the Light. 2000. (Attorney Sarah Fortune Mysteries Ser.). 288p. 23.95 o.s.i (*0-670-88730-7*) Viking Penguin.
—Trial by Fire. l.t. ed. 1992. 18.95 o.p. (*0-7927-1200-5*); pap. 16.95 o.p. (*0-7927-1174-2*); 69.95 incl. audio (*0-7451-4025-4*, CAB 722) BBC Audiobooks America.
—Trial by Fire. unabr. ed. 2000. (West & Bailey Mystery Ser.). audio 59.95 Chivers Audio Bks. GBR. *Dist:* BBC Audiobooks America.
—Without Consent. unabr. ed. 1997. (West & Bailey Mystery Ser.). audio 59.95 (*0-7451-6799-3*, CAB 1415) Chivers Audio Bks. GBR. *Dist:* BBC Audiobooks America.
—Without Consent. 1998. 272p. mass mkt. 5.99 (*0-14-027477-4*) Penguin Group (USA) Inc.
—Without Consent. l.t. ed. 1998. (Mystery Ser.). 325p. 26.95 (*0-7838-8437-0*) Thorndike Pr.

—Without Consent. 1997. (Helen West Mystery Ser.). 224p. 21.95 o.p. (*0-670-87682-8*) Viking Penguin.

Fyfield, Frances, ed. Staring at the Light. 2001. 288p. mass mkt. 5.99 (*0-14-029845-2*) Penguin Group (USA) Inc.

Gabaldon, Diana. Lord John & the Private Matter. 2003. E-Book (*0-440-33452-7*); 320p. 23.95 (*0-385-33747-7*, Delacorte Pr.) Dell Publishing.

—Lord John & the Private Matter. 2003. 336p. (*0-385-66022-7*) Doubleday Canada, Ltd. CAN. *Dist:* Random Hse., Inc.

Gadney, Reg. Nightshade. 1988. 240p. 15.95 o.p. (*0-312-02261-1*) St. Martin's Pr.

Gaiman, Neil. Neverwhere. abr. ed. 1997. audio 16.95 (*1-56511-231-8*) HighBridge Co.

—Neverwhere. 1998. 400p. mass mkt. 7.99 (*0-380-78901-9*, Avon Bks.); 1997. 352p. 24.00 (*0-380-97363-4*, Morrow, William & Co.) Morrow/Avon.

—Neverwhere: A Novel. 2003. 400p. pap. 13.95 (*0-06-055781-8*, Perennial) HarperTrade.

Galford, Ellen. The Dyke & the Dybbuk. 1994. 248p. reprint ed. pap. 10.95 o.p. (*1-878067-51-6*, Seal Pr.) Avalon Publishing Group.

Gardam, Jane. The Queen of the Tambourine. 1996. 240p. pap. 11.00 o.s.i (*0-312-14398-2*) Picador.

—The Queen of the Tambourine. 1995. 240p. 20.95 o.p. (*0-312-13151-8*) St. Martin's Pr.

Gardner, Ashley. A Regimental Murder. 2004. 256p. mass mkt. 5.99 (*0-425-19612-7*) Berkley Publishing Group.

Gardner, John. Bottled Spider. 29.99 (*0-7278-7200-1*); 2002. 384p. 26.99 (*0-7278-5829-7*) Severn Hse. Pubs., Ltd.

Garfield, Leon. Black Jack, RS. 2000. 197p. (YA). (gr. 7 up). 18.00 (*0-374-30827-6*, Farrar, Straus & Giroux (BYR)) Farrar, Straus & Giroux.

Gash, Jonathan. Different Women Dancing. l.t. ed. 1997. (Large Print Book Ser.). pap. 23.95 o.p. (*1-56895-512-X*, Wheeler Publishing, Inc.) Gale Group.

—Different Women Dancing. 1998. 304p. pap. 5.99 o.s.i (*0-14-026411-6*) Penguin Group (USA) Inc.

—Different Women Dancing. 1997. 320p. 21.95 o.s.i (*0-670-87369-1*) Viking Penguin.

—Prey Dancing. l.t. ed. 1999. (Dr. Clare Burtonall Mysteries Ser.). pap. 24.95 (*1-56895-626-6*, Wheeler Publishing, Inc.) Gale Group.

—Prey Dancing. 1999. (Dr. Clare Burtonall Mysteries Ser.). 288p. pap. 5.99 o.s.i (*0-14-028016-2*, Penguin Bks.) Penguin Group (USA) Inc.

—Prey Dancing. 1998. (Dr. Clare Burtonall Mysteries Ser.). 288p. 21.95 o.p. (*0-670-87764-6*) Viking Penguin.

—A Rag, a Bone & a Hank of Hair. 2000. (Lovejoy Mystery Ser.). 256p. 23.95 o.s.i (*0-670-88598-3*, Viking) Viking Penguin.

Gayle, Mike. Mr. Commitment: A Novel. 2002. 336p. reprint ed. pap. 12.95 (*0-7679-0654-3*) Broadway Bks.

—My Legendary Girlfriend. 2001. (*0-385-50103-X*) Doubleday Publishing.

Gee, Maggie. The White Family. 2003. (Saqi Bks.). 280p. pap. 14.95 (*0-86356-380-5*) I.B.Tauris & Co., Ltd. GBR. *Dist:* Holtzbrinck Pubs., Palgrave Macmillan.

Gentle, Mary. The Architecture of Desire. 208p. 1994. mass mkt. 4.99 o.s.i (*0-451-45353-0*); 1993. 19.00 o.p. (*0-451-45234-8*) NAL. (ROC).

—The Architecture of Desire. 1999. pap. (*0-670-84582-5*) Viking Penguin.

George, Sara. The Journal of Mrs. Pepys: Portrait of a Marriage. 2000. 352p. pap. 11.95 (*0-312-26347-3*, Saint Martin's Griffin); 1999. 340p. 21.95 o.p. (*0-312-20554-6*) St. Martin's Pr.

Gibson, William. Pattern Recognition. 2003. 368p. 25.95 (*0-399-14986-4*, Putnam & Grosset) Putnam Publishing Group, The.

—Pattern Recognition. 2004. 368p. pap. 14.00 (*0-425-19293-8*) Berkley Publishing Group.

Gifford, Thomas. Praetorian. 1994. 736p. mass mkt. 6.50 o.s.i (*0-553-56502-8*) Bantam Bks.

Gilbert, Michael. Ring of Terror. 1995. 256p. 20.00 o.p. (*0-7867-0193-5*, Carroll & Graf Pubs.) Avalon Publishing Group.

—Ring of Terror. l.t. ed. 1996. pap. 17.95 o.p. (*0-7838-1537-9*, Macmillan Reference USA) Gale Group.

—Roller-Coaster. 1994. 256p. 19.95 o.p. (*0-88184-996-0*, Carroll & Graf Pubs.) Avalon Publishing Group.

Gilpin, T. G. Death of a Fantasy Life. 1993. 176p. 16.95 o.p. (*0-312-09270-9*, Saint Martin's Minotaur) St. Martin's Pr.

Girard, Paula Tanner. The Seventh Sister. 2001. (Five Star Romance Ser.). 219p. 25.95 (*0-7862-3503-9*, Five Star) Gale Group.

Giroux, E. X. A Death for a Dancer: A Robert Forsythe Mystery. 1986. mass mkt. 2.95 o.s.i (*0-345-33408-6*) Ballantine Bks.

—A Death for a Dancer: A Robert Forsythe Mystery. 1985. 192p. 12.95 o.p. (*0-312-18868-4*) St. Martin's Pr.

—A Death for a Darling. 1986. 192p. mass mkt. 3.50 o.s.i (*0-345-33024-2*) Ballantine Bks.

—A Death for a Darling. 1985. 192p. 13.95 o.p. (*0-312-18607-X*) St. Martin's Pr.

—A Death for a Dietician. 1989. 192p. mass mkt. 3.95 o.s.i (*0-345-35767-1*) Ballantine Bks.

—A Death for a Dietitian. 1988. 176p. 13.95 o.p. (*0-312-01417-1*, Saint Martin's Minotaur) St. Martin's Pr.

—A Death for a Dilettante. 1987. 176p. mass mkt. 3.50 o.s.i (*0-345-34758-7*) Ballantine Bks.

—A Death for a Dilettante. 1987. (Robert Forsythe Mystery Ser.). 208p. 13.95 o.p. (*0-312-00044-8*) St. Martin's Pr.

—A Death for a Doctor: A Robert Forsythe Mystery. 1986. 208p. 13.95 o.p. (*0-312-18603-7*) St. Martin's Pr.

—A Death for a Dodo. 1993. 17.95 o.p. (*0-312-08762-4*, Saint Martin's Minotaur) St. Martin's Pr.

—A Death for a Double. 1991. 192p. mass mkt. 3.95 o.s.i (*0-345-36833-9*) Ballantine Bks.

—A Death for a Double. 1992. 2.99 o.p. (*0-517-09039-2*) Random Hse. Value Publishing.

—A Death for a Double. 1990. 208p. 15.95 o.p. (*0-312-03809-7*, Saint Martin's Minotaur) St. Martin's Pr.

—A Death for a Dreamer. 1990. (Death Ser.). 192p. mass mkt. 3.95 o.s.i (*0-345-36528-3*) Ballantine Bks.

—A Death for a Dreamer. 1989. 14.95 o.p. (*0-312-02901-2*, Saint Martin's Minotaur) St. Martin's Pr.

—A Death for Adonis. 1985. 160p. mass mkt. 4.95 o.s.i (*0-345-32889-2*) Ballantine Bks.

—A Death for Adonis. 1984. 160p. 11.95 o.p. (*0-312-18610-X*) St. Martin's Pr.

Giroux, E. X. & Giroux, Leo. A Death for a Doctor: A Robert Forsythe Mystery. 1987. 192p. mass mkt. 4.95 o.s.i (*0-345-34231-3*) Ballantine Bks.

Gissing, George R. Born in Exile: A Novel, 3 vols. in 1. reprint ed. 37.50 (*0-404-02786-5*) AMS Pr., Inc.

—Born in Exile: A Novel. Coustillas, Pierre, ed. 1978. (Society & the Victorians Ser.). text 22.25 o.p. (*0-85527-872-2*) Brill Academic Pubs., Inc.

—Born in Exile: A Novel. 1993. 544p. pap. 6.95 (*0-460-87241-9*, Everyman's Classic Library in Paperback) Tuttle Publishing.

—The Emancipated, 3 vols. in 1. reprint ed. 115.00 (*0-404-02785-7*) AMS Pr., Inc.

—The Emancipated. Coustillas, Pierre, ed. 1978. 469p. 22.50 o.p. (*0-8386-2171-6*) Fairleigh Dickinson Univ. Pr.

Gleeson, Janet. The Grenadillo Box. 2004. (Illus.). 352p. 25.00 (*0-7432-4686-1*, Simon & Schuster) Simon & Schuster.

Godden, Rumer. Cromartie vs. the God Shiva: Acting Through the Government of India. 1998. 176p. pap. 13.00 o.s.i (*0-688-16343-2*, Quill) HarperTrade.

—Cromartie vs. the God Shiva: Acting Through the Government of India. l.t. ed. 1997. 208p. 22.00 o.p. (*0-688-15550-2*, Morrow, William & Co.) Morrow/Avon.

—Cromartie vs. the God Shiva: Acting Through the Government of India. l.t. ed. 1998. (Basic Ser.). 200p. 29.95 (*0-7862-1347-7*) Thorndike Pr.

—An Episode of Sparrows. 1989. 256p. (YA). (gr. 7 up). pap. 4.95 o.p. (*0-14-034024-6*, Puffin Bks.) Penguin Putnam Bks. for Young Readers.

—The Kitchen Madonna. 1967. (Illus.). (J). 5.95 o.p. (*0-670-41399-2*) Viking Penguin.

Gooden, Philip. Alms for Oblivion: A Shakespearean Murder Mystery. 2003. 288p. 24.00 (*0-7867-1142-6*, Carroll & Graf Pubs.) Avalon Publishing Group.

Goodman, Allegra. Total Immersion: Stories. 1989. 16.95 o.p. (*0-06-015998-7*) HarperTrade.

Gosling, Paula. Death Penalties. 1991. 297p. 25.00 (*0-89296-458-8*) Mysterious Pr.

—Death Penalties. 1992. 304p. mass mkt. 4.99 o.s.i (*0-446-40189-7*) Warner Bks., Inc.

—The Wychford Murders. 1986. (Crime Club Ser.). 192p. 12.95 o.p. (*0-385-23551-8*) Doubleday Publishing.

—The Wychford Murders. 1988. 224p. reprint ed. mass mkt. (*0-373-26009-1*, Harlequin Bks.) Harlequin Enterprises, Ltd.

—The Wychford Murders. unabr. ed. 1993. audio 69.95 (*1-85089-757-3*, 9008X) ISIS Audio Bks. GBR. *Dist:* Ulverscroft Large Print Bks., Ltd.

—The Wychford Murders. l.t. ed. 1987. (Ulverscroft Large Print Ser.). 528p. o.p. (*0-7089-1709-7*, Ulverscroft) Thorpe, F. A. Pubs. GBR. *Dist:* Ulverscroft Large Print Canada, Ltd.

Granger, Pip. Not All Tarts Are Apple. 2003. 336p. mass mkt. (*0-552-14895-4*, Corgi) Bantam Bks.

—Not All Tarts Are Apple. 2003. 224p. pap. 12.00 (*0-14-200332-8*) Penguin Group (USA) Inc.

—Not All Tarts Are Apple. 2nd rev. ed. 2003. 205p. pap. 14.95 (*1-59058-043-5*) Poisoned Pen Pr.

—The Widow Ginger. l.t. ed. 2003. (Magna Large Print Ser.). 368p. (*0-7505-2095-7*) Magna Large Print Bks. GBR. *Dist:* Ulverscroft Large Print Canada, Ltd.

—The Widow Ginger. 2003. 278p. 24.95 o.s.i (*1-59058-057-5*) Poisoned Pen Pr.

Grant-Adamson, Lesley. Too Many Questions. 1993. mass mkt. 4.50 o.s.i (*0-449-22104-0*, Fawcett) Ballantine Bks.

—Too Many Questions. 1991. 15.95 o.p. (*0-312-05434-3*, Saint Martin's Minotaur) St. Martin's Pr.

Grant, Tracy. Daughter of the Game. 496p. 2003. mass mkt. 6.99 (*0-06-103206-9*, HarperTorch); 2002. 24.95 (*0-06-621133-6*, Morrow, William & Co.) Morrow/Avon.

Gray, John MacLachlan. The Fiend in Human. 2003. 352p. 24.95 (*0-312-28284-2*) St. Martin's Pr.

Green, Jane. Bookends: A Novel. 2002. 368p. 21.00 (*0-7679-0780-9*) Broadway Bks.

—Bookends: A Novel. 2002. audio compact disk 29.95 (*0-553-71307-8*, RH Audio) Random Hse. Audio Publishing Group.

—Bookends: A Novel. unabr. ed. 2001. audio 82.00 (*1-84197-194-4*, H1177E7, Clipper Audio) Recorded Bks., LLC.

—Bookends: A Novel. 2000. 393p. (*0-7181-4456-2*, Joseph, Michael) Viking Penguin.

—Mr. Maybe. 2001. E-Book 16.00 (*1-59061-361-9*); E-Book 16.00 (*1-59061-495-X*) Adobe Systems, Inc.

—Mr. Maybe. 368p. 2001. 19.95 o.s.i (*0-7679-0519-9*); 2002. reprint ed. pap. 11.95 (*0-7679-0520-2*) Broadway Bks.

—Straight Talking. 2003. 320p. pap. 11.95 (*0-7679-1559-3*) Broadway Bks.

Greene, Graham. The Captain & the Enemy. 1991. pap. text 22.25 (*0-582-06024-9*) Addison-Wesley Longman, Ltd. GBR. *Dist:* Trans-Atlantic Pubns., Inc.

—The Captain & the Enemy. l.t. ed. 1989. (General Ser.). 256p. 13.95 o.p. (*0-8161-4932-1*); lib. bdg. 19.95 o.p. (*0-8161-4799-X*) Gale Group. (Macmillan Reference USA).

—The Captain & the Enemy. 1992. 2.99 o.p. (*0-517-07986-0*) Random Hse. Value Publishing.

—The Captain & the Enemy. 192p. 1989. pap. 7.95 o.s.i (*0-14-012418-7*, Penguin Bks.); 1988. 17.95 o.p. (*0-670-82405-4*) Viking Penguin.

—The End of the Affair. l.t. ed. 2001. (G. K. Hall Perennial Bestsellers Ser. ). 186p. 28.95 (*0-7838-9528-3*, Macmillan Reference USA) Gale Group.

—The End of the Affair. 1999. 192p. pap. 11.95 (*0-14-029109-1*, Penguin Bks.) Penguin Group (USA) Inc.

—The End of the Affair. 9999. 14.95 o.p. (*0-559-35055-4*) Putnam Publishing Group, The.

—The End of the Affair. 1975. 240p. mass mkt. 2.95 o.s.i (*0-671-44535-9*, Pocket) Simon & Schuster.

—The End of the Affair. (Penguin Twentieth-Century Classics Ser.). 1991. 192p. 13.00 (*0-14-018495-3*, Penguin Classics); 1977. 256p. pap. 6.95 o.p. (*0-14-004696-8*, Penguin Bks.); 1951. 16.95 o.p. (*0-670-29457-8*) Viking Penguin.

Griesemer, John. Signal & Noise: A Novel. 2004. 608p. pap. 15.00 (*0-312-42334-9*); 2003. 640p. 26.00 (*0-312-30082-4*) Picador.

Griffin, Nicholas. The House of Sight & Shadow. 2001. E-Book 10.00 (*1-58945-860-5*) Adobe Systems, Inc.

—The House of Sight & Shadow: A Novel. 2002. 320p. pap. 12.95 (*0-375-75939-5*) Random House Adult Trade Publishing Group.

Gunesekera, Romesh. The Sandglass. 1998. 288p. 21.95 (*1-56584-484-X*) New Pr., The.

—The Sandglass. 1999. 288p. 12.95 o.s.i (*1-57322-758-7*, Riverhead Bks. (Hardcovers)) Putnam Publishing Group, The.

—The Sandglass. 1998. 278p. 22.00 (*0-670-88173-2*, Viking) Viking Penguin.

Gupta, Sunetra. Memories of Rain: A Novel. 1992. 17.95 o.p. (*0-8021-1448-2*) Grove/Atlantic, Inc.

—A Sin of Color: A Novel of Obsession. 2001. 288p. pap. 15.00 (*1-57071-856-3*, Sourcebooks Landmark) Sourcebooks, Inc.

Guresekera, Romesh. The Reef. 1996. 192p. 11.00 o.s.i (*1-57322-533-9*, Riverhead Trade (Paperbacks)) Berkley Publishing Group.

H. D. Pilate's Wife. Burke, Joan, ed. & intro. by. 2000. xvii, 135p. pap. 12.95 (*0-8112-1433-8*) New Directions Publishing Corp.

Haasler, Sue. Time after Time. 2002. 272p. 23.95 (*0-312-30642-3*) St. Martin's Pr.

Haaster, Sue. Time after Time. E-Book 23.95 (*0-312-70509-3*); 2004. 272p. pap. 13.95 (*0-312-30643-1*, Saint Martin's Griffin) St. Martin's Pr.

Hall, John. Sherlock Holmes & the Disgraced Inspector. 1998. 140p. pap. 14.95 (*0-947533-88-5*) Breese Bks., Ltd. GBR. *Dist:* Midpoint Trade Bks., Inc.

—Sherlock Holmes & the Disgraced Inspector. l.t. ed. 2000. (Linford Mystery Large Print Ser.). 248p. pap. 18.99 (*0-7089-5783-8*, Linford) Thorpe, F. A. Pubs. GBR. *Dist:* Ulverscroft Large Print Bks., Ltd., Ulverscroft Large Print Canada, Ltd.

Hall, Patricia. Dead on Arrival. l.t. ed. 2000. (Dales Large Print Ser.). 400p. pap. (*1-84262-012-6*) Dales Large Print Bks. GBR. *Dist:* Ulverscroft Large Print Canada, Ltd.

—Dead on Arrival. 2001. (Yorkshire Mystery Ser.). 224p. 22.95 (*0-312-26572-7*, Saint Martin's Minotaur) St. Martin's Pr.

Hall, Robert L. Benjamin Franklin & a Case of Artful Murder. 1995. mass mkt. 4.99 (*0-312-95419-0*, St. Martin's Paperbacks) St. Martin's Pr.

—Benjamin Franklin & a Case of Christmas Murder. l.t. ed. 1998. 413p. reprint ed. text 15.00 (*0-7881-5175-4*) DIANE Publishing Co.

—Benjamin Franklin & a Case of Christmas Murder. 1991. 288p. mass mkt. 3.99 o.p. (*0-312-92670-7*, St. Martin's Paperbacks); 1990. 17.95 o.p. (*0-312-05383-5*, Saint Martin's Minotaur) St. Martin's Pr.

—Benjamin Franklin Takes the Case: The American Agent Investigates Murder in the Dark Byways of London. 1993. mass mkt. 3.99 o.p. (*0-312-95047-0*, St. Martin's Paperbacks) St. Martin's Pr.

—London Blood: Further Adventures of the American Agent Abroad: A Benjamin Franklin Mystery. 1997. (Benjamin Franklin Mystery Ser.). 256p. 21.95 (*0-312-16908-6*, Saint Martin's Minotaur) St. Martin's Pr.

—Murder at Drury Lane: Further Adventures of the American Agent in London. 1993. mass mkt. 4.50 (*0-312-95112-4*, St. Martin's Paperbacks); 1992. 288p. 18.95 o.p. (*0-312-08266-5*, Saint Martin's Minotaur) St. Martin's Pr.

—Murder by the Waters: A Benjamin Franklin Mystery. pap. 15.95 (*0-312-30104-9*, Saint Martin's Griffin); 1995. 272p. 21.95 (*0-312-13568-8*, Saint Martin's Minotaur) St. Martin's Pr.

Hall, Robert Lee. Benjamin Franklin Takes the Case. 2001. 227p. reprint ed. pap. 14.95 (*0-8122-1789-6*) Univ. of Pennsylvania Pr.

Halpern, Chaiky. The House on Kyverdale Road. 1995. 16.95 (*0-87306-737-1*); pap. 12.95 (*0-87306-738-X*) Feldheim, Philipp Inc.

Hamilton, Ruth. Billy London's Girls. 2000. (J). pap. 9.95 (*0-552-13897-5*) Transworld Publishers Ltd. GBR. *Dist:* Trafalgar Square.

Hammick, Georgina. Green Man Running. 2002. 296p. (*0-7011-6677-0*) Random Hse. of Canada, Ltd. CAN. *Dist:* Random Hse., Inc.

Hansen, Brooks. Perlman's Ordeal. 1999. (Illus.). 400p. 24.00 o.p. (*0-374-23078-1*) Farrar, Straus & Giroux.

Harcourt, Palma. Limited Options. 1987. 224p. 15.95 o.p. (*0-8253-0419-9*) Beaufort Bks., Inc.

—Limited Options. l.t. ed. 1988. (Ulverscroft Large Print Ser.). 400p. 29.99 o.p. (*0-7089-1847-6*, Ulverscroft) Thorpe, F. A. Pubs. GBR. *Dist:* Ulverscroft Large Print Bks., Ltd., Ulverscroft Large Print Canada, Ltd.

Hardwick, Michael & Hardwick, Mollie. The Private Life of Sherlock Holmes. 1993. 200p. 25.00 (*0-86025-277-9*) Henry, Ian Pubns. GBR. *Dist:* Empire Publishing Service.

Hardy, Jules. Altered Land: A Novel. 2002. 336p. 24.95 (*1-55970-642-2*) Arcade Publishing, Inc.

Harkness, Lucy. The Happy Pigs. 2001. 160p. pap. 16.95 (*0-85640-656-2*) Blackstaff Pr., The IRL. *Dist:* Dufour Editions, Inc.

—The Happy Pigs. 2002. 256p. 23.95 (*0-312-28286-9*) St. Martin's Pr.

Harper, Karen. The Tidal Poole: An Elizabeth I Mystery. (Elizabeth I Mysteries Ser.). 2001. 336p. mass mkt. 6.50 (*0-440-22593-0*); 2000. (Illus.). 304p. 22.95 o.s.i (*0-385-33284-X*, Delacorte Pr.) Dell Publishing.

—The Tidal Poole: An Elizabeth I Mystery. l.t. ed. 2000. (Wheeler Large Print Book Ser.). 306p. 28.95 (*1-56895-894-3*, Wheeler Publishing, Inc.) Gale Group.

Harrod-Eagles, Cynthia. Blood Lines. 1996. 281p. o.s.i (*0-316-91420-7*) Little Brown & Co.

—Blood Lines. 1997. (Inspector Bill Slider Mysteries Ser.). mass mkt. 5.50 (*0-380-73052-9*, Avon Bks.) Morrow/Avon.

—Blood Lines. 1996. 281p. 20.50 o.p. (*0-684-80047-0*, Scribner) Simon & Schuster.

—Blood Sinister. l.t. ed. 2001. (Magna Large Print Ser.). 384p. (*0-7505-1599-6*) Magna Large Print Bks. GBR. *Dist:* Ulverscroft Large Print Canada, Ltd.

—Blood Sinister. E-Book 23.95 (*0-312-70251-5*); 2001. 308p. 23.95 (*0-312-27485-8*, Saint Martin's Minotaur) St. Martin's Pr.

—Dead End. 1996. 234p. mass mkt. o.s.i (*0-7515-1354-7*) Little Brown & Co.

—Dead End. unabr. ed. 2000. audio 79.95 (*1-86042-433-3*, 24333) Soundings, Ltd. GBR. *Dist:* Ulverscroft Large Print Bks., Ltd.

—Death to Go. l.t. ed. 1994. 413p. reprint ed. pap. 18.95 (*0-8161-5977-7*, Macmillan Reference USA) Gale Group.

—Death to Go. 1995. 288p. mass mkt. 4.99 o.s.i (*0-380-72346-8*, Avon Bks.) Morrow/Avon.

—Death to Go: An Inspector Bill Slider Mystery. 1994. 288p. 20.00 (*0-684-19650-6*, Macmillan Reference USA) Gale Group.
—Death Watch. 1994. 288p. mass mkt. 4.99 (*0-380-72065-5*, Avon Bks.) Morrow/Avon.
—Death Watch: An Inspector Bill Slider Mystery. 1993. 288p. 20.00 o.p. (*0-684-19519-4*, Macmillan Reference USA) Gale Group.
—Gone Tomorrow: A Bill Slider Mystery. 2001. 288p. (*0-316-85741-6*) Little Brown & Co.
—Gone Tomorrow: A Bill Slider Mystery. l.t. ed. 2002. (Magna Large Print Ser.). 496p. (*0-7505-1903-7*) Magna Large Print Bks. GBR. *Dist:* Ulverscroft Large Print Canada, Ltd.
—Gone Tomorrow: A Bill Slider Mystery. 2002. 368p. 24.95 (*0-312-30046-8*, Saint Martin's Minotaur) St. Martin's Pr.
—Grave Music. 1996. 256p. mass mkt. 5.50 o.s.i (*0-380-72636-X*, Avon Bks.) Morrow/Avon.
—Grave Music: An Inspector Bill Slider Mystery. l.t. ed. 1995. 370p. 23.95 o.p. (*0-7838-1469-0*, Macmillan Reference USA) Gale Group.
—Grave Music: An Inspector Bill Slider Mystery. 1995. 234p. 20.00 (*0-684-80046-2*, Scribner) Simon & Schuster.
—The Homecoming. 2002. (Morland Dynasty Ser.). mass mkt. 6.95 (*0-7515-2531-6*) Trafalgar Square.
—Killing Time. 1996. 313p. o.s.i (*0-316-88103-1*) Little Brown & Co.
—Killing Time. l.t. ed. 2000. (Magna Large Print Ser.). 464p. (*0-7505-1597-X*) Magna Large Print Bks. GBR. *Dist:* Ulverscroft Large Print Canada, Ltd.
—Killing Time: An Inspector Bill Slider Mystery. 1998. (Inspector Bill Slider Mysteries Ser.). 320p. 22.00 (*0-684-83776-5*, Scribner) Simon & Schuster.
—Necrochip. l.t. ed. 1994. (Magna Large Print Ser.). 462p. o.p. (*0-7505-0638-5*) Magna Large Print Bks. GBR. *Dist:* Ulverscroft Large Print Canada, Ltd.
—Orchestrated Death. 1993. 272p. mass mkt. 5.50 o.s.i (*0-380-71967-3*, Avon Bks.) Morrow/Avon.
—Orchestrated Death: A Mystery Introducing Inspector Bill Slider. 1992. 256p. text 19.95 (*0-684-19388-4*, Macmillan Reference USA) Gale Group.
—Shallow Grave. l.t. ed. 2001. (Magna Large Print Ser.). 464p. (*0-7505-1598-8*) Magna Large Print Bks. GBR. *Dist:* Ulverscroft Large Print Canada, Ltd.
—Shallow Grave. 1999. (Inspector Bill Slider Mysteries Ser.). 320p. 22.00 (*0-684-83777-3*, Scribner) Simon & Schuster.
—Shallow Grave. unabr. ed. 2000. audio 84.95 (*1-86042-521-6*, 25216) Soundings, Ltd. GBR. *Dist:* Ulverscroft Large Print Bks., Ltd.
—Shallow Grave. l.t. ed. 2000. (Mystery Ser.). 505p. 28.95 (*0-7862-2342-1*) Thorndike Pr.
Hart, Christopher. Rescue Me! 2001. 272p. pap. (*0-571-20625-5*) Faber & Faber, Inc.
Hart, Josephine. The Reconstructionist. l.t. ed. 2002. 256p. pap. 24.95 (*0-7862-3726-0*) Gale Group.
—The Reconstructionist. 2001. 288p. 26.95 (*1-58567-170-3*) Overlook Pr., The.
Hartland, Michael. The Third Betrayal. 1990. mass mkt. 3.95 o.p. (*0-425-11977-7*) Berkley Publishing Group.
—The Third Betrayal. l.t. ed. 1988. (Ulverscroft Large Print Ser.). 384p. 29.99 (*0-7089-1787-9*, Ulverscroft) Thorpe, F. A. Pubs. GBR. *Dist:* Ulverscroft Large Print Bks., Ltd., Ulverscroft Large Print Canada, Ltd.
Hartnett, P. Call Me. 1997. (Stonewall Inn Editions Ser.). 192p. pap. 11.95 (*0-312-18063-2*, Saint Martin's Griffin) St. Martin's Pr.
Hartnett, P. -P. Call Me. 1997. 184p. (Orig.). pap. 16.95 (*1-901072-00-2*) Pulp Faction GBR. *Dist:* AK Pr. Distribution.
Harvey, John. Last Rites: A Novel. l.t. ed. 1999. (Core Ser.). 396p. 27.95 (*0-7838-8674-8*, Macmillan Reference USA) Gale Group.
—Last Rites: A Novel. 1999. (Charles Resnick Novels Ser.). 312p. 25.00 o.s.i (*0-8050-4150-8*) Holt, Henry & Co.
—Last Rites: A Novel. unabr. ed. 2000. audio 71.00 (*1-84197-042-5*, H1056E7, Clipper Audio) Recorded Bks., LLC.
Hattersley, Ray, told to. Buster's Diaries: The True Story of a Dog & His Man. 2001. 192p. reprint ed. pap. 11.95 (*0-446-67781-7*) Warner Bks., Inc.
Hattersley, Roy, told to. Buster's Diaries: A True Story of a Dog & His Man. l.t. ed. 2000. (Basic Ser.). 184p. 27.95 (*0-7862-2869-5*) Thorndike Pr.
—Buster's Diaries: The True Story of a Dog & His Man. 2000. (Illus.). 192p. 15.95 o.p. (*0-446-52662-2*) Warner Bks., Inc.
Hawes, James. A White Merc with Fins. 1997. 304p. pap. 12.00 o.s.i (*0-679-77615-X*) Random Hse., Inc.
Hawke, Simon. Much Ado about Murder. E-Book 23.95 (*0-312-70933-1*, Tor Bks.); 2004. 240p. pap. 13.95 (*0-7653-0836-3*, Forge Bks.); 2002. 304p. 23.95 (*0-7653-0241-1*, Forge Bks.) Doherty, Tom Assocs., LLC.
Hayder, Mo. Birdman. 2000. 448p. mass mkt. 6.99 (*0-440-23616-9*) Dell Publishing.
Headley, Victor. Yardie. 1993. 192p. 18.00 o.p. (*0-87113-550-7*, Atlantic Monthly Pr.) Grove/Atlantic, Inc.
Heald, Tim. Blue Blood Will Out. 1980. 192p. mass mkt. 2.25 o.s.i (*0-345-28904-8*) Ballantine Bks.
—Blue Blood Will Out. 1974. 192p. 15.95 o.p. (*0-8128-1688-9*, Scarborough Hse.) Madison Bks., Inc.
—Business Unusual. 1990. 14.95 o.s.i (*0-385-41337-8*) Doubleday Publishing.
—Business Unusual, Set. unabr. ed. 1998. audio 63.95 o.p. (*1-872672-99-X*) Magna Story Sound GBR. *Dist:* Ulverscroft Large Print Bks., Ltd.
—Deadline. 1980. mass mkt. 2.25 o.s.i (*0-345-28905-6*) Ballantine Bks.
—Deadline. 1975. 192p. 6.95 o.p. (*0-8128-1757-5*, Scarborough Hse.) Madison Bks., Inc.
—Let Sleeping Dogs Die. 1981. 192p. mass mkt. 2.25 o.p. (*0-345-28903-X*) Ballantine Bks.
—Murder at Moosejaw. 1981. (Crime Club Ser.). 192p. 10.95 o.p. (*0-385-17754-2*) Doubleday Publishing.
—Red Herrings. 1986. (Crime Club Ser.). 192p. 12.95 o.p. (*0-385-23354-X*) Doubleday Publishing.
—Red Herrings. l.t. ed. 1987. lib. bdg. 18.50 o.p. (*0-7451-0581-5*, Macmillan Reference USA) Gale Group.
—A Small Masterpiece. 1982. (Crime Club Ser.). 192p. 10.95 o.p. (*0-385-17942-1*) Doubleday Publishing.
Healy, Dermot. Sudden Times. 2000. 352p. 23.00 o.s.i (*0-15-100578-8*) Harcourt Trade Pubs.
Heath, Lorraine. To Marry an Heiress. 2002. 384p. mass mkt. 5.99 (*0-380-81742-X*, Avon Bks.) Morrow/Avon.
Hegarty, Frances. Half Light. Chelius, Jane, ed. 1993. 288p. 20.00 o.p. (*0-671-78967-8*, Atria) Simon & Schuster.
—The Playroom. unabr. ed. 1995. audio 84.95 (*0-7862-9945-2*, SAB 062, Sterling Audio Bks.) BBC Audiobooks America.
—The Playroom. Chelius, Jane, ed. 1991. 304p. 20.00 o.p. (*0-671-73582-9*, Atria) Simon & Schuster.
Heley, Veronica. Murder by Suicide. 2003. 240p. mass mkt. 7.95 (*0-00-712294-2*); 2002. 266p. 27.50 (*0-00-712293-4*) HarperCollins Pubs. Ltd. GBR. *Dist:* Trafalgar Square.
Heller, Keith. Man's Storm: A Novel of Crime Set in London, 1703. 1986. 196p. 13.95 o.p. (*0-684-18653-5*, Macmillan Reference USA) Gale Group.
—Man's Storm: A Novel of Crime Set in London 1703. 1998. 218p. mass mkt. 9.95 (*0-7472-5684-5*) Headline Bk. Publishing, Ltd. GBR. *Dist:* Trafalgar Square.
Heller, Zoe. Everything You Know. 2000. 224p. 22.00 o.s.i (*0-375-40724-3*) Knopf, Alfred A. Inc.
—Everything You Know. 2001. (Illus.). 224p. reprint ed. pap. 12.95 (*0-7434-1195-1*, Washington Square Pr.) Simon & Schuster.
Henderson, Lauren. Black Rubber Dress. E-Book 11.50 (*1-58945-549-5*) Adobe Systems, Inc.
—Black Rubber Dress. 1999. E-Book 11.50 (*0-609-60715-4*) Random Hse., Inc.
—Black Rubber Dress: A Sam Jones Novel. 1999. 304p. pap. 12.95 (*0-609-80438-3*, Three Rivers Pr.) Crown Publishing Group.
—Chained! 2000. 249p. (*0-09-180045-5*) Hutchinson, Fred Cancer Research Ctr.
—Chained! 2000. 256p. pap. o.p. (*0-09-180050-1*) Random Hse. of Canada, Ltd. CAN. *Dist:* Random Hse., Inc.
—Chained! A Novel. 2002. 336p. pap. 12.95 (*0-609-80865-6*, Three Rivers Pr.) Crown Publishing Group.
—Freeze My Margarita. E-Book 11.50 (*1-58945-594-0*) Adobe Systems, Inc.
—Freeze My Margarita. 2000. E-Book 11.50 (*0-609-60882-7*, Crown); 22.00 (*0-609-60744-8*); 288p. pap. 12.95 (*0-609-80487-1*, Crown) Crown Publishing Group.
—Freeze My Margarita: A Sam Jones Novel. 2000. 320p. pap. 13.00 (*0-609-80684-X*, Three Rivers Pr.) Crown Publishing Group.
Herbert, James. '48. 1997. 280p. 22.00 o.p. (*0-06-105293-0*, Eos) Morrow/Avon.
Hiatt, Brenda. Rogue's Honor. 2001. 384p. mass mkt. 5.99 (*0-380-81777-2*, Avon Bks.) Morrow/Avon.
Higson, Charles. Getting Rid of Mister Kitchen. 2001. 219p. pap. 12.00 (*0-349-10815-3*) Little Brown U.K. GBR. *Dist:* Trafalgar Square.
Hill, Reginald. Traitor's Blood. 1986. 256p. 16.95 o.p. (*0-88150-076-3*) Countryman Pr.
—Traitor's Blood. l.t. ed. 1985. (Ulverscroft Large Print Ser.). 504p. 29.99 o.p. (*0-7089-1297-4*, Ulverscroft) Thorpe, F. A. Pubs. GBR. *Dist:* Ulverscroft Large Print Bks., Ltd., Ulverscroft Large Print Canada, Ltd.
—Traitor's Blood. 1987. 256p. mass mkt. 3.95 (*0-446-34719-1*) Warner Bks., Inc.
Hill, Tobias. The Love of Stones. 2001. 400p. pap. (*0-571-19454-0*) Faber & Faber, Inc.
—The Love of Stones. 2002. 416p. 25.00 (*0-312-28773-9*) Picador.
—The Love of Stones: A Novel. 2003. 400p. pap. 14.00 (*0-312-31131-1*) Picador.
Hinshaw, Victoria. The Fontainebleau Fan. l.t. ed. 2003. (Thorndike Romance Ser.). 325p. 27.95 (*0-7862-4989-7*) Gale Group.
—The Fontainebleau Fan. 2002. 224p. mass mkt. 4.99 o.s.i (*0-8217-7404-2*) Kensington Publishing Corp.
Hoban, Russell. Turtle Diary. 1982. pap. 1.95 o.p. (*0-380-39081-7*, 39081, Avon Bks.) Morrow/Avon.
—Turtle Diary. 1976. 7.95 o.p. (*0-394-40199-9*) Random Hse., Inc.
—Turtle Diary. 1986. mass mkt. 3.95 o.s.i (*0-671-61833-4*, Pocket) Simon & Schuster.
Hocker, Karla. A Bid for Independence. 2000. 276p. E-Book 5.50 (*1-58200-545-1*) Hard Shell Word Factory.
—The Impertinent Miss Bancroft. 2002. (Zebra Regency Romance Ser.). 256p. mass mkt. 4.99 o.s.i (*0-8217-7360-7*) Kensington Publishing Corp.
—The Impertinent Miss Bancroft. 1991. 224p. 18.95 (*0-8027-1164-2*) Walker & Co.
—The Incorrigible Sophia: A Regency Intrigue. 1992. 208p. 19.95 o.p. (*0-8027-1208-8*) Walker & Co.
Hoeg, Peter. The Woman & the Ape. 1997. 272p. mass mkt. 7.50 (*0-7704-2756-1*) Bantam Bks.
—The Woman & the Ape. Haveland, Barbara, tr. l.t. ed. 1996. 256p. 23.00 o.p. (*0-374-29203-5*) Farrar, Straus & Giroux.
—The Woman & the Ape. Haveland, Barbara, tr. l.t. ed. 1997. (G. K. Hall Core Ser.). 364p. 25.95 (*0-7838-8068-5*, Macmillan Reference USA) Gale Group.
—The Woman & the Ape. l.t. ed. 1997. 272p. pap. 12.95 o.s.i (*0-14-026844-8*) Penguin Group (USA) Inc.
—The Woman & the Ape. unabr. ed. 1997. audio 56.00 (*0-7887-0856-2*, 95002E7) Recorded Bks., LLC.
Holden, Wendy. Gossip Hound. 2003. 304p. pap. 13.00 (*0-452-28393-0*, Plume) Dutton/Plume.
—Simply Divine. 2000. 304p. pap. 12.95 (*0-452-28167-9*, Plume) Dutton/Plume.
—Simply Divine. unabr. ed. 2001. audio compact disk 124.00 (*0-7887-7169-8*, C1422); 2000. audio 88.00 (*0-7887-4858-0*, 96427E7) Recorded Bks., LLC.
Holland, David. The Devil's Acre. Date not set. mass mkt. (*0-312-99197-5*, St. Martin's Paperbacks); 2003. 256p. 23.95 (*0-312-31866-9*) St. Martin's Pr.
—Murcheston: The Wolf's Tale. E-Book 23.95 (*0-312-87699-8*, Tor Bks.); 2000. 349p. 23.95 (*0-312-87213-5*, Forge Bks.) Doherty, Tom Assocs., LLC.
Holland, Jamie. An Almost Perfect Moon. 2001. 332p. (*0-00-651416-2*) HarperCollins Pubs.
Hollinghurst, Alan. The Swimming-Pool Library. 1989. (Vintage International Ser.). 352p. pap. 14.00 (*0-679-72256-4*, Vintage) Knopf Publishing Group.
Holt, Hazel. Mrs. Malory & the Fatal Legacy: A Sheila Malory Mystery. l.t. ed. 2000. (Mystery Ser.). 344p. 27.95 (*0-7862-2842-3*) Thorndike Pr.
Home, Stewart. Slow Death. 1996. (High Risk Ser.). 296p. (Orig.). (*1-85242-519-9*) Serpent's Tail Ltd.
Hope, Christopher. The Hottentot Room. 1987. 218p. 16.95 o.p. (*0-374-17284-6*) Farrar, Straus & Giroux.
Hornby, Nick. About a Boy. l.t. ed. 1998. 424p. (*0-7540-1206-9*) BBC Audiobooks America.
—About a Boy. movie tie-in ed. 320p. 2002. pap. 12.95 (*1-57322-957-1*); 1999. reprint ed. pap. 12.95 (*1-57322-733-1*) Berkley Publishing Group. (Riverhead Trade (Paperbacks)).
—About a Boy. 2002. pap. (*1-57322-961-X*) Penguin Group (USA) Inc.
—About a Boy. 1998. 288p. 22.95 o.s.i (*1-57322-087-6*, Riverhead Bks. (Hardcovers)); audio 17.95 o.p. (*1-57322-101-5*) Putnam Publishing Group, The.
—About a Boy. l.t. ed. 1998. (Basic Ser.). 424p. 28.95 (*0-7862-1606-9*) Thorndike Pr.
—How to Be Good. 2002. 320p. pap. 13.00 (*1-57322-932-6*, Riverhead Trade (Paperbacks)) Berkley Publishing Group.
—How to Be Good. 2001. 320p. 24.95 o.s.i (*1-57322-193-7*, Riverhead Bks. (Hardcovers)) Putnam Publishing Group, The.
House, Richard. Uninvited. 2002. 224p. reprint ed. pap. 15.00 (*1-85242-438-9*) Serpent's Tail Ltd. GBR. *Dist:* Consortium Bk. Sales & Distribution.
Howatch, Susan. The Heartbreaker: A Novel. 2004. 496p. 25.00 (*1-4000-4147-3*) Knopf, Alfred A. Inc.
—A Question of Integrity. 1997. 615p. (*0-316-64137-5*) Little Brown & Co.
Howlett, John. Murder of a Moderate Man. 1988. 352p. reprint ed. pap. (*0-373-97083-8*, Harlequin Bks.) Harlequin Enterprises, Ltd.
—Murder of a Moderate Man. 1986. 272p. 15.95 o.p. (*0-312-00055-3*) St. Martin's Pr.
Hoyt, Sarah A. All Night Awake. 2003. 368p. mass mkt. 6.50 (*0-441-01112-8*); 2002. 320p. 22.95 (*0-441-00973-5*) Ace Bks.
Huggins, David. The Big Kiss: An Arcade Mystery. 1997. 240p. pap. 21.95 (*1-55970-409-8*) Arcade Publishing, Inc.
Hughes, Richard. Lost in London. Wheeler, Jill, ed. 1988. (Great Cities Adventures Ser.). (Illus.). 48p. (J). (gr. 4). lib. bdg. 10.95 o.p. (*0-939179-47-4*) ABDO Publishing Co.
Hughes, Sean. It's What He Would've Wanted: A Novel. 2001. (Illus.). 304p. 25.00 o.s.i (*0-7432-0159-0*, Scribner) Simon & Schuster.
Hull, Richard. Keep It Quiet. 1983. (Detective Stories Ser.). 192p. reprint ed. pap. 5.95 (*0-486-24520-9*) Dover Pubns., Inc.
Hunt, Kyle, pseud. As Merry as Hell. 1974. 192p. 13.95 o.p. (*0-8128-1662-5*, Scarborough Hse.) Madison Bks., Inc.
—This Man Did I Kill? 1985. 256p. pap. 2.95 o.p. (*0-8128-8133-8*, Scarborough Hse.) Madison Bks., Inc.
Hunter, Jillian. The Husband Hunt. 2002. 384p. pap. 6.99 (*0-7434-1791-7*, Pocket) Simon & Schuster.
Hunter, Matthew. The Gibraltar Factor. 1993. 234p. 19.95 (*0-8027-1274-6*) Walker & Co.
Huxley, Aldous. Antic Hay. 1997. 208p. reprint ed. pap. 12.50 (*1-56478-149-6*) Dalkey Archive Pr.
Hyde, Christopher. A Gathering of Saints. abr. ed. 1997. audio 7.99 o.p. (*1-56740-174-0*, 654, Paperback Nova Audio Bks.); 1996. audio 16.95 o.p. (*1-56100-906-7*, 878, Nova Audio Bks.); 1996. audio 25.95 o.p. (*1-56100-697-1*, 119, Bookcassette); 1996. audio 89.25 o.p. (*1-56100-322-0*, 1208, Unabridged Library Editions) Brilliance Audio.
—A Gathering of Saints. 1997. 438p. per. 6.99 (*0-671-87581-7*, Pocket); 1996. 432p. 24.00 (*0-671-87580-9*, Atria) Simon & Schuster.
Innes, Michael. The Ampersand Papers. 2000. 174p. pap. 9.95 (*1-84232-871-9*) House of Stratus, Inc. GBR. *Dist:* Midpoint Trade Bks., Inc.
—The Ampersand Papers. 1980. (Crime Monthly Ser.). 192p. pap. 3.95 o.p. (*0-14-005163-5*, Penguin Bks.) Viking Penguin.
—Appleby & Honeybath. l.t. ed. 2003. (Dales Large Print Ser.). 304p. pap. 21.99 (*1-84262-221-8*) Dales Large Print Bks. GBR. *Dist:* Ulverscroft Large Print Bks., Ltd., Ulverscroft Large Print Canada, Ltd.
—Appleby & Honeybath. 2000. 176p. pap. 9.95 (*1-84232-718-6*) House of Stratus, Inc. GBR. *Dist:* Midpoint Trade Bks., Inc.
—Appleby & Honeybath. 1984. 160p. pap. 3.95 o.p. (*0-14-007307-8*, Penguin Bks.) Viking Penguin.
—Appleby & the Ospreys. 2001. 170p. pap. 9.95 (*1-84232-719-4*) House of Stratus, Inc. GBR. *Dist:* Midpoint Trade Bks., Inc.
—Appleby & the Ospreys. 1988. 39.50 o.p. (*0-14-778337-2*) Penguin Group (USA) Inc.
—Appleby & the Ospreys. 1988. (Crime Ser.). 192p. pap. 3.95 o.p. (*0-14-011092-5*, Penguin Bks.) Viking Penguin.
—The Appleby File. 2001. 204p. pap. 9.95 (*1-84232-717-8*) House of Stratus, Inc. GBR. *Dist:* Midpoint Trade Bks., Inc.
—The Appleby File. l.t. ed. 1978. (Ulverscroft Large Print Ser.). 29.99 o.p. (*0-7089-0224-3*, Ulverscroft) Thorpe, F. A. Pubs. GBR. *Dist:* Ulverscroft Large Print Bks., Ltd., Ulverscroft Large Print Canada, Ltd.
—Appleby on Ararat: A Sir John Appleby Mystery. 1971. 254p. reprint ed. 69.95 (*0-8371-3377-7*, STAO, Greenwood Pr.) Greenwood Publishing Group, Inc.
—Appleby on Ararat: A Sir John Appleby Mystery. 1983. 288p. reprint ed. pap. 5.95 o.p. (*0-06-080648-6*, Perennial) HarperTrade.
—Appleby on Ararat: A Sir John Appleby Mystery. 2001. 192p. pap. 9.95 (*1-84232-715-1*) House of Stratus, Inc. GBR. *Dist:* Midpoint Trade Bks., Inc.
—Appleby Talks Again. 1977. (Short Story Index Reprint Ser.). 19.95 (*0-8369-3029-0*) Ayer Co. Pubs., Inc.
—Appleby Talks Again. 2001. 185p. pap. 9.95 (*1-84232-723-2*) House of Stratus, Inc. GBR. *Dist:* Midpoint Trade Bks., Inc.
—Appleby's Answer. 2000. 190p. pap. 9.95 (*1-84232-714-3*) House of Stratus, Inc. GBR. *Dist:* Midpoint Trade Bks., Inc.
—Appleby's Answer. 1985. (Crime Monthly Ser.). 160p. pap. 3.95 o.p. (*0-14-003981-3*, Penguin Bks.) Viking Penguin.
—Appleby's End. 1975. 224p. mass mkt. 1.25 o.s.i (*0-345-24409-5*) Ballantine Bks.
—Appleby's End. 1970. 211p. reprint ed. 69.95 (*0-8371-3376-9*, STAE, Greenwood Pr.) Greenwood Publishing Group, Inc.
—Appleby's End. 1983. 224p. pap. 2.95 o.p. (*0-06-080649-4*, P 649, Perennial) HarperTrade.
—Appleby's End. 2001. 218p. pap. 9.95 (*1-84232-716-X*) House of Stratus, Inc. GBR. *Dist:* Midpoint Trade Bks., Inc.
—Appleby's Other Story: A Sir John Appleby Mystery. 1975. 192p. mass mkt. 1.25 o.s.i (*0-345-24505-9*) Ballantine Bks.

—Appleby's Other Story: A Sir John Appleby Mystery. 2001. 179p. pap. 9.95 (*1-84232-720-8*) House of Stratus, Inc. GBR. *Dist:* Midpoint Trade Bks., Inc.

—Appleby's Other Story: A Sir John Appleby Mystery. 1993. (Classic Crime Ser.). 208p. pap. 6.00 o.p. (*0-14-014679-2*, Penguin Bks.) Penguin Group (USA) Inc.

—Appleby's Other Story: A Sir John Appleby Mystery. 1986. (Crime Ser.). 208p. pap. 3.95 o.p. (*0-14-004159-1*, Penguin Bks.) Viking Penguin.

—An Awkward Lie. 2001. 180p. pap. 9.95 (*1-84232-724-0*) House of Stratus, Inc. GBR. *Dist:* Midpoint Trade Bks., Inc.

—An Awkward Lie. 1991. (Classic Crime Ser.). 176p. reprint ed. pap. 4.95 o.p. (*0-14-012785-2*, Penguin Bks.) Penguin Group (USA) Inc.

—An Awkward Lie. 1974. (Crime Ser.). 176p. pap. 3.95 o.p. (*0-14-003664-4*, Penguin Bks.) Viking Penguin.

—The Bloody Wood. 1986. 224p. reprint ed. pap. 4.95 o.p. (*0-06-080811-X*, P 811, Perennial) HarperTrade.

—The Bloody Wood. 2001. 182p. pap. (*1-84232-725-9*) House of Stratus, Inc.

—The Bloody Wood. 1990. 192p. (C). reprint ed. lib. bdg. 19.95 o.p. (*0-8095-9028-X*) Millefleurs.

—Carson's Conspiracy: A Sir John Appleby Mystery Novel. 2001. 174p. pap. 9.95 (*1-84232-726-7*) House of Stratus, Inc. GBR. *Dist:* Midpoint Trade Bks., Inc.

—Carson's Conspiracy: A Sir John Appleby Mystery Novel. 1986. (Crime Monthly Ser.). 192p. pap. 3.95 o.p. (*0-14-008444-4*, Penguin Bks.) Viking Penguin.

—A Comedy of Terrors. 1989. pap. 4.95 o.p. (*0-14-012919-7*); 1987. 256p. mass mkt. 3.95 o.p. (*0-14-010090-3*, Penguin Bks.) Viking Penguin.

—A Connoisseur's Case. 2001. 180p. pap. 9.95 (*1-84232-729-1*) House of Stratus, Inc. GBR. *Dist:* Midpoint Trade Bks., Inc.

—A Connoisseur's Case. l.t. ed. 1980. (Ulverscroft Large Print Ser.). 29.99 o.p. (*0-7089-0421-1*, Ulverscroft) Thorpe, F. A. Pubs. GBR. *Dist:* Ulverscroft Large Print Bks., Ltd., Ulverscroft Large Print Canada, Ltd.

—The Crabtree Affair: A Sir John Appleby Mystery. 1984. 240p. reprint ed. pap. 5.95 o.p. (*0-06-080706-7*, Perennial) HarperTrade.

—The Daffodil Affair. 1976. (Crime Fiction Ser). reprint ed. lib. bdg. 21.00 o.p. (*0-8240-2378-1*) Garland Publishing, Inc.

—The Daffodil Affair. 2001. 230p. pap. 9.95 (*1-84232-730-5*) House of Stratus, Inc. GBR. *Dist:* Midpoint Trade Bks., Inc.

—The Daffodil Affair. (Crime Ser.). 1990. 208p. pap. 5.00 o.p. (*0-14-011498-X*, Penguin Bks.); 1984. 208p. pap. 3.95 o.p. (*0-14-002202-3*, Penguin Bks.); 1983. Viking Penguin.

—Death at the Chase. 2000. 186p. pap. 9.95 (*1-84232-731-3*) House of Stratus, Inc. GBR. *Dist:* Midpoint Trade Bks., Inc.

—Death at the Chase. 1986. (Crime Monthly Ser.). 192p. pap. 3.95 o.p. (*0-14-003243-6*); reprint ed. pap. 6.00 o.p. (*0-14-017242-4*) Viking Penguin. (Penguin Bks.).

—Death at the President's Lodging. 2000. (Illus.). 254p. pap. 9.95 (*1-84232-732-1*) House of Stratus, Inc. GBR. *Dist:* Midpoint Trade Bks., Inc.

—Death at the President's Lodging. 1992. (Penguin Crime Fiction Ser.). 288p. pap. 6.95 o.s.i (*0-14-010555-7*, Penguin Bks.) Penguin Group (USA) Inc.

—Death at the President's Lodging. l.t. ed. 1989. (Ulverscroft Large Print Ser.). 448p. 29.99 o.p. (*0-7089-2012-8*, Ulverscroft) Thorpe, F. A. Pubs. GBR. *Dist:* Ulverscroft Large Print Bks., Ltd., Ulverscroft Large Print Canada, Ltd.

—Death at the President's Lodging. 1983. Viking Penguin.

—Death by Water: A Sir John Appleby Mystery. 1982. 224p. reprint ed. pap. 5.95 o.p. (*0-06-080574-9*, Perennial) HarperTrade.

—Death on a Quiet Day: A Sir John Appleby Mystery. 1983. 224p. pap. o.p. (*0-06-080677-X*, P677) HarperCollins Pubs.

—Death on a Quiet Day: A Sir John Appleby Mystery. 1991. 288p. reprint ed. pap. 8.00 o.p. (*0-06-092137-4*, Perennial) HarperTrade.

—Death on a Quiet Day: A Sir John Appleby Mystery. 1994. 2.99 o.p. (*0-517-12586-2*) Random Hse. Value Publishing.

—The Gay Phoenix. 2001. 184p. pap. 9.95 (*1-84232-735-6*) House of Stratus, Inc. GBR. *Dist:* Midpoint Trade Bks., Inc.

—The Gay Phoenix. l.t. ed. 1992. (Adventure Suspense Ser.). 279p. 29.99 o.p. (*0-7505-0048-4*) Magna Large Print Bks. GBR. *Dist:* Ulverscroft Large Print Bks., Ltd., Ulverscroft Large Print Canada, Ltd.

—The Gay Phoenix. 1981. 192p. pap. 3.50 o.p. (*0-14-004701-8*, Penguin Bks.) Viking Penguin.

—Hamlet, Revenge! 2001. 316p. pap. 9.95 (*1-84232-737-2*) House of Stratus, Inc. GBR. *Dist:* Midpoint Trade Bks., Inc.

—Hamlet, Revenge! l.t. ed. 1994. (Magna Large Print Ser.). 498p. 29.99 o.p. (*0-7505-0493-5*) Magna Large Print Bks. GBR. *Dist:* Ulverscroft Large Print Bks., Ltd., Ulverscroft Large Print Canada, Ltd.

—Hamlet, Revenge! (Classic Crime Ser.). 1990. 288p. pap. 6.00 o.p. (*0-14-011497-1*, Penguin Bks.); 1983.; 1976. 288p. pap. 3.50 o.p. (*0-14-001640-6*, Penguin Bks.) Viking Penguin.

—Hare Sitting Up: A Sir John Appleby Mystery. 1982. 256p. reprint ed. pap. 5.95 o.p. (*0-06-080590-0*, Perennial) HarperTrade.

—Hare Sitting Up: A Sir John Appleby Mystery. 2001. 182p. pap. (*1-84232-738-0*) House of Stratus, Inc.

—Hare Sitting Up: A Sir John Appleby Mystery. l.t. ed. 1992. (Magna Large Print Ser.). 280p. 29.99 (*0-7505-0276-2*) Magna Large Print Bks. GBR. *Dist:* Ulverscroft Large Print Bks., Ltd., Ulverscroft Large Print Canada, Ltd.

—Lament for a Maker: A Sir John Appleby Mystery. 1985. 256p. mass mkt. 9.95 o.p. (*0-553-06514-9*) Bantam Bks.

—Lament for a Maker: A Sir John Appleby Mystery. 1985. 288p. mass mkt. 3.50 o.p. (*0-06-080729-6*, P729); 1990. 272p. reprint ed. pap. 4.95 o.p. (*0-06-081041-6*) HarperTrade. (Perennial).

—Lament for a Maker: A Sir John Appleby Mystery. 2001. 286p. pap. 9.95 (*1-84232-741-0*) House of Stratus, Inc. GBR. *Dist:* Midpoint Trade Bks., Inc.

—Lament for a Maker: A Sir John Appleby Mystery. 1990. 272p. (C). reprint ed. lib. bdg. 19.95 o.p. (*0-8095-9029-8*) Millefleurs.

—The Long Farewell. l.t. ed. 1991. pap. 17.95 o.p. (*0-7927-0142-9*, C0012) BBC Audiobooks America.

—The Long Farewell. 1982. (Sir John Appleby Mystery Ser.). 240p. reprint ed. pap. 5.95 o.p. (*0-06-080575-7*, Perennial) HarperTrade.

—The Long Farewell. 2001. 190p. pap. 9.95 (*1-84232-742-9*) House of Stratus, Inc. GBR. *Dist:* Midpoint Trade Bks., Inc.

—A Night of Errors: A Sir John Appleby Mystery. 1989. 304p. reprint ed. pap. 3.95 o.p. (*0-06-080877-2*, P 877, Perennial) HarperTrade.

—A Night of Errors: A Sir John Appleby Mystery. 2000. 234p. pap. 9.95 (*1-84232-748-8*) House of Stratus, Inc. GBR. *Dist:* Midpoint Trade Bks., Inc.

—One Man Show. Barzun, Jacques & Taylor, W. H., eds. 1983. (Crime Fiction 1950-1975 Ser.). 192p. lib. bdg. 18.00 o.p. (*0-8240-4994-2*) Garland Publishing, Inc.

—One Man Show. 1983. 400p. pap. 5.95 o.p. (*0-06-080672-9*, Perennial) HarperTrade.

—Open House. 1982. pap. 2.95 o.p. (*0-14-003663-6*, Penguin Bks.) Viking Penguin.

—Operation Pax. 2001. 346p. pap. 9.95 (*1-84232-751-8*) House of Stratus, Inc. GBR. *Dist:* Midpoint Trade Bks., Inc.

—The Paper Thunderbolt. 1987. 352p. mass mkt. 3.95 o.p. (*0-14-010089-X*, Penguin Bks.) Viking Penguin.

—Picture of Guilt: A Sir John Appleby Mystery. 1988. 224p. reprint ed. pap. 3.95 o.p. (*0-06-080878-0*, P-878, Perennial) HarperTrade.

—The Secret Vanguard: A Sir John Appleby Mystery. 1982. 288p. reprint ed. pap. 4.95 o.p. (*0-06-080584-6*, Perennial) HarperTrade.

—The Secret Vanguard: A Sir John Appleby Mystery. l.t. ed. 1991. (Magna Large Print Ser.). 284p. o.p. (*1-85057-864-8*) Magna Large Print Bks. GBR. *Dist:* Ulverscroft Large Print Canada, Ltd.

—The Secret Vanguard: A Sir John Appleby Mystery. 2001. 190p. pap. 9.95 (*1-84232-753-4*) Midpoint Trade Bks., Inc.

—Seven Suspects. 1984. (Crime Ser.). 288p. pap. 3.95 o.p. (*0-14-006886-4*, Penguin Bks.) Viking Penguin.

—Sheiks & Adders: A Sir John Appleby Mystery Novel. 1983. 160p. pap. 2.95 o.p. (*0-14-006520-2*, Penguin Bks.) Viking Penguin.

—There Came Both Mist & Snow. 2001. 198p. pap. 9.95 (*1-84232-757-7*) House of Stratus, Inc. GBR. *Dist:* Midpoint Trade Bks., Inc.

—There Came Both Mist & Snow. l.t. ed. 1991. (Magna Large Print Ser.). 302p. o.p. (*1-85057-862-1*) Magna Large Print Bks. GBR. *Dist:* Ulverscroft Large Print Canada, Ltd.

Ireland, Kevin. The Craymore Affair: A Novel. 2000. (Illus.). 223p. (*1-86941-426-8*, Vintage) Knopf Publishing Group.

Irwin, Robert. Exquisite Corpse. 1999. pap. (*0-679-77916-7*, Vintage) Knopf Publishing Group.

—Exquisite Corpse. 2003. 235p. 14.95 (*1-58567-386-2*) Overlook Pr., The.

Isherwood, Christopher. Prater Violet. 2001. 144p. reprint ed. pap. 14.95 (*0-8166-3861-6*) Univ. of Minnesota Pr.

Innes, Michael. Silence Observed. 1975. 160p. mass mkt. 1.25 o.s.i (*0-345-24627-6*) Ballantine Bks.

Ivory, Judith. The Proposition. 1999. 384p. mass mkt. 6.50 (*0-380-80260-0*, Avon Bks.) Morrow/Avon.

—The Proposition. l.t. ed. 2000. (Core Ser.). 472p. 29.95 (*0-7838-9057-5*) Thorndike Pr.

Jaffe, Michele. Lady Killer/Secret Admirer. 2002. 896p. mass mkt. 6.99 (*0-345-45562-2*, Ballantine Bks.) Ballantine Bks.

Jagendorf, Zvi. Wolfy & the Strudelbakers. 2002. 192p. pap. 13.95 (*1-899235-38-8*) Lewis, Dewi Publishing GBR. *Dist:* Consortium Bk. Sales & Distribution.

Jakeman, Jane. In the Kingdom of Mists. 2004. 368p. 23.95 (*0-425-19512-0*, Prime Crime) Berkley Publishing Group.

—In the Kingdom of Mists. l.t. ed. 2003. (Magna Large Print Ser.). 512p. 32.50 (*0-7505-2045-0*) Magna Large Print Bks. GBR. *Dist:* Ulverscroft Large Print Bks., Ltd., Ulverscroft Large Print Canada, Ltd.

James, Eloisa. Enchanting Pleasures. 2001. 352p. 21.95 o.s.i (*0-385-33362-5*, Delacorte Pr.); 2002. 432p. reprint ed. mass mkt. 6.50 (*0-440-23458-1*) Dell Publishing.

James, Henry. The Princess Casamassima. 1991. (Everyman's Library). 640p. 20.00 (*0-679-40672-7*) Random Hse., Inc.

—The Wings of the Dove. abr. ed. 1992. audio 15.95 o.p. (*0-88646-333-5*, 7333) Durkin Hayes Publishing Ltd.

—The Wings of the Dove. 1997. (Illus.). 528p. (J). pap. 12.95 (*0-7868-8251-4*) Hyperion Pr.

—The Wings of the Dove. 1997. (Everyman's Library). 544p. 20.00 (*0-679-45512-4*) Knopf, Alfred A. Inc.

—The Wings of the Dove. 2000. (Cloth Bound Pocket Ser.). 7.95 (*3-8290-5387-8*, 522085) Konemann.

—The Wings of the Dove. (Signet Classics). 1999. 512p. mass mkt. 6.95 (*0-451-52728-3*, Signet Classics); 1964. pap. 4.50 o.p. (*0-452-00858-1*, Meridian Bks.); 1964. mass mkt. 3.95 o.p. (*0-451-51872-1*, CE1872, Signet Classics) NAL.

—The Wings of the Dove. Crowley, Joseph Donald & Hocks, Richard A., eds. 1978. (Critical Editions Ser.). (C). o.p. (*0-393-04478-5*); 583p. pap. text 12.00 (*0-393-09088-4*) Norton, W. W. & Co., Inc.

—The Wings of the Dove. Brooks, Peter, ed. & intro. by. 1998. (Oxford World's Classics Ser.). 592p. pap. 8.95 (*0-19-283861-X*) Oxford Univ. Pr., Inc.

—The Wings of the Dove. Brooks, Peter, ed. 1985. (Oxford World's Classics Ser.). 584p. pap. 6.95 o.p. (*0-19-281631-4*) Oxford Univ. Pr., Inc.

—The Wings of the Dove. 1974. pap. 3.95 o.p. (*0-14-002320-8*) Penguin Group (USA) Inc.

—The Wings of the Dove. 2003. 768p. pap. 9.95 (*0-8129-6719-4*); 2000. E-Book 4.95 (*0-679-64156-4*) Random House Adult Trade Publishing Group. (Modern Library).

—The Wings of the Dove. 1993. (Modern Library Ser.). 712p. 19.00 o.s.i (*0-679-60067-1*) Random Hse., Inc.

—The Wings of the Dove. 1997. (Everyman Paperback Classics Ser.). 464p. pap. 5.95 (*0-460-87617-1*, Everyman's Classic Library in Paperback) Tuttle Publishing.

—The Wings of the Dove. Bayley, John, ed. & intro. by. 1986. (Penguin Classics Ser.). 528p. pap. 9.95 (*0-14-043263-9*, Penguin Classics) Viking Penguin.

—The Wings of the Dove. abr. ed. 1997. (Classic Fiction Ser.). audio 17.98 o.p. (*962-634-612-4*, NA311214); audio compact disk 19.98 o.p. (*962-634-112-2*, NA311212) Naxos of America, Inc. (Naxos AudioBooks).

—The Wings of the Dove, Set. unabr. ed. 1993. audio 77.95 (*1-55685-286-X*) Audio Bk. Contractors, Inc.

—The Wings of the Dove. unabr. ed. 1999. audio 89.95 (*0-7861-1525-4*, 2375) Blackstone Audio Bks., Inc.

—The Wings of the Dove. 1977. (Novels & Tales of Henry James Ser.: Vol. 19). reprint ed. xxii, 301p. lib. bdg. 37.50 o.p. (*0-678-02819-2*);Vol. 2. 404p. lib. bdg. 37.50 (*0-678-02820-6*) Kelley, Augustus M. Pubs.

—The Wings of the Dove. (BCL1-PS American Literature Ser.). reprint ed. 1993. 329p. lib. bdg. 89.00 (*0-7812-6978-4*); 1992. lib. bdg. 75.00 (*0-7812-3429-8*) Reprint Services Corp.

James, P. D. The Black Tower. unabr. ed. 1993. audio 72.00 (*0-7366-2509-7*, 3265) Books on Tape, Inc.

—The Black Tower. (Paperback Ser.). 1990. 464p. 13.95 o.p. (*0-8161-4983-6*); 1981. 14.95 o.p. (*0-8161-6789-3*) Gale Group. (Macmillan Reference USA).

—The Black Tower. 2001. 352p. pap. 12.00 (*0-7432-1961-9*, Touchstone) Simon & Schuster.

—The Black Tower. 1990. audio 69.95 o.p. (*0-8161-9622-2*) Thorndike Pr.

—The Black Tower. 1988. 288p. mass mkt. 6.99 o.p. (*0-446-31502-8*) Warner Bks., Inc.

—A Certain Justice: An Adam Dalgliesh Mystery. 2003. 448p. pap. 13.95 (*0-345-42532-4*); 1999. 7.99 (*0-345-91605-0*); 1998. mass mkt. 5.99 (*0-345-42533-2*); 1998. 448p. mass mkt. 7.99 (*0-345-43057-3*); 1998. mass mkt. 6.99 (*0-345-42564-2*, Del Rey) Ballantine Bks.

—A Certain Justice: An Adam Dalgliesh Mystery. unabr. ed. 1998. audio 104.00 (*0-7366-4067-3*, 4578) Books on Tape, Inc.

—A Certain Justice: An Adam Dalgliesh Mystery. unabr. ed. 2000. audio 79.95 (*0-7540-0079-6*, CAB 1502) Chivers Audio Bks. GBR. *Dist:* BBC Audiobooks America.

—A Certain Justice: An Adam Dalgliesh Mystery. 1997. 390p. (*0-571-19164-9*) Faber & Faber, Inc.

—A Certain Justice: An Adam Dalgliesh Mystery. l.t. ed. pap. 25.00 o.p. (*0-7838-8251-3*, Macmillan Reference USA) Gale Group.

—A Certain Justice: An Adam Dalgliesh Mystery. 1997. 364p. 25.00 o.s.i (*0-375-40109-1*) Knopf, Alfred A. Inc.

—A Certain Justice: An Adam Dalgliesh Mystery. unabr. ed. 1997. audio 44.95 (*0-679-46085-3*, 115588, RH Audio) Random Hse. Audio Publishing Group.

—A Certain Justice: An Adam Dalgliesh Mystery. l.t. ed. 1997. 640p. pap. 25.00 (*0-679-77452-1*) Random Hse. Large Print.

—A Certain Justice: An Adam Dalgliesh Mystery. 1999. (Remainder Ser.). 5.99 o.s.i (*0-517-46309-1*) Random Hse. Value Publishing.

—A Certain Justice: An Adam Dalgliesh Mystery. unabr. ed. 1998. (Inspector Dalgliesh Mystery Ser.: Vol. 10). audio 97.00 (*0-7887-1966-1*, 95354E7) Recorded Bks., LLC.

—A Certain Justice: An Adam Dalgliesh Mystery. 2003. E-Book 8.99 (*0-7953-2798-6*) RosettaBooks.

—Cover Her Face. unabr. ed. 1993. audio 56.00 (*0-7366-2330-2*, 3110) Books on Tape, Inc.

—Cover Her Face. unabr. ed. 2000. audio 49.95 (*0-7451-6065-4*, CAB 138) Chivers Audio Bks. GBR. *Dist:* BBC Audiobooks America.

—Cover Her Face. 1979. (General Ser.). lib. bdg. 12.95 o.p. (*0-8161-6793-1*, Macmillan Reference USA) Gale Group.

—Cover Her Face. Barzun, Jacques & Taylor, W. H., eds. 1982. (Crime Fiction 1950-1975 Ser.). 254p. lib. bdg. 18.00 o.p. (*0-8240-4983-7*) Garland Publishing, Inc.

—Cover Her Face. unabr. ed. 1992. (Inspector Dalgliesh Mystery Ser.: Vol. 1). audio 51.00 (*1-55690-676-5*, 92329E7) Recorded Bks., LLC.

—Cover Her Face. 2001. 256p. pap. 12.00 (*0-7432-1957-0*, Touchstone) Simon & Schuster.

—Cover Her Face. 1990. 18.05 (*0-606-22453-X*) Turtleback Bks.

—Cover Her Face. 1989. 256p. mass mkt. 6.99 o.p. (*0-446-31221-5*); 1987. mass mkt. 3.50 (*0-446-31437-4*) Warner Bks., Inc.

—Death of An Expert Witness. 1978. lib. bdg. 13.95 o.p. (*0-8161-6600-5*, Macmillan Reference USA) Gale Group.

—Death of An Expert Witness. 2003. 496p. mass mkt. (*0-7704-2915-7*) Seal Bks. CAN. *Dist:* Random Hse. of Canada, Ltd.

—Death of An Expert Witness. 2001. 368p. pap. 12.00 (*0-7432-1962-7*, Touchstone) Simon & Schuster.

—Death of An Expert Witness. 1988. 352p. mass mkt. 6.99 o.p. (*0-446-31472-2*) Warner Bks., Inc.

—Death of an Expert Witness. l.t. ed. 1992. (General Ser.). 443p. pap. 18.95 (*0-8161-5575-5*, Macmillan Reference USA) Gale Group.

—Death of An Expert Witness. unabr. ed. 1993. audio 72.00 (*0-7366-2569-0*, 3318) Books on Tape, Inc.

—Death of An Expert Witness. unabr. ed. 2000. audio 59.95 (*0-7451-6066-2*, CAB 311) Chivers Audio Bks. GBR. *Dist:* BBC Audiobooks America.

—Death of An Expert Witness. unabr. ed. 1993. (Inspector Dalgliesh Mystery Ser.: Vol. 6). audio 70.00 (*1-55690-884-9*, 93326E7) Recorded Bks., LLC.

—Devices & Desires. unabr. collector's ed. 1990. audio 96.00 (*0-7366-1819-8*, 2655) Books on Tape, Inc.

—Devices & Desires. l.t. ed. 1990. (General Ser.). 608p. pap. 15.95 o.p. (*0-8161-5045-1*); lib. bdg. 14.95 o.p. (*0-8161-5044-3*) Gale Group. (Macmillan Reference USA).

—Devices & Desires. 2004. 480p. pap. 12.95 (*1-4000-7624-2*, Vintage) Knopf Publishing Group.

—Devices & Desires. 1992. 5.99 o.p. (*0-517-08846-0*); 1991. 4.99 o.p. (*0-517-07898-8*) Random Hse. Value Publishing.

—Devices & Desires. unabr. ed. 1990. (Inspector Dalgliesh Mystery Ser.: Vol. 8). audio 97.00 (*1-55690-141-0*, 90089E7) Recorded Bks., LLC.

—Devices & Desires. 1992. audio 96.95 o.p. (*0-8161-3212-7*, 90089) Thorndike Pr.

—Devices & Desires. 480p. 1991. mass mkt. 7.99 (*0-446-35975-0*); 2002. reprint ed. pap. 13.95 (*0-446-67919-4*) Warner Bks., Inc.

—Innocent Blood. 1988. 352p. mass mkt. 6.99 o.p. (*0-446-31177-4*) Warner Bks., Inc.

—A Mind to Murder. unabr. ed. 1993. audio 56.00 (*0-7366-2396-5*, 3165) Books on Tape, Inc.

—A Mind to Murder. (General Ser.). 1980. lib. bdg. 12.95 o.p. (*0-8161-3057-4*); 1994. 304p. pap. 17.95 (*0-8161-5645-X*) Gale Group. (Macmillan Reference USA).

—A Mind to Murder. 2001. 256p. pap. 12.00 (*0-7432-1958-9*, Touchstone) Simon & Schuster.
—A Mind to Murder. 1986. audio 49.95 o.s.i (*0-8161-9903-5*) Thorndike Pr.
—A Mind to Murder. 1991. 18.05 (*0-606-22454-8*) Turtleback Bks.
—A Mind to Murder. 1988. 256p. mass mkt. 6.99 o.p. (*0-446-31480-3*); 1987. mass mkt. 3.95 (*0-446-34828-7*); 1985. mass mkt. 3.50 (*0-446-31395-5*) Warner Bks., Inc.
—The Murder Room. unabr. ed. 2003. audio 72.00 (*0-7366-9445-5*); audio compact disk (*0-7366-9606-7*) Books on Tape, Inc.
—The Murder Room. 2003. 432p. 25.95 (*1-4000-4141-4*, Everyman's Library) Knopf Publishing Group.
—The Murder Room. unabr. ed. 2003. audio 39.95 (*0-7393-0670-7*); audio compact disk 44.95 (*0-7393-0756-8*) Random Hse. Audio Publishing Group. (Listening Library).
—The Murder Room. l.t. ed. 2003. 691p. 27.95 (*0-375-43223-X*) Random Hse. Large Print.
—Original Sin. unabr. ed. 1995. audio 120.00 (*0-7366-3044-9*, 3726) Books on Tape, Inc.
—Original Sin. unabr. ed. 2000. 14p. audio compact disk 115.95 (*0-7540-5357-1*, CCD 048) Chivers Audio Bks. GBR. *Dist:* BBC Audiobooks America.
—Original Sin. l.t. ed. 1995. 23.00 o.s.i (*0-679-76033-4*) Random Hse., Inc.
—Original Sin. unabr. ed. audio. 2000. (Inspector Dalgliesh Mystery Ser.: Vol. 9). audio 97.00 (*0-7887-0273-4*, 94484E7) Recorded Bks., LLC.
—Original Sin. 1996. 560p. mass mkt. 7.99 (*0-446-60234-5*); 2002. 512p. reprint ed. pap. 13.95 (*0-446-67922-4*) Warner Bks., Inc.
—Shroud for a Nightingale. unabr. ed. 1993. audio 72.00 (*0-7366-2443-0*, 3208) Books on Tape, Inc.
—Shroud for a Nightingale. unabr. ed. 2000. audio 59.95 (*0-7451-6069-7*, CAB 388) Chivers Audio Bks. GBR. *Dist:* BBC Audiobooks America.
—Shroud for a Nightingale. (Paperback Ser.). 1991. 448p. pap. 15.95 o.p. (*0-8161-5032-X*); 1982. lib. bdg. 14.95 o.p. (*0-8161-6791-5*) Gale Group. (Macmillan Reference USA).
—Shroud for a Nightingale. 2002. (Best Mysteries of All Time Ser.). 310p. (*0-7621-8879-0*, Impress) Scriptorium Pr., The.
—Shroud for a Nightingale. 2001. 368p. pap. 13.00 (*0-7432-1960-0*, Touchstone) Simon & Schuster.
—Shroud for a Nightingale. 1988. 288p. mass mkt. 6.99 o.p. (*0-446-31303-3*) Warner Bks., Inc.
—The Skull Beneath the Skin. unabr. ed. 1994. audio 88.00 (*0-7366-2647-6*, 3384) Books on Tape, Inc.
—The Skull Beneath the Skin. unabr. ed. 2000. (Cordelia Gray Mystery Ser.: Bk. 2). audio 69.95 (*0-7451-6838-8*, CAB 330) Chivers Audio Bks. GBR. *Dist:* BBC Audiobooks America.
—The Skull Beneath the Skin. l.t. ed. 1983. 571p. 18.95 o.p. (*0-8161-3508-8*); 9.95 o.p. (*0-8161-3569-X*) Gale Group. (Macmillan Reference USA).
—The Skull Beneath the Skin. 1988. mass mkt. 4.95 (*0-446-35272-1*) Little Brown & Co.
—The Skull Beneath the Skin. Set. abr. ed. 1994. audio 15.99 o.s.i (*0-553-47223-2*, 391595, RH Audio) Random Hse. Audio Publishing Group.
—The Skull Beneath the Skin. 2001. 448p. pap. 12.00 (*0-7432-1956-2*, Touchstone); 1982. 352p. 13.95 o.s.i (*0-684-17773-0*, Scribner) Simon & Schuster.
—The Skull Beneath the Skin. 1988. 432p. mass mkt. 7.99 o.p. (*0-446-35372-8*) Warner Bks., Inc.
—A Taste for Death. audio 8.95 American Audio Prose Library, Inc.
—A Taste for Death. 2003. 480p. pap. 13.95 (*0-345-46938-0*); 1999. mass mkt. 6.99 (*0-345-42916-8*); 1998. 480p. mass mkt. 7.99 (*0-345-43058-1*) Ballantine Bks.
—A Taste for Death, Pt. 1. unabr. ed. 1994. audio 64.00 (*0-7366-2703-0*, 3437-A) Books on Tape, Inc.
—A Taste for Death. l.t. ed. 1987. 713p. 20.95 o.p. (*0-8161-4265-3*); 12.95 o.p. (*0-8161-4266-1*) Gale Group. (Macmillan Reference USA).
—A Taste for Death. 1987. 512p. mass mkt. 6.50 (*0-446-32352-7*) Warner Bks., Inc.
—Unnatural Causes. unabr. ed. 1993. 54.95 incl. audio (*0-7451-6071-9*, CAB 072) BBC Audiobooks America.
—Unnatural Causes. unabr. ed. 1992. audio 56.00 (*0-7366-2318-3*, 3098) Books on Tape, Inc.
—Unnatural Causes. l.t. ed. 1993. 340p. pap. 16.95 o.p. (*0-8161-5646-8*, Macmillan Reference USA) Gale Group.
—Unnatural Causes. unabr. ed. 1993. (Inspector Dalgliesh Mystery Ser.: Vol. 3). audio 51.00 (*1-55690-832-6*, 93128E7) Recorded Bks., LLC.
—Unnatural Causes. 2003. 352p. mass mkt. (*0-7704-2912-2*) Seal Bks. CAN. *Dist:* Random Hse. of Canada, Ltd.
—Unnatural Causes. 2001. 18.05 (*0-606-22455-6*) Turtleback Bks.
—Unnatural Causes. 1988. 256p. mass mkt. 7.50 o.p. (*0-446-31219-3*) Warner Bks., Inc.
—An Unsuitable Job for a Woman. unabr. ed. 1993. audio 56.00 (*0-7366-2497-X*, 3255) Books on Tape, Inc.
—An Unsuitable Job for a Woman. unabr. ed. 2000. (Cordelia Gray Mystery Ser.: Bk. 1). audio 49.95 (*0-7451-6064-6*, CAB 180) Chivers Audio Bks. GBR. *Dist:* BBC Audiobooks America.
—An Unsuitable Job for a Woman. 1980. (General Ser.). lib. bdg. 13.95 o.p. (*0-8161-6788-5*, Macmillan Reference USA) Gale Group.
—An Unsuitable Job for a Woman. unabr. ed. 1992. audio 51.00 (*1-55690-737-0*, 92110E7) Recorded Bks., LLC.
—An Unsuitable Job for a Woman. 2001. (Classic Ser.). 208p. 25.00 (*0-7432-2204-0*, Scribner); 256p. pap. 12.00 (*0-7432-1955-4*, Touchstone); 320p. 25.00 o.p. (*0-7432-2492-2*, Scribner) Simon & Schuster.
—An Unsuitable Job for a Woman. 1988. 288p. reprint ed. mass mkt. 6.99 o.p. (*0-446-31517-6*) Warner Bks., Inc.
James, Russell. Payback: A Novel of Suspense. 1993. 224p. 19.00 o.p. (*0-88150-267-7*) Countryman Pr.
Jarrett, Miranda. Star Bright. 2000. 336p. pap. 6.50 (*0-7434-0356-8*, Pocket) Simon & Schuster.
—Starlight. 2000. (Illus.). 384p. pap. 6.50 (*0-7434-0355-X*, Pocket) Simon & Schuster.
Jensen, Emma. His Grace Endures. 1998. (Regency Romance Ser.). 213p. mass mkt. 4.99 o.s.i (*0-449-00233-0*, Fawcett) Ballantine Bks.
Jewell, Lisa. One-Hit Wonder. 2002. 352p. 23.95 o.s.i (*0-525-94653-5*, Dutton) Dutton/Plume.
—Ralph's Party: A Novel. 2000. 288p. pap. 12.95 (*0-452-28163-6*, Plume) Dutton/Plume.
—Ralph's Party: A Novel. 368p. 25.99 (*0-7278-5836-X*) Severn Hse. Pubs., Ltd.
—Thirtynothing: A Novel. 2001. 336p. pap. 13.00 (*0-452-28212-8*, Plume) Dutton/Plume.
Jhabvala, Ruth Prawer. Shards of Memory. 224p. 1996. pap. 11.00 (*0-385-47723-6*); 1995. 22.95 o.s.i (*0-385-47722-8*) Doubleday Publishing.
John, Katherine. Murder of a Dead Man. 1996. 314p. 23.95 o.p. (*0-312-15369-4*, Saint Martin's Minotaur) St. Martin's Pr.
—Six Foot Under. 1996. 384p. 23.95 o.p. (*0-312-14416-4*, Saint Martin's Minotaur) St. Martin's Pr.
—Six Foot Under. l.t. ed. 1996. (Large Print Ser.). 752p. 29.99 o.p. (*0-7089-3554-0*, Ulverscroft) Thorpe, F. A. Pubs. GBR. *Dist:* Ulverscroft Large Print Bks., Ltd., Ulverscroft Large Print Canada, Ltd.
—Without Trace. 1995. 426p. 24.95 o.p. (*0-312-13218-2*, Saint Martin's Minotaur) St. Martin's Pr.
Johnston, Linda. Once a Cavalier. 2000. (Time Passages Romance Ser.). 304p. mass mkt. 5.99 o.s.i (*0-515-12847-3*, Jove) Berkley Publishing Group.
Jones, Dylan. Outside the Rules. l.t. ed. 2003. (Magna Large Print Ser.). 448p. 32.50 (*0-7505-2053-1*) Magna Large Print Bks. GBR. *Dist:* Ulverscroft Large Print Bks., Ltd., Ulverscroft Large Print Canada, Ltd.
—Outside the Rules. 1995. 21.00 o.p. (*0-312-11873-2*, Saint Martin's Minotaur) St. Martin's Pr.
Jones, Elwyn. Barlow Exposed. 1977. 7.95 o.p. (*0-312-06685-6*) St. Martin's Pr.
Jong, Erica. Fanny: Being the True History of the Adventures of Fanny Hackabout-Jones. 1981. pap. 6.95 o.p. (*0-452-25273-3*, Z5273, Plume) Dutton/Plume.
—Fanny: Being the True History of the Adventures of Fanny Hackabout-Jones. 1984. mass mkt. 1.95 o.p. (*0-451-13370-6*, Signet Bks.) NAL.
—Fanny: Being the True History of the Adventures of Fanny Hackabout-Jones. 2003. (Illus.). 512p. pap. 14.95 (*0-393-32435-4*) Norton, W. W. & Co., Inc.
Jordan, Penny. Power Play. 2000. mass mkt. (*1-55166-587-5*, 1-66587-6, Mira Bks.); 1990. mass mkt. o.s.i (*0-373-97108-7*, Harlequin Bks.) Harlequin Enterprises, Ltd.
Joseph, Alison. Sacred Hearts: A Mystery Introducing Sister Agnes. 1996. 256p. 22.95 o.p. (*0-312-14405-9*, Saint Martin's Minotaur) St. Martin's Pr.
Joyce, Brenda. The Third Heiress. l.t. ed. 2000. 27.95 (*1-56895-838-2*, Wheeler Publishing, Inc.) Gale Group.
—The Third Heiress. 2000. 512p. mass mkt. 6.99 (*0-312-97419-1*, St. Martin's Paperbacks); 1999. 416p. 19.95 o.p. (*0-312-20387-X*) St. Martin's Pr.
Kane, Jessica Francis. Bending Heaven: Stories. 2002. 208p. text 23.00 (*1-58243-206-6*, Counterpoint Pr.) Basic Bks.
Kaste, Harry, ed. CliffsNotes TM Oliver Twist. 1999. E-Book 5.99 (*0-8220-7152-5*, Cliff Notes) Wiley, John & Sons, Inc.
Keating, H. R. F. A Detective under Fire. l.t. ed. 2003. (Magna Large Print Ser.). 320p. (*0-7505-2072-8*) Magna Large Print Bks. GBR. *Dist:* Ulverscroft Large Print Canada, Ltd.
—A Detective under Fire. Date not set. pap. (*0-312-31658-5*); mass mkt. (*0-312-99057-X*) St. Martin's Pr. (St. Martin's Paperbacks).
—A Long Walk to Wimbledon. l.t. ed. 2002. 300p. pap. 24.95 (*0-7862-3960-3*) Gale Group.
—The Soft Detective. 1998. 272p. 22.95 o.p. (*0-312-19335-1*, Saint Martin's Minotaur) St. Martin's Pr.
—The Soft Detective. l.t. ed. 1998. (Mystery Ser.). 343p. 26.95 (*0-7862-1565-8*) Thorndike Pr.
Kellogg, Marne Davis. Brilliant. l.t. ed. 2003. 444p. 30.95 (*1-58724-543-4*, Wheeler Publishing, Inc.) Gale Group.
—Brilliant. 2003. 352p. 24.95 (*0-312-30347-5*) St. Martin's Pr.
Kelly, Nora. Hot Pursuit. 2002. 200p. 24.95 o.s.i (*1-59058-014-1*); 325p. pap. (*1-59058-018-4*) Poisoned Pen Pr.
Kendrick, Stephen. Night Watch: A Long-Lost Adventure in Which Sherlock Holmes Meets Father Brown. 2001. (Illus.). 272p. 23.00 (*0-375-40367-1*, Pantheon) Knopf Publishing Group.
Kennedy, Shirley. The London Belle. 1999. (Signet Regency Romance Ser.). 224p. mass mkt. 4.99 o.s.i (*0-451-19836-0*) NAL.
Kenyon, Michael. The Elgar Variation. 1981. 360p. 13.95 o.p. (*0-698-11057-9*) Putnam Publishing Group, The.
—A Free-Range Wife. 1988. 208p. pap. 3.50 o.p. (*0-380-70382-3*, Avon Bks.) Morrow/Avon.
—A Free Range Wife. 1983. (Crime Club Ser.). (Illus.). 192p. 11.95 o.p. (*0-385-18838-2*) Doubleday Publishing.
—A Healthy Way to Die. 1986. (Crime Club Ser.). 192p. 12.95 o.p. (*0-385-23355-8*) Doubleday Publishing.
—A Healthy Way to Die. 1987. 192p. pap. 2.95 o.p. (*0-380-70380-7*, Avon Bks.) Morrow/Avon.
—Kill the Butler. 1993. 221p. 17.95 o.p. (*0-312-08833-7*, Saint Martin's Minotaur) St. Martin's Pr.
—Man at the Wheel. 1982. (Crime Club Ser.). 11.95 o.p. (*0-385-18299-6*) Doubleday Publishing.
—Man at the Wheel. 1988. 192p. pap. 3.50 (*0-380-70381-5*, Avon Bks.) Morrow/Avon.
—Peckover & the Bog Man: An Inspector Peckover Mystery. 1995. 208p. 20.95 o.p. (*0-312-13582-3*, Saint Martin's Minotaur) St. Martin's Pr.
—Peckover Holds the Baby. 1988. (Crime Club Ser.). 192p. pap. 12.95 o.s.i (*0-385-24324-3*) Doubleday Publishing.
—Peckover Holds the Baby. 1988. pap. 3.50 (*0-380-70636-9*, Avon Bks.) Morrow/Avon.
—Peckover Joins the Choir. 1994. 224p. 19.95 o.p. (*0-312-10523-1*, Saint Martin's Minotaur) St. Martin's Pr.
Kerr, Philip. Dark Matter: The Private Life of Sir Isaac Newton: A Novel. (Illus.). 352p. 2003. pap. 14.00 (*1-4000-4949-0*, Three Rivers Pr.); 2002. 24.00 (*0-609-60981-5*, Crown) Crown Publishing Group.
—A Philosophical Investigation. 1995. 384p. mass mkt. 8.99 o.s.i (*0-7704-2592-5*) Bantam Bks.
—A Philosophical Investigation. 1994. 336p. pap. 14.00 o.s.i (*0-452-27140-1*, Plume) Dutton/Plume.
—A Philosophical Investigation. 1993. 329p. 20.00 o.p. (*0-374-23176-1*) Farrar, Straus & Giroux.
Kerstan, Lynn. Celia's Grand Passion. 1998. (Regency Romance Ser.). 214p. mass mkt. 5.99 o.s.i (*0-449-00183-0*, Fawcett) Ballantine Bks.
Keyes, Marian. Last Chance Saloon. 2003. 528p. pap. 13.95 (*0-06-008624-6*, Perennial) HarperTrade.
—Last Chance Saloon. 2002. 544p. mass mkt. 7.99 (*0-380-82029-3*); 2001. 384p. 25.00 (*0-688-18072-8*, Morrow, William & Co.) Morrow/Avon.
—Last Chance Saloon. 1999. 505p. (*1-85371-965-X*) Poolbeg Pr. IRL. *Dist:* Dufour Editions, Inc.
—Lucy Sullivan Is Getting Married. 2002. 624p. pap. 13.95 (*0-06-009037-5*, Perennial) HarperTrade.
—Lucy Sullivan Is Getting Married. 2000. 624p. mass mkt. 6.99 (*0-380-79610-4*); 1999. 448p. 24.00 (*0-380-97618-8*) Morrow/Avon. (Avon Bks.).
—Lucy Sullivan Is Getting Married. 1996. 740p. pap. 12.95 (*1-85371-615-4*) Poolbeg Pr. IRL. *Dist:* Dufour Editions, Inc.
King, Laurie R. The Beekeeper's Apprentice. 1996. 448p. reprint ed. mass mkt. 6.99 (*0-553-57165-6*) Bantam Bks.
—The Beekeeper's Apprentice. abr. ed. 1996. 6p. audio 16.99 (*0-88646-388-2*, 7388) Durkin Hayes Publishing Ltd.
—The Beekeeper's Apprentice. l.t. ed. 1996. 574p. 24.95 (*0-7838-1932-3*, Macmillan Reference USA) Gale Group.
—The Beekeeper's Apprentice. unabr. ed. (Mary Russell Mystery Ser.: Vol. 1). 2001. audio compact disk 124.00; 1995. audio 85.00 (*0-7887-0319-6*, 94511E7) Recorded Bks., LLC.
—The Beekeeper's Apprentice. 1994. xvii, 347p. 23.95 (*0-312-10423-5*, Saint Martin's Minotaur) St. Martin's Pr.
—A Letter of Mary. 1998. (Mary Russell Novels Ser.). 336p. reprint ed. mass mkt. 6.99 (*0-553-57780-8*) Bantam Bks.
—A Letter of Mary. abr. ed. 1997. audio 16.99 (*0-88646-420-X*, 7420) Durkin Hayes Publishing Ltd.
—A Letter of Mary. 1999. E-Book 23.95 (*0-312-20728-X*) St. Martin's Pr.
—A Monstrous Regiment of Women. 1996. (Mary Russell Ser.: No. 2). 368p. mass mkt. 6.99 (*0-553-57456-6*, Crimeline) Bantam Bks.
—A Monstrous Regiment of Women. abr. ed. 1995. audio 16.99 (*0-88646-390-4*, 7390) Durkin Hayes Publishing Ltd.
—A Monstrous Regiment of Women. unabr. ed. 1996. (Mary Russell Mystery Ser.: Vol. 2). audio 78.00 (*0-7887-0493-1*, 94685E7) Recorded Bks., LLC.
—A Monstrous Regiment of Women. 1995. viii, 326p. 22.95 (*0-312-13565-3*, Saint Martin's Minotaur) St. Martin's Pr.
—The Moor. 1999. (Mary Russell Novels Ser.). 400p. (gr. 5 up). mass mkt. 6.99 (*0-553-57952-5*) Bantam Bks.
—The Moor. l.t. ed. 1998. (G. K. Hall Mystery Ser.). 419p. 27.95 (*0-7838-0162-9*, Macmillan Reference USA) Gale Group.
—The Moor. unabr. ed. 1998. (Mary Russell Mystery Ser.: Vol. 4). audio 75.00 (*0-7887-1979-3*, 95366E7 ) Recorded Bks., LLC.
—The Moor. 1999. E-Book 23.95 (*0-312-20731-X*); 1997. (Illus.). 307p. 23.95 o.p. (*0-312-16934-5*, Saint Martin's Minotaur) St. Martin's Pr.
—O Jerusalem. 2000. (Mary Russell Novels Ser.). 464p. mass mkt. 6.99 (*0-553-58105-8*) Bantam Bks.
—O Jerusalem. 1999. (Mary Russell Novels Ser.). (Illus.). 384p. 23.95 o.s.i (*0-553-11093-4*) Broadway Bks.
—O Jerusalem. unabr. ed. 1999. (Mary Russell Mystery Ser.: Vol. 5). audio 83.00 (*0-7887-3746-5*, 95781E7) Recorded Bks., LLC.
King, Martin. The Estate: A Novel. 2002. 191p. pap. 14.95 (*1-84018-410-8*) Mainstream Publishing Co., Ltd. GBR. *Dist:* Trafalgar Square.
King, Peter. Death Al Dente: A Gourmet Detective Mystery. 2000. (Culinary Mysteries Ser.). 256p. mass mkt. 5.99 (*0-312-97038-2*, St. Martin's Paperbacks); 1999. (Gourmet Detective Mystery Ser.: Vol. 4). 240p. 22.95 o.p. (*0-312-19891-4*, Saint Martin's Minotaur) St. Martin's Pr.
—Death & the Celestial Spice. 1997. (*0-312-15137-3*) St. Martin's Pr.
—Dying on the Vine: A Further Adventure of the Gourmet Detective. (Culinary Mysteries Ser.). 1999. 288p. mass mkt. 5.99 (*0-312-96683-0*, St. Martin's Paperbacks); 1998. 304p. 22.95 o.p. (*0-312-18090-X*, Saint Martin's Minotaur) St. Martin's Pr.
—The Gourmet Detective. 256p. 1996. 22.95 (*0-312-14346-X*, Saint Martin's Minotaur); Vol. 1. 1997. mass mkt. 5.99 o.s.i (*0-312-96260-6*, St. Martin's Paperbacks) St. Martin's Pr.
—A Healthy Place to Die: A Gourmet Detective Mystery. (Gourmet Detective Mystery Ser.). 2001. 240p. mass mkt. 5.99 (*0-312-97683-6*, St. Martin's Paperbacks); 2000. 230p. 22.95 (*0-312-24269-7*, Saint Martin's Minotaur) St. Martin's Pr.
—Spiced to Death. (Culinary Mysteries Ser.). 1998. 304p. mass mkt. 5.99 (*0-312-96500-1*, St. Martin's Paperbacks); 1997. 352p. text 23.95 o.p. (*0-312-15661-8*, Saint Martin's Minotaur) St. Martin's Pr.
King, Ross. Domino. 2003. 448p. pap. 14.00 (*0-14-200336-0*) Penguin Group (USA) Inc.
—Domino. 2002. 448p. 26.00 (*0-8027-3378-6*) Walker & Co.
King, Valerie. A London Flirtation. 2000. (Zebra Regency Romance Ser.). 256p. mass mkt. 4.99 o.s.i (*0-8217-6535-3*) Kensington Publishing Corp.
Kingsley, Katherine. Lilies on the Lake. 2001. 336p. mass mkt. 6.50 (*0-440-23602-9*) Dell Publishing.
Kinsella, Sophie. Confessions of a Shopaholic. 2003. 384p. mass mkt. 6.99 (*0-440-24141-3*, Dell Bks.); 2001. (Illus.). 320p. pap. 11.95 (*0-385-33548-2*, Delta) Dell Publishing.
—Confessions of a Shopaholic. audio 29.99 (*1-4025-3603-8*) Recorded Bks., LLC.
Kleypas, Lisa. The Eye of Horus: Someon. 2001. 432p. mass mkt. 6.99 (*0-380-80223-6*, HarperTorch) Morrow/Avon.
—Someone to Watch over Me. 1999. 384p. mass mkt. 7.50 (*0-380-80230-9*, Avon Bks.) Morrow/Avon.
—Suddenly You. l.t. ed. 2001. (Wheeler Large Print Book Ser.). 363p. 30.95 (*1-58724-130-7*, Wheeler Publishing, Inc.) Gale Group.
—Where Dreams Begin. l.t. ed. 2002. (Wheeler Large Print Book Ser.). 28.95 (*1-58724-192-7*, Wheeler Publishing, Inc.) Gale Group.
—Where Dreams Begin. 2000. 384p. mass mkt. 6.99 (*0-380-80231-7*, Avon Bks.) Morrow/Avon.
Krahn, Betina. The Mermaid. 1997. 368p. mass mkt. 5.99 (*0-553-57617-8*, Spectra) Bantam Bks.
Krahn, Betina M. The Last Bachelor. 1994. 528p. mass mkt. 6.50 (*0-553-56522-2*) Bantam Bks.
—The Last Bachelor. l.t. ed. 1995. (Large Print Bks.). 23.95 o.p. (*1-56895-170-1*, Wheeler Publishing, Inc.) Gale Group.
—The Perfect Mistress. l.t. ed. 1995. pap. 21.95 o.p. (*1-56895-274-0*, Wheeler Publishing, Inc.) Gale Group.

Settings

Kureishi, Hanif. The Black Album. 288p. 1996. pap. 13.00 (*0-684-82540-6*); 1995. 22.00 (*0-684-81342-4*) Simon & Schuster. (Scribner).

—The Black Album. abr. ed. 1997. (Audio Ser.). pap. 16.95 o.s.i incl. audio (*0-14-086414-8*, Penguin AudioBooks) Viking Penguin.

La Plante, Lynda. Prime Suspect, No. 3. 1994. 320p. mass mkt. 4.99 o.s.i (*0-440-21496-3*) Dell Publishing.

Lake, Deryn. Death at St. James Palace: A John Rawlings Mystery. 2002. (John Rawlings Mystery Ser.). 274p. 24.95 (*0-7490-0583-1*) Allison & Busby, Ltd. GBR. *Dist:* International Publishers Marketing.

Laker, Rosalind, pseud. The Silver Touch. 1990. mass mkt. 4.50 o.s.i (*0-553-28336-7*) Bantam Bks.

—The Silver Touch. l.t. ed. 1989. (Magna Large Print Ser.). 551p. o.p. (*1-85057-461-8*) Magna Large Print Bks. GBR. *Dist:* Ulverscroft Large Print Canada, Ltd.

Lamb, Charlotte. In the Still of the Night. l.t. ed. 1997. 431p. 24.95 o.p. (*0-7838-1944-7*, Macmillan Reference USA) Gale Group.

Lang, Adele. Confessions of a Sociopathic Social Climber: The Katya Livingston Chronicles. Orig. Title: What Katya Did Next: Chronicles of a Sociopathic Social Climber. 196p. 2002. 22.95 (*0-312-28811-5*); 2003. reprint ed. pap. 12.95 (*0-312-31361-6*, Saint Martin's Griffin) St. Martin's Pr.

Langley, Lee. Distant Music. 2003. 322p. 22.00 (*1-57131-040-1*) Milkweed Editions.

Laurence, Janet. Canaletto & the Case of the Westminster Bridge, Vol. 1. 1998. (Canaletto & the Case of the Westminster Bridge Ser.: Vol. 1). 400p. 24.95 o.p. (*0-312-18551-0*, Saint Martin's Minotaur) St. Martin's Pr.

—Canaletto & the Case of Westminster Bridge. l.t. ed. 1999. (Magna Large Print Ser.). 416p. (*0-7505-1370-5*) Magna Large Print Bks. GBR. *Dist:* Ulverscroft Large Print Canada, Ltd.

Laurens, Stephanie. Four in Hand. 2002. 304p. mass mkt. (*0-373-83539-6*, Harlequin Bks.) Harlequin Enterprises, Ltd.

—Four in Hand. l.t. ed. 1993. (Masquerade Historical Romance Ser.). 18.95 o.p. (*0-263-13751-1*) Harlequin Mills & Boon, Ltd. GBR. *Dist:* BBC Audiobooks America.

—A Season for Scandal: Tangled Reins & Fair Juno. 2001. 480p. mass mkt. (*0-373-83479-9*, Harlequin Bks.) Harlequin Enterprises, Ltd.

Laurie, Hugh. The Gun Seller. 1998. 368p. pap. 14.00 (*0-671-02082-X*, Washington Square Pr.) Simon & Schuster.

—The Gun Seller. 1997. 340p. 24.00 (*1-56947-087-1*) Soho Pr., Inc.

Lawrence, David. The Dead Sit Round in a Ring. Date not set. pap. (*0-312-32711-0*); pap. (*0-312-32712-9*); mass mkt. (*0-312-99629-2*) St. Martin's Pr. (St. Martin's Paperbacks).

Lawton, John. Black Out. 1996. 352p. pap. 11.95 o.s.i (*0-14-024081-0*, Penguin Bks.) Penguin Group (USA) Inc.

—Black Out. 2002. 432p. 6.99 (*0-14-200276-3*); 1995. 352p. 22.95 o.p. (*0-670-85767-X*, Viking) Viking Penguin.

—Bluffing Mr. Churchill. 2005. 336p. 24.00 (*0-87113-907-3*, Atlantic Monthly Pr.) Grove/Atlantic, Inc.

Le Carré, John. The Night Manager. (George Smiley Ser.). 1997. pap. 12.00 o.p. (*0-345-41830-1*); 1994. 480p. mass mkt. 6.99 (*0-345-38576-4*) Ballantine Bks.

—The Night Manager. unabr. collector's ed. 1994. (George Smiley Novels Ser.). audio 104.00 (*0-7366-2789-8*, 3505) Books on Tape, Inc.

—The Night Manager. 1993. (George Smiley Novels Ser.). 24.00 o.s.i (*0-679-42513-6*) Knopf, Alfred A. Inc.

—The Night Manager. l.t. ed. 1993. (George Smiley Ser.). 22.00 o.s.i (*0-679-74728-1*) Random Hse. Large Print.

Leather, Stephen. The Chinaman. Grose, Bill, ed. 1992. 320p. 20.00 (*0-671-74301-5*, Atria) Simon & Schuster.

—Tango One. 2002. 406p. pap. (*0-340-73405-1*) Coronet GBR. *Dist:* Trafalgar Square.

Lee, Mark. The Canal House. 2003. 368p. tchr. ed. 23.95 (*1-56512-379-4*, 72379) Algonquin Bks. of Chapel Hill.

—The Canal House. 2004. 368p. pap. 14.00 (*0-15-602954-5*, Harvest Bks.) Harcourt Trade Pubs.

Leebron, Fred G. In the Middle of All This. 264p. 2004. pap. 13.00 (*0-15-602742-9*, Harvest Bks.); 2002. 24.00 (*0-15-100834-5*) Harcourt Trade Pubs.

Lefebure, Molly. Blitz! 1989. 18.95 o.p. (*0-312-02873-3*) St. Martin's Pr.

Leith, Prue. Leaving Patrick. 2001. 320p. 23.95 (*0-312-28258-3*) St. Martin's Pr.

—Leaving Patrick. l.t. ed. 2000. (General Ser.). viii, 429p. pap. 23.95 (*0-7862-2419-3*) Thorndike Pr.

—Sisters: A Novel. 2002. 304p. 23.95 (*0-312-28779-8*) St. Martin's Pr.

Lennox, Charlotte. The Life of Harriot Stuart, Written by Herself. Kubica, Susan, ed. & intro. by. 1995. 328p. 45.00 (*0-8386-3579-2*) Fairleigh Dickinson Univ. Pr.

Leroy, Margaret. Postcards from Berlin. 2003. 400p. 22.95 (*0-316-73813-1*) Little Brown & Co.

Lessing, Doris. Ben, in the World. 2000. 192p. 23.00 (*0-06-019628-9*, HarperCollins) HarperTrade.

—The Golden Notebook. 1999. (Perennial Classics Ser.). 672p. pap. 15.00 (*0-06-093140-X*, Perennial) HarperTrade.

—The Golden Notebook. 1984. 24.45 o.p. (*0-671-28770-2*, Simon & Schuster) Simon & Schuster.

—The Golden Notebook: A Novel. 1994. 656p. reprint ed. pap. 14.00 o.p. (*0-06-097590-3*, Perennial) HarperTrade.

—The Golden Notebook: A Novel. 1994. 576p. lib. bdg. 33.00 o.p. (*0-8095-9146-4*) Millefleurs.

—Love, Again. l.t. ed. 1996. (Large Print Bks.). 25.95 o.p. (*1-56895-341-0*, Wheeler Publishing, Inc.) Gale Group.

—Love, Again. 1996. 352p. 24.00 o.p. (*0-06-017687-3*) HarperCollins Pubs.

—Love, Again: A Novel. 1997. 368p. pap. 13.00 (*0-06-092796-8*, Perennial) HarperTrade.

—The Real Thing. 1992. 214p. 20.00 o.p. (*0-06-016853-6*) HarperTrade.

—The Sweetest Dream. 2002. E-Book 19.95 (*0-06-008494-4*); E-Book 19.95 (*0-06-008493-6*); E-Book 19.95 (*0-06-008492-8*); E-Book 19.95 (*0-06-050455-2*) HarperCollins General Bks. Group. (PerfectBound).

—The Sweetest Dream. 2002. 496p. 26.95 (*0-06-621334-7*) HarperCollins Pubs.

—The Sweetest Dream. 2003. 496p. pap. 13.95 (*0-06-093755-6*, Perennial) HarperTrade.

Lette, Kathy. Altar Ego. 1999. ix, 353p. 23.00 (*0-688-17145-1*, Morrow, William & Co.) Morrow/Avon.

—Altar Ego. 1998. 353p. (*0-330-36116-3*) Picador.

Lindsey, Johanna. Home for the Holidays. l.t. ed. 2000. 272p. pap. 20.00 o.s.i (*0-06-019909-1*) HarperCollins Pubs.

—Home for the Holidays. 2000. 240p. 18.00 (*0-380-97856-3*, Morrow, William & Co.) Morrow/Avon.

—Secret Fire. l.t. ed. 1996. (Americana Ser.). 505p. lib. bdg. 26.95 o.p. (*0-7862-0725-6*) Thorndike Pr.

Linscott, Gillian. Dead Man's Sweetheart. 1996. 272p. 21.95 o.p. (*0-312-14579-9*, Saint Martin's Minotaur) St. Martin's Pr.

—Stage Fright. l.t. ed. 1994. 20.95 o.p. (*0-7927-2044-X*); pap. 19.95 o.p. (*0-7927-2043-1*) BBC Audiobooks America.

—Stage Fright. 1993. 192p. 17.95 o.p. (*0-312-09812-X*, Saint Martin's Minotaur) St. Martin's Pr.

Lippincott, Robin. Mr. Dalloway. 1999. 232p. 21.95 o.p. (*1-889330-28-0*); (Illus.). pap. 13.95 (*1-889330-29-9*) Sarabande Bks., Inc.

Liss, David. A Conspiracy of Paper. E-Book 19.95 (*1-58945-562-2*) Adobe Systems, Inc.

—A Conspiracy of Paper. 2001. (Reader's Circle Ser.). 464p. pap. 14.95 (*0-8041-1912-0*, Ballantine Bks.) Ballantine Bks.

—A Conspiracy of Paper. 2000. E-Book 19.95 (*0-375-50504-0*) Random Hse., Inc.

—A Conspiracy of Paper. l.t. ed. 2000. (Basic Ser.). 781p. pap. 28.95 (*0-7862-2665-X*) Thorndike Pr.

—A Spectacle of Corruption. 2004. audio 97.25 (*1-59355-655-1*); audio 24.95 (*1-59355-658-6*, 5283); audio compact disk 26.95 (*1-59355-656-X*, 5281); audio 34.95 (*1-59355-654-3*, 5279) Brilliance Audio.

—A Spectacle of Corruption. 2004. 400p. 24.95 (*0-375-50855-4*) Random Hse., Inc.

Lively, Penelope. City of the Mind: A Novel. 1991. 240p. 20.00 o.p. (*0-06-016666-5*) HarperTrade.

Livingston, Nancy. Quiet Murder. l.t. ed. 1993. 23.95 o.p. (*0-7927-1797-X*); pap. 21.95 o.p. (*0-7927-1796-1*) BBC Audiobooks America.

—Quiet Murder. 1995. 253p. per. (*0-373-26186-1*, 1-26186-6, Worldwide Library) Harlequin Enterprises, Ltd.

—Quiet Murder. l.t. ed. 1993. (Magna Large Print Ser.). 388p. o.p. (*0-7505-0582-6*) Magna Large Print Bks. GBR. *Dist:* Ulverscroft Large Print Canada, Ltd.

—Quiet Murder. 1993. 17.95 o.p. (*0-312-08878-7*, Saint Martin's Minotaur) St. Martin's Pr.

Lloyd, Josie. The Boy Next Door. 2001. (Illus.). 416p. pap. (*0-434-00834-6*) Random Hse. of Canada, Ltd. CAN. *Dist:* Random Hse., Inc.

Lock, Joan. Dead Letters: A Victorian Murder Mystery. 2003. 192p. 26.99 (*0-7278-5969-2*) Severn Hse. Pubs., Ltd.

Lodge, David. The British Museum Is Falling Down. 1989. (King Penguin Ser.). 182p. pap. 14.00 (*0-14-012419-5*, Penguin Bks.) Penguin Group (USA) Inc.

—Home Truths: A Novella. 2000. 128p. 11.95 (*0-14-029180-6*) Viking Penguin.

—Therapy. unabr. ed. 1998. audio 84.95 (*1-85089-879-0*, 951106) ISIS Audio Bks. GBR. *Dist:* Ulverscroft Large Print Bks., Ltd.

—Therapy. 1996. 336p. 14.00 (*0-14-024900-1*); 1995. 368p. 22.95 o.p. (*0-670-86358-0*, Viking); 1996. 2p. audio 16.95 o.s.i (*0-14-086356-7*, Penguin AudioBooks) Viking Penguin.

London, Julia. The Secret Lover. 2002. 400p. mass mkt. 5.99 (*0-440-23694-0*) Dell Publishing.

Longworth, Gay. Dead Alone: A Mystery. 2003. 336p. 24.95 (*0-312-31061-7*, Saint Martin's Minotaur) St. Martin's Pr.

Lott, Tim. Rumours of a Hurricane. 2002. 336p. text (*0-670-88661-0*, Viking) Viking Penguin.

Lovell, Marc. And They Say You Can't Buy Happiness. 2001. 190p. reprint ed. pap. 19.95 (*1-930067-07-0*) Vineyard Pr.

Lovesey, Peter. Abracadaver. 1994. 224p. 16.95 o.p. (*0-7451-8645-9*, Black Dagger); 1996. audio 54.95 (*0-7451-6110-3*, CAB294) BBC Audiobooks America.

—Abracadaver. 1989. 256p. reprint ed. pap. 4.50 o.p. (*0-06-081000-9*, Perennial) HarperTrade.

—Abracadaver. 1981. 224p. pap. 3.95 o.p. (*0-14-005803-6*, Penguin Bks.) Viking Penguin.

—Bertie & the Crime of Passion. 1995. 256p. 19.95 o.s.i (*0-89296-550-9*) Mysterious Pr.

—Bertie & the Crime of Passion. 1995. 240p. mass mkt. 5.50 o.s.i (*0-446-40368-7*) Warner Bks., Inc.

—Bertie & the Seven Bodies, Set. unabr. ed. 1993. (Detective Memoirs of King Edward the Eighth Ser.). 54.95 incl. audio (*0-7451-6111-1*, CAB 623) BBC Audiobooks America.

—Bertie & the Seven Bodies. 1990. 208p. 16.95 o.p. (*0-89296-399-9*) Mysterious Pr.

—Bertie & the Seven Bodies. 1991. (Audio Books Ser.). audio 53.95 o.p. (*0-8161-9247-2*) Thorndike Pr.

—Bertie & the Seven Bodies. 1991. mass mkt. 4.95 o.s.i (*0-445-40858-8*) Warner Bks., Inc.

—Bertie & the Tinman. 1988. 15.95 o.p. (*0-89296-196-1*) Mysterious Pr.

—Bertie & the Tinman. 1989. mass mkt. 3.95 (*0-445-40592-9*, Mysterious Pr. Paperback Bks.) Warner Bks., Inc.

—A Case of Spirits. l.t. ed. 2002. (General Ser.). 280p. pap. 24.95 (*0-7862-4224-8*) Thorndike Pr.

—A Case of Spirits. 1977. (Crime Ser.). 192p. pap. 3.95 o.p. (*0-14-004333-0*, Penguin Bks.) Viking Penguin.

—The Detective Wore Silk Drawers. 1988. audio 35.95 o.p. (*0-8161-9452-1*) Thorndike Pr.

—The Detective Wore Silk Drawers. 1980. (Crime Monthly Ser.). pap. 3.95 o.p. (*0-14-005558-4*, Penguin Bks.) Viking Penguin.

—The Detective Wore Silk Drawers: A Sergeant Cribb Adventure. unabr. ed. 1995. audio 39.95 (*0-7451-6112-X*, CAB 338) BBC Audiobooks America.

—The Detective Wore Silk Drawers: A Sergeant Cribb Mystery. 1989. 208p. reprint ed. pap. 4.50 o.p. (*0-06-080999-X*, Perennial) HarperTrade.

—The Detective Wore Silk Drawers: A Sergeant Cribb Mystery. l.t. ed. 2000. (General Ser.). 268p. pap. 23.95 (*0-7862-2426-6*) Thorndike Pr.

—Invitation to a Dynamite Party. 1981. 176p. pap. 3.95 o.p. (*0-14-004029-3*, Penguin Bks.) Viking Penguin.

—Rough Cider. unabr. ed. 2001. audio 54.95 (*1-85089-785-9*, 88022) ISIS Audio Bks. GBR. *Dist:* Ulverscroft Large Print Bks., Ltd.

—Rough Cider. l.t. ed. 1987. (Mainstream Ser.). 242p. reprint ed. 15.95 o.p. (*1-85089-149-4*) ISIS Large Print Bks. GBR. *Dist:* Transaction Pubs.

—Rough Cider. 1987. 224p. 15.95 (*0-89296-194-5*) Mysterious Pr.

—Rough Cider. 2001. 206p. pap. 13.00 (*1-56947-228-9*) Soho Pr., Inc.

—Rough Cider. 1988. mass mkt. 3.95 (*0-445-40545-7*, Mysterious Pr. Paperback Bks.) Warner Bks., Inc.

—Swing, Swing Together. 1976. 21.95 (*0-89190-093-4*) Amereon, Ltd.

—Swing, Swing Together. 1990. 352p. (C). reprint ed. lib. bdg. 20.00 o.p. (*0-8095-9023-9*) Millefleurs.

—Swing, Swing Together. 1978. (Crime Ser.). pap. 3.95 o.p. (*0-14-004618-6*, Penguin Bks.) Viking Penguin.

—Swing, Swing Together: A Sergeant Cribb Mystery. 1990. 352p. reprint ed. pap. 4.50 o.p. (*0-06-081023-8*, Perennial) HarperTrade.

—Swing, Swing Together: A Sergeant Cribb Mystery. 2002. (General Ser.). 24.95 (*0-7862-4408-9*) Thorndike Pr.

—Waxwork. l.t. ed. 1978. 12.95 o.p. (*0-8161-6651-X*, Macmillan Reference USA) Gale Group.

—Waxwork. 1978. 7.95 o.p. (*0-394-50066-0*, Pantheon) Knopf Publishing Group.

—Waxwork. 1980. (Crime Monthly Ser.). pap. 3.95 o.p. (*0-14-004887-1*, Penguin Bks.) Viking Penguin.

—Wobble to Death. l.t. ed. 1999. (General Ser.). 272p. pap. 23.95 (*0-7862-1868-1*) Thorndike Pr.

—Wobble to Death. 1980. pap. 3.95 o.p. (*0-14-005557-6*, Penguin Bks.) Viking Penguin.

Lowndes, Marie B. The Lodger. Marcus, Laura, ed. 1996. (Oxford Popular Fiction Ser.). 228p. pap. 8.95 o.p. (*0-19-282371-X*) Oxford Univ. Pr., Inc.

Lowndes, Natalya. Snow Red. 1992. 272p. 24.95 o.p. (*0-340-55977-2*) Hodder & Stoughton, Ltd. GBR. *Dist:* Lubrecht & Cramer, Ltd., Trafalgar Square.

Lynne, Victoria. With This Kiss. 1999. 368p. mass mkt. 5.99 o.s.i (*0-440-22334-2*) Dell Publishing.

Lytton, Edward Bulwer & Ainsworth, William Harrison. Cult Criminals: The Newgate Novels, 1830-1847, 6 vols. John, Juliet, ed. 1998. (Subcultures & Subversions: 1750-1850 Ser.). 2712p. (C). lib. bdg. 715.00 (*0-415-14383-7*) Routledge.

MacDonald, George. Home Again. Hamilton, Dan, ed. 1988. 192p. pap. text 5.95 o.p. (*0-89693-464-0*) Cook Communications Ministries.

—Home Again. 2003. (George MacDonald Original Works Ser.: Series II). 373p. reprint ed. 24.00 (*1-881084-11-6*) Johannesen Printing & Publishing.

MacDonald, George & Phillips, Michael R. The Poet's Homecoming. 1990. 192p. pap. 7.99 o.p. (*1-55661-135-8*) Bethany Hse. Pubs.

Macdonald, Malcolm. Tessa D'Arblay. 1985. 320p. 15.95 o.p. (*0-312-79350-2*) St. Martin's Pr.

MacDonald, Marianne. Death's Autograph. abr. ed. 1998. audio 54.95 (*0-7540-0089-3*, CAB1512) BBC Audiobooks America.

—Death's Autograph: A Mystery. 1999. (Antiquarian Book Mysteries Ser.). 352p. mass mkt. 5.99 (*0-06-109742-X*, HarperTorch) Morrow/Avon.

—Death's Autograph: A Mystery. 1997. (Dido Hoare Mysteries Ser.). 224p. 22.95 o.p. (*0-312-16815-2*, Saint Martin's Minotaur) St. Martin's Pr.

—Ghost Walk. 2000. (Antiquarian Book Mysteries Ser.). 304p. mass mkt. 5.99 (*0-06-101426-5*) HarperCollins Pubs.

—Ghost Walk. 1998. (Dido Hoare Mysteries Ser.). 256p. 21.95 o.p. (*0-312-19417-X*, Saint Martin's Minotaur) St. Martin's Pr.

—Smoke Screen. 1999. 255p. 23.95 o.p. (*0-312-24243-3*, Saint Martin's Minotaur) St. Martin's Pr.

MacInnes, Colin. Absolute Beginners. 2001. 203p. pap. 10.95 (*0-7490-0540-8*) Allison & Busby, Ltd. GBR. *Dist:* International Publishers Marketing.

—Absolute Beginners. 1980. 208p. 13.95 o.p. (*0-8052-8039-1*); pap. 5.95 o.p. (*0-8052-8038-3*) Knopf Publishing Group. (Schocken).

—Absolute Beginners. 1985. pap. 7.95 o.p. (*0-525-48189-3*, Obelisk) NAL.

—City of Spades. 1985. pap. 8.95 o.p. (*0-525-48188-5*, Obelisk) NAL.

Macintyre, F. Gwynplaine. The Woman Between the Worlds. 2000. (Illus.). 324p. pap. 19.95 (*0-595-08884-8*, Backinprint.com) iUniverse, Inc.

Mackay, Sheena. Dunedin. 1993. 296p. reprint ed. 21.95 o.p. (*1-55921-093-1*) Moyer Bell.

Mackay, Shena. The Artist's Widow. 1999. 176p. 21.95 (*1-55921-229-2*) Moyer Bell.

—Dunedin. 1994. pap. 5.95 o.p. (*1-55921-119-9*) Moyer Bell.

MacKenzie, Donald. Loose Cannon. l.t. ed. 1994. (Nightingale Mystery in Large Print Ser.). 269p. lib. bdg. 16.95 (*0-8161-5859-2*, Macmillan Reference USA) Gale Group.

—Loose Cannon: A John Raven Mystery. 1993. 160p. 17.95 o.p. (*0-312-09863-4*, Saint Martin's Minotaur) St. Martin's Pr.

—Raven after Dark, 001. 1979. 7.95 o.p. (*0-395-28209-8*) Houghton Mifflin Co.

—Raven Settles a Score, 001. 1978. 7.95 o.p. (*0-395-27100-2*) Houghton Mifflin Co.

Mackenzie, Donald. Raven's Revenge, 001. 1982. 192p. 10.95 o.p. (*0-395-32050-X*) Houghton Mifflin Co.

Maitland, Barry. Babel. 2003. (Illus.). 288p. 24.95 (*1-55970-668-6*) Arcade Publishing, Inc.

—The Malcontenta. 2000. 348p. 24.95 (*1-55970-527-2*) Arcade Publishing, Inc.

Maitland, Sara. Daughter of Jerusalem: A Novel. 1995. 88p. pap. 12.00 o.p. (*0-8050-3810-8*, Owl Bks.) Holt, Henry & Co.

Malcolm, John. A Back Room in Somers Town. 1986. 160p. mass mkt. 2.95 o.s.i (*0-345-33032-3*) Ballantine Bks.

—A Back Room in Somers Town. 1985. 160p. 12.95 o.s.i (*0-684-18301-3*, Macmillan Reference USA) Gale Group.

—A Deceptive Appearance. (Tim Simpson Mystery Ser.). 1992. 224p. text 20.00 o.s.i (*0-684-19508-9*); 1993. 318p. lib. bdg. 15.95 (*0-8161-5780-4*) Gale Group. (Macmillan Reference USA).

—The Godwin Sideboard. 1986. mass mkt. 2.95 o.s.i (*0-345-33371-3*) Ballantine Bks.

—The Godwin Sideboard. 1985. (Tim Simpson Mystery Ser.). 176p. 13.95 o.s.i (*0-684-18398-6*, Macmillan Reference USA) Gale Group.

—Gothic Pursuit. 1987. (Tim Simpson Mystery Ser.). 208p. 14.95 o.p. (*0-684-18833-3*, Macmillan Reference USA) Gale Group.

—The Gwen John Sculpture. 1987. mass mkt. 2.95 o.s.i (*0-345-33618-6*) Ballantine Bks.

—The Gwen John Sculpture. 1986. 208p. 13.95 o.p. (0-684-18574-1, Macmillan Reference USA) Gale Group.
—Hung Over. 1995. 240p. 19.95 o.p. (0-312-13514-9, Saint Martin's Minotaur) St. Martin's Pr.
—Into the Vortex, Vol. 1. 1997. (Into the Vortex Ser.: Vol. 1). 240p. 21.95 o.p. (0-312-15555-7, Saint Martin's Minotaur) St. Martin's Pr.
—Mortal Ruin. 1988. 208p. 15.95 o.s.i (0-684-18958-5, Macmillan Reference USA) Gale Group.
—Sheep, Goats & Soap: A Tim Simpson Mystery. l.t. ed. 1992. 275p. pap. 14.95 o.p. (0-8161-5475-9, Macmillan Reference USA) Gale Group.
—Sheep, Goats & Soap: A Tim Simpson Mystery. 1992. 224p. 19.95 o.s.i (0-684-19384-1, Scribner) Simon & Schuster.
—Whistler in the Dark. 1988. mass mkt. 3.50 o.s.i (0-345-34292-5) Ballantine Bks.
—Whistler in the Dark. 1987. 160p. 14.95 o.p. (0-684-18701-9, Scribner) Simon & Schuster.
—The Wrong Impression: A Tim Simpson Mystery. 1990. 224p. 18.95 o.p. (0-684-19252-7, Scribner) Simon & Schuster.
Mann, Jessica. Under a Dark Sun. l.t. ed. 2001. (Thorndike General Ser.). 271p. pap. 22.95 o.p. (0-7862-3221-8); (0-7540-4422-X); (0-7540-4423-8) Thorndike Pr.
Mantle, John. The Bloody War, Mate. 2003. 320p. pap. 16.95 (0-9713318-7-1) Lucky Pr., LLC.
Marechera, Dambudzo, et al, contrib. by. Scrapiron Blues. 1999. (African Writers Library). (ENG & SHO., Illus.). 266p. text 29.95 (0-86543-730-0) Africa World Pr.
Marechera, Dambudzo & Veit-Wild, Flora. Scrapiron Blues. 1999. (African Writers Library). (ENG & SHO., Illus.). 266p. pap. 16.95 (0-86543-731-9) Africa World Pr.
Margolis, Sue. Apocalipstick. 2003. 320p. pap. 11.95 (0-385-33656-X, Delta) Dell Publishing.
Marquis, Max. Undignified Death: A Detective Inspector Harry Timberlake Mystery. 1994. 192p. 18.95 o.p. (0-312-11087-1) St. Martin's Pr.
Marsh, Jean. Iris. l.t. ed. 2001. (Magna Large Print Ser.). (0-7505-1612-7) Magna Large Print Bks. GBR. Dist: Ulverscroft Large Print Canada, Ltd.
—Iris. 2000. 352p. 24.95 (0-312-26182-9) St. Martin's Pr.
Marshall, Paula. Dear Lady Disdain. 2000. 256p. mass mkt. (0-373-51115-9, 1-51115-3, Harlequin Bks.) Harlequin Enterprises, Ltd.
—Dear Lady Disdain. l.t. ed. 1995. (Mills & Boon Large Print Ser.). 350p. 25.99 (0-263-14425-9) Harlequin Mills & Boon, Ltd. GBR. Dist: Ulverscroft Large Print Bks., Ltd., Ulverscroft Large Print Canada, Ltd.
Marston, Edward. The Devil's Apprentice: An Elizabethan Theater Mystery Featuring Nicholas Bracewell. 2001. 288p. 23.95 (0-312-26574-3, Saint Martin's Minotaur) St. Martin's Pr.
Martin, Kat. Fanning the Flame. 2002. (Illus.). 400p. pap. 6.99 (0-7434-1916-2, Pocket) Simon & Schuster.
—Fanning the Flame. l.t. ed. 2003. (Core Ser.). 423p. 30.95 (0-7862-4965-X) Thorndike Pr.
Martin, S. I. Incomparable World. 1998. 213p. 22.50 (0-8076-1436-X) Braziller, George Inc.
Martin, Valerie. Mary Reilly. 1990. 272p. 18.95 o.s.i (0-385-24968-3) Doubleday Publishing.
Matthews, Carole. A Minor Indiscretion. 2003. (Red Dress Ink Ser.: No. 22). 400p. pap. (0-373-25033-9, Red Dress Ink) Harlequin Enterprises, Ltd.
Maugham, Robin. The Servant. 2000. (Film Ink Ser.). xiv, 75p. pap. 12.00 (1-85375-389-0) Prion GBR. Dist: Trafalgar Square.
Mawer, Simon. The Fall. 2004. 400p. pap. 13.95 (0-316-73559-0, Back Bay); 2003. 384p. 24.95 (0-316-09780-2) Little Brown & Co.
Maxted, Anna. Getting over It. 2001. 416p. pap. 14.00 (0-06-098824-X); 2000. 288p. 25.00 (0-06-039320-3) HarperTrade. (ReganBooks).
McCabe, Patrick. Breakfast on Pluto. 1998. 224p. 22.00 o.p. (0-06-019340-9) HarperCollins Pubs.
—Breakfast on Pluto: A Novel. 1999. 224p. pap. 13.00 (0-06-093158-2, Perennial) HarperTrade.
McDermid, Val. Booked for Murder. 2nd ed. 2000. (Lindsay Gordon Mystery Ser.). 260p. pap. 12.00 (1-883523-37-0) Spinsters Ink Bks.
—Common Murder. 2nd ed. 1995. 264p. pap. 10.95 (1-883523-08-7) Spinsters Ink Bks.
—Common Murder. l.t. ed. 2001. 286p. 32.50 (0-7531-6538-4) Thorpe, F. A. Pubs. GBR. Dist: Ulverscroft Large Print Bks., Ltd., Ulverscroft Large Print Canada, Ltd.
—Conferences Are Murder: A Lindsay Gordon Mystery. 1999. (Lindsay Gordon Mystery Ser.: Vol. 4). (Illus.). 264p. pap. 12.00 (1-883523-30-3) Spinsters Ink Bks.
—Deadline for Murder: A Lindsay Gordon Mystery. 2nd ed. 1997. (Kate Brannigan Mystery Ser.). 264p. (Orig.). pap. 10.95 (1-883523-17-6) Spinsters Ink Bks.
—Final Edition. l.t. ed. 2001. 288p. 32.50 (0-7531-6540-6) Thorpe, F. A. Pubs. GBR. Dist: Ulverscroft Large Print Bks., Ltd., Ulverscroft Large Print Canada, Ltd.
—Report for Murder. l.t. ed. 2001. (Magna Large Print Ser.). 400p. 32.50 (0-7505-1699-2) Magna Large Print Bks. GBR. Dist: Ulverscroft Large Print Bks., Ltd., Ulverscroft Large Print Canada, Ltd.
—Report for Murder. 224p. 25.00 (0-7278-5554-9) Severn Hse. Pubs., Ltd.
—Report for Murder. 2nd ed. 1998. 264p. pap. 10.95 (1-883523-24-9) Spinsters Ink Bks.
—Report for Murder. 1989. 208p. 16.95 o.p. (0-312-03888-7, Saint Martin's Minotaur) St. Martin's Pr.
McEwan, Ian. Amsterdam: A Novel. unabr. ed. 1999. audio 24.00 (0-7366-4451-2, 4896) Books on Tape, Inc.
—Amsterdam: A Novel. Oeser, Hans-Christian, tr. from ENG. 1999. (GER.). 224p. (3-257-06220-6) Diogenes Verlag AG CHE. Dist: International Bk. Import Service, Inc.
—Amsterdam: A Novel. 1998. 208p. 21.00 o.s.i (0-385-49423-8, Talese, Nan A.) Doubleday Publishing.
—Amsterdam: A Novel. unabr. ed. 1999. audio 24.95 (1-57511-060-1) Publishing Mills, Inc., The.
—Amsterdam: A Novel. 1999. 208p. pap. 13.00 (0-385-49424-6, Knopf Bks. for Young Readers) Random Hse. Children's Bks.
—Amsterdam: A Novel. l.t. ed. 1999. (Basic Ser.). 232p. 29.95 (0-7862-1796-0) Thorndike Pr.
—Amsterdam: A Novel. abr. ed. 1999. audio 18.70 (0-00-105566-6) Ulverscroft Audio (U.S.A.).
McSmith, Andy. Innocent in the House. 2002. 320p. reprint ed. pap. 11.00 (1-85984-491-X) Verso.
—The Innocent in the House: A Novel. 2001. 240p. 23.00 (1-85984-643-2) Verso.
Melville, Jennie. Dead Set: A Charmian Daniels Mystery. 1995. (WWL Mystery Ser.). 252p. per. (0-373-26174-8, 1-26174-2, Harlequin Bks.) Harlequin Enterprises, Ltd.
—Dead Set: A Charmian Daniels Mystery. 1992. 17.95 (0-312-08757-8, Saint Martin's Minotaur) St. Martin's Pr.
—Death in the Family. 1995. 277p. 21.00 (0-312-11772-8, Saint Martin's Minotaur) St. Martin's Pr.
—A Different Kind of Summer. l.t. ed. 1993. 18.95 o.p. (0-7451-6437-4); 1992. audio 39.95 (0-7451-2401-1, CD 002) BBC Audiobooks America.
—A Different Kind of Summer. (Black Dagger Crime Ser.). 12.95 o.p. (0-86220-800-9, BD005) Chivers Pr. GBR. Dist: BBC Audiobooks America.
—Footsteps in the Blood. pap. 15.95 (0-312-29187-6, Saint Martin's Griffin); 1993. 192p. 17.95 (0-312-09813-8, Saint Martin's Minotaur) St. Martin's Pr.
—Making Good Blood. 1990. 15.95 o.p. (0-312-04344-9, Saint Martin's Minotaur) St. Martin's Pr.
—The Morbid Kitchen. 208p. 1996. 20.95 (0-312-14681-7, Saint Martin's Minotaur); 1995. per. 15.95 (0-312-29172-8, Saint Martin's Griffin) St. Martin's Pr.
—Murder Has a Pretty Face. 1991. reprint ed. per. (0-373-26079-2, Harlequin Bks.) Harlequin Enterprises, Ltd.
—Murder Has a Pretty Face. l.t. ed. 1996. (Magna Large Print Ser.). 400p. 29.99 (0-7505-1047-1) Magna Large Print Bks. GBR. Dist: Ulverscroft Large Print Bks., Ltd., Ulverscroft Large Print Canada, Ltd.
—Murder Has a Pretty Face. 1989. 256p. 16.95 o.p. (0-312-03405-9, Saint Martin's Minotaur) St. Martin's Pr.
—Murder in the Garden. 1991. 2.99 o.p. (0-517-07814-7) Random Hse. Value Publishing.
—Murder in the Garden. pap. 15.95 (0-312-29185-X, Saint Martin's Griffin); 1990. 224p. 15.95 (0-312-03895-X, Saint Martin's Minotaur) St. Martin's Pr.
—Revengeful Death. l.t. ed. 1998. (Magna Large Print Ser.). 272p. (0-7505-1232-6) Magna Large Print Bks. GBR. Dist: Ulverscroft Large Print Canada, Ltd.
—Tarot's Tower. 1979. mass mkt. 1.75 o.s.i (0-449-24001-0, Fawcett) Ballantine Bks.
—Tarot's Tower. 1978. 8.95 o.s.i (0-671-22905-2, Simon & Schuster) Simon & Schuster.
—Whoever Has the Heart. 218p. 3.95 o.p. (0-8317-5152-5) Smithmark Pubs., Inc.
—Whoever Has the Heart. 1994. 224p. 19.95 (0-312-11099-5, Saint Martin's Minotaur) St. Martin's Pr.
—Windsor Red. pap. 9.95 (1-902002-01-6) CT Publishing GBR. Dist: Trafalgar Square.
—Windsor Red. 1990. mass mkt. (0-373-26051-2, Harlequin Bks.) Harlequin Enterprises, Ltd.
—Windsor Red. 1988. 256p. 16.95 o.p. (0-312-01846-0, Saint Martin's Minotaur) St. Martin's Pr.
—Witching Murder. 1991. (Lythway Adult Ser.). 280p. 20.50 o.p. (0-7451-1374-5) Chivers Pr. GBR. Dist: BBC Audiobooks America.
—Witching Murder. pap. 15.95 (0-312-29186-8, Saint Martin's Griffin); 1991. 15.95 (0-312-05999-X, Saint Martin's Minotaur) St. Martin's Pr.
Michaels, Barbara, pseud. The Wizard's Daughter. (0-7540-1029-5); (0-7540-2013-4) BBC Audiobooks America.
—The Wizard's Daughter. 1982. 256p. mass mkt. 2.95 o.s.i (0-449-20113-9, Fawcett) Ballantine Bks.
—The Wizard's Daughter. l.t. ed. 1995. 336p. mass mkt. 7.50 o.s.i (0-425-14642-1) Berkley Publishing Group.
—The Wizard's Daughter. 1981. (General Ser.). lib. bdg. 13.95 o.p. (0-8161-3248-8, Macmillan Reference USA) Gale Group.
—The Wizard's Daughter. 1996. 336p. reprint ed. 24.00 (0-7278-4917-4) Severn Hse. Pubs., Ltd.
—The Wizard's Daughter. l.t. ed. 1997. (Americana Ser.). 479p. 26.95 (0-7862-1025-7) Thorndike Pr.
Michaels, Kasey. Indiscreet. l.t. ed. 2000. (Wheeler Large Print Book Ser.). 413p. 26.95 (1-56895-843-9, Wheeler Publishing, Inc.) Gale Group.
—Indiscreet. 1998. 400p. reprint ed. mass mkt. 6.50 (0-446-60582-4, Warner Romance) Warner Bks., Inc.
Mieville, China. King Rat. 1999. 320p. 23.95 (0-312-89073-7); 2nd ed. 2000. 318p. pap. 14.95 (0-312-89072-9, CPB1120) Doherty, Tom Assocs., LLC. (Tor Bks.).
Miller, Hugh. Skin Deep. 1992. 192p. 16.95 o.p. (0-312-08293-2, Saint Martin's Minotaur) St. Martin's Pr.
Millner, Denene & Chiles, Nick. In Love & War. 2003. 352p. 23.95 (0-525-94709-4) Dutton/Plume.
—In Love & War. 2004. 352p. pap. 14.00 (0-451-21115-4) NAL.
Milne, John. Daddy's Girl. 201p. pap. 13.00 (1-874061-90-4) No Exit Pr. GBR. Dist: Trafalgar Square.
—Daddy's Girl. 1989. 15.95 o.p. (0-312-02893-8, Saint Martin's Minotaur) St. Martin's Pr.
—The Moody Man. 249p. pap. 13.00 (1-874061-89-0) No Exit Pr. GBR. Dist: Trafalgar Square.
—The Moody Man. 1989. 256p. pap. 3.95 o.p. (0-14-010145-4, Penguin Bks.); 1988. 15.95 o.p. (0-670-81728-7) Viking Penguin.
Mina, Denise. Exile. 2001. 364p. 25.00 (0-7867-0838-7); 2002. 368p. reprint ed. pap. 14.00 (0-7867-0962-6) Avalon Publishing Group. (Carroll & Graf Pubs.).
Minds Eye Staff. Rumpole 2. 14.95 (0-559-35014-7) Penguin Group (USA) Inc.
Mitchell, Gladys. Cold, Lone & Still. l.t. ed. 1987. (Nightingale Paperbacks Ser.). 304p. 11.95 o.p. (0-8161-4374-9, Macmillan Reference USA) Gale Group.
—The Dancing Druids. 1986. 239p. 14.95 o.p. (0-312-18207-4) St. Martin's Pr.
—Death at the Opera. 1992. 248p. reprint ed. 14.95 o.p. (0-86220-835-1, Black Dagger) BBC Audiobooks America.
—The Death-Cap Dancers. (Fingerprint Mysteries Ser.). 192p. 1983. pap. 5.95 o.p. (0-312-18609-6, Saint Martin's Griffin); 1981. 9.95 o.p. (0-312-18608-8) St. Martin's Pr.
—Faintley Speaking. 1986. 224p. 14.95 o.p. (0-312-27957-4) St. Martin's Pr.
—Here Lies Gloria Mundy. 1983. 192p. 9.95 o.p. (0-312-36986-7) St. Martin's Pr.
—Late, Late in the Evening. 1995. 192p. reprint ed. 19.00 o.p. (0-7278-4793-7) Severn Hse. Pubs., Ltd.
—Late, Late in the Evening. l.t. ed. 1996. (Linford Mystery Library). 400p. pap. 17.99 o.p. (0-7089-7941-6, Ulverscroft) Thorpe, F. A. Pubs. GBR. Dist: Ulverscroft Large Print Bks., Ltd., Ulverscroft Large Print Canada, Ltd.
—No Winding-Sheet. l.t. ed. 1989. (Popular Ser.). lib. bdg. 11.95 o.p. (1-85057-319-0, Macmillan Reference USA) Gale Group.
—The Rising of the Moon. 1984. 11.95 o.p. (0-312-68442-8) St. Martin's Pr.
—Speedy Death. 1999. 21.95 (0-7540-8547-3, Black Dagger) BBC Audiobooks America.
—Spotted Hemlock: A Murder Mystery. 1985. 240p. 14.95 o.p. (0-312-75350-0) St. Martin's Pr.
—St. Peter's Finger. 1986. 352p. 15.95 (0-312-00192-4) St. Martin's Pr.
—Three Quick & Five Dead, Set. unabr. ed. 1999. audio 47.95 (1-86015-418-2) Beeler, Thomas T. Publisher.
—Uncoffin'd Clay. 1982. 189p. 9.95 o.p. (0-312-82857-8) St. Martin's Pr.
—Watson's Choice. 1976. 6.95 o.p. (0-679-50658-6) McKay, David Co., Inc.
—Winking at the Brim. 1977. (McKay-Washburn Mystery Ser.). 6.95 o.p. (0-679-50732-9) McKay, David Co., Inc.
Modiano, Patrick. Out of the Dark. Stump, Jordan, tr. from FRE. 1998. Orig. Title: Du Plus Loin de L'Oubli. 139p. text 50.00 (0-8032-3196-2) Univ. of Nebraska Pr.
Moggach, Deborah. Close to Home. 1998. 249p. mass mkt. o.p. (0-7493-1229-7) Random Hse. of Canada, Ltd.
—Close to Home. l.t. ed. 2001. 273p. pap. 24.95 (0-7862-3485-7) Thorndike Pr.
—The Ex-Wives. l.t. ed. 2001. (Thorndike General Ser.). 354p. 25.95 (0-7862-3199-8) Thorndike Pr.
Moline, Karen. Lunch. 1994. 287p. 22.00 o.p. (0-688-13320-7, Morrow, William & Co.) Morrow/Avon.
Monahan, Brent. The Sceptered Isle Club. 2002. 288p. 24.95 (0-312-28803-4, Saint Martin's Minotaur) St. Martin's Pr.
Moorcock, Michael. Mother London. 1990. 496p. reprint ed. pap. 8.95 o.p. (0-06-097309-9, Perennial) HarperTrade.
Moorings. Baker St. Mysteries, Vol. 4. 1996. (Baker St. Mysteries Ser.). pap. 5.99 o.s.i (0-345-39558-1) Ballantine Bks.
Morgan, Fidelis. The Rival Queens: A Novel of Artifice, Gunpowder & Murder in Eighteenth-Century London. 2002. 352p. 23.95 (0-688-17684-4, Morrow, William & Co.) Morrow/Avon.
Morgan, Robert. All Things under the Moon. 1994. 224p. (Orig.). mass mkt. 4.99 o.p. (0-425-14302-3, Prime Crime) Berkley Publishing Group.
—The Only Thing to Fear. 1994. 256p. mass mkt. 4.99 o.s.i (0-425-14468-2, Prime Crime) Berkley Publishing Group.
—Some Things Come Back. 1995. 256p. (Orig.). mass mkt. 4.99 o.s.i (0-425-14690-1, Prime Crime) Berkley Publishing Group.
—Some Things Never Die. 1993. 208p. (Orig.). 3.99 o.p. (1-55773-887-4, Diamond Bks.) Ace Bks.
—Thing That Darkness Hides. 1993. 4.50 o.p. (1-55773-960-9, Diamond Bks.) Ace Bks.
—Things That Are Not There. 1992. 208p. (Orig.). 3.99 o.p. (1-55773-827-0, Diamond Bks.) Ace Bks.
Morice, Anne. Dead on Cue. l.t. ed. 1986. (Nightingale Ser.). 291p. 11.95 o.p. (0-8161-4118-5, Macmillan Reference USA) Gale Group.
—Dead on Cue. 1985. 208p. 12.95 o.p. (0-312-18519-7) St. Martin's Pr.
—Death & the Dutiful Daughter. l.t. ed. 1986. (Nightingale Ser.). 288p. 10.95 o.p. (0-8161-3866-4, Macmillan Reference USA) Gale Group.
—Death in the Round. 1980. 192p. 8.95 o.p. (0-312-18616-9) St. Martin's Pr.
—Death of a Wedding Guest. 1976. 7.95 o.p. (0-312-18830-7) St. Martin's Pr.
—Fatal Charm. 1989. 192p. 14.95 o.p. (0-312-03338-9, Saint Martin's Minotaur) St. Martin's Pr.
—Getting Away with Murder? l.t. ed. 1985. (Nightingale Ser.). 304p. 10.95 o.p. (0-8161-3865-6, Macmillan Reference USA) Gale Group.
—Getting Away with Murder? 1984. 11.95 o.p. (0-312-32633-5) St. Martin's Pr.
—The Men in Her Death. 1981. 224p. 9.95 o.p. (0-312-52939-2) St. Martin's Pr.
—Murder by Proxy. 1978. 7.95 o.p. (0-312-55292-0) St. Martin's Pr.
—Murder in Outline. 1986. 176p. mass mkt. 2.95 o.s.i (0-553-25647-5) Bantam Bks.
—Murder in Outline. 1979. 8.95 o.p. (0-312-55303-X) St. Martin's Pr.
—Murder Post-Dated. 1984. 192p. 10.95 o.p. (0-312-55321-8) St. Martin's Pr.
—Nursery Tea & Poison, Vol. 1. 1975. 6.95 o.p. (0-312-58030-4) St. Martin's Pr.
—Planning for Murder. 1991. 15.95 o.p. (0-312-04869-6, Saint Martin's Minotaur) St. Martin's Pr.
—Publish & Be Killed. 1986. 192p. 12.95 o.p. (0-312-00178-9) St. Martin's Pr.
—Scared to Death. 1986. mass mkt. 2.95 o.s.i (0-553-25628-9) Bantam Bks.
—Scared to Death. 1978. (General Ser.). lib. bdg. 10.95 o.p. (0-8161-6584-X, Macmillan Reference USA) Gale Group.
—Scared to Death. (Mystery Bookshelf Selection Ser.). 1978. pap. 2.95 o.p. (0-312-70044-X, Saint Martin's Griffin); 1977. 7.95 o.p. (0-312-70043-1) St. Martin's Pr.
—Sleep of Death. 1986. mass mkt. 2.95 o.s.i (0-553-25877-X) Bantam Bks.
—Sleep of Death. 1982. 176p. 10.95 o.p. (0-312-72863-8) St. Martin's Pr.
—Treble Exposure. 1988. 192p. 13.95 o.p. (0-312-01525-9, Saint Martin's Minotaur) St. Martin's Pr.
Morrison, Arthur. A Child of the Jago. (Academy Book Ser.). 208p. 1995. pap. 12.00 (0-89733-392-6); 1983. pap. 8.95 o.p. (0-85115-203-1) Academy Chicago Pubs., Ltd.
—Tales of Mean Streets. 1997. (Academy Book Ser.). 175p. pap. text 12.00 (0-89733-440-X) Academy Chicago Pubs., Ltd.
—Tales of Mean Streets. 1977. (Short Story Index Reprint Ser.). 19.95 (0-8369-3633-7) Ayer Co. Pubs., Inc.
Mortimer, John. Rumpole a la Carte. l.t. ed. 1992. pap. 14.95 o.p. (0-7927-1002-9); 18.95 o.p. (0-7927-1001-0, E0023) BBC Audiobooks America.
—Rumpole a la Carte. unabr. ed. 1992. audio 49.95 (0-7861-0351-5, 1308) Blackstone Audio Bks., Inc.
—Rumpole a la Carte. unabr. ed. 1992. audio 4.99 (0-88646-608-3); Set. 1991. audio 16.99 (0-88646-276-2, LFP 7276) Durkin Hayes Publishing Ltd.

Settings

Settings

—Rumpole a la Carte. (Rumpole Ser.). 256p. 1993. pap. 10.00 o.p. (*0-14-017981-X*); 1991. reprint ed. pap. 12.00 (*0-14-015609-7*) Penguin Group (USA) Inc. (Penguin Bks.).
—Rumpole a la Carte. 1990. (Rumpole Ser.). 256p. 18.95 o.p. (*0-670-83284-7*) Viking Penguin.
—Rumpole & the Age of Miracles. l.t. ed. 1995. pap. 19.95 o.p. (*0-7838-1188-8*, Macmillan Reference USA) Gale Group.
—Rumpole & the Age of Miracles. 1989. (Rumpole Ser.). 240p. pap. 10.95 o.s.i (*0-14-013116-7*, Penguin Bks.) Penguin Group (USA) Inc.
—Rumpole & the Age of Miracles. unabr. ed. 1988. audio 62.00 (*0-7887-3483-0*, 95892E7) Recorded Bks., LLC.
—Rumpole & the Age of Retirement. unabr. ed. 1994. audio 4.99 (*0-88646-700-4*) Durkin Hayes Publishing Ltd.
—Rumpole & the Angel of Death. unabr. ed. 1996. audio 49.95 (*0-7861-0974-2*, 1751) Blackstone Audio Bks., Inc.
—Rumpole & the Angel of Death. l.t. ed. 1996. 426p. lib. bdg. 22.95 o.p. (*0-7838-1794-0*, Macmillan Reference USA) Gale Group.
—Rumpole & the Angel of Death. 1997. 272p. reprint ed. pap. 9.95 o.s.i (*0-14-026314-4*) Penguin Group (USA) Inc.
—Rumpole & the Angel of Death. unabr. ed. 1996. (Rumpole of the Bailey Ser.: Vol. 7). audio 70.00 (*0-7887-0514-8*, 94708E7) Recorded Bks., LLC.
—Rumpole & the Angel of Death. 1996. 272p. 22.95 o.p. (*0-670-86451-X*); 2p. audio 16.95 (*0-14-086197-1*, Penguin AudioBooks) Viking Penguin.
—Rumpole & the Golden Thread. l.t. ed. 1993. pap. 16.95 o.p. (*0-7927-1370-2*); 1992. 18.95 o.p. (*0-7927-1371-0*) BBC Audiobooks America.
—Rumpole & the Golden Thread. unabr. ed. 1995. audio 49.95 (*0-7861-0855-X*, 1653) Blackstone Audio Bks., Inc.
—Rumpole & the Golden Thread. unabr. ed. 1991. (Rumpole of the Bailey Ser.: Vol. 5). audio 60.00 (*1-55690-451-7*, 91211E7) Recorded Bks., LLC.
—Rumpole & the Golden Thread. 1984. (Crime Ser.). 256p. pap. 5.95 o.p. (*0-14-006331-5*, Penguin Bks.); pap. 9.95 o.s.i (*0-14-025014-X*, Penguin Classics) Viking Penguin.
—Rumpole & the Judge's Elbow. unabr. ed. 1992. audio 5.99 (*0-88646-607-5*, PAC-7607) Durkin Hayes Publishing Ltd.
—Rumpole & the Man of God. abr. ed. 1996. (Paperback Audio Ser.). audio 9.99 (*0-88646-882-5*, 7882) Durkin Hayes Publishing Ltd.
—Rumpole & the Primrose Path. 2003. (Rumpole Ser.). 224p. 24.95 (*0-670-03146-1*, Viking) Viking Penguin.
—Rumpole & the Younger Generation. 1995. 64p. pap. 0.95 o.p. (*0-14-600006-4*) Penguin Group (USA) Inc.
—Rumpole at the Bar. abr. ed. 1989. audio 16.99 (*0-88646-238-X*, LFP 7238) Durkin Hayes Publishing Ltd.
—The Rumpole Collection, 2 bks., Set. deluxe ed. 1992. (Rumpole Ser.). pap. 22.00 o.p. (*0-14-095385-X*, Penguin Bks.) Penguin Group (USA) Inc.
—Rumpole for the Defence. l.t. ed. 1994. pap. 16.95 o.p. (*0-7927-1604-3*); 1993. 18.95 o.p. (*0-7927-1605-1*) BBC Audiobooks America.
—Rumpole for the Defence. unabr. ed. 1991. audio 39.95 (*0-7861-0236-5*, 1206) Blackstone Audio Bks., Inc.
—Rumpole for the Defence. 1984. 192p. pap. 9.95 o.s.i (*0-14-025013-1*) Penguin Group (USA) Inc.
—Rumpole for the Defence. unabr. ed. 1991. (Rumpole of the Bailey Ser.: Vol. 4). audio 51.00 (*1-55690-452-5*, 91108E7) Recorded Bks., LLC.
—Rumpole for the Defence. 1984. (Crime Monthly Ser.). 192p. pap. 5.95 o.p. (*0-14-006060-X*, Penguin Bks.) Viking Penguin.
—Rumpole for the Prosecution, Set. unabr. ed. 1992. audio 16.99 (*0-88646-283-5*, 7283) Durkin Hayes Publishing Ltd.
—Rumpole of the Bailey. 17.95 (*0-89190-275-9*) Amereon, Ltd.
—Rumpole of the Bailey. l.t. ed. 1993. (Eagle Large Print Ser.). 19.95 o.p. (*0-7927-1532-2*); pap. o.p. (*0-7927-1531-4*) BBC Audiobooks America.
—Rumpole of the Bailey, unabr. ed. 1991. audio 44.95 (*0-7861-0255-1*, 1223) Blackstone Audio Bks., Inc.
—Rumpole of the Bailey. abr. ed. 1983. audio 16.99 (*0-88646-084-0*, TC-LFP 7110) Durkin Hayes Publishing Ltd.
—Rumpole of the Bailey. unabr. ed. 1993. (Rumpole of the Bailey Ser.: Vol. 1). audio 51.00 (*1-55690-920-9*, 93416E7) Recorded Bks., LLC.
—Rumpole of the Bailey. 1980. (Rumpole Ser.). 208p. pap. 5.95 o.p. (*0-14-004670-4*, Penguin Bks.); pap. 9.95 o.s.i (*0-14-025012-3*) Viking Penguin.
—Rumpole on Trial. unabr. ed. 1995. audio 69.95 (*0-7451-4289-3*, CAB 972) BBC Audiobooks America.
—Rumpole on Trial. unabr. ed. 2000. 8p. audio compact disk 79.95 (*0-7540-5361-X*, CCD 052) Chivers Audio Bks. GBR. *Dist:* BBC Audiobooks America.
—Rumpole on Trial. 1993. (Rumpole Ser.). 256p. reprint ed. pap. 10.00 o.s.i (*0-14-017510-5*, Penguin Bks.) Penguin Group (USA) Inc.
—Rumpole on Trial. abr. ed. 1992. (Rumpole Ser.). 15.95 o.p. incl. audio (*0-453-00794-5*) Penguin/HighBridge.
—Rumpole on Trial. 1992. (Rumpole Ser.). 256p. 21.00 o.p. (*0-670-84459-4*, Viking) Viking Penguin.
—Rumpole Rests His Case. 2002. 224p. 24.95 (*0-670-03139-9*, Viking) Viking Penguin.
—Rumpole Unabridged, Set. unabr. ed. lib. bdg. 29.99 incl. audio (*1-55204-723-7*, PAUB-024) Durkin Hayes Publishing Ltd.
—Rumpole's Last Case. unabr. ed. 1995. audio 44.95 (*0-7861-0801-0*, 1625) Blackstone Audio Bks., Inc.
—Rumpole's Last Case. abr. ed. 1988. audio 16.99 (*0-88646-233-9*, LFP 7233); 1993. audio 4.99 (*0-88646-652-0*) Durkin Hayes Publishing Ltd.
—Rumpole's Last Case. l.t. ed. 1988. (General Ser.). 393p. 18.95 o.p. (*0-8161-4660-8*, Macmillan Reference USA) Gale Group.
—Rumpole's Last Case. 140th ed. 1990. (Rumpole Ser.). 288p. pap. 10.95 o.s.i (*0-14-012695-3*, Penguin Bks.) Penguin Group (USA) Inc.
—Rumpole's Last Case. unabr. ed. 1994. (Rumpole of the Bailey Ser.: Vol. 6). audio 60.00 (*0-7887-0057-X*, 94256E7) Recorded Bks., LLC.
—Rumpole's Last Case. 1988. (Rumpole Ser.). 288p. pap. 3.95 o.p. (*0-14-010447-X*, Penguin Bks.) Viking Penguin.
—Rumpole's Return. 18.95 (*0-89190-277-5*) Amereon, Ltd.
—Rumpole's Return, Set. abr. ed. 1990. audio 16.99 (*0-88646-162-6*, 7163) Durkin Hayes Publishing Ltd.
—Rumpole's Return. unabr. ed. 1991. (Rumpole of the Bailey Ser.: Vol. 3). audio 35.00 (*1-55690-453-3*, 91102E7) Recorded Bks., LLC.
—Rumpole's Return. 1982. (Rumpole Ser.). 160p. pap. 6.00 o.p. (*0-14-005571-1*, Penguin Bks.); pap. 9.95 o.s.i (*0-14-024698-3*, Penguin Classics) Viking Penguin.
Moses, Kate. Wintering: A Novel of Sylvia Plath. 2003. 336p. pap. 13.00 (*1-4000-3500-7*, Anchor) Knopf Publishing Group.
—Wintering: A Novel of Sylvia Plath. 2003. 272p. 23.95 o.s.i (*0-312-28375-X*) St. Martin's Pr.
Moyes, Patricia. Angel Death. 1982. (Henry Tibbett Mystery Ser.). 240p. pap. 5.95 o.s.i (*0-8050-0505-6*, Owl Bks.) Holt, Henry & Co.
—Angel Death. l.t. ed. 1982. (Henry Tibbett Mystery Ser.). 457p. 12.50 o.p. (*0-7089-0746-6*, Ulverscroft) Thorpe, F. A. Pubs. GBR. *Dist:* Ulverscroft Large Print Bks., Ltd., Ulverscroft Large Print Canada, Ltd.
—Black Girl, White Girl. unabr. ed. 1993. (Henry Tibbett Mystery Ser.). audio 36.00 (*0-7366-2327-2*, 3107) Books on Tape, Inc.
—Black Girl, White Girl. l.t. ed. 1991. (Henry Tibbett Mystery Ser.). 326p. lib. bdg. 19.95 o.p. (*0-8161-5011-7*, Macmillan Reference USA) Gale Group.
—Black Girl, White Girl. (Henry Tibbett Mystery Ser.). 224p. 1990. pap. 5.95 o.s.i (*0-8050-1149-8*, Owl Bks.); 1989. 15.95 o.p. (*0-8050-1148-X*) Holt, Henry & Co.
—Black Widower. unabr. ed. 1992. (Henry Tibbett Mystery Ser.). audio 42.00 (*0-7366-2272-1*, 3060) Books on Tape, Inc.
—Black Widower. 1985. (Henry Tibbett Mystery Ser.). 224p. pap. 5.95 o.s.i (*0-8050-0243-X*, Owl Bks.) Holt, Henry & Co.
—Black Widower. 1977. (Henry Tibbett Mystery Ser.). 224p. pap. 2.95 o.p. (*0-14-004334-9*, Penguin Bks.) Viking Penguin.
—The Coconut Killings. (Henry Tibbett Mystery Ser.). 1985. 224p. pap. 5.95 o.s.i (*0-8050-0754-7*, Owl Bks.); 1985. pap. o.p. (*0-03-005608-X*, Owl Bks.); 1977. o.p. (*0-03-018481-9*) Holt, Henry & Co.
—The Coconut Killings. 1979. (Henry Tibbett Mystery Ser.). pap. 1.95 o.p. (*0-14-004593-7*, Penguin Bks.) Viking Penguin.
—The Curious Affair of the Third Dog. unabr. ed. 1993. (Henry Tibbett Mystery Ser.). audio 44.95 (*0-7861-0428-7*, 1380) Blackstone Audio Bks., Inc.
—The Curious Affair of the Third Dog. 1986. (Henry Tibbett Mystery Ser.). 224p. pap. 5.95 o.s.i (*0-8050-0503-X*); pap. o.p. (*0-03-009534-4*) Holt, Henry & Co. (Owl Bks.).
—The Curious Affair of the Third Dog. 1976. (Henry Tibbett Mystery Ser.). 208p. pap. 1.95 o.p. (*0-14-004027-7*, Penguin Bks.) Viking Penguin.
—Dead Men Don't Ski. 1984. (Henry Tibbett Mystery Ser.). 288p. pap. 5.95 o.s.i (*0-8050-0705-9*, Owl Bks.) Holt, Henry & Co.
—Dead Men Don't Ski. l.t. ed. 1983. (Ulverscroft Large Print Ser.). 496p. 29.99 o.p. (*0-7089-1006-8*, Ulverscroft) Thorpe, F. A. Pubs. GBR. *Dist:* Ulverscroft Large Print Bks., Ltd., Ulverscroft Large Print Canada, Ltd.
—Death & the Dutch Uncle. 1983. (Henry Tibbett Mystery Ser.). 256p. pap. 5.95 o.s.i (*0-8050-0506-4*, Owl Bks.) Holt, Henry & Co.
—Death on the Agenda. 1984. (Henry Tibbett Mystery Ser.). 192p. pap. 5.95 o.s.i (*0-8050-0507-2*, Owl Bks.) Holt, Henry & Co.
—Down among the Dead Men. (Henry Tibbett Mystery Ser.). 18.50 o.p. (*0-86220-823-8*, BD022, Black Dagger); 1994. 18.95 o.p. (*0-7451-6461-7*) BBC Audiobooks America.
—Down among the Dead Men. 1982. (Henry Tibbett Mystery Ser.). 240p. pap. 2.50 o.p. (*0-440-11627-9*) Dell Publishing.
—Down among the Dead Men. 1986. (Henry Tibbett Mystery Ser.). 240p. pap. 5.95 o.s.i (*0-8050-0117-4*, Owl Bks.) Holt, Henry & Co.
—Falling Star. 1982. (Henry Tibbett Mystery Ser.). (Orig.). 256p. pap. 5.95 o.s.i (*0-8050-0755-5*); pap. o.p. (*0-03-059784-6*) Holt, Henry & Co. (Owl Bks.).
—Johnny under Ground. (Henry Tibbett Mystery Ser.). 18.50 o.p. (*0-86220-789-4*, C1029, Black Dagger); 1993. 18.95 o.p. (*0-7451-6441-2*); 1996. audio 54.95 (*0-7451-2414-3*, CDA015) BBC Audiobooks America.
—Johnny under Ground. 1983. (Henry Tibbett Mystery Ser.). pap. 2.95 o.p. (*0-440-14211-3*) Dell Publishing.
—Johnny under Ground. Barzun, Jacques & Taylor, W. H., eds. 1983. (Henry Tibbett Mystery Ser.). 253p. lib. bdg. 18.00 o.p. (*0-8240-4987-X*) Garland Publishing, Inc.
—Johnny under Ground: An Inspector Henry Tibbett Mystery. 1987. (Henry Tibbett Mystery Ser.). 256p. pap. 5.95 o.s.i (*0-8050-0270-7*, Owl Bks.) Holt, Henry & Co.
—Many Deadly Returns. unabr. ed. 1994. (Henry Tibbett Mystery Ser.). audio 49.95 (*0-7861-0433-3*, 1385) Blackstone Audio Bks., Inc.
—Many Deadly Returns. 1981. (Henry Tibbett Mystery Ser.). pap. 2.25 o.p. (*0-440-16172-X*) Dell Publishing.
—Many Deadly Returns: An Inspector Henry Tibbett Mystery. 1987. (Henry Tibbett Mystery Ser.). 256p. pap. 5.95 o.s.i (*0-8050-0598-6*, Owl Bks.) Holt, Henry & Co.
—Murder a la Mode. 1983. (Henry Tibbett Mystery Ser.). 224p. pap. 5.95 o.s.i (*0-8050-0706-7*, Owl Bks.) Holt, Henry & Co.
—Murder Fantastical. (Henry Tibbett Mystery Ser.). 189p. 12.95 o.p. (*0-86220-722-3*) Chivers Pr. GBR. *Dist:* BBC Audiobooks America.
—Murder Fantastical. 1984. (Henry Tibbett Mystery Ser.). 256p. pap. 5.95 o.s.i (*0-8050-0504-8*, Owl Bks.) Holt, Henry & Co.
—Night Ferry to Death. (Henry Tibbett Mystery Ser.). 192p. 1986. pap. 5.95 o.s.i (*0-8050-0116-6*, Owl Bks.); 1985. o.p. (*0-03-004477-4*) Holt, Henry & Co.
—Night Ferry to Death. l.t. ed. 1987. (Henry Tibbett Mystery Ser.). 336p. 29.99 o.p. (*0-7089-1615-5*, Ulverscroft) Thorpe, F. A. Pubs. GBR. *Dist:* Ulverscroft Large Print Bks., Ltd., Ulverscroft Large Print Canada, Ltd.
—Season of Snows & Sins. (Henry Tibbett Mystery Ser.). 1988. 224p. pap. 6.95 o.s.i (*0-8050-0849-7*); 1983. pap. o.p. (*0-03-063542-X*) Holt, Henry & Co. (Owl Bks.).
—A Six-Letter Word for Death. 1985. (Henry Tibbett Mystery Ser.). 256p. pap. 5.95 o.s.i (*0-8050-0244-8*, Owl Bks.) Holt, Henry & Co.
—A Six-Letter Word for Death. l.t. ed. 1984. (Henry Tibbett Mystery Ser.). 432p. 29.99 o.p. (*0-7089-1163-3*, Ulverscroft) Thorpe, F. A. Pubs. GBR. *Dist:* Ulverscroft Large Print Bks., Ltd., Ulverscroft Large Print Canada, Ltd.
—To Kill a Coconut. l.t. ed. 1981. (Ulverscroft Large Print Ser.). 336p. 29.99 o.p. (*0-7089-0632-X*, Ulverscroft) Thorpe, F. A. Pubs. GBR. *Dist:* Ulverscroft Large Print Bks., Ltd., Ulverscroft Large Print Canada, Ltd.
—Twice in a Blue Moon. (Henry Tibbett Mystery Ser.). 1994. pap. 5.95 o.s.i (*0-8050-2948-6*, Owl Bks.); 1993. 192p. 19.95 o.p. (*0-8050-2823-4*) Holt, Henry & Co.
—Who Is Simon Warwick? (Henry Tibbett Mystery Ser.). 1982. pap. o.p. (*0-03-059783-8*, Owl Bks.); 1982. 176p. pap. 5.95 o.s.i (*0-8050-0719-9*, Owl Bks.); 1979. 180p. o.p. (*0-03-044726-7*) Holt, Henry & Co.
Murdoch, Iris. The Green Knight. 1994. 480p. 23.95 o.p. (*0-670-85229-5*, Viking) Viking Penguin.
—The Sea, the Sea. 2001. pap. (*0-14-771593-8*); 2001. 528p. pap. 15.00 (*0-14-118616-X*, Penguin Classics); 1980. 512p. pap. 14.95 o.s.i (*0-14-005199-6*, Penguin Bks.); 1978. 12.95 o.p. (*0-670-62651-1*) Viking Penguin.
Myers, Amy. Murder at Plum's. pap. 9.95 (*0-7472-3397-7*) Headline Bk. Publishing, Ltd. GBR. *Dist:* Trafalgar Square.
—Murder at Plum's. 1993. 224p. mass mkt. 4.50 (*0-380-76586-1*, Avon Bks.) Morrow/Avon.
—Murder at Plum's. l.t. ed. 1993. (General Ser.). 432p. 29.99 o.p. (*0-7089-2847-1*, Ulverscroft) Thorpe, F. A. Pubs. GBR. *Dist:* Ulverscroft Large Print Bks., Ltd., Ulverscroft Large Print Canada, Ltd.
—Murder at the Masque. 1993. 256p. mass mkt. 4.99 (*0-380-76584-5*, Avon Bks.) Morrow/Avon.
—Murder at the Music Hall. 1999. 345p. pap. 11.00 (*0-7472-4843-5*) Headline Bk. Publishing, Ltd. GBR. *Dist:* Trafalgar Square.
—Murder in Pug's Parlour. 1992. 256p. mass mkt. 4.50 (*0-380-76587-X*, Avon Bks.) Morrow/Avon.
—Murder in Pug's Parlour. l.t. ed. 1992. (Ulverscroft Large Print Ser.). 432p. 29.99 o.p. (*0-7089-2732-7*, Ulverscroft) Thorpe, F. A. Pubs. GBR. *Dist:* Ulverscroft Large Print Bks., Ltd., Ulverscroft Large Print Canada, Ltd.
—Murder in the Limelight. 1992. 224p. mass mkt. 4.50 (*0-380-76585-3*, Avon Bks.) Morrow/Avon.
—Murder in the Limelight. l.t. ed. 1991. (General Ser.). 29.99 o.p. (*0-7089-2435-2*, Ulverscroft) Thorpe, F. A. Pubs. GBR. *Dist:* Ulverscroft Large Print Bks., Ltd., Ulverscroft Large Print Canada, Ltd.
—Murder in the Motor Stable. 1999. 311p. pap. 11.00 (*0-7472-4844-3*) Headline Bk. Publishing, Ltd. GBR. *Dist:* Trafalgar Square.
—Murder in the Queen's Boudoir. l.t. ed. 28.99 (*0-7278-7159-5*); 2000. 256p. 26.00 (*0-7278-5561-1*) Severn Hse. Pubs., Ltd.
—Murder in the Smokehouse: An Auguste Didier Whodunit. 1997. 312p. 23.95 o.p. (*0-312-15598-0*, Saint Martin's Minotaur) St. Martin's Pr.
—Murder Makes an Entree. 1996. 288p. 21.95 o.p. (*0-312-14376-1*, Saint Martin's Minotaur) St. Martin's Pr.
—Murder with Majesty. 1999. 288p. 25.00 (*0-7278-5415-1*) Severn Hse. Pubs., Ltd.
Myerson, Julie. Laura Blundy. 272p. 2000. 22.95 o.s.i (*1-57322-168-6*); 2001. reprint ed. pap. 13.00 (*1-57322-884-2*) Putnam Publishing Group, The. (Riverhead Bks. (Hardcovers)).
—The Touch. 1996. 320p. 21.95 o.s.i (*0-385-47507-1*, Talese, Nan A.) Doubleday Publishing.
Nadelson, Reggie. Bloody London. 2000. 308p. 24.95 o.p. (*0-312-24372-3*, Saint Martin's Minotaur) St. Martin's Pr.
Naipaul, V. S. Half a Life. 2001. 224p. 24.00 (*0-375-40737-5*) Knopf, Alfred A. Inc.
—Half a Life: A Novel. 2002. 224p. pap. 13.00 (*0-375-70728-X*) Knopf, Alfred A. Inc.
Nathan, Melissa. The Nanny. 2003. 352p. pap. 13.95 (*0-06-056011-8*, Avon Bks.) Morrow/Avon.
—Pride, Prejudice & Jasmin Field. 2001. 280p. pap. 6.50 (*0-06-107233-8*) HarperCollins Pubs.
—Pride, Prejudice, & Jasmine Field: A Novel. 2001. 288p. pap. 14.00 (*0-06-018495-7*, Avon Bks.) Morrow/Avon.
Nattel, Lilian. The Singing Fire. 2004. 352p. (*0-676-97600-X*) Knopf Canada CAN. *Dist:* Random Hse. of Canada, Ltd., Random Hse., Inc.
Navin, Jacqueline. Princess of Park Lane. 2003. 352p. mass mkt. 5.99 (*0-425-19326-8*) Berkley Publishing Group.
Neale, Jonathan. Laughter of Heroes. 1993. 128p. pap. (*1-85242-279-3*) Serpent's Tail Ltd.
Neate, Patrick. The London Pigeon Wars. 2004. 272p. 24.00 (*0-374-19205-7*) Farrar, Straus & Giroux.
—The London Pigeon Wars. 2003. 304p. (*0-670-91264-6*, Viking) Viking Penguin.
Neel, Janet. Death among the Dons. l.t. ed. 1994. 369p. lib. bdg. 21.95 (*0-8161-7439-3*, Macmillan Reference USA) Gale Group.
—Death among the Dons. 1995. (Illus.). 272p. (J). mass mkt. 5.50 (*0-671-89952-X*, Pocket) Simon & Schuster.
—Death among the Dons. 1993. 240p. 19.95 o.p. (*0-312-10450-2*, Saint Martin's Minotaur) St. Martin's Pr.
—Death of a Partner. l.t. ed. 1996. 384p. pap. 20.95 (*0-7838-1641-3*, Macmillan Reference USA) Gale Group.
—Death of a Partner. Chelius, Jane, ed. 1994. 256p. reprint ed. mass mkt. 4.99 (*0-671-74839-4*, Pocket) Simon & Schuster.
—Death of a Partner. 1991. 16.95 o.p. (*0-312-05411-4*, Saint Martin's Minotaur) St. Martin's Pr.
—Death on Site. l.t. ed. 1996. 363p. pap. 20.95 o.p. (*0-7838-1640-5*, Macmillan Reference USA) Gale Group.
—Death on Site. Chelius, Jane, ed. 1993. 288p. reprint ed. mass mkt. 4.99 (*0-671-73581-0*, Pocket) Simon & Schuster.
—Death on Site. 1990. 256p. 16.95 o.p. (*0-312-04298-1*, Saint Martin's Minotaur) St. Martin's Pr.
—Death's Bright Angel. Chelius, Jane, ed. 1991. 288p. reprint ed. mass mkt. 4.99 (*0-671-73579-9*, Pocket) Simon & Schuster.

—Death's Bright Angel. l.t. ed. 1998. (General Ser.). 365p. pap. 23.95 (*0-7862-1289-6*) Thorndike Pr.
—A Timely Death. l.t. ed. 1997. 382p. pap. 21.95 (*0-7838-8140-1*, Macmillan Reference USA) Gale Group.
—A Timely Death. 1996. 219p. text 21.95 o.p. (*0-312-15223-X*, Saint Martin's Minotaur) St. Martin's Pr.
Nelson, Casey. Nothing Gold Can Stay. 2000. 212p. pap. 12.95 o.p. (*1-55583-492-2*, Alyson Bks.) Alyson Pubns.
Newman, Kim. Anno Dracula. 1993. 400p. 21.00 o.p. (*0-88184-967-7*, Carroll & Graf Pubs.) Avalon Publishing Group.
—The Quorum. 1994. 310p. 21.00 o.p. (*0-7867-0132-3*, Carroll & Graf Pubs.) Avalon Publishing Group.
Nicholson, Geoff. Bleeding London. 320p. 1998. 13.95 (*0-87951-886-3*); 1997. 23.95 (*0-87951-807-3*) Overlook Pr., The.
—Everything & More. 1999. 249p. 13.95 (*0-87951-710-7*) Overlook Pr., The.
—Everything & More. 1995. 256p. 21.95 o.p. (*0-312-13069-4*) St. Martin's Pr.
Niles, Chris. Spike It. 1998. 272p. mass mkt. 5.99 o.s.i (*0-425-16565-5*, Prime Crime) Berkley Publishing Group.
Norfolk, Lawrence. Lempriere's Dictionary. 2003. 432p. pap. 15.00 (*0-8021-3987-6*, Grove Pr.) Grove/Atlantic, Inc.
—Lempriere's Dictionary: A Novel. 1993. 432p. pap. 19.00 (*0-345-38423-7*, Ballantine Bks.) Ballantine Bks.
Norman, Diana. A Catch of Consequence. 2003. 400p. pap. 14.00 (*0-425-19015-3*) Berkley Publishing Group.
Nunez, Sigrid. Mitz: The Marmoset of Bloomsbury. unabr. ed. 1999. audio 19.95 (*0-7861-1533-5*); 1998. audio 23.95 (*0-7861-1436-3*, 2322) Blackstone Audio Bks., Inc.
—Mitz: The Marmoset of Bloomsbury. 1998. 128p. 18.00 o.s.i (*0-06-017407-2*) HarperCollins Pubs.
O'Brien, Maureen. Unauthorized Departure: A Mystery. 2003. 288p. 23.95 (*0-312-31600-3*, Saint Martin's Minotaur) St. Martin's Pr.
O'Connor, Kathleen Sheehan. Different Kinds of Loving. 2000. 346p. (*1-902011-14-7*) Mount Eagle Pubns., Ltd.
O'Farrell, John. The Best a Man Can Get: A Novel. 2002. 272p. reprint ed. pap. 12.95 (*0-7679-0714-0*) Broadway Bks.
—The Best a Man Can Get: A Novel of Fatherhood & Its Discontents. 2001. E-Book 15.95 (*1-59061-574-3*) Adobe Systems, Inc.
O'Farrell, Maggie. After You'd Gone. l.t. ed. 2001. (Magna Large Print Ser.). 432p. (*0-7505-1722-0*) Magna Large Print Bks. GBR. *Dist:* Ulverscroft Large Print Canada, Ltd.
—After You'd Gone. 2002. 384p. 13.00 (*0-14-200032-9*); 2001. 372p. 24.95 o.s.i (*0-670-89448-6*, Viking) Viking Penguin.
—My Lover's Lover: A Novel. 2003. 288p. 24.95 (*0-670-03215-8*, Viking) Viking Penguin.
O'Hagan, Andrew. Personality. 320p. 2004. pap. (*0-15-602967-7*, Harvest Bks.); 2003. 25.00 (*0-15-101000-5*) Harcourt Trade Pubs.
Oldfield, Jenny. All Fall Down. 1998. 551 p. (*0-7540-2120-3*, Macmillan Reference USA) Gale Group.
—All Fall Down. 2003. 392p. pap. (*0-330-34843-4*) Pan Macmillan.
—All Fall Down. l.t. ed. 1998. (Romance Ser.). 552p. 26.95 (*0-7862-1393-0*) Thorndike Pr.
—Paradise Court. l.t. ed. 1997. 603 p. (*0-7540-2011-8*, Galaxy Children's Large Print) BBC Audiobooks America.
—Paradise Court. 2003. 421p. pap. (*0-330-33886-2*) Macmillan Children's Bks.
O'Riordan, Kate. Angel in the House. 2000. 336p. pap. (*0-00-225880-3*) HarperCollins Pubs.
Ormerod, Roger. The Second Jeopardy. 1988. (Crime Club Ser.). 12.95 o.s.i (*0-385-24613-7*) Doubleday Publishing.
—The Second Jeopardy. l.t. ed. 2001. (General Ser.). 313p. pap. 22.95 o.p. (*0-7862-2986-1*) Thorndike Pr.
Owen, Ruth. Midnight Mistress. 2000. (Meet Me at Midnight Ser.). 320p. mass mkt. 5.99 o.s.i (*0-553-57746-8*) Bantam Bks.
Paige, Robin. Death at Epsom Downs. 2002. 304p. reprint ed. mass mkt. 6.50 (*0-425-18384-X*, Prime Crime) Berkley Publishing Group.
—Death in Hyde Park: A Victorian Mystery. 2004. 304p. 23.95 (*0-425-19419-1*) Berkley Publishing Group.
Palmer, Elizabeth. Flowering Judas. unabr. ed. 1997. audio 69.95 (*0-7540-0058-3*, CAB 1481) BBC Audiobooks America.
—Flowering Judas. 2000. 408p. mass mkt. (*1-55166-593-X*, 1-66593-4, Mira Bks.) Harlequin Enterprises, Ltd.
—Flowering Judas. 1997. 280p. 22.95 o.p. (*0-312-16843-8*) St. Martin's Pr.
—Flowering Judas. l.t. ed. 1998. (Core Ser.). 442p. 28.95 (*0-7838-8401-X*) Thorndike Pr.
—Old Money. 1999. mass mkt. (*1-55166-547-6*, 1-66547-0, Mira Bks.) Harlequin Enterprises, Ltd.
—Plucking the Apple. 1999. (Mira Bks.). 378p. mass mkt. (*1-55166-493-3*, 1-66493-7, Mira Bks.) Harlequin Enterprises, Ltd.
—Plucking the Apple. 1994. 272p. 20.95 o.p. (*0-312-11326-9*) St. Martin's Pr.
Palmer, Elizabeth, contrib. by. Plucking the Apple. 1999. (*0-7540-1300-6*) BBC Audiobooks America.
Palmer, William J. The Hoydens & Mr. Dickens. 1996. 256p. 21.95 o.p. (*0-312-15145-4*) St. Martin's Pr.
Parks, Tim. Loving Roger. 1987. 160p. 15.95 o.p. (*0-8021-0016-3*) Grove/Atlantic, Inc.
—Loving Roger. 1989. 160p. pap. 6.95 o.p. (*0-14-011459-9*, Penguin Bks.) Viking Penguin.
Parsons, Tony. Man & Wife. 2004. 368p. pap. 13.00 (*0-7432-3614-9*, Touchstone); 2003. 352p. 23.00 (*0-7434-5665-3*, Atria) Simon & Schuster.
—One for My Baby. 2001. 330p. (*0-00-712614-X*); (*0-00-226182-0*) HarperCollins Pubs.
—One for My Baby. 2005. 336p. pap. 12.00 (*0-7432-3609-2*, Touchstone) Simon & Schuster.
Paston, George. A Writer of Books. 1999. 258p. 35.00 (*0-89733-466-3*); pap. 15.95 (*0-89733-465-5*) Academy Chicago Pubs., Ltd.
Paton Walsh, Jill & Sayers, Dorothy L. A Presumption of Death. unabr. ed. 2003. (Lord Peter Wimsey Mystery Ser.). audio 29.95 (*1-57270-322-9*); audio compact disk 34.95 (*1-57270-323-7*) Audio Partners Publishing Corp. (Audio Editions Mystery Masters).
—A Presumption of Death. 2003. audio 69.95 (*0-7540-8309-8*); audio compact disk 79.95 (*0-7540-8752-2*) Chivers Audio Bks. GBR. *Dist:* BBC Audiobooks America.
Pearson, Allison. I Don't Know How She Does It: The Life of Kate Reddy, Working Mother. l.t. ed. 2003. 31.95 (*1-58724-401-2*, Wheeler Publishing, Inc.) Gale Group.
—I Don't Know How She Does It: The Life of Kate Reddy, Working Mother. 2003. 352p. pap. 13.95 (*0-375-71375-1*) Knopf, Alfred A. Inc.
—I Don't Know How She Does It: The Life of Kate Reddy, Working Mother. 2002. 352p. 23.00 (*0-375-41405-3*) Random Hse., Inc.
Peck, Richard. London Holiday. 1999. 272p. pap. 14.00 (*0-14-027857-5*) Penguin Group (USA) Inc.
—London Holiday. l.t. ed. 1998. (Basic Ser.). 360p. 28.95 (*0-7862-1635-2*) Thorndike Pr.
Pemberton, Margaret A. The Londoners. l.t. ed. 1996. (Magna Large Print Ser.). 675p. 29.99 (*0-7505-0907-4*) Magna Large Print Bks. GBR. *Dist:* Ulverscroft Large Print Bks., Ltd.
—The Londoners. 2000. 431p. pap. 8.95 (*0-552-14123-2*) Transworld Publishers Ltd. GBR. *Dist:* Trafalgar Square.
Perera, Shyama, contrib. by. Haven't Stopped Dancing Yet. 1999. 248p. pap. (*0-340-72820-5*) Sceptre.
Perriam, Wendy. Devils for a Change. 1990. 480p. 19.95 o.p. (*0-312-04300-7*) St. Martin's Pr.
Perry, Anne. Ashworth Hall. 1998. 384p. mass mkt. 7.50 (*0-449-00086-9*, Fawcett) Ballantine Bks.
—Bedford Square. 2000. 336p. mass mkt. 6.99 (*0-449-00582-8*, Ballantine Bks.); 1995. o.p. (*0-449-90633-7*, Fawcett) Ballantine Bks.
—Bedford Square. l.t. ed. 1999. (Basic Ser.). 571p. 30.95 (*0-7862-2018-X*) Thorndike Pr.
—Belgrave Square. 1993. 384p. mass mkt. 6.99 (*0-449-22227-6*, Fawcett) Ballantine Bks.
—Belgrave Square. 1994. 4.99 o.p. (*0-517-12853-5*) Random Hse. Value Publishing.
—Bethlehem Road. 1991. 320p. mass mkt. 5.99 o.p. (*0-449-45316-2*); mass mkt. 6.99 (*0-449-21914-3*) Ballantine Bks. (Fawcett).
—Bethlehem Road. l.t. ed. 2001. (Dales Large Print Ser.). 464p. pap. (*1-84262-093-2*) Dales Large Print Bks. GBR. *Dist:* Ulverscroft Large Print Canada, Ltd.
—Bethlehem Road. 1990. 17.95 o.p. (*0-312-04266-3*, Saint Martin's Minotaur) St. Martin's Pr.
—Bethlehem Road. l.t. ed. 1993. (Mystery Ser.). 592p. 29.99 o.p. (*0-7089-2939-7*, Ulverscroft) Thorpe, F. A. Pubs. GBR. *Dist:* Ulverscroft Large Print Bks., Ltd., Ulverscroft Large Print Canada, Ltd.
—Bluegate Fields. 1985. 288p. mass mkt. 5.99 o.p. (*0-449-45317-0*); mass mkt. 6.99 (*0-449-20766-8*) Ballantine Bks. (Fawcett).
—Bluegate Fields. l.t. ed. 2000. 398p. lib. bdg. 28.95 (*1-58547-017-1*) Ctr. Point Large Print.
—Bluegate Fields. l.t. ed. 2001. (Magna Large Print Ser.). 384p. (*0-7505-1709-3*) Magna Large Print Bks. GBR. *Dist:* Ulverscroft Large Print Canada, Ltd.
—Bluegate Fields. unabr. ed. 2002. audio 72.00 (*1-4025-3604-6*, Clipper Audio) Recorded Bks., LLC.
—Bluegate Fields. 1984. 320p. 13.95 o.p. (*0-312-08718-7*) St. Martin's Pr.
—A Breach of Promise. (William Monk Novels Ser.). 1999. 384p. mass mkt. 6.99 (*0-8041-1855-8*, Ivy Bks.); 1998. 384p. 25.00 o.s.i (*0-449-90849-6*, Fawcett); 1998. mass mkt. 6.99 (*0-8041-1888-4*, Ivy Bks.) Ballantine Bks.
—A Breach of Promise. abr. ed. 1998. audio 18.00 o.s.i (*0-375-40275-6*, 396111, RH Audio) Random Hse. Audio Publishing Group.
—A Breach of Promise. l.t. ed. 1998. (Basic Ser.). 639p. 29.95 (*0-7862-1465-1*) Thorndike Pr.
—Brunswick Gardens. 1999. 416p. mass mkt. 7.50 (*0-449-00318-3*, Fawcett) Ballantine Bks.
—Brunswick Gardens. l.t. ed. 1998. (Basic Ser.). 656p. 30.95 (*0-7862-1464-3*) Thorndike Pr.
—Cain His Brother. 1996. 416p. mass mkt. 7.50 (*0-8041-1507-9*); mass mkt. 6.99 o.s.i (*0-8041-1504-4*) Ballantine Bks. (Ivy Bks.).
—Cain His Brother. abr. ed. 1997. (William Monk Mystery Ser.). audio 8.99 o.s.i (*0-679-46025-X*, 393145, RH Audio) Random Hse. Audio Publishing Group.
—Cain His Brother. l.t. ed. 1996. (Cloak & Dagger Ser.). 629p. 26.95 (*0-7862-0607-1*) Thorndike Pr.
—Callander Square. 1998. mass mkt. 3.99 o.s.i (*0-449-00461-9*); 1985. 256p. mass mkt. 6.99 (*0-449-20999-7*); 1981. mass mkt. 2.25 o.p. (*0-449-24365-6*) Ballantine Bks. (Fawcett).
—Callander Square. 1980. 10.00 o.p. (*0-312-11430-3*) St. Martin's Pr.
—Callander Square. l.t. ed. 1981. 447p. 12.00 o.p. (*0-7089-0718-0*, Ulverscroft) Thorpe, F. A. Pubs. GBR. *Dist:* Ulverscroft Large Print Bks., Ltd.
—Cardington Crescent. 1988. 304p. reprint ed. mass mkt. 6.99 (*0-449-21442-7*, Fawcett) Ballantine Bks.
—Cardington Crescent. l.t. ed. 2001. 375p. lib. bdg. 28.95 (*1-58547-015-5*) Ctr. Point Large Print.
—Cardington Crescent. unabr. ed. 1998. audio 83.95 (*1-85903-217-6*) Magna Story Sound GBR. *Dist:* Ulverscroft Large Print Bks., Ltd.
—Cardington Crescent. 1987. 304p. 15.95 o.p. (*0-312-00113-4*) St. Martin's Pr.
—The Cater Street Hangman. 1998. mass mkt. 3.99 o.s.i (*0-449-00460-0*); 1985. 288p. mass mkt. 6.99 (*0-449-20867-2*); 1980. mass mkt. 2.25 o.s.i (*0-449-24327-3*) Ballantine Bks. (Fawcett).
—The Cater Street Hangman. l.t. ed. 2000. 364p. lib. bdg. 27.95 (*1-58547-002-3*) Ctr. Point Large Print.
—The Cater Street Hangman. 1979. 8.95 o.p. (*0-312-12385-X*) St. Martin's Pr.
—A Dangerous Mourning. 1992. 352p. mass mkt. 6.99 (*0-8041-1037-9*, Ivy Bks.) Ballantine Bks.
—A Dangerous Mourning. unabr. ed. 1995. (Inspector Monk Ser.: Vol. 2). audio 91.00 (*0-7887-0417-6*, 94609E7) Recorded Bks., LLC.
—Death in the Devil's Acre. 1987. 272p. mass mkt. 6.99 (*0-449-21095-2*, Fawcett) Ballantine Bks.
—Death in the Devil's Acre. l.t. ed. 2001. lib. bdg. 27.95 (*1-58547-016-3*) Ctr. Point Large Print.
—Death in the Devil's Acre. 1985. 288p. 14.95 o.p. (*0-312-18869-2*) St. Martin's Pr.
—Death of a Stranger. 2003. 352p. mass mkt. 7.50 (*0-345-44006-4*); 2002. 352p. 25.95 (*0-345-44005-6*, Ballantine Bks.); 2002. E-Book 18.00 (*0-345-45865-6*, Ballantine Bks.) Ballantine Bks.
—Death of a Stranger. l.t. ed. 2003. (Basic Ser.). 570p. 32.95 (*0-7862-4939-0*) Thorndike Pr.
—Defend & Betray. 1993. 448p. mass mkt. 7.50 (*0-8041-1188-X*, Ivy Bks.); 1992. 18.00 o.p. (*0-449-90555-1*, Fawcett); 1992. 368p. 18.00 o.p. (*0-449-90755-4*, Fawcett) Ballantine Bks.
—Defend & Betray. unabr. ed. 2000. (Inspector Monk Ser.: Vol. 3). audio 97.00 (*0-7887-0403-6*, 94595E7) Recorded Bks., LLC.
—The Face of a Stranger. 1998. mass mkt. 3.99 o.s.i (*0-8041-1885-X*); 1991. 352p. mass mkt. 6.99 (*0-8041-0858-7*) Ballantine Bks. (Ivy Bks.).
—The Face of a Stranger. unabr. ed. 1995. (Inspector Monk Ser.: Vol. 1). audio 78.00 (*0-7887-0321-8*, 94513E7) Recorded Bks., LLC.
—Farriers' Lane. 1994. 432p. mass mkt. 7.50 (*0-449-21961-5*, Fawcett) Ballantine Bks.
—Funeral in Blue. 2001. 352p. 25.00 (*0-345-44001-3*, Ballantine Bks.) Ballantine Bks.
—Funeral in Blue. l.t. ed. 2002. (Basic Ser.). 574p. 30.95 (*0-7862-3640-X*) Gale Group.
—Half Moon Street. 2001. 320p. mass mkt. 6.99 (*0-449-00655-7*, Ballantine Bks.) Ballantine Bks.
—Half Moon Street. l.t. ed. 2000. 439p. 27.95 (*1-56895-857-9*, Wheeler Publishing, Inc.) Gale Group.
—Half Moon Street. abr. ed. 2000. (Charlotte & Thomas Pitt Novel Ser.). audio 18.00 (*0-553-52710-X*, RH Audio) Random Hse. Audio Publishing Group.
—Highgate Rise. 1992. 352p. mass mkt. 7.50 (*0-449-21959-3*, Fawcett) Ballantine Bks.
—Highgate Rise. l.t. ed. 1994. (Ulverscroft Ser.). 672p. 21.95 o.p. (*0-7089-3013-1*, Ulverscroft) Thorpe, F. A. Pubs. GBR. *Dist:* Ulverscroft Large Print Bks., Ltd., Ulverscroft Large Print Canada, Ltd.
—The Hyde Park Headsman. 1995. 352p. mass mkt. 7.50 (*0-449-22350-7*); 1994. 432p. 21.00 o.s.i (*0-449-90636-1*) Ballantine Bks. (Fawcett).
—Paragon Walk. 1986. 256p. mass mkt. 6.99 (*0-449-21168-1*); 1986. mass mkt. 5.99 (*0-449-45319-7*); 1982. mass mkt. 2.50 o.p. (*0-449-20110-4*); 1982. 224p. mass mkt. 2.50 o.p. (*0-449-24497-0*) Ballantine Bks. (Fawcett).
—Paragon Walk. l.t. ed. 2000. 308p. lib. bdg. 27.95 (*1-58547-005-8*) Ctr. Point Large Print.
—Paragon Walk. 1981. 224p. 9.95 o.p. (*0-312-59598-0*) St. Martin's Pr.
—Pentecost Alley. 1997. (Charlotte & Thomas Pitt Novel Ser.). 416p. mass mkt. 6.99 (*0-449-22566-6*, Fawcett) Ballantine Bks.
—Pentecost Alley. l.t. ed. 1996. (Cloak & Dagger Ser.). 708p. 27.95 (*0-7862-0812-0*) Thorndike Pr.
—Resurrection Row. 1986. 224p. mass mkt. 6.99 (*0-449-21067-7*, Fawcett) Ballantine Bks.
—Resurrection Row. l.t. ed. 2000. 312p. lib. bdg. 27.95 (*1-58547-009-0*) Ctr. Point Large Print.
—Resurrection Row. 1981. 224p. 9.95 o.p. (*0-312-67797-9*) St. Martin's Pr.
—Rutland Place. 1986. 224p. mass mkt. 6.99 (*0-449-21285-8*); 1986. 224p. mass mkt. 5.99 o.p. (*0-449-45318-9*); 1984. mass mkt. 2.50 o.p. (*0-449-20474-X*) Ballantine Bks. (Fawcett).
—Rutland Place. l.t. ed. 2000. 319p. lib. bdg. 27.95 (*1-58547-013-9*) Ctr. Point Large Print.
—Rutland Place. 224p. (*0-7278-5864-5*) Severn Hse. Pubs., Ltd.
—Rutland Place. 1983. 256p. 12.95 o.p. (*0-312-69621-3*) St. Martin's Pr.
—Seven Dials. 2004. 352p. mass mkt. 7.50 (*0-345-44008-0*); 2003. 352p. 25.95 (*0-345-44007-2*, Ballantine Bks.); 2003. E-Book 17.85 (*0-345-46352-8*, Ballantine Bks.) Ballantine Bks.
—Seven Dials. 2003. (Basic Ser.). 552p. 32.95 (*0-7862-5210-3*) Thorndike Pr.
—The Silence in Hanover Close. 1989. 352p. mass mkt. 7.50 (*0-449-21686-1*, Fawcett) Ballantine Bks.
—The Silence in Hanover Close. 1988. 384p. 17.95 o.p. (*0-312-01824-X*, Saint Martin's Minotaur) St. Martin's Pr.
—The Silence in Hanover Close. l.t. ed. 1990. (Mystery Ser.). 29.99 o.p. (*0-7089-2324-0*, Ulverscroft) Thorpe, F. A. Pubs. GBR. *Dist:* Ulverscroft Large Print Bks., Ltd., Ulverscroft Large Print Canada, Ltd.
—The Silent Cry. 368p. 1998. (William Monk Novels Ser.: Vol. 8). mass mkt. 6.99 (*0-8041-1793-4*, Ivy Bks.); 1997. 24.95 o.s.i (*0-449-90848-8*, Fawcett) Ballantine Bks.
—The Silent Cry. l.t. ed. 1998. (Basic Ser.). 616p. 30.95 (*0-7862-1301-9*) Thorndike Pr.
—The Sins of the Wolf. 1995. 448p. mass mkt. 6.99 (*0-8041-1383-1*, Ivy Bks.) Ballantine Bks.
—The Sins of the Wolf. unabr. ed. 2000. (Inspector Monk Ser.: Vol. 5). audio 91.00 (*0-7887-0272-6*, 94481E7) Recorded Bks., LLC.
—Southampton Row. 2003. 352p. mass mkt. 7.50 (*0-345-44004-8*); 2002. 336p. 25.00 (*0-345-44003-X*) Ballantine Bks. (Ballantine Bks.).
—Southampton Row. 2002. E-Book 20.00 (*1-4014-9974-0*) Barnes & Noble Digital.
—Southampton Row. abr. ed. (Thomas & Charlotte Pitt Ser.). 2005. audio compact disk 16.99 (*1-59355-704-3*, 5322, Brilliance Audio on CD Value Priced); 2003. audio 12.99 (*1-58788-918-8*, 3436, Brilliance Audio Paperback Audiobooks); 2002. audio 24.95 (*1-58788-915-3*, 3433, Nova Audio Bks.); 2002. audio compact disk 29.95 (*1-58788-916-1*, 3434, CD); 2002. audio compact disk 69.25 (*1-58788-917-X*, 3435, CD Library Edition); 2002. audio 34.95 (*1-58788-913-7*, 3431, Brilliance Audio Unabridged); 2002. audio 89.25 (*1-58788-914-5*, 3432, Unabridged Library Editions) Brilliance Audio.
—Southampton Row. unabr. ed. 2003. (Thomas & Charlotte Pitt Ser.). audio 19.99 (*1-59335-166-6*, 30262) Soulmate Audio Bks., Inc.
—Southampton Row. l.t. ed. 13.95 (*1-4104-0092-1*, Large Print Pr.); 2003. 571p. pap. 27.95 (*0-7862-4502-6*); 2002. 588p. 30.95 (*0-7862-4066-0*) Thorndike Pr.
—A Sudden, Fearful Death. 1994. 464p. mass mkt. 6.99 (*0-8041-1283-5*, Ivy Bks.) Ballantine Bks.
—A Sudden, Fearful Death. unabr. ed. 2000. (Inspector Monk Ser.: Vol. 4). audio 97.00 (*0-7887-0499-0*, 94692E7) Recorded Bks., LLC.
—Traitor's Gate. 1996. 432p. mass mkt. 7.50 (*0-449-22439-2*, Fawcett) Ballantine Bks.
—The Twisted Root. 2000. (William Monk Novels Ser.). 368p. mass mkt. 7.50 (*0-8041-1936-8*, Ballantine Bks.) Ballantine Bks.
—The Twisted Root. l.t. ed. 1999. pap. 25.00 o.p. (*0-7838-8698-5*, Macmillan Reference USA) Gale Group.
—The Twisted Root, Set. abr. ed. 1999. audio 25.00 Highsmith Inc.
—The Twisted Root, Set. abr. ed. 1999. audio 25.00 o.s.i (*0-375-40810-X*, RH Audio) Random Hse. Audio Publishing Group.
—The Twisted Root. l.t. ed. 1999. 496p. 25.00 (*0-375-40857-6*) Random Hse. Large Print.

Settings

—Weighed in the Balance. 1996. mass mkt. 6.99 o.s.i (0-8041-1619-9); 1997. 384p. mass mkt. 7.50 (0-8041-1562-1) Ballantine Bks. (Ivy Bks.).
—The Whitechapel Conspiracy. unabr. ed. 2003. 10p. audio 84.95 (0-7540-0858-4, CAB 2280); audio compact disk 99.95 (0-7540-5597-3, CCD 288) BBC Audiobooks America.
—The Whitechapel Conspiracy. 2002. (Thomas & Charlotte Pitt Ser.). 352p. reprint ed. mass mkt. 6.99 (0-449-00656-5, Ballantine Bks.) Ballantine Bks.
—The Whitechapel Conspiracy. l.t. ed. 2001. 515p. 31.95 (0-7838-9513-5, Macmillan Reference USA) Gale Group.
—The Whitechapel Conspiracy. abr. ed. 2001. audio 25.95 (0-553-52789-4, RH Audio) Random Hse. Audio Publishing Group.
Peters, Elizabeth, pseud. The Deeds of the Disturber. 2000. (Amelia Peabody Mystery Ser.: No. 5). 400p. mass mkt. 7.50 (0-380-73195-9, Avon Bks.) Morrow/Avon.
—The Deeds of the Disturber. 1988. (Amelia Peabody Mystery Ser.: No. 5). 320p. 16.95 o.s.i (0-689-11907-0, Scribner) Simon & Schuster.
—The Deeds of the Disturber. 1989. (Amelia Peabody Mystery Ser.: No. 5). 304p. mass mkt. 5.99 (0-446-35333-7) Warner Bks., Inc.
Petit, Chris. Robinson. 1994. 208p. 20.95 o.p. (0-670-84925-1, Viking) Viking Penguin.
Phillips, Mike. Blood Rights. 1990. 208p. reprint ed. mass mkt. 3.95 o.s.i (0-440-20702-9) Dell Publishing.
—Blood Rights. 1989. 15.95 o.p. (0-312-02874-1, Saint Martin's Minotaur) St. Martin's Pr.
—Image to Die For: A Sam Dean Mystery. 1997. 239p. 22.95 o.p. (0-312-15147-0, Saint Martin's Minotaur) St. Martin's Pr.
—The Late Candidate. 1991. 320p. mass mkt. 3.99 o.s.i (0-440-20942-0) Dell Publishing.
—The Late Candidate. 1990. 256p. 17.95 o.p. (0-312-04866-1, Saint Martin's Minotaur) St. Martin's Pr.
Pianka, Phyllis T. Heather Wild. l.t. ed. 1990. pap. 17.95 o.p. (0-7927-0395-2, C0482); 19.95 o.p. (0-7927-0394-4, C0254) BBC Audiobooks America.
Plaidy, Jean. Beyond the Blue Mountains. 1981. 480p. mass mkt. 2.95 o.s.i (0-449-24451-2, Fawcett) Ballantine Bks.
Plante, David. Annunciation. 1994. 346p. 21.95 o.p. (0-395-68091-3) Houghton Mifflin Co.
Porter, Margaret E. Toast of the Town. l.t. ed. 2001. 395p. (Orig.). 27.95 (0-7862-3345-1) Thorndike Pr.
Priestley, J. B. Angel Pavement. 1983. (Phoenix Fiction Ser.). iv, 494p. pap. 8.95 o.s.i (0-226-68210-2) Univ. of Chicago Pr.
Prince, Maggie. The House on Hound Hill. (YA). 2003. 256p. (gr. 5). pap. 6.95 (0-618-33124-7); 1998. 242p. (gr. 7-9). tchr. ed. 16.00 (0-395-90702-0) Houghton Mifflin Co.
Prince, Peter. Bubbles. 2000. 246p. (0-7475-4917-6) Bloomsbury Pr.
Pritchard, Melissa. Selene of the Spirits. 1998. 217p. 22.00 (0-86538-094-5) Ontario Review Pr.
Putney, Mary Jo. Silk & Shadows. l.t. ed. 2001. (Large Print Bks.). 555p. 28.95 o.p. (1-56895-132-9, Wheeler Publishing, Inc.) Gale Group.
—Silk & Shadows. 432p. 2000. mass mkt. 6.99 (0-451-20206-6, Signet Bks.); 1991. mass mkt. 6.99 o.s.i (0-451-40277-4, Onyx) NAL.
Pye, Frances. Sharing Sean: A Novel. 2004. 480p. (0-06-054556-9, Morrow, William & Co.) Morrow/Avon.
Pykare, Nina Coombs. Death Rides a Pink Horse. 2001. (First Edition Romance Ser.). 183p. 25.95 (0-7862-3108-4, Five Star) Gale Group.
Pym, Barbara. Less Than Angels. 1981. 256p. 13.95 o.p. (0-525-14440-4, Dutton) Dutton/Plume.
—Less Than Angels. l.t. ed. 1986. (General Ser.). 432p. 15.95 o.p. (0-8161-3842-7, Macmillan Reference USA) Gale Group.
—Less Than Angels. 1987. 256p. pap. 6.95 o.p. (0-06-097117-7, Perennial) HarperTrade.
—An Unsuitable Attachment. 1982. 224p. 13.95 o.p. (0-525-24117-5, Dutton) Dutton/Plume.
—An Unsuitable Attachment. 256p. 1983. mass mkt. o.p. (0-06-080653-2, P 653); 1986. reprint ed. pap. 7.95 o.p. (0-06-097055-3, PL/7055) HarperTrade. (Perennial).
—An Unsuitable Attachment. unabr. ed. 1996. audio 61.95 (1-85695-687-3, 89116) ISIS Audio Bks. GBR. *Dist:* Ulverscroft Large Print Bks., Ltd.
Queen, Ellery. A Study in Terror. l.t. ed. 2001. 192p. pap. 24.95 (0-7838-9485-6, Macmillan Reference USA) Gale Group.
Quick, Amanda, pseud. Slightly Shady. l.t. ed. 2001. (Large Print Book Ser.). 391p. 31.95 (1-58724-026-2, Wheeler Publishing, Inc.) Gale Group.
—Wicked Widow. abr. ed. 2000. audio 18.00 (0-553-52682-0, RH Audio) Random Hse. Audio Publishing Group.
—Wicked Widow. l.t. ed. 2001. pap. 29.95 (0-7862-2598-X); 2000. 453p. 31.95 (0-7862-2596-3) Thorndike Pr.
Rabley, Stephen. Dino's Day in London. 2002. (Illus.). 16p. pap. (0-582-40281-6) Penguin Putnam Bks. for Young Readers.
Raison, Jennifer & Goldie, Michael. Caraboo: The Servant Girl Princess: The Real Story of the Grand Hoax. 1995. (Illus.). 220p. pap. 13.95 (1-56656-179-5) Interlink Publishing Group, Inc.
Randall, Charlotte. The Curative. 2000. 264p. pap. (0-14-029753-7) Penguin Group (USA) Inc.
Ransome, Arthur. Bohemia in London. 1984. (Oxford Paperbacks Ser.). (Illus.). pap. 5.95 o.p. (0-19-281412-5) Oxford Univ. Pr., Inc.
Rayner, Claire. First Blood. l.t. ed. 1995. (Charnwood Large Print Ser.). 480p. 29.99 o.p. (0-7089-8825-3, Charnwood) Thorpe, F. A. Pubs. GBR. *Dist:* Ulverscroft Large Print Bks., Ltd., Ulverscroft Large Print Canada, Ltd.
—Fourth Attempt. l.t. ed. 1997. (Charnwood Large Print Ser.). 496p. 29.99 o.p. (0-7089-8975-6, Ulverscroft) Thorpe, F. A. Pubs. GBR. *Dist:* Ulverscroft Large Print Bks., Ltd., Ulverscroft Large Print Canada, Ltd.
—Second Opinion. unabr. ed. 1995. audio 84.95 (0-7451-6539-7, CAB 1155) BBC Audiobooks America.
—Second Opinion. l.t. ed. 1996. (Charnwood Large Print Ser.). 528p. 29.99 o.p. (0-7089-8897-0, Ulverscroft) Thorpe, F. A. Pubs. GBR. *Dist:* Ulverscroft Large Print Bks., Ltd., Ulverscroft Large Print Canada, Ltd.
Redfern, Elizabeth. Auriel Rising. 2004. 400p. 24.95 (0-399-15105-2) Putnam Publishing Group, The.
—The Music of the Spheres. 2001. 400p. 24.95 o.p. (0-399-14763-2, Putnam & Grosset) Penguin Group (USA) Inc.
—The Music of the Spheres. abr. ed. 2001. audio 26.00 (0-7435-0781-9); audio compact disk 32.00 (0-7435-0782-7) Simon & Schuster Audio. (Simon & Schuster Audioworks).
Rees, Emlyn & Lloyd, Josie. Come Together: A Novel. 1999. 304p. 21.95 o.s.i (0-375-50232-7, Villard Bks.) Random House Adult Trade Publishing Group.
Renault, Mary. The Friendly Young Ladies. 2003. 304p. pap. 13.00 (0-375-71421-9, Vintage) Knopf Publishing Group.
Rendell, Ruth. Adam & Eve & Pinch Me. 2003. 368p. pap. 13.00 (1-4000-3118-4, Vintage) Knopf Publishing Group.
—Adam & Eve & Pinch Me. l.t. ed. 2002. 604p. 29.95 (0-7862-3815-1) Thorndike Pr.
—Going Wrong. l.t. ed. 1992. pap. 15.95 o.p. (0-7927-0822-9); 302p. 19.95 o.p. (0-7927-0821-0, E0016) BBC Audiobooks America.
—Going Wrong. 1991. 272p. mass mkt. 6.99 (0-7704-2435-X) Bantam Bks.
—Going Wrong. unabr. collector's ed. 1991. audio 48.00 (0-7366-1920-8, 2744) Books on Tape, Inc.
—Going Wrong. 1990. 256p. 24.95 o.p. (0-385-25281-1) Doubleday Publishing.
—Going Wrong. 1990. 304p. 18.95 o.p. (0-89296-389-1) Mysterious Pr.
—Going Wrong. 1993. 3.99 o.p. (0-517-09872-5) Random Hse. Value Publishing.
—Going Wrong. 1991. mass mkt. 4.99 o.s.i (0-446-40028-9) Warner Bks., Inc.
—The Keys to the Street. 1997. 400p. mass mkt. 8.99 (0-7704-2760-X) Bantam Bks.
—The Keys to the Street. 1997. 384p. mass mkt. 6.50 (0-440-22392-X) Dell Publishing.
—The Keys to the Street. l.t. ed. 1996. 576p. pap. 24.00 o.p. (0-7838-1917-X) Random Hse. Large Print.
—The Killing Doll. 1985. 288p. mass mkt. 4.95 o.s.i (0-345-31199-X) Ballantine Bks.
—The Killing Doll. l.t. ed. 1984. (General Ser.). 354p. 15.95 o.p. (0-8161-3720-X, Macmillan Reference USA) Gale Group.
—The Killing Doll. 1984. 258p. 12.95 o.s.i (0-394-53097-7, Pantheon) Knopf Publishing Group.
—One Across, Two Down. 2001. 192p. pap. 11.00 (0-375-70494-9, Vintage) Knopf Publishing Group.
Richards, Ben. The Silver River. 1998. 310p. (0-7472-7567-X) Review.
Richmond, Grace. The Doctor's Secret. l.t. ed. 1994. 19.95 o.p. (0-7927-1911-5); pap. 17.95 o.p. (0-7927-1910-7) BBC Audiobooks America.
Riddell, Marjorie. M for Mother. 2000. (Illus.). 173p. pap. 12.95 (0-552-99747-1) Transworld Publishers Ltd. GBR. *Dist:* Trafalgar Square.
Ridpath, Michael. Free to Trade: A Novel of Suspense. 1994. 346p. 23.00 o.p. (0-06-017630-X) HarperTrade.
—The Marketmaker. 1998. 342p. (0-7181-4316-7); pap. (0-7181-4317-5) Joseph, Michael Ltd. GBR. *Dist:* Trafalgar Square.
Ripley, Mike. Angel City. 1995. 192p. 18.95 o.p. (0-312-11742-6, Saint Martin's Minotaur) St. Martin's Pr.
Rizzolo, S. K. The Rose in the Wheel. 2003. 226p. pap. 14.95 o.s.i (1-890208-89-2) Poisoned Pen Pr.
Roberts, Michele. The Mistressclass. 2003. 304p. 23.00 (0-8050-7440-6) Holt, Henry & Co.
Robins, Madeline E. Point of Honour. 2003. (Sarah Tolerance Ser.). 352p. 24.95 (0-312-87202-X, Tor Bks.) Doherty, Tom Assocs., LLC.
Robinson, Randall. The Debt: What America Owes to Blacks. 2001. 272p. pap. 13.00 (0-452-28210-1) Dutton/Plume.
Robinson, Suzanne. Just Before Midnight. 2000. (Meet Me at Midnight Ser.). 336p. mass mkt. 5.99 o.s.i (0-553-57961-4) Bantam Bks.
—The Rescue. 1998. 304p. pap. 19.00 (0-553-76274-5); mass mkt. 5.99 (0-553-56347-5) Bantam Bks.
Roffey, Monique. August Frost. 2003. 24.00 (0-87113-869-7, Atlantic Monthly Pr.) Grove/Atlantic, Inc.
Rogers, Evelyn. Raven. 1995. 384p. mass mkt. 4.99 o.s.i (0-8217-4800-9, Zebra Bks.) Kensington Publishing Corp.
Rogers, James. Savage Life. 1998. 262p. pap. 12.99 o.p. (1-85242-384-6) Serpent's Tail Ltd. GBR. *Dist:* Consortium Bk. Sales & Distribution.
Rogow, Roberta. The Problem of the Evil Editor: A Charles Dodgson/Arthur Conan Doyle Mystery. 2000. (Charles Dodgson/Arthur Conan Doyle Mysteries Ser.). 298p. 23.95 (0-312-20903-7, Saint Martin's Minotaur) St. Martin's Pr.
Rolfe, Lionel. Death & Redemption in London & LA. 2000. E-Book 10.99 (1-929429-59-2); E-Book 10.99 (1-929429-60-6) Dead End Street, LLC.
Romkey, Michael. The London Vampire Panic. 2001. 304p. mass mkt. 6.99 (0-449-00573-9) Ballantine Bks.
Ross, Kate. A Broken Vessel. 1995. (Crime Ser.). 304p. pap. 6.99 (0-14-023453-5, Penguin Bks.) Penguin Group (USA) Inc.
—A Broken Vessel. 1994. (Julian Kestrel Mystery Ser.). 304p. 18.95 o.p. (0-670-84999-5, Viking) Viking Penguin.
—Cut to the Quick. 1994. (Crime Ser.). 352p. pap. 6.99 (0-14-023394-6, Penguin Bks.) Penguin Group (USA) Inc.
—Cut to the Quick. 1993. 352p. 19.00 o.p. (0-670-84847-6, Viking) Viking Penguin.
—The Devil in Music. 1998. (Julian Kestrel Mystery Ser.). 480p. pap. 6.99 (0-14-026364-0) Penguin Group (USA) Inc.
—The Devil in Music. 1997. (Julian Kestrel Mystery Ser.). 464p. 24.95 o.s.i (0-670-86359-9) Viking Penguin.
—Whom the Gods Love. 1996. (Julian Kestrel Mystery Ser.). 400p. pap. 6.99 (0-14-024767-X, Penguin Bks.) Penguin Group (USA) Inc.
—Whom the Gods Love. 1995. (Julian Kestrel Mystery Ser.). 400p. 20.95 o.p. (0-670-86207-X, Viking) Viking Penguin.
Roth, Philip. The Professor of Desire. 1977. 263p. 8.95 o.p. (0-374-23756-5) Farrar, Straus & Giroux.
—The Professor of Desire. 1994. 272p. pap. 13.00 (0-679-74900-4, Vintage) Knopf Publishing Group.
Roy, Lucinda. Lady Moses: A Novel. 1998. 400p. 24.00 o.s.i (0-06-018244-X) HarperCollins Pubs.
—Lady Moses: A Novel. 1998. 400p. pap. 13.00 (0-06-093084-5, Perennial) HarperTrade.
Royle, Nicholas. The Matter of the Heart. 1998. 256p. pap. o.s.i (0-349-10956-7) Little Brown & Co.
Rushdie, Salman. The Satanic Verses. 1992. 546p. pap. 14.00 (0-9632707-0-2) Consortium, Inc.
—The Satanic Verses. 1997. 576p. pap. 16.00 o.s.i (0-8050-5309-3, Owl Bks.) Holt, Henry & Co.
—The Satanic Verses. 2000. 576p. pap. 16.00 (0-312-27082-8) Picador.
—The Satanic Verses. 1989. 496p. 27.95 (0-670-82537-9) Viking Penguin.
Rutherfurd, Edward. London. 1152p. 2002. pap. 18.95 (0-345-45568-1); 1998. mass mkt. 7.99 (0-449-00263-2, Fawcett) Ballantine Bks.
Sagastizabal, Patricia. A Secret for Julia: A Novel. Zatz, Asa, tr. from SPA. 2001. 256p. 23.95 (0-393-05044-0) Norton, W. W. & Co., Inc.
Samson, Polly. Out of the Picture. 2002. 256p. (Orig.). pap. 12.00 (1-86049-864-7) Virago Pr., Ltd. GBR. *Dist:* Trafalgar Square.
Sanderson, Mark. Audacious Perversion. 1999. 236p. pap. 14.95 (1-899344-32-2) DuFour, Howard.
Satterthwait, Walter. Escapade. 1996. 355p. mass mkt. 5.99 (0-312-95920-6, St. Martin's Paperbacks); 1995. 336p. 22.95 o.p. (0-312-13068-6, Saint Martin's Minotaur) St. Martin's Pr.
Saunders, Kate. The Marrying Game: A Novel. 2003. 384p. 24.95 (0-312-31043-9) St. Martin's Pr.
Sayers, Dorothy L. A Presumption of Death. Date not set. mass mkt. (0-312-99138-X, St. Martin's Paperbacks) St. Martin's Pr.
Sayers, Dorothy L. & Paton Walsh, Jill. A Presumption of Death. 2003. (Lord Peter Wimsey Mystery Ser.). 384p. 24.95 (0-312-29100-0, Saint Martin's Minotaur) St. Martin's Pr.
Scholefield, Alan. Night Child. 1993. 256p. 19.95 o.p. (0-312-08863-9, Saint Martin's Minotaur) St. Martin's Pr.
—Night Child. l.t. ed. 1994. (Ulverscroft Large Print Ser.). 480p. 29.99 o.p. (0-7089-3082-4, Ulverscroft) Thorpe, F. A. Pubs. GBR. *Dist:* Ulverscroft Large Print Bks., Ltd., Ulverscroft Large Print Canada, Ltd.
Self, Will. Dorian. 2004. 288p. pap. 13.00 (0-8021-4047-5, Grove Pr.) Grove/Atlantic, Inc.
—How the Dead Live. 2001. 416p. pap. 13.00 (0-8021-3848-9); 2000. 404p. 24.00 o.p. (0-8021-1671-X, Grove Pr.) Grove/Atlantic, Inc.
Selvon, Samuel. The Lonely Londoners. 1989. (Longman Caribbean Writers Ser.). 141p. (C). pap. 16.00 (0-582-64264-7, TG7161) Longman Publishing Group.
—The Lonely Londoners. 1991. pap. (0-920661-16-5) TSAR Pubns.
Selwyn, Francis. Sergeant Verity & the Imperial Diamond. 1976. 252p. 7.95 o.p. (0-8128-1917-9); No. 1. 1984. 256p. pap. 2.95 o.p. (0-8128-8038-2) Madison Bks., Inc. (Scarborough Hse.).
—Sergeant Verity Presents His Compliments. 1977. 7.95 o.p. (0-8128-2148-3, Scarborough Hse.) Madison Bks., Inc.
Seth, Vikram. An Equal Music. abr. ed. 1999. audio 25.00 o.s.i (0-553-52636-7, RH Audio) Random Hse. Audio Publishing Group.
—An Equal Music. unabr. ed. 2000. audio 102.00 (0-7887-4493-3, H1080E7, Clipper Audio) Recorded Bks., LLC.
—An Equal Music: A Novel. 2000. (International Ser.). 400p. pap. 14.00 (0-375-70924-X, Vintage) Knopf Publishing Group.
Seymour, Gerald. The Running Target. 1991. 592p. mass mkt. 4.95 o.p. (0-06-100143-0, Perennial) HarperTrade.
—The Running Target. 1990. 19.95 o.p. (0-688-05201-0, Morrow, William & Co.) Morrow/Avon.
Shakespeare, L. M. Question of Risk. 1990. 17.95 o.p. (0-312-04407-0, Saint Martin's Minotaur) St. Martin's Pr.
Shamsie, Kamila. Kartography. 2002. (Illus.). 352p. pap. (0-7475-5730-6) Bloomsbury Pr.
—Kartography. 320p. 2004. pap. (0-15-602973-1, Harvest Bks.); 2003. 24.00 (0-15-101010-2) Harcourt Trade Pubs.
—Kartography. 2002. 343p. (0-19-579833-3) Oxford Univ. Pr., Inc.
Shaw, Simon. The Company of Knaves. 1997. (Philip Fletcher Mystery Ser.). 224p. 22.95 (0-312-18069-1, Saint Martin's Minotaur) St. Martin's Pr.
—Dead for a Ducat. 1996. 224p. 20.95 o.p. (0-312-14309-5, Saint Martin's Minotaur) St. Martin's Pr.
—Murder Out of Tune. unabr. ed. 1993. audio 54.95 (0-7451-4094-7, CAB 782) BBC Audiobooks America.
—Murder Out of Tune. 1992. 256p. mass mkt. 4.50 o.s.i (0-553-29592-6) Bantam Bks.
—Murder Out of Tune. 1988. 192p. o.s.i (0-385-24602-1) Doubleday Publishing.
—The Villain of the Earth. 1995. 189p. 19.95 o.p. (0-312-13201-8, Saint Martin's Minotaur) St. Martin's Pr.
Sherrod, Barbara. The Players. 2001. (Five Star Romance Ser.). 248p. 26.95 (0-7862-3709-0, Five Star) Gale Group.
—The Players. 1989. 256p. mass mkt. 3.95 (0-446-35870-3) Warner Bks., Inc.
Sherwood, John. A Bouquet of Thorns. 1991. mass mkt. 3.95 o.s.i (0-345-36525-9) Ballantine Bks.
—A Bouquet of Thorns. 1989. 224p. 16.95 o.s.i (0-684-19091-5, Macmillan Reference USA) Gale Group.
—Creeping Jenny: A Celia Grant Mystery. 1993. 256p. 20.00 o.p. (0-684-19613-1, Macmillan Reference USA) Gale Group.
—Flowers of Evil. 1990. 224p. mass mkt. 3.95 o.s.i (0-345-35342-0) Ballantine Bks.
—Flowers of Evil. 1988. (Celia Grant Mystery Ser.). 204p. 14.95 o.p. (0-684-18867-8, Macmillan Reference USA) Gale Group.
—Flowers of Evil. l.t. ed. 1989. (Ulverscroft Large Print Ser.). 379p. 29.99 o.p. (0-7089-1980-4, Ulverscroft) Thorpe, F. A. Pubs. GBR. *Dist:* Ulverscroft Large Print Bks., Ltd., Ulverscroft Large Print Canada, Ltd.
—Green Trigger Finger. 1986. 176p. mass mkt. 2.95 o.s.i (0-345-32890-6) Ballantine Bks.
—The Mantrap Garden. 1987. 192p. mass mkt. 2.95 o.s.i (0-345-34306-9) Ballantine Bks.
—The Mantrap Garden. 1986. 224p. 13.95 o.p. (0-684-18726-4, Macmillan Reference USA) Gale Group.
—The Mantrap Garden. l.t. ed. 1990. (Magna Large Print Ser.). 327p. o.p. (1-85057-560-6) Magna Large Print Bks. GBR. *Dist:* Ulverscroft Large Print Canada, Ltd.
—A Shot in the Arm: Death at the BBC. 1983. 176p. 12.95 o.s.i (0-684-17990-3, Macmillan Reference USA) Gale Group.
—A Shot in the Arm: Death at the BBC. 1985. 172p. pap. 4.95 (0-930330-25-0) International Polygonics, Ltd.
—The Sunflower Plot. l.t. ed. 1992. 18.95 o.p. (0-7451-8332-8); pap. 16.95 o.p. (0-7927-1018-5) BBC Audiobooks America.
—The Sunflower Plot. 1991. 256p. 18.95 o.s.i (0-684-19270-5, Scribner) Simon & Schuster.

Shirley, Edna I. As I Like It: A Tale of Shakespeare & His Associates. 1996. 196p. pap. 16.95 o.p. (1-85756-295-X) Janus Publishing Co. GBR. Dist: Paul & Co. Pubs. Consortium, Inc.
Shreve, Anita. The Pilot's Wife. l.t. ed. 2001. pap. 11.95 (1-56895-146-9); 1998. 337p. 27.95 (1-56895-686-X) Gale Group. (Wheeler Publishing, Inc.).
—The Pilot's Wife. (Oprah's Book Club Selection Ser. ). 2001. 320p. mass mkt. 7.99 (0-316-78822-8); 2000. 304p. pap. 7.99 (0-316-78915-1); 1999. 320p. pap. 13.95 (0-316-78990-9); 1999. 23.95 (0-316-60194-2); 1998. 304p. 23.95 o.p. (0-316-78908-9); 1999. 304p. reprint ed. pap. 13.95 (0-316-60195-0, Back Bay) Little Brown & Co.
—The Pilot's Wife. 1999. 19.75 (0-606-19029-5) Turtleback Bks.
Sigerson, Davitt. Faithful: A Novel. 2004. 224p. 23.95 (0-385-51050-0, Talese, Nan A.) Doubleday Publishing.
Silva, Daniel. The Unlikely Spy. 2000. mass mkt. 6.99 (0-449-45938-1); 1998. 544p. mass mkt. 7.99 o.s.i (0-449-00264-0) Ballantine Bks. (Fawcett).
—The Unlikely Spy. 2003. 544p. mass mkt. 7.99 (0-451-20930-3, Signet Bks.) NAL.
Simmons, Steven J. Percy to the Rescue. 1998. (Illus.). 32p. (J). (ps-3). 15.95 (0-88106-390-8, Talewinds) Charlesbridge Publishing, Inc.
Sims, Ruth. The Phoenix. 2004. pap. 16.95 (1-932133-40-2); 2003. E-Book 7.50 (0-9716734-6-2) Writers' Collective, The.
Sinclair, Ian & McKean, Dave. Slow Chocolate Autopsy: Incidents from the Notorious Career of Norton, Prisoner of London. 1997. (Illus.). 240p. (1-86159-088-1) Phoenix Hse.
Sizemore, Susan. The Price of Innocence. 1999. 384p. mass mkt. 5.99 (0-380-80418-2, Avon Bks.) Morrow/Avon.
Skinner, Melynda Beth. Lord Logic & the Wedding Wish. 2003. (Zebra Regency Romance Ser.). 256p. mass mkt. 4.99 (0-8217-7419-0) Kensington Publishing Corp.
Slaughter, Carolyn. The Banquet. 1984. 192p. 13.95 o.p. (0-89919-274-2) Houghton Mifflin Co.
—The Banquet. 1987. 208p. pap. 4.95 o.p. (0-14-006662-4, Penguin Bks.) Viking Penguin.
Slovo, Gillian. Catnap. 1996. 288p. 23.95 o.p. (0-312-14561-6, Saint Martin's Minotaur) St. Martin's Pr.
—Catnap. 1995. 276p. pap. o.s.i (1-85381-815-1) Virago Pr., Ltd. GBR. Dist: Little Brown & Co.
—Close Call: A Kate Baeier Mystery. 1996. 314p. mass mkt. o.s.i (1-85381-816-X) Virago Pr., Ltd. GBR. Dist: Little Brown & Co.
—Death Comes Staccato. 1988. 12.95 o.s.i (0-385-24609-9) Doubleday Publishing.
Smith, Barbara Dawson. Never a Lady. 1996. 338p. mass mkt. 6.99 (0-312-95936-2, St. Martin's Paperbacks) St. Martin's Pr.
Smith, Carol. Friends for Life. 480p. 2001. pap. 4.95 (0-446-52004-7); 1997. mass mkt. 6.50 (0-446-60445-3) Warner Bks., Inc.
—The Neighbors. 2001. 512p. mass mkt. 7.50 o.s.i (0-446-60926-9); 496p. E-Book 14.95 (0-446-96032-2); 496p. E-Book 14.95 (0-446-91463-0) Warner Bks., Inc.
Smith, Joan. Kissing Cousins. 1995. mass mkt. 4.50 o.s.i (0-449-22381-7, Fawcett) Ballantine Bks.
—Murder & Misdeeds. 1997. mass mkt. 4.50 o.s.i (0-449-28791-2, Fawcett) Ballantine Bks.
—Murder Comes to Mind. 1998. mass mkt. 4.99 o.s.i (0-449-00287-X, Fawcett) Ballantine Bks.
—Murder While I Smile. 1997. mass mkt. 4.99 o.s.i (0-449-22494-5, Fawcett) Ballantine Bks.
—Murder Will Speak. 1997. mass mkt. 4.50 o.s.i (0-449-22465-1, Fawcett) Ballantine Bks.
—Murder Will Speak. 1996. 208p. 21.95 o.p. (0-312-14378-8, Saint Martin's Minotaur) St. Martin's Pr.
Smith, Kathryn. For the First Time. 2003. 384p. mass mkt. 5.99 (0-06-052741-2, Avon Bks.) Morrow/ Avon.
Smith, Stevie. Novel on Yellow Paper. 1994. (Revived Modern Classic Ser.: Vol. 778). 256p. reprint ed. pap. 10.95 (0-8112-1239-4, NDP778) New Directions Publishing Corp.
Smith, Zadie. White Teeth. E-Book 19.95 (1-58945-566-5) Adobe Systems, Inc.
—White Teeth. l.t. ed. 2000. 717p. 28.95 o.p. (1-56895-950-8, Wheeler Publishing, Inc.) Gale Group.
—White Teeth. 2001. E-Book 19.95 (0-375-50561-X) Random Hse., Inc.
—White Teeth, 14 cass. 2002. audio 39.99 (1-4025-0218-4, 00634) Recorded Bks., LLC.
—White Teeth: A Novel. 2001. (International Ser.). 464p. reprint ed. pap. 14.00 (0-375-70386-1, Vintage) Knopf Publishing Group.
—White Teeth: A Novel. 2000. (Illus.). 464p. 24.95 (0-375-50185-1) Random Hse., Inc.
Sole, Linda. Bridget. 2002. 256p. 26.99 (0-7278-5868-8) Severn Hse. Pubs., Ltd.
Solmssen, Arthur R. G. The Wife of Shore: A Search. 2000. (Illus.). vi, 284p. (Orig.). pap. 20.00 (0-9705336-0-8) Mill Creek Pr.
Solomon, Andrew. A Stone Boat. 1996. 256p. pap. 13.00 (0-452-27498-2, Plume) Dutton/Plume.
—A Stone Boat. 1994. 288p. 22.95 o.p. (0-571-17240-7) Faber & Faber, Inc.
Spark, Muriel. The Ballad of Peckham Rye. 1990. pap. 7.95 (0-380-70936-8, Avon Bks.) Morrow/Avon.
—The Ballad of Peckham Rye. 1999. (Classics Ser.). 143p. reprint ed. pap. 11.95 (0-8112-1408-7, NDP877) New Directions Publishing Corp.
—The Ballad of Peckham Rye. 1982. 208p. pap. 5.95 o.p. (0-399-50650-0) Putnam Publishing Group, The.
—A Far Cry from Kensington. 1988. 192p. 17.95 o.p. (0-395-47694-1) Houghton Mifflin Co.
—A Far Cry from Kensington. 1990. 192p. pap. 7.95 (0-380-70786-1, Avon Bks.) Morrow/Avon.
—A Far Cry from Kensington. 2000. (Classics Ser.). 189p. pap. 12.95 (0-8112-1457-5) New Directions Publishing Corp.
—A Far Cry from Kensington. 1990. 3.99 o.p. (0-517-05284-9) Random Hse. Value Publishing.
—The Girls of Slender Means. l.t. ed. 1986. (Mainstream Ser.). 148p. reprint ed. lib. bdg. 15.50 o.p. (1-85089-053-6) ISIS Large Print Bks. GBR. Dist: Transaction Pubs.
—The Girls of Slender Means. 1990. 128p. pap. 7.95 (0-380-70937-6, Avon Bks.) Morrow/Avon.
—The Girls of Slender Means. 1998. (Classics Ser.). 144p. pap. 10.95 (0-8112-1379-X, NDP859) New Directions Publishing Corp.
—The Girls of Slender Means. 1982. 192p. pap. 5.95 o.p. (0-399-50659-4) Putnam Publishing Group, The.
—The Girls of Slender Means. 1963. 4.95 o.p. (0-394-42637-1, Knopf Bks. for Young Readers) Random Hse. Children's Bks.
—Memento Mori. 1990. pap. 9.00 o.p. (0-380-70938-4, Avon Bks.) Morrow/Avon.
—Memento Mori. 2000. (Classics Ser.). 228p. pap. 11.95 (0-8112-1438-9) New Directions Publishing Corp.
—Memento Mori. 1982. 224p. pap. 8.95 o.p. (0-399-50665-9) Putnam Publishing Group, The.
Spencer, Sally. Murder at Swann's Lake. l.t. ed. 2000. (Dales Large Print Ser.). 400p. pap. 20.99 o.p. (1-84137-001-0) Magna Large Print Bks. GBR. Dist: Ulverscroft Large Print Bks., Ltd.
—Murder at Swann's Lake. 1999. 224p. 25.00 (0-7278-2285-3) Severn Hse. Pubs., Ltd.
St. John, Madeleine. A Pure Clear Light. 2000. 240p. 22.00 (0-7867-0756-9, Carroll & Graf Pubs.) Avalon Publishing Group.
—A Pure Clear Light. 1996. 233p. (1-85702-387-0) Fourth Estate, Ltd.
—A Stairway to Paradise. 1999. 185p. 22.00 o.p. (0-7867-0662-7); 2000. 192p. reprint ed. pap. 11.95 (0-7867-0795-X) Avalon Publishing Group. (Carroll & Graf Pubs.).
—A Stairway to Paradise. 1999. 185p. pap. (1-85702-881-3) Fourth Estate, Ltd.
Stableford, Brian M. The Werewolves of London. 1992. 392p. 21.00 o.p. (0-88184-916-2, Carroll & Graf Pubs.) Avalon Publishing Group.
—Year Zero. 2003. 335p. pap. 13.95 (1-4104-0156-1, Five Star Trade); 314p. 25.95 (0-7862-5333-9, Five Star) Gale Group.
Staples, Mary Jane. Changing Times. 2002. (Illus.). 384p. 29.95 o.s.i (0-593-05098-3) Bantam Bks.
—Changing Times. 2002. (Illus.). 384p. pap. (0-552-15046-0) Black Swan GBR. Dist: Random Hse. of Canada, Ltd.
—Changing Times. l.t. ed. 2003. (Magna Large Print Ser.). 432p. (0-7505-2003-5) Magna Large Print Bks. GBR. Dist: Ulverscroft Large Print Canada, Ltd.
Starling, Boris. Messiah. 1999. 464p. mass mkt. 7.50 (0-451-40900-0, Onyx) NAL.
Steel, Danielle. The Kiss. 2001. 360p. 26.95 (0-385-33540-7, Delacorte Pr.) Dell Publishing.
Stevens, Rosemary. Miss Pembroke's Rules. 2003. (Cats of Mayfair Ser.). 186p. 25.95 (0-7862-5151-4, Five Star) Gale Group.
Stevenson, Jane. London Bridges. 2001. 304p. 24.00 (0-618-04934-7) Houghton Mifflin Co.
Stevenson, Robert Louis. Dr. Jekyll & Mr. Hyde. (Illus.). lib. bdg. 19.95 (0-88411-994-7, Aeonian Pr.) Amereon, Ltd.
—Dr. Jekyll & Mr. Hyde. 1987. (Running Press Classics Ser.). 63p. pap. 2.95 o.p. (0-89471-491-0); lib. bdg. 12.90 o.p. (0-89471-492-9) Running Pr. Bk. Pubs.
—Dr. Jekyll & Mr. Hyde. 1998. 135p. text 27.95 (1-56000-517-3) Transaction Pubs.
—Dr. Jekyll & Mr. Hyde & Other Stories. Calder, Jenni, ed. & intro. by. 1980. (Penguin English Library). 304p. pap. 6.95 o.s.i (0-14-043117-9, Penguin Classics) Viking Penguin.
—Dr. Jekyll & Mr. Hyde & Weir of Hermiston. Letley, Emma, ed. & intro. by. 1987. (Oxford World's Classics Ser.). 256p. pap. 5.95 o.p. (0-19-281740-X) Oxford Univ. Pr., Inc.
—The Strange Case of Dr. Jekyll & Mr. Hyde. 1991. (Dover Thrift Editions Ser.). 64p. pap. 1.00 (0-486-26688-5) Dover Pubns., Inc.
—The Strange Case of Dr. Jekyll & Mr. Hyde. Qualls, Barry V., ed. & intro. by. 1995. 144p. mass mkt. 3.99 (0-671-53210-3, Pocket) Simon & Schuster.
—The Strange Case of Dr. Jekyll & Mr. Hyde. 1990. (Illus.). 164p. reprint ed. 25.00 o.p. (0-8032-4212-3) Univ. of Nebraska Pr.
Stirling. Drums of Time. 1979. 12.95 o.p. (0-312-22019-7) St. Martin's Pr.
Stirling, Jessica. The Gates of Midnight. 1983. 256p. 13.95 o.p. (0-312-31763-8) St. Martin's Pr.
Struther. Mrs. Miniver. 1989. xxi, 153p. o.s.i (1-85381-090-8) Virago Pr., Ltd. GBR. Dist: Little Brown & Co.
Struther, Jan. Mrs. Miniver. 23.95 (0-88411-677-8) Amereon, Ltd.
—Mrs. Miniver. 1990. reprint ed. lib. bdg. 19.95 (0-89968-554-4) Buccaneer Bks., Inc.
—Mrs. Miniver. l.t. ed. 2001. 175p. 28.95 (0-7838-9635-2, Hall, G. K. & Co.) Gale Group.
—Mrs. Miniver. 1990. 162p. pap. 8.95 (0-15-663140-7); 1966. pap. 0.50 o.p. (0-15-663138-5) Harcourt Trade Pubs. (Harvest Bks.).
—Mrs. Miniver. 1985. 320p. reprint ed. mass mkt. 3.95 o.p. (0-06-080761-X, P 761, Perennial) Harper-Trade.
—Mrs. Miniver. l.t. ed. 1991. 145p. 21.95 o.p. (1-85089-364-0) ISIS Large Print Bks. GBR. Dist: Transaction Pubs.
Stuart, Anne. Prince of Swords. 1997. (Romance Ser.). 270p. lib. bdg. 22.95 (0-7862-1116-4, Five Star) Gale Group.
—Prince of Swords. 1996. 384p. mass mkt. 5.99 o.s.i (0-8217-5397-5, Zebra Bks.) Kensington Publishing Corp.
Sturtevant, Katherine. A Mistress Moderately Fair. 1988. 249p. (Orig.). pap. 8.95 o.p. (1-55583-137-0) Alyson Pubns.
Summerson, Rachel. Belgrave Square. 1981. 300p. 11.95 o.p. (0-312-07427-1) St. Martin's Pr.
Sutcliffe, William. The Love Hexagon. 2000. 224p. pap. 12.00 o.s.i (0-14-029609-3) Penguin Group (USA) Inc.
—The Love Hexagon. 2000. 215p. pap. (0-241-14066-8, Hamilton, Hamish) Viking Penguin.
Sutherland, Luke. Sweetmeat. 2002. 448p. pap. (0-552-99920-2) Black Swan GBR. Dist: Random Hse. of Canada, Ltd.
—Sweetmeat. 2002. 384p. pap. (0-385-60232-4) Doubleday Publishing.
Sweeney, Eamonn. Waiting for the Healer. 1999. 320p. pap. 13.00 (0-312-20046-3); 1998. 308p. 23.00 (0-312-18206-6) Picador.
Swift, Graham. Shuttlecock. 1992. 220p. pap. 11.00 (0-679-73933-5, Vintage) Knopf Publishing Group.
Syal, Meera. Life Isn't All Ha Ha Hee Hee. 2000. 336p. text 22.95 (1-56584-614-1) New Pr., The.
Tambling, Jeremy, ed. Bleak House: Charles Dickens. 1998. (New Casebooks Ser.). 272p. 59.95 (0-312-21120-1) Palgrave Macmillan.
Taylor, Andrew. The Four Last Things. 1997. (Roth Trilogy Ser.: Vol. 1). 304p. 22.95 (0-312-16845-4, Saint Martin's Minotaur) St. Martin's Pr.
—Judgement of Strangers. pap. 14.95 (0-312-28730-5, Saint Martin's Griffin); 1998. (Roth Trilogy Ser.: Vol. 2). 304p. 22.95 o.p. (0-312-19292-4, Saint Martin's Minotaur) St. Martin's Pr.
—The Office of the Dead. 2000. (Roth Trilogy Ser.: Vol. 3). 352p. 24.95 (0-312-20348-9, Saint Martin's Minotaur) St. Martin's Pr.
—An Unpardonable Crime. abr. ed. 2004. audio 25.98 (1-4013-9802-2) Hyperion Pr.
Taylor, Domini. Teacher's Pet. 1989. mass mkt. 3.95 o.s.i (0-515-10029-3, Jove) Berkley Publishing Group.
—Teacher's Pet. 1987. 288p. 18.95 o.p. (0-689-11933-X, Scribner) Simon & Schuster.
Tel, Jonathan. Freud's Alphabet. 2003. 192p. text 24.00 (1-58243-219-8, Counterpoint Pr.) Basic Bks.
Templeton, Edith. Gordon. 2003. 240p. 22.00 (0-375-42194-7, Pantheon) Knopf Publishing Group.
—Gordon: A Novel. 2004. 240p. pap. 13.00 (1-4000-3029-3, Vintage) Knopf Publishing Group.
Tessaro, Kathleen. Elegance. 2004. 352p. pap. 10.95 (0-06-052227-5, Avon Bks.); 2003. 320p. 23.95 (0-06-052225-9, Morrow, William & Co.) Morrow/ Avon.
Tey, Josephine. The Man in the Queue. l.t. ed. 2000. (Mystery Ser.). 392p. 26.95 o.p. (0-7862-2345-6) Thorndike Pr.
Theroux, Marcel. A Stranger in the Earth. 288p. 2001. pap. 13.00 (0-15-601195-6); 1999. 23.00 o.s.i (0-15-100408-0) Harcourt Trade Pubs. (Harvest Bks.).
Theroux, Paul. The Family Arsenal. 1977. mass mkt. 2.25 o.s.i (0-345-25751-0) Ballantine Bks.
—The Family Arsenal, 001. 1976. 8.95 o.p. (0-395-24400-5) Houghton Mifflin Co.
—The Family Arsenal. 1996. 288p. pap. 14.00 (0-14-004465-5, Penguin Bks.) Penguin Group (USA) Inc.
—The Family Arsenal. 1984. mass mkt. 4.95 o.s.i (0-671-49824-X, Pocket) Simon & Schuster.
—Half Moon Street. 1984. 14.95 o.p. (0-395-36511-2) Houghton Mifflin Co.
—My Other Life. 1996. 448p. 24.95 o.p. (0-395-82527-X) Houghton Mifflin Co.
—My Other Life. 1997. 464p. pap. 15.00 (0-395-87752-0, Mariner Bks.) Houghton Mifflin Co. Trade & Reference Div.
—My Other Life. 1996. 488p. 33.99 (0-7710-8575-3) McClelland & Stewart/Tundra Bks.
—My Other Life. abr. ed. 1996. 24.95 o.p. (0-7871-1126-0); 12p. pap. 49.95 o.p. (0-7871-1127-9, 134321) NewStar Media, Inc.
—My Other Life. 1999. text 22.95 (0-670-86583-4) Viking Penguin.
Thirlwell, Adam. Politics. 2003. 288p. 22.95 (0-00-716366-5, Fourth Estate) HarperTrade.
Thoene, Jake. The Mystery of the Yellow Hands. 1997. (Baker Street Ser.: Vol. 1). pap. 5.99 o.p. (0-8499-4005-2) W Publishing Group.
Thoene, Jake & Thoene, Luke. The Mystery of the Yellow Hands. 1995. (Baker Street Brigade Ser.: No. 1). 160p. pap. 5.99 o.s.i (0-345-39561-1, Ballantine Bks.) Ballantine Bks.
Thomas, D. M. Pictures at an Exhibition. 1994. 278p. pap. 10.95 (0-7867-0147-1, Carroll & Graf Pubs.) Avalon Publishing Group.
—Pictures at an Exhibition. 1993. (Robert Stewart Bk.). 272p. 22.00 o.p. (0-684-19586-0, Scribner) Simon & Schuster.
Thomas, Graham. Malice in London: An Erskine Powell Mystery. 2000. (Erskine Powell Mysteries Ser.). 240p. mass mkt. 6.50 (0-8041-1840-X, Fawcett) Ballantine Bks.
Thomas, Jerry D. Detective Zack Trapped in Darkmoor Manor. 1997. (Detective Zack Ser.: Vol. 9). (J). pap. 6.99 (0-8163-1394-6) Pacific Pr. Publishing Assn.
Thomas, Rosie. Bad Girls, Good Women. 1990. 688p. mass mkt. 5.95 o.s.i (0-553-28394-4) Bantam Bks.
—Strangers. 1987. 324p. 17.45 o.s.i (0-671-62875-5, Simon & Schuster) Simon & Schuster.
Thomas, Ross. Voodoo, Ltd. l.t. ed. 1993. (General Ser.). 367p. lib. bdg. 21.95 (0-8161-5679-4, Macmillan Reference USA) Gale Group.
—Voodoo, Ltd. 1992. 288p. 19.95 (0-89296-451-0) Mysterious Pr.
—Voodoo, Ltd., unabr. ed. 1993. (Durant & Wu Ser.). audio 51.00 (1-55690-785-0, 93105E7) Recorded Bks., LLC.
—Voodoo, Ltd. 1993. 320p. mass mkt. 5.99 (0-446-40030-0, Mysterious Pr. Paperback Bks.) Warner Bks., Inc.
Thompson, Brian. Ladder of Angels. 1999. (Slow Dancer Crime Ser.). 237p. (Orig.). pap. 14.95 (1-871033-48-9) Slow Dancer Pr. GBR. Dist: Dufour Editions, Inc.
Thompson, Kate. Down among the Gods. 1997. 281p. (1-86049-349-1) Virago Pr., Ltd.
Thomson, June. The Secret Documents of Sherlock Holmes. 1999. 233p. mass mkt. (0-7490-0407-X) Allison & Busby, Ltd. GBR. Dist: International Publishers Marketing.
Todd, Charles. A Fearsome Doubt: An Inspector Ian Rutledge Mystery. 2003. 384p. mass mkt. 6.99 (0-553-58317-4); 2002. 304p. 24.95 (0-553-80180-5); 2002. E-Book 19.99 (0-553-89709-8) Bantam Bks.
—Search the Dark. unabr. ed. 2001. audio compact disk 94.00 (1-84197-099-9, C1144E7); 1999. audio 79.00 (1-84197-039-5, H1039E7) Recorded Bks., LLC. (Clipper Audio).
—Search the Dark. E-Book 5.99 (0-312-26467-4); 1999. 336p. 24.95 o.p. (0-312-20000-5, Saint Martin's Minotaur) St. Martin's Pr.
—A Test of Wills. l.t. ed. 1998. 336p. mass mkt. 6.99 (0-553-57759-X) Bantam Bks.
—A Test of Wills. unabr. ed. 1999. audio compact disk 81.00 (1-84197-092-1, C1128E7, Clipper Audio); audio 71.00 (1-84197-006-9, H1006E7);Set. audio 71.00 Recorded Bks., LLC.
—A Test of Wills. 4th l.t. ed. 1996. 320p. 22.95 o.p. (0-312-14431-8, Saint Martin's Minotaur) St. Martin's Pr.
—A Test of Wills. l.t. ed. 1997. (Mystery Ser.). 416p. lib. bdg. 25.95 o.p. (0-7838-2023-2) Thorndike Pr.
—Wings of Fire. unabr. ed. 1999. audio 71.00 (1-84197-023-9, H1023E7);Set. audio 71.00 Recorded Bks., LLC.
—Wings of Fire. 1999. (Wings of Fire Ser.: Vol. 1). 320p. mass mkt. 6.99 (0-312-96568-0, St. Martin's Paperbacks); 1999. E-Book 23.95 (0-312-20751-4); 1998. (Inspector Ian Rutledge Mysteries Ser.). 294p. (gr. 5 up). 23.95 (0-312-17064-5, Saint Martin's Minotaur) St. Martin's Pr.
Tolkien, Simon. Final Witness: A Novel. 2002. 304p. 24.95 (0-375-50882-1) Random Hse., Inc.

Settings

Tonkin, Peter. One Head Too Many. 2002. (Master of Defence Ser.). 288p. 26.99 (*0-7278-5724-X*) Severn Hse. Pubs., Ltd.

Townsend, Sue. Number Ten. 2003. 288p. 24.00 (*1-56947-349-8*) Soho Pr., Inc.

Treadwell, Lawrence P. The Bulldog Drummond Encyclopedia. 2001. (Illus.). 223p. lib. bdg. 45.00 (*0-7864-0769-7*) McFarland & Co., Inc. Pubs.

Trevor, William. Miss Gomez & the Brethren. 1997. 256p. pap. 11.95 (*0-14-025264-9*, Penguin Bks.) Penguin Group (USA) Inc.

Trollope, Anthony. Can You Forgive Her? 1994. (Everyman's Library). 960p. 23.00 (*0-679-43595-6*) Knopf, Alfred A. Inc.

—Can You Forgive Her? Swarbrick, Andrew, ed. (Palliser Novels Ser.). (Illus.). 1991. 928p. 21.00 o.p. (*0-19-520895-1*); 1984. 916p. pap. 8.95 o.p. (*0-19-281585-7*) Oxford Univ. Pr., Inc.

—Can You Forgive Her? Wall, Stephen, ed. 1975. (English Library). 848p. 11.95 (*0-14-043086-5*, Penguin Classics) Viking Penguin.

—The Duke's Children. 1991. (Palliser Novels Ser.). (Illus.). 704p. 21.00 o.p. (*0-19-520900-1*) Oxford Univ. Pr., Inc.

—The Duke's Children. Lee, Hermione, ed. 1984. (Oxford World's Classics Ser.). (Illus.). 704p. pap. 6.95 o.p. (*0-19-281586-5*) Oxford Univ. Pr., Inc.

—The Duke's Children. Birch, Dinah, ed. & intro. by. 1996. (Penguin Classics Ser.). 560p. pap. 10.95 o.p. (*0-14-043344-9*) Viking Penguin.

—The Eustace Diamonds. unabr. ed. Pt. 1. 1994. audio 53.95 (*1-55685-313-0*); Pt. 2. 1999. audio 59.95 Audio Bk. Contractors, Inc.

—The Eustace Diamonds. unabr. ed. (Palliser Novels: Vol. 3). audio 124.95 o.p. (*1-85549-938-X*, CTC 129) BBC Audiobooks America.

—The Eustace Diamonds, Pt. 1. unabr. collector's ed. 1993. audio 72.00 (*0-7366-2638-7*, 3377-A ) Books on Tape, Inc.

—The Eustace Diamonds, 3. reprint ed. lib. bdg. 294.00 (*0-7426-2468-4*); 2001. pap. text 84.00 (*0-7426-7468-1*) Classic Bks.

—The Eustace Diamonds. 1992. (Everyman's Library). 20.00 (*0-679-41745-1*) Knopf, Alfred A. Inc.

—The Eustace Diamonds. McCormack, W. J., ed. (Palliser Novels Ser.). (Illus.). 1991. 830p. 21.00 (*0-19-520897-8*); 1984. 818p. pap. 7.95 o.p. (*0-19-281588-1*) Oxford Univ. Pr., Inc.

—The Eustace Diamonds. 1973. pap. 5.95 o.p. (*0-19-281145-2*); 1968. (Oxford World's Classics Ser.: No. 357). 15.95 o.p. (*0-19-250357-X*) Oxford Univ. Pr., Inc.

—The Eustace Diamonds. McCormack, W. J., ed. & intro. by. 1998. (Oxford World's Classics Ser.). (Illus.). 832p. reprint ed. pap. 8.95 (*0-19-283466-5*) Oxford Univ. Pr., Inc.

—The Eustace Diamonds. (Trollope Ser.). 1994. 624p. pap. 8.95 o.p. (*0-14-043832-7*); 1976. lib. bdg. 14.95 (*0-89968-140-9*) Viking Penguin. (Penguin Classics).

—The Eustace Diamonds. Gillers, Stephen & Sutherland, John, eds. 1969. (Penguin English Library). 784p. pap. 10.00 (*0-14-043041-5*, Penguin Classics) Viking Penguin.

—Phineas Finn. unabr. ed. 1993. audio 101.95 (*1-55685-267-3*) Audio Bk. Contractors, Inc.

—Phineas Finn. unabr. ed. audio 114.95 o.p. (*1-85549-937-1*, CTC 102) BBC Audiobooks America.

—Phineas Finn. unabr. ed. 2000. audio 99.95 (*0-7861-1782-6*, 2581) Blackstone Audio Bks., Inc.

—Phineas Finn, Pt. 1. unabr. collector's ed. 1994. audio 72.00 (*0-7366-2618-2*, 3359-A) Books on Tape, Inc.

—Phineas Finn. 1973. pap. 5.95 o.p. (*0-19-281144-4*); 1968. 17.95 o.p. (*0-19-250447-9*) Oxford Univ. Pr., Inc.

—Phineas Finn. MacCormack, Bill, ed. 1997. (Everyman Paperback Classics Ser.). (Illus.). 432p. pap. 6.95 (*0-460-87497-7*, Everyman's Classic Library in Paperback) Tuttle Publishing.

—Phineas Finn. Sutherland, John, ed. 1975. (Penguin Classics Ser.). 752p. pap. 8.95 o.p. (*0-14-043085-7*, Penguin Classics) Viking Penguin.

—Phineas Finn: The Irish Member, 2. reprint ed. lib. bdg. 98.00 (*0-7426-2460-9*); 2001. pap. text 28.00 (*0-7426-7460-6*) Classic Bks.

—Phineas Finn: The Irish Member. 1991. (Palliser Novels Ser.). (Illus.). 323p. 21.00 o.p. (*0-19-520896-X*) Oxford Univ. Pr., Inc.

—Phineas Finn: The Irish Member. Berthoud, Jacques, ed. 1984. (Oxford World's Classics Ser.). (Illus.). 776p. pap. 6.95 o.p. (*0-19-281587-3*) Oxford Univ. Pr., Inc.

—Phineas Finn: The Irish Member. Berthoud, Jacques, ed. & intro. by. 1999. (Oxford World's Classics Ser.). (Illus.). 776p. reprint ed. pap. 7.95 (*0-19-283533-5*) Oxford Univ. Pr., Inc.

—Phineas Finn: The Irish Member. 1994. (Trollope Ser.). 688p. pap. 8.95 o.p. (*0-14-043825-4*, Penguin Classics) Viking Penguin.

—Phineas Redux. unabr. ed. Pt. 1. 1994. audio 59.95 (*1-55685-312-2*); Pt. 2. 1999. audio 59.95 Audio Bk. Contractors, Inc.

—Phineas Redux. unabr. ed. (Palliser Novels: Vol. 4). audio 114.95 o.p. (*1-85549-939-8*, CTC 130) BBC Audiobooks America.

—Phineas Redux, Pt. 1. unabr. collector's ed. 1994. audio 72.00 (*0-7366-2790-1*, 3506-A) Books on Tape, Inc.

—Phineas Redux, 2. reprint ed. lib. bdg. 196.00 (*0-7426-2471-4*); 2001. pap. text 56.00 (*0-7426-7471-1*) Classic Bks.

—Phineas Redux. 2002. (Oxford World's Classics Ser.). (Illus.). 768p. pap. 8.95 (*0-19-283559-9*) Oxford Univ. Pr., Inc.

—Phineas Redux. Whale, John C., ed. (Palliser Novels Ser.). (Illus.). 1991. 784p. 21.00 o.p. (*0-19-520898-6*); 1984. 768p. pap. 7.95 o.p. (*0-19-281589-X*) Oxford Univ. Pr., Inc.

—Phineas Redux. 1968. (Oxford World's Classics Ser.: No. 450). 14.95 o.p. (*0-19-250450-9*) Oxford Univ. Pr., Inc.

—Phineas Redux. 1994. (Trollope Ser.). 896p. pap. 8.95 o.s.i (*0-14-043833-5*) Penguin Group (USA) Inc.

—Phineas Redux. 2003. (Illus.). 688p. pap. 11.00 (*0-14-043762-2*, Penguin Classics) Viking Penguin.

—The Prime Minister. Uglow, Jennifer, ed. (Palliser Novels Ser.). (Illus.). 1991. 864p. 21.00 o.p. (*0-19-520899-4*); 1984. 852p. pap. 8.95 o.p. (*0-19-281590-3*) Oxford Univ. Pr., Inc.

—The Prime Minister. Skilton, David, ed. & intro. by. 1996. (Classics Ser.). 736p. 14.00 (*0-14-043349-X*, Penguin Classics) Viking Penguin.

—The Three Clerks. 1981. 497p. reprint ed. pap. 8.95 (*0-486-24099-1*) Dover Pubns., Inc.

—The Three Clerks. Handley, Graham, ed. 1990. (Oxford World's Classics Ser.). (Illus.). 646p. pap. 9.95 o.p. (*0-19-281829-5*) Oxford Univ. Pr., Inc.

Trollope, Joanna. Girl from the South. 2003. 352p. pap. 14.00 (*0-425-19350-0*) Berkley Publishing Group.

—Girl from the South. 2002. 304p. 24.95 (*0-670-03097-X*, Viking) Viking Penguin.

Trow, M. J. The Adventures of Inspector Lestrade. (Lestrade Mysteries Ser.: Vol. 1). 2000. 224p. pap. 9.95 (*0-89526-291-6*); 1998. 208p. 19.95 (*0-89526-343-2*) Regnery Publishing, Inc., An Eagle Publishing Co. (Gateway Editions).

—Brigade: The Further Adventures of Lestrade. (Lestrade Mystery Ser.: Vol. 2). 2000. 219p. pap. 9.95 (*0-89526-290-8*); 1998. 208p. 19.95 (*0-89526-342-4*) Regnery Publishing, Inc., An Eagle Publishing Co. (Gateway Editions).

—Lestrade & the Brother of Death. 1999. (Lestrade Mysteries Ser.: Vol. 7). 224p. 19.95 (*0-89526-268-1*) Regnery Publishing, Inc., An Eagle Publishing Co.

—Lestrade & the Dead Man's Hand. 2000. (Gateway Mystery Ser.: Vol. XI). 237p. 19.95 (*0-89526-288-6*, Gateway Editions) Regnery Publishing, Inc., An Eagle Publishing Co.

—Lestrade & the Deadly Game. 1999. (Lestrade Mysteries Ser.: Vol. 5). 224p. 19.95 (*0-89526-312-2*, Gateway Editions) Regnery Publishing, Inc., An Eagle Publishing Co.

—Lestrade & the Devil's Own. 2001. (Lestrade Mystery Ser.: Vol. 16). 190p. 19.95 (*0-89526-215-0*) Regnery Publishing, Inc., An Eagle Publishing Co.

—Lestrade & the Gift of the Prince. 2000. (Lestrade Mysteries Ser.). 208p. 19.95 (*0-89526-253-3*, Gateway Editions) Regnery Publishing, Inc., An Eagle Publishing Co.

—Lestrade & the Guardian Angel. 1999. (Lestrade Mysteries Ser.: Vol. 8). 240p. 19.95 (*0-89526-267-3*) Regnery Publishing, Inc., An Eagle Publishing Co.

—Lestrade & the Hallowed House. 208p. 2001. (Lestrade Mystery Ser.). pap. 12.95 (*0-89526-213-4*); 1999. (Lestrade Mysteries Ser.: Vol. 3). 19.95 (*0-89526-341-6*, Gateway Editions) Regnery Publishing, Inc., An Eagle Publishing Co.

—Lestrade & the Leviathan. 1999. (Lestrade Mysteries Ser.: Vol. 4). 208p. 19.95 (*0-89526-340-8*, Gateway Editions) Regnery Publishing, Inc., An Eagle Publishing Co.

—Lestrade & the Magpie. 2000. (Gateway Mystery Ser.: Vol. X). 224p. 19.95 (*0-89526-289-4*, Gateway Editions) Regnery Publishing, Inc., An Eagle Publishing Co.

—Lestrade & the Mirror of Murder. 2001. (Lestrade Mystery Ser.: Vol. 14). 250p. 19.95 (*0-89526-233-9*) Regnery Publishing, Inc., An Eagle Publishing Co.

—Lestrade & the Ripper. 1999. (Lestrade Mysteries Ser.: Vol. 6). 287p. 19.95 (*0-89526-311-4*, Gateway Editions) Regnery Publishing, Inc., An Eagle Publishing Co.

—Lestrade & the Sawdust Ring. 2000. (Lestrade Mystery Ser.: Vol. 13). 224p. 19.95 (*0-89526-245-2*, Gateway Editions) Regnery Publishing, Inc., An Eagle Publishing Co.

—Lestrade & the Sign of Nine. 2000. (Lestrade Mystery Ser.: Vol. 12). 224p. 19.95 (*0-89526-246-0*) Regnery Publishing, Inc., An Eagle Publishing Co.

Truman, Margaret. Murder in the CIA. 1999. 6.99 (*0-449-45925-X*); 1988. 320p. reprint ed. mass mkt. 6.99 (*0-449-21275-0*) Ballantine Bks. (Fawcett).

—Murder in the CIA. l.t. ed. 1988. (General Ser.). 412p. 19.95 o.p. (*0-8161-4406-0*); 11.95 o.p. (*0-8161-4407-9*) Gale Group. (Macmillan Reference USA).

—Murder in the CIA. 1993. audio. audio 49.00 (*1-56544-013-7*, 250030) Literate Ear, Inc.

—Murder in the CIA. abr. ed. 1988. audio 16.00 o.s.i (*0-394-57184-3*); Set. 1996. audio 8.99 o.s.i (*0-679-45597-3*, 391229) Random Hse. Audio Publishing Group. (RH Audio).

—Murder in the CIA. unabr. ed. 1991. audio 70.00 (*1-55690-364-2*, 91219E7) Recorded Bks., LLC.

Twain, Mark. The Prince & the Pauper. 1983. mass mkt. 1.95 o.s.i (*0-553-21150-1*, Bantam Classics) Bantam Bks.

—The Prince & the Pauper. 1988. mass mkt. 4.95 (*0-938819-84-4*, Aerie) Doherty, Tom Assocs., LLC.

—The Prince & the Pauper. Exams Unlimited, Inc. Staff, ed. 2002. (Illus.). 245p. (C). reprint ed. cd-rom 6.95 (*1-59132-073-9*) Exams Unlimited, Inc.

—The Prince & the Pauper. Stemach, Jerry, ed. l.t. ed. 2000. (Illus.). 120p. text 50.00 (*1-58702-517-5*); text 65.00 incl. audio, cd-rom (*1-58702-397-0*); text 10.00 (*1-58702-361-X*) Johnston, Don Inc.

—The Prince & the Pauper, Level 2. 2001. pap. 7.93 (*0-582-42179-9*) Longman Publishing Group.

—The Prince & the Pauper. 2002. 224p. mass mkt. 3.95 (*0-451-52835-2*, Signet Classics); 1976. mass mkt. 1.25 o.p. (*0-451-07383-5*, Signet Bks.); 1968. mass mkt. 0.60 o.p. (*0-451-50447-X*, Signet Classics); 1968. mass mkt. 0.50 o.p. (*0-451-50230-2*, Signet Classics); 1964. mass mkt. 1.75 o.p. (*0-451-51407-6*, Signet Classics); 1964. mass mkt. 1.50 o.p. (*0-451-51138-7*, Signet Classics); 1964. mass mkt. 1.25 o.p. (*0-451-50873-4*, Signet Classics); 1964. mass mkt. 0.95 o.p. (*0-451-50739-8*, Signet Classics); 1964. mass mkt. 0.75 o.p. (*0-451-50602-2*, Signet Classics); 1964. mass mkt. 1.95 o.p. (*0-451-51777-6*, Signet Classics) NAL.

Underwood, Michael. Guilty Conscience. 1999. audio 54.95 Soundings, Ltd. GBR. *Dist:* Ulverscroft Large Print Bks., Ltd.

—Guilty Conscience. 1993. 208p. 18.95 o.p. (*0-312-09824-3*, Saint Martin's Minotaur) St. Martin's Pr.

—Guilty Conscience. l.t. ed. 1994. (Ulverscroft Large Print Ser.). 432p. 29.99 o.p. (*0-7089-3103-0*, Ulverscroft) Thorpe, F. A. Pubs. GBR. *Dist:* Ulverscroft Large Print Bks., Ltd., Ulverscroft Large Print Canada, Ltd.

Vickers, Salley. Instances of the Number 3. 2002. E-Book 15.00 (*0-374-70400-7*); E-Book 15.00 (*0-374-70398-1*); E-Book 15.00 o.p. (*0-374-70401-5*); E-Book 15.00 (*0-374-70402-3*); E-Book (*0-374-70403-1*); 320p. 23.00 (*0-374-17702-3*) Farrar, Straus & Giroux.

—Instances of the Number 3. l.t. ed. 2002. (Core Collection). 375p. 30.95 (*0-7862-4492-5*) Thorndike Pr.

—Instances of the Number 3: A Novel. 2003. (Illus.). 320p. pap. 14.00 (*0-312-42112-5*) Picador.

Victor, Cynthia. Consequences. l.t. ed. 2000. (Wheeler Large Print Book Ser.). 435p. 27.95 (*1-56895-904-4*, Wheeler Publishing, Inc.) Gale Group.

—Consequences. 2000. 352p. mass mkt. 6.99 o.s.i (*0-451-40901-9*, Onyx) NAL.

—Consequences. 1989. 320p. mass mkt. 5.50 (*0-671-66886-2*, Pocket) Simon & Schuster.

Vine, Barbara, pseud. Anna's Book. 1994. 384p. mass mkt. 6.99 (*0-451-40549-8*, Onyx) NAL.

—King Solomon's Carpet. l.t. ed. 1992. pap. 15.95 o.p. (*0-7927-1059-2*); 396p. 19.95 o.p. (*0-7927-1058-4*, E0026) BBC Audiobooks America.

—King Solomon's Carpet. 1993. 384p. mass mkt. 5.99 o.s.i (*0-451-40388-6*, Onyx) NAL.

Virtue, Noel. Lady Jean. 2001. 202p. 21.95 (*0-7206-1133-4*) Owen, Peter Ltd. GBR. *Dist:* Dufour Editions, Inc.

Waites, M. Candleland. 2000. 256p. 26.95 (*0-7490-0464-9*) Allison & Busby, Ltd. GBR. *Dist:* International Publishers Marketing.

Wakefield, Hannah. The Price You Pay. 1990. 16.95 o.p. (*0-312-04989-7*, Saint Martin's Minotaur) St. Martin's Pr.

Wakling, Christopher. The Immortal Part: A Novel of Suspense. 2003. 320p. 24.95 (*1-57322-239-9*, Riverhead Bks. (Hardcovers)) Putnam Publishing Group, The.

Walker, Fiona. Between Males. 697p. mass mkt. 13.95 (*0-340-68229-9*); 2000. 560p. 35.00 (*0-340-68228-0*) Hodder & Stoughton, Ltd. GBR. *Dist:* Lubrecht & Cramer, Ltd., Trafalgar Square.

—Snap Happy. 566p. text 35.00 o.p. (*0-340-68226-4*); 1999. mass mkt. 12.00 (*0-340-68227-2*) Hodder & Stoughton, Ltd. GBR. *Dist:* Lubrecht & Cramer, Ltd., Trafalgar Square.

Walker, Robert W. Blind Instinct: A Jessica Coren Novel. 2000. 369p. 21.95 o.s.i (*0-425-17234-1*) Berkley Publishing Group.

Wall, Alan. China. Date not set. (*0-312-32779-X*); pap. (*0-312-32780-3*, St. Martin's Paperbacks); mass mkt. (*0-312-99648-9*, St. Martin's Paperbacks) St. Martin's Pr.

—The Lightning Cage. 1999. 300p. (*0-436-20491-6*) Secker, Martin & Warburg, Ltd.

—The Lightning Cage: A Novel. 2003. 320p. 24.95 (*0-312-28772-0*) St. Martin's Pr.

Waller, Leslie. Embassy. 1988. 432p. pap. text 5.95 o.p. (*0-07-067944-4*); 1987. 256p. 15.95 o.p. (*0-07-067941-X*) McGraw-Hill Cos., The.

Walters, Minette. The Echo. 1998. 368p. mass mkt. 7.99 (*0-515-12256-4*, Jove) Berkley Publishing Group.

—The Echo. l.t. ed. 1997. (Large Print Book Ser.). (Illus.). 449p. 25.95 o.p. (*1-56895-471-9*, Wheeler Publishing, Inc.) Gale Group.

—The Echo. 1998. 424p. mass mkt. 8.99 o.s.i (*0-7710-8754-3*) McClelland & Stewart/Tundra Bks.

—The Echo. 1997. (Illus.). 338p. 23.95 o.s.i (*0-399-14251-7*, G. P. Putnam's Sons) Penguin Group (USA) Inc.

—The Echo. unabr. ed. 1997. audio 70.00 (*0-7887-4044-X*, 96153E7) Recorded Bks., LLC.

—The Shape of Snakes. 2002. 384p. reprint ed. mass mkt. 7.99 (*0-515-13306-X*, Jove) Berkley Publishing Group.

—The Shape of Snakes. l.t. ed. 2002. 27.95 (*1-58724-156-0*, Wheeler Publishing, Inc.) Gale Group.

—The Shape of Snakes. 2001. (Illus.). 352p. 24.95 o.s.i (*0-399-14733-0*) Penguin Group (USA) Inc.

Warady, Phylis A. The Earl's Comeuppance. 1991. 224p. 18.95 (*0-8027-1186-3*) Walker & Co.

Warmington, Mary Jane. Pyramid of Love. l.t. ed. 1997. (Nightingale Ser.). 245p. lib. bdg. 17.95 o.p. (*0-7838-8110-X*, Macmillan Reference USA) Gale Group.

Waters, Sarah. Affinity. 2000. 352p. 24.95 o.s.i (*1-57322-156-2*, Riverhead Bks. (Hardcovers)) Putnam Publishing Group, The.

—Fingersmith. 2002. 592p. pap. 15.00 (*1-57322-972-5*); 352p. 25.95 o.s.i (*1-57322-203-8*) Putnam Publishing Group, The. (Riverhead Bks. (Hardcovers)).

Weldon, Fay. The Bulgari Connection. l.t. ed. 2002. 285p. 29.95 (*0-7862-3857-7*) Gale Group.

—The Bulgari Connection. 2002. 192p. pap. 12.00 (*0-8021-3930-2*, Grove Pr.) Grove/Atlantic, Inc.

—The Bulgari Connection. l.t. ed. 2002. 285p. 29.95 (*0-7540-1733-8*) Thorndike Pr.

—Trouble. 1993. 240p. 21.00 o.p. (*0-670-84148-X*, Viking) Viking Penguin.

Wells, Dee. Jane. 1987. 288p. reprint ed. pap. 7.95 o.p. (*0-06-097078-2*, PL 7078, Perennial) HarperTrade.

Wentworth, Patricia. The Alington Inheritance. 21.95 (*0-88411-730-8*) Amereon, Ltd.

—The Alington Inheritance. unabr. ed. 1992. audio 39.95 (*0-7861-0318-3*, 1279) Blackstone Audio Bks., Inc.

—The Alington Inheritance. 1992. 320p. reprint ed. pap. 8.00 o.p. (*0-06-092297-4*, Perennial) HarperTrade.

—The Alington Inheritance. 1990. 256p. (C). reprint ed. lib. bdg. 19.95 o.p. (*0-8095-9024-7*) Millefleurs.

—The Alington Inheritance. 1996. 272p. mass mkt. 4.99 o.p. (*0-06-104408-3*, HarperTorch) Morrow/Avon.

—The Alington Inheritance. l.t. ed. 1983. (Ulverscroft Large Print Ser.). 448p. 29.99 o.p. (*0-7089-1051-3*, Ulverscroft) Thorpe, F. A. Pubs. GBR. *Dist:* Ulverscroft Large Print Bks., Ltd., Ulverscroft Large Print Canada, Ltd.

—Anna, Where Are You? 21.95 (*0-88411-728-6*) Amereon, Ltd.

—Anna, Where Are You?, unabr. ed. 1992. audio 44.95 (*0-7861-0317-5*, 1278) Blackstone Audio Bks., Inc.

—Anna, Where Are You? (Miss Silver Mystery Ser.). 352p. 1992. pap. 8.00 o.p. (*0-06-092335-0*); 1991. reprint ed. pap. 5.95 o.p. (*0-06-081057-2*) Harper-Trade. (Perennial).

—The Benevent Treasure. 1976. reprint ed. lib. bdg. 23.95 (*0-88411-731-6*) Amereon, Ltd.

—The Benevent Treasure. 1992. 224p. pap. 8.00 o.p. (*0-06-092336-9*); 1990. 256p. reprint ed. mass mkt. 4.95 o.p. (*0-06-081225-7*) HarperTrade. (Perennial).

—The Benevent Treasure. 1996. 288p. mass mkt. 4.99 o.s.i (*0-06-104406-7*, HarperTorch) Morrow/Avon.

—The Benevent Treasure. l.t. ed. 1982. 448p. 15.95 o.p. (*0-7089-0886-1*, Ulverscroft) Thorpe, F. A. Pubs. GBR. *Dist:* Ulverscroft Large Print Bks., Ltd.

—The Brading Collection. 22.95 (*0-88411-729-4*) Amereon, Ltd.

—The Brading Collection. 256p. 1992. pap. 8.00 o.p. (*0-06-092337-7*); 1990. reprint ed. mass mkt. 4.95 o.p. (*0-06-081226-5*) HarperTrade. (Perennial).

—The Brading Collection. l.t. ed. 1978. (Ulverscroft Large Print Ser.). 29.99 o.p. (*0-7089-0108-5*, Ulverscroft) Thorpe, F. A. Pubs. GBR. *Dist:* Ulverscroft Large Print Bks., Ltd., Ulverscroft Large Print Canada, Ltd.
—The Case Is Closed. 22.95 (*0-8488-0326-4*) Amereon, Ltd.
—The Case Is Closed. 1986. 256p. mass mkt. 3.99 o.s.i (*0-446-34471-0*) Warner Bks., Inc.
—The Case of William Smith. 24.95 (*0-88411-746-4*) Amereon, Ltd.
—The Case of William Smith. (Miss Silver Mystery Ser.). 352p. 1992. pap. 8.00 o.p. (*0-06-092340-7*); 1991. reprint ed. pap. 5.95 o.p. (*0-06-081058-0*) HarperTrade. (Perennial).
—The Catherine Wheel. 22.95 (*0-88411-747-2*) Amereon, Ltd.
—The Catherine Wheel. 1991. 352p. reprint ed. pap. 9.00 o.p. (*0-06-097441-9*, Perennial) HarperTrade.
—The Catherine Wheel. l.t. ed. 1977. (Ulverscroft Large Print Ser.). 12.00 o.p. (*0-85456-534-5*, Ulverscroft) Thorpe, F. A. Pubs. GBR. *Dist:* Ulverscroft Large Print Bks., Ltd., Ulverscroft Large Print Canada, Ltd.
—The Chinese Shawl. l.t. ed. 1992. (General Ser.). 305p. lib. bdg. 14.95 o.p. (*0-8161-5314-0*, Macmillan Reference USA) Gale Group.
—The Chinese Shawl. 1996. 272p. mass mkt. 4.99 o.p. (*0-06-104397-4*) HarperCollins Pubs.
—The Chinese Shawl. (Miss Silver Mystery Ser.). 256p. 1992. pap. 8.00 o.p. (*0-06-092339-3*); 1990. reprint ed. 5.95 o.p. (*0-06-081047-5*) HarperTrade. (Perennial).
—The Clock Strikes Twelve. 21.95 (*0-89190-923-0*) Amereon, Ltd.
—The Clock Strikes Twelve. 1996. 288p. mass mkt. 4.99 o.p. (*0-06-104400-8*) HarperCollins Pubs.
—The Clock Strikes Twelve. 1993. 256p. pap. 8.00 o.p. (*0-06-092408-X*, Perennial) HarperTrade.
—The Clock Strikes Twelve. l.t. ed. 1981. (Ulverscroft Large Print Ser.). 424p. o.p. (*0-7089-0604-4*, Ulverscroft) Thorpe, F. A. Pubs. GBR. *Dist:* Ulverscroft Large Print Canada, Ltd.
—The Clock Strikes Twelve. 1988. 295p. mass mkt. 3.95 o.s.i (*0-446-34905-4*) Warner Bks., Inc.
—Danger Point. l.t. ed. 1975. 12.00 o.p. (*0-85456-320-2*, Ulverscroft) Thorpe, F. A. Pubs. GBR. *Dist:* Ulverscroft Large Print Bks., Ltd.
—The Eternity Ring. 22.95 (*0-88411-748-0*) Amereon, Ltd.
—The Eternity Ring. 1991. 336p. reprint ed. pap. 9.00 o.p. (*0-06-097442-7*, Perennial) HarperTrade.
—The Fingerprint. 23.95 (*0-88411-727-8*) Amereon, Ltd.
—The Fingerprint. 1985. 240p. pap. 2.95 o.p. (*0-553-24986-X*) Bantam Bks.
—The Fingerprint. l.t. ed. 1990. (Ulverscroft Large Print Ser.). 29.99 o.p. (*0-7089-2265-1*, Ulverscroft) Thorpe, F. A. Pubs. GBR. *Dist:* Ulverscroft Large Print Bks., Ltd., Ulverscroft Large Print Canada, Ltd.
—The Fingerprint. 1988. 240p. mass mkt. 3.95 o.s.i (*0-446-34859-7*) Warner Bks., Inc.
—The Gazebo. 20.95 (*0-88411-725-1*) Amereon, Ltd.
—The Gazebo. (Miss Silver Mystery Ser.). 304p. 1992. pap. 8.00 o.p. (*0-06-092338-5*); 1990. reprint ed. 5.95 o.p. (*0-06-081048-3*) HarperTrade. (Perennial).
—The Gazebo. 1996. 288p. mass mkt. 4.99 o.p. (*0-06-104405-9*, HarperTorch) Morrow/Avon.
—The Girl in the Cellar. 20.95 (*0-89190-920-6*) Amereon, Ltd.
—The Girl in the Cellar. 1992. 192p. reprint ed. pap. 8.00 o.p. (*0-06-097445-1*, Perennial) HarperTrade.
—Grey Mask. 24.95 (*0-88411-726-X*) Amereon, Ltd.
—Grey Mask. 1996. 272p. mass mkt. 4.99 o.p. (*0-06-104398-2*) HarperCollins Pubs.
—Grey Mask. 1993. 224p. pap. 8.00 o.p. (*0-06-092364-4*, Perennial) HarperTrade.
—Grey Mask. l.t. ed. 1984. 432p. 12.50 o.p. (*0-7089-1221-4*, Ulverscroft) Thorpe, F. A. Pubs. GBR. *Dist:* Ulverscroft Large Print Bks., Ltd.
—Grey Mask. 1986. 256p. mass mkt. 3.95 o.s.i (*0-446-30135-3*) Warner Bks., Inc.
—The Ivory Dagger. 1976. reprint ed. lib. bdg. 21.95 (*0-88411-735-9*) Amereon, Ltd.
—The Ivory Dagger. 1981. 240p. mass mkt. 2.95 o.s.i (*0-553-25128-7*) Bantam Bks.
—The Ivory Dagger. 1992. 352p. reprint ed. pap. 8.00 o.p. (*0-06-092299-0*, Perennial) HarperTrade.
—The Ivory Dagger. 1996. 272p. mass mkt. 4.99 o.s.i (*0-06-104403-2*, HarperTorch) Morrow/Avon.
—The Ivory Dagger. l.t. ed. 1977. 12.00 o.p. (*0-85456-525-6*, Ulverscroft) Thorpe, F. A. Pubs. GBR. *Dist:* Ulverscroft Large Print Bks., Ltd.
—The Key. 1992. 224p. reprint ed. pap. 8.00 o.p. (*0-06-097446-X*, Perennial) HarperTrade.
—Ladies' Bane. 1976. reprint ed. lib. bdg. 21.95 (*0-88411-737-5*) Amereon, Ltd.
—Ladies' Bane. (Miss Silver Mystery Ser.). 1991. 368p. reprint ed. mass mkt. 5.95 o.p. (*0-06-081059-9*); 2nd ed. 1993. 336p. pap. 8.00 o.p. (*0-06-092361-X*) HarperTrade. (Perennial).
—Latter End. 25.95 (*0-89190-924-9*) Amereon, Ltd.
—Latter End. (Miss Silver Mystery Ser.). 272p. 1992. pap. 8.00 o.p. (*0-06-092334-2*); 1990. reprint ed. 5.95 o.p. (*0-06-081049-1*) HarperTrade. (Perennial).
—Latter End. l.t. ed. 1974. (Ulverscroft Large Print Ser.). 29.99 o.p. (*0-85456-252-4*, Ulverscroft) Thorpe, F. A. Pubs. GBR. *Dist:* Ulverscroft Large Print Bks., Ltd., Ulverscroft Large Print Canada, Ltd.
—The Listening Eye. 1976. reprint ed. lib. bdg. 23.95 (*0-88411-738-3*) Amereon, Ltd.
—The Listening Eye. 1985. mass mkt. 2.95 o.s.i (*0-553-24885-5*) Bantam Bks.
—The Listening Eye. l.t. ed. 1981. 405p. o.p. (*0-7089-0661-3*, Ulverscroft) Thorpe, F. A. Pubs.
—The Listening Eye. 1990. mass mkt. 4.50 (*0-446-34857-0*) Warner Bks., Inc.
—Lonesome Road. 1993. 320p. pap. 8.00 o.p. (*0-06-092406-3*, Perennial) HarperTrade.
—Lonesome Road. 1988. 208p. mass mkt. 3.50 o.s.i (*0-446-31466-8*) Warner Bks., Inc.
—Miss Silver Comes to Stay. 22.95 (*0-88411-749-9*) Amereon, Ltd.
—Miss Silver Comes to Stay. 1985. (Mystery Ser.). 208p. mass mkt. 2.95 o.s.i (*0-553-25362-X*) Bantam Bks.
—Miss Silver Comes to Stay. 320p. reprint ed. 1992. pap. 8.00 o.p. (*0-06-092300-8*); 1989. mass mkt. 3.95 o.p. (*0-06-080978-7*, P 978) HarperTrade. (Perennial).
—Miss Silver Comes to Stay. 1996. 288p. mass mkt. 4.99 o.p. (*0-06-104404-0*, HarperTorch) Morrow/Avon.
—Miss Silver Comes to Stay. l.t. ed. 1977. (Ulverscroft Large Print Ser.). 12.00 o.p. (*0-7089-0064-X*, Ulverscroft) Thorpe, F. A. Pubs. GBR. *Dist:* Ulverscroft Large Print Bks., Ltd., Ulverscroft Large Print Canada, Ltd.
—Miss Silver Deals with Death. 21.95 (*0-8488-1218-2*) Amereon, Ltd.
—Miss Silver Deals with Death. 1991. 336p. reprint ed. pap. 8.00 o.p. (*0-06-097443-5*, Perennial) HarperTrade.
—Out of the Past. 21.95 (*0-89190-922-2*) Amereon, Ltd.
—Out of the Past. (Miss Silver Mystery Ser.). 1991. 320p. reprint ed. mass mkt. 5.95 o.p. (*0-06-081060-2*); 2nd ed. 1993. 336p. pap. 8.00 o.p. (*0-06-092363-6*) HarperTrade. (Perennial).
—Out of the Past. l.t. ed. 1974. (Ulverscroft Large Print Ser.). 12.00 o.p. (*0-85456-235-4*, Ulverscroft) Thorpe, F. A. Pubs. GBR. *Dist:* Ulverscroft Large Print Bks., Ltd., Ulverscroft Large Print Canada, Ltd.
—Pilgrim's Rest. 25.95 (*0-88411-721-9*) Amereon, Ltd.
—Pilgrim's Rest. 1993. 256p. pap. 8.00 o.p. (*0-06-092407-1*, Perennial) HarperTrade.
—Pilgrim's Rest. 1996. 288p. mass mkt. 4.99 o.p. (*0-06-104402-4*, HarperTorch) Morrow/Avon.
—Pilgrim's Rest. l.t. ed. 1983. (Ulverscroft Large Print Ser.). 464p. 29.99 o.p. (*0-7089-0938-8*, Ulverscroft) Thorpe, F. A. Pubs. GBR. *Dist:* Ulverscroft Large Print Bks., Ltd., Ulverscroft Large Print Canada, Ltd.
—Pilgrim's Rest. 1988. 240p. mass mkt. 3.50 o.s.i (*0-446-31463-3*) Warner Bks., Inc.
—Poison in the Pen. 1976. reprint ed. lib. bdg. 23.95 (*0-88411-739-1*) Amereon, Ltd.
—Poison in the Pen. 1985. 208p. mass mkt. 2.95 o.s.i (*0-553-25067-1*) Bantam Bks.
—Poison in the Pen, unabr. ed. 1992. audio 39.95 (*0-7861-0320-5*, 752375) Blackstone Audio Bks., Inc.
—Poison in the Pen. l.t. ed. 1991. (Paperback Ser.). 315p. pap. 15.95 o.p. (*0-8161-5137-7*, Macmillan Reference USA) Gale Group.
—Poison in the Pen. 1992. 320p. reprint ed. pap. 8.00 o.p. (*0-06-092302-4*, Perennial) HarperTrade.
—Poison in the Pen. 1990. 352p. (C). reprint ed. lib. bdg. 20.00 o.p. (*0-8095-9025-5*) Millefleurs.
—Poison in the Pen. 1996. 79p. mass mkt. 4.99 o.p. (*0-06-104407-5*, HarperTorch) Morrow/Avon.
—She Came Back. 20.95 (*0-88411-744-8*) Amereon, Ltd.
—She Came Back. 1985. 208p. pap. 2.95 o.p. (*0-553-25173-2*) Bantam Bks.
—She Came Back, unabr. ed. 1993. audio 39.95 (*0-7861-0319-1*, 752406) Blackstone Audio Bks., Inc.
—She Came Back. 1996. 256p. mass mkt. 4.99 o.p. (*0-06-104399-0*) HarperCollins Pubs.
—She Came Back. 1992. 320p. reprint ed. pap. 8.00 o.p. (*0-06-092301-6*, Perennial) HarperTrade.
—The Silent Pool. 1980. reprint ed. lib. bdg. 20.95 (*0-88411-740-5*) Amereon, Ltd.
—The Silent Pool. (Miss Silver Mystery Ser.). 288p. 1992. pap. 8.00 o.p. (*0-06-092333-4*); 1990. reprint ed. 5.95 o.p. (*0-06-081050-5*) HarperTrade. (Perennial).
—The Silent Pool. l.t. ed. 1980. (Ulverscroft Large Print Ser.). 424p. 12.00 o.p. (*0-7089-0549-8*, Ulverscroft) Thorpe, F. A. Pubs. GBR. *Dist:* Ulverscroft Large Print Bks., Ltd., Ulverscroft Large Print Canada, Ltd.
—Spotlight. 22.95 (*0-88411-722-7*) Amereon, Ltd.
—Through the Wall. 22.95 (*0-88411-723-5*) Amereon, Ltd.
—Through the Wall. 1982. 240p. mass mkt. 2.95 o.s.i (*0-553-25255-0*) Bantam Bks.
—Through the Wall, unabr. ed. 1992. audio 44.95 (*0-7861-0321-3*, 892528) Blackstone Audio Bks., Inc.
—Through the Wall. reprint ed. 1992. 368p. pap. 8.00 o.p. (*0-06-092298-2*); 1989. 352p. mass mkt. 3.95 o.p. (*0-06-080979-5*, P979) HarperTrade. (Perennial).
—Through the Wall. l.t. ed. 1988. (Ulverscroft Large Print Ser.). 496p. 29.99 o.p. (*0-7089-1826-3*, Ulverscroft) Thorpe, F. A. Pubs. GBR. *Dist:* Ulverscroft Large Print Bks., Ltd., Ulverscroft Large Print Canada, Ltd.
—The Traveller Returns. 21.95 (*0-89190-921-4*) Amereon, Ltd.
—The Traveller Returns. l.t. ed. 1993. 21.95 o.p. (*0-7927-1638-8*); pap. 19.95 o.p. (*0-7927-1637-X*) BBC Audiobooks America.
—Vanishing Point. 1976. reprint ed. lib. bdg. 22.95 (*0-88411-742-1*) Amereon, Ltd.
—Vanishing Point. 1991. 368p. reprint ed. pap. 8.00 o.p. (*0-06-097444-3*, Perennial) HarperTrade.
—The Watersplash. 1976. reprint ed. lib. bdg. 22.95 (*0-88411-741-3*, 741) Amereon, Ltd.
—The Watersplash. 1994. reprint ed. lib. bdg. 32.95 (*1-56849-359-2*) Buccaneer Bks., Inc.
—The Watersplash. l.t. ed. 1976. o.p. (*0-85456-489-6*, Ulverscroft) Thorpe, F. A. Pubs.
—The Watersplash. 1989. 256p. mass mkt. 4.50 o.s.i (*0-446-35699-9*); 1987. mass mkt. 3.50 (*0-446-34448-6*) Warner Bks., Inc.
—Wicked Uncle. 22.95 (*0-88411-724-3*) Amereon, Ltd.
—Wicked Uncle. 1993. 288p. pap. 8.00 o.p. (*0-06-092362-8*, Perennial) HarperTrade.
—Wicked Uncle. 1996. 288p. mass mkt. 4.99 o.s.i (*0-06-104401-6*, HarperTorch) Morrow/Avon.
—Wicked Uncle. 1986. 272p. mass mkt. 3.99 o.s.i (*0-446-30083-7*) Warner Bks., Inc.
Wesley, Mary. The Camomile Lawn. 1986. 336p. pap. 10.95 o.p. (*0-552-99126-0*) Bantam Bks.
—The Camomile Lawn. 1990. (King Penguin Ser.). 336p. pap. 14.00 (*0-14-012392-X*, Penguin Bks.) Penguin Group (USA) Inc.
—The Camomile Lawn. 1984. 297p. 15.50 o.p. (*0-671-50461-4*) Summit Bks.
—The Camomile Lawn. abr. ed. 1997. mass mkt. 16.95 (*1-85998-864-4*) Trafalgar Square.
Westleigh, Sarah. A Most Exceptional Quest. 2000. 256p. mass mkt. (*0-373-51114-0*, 1-51114-6, Harlequin Bks.) Harlequin Enterprises, Ltd.
—A Most Exceptional Quest. l.t. ed. 1994. 18.95 o.p. (*0-263-13760-0*) Harlequin Mills & Boon, Ltd. GBR. *Dist:* BBC Audiobooks America.
Whalley, Peter. Crooks. 1990. 192p. pap. 3.50 (*0-380-70617-2*, Avon Bks.) Morrow/Avon.
—Crooks. 1988. 15.95 (*0-8027-1038-7*) Walker & Co.
Wharton, Thomas. Salamander. 2002. 400p. pap. 14.00 (*0-7434-4415-9*, Washington Square Pr.) Simon & Schuster.
Whitmee, Jeanne. A Lobster & a Lady. 1980. 8.95 o.p. (*0-312-49410-6*) St. Martin's Pr.
—A Lobster & a Lady. l.t. ed. 2000. (General Ser.). 304p. pap. 22.95 (*0-7862-2810-5*); (*0-7540-4253-7*); (*0-7540-4254-5*) Thorndike Pr.
Wick, Lori. Who Brings Forth the Wind? 1994. (Kensington Chronicles Ser.). 396p. pap. 9.99 (*1-56507-229-4*) Harvest Hse. Pubs.
—Who Brings Forth the Wind? l.t. ed. 2001. (Thorndike Christian Fiction Ser.). 568p. 26.95 (*0-7862-2957-8*) Thorndike Pr.
Wickham, Madeleine. Cocktails for Three. 2000. (Illus.). 300p. 13.00 (*0-552-99834-6*) Corgi Bks. Ltd. GBR. *Dist:* Trafalgar Square.
—Cocktails for Three. l.t. ed. 2002. (Women's Fiction Ser.). 28.95 (*0-7862-3906-9*) Gale Group.
—Cocktails for Three. Date not set. E-Book 23.95 (*0-312-70151-9*); 2002. 304p. mass mkt. 6.50 (*0-312-98499-5*, St. Martin's Paperbacks); 2001. 304p. 23.95 (*0-312-28192-7*) St. Martin's Pr.
Williams, Nigel. Wimbledon Poisoner. 1991. 320p. 19.95 o.p. (*0-571-14242-7*) Faber & Faber, Inc.
Willsher, Audrey. The Sower Went Forth. l.t. ed. 2000. (Magna Large Print Ser.). 384p. 31.99 (*0-7505-1570-8*) Magna Large Print Bks. GBR. *Dist:* Ulverscroft Large Print Bks., Ltd., Ulverscroft Large Print Canada, Ltd.
—The Sower Went Forth. 1999. 281p. 25.00 (*0-7278-5420-8*) Severn Hse. Pubs., Ltd.
Wilson, A. N. A Bottle in the Smoke. 1991. 288p. pap. 8.95 o.p. (*0-14-013165-5*, Penguin Bks.) Penguin Group (USA) Inc.
—A Bottle in the Smoke. 1990. 288p. 18.95 o.p. (*0-670-83221-9*, Viking) Viking Penguin.
—Daughters of Albion. 1993. 304p. pap. 10.00 o.p. (*0-14-013166-3*, Penguin Bks.); pap. 10.00 o.p. (*0-14-017509-1*) Penguin Group (USA) Inc.
—Daughters of Albion. 1992. 304p. 21.00 o.p. (*0-670-83959-0*, Viking) Viking Penguin.
—Dream Children. 2000. 224p. pap. 13.00 (*0-393-31993-8*) Norton, W. W. & Co., Inc.
—Dream Children: A Novel. 1998. 224p. 23.95 (*0-393-02740-6*) Norton, W. W. & Co., Inc.
—A Watch in the Night. 1998. 224p. pap. 12.00 (*0-393-31725-0*); 1996. 256p. 23.00 o.p. (*0-393-04042-9*) Norton, W. W. & Co., Inc.
Wilson, Barbara. Gaudi Afternoon: A Cassandra Reilly Mystery. 1990. (Cassandra Reilly Mysteries Ser.). 172p. pap. 11.95 (*0-931188-89-X*, Seal Pr.) Avalon Publishing Group.
Wingfield, R. D. Winter Frost. 2000. audio 94.95 (*0-7531-0689-2*, 000202); 14p. audio compact disk 99.95 (*0-7531-0886-0*, 108860) ISIS Audio Bks. GBR. *Dist:* Ulverscroft Large Print Bks., Ltd.
—Winter Frost. l.t. ed. 2000. (Magna Large Print Ser.). 592p. o.p. (*0-7505-1559-7*) Magna Large Print Bks. GBR. *Dist:* Ulverscroft Large Print Canada, Ltd.
—Winter Frost. 2001. 508p. pap. 9.95 (*0-552-14778-8*) Transworld Publishers Ltd. GBR. *Dist:* Trafalgar Square.
Winsor, Kathleen. Forever Amber. 1993. 800p. pap. 12.00 o.s.i (*0-345-37941-1*) Ballantine Bks.
—Forever Amber. 1991. 400p. reprint ed. lib. bdg. 54.95 (*0-89966-866-6*) Buccaneer Bks., Inc.
—Forever Amber. 2000. 976p. pap. 18.95 (*1-55652-404-8*) Chicago Review Pr., Inc.
—Forever Amber. mass mkt. 0.50 o.p. (*0-451-00809-X*); 1977. mass mkt. 1.95 o.p. (*0-451-07360-6*); 1971. mass mkt. 1.50 o.p. (*0-451-04540-8*); 1971. mass mkt. 0.50 o.p. (*0-451-01169-4*); 1971. mass mkt. 0.75 o.p. (*0-451-01567-3*); 1971. mass mkt. 0.95 o.p. (*0-451-02332-3*); 1971. mass mkt. 1.25 o.p. (*0-451-02717-5*); 1950. mass mkt. 2.95 o.p. (*0-451-09234-1*); 1950. mass mkt. 2.75 o.p. (*0-451-08278-8*); 1950. mass mkt. 3.95 o.p. (*0-451-12164-3*); 1950. 728p. mass mkt. 5.50 o.p. (*0-451-14697-2*); 1950. mass mkt. 2.25 o.p. (*0-451-07675-3*); 1950. mass mkt. 1.95 o.p. (*0-451-06822-X*); 1950. mass mkt. 1.75 o.p. (*0-451-05960-3*) NAL. (Signet Bks.).
Winspear, Jacqueline. Maisie Dobbs. l.t. ed. 2004. lib. bdg. 28.95 (*1-58547-406-1*, Platinum) Ctr. Point Large Print.
—Maisie Dobbs. 2003. 336p. 24.00 (*1-56947-330-7*) Soho Pr., Inc.
Wintering. Date not set. pap. (*0-312-28376-8*, Saint Martin's Griffin) St. Martin's Pr.
Winterson, Jeanette. Sexing the Cherry. 1990. 19.95 o.p. (*0-87113-350-4*); 1998. 176p. reprint ed. pap. 12.00 (*0-8021-3578-1*) Grove/Atlantic, Inc.
—Sexing the Cherry. 1991. 192p. pap. 11.00 o.s.i (*0-679-73316-7*, Vintage) Knopf Publishing Group.
—Sexing the Cherry. 2000. 160p. pap. (*0-676-97348-5*, Vintage) Random Hse. of Canada, Ltd. CAN. *Dist:* Random Hse., Inc.
Wodehouse, P. G. Tales from the Drones Club. reprint ed. 1992. 360p. pap. 14.95 o.p. (*1-55882-118-X*); 1991. 352p. 21.95 o.p. (*1-55882-088-4*) International Polygonics, Ltd. (Library of Crime Classics).
Woodcraft, Elizabeth. Good Bad Woman: A Frankie Richmond Mystery. 2002. 352p. 22.00 (*0-7582-0258-X*) Kensington Publishing Corp.
Woodiwiss, Kathleen E. The Elusive Flame. abr. ed. 1999. audio 7.99 o.s.i (*1-56740-316-6*, 1866, Paperback Nova Audio Bks.); 1998. audio 39.95 (*1-56740-407-3*, 1492, Brilliance Audio Unabridged); 1998. 16p. audio 89.25 (*1-56740-605-X*, 1632, Unabridged Library Editions) Brilliance Audio.
—The Elusive Flame. l.t. ed. 1998. (Large Print Book Ser.). 27.95 o.p. (*1-56895-692-4*, Wheeler Publishing, Inc.) Gale Group.
—The Elusive Flame. 1999. 496p. mass mkt. 7.50 (*0-380-80786-6*); 1998. 432p. pap. 14.00 o.p. (*0-380-76655-8*) Morrow/Avon. (Avon Bks.).
Woolf, Virginia. Night & Day. reprint ed. lib. bdg. 98.00 (*0-7426-3271-7*); 2001. 538p. pap. text 28.00 (*0-7426-8271-4*) Classic Bks.
—Night & Day. 1999. E-Book 2.49 (*1-58627-475-9*) Electric Umbrella Publishing.
—Night & Day. 1973. (Harvest Book Ser.). 516p. reprint ed. pap. 16.00 o.s.i (*0-15-665600-0*, HB263, Harvest Bks.) Harcourt Trade Pubs.
—Night & Day. Raitt, Suzanne, ed. 1992. (Oxford World's Classics Ser.). 582p. pap. (*0-19-281842-2*) Oxford Univ. Pr., Inc.
—Night & Day. l.t. ed. 2000. 590p. 37.95 (*0-7658-0782-3*) Transaction Pubs.

—Night & Day. Briggs, Julia, ed. & intro. by. 1996. (Twentieth Century Classics Ser.). (Illus.). 496p. 13.95 (0-14-018568-2, Penguin Classics) Viking Penguin.

Wrede, Patricia C. Magician's Ward. 1997. 320p. 22.95 (0-312-85369-6, Tor Bks.) Doherty, Tom Assocs., LLC.

—The Magician's Ward. 1998. (Tor Fantasy Ser.). 288p. mass mkt. 5.99 o.s.i (0-8125-2085-8, Tor Bks.) Doherty, Tom Assocs., LLC.

Yorke, Margaret. Crime in Question. l.t. ed. 272p. 2003. pap. 21.99 (0-7531-6778-6); 2002. 32.50 (0-7531-6777-8) ISIS Large Print Bks. GBR. *Dist:* Ulverscroft Large Print Bks., Ltd., Ulverscroft Large Print Bks., Ltd., Ulverscroft Large Print Canada, Ltd.

—Crime in Question. 240p. 1990. pap. 3.95 o.p. (0-14-012435-7, Penguin Bks.); 1989. 16.95 o.p. (0-670-82932-3) Viking Penguin.

Zangwill, Israel. Children of the Ghetto. 1977. (Victorian Library Ser.). (Illus.). 448p. reprint ed. text 15.75 o.p. (0-7185-5028-5) Brill Academic Pubs., Inc.

—Children of the Ghetto. 2001. (Works of Israel Zangwill). pap. text 56.00 (0-7426-8780-5) Classic Bks.

—Children of the Ghetto. 1998. 512p. reprint ed. pap. 27.95 (0-8143-2593-9) Wayne State Univ. Pr.

**LONG ISLAND (N.Y.)—FICTION**

Andrews, Russell. Aphrodite. 2004. 23.95 (0-89296-784-6) Mysterious Pr.

Ashe, Penelope. Naked Came the Stranger. 2003. 220p. pap. 12.00 (1-56980-262-9) Barricade Bks., Inc.

Auchincloss, Louis. The Scarlet Letters. 2003. 192p. tchr. ed. 24.00 (0-618-34159-5) Houghton Mifflin Co.

Blume, Judy. Then Again, Maybe I Won't. unabr. ed. 1990. (YA). (gr. 7 up). audio 24.00 (0-8072-7295-7, YA827CX, Listening Library) Random Hse. Audio Publishing Group.

Brady, James. Gin Lane: A Novel of Southampton. 1999. (Gin Lane Ser.: Vol. 1). 314p. mass mkt. 6.99 (0-312-96706-3, St. Martin's Paperbacks); 1998. 256p. 22.95 (0-312-18579-0) St. Martin's Pr.

—A Hampton's Christmas. 2000. (Illus.). 211p. 23.95 (0-312-26604-9) St. Martin's Pr.

Cantor, Jay. Great Neck: A Novel. 720p. 2004. pap. 15.00 (0-375-71339-5); 2003. 27.95 (0-375-41394-4) Knopf, Alfred A. Inc.

DeMaria, Robert. The White Road. 2000. 272p. 25.00 (1-57962-073-6) Permanent Pr., The.

DeMille, Nelson. Plum Island. abr. ed. 1997. audio 24.00 o.s.i (0-394-58389-2, 495350, RH Audio) Random Hse. Audio Publishing Group.

—Plum Island. l.t. ed. 1998. (Paperback Bestsellers Ser.). 821p. pap. 28.95 (0-7862-0980-1) Thorndike Pr.

—Plum Island. 2001. 576p. E-Book 6.95 (0-7595-4260-0); 2001. 576p. E-Book 6.95 (0-7595-9290-X); 2001. 576p. E-Book 6.95 (0-7595-6257-1); 2001. 576p. E-Book 6.95 (0-7595-8263-7); 2001. 576p. E-Book 6.95 (0-7595-0257-9); 1998. mass mkt. 287.64 (0-446-16544-1); 1997. 528p. 24.50 o.p. (0-446-51506-X); 2002. 592p. reprint ed. pap. 15.95 (0-446-67908-9); 1998. 592p. reprint ed. mass mkt. 7.99 (0-446-60540-9) Warner Bks., Inc.

Dworkin, Susan. The Book of Candy. 1996. 360p. 20.00 (1-56858-078-9) Four Walls Eight Windows.

Eberhart, Mignon G. Danger Money. 1989. 224p. mass mkt. 5.99 (0-446-35565-8) Warner Bks., Inc.

Ephron, Delia. Big City Eyes. 2001. 256p. reprint ed. pap. 12.95 (0-345-44345-4, Ballantine Bks.) Ballantine Bks.

—Big City Eyes. 2000. 256p. 23.95 o.s.i (0-399-14391-2) Penguin Group (USA) Inc.

—Big City Eyes. l.t. ed. 2001. (Thorndike Americana Ser.). 339p. 30.95 (0-7862-3175-0) Thorndike Pr.

Fletcher, Jessica. A Palette for Murder: A Murder, She Wrote Mystery. 1996. (Murder She Wrote Ser.: Vol. 6). 304p. mass mkt. 6.50 (0-451-18820-9, Signet Bks.) NAL.

Glass, Julia. Three Junes: A Novel. l.t. ed. 2003. (Romance Ser.). 28.95 (1-58724-379-2, Wheeler Publishing, Inc.) Gale Group.

—Three Junes: A Novel. 368p. 2002. 25.00 (0-375-42144-0, Pantheon); 2003. reprint ed. pap. 14.00 (0-385-72142-0, Anchor) Knopf Publishing Group.

—Three Junes: A Novel. 2002. 368p. 25.00 (0-375-42241-2) Knopf, Alfred A. Inc.

Hitchcock, Jane S. Trick of the Eye. l.t. ed. 1993. 23.95 o.p. (0-7927-1482-2); pap. 21.95 o.p. (0-7927-1481-4) BBC Audiobooks America.

—Trick of the Eye. 1992. 288p. 19.00 o.p. (0-525-93529-0, Dutton) Dutton/Plume.

—Trick of the Eye. 1993. 256p. pap. o.p. (0-451-17480-1); 368p. mass mkt. 5.50 o.s.i (0-451-17673-1) NAL. (Signet Bks.).

Hitchcock, Jane Stanton. Social Crimes. l.t. ed. 2002. 28.95 (1-58724-337-7, Wheeler Publishing, Inc.) Gale Group.

—Social Crimes. 2002. 368p. 22.95 (0-7868-6815-5) Hyperion Pr.

—Social Crimes. Date not set. pap. 12.95 (0-7868-8848-2) Talk Miramax Bks.

Hoffman, Alice. Local Girls. 2000. 208p. pap. 12.95 (0-425-17434-4) Berkley Publishing Group.

—Local Girls. 1999. 197p. 22.95 o.s.i (0-399-14507-9) Penguin Group (USA) Inc.

—Local Girls. l.t. ed. (Thorndike/G. K. Hall Paperback Bestsellers Ser.). 208p. 2000. pap. 28.95 (0-7862-2010-4); 1999. 29.95 (0-7862-2009-0) Thorndike Pr.

—Local Girls. 2000. 19.00 (0-606-20422-9) Turtleback Bks.

Hollander, David. L. I. E. E-Book 18.50 (1-58945-595-9) Adobe Systems, Inc.

—L. I. E. 2001. E-Book 11.50 (0-375-50641-1) Random Hse., Inc.

Isaacs, Susan. Lily White. 1996. 480p. 25.00 o.p. (0-06-017607-5) HarperCollins Pubs.

—Lily White. l.t. ed. 1997. 656p. mass mkt. 7.99 (0-06-109309-2, HarperTorch) Morrow/Avon.

—Lily White. l.t. ed. (Paperback Bestsellers Ser.). 738p. 1997. pap. 27.95 (0-7862-0829-5); 1996. 28.95 o.p. (0-7862-0828-7) Thorndike Pr.

—Long Time No See. 2001. 368p. 26.00 (0-06-019570-3); 496p. pap. 26.00 (0-06-621404-1) HarperCollins Pubs.

Kraft, Eric. At Home with the Glynns: The Personal History, Experiences & Observations of Peter Leroy (Continued) 1996. pap. 11.00 (0-312-14279-X) Picador.

—Do Clams Bite? 1982. (Peter Leroy Ser.: Vol. 1, No. 2). (Illus.). 96p. pap. 4.95 o.p. (0-918222-45-1) Applewood Bks.

—Do Clams Bite? 1986. 96p. mass mkt. 4.95 o.p. (0-446-38353-8) Warner Bks., Inc.

—The Fox & the Clam. 1984. (Personal History, Adventures, Experiences & Observations of Peter Leroy Ser.). pap. 4.95 o.p. (0-918222-53-2) Applewood Bks.

—Inflating a Dog: The Story of Ella's Lunch Launch. 2003. (Illus.). 256p. pap. 14.00 (0-312-42221-0); 2002. 336p. 25.00 (0-312-28804-2) Picador.

—Leaving Small's Hotel. 1999. 352p. pap. 14.00 (0-312-20660-7); 1998. 336p. 23.00 o.p. (0-312-18689-4) Picador.

—Life on the Bolotomy. 1983. (Peter Leroy Ser.: Vol. 1, No. 3). (Illus.). 96p. pap. 4.95 o.p. (0-918222-48-6) Applewood Bks.

—Life on the Bolotomy. 1986. 96p. mass mkt. 4.95 o.p. (0-446-38354-6) Warner Bks., Inc.

—The Little Follies: The Personal History, Adventure, Experiences & Observations of Peter Leroy (So Far) 1995. pap. 13.00 (0-312-11928-3) Picador.

—Mutiny!, No. 10. 1985. 96p. pap. 4.95 o.p. (0-918222-76-1) Applewood Bks.

—My Mother Takes a Tumble. 1982. (Portable Peter Leroy Ser.: Vol. 1 No. 1). 96p. pap. 4.95 o.p. (0-918222-40-0) Applewood Bks.

—My Mother Takes a Tumble. 1986. 96p. mass mkt. 4.95 o.p. (0-446-38350-3) Warner Bks., Inc.

—The Personal History, Adventures, Experiences, & Observations of Peter Leroy, Vol. 1. 1983. (Peter Leroy Ser.). 400p. 17.95 o.p. (0-918222-50-8) Applewood Bks.

—Peter Leroy: Take the Long Way Home. 1984. (Peter Leroy Ser.: No. 7). pap. 4.95 o.p. (0-918222-61-3) Applewood Bks.

—The Static of the Spheres. 1983. (Peter Leroy Ser.: Vol. 1, No. 4). pap. 4.95 o.p. (0-918222-49-4) Applewood Bks.

—The Static of the Spheres. 1986. 96p. mass mkt. 4.95 o.p. (0-446-38356-2) Warner Bks., Inc.

—What a Piece of Work I Am. 3rd ed. 1995. 288p. pap. 11.00 (0-312-13211-5) Picador.

—What a Piece of Work I Am: A Novel. 1994. 275p. 22.00 o.s.i (0-517-59612-1, Crown) Crown Publishing Group.

—Where Do You Stop? The Personal History, Adventures, Experiences, & Observations of Peter Leroy. 1992. (Illus.). 192p. 15.00 o.s.i (0-517-58544-8, Crown) Crown Publishing Group.

—Where Do You Stop? The Personal History, Adventures, Experiences & Observations of Peter Leroy. 1995. pap. 10.00 (0-312-11932-1) Picador.

—The Young Tars, No. 9. 1985. 96p. pap. 4.95 o.p. (0-918222-68-0) Applewood Bks.

Lardo, Vincent. The Hampton Affair. 2000. 352p. mass mkt. 6.99 o.s.i (0-425-17482-4) Berkley Publishing Group.

—The Hampton Affair. 1999. 311p. 23.95 o.p. (0-399-14476-5, G. P. Putnam's Sons) Penguin Group (USA) Inc.

—The Hampton Connection. 2002. 320p. mass mkt. 7.50 o.s.i (0-425-18447-1) Berkley Publishing Group.

—The Hampton Connection. 2001. 292p. 24.95 o.p. (0-399-14631-8) Penguin Group (USA) Inc.

Lawrence, Rae. Jacqueline Susann's Shadow of the Dolls. 2001. 320p. 22.00 o.s.i (0-609-60585-2) Crown Publishing Group.

—Jacqueline Susann's Shadow of the Dolls. 2002. 368p. mass mkt. 7.99 o.s.i (0-7582-0272-5) Kensington Publishing Corp.

Logue, John. On a Par with Murder. 1999. (Morris & Sullivan Mystery Ser.: Vol. 5). 288p. mass mkt. 5.99 o.s.i (0-440-22400-4) Dell Publishing.

Maclean, Charles. The Silence. 1997. 336p. mass mkt. 5.99 o.s.i (0-06-101233-5) HarperCollins Pubs.

McDermott, Alice. Child of My Heart. l.t. ed. 2003. lib. bdg. 29.95 (1-58547-290-5, Platinum) Ctr. Point Large Print.

—Child of My Heart. 2002. 256p. 23.00 (0-374-12123-0); E-Book 9.00 (0-374-70377-9); E-Book 15.00 o.p. (0-374-70379-5); E-Book 9.00 (0-374-70380-9); E-Book 9.00 (0-374-70378-7); E-Book (0-374-70381-7) Farrar, Straus & Giroux.

—Child of My Heart. 2003. 256p. pap. 13.00 (0-312-42291-1) Picador.

Peck, Dale. What We Lost: Based on a True Story. 2003. 240p. 23.00 (0-618-25128-6) Houghton Mifflin Co.

Pellegrino, Charles. Dust. 1999. 464p. mass mkt. 6.99 (0-380-78742-3); 1998. 400p. 15.95 (0-380-97308-1) Morrow/Avon. (Avon Bks.).

Pilcher, Robin. An Ocean Apart. unabr. ed. 1999. audio 44.00 (0-7871-1868-0, Dove Audio) NewStar Media, Inc.

Pilcher, Robin. An Ocean Apart. abr. ed. 1999. audio 25.00 (0-7871-1867-2, 698452, Dove Audio) NewStar Media, Inc.

—An Ocean Apart. 1999. 512p. mass mkt. 6.99 (0-312-97184-2, St. Martin's Paperbacks); 1998. 470p. 24.95 o.p. (0-312-19995-3) St. Martin's Pr.

—An Ocean Apart. l.t. ed. 1999. (Basic Ser.). 699p. 30.95 (0-7862-1911-4) Thorndike Pr.

Rogan, Barbara. Suspicion. l.t. ed. 2000. pap. 23.95 (1-56895-874-9, Wheeler Publishing, Inc.) Gale Group.

—Suspicion. 1999. 352p. 24.00 (0-684-81415-3, Simon & Schuster); 2000. 432p. reprint ed. pap. 6.99 (0-7434-0057-7, Pocket) Simon & Schuster.

Ross, Clarissa. Beware the Kindly Stranger. l.t. ed. 2000. (G. K. Hall Romance Ser.). 246p. 27.95 (0-7838-8980-1, Macmillan Reference USA) Gale Group.

Scoppettone, Sandra. Gonna Take a Homicidal Journey: A Lauren Laurano Mystery. 1999. (Lauren Laurano Mystery Ser.). 288p. mass mkt. 6.99 (0-345-43118-9) Ballantine Bks.

—Gonna Take a Homicidal Journey: A Lauren Laurano Mystery. 1998. 240p. (gr. 8). 22.95 o.p. (0-316-77665-3) Little Brown & Co.

Spitz, Marc. How Soon Is Never? 2003. 368p. pap. 13.00 (0-609-81040-5, Three Rivers Pr.) Crown Publishing Group.

Stahl, Maryanne. Forgive the Moon. 2002. (Illus.). 304p. pap. 12.95 (0-451-20633-9, NAL Bks.) NAL.

Upcher, Caroline. Down by the Water. 2002. 384p. mass mkt. 7.50 (0-06-103152-6); 2001. 400p. 25.00 (0-06-018568-6) HarperCollins Pubs.

Vachss, Andrew. Only Child: A Burke Novel. 2002. 288p. 24.00 (0-375-41487-8) Knopf, Alfred A. Inc.

Watson, Clarissa. The Bishop in the Back Seat. 1986. 256p. mass mkt. 2.95 o.s.i (0-345-33084-6) Ballantine Bks.

—The Bishop in the Back Seat. 1979. 9.95 o.p. (0-689-11012-X, Scribner) Simon & Schuster.

—The Fourth Stage of Gainsborough Brown. 1986. 224p. mass mkt. 2.95 o.s.i (0-345-33531-7) Ballantine Bks.

—The Fourth Stage of Gainsborough Brown. 1977. 7.95 o.p. (0-679-50667-5) McKay, David Co., Inc.

—The Fourth Stage of Gainsborough Brown. 1978. (Crime Ser.). pap. 1.95 o.p. (0-14-004789-1, Penguin Bks.) Viking Penguin.

—Last Plane from Nice. 1988. (Persis Willum Mystery Ser.). 224p. 16.95 o.s.i (0-689-11835-X, Scribner) Simon & Schuster.

—Runaway. l.t. ed. 1989. (Atlantic Mystery Ser.). pap. 14.95 o.p. (1-55504-739-4, 838) BBC Audiobooks America.

—Runaway. 1986. 208p. mass mkt. 2.95 o.s.i (0-345-33114-1) Ballantine Bks.

—Runaway. 1985. 250p. 12.95 o.p. (0-689-11521-0, Scribner) Simon & Schuster.

—Somebody Killed the Messenger. 1988. 224p. 16.95 o.s.i (0-689-11963-1, Scribner) Simon & Schuster.

Westermann, John. Exit Wounds. McCarthy, Paul, ed. 1991. 320p. reprint ed. mass mkt. 5.99 (0-671-72935-7, Pocket) Simon & Schuster.

—Exit Wounds. 2000. 304p. pap. 12.00 (1-56947-223-8); 1989. 273p. 18.95 o.p. (0-939149-27-3) Soho Pr., Inc.

—High Crimes. McCarthy, Paul, ed. 1989. 256p. mass mkt. 5.99 (0-671-67968-6, Pocket) Simon & Schuster.

—High Crimes. 2001. 208p. pap. 12.00 (1-56947-244-0); 1988. 234p. 15.95 (0-939149-15-X) Soho Pr., Inc.

—The Honor Farm. 2000. 320p. pap. 6.99 (0-671-87126-9, Pocket Star); 1997. (Illus.). 368p. pap. 6.99 (0-671-87123-4, Pocket); 1996. 320p. 22.00 o.p. (0-671-87122-6, Atria) Simon & Schuster.

—Ladies of the Night. 1998. 288p. 23.00 (0-671-87124-2, Atria) Simon & Schuster.

Wishnia, K. J. A. The Glass Factory: A Filomena Buscarsela Mystery. 2000. (Filomena Buscarsela Mysteries Ser.). 224p. 23.95 o.s.i (0-525-94545-8, Dutton) Dutton/Plume.

—The Glass Factory: A Filomena Buscarsela Mystery. 2001. 256p. reprint ed. mass mkt. 5.99 o.s.i (0-451-19751-8, Signet Bks.) NAL.

—The Glass Factory: A Filomena Buscarsela Mystery. l.t. ed. 2000. (Mystery Ser.). 375p. 27.95 (0-7862-2841-5) Thorndike Pr.

Wolitzer, Meg. Surrender, Dorothy. 1999. 224p. 22.00 (0-684-84844-9); 2000. 240p. reprint ed. pap. 12.95 (0-671-04254-8) Simon & Schuster. (Scribner).

**LOS ANGELES (CALIF.)—FICTION**

Abella, Alex. Dead of Night. 1998. 304p. 23.00 (0-684-81426-9, Simon & Schuster) Simon & Schuster.

—Final Acts: A Novel. 2000. 304p. 25.00 o.s.i (0-684-85989-0, Simon & Schuster) Simon & Schuster.

—The Killing of the Saints. 1993. (Crime Ser.). 320p. pap. 5.95 o.p. (0-14-017419-2, Penguin Bks.) Penguin Group (USA) Inc.

Abu-Jaber, Diana. Crescent. 2003. 352p. 24.95 (0-393-05747-X) Norton, W. W. & Co., Inc.

Adler, Bill, Jr., et al. Murder in Los Angeles. 1987. 320p. 16.95 o.p. (0-688-06684-4, Morrow, William & Co.) Morrow/Avon.

Adler, Dick. The Mozart Code. 1999. 168p. E-Book 6.00 (1-58200-107-3); E-Book 6.00 (1-58200-227-4) Hard Shell Word Factory.

Adler, Elizabeth A. All or Nothing. 2000. 368p. mass mkt. 6.99 (0-440-23496-4, Dell Bks.) Dell Publishing.

—All or Nothing. l.t. ed. 1999. 27.95 (1-56895-825-0, Wheeler Publishing, Inc.) Gale Group.

Alcala, Kathleen. The Flower in the Skull: A Novel. 1998. 182p. 22.95 o.p. (0-8118-1916-7) Chronicle Bks. LLC.

—The Flower in the Skull: A Novel. 1999. 192p. pap. 13.00 (0-15-600634-0, Harvest Bks.) Harcourt Trade Pubs.

Alder, Elizabeth A. All or Nothing. E-Book 6.99 (1-930161-75-1) Adobe Systems, Inc.

Allegretto, Michael. The Watchman. 1991. 288p. 20.00 o.p. (0-671-73643-4, Simon & Schuster) Simon & Schuster.

Allende, Isabel. The Infinite Plan: A Novel. Peden, Margaret Sayers, tr. from ENG. 1993. 384p. 23.00 o.p. (0-06-017016-6) HarperTrade.

Allman, Kevin. Hot Shot. 1998. 256p. 22.95 (0-312-16866-7, Saint Martin's Minotaur) St. Martin's Pr.

—Tight Shot. 1995. 262p. 21.00 o.p. (0-312-11904-6, Saint Martin's Minotaur) St. Martin's Pr.

Alvarez, Margaret. Glimpse of Death. 2000. 176p. pap. 20.99 (0-7388-2406-2); text 30.99 (0-7388-2405-4) Xlibris Corp.

Anobile, Richard J., ed. The Maltese Falcon. 1974. (Film Classics Library). (Illus.). 256p. mass mkt. 5.50 o.p. (0-380-01485-8, 19109-1, Avon Bks.) Morrow/Avon.

Appelman, William. Claim to Fame. 1993. 256p. 19.95 o.p. (0-88184-935-9, Carroll & Graf Pubs.) Avalon Publishing Group.

Bagshawe, Louise. The Devil You Know: A Novel. 2003. 384p. 24.95 (0-312-27305-3) St. Martin's Pr.

Bain, Donald & Fletcher, Jessica. Murder, She Wrote: Martinis & Mayhem. l.t. ed. 1999. (Nightingale Ser.). 280p. pap. 21.95 (0-7838-8665-9) Thorndike Pr.

Bakeer, Donald. Crips: The Story of a South Central L.A. Street Gang. 1992. 195p. reprint ed. 19.95 (0-9634969-0-5) Precocious Publishing Co.

Baker, James Robert. Fuel Injected Dreams. 2003. 14.95 (1-56025-535-8, Thunder's Mouth Pr.) Avalon Publishing Group.

—Testosterone: A Novel. viii, 200p. 2001. pap. 12.95 (1-55583-714-X); 2000. 22.95 o.p. (1-55583-567-8, Alyson Bks.) Alyson Pubns.

Banbury, Jen. Like a Hole in the Head: A Novel. 1998. 304p. (YA). (gr. 8 up). 21.95 o.p. (0-316-17110-7) Little Brown & Co.

—Like a Hole in the Head: A Novel. 1999. 304p. pap. 12.00 o.s.i (0-446-67517-2) Warner Bks., Inc.

Barkhordar-Nahai, Gina. Moonlight on the Avenue of Faith. 2000. 400p. reprint ed. pap. 13.95 (0-671-04283-1, Washington Square Pr.) Simon & Schuster.

Barnes, Joanna. The Deceivers. 1970. 6.95 o.p. (0-87795-007-5, Morrow, William & Co.) Morrow/Avon.

Barnes, Steven. Firedance. 1993. 416p. 21.95 o.p. (0-312-85094-8, Tor Bks.) Doherty, Tom Assocs., LLC.

Barre, Richard. Bearing Secrets: A Wil Hardesty Mystery. 1998. (Wil Hardesty Ser.: Vol. 2). 288p. reprint ed. mass mkt. 5.99 o.s.i (0-425-16641-4) Berkley Publishing Group.

—Bearing Secrets: A Wil Hardesty Mystery. 1996. (Wil Hardesty Ser.). 312p. 22.95 (0-8027-3280-1) Walker & Co.

—Blackheart Highway. (Wil Hardesty Ser.: Vol. 4). 2000. 326p. mass mkt. 6.99 o.s.i (*0-425-17467-0*); 1999. 336p. 21.95 o.s.i (*0-425-16903-0*, Prime Crime) Berkley Publishing Group.
—The Ghosts of Morning: A Will Hardesty Mystery. 1998. 336p. 21.95 o.s.i (*0-425-16300-8*); 1999. 320p. reprint ed. mass mkt. 6.50 o.s.i (*0-425-16931-6*, Prime Crime) Berkley Publishing Group.
—The Innocents. 1997. (Wil Hardesty Ser.: Vol. 1). 288p. mass mkt. 6.50 o.s.i (*0-425-16109-9*, Prime Crime) Berkley Publishing Group.
—The Innocents. 1995. 332p. 19.95 (*0-8027-3261-5*) Walker & Co.
—The Star. 2002. 48p. 17.95 (*1-59266-008-8*); 43p. 85.00 (*1-59266-009-6*); 43p. 125.00 (*1-59266-010-X*) Capra Pr.
Barry, Max. Syrup. 2000. 304p. pap. 11.95 (*0-14-029187-3*) Penguin Group (USA) Inc.
—Syrup. 1999. 320p. 23.95 o.p. (*0-670-88640-8*) Viking Penguin.
Barth, Nadine. Abgedreht: Roman. 2003. (GER.). 256p. pap. 19.00 (*1-4000-3984-3*) Random Hse. Information Group.
Bates, Karen Grigsby. Plain Brown Wrapper: An Alex Powell Novel. 2001. 336p. pap. 13.00 (*0-380-80890-0*, Avon Bks.) Morrow/Avon.
Baxt, George. The Mae West Murder Case. 1993. 208p. 17.95 o.p. (*0-312-09864-2*, Saint Martin's Minotaur) St. Martin's Pr.
—The Marlene Dietrich Murder Case. 1993. 224p. 17.95 o.p. (*0-312-09334-9*, Saint Martin's Minotaur) St. Martin's Pr.
—The Talking Pictures Murder Case. 1990. 208p. 15.95 o.p. (*0-312-05043-7*, Saint Martin's Minotaur) St. Martin's Pr.
—The Tallulah Bankhead Murder Case. 1987. 240p. 15.95 o.p. (*0-312-01098-2*, Saint Martin's Minotaur) St. Martin's Pr.
—The William Powell & Myrna Loy Murder Case. 1996. 208p. 20.95 o.p. (*0-312-14071-1*, Saint Martin's Minotaur) St. Martin's Pr.
Bear, Greg. Infinity Concerto. 1987. mass mkt. 3.95 o.s.i (*0-441-37059-4*) Ace Bks.
—Infinity Concerto. 1986. 352p. 3.50 o.s.i (*0-425-09536-3*); 1984. 2.95 o.s.i (*0-425-07308-4*) Berkley Publishing Group.
—The Serpent Mage. (Orig.). 1987. mass mkt. 3.95 o.s.i (*0-441-75910-6*); 1986. mass mkt. 2.75 o.s.i (*0-441-79066-6*) Ace Bks.
—The Serpent Mage. 1986. 352p. (Orig.). 3.50 o.s.i (*0-425-09337-9*) Berkley Publishing Group.
—Songs of Earth & Power. 1996. 695p. pap. text 6.99 (*0-8125-3603-7*); 1994. 560p. 24.95 o.p. (*0-312-85669-5*) Doherty, Tom Assocs., LLC. (Tor Bks.).
—Songs of Earth & Power. 1992. (*0-7126-5494-1*) Random Hse. UK, Ltd. GBR. *Dist:* Random Hse. of Canada, Ltd.
Beatty, Paul. The White Boy Shuffle. 2001. 240p. pap. 13.00 (*0-312-28019-X*) Picador.
Bell, James S. Circumstantial Evidence. 1997. 480p. pap. 13.99 o.p. (*0-8054-6359-3*) Broadman & Holman Pubs.
Bell, James Scott. A Greater Glory. 2003. (Trials of Kit Shannon Ser.). 304p. pap. 12.99 (*0-7642-2645-2*) Bethany Hse. Pubs.
—A Higher Justice. 2003. (Trials of Kit Shannon Ser.). 304p. pap. 12.99 (*0-7642-2646-0*) Bethany Hse. Pubs.
Berrenson, Marc. Bodily Harm. 1992. 224p. (Orig.). mass mkt. 4.50 (*0-380-76613-2*, Avon Bks.) Morrow/Avon.
—L. A. Snitch. 1991. 256p. (Orig.). pap. 3.95 (*0-380-76324-9*, Avon Bks.) Morrow/Avon.
Bishop, Paul. Chalk Whispers. 2000. 368p. 25.00 (*0-684-87157-2*, Scribner) Simon & Schuster.
—Chalk Whispers: A Fey Croaker LAPD Crime Novel. (Fey Croaker Novels Ser.). 2000. 368p. 25.00 o.s.i (*0-684-83010-8*, Scribner); 2001. 400p. reprint ed. mass mkt. 6.99 (*0-7434-1207-9*, Pocket) Simon & Schuster.
—Chapel of the Ravens, Bk. 3. unabr. ed. 1998. audio 64.95 (*1-55686-781-6*) Books in Motion.
—Chapel of the Ravens. 1992. 352p. mass mkt. 4.99 o.p. (*0-8125-0583-2*); 1991. 18.95 o.p. (*0-312-93155-7*) Doherty, Tom Assocs., LLC. (Tor Bks.).
—Kill Me Again. unabr. ed. 1996. (Fey Croaker Mystery Ser.: Bk. 1). audio 49.95 (*1-55686-614-3*) Books in Motion.
—Kill Me Again. 1994. 288p. mass mkt. 4.99 (*0-380-76890-9*, Avon Bks.) Morrow/Avon.
—Tequila Mockingbird. 1998. (Fey Croaker Novels Ser.). 400p. pap. 6.99 (*0-671-02531-7*, Pocket) Simon & Schuster.
—Tequila Mockingbird: A Fey Croaker Novel. 1997. (Fey Croaker Novels Ser.). 400p. 23.00 o.s.i (*0-684-83009-4*, Scribner) Simon & Schuster.
—Twice Dead. unabr. ed. 1996. (Fey Croaker Mystery Ser.: Bk. 2). audio 64.95 (*1-55686-710-7*) Books in Motion.
—Twice Dead. 1996. 336p. mass mkt. 5.50 (*0-380-77862-9*, Avon Bks.) Morrow/Avon.
Blatty, William P. Demons Five, Exorcists Nothing: A Fable. 1996. 188p. 18.95 o.p. (*1-55611-501-6*) Fine, Donald I. Bks.
Bloom, Rebecca. Girl Anatomy: A Novel. 2003. 272p. pap. 12.95 (*0-06-093680-0*, Perennial) HarperTrade.
—Girl Anatomy: A Novel. 2002. 272p. 24.95 (*0-06-621257-X*, Morrow, William & Co.) Morrow/Avon.
—Tangled up in Daydreams. 2003. 288p. 24.95 (*0-06-621258-8*, Morrow, William & Co.) Morrow/Avon.
Blum, Bill. The Face of Justice. 1999. pap. 19.95 (*0-525-93906-7*); 1998. 400p. mass mkt. 6.99 o.s.i (*0-451-40803-9*, Onyx) NAL.
—The Last Appeal. 1997. 416p. mass mkt. 6.99 o.s.i (*0-451-18311-8*, Signet Bks.) NAL.
—Prejudicial Error. 1995. 304p. 21.95 o.p. (*0-525-93905-9*, Dutton) Dutton/Plume.
—Prejudicial Error. 1996. 368p. mass mkt. 5.99 o.s.i (*0-451-18309-6*, Signet Bks.) NAL.
Bogart, Humphrey, et al. The Maltese Falcon. 1946. audio 7.95 National Recording Co.
Bogner, Norman. The Deadliest Art. 2001. 384p. 25.95 (*0-312-86856-1*, Forge Bks.) Doherty, Tom Assocs., LLC.
Boorstin, Jon. Pay or Play. 1997. 256p. 22.00 o.p. (*0-7867-0359-8*, Carroll & Graf Pubs.) Avalon Publishing Group.
—Pay or Play. 2000. 278p. pap. 12.95 (*1-890085-04-9*) Siles Pr.
Boucher, Anthony. Nine Times Nine. 1986. 254p. pap. 4.95 o.p. (*0-930330-37-4*) International Polygonics, Ltd.
—Rocket to the Morgue. 1988. 176p. pap. 4.95 (*0-930330-82-X*) International Polygonics, Ltd.
Boyd, William. The New Confessions. 1989. 480p. pap. 8.95 o.p. (*0-14-010699-5*, Penguin Bks.) Viking Penguin.
Boyle, Alistair. The Con: A Gil Yates Private Investigator Novel. 1996. 222p. 19.95 (*0-9627297-9-5*) Knoll, Allen A. Pubs.
Boyle, Dan. Huddle. 2003. 244p. pap. 16.95 (*1-56023-459-8*, Southern Tier Editions) Haworth Pr., Inc., The.
Boyle, T. Coraghessan. The Tortilla Curtain, Set. abr. ed. 1995. audio 16.95 (*1-55927-353-4*, 393174) Audio Renaissance.
—The Tortilla Curtain. unabr. ed. 1996. audio 80.00 (*0-7366-3300-6*, 3955) Books on Tape, Inc.
—The Tortilla Curtain. l.t. ed. 1996. 25.95 (*1-56895-287-2*, Wheeler Publishing, Inc.) Gale Group.
—The Tortilla Curtain. 1996. 368p. pap. 14.00 (*0-14-023828-X*) Penguin Group (USA) Inc.
—The Tortilla Curtain. unabr. ed. audio 85.00 (*0-7887-0457-5*, 94650E7) Recorded Bks., LLC.
—The Tortilla Curtain. 1995. 368p. 23.95 o.s.i (*0-670-85604-5*, Viking) Viking Penguin.
Braudy, Susan. Who Killed Sal Mineo? 1982. 14.50 o.s.i (*0-671-61009-0*, Simon & Schuster) Simon & Schuster.
Braverman, Kate. Lithium for Medea. 1989. 256p. pap. 8.95 o.p. (*0-14-012641-4*, Penguin Bks.) Viking Penguin.
—Palm Latitudes. 2003. 384p. reprint ed. pap. 14.95 (*1-58322-572-2*) Seven Stories Pr.
—Palm Latitudes. 1988. 18.95 o.p. (*0-671-64542-0*, Simon & Schuster) Simon & Schuster.
—Palm Latitudes. 1989. 384p. pap. 8.95 o.p. (*0-14-012640-6*, Penguin Bks.) Viking Penguin.
Bray, Marian F. Stars over East L. A. 1993. (Young Adult Fiction Ser.). 216p. (Orig.). (YA). (gr. 8-12). pap. 6.99 o.p. (*0-87788-798-5*, Shaw) WaterBrook Pr.
Breen, Jon. The Gathering Place. 1984. (Mysteries Ser.). 192p. 12.95 o.p. (*0-8027-5575-5*) Walker & Co.
Breen, Jon L. Touch of the Past. l.t. ed. 1990. 16.95 o.p. (*0-7451-9711-6*, C0053); pap. 14.95 o.p. (*0-7927-0123-2*, C0201) BBC Audiobooks America.
—Touch of the Past. 1988. 192p. 16.95 o.p. (*0-8027-5704-9*) Walker & Co.
Brennan, Carol. In the Dark. l.t. ed. 1995. 288p. lib. bdg. 23.95 (*1-57490-029-3*, Beeler Large Print Bks.) Beeler, Thomas T. Publisher.
—In the Dark. 1995. 256p. mass mkt. 4.99 o.p. (*0-425-14579-4*, Prime Crime) Berkley Publishing Group.
—In the Dark. 1994. 288p. 21.95 o.p. (*0-399-13940-0*, G. P. Putnam's Sons) Penguin Group (USA) Inc.
Britto, Anthony. Tattoo. pap. 15.95 (*0-312-30230-4*, Saint Martin's Griffin); 1997. 400p. 24.95 o.p. (*0-312-15220-5*, Saint Martin's Minotaur) St. Martin's Pr.
Brookmyre, Christopher. Not the End of the World. 2001. 388p. 23.00 (*0-87113-787-9*, Atlantic Monthly Pr.) Grove/Atlantic, Inc.
Brown, Sandra. Send No Flowers. 2000. 256p. mass mkt. 6.99 (*0-553-57601-1*); 1984. 192p. mass mkt. 2.25 o.s.i (*0-553-21659-7*) Bantam Bks.
—Send No Flowers. l.t. ed. (Wheeler Press Paperback Ser.). 2000. pap. 10.95 (*1-56895-974-5*); 1999. 27.95 (*1-56895-720-3*) Gale Group. (Wheeler Publishing, Inc.).
—Send No Flowers, abr. ed. 1999. audio 18.00 Highsmith Inc.
Buffa, D. W. The Legacy. 2004. 480p. mass mkt. 8.00 (*0-446-61013-5*) Warner Bks., Inc.
Bukowski, Charles. Ham on Rye. 2001. 336p. pap. 9.83 (*1-84195-163-3*) Canongate Bks. GBR. *Dist:* Grove/Atlantic, Inc.
—Ham on Rye. 1998. 288p. reprint ed. 25.00 (*0-87685-558-3*); pap. 16.00 (*0-87685-557-5*) HarperCollins Pubs.
—Hollywood. 1989. 35.00 o.p. (*0-87685-765-9*, Black Sparrow Pr.) Godine, David R. Pub.
—Hollywood. 1998. reprint ed. 244p. 25.00 (*0-87685-764-0*); 248p. pap. 16.00 (*0-87685-763-2*) HarperCollins Pubs.
—Post Office. 1998. reprint ed. 192p. 25.00 (*0-87685-087-5*); 200p. pap. 15.00 (*0-87685-086-7*) HarperCollins Pubs.
—Pulp. deluxe ed. 1994. 200p. 40.00 o.p. (*0-87685-928-7*, Black Sparrow Pr.) Godine, David R. Pub.
—Pulp. 1998. reprint ed. 202p. 25.00 (*0-87685-927-9*); 208p. pap. 15.00 (*0-87685-926-0*) HarperCollins Pubs.
Bunker, Edward. No Beast So Fierce: A Novel. 1993. (Vintage Crime/Black Lizard Ser.). pap. 10.00 o.s.i (*0-679-74155-0*, Vintage) Knopf Publishing Group.
Bunting, Eve. Will You Be My POSSLQ. 1987. 160p. (YA). (gr. 7 up). 12.95 (*0-15-297399-0*) Harcourt Children's Bks.
Burke, Jan. Nine. 2003. 544p. mass mkt. 7.50 (*0-7434-4454-X*, Pocket); 2002. 384p. 24.00 (*0-7432-2389-6*, Simon & Schuster); 2002. E-Book 14.99 (*0-7432-3334-4*, Simon & Schuster) Simon & Schuster.
Byrd, Max. Fuse Time. 1991. 288p. mass mkt. 4.95 o.s.i (*0-553-28816-4*) Bantam Bks.
Cameron, Carey. Daddy Boy. 1989. 377p. 15.95 o.p. (*0-912697-84-9*) Algonquin Bks. of Chapel Hill.
Cameron, Sue. Honey Dust. 1993. 368p. 18.95 o.s.i (*0-446-51513-2*) Warner Bks., Inc.
Campbell, Bebe Moore. Brothers & Sisters. abr. ed. 1994. audio 19.95 (*1-55927-303-8*, 492032) Audio Renaissance.
—Brothers & Sisters. 2000. 480p. pap. 13.95 (*0-425-17267-8*); 1995. 560p. mass mkt. 7.99 (*0-425-14940-4*) Berkley Publishing Group.
—Brothers & Sisters. unabr. ed. 1996. audio 112.00 (*0-7366-3202-6*, 3866) Books on Tape, Inc.
—Brothers & Sisters. l.t. ed. 1995. (Large Print Bks.). 26.95 o.p. (*1-56895-211-2*, Wheeler Publishing, Inc.) Gale Group.
—Brothers & Sisters. 1994. 480p. 22.95 o.p. (*0-399-13929-X*, G. P. Putnam's Sons) Penguin Group (USA) Inc.
—Brothers & Sisters. 476p. pap. 22.95 o.p. (*0-7651-0630-2*) Smithmark Pubs., Inc.
—Brothers & Sisters. 1995. 14.04 (*0-606-19295-6*) Turtleback Bks.
—Brothers & Sisters. 1997. 4.98 (*0-681-56088-6*) Waldenbooks, Inc.
—Singing in the Comeback Choir. 1999. 400p. reprint ed. mass mkt. 7.99 (*0-425-16662-7*) Berkley Publishing Group.
—Singing in the Comeback Choir. l.t. ed. 1998. (Large Print Book Ser.). 27.95 (*1-56895-613-4*, Wheeler Publishing, Inc.) Gale Group.
—Singing in the Comeback Choir. 1998. 320p. 24.95 o.p. (*0-399-14298-3*, G. P. Putnam's Sons) Penguin Group (USA) Inc.
—Singing in the Comeback Choir. 1999. 13.55 (*0-606-19302-2*) Turtleback Bks.
Campbell, Robert. Alice in La-La Land. 1999. 232p. pap. 17.95 (*1-58444-024-4*) Disc-Us Bks., Inc.
—Alice in La-La Land. Chelius, Jane, ed. 1990. mass mkt. 4.95 (*0-671-73343-5*, Pocket) Simon & Schuster.
—Alice in La-La Land. 1987. 256p. 16.45 o.p. (*0-671-64483-1*, Simon & Schuster) Simon & Schuster.
—In La-La Land We Trust. 2000. E-Book 19.95 incl. cd-rom (*1-58444-076-7*); 1999. 230p. pap. 17.95 (*1-58444-051-1*) Disc-Us Bks., Inc.
—In La-La Land We Trust. 1986. 15.45 o.p. (*0-89296-170-8*) Mysterious Pr.
—In La-La Land We Trust. 1987. mass mkt. 4.95 o.p. (*0-445-40596-1*, Mysterious Pr. Paperback Bks.) Warner Bks., Inc.
—Juice. Chelius, Jane, ed. 1990. 320p. mass mkt. 4.95 (*0-671-67454-4*, Pocket) Simon & Schuster.
—Juice. 1989. pap. 18.95 o.p. (*0-671-66624-X*, Simon & Schuster) Simon & Schuster.
—The La-La Land Quartet: Contains 4 Titles- Alice in La-La Land, in La-La Land We Trust, Sweet La-La Land, & Wizard of La-La Land. 2000. E-Book 24.95 incl. cd-rom (*1-58444-083-X*) Disc-Us Bks., Inc.
—Sweet La-La Land. 2000. E-Book 16.95 incl. cd-rom (*1-58444-075-9*); 1999. 232p. pap. 17.95 (*1-58444-050-3*) Disc-Us Bks., Inc.
—Sweet La-La Land. 1990. 18.95 o.p. (*0-671-64484-X*, Simon & Schuster) Simon & Schuster.
—Sweet La-La Land. Chelius, Jane, ed. 1991. 320p. reprint ed. mass mkt. 4.99 (*0-671-73236-6*, Pocket) Simon & Schuster.
—The Wizard of La-La Land. 1999. 244p. pap. 17.95 (*1-58444-052-X*) Disc-Us Bks., Inc.
—The Wizard of La-La Land. Chelius, Jane, ed. 1995. 288p. 20.00 o.p. (*0-671-70321-8*, Atria) Simon & Schuster.
Cannell, Stephen J. Hollywood Tough: A Shane Scully Novel. 2004. 448p. mass mkt. 6.99 (*0-312-98942-3*, St. Martin's Paperbacks) St. Martin's Pr.
—The Tin Collectors. l.t. ed. 2001. (Wheeler Large Print Book Ser.). viii, 467p. 29.95 o.p. (*1-58724-080-7*, Wheeler Publishing, Inc.) Gale Group.
—The Tin Collectors. E-Book 24.95 (*0-312-70062-8*); 2001. E-Book 24.95 (*0-312-27411-4*); 2001. viii, 389p. 24.95 o.p. (*0-312-26959-5*) St. Martin's Pr.
—Vertical Coffin: A Shane Scully Novel. 2004. 400p. 24.95 (*0-312-30425-0*) St. Martin's Pr.
—The Viking Funeral. l.t. ed. 2002. (Wheeler Large Print Book Ser.). 27.95 (*1-58724-169-2*, Wheeler Publishing, Inc.) Gale Group.
—The Viking Funeral. 2002. 400p. 24.95 (*0-312-26960-9*) St. Martin's Pr.
Cannon, Taffy. Open Season on Lawyers: A Novel of Suspense. 2002. 13.95 (*1-880284-51-0*) Daniel, John & Co., Pubs.
Carroll, Jonathan. Sleeping in Flame. 1990. 288p. pap. 13.00 (*0-679-72777-9*, Vintage) Knopf Publishing Group.
—Sleeping in Flames. 1989. 288p. 17.95 o.s.i (*0-385-24957-8*) Doubleday Publishing.
Cebulash, Mel. Dirty Money. 1993. 3.95 (*1-56420-002-7*) New Readers Pr.
—Dirty Money: A Sully Gomez Mystery. 1993. (J). audio 10.95 (*1-56420-003-5*) New Readers Pr.
—Knockout Punch: A Sully Gomez Mystery. 1993. audio 9.95 o.p. (*1-56420-009-4*); 3.95 o.p. (*1-56420-008-6*) New Readers Pr.
—Set to Explode: A Sully Gomez Mystery. 1993. 3.95 o.p. (*1-56420-004-3*) New Readers Pr.
—Set to Explode: A/Sully Gomez Mystery. 1993. (J). audio 10.00 o.p. (*1-56420-005-1*) New Readers Pr.
—A Sucker for Redheads: A Sully Gomez Mystery. 1993. audio 9.95 o.p. (*1-56420-007-8*); 3.95 o.p. (*1-56420-006-X*) New Readers Pr.
Chan, David Marshall. Goblin Fruit. 2003. 226p. 21.95 (*1-893956-32-6*) Context Bks.
Chandler, Raymond. Adieu, Ma Jolie. 1988. Orig. Title: Farewell, My Lovely. (FRE.). 301p. pap. 11.95 (*0-7859-2102-8*, 2070380793) French & European Pubns., Inc.
—The Adventures of Philip Marlowe, Vol. 1. collector's ed. 1999. 34.98 incl. audio Radio Spirits, Inc.
—The Big Sleep. deluxe ltd. ed. 1986. (Illus.). 250p. 425.00 o.p. (*0-910457-09-3*) Arion Pr.
—The Big Sleep. 1975. 224p. mass mkt. 1.50 o.s.i (*0-345-24565-2*); 1973. mass mkt. 0.95 o.s.i (*0-345-22201-6*) Ballantine Bks.
—The Big Sleep. 1986. (Mystery Ser.). mass mkt. 9.95 o.p. (*0-553-06513-0*) Bantam Bks.
—The Big Sleep. 1994. reprint ed. lib. bdg. 29.95 o.p. (*1-56849-261-8*) Buccaneer Bks., Inc.
—The Big Sleep. l.t. ed. 2002. 232p. lib. bdg. 27.95 (*1-58547-164-X*) Ctr. Point Large Print.
—The Big Sleep. abr. ed. audio 15.95 o.p. (*0-88646-007-7*, 7009) Durkin Hayes Publishing Ltd.
—The Big Sleep. 1989. (Illus.). 256p. reprint ed. 22.95 o.p. (*0-86547-402-8*, North Point Pr.) Farrar, Straus & Giroux.
—The Big Sleep. Garrett, George P. et al, eds. 1989. (Film Scripts Ser.). reprint ed. pap. 19.95 (*0-89197-677-9*) Irvington Pubs.
—The Big Sleep. 1992. pap. 9.00 (*0-394-23906-7*); 1988. 240p. reprint ed. pap. 12.00 (*0-394-75828-5*) Knopf Publishing Group. (Vintage).
—The Big Sleep. abr. ed. 1993. 16.95 o.p. (*1-55800-690-7*); audio 29.95 o.p. (*1-55800-848-9*, 752391) NewStar Media, Inc.
—The Big Sleep. 1992. pap. 9.00 o.p. (*0-679-74091-0*); 1978. pap. 3.95 o.p. (*0-394-72631-6*) Random Hse., Inc.
—The Big Sleep. 2002. (Best Mysteries of All Time Ser.). 261p. (*0-7621-8880-4*, Impress) Scriptorium Pr., The.
—The Big Sleep. 1995. 288p. reprint ed. 35.00 (*1-883402-16-6*, Scribner) Simon & Schuster.
—The Big Sleep & Farewell, My Lovely. 1995. (Modern Library Ser.). 544p. 18.95 (*0-679-60140-6*) Random Hse., Inc.
—The Big Sleep & The High Window. abr. ed. 1999. audio 16.85 (*0-563-55892-X*) BBC Bk. Publishing GBR. *Dist:* Ulverscroft Large Print Bks., Ltd.
—La Dame du Lac. 1988. Orig. Title: Lady of the Lake. (FRE.). 258p. pap. 10.95 (*0-7859-2088-9*, 2070379434) French & European Pubns., Inc.
—Farewell, My Lovely. 1983. 256p. mass mkt. 2.25 o.s.i (*0-345-31528-6*, Ballantine Bks.); 1973. mass mkt. 0.95 o.s.i (*0-345-22202-4*) Ballantine Bks.

—Farewell, My Lovely. 1992. pap. 10.00 (*0-394-23907-5*); 1988. 304p. reprint ed. pap. 12.00 (*0-394-75827-7*) Knopf Publishing Group. (Vintage).

—Farewell, My Lovely. abr. ed. 1993. 16.95 o.p. (*1-55800-672-9*); audio 29.95 o.p. (*1-55800-769-5*) NewStar Media, Inc.

—Farewell, My Lovely. 1986. audio 14.95 o.p. (*0-394-55466-3*); 1985. audio 16.00 o.p. (*0-394-55048-X*) Random Hse. Audio Publishing Group. (RH Audio).

—Farewell, My Lovely. 1992. pap. 10.00 (*0-679-74090-2*); 1976. pap. 3.95 o.p. (*0-394-72138-1*) Random Hse., Inc.

—Farewell, My Lovely & The Lady in the Lake. abr. ed. 1999. audio 16.85 (*0-563-55897-0*) BBC Bk. Publishing GBR. *Dist:* Ulverscroft Large Print Bks., Ltd.

—La Grande Fenetre. 1989. Orig. Title: High Window. (FRE.). 276p. pap. 10.95 (*0-7859-2236-9*, 207038103X) French & European Pubns., Inc.

—Le Grande Sommeil. 1987. Orig. Title: Big Sleep. (FRE.). 252p. pap. 10.95 (*0-7859-2071-4*, 2070378659) French & European Pubns., Inc.

—The High Window. 1971. mass mkt. 0.95 o.s.i (*0-345-22203-2*) Ballantine Bks.

—The High Window. l.t. ed. 23.95 (*1-85695-367-X*) ISIS Large Print Bks. GBR. *Dist:* Transaction Pubs.

—The High Window. 1992. pap. 10.00 (*0-394-23908-3*); 1976. pap. 3.95 o.p. (*0-394-72141-1*); 1988. 272p. reprint ed. pap. 12.00 (*0-394-75826-9*) Knopf Publishing Group. (Vintage).

—The High Window. abr. ed. 1993. audio 15.95 o.p. (*1-55800-091-7*, 40290, Dove Audio) NewStar Media, Inc.

—Killer in the Rain. 1987. mass mkt. 3.95 o.s.i (*0-345-35185-1*); 1986. mass mkt. 2.95 o.s.i (*0-345-34195-3*); 1984. mass mkt. 2.50 o.s.i (*0-345-32020-4*); 1980. mass mkt. 2.25 o.s.i (*0-345-28858-0*); 1977. mass mkt. 1.95 o.s.i (*0-345-25728-6*) Ballantine Bks.

—Killer in the Rain & Other Stories. abr. ed. 1996. 24.95 o.p. (*0-7871-0555-4*, 693446) NewStar Media, Inc.

—The Lady in the Lake. Date not set. lib. bdg. 20.95 (*0-8488-2136-X*) Amereon, Ltd.

—The Lady in the Lake. 1976. (Crime Fiction Ser). reprint ed. lib. bdg. 21.00 o.p. (*0-8240-2358-7*) Garland Publishing, Inc.

—The Lady in the Lake. l.t. ed. 23.95 (*1-85695-362-9*) ISIS Large Print Bks. GBR. *Dist:* Transaction Pubs.

—The Lady in the Lake. 1992. pap. 10.00 (*0-394-23909-1*); 1988. 272p. pap. 12.00 (*0-394-75825-0*); 1976. pap. 3.95 o.p. (*0-394-72145-4*) Knopf Publishing Group. (Vintage).

—The Lady in the Lake. abr. ed. 1993. audio 8.99 o.p. (*1-55800-916-7*); audio 15.95 o.p. (*1-55800-069-0*, 40240) NewStar Media, Inc. (Dove Audio).

—The Lady in the Lake. 1992. pap. 10.00 (*0-679-74088-0*) Random Hse., Inc.

—The Lady in the Lake. 1994. 288p. 35.00 (*1-883402-94-8*, Scribner) Simon & Schuster.

—Later Novels & Other Writings: The Lady in the Lake; The Little Sister; The Long Goodbye; Playback; Double Indemnity; Essays & Letters. MacShane, Frank, ed. 1995. 1088p. 35.00 (*1-883011-08-6*) Library of America, The.

—The Little Sister. l.t. ed. 1993. 21.95 o.p. (*0-7927-1654-X*); pap. 19.95 o.p. (*0-7927-1653-1*); audio 54.95 (*0-7451-5823-4*, CAB 057) BBC Audiobooks America.

—The Little Sister. 1985. mass mkt. 2.95 o.s.i (*0-345-32217-7*); 1983. mass mkt. 2.25 o.s.i (*0-345-31643-6*); 1977. mass mkt. 1.95 o.s.i (*0-345-25727-8*) Ballantine Bks.

—The Little Sister. 1988. (Vintage Crime Ser.). 256p. pap. 12.00 (*0-394-75767-X*, Vintage) Knopf Publishing Group.

—The Little Sister. abr. ed. 1993. pap. 15.95 o.p. incl. audio (*1-55800-082-8*, 40270) NewStar Media, Inc.

—The Little Sister. 1994. 256p. 35.00 (*1-883402-79-4*, Scribner) Simon & Schuster.

—The Little Sister. unabr. ed. 1983. (J). audio 49.95 o.p. (*0-8161-9777-6*) Thorndike Pr.

—The Long Goodbye. 1987. mass mkt. 3.95 o.s.i (*0-345-34938-5*); 1985. mass mkt. 2.95 o.s.i (*0-345-32132-4*); 1982. mass mkt. 2.50 o.s.i (*0-345-30582-5*); 1980. mass mkt. 2.25 o.s.i (*0-345-28859-9*); 1977. mass mkt. 1.95 o.s.i (*0-345-25734-0*) Ballantine Bks.

—The Long Goodbye. 1992. pap. 10.00 (*0-394-23910-5*); 1988. 384p. pap. 13.00 (*0-394-75768-8*) Knopf Publishing Group. (Vintage).

—The Long Goodbye. abr. ed. 1993. audio 15.95 o.p. (*1-55800-002-X*, 40010, Dove Audio) NewStar Media, Inc.

—The Long Goodbye. 1992. pap. 10.00 (*0-679-74087-2*) Random Hse., Inc.

—The Long Goodbye & The Little Sister. abr. ed. 1999. audio 16.85 (*0-563-55803-2*) BBC Bk. Publishing GBR. *Dist:* Ulverscroft Large Print Bks., Ltd.

—Midnight Raymond Chandler, 001. 1971. 10.25 o.p. (*0-395-13152-9*) Houghton Mifflin Co.

—Philip Marlowe. 1999. (Illus.). 416p. pap. 16.00 (*0-671-03890-7*) ibooks, Inc.

—Playback. 1987. mass mkt. 2.95 o.s.i (*0-345-32226-6*); 1987. mass mkt. 3.95 o.s.i (*0-345-34933-4*); 1984. mass mkt. 2.50 o.s.i (*0-345-31961-3*); 1980. mass mkt. 2.25 o.s.i (*0-345-28857-2*); 1976. mass mkt. 1.50 o.s.i (*0-345-25169-5*) Ballantine Bks.

—Playback. l.t. ed. 2001. (Dales Large Print Ser.). 240p. pap. 20.99 (*1-84262-094-0*) Dales Large Print Bks. GBR. *Dist:* Ulverscroft Large Print Bks., Ltd., Ulverscroft Large Print Canada, Ltd.

—Playback. 1988. (Vintage Crime Ser.). 176p. pap. 11.00 (*0-394-75766-1*, Vintage) Knopf Publishing Group.

—Playback. unabr. ed. 1993. pap. 24.95 o.p. (*1-55800-270-7*) NewStar Media, Inc.

—Raymond Chandler: Four Complete Philip Marlowe Novels. 1986. 8.99 o.s.i (*0-517-61811-7*) Random Hse. Value Publishing.

—Stories & Early Novels: Pulp Stories; The Big Sleep; Farewell, My Lovely; The High Window. MacShane, Frank, ed. 1995. 1216p. 35.00 (*1-883011-07-8*) Library of America, The.

—Trouble Is My Business. 1987. mass mkt. 3.95 o.s.i (*0-345-35494-X*); 1984. mass mkt. 2.50 o.s.i (*0-345-32021-2*); 1980. mass mkt. 2.25 o.s.i (*0-345-28862-9*) Ballantine Bks.

—Trouble Is My Business. 1992. pap. 9.00 (*0-394-23911-3*); 1988. 224p. pap. 12.00 (*0-394-75764-5*) Knopf Publishing Group. (Vintage).

—Trouble Is My Business. unabr. ed. 1993. audio 15.95 o.p. (*1-55800-090-9*, 40320, Dove Audio) NewStar Media, Inc.

—Trouble Is My Business. 1992. pap. 9.00 (*0-679-74086-4*) Random Hse., Inc.

—Un Tueur sous la Pluie. 1988. Orig. Title: Killer in the Rain. (FRE.). 245p. pap. 10.95 (*0-7859-2082-X*, 2070379108) French & European Pubns., Inc.

Chandler, Raymond & Parker, Robert B. Farewell, My Lovely & Poodle Springs. abr. ed. 1993. audio 17.95 (*1-55800-778-4*, Dove Audio) NewStar Media, Inc.

—Poodle Springs. 1990. (J). mass mkt. 7.50 o.s.i (*0-425-12343-X*) Berkley Publishing Group.

—Poodle Springs. abr. ed. 1993. audio 14.95 o.p. (*1-55800-168-9*, Dove Audio) NewStar Media, Inc.

—Poodle Springs. 1989. 18.95 o.p. (*0-399-13482-4*, G. P. Putnam's Sons) Penguin Putnam Bks. for Young Readers.

Chang, Leonard. Underkill: An Allen Choice Novel. 2003. 336p. 24.95 (*0-312-30843-4*, Saint Martin's Minotaur) St. Martin's Pr.

Charbonneau, Louis. The Devil's Menagerie. 1996. 288p. 23.95 o.p. (*1-55611-494-X*, Dutton) Fine, Donald I. Bks.

Chin, Frank. Gunga Din Highway. 400p. 1995. pap. 14.95 (*1-56689-037-3*); 1994. 24.95 (*1-56689-024-1*) Coffee Hse. Pr.

Clare, Baxter. Cry Havoc: A Detective Franco Mystery. 2003. 256p. pap. 12.95 (*1-931513-31-7*) Bella Bks., Inc.

Clark, Carol Higgins. Jinxed: A Reagan Reilly Mystery. 2002. 272p. 23.00 (*0-7432-0582-0*); 272p. 23.00 (*0-7432-4625-X*); 352p. 23.00 (*0-7432-3519-3*) Simon & Schuster. (Scribner).

—Popped: A Regan Reilly Mystery. 2003. 288p. 23.00 (*0-7432-4937-2*, Scribner) Simon & Schuster.

Clark, Leigh. Shock Radio. 1998. 352p. mass mkt. 6.99 (*0-8125-2372-5*, Tor Bks.); 1996. 381p. 24.95 o.p. (*0-312-85724-1*, Forge Bks.) Doherty, Tom Assocs., LLC.

Coleman, Wanda. Mambo Hips & Make Believe. ltd. ed. 1999. 250p. 35.00 o.p. (*1-57423-096-4*, Black Sparrow Pr.) Godine, David R. Pub.

—Mambo Hips & Make Believe: A Novel. 1999. 403p. 25.00 o.p. (*1-57423-095-6*, Black Sparrow Pr.) Godine, David R. Pub.

—Mambo Hips & Make Believe: A Novel. 1999. 403p. pap. 16.00 (*1-57423-094-8*) HarperCollins Pubs.

Collins, Jackie. Chances. abr. ed. 1991. audio 15.95 (*0-671-73807-0*); Pt. 2. 1995. audio 15.95 (*0-671-75510-2*) Simon & Schuster Audio. (Simon & Schuster Audioworks).

—Chances. 816p. 1981. 14.95 o.s.i (*0-446-51237-0*); 1991. reprint ed. mass mkt. 7.99 (*0-446-35717-0*) Warner Bks., Inc.

—Dangerous Kiss: A Lucky Santangelo Novel. l.t. ed. 2000. (Thorndike/G. K. Hall Paperback Bestsellers Ser.). 620p. pap. 28.95 (*0-7838-8748-5*, Macmillan Reference USA) Gale Group.

—Dangerous Kiss: A Lucky Santangelo Novel, Set. abr. ed. 1999. audio 25.00 Highsmith Inc.

—Dangerous Kiss: A Lucky Santangelo Novel. abr. ed. 2001. audio (*0-333-78160-0*) Macmillan U.K. GBR. *Dist:* Macmillan Publishing Co., Inc.

—Dangerous Kiss: A Lucky Santangelo Novel. unabr. ed. 2001. audio 94.00 (*0-7887-4979-X*, 96486L8) Recorded Bks., LLC.

—Dangerous Kiss: A Lucky Santangelo Novel. 2000. E-Book 25.00 (*0-684-87371-0*, Simon & Schuster); 1999. 528p. 25.00 (*0-684-85030-3*, Simon & Schuster); 2000. (Illus.). 592p. reprint ed. pap. 7.99 (*0-671-02095-1*, Pocket) Simon & Schuster.

—Dangerous Kiss: A Lucky Santangelo Novel. abr. ed. 1999. audio 25.00 (*0-671-58199-6*, Simon & Schuster Audioworks) Simon & Schuster Audio.

—Dangerous Kiss: A Lucky Santangelo Novel. l.t. ed. 1999. (Core Ser.). 620p. 31.95 (*0-7838-8747-7*) Thorndike Pr.

—Hollywood Husbands. 1986. 512p. 18.45 o.p. (*0-671-52500-X*, Simon & Schuster) Simon & Schuster.

—Hollywood Kids. l.t. ed. 1995. (G. K. Hall Core Ser.). 850p. 25.95 (*0-7838-1211-6*); 733p. 20.95 o.p. (*0-7838-1212-4*) Gale Group. (Macmillan Reference USA).

—Hollywood Kids. 1999. per. 7.99 (*0-671-02356-X*, Pocket); 1995. pap. 6.50 (*0-671-89856-6*, Pocket); 1994. 624p. 23.50 (*0-671-66627-4*, Simon & Schuster); 1995. 624p. reprint ed. mass mkt. 7.99 (*0-671-89849-3*, Pocket) Simon & Schuster.

—Hollywood Kids. abr. ed. 1999. 5p. audio 23.00 (*0-671-88859-5*, 492040, Simon & Schuster Audioworks) Simon & Schuster Audio.

—Hollywood Wives: The New Generation. 2001. 528p. 26.00 (*0-7432-1634-2*, Simon & Schuster); 1999. per. 7.99 (*0-671-02355-1*, Pocket); 1986. 560p. mass mkt. 4.95 o.s.i (*0-671-62425-3*, Pocket); 1985. mass mkt. 4.50 o.s.i (*0-671-54764-X*, Pocket); 1984. mass mkt. 4.50 o.s.i (*0-671-49227-6*, Pocket); 1983. 512p. 16.50 o.p. (*0-671-47406-5*, Simon & Schuster); 1987. 560p. reprint ed. mass mkt. 7.99 (*0-671-70459-1*, Pocket) Simon & Schuster.

—Lady Boss. l.t. ed. 1991. (General Ser.). 760p. 16.95 o.p. (*0-8161-5189-X*); lib. bdg. 22.95 o.p. (*0-8161-5193-8*) Gale Group. (Macmillan Reference USA).

—Lady Boss. Peters, Sally, ed. 1992. mass mkt. 5.99 (*0-671-79571-6*, Pocket) Simon & Schuster.

—Lady Boss. 1990. 21.95 o.p. (*0-671-61937-3*); 21.95 (*0-671-94826-1*) Simon & Schuster. (Simon & Schuster).

—Lady Boss. Grose, Bill, ed. 1991. 640p. reprint ed. mass mkt. 7.99 (*0-671-74418-6*, Pocket) Simon & Schuster.

—Lady Boss. rev. ed. 1998. 640p. mass mkt. 7.99 (*0-671-02347-0*, Pocket) Simon & Schuster.

—Lady Boss. abr. ed. 1990. audio 15.95 (*0-671-73710-4*, Simon & Schuster Audioworks) Simon & Schuster Audio.

—Lucky. 1990. 608p. mass mkt. 5.95 o.s.i (*0-671-63845-9*); 1987. mass mkt. 6.99 (*0-671-70419-2*); 1986. 608p. mass mkt. 4.95 o.s.i (*0-671-52496-8*); 1998. 624p. mass mkt. 7.99 (*0-671-02348-9*) Simon & Schuster. (Pocket).

—Lucky. abr. ed. 1991. audio 15.95 (*0-671-73808-9*, Simon & Schuster Audioworks) Simon & Schuster Audio.

—Vendetta: Lucky's Revenge. l.t. ed. 1997. (Large Print Book Ser.). 28.95 (*1-56895-435-2*, Wheeler Publishing, Inc.) Gale Group.

—Vendetta: Lucky's Revenge. 1997. 544p. 25.00 o.p. (*0-06-039209-6*, ReganBooks); audio 25.00 o.p. (*0-694-51809-3*, CPN 4048, HarperAudio) HarperTrade.

—Vendetta: Lucky's Revenge. 1998. 5.98 o.p. (*0-7651-0824-0*) Smithmark Pubs., Inc.

Collins, Joan. Infamous. 1996. 320p. 23.95 o.p. (*0-525-94129-0*, Dutton) Dutton/Plume.

Collins, Max Allan. Angel in Black. 2001. (Nathan Heller Ser.). 352p. 21.95 o.s.i (*0-451-20263-5*, Signet Bks.) NAL.

Comfort, Bonnie. Denial. 1996. pap. 5.99 (*0-380-72716-1*, Avon Bks.) Morrow/Avon.

—Denial. 1995. 302p. 22.00 o.p. (*0-671-89696-2*, Simon & Schuster) Simon & Schuster.

Compo, Susan. Life after Death & Other Stories. (New American Fiction Ser.). 1991. 214p. pap. 9.95 o.p. (*0-571-12914-5*); 1990. 224p. 18.95 o.p. (*0-571-12902-1*) Faber & Faber, Inc.

—Malingering: Short Stories. 1993. 220p. (Orig.). pap. 13.95 o.p. (*0-571-19818-X*) Faber & Faber, Inc.

Conn, Nicole. She Walks in Beauty. 2002. 320p. pap. 14.95 (*1-56280-269-0*) Naiad Pr., Inc.

Connelly, Michael. Angels Flight. 1999. (*0-7540-2211-0*) BBC Audiobooks America.

—Angels Flight. unabr. ed. 1999. (Harry Bosch Novel Ser.). audio 39.95 (*1-56740-410-3*, 1512, Brilliance Audio Unabridged) Brilliance Audio.

—Angels Flight, unabr. ed. 1999. audio 73.25 Highsmith Inc.

—Angels Flight. 1999. (Detective Harry Bosch Mysteries Ser.). 400p. (YA). (gr. 8 up). 25.00 o.p. (*0-316-15219-6*) Little Brown & Co.

—Angels Flight. l.t. ed. (Thorndike/G. K. Hall Paperback Bestsellers Ser.). 595p. 2000. pap. 27.95 (*0-7862-1865-7*); 1999. 30.95 (*0-7862-1864-9*) Thorndike Pr.

—Angels Flight. abr. ed. 1999. (Detective Harry Bosch Mysteries Ser.). (gr. 8 up). audio 24.00 (*1-57042-645-7*) Time Warner AudioBooks.

—Angels Flight. 2000. 480p. reprint ed. mass mkt. 7.99 (*0-446-60727-4*) Warner Bks., Inc.

—The Black Echo. 1992. 19.95 o.p. (*0-316-15361-3*) Little Brown & Co.

—The Black Echo. 10th ed. 1993. 418p. mass mkt. 7.99 (*0-312-95048-9*, St. Martin's Paperbacks) St. Martin's Pr.

—The Black Echo. l.t. ed. 2001. 647p. 30.95 (*0-7862-3309-5*); 584p. (*0-7540-1659-5*); 584p. (*0-7540-9073-6*) Thorndike Pr.

—The Black Echo. 2002. 496p. reprint ed. mass mkt. 7.99 (*0-446-61273-1*) Warner Bks., Inc.

—The Black Ice. unabr. ed. 1998. (Harry Bosch Ser.). audio 26.95 (*1-56740-095-7*, 1479, Bookcassette); 11p. audio 73.25 (*1-56740-624-6*, 1480, Unabridged Library Editions) Brilliance Audio.

—The Black Ice. l.t. ed. 1994. 90.95 o.p. (*0-7862-9985-1*, Macmillan Reference USA) Gale Group.

—The Black Ice. 1993. 322p. 19.95 o.p. (*0-316-15382-6*) Little Brown & Co.

—The Black Ice. 1994. 374p. mass mkt. 7.99 o.s.i (*0-312-95281-3*, St. Martin's Paperbacks) St. Martin's Pr.

—The Black Ice. 2003. 448p. mass mkt. 7.99 (*0-446-61344-4*, Warner Vision) Warner Bks., Inc.

—Blood Work. abr. ed. 1998. audio 7.99 (*1-56740-279-8*, 1679, Paperback Nova Audio Bks.); audio 25.95 o.p. (*1-56100-763-3*, 50, Bookcassette); 15p. audio 89.25 (*1-56100-838-9*, 813, Unabridged Library Editions);Set. audio 17.95 o.p. (*1-56100-988-1*, 461, Nova Audio Bks.) Brilliance Audio.

—Blood Work. l.t. ed. 1998. (Large Print Book Ser.). 26.95 o.p. (*1-56895-622-3*, Wheeler Publishing, Inc.) Gale Group.

—Blood Work, Set. unabr. ed. 1999. audio 89.25 Highsmith Inc.

—Blood Work, Vol. 1. 1998. (Blood Work Ser.: Vol. 1). 400p. (gr. 8). 23.95 (*0-316-15399-0*) Little Brown & Co.

—Blood Work. 2003. E-Book 5.95 (*0-7595-4786-6*) Time Warner Bk. Group.

—Blood Work. reprint ed. 2002. 480p. pap. 14.95 (*0-446-69044-9*); 1998. 528p. mass mkt. 7.99 (*0-446-60262-0*) Warner Bks., Inc.

—Chasing the Dime. 2002. 384p. 25.95 (*0-316-15391-5*); E-Book 14.95 (*0-7595-4710-6*); (Illus.). 544p. 25.95 (*0-316-16046-6*) Little Brown & Co.

—Chasing the Dime. 2003. 448p. mass mkt. 7.99 (*0-446-61162-X*, Warner Vision) Warner Bks., Inc.

—City of Bones. 2002. 400p. 25.95 (*0-316-15405-9*); E-Book 14.95 (*0-7595-8691-8*); 528p. 25.95 (*0-316-15431-8*) Little Brown & Co.

—City of Bones. abr. ed. 2002. audio 31.98 (*1-58621-202-8*); audio 26.98 (*1-58621-201-X*); audio 39.98 (*1-58621-203-6*, 2C362) Time Warner AudioBooks.

—City of Bones. 2003. 448p. mass mkt. 7.99 (*0-446-61161-1*, Warner Vision) Warner Bks., Inc.

—City of Bones. 2002. E-Book 14.95 (*0-7595-6682-8*) ereads.com.

—The Concrete Blonde. abr. ed. 1994. (Harry Bosch Ser.). audio 16.95 o.p. (*1-56100-375-1*, 1642, Nova Audio Bks.); 13p. audio 89.25 (*1-56100-198-8*, 1160, Unabridged Library Editions); 13p. audio 25.95 (*1-56100-572-X*, 67, Bookcassette) Brilliance Audio.

—The Concrete Blonde. 1994. 382p. 21.95 o.p. (*0-316-15383-4*) Little Brown & Co.

—The Concrete Blonde. abr. ed. 2000. audio 7.95 (*1-57815-004-3*, 1031, Media Bks. Audio Publishing) Media Bks., L. L. C.

—The Concrete Blonde. 1995. 397p. mass mkt. 7.99 (*0-312-95500-6*, St. Martin's Paperbacks) St. Martin's Pr.

—A Darkness More Than Night. 2001. 432p. 25.95 o.p. (*0-316-15407-5*); 400p. E-Book 14.95 (*0-7595-4069-1*); 400p. E-Book 14.95 (*0-7595-0067-3*); 400p. E-Book 14.95 (*0-7595-9076-1*) Little Brown & Co.

—A Darkness More Than Night. l.t. ed. 608p. 2002. 30.95 (*0-7862-2821-0*); 2001. 31.95 (*0-7862-2820-2*) Thorndike Pr.

—A Darkness More Than Night. deluxe ltd. ed. 2000. 150.00 (*1-890885-10-X*) Trice, B.E. Publishing.

—A Darkness More Than Night. 2002. 488p. reprint ed. mass mkt. 7.99 (*0-446-66790-0*) Warner Bks., Inc.

—The Harry Bosch Novels: The Black Echo; The Black Ice; The Concrete Blonde. 2001. 800p. 16.95 (*0-316-15497-0*) Little Brown & Co.

—The Last Coyote. abr. ed. (Harry Bosch Novel Ser.). 1996. audio 7.99 o.s.i (*1-56740-118-X*, 671, Paperback Nova Audio Bks.); 1995. audio 16.95 o.p. (*1-56100-409-X*, 1270, Nova Audio Bks.); 1995. 13p. audio 89.25 (*1-56100-241-0*, 922, Unabridged Library Editions); 1995. audio 25.95 (*1-56100-616-5*, 157, Bookcassette) Brilliance Audio.

—The Last Coyote. l.t. ed. 1995. (Large Print Bks.). pap. 24.95 (*1-56895-272-4*, Wheeler Publishing, Inc.) Gale Group.

—The Last Coyote. l.t. ed. 1995. 383p. 22.95 o.p. (*0-316-15390-7*) Little Brown & Co.
—The Last Coyote. 5th ed. 1996. 416p. reprint ed. mass mkt. 7.99 (*0-312-95845-5*, St. Martin's Paperbacks) St. Martin's Pr.
—Lost Light. 2003. 368p. 25.95 (*0-316-15460-1*); 496p. 25.95 (*0-316-71117-9*) Little Brown & Co.
—Lost Light. 2003. E-Book 15.95 (*0-7595-8757-4*); E-Book 15.95 (*0-7595-4750-5*) Time Warner Bk. Group.
—Lost Light. aut. ltd. num. ed. 2003. 150.00 (*1-890885-16-9*) Trice, B.E. Publishing.
—Lost Light. 2004. mass mkt. 7.99 (*0-446-61163-8*, Warner Vision) Warner Bks., Inc.
—Trunk Music. abr. ed. 1997. (Harry Bosch Novel Ser.). audio 7.99 o.s.i (*1-56740-201-1*, 713, Paperback Nova Audio Bks.); audio 25.95 o.s.i (*1-56100-724-2*, 301, Bookcassette); 15p. audio 89.25 (*1-56100-801-X*, 1110, Unabridged Library Editions) Brilliance Audio.
—Trunk Music. l.t. ed. 1997. 27.95 (*1-56895-440-9*, Wheeler Publishing, Inc.) Gale Group.
—Trunk Music. 1997. 400p. 23.45 o.p. (*0-316-15244-7*) Little Brown & Co.
—Trunk Music. 1998. 438p. mass mkt. 7.99 (*0-312-96329-7*, St. Martin's Paperbacks) St. Martin's Pr.
Cook, Bruce. Death As a Career Move. 1992. 272p. 18.95 o.p. (*0-312-06946-4*, Saint Martin's Minotaur) St. Martin's Pr.
—Mexican Standoff. 1988. 256p. 16.95 o.p. (*0-531-15089-5*, Watts, Franklin) Scholastic Library Publishing.
—Mexican Standoff. 1990. mass mkt. 3.95 (*0-312-92114-4*, St. Martin's Paperbacks) St. Martin's Pr.
—Rough Cut. 1992. 2.99 o.p. (*0-517-09052-X*) Random Hse. Value Publishing.
—Rough Cut. 1990. 240p. 16.95 o.p. (*0-312-05149-2*, Saint Martin's Minotaur) St. Martin's Pr.
—The Sidewalk Hilton. 1994. 320p. 21.95 o.p. (*0-312-11062-6*, Saint Martin's Minotaur) St. Martin's Pr.
Copeland, Sheila. A Chocolate Affair. 288p. mass mkt. 6.99 (*1-58314-441-2*, Arabesque); 2001. 240p. pap. 15.00 (*1-58314-234-7*, Sepia) BET Bks.
Copper, Basil. Bad Scene. l.t. ed. 2000. (G. K. Hall Nightingale Ser.). 217p. pap. 20.95 (*0-7838-8997-6*, Macmillan Reference USA) Gale Group.
—Bad Scene. l.t. ed. 1991. (Linford Mystery Large Print Ser.). pap. 17.99 o.p. (*0-7089-7021-4*, Ulverscroft) Thorpe, F. A. Pubs. GBR. *Dist:* Ulverscroft Large Print Bks., Ltd., Ulverscroft Large Print Canada, Ltd.
—The Breaking Point. l.t. ed. 1995. (Linford Mystery Large Print Ser.). 320p. pap. 17.99 o.p. (*0-7089-7805-3*, Linford) Thorpe, F. A. Pubs. GBR. *Dist:* Ulverscroft Large Print Bks., Ltd., Ulverscroft Large Print Canada, Ltd.
—The Caligari Complex. l.t. ed. 1999. (Linford Mystery Large Print Ser.). 304p. pap. 18.99 (*0-7089-5504-5*, Linford) Thorpe, F. A. Pubs. GBR. *Dist:* Ulverscroft Large Print Bks., Ltd., Ulverscroft Large Print Canada, Ltd.
—Crack in the Sidewalk. l.t. ed. 1997. (Linford Mystery Library). 320p. pap. 17.99 o.p. (*0-7089-5065-5*, Linford) Thorpe, F. A. Pubs. GBR. *Dist:* Ulverscroft Large Print Bks., Ltd., Ulverscroft Large Print Canada, Ltd.
—The Dark Mirror. (Black Dagger Crime Ser.). 16.50 o.p. (*0-86220-796-7*, BD001, Black Dagger) BBC Audiobooks America.
—The Dark Mirror. l.t. ed. 1997. (Linford Mystery Library). 416p. pap. 17.99 o.p. (*0-7089-5101-5*, Linford) Thorpe, F. A. Pubs. GBR. *Dist:* Ulverscroft Large Print Bks., Ltd., Ulverscroft Large Print Canada, Ltd.
—Dead File. l.t. ed. 1991. (Linford Mystery Large Print Ser.). pap. 17.99 o.p. (*0-7089-7001-X*, Ulverscroft) Thorpe, F. A. Pubs. GBR. *Dist:* Ulverscroft Large Print Bks., Ltd., Ulverscroft Large Print Canada, Ltd.
—Death Squad. l.t. ed. 1999. (Linford Mystery Large Print Ser.). 304p. pap. 18.99 (*0-7089-5460-X*, Linford) Thorpe, F. A. Pubs. GBR. *Dist:* Ulverscroft Large Print Bks., Ltd., Ulverscroft Large Print Canada, Ltd.
—Die Now, Live Later. l.t. ed. 1993. (Linford Mystery Library). 336p. pap. 17.99 o.p. (*0-7089-7341-8*, Ulverscroft) Thorpe, F. A. Pubs. GBR. *Dist:* Ulverscroft Large Print Bks., Ltd., Ulverscroft Large Print Canada, Ltd.
—Don't Bleed on Me. l.t. ed. 1991. (Linford Mystery Library). pap. 17.99 o.p. (*0-7089-7081-8*, Ulverscroft) Thorpe, F. A. Pubs. GBR. *Dist:* Ulverscroft Large Print Bks., Ltd., Ulverscroft Large Print Canada, Ltd.
—The Far Horizon. 2001. 219p. (*0-7540-4399-1*); (*0-7540-4400-9*) Gale Group. (Macmillan Reference USA).
—The Far Horizon. l.t. ed. 2001. (G. K. Hall Nightingale Ser.). 219p. pap. 23.95 (*0-7838-9327-2*) Thorndike Pr.
—The Far Horizon. l.t. ed. 1993. (Linford Mystery Library). 336p. pap. 17.99 o.p. (*0-7089-7378-7*, Ulverscroft) Thorpe, F. A. Pubs. GBR. *Dist:* Ulverscroft Large Print Bks., Ltd., Ulverscroft Large Print Canada, Ltd.
—Feedback. l.t. ed. 2001. 225p. pap. 23.95 (*0-7838-9592-5*) Thorndike Pr.
—Feedback. l.t. ed. 1991. (Linford Mystery Library). pap. 17.99 o.p. (*0-7089-7129-6*, Ulverscroft) Thorpe, F. A. Pubs. GBR. *Dist:* Ulverscroft Large Print Bks., Ltd., Ulverscroft Large Print Canada, Ltd.
—A Good Place to Die. l.t. ed. 1989. (Linford Mystery Library). pap. 17.99 o.p. (*0-7089-6742-6*, Ulverscroft) Thorpe, F. A. Pubs. GBR. *Dist:* Ulverscroft Large Print Bks., Ltd., Ulverscroft Large Print Canada, Ltd.
—A Great Year for Dying. l.t. ed. 1993. (Linford Mystery Library). 352p. pap. 17.99 o.p. (*0-7089-7349-3*, Ulverscroft) Thorpe, F. A. Pubs. GBR. *Dist:* Ulverscroft Large Print Bks., Ltd., Ulverscroft Large Print Canada, Ltd.
—The High Wall. l.t. ed. 1987. (Linford Mystery Library). 304p. pap. 17.99 o.p. (*0-7089-6455-9*, Linford) Thorpe, F. A. Pubs. GBR. *Dist:* Ulverscroft Large Print Bks., Ltd., Ulverscroft Large Print Canada, Ltd.
—Impact. l.t. ed. 1997. (Linford Mystery Library). 320p. pap. 17.99 o.p. (*0-7089-5070-1*, Linford) Thorpe, F. A. Pubs. GBR. *Dist:* Ulverscroft Large Print Bks., Ltd., Ulverscroft Large Print Canada, Ltd.
—The Lonely Place. l.t. ed. 1997. (Linford Mystery Library). 304p. pap. 17.99 o.p. (*0-7089-5060-4*, Ulverscroft) Thorpe, F. A. Pubs. GBR. *Dist:* Ulverscroft Large Print Bks., Ltd., Ulverscroft Large Print Canada, Ltd.
—The Long Rest. l.t. ed. 1994. 221p. lib. bdg. 16.95 (*0-8161-7421-0*, Macmillan Reference USA) Gale Group.
—The Marble Orchard. l.t. ed. 1998. (Linford Mystery Large Print Ser.). 256p. pap. 17.99 (*0-7089-5265-8*, Linford) Thorpe, F. A. Pubs. GBR. *Dist:* Ulverscroft Large Print Bks., Ltd., Ulverscroft Large Print Canada, Ltd.
—Night Frost. l.t. ed. 1996. (Linford Mystery Library). 368p. pap. 17.99 o.p. (*0-7089-7868-1*, Linford) Thorpe, F. A. Pubs. GBR. *Dist:* Ulverscroft Large Print Bks., Ltd., Ulverscroft Large Print Canada, Ltd.
—No Letters from the Grave. l.t. ed. 1998. (Linford Mystery Library). 240p. pap. 17.99 (*0-7089-5223-2*, Linford) Thorpe, F. A. Pubs. GBR. *Dist:* Ulverscroft Large Print Bks., Ltd., Ulverscroft Large Print Canada, Ltd.
—Print-Out. l.t. ed. 1993. (Dales Mystery Ser.). 246p. pap. 19.99 o.p. (*1-85389-380-3*) Dales Large Print Bks. GBR. *Dist:* Ulverscroft Large Print Bks., Ltd., Ulverscroft Large Print Canada, Ltd.
—Print-Out. l.t. ed. 1996. (Linford Mystery Library). 304p. pap. 17.99 o.p. (*0-7089-7861-4*, Linford) Thorpe, F. A. Pubs. GBR. *Dist:* Ulverscroft Large Print Bks., Ltd., Ulverscroft Large Print Canada, Ltd.
—A Quiet Room in Hell. l.t. ed. 1998. (Linford Mystery Large Print Ser.). 288p. pap. 17.99 (*0-7089-5294-1*, Linford) Thorpe, F. A. Pubs. GBR. *Dist:* Ulverscroft Large Print Bks., Ltd., Ulverscroft Large Print Canada, Ltd.
—Ricochet. l.t. ed. 1993. (Linford Mystery Library). 304p. pap. 17.99 o.p. (*0-7089-7382-5*, Linford) Thorpe, F. A. Pubs. GBR. *Dist:* Ulverscroft Large Print Bks., Ltd., Ulverscroft Large Print Canada, Ltd.
—Scratch on the Dark. 2002. 192p. 21.95 (*0-7540-8610-0*, Black Dagger) BBC Audiobooks America.
—Scratch on the Dark. l.t. ed. 2000. (Linford Mystery Large Print Ser.). 264p. pap. 18.99 (*0-7089-5767-6*, Ulverscroft) Thorpe, F. A. Pubs. GBR. *Dist:* Ulverscroft Large Print Bks., Ltd., Ulverscroft Large Print Canada, Ltd.
—Shock-Wave. l.t. ed. 1994. (Linford Mystery Library). 320p. pap. 17.99 o.p. (*0-7089-7629-8*, Linford) Thorpe, F. A. Pubs. GBR. *Dist:* Ulverscroft Large Print Bks., Ltd., Ulverscroft Large Print Canada, Ltd.
—Strong-Arm. l.t. ed. 1989. (Linford Mystery Library). 319p. pap. 17.99 o.p. (*0-7089-6629-2*, Linford) Thorpe, F. A. Pubs. GBR. *Dist:* Ulverscroft Large Print Bks., Ltd., Ulverscroft Large Print Canada, Ltd.
—Tight Corner. l.t. ed. 1994. (Linford Mystery Library). 304p. pap. 17.99 o.p. (*0-7089-7564-X*, Linford) Thorpe, F. A. Pubs. GBR. *Dist:* Ulverscroft Large Print Bks., Ltd., Ulverscroft Large Print Canada, Ltd.
—Trigger-Man. l.t. ed. 1994. (Linford Mystery Library). 320p. pap. 17.99 o.p. (*0-7089-7561-5*, Linford) Thorpe, F. A. Pubs. GBR. *Dist:* Ulverscroft Large Print Bks., Ltd., Ulverscroft Large Print Canada, Ltd.
—A Voice from the Dead. l.t. ed. 1998. (Linford Mystery Large Print Ser.). 304p. pap. 17.99 (*0-7089-5287-9*, Linford) Thorpe, F. A. Pubs. GBR. *Dist:* Ulverscroft Large Print Bks., Ltd., Ulverscroft Large Print Canada, Ltd.
—The Year of the Dragon. l.t. ed. 1991. (Linford Mystery Library). pap. 17.99 o.p. (*0-7089-7077-X*, Linford) Thorpe, F. A. Pubs. GBR. *Dist:* Ulverscroft Large Print Bks., Ltd., Ulverscroft Large Print Canada, Ltd.
Coscarelli, Kate. Leading Lady. 1991. 19.95 o.p. (*0-312-05889-6*) St. Martin's Pr.
Cosin, Elizabeth M. Zen & the Art of Murder. (St. Martin's Minotaur Mysteries Ser.). 1999. 304p. mass mkt. 5.99 (*0-312-96948-1*, St. Martin's Paperbacks); 1998. 288p. 22.95 o.p. (*0-312-19376-9*, Saint Martin's Minotaur) St. Martin's Pr.
—Zen & the City of Angels. E-Book 23.95 (*0-312-26859-9*); 2000. 304p. mass mkt. 5.99 (*0-312-97446-9*, St. Martin's Paperbacks); 1999. 288p. 23.95 o.p. (*0-312-20611-9*, Saint Martin's Minotaur) St. Martin's Pr.
Covino, Michael. The Negative. 1993. 368p. 21.00 o.p. (*0-670-85078-0*, Viking) Viking Penguin.
Crais, Robert. Demolition Angel. 2001. 400p. mass mkt. 6.99 (*0-345-43448-X*, Ballantine Bks.) Ballantine Bks.
—Demolition Angel. l.t. ed. 2000. (Wheeler Large Print Book Ser.). 474p. 29.95 (*1-56895-921-4*, Wheeler Publishing, Inc.) Gale Group.
—The Devil's Cantina. 1999. 288p. 22.95 (*0-7868-6355-2*) Hyperion Pr.
—Free Fall. 1994. (Elvis Cole Mystery Ser.). mass mkt. 4.99 o.s.i (*0-553-56831-0*, Crimeline); 304p. mass mkt. 6.99 (*0-553-56509-5*) Bantam Bks.
—Hostage: A Novel. l.t. ed. 2001. (Hardcover Ser.). 477p. 31.95 (*1-58724-076-9*, Wheeler Publishing, Inc.) Gale Group.
—Indigo Slam. 2003. (Elvis Cole Mystery Ser.). 320p. mass mkt. 7.99 (*0-345-43564-8*, Ballantine Bks.) Ballantine Bks.
—Indigo Slam. unabr. ed. 1997. (Elvis Cole Mystery Ser.). audio 48.00 (*0-7366-3833-4*, 4553) Books on Tape, Inc.
—Indigo Slam. abr. ed. (Elvis Cole Mystery Ser.). 2000. audio 7.99 o.s.i (*1-58788-097-0*, 2352, Paperback Nova Audio Bks.); 1998. audio 7.99 o.s.i (*1-56740-252-6*, 2379, Nova Audio Bks.); 1997. audio 16.95 o.p. (*1-56100-977-6*, 1236, Nova Audio Bks.); 1997. audio 16.95 o.p.; 1997. audio 23.95 (*1-56100-752-8*, 144, Bookcassette); 1997. audio 57.25 (*1-56100-827-3*, 907, Unabridged Library Editions) Brilliance Audio.
—Indigo Slam. (Elvis Cole Mystery Ser.). 1999. 384p. mass mkt. 5.99 (*0-7868-8929-2*); 1997. 304p. 22.95 (*0-7868-6261-0*) Hyperion Pr.
—L. A. Requiem. 2000. (Elvis Cole Mystery Ser.). 416p. mass mkt. 6.99 (*0-345-43447-1*, Ballantine Bks.) Ballantine Bks.
—L. A. Requiem. l.t. ed. 2000. (Elvis Cole Mystery Ser.). 538p. 27.95 (*1-56895-881-1*, Wheeler Publishing, Inc.) Gale Group.
—L. A. Requiem, Set. abr. ed. 1999. (Elvis Cole Mystery Ser.). audio 25.00 Highsmith Inc.
—L. A. Requiem. abr. ed. 1999. (Elvis Cole Mystery Ser.). audio 25.00 (*0-553-52648-0*, RH Audio) Random Hse. Audio Publishing Group.
—Lullaby Town. (Elvis Cole Mystery Ser.). 1993. 352p. mass mkt. 6.99 (*0-553-29951-4*); 1992. 304p. 20.00 o.s.i (*0-553-08197-7*) Bantam Bks.
—The Monkey's Raincoat. (Elvis Cole Mystery Ser.). 1987. 208p. mass mkt. 2.95 o.s.i (*0-553-26336-6*); 1992. 224p. reprint ed. mass mkt. 7.50 (*0-553-27585-2*) Bantam Bks.
—Stalking the Angel. 1992. (Elvis Cole Mystery Ser.). 288p. mass mkt. 7.50 (*0-553-28644-7*) Bantam Bks.
—Sunset Express. unabr. ed. 1997. (Elvis Cole Mystery Ser.). audio 56.00 (*0-913369-89-6*, 4389) Books on Tape, Inc.
—Sunset Express. abr. ed. (Elvis Cole Mystery Ser.). 1997. audio 7.99 o.p. (*1-56740-166-X*, 707, Nova Audio Bks.); 1996. audio 16.95 o.p. (*1-56100-905-9*, 1066, Nova Audio Bks.); 1996. audio 57.25 o.p. (*1-56100-320-4*, 1065, Unabridged Library Editions); 1996. audio 23.95 o.p. (*1-56100-695-5*, 284, Bookcassette) Brilliance Audio.
—Sunset Express. (Elvis Cole Mystery Ser.). 1996. 288p. 21.95 o.p. (*0-7868-6096-0*); 2002. 416p. reprint ed. mass mkt. 6.99 (*0-7868-8915-2*) Hyperion Pr.
—Sunset Express. l.t. ed. 2001. (Elvis Cole Mystery Ser.). 288p. 28.95 (*0-7862-3401-6*); 485p. (*0-7540-1644-7*); 485p. (*0-7540-2496-2*) Thorndike Pr.
—Voodoo River. l.t. ed. 2002. (Elvis Cole Mystery Ser.). 499p. 29.95 (*0-7862-3404-0*) Gale Group.
—Voodoo River. (Elvis Cole Mystery Ser.). 1995. 304p. 21.95 (*0-7868-6076-6*); 2003. 416p. reprint ed. mass mkt. 7.99 (*0-7868-8905-5*) Hyperion Pr.
Crichton, Michael. Rising Sun. 1997. pap. 12.00 o.s.i (*0-345-41896-4*); 1992. mass mkt. 6.99 o.p. (*0-345-90226-2*); 1992. 416p. mass mkt. 7.99 (*0-345-38037-1*) Ballantine Bks.
—Rising Sun. 1992. 355p. 26.00 (*0-394-58942-4*) Knopf, Alfred A. Inc.
—Rising Sun. abr. ed. 1999. audio 8.99 o.s.i (*0-375-40575-5*); 1992. audio 16.00 o.s.i (*0-679-41099-6*, 391477) Random Hse. Audio Publishing Group. (RH Audio).
—Rising Sun. l.t. ed. 1992. 24.00 o.s.i (*0-679-41017-1*) Random Hse. Large Print.
Culea, John. Light the Night. 1997. 389p. pap. 11.99 o.p. (*0-7814-0296-4*) Cook Communications Ministries.
Cunningham, E. V., pseud. The Case of the Murdered MacKenzie. 1984. (Masao Masuto Mystery Ser.). 192p. 11.95 o.s.i (*0-385-29337-2*, Delacorte Pr.) Dell Publishing.
Cutler, Stan. Best Performance by a Patsy. 1991. (Goodman-Bradley Mystery Ser.). 352p. 18.95 o.p. (*0-525-93317-4*) Dutton/Plume.
—Best Performance by a Patsy. 1993. (Goodman-Bradley Mystery Ser.). 336p. mass mkt. 4.50 o.p. (*0-451-40359-2*, Onyx) NAL.
—The Face on the Cutting Room Floor. 1991. 320p. 18.95 o.p. (*0-525-93381-6*, Dutton) Dutton/Plume.
—The Face on the Cutting Room Floor. 1993. (Goodman-Bradley Mystery Ser.). 272p. mass mkt. 4.50 o.s.i (*0-451-40394-0*, Signet Bks.) NAL.
—Rough Cut. 1994. 336p. (Orig.). mass mkt. 4.99 o.s.i (*0-451-18253-7*) NAL.
—Shot on Location. 1993. (Goodman-Bradley Mystery Ser.). 352p. 19.00 o.p. (*0-525-93576-2*) Dutton/Plume.
—Shot on Location. 1994. (Goodman-Bradley Mystery Ser.). 336p. mass mkt. 4.99 o.p. (*0-451-40391-6*, Signet Bks.) NAL.
Dana, Richard & Paine, Lauran. Death Was the Echo. l.t. ed. 2000. (G. K. Hall Nightingale Ser.). 184p. pap. 20.95 (*0-7838-8846-5*, Macmillan Reference USA) Gale Group.
Danks, Denise. Torso. 2003. 249p. pap. 9.95 (*0-575-40257-1*) Orion Publishing Group, Ltd. GBR. *Dist:* Trafalgar Square.
Dann, Joshua. Timeshare: ATime for War. 1999. (Timeshare Trilogy Ser.). 288p. mass mkt. 5.99 o.s.i (*0-441-00638-8*) Ace Bks.
—Timeshare: Do You Believe in Yesterday? 1997. 256p. mass mkt. 5.99 o.s.i (*0-441-00457-1*) Ace Bks.
—Timeshare: Second Time Around. 1998. (Timeshare Trilogy Ser.). 256p. mass mkt. 5.99 o.s.i (*0-441-00567-5*) Ace Bks.
Darden, Christopher. The Last Defense. 2004. 400p. mass mkt. 7.99 (*0-451-41122-6*, Onyx) NAL.
—Lawless. 2004. 368p. 24.95 (*0-451-21109-X*) NAL.
Darden, Christopher A. L. A. Justice. 2002. 464p. reprint ed. mass mkt. 6.99 o.s.i (*0-451-20541-3*, Signet Bks.) NAL.
Darden, Christopher A. & Lochte, Dick. L. A. Justice. 2001. 448p. 25.95 o.p. (*0-446-52327-5*) Warner Bks., Inc.
—The Last Defense. 2002. 368p. 24.95 (*0-451-20732-7*) NAL.
—The Trials of Nikki Hill. 2001. 496p. mass mkt. 7.50 o.s.i (*0-446-60798-3*); 1999. 448p. 25.00 (*0-446-52326-7*) Warner Bks., Inc.
Dart, Iris Rainer. I'll Be There. l.t. ed. 1994. 22.95 o.p. (*0-7927-2087-3*); pap. 21.95 o.p. (*0-7927-2086-5*) BBC Audiobooks America.
—I'll Be There. 1991. 19.95 o.p. (*0-316-17328-2*) Little Brown & Co.
—I'll Be There. 1993. 15.95 o.p. (*1-55800-414-9*) NewStar Media, Inc.
—Show Business Kills. 1995. 310p. 21.95 o.p. (*0-316-17334-7*) Little Brown & Co.
—Show Business Kills. 1996. 400p. mass mkt. 6.50 o.p. (*0-446-36511-4*) Warner Bks., Inc.
—The Stork Club. l.t. ed. 1993. 22.95 o.p. (*0-7927-1670-1*); pap. 20.95 o.p. (*0-7927-1669-8*) BBC Audiobooks America.
—The Stork Club. 1992. 400p. 21.95 o.p. (*0-316-17332-0*) Little Brown & Co.
—When I Fall in Love. abr. ed. 1999. audio 7.99 o.s.i (*1-56740-336-0*, 1951, Paperback Nova Audio Bks.); audio 17.95 o.p. (*1-56100-833-8*, 1667, Nova Audio Bks.); audio 35.95 (*1-56740-420-0*, 1664, Brilliance Audio Unabridged); 7p. audio 57.25 (*1-56740-646-7*, 1665, Unabridged Library Editions) Brilliance Audio.
—When I Fall in Love. l.t. ed. 1999. 27.95 (*1-56895-734-3*, Wheeler Publishing, Inc.) Gale Group.
—When I Fall in Love. abr. ed. 1999. audio 17.95 Highsmith Inc.
—When I Fall in Love. 1999. 352p. mass mkt. 6.99 (*0-380-73198-3*, Avon Bks.); 258p. 25.00 (*0-688-16034-4*, Morrow, William & Co.) Morrow/Avon.
De Felitta, Frank. Funeral March. 1991. 352p. mass mkt. 4.95 o.s.i (*0-553-28927-6*) Bantam Bks.
Debin, David. The Big O: An Albie Marx Caper. 1994. 256p. 19.95 o.p. (*0-7867-0005-X*, Carroll & Graf Pubs.) Avalon Publishing Group.
—Murder Live at Five. 1995. 304p. 21.00 o.p. (*0-7867-0190-0*, Carroll & Graf Pubs.) Avalon Publishing Group.

Settings

Dedman, Stephen. The Art of Arrow Cutting. 2001. 304p. mass mkt. 6.99 (0-8125-4534-6); 1999. 284p. pap. 13.95 (0-312-86832-4); 1997. 320p. 22.95 (0-312-86320-9) Doherty, Tom Assocs., LLC. (Tor Bks.).

Deighton, Len. Violent Ward. l.t. ed. 1995. pap. 18.95 o.p. (0-7927-2022-9); 1994. 19.95 o.p. (0-7927-2023-7) BBC Audiobooks America.

Delacorte, Peter. Time on My Hands. 2000. E-Book 23.00 (0-684-86459-2); 1998. (Illus.). 400p. pap. 14.00 o.s.i (0-671-02324-1) Simon & Schuster. (Scribner).

—Time on My Hands: A Novel with Photographs. 1997. 397p. 23.00 (0-684-82651-8, Scribner) Simon & Schuster.

DeMarinis, Rick. The Year of the Zinc Penny. l.t. ed. 1990. (General Ser.). 288p. lib. bdg. 19.95 o.p. (0-8161-5056-7, Macmillan Reference USA) Gale Group.

—The Year of the Zinc Penny. 1990. 176p. reprint ed. pap. 9.00 o.p. (0-06-097339-0, Perennial) HarperTrade.

—The Year of the Zinc Penny. 1989. 17.95 o.p. (0-393-02758-9) Norton, W. W. & Co., Inc.

—The Year of the Zinc Penny. 1999. pap. 18.95 (0-670-82575-1) Viking Penguin.

Dentinger, Jane. Dead Pan: A Jocelyn O'Roarke Mystery. 1992. (Jocelyn O'Roarke Mystery Ser.). 256p. 19.00 o.p. (0-670-84108-0, Viking) Viking Penguin.

Dexter, Pete. Train. 2003. 288p. 26.00 (0-385-50591-4) Doubleday Publishing.

Dickey, Eric Jerome. Cheaters. 1999. 224p. 24.95 o.s.i (0-525-94386-2) Dutton/Plume.

—Cheaters. 2000. 448p. mass mkt. 7.50 (0-451-19407-1, Signet Bks.) NAL.

—Cheaters. abr. ed. 1999. audio 18.95 (0-14-180024-0, Penguin AudioBooks) Viking Penguin.

—Liar's Game. 2000. 336p. 23.95 o.s.i (0-525-94483-4) Dutton/Plume.

—Liar's Game. l.t. ed. 2000. (Wheeler Large Print Book Ser.). 28.95 (1-56895-986-9, Wheeler Publishing, Inc.) Gale Group.

—Liar's Game. 2001. 400p. reprint ed. mass mkt. 7.50 (0-451-20134-5, Signet Bks.) NAL.

—Naughty or Nice. 2003. 176p. 17.95 (0-525-94776-0, Dutton) Dutton/Plume.

—The Other Woman: A Novel. 2003. 304p. 23.95 (0-525-94724-8, Dutton) Dutton/Plume.

—Sister, Sister. 1996. 256p. 23.95 (0-525-94126-6) Dutton/Plume.

—Sister, Sister. 1997. 368p. mass mkt. 7.50 (0-451-18802-0, Signet Bks.) NAL.

—Sister, Sister. 1997. 13.04 (0-606-15705-0) Turtleback Bks.

—Sister Sister. 2000. 256p. pap. 13.95 (0-451-20101-9, Signet Bks.) NAL.

—Thieves' Paradise. l.t. ed. 2002. (African American Ser.). 645p. 29.95 (0-7862-4768-1) Thorndike Pr.

—Thieves' Paradise: A Novel. 2002. 320p. 19.95 (0-525-94663-2, Dutton) Dutton/Plume.

Didion, Joan. Play It As It Lays. 1983. 266p. mass mkt. 3.95 o.s.i (0-671-49590-9, Pocket) Simon & Schuster.

Donahue, Marilyn. Reach with All Your Heart. 1988. (Quick Fox Line Ser.). Orig. Title: To Catch a Golden Ring. 224p. (YA). pap. 4.49 o.p. (1-55513-755-5) Cook Communications Ministries.

—To Catch a Golden Ring. 1980. (J). (gr. 4-9). pap. 2.95 o.p. (0-89191-330-0) Cook Communications Ministries.

Donald, Roger James. Answer by Fire. Edit Ink Staff, ed. 1997. 260p. pap. 11.95 (0-9742655-0-0) Galaxy Publishing.

Donner, Rebecca. Sunset Terrace. 2003. 312p. 22.00 (1-931561-34-6) MacAdam/Cage Publishing, Inc.

Douglas, Kirk. Dance with the Devil. l.t. ed. 1994. 554p. lib. bdg. 23.95 o.p. (0-8161-7464-4, Macmillan Reference USA) Gale Group.

—Dance with the Devil. abr. ed. 1993. 15.95 o.p. (1-55800-406-8) NewStar Media, Inc.

—Dance with the Devil. 1992. 3.99 o.p. (0-517-08346-9) Random Hse. Value Publishing.

—Dance with the Devil. 1991. 384p. mass mkt. 5.99 o.s.i (0-446-36191-7) Warner Bks., Inc.

Doumani, Carol. Indiscretions. unabr. ed. 1999. audio 29.95 (0-7366-4480-6) Books on Tape, Inc.

—Indiscretions. 1999. 336p. 25.00 (0-9642359-9-4) Wave Publishing.

Downing, Warwick. A Lingering Doubt. Isaacson, Dana, ed. 1993. 320p. (Orig.). mass mkt. 4.99 (0-671-76034-3, Pocket) Simon & Schuster.

Duchin, Peter & Wilson, John Morgan. Good Morning, Heartache. 2003. 304p. 22.95 (0-425-19180-X, Prime Crime) Berkley Publishing Group.

Dukore, Margaret M. Bloom: A Novel. 1985. 304p. 17.95 o.p. (0-531-09708-0, Watts, Franklin) Scholastic Library Publishing.

Dunne, Dominick. Another City, Not My Own: A Novel in the Form of a Memoir. 1999. mass mkt. 7.99 (0-449-00419-8, Fawcett); 1998. 406p. mass mkt. 7.99 (0-345-43051-4); 1998. mass mkt. o.p. (0-345-42703-3) Ballantine Bks.

—Another City, Not My Own: A Novel in the Form of a Memoir. 1998. mass mkt. o.s.i (0-553-57986-X) Bantam Bks.

—Another City, Not My Own: A Novel in the Form of a Memoir, unabr. ed. 1998. audio 64.00 (0-7366-4111-4, 106016) Books on Tape, Inc.

—Another City, Not My Own: A Novel in the Form of a Memoir. l.t. ed. 1997. pap. 25.00 o.p. (0-7838-8248-3, Macmillan Reference USA) Gale Group.

—Another City, Not My Own: A Novel in the Form of a Memoir. abr. ed. 1997. 25.00 o.p. (0-7871-1612-2) NewStar Media, Inc.

Dunne, John Gregory. Playland. 1995. 512p. pap. 13.95 o.s.i (0-452-27495-8, Plume) Dutton/Plume.

Eberhardt, Michael C. Body of a Crime. 1994. 368p. 19.95 o.p. (0-525-93623-8, Dutton) Dutton/Plume.

—Body of a Crime. unabr. ed. 1998. audio 103.95 (1-85903-136-6) Magna Story Sound GBR. Dist: Ulverscroft Large Print Bks., Ltd.

—Body of a Crime. 1995. 448p. mass mkt. 5.99 o.s.i (0-451-40569-2, Onyx) NAL.

—Body of a Crime. l.t. ed. 1997. (Niagara Large Print Ser.). 546p. 29.50 o.p. (0-7089-5803-6, Ulverscroft) Thorpe, F. A. Pubs. GBR. Dist: Ulverscroft Large Print Bks., Ltd., Ulverscroft Large Print Canada, Ltd.

Egan, Lesley. Chain of Violence. 1985. (Crime Club Ser.). 192p. 12.95 o.p. (0-385-19807-8) Doubleday Publishing.

—Little Boy Lost. 1983. (Crime Club Ser.). (Illus.). 192p. 11.95 o.p. (0-385-18840-4) Doubleday Publishing.

—Little Boy Lost. l.t. ed. 1986. (Ulverscroft Large Print Ser.). 384p. 29.99 o.p. (0-7089-1417-9, Ulverscroft) Thorpe, F. A. Pubs. GBR. Dist: Ulverscroft Large Print Bks., Ltd., Ulverscroft Large Print Canada, Ltd.

—Look Back on Death. 1978. 7.95 o.p. (0-385-14303-6) Doubleday Publishing.

—Look Back on Death. l.t. ed. 1981. reprint ed. 9.95 o.p. (0-89621-267-X) Thorndike Pr.

—The Miser. 1981. (Crime Club Ser.). 192p. 9.95 o.p. (0-385-17626-0) Doubleday Publishing.

—The Miser. l.t. ed. 1984. 368p. o.p. (0-7089-1069-6, Ulverscroft) Thorpe, F. A. Pubs.

—Motive in Shadow. 1980. (Crime Club Ser.). 10.95 o.p. (0-385-15605-7) Doubleday Publishing.

—Motive in Shadow. l.t. ed. 1986. (Ulverscroft Large Print Ser.). 384p. 29.99 o.p. (0-7089-1471-3, Ulverscroft) Thorpe, F. A. Pubs. GBR. Dist: Ulverscroft Large Print Bks., Ltd., Ulverscroft Large Print Canada, Ltd.

Elliott, Bruce. Still Life. 2001. 384p. mass mkt. 6.99 o.s.i (0-451-40984-1, Onyx) NAL.

Ellis, Bret Easton. The Informers. 1994. 240p. 22.00 o.s.i (0-679-43587-5) Knopf, Alfred A. Inc.

—The Informers. 1995. 240p. pap. 12.00 (0-679-74324-3); pap. 7.00 o.p. (0-679-76085-7) Random Hse., Inc.

—Less Than Zero. 1998. 208p. pap. 12.00 (0-679-78149-8, Vintage) Knopf Publishing Group.

—Less Than Zero. 1985. 15.45 o.p. (0-671-54329-6, Simon & Schuster) Simon & Schuster.

—Less Than Zero. 1986. 14.95 o.p. (0-671-62140-8, Simon & Schuster Audioworks) Simon & Schuster Audio.

—Less Than Zero. 208p. 1987. mass mkt. 3.95 o.p. (0-14-010927-7, Penguin Bks.); 1986. pap. 11.95 o.s.i (0-14-008894-6) Viking Penguin.

Ellroy, James. Because the Night. 1987. pap. 5.99 (0-380-70063-8, Avon Bks.) Morrow/Avon.

—Because the Night. 1986. 15.95 (0-89296-071-X) Mysterious Pr.

—The Big Nowhere. 1988. 416p. 17.95 o.s.i (0-89296-283-6) Mysterious Pr.

—The Big Nowhere. 1989. 60.00 (0-89366-239-9) Ultramarine Publishing Co., Inc.

—The Big Nowhere. 1998. 416p. pap. 13.95 (0-446-67437-0); 1990. mass mkt. 4.95 (0-445-77285-9); 1989. 496p. mass mkt. 6.99 (0-445-40832-4) Warner Bks., Inc.

—The Black Dahlia. unabr. collector's ed. 1990. (L. A. Quartet). audio 88.00 (0-7366-1816-3, 2652) Books on Tape, Inc.

—The Black Dahlia. 1987. 336p. 16.95 (0-89296-206-2) Mysterious Pr.

—The Black Dahlia. 1998. 336p. pap. 13.99 (0-446-67436-2); 1988. 384p. mass mkt. 5.99 (0-445-40525-2) Warner Bks., Inc.

—Blood on the Moon. 1986. 14.45 o.p. (0-89296-069-8) Mysterious Pr.

—Brown's Requiem. 1998. 256p. pap. 13.00 (0-380-73177-0); 1981. pap. 4.99 (0-380-78741-5) Morrow/Avon. (Avon Bks.).

—Clandestine. 1999. 336p. pap. 12.95 (0-380-80529-4); 1982. 352p. mass mkt. 5.99 (0-380-81141-3) Morrow/Avon. (Avon Bks.).

—Crime Wave: Auf der Nachseite von L. A. 2001. (GER.). 336p. pap. (3-548-24972-8) Ullstein-Taschenbuch-Verlag DEU. Dist: International Bk. Import Service, Inc.

—Hollywood Nocturnes. unabr. collector's ed. 1996. audio 48.00 (0-7366-3255-7, 3912) Books on Tape, Inc.

—Hollywood Nocturnes. 1995. 368p. mass mkt. 5.99 o.s.i (0-440-22098-X) Dell Publishing.

—Hollywood Nocturnes. 1994. (Illus.). 272p. bds. 20.00 o.s.i (1-883402-54-9, Scribner) Simon & Schuster.

—L. A. Confidential. unabr. collector's ed. 1991. (L. A. Quartet). audio 80.00 (0-7366-2012-5, 116014) Books on Tape, Inc.

—L. A. Confidential. 1990. 75.00 o.p. (0-89296-424-3); 19.95 (0-89296-293-3) Mysterious Pr.

—L. A. Confidential. abr. ed. 2001. audio 9.99 (0-553-70244-0); Set. 1997. audio 18.00 o.s.i (0-375-40213-6, 390277) Random Hse. Audio Publishing Group. (RH Audio).

—L. A. Confidential. 1997. 480p. pap. text 9.23 (0-09-925508-1) Random Hse. Value Publishing.

—L. A. Confidential. 1997. (0-446-60605-7); 1997. 512p. pap. 14.95 (0-446-67424-9); 1991. mass mkt. 5.99 (0-446-40010-6) Warner Bks., Inc.

—L. A. Noir. 2000. 648p. 25.00 (0-89296-686-6); E-Book 14.95 (0-7595-6040-4); 600p. E-Book 14.95 (0-7595-8042-1); 600p. E-Book 14.95 (0-7595-9046-X); 600p. E-Book 14.95 (0-7595-4041-1); 600p. E-Book 14.95 (0-7595-0040-1) Mysterious Pr.

—Suicide Hill. 1986. 288p. 15.95 (0-89296-235-6) Mysterious Pr.

—Suicide Hill. 1989. mass mkt. 5.99 o.s.i (0-445-40852-9); 1987. mass mkt. 3.95 (0-445-40585-6, Mysterious Pr. Paperback Bks.) Warner Bks., Inc.

—White Jazz. 1997. 368p. pap. 13.00 o.s.i (0-449-00088-5, Fawcett) Ballantine Bks.

—White Jazz. unabr. collector's ed. 1992. (L. A. Quartet). audio 64.00 (0-7366-2323-X, 3103) Books on Tape, Inc.

—White Jazz. 2001. 368p. pap. 13.00 (0-375-72736-1, Vintage) Knopf Publishing Group.

—White Jazz: A Novel. 1993. (Los Angeles Mysteries Ser.). 368p. mass mkt. 5.99 o.s.i (0-449-14841-6, Fawcett) Ballantine Bks.

Ellroy, James, et al. Hollywood Nocturnes. 1998. 304p. pap. 13.95 (0-385-33328-5) Dell Publishing.

Elton, Ben. Popcorn. 2003. 320p. mass mkt. (0-552-15101-7, Corgi) Bantam Bks.

—Popcorn. 1998. 304p. pap. 13.95 (0-312-19472-2, Saint Martin's Griffin); 1997. 298p. 22.95 (0-312-16965-5) St. Martin's Pr.

Ephron, Delia. Hanging Up. 2000. 288p. mass mkt. 6.99 (0-345-43782-9); 1996. 320p. pap. 12.00 o.s.i (0-345-40444-0) Ballantine Bks.

—Hanging Up. l.t. ed. 1996. 320p. lib. bdg. 23.95 (1-57490-064-1, Beeler Large Print Bks.) Beeler, Thomas T. Publisher.

—Hanging Up. pap. 17.95 o.p. (0-7871-0537-6, NewStar Pr.) NewStar Media, Inc.

—Hanging Up. 1995. 336p. 23.95 o.s.i (0-399-14052-2, G. P. Putnam's Sons) Penguin Group (USA) Inc.

—Hanging Up. unabr. ed. 1995. audio 58.00 (0-7887-4082-2, 96169E5) Recorded Bks., LLC.

Epstein, Leslie. Pandaemonium. 1998. 416p. pap. 14.95 (0-312-18752-1, Saint Martin's Griffin); 1997. 384p. 24.95 o.p. (0-312-15622-7) St. Martin's Pr.

Erickson, Steve. Amnesiascope. 1997. 240p. pap. 12.00 o.p. (0-8050-5361-1, Owl Bks.) Holt, Henry & Co.

—Amnesiascope: A Novel. 1996. 88p. 23.00 o.p. (0-8050-3503-6) Holt, Henry & Co.

Escandon, Maria Amparo. Santitos: Sexo, Humor y Realismo en una Novela Magica. 1999. (SPA.). 288p. pap. 14.95 o.s.i (0-553-06098-8) Bantam Bks.

Estleman, Loren D. The Rocky Mountain Moving Picture Association. 2000. (Illus.). 308p. mass mkt. 6.99 (0-8125-4154-5); 2nd ed. 1999. 288p. 22.95 (0-312-86676-3) Doherty, Tom Assocs., LLC. (Forge Bks.).

—The Rocky Mountain Moving Picture Association. l.t. ed. 2001. (Wheeler Large Print Book Ser.). 19.95 (1-58724-103-X, Wheeler Publishing, Inc.) Gale Group.

—Something Borrowed, Something Black. E-Book 24.95 (0-312-70606-5, Tor Bks.); 2003. 224p. mass mkt. 6.99 (0-8125-4546-X, Tor Bks.); 2002. 236p. 24.95 (0-312-87863-X, CPHC0630, Forge Bks.) Doherty, Tom Assocs., LLC.

Eulo, Ken & Mauck, Joe. Claw. 1994. 22.00 o.s.i (0-671-79963-0, Simon & Schuster) Simon & Schuster.

—Claw. 1995. 319p. pap. text 5.50 (0-312-95595-2, St. Martin's Paperbacks) St. Martin's Pr.

Eversz, Robert M. Burning Garbo: A Nina Zero Novel. 2003. 288p. 23.00 (0-7432-5013-3); E-Book (0-7432-5356-6) Simon & Schuster. (Simon & Schuster).

Faherty, Terence. Raise the Devil. 2000. (Scott Elliott Mysteries Ser.). 264p. 23.95 (0-312-26640-5, Saint Martin's Minotaur) St. Martin's Pr.

Farmer, Jerrilyn. Mumbo Gumbo: A Madeline Bean Novel. 2004. 368p. mass mkt. 6.99 (0-380-81719-5, Avon Bks.); 2003. 272p. 19.95 (0-380-97889-X, Morrow, William & Co.) Morrow/Avon.

—Perfect Sax: A Madeline Bean Novel. 2004. 304p. 22.95 (0-380-97890-3, Morrow, William & Co.) Morrow/Avon.

Farren, Mick. Darklost. 2000. 412p. 24.95 (0-312-86979-7, Tor Bks.) Doherty, Tom Assocs., LLC.

Fast, Howard. Masuto: The Hollywood Murders, Vol. 2. 2001. 416p. pap. 14.00 (0-7434-1305-9) ibooks, Inc.

Feinsod, Ethan. The Habits of a Lifetime. 1992. 240p. 17.95 o.p. (0-312-08205-3, Saint Martin's Minotaur) St. Martin's Pr.

Ferrigno, Robert. Flinch: A Novel. 2003. 320p. pap. 12.95 (1-4000-3024-2, Random House) Random House Adult Trade Publishing Group.

—Heartbreaker. 2000. 368p. mass mkt. 7.50 (0-446-60891-2) Warner Bks., Inc.

—Heartbreaker Signed Edition. 1999. 24.00 o.s.i (0-676-58995-2) Knopf, Alfred A. Inc.

Files, Lolita. Blind Ambitions. 288p. 2000. 23.00 o.s.i (0-684-87144-0); 2001. reprint ed. pap. 13.00 (0-684-87145-9) Simon & Schuster. (Simon & Schuster).

Fisher, David E. Hostage One. 1990. mass mkt. 4.95 o.p. (0-312-92144-6, St. Martin's Paperbacks) St. Martin's Pr.

Fitch, Janet. White Oleander, Set. abr. ed. 1999. audio 24.98 Highsmith Inc.

—White Oleander. (Oprah's Book Club Selection Ser. ). 1999. pap. 7.99 (0-316-28508-0, Back Bay); 1999. 390p. (gr. 8). 24.95 (0-316-56932-1); 1999. 400p. 24.00 o.p. (0-316-28526-9); 2000. 464p. pap. 13.95 (0-316-28495-5, Back Bay) Little Brown & Co.

—White Oleander. unabr. ed. 1999. audio 96.00 (0-7887-3471-7, 95890E7); audio compact disk 112.00 (0-7887-3970-0, C1089E7) Recorded Bks., LLC.

—White Oleander. l.t. ed. 2002. 14.00 (1-4104-0081-6, Large Print Pr.); 2000. 613p. pap. 27.95 (0-7862-2166-6); 1999. 613p. 30.95 (0-7862-2095-3) Thorndike Pr.

—White Oleander. abr. ed. 1999. audio 24.98 (1-57042-821-2) Time Warner AudioBooks.

—White Oleander. 2000. 19.75 (0-606-19031-7) Turtleback Bks.

Fitzgerald, F. Scott. F. Scott Fitzgerald: The Love of The Last Tycoon. Bruccoli, Matthew J., ed. 1993. (Works of F. Scott Fitzgerald). (Illus.). 448p. 45.00 (0-521-40231-X) Cambridge Univ. Pr.

—The Love of the Last Tycoon. 1995. 17.05 (0-606-20777-5) Turtleback Bks.

Fluke, Joanne. Deadly Memories. 1995. 352p. mass mkt. 4.50 o.s.i (0-8217-4841-6, Zebra Bks.) Kensington Publishing Corp.

Forrest, Katherine V. Amateur City. 1984. (Kate Delafield Mystery Ser.: Vol. 1). 224p. pap. 11.95 (0-930044-55-X) Naiad Pr., Inc.

—Apparition Alley. (Kate Delafield Mystery Ser.). 256p. 1997. 21.95 o.s.i (0-425-15966-3); 1998. reprint ed. mass mkt. 5.99 o.s.i (0-425-16632-5) Berkley Publishing Group. (Prime Crime).

—The Beverly Malibu. (Kate Delafield Mystery Ser.). 1989. 16.95 o.p. (0-941483-47-9); 1991. 288p. reprint ed. pap. 11.95 (0-941483-48-7) Naiad Pr., Inc.

—The Beverly Malibu: A Kate Delafield Mystery. 2003. (Kate Delafield Mystery Ser.). 280p. pap. 12.95 (1-55583-716-6, Alyson Bks.) Alyson Pubns.

—Flashpoint. 256p. 1995. pap. 10.95 o.p. (1-56280-079-5); 1994. 22.95 (1-56280-043-4) Naiad Pr., Inc.

—Murder at the Nightwood Bar. 1987. (Kate Delafield Mystery Ser.: Vol. 2). 240p. pap. 11.95 o.p. (0-930044-92-4) Naiad Pr., Inc.

—Murder at the Nightwood Bar: A Kate Delafield Mystery. 2003. (Kate Delafield Mystery Ser.). 216p. pap. 12.95 (1-55583-717-4) Alyson Pubns.

—Murder by Tradition. 288p. 1991. text 18.95 o.p. (0-941483-89-4); 1993. (Kate Delafield Mystery Ser.: Vol. 4). reprint ed. pap. 11.95 (1-56280-002-7) Naiad Pr., Inc.

—Sleeping Bones: A Kate Delafield Mystery. (Kate Delafield Mystery Ser.). 272p. 1999. 21.95 o.s.i (0-425-17029-2); 2000. reprint ed. pap. 13.00 (0-425-17484-0, Prime Crime) Berkley Publishing Group.

Forster, R. A. Character Witness. 1997. 304p. mass mkt. 5.99 o.s.i (0-7860-0378-2, Pinnacle Bks.) Kensington Publishing Corp.

Forster, Suzanne. Come Midnight. (Orig.). mass mkt. 6.99 o.s.i (0-515-12946-1, Jove); 1995. 304p. mass mkt. 5.99 o.s.i (0-425-14565-4) Berkley Publishing Group.

Foster, Alan Dean. The Mocking Program. 2003. 336p. mass mkt. 6.99 (0-446-61307-X); 2002. 288p. 24.95 (0-446-52774-2) Warner Bks., Inc. (Aspect).

Fowles, John. Daniel Martin. 1997. 640p. pap. 12.95 (0-316-29039-4); 1977. 19.95 o.p. (0-316-28959-0) Little Brown & Co.

—Daniel Martin. 1978. mass mkt. 2.95 o.p. (*0-451-08249-4*); mass mkt. 4.50 o.p. (*0-451-12210-0*, AE2210); mass mkt. 3.50 o.p. (*0-451-11484-1*); 688p. mass mkt. 5.95 o.p. (*0-451-16761-9*) NAL. (Signet Bks.).

Frank, Larry. Fragments of a Mask: A Novel. 2002. 192p. 26.95 (*0-86534-370-5*); pap. 18.95 (*0-86534-359-4*) Sunstone Pr.

Freadhoff, Chuck. Blue Rain. 2000. 368p. mass mkt. 6.99 (*0-06-109727-6*); 1999. 336p. 24.00 o.p. (*0-06-019217-8*) HarperCollins Pubs.

—Blue Rain. l.t. ed. 1999. (Americana Ser.). 493p. 26.95 (*0-7862-2068-6*) Thorndike Pr.

—A Permanent Twilight. 2000. 352p. 25.00 (*0-06-019216-X*) HarperCollins Pubs.

Freeman, David. A Hollywood Education: Tales of Movie Dreams & Easy Money. 1992. 288p. pap. 10.95 (*0-88184-870-0*, Carroll & Graf Pubs.) Avalon Publishing Group.

—A Hollywood Education: Tales of Movie Dreams & Easy Money. 1987. pap. 6.95 o.s.i (*0-440-53738-X*, Laurel) Dell Publishing.

—A Hollywood Education: Tales of Movie Dreams & Easy Money. 1986. 256p. 17.95 o.p. (*0-399-13044-6*) Putnam Publishing Group, The.

—A Hollywood Life. 1991. 19.95 o.p. (*0-671-72738-9*, Simon & Schuster) Simon & Schuster.

Freeman, Judith. The Chinchilla Farm. 1990. (Vintage Contemporaries Ser.). 320p. pap. 14.00 o.s.i (*0-679-73052-4*, Vintage) Knopf Publishing Group.

—Chinchilla Farm. 1989. 19.95 o.p. (*0-393-02722-8*) Norton, W. W. & Co., Inc.

—The Chinchilla Farm: A Novel. 2003. 320p. pap. 13.95 (*0-393-32426-5*) Norton, W. W. & Co., Inc.

Friedman. A-Hunting We Will Go. 1998. 448p. mass mkt. 6.99 o.s.i (*0-06-109590-7*) HarperCollins Pubs.

Friedman, Hal. A Hunting We Will Go. 1998. 368p. 23.00 o.p. (*0-06-018264-4*) HarperCollins Pubs.

—Over the Edge. 1999. 416p. mass mkt. 6.99 o.s.i (*0-06-109367-X*); 1998. 320p. 24.00 (*0-06-018265-2*) HarperCollins Pubs.

Furutani, Dale. Death in Little Tokyo. unabr. collector's ed. 1999. (Ken Tanaka Ser.). audio 32.00 (*0-7366-4414-8*, 4875) Books on Tape, Inc.

—Death in Little Tokyo. 1996. 256p. 21.95 o.p. (*0-312-14580-2*, Saint Martin's Minotaur); Vol. 1. 1997. (Death in Little Tokyo Ser.: Vol. 1). 224p. mass mkt. 5.99 o.p. (*0-312-96323-8*, St. Martin's Paperbacks) St. Martin's Pr.

—The Toyotomi Blades, Vol. 1. 1998. (Toyotomi Blades Ser.: Vol. 1). 240p. mass mkt. 5.99 (*0-312-96667-9*, St. Martin's Paperbacks) St. Martin's Pr.

—The Toyotomi Blades: A Ken Tanaka Mystery. 1997. (Ken Tanaka Mystery Ser.). 224p. 21.95 (*0-312-17050-5*, Saint Martin's Minotaur) St. Martin's Pr.

Gage, Elizabeth. Taboo. l.t. ed. 1994. pap. 23.95 o.p. (*0-7927-1731-7*); 1993. 25.95 o.p. (*0-7927-1732-5*) BBC Audiobooks America.

—Taboo. abr. ed. 1993. 16.95 o.p. (*1-55800-698-2*); audio 8.99 o.p. (*1-55800-905-1*, Dove Audio) NewStar Media, Inc.

—Taboo. Zion, Claire, ed. 1993. 480p. 22.00 (*0-671-78641-5*, Atria); 576p. reprint ed. mass mkt. 5.99 (*0-671-78644-X*, Pocket) Simon & Schuster.

Galbraith, Liam Patrick. Honda Dream. 2000. 256p. pap. 24.50 (*0-88739-222-9*) Creative Arts Bk. Co.

Gardner, Erle Stanley. The Case of the Amorous Aunt. 1994. mass mkt. 4.50 o.s.i (*0-345-37878-4*) Ballantine Bks.

—The Case of the Amorous Aunt. l.t. ed. 1985. (Nightingale Ser.). 11.95 o.p. (*0-8161-3752-8*, Macmillan Reference USA) Gale Group.

—The Case of the Angry Mourner. 1989. (*1-55504-971-0*); 1991. 12.95 o.p. (*1-55504-970-2*, 215) BBC Audiobooks America.

—The Case of the Angry Mourner. 1993. mass mkt. 4.50 o.s.i (*0-345-37870-9*) Ballantine Bks.

—The Case of the Baited Hook. (Perry Mason Bks.). 288p. reprint ed. lib. bdg. 23.95 (*0-88411-416-3*) Amereon, Ltd.

—The Case of the Baited Hook. (Perry Mason Mysteries Ser.). 1999. mass mkt. 4.99 (*0-345-91478-3*); 1995. 224p. pap. 15.00 (*0-345-46896-1*); 1986. 224p. mass mkt. 5.99 (*0-345-32942-2*) Ballantine Bks.

—The Case of the Beautiful Beggar. 1976. 21.95 (*0-8488-0498-8*) Amereon, Ltd.

—The Case of the Beautiful Beggar. 1986. mass mkt. 3.50 o.s.i (*0-345-34318-2*) Ballantine Bks.

—The Case of the Beautiful Beggar. l.t. ed. 1998. (G. K. Hall Paperback Ser.). 272p. 22.95 o.p. (*0-7838-0269-2*, Macmillan Reference USA) Gale Group.

—The Case of the Beautiful Beggar. abr. ed. 1988. audio 14.95 (*1-55800-118-2*, 40450, Dove Audio) NewStar Media, Inc.

—The Case of the Bigamous Spouse. l.t. ed. 1988. pap. 18.95 o.p. (*1-55504-668-1*); lib. bdg. 20.95 o.p. (*1-55504-687-8*) BBC Audiobooks America.

—The Case of the Bigamous Spouse. 1987. mass mkt. 2.95 o.s.i (*0-345-34378-6*) Ballantine Bks.

—The Case of the Bigamous Spouse. 1972. pap. 0.95 o.p. (*0-671-77865-X*, Pocket) Simon & Schuster.

—The Case of the Black-Eyed Blonde. 1976. 21.95 (*0-8488-0271-3*) Amereon, Ltd.

—The Case of the Black-Eyed Blonde. 1985. 208p. mass mkt. 3.50 o.s.i (*0-345-32311-4*) Ballantine Bks.

—The Case of the Black-Eyed Blonde. 1975. pap. 1.50 o.p. (*0-671-78782-9*, Pocket) Simon & Schuster.

—The Case of the Blonde Bonanza. 1994. mass mkt. 4.50 o.s.i (*0-345-37877-6*) Ballantine Bks.

—The Case of the Blonde Bonanza. l.t. ed. 1987. (Nightingale Ser.). 291p. pap. 11.95 o.p. (*0-8161-4283-1*, Macmillan Reference USA) Gale Group.

—The Case of the Borrowed Brunette. 1987. 224p. mass mkt. 4.99 o.s.i (*0-345-34374-3*) Ballantine Bks.

—The Case of the Borrowed Brunette. 1976. pap. 1.95 o.p. (*0-671-80470-7*, Pocket) Simon & Schuster.

—The Case of the Buried Clock. 1976. 22.95 (*0-8488-0273-X*) Amereon, Ltd.

—The Case of the Buried Clock. 1997. mass mkt. 4.99 (*0-345-90799-X*); 1986. mass mkt. 3.95 o.s.i (*0-345-33691-7*); 1983. mass mkt. 4.99 o.s.i (*0-345-31013-6*, Ballantine Bks.) Ballantine Bks.

—The Case of the Buried Clock. l.t. ed. 1998. (Paperback Ser.). 312p. pap. 24.95 (*0-7838-0366-4*) Thorndike Pr.

—The Case of the Calendar Girl. 1976. 21.95 (*0-8488-0499-6*) Amereon, Ltd.

—The Case of the Calendar Girl. 1987. 224p. mass mkt. 4.99 o.s.i (*0-345-34375-1*) Ballantine Bks.

—The Case of the Careless Cupid. 1995. mass mkt. 4.99 o.s.i (*0-345-39226-4*) Ballantine Bks.

—The Case of the Careless Cupid. l.t. ed. 2003. (Dales Large Print Ser.). 304p. pap. 21.99 (*1-84262-216-1*) Dales Large Print Bks. GBR. *Dist:* Ulverscroft Large Print Bks., Ltd., Ulverscroft Large Print Canada, Ltd.

—The Case of the Careless Cupid. 1977. lib. bdg. 9.95 o.p. (*0-8161-6447-9*, Macmillan Reference USA) Gale Group.

—The Case of the Careless Kitten. 1976. 23.95 (*0-8488-0272-1*) Amereon, Ltd.

—The Case of the Careless Kitten. 1989. (Perry Mason Mysteries Ser.). 224p. mass mkt. 4.99 o.s.i (*0-345-36223-3*) Ballantine Bks.

—The Case of the Caretaker's Cat. 1976. (Perry Mason Bks.). reprint ed. lib. bdg. 24.95 (*0-88411-407-4*) Amereon, Ltd.

—The Case of the Caretaker's Cat. 1985. (Perry Mason Mysteries Ser.). reprint ed. mass mkt. 4.99 o.s.i (*0-345-32156-1*) Ballantine Bks.

—The Case of the Caretaker's Cat. l.t. ed. 1998. (Perry Mason Mysteries Ser.). 283p. 21.95 o.p. (*0-7838-8439-7*, Macmillan Reference USA) Gale Group.

—The Case of the Cautious Coquette. 1997. 18.95 (*0-88411-440-6*); 1976. 21.95 (*0-8488-0500-3*) Amereon, Ltd.

—The Case of the Cautious Coquette. l.t. ed. 1991. 19.95 o.p. (*0-7927-0847-4*, CS0189); pap. 17.95 o.p. (*0-7927-0848-2*) BBC Audiobooks America.

—The Case of the Cautious Coquette. 1988. 240p. reprint ed. mass mkt. 4.99 o.s.i (*0-345-35202-5*) Ballantine Bks.

—The Case of the Counterfeit Eye. 1976. (Perry Mason Books Ser.). reprint ed. lib. bdg. 24.95 (*0-88411-406-6*) Amereon, Ltd.

—The Case of the Counterfeit Eye. (*0-7540-3701-0*); 1999. 296 p. (*0-7540-3702-9*) BBC Audiobooks America.

—The Case of the Counterfeit Eye. (Perry Mason Mysteries Ser.). 1998. mass mkt. 4.99 (*0-345-91229-2*); 1986. 256p. mass mkt. 4.99 o.s.i (*0-345-33195-8*) Ballantine Bks.

—The Case of the Counterfeit Eye. 1974. pap. 0.95 o.p. (*0-671-77895-1*, Pocket) Simon & Schuster.

—The Case of the Counterfeit Eye. l.t. ed. 1999. (Paperback Ser.). 296p. pap. 23.95 o.p. (*0-7838-8522-9*) Thorndike Pr.

—The Case of the Crimson Kiss. 1972. pap. 0.95 o.p. (*0-671-77881-1*, Simon Pulse) Simon & Schuster Children's Publishing.

—The Case of the Crooked Candle. 1976. 21.95 (*0-8488-0275-6*) Amereon, Ltd.

—The Case of the Crooked Candle. l.t. ed. 1989. vi, 339 p. (*1-55504-787-4*) BBC Audiobooks America.

—The Case of the Crooked Candle. 1989. mass mkt. 3.99 o.p. (*0-345-01834-6*); 1987. mass mkt. 3.99 o.s.i (*0-345-34164-3*) Ballantine Bks.

—The Case of the Crooked Candle. 1976. (Crime Fiction Ser.). reprint ed. lib. bdg. 21.00 o.p. (*0-8240-2368-4*) Garland Publishing, Inc.

—The Case of the Crying Swallow: A Perry Mason Novelette & Other Stories. l.t. ed. 1987. (Nightingale Ser.). 295p. 11.95 o.p. (*0-8161-4284-X*, Macmillan Reference USA) Gale Group.

—The Case of the Curious Bride. 1976. (Perry Mason Bks.). reprint ed. lib. bdg. 23.95 (*0-88411-405-8*) Amereon, Ltd.

—The Case of the Curious Bride. (Perry Mason Mysteries Ser.). 2000. 192p. mass mkt. 5.99 o.s.i (*0-345-43783-7*, Fawcett); 1989. 224p. mass mkt. 4.99 o.s.i (*0-345-36222-5*) Ballantine Bks.

—The Case of the Curious Bride. l.t. ed. 2001. (G. K. Hall Paperback Ser.). 319p. pap. 24.95 (*0-7838-9432-5*); (*0-7540-4535-8*); (*0-7540-4536-6*) Gale Group. (Macmillan Reference USA).

—The Case of the Curious Bride. 1992. pap. 46.00 o.p. (*0-671-82708-1*, Pocket) Simon & Schuster.

—The Case of the Dangerous Dowager. 1976. (Perry Mason Bks.). reprint ed. lib. bdg. 19.95 (*0-88411-410-4*) Amereon, Ltd.

—The Case of the Dangerous Dowager. (Perry Mason Mysteries Ser.). 1998. mass mkt. 4.99 (*0-345-91231-4*); 1986. 224p. mass mkt. 4.99 o.s.i (*0-345-33192-3*) Ballantine Bks.

—The Case of the Dangerous Dowager. l.t. ed. 2000. (G. K. Hall Paperback Ser.). 299p. pap. 23.95 (*0-7838-9225-X*, Macmillan Reference USA) Gale Group.

—The Case of the Daring Decoy. 1989. (Perry Mason Mysteries Ser.). 224p. mass mkt. 4.99 o.s.i (*0-345-36220-9*) Ballantine Bks.

—The Case of the Daring Divorcee. 1984. 192p. mass mkt. 3.95 o.s.i (*0-345-32003-4*) Ballantine Bks.

—The Case of the Deadly Toy. (Perry Mason Mysteries Ser.). 224p. 2000. mass mkt. 6.99 (*0-345-43784-5*, Fawcett); 1985. mass mkt. 3.50 o.s.i (*0-345-33494-9*) Ballantine Bks.

—The Case of the Deadly Toy. 1981. 288p. reprint ed. lib. bdg. 18.00 (*0-8376-0397-8*) Bentley Pubs.

—The Case of the Deadly Toy. l.t. ed. 1993. (Nightingale Ser.). 378p. lib. bdg. 15.95 o.p. (*0-8161-5632-8*, Macmillan Reference USA) Gale Group.

—The Case of the Demure Defendant. 1991. 192p. mass mkt. 3.95 o.s.i (*0-345-37148-8*, Ballantine Bks.) Ballantine Bks.

—The Case of the Demure Defendant. l.t. ed. 1988. 336p. 15.95 o.p. (*0-7089-1785-2*, Ulverscroft) Thorpe, F. A. Pubs. GBR. *Dist:* Ulverscroft Large Print Bks., Ltd.

—The Case of the Drowning Duck. (Perry Mason Bks.). 284p. reprint ed. lib. bdg. 23.95 (*0-88411-420-1*) Amereon, Ltd.

—The Case of the Drowning Duck. l.t. ed. 1990. (Perry Mason Mystery Ser.). 21.95 o.p. (*0-7927-0635-8*, C0595); pap. 19.95 o.p. (*0-7927-0636-6*) BBC Audiobooks America.

—The Case of the Drowning Duck. 1993. reprint ed. mass mkt. 4.50 o.s.i (*0-345-37868-7*) Ballantine Bks.

—The Case of the Drowning Duck. 1976. pap. 1.95 o.p. (*0-671-80281-X*, Pocket) Simon & Schuster.

—The Case of the Drowsy Mosquito. 1976. 22.95 (*0-8488-0274-8*) Amereon, Ltd.

—The Case of the Drowsy Mosquito. 1994. reprint ed. mass mkt. 4.99 o.s.i (*0-345-37869-5*) Ballantine Bks.

—The Case of the Drowsy Mosquito. 1976. (Two-in-One Ser.). pap. 1.95 o.p. (*0-671-80390-5*, Pocket) Simon & Schuster.

—The Case of the Drowsy Mosquito. l.t. ed. 1978. 12.00 o.p. (*0-7089-0235-9*, Ulverscroft) Thorpe, F. A. Pubs. GBR. *Dist:* Ulverscroft Large Print Bks., Ltd.

—The Case of the Dubious Bridegroom. l.t. ed. 1994. 22.95 o.p. (*0-7927-2103-9*); pap. 21.95 o.p. (*0-7927-2102-0*) BBC Audiobooks America.

—The Case of the Dubious Bridegroom. 1986. 224p. mass mkt. 3.50 o.s.i (*0-345-34186-4*); 1984. mass mkt. 2.50 o.p. (*0-345-31811-0*); 1983. mass mkt. 4.99 o.s.i (*0-345-30881-6*) Ballantine Bks.

—The Case of the Duplicate Daughter. 1988. mass mkt. 3.50 o.s.i (*0-345-35681-0*) Ballantine Bks.

—The Case of the Duplicate Daughter. 1975. pap. 1.50 o.p. (*0-671-78779-9*, Pocket) Simon & Schuster.

—The Case of the Empty Tin. (Perry Mason Bks.). 282p. reprint ed. lib. bdg. 23.95 (*0-88411-419-8*) Amereon, Ltd.

—The Case of the Empty Tin. 1985. 240p. mass mkt. 4.99 o.s.i (*0-345-33198-2*); 1996. reprint ed. mass mkt. 4.99 (*0-345-90798-1*) Ballantine Bks.

—The Case of the Empty Tin. l.t. ed. 1979. (Ulverscroft Large Print Ser.). 12.00 o.p. (*0-7089-0244-8*, Ulverscroft) Thorpe, F. A. Pubs. GBR. *Dist:* Ulverscroft Large Print Bks., Ltd., Ulverscroft Large Print Canada, Ltd.

—The Case of the Fabulous Fake. l.t. ed. 1990. (Perry Mason Mystery Ser.). pap. 10.95 o.p. (*0-89340-024-6*, C0148) BBC Audiobooks America.

—The Case of the Fabulous Fake. 1986. mass mkt. 3.95 o.s.i (*0-345-33548-1*) Ballantine Bks.

—The Case of the Fabulous Fake. 1969. 7.95 o.p. (*0-688-01276-0*, Morrow, William & Co.) Morrow/Avon.

—The Case of the Fan-Dancer's Horse. 1992. reprint ed. mass mkt. 4.99 o.s.i (*0-345-37144-5*) Ballantine Bks.

—The Case of the Fan-Dancer's Horse & the Case of the Hesitant Hostess. 1977. pap. 1.95 o.p. (*0-671-81386-2*, Pocket) Simon & Schuster.

—The Case of the Fenced-In Woman. 1994. (Perry Mason Mysteries Ser.). 224p. mass mkt. 5.99 o.s.i (*0-345-39223-X*) Ballantine Bks.

—The Case of the Fiery Fingers. 1987. mass mkt. 3.50 o.s.i (*0-345-35161-4*) Ballantine Bks.

—The Case of the Fiery Fingers. 1975. pap. 1.50 o.p. (*0-671-78783-7*, Pocket) Simon & Schuster.

—The Case of the Foot-Loose Doll. 1975. pap. 24.95 o.p. (*0-671-78787-X*, Atria) Simon & Schuster.

—The Case of the Fugitive Nurse. 1993. mass mkt. 4.99 o.s.i (*0-345-37873-3*) Ballantine Bks.

—The Case of the Gilded Lily. l.t. ed. 1991. 8.95 o.p. (*1-55504-899-4*, 16) BBC Audiobooks America.

—The Case of the Gilded Lily. 1999. mass mkt. 4.99 (*0-345-91480-5*); 1985. 199p. mass mkt. 5.99 o.s.i (*0-345-32318-1*) Ballantine Bks.

—The Case of the Gilded Lily. 1981. (Perry Mason Mysteries Ser.). 256p. reprint ed. lib. bdg. 18.00 (*0-8376-0396-X*) Bentley Pubs.

—The Case of the Glamorous Ghost. l.t. ed. 1992. pap. 20.95 o.p. (*0-7927-1044-4*, CS0279); 1991. 22.95 o.p. (*0-7927-1043-6*, CH0211) BBC Audiobooks America.

—The Case of the Glamorous Ghost. 240p. 2000. mass mkt. 5.99 (*0-345-43786-1*, Fawcett); 1986. mass mkt. 3.95 o.s.i (*0-345-34440-5*) Ballantine Bks.

—The Case of the Glamorous Ghost. 1977. pap. 1.95 o.p. (*0-671-81691-8*, Pocket) Simon & Schuster.

—The Case of the Golddigger's Purse. 1997. mass mkt. 4.99 (*0-345-90800-7*); 1984. 224p. mass mkt. 4.99 o.s.i (*0-345-31680-0*, Ballantine Bks.) Ballantine Bks.

—The Case of the Golddigger's Purse. l.t. ed. 2002. 370p. pap. 25.95 (*0-7862-4251-5*) Gale Group.

—The Case of the Green-Eyed Sister. 1978. xii, 426p. (*0-89340-140-4*) BBC Audiobooks America.

—The Case of the Green-Eyed Sister. 1993. mass mkt. 4.50 o.s.i (*0-345-37872-5*) Ballantine Bks.

—The Case of the Green-Eyed Sister. 1975. pap. 1.50 o.p. (*0-671-80074-4*, Pocket) Simon & Schuster.

—The Case of the Grinning Gorilla. 1986. mass mkt. 2.95 o.s.i (*0-345-34187-2*) Ballantine Bks.

—The Case of the Grinning Gorilla. 1973. pap. 0.95 o.p. (*0-671-77889-7*, Star Trek) Simon & Schuster.

—The Case of the Half-Wakened Wife. 1991. 256p. mass mkt. 4.99 o.s.i (*0-345-37147-X*, Ballantine Bks.) Ballantine Bks.

—The Case of the Haunted Husband. 281p. reprint ed. lib. bdg. 23.95 (*0-88411-418-X*) Amereon, Ltd.

—The Case of the Haunted Husband. 1986. vii, 374 p. (*1-55504-067-5*) BBC Audiobooks America.

—The Case of the Haunted Husband. 1985. 208p. mass mkt. 4.99 o.s.i (*0-345-33495-7*) Ballantine Bks.

—The Case of the Haunted Husband. abr. ed. 1991. 2p. audio 16.99 (*0-88646-299-1*) Durkin Hayes Publishing Ltd.

—The Case of the Hesitant Hostess. 1993. mass mkt. 4.50 o.s.i (*0-345-37871-7*) Ballantine Bks.

—The Case of the Hesitant Hostess. l.t. ed. 1991. 377p. pap. 15.95 o.p. (*0-8161-5064-8*, Macmillan Reference USA) Gale Group.

—The Case of the Horrified Heirs. 1995. 192p. mass mkt. 5.99 (*0-345-39227-2*); pap. 15.00 (*0-345-47043-5*) Ballantine Bks.

—The Case of the Howling Dog. 1976. (Perry Mason Bks.). reprint ed. lib. bdg. 24.95 (*0-88411-404-X*) Amereon, Ltd.

—The Case of the Howling Dog. 1987. mass mkt. 4.99 o.s.i (*0-345-34783-8*); 1984. mass mkt. 2.50 o.p. (*0-345-31679-7*) Ballantine Bks.

—The Case of the Howling Dog. l.t. ed. 1999. (Paperback Ser.). 279p. pap. 23.95 (*0-7838-8775-2*, Macmillan Reference USA) Gale Group.

—The Case of the Ice-Cold Hands. 1989. mass mkt. 3.95 o.s.i (*0-345-35939-9*) Ballantine Bks.

—The Case of the Ice-Cold Hands. 1980. (General Ser.). lib. bdg. 11.95 o.p. (*0-8161-3174-0*, Macmillan Reference USA) Gale Group.

—The Case of the Irate Witness. 1973. pap. 0.95 o.p. (*0-671-77883-8*, Pocket) Simon & Schuster.

—The Case of the Lame Canary. (Perry Mason Bks.). 281p. reprint ed. lib. bdg. 23.95 (*0-88411-411-2*) Amereon, Ltd.

—The Case of the Lame Canary. 1996. mass mkt. 4.99 (*0-345-90796-5*); 1987. 256p. mass mkt. 4.99 o.s.i (*0-345-35162-2*); 1984. mass mkt. 2.50 o.s.i (*0-345-31547-2*) Ballantine Bks.

—The Case of the Lazy Lover. l.t. ed. 1982. vii, 438 p. (*0-89340-362-8*) BBC Audiobooks America.

—The Case of the Lazy Lover. 1997. mass mkt. 4.99 (*0-345-90801-5*); 1987. mass mkt. 2.95 o.s.i (*0-345-35007-3*); 1981. mass mkt. 4.99 o.s.i (*0-345-29496-3*) Ballantine Bks.

—The Case of the Lazy Lover. l.t. ed. 1997. 21.95 (*0-7838-8348-X*, Macmillan Reference USA) Gale Group.

—The Case of the Lazy Lover. abr. ed. 1989. audio 14.95 (*1-55800-119-0*, 40460, Dove Audio) NewStar Media, Inc.

—The Case of the Lonely Heiress. (Perry Mason Mysteries Ser.). 1997. mass mkt. 4.99 (*0-345-90802-3*); 1986. 224p. mass mkt. 3.95 o.s.i (*0-345-34012-4*); 1984. mass mkt. 2.50 o.p. (*0-345-31797-1*); 1983. 224p. mass mkt. 5.99 o.s.i (*0-345-31012-8*, Ballantine Bks.) Ballantine Bks.

—The Case of the Lonely Heiress. l.t. ed. 2001. 216p. pap. 24.95 (*0-7838-9506-2*, Macmillan Reference USA) Gale Group.

—The Case of the Lonely Heiress. 1973. pap. 0.95 o.p. (*0-671-77886-2*, Atria) Simon & Schuster.
—The Case of the Long-Legged Models. 1994. mass mkt. 4.99 o.s.i (*0-345-37876-8*) Ballantine Bks.
—The Case of the Long-Legged Models. 1971. pap. 0.75 o.p. (*0-671-75556-0*, Pimsleur) Simon & Schuster Audio.
—The Case of the Lucky Loser. l.t. ed. 1991. 12.95 o.p. (*0-7927-0227-1*, 4764); 1990. pap. 17.95 o.p. (*0-7927-0228-X*, C0247) BBC Audiobooks America.
—The Case of the Lucky Loser. 1990. 192p. mass mkt. 4.99 o.s.i (*0-345-36497-X*) Ballantine Bks.
—The Case of the Mischievous Doll. 1989. mass mkt. 4.99 o.s.i (*0-345-35940-2*) Ballantine Bks.
—The Case of the Mischievous Doll. 1981. (General Ser.). lib. bdg. 11.95 o.p. (*0-8161-3215-1*, Macmillan Reference USA) Gale Group.
—The Case of the Moth-Eaten Mink. 1990. (Perry Mason Mysteries Ser.: No. 57). 240p. mass mkt. 3.95 o.p. (*0-345-36928-9*) Ballantine Bks.
—The Case of the Moth-Eaten Mink. l.t. ed. 1992. (General Ser.). 365p. lib. bdg. 19.95 o.p. (*0-8161-5063-X*, Macmillan Reference USA) Gale Group.
—The Case of the Moth-Eaten Mink. 1971. pap. 0.75 o.p. (*0-671-75539-0*, Star Trek) Simon & Schuster.
—The Case of the Mythical Monkeys. 1984. mass mkt. 3.95 o.s.i (*0-345-31404-2*) Ballantine Bks.
—The Case of the Mythical Monkeys. 1981. 288p. reprint ed. lib. bdg. 18.00 (*0-8376-0398-6*) Bentley Pubs.
—The Case of the Mythical Monkeys. l.t. ed. 1993. 13.95 o.p. (*0-8161-3384-0*, Macmillan Reference USA) Gale Group.
—The Case of the Negligent Nymph. 1986. 176p. mass mkt. 3.95 o.s.i (*0-345-34013-2*) Ballantine Bks.
—The Case of the Negligent Nymph. 1973. pap. 0.95 o.p. (*0-671-77892-7*, Pocket) Simon & Schuster.
—The Case of the Nervous Accomplice. 1992. mass mkt. 3.99 o.s.i (*0-345-37874-1*) Ballantine Bks.
—The Case of the Nervous Accomplice. 1974. pap. 0.95 o.p. (*0-671-77926-5*, Pocket) Simon & Schuster.
—The Case of the One-Eyed Witness. 1995. 240p. mass mkt. 5.99 (*0-345-39225-6*) Ballantine Bks.
—The Case of the One-Eyed Witness. l.t. ed. 1990. pap. 15.95 o.p. (*0-8161-5062-1*, Macmillan Reference USA) Gale Group.
—The Case of the One-Eyed Witness. 1971. pap. 0.75 o.p. (*0-671-75536-6*, Star Trek) Simon & Schuster.
—The Case of the Perjured Parrot. (Perry Mason Bks.). 288p. reprint ed. lib. bdg. 23.95 (*0-88411-414-7*) Amereon, Ltd.
—The Case of the Perjured Parrot. (Perry Mason Mysteries Ser.). 1987. mass mkt. 4.99 o.s.i (*0-345-34685-8*); 1982. mass mkt. 2.25 o.p. (*0-345-30396-2*) Ballantine Bks.
—The Case of the Perjured Parrot. l.t. ed. 2001. 253p. (*0-7540-4401-7*); (*0-7540-4402-5*) Gale Group. (Macmillan Reference USA).
—The Case of the Perjured Parrot. 1975. pap. 1.50 o.p. (*0-671-78944-9*, Pocket) Simon & Schuster.
—The Case of the Perjured Parrot. l.t. ed. 2001. (G. K. Hall Nightingale Ser.). 253p. pap. 23.95 (*0-7838-9322-1*) Thorndike Pr.
—The Case of the Phantom Fortune. 1986. mass mkt. 3.50 o.s.i (*0-345-33191-5*) Ballantine Bks.
—The Case of the Phantom Fortune. l.t. ed. 1984. (Nightingale Ser.). 9.95 o.p. (*0-8161-3754-4*, Macmillan Reference USA) Gale Group.
—The Case of the Phantom Fortune. 1974. pap. 0.95 o.p. (*0-671-77896-X*, Pocket) Simon & Schuster.
—The Case of the Postponed Murder. 1995. mass mkt. 4.99 o.s.i (*0-345-39229-9*) Ballantine Bks.
—The Case of the Postponed Murder. 1973. (General Ser.). reprint ed. lib. bdg. 8.95 o.p. (*0-8161-6090-2*, Macmillan Reference USA) Gale Group.
—The Case of the Postponed Murder. 1973. 7.95 o.p. (*0-688-00033-9*, Morrow, William & Co.) Morrow/Avon.
—The Case of the Postponed Murder. 1974. pap. 0.95 o.p. (*0-671-77894-3*, Pocket) Simon & Schuster.
—The Case of the Queenly Contestant. l.t. ed. 1990. (Perry Mason Mystery Ser.). pap. 18.95 o.p. (*0-89340-025-4*, C0160) BBC Audiobooks America.
—The Case of the Queenly Contestant. 1993. reprint ed. mass mkt. 4.50 o.s.i (*0-345-37879-2*) Ballantine Bks.
—The Case of the Reluctant Model. 1990. 208p. mass mkt. 3.95 o.s.i (*0-345-36689-1*) Ballantine Bks.
—The Case of the Reluctant Model, abr. ed. audio 16.99 (*0-88646-301-7*, DHA7301) Durkin Hayes Publishing Ltd.
—The Case of the Restless Redhead. 1980. xiv, 435 p. (*0-89340-261-3*) BBC Audiobooks America.
—The Case of the Restless Redhead. 1985. mass mkt. 3.95 o.s.i (*0-345-33199-0*) Ballantine Bks.
—The Case of the Rolling Bones. (Perry Mason Bks.). 288p. reprint ed. lib. bdg. 23.95 (*0-88411-415-5*) Amereon, Ltd.
—The Case of the Rolling Bones. 1999. 4.99 (*0-345-91481-3*); 1985. 208p. reprint ed. mass mkt. 4.99 o.s.i (*0-345-32979-1*) Ballantine Bks.
—The Case of the Rolling Bones. l.t. ed. 1986. (Nightingale Ser.). 350p. 11.95 o.p. (*0-8161-4080-4*, Macmillan Reference USA) Gale Group.
—The Case of the Rolling Bones. 1976. (Two-in-One Ser.). pap. 1.95 o.p. (*0-671-80583-5*, Pocket) Simon & Schuster.
—The Case of the Runaway Corpse. 1990. 224p. mass mkt. 4.99 o.s.i (*0-345-36498-8*) Ballantine Bks.
—The Case of the Runaway Corpse. l.t. ed. 1988. lib. bdg. 14.95 o.p. (*1-85057-453-7*, Macmillan Reference USA) Gale Group.
—The Case of the Screaming Woman. l.t. ed. 1992. pap. 18.95 o.p. (*0-7927-0969-1*) BBC Audiobooks America.
—The Case of the Screaming Woman. 1994. mass mkt. 4.99 o.s.i (*0-345-37875-X*); 1992. 20.95 o.p. (*0-7927-1228-5*, CH0260) Ballantine Bks.
—The Case of the Shapely Shadow. 1986. mass mkt. 3.50 o.s.i (*0-345-33496-5*) Ballantine Bks.
—The Case of the Shoplifter's Shoe. (Perry Mason Bks.). 312p. reprint ed. lib. bdg. 24.95 (*0-88411-413-9*) Amereon, Ltd.
—The Case of the Shoplifter's Shoe. 1998. mass mkt. 4.99 (*0-345-91233-0*); 1986. 224p. mass mkt. 5.99 o.s.i (*0-345-32943-0*) Ballantine Bks.
—The Case of the Shoplifter's Shoe. 1973. pap. 0.95 o.p. (*0-671-77888-9*, Pocket) Simon & Schuster.
—The Case of the Silent Partner. (Perry Mason Bks.). reprint ed. lib. bdg. 23.95 (*0-88411-417-1*) Amereon, Ltd.
—The Case of the Silent Partner. 1999. 4.99 (*0-345-91482-1*); 1986. 224p. mass mkt. 4.99 o.s.i (*0-345-33684-4*) Ballantine Bks.
—The Case of the Silent Partner. 2003. (Paperback Ser.). pap. 25.95 (*0-7862-5047-X*) Thorndike Pr.
—The Case of the Singing Skirt. 1992. mass mkt. 3.99 o.s.i (*0-345-37149-6*) Ballantine Bks.
—The Case of the Singing Skirt. 1981. 256p. reprint ed. 18.00 (*0-8376-0399-4*) Bentley Pubs.
—The Case of the Singing Skirt. l.t. ed. 1988. (Nightingale Ser.). 183p. 12.95 o.p. (*0-8161-4515-6*, Macmillan Reference USA) Gale Group.
—The Case of the Sleepwalker's Niece. 1976. (Perry Mason Bks.). reprint ed. lib. bdg. 21.95 (*0-88411-408-2*) Amereon, Ltd.
—The Case of the Sleepwalker's Niece. 1991. (Perry Mason Mysteries Ser.). mass mkt. 3.99 o.s.i (*0-345-37146-1*, Ballantine Bks.) Ballantine Bks.
—The Case of the Sleepwalker's Niece. l.t. ed. 1993. (Nightingale Ser.). 344p. 14.95 o.p. (*0-8161-5633-6*, Macmillan Reference USA) Gale Group.
—The Case of the Sleepwalker's Niece. 1973. pap. 0.95 o.p. (*0-671-77893-5*, Pocket) Simon & Schuster.
—The Case of the Spurious Spinster. 1988. mass mkt. 3.50 o.s.i (*0-345-35203-3*) Ballantine Bks.
—The Case of the Stepdaughter's Secret. 1989. (Perry Mason Mysteries Ser.). 192p. mass mkt. 3.95 o.s.i (*0-345-36221-7*) Ballantine Bks.
—The Case of the Stepdaughter's Secret. l.t. ed. 1985. (Nightingale Ser.). 288p. 9.95 o.p. (*0-8161-3753-6*, Macmillan Reference USA) Gale Group.
—The Case of the Stepdaughter's Secret. 1977. pap. 1.95 o.p. (*0-671-80968-7*, Pocket) Simon & Schuster.
—The Case of the Stuttering Bishop. 1976. (Perry Mason Bks.). reprint ed. lib. bdg. 23.95 (*0-88411-409-0*) Amereon, Ltd.
—The Case of the Stuttering Bishop. l.t. ed. 1994. 21.95 o.p. (*0-7927-1907-7*); pap. 19.95 o.p. (*0-7927-1906-9*) BBC Audiobooks America.
—The Case of the Stuttering Bishop. 1998. mass mkt. 4.99 (*0-345-91230-6*); 1988. 192p. mass mkt. 6.99 (*0-345-35680-2*) Ballantine Bks.
—The Case of the Substitute Face. (Perry Mason Bks.). 310p. reprint ed. lib. bdg. 24.95 (*0-88411-412-0*) Amereon, Ltd.
—The Case of the Substitute Face. l.t. ed. 1993. 22.95 o.p. (*0-7927-1562-4*); pap. 20.95 o.p. (*0-7927-1561-6*) BBC Audiobooks America.
—The Case of the Substitute Face. (Perry Mason Mysteries Ser.). 1998. mass mkt. 4.99 (*0-345-91232-2*); 1987. pap. o.s.i (*0-345-01849-4*); 1987. 256p. mass mkt. 4.99 o.s.i (*0-345-34377-8*) Ballantine Bks.
—The Case of the Substitute Face. 1974. pap. 1.25 o.p. (*0-671-78448-X*, Pocket) Simon & Schuster.
—The Case of the Sulky Girl. 1976. (Perry Mason Books Ser.). reprint ed. lib. bdg. 24.95 (*0-88411-402-3*) Amereon, Ltd.
—The Case of the Sulky Girl. 1992. mass mkt. 4.99 o.s.i (*0-345-37145-3*) Ballantine Bks.
—The Case of the Sulky Girl, unabr. ed. 1991. (Listen for Pleasure Ser.). audio 16.99 (*0-88646-298-3*, LFP 7298) Durkin Hayes Publishing Ltd.
—The Case of the Sun Bather's Diary. 1995. 244p. pap. 15.00 (*0-345-47042-7*, Fawcett); 1985. 208p. mass mkt. 2.95 o.s.i (*0-345-33503-1*) Ballantine Bks.
—The Case of the Sun Bather's Diary. 1971. pap. 1.25 o.p. (*0-671-82704-9*, Pocket) Simon & Schuster.
—The Case of the Sun Bather's Diary. l.t. ed. 2001. (Paperback Ser.). 328p. 24.95 (*0-7838-9338-8*) Thorndike Pr.
—The Case of the Sun Bather's Diary: A Perry Mason Mystery. 2000. (Perry Mason Mysteries Ser.). 240p. mass mkt. 5.99 (*0-345-43788-8*, Fawcett) Ballantine Bks.
—The Case of the Terrified Typist. 1999. 4.99 (*0-345-91483-X*); 1987. 192p. mass mkt. 5.99 o.s.i (*0-345-34165-1*) Ballantine Bks.
—The Case of the Terrified Typist. l.t. ed. 1989. 296p. 14.95 o.p. (*0-8161-4514-8*, Macmillan Reference USA) Gale Group.
—The Case of the Terrified Typist. 1975. pap. 1.50 o.p. (*0-671-78780-2*, Simon Pulse) Simon & Schuster Children's Publishing.
—The Case of the Troubled Trustee. 1995. mass mkt. 4.99 o.s.i (*0-345-39224-8*) Ballantine Bks.
—The Case of the Vagabond Virgin. l.t. ed. 1990. pap. 17.95 o.p. (*0-7927-0534-3*, C0794); 19.95 o.p. (*0-7927-0533-5*, C0286) BBC Audiobooks America.
—The Case of the Vagabond Virgin. 1997. pap. 4.99 (*0-345-90803-1*); 1986. mass mkt. 3.50 o.s.i (*0-345-34319-0*); 1982. mass mkt. 4.99 o.s.i (*0-345-30393-8*) Ballantine Bks.
—The Case of the Vagabond Virgin. 1973. pap. 0.95 o.p. (*0-671-77885-4*, Simon Pulse) Simon & Schuster Children's Publishing.
—The Case of the Velvet Claws. 1976. (Perry Mason Books Ser.). reprint ed. lib. bdg. 24.95 (*0-88411-401-5*) Amereon, Ltd.
—The Case of the Velvet Claws. 1996. mass mkt. 4.99 (*0-345-90793-0*); 1985. 224p. mass mkt. 5.99 o.s.i (*0-345-32317-3*) Ballantine Bks.
—The Case of the Velvet Claws. 2002. (Best Mysteries of All Time Ser.). 261p. (*0-7621-8878-2*, IM Pr.) Reader's Digest Assn., Inc., The.
—The Case of the Waylaid Wolf. 1990. (Perry Mason Mysteries Ser.). 208p. mass mkt. 3.95 o.s.i (*0-345-36690-5*) Ballantine Bks.
—The Case of the Waylaid Wolf. 1976. pap. 1.95 o.p. (*0-671-80860-5*, Pocket) Simon & Schuster.
—The Case of the Worried Waitress. 1986. 160p. mass mkt. 2.95 o.s.i (*0-345-33193-1*) Ballantine Bks.
Gardner, Theodore R., 2nd. Flip Side: A Novel of Suspense. 1997. 269p. 22.00 (*1-888310-96-0*) Knoll, Allen A. Pubs.
Garnett, Edward H. Malcolm from a Distance. 2001. pap. 14.95 o.p. (*0-595-19842-2*) iUniverse, Inc.
Garrison, Zoe. Golden Triple Time. 1986. mass mkt. 2.95 o.p. (*0-451-15163-1*, Signet Bks.); 1986. mass mkt. 3.95 o.p. (*0-451-14150-4*, Signet Bks.); 1985. 448p. 15.95 o.p. (*0-453-00478-4*) NAL.
Gault, William C. Cat & Mouse. 1988. 176p. 12.95 o.p. (*0-312-01398-1*, Saint Martin's Minotaur) St. Martin's Pr.
—Death in Donegal Bay. 1984. 192p. 12.95 o.p. (*0-8027-5591-7*) Walker & Co.
Geller, Shari P. Fatal Convictions. 1996. 416p. 24.00 o.p. (*0-06-039181-2*) HarperCollins Pubs.
—Fatal Convictions. 1998. 544p. mass mkt. 6.50 o.s.i (*0-06-101223-8*, HarperTorch) Morrow/Avon.
Gerber, Merrill J. Anna in Chains. 1997. (Library of Modern Jewish Literature). 136p. 19.95 (*0-8156-0484-X*) Syracuse Univ. Pr.
Gerber, Merrill Joan. Anna in the Afterlife: A Novel. 2001. (Library of Modern Jewish Literature). 130p. pap. 22.95 (*0-8156-0699-0*) Syracuse Univ. Pr.
Gilb, Dagoberto. The Magic of Blood. 1994. 304p. pap. 12.00 (*0-8021-3399-1*, Grove Pr.) Grove/Atlantic, Inc.
—The Magic of Blood. 1993. 289p. reprint ed. 10.95 o.p. (*0-8263-1436-8*) Univ. of New Mexico Pr.
—The Magic of Blood. 1993. E-Book 10.95 (*0-585-18787-8*) netLibrary, Inc.
Gilbar, Steven, ed. L. A. Shorts. 2000. viii, 278p. pap. 14.95 (*1-890771-29-5*) Heyday Bks.
Gilmore, Monique. Soul Deep. 1997. 256p. mass mkt. 4.99 o.s.i (*0-7860-0395-2*, Pinnacle Bks.) Kensington Publishing Corp.
Gilmour, H. B. Billy Moon. 1993. 17.95 (*0-932279-44-9*) World Citizens.
Gold, Herbert. She Took My Arm As If She Loved Me. 1998. 256p. pap. 12.95 (*0-312-19525-7*, Saint Martin's Griffin) St. Martin's Pr.
Goldberg, Lee. My Gun Has Bullets. 1995. 262p. 21.00 o.p. (*0-312-11862-7*, Saint Martin's Minotaur) St. Martin's Pr.
Goldberg, Leonard S. Deadly Care. 1996. 336p. 23.95 o.s.i (*0-525-94092-8*, Dutton) Dutton/Plume.
—Deadly Care. 1997. 416p. mass mkt. 6.99 o.s.i (*0-451-18742-3*, Signet Bks.) NAL.
—Deadly Harvest. 1997. 320p. 23.95 o.s.i (*0-525-94093-6*) Dutton/Plume.
—Deadly Harvest. 1998. 416p. mass mkt. 6.99 o.s.i (*0-451-18743-1*, Signet Bks.) NAL.
—Deadly Medicine. 1992. 352p. (Orig.). mass mkt. 6.99 (*0-451-17439-9*, Signet Bks.) NAL.
—Deadly Practice. 1994. 320p. (Orig.). mass mkt. 6.99 (*0-451-17945-5*) NAL.
Goldberg, Tod B. Fake Liar Cheat. 2000. 176p. pap. 12.95 (*0-7434-0056-9*, MTV) Simon & Schuster.
Goldemberg, Rose Leiman. Adios, Hollywood: My Story by Dick, Dog of Oaxaca As Told to Rose Leiman Goldemberg. 2000. 180p. pap. 16.95 (*0-595-08907-0*) iUniverse, Inc.
Goldemberg, Rose Leiman, told to. Adios, Hollywood: My Story by Dick, Dog of Oaxaca As Told to Rose Leiman Goldemberg. 1994. 176p. 18.95 o.p. (*0-312-10455-3*) St. Martin's Pr.
Goldhirsh, Martha. Butterflies. 1999. 368p. mass mkt. 6.99 o.s.i (*0-515-12563-6*, Jove) Berkley Publishing Group.
Goldman, William. Tinsel. 1980. mass mkt. 2.75 o.s.i (*0-440-18735-4*); 1979. pap. 10.95 o.s.i (*0-385-29031-4*, Delacorte Pr.) Dell Publishing.
Goldsmith, Olivia. Flavor of the Month. 1993. 704p. 23.00 o.p. (*0-671-79449-3*, Simon & Schuster) Simon & Schuster.
Gomez, Jeff. Geniuses of Crack. 1997. 432p. pap. 12.00 o.s.i (*0-684-83194-5*, Touchstone) Simon & Schuster.
Goodbye, Saigon. audio Thorsons.
Gouge, Louise M. The Homecoming. 1997. 192p. pap. 8.99 (*0-89107-982-3*) Crossway Bks.
—The Homecoming. l.t. ed. 1998. (Candlelight Romance Ser.). 275p. 20.95 (*0-7862-1656-5*) Thorndike Pr.
Graham, Heather. Dying to Have Her. l.t. ed. 2001. (Wheeler Large Print Book Ser.). 428p. 29.95 (*1-58724-085-8*, Wheeler Publishing, Inc.) Gale Group.
—Long, Lean & Lethal. l.t. ed. 2000. (Large Print Book Ser.). 410p. 28.95 (*1-56895-928-1*, Wheeler Publishing, Inc.) Gale Group.
—Long, Lean & Lethal. 2000. 400p. mass mkt. 6.99 o.s.i (*0-451-40915-9*, Onyx) NAL.
Green, Kate. Black Dreams: A Theresa Fortunato Mystery. 1993. 288p. 20.00 o.p. (*0-06-017984-8*) HarperTrade.
—Black Dreams: A Theresa Fortunato Mystery. 1994. 464p. mass mkt. 5.99 o.p. (*0-06-109103-0*, Harper-Torch) Morrow/Avon.
Greenberg, Martin H. & Waugh, Charles, eds. Hollywood Unreel: Fantasies About Hollywood & the Movies. 1982. 304p. 14.95 o.s.i (*0-8008-3197-7*) Taplinger Publishing Co., Inc.
Grenville, Hilary. Past Imperfect. l.t. ed. 2001. (Nightingale Ser.). 332p. pap. 23.95 (*0-7838-9325-6*) Thorndike Pr.
Grobeson, Mitchell. Outside the Badge. 2000. pap. 14.95 o.p. (*0-533-11559-0*) Vantage Pr., Inc.
Groom, Winston. Such a Pretty, Pretty Girl. l.t. ed. 1999. 30.00 o.p. (*0-7838-8485-0*, Macmillan Reference USA) Gale Group.
—Such a Pretty, Pretty Girl. abr. ed. 1999. audio 24.00 o.s.i (*0-375-40588-7*, 494172, RH Audio) Random Hse. Audio Publishing Group.
Gross, Shelly. Stardust. 1985. 448p. 18.95 o.p. (*0-312-75588-0*) St. Martin's Pr.
Gummerman, Jay. Chez Chance. 1996. pap. o.p. (*0-679-75845-3*) Knopf, Alfred A. Inc.
—Chez Chance: A Novel. 1997. (California Fiction Ser.). 211p. pap. 15.95 (*0-520-21080-8*) Univ. of California Pr.
Hagberg, David. Critical Mass. unabr. ed. 1992. audio 23.95 o.p. (*1-56100-466-9*, 73, Bookcassette); audio 73.25 o.p. (*1-56100-100-7*, 1158, Unabridged Library Editions) Brilliance Audio.
—Critical Mass. 1999. 472p. mass mkt. 6.99 (*0-8125-2497-7*); 1992. 384p. 4.99 o.p. (*0-312-85255-X*) Doherty, Tom Assocs., LLC. (Tor Bks.).
Hall, Jennifer. Star Quality: A Novel. 1993. 21.00 o.p. (*1-55611-346-3*) Fine, Donald I. Bks.
Hallinan, Timothy. Bone Polisher. 1995. 305p. 22.00 o.p. (*0-688-10345-6*, Morrow, William & Co.) Morrow/Avon.
—Everything but the Squeal: A Simeon Grist Suspense Novel. 1990. (Simeon Grist Mystery Ser.). 352p. 17.95 o.p. (*0-453-00694-9*) NAL.
—The Four Last Things. 1989. (Simeon Grist Mystery Ser.). 336p. 16.95 o.p. (*0-453-00650-7*) NAL.
—Incinerator. 1993. 304p. mass mkt. 4.99 (*0-380-71370-5*, Avon Bks.) Morrow/Avon.
—Incinerator: A Simeon Grist Mystery. 1992. 288p. 19.00 o.p. (*0-688-10343-X*, Morrow, William & Co.) Morrow/Avon.
—The Man with No Time: A Simeon Grist Mystery. 1993. 22.00 o.p. (*0-688-10344-8*, Morrow, William & Co.) Morrow/Avon.
—Skin Deep: A Simeon Grist Suspense Novel. 1991. (Simeon Grist Mystery Ser.). 336p. 18.95 o.p. (*0-525-24978-8*, Dutton) Dutton/Plume.
Hamilton, Denise. The Jasmine Trade: A Novel of Suspense Introducing Eve Diamond. 2001. 288p. 24.00 (*0-7432-1269-X*); E-Book 9.99 (*0-7432-1477-3*) Simon & Schuster. (Scribner).

—Sugar Skull: An Eve Diamond Novel. 2004. (Illus.). 400p. mass mkt. 6.99 (*0-7434-8221-2*, Pocket Star); 2003. 304p. 25.00 (*0-7432-4539-3*, Scribner); 2003. 304p. 25.00 (*0-7432-4784-1*, Scribner) Simon & Schuster.

Hamilton, Laurell K. A Caress of Twilight. 2003. 368p. mass mkt. 7.50 (*0-345-42342-9*, Fawcett); 2002. 336p. 23.95 o.s.i (*0-345-43527-3*) Ballantine Bks.

—A Caress of Twilight. abr. ed. (Meredith Gentry Ser.: Vol. 2). 2003. audio 12.99 (*1-59086-037-3*, 3580, Brilliance Audio Paperback Audiobooks); 2002. audio 24.95 o.p. (*1-59086-036-5*, 3579, Nova Audio Bks.); 2002. audio 87.25 (*1-59086-035-7*, 3578, Unabridged Library Editions); 2002. audio 32.95 (*1-59086-034-9*, 3577, Brilliance Audio Unabridged) Brilliance Audio.

—A Caress of Twilight. unabr. ed. 2003. (Meredith Gentry Ser.). audio 19.99 (*1-59335-055-4*, 30140) Soulmate Audio Bks., Inc.

—Seduced by Moonlight. 2004. 336p. 23.95 (*0-345-44356-X*) Ballantine Bks.

Hammett, Dashiell. The Maltese Falcon. Date not set. 148p. 18.95 (*0-8488-2436-9*) Amereon, Ltd.

—The Maltese Falcon. 1987. (Illus.). 352p. reprint ed. pap. 9.95 o.p. (*0-86547-157-6*, North Point Pr.) Farrar, Straus & Giroux.

—The Maltese Falcon. 1989. (Vintage Crime Ser.). 16.05 (*0-606-12411-X*) Turtleback Bks.

Handler, David. The Boy Who Never Grew Up. 1993. 384p. mass mkt. 4.99 o.s.i (*0-553-29739-2*) Bantam Bks.

—The Boy Who Never Grew Up. unabr. ed. 1998. (Stewart Hoag Mystery Ser.: Vol. 5). audio 85.00 (*0-7887-2283-2*, 95534E7) Recorded Bks., LLC.

Hannah, Kristin. Summer Island. 2002. 416p. mass mkt. 6.99 (*0-345-44113-3*) Ballantine Bks.

—Summer Island. unabr. ed. 2001. audio 69.25 (*1-58788-301-5*, 2539, Unabridged Library Editions) Brilliance Audio.

—Summer Island. l.t. ed. 2001. 368p. lib. bdg. 29.95 (*1-58547-107-0*); 367p. 17.97 (*1-74030-498-5*) Ctr. Point Large Print.

—Summer Island: A Novel. 2001. 336p. 21.00 o.s.i (*0-609-60737-5*, Crown) Crown Publishing Group.

Hansen, Joseph. The Boy Who Was Buried This Morning. 1991. 192p. reprint ed. pap. 5.95 o.p. (*0-452-26617-3*, Plume) Dutton/Plume.

—The Boy Who Was Buried This Morning. 1990. 176p. 16.95 o.p. (*0-670-83324-X*) Viking Penguin.

—Country of Old Men: The Last Dave Brandstetter Mystery. 1992. 192p. pap. 7.00 o.p. (*0-452-26805-2*, Plume) Dutton/Plume.

—Country of Old Men: The Last Dave Brandstetter Mystery. 1991. 192p. 17.95 o.p. (*0-670-83826-8*) Viking Penguin.

—Fadeout. 2000. (Dave Brandstetter Mysteries Ser.). 256p. reprint ed. pap. 11.95 o.p. (*1-55583-552-X*, Alyson Bks.) Alyson Pubns.

—Fadeout. unabr. ed. 1995. (Dave Brandstetter Mystery Ser.: No. 1). audio 24.95 (*1-888348-01-1*, HCB201) Hall Closet Bk. Co.

—Fadeout. 1980. 88p. pap. 5.95 o.p. (*0-8050-1054-8*);Vol. 1. pap. 3.95 o.p. (*0-03-057486-2*) Holt, Henry & Co. (Owl Bks.).

—Living Upstairs. 1993. 224p. (J). (gr. 5 up). 20.00 o.p. (*0-525-93682-3*, Dutton) Dutton/Plume.

Harper, Brian. Shatter. 1995. 384p. mass mkt. 4.99 o.s.i (*0-451-17338-4*, Signet Bks.) NAL.

—Shudder. 1994. 416p. mass mkt. 4.99 o.s.i (*0-451-17693-6*, Signet Bks.) NAL.

Harrington, William. Columbo: The Game Show Killer. 1996. 224p. 21.95 o.p. (*0-312-86178-8*, Forge Bks.) Doherty, Tom Assocs., LLC.

—Columbo: The Game Show Killer. l.t. ed. 1999. (Nightingale Ser.). 256p. pap. 20.95 (*0-7838-8595-4*) Thorndike Pr.

—Columbo: The Grassy Knoll. l.t. ed. 1994. 22.95 o.p. (*0-7927-2032-6*); pap. 21.95 o.p. (*0-7927-2031-8*) BBC Audiobooks America.

—Columbo: The Grassy Knoll. 1994. 320p. mass mkt. 4.99 (*0-8125-3024-1*, Tor Bks.); 1993. 288p. 18.95 o.p. (*0-312-85536-2*, Forge Bks.) Doherty, Tom Assocs., LLC.

—Columbo: The Helter Skelter Murders. (Columbo Ser.). 1995. 303p. mass mkt. 5.99 (*0-8125-3026-8*); 1994. 288p. 19.95 o.p. (*0-312-85537-0*) Doherty, Tom Assocs., LLC. (Forge Bks.).

—Columbo: The Hoffa Connection. 1995. 288p. 21.95 o.p. (*0-312-85816-7*, Forge Bks.) Doherty, Tom Assocs., LLC.

—Columbo: The Hoover Files. (Columbo Ser.). 224p. 1999. mass mkt. 5.99 (*0-8125-6274-7*); 1997. 21.95 o.p. (*0-312-86027-7*) Doherty, Tom Assocs., LLC. (Forge Bks.).

—Columbo: The Hoover Files. l.t. ed. 2000. (G. K. Hall Nightingale Ser.). 272p. pap. 21.95 (*0-7838-8925-9*, Macmillan Reference USA) Gale Group.

—The Game Show Killer. 1997. (Columbo Ser.: Vol. 4). 211p. pap. 5.99 (*0-8125-5080-3*, Forge Bks.) Doherty, Tom Assocs., LLC.

—Hoffa Connection. 1996. (Columbo Ser.). 245p. mass mkt. 5.99 (*0-8125-5078-1*, Forge Bks.) Doherty, Tom Assocs., LLC.

Hart, William. Never Fade Away: A Novel. 2002. 202p. pap. 12.95 (*1-56474-386-1*) Fithian Pr.

Hartman, Melissa. The Sure Thing. 1994. 208p. pap. 9.95 o.p. (*1-56280-078-7*) Naiad Pr., Inc.

Hayes, Helen & Chastain, Thomas. Where the Truth Lies. 1988. 288p. 16.95 o.p. (*0-688-06933-9*, Morrow, William & Co.) Morrow/Avon.

Haywood, Gar Anthony. All the Lucky Ones Are Dead: An Aaron Gunner Mystery. 2000. 240p. 23.95 o.s.i (*0-399-14540-0*, G. P. Putnam's Sons) Penguin Group (USA) Inc.

—Fear of the Dark. 1988. 192p. 13.95 o.p. (*0-312-01796-0*, Saint Martin's Minotaur) St. Martin's Pr.

—Fear of the Dark. 1990. 192p. pap. 3.95 o.p. (*0-14-013153-1*, Penguin Bks.) Viking Penguin.

—It's Not a Pretty Sight: An Aaron Gunner Mystery. 1998. 256p. mass mkt. 5.99 o.s.i (*0-425-16196-X*, Prime Crime) Berkley Publishing Group.

—It's Not a Pretty Sight: An Aaron Gunner Mystery. 1996. 240p. 22.95 o.p. (*0-399-14132-4*, G. P. Putnam's Sons) Penguin Group (USA) Inc.

—Not Long for This World. 1991. (Crime Monthly Ser.). 272p. pap. 4.95 o.p. (*0-14-015265-2*, Penguin Bks.) Penguin Group (USA) Inc.

—Not Long for This World. 1990. 17.95 o.p. (*0-312-04398-8*, Saint Martin's Minotaur) St. Martin's Pr.

—When Last Seen Alive. 1999. 256p. mass mkt. 5.99 o.s.i (*0-425-17027-6*) Berkley Publishing Group.

—When Last Seen Alive. 1997. 240p. 22.95 o.p. (*0-399-14303-3*, G. P. Putnam's Sons) Penguin Group (USA) Inc.

—You Can Die Trying. 1993. 224p. 17.95 o.p. (*0-312-09425-6*, Saint Martin's Minotaur) St. Martin's Pr.

—You Can Die Trying: An Aaron Gunner Mystery. 1994. (Crime Ser.). 224p. reprint ed. pap. 5.95 o.p. (*0-14-023946-4*, Penguin Bks.) Penguin Group (USA) Inc.

Heller, Zoe. Everything You Know. 2000. 224p. 22.00 o.s.i (*0-375-40724-3*) Knopf, Alfred A. Inc.

—Everything You Know. 2001. (Illus.). 224p. reprint ed. pap. 12.95 (*0-7434-1195-1*, Washington Square Pr.) Simon & Schuster.

Hensley, Dennis. Misadventures in the (213). abr. ed. 1999. audio 18.00 (*1-57511-063-6*) Publishing Mills, Inc., The.

Hillerman, Tony. The Ghostway. unabr. ed. 1994. audio 42.00 (*0-7366-2748-0*, 3473) Books on Tape, Inc.

—The Ghostway. 1985. 224p. 13.95 o.p. (*0-06-015396-2*); 1992. 3p. audio 18.00 (*1-55994-606-7*, CPN 2301, HarperAudio) HarperTrade.

—The Ghostway. 1993. audio. audio 47.20 (*1-56544-040-4*, 250033) Literate Ear, Inc.

—The Ghostway. 1992. 320p. mass mkt. 6.99 (*0-06-100345-X*, HarperTorch); 1986. 208p. mass mkt. 4.95 (*0-380-70024-7*, Avon Bks.) Morrow/Avon.

—The Ghostway. unabr. ed. 1990. (Jim Chee Mystery Ser.: Vol. 3). audio 44.00 (*1-55690-194-1*, 90098E7) Recorded Bks., LLC.

—The Ghostway. 1984. (J). 12.55 (*0-606-01124-2*) Turtleback Bks.

Himes, Chester B. The Lonely Crusade. 1986. (Classic Reprint Ser.). 408p. (C). reprint ed. pap. 14.95 o.p. (*0-938410-37-7*, Thunder's Mouth Pr.) Avalon Publishing Group.

—Lonely Crusade. 1973. reprint ed. 9.50 o.p. (*0-911860-35-5*) Chatham Bookseller.

—The Lonely Crusade: A Novel. 2nd ed. 1997. 398p. reprint ed. pap. 14.95 (*1-56025-142-5*, Thunder's Mouth Pr.) Avalon Publishing Group.

Hoffman, Lauran. Bar Girls. 1995. pap. text 10.95 o.p. (*1-56280-115-5*) Naiad Pr., Inc.

Holmes, Rupert. Where the Truth Lies. 2003. 400p. 24.95 (*0-679-45220-6*); E-Book 17.50 (*1-58836-328-7*) Random Hse., Inc.

Hornsby, Wendy. Bad Intent: A Maggie MacGowen Mystery. 1994. (Maggie MacGowen Mystery Ser.). 304p. 18.95 o.p. (*0-525-93817-6*, Dutton) Dutton/Plume.

—Bad Intent: A Maggie MacGowen Mystery. 1995. (Maggie MacGowen Mystery Ser.). 384p. mass mkt. 5.50 o.s.i (*0-451-18501-3*, Onyx) NAL.

—A Hard Light: A Maggie MacGowen Mystery. 1997. (Maggie MacGowen Mystery Ser.). 272p. 22.95 o.p. (*0-525-94067-7*) Dutton/Plume.

—A Hard Light: A Maggie MacGowen Mystery. 1998. (Maggie Macgowen Mystery Ser.). 272p. mass mkt. 5.99 o.s.i (*0-451-18690-7*, Signet Bks.) NAL.

—Midnight Baby: A Maggie MacGowen Mystery. 1993. (Maggie MacGowen Mystery Ser.). 272p. 19.00 o.p. (*0-525-93615-7*, Dutton) Dutton/Plume.

—Midnight Baby: A Maggie MacGowen Mystery. 1994. (Maggie MacGowen Mystery Ser.). 304p. mass mkt. 5.99 o.s.i (*0-451-18136-0*, Signet Bks.) NAL.

—Telling Lies: A Maggie MacGowen Mystery. 1992. 256p. 18.00 o.p. (*0-525-93472-3*, Dutton) Dutton/Plume.

—Telling Lies: A Maggie MacGowen Mystery. 1993. (Maggie MacGowen Mystery Ser.). 288p. mass mkt. 5.99 o.s.i (*0-451-40380-0*, Onyx) NAL.

—77th Street Requiem: A Maggie MacGowan Mystery. 1996. (Maggie MacGowen Mystery Ser.). 384p. mass mkt. 5.99 o.s.i (*0-451-40675-3*, Signet Bks.) NAL.

—77th Street Requiem: A Maggie MacGowen Mystery. 1995. (Maggie MacGowen Mystery Ser.). 288p. 21.95 o.p. (*0-525-93998-9*, Dutton) Dutton/Plume.

—77th Street Requiem: A Maggie MacGowen Mystery. l.t. ed. 1996. (Large Print Bks.). pap. 21.95 (*1-56895-334-8*, Wheeler Publishing, Inc.) Gale Group.

Howe, Melodie J. Beauty Dies. 1996. (Crime Ser.). 272p. pap. 5.95 o.s.i (*0-14-023565-5*) Penguin Group (USA) Inc.

—Beauty Dies: A Claire Conrad - Maggie Hill Mystery. 1994. 272p. 19.95 o.p. (*0-670-85449-2*, Viking) Viking Penguin.

—The Mother Shadow. (Crime Ser.). 272p. 1990. pap. 5.95 o.p. (*0-14-011778-4*, Penguin Bks.); 1989. 16.95 o.p. (*0-670-82602-2*) Viking Penguin.

Huggins, David. Me Me Me. 2001. 256p. pap. (*0-571-20936-X*) Faber & Faber, Inc.

Hughes, Dorothy B. In a Lonely Place. 1984. 240p. pap. 3.50 o.p. (*0-88184-079-3*, Carroll & Graf Pubs.) Avalon Publishing Group.

—In a Lonely Place. 2003. (Femmes Fatales Ser.). 256p. pap. 14.95 (*1-55861-455-9*); lib. bdg. 39.00 (*1-55861-461-3*) Feminist Pr. at The City Univ. of New York.

Huxley, Aldous. After Many a Summer Dies the Swan. 1977. reprint ed. lib. bdg. 25.95 (*0-89190-395-X*, Queens Hse., Inc.) Amereon, Ltd.

—After Many a Summer Dies the Swan. 1993. 95p. reprint ed. pap. 14.95 (*1-56663-018-5*, Elephant Paperbacks) Dee, Ivan R. Pub.

—After Many a Summer Dies the Swan. 1965. pap. 2.25 o.p. (*0-06-083046-8*, P3046) HarperCollins Pubs.

—After Many a Summer Dies the Swan. 1983. 256p. mass mkt. 5.95 o.p. (*0-06-091063-1*, CN1063, Perennial) HarperTrade.

Hynd, Noel. Cemetery of Angels. 2002. 416p. mass mkt. 6.99 o.s.i (*0-7860-1487-3*); 1996. 416p. mass mkt. 5.99 o.s.i (*0-7860-0261-1*, Pinnacle Bks.); 1995. 368p. mass mkt. 19.95 o.p. (*0-8217-5029-1*, Zebra Bks.) Kensington Publishing Corp.

Isenberg, Lynn. My Life Uncovered. 2003. 336p. pap. (*0-373-25043-6*, Red Dress Ink) Harlequin Enterprises, Ltd.

Jackson, Brenda. One Special Moment. 2001. (Arabesque Ser.). 304p. mass mkt. 5.99 (*1-58314-227-4*) BET Bks.

Jackson, Sheneska. Blessings. 2003. mass mkt. 6.99 (*0-7434-8246-8*); 1999. 400p. pap. 13.00 (*0-684-85312-4*); 1998. 400p. 23.00 (*0-684-85035-4*) Simon & Schuster. (Simon & Schuster).

—Caught up in the Rapture. 1996. 272p. 20.50 (*0-684-81487-0*, Simon & Schuster) Simon & Schuster.

—Caught up in the Rapture: A Novel. 1997. 272p. pap. 13.00 (*0-684-83153-8*, Simon & Schuster) Simon & Schuster.

Jacobsen, Clay. The Lasko Interview. 1998. 412p. pap. 12.99 (*0-8054-1660-9*) Broadman & Holman Pubs.

Johs, Maria. The Mysterious Visitor. 2001. 116p. 22.95 (*0-7596-4012-2*); pap. 14.95 (*0-7596-4011-4*) 1stBooks Library.

Jong, Erica. How to Save Your Own Life. 1995. 320p. pap. 11.95 o.p. (*0-452-27454-0*, Plume) Dutton/Plume.

—How to Save Your Own Life. 1977. 8.95 o.p. (*0-03-017726-X*) Holt, Henry & Co.

Kadohata, Cynthia. In the Heart of the Valley of Love. 1993. 240p. pap. 10.00 o.p. (*0-14-013449-2*, Penguin Bks.) Penguin Group (USA) Inc.

—In the Heart of the Valley of Love. 1997. (California Fiction Ser.). 224p. pap. text 15.95 (*0-520-20728-9*) Univ. of California Pr.

—In the Heart of the Valley of Love. 1992. 240p. 20.00 o.p. (*0-670-83415-7*, Viking) Viking Penguin.

Kagan, Elaine. Losing Mr. North: A Novel. 2002. 272p. 24.95 (*0-06-018474-4*, Morrow, William & Co.) Morrow/Avon.

Kahn, James. The Echo Vector. 1988. 240p. 15.95 o.p. (*0-312-01023-0*); Vol. 1. 1989. pap. 3.95 o.p. (*0-312-91049-5*, St. Martin's Paperbacks) St. Martin's Pr.

Kaiser, R. J. Glamourpuss. 2000. 448p. mass mkt. (*1-55166-614-6*, 1-66614-8, Mira Bks.) Harlequin Enterprises, Ltd.

Kaminsky, Stuart M. A Few Minutes Past Midnight. l.t. ed. 2002. 347p. 29.95 (*0-7862-4118-7*) Gale Group.

Kanin, Garson. Moviola. 1979. 12.95 o.s.i (*0-671-24822-7*, Simon & Schuster) Simon & Schuster.

Karbo, Karen. The Diamond Lane. 1991. 320p. 21.95 o.p. (*0-399-13597-9*, G. P. Putnam's Sons) Penguin Group (USA) Inc.

Kaye, John. The Dead Circus: A Novel. 2003. 336p. pap. 14.00 (*0-8021-4017-3*); 2002. 320p. 24.00 (*0-87113-849-2*, Atlantic Monthly Pr.) Grove/Atlantic, Inc.

—Stars Screaming. 336p. 1997. 25.00 o.p. (*0-87113-691-0*, Atlantic Monthly Pr.); 1999. reprint ed. pap. 13.00 (*0-87113-742-9*) Grove/Atlantic, Inc.

Kellerman, Faye. Day of Atonement: A Peter Decker & Rina Lazarus Novel. 1998. 368p. mass mkt. 6.99 o.s.i (*0-449-00323-X*); 1992. mass mkt. 6.99 o.s.i (*0-449-14824-6*) Ballantine Bks. (Fawcett).

—Day of Atonement: A Peter Decker & Rina Lazarus Novel. l.t. ed. 1992. (Large Print Bks.). 401p. lib. bdg. 21.95 (*0-8161-5351-5*, Macmillan Reference USA) Gale Group.

—Day of Atonement: A Peter Decker & Rina Lazarus Novel. 2004. 400p. mass mkt. 7.99 (*0-06-055489-4*, HarperTorch); 1991. 359p. 20.00 o.p. (*0-688-08604-7*, Morrow, William & Co.) Morrow/Avon.

—False Prophet: A Peter Decker & Rina Lazarus Novel. 1998. 416p. mass mkt. 7.99 (*0-449-00329-9*); 1994. mass mkt. 5.99 o.p. (*0-449-45337-5*); 1993. mass mkt. 5.99 o.s.i (*0-449-14840-8*); 1993. mass mkt. 5.99 o.s.i (*0-449-14898-X*) Ballantine Bks. (Fawcett).

—False Prophet: A Peter Decker & Rina Lazarus Novel. l.t. ed. 1994. (Large Print Bks.). 554p. lib. bdg. 23.95 (*0-8161-7458-X*, Macmillan Reference USA) Gale Group.

—False Prophet: A Peter Decker & Rina Lazarus Novel. 1992. 367p. 20.00 o.p. (*0-688-10553-X*, Morrow, William & Co.) Morrow/Avon.

—Grievous Sin: A Peter Decker & Rina Lazarus Novel. 1998. 400p. mass mkt. 7.99 (*0-449-00330-2*); 1994. mass mkt. 6.99 o.s.i (*0-449-14839-4*) Ballantine Bks. (Fawcett).

—Grievous Sin: A Peter Decker & Rina Lazarus Novel. unabr. ed. 1996. audio 72.00 (*0-7366-3321-9*, 3973) Books on Tape, Inc.

—Grievous Sin: A Peter Decker & Rina Lazarus Novel. unabr. ed. 1993. audio 23.95 o.p. (*1-56100-518-5*, 129, Bookcassette); audio 73.25 (*1-56100-150-3*, 885, Unabridged Library Editions) Brilliance Audio.

—Grievous Sin: A Peter Decker & Rina Lazarus Novel. l.t. ed. 1994. (Large Print Bks.). 552p. lib. bdg. 24.95 (*0-8161-7460-1*, Macmillan Reference USA) Gale Group.

—Grievous Sin: A Peter Decker & Rina Lazarus Novel. 1993. 368p. 20.00 o.p. (*0-688-10554-8*, Morrow, William & Co.) Morrow/Avon.

—Jupiter's Bones: A Peter Decker & Rina Lazarus Novel. l.t. ed. 552p. 2000. pap. 28.95 (*0-7838-8783-3*); 1999. 31.95 (*0-7838-8782-5*) Gale Group. (Macmillan Reference USA).

—Jupiter's Bones: A Peter Decker & Rina Lazarus Novel. Feron, C. F., ed. 2000. 448p. mass mkt. 7.50 (*0-380-73082-0*, Avon Bks.) Morrow/Avon.

—Jupiter's Bones: A Peter Decker & Rina Lazarus Novel. 1999. 375p. 25.00 o.p. (*0-688-15612-6*, Morrow, William & Co.) Morrow/Avon.

—Jupiter's Bones: A Peter Decker & Rina Lazarus Novel. abr. ed. 1999. audio 25.00 (*0-671-57759-X*, Simon & Schuster Audioworks) Simon & Schuster Audio.

—Justice: A Peter Decker & Rina Lazarus Novel. unabr. ed. 1996. audio 80.00 (*0-7366-3275-1*, 3931) Books on Tape, Inc.

—Justice: A Peter Decker & Rina Lazarus Novel. abr. ed. 1996. audio 7.99 o.p. (*1-56740-129-5*, 665, Paperback Nova Audio Bks.); 1995. audio 16.95 o.p. (*1-56100-850-8*, 1258, Nova Audio Bks.); 1995. audio 89.25 o.p. (*1-56100-283-6*, 914, Unabridged Library Editions); 1995. audio 25.95 o.p. (*1-56100-658-0*, 150, Bookcassette) Brilliance Audio.

—Justice: A Peter Decker & Rina Lazarus Novel. l.t. ed. 1995. 563p. 26.95 (*0-7838-1494-1*, Macmillan Reference USA) Gale Group.

—Justice: A Peter Decker & Rina Lazarus Novel. abr. ed. 2000. audio 7.95 (*1-57815-172-4*, 1115, Media Bks. Audio Publishing) Media Bks., L. L. C.

—Justice: A Peter Decker & Rina Lazarus Novel. 1996. 465p. mass mkt. 7.99 (*0-380-72498-7*); 1995. 388p. 23.00 o.p. (*0-688-04613-4*, Morrow, William & Co.) Morrow/Avon.

—Milk & Honey: A Peter Decker & Rina Lazarus Novel. 384p. 1998. mass mkt. 6.99 o.s.i (*0-449-00313-2*); 1991. mass mkt. 5.99 o.s.i (*0-449-14728-2*) Ballantine Bks. (Fawcett).

—Milk & Honey: A Peter Decker & Rina Lazarus Novel. 1990. 384p. 18.95 o.p. (*0-688-08603-9*, Morrow, William & Co.) Morrow/Avon.

—Prayers for the Dead: A Peter Decker & Rina Lazarus Novel. unabr. ed. 1997. audio 80.00 Books on Tape, Inc.

—Prayers for the Dead: A Peter Decker & Rina Lazarus Novel. abr. ed. 1997. audio 7.99 o.p. (*1-56740-181-3*, 689, Nova Audio Bks.); 1996. audio 16.95 o.p. (*1-56100-919-9*, 1349, Nova Audio Bks.); 1996. audio 25.95 o.p. (*1-56100-709-9*, 218, Bookcassette); 1996. audio 89.25 o.p. (*1-56100-334-4*, 991, Unabridged Library Editions) Brilliance Audio.

Settings

—Prayers for the Dead: A Peter Decker & Rina Lazarus Novel. l.t. ed. 1996. (Large Print Bks.). 586p. 26.95 (0-7838-1910-2, Macmillan Reference USA) Gale Group.

—Prayers for the Dead: A Peter Decker & Rina Lazarus Novel. 1997. 424p. mass mkt. 7.99 (0-380-72624-6); 1996. 406p. 24.00 o.p. (0-688-14367-9, Morrow, William & Co.) Morrow/Avon.

—The Ritual Bath: A Peter Decker & Rina Lazarus Novel. 1998. mass mkt. 6.99 (0-449-45814-8); 1987. 288p. mass mkt. 6.99 o.s.i (0-449-21373-0) Ballantine Bks. (Fawcett).

—The Ritual Bath: A Peter Decker & Rina Lazarus Novel. l.t. ed. 2000. (G. K. Hall Core Ser.). 368p. 30.95 (0-7838-9046-X, Macmillan Reference USA) Gale Group.

—The Ritual Bath: A Peter Decker & Rina Lazarus Novel. 2004. 352p. pap. 12.95 (0-06-056375-3, Perennial) HarperTrade.

—The Ritual Bath: A Peter Decker & Rina Lazarus Novel. 1999. 384p. mass mkt. 6.99 (0-380-73266-1) Morrow/Avon.

—Sacred & Profane: A Peter Decker & Rina Lazarus Novel. 1998. mass mkt. 6.99 (0-449-45815-6); 1988. mass mkt. 6.99 o.s.i (0-449-21502-4, Fawcett) Ballantine Bks.

—Sacred & Profane: A Peter Decker & Rina Lazarus Novel. l.t. ed. 2001. (Magna Large Print Ser.). 400p. (0-7505-1667-4) Magna Large Print Bks. GBR. *Dist:* Ulverscroft Large Print Canada, Ltd.

—Sacred & Profane: A Peter Decker & Rina Lazarus Novel. 1999. 384p. mass mkt. 6.99 (0-380-73267-X, Avon Bks.); 1987. 311p. 16.95 o.p. (0-87795-887-4, Morrow, William & Co.) Morrow/Avon.

—Sacred & Profane: A Peter Decker & Rina Lazarus Novel. 1990. 3.99 o.p. (0-517-05799-9) Random Hse. Value Publishing.

—Sanctuary: A Peter Decker & Rina Lazarus Novel. unabr. ed. 1996. audio 72.00 (0-7366-3355-3, 4006) Books on Tape, Inc.

—Sanctuary: A Peter Decker & Rina Lazarus Novel. abr. ed. 1994. audio 16.95 o.p. (1-56100-386-7, 1359, Nova Audio Bks.); audio 89.25 o.p. (1-56100-221-6, 1023, Unabridged Library Editions); audio 25.95 o.p. (1-56100-596-7, 246, Bookcassette) Brilliance Audio.

—Sanctuary: A Peter Decker & Rina Lazarus Novel. l.t. ed. 1995. 509p. pap. 23.95 o.p. (1-56895-090-X, Wheeler Publishing, Inc.) Gale Group.

—Sanctuary: A Peter Decker & Rina Lazarus Novel. abr. ed. 2000. audio 7.95 (1-57815-022-1, 1006, Media Bks. Audio Publishing) Media Bks., L. L. C.

—Sanctuary: A Peter Decker & Rina Lazarus Novel. 1994. 396p. 22.00 o.p. (0-688-04612-6, Morrow, William & Co.); 1995. 428p. reprint ed. pap. 6.99 (0-380-72497-9, Avon Bks.) Morrow/Avon.

—Serpent's Tooth: A Peter Decker & Rina Lazarus Novel. unabr. ed. 1997. audio 72.00 (0-7366-4049-5, 4548) Books on Tape, Inc.

—Serpent's Tooth: A Peter Decker & Rina Lazarus Novel. l.t. ed. 539p. 2001. pap. 30.00 (0-7838-8323-4); 1997. lib. bdg. 28.95 o.p. (0-7838-8322-6) Gale Group. (Macmillan Reference USA).

—Serpent's Tooth: A Peter Decker & Rina Lazarus Novel. 1998. 432p. mass mkt. 6.99 (0-380-72625-4, Avon Bks.); 1997. 416p. 24.50 (0-688-14368-7, Morrow, William & Co.); 1997. 416p. 294.00 (0-688-15649-5, Morrow, William & Co.) Morrow/Avon.

—Serpent's Tooth: A Peter Decker & Rina Lazarus Novel. abr. ed. 1997. audio 24.00 (0-671-57757-3, 495448, Simon & Schuster Audioworks) Simon & Schuster Audio.

—Stalker: A Peter Decker & Rina Lazarus Novel. unabr. ed. 2001. audio compact disk 115.95 (0-7927-9987-9, SLD 038, Chivers Sound Library) BBC Audiobooks America.

—Stalker: A Peter Decker & Rina Lazarus Novel. l.t. ed. 2000. 624p. pap. 25.00 (0-06-019729-3, HarperLargePrint) HarperTrade.

—Stalker: A Peter Decker & Rina Lazarus Novel. 2001. 448p. mass mkt. 7.99 (0-380-81769-1, Avon Bks.); 2000. 416p. 25.00 (0-688-15613-4, Morrow, William & Co.) Morrow/Avon.

—Stalker: A Peter Decker & Rina Lazarus Novel. abr. ed. 2000. audio 25.00 (0-671-57760-3, Simon & Schuster Audioworks) Simon & Schuster Audio.

—Stone Kiss. 2003. 528p. mass mkt. 7.99 (0-446-61147-6, Warner Vision); 2002. 400p. 25.95 (0-446-53038-7); 2002. 668p. 25.95 (0-446-53078-6) Warner Bks., Inc.

—Street Dreams. 2004. 560p. mass mkt. 8.00 (0-446-61404-1); 2003. 432p. 25.95 (0-446-53131-6); 2003. 624p. 25.95 (0-446-53232-0) Warner Bks., Inc.

Kellerman, Jonathan. Bad Love. 2003. 512p. mass mkt. 7.99 (0-345-46072-3, Ballantine Bks.) Ballantine Bks.

—Bad Love. 1994. 496p. mass mkt. 6.99 o.s.i (0-553-18118-1); 512p. mass mkt. 7.99 o.s.i (0-553-56870-1); 27.50 o.s.i (0-553-09636-2) Bantam Bks.

—Bad Love. l.t. ed. 2001. 386p. 31.95 (0-7838-9456-2, Macmillan Reference USA) Gale Group.

—Bad Love. 1994. audio 13.59 o.s.i (0-553-70076-6, RH Audio) Random Hse. Audio Publishing Group.

—Billy Straight. 1999. 448p. mass mkt. 7.99 (0-345-41386-5) Ballantine Bks.

—Billy Straight. 1998. pap. 25.95 o.p. (0-7838-0268-4, Macmillan Reference USA) Gale Group.

—Billy Straight: A Novel. l.t. ed. 1998. 663p. pap. 25.95 (0-375-70422-1) Random Hse. Large Print.

—Billy Straight: A Novel. 1998. 467p. 25.95 o.s.i (0-679-45959-6) Random Hse., Inc.

—Blood Test. 2003. 320p. mass mkt. 7.99 (0-345-46661-6, Ballantine Bks.) Ballantine Bks.

—Blood Test. 1995. (Alex Delaware Novel Ser.). 320p. mass mkt. 7.99 o.s.i (0-553-56963-5) Bantam Bks.

—Blood Test. l.t. ed. 2002. (Famous Authors Ser.). 405p. 29.95 (0-7862-3753-8) Gale Group.

—Blood Test. 1987. mass mkt. 4.50 o.p. (0-451-15434-7, Signet Bks.); mass mkt. 4.50 o.p. (0-451-14737-5, Signet Bks.); 352p. mass mkt. 5.99 o.p. (0-451-15929-2, Signet Bks.); mass mkt. 5.99 o.s.i (0-451-17802-5) NAL.

—Blood Test. 1986. 258p. bds. 14.95 o.s.i (0-689-11634-9, Scribner) Simon & Schuster.

—The Clinic. 2003. 496p. mass mkt. 7.99 (0-345-46074-X, Ballantine Bks.) Ballantine Bks.

—The Clinic. 1997. (Alex Delaware Novel Ser.). 496p. mass mkt. 7.99 o.s.i (0-553-57230-X); mass mkt. 6.99 (0-553-84009-6) Bantam Bks.

—The Clinic. unabr. ed. 1997. (Alex Delaware Mystery Ser.). audio 64.00 (0-913369-47-0, 4251) Books on Tape, Inc.

—The Clinic. abr. ed. 1997. (Alex Delaware Mystery Ser.). audio compact disk 29.95 (0-553-45552-4, RH Audio) Random Hse. Audio Publishing Group.

—The Clinic. l.t. ed. 1998. (Thorndike/G. K. Hall Paperback Bestsellers Ser.). 600p. pap. 28.95 (0-7862-0983-6) Thorndike Pr.

—A Cold Heart. 2003. 432p. mass mkt. 7.99 (0-345-45256-9); 400p. 26.95 (0-345-45255-0, Ballantine Bks.); E-Book 18.85 (0-345-46365-X, Ballantine Bks.) Ballantine Bks.

—Devil's Waltz. 2003. 528p. mass mkt. 7.99 (0-345-46071-5, Ballantine Bks.) Ballantine Bks.

—Devil's Waltz. 1993. (Alex Delaware Novel Ser.). 528p. mass mkt. 7.99 (0-553-56352-1); 512p. mass mkt. 6.50 o.s.i (0-553-18101-7) Bantam Bks.

—Devil's Waltz. unabr. ed. 1993. audio 72.00 (0-7366-2424-4, 3189) Books on Tape, Inc.

—Devil's Waltz. 1993. audio 15.95 o.s.i (0-553-74528-X); 1993. audio 12.79 o.s.i (0-553-70060-X); 1999. audio 9.99 o.s.i (0-553-70211-4) Random Hse. Audio Publishing Group. (RH Audio).

—Devil's Waltz. 6.98 o.p. (0-8317-4339-5) Smithmark Pubs., Inc.

—Flesh & Blood. abr. ed. 2001. audio 25.95 (0-375-41940-3); audio compact disk 29.95 (0-375-41941-1); audio 39.95 (0-375-41942-X) Random Hse. Audio Publishing Group. (RH Audio).

—Flesh & Blood. l.t. ed. 2001. 592p. 26.95 (0-375-43129-2) Random Hse. Large Print.

—Monster. 2000. 416p. mass mkt. (0-345-44172-9); mass mkt. 7.99 (0-345-41387-3, Ballantine Bks.) Ballantine Bks.

—Monster. l.t. ed. 512p. 2000. pap. 14.95 (0-375-72794-9); 1999. 25.95 (0-375-40868-1) Random Hse. Large Print.

—The Murder Book. 2003. 544p. mass mkt. 7.99 (0-345-41390-3); 2002. 416p. 26.95 (0-345-45253-4); 2002. E-Book 18.95 (0-345-45864-8) Ballantine Bks. (Ballantine Bks.).

—The Murder Book. l.t. ed. 2002. 672p. 28.95 (0-375-43173-X) Random Hse. Large Print.

—Over the Edge. 1988. 448p. mass mkt. 5.99 o.p. (0-451-15219-0); mass mkt. 7.99 o.s.i (0-451-17801-7) NAL. (Signet Bks.).

—Over the Edge. 1987. 384p. bds. 17.95 o.s.i (0-689-11635-7, Scribner) Simon & Schuster.

—Private Eyes. 2003. 560p. mass mkt. 7.99 (0-345-46070-7, Ballantine Bks.) Ballantine Bks.

—Private Eyes. audio 15.99. 1992. 560p. mass mkt. 7.99 o.s.i (0-553-29950-6); 1992. pap. 5.50 (0-553-18085-1) Bantam Bks.

—Private Eyes. l.t. ed. 1992. 720p. 25.00 o.s.i (0-385-42283-0, Bantam Large Type) Bantam Doubleday Dell Large Print Group, Inc.

—Private Eyes. unabr. ed. 1993. audio 88.00 (0-7366-2351-5, 3128) Books on Tape, Inc.

—Private Eyes. 1992. audio 12.79 o.s.i (0-553-70022-7, RH Audio); 2004. audio compact disk 14.99 (0-7393-1223-5, RH Audio Price-Less); 1999. audio 9.99 o.s.i (0-553-70201-7, RH Audio) Random Hse. Audio Publishing Group.

—Self-Defense. 1995. 528p. mass mkt. 6.99 o.s.i (0-553-84002-9); (Illus.). reprint ed. mass mkt. 7.99 o.s.i (0-553-57220-2) Bantam Bks.

—Self-Defense. unabr. ed. 1995. audio 64.00 (0-7366-2958-0, 3651) Books on Tape, Inc.

—Self-Defense. l.t. ed. 1995. (Large Print Bks.). 556p. 26.95 o.p. (1-56895-206-6, Wheeler Publishing, Inc.) Gale Group.

—Self-Defense. abr. ed. 1995. audio 16.98 o.s.i (0-553-74598-0, RH Audio) Random Hse. Audio Publishing Group.

—Self-Defense. 2002. (Illus.). 528p. mass mkt. 7.99 (0-345-45883-4) Random Hse., Inc.

—Silent Partner. 2003. 512p. mass mkt. 7.99 (0-345-46068-5, Ballantine Bks.) Ballantine Bks.

—Silent Partner. 1990. 512p. mass mkt. 5.50 o.s.i (0-553-17339-1); mass mkt. 7.99 o.s.i (0-553-28592-0) Bantam Bks.

—Silent Partner. unabr. ed. 1992. (Alex Delaware Mystery Ser.). audio 88.00 (0-7366-2266-7, 3054) Books on Tape, Inc.

—Silent Partner. l.t. ed. 1996. (Large Print Bks.). 585p. pap. 23.95 o.p. (1-56895-362-3, Wheeler Publishing, Inc.) Gale Group.

—Silent Partner. 1989. audio 15.95 o.s.i (0-553-74579-4, RH Audio); 2003. audio compact disk 14.99 (0-7393-0376-7, RH Audio Price-Less); 1999. audio 9.99 o.s.i (0-553-70196-7, RH Audio); 1989. audio 16.99 o.s.i (0-553-45191-X, RH Audio) Random Hse. Audio Publishing Group.

—Survival of the Fittest. l.t. ed. 1998. 621p. (0-7540-2083-5) BBC Audiobooks America.

—Survival of the Fittest. 1998. (Alex Delaware Novel Ser.). 544p. mass mkt. 7.99 o.s.i (0-553-57232-6) Bantam Bks.

—Survival of the Fittest. unabr. ed. 1998. audio 72.00 (0-7366-3995-0, 4461) Books on Tape, Inc.

—Survival of the Fittest. abr. ed. 1997. (Alex Delaware Mystery Ser.). audio compact disk 29.95 o.s.i (0-553-45569-9, , RH Audio) Random Hse. Audio Publishing Group.

—Survival of the Fittest. 2002. (Illus.). 544p. mass mkt. 7.99 (0-345-45884-2) Random Hse., Inc.

—Survival of the Fittest. l.t. ed. (Paperback Bestsellers Ser.). 667p. 1999. 27.95 o.p. (0-7862-1283-7); 1998. 30.95 (0-7862-1282-9) Thorndike Pr.

—Time Bomb. 2003. 496p. mass mkt. 7.99 (0-345-46069-3, Ballantine Bks.) Ballantine Bks.

—Time Bomb. 1991. (Alex Delaware Novel Ser.). 496p. mass mkt. 7.99 o.s.i (0-553-29170-X); 480p. mass mkt. 5.95 o.s.i (0-553-18041-X) Bantam Bks.

—Time Bomb. unabr. ed. 1992. audio 88.00 (0-7366-2267-5, 3055) Books on Tape, Inc.

—Time Bomb. abr. ed. 1990. audio 16.99 o.s.i (0-553-45237-1, RH Audio) Random Hse. Audio Publishing Group.

—The Web. 2003. 448p. mass mkt. 7.99 (0-345-46073-1, Ballantine Bks.) Ballantine Bks.

—The Web. 1996. 448p. mass mkt. 7.99 o.s.i (0-553-57227-X) Bantam Bks.

—The Web. unabr. ed. 1996. (Alex Delaware Mystery Ser.). audio 64.00 (0-7366-3277-8, 3933) Books on Tape, Inc.

—The Web. l.t. ed. 1996. (Alex Delaware Ser.). 454p. 26.95 o.p. (1-56895-311-9, Wheeler Publishing, Inc.) Gale Group.

—The Web. abr. ed. 1996. (Alex Delaware Mystery Ser.). audio 23.95 o.s.i (0-553-47430-8, 693452, RH Audio) Random Hse. Audio Publishing Group.

—When the Bough Breaks. 2003. 448p. mass mkt. 7.99 (0-345-46660-8, Ballantine Bks.) Ballantine Bks.

—When the Bough Breaks. 1994. (Alex Delaware Novel Ser.). 448p. mass mkt. 7.99 o.s.i (0-553-56961-9) Bantam Bks.

—When the Bough Breaks. 1986. mass mkt. 4.95 o.p. (0-451-15874-1); mass mkt. 4.50 o.p. (0-451-14870-3); mass mkt. 3.95 o.p. (0-451-14249-7); 352p. mass mkt. 5.99 o.p. (0-451-16862-3); mass mkt. 5.99 o.s.i (0-451-17803-3) NAL. (Signet Bks.).

—When the Bough Breaks. 1985. 304p. bds. 15.95 o.s.i (0-689-11519-9, Scribner) Simon & Schuster.

—When the Bough Breaks. l.t. ed. 2001. 608p. 28.95 o.p. (0-7862-3752-X); (0-7540-1721-4); (0-7540-9118-X) Thorndike Pr.

Kenner, Julie. L. A. Confidential. 2001. (Harlequin Blaze Ser.: No. 16). 249p. mass mkt. (0-373-79020-1, 1-79020-3, Harlequin Bks.) Harlequin Enterprises, Ltd.

Kerr, Larry L. The Neon Nightmare. l.t. ed. 1999. E-Book 14.99 incl. cd-rom (1-929077-71-8, Books OnScreen) PageFree Publishing, Inc.

—The Neon Nightmare. deluxe unabr. ed. 2002. lib. bdg. 35.00 incl. audio (0-932079-26-1, 79261) TimeFare Audio Bk. Productions.

Kerr, Philip. The Grid. l.t. ed. 1996. 578p. 25.95 o.p. (0-7838-1654-5, Macmillan Reference USA) Gale Group.

—The Grid. abr. ed. 1996. audio 12.98 (1-57042-406-3, 394054) Time Warner AudioBooks.

—The Grid. 1997. 464p. mass mkt. 6.99 (0-446-60340-6); 1996. 82p. 21.95 o.s.i (0-446-52053-5) Warner Bks., Inc.

Kerr, Philip. The Grid. unabr. ed. 1996. audio 72.00 (0-7366-3468-1, 4112) Books on Tape, Inc.

Keyes, Marian. Angels. 2004. 400p. pap. 13.95 (0-06-051214-8, Perennial) HarperTrade.

—Angels. 2003. 464p. mass mkt. 7.99 (0-06-000803-2, HarperTorch); 2002. 400p. 24.95 (0-06-000802-4, Morrow, William & Co.) Morrow/Avon.

Kincaid, Tim. Today, Tomorrow & Always. 1997. 480p. mass mkt. 5.99 o.s.i (1-57566-187-X); 1996. 432p. 22.00 o.p. (1-57566-077-6, Kensington Bks.) Kensington Publishing Corp.

Kingsbury, Karen. One Tuesday Morning. l.t. ed. 2004. 689p. 27.95 (0-7862-6111-0) Thorndike Pr.

—One Tuesday Morning. 2003. 352p. pap. 12.99 (0-310-24752-7) Zondervan.

Kizis, Deanna. How to Meet Cute Boys: A Novel. 2003. (Illus.). 272p. 21.95 (0-446-53072-7) Warner Bks., Inc.

Knoerle, John. Crystal Meth Cowboys. 2003. 204p. pap. 12.95 (0-9743199-0-2) Blue Steel Pr.

Koontz, Dean. Winter Moon. 1997. pap. 12.95 o.p. (0-345-41949-9); 1993. 480p. mass mkt. 7.99 o.s.i (0-345-38610-8) Ballantine Bks.

Kotzwinkle, William. The Exile. 1998. 277p. pap. 12.95 (1-56924-728-5, Marlowe & Co.) Avalon Publishing Group.

—The Exile. 1988. 288p. pap. 7.95 o.p. (0-525-48378-0, Obelisk); 1987. 17.95 o.p. (0-525-24526-X, Seymour Lawrence) NAL.

—The Exile. 1990. 4.99 o.p. (0-517-02758-5) Random Hse. Value Publishing.

Krantz, Judith. Lovers. 1995. 544p. mass mkt. 7.99 (0-553-56135-9) Bantam Bks.

—Lovers. unabr. ed. 1997. audio 99.95 (1-85695-924-4, 950304) ISIS Audio Bks. GBR. *Dist:* Ulverscroft Large Print Bks., Ltd.

—Lovers. abr. ed. 1995. audio 8.99 o.s.i (0-679-44348-7, 391115, RH Audio) Random Hse. Audio Publishing Group.

—Lovers. l.t. ed. Date not set. pap. 4.99 (0-517-19680-8) Random Hse. Large Print.

Krich, Rochelle Majer. Angel of Death. 1994. 384p. 27.00 (0-89296-508-8) Mysterious Pr.

—Angel of Death. 372p. pap. 4.98 o.p. (0-7651-0305-2) Smithmark Pubs., Inc.

—Angel of Death. 1996. 368p. mass mkt. 5.99 o.s.i (0-446-40311-3) Warner Bks., Inc.

—Blood Money: A Mystery. 2000. 352p. mass mkt. 6.99 (0-380-78954-X); 1999. 341p. 23.00 (0-380-97378-0) Morrow/Avon. (Avon Bks.).

—Blues in the Night. 352p. 2003. mass mkt. 6.99 (0-449-00726-X); 2002. 23.95 (0-345-44971-1, Ballantine Bks.) Ballantine Bks.

—Blues in the Night. unabr. ed. 2002. (Molly Blume Ser.). audio 74.25 (1-59086-425-5, 4017, Unabridged Library Editions) Brilliance Audio.

—Blues in the Night. 2003. (Women's Fiction Ser.). 29.95 (0-7862-5188-3) Thorndike Pr.

—Dead Air: A Jessie Drake Mystery. 2001. 416p. mass mkt. 6.99 (0-380-80701-7); 2000. 304p. 23.00 (0-380-97769-9) Morrow/Avon. (Avon Bks.).

—Dream House. 2003. 400p. 24.95 (0-345-44972-X, Ballantine Bks.) Ballantine Bks.

—Dream House. abr. ed. 2004. (Molly Blume Ser.). audio 12.99 (1-59086-456-5, 4051, Brilliance Audio Paperback Audiobooks); 2003. (The Molly Blume Ser.: Vol. 2). audio 24.95 (1-59086-455-7, 4049, Brilliance Audio Unabridged); 2003. (The Molly Blume Ser.: Vol. 2). audio 32.95 (1-59086-453-0, 4047, Brilliance Audio Unabridged); 2003. (The Molly Blume Ser.: Vol. 2). audio 82.25 (1-59086-454-9, 4048, Unabridged Library Editions) Brilliance Audio.

—Fair Game. 1994. 320p. mass mkt. 5.50 o.s.i (0-446-40310-5) Warner Bks., Inc.

—Fertile Ground: A Mystery. 1999. mass mkt. 6.99 (0-380-78953-1); 1998. 352p. mass mkt. 22.00 (0-380-97378-2) Morrow/Avon. (Avon Bks.).

—Speak No Evil. 1996. 82p. 21.95 o.p. (0-89296-584-3) Mysterious Pr.

—Speak No Evil. 1997. 384p. mass mkt. 6.50 o.p. (0-446-40505-1) Warner Bks., Inc.

Kyne, Jon. Henrietta. 2002. 156p. per. 19.95 (1-930859-07-4) Elderberry Pr., LLC.

La Plante, Lynda. Cold Blood. 1999. 480p. mass mkt. 6.99 o.s.i (0-515-12479-6, Jove) Berkley Publishing Group.

—Cold Blood. unabr. ed. 2000. (Lorraine Page Mystery Ser.). audio 89.95 (0-7451-8782-X, CAB 1417) Chivers Audio Bks. GBR. *Dist:* BBC Audiobooks America.

—Cold Heart. unabr. ed. 1998. audio 84.95 (0-7540-0213-6, CAB 1636) BBC Audiobooks America.

—Cold Shoulder. 1997. 464p. mass mkt. 6.99 o.s.i (0-515-12128-2, Jove) Berkley Publishing Group.

—Cold Shoulder. unabr. ed. 2000. (Lorraine Page Mystery Ser.). audio 79.95 (0-7451-6511-7, CAB 1127) Chivers Audio Bks. GBR. *Dist:* BBC Audiobooks America.

Lafferty, Perry. Jablonski & the Erotomaniac: A Jack Jablonski Thriller. 1992. 19.95 o.p. (1-55611-323-4) Fine, Donald I. Bks.

Laidlaw, Marc. The Orchid Eater. 1994. 240p. 19.95 o.p. (0-312-10515-0) St. Martin's Pr.

Lambert, Mercedes. Dogtown: A Whitney Logan Mystery. 1991. (Whitney Logan Mystery Ser.). 272p. 18.95 o.p. (0-670-83479-3) Viking Penguin.

Settings

—Soultown. 1997. (Whitney Logan Mystery Ser.). 256p. pap. 5.95 o.s.i (*0-14-025492-7*) Penguin Group (USA) Inc.

—Soultown: A Whitney Logan Mystery. 1996. (Whitney Logan Mystery Ser.). 256p. 21.95 o.s.i (*0-670-86684-9*, Viking) Viking Penguin.

L'Amour, Louis. The Lonesome Gods. 1984. 464p. reprint ed. mass mkt. 5.50 (*0-553-27518-6*) Bantam Bks.

Lange, Kelly. Dead File. 2003. 320p. 24.95 (*0-89296-751-X*) Mysterious Pr.

—Dead File. 2004. mass mkt. (*0-446-61387-8*) Warner Bks., Inc.

Lankford, Terrill. Angry Moon, unabr. ed. 1998. audio 49.95 (*0-7861-1347-2*, 2250) Blackstone Audio Bks., Inc.

—Angry Moon. 317p. 1999. mass mkt. 5.99 (*0-8125-4834-5*, Tor Bks.); 1997. 22.95 (*0-312-85726-8*, Forge Bks.) Doherty, Tom Assocs., LLC.

—Shooters. 224p. 1998. mass mkt. 5.99 (*0-8125-5538-4*); 1996. 20.95 o.p. (*0-312-86272-5*) Doherty, Tom Assocs., LLC. (Forge Bks.).

—Shooters. abr. ed. 1997. audio 17.00 (*1-56876-068-X*) Soundlines Entertainment, Inc.

Lark, Michael. Graphic Comic Book: Raymond Chandler's 'The Little Sister' 1997. (Illus.). 136p. pap. 15.00 o.s.i (*0-684-82933-9*, Fireside) Simon & Schuster.

Larsen, Michael. Uncertainty. 1998. Tr. of Uden Sikker Viden. 272p. pap. 12.00 o.s.i (*0-449-91236-1*, Fawcett) Ballantine Bks.

—Uncertainty. Blecher, Lone T. & Blecher, George, trs. from DAN. 1996. Tr. of Uden Sikker Viden. 272p. 22.00 o.s.i (*0-15-100202-9*) Harcourt Trade Pubs.

Latt, Mimi. Powers of Attorney. 1993. 512p. 23.00 o.p. (*0-671-78708-X*, Simon & Schuster) Simon & Schuster.

—Powers of Attorney. Rubenstein, Julie, ed. 1994. 544p. reprint ed. mass mkt. 6.99 (*0-671-86916-7*, Pocket) Simon & Schuster.

—Pursuit of Justice. l.t. ed. 1998. (Large Print Bks.). pap. 24.95 (*1-56895-589-8*, Wheeler Publishing, Inc.) Gale Group.

—Pursuit of Justice. 1999. (Illus.). 480p. mass mkt. 6.99 o.s.i (*0-671-03411-1*, Pocket); 1998. 384p. 23.00 (*0-684-81184-7*, Simon & Schuster) Simon & Schuster.

Lawrence, Cynthia. Take-Out City. 1993. 208p. 18.95 o.p. (*0-88184-942-1*, Carroll & Graf Pubs.) Avalon Publishing Group.

Laymon, Richard. The Quake. 1995. 400p. 22.95 o.p. (*0-312-13150-X*) St. Martin's Pr.

LaZebnik, Claire Scovell. Same As It Never Was: A Novel. 2003. 352p. 24.95 (*0-312-31249-0*) St. Martin's Pr.

Lehman, Ernest. Sweet Smell of Success: Short Fiction of Ernest Lehman. 2000. 272p. 15.95 (*1-58567-047-2*) Overlook Pr., The.

Leigh, Janet. House of Destiny. 1996. 507p. mass mkt. (*1-55166-159-4*, 1-66159-4); 1995. 512p. (*1-55166-125-X*) Harlequin Enterprises, Ltd. (Mira Bks.).

LeMone, Charles S. A Dance in the Street. 1993. 256p. (Orig.). mass mkt. 3.99 (*0-380-76713-9*, Avon Bks.) Morrow/Avon.

Lemus, Felicia Luna. The Trace Elements of Random Tea Parties. 2003. 256p. 23.00 (*0-374-27856-3*) Farrar, Straus & Giroux.

Leonard, Elmore. Be Cool. 1999. (*0-7540-1295-6*) BBC Audiobooks America.

—Be Cool. unabr. ed. 1999. audio 40.00 (*0-7366-4449-0*, 4894) Books on Tape, Inc.

—Be Cool. 2000. 368p. mass mkt. 7.50 o.s.i (*0-440-23505-7*); 1999. mass mkt. 7.99 (*0-440-29577-7*) Dell Publishing.

—Be Cool. abr. ed. 1999. audio 25.00 o.s.i (*0-553-52604-9*, RH Audio) Random Hse. Audio Publishing Group.

—Be Cool. 2000. E-Book 7.50 (*0-440-33423-3*) Random Hse., Inc.

—Be Cool, unabr. ed. 1999. audio 51.00 (*0-7887-2916-0*, 95708E7) Recorded Bks., LLC.

—Be Cool. l.t. ed. (Thorndike/G. K. Hall Paperback Bestsellers Ser.). 383p. 2000. pap. 27.95 (*0-7862-1839-8*); 1999. lib. bdg. 30.95 (*0-7862-1838-X*) Thorndike Pr.

—Get Shorty. unabr. ed. 1992. audio 48.00 (*0-7366-2222-5*, 3012) Books on Tape, Inc.

—Get Shorty. 2000. 368p. mass mkt. 4.99 o.s.i (*0-440-23614-2*); 1998. 304p. pap. 9.95 o.s.i (*0-385-32398-0*); 1995. 304p. pap. 8.95 o.s.i (*0-385-31567-8*, Delacorte Pr.); 1991. 384p. mass mkt. 6.99 o.s.i (*0-440-20980-3*); 1991. 368p. mass mkt. 5.50 o.s.i (*0-440-29515-7*) Dell Publishing.

—Get Shorty. l.t. ed. 1993. pap. 18.95 (*0-8161-5809-6*, Macmillan Reference USA) Gale Group.

—Get Shorty. 1990. audio 14.98 o.s.i (*0-553-74582-4*); audio 12.79 o.s.i (*0-553-19964-1*) Random Hse. Audio Publishing Group. (RH Audio).

Leonard, Elmore, contrib. by. Be Cool. 1999. (*0-7540-2221-8*) BBC Audiobooks America.

Levinson, Robert S. Hot Paint: A Neil Gulliver & Stevie Marriner Novel. 2002. 352p. 26.95 (*0-7653-0231-4*, Forge Bks.) Doherty, Tom Assocs., LLC.

—The John Lennon Affair. 2001. (Neil Gulliver & Steve Marriner Novels Ser.). 320p. 24.95 (*0-312-87902-4*, Forge Bks.) Doherty, Tom Assocs., LLC.

Lewis, Fiona. Between Men: A Novel. 1995. 304p. 21.00 o.p. (*0-87113-586-8*, Atlantic Monthly Pr.) Grove/Atlantic, Inc.

Lita, Lita. 2003. (Illus.). 352p. 26.00 (*0-7434-7398-1*, WWE) Simon & Schuster.

Lochte, Dick. Laughing Dog. 1988. (Leo Bloodworth-Serendipity Dahlquist Mystery Ser.: Bk. 2). 272p. 17.95 o.p. (*0-87795-941-2*, Morrow, William & Co.) Morrow/Avon.

—Laughing Dog. 1989. 400p. reprint ed. mass mkt. 3.95 o.s.i (*0-446-35724-3*) Warner Bks., Inc.

—Lucky Dog & Other Tales of Murder. 2000. (Five Star Mystery Ser.). 207p. 20.95 (*0-7862-2688-9*, Five Star) Gale Group.

—Sleeping Dog. 1985. 288p. 15.95 o.p. (*0-87795-738-X*, Morrow, William & Co.) Morrow/Avon.

—Sleeping Dog. 2001. (Missing Mystery Ser.: Vol. 29). 292p. pap. 14.95 (*1-890208-51-5*) Poisoned Pen Pr.

—Sleeping Dog. 1986. 288p. mass mkt. 3.95 o.s.i (*0-446-32661-5*) Warner Bks., Inc.

Loh, Sandra Tsing. If You Lived Here, You'd Be Home by Now: A Novel. 1998. 240p. 13.00 o.s.i (*1-57322-695-5*, Riverhead Trade (Paperbacks)) Berkley Publishing Group.

—If You Lived Here, You'd Be Home by Now: A Novel. 1997. 224p. 23.95 o.p. (*1-57322-068-X*, Riverhead Bks. (Hardcovers)) Putnam Publishing Group, The.

Lovett, Sarah. Dark Alchemy. 2003. 304p. 24.00 (*0-684-85599-2*, Simon & Schuster) Simon & Schuster.

Lowell, Elizabeth. Moving Target. 2002. E-Book 19.95 (*0-06-001063-0*); 2001. E-Book 19.95 (*0-06-001065-7*); 2001. 592p. pap. 24.00 (*0-06-620962-5*) HarperCollins Pubs.

—Moving Target. abr. ed. 2001. audio 25.95 (*0-694-52562-6*, HarperAudio) HarperTrade.

—Moving Target. 464p. 2002. mass mkt. 7.99 (*0-06-103107-0*, Avon Bks.); 2001. 24.00 (*0-06-019875-3*, Morrow, William & Co.) Morrow/Avon.

Lucas, Frances. If Looks Could Kill. 1995. 190p. (Orig.). pap. 9.95 (*0-934678-63-4*) New Victoria Pubs., Inc.

Lucier, Charles B. Of My Flesh & This Wicked World. 1999. 288p. 21.95 (*1-56167-491-5*) Noble Hse.

Lynch, Patrick. Omega. 1997. 384p. 23.95 o.s.i (*0-525-94327-7*) Dutton/Plume.

—Omega. 1998. 432p. mass mkt. 6.99 o.s.i (*0-451-19323-7*, Signet Bks.) NAL.

Lyons. Castles Burning. 1981. mass mkt. 2.50 (*0-671-41864-5*, Pocket) Simon & Schuster.

Lyons, Arthur. All God's Children. 1976. mass mkt. 1.50 o.s.i (*0-345-25020-6*) Ballantine Bks.

—All God's Children. 1982. 224p. pap. o.p. (*0-03-060394-3*, Owl Bks.) Holt, Henry & Co.

—At the Hands of Another. 240p. 1986. pap. o.p. (*0-03-008533-0*, Owl Bks.); 1983. o.p. (*0-03-059616-5*) Holt, Henry & Co.

—Castles Burning. 1982. (Rinehart Suspense Novel Ser.). 224p. pap. o.p. (*0-03-062417-7*, Owl Bks.) Holt, Henry & Co.

—The Dead Are Discreet. 1983. 224p. pap. o.p. (*0-03-060393-5*, Owl Bks.) Holt, Henry & Co.

—Dead Ringer. 1983. 240p. pap. o.p. (*0-03-060396-X*, Owl Bks.) Holt, Henry & Co.

—False Pretenses. 1994. 240p. 18.95 o.s.i (*0-89296-220-8*) Mysterious Pr.

—False Pretenses. 1995. 224p. mass mkt. 5.50 o.s.i (*0-446-40422-5*) Warner Bks., Inc.

—Fast Fade: A Jacob Asch Mystery. 1987. 224p. 15.45 (*0-89296-216-X*) Mysterious Pr.

—Fast Fade: A Jacob Asch Mystery. 1988. 208p. mass mkt. 3.95 o.s.i (*0-445-40703-4*, Mysterious Pr. Paperback Bks.) Warner Bks., Inc.

—Hard Trade. 264p. 1983. pap. o.p. (*0-03-063333-8*, Owl Bks.); 1981. o.p. (*0-03-053621-9*) Holt, Henry & Co.

—The Killing Floor. 1982. pap. o.p. (*0-03-060397-8*, Owl Bks.) Holt, Henry & Co.

—Other People's Money. 1989. 213p. 17.95 o.s.i (*0-89296-218-6*) Mysterious Pr.

—Other People's Money. 1990. 224p. mass mkt. 4.95 o.s.i (*0-445-40903-7*, Mysterious Pr. Paperback Bks.) Warner Bks., Inc.

—Three with a Bullet. 240p. 1986. pap. 3.95 o.p. (*0-03-008539-X*, Owl Bks.); 1985. o.p. (*0-03-059617-3*) Holt, Henry & Co.

MacDonald, Ross, pseud. Archer in Jeopardy, 3 bks., Set. Incl. Zebra-Striped Hearse. 1979. (Lew Archer Mystery Ser.). 1979. 24.95 o.s.i (*0-394-50804-1*) Knopf, Alfred A. Inc.

—The Barbarous Coast. 1975. (Lew Archer Mystery Ser.). 192p. pap. 2.95 o.s.i (*0-553-12249-5*) Bantam Bks.

—The Barbarous Coast. unabr. ed. (Lew Archer Mystery Ser.). 2000. audio compact disk 48.00 (*0-7861-9916-4*, z1819); 1996. audio 39.95 (*0-7861-1047-3*, 1819) Blackstone Audio Bks., Inc.

—The Barbarous Coast. 1990. (Lew Archer Mystery Ser.). 240p. mass mkt. 3.95 o.s.i (*0-446-35882-7*) Warner Bks., Inc.

—Blue City. 1988. 2.99 o.p. (*0-517-68432-2*) Random Hse. Value Publishing.

—Blue City. 1992. (Lew Archer Mystery Ser.). 224p. mass mkt. 4.50 o.s.i (*0-446-35884-3*) Warner Bks., Inc.

—The Blue Hammer. Date not set. (Lew Archer Mystery Ser.). pap. 16.95 (*0-8488-1722-2*); 23.95 (*0-89190-095-0*) Amereon, Ltd.

—The Blue Hammer. 1988. (Lew Archer Mystery Ser.). pap. 3.95 o.s.i (*0-553-27548-8*) Bantam Bks.

—The Blue Hammer, unabr. ed. 1999. (Lew Archer Mystery Ser.). audio 44.95 (*0-7861-1031-7*, 894402) Blackstone Audio Bks., Inc.

—The Blue Hammer. 1976. (Lew Archer Mystery Ser.). reprint ed. lib. bdg. 13.50 o.p. (*0-8161-6431-2*, Macmillan Reference USA) Gale Group.

—The Blue Hammer. 1990. (Lew Archer Mystery Ser.). mass mkt. 3.95 o.s.i (*0-446-35885-1*) Warner Bks., Inc.

—The Chill, unabr. ed. 1996. (Lew Archer Mystery Ser.). audio 44.95 (*0-7861-1066-X*, 894596) Blackstone Audio Bks., Inc.

—The Chill. 2001. 288p. pap. 8.42 (*1-84195-118-8*) Canongate Bks. GBR. *Dist:* Grove/Atlantic, Inc.

—The Chill. 1996. (Lew Archer Mystery Ser.). 288p. pap. 12.00 (*0-679-76807-6*) Random Hse., Inc.

—The Chill. 1990. (Lew Archer Mystery Ser.). mass mkt. 3.95 o.s.i (*0-446-35887-8*) Warner Bks., Inc.

—The Doomsters. 1990. (Lew Archer Mystery Ser.). mass mkt. 3.95 o.s.i (*0-446-35888-6*) Warner Bks., Inc.

—The Drowning Pool. 1975. (Lew Archer Mystery Ser.). 224p. pap. 2.75 o.p. (*0-553-24135-4*) Bantam Bks.

—The Drowning Pool. l.t. ed. 2002. pap. 25.95 (*0-7838-9783-9*) Gale Group.

—The Drowning Pool. Barzun, Jacques & Taylor, Wendell H., eds. 1976. (Lew Archer Mystery Ser.). reprint ed. lib. bdg. 21.00 o.p. (*0-8240-2382-X*) Garland Publishing, Inc.

—The Drowning Pool. 1996. (Lew Archer Mystery Ser.). 256p. pap. 12.00 (*0-679-76806-8*) Random Hse., Inc.

—The Drowning Pool. 1993. (Lew Archer Mystery Ser.). 224p. mass mkt. 4.99 o.s.i (*0-446-35889-4*) Warner Bks., Inc.

—The Far Side of the Dollar. (Lew Archer Mystery Ser.). 2000. audio compact disk 56.00 (*0-7861-9889-3*, ZP1769); 1996. audio 44.95 (*0-7861-0990-4*, 1767) Blackstone Audio Bks., Inc.

—The Far Side of the Dollar. 1990. (Lew Archer Mystery Ser.). mass mkt. 4.99 o.s.i (*0-446-35890-8*) Warner Bks., Inc.

—Find a Victim, unabr. ed. 1999. (Lew Archer Mystery Ser.). audio 39.95 (*0-7861-1493-2*, 758945) Blackstone Audio Bks., Inc.

—Find a Victim, Set. unabr. ed. 1999. (Lew Archer Mystery Ser.). audio 39.95 Highsmith Inc.

—Find a Victim. 2001. (Lew Archer Mystery Ser.). 224p. pap. 12.00 (*0-375-70867-7*, Vintage) Knopf Publishing Group.

—Find a Victim. 1991. (Lew Archer Mystery Ser.). mass mkt. 4.50 o.s.i (*0-446-35892-4*) Warner Bks., Inc.

—The Galton Case. 1980. (Lew Archer Mystery Ser.). pap. 2.75 o.p. (*0-553-22621-5*) Bantam Bks.

—The Galton Case. 1990. (Lew Archer Mystery Ser.). mass mkt. 3.95 o.s.i (*0-446-35893-2*) Warner Bks., Inc.

—The Galton Case: A Lew Archer Novel. 1996. (Lew Archer Mystery Ser.). 256p. pap. 12.00 (*0-679-76864-5*) McKay, David Co., Inc.

—The Goodbye Look. 2000. (Lew Archer Mystery Ser.). 256p. pap. 12.00 (*0-375-70865-0*, Vintage) Knopf Publishing Group.

—The Goodbye Look. 1992. (Lew Archer Mystery Ser.). 224p. mass mkt. 4.50 o.s.i (*0-446-35894-0*) Warner Bks., Inc.

—The Instant Enemy. 1985. (Lew Archer Mystery Ser.). 208p. pap. 2.95 o.p. (*0-553-24738-7*) Bantam Bks.

—The Instant Enemy. 1991. (Lew Archer Mystery Ser.). 224p. mass mkt. 4.50 o.s.i (*0-446-35895-9*) Warner Bks., Inc.

—The Ivory Grin. 1998. (Lew Archer Mystery Ser.). 192p. 19.50 (*0-7540-8519-8*, Black Dagger) BBC Audiobooks America.

—The Ivory Grin. 1992. (Lew Archer Mystery Ser.). 224p. reprint ed. mass mkt. 4.50 o.s.i (*0-446-35896-7*) Warner Bks., Inc.

—Lew Archer Private Investigator. l.t. ed. 1988. (Lew Archer Mystery Ser.). 20.95 o.p. (*1-55504-639-8*); pap. 18.95 o.p. (*1-55504-640-1*) BBC Audiobooks America.

—Lew Archer Private Investigator. 1986. (Lew Archer Mystery Ser.). 10.00 o.p. (*0-89296-033-7*) Mysterious Pr.

—Lew Archer Private Investigator II. l.t. ed. 1988. (Lew Archer Mystery Ser.). pap. 17.95 o.p. (*1-55504-703-3*); lib. bdg. 19.95 o.p. (*1-55504-727-0*) BBC Audiobooks America.

—The Moving Target. l.t. ed. 1991. (Lew Archer Mystery Ser.). pap. 10.95 o.p. (*0-89340-171-4*, C0096) BBC Audiobooks America.

—The Moving Target. 1979. (Lew Archer Mystery Ser.). lib. bdg. 9.95 o.p. (*0-8398-2538-2*, Macmillan Reference USA) Gale Group.

—The Moving Target. 1998. (Lew Archer Mystery Ser.). 256p. pap. 11.00 (*0-375-70146-X*, Vintage) Knopf Publishing Group.

—The Moving Target. 1990. (Lew Archer Mystery Ser.). mass mkt. 4.99 o.s.i (*0-446-35898-3*) Warner Bks., Inc.

—Sleeping Beauty. (Lew Archer Mystery Ser.). 23.95 (*0-89190-096-9*) Amereon, Ltd.

—Sleeping Beauty, unabr. ed. 1997. (Lew Archer Mystery Ser.). audio 29.95 (*1-57270-049-1*, N61049u) Audio Partners Publishing Corp.

—Sleeping Beauty. 1984. mass mkt. 3.50 o.s.i (*0-553-27101-6*) Bantam Bks.

—Sleeping Beauty. unabr. ed. 1998. (Lew Archer Mystery Ser.). audio 44.95 (*0-7861-1320-0*, 2245) Blackstone Audio Bks., Inc.

—Sleeping Beauty. 2000. (Lew Archer Mystery Ser.). 288p. pap. 12.00 (*0-375-70866-9*, Vintage) Knopf Publishing Group.

—Sleeping Beauty. 1973. (Lew Archer Mystery Ser). 5.95 o.p. (*0-394-48474-6*, Knopf Bks. for Young Readers) Random Hse. Children's Bks.

—Sleeping Beauty. 1991. (Lew Archer Mystery Ser.). mass mkt. 4.50 o.s.i (*0-446-35899-1*) Warner Bks., Inc.

—The Underground Man. 1984. (Lew Archer Mystery Ser.). mass mkt. 3.95 o.s.i (*0-553-27183-0*) Bantam Bks.

—The Underground Man. 1992. (Lew Archer Mystery Ser.). mass mkt. 4.50 o.s.i (*0-446-35901-7*) Warner Bks., Inc.

—The Underground Man: A Lew Archer Novel. 1996. (Lew Archer Mystery Ser.). (SPA.). 288p. pap. 12.00 (*0-679-76808-4*, Vintage) Knopf Publishing Group.

—The Way Some People Die. 1990. (Lew Archer Mystery Ser.). mass mkt. 3.95 o.s.i (*0-446-35902-5*) Warner Bks., Inc.

—The Wycherly Woman. 1984. (Lew Archer Mystery Ser.). mass mkt. 2.95 o.s.i (*0-553-23855-8*) Bantam Bks.

—The Wycherly Woman. 1998. (Lew Archer Mystery Ser.). 288p. pap. 12.00 (*0-375-70144-3*, Vintage) Knopf Publishing Group.

—The Wycherly Woman. 1990. (Lew Archer Mystery Ser.). mass mkt. 3.95 o.s.i (*0-446-35903-3*) Warner Bks., Inc.

—The Zebra-Striped Hearse. 1998. (Lew Archer Mystery Ser.). 19.50 o.p. (*0-7540-8511-2*, Black Dagger) BBC Audiobooks America.

—The Zebra-Striped Hearse. 1984. (Lew Archer Mystery Ser.). 224p. mass mkt. 3.95 o.s.i (*0-553-27362-0*) Bantam Bks.

—The Zebra-Striped Hearse. 1998. (Lew Archer Mystery Ser.). 288p. pap. 12.00 (*0-375-70145-1*, Vintage) Knopf Publishing Group.

—The Zebra-Striped Hearse. 1979. (Lew Archer Mystery Ser.). Knopf, Alfred A. Inc.

—The Zebra-Striped Hearse. 1993. (Lew Archer Mystery Ser.). 272p. mass mkt. 4.99 o.s.i (*0-446-35904-1*) Warner Bks., Inc.

MacDonald, Ross, pseud, ed. The Ivory Grin. 1988. (Lew Archer Mystery Ser.). 256p. mass mkt. 3.95 o.s.i (*0-553-27352-3*) Bantam Bks.

MacDonald, Shari. A Match Made in Heaven. 2001. (Salinger Sisters Ser.: Vol. 3). 231p. 23.95 (*0-7862-3094-0*, Five Star) Gale Group.

Magallanes, Marcus. County. 2001. 224p. pap. 13.95 (*0-87714-208-4*) Denlingers Pubs., Ltd.

Majer Krich, Rochelle. Fair Game. 1993. 384p. 29.00 (*0-89296-507-X*) Mysterious Pr.

Mallory, Carole. Flash. 1991. 2.99 o.p. (*0-517-07575-X*) Random Hse. Value Publishing.

—Flash. 1989. mass mkt. 4.50 o.s.i (*0-671-64465-3*, Pocket); 1988. 16.95 o.p. (*0-671-64464-5*, Simon & Schuster) Simon & Schuster.

Manaster, Benjamin. Skyla. Caso, Adolph, ed. 1995. 246p. 21.95 (*0-8283-2002-0*) Branden Bks.

Markoe, Merrill. It's My F—ing Birthday: A Novel. 2002. 224p. pap. 11.95 (*0-8129-6724-0*); 21.95 (*0-375-50712-4*) Random House Adult Trade Publishing Group. (Villard Bks.).

Marshall, Michael. The Straw Men. 2002. 373p. pap. (*0-00-715186-1*) HarperCollins Pubs.

Marx, Pat. Blockbuster. 1988. 224p. pap. 15.00 (*0-553-34498-6*) Bantam Bks.

Matinez, Manuel Luis. Drift. 2003. 256p. pap. 14.00 o.s.i (*0-312-30995-3*) Picador.

Matthews, Greg. Far from Heaven: A Keith Moody Mystery. 1997. (Keith Moody Mystery Ser.). 276p. 20.95 (*0-8027-3303-4*) Walker & Co.

Maupin, Armistead. Maybe the Moon: A Novel. ltd. ed. 1992. 320p. 100.00 o.p. (*0-06-016947-8*) HarperTrade.

Mayersberg, Paul. Homme Fatale. 1992. 352p. 19.95 o.p. (*0-312-06996-0*) St. Martin's Pr.

McCabe, Peter. Wasteland: A Novel. 1994. 258p. 20.00 (*0-684-19681-6*, Scribner) Simon & Schuster.

McCall, Dinah. The Perfect Lie. l.t. ed. 2003. 374p. pap. 25.95 (*1-58724-499-3*, Wheeler Publishing, Inc.) Gale Group.

—The Perfect Lie. 2003. 384p. mass mkt. (*1-55166-675-8*, Mira Bks.) Harlequin Enterprises, Ltd.

McCoy, Horace. I Should Have Stayed Home. Kupelnick, Bruce S., ed. 1978. (Classics of Film Literature Ser.). lib. bdg. 21.00 o.p. (*0-8240-2883-X*) Garland Publishing, Inc.

McDonald, Ian. Terminal Cafe. 1994. 277p. pap. 19.00 (*0-553-37416-8*) Bantam Bks.

McGrady, Sean. Dead Letter. Chelius, Jane, ed. 1992. 240p. (Orig.). mass mkt. 4.99 (*0-671-74267-1*, Pocket) Simon & Schuster.

McKay, Gardner. Toyer. unabr. ed. 1999. audio 39.95 (*1-56740-424-3*, 1677, Brilliance Audio Unabridged); audio 73.25 (*1-56740-650-5*, 1678, Unabridged Library Editions) Brilliance Audio.

—Toyer. abr. ed. 1999. audio 17.98 (*1-57042-626-0*) Time Warner AudioBooks.

—Toyer. 1999. 496p. mass mkt. 7.50 (*0-446-60773-8*) Warner Bks., Inc.

—Toyer: A Novel. 1999. 464p. (YA). (gr. 8 up). 24.00 o.p. (*0-316-56118-5*) Little Brown & Co.

McLaughlin, Christian. Glamourpuss. 1994. 256p. 19.95 o.p. (*0-525-93866-4*) Dutton/Plume.

McMahon, Kevin. Weekend in Silverlake: A Pastoral Comedy. 2001. 256p. 25.00 (*1-85984-791-9*) Verso.

Meallet, Sandro. Edgewater Angels: A Novel. 2002. 336p. pap. 13.00 (*0-375-72561-X*, Vintage) Knopf Publishing Group.

Mercer, Judy. Blind Spot. 2000. 480p. 23.95 (*0-671-03424-3*, Atria) Simon & Schuster.

—Fast Forward. l.t. ed. 1996. (G. K. Hall Mystery Ser.). 593p. 22.95 o.p. (*0-7838-1495-X*, Macmillan Reference USA) Gale Group.

—Fast Forward. Date not set. pap. 3.99 (*0-671-02431-0*); 1997. (Illus.). 400p. pap. 6.99 (*0-671-89961-9*) Simon & Schuster. (Pocket).

—Fast Forward. Chernoff, Dona, ed. 1995. 352p. 22.00 o.p. (*0-671-89960-0*, Atria) Simon & Schuster.

Mickelbury, Penny. Where to Choose. 1999. 256p. 22.00 (*0-684-83742-0*, Simon & Schuster) Simon & Schuster.

—Where to Choose. 2001. 240p. reprint ed. mass mkt. 6.50 (*0-312-97708-5*, 20-3261, St. Martin's Paperbacks) St. Martin's Pr.

Miller, Andrew. Oxygen. 2003. 352p. pap. 14.00 (*0-15-602740-2*, Harvest Bks.); 2002. 336p. 24.00 (*0-15-100721-7*) Harcourt Trade Pubs.

Miller, Geoffrey. The Black Glove. 1984. 254p. pap. 3.50 o.p. (*0-88184-080-7*, Carroll & Graf Pubs.) Avalon Publishing Group.

—The Black Glove. 1981. 276p. 12.95 o.p. (*0-670-17166-2*) Viking Penguin.

Miller, J. M. The Big Lie: A Weatherby Mystery. 1994. pap. 10.99 (*0-8407-6357-3*) Nelson, Thomas Inc.

Miller, Joshua. The Mao Game. 1997. 224p. 21.00 o.s.i (*0-06-039185-5*, ReganBooks) HarperTrade.

—The Mao Game. 1998. pap. 12.00 (*0-380-73182-7*, Avon Bks.) Morrow/Avon.

Millhiser, Marlys. Death of the Office Witch. 1995. (Charlie Green Mystery Ser.). 304p. pap. 5.95 o.p. (*0-14-024340-2*, Penguin Bks.) Penguin Group (USA) Inc.

—Death of the Office Witch. 1993. 289p. 20.00 (*1-883402-02-6*, Scribner) Simon & Schuster.

—Nobody Dies in a Casino. 1999. 288p. 22.95 (*0-312-20344-6*, Saint Martin's Minotaur) St. Martin's Pr.

Miner, Valerie. Winter's Edge: A Novel. 1985. (Feminist Ser.). 184p. (Orig.). (C). pap. 7.95 o.p. (*0-89594-175-9*) Crossing Pr., Inc., The.

Monette, Paul. Taking Care of Mrs. Carroll. 1978. 8.95 o.p. (*0-316-57821-5*) Little Brown & Co.

—Taking Care of Mrs. Carroll. 1979. pap. 2.75 o.p. (*0-380-45161-1*, 45161-1, Avon Bks.) Morrow/Avon.

—Taking Care of Mrs. Carroll. 1988. (Stonewall Inn Editions Ser.). 288p. pap. 12.95 (*0-312-01515-1*, Saint Martin's Griffin) St. Martin's Pr.

Montecino, Marcel. The Crosskiller. 1988. 352p. 18.95 o.p. (*0-87795-908-0*, Morrow, William & Co.) Morrow/Avon.

—Crosskiller. 1990. 3.99 o.p. (*0-517-03359-3*) Random Hse. Value Publishing.

—Crosskiller. 1989. 592p. mass mkt. 6.99 (*0-671-67894-9*, Pocket) Simon & Schuster.

Monteilh, Marissa. Hot Boyz. 2004. 352p. pap. 13.95 (*0-06-059094-7*, Avon Bks.) Morrow/Avon.

Montgomery, Lee. Absolute Disaster: New Fiction from Los Angeles. 1996. 352p. pap. 15.95 o.p. (*0-7871-1052-3*) NewStar Media, Inc.

Moody, Bill. Solo Hand. 1996. 304p. mass mkt. 5.50 o.s.i (*0-440-22322-9*) Dell Publishing.

—Solo Hand. 2003. 193p. pap. 13.95 (*0-9644138-3-3*, Dark City Bks.) OffByOne Pr.

—Solo Hand. 1994. 19.95 (*0-8027-3248-8*) Walker & Co.

Morris, Gilbert. The Silver Star, Vol. 20. 1997. (House of Winslow Ser.: Vol. 20). 336p. pap. 11.99 (*1-55661-688-0*) Bethany Hse. Pubs.

Morris, Wright. Love among the Cannibals. 1977. 253p. reprint ed. pap. 8.95 o.p. (*0-8032-5842-9*, Bison Bks.) Univ. of Nebraska Pr.

Mosley, Walter. Always Outnumbered, Always Outgunned. abr. ed. 1997. (Easy Rawlins Mystery Ser.). 25.00 o.p. (*0-7871-1646-7*, 695538) NewStar Media, Inc.

—Always Outnumbered, Always Outgunned. 1997. 224p. 23.00 (*0-393-04539-0*) Norton, W. W. & Co., Inc.

—Always Outnumbered, Always Outgunned. 1998. 208p. pap. 14.00 (*0-671-01499-4*, Washington Square Pr.) Simon & Schuster.

—Always Outnumbered, Always Outgunned. l.t. ed. 1998. (Basic Ser.). 360p. 30.95 (*0-7862-1268-3*) Thorndike Pr.

—Bad Boy Brawly Brown: An Easy Rawlins Mystery. 2002. 320p. 24.95 (*0-316-07301-6*) Little Brown & Co.

—Bad Boy Brawly Brown: An Easy Rawlins Mystery. (Illus.). mass mkt. 0.00 (*0-671-88430-1*); 1900. pap. (*0-671-03839-7*) Simon & Schuster. (Pocket).

—Black Betty. abr. ed. 1994. (Easy Rawlins Mystery Ser.: No. 4). 3p. audio 16.95 (*1-55927-290-2*, 390399) Audio Renaissance.

—Black Betty. unabr. ed. 1994. (Easy Rawlins Mystery Ser.). audio 56.00 (*0-7366-2853-3*, 3561) Books on Tape, Inc.

—Black Betty. 1994. (Easy Rawlins Mystery Ser.). 255p. 19.95 (*0-393-03644-8*) Norton, W. W. & Co., Inc.

—Black Betty. 368p. 1997. pap. 14.00 (*0-671-01983-X*, Pocket); 1995. (Illus.). mass mkt. 6.99 (*0-671-88427-1*, Pocket); 2002. reprint ed. pap. 14.00 (*0-7434-5178-3*, Washington Square Pr.) Simon & Schuster.

—Black Betty: Library Edition, Set. unabr. ed. 1994. audio 59.95 o.p. (*1-55927-302-X*) Audio Renaissance.

—Devil in a Blue Dress. abr. ed. 1993. (Easy Rawlins Mystery Ser.). audio 16.95 (*1-55927-238-4*, 390653) Audio Renaissance.

—Devil in a Blue Dress. unabr. ed. 1994. (Easy Rawlins Mystery Ser.). audio 36.00 (*0-7366-2810-X*, 3524) Books on Tape, Inc.

—Devil in a Blue Dress. 1990. (Easy Rawlins Mystery Ser.). 219p. 19.95 (*0-393-02854-2*) Norton, W. W. & Co., Inc.

—Devil in a Blue Dress. (Easy Rawlins Mystery Ser.). 1997. 240p. pap. 14.00 (*0-671-01982-1*); 2002. 272p. reprint ed. pap. 14.00 (*0-7434-5179-1*) Simon & Schuster. (Washington Square Pr.).

—Devil in a Blue Dress. Ryan, Kevin, ed. 1995. (Easy Rawlins Mystery Ser.). 240p. reprint ed. mass mkt. 6.99 (*0-671-51142-4*, Pocket) Simon & Schuster.

—Devil in a Blue Dress. Chelius, Jane, ed. 1991. 224p. reprint ed. mass mkt. 5.99 (*0-671-74050-4*, Pocket) Simon & Schuster.

—Devil in a Blue Dress: Library Edition, Set. unabr. ed. 1994. audio 39.95 o.p. (*1-55927-269-4*) Audio Renaissance.

—Fearless Jones. l.t. ed. 2001. (Hardcover Ser.). 322p. 31.95 (*1-58724-050-5*, Wheeler Publishing, Inc.) Gale Group.

—Fearless Jones. Pietsch, Michael, ed. 2001. 320p. 24.95 o.p. (*0-316-59238-2*) Little Brown & Co.

—Gone Fishin' 1997. 208p. 22.00 o.p. (*1-57478-025-5*) Black Classic Pr.

—Gone Fishin', Set. abr. ed. 1997. (Easy Rawlins Mystery Ser.). 17.95 o.p. (*0-7871-1402-2*, 394867) NewStar Media, Inc.

—Gone Fishin' (Easy Rawlins Mystery Ser.). 1998. 272p. mass mkt. 6.50 (*0-671-01011-5*, Pocket); 1999. 256p. reprint ed. pap. 14.00 (*0-671-02746-8*, Washington Square Pr.) Simon & Schuster.

—Gone Fishin' l.t. ed. 1997. (Americana Ser.). 203p. 29.95 (*0-7862-1060-5*) Thorndike Pr.

—A Little Yellow Dog. unabr. ed. 1997. (Easy Rawlins Mystery Ser.). audio 48.00 (*0-7366-3732-X*, 4410) Books on Tape, Inc.

—A Little Yellow Dog. (Easy Rawlins Mystery Ser.). 1997. 336p. pap. 14.00 (*0-671-01986-4*, Washington Square Pr.); 1997. 336p. mass mkt. 6.50 (*0-671-88429-8*, Pocket); 2002. 384p. reprint ed. pap. 14.00 (*0-7434-5180-5*, Washington Square Pr.) Simon & Schuster.

—A Little Yellow Dog: An Easy Rawlins Mystery. abr. ed. 1996. (Easy Rawlins Mystery Ser.). audio 16.95 (*1-55927-374-7*, 394056) Audio Renaissance.

—A Little Yellow Dog: An Easy Rawlins Mystery. (Easy Rawlins Mystery Ser.). 1996. 300p. 23.00 (*0-393-03924-2*); 100.00 (*0-393-03978-1*) Norton, W. W. & Co., Inc.

—A Little Yellow Dog: An Easy Rawlins Mystery. l.t. ed. 1996. (Basic Ser.). 447p. 28.95 (*0-7862-0810-4*) Thorndike Pr.

—A Red Death. abr. ed. (Easy Rawlins Mystery Ser.). 1993. audio 16.95 (*1-55927-234-1*, 391455); Set. 1994. audio 59.95 o.p. (*1-55927-270-8*) Audio Renaissance.

—A Red Death. unabr. ed. 1994. audio 48.00 (*0-7366-2833-9*, 3541) Books on Tape, Inc.

—A Red Death. 1991. (Easy Rawlins Mystery Ser.). 284p. 19.95 (*0-393-02998-0*) Norton, W. W. & Co., Inc.

—A Red Death. 1997. (Easy Rawlins Mystery Ser.). 272p. pap. 14.00 (*0-671-01984-8*, Washington Square Pr.); pap. 3.99 (*0-671-01006-9*, Pocket) Simon & Schuster.

—A Red Death. Chelius, Jane, ed. 1992. (Easy Rawlins Mystery Ser.). 256p. reprint ed. mass mkt. 6.99 (*0-671-74989-7*, Pocket) Simon & Schuster.

—Walkin' the Dog. l.t. ed. 2000. (Core Ser.). 301p. 31.95 (*0-7838-8961-5*, Macmillan Reference USA) Gale Group.

—Walkin' the Dog. 2000. 288p. pap. 13.95 (*0-316-88171-6*, Back Bay); 2000. 14.95 (*0-316-57054-0*); 1999. 272p. 24.95 o.p. (*0-316-96620-7*) Little Brown & Co.

—Walkin' the Dog. l.t. ed. 2001. (G. K. Hall Paperback Ser.). 301p. pap. 29.95 (*0-7838-8962-3*) Thorndike Pr.

—White Butterfly. abr. ed. 1993. (Easy Rawlins Mystery Ser.). audio 16.95 (*1-55927-224-4*, 391901) Audio Renaissance.

—White Butterfly. unabr. ed. 1994. (Easy Rawlins Mystery Ser.). audio 48.00 (*0-7366-2798-7*, 3513) Books on Tape, Inc.

—White Butterfly. 1992. (Easy Rawlins Mystery Ser.). 256p. 19.95 (*0-393-03366-X*) Norton, W. W. & Co., Inc.

—White Butterfly. (Easy Rawlins Mystery Ser.). 2002. 320p. pap. 14.00 (*0-7434-5177-5*); 1997. pap. 14.00 (*0-671-01985-6*) Simon & Schuster. (Washington Square Pr.).

—White Butterfly. Chelius, Jane, ed. 1993. (Easy Rawlins Mystery Ser.). 304p. reprint ed. mass mkt. 6.50 (*0-671-86787-3*, Pocket) Simon & Schuster.

—White Butterfly: Library Edition. unabr. ed. 1994. (Easy Rawlins Mystery Ser.). audio 59.95 o.p. (*1-55927-271-6*) Audio Renaissance.

Muller, Marcia. The Cheshire Cat's Eye: A Sharon McCone Mystery. l.t. ed. 1988. (Nightingale Ser.). 278p. pap. 12.95 o.p. (*0-8161-4396-X*, Macmillan Reference USA) Gale Group.

—A Wild & Lonely Place: A Sharon McCone Mystery. 1995. 300p. 19.95 o.s.i (*0-89296-526-6*) Mysterious Pr.

Munson, Douglas A. El Nino. 1990. 256p. 18.95 o.p. (*0-670-83134-4*, Viking) Viking Penguin.

Murray, Victoria Christopher. Joy. l.t. ed. 2002. (African American Ser.). 643p. 29.95 (*0-7862-3864-X*) Thorndike Pr.

—Joy. 2002. 400p. pap. 13.95 (*0-446-67944-5*); 2001. 384p. 23.95 o.p. (*0-446-52875-7*) Warner Bks., Inc. (Walk Worthy Pr.).

Murray, Yxta M. Locas. 1997. 256p. 22.00 o.p. (*0-8021-1605-1*, Grove Pr.) Grove/Atlantic, Inc.

Murray, Yxta Maya. The Conquest. 2003. 320p. pap. 12.95 (*0-06-009360-9*); 2002. 304p. 24.95 (*0-06-009359-5*) HarperTrade. (Rayo).

Mystery Scene Magazine Editors. Hollywood Kills. 1993. 416p. 21.00 o.p. (*0-88184-879-4*, Carroll & Graf Pubs.) Avalon Publishing Group.

Nagy, Gloria. Marriage: A Novel. 1995. 448p. 22.95 o.p. (*0-316-59675-2*) Little Brown & Co.

Nahai, Gina B. Moonlight on the Avenue of Faith. 1999. 384p. 24.00 o.s.i (*0-15-100388-2*) Harcourt Trade Pubs.

Nava, Michael. The Burning Plain. 1999. 432p. mass mkt. 5.99 o.s.i (*0-553-58085-X*) Bantam Bks.

—The Burning Plain. 1998. 240p. 23.95 o.p. (*0-399-14310-6*, G. P. Putnam's Sons) Penguin Group (USA) Inc.

—Death of Friends. 1996. 288p. 22.95 o.p. (*0-399-13977-X*, G. P. Putnam's Sons) Penguin Group (USA) Inc.

—The Death of Friends. 1998. 256p. reprint ed. mass mkt. 5.99 o.s.i (*0-553-57763-8*) Bantam Bks.

—Goldenboy. 1988. 216p. 5.95 o.p. (*1-55583-141-9*); 1996. 224p. reprint ed. pap. 10.00 o.p. (*1-55583-366-7*); 1991. 215p. reprint ed. pap. 8.95 o.p. (*1-55583-130-3*) Alyson Pubns.

—The Hidden Law. 2003. (Henry Rios Mystery Ser.). 232p. pap. 12.95 (*1-55583-778-6*, Alyson Bks.) Alyson Pubns.

—The Hidden Law. 1994. (Los Angeles Mysteries Ser.). 192p. mass mkt. 4.99 o.s.i (*0-345-38406-7*) Ballantine Bks.

—The Hidden Law. 1992. 288p. 19.00 o.p. (*0-06-016783-1*) HarperTrade.

—How Town. 1991. (Los Angeles Mysteries Ser.). 240p. mass mkt. 4.99 o.s.i (*0-345-36987-4*) Ballantine Bks.

—How Town. 1990. 224p. 16.95 o.p. (*0-06-016207-4*) HarperTrade.

—Howtown. 2003. (Henry Rios Mystery Ser.). 232p. pap. 12.95 (*1-55583-779-4*, Advocate Bks.) Alyson Pubns.

—The Little Death. 1997. 165p. reprint ed. pap. 9.95 o.p. (*1-55583-388-8*) Alyson Pubns.

—Rag & Bone: A Henry Rios Novel. 2001. 304p. 24.95 o.s.i (*0-399-14708-X*) Penguin Group (USA) Inc.

Nietzke, Ann. Windowlight. 1996. 200p. 12.00 o.p. (*1-56947-060-X*) Soho Pr., Inc.

—Windowlight: A Woman's Journal from the Edge of America. 1988. 224p. (Orig.). (C). reprint ed. pap. text 22.95 o.p. (*0-8095-4052-5*) Millefleurs.

Noguchi, Thomas T. & Lyons, Arthur. Unnatural Causes. 1989. 4.95 (*1-55773-264-7*, Diamond Bks.) Berkley Publishing Group.

—Unnatural Causes. 1988. 320p. 17.95 o.p. (*0-399-13354-2*) Putnam Publishing Group, The.

Norman, Barry. Birddog Tape. 1995. 236 p. 19.95 o.p. (*0-312-11753-1*, Saint Martin's Minotaur) St. Martin's Pr.

Nova, Craig. The Book of Dreams. 1994. 336p. 22.95 o.p. (*0-395-63650-7*) Houghton Mifflin Co.

—The Universal Donor. 1997. 288p. tchr. ed. 23.00 o.p. (*0-395-70938-5*) Houghton Mifflin Co.

—The Universal Donor. 1998. (Norton Paperback Fiction Ser.). 256p. pap. 13.00 (*0-393-31845-1*, Norton Paperbacks) Norton, W. W. & Co., Inc.

Noyola, Robert. City of Losers: Los Angeles Stories. 2000. 168p. pap. 20.99 (*0-7388-2806-8*); E-Book 8.00 (*0-7388-7248-2*) Xlibris Corp.

O'Brien, Darcy. Margaret in Hollywood. 1991. 320p. 20.95 o.p. (*0-688-09169-5*, Morrow, William & Co.) Morrow/Avon.

O'Rourke, F. M. The Poison Tree: A Novel. 1996. 368p. 23.00 o.p. (*0-684-80214-7*, Simon & Schuster) Simon & Schuster.

Osborne, Denise. Murder Offscreen. 1994. 310p. 19.95 o.p. (*0-8050-3113-8*) Holt, Henry & Co.

Parker, Robert B. Perchance to Dream. 1993. 288p. mass mkt. 6.99 o.s.i (*0-425-13131-9*) Berkley Publishing Group.

—Perchance to Dream. unabr. ed. 1994. (Spenser Ser.). audio 30.00 (*0-7366-2694-8*, 3428) Books on Tape, Inc.

—Perchance to Dream. abr. ed. 1993. 15.95 o.p. (*1-55800-291-X*, 41250) NewStar Media, Inc.

—Perchance to Dream. 1991. (Spenser Thriller Ser.). 272p. 19.95 o.p. (*0-399-13580-4*, G. P. Putnam's Sons) Penguin Group (USA) Inc.

Parker, Robert B. & Chandler, Raymond. Poodle Springs & Pastime. abr. ed. 1999. audio 25.00 (*0-7871-1894-X*, Dove Audio) NewStar Media, Inc.

Passman, Don. The Visionary. 2000. 432p. mass mkt. 7.99 o.s.i (*0-446-60831-9*) Warner Bks., Inc.

Passman, Donald S. Mirage. 2000. (Illus.). 336p. 25.95 o.p. (*0-446-52724-6*) Warner Bks., Inc.

—The Visionary. 1999. 448p. 25.00 o.p. (*0-446-52159-0*) Warner Bks., Inc.

Patchett, Ann. The Magician's Assistant. 368p. 1998. pap. 14.00 (*0-15-600621-9*, Harvest Bks.); 1997. 23.00 (*0-15-100263-0*) Harcourt Trade Pubs.

Paul, Jim. Medieval in L. A. A Delightful Romp Through Los Angeles as Seen Through the Mind of a Medieval Man. 1997. (Harvest Book Ser.). 240p. pap. 12.00 (*0-15-600537-9*, Harvest Bks.) Harcourt Trade Pubs.

—Medieval in L. A. A Fiction. 1988. 240p. text 21.00 o.p. (*1-887178-15-5*, Counterpoint Pr.) Basic Bks.

Pears, Iain. The Bernini Bust. 2003. 288p. pap. 13.00 (*0-425-19189-3*); 2001. 272p. reprint ed. mass mkt. 6.50 (*0-425-17884-6*) Berkley Publishing Group. (Prime Crime).

Pearson, Ridley. Hard Fall. unabr. ed. 1993. audio 80.00 (*0-7366-2528-3*, 3280) Books on Tape, Inc.

—Hard Fall. 1992. 416p. mass mkt. 6.99 o.s.i (*0-440-21262-6*) Dell Publishing.

Pendleton, Don. Copp for Hire. 1987. 272p. 16.95 o.p. (*1-55611-064-2*) Fine, Donald I. Bks.

—Copp in Deep. 1989. 252p. 17.95 o.p. (*1-55611-141-X*) Fine, Donald I. Bks.

—Copp in Deep. 1991. 256p. mass mkt. 4.50 o.p. (*0-06-100248-8*, HarperTorch) Morrow/Avon.

—Copp in Shock. 1992. 256p. 19.95 o.p. (*1-55611-287-4*) Fine, Donald I. Bks.

—Copp in Shock. 1993. 256p. mass mkt. 4.99 o.p. (*0-06-100459-6*, HarperTorch) Morrow/Avon.

—Copp in the Dark. l.t. ed. 1991. 19.95 o.p. (*0-7927-0982-9*, CH0157); pap. 17.95 o.p. (*0-7927-0983-7*, CS0256) BBC Audiobooks America.

—Copp in the Dark. 1990. (Joe Copp Ser.: No. 4). 18.95 o.p. (*1-55611-210-6*) Fine, Donald I. Bks.

—Copp in the Dark. 1992. 256p. mass mkt. 4.99 o.p. (*0-06-100347-6*, HarperTorch) Morrow/Avon.

—Copp on Fire. 1988. 16.95 o.p. (*1-55611-088-X*) Fine, Donald I. Bks.

—Copp on Fire. 1990. 256p. mass mkt. 4.50 o.p. (*0-06-100036-1*, HarperTorch) Morrow/Avon.
—Copp on Ice. 1991. 18.95 o.p. (*1-55611-235-1*) Fine, Donald I. Bks.
—Copp on Ice. 1992. 240p. mass mkt. 4.99 o.p. (*0-06-100458-8*, HarperTorch) Morrow/Avon.
—Termination Point: Four Horsemen Trilogy. 1999. (SuperBolan Ser.: No. 66). per. (*0-373-61466-7*, 1-61466-8, Worldwide Library) Harlequin Enterprises, Ltd.
Penn, W. S. The Absence of Angels: A Novel. 1995. (American Indian Literature & Critical Studies Ser.: Vol. 14). 272p. pap. 19.95 (*0-8061-2714-7*) Univ. of Oklahoma Pr.
Penn, William. The Absence of Angels. 1994. 274p. 28.00 (*1-877946-42-7*) Permanent Pr., The.
Pete, Eric E. Real for Me. 2000. 214p. pap. 14.95 (*0-9704995-2-3*) E-fect Publishing.
Peterson, Tracie & Bell, James Scott. Angels Flight. 2001. (Shannon Saga Ser.). 384p. pap. 12.99 (*0-7642-2419-0*) Bethany Hse. Pubs.
—City of Angels #1: Shannon Saga. 2000. (Shannon Saga Ser.: Vol. 1). 384p. pap. 12.99 (*0-7642-2418-2*) Bethany Hse. Pubs.
Petievich, Gerald. Earth Angels. 1991. 320p. mass mkt. 4.99 o.p. (*0-451-16885-2*); 1989. 288p. 17.95 o.p. (*0-453-00680-9*) NAL.
—Earth Angels. 2001. 308p. pap. 15.95 (*1-930916-15-9*) Virtual Publishing Group, Inc.
Phillips, Gary. Bad Night Is Falling. 1998. (Ivan Monk Mysteries Ser.). 320p. 21.95 o.s.i (*0-425-16302-4*) Berkley Publishing Group.
—Only the Wicked. 2000. 342p. 24.95 (*1-885173-64-4*) Write Way Publishing.
—Perdition, U. S. A. 1997. 272p. mass mkt. 5.99 o.s.i (*0-425-15900-0*, Prime Crime) Berkley Publishing Group.
—Perdition, U. S. A. 1994. 260p. pap. 13.00 o.p. (*0-9639050-6-6*, West Coast Crime) Blue Heron Publishing.
—Violent Spring. 1997. 27p. reprint ed. mass mkt. 5.99 o.s.i (*0-425-15625-7*, Prime Crime) Berkley Publishing Group.
—Violent Spring. 1994. 275p. pap. 9.00 o.p. (*1-883303-13-3*, West Coast Crime) Blue Heron Publishing.
Pierce, David M. As She Rides By. 1996. 224p. 20.95 o.p. (*0-312-13924-1*, Saint Martin's Minotaur) St. Martin's Pr.
Pike, Christopher, pseud. The Cold One. 1995. 394p. pap. text 5.99 o.s.i (*0-8125-1245-6*); 1994. 352p. 21.00 o.p. (*0-312-85117-0*) Doherty, Tom Assocs., LLC. (Tor Bks.).
Pillsbury, Samuel H. Conviction: A Novel. 1992. 213p. 21.95 o.p. (*0-8027-1225-8*) Walker & Co.
Platt, Randall Beth. The Royalscope Fe-As-Ko. 1997. 288p. 21.95 (*0-945774-35-4*, PS3566.L293R68) Catbird Pr.
Plesko, Les. The Last Bongo Sunset: A Novel. 1995. 269p. 21.00 o.s.i (*0-671-88049-7*, Simon & Schuster) Simon & Schuster.
Power, T. P. Proud Flesh. 2000. 192p. pap. 20.99 (*0-7388-2459-3*) Xlibris Corp.
Powers, Richard. Operation Wandering Soul. 2002. 352p. reprint ed. pap. 13.95 (*0-06-097611-X*, Perennial) HarperTrade.
—Operation Wandering Soul: A Novel. 1993. 352p. 23.00 o.p. (*0-688-11548-9*, Morrow, William & Co.) Morrow/Avon.
Powers, Tim. Expiration Date. 1995. 384p. 23.95 o.p. (*0-312-86086-2*); 1996. 534p. pap. text 6.99 (*0-8125-5517-1*) Doherty, Tom Assocs., LLC. (Tor Bks.).
—Expiration Date. 1924. o.s.i (*0-688-10733-8*, Morrow, William & Co.) Morrow/Avon.
Prather, Richard S. Shellshock. 1987. 352p. 16.95 o.p. (*0-312-93034-8*, Tor Bks.) Doherty, Tom Assocs., LLC.
Preiss, Byron. Raymond Chandler's Philip Marlowe. 1990. 6.99 o.p. (*0-517-05641-0*) Random Hse. Value Publishing.
Preiss, Byron, ed. Raymond Chandler's Philip Marlowe. 1990. 384p. reprint ed. pap. 12.95 o.p. (*0-399-51616-6*) Putnam Publishing Group, The.
—Raymond Chandler's Philip Marlowe: A Centennial Celebration. unabr. ed. 1993. 24.95 o.p. (*1-55800-485-8*) NewStar Media, Inc.
Pronzini, Bill. Sentinels: A "Nameless Detective" Mystery. 1996. 288p. 20.00 (*0-7867-0311-3*, Carroll & Graf Pubs.) Avalon Publishing Group.
—Sentinels: A "Nameless Detective" Mystery. l.t. ed. 1996. lib. bdg. 23.95 (*1-57490-074-9*, Beeler Large Print Bks.) Beeler, Thomas T. Publisher.
—Sentinels: A "Nameless Detective" Mystery. unabr. ed. 2000. (Nameless Detective Mystery Ser.). audio 49.95 (*0-7927-2207-8*, CSL 096) Chivers Audio Bks. GBR. *Dist:* BBC Audiobooks America.
Pryor, Josh. Monkey in the Middle. 2003. 288p. 24.00 (*0-7867-1173-6*, Carroll & Graf Pubs.) Avalon Publishing Group.
Pugh, Dianne G. Cold Call. Isaacson, Dana, ed. 1993. 288p. 20.00 (*0-671-77841-2*, Atria) Simon & Schuster.
—Fast Friends. 1997. 320p. 22.00 (*0-671-51912-3*, Atria) Simon & Schuster.
—Foolproof. 1998. (Iris Thorne Mystery Ser.). 344p. 23.00 (*0-671-01424-2*, Atria) Simon & Schuster.
—Slow Squeeze. Isaacson, Dana, ed. 1994. 320p. 20.00 o.p. (*0-671-77843-9*, Atria) Simon & Schuster.
—Slow Squeeze: An Iris Thorne Mystery. 1995. 288p. mass mkt. 5.99 (*0-671-77844-7*, Pocket) Simon & Schuster.
Queen, Ellery. The Four of Hearts: An Ellery Queen Mystery. 1994. 224p. reprint ed. pap. 8.00 o.p. (*0-06-097604-7*, Perennial) HarperTrade.
Randall, Stephen. The Other Side of Mulholland. 2001. 277p. 23.95 (*0-312-26216-7*, L. A. Weekly Bks.) St. Martin's Pr.
Rawles, Nancy. Crawfish Dreams. 2004. 368p. pap. 13.00 (*0-385-72213-3*, Anchor) Knopf Publishing Group.
—Crawfish Dreams: A Novel. 2003. 368p. 21.95 (*0-385-50418-7*) Doubleday Publishing.
—Love Like Gumbo. 1997. (Discoveries Ser.: No. 2). 272p. pap. 14.00 (*0-940242-75-3*) Fjord Pr.
Rayner, Richard. Los Angeles Without a Map: A Love Story. 1990. 208p. pap. 7.95 o.p. (*0-452-26370-0*, Plume) Dutton/Plume.
— Los Angeles Without a Map: A Love Story. 1988. 16.95 o.p. (*1-55584-268-2*) Grove/Atlantic, Inc.
— Los Angeles Without a Map: A Love Story. 1997. (Illus.). 192p. pap. 12.00 o.p. (*0-395-83809-6*, Mariner Bks.) Houghton Mifflin Co. Trade & Reference Div.
—Murder Book. 1999. 432p. mass mkt. 5.99 o.s.i (*0-06-109737-3*) HarperCollins Pubs.
—Murder Book. 2001. 384p. pap. 14.00 (*0-06-093828-5*, Perennial) HarperTrade.
—Murder Book. 1997. 384p. tchr. ed. 25.00 o.p. (*0-395-83625-5*) Houghton Mifflin Co.
Reaves, Michael. Night Hunter. 1997. 276p. mass mkt. 5.99 (*0-8125-1994-9*); 1995. 256p. 21.95 o.p. (*0-312-85318-1*) Doherty, Tom Assocs., LLC. (Tor Bks.).
Rechy, John. Bodies & Souls: A Novel. 2001. 448p. pap. 14.00 (*0-8021-3846-2*, Grove Pr.) Grove/Atlantic, Inc.
—The Coming of the Night. 256p. 1999. 23.00 o.p. (*0-8021-1650-7*); 2000. reprint ed. pap. 12.00 (*0-8021-3742-3*) Grove/Atlantic, Inc. (Grove Pr.).
—The Life & Adventures of Lyle Clemens. 2003. (Illus.). 352p. 24.00 (*0-8021-1746-5*, Grove Pr.) Grove/Atlantic, Inc.
—The Miraculous Day of Amalia Gomez: A Novel. 2001. 224p. pap. 13.00 (*0-8021-3847-0*, Grove Pr.) Grove/Atlantic, Inc.
Reed, Philip. Bird Dog. (Car Noir Thrillers Ser.). 1998. 336p. pap. 6.50 (*0-671-00165-5*, Pocket Star); 1997. 304p. 22.00 (*0-671-00163-9*, Atria) Simon & Schuster.
—Low Rider. 1998. (Car Noir Thrillers Ser.). 336p. 23.00 (*0-671-00166-3*, Atria) Simon & Schuster.
—Low Rider. l.t. ed. 1999. (Americana Ser.). 456p. 27.95 (*0-7862-1758-8*) Thorndike Pr.
Reese, Robert. Flying with One Wing. 1992. 176p. (Orig.). pap. 8.95 (*0-9633351-2-X*) Blue Pacific Pr.
Resnick, Rachel. Go West Young F*cked-Up Chick: A Novel of Separation. 256p. 2000. pap. 12.95 (*0-312-26329-5*, Saint Martin's Griffin); 1999. 22.95 o.p. (*0-312-19889-2*) St. Martin's Pr.
Revoyr, Nina. The Necessary Hunger. 1997. 368p. 22.50 (*0-684-83234-8*, Simon & Schuster) Simon & Schuster.
—The Necessary Hunger. 1998. 368p. pap. 14.95 (*0-312-18142-6*, Saint Martin's Griffin) St. Martin's Pr.
—Southland. 2003. 348p. pap. 15.95 (*1-888451-41-6*) Akashic Bks.
Ridley, John. Those Who Walk in Darkness. 2003. 320p. 24.95 (*0-446-53093-X*, Aspect) Warner Bks., Inc.
Rifkin, Alan. Signal Hill. 2003. 152p. pap. 12.95 (*0-87286-424-3*) City Lights Bks.
Robbins, Harold. The Storyteller. l.t. ed. 1987. 8.95 o.p. (*1-55504-244-9*); pap. 18.95 o.p. (*1-55504-359-3*) BBC Audiobooks America.
—The Storyteller. 1985. 17.45 o.p. (*0-671-55749-1*, Simon & Schuster) Simon & Schuster.
Roberts, Les. A Carrot for the Donkey: A Saxon Mystery. 1989. 256p. 16.95 o.p. (*0-312-02554-8*, Saint Martin's Minotaur) St. Martin's Pr.
—An Infinite Number of Monkeys. 1988. mass mkt. 2.95 (*0-312-91095-9*, St. Martin's Paperbacks); 1987. 176p. 12.95 o.p. (*0-312-00610-1*) St. Martin's Pr.
—The Lemon Chicken Jones. 1993. 288p. 20.95 o.p. (*0-312-10490-1*, Saint Martin's Minotaur) St. Martin's Pr.
—Not Enough Horses. 1988. 224p. mass mkt. 3.50 o.p. (*0-312-91225-0*, St. Martin's Paperbacks); 256p. 15.95 o.p. (*0-312-01485-6*, Saint Martin's Minotaur) St. Martin's Pr.
—Seeing the Elephant. 1992. 352p. 18.95 o.p. (*0-312-07081-0*, Saint Martin's Minotaur) St. Martin's Pr.
—Snake Oil. 1990. 17.95 o.p. (*0-312-04424-0*, Saint Martin's Minotaur) St. Martin's Pr.
Roberts, Paul W. Palace of Fears. 1997. 23.00 o.s.i (*0-679-43077-6*) Random Hse., Inc.
Robinson, Jill. Star Country. 9999. mass mkt. o.p. (*0-449-22257-8*, Fawcett); 1997. mass mkt. 6.50 o.s.i (*0-8041-1551-6*, Ivy Bks.) Ballantine Bks.
Rodriguez, Luis. The Republic of East L. A. Stories. 2002. 256p. 23.95 (*0-06-621263-4*) HarperCollins Pubs.
—The Republic of East L. A. Stories. 2003. 256p. pap. 12.95 (*0-06-093686-X*, Rayo) HarperTrade.
Rolfe, Lionel. Death & Redemption in London & LA. 2000. E-Book 10.99 (*1-929429-59-2*); E-Book 10.99 (*1-929429-60-6*) Dead End Street, LLC.
Rooney, Mickey. The Search for Sonny Skies: A Novel. l.t. ed. 1995. 314p. lib. bdg. 22.95 (*0-7838-1254-X*, Macmillan Reference USA) Gale Group.
Rosen, Marion. Death by Education. 1993. 224p. 17.95 o.p. (*0-312-09268-7*, Saint Martin's Minotaur) St. Martin's Pr.
Ross, JoAnn. Magnolia Moon. l.t. ed. 2003. 392p. 30.95 (*1-58724-467-5*, Wheeler Publishing, Inc.) Gale Group.
—Magnolia Moon. 2003. (Illus.). 384p. mass mkt. 6.99 (*0-7434-5743-9*, Pocket) Simon & Schuster.
Rossner, Judith. His Little Women. 1990. 19.95 o.p. (*0-671-64858-6*, Simon & Schuster) Simon & Schuster.
—His Little Women. Rubenstein, Julie, ed. 1991. 448p. reprint ed. mass mkt. 5.95 (*0-671-70124-X*, Pocket) Simon & Schuster.
Rovin, Jeff. Fatalis. 2000. 355p. 25.95 (*0-312-24103-8*); 2001. 368p. reprint ed. mass mkt. 6.99 (*0-312-98120-1*, St. Martin's Paperbacks) St. Martin's Pr.
Rubin, Charles. 4-F Blues: A Novel of WWII Hollywood. 2002. 308p. pap. 14.00 (*0-9679790-0-5*) NewCentury Pubs.
Rubin, Mann. Fast Friends Die Slow. 1998. 184p. per. 14.95 (*0-9668043-3-3*) Mesa Vista Pr.
Rucker, Lance. Intimate Falls: A Brandon Drake Novel. 2001. (Brandon Drake Mysteries). 405p. pap. (*0-9688274-0-3*) Lochenlode Publishing.
Russell, Jay. Greed & Stuff. 2001. 264p. 23.95 (*0-312-26168-3*, Saint Martin's Minotaur) St. Martin's Pr.
Russell, Jay S. Burning Bright. 1998. 288p. 23.95 o.p. (*0-312-18545-6*) St. Martin's Pr.
—Celestial Dogs. 1997. 272p. 22.95 o.p. (*0-312-15076-8*, Saint Martin's Minotaur) St. Martin's Pr.
Rust, Megan Mallory. Coffin Corner. 2000. (Alaskan Mystery Ser.). 224p. mass mkt. 5.99 o.s.i (*0-425-17508-1*) Berkley Publishing Group.
Ryman, Geoff. Was. 1993. 384p. pap. 13.95 (*0-14-017872-4*, Penguin Bks.) Penguin Group (USA) Inc.
—Was. 1994. 4.99 o.p. (*0-517-11656-1*) Random Hse. Value Publishing.
Saban, Cheryl. Sins of the Mother. abr. ed. 1997. 18.00 o.p. (*0-7871-1398-0*) NewStar Media, Inc.
Sadownick, Douglas. Sacred Lips of the Bronx. 1995. pap. 9.95 o.p. (*0-312-13165-8*, Saint Martin's Griffin); 1994. 240p. 21.95 o.p. (*0-312-11052-9*) St. Martin's Pr.
Sahgal, Ajay. Pool: A Novel. 224p. 1995. pap. 10.00 (*0-8021-3343-6*, Grove Pr.); 1994. 20.00 o.p. (*0-87113-559-0*, Atlantic Monthly Pr.) Grove/Atlantic, Inc.
Salzman, Mark. Lying Awake. 2001. (Illus.). 192p. reprint ed. pap. 12.00 (*0-375-70606-2*, Vintage) Knopf Publishing Group.
—Lying Awake, 4 cass. 2002. audio 19.99 (*1-4025-0174-9*, 00604) Recorded Bks., LLC.
—Lying Awake: A Novel. 2000. (Illus.). 192p. 22.00 (*0-375-40632-8*) Knopf, Alfred A. Inc.
—Lying Awake: A Novel. l.t. ed. 2001. (G. K. Hall Inspirational Ser.). 183p. 27.95 (*0-7838-9395-7*) Thorndike Pr.
Sanders, Lawrence. Stolen Blessings. l.t. ed. 1992. pap. 14.95 o.p. (*0-7927-0558-0*) BBC Audiobooks America.
Sandford, John, pseud. The Night Crew. 1998. 368p. mass mkt. 7.99 (*0-425-16338-5*) Berkley Publishing Group.
—The Night Crew. l.t. ed. 1997. 25.95 o.p. (*1-56895-497-2*, Wheeler Publishing, Inc.) Gale Group.
—The Night Crew. 1997. 368p. 23.95 o.s.i (*0-399-14237-1*, G. P. Putnam's Sons) Penguin Group (USA) Inc.
—The Night Crew. 23.95 o.s.i (*0-399-14552-4*) Putnam Publishing Group, The.
Sawyer, Robert J. Illegal Alien. 1997. 304p. 21.95 o.s.i (*0-441-00476-8*); 1999. 320p. reprint ed. mass mkt. 5.99 o.s.i (*0-441-00592-6*) Ace Bks.
Schempp, Mark A. Disintegration of the Mind: A Comedy for the Confused. 2000. 160p. pap. 20.99 (*0-7388-2737-1*) Xlibris Corp.
Schiller, Gerald A. Death Underground. unabr. ed. 1999. 220p. pap. 9.95 (*1-881164-84-5*) Intercontinental Publishing, Inc.
Schine, Cathleen. She Is Me: A Novel. 2003. 272p. 23.95 (*0-316-78609-8*) Little Brown & Co.
Schmidt, Carol. Cabin Fever. 1995. (Laney Samms Mysteries Ser.). 224p. pap. 10.95 (*1-56280-098-1*) Naiad Pr., Inc.
—Silverlake Heat. 1993. 224p. pap. 9.95 o.p. (*1-56280-031-0*) Naiad Pr., Inc.
—Sweet Cherry Wine. 1994. (Laney Samms Mysteries Ser.). 272p. pap. 9.95 (*1-56280-063-9*) Naiad Pr., Inc.
Schulberg, Budd. The Disenchanted. 1975. 416p. pap. 3.95 o.p. (*0-670-00584-3*, Penguin Bks.) Viking Penguin.
—What Makes Sammy Run? 1979. reprint ed. lib. bdg. 16.00 (*0-8376-0435-4*) Bentley Pubs.
—What Makes Sammy Run? 1994. reprint ed. lib. bdg. 32.95 (*1-56849-333-9*) Buccaneer Bks., Inc.
—What Makes Sammy Run? 1993. 352p. pap. 14.00 (*0-679-73422-8*, Vintage) Knopf Publishing Group.
—What Makes Sammy Run? 1990. 19.95 o.s.i (*0-394-57618-7*) Random Hse., Inc.
—What Makes Sammy Run? 1978. pap. 3.95 o.p. (*0-14-004795-6*, Penguin Bks.) Viking Penguin.
See, Carolyn. Golden Days. 1987. mass mkt. 3.95 o.s.i (*0-449-21437-0*, Fawcett) Ballantine Bks.
—Golden Days. 1987. 208p. text 15.95 o.p. (*0-07-056120-6*) McGraw-Hill Cos., The.
—Golden Days. 1996. (California Fiction Ser.). 196p. (C). pap. 15.95 (*0-520-20673-8*) Univ. of California Pr.
—Golden Days. 1996. E-Book 29.95 (*0-585-28774-0*) netLibrary, Inc.
—The Handyman. 2000. 272p. pap. 13.95 (*0-345-42660-6*, Ballantine Bks.) Ballantine Bks.
—The Handyman, unabr. ed. 1999. audio 24.95 (*1-57511-059-8*) Publishing Mills, Inc., The.
—The Handyman. l.t. ed. 1999. (Basic Ser.). 345p. 27.95 (*0-7862-2078-3*) Thorndike Pr.
—The Handyman: A Novel. 1999. 240p. 22.95 o.s.i (*0-375-50155-X*) Random Hse., Inc.
Sennett, Frank. Nash, Rambler. 2003. (Five Star First Edition Mystery Ser.). 339p. 25.95 (*0-7862-5034-8*, Five Star) Gale Group.
Seranella, Barbara. No Man Standing: A Munch Mancini Crime Novel. 2002. 304p. 24.00 (*0-7432-1386-6*, Scribner) Simon & Schuster.
—Unfinished Business: A Munch Mancini Crime Novel. 2001. 272p. 24.00 (*0-7432-1266-5*, Scribner) Simon & Schuster.
—Unpaid Dues. 2004. 320p. mass mkt. 6.99 (*0-7434-6637-3*, Pocket); 2003. 304p. 25.00 (*0-7432-4500-8*, Scribner) Simon & Schuster.
Shagan, Steve. A Cast of Thousands. l.t. ed. 1993. 22.95 o.p. (*1-56895-021-7*, Wheeler Publishing, Inc.) Gale Group.
—A Cast of Thousands. Grose, Bill, ed. 1993. 368p. 22.00 (*0-671-74132-2*, Atria); 1994. 384p. reprint ed. mass mkt. 5.99 (*0-671-74133-0*, Pocket) Simon & Schuster.
—Vendetta: High-Voltage Tension from the Streets of L. A. to the Jungles of Colombia. 1987. 288p. mass mkt. 4.50 o.s.i (*0-553-26733-7*) Bantam Bks.
Shah, Diane K. Dying Cheek to Cheek. 1992. 464p. 18.50 o.s.i (*0-385-42250-4*) Doubleday Publishing.
—High Heel Blue. 1997. 318p. 22.50 (*0-684-81431-5*, Simon & Schuster) Simon & Schuster.
Shannon, Dell. The Ace of Spades. l.t. ed. 1992. 18.95 o.p. (*0-7451-8385-9*); pap. 16.95 o.p. (*0-7927-1151-3*) BBC Audiobooks America.
—The Ace of Spades. 1984. reprint ed. pap. 3.95 o.p. (*0-89296-078-7*) Mysterious Pr.
—Appearances of Death. 1980. 208p. pap. 1.95 o.p. (*0-553-13953-3*) Bantam Bks.
—Appearances of Death. l.t. ed. 1981. 319p. reprint ed. 12.95 o.p. (*0-89621-319-6*) Thorndike Pr.
—Blood Count. 1988. 224p. mass mkt. (*0-373-26006-7*, Harlequin Bks.) Harlequin Enterprises, Ltd.
—Blood Count. 1989. 2.99 o.p. (*0-517-69441-7*) Random Hse. Value Publishing.
—Blood Count: The 37th Volume of a Detective Series. 1986. 224p. 15.95 o.p. (*0-688-06394-2*, Morrow, William & Co.) Morrow/Avon.
—Case Pending. l.t. ed. 1991. pap. 14.95 o.p. (*0-7927-0173-9*, C0214); 1990. 16.95 o.p. (*0-7451-9742-6*, C0066) BBC Audiobooks America.
—Case Pending. 1984. reprint ed. pap. 3.95 o.p. (*0-89296-076-0*) Mysterious Pr.
—Chaos of Crime. l.t. ed. 1988. lib. bdg. 14.95 o.p. (*1-85057-443-X*, Macmillan Reference USA) Gale Group.
—Chaos of Crime. 1988. 224p. reprint ed. pap. (*0-373-26015-6*, Harlequin Bks.) Harlequin Enterprises, Ltd.
—Chaos of Crime. 1985. 256p. 14.95 o.p. (*0-688-02297-9*, Morrow, William & Co.) Morrow/Avon.
—Cold Trail. 1989. 224p. reprint ed. mass mkt. (*0-373-26027-X*, Harlequin Bks.) Harlequin Enterprises, Ltd.
—The Death Bringers. l.t. ed. 1993. 21.95 o.p. (*0-7927-1513-6*) BBC Audiobooks America.

Settings

—The Death-Bringers. l.t. ed. 1993. pap. 19.95 o.p. (*0-7927-1512-8*); 1996. audio 54.95 (*0-7927-2205-1*, CSL094, Chivers Sound Library) BBC Audiobooks America.
—Death by Inches. l.t. ed. 1992. 18.95 o.p. (*0-7451-8425-1*); pap. 16.95 o.p. (*0-7927-1343-5*) BBC Audiobooks America.
—Death of a Busybody. l.t. ed. 1991. 17.95 o.p. (*0-7451-8024-8*, AH083); pap. 15.95 o.p. (*0-7927-0500-9*, AS0119) BBC Audiobooks America.
—Death of a Busybody. 1985. (Lt. Luis Mendoza Mystery Ser.). pap. 3.95 o.s.i (*0-89296-149-X*) Mysterious Pr.
—Destiny of Death. 1984. 227p. 14.95 o.p. (*0-688-03109-9*, Morrow, William & Co.) Morrow/Avon.
—Destiny of Death: A Luis Mendoza Mystery. 1991. 224p. reprint ed. mass mkt. (*0-373-26073-3*, Harlequin Bks.) Harlequin Enterprises, Ltd.
—The Dispossessed. 1988. 352p. 18.95 o.p. (*0-688-07998-9*, Morrow, William & Co.) Morrow/Avon.
—Double Bluff. l.t. ed. 1991. 17.95 o.p. (*0-7451-8173-2*, AH0227); pap. 15.95 o.p. (*0-7927-0708-7*, AS0263) BBC Audiobooks America.
—Double Bluff. 1985. (Lt. Luis Mendoza Mystery Ser.). pap. 3.95 o.p. (*0-89296-150-3*) Mysterious Pr.
—Exploit of Death. 1990. mass mkt. (*0-373-26061-X*, Harlequin Bks.) Harlequin Enterprises, Ltd.
—Exploit of Death. l.t. ed. 1983. (Luis Mendoza Mystery Ser.). 349p. reprint ed. 12.95 o.p. (*0-89621-493-1*) Thorndike Pr.
—Extra Kill. 1984. 256p. reprint ed. pap. 3.95 o.p. (*0-89296-080-9*) Mysterious Pr.
—Felony at Random. 1980. 224p. pap. 1.95 o.p. (*0-553-13954-1*) Bantam Bks.
—Felony at Random. l.t. ed. 1981. (Ulverscroft Large Print Ser.). 355p. 29.99 o.p. (*0-7089-0660-5*, Ulverscroft) Thorpe, F. A. Pubs. GBR. *Dist:* Ulverscroft Large Print Bks., Ltd., Ulverscroft Large Print Canada, Ltd.
—Felony File. l.t. ed. 1981. 374p. reprint ed. 10.95 o.p. (*0-89621-281-5*) Thorndike Pr.
—Knave of Hearts. 1984. reprint ed. pap. 3.95 o.p. (*0-89296-082-5*) Mysterious Pr.
—The Manson Curse. l.t. ed. 1992. 18.95 o.p. (*0-7451-8253-4*, AH0264); pap. 16.95 o.p. (*0-7927-0814-8*, AS0300) BBC Audiobooks America.
—The Manson Curse. 1990. 288p. 17.95 o.p. (*0-688-10119-4*, Morrow, William & Co.) Morrow/Avon.
—Mark of Murder. 1994. 256p. mass mkt. 4.50 o.p. (*0-7867-0043-2*, Carroll & Graf Pubs.) Avalon Publishing Group.
—Mark of Murder. l.t. ed. 1991. 12.95 o.p. (*0-7927-0147-X*, 4662); pap. 17.95 o.p. (*0-7927-0148-8*, C0079) BBC Audiobooks America.
—Mark of Murder: A Lieutenant Luis Mendoza Mystery. 1986. 240p. mass mkt. 3.95 (*0-445-40262-8*, Mysterious Pr. Paperback Bks.) Warner Bks., Inc.
—Motive on Record. 1990. mass mkt. (*0-373-26049-0*, Harlequin Bks.) Harlequin Enterprises, Ltd.
—The Motive on Record. l.t. ed. 1982. 364p. reprint ed. 12.95 o.p. (*0-89621-394-3*) Thorndike Pr.
—Murder by the Tale. 1987. 224p. 16.95 o.p. (*0-688-07538-X*, Morrow, William & Co.) Morrow/Avon.
—Murder by the Tale. 1989. 2.99 o.p. (*0-517-69454-9*) Random Hse. Value Publishing.
—Murder Most Strange. 1989. mass mkt. (*0-373-26037-7*, Harlequin Bks.) Harlequin Enterprises, Ltd.
—Murder Most Strange. l.t. ed. 1982. 354p. 12.95 o.p. (*0-89621-377-3*) Thorndike Pr.
—Root of All Evil. 1993. 208p. mass mkt. 3.95 o.p. (*0-88184-978-2*, Carroll & Graf Pubs.) Avalon Publishing Group.
—Root of All Evil. l.t. ed. 1993. 21.95 o.p. (*0-7927-1771-6*); pap. 19.95 o.p. (*0-7927-1770-8*) BBC Audiobooks America.
—Root of All Evil. 1986. 288p. reprint ed. mass mkt. 3.95 (*0-445-40259-8*, Mysterious Pr. Paperback Bks.) Warner Bks., Inc.
—The Scalpel & the Sword. 1987. 416p. 18.95 o.p. (*0-688-07216-X*, Morrow, William & Co.) Morrow/Avon.
—Sorrow to the Grave. 1992. 18.00 o.p. (*0-688-11577-2*, Morrow, William & Co.) Morrow/Avon.
—Streets of Death. 1980. 192p. pap. 1.95 o.p. (*0-553-13952-5*) Bantam Bks.
—Streets of Death. l.t. ed. 1980. 315p. reprint ed. 9.95 o.p. (*0-89621-250-5*) Thorndike Pr.
Shannon, John. The Concrete River. 1998. (Jack Liffey Mystery Ser.). 240p. reprint ed. mass mkt. 5.99 o.s.i (*0-425-16193-5*, Prime Crime) Berkley Publishing Group.
—The Concrete River. 1996. 192p. pap. 12.00 o.p. (*0-9639050-5-8*, West Coast Crime) Blue Heron Publishing.
—The Cracked Earth. 1999. (Jack Liffey Mystery Ser.). 288p. mass mkt. 5.99 o.s.i (*0-425-16732-1*) Berkley Publishing Group.
—The Poison Sky. 2000. (Jack Liffey Mystery Ser.). 241p. mass mkt. 5.99 o.s.i (*0-425-17424-7*, Prime Crime) Berkley Publishing Group.
—Streets on Fire: A Jack Liffey Mystery. Penzler, Otto, ed. 2002. 240p. 24.00 (*0-7867-1018-7*, Carroll & Graf Pubs.) Avalon Publishing Group.
Shayne, Maggie B. Kiss of the Shadow Man. 1994. (Shadows Ser.). mass mkt. (*0-373-27038-0*, 1-27038-8, Harlequin Bks.) Harlequin Enterprises, Ltd.
Sheldon, Mary. Reflection. 2004. 30p. mass mkt. 6.99 (*0-7582-0311-X*, Kensington Bks.); 2003. 320p. 23.00 (*0-7582-0308-X*) Kensington Publishing Corp.
Sherman, David J. The Dark Side. 2002. 348p. pap. 12.95 o.p. (*1-892343-26-6*, Oak Tree Pr.) Oak Tree Publishing.
—The Dark Side: A Jack Murphy Novel. 2002. 352p. per. 14.95 (*1-932306-51-X*) Bloody Mist Pr.
Shirley, John. Wetbones. 1999. 352p. mass mkt. 5.50 (*0-8439-4525-7*, Leisure Bks.) Dorchester Publishing Co., Inc.
—Wetbones. 1992. 25.00 o.p. (*0-929480-63-5*); 65.00 o.p. (*0-929480-64-3*) Ziesing, Mark V.
—Wetbones. 1999. E-Book 9.95 (*0-585-29892-0*) netLibrary, Inc.
Shoemaker, Bill. Fire Horse. 1996. mass mkt. 5.99 o.s.i (*0-449-14974-9*, Fawcett) Ballantine Bks.
—Fire Horse. l.t. ed. 1995. (Niagara Large Print Ser.). 415p. 29.50 o.p. (*0-7089-5802-8*, Ulverscroft) Thorpe, F. A. Pubs. GBR. *Dist:* Ulverscroft Large Print Bks., Ltd.
Shuken, Julia. In the House of My Pilgrimage. 1995. 256p. pap. 10.99 (*0-89107-839-8*) Crossway Bks.
Silver, Marisa. Babe in Paradise. 2001. 224p. 23.95 (*0-393-02003-7*) Norton, W. W. & Co., Inc.
Simon, Roger L. The Big Fix. 1924. o.s.i (*1-55710-050-0*, Morrow, William & Co.) Morrow/Avon.
—The Big Fix. 1978. pap. 1.95 o.p. (*0-671-82010-9*, Pocket) Simon & Schuster.
—The Big Fix. 1986. 208p. mass mkt. 3.50 o.s.i (*0-446-30043-8*) Warner Bks., Inc.
—The Big Fix. 2000. (Moses Wine Mystery Ser.). (Illus.). 192p. reprint ed. pap. 14.00 (*0-671-03906-7*) ibooks, Inc.
—California Roll. 1986. 208p. mass mkt. 3.50 o.s.i (*0-446-32965-7*) Warner Bks., Inc.
—The Lost Coast. 1997. 79p. 22.50 o.p. (*0-06-017707-1*) HarperTrade.
—The Lost Coast. 272p. 2003. mass mkt. 6.99 (*0-7434-5913-X*); 2000. reprint ed. pap. 14.00 (*0-671-03904-0*) ibooks, Inc.
—The Straight Man. 1987. 240p. mass mkt. 3.95 (*0-446-34389-7*) Warner Bks., Inc.
—Wild Turkey: A Moses Wine Mystery. 1986. 240p. mass mkt. 3.50 o.s.i (*0-446-30044-6*) Warner Bks., Inc.
—Wild Turkey: A Moses Wine Mystery. 2000. (Moses Wine Mysteries Ser.). 208p. pap. 14.00 (*0-7434-0012-7*) ibooks, Inc.
Sisters in Crime, Los Angeles Chapter Staff. Murder by Thirteen. English, Priscilla et al, eds. 1997. 176p. pap. 10.95 (*0-9647945-3-5*, Intrigue Pr.) Corvus Publishing.
Slim, Iceberg. Doom Fox. 1998. 256p. pap. 12.00 (*0-8021-3588-9*, Grove Pr.) Grove/Atlantic, Inc.
—Doom Fox. viii, 260p. pap. 11.95 (*0-86241-762-7*) Payback Pr. GBR. *Dist:* AK Pr. Distribution.
Smith, April. North of Montana. 1995. 368p. mass mkt. 6.99 (*0-449-22502-X*, Fawcett) Ballantine Bks.
—North of Montana. l.t. ed. 1995. (Large Print Ser.). 352p. lib. bdg. 23.95 (*1-57490-035-8*, Beeler Large Print Bks.) Beeler, Thomas T. Publisher.
—North of Montana. abr. ed. 1994. audio 17.00 o.s.i (*0-679-43652-9*, RH Audio) Random Hse. Audio Publishing Group.
Smith, Charlie. Chimney Rock: A Novel. 1997. 352p. pap. 14.00 o.p. (*0-8050-5592-4*, Owl Bks.); 1993. 400p. 22.50 o.p. (*0-8050-2244-9*) Holt, Henry & Co.
Smith, Mark Haskell. Moist: A Novel. 2002. 320p. 24.95 (*0-312-30364-5*, L. A. Weekly Bks.) St. Martin's Pr.
Snyder, Keith. Coffin's Got the Dead Guy on the Inside. 1999. mass mkt. 5.99 (*0-440-23536-7*); 320p. mass mkt. 5.99 o.s.i (*0-440-23541-3*) Dell Publishing.
—Coffin's Got the Dead Guy on the Inside. l.t. ed. 1998. (Jason Keltner Mysteries Ser.). 300p. 22.95 (*0-8027-3320-4*) Walker & Co.
—The Night Men: A Jason Keltner Mystery. 2001. 312p. 23.95 (*0-8027-3370-0*) Walker & Co.
—Show Control. 1996. 267p. 20.95 o.p. (*1-885173-11-3*) Write Way Publishing.
—Trouble Comes Back. 1999. (Jason Keltner Mysteries Ser.). 318p. 22.95 (*0-8027-3338-7*) Walker & Co.
Songer, C. J. Bait. 1999. 384p. mass mkt. 6.99 (*0-06-101424-9*, HarperTorch) Morrow/Avon.
—Bait. 1998. 320p. 23.00 (*0-684-85042-7*, Scribner) Simon & Schuster.
—Hook. 1999. 304p. 24.00 o.s.i (*0-684-85043-5*, Scribner) Simon & Schuster.
Sonnett, Sherry. Restraint. 1996. 320p. mass mkt. 5.99 o.s.i (*0-451-18642-7*, Signet Bks.) NAL.
Sonnett, Shery. Restraint. 1995. 319p. 21.00 (*0-671-87958-8*, Simon & Schuster) Simon & Schuster.
Southern, Terry. Blue Movie. 6.95 o.p. (*0-453-00331-1*, Dutton); 1985. pap. 7.95 o.p. (*0-452-25723-9*, Plume) Dutton/Plume.
—Blue Movie. 2001. 256p. reprint ed. pap. 12.00 (*0-8021-3466-1*) Grove/Atlantic, Inc.
—Blue Movie. 1971. mass mkt. 1.50 o.p. (*0-451-06173-X*, W6173); mass mkt. 1.25 o.p. (*0-451-04608-0*) NAL. (Signet Bks.).
Spencer, John B. Quake City. 1997. 158p. pap. 12.95 (*1-899344-02-0*) Dufour Editions, Inc.
Spies, Sidney. Vacant Eyes. 1992. 400p. mass mkt. 4.99 o.s.i (*0-440-20985-4*) Dell Publishing.
Spillane, Mickey. Kiss Me Deadly. 1953. mass mkt. 2.95 o.p. (*0-451-13602-0*); reprint ed. mass mkt. 3.95 o.p. (*0-451-16593-4*) NAL. (Signet Bks.).
Spiotta, Dana. Lightning Field. 224p. 2002. pap. 12.00 (*0-7432-2375-6*); 2001. 23.00 (*0-7432-1261-4*) Simon & Schuster. (Scribner).
Stebel, S. L. The Boss's Wife. 1992. 252p. 19.95 o.p. (*0-8027-1198-7*) Walker & Co.
Steel, Danielle. Secrets. 1985. 336p. 19.95 o.s.i (*0-385-29418-2*, Delacorte Pr.) Dell Publishing.
—Secrets. l.t. ed. 1986. (Special Editions Ser.). 18.95 o.p. (*0-8161-4013-8*, Macmillan Reference USA) Gale Group.
—The Wedding. 2000. 408p. 200.00 (*0-385-31830-8*, Dial Bks.); 2001. 528p. reprint ed. mass mkt. 7.99 (*0-440-23685-1*) Dell Publishing.
—The Wedding. l.t. ed. 2001. 576p. pap. 13.95 (*0-375-72806-6*) Random Hse. Large Print.
Stewart, Ed. Doomsday Flight. 1995. 475p. pap. 11.99 (*1-56476-482-6*, 6-3482) Cook Communications Ministries.
—Millennium's Dawn. 1994. 480p. pap. 11.99 o.p. (*1-56476-345-5*, 6-3345) Cook Communications Ministries.
—Millennium's Eve. 1993. 448p. pap. 12.99 (*1-56476-133-9*, 6-3133) Cook Communications Ministries.
Stone, Katherine. Happy Endings. l.t. ed. 1995. 23.95 o.p. (*1-56895-216-3*, Wheeler Publishing, Inc.) Gale Group.
—Happy Endings. 1996. 384p. mass mkt. 6.99 (*0-8217-5250-2*); 1995. 384p. mass mkt. 5.99 o.s.i (*0-8217-4856-4*); 1994. 368p. mass mkt. 15.95 o.p. (*0-8217-4646-4*) Kensington Publishing Corp. (Zebra Bks.).
—Illusions. l.t. ed. 1994. 512p. reprint ed. lib. bdg. 20.95 o.p. (*0-8161-5946-7*, Macmillan Reference USA) Gale Group.
—Illusions. 1996. 418p. mass mkt. 6.99 (*0-8217-5247-2*, Zebra Bks.); 1994. 448p. mass mkt. 5.99 o.s.i (*0-8217-4617-0*); 1994. mass mkt. 18.95 o.s.i (*0-8217-4453-4*, Zebra Bks.) Kensington Publishing Corp.
Stromme, Elizabeth. Joe's Word: An Echo Park Novel. 2003. (City Lights Noir Ser.). 224p. pap. 11.95 (*0-87286-425-1*) City Lights Bks.
Sublett, Jesse. Boiled in Concrete. 1999. pap. 3.95 (*0-14-015230-X*); 1992. 320p. 20.00 o.p. (*0-670-83888-8*) Viking Penguin. (Viking).
Swart, Carter. Insufficient Evidence. 2001. 304p. 27.95 (*0-9704304-4-2*); 372p. pap. 16.95 (*0-9704304-5-0*) Hilliard & Harris.
Swindle, Renee. Please Please Please. 2000. 336p. mass mkt. 6.99 (*0-440-22376-8*) Dell Publishing.
Tanney, Katherine. Carousel of Progress. 2001. 272p. pap. 19.00 (*0-8129-9254-7*, Villard Bks.) Random House Adult Trade Publishing Group.
Taylor, Erika. The Sun Maiden. 1991. 288p. 19.95 o.p. (*0-689-12130-X*, Scribner) Simon & Schuster.
Telushkin, Joseph. An Eye for an Eye. 1992. 288p. mass mkt. 4.99 o.s.i (*0-553-29620-5*) Bantam Bks.
—An Eye for an Eye. 1991. 272p. 15.00 o.s.i (*0-385-42116-8*) Doubleday Publishing.
Teran, Boston. Never Count Out the Dead. 2001. E-Book 23.95 (*1-58945-789-7*) Adobe Systems, Inc.
—Never Count Out the Dead. E-Book 23.95 (*0-312-70156-X*); 2002. 384p. mass mkt. 6.99 (*0-312-98020-5*, St. Martin's Paperbacks); 2001. 366p. 23.95 (*0-312-27115-8*, Saint Martin's Minotaur) St. Martin's Pr.
Tervalon, Jervey. Understand This. 1999. pap. 15.00 (*0-385-50021-1*) Doubleday Publishing.
—Understand This. 1995. 272p. pap. 19.00 o.s.i (*0-385-47824-0*) Knopf, Alfred A. Inc.
—Understand This. 1994. 271p. 20.00 o.p. (*0-688-04560-X*, Morrow, William & Co.) Morrow/Avon.
—Understand This. 2000. (California Fiction Ser.). 271p. pap. text 15.95 (*0-520-22355-1*) Univ. of California Pr.
Thomas, Ross. Ah, Treachery! 1994. 288p. 21.95 o.s.i (*0-89296-452-9*) Mysterious Pr.
—Ah, Treachery!, unabr. ed. audio 51.00 (*0-7887-0260-2*, 94469E7) Recorded Bks., LLC.
—Ah, Treachery! 2004. 288p. pap. 13.95 (*0-312-32704-8*, Saint Martin's Griffin) St. Martin's Pr.
—Ah, Treachery! 1995. 272p. mass mkt. 5.99 o.s.i (*0-446-40031-9*) Warner Bks., Inc.
Thomas, Trisha R. Roadrunner: A Novel. 2003. 288p. pap. 12.00 (*1-4000-4791-9*) Crown Publishing Group.
—Roadrunner: A Novel. 2002. 288p. 22.95 (*0-609-60584-4*, Compass American Guides, Inc.) Fodor's Travel Pubns.
—Would I Lie to You? A Novel. 2004. (Illus.). 304p. 22.00 (*1-4000-4874-5*, Crown) Crown Publishing Group.
Thompson, Jim. The Grifters. 1985. 196p. reprint ed. pap. 3.95 o.p. (*0-916870-90-1*, Black Mask) Creative Arts Bk. Co.
—The Grifters. 1990. (Vintage Crime/Black Lizard Ser.). 208p. pap. 11.00 (*0-679-73248-9*, Vintage) Knopf Publishing Group.
Thorp, Roderick. Nothing Lasts Forever. 1983. mass mkt. 2.50 o.s.i (*0-345-28781-9*) Ballantine Bks.
—Nothing Lasts Forever. 1979. 9.95 o.p. (*0-393-01249-2*) Norton, W. W. & Co., Inc.
—Rainbow Drive. 1987. mass mkt. 4.99 o.s.i (*0-8041-0170-1*, Ivy Bks.) Ballantine Bks.
—Rainbow Drive. 1986. 320p. 18.45 o.p. (*0-671-49981-5*) Summit Bks.
Tobar, Hector. Tattooed Soldier: A Novel. 2000. 320p. 23.00 (*1-883285-15-1*) Delphinium Bks., Inc.
—Tattooed Soldier: A Novel. 2000. 320p. 12.95 (*0-14-028861-9*) Viking Penguin.
Tolkin, Michael. The Player. 1997. 208p. pap. 12.00 (*0-8021-3513-7*, Grove Pr.); 1988. 204p. 17.95 o.p. (*0-87113-228-1*) Grove/Atlantic, Inc.
—The Player. 1992. pap. 10.00 (*0-394-23924-5*); 1989. pap. 10.00 o.s.i (*0-679-72254-8*) Knopf Publishing Group. (Vintage).
—The Player. 1992. audio 16.00 o.p. (*0-679-41849-0*, RH Audio) Random Hse. Audio Publishing Group.
—The Player. 1993. 3.99 o.p. (*0-517-10912-3*) Random Hse. Value Publishing.
Townsend, Larry. The Case of the Severed Head. 1994. 239p. (Orig.). pap. 8.95 (*1-881684-04-0*) L.T. Pubns.
—One for the Master, Two for the Fool: A Bruce MacLeod Mystery. 1992. 214p. pap. 9.95 (*1-55583-209-1*) Alyson Pubns.
Traylor, James L., ed. Hollywood Troubleshooter: W. T. Ballards Bill Lennox Stories. 1985. 156p. 19.95 (*0-87972-316-5*, Popular Pr.) Univ. of Wisconsin Pr.
Trevino, Jesus. The Fabulous Sinkhole & Other Stories. 1995. 164p. pap. 9.95 o.p. (*1-55885-129-1*) Arte Publico Pr.
Vanderhaeghe, Guy. The Englishman's Boy. 1998. 352p. pap. 14.00 (*0-312-19544-3*); 1997. 336p. 24.00 o.p. (*0-312-16823-3*) Picador.
Ventura, Michael. The Zoo Where You're Fed to God: A Novel. 1994. 256p. 21.00 o.s.i (*0-671-89222-3*, Simon & Schuster) Simon & Schuster.
Vida. Goodbye, Saigon. Date not set. mass mkt. (*0-449-22404-X*, Fawcett) Ballantine Bks.
Vida, Nina. Goodbye, Saigon. 1995. mass mkt. 5.99 o.s.i (*0-449-22422-8*, Fawcett) Ballantine Bks.
—Goodbye, Saigon. Set. abr. ed. 1994. 17.95 o.p. (*0-7871-0218-0*) NewStar Media, Inc.
Vidal, Gore. Hollywood: A Novel of America in the 1920's. 1991. (American Chronicle Ser.). 432p. mass mkt. 7.99 o.s.i (*0-345-37013-9*, Ballantine Bks.) Ballantine Bks.
—Hollywood: A Novel of America in the 1920's. unabr. ed. 1993. (American Chronicles Ser.). audio 104.00 (*0-7366-2529-1*, 3281) Books on Tape, Inc.
—Hollywood: A Novel of America in the 1920's. 2000. (International Ser.). 448p. pap. 15.00 (*0-375-70875-8*, Vintage) Knopf Publishing Group.
—Hollywood: A Novel of America in the 1920's. aut. ed. 1999. 24.95 (*0-676-58932-4*, Modern Library) Random House Adult Trade Publishing Group.
—Hollywood: A Novel of America in the 1920's. 1993. 4.99 o.p. (*0-517-10710-4*); 1992. 5.99 o.p. (*0-517-08085-0*) Random Hse. Value Publishing.
—Hollywood: A Novel of America in the 1920's. 1999. (Modern Library Ser.). 640p. 24.95 o.s.i (*0-679-60292-5*) Random Hse., Inc.
—Myron. 1975. mass mkt. 1.75 o.s.i (*0-345-24625-X*, Ballantine Bks.) Ballantine Bks.
Wagman, Diana. Bump. 2004. 336p. pap. 13.00 (*0-7867-1276-7*); 2003. 288p. 24.00 (*0-7867-1106-X*) Avalon Publishing Group. (Carroll & Graf Pubs.).
—Spontaneous. 2000. 261p. 23.95 (*0-312-26234-5*); 2001. 272p. reprint ed. pap. 13.95 (*0-312-28349-0*) St. Martin's Pr. (L. A. Weekly Bks.).
Wagner, Bruce. I'll Let You Go: A Novel. 576p. 2003. pap. 13.95 (*0-8129-6847-6*); 2002. (Illus.). 25.95 (*0-375-50002-2*, Villard Bks.) Random House Adult Trade Publishing Group.
—I'm Losing You. 1997. 336p. pap. 12.95 (*0-452-27868-6*, Signet Bks.) Dutton/Plume.
Waldman, Ayelet. The Big Nap: A Mommy Track Mystery. 240p. 2001. 21.95 o.s.i (*0-425-17949-4*); 2002. reprint ed. mass mkt. 6.99 (*0-425-18452-8*) Berkley Publishing Group. (Prime Crime).

—Nursery Crimes: A Mommy Track Mystery. (Mommy-Track Mysteries Ser.). 2000. 215p. 21.95 o.s.i (*0-425-17469-7*); 2001. 240p. reprint ed. mass mkt. 6.99 (*0-425-18000-X*, Prime Crime) Berkley Publishing Group.
—A Playdate with Death: A Mommy Track Mystery. 2002. 240p. 22.95 (*0-425-18473-0*, Prime Crime) Berkley Publishing Group.
Wallace, Connie. Any Way the Wind Blows. 1999. 351p. mass mkt. 6.99 (*0-9668039-0-6*) Wallace, Connie.
Walpow, Nathan. One Last Hit. 2003. 377p. pap. 14.95 (*0-9724412-0-4*) UglyTown.
Wambaugh, Joseph. The Choirboys. unabr. ed. 1976. audio 64.00 (*0-7366-0014-0*, 1024) Books on Tape, Inc.
—The Choirboys. 1987. 384p. mass mkt. 7.50 (*0-440-11188-9*); 1975. 8.95 o.p. (*0-440-05363-3*, Delacorte Pr.) Dell Publishing.
—The Glitter Dome. 1984. mass mkt. 4.50 o.s.i (*0-553-26302-1*); 1982. 352p. mass mkt. 6.99 (*0-553-27259-4*) Bantam Bks.
—The New Centurions. unabr. ed. audio 59.50 Audio Bk. Co.
—The New Centurions. 1987. 368p. mass mkt. 7.50 (*0-440-16417-6*) Dell Publishing.
—The New Centurions. 1971. 30.00 o.p. (*0-316-92145-9*) Little Brown & Co.
—The Secrets of Harry Bright. 1986. 352p. pap. 19.00 (*0-553-76287-7*) Bantam Bks.
—The Secrets of Harry Bright. l.t. ed. 1986. 444p. 18.95 o.p. (*0-8161-4066-9*); pap. 10.95 o.p. (*0-8161-4069-3*) Gale Group. (Macmillan Reference USA).
—The Secrets of Harry Bright. 1985. 345p. 17.95 o.p. (*0-688-05958-9*, Morrow, William & Co.) Morrow/Avon.
Ward, Robert. The Cactus Garden. 1996. 320p. mass mkt. 6.99 (*0-671-88266-X*, Pocket) Simon & Schuster.
—The Cactus Garden. Grose, William, ed. 1995. 304p. 22.00 o.p. (*0-671-88265-1*, Atria) Simon & Schuster.
Waugh, Evelyn. The Loved One. unabr. collector's ed. 1992. audio 24.00 (*0-7366-2108-3*, 2912) Books on Tape, Inc.
—The Loved One. 1994. reprint ed. lib. bdg. 27.95 (*1-56849-358-4*) Buccaneer Bks., Inc.
—The Loved One. rev. ed. 1977. 13.95 o.s.i (*0-316-92618-3*) Little Brown & Co.
—The Loved One. l.t. ed. 1999. (Perennial Bestsellers Ser.). 131p. 27.95 (*0-7838-8787-6*) Thorndike Pr.
—The Loved One. lib. bdg. 20.95 (*1-56723-177-2*) Yestermorrow, Inc.
—The Loved One: A Novel. rev. ed. 1977. (Illus.). 176p. pap. 13.95 (*0-316-92608-6*, Back Bay) Little Brown & Co.
West, Nathanael. A Cool Million & the Dream Life of Balso Snell. Date not set. lib. bdg. 18.95 (*0-8488-2174-2*) Amereon, Ltd.
White, Curtis. The Idea of Home. 1992. (New American Fiction Ser.: No. 27). 208p. (Orig.). pap. 12.95 (*1-55713-144-9*) Sun & Moon Pr.
White, Teri. Tightrope. 228p. 1987. mass mkt. 3.95 o.s.i (*0-445-40579-1*); 1986. 15.95 o.p. (*0-89296-234-8*) Mysterious Pr.
Wicinas, David. Sagebrush & Cappuccino: Confessions of an L. A. Naturalist. 2000. 228p. pap. 14.95 (*0-595-00198-X*) iUniverse, Inc.
—Sagebrush & Cappuccino: Confessions of an LA Naturalist. 1995. 160p. (Orig.). pap. 13.00 o.p. (*0-87156-435-1*) Sierra Club Bks.
Wilkins, Barbara. In Name Only: A Novel. 1992. 432p. 20.00 o.p. (*0-06-017957-0*) HarperTrade.
Williams, Billy Dee. Twilight. Date not set. E-Book (*0-312-70749-5*, Tor Bks.) Doherty, Tom Assocs., LLC.
Williams, Billy Dee & Bowman, Elizabeth Atkins. Twilight. 2002. 432p. 25.95 (*0-312-87909-1*, Forge Bks.) Doherty, Tom Assocs., LLC.
Willis, Connie. Remake. 1996. 176p. mass mkt. 5.99 (*0-553-57441-8*) Bantam Bks.
—Remake. ltd. ed. 1994. 45.00 (*0-929480-48-1*) Ziesing, Mark V.
Wilson, John Morgan. Blind Eye: A Benjamin Justice Novel. 2003. 288p. 23.95 (*0-312-30919-8*, Saint Martin's Minotaur) St. Martin's Pr.
—Justice at Risk: A Benjamin Justice Mystery. 2000. (Benjamin Justice Mystery Ser.). 368p. mass mkt. 6.50 (*0-553-57860-X*) Bantam Bks.
—Justice at Risk: A Benjamin Justice Mystery. 1999. (Benjamin Justice Mystery Ser.). 304p. 22.95 o.s.i (*0-385-49116-6*) Doubleday Publishing.
—Revision of Justice: A Benjamin Justice Mystery. 1999. (Benjamin Justice Mystery Ser.). 416p. mass mkt. 5.99 (*0-553-57533-3*) Bantam Bks.
—Simple Justice: A Benjamin Justice Mystery. 1997. (Benjamin Justice Mystery Ser.). 304p. mass mkt. 6.50 o.s.i (*0-553-57532-5*) Bantam Bks.
—Simple Justice: A Benjamin Justice Mystery. 1996. 256p. 21.00 o.s.i (*0-385-48234-5*) Doubleday Publishing.
Wolitzer, Hilma. Tunnel of Love. 384p. 1995. pap. 12.00 o.p. (*0-06-118010-6*, Perennial); 1994. 20.00 o.p. (*0-06-118007-6*) HarperTrade.
Wolper, Carol. The Cigarette Girl. 1999. 208p. 22.95 o.p. (*1-57322-137-6*, Riverhead Bks. (Hardcovers)) Putnam Publishing Group, The.
—The Cigarette Girl: A Novel. 2000. 288p. pap. 12.95 (*1-57322-818-4*, Riverhead Trade (Paperbacks)) Berkley Publishing Group.
—Secret Celebrity. 2002. 336p. 24.95 o.s.i (*1-57322-214-3*, Riverhead Bks. (Hardcovers)) Putnam Publishing Group, The.
Wood, William P. Stay of Execution. Zion, Claire, ed. 1994. 416p. mass mkt. 5.99 (*0-671-73179-3*, Pocket) Simon & Schuster.
—Stay of Execution. 1993. o.s.i (*0-671-73178-5*, Atria) Simon & Schuster.
Woods, Paula L. Inner City Blues: A Charlotte Justice Novel. 1999. 316p. 23.95 (*0-393-04680-X*) Norton, W. W. & Co., Inc.
—Stormy Weather. 304p. 2003. mass mkt. 6.99 (*0-449-00724-3*, One World/Ballantine); 2002. pap. 14.00 (*0-345-44908-8*, Ballantine Bks.) Ballantine Bks.
—Stormy Weather: A Charlotte Justice Novel. 2001. 320p. 24.95 (*0-393-02021-5*) Norton, W. W. & Co., Inc.
Woods, Stuart. Dead Eyes. 1994. 320p. 22.00 o.p. (*0-06-017715-2*) HarperTrade.
—Dead Eyes. 368p. 1995. mass mkt. 3.99 o.p. (*0-06-109480-3*); 1994. mass mkt. 7.99 (*0-06-109157-X*) Morrow/Avon. (HarperTorch).
—Dead Eyes. unabr. ed. 1995. audio 60.00 (*0-7887-0161-4*, 94386E7) Recorded Bks., LLC.
—L. A. Dead. l.t. ed. 2000. (Hardcover Ser.). 409p. 29.95 (*1-56895-999-0*, Wheeler Publishing, Inc.) Gale Group.
—L. A. Dead. 2000. (Stone Barrington Ser.). 352p. 24.95 o.s.i (*0-399-14664-4*) Penguin Group (USA) Inc.
Woolner, Ann. Washed Gold. 1994. 391p. 25.00 o.s.i (*0-671-74194-2*, Simon & Schuster) Simon & Schuster.
Wright, Edward. Clea's Moon. 2004. 336p. mass mkt. 6.99 (*0-425-19522-8*) Berkley Publishing Group.
—Clea's Moon. 2003. 320p. 23.95 (*0-399-15047-1*) Putnam Publishing Group, The.
Wurlitzer, Rudolph. Quake. 2nd ed. 1995. (Midnight Classics Ser.). 158p. pap. (*1-85242-409-5*) Serpent's Tail Ltd.
—Slow Fade. 1984. 209p. (Orig.). 13.95 o.p. (*0-394-53610-X*) Knopf, Alfred A. Inc.
Wurlitzer, Rudy. Quake. 2000. 158p. pap. 39.95 o.p. (*1-56649-116-9*) Welcome Rain Pubs.
Yamashita, Karen T. Tropic of Orange. 1997. 280p. (Orig.). pap. 14.95 (*1-56689-064-0*) Coffee Hse. Pr.
Yardley, Cathy. L. A. Woman: A Novel. 2002. 288p. pap. (*0-373-25016-9*, Red Dress Ink) Harlequin Enterprises, Ltd.
Ybarra, Ricardo M. Brotherhood of Dolphins. 1997. 160p. pap. 12.95 (*1-55885-215-8*) Arte Publico Pr.
Young & Dead. 2001. mass mkt. (*1-931297-55-X*); E-Book 7.99 net. (*1-931297-47-9*) Bookbooters Pr.
Zappa, Moon Unit. America the Beautiful: A Novel. 2001. 304p. pap. 14.00 (*0-7432-1383-1*); E-Book 9.99 (*0-7432-1913-9*) Simon & Schuster. (Touchstone).
Zelman, Anita. Dead down Under: A Rebecca Lewis Mystery. 2002. 188p. 12.95 (*1-56474-398-5*) Fithian Pr.

**LOS SANTOS (TEX.: IMAGINARY PLACE)—FICTION**

Herndon, Nancy. C. O. P. Out. 1998. (Elena Jarvis Ser.). 304p. mass mkt. 5.99 o.s.i (*0-425-16293-1*, Prime Crime) Berkley Publishing Group.
—Casanova Crimes. 1999. 288p. mass mkt. 5.99 o.s.i (*0-425-16812-3*, Prime Crime) Berkley Publishing Group.
—Hunting Game. 1996. 288p. (Orig.). mass mkt. 5.99 o.s.i (*0-425-15579-X*, Prime Crime) Berkley Publishing Group.
—Lethal Statues. 1996. 304p. mass mkt. 5.99 o.s.i (*0-425-15384-3*) Berkley Publishing Group.
—Time Bombs. 1997. 320p. mass mkt. 5.99 o.s.i (*0-425-15965-5*, Prime Crime) Berkley Publishing Group.
—Widow's Watch. 1995. 304p. mass mkt. 5.50 o.s.i (*0-425-14900-5*) Berkley Publishing Group.
—Widow's Watch. 260p. 2002. pap. 6.99 (*0-7592-3636-4*); 2002. E-Book 6.99 (*0-7592-3633-X*); 2002. E-Book 6.99 (*0-7592-3632-1*); 2001. E-Book 6.99 (*0-7592-3631-3*) ereads.com.

**LOUISIANA—FICTION**

Aarons, Edward S. Death Is My Shadow. l.t. ed. 1990. 17.95 o.p. (*0-7451-9760-4*, C0077); pap. 15.95 o.p. (*0-7927-0217-4*, C0225) BBC Audiobooks America.
Abel, Kenneth. The Burying Field. 2002. 400p. 26.95 o.s.i (*0-399-14796-9*) Penguin Group (USA) Inc.
—The Burying Field. l.t. ed. 2002. (Core Collection). 538p. 29.95 (*0-7862-4672-3*) Thorndike Pr.
—Cold Steel Rain. l.t. ed. 2001. 439p. lib. bdg. 28.95 (*1-58547-077-5*) Ctr. Point Large Print.
—Cold Steel Rain. 2000. 448p. 24.95 o.p. (*0-399-14662-8*) Penguin Group (USA) Inc.
Adams, Pepper. That Old Black Magic. 1991. (Harlequin Romance Ser.: No. 842). pap. (*0-373-08842-6*, 5-08842-2, Silhouette) Harlequin Enterprises, Ltd.
Algren, Nelson. A Walk on the Wild Side. 1990. (Classic Reprint Ser.). 368p. reprint ed. pap. 12.95 (*0-938410-80-6*, Thunder's Mouth Pr.) Avalon Publishing Group.
—A Walk on the Wild Side. 1998. 368p. pap. 14.00 (*0-374-52532-3*) Farrar, Straus & Giroux.
—A Walk on the Wild Side. 1978. 346p. reprint ed. 57.95 (*0-313-20294-X*, ALWW, Greenwood Pr.) Greenwood Publishing Group, Inc.
—A Walk on the Wild Side. 1992. 21.50 o.p. (*0-8446-6532-0*) Smith, Peter Pub., Inc.
—A Walk on the Wild Side. 1977. 352p. pap. 6.95 o.p. (*0-14-003565-6*, Penguin Bks.) Viking Penguin.
Allen, Danice. Arms of a Stranger. 1995. 384p. (Orig.). mass mkt. 4.50 (*0-380-77726-6*, Avon Bks.) Morrow/Avon.
Ambler, Eric. Cause for Alarm. 246p. reprint ed. lib. bdg. 22.95 (*0-89190-466-2*, Rivercity Pr.) Amereon, Ltd.
—Cause for Alarm. 1990. 264p. mass mkt. 3.95 o.p. (*0-88184-664-3*, Carroll & Graf Pubs.) Avalon Publishing Group.
—Cause for Alarm. 1978. mass mkt. 1.95 o.s.i (*0-345-25909-2*) Ballantine Bks.
—Cause for Alarm. 1984. 256p. mass mkt. 2.95 o.s.i (*0-425-07029-8*) Berkley Publishing Group.
—Cause for Alarm. unabr. ed. 1995. audio 44.95 (*0-7861-0772-3*, 1621) Blackstone Audio Bks., Inc.
—Cause for Alarm. unabr. collector's ed. 1987. audio 48.00 (*0-7366-1182-7*, 2102) Books on Tape, Inc.
—Cause for Alarm. 1990. reprint ed. lib. bdg. 22.95 o.p. (*0-89968-470-X*) Buccaneer Bks., Inc.
—Cause for Alarm. 2002. 304p. pap. 12.00 (*0-375-72674-8*, Vintage) Knopf Publishing Group.
—Cause for Alarm. 1942. mass mkt. 0.25 o.p. (*0-451-00511-2*, Signet Bks.) NAL.
Andersen, Susan. Be My Baby. 1999. 384p. mass mkt. 6.99 (*0-380-79512-4*, Avon Bks.) Morrow/Avon.
Andrews, V. C. All That Glitters. l.t. ed. 2000. 26.95 (*1-56895-236-8*, Wheeler Publishing, Inc.) Gale Group.
—All That Glitters. 1995. (Landry Ser.). 352p. mass mkt. 7.99 (*0-671-87319-9*, Pocket) Simon & Schuster.
—All That Glitters. Marrow, Linda, ed. 1995. 352p. 23.00 o.p. (*0-671-87574-4*, Atria) Simon & Schuster.
—Hidden Jewel. l.t. ed. (Paperback Bestsellers Ser.). 1997. 459p. pap. 24.95 o.p. (*0-7838-1696-0*); 1996. 26.95 o.p. (*0-7838-1695-2*) Gale Group. (Macmillan Reference USA).
—Hidden Jewel. Marrow, Linda, ed. 1995. 384p. 23.00 o.p. (*0-671-87575-2*, Atria) Simon & Schuster.
—Hidden Jewel. l.t. ed. 1995. (Landry Ser.). 384p. mass mkt. 7.99 (*0-671-87320-2*, Pocket) Simon & Schuster.
—Pearl in the Mist. l.t. ed. 1995. 555p. 19.95 o.p. (*0-7838-1165-9*); 514p. 24.95 (*0-7838-1164-0*) Gale Group. (Macmillan Reference USA).
—Pearl in the Mist. Marrow, Linda, ed. 1994. 384p. 23.00 (*0-671-75937-X*, Atria); mass mkt. 7.99 (*0-671-75936-1*, Pocket) Simon & Schuster.
—Pearl in the Mist. 1994. 14.04 (*0-606-07067-2*) Turtleback Bks.
—Ruby. l.t. ed. 2000. 25.95 o.p. (*1-56895-074-8*, Wheeler Publishing, Inc.) Gale Group.
—Ruby. 1998. (SPA., Illus.). 544p. 12.95 (*84-01-49795-7*, PJ9450) Plaza & Janés Editories, S.A. ESP. *Dist:* Lectorum Pubns., Inc.
—Ruby. unabr. ed. 1997. (Landry Ser.: Vol. 1). audio 97.00 (*0-7887-1088-5*, 94981E7) Recorded Bks., LLC.
—Ruby. 1994. 448p. 22.00 (*0-671-75935-3*, Atria) Simon & Schuster.
—Ruby. Marrow, Linda, ed. 1994. (Landry Ser.). 448p. mass mkt. 7.99 (*0-671-75934-5*, Pocket) Simon & Schuster.
—Ruby. 1994. 14.04 (*0-606-05989-X*) Turtleback Bks.
—Tarnished Gold. l.t. ed. 2000. (Large Print Bks.). 26.95 o.p. (*1-56895-338-0*, Wheeler Publishing, Inc.) Gale Group.
—Tarnished Gold. 1996. (Landry Ser.). 352p. mass mkt. 6.99 (*0-671-87321-0*, Pocket) Simon & Schuster.
—Tarnished Gold. Marrow, Linda, ed. 1996. 320p. 23.00 o.p. (*0-671-87576-0*, Atria) Simon & Schuster.
At the Bend of the Red. unabr. ed. 1998. 175p. pap. 24.95 (*0-9666111-1-X*, BI-3) Baggetts Investigative Enterprises, Ltd.
Barnes, Linda. Cities of the Dead. l.t. ed. 1991. 8.95 o.p. (*0-7451-9581-4*, 5059); pap. 10.95 o.p. (*0-7927-0009-0*, 4616) BBC Audiobooks America.
—Cities of the Dead. 1987. mass mkt. 4.99 o.s.i (*0-449-21188-6*, Fawcett) Ballantine Bks.
—Cities of the Dead. 1996. 272p. mass mkt. 5.99 o.s.i (*0-440-22095-5*) Dell Publishing.
—Cities of the Dead. 1985. 224p. 14.95 o.p. (*0-312-13940-3*) St. Martin's Pr.
Battle, Lois. Storyville. 1993. 496p. mass mkt. 5.99 o.s.i (*0-440-21690-7*) Dell Publishing.
—Storyville. 1997. 448p. pap. 15.00 (*0-14-026769-7*) Penguin Group (USA) Inc.
—Storyville. 1993. 432p. 22.00 o.p. (*0-670-83867-5*, Viking) Viking Penguin.
Benoit, Brent. All Saints' Day. 2002. (Sewanee Writers' Ser.). 345p. 26.95 (*1-58567-312-9*) Overlook Pr., The.
Bevill, Caren. Bayou Moon: A Mystery. 2002. 304p. 23.95 (*0-312-28207-9*, Saint Martin's Minotaur) St. Martin's Pr.
Bicos, Olga. Wrapped in Wishes. l.t. ed. 1999. 26.95 (*1-56895-759-9*, Wheeler Publishing, Inc.) Gale Group.
—Wrapped in Wishes. 1996. 432p. mass mkt. 5.50 o.s.i (*0-8217-5370-3*, Zebra Bks.) Kensington Publishing Corp.
Biguenet, John. Oyster: A Novel. 304p. 2003. pap. 12.95 (*0-06-051447-7*); 2002. 23.95 (*0-06-019836-2*) HarperTrade. (Ecco).
Bizier, Richard & Nadeau, Roch. Louisiana. 2nd ed. 2001. 432p. pap. (*2-89464-337-3*) Ulysses Travel Guides.
Blackstock, Terri. Blind Trust. 1997. (Second Chances Ser.: Vol. 3). 256p. pap. 10.99 (*0-310-20710-X*) Zondervan.
—Never Again Good-Bye. 1996. (Second Chances Ser.: No. 1). 240p. pap. 10.99 (*0-310-20707-X*) Zondervan.
—Never Again Goodbye. l.t. ed. 1999. (Christian Fiction Ser.). 312p. 24.95 (*0-7862-1675-1*) Thorndike Pr.
—Private Justice. 1999. pap. text 23.95 (*0-7862-1823-1*, Macmillan Reference USA) Gale Group.
—Private Justice. 1998. (Newpointe 911 Ser.: Bk. 1). 384p. pap. 12.99 (*0-310-21757-1*) Zondervan.
—Trial by Fire. 2000. (Newpointe 911 Ser.: Bk. 4). (Illus.). 352p. pap. 12.99 (*0-310-21760-1*) Zondervan.
Blackstone, Terri. Shadow of Doubt Bk. 2: New Pointe 911. 1999. (Christian Fiction Ser.: Vol. 2). 22.95 o.p. (*0-7862-2097-X*, Five Star) Gale Group.
Blake, James Carlos. A World of Thieves: A Novel. 2002. 304p. 25.95 (*0-380-97750-8*, Morrow, William & Co.) Morrow/Avon.
Blake, Jennifer. Arrow to the Heart. 1995. mass mkt. 5.99 o.s.i (*0-449-14734-7*); 1993. 368p. 19.00 o.s.i (*0-449-90824-0*) Ballantine Bks. (Fawcett).
—Arrow to the Heart. l.t. ed. 1997. (Large Print Bks.). pap. 24.95 (*1-56895-404-2*, Wheeler Publishing, Inc.) Gale Group.
—Clay. 2001. 384p. mass mkt. (*1-55166-819-X*, Mira Bks.) Harlequin Enterprises, Ltd.
—Fierce Eden. 304p. 2002. pap. 6.99 (*1-58586-097-2*); 1999. E-Book 6.99 (*1-58586-095-6*) ereads.com.
—Kane. 1998. (Mira Bks.). 384p. mass mkt. (*1-55166-429-1*, 1-66429-1, Mira Bks.) Harlequin Enterprises, Ltd.
—Kane. l.t. ed. 2000. (Basic Ser.). 491p. 28.95 (*0-7862-2611-0*) Thorndike Pr.
—Love's Wild Desire. 1996. mass mkt. 4.99 o.s.i (*0-449-14878-5*, Fawcett) Ballantine Bks.
—Love's Wild Desire. l.t. ed. 1997. (Large Print Book Ser.). 26.95 (*1-56895-419-0*, Wheeler Publishing, Inc.) Gale Group.
—Love's Wild Desire. 1991. reprint ed. 20.00 o.p. (*0-7278-4238-2*) Severn Hse. Pubs., Ltd.
—Love's Wild Desire. 1983. 384p. pap. 3.50 o.s.i (*0-446-31067-0*) Warner Bks., Inc.
—Luke. 1999. (Benedict Trilogy Ser.). 376p. mass mkt. (*1-55166-490-9*, 1-66490-3, Mira Bks.) Harlequin Enterprises, Ltd.
—Luke. l.t. ed. 2001. (Basic Ser.). 474p. 29.95 (*0-7862-2620-X*) Thorndike Pr.
—Roan. 2000. (Benedict Trilogy Ser.). 384p. mass mkt. (*1-55166-630-8*, 1-66630-4, Mira Bks.) Harlequin Enterprises, Ltd.
—Shameless. 1997. mass mkt. 5.99 o.s.i (*0-449-15002-X*, Fawcett) Ballantine Bks.
—Silver-Tongued Devil. 1995. 336p. mass mkt. 4.99 o.s.i (*0-449-14938-2*, Fawcett) Ballantine Bks.
—Silver-Tongued Devil. 1996. 384p. 24.00 (*0-7278-5114-4*) Severn Hse. Pubs., Ltd.
—Wade. 2002. 384p. mass mkt. (*1-55166-898-X*, Mira Bks.) Harlequin Enterprises, Ltd.
—Wade. l.t. ed. 2003. (Basic Ser.). 449p. 28.95 (*0-7862-4938-2*) Thorndike Pr.
—Wildest Dreams. 1995. 341p. pap. 19.00 (*0-449-91264-7*); 1993. mass mkt. 5.99 o.s.i (*0-449-14739-8*, Fawcett) Ballantine Bks.
Bloodline. unabr. collector's ed. Incl. Just Like a Tree. audio Long Day in November. audio Sky in Gray. audio Three Men. audio 1982. Set audio 42.00 (*0-7366-0515-0*, 1489) Books on Tape, Inc.

Bosworth, Sheila. Almost Innocent. 1996. (Voices of the South Ser.). 268p. (C). pap. 16.95 (0-8071-2066-9) Louisiana State Univ. Pr.
—Almost Innocent. 1984. 320p. 16.45 o.p. (0-671-50365-0, Simon & Schuster) Simon & Schuster.
—Almost Innocent. 1986. (Contemporary American Fiction Ser.). 272p. pap. 6.95 o.p. (0-14-008443-6, Penguin Bks.) Viking Penguin.
—Slow Poison. 1993. mass mkt. 4.99 o.s.i (0-8041-1124-3, Ivy Bks.) Ballantine Bks.
—Slow Poison. 1998. (Voices of the South Ser.). 336p. pap. 17.95 (0-8071-2278-5) Louisiana State Univ. Pr.
Bradley, John Ed. Smoke. unabr. ed. 1998. audio 69.95 (0-7861-1368-5, 2276) Blackstone Audio Bks., Inc.
—Smoke, Set. unabr. ed. 1999. audio 69.95 Highsmith Inc.
—Smoke. 1994. 400p. 23.00 o.p. (0-8050-2421-2) Holt, Henry & Co.
—Smoke. 1995. 416p. 20.00 (0-14-024759-9) Viking Penguin.
Brandt, Nat & Brandt, Yanna. A Death in the Bulloch Parish: A Mitch Stevens Mystery. 1993. (Mitch Stevens Ser.). 224p. 19.00 o.p. (0-88150-265-0) Countryman Pr.
Breaux, Magdalene. The Family Curse. 2000. 244p. pap. 15.00 (0-9701709-0-4) Breaux Bks., LLC.
—The Family Curse. 2000. 248p. pap. 17.95 o.p. (1-887617-00-0) St. Barthelemey Pr., Ltd.
Brite, Poppy Z. The Lazarus Heart. 1998. (Crow Ser.). 224p. pap. 13.00 (0-06-105824-6, HarperEntertainment) Morrow/Avon.
Brodber, Erna. Louisiana: A Novel. 1997. 168p. (Orig.). pap. 17.00 (1-57806-031-1) Univ. Pr. of Mississippi.
Brown, John G. The Wrecked, Blessed Body of Shelton Lafleur. l.t. ed. 1997. (Paperback Ser.). 361p. pap. 21.95 (0-7838-8198-3, Macmillan Reference USA) Gale Group.
—The Wrecked, Blessed Body of Shelton Lafleur. 1996. 256p. 21.95 o.p. (0-395-72988-2) Houghton Mifflin Co.
—The Wrecked, Blessed Body of Shelton Lafleur. 1997. pap. 12.00 (0-380-72965-2, Avon Bks.) Morrow/Avon.
Brown, John Gregory. Audubon's Watch: A Novel. 2001. 224p. tchr. ed. 24.00 (0-395-78607-X) Houghton Mifflin Co.
—Audubon's Watch: A Novel. 2002. 224p. pap. 13.00 (0-618-25731-4, Mariner Bks.) Houghton Mifflin Co. Trade & Reference Div.
Brown, Sandra. French Silk. l.t. ed. 1993. (General Ser.). 522p. lib. bdg. 17.95 o.p. (0-8161-5445-7, Macmillan Reference USA) Gale Group.
—French Silk. 1992. 18.95 o.s.i (0-446-51654-6) Warner Bks., Inc.
Burke, James Lee. Black Cherry Blues. l.t. ed. 1996. lib. bdg. 24.95 (1-57490-070-6, Beeler Large Print Bks.) Beeler, Thomas T. Publisher.
—Black Cherry Blues. 1989. 17.95 o.p. (0-316-11699-8) Little Brown & Co.
—Black Cherry Blues. 1990. 384p. reprint ed. mass mkt. 7.99 (0-380-71204-0, Avon Bks.) Morrow/Avon.
—Black Cherry Blues. unabr. ed. 2000. audio 78.00 (1-55690-791-5, 93106E7) Recorded Bks., LLC.
—Black Cherry Blues. abr. ed. 2001. audio 9.98 (0-7435-2302-4); 1991. audio 16.00 (0-671-73610-8); Set. 1998. audio 9.98 (0-671-58255-0, 390401) Simon & Schuster Audio. (Simon & Schuster Audioworks).
—Burning Angel. l.t. ed. 1995. 502p. 25.95 o.p. (0-7838-1492-5, Macmillan Reference USA) Gale Group.
—Burning Angel. 1995. 352p. 22.95 o.p. (0-7868-6082-0); 2002. 464p. reprint ed. mass mkt. 7.99 (0-7868-8904-7) Hyperion Pr.
—Burning Angel. unabr. ed. 2000. (Dave Robicheaux Ser.: Vol. 8). audio 85.00 (0-7887-0345-5, 94537E7) Recorded Bks., LLC.
—Burning Angel. 2001. audio 9.98 (0-7435-2309-1); 1998. audio 9.98 (0-671-58254-2); 1995. audio 17.00 (0-671-52927-7, 393120) Simon & Schuster Audio. (Simon & Schuster Audioworks).
—Burning Angel. deluxe ltd. num. ed. 1995. 340p. 125.00 o.s.i (0-9631925-3-1) Trice, B.E. Publishing.
—Cadillac Jukebox. l.t. ed. 1996. (Large Print Bks.). 27.95 o.p. (1-56895-375-5, Wheeler Publishing, Inc.) Gale Group.
—Cadillac Jukebox. 1996. 352p. 22.95 (0-7868-6175-4); 2002. 464p. reprint ed. mass mkt. 6.99 (0-7868-8918-7) Hyperion Pr.
—Cadillac Jukebox. unabr. ed. 1996. (Dave Robicheaux Ser.: Vol. 9). audio 83.00 (0-7887-0725-6, 94902E7) Recorded Bks., LLC.
—Cadillac Jukebox. abr. ed. 1998. audio 14.40 (0-671-57732-8, 908764); 1996. audio 18.00 (0-671-57365-9, 394156) Simon & Schuster Audio. (Simon & Schuster Audioworks).
—Cadillac Jukebox. deluxe ltd. num. ed. 1996. 303p. 150.00 (0-9631925-5-8) Trice, B.E. Publishing.
—The Convict: And Other Stories. 1990. pap. 9.95 o.p. (0-316-11728-5) Little Brown & Co.
—The Convict: And Other Stories. 1985. 145p. text 15.95 o.p. (0-8071-1273-9) Louisiana State Univ. Pr.
—Dixie City Jam. l.t. ed. 1994. 590p. lib. bdg. 22.95 o.p. (0-8161-7488-1, Macmillan Reference USA) Gale Group.
—Dixie City Jam. 1994. 352p. 22.95 (0-7868-6019-7); 2002. 512p. reprint ed. mass mkt. 7.99 (0-7868-8900-4) Hyperion Pr.
—Dixie City Jam. unabr. ed. 1994. audio. (Dave Robicheaux Ser.: Vol. 7). audio 85.00 (0-7887-0060-X, 94316E7) Recorded Bks., LLC.
—Dixie City Jam. 2001. audio 9.98 o.s.i (0-7435-0476-3); 1998. audio 9.98 (0-671-58252-6); 1994. audio 17.00 o.s.i (0-671-88761-0, 390665) Simon & Schuster Audio. (Simon & Schuster Audioworks).
—Half of Paradise. Date not set. lib. bdg. 24.95 (0-8488-1778-8) Amereon, Ltd.
—Half of Paradise. 1998. 469p. mass mkt. 6.50 (0-7868-8946-2); 1995. 288p. pap. 10.95 (0-7868-8117-8) Hyperion Pr.
—Half of Paradise. l.t. ed. 2001. 482p. 29.95 (0-7862-3398-2); 487p. (0-7540-1683-8); 487p. (0-7540-9079-5) Thorndike Pr.
—Heaven's Prisoners. l.t. ed. 1997. lib. bdg. 24.95 (1-57490-086-2, Beeler Large Print Bks.) Beeler, Thomas T. Publisher.
—Heaven's Prisoners. 1988. 17.95 o.p. (0-8050-0665-6) Holt, Henry & Co.
—Heaven's Prisoners. unabr. ed. 1996. (Dave Robicheaux Ser.: Vol. 2). audio 70.00 (0-7887-0623-3, 94797E7) Recorded Bks., LLC.
—Heaven's Prisoners. 288p. 1989. mass mkt. 5.99 o.s.i (0-671-67629-6); 1996. pap. 7.99 (0-671-51741-4) Simon & Schuster. (Pocket).
—Heaven's Prisoners. abr. ed. 1996. (Dave Robicheaux Mystery Ser.). 3p. audio 17.00 (0-671-73608-6, 392196, Simon & Schuster Audioworks) Simon & Schuster Audio.
—In the Electric Mist with Confederate Dead. unabr. collector's ed. 1995. audio 72.00 (0-7366-2940-8, 3636) Books on Tape, Inc.
—In the Electric Mist with Confederate Dead. l.t. ed. 1995. 483p. 23.95 o.p. (0-8161-7487-3, Macmillan Reference USA) Gale Group.
—In the Electric Mist with Confederate Dead. 1993. 352p. 19.95 o.p. (1-56282-882-7) Hyperion Pr.
—In the Electric Mist with Confederate Dead. 1994. 384p. reprint ed. mass mkt. 7.50 (0-380-72121-X, Avon Bks.) Morrow/Avon.
—In the Electric Mist with Confederate Dead. abr. ed. 1993. (Dave Robicheaux Mystery Ser.). 3p. audio 17.00 (0-671-86816-0, 390972, Simon & Schuster Audioworks) Simon & Schuster Audio.
—The Intruders. abr. ed. 1999. audio 9.98 (0-671-04407-9, Simon & Schuster Audioworks) Simon & Schuster Audio.
—Jolie Blon's Bounce. l.t. ed. 2002. (Wheeler Hardcover Ser.). 566p. 30.95 (1-58724-273-7, Wheeler Publishing, Inc.) Gale Group.
—Jolie Blon's Bounce. unabr. ed. 2002. audio 49.95 (1-4025-2396-3, RG088); audio compact disk 124.00 (1-4025-2966-X, C1855) Recorded Bks., LLC.
—Jolie Blon's Bounce. 2003. 480p. mass mkt. 7.99 (0-7434-1144-7, Pocket Star); 2003. E-Book (0-7432-4462-1, Simon & Schuster); 2002. 352p. 25.00 (0-7432-0484-0, Simon & Schuster); 2002. 48p. mass mkt. 7.99 (0-7434-5599-1, Pocket); 2002. 352p. 25.00 (0-7432-3379-4, Simon & Schuster) Simon & Schuster.
—Jolie Blon's Bounce. abr. ed. 2002. audio 26.00 (0-7435-2463-2); audio compact disk 30.00 (0-7435-2460-8); audio 45.00 (0-7435-2594-9); audio compact disk 49.95 (0-7435-2595-7) Simon & Schuster Audio. (Simon & Schuster Audioworks).
—Jolie Blon's Bounce. aut. ltd. num. ed. 2002. 349p. 150.00 (1-890885-13-4) Trice, B.E. Publishing.
—A Morning for Flamingos. l.t. ed. 1998. 353p. 24.95 (1-57490-155-9, Beeler Large Print Bks.) Beeler, Thomas T. Publisher.
—A Morning for Flamingos. 1990. (Dave Robicheaux Ser.). 18.95 o.p. (0-316-11721-8) Little Brown & Co.
—A Morning for Flamingos. 1991. 384p. reprint ed. mass mkt. 7.50 (0-380-71360-8, Avon Bks.) Morrow/Avon.
—A Morning for Flamingos. unabr. ed. 1993. (Dave Robicheaux Ser.: Vol. 4). audio 75.00 (1-55690-940-3, 93436) Recorded Bks., LLC.
—A Morning for Flamingos. 1999. pap. 9.98 (0-671-04408-7); 1991. audio 16.00 (0-671-73611-6, 391205) Simon & Schuster Audio. (Simon & Schuster Audioworks).
—The Neon Rain: A Novel. 1987. 16.95 o.p. (0-8050-0053-4) Holt, Henry & Co.
—The Neon Rain: A Novel. l.t. ed. 1991. 377p. 21.95 (1-85089-413-2) ISIS Large Print Bks. GBR. *Dist:* Transaction Pubs.
—The Neon Rain: A Novel. 288p. reprint ed. 2002. (Illus.). pap. 14.00 (0-7434-4920-7); 1992. mass mkt. 6.99 (0-671-75644-3) Simon & Schuster. (Pocket).
—Purple Cane Road. l.t. ed. 2000. 512p. 24.95 (0-375-43055-5) Random Hse. Large Print.
—A Stained White Radiance. l.t. ed. 1993. (General Ser.). 465p. pap. 16.95 o.p. (0-8161-5612-3, Macmillan Reference USA) Gale Group.
—A Stained White Radiance. 1992. 384p. 19.95 o.p. (1-56282-980-7) Hyperion Pr.
—A Stained White Radiance. 1993. 384p. reprint ed. mass mkt. 7.50 (0-380-72047-7, Avon Bks.) Morrow/Avon.
—A Stained White Radiance. unabr. ed. 1994. (Dave Robicheaux Ser.: No. 5). audio 78.00 (1-55690-999-3, 94138E7) Recorded Bks., LLC.
—A Stained White Radiance. 1998. audio 9.98 (0-671-58249-6); 1996. audio 17.00 (0-671-86817-9, 394196) Simon & Schuster Audio. (Simon & Schuster Audioworks).
—Sunset Limited. 1999. (Dave Robicheaux Mysteries Ser.). 416p. mass mkt. 7.50 (0-440-22398-9) Dell Publishing.
—Sunset Limited, Set. abr. ed. 1999. audio 25.00 Highsmith Inc.
—Sunset Limited. (Dave Robicheaux Ser.: Vol. 10). 2001. audio compact disk 99.00 (0-7887-3399-0, C1005E7); 1998. audio 83.00 (0-7887-2592-0, 95498E7) Recorded Bks., LLC.
—Sunset Limited. abr. ed. 1998. (Dave Robicheaux Mystery Ser.). audio 25.00 (0-671-58106-6, 696022, Simon & Schuster Audioworks) Simon & Schuster Audio.
—Sunset Limited. l.t. ed. (Paperback Bestsellers Ser.). 429p. 1999. pap. 27.95 (0-7838-0332-X); 1998. 30.95 (0-7838-0331-1) Thorndike Pr.
—Sunset Limited. ltd. ed. 1998. 309p. 150.00 o.p. (1-890885-03-7) Trice, B.E. Publishing.
—White Doves at Morning. 2004. 502p. pap. 12.95 (1-4104-0173-1, Wheeler Publishing, Inc.) Gale Group.
—White Doves at Morning. 2004. 448p. mass mkt. 7.99 (0-7434-6662-4, Pocket Star); 2002. 320p. 25.00 (0-7432-4471-0, Simon & Schuster) Simon & Schuster.
—White Doves at Morning. l.t. ed. 2003. (Core Ser.). 537p. 32.95 (0-7862-4924-2) Thorndike Pr.
Butler, Robert Olen. A Good Scent from a Strange Mountain: Stories. 1994. (American Audio Prose Library Reading). audio 13.95 (1-55644-398-6, 14011); audio 25.00 (1-55644-400-1, 14013); audio 13.95 (1-55644-399-4, 14012) American Audio Prose Library, Inc.
—A Good Scent from a Strange Mountain: Stories. 1992. 256p. 19.95 o.s.i (0-8050-1986-3) Holt, Henry & Co.
—A Good Scent from a Strange Mountain: Stories. 1993. 272p. pap. 12.95 o.s.i (0-14-017664-0, Penguin Bks.) Penguin Group (USA) Inc.
Cable, George W. Bylow Hill. (BCL Ser. I). (Illus.). reprint ed. 29.50 (0-404-01355-4) AMS Pr., Inc.
—Bylow Hill. 1990. (Works of George Washington Cable). reprint ed. lib. bdg. 79.00 (0-7812-1144-1) Reprint Services Corp.
—Bylow Hill. 2002. 13.00 (0-403-00106-4) Scholarly Pr., Inc.
—Bylow Hill. 1902. reprint ed. 14.00 (0-403-02297-5) Somerset Pubs., Inc.
—The Grandissimes. E-Book 3.95 (0-594-06011-7) 1873 Pr.
—The Grandissimes. 25.95 (0-88411-796-0) Amereon, Ltd.
—The Grandissimes. 1957. pap. 5.95 o.p. (0-8090-0025-3, Hill & Wang) Farrar, Straus & Giroux.
—The Grandissimes. 1983. 7.50 o.p. (0-8446-1791-1) Smith, Peter Pub., Inc.
—The Grandissimes. 1988. (Classics Ser.). 384p. 14.95 (0-14-043322-8, Penguin Classics) Viking Penguin.
—Old Creole Days. E-Book 3.95 (0-594-04343-3) 1873 Pr.
—Old Creole Days, Set, Pts. 1 & 2. 1977. (Black Heritage Library Collection). 27.95 (0-8369-8530-3) Ayer Co. Pubs., Inc.
—Old Creole Days. 1883. 300p. (YA). reprint ed. pap. text 28.00 (1-4047-1132-5) Classic Textbooks.
—Old Creole Days. 1972. reprint ed. lib. bdg. 9.00 o.p. (0-8422-8184-3) Irvington Pubs.
—Old Creole Days. 1989. mass mkt. 3.95 o.p. (0-451-52349-0, Signet Classics) NAL.
—Old Creole Days. 1990. (Pelican Pouch Ser.). 312p. (YA). (gr. 10-12). reprint ed. pap. 6.99 (0-88289-780-2) Pelican Publishing Co., Inc.
—Old Creole Days. 1990. (Works of George Washington Cable). reprint ed. lib. bdg. 79.00 (0-7812-1132-8) Reprint Services Corp.
—Old Creole Days. 1974. reprint ed. 10.00 (0-403-03056-0) Somerset Pubs., Inc.
—Strange True Stories of Louisiana. 1977. (Short Story Index Reprint Ser.). 29.95 (0-8369-3446-6) Ayer Co. Pubs., Inc.
—Strange True Stories of Louisiana. 1994. 368p. pap. 6.99 (1-56554-038-7) Pelican Publishing Co., Inc.
—Strange True Stories of Louisiana. 1974. reprint ed. 69.00 (0-403-02952-X) Somerset Pubs., Inc.
Cable, George Washington. The Grandissimes. 2001. (Illus.). 528p. pap. 7.99 (1-56554-901-5) Pelican Publishing Co., Inc.
—The Grandissimes. 1990. (Works of George Washington Cable). reprint ed. lib. bdg. 79.00 (0-7812-1133-6) Reprint Services Corp.
—The Grandissimes. 1974. reprint ed. 79.00 (0-403-02979-1) Somerset Pubs., Inc.
—The Grandissimes. 1988. (Brown Thrasher Bks.). 360p. reprint ed. pap. 15.95 (0-8203-1020-4) Univ. of Georgia Pr.
Cameron, Stella. French Quarter. l.t. ed. 1999. 27.95 (1-56895-643-6, Wheeler Publishing, Inc.) Gale Group.
—French Quarter. 1999. 445p. mass mkt. 6.99 o.s.i (0-8217-6251-6); 1998. (Illus.). 384p. 16.95 o.s.i (1-57566-312-0, Kensington Bks.) Kensington Publishing Corp.
Cannon, C. W. Soul Resin. 2002. 304p. pap. 13.95 (1-57366-099-X) Fiction Collective Two, Inc.
Catling, Patrick Skene. Jazz, Jazz, Jazz. 1981. 322p. 11.95 o.p. (0-312-44073-1) St. Martin's Pr.
Cawood, Chris. 1998: The Year of the Beast. Seale, Gaynell, ed. 1996. 312p. (Orig.). pap. 12.95 (0-9642231-9-8) Magnolia Hill Pr.
Chance, Megan. The Gentleman Caller. l.t. ed. 1999. (Large Print Book Ser.). pap. 23.95 (1-56895-729-7, Wheeler Publishing, Inc.) Gale Group.
—The Gentleman Caller. 1998. 432p. mass mkt. 6.99 (0-06-108704-1, HarperTorch) Morrow/Avon.
Chesnutt, Charles Waddell. Paul Marchand: Free Man of Color. 1998. 144p. 20.00 (1-57806-055-9) Univ. Pr. of Mississippi.
Chesnutt, Charles Waddell & McWilliams, Dean. Paul Marchand, F. M. C. 1999. 223p. text 49.95 (0-691-05993-4); pap. text 20.95 o.p. (0-691-05994-2) Princeton Univ. Pr.
Chopin, Kate. At Fault: A Scholarly Edition with Background Readings. Green, Suzanne Disheroon & Caudle, David J., eds. 2001. (Illus.). xxxii, 304p. 30.00 (1-57233-120-8); 336p. reprint ed. pap. 28.00 (1-57233-121-6) Univ. of Tennessee Pr.
—The Awakening. 2000. 252p. E-Book 9.95 (0-594-05221-1) 1873 Pr.
—The Awakening. unabr. ed. 1986. audio 29.95 (1-55685-000-X) Audio Bk. Contractors, Inc.
—The Awakening. 1985. mass mkt. 2.95 o.s.i (0-553-21194-3) Bantam Bks.
—The Awakening. E-Book (0-7607-1303-0); 1997. (Illus.). (0-7607-0590-9) Barnes & Noble, Inc.
—The Awakening. 1995. 256p. 9.00 o.s.i (1-57322-511-8, Riverhead Trade (Paperbacks)); 1974. pap. 5.95 o.s.i (0-399-50031-6, Perigee Bks.) Berkley Publishing Group.
—The Awakening. unabr. ed. 1994. audio 32.95 (0-7861-0848-7, 1517) Blackstone Audio Bks., Inc.
—The Awakening. unabr. ed. 1991. audio 39.95 (1-55686-377-2, 377) Books in Motion.
—The Awakening. unabr. collector's ed. 1995. audio 30.00 (0-7366-2968-8, 3659) Books on Tape, Inc.
—The Awakening. 1992. reprint ed. lib. bdg. 21.95 (0-89968-270-7, Lightyear Pr.) Buccaneer Bks., Inc.
—The Awakening. l.t. ed. 2000. 329p. pap. 24.95 (1-58855-004-4) Cyber Classics, Inc.
—The Awakening. 1993. 128p. reprint ed. pap. text 1.00 (0-486-27786-0) Dover Pubns., Inc.
—The Awakening. l.t. ed. 903p. pap. 71.39 (0-7583-0319-X); 777p. pap. 62.47 (0-7583-0318-1); 634p. pap. 51.01 (0-7583-0317-3); 402p. pap. 34.44 (0-7583-0315-7); 231p. pap. 22.08 (0-7583-0313-0); 315p. pap. 27.70 (0-7583-0314-9); 231p. lib. bdg. 28.08 (0-7583-0305-X); 315p. lib. bdg. 33.70 (0-7583-0306-8); 402p. lib. bdg. 40.44 (0-7583-0307-6); 515p. lib. bdg. 48.52 (0-7583-0308-4); 634p. lib. bdg. 57.01 (0-7583-0309-2); 777p. lib. bdg. 79.57 (0-7583-0310-6); 903p. lib. bdg. 87.76 (0-7583-0311-4); 2000. 185p. pap. 19.58 (0-7583-0312-2) Huge Print Pr.
—The Awakening. unabr. ed. 1981. audio 26.00 Jimcin Recordings.
—The Awakening. 1992. (Everyman's Library). 272p. 15.00 (0-679-41721-4) Knopf, Alfred A. Inc.
—The Awakening. 1982. 192p. mass mkt. 4.50 (0-380-00245-0, Avon Bks.) Morrow/Avon.
—The Awakening. abr. ed. 1997. audio 13.98 (962-634-608-6, NA210814); audio compact disk 15.98 (962-634-108-4, NA210812) Naxos of America, Inc. (Naxos AudioBooks).
—The Awakening. l.t. ed. 1995. 266p. lib. bdg. 25.00 (0-939495-83-X); 1998. 172p. reprint ed. lib. bdg. 24.00 (1-58287-017-9) North Bks.
—The Awakening. Culley, Margaret, ed. 1977. (Critical Editions Ser.). 256p. (C). pap. o.p. (0-393-09172-4) Norton, W. W. & Co., Inc.
—The Awakening. 2nd ed. (Critical Editions Ser.). (C). 1999. pap. text 35.85 (0-393-99009-5); 1993. pap. text (0-393-96057-9) Norton, W. W. & Co., Inc.
—The Awakening. 1997. (0-14-771200-9) Penguin Group (USA) Inc.

—The Awakening. 1996. (Literary Classics). 182p. pap. 10.00 (1-57392-098-3) Prometheus Bks., Pubs.
—The Awakening, unabr. ed. 1986. audio 35.00 (1-55690-583-1, 86850E7) Recorded Bks., LLC.
—The Awakening. 1988. reprint ed. lib. bdg. 79.00 (0-7812-1102-6) Reprint Services Corp.
—The Awakening. 1996. 140p. 21.50 o.p. (0-684-81912-0, Simon & Schuster); 1998. (Illus.). 256p. reprint ed. mass mkt. 5.99 (0-671-01547-8, Pocket) Simon & Schuster.
—The Awakening. 1996. pap. text 14.95 o.p. (0-312-13856-3) St. Martin's Pr.
—The Awakening: And Other Stories. Knights, Pamela, ed. 2000. (Oxford World's Classics Ser.). 480p. pap. 7.95 (0-19-282300-0) Oxford Univ. Pr., Inc.
—The Awakening & Other Stories. 1976. 24.95 (0-8488-0457-0) Amereon, Ltd.
—The Awakening & Other Stories. Baxter, Judith, ed. 1996. (Cambridge Literature Ser.). (Illus.). 256p. pap. text 11.95 (0-521-56766-1) Cambridge Univ. Pr.
—The Awakening & Other Stories. Leary, Lewis Gaston, ed. 1970. (Rinehart Editions Ser.: Vol. 142). (C). pap. text 29.00 o.p. (0-03-078395-X) Harcourt College Pubs.
—The Awakening & Other Stories. annuals Baym, Nina, ed. & anno. by. 2000. (Modern Library Classics). 448p. pap. 7.95 (0-679-78333-4, Modern Library) Random House Adult Trade Publishing Group.
—The Awakening & Other Stories. 1987. 18.75 o.p. (0-8446-0544-1) Smith, Peter Pub., Inc.
—The Awakening & Other Stories. 1998. (Classics Library). pap. 3.95 (1-85326-556-X, 556XWW) Wordsworth Editions, Ltd. GBR. *Dist:* Combined Publishing.
—The Awakening & Selected Stories. 1976. mass mkt. 1.50 o.p. (0-451-50882-3); mass mkt. 1.95 o.p. (0-451-51234-0); mass mkt. 2.75 o.p. (0-451-51561-7); mass mkt. 2.95 o.p. (0-451-51749-0) NAL. (Signet Classics).
—The Awakening & Selected Stories. 1993. (Modern Library Ser.). 420p. 17.95 o.s.i (0-679-42469-5, Modern Library) Random House Adult Trade Publishing Group.
—The Awakening & Selected Stories. 2003. (Penguin Classics Ser.). 288p. pap. 8.00 (0-14-243732-8, Penguin Classics) Viking Penguin.
—Bayou Folk. 1972. reprint ed. 18.95 o.p. (0-8422-8170-3) Irvington Pubs.
—Bayou Folk. 2000. (Works of Kate Chopin). reprint ed. lib. bdg. 79.00 (0-7812-1103-4) Reprint Services Corp.
—Bayou Folk. reprint ed. 65.00 (0-403-04559-2) Somerset Pubs., Inc.
—A Pair of Silk Stockings & Other Stories. 1998. (Thrift Editions Ser.). 64p. reprint ed. pap. text 1.00 (0-486-29264-9) Dover Pubns., Inc.
—A Vocation & a Voice. 1993. 23.25 (0-8446-6708-0) Smith, Peter Pub., Inc.
—A Vocation & a Voice. Toth, Emily, ed. & intro. by. 1991. (Classics Ser.). 192p. 10.95 (0-14-039078-2, Penguin Classics) Viking Penguin.
Chopin, Kate & Collier, John, contrib. by. The Awakening. 1997. (Illus.). 88.24 (0-7607-0815-0) Barnes & Noble, Inc.
Chopin, Kate & Koloski, Bernard. Bayou Folk: And a Night in Acadie. 1999. (Classics Ser.). 416p. 11.95 (0-14-043681-2, Penguin Classics) Viking Penguin.
Christovich, Mary-Louise & Toledano, Roulhac. Nankowetco. the Natchez Odyssey, 1716-1734: The Natchez Odyssey, 1716-1734. 2001. (Illus.). xxiii, 391p. pap. 29.95 (1-889431-90-7) Univ. Pr. of the South, Inc.
Claire, Cherie. The Acadians: Emilie. 2000. (Acadians Ser.). 320p. mass mkt. 5.50 o.s.i (0-8217-6648-1, Zebra Bks.) Kensington Publishing Corp.
—The Acadians: Rose. 2000. (Ballad Romances Ser.). 320p. mass mkt. 5.50 o.s.i (0-8217-6716-X) Kensington Publishing Corp.
—Gabrielle. 2001. (Acadians Ser.). (Illus.). 32p. mass mkt. 5.50 o.s.i (0-8217-6802-6) Kensington Publishing Corp.
Colbert, James. All I Have Is Blue. unabr. ed. 1994. audio 51.00 (0-7887-0033-2, 94232E7) Recorded Bks., LLC.
—No Special Hurry. 1988. 192p. 16.95 o.p. (0-395-47016-1) Houghton Mifflin Co.
—No Special Hurry. 1989. 224p. pap. 3.95 o.p. (0-14-012399-7, Penguin Bks.) Viking Penguin.
—Skinny Man. unabr. ed. 1993. audio 44.00 (1-55690-930-6, 93426E7) Recorded Bks., LLC.
—Skinny Man. 1991. 224p. text 18.95 o.p. (0-689-12098-2, Scribner) Simon & Schuster.
Collins, Max Allan. Blood & Thunder. Landt, Fran, ed. abr. ed. 1999. audio 16.95 (1-882071-57-3) B&B Audio, Inc.
—Blood & Thunder, Set. unabr. ed. 1997. audio 69.95 (0-7927-2211-6, CSL 100, Chivers Sound Library) BBC Audiobooks America.
—Blood & Thunder. 1999. 320p. reprint ed. text 22.00 (0-7881-6601-8) DIANE Publishing Co.
—Blood & Thunder. 1995. 336p. 21.95 o.s.i (0-525-93759-5, Dutton) Dutton/Plume.
—Blood & Thunder. 1996. 368p. mass mkt. 5.99 o.s.i (0-451-17976-5, Signet Bks.) NAL.
—Dying in the Post-War World: A Nathan Heller Casebook. 1991. (Nate Heller Ser.). 280p. 19.95 o.p. (0-88150-210-3) Countryman Pr.
—Dying in the Post-War World: A Nathan Heller Casebook. 1993. 3.99 o.p. (0-517-10403-2) Random Hse. Value Publishing.
Coner, Kenyetta. The Mockingbirds. Richards, Lyn, ed. 1988. 250p. pap. 11.00 (0-9665005-0-4) 52 Weeks Publishing Hse.
Connolly, John. Every Dead Thing. 1999. 400p. 25.00 (0-684-85714-6, Simon & Schuster) Simon & Schuster.
Corrington, John W. A Civil Death. 1988. mass mkt. 3.50 o.s.i (0-449-21630-6, Fawcett) Ballantine Bks.
—Shad Sentell. 1992. mass mkt. 107.73 (0-312-92765-7) St. Martin's Pr.
Corrington, John W. & Corrington, Joyce H. A Civil Death. 1987. 15.95 o.p. (0-670-81490-3) Viking Penguin.
Crais, Robert. Voodoo River. l.t. ed. 2002. (Elvis Cole Mystery Ser.). 499p. 29.95 (0-7862-3404-0) Gale Group.
—Voodoo River. (Elvis Cole Mystery Ser.). 1995. 304p. 21.95 (0-7868-6076-6); 2003. 416p. reprint ed. mass mkt. 7.99 (0-7868-8905-5) Hyperion Pr.
Cushman, Jerome. Tom B. & the Joyful Noise. 1970. (Illus.). (J). (gr. 4-7). 4.25 o.p. (0-664-32467-3) Westminster John Knox Pr.
Cuviep, Remi. The Superdome Murders. unabr. ed. 1998. (New Orleans Murder Ser.: No. 1). 100p. pap. 6.95 (1-892651-05-X) Columbia Pubns.
Dancer, Rex. Bad Girl Blues. 2001. 304p. pap. 19.95 (0-7432-3345-X); 1994. 301p. 20.00 (0-671-88007-1) Simon & Schuster. (Simon & Schuster).
—Postcard from Hell. 1995. 297p. 21.00 (0-671-88009-8, Simon & Schuster) Simon & Schuster.
—Postcard from Hell: Andy Derain Novel. 1995. 320p. 22.00 (0-684-80362-3, Simon & Schuster) Simon & Schuster.
Daniell, Rosemary. The Hurricane Season: A Novel. 1992. 416p. 20.00 o.p. (0-688-08860-0, Morrow, William & Co.) Morrow/Avon.
Davis, Albert B. Marquis at Bay. 1992. 336p. 24.95 (0-8071-1737-4) Louisiana State Univ. Pr.
Davis, J. Madison. Red Knight: A Novel. 1992. 232p. 19.95 o.p. (0-8027-1199-5) Walker & Co.
Davis, Kathleen Legeia. Serpentina: A Novel. 2003. (Illus.). 323p. 18.50 (0-9715402-1-7, 410-707-6686) Barnhardt & Ashe Publishing, Inc.
De Noux, O'Neil. The Big Show. 1998. 320p. pap. 5.95 (0-9653145-8-8, Autumn Bks.) Pontalba Pr.
—Crescent City Kills. 1992. mass mkt. 4.50 o.s.i (0-8217-3752-X, Zebra Bks.) Kensington Publishing Corp.
Despres, Loraine. The Scandalous Summer of Sissy LeBlanc. 2001. 352p. 24.00 (0-688-17389-6, Morrow, William & Co.) Morrow/Avon.
—The Scandalous Summer of Sissy LeBlanc. l.t. ed. 2002. 28.95 (0-7862-4098-9) Thorndike Pr.
—The Scandalous Summer of Sissy LeBlanc: A Novel. 2002. 352p. pap. 12.95 (0-06-050588-5, Perennial) HarperTrade.
Dobie, Ann B., ed. Something in Common: Contemporary Louisiana Stories. 1991. 302p. 19.95 (0-8071-1644-0) Louisiana State Univ. Pr.
Donachie, David. The Scent of Betrayal. 2003. (Privateersman Mysteries Ser.: No. 5). 448p. pap. 17.95 (1-59013-031-6) McBooks Pr., Inc.
Donaldson, D. J. Blood on the Bayou. 1991. 16.95 o.p. (0-312-05387-8, Saint Martin's Minotaur) St. Martin's Pr.
—Cajun Nights. 1989. pap. 3.95 o.p. (0-312-91610-8, St. Martin's Paperbacks); 1988. 256p. 16.95 o.p. (0-312-02175-5, Saint Martin's Minotaur) St. Martin's Pr.
—Louisiana Fever. (Andy Broussard/Kit Franklyn Mysteries Ser.). 288p. 1997. mass mkt. 5.99 o.p. (0-312-96257-6, St. Martin's Paperbacks); 1996. 21.95 o.p. (0-312-14362-1, Saint Martin's Minotaur) St. Martin's Pr.
—New Orleans Requiem. 1995. (Mystery Ser.). 250p. per. (0-373-26188-8, 1-26188-2, Worldwide Library) Harlequin Enterprises, Ltd.
—New Orleans Requiem. 1994. 240p. 19.95 o.p. (0-312-10495-2, Saint Martin's Minotaur) St. Martin's Pr.
—No Mardi Gras for the Dead. 1995. (WWL Mystery Ser.). mass mkt. (0-373-26163-2, 1-26163-5, Harlequin Bks.) Harlequin Enterprises, Ltd.
—No Mardi Gras for the Dead. 1992. (Andy Broussard - Kit Franklyn Mystery Ser.). 216p. 17.95 o.p. (0-312-08271-1) St. Martin's Pr.
—Sleeping with the Crawfish: An Andy Broussard & Kit Franklyn Mystery. (Andy Broussard/Kit Franklyn Mysteries Ser.). 272p. 1998. mass mkt. 5.99 (0-312-96681-4, St. Martin's Paperbacks); 1997. 21.95 o.p. (0-312-17025-4, Saint Martin's Minotaur) St. Martin's Pr.
Donovan, David Michael. Evil Down in the Alley: A Novel. 1999. 438p. 26.00 (0-9669259-3-9) J-D Publishing Co.
Doucet, Sharon Arms. Back Before Dark. 2004. 272p. pap. 12.95 (0-451-21104-9) NAL.
Drake, Shannon. When Darkness Falls. 2000. 432p. mass mkt. 6.99 (0-8217-6692-9, Zebra Bks.) Kensington Publishing Corp.
Dufresne, John. Deep in the Shade of Paradise: A Novel. 2003. 368p. pap. 14.00 (0-452-28406-6) Dutton/Plume.
—Deep in the Shade of Paradise: A Novel. 2002. 416p. 25.95 (0-393-02020-7) Norton, W. W. & Co., Inc.
—Louisiana Power & Light. 1995. 320p. pap. 13.95 (0-452-27502-4, Plume) Dutton/Plume.
—Louisiana Power & Light. 1994. xi, 306p. 22.00 o.p. (0-393-03648-0) Norton, W. W. & Co., Inc.
Dunbar, Alice. The Goodness of St. Rocque. 1977. (Black Heritage Library Collection). reprint ed. 22.95 (0-8369-8817-5) Ayer Co. Pubs., Inc.
Dunbar, Sophie. A Bad Hair Day: An Eclaire Mystery. 295th ed. 1998. (Eclaire Mysteries Ser.: No. 3). 296p. reprint ed. mass mkt. 5.95 (1-890768-08-1, Intrigue Pr.) Corvus Publishing.
—A Bad Hair Day: An Eclaire Mystery. 1996. 272p. 22.95 o.p. (0-312-13926-8, Saint Martin's Minotaur) St. Martin's Pr.
—Behind Eclaire's Doors. unabr. ed. 1998. (Claire & Dan Claiborne Eclaire Mystery Ser.: Bk. 1). audio 39.95 (1-55686-804-9) Books in Motion.
—Behind Eclaire's Doors. 1994. mass mkt. 4.99 o.p. (0-312-95259-7, St. Martin's Paperbacks) St. Martin's Pr.
—Behind Eclaire's Doors: A Tale of Murder & Mayhem in New Orleans. 1993. 224p. 17.95 o.p. (0-312-09280-6, Saint Martin's Minotaur) St. Martin's Pr.
—Behind Eclaire's Doors: An Eclaire Mystery. 1998. (Eclaire Mysteries Ser.: No. 1). 296p. reprint ed. mass mkt. 5.95 (1-890768-10-3, Intrigue Pr.) Corvus Publishing.
—Shiveree. (Eclaire Mysteries Ser.: 4). 416p. 2000. mass mkt. 5.95 (1-890768-24-3); 1999. 22.95 (1-890768-11-1) Corvus Publishing. (Intrigue Pr.).
Dunbar, Tony. City of Beads. 1996. 256p. mass mkt. 5.99 o.s.i (0-425-15578-1, Prime Crime) Berkley Publishing Group.
—City of Beads. 1996. 256p. 21.95 o.p. (0-399-14081-6, G. P. Putnam's Sons) Penguin Group (USA) Inc.
—The Crime Czar: A Tubby Dubonnet Mystery. 1998. (Tubby Dubonnet Mysteries Ser.). 240p. mass mkt. 5.99 o.s.i (0-440-22658-9) Dell Publishing.
—Crooked Man. 1996. 208p. mass mkt. 4.99 o.s.i (0-425-15138-7) Berkley Publishing Group.
—Crooked Man. 1994. 240p. 21.95 o.p. (0-399-13973-7, G. P. Putnam's Sons) Penguin Group (USA) Inc.
—Lucky Man. 1999. (Tubby Dubonnet Mysteries Ser.). 240p. mass mkt. 5.99 o.s.i (0-440-22662-7) Dell Publishing.
—Shelter from the Storm. 1998. 224p. mass mkt. 5.99 o.s.i (0-425-16644-9) Berkley Publishing Group.
—Shelter from the Storm. l.t. ed. 1998. (Large Print Book Ser.). pap. 23.95 (1-56895-607-X, Wheeler Publishing, Inc.) Gale Group.
—Shelter from the Storm. 1997. 256p. 24.95 o.p. (0-399-14301-7, G. P. Putnam's Sons) Penguin Group (USA) Inc.
—Trick Question. l.t. ed. 1997. (Tubby Dubonnet Mysteries Ser.). 224p. mass mkt. 5.99 o.s.i (0-425-16092-0, Prime Crime) Berkley Publishing Group.
—Trick Question. 1997. 256p. 22.95 o.p. (0-399-14184-7, G. P. Putnam's Sons) Penguin Group (USA) Inc.
Edwards, Cassie. Savage Destiny. 2003. 384p. mass mkt. 6.99 (0-8439-5051-X) Dorchester Publishing Co., Inc.
—Savage Destiny. 2003. (Basic Ser.). 389p. 28.95 (0-7862-5394-0) Thorndike Pr.
Edwards, Louis. N: A Romantic Mystery. 240p. 1998. pap. 12.95 o.s.i (0-452-27788-4, Plume); 1997. 22.95 o.p. (0-525-94182-7) Dutton/Plume.
Ellis, Julie. Kara. 2000. (Five Star Romance Ser.). 328p. 27.95 (0-7862-2839-3, Five Star) Gale Group.
—Savage Oaks. 1981. mass mkt. 2.25 o.s.i (0-449-23996-9, Fawcett) Ballantine Bks.
—Savage Oaks. l.t. ed. 2000. (G. K. Hall Romance Ser.). 453p. 26.95 (0-7838-9158-X, Macmillan Reference USA) Gale Group.
Emery, Lynn. All I Want Is Forever. 2002. 384p. mass mkt. 6.50 (0-06-008928-8) Morrow/Avon.
—Gotta Get Next to You. 2001. 384p. mass mkt. 6.50 (0-380-81304-1) Morrow/Avon.
—A Time to Love. 1999. mass mkt. 4.99 (1-58314-008-5); 304p. mass mkt. 4.99 o.s.i (0-7860-0641-2) Kensington Publishing Corp.
Fennelly, Tony. The Closet Hanging. 1987. (Matt Sinclair Ser.). 224p. 14.95 o.p. (0-88184-306-7); pap. 3.50 o.p. (0-88184-393-8) Avalon Publishing Group. (Carroll & Graf Pubs.).
—The Hippie in the Wall. 1994. 240p. 19.95 o.p. (0-312-10475-8, Saint Martin's Minotaur) St. Martin's Pr.
—Murder with a Twist: The Glory Hole Murders & the Closet Hanging. 1991. 432p. pap. 4.95 o.p. (0-88184-783-6, Carroll & Graf Pubs.) Avalon Publishing Group.
—1 (900) D-E-A-D: A Margo Fortier Mystery. 1996. 240p. 21.95 (0-312-14267-6, Saint Martin's Minotaur) St. Martin's Pr.
Folse, Pamela. A Sweet Surprise. 1995. (Illus.). 32p. (J). (ps-7). lib. bdg. 10.00 (1-884725-11-2) Blue Heron Pr.
Fontenot, Mary Alice. Clovis Crawfish & Fedora Field Mouse. 1998. (Clovis Crawfish Ser.). (Illus.). 32p. (J). (ps-3). 14.95 (1-56554-335-1) Pelican Publishing Co., Inc.
Forkner, Ben, ed. Louisiana Stories. 1990. 400p. (gr. 7-12). pap. 15.95 (0-88289-737-3); (YA). 15.95 (0-88289-784-5) Pelican Publishing Co., Inc.
Foster, B. J. Bayou Shadows. 2000. 267p. 21.95 (0-9675884-5-6) Cresent Hse. Publishing.
Fox, Frank G. Funky Butt Blues. 1996. 213p. (Orig.). pap. 10.00 (0-9652052-0-7) St. Expedite Pr.
Francois, John. The March. 1999. (Illus.). vi, 164p. 17.95 (0-9667806-0-4) Attakapas Pr.
Friedmann, Patty. Eleanor Rushing: A Novel. 288p. 2000. pap. text 14.00 (1-58243-077-2); 1999. text 23.00 o.p. (1-58243-003-9) Basic Bks. (Counterpoint Pr.).
Funderburk, Robert. All the Days Were Summer, Vol. 2. 1997. (Dylan St John Ser.: Vol. 2). 208p. pap. 8.99 o.p. (1-55661-615-5) Bethany Hse. Pubs.
—The Fires of Autumn. l.t. ed. 1996. (Dylan St John Ser.: Vol. 1). 256p. pap. 8.99 o.p. (1-55661-614-7) Bethany Hse. Pubs.
—Heart & Soul. 1995. (Innocent Years Ser.: Bk. 3). 304p. pap. 8.99 o.p. (1-55661-462-4) Bethany Hse. Pubs.
—Love & Glory. 1994. (Innocent Years Ser.: No. 1). 304p. pap. 8.99 o.p. (1-55661-460-8) Bethany Hse. Pubs.
—Love & Glory. l.t. ed. 2000. (Christian Fiction Ser.). 397p. 24.95 (0-7862-2375-8) Thorndike Pr.
—The Spring of Our Exile. 1999. (Dylan St John Ser.: Vol. 4). 224p. pap. 8.99 o.p. (1-55661-617-1) Bethany Hse. Pubs.
—Tenderness & Fire, Vol. 5. 1997. (Innocent Years Ser.: Vol. 5). 288p. pap. 8.99 o.p. (1-55661-464-0) Bethany Hse. Pubs.
—Tenderness & Fire. l.t. ed. 1998. (Christian Fiction Ser.: Vol. 5). 373p. 25.95 (0-7862-1299-3) Thorndike Pr.
—Winter of Grace. 1998. (Dylan St John Ser.: Vol. 3). 224p. (YA). (gr. 10 up). pap. 8.99 o.p. (1-55661-616-3) Bethany Hse. Pubs.
—Winter of Grace. l.t. ed. 1999. (Thorndike Christian Mystery Ser.). 355p. pap. 22.95 (0-7862-2067-8, Macmillan Reference USA) Gale Group.
Gaines, Ernest J. The Autobiography of Miss Jane Pittman. 1982. (Illus.). 272p. mass mkt. 6.50 (0-553-26357-9) Bantam Bks.
—The Autobiography of Miss Jane Pittman. unabr. ed. 1997. audio 44.95 (0-7861-1053-8, 1856) Blackstone Audio Bks., Inc.
—The Autobiography of Miss Jane Pittman. unabr. collector's ed. 1982. audio 56.00 (0-7366-0513-4, 1487) Books on Tape, Inc.
—The Autobiography of Miss Jane Pittman. 1987. 255p. 16.95 o.s.i (0-385-24017-1); 1971. 12.95 o.p. (0-385-27009-7) Doubleday Publishing.
—The Autobiography of Miss Jane Pittman. 1972. (Illus.). 13.55 (0-88103-562-9) Econo-Clad Bks.
—The Autobiography of Miss Jane Pittman. 1977. (Adult Ser.). reprint ed. lib. bdg. 10.95 o.p. (0-8161-6010-4, Macmillan Reference USA) Gale Group.
—The Autobiography of Miss Jane Pittman. unabr. ed. audio 19.95 o.p. (0-694-50413-0, SWC 2058, Caedmon) HarperTrade.
—The Autobiography of Miss Jane Pittman. unabr. ed. 1994. audio 60.00 (0-7887-0072-3, 94305E7) Recorded Bks., LLC.
—The Autobiography of Miss Jane Pittman. 1972. 12.04 (0-606-02213-9) Turtleback Bks.
—Bloodline: Five Stories. 1997. 256p. pap. 12.00 (0-679-78165-X, Vintage) Knopf Publishing Group.
—Catherine Carmier. unabr. ed. 1997. audio 32.95 Blackstone Audio Bks., Inc.
—Catherine Carmier. 1987. 256p. reprint ed. pap. 9.95 o.p. (0-86547-022-7, North Point Pr.) Farrar, Straus & Giroux.
—Catherine Carmier. 1993. (Vintage Contemporaries Ser.). 256p. pap. 12.95 (0-679-73891-6, Vintage) Knopf Publishing Group.
—A Gathering of Old Men. 1986. audio 13.95 (1-55644-155-X, 6051) American Audio Prose Library, Inc.
—A Gathering of Old Men. unabr. collector's ed. 1987. audio 42.00 (0-7366-1184-3, 2104) Books on Tape, Inc.
—A Gathering of Old Men. 1984. 224p. pap. 8.00 o.p. (0-394-72591-3, Vintage) Knopf Publishing Group.



 

—A Gathering of Old Men. 224p. 1992. pap. 11.00 (*0-679-73890-8*); 1983. 23.00 o.s.i (*0-394-51468-8*) Knopf, Alfred A. Inc.

—A Gathering of Old Men, unabr. ed. 2001. audio 51.00 (*0-7887-0399-4*, 94591E7) Recorded Bks., LLC.

—A Gathering of Old Men. 1992. 17.05 (*0-606-01027-0*) Turtleback Bks.

—In My Father's House. unabr. collector's ed. 1982. audio 36.00 (*0-7366-0514-2*, 1488) Books on Tape, Inc.

—In My Father's House. l.t. ed. 1993. 12.50 o.p. (*0-8161-6648-X*, Macmillan Reference USA) Gale Group.

—In My Father's House. 1978. 13.95 o.s.i (*0-394-47938-6*) Knopf, Alfred A. Inc.

—In My Father's House. 1983. 224p. reprint ed. pap. 6.95 o.p. (*0-393-30124-9*) Norton, W. W. & Co., Inc.

—In My Father's House. 1992. (Vintage Contemporaries Ser.). 224p. pap. 11.95 (*0-679-72791-4*) Random Hse., Inc.

—In My Father's House. unabr. ed. 1994. audio 44.00 (*0-7887-0041-3*, 94240E7) Recorded Bks., LLC.

—A Lesson Before Dying. l.t. ed. 1993. 25.95 o.p. (*0-7927-1795-3*); pap. 23.95 o.p. (*0-7927-1794-5*) BBC Audiobooks America.

—A Lesson Before Dying. unabr. collector's ed. 1994. audio 48.00 (*0-7366-2688-3*, 3423) Books on Tape, Inc.

—A Lesson Before Dying. 1994. 272p. pap. 12.00 o.p. (*0-679-74166-6*, Vintage) Knopf Publishing Group.

—A Lesson Before Dying. 1993. (Borzoi Reader Ser.). 25.00 o.p. (*0-679-41477-0*) Knopf, Alfred A. Inc.

—A Lesson Before Dying. unabr. ed. 1997. audio 32.95 (*0-375-40258-6*, RH Audio) Random Hse. Audio Publishing Group.

—A Lesson Before Dying. 1997. 272p. 26.00 (*0-679-45561-2*) Random Hse., Inc.

—A Lesson Before Dying. abr. ed. 1995. audio 17.00 (*1-57042-223-0*) Time Warner AudioBooks.

—A Lesson Before Dying. 1994. (Vintage Contemporaries Ser.). 18.05 (*0-606-07150-4*) Turtleback Bks.

—A Lesson Before Dying: A Novel. 1997. (Vintage Contemporaries Ser.). 272p. pap. 12.95 (*0-375-70270-9*, Vintage) Knopf Publishing Group.

—Of Love & Dust. unabr. collector's ed. 1982. audio 42.00 (*0-7366-0516-9*, 1490) Books on Tape, Inc.

—Of Love & Dust. 1994. 288p. pap. 12.95 (*0-679-75248-X*, Vintage) Knopf Publishing Group.

—Of Love & Dust. 1979. reprint ed. pap. 8.95 o.p. (*0-393-00914-9*) Norton, W. W. & Co., Inc.

Garwood, Julie. Heartbreaker. 2000. 432p. 24.95 o.s.i (*0-671-03299-2*, Atria) Simon & Schuster.

Gautreaux, Tim. Next Step in the Dance. 352p. 1999. pap. 14.00 (*0-312-19936-8*); 1998. 23.00 o.p. (*0-312-18143-4*) Picador.

—Same Place, Same Things. 1996. 224p. 20.95 o.p. (*0-312-14727-9*) St. Martin's Pr.

Gear, Kathleen O'Neal & Gear, W. Michael. People of the Owl: A Novel of Prehistoric North America. 2003. (First North Americans Ser.). (Illus.). 560p. 25.95 (*0-312-87741-2*, Forge Bks.) Doherty, Tom Assocs., LLC.

Gifford, Barry. Arise & Walk: A Novel. 1994. 176p. (J). 19.95 (*0-7868-6013-8*) Hyperion Pr.

—Baby Cat-Face. 1997. 192p. pap. 11.00 (*0-15-600525-5*, Harvest Bks.) Harcourt Trade Pubs.

Gifford, Barry, ed. Baby Cat-Face: A Novel. 1995. 192p. 20.00 o.s.i (*0-15-100183-9*) Harcourt Trade Pubs.

Gilchrist, Ellen. In the Land of Dreamy Dreams. unabr. collector's ed. 1989. audio 42.00 (*0-7366-1542-3*, 2411) Books on Tape, Inc.

—In the Land of Dreamy Dreams. 1985. 14.95 o.s.i (*0-316-31304-1*); 167p. pap. 11.95 o.p. (*0-316-31306-8*) Little Brown & Co.

—In the Land of Dreamy Dreams. 1981. 14.95 o.p. (*0-938626-02-7*); pap. 5.95 o.p. (*0-938626-03-5*) Univ. of Arkansas Pr.

Girardi, Robert. Madeleine's Ghost: A Novel of New York, New Orleans & the Next World. l.t. ed. 1996. 530p. 24.95 o.p. (*0-7838-1507-7*, Macmillan Reference USA) Gale Group.

—Madeleine's Ghost: A Novel of New York, New Orleans & the Next World. 1999. E-Book 11.95 (*0-440-33399-7*) Random Hse., Inc.

—Madeleine's Ghost: A Novel of New York, New Orleans & the Next World. unabr. ed. 1997. audio 85.00 (*0-7887-0932-1*, 95072E7) Recorded Bks., LLC.

Glancy, Diane H. The Only Piece of Furniture in the House. 2001. 160p. pap. 10.95 (*1-55921-294-2*); 1996. 124p. 18.95 o.p. (*1-55921-183-0*) Moyer Bell.

Goodman, Joanna. Belle of the Bayou. 1998. 168p. pap. 16.95 (*0-88984-198-5*) Porcupine's Quill, Inc. CAN. *Dist:* Univ. of Toronto Pr.

Gores, Joe. Dead Man, set. unabr. ed. 1995. audio 69.95 (*0-7862-9974-6*, CSL 083) BBC Audiobooks America.

—Dead Man. 1993. 272p. 18.95 (*0-89296-541-X*) Mysterious Pr.

—Dead Man. 1994. 272p. mass mkt. 5.50 o.s.i (*0-446-40391-1*) Warner Bks., Inc.

Graf, Herb R. Memoirs & Murder: A Louisiana Reconstruction Mystery. 1995. 176p. pap. 8.00 (*1-884725-06-6*) Blue Heron Pr.

—Memoirs & Murder: A Louisiana Reconstruction Mystery. Gorman, Carolyn P., ed. 1995. 176p. 10.00 o.p. (*1-884725-15-5*) Blue Heron Pr.

Grant, Elaine. Roses for Chloe. 1998. (Haunting Hearts Ser.). 320p. mass mkt. 5.99 o.s.i (*0-515-12439-7*, Jove) Berkley Publishing Group.

Grau, Shirley Ann. The Hard Blue Sky. 2001. (Voices of the South Ser.). 480p. pap. 17.95 (*0-8071-2690-X*) Louisiana State Univ. Pr.

Greenburg, Martin H. & Davis, Russell, eds. Mardi Gras Madness: Stories of Murder & Mayhem in New Orleans. 2000. 239p. pap. 16.95 (*1-58182-077-1*, Cumberland Hearthside) Cumberland Hse. Publishing.

Greenough, Malcolm W., Jr. Dear Lily: A Love Story. Silitch, Clarissa M., ed. 1987. (Illus.). 240p. 15.95 o.p. (*0-89909-136-9*) Yankee Bks.

Grimsley, Jim. Boulevard. 2002. 304p. tchr. ed. 23.95 (*1-56512-251-8*) Algonquin Bks. of Chapel Hill.

Grisham, John. The Client. l.t. ed. 1993. 432p. 29.95 (*0-385-42471-X*); (YA). 26.00 o.s.i (*0-385-46865-2*); 432p. 200.00 o.s.i (*0-385-47015-0*) Bantam Doubleday Dell Large Print Group, Inc. (Doubleday Large Type).

—The Client. unabr. ed. 1993. audio 80.00 (*0-7366-2464-3*, 3228) Books on Tape, Inc.

—The Client. 1994. 576p. mass mkt. 7.99 (*0-440-21352-5*); mass mkt. (*0-440-21807-1*) Dell Publishing.

—The Client. 1994. audio 27.50 o.s.i (*0-553-54152-8*); 1993. audio 18.80 o.s.i (*0-553-70058-8*); 1993. 360p. pap. 23.50 incl. audio (*0-553-47139-2*, 692172) Random Hse. Audio Publishing Group. (RH Audio).

—The Client. 1994. (Illus.). 14.04 (*0-606-18101-6*) Turtleback Bks.

—The Client: International Edition. 1993. 512p. mass mkt. 6.99 o.s.i (*0-440-29526-2*) Dell Publishing.

—El Cliente. 2nd ed. 1998. (SPA.). 424p. (*84-08-02141-9*) GeoPlaneta, Editorial, S. A.

—El Cliente. 1994. (SPA.). 16.30 (*0-606-18347-7*) Turtleback Bks.

—Tiempo de Matar. 1995. (SPA., Illus.). 472p. 9.95 (*84-08-01475-7*, PT9159) GeoPlaneta, Editorial, S. A. ESP. *Dist:* Lectorum Pubns., Inc., Planeta Publishing Corp.

Guidry, Jacqueline. The Year the Colored Sisters Came to Town. 256p. 2003. pap. 15.00 (*1-56649-256-4*); 2001. 25.00 (*1-56649-200-9*) Welcome Rain Pubs.

Haines, Carolyn. Buried Bones. 2000. 368p. mass mkt. 5.99 (*0-553-58172-4*) Bantam Bks.

—Buried Bones. l.t. ed. 2003. 588p. 25.95 (*0-375-43270-1*, Random House Large Print) Random Hse. Large Print.

Hall, Martha L. Apple-Green Triumph & Other Stories. 1990. 152p. 17.95 (*0-8071-1608-4*) Louisiana State Univ. Pr.

Hambly, Barbara. A Free Man of Color. 1998. 432p. reprint ed. mass mkt. 6.99 (*0-553-57526-0*) Bantam Bks.

—Wet Grave. 2003. 384p. mass mkt. 6.50 (*0-553-58159-7*); 2002. (Illus.). 304p. 23.95 (*0-553-10935-9*) Bantam Bks.

—Wet Grave. l.t. ed. 2003. 486p. 25.95 (*0-375-43274-4*, Random House Large Print) Random Hse. Large Print.

Haymaker, Lafayette. Nola 46. 1995. (Illus.). 211p. (Orig.). pap. 14.00 (*0-9641632-2-5*) Mainesburg Pr.

Hearn, Lafcadio. Chita: A Memory of Last Island. LaBarre, Delia, ed. 2003. 128p. 20.00 (*1-57806-558-5*, A Banner Bk.) Univ. Pr. of Mississippi.

Hearon, Shelby. Ella in Bloom. l.t. ed. 2001. (Thorndike Press Large Print Women's Fiction Ser.). 336p. 29.95 (*0-7862-3302-8*) Thorndike Pr.

—Ella in Bloom: A Novel. 2002. 272p. reprint ed. 13.00 (*0-14-200088-4*) Viking Penguin.

Hebert, Charles J. Swimming to Atlantis. Neil, Winter C., ed. unabr. ed. 1997. 296p. 17.95 (*0-9653145-0-2*, 97-01, Autumn Bks.) Pontalba Pr.

Hegwood, Martin. Big Easy Backroad. E-Book 22.95 (*0-312-26441-0*); 2000. 256p. mass mkt. 5.99 (*0-312-97141-9*, St. Martin's Paperbacks); 3rd ed. 1999. 247p. 22.95 (*0-312-20277-6*, Saint Martin's Minotaur) St. Martin's Pr.

Helms, Richard. Juicy Watusi. 2002. (Pat Gallegher Mystery Ser.). 320p. pap. 15.95 (*0-9710159-1-0*, Back Alley Bks.) Barbadoes Hall Communications.

Hess, Joan. Death by the Light of the Moon. 208p. 1995. pap. 15.00 (*0-345-47171-7*); 1994. mass mkt. 6.50 (*0-345-37838-5*) Ballantine Bks.

—Death by the Light of the Moon. (Claire Malloy Mystery Ser.). 240p. 2003. mass mkt. 6.99 (*0-312-99101-0*, St. Martin's Paperbacks); 1992. 18.95 o.p. (*0-312-06949-9*, Saint Martin's Minotaur) St. Martin's Pr.

Hicks, Jimmy G. Eight, Skate & Donate. 2001. pap. 21.95 (*0-595-16869-8*) iUniverse, Inc.

Hill, Ernest. Cry Me a River. 2004. 304p. pap. 15.00 (*0-7582-0277-6*, Kensington Bks.); 2003. 24.00 (*0-7582-0276-8*) Kensington Publishing Corp.

—Satisfied with Nothin' 1996. 304p. 21.50 o.p. (*0-684-82259-8*, Simon & Schuster) Simon & Schuster.

Hill, Sandra. Frankly My Dear. (Timeswept Ser.). 2003. 368p. mass mkt. 5.99 (*0-8439-4617-2*); 1996. 400p. pap. 5.50 (*0-8439-4042-5*) Dorchester Publishing Co., Inc. (Leisure Bks.).

—Frankly, My Dear. 1999. E-Book 9.95 (*0-585-29855-6*) netLibrary, Inc.

Hoag, Tami. Cry Wolf. 1997. 560p. mass mkt. 7.99 (*0-553-56160-X*) Bantam Bks.

—Lucky's Lady. 2003. 400p. mass mkt. 7.99 (*0-553-58718-8*); 1992. 368p. mass mkt. 6.99 o.s.i (*0-553-29534-9*) Bantam Bks.

—Lucky's Lady. 1992. 272p. 15.00 o.s.i (*0-385-42289-X*) Doubleday Publishing.

—A Thin Dark Line. 1998. 608p. reprint ed. mass mkt. 7.99 (*0-553-57188-5*) Bantam Bks.

—A Thin Dark Line. 2002. pap. incl. audio (*0-7435-2754-2*) Encore Performance Publishing.

—A Thin Dark Line. l.t. ed. 1997. (Large Print Book Ser.). 26.95 o.p. (*1-56895-450-6*, Wheeler Publishing, Inc.) Gale Group.

—A Thin Dark Line, unabr. ed. 1997. audio 117.00 (*0-7887-1766-9*, 95244E7) Recorded Bks., LLC.

—A Thin Dark Line. abr. ed. 1997. audio 23.00 (*0-671-57477-9*, 495077, Simon & Schuster Audioworks) Simon & Schuster Audio.

Hotchner, A. E. Louisiana Purchase. 1996. 400p. 24.00 o.p. (*0-7867-0309-1*, Carroll & Graf Pubs.) Avalon Publishing Group.

—Louisiana Purchase. 1997. 384p. reprint ed. pap. 14.95 (*1-891442-00-7*) Virginia Publishing Corp.

Howard, Linda. After the Night. 352p. 1995. mass mkt. 6.50 (*0-671-79936-3*); 1997. reprint ed. pap. 7.99 (*0-671-01970-8*) Simon & Schuster. (Pocket).

—After the Night. l.t. ed. 2001. (Thorndike Press Large Print Famous Authors Ser.). 565p. 28.95 o.p. (*0-7862-2853-9*) Thorndike Pr.

—Kill & Tell. l.t. ed. 1998. pap. 23.95 o.p. (*1-56895-554-5*, Wheeler Publishing, Inc.) Gale Group.

—Kill & Tell. 1998. 320p. mass mkt. 7.99 (*0-671-56883-3*, Pocket) Simon & Schuster.

Jackson, Brian Keith. Walking Through Mirrors. 1999. 272p. pap. 14.00 (*0-671-56894-9*, Washington Square Pr.); 1998. 258p. 23.00 (*0-671-56893-0*, Atria) Simon & Schuster.

—Walking Through Mirrors. 1999. 20.05 (*0-606-19129-1*) Turtleback Bks.

Jackson, Lisa. Cold Blooded. 2002. 352p. mass mkt. 6.99 (*0-8217-6934-0*) Kensington Publishing Corp.

Jekel, Pamela. Bayou. 1992. mass mkt. 5.99 o.s.i (*0-8217-3740-6*); 1991. mass mkt. 20.00 o.s.i (*0-8217-3490-3*) Kensington Publishing Corp. (Zebra Bks.).

—Natchez. 1996. mass mkt. 6.99 o.s.i (*1-57566-026-1*); 1995. 482p. mass mkt. 19.95 o.s.i (*0-8217-5061-5*) Kensington Publishing Corp.

Johansen, Iris. Body of Lies: A Novel. 2003. 400p. mass mkt. 7.50 (*0-553-58214-3*); 2002. 352p. 24.95 (*0-553-80097-3*) Bantam Bks.

—Body of Lies: A Novel. abr. ed. 2002. audio 25.95 (*0-553-71496-1*); audio compact disk 29.95 (*0-553-71497-X*) Random Hse. Audio Publishing Group.

—Body of Lies: A Novel. l.t. ed. 2002. 480p. 24.95 (*0-375-43158-6*) Random Hse. Large Print.

Johnson, Guy. Standing at the Scratch Line. 2001. E-Book 11.95 (*1-58945-866-4*) Adobe Systems, Inc.

—Standing at the Scratch Line. 2001. E-Book 11.95 (*0-375-50656-X*) Random Hse., Inc.

—Standing at the Scratch Line: A Novel. 1998. 432p. 24.95 o.s.i (*0-375-50158-4*) Random Hse. Information Group.

Karl, M. S. The Deerslayer. 1991. 208p. 17.95 o.p. (*0-312-06336-9*, Saint Martin's Minotaur) St. Martin's Pr.

Kein, Sybil. An American South. 1996. 60p. pap. 10.00 o.p. (*0-87013-412-4*) Lotus Pr., Inc.

Kemper, Marjorie. Until That Good Day: A Novel. 2003. 320p. 24.95 (*0-312-29079-9*) St. Martin's Pr.

King, Atticus. Pretense . . . of Innocence. 1996. 256p. (Orig.). pap. 12.95 (*1-56184-081-5*) New Falcon Pubns.

King, Grace E. Tales of a Time & Place. reprint ed. 27.50 (*0-404-03690-2*) AMS Pr., Inc.

—Tales of a Time & Place. 1972. lib. bdg. 17.00 (*0-8422-8086-3*); reprint ed. pap. text 6.95 (*0-8290-0675-3*) Irvington Pubs.

—Tales of a Time & Place. 1992. (BCL1-PS American Literature Ser.). 303p. reprint ed. lib. bdg. 89.00 (*0-7812-6778-1*) Reprint Services Corp.

—Tales of a Time & Place. 19.00 o.p. (*0-403-04304-2*) Somerset Pubs., Inc.

Knight, Eric. Way of the Wolf: Book One of the Vampire Earth. 2003. 400p. mass mkt. 6.50 (*0-451-45939-3*, ROC) NAL.

Lanigan, Catherine. California Moon. 2000. 376p. per. (*1-55166-578-6*, Harlequin Bks.) Harlequin Enterprises, Ltd.

Lawrence, Carole. Looking for Mary Gabriel. E-Book 23.95 (*0-312-70677-4*); 2002. 320p. 23.95 (*0-312-28541-8*) St. Martin's Pr.

Leblance, Whitney J. Blues in the Wind. 2002. 330p. 23.95 (*0-913515-47-7*) River City Publishing.

Leonard, Elmore. Bandits. l.t. ed. 1987. 382p. 18.95 o.p. (*0-8161-4297-1*); 10.95 o.p. (*0-8161-4298-X*) Gale Group. (Macmillan Reference USA).

—Bandits. 1987. 17.95 o.p. (*0-87795-841-6*, Morrow, William & Co.) Morrow/Avon.

Lewis, Henry C. Odd Leaves from the Life of a Louisiana Swamp Doctor. 1985. reprint ed. lib. bdg. 18.75 o.p. (*0-8398-1160-8*) Irvington Pubs.

—Odd Leaves from the Life of a Louisiana Swamp Doctor. 1997. (Library of Southern Civilization). (Illus.). 240p. 24.95 (*0-8071-2185-1*); pap. 12.95 (*0-8071-2167-3*) Louisiana State Univ. Pr.

Lewis, John-Paul. Buffalo Gordon. 2001. 528p. 25.95 o.p. (*0-312-87376-X*, Forge Bks.) Doherty, Tom Assocs., LLC.

Llwellyn, Michael. Twelfth Night. 1997. 384p. (YA). 21.95 o.p. (*1-57566-082-2*, Kensington Bks.) Kensington Publishing Corp.

Lochte, Dick. Blue Bayou. 1993. (Southern Mysteries Ser.). mass mkt. 4.99 o.s.i (*0-8041-1145-6*, Ivy Bks.) Ballantine Bks.

—Blue Bayou. 1992. 304p. 20.00 o.p. (*0-671-74711-8*, Simon & Schuster) Simon & Schuster.

—The Neon Smile. 1996. mass mkt. 5.99 o.s.i (*0-8041-1405-6*, Ivy Bks.) Ballantine Bks.

—The Neon Smile. 1995. (Illus.). 304p. 21.00 (*0-671-74712-6*, Simon & Schuster) Simon & Schuster.

Lovelace, Merline. A Savage Beauty. 2003. 384p. mass mkt. (*1-55166-707-X*, Mira Bks.) Harlequin Enterprises, Ltd.

—A Savage Beauty. l.t. ed. 2003. 444p. 28.95 (*0-7862-6072-6*, Large Print Pr.) Thorndike Pr.

Lyles, Milton. The Cruelest Lie. 1996. 224p. 21.95 o.p. (*0-935016-49-X*) Zinn Publishing Group.

—Cruelest Lie. 1998. 320p. (YA). pap. 14.95 (*1-887492-01-1*) Hi.J.Que Publishing.

MacBride, Roger Lea. On the Banks of the Bayou. 1998. (Little House Ser.: Vol. 1). (Illus.). 240p. (J). (gr. 3-6). pap. 5.99 (*0-06-440582-6*) HarperCollins Pubs.

Maiman, Jaye. Old Black Magic: A Robin Miller Mystery. 1997. (Robin Miller Mysteries Ser.: Vol. 6). 288p. pap. 11.95 o.p. (*1-56280-175-9*) Naiad Pr., Inc.

Martin, Gilbert E. Passe Pour Blanc: Creole Secrets. 2001. 197p. (*1-55212-736-2*) Trafford Publishing.

Martin, Valerie. Property. l.t. ed. 2003. lib. bdg. 28.95 (*1-58547-327-8*, Platinum) Ctr. Point Large Print.

—Property. 2003. 208p. 23.95 (*0-385-50408-X*, Talese, Nan A.) Doubleday Publishing.

—Property. 2004. 208p. pap. 12.00 (*0-375-71330-1*, Vintage) Knopf Publishing Group.

Matthews, Christine & Randisi, Robert J. The Masks of Auntie Laveau: A Gil & Claire Hunt Mystery. 2002. 208p. 23.95 (*0-312-26898-X*, Saint Martin's Minotaur) St. Martin's Pr.

McCammon, Robert R. Gone South. l.t. ed. 1993. 22.95 o.p. (*1-56895-018-7*, Wheeler Publishing, Inc.) Gale Group.

—Gone South. Peters, Sally, ed. 1992. 368p. 22.00 (*0-671-74306-6*, Atria) Simon & Schuster.

McClafferty, Susan. Don't Tell a Soul. 2003. 352p. mass mkt. 5.99 (*0-8217-7299-6*) Kensington Publishing Corp.

McCloskey, Walter. Risking Elizabeth. 1998. 320p. mass mkt. 6.99 o.s.i (*0-425-16413-6*) Berkley Publishing Group.

—Risking Elizabeth. 1997. 288p. 21.50 (*0-684-82434-5*, Simon & Schuster) Simon & Schuster.

McGaughey, Neil. Otherwise Known As Murder. 1994. 224p. text 20.00 (*0-684-19674-3*, Macmillan Reference USA) Gale Group.

McKinney, Meagan. A Man to Slay Dragons. l.t. ed. 1996. 440p. lib. bdg. 23.95 (*1-57490-063-3*, Beeler Large Print Bks.) Beeler, Thomas T. Publisher.

—A Man to Slay Dragons. 1996. 416p. mass mkt. 5.99 o.s.i (*0-8217-5345-2*, Zebra Bks.); 384p. pap. 21.95 o.p. (*1-57566-009-1*) Kensington Publishing Corp.

—My Wicked Enchantress. 1988. 416p. mass mkt. 5.50 o.s.i (*0-440-20301-5*) Dell Publishing.

—My Wicked Enchantress. 1997. (Romance Ser.). 408p. pap. 23.95 (*0-7862-1206-3*, Five Star) Gale Group.

—My Wicked Enchantress. 1997. 416p. mass mkt. 5.99 o.s.i (*0-8217-5661-3*) Kensington Publishing Corp.

—Still of the Night. 2001. 32p. 23.00 o.s.i (*1-57566-615-4*) Kensington Publishing Corp.

McVoy, L. C. Louisiana in the Short Story. 1970. (American History & Americana Ser.: No. 47). reprint ed. lib. bdg. 75.00 (*0-8383-1171-7*) M.S.G. Haskell Hse.

Michaels, Fern. Listen to Your Heart. abr. ed. 2000. audio 17.95 o.p. (*1-56740-907-5*, 2120, Nova Audio Bks.); audio 24.95 (*1-56740-366-2*, 2119,

Brilliance Audio Unabridged); 6p. audio 44.25 (*1-56740-733-1*, 2121, Unabridged Library Editions) Brilliance Audio.
—Listen to Your Heart. l.t. ed. 2000. 27.95 (*1-56895-876-5*, Wheeler Publishing, Inc.) Gale Group.
—Listen to Your Heart. 2004. 256p. mass mkt. 6.99 (*0-8217-7463-8*, Zebra Bks.); 2000. 214p. 20.00 o.s.i (*1-57566-572-7*) Kensington Publishing Corp.
—Listen to Your Heart. l.t. ed. 2004. 229p. pap. 13.95 (*1-59413-027-2*, Large Print Pr.) Thorndike Pr.
—Plain Jane. l.t. ed. 2001. 532p. 31.95 o.p. (*0-7862-3434-2*) Gale Group.
—Plain Jane. 2002. 384p. mass mkt. 7.99 (*0-8217-6927-8*); 2001. 34p. 24.00 o.s.i (*1-57566-673-1*, Kensington Bks.) Kensington Publishing Corp.
—Plain Jane. l.t. ed. 2002. 568p. pap. 13.95 (*0-7862-3435-0*) Thorndike Pr.
Miller, Brenda Rhodes. The Laying on of Hands. 2004. 256p. pap. 12.95 (*0-7679-1556-9*) Broadway Bks.
Million, Leslie. Duke Dunbar: Louisiana Man. 1996. 192p. 15.95 o.p. (*0-944957-58-7*) Rivercross Publishing, Inc.
Moores, Amanda. Dream Palace. 1994. 288p. 20.00 o.p. (*0-7867-0125-0*, Carroll & Graf Pubs.) Avalon Publishing Group.
—Dream Palace. 1993. 288p. 21.00 (*0-671-75919-1*, Simon & Schuster) Simon & Schuster.
Morris, Gilbert. And Then There Were Two. l.t. ed. 2002. 431p. pap. 16.95 (*1-4104-0015-8*, Walker Large Print) Gale Group.
—And Then There Were Two. l.t. ed. 2001. (Dani Ross Mysteries Ser.). 463p. 24.95 o.p. (*0-7862-3088-6*) Thorndike Pr.
—Deadly Deception. 1991. (Danielle Ross Mystery Ser.: No. 3). 320p. (gr. 10). pap. 9.99 o.p. (*0-8007-5419-0*) Revell, Fleming H. Co.
Morris, Lynn & Morris, Gilbert. The Secret Place of Thunder. 1996. (Cheney Duvall, M. D. Ser.: No. 5). 336p. pap. 11.99 (*1-55661-426-8*) Bethany Hse. Pubs.
—The Secret Place of Thunder. l.t. ed. 1998. (Cheney Duvall, M. D. Ser.: Vol. 5). 393p. 24.95 (*0-7862-1514-3*) Thorndike Pr.
Morsi, Pamela. The Love Charm. 1996. mass mkt. 5.99 (*0-380-78641-9*, Avon Bks.) Morrow/Avon.
—The Love Charm. l.t. ed. 1998. (G. K. Hall Romance Ser.). 424 p. 27.95 (*0-7838-0307-9*) Thorndike Pr.
Moser, Kay. Belle Saint Marie. 1996. 288p. mass mkt. 5.99 o.p. (*0-7852-7539-8*) Nelson, Thomas Inc.
Nance, Kathleen. The Trickster. 2000. (Time of Your Life Ser.). 400p. mass mkt. 5.99 (*0-505-52382-5*, Love Spell) Dorchester Publishing Co., Inc.
Neihart, Ben. Hey, Joe: A Novel. 1996. 208p. 21.00 o.p. (*0-684-81316-5*, Simon & Schuster) Simon & Schuster.
Nicholls, Josephine H. Bayou Triste: A Story of Louisiana. 1977. (Black Heritage Library Collection). reprint ed. 26.95 (*0-8369-9040-4*) Ayer Co. Pubs., Inc.
Olivier, Robert L. Tidoon. 1972. 104p. 14.95 (*0-911116-62-1*); pap. 12.95 (*1-56554-642-3*) Pelican Publishing Co., Inc.
—Tinonc: Son of the Cajun Teche. 1974. (Illus.). 122p. 14.95 (*0-88289-054-9*) Pelican Publishing Co., Inc.
Ondaatje, Michael. Coming Through Slaughter. 1996. 160p. pap. 11.00 (*0-679-76785-1*, Vintage) Knopf Publishing Group.
—Coming Through Slaughter. 1983. pap. 2.25 o.p. (*0-380-42911-X*, Avon Bks.) Morrow/Avon.
—Coming Through Slaughter. 1977. 9.95 o.p. (*0-393-08765-4*) Norton, W. W. & Co., Inc.
—Coming Through Slaughter. 1984. 158p. pap. 10.95 o.p. (*0-14-007281-0*, Penguin Bks.) Viking Penguin.
Parker, F. M. The Assassins. l.t. ed. 1990. (General Ser.). 350p. lib. bdg. 18.95 o.p. (*0-8161-4999-2*, Macmillan Reference USA) Gale Group.
—The Assassins. 1989. 16.95 o.p. (*0-453-00701-5*); 1990. 256p. reprint ed. mass mkt. 3.95 o.p. (*0-451-16846-1*, Signet Bks.) NAL.
—Distant Thunder. l.t. ed. 2002. (Western Ser.). 415p. pap. 19.95 (*1-58724-269-9*, Wheeler Publishing, Inc.) Gale Group.
—Distant Thunder. 1999. 384p. mass mkt. 5.99 o.s.i (*0-7860-0647-1*, Pinnacle Bks.) Kensington Publishing Corp.
Parrish, Timothy A. Red Stick Men: Stories. 2001. 227p. reprint ed. pap. 16.00 (*1-57806-421-X*) Univ. Pr. of Mississippi.
Pavie, Theodore. Tales of the Sabine Borderlands: Early Louisiana & Texas Fiction. Klier, Betje B., ed. & tr. by. Marsh, Anne C. et al, trs. 1998. (Centennial Series of the Association of Former Students: No. 79). (Illus.). 144p. 29.95 (*0-89096-837-3*); pap. 15.95 (*0-89096-854-3*) Texas A&M Univ. Pr.
Peart, Jane. The House of Haunted Dreams. 1992. 3.99 o.p. (*1-55773-649-9*, Diamond Bks.) Ace Bks.
Pitre, Glen. Belizaire the Cajun. Shapiro, Dean, ed. 1988. (Illus.). 144p. 15.95 o.p. (*0-88289-711-X*); pap. 10.95 (*0-88289-671-7*) Pelican Publishing Co., Inc.
Plain, Belva. Crescent City. 1984. 432p. 16.95 o.p. (*0-385-29354-2*, Delacorte Pr.) Dell Publishing.
—Crescent City. l.t. ed. 1985. (General Ser.). 18.95 o.p. (*0-8161-3775-7*, Macmillan Reference USA) Gale Group.
Postell, Catherine. On Toplecote Bayou. 1977. (Black Heritage Library Collection). reprint ed. 15.95 (*0-8369-9048-X*) Ayer Co. Pubs., Inc.
Pousson, Martin. No Place, Louisiana. 2003. 272p. reprint ed. pap. 14.00 (*1-57322-976-8*, Riverhead Trade (Paperbacks)) Berkley Publishing Group.
—No Place, Louisiana. 2002. 240p. 24.95 o.s.i (*1-57322-200-3*); (*1-57322-199-6*) Putnam Publishing Group, The. (Riverhead Bks. (Hardcovers)).
Poyer, David. Louisiana Blue: A Tiller Gallaway Underwater Thriller. 1994. 304p. 22.00 o.p. (*0-312-10494-4*); Vol. 1. 1995. (Louisiana Blue Ser.: Vol. 1). mass mkt. 5.99 (*0-312-95422-0*, St. Martin's Paperbacks) St. Martin's Pr.
Reaves, Michael. Voodoo Child. 352p. 1999. pap. text 6.99 (*0-8125-1993-0*); 1998. 25.95 o.p. (*0-312-85608-3*) Doherty, Tom Assocs., LLC. (Tor Bks.).
Redmann, J. M. Death by the Riverside. 1990. 256p. (Orig.). pap. 9.95 o.p. (*0-934678-27-8*) New Victoria Pubs., Inc.
—Death of Jocasta. 1992. 288p. (Orig.). pap. 10.95 o.p. (*0-934678-39-1*) New Victoria Pubs., Inc.
—The Intersection of Law & Desire. 1997. mass mkt. 5.99 (*0-380-72819-2*, Avon Bks.) Morrow/Avon.
—The Intersection of Law & Desire. 1995. 336p. 22.00 o.p. (*0-393-03793-2*) Norton, W. W. & Co., Inc.
—Lost Daughters: A Micky Knight Mystery. 1999. (Mickey Knight Mystery Ser.). 320p. text 24.95 o.p. (*0-393-04028-3*) Norton, W. W. & Co., Inc.
Rhodes, Jewell P. Voodoo Dreams: A Novel of Marie. 1993. 436p. 22.95 o.p. (*0-312-09869-3*) St. Martin's Pr.
Rhodes, Jewell Parker. Voodoo Dreams: A Novel of Marie Laveau. 4th ed. 1995. 448p. pap. 14.00 (*0-312-11931-3*) Picador.
Rice, Anne. Blackwood Farm. 2002. 544p. (*0-676-97542-9*); 26.95 (*0-375-41199-2*) Knopf, Alfred A. Inc.
—Blackwood Farm: The Vampire Chronicles. 2002. E-Book 6.99 (*1-4000-4020-5*) Knopf Publishing Group.
—The Feast of All Saints. 1992. 576p. pap. 15.00 (*0-345-37604-8*); 1986. 640p. mass mkt. 7.99 (*0-345-33453-1*); 1985. mass mkt. 4.95 o.s.i (*0-449-21063-4*, Fawcett); 1981. 640p. mass mkt. 2.95 o.p. (*0-449-24378-8*) Ballantine Bks.
—The Feast of All Saints. abr. ed. 1994. audio 8.99 o.s.i (*0-679-43413-5*, 390765); 1992. audio 16.00 o.p. (*0-394-58812-6*) Random Hse. Audio Publishing Group. (RH Audio).
—The Feast of All Saints. 1980. 14.95 o.p. (*0-671-24755-7*, Simon & Schuster) Simon & Schuster.
—Lasher. (SPA.). 26.95 (*950-08-1316-5*, AA9101) Atlantida ARG. *Dist:* Lectorum Pubns., Inc.
—Lasher. (Lives of the Mayfair Witches Ser.). 1995. 640p. mass mkt. 7.99 (*0-345-39781-9*); 1994. 592p. pap. 14.95 (*0-345-37764-8*) Ballantine Bks.
—Lasher. 1993. 592p. 30.00 (*0-679-41295-6*); 22.00 o.s.i (*0-394-28021-0*) Knopf, Alfred A. Inc.
—Lasher, abr. ed. 1993. audio 17.00 (*0-679-42173-4*, 391044, RH Audio) Random Hse. Audio Publishing Group.
—Merrick. 2000. 320p. o.s.i (*0-676-97331-0*) Knopf Canada CAN. *Dist:* Random Hse. of Canada, Ltd., Random Hse., Inc.
—Merrick. 2000. (Vampire Chronicles). 320p. 26.95 (*0-679-45448-9*) Knopf, Alfred A. Inc.
—Merrick. l.t. ed. 2000. 544p. 26.95 (*0-375-43077-6*) Random Hse. Large Print.
—Taltos. 2000. 12.95 B Ediciones S.A. ESP. *Dist:* Distribooks, Inc.
—Taltos. 1996. 576p. mass mkt. 7.99 (*0-345-40431-9*); 1995. 480p. pap. 14.95 (*0-345-39471-2*); 1995. mass mkt. (*0-345-40006-2*, Ballantine Bks.) Ballantine Bks.
—Taltos. 1994. 467p. 25.00 (*0-679-42573-X*) Knopf, Alfred A. Inc.
—Taltos. (FRE.). pap. 12.95 (*2-266-07477-6*) Presses Pocket FRA. *Dist:* Distribooks, Inc.
—Taltos, Set. abr. ed. 1994. audio 22.50 (*0-679-43654-5*, 492019, RH Audio) Random Hse. Audio Publishing Group.
—Taltos. deluxe ltd. num. ed. 1994. 467p. 150.00 (*0-9631925-1-5*) Trice, B.E. Publishing.
—The Violin. 2002. (SPA.). pap. 17.95 (*950-08-2295-4*, AA11960) Atlantida ARG. *Dist:* Lectorum Pubns., Inc.
—The Violin. 1999. 384p. mass mkt. 7.99 (*0-345-42530-8*); 1998. 304p. pap. 14.00 (*0-345-38942-5*); 1998. 7.50 (*0-345-42446-8*, Del Rey) Ballantine Bks.
—The Violin. unabr. ed. 1997. audio 64.00 (*0-7366-3771-0*, 4444) Books on Tape, Inc.
—The Violin. l.t. ed. 1997. pap. 25.95 o.p. (*0-7838-8247-5*, Macmillan Reference USA) Gale Group.
—The Violin. 1997. 289p. 25.95 (*0-679-43302-3*) Knopf, Alfred A. Inc.
—The Violin. unabr. ed. 1997. audio 39.95 (*0-679-46066-7*, 105975);Set. audio compact disk 27.50 (*0-679-46065-9*) Random Hse. Audio Publishing Group. (RH Audio).
—The Violin. l.t. ed. 1997. (Large Print Ser.). 496p. pap. 25.95 (*0-679-77444-0*) Random Hse. Large Print.
—The Violin. deluxe ltd. ed. 1997. 304p. 150.00 (*1-890885-00-2*) Trice, B.E. Publishing.
—The Witching Hour. (Lives of the Mayfair Witches Ser.). 1993. 1056p. mass mkt. 7.99 (*0-345-38446-6*); 1991. 976p. pap. 15.95 (*0-345-36789-8*) Ballantine Bks.
—The Witching Hour. 1998. pap. o.s.i (*0-394-25663-8*); 1990. 976p. 29.95 (*0-394-58786-3*) Knopf, Alfred A. Inc.
—The Witching Hour. abr. ed. 2002. audio 9.99 (*0-553-71352-3*); Set. 1990. audio 18.00 o.s.i (*0-394-58789-8*) Random Hse. Audio Publishing Group. (RH Audio).
Rice, Christopher. A Density of Souls. abr. ed. 2000. audio 17.95 o.p. (*1-56740-399-9*, 2233, Nova Audio Bks.); 9p. audio 57.25 (*1-56740-398-0*, 2232, Unabridged Library Editions); audio 29.95 (*1-56740-475-8*, 2231, Brilliance Audio Unabridged) Brilliance Audio.
Rice, James. Gaston Goes to Mardi Gras. 2nd ed. 1999. (Illus.). 40p. (J). (ps-3). 14.95 (*1-56554-286-X*) Pelican Publishing Co., Inc.
—The Ghost of Pont Diable. 1996. (Illus.). 176p. (J). (gr. 5-8). 14.95 o.p. (*1-57168-109-4*); pap. 8.95 o.p. (*1-57168-130-2*) Eakin Pr.
Rice, Luanne. Dream Country. 2002. 544p. mass mkt. 7.50 (*0-553-58264-X*) Bantam Bks.
Ridout, James W. The Man Pilot. 2003. 366p. pap. 17.95 (*1-56023-460-1*, Southern Tier Editions) Haworth Pr., Inc., The.
Ridout, James W., IV. Plantation Secrets. 2000. 377p. 23.95 (*0-9678838-0-6*) Pilot Bks.
Robards, Karen. Ghost Moon. abr. ed. 2001. audio 12.99 o.s.i (*1-58788-085-7*, 2334, Paperback Nova Audio Bks.); 2000. audio 24.95 o.p. (*1-56740-896-6*, 2060, Nova Audio Bks.); 2000. audio 26.95 (*1-56740-351-4*, 2059, Bookcassette); 2000. audio 73.25 (*1-56740-719-6*, 2061, Unabridged Library Editions) Brilliance Audio.
—Ghost Moon. l.t. ed. 517p. 2001. pap. 28.95 (*0-7838-9114-8*); 2000. 30.95 (*0-7838-9110-5*) Gale Group. (Macmillan Reference USA).
Robbins, Dorothy Dodge & Robbins, Kenn, eds. Christmas Stories from Louisiana. 2003. 28.00 (*1-57806-588-7*) Univ. Pr. of Mississippi.
Roberts, Walter A. Royal Street, a Novel of Old New Orleans. reprint ed. 42.50 (*0-404-11415-6*) AMS Pr., Inc.
Ryan, Marah E. A Flower of France: A Story of Old Louisiana. 1977. (Black Heritage Library Collection). reprint ed. 29.95 (*0-8369-9078-1*) Ayer Co. Pubs., Inc.
Ryan, Nan. The Countess Misbehaves. 2000. 384p. mass mkt. (*1-55166-591-3*, 1-66591-8, Mira Bks.) Harlequin Enterprises, Ltd.
Sallis, James. Black Hornet. 1994. 208p. 18.95 o.p. (*0-7867-0118-8*, Carroll & Graf Pubs.) Avalon Publishing Group.
—Black Hornet. 1996. (New Orleans Mystery Ser.: No. 3). 192p. mass mkt. 5.50 (*0-380-72515-0*, Avon Bks.) Morrow/Avon.
—Bluebottle. (Lew Griffin Mysteries Ser.). 161p. 2000. pap. 8.95 (*0-8027-7595-0*); 1999. (Illus.). pap. 22.95 (*0-8027-3323-9*) Walker & Co.
—Eye of the Cricket. 2000. (Lew Griffin Mysteries Ser.). 196p. reprint ed. pap. 8.95 (*0-8027-7581-0*) Walker & Co.
—Eye of the Cricket: A Lew Griffin Mystery. 1997. (Lew Griffin Mysteries Ser.). 204p. 21.95 (*0-8027-3313-1*) Walker & Co.
—The Long-Legged Fly. 1992. 208p. 17.95 o.p. (*0-88184-810-7*, Carroll & Graf Pubs.) Avalon Publishing Group.
—The Long-Legged Fly. 1994. 192p. mass mkt. 4.99 (*0-380-72242-9*, Avon Bks.) Morrow/Avon.
—The Long-Legged Fly. 183p. pap. 15.00 (*1-901982-41-6*) No Exit Pr. GBR. *Dist:* Trafalgar Square.
—Moth. 1993. 208p. 18.95 o.p. (*0-88184-945-6*, Carroll & Graf Pubs.) Avalon Publishing Group.
—Moth. 1995. (Lew Griffin Ser.). reprint ed. pap. 4.99 o.p. (*0-380-72377-8*, Avon Bks.) Morrow/Avon.
Saul, John. The Right Hand of Evil. 2000. 448p. mass mkt. 7.99 (*0-449-00583-6*, Ballantine Bks.); E-Book 7.99 (*0-345-43979-1*) Ballantine Bks.
—The Right Hand of Evil. unabr. ed. 1999. audio 39.95 (*1-56740-419-7*, 1658, Brilliance Audio Unabridged); audio 73.25 (*1-56740-645-9*, 1659, Unabridged Library Editions) Brilliance Audio.
—The Right Hand of Evil. abr. ed. 1999. audio 24.00. audio 39.95 Highsmith Inc.
—The Right Hand of Evil: A Novel. abr. ed. 1999. audio 24.00 (*0-375-40303-5*, RH Audio) Random Hse. Audio Publishing Group.
Schilling, Vivian. Sacred Prey. 1996. 279p. pap. 5.50 (*0-312-95693-2*, St. Martin's Paperbacks) St. Martin's Pr.
—Sacred Prey. Lovendahl, Shari, ed. 2nd ed. 1994. 245p. 9.95 (*0-9637846-0-9*, 784605) Truman Pr., Inc.
Segura, Chris. Marshland Brace: Two Louisiana Stories. 1982. viii, 289p. 16.95 o.p. (*0-8071-1040-X*) Louisiana State Univ. Pr.
—Marshland Trinity. unabr. ed. 1997. 497p. 29.95 (*0-9655342-0-0*) Win or Lose Ink.
Shaik, Fatima. The Mayor of New Orleans: Just Talking Jazz. 1989. 160p. 9.95 (*0-88739-050-1*); pap. 9.95 (*0-88739-071-4*) Creative Arts Bk. Co.
—On Mardi Gras Day. Kane, Cindy, ed. (Illus.). 32p. (J). (ps-3). 2015. 16.89 o.s.i (*0-8037-1443-2*); 1999. 16.99 o.p. (*0-8037-1442-4*) Penguin Putnam Bks. for Young Readers. (Dial Bks. for Young Readers).
Shankman, Sarah. Now Let's Talk of Graves. Chelius, Jane, ed. 1990. 304p. 18.95 o.p. (*0-671-68456-6*, Atria); 1991. 320p. reprint ed. mass mkt. 5.99 (*0-671-68457-4*, Pocket) Simon & Schuster.
Sharpe, Jon. Louisiana Gold Race. 1993. (Canyon O'Grady Ser.: No. 23). 176p. (Orig.). mass mkt. 3.50 o.s.i (*0-451-17376-7*, Signet Bks.) NAL.
Shepard, Lucius. Louisiana Breakdown. 2003. (Illus.). 144p. 21.95 (*1-930846-14-2*) Golden Gryphon Pr.
Sheridan, Barbara. Silver Rain. 2000. (Magical Love Ser.). 320p. mass mkt. 5.99 o.s.i (*0-515-12804-X*, Jove) Berkley Publishing Group.
Shoemaker, Bill. Stalking Horse. 1994. (Los Angeles Mysteries Ser.). mass mkt. 5.99 o.s.i (*0-449-14936-6*, Fawcett) Ballantine Bks.
—Stalking Horse. l.t. ed. 1995. 481p. pap. 19.95 o.p. (*0-7838-1296-5*, Macmillan Reference USA) Gale Group.
—Stalking Horse. abr. ed. 1993. 16.95 o.p. (*0-7871-0025-0*) NewStar Media, Inc.
Shuman, M. K. Caesar Clue. 1990. 16.95 o.p. (*0-312-04275-2*, Saint Martin's Minotaur) St. Martin's Pr.
—Deep Kill. 1993. 2.99 o.p. (*0-517-09907-1*) Random Hse. Value Publishing.
—Deep Kill. 1991. 16.95 o.p. (*0-312-05854-3*, Saint Martin's Minotaur) St. Martin's Pr.
—Frenchman's Blood: A Louisiana Bayou Mystery. 1987. 15.95 o.p. (*0-8253-0448-2*) Beaufort Bks., Inc.
—The Last Man to Die: A Micah Dunn Mystery. 1992. 240p. 17.95 o.p. (*0-312-07858-7*, Saint Martin's Minotaur) St. Martin's Pr.
—The Maya Stone Murders. 1989. 256p. 16.95 o.p. (*0-312-02608-0*, Saint Martin's Minotaur) St. Martin's Pr.
Shuman, Malcolm. Assassin's Blood. 1999. 224p. mass mkt. 5.99 (*0-380-80485-9*) Morrow/Avon.
—Burial Ground. 1998. 224p. mass mkt. 5.50 (*0-380-79423-3*, Avon Bks.) Morrow/Avon.
—Meriweather Murder. 1998. (Alan Graham Mysteries Ser.: No. 2). 272p. mass mkt. 5.99 (*0-380-79424-1*, Avon Bks.) Morrow/Avon.
—Past Dying. 2000. (Alan Graham Mysteries Ser.). 224p. mass mkt. 5.99 (*0-380-80486-7*, Avon Bks.) Morrow/Avon.
Skinner, Robert E. Cat-Eyed Trouble. 1999. 256p. mass mkt. 5.99 o.s.i (*1-57566-381-3*); 1998. 288p. 19.95 o.s.i (*1-57566-250-7*) Kensington Publishing Corp.
—Daddy's Gone A-Hunting: A Wesley Farrell Novel. 1999. 256p. 22.00 o.s.i (*1-57566-376-7*) Kensington Publishing Corp.
—Daddy's Gone A-Hunting: A Wesley Farrell Novel. 2000. (Illus.). 306p. 23.95 (*1-890208-17-5*) Poisoned Pen Pr.
—Skin Deep, Blood Red. 1998. 256p. mass mkt. 5.99 o.s.i (*1-57566-254-X*); 1997. 288p. 19.95 o.s.i (*1-57566-092-X*, Kensington Bks.) Kensington Publishing Corp.
Smith, Julie. The Axeman's Jazz. 1992. (Skip Langdon Novel Ser.). 368p. mass mkt. 6.99 (*0-8041-0954-0*, Ivy Bks.) Ballantine Bks.
—The Axeman's Jazz. 1991. 384p. 19.95 o.p. (*0-312-06295-8*, Saint Martin's Minotaur) St. Martin's Pr.
—Crescent City Kill. (Skip Langdon Novel Ser.). 1998. 368p. mass mkt. 6.50 o.s.i (*0-8041-1397-1*, Ivy Bks.); 1997. 326p. 4.99 o.s.i (*0-449-91000-8*, Fawcett) Ballantine Bks.
—House of Blues. 1996. (Skip Langdon Novel Ser.). 352p. reprint ed. mass mkt. 6.99 o.s.i (*0-8041-1342-4*, Ivy Bks.) Ballantine Bks.
—Jazz Funeral. 1994. (Skip Langdon Novel Ser.). 368p. mass mkt. 5.99 o.s.i (*0-8041-1252-5*, Ivy Bks.) Ballantine Bks.
—The Kindness of Strangers. 1997. (Skip Langdon Novel Ser.). mass mkt. 5.99 o.s.i (*0-8041-1273-8*, Ivy Bks.) Ballantine Bks.
—Louisiana Bigshot. 2003. (Talba Wallis Ser.). 320p. mass mkt. 6.99 (*0-7653-4380-0*, Tor Bks.) Doherty, Tom Assocs., LLC.
—Louisiana Hotshot. 2002. pap. 6.99 (*0-7653-4292-8*, Tor Bks.); 2001. 335p. 24.95 (*0-7653-0058-3*, Forge Bks.) Doherty, Tom Assocs., LLC.
—New Orleans Beat: A Skip Langdon Mystery. 1995. (Skip Langdon Novel Ser.). 368p. mass mkt. 6.50 o.s.i (*0-8041-1336-X*, Ivy Bks.) Ballantine Bks.

Settings

—New Orleans Mourning. 1990. (Skip Langdon Novel Ser.). 352p. mass mkt. 6.99 (*0-8041-0738-6*, Ivy Bks.) Ballantine Bks.
—New Orleans Mourning, unabr. ed. 1999. (Skip Langdon Mysteries Ser. ). audio 87.00 (*0-7887-3480-6*, 95775E7) Recorded Bks., LLC.
—New Orleans Mourning. 1990. 384p. 17.95 o.p. (*0-312-03892-5*, Saint Martin's Minotaur) St. Martin's Pr.
—82 Desire. (Skip Langdon Novel Ser.). 1999. 352p. mass mkt. 6.99 (*0-8041-1699-7*, Ivy Bks.); 1998. 320p. 24.00 o.s.i (*0-449-00060-5*, Fawcett) Ballantine Bks.
—82 Desire. l.t. ed. 1999. (Large Print Book Ser.). pap. 24.95 (*1-56895-628-2*, Wheeler Publishing, Inc.) Gale Group.
Speart, Jessica. Bird Brained. l.t. ed. 2002. (Paperback Ser.). 502p. pap. 24.95 (*0-7862-4979-X*) Gale Group.
—Bird Brained. 1999. (Rachel Porter Mysteries Ser.). 288p. mass mkt. 5.99 (*0-380-79290-7*, Avon Bks.) Morrow/Avon.
—Gator Aide. 1997. (Rachel Porter Mysteries Ser.). 304p. mass mkt. 5.99 (*0-380-79288-5*, Avon Bks.) Morrow/Avon.
—Tortoise Soup. 1998. (Rachel Porter Mysteries Ser.). 304p. mass mkt. 5.99 (*0-380-79289-3*, Avon Bks.) Morrow/Avon.
Spencer, Elizabeth. The Snare. 1972. 384p. o.p. (*0-07-060178-X*) McGraw-Hill Cos., The.
—The Snare. 1993. (Banner Bks.). 448p. reprint ed. pap. 20.00 (*0-87805-666-1*) Univ. Pr. of Mississippi.
Spindler, Erica. In Silence. 2004. 480p. mass mkt. (*0-7783-2037-5*); 2003. 384p. (*1-55166-699-5*) Harlequin Enterprises, Ltd. (Mira Bks.).
—In Silence. l.t. ed. 2003. 665p. 28.95 (*0-7862-5959-0*, Large Print Pr.) Thorndike Pr.
Stone, Duel. The Huey P. Long Assassination Conspiracy Unveiled: The Jessica Lauren Fields Story. unabr. ed. 1997. xvi, 290p. 26.95 (*0-9660305-0-8*) Lloyds of Louisiana.
—The Huey P. Long Assassination Conspiracy Unveiled: The Unforgettable & Unfortunate Life of Jessica Lauren Fields. 1997. xii, 290p. (*0-9660305-1-6*) Lloyds of Louisiana.
Stuart, Ruth M. Aunt Amity's Silver Wedding, & Other Stories. 1977. (Short Story Index Reprint Ser.). 19.95 (*0-8369-3736-8*) Ayer Co. Pubs., Inc.
—Haunted Photograph. 1977. (Short Story Index Reprint Ser.). (Illus.). 16.95 (*0-8369-3684-1*) Ayer Co. Pubs., Inc.
—Holly & Pizen & Other Stories. 1977. (Short Story Index Reprint Ser.). 19.95 (*0-8369-3173-4*) Ayer Co. Pubs., Inc.
—Moriah's Mourning & Other Half Hour Sketches. 1977. (Short Story Index Reprint Ser.). 19.95 (*0-8369-3175-0*) Ayer Co. Pubs., Inc.
—Moriah's Mourning & Other Half Hour Sketches. (Illus.). reprint ed. pap. text 6.95 (*0-89197-859-3*); lib. bdg. 18.50 (*0-8398-1878-5*) Irvington Pubs.
Tademy, Lalita. Cane River: A Novel. l.t. ed. (Americana Ser.). (Illus.). 2002. 645p. pap. 13.95 (*0-7862-3373-7*); 2001. 672p. 31.95 (*0-7862-3372-9*) Thorndike Pr.
—Cane River: A Novel. abr. ed. 2001. audio 29.98 (*1-58621-262-1*); audio 24.98 (*1-58621-062-9*) Time Warner AudioBooks.
—Cane River: A Novel. (Oprah's Book Club Selection Ser.). 2002. (Illus.). 560p. pap. 13.95 (*0-446-67845-7*); 2001. 432p. 24.95 o.p. (*0-446-53052-2*); 2001. 432p. E-Book 14.95 (*0-7595-4242-2*); 2001. 432p. E-Book 14.95 (*0-7595-9271-3*); 2001. 432p. E-Book 14.95 (*0-7595-6239-3*); 2001. 432p. E-Book 14.95 (*0-7595-8245-9*); 2001. 432p. E-Book 14.95 (*0-7595-0239-0*); 2001. (Illus.). 432p. 24.95 o.p. (*0-446-52732-7*) Warner Bks., Inc.
Tallant, Robert. The Voodoo Queen. 1983. 320p. reprint ed. pap. 5.95 (*0-88289-332-7*) Pelican Publishing Co., Inc.
Tarlton, John S. The Cost of Doing Business: A Novel. 2001. 272p. 22.95 (*1-882593-42-1*); 2003. 406p. reprint ed. pap. 15.95 (*1-882593-72-3*) Bridge Works Publishing Co., Inc.
—A Window Facing West: A Novel. 1999. 211p. 22.95 (*1-882593-30-8*); 2001. 208p. reprint ed. 13.95 (*1-882593-46-4*) Bridge Works Publishing Co., Inc.
Taylor, Mel. The Mitt Man. 1999. 352p. 24.00 (*0-688-16094-8*, Morrow, William & Co.) Morrow/Avon.
Temple, Lou Jane. Red Beans & Vice. mass mkt. o.p. (*0-312-98100-7*, St. Martin's Paperbacks); 2001. 288p. 23.95 (*0-312-28013-0*, Saint Martin's Minotaur) St. Martin's Pr.
Tervalon, Jervey. Dead above Ground. 2001. (Illus.). 240p. pap. 12.95 (*0-671-03469-3*, Washington Square Pr.); 2000. 272p. 23.95 o.s.i (*0-671-03468-5*, Atria) Simon & Schuster.
Toole, John Kennedy. A Confederacy of Dunces. 21.95 (*0-8488-1207-7*) Amereon, Ltd.
—A Confederacy of Dunces. unabr. ed. 1997. audio 69.95 (*0-7861-1232-8*, 1978) Blackstone Audio Bks., Inc.
—A Confederacy of Dunces. 416p. 1982. pap. 4.50 o.s.i (*0-394-17969-2*, B-474); 20th anniv. ed. 1987. pap. 14.00 (*0-8021-3020-8*, Grove Pr.) Grove/Atlantic, Inc.
—A Confederacy of Dunces. 1980. 352p. 24.95 (*0-8071-0657-7*); 20th anniv. ed. 2000. 338p. 24.95 (*0-8071-2606-3*); 20th anniv. ltd. ed. 2000. (Illus.). 338p. 75.00 (*0-8071-2607-1*) Louisiana State Univ. Pr.
—A Confederacy of Dunces. abr. ed. 1993. audio 16.95 o.p. (*1-55800-145-X*, 40560); Set. 1998. 3p. audio 18.00 (*0-7871-1766-8*, 390552) NewStar Media, Inc. (Dove Audio).
—A Confederacy of Dunces. 1994. 480p. 10.99 o.s.i (*0-517-12270-7*) Random Hse. Value Publishing.
—A Confederacy of Dunces. 1987. 18.00 (*0-606-20071-1*) Turtleback Bks.
Turner, Louise Kreher. Margaretha's Trunk. 2003. pap. (*1-58838-153-6*, Court Street Pr.) NewSouth, Inc.
Van Horne, Hollie. When We Do Meet Again. 1999. (Time Travelers Ser.: Vol. 4). 509p. 16.50 (*0-9674552-0-0*) Time Travelers.
Victor, Metta V. Maum Guinea, & Her Plantation "Children": or Holiday-Week on a Louisiana Estate: A Slave Romance. 1977. (Black Heritage Library Collection). reprint ed. 25.95 (*0-8369-9087-0*) Ayer Co. Pubs., Inc.
Walker, Laura. When Love Beckons. 2001. 263p. pap. 19.95 (*1-58851-928-7*) PublishAmerica, Inc.
Ware, Ciji. Midnight on Julia Street. 1999. 470p. mass mkt. 6.99 (*0-449-00187-3*, Fawcett) Ballantine Bks.
Wells, Ken. Logan's Storm: A Novel. 2003. 304p. pap. 12.95 (*0-375-76067-9*) Random House Adult Trade Publishing Group.
—Logan's Storm: A Novel. 2002. 304p. 21.95 (*0-375-50525-3*) Random Hse., Inc.
—Meely LaBauve: A Novel. 2001. 272p. pap. 11.95 (*0-375-75816-X*); 2000. 256p. 19.95 o.s.i (*0-375-50311-0*) Random Hse., Inc.
—Meely LaBauve: A Novel. l.t. ed. 2001. (Americana Ser.). 309p. 28.95 (*0-7862-3023-1*) Thorndike Pr.
Wells, Rebecca. Divine Secrets of the Ya-Ya Sisterhood. l.t. ed. 2002. 12.95 (*1-56895-199-X*); 1998. 27.95 o.p. (*1-56895-621-5*, Wheeler Publishing, Inc.) Gale Group.
—Divine Secrets of the Ya-Ya Sisterhood. 2002. 480p. mass mkt. 7.99 (*0-06-000810-5*); 1996. 368p. 24.00 (*0-06-017328-9*); 1998. 256p. 22.00 (*0-06-019345-X*) HarperCollins Pubs.
—Divine Secrets of the Ya-Ya Sisterhood. 2000. 368p. mass mkt. 7.99 (*0-06-101507-5*, HarperTorch) Morrow/Avon.
—Divine Secrets of the Ya-Ya Sisterhood: A Novel. 1997. 368p. pap. 14.00 (*0-06-092833-6*, Perennial) HarperTrade.
—Divine Secrets of the Ya-Ya Sisterhood: A Novel. 2002. 480p. mass mkt. 7.99 (*0-06-050225-8*) Morrow/Avon.
—Les Divins Secrets des Petits Ya Ya. 2000. Tr. of Divine Secrets of the Ya Ya Sisterhood. (FRE.). pap. 12.95 (*2-266-09548-X*) Presses Pocket FRA. *Dist:* Distribooks, Inc.
—Little Altars Everywhere. 1998. 240p. 22.00 (*0-06-019362-X*); 1999. 352p. pap. 20.00 (*0-06-093318-6*) HarperCollins Pubs.
—Little Altars Everywhere. 1999. audio compact disk 22.00 (*0-694-52122-1*, HarperAudio); 1998. 224p. 22.00 (*0-06-019349-2*, HarperCollins); 1996. 240p. pap. 13.00 (*0-06-097684-5*, Perennial) HarperTrade.
—Little Altars Everywhere: A Novel. 2003. 400p. mass mkt. 7.99 (*0-06-051779-4*, HarperTorch) Morrow/Avon.
West, Michael L. She Flew the Coop. 1994. 384p. 22.00 o.p. (*0-06-018348-9*) HarperTrade.
Wilcox, James. Heavenly Days. 2003. 208p. (*0-670-03247-6*) Viking Penguin.
—Miss Undine's Living Room. 1994. reprint ed. lib. bdg. 21.95 (*1-56849-522-6*) Buccaneer Bks., Inc.
—Miss Undine's Living Room. 1988. 288p. pap. 6.95 o.p. (*0-06-091502-1*, PL-1502, Perennial) HarperTrade.
—Miss Undine's Living Room. 2001. (Voices of the South Ser.). 275p. pap. 15.95 (*0-8071-2699-3*) Louisiana State Univ. Pr.
—North Gladiola. 1994. reprint ed. lib. bdg. 21.95 (*1-56849-523-4*) Buccaneer Bks., Inc.
—North Gladiola. 1985. 288p. 15.95 o.p. (*0-06-015441-1*); 1986. 272p. reprint ed. pap. 5.95 o.p. (*0-06-091345-2*, PL1345, Perennial) HarperTrade.
—North Gladiola. 2000. (Voices of the South Ser.). 264p. pap. 15.95 (*0-8071-2565-2*) Louisiana State Univ. Pr.
—Sort of Rich. 1989. 17.95 o.p. (*0-06-016099-3*) HarperTrade.
—Sort of Rich: A Novel. 1990. 288p. reprint ed. pap. 12.00 o.p. (*0-06-091707-5*, Perennial) HarperTrade.
—Sort of Rich: A Novel. 1999. 288p. pap. 12.95 (*0-316-94044-5*, Back Bay) Little Brown & Co.
Williams, Deborah K. Cameroon. 1999. 88p. pap. 9.95 (*1-56002-823-8*, University Editions) Aegina Pr., Inc.
Williamson, Penelope. Mortal Sins. 2003. 496p. mass mkt. 7.50 (*0-446-60950-1*) Warner Bks., Inc.
Williamson, Penn. Mortal Sins. abr. ed. 2000. audio 24.98 (*1-57042-924-3*); audio 24.98 Time Warner AudioBooks.
—Mortal Sins. 2000. 432p. 23.95 o.p. (*0-446-52154-X*) Warner Bks., Inc.
Wilson, Charles. Deep Sleep. 2001. 290p. 24.95 o.p. (*0-312-26696-0*); 304p. reprint ed. mass mkt. 6.99 (*0-312-97765-4*, St. Martin's Paperbacks) St. Martin's Pr.
Wiltz, Chris. A Diamond Before You Die. (Neal Rafferty Mystery Ser.). 208p. 1988. mass mkt. 3.95 o.s.i (*0-445-40536-8*); 1987. 15.95 o.p. (*0-89296-192-9*) Mysterious Pr.
—A Diamond Before You Die. l.t. ed. 1990. (Ulverscroft Large Print Ser.). 29.99 o.p. (*0-7089-2194-9*, Ulverscroft) Thorpe, F. A. Pubs. GBR. *Dist:* Ulverscroft Large Print Bks., Ltd., Ulverscroft Large Print Canada, Ltd.
—The Emerald Lizard: A Neal Rafferty Mystery. 1991. 224p. 17.95 o.p. (*0-525-24945-1*, Dutton) Dutton/Plume.
—The Killing Circle. l.t. ed. 1991. 8.95 o.p. (*0-7451-9395-1*, 1599); 1988. pap. 14.95 o.p. (*1-55504-628-2*, 333) BBC Audiobooks America.
—The Killing Circle. 1985. pap. 2.95 o.p. (*0-523-41933-3*, Pinnacle Bks.) Kensington Publishing Corp.
Wiltz, Christine. Glass House: Voices of the South. (Voices of the South Ser.). 2001. 189p. pap. 14.95 (*0-8071-2683-7*); 1994. 208p. (C). 19.95 (*0-8071-1864-8*) Louisiana State Univ. Pr.
Womack, Steven. Murphy's Fault. 1990. 320p. 17.95 o.p. (*0-312-03896-8*, Saint Martin's Minotaur); Vol. 1. 1991. mass mkt. 3.99 o.p. (*0-312-92539-5*, St. Martin's Paperbacks) St. Martin's Pr.
—Smash Cut. 3.98 o.s.i (*0-8317-4629-7*) Smithmark Pubs., Inc.
—Smash Cut. 1991. 304p. 18.95 o.p. (*0-312-06467-5*, Saint Martin's Minotaur) St. Martin's Pr.
—The Software Bomb. 3.98 o.p. (*0-8317-4632-7*) Smithmark Pubs., Inc.
—The Software Bomb. 1993. 288p. 19.95 o.p. (*0-312-09390-X*, Saint Martin's Minotaur) St. Martin's Pr.
Woodrell, Daniel. Muscle for the Wing: A Rene Shade Mystery. 1988. 16.95 o.p. (*0-8050-0788-1*) Holt, Henry & Co.
—Muscle for the Wing: A Rene Shade Mystery. 1990. 224p. mass mkt. 4.50 o.p. (*0-451-16569-1*, Signet Bks.) NAL.
—Muscle for the Wing: A Rene Shade Mystery. 1998. 224p. pap. 14.00 (*0-671-00137-X*, Pocket) Simon & Schuster.
—The Ones You Do. 1992. 224p. 19.95 o.p. (*0-8050-0972-8*) Holt, Henry & Co.
—The Ones You Do. 1993. 256p. mass mkt. 4.99 o.p. (*0-451-40385-1*, Onyx) NAL.
—The Ones You Do. 1998. 224p. pap. 17.95 (*0-671-00135-3*, Pocket) Simon & Schuster.
—Under the Bright Lights. 1986. o.p. (*0-03-008514-4*) Holt, Henry & Co.
—Under the Bright Lights. 1988. 192p. pap. 3.50 (*0-380-70456-0*, Avon Bks.) Morrow/Avon.
Worth, Lenora. When Love Came to Town. 2001. (Steeple Hill Love Inspired Ser.: Vol. 142). 256p. mass mkt. (*0-373-87149-X*, Harlequin Bks.) Harlequin Enterprises, Ltd.

### LOUISVILLE (KY.)—FICTION

Allen, Dwight. Judge: A Novel. 2003. 320p. tchr. ed. 23.95 (*1-56512-369-7*, 72369) Algonquin Bks. of Chapel Hill.
McCafferty, Barbara Taylor. Double Cross. (Bert & Nan Tatum Mystery Ser.). 2000. 256p. mass mkt. 5.99 o.s.i (*1-57566-511-5*); 1998. 240p. 20.00 o.s.i (*1-57566-338-4*) Kensington Publishing Corp.
—Double Dealer. 2000. (Bert & Nan Tatum Mystery Ser.). 250p. 20.00 o.s.i (*1-57566-507-7*, Kensington Bks.) Kensington Publishing Corp.
—Double Murder. 1996. 288p. 18.95 o.s.i (*1-57566-084-9*, Kensington Bks.) Kensington Publishing Corp.
McCafferty, Barbara Taylor & Herald, Beverly Taylor. Double Date. 2002. (Partners in Crime Ser.). 288p. mass mkt. 5.99 (*1-57566-732-0*) Kensington Publishing Corp.
—Double Date. l.t. ed. 2001. 336p. 28.95 (*0-7862-3326-5*) Thorndike Pr.
—Double Dealer. 2000. 272p. mass mkt. 5.99 o.s.i (*1-57566-642-1*) Kensington Publishing Corp.
—Double Dealer. l.t. ed. 2000. (Mystery Ser.). 352p. 26.95 (*0-7862-2835-0*) Thorndike Pr.
—Double Exposure. annuals 1997. (Bert & Nan Tatum Mystery Ser.). 288p. 18.95 o.s.i (*1-57566-207-8*) Kensington Publishing Corp.
—Double Murder. 1997. (Bert & Nan Tatum Mystery Ser.). 288p. mass mkt. 5.50 (*1-57566-212-4*) Kensington Publishing Corp.
McClellan, Tierney. Closing Statement: A Schuyler Ridgway Mystery. 1995. 304p. (Orig.). mass mkt. 4.99 o.s.i (*0-451-18464-5*, Signet Bks.) NAL.
—Heir Condition. 1995. 256p. (Orig.). mass mkt. 5.50 o.s.i (*0-451-18144-1*, Signet Bks.) NAL.
—Killing in Real Estate. 1996. (Schuyler Ridgway Mystery Ser.). 256p. mass mkt. 5.50 o.s.i (*0-451-18765-2*) NAL.
—Two-Story Frame. 1997. (Schuyler Ridgway Mystery Ser.). 256p. mass mkt. 5.99 o.s.i (*0-451-19197-8*, Signet Bks.) NAL.
Schneider, Jeff. The Fix. 2001. 324p. pap. 16.00 (*1-58776-119-X*) Vivisphere Publishing.

### LUSITANIA (IMAGINARY PLACE)—FICTION

Card, Orson Scott. Speaker for the Dead. abr. ed. audio 15.95 o.p. (*1-55927-160-4*) Audio Renaissance.
—Speaker for the Dead. (Ender Ser.: Bk. 2). 1994. 382p. mass mkt. 7.99 (*0-8125-5075-7*); 1992. 280p. pap. 13.95 (*0-312-85325-4*); 1991. 432p. mass mkt. 4.95 o.s.i (*0-8125-1350-9*); 1987. mass mkt. 3.95 o.s.i (*0-8125-3257-0*); rev. ed. 1991. 416p. mass mkt. 5.99 o.s.i (*0-8125-2015-7*); 2nd ed. 1986. 280p. 24.95 (*0-312-93738-5*) Doherty, Tom Assocs., LLC. (Tor Bks.).
—Speaker for the Dead. 1993. audio. audio 63.40 (*1-56544-044-7*, 550002) Literate Ear, Inc.
—Speaker for the Dead. 1994. (Ender Ser.: Bk. 2). 14.04 (*0-606-11866-7*) Turtleback Bks.
—Xenocide. abr. ed. 1991. audio 15.95 o.p. (*1-55927-161-2*) Audio Renaissance.
—Xenocide. (Ender Ser.: Bk. 3). 1992. 592p. mass mkt. 7.99 (*0-8125-0925-0*); 1991. 21.95 o.p. (*0-312-85056-5*); 2nd ed. 1996. 394p. pap. 14.95 (*0-312-86187-7*) Doherty, Tom Assocs., LLC. (Tor Bks.).
—Xenocide. 2002. 16.15 (*0-7857-1634-3*) Econo-Clad Bks.
—Xenocide. 1993. audio 78.60 (*1-56544-045-5*, 550006); audio Literate Ear, Inc.
—Xenocide. 1992. (Ender Ser.: Bk. 3). 14.04 (*0-606-12119-6*) Turtleback Bks.

### LYDMOUTH (ENGLAND: IMAGINARY PLACE)—FICTION

Taylor, Andrew. An Air That Kills. 1995. 266p. 19.95 o.p. (*0-312-11739-6*, Saint Martin's Minotaur) St. Martin's Pr.
—The Lover of the Grave. 1997. 309p. 22.95 o.p. (*0-312-15573-5*, Saint Martin's Minotaur) St. Martin's Pr.
—The Mortal Sickness. 1996. 304p. 22.95 o.p. (*0-312-14371-0*, Saint Martin's Minotaur) St. Martin's Pr.
—The Suffocating Night. l.t. ed. 2000. (Ulverscroft Large Print Ser.). 392p. 31.99 (*0-7089-4188-5*, Ulverscroft) Thorpe, F. A. Pubs. GBR. *Dist:* Ulverscroft Large Print Bks., Ltd., Ulverscroft Large Print Canada, Ltd.

### LYRA (IMAGINARY PLACE)—FICTION

Wrede, Patricia C. Caught in Crystal. 1987. mass mkt. 3.50 o.s.i (*0-441-76006-6*) Ace Bks.
—Daughter of Witches. 1987. mass mkt. 3.50 o.s.i (*0-441-13899-3*); 1987. mass mkt. 2.95 o.s.i (*0-441-13912-4*); 1985. mass mkt. 2.95 o.s.i (*0-441-13897-7*); 1984. mass mkt. 2.75 o.s.i (*0-441-13895-0*); 1983. mass mkt. 2.50 o.s.i (*0-441-13894-2*) Ace Bks.
—The Harp of Imach Thyssel. 1986. 240p. mass mkt. 2.95 o.s.i (*0-441-31759-6*) Ace Bks.
—The Raven Ring. (Tor Fantasy Ser.). 1995. 348p. mass mkt. 5.99 o.s.i (*0-8125-1432-7*); 1994. 352p. 14.99 o.p. (*0-312-85040-9*) Doherty, Tom Assocs., LLC. (Tor Bks.).
—Shadow Magic. 1986. (Lyra Ser.: Bk. 1). (Illus.). 256p. mass mkt. 3.50 o.s.i (*0-441-76014-7*); 1984. mass mkt. 2.95 o.s.i (*0-441-76013-9*); 1982. mass mkt. 2.50 o.s.i (*0-441-76012-0*) Ace Bks.
—Shadows over Lyra, Vol. 1. 1997. 535p. pap. 11.99 (*0-8125-6759-5*, Tor Bks.) Doherty, Tom Assocs., LLC.

## M

### MACONDO (IMAGINARY PLACE)—FICTION

Garcia Márquez, Gabriel. Cien Anos de Soledad. Joset, Jacques, ed. 8th ed. 1989. (Letras Hispanicas Ser.: Vol. 215). (SPA., Illus.). 559p. pap. 16.95 (*84-376-0494-X*) Ediciones Cátedra ESP. *Dist:* Continental Bk. Co., Inc., Distribooks, Inc., Lectorum Pubns., Inc.
—Cien Anos de Soledad. annot. ed. (Coleccion Centro Literario). (SPA.). pap., stu. ed. 7.95 (*958-02-0503-5*, CAR034) Editorial Voluntad S.A. COL. *Dist:* Continental Bk. Co., Inc.
—Cien Anos de Soledad. 18th ed. 2000. (Nueva Austral Ser.: Vol. 100). (SPA., Illus.). 456p. 14.95 (*84-239-1900-5*) Elliot's Bks.
—Cien Anos de Soledad. (SPA.). 1986. 12.50 o.p. (*0-8288-2516-5*); 11th ed. 1990. 448p. 15.95 o.p. (*0-8288-2567-X*, S7542); 11th ed. 1990. 448p. pap. 19.95 (*0-7859-5010-9*) French & European Pubns., Inc.
—Cien Anos de Soledad. 1997. (SPA.). pap. text 25.98 o.s.i (*968-13-1574-X*) Libros Sin Fronteras.

—Cien Anos de Soledad. (SPA.). 14.00 (*958-04-3952-4*) Norma S.A. COL. *Dist:* Distribuidora Norma, Inc.
—Cien Anos de Soledad. 7th ed. (SPA., Illus.). 496p. 16.95 (*84-01-24226-6*, PJ2266) Plaza & Janés Editories, S.A. ESP. *Dist:* Continental Bk. Co., Inc., Lectorum Pubns., Inc.
—One Hundred Years of Solitude. 1997. Tr. of Cien Anos de Soledad. (C). text 9.38 o.p. (*0-06-502396-X*) Addison-Wesley Longman, Inc.
—One Hundred Years of Solitude. 1976. Tr. of Cien Anos de Soledad. 25.95 (*0-8488-1429-0*) Amereon, Ltd.
—One Hundred Years of Solitude. 1990. Tr. of Cien Anos de Soledad. reprint ed. lib. bdg. 24.95 (*0-89966-703-1*) Buccaneer Bks., Inc.
—One Hundred Years of Solitude. Rabassa, Gregory, tr. from SPA. l.t. ed. 1993. (General Ser.).Tr. of Cien Anos de Soledad. 533p. lib. bdg. 21.95 o.p. (*0-8161-5483-X*, Macmillan Reference USA) Gale Group.
—One Hundred Years of Solitude.Tr. of Cien Anos de Soledad. 2003. 432p. 24.95 (*0-06-053104-5*, HarperCollins); 1998. 464p. pap. 14.00 (*0-06-092979-0*, Perennial) HarperTrade.
—One Hundred Years of Solitude. Rabassa, Gregory, tr. Tr. of Cien Anos de Soledad. 432p. 1970. 30.00 (*0-06-011418-5*); 1991. reprint ed. pap. 13.50 o.p. (*0-06-091965-5*, Perennial) HarperTrade.
—One Hundred Years of Solitude. 1995. Tr. of Cien Anos de Soledad. 480p. 20.00 (*0-679-44465-3*, RH4653) Knopf, Alfred A. Inc.
—One Hundred Years of Solitude. 1976. Tr. of Cien Anos de Soledad. mass mkt. 5.95 o.p. (*0-380-01503-X*, Avon Bks.) Morrow/Avon.
—One Hundred Years of Solitude. 1988. (Monarch Ser.).Tr. of Cien Anos de Soledad. pap. 3.95 o.p. (*0-671-64756-3*) Simon & Schuster.
—One Hundred Years of Solitude. 1998. Tr. of Cien Anos de Soledad. 19.55 (*0-606-20288-9*) Turtleback Bks.

**MADRID (SPAIN)—FICTION**

Buitrago, Fanny. Senora Honeycomb. Peden, Margaret Sayers, tr. 1996. 232p. 18.00 o.p. (*0-06-017365-3*) HarperCollins Pubs.
Cela, Camilo José. San Camilo, 1936: The Eve, Feast, & Octave of St. Camillus of the Year 1936 in Madrid. Polt, John H., tr. 1991. 327p. pap. 21.95 (*0-8223-1196-8*); lib. bdg. 69.95 (*0-8223-1179-8*) Duke Univ. Pr.
Crawford, F. Marion. In the Palace of the King. E-Book 3.95 (*0-594-04328-X*) 1873 Pr.
—In the Palace of the King. collector's ed. 2002. (Illus.). im. lthr. 38.85 (*1-4115-1193-X*); pap. 19.95 (*1-4115-0517-4*); 25.95 (*1-4115-0843-2*); pap. 17.95 (*1-4115-0248-5*) Polyglot Pr., Inc.
—In the Palace of the King. 1990. (Works of Francis Marion Crawford). reprint ed. lib. bdg. 79.00 (*0-7812-2551-5*) Reprint Services Corp.
Donoso, José. The Garden Next Door: A Novel. 1992. 243p. 18.95 o.p. (*0-8021-1238-2*) Grove/Atlantic, Inc.
Doyle, Peter R. Chased by the Jewel Thieves. 1997. (Daring Adventure Ser.: Bk. 11). (J). (gr. 4). pap. 5.99 o.p. (*1-56179-547-X*) Focus on the Family Publishing.
Fitzpatrick, Christina. What's the Girl Worth? 2002. 416p. 24.95 (*0-06-019910-5*) HarperCollins Pubs.
Jacobs, Mark. A Handful of Kings. 2004. 288p. 24.00 (*0-7432-4590-3*, Simon & Schuster) Simon & Schuster.
Lewis, M. G. The Monk. 2003. (Dover Thrift Editions Ser.). 288p. pap. 3.50 (*0-486-43214-9*) Dover Pubns., Inc.
Marias, Javier. Tomorrow in the Battle Think of Me. Costa, Margaret Jull, tr. from SPA. 1997. 320p. 24.00 o.s.i (*0-15-100276-2*) Harcourt Trade Pubs.
—Tomorrow in the Battle Think on Me. Costa, Margaret Jull, tr. from SPA. 2001. 320p. reprint ed. pap. 15.95 (*0-8112-1482-6*, NDP923) New Directions Publishing Corp.
Pérez-Reverte, Arturo. The Fencing Master. Costa, Margaret Jull, tr. from SPA. 1999. 256p. 24.00 o.s.i (*0-15-100181-2*) Harcourt Trade Pubs.
—The Fencing Master. unabr. ed. 1999. audio 26.95 (*0-7871-1909-1*) Simon & Schuster Audio.
—The Fencing Master: A Novel. 2000. (Illus.). 256p. pap. 13.00 (*0-15-600684-7*, Harvest Bks.) Harcourt Trade Pubs.
—Flanders Panel. 1994. 294p. 21.95 o.s.i (*0-15-148926-2*) Harcourt Trade Pubs.
—The Flanders Panel. Costa, Margaret Jull, tr. from SPA. 1996. Tr. of Tabla de Flandes. (Illus.). 304p. pap. 13.95 (*0-553-37786-8*) Bantam Bks.
Serafin, David. Madrid Underground. 1984. 224p. 11.95 o.p. (*0-312-50401-2*) St. Martin's Pr.

**MAGGODY (ARK.: IMAGINARY PLACE)—FICTION**

Hess, Joan. Madness in Maggody. 1992. (Arly Hanks Mystery Ser.). 240p. mass mkt. 5.99 o.s.i (*0-451-40299-5*, Onyx) NAL.
—Madness in Maggody. 1990. 16.95 o.p. (*0-312-05465-3*, Saint Martin's Minotaur) St. Martin's Pr.
—Maggody & the Moonbeams. 2001. 256p. 23.00 (*0-7432-0229-5*, Simon & Schuster) Simon & Schuster.
—Maggody in Manhattan. 1992. (Arly Hanks Mystery Ser.). 272p. 18.00 o.p. (*0-525-93519-3*, Dutton) Dutton/Plume.
—Maggody in Manhattan. 1993. (Arly Hanks Mystery Ser.). 256p. reprint ed. mass mkt. 5.50 o.s.i (*0-451-40376-2*, Onyx) NAL.
—The Maggody Militia. 1997. (Arly Hanks Mystery Ser.). 320p. 21.95 o.s.i (*0-525-94236-X*) Dutton/Plume.
—The Maggody Militia. 1998. (Arly Hanks Mystery Ser.). 224p. mass mkt. 5.99 o.s.i (*0-451-40726-1*, Onyx) NAL.
—Malice in Maggody. 1991. (Arly Hanks Mystery Ser.). 240p. mass mkt. 5.99 o.s.i (*0-451-40236-7*, Onyx) NAL.
—Martians in Maggody. 1994. (Arly Hanks Mystery Ser.). 256p. 18.95 o.s.i (*0-525-93840-0*) Dutton/Plume.
—Martians in Maggody. 1995. (Arly Hanks Mystery Ser.). 304p. mass mkt. 5.50 o.s.i (*0-451-40592-7*, Onyx) NAL.
—Miracles in Maggody, unabr. ed. 1999. audio 39.95 Blackstone Audio Bks., Inc.
—Miracles in Maggody. 1995. (Arly Hanks Mystery Ser.). 288p. 20.95 o.p. (*0-525-94051-0*, Dutton) Dutton/Plume.
—Miracles in Maggody. 1996. (Arly Hanks Mystery Ser.). 288p. mass mkt. 5.99 o.s.i (*0-451-40656-7*) NAL.
—Mischief in Maggody. 1991. (Arly Hanks Mystery Ser.). 256p. mass mkt. 5.99 o.s.i (*0-451-40253-7*, Onyx) NAL.
—Mischief in Maggody. 1988. 176p. 14.95 o.p. (*0-312-01792-8*, Saint Martin's Minotaur) St. Martin's Pr.
—Misery Loves Maggody. 1999. 288p. 22.00 (*0-684-84562-8*, Simon & Schuster); 2000. (Illus.). 304p. reprint ed. pap. 6.99 (*0-671-01684-9*, Pocket) Simon & Schuster.
—Mortal Remains in Maggody. 1991. (Arly Hanks Mystery Ser.). 304p. 18.95 o.p. (*0-525-93368-9*, Dutton) Dutton/Plume.
—Mortal Remains in Maggody. 1992. (Arly Hanks Mystery Ser.). 272p. mass mkt. 4.50 o.s.i (*0-451-40326-6*, Onyx) NAL.
—Much Ado in Maggody. 1991. (Arly Hanks Mystery Ser.). 256p. mass mkt. 5.99 o.s.i (*0-451-40268-5*, Onyx) NAL.
—Much Ado in Maggody. 1989. 15.95 o.p. (*0-312-02952-7*, Saint Martin's Minotaur) St. Martin's Pr.
—Murder@Maggody.com. l.t. ed. 2000. (Wheeler Large Print Book Ser.). 312p. pap. 24.95 (*1-56895-886-2*, Wheeler Publishing, Inc.) Gale Group.
—Murder@Maggody.com. 2000. 256p. 22.00 o.s.i (*0-684-84563-6*, Simon & Schuster); 2001. (Illus.). 304p. reprint ed. mass mkt. 6.99 (*0-671-01685-7*, Pocket) Simon & Schuster.
—O Little Town of Maggody. 1993. (Arly Hanks Mystery Ser.). 256p. 19.00 o.p. (*0-525-93654-8*, Dutton) Dutton/Plume.
—O Little Town of Maggody. abr. ed. 1994. (Arly Hanks Mystery Ser.). audio 16.00 o.p. (*0-453-00871-2*, Penguin AudioBooks) HighBridge Co.
—O Little Town of Maggody. 1994. (Arly Hanks Mystery Ser.). 256p. mass mkt. 4.50 o.s.i (*0-451-40457-2*, Onyx) NAL.

**MAGIC KINGDOM OF LANDOVER (IMAGINARY PLACE)—FICTION**

Brooks, Terry. The Black Unicorn. 1988. (Magic Kingdom of Landover Ser.: No. 2). 320p. mass mkt. 7.99 (*0-345-33528-7*, Del Rey) Ballantine Bks.
—The Black Unicorn. 1988. (Magic Kingdom of Landover Ser.: No. 2). 13.04 (*0-606-01234-6*) Turtleback Bks.
—Magic Kingdom for Sale - Sold! 1987. (Magic Kingdom of Landover Ser.: No. 1). 384p. mass mkt. 7.99 (*0-345-31758-0*, Ballantine Bks.) Ballantine Bks.
—Magic Kingdom for Sale - Sold! 1988. 3.99 o.p. (*0-517-67355-X*) Random Hse. Value Publishing.
—Magic Kingdom for Sale - Sold! 1986. (Magic Kingdom of Landover Ser.: No. 1). 13.04 (*0-606-02550-2*) Turtleback Bks.
—The Tangle Box. 1995. (Magic Kingdom of Landover Ser.: No. 4). 368p. reprint ed. mass mkt. 7.99 (*0-345-38700-7*, Del Rey) Ballantine Bks.
—Witches' Brew. 1996. (Magic Kingdom of Landover Ser.: No. 5). 352p. mass mkt. 6.99 (*0-345-38702-3*) Ballantine Bks.
—Wizard at Large. 1989. (Magic Kingdom of Landover Ser.: No. 3K.). 320p. mass mkt. 7.99 (*0-345-36227-6*, Del Rey) Ballantine Bks.
—Wizard at Large. 1989. (Magic Kingdom of Landover Ser.: No. 3). 13.04 (*0-606-01235-4*) Turtleback Bks.

**MAINE—FICTION**

Amos, Diane. Getting Personal. 2004. 323p. pap. 13.95 (*1-4104-0195-2*, Five Star Trade); 2003. 325p. 26.95 (*0-7862-5169-7*, Five Star) Gale Group.
Andrews, Donna. Murder with Puffins. l.t. ed. 2002. 26.95 (*1-57490-415-9*) Beeler, Thomas T. Publisher.
—Murder with Puffins. 2001. 320p. mass mkt. 6.50 o.s.i (*0-312-97886-3*, St. Martin's Paperbacks); 2000. 281p. 24.95 (*0-312-26221-3*, Saint Martin's Minotaur) St. Martin's Pr.
Arensberg, Ann. Incubus. 2000. 336p. pap. 14.00 (*0-345-43816-7*, Ballantine Bks.) Ballantine Bks.
Askari, Brent. Not Ready for Prime Time. 1999. 234p. 24.95 (*0-7867-0648-1*, Carroll & Graf Pubs.) Avalon Publishing Group.
Azzolina, Ronald. Suicide Inc. E-Book 8.95 (*1-58820-061-2*); 1999. 234p. pap. 13.95 (*1-58500-474-X*) 1stBooks Library.
Bain, Donald. Brandy & Bullets: Murder, She Wrote. l.t. ed. 1999. (G. K. Hall Nightingale Ser.). 288p. pap. 20.95 (*0-7838-8596-2*) Thorndike Pr.
Bain, Donald & Fletcher, Jessica. A Little Yuletide Murder. 1998. (Murder She Wrote Ser.: Vol. 10). 304p. mass mkt. 6.50 (*0-451-19475-6*, Signet Bks.) NAL.
—A Little Yuletide Murder: A Murder, She Wrote, Mystery. l.t. ed. 2000. (Nightingale Ser.). 279p. pap. 21.95 (*0-7838-9101-6*) Thorndike Pr.
Baker-Kline, Christina. Desire Lines: A Novel. 1999. 320p. 24.00 (*0-688-15107-8*, Morrow, William & Co.) Morrow/Avon.
Blanchard, Alice. Darkness Peering. 2000. 336p. mass mkt. 6.99 (*0-553-58129-5*) Bantam Bks.
—Darkness Peering. l.t. ed. 2000. 26.95 o.p. (*1-56895-829-3*, Wheeler Publishing, Inc.) Gale Group.
Bodner, Elizabeth L. Uncompromising Vol. 1: Family Style. 1997. 235p. (Orig.). pap. 14.95 (*0-9657162-0-1*) EBW Assocs.
Bonnie, Fred. Too Hot, & Other Maine Stories. 1987. 208p. (Orig.). 16.95 o.p. (*0-937966-21-5*); pap. 9.95 o.p. (*0-937966-22-3*) Tilbury Hse. Pubs.
Borthwick, J. S. Bodies of Water. 1990. 17.95 o.p. (*0-312-04269-8*, Saint Martin's Minotaur) St. Martin's Pr.
—The Bridled Groom: A Dead Letter Mystery. 1995. 336p. mass mkt. 6.50 (*0-312-95505-7*, St. Martin's Paperbacks) St. Martin's Pr.
—The Bridled Groom: A Mystery. 1994. 304p. 20.95 o.p. (*0-312-10435-9*, Saint Martin's Minotaur) St. Martin's Pr.
—Dolly Is Dead. 324p. 1996. mass mkt. 6.50 (*0-312-95675-4*, St. Martin's Paperbacks); 1995. 22.95 o.p. (*0-312-13052-X*, Saint Martin's Minotaur) St. Martin's Pr.
—The Down-East Murders: A Mystery Set on the Coast of Maine. 1985. 288p. 14.95 o.p. (*0-312-21855-9*) St. Martin's Pr.
—The Garden Plot. (Dead Letter Mysteries Ser.). 1998. 336p. pap. 6.50 (*0-312-96291-6*, St. Martin's Paperbacks); 1997. 352p. 23.95 (*0-312-15131-4*, Saint Martin's Minotaur) St. Martin's Pr.
—Murder in the Rough. 2003. 352p. mass mkt. 6.50 (*0-312-98453-7*, St. Martin's Paperbacks); 2002. (Illus.). 336p. 24.95 (*0-312-28829-8*, Saint Martin's Minotaur) St. Martin's Pr.
—My Body Lies over the Ocean. (Sarah Deane Mysteries Ser.). 304p. 2000. mass mkt. 6.50 (*0-312-97040-4*, St. Martin's Paperbacks); 1998. 22.95 o.p. (*0-312-19991-0*, Saint Martin's Minotaur) St. Martin's Pr.
Bourjaily, Vance N. Old Soldier. 1990. 18.95 o.s.i (*1-55611-198-3*) Fine, Donald I. Bks.
Bowkett, Stephen. Dreamcatcher. 128p. pap. 7.95 (*1-85881-652-1*) Orion Publishing Group, Ltd. GBR. *Dist:* Trafalgar Square.
Boyle, Gerry. Bloodline. 1996. 336p. mass mkt. 5.99 o.s.i (*0-425-15182-4*) Berkley Publishing Group.
—Bloodline. 1995. 21.95 o.p. (*0-399-14030-1*, G. P. Putnam's Sons) Penguin Group (USA) Inc.
—Borderline. (Jack McMorrow Mystery Ser.). 368p. 1998. 22.95 o.s.i (*0-425-16147-1*); 2000. reprint ed. mass mkt. 6.99 o.s.i (*0-425-16964-2*, Prime Crime) Berkley Publishing Group.
—Deadline: A Jack McMorrow Mystery. 1995. 288p. mass mkt. 6.50 o.s.i (*0-425-14637-5*, Prime Crime) Berkley Publishing Group.
—Deadline: A Jack McMorrow Mystery. 1993. 17.95 (*0-945980-44-2*) North Country Pr.
—Lifeline. 1997. (Jack McMorrow Mystery Ser.). 368p. mass mkt. 5.99 o.s.i (*0-425-15688-5*) Berkley Publishing Group.
—Lifeline. 1996. 288p. 22.95 o.s.i (*0-399-14150-2*, G. P. Putnam's Sons) Penguin Group (USA) Inc.
—Potshot. 1998. (Jack McMorrow Mystery Ser.). 336p. mass mkt. 5.99 o.s.i (*0-425-16233-8*) Berkley Publishing Group.
—Potshot. 1997. 304p. 23.95 o.p. (*0-399-14259-2*, G. P. Putnam's Sons) Penguin Group (USA) Inc.
Brahms, Ann. Run for Your Life. 1993. 352p. mass mkt. 4.50 o.s.i (*0-8217-4193-4*, Zebra Bks.) Kensington Publishing Corp.
Bretton, Barbara. At Last. 2000. 320p. mass mkt. 6.99 (*0-425-17737-8*) Berkley Publishing Group.
Bryant, Sally S. Here's Juggins. 1996. (Illus.). 176p. (J). (gr. 4-7). 19.95 (*0-945980-62-0*) North Country Pr.
Bryers, Paul. The Prayer of the Bone. 2000. 256p. pap. 13.95 (*1-58234-075-7*); 1999. 23.95 (*1-58234-022-6*) Bloomsbury Publishing.
Caldwell, Erskine. Midsummer Passion & Other Tales of Maine Cussedness. 1990. pap. 11.95 o.p. (*0-89909-214-4*, 80-951-3) Rodale Pr., Inc.
Carey, Lisa. In the Country of the Young. 2002. 304p. pap. 12.95 (*0-06-093774-2*, Perennial) HarperTrade.
—In the Country of the Young. Hershey, J. H., ed. 2001. mass mkt. (*0-380-79967-7*, Avon Bks.) Morrow/Avon.
—In the Country of the Young. 2000. 304p. 24.00 (*0-380-97675-7*, Morrow, William & Co.) Morrow/Avon.
Carpenter, Mimi G. What the Sea Left Behind. 1981. (Illus.). 32p. (J). (gr. k-2). pap. 9.95 (*0-89272-123-5*) Down East Bks.
Chapman, Janet. Loving the Highlander. 2003. 384p. mass mkt. 6.99 (*0-7434-5307-7*); E-Book 5.99 (*0-7434-6691-8*) Simon & Schuster. (Pocket).
Child, Lee. Persuader: A Jack Reacher Novel. 2003. 352p. 24.95 (*0-385-33666-7*, Delacorte Pr.) Dell Publishing.
—Persuader: A Jack Reacher Novel. l.t. ed. 2003. (Jack Reacher Novel Ser.). 648p. 31.95 (*0-7862-5684-2*) Thorndike Pr.
Chute, Carolyn. The Beans of Egypt, Maine. l.t. ed. 1985. 14.95 o.p. (*0-8161-3956-3*, Macmillan Reference USA) Gale Group.
—The Beans of Egypt, Maine. 228p. 1985. 15.95 o.p. (*0-89919-314-5*); 1984. pap. 7.95 o.p. (*0-89919-362-5*) Houghton Mifflin Co.
—The Beans of Egypt, Maine. 1987. 14.95 o.s.i (*0-671-64104-2*, Simon & Schuster Audioworks) Simon & Schuster Audio.
—The Beans of Egypt, Maine. 1986. 256p. mass mkt. 6.50 o.s.i (*0-446-30010-1*) Warner Bks., Inc.
—The Beans of Egypt, Maine: The Finished Version. 1995. (Harvest American Writing Ser.). 304p. pap. 13.00 (*0-15-600188-8*, Harvest Bks.) Harcourt Trade Pubs.
—Letourneau's Used Auto Parts. 1995. (Harvest American Writing Ser.). 256p. pap. 11.00 (*0-15-600189-6*, Harvest Bks.) Harcourt Trade Pubs.
—Letourneau's Used Auto Parts. 1989. 256p. reprint ed. pap. 7.95 o.p. (*0-06-097225-4*, PL 7225, Perennial) HarperTrade.
—Letourneau's Used Auto Parts. 1988. 224p. 16.45 (*0-89919-500-8*) Houghton Mifflin Co.
—Merry Men. 1995. 712p. pap. 17.00 (*0-15-600191-8*, Harvest Bks.); 1994. x, 695p. (C). 24.95 o.s.i (*0-15-159270-5*) Harcourt Trade Pubs.
Chute, Carolyn, et al. Inside Vacationland: New Fiction from the Real Maine. Melnicove, Mark, ed. 1985. 192p. (Orig.). pap. 8.95 o.p. (*0-937966-18-5*) Tilbury Hse. Pubs.
Clark, A. Carman. The Maine Mulch Murder. 2004. (WWL Mystery Ser.: No. 483). 256p. mass mkt. (*0-373-26483-6*, Worldwide Library) Harlequin Enterprises, Ltd.
—The Maine Mulch Murder. 2001. 236p. 22.00 (*0-9678199-3-8*) Larcom Pr.
Clark, Bruce. Tales of Maritime Maine: The Vanished Years of the Maine Coast Brought to Life in Three Absorbing Tales. Mason, Jill, ed. 1987. 168p. 12.95 o.p. (*0-89909-122-9*) Yankee Bks.
Clark, William M. The Hills of Maine: And Other Stories. 1990. 122p. (Orig.). pap. 12.95 (*0-945980-17-5*) North Country Pr.
Cleveland, George A. Maine in Verse & Story. 1986. 288p. o.p. (*0-941216-29-2*); pap. o.p. (*0-941216-28-4*) Cay-Bel Publishing Co.
Colbert, Jaimee W. Climbing the God Tree: A Novel in 24 Stories. 1998. (Winner of the 1997 Willa Cather Fiction Prize Ser.). 208p. pap. 12.95 (*1-884235-25-5*) Helicon 9 Editions.
Connolly, John. Dark Hollow: A Novel. 2001. 448p. 25.00 (*0-7432-0332-1*, Simon & Schuster) Simon & Schuster.
—The Killing Kind. 2001. (Illus.). 388p. pap. (*0-340-77121-6*) Hodder & Stoughton, Ltd. GBR. *Dist:* Trafalgar Square.
—The Killing Kind. 2003. 448p. pap. 6.99 (*0-7434-5637-8*, Pocket Star); 2002. 384p. 25.00 (*0-7434-5334-4*, Atria) Simon & Schuster.
Cook, Thomas H. Places in the Dark. 2001. 304p. reprint ed. mass mkt. 6.50 (*0-553-58067-1*, Spectra) Bantam Bks.
—Places in the Dark. l.t. ed. 2000. (Americana Ser.). 373p. 28.95 (*0-7862-2556-4*) Thorndike Pr.
Crossman, David A. Dead of Winter: A Winston Crisp Maine Island Mystery. 1999. 349p. 22.95 (*0-89272-445-5*) Down East Bks.
—A Show of Hands. 288p. 1998. pap. 14.95 (*0-89272-398-X*); 1997. 22.95 o.p. (*0-89272-412-9*) Down East Bks.

Dailey, Janet. Summer Mahogany: Maine. 2002. 120p. pap. 6.99 (*0-7592-3830-8*); E-Book 6.99 (*0-7592-0168-4*); E-Book 6.99 (*1-58586-386-6*); E-Book 6.99 (*0-7592-0912-X*) ereads.com.

Delinsky, Barbara. For My Daughters. l.t. ed. 1994. 445p. lib. bdg. 23.95 o.p. (*0-8161-7403-2*, Macmillan Reference USA) Gale Group.

—For My Daughters. 1994. 288p. 20.00 o.p. (*0-06-017618-0*) HarperCollins Pubs.

—For My Daughters. 1995. 416p. mass mkt. 7.99 (*0-06-109280-0*, HarperTorch) Morrow/Avon.

—Through My Eyes. 2003. 256p. mass mkt. (*1-55166-653-7*, Mira Bks.) Harlequin Enterprises, Ltd.

—Within Reach. 1997. (Romance Ser.). 386p. 24.95 (*0-7862-0848-1*, Five Star) Gale Group.

—Within Reach. 1986. 400p. mass mkt. (*0-373-97018-8*, Harlequin Bks.) Harlequin Enterprises, Ltd.

—Within Reach. 1992. 528p. mass mkt. 7.99 (*0-06-104174-2*, HarperTorch) Morrow/Avon.

—Within Reach. 1991. reprint ed. 21.95 o.p. (*0-7278-4251-X*) Severn Hse. Pubs., Ltd.

DeMarco, Tom. Dark Harbor House. 2000. viii, 280p. pap. 15.95 (*0-89272-511-7*) Down East Bks.

Dethier, Vincent G. Newberry: The Life & Times of a Maine Clam. 1981. (Illus.). 86p. (J). (gr. 1-4). pap. 6.95 o.p. (*0-89272-085-9*) Down East Bks.

DeVries, Douglas. Muscles Visits Anchorage. 1990. (Illus.). 32p. (Orig.). (J). (ps-3). pap. text 10.00 (*1-877721-01-8*) Jade Ram Publishing.

Dickson, Margaret. Cliff Walk, 001. 1987. 256p. 16.95 o.p. (*0-395-41106-8*) Houghton Mifflin Co.

Dobyns, Stephen. A Boat off the Coast. l.t. ed. 1988. 21.95 o.p. (*1-55504-641-X*); pap. 19.95 o.p. (*1-55504-642-8*) BBC Audiobooks America.

—A Boat off the Coast. 1989. 272p. pap. 3.95 o.p. (*0-14-010047-4*, Penguin Bks.); 1987. 16.95 o.p. (*0-670-81668-X*) Viking Penguin.

Ellis, Julie. Walk a Tightrope. l.t. ed. 2002. (Hall Romance Ser.). 225p. 28.95 (*0-7838-9737-5*) Gale Group.

Emerson, Kathy Lynn. The Mystery of Hilliard's Castle. 1985. (J). (gr. 6-9). pap. 7.95 o.p. (*0-89272-213-4*) Down East Bks.

Ensor, Eloise & Ensor, Robert. Good Golly Miss Molly. Weinberger, Jane, ed. 1997. (Illus.). 40p. (Orig.). (J). (ps-6). pap. 9.95 (*1-883650-37-2*) Windswept Hse. Pubs.

Ensor, Robert. Nellie, the Flying Instructor. 1995. (Illus.). 40p. (J). (ps up). pap. 9.95 (*1-883650-21-6*) Windswept Hse. Pubs.

Fahy, Christopher. One Day in the Short Happy Life of Anna Banana: And Other Maine Stories. 1988. 62p. (Orig.). pap. 5.95 o.p. (*0-9618592-0-2*) Maine Writers & Pubs. Alliance.

Fickett, David. Nectar. 2002. 320p. 23.95 (*0-7653-0174-1*, Forge Bks.) Doherty, Tom Assocs., LLC.

Fister, Barbara. On Edge. 2002. 288p. mass mkt. 6.50 (*0-440-23751-3*, Delta) Dell Publishing.

Flanagan, James M. Builders of Maine. 1994. 400p. (YA). pap. 10.00 (*0-932433-86-3*) Windswept Hse. Pubs.

Flanagan, Mary. Rose Reason. 1992. 388p. 23.95 (*0-15-179015-9*) Harcourt Trade Pubs.

Fletcher, Jessica. Gin & Daggers: Jessica Fletcher & Donald Bain Mystery. 2000. (Murder She Wrote Ser.). 272p. mass mkt. 6.50 (*0-451-19998-7*, Signet Bks.) NAL.

—Murder She Wrote: Knock 'em Dead, Vol. 12. 1999. (Murder She Wrote Ser.). 288p. mass mkt. 6.50 (*0-451-19477-2*, Signet Bks.) NAL.

—Murder She Wrote: Trick or Treachery. 2000. (Murder She Wrote Ser.). 272p. mass mkt. 6.50 (*0-451-20152-3*, Signet Bks.) NAL.

Fletcher, Jessica & Bain, Donald. Brandy & Bullets. 1995. (Murder She Wrote Ser.: Vol. 3). 288p. (Orig.). mass mkt. 6.50 (*0-451-18491-2*, Signet Bks.) NAL.

—Deadly Judgement. 1996. (Murder She Wrote Ser.). 304p. mass mkt. 6.50 (*0-451-18771-7*) NAL.

—Gin & Daggers. 1990. reprint ed. pap. 3.50 (*0-380-71166-4*, Avon Bks.) Morrow/Avon.

—Gin & Daggers: A Murder, She Wrote Mystery. 1989. 272p. text 17.95 o.p. (*0-07-003239-4*) McGraw-Hill Cos., The.

Ford, Elaine. Monkey Bay. 256p. 1990. pap. 7.95 o.p. (*0-14-012057-2*, Penguin Bks.); 1989. 17.95 o.p. (*0-670-82752-5*) Viking Penguin.

Fox, Elaine S. If the Slipper Fits. 2003. 384p. mass mkt. 5.99 (*0-06-051721-2*, Avon Bks.) Morrow/Avon.

Gage, Elizabeth. The Hourglass. 1999. 304p. mass mkt. (*1-55166-546-8*, 1-66546-2); 240p. pap. (*1-55166-503-4*, 1-66503-3) Harlequin Enterprises, Ltd. (Mira Bks.).

Garrett, Annie. After You. 1999. E-Book 5.99 o.s.i (*0-312-24604-8*) St. Martin's Pr.

—After You: A Novel. l.t. ed. 1998. 210p. 23.95 (*1-57490-167-2*, Beeler Large Print Bks.) Beeler, Thomas T. Publisher.

—After You: A Novel. 1999. 288p. mass mkt. 5.99 (*0-312-96926-0*, St. Martin's Paperbacks); 1998. 224p. 20.95 o.p. (*0-312-19671-7*) St. Martin's Pr.

Gautreau, Norman G. Sea Room. 314p. 2003. pap. 12.50 (*1-931561-38-9*); 2002. pap. 25.00 (*1-931561-07-9*) MacAdam/Cage Publishing, Inc.

Gerritsen, Tess. Bloodstream. 1999. (Illus.). 512p. mass mkt. 7.99 (*0-671-01676-8*, Pocket); 1998. 324p. (YA). 23.00 (*0-671-01675-X*, Atria) Simon & Schuster.

—Bloodstream. l.t. ed. 1998. (Mystery Ser.). 560p. 30.95 o.p. (*0-7862-1617-4*) Thorndike Pr.

—Keeper of the Bride. 2002. 256p. mass mkt. (*1-55166-935-8*, Mira Bks.) Harlequin Enterprises, Ltd.

Gideon, Melanie. The Girl Who Swallowed the Moon. 1995. 194p. pap. 12.95 (*0-9624626-9-1*) Astarte Shell Pr.

Gilbert, Elizabeth. Stern Men. 2000. 304p. tchr. ed. 24.00 (*0-395-83622-0*) Houghton Mifflin Co.

—Stern Men. 2001. 304p. pap. 13.00 (*0-618-12733-X*, Mariner Bks.) Houghton Mifflin Co. Trade & Reference Div.

—Stern Men. l.t. ed. 2000. (Americana Ser.). 566p. 26.95 (*0-7862-2988-8*) Thorndike Pr.

Gjelfriend, George E. High Island Treasure. Little, Carl, ed. 2nd ed. 1992. (Illus.). 120p. (J). (gr. 3-8). reprint ed. pap. 8.95 (*0-932433-84-7*) Windswept Hse. Pubs.

Gould, John. The Wines of Pentagoet. 1986. 14.95 o.p. (*0-393-02303-6*) Norton, W. W. & Co., Inc.

Graves, Sarah. The Dead Cat Bounce. 1998. 336p. mass mkt. 6.99 (*0-553-57857-X*) Bantam Bks.

—Triple Witch. 1999. 304p. mass mkt. 5.99 (*0-553-57858-8*) Bantam Bks.

—Unhinged: A Home Repair Is Homicide Mystery. 2003. 368p. mass mkt. 6.50 (*0-553-58227-5*); 272p. 19.95 (*0-553-80229-1*) Bantam Bks.

—Wicked Fix. 2000. 304p. mass mkt. 6.50 (*0-553-57859-6*) Bantam Bks.

Griesemer, John. Signal & Noise: A Novel. 2004. 608p. pap. 15.00 (*0-312-42334-9*); 2003. 640p. 26.00 (*0-312-30082-4*) Picador.

Guild, Nicholas. Chain Reaction. 1986. 320p. mass mkt. 3.95 o.p. (*0-425-08778-6*) Berkley Publishing Group.

—Chain Reaction. 1983. 384p. 13.95 o.p. (*0-312-12785-5*) St. Martin's Pr.

Gutman, Amy. The Anniversary. 2003. 352p. 21.95 (*0-316-38120-9*) Little Brown & Co.

—The Anniversary. 2004. 432p. mass mkt. 7.50 (*0-446-61417-3*) Warner Bks., Inc.

Haddam, Jane. And One to Die On: A Birthday Mystery. 1997. 304p. mass mkt. 5.99 o.s.i (*0-553-56448-X*) Bantam Bks.

Hall, Linda. Chat Room. 2003. (Teri Blake-Addision Mystery Series, Book 2 Ser.). 290p. pap. 11.99 (*1-59052-200-1*) Multnomah Pubs., Inc.

—Island of Refuge. 1999. 310p. pap. 10.99 (*1-57673-397-1*) Multnomah Pubs., Inc.

—Margaret's Peace. 1998. (Christian Fiction Ser.). 311p. 23.95 (*0-7862-1652-2*, Five Star) Gale Group.

—Margaret's Peace. 1998. 308p. pap. 9.99 (*1-57673-216-9*, Multnomah Fiction) Multnomah Pubs., Inc.

—Sadie's Song. 2001. 304p. pap. 10.99 (*1-57673-659-8*) Multnomah Pubs., Inc.

—Steal Away. 2003. (Teri Blake-Addison Mystery Series, Book One Ser.). 290p. pap. 11.99 (*1-59052-072-6*) Multnomah Pubs., Inc.

Harnum, Robert. Exile in the Kingdom. 2001. (Hardscrabble Bks.). 176p. 19.95 (*1-58465-148-2*, Hardscrabble Bks.) Univ. Pr. of New England.

Harrison, Constance C. Virginia Cousin & Bar Harbor Tales. 1977. (Short Story Index Reprint Ser.). 19.95 (*0-8369-3110-6*) Ayer Co. Pubs., Inc.

Harrison, Stuart. Still Water. 2000. 373p. (*0-00-226153-7*); (*0-00-710751-X*) HarperCollins Pubs.

Hatcher, Maynard. The Liberty Pole. Weinberger, Jane, ed. 1987. 200p. (Orig.). pap. 5.00 (*0-932433-32-4*) Windswept Hse. Pubs.

Hautala, Rick. The Mountain King. 1996. 276p. 50.00 o.p. (*1-881475-16-6*) Cemetery Dance Pubns.

—The Mountain King. 2001. 384p. mass mkt. 5.99 (*0-8439-4887-6*, Leisure Bks.) Dorchester Publishing Co., Inc.

Holmes, Edward M. A Part of the Main: Short Stories of the Maine Coast. 1976. pap. 9.95 (*0-89101-031-9*) Univ. of Maine Pr.

Hulbert, Elizabeth M. The Memory Quilt. 1996. (Illus.). 52p. (Orig.). (J). (ps up). pap. 6.95 (*0-932433-42-1*) Windswept Hse. Pubs.

Irving, John. The Cider House Rules. 1999. mass mkt. 7.99 (*0-345-91638-7*); 1999. 7.99 (*0-345-91557-7*); 1999. pap. 12.95 (*0-345-91558-5*); 1994. 608p. mass mkt. 7.99 (*0-345-38765-1*, Ballantine Bks.); 1997. 576p. reprint ed. pap. 14.95 (*0-345-41794-1*, Ballantine Bks.) Ballantine Bks.

—The Cider House Rules. 608p. 1991. mass mkt. 2.99 o.s.i (*0-553-19648-0*); 1986. mass mkt. 5.95 o.s.i (*0-553-25800-1*) Bantam Bks.

—The Cider House Rules. 1985. 640p. 18.95 o.p. (*0-688-03036-X*, Morrow, William & Co.) Morrow/Avon.

—The Cider House Rules. 1999. (Modern Library Ser.). 592p. 21.95 (*0-679-60335-2*) Random Hse., Inc.

—The Cider House Rules. 1999. 144p. 10.95 (*0-7868-8523-8*) Talk Miramax Bks.

—The Cider House Rules. l.t. ed. (Basic Ser.). 2001. 28.95 (*0-7862-2675-7*); 2000. 1064p. 30.95 (*0-7862-2674-9*) Thorndike Pr.

—The Cider House Rules. 1993. 14.04 (*0-606-20389-3*) Turtleback Bks.

Jackson, Faith Reyher. Meadow Fugue & Descant: A Novel. 2002. (*0-931846-66-8*); pap. (*0-931846-64-1*) Washington Writers' Publishing Hse.

Jensen, Muriel. That Summer in Maine. 2003. (Harlequin American Romance Ser.: No. 965). (Illus.). 256p. mass mkt. (*0-373-16965-5*, Harlequin Bks.) Harlequin Enterprises, Ltd.

Jewett, Sarah Orne. The Country of the Pointed Firs. 24.95 (*0-8488-1062-7*) Amereon, Ltd.

—The Country of the Pointed Firs. 1910. E-Book (*1-58734-026-7*) Bartleby.com.

—The Country of the Pointed Firs. 1927. 253p. (YA). reprint ed. pap. text 28.00 (*1-4047-1313-1*) Classic Textbooks.

—The Country of the Pointed Firs. 1999. (Illus.). 141p. reprint ed. pap. text 22.00 (*0-7881-6205-5*) DIANE Publishing Co.

—The Country of the Pointed Firs. unabr. ed. 1998. (Thrift Editions Ser.). 96p. (J). pap. 2.00 (*0-486-28196-5*) Dover Pubns., Inc.

—The Country of the Pointed Firs. (Illus.). 1991. 198p. 20.00 o.s.i (*0-87923-894-1*); 2000. 224p. reprint ed. pap. 20.00 (*1-56792-140-X*) Godine, David R. Pub.

—The Country of the Pointed Firs. 1994. pap. 11.00 (*0-393-31137-6*) Norton, W. W. & Co., Inc.

—The Country of the Pointed Firs. 1988. (Collected Works of Sarah Orne Jewett). reprint ed. lib. bdg. 79.00 (*0-7812-1313-4*) Reprint Services Corp.

—The Country of the Pointed Firs. 1981. (Keith Jennison Large Type Bks.). (gr. 7 up). lib. bdg. 7.95 o.p. (*0-531-00177-6*, Watts, Franklin) Scholastic Library Publishing.

—The Country of the Pointed Firs. 1997. (Illus.). 141p. 21.50 o.p. (*0-684-81909-0*, Simon & Schuster) Simon & Schuster.

—The Country of the Pointed Firs. reprint ed. 59.00 (*0-403-03174-5*) Somerset Pubs., Inc.

—The Country of the Pointed Firs: And Other Stories. 1954. 320p. reprint ed. pap. 10.95 (*0-385-09214-8*, A26) Doubleday Publishing.

—The Country of the Pointed Firs & Other Fiction. Heller, Terry, ed. & intro. by. 1996. (Oxford World's Classics Ser.). 386p. (C). pap. 8.95 o.p. (*0-19-283190-9*) Oxford Univ. Pr., Inc.

—The Country of the Pointed Firs & Other Stories. E-Book 4.95 (*1-931208-60-3*) Adobe Systems, Inc.

—The Country of the Pointed Firs & Other Stories. 2000. (Classics Ser.). 256p. mass mkt. 3.95 (*0-451-52757-7*, Signet Classics) NAL.

—The Country of the Pointed Firs & Other Stories. 1982. (Illus.). 336p. pap. 8.95 o.p. (*0-393-00048-6*) Norton, W. W. & Co., Inc.

—The Country of the Pointed Firs & Other Stories. (Classics Ser.). 2001. 304p. pap. 8.95 (*0-375-75671-X*); 2000. E-Book 4.95 (*0-679-64159-9*) Random House Adult Trade Publishing Group. (Modern Library).

—The Country of the Pointed Firs & Other Stories. 1995. (Modern Library Ser.). 196p. 13.50 o.s.i (*0-679-60173-2*) Random Hse., Inc.

—The Country of the Pointed Firs & Other Stories. 1990. 19.50 (*0-8446-2325-3*) Smith, Peter Pub., Inc.

—The Country of the Pointed Firs & Other Stories. Easton, Alison, ed. & intro. by. 1996. (Penguin Classics Ser.). (Illus.). 304p. 8.95 (*0-14-043476-3*) Viking Penguin.

—The Country of the Pointed Firs & Other Stories: Centennial Edition. Sherman, Sarah W., ed. & intro. by. anniv. ed. 1997. 326p. pap. 15.95 (*0-87451-826-1*, Hardscrabble Bks.) Univ. Pr. of New England.

—Deephaven. 1976. 14.95 (*0-8488-1389-8*) Amereon, Ltd.

—Deephaven. 1980. 255p. reprint ed. lib. bdg. 13.50 (*0-89968-211-1*, Lightyear Pr.) Buccaneer Bks., Inc.

—Deephaven. 1993. (Illus.). 310p. reprint ed. 20.00 (*0-9636111-0-0*) Old Berwick Historical Society.

—Deephaven. 1988. reprint ed. lib. bdg. 79.00 (*0-7812-1302-9*) Reprint Services Corp.

—Deephaven. reprint ed. 59.00 (*0-403-03190-7*) Somerset Pubs., Inc.

—An Edited Edition of Sarah Orne Jewett's the Country of the Pointed Firs. Morgan, Jeff, tr. & intro. by. 2003. (Studies in American Literature Ser.). 176p. text 99.95 (*0-7734-6588-X*) Mellen, Edwin Pr., The.

—Novels & Stories: Deephaven; A Country Doctor; The Country of the Pointed Firs; Dunnet Landing Stories; Selected Stories & Sketches. Bell, Michael D., ed. 1994. (Library of America: Vol. 69). 950p. 35.00 (*0-940450-74-7*) Library of America, The.

Johnson, Willis. The Girl Who Would Be Russian: And Other Stories. 1991. 180p. reprint ed. pap. 10.95 o.p. (*0-88448-096-8*) Tilbury Hse. Pubs.

—The Girl Who Would Be Russian & Other Stories. 1986. 192p. 15.95 o.p. (*0-15-135691-2*) Harcourt Trade Pubs.

Johnstone, William W. Slaughter in the Ashes. abr. ed. 1998. audio 16.95 (*1-882071-94-8*) B&B Audio, Inc.

—Slaughter in the Ashes, No. 23. 1997. (Slaughter in the Ashes Ser.: Vol. 23). 288p. mass mkt. 5.99 (*0-7860-0380-4*, Pinnacle Bks.) Kensington Publishing Corp.

Jones, Able. Country Living, Country Dying: A Witty Tale of Secrets Unburied. 1996. 176p. reprint ed. pap. 10.95 (*0-89272-378-5*) Down East Bks.

Kean, Rob. The Pledge. 2000. 736p. (gr. 8 up). mass mkt. 7.50 (*0-446-60848-3*); 1999. 528p. 24.95 (*0-446-52497-2*) Warner Bks., Inc.

Kenney, Susan. Sailing. l.t. ed. 1989. (General Ser.). 480p. 19.95 o.p. (*0-8161-4726-4*, Macmillan Reference USA) Gale Group.

—Sailing. 1989. 336p. pap. 8.95 o.p. (*0-14-009333-8*, Penguin Bks.); 1988. 318p. 18.95 o.p. (*0-670-81229-3*) Viking Penguin.

Kenvin, Roger Lee. Harpo's Garden. 123p. (Orig.). unabr. ed. 1997. pap. 14.95 (*0-9656635-0-7*); 2nd unabr. ed. 1998. pap. 14.95 (*0-9656635-3-1*) July Blue Pr.

Ketchum, Jack. Hide & Seek. 2000. 192p. 40.00 o.p. (*1-58767-004-6*) Cemetery Dance Pubns.

Kimball, Michael. Undone. 1997. 416p. mass mkt. 5.99 (*0-380-78670-2*); 1996. 352p. 23.00 o.p. (*0-380-97305-7*) Morrow/Avon. (Avon Bks.).

King, Stephen. Bag of Bones. 2000. (RUS.). Vol. 1. pap. 14.95 (*5-237-01450-X*); Vol. 2. pap. 14.95 (*5-237-01451-8*) AST, Izdatel'stvo, OOO, firma RUS. *Dist:* Distribooks, Inc.

—Bag of Bones. 2002. E-Book 9.99 (*1-59061-785-1*) Adobe Systems, Inc.

—Bag of Bones. unabr. ed. 1999. audio 59.95 Highsmith Inc.

—Bag of Bones. unabr. ed. 1999. audio 56.00 (*1-84032-192-X*) Hodder Headline Audiobooks GBR. *Dist:* Ulverscroft Large Print Bks., Ltd.

—Bag of Bones. 1999. E-Book 28.00 (*0-684-83541-X*, Scribner); 1998. 544p. 28.00 (*0-684-85350-7*, Scribner); 1988. pap. 7.99 (*0-671-02607-0*, Pocket); 1999. 752p. reprint ed. mass mkt. 7.99 (*0-671-02423-X*, Pocket) Simon & Schuster.

—Bag of Bones. unabr. ed. 1998. audio 59.95 (*0-671-58234-8*, 136013); audio compact disk 79.95 (*0-671-04306-4*) Simon & Schuster Audio. (Simon & Schuster Audioworks).

—Bag of Bones. l.t. ed. 1999. (Thorndike/G. K. Hall Paperback Bestsellers Ser.). 901p. pap. 28.95 (*0-7862-1721-9*); 30.95 o.p. (*0-7862-1720-0*) Thorndike Pr.

—Bag of Bones. 1999. 14.04 (*0-606-17066-9*) Turtleback Bks.

—Carrie. 1990. 192p. 32.50 (*0-385-08695-4*) Doubleday Publishing.

—Carrie. 1991. (Stephen King Collectors Editions Ser.). 176p. pap. 12.95 o.p. (*0-452-26719-6*, Plume) Dutton/Plume.

—Carrie. 1992. (SPA.). 288p. pap. 3.95 (*1-56780-057-2*) La Costa Pr., Inc.

—Carrie. 1975. mass mkt. 3.95 o.p. (*0-451-15071-6*); 256p. reprint ed. mass mkt. 7.99 o.s.i (*0-451-15744-3*) NAL. (Signet Bks.).

—Carrie. 1999. (SPA., Illus.). 288p. (*84-01-49966-6*) Plaza & Janés Editories, S.A.

—Carrie. (SPA.). 288p. 12.95 (*84-01-49888-0*) Plaza & Janés Editories, S.A. ESP. *Dist:* Distribooks, Inc.

—Carrie. 2002. 272p. pap. 7.99 (*0-671-03972-5*); 2000. 208p. pap. 12.95 (*0-671-03973-3*) Simon & Schuster. (Pocket).

—Carrie. 1975. 14.04 (*0-606-00823-3*) Turtleback Bks.

—Cujo. 1994. (Collectors' Editions Ser.). 304p. pap. 14.95 o.p. (*0-452-27328-5*, Plume) Dutton/Plume.

—Cujo. l.t. ed. 1993. 497p. 23.95 (*0-8161-5667-0*, Macmillan Reference USA) Gale Group.

—Cujo. 1983. (SPA.). (*970-05-0888-9*) Grijalbo, Editorial.

—Cujo. 1983. mass mkt. 3.95 o.p. (*0-451-12650-5*); 1983. mass mkt. 3.95 o.p. (*0-451-13970-4*); 1982. mass mkt. 3.95 o.p. (*0-451-11729-8*); 1982. mass mkt. 4.50 o.p. (*0-451-14507-0*); 1982. mass mkt. 4.50 o.p. (*0-451-15064-3*); 1982. 320p. reprint ed. mass mkt. 7.99 (*0-451-16135-1*) NAL. (Signet Bks.).

—Cujo. l.t. ed. 1983. 496p. 13.95 o.p. (*0-7089-8123-2*, Charnwood) Thorpe, F. A. Pubs. GBR. *Dist:* Ulverscroft Large Print Bks., Ltd.

—Cujo. 1981. 14.04 (*0-606-02861-7*) Turtleback Bks.

—Cujo. 1981. 336p. 29.95 (*0-670-45193-2*) Viking Penguin.

—Dolores Claiborne. (FRE.). pap. 12.95 (*2-277-04742-2*) 84, Editions FRA. *Dist:* Distribooks, Inc.
—Dolores Claiborne. l.t. ed. (General Ser.). 355p. 1993. pap. 17.95 (*0-8161-5641-7*); 1992. lib. bdg. 25.00 o.p. (*0-8161-5640-9*) Gale Group. (Macmillan Reference USA).
—Dolores Claiborne. 384p. 1995. mass mkt. 6.99 o.p. (*0-451-18411-4*); 1993. reprint ed. mass mkt. 7.99 (*0-451-17709-6*) NAL. (Signet Bks.).
—Dolores Claiborne. unabr. ed. 1995. (SPA.). 29.95 o.p. (*0-7871-0643-7*, 893235) NewStar Media, Inc.
—Dolores Claiborne. abr. unabr. ed. 1995. pap. 30.00 o.p. incl. audio (*0-453-00957-3*); Set. 1993. 30.00 o.p. incl. audio (*0-453-00803-8*, 892486) Penguin/HighBridge.
—Dolores Claiborne. 6.98 o.p. (*0-8317-1186-8*) Smithmark Pubs., Inc.
—Dolores Claiborne. 1993. 14.04 (*0-606-05811-7*) Turtleback Bks.
—Dolores Claiborne. 1993. 320p. 23.50 o.s.i (*0-670-84452-7*); 352p. 25.00 o.p. (*0-670-84936-7*) Viking Penguin. (Viking).
—Dreamcatcher. 2001. E-Book 28.00 (*1-58945-621-1*) Adobe Systems, Inc.
—Dreamcatcher. 2003. 896p. mass mkt. 7.99 (*0-7434-6752-3*, Pocket); 2001. mass mkt. 7.99 (*0-7434-3628-8*, Pocket); 2001. 896p. mass mkt. 7.99 (*0-7434-3627-X*, Pocket); 2001. 624p. 28.00 (*0-7432-1138-3*, Scribner); 2001. E-Book 28.00 (*0-7432-2188-5*, Scribner); 2001. E-Book 28.00 (*0-7410-0369-4*) Simon & Schuster.
—Dreamcatcher. l.t. ed. 2001. 928p. 32.50 o.p. (*0-7432-1644-X*) Thorpe, F. A. Pubs. GBR. *Dist:* Ulverscroft Large Print Bks., Ltd.
—Gerald's Game. 1993. 448p. mass mkt. 7.99 (*0-451-17646-4*); pap. 6.99 (*0-451-17811-4*) NAL. (Signet Bks.).
—Gerald's Game. abr. unabr. ed. 1992. audio 34.95 (*0-453-00800-3*) Penguin/HighBridge.
—Gerald's Game. 1992. pap. 6.98 o.p. (*0-8317-2752-7*) Smithmark Pubs., Inc.
—Gerald's Game. 1992. 14.04 (*0-606-05310-7*) Turtleback Bks.
—Gerald's Game. 1992. 352p. 23.50 o.s.i (*0-670-84650-3*) Viking Penguin.
—Hearts in Atlantis. 2001. E-Book 9.99 (*1-59061-258-2*) Adobe Systems, Inc.
—Hearts in Atlantis. l.t. ed. (Thorndike/G. K. Hall Paperback Bestsellers Ser.). 2000. 760p. pap. 28.95 (*0-7838-8738-8*); 1999. 732p. 31.95 (*0-7838-8737-X*) Gale Group. (Macmillan Reference USA).
—Hearts in Atlantis. 1999. 528p. 28.00 (*0-684-85351-5*, Scribner); 1999. E-Book 28.00 (*0-684-84490-7*, Scribner); 2000. 688p. reprint ed. pap. 7.99 (*0-671-02424-8*, Pocket); 2000. 528p. reprint ed. 7.99 (*0-671-04214-9*, Pocket); 2001. 688p. reprint ed. mass mkt. 7.99 o.s.i (*0-7434-3621-0*, Pocket) Simon & Schuster.
—Hearts in Atlantis. 2001. pap. 49.95 incl. audio compact disk (*0-7435-0987-0*, Simon & Schuster Audioworks) Simon & Schuster Audio.
—Hearts in Atlantis. 2000. 14.04 (*0-606-19496-7*) Turtleback Bks.
—Insomnia. 1995. (SPA., Illus.). 610p. (*84-253-2703-2*) Grijalbo, Editorial.
—Insomnia. 1995. pap. 6.99 o.s.i (*0-451-18612-5*); (Illus.). 672p. mass mkt. 7.99 (*0-451-18496-3*, Signet Bks.) NAL.
—Insomnia. abr. unabr. ed. 1994. audio 79.95 (*0-453-00910-7*) Penguin/HighBridge.
—Insomnia. 788p. 7.98 o.p. (*0-8317-3612-7*) Smithmark Pubs., Inc.
—Insomnia. l.t. ed. 1995. (Core Collection). 951p. 31.95 (*0-7838-1183-7*) Thorndike Pr.
—Insomnia. 1995. 14.04 (*0-606-07708-1*) Turtleback Bks.
—Insomnia. 1994. (Illus.). 832p. 27.95 (*0-670-85503-0*, Viking) Viking Penguin.
—Insomnia. deluxe ed. 1994. (Illus.). 591p. 75.00 (*0-929480-37-6*) Ziesing, Mark V.
—El Juego de Gerald. unabr. ed. 1995. Tr. of Gerald's Game. (SPA.). audio 49.95 o.p. (*0-7871-0601-1*, 113236) NewStar Media, Inc.
—Needful Things. l.t. ed. 1992. (General Ser.). 1044p. pap. 19.95 o.p. (*0-8161-5477-5*); lib. bdg. 25.95 o.p. (*0-8161-5476-7*) Gale Group. (Macmillan Reference USA).
—Needful Things. abr. unabr. ed. Pt. 1. 1991. 704p. 29.95 o.p. incl. audio (*0-453-00759-7*, Penguin Bks.); Pt. 2. 1991. 704p. 29.95 o.p. incl. audio (*0-453-00760-0*, Penguin Bks.); Pt. 2. audio 29.95 o.p.; Pt. 3. 1991. audio 29.95 o.p. (*0-453-00761-9*); Pt. 3. audio 29.95 o.p. HighBridge Co.
—Needful Things. 752p. 1993. mass mkt. 6.99 o.p. (*0-451-17859-9*); 1992. mass mkt. 7.99 (*0-451-17281-7*) NAL. (Signet Bks.).
—Needful Things. abr. unabr. ed. 1993. 49.95 incl. audio (*0-453-00859-3*) Penguin/HighBridge.
—Needful Things. 1992. 14.04 (*0-606-01485-3*) Turtleback Bks.
—Needful Things. 1991. 704p. text 35.00 (*0-670-83953-1*, Penguin Bks.) Viking Penguin.
—El Perro del Sol. 1999. pap. 5.99 (*0-451-18661-3*, Signet Bks.) NAL.
—El Perro del Sol. unabr. ed. 1995. (SPA.). 22.95 o.p. (*0-7871-0606-2*, 394029) NewStar Media, Inc.
—Pet Sematary. 1994. reprint ed. lib. bdg. 29.95 (*1-56849-545-5*) Buccaneer Bks., Inc.
—Pet Sematary. 1983. 384p. 30.00 o.s.i (*0-385-18244-9*) Doubleday Publishing.
—Pet Sematary. l.t. ed. (General Ser.). x, 634p. 1985. 9.95 o.p. (*0-8161-3756-0*); 1984. 18.95 o.p. (*0-8161-3691-2*) Gale Group. (Macmillan Reference USA).
—Pet Sematary. 1984. (J). mass mkt. 4.50 o.p. (*0-451-13975-5*); (J). mass mkt. 4.50 o.p. (*0-451-15024-4*); (J). mass mkt. 4.50 o.p. (*0-451-13237-8*); 416p. (YA). mass mkt. 4.95 o.p. (*0-451-15775-3*); 416p. reprint ed. mass mkt. 7.99 o.s.i (*0-451-16207-2*) NAL. (Signet Bks.).
—Pet Sematary. abr. ed. 1998. audio 18.00 (*0-671-58227-5*, 393645, Simon & Schuster Audioworks) Simon & Schuster Audio.
—Pet Sematary. 1984. 14.04 (*0-606-01108-0*) Turtleback Bks.
—The Shawshank Redemption. 1994. mass mkt. 7.99 o.s.i (*0-451-18394-0*, Signet Bks.) NAL.
—The Shawshank Redemption. abr. unabr. ed. 1995. 3p. audio 24.95 (*0-14-086213-7*, Penguin AudioBooks) Viking Penguin.
—The Tommyknockers. 752p. 1993. mass mkt. 6.99 o.p. (*0-451-17842-4*, Signet Bks.); 1988. reprint ed. mass mkt. 7.99 (*0-451-15660-9*) NAL.
—The Tommyknockers. 19.95 (*0-399-13699-1*) Penguin Group (USA) Inc.
—The Tommyknockers. 1987. 544p. 19.95 o.p. (*0-399-13314-3*, G. P. Putnam's Sons) Penguin Putnam Bks. for Young Readers.
—The Tommyknockers. 2nd ed. 1999. (Nevedomoe, Neobiasnimoe, Neveroitnoe Ser.: Vol. 102). (SPA., Illus.). 968p. (*84-01-47465-5*) Plaza & Janés Editories, S.A.
—The Tommyknockers. 1992. (SPA.). 704p. 15.50 (*84-01-49998-4*) Plaza & Janés Editories, S.A. ESP. *Dist:* Distribooks, Inc.
—The Tommyknockers. 1987. 14.04 (*0-606-04113-3*) Turtleback Bks.
—La Tormenta del Siglo. 2000. Tr. of Storm of the Century. (SPA., Illus.). 576p. 17.95 (*84-01-47475-2*) Plaza & Janés Editories, S.A. ESP. *Dist:* Distribooks, Inc., Libros Sin Fronteras.
King, Tabitha. The Book of Reuben. 1994. 368p. 22.95 o.p. (*0-525-93766-8*, Dutton) Dutton/Plume.
—Caretakers. 1984. mass mkt. 3.95 o.p. (*0-451-13156-8*); 352p. mass mkt. 5.99 o.s.i (*0-451-16169-6*) NAL. (Signet Bks.).
—One on One. 1993. 496p. 23.00 o.p. (*0-525-93590-8*) Dutton/Plume.
—Pearl. 1988. 324p. 18.95 o.p. (*0-453-00626-4*) NAL.
—Survivor. 1997. 448p. 24.95 o.p. (*0-525-94241-6*) Dutton/Plume.
—Survivor. 1998. 496p. mass mkt. 7.99 o.p. (*0-451-19090-4*, Signet Bks.) NAL.
Knight, Phyllis. Shattered Rhythms: A Lil Ritchie Mystery. 1994. 256p. 20.95 o.p. (*0-312-10548-7*, Saint Martin's Minotaur) St. Martin's Pr.
Knowles, Ardeana H. Pink Chimneys: A Novel of 19th Century Maine. 1999. 312p. pap. 12.95 (*0-88448-056-9*); 1988. 320p. 15.95 o.p. (*0-88448-041-0*) Tilbury Hse. Pubs.
Landay, William. Mission Flats. 2003. 384p. 23.95 (*0-385-33614-4*, Delacorte Pr.); E-Book (*0-440-33455-1*) Dell Publishing.
Lawrence, Margaret. Blood Red Roses: A Novel of Historical Suspense. 1998. 416p. mass mkt. 6.50 (*0-380-78880-2*); 1997. 368p. 23.00 (*0-380-97352-9*) Morrow/Avon. (Avon Bks.).
—The Burning Bride. 400p. 1999. mass mkt. 6.99 (*0-380-79612-0*); 1998. 23.00 (*0-380-97620-X*) Morrow/Avon. (Avon Bks.).
—Hearts & Bones. 1997. 352p. mass mkt. 6.50 (*0-380-78879-9*); 1996. 304p. 23.00 (*0-380-97351-0*) Morrow/Avon. (Avon Bks.).
Lea, Sydney. A Place in Mind. 1993. 3.99 o.p. (*0-517-09600-5*) Random Hse. Value Publishing.
—A Place in Mind. 1989. 256p. 17.95 o.s.i (*0-684-19054-0*, Scribner) Simon & Schuster.
—A Place in Mind. 1997. (Fiction Ser.). 240p. reprint ed. pap. 12.95 (*1-885266-39-1*) Story Line Pr.
Lewis, Gerald E. So Long, Scout, & Other Stories. 1988. (Illus.). 161p. (Orig.). pap. 9.95 (*0-945432-00-3*) North Country Pr.
Madison, Susan. The Color of Hope. E-Book 24.95 (*0-312-27408-4*) St. Martin's Pr.
Manfredi, Renee. Above the Thunder. 2004. 24.00 (*1-931561-59-1*) MacAdam/Cage Publishing, Inc.
Mark, Andrew, et al. Falling Bodies: Novel. 1999. 272p. 22.95 o.s.i (*0-399-14447-1*, G. P. Putnam's Sons) Penguin Group (USA) Inc.
Mars, Peter. A Taste for Money: A Novel Based on the True Story of a Dirty Boston Cop. 1999. (Illus.). 320p. pap. 14.95 (*0-9664475-1-4*) Commonwealth Publishing.
Martin, Sally. The Shape of Dark. 2002. 28.95 (*1-4033-5749-8*); pap. 18.95 (*1-4033-5748-X*) 1stBooks Library.
—The Shape of Dark. 2003. 376p. pap. 14.50 (*0-9726510-0-4*) sa martin assocs.
Matteson, Stefanie. Murder on High. l.t. ed. 2000. (Beeler Large Print Mystery Ser.). 25.95 (*1-57490-261-X*, Beeler Large Print Bks.) Beeler, Thomas T. Publisher.
—Murder on High. 1995. 272p. mass mkt. 5.99 o.s.i (*0-425-15050-X*); 1994. 18.95 o.p. (*0-425-14355-4*, Prime Crime) Berkley Publishing Group.
McKinnon, K. C. Candles on Bay Street. 2000. 272p. mass mkt. 6.99 o.s.i (*0-449-00555-0*, Ballantine Bks.) Ballantine Bks.
—Candles on Bay Street. l.t. ed. 1999. pap. 26.95 (*1-56895-721-1*, Wheeler Publishing, Inc.) Gale Group.
Meier, Leslie. Back to School Murder: A Lucy Stone Mystery. (Lucy Stone Mysteries Ser.). 1998. 272p. mass mkt. 5.99 (*1-57566-330-9*); 1997. 256p. 18.95 o.s.i (*1-57566-216-7*) Kensington Publishing Corp.
—Christmas Cookie Murder, Vol. 1. 1999. (Lucy Stone Mysteries Ser.). 256p. (J). pap. 20.00 o.s.i (*1-57566-476-3*) Kensington Publishing Corp.
—Father's Day Murder. 2004. 256p. mass mkt. 6.50 (*1-57566-835-1*, Kensington Bks.) Kensington Publishing Corp.
—Father's Day Murder. l.t. ed. 2003. (Lucy Stone Mystery Ser.). 307p. 28.95 (*0-7862-5617-6*) Thorndike Pr.
—Mail-Order Murder. 1999. pap. 5.95 (*0-14-015832-4*, Viking) Viking Penguin.
—Mail-Order Murder: A Christmas Mystery. 1991. 192p. 18.95 o.p. (*0-670-84111-0*, Viking) Viking Penguin.
—Mail Order Murders. 1993. 256p. mass mkt. 4.99 o.s.i (*0-440-21452-1*) Dell Publishing.
—Mistletoe Murder. 1998. Orig. Title: Mail-Order Murder. 224p. mass mkt. 6.50 (*0-7582-0337-3*); mass mkt. 5.99 o.s.i (*1-57566-370-8*, Kensington Bks.) Kensington Publishing Corp.
—Tippy Toe Murder. (Lucy Stone Mysteries Ser.). 1999. 352p. mass mkt. 5.99 (*1-57566-392-9*); 1996. 256p. mass mkt. 4.99 o.s.i (*1-57566-099-7*) Kensington Publishing Corp.
—Tippy Toe Murder. 1994. 240p. 18.95 o.p. (*0-670-84791-7*, Viking) Viking Penguin.
—Tippy-Toe Murder: A Lucy Stone Mystery. 2003. (Paperback Ser.). lib. bdg. 24.95 (*0-7862-5025-9*) Thorndike Pr.
—Trick or Treat Murder. (Lucy Stone Mysteries Ser.). 256p. 1997. mass mkt. 5.99 (*1-57566-219-1*); 1996. 18.95 o.s.i (*1-57566-093-8*, Kensington Bks.) Kensington Publishing Corp.
—Valentine Murder. (Lucy Stone Mysteries Ser.). 2000. 272p. mass mkt. 5.99 (*1-57566-499-2*); 1999. 248p. 20.00 o.s.i (*1-57566-390-2*) Kensington Publishing Corp.
—Wedding Day Murder. 2002. 256p. mass mkt. 6.50 (*1-57566-734-7*); 2001. 24p. 22.00 o.s.i (*1-57566-652-9*, Kensington Bks.) Kensington Publishing Corp.
—Wedding Day Murder. l.t. ed. 2003. (Lucy Stone Mystery Ser.). 391p. 24.95 (*0-7862-5597-8*) Thorndike Pr.
Michaels, Barbara, pseud. The Crying Child. 1989. mass mkt. 7.50 o.s.i (*0-425-11584-4*) Berkley Publishing Group.
—The Crying Child. l.t. ed. 1981. 350p. 12.00 o.p. (*0-7089-0568-4*, Ulverscroft) Thorpe, F. A. Pubs. GBR. *Dist:* Ulverscroft Large Print Bks., Ltd.
Michaels, Fern. Beyond Tomorrow. l.t. ed. 1985. 9.95 o.p. (*0-8161-3741-2*, Macmillan Reference USA) Gale Group.
—Beyond Tomorrow. 2001. 256p. mass mkt. (*1-55166-858-0*, 1-66858-1, Mira Bks.) Harlequin Enterprises, Ltd.
—Beyond Tomorrow (Best of the Best). 1994. per. (*0-373-48302-3*, 5-48302-9, Silhouette) Harlequin Enterprises, Ltd.
Minot, Susan. Evening. l.t. ed. 1999. (Americana Ser.). 351p. 28.95 o.p. (*0-7862-1891-6*) Thorndike Pr.
Mitcheltree, Tom. Katie's Gold: A Paul Fischer Mystery. 2003. 24.95 (*1-890768-48-0*, Intrigue Pr.) Corvus Publishing.
Moore, Elizabeth J. Cold Times. 1992. 416p. 22.00 o.p. (*0-671-63860-2*) Summit Bks.
Moore, Jim. Official Secrets. 1997. 224p. 24.95 (*0-945980-64-7*); 1996. 214p. pap. 19.95 (*0-945980-58-2*) North Country Pr.
Morison, B. J. Beer & Skittles. 1985. 256p. 15.95 o.s.i (*0-89621-094-4*) North Country Pr.
—Champagne & a Gardener. 1982. 229p. 10.95 o.s.i (*0-89621-069-3*) North Country Pr.
—The Martini Effect. 1992. (Little Maine Murder Ser.). 17.95 (*0-945980-38-8*) North Country Pr.
—Port & a Star Boarder. 1984. 244p. 12.95 (*0-89621-081-2*) North Country Pr.
—The Voyage of the Chianti. 1987. 300p. 15.95 (*0-89621-110-X*); pap. 8.95 (*0-89621-112-6*) North Country Pr.
Murphy, Dallas. Don't Explain. Grose, Bill, ed. 1996. 304p. 22.00 o.p. (*0-671-86687-7*, Atria) Simon & Schuster.
Neely, Barbara. Blanche among the Talented Tenth. 1995. 240p. pap. 5.99 (*0-14-025036-0*, Penguin Bks.) Penguin Group (USA) Inc.
—Blanche among the Talented Tenth. 1994. 240p. 19.95 o.p. (*0-312-11248-3*, Saint Martin's Minotaur) St. Martin's Pr.
Neggers, Carla. The Harbor. 2003. 384p. mass mkt. (*1-55166-651-0*, Mira Bks.) Harlequin Enterprises, Ltd.
—The Harbor. l.t. ed. 2003. 28.95 (*0-7862-5461-0*) Thorndike Pr.
—On Fire. unabr. ed. 1999. audio 7.99 (*1-55204-192-1*, MIR-1192) Durkin Hayes Publishing Ltd.
—On Fire. 384p. 2003. mass mkt. (*1-55166-970-6*); 1999. per. (*1-55166-541-7*, 1-66541-3) Harlequin Enterprises, Ltd. (Mira Bks.).
Ogilvie, Elisabeth. An Answer in the Tide. 1976. 23.95 (*0-8488-1117-8*) Amereon, Ltd.
—An Answer in the Tide. 1991. (Bennett's Island Saga Ser.). 288p. reprint ed. pap. 12.95 (*0-89272-311-4*) Down East Bks.
—An Answer in the Tide. 1979. (General Ser.). lib. bdg. 15.95 o.p. (*0-8161-6751-6*, Macmillan Reference USA) Gale Group.
—An Answer in the Tide. 1978. text 9.95 o.p. (*0-07-047664-0*) McGraw-Hill Cos., The.
—The Day Before Winter. (Bennett's Island Saga Ser.). 304p. 1999. pap. 15.95 (*0-89272-429-3*); 1997. 23.95 (*0-89272-411-0*) Down East Bks.
—The Ebbing Tide. 1985. (Tide Trilogy Ser.: Bk. 3). 280p. reprint ed. pap. 12.95 (*0-89272-218-5*) Down East Bks.
—The Ebbing Tide. l.t. ed. 2000. (Perennial Bestsellers Ser.). 464p. 28.95 (*0-7838-8801-5*) Thorndike Pr.
—The Ebbing Tide. Schaub, Rick, ed. 1996. 69.95 o.s.i (*1-57553-068-6*) Watermark Pr.
—Ebbing Tide. 1976. reprint ed. lib. bdg. 24.95 (*0-88411-185-7*) Amereon, Ltd.
—High Tide at Noon. l.t. ed. 1999. (Perennial Bestsellers Ser.). 599p. 26.95 (*0-7838-8554-7*) Thorndike Pr.
—Jennie about to Be. 1994. (Jennie Glenroy Trilogy Ser.: Bk. 1). 352p. pap. 13.95 (*0-89272-345-9*) Down East Bks.
—Jennie about to Be. 1984. (McGraw-Hill Paperbacks). 360p. text 14.95 o.p. (*0-07-047769-8*) McGraw-Hill Cos., The.
—Jennie Glenroy. 1993. (Jennie Glenroy Trilogy Ser.: Bk. 3). 512p. 24.95 (*0-89272-326-2*) Down East Bks.
—Storm Tide. 1985. (Tide Trilogy Ser.: Bk. 2). 368p. reprint ed. pap. 12.95 (*0-89272-217-7*) Down East Bks.
—Storm Tide. l.t. ed. 2000. (Perennial Bestsellers Ser.). 573p. 27.95 (*0-7838-8800-7*) Thorndike Pr.
—The World of Jennie G. 1994. (Jennie Glenroy Trilogy Ser.: Bk. 2). 368p. reprint ed. pap. 13.95 (*0-89272-346-7*) Down East Bks.
—The World of Jennie G. 368p. 1987. pap. text 5.95 o.p. (*0-07-047789-2*); 1986. text 16.95 o.p. (*0-07-047783-3*) McGraw-Hill Cos., The.
Ogilvie, Elizabeth. Dawning of the Day. 1976. reprint ed. lib. bdg. 24.95 (*0-88411-186-5*) Amereon, Ltd.
—High Tide at Noon. 1976. reprint ed. lib. bdg. 27.95 (*0-88411-183-0*) Amereon, Ltd.
—Storm Tide. 1976. reprint ed. lib. bdg. 25.95 (*0-88411-184-9*) Amereon, Ltd.
Packie, Robert M. Storm Treasure. 1981. (Illus.). 160p. (Orig.). (J). (gr. 6). 8.95 o.p. (*0-89272-082-4*) Down East Bks.
Page, Katherine Hall. The Body in the Basement. l.t. ed. 1999. (Beeler Large Print Mystery Ser.). 25.95 (*1-57490-206-7*, Beeler Large Print Bks.) Beeler, Thomas T. Publisher.
—The Body in the Basement. 1995. (Faith Fairchild Mystery Ser.). 368p. reprint ed. mass mkt. 6.99 (*0-380-72339-5*, Avon Bks.) Morrow/Avon.
—The Body in the Basement. 1994. 272p. 20.95 o.p. (*0-312-11470-2*, Saint Martin's Minotaur) St. Martin's Pr.
—The Body in the Kelp. l.t. ed. 1998. (Beeler Large Print Mystery Ser.). (Illus.). 246p. 25.95 (*1-57490-188-5*, Beeler Large Print Bks.) Beeler, Thomas T. Publisher.
—The Body in the Kelp. 1992. 304p. mass mkt. 6.99 (*0-380-71329-2*, Avon Bks.) Morrow/Avon.
—The Body in the Kelp. 1990. 16.95 o.p. (*0-312-05392-4*, Saint Martin's Minotaur) St. Martin's Pr.
Paisner, Daniel. Mourning Wood: A Novel. 2004. 21.95 (*1-56625-209-1*) Bonus Bks., Inc.
Paretti, Sandra. The Magic Ship. Hein, Ruth, tr. from GER. 1999. Tr. of Zauberschiff. 314p. reprint ed. pap. 16.95 (*0-89272-463-3*) Down East Bks.
—The Magic Ship. Hein, Ruth, tr. 1979. Tr. of Zauberschiff. 10.95 o.p. (*0-312-50419-5*) St. Martin's Pr.
Parker, Robert B. Wilderness. l.t. ed. 1994. 19.95 o.p. (*0-7927-1726-0*); pap. 18.95 o.p. (*0-7927-1725-2*) BBC Audiobooks America.

—Wilderness. 1979. 8.95 o.s.i (*0-440-09328-7*, Delacorte Pr.) Dell Publishing.

Pelletier, Cathie. The Bubble Reputation. 1994. 304p. reprint ed. pap. (*0-671-89010-7*, Washington Square Pr.) Simon & Schuster.

—The Funeral Makers. 1997. 256p. reprint ed. pap. 16.95 (*0-684-82614-3*, Scribner) Simon & Schuster.

—Once upon a Time on the Banks. Rosenman, Jane, ed. 1991. 384p. reprint ed. pap. (*0-671-72447-9*, Washington Square Pr.) Simon & Schuster.

—Once upon a Time on the Banks. 1989. 368p. 19.95 o.p. (*0-670-82776-2*) Viking Penguin.

—The Weight of Winter. 1993. 432p. reprint ed. pap. (*0-671-79387-X*, Washington Square Pr.) Simon & Schuster.

—The Weight of Winter. 1991. 432p. 22.95 o.p. (*0-670-84090-4*, Viking) Viking Penguin.

Phippen, Sanford, et al, eds. The Best Maine Stories. 1994. 320p. (Orig.). pap. 12.95 (*0-89272-351-3*) Down East Bks.

—The Best Maine Stories. 1986. 316p. (Orig.). (C). pap. 10.95 o.p. (*0-912769-07-6*, 80-550-9) Rodale Pr., Inc.

Picoult, Jodi. A Perfect Match. 2002. 368p. 25.00 (*0-7434-1872-7*, Atria) Simon & Schuster.

—Perfect Match: A Novel. 2002. E-Book 9.99 (*0-7434-2280-5*, Atria) Simon & Schuster.

Preston, Douglas J. & Child, Lincoln. Riptide. 1998. 420p. 32.00 o.p. (*0-446-52336-4*); 1999. 496p. reprint ed. mass mkt. 7.50 (*0-446-60717-7*) Warner Bks., Inc.

Rawson, David. Murder on Mount Desert. 304p. 1996. pap. 15.95 (*0-89272-363-7*); 1995. 24.95 o.p. (*0-89272-373-4*) Down East Bks.

Reid, Van. Cordelia Underwood: Or the Marvelous Beginnings of the Moosepath League. l.t. ed. 1999. 26.95 (*1-56895-649-5*, Wheeler Publishing, Inc.) Gale Group.

—Cordelia Underwood: Or the Marvelous Beginnings of the Moosepath League. 1999. 448p. pap. 14.00 (*0-14-028010-3*) Penguin Group (USA) Inc.

—Cordelia Underwood: Or the Marvelous Beginnings of the Moosepath League. 1998. 480p. 24.95 o.p. (*0-670-88097-3*) Viking Penguin.

—Daniel Plainway: Or the Holiday Haunting of the Moosepath League. 2000. 416p. 24.95 o.s.i (*0-670-89171-1*, Viking) Viking Penguin.

—Fiddler's Green. 2004. 320p. 25.95 (*0-670-03320-0*) Viking Penguin.

—Mollie Peer: Or the Underground Adventures of the Moosepath League. 2000. 368p. pap. 14.00 (*0-14-029185-7*) Penguin Group (USA) Inc.

—Mollie Peer: Or the Underground Adventures of the Moosepath League. 1999. 416p. 24.95 o.p. (*0-670-88633-5*, Viking) Viking Penguin.

Rice, Luanne. Cloud Nine. 2000. 400p. mass mkt. 7.50 (*0-553-58099-X*); 1999. 21.95 (*0-553-09729-6*) Bantam Bks.

—Cloud Nine. abr. ed. 2000. audio 7.99 o.s.i (*1-56740-326-3*, 1886, Paperback Nova Audio Bks.) Brilliance Audio.

—Cloud Nine. l.t. ed. 1999. 26.95 o.p. (*1-56895-708-4*, Wheeler Publishing, Inc.) Gale Group.

Rich, Virginia. The Baked Bean Supper Murders. 1983. 12.95 o.p. (*0-525-24185-X*, Dutton) Dutton/Plume.

Rickards, John. Winter's End. mass mkt. (*0-312-98795-1*, St. Martin's Paperbacks); 2003. 304p. 23.95 (*0-312-31097-8*) St. Martin's Pr.

Rittenhouse, Caroline S. Stonington Scraps: A Story of Stonington, Maine in the 1920s. 2002. (Illus.). 88p. 15.00 (*0-9665183-1-4*) Mitten, Peg Pr.

Roberts, Kenneth. Lydia Bailey. 1988. 14.95 o.p. (*0-385-04271-X*) Doubleday Publishing.

—Lydia Bailey. 2000. 488p. pap. 17.95 (*0-89272-514-1*) Down East Bks.

Roberts, Kenneth Lewis. The Lively Lady: A Chronicle of Arundel, of Privateering, & of the Circular Prison on Dartmoor. Date not set. 282p. 23.95 (*0-8488-2591-8*) Amereon, Ltd.

—The Lively Lady: A Chronicle of Arundel, of Privateering, & of the Circular Prison on Dartmoor. 1988. 15.95 o.p. (*0-385-04261-2*) Doubleday Publishing.

—The Lively Lady: A Chronicle of Arundel, of Privateering & of the Circular Prison on Dartmoor. 1982. mass mkt. 2.95 o.s.i (*0-449-24482-2*, Fawcett) Ballantine Bks.

—The Lively Lady: A Chronicle of Arundel, of Privateering, & of the Circular Prison on Dartmoor. 1997. 288p. reprint ed. pap. 15.95 (*0-89272-425-0*) Down East Bks.

—The Lively Lady: A Chronicle of Arundel, of Privateering, & of the Circular Prison on Dartmoor. l.t. ed. 1994. 405p. lib. bdg. 22.95 (*0-8161-5996-3*) Thorndike Pr.

Roberts, Nora. Courting Catherine. l.t. ed. 1992. 231p. 14.95 o.p. (*0-8161-5403-1*, Macmillan Reference USA) Gale Group.

—Homeport. 1999. 496p. reprint ed. mass mkt. 7.99 (*0-515-12489-3*, Jove) Berkley Publishing Group.

—Homeport. abr. ed. 1999. audio 7.99 (*1-56740-283-6*, 1751, Paperback Nova Audio Bks.); 1998. audio 17.95 o.p. (*1-56740-761-7*, 477, Nova Audio Bks.); 1998. audio 25.95 (*1-56100-786-2*, 136, Bookcassette); 1998. audio 89.25 (*1-56740-565-7*, 899, Unabridged Library Editions) Brilliance Audio.

—Homeport. 1998. 448p. 23.95 o.s.i (*0-399-14387-4*, Grosset & Dunlap) Penguin Group (USA) Inc.

—Homeport. l.t. ed. (Paperback Bestsellers Ser.). 717p. 1999. pap. 26.95 (*0-7862-1427-9*); 1998. 29.95 (*0-7862-1426-0*) Thorndike Pr.

Robinson, Lewis. Officer Friendly: And Other Stories. 2003. 240p. 23.95 (*0-06-051368-3*) HarperCollins Pubs.

—Officer Friendly: And Other Stories. 2005. pap. (*0-06-051369-1*, Perennial) HarperTrade.

—Officer Friendly: And Other Stories. 2004. 240p. pap. 12.95 (*0-8129-7227-9*, Random Hse. Trade Paperbacks) Random House Adult Trade Publishing Group.

Rogers, John A. The Elephant on the Tracks & Other Stories. 1992. 66p. pap. 8.00 (*1-882265-01-7*) Maine Writers & Pubs. Alliance.

Rose, M. L. The Road to Eden's Ridge. 2002. 256p. 21.99 (*1-55853-993-X*) Rutledge Hill Pr.

Ross, Clarissa. Out of the Fog. l.t. ed. 2002. 268p. 27.95 (*0-7862-4037-7*) Gale Group.

Russo, Richard. Empire Falls. unabr. ed. 2001. audio 42.95 (*0-694-52559-6*, HarperAudio) HarperTrade.

—Empire Falls. 2002. 496p. pap. 14.95 (*0-375-72640-3*, Vintage) Knopf Publishing Group.

—Empire Falls. 2001. 496p. 25.95 (*0-679-43247-7*) Knopf, Alfred A. Inc.

—Empire Falls. unabr. ed. 2001. audio 122.00 (*0-7887-8928-7*) Recorded Bks., LLC.

—Empire Falls. l.t. ed. 2001. (Thorndike Press Large Print Americana Ser.). 902p. 30.95 (*0-7862-3651-5*) Thorndike Pr.

Sala, Sharon. Dark Water. 2002. 384p. mass mkt. (*1-55166-939-0*, Mira Bks.) Harlequin Enterprises, Ltd.

Sanders, Lawrence. Love Songs. 1989. 400p. mass mkt. 7.50 (*0-425-11273-X*) Berkley Publishing Group.

Sargent, Ruth. The Tunnel Beneath the Sea. Weinberger, Jane, ed. 1993. (Illus.). 120p. (J). (gr. 3-6). pap. 9.95 (*0-932433-11-1*) Windswept Hse. Pubs.

Saum, Karen. I Never Read Thoreau. 1996. 200p. (Orig.). pap. 10.95 (*0-934678-76-6*) New Victoria Pubs., Inc.

—Murder Is Germane. 1991. (Brigid Donovan Mystery Ser.). 288p. (Orig.). pap. 8.95 o.p. (*0-941483-98-3*) Naiad Pr., Inc.

—Murder Is Germane. 1991. (Brigid Donovan Mystery Ser.). 224p. (Orig.). pap. 8.95 (*0-934678-56-1*) New Victoria Pubs., Inc.

—Murder Is Material. 1994. (Brigid Donovan Mystery Ser.). 192p. (Orig.). pap. 9.95 (*0-934678-57-X*) New Victoria Pubs., Inc.

—Murder Is Relative. 1990. 256p. pap. 8.95 o.p. (*0-941483-70-3*) Naiad Pr., Inc.

—Murder Is Relative. 1990. (Brigid Donovan Mystery Ser.). 256p. pap. 8.95 (*0-934678-55-3*) New Victoria Pubs., Inc.

Scarpino, Jane. Nellie, the Light House Dog. Weinberger, Jane, ed. 1993. (Picture Bk.). (Illus.). 40p. (J). (ps up). pap. 9.95 (*0-932433-23-5*) Windswept Hse. Pubs.

Scott, Peter. Something in the Water. 2000. 301p. pap. 16.95 (*0-89272-517-6*) Down East Bks.

Shea, Christina. Moira's Crossing. 2001. (Illus.). 256p. pap. 12.95 (*0-7434-1057-2*, Pocket) Simon & Schuster.

—Moira's Crossing. 2000. 248p. 22.95 (*0-312-20347-0*); E-Book 12.95 (*0-312-27345-2*) St. Martin's Pr.

Shreve, Anita. Strange Fits of Passion. unabr. collector's ed. 1999. audio 48.00 (*0-7366-4497-0*, 4933) Books on Tape, Inc.

—Strange Fits of Passion. l.t. ed. 2000. 350p. lib. bdg. 25.95 (*1-58547-045-7*) Ctr. Point Large Print.

—Strange Fits of Passion. (Harvest Book Ser.). 1999. 352p. pap. 13.00 (*0-15-600710-X*, Harvest Bks.); 1991. 336p. 18.95 (*0-15-185760-1*) Harcourt Trade Pubs.

—Strange Fits of Passion. 1992. 384p. mass mkt. 5.99 o.s.i (*0-451-40300-2*, Onyx) NAL.

Siddons, Anne Rivers. Colony. l.t. ed. 1993. 705p. lib. bdg. 18.95 (*0-8161-5616-6*); 24.95 o.p. (*0-8161-5615-8*) Gale Group. (Macmillan Reference USA).

—Colony. 1992. 400p. 311.88 o.p. (*0-06-017991-0*) HarperCollins Pubs.

—Colony. 2004. audio 9.99 (*0-06-059039-4*, HarperAudio); 1992. 400p. 20.00 o.p. (*0-06-017933-3*); audio 16.00 o.s.i (*1-55994-593-1*, HarperAudio) HarperTrade.

—Colony. 1993. 640p. mass mkt. 7.99 (*0-06-109970-8*, HarperTorch) Morrow/Avon.

—Colony. unabr. ed. 1999. audio 128.00 (*1-55690-867-9*, 93309E7) Recorded Bks., LLC.

Smith, Edmund Ware. To Fish & Hunt in Maine: The Classic Stories of Edmund Ware Smith. 1991. 192p. pap. 12.95 o.p. (*0-89909-336-1*, 80-551-9) Rodale Pr., Inc.

Snyder, Don J. Fallen Angel. 2003. 304p. pap. 12.00 (*0-7434-2232-5*, Washington Square Pr.); 2001. 304p. 20.00 (*0-7434-2231-7*, Atria); 2001. E-Book 20.00 (*0-7434-2369-0*, Atria) Simon & Schuster.

Spencer, LaVyrle. That Camden Summer. 1997. 416p. reprint ed. mass mkt. 7.99 (*0-515-11992-X*, Jove) Berkley Publishing Group.

—That Camden Summer. l.t. ed. 1997. pap. 24.95 o.p. (*0-7838-1606-5*, Macmillan Reference USA) Gale Group.

—That Camden Summer. 1996. 384p. 23.95 o.p. (*0-399-14120-0*, G. P. Putnam's Sons) Penguin Group (USA) Inc.

—That Camden Summer. l.t. ed. pap. (*0-07-838160-6*, G. P. Putnam's Sons) Penguin Putnam Bks. for Young Readers.

—That Camden Summer. l.t. ed. 1996. (Core Ser.). 439p. 28.95 incl. reel tape (*0-7838-1604-9*) Thorndike Pr.

Stephens, C. A. Sailing on Ice: And Other Stories from Old Squire's Farm. Waugh, Charles G. & Glatz, Larry S., eds. 1996. 384p. 18.95 o.s.i (*1-55853-424-5*) Rutledge Hill Pr.

—Stories from the Old Squire's Farm. 2001. 420p. pap. 17.98 (*1-55853-959-X*) Rutledge Hill Pr.

—Stories from the Old Squire's Farm. Waugh, Eric J. & Waugh, Charles, eds. 1995. 288p. 18.95 o.p. (*1-55853-334-6*) Rutledge Hill Pr.

Stephens, Charles A. My Folks in Maine, Vol. 1. 1977. (Short Story Index Reprint Ser.). reprint ed. 22.95 (*0-8369-4161-6*) Ayer Co. Pubs., Inc.

Stockenberg, Antoinette. Embers. 1994. 432p. mass mkt. 4.99 o.s.i (*0-440-21673-7*) Dell Publishing.

—Embers. l.t. ed. 1995. 577p. 22.95 (*0-7838-1136-5*, Macmillan Reference USA) Gale Group.

Stowe, Harriet Beecher. The Pearl of Orr's Island: A Story of the Coast of Maine. 1862. (YA). reprint ed. 402p. pap. text 28.00 (*1-4047-6874-2*); pap. text 28.00 (*1-4047-8960-X*) Classic Textbooks.

—The Pearl of Orr's Island: A Story of the Coast of Maine. 2001. 400p. reprint ed. pap. 13.00 o.s.i (*0-618-08347-2*, Mariner Bks.) Houghton Mifflin Co. Trade & Reference Div.

—The Pearl of Orr's Island: A Story of the Coast of Maine. 1986. (Americans in Fiction Ser.). reprint ed. pap. text 5.95 o.p. (*0-89197-879-8*); lib. bdg. 13.00 o.p. (*0-8398-1876-9*) Irvington Pubs.

—The Pearl of Orr's Island: A Story of the Coast of Maine. (Notable American Authors Ser.). reprint ed. 1999. lib. bdg. 125.00 (*0-7812-8960-2*); 1992. 437p. lib. bdg. 99.00 (*0-7812-6874-5*) Reprint Services Corp.

—The Pearl of Orr's Island: A Story of the Coast of Maine. reprint ed. 14.00 (*0-403-00280-X*) Scholarly Pr., Inc.

—The Pearl of Orr's Island: A Story of the Coast of Maine. 1979. (Illus.). pap. 9.95 (*0-917482-18-2*) Stowe-Day Foundation.

Thayer, Cynthia. Certain Slant of Light. 2000. 259p. 23.95 (*0-312-26132-2*) St. Martin's Pr.

—A Certain Slant of Light. E-Book 23.95 (*0-312-27591-9*); 2001. 288p. pap. 12.95 (*0-312-27564-1*, Saint Martin's Griffin) St. Martin's Pr.

—Strong for Potatoes. 1997. 248p. 22.95 o.p. (*0-312-18187-6*); 1999. 256p. reprint ed. pap. 12.95 (*0-312-20027-7*, NPB 0336, Saint Martin's Griffin) St. Martin's Pr.

Tracy, Ann. What Do Cowboys Like? 1995. 160p. 22.00 o.p. (*1-877946-52-4*) Permanent Pr., The.

Van Arsdale, Sarah. Blue: A Novel. 2003. 29.95 (*1-57233-238-7*) Univ. of Tennessee Pr.

Van de Wetering, Janwillem. The Maine Massacre, 001. 1978. 8.95 o.p. (*0-395-27395-1*) Houghton Mifflin Co.

—The Maine Massacre. 1996. 231p. pap. 12.00 (*1-56947-064-2*) Soho Pr., Inc.

Wait, Lea. Shadows on the Coast of Maine: An Antique Print Mystery. unabr. ed. 2003. audio 49.95 (*0-7861-2513-6*); audio compact disk 14.95 (*0-7861-9144-9*); audio compact disk 24.95 (*0-7861-8909-6*) Blackstone Audio Bks., Inc.

—Shadows on the Coast of Maine: An Antique Print Mystery. 2004. 272p. mass mkt. 6.99 (*0-7434-5621-1*, Pocket); 2003. 288p. 24.00 (*0-7432-2554-6*, Scribner) Simon & Schuster.

Waters, John F. Summer of the Seals. 1978. (Illus.). (J). (gr. 3-6). 6.95 o.p. (*0-7232-6155-5*, Warne, Frederick) Penguin Putnam Bks. for Young Readers.

Watkins, Paul. Archangel. 1996. 336p. pap. 13.00 (*0-312-15055-5*) Picador.

Waugh, Charles G. Murder & Mystery in Maine. 1990. 3.99 o.p. (*0-517-06158-9*) Random Hse. Value Publishing.

Waugh, Charles G., et al, eds. Murder & Mystery in Maine. 1989. 16.95 o.p. (*0-942637-10-0*, Dembner Bks.) Barricade Bks., Inc.

—Strange Maine. 1986. (Illus.). 295p. (Orig.). pap. 10.95 o.p. (*0-912769-10-6*) Yankee Bks.

Weesner, Theodore. Harbor Lights: A Novel. 2000. 240p. 23.00 o.p. (*0-87113-766-6*, Atlantic Monthly Pr.) Grove/Atlantic, Inc.

Weinberger, Jane. Stormy. 1985. (Illus.). 54p. (J). (gr. 1-6). pap. 5.95 o.p. (*0-932433-13-8*) Windswept Hse. Pubs.

White, Michael C. A Brother's Blood: A Novel. 1996. 336p. 22.50 o.p. (*0-06-018667-4*) HarperCollins Pubs.

—A Brother's Blood: A Novel. 1997. 336p. pap. 13.00 (*0-06-092859-X*, Perennial) HarperTrade.

Whittlesey, Marjorie. Growing up Summer. 1990. 176p. 3.00 (*0-934745-14-5*) Acadia Publishing Co.

Wick, Lori. Wings of the Morning. (Kensington Chronicles Ser.). 1994. 273p. pap. 9.99 (*1-56507-177-8*); 2nd ed. 2004. reprint ed. pap. 10.99 (*0-7369-1321-1*) Harvest Hse. Pubs.

—Wings of the Morning. l.t. ed. 2001. (Christian Fiction Ser.). 402p. 27.95 (*0-7862-2958-6*) Thorndike Pr.

Wiggin, Eric. The Hills of God. 1993. pap. 8.99 o.p. (*1-56507-136-0*) Harvest Hse. Pubs.

Wiggin, Eric E. The Hills of God. l.t. ed. 1998. (Christian Fiction Ser.). 383p. 24.95 (*0-7862-1540-2*) Thorndike Pr.

Wilson, Robley. The Victim's Daughter: A Novel. 1991. 224p. 19.00 o.p. (*0-671-72618-8*, Simon & Schuster) Simon & Schuster.

Wilson, Susan. Hawke's Cove. 2000. 282p. 23.95 (*0-671-03573-8*, Atria) Simon & Schuster.

Winnefeld, James A. To Maine with a Vengence. 2002. pap. 9.95 (*0-87714-270-X*) Denlingers Pubs., Ltd.

Winston, Anne Marie. Billionaire Bachelors: Garrett. 2002. (Silhouette Desire Ser.: No. 1440). 192p. mass mkt. o.s.i (*0-373-76440-5*, Silhouette) Harlequin Enterprises, Ltd.

Wuori, G. K. An American Outrage: A Novel of Quillifarkeag, Maine. 2000. 288p. tchr. ed. 22.95 (*1-56512-292-5*) Algonquin Bks. of Chapel Hill.

—Nude in Tub: Stories of Quillifarkeag, Maine. 1999. xiii, 273p. tchr. ed. 18.95 (*1-56512-223-2*, 72223) Algonquin Bks. of Chapel Hill.

## MAJIPOOR (IMAGINARY PLACE)—FICTION

Silverberg, Robert. The King of Dreams. 2001. E-Book 19.95 (*0-06-008729-3*); E-Book 19.95 (*0-06-008728-5*); E-Book 19.95 (*0-06-008727-7*); E-Book 19.95 (*0-06-050294-0*) HarperCollins General Bks. Group. (PerfectBound).

—The King of Dreams, Bk. 3. 2001. (Prestimion Trilogy Ser.: Vol. 3). 464p. 25.00 (*0-06-105171-3*, Eos) Morrow/Avon.

—The King of Dreams Vol. 3 of the Prestimion Trilogy: A Majipoor Novel. 2002. 496p. mass mkt. 7.50 (*0-06-102052-4*, Eos) Morrow/Avon.

—Lord Prestimion: The Majipoor Cycle Continues. 1999. (Illus.). 432p. 25.00 (*0-06-105028-8*) HarperCollins Pubs.

—Lord Prestimion: The Majipoor Cycle Continues. 2000. (Prestimion Trilogy Ser.: Vol. 2). 512p. mass mkt. 6.99 (*0-06-105810-6*, Eos) Morrow/Avon.

—Lord Valentine's Castle. 1984. 480p. mass mkt. 3.95 o.s.i (*0-553-25097-3*) Bantam Bks.

—Lord Valentine's Castle. 1980. o.p. (*0-06-014026-7*) HarperCollins Pubs.

—Lord Valentine's Castle. 1995. (Majipoor Ser.: Vol. 1). 528p. mass mkt. 7.99 (*0-06-105487-9*, Eos) Morrow/Avon.

—Majipoor Chronicles. 1983. 304p. mass mkt. 4.50 o.s.i (*0-553-25530-4*) Bantam Bks.

—Majipoor Chronicles. 2001. E-Book 6.99 (*0-06-050269-X*); E-Book 6.99 (*0-06-050268-1*); E-Book 6.99 (*0-06-050266-5*); E-Book 6.99 (*0-06-050267-3*) HarperCollins General Bks. Group. (PerfectBound).

—Majipoor Chronicles. 1996. (Majipoor Ser.: Vol. 3). 400p. mass mkt. 6.99 (*0-06-105485-2*, Eos); 1982. 304p. 12.95 o.p. (*0-87795-358-9*, Morrow, William & Co.); 1982. 304p. pap. 5.95 o.p. (*0-87795-359-7*, Morrow, William & Co.) Morrow/Avon.

—The Mountains of Majipoor. E-Book 5.99 (*1-930936-00-1*) Fictionwise, Inc.

—The Mountains of Majipoor. l.t. ed. 1996. (Large Print Ser.). 304p. 29.99 o.p. (*0-7089-3580-X*, Ulverscroft) Thorpe, F. A. Pubs. GBR. *Dist:* Ulverscroft Large Print Bks., Ltd., Ulverscroft Large Print Canada, Ltd.

—Sorcerers of Majipoor. 2001. E-Book 6.99 (*0-06-050265-7*); E-Book 6.99 (*0-06-050264-9*); E-Book 6.99 (*0-06-050262-2*); E-Book 6.99 (*0-06-050263-0*) HarperCollins General Bks. Group. (PerfectBound).

—Sorcerers of Majipoor. 1997. 480p. mass mkt. 23.00 o.p. (*0-06-105254-X*) HarperCollins Pubs.

—Sorcerers of Majipoor. 1998. (Majipoor Ser.: Vol. 4). (Illus.). 624p. mass mkt. 6.99 (*0-06-105780-0*, Eos) Morrow/Avon.

—Valentine Pontifex. 1984. (Majipoor Trilogy Ser.: No. 3). 384p. mass mkt. 4.50 o.s.i (*0-553-24494-9*, Spectra) Bantam Bks.

—Valentine Pontifex. 2001. E-Book 6.99 (0-06-050261-4); E-Book 6.99 (0-06-050260-6); E-Book 6.99 (0-06-050258-4); E-Book 6.99 (0-06-050259-2) HarperCollins General Bks. Group. (PerfectBound).

—Valentine Pontifex. 1996. (Majipoor Ser.: Vol. 2). 496p. mass mkt. 6.99 (0-06-105486-0, Eos); 1983. 15.95 o.p. (0-87795-544-1, Morrow, William & Co.); 1983. 35.00 o.p. (0-87795-561-1, Morrow, William & Co.) Morrow/Avon.

**MALAYSIA—FICTION**

Carey, Peter. My Life As a Fake. 2003. (Illus.). 288p. 24.00 (0-375-41498-3) Knopf, Alfred A. Inc.

Conrad, Joseph & Kalnins, Mara. Victory. Kalnins, Mara, ed. 2nd ed. 2004. (Oxford World's Classics Ser.). (Illus.). 416p. (Orig.). pap. 9.95 (0-19-280175-9) Oxford Univ. Pr., Inc.

Eggers, Paul. How the Water Feels: Stories. 2002. 192p. 19.95 (0-87074-473-9) Southern Methodist Univ. Pr.

Geok-Lin Lim, Shirley. Joss & Gold. 2001. 240p. 24.95 (1-55861-265-3) Feminist Pr. at The City Univ. of New York.

Godshalk, C. S. Kalimantaan. 1999. 480p. pap. o.s.i (0-385-25769-4) Doubleday Canada, Ltd. CAN. *Dist:* Random Hse. of Canada, Ltd., Random Hse., Inc.

—Kalimantaan. 1998. 472p. 25.00 o.s.i (0-8050-5533-9) Holt, Henry & Co.

Lim, Shirley G. Two Dreams: New & Selected Stories. 1997. 240p. 24.00 (1-55861-164-9); pap. 10.95 o.p. (1-55861-168-1) Feminist Pr. at The City Univ. of New York.

Lim, Shirley Geok-Lin. Joss & Gold. 2002. pap. 15.95 (1-55861-401-X) Feminist Pr. at The City Univ. of New York.

Manicka, Rani. The Rice Mother. 2003. 448p. 24.95 (0-670-03192-5, Viking) Viking Penguin.

**MALLOREA (IMAGINARY PLACE)—FICTION**

Eddings, David. Demon Lord of Karanda. (Mallorean Ser.: Bk. 3). 1997. pap. 12.95 o.s.i (0-345-41918-9); 1989. 416p. mass mkt. 7.50 (0-345-36331-0) Ballantine Bks. (Del Rey).

—Demon Lord of Karanda. 1991. 3.99 o.p. (0-517-06775-7) Random Hse. Value Publishing.

—Demon Lord of Karanda. 1989. (Malloreon: Bk. 3). 13.04 (0-606-01247-8) Turtleback Bks.

—Guardians of the West. (Mallorean Ser.: Bk. 1). 1997. pap. 12.95 o.s.i (0-345-41919-7); 1988. 448p. mass mkt. 7.50 (0-345-35266-1); 1987. 16.95 o.s.i (0-345-33000-5) Ballantine Bks. (Del Rey).

—Guardians of the West. 1988. (Malloreon: Bk. 1). 13.04 (0-606-01245-1) Turtleback Bks.

—King of the Murgos. (Mallorean Ser.: Bk. 2). 1997. pap. 12.95 o.s.i (0-345-41920-0); 1989. 416p. mass mkt. 7.50 (0-345-35880-5) Ballantine Bks. (Del Rey).

—King of the Murgos. 1989. (Malloreon: Bk. 2). 13.04 (0-606-01246-X) Turtleback Bks.

—The Seeress of Kell. (Mallorean Ser.: Bk. 5). 1997. pap. 12.95 o.s.i (0-345-41922-7); 1992. 384p. mass mkt. 6.99 (0-345-37759-1) Ballantine Bks. (Del Rey).

—Sorceress of Darshiva. (Mallorean Ser.: Bk. 4). 1997. 227p. pap. 12.95 o.s.i (0-345-41921-9); 1990. 384p. mass mkt. 7.50 (0-345-36935-1) Ballantine Bks. (Del Rey).

—Sorceress of Darshiva. 1991. 3.99 o.p. (0-517-06791-9) Random Hse. Value Publishing.

**MALTA—FICTION**

Ball, David. Ironfire. 2003. (Illus.). 688p. 24.95 (0-385-33601-2) Dell Publishing.

Hamilton, Lyn. The Maltese Goddess: An Archaeological Mystery. 1998. (Archaeological Mystery Ser.). 256p. mass mkt. 6.50 (0-425-16240-0, Prime Crime) Berkley Publishing Group.

Harvey, Caroline, pseud. The Brass Dolphin. (Illus.). 1998. 413p. mass mkt. 8.99 (0-552-14553-X); 1997. 352p. 32.95 o.s.i (0-385-40890-0) Bantam Bks.

—The Brass Dolphin. l.t. ed. 1998. (Charnwood Large Print Ser.). 448p. 29.99 o.p. (0-7089-8987-X, Ulverscroft) Thorpe, F. A. Pubs. GBR. *Dist:* Ulverscroft Large Print Bks., Ltd., Ulverscroft Large Print Canada, Ltd.

—The Brass Dolphin. 1999. 336p. 24.95 o.s.i (0-670-88518-5, Viking) Viking Penguin.

MacLeod, Robert. A Killing in Malta. l.t. ed. 1979. (Ulverscroft Large Print Ser.). 29.99 o.p. (0-7089-0320-7, Ulverscroft) Thorpe, F. A. Pubs. GBR. *Dist:* Ulverscroft Large Print Bks., Ltd., Ulverscroft Large Print Canada, Ltd.

Monsarrat, Nicholas. The Kappillan of Malta. 2001. (Cassell Military Paperbacks Ser.). (Illus.). 464p. pap. 9.95 (0-304-35844-4) Sterling Publishing Co., Inc.

—The Kappillan of Malta. l.t. ed. 1976. (Ulverscroft Large Print Ser.). 29.99 o.p. (0-85456-564-7, Ulverscroft) Thorpe, F. A. Pubs. GBR. *Dist:* Ulverscroft Large Print Bks., Ltd., Ulverscroft Large Print Canada, Ltd.

Prata, Nicholas C. Angels in Iron. 1997. x, 305p. 29.00 (1-889758-04-3) Arx Publishing.

Rinaldi, Nicholas M. The Jukebox Queen of Malta. 368p. 2000. pap. 13.00 (0-684-86742-7); 1999. (Illus.). 25.00 (0-684-85612-3) Simon & Schuster. (Simon & Schuster).

Styles, Showell. The Malta Frigate. 1986. 192p. 15.95 o.p. (0-8027-0891-9) Walker & Co.

Terpening, Ron. Storm Track. 1989. 360p. 22.95 (0-8027-1069-7) Walker & Co.

**MANITOBA—FICTION**

Birdsell, Sandra. Agassiz: A Novel in Stories. 1991. (Illus.). 352p. 18.95 (0-915943-61-1) Milkweed Editions.

—Agassiz: A Novel in Stories. 1997. pap. 14.95 (0-88801-123-7) Turnstone Pr. CAN. *Dist:* General Distribution Services, Inc.

Coggins, James Robert. Who's Grace? A John Smyth Mystery. 2004. 10.99 (0-8024-1764-7) Moody Pr.

Mindus, Selena. Oh Susannah. l.t. ed. 2000. (Candlelight Romance Ser.). 208p. 19.95 (0-7862-2800-8) Thorndike Pr.

Norman, Howard. The Haunting of L. 2002. E-Book 9.00 (0-374-70353-1); E-Book 9.00 (0-374-70355-8); E-Book 9.00 o.p. (0-374-70356-6); E-Book (0-374-70358-2); 336p. 24.00 (0-374-16825-3); E-Book 9.00 (0-374-70357-4) Farrar, Straus & Giroux.

—The Haunting of L. 2003. 336p. pap. (0-676-97500-3, Vintage) Random Hse. of Canada, Ltd. CAN. *Dist:* Random Hse., Inc.

Patterson, Kevin. Country of Cold: Stories. 2004. 272p. pap. 13.00 (0-385-72217-6, Anchor) Knopf Publishing Group.

Rougeau, Remy. All We Know of Heaven. 2001. 240p. tchr. ed. 23.00 (0-618-09499-7) Houghton Mifflin Co.

—All We Know of Heaven: A Novel. 2002. 240p. pap. 13.00 (0-618-21922-6, Mariner Bks.) Houghton Mifflin Co. Trade & Reference Div.

Roy, Gabrielle. The Road Past Altamont. 1996. (New Canadian Library). 160p. mass mkt. 6.95 (0-7710-9856-1) McClelland & Stewart/Tundra Bks.

—The Road Past Altamont. Marshall, Joyce, tr. 1993. 147p. pap. 7.95 (0-8032-8948-0, Bison Bks.) Univ. of Nebraska Pr.

Valgardson, W. D. Sarah & the People of Sand River. 1996. (Illus.). 44p. (J). (ps-3). 16.95 (0-88899-255-6) Groundwood Bks. CAN. *Dist:* Publishers Group West.

**MARIN COUNTY (CALIF.)—FICTION**

Dick, Philip K. Dr. Bloodmoney. 1984. 304p. pap. 7.95 o.p. (0-312-94105-6) Bluejay Bks.

—Dr. Bloodmoney. 1980. pap. 2.25 o.p. (0-440-11489-6) Dell Publishing.

—Dr. Bloodmoney. 1977. reprint ed. lib. bdg. 11.50 o.p. (0-8398-2365-7, Macmillan Reference USA) Gale Group.

—Dr. Bloodmoney. 2002. 304p. pap. 13.00 (0-375-71929-6, Vintage) Knopf Publishing Group.

Girdner, Jaqueline. A Cry for Self-Help. (Kate Jasper Mysteries Ser.). 288p. 1998. mass mkt. 5.99 o.s.i (0-425-16265-6); 1997. 21.95 o.s.i (0-425-15630-3, Prime Crime) Berkley Publishing Group.

—Death Hits the Fan. 1999. (Kate Jasper Mystery Ser.). 288p. reprint ed. mass mkt. 5.99 o.s.i (0-425-16808-5, Prime Crime) Berkley Publishing Group.

—Death Hits the Fan: A Kate Jasper Mystery. 1998. (Kate Jasper Mysteries Ser.). 288p. 21.95 o.s.i (0-425-16148-X) Berkley Publishing Group.

—Fat-Free & Fatal. 1993. (Orig.). 3.99 o.s.i (1-55773-917-X) Ace Bks.

—Fat-Free & Fatal. 1993. 224p. (Orig.). mass mkt. 5.99 o.s.i (0-425-15811-X, Prime Crime) Berkley Publishing Group.

—Murder, My Deer: A Kate Jasper Mystery. 2000. (Kate Jasper Mysteries Ser.). (Illus.). 275p. 21.95 o.s.i (0-425-17328-3) Berkley Publishing Group.

Griffin, Annie. Date with the Perfect Dead Man. 1999. (Hannah & Kiki Mysteries Ser.: Vol. 2). 288p. mass mkt. 5.99 o.s.i (0-425-16985-5) Berkley Publishing Group.

—Love & the Single Corpse. 2000. (Hannah & Kiki Mysteries Ser.). 288p. mass mkt. 5.99 o.s.i (0-425-17612-6, Prime Crime) Berkley Publishing Group.

—A Very Eligible Corpse. 1998. (Hannah & Kiki Mysteries Ser.). 272p. mass mkt. 5.99 o.s.i (0-425-16535-3) Berkley Publishing Group.

Nelson-Weyh, Christie. Woodacre: A Novel. 1998. 258p. (0-9654951-2-4) Thumbprint Pr.

Roberts, Gillian. Time & Trouble. 1999. 336p. mass mkt. 5.99 (0-312-96996-1, St. Martin's Paperbacks); 1998. 384p. 24.95 (0-312-18673-8, Saint Martin's Minotaur) St. Martin's Pr.

—Whatever Doesn't Kill You: An Emma Howe & Billie August Mystery. 2001. 312p. 23.95 (0-312-26269-8, Saint Martin's Minotaur) St. Martin's Pr.

**MARTHA'S VINEYARD (MASS.)—FICTION**

Bates, Karen Grigsby. Plain Brown Wrapper: An Alex Powell Novel. 2001. 336p. pap. 13.00 (0-380-80890-0, Avon Bks.) Morrow/Avon.

Begley, Louis. Shipwreck. 2003. 256p. 23.00 (1-4000-4098-1) Knopf, Alfred A. Inc.

Blume, Judy. Summer Sisters: A Novel. l.t. ed. 1998. 441p. (0-7540-1203-4) BBC Audiobooks America.

—Summer Sisters: A Novel. unabr. ed. 1998. audio 48.00 (0-7366-4211-0, 4709) Books on Tape, Inc.

—Summer Sisters: A Novel. 416p. 1999. mass mkt. 7.99 (0-440-22643-0); 1998. 21.95 o.s.i (0-385-32405-7, Delacorte Pr.) Dell Publishing.

—Summer Sisters: A Novel. abr. ed. 1998. audio 18.00 (0-671-58245-3, 396066, Simon & Schuster Audioworks) Simon & Schuster Audio.

—Summer Sisters: A Novel. l.t. ed. 1998. (Basic Ser.). 443p. 30.95 (0-7862-1536-4) Thorndike Pr.

—Summer Sisters: A Novel. 1999. 13.55 (0-606-16457-X) Turtleback Bks.

Craig, Philip R. A Beautiful Place to Die: A Martha's Vineyard Mystery. 1989. 224p. 18.95 o.s.i (0-684-19122-9, Macmillan Reference USA) Gale Group.

—A Beautiful Place to Die: A Martha's Vineyard Mystery. 1991. 224p. mass mkt. 6.99 (0-380-71155-9, Avon Bks.) Morrow/Avon.

—A Case of Vineyard Poison. 1996. 224p. mass mkt. 5.99 (0-380-72679-3, Avon Bks.) Morrow/Avon.

—A Case of Vineyard Poison: A Martha's Vineyard Mystery. 1995. 253p. 20.00 o.p. (0-684-19616-6, Scribner) Simon & Schuster.

—Cliff Hanger: A Martha's Vineyard Mystery. 1993. 256p. 20.00 o.p. (0-684-19552-6, Macmillan Reference USA) Gale Group.

—Cliff Hanger: A Martha's Vineyard Mystery. 1994. 224p. mass mkt. 4.99 (0-380-72240-2, Avon Bks.) Morrow/Avon.

—A Deadly Vineyard Holiday. 1998. (Martha's Vineyard Mysteries Ser.). 240p. mass mkt. 6.50 (0-380-73110-X, Avon Bks.) Morrow/Avon.

—A Deadly Vineyard Holiday: A Martha's Vineyard Mystery. 1997. 282p. 20.50 (0-684-19718-9, Scribner) Simon & Schuster.

—A Deadly Vineyard Holiday: A Martha's Vineyard Mystery. l.t. ed. 1997. (Core Ser.). 344p. lib. bdg. 26.95 (0-7838-8278-5) Thorndike Pr.

—Death on a Vineyard Beach. 1997. 224p. mass mkt. 6.50 (0-380-72873-7, Avon Bks.) Morrow/Avon.

—Death on a Vineyard Beach: A Martha's Vineyard Mystery. 1996. 288p. 21.00 o.p. (0-684-19717-0, Scribner) Simon & Schuster.

—The Double Minded Men: A Martha's Vineyard Mystery. 1992. (Martha's Vineyard Mystery Ser.: No. 3). 256p. text 20.00 (0-684-19396-5, Macmillan Reference USA) Gale Group.

—The Double Minded Men: A Martha's Vineyard Mystery. 1993. 256p. pap. 4.99 (0-380-71973-8, Avon Bks.) Morrow/Avon.

—A Fatal Vineyard Season. 2000. (Martha's Vineyard Mysteries Ser.). 224p. mass mkt. 5.99 (0-380-73289-0, Avon Bks.) Morrow/Avon.

—A Fatal Vineyard Season: A Martha's Vineyard Mystery. 1999. (Martha's Vineyard Mysteries Ser.). (Illus.). 224p. 22.00 o.s.i (0-684-85544-5, Scribner) Simon & Schuster.

—A Fatal Vineyard Season: A Martha's Vineyard Mystery. l.t. ed. 1999. (Mystery Ser.). (Illus.). 324p. 28.95 (0-7862-2207-7) Thorndike Pr.

—Martha's Vineyard Mystery, No. 8. 2005. 256p. 24.00 (0-7432-4677-2, Scribner) Simon & Schuster.

—Murder at a Vineyard Mansion: A Martha's Vineyard Mystery, No. 7. 2004. 256p. 24.00 (0-7432-4676-4, Scribner) Simon & Schuster.

—Off Season. 1996. (Martha's Vineyard Ser.: No. 5). 224p. mass mkt. 5.99 (0-380-72588-6, Avon Bks.) Morrow/Avon.

—Off Season: A Martha's Vineyard Mystery. 1994. 256p. 20.00 (0-684-19617-4, Macmillan Reference USA) Gale Group.

—A Shoot on Martha's Vineyard. 1999. (Martha's Vineyard Mysteries Ser.). 256p. mass mkt. 5.99 (0-380-73201-7, Avon Bks.) Morrow/Avon.

—Shoot on Martha's Vineyard: A Martha's Vineyard Mystery. 1998. (Martha's Vineyard Mysteries Ser.). 288p. 22.00 (0-684-83454-5, Scribner) Simon & Schuster.

—A Shoot on Martha's Vineyard: A Martha's Vineyard Mystery. l.t. ed. 1999. (Mystery Ser.). 427p. 27.95 (0-7862-1614-X) Thorndike Pr.

—Vineyard Blues: A Martha's Vineyard Mystery. 2001. 224p. mass mkt. 5.99 (0-380-81859-0, Avon Bks.) Morrow/Avon.

—Vineyard Blues: A Martha's Vineyard Mystery. 2000. (Martha's Vineyard Mysteries Ser.). (Illus.). 224p. 23.00 o.s.i (0-684-83455-3, Scribner) Simon & Schuster.

—Vineyard Blues: A Martha's Vineyard Mystery. l.t. ed. 2000. (Mystery Ser.). (Illus.). 339p. 29.95 (0-7862-2591-2) Thorndike Pr.

—Vineyard Enigma. l.t. ed. 2002. (Mystery Ser.). 305p. 30.45 (0-7862-4788-6) Gale Group.

—Vineyard Enigma. 2003. 256p. mass mkt. 6.99 (0-06-051188-5) Morrow/Avon.

—Vineyard Enigma: A Martha Vineyard Mystery. 2002. (Illus.). 256p. 24.00 (0-7432-0523-5, Scribner) Simon & Schuster.

—A Vineyard Killing. l.t. ed. 2003. (Martha's Vineyard Mystery Ser.). 292p. 30.45 (0-7862-5594-3) Thorndike Pr.

—A Vineyard Killing: A Martha's Vineyard Mystery. 2003. (Illus.). 240p. 24.00 (0-7432-0524-3, Scribner) Simon & Schuster.

—Vineyard Shadows. 2001. (Martha's Vineyard Mysteries Ser.). 256p. 24.00 o.s.i (0-684-85545-3, Scribner) Simon & Schuster.

—Vineyard Shadows: A Martha's Vineyard Mystery. 2002. 256p. mass mkt. 6.50 (0-380-82099-4) Morrow/Avon.

—Vineyard Shadows: A Martha's Vineyard Mystery. l.t. ed. 2001. 334p. 29.95 (0-7862-3646-9) Thorndike Pr.

—The Woman Who Walked into the Sea: A Martha's Vineyard Mystery. 1993. 224p. reprint ed. mass mkt. 4.99 (0-380-71536-8, Avon Bks.) Morrow/Avon.

—The Woman Who Walked into the Sea: A Martha's Vineyard Mystery. 1991. 224p. 17.95 o.s.i (0-684-19228-4, Scribner) Simon & Schuster.

Craig, Philip R. & Tapply, William G. First Light. l.t. ed. 2002. 443p. 29.95 (0-7862-4185-3) Gale Group.

—First Light: The First Ever Brady Coyne/J. W. Jackson Novel. 2002. 352p. E-Book 24.00 (0-7432-3484-7); 24.00 (0-7432-2208-3) Simon & Schuster. (Scribner).

Daniel, David. The Tuesday Man. 1991. 320p. 19.95 o.p. (0-525-93318-2) Dutton/Plume.

—The Tuesday Man. 1992. 320p. mass mkt. 4.99 o.p. (0-451-17310-4, Signet Bks.) NAL.

Gordon, Neil. The Gun Runner's Daughter. 2000. 416p. reprint ed. mass mkt. 6.99 o.s.i (0-553-58211-9) Bantam Bks.

Hoffman, Alice. Illumination Night. 1988. 256p. mass mkt. 6.99 o.s.i (0-449-21594-6, Fawcett) Ballantine Bks.

—Illumination Night. 2002. 272p. reprint ed. pap. 13.00 (0-425-18326-2) Berkley Publishing Group.

Hutton, Carol. Eternal Journey. 2000. 149p. E-Book 14.95 (0-7595-8018-9); 149p. E-Book 14.95 (0-7595-9018-4); 149p. E-Book 14.95 (0-7595-0018-5); (Illus.). 160p. 19.95 o.p. (0-446-52657-6) Warner Bks., Inc.

—The Eternal Journey. 2001. 160p. reprint ed. pap. 12.95 (0-446-67731-0) Warner Bks., Inc.

—Eternal Journey: A Novel. l.t. ed. 2001. 102p. 24.95 (1-57490-354-3, Beeler Large Print Bks.) Beeler, Thomas T. Publisher.

Riggs, Cynthia. The Cemetery Yew. 2003. 208p. 22.95 (0-312-32126-0) St. Martin's Pr.

—The Cemetery Yew. l.t. ed. 2003. (Martha's Vineyard Mystery Ser.). 377p. 28.95 (0-7862-5929-9) Thorndike Pr.

—The Cranefly Orchid Murders. 2004. 272p. mass mkt. 5.99 (0-451-20961-3, Signet Bks.) NAL.

—The Cranefly Orchid Murders. E-Book 23.95 (0-312-70620-0); 2002. 272p. 23.95 (0-312-30145-6, Saint Martin's Minotaur) St. Martin's Pr.

—The Cranefly Orchid Murders. l.t. ed. 2002. (Senior Lifestyles Ser.). 398p. 28.95 (0-7862-4544-1) Thorndike Pr.

—Deadly Nightshade. 2003. 272p. mass mkt. 5.99 (0-451-20816-1, Signet Bks.) NAL.

—Deadly Nightshade. 2001. ix, 276p. 23.95 (0-312-27252-9, Saint Martin's Minotaur) St. Martin's Pr.

—Deadly Nightshade. l.t. ed. 2001. (Thorndike Press Large Print Senior Lifestyles Ser.). 437p. 28.95 (0-7862-3754-6) Thorndike Pr.

Siddons, Anne Rivers. Up Island. unabr. ed. 1997. audio 80.00 (0-7366-3709-5, 4393) Books on Tape, Inc.

—Up Island. l.t. ed. 1997. (Wheeler Large Print Book Ser.). 27.95 (1-56895-485-9, Wheeler Publishing, Inc.) Gale Group.

—Up Island. 1997. 352p. 24.00 o.s.i (0-06-017615-6) HarperCollins Pubs.

—Up Island. abr. ed. 1997. audio 25.00 (0-694-51843-3, 695952, HarperAudio) HarperTrade.

—Up Island. 1998. 512p. mass mkt. 7.99 (0-06-109921-X, HarperTorch) Morrow/Avon.

—Up Island. unabr. ed. 1997. audio 91.00 (0-7887-1295-0, 95129E7) Recorded Bks., LLC.

Stone, Jean. Beach Roses. 2003. 336p. mass mkt. 6.50 (0-553-58412-X) Bantam Bks.

—The Off Season. 2001. 368p. mass mkt. 5.99 (0-553-58086-8) Bantam Bks.

Sullivan, Mary. Stay. 2000. 183p. pap. 13.00 o.p. (1-58195-025-X, Zoland Bks., Inc.) Steerforth Pr.

**MARTINIQUE—FICTION**

Confiant, Raphael. Mamzelle Dragonfly. Coverdale, Linda, tr. from CRP. 2000. 160p. 22.00 (0-374-19932-9) Farrar, Straus & Giroux.

—Mamzelle Dragonfly. Coverdale, Linda, tr. from CRP. 2001. 169p. pap. 12.95 (0-8032-6418-6) Univ. of Nebraska Pr.

Ford, Bette. Island Magic. 2000. (Arabesque Ser.). 320p. mass mkt. 5.99 (1-58314-113-8) BET Bks.

Glissant, Edouard. The Fourth Century. Wing, Betsy, tr. from FRE. 2001. 295p. pap. 20.00 (*0-8032-7083-6*, Bison Bks.) Univ. of Nebraska Pr.

Zobel, Joseph. Black Shack Alley. Warner, Keith Q., tr. from FRE. Orig. Title: La Rue Cases-Negres. (Illus.). 184p. reprint ed. 1991. 25.00 o.s.i (*0-914478-67-2*); 1980. pap. 14.50 (*0-914478-68-0*) Rienner, Lynne Pubs., Inc. (Three Continents).

**MARYLAND—FICTION**

Abresch, Peter. Killing Thyme. l.t. ed. 2002. 386p. pap. 25.95 (*0-7862-4336-8*) Gale Group.

—Killing Thyme. 2000. (James P. Dandy Elderhostel Mysteries Ser.). 256p. mass mkt. (*0-373-26356-2*, 1-26356-5, Harlequin Bks.) Harlequin Enterprises, Ltd.

—Killing Thyme. 1999. (Jim Dandy Elderhostel Mystery Ser.: No. 2). 279p. 23.95 (*1-885173-68-7*) Write Way Publishing.

Allison, Margaret. The Last Curve. 1999. 400p. pap. 6.50 (*0-671-56326-2*, Pocket) Simon & Schuster.

Alvarez, Rafael. The Fountain of Highlandtown: Stories. 1997. 192p. pap. 14.95 o.p. (*0-9656342-8-0*) Woodholme Hse. Pubs.

Amidon, Stephen. The New City: A Novel. 2001. (Illus.). 464p. reprint ed. pap. 14.00 (*0-385-49763-6*) Doubleday Publishing.

Auster, Paul. Timbuktu. 1999. 192p. 22.00 o.s.i (*0-8050-5407-3*) Holt, Henry & Co.

—Timbuktu. 2000. 192p. pap. 11.00 (*0-312-26399-6*); mass mkt. 7.99 o.s.i (*0-312-97528-7*) Picador.

Barth, John. Sabbatical. 1984. audio 8.95 American Audio Prose Library, Inc.

—Sabbatical: A Romance. 1983. 366p. pap. 5.95 o.p. (*0-14-006619-5*); 1982. 352p. 14.95 o.p. (*0-399-12717-8*); 1982. 50.00 o.p. (*0-399-12723-2*) Putnam Publishing Group, The.

—Sabbatical: A Romance. 1996. 366p. reprint ed. pap. 12.95 (*1-56478-096-1*) Dalkey Archive Pr.

—The Sot-Weed Factor. 1969. mass mkt. 4.95 o.p. (*0-553-23400-5*) Bantam Bks.

—The Sot-Weed Factor. 1987. (Anchor Literary Library). 768p. reprint ed. pap. 18.95 (*0-385-24088-0*) Doubleday Publishing.

—The Tidewater Tales: A Novel. 1988. 656p. pap. 15.00 o.s.i (*0-449-90293-5*, Fawcett) Ballantine Bks.

—The Tidewater Tales: A Novel. 1987. 624p. 21.95 o.p. (*0-399-13247-3*, G. P. Putnam's Sons) Penguin Putnam Bks. for Young Readers.

Barth, John & Johnston, Mary. The Tidewater Tales: A Novel. 1997. (Maryland Paperback Bookshelf Ser.). (Illus.). 655p. reprint ed. pap. 19.95 (*0-8018-5556-X*) Johns Hopkins Univ. Pr.

Bell, Madison Smartt. Ten Indians. 1996. 264p. 23.00 o.s.i (*0-679-44246-4*) McKay, David Co., Inc.

—Ten Indians. 1997. 272p. pap. 12.95 o.s.i (*0-14-026846-4*) Penguin Group (USA) Inc.

Bennet, Rick. King of a Small World. 1995. 288p. 21.95 (*1-55970-284-2*) Arcade Publishing, Inc.

Berenson, Laurien. Best in Show. l.t. ed. 2003. 400p. 28.95 (*0-7862-6002-5*) Gale Group.

—Best in Show: A Melanie Travis Mystery. 2003. 288p. 22.00 (*1-57566-783-5*) Kensington Publishing Corp.

Boland, John. Rich Man's Blood. 1993. 240p. 17.95 o.p. (*0-312-09371-3*, Saint Martin's Minotaur) St. Martin's Pr.

Briscoe, Connie. P. G. County. 2003. 336p. pap. 13.95 (*0-345-44413-2*, One World/Ballantine) Ballantine Bks.

—P. G. County. 2002. 336p. 24.95 (*0-385-50161-7*) Doubleday Publishing.

—P. G. County. l.t. ed. 2003. (Basic Ser.). 469p. 29.95 (*0-7862-4931-5*) Thorndike Pr.

Brown, Rita Mae. Loose Lips. 2000. 384p. pap. 14.95 (*0-553-38067-2*, Spectra) Bantam Bks.

Byron, Gilbert. Chesapeake Duke. 1975. (Illus.). 167p. pap. 5.00 o.p. (*0-87033-210-4*, Tidewater Pubs.) Cornell Maritime Pr., Inc.

—Done Crabbin' Noah Leaves the River. 208p. 2000. pap. 16.95 (*0-8018-6528-X*); 1957. (gr. 9-12). text 40.00 o.p. (*0-8018-3988-2*) Johns Hopkins Univ. Pr.

Cannell, Stephen J. The Devil's Workshop, Set. abr. ed. 1999. audio 25.00 Highsmith Inc.

—The Devil's Workshop. 1999. viii, 421p. 25.00 (*0-688-16618-0*, Morrow, William & Co.); 2000. 448p. reprint ed. mass mkt. 6.99 (*0-380-73221-1*) Morrow/Avon.

Chamberlain, Diane. The Escape Artist. 1998. 400p. mass mkt. 6.50 o.s.i (*0-06-109073-5*); 1997. 336p. 24.00 o.p. (*0-06-017651-2*) HarperCollins Pubs.

Chappell, Helen. Dead Duck. 1997. (Sam & Hollis Mystery Ser.). mass mkt. 5.50 o.s.i (*0-449-15001-1*, Fawcett) Ballantine Bks.

—Dead Duck. l.t. ed. 2000. (Beeler Large Print Mystery Ser.). 231p. 25.95 (*1-57490-320-9*, Beeler Large Print Bks.) Beeler, Thomas T. Publisher.

—Ghost of a Chance. l.t. ed. 1999. (Beeler Large Print Mystery Ser.). 25.95 (*1-57490-202-4*, Beeler Large Print Bks.) Beeler, Thomas T. Publisher.

—Ghost of a Chance. 1998. (Sam & Hollis Mystery Ser.: No. 3). 256p. mass mkt. 5.99 o.s.i (*0-440-22567-1*) Doubleday Publishing.

—Giving up the Ghost. l.t. ed. 2001. (Beeler Large Print Mystery Ser.). 188p. 25.95 (*1-57490-350-0*, Beeler Large Print Bks.) Beeler, Thomas T. Publisher.

—Giving up the Ghost: A Sam & Hollis Mystery. 1999. (Sam & Hollis Mystery Ser.). 256p. mass mkt. 5.99 o.s.i (*0-440-22575-2*) Dell Publishing.

—Oysterback Spoken Here. 1998. (Illus.). 208p. pap. 14.95 (*1-891521-01-2*) Woodholme Hse. Pubs.

—The Oysterback Tales. 1980. 128p. 22.95 (*0-8018-4815-6*) Johns Hopkins Univ. Pr.

—Slow Dancing with the Angel of Death. 1996. mass mkt. 5.50 o.s.i (*0-449-14983-8*, Fawcett) Ballantine Bks.

—A Whole World of Trouble. 2003. (Illus.). 224p. 23.00 (*0-7432-1529-X*, Simon & Schuster) Simon & Schuster.

Charbeneau, James A. Shouts & Whispers: Stories from the Southern Chesapeake Bay. 1997. (Illus.). 175p. (Orig.). pap. 12.95 (*1-883911-11-7*) Brandylane Pubs., Inc.

Churchman, Deborah. Cross a Dark Bridge: A Novel. 1996. 130p. 14.95 (*0-918056-08-X*) Ariadne Pr.

Clayton, Meg Waite. The Language of Light. Date not set. pap. (*0-312-31803-0*, St. Martin's Paperbacks); Date not set. mass mkt. (*0-312-99126-6*, St. Martin's Paperbacks); 2003. 352p. 24.95 (*0-312-31801-4*) St. Martin's Pr.

Cockey, Tim. Hearse of a Different Color. 2003. (*1-57490-536-8*, Beeler Large Print Bks.) Beeler, Thomas T. Publisher.

—Hearse of a Different Color. 2002. E-Book 5.95 (*0-7868-6955-0*); 2001. 318p. 23.95 (*0-7868-6571-7*); 2003. 416p. reprint ed. mass mkt. 7.99 (*0-7868-8963-2*) Hyperion Pr.

—The Hearse You Came in On. l.t. ed. 28.95 (*1-58724-216-8*, Wheeler Publishing, Inc.) Gale Group.

—The Hearse You Came in On. 2002. E-Book 5.95 (*0-7868-6961-5*); 2000. viii, 308p. 22.95 (*0-7868-6570-9*); 2003. 416p. reprint ed. mass mkt. 6.99 (*0-7868-8962-4*) Hyperion Pr.

Coulter, Catherine. Hemlock Bay. 2001. 300p. 23.95 o.s.i (*0-399-14800-0*) Penguin Group (USA) Inc.

—Hemlock Bay. 2001. 432p. 24.95 o.p. (*0-399-14738-1*) Putnam Publishing Group, The.

—Hemlock Bay. l.t. ed. 2001. 496p. 24.95 (*0-375-43115-2*) Random Hse. Large Print.

Crone, Moira. A Period of Confinement. 1987. 304p. reprint ed. pap. 6.95 o.p. (*0-06-097108-8*, PL 7108, Perennial) HarperTrade.

—A Period of Confinement. 1986. 336p. 19.95 o.p. (*0-399-13136-1*, G. P. Putnam's Sons) Penguin Putnam Bks. for Young Readers.

Dailey, Janet. Bed of Grass: Maryland, No. 20. 1987. pap. (*0-373-89820-7*, Harlequin Bks.) Harlequin Enterprises, Ltd.

—Bed of Grass: Maryland. l.t. ed. 2000. (Americana Ser.). 237p. 26.95 o.p. (*0-7862-2692-7*); (*0-7540-4273-1*); (*0-7540-4274-X*) Thorndike Pr.

—Bed of Grass: Maryland. E-Book 6.99 (*1-58586-464-1*); 2001. 124p. pap. 12.99 (*0-7592-3800-6*); 2001. E-Book 6.99 (*0-7592-0093-9*); 2001. E-Book 6.99 (*1-58586-466-8*); 2001. E-Book 6.99 (*0-7592-0838-7*) ereads.com.

D'Arnuk, Nanisi B. Outside In: A Cameron Andrews Mystery. 1996. 200p. (Orig.). pap. 10.95 (*0-934678-75-8*) New Victoria Pubs., Inc.

Dawson, David L. Double Blind. 1991. 240p. 17.95 o.p. (*0-312-07085-3*, Saint Martin's Minotaur) St. Martin's Pr.

Duffy, Bruce. Last Comes the Egg. 2000. (Nonpareil Ser.: Vol. 91). 359p. pap. 16.95 (*1-56792-124-8*, Non Pareil Bks.) Godine, David R. Pub.

—Last Comes the Egg. 1997. 368p. 23.00 (*0-684-80883-8*, Simon & Schuster) Simon & Schuster.

Durham, David Anthony. A Walk Through Darkness. l.t. ed. 2002. 28.95 (*1-58724-242-7*, Wheeler Publishing, Inc.) Gale Group.

—A Walk Through Darkness. 2003. 304p. reprint ed. pap. 13.00 (*0-385-72036-X*, Anchor) Knopf Publishing Group.

—A Walk Through Darkness: A Novel. 2002. 304p. 23.95 (*0-385-49925-6*) Doubleday Publishing.

Ehrman, Kit. At Risk. 2002. 299p. 24.95 o.s.i (*1-59058-036-2*); 292p. pap. (*1-59058-045-1*) Poisoned Pen Pr.

—At Risk. 2003. 304p. mass mkt. 6.99 (*0-7434-7506-2*) ibooks, Inc.

—Dead Man's Touch. 2003. 24.95 (*1-59058-089-3*); pap. 22.95 (*1-59058-090-7*) Poisoned Pen Pr.

Feinstein, John. Running Mates. 1993. 336p. mass mkt. 4.50 o.p. (*0-06-104248-X*, HarperTorch) Morrow/Avon.

—Running Mates. 1994. 3.99 o.p. (*0-517-11763-0*) Random Hse. Value Publishing.

Forster, Gwynne. Against the Wind. 1999. (Love Spectrum Romance Ser.). 257p. pap. text 8.95 (*1-885478-90-9*) Genesis Pr., Inc.

Freedman, J. F. Bird's-Eye View. 2001. 432p. 24.95 o.p. (*0-446-52823-4*) Warner Bks., Inc.

—The Obstacle Course. 1994. 368p. 21.95 o.p. (*0-670-85346-1*, Viking) Viking Penguin.

Fuqua, Jonathon Scott. The Re-Appearance of Sam Webber. 1999. 240p. 23.95 (*1-890862-02-9*) Bancroft Pr.

Gaffney, Patricia. Flight Lessons. 2002. 400p. 24.95 (*0-06-018528-7*); 608p. pap. 24.95 (*0-06-009392-7*) HarperCollins Pubs.

—Flight Lessons. abr. ed. 2002. audio 25.95 (*0-06-009562-8*, Caedmon) HarperTrade.

—Flight Lessons. 2003. 464p. mass mkt. 7.99 (*0-06-103144-5*, HarperTorch) Morrow/Avon.

Gear, Kathleen O'Neal & Gear, W. Michael. People of the Mist. (First North Americans Ser.). 1998. (Illus.). 553p. mass mkt. 7.99 (*0-8125-1560-9*, Tor Bks.); 1997. 480p. 26.95 o.p. (*0-312-85854-X*, Forge Bks.) Doherty, Tom Assocs., LLC.

—People of the Mist. l.t. ed. 1998. (Western Ser.). 679p. 26.95 (*0-7838-0251-X*) Thorndike Pr.

Grimes, Martha. The Horse You Came in On. 1994. 384p. mass mkt. 7.99 (*0-345-38755-4*) Ballantine Bks.

—The Horse You Came in On. l.t. ed. 1993. 19.00 o.s.i (*0-679-74770-2*) Random Hse. Large Print.

—The Horse You Came in On. unabr. ed. 1994. audio 70.00 (*0-7887-0003-0*, 94142E7) Recorded Bks., LLC.

—The Horse You Came in On. abr. ed. 1993. (Inspector Richard Jury Ser.). audio 17.00 (*0-671-87223-0*, 390934, Simon & Schuster Audioworks) Simon & Schuster Audio.

Hamilton, Alexander. The History of the Ancient & Honorable Tuesday Club, 3 Vols. Micklus, Robert, ed. 1990. (Institute of Early American History & Culture Ser.). (Illus.). cxxviii, 1288p. (C). 250.00 (*0-8078-1851-8*) Univ. of North Carolina Pr.

—The Tuesday Club: A Shorter Edition of the History of the Ancient & Honorable Tuesday Club by Dr. Alexander Hamilton. Micklus, Robert, ed. (Maryland Paperback Bookshelf Ser.). (Illus.). 368p. 1995. text 52.00 o.p. (*0-8018-5008-8*); 1988. pap. text 19.95 o.p. (*0-8018-4968-3*) Johns Hopkins Univ. Pr.

Heidish, Marcy. The Torching: A Novel. 1992. 208p. 19.00 o.p. (*0-671-74375-9*, Simon & Schuster) Simon & Schuster.

Hollyday, Thomas. Slave Graves. 2003. 284p. pap. 12.95 (*0-9741287-0-8*); E-Book 12.95 (*0-9741287-1-6*) Happy Bird Corp.

Junkin, Tim. The Waterman. 1999. 300p. tchr. ed. 22.95 (*1-56512-230-5*) Algonquin Bks. of Chapel Hill.

Karlin, Wayne. The Wished-For Country. 2002. (Illus.). 340p. pap. 16.95 (*1-880684-89-6*) Curbstone Pr.

Keech, Thomas. The Crawlspace Conspiracy. 1995. 328p. 22.00 (*1-880909-34-0*) Baskerville Pubs., Inc.

Kotlowitz, Robert. His Master's Voice. 1992. 21.00 o.s.i (*0-679-40868-1*) Knopf, Alfred A. Inc.

Lacy, Al. Joy from Ashes: Fredericksburg, 8 vols. 2003. (Battles of Destiny Ser.: Vol. 5). 308p. pap. 9.99 (*0-88070-720-8*) Multnomah Pubs., Inc.

Lacy, Al & Lacy, Lew A. Wings of the Wind, 8 vols. 2003. (Battles of Destiny Ser.: Vol. 7). 366p. pap. 9.99 (*1-57673-032-8*, Multnomah Bks.) Multnomah Pubs., Inc.

Lawrence, Charlotte. Ragbone Man. 1994. (Psi-Fi Ser.). 336p. pap. 4.99 (*1-56718-412-X*) Llewellyn Pubns.

Lee, Barbara. Dead Man's Fingers. 1999. (Chesapeake Bay Mysteries Ser.). 276p. 22.95 o.p. (*0-312-20524-4*, Saint Martin's Minotaur) St. Martin's Pr.

—Death in Still Waters: A Chesapeake Bay Mystery. 1996. 226p. pap. text 5.50 (*0-312-95780-7*, St. Martin's Paperbacks); 1995. 240p. 20.95 o.p. (*0-312-13048-1*, Saint Martin's Minotaur) St. Martin's Pr.

—Final Closing. 1999. (WWL Mystery Ser.: No. 304). per. (*0-373-26304-X*, 1-26304-5, Worldwide Library) Harlequin Enterprises, Ltd.

—Final Closing: An Eve Elliot Mystery. 1997. (Eve Elliot Mystery Ser.). 304p. 22.95 o.p. (*0-312-16762-8*, Saint Martin's Minotaur) St. Martin's Pr.

Linz, Cathie. Tender Guardian. 1985. (Candlelight Regency Romance Ser.: No. 364). pap. 2.25 o.p. (*0-440-18645-5*) Dell Publishing.

Lippman, Laura. Baltimore Blues. 1997. 304p. mass mkt. 6.99 (*0-380-78875-6*, Avon Bks.) Morrow/Avon.

—Butcher's Hill. 1998. (Tess Monaghan Mysteries Ser.: Vol. 3). 288p. mass mkt. 5.99 (*0-380-79846-8*, Avon Bks.) Morrow/Avon.

—Charm City. l.t. ed. 2002. (Wheeler Large Print Book Ser.). 27.95 (*1-58724-214-1*, Wheeler Publishing, Inc.) Gale Group.

—Charm City. 1997. (Tess Monaghan Mysteries Ser.: Vol. 2). 304p. mass mkt. 6.99 (*0-380-78876-4*, Avon Bks.) Morrow/Avon.

—In a Strange City. 16th l.t. ed. 2002. 368p. lib. bdg. 27.95 (*1-58547-171-2*) Ctr. Point Large Print.

—In a Strange City. 2002. 400p. mass mkt. 6.99 (*0-380-81023-9*); 2001. 320p. 24.00 (*0-380-97818-0*, Morrow, William & Co.) Morrow/Avon.

—In Big Trouble. 1999. (Tess Monaghan Mysteries Ser.). 352p. mass mkt. 6.99 (*0-380-79847-6*, Avon Bks.) Morrow/Avon.

—The Last Place. 2003. 432p. mass mkt. 7.50 (*0-380-81024-7*, Avon Bks.); 2002. 352p. 23.95 (*0-380-97819-9*, Morrow, William & Co.) Morrow/Avon.

—The Sugar House. 2000. (Tess Monaghan Mysteries Ser.). 320p. 24.00 (*0-380-97817-2*, Morrow, William & Co.) Morrow/Avon.

Lockhart, Barbara M. Requiem for a Summer Cottage: A Novel. 2002. 360p. 22.50 (*0-87074-476-3*) Southern Methodist Univ. Pr.

MacDonald, Patricia. Not Guilty. 2003. (Illus.). 464p. mass mkt. 7.50 (*0-7434-2356-9*, Pocket); 2002. 368p. 24.00 (*0-7434-2355-0*, Atria) Simon & Schuster.

Martin, David. Cul-de-Sac. 1998. 352p. mass mkt. 6.99 (*0-312-96730-6*, St. Martin's Paperbacks) St. Martin's Pr.

Martin, William, Jr. Annapolis, Pt. 1. unabr. ed. 1997. audio 64.00 (*0-7366-3589-0*, 4243A) Books on Tape, Inc.

—Annapolis. abr. ed. 1996. audio 17.00 (*1-57042-410-1*, 394222) Time Warner AudioBooks.

—Annapolis. 1996. 82p. 24.95 o.s.i (*0-446-51511-6*); 1997. 800p. reprint ed. mass mkt. 7.99 (*0-446-60420-8*) Warner Bks., Inc.

Maxwell, John. Point Fury. 2003. 384p. mass mkt. 6.99 (*0-7434-5340-9*, Pocket Star); 2002. 320p. 25.00 (*0-7432-2207-5*, Scribner) Simon & Schuster.

McKinney, Meagan. In the Dark. 1999. 304p. mass mkt. 6.99 o.s.i (*0-8217-6341-5*, Zebra Bks.); 1998. (Illus.). 288p. 23.00 o.s.i (*1-57566-371-6*) Kensington Publishing Corp.

—In the Dark. l.t. ed. 2000. (Basic Ser.). 448p. 27.95 (*0-7862-2452-5*) Thorndike Pr.

Mewshaw, Michael. True Crime. 1993. reprint ed. mass mkt. 5.99 o.s.i (*0-449-22132-6*, Fawcett) Ballantine Bks.

—True Crime. 1991. 19.95 o.p. (*0-671-73204-8*, Simon & Schuster) Simon & Schuster.

Michaels, Barbara, pseud. Here I Stay. l.t. ed. 1994. 21.95 o.p. (*0-7927-2172-1*); pap. 20.95 o.p. (*0-7927-2171-3*) BBC Audiobooks America.

—Here I Stay. 1992. 317p. mass mkt. 4.99 (*0-8125-2140-4*); 1988. 320p. pap. 3.95 o.s.i (*0-8125-0679-0*); 1985. reprint ed. pap. 3.50 o.s.i (*0-8125-2250-8*) Doherty, Tom Assocs., LLC. (Tor Bks.).

—Here I Stay. l.t. ed. 1984. (General Ser.). lib. bdg. 16.95 o.p. (*0-8161-3619-X*, Macmillan Reference USA) Gale Group.

—Here I Stay. 1999. 352p. mass mkt. 7.50 (*0-06-104470-9*) HarperCollins Pubs.

—Here I Stay. 1994. 352p. mass mkt. 5.99 (*0-06-100726-9*, HarperTorch) Morrow/Avon.

—Here I Stay. 1993. 320p. reprint ed. lib. bdg. 20.00 o.p. (*0-7278-4448-2*) Severn Hse. Pubs., Ltd.

Michener, James A. Chesapeake. 1986. 1024p. mass mkt. 7.99 (*0-449-21158-4*); 1984. mass mkt. 4.95 o.p. (*0-449-20668-8*); 1983. mass mkt. 3.95 o.p. (*0-449-20315-8*) Ballantine Bks. (Fawcett).

—Chesapeake. 1993. audio 96.00 (*0-7366-2421-X*); audio 96.00 (*0-7366-2422-8*);Pt. 1. audio 96.00 (*0-7366-2420-1*, 3187A);Pt. 2. audio 96.00Pt. 3. audio 96.00 Books on Tape, Inc.

—Chesapeake. 2003. (Illus.). 888p. pap. 14.95 (*0-8129-7043-8*, Random Hse. Trade Paperbacks) Random House Adult Trade Publishing Group.

—Chesapeake. 1987. audio 14.95 o.p. (*0-394-56383-2*); Set. 1986. audio 16.00 o.s.i (*0-394-55695-X*) Random Hse. Audio Publishing Group. (RH Audio).

—Chesapeake. 1978. 45.00 o.s.i (*0-394-50079-2*) Random Hse., Inc.

Miller, Dinah. Monday at the Charm. 2001. 214p. pap. 19.95 (*1-58851-558-3*) PublishAmerica, Inc.

Morris, Gilbert. The Soldier Boy's Discovery. 1996. (Bonnets & Bugles Ser.: No. 4). (J). (gr. 7 up). pap. 5.99 (*0-8024-0914-8*, 571) Moody Pr.

Neihart, Ben. Burning Girl. 2000. 256p. pap. 13.00 (*0-688-17689-5*); 1999. 245p. 24.00 (*0-688-15691-6*) Morrow/Avon. (Morrow, William & Co.).

Oke, Janette & Bunn, T. Davis. Another Homecoming. 1997. 256p. pap. 11.99 (*1-55661-934-0*); 256p. text 15.99 o.p. (*1-55661-978-2*); 1p. audio 15.99 o.p. (*1-55661-980-4*); 384p. pap. 14.99 o.p. (*1-55661-979-0*) Bethany Hse. Pubs.

—Another Homecoming. l.t. ed. 1997. 25.95 (*0-7838-8332-3*, Macmillan Reference USA) Gale Group.

Olshaker, Mark. Unnatural Causes. 1986. 480p. 18.95 o.p. (*0-688-05896-5*, Morrow, William & Co.) Morrow/Avon.

—Unnatural Causes. 1989. mass mkt. 4.50 o.s.i (*0-671-64435-1*, Pocket) Simon & Schuster.

Osborn, David. Murder on the Chesapeake. unabr. ed. 1993. audio 36.00 (*0-7366-2437-6*, 3202) Books on Tape, Inc.

—Murder on the Chesapeake. 2000. 208p. pap. 19.00 (*0-7432-1271-1*); 1992. 320p. 19.00 o.s.i (*0-671-70486-9*) Simon & Schuster. (Simon & Schuster).

—Murder on the Chesapeake: A Margaret Barlow Mystery. 1993. 304p. mass mkt. 3.99 o.s.i (*0-8217-4165-9*, Zebra Bks.) Kensington Publishing Corp.

Pairo, Preston. Beach Money. 1991. 208p. 18.95 o.p. (*0-8027-5786-3*) Walker & Co.

—Breach of Trust. 1995. 342p. 22.95 o.p. (*0-312-13034-1*, Saint Martin's Minotaur) St. Martin's Pr.

—Bright Eyes. 1996. 320p. mass mkt. 5.99 o.s.i (*0-451-40706-7*, Onyx) NAL.

—One Dead Judge. 1993. 204p. 19.95 o.p. (*0-8027-1250-9*) Walker & Co.

Pease, William D. The Rage of Innocence. 1993. 448p. 22.00 o.p. (*0-670-83519-6*, Viking) Viking Penguin.

Pelecanos, George P. Shoedog. 1994. 216p. 19.95 o.p. (*0-312-11061-8*, Saint Martin's Minotaur) St. Martin's Pr.

Perry, Marta. The Doctor's Christmas. 2003. (Steeple Hill Love Inspired Ser.: No. 232). 256p. mass mkt. (*0-373-87242-9*, Steeple Hill) Harlequin Enterprises, Ltd.

Peters, Elizabeth, pseud. The Love Talker. 1981. 256p. mass mkt. 2.50 o.s.i (*0-449-24468-7*, Fawcett) Ballantine Bks.

—The Love Talker. unabr. ed. 1995. audio 44.95 (*0-7861-0709-X*, 894078) Blackstone Audio Bks., Inc.

—The Love Talker. 1990. 255p. mass mkt. 4.99 (*0-8125-0727-4*, Tor Bks.) Doherty, Tom Assocs., LLC.

—The Love Talker. 1980. (General Ser.). lib. bdg. 13.95 o.p. (*0-8161-3135-X*, Macmillan Reference USA) Gale Group.

—The Love Talker. 2001. 368p. mass mkt. 6.99 (*0-380-73340-4*, Avon Bks.) Morrow/Avon.

—The Love Talker. 1994. 255p. 20.00 o.p. (*0-7278-4579-9*) Severn Hse. Pubs., Ltd.

Phillips, Doc'. Internal Principles. 1999. 280p. pap. 21.99 (*0-7388-0653-6*); text 31.99 (*0-7388-0652-8*) Xlibris Corp.

Poyer, David. The Return of Philo T. McGiffin: The Comic Novel of Annapolis. 1997. (Bluejacket Bks.). 288p. pap. 19.95 (*1-55750-689-2*) Naval Institute Pr.

—The Return of Philo T. McGiffin: The Comic Novel of Annapolis. 1983. 288p. 13.95 o.p. (*0-312-67907-6*) St. Martin's Pr.

Price, Hugh B. & Walker, Blair S. Up Jumped the Devil. 1997. 292p. 22.00 o.s.i (*0-380-97420-7*, Avon Bks.) Morrow/Avon.

Pynchon, Thomas. Mason & Dixon, Pt. 2. unabr. collector's ed. 1997. audio 80.00 (*0-7366-3782-6*, 4454-B) Books on Tape, Inc.

—Mason & Dixon. 1998. 0.01 o.s.i (*0-8050-5850-8*, Owl Bks.); 1998. 773p. pap. 17.00 (*0-8050-5837-0*, Owl Bks.); 1997. 784p. 27.50 o.s.i (*0-8050-3758-6*) Holt, Henry & Co.

—Mason & Dixon. 2004. 784p. pap. 15.00 (*0-312-42320-9*) Picador.

Richardson, Brenda L. Chesapeake Song. 371p. 1999. pap. 19.95 (*1-56743-040-6*); 1994. pap. 10.95 (*1-56743-063-5*) HarperTrade. (Amistad Pr.).

—Chesapeake Song. 1996. 480p. mass mkt. 5.99 o.s.i (*0-7860-0304-9*, Pinnacle Bks.) Kensington Publishing Corp.

Roberts, Nora. Chesapeake Blue. 2004. 368p. mass mkt. 7.99 (*0-515-13626-3*, Jove) Berkley Publishing Group.

—Chesapeake Blue. 2002. (Chesapeake Bay Ser.: Bk. 4). 384p. 25.95 (*0-399-14939-2*, Putnam & Grosset) Putnam Publishing Group, The.

—Chesapeake Blue. (Basic Ser.). 2003. 32.95 (*0-7862-5128-X*); 2004. 500p. pap. 14.95 (*1-59413-031-0*, Large Print Pr.) Thorndike Pr.

—Divine Evil. 1992. 512p. mass mkt. 7.50 (*0-553-29490-3*) Bantam Bks.

—Divine Evil. l.t. ed. 24.95 o.p. (*1-56895-118-3*, Wheeler Publishing, Inc.) Gale Group.

—Divine Evil. l.t. ed. 2004. 800p. 24.00 (*0-375-43377-5*) Random Hse. Large Print.

—Inner Harbor. 1999. (Chesapeake Bay Ser.: Bk. 3). 352p. mass mkt. 7.99 (*0-515-12421-4*, Jove) Berkley Publishing Group.

—Inner Harbor. abr. ed. (Chesapeake Bay Ser.: Bk. 3). 1999. audio 7.99 o.s.i (*1-56740-323-9*, 1883, Paperback Nova Audio Bks.); 1998. audio 17.95 o.p. (*1-56740-758-7*, 1276, Nova Audio Bks.); 1998. audio 24.95 (*1-56100-780-3*, 1275, Bookcassette); 1998. 9p. audio 57.25 (*1-56740-559-2*, 1277, Unabridged Library Editions) Brilliance Audio.

—Inner Harbor. abr. ed. 1999. (Chesapeake Bay Ser.: Bk. 3). audio 17.95. audio 73.25 Highsmith Inc.

—Inner Harbor. l.t. ed. 1999. (Chesapeake Bay Ser.: Bk. 3). 488p. 29.95 (*0-7862-1442-2*) Thorndike Pr.

Robson, Lucia St Clair. Mary's Land. 1996. mass mkt. 5.99 o.s.i (*0-345-40628-1*) Ballantine Bks.

Rogers, Rosemary. Return to Me. 2003. 480p. mass mkt. (*1-55166-748-7*, Mira Bks.) Harlequin Enterprises, Ltd.

Schechter, Harold. Nevermore. 2000. 480p. reprint ed. pap. 6.99 (*0-671-79856-1*, Pocket) Simon & Schuster.

—Nevermore: A Novel. 1999. 352p. 23.00 (*0-671-79855-3*, Atria) Simon & Schuster.

Schott, Carolyn J. & Smith, Phillipa A. The Cracker Crumb Rescue. 1992. 40p. (J). (gr. 3-6). lib. bdg. 16.95 (*0-9632461-0-0*) Harbour Duck Specialties, Inc.

Talley, Marcia. Sing It to Her Bones. l.t. ed. 2000. 27.95 (*1-57490-301-2*, Beeler Large Print Bks.) Beeler, Thomas T. Publisher.

—Sing It to Her Bones: A Hannah Ives Mystery. 1999. (Hannah Ives Mysteries Ser.). 304p. mass mkt. 5.99 (*0-440-23517-0*) Dell Publishing.

Taube, Herman. My Baltimore Landsmen: A Documentary Novel. 1995. (Orig.). pap. 12.95 o.p. (*0-931848-90-3*) Dryad Pr.

Tawes, Natalie L. Camellia Stephens. 1996. 344p. 19.00 (*0-8059-3988-1*) Dorrance Publishing Co., Inc.

Tilghman, Christopher. Mason's Retreat. Date not set. (*0-679-45240-0*) McKay, David Co., Inc.

—Mason's Retreat. 1997. 304p. pap. 13.00 o.p. (*0-312-15586-7*) Picador.

—Mason's Retreat. 1995. 290p. 22.00 o.s.i (*0-679-45143-9*) Random Hse., Inc.

—The Way People Run: Stories. 2000. 224p. pap. 12.00 o.p. (*0-312-26791-6*) Picador.

—The Way People Run: Stories. l.t. ed. 1999. (Americana Ser.). 254p. 26.95 (*0-7862-2170-4*) Thorndike Pr.

Tucker, Augusta. Miss Susie Slagle's. 1968. (Maryland Paperback Bookshelf Ser.). 352p. reprint ed. pap. 17.95 (*0-8018-3419-8*) Johns Hopkins Univ. Pr.

Turchi, Peter. The Girls Next Door. 1989. 320p. 18.95 o.p. (*0-453-00665-5*) NAL.

Tyler, Anne. Back When We Were Grownups. 2001. 288p. 25.00 (*0-375-41253-0*) Knopf, Alfred A. Inc.

—Back When We Were Grownups. l.t. ed. 2001. 416p. 25.00 (*0-375-43118-7*) Random Hse. Large Print.

—The Clock Winder. 1996. (First Ballantine Books Trade Ed). 320p. pap. 14.95 (*0-449-91179-9*, Fawcett) Ballantine Bks.

—A Patchwork Planet. 1999. 304p. pap. 13.95 (*0-449-00398-1*, Fawcett) Ballantine Bks.

—A Patchwork Planet. unabr. ed. 1998. audio 64.00 (*0-7366-4250-1*, 4749) Books on Tape, Inc.

—A Patchwork Planet. abr. ed. 1998. audio 24.00 (*0-375-40308-6*, 595762, RH Audio) Random Hse. Audio Publishing Group.

—A Patchwork Planet. aut. ed. 1998. 24.00 o.p. (*0-676-54925-X*) Random Hse., Inc.

—A Patchwork Planet. unabr. ed. 1999. audio 60.00 (*0-7887-2020-1*, 95397E7) Recorded Bks., LLC.

—A Patchwork Planet. l.t. ed. 1999. (Charnwood Large Print Ser.). 352p. 31.99 o.p. (*0-7089-9085-1*, Ulverscroft) Thorpe, F. A. Pubs. GBR. *Dist:* Ulverscroft Large Print Bks., Ltd., Ulverscroft Large Print Canada, Ltd.

—A Patchwork Planet, Set. abr. ed. 1999. audio 24.35 (*1-85686-711-0*) Ulverscroft Audio (U.S.A.).

Wade, Brent. Company Man. 1993. 240p. pap. 10.95 o.s.i (*0-385-42563-5*) Doubleday Publishing.

—Company Man: A Novel. 1992. 240p. 18.95 o.p. (*0-945575-73-4*) Algonquin Bks. of Chapel Hill.

Walbert, Kate. The Gardens of Kyoto: A Novel. 288p. 2002. pap. 13.00 (*0-684-86949-7*); 2001. 24.00 (*0-684-86948-9*) Simon & Schuster. (Scribner).

—The Gardens of Kyoto: A Novel. l.t. ed. 2001. (Women's Fiction Ser.). 461p. 29.95 (*0-7862-3477-6*) Thorndike Pr.

Walker, Blair S. Hidden in Plain View. abr. ed. 2001. audio 12.99 (*1-57815-207-0*, Media Bks. Audio Publishing) Media Bks., L. L. C.

—Hidden in Plain View. 1999. (Easy Rawlins Mystery Ser.). 240p. 22.00 o.s.i (*0-380-97421-5*, Avon Bks.) Morrow/Avon.

—Hidden in Plain View. abr. ed. 1999. audio 24.95 (*1-57511-061-X*) Publishing Mills, Inc., The.

—Hidden in Plain View: A Darryl Billups Mystery. 2000. (Darryl Billups Ser.). 240p. mass mkt. 5.99 o.s.i (*0-380-79026-2*, Avon Bks.) Morrow/Avon.

—Up Jumped the Devil. abr. ed. 2001. audio 12.99 (*1-57815-210-0*, Media Bks. Audio Publishing) Media Bks., L. L. C.

—Up Jumped the Devil. 1999. 272p. mass mkt. 5.99 o.s.i (*0-380-79025-4*, Avon Bks.) Morrow/Avon.

—Up Jumped the Devil, Set. abr. ed. 1997. audio 24.95 (*1-57511-027-X*) Publishing Mills, Inc., The.

Ward, Robert. Grace: A Fictional Memoir. 2000. (Illus.). 240p. pap. 12.95 (*0-312-25390-7*, Golden Guides from Saint Martin's Pr.); 1998. 224p. 20.00 (*0-307-44007-9*, Golden Bks. Adult Publishing Group) St. Martin's Pr.

—Grace: A Fictional Memoir. l.t. ed. 1999. (Core Ser.). 352p. 28.95 (*0-7838-0427-X*) Thorndike Pr.

—The King of Cards. Rosenman, Jane, ed. 1993. 336p. 20.00 (*0-671-79568-6*, Atria) Simon & Schuster.

Warfield, Gallatin. Raising Cain. 1998. 400p. mass mkt. 6.99 (*0-446-60513-1*); 1996. 352p. 23.45 o.p. (*0-446-51850-6*) Warner Bks., Inc.

—Silent Son. 1994. 336p. 21.95 o.s.i (*0-446-51725-9*) Warner Bks., Inc.

—The Silent Son. 1995. 384p. mass mkt. 5.99 o.s.i (*0-446-60199-3*) Warner Bks., Inc.

—State vs. Justice, Set. unabr. ed. 1998. audio 103.95 (*1-85903-130-7*) Magna Story Sound GBR. *Dist:* Ulverscroft Large Print Bks., Ltd.

—State vs. Justice. 1993. 384p. mass mkt. 5.99 o.s.i (*0-446-36477-0*); 1992. 336p. 18.95 o.p. (*0-446-51688-0*) Warner Bks., Inc.

Wright, Sarah E. This Child's Gonna Live. 1986. 304p. (C). reprint ed. pap. 10.95 o.p. (*0-935312-67-6*); 2nd ed. 2002. 320p. pap. 15.95 (*1-55861-397-8*) Feminist Pr. at The City Univ. of New York.

**MASSACHUSETTS—FICTION**

Ablow, Keith Russell. Compulsion: A Novel. E-Book 24.95 (*0-312-70706-1*); 2002. 320p. 24.95 (*0-312-26641-3*); 2003. 384p. reprint ed. mass mkt. 6.99 (*0-312-98824-9*, St. Martin's Paperbacks) St. Martin's Pr.

—Denial. 1998. (Denial Ser.: Vol. 1). 368p. mass mkt. 6.99 o.s.i (*0-312-96596-6*, St. Martin's Paperbacks) St. Martin's Pr.

Abrahams, Peter. Revolution, No. 9. 2002. 320p. mass mkt. 6.99 (*0-345-44580-5*, Fawcett) Ballantine Bks.

—Revolution, No. 9. 1992. 336p. 18.95 o.p. (*0-89296-481-2*) Mysterious Pr.

—Revolution, No. 9. 1993. 320p. mass mkt. 5.50 o.p. (*0-446-40156-0*, Mysterious Pr. Paperback Bks.) Warner Bks., Inc.

Adamson, Lydia. A Cat with a Fiddle. 1993. (Alice Nestleton Mystery Ser.: No. 6). 224p. mass mkt. 5.50 o.s.i (*0-451-17586-7*, Signet Bks.) NAL.

—A Cat with a Fiddle: An Alice Nestleton Mystery. l.t. ed. 2002. (Mystery Ser.). 270p. 29.45 (*0-7862-3895-X*) Gale Group.

Allen, Irene. Quaker Silence: An Elizabeth Elliot Mystery. 1992. 210p. 17.00 o.s.i (*0-679-41414-2*, Villard Bks.) Random House Adult Trade Publishing Group.

—Quaker Testimony. 272p. 1996. text 21.95 o.p. (*0-312-14709-0*, Saint Martin's Minotaur); Vol. 1. 1998. (Quaker Testimony Ser.: Vol. 1). (Illus.). mass mkt. 5.99 (*0-312-96424-2*, St. Martin's Paperbacks) St. Martin's Pr.

—Quaker Witness. 1993. 254p. 18.00 o.s.i (*0-679-41415-0*, Villard Bks.) Random House Adult Trade Publishing Group.

—Quaker Witness. 2001. 272p. mass mkt. 5.99 (*0-312-97285-7*, St. Martin's Paperbacks) St. Martin's Pr.

Anastas, Benjamin. The Faithful Narrative of a Pastor's Disappearance. 2001. 24.00 o.p. (*0-374-15214-4*) Farrar, Straus & Giroux.

—The Faithful Narrative of a Pastor's Disappearance. 2002. 288p. pap. 13.00 (*0-312-42068-4*); pap. (*0-312-42108-7*) Picador.

Andrews, V. C. Heart Song. 1997. 384p. 23.00 (*0-671-53468-8*, Atria); pap. 7.99 (*0-671-53472-6*, Pocket) Simon & Schuster.

—Heart Song. l.t. ed. 1998. (Core Ser.). 477p. 29.95 (*0-7838-8346-3*) Thorndike Pr.

—Heart Song. 1997. 14.04 (*0-606-13471-9*) Turtleback Bks.

—Melody. 1999. 15.70 (*0-613-01437-5*) CRC Pr. LLC.

—Melody. l.t. ed. 1996. (G. K. Hall Core Ser.). 451p. 25.95 (*0-7838-1906-4*, Macmillan Reference USA) Gale Group.

—Melody. 1996. 384p. 23.00 o.p. (*0-671-53470-X*, Atria); pap. 7.99 (*0-671-53471-8*, Pocket) Simon & Schuster.

—Melody. 1996. 14.04 (*0-606-13603-7*) Turtleback Bks.

—Music in the Night. 1998. (Logan Ser.). 320p. 24.00 o.s.i (*0-671-53467-X*, Atria); (Illus.). 336p. pap. 7.99 (*0-671-53474-2*, Pocket) Simon & Schuster.

—Music in the Night. 1998. 14.04 (*0-606-13627-4*) Turtleback Bks.

—Olivia. 1999. (Logan Ser.). 384p. 24.00 (*0-671-00760-2*, Atria); pap. 7.99 (*0-671-00761-0*, Pocket) Simon & Schuster.

—Olivia. l.t. ed. 1999. (Core Ser.). 456p. 28.95 (*0-7838-8592-X*) Thorndike Pr.

—Olivia. 1999. 14.04 (*0-606-17529-6*) Turtleback Bks.

—Unfinished Symphony. 1997. (Logan Ser.). 352p. 24.00 o.s.i (*0-671-53469-6*, Atria); 384p. mass mkt. 7.99 (*0-671-53473-4*, Pocket) Simon & Schuster.

—Unfinished Symphony. l.t. ed. 1998. (Core Ser.). 479p. 30.95 (*0-7838-8407-9*) Thorndike Pr.

—Unfinished Symphony. 1997. 14.04 (*0-606-13883-8*) Turtleback Bks.

Angoff, Charles. When I Was a Boy in Boston. 1977. (Short Story Index Reprint Ser.). (Illus.). 19.95 (*0-8369-3668-X*) Ayer Co. Pubs., Inc.

Arnold, Margot, pseud. The Cape Cod Conundrum. 1992. (Penny Spring & Sir Toby Glendower Mystery Ser.). 224p. text 20.00 o.p. (*0-88150-244-8*, Foul Play) Norton, W. W. & Co., Inc.

Arsenault, Mark. Spiked. 2003. 240p. 24.95 o.s.i (*1-59058-059-1*); 420p. pap. 22.95 o.s.i (*1-59058-085-0*) Poisoned Pen Pr.

Athey, Miles. The Great Cause. 2003. pap. 12.50 (*1-4033-4275-X*) 1stBooks Library.

—The Great Cause. 1991. 190p. pap. 9.95 (*1-880144-44-1*) Arrowmist Publishing, Inc.

August, Elizabeth. A Wedding for Emily Smytheshire. 1993. (Harlequin Romance Ser.). per. (*0-373-08953-8*, 5-08953-7, Silhouette) Harlequin Enterprises, Ltd.

Austin, Jane G. Standish of Standish. 2000. 252p. E-Book 3.95 (*0-594-06371-X*) 1873 Pr.

—Standish of Standish. 1989. (Works of Jane Austin). reprint ed. lib. bdg. 79.00 (*0-7812-1831-4*) Reprint Services Corp.

Bacon, Josephine D. Smith College Stories. 1977. (Short Story Index Reprint Ser.). 23.95 (*0-8369-3079-7*) Ayer Co. Pubs., Inc.

Barlow, Linda. Leaves of Fortune. 1990. 560p. reprint ed. mass mkt. 4.95 o.s.i (*0-440-20471-2*) Dell Publishing.

Barnes, Linda. Bitter Finish. 1985. 208p. mass mkt. 4.95 o.s.i (*0-449-20690-4*, Fawcett) Ballantine Bks.

—Bitter Finish. l.t. ed. 2000. 263p. lib. bdg. 28.95 (*1-58547-031-7*) Ctr. Point Large Print.

—Bitter Finish. 1994. 272p. mass mkt. 5.99 o.s.i (*0-440-21606-0*) Dell Publishing.

—Bitter Finish. 1983. 192p. 11.95 o.p. (*0-312-08236-3*) St. Martin's Pr.

—Blood Will Have Blood. 1986. 192p. mass mkt. 5.99 o.s.i (*0-449-20901-6*, Fawcett) Ballantine Bks.

—Blood Will Have Blood. 1985. 192p. pap. 2.25 o.p. (*0-380-79368-7*, 79368, Avon Bks.) Morrow/Avon.

—Cold Case. 1998. 496p. mass mkt. 5.99 o.s.i (*0-440-21226-X*, Dell Bks.) Dell Publishing.

—Cold Case. l.t. ed. 1997. (Large Print Book Ser.). 27.95 (*1-56895-427-1*, Wheeler Publishing, Inc.) Gale Group.

—Coyote. 1991. 304p. mass mkt. 5.99 o.s.i (*0-440-21089-5*) Dell Publishing.

—Coyote. l.t. ed. 1991. (General Ser.). 332p. lib. bdg. 20.95 (*0-8161-5197-0*, Macmillan Reference USA) Gale Group.

—Coyote. unabr. ed. 1994. audio. (Carlotta Carlyle Mysteries Ser. : No. 3). audio 44.00 (*0-7887-0036-7*, 94235E7) Recorded Bks., LLC.

—Dead Heat. 1985. 256p. mass mkt. 4.99 o.s.i (*0-449-20689-0*, Fawcett) Ballantine Bks.

—Dead Heat. 1995. 288p. mass mkt. 5.99 o.s.i (*0-440-21862-4*) Dell Publishing.

—Dead Heat. 1984. 224p. 11.95 o.p. (*0-312-18498-0*) St. Martin's Pr.

—Flashpoint. l.t. ed. 2000. (Wheeler Large Print Book Ser.). 354p. 26.95 (*1-56895-856-0*, Wheeler Publishing, Inc.) Gale Group.

—Flashpoint. 2001. 432p. mass mkt. 6.99 (*0-7868-8948-9*); 1999. 288p. 22.95 (*0-7868-6317-X*) Hyperion Pr.

—Hardware. 1996. 400p. mass mkt. 5.99 o.s.i (*0-440-21223-5*) Dell Publishing.

—Hardware. unabr. ed. 2000. (Carlotta Carlyle Mysteries Ser. : No. 6). audio 70.00 (*0-7887-0262-9*, 94471E7) Recorded Bks., LLC.

—The Snake Tattoo. 1990. 208p. mass mkt. 5.99 o.s.i (*0-449-21759-0*, Fawcett) Ballantine Bks.

—The Snake Tattoo. l.t. ed. 1990. (General Ser.). 350p. lib. bdg. 19.95 o.p. (*0-8161-4866-X*, Macmillan Reference USA) Gale Group.

—The Snake Tattoo. unabr. ed. 1993. (Carlotta Carlyle Mysteries Ser. : No. 2). audio 44.00 (*1-55690-923-3*, 93419E7) Recorded Bks., LLC.

—The Snake Tattoo. 2004. 320p. mass mkt. 6.99 (*0-312-99355-2*, St. Martin's Paperbacks); 1989. 288p. 17.95 o.p. (*0-312-02643-9*) St. Martin's Pr.

—Snapshot. 1994. 400p. mass mkt. 5.99 o.s.i (*0-440-21220-0*) Dell Publishing.

—Snapshot. l.t. ed. 1994. (Magna Large Print Ser.). 530p. (*0-7505-0706-3*) Magna Large Print Bks. GBR. *Dist:* Ulverscroft Large Print Canada, Ltd.

—Snapshot. unabr. ed. 1994. (Carlotta Carlyle Mysteries Ser. : No. 5). audio 70.00 (*1-55690-969-1*, 94112E7) Recorded Bks., LLC.

—Steel Guitar. 1992. 272p. pap. 19.00 o.s.i (*0-440-61399-X*); mass mkt. 5.99 o.s.i (*0-440-21268-5*) Dell Publishing.

—Steel Guitar. unabr. ed. 1993. (Carlotta Carlyle Mysteries Ser. : No. 4). audio 44.00 (*1-55690-787-7*, 93102E7) Recorded Bks., LLC.

—A Trouble of Fools. 1988. mass mkt. 5.99 o.s.i (*0-449-21640-3*, Fawcett) Ballantine Bks.

—A Trouble of Fools. l.t. ed. 1989. (General Ser.). 370p. lib. bdg. 19.95 o.p. (*0-8161-4714-0*, Macmillan Reference USA) Gale Group.

—A Trouble of Fools. 2001. 224p. mass mkt. 4.50 (*0-7868-8953-5*) Hyperion Pr.

—A Trouble of Fools. unabr. ed. 2000. (Carlotta Carlyle Mysteries Ser. : No. 1). audio 51.00 (*1-55690-834-2*, 93202E7) Recorded Bks., LLC.

—A Trouble of Fools. 1987. 228p. 15.95 o.p. (*0-312-01100-8*) St. Martin's Pr.

Bates, Karen Grigsby. Plain Brown Wrapper: An Alex Powell Novel. 2001. 336p. pap. 13.00 (*0-380-80890-0*, Avon Bks.) Morrow/Avon.

Begiebing, Robert J. The Strange Death of Mistress Coffin. 1996. 240p. pap. 9.95 (*1-56512-145-7*, 72145); 1991. 252p. 17.95 o.p. (*0-945575-56-4*) Algonquin Bks. of Chapel Hill.
—The Strange Death of Mistress Coffin. 1994. 3.99 o.p. (*0-517-12663-X*) Random Hse. Value Publishing.
Benedict, Elizabeth. Almost. 2001. 256p. tchr. ed. 24.00 (*0-618-14332-7*) Houghton Mifflin Co.
Berg, Elizabeth. Until the Real Thing Comes Along. unabr. ed. 1999. (Chivers Sound Library American Collections). 56p. audio 39.95 (*0-7927-2342-2*, CSL 231, Chivers Sound Library) BBC Audiobooks America.
—Until the Real Thing Comes Along. 2000. 272p. pap. 14.00 (*0-345-43739-X*) Ballantine Bks.
—Until the Real Thing Comes Along. l.t. ed. 1999. 27.95 (*1-56895-764-5*, Wheeler Publishing, Inc.) Gale Group.
Bernays, Anne. Professor Romeo. 1989. 288p. 18.95 o.p. (*1-55584-218-6*) Grove/Atlantic, Inc.
—Professor Romeo. 1997. 287p. reprint ed. pap. 15.95 (*0-87451-809-1*, Hardscrabble Bks.) Univ. Pr. of New England.
—Professor Romeo. 1990. 288p. reprint ed. pap. 7.95 o.p. (*0-14-014416-1*, Penguin Bks.) Viking Penguin.
Berry, Carole. Nightmare Point. 1993. 264p. 18.95 o.p. (*0-312-08889-2*, Saint Martin's Minotaur) St. Martin's Pr.
Bigsby, Christopher W. Hester: A Novel about the Early Hester Prynne. 1994. 208p. 21.95 o.p. (*0-670-85588-X*, Viking) Viking Penguin.
Birchard, Harry. Massachusetts Bay: An Historical Novel. 2000. 464p. pap. 24.99 (*0-7388-2028-8*); text 34.99 (*0-7388-2027-X*); E-Book 8.00 (*0-7388-8678-5*) Xlibris Corp.
Bittle, Camilla R. Dear Family. 1991. 272p. 17.95 o.p. (*0-312-05847-0*) St. Martin's Pr.
—Friends of the Family. 1993. 240p. 19.95 o.p. (*0-312-10464-2*) St. Martin's Pr.
Black, Veronica. My Pilgrim Love. l.t. ed. 1997. pap. 18.95 o.p. (*0-7838-1971-4*, Macmillan Reference USA) Gale Group.
Blake, Cindy. Second Wives. 2000. 432p. mass mkt. 6.99 (*0-312-97121-4*, St. Martin's Paperbacks); 2000. mass mkt. (*0-312-97568-6*); 1999. 336p. 24.95 o.p. (*0-312-19328-9*) St. Martin's Pr.
Blake, Michelle. Earth Has No Sorrow. 2001. 272p. 23.95 o.p. (*0-399-14747-0*, Putnam & Grosset) Penguin Group (USA) Inc.
Blanc, Nero. Corpus de Crossword. 2003. 320p. pap. 13.00 (*0-425-19021-8*, Prime Crime) Berkley Publishing Group.
—The Crossword Connection. 2001. (Illus.). 256p. pap. 12.00 (*0-425-17950-8*, Prime Crime) Berkley Publishing Group.
—The Crossword Murder. 320p. 2000. mass mkt. 5.99 (*0-425-17701-7*); 1999. pap. 13.00 (*0-425-16977-4*, Prime Crime) Berkley Publishing Group.
—A Crossworder's Holiday. 208p. 2003. pap. 13.00 (*0-425-19260-1*); 2002. 22.95 (*0-425-18733-0*) Berkley Publishing Group. (Prime Crime).
—Two Down: A New Crossword Murder Mystery with Crosswords included. 2000. (Illus.). 304p. pap. 13.00 (*0-425-17510-3*, Prime Crime) Berkley Publishing Group.
Blume, Judy. Summer Sisters: A Novel. l.t. ed. 1998. 441p. (*0-7540-1203-4*) BBC Audiobooks America.
—Summer Sisters: A Novel. unabr. ed. 1998. audio 48.00 (*0-7366-4211-0*, 4709) Books on Tape, Inc.
—Summer Sisters: A Novel. 416p. 1999. mass mkt. 7.99 (*0-440-22643-0*); 1998. 21.95 o.s.i (*0-385-32405-7*, Delacorte Pr.) Dell Publishing.
—Summer Sisters: A Novel. abr. ed. 1998. audio 18.00 (*0-671-58245-3*, 396066, Simon & Schuster Audioworks) Simon & Schuster Audio.
—Summer Sisters: A Novel. l.t. ed. 1998. (Basic Ser.). 443p. 30.95 (*0-7862-1536-4*) Thorndike Pr.
—Summer Sisters: A Novel. 1999. 13.55 (*0-606-16457-X*) Turtleback Bks.
Blumenthal, Michael. Weinstock among the Dying. 1993. 386p. 22.95 o.p. (*0-944072-34-8*, Zoland Bks., Inc.) Steerforth Pr.
Boyer, Rick. Billingsgate Shoal. 1989. 320p. mass mkt. 5.99 o.s.i (*0-8041-0551-0*, Ivy Bks.) Ballantine Bks.
—Billingsgate Shoal. unabr. ed. 1997. audio 56.95 Blackstone Audio Bks., Inc.
—Billingsgate Shoal, 001. 1982. 288p. 11.95 o.p. (*0-395-32041-0*) Houghton Mifflin Co.
—Billingsgate Shoal. 1985. 258p. mass mkt. 3.50 o.s.i (*0-446-32739-5*) Warner Bks., Inc.
—The Daisy Ducks. 1988. 288p. reprint ed. mass mkt. 3.50 o.s.i (*0-8041-0293-7*, Ivy Bks.) Ballantine Bks.
—The Daisy Ducks, 001. 1986. 276p. 15.95 o.p. (*0-395-35289-4*) Houghton Mifflin Co.
—Gone to Earth. 1991. (Boston Mysteries Ser.). mass mkt. 4.99 o.s.i (*0-8041-0611-8*, Ivy Bks.) Ballantine Bks.
—The Man Who Whispered. 1998. (Doc Adams Mysteries Ser.). 272p. mass mkt. 6.50 o.s.i (*0-8041-1044-1*, Ivy Bks.) Ballantine Bks.
—Moscow Metal. l.t. ed. 1991. pap. 8.95 o.p. (*1-55504-884-6*, 182); 1989. 21.95 o.p. (*1-55504-883-8*, 699) BBC Audiobooks America.
—Moscow Metal. 1988. 288p. reprint ed. mass mkt. 3.95 o.s.i (*0-8041-0292-9*, Ivy Bks.) Ballantine Bks.
—Moscow Metal: A Doc Adams Suspense Novel. 1987. 15.95 o.p. (*0-395-42737-1*) Houghton Mifflin Co.
—The Penny Ferry. 1990. 304p. mass mkt. 4.99 o.s.i (*0-8041-0550-2*, Ivy Bks.) Ballantine Bks.
—The Penny Ferry, 001. 1984. 13.95 o.p. (*0-395-35288-6*) Houghton Mifflin Co.
—The Penny Ferry. 1986. 272p. mass mkt. 3.50 o.s.i (*0-446-32741-7*) Warner Bks., Inc.
—Pirate Trade. 1994. (Doc Adams Mysteries Ser.). mass mkt. 4.99 o.s.i (*0-8041-0612-6*, Ivy Bks.) Ballantine Bks.
—The Whale's Footprints. 1989. 288p. mass mkt. 4.99 o.s.i (*0-8041-0450-6*, Ivy Bks.) Ballantine Bks.
—The Whale's Footprints. l.t. ed. 1989. (General Ser.). 392p. lib. bdg. 18.95 o.p. (*0-8161-4764-7*, Macmillan Reference USA) Gale Group.
—The Whale's Footprints. 1988. 288p. 17.95 o.p. (*0-395-42738-X*) Houghton Mifflin Co.
—Yellow Bird. (Boston Mysteries Ser.). 1992. mass mkt. 4.99 o.s.i (*0-8041-1036-0*, Ivy Bks.); 1991. 352p. 17.00 o.p. (*0-449-90506-3*, Fawcett) Ballantine Bks.
Bradley, Don. Angels in a Harsh World. 1997. pap. text 17.95 (*1-888298-02-2*) Native Planet Publishing.
—Angels in a Harsh World. 1998. 19.95 o.p. (*0-399-14359-9*, G. P. Putnam's Sons) Penguin Group (USA) Inc.
Bradley, Don & Olsten, Haley. Angels in a Harsh World: A Novel. 1999. 320p. reprint ed. pap. 13.00 o.s.i (*0-425-16690-2*) Berkley Publishing Group.
Braver, Gary. Elixir. 2000. 352p. 25.95 (*0-312-87308-5*, Forge Bks.); 2001. 448p. reprint ed. mass mkt. 7.99 (*0-8125-7591-1*, Tor Bks.) Doherty, Tom Assocs., LLC.
Burke, Arleen Carroll. The Motherhood of Man: And Other Tales of the Heart. 124p. pap. 7.95 (*0-9721881-0-X*) Burke, Arleen.
Butler, Pierce. A Riddle of Stars. 1999. 287p. pap. o.p. (*1-58195-007-1*, Zoland Bks., Inc.) Steerforth Pr.
Callahan, Sheila M. Forty Whacks. 1994. (Brian Donodio Mystery Ser.). 208p. 18.95 o.p. (*0-312-11362-5*, Saint Martin's Minotaur) St. Martin's Pr.
Carlisle, Henry. The Jonah Man. 1984. (Illus.). 260p. 13.95 o.s.i (*0-394-52942-1*) Knopf, Alfred A. Inc.
—The Jonah Man. 1985. 272p. pap. 5.95 o.p. (*0-14-008110-0*, Penguin Bks.) Viking Penguin.
Carpenter, William. A Keeper of Sheep. 340p. 1994. 21.95 (*1-57131-000-2*); 1996. reprint ed. pap. 13.95 (*1-57131-007-X*) Milkweed Editions.
Carroll, James. The City Below. 1996. 432p. pap. 14.00 (*0-395-82522-9*); 1994. 422p. 22.95 o.s.i (*0-395-59070-1*) Houghton Mifflin Co.
Carter, Stephen L. The Emperor of Ocean Park: A Novel. unabr. ed. 2002. audio compact disk 160.00 (*0-7366-8646-0*);Pt. 1. audio 80.00 (*0-7366-8645-2*);Pt. 2. audio 80.00 (*0-7366-8740-8*) Books on Tape, Inc.
—The Emperor of Ocean Park: A Novel. 2003. 672p. reprint ed. pap. 14.00 (*0-375-71292-5*, Vintage) Knopf Publishing Group.
—The Emperor of Ocean Park: A Novel. 2002. 672p. 26.95 (*0-375-41363-4*) Knopf, Alfred A. Inc.
—The Emperor of Ocean Park: A Novel. abr. ed. 2002. audio 26.95 (*0-553-71337-X*); audio compact disk 29.95 (*0-553-71338-8*) Random Hse. Audio Publishing Group. (RH Audio).
—The Emperor of Ocean Park: A Novel. l.t. ed. 2002. 1152p. 26.95 (*0-375-43165-9*) Random Hse. Large Print.
Cashdan, Linda. It's Only Love: A Novel. 1992. 336p. 19.95 o.p. (*0-312-07811-0*) St. Martin's Pr.
Cassara, Ernest. Murder on Beacon Hill. 1995. 201p. (Orig.). pap. 10.00 (*0-9625794-6-7*) Miniver, Anne Pr.
—Murder on Boston Common: A Father Ballou & His Dog Spot Mystery. 1998. 174p. pap. 9.95 (*0-9662870-0-2*) Cambridge Cornerstone Pr.
Cavanaugh, Jack. The Colonists. (American Family Portrait Ser.). 500p. (Orig.). pap. 13.99 (*1-56476-346-3*, 6-3346) Cook Communications Ministries.
—The Puritans. 1994. (American Family Portrait Ser.). 426p. (Orig.). pap. 11.99 o.p. (*1-56476-239-4*, 6-3239) Cook Communications Ministries.
—Puritans: An American Family Portrait. rev. ed. (American Family Portrait Ser.: Vol. 1). 432p. pap. 13.99 (*1-56476-440-0*) Cook Communications Ministries.
Ceremony. 1982. 12.95 o.s.i (*0-385-28127-7*) Doubleday Publishing.
Chance, Megan. Susannah Morrow. 2003. 480p. mass mkt. 7.50 (*0-446-61323-1*); 2002. 416p. 24.95 (*0-446-52953-2*) Warner Bks., Inc.
Charyn, Jerome. The Seventh Babe. 1984. 352p. pap. 2.95 o.p. (*0-380-51540-7*, 51540, Avon Bks.); 1979. 9.95 o.p. (*0-87795-220-5*, Morrow, William & Co.) Morrow/Avon.
—The Seventh Babe. 1996. 352p. (C). 46.00 (*0-87805-898-2*); pap. 16.95 (*0-87805-882-6*) Univ. Pr. of Mississippi.
Child, Lydia M. Hobomok: A Tale of Early Times. 1972. reprint ed. 16.50 o.p. (*0-8422-8185-1*) Irvington Pubs.
Child, Lydia Maria. Hobomok & Other Writings on Indians. Karcher, Carolyn L., ed. 1986. (American Women Writers Ser.). 350p. (C). pap. 15.00 (*0-8135-1164-X*); text 40.00 (*0-8135-1163-1*) Rutgers Univ. Pr.
Clapp, Patricia C. Constance: A Story of Early Plymouth. 1993. (J). (gr. 5-9). 20.25 (*0-8446-6647-5*) Smith, Peter Pub., Inc.
Clark, Mary Higgins. Remember Me. unabr. ed. 1995. audio 56.00 (*0-7366-2920-3*, 3618) Books on Tape, Inc.
—Remember Me. 1997. reprint ed. lib. bdg. 15.95 (*1-56849-589-7*) Buccaneer Bks., Inc.
—Remember Me. 2000. E-Book 9.95 (*0-7432-0622-3*, Simon & Schuster); 1995. 352p. mass mkt. 7.99 (*0-671-86709-1*, Pocket); 1994. 304p. 23.50 o.s.i (*0-671-86708-3*, Simon & Schuster); 1994. 26.00 (*0-671-89468-4*, Simon & Schuster) Simon & Schuster.
—Remember Me. abr. ed. 1994. audio 18.00 (*0-671-88793-9*, 391464, Simon & Schuster Audioworks) Simon & Schuster Audio.
—Where Are the Children? E-Book 9.95 (*1-930161-68-9*) Adobe Systems, Inc.
—Where Are the Children? 2000. E-Book 9.95 (*0-7432-0611-8*); 1999. (Illus.). 272p. 25.00 (*0-684-86356-1*) Simon & Schuster. (Simon & Schuster).
Cluster, Dick. Obligations of the Bone. 1992. 18.95 o.p. (*0-312-08274-6*, Saint Martin's Minotaur) St. Martin's Pr.
Coburn, Andrew. No Way Home. 1992. 288p. 20.00 o.p. (*0-525-93470-7*, Dutton) Dutton/Plume.
—No Way Home. 1993. 352p. mass mkt. 4.99 o.s.i (*0-451-17675-8*, Signet Bks.) NAL.
—Voices in the Dark. 1994. 304p. 19.95 o.p. (*0-525-93644-0*, Dutton) Dutton/Plume.
—Voices in the Dark. 1995. 304p. mass mkt. 4.99 o.p. (*0-451-40590-0*, Onyx) NAL.
Conant, Susan. Animal Appetite: A Dog Lover's Mystery. 1998. (Dog Lover's Mysteries Ser.). 304p. reprint ed. mass mkt. 5.99 o.s.i (*0-553-57186-9*, Crimeline) Bantam Bks.
—Animal Appetite: A Dog Lover's Mystery. 1997. 288p. 21.95 o.s.i (*0-385-47725-2*) Doubleday Publishing.
—The Barker Street Regulars: A Dog Lover's Mystery. 1999. (Dog Lover's Mysteries Ser.). 288p. mass mkt. 6.99 (*0-553-57655-0*) Bantam Bks.
—The Barker Street Regulars: A Dog Lover's Mystery. l.t. ed. 1998. (Large Print Book Ser.). pap. 23.95 (*1-56895-609-6*, Wheeler Publishing, Inc.) Gale Group.
—Bite of Death. 1991. 4.50 (*1-55773-490-9*) Ace Bks.
—Bite of Death. 1994. mass mkt. 5.99 o.s.i (*0-425-14542-5*) Berkley Publishing Group.
—Black Ribbon: A Dog Lover's Mystery. 1995. (Dog Lover's Mysteries Ser.). 288p. reprint ed. mass mkt. 5.99 o.s.i (*0-553-29875-5*, Crimeline) Bantam Bks.
—Bloodlines. 1993. (Dog Lover's Mysteries Ser.). 272p. mass mkt. 5.99 (*0-553-29886-0*) Bantam Bks.
—Creature Discomforts. 2001. (Dog Lover's Mysteries Ser.). 224p. mass mkt. 6.99 (*0-553-58059-0*, Spectra) Bantam Bks.
—Creature Discomforts: A Dog Lover's Mystery. l.t. ed. 2001. (Beeler Large Print Mystery Ser.). 228p. 25.95 (*1-57490-360-8*, Beeler Large Print Bks.) Beeler, Thomas T. Publisher.
—Creature Discomforts: A Dog Lover's Mystery. 2000. 256p. 22.95 o.s.i (*0-385-49446-7*) Doubleday Publishing.
—Dead & Doggone. 2003. (Mystery Ser.). 27.95 (*1-57490-466-3*) Beeler, Thomas T. Publisher.
—Dead & Doggone. 1990. mass mkt. 5.99 o.s.i (*0-425-14429-1*, Prime Crime) Berkley Publishing Group.
—Evil Breeding. 2000. (Dog Lover's Mysteries Ser.). 224p. reprint ed. mass mkt. 6.99 (*0-553-58052-3*) Bantam Bks.
—Gone to the Dogs: A Dog Lover's Mystery. 1992. (Dog Lover's Mysteries Ser.). 272p. mass mkt. 5.99 (*0-553-29734-1*) Bantam Bks.
—Gone to the Dogs: A Dog Lover's Mystery. l.t. ed. 2003. (Mystery Ser.). 27.95 (*1-57490-488-4*, Beeler Large Print Bks.) Beeler, Thomas T. Publisher.
—Gone to the Dogs: A Dog Lover's Mystery. 1992. 224p. 16.50 o.s.i (*0-385-42378-0*) Doubleday Publishing.
—New Leash on Death. 1990. 4.50 (*1-55773-385-6*) Berkley Publishing Group.
—A New Leash on Death. 1994. 192p. mass mkt. 5.99 (*0-425-14622-7*) Berkley Publishing Group.
—Paws Before Dying. 1991. 4.50 (*1-55773-550-6*) Ace Bks.
—Paws Before Dying. 1991. mass mkt. 5.99 o.s.i (*0-425-14430-5*) Berkley Publishing Group.
—Ruffly Speaking: A Dog Lover's Mystery. 1994. (Dog Lover's Mysteries Ser.). 304p. mass mkt. 6.99 (*0-553-29484-9*) Bantam Bks.
—Stud Rites: A Dog Lover's Mystery. 1997. (Dog Lover's Mysteries Ser.). 272p. mass mkt. 5.99 o.s.i (*0-553-57300-4*, Crimeline) Bantam Bks.
—The Wicked Flea. 304p. 2002. 22.95 (*0-425-18334-3*); 2003. reprint ed. mass mkt. 6.99 (*0-425-18885-X*) Berkley Publishing Group. (Prime Crime).
Conde, Maryse. I, Tituba, Black Witch of Salem. Philcox, Richard, tr. from FRE. 1992. (CARAF Ser.). 248p. (C). text 19.95 o.p. (*0-8139-1398-5*) Univ. Pr. of Virginia.
—Moi, Tituba Sorciere. 1988. (FRE.). 276p. pap. 11.95 (*0-7859-2087-0*, 2070379299) French & European Pubns., Inc.
Connolly, James B. Out of Gloucester. 2000. 252p. E-Book 9.95 (*0-594-03638-0*) 1873 Pr.
—Out of Gloucester. 1977. (Short Story Index Reprint Ser.). 26.95 (*0-8369-3091-6*) Ayer Co. Pubs., Inc.
Connors, Rose. Absolute Certainty. 2003. 304p. E-Book 24.00 (*0-7432-3366-2*, Scribner); 2003. (Illus.). 320p. mass mkt. 6.99 (*0-7434-4881-2*, Pocket Star); 2002. 304p. 24.00 (*0-7432-2906-1*, Scribner) Simon & Schuster.
—Absolute Certainty. 2002. (Basic Ser.). 27.95 (*0-7862-4791-6*) Thorndike Pr.
—Temporary Sanity. 2003. 320p. 24.00 (*0-7432-2907-X*, Scribner) Simon & Schuster.
—Temporary Sanity. l.t. ed. 2003. 467p. 28.95 (*0-7862-5907-8*) Thorndike Pr.
Cook, Robin. Harmful Intent. 1991. 368p. mass mkt. 7.99 (*0-425-12546-7*) Berkley Publishing Group.
—Harmful Intent. 1990. 368p. 18.95 o.p. (*0-399-13481-6*, G. P. Putnam's Sons) Penguin Putnam Bks. for Young Readers.
—Harmful Intent. 18.95 o.s.i (*0-399-13700-9*) Putnam Publishing Group, The.
—Harmful Intent. l.t. ed. 2000. (Famous Authors Ser.). 663p. 28.95 (*0-7862-2504-1*) Thorndike Pr.
—Harmful Intent. 1991. 14.04 (*0-606-00927-2*) Turtleback Bks.
—Shock. 2002. pap. 7.99 (*0-425-17714-9*) Berkley Publishing Group.
—Shock. 2001. 368p. 24.95 o.p. (*0-399-14600-8*) Penguin Group (USA) Inc.
Cook, Thomas H. The Chatham School Affair. 1997. 336p. mass mkt. 6.99 (*0-553-57193-1*) Bantam Bks.
—The Chatham School Affair. unabr. ed. 2000. audio 60.00 (*0-7887-0622-5*, 94796E7) Recorded Bks., LLC.
Cooke, Elizabeth & Wharton, Edith. Zeena. 1996. 352p. 23.95 o.p. (*0-312-14775-9*) St. Martin's Pr.
Cooper, James Fenimore. Lionel Lincoln: Or, The Leaguer of Boston. 1985. (Writings of James Fenimore Cooper Ser.). 437p. (C). text 25.50 (*0-87395-416-5*); pap. text 24.95 (*0-87395-671-0*) State Univ. of New York Pr.
Craig, Philip R. A Beautiful Place to Die: A Martha's Vineyard Mystery. 1989. 224p. 18.95 o.s.i (*0-684-19122-9*, Macmillan Reference USA) Gale Group.
—A Beautiful Place to Die: A Martha's Vineyard Mystery. 1991. 224p. mass mkt. 6.99 (*0-380-71155-9*, Avon Bks.) Morrow/Avon.
—A Case of Vineyard Poison. 1996. 224p. mass mkt. 5.99 (*0-380-72679-3*, Avon Bks.) Morrow/Avon.
—A Case of Vineyard Poison: A Martha's Vineyard Mystery. 1995. 253p. 20.00 o.p. (*0-684-19616-6*, Scribner) Simon & Schuster.
—Cliff Hanger: A Martha's Vineyard Mystery. 1993. 256p. 20.00 o.p. (*0-684-19552-6*, Macmillan Reference USA) Gale Group.
—Cliff Hanger: A Martha's Vineyard Mystery. 1994. 224p. mass mkt. 4.99 (*0-380-72240-2*, Avon Bks.) Morrow/Avon.
—A Deadly Vineyard Holiday. 1998. (Martha's Vineyard Mysteries Ser.). 240p. mass mkt. 6.50 (*0-380-73110-X*, Avon Bks.) Morrow/Avon.
—A Deadly Vineyard Holiday: A Martha's Vineyard Mystery. 1997. 282p. 20.50 (*0-684-19718-9*, Scribner) Simon & Schuster.
—A Deadly Vineyard Holiday: A Martha's Vineyard Mystery. l.t. ed. 1997. (Core Ser.). 344p. lib. bdg. 26.95 (*0-7838-8278-5*) Thorndike Pr.
—Death on a Vineyard Beach. 1997. 224p. mass mkt. 6.50 (*0-380-72873-7*, Avon Bks.) Morrow/Avon.
—Death on a Vineyard Beach: A Martha's Vineyard Mystery. 1996. 288p. 21.00 o.p. (*0-684-19717-0*, Scribner) Simon & Schuster.
—The Double Minded Men: A Martha's Vineyard Mystery. 1992. (Martha's Vineyard Mystery Ser.: No. 3). 256p. text 20.00 (*0-684-19396-5*, Macmillan Reference USA) Gale Group.

Settings

—The Double Minded Men: A Martha's Vineyard Mystery. 1993. 256p. pap. 4.99 (*0-380-71973-8*, Avon Bks.) Morrow/Avon.
—A Fatal Vineyard Season. 2000. (Martha's Vineyard Mysteries Ser.). 224p. mass mkt. 5.99 (*0-380-73289-0*, Avon Bks.) Morrow/Avon.
—A Fatal Vineyard Season: A Martha's Vineyard Mystery. 1999. (Martha's Vineyard Mysteries Ser.). (Illus.). 224p. 22.00 o.s.i (*0-684-85544-5*, Scribner) Simon & Schuster.
—A Fatal Vineyard Season: A Martha's Vineyard Mystery. l.t. ed. 1999. (Mystery Ser.). (Illus.). 324p. 28.95 (*0-7862-2207-7*) Thorndike Pr.
—Off Season. 1996. (Martha's Vineyard Ser.: No. 5). 224p. mass mkt. 5.99 (*0-380-72588-6*, Avon Bks.) Morrow/Avon.
—Off Season: A Martha's Vineyard Mystery. 1994. 256p. 20.00 (*0-684-19617-4*, Macmillan Reference USA) Gale Group.
—A Shoot on Martha's Vineyard. 1999. (Martha's Vineyard Mysteries Ser.). 256p. mass mkt. 5.99 (*0-380-73201-7*, Avon Bks.) Morrow/Avon.
—Shoot on Martha's Vineyard: A Martha's Vineyard Mystery. 1998. (Martha's Vineyard Mysteries Ser.). 288p. 22.00 (*0-684-83454-5*, Scribner) Simon & Schuster.
—A Shoot on Martha's Vineyard: A Martha's Vineyard Mystery. l.t. ed. 1999. (Mystery Ser.). 427p. 27.95 (*0-7862-1614-X*) Thorndike Pr.
—Vineyard Blues: A Martha's Vineyard Mystery. 2001. 224p. mass mkt. 5.99 (*0-380-81859-0*, Avon Bks.) Morrow/Avon.
—Vineyard Blues: A Martha's Vineyard Mystery. 2000. (Martha's Vineyard Mysteries Ser.). (Illus.). 224p. 23.00 o.s.i (*0-684-83455-3*, Scribner) Simon & Schuster.
—Vineyard Blues: A Martha's Vineyard Mystery. l.t. ed. 2000. (Mystery Ser.). (Illus.). 339p. 29.95 (*0-7862-2591-2*) Thorndike Pr.
—Vineyard Enigma: A Martha Vineyard Mystery. 2002. (Illus.). 256p. 24.00 (*0-7432-0523-5*, Scribner) Simon & Schuster.
—Vineyard Shadows: A Martha's Vineyard Mystery. 2002. 256p. mass mkt. 6.50 (*0-380-82099-4*) Morrow/Avon.
—Vineyard Shadows: A Martha's Vineyard Mystery. l.t. ed. 2001. 334p. 29.95 (*0-7862-3646-9*) Thorndike Pr.
—The Woman Who Walked into the Sea: A Martha's Vineyard Mystery. 1993. 224p. reprint ed. mass mkt. 4.99 (*0-380-71536-8*, Avon Bks.) Morrow/Avon.
—The Woman Who Walked into the Sea: A Martha's Vineyard Mystery. 1991. 224p. 17.95 o.s.i (*0-684-19228-4*, Scribner) Simon & Schuster.
Craig, Philip R. & Tapply, William G. First Light: The First Ever Brady Coyne/J. W. Jackson Novel. 2002. 352p. E-Book 24.00 (*0-7432-3484-7*); 24.00 (*0-7432-2208-3*) Simon & Schuster. (Scribner).
Creamer, Hannah Gardner. Delia's Doctors; or, a Glance Behind the Scenes. 2003. 296p. text 39.95 (*0-252-02807-4*); pap. text 14.95 (*0-252-07108-5*) Univ. of Illinois Pr.
Curran, Mary Doyle. The Parish & the Hill. (Contemporary Classics by Women Ser.). 2002. 280p. pap. 15.95 (*1-55861-396-X*); 1986. 272p. reprint ed. pap. 12.95 o.p. (*0-935312-58-7*) Feminist Pr. at The City Univ. of New York.
Dailey, Janet. That Boston Man: Massachusetts. l.t. ed. 2000. (G. K. Hall Core Ser.). 216p. 29.95 (*0-7838-9122-9*, Macmillan Reference USA) Gale Group.
—That Boston Man: Massachusetts. 1991. (Americana Ser.: No. 871). mass mkt. (*0-373-89871-1*); 1987. pap. (*0-373-89821-5*) Harlequin Enterprises, Ltd. (Harlequin Bks.).
—That Boston Man: Massachusetts. 2002. 128p. pap. 6.99 (*0-7592-3831-6*); E-Book 6.99 (*0-7592-0172-2*); E-Book 6.99 (*1-58586-392-0*); E-Book 6.99 (*0-7592-0916-2*) ereads.com.
Dandola, John. Wicked Is the Wind: A Jeffrey Devereaux—Kirsten Eriksson Novel. 2001. (Illus.). 222p. pap. 11.95 (*1-878452-28-2*, Compass Point Mysteries) Quincannon Publishing Group.
Daniel, David. The Heaven Stone. 1994. 256p. 20.95 o.p. (*0-312-11282-3*, Saint Martin's Minotaur) St. Martin's Pr.
—The Skelly Man: An Alex Rasmussen Mystery. 1995. 208p. 20.95 o.p. (*0-312-13602-1*, Saint Martin's Minotaur) St. Martin's Pr.
David, Lawrence. Family Values: A Novel. 1993. 256p. 20.00 o.s.i (*0-671-73215-3*, Simon & Schuster) Simon & Schuster.
De Forest, John W. Witching Times. 1976. (Monument Edition Ser.). 24.50 o.p. (*0-271-00505-X*) Pennsylvania State Univ. Pr.
—Witching Times. Appel, Alfred, Jr., ed. 1967. 416p. pap. 26.95 (*0-8084-0333-8*) Rowman & Littlefield Pubs., Inc.
Degenhard, William. The Regulators. 1981. 598p. reprint ed. 28.00 (*0-933256-22-1*); pap. 16.00 o.p. (*0-933256-23-X*) Second Chance Pr.
Delinsky, Barbara. Dreams. 1999. 448p. pap. (*1-55166-627-8*, Mira Bks.) Harlequin Enterprises, Ltd.
—Passion & Illusion. l.t. ed. 1996. (Large Print Bks.). 23.95 o.p. (*1-56895-278-3*, Wheeler Publishing, Inc.) Gale Group.
—Passion & Illusion. 1994. 336p. mass mkt. 7.99 (*0-06-104232-3*) Morrow/Avon.
—Together Alone. 1995. 384p. 20.00 o.p. (*0-06-017780-2*) HarperCollins Pubs.
Dershowitz, Alan M. The Advocate's Devil. abr. ed. 1994. audio 17.95 o.p. (*0-7871-0408-6*, Dove Audio) NewStar Media, Inc.
—The Advocate's Devil. 1999. 352p. reprint ed. lib. bdg. 35.95 (*0-7351-0066-7*) Replica Bks.
—The Advocate's Devil. 384p. 2001. pap. 4.95 (*0-446-51759-3*); 1995. mass mkt. 6.50 (*0-446-60291-4*) Warner Bks., Inc.
Desai, Anita. Fasting, Feasting. 2000. 240p. pap. 13.00 (*0-618-06582-2*, Mariner Bks.) Houghton Mifflin Co. Trade & Reference Div.
—Fasting, Feasting. 1999. 227p. (*0-7011-6894-3*) Random Hse. of Canada, Ltd. CAN. *Dist:* Random Hse., Inc.
—Fasting, Feasting. l.t. ed. 2000. (Basic Ser.). 323p. 27.95 (*0-7862-2638-2*); (*0-7540-4239-1*); (*0-7540-4240-5*) Thorndike Pr.
Devane, Terry. Juror Number Eleven: A Novel. 2003. 336p. mass mkt. 6.99 (*0-425-19066-8*) Berkley Publishing Group.
—Juror Number Eleven: A Novel. 2002. 320p. 24.95 o.s.i (*0-399-14886-8*) Penguin Group (USA) Inc.
—Uncommon Justice. 2002. 352p. reprint ed. mass mkt. 6.99 (*0-425-18424-2*) Berkley Publishing Group.
—Uncommon Justice. 2001. 240p. 24.95 o.p. (*0-399-14717-9*) Penguin Group (USA) Inc.
Devereaux, Margaret. Ride the Restless Tide: A Story of Old Marblehead. 2000. 416p. pap. 24.99 (*0-7388-1135-1*); text 34.99 (*0-7388-1134-3*) Xlibris Corp.
Dew, Robb Forman. Fortunate Lives: A Novel. 1993. 288p. pap. 11.00 o.p. (*0-06-097536-9*, Perennial) HarperTrade.
—Fortunate Lives: A Novel. 1992. 288p. 20.00 o.p. (*0-688-10781-8*, Morrow, William & Co.) Morrow/Avon.
—Fortunate Lives: A Novel. unabr. ed. 1992. audio 60.00 (*1-55690-704-4*, 92429E7) Recorded Bks., LLC.
—Fortunate Lives: A Novel. pap. 4.98 o.p. (*0-8317-4358-1*) Smithmark Pubs., Inc.
Diamant, Anita. Good Harbor: A Novel. l.t. ed. 2001. 31.95 (*1-58724-140-4*, Wheeler Publishing, Inc.) Gale Group.
—Good Harbor: A Novel. 256p. 2002. E-Book (*0-7432-2976-2*); 2001. 25.00 (*0-7432-2532-5*); 2002. reprint ed. pap. 13.00 (*0-7432-2572-4*) Simon & Schuster. (Scribner).
Dix, Beulah Marie. Soldier Rigdale. 2000. 252p. E-Book 3.95 (*0-594-02109-X*) 1873 Pr.
Dobson, Joanne. Cold & Pure & Very Dead. 2001. 304p. mass mkt. 6.99 (*0-553-58002-7*) Bantam Bks.
—Cold & Pure & Very Dead: A Karen Pelletier Mystery. 2000. 272p. 22.95 o.s.i (*0-385-49340-1*) Doubleday Publishing.
—Quieter Than Sleep. 1998. 336p. reprint ed. mass mkt. 6.99 (*0-553-57660-7*) Bantam Bks.
Doolittle, Jerome. Kill Story. 304p. 1996. mass mkt. 5.99 (*0-671-79981-9*, Pocket); 1995. 22.00 o.p. (*0-671-79980-0*, Atria) Simon & Schuster.
—Strangle Hold. Grose, Bill, ed. 1992. 304p. reprint ed. mass mkt. 4.99 (*0-671-74571-9*, Pocket) Simon & Schuster.
—Stranglehold: A Tom Bethany Mystery. 1991. 304p. 20.00 (*0-671-70754-X*, Atria) Simon & Schuster.
Downing, Michael. Perfect Agreement. 1997. 224p. 22.00 (*1-887178-45-7*, Counterpoint Pr.) Basic Bks.
—Perfect Agreement. 1998. 288p. reprint ed. pap. 12.95 o.s.i (*0-425-16628-7*) Berkley Publishing Group.
Dubus, Andre, III. Bluesman: A Novel. 276p. 1994. pap. 12.95 o.p. (*0-571-19841-4*); 1993. text 22.95 o.p. (*0-571-19812-0*) Faber & Faber, Inc.
—Bluesman: A Novel. 2001. 336p. pap. 13.00 (*0-375-72516-4*, Vintage) Knopf Publishing Group.
Dwyer, Kelly. The Tracks of Angels. 1994. 22.95 o.p. (*0-399-13882-X*, G. P. Putnam's Sons) Penguin Group (USA) Inc.
—The Tracks of Angels. 1995. 272p. pap. 17.99 (*0-446-67052-9*) Warner Bks., Inc.
Eastlake, William. The Long Naked Descent into Boston. 1977. (Richard Seaver Bks.). 10.00 o.p. (*0-670-43852-9*) Viking Penguin.
Edward, Jonathan. Yankee Doodle. 1993. 176p. 22.00 (*1-881119-63-7*); 1993. 176p. pap. 13.00 (*1-881119-79-3*); 1994. 173p. 95.00 o.p. (*1-881119-14-9*) Pyncheon Hse.
Eidson, Bill. Dangerous Waters. 1991. 304p. 19.95 o.p. (*0-8050-1767-4*) Holt, Henry & Co.
—The Guardian. 1996. 288p. 22.95 o.p. (*0-312-86115-X*, Forge Bks.) Doherty, Tom Assocs., LLC.
—Guardian. 1998. 288p. mass mkt. 5.99 (*0-8125-4444-7*, Tor Bks.) Doherty, Tom Assocs., LLC.
—The Little Brother. 1990. 272p. 18.95 o.p. (*0-8050-1236-2*) Holt, Henry & Co.
—The Little Brother. 1991. 288p. mass mkt. 4.50 o.s.i (*0-8217-3397-4*, Zebra Bks.) Kensington Publishing Corp.
Elkins, Aaron. Loot. l.t. ed. 1999. 26.95 (*1-56895-750-5*, Wheeler Publishing, Inc.) Gale Group.
—Loot. 1999. 384p. mass mkt. 6.99 (*0-380-73162-2*, Avon Bks.); 320p. 24.00 (*0-688-15927-3*, Morrow, William & Co.) Morrow/Avon.
Engel, Monroe. Fish. 1981. 12.95 o.p. (*0-689-11219-X*, Scribner) Simon & Schuster.
—Fish. 1985. (Phoenix Fiction Ser.). vi, 218p. pap. 6.95 o.s.i (*0-226-20835-4*) Univ. of Chicago Pr.
Engstrom, Elizabeth. Lizzie Borden. 1997. 352p. pap. 14.95 (*0-312-86154-0*, Forge Bks.); 1992. 352p. mass mkt. 4.99 (*0-8125-0591-3*, Tor Bks.); 1990. 18.95 o.p. (*0-312-93204-9*, Tor Bks.) Doherty, Tom Assocs., LLC.
Ephron, G. H. Amnesia. 2000. 295p. 23.95 (*0-312-26867-X*, Saint Martin's Minotaur) St. Martin's Pr.
Faherty, Terence. Orion Rising: An Owen Keane Mystery. 1999. (Owen Keane Mysteries Ser.). 256p. 22.95 (*0-312-20351-9*, Saint Martin's Minotaur) St. Martin's Pr.
Fallis, Gregory. Lightning in the Blood. 1993. 272p. 18.95 o.p. (*0-312-09340-3*, Saint Martin's Minotaur) St. Martin's Pr.
Farber, Thomas. Learning to Love It: Seven Stories & a Novella. 1993. 134p. (Orig.). lib. bdg. 31.00 o.p. (*0-8095-4121-1*) Millefleurs.
Fast, Howard. April Morning. 1987. mass mkt. o.s.i (*0-553-16786-3*); 1983. mass mkt. 3.50 o.s.i (*0-553-25681-5*) Bantam Bks.
—April Morning. 1982. 8.95 o.s.i (*0-517-50681-5*, Crown) Crown Publishing Group.
—April Morning. 1962. 12.55 (*0-606-00355-X*) Turtleback Bks.
Fielding, Joy. Don't Cry Now. 1996. 480p. mass mkt. 7.99 (*0-7704-2721-9*) Bantam Bks.
—Don't Cry Now. abr. ed. 1996. audio 7.99 o.p. (*1-56740-111-2*, 1578, Paperback Nova Audio Bks.); 1995. audio 17.95 o.p. (*1-56100-422-7*, 1576, Nova Audio Bks.); 1995. audio 73.25 o.p. (*1-56100-254-2*, 868); 1995. audio 23.95 o.p. (*1-56100-629-7*, 93, Bookcassette) Brilliance Audio.
—Don't Cry Now. l.t. ed. 1995. pap. 21.95 o.p. (*1-56895-259-7*, Wheeler Publishing, Inc.) Gale Group.
—Don't Cry Now. 1996. 400p. mass mkt. 7.99 (*0-380-71153-2*, Avon Bks.); 1995. 356p. (YA). 23.00 o.p. (*0-688-12673-1*, Morrow, William & Co.) Morrow/Avon.
—See Jane Run. unabr. ed. 1991. audio 23.95 o.p. (*0-930435-82-6*, 419, Bookcassette); audio 73.25 o.p. (*1-56100-076-0*, 601, Unabridged Library Editions) Brilliance Audio.
—See Jane Run. l.t. ed. 1992. (Magna Large Print Ser.). 624p. o.p. (*0-7505-0333-5*) Magna Large Print Bks. GBR. *Dist:* Ulverscroft Large Print Canada, Ltd.
—See Jane Run. 1991. 420p. 20.00 o.p. (*0-688-08867-8*, Morrow, William & Co.); 1992. 416p. reprint ed. mass mkt. 7.99 (*0-380-71152-4*, Avon Bks.) Morrow/Avon.
—See Jane Run. abr. ed. 1993. 15.95 o.p. (*1-55800-408-4*) NewStar Media, Inc.
Finder, Joseph. Extraordinary Powers. 1995. 448p. mass mkt. 6.99 o.s.i (*0-345-39436-4*); 1994. 464p. 22.00 o.s.i (*0-345-38621-3*) Ballantine Bks.
—Extraordinary Powers. abr. ed. 1995. audio 8.99 o.s.i (*0-679-44352-5*) Knopf, Alfred A. Inc.
—Extraordinary Powers. 1994. audio 17.00 o.p. (*0-679-43051-2*, RH Audio) Random Hse. Audio Publishing Group.
—High Crimes. abr. ed. 1998. audio 7.99 o.s.i (*1-56740-274-7*, 1682, Paperback Nova Audio Bks.); audio 24.95 o.p. (*1-56100-789-7*, 134, Bookcassette); audio 57.25 (*1-56740-568-1*, 896, Unabridged Library Editions) Brilliance Audio.
—High Crimes. 1999. 400p. mass mkt. 7.99 (*0-380-72880-X*, Avon Bks.); 1998. 352p. 24.95 (*0-688-14962-6*, Morrow, William & Co.) Morrow/Avon.
—High Crimes. l.t. ed. 2000. (Charnwood Large Print Ser.). 440p. (*0-7089-9128-9*, Ulverscroft) Thorpe, F. A. Pubs. GBR. *Dist:* Ulverscroft Large Print Bks., Ltd., Ulverscroft Large Print Canada, Ltd.
—High Crimes. 1999. 13.04 (*0-606-19265-4*) Turtleback Bks.
Fitch, Stona. Strategies for Success. 1992. 288p. 21.95 o.p. (*0-399-13735-1*, G. P. Putnam's Sons) Penguin Group (USA) Inc.
Flood, John. Bag Men. 1997. 256p. pap. 9.95 o.s.i (*0-385-32000-0*) Doubleday Publishing.
—Bag Men: A Novel. 1997. 240p. 24.00 o.p. (*0-393-03998-6*) Norton, W. W. & Co., Inc.
Flora, Kate. Chosen for Death. 2003. 256p. pap. 13.00 (*1-932325-00-X*) Crum Creek Pr.
—Chosen for Death. 288p. 1995. mass mkt. 4.99 (*0-8125-3429-8*); 1994. 20.95 o.p. (*0-312-85598-2*) Doherty, Tom Assocs., LLC. (Forge Bks.).
—Death at the Wheel. (Thea Kozak Mystery Ser.). 320p. 1998. mass mkt. 5.99 (*0-8125-6484-7*); 1996. 22.95 o.p. (*0-312-85599-0*) Doherty, Tom Assocs., LLC. (Forge Bks.).
—Death in a Funhouse Mirror. 1995. 352p. 23.95 o.p. (*0-312-85600-8*); Vol. 1. 1996. mass mkt. 5.99 o.p. (*0-8125-3432-8*) Doherty, Tom Assocs., LLC. (Forge Bks.).
—An Educated Death. 384p. 1999. mass mkt. 6.99 (*0-8125-7156-8*); 1997. 23.95 (*0-312-86079-X*) Doherty, Tom Assocs., LLC. (Forge Bks.).
Flynn, Jack. Buddy Reardon in Pursuit of the Lone Ranger. 2002. 29.45 (*1-4033-1909-X*); 2001. 276p. pap. 18.67 (*0-7596-2252-3*) 1stBooks Library.
Flynn, Raymond & Moore, Robin. The Accidental Pope. 2000. 394p. 24.95 (*0-312-26801-7*) St. Martin's Pr.
Forbes, Esther. A Mirror for Witches. 1985. (Cassandra Editions Ser.). (Illus.). 215p. reprint ed. pap. 12.95 (*0-89733-154-0*) Academy Chicago Pubs., Ltd.
—A Mirror for Witches. 21.95 (*0-8488-0050-8*) Amereon, Ltd.
—A Mirror for Witches. 1960. (C). pap. o.p. Harcourt College Pubs.
Ford, Elaine. Life Designs. 1997. 192p. 22.95 o.p. (*0-944072-80-1*, Zoland Bks., Inc.) Steerforth Pr.
Franzen, Jonathan. Strong Motion: A Novel. 1992. 508p. 22.95 o.p. (*0-374-27105-4*) Farrar, Straus & Giroux.
—Strong Motion: A Novel. 1993. 512p. pap. 10.95 (*0-393-30996-7*) Norton, W. W. & Co., Inc.
—Strong Motion: A Novel. 2001. 512p. pap. 14.00 (*0-312-42051-X*) Picador.
Frede, Richard. The Nurses, 001. 1985. 480p. 17.95 o.p. (*0-395-38169-X*) Houghton Mifflin Co.
Fredrickson, Michael. A Cinderella Affidavit. 2000. 450p. mass mkt. 6.99 (*0-8125-8013-3*, Tor Bks.); 1999. 384p. 25.95 (*0-312-86723-9*, Forge Bks.) Doherty, Tom Assocs., LLC.
—A Cinderella Affidavit. unabr. ed. 2000. audio compact disk 119.00 (*0-7887-4210-8*, C1139E7); 1999. audio 96.00 (*0-7887-3764-3*, 95981E7) Recorded Bks., LLC.
Galbraith, John Kenneth. A Tenured Professor. 1991. 208p. pap. 12.95 o.p. (*0-395-57424-2*); 1990. 224p. 19.95 o.p. (*0-395-47100-1*) Houghton Mifflin Co.
Gardner, Barbara. The Sai Prophecy: A Novel. 1999. (Illus.). 260p. pap. 14.95 (*1-55874-679-X*) Health Communications, Inc.
—The Sai Prophecy: A Novel. 1998. 260p. 21.95 (*0-935699-12-0*) Illumination Arts Publishing Co., Inc.
—The Sai Prophecy: A Novel. 1997. E-Book 14.95 (*0-585-10258-9*) netLibrary, Inc.
Gardner, Lisa. The Other Daughter. 10p. 2003. pap. 94.95 incl. audio compact disk (*0-7927-2901-3*); 2000. audio 84.95 (*0-7927-2356-2*, CSL 245, Chivers Sound Library) BBC Audiobooks America.
—The Other Daughter. 1999. 416p. mass mkt. 7.50 (*0-553-57679-8*) Bantam Bks.
—The Other Daughter. l.t. ed. (Thorndike/G. K. Hall Paperback Bestsellers Ser.). 2000. 523p. 28.95 (*0-7862-2291-3*); 1999. 619p. 31.95 (*0-7862-2290-5*) Thorndike Pr.
Geary, Nancy. Redemption. 2004. mass mkt. (*0-446-61389-4*); 2003. 336p. 23.95 (*0-446-52754-8*) Warner Bks., Inc.
Gerritsen, Tess. Harvest. unabr. ed. 1999. audio compact disk 96.00 (*0-7887-3716-3*, C1073E7); 1997. audio 80.00 (*0-7887-0790-6*, 94940E7) Recorded Bks., LLC.
—Harvest. 1997. (Illus.). 368p. mass mkt. 7.99 (*0-671-55302-X*, Pocket); 1996. 352p. 22.00 (*0-671-55301-1*, Atria) Simon & Schuster.
—Harvest. 2003. audio 9.95 (*0-7435-3286-4*, Encore); 1996. audio 18.00 o.s.i (*0-671-57067-6*, 394242, Simon & Schuster Audioworks) Simon & Schuster Audio.
—Harvest Export. 1997. per. 6.99 (*0-671-01370-X*, Pocket) Simon & Schuster.
Giardina, Anthony. Recent History. 2001. E-Book 19.50 (*1-58945-783-8*) Adobe Systems, Inc.
—Recent History. 2002. 272p. pap. 13.95 (*0-375-75938-7*) Random House Adult Trade Publishing Group.
—Recent History: A Novel. 2001. E-Book 19.50 (*0-375-50694-2*) Random Hse., Inc.
Gilman, Charlotte Perkins. The Crux. 2003. 168p. 49.95 (*0-8223-3179-9*); pap. 16.95 (*0-8223-3167-5*) Duke Univ. Pr.
—The Crux. Tuttle, Jennifer S., ed. & intro. by. 2002. (Illus.). 248p. 42.50 (*0-87413-771-3*) Univ. of Delaware Pr.
Gilman, Dorothy. Thale's Folly. 2000. 224p. mass mkt. 6.99 (*0-449-00365-5*); 1999. (*0-449-00364-7*, Fawcett) Ballantine Bks.
—Thale's Folly. l.t. ed. 1999. 26.95 (*1-56895-741-6*, Wheeler Publishing, Inc.) Gale Group.
Giroux, Leo, Jr. The Rishi: A Novel. 1985. 372p. 16.46 o.p. (*0-87131-463-0*) Holt, Henry & Co.

Goldberg, Myra. Rosalind: A Family Romance. 1998. 128p. pap. 13.00 o.p. (0-944072-60-7); 1996. 304p. 22.95 o.p. (0-944072-59-3) Steerforth Pr. (Zoland Bks., Inc.).

Goldstone, Nancy. Mommy & the Money: A Novel. 1997. 240p. 22.50 o.p. (0-06-017526-5) HarperCollins Pubs.

Gordon, Mary. Spending: A Utopian Divertimento. 304p. 1999. pap. 13.00 (0-684-85204-7); 1998. 24.00 (0-684-83945-8) Simon & Schuster. (Scribner).

—Spending: A Utopian Divertimento. 1999. 18.00 (0-671-57994-0, Simon & Schuster Audioworks) Simon & Schuster Audio.

Gordon, Neil. The Gun Runner's Daughter. 2000. 416p. reprint ed. mass mkt. 6.99 o.s.i (0-553-58211-9) Bantam Bks.

Gordon, Noah. Matters of Choice. 1996. 368p. 24.95 o.p. (0-525-94080-4, Dutton) Dutton/Plume.

—Matters of Choice. 1997. 448p. mass mkt. 6.99 o.s.i (0-451-18726-1, Signet Bks.); 1996. pap. 12.95 (0-452-27635-7) NAL.

Goshgarian, Gary. Stone Circle. 1997. 296p. 24.95 o.p. (1-55611-533-4) Fine, Donald I. Bks.

Gotti, Victoria. The Senator's Daughter. 1998. 320p. mass mkt. 6.99 o.p. (0-8125-7176-2); 1997. 304p. 23.95 o.p. (0-312-86323-3) Doherty, Tom Assocs., LLC. (Forge Bks.).

—The Senator's Daughter. l.t. ed. 1997. (Core Ser.). 464p. 26.95 (0-7838-8196-7, Macmillan Reference USA) Gale Group.

—The Senator's Daughter. abr. ed. 1997. audio 23.00 (1-56876-065-5) Soundlines Entertainment, Inc.

—The Senator's Daughter. 1999. 6.99 (0-312-87111-2) St. Martin's Pr.

Graham, Brendan. Element of Fire. 2001. 356p. (0-00-225977-X) HarperCollins Pubs.

Greeley, Andrew M. Star Bright! A Christmas Story. l.t. ed. 1998. 19.95 (1-57490-166-4) Beeler, Thomas T. Publisher.

—Star Bright! A Christmas Story. 1997. 127p. 13.95 (0-312-86387-X); 128p. 111.60 o.s.i (0-312-86500-7) Doherty, Tom Assocs., LLC. (Forge Bks.).

—Star Bright! A Christmas Story. 1999. 13.95 (0-312-87116-3) St. Martin's Pr.

Greene, J. R. More Strange Tales from Old Quabbin. 1999. (Illus.). 126p. pap. 11.95 (1-884132-05-7) Greene, J. R.

—Strange Tales from Old Quabbin. 1993. (Illus.). 136p. (Orig.). pap. 11.95 (1-884132-00-6) Greene, J. R.

Gunning, Sally. Deep Water. 1996. mass mkt. 5.99 (0-671-56313-0, Pocket) Simon & Schuster.

—Dirty Water. 1998. (Peter Bartholomew Mysteries Ser.: Vol. 9). 288p. per. 6.50 o.s.i (0-671-01736-5, Pocket) Simon & Schuster.

—Fire Water. 1999. (Peter Bartholomew Mysteries Ser.: Vol. 7). 304p. pap. 6.50 (0-671-01737-3, Pocket) Simon & Schuster.

—Hot Water. Chelius, Jane, ed. 1990. 256p. (Orig.). mass mkt. 5.99 (0-671-72804-0, Pocket) Simon & Schuster.

—Ice Water. Chelius, Jane, ed. 1993. 256p. (Orig.). mass mkt. 5.50 (0-671-76005-X, Pocket) Simon & Schuster.

—Muddy Water. 1997. (Peter Bartholomew Mysteries Ser.). 256p. mass mkt. 6.50 (0-671-56314-9, Pocket) Simon & Schuster.

—Rough Water. Chelius, Jane, ed. 1994. 304p. (Orig.). mass mkt. 5.50 (0-671-87137-4, Pocket) Simon & Schuster.

—Still Water. 1995. 288p. mass mkt. 5.99 (0-671-87138-2, Pocket) Simon & Schuster.

—Troubled Water. Chelius, Jane, ed. 1993. 240p. (Orig.). mass mkt. 5.50 (0-671-76006-8, Pocket) Simon & Schuster.

—Under Water. Chelius, Jane, ed. 1992. 224p. (Orig.). mass mkt. 5.99 (0-671-72805-9, Pocket) Simon & Schuster.

Habegger, Alfred, ed. The Bostonians. 1985. 496p. pap. text 17.33 o.p. (0-02-348560-4, Macmillan College) Prentice Hall PTR.

Hawthorne, Nathaniel. The Blithedale Romance. 2003. (Dover Thrift Editions Ser.). 176p. pap. 2.50 (0-486-42684-X) Dover Pubns., Inc.

—The Blithedale Romance. 1981. mass mkt. 1.95 o.p. (0-451-51488-2, Signet Classics) NAL.

—The Blithedale Romance. 2001. (Paperback Classics Ser.). 272p. pap. 7.95 (0-375-75720-1, Modern Library) Random House Adult Trade Publishing Group.

—The Scarlet Letter. 2002. pap. 3.95 (1-59109-017-2) Booksurge, LLC.

—The Scarlet Letter. 1972. 3.95 o.p. (0-460-01122-7); 1957. 11.50 o.p. (0-460-00122-1) Dutton/Plume. (Dutton).

—The Scarlet Letter. 2002. (Illus.). 410p. (0-9710756-1-1) Everbind/Marco Bk. Co.

—The Scarlet Letter. 2003. (Barnes & Noble Classics Ser.). 320p. pap. 3.95 (1-59308-012-3) Fine Communications.

—The Scarlet Letter. 1992. (Everyman's Library). 304p. 17.00 (0-679-41731-1) Knopf, Alfred A. Inc.

—The Scarlet Letter. 1977. mass mkt. 1.25 o.p. (0-451-07499-8, Signet Bks.); 1973. mass mkt. 0.95 o.p. (0-451-05362-1, Signet Bks.); 1959. mass mkt. 1.50 o.p. (0-451-51188-3, Signet Classics); 1959. mass mkt. 0.95 o.p. (0-451-50910-2, Signet Classics); 1959. mass mkt. 1.25 o.p. (0-451-51067-4, Signet Classics); 1959. mass mkt. 0.50 o.p. (0-451-50008-3, Signet Classics); 1959. mass mkt. 1.50 o.p. (0-451-51232-4, Signet Classics); 1959. mass mkt. 1.75 o.p. (0-451-51431-9, Signet Classics); 1959. mass mkt. 0.60 o.p. (0-451-50650-2, Signet Classics) NAL.

—The Scarlet Letter. abr. ed. 1995. 29.95 o.p. (0-7871-0119-2) NewStar Media, Inc.

—The Scarlet Letter. 1991. (Literary Classics Ser.). 208p. text 5.98 o.p. (1-56138-036-9, Courage Bks.) Running Pr. Bk. Pubs.

—The Scarlet Letter. 2004. 352p. mass mkt. 3.95 (0-7434-8756-7, Pocket) Simon & Schuster.

—The Scarlet Letter. (Ebook Classic Ser.). E-Book 5.00 (0-7410-0475-5) SoftBook Pr.

—The Scarlet Letter. l.t. ed. 2002. (Perennial Bestsellers Ser.). 435p. 28.95 (0-7862-4628-6) Thorndike Pr.

—The Scarlet Letter. 2000. (Signature Classics Ser.). xiv, 298p. 24.95 (1-58279-071-X); (1-58279-077-9) Trident Pr. International.

—The Scarlet Letter. 2002. 272p. pap. 6.00 (0-14-243726-3, Penguin Classics) Viking Penguin.

Healy, Jeremiah. Act of God. Chelius, Jane, ed. 1995. 336p. mass mkt. 5.50 (0-671-79559-7, Pocket); 1994. 352p. 20.00 (0-671-79558-9, Atria) Simon & Schuster.

—Blunt Darts. l.t. ed. 1985. lib. bdg. 16.95 o.p. (0-89340-918-9, 482) BBC Audiobooks America.

—Blunt Darts. Chelius, Jane, ed. 1991. 192p. reprint ed. mass mkt. 5.50 (0-671-73742-2, Pocket) Simon & Schuster.

—Blunt Darts. 1984. 192p. 12.95 o.s.i (0-8027-5570-4) Walker & Co.

—The Concise Cuddy: A Collection of John Francis Cuddy Stories. 1998. 293p. pap. 17.00 (1-885941-27-7); 42.00 o.p. (1-885941-26-9) Crippen & Landru, Pubs.

—Foursome. 1993. 352p. 20.00 (0-671-79556-2, Atria) Simon & Schuster.

—Foursome. Chelius, Jane, ed. 1994. 352p. reprint ed. mass mkt. 5.99 (0-671-79557-0, Pocket) Simon & Schuster.

—Invasion of Privacy. l.t. ed. 1997. (Large Print Book Ser.). pap. 23.95 (1-56895-484-0, Wheeler Publishing, Inc.) Gale Group.

—Invasion of Privacy. (John Francis Cuddy Mystery Ser.). 1997. 320p. pap. 5.99 (0-671-89874-4, Pocket); 1996. 352p. 21.00 o.p. (0-671-89876-0, Atria) Simon & Schuster.

—The Only Good Lawyer. (John Francis Cuddy Mystery Ser.). 1998. 304p. 23.00 o.s.i (0-671-00953-2, Atria); 1999. (Illus.). 400p. reprint ed. pap. 6.99 (0-671-00954-0, Pocket) Simon & Schuster.

—Rescue. 1996. 384p. pap. 5.99 (0-671-89875-2, Pocket) Simon & Schuster.

—Rescue. Chelius, Jane, ed. 1995. 368p. 20.00 o.p. (0-671-89877-9, Atria) Simon & Schuster.

—Right to Die. Chelius, Jane, ed. 1991. 256p. 18.95 o.p. (0-671-70809-0, Atria); 1992. 288p. reprint ed. mass mkt. 5.99 (0-671-70810-4, Pocket) Simon & Schuster.

—Shallow Graves. Chelius, Jane, ed. 1992. 288p. 19.00 (0-671-70811-2, Atria) Simon & Schuster.

—Shallow Graves. 1993. 288p. reprint ed. mass mkt. 5.99 (0-671-70812-0, Pocket) Simon & Schuster.

—So Like Sleep. 1987. 256p. 15.95 o.p. (0-06-015693-7) HarperTrade.

—So Like Sleep. 1991. mass mkt. 4.50 (0-671-74328-7, Pocket) Simon & Schuster.

—Spiral: A John Frances Cuddy Mystery. (John Francis Cuddy Mystery Ser.). 1999. 368p. 23.00 o.s.i (0-671-00955-9, Atria); 2000. 400p. reprint ed. pap. 6.99 (0-671-00956-7, Pocket) Simon & Schuster.

—The Staked Goat. 1986. 224p. 14.95 o.p. (0-06-015515-9) HarperTrade.

—Swan Dive. 1991. mass mkt. 5.99 (0-671-74329-5); 1989. mass mkt. 3.95 (0-671-67185-5) Simon & Schuster. (Pocket).

—Swan Dive: A Novel of Suspense. 1988. 224p. 16.95 o.p. (0-06-015921-9) HarperTrade.

—Yesterday's News: A Novel of Suspense. l.t. ed. 1990. 19.95 o.p. (0-7927-0586-6, C0581); pap. 17.95 o.p. (0-7927-0587-4) BBC Audiobooks America.

—Yesterday's News: A Novel of Suspense. 1989. 16.95 o.p. (0-06-015922-7) HarperTrade.

—Yesterday's News: A Novel of Suspense. Chelius, Jane, ed. 1990. 256p. reprint ed. mass mkt. 5.50 (0-671-69584-3, Pocket) Simon & Schuster.

Heidish, Marcy. Witnesses, 001. 1980. 10.95 o.p. (0-395-29196-8) Houghton Mifflin Co.

Higgins, George V. The Agent. 1999. 352p. 24.00 o.s.i (0-15-100357-2) Harcourt Trade Pubs.

—At End of Day. 2001. 392p. reprint ed. pap. 14.00 (0-15-601190-5, Harvest Bks.) Harcourt Trade Pubs.

—At End of Day: A Novel of Suspense. 2000. 392p. 24.00 (0-15-100358-0); (0-15-100532-X) Harcourt Trade Pubs.

—Bomber's Law. unabr. ed. 1994. audio 72.00 (0-7366-2805-3, 3519) Books on Tape, Inc.

—Bomber's Law. unabr. ed. 1997. audio 85.00 (0-7887-0668-3, 94845E7) Recorded Bks., LLC.

—Bomber's Law: A Novel. 304p. 1994. pap. 11.00 o.s.i (0-8050-3566-4, Owl Bks.); 1993. 22.50 o.p. (0-8050-2329-1) Holt, Henry & Co.

—A Change of Gravity. unabr. ed. 1998. audio 112.00 (0-7366-4050-9, 4549) Books on Tape, Inc.

—A Change of Gravity. 1997. 464p. 25.00 o.s.i (0-8050-4815-4) Holt, Henry & Co.

—Defending Billy Ryan. unabr. ed. 1997. audio 39.95 (0-7861-1234-4) Blackstone Audio Bks., Inc.

—Defending Billy Ryan. l.t. ed. 1993. 50.95 (0-7838-1112-8, Macmillan Reference USA) Gale Group.

—Defending Billy Ryan. 1992. 320p. 21.95 o.p. (0-8050-1677-5) Holt, Henry & Co.

—Defending Billy Ryan. 1994. 304p. mass mkt. 4.99 o.s.i (0-8217-4586-7) Kensington Publishing Corp.

—The Friends of Eddie Coyle. 1980. 176p. mass mkt. 2.50 o.s.i (0-345-28635-9) Ballantine Bks.

—The Friends of Eddie Coyle. unabr. collector's ed. 1990. audio 36.00 (0-7366-1859-7, 2690) Books on Tape, Inc.

—The Friends of Eddie Coyle. (John MacRae Bks.). 192p. 2000. pap. 13.00 (0-8050-6598-9); 1995. pap. 13.00 o.s.i (0-8050-4152-4) Holt, Henry & Co. (Owl Bks.).

—The Friends of Eddie Coyle. 1972. 15.95 o.s.i (0-394-47327-2) Knopf, Alfred A. Inc.

—The Friends of Eddie Coyle. unabr. ed. 1996. audio. audio 35.00 (0-7887-0643-8, 94820E7) Recorded Bks., LLC.

—The Friends of Eddie Coyle. 1987. 192p. mass mkt. 3.95 o.p. (0-14-010232-9, Penguin Bks.) Viking Penguin.

—The Judgment of Deke Hunter. 1978. mass mkt. 1.95 o.s.i (0-345-25862-2) Ballantine Bks.

—The Judgment of Deke Hunter: A Novel. 1994. pap. 11.00 o.p. (0-8050-3557-5, Owl Bks.) Holt, Henry & Co.

—Kennedy for the Defense. 1985. 224p. mass mkt. 2.95 o.p. (0-345-32612-1) Ballantine Bks.

—Kennedy for the Defense. 1992. mass mkt. 4.50 o.s.i (0-8217-3724-4, Zebra Bks.) Kensington Publishing Corp.

—Kennedy for the Defense. 1980. 9.95 o.p. (0-394-42406-9, Knopf Bks. for Young Readers) Random Hse. Children's Bks.

—Kennedy for the Defense: A Novel. 1995. pap. 12.00 o.p. (0-8050-4182-6, Owl Bks.) Holt, Henry & Co.

—Penance for Jerry Kennedy. 1986. 320p. pap. 3.50 o.p. (0-88184-224-9, Carroll & Graf Pubs.) Avalon Publishing Group.

—Sandra Nichols Found Dead: A Jerry Kennedy Novel. 1997. 256p. pap. 12.00 o.s.i (0-8050-5222-4, Owl Bks.); 1996. 89p. 23.00 o.p. (0-8050-3747-0) Holt, Henry & Co.

Hilderbrand, Elin. The Beach Club. 2000. 357p. 23.95 (0-312-26125-X); E-Book 23.95 (0-312-27424-6) St. Martin's Pr.

—Nantucket Nights: A Novel. 2002. 288p. 23.95 (0-312-28335-0) St. Martin's Pr.

Hobbie, Douglas. Boomfell. 1993. 448p. pap. 10.95 o.p. (0-8050-2663-0, Owl Bks.); 1991. 288p. 19.95 o.p. (0-8050-1534-5) Holt, Henry & Co.

—Boomfell. 1994. 3.99 o.p. (0-517-11417-8) Random Hse. Value Publishing.

Hoffman, Alice. Blue Diary. 2002. 304p. pap. 13.00 (0-425-18494-3); pap. 7.99 (0-425-18444-7) Berkley Publishing Group.

—Blue Diary. l.t. ed. 2001. (Wheeler Large Print Book Ser.). 361p. 31.95 (1-58724-136-6, Wheeler Publishing, Inc.) Gale Group.

—Blue Diary. 2001. 336p. 24.95 o.p. (0-399-14802-7) Penguin Group (USA) Inc.

—Blue Diary. l.t. ed. 2002. pap. 12.95 (1-56895-196-5, Large Print Pr.) Thorndike Pr.

—Here on Earth. 2015. 336p. mass mkt. 7.50 o.s.i (0-425-16430-6); 1998. 304p. pap. 13.00 (0-425-16731-3); 1999. 336p. reprint ed. mass mkt. 7.99 (0-425-16969-3) Berkley Publishing Group.

—Here on Earth. abr. ed. 1999. audio 7.99 o.s.i (1-56740-254-2, 1750, Paperback Nova Audio Bks.); 1997. audio 16.95 o.p. (1-56100-981-4, 475, Nova Audio Bks.); 1997. audio 23.95 (1-56100-755-2, 133, Bookcassette); 1997. audio 73.25 (1-56100-830-3, 893, Unabridged Library Editions) Brilliance Audio.

—Here on Earth. 2001. 23.95 o.s.i (0-399-14901-5); 1997. 304p. 23.95 o.p. (0-399-14313-0, G. P. Putnam's Sons) Penguin Group (USA) Inc.

—Here on Earth. 1999. 14.04 (0-606-16392-1) Turtleback Bks.

—Illumination Night. l.t. ed. 1994. 22.95 o.p. (0-7927-2034-2); pap. 21.95 o.p. (0-7927-2033-4) BBC Audiobooks America.

—Illumination Night. 1988. 256p. mass mkt. 6.99 o.s.i (0-449-21594-6, Fawcett) Ballantine Bks.

—Illumination Night. 1987. 224p. 18.95 o.s.i (0-399-13282-1, G. P. Putnam's Sons) Penguin Putnam Bks. for Young Readers.

—Practical Magic. 2003. 304p. pap. 13.00 (0-425-19037-4); 1998. 304p. pap. 13.00 (0-425-16320-2); 1998. 336p. mass mkt. 7.99 o.s.i (0-425-16846-8); 1996. 336p. reprint ed. mass mkt. 7.99 (0-425-15249-9) Berkley Publishing Group.

—Practical Magic. 1995. 244p. 22.95 o.p. (0-399-14055-7, G. P. Putnam's Sons) Penguin Group (USA) Inc.

—Practical Magic. unabr. ed. 1999. audio compact disk 73.00 (0-7887-3396-6, C1002E7); 1995. audio 60.00 (0-7887-0337-4, 94529E7) Recorded Bks., LLC.

—Practical Magic. abr. ed. 1998. audio (0-671-04332-3, 393059); 1995. 17.00 incl. audio (0-671-53540-4) Simon & Schuster Audio. (Simon & Schuster Audioworks).

—Practical Magic. 244p. pap. 5.98 o.p. (0-7651-0631-0) Smithmark Pubs., Inc.

—Practical Magic. 1996. 14.04 (0-606-15822-7) Turtleback Bks.

—The River King. 2001. 352p. reprint ed. pap. 14.00 (0-425-17967-2) Berkley Publishing Group.

—The River King. 2001. 23.95 o.s.i (0-399-14908-2); 2000. 304p. 23.95 o.s.i (0-399-14599-0) Penguin Group (USA) Inc.

—The River King. l.t. ed. 471p. 2001. 28.95 (0-7862-2798-2); 2000. 30.95 (0-7862-2788-5) Thorndike Pr.

Howells, William Dean. A Modern Instance. unabr. ed. 1997. (J). (gr. 10 up). audio 65.95 (1-55685-461-7, 461-7) Audio Bk. Contractors, Inc.

—A Modern Instance. 1882. 255p. (YA). reprint ed. pap. text 28.00 (1-4047-3235-7) Classic Textbooks.

—A Modern Instance, 001. Gibson, W., ed. 1957. (YA). (gr. 9 up). pap. 13.16 o.p. (0-395-05119-3, Riverside Editions) Houghton Mifflin Co.

—A Modern Instance. 1977. (Selected Edition of W. D. Howells Ser.: Vol. 10). 608p. 20.00 o.p. (0-253-33864-6) Indiana Univ. Pr.

—A Modern Instance. mass mkt. 0.75 o.p. (0-451-50249-3, Signet Classics) NAL.

—A Modern Instance. 2003. (Twelve-Point Ser.). lib. bdg. 25.00 (1-58287-220-1); lib. bdg. 26.00 (1-58287-704-1) North Bks.

—A Modern Instance. 1992. (Notable American Authors Ser.). reprint ed. lib. bdg. 75.00 (0-7812-3235-X) Reprint Services Corp.

—A Modern Instance. l.t. ed. 1999. 524p. text 27.95 (1-56000-487-8) Transaction Pubs.

—A Modern Instance. 1984. (Classics Ser.). 480p. (C). 14.00 (0-14-039027-8, Penguin Classics) Viking Penguin.

—The Rise of Silas Lapham. reprint ed. lib. bdg. 25.95 (0-89190-456-5, Rivercity Pr.) Amereon, Ltd.

—The Rise of Silas Lapham. 1990. audio 53.95 (1-55685-168-5) Audio Bk. Contractors, Inc.

—The Rise of Silas Lapham. reprint ed. 1992. lib. bdg. 21.95 (0-89968-261-8, Lightyear Pr.); 1990. lib. bdg. 21.95 (0-89968-528-5) Buccaneer Bks., Inc.

—The Rise of Silas Lapham. 1971. (Selected Edition of W. D. Howells Ser.: Vol. 12). 434p. 29.95 o.p. (0-253-35016-6) Indiana Univ. Pr.

—The Rise of Silas Lapham. unabr. ed. 1993. audio 49.00 Jimcin Recordings.

—The Rise of Silas Lapham. 1991. 368p. pap. 10.50 o.s.i (0-679-72517-2, Vintage) Knopf Publishing Group.

—The Rise of Silas Lapham. 1998. (Cloth Bound Pocket Ser.). 7.95 (3-8290-0874-0, 520657) Konemann.

—The Rise of Silas Lapham. Cook, Don L., ed. 1982. (Critical Editions Ser.). (C). 24.95 o.p. (0-393-04433-5); 519p. pap. text 12.00 (0-393-09165-1) Norton, W. W. & Co., Inc.

—The Rise of Silas Lapham. 1977. reprint ed. lib. bdg. 21.95 o.s.i (0-89244-043-0) Queens Hse./Focus Service.

—The Rise of Silas Lapham. 1992. (Notable American Authors Ser.). reprint ed. lib. bdg. 75.00 (0-7812-3237-6) Reprint Services Corp.

—The Rise of Silas Lapham. 1983. (American Library). 400p. pap. 12.00 (0-14-039030-8, Penguin Classics) Viking Penguin.

Hughes, Dean. Lucky Fights Back. 1991. (Lucky Ladd Ser.: Bk. 4). 150p. (Orig.). (J). (gr. 3-6). pap. text 4.95 (0-87579-559-5, Cinnamon Tree) Deseret Bk. Co.

Hughes, Judith E. A Faraway Place. 2000. 512p. pap. 26.99 (0-7388-2452-6) Xlibris Corp.

Hughes, Richard. Bound for Boston. Wheeler, Jill, ed. 1989. (Great Cities Adventures Ser.). (Illus.). 48p. (J). (gr. 4). lib. bdg. 10.95 o.p. (0-939179-44-X) ABDO Publishing Co.

Hunter, Evan. Lizzie. 1984. 430p. 16.95 o.p. (0-87795-570-0, Morrow, William & Co.) Morrow/Avon.

Ikeda, Stewart D. What the Scarecrow Said: A Novel. 1996. (Illus.). 464p. 24.00 o.p. (*0-06-039164-2*) HarperCollins Pubs.

James, Henry. The Bostonians. 2000. 252p. E-Book 3.95 (*0-594-06195-4*) 1873 Pr.

—The Bostonians. 1976. 27.95 (*0-8488-0542-9*) Amereon, Ltd.

—The Bostonians. 1984. 416p. mass mkt. 2.95 o.s.i (*0-553-21153-6*, Bantam Classics) Bantam Bks.

—The Bostonians. 1999. 462p. pap. 9.95 o.p. (*1-930128-02-9*, JNMedia Bks.) JNMedia, Inc.

—The Bostonians. 1992. 17.00 (*0-679-47150-2*, Everyman's Library); 1991. 448p. pap. 10.50 o.s.i (*0-679-73381-7*, Vintage) Knopf Publishing Group.

—The Bostonians. 1992. (Everyman's Library: Vol. 82). 442p. 20.00 (*0-679-41750-8*) Knopf, Alfred A. Inc.

—The Bostonians. 1964. (Modern Library College Editions Ser.). 464p. (C). pap. 10.63 o.p. (*0-07-553642-0*, T59, McGraw-Hill Humanities, Social Sciences & World Languages) McGraw-Hill Higher Education.

—The Bostonians. 1984. 384p. mass mkt. 3.50 o.p. (*0-451-52550-7*, CE1285, Signet Classics) NAL.

—The Bostonians. Gooder, R. D., ed. & intro. by. 1998. (Oxford World's Classics Ser.). (Illus.). 504p. pap. 7.95 (*0-19-283442-8*) Oxford Univ. Pr., Inc.

—The Bostonians. 1994. 464p. pap. 4.95 (*0-460-87493-4*, Everyman's Classic Library in Paperback) Tuttle Publishing.

—The Bostonians. 2001. (Classics Ser.). 480p. pap. 9.00 (*0-14-043766-5*, Penguin Classics) Viking Penguin.

—The Bostonians. Anderson, Charles, ed. & intro. by. 1984. (Penguin Classics Ser.). 448p. pap. 8.95 o.s.i (*0-14-043225-6*, Penguin Classics) Viking Penguin.

—The Bostonians. 1974. 400p. pap. 2.95 o.p. (*0-14-002450-6*, Penguin Bks.) Viking Penguin.

—The Bostonians. Gooder, R. D., ed. & intro. by. 1985. 498p. (C). pap. 5.95 o.p. (*0-19-281639-X*) Oxford Univ. Pr., Inc.

—The Bostonians, Set. unabr. ed. 1989. audio 71.95 (*1-55685-150-2*) Audio Bk. Contractors, Inc.

—The Bostonians. 1986. 384p. reprint ed. lib. bdg. 25.95 (*0-89966-522-5*) Buccaneer Bks., Inc.

—The Bostonians. l.t. ed. 2000. (Large Print Ser.). 606p. lib. bdg. 28.00 (*1-58287-608-8*); 250p. reprint ed. lib. bdg. 25.00 (*1-58287-131-0*) North Bks.

—The Bostonians. 1992. (Notable American Authors Ser.). reprint ed. lib. bdg. 75.00 (*0-7812-3387-9*) Reprint Services Corp.

—The Europeans. l.t. ed. 2001. per. 15.50 (*1-58396-136-4*); 200p. per. 9.90 (*1-58396-039-2*) Blue Unicorn Editions.

—The Europeans. 1987. 166p. reprint ed. lib. bdg. 25.95 (*0-89966-608-6*) Buccaneer Bks., Inc.

—The Europeans. 1999. E-Book 2.49 (*1-58627-944-0*) Electric Umbrella Publishing.

—The Europeans. l.t. ed. 723p. pap. 57.18 (*0-7583-0862-0*); 478p. pap. 40.76 (*0-7583-0860-4*); 374p. pap. 32.97 (*0-7583-0859-0*); 839p. pap. 66.86 (*0-7583-0863-9*); 292p. pap. 26.47 (*0-7583-0858-2*); 213p. pap. 21.06 (*0-7583-0857-4*); 170p. pap. 18.64 (*0-7583-0856-6*); 588p. pap. 48.94 (*0-7583-0861-2*); 213p. lib. bdg. 27.06 (*0-7583-0849-3*); 170p. lib. bdg. 24.64 (*0-7583-0848-5*); 374p. lib. bdg. 38.97 (*0-7583-0851-5*); 478p. lib. bdg. 46.76 (*0-7583-0852-3*); 588p. lib. bdg. 54.94 (*0-7583-0853-1*); 839p. lib. bdg. 85.08 (*0-7583-0855-8*); 292p. lib. bdg. 32.47 (*0-7583-0850-7*); 723p. lib. bdg. 63.18 (*0-7583-0854-X*) Huge Print Pr.

—The Europeans. 1964. pap. 4.95 o.p. (*0-452-01021-7*, Meridian Bks.); mass mkt. 1.75 o.p. (*0-451-51351-7*, CE 1351, Signet Classics); mass mkt. 0.60 o.p. (*0-451-50232-9*, Signet Classics) NAL.

—The Europeans. Ross, Ain C., ed. 2nd ed. 1985. (Oxford World's Classics Ser.). 208p. (C). reprint ed. pap. 5.95 o.p. (*0-19-281683-7*) Oxford Univ. Pr., Inc.

—The Europeans. 1979. pap. 2.50 o.p. (*0-14-005398-0*); 1975. pap. 2.50 o.p. (*0-14-002070-5*) Penguin Group (USA) Inc.

—The Europeans. 1976. 176p. reprint ed. lib. bdg. 18.95 (*0-89244-018-X*) Queens Hse./Focus Service.

—The Europeans. 1992. (Notable American Authors Ser.). reprint ed. lib. bdg. 75.00 (*0-7812-3372-0*) Reprint Services Corp.

—The Europeans. 1980. 8.00 o.p. (*0-8446-5205-9*) Smith, Peter Pub., Inc.

—The Europeans. (Ebook Classic Ser.). E-Book 5.00 (*0-7410-0438-0*) SoftBook Pr.

—The Europeans. l.t. ed. 2000. (Perennial Bestsellers Ser.). 255p. 26.95 (*0-7838-9060-5*) Thorndike Pr.

—The Europeans. Tanner, Tony, ed. & intro. by. 1985. (Classics Ser.). 576p. 7.95 (*0-14-043232-9*, Penguin Classics) Viking Penguin.

—The Europeans. 1998. (Classics Library). 160p. pap. 3.95 (*1-85326-262-5*, 2625WW) Wordsworth Editions, Ltd. GBR. *Dist:* Combined Publishing.

—The Europeans: A Sketch. Ross, Ian C., ed. & intro. by. 2000. (Oxford World's Classics Ser.). 208p. pap. 7.95 (*0-19-283500-9*) Oxford Univ. Pr., Inc.

Jarrett, Miranda. Wishing. 1999. 368p. pap. 6.50 (*0-671-00341-0*, Pocket) Simon & Schuster.

Jensen, Muriel. Man with a Miracle. 2002. (Harlequin Superromance Ser.). 304p. mass mkt. o.s.i (*0-373-71093-3*, Harlequin Bks.) Harlequin Enterprises, Ltd.

Johnstone, William W. Rage of the Mountain Man. 1996. mass mkt. 4.99 o.s.i (*0-8217-5361-4*); 1994. 288p. mass mkt. 3.99 o.s.i (*0-8217-4567-0*) Kensington Publishing Corp. (Zebra Bks.).

—Rage of the Mountain Man. 2003. (Western Ser.). 25.95 (*0-7862-4633-2*) Thorndike Pr.

Juniper, Alex. A Very Proper Death. l.t. ed. 1992. 18.95 o.p. (*0-7451-8384-0*); pap. 16.95 o.p. (*0-7927-1124-6*) BBC Audiobooks America.

—A Very Proper Death. 1991. 256p. 18.95 o.s.i (*0-684-19301-9*, Scribner) Simon & Schuster.

Karp, Catherine. Gilded. 2000. 344p. pap. 22.99 o.p. (*0-7388-2553-0*); text 32.99 o.p. (*0-7388-2552-2*) Xlibris Corp.

Katz, Jamie. Dead Low Tide. 1998. (Dan Kardon Mysteries Ser.). 384p. mass mkt. 5.99 (*0-06-109711-X*, HarperTorch) Morrow/Avon.

Kava, Alex. The Soul Catcher: A Maggie O'Dell Novel. 2003. 416p. mass mkt. (*1-55166-701-0*, Mira Bks.) Harlequin Enterprises, Ltd.

—The Soul Catcher: A Maggie O'Dell Novel. l.t. ed. 2003. (Basic Ser.). 628p. 28.95 (*0-7862-4925-0*) Thorndike Pr.

Kelly, Susan. The Gemini Man. 1986. 304p. mass mkt. 2.95 o.s.i (*0-345-33113-3*) Ballantine Bks.

—The Gemini Man. 1985. 221p. 14.95 o.s.i (*0-8027-5613-1*) Walker & Co.

—Out of the Darkness. unabr. ed. 1992. audio 21.95 o.p. (*1-56100-478-2*, 204, Bookcassette); audio 57.25 o.p. (*1-56100-112-0*, 974, Unabridged Library Editions) Brilliance Audio.

—Out of the Darkness. 1994. 352p. mass mkt. 4.50 o.s.i (*0-8217-4620-0*) Kensington Publishing Corp.

—Out of the Darkness. 1992. 278p. 18.00 o.s.i (*0-679-41131-3*, Villard Bks.) Random House Adult Trade Publishing Group.

—The Summertime Soldiers. 1986. 192p. 14.95 o.p. (*0-8027-5646-8*) Walker & Co.

—Trail of the Dragon. 1990. 256p. mass mkt. 3.95 o.s.i (*0-345-35749-3*) Ballantine Bks.

—Trail of the Dragon. 1988. 282p. 17.95 (*0-8027-5696-4*) Walker & Co.

—Until Proven Innocent. unabr. ed. 1991. audio 57.25 o.p. (*1-56100-067-1*, 593); audio 21.95 o.p. (*0-930435-73-7*, 411) Brilliance Audio.

—Until Proven Innocent. 1990. 288p. 16.95 o.s.i (*0-394-58414-7*, Villard Bks.) Random House Adult Trade Publishing Group.

Kemelman, Harry. The Day the Rabbi Resigned. l.t. ed. 1993. (Large Print Mystery Ser.). 345p. 24.95 o.p. (*0-7927-1414-8*); pap. 19.95 o.p. (*0-7927-1413-X*) BBC Audiobooks America.

—The Day the Rabbi Resigned. 1992. mass mkt. 5.99 o.s.i (*0-449-21908-9*); 273p. 20.00 o.s.i (*0-449-90681-7*) Ballantine Bks. (Fawcett).

—The Day the Rabbi Resigned. 2004. 288p. mass mkt. 6.99 (*0-7434-7979-3*) ibooks, Inc.

—Friday the Rabbi Slept Late. 1993. pap. o.p. (*0-449-45127-5*); 1986. mass mkt. 5.99 o.s.i (*0-449-21180-0*) Ballantine Bks. (Fawcett).

—Friday the Rabbi Slept Late. l.t. ed. 1983. (General Ser.). 339p. lib. bdg. 13.95 o.p. (*0-8161-3537-1*, Macmillan Reference USA) Gale Group.

—Monday the Rabbi Took Off. 1988. mass mkt. o.s.i (*0-449-20785-4*); 1986. 288p. mass mkt. 5.99 o.s.i (*0-449-21001-4*, Fawcett); 1981. mass mkt. 2.50 o.s.i (*0-449-23872-5*, Fawcett) Ballantine Bks.

—Monday the Rabbi Took Off. 1972. 316p. 5.95 o.p. (*0-399-10550-6*) Putnam Publishing Group, The.

—Monday the Rabbi Took Off. 2002. 368p. pap. 6.99 (*0-7434-5271-2*) ibooks, Inc.

—One Fine Day the Rabbi Bought a Cross. 1988. (Boston Mysteries Ser.). mass mkt. 5.99 o.s.i (*0-449-20687-4*, Fawcett) Ballantine Bks.

—One Fine Day the Rabbi Bought a Cross. l.t. ed. 1988. (Large Print Bks.). 353p. 18.95 o.p. (*0-8161-4347-1*, Macmillan Reference USA) Gale Group.

—One Fine Day the Rabbi Bought a Cross. 1987. 234p. 15.95 o.p. (*0-688-05631-8*, Morrow, William & Co.) Morrow/Avon.

—One Fine Day the Rabbi Bought a Cross. 1990. 3.99 o.p. (*0-517-05752-2*) Random Hse. Value Publishing.

—One Fine Day the Rabbi Bought a Cross. 2003. 320p. pap. 6.99 (*0-7434-7478-3*) ibooks, Inc.

—Rabbi Small, Bk. 2. 1924. o.s.i (*0-688-05617-2*, Morrow, William & Co.) Morrow/Avon.

—Saturday the Rabbi Went Hungry. 1987. 224p. mass mkt. 5.99 o.s.i (*0-449-21392-7*, Fawcett) Ballantine Bks.

—Saturday the Rabbi Went Hungry. 1988. 4.95 o.s.i (*0-517-01307-X*) Crown Publishing Group.

—Saturday the Rabbi Went Hungry. l.t. ed. 1983. 14.95 o.p. (*0-8161-3531-2*, Macmillan Reference USA) Gale Group.

—Someday the Rabbi Will Leave. 1986. 288p. mass mkt. 5.99 o.s.i (*0-449-20945-8*, Fawcett) Ballantine Bks.

—Someday the Rabbi Will Leave. 1985. 264p. 15.95 o.p. (*0-688-04174-4*, Morrow, William & Co.) Morrow/Avon.

—Someday the Rabbi Will Leave. 2003. 288p. pap. 6.99 (*0-7434-5911-3*) ibooks, Inc.

—Sunday the Rabbi Stayed Home. Date not set. mass mkt. (*0-449-20784-6*); 1985. 224p. mass mkt. 5.99 o.s.i (*0-449-21000-6*) Ballantine Bks. (Fawcett).

—Sunday the Rabbi Stayed Home. l.t. ed. 1977. (General Ser.). 420p. lib. bdg. 11.95 o.p. (*0-8161-6499-1*, Macmillan Reference USA) Gale Group.

—Sunday the Rabbi Stayed Home. 2002. (Rabbi Small Mystery Ser.). (Illus.). 304p. pap. 6.99 (*0-7434-5238-0*) ibooks, Inc.

—That Day the Rabbi Left Town. (Rabbi Small Mystery Ser.). 1997. 263p. mass mkt. 5.99 o.s.i (*0-449-22570-4*); 1996. 256p. 22.00 o.s.i (*0-449-91002-4*); 1996. 233p. lib. bdg. 22.95 (*1-57490-040-4*) Ballantine Bks. (Fawcett).

—Thursday the Rabbi Walked Out. 1986. mass mkt. 5.99 o.s.i (*0-449-21157-6*, Fawcett) Ballantine Bks.

—Thursday the Rabbi Walked Out. 2003. 256p. mass mkt. 6.99 (*0-7434-5860-5*) ibooks, Inc.

—Tuesday the Rabbi Saw Red. 1986. (Rabbi Ser.). mass mkt. 5.99 o.s.i (*0-449-21321-8*, Fawcett) Ballantine Bks.

—Tuesday the Rabbi Saw Red. 1974. (Adult Ser.). 508p. reprint ed. lib. bdg. 11.95 o.p. (*0-8161-6230-1*, Macmillan Reference USA) Gale Group.

—Tuesday the Rabbi Saw Red. 2003. 352p. pap. 6.99 (*0-7434-4534-1*) ibooks, Inc.

—Wednesday the Rabbi Got Wet. 1986. (Rabbi Ser.). mass mkt. 5.99 o.s.i (*0-449-21328-5*, Fawcett) Ballantine Bks.

Kemmer, Brenton C. War, Hell & Honor: A Novel of the French & Indian War. 2001. (Illus.). 173p. pap. 14.95 (*0-7884-1875-0*) Heritage Bks.

Kemprecos, Paul. Bluefin Blues: An Aristotle "Soc" Socarides Mystery. 1997. 224p. 20.95 o.p. (*0-312-16787-3*, Saint Martin's Minotaur) St. Martin's Pr.

—Cool Blue Tomb. 1991. 288p. mass mkt. 4.50 o.s.i (*0-553-28881-4*) Bantam Bks.

—Death in Deep Water. 1993. 336p. mass mkt. 4.99 o.s.i (*0-553-29735-X*) Bantam Bks.

—Death in Deep Water: An Aristotle "Soc" Socraides Mystery. 1992. 368p. 16.50 o.s.i (*0-385-42379-9*) Doubleday Publishing.

—A Feeding Frenzy. 1994. 336p. mass mkt. 4.99 o.s.i (*0-553-56774-8*) Bantam Bks.

—Mayflower Murder. 1996. 22.95 (*0-312-14852-6*, Saint Martin's Minotaur) St. Martin's Pr.

—Neptune's Eye. 1991. 320p. mass mkt. 4.50 o.s.i (*0-553-29353-2*) Bantam Bks.

Kennedy, Raymond. Lulu Incognito. 1988. (Vintage Contemporaries Ser.). 320p. pap. 7.95 o.s.i (*0-394-75641-X*, Vintage) Knopf Publishing Group.

Kennedy, Raymond A. The Romance of Eleanor Gray: A Novel. 2003. (Hardscrabble Books). (Illus.). 255p. text 24.95 (*1-58465-291-8*) Univ. Pr. of New England.

Kenney, Charles. Code of Vengeance. 1997. mass mkt. 5.99 o.s.i (*0-449-28779-3*, Fawcett) Ballantine Bks.

—Code of Vengeance. 1995. 303p. 22.00 (*0-671-89697-0*, Simon & Schuster) Simon & Schuster.

Kerouac, Jack. Maggie Cassidy. (FRE.). pap. 13.95 (*2-02-009302-2*) Editions du Seuil FRA. *Dist:* Distribooks, Inc.

—Maggie Cassidy. 1978. 194p. reprint ed. pap. text 4.95 o.p. (*0-07-034203-2*) McGraw-Hill Cos., The.

—Maggie Cassidy. 1993. 202p. 14.00 (*0-14-017906-2*) Viking Penguin.

Kilmer, Nicholas. Dirty Linen. 1999. (Fred Taylor Mystery Ser.). 256p. 25.00 o.s.i (*0-8050-5034-5*) Holt, Henry & Co.

—Dirty Linen. 2001. 218p. pap. 14.95 o.s.i (*1-890208-53-1*) Poisoned Pen Pr.

—Harmony in Flesh & Black. 1995. 261p. 21.00 o.p. (*0-8050-3663-6*) Holt, Henry & Co.

—Harmony in Flesh & Black. 1996. 272p. mass mkt. 4.99 o.p. (*0-06-104425-3*, HarperTorch) Morrow/Avon.

—Man with a Squirrel. unabr. ed. 1997. audio 44.95 (*0-7861-1226-3*, 1969) Blackstone Audio Bks., Inc.

—Man with a Squirrel. 1996. 88p. 22.50 o.p. (*0-8050-3666-0*) Holt, Henry & Co.

—O Sacred Head. 1997. 288p. 23.00 o.p. (*0-8050-5033-7*) Holt, Henry & Co.

Kinsman, Lawrence. Birds of Prey: A Detective Novel. 2nd ed. 2002. 330p. 25.00 (*0-9648817-4-8*); 350p. pap. 15.00 (*0-9648817-5-6*) Abelard Pr., The.

Klavan, Andrew. Hunting down Amanda. 2000. 448p. reprint ed. mass mkt. 7.99 (*0-7434-0338-X*, Pocket) Simon & Schuster.

Knight, Kathryn L. Dark Swan. 1996. (WWL Mystery Ser.). per. (*0-373-26203-5*, 1-26203-9, Worldwide Library) Harlequin Enterprises, Ltd.

—Dark Swan. 1994. 224p. 19.95 o.p. (*0-312-10961-X*, Saint Martin's Minotaur) St. Martin's Pr.

—Mortal Words. 1990. 17.95 o.p. (*0-671-68446-9*, Simon & Schuster) Simon & Schuster.

—Mortal Words. Chelius, Jane, ed. 1991. 352p. reprint ed. mass mkt. 4.50 (*0-671-68449-3*, Pocket) Simon & Schuster.

—Trace Elements. 1986. 15.95 o.p. (*0-393-02333-8*) Norton, W. W. & Co., Inc.

—Trace Elements. 1987. mass mkt. 3.50 (*0-671-64089-5*, Pocket) Simon & Schuster.

Kraft, Eric. Reservations Recommended. 1995. 288p. pap. 12.00 (*0-312-13597-1*) Picador.

—Reservations Recommended. 1992. 2.99 o.p. (*0-517-08814-2*); 1991. 2.99 o.p. (*0-517-07617-9*) Random Hse. Value Publishing.

Kraus, Jim & Kraus, Terri. The Quest: A Novel. 2002. (Circle of Destiny Ser.). 384p. pap. 10.99 o.p. (*0-8423-1838-0*) Tyndale Hse. Pubs.

Kricorian, Nancy. Zabelle. 1998. 256p. 23.00 o.p. (*0-87113-705-4*, Atlantic Monthly Pr.) Grove/Atlantic, Inc.

—Zabelle. 1999. 256p. reprint ed. pap. 12.95 (*0-380-73211-4*, Avon Bks.) Morrow/Avon.

Lahiri, Jhumpa. The Namesake: A Novel. l.t. ed. 2003. 413p. 31.95 (*1-58724-516-7*, Wheeler Publishing, Inc.) Gale Group.

—The Namesake: A Novel. 2003. 304p. 24.00 (*0-395-92721-8*) Houghton Mifflin Co.

Lamb, J. Dayne. A Question of Preference: A Teal Stewart Mystery. 1995. mass mkt. 4.99 o.s.i (*0-8217-5099-2*); 1994. 304p. mass mkt. 16.95 o.s.i (*0-8217-4631-6*) Kensington Publishing Corp.

—Questionable Behavior. 1993. 288p. mass mkt. 3.99 o.s.i (*0-8217-4333-3*, Zebra Bks.) Kensington Publishing Corp.

—Unquestioned Loyalty: A Teal Stewart Mystery. 1996. 352p. mass mkt. 4.99 o.s.i (*1-57566-054-7*); 1995. mass mkt. 16.95 o.s.i (*0-8217-5090-9*) Kensington Publishing Corp.

Landesman, Peter. The Raven. 1995. 356p. 23.00 (*1-880909-37-5*) Baskerville Pubs., Inc.

—Raven. 1997. 368p. pap. 11.95 (*0-14-026345-4*) Penguin Group (USA) Inc.

Langton, Jane. Dark Nantucket Noon. 1993. (Black Dagger Crime Ser.). (Illus.). 304p. 16.50 o.p. (*0-7451-8604-1*, Black Dagger) BBC Audiobooks America.

—Dark Nantucket Noon. unabr. ed. 1982. audio 48.00 (*0-7366-0630-0*, 1591) Books on Tape, Inc.

—Dark Nantucket Noon. 1981. (Fiction Ser.). 304p. pap. 5.99 (*0-14-005836-2*, Penguin Bks.) Penguin Group (USA) Inc.

—Divine Inspiration: A Homer Kelly Mystery. unabr. collector's ed. 1994. audio 56.00 (*0-7366-2722-7*, 3452) Books on Tape, Inc.

—Divine Inspiration: A Homer Kelly Mystery. abr. ed. 1994. (Homer Kelly Mystery Ser.). audio 16.00 o.p. (*0-453-00888-7*, Penguin AudioBooks) HighBridge Co.

—Divine Inspiration: A Homer Kelly Mystery. 1994. (Homer Kelly Mystery Ser.). (Illus.). 416p. reprint ed. pap. 5.99 o.s.i (*0-14-017376-5*, Penguin Bks.) Penguin Group (USA) Inc.

—Divine Inspiration: A Homer Kelly Mystery. 1993. (Homer Kelly Mystery Ser.). (Illus.). 416p. 20.00 o.p. (*0-670-84709-7*, Viking) Viking Penguin.

—Emily Dickinson Is Dead. unabr. collector's ed. 1987. audio 48.00 (*0-7366-1077-4*, 2004) Books on Tape, Inc.

—Emily Dickinson Is Dead. 1984. 256p. 13.95 o.p. (*0-312-24434-7*) St. Martin's Pr.

—Emily Dickinson Is Dead. l.t. ed. 1992. (Linford Mystery Large Print Ser.). 448p. pap. 17.99 o.p. (*0-7089-7162-8*, Ulverscroft) Thorpe, F. A. Pubs. GBR. *Dist:* Ulverscroft Large Print Bks., Ltd., Ulverscroft Large Print Canada, Ltd.

—Emily Dickinson Is Dead. 1985. (Crime Ser.). 256p. pap. 5.95 o.p. (*0-14-007771-5*, Penguin Bks.) Viking Penguin.

—The Face on the Wall: A Homer Kelly Mystery. l.t. ed. 1999. (Large Print Mystery Ser.). 25.95 (*1-57490-205-9*, Beeler Large Print Bks.) Beeler, Thomas T. Publisher.

—The Face on the Wall: A Homer Kelly Mystery, , unabr. ed. 1999. audio 48.00 (*0-7366-4369-9*, 4827) Books on Tape, Inc.

—The Face on the Wall: A Homer Kelly Mystery. 1999. (Homer Kelly Mystery Ser.). (Illus.). 304p. pap. 5.99 o.s.i (*0-14-028157-6*) Penguin Group (USA) Inc.

—The Face on the Wall: A Homer Kelly Mystery. 1998. (Homer Kelly Mystery Ser.). (Illus.). 288p. 21.95 o.p. (*0-670-87674-7*) Viking Penguin.

—God in Concord: A Homer Kelly Mystery. 1993. (Homer Kelly Mystery Ser.). (Illus.). 352p. pap. 6.99 (*0-14-016594-0*, Penguin Bks.) Penguin Group (USA) Inc.

—God in Concord: A Homer Kelly Mystery. 1992. (Homer Kelly Mystery Ser.). 384p. 19.00 o.p. (*0-670-84260-5*, Viking) Viking Penguin.

—Good & Dead. unabr. collector's ed. 1992. audio 48.00 (*0-7366-2223-3*, 3013) Books on Tape, Inc.

—Good & Dead. 1986. 320p. 15.95 o.p. (*0-312-33865-1*) St. Martin's Pr.

—Good & Dead. (Homer Kelly Mystery Ser.). 256p. 1989. pap. 5.95 o.s.i (*0-14-012687-2*); 1987. pap. 3.95 o.p. (*0-14-010088-1*) Viking Penguin. (Penguin Bks.).

—The Memorial Hall Murder. unabr. ed. 1982. audio 48.00 (*0-7366-0631-9*, 1592) Books on Tape, Inc.

—The Memorial Hall Murder. 1996. pap. (*0-14-771166-5*) Penguin Group (USA) Inc.

—The Memorial Hall Murder. 1981. (Fiction Ser.). 272p. pap. 5.95 o.p. (*0-14-005704-8*, Penguin Bks.) Viking Penguin.

—Murder at the Gardner. unabr. collector's ed. 1990. audio 56.00 (*0-7366-1741-8*, 2581) Books on Tape, Inc.

—Murder at the Gardner. 1989. (Penguin Crime Fiction Ser.). 368p. pap. 6.99 (*0-14-011382-7*, Penguin Bks.) Penguin Group (USA) Inc.

—Murder at the Gardner. 1988. (Illus.). 288p. 17.95 o.p. (*0-312-01479-1*, Saint Martin's Minotaur) St. Martin's Pr.

—Natural Enemy. unabr. collector's ed. 1992. audio 48.00 (*0-7366-2231-4*, 3021) Books on Tape, Inc.

—Natural Enemy. 1982. (Joan Kahn Bk.). (Illus.). 288p. 11.95 o.p. (*0-89919-081-2*) Houghton Mifflin Co.

—Natural Enemy. (Homer Kelly Mystery Ser.). 1990. 28p. pap. 5.95 o.p. (*0-14-013393-3*); 1987. (Illus.). 228p. pap. 3.95 o.p. (*0-14-009345-1*) Viking Penguin. (Penguin Bks.).

—The Shortest Day: Murder at the Revels. 1996. (Homer Kelly Mystery Ser.). (Illus.). 272p. pap. 5.95 o.s.i (*0-14-017377-3*, Viking) Penguin Group (USA) Inc.

—The Shortest Day: Murder at the Revels. 1995. (Homer Kelly Mystery Ser.). (Illus.). 272p. 19.95 o.p. (*0-670-84710-0*) Viking Penguin.

—The Transcendental Murder. unabr. collector's ed. 1982. audio 48.00 (*0-7366-0499-5*, 1473) Books on Tape, Inc.

—The Transcendental Murder. (Homer Kelly Mystery Ser.). 1990. 36p. pap. 6.95 o.p. (*0-14-014852-3*); 1989. 288p. pap. 3.95 o.p. (*0-14-011384-3*) Viking Penguin. (Penguin Bks.).

LeClaire, Anne D. Entering Normal. 2002. 336p. pap. 14.00 (*0-345-44573-2*, Ballantine Bks.) Ballantine Bks.

—Entering Normal. l.t. ed. 2001. (Women's Fiction Ser.). 582p. 29.95 (*0-7862-3567-5*) Thorndike Pr.

—Sideshow. 1995. 400p. mass mkt. 5.99 o.s.i (*0-451-40610-9*, Onyx) NAL.

—Sideshow. 308p. 3.98 o.p. (*0-8317-4551-7*) Smithmark Pubs., Inc.

—Sideshow. 1994. 320p. 20.95 o.p. (*0-670-84328-8*, Viking) Viking Penguin.

Lee, Linda Francis. Swan's Grace. 2000. 352p. mass mkt. 6.99 (*0-449-00206-3*, Ivy Bks.) Ballantine Bks.

Lee, Marie G. The Curious Cape Cod Skull. 1995. (Cape Cod Mystery Ser.: Bk. 1). 224p. 18.95 (*0-8034-9109-3*, Avalon Bks.) Bouregy, Thomas & Co., Inc.

Lee, Wendi. Crazy Like a Fox: An Angela Matelli Mystery. 2002. 240p. 22.95 (*0-312-26139-X*, Saint Martin's Minotaur) St. Martin's Pr.

—Deadbeat. 2000. 256p. mass mkt. (*0-373-26339-2*, Harlequin Bks.) Harlequin Enterprises, Ltd.

—Deadbeat. 1999. (Angela Matelli Mysteries Ser.). 256p. 22.95 o.p. (*0-312-16812-8*, Saint Martin's Minotaur) St. Martin's Pr.

—The Good Daughter. 1996. pap. 4.99 (*0-312-95696-7*, St. Martin's Paperbacks); 1994. 224p. 19.95 o.p. (*0-312-11259-9*, Saint Martin's Minotaur) St. Martin's Pr.

—He Who Dies. 2001. (WWL Mystery Ser.: No. 386). 252p. mass mkt. (*0-373-26386-4*, Worldwide Library) Harlequin Enterprises, Ltd.

—He Who Dies. E-Book 5.99 (*0-312-27437-8*) St. Martin's Pr.

—He Who Dies: An Angela Matelli Mystery. 2000. (Angela Matelli Mysteries Ser.). 247p. 23.95 (*0-312-20894-4*, Saint Martin's Minotaur) St. Martin's Pr.

—Missing Eden. 1999. per. (*0-373-26301-5*, Harlequin Bks.) Harlequin Enterprises, Ltd.

—Missing Eden. 1996. 240p. 21.95 o.p. (*0-312-14370-2*, Saint Martin's Minotaur) St. Martin's Pr.

Lehane, Dennis. Darkness, Take My Hand. 1996. 320p. 24.00 (*0-688-14380-6*, Morrow, William & Co.) Morrow/Avon.

—A Drink Before the War. 1994. 288p. 22.95 (*0-15-100093-X*) Harcourt Trade Pubs.

—A Drink Before the War. 1996. 320p. mass mkt. 7.99 (*0-380-72623-8*, Avon Bks.) Morrow/Avon.

—A Drink Before the War. 336p. (*0-7278-5537-9*) Severn Hse. Pubs., Ltd.

—Gone, Baby, Gone. abr. ed. 1999. audio 7.99 o.s.i (*1-56740-305-0*, 1869, Paperback Nova Audio Bks.); 1998. audio 17.95 o.p. (*1-56740-783-8*, 450, Nova Audio Bks.); 1998. audio 26.95 (*1-56740-058-2*, 18, Bookcassette); 1998. audio 73.25 (*1-56740-587-8*, 881, Unabridged Library Editions) Brilliance Audio.

—Gone, Baby, Gone. 1999. 448p. mass mkt. 7.99 (*0-380-73035-9*, Avon Bks.); 1998. 256p. 24.00 (*0-688-15332-1*, Morrow, William & Co.) Morrow/Avon.

—Prayers for Rain. abr. ed. 1999. audio 17.95 o.p. (*1-56740-840-0*, 1698, Nova Audio Bks.); audio 35.95 (*1-56740-428-6*, 1696, Brilliance Audio Unabridged); audio 57.25 (*1-56740-654-8*, 1697, Unabridged Library Editions) Brilliance Audio.

—Prayers for Rain, Set. abr. ed. 1999. audio 17.95. audio 35.95 Highsmith Inc.

—Prayers for Rain. 2000. 416p. mass mkt. 7.99 (*0-380-73036-7*); 1999. 352p. 25.00 (*0-688-15333-X*, Morrow, William & Co.) Morrow/Avon.

—Prayers for Rain. l.t. ed. 1999. (Core Ser.). 570p. 29.95 (*0-7838-8786-8*) Thorndike Pr.

—Sacred. abr. ed. 1998. audio 7.99 o.p. (*1-56740-238-0*, 1650, Nova Audio Bks.); 1997. audio 16.95 o.p. (*1-56100-979-2*, 505, Nova Audio Bks.); 1997. audio 73.25 o.p. (*1-56100-829-X*, 1022, Unabridged Library Editions); 1997. audio 23.95 (*1-56100-754-4*, 244, Bookcassette) Brilliance Audio.

—Sacred. 1998. 400p. mass mkt. 7.99 (*0-380-72629-7*, Avon Bks.); 1997. 256p. 23.00 (*0-688-14381-4*, Morrow, William & Co.) Morrow/Avon.

—Shutter Island. 2003. 336p. 25.95 (*0-688-16317-3*, Morrow, William & Co.) Morrow/Avon.

Lesourd, Leonard. The Rookie. 1996. 18.99 (*0-345-40504-8*) Ballantine Bks.

Lewis, Stephen. The Blind in Darkness. 2000. (Mystery of Colonial Times Ser.). 272p. mass mkt. 5.99 o.s.i (*0-425-17466-2*, Prime Crime) Berkley Publishing Group.

—The Dumb Shall Sing: A Mystery of Colonial Times. 1999. 272p. mass mkt. 5.99 o.s.i (*0-425-16997-9*, Prime Crime) Berkley Publishing Group.

L'Heureux, John. The Miracle: A Novel. 2002. 240p. 24.00 (*0-87113-857-3*, Atlantic Monthly Pr.) Grove/Atlantic, Inc.

Lipman, Elinor. The Ladies' Man. l.t. ed. 2000. 26.95 (*1-56895-837-4*, Wheeler Publishing, Inc.) Gale Group.

—The Ladies' Man. 2000. (Contemporaries Ser.). 272p. pap. 13.00 (*0-375-70731-X*, Vintage) Knopf Publishing Group.

Loeschke, Maravene S. The Path Between: An Historical Novel of the Dickinson Family of Amherst. 1988. (Illus.). 300p. (Orig.). (C). pap. 15.95 (*0-935132-11-2*) Fairfax, C.H. Co., Inc.

Logan, Margaret. The End of an Altruist. 1993. 288p. 21.95 o.p. (*0-312-10459-6*, Saint Martin's Minotaur) St. Martin's Pr.

—Never Let a Stranger in Your House. 1995. 256p. 21.95 o.p. (*0-312-13130-5*, Saint Martin's Minotaur) St. Martin's Pr.

Lonsdale, Harry Paul. Up in Smoke. 2001. (Nicholas Chase Cigar Mysteries Ser.). 256p. mass mkt. 5.99 (*0-380-80300-3*, Avon Bks.) Morrow/Avon.

Lott, Bret. The Man Who Owned Vermont. 1999. 240p. pap. 12.00 (*0-671-03820-6*); 1988. 224p. pap. (*0-671-64587-0*) Simon & Schuster. (Washington Square Pr.).

—The Man Who Owned Vermont. 1987. 231p. 16.95 o.p. (*0-670-81582-9*) Viking Penguin.

—A Stranger's House. 1999. 256p. pap. 12.00 (*0-671-03822-2*); 1990. 272p. pap. (*0-671-68328-4*) Simon & Schuster. (Washington Square Pr.).

—A Stranger's House. 1988. 272p. 17.95 o.p. (*0-670-82246-9*) Viking Penguin.

Lowry, Lois. Taking Care of Terrific, 001. 1983. 176p. (J). (gr. 4-6). 16.00 (*0-395-34070-5*) Houghton Mifflin Co.

—Taking Care of Terrific. l.t. ed. 1989. 208p. (YA). reprint ed. lib. bdg. 16.95 o.s.i (*1-55736-119-3*, Cornerstone Bks.) Pages, Inc.

Luber, Philip. Deliver Us from Evil. 1997. 324p. mass mkt. 5.99 (*0-449-14940-4*, Fawcett) Ballantine Bks.

—Forgive Us Our Sins. 1994. (Boston Mysteries Ser.). mass mkt. 5.99 o.s.i (*0-449-14849-1*, Fawcett) Ballantine Bks.

—Pray for Us Sinners. 1997. 294p. (Orig.). mass mkt. 5.99 o.s.i (*0-449-18329-7*, Fawcett) Ballantine Bks.

Mac, Gerard. Pilgrims a Novel of the Mayflower. 1994. 21.95 o.p. (*0-312-11551-2*) St. Martin's Pr.

MacDonald, Patricia. Mother's Day. l.t. ed. 1994. 23.95 o.p. (*0-7927-1962-X*); pap. o.p. (*0-7927-1961-1*) BBC Audiobooks America.

—Mother's Day. 1994. 304p. 29.00 (*0-446-51685-6*) Warner Bks., Inc.

MacLeod, Charlotte. The Balloon Man. 1998. (Sarah Kelling & Max Bittersohn Mysteries Ser.). 240p. 23.00 o.s.i (*0-89296-657-2*) Mysterious Pr.

—The Balloon Man. 2000. 288p. mass mkt. 6.50 (*0-446-60835-1*) Warner Bks., Inc.

—The Bilbao Looking Glass. 1983. (Crime Club Ser.). 192p. 11.95 o.p. (*0-385-18336-4*) Doubleday Publishing.

—The Bilbao Looking Glass. 1984. 208p. pap. 3.50 (*0-380-67454-8*, Avon Bks.) Morrow/Avon.

—The Bilbao Looking Glass. 2003. 192p. pap. 6.99 (*0-7434-7492-9*) ibooks, Inc.

—The Convivial Codfish. 1984. (Crime Club Ser.). 192p. 11.95 o.p. (*0-385-19333-5*) Doubleday Publishing.

—The Convivial Codfish. 1985. 224p. pap. 3.50 (*0-380-69865-X*, Avon Bks.) Morrow/Avon.

—The Corpse in Oozak's Pond. 1987. 224p. 15.45 o.p. (*0-89296-188-0*) Mysterious Pr.

—The Corpse in Oozak's Pond. 1989. 2.99 o.p. (*0-517-00184-5*) Random Hse. Value Publishing.

—The Corpse in Oozak's Pond. 1988. 203p. mass mkt. 5.99 o.p. (*0-445-40683-6*, Mysterious Pr. Paperback Bks.) Warner Bks., Inc.

—Curse of the Giant Hogweed. 1986. (Peter Shandy Ser.). 176p. pap. 3.50 (*0-380-70051-4*, Avon Bks.) Morrow/Avon.

—Exit the Milkman. l.t. ed. 1996. 22.95 o.p. (*1-56895-388-7*, Wheeler Publishing, Inc.) Gale Group.

—Exit the Milkman. 1996. 364p. 21.95 o.s.i (*0-89296-572-X*) Mysterious Pr.

—Exit the Milkman. 1997. 256p. mass mkt. 5.99 o.p. (*0-446-40398-9*) Warner Bks., Inc.

—Exit the Milkman. 2003. 320p. pap. 6.99 (*0-7434-4537-6*) ibooks, Inc.

—The Family Vault. 1979. 10.95 o.p. (*0-385-14871-2*) Doubleday Publishing.

—The Family Vault. 1980. 240p. mass mkt. 4.50 (*0-380-49080-3*, Avon Bks.) Morrow/Avon.

—The Gladstone Bag: A Sarah Kelling Mystery. 1990. 16.95 o.p. (*0-89296-370-0*) Mysterious Pr.

—The Gladstone Bag: A Sarah Kelling Mystery. 1992. 3.99 o.p. (*0-517-08076-1*) Random Hse. Value Publishing.

—The Gladstone Bag: A Sarah Kelling Mystery. 1991. mass mkt. 5.99 o.p. (*0-446-40002-5*, Mysterious Pr. Paperback Bks.) Warner Bks., Inc.

—The Luck Runs Out. 1981. 192p. pap. 3.50 (*0-380-54171-8*, Avon Bks.) Morrow/Avon.

—The Odd Job. l.t. ed. 1995. 352p. reprint ed. 21.95 o.p. (*0-7838-1374-0*, Macmillan Reference USA) Gale Group.

—The Odd Job. 1995. 288p. 18.95 o.s.i (*0-89296-571-1*) Mysterious Pr.

—The Odd Job. 1996. 272p. mass mkt. 5.99 o.p. (*0-446-40397-0*) Warner Bks., Inc.

—An Owl Too Many. l.t. ed. 1991. (General Ser.). 355p. lib. bdg. 20.95 (*0-8161-5235-7*, Macmillan Reference USA) Gale Group.

—An Owl Too Many. 1991. 17.95 o.p. (*0-89296-431-6*) Mysterious Pr.

—An Owl Too Many. 1992. 240p. mass mkt. 4.99 o.p. (*0-446-40101-3*, Mysterious Pr. Paperback Bks.) Warner Bks., Inc.

—The Palace Guard. 1981. 192p. 10.95 o.p. (*0-385-17533-7*) Doubleday Publishing.

—The Palace Guard. 1982. 176p. mass mkt. 3.99 (*0-380-59857-4*, Avon Bks.) Morrow/Avon.

—The Palace Guard. l.t. ed. 1982. 325p. reprint ed. 11.95 o.p. (*0-89621-345-5*) Thorndike Pr.

—The Palace Guard. 2003. 192p. mass mkt. 6.99 (*0-7434-5912-1*) ibooks, Inc.

—The Plain Old Man. 1985. (Crime Club Ser.). 192p. 12.95 o.p. (*0-385-23003-6*) Doubleday Publishing.

—The Plain Old Man. l.t. ed. 1986. (Nightingale Ser.). 336p. 10.95 o.p. (*0-8161-4025-1*, Macmillan Reference USA) Gale Group.

—The Plain Old Man. 1986. 224p. mass mkt. 3.99 (*0-380-70148-0*, Avon Bks.) Morrow/Avon.

—The Plain Old Man. 2003. 224p. mass mkt. 6.99 (*0-7434-7479-1*) ibooks, Inc.

—The Recycled Citizen. l.t. ed. 1989. (General Ser.). 352p. lib. bdg. 19.95 o.p. (*0-8161-4777-9*, Macmillan Reference USA) Gale Group.

—The Recycled Citizen. 1988. 208p. 15.45 o.p. (*0-89296-187-2*) Mysterious Pr.

—The Recycled Citizen. 1992. 4.50 (*0-446-77518-5*); 1989. 272p. mass mkt. 4.99 o.p. (*0-445-40689-5*, Mysterious Pr. Paperback Bks.) Warner Bks., Inc.

—Rest You Merry. 1979. (General Ser.). lib. bdg. 13.50 o.p. (*0-8161-3000-0*, Macmillan Reference USA) Gale Group.

—Rest You Merry. 1980. 224p. reprint ed. mass mkt. 4.99 o.p. (*0-380-47530-8*, Avon Bks.) Morrow/Avon.

—The Resurrection Man: A Sarah Kelling & Max Bittersohn Mystery. l.t. ed. 1993. (Magna Large Print Ser.). 381p. o.p. (*0-7505-0496-X*) Magna Large Print Bks. GBR. *Dist:* Ulverscroft Large Print Canada, Ltd.

—The Resurrection Man: A Sarah Kelling & Max Bittersohn Mystery. 1992. 256p. 17.95 o.p. (*0-89296-443-X*) Mysterious Pr.

—The Resurrection Man: A Sarah Kelling & Max Bittersohn Mystery. 1993. 256p. mass mkt. 5.99 o.p. (*0-446-40332-6*, Mysterious Pr. Paperback Bks.) Warner Bks., Inc.

—The Silver Ghost: A Sarah Kelling Mystery. l.t. ed. 1990. (Magna Large Print Ser.). 339p. 29.99 o.p. (*1-85057-592-4*) Magna Large Print Bks. GBR. *Dist:* Ulverscroft Large Print Bks., Ltd., Ulverscroft Large Print Canada, Ltd.

—The Silver Ghost: A Sarah Kelling Mystery. 1988. (Sarah Kelling Mystery Ser.). 224p. 15.95 (*0-89296-189-9*) Mysterious Pr.

—The Silver Ghost: A Sarah Kelling Mystery. 1989. 224p. reprint ed. mass mkt. 4.99 o.p. (*0-445-40828-6*, Mysterious Pr. Paperback Bks.) Warner Bks., Inc.

—Something in the Water. 1994. 272p. 18.95 o.s.i (*0-89296-430-8*) Mysterious Pr.

—Something in the Water. 1995. 240p. mass mkt. 5.50 o.p. (*0-446-40446-2*, Mysterious Pr. Paperback Bks.) Warner Bks., Inc.

—Something the Cat Dragged In. l.t. ed. 1984. (Nightingale Ser.). 10.95 o.p. (*0-8161-3710-2*, Macmillan Reference USA) Gale Group.

—Something the Cat Dragged In. 1984. 208p. mass mkt. 3.99 (*0-380-69096-9*, Avon Bks.) Morrow/Avon.

—Vane Pursuit: A Peter Shandy Mystery. l.t. ed. 1990. 368p. lib. bdg. 19.95 o.p. (*0-8161-4850-3*, Macmillan Reference USA) Gale Group.

—Vane Pursuit: A Peter Shandy Mystery. 1989. 15.95 o.p. (*0-89296-369-7*) Mysterious Pr.

—Vane Pursuit: A Peter Shandy Mystery. 1990. 224p. mass mkt. 5.50 o.p. (*0-445-40780-8*, Mysterious Pr. Paperback Bks.) Warner Bks., Inc.

—The Withdrawing Room. 1980. (Crime Club Ser.). 192p. 8.95 o.p. (*0-385-17181-1*) Doubleday Publishing.

—The Withdrawing Room. 1982. 192p. mass mkt. 3.99 (*0-380-56473-4*, Avon Bks.) Morrow/Avon.

—The Withdrawing Room. 2002. 192p. pap. 6.99 (*0-7434-5258-5*) ibooks, Inc.

—Wrack & Rune. 1983. 208p. mass mkt. 3.99 (*0-380-61911-3*, Avon Bks.) Morrow/Avon.

—Wrack & Rune. l.t. ed. 1982. 322p. reprint ed. 11.95 o.p. (*0-89621-372-2*) Thorndike Pr.

Maness, Larry. Nantucket Revenge: A Jake Eaton Mystery. 1995. 208p. 19.95 o.s.i (*0-89141-566-1*, Presidio Pr.) Ballantine Bks.

—A Once Perfect Place: A Jake Eaton Mystery. 1996. 208p. 19.95 o.s.i (*0-89141-567-X*, Presidio Pr.) Ballantine Bks.

—Strangler: A Jake Eaton Mystery. 1998. 192p. 19.95 o.p. (*0-89141-568-8*, Presidio Pr.) Ballantine Bks.

Marcoux, Alex, ed. Back to Salem. (C). 2003. 323p. 27.95 (*1-56023-224-2*); 2001. 324p. pap. 17.95 (*1-56023-225-0*) Haworth Pr., Inc., The. (Alice Street Editions).

Markham, Gretchen. A Gift for Dempsey: The Christmas Adventure of a Cape Cod Dog. 1995. (Illus.). 30p. (Orig.). (J). (gr. 1-3). pap. 9.95 (*1-887146-00-8*) Ark Works, Inc.

Marquand, John P. The Late George Apley. 1937. 18.95 o.s.i (*0-316-54652-6*) Aspen Pubs., Inc.

—The Late George Apley. 1994. lib. bdg. 24.95 (*1-56849-446-7*) Buccaneer Bks., Inc.

—The Late George Apley. 2004. 368p. pap. 14.95 (*0-316-73567-1*, Back Bay) Little Brown & Co.

—The Late George Apley. 1982. mass mkt. 3.95 o.s.i (*0-671-45929-5*, Pocket) Simon & Schuster.

Mars, Peter. A Taste for Money: A Novel Based on the True Story of a Dirty Boston Cop. 1999. (Illus.). 320p. pap. 14.95 (*0-9664475-1-4*) Commonwealth Publishing.

Martin, William. Cape Cod. abr. ed. 1993. 15.95 o.p. (*1-55800-399-1*, 41500) NewStar Media, Inc.

—Cape Cod. 2003. 864p. pap. 14.00 (*0-446-69260-3*); 1991. 672p. 21.95 o.p. (*0-446-51510-8*); 1992. 736p. reprint ed. mass mkt. 7.99 (*0-446-36317-0*) Warner Bks., Inc.

—Harvard Yard: A Novel. 2003. 592p. 25.95 (*0-446-53084-0*) Warner Bks., Inc.

Maso, Carole. Defiance. 272p. 1999. pap. 12.95 o.s.i (*0-452-27829-5*, Plume); 1998. 23.95 o.p. (*0-525-94307-2*) Dutton/Plume.

Mathews, Francine. Death in a Cold Hard Light. 1999. (Indigo Ser.). 352p. reprint ed. mass mkt. 5.99 (*0-553-57625-9*) Bantam Bks.

—Death in a Cold Hard Light. unabr. collector's ed. 1998. (Merry Folger Ser.). audio 64.00 (*0-7366-4262-5*, 4761) Books on Tape, Inc.

—Death in a Mood Indigo. 1998. 352p. mass mkt. 5.99 (*0-553-57624-0*) Bantam Bks.

—Death in a Mood Indigo. unabr. collector's ed. 1997. (Merry Folger Ser.). audio 64.00 (*0-7366-4006-1*, 4504) Books on Tape, Inc.

—Death in Rough Water. unabr. collector's ed. 1997. (Merry Folger Ser.: Vol. 2). audio 56.00 (*0-7366-3631-5*, 4292) Books on Tape, Inc.

—Death in Rough Water: A Merry Folger Mystery. 1996. 288p. mass mkt. 5.50 (*0-380-72335-2*, Avon Bks.); 1995. 320p. 22.00 o.p. (*0-688-13473-4*, Morrow, William & Co.) Morrow/Avon.

—Death in the Off-Season. unabr. collector's ed. 1997. (Merry Folger Ser.: Vol. 1). audio 64.00 (*0-7366-3600-5*, 4255) Books on Tape, Inc.

—Death in the Off-Season. 1995. 352p. mass mkt. 4.99 (*0-380-72334-4*, Avon Bks.); 1994. 318p. 23.00 o.p. (*0-688-13443-2*, Morrow, William & Co.) Morrow/Avon.
Matson, Suzanne. The Hunger Moon: A Novel. 1999. 272p. pap. 12.00 (*0-345-42553-7*) Ballantine Bks.
—The Hunger Moon: A Novel. 1997. 252p. 23.00 (*0-393-04099-2*) Norton, W. W. & Co., Inc.
McCracken, Elizabeth. The Giant's House: A Romance. 1997. 304p. pap. 13.00 (*0-380-73020-0*, Avon Bks.) Morrow/Avon.
McDaniel, Judith. Just Say Yes: A Novel. 1991. 176p. pap. 10.95 (*0-932379-96-6*); lib. bdg. 22.95 (*0-932379-97-4*) Firebrand Bks.
Mcdonald, Gregory. The Buck Passes Flynn. 1986. 224p. mass mkt. 4.95 o.s.i (*0-345-33690-9*); 1983. mass mkt. 2.50 o.s.i (*0-345-31610-X*); 1981. mass mkt. 2.25 o.s.i (*0-345-30029-7*) Ballantine Bks.
—The Buck Passes Flynn. 2000. E-Book (*1-930351-03-8*) FairHillBooks.com.
—The Buck Passes Flynn. l.t. ed. 1993. 12.95 o.p. (*0-8161-3394-8*, Macmillan Reference USA) Gale Group.
—The Buck Passes Flynn. 2004. 224p. pap. 12.00 (*0-375-71360-3*, Vintage) Knopf Publishing Group.
—Flynn. 2000. E-Book (*1-930351-04-6*) FairHillBooks.com.
—Flynn. 2003. (Vintage Crime/Black Lizard Ser.). 256p. pap. 12.00 (*0-375-71357-3*, Vintage) Knopf Publishing Group.
—Flynn. 1977. 1977p. pap. 3.95 (*0-380-01764-4*, Avon Bks.) Morrow/Avon.
—Flynn's In. 2000. E-Book (*1-930351-02-X*) FairHillBooks.com.
—Flynn's In. 2004. 208p. pap. 12.00 (*0-375-71361-1*, Vintage) Knopf Publishing Group.
—Flynn's In. ("Flynn" Ser.). 1999. 15.45 o.s.i (*0-89296-085-X*); 1987. 45.00 o.p. (*0-89296-086-8*) Mysterious Pr.
—Flynn's In. 1988. mass mkt. 4.95 o.s.i (*0-445-20864-3*) Warner Bks., Inc.
—Flynn's World. E-Book 23.50 (*1-930351-05-4*) FairHillBooks.com.
—Skylar in Yankeeland. 1997. 275p. 23.00 o.p. (*0-688-14164-1*, Morrow, William & Co.) Morrow/Avon.
McInerney, Merry. Dog People. 287p. 2000. pap. 14.95 (*0-312-87292-5*); 1998. 22.95 (*0-312-85699-7*) Doherty, Tom Assocs., LLC. (Forge Bks.).
Merullo, Roland. In Revere, in Those Days: A Novel. 2002. 320p. 22.00 (*0-609-61032-5*) Crown Publishing Group.
—In Revere, in Those Days: A Novel. 2003. 320p. pap. 13.00 (*0-375-71405-7*, Vintage) Knopf Publishing Group.
—In Revere, in Those Days: A Novel. 2002. (Americana Ser.). 28.95 (*0-7862-4823-8*) Thorndike Pr.
—Revere Beach Boulevard: A Novel. 336p. 1999. (Revere Beach Trilogy Ser.: Vol. 1). pap. 13.00 o.s.i (*0-8050-6006-5*, Owl Bks.); 1998. (Book One of the Revere Beach Trilogy Ser.). 23.00 o.s.i (*0-8050-6005-7*) Holt, Henry & Co.
Michaels, Grant. Body to Dye For. 1991. (Stonewall Inn Editions Ser.: Vol. 1). 241p. pap. 11.95 (*0-312-05825-X*, Saint Martin's Griffin); 1990. 17.95 o.p. (*0-312-04273-6*, Saint Martin's Minotaur) St. Martin's Pr.
—Dead As a Doornail. (Stan Kraychik Mystery Ser.). 256p. 1999. pap. 12.95 (*0-312-20644-5*, Saint Martin's Griffin); 1998. 22.95 o.p. (*0-312-18077-2*, Saint Martin's Minotaur) St. Martin's Pr.
—Dead on Your Feet. 256p. 1993. 12.99 o.p. (*0-312-09781-6*, Saint Martin's Minotaur); 4th ed. 1994. (Stonewall Inn Editions Ser.: Vol. 1). pap. 11.95 (*0-312-11457-5*, Saint Martin's Griffin) St. Martin's Pr.
—Love You to Death. (Stonewall Inn Editions Ser.). 1993. 10.95 (*0-312-08841-8*, Saint Martin's Griffin); 1992. 256p. 18.95 (*0-312-07027-6*, Saint Martin's Minotaur) St. Martin's Pr.
—Mask for a Diva. 1996. 304p. pap. 10.95 (*0-312-14120-3*, Saint Martin's Griffin); 1994. 272p. 20.95 o.p. (*0-312-11462-1*, Saint Martin's Minotaur) St. Martin's Pr.
—Time to Check Out: A Stan Kraychik Mystery. 1996. 272p. 21.95 o.p. (*0-312-14434-2*, Saint Martin's Minotaur); 1997. 256p. reprint ed. pap. 12.95 (*0-312-15673-1*, NPB 0273, Saint Martin's Griffin) St. Martin's Pr.
Miles, Margaret. Too Soon for Flowers. 1999. 320p. mass mkt. 5.99 (*0-553-57863-4*) Bantam Bks.
Miller, John & Smith, Tim, eds. Cape Cod Stories: Tales from Cape Cod, Nantucket, & Martha's Vineyard. 1996. 224p. pap. 12.95 o.p. (*0-8118-1080-1*) Chronicle Bks. LLC.
Miller, Sue. While I Was Gone. 2002. 352p. mass mkt. 7.99 (*0-345-42074-8*); 2000. 304p. pap. 14.00 (*0-345-44328-4*); 2000. 304p. pap. 12.95 o.s.i (*0-345-43500-1*) Ballantine Bks.
—While I Was Gone. l.t. ed. 1999. 30.00 o.p. (*0-7838-8481-8*, Macmillan Reference USA) Gale Group.
—While I Was Gone. l.t. ed. 1999. 448p. 24.00 o.s.i (*0-375-70571-6*) Knopf, Alfred A. Inc.
—While I Was Gone. abr. ed. 2000. audio 25.95 (*0-375-41664-1*); 2000. audio compact disk 29.95 (*0-375-41665-X*); 1999. audio 24.00 o.s.i (*0-375-40563-1*, 691584) Random Hse. Audio Publishing Group. (RH Audio).
—While I Was Gone. l.t. ed. 2000. 448p. pap. 12.95 o.s.i (*0-375-72801-5*) Random Hse. Large Print.
—While I Was Gone. 2000. (Oprah's Book Club Ser.). 288p. 24.00 (*0-375-41178-X*) Random Hse., Inc.
—While I Was Gone. 2000. 19.00 (*0-606-22790-3*) Turtleback Bks.
Minichino, Camille. The Boric Acid Murder. 2002. (Gloria Lamerino Mystery Ser.). 288p. 23.95 (*0-312-28502-7*, Saint Martin's Minotaur) St. Martin's Pr.
—The Boric Acid Murder. 2002. (Senior Lifestyles Ser.). 28.95 (*0-7862-4810-6*) Thorndike Pr.
Minot, Eliza. The Tiny One: A Novel. 2000. (Vintage Contemporaries Ser.). 272p. pap. 13.00 (*0-375-70633-X*, Vintage) Knopf Publishing Group.
—The Tiny One: A Novel. 1999. 272p. 22.00 o.s.i (*0-375-40645-X*) Knopf, Alfred A. Inc.
Minot, Susan. Folly. l.t. ed. 1993. 21.95 o.p. (*0-7927-1566-7*); pap. o.p. (*0-7927-1565-9*) BBC Audiobooks America.
—Folly. 1992. 256p. 19.95 o.p. (*0-395-60339-0*) Houghton Mifflin Co. Trade & Reference Div.
—Folly. Rosenman, Jane, ed. 1994. 288p. reprint ed. pap. 12.00 (*0-671-74951-X*, Pocket) Simon & Schuster.
Montague, Dan. White Wings. 1998. 464p. mass mkt. 6.99 o.s.i (*0-451-19565-5*, Signet Bks.) NAL.
Montague, Daniel F. White Wings. 1997. 480p. 24.95 o.p. (*0-525-94303-X*) Dutton/Plume.
Moodie, Craig. A Sailor's Valentine. 1994. 208p. 17.95 o.p. (*0-312-11053-7*) St. Martin's Pr.
—A Sailor's Valentine: Stories. 1999. pap. text 14.95 (*0-940160-80-3*) Parnassus Imprints.
Moore, Christine P. The Virgin Knows. 1995. 320p. 22.95 o.p. (*0-312-13203-4*) St. Martin's Pr.
Morris, Mary McGarry. Fiona Range. l.t. ed. 2000. 28.95 (*1-56895-882-X*, Wheeler Publishing, Inc.) Gale Group.
—Fiona Range. 2000. 400p. 24.95 o.s.i (*0-670-89156-8*, Viking); 2001. 432p. reprint ed. 14.00 (*0-14-100184-4*) Viking Penguin.
Morris, Sandra A. By the Sea Shore: A Jess Shore Mystery. 2000. 219p. pap. 12.00 (*1-883061-32-6*) Rising Tide Pr.
Munson, Ronald. Night Vision. 1995. 336p. 21.95 o.p. (*0-525-93781-1*, Dutton) Dutton/Plume.
—Night Vision. 1996. pap. 5.99 o.s.i (*0-451-40659-1*, Onyx); 416p. mass mkt. 5.99 o.s.i (*0-451-18013-5*, Signet Bks.) NAL.
Murphy, Gloria. Down Will Come Baby. 1991. 18.95 o.p. (*1-55611-196-7*) Fine, Donald I. Bks.
Murphy, Timothy. Getting off Clean. (Stonewall Inn Editions Ser.). 1998. 336p. pap. 13.95 (*0-312-18720-3*, Saint Martin's Griffin); 1997. 272p. 23.95 (*0-312-15132-2*) St. Martin's Pr.
Neal, John. Rachel Dyer. 1996. (Literary Classics). 284p. pap. 10.00 (*1-57392-049-5*) Prometheus Bks., Pubs.
—Rachel Dyer. 1979. 288p. reprint ed. 50.00 (*0-8201-1263-1*) Scholars' Facsimiles & Reprints.
—Rachel Dyer, a North American Story. 1988. reprint ed. lib. bdg. 49.00 (*0-7812-0003-2*) Reprint Services Corp.
—Rachel Dyer, a North American Story. reprint ed. 21.00 o.p. (*0-403-01978-8*) Somerset Pubs., Inc.
Neggers, Carla. On Fire. unabr. ed. 1999. audio 7.99 (*1-55204-192-1*, MIR-1192) Durkin Hayes Publishing Ltd.
—On Fire. 384p. 2003. mass mkt. (*1-55166-970-6*); 1999. per. (*1-55166-541-7*, 1-66541-3) Harlequin Enterprises, Ltd. (Mira Bks.).
Nevins, Linda M. Commonwealth Avenue. 1996. 432p. 24.95 o.p. (*0-312-13949-7*) St. Martin's Pr.
Norton, Andre & Hogarth, Grace A. Sneeze on Sunday. 1991. 256p. 18.95 o.p. (*0-312-85222-3*, Tor Bks.) Doherty, Tom Assocs., LLC.
O'Connell, Jack. Word Made Flesh. 1999. 336p. 24.00 o.p. (*0-06-019209-7*) HarperCollins Pubs.
—Word Made Flesh. 2000. 336p. pap. 13.00 (*0-06-109722-5*, Perennial) HarperTrade.
Oleksiw, Susan. Friends & Enemies: A Mellingham Mystery. l.t. ed. 2001. (Mystery Ser.). 232p. 24.95 (*0-7862-3009-6*, Five Star) Gale Group.
Oleksiw, Susan P. Double Take. 1994. (Chief Joe Silva Ser.). 256p. text 20.00 (*0-684-19656-5*, Macmillan Reference USA) Gale Group.
—Family Album. 1995. (Chief Joe Silva Ser.). 287p. 20.00 (*0-684-19731-6*, Scribner) Simon & Schuster.
—Murder in Mellingham. 1993. 288p. 20.00 o.p. (*0-684-19528-3*, Macmillan Reference USA) Gale Group.
Olson, Toby. At Sea. 1993. 256p. 19.00 o.p. (*0-671-73641-8*, Simon & Schuster) Simon & Schuster.
Osborn, David. Murder on Martha's Vineyard. unabr. ed. 1992. audio 42.00 (*0-7366-2188-1*, 2983) Books on Tape, Inc.
Packer, George. Central Square. 1998. 304p. 24.95 (*1-55597-277-2*) Graywolf Pr.
Page, Katherine Hall. The Body in the Belfry. 1991. 320p. reprint ed. mass mkt. 6.99 (*0-380-71328-4*, Avon Bks.) Morrow/Avon.
—The Body in the Belfry. 1990. 272p. 16.95 (*0-312-03798-8*, Saint Martin's Minotaur) St. Martin's Pr.
—The Body in the Bog. l.t. ed. 1997. 299p. lib. bdg. 23.95 (*1-57490-087-0*, Beeler Large Print Bks.) Beeler, Thomas T. Publisher.
—The Body in the Bog. 1997. 384p. mass mkt. 6.99 (*0-380-72712-9*, Avon Bks.); 1996. 256p. 22.00 o.p. (*0-688-14573-6*, Morrow, William & Co.) Morrow/Avon.
—The Body in the Bonfire. 2002. 256p. 23.95 (*0-380-97843-1*, Morrow, William & Co.) Morrow/Avon.
—The Body in the Bookcase. l.t. ed. 2001. (Wheeler Large Print Book Ser.). 333p. pap. 22.95 (*1-58724-018-1*, Wheeler Publishing, Inc.) Gale Group.
—The Body in the Bookcase. (Faith Fairchild Mysteries Ser.). 1999. 384p. mass mkt. 6.99 (*0-380-73237-8*, Avon Bks.); 1998. 272p. 22.00 (*0-688-15747-5*, Morrow, William & Co.) Morrow/Avon.
—The Body in the Cast. l.t. ed. 1999. (Beeler Large Print Mystery Ser.). 24.95 (*1-57490-239-3*, Beeler Large Print Bks.) Beeler, Thomas T. Publisher.
—The Body in the Cast. 1994. 368p. mass mkt. 6.99 (*0-380-72338-7*, Avon Bks.) Morrow/Avon.
—The Body in the Cast. 1993. 224p. 19.95 o.p. (*0-312-09755-7*, Saint Martin's Minotaur) St. Martin's Pr.
—The Body in the Lighthouse. l.t. ed. 2003. (Mystery Ser.). 28.95 (*1-57490-508-2*) Beeler, Thomas T. Publisher.
—The Body in the Lighthouse. 2004. 352p. mass mkt. 6.99 (*0-380-81386-6*, Avon Bks.); 2003. 256p. 23.95 (*0-380-97844-X*, Morrow, William & Co.) Morrow/Avon.
—The Body in the Moonlight. 2001. (Faith Fairchild Mysteries Ser.). 256p. 23.00 (*0-380-97842-3*, Morrow, William & Co.) Morrow/Avon.
Palmer, Michael. Michael Palmer: Three Complete Novels. 1996. 784p. 13.99 (*0-517-14959-1*) Random Hse. Value Publishing.
—Miracle Cure. 1998. 416p. 23.95 o.s.i (*0-553-10523-X*); 1999. 448p. reprint ed. mass mkt. 7.50 (*0-553-57662-3*) Bantam Bks.
—Miracle Cure. unabr. ed. 1998. audio 64.00 (*0-7366-4158-0*, 4661) Books on Tape, Inc.
—Miracle Cure. l.t. ed. 1998. 27.95 o.p. (*1-56895-612-6*, Wheeler Publishing, Inc.) Gale Group.
—Miracle Cure. abr. ed. 1998. audio 23.95 (*0-553-47816-8*); audio compact disk 29.95 (*0-553-45591-5*, ) Random Hse. Audio Publishing Group. (RH Audio).
—Miracle Cure. unabr. ed. 1998. audio 78.00 (*0-7887-1897-5*, 95319E7) Recorded Bks., LLC.
—Natural Causes. 1994. 496p. mass mkt. 7.50 (*0-553-56876-0*) Bantam Bks.
—Natural Causes. abr. ed. 2000. audio 9.99 (*0-553-52727-4*, RH Audio) Random Hse. Audio Publishing Group.
—Natural Causes. unabr. ed. 1994. audio audio 91.00 (*0-7887-0085-5*, 94325E7) Recorded Bks., LLC.
Parker, Robert B. A Catskill Eagle. unabr. collector's ed. 1990. (Spenser Ser.). audio 40.00 (*0-7366-1676-4*, 2524) Books on Tape, Inc.
—A Catskill Eagle. 1986. (Spencer Mystery Ser.). 384p. mass mkt. 7.50 (*0-440-11132-3*) Dell Publishing.
—A Catskill Eagle. l.t. ed. 1985. (Spencer Mystery Ser.). 16.95 o.p. (*0-8161-3892-3*, Macmillan Reference USA) Gale Group.
—Ceremony. unabr. collector's ed. 1989. (Spenser Ser.). audio 30.00 (*0-7366-1628-4*, 2486) Books on Tape, Inc.
—Ceremony. 1992. (Spencer Mystery Ser.). 224p. mass mkt. 7.50 (*0-440-10993-0*) Dell Publishing.
—Ceremony. l.t. ed. 1985. (Nightingale-Lythway Ser.). 9.95 o.p. (*0-8161-3833-8*, Macmillan Reference USA) Gale Group.
—Chance. 1997. (Spenser Mystery Ser.). 336p. reprint ed. mass mkt. 7.99 (*0-425-15747-4*) Berkley Publishing Group.
—Chance. l.t. ed. 1996. (Spenser Mystery Ser.). 26.95 o.p. (*1-56895-335-6*, Wheeler Publishing, Inc.) Gale Group.
—Chance. unabr. ed. 1996. (Spenser Mystery Ser.). 24.95 o.p. (*0-7871-0712-3*, 693925) NewStar Media, Inc.
—Chance. 1996. 21.95 (*0-399-14688-1*); 1996. 320p. 21.95 o.p. (*0-399-14134-0*, G. P. Putnam's Sons); 2015. 100.00 (*0-399-14167-7*) Penguin Group (USA) Inc.
—Crimson Joy. unabr. collector's ed. 1990. (Spenser Ser.). audio 30.00 (*0-7366-1758-2*, 2597) Books on Tape, Inc.
—Crimson Joy. (Spencer Mystery Ser.). 1989. 304p. mass mkt. 7.99 (*0-440-20343-0*); 1988. 75.00 o.s.i (*0-385-29668-1*, Delacorte Pr.) Dell Publishing.
—Crimson Joy. abr. ed. 1988. (Spencer Mystery Ser.). audio 14.95 (*0-671-66617-7*, Simon & Schuster Audioworks) Simon & Schuster Audio.
—Death in Paradise. 2002. 304p. reprint ed. mass mkt. 7.99 (*0-425-18706-3*) Berkley Publishing Group.
—Death in Paradise. l.t. ed. 2002. 382p. 31.95 (*0-7862-3850-X*) Gale Group.
—Death in Paradise. 2001. 320p. 23.95 o.s.i (*0-399-14779-9*) Penguin Group (USA) Inc.
—Death in Paradise. l.t. ed. 13.95 (*1-4104-0054-9*, Large Print Pr.); 2003. pap. 13.95 (*0-7862-3851-8*) Thorndike Pr.
—Double Deuce. 1993. (Spenser Mystery Ser.). 256p. mass mkt. 7.99 (*0-425-13793-7*) Berkley Publishing Group.
—Double Deuce. unabr. ed. 2000. (Spenser Mystery Ser.). audio (*1-56054-857-6*, SAB 053) Chivers Audio Bks. GBR. *Dist:* BBC Audiobooks America.
—Double Deuce. l.t. ed. 1993. (Spencer Mystery Ser.). 233p. pap. 17.95 o.p. (*0-8161-5597-6*); 20.95 o.p. (*0-8161-5596-8*) Gale Group. (Macmillan Reference USA).
—Double Deuce. unabr. ed. 1993. (Spenser Mystery Ser.). 24.95 o.p. (*1-55800-473-4*, 492065) NewStar Media, Inc.
—Double Deuce. 1992. (Spenser Mystery Ser.). 224p. 100.00 o.p. (*0-399-13754-8*); 19.95 o.s.i (*0-399-13721-1*) Penguin Group (USA) Inc. (G. P. Putnam's Sons).
—Early Autumn. unabr. collector's ed. 1989. (Spenser Ser.). audio 30.00 (*0-7366-1589-X*, 2452) Books on Tape, Inc.
—Early Autumn. (Spencer Mystery Ser.). 1992. 224p. mass mkt. 2.99 o.s.i (*0-440-21387-8*); 1992. 224p. mass mkt. 7.99 (*0-440-12214-7*); 1981. 10.95 o.s.i (*0-440-02248-7*, Delacorte Pr.) Dell Publishing.
—The Early Spenser - Three Complete Novels: The Godwulf Manuscript, God Save the Child, Mortal Stakes. 1989. 504p. 13.95 o.s.i (*0-385-29728-9*, Delacorte Pr.) Dell Publishing.
—Family Honor. 2000. (Sunny Randall Ser.). 338p. mass mkt. 7.50 (*0-425-17706-8*) Berkley Publishing Group.
—Family Honor. l.t. ed. (Wheeler Press Paperback Ser.). 2000. 10.95 (*1-56895-977-X*); 1999. 27.95 (*1-56895-788-2*) Gale Group. (Wheeler Publishing, Inc.).
—Family Honor, Set. abr. ed. 1999. audio 18.00 Highsmith Inc.
—Family Honor. 1999. audio 30.00 (*0-7871-2354-4*); audio compact disk 36.00 (*0-7871-2369-2*); audio 18.00 (*0-7871-2355-2*, Dove Audio); audio 30.00 NewStar Media, Inc.
—Family Honor. l.t. ed. 1999. (Sunny Randall Ser.). 322p. 22.95 o.p. (*0-399-14566-4*, G. P. Putnam's Sons) Penguin Group (USA) Inc.
—God Save the Child. unabr. collector's ed. 1988. (Spenser Ser.). audio 36.00 (*0-7366-1381-1*, 2274) Books on Tape, Inc.
—God Save the Child. 1987. (Spencer Mystery Ser.). 208p. mass mkt. 7.99 (*0-440-12899-4*) Dell Publishing.
—God Save the Child. 1974. (Spenser Mystery Ser.). 192p. 5.95 o.p. (*0-395-19955-7*) Houghton Mifflin Co.
—God Save the Child. 1995. (Spenser Mystery Ser.). Random Hse., Inc.
—The Godwulf Manuscript. l.t. ed. 1994. (Spenser Mystery Ser.). pap. 18.95 o.p. (*0-7927-1883-6*); 19.95 o.p. (*0-7927-1884-4*) BBC Audiobooks America.
—The Godwulf Manuscript. 1978. (Spenser Mystery Ser.). 1.50 o.s.i (*0-425-03967-6*) Berkley Publishing Group.
—The Godwulf Manuscript. unabr. collector's ed. 1988. (Spenser Ser.). audio 36.00 (*0-7366-1353-6*, 2254) Books on Tape, Inc.
—The Godwulf Manuscript. 1994. (Spenser Mystery Ser.). 192p. reprint ed. lib. bdg. 29.95 (*1-56849-317-7*) Buccaneer Bks., Inc.
—The Godwulf Manuscript. 1992. (Spencer Mystery Ser.). 208p. mass mkt. 7.99 (*0-440-12961-3*) Dell Publishing.
—The Godwulf Manuscript. 1974. (Spenser Mystery Ser.). 5.95 o.p. (*0-395-18011-2*) Houghton Mifflin Co.
—The Godwulf Manuscript. 1995. (Spenser Mystery Ser.). Random Hse., Inc.
—Hush Money. 2000. (Spenser Mystery Ser.). 336p. pap. 7.99 (*0-425-17401-8*) Berkley Publishing Group.
—Hush Money. l.t. ed. 1999. (Spenser Mystery Ser.). 27.95 (*1-56895-739-4*, Wheeler Publishing, Inc.) Gale Group.
—Hush Money. abr. ed. 1999. (Spenser Mystery Ser.). audio 18.00 (*0-7871-1898-2*, 394162); audio 30.00 (*0-7871-1870-2*, 890100) NewStar Media, Inc.
—Hush Money. 1999. (Spenser Mystery Ser.). 336p. 22.95 o.p. (*0-399-14458-7*) Penguin Group (USA) Inc.
—Hush Money. 2000. 13.55 (*0-606-20394-X*); 13.55 (*0-606-20098-3*) Turtleback Bks.
—The Judas Goat. (Spenser Mystery Ser.). 20.95 (*0-89190-371-2*) Amereon, Ltd.
—The Judas Goat. 1979. (Spenser Mystery Ser.). 1.95 o.p. (*0-425-04204-9*) Berkley Publishing Group.

Settings

—The Judas Goat. unabr. collector's ed. 1989. (Spenser Ser.). audio 36.00 (*0-7366-1571-7*, 2438) Books on Tape, Inc.

—The Judas Goat. 1992. (Spencer Mystery Ser.). 208p. mass mkt. 7.99 (*0-440-14196-6*) Dell Publishing.

—The Judas Goat, 001. 1978. (Spenser Mystery Ser.). 7.95 o.p. (*0-395-26682-3*) Houghton Mifflin Co.

—Looking for Rachel Wallace. unabr. collector's ed. 1989. (Spenser Ser.). audio 36.00 (*0-7366-1597-0*, 2458) Books on Tape, Inc.

—Looking for Rachel Wallace. (Spencer Mystery Ser.). 1987. 224p. mass mkt. 7.50 (*0-440-15316-6*); 1980. 10.95 o.s.i (*0-440-04764-1*, Delacorte Pr.) Dell Publishing.

—Mortal Stakes. unabr. collector's ed. 1989. (Spenser Ser.). audio 36.00 (*0-7366-1530-X*, 2400) Books on Tape, Inc.

—Mortal Stakes. 1994. (Spenser Mystery Ser.). reprint ed. lib. bdg. 32.95 (*1-56849-316-9*) Buccaneer Bks., Inc.

—Mortal Stakes. 1987. (Spencer Mystery Ser.). 336p. mass mkt. 7.50 (*0-440-15758-7*) Dell Publishing.

—Mortal Stakes, 001. 1975. (Spenser Mystery Ser.). 192p. 6.95 o.p. (*0-395-21969-8*) Houghton Mifflin Co.

—Night Passage. 336p. 2001. mass mkt. 7.99 (*0-425-18396-3*); 1998. reprint ed. mass mkt. 7.50 o.s.i (*0-515-12349-8*, Jove) Berkley Publishing Group.

—Night Passage. l.t. ed. 1998. (Large Print Book Ser.). 26.95 o.p. (*1-56895-530-8*, Wheeler Publishing, Inc.) Gale Group.

—Night Passage. 1997. 21.95 o.s.i (*0-399-14694-6*); 320p. 21.95 o.p. (*0-399-14304-1*, G. P. Putnam's Sons) Penguin Group (USA) Inc.

—Pale Kings & Princes. unabr. collector's ed. 1990. (Spenser Ser.). audio 30.00 (*0-7366-1772-8*, 2611) Books on Tape, Inc.

—Pale Kings & Princes. (Spencer Mystery Ser.). 1993. 320p. mass mkt. 3.99 o.s.i (*0-440-21584-6*); 1987. 288p. 75.00 o.s.i (*0-385-29568-5*, Delacorte Pr.); 1988. 320p. reprint ed. mass mkt. 7.99 (*0-440-20004-0*) Dell Publishing.

—Pale Kings & Princes. abr. ed. 1988. (Spencer Mystery Ser.). 14.95 incl. audio (*0-671-66073-X*, Simon & Schuster Audioworks) Simon & Schuster Audio.

—Paper Doll. 1994. (Spenser Mystery Ser.). 288p. mass mkt. 7.99 (*0-425-14155-1*) Berkley Publishing Group.

—Paper Doll. unabr. ed. 1993. (Spenser Ser.). audio 36.00 (*0-7366-2636-0*, 3375) Books on Tape, Inc.

—Paper Doll. unabr. ed. 2000. (Spenser Mystery Ser.). audio (*0-7862-9942-8*, SAB 072) Chivers Audio Bks. GBR. *Dist:* BBC Audiobooks America.

—Paper Doll. unabr. ed. 1993. (Spenser Mystery Ser.). 24.95 o.p. (*1-55800-707-5*, 592092) NewStar Media, Inc.

—Paper Doll. 1993. (Spenser Mystery Ser.). 224p. 19.95 o.p. (*0-399-13818-8*, G. P. Putnam's Sons) Penguin Group (USA) Inc.

—Paper Doll. (Spencer Mystery Ser.). 5.98 o.p. (*0-8317-5332-3*) Smithmark Pubs., Inc.

—Pastime. 1992. (Spenser Mystery Ser.). 352p. reprint ed. mass mkt. 7.99 (*0-425-13293-5*) Berkley Publishing Group.

—Pastime. unabr. ed. 2000. (Spenser Mystery Ser.). audio 49.95 (*1-56054-910-6*, SAB 035) Chivers Audio Bks. GBR. *Dist:* BBC Audiobooks America.

—Pastime. l.t. ed. 1992. (Spencer Mystery Ser.). 269p. lib. bdg. 20.95 o.p. (*0-8161-5347-7*, Macmillan Reference USA) Gale Group.

—Pastime. abr. ed. 1993. (Spencer Mystery Ser.). 15.95 o.p. (*1-55800-272-3*, 41180); audio 8.99 o.p. (*1-55800-902-7*, Dove Audio); 24.95 o.p. (*1-55800-433-5*, 692282) NewStar Media, Inc.

—Pastime. (Select Sound, Dove Ser.). 1995. pap. 4.99 o.p. (*0-7871-0305-5*); 1991. 224p. 19.95 o.s.i (*0-399-13628-2*, G. P. Putnam's Sons); 1991. 100.00 o.p. (*0-399-13630-4*) Penguin Group (USA) Inc.

—Pastime. 1992. (Spencer Mystery Ser.). 5.99 o.p. (*0-517-09584-X*) Random Hse. Value Publishing.

—Perish Twice. 2001. 352p. reprint ed. mass mkt. 7.99 (*0-425-18215-0*) Berkley Publishing Group.

—Perish Twice. l.t. ed. (Wheeler Press Paperback Ser.). 2001. 12.95 (*1-56895-180-9*); 2000. 279p. 28.95 (*1-56895-992-3*) Gale Group. (Wheeler Publishing, Inc.).

—Perish Twice. 2000. 320p. 23.95 o.s.i (*0-399-14668-7*) Penguin Group (USA) Inc.

—Playmates. 1990. (Spenser Mystery Ser.). 288p. mass mkt. 7.99 (*0-425-12001-5*) Berkley Publishing Group.

—Playmates. unabr. collector's ed. 1990. (Spenser Ser.). audio 30.00 (*0-7366-1774-4*, 2613) Books on Tape, Inc.

—Playmates. 1989. (Spencer Mystery Ser.). 17.95 o.p. (*0-399-13425-5*, G. P. Putnam's Sons) Penguin Putnam Bks. for Young Readers.

—Playmates. abr. ed. 1989. (Spencer Mystery Ser.). audio 14.95 (*0-671-67832-9*, Simon & Schuster Audioworks) Simon & Schuster Audio.

—Promised Land. 1978. (Spenser Mystery Ser.). 1.75 o.p. (*0-425-03614-6*) Berkley Publishing Group.

—Promised Land. unabr. collector's ed. 1989. (Spenser Ser.). audio 36.00 (*0-7366-1551-2*, 2420) Books on Tape, Inc.

—Promised Land. 1992. (Spencer Mystery Ser.). 224p. mass mkt. 7.50 (*0-440-17197-0*) Dell Publishing.

—Promised Land. 2002. E-Book 6.99 (*0-7953-0732-2*) RosettaBooks.

—A Savage Place. unabr. collector's ed. 1989. (Spenser Ser.). audio 30.00 (*0-7366-1621-7*, 2481) Books on Tape, Inc.

—A Savage Place. (Spencer Mystery Ser.). 1982. 192p. mass mkt. 6.99 (*0-440-18095-3*); 1981. 6.99 (*0-440-08094-0*); 1981. 14.95 o.s.i (*0-385-28951-0*, Delacorte Pr.) Dell Publishing.

—A Savage Place. l.t. ed. 1982. (Spenser Mystery Ser.). 264p. reprint ed. 12.95 o.p. (*0-89621-343-9*) Thorndike Pr.

—Small Vices. 1998. (Spenser Mystery Ser.). 352p. mass mkt. 7.99 (*0-425-16248-6*) Berkley Publishing Group.

—Small Vices. l.t. ed. 1997. (Spenser Mystery Ser.). 25.95 o.p. (*1-56895-466-2*, Wheeler Publishing, Inc.) Gale Group.

—Small Vices. unabr. ed. 1997. (Spenser Mysteries Ser.). 29.95 o.p. (*0-7871-1133-3*, 754969) NewStar Media, Inc.

—Small Vices. 1997. (Spenser Mystery Ser.). 320p. (J). 21.95 o.p. (*0-399-14244-4*, G. P. Putnam's Sons) Penguin Group (USA) Inc.

—Stardust. Set. unabr. ed. 1995. (Spenser Mystery Ser.). audio 54.95 (*1-56054-968-8*, SAB 012, Sterling Audio Bks.) BBC Audiobooks America.

—Stardust. 1991. (Spenser Mystery Ser.). 304p. mass mkt. 7.99 (*0-425-12723-0*) Berkley Publishing Group.

—Stardust. unabr. collector's ed. 1990. (Spenser Ser.). audio 36.00 (*0-7366-1840-6*, 2673) Books on Tape, Inc.

—Stardust. 1990. (Spencer Mystery Ser.). 224p. 18.95 o.s.i (*0-399-13537-5*); 75.00 o.p. (*0-399-13514-6*) Penguin Putnam Bks. for Young Readers. (G. P. Putnam's Sons).

—Stardust. 1992. (Spencer Mystery Ser.). 4.99 o.p. (*0-517-08606-9*) Random Hse. Value Publishing.

—Stardust. abr. ed. 1990. (Spencer Mystery Ser.). audio 14.95 (*0-671-70481-8*, Simon & Schuster Audioworks) Simon & Schuster Audio.

—Stone Cold: A Jesse Stone Novel. 2003. 336p. 24.95 (*0-399-15087-0*, Putnam & Grosset) Putnam Publishing Group, The.

—Stone Cold: A Jesse Stone Novel. l.t. ed. 2003. 323p. 32.95 (*0-7862-6079-3*, Large Print Pr.) Thorndike Pr.

—Sudden Mischief. l.t. ed. 1998. (Spenser Mystery Ser.). 27.95 (*1-56895-569-3*, Wheeler Publishing, Inc.) Gale Group.

—Sudden Mischief. 1998. 22.95 o.s.i (*0-399-14696-2*); 304p. 22.95 o.p. incl. audio (*0-399-14370-X*, G. P. Putnam's Sons) Penguin Group (USA) Inc.

—Taming a Seahorse. unabr. collector's ed. 1990. (Spenser Ser.). audio 30.00 (*0-7366-1750-7*, 2589) Books on Tape, Inc.

—Taming a Seahorse. 1987. (Spencer Mystery Ser.). 320p. mass mkt. 7.99 (*0-440-18841-5*) Dell Publishing.

—Taming a Seahorse. l.t. ed. 1987. (Spencer Mystery Ser.). 362p. 18.95 o.p. (*0-8161-4166-5*, Macmillan Reference USA) Gale Group.

—Thin Air. 1996. (Spenser Mystery Ser.). 304p. reprint ed. mass mkt. 7.99 (*0-425-15290-1*) Berkley Publishing Group.

—Thin Air. l.t. ed. 1995. (Spencer Mystery Ser.). 26.95 o.p. (*1-56895-212-0*, Wheeler Publishing, Inc.) Gale Group.

—Thin Air. unabr. ed. 1995. (Spenser Mystery Ser.). 24.95 o.p. (*0-7871-0277-6*, 692871) NewStar Media, Inc.

—Thin Air. (*0-399-19276-X*); 1995. 293p. 21.95 o.p. (*0-399-14020-4*, G. P. Putnam's Sons); 1995. 125.00 o.p. (*0-399-14063-8*, G. P. Putnam's Sons) Penguin Group (USA) Inc.

—Three Complete Novels, 3 vols. Incl. God Save the Child. 1995. Godwulf Manuscript. 1995. Mortal Stakes. 192p. 1975. 6.95 o.p. (*0-395-21969-8*); 560p. 1995. 13.99 o.s.i (*0-517-14802-1*) Random Hse., Inc.

—Trouble in Paradise. 1999. (Jesse Stone Ser.). 320p. reprint ed. mass mkt. 7.99 (*0-515-12649-7*, Jove) Berkley Publishing Group.

—Trouble in Paradise. l.t. ed. 1998. 27.95 (*1-56895-681-9*, Wheeler Publishing, Inc.) Gale Group.

—Trouble in Paradise. 1998. 336p. 22.95 o.p. (*0-399-14433-1*, G. P. Putnam's Sons) Penguin Group (USA) Inc.

—Trouble in Paradise. l.t. ed. 2000. (Charnwood Large Print Ser.). 304p. (*0-7089-9137-8*, Ulverscroft) Thorpe, F. A. Pubs. GBR. *Dist:* Ulverscroft Large Print Bks., Ltd., Ulverscroft Large Print Canada, Ltd.

—Valediction. unabr. collector's ed. 1989. (Spenser Ser.). audio 30.00 (*0-7366-1670-5*, 2519) Books on Tape, Inc.

—Valediction. (Spencer Mystery Ser.). 1992. 288p. mass mkt. 7.50 (*0-440-19246-3*); 1984. 240p. 12.95 o.s.i (*0-385-29330-5*, Delacorte Pr.) Dell Publishing.

—Valediction. 1985. (Spencer Mystery Ser.). mass mkt. 3.50 o.s.i (*0-440-19247-1*) Doubleday Publishing.

—Valediction. l.t. ed. 1984. (Spencer Mystery Ser.). 14.95 o.p. (*0-8161-3702-1*, Macmillan Reference USA) Gale Group.

—Walking Shadow. 1995. (Spenser Mystery Ser.). 304p. mass mkt. 7.99 (*0-425-14774-6*) Berkley Publishing Group.

—Walking Shadow. unabr. ed. 1995. (Spenser Ser.). audio 48.00 (*0-7366-2924-6*, 3622) Books on Tape, Inc.

—Walking Shadow. l.t. ed. 1994. (Spencer Mystery Ser.). 25.95 o.p. (*1-56895-106-X*, Wheeler Publishing, Inc.) Gale Group.

—Walking Shadow. abr. ed. 1993. (Spencer Mystery Ser.). audio 24.95 o.p. (*1-55800-999-X*, Dove Audio) NewStar Media, Inc.

—Walking Shadow. 1994. (Spenser Mystery Ser.). 224p. 19.95 o.p. (*0-399-13920-6*); 100.00 o.p. (*0-399-13961-3*) Penguin Group (USA) Inc. (G. P. Putnam's Sons).

—The Widening Gyre. unabr. collector's ed. 1989. (Spenser Ser.). audio 30.00 (*0-7366-1655-1*, 2506) Books on Tape, Inc.

—The Widening Gyre. (Spencer Mystery Ser.). 192p. 1992. mass mkt. 7.99 (*0-440-19535-7*); 1983. 13.95 o.p. (*0-385-29220-1*, Delacorte Pr.) Dell Publishing.

Parker, Robert B. & Cohen, Stan. Sudden Mischief. 1999. (Spenser Mystery Ser.). 306p. reprint ed. pap. 7.99 (*0-425-16828-X*) Berkley Publishing Group.

Parker, Virginia Bailey. The Water's Edge. 2001. (Illus.). xiv, 366p. 18.95 (*0-9703497-0-X*) Snowy Creek Pr.

Passarella, J. G. Wither. 1999. 320p. 23.00 o.s.i (*0-671-02480-9*, Atria); 2000. 448p. reprint ed. mass mkt. 7.99 (*0-671-02481-7*, Pocket) Simon & Schuster.

Patterson, James. Cradle & All. l.t. ed. 2000. (Large Print Book Ser.). 305p. 31.95 (*1-56895-879-X*, Wheeler Publishing, Inc.) Gale Group.

—Cradle & All. 2000. 368p. 25.95 o.p. (*0-316-69061-9*) Little Brown & Co.

—Cradle & All. 2001. 384p. reprint ed. mass mkt. 7.99 (*0-446-60940-4*) Warner Bks., Inc.

Peale, Cynthia. The Death of Colonel Mann. 2001. (Beacon Hill Mysteries Ser.). 352p. mass mkt. 6.50 (*0-440-23565-0*) Dell Publishing.

—The Death of Colonel Mann. l.t. ed. 2002. (Ulverscroft Large Print Ser.). 488p. 32.50 (*0-7089-4655-0*, Ulverscroft) Thorpe, F. A. Pubs. GBR. *Dist:* Ulverscroft Large Print Bks., Ltd., Ulverscroft Large Print Canada, Ltd.

—The White Crow. 2003. 336p. mass mkt. 6.50 (*0-440-23566-9*) Dell Publishing.

—The White Crow. 2002. 336p. 24.95 (*0-385-49638-9*) Doubleday Publishing.

Peterson, Tracie & Miller, Judith. Daughter of the Loom. 2003. (Bells of Lowell Ser.). 384p. pap. 12.99 (*0-7642-2688-6*) Bethany Hse. Pubs.

—A Fragile Design. 2003. (Bells of Lowell Ser.). 400p. pap. 12.99 (*0-7642-2689-4*) Bethany Hse. Pubs.

—These Tangled Threads. 2003. (Bells of Lowell Ser.). 384p. pap. 12.99 (*0-7642-2690-8*) Bethany Hse. Pubs.

Phillips, Carly. Simply Scandalous. 2003. 304p. mass mkt. (*0-373-83579-5*, Harlequin Bks.) Harlequin Enterprises, Ltd.

Pickard, Nancy. Confession. (Jenny Cain Mystery Ser.). 1995. 336p. mass mkt. 5.99 (*0-671-78262-2*, Pocket); 1994. 320p. 20.00 o.p. (*0-671-78261-4*, Atria) Simon & Schuster.

—Dead Crazy. 1988. (Jenny Cain Mystery Ser.). 256p. 16.95 o.s.i (*0-684-18761-2*, Macmillan Reference USA) Gale Group.

—Dead Crazy. (Jenny Cain Mystery Ser.). 1990. mass mkt. 3.95 (*0-671-70267-X*); 1989. mass mkt. 3.50 (*0-671-64337-1*) Simon & Schuster. (Pocket).

—Dead Crazy. Marrow, Linda, ed. 1989. 320p. mass mkt. 6.50 (*0-671-73430-X*, Pocket) Simon & Schuster.

—I. O. U. 1993. (Jenny Cain Mystery Ser.). 3.99 o.p. (*0-517-09728-1*) Random Hse. Value Publishing.

—I. O. U. Marrow, Linda, ed. (Jenny Cain Mystery Ser.). 1992. 240p. mass mkt. 4.99 (*0-671-68043-9*, Pocket); 1991. 17.95 o.p. (*0-671-68041-2*, Atria) Simon & Schuster.

—Marriage Is Murder. Marrow, Linda, ed. 1988. (Jenny Cain Mystery Ser.). mass mkt. 5.50 (*0-671-73428-8*, Pocket) Simon & Schuster.

—No Body. 1986. (Jenny Cain Mystery Ser.). 224p. 13.95 o.p. (*0-684-18593-8*, Macmillan Reference USA) Gale Group.

—No Body. (Jenny Cain Mystery Ser.). 1989. mass mkt. 3.95 (*0-671-69179-1*); 1987. mass mkt. (*0-671-64335-5*); 1987. mass mkt. 5.99 (*0-671-73429-6*) Simon & Schuster. (Pocket).

—Say No to Murder. 1999. (Jenny Cain Mystery Ser.). 242p. 20.95 (*0-7862-1703-0*, Five Star) Gale Group.

—Say No to Murder. 1985. (Jenny Cain Mystery Ser.). 192p. pap. 2.95 o.p. (*0-380-89642-7*, Avon Bks.) Morrow/Avon.

—Say No to Murder. (Jenny Cain Mystery Ser.). 1990. mass mkt. 3.95 (*0-671-70269-6*); 1988. mass mkt. 3.50 (*0-671-66396-8*) Simon & Schuster. (Pocket).

—Say No to Murder. Marrow, Linda, ed. 1988. (Jenny Cain Mystery Ser.). mass mkt. 5.50 (*0-671-73431-8*, Pocket) Simon & Schuster.

—Twilight. Set. unabr. ed. 1999. (Jenny Cain Mystery Ser.). audio 96.95 (*0-7927-2302-3*, CSL191, Chivers Sound Library) BBC Audiobooks America.

—Twilight. 1996. (Jenny Cain Mystery Ser.). 320p. pap. 6.99 (*0-671-78290-8*, Pocket) Simon & Schuster.

—Twilight. Marrow, Linda, ed. 1995. (Jenny Cain Mystery Ser.). 320p. 22.00 o.p. (*0-671-78271-1*, Atria) Simon & Schuster.

Picoult, Jodi. Mercy. 2002. E-Book 9.99 (*1-4014-9981-3*) Barnes & Noble Digital.

—Mercy. l.t. ed. 1997. (Core Ser.). 662p. lib. bdg. 26.95 (*0-7838-2003-8*, Macmillan Reference USA) Gale Group.

—Mercy. 1996. 400p. 24.95 o.p. (*0-399-14160-X*, G. P. Putnam's Sons) Penguin Group (USA) Inc.

—Mercy. 2001. reprint ed. 416p. pap. 13.95 (*0-7434-2244-9*); E-Book 13.95 (*0-7434-3736-5*) Simon & Schuster. (Washington Square Pr.).

Piercy, Marge. The Longings of Women. 1995. 448p. mass mkt. 6.99 o.s.i (*0-449-22349-3*, Fawcett) Ballantine Bks.

—The Longings of Women. l.t. ed. 1994. (G. K. Hall Core Ser.). 752p. lib. bdg. 25.95 (*0-8161-7457-1*, Macmillan Reference USA) Gale Group.

—The Longings of Women. abr. ed. 1994. audio 17.00 o.s.i (*1-57042-044-0*, 4-520440) Time Warner AudioBooks.

—Summer People. 1990. mass mkt. 5.95 o.s.i (*0-449-21904-6*); 416p. reprint ed. mass mkt. 5.95 o.s.i (*0-449-21842-2*, Fawcett) Ballantine Bks.

—Summer People. 2002. 384p. pap. 21.95 (*0-7432-4185-1*, Simon & Schuster) Simon & Schuster.

—Summer People. 1989. 400p. 19.95 o.p. (*0-671-67856-6*) Summit Bks.

Poe, Edgar Allan. The Narrative of Arthur Gordon Pym. 1838. (YA). reprint ed. pap. text 28.00 (*1-4047-8752-6*) Classic Textbooks.

—The Narrative of Arthur Gordon Pym. 1974. (Illus.). 190p. pap. 8.50 o.p. (*0-87923-147-5*); 1973. xxv, 157 p. o.p. (*0-87923-062-2*, Hoc Volo) Godine, David R. Pub.

—The Narrative of Arthur Gordon Pym. 1989. audio 34.00 Jimcin Recordings.

—The Narrative of Arthur Gordon Pym. unabr. ed. 1988. audio 44.00 (*1-55690-369-3*, 88390E7) Recorded Bks., LLC.

—The Narrative of Arthur Gordon Pym. 1999. (Notable American Authors Ser.). reprint ed. lib. bdg. 125.00 (*0-7812-8752-9*) Reprint Services Corp.

—The Narrative of Arthur Gordon Pym of Nantucket. unabr. ed. 1994. audio 44.95 (*0-7861-0625-5*, 2115) Blackstone Audio Bks., Inc.

—The Narrative of Arthur Gordon Pym of Nantucket. unabr. collector's ed. 1988. audio 48.00 (*0-7366-3928-4*, 9166) Books on Tape, Inc.

—The Narrative of Arthur Gordon Pym of Nantucket. abr. ed. 1990. audio 16.99 (*0-88646-269-X*, 7269) Durkin Hayes Publishing Ltd.

—The Narrative of Arthur Gordon Pym of Nantucket. 2002. (Paperback Classics Ser.). (Illus.). 224p. pap. 9.95 (*0-375-76007-5*, Modern Library) Random House Adult Trade Publishing Group.

—The Narrative of Arthur Gordon Pym of Nantucket. Kopley, Richard, ed. & intro. by. 1999. (Classics Ser.). 320p. pap. 10.00 (*0-14-043748-7*, Penguin Classics) Viking Penguin.

—The Narrative of Arthur Gordon Pym of Nantucket. Beaver, Harold, ed. & comment by. 1976. (Penguin Classics Ser.). 320p. pap. 9.95 o.s.i (*0-14-043097-0*, Penguin Classics) Viking Penguin.

—The Narrative of Arthur Gordon Pym of Nantucket & Related Tales. 1960. (American Century Ser.). 198p. pap. 6.25 o.p. (*0-8090-0029-6*, Hill & Wang) Farrar, Straus & Giroux.

—The Narrative of Arthur Gordon Pym of Nantucket & Related Tales. Kennedy, J. Gerald, ed. 1998. (Oxford World's Classics Ser.). 336p. pap. 9.95 (*0-19-283771-0*) Oxford Univ. Pr., Inc.

—The Narrative of Arthur Gordon Pym of Nantucket & Related Tales. Kennedy, J. Gerald, ed. & intro. by. 1994. (Oxford World's Classics Ser.). 326p. pap. 7.95 o.p. (*0-19-282844-4*) Oxford Univ. Pr., Inc.

Post, Waldron K. Harvard Stories. 1977. (Short Story Index Reprint Ser.). 22.95 (*0-8369-3072-X*) Ayer Co. Pubs., Inc.
Pozzessere, Heather G. An Angel's Touch. 1996. 192p. mass mkt. 5.99 o.s.i (*0-8217-5442-4*, Zebra Bks.); 1995. mass mkt. 17.95 o.s.i (*0-8217-5126-3*) Kensington Publishing Corp.
Pratt, James Michael. The Lighthouse Keeper. l.t. ed. 2000. (Wheeler Large Print Book Ser.). 277p. 28.95 (*1-56895-896-X*, Wheeler Publishing, Inc.) Gale Group.
—The Lighthouse Keeper. 2000. ix, 257p. 23.95 o.s.i (*0-312-24113-5*); 2001. 336p. reprint ed. mass mkt. 6.99 o.s.i (*0-312-97469-8*, 20-3283, St. Martin's Paperbacks) St. Martin's Pr.
Press, Margaret. Elegy for a Thief. 1993. 208p. 18.95 o.p. (*0-88184-949-9*, Carroll & Graf Pubs.) Avalon Publishing Group.
—Requiem for a Postman. 1992. 224p. 18.95 o.p. (*0-88184-750-X*, Carroll & Graf Pubs.) Avalon Publishing Group.
Preston, Douglas J. Jennie. 1994. 336p. text 21.95 o.p. (*0-312-11294-7*) St. Martin's Pr.
Preston, John. Franny, Queen of Provincetown. 1995. 15.95 o.p. (*0-312-11792-2*) St. Martin's Pr.
—Franny, the Queen of Provincetown. 1983. 96p. pap. 4.95 o.p. (*0-932870-31-7*) Alyson Pubns.
—Franny, the Queen of Provincetown. 1995. 112p. pap. 8.95 o.p. (*0-312-14106-8*, Saint Martin's Griffin) St. Martin's Pr.
Ray, Jeanne. Julie & Romeo. abr. ed. 2000. audio 17.95 (*1-56740-900-8*, Nova Audio Bks.); audio 44.25 (*1-56740-722-6*, 2076, Unabridged Library Editions); audio 24.95 (*1-56740-355-7*, 2075, Brilliance Audio Unabridged) Brilliance Audio.
—Julie & Romeo. 2000. (Illus.). 240p. 21.00 (*0-609-60672-7*, Harmony) Crown Publishing Group.
—Juliet & Romeo: A Novel. l.t. ed. 2000. (Basic Ser.). 303p. 29.95 (*0-7862-2660-9*) Thorndike Pr.
Reed, Barry. The Deception. l.t. ed. 1997. (Niagara Large Print Ser.). 592p. 29.50 o.p. (*0-7089-5884-2*, Ulverscroft) Thorpe, F. A. Pubs. GBR. *Dist:* Ulverscroft Large Print Bks., Ltd.
—The Deception: Courtroom Drama. 1998. 432p. mass mkt. 6.99 (*0-312-96494-3*, St. Martin's Paperbacks) St. Martin's Pr.
—The Indictment. 1995. 436p. mass mkt. 6.99 (*0-312-95416-6*, St. Martin's Paperbacks) St. Martin's Pr.
Reed, Kelvin L. Rookie Year: Journey of a First-Year Teacher. 1999. 336p. 21.95 (*0-9667631-2-2*) Peralta Publishing Co.
Reed, Kit. J. Eden: A Novel. 1996. 315p. text 24.95 o.p. (*0-87451-746-X*, Hardscrabble Bks.) Univ. Pr. of New England.
Reynolds, John L. And Leave Her Lay Dying. 1992. (Crime Ser.). 272p. pap. 4.95 o.p. (*0-14-012298-2*, Penguin Bks.) Penguin Group (USA) Inc.
—And Leave Her Lay Dying. 1990. 304p. 16.95 o.p. (*0-670-82875-0*) Viking Penguin.
—The Man Who Murdered God. 272p. 1989. 16.95 o.p. (*0-670-82736-3*); 1990. reprint ed. pap. 4.50 o.p. (*0-14-012037-8*, Penguin Bks.) Viking Penguin.
—Whisper Death. 1992. 256p. 18.95 o.p. (*0-670-83669-9*, Viking) Viking Penguin.
Rich, Virginia. The Baked Bean Supper Murders. l.t. ed. 1983. 499p. reprint ed. 14.95 o.p. (*0-89621-487-7*) Thorndike Pr.
—The Nantucket Diet Murders. (Eugenia Potter Mysteries Ser.). 1986. 288p. mass mkt. 6.99 (*0-440-16264-5*); 1985. 224p. 13.95 o.s.i (*0-385-29386-0*, Delacorte Pr.) Dell Publishing.
—The Nantucket Diet Murders. 1985. 13.95 o.p. (*0-525-24233-3*, Dutton) Dutton/Plume.
Richardson, Judith Benet. David's Landing. 1984. (Illus.). 150p. (J). (gr. 3-7). 10.95 (*0-9611374-1-X*) Woods Hole Historical Collection.
Riggs, Cynthia. The Cranefly Orchid Murders. 2002. 272p. 23.95 (*0-312-30145-6*, Saint Martin's Minotaur) St. Martin's Pr.
Rimmer, Robert H. The Resurrection of Anne Hutchinson. 1987. 425p. 16.00 (*0-87975-370-6*) Prometheus Bks., Pubs.
Roberts, Nora. Heaven & Earth. l.t. ed. 2002. 32.95 (*0-7838-9618-2*) Gale Group.
—Heaven & Earth. l.t. ed. 2002. 424p. pap. 29.95 (*0-7838-9621-2*) Thorndike Pr.
Roos, Kelley. Murder on Martha's Vineyard. l.t. ed. 1981. 279p. reprint ed. 11.95 o.p. (*0-89621-320-X*) Thorndike Pr.
Roos, Kelly. Murder in Martha's Vineyard. 1981. 190p. 12.95 o.s.i (*0-8027-5436-8*) Walker & Co.
—Murder on Martha's Vineyard. 1986. pap. 2.95 o.s.i (*0-8027-3164-3*) Walker & Co.
Rosen, Dorothy & Rosen, Sidney. Death & Blintzes. 1998. 180p. reprint ed. pap. 10.95 (*0-89733-450-7*) Academy Chicago Pubs., Ltd.
—Death & Blintzes. 1985. 192p. 14.95 o.p. (*0-8027-5625-5*) Walker & Co.
—Death & Strudel. 1999. 272p. 23.00 (*0-89733-478-7*) Academy Chicago Pubs., Ltd.
Rosen, Richard D. Fadeaway. 1986. 256p. 15.95 o.p. (*0-06-015599-X*) HarperTrade.
—Fadeaway. 1987. mass mkt. 3.95 o.p. (*0-451-40046-1*); 288p. mass mkt. 3.95 o.p. (*0-451-40148-4*) NAL. (Onyx).
—Saturday Night Dead. 1989. mass mkt. 3.95 o.p. (*0-451-40134-4*, Onyx) NAL.
—Saturday Night Dead. 1988. 28p. 16.95 o.p. (*0-670-81977-8*) Viking Penguin.
—Strike Three, You're Dead. l.t. ed. 1986. 19.95 o.p. (*1-55504-143-4*) BBC Audiobooks America.
—Strike Three, You're Dead. 1986. mass mkt. 2.95 o.p. (*0-451-14233-0*, Signet Bks.); 256p. mass mkt. 3.95 o.p. (*0-451-40142-5*, Onyx) NAL.
—Strike Three, You're Dead. 1984. 192p. 12.95 o.s.i (*0-8027-5587-9*) Walker & Co.
—World of Hurt. 1994. 264p. 20.95 (*0-8027-3251-8*) Walker & Co.
Rosenburg, Vivan. Lonely Love. 2000. 480p. pap. 24.99 (*0-7388-1718-X*); text 34.99 (*0-7388-1717-1*) Xlibris Corp.
Russell, E. S. Dead Easy. 1992. 202p. 19.95 o.p. (*0-8027-3214-3*) Walker & Co.
—Death of a Cloudwalker. 1991. 192p. 18.95 (*0-8027-5784-7*) Walker & Co.
Ryan, Conall. The House of Cards. 2002. 298p. reprint ed. pap. 14.95 (*1-902881-61-3*) Toby Pr.
Sarton, May. The Education of Harriet Hatfield. 1989. 18.95 o.p. (*0-393-02695-7*) Norton, W. W. & Co., Inc.
Satterthwait, Walter. Miss Lizzie. 1989. 17.95 o.p. (*0-312-03400-8*) St. Martin's Pr.
Scott, Holden. Skeptic. E-Book 6.99 (*0-312-26468-2*); 2000. 400p. mass mkt. 6.99 (*0-312-96928-7*, St. Martin's Paperbacks); 1999. 322p. 24.95 o.p. (*0-312-19334-3*) St. Martin's Pr.
Searles, John. Boy Still Missing. 2002. 304p. pap. 12.95 (*0-06-000780-X*, Perennial) HarperTrade.
—Boy Still Missing. 2001. 304p. 25.00 (*0-688-17570-8*, Morrow, William & Co.) Morrow/Avon.
Sedgwick, Catharine Maria. Hope Leslie. Kelley, Mary, ed. 1987. (American Women Writers Ser.). 365p. text 40.00 (*0-8135-1221-2*); pap. text 15.00 (*0-8135-1222-0*) Rutgers Univ. Pr.
—Hope Leslie: Or, Early Times in the Massachusetts. 1972. reprint ed. lib. bdg. 29.50 o.p. (*0-8422-8107-X*) Irvington Pubs.
—Hope Leslie: Or Early Times in the Massachusetts. reprint ed. 20.00 o.p. (*0-403-02083-2*) Somerset Pubs., Inc.
Sedgwick, Catharine Maria & Karcher, Carolyn L. Hope Leslie. 1998. (Classics Ser.). 448p. pap. 13.95 (*0-14-043676-6*, Penguin Classics) Viking Penguin.
Sedgwick, John. The Dark House: A Novel. 2000. 432p. 25.00 (*0-06-019560-6*, HarperCollins) HarperTrade.
—The Education of Mrs. Bemis. 2002. 400p. 24.95 (*0-06-019565-7*) HarperCollins Pubs.
—The Education of Mrs. Bemis: A Novel. 2003. 400p. pap. 13.95 (*0-06-051259-8*, Perennial) HarperTrade.
Senna, Danzy. Caucasia. 1998. 353p. 24.95 o.s.i (*1-57322-091-4*); 1999. 432p. reprint ed. pap. 14.00 (*1-57322-716-1*) Berkley Publishing Group. (Riverhead Trade (Paperbacks)).
—Caucasia. pap. (*1-57322-772-2*, Riverhead Bks. (Hardcovers)) Putnam Publishing Group, The.
—Caucasia. 1999. 19.00 (*0-606-18969-6*) Turtleback Bks.
Seton, Anya. Winthrop Woman. 1985. mass mkt. 4.50 o.s.i (*0-449-21006-5*, Fawcett) Ballantine Bks.
—Winthrop Woman, 001. 1958. 10.00 o.p. (*0-395-08176-9*) Houghton Mifflin Co.
Shapiro, Barbara. The Safe Room. 2003. 303p. pap. 13.95 (*1-4104-0109-X*, Five Star Trade); 2002. (Illus.). 308p. 25.95 (*0-7862-3012-6*, Five Star) Gale Group.
Shapiro, Dani. Family History. 288p. 2004. pap. 13.00 (*1-4000-3211-3*); 2003. 23.00 (*0-375-41547-5*) Knopf, Alfred A. Inc.
—Family History. l.t. ed. 2003. 460p. 25.00 (*0-375-43279-5*) Random Hse. Large Print.
Shea, Suzanne Strempek. Around Again. 320p. 2002. pap. 14.00 (*0-7434-0376-2*, Washington Square Pr.); 2001. (Illus.). 23.95 (*0-7434-0375-4*, Atria) Simon & Schuster.
—Lily of the Valley. 288p. 2000. (Illus.). pap. 13.95 (*0-671-02711-5*, Washington Square Pr.); 1999. 22.00 o.s.i (*0-671-02710-7*, Atria) Simon & Schuster.
—Selling the Lite of Heaven. 1995. 288p. pap. 12.95 (*0-671-79865-0*, Washington Square Pr.) Simon & Schuster.
—Selling the Lite of Heaven. Rosenman, Jane, ed. 1994. 288p. 20.00 o.s.i (*0-671-79864-2*, Atria) Simon & Schuster.
Sherwood, Ben. The Death & Life of Charlie St. Cloud. 2004. 288p. 22.95 (*0-553-80220-8*) Bantam Bks.
Siddons, Anne Rivers. Up Island. unabr. ed. 1997. audio 80.00 (*0-7366-3709-5*, 4393) Books on Tape, Inc.
—Up Island. l.t. ed. 1997. (Wheeler Large Print Book Ser.). 27.95 (*1-56895-485-9*, Wheeler Publishing, Inc.) Gale Group.
—Up Island. 1997. 352p. 24.00 o.s.i (*0-06-017615-6*) HarperCollins Pubs.
—Up Island. abr. ed. 1997. audio 25.00 (*0-694-51843-3*, 695952, HarperAudio) HarperTrade.
—Up Island. 1998. 512p. mass mkt. 7.99 (*0-06-109921-X*, HarperTorch) Morrow/Avon.
—Up Island. unabr. ed. 1997. audio 91.00 (*0-7887-1295-0*, 95129E7) Recorded Bks., LLC.
Sinclair, Upton. Boston: A Documentary Novel of the Sacco-Vanzetti Case. 1978. reprint ed. 32.00 (*0-8376-0420-6*) Bentley Pubs.
—Boston: A Documentary Novel of the Sacco-Vanzetti Case. 1999. (Works of Upton Sinclair). 148.00 (*1-58201-826-X*) Classic Bks.
—Boston: A Documentary Novel of the Sacco-Vanzetti Case, 2 vols. 1928. reprint ed. 59.00 (*0-403-00295-8*) Scholarly Pr., Inc.
Smith, David A. In the Cube: A Novel of Future Boston. 1993. 288p. (YA). 18.95 o.p. (*0-312-85448-X*, Tor Bks.) Doherty, Tom Assocs., LLC.
Smith, David A., ed. Future Boston. 384p. 1995. pap. 13.95 (*0-312-89028-1*, Orb Bks.); 1993. 22.95 o.p. (*0-312-85589-3*, Tor Bks.) Doherty, Tom Assocs., LLC.
Smith, J. P. Breathless. unabr. ed. 1995. audio 64.00 (*0-7366-3128-3*, 3803); audio compact disk 12.95 Books on Tape, Inc.
—Breathless. 1999. pap. 9.95 (*0-14-024524-3*); 1995. 336p. 23.95 o.p. (*0-670-86046-8*) Viking Penguin. (Viking).
Smith, Mitchell. Reprisal. 1999. 400p. 24.95 o.p. (*0-525-93979-2*) Dutton/Plume.
—Reprisal. 2000. 400p. mass mkt. 6.99 o.s.i (*0-451-18476-9*, Signet Bks.) NAL.
Smolens, John. Angel's Head: A Novel of Suspense. 1994. 240p. 19.00 o.p. (*0-88150-297-9*) Countryman Pr.
Soos, Troy. Murder at Fenway Park. 1995. 256p. mass mkt. 4.99 o.s.i (*0-8217-4909-9*, Zebra Bks.); 1994. mass mkt. 14.95 o.s.i (*0-8217-4518-2*) Kensington Publishing Corp.
—Murder at Fenway Park. unabr. ed. (Mickey Rawlings Baseball Ser.: Vol. 1). 1999. audio compact disk 58.00 (*0-7887-3418-0*, C1024E7); 1997. audio 51.00 (*0-7887-0874-0*, 95009E7) Recorded Bks., LLC.
—Murder at Fenway Park. l.t. ed. 1995. (Niagara Large Print Ser.). 277p. 29.50 o.p. (*0-7089-5813-3*, Ulverscroft) Thorpe, F. A. Pubs. GBR. *Dist:* Ulverscroft Large Print Bks., Ltd.
Sparks, Nicholas. Message in a Bottle. 2000. 288p. E-Book 5.95 (*0-446-96104-3*); 2000. 214p. E-Book 5.95 (*0-446-96076-4*); 2000. 214p. E-Book 5.95 (*0-446-92009-6*); 2000. E-Book 5.95 (*0-446-93041-5*); 1998. 336p. 20.00 (*0-446-52356-9*) Warner Bks., Inc.
Spencer, LaVyrle. Twice Loved. 1986. 416p. mass mkt. 7.50 (*0-515-09065-4*); 1985. mass mkt. 3.95 o.s.i (*0-515-08550-2*); 1984. mass mkt. 3.95 o.s.i (*0-515-07891-3*); 1984. mass mkt. 3.50 o.s.i (*0-515-07622-8*) Berkley Publishing Group. (Jove).
—Twice Loved. l.t. ed. 1993. (General Ser.). 513p. 23.95 o.p. (*0-8161-5299-3*); 16.95 o.p. (*0-8161-5325-6*) Gale Group. (Macmillan Reference USA).
St. John, Nicole. The Medici Ring. 1975. 6.95 o.p. (*0-394-49342-7*) Random Hse., Inc.
—The Medici Ring. 1976. pap. 1.95 o.s.i (*0-671-80444-8*, Pocket) Simon & Schuster.
—The Medici Ring. l.t. ed. 1978. (Ulverscroft Large Print Ser.). 29.99 o.p. (*0-7089-0160-3*, Ulverscroft) Thorpe, F. A. Pubs. GBR. *Dist:* Ulverscroft Large Print Bks., Ltd., Ulverscroft Large Print Canada, Ltd.
—The Medici Ring. 1999. 286p. reprint ed. pap. 16.00 (*1-892323-25-7*) Vivisphere Publishing.
Stanton, Cathy. Trouble in Tow. 1993. (Illus.). 104p. (Orig.). pap. 7.50 o.p. (*0-9626308-2-9*) Haley's.
Steel, Danielle. The Ghost. 1998. 432p. mass mkt. 7.99 (*0-440-22485-3*); 1997. 360p. 200.00 (*0-385-32353-0*, Delacorte Pr.); 1997. 360p. 25.95 (*0-385-31695-X*, Delacorte Pr.); 1997. 592p. 29.95 o.s.i (*0-385-31982-7*, Delacorte Pr.) Dell Publishing.
—The Ghost. abr. ed. 1997. audio 25.95 (*0-553-47882-6*, 695424); audio compact disk 29.95 (*0-553-45563-X*) Random Hse. Audio Publishing Group. (RH Audio).
—The Ghost. l.t. ed. 2004. 576p. 27.95 (*0-375-43322-8*) Random Hse. Large Print.
Stewart, Eleanor. The Fair Vision: A Frontier Story. (Western Ser.). 1999. 215p. 19.95 (*0-7862-1897-5*, Five Star); 2000. 269p. pap. 23.95 (*0-7838-9135-0*, Macmillan Reference USA) Gale Group.
Stone, Andrew K. All Flowers Die. 1999. 240p. pap. 13.00 (*0-9679073-0-6*) So There Bks.
Stone, Jean. The Off Season. 2001. 368p. mass mkt. 5.99 (*0-553-58086-8*) Bantam Bks.
Stuart, Sarah P. The Year Roger Wasn't Well: A Novel. 1994. 256p. 20.00 o.p. (*0-06-017079-4*) HarperTrade.
Sullivan, Mary. Stay. 2000. 183p. pap. 13.00 o.p. (*1-58195-025-X*, Zoland Bks., Inc.) Steerforth Pr.
Sullivan, Winona. A Sudden Death at the Norfolk Cafe: A Sister Cecile Mystery. 1995. (Sister Cecile Mystery Ser.). mass mkt. 5.99 o.s.i (*0-8041-1213-4*, Ivy Bks.) Ballantine Bks.
—A Sudden Death at the Norfolk Cafe: A Sister Cecile Mystery. 1993. 214p. 17.95 o.p. (*0-312-08899-X*, Saint Martin's Minotaur) St. Martin's Pr.
Swann, E. L. Night Gardening. unabr. ed. 1999. audio 24.95 (*1-56740-825-7*, 1592, Brilliance Audio Unabridged) Brilliance Audio.
—Night Gardening. l.t. ed. 2000. (G. K. Hall Core Ser.). 256p. 28.95 (*0-7838-9036-2*, Macmillan Reference USA) Gale Group.
—Night Gardening. 2000. (Illus.). 208p. mass mkt. 6.50 o.s.i (*0-7868-8952-7*) Hyperion Pr.
—Night Gardening: A Novel. 1999. 215p. 16.95 (*0-7868-6498-2*) Hyperion Pr.
Tanger, Woody. The Dead Cure. Caso, Adolph, ed. 1996. 180p. pap. 13.95 (*0-8283-2021-7*) Branden Bks.
Tapply, William G. Client Privilege. l.t. ed. 1991. 23.95 o.p. (*0-7927-0888-1*, CH099); pap. 21.95 o.p. (*0-7927-0889-X*, CS0199) BBC Audiobooks America.
—Client Privilege. 1991. 288p. mass mkt. 4.50 o.s.i (*0-440-20866-1*) Dell Publishing.
—Close to the Bone. 1996. 224p. 20.95 o.p. (*0-312-14567-5*, Saint Martin's Minotaur) St. Martin's Pr.
—Close to the Bone: A Brady Coyne Mystery. unabr. ed. 2000. audio 49.95 (*0-7927-2212-4*, CSL 101) Chivers Audio Bks. GBR. *Dist:* BBC Audiobooks America.
—Cutter's Run. l.t. ed. 1999. pap. 24.95 (*1-56895-706-8*, Wheeler Publishing, Inc.) Gale Group.
—Cutter's Run. 1998. (Brady Coyne Mysteries Ser.). 274p. 23.95 (*0-312-18561-8*, Saint Martin's Minotaur) St. Martin's Pr.
—Dead Meat. l.t. ed. 1991. pap. 8.95 o.p. (*1-55504-857-9*, 162); 1989. 15.95 o.p. (*0-7451-9473-7*, 546) BBC Audiobooks America.
—Dead Meat. 1988. 240p. mass mkt. 3.50 o.s.i (*0-345-34730-7*) Ballantine Bks.
—Dead Meat: A Brady Coyne Mystery. 1987. 14.95 o.p. (*0-684-18682-9*, Macmillan Reference USA) Gale Group.
—Dead Winter. 1990. 240p. mass mkt. 3.95 o.s.i (*0-440-20566-2*); 1989. 16.95 o.s.i (*0-440-50171-7*, Delacorte Pr.) Dell Publishing.
—Dead Winter. l.t. ed. 1991. (General Ser.). 350p. lib. bdg. 18.95 o.p. (*0-8161-5003-6*, Macmillan Reference USA) Gale Group.
—Dead Winter. l.t. ed. 1991. (Magna Large Print Ser.). 318p. o.p. (*0-7505-0126-X*) Magna Large Print Bks. GBR. *Dist:* Ulverscroft Large Print Canada, Ltd.
—Death at Charity's Point. l.t. ed. 1991. pap. 10.95 o.p. (*0-7927-0109-7*, C0136) BBC Audiobooks America.
—Death at Charity's Point. 1985. 240p. mass mkt. 2.95 o.s.i (*0-345-32014-X*) Ballantine Bks.
—Death at Charity's Point. 1984. 224p. 12.95 o.p. (*0-684-18056-1*, Macmillan Reference USA) Gale Group.
—Death at Charity's Point. 1997. (Missing Mysteries Ser.: Vol. 2). 244p. reprint ed. pap. 7.95 (*1-890208-02-7*) Poisoned Pen Pr.
—The Dutch Blue Error. 1985. 224p. mass mkt. 2.95 o.s.i (*0-345-32341-6*) Ballantine Bks.
—The Dutch Blue Error. 1984. 240p. 12.95 o.s.i (*0-684-18213-0*, Macmillan Reference USA) Gale Group.
—Dutch Blue Error. l.t. ed. 1986. 321p. 16.95 o.p. (*0-89340-937-5*) BBC Audiobooks America.
—Follow the Sharks. 1985. (Brady Coyne Mystery Ser.). 224p. 13.95 o.p. (*0-684-18446-X*, Macmillan Reference USA) Gale Group.
—Follow the Sharks! 1986. mass mkt. 4.99 o.s.i (*0-345-32906-6*) Ballantine Bks.
—Follow the Sharks. l.t. ed. 1988. pap. 8.95 o.p. (*1-55504-346-1*) BBC Audiobooks America.
—The Marine Corpse. 1987. 240p. mass mkt. 3.95 o.s.i (*0-345-34057-4*) Ballantine Bks.
—The Marine Corpse: A Brady Coyne Mystery. 1986. 240p. 13.95 o.s.i (*0-684-18681-0*, Macmillan Reference USA) Gale Group.
—Rodent of Doubt. l.t. ed. 1988. pap. 13.95 o.p. (*1-55504-548-0*) BBC Audiobooks America.
—Scar Tissue. 2000. 276p. 24.95 (*0-312-26679-0*, Saint Martin's Minotaur) St. Martin's Pr.
—Seventh Enemy: A Brady Coyne Mystery. 1995. 234p. 21.00 (*1-883402-99-9*, Scribner) Simon & Schuster.
—The Snake Eater. 1993. 273p. 20.00 o.p. (*1-883402-04-2*, Scribner) Simon & Schuster.
—The Spotted Cats: A Brady Coyne Mystery. 1992. 256p. mass mkt. 4.50 o.s.i (*0-440-21191-3*) Dell Publishing.
—Tight Lines. l.t. ed. 1995. (Magna Large Print Ser.). 421p. (*0-7505-0796-9*) Magna Large Print Bks. GBR. *Dist:* Ulverscroft Large Print Canada, Ltd.

—Tight Lines: A Brady Coyne Mystery. 1993. 288p. mass mkt. 4.99 o.s.i (*0-440-21410-6*) Dell Publishing.

—A Void in Hearts. 1990. 192p. mass mkt. 3.95 o.s.i (*0-345-35868-6*) Ballantine Bks.

—A Void in Hearts. l.t. ed. 1990. (General Ser.). 427p. lib. bdg. 18.95 o.p. (*0-8161-4822-8*, Macmillan Reference USA) Gale Group.

—A Void in Hearts. 1988. (Brady Coyne Mystery Ser.: No. 7). 224p. 16.95 o.s.i (*0-684-18793-0*, Scribner) Simon & Schuster.

—The Vulgar Boatman. l.t. ed. 1991. 8.95 o.p. (*0-7451-9583-0*, 5054); pap. 10.95 o.p. (*0-7927-0011-2*, 618) BBC Audiobooks America.

—The Vulgar Boatman. 1989. 256p. mass mkt. 3.95 o.s.i (*0-345-35577-6*) Ballantine Bks.

—The Vulgar Boatman. l.t. ed. 1989. viii, 315 p. pap. (*0-7451-9595-4*) Chivers Pr.

—The Vulgar Boatman. 1988. (Brady Coyne Mystery Ser.). 240p. 14.95 o.s.i (*0-684-18792-2*, Scribner) Simon & Schuster.

Taylor, Phoebe Atwood. The Annulet of Gilt. 1986. (Asey Mayo Cape Cod Mystery Ser.). 288p. reprint ed. pap. 6.95 (*0-88150-078-X*, Foul Play) Norton, W. W. & Co., Inc.

—The Asey Mayo Trio. 1990. 256p. reprint ed. pap. 7.95 (*0-88150-171-9*, Foul Play) Norton, W. W. & Co., Inc.

—Banbury Bog. 1978. reprint ed. lib. bdg. 16.95 o.p. (*0-89966-247-1*) Buccaneer Bks., Inc.

—Banbury Bog. 1987. (Asey Mayo Cape Cod Mystery Ser.). 176p. reprint ed. pap. 5.95 (*0-88150-090-9*, Foul Play) Norton, W. W. & Co., Inc.

—The Cape Cod Mystery. 1985. (Asey Mayo Cape Cod Mystery Ser.). 192p. pap. 7.95 (*0-88150-046-1*, Foul Play) Norton, W. W. & Co., Inc.

—The Deadly Sunshade. l.t. ed. 1992. 19.95 o.p. (*0-7927-1318-4*); pap. 17.95 o.p. (*0-7927-1317-6*) BBC Audiobooks America.

—The Deadly Sunshade. 1989. (Asey Mayo Cape Cod Mystery Ser.). 300p. reprint ed. pap. 6.00 o.p. (*0-88150-136-0*) Countryman Pr.

—Death Lights a Candle. 1989. (Asey Mayo Cape Cod Mystery Ser.). 304p. reprint ed. pap. 7.95 (*0-88150-145-X*, Foul Play) Norton, W. W. & Co., Inc.

—Deathblow Hill. 1993. (Asey Mayo Cape Cod Mystery Ser.). 286p. pap. 6.50 (*0-88150-262-6*, Foul Play) Norton, W. W. & Co., Inc.

—Diplomatic Corpse. 1989. (Asey Mayo Cape Cod Mystery Ser.). 244p. reprint ed. pap. 5.95 o.p. (*0-88150-146-8*) Countryman Pr.

—Figure Away. 1979. (Foul Play Press Bks.). reprint ed. pap. 4.50 o.p. (*0-914378-48-1*) Countryman Pr.

—Figure Away. 1991. (Asey Mayo Cape Cod Mystery Ser.). 286p. reprint ed. pap. 5.95 o.p. (*0-88150-206-5*, Foul Play) Norton, W. W. & Co., Inc.

—Going, Going, Gone. 21.95 (*0-8488-1201-8*) Amereon, Ltd.

—The Iron Clew. 1992. (Leonidas Witherall Mystery Ser.). 216p. pap. 6.00 (*0-88150-241-3*, Foul Play) Norton, W. W. & Co., Inc.

—The Mystery of the Cape Cod Players. 1987. (Asey Mayo Cape Cod Mystyery Ser.). 272p. reprint ed. pap. 6.00 o.p. (*0-88150-091-7*) Countryman Pr.

—The Mystery of the Cape Cod Tavern. 1985. (Asey Mayo Cape Cod Mystery Ser.). 288p. pap. 7.95 (*0-88150-047-X*, Foul Play) Norton, W. W. & Co., Inc.

—Octagon House. 1983. pap. 4.50 o.p. (*0-914378-47-3*) Countryman Pr.

—Octagon House. 1991. (Asey Mayo Cape Cod Mystery Ser.). 296p. pap. 6.95 (*0-88150-194-8*, Foul Play) Norton, W. W. & Co., Inc.

—Octagon House. 1999. lib. bdg. 22.95 (*1-56723-139-X*, 148) Yestermorrow, Inc.

—Proof of the Pudding. 1979. (Foul Play Press Bks.). reprint ed. pap. 4.95 o.p. (*0-914378-55-4*) Countryman Pr.

—Proof of the Pudding. 1991. 192p. pap. 6.00 (*0-88150-193-X*, Foul Play) Norton, W. W. & Co., Inc.

—Punch with Care. 21.95 (*0-8488-1202-6*) Amereon, Ltd.

—Punch with Care. 1992. (Asey Mayo Cape Cod Mystery Ser.). 224p. pap. 7.95 (*0-88150-229-4*, Foul Play) Norton, W. W. & Co., Inc.

—The Six Iron Spiders. 1979. (Foul Play Press Bks.). reprint ed. pap. 4.95 o.p. (*0-914378-53-8*) Countryman Pr.

—The Six Iron Spiders. 1992. (Asey Mayo Cape Cod Mystery Ser.). 288p. pap. 6.95 (*0-88150-230-8*, Foul Play) Norton, W. W. & Co., Inc.

—Three Plots for Asey Mayo. 1969. 5.95 o.p. (*0-393-08534-1*); 1991. 320p. reprint ed. pap. 6.95 o.p. (*0-88150-205-7*, Foul Play) Norton, W. W. & Co., Inc.

—The Tinkling Symbol. 1993. (Asey Mayo Cape Cod Mystery Ser.). 288p. pap. 7.95 (*0-88150-263-4*, Foul Play) Norton, W. W. & Co., Inc.

Thayer, Nancy. Belonging. 1995. 336p. 22.95 o.p. (*0-312-13026-0*); Vol. 1. 1996. (Belonging Ser.: Vol. 1). 388p. mass mkt. 6.99 (*0-312-95892-7*, St. Martin's Paperbacks) St. Martin's Pr.

—Between Husbands & Friends. l.t. ed. 1999. 26.95 (*1-56895-776-9*, Wheeler Publishing, Inc.) Gale Group.

—Between Husbands & Friends. 2001. 320p. mass mkt. 6.99 (*0-312-97422-1*, St. Martin's Paperbacks); 1999. 256p. 23.95 o.p. (*0-312-20613-5*) St. Martin's Pr.

—Custody. l.t. ed. 2002. (Basic Ser.). 605p. 30.95 (*0-7862-3907-7*) Gale Group.

—Custody. E-Book 23.95 (*0-312-70324-4*); 2001. 320p. 24.95 (*0-312-27734-2*) St. Martin's Pr.

Thomas-Graham, Pamela. A Darker Shade of Crimson: An Ivy League Mystery. (Ivy League Mysteries Ser.). 1999. (Illus.). 416p. pap. 6.99 (*0-671-01670-9*, Pocket); 1998. 288p. 23.00 (*0-684-84526-1*, Simon & Schuster) Simon & Schuster.

Thomson, Maynard F. Dreams of Gold. 2001. 464p. E-Book 4.95 (*0-7595-0628-0*); 2001. 464p. E-Book 4.95 (*0-7595-6629-1*); 2001. 464p. E-Book 4.95 (*0-7595-8638-1*); 2001. 464p. E-Book 4.95 (*0-7595-9699-9*); 2001. 464p. E-Book 4.95 (*0-7595-4631-2*); 2000. 464p. mass mkt. 6.99 (*0-446-60775-4*); 1999. 452p. 22.00 o.p. (*0-446-52445-X*) Warner Bks., Inc.

Title, Elise. Inside Out: A Mystery. 2003. 368p. 24.95 (*0-312-28582-5*) St. Martin's Pr.

—Killing Time. Date not set. E-Book 23.95 (*0-312-70748-7*); 2002. 256p. 24.95 (*0-312-28566-3*, Saint Martin's Minotaur) St. Martin's Pr.

Torra, Joseph. Gas Station. 1996. 144p. (Orig.). pap. 11.95 o.p. (*0-944072-67-4*, Zoland Bks., Inc.) Steerforth Pr.

Tripp, Dawn Clifton. Moon Tide: A Novel. 2004. 304p. pap. 13.95 (*0-375-76116-0*, Random Hse. Trade Paperbacks) Random House Adult Trade Publishing Group.

—Moon Tide: A Novel. 2003. 304p. 24.95 (*0-375-50844-9*) Random Hse., Inc.

Tucker, Kerry. Drift Away: A Libby Kincaid Mystery. 1995. 240p. mass mkt. 4.99 o.p. (*0-06-109176-6*); 1994. 224p. 20.00 o.p. (*0-06-017999-6*) HarperCollins Pubs.

Turkle, Brinton. Thy Friend, Obadiah. 1982. (Picture Puffins Ser.). (Illus.). 40p. (J). (gr. 4-7). pap. 5.99 (*0-14-050393-5*, Puffin Bks.) Penguin Putnam Bks. for Young Readers.

Ullman, John A. Fried Fog & Other Cape Cod Yarns. 1990. (Illus.). 160p. (Orig.). pap. 9.95 o.p. (*0-936784-82-2*) Daniel, John & Co., Pubs.

Updike, John. Toward the End of Time. 1998. 352p. pap. 12.95 (*0-449-00041-9*, Fawcett); mass mkt. (*0-449-00305-1*, Ballantine Bks.) Ballantine Bks.

—Toward the End of Time. 1997. 334p. 25.00 (*0-375-40006-0*) Knopf, Alfred A. Inc.

Van Dine, Lynn. The Search for Peter Hunt. 2003. (ENG., Illus.). xiv, 248p. 34.95 (*0-9711835-4-6*) Local History Co., The.

Wagman, Fredrica. Peachy. 1993. 220p. 18.95 o.s.i (*0-939149-72-9*) Soho Pr., Inc.

Walker, Walter. The Immediate Prospect of Being Hanged. 1990. mass mkt. 4.50 o.p. (*0-451-40207-3*, Onyx) NAL.

—The Immediate Prospect of Being Hanged. 1989. 304p. 17.95 o.p. (*0-670-82247-7*) Viking Penguin.

Warren, Roland L. Mary Coffin Starbuck & the Early History of Nantucket. 1987. (Illus.). 300p. 19.95 o.p. (*0-942861-00-0*) Pingry Pr.

Warsh, Lewis. Ted's Favorite Skirt. 2002. 220p. pap. 14.00 (*1-881471-78-0*) Spuyten Duyvil.

Watkins, Dawn L. Nantucket Cats. 1998. (Illus.). 32p. (J). (ps-1). pap. 5.49 (*0-89084-975-7*) Jones, Bob Univ. Pr.

Waugh, Carol-Lynn R., et al, eds. Murder & Mystery in Boston. 1987. (Murder & Mystery in Ser.). 304p. 15.95 o.p. (*0-934878-95-1*, Dembner Bks.) Barricade Bks., Inc.

Waugh, Charles G. Massachusetts Madness. 1991. pap. 11.95 o.p. (*0-89909-344-2*) Rodale Pr., Inc.

Weber, Janice. Devil's Food. 1996. 480p. 22.95 o.p. (*0-446-51772-0*) Warner Bks., Inc.

Weld, William F. Stillwater. 2003. 240p. pap. 13.00 (*0-15-602723-2*) Harcourt Trade Pubs.

—Stillwater: A Novel. l.t. ed. 2002. 275p. 28.95 (*0-7862-4170-5*) Gale Group.

—Stillwater: A Novel. 2002. 240p. 23.00 (*0-7432-0598-7*); E-Book 9.99 (*0-7432-1770-5*) Simon & Schuster. (Simon & Schuster).

Wensberg, Peter C. The Last Bastion. 1995. 224p. 22.00 o.p. (*1-877946-58-3*); pap. 16.00 (*1-57962-001-9*) Permanent Pr., The.

West, Dorothy. Living Is Easy. 1970. (American Negro). reprint ed. 45.95 (*0-405-01942-4*) Ayer Co. Pubs., Inc.

—Living Is Easy. 1982. 376p. (C). reprint ed. pap. 14.95 o.p. (*0-912670-97-5*) Feminist Pr. at The City Univ. of New York.

—The Wedding. 1995. 20.00 o.s.i (*0-385-47143-2*); 200.00 o.s.i (*0-385-47915-8*) Doubleday Publishing.

—The Wedding. 1996. 256p. pap. 12.00 (*0-385-47144-0*, Knopf Bks. for Young Readers) Random Hse. Children's Bks.

—The Wedding. abr. ed. 1998. audio 18.00 (*0-671-53562-5*, 908771, Simon & Schuster Audioworks) Simon & Schuster Audio.

Wharton, Edith. Ethan Frome. 20.95 (*0-89190-509-X*) Amereon, Ltd.

—Ethan Frome. E-Book 5.00 (*0-7607-1307-3*) Barnes & Noble, Inc.

—Ethan Frome. 2002. 110p. pap. 3.95 (*1-59109-098-9*) Booksurge, LLC.

—Ethan Frome. 1995. reprint ed. lib. bdg. 19.95 (*1-56849-636-2*) Buccaneer Bks., Inc.

—Ethan Frome. Peel, Edith, ed. 1999. (Literature Ser.). (Illus.). 172p. pap. text 11.95 (*0-521-64529-8*) Cambridge Univ. Pr.

—Ethan Frome. (Collected Works of Edith Wharton). 195p. 2001. pap. text 28.00 (*0-7426-5976-3*); 1998. reprint ed. lib. bdg. 88.00 (*1-58201-976-2*) Classic Bks.

—Ethan Frome. 1991. (Illus.). 96p. pap. 1.00 (*0-486-26690-7*) Dover Pubns., Inc.

—Ethan Frome. 1987. 192p. pap. 8.00 (*0-684-18906-2*); 1982. 192p. pap. 1.95 o.s.i (*0-684-17487-1*); 1977. 192p. 30.00 (*0-684-15326-2*); 1977. text 11.25 o.s.i (*0-684-51564-4*); 1977. pap. text (*0-684-51565-2*); 1910. pap. 5.95 o.s.i (*0-684-71927-4*, SL8) Gale Group. (Macmillan Reference USA).

—Ethan Frome. l.t. ed. 360p. pap. 32.97 (*0-7583-0846-9*); 420p. pap. 37.22 (*0-7583-0847-7*); 80p. pap. 13.16 (*0-7583-0840-X*); 294p. pap. 28.30 (*0-7583-0845-0*); 107p. pap. 15.07 (*0-7583-0841-8*); 240p. pap. 24.48 (*0-7583-0844-2*); 145p. pap. 17.76 (*0-7583-0842-6*); 187p. pap. 20.73 (*0-7583-0843-4*); 294p. lib. bdg. 39.55 (*0-7583-0837-X*); 240p. lib. bdg. 35.73 (*0-7583-0836-1*); 187p. lib. bdg. 31.98 (*0-7583-0835-3*); 360p. lib. bdg. 44.22 (*0-7583-0838-8*); 420p. lib. bdg. 48.47 (*0-7583-0839-6*); 80p. lib. bdg. 19.76 (*0-7583-0832-9*); 107p. lib. bdg. 23.06 (*0-7583-0833-7*); 145p. lib. bdg. 27.67 (*0-7583-0834-5*) Huge Print Pr.

—Ethan Frome. 1999. 110p. pap. 9.95 o.p. (*1-930128-05-3*, JNMedia Bks.) JNMedia, Inc.

—Ethan Frome. (Signet Classics). 2000. 176p. mass mkt. 4.95 (*0-451-52766-6*); 1996. pap., instr.'s gde. ed. (*0-451-16661-2*); 1992. 160p. mass mkt. 3.95 o.p. (*0-451-52580-9*); 1987. 160p. mass mkt. 4.95 o.s.i (*0-451-52227-3*); 1987. mass mkt. 2.50 o.p. (*0-451-52079-3*) NAL. (Signet Classics).

—Ethan Frome. 1991. 96p. (C). reprint ed. pap. text 2.75 (*0-914061-23-2*) Orchises Pr.

—Ethan Frome. Showalter, Elaine, ed. & intro. by. (Oxford World's Classics Ser.). 1998. 160p. pap. 7.95 (*0-19-283496-7*); 1996. 156p. pap. 6.95 o.p. (*0-19-282515-1*) Oxford Univ. Pr., Inc.

—Ethan Frome. 1911. 178p. text 9.50 o.s.i (*0-02-426690-6*, Macmillan College) Prentice Hall PTR.

—Ethan Frome. 1999. (Illus.). 182p. reprint ed. lib. bdg. 29.95 (*0-7351-0119-1*) Replica Bks.

—Ethan Frome. 1997. 160p. pap. 10.00 (*0-684-82591-0*, Scribner) Simon & Schuster.

—Ethan Frome. 1997. 16.05 (*0-606-00613-3*) Turtleback Bks.

—Ethan Frome. (Great Books of the 20th Century Ser.). 1994. 208p. 7.95 (*0-14-018736-7*); 1987. 224p. pap. 6.95 o.p. (*0-14-039058-8*) Viking Penguin. (Penguin Classics).

—Ethan Frome. 1993. 4.99 o.s.i (*1-85381-672-8*); 1991. 9.95 (*1-85381-228-5*) Virago Pr., Ltd. GBR. *Dist:* Random Hse. of Canada, Ltd., Trafalgar Square.

—Ethan Frome. 1999. E-Book 5.99 (*0-8220-7064-2*, Cliff Notes) Wiley, John & Sons, Inc.

—Ethan Frome. (Classics Library). 96p. pap. 3.95 (*1-84022-408-8*); 1998. pap. 3.95 (*1-85326-555-1*, 5551WW) Wordsworth Editions, Ltd. GBR. *Dist:* Combined Publishing.

—Ethan Frome: Authoritative Text, Backgrounds & Contexts, Criticism. Lauer, Kristin O. & Wolff, Cynthia G., eds. 1994. (Critical Editions Ser.). (C). pap. text 7.50 (*0-393-96635-6*) Norton, W. W. & Co., Inc.

—Ethan Frome & Other Short Fiction. 1987. (Classics Ser.). 256p. mass mkt. 5.50 (*0-553-21255-9*, Bantam Classics) Bantam Bks.

—Ethan Frome & Other Stories. 1996. 176p. text 5.98 o.p. (*1-56138-763-0*, Courage Bks.) Running Pr. Bk. Pubs.

—Ethan Frome & Summer. (Twelve-Point Ser.). 1998. lib. bdg. 25.00 (*1-58287-027-6*); 1993. 449p. reprint ed. lib. bdg. 26.00 (*0-939495-27-9*) North Bks.

—Ethan Frome & Summer. 2001. (Modern Library Classics). 304p. pap. 7.95 (*0-375-75728-7*, Modern Library) Random House Adult Trade Publishing Group.

—Summer. lib. bdg. 20.95 (*0-8488-1876-8*) Amereon, Ltd.

—Summer. unabr. ed. 1986. audio 29.95 (*1-55685-038-7*) Audio Bk. Contractors, Inc.

—Summer. 1993. 224p. mass mkt. 4.95 (*0-553-21422-5*) Bantam Bks.

—Summer. unabr. ed. 1994. audio 32.95 (*0-7861-0691-3*, 1476) Blackstone Audio Bks., Inc.

—Summer. unabr. ed. 1992. audio 26.95 (*1-55686-440-X*, 440) Books in Motion.

—Summer. 1998. (Collected Works of Edith Wharton). 290p. reprint ed. lib. bdg. 88.00 (*1-58201-994-0*) Classic Bks.

—Summer. 1980. pap. 6.50 o.p. (*0-06-080507-2*, P 507, Perennial) HarperTrade.

—Summer, Set. unabr. ed. 1999. audio 32.95 Highsmith Inc.

—Summer. 1991. 318p. reprint ed. lib. bdg. 25.00 o.p. (*0-8095-9073-5*) Millefleurs.

—Summer. 1993. 216p. mass mkt. 4.95 (*0-451-52566-3*, Signet Classics) NAL.

—Summer. 1970. reprint ed. 59.00 (*0-403-00259-1*) Scholarly Pr., Inc.

—Summer. 1998. 256p. pap. 10.00 (*0-684-84258-0*, Scribner) Simon & Schuster.

—Summer. l.t. ed. 1996. (Perennial Bestsellers Ser.). lib. bdg. 22.95 (*0-7838-1831-9*) Thorndike Pr.

—Summer. 1993. (Great Books of the 20th Century Ser.). 224p. 9.95 (*0-14-018679-4*, Penguin Classics) Viking Penguin.

Wharton, Edith & Showalter, Elaine. Ethan Frome. 1996. E-Book 7.30 (*0-585-35118-X*) netLibrary, Inc.

White, Michael C. The Blind Side of the Heart: A Novel. 1999. 368p. 24.00 (*0-06-019431-6*) HarperCollins Pubs.

Wiggs, Susan. The Charm School. abr. ed. 2001. audio 7.99 (*1-55204-174-3*, MIR-1174) Durkin Hayes Publishing Ltd.

—The Charm School. 1999. (Mira Bks.). 408p. per. (*1-55166-491-7*, 1-66491-1, Mira Bks.) Harlequin Enterprises, Ltd.

Willett, Sabin. The Deal. 1997. 496p. mass mkt. 6.99 o.s.i (*0-515-12182-7*, Jove) Berkley Publishing Group.

Williams, William Carlos. White Mule. 1967. (Stecher Trilogy: Vol. 1). pap. 12.95 (*0-8112-0238-0*, NDP226) New Directions Publishing Corp.

Winston, Daoma. The Fall River Line. 1986. mass mkt. 4.95 (*0-312-90184-4*, St. Martin's Paperbacks); 1984. 576p. 16.95 o.p. (*0-312-27986-8*) St. Martin's Pr.

Wittlinger, Ellen. What's in a Name. 2001. (Illus.). 192p. (YA). mass mkt. 4.99 (*0-689-84532-4*, Simon Pulse) Simon & Schuster Children's Publishing.

**MATTAGASH (ME.: IMAGINARY PLACE)—FICTION**

Pelletier, Cathie. The Funeral Makers. 1997. 256p. reprint ed. pap. 16.95 (*0-684-82614-3*, Scribner) Simon & Schuster.

—Once upon a Time on the Banks. Rosenman, Jane, ed. 1991. 384p. reprint ed. pap. (*0-671-72447-9*, Washington Square Pr.) Simon & Schuster.

—Once upon a Time on the Banks. 1989. 368p. 19.95 o.p. (*0-670-82776-2*) Viking Penguin.

—The Weight of Winter. 1993. 432p. reprint ed. pap. (*0-671-79387-X*, Washington Square Pr.) Simon & Schuster.

—The Weight of Winter. 1991. 432p. 22.95 o.p. (*0-670-84090-4*, Viking) Viking Penguin.

**MAURITIUS—FICTION**

Blackburn, Julia. The Book of Color. 1996. 192p. pap. 15.00 (*0-679-75837-2*) Random Hse., Inc.

De Saint-Pierre, Bernardin J. Paul & Virginia. Lang, Andrew, tr. from FRE. 1987. 152p. reprint ed. lib. bdg. 29.50 (*0-86527-363-4*) Fertig, Howard Inc.

—Paul & Virginia. Donovan, John, tr. & intro. by. 1983. 29.95 (*0-7206-0598-9*) Owen, Peter Ltd. GBR. *Dist:* Dufour Editions, Inc.

—Paul & Virginia. 1989. 144p. pap. 5.95 o.p. (*0-14-044546-3*, Penguin Classics) Viking Penguin.

—Paul & Virginia. 1989. 248p. reprint ed. o.p. (*1-85477-009-8*) Woodstock Books.

Le Clezio, J. M. G. The Prospector. Marks, Carol, tr. from FRE. 1993. (Verba Mundi Ser.). 352p. 22.95 (*0-87923-976-X*) Godine, David R. Pub.

**MEDITERRANEAN REGION—FICTION**

Coonts, Stephen. Final Flight. unabr. ed. 1988. audio 72.00 (*0-7366-1525-3*, 2396) Books on Tape, Inc.

—Final Flight. 1989. 400p. mass mkt. 7.99 (*0-440-20447-X*) Dell Publishing.

—Final Flight. l.t. ed. 1990. (Magna Large Print Ser.). 601p. o.p. (*1-85057-718-8*) Magna Large Print Bks. GBR. *Dist:* Ulverscroft Large Print Canada, Ltd.

Edwards, Jonathan. Tales in the Key of Sea. 2001. 185p. pap. 13.95 (*0-595-16841-8*) iUniverse, Inc.

Graham, Lynne. A Mediterranean Marriage. 2003. (Harlequin Presents Ser.: No. 2295). 192p. mass mkt. o.s.i (*0-373-12295-0*, Harlequin Bks.) Harlequin Enterprises, Ltd.

—A Mediterranean Marriage. l.t. ed. 2003. (Harlequin I Romance Ser.). 25.95 (*0-263-17899-4*) Harlequin Mills & Boon, Ltd. GBR. *Dist:* Thorndike Pr.

Gray, Suzanne. Circe, Goodnight: A Novel. 2001. 188p. 24.95 (*1-56474-357-8*) Fithian Pr.

Hawkes, John. The Blood Oranges. 1972. 9.95 o.p. (*0-8112-0285-2*); pap. 12.95 (*0-8112-0061-2*, NDP338) New Directions Publishing Corp.

—The Blood Oranges. 1998. 288p. pap. 11.95 o.s.i (*0-14-026734-4*) Penguin Group (USA) Inc.

Maalouf, Amin. Balthasar's Odyssey: A Novel. 2003. 392p. pap. 14.95 (*1-55970-702-X*) Arcade Publishing, Inc.

—Balthasar's Odyssey: A Novel. Bray, Barbara, tr. from FRE. 2002. (Illus.). 384p. 25.95 (*1-55970-666-X*) Arcade Publishing, Inc.

Morris, Jan. Last Letters from Hav. 1989. pap. 6.95 o.s.i (*0-394-75564-2*, Vintage) Knopf Publishing Group.

—Last Letters from Hav: Notes from a Lost City. 1985. 193p. 14.95 o.p. (*0-394-53262-7*) Random Hse., Inc.

O'Brien, Edna. The High Road. 1989. 22p. pap. 8.95 o.p. (*0-452-26306-9*, Plume) Dutton/Plume.

—The High Road. 1988. 256p. 18.95 o.s.i (*0-374-29273-6*) Farrar, Straus & Giroux.

Rubens, Bernice. Birds of Passage. 1984. mass mkt. 3.95 o.s.i (*0-671-50282-4*, Pocket) Simon & Schuster.

—Birds of Passage. Silberman, J., ed. 1982. 224p. 12.95 o.p. (*0-671-44798-X*) Summit Bks.

Skármeta, Antonio. The Poet's Wedding. Rascon, Susan G., tr. from SPA. 2004. 256p. 26.95 (*1-56649-249-1*) Welcome Rain Pubs.

Smith, Debra White. To Rome with Love. 2001. (Seven Sisters Ser.: No. 4). 298p. pap. 10.99 (*0-7369-0660-6*) Harvest Hse. Pubs.

Wadham, Lucy. Lost. 2000. 320p. 24.95 (*0-7867-0785-2*, Carroll & Graf Pubs.) Avalon Publishing Group.

**MELNIBONE (IMAGINARY PLACE)—FICTION**

Moorcock, Michael. The Bane of the Black Sword. 1987. (Elric Saga). 160p. mass mkt. 5.99 o.s.i (*0-441-04885-4*) Ace Bks.

—The Bane of the Black Sword. 1986. 160p. 2.95 o.s.i (*0-425-10132-0*); 1986. 2.95 o.s.i (*0-425-09281-X*); 1985. 2.95 o.s.i (*0-425-08503-1*); 1984. 2.75 o.s.i (*0-425-07636-9*); 1984. 2.50 o.s.i (*0-425-06537-5*) Berkley Publishing Group.

—The Bane of the Black Sword. 1977. mass mkt. 1.25 o.p. (*0-87997-316-1*); mass mkt. 1.50 o.p. (*0-87997-421-4*); mass mkt. 1.75 o.p. (*0-87997-515-6*); mass mkt. 1.95 o.p. (*0-87997-628-4*);No. 5. mass mkt. 2.25 o.p. (*0-87997-805-8*, UE1805) DAW Bks., Inc.

—Elric at the End of Time. 1985. (Elric Saga). mass mkt. 2.95 o.p. (*0-88677-040-8*); 224p. mass mkt. 4.50 o.p. (*0-88677-228-1*) DAW Bks., Inc.

—Elric at the End of Time. 1985. (Elric Saga). 224p. mass mkt. 4.50 o.s.i (*0-88677-410-1*, Abrahams, William Bks.) Dutton/Plume.

—Elric of Melnibone. 1987. (Elric Saga: Bk. 1). 192p. mass mkt. 5.99 o.s.i (*0-441-20398-1*) Ace Bks.

—Elric of Melnibone. (Elric Saga). 1986. 192p. 2.95 o.s.i (*0-425-09957-1*); 1985. 2.95 o.s.i (*0-425-08843-X*); 1985. 2.95 o.s.i (*0-425-08195-8*); 1984. 2.75 o.s.i (*0-425-07634-2*); 1983. 2.50 o.s.i (*0-425-06044-6*) Berkley Publishing Group.

—Elric of Melnibone. 1976. (Elric Saga). mass mkt. 1.25 o.p. (*0-87997-259-9*); mass mkt. 1.95 o.p. (*0-87997-644-6*); mass mkt. 2.25 o.p. (*0-87997-734-5*); mass mkt. 1.50 o.p. (*0-87997-356-0*, UW1356) DAW Bks., Inc.

—The Fortress of the Pearl. (Elric Saga: Bk. 7). 1990. mass mkt. 4.99 o.s.i (*0-441-24866-7*); 1989. 16.95 o.p. (*0-441-19123-1*) Ace Bks.

—The Revenge of the Rose. 1994. 256p. mass mkt. 5.99 o.s.i (*0-441-00106-8*); 1991. 17.95 o.p. (*0-441-71844-2*) Ace Bks.

—The Sailor on the Seas of Fate. 1987. (Elric Saga: Bk. 2). 160p. mass mkt. 5.99 o.s.i (*0-441-74863-5*) Ace Bks.

—The Sailor on the Seas of Fate. 1987. 160p. 2.95 o.s.i (*0-425-10329-3*) Berkley Publishing Group.

—The Skrayling Tree: The Albino in America. (Elric Noel Book Ser.: No. 2). 2004. mass mkt. (*0-446-61340-1*); 2003. 336p. 24.95 (*0-446-53104-9*) Warner Bks., Inc. (Aspect).

—Stormbringer. 1987. (Elric Saga: Vol. 6). mass mkt. 5.50 o.s.i (*0-441-78754-1*) Ace Bks.

—Stormbringer. (Elric Saga: No. 6). 1986. 224p. 2.95 o.s.i (*0-425-10249-1*); 1986. 2.95 o.s.i (*0-425-09280-1*); 1984. 2.50 o.s.i (*0-425-06559-6*) Berkley Publishing Group.

—Stormbringer. 1977. (Elric Saga). mass mkt. 1.50 o.p. (*0-87997-335-8*); mass mkt. 2.50 o.p. (*0-87997-755-8*); mass mkt. 2.75 o.p. (*0-87997-842-2*); mass mkt. 1.75 o.p. (*0-87997-574-1*); mass mkt. 2.25 o.p. (*0-87997-691-8*) DAW Bks., Inc.

—The Vanishing Tower. 1987. (Elric Saga: Vol. 4). 176p. mass mkt. 5.99 o.s.i (*0-441-86039-7*) Ace Bks.

—The Vanishing Tower. 1986. 2.95 o.s.i (*0-425-10171-1*); 1986. 2.95 o.s.i (*0-425-09535-5*); 1984. 2.75 o.s.i (*0-425-07762-4*); 1983. 2.50 o.s.i (*0-425-06406-9*) Berkley Publishing Group.

—The Vanishing Tower. 1977. mass mkt. 1.25 o.p. (*0-87997-304-8*); mass mkt. 1.50 o.p. (*0-87997-406-0*); mass mkt. 1.75 o.p. (*0-87997-553-9*); mass mkt. 2.25 o.p. (*0-87997-693-4*); mass mkt. 2.50 o.p. (*0-87997-796-5*) DAW Bks., Inc.

—The Weird of the White Wolf, Vol. 3. 1988. (Elric Saga: Bk. 3). 160p. mass mkt. 5.99 o.s.i (*0-441-88805-4*) Ace Bks.

—The Weird of the White Wolf. 1985. 2.95 o.s.i (*0-425-08904-5*); 1985. 2.95 o.s.i (*0-425-08267-9*); 1984. 2.50 o.s.i (*0-425-07176-6*); 1983. 2.50 o.s.i (*0-425-06289-9*) Berkley Publishing Group.

—The Weird of the White Wolf. 1977. mass mkt. 1.25 o.p. (*0-87997-286-6*); mass mkt. 1.50 o.p. (*0-87997-390-0*); mass mkt. 1.75 o.p. (*0-87997-528-8*) DAW Bks., Inc.

Moorcock, Michael & Matthews, Rodney. Elric at the End of Time. 9999. (Illus.). 128p. pap. 17.95 o.p. (*1-85028-032-0*) Penguin Group (USA) Inc.

**MENSANDOR (IMAGINARY PLACE)—FICTION**

Lawhead, Stephen R. In the Hall of the Dragon King. (Dragon King Trilogy ). (YA). (gr. 7-12). 1990. pap. 9.99 o.p. (*0-89107-563-1*); Bk. I. 1982. 348p. pap. 9.95 o.p. (*0-89107-257-8*) Crossway Bks.

—In the Hall of the Dragon King. 2003. (Illus.). 384p. pap. 6.95 (*0-7459-4618-6*) Lion Publishing PLC GBR. *Dist:* Trafalgar Square.

—In the Hall of the Dragon King. 1992. (Dragon King Trilogy : Bk. 1). (YA). pap. 6.50 (*0-380-71629-1*, Avon Bks.) Morrow/Avon.

—In the Hall of the Dragon King. 1996. (Dragon King Trilogy : Bk. 1). 352p. (YA). pap. 24.99 (*0-310-20502-6*) Zondervan.

—The Sword & the Flame. (Dragon King Trilogy : Bk. 3). (YA). (gr. 7-12). 1990. pap. 9.99 o.p. (*0-89107-565-8*); 1984. 348p. pap. 9.95 o.p. (*0-89107-310-8*) Crossway Bks.

—The Sword & the Flame. 2003. (Dragon King Saga: Bk. 3). (Illus.). 320p. (J). pap. 6.95 (*0-7459-4619-4*) Lion Publishing PLC GBR. *Dist:* Trafalgar Square.

—The Sword & the Flame. 1992. (Dragon King Trilogy : Bk. 3). 384p. (YA). mass mkt. 5.99 (*0-380-71631-3*, Avon Bks.) Morrow/Avon.

—The Sword & the Flame. 1996. (Dragon King Trilogy : Bk. 3). 320p. (YA). pap. 24.99 (*0-310-20504-2*) Zondervan.

—The Warlords of Nin. (Dragon King Saga: Bk. 2). (YA). (gr. 7-12). 1983. 488p. pap. 9.95 o.p. (*0-89107-278-0*); Bk. 2. 1990. pap. 9.99 o.p. (*0-89107-564-X*) Crossway Bks.

—The Warlords of Nin. 2003. (Illus.). 352p. pap. 6.95 (*0-7459-4620-8*) Lion Publishing PLC GBR. *Dist:* Trafalgar Square.

—The Warlords of Nin. 1992. (Dragon King Saga: Bk. 2). 416p. (YA). pap. 5.99 (*0-380-71630-5*, Avon Bks.) Morrow/Avon.

—The Warlords of Nin. 1996. (Dragon King Saga: Bk. 2). 400p. (YA). pap. 24.99 (*0-310-20503-4*) Zondervan.

**METROPOLIS (IMAGINARY PLACE)—FICTION**

Cherryh, C. J. Lois & Clark: A Superman Novel. 288p. 1997. pap. 12.00 o.s.i (*0-7615-1169-5*); 1996. 20.00 o.p. (*0-7615-0482-6*) Crown Publishing Group. (Prima Lifestyles).

Stern, Roger. The Death & Life of Superman. 1994. 544p. mass mkt. 5.99 o.s.i (*0-553-56930-9*) Bantam Bks.

—The Death & Life of Superman. 4.98 o.p. (*0-8317-7733-8*) Smithmark Pubs., Inc.

**MEXICO—FICTION**

Abish, Walter. Eclipse Fever. 1995. (Nonpareil Bks.: Vol. 76). 352p. pap. 15.95 (*1-56792-036-5*) Godine, David R. Pub.

—Eclipse Fever. 1994. 4.99 o.p. (*0-517-11769-X*) Random Hse. Value Publishing.

Abreu Gomez, Emilio. Canek, History & Legend of a Maya Hero. Davila, Mario L. & Wilson, Carter, trs. from SPA. 1979. 45.00 o.p. (*0-520-03148-2*); pap. 8.95 o.p. (*0-520-03982-3*) Univ. of California Pr.

Alcala, Kathleen. Mrs. Vargas & the Dead Naturalist. 1992. 192p. 19.95 (*0-934971-26-9*); pap. 9.95 (*0-934971-25-0*) Calyx Bks.

—Treasures in Heaven: A Novel. 2000. 210p. 22.95 (*0-8118-2953-7*) Chronicle Bks. LLC.

All the Pretty Horses. 2000. 11.95 (*1-56137-914-X*) Novel Units, Inc.

Anaya, Rudolfo A. The Legend of la Llorona. 95p. 1984. pap. 6.00 o.p. (*0-89229-015-3*); 2nd ed. 1994. pap. 8.00 o.p. (*0-89229-025-0*) TQS Pubns., Eclectic Chicano Literature.

Anaya, Rudolfo A. & Johnson, David. Lord of the Dawn: The Legend of Quetzalcoatl. 1987. 164p. 15.95 o.p. (*0-8263-1001-X*) Univ. of New Mexico Pr.

Anderson, Kevin J. Ruins. 1996. (X-Files Ser.). 304p. mass mkt. 22.00 o.p. (*0-06-105247-7*) HarperCollins Pubs.

—Ruins. (X-Files Ser.: Vol. 4). 1997. 272p. mass mkt. 6.50 o.s.i (*0-06-105736-3*, HarperEntertainment); 1996. 304p. 50.00 o.s.i (*0-06-105273-6*, Eos) Morrow/Avon.

Anderson, Mary. The Curse of the Demon. 1989. (Mostly Monsters Ser.: No. 4). 128p. (J). (gr. k-6). pap. 2.95 o.s.i (*0-440-40203-4*, Yearling) Random Hse. Children's Bks.

Antonio-Villarreal, Jose. The Fifth Horseman. 2nd ed. 1984. xxvi, 410p. pap. 19.00 (*0-916950-49-2*) Bilingual Pr./Editorial Bilingue.

Avila, Alfred. Mexican Ghost Tale of the Southwest. Avila, Kat, ed. 1994. 172p. (YA). (gr. 7-12). pap. 9.95 (*1-55885-107-0*, Piñata Books) Arte Publico Pr.

—Mexican Ghost Tale of the Southwest. 1994. 16.00 (*0-606-16088-4*) Turtleback Bks.

Azuela, Arturo. Shadows of Silence. Murray, Elena C., tr. 1985. 304p. (C). text 26.95 o.p. (*0-268-01716-6*) Univ. of Notre Dame Pr.

Azuela, Mariano. Three Novels by Mariano Azuela: The Trials of a Respectable Family; The Underdogs; The Firefly. Hendricks, Frances K. & Berler, Bernice, trs. from SPA. 2nd ed. 373p. 25.00 (*0-911536-78-7*) Trinity Univ. Pr.

—The Underdogs: A Novel of the Mexican Revolution. Date not set. Tr. of De abajo. 149p. 18.95 (*0-8488-2559-4*) Amereon, Ltd.

—The Underdogs: A Novel of the Mexican Revolution. 1986. Tr. of De abajo. 160p. reprint ed. lib. bdg. 21.95 (*0-89966-515-2*) Buccaneer Bks., Inc.

—The Underdogs: A Novel of the Mexican Revolution.Tr. of De abajo. E-Book 2.49 (*1-58627-010-9*) Electric Umbrella Publishing.

—The Underdogs: A Novel of the Mexican Revolution. 1996. Tr. of De abajo. 176p. mass mkt. 6.95 (*0-451-52625-2*, MS6252, Signet Classics) NAL.

—The Underdogs: A Novel of the Mexican Revolution. Munguia, E., Jr., tr. 1963. Tr. of De abajo. mass mkt. 3.50 o.p. (*0-451-52102-1*, CE1741, Signet Classics) NAL.

—The Underdogs: A Novel of the Mexican Revolution. Fornoff, Frederick H., tr. 1992. (Latin American Ser.).Tr. of De abajo. (ENG & SPA.). 184p. (C). 49.95 o.p. (*0-8229-3728-X*); (Illus.). pap. 14.95 o.p. (*0-8229-5484-2*) Univ. of Pittsburgh Pr.

Azulea, Mariano. The Underdogs. 1963. 152p. mass mkt. 4.95 o.p. (*0-451-52255-9*) NAL.

Bean, Frederic. Pancho & Black Jack. 1995. 384p. mass mkt. 5.50 (*0-671-88691-6*, Pocket) Simon & Schuster.

Bedford, Sybille. A Visit to Don Otavio. 2003. 384p. pap. text 16.00 (*1-58243-171-X*, Counterpoint Pr.) Basic Bks.

Bellow, Saul. The Adventures of Augie March. 1995. (Everyman's Library: Vol. 215). 656p. 20.00 (*0-679-44460-2*) Knopf, Alfred A. Inc.

—The Adventures of Augie March. 1977. pap. 3.50 o.p. (*0-380-00961-7*, 64600-5, Avon Bks.) Morrow/Avon.

—The Adventures of Augie March. (Penguin Great Books of the 20th Century Ser.). 1999. 592p. pap. 14.95 (*0-14-028160-6*); 1960. pap. 2.95 o.p. (*0-670-00069-8*) Penguin Group (USA) Inc.

—The Adventures of Augie March. 2003. 608p. 29.95 (*0-670-03242-5*); 1996. 544p. 15.00 (*0-14-018941-6*, Penguin Classics); 1984. 544p. pap. 11.95 o.p. (*0-14-007272-1*, Penguin Bks.) Viking Penguin.

Benitez, Sandra. Night of the Radishes. 2004. 22.95 (*0-7868-6400-1*) Hyperion Pr.

—A Place Where the Sea Remembers. 1993. 160p. (YA). (gr. 10-12). 19.95 (*1-56689-011-X*) Coffee Hse. Pr.

—A Place Where the Sea Remembers. 1995. 176p. pap. 11.00 (*0-671-89267-3*, Touchstone) Simon & Schuster.

Berman, Sabina. Bubbeh. Labinger, Andrea G., tr. from SPA. 1998. (Discoveries Ser.). 96p. pap. 12.95 (*0-935480-93-5*) Latin American Literary Review Pr.

Bittrich, Louis E. & Lewis, Theresia J. Betrayal in Mexico: A True Story of Romance & Adventure in the Early Days of Exotic Puerto Vallarta. 1994. pap. 14.95 (*1-56875-072-2*) R & E Pubs., Inc.

Blackburn, Steve. The Extinction of Rhinos in Mexico: 9 Tales of Life & Death. 2001. 200p. E-Book 8.00 (*0-7388-9834-1*) Xlibris Corp.

Blair, Kathryn S. In the Shadow of the Angel. 2001. 636p. pap. 29.60 (*0-7596-0631-5*) 1stBooks Library.

Blake, James C. The Friends of Pancho Villa. 1998. 288p. mass mkt. 5.99 o.s.i (*0-425-16235-4*); 1996. 272p. pap. 13.00 o.s.i (*0-425-15304-5*) Berkley Publishing Group.

Blom, Suzanne Alles. Inca: The Scarlet Fringe. 2001. (Illus.). 367p. mass mkt. 7.99 (*0-8125-7883-X*, Tor Bks.) Doherty, Tom Assocs., LLC.

Bly, Stephen A. Final Justice at Adobe Wells. 1993. (Stuart Brannon Western Adventure Ser.: No. 5). 192p. pap. 8.99 (*0-89107-744-8*) Crossway Bks.

Bonds, Parris Afton. Blue Moon. 1988. mass mkt. 4.50 o.s.i (*0-449-14568-9*, Fawcett); 1985. pap. o.s.i (*0-449-90154-8*) Ballantine Bks.

Brand, Max. The Song of the Whip. 1975. 261p. reprint ed. lib. bdg. 20.95 (*0-89190-210-4*, Rivercity Pr.) Amereon, Ltd.

—The Song of the Whip. 1990. reprint ed. lib. bdg. 16.95 (*0-89968-486-6*) Buccaneer Bks., Inc.

—The Survival of Juan Oro. 1999. (Western Ser.). 259p. 19.95 (*0-7862-1325-6*, Five Star) Gale Group.

—The Survival of Juan Oro. l.t. ed. 1999. (Western Ser.). 373p. 24.95 (*0-7862-1336-1*) Thorndike Pr.

Brandel, Marc. An Ear for Danger. 1989. (Three Investigators Crimebusters Ser.: No. 5). 144p. (J). (gr. 3-7). pap. 2.95 o.s.i (*0-394-89943-1*, Knopf Bks. for Young Readers) Random Hse. Children's Bks.

Braverman, Kate. The Incantation of Frida K. 240p. 2002. 23.95 (*1-58322-469-6*); 2003. reprint ed. pap. 11.95 (*1-58322-571-4*) Seven Stories Pr.

Britton, Vickie & Jackson, Loretta. Path of the Jaguar. 1989. 13.95 o.p. (*0-8034-8748-7*) Bouregy, Thomas & Co., Inc.

—Path of the Jaguar. l.t. ed. 2002. 200p. 23.95 (*0-7862-4085-7*) Gale Group.

Brouwer, Sigmund. Sunrise at the Mayan Temple. (Accidental Detective Ser.: Vol. 10). (J). (gr. 3-7). 1995. 132p. pap. 5.99 o.p. (*1-56476-379-X*, 6-3379); 1992. pap. 4.99 (*0-89693-057-2*) Cook Communications Ministries.

Brown, J. P. S. The Cinnamon Colt & Other Stories. 1992. 192p. 15.00 o.s.i (*0-385-41499-4*) Doubleday Publishing.

Bryan, Diane Brenda. Soldier of God: Novel. 2001. 192p. pap. 11.95 (*1-56315-247-9*) SterlingHouse Pubs., Inc.

Bunting, Eve. A Part of the Dream. 1992. (Eve Bunting Collection). (Illus.). 48p. (J). (gr. 2-6). lib. bdg. 12.79 o.p. (*0-89565-771-6*) Child's World, Inc.

Burroway, Janet. Cutting Stone. 1992. 400p. 21.95 o.p. (*0-395-59300-X*) Houghton Mifflin Co.

—Cutting Stone. 1993. 480p. mass mkt. 4.50 o.s.i (*1-55817-757-4*) Kensington Publishing Corp.

—Cutting Stone. 404p. 4.98 o.p. (*0-8317-9071-7*) Smithmark Pubs., Inc.

Camin, Hector Aguilar. El Resplandor de la Madera. 2001. (SPA., Illus.). 512p. 19.95 (*84-204-4191-0*) Alfaguara, Ediciones, S.A.- Grupo Santillana ESP. *Dist:* Santillana USA Publishing Co., Inc.

Camp, Roderic A. Memoirs of a Mexican Politician. 1988. (Illus.). 248p. reprint ed. pap. 76.90 (*0-608-04128-9*, 206486100011) Bks. on Demand.

—Memoirs of a Mexican Politician. 1988. (Illus.). 247p. 12.95 o.p. (*0-8263-1041-9*); pap. 12.95 o.p. (*0-8263-1042-7*) Univ. of New Mexico Pr.

Campobello, Nellie. Cartucho & My Mother's Hands. Meyer, Doris & Matthews, Irene, trs. 1988. (Texas Pan American Ser.). 143p. pap. 10.95 o.p. (*0-292-71111-5*); 19.95 o.p. (*0-292-71110-7*) Univ. of Texas Pr.

Cano, Daniel. Pepe Rios. 1991. (SPA.). 250p. pap. 9.50 o.p. (*1-55885-023-6*) Arte Publico Pr.

Castellanos, Rosario. Nine Guardians. Nicholson, Irene, tr. from SPA. 1992. 272p. 19.95 o.p. (*0-930523-89-X*); pap. 14.95 (*0-930523-90-3*) Readers International.

—Oficio de Tinieblas. 2003. Tr. of Book of Lamentations. (SPA.). 368p. 18.95 (*968-27-0902-4*) Ediciones Joaquin Mortiz MEX. *Dist:* Planeta Publishing Corp.

—Oficio de Tinieblas. 1998. Tr. of Book of Lamentations. (SPA.). 368p. 20.00 (*0-14-026833-2*) Viking Penguin.

Center for Learning Network Staff. All the Pretty Horses: Curriculum Unit —Novel Series — Grades 9-12. 2001. (Novel Ser.). 60p. tchr. ed., spiral bd. 18.95 (*1-56077-667-6*) Ctr. for Learning, The.

Champlin, Tim. The Last Campaign. l.t. ed. (Western Ser.). 1997. 287p. lib. bdg. 22.95 o.p. (*0-7838-1541-7*, Macmillan Reference USA); 1996. 246p. 17.95 (*0-7862-0566-0*, Five Star) Gale Group.

Chaney, J. D. Tito's Whore. 1999. 144p. pap. 13.50 (*0-88739-184-2*) Creative Arts Bk. Co.

Chin, Frank. Gunga Din Highway. 400p. 1995. pap. 14.95 (*1-56689-037-3*); 1994. 24.95 (*1-56689-024-1*) Coffee Hse. Pr.

Chiu, Tony. Positive Match. 1998. 480p. mass mkt. 6.50 (*0-553-57546-5*) Bantam Bks.

Cisneros, Sandra. Caramelo. unabr. ed. 2002. 112p. audio 39.95 (*0-06-051591-0*, HarperAudio) HarperTrade.

—Caramelo. 2003. (SPA.). 496p. pap. 13.95 (*1-4000-3099-4*, Vintage); 464p. pap. 13.95 (*0-679-74258-1*, Vintage); 464p. 24.00 (*1-4000-4150-3*) Knopf Publishing Group.

—Caramelo. 2002. 464p. 24.00 (*0-679-43554-9*) Knopf, Alfred A. Inc.

—Caramelo. 2002. (SPA.). 496p. 24.00 (*0-375-41509-2*) Random Hse., Inc.

—Caramelo. 2003. (Spanish Language Ser.). (SPA.). 28.95 (*0-7862-5124-7*); 30.95 (*0-7862-5138-7*) Thorndike Pr.

Settings

Clymer, Eleanor. Santiago's Silver Mine. 1989. 80p. (gr. k-6). pap. text 2.75 o.p. (0-440-40157-7, Yearling) Random Hse. Children's Bks.

Coker, Elizabeth B. The Grasshopper King: A Story of Two Confederate Exiles in Mexico During the Reign of Maximillian & Carlota. 1981. 336p. 13.50 o.p. (0-525-10716-9, 01311-390, Dutton) Dutton/Plume.

Collins, Joan. Love & Desire & Hate. l.t. ed. 1994. 23.95 o.p. (0-7927-1957-3); 24.95 o.p. (0-7927-1958-1) BBC Audiobooks America.

—Love & Desire & Hate. 1991. 368p. 21.95 o.p. (0-671-66580-4, Simon & Schuster) Simon & Schuster.

Conner, K. Patrick. Kingdom Road. 1991. 192p. 18.95 o.p. (1-55611-302-1) Fine, Donald I. Bks.

Cowart, John L. Pancho Villa's Revenge. 2001. pap. 15.54 (0-7596-1494-6) 1stBooks Library.

Crespi, Camilla T. The Trouble with Too Much Sun. 1992. (Simona Griffo Mystery Ser.). mass mkt. 3.99 o.s.i (0-8217-3776-7, Zebra Bks.) Kensington Publishing Corp.

Cunningham, John. The Rainbow Runner. 288p. 1993. mass mkt. 4.99 (0-8125-1359-2); 1992. 19.95 o.p. (0-312-85163-4) Doherty, Tom Assocs., LLC. (Tor Bks.).

Curley, Daniel. Mummy. 1987. 256p. 16.95 o.p. (0-395-42507-7) Houghton Mifflin Co.

Curry, Edna. Traveling Bug. E-Book 3.50 (1-58495-070-6); 2000. E-Book 3.50 (1-58495-063-3) DiskUs Publishing.

Curtis, Sandra. Zorro Unmasked: The Official History. 1998. (Illus.). 320p. pap. 14.95 o.p. (0-7868-8285-9) Hyperion Pr.

Cutler, Bruce. At War with Mexico: A Fictional Mosaic. 2001. (Literature of the American West Ser.: Vol. 6). x, 209p. 24.95 (0-8061-3264-7) Univ. of Oklahoma Pr.

Czernecki, Stefan & Rhodes, Timothy. The Hummingbirds' Gift. 1994. (Illus.). 32p. (J). (gr. k-4). 14.95 (1-56282-604-2); lib. bdg. 15.49 o.s.i (1-56282-605-0) Hyperion Bks. for Children.

—The Hummingbirds' Gift. l.t. ed. 1994. (Illus.). 32p. (J). (gr. k-4). (0-920534-99-6) Hyperion Pr., Ltd.

Dalton, Richard Merrill, Jr. Cattle War: A Novel about the Border War with Mexico in the 1870's. 2000. 256p. pap. 21.99 (0-7388-4385-7); text 31.99 (0-7388-4384-9); E-Book 8.00 (0-7388-9506-7) Xlibris Corp.

Dawson, Clarence W. Return of Montezuma: A Novel. 1991. 128p. pap. 10.95 (0-86534-162-1) Sunstone Pr.

Day, A. Steven. Generations. Diaz, Arthur S., ed. 2001. pap. 8.99 (0-9705259-2-3); (Illus.). ix, 545p. 27.95 (0-9705259-4-X) St. Aztec Publishing.

Day, Douglas. The Prison Notebooks of Ricardo Flores Magon. 1991. 21.95 (0-15-174598-6) Harcourt Trade Pubs.

De Aragon, Ray J. Hermanos de la Luz: Living Tradition of the Penitente Faith. 1994. (Illus.). 258p. 24.95 o.p. (0-940666-42-1); 120p. pap. 24.95 o.p. (0-940666-54-5) Clear Light Pubs.

Deighton, Len. Mexico Set. 1997. pap. 12.95 o.p. (0-345-41836-0); 1985. 408p. mass mkt. 6.99 o.s.i (0-345-31499-9, Ballantine Bks.) Ballantine Bks.

Del Paso, Fernando. Palinuro of Mexico. Plaister, Elisabeth, tr. 1996. 557p. pap. 14.95 (1-56478-095-3) Dalkey Archive Pr.

Delahunt, Meaghan. In the Blue House. 2001. 308p. (0-7475-5236-3); pap. (0-7475-5359-9) Bloomsbury Pr.

—In the Casa Azul: A Novel of Revolution & Betrayal. 2003. 320p. pap. 14.00 (0-312-29107-8) Picador.

—In the Casa Azul: A Novel of Revolution & Betrayal. 2002. 320p. 23.95 (0-312-29106-X) St. Martin's Pr.

Delinsky, Barbara. First Things First. 1992. mass mkt. (0-373-83249-4, 1-83249-2); 1985. mass mkt. (0-373-25187-4) Harlequin Enterprises, Ltd. (Harlequin Bks.).

—First Things First. l.t. ed. 2001. (Large Print Famous Authors Ser.). 334p. 29.95 (0-7862-3101-7) Thorndike Pr.

Denton, Anne. Heart of Stone. Smith, James C., Jr., ed. 1994. 196p. pap. 12.95 o.p. (0-86534-224-5) Sunstone Pr.

Dillon, Millicent. A Version of Love: A Novel. 2003. 288p. 23.95 (0-393-05216-8) Norton, W. W. & Co., Inc.

Doerr, Harriet. Consider This, Senora. l.t. ed. 1994. 25.95 o.p. (0-7927-1840-2); pap. 24.95 o.p. (0-7927-1839-9) BBC Audiobooks America.

—Consider This, Senora. (Harvest American Writing Ser.). 1994. 256p. (C). pap. 13.00 (0-15-600002-4); 1993. 241p. 21.95 o.s.i (0-15-193103-8) Harcourt Trade Pubs.

Dold, Gaylord. Six White Horses: A Thriller. 2002. 304p. 23.95 (0-312-29025-X, Saint Martin's Minotaur) St. Martin's Pr.

Domecq, Brianda. Eleven Days. 1995. 226p. (C). pap. 10.95 (0-8263-1606-9) Univ. of New Mexico Pr.

Domecq, Brianda & Garcia, Kay S. Eleven Days. 1995. E-Book 10.95 (0-585-18745-2) netLibrary, Inc.

Donoghue, P. S. Mazatlan: A Jack Novak Thriller. 1993. 256p. 20.95 o.p. (1-55611-369-2) Fine, Donald I. Bks.

Dorantes, Jorge. Nada que Ver. 2001. Tr. of Nothing to See. (SPA.). 125p. pap. 13.10 (968-411-513-X) Ediciones Era MEX. *Dist:* Continental Bk. Co., Inc.

Ducornet, Rikki. The Fan-Maker's Inquisition: A Novel of the Marquis de Sade. 2000. 240p. pap. 14.00 (0-345-44104-4, Ballantine Bks.) Ballantine Bks.

—The Fan-Maker's Inquisition: A Novel of the Marquis de Sade. 1999. 224p. 22.00 o.s.i (0-8050-5926-1) Holt, Henry & Co.

Dunkel, Elizabeth. Under the Mosquito Net. 1993. 224p. 19.95 o.p. (1-55611-365-X) Fine, Donald I. Bks.

Dunne, Wilbert V. Honeymoon in Merida. 1995. (Illus.). 64p. (Orig.). pap. 10.00 (1-56474-123-0) Fithian Pr.

Elkins, Aaron. Curses! 1989. 208p. 15.95 o.p. (0-89296-263-1) Mysterious Pr.

—Curses! 1990. 254p. mass mkt. 5.99 o.p. (0-445-40864-2, Mysterious Pr. Paperback Bks.) Warner Bks., Inc.

Embree, Charles Fleming. A Dream of a Throne. 2000. 252p. E-Book 3.95 (0-594-02185-5) 1873 Pr.

Escandon, Maria Amparo. Esperanza's Box of Saints: A Novel. 1999. 256p. pap. 12.00 (0-684-85614-X, Touchstone) Simon & Schuster.

—Esperanza's Box of Saints: A Novel. 1999. 18.05 (0-606-16079-5) Turtleback Bks.

—Santitos: Sexo, Humor y Realismo en una Novela Magica. 1999. (SPA.). 288p. pap. 14.95 o.s.i (0-553-06098-8) Bantam Bks.

Esquivel, Laura. The Law of Love. 1997. Tr. of Ley del Amor. (Illus.). 288p. pap. 18.95 (0-609-80127-9) Random Hse. Value Publishing.

—Like Water for Chocolate: A Novel in Monthly Installments, with Recipes, Romances & Home Remedies. l.t. ed. 1993. Tr. of Como Agua para Chocolate. 21.95 o.p. (0-7927-1785-6); pap. 19.95 o.p. (0-7927-1784-8) BBC Audiobooks America.

—Like Water for Chocolate: A Novel in Monthly Installments, with Recipes, Romances & Home Remedies. 1994. Tr. of Como Agua para Chocolate. mass mkt. 5.99 o.s.i (0-385-42685-2) Bantam Bks.

—Like Water for Chocolate: A Novel in Monthly Installments, with Recipes, Romances & Home Remedies.Tr. of Como Agua para Chocolate. 1994. 256p. mass mkt. 5.99 o.s.i (0-385-47401-6); 1994. mass mkt. 5.99 o.s.i (0-385-47486-5); 1992. 256p. 25.00 (0-385-42016-1) Doubleday Publishing.

—Like Water for Chocolate: A Novel in Monthly Installments, with Recipes, Romances & Home Remedies. Christensen, Carol & Christensen, Thomas, trs. from SPA. 1995. Tr. of Como Agua para Chocolate. 256p. reprint ed. pap. 11.95 (0-385-42017-X, BT017X) Doubleday Publishing.

—Like Water for Chocolate: A Novel in Monthly Installments, with Recipes, Romances & Home Remedies. 2000. Tr. of Como Agua para Chocolate. E-Book 10.95 (0-385-49747-4) Random Hse., Inc.

—Like Water for Chocolate: A Novel in Monthly Installments, with Recipes, Romances & Home Remedies. 1995. Tr. of Como Agua para Chocolate. 18.00 (0-606-09556-X) Turtleback Bks.

Falconer, Colin. Feathered Serpent: A Novel of the Mexican Conquest. 2003. 432p. pap. 13.95 (1-4000-4957-1, Three Rivers Pr.) Crown Publishing Group.

Farcau, Bruce W. A Little Empire of Their Own: A Novel of Old Mexico. 2000. 356p. 21.95 (0-918339-54-5) Vandamere Pr.

Ford, Richard. The Ultimate Good Luck. 1981. 216p. 9.95 o.p. (0-395-30373-7) Houghton Mifflin Co.

—The Ultimate Good Luck. 1996. pap. 12.00 (0-676-51110-4); 1987. 208p. pap. 12.00 (0-394-75089-6) Knopf Publishing Group. (Vintage).

Forsman, Bettie. From Lupita's Hill. 1973. 272p. (J). (gr. 4-6). 1.49 o.p. (0-689-30085-9, Atheneum) Simon & Schuster Children's Publishing.

Francisco, Ruth. Confessions of a Deathmaiden: A Novel. 2003. 352p. 23.95 (0-89296-773-0) Mysterious Pr.

Freedom's Fire: An Historical Novel Based upon the True Story of the Palm Sunday Massacre on March 27, 1836, at Fort La Bahia, Goliad, Texas. 1999. (Illus.). lxxv, 180p. (gr. 7-12). 30.00 (0-9675023-0-6) Kalcolby, Pat.

Freschet, Gina. La Procesion de Naty, RS. 2000. (SPA., Illus.). 32p. (J). (gr. 1-3). 16.00 (0-374-36136-3, FS0466, Mirasol/Libros Juveniles) Farrar, Straus & Giroux.

Frias, Heriberto. Tomochic: A Novel. Saborit, Antonio, ed. Jamison, Barbara, tr. from SPA. 2005. (Library of Latin America). 160p. text 25.00 (0-19-511742-5); pap. text 11.95 (0-19-511743-3) Oxford Univ. Pr., Inc.

Fuentes, Carlos. Burnt Water. Peden, Margaret Sayers, tr. from SPA. Tr. of Agua Quemada. 1986. 231p. pap. 12.00 o.s.i (0-374-51988-9, ND9889); 1980. 11.95 o.p. (0-374-11741-1) Farrar, Straus & Giroux.

—Constancia: And Other Stories for Virgins. Christensen, Thomas, tr. 1990. 204p. 19.95 o.s.i (0-374-12886-3) Farrar, Straus & Giroux.

—Constancia: And Other Stories for Virgins. 1992. 352p. pap. 13.00 o.p. (0-06-097387-0, Perennial) HarperTrade.

—The Death of Artemio Cruz. Hileman, Sam, tr. from SPA. 1964. Tr. of Muerte de Artemio Cruz. 306p. pap. 8.95 o.p. (0-374-50540-3) Farrar, Straus & Giroux.

—El Gringo Viejo. 1991. (Coleccion Tierra Firme Ser.).Tr. of Old Gringo. (SPA.). 191p. pap. 14.95 (968-16-1782-7, FC1105) Fondo de Cultura Economica MEX. *Dist:* Continental Bk. Co., Inc.

—The Old Gringo. 1997. Tr. of Grinjo Viejo. 208p. pap. 13.00 (0-374-52522-6) Farrar, Straus & Giroux.

—The Old Gringo. Peden, Margaret Sayers, tr. from SPA. 1985. Tr. of Grinjo Viejo. 180p. 14.95 o.s.i (0-374-22578-8) Farrar, Straus & Giroux.

—The Old Gringo.Tr. of Grinjo Viejo. 208p. reprint ed. 1991. pap. 12.00 o.p. (0-06-097063-4, PL/7063); 1989. pap. 7.95 o.p. (0-06-097258-0) HarperTrade. (Perennial).

—The Old Gringo. 1994. Tr. of Grinjo Viejo. 200p. lib. bdg. 33.00 o.p. (0-8095-9136-7) Millefleurs.

—The Years with Laura Diaz. MacAdam, Alfred, tr. from SPA. 2000. 516p. 26.00 o.p. (0-374-29341-4); 544p. pap. (0-374-98836-6) Farrar, Straus & Giroux.

Galindo, Sergio. Otilia's Body. Brushwood, Carolyn & Brushwood, John S., trs. from SPA. 1994. (Texas Pan American Ser.). (Illus.). 235p. (Orig.). 37.50 o.p. (0-292-72769-0); pap. 15.95 (0-292-72770-4) Univ. of Texas Pr.

Gerritsen, Tess & Erickson, Lynn. Something to Hide: Thief of Hearts; Shadow on the Sun, 2 bks. in 1. 1999. 520p. per. (0-373-83414-4, 1-83414-2, Harlequin Bks.) Harlequin Enterprises, Ltd.

Gershten, Donna M. Kissing the Virgin's Mouth. 2001. 240p. 23.00 (0-06-018567-8) HarperCollins Pubs.

Gilman, Dorothy. The Unexpected Mrs. Pollifax. 1972. 216p. 6.95 o.p. (0-385-05974-4) Doubleday Publishing.

—The Unexpected Mrs. Pollifax. 1984. (Nightingale Paperbacks Ser.). 342p. pap. 9.95 o.p. (0-8161-3368-9, Macmillan Reference USA) Gale Group.

Gobineau, Conte D. Romances of the East. 1973. (Middle East Ser.). reprint ed. 26.95 (0-405-05340-1) Ayer Co. Pubs., Inc.

Gomez, Ermilo A. Canek: History & Legend of a Maya Hero. 1983. 80p. pap. 2.50 o.p. (0-380-61937-7, 61937-7, Avon Bks.) Morrow/Avon.

Gonzalbo, Pablo Escalante. Los Cazadores de la Banda del Valle. 2000. (Historias de Mexico: Vol. 1). Tr. of Hunters of the Valley Tribe. (SPA., Illus.). 74p. 12.99 (968-16-5620-2) Fondo de Cultura Economica USA.

Gonzales, Laurence. El Vago. 1983. 320p. 16.95 o.p. (0-689-11330-7, Scribner) Simon & Schuster.

Gonzalez-Rubio, Javier. Loving You Was My Undoing: A Novel. Arizmendi, Yareli & Lytle, Stephen, trs. from SPA. 1999. 160p. 22.00 o.s.i (0-8050-4878-2) Holt, Henry & Co.

Gordon, Helen Heightsman. Voice of the Vanquished: The Story of the Slave Marina & Hernan Cortes. 1996. 475p. pap. 15.00 (1-56002-530-1) Anacade International.

Grant, Reg. Ebony Moon. 1993. 352p. (Orig.). pap. 10.00 o.p. (0-89109-745-7, Discipleship Journal) NavPress Publishing Group.

Greene, Graham. The Power & the Glory. 24.95 (0-88411-656-5) Amereon, Ltd.

—The Power & the Glory. l.t. ed. 1992. pap. 21.95 o.p. (0-7927-1142-4, CS0307); 1991. 23.95 o.p. (0-7927-1141-6, CH0235) BBC Audiobooks America.

—The Power & the Glory. l.t. ed. 2002. 28.95 (0-7862-4131-4) Gale Group.

—The Power & the Glory. 1977. 19.00 (0-606-12485-3) Turtleback Bks.

—The Power & the Glory. 2003. (Twentieth Century Classics Ser.). 240p. pap. 14.00 (0-14-243730-1, Penguin Classics); 1991. (Penguin Twentieth-Century Classics Ser.). 240p. pap. 14.00 o.s.i (0-14-018499-6, Penguin Classics); 1977. (Critical Studies: No. 6). (Illus.). 224p. pap. 6.00 o.p. (0-14-001791-7, Penguin Bks.); 1946. 276p. 16.95 o.p. (0-670-56979-8); 1990. 320p. 25.00 o.p. (0-670-83536-6); 1968. 8.50 o.p. (0-670-57012-5, LT3) Viking Penguin.

Grey, Zane. Ken Ward in the Jungle. 312p. reprint ed. lib. bdg. 24.95 (0-89190-763-7, Rivercity Pr.) Amereon, Ltd.

—Ken Ward in the Jungle. 1998. 245p. mass mkt. 4.99 (0-8125-8041-9, Forge Bks.) Doherty, Tom Assocs., LLC.

—Ken Ward in the Jungle. l.t. ed. 1999. (Paperback Ser.). 272p. pap. 23.95 (0-7838-0439-3) Thorndike Pr.

Grifalconi, Ann, illus. The Toy Trumpet. 2nd ed. 1995. (J). (ps-3). 15.95 (0-316-32858-8) Little Brown & Co.

Grove, Fred. Man on a Red Horse. 2000. 272p. mass mkt. 4.50 (0-8439-4771-3, Leisure Bks.) Dorchester Publishing Co., Inc.

—Man on a Red Horse. 1998. (Western Ser.). 270p. 19.95 (0-7862-1157-1, Five Star) Gale Group.

—Man on a Red Horse. l.t. ed. 1999. (Western Ser.). 384p. 21.95 (0-7862-1169-5) Thorndike Pr.

Guerard, Albert J. The Hotel in the Jungle. 1996. 392p. 23.00 (1-880909-45-6) Baskerville Pubs., Inc.

Hambly, Barbara. Days of the Dead. 2004. 448p. mass mkt. 6.99 (0-553-58162-7); 2003. (Illus.). 336p. 23.95 (0-553-10954-5) Bantam Bks.

—Days of the Dead. l.t. ed. 2004. 544p. 25.95 (0-375-43250-7) Random Hse. Large Print.

Hamilton, Lyn. The Xibalba Murders: An Archeological Mystery. 1997. (Archaeological Mystery Ser.). 304p. mass mkt. 6.50 (0-425-15722-9, Prime Crime) Berkley Publishing Group.

Hansen, Ron. Atticus. 256p. 1997. pap. 13.00 (0-06-092786-0, Perennial); 1996. 22.00 o.p. (0-06-018217-2) HarperTrade.

—Atticus. unabr. ed. 1997. audio 44.00 (0-7887-0943-7, 95076E7) Recorded Bks., LLC.

Harlan, Thomas. Wasteland of Flint. 2003. 432p. 27.95 (0-7653-0192-X, Tor Bks.) Doherty, Tom Assocs., LLC.

Harper, Richard. Death Raid. 1986. pap. 3.50 o.p. (0-440-11685-6) Dell Publishing.

Harrigan, Lana M. K'atsina: A Novel of Rebellion. (Tom Doherty Associates Book Ser.). 350p. 2000. (Illus.). pap. 16.95 (0-312-87277-1); 1998. 25.95 o.p. (0-312-86260-1) Doherty, Tom Assocs., LLC. (Forge Bks.).

Harrington, Kent. Dia de los Muertos. 1997. Tr. of Day of the Dead. (SPA.). 244p. 30.00 (0-939767-30-9) McMillan, Dennis Pubns.

—Dia de los Muertos. 2003. 250p. pap. 17.95 (1-59266-035-5) Capra Pr.

Hearon, Shelby. Five Hundred Scorpions. 1993. 320p. pap. 9.99 o.s.i (0-446-39478-5) Warner Bks., Inc.

Heller, Zoe. Everything You Know. 2000. 224p. 22.00 o.s.i (0-375-40724-3) Knopf, Alfred A. Inc.

—Everything You Know. 2001. (Illus.). 224p. reprint ed. pap. 12.95 (0-7434-1195-1, Washington Square Pr.) Simon & Schuster.

Hennessy, Max. The Crimson Wind. 1985. 256p. 13.95 o.p. (0-689-11530-X, Scribner) Simon & Schuster.

—Crimson Wind. l.t. ed. 1988. lib. bdg. 15.95 o.p. (1-85057-149-X, Macmillan Reference USA) Gale Group.

Higgins, Jack & Graham, James. The Wrath of God. 1985. 224p. mass mkt. 3.50 o.s.i (0-425-07748-9) Berkley Publishing Group.

Highsmith, Patricia. A Game for the Living. 1988. 288p. pap. 12.00 (0-87113-210-9, Atlantic Monthly Pr.) Grove/Atlantic, Inc.

Hogan, Ray. Texas Guns. 1980. mass mkt. 1.75 o.p. (0-451-09257-0, Signet Bks.) NAL.

—Texas Guns: And the Hell Raiser. 1986. mass mkt. 3.50 o.p. (0-451-14445-7, Signet Bks.) NAL.

A House Far South in Mexico. 2000. 271p. pap. 19.85 (1-893518-00-0) Perception Pr.

Howard, Linda. Cry No More. 2003. 384p. 25.95 (0-345-45341-7); E-Book 25.95 (0-345-46989-5) Ballantine Bks. (Ballantine Bks.).

—Cry No More. l.t. ed. 2003. 512p. 27.95 (0-375-43290-6) Random Hse. Large Print.

Humphreys, J. R. Maya Red. 1989. 254p. (Orig.). (C). pap. 9.95 (0-943433-01-0) Cane Hill Pr.

Hunt, E. Howard. Ixtapa. 1994. (Jack Novak Ser.). 224p. 19.95 o.p. (1-55611-404-4) Fine, Donald I. Bks.

—Sonora. 2000. 315p. 23.95 (0-312-87205-4, Forge Bks.) Doherty, Tom Assocs., LLC.

—Sonora. 1999. pap. 24.95 (1-55611-535-0) Fine, Donald I. Bks.

Ing, Dean. The Nemesis Mission. 1992. 468p. mass mkt. 5.99 (0-8125-1173-5); 1991. 384p. 19.95 o.p. (0-312-85105-7) Doherty, Tom Assocs., LLC. (Tor Bks.).

Innis, W. Joe. Also Rising. 1998. 22.95 o.p. (1-57168-196-5) Eakin Pr.

—Also Rising. 2000. 268p. pap. 16.95 (0-595-15200-7, Backinprint.com) iUniverse, Inc.

Jacobs, Barbara. The Dead Leaves: A Novel. Unger, David, tr. from SPA. 1993. 126p. pap. 10.95 (1-880684-08-X) Curbstone Pr.

Jarrard, Kyle. Rolling the Bones. 2001. 336p. 26.00 (1-58642-026-7) Steerforth Pr.

Jenkins, Amy. Honeymoon. 2001. 304p. pap. 13.95 (0-316-65588-0, Back Bay) Little Brown & Co.

—Honeymoon: A Romantic Rampage. 2000. 288p. 24.95 o.p. (0-316-65570-8) Little Brown & Co.

Jennings, Gary. Aztec. 1995. lib. bdg. 49.95 (1-56849-410-6) Buccaneer Bks., Inc.

—Aztec. 1997. 1038p. mass mkt. 7.99 (*0-8125-2146-3*, Tor Bks.) Doherty, Tom Assocs., LLC.

—Aztec Autumn. 1998. 468p. mass mkt. 6.99 (*0-8125-9096-1*, Tor Bks.); 1997. 378p. mass mkt. 295.48 (*0-8125-3948-6*, Forge Bks.); 1997. 384p. 24.95 o.p. (*0-312-86250-4*, Forge Bks.) Doherty, Tom Assocs., LLC.

—Aztec Autumn. abr. ed. 1997. 25.00 o.p. (*0-7871-1459-6*) NewStar Media, Inc.

—Aztec Autumn. 1999. 6.99 (*0-312-87131-7*) St. Martin's Pr.

—Aztec Blood. 2001. 384p. 27.95 (*0-312-86251-2*, Forge Bks.); 2002. 768p. reprint ed. mass mkt. 7.99 (*0-8125-9098-8*, Tor Bks.) Doherty, Tom Assocs., LLC.

—Azteca. Correa, Maria de los Angeles, tr. 2003. (SPA.). 872p. 34.95 (*84-08-04841-4*) Editorial Planeta, S. A. ESP. *Dist:* Giron Bks.

—Azteca. 1999. (SPA.). 880p. pap. (*84-08-03362-X*) GeoPlaneta, Editorial, S. A.

—Azteca. 2001. (SPA.). 880p. 18.98 (*84-08-03998-9*, PT13487); 1998. pap. (*84-08-01207-X*) GeoPlaneta, Editorial, S. A. ESP. *Dist:* Continental Bk. Co., Inc., Lectorum Pubns., Inc., Planeta Publishing Corp.

—Azteca. 1995. (SPA.). pap. 10.00 o.s.i (*968-406-032-7*) Planeta Publishing Corp.

Johansen, Iris. And Then You Die. 1998. 352p. mass mkt. 7.50 (*0-553-57998-3*) Bantam Bks.

—And Then You Die. abr. ed. 1997. audio o.p. Random Hse. Audio Publishing Group.

—And Then You Die. unabr. ed. 1998. audio 56.00 (*0-7887-1975-0*, 95362E7) Recorded Bks., LLC.

—And Then You Die. l.t. ed. 1998. (Romance Ser.). 448p. 28.95 (*0-7862-1310-8*) Thorndike Pr.

Johnson, Denny. Oaxaca Connection. 2000. 192p. E-Book 8.00 (*0-7388-9572-5*) Xlibris Corp.

Johnson, Guy. Echoes of a Distant Summer: A Novel. 2002. 688p. 24.95 (*0-375-50567-9*) Random Hse., Inc.

Johnston, Tony. Isabel's House of Butterflies. 2003. (Illus.). 32p. (J). (ps-3). 15.95 (*0-87156-409-2*) Sierra Club Bks. for Children.

Jones, Thomas F. Rebel Gold. 1975. 160p. (YA). (gr. 8 up). 5.95 o.p. (*0-664-32571-8*) Westminster John Knox Pr.

Juarez, Tina. Call No Man Master. 1995. 334p. (YA). (gr. 8-12). 11.50 (*1-55885-124-0*) Arte Publico Pr.

—South Wind Come. 1998. 384p. pap. 14.95 (*1-55885-231-X*) Arte Publico Pr.

—South Wind Come. 1998. pap. text 21.00 (*1-55855-231-6*) Educational Developmental Laboratories, Inc.

Kalechofsky, Roberta. Justice, My Brother, My Sister: Life & Death in a Mexican Family. 1993. 148p. pap. 11.95 (*0-916288-37-4*) Micah Pubns.

Kalnay, Francis. It Happened in Chichipica. 1971. (Illus.). 127p. (J). (gr. 4-6). 4.95 o.p. (*0-15-239340-4*) Harcourt Children's Bks.

Kelton, Elmer. Bitter Trail. 1986. 2.50 o.s.i (*0-441-06364-0*); 1984. 2.50 o.s.i (*0-441-06363-2*); 1981. 2.25 o.s.i (*0-441-06362-4*) Ace Bks.

—Bitter Trail. l.t. ed. 2002. lib. bdg. 28.95 (*1-58547-190-9*, Western) Ctr. Point Large Print.

—Bitter Trail. 1997. 217p. pap. 5.99 (*0-8125-5118-4*, Forge Bks.) Doherty, Tom Assocs., LLC.

—Bitter Trail. 1999. 12.04 (*0-606-19645-5*) Turtleback Bks.

Kira, Gene. King of the Moon: A Novel of Baja California. 1997. 342p. 21.95 (*0-929637-03-8*) Apples & Oranges, Inc.

Lakin, Charles. 'Tzin: A Novel of Ancient Mexico. 2000. 524p. pap. 26.99 (*0-7388-2331-7*) Xlibris Corp.

—Tzin: A Novel of Ancient Mexico. 2000. 376p. E-Book 8.00 (*0-7388-8959-8*); 524p. E-Book 8.00 (*0-7388-8879-6*) Xlibris Corp.

—'Tzin Pt. 2: A Novel of Ancient Mexico. 2000. 376p. pap. 22.99 (*0-7388-2454-2*) Xlibris Corp.

—'Tzin Pt. 3: A Novel of Ancient Mexico. 2000. 352p. pap. 22.99 (*0-7388-2562-X*) Xlibris Corp.

—Tzin, Part Three: A Novel of Ancient Mexico. 2000. 352p. E-Book 8.00 (*0-7388-9029-4*) Xlibris Corp.

Lansdale, Joe R. Captains Outrageous. 2001. 336p. 24.45 o.p. (*0-89296-728-5*) Mysterious Pr.

—Captains Outrageous. 2003. 336p. pap. 12.95 (*0-446-67963-1*, Mysterious Pr. Paperback Bks.) Warner Bks., Inc.

Lawrence, D. H. The Plumed Serpent. Clark, L. D., ed. 1987. (Cambridge Edition of the Works of D. H. Lawrence). (Illus.). 624p. 115.00 o.p. (*0-521-22262-1*); 619p. pap. 50.00 (*0-521-29422-3*) Cambridge Univ. Pr.

—The Plumed Serpent. 1955. pap. 10.00 o.p. (*0-394-70023-6*, Vintage) Knopf Publishing Group.

—The Plumed Serpent. 1992. 464p. pap. 16.00 (*0-679-73493-7*) McKay, David Co., Inc.

—Quetzalcoatl. 1995. (Illus.). 333p. 30.00 o.p. (*0-933806-60-4*) Black Swan Bks., Ltd.

—Quetzalcoatl. Martz, Louis L., ed. & intro. by. 1998. (Paperbook Ser.: Vol. 864). 358p. pap. 14.95 (*0-8112-1385-4*, NDP864) New Directions Publishing Corp.

Lea, Tom. The Brave Bulls: A Novel. 2002. (Southwestern Writers Collection). (Illus.). 296p. pap. 16.95 (*0-292-74733-0*) Univ. of Texas Pr.

—The Wonderful Country. 1979. lib. bdg. 9.95 o.p. (*0-8398-2587-0*, Macmillan Reference USA) Gale Group.

—The Wonderful Country. 1984. (Illus.). 400p. reprint ed. 15.95 o.p. (*0-89096-185-9*) Texas A&M Univ. Pr.

—The Wonderful Country. 2002. (Texas Tradition Ser.: No. 33). (Illus.). 400p. 24.95 (*0-87565-261-1*); pap. 17.95 (*0-87565-255-7*) Texas Christian Univ. Pr.

Lida, David. Travel Advisory: Stories of Mexico. 2000. 208p. 24.00 (*0-688-17406-X*, Morrow, William & Co.) Morrow/Avon.

Limon, Graciela. The Day of the Moon. 1999. 228p. pap. 12.95 (*1-55885-274-3*) Arte Publico Pr.

—Erased Faces. 2001. 208p. pap. 14.95 (*1-55885-342-1*) Arte Publico Pr.

—Song of the Hummingbird. 1996. 217p. 19.95 o.p. (*1-55885-157-7*); pap. 12.95 (*1-55885-091-0*) Arte Publico Pr.

Loring, Emilie Baker. Stars in Your Eyes. l.t. ed. 1999. (Candlelight Romance Ser.). 445p. 22.95 (*0-7862-2299-9*) Thorndike Pr.

Luceno, James. Zorro. 1998. 224p. pap. 6.50 (*0-671-51989-1*, Pocket) Simon & Schuster.

Markson, David. Going Down. 2002. 278p. pap. 15.00 (*1-928746-27-6*) Herodias.

Martin, Allana. Death of a Saint Maker. 1999. (gr. 3). per. (*0-373-26299-X*, Harlequin Bks.) Harlequin Enterprises, Ltd.

—Death of an Evangelista. 2000. (WWL Mystery Ser.: No. 335). mass mkt. (*0-373-26335-X*, 1-26335-9, Worldwide Library) Harlequin Enterprises, Ltd.

Masters, Hilary. Home Is the Exile. 1996. 288p. 28.00 (*1-877946-73-7*) Permanent Pr., The.

Mastretta, Angeles. Lovesick: A Novel. abr. ed. 1997. audio 21.95 (*1-57453-178-6*) Audio Literature.

—Lovesick: A Novel. Peden, Margaret Sayers, tr. l.t. ed. 1998. (Illus.). 384p. 13.00 o.s.i (*1-57322-655-6*, Riverhead Trade (Paperbacks)) Berkley Publishing Group.

—Lovesick: A Novel. Peden, Margaret Sayers, tr. from SPA. l.t. ed. 1997. 288p. 22.00 o.s.i (*1-57322-062-0*, Riverhead Bks. (Hardcovers)) Putnam Publishing Group, The.

—Tear This Heart Out. Peden, Margaret, tr. from SPA. 1997. 288p. 12.00 (*1-57322-602-5*, Riverhead Trade (Paperbacks)) Berkley Publishing Group.

May, Janis S. Where Shadows Linger. l.t. ed. 1993. 19.95 o.p. (*0-7927-1767-8*); pap. 18.95 o.p. (*0-7927-1766-X*) BBC Audiobooks America.

Mayo, C. M. Sky over El Nido. 1995. 176p. 22.95 (*0-8203-1766-7*) Univ. of Georgia Pr.

—Sky over El Nido: Stories. 1999. 176p. pap. 12.95 (*0-8203-2119-2*) Univ. of Georgia Pr.

McAndrews, Anita. Conquistador's Lady. 1990. 240p. (Orig.). pap. 10.95 (*0-931832-48-9*) Fithian Pr.

McCarthy, Cormac. All the Pretty Horses. l.t. ed. 1993. 24.95 o.p. (*0-7927-1576-4*); pap. 22.95 o.p. (*0-7927-1575-6*) BBC Audiobooks America.

—All the Pretty Horses. unabr. collector's ed. 1993. audio 48.00 (*0-7366-2416-3*, 3183) Books on Tape, Inc.

—All the Pretty Horses. unabr. ed. 2000. audio 34.95 (*0-694-52280-5*); (Border Trilogy: Vol. 1). audio compact disk 50.00 (*0-694-52344-5*) HarperTrade. (HarperAudio).

—All the Pretty Horses. movie tie-in ed. 1993. (Border Trilogy: Vol. 1). 320p. pap. 14.00 (*0-679-74439-8*, Vintage) Knopf Publishing Group.

—All the Pretty Horses. abr. ed. 2000. (Border Trilogy: Vol. 1). audio 18.00 (*0-679-42568-3*, 390333);Set. audio compact disk 21.95 (*0-375-41587-4*) Random Hse. Audio Publishing Group. (RH Audio).

—All the Pretty Horses. 1992. (Border Trilogy: Vol. 1). 320p. 27.50 (*0-394-57474-5*) Random Hse., Inc.

—All the Pretty Horses. unabr. ed. 1999. (Border Trilogy: Vol. 1). audio 60.00 (*1-55690-660-9*, 92403E7) Recorded Bks., LLC.

—All the Pretty Horses. 1993. 19.05 (*0-606-20069-X*) Turtleback Bks.

—All the Pretty Horses. 2000. (CliffsNotes Ser.). (Illus.). 80p. pap. 5.99 (*0-7645-8551-7*, Cliff Notes) Wiley, John & Sons, Inc.

McCarthy, Patrick A., ed. Malcolm Lowry's "La Mordida" 1996. xxiii, 400p. 75.00 (*0-8203-1763-2*) Univ. of Georgia Pr.

McGahan, Jerry. A Condor Brings the Sun: A Novel. 1996. 276p. 25.00 o.p. (*0-87156-354-1*) Sierra Club Bks.

McKinty, A. G. Dead I Well May Be. 2004. 288p. mass mkt. 6.99 (*0-7434-7056-7*, Pocket); 2003. 320p. 24.00 (*0-7432-4699-3*, Scribner) Simon & Schuster.

Mena, Maria C. The Collected Stories of Maria Cristina Mena. Doherty, Amy, ed. 1997. (Recovering the U. S. - Hispanic Literary Heritage Ser.). 208p. pap. 12.95 (*1-55885-211-5*) Arte Publico Pr.

Michael, Emory J. Queen of the Sun. 1995. 120.00 o.p. (*0-06-251366-4*) HarperSanFrancisco.

—Queen of the Sun: A Modern Revelation. 1995. (Illus.). (Orig.). xii, 225p. pap. 10.00 (*0-06-251356-7*); 240p. 20.00 o.p. (*0-06-251355-9*) HarperSanFrancisco.

—Queen of the Sun: A Modern Revelation. (Illus.). (Orig.). 1994. pap. 12.95 o.p. (*0-9642147-0-9*); 2nd rev. ed. 1995. 250p. pap. 12.95 (*0-9642147-8-4*) Mountain Rose Publishing.

Millar, Margaret. Ask for Me Tomorrow. l.t. ed. 1989. (Atlantic Mystery Ser.). 265p. pap. 14.95 o.p. (*1-55504-738-6*, 833) BBC Audiobooks America.

—Ask for Me Tomorrow. (Library of Crime Classics). 1991. 184p. pap. 8.95 o.p. (*1-55882-115-5*); 1985. 179p. reprint ed. pap. 4.95 o.p. (*0-930330-15-3*) International Polygonics, Ltd.

—Ask for Me Tomorrow. 1978. pap. 1.50 o.p. (*0-380-01805-5*, 35618, Avon Bks.) Morrow/Avon.

Molina, Silvia. El Amor Que Me Juraste. 1998. (SPA., Illus.). 170p. pap. text (*968-27-0724-2*) Ediciones Joaquin Mortiz.

Montecino, Marcel. Sacred Heart. 1998. mass mkt. 6.99 (*0-671-01540-0*, Pocket Star); 1997. 375p. 23.00 (*0-671-01539-7*, Atria) Simon & Schuster.

Montemayor, Carlos. Blood Relations. Carter, Dale & González, Alfonso, trs. from SPA. 1995. (Contemporary Latin-American Classics in English Translation Ser.).Tr. of Mal de Piedra. 111p. 17.95 (*0-917635-16-7*) Plover Pr.

—Gambusino. Copeland, John, tr. from SPA. 1997. Orig. Title: Minas del Retorno. 120p. 17.95 (*0-917635-21-3*); pap. 8.95 (*0-917635-24-8*) Plover Pr.

Mooney, Ted. Singing into the Piano. 1999. 368p. pap. 19.00 (*0-679-74306-5*) Knopf, Alfred A. Inc.

Moore, Rod V. Igloo among Palms. 1997. 216p. pap. 11.00 (*0-9660829-0-7*) Hinterlands Pr.

—Igloo among Palms. 1994. (Iowa Short Fiction Award Ser.). 145p. 11.50 (*0-87745-475-2*) Univ. of Iowa Pr.

Morrell, David. Assumed Identity. l.t. ed. 1994. 23.95 o.p. (*0-7927-1959-X*) BBC Audiobooks America.

—Assumed Identity. 5.98 o.p. (*0-8317-5371-4*) Smithmark Pubs., Inc.

—Assumed Identity. 1993. 469p. 21.95 (*0-446-51669-4*); 1999. reprint ed. mass mkt. 3.99 (*0-446-60749-5*); 1994. 512p. reprint ed. mass mkt. 7.50 (*0-446-60070-9*) Warner Bks., Inc.

Morris, Chris. Locoland. 1998. 180p. pap. 13.50 (*0-88739-163-X*) Creative Arts Bk. Co.

Morris, Joe Edd. Land Where My Fathers Died. 2002. (Illus.). 288p. 24.95 (*1-893956-27-X*) Context Bks.

Mujica, Bárbara. Frida. 2001. (Illus.). 320p. 26.95 (*1-58567-074-X*) Overlook Pr., The.

Neal, Wayne. The Music Box. 2003. 197p. pap. 19.95 (*1-59286-223-3*) PublishAmerica, Inc.

Nicholson, Joy. Road to Esmeralda. Date not set. (*0-312-26863-7*) St. Martin's Pr.

Niggli, Josephina. Mexican Village. 1994. 526p. (C). reprint ed. pap. 12.95 o.p. (*0-8263-1338-8*) Univ. of New Mexico Pr.

Pacheco, Jose E. Battles in the Desert & Other Stories. Silver, Katherine, tr. from SPA. 1987. 128p. 11.95 (*0-8112-1019-7*); pap. 8.95 o.s.i (*0-8112-1020-0*, NDP637) New Directions Publishing Corp.

Paine, Lauran. The Bandoleros. 1990. mass mkt. 3.50 o.s.i (*0-449-14663-4*, Fawcett) Ballantine Bks.

—The Bandoleros. l.t. ed. 2000. 261p. 20.95 (*1-57490-287-3*, Sagebrush Large Print Westerns) Beeler, Thomas T. Publisher.

—The Bandoleros. l.t. ed. 2000. 261p. (*0-7531-6260-1*); (*1-74030-011-4*) Sagebrush Large Print Westerns.

Paredes, Americo. The Shadow. 1998. (Pioneers of Modern U.S. Hispanic Literature Ser.). 114 p. pap. 9.95 (*1-55885-230-1*) Arte Publico Pr.

Parker, F. M. The Slavers. l.t. ed. 1992. (General Ser.). 352p. lib. bdg. 19.95 o.p. (*0-8161-5482-1*, Macmillan Reference USA) Gale Group.

—The Slavers. 256p. 1990. mass mkt. 3.95 o.p. (*0-451-16400-8*, Signet Bks.); 1989. 17.95 o.p. (*0-453-00655-8*) NAL.

Pestum, Jo. Maya y el Truco Para Hacer la Tarea. 1995. (SPA., Illus.). 43p. (J). (gr. 3-4). 5.99 (*968-16-4727-0*) Fondo de Cultura Economica MEX. *Dist:* Continental Bk. Co., Inc.

Peters, Elizabeth, pseud. The Night of Four Hundred Rabbits. l.t. ed. 1992. pap. 15.95 o.p. (*0-7927-1000-2*); 18.95 o.p. (*0-7927-0974-8*, E0022) BBC Audiobooks America.

—The Night of Four Hundred Rabbits. unabr. ed. 1997. audio 44.95 (*0-7861-1098-8*, 1862) Blackstone Audio Bks., Inc.

—The Night of Four Hundred Rabbits. 1996. mass mkt. 5.99 o.s.i (*0-8125-6360-3*); 1989. 247p. mass mkt. 5.99 (*0-8125-0773-8*) Doherty, Tom Assocs., LLC. (Tor Bks.).

—The Night of Four Hundred Rabbits. 1992. 18.95 o.p. (*0-7278-4306-0*); 256p. reprint ed. 18.95 o.p. (*0-7278-4303-6*) Severn Hse. Pubs., Ltd.

Pierce, David M. Angels in Heaven. 1992. 240p. 17.95 o.p. (*0-89296-483-9*) Mysterious Pr.

—Angels in Heaven. 1993. 208p. mass mkt. 4.99 (*0-446-40163-3*, Mysterious Pr. Paperback Bks.) Warner Bks., Inc.

Poniatowska, Elena. Dear Diego. Silver, Katherine, tr. 1986. 63p. 10.95 o.s.i (*0-394-55383-7*, Pantheon) Knopf Publishing Group.

—Here's to You, Jesusa! Heikkinen, Deanna, tr. from SPA. 2001. Tr. of Hasta No Verte Jesus Mio. xxx, 303p. 24.00 (*0-374-16819-9*) Farrar, Straus & Giroux.

—Here's to You, Jesusa! 2002. Tr. of Hasta No Verte Jesus Mio. 336p. pap. 14.00 (*0-14-200122-8*) Penguin Group (USA) Inc.

Portillo y Pacheco, Jose L. They Are Coming: The Conquest of Mexico. Berler, Beatrice, tr. from SPA. 1992. (Illus.). 375p. 34.50 (*0-929398-35-1*) Univ. of North Texas Pr.

Portis, Charles. Gringos. 2000. 269p. 14.95 (*1-58567-093-6*) Overlook Pr., The.

—Gringos: A Novel. 1991. 272p. 18.95 o.p. (*0-671-72457-6*, Simon & Schuster) Simon & Schuster.

Pronzini, Bill. Border Fever. (Gunsmoke Western Ser.). 12.95 o.p. (*0-86220-977-3*, C1146) Chivers Pr. GBR. *Dist:* BBC Audiobooks America.

Pronzini, Bill & Wallmann, Jeffrey M. Border Fever. l.t. ed. 2001. (G.K. Hall Large Print Western Ser.). 176p. 24.95 (*0-7838-9540-2*, Macmillan Reference USA) Gale Group.

Pérez-Reverte, Arturo. La Reina del Sur. 2002. (SPA., Illus.). 552p. pap. 19.95 (*84-204-6435-X*) Alfaguara, Ediciones, S.A.- Grupo Santillana ESP. *Dist:* Lectorum Pubns., Inc., Santillana USA Publishing Co., Inc.

Rabasa, George. Floating Kingdom. 1997. 278p. 21.95 (*1-56689-063-2*) Coffee Hse. Pr.

Reay, James. Tale of Three Cities: A Mexican Trilogy. 2001. 245p. pap. 21.99 (*1-4010-0252-8*); text 31.99 (*1-4010-0251-X*); E-Book 8.00 (*1-4010-0253-6*) Xlibris Corp.

Reveles, Daniel. Enchiladas, Rice & Beans. 1996. pap. 10.00 o.s.i (*0-345-91102-4*) Ballantine Bks.

—Enchiladas, Rice, & Beans. 1994. 272p. pap. 19.00 (*0-345-38426-1*, One World/Ballantine) Ballantine Bks.

Revueltas, Jose. Human Mourning. 1990. 229p. pap. 9.95 o.p. (*0-8166-1810-0*); text 24.95 o.p. (*0-8166-1809-7*) Univ. of Minnesota Pr.

Rios, Alberto. The Iguana Killer: Twelve Stories of the Heart. 1998. 120p. pap. 13.95 (*0-8263-1922-X*) Univ. of New Mexico Pr.

Rios, Alberto Alvaro. The Iguana Killer: Twelve Stories of the Heart. 1984. (Illus.). 144p. 14.95 o.p. (*0-933188-28-5*); pap. 11.00 o.p. (*0-933188-29-3*) Blue Moon Pr., Inc.

Rogers, Rosemary. Savage Desire. 2000. 448p. mass mkt. (*1-55166-621-9*, Mira Bks.) Harlequin Enterprises, Ltd.

Romo, Ito. El Puente - The Bridge. 2002. 128p. pap. 12.95 (*0-8263-2253-0*); 2000. (SPA.). 149p. 18.95 (*0-8263-2252-2*) Univ. of New Mexico Pr.

Rulfo, Juan. The Burning Plain & Other Stories. Schade, George D., tr. from SPA. (Pelican Book Ser.).Tr. of Llano en Llamas y Otras Historias. (Illus.). 191p. 1971. pap. 15.95 (*0-292-70132-2*, UT1322); 1967. 12.95 o.p. (*0-292-73685-1*) Univ. of Texas Pr.

—Pedro Paramo. 11th ed. (SPA., Illus.). 200p. 13.95 (*84-376-0418-4*) Ediciones Cátedra ESP. *Dist:* Continental Bk. Co., Inc., Lectorum Pubns., Inc.

—Pedro Paramo. annot. ed. (Coleccion Centro Literario). (SPA.). pap., stu. ed. 7.95 (*958-02-0492-6*, CAR025) Editorial Voluntad S.A. COL. *Dist:* Continental Bk. Co., Inc.

—Pedro Paramo. 1981. (Coleccion Popular Ser.: Vol. 58). (SPA.). 160p. pap. 9.99 (*968-16-0502-0*) Fondo de Cultura Economica USA.

—Pedro Paramo. 1989. (SPA.). 6.50 (*0-8288-2575-0*) French & European Pubns., Inc.

—Pedro Paramo. 1983. pap. 5.95 o.p. (*0-8021-3119-0*) Grove/Atlantic, Inc.

—Pedro Paramo. 1984. pap. 6.95 o.p. (*0-8437-6018-4*) Hammond World Atlas Corp.

—Pedro Paramo. 2000. (SPA., Illus.). 144p. (*84-01-01375-5*) Plaza & Janés Editories, S.A.

—Pedro Paramo. Peden, Margaret Sayers, tr. from SPA. 2002. (Wittliff Gallery Ser.). (Illus.). 164p. 35.00 (*0-292-77121-5*) Univ. of Texas Pr.

Runcie, James. The Discovery of Chocolate. 2001. 272p. 25.00 (*0-06-018481-7*) HarperCollins Pubs.

Ryan, James. The Last Cartridge: The French Foreign Legion in Mexico. 2000. 280p. E-Book 8.00 (*0-7388-8820-6*) Xlibris Corp.

Samperio, Guillermo. Beatle Dreams & Other Stories. Miller, Yvette E., ed. Quackenbush, L. Howard & Cluff, Russell M., trs. from SPA. 1993. (Discoveries Ser.). 169p. pap. 15.95 (*0-935480-60-9*) Latin American Literary Review Pr.

Sanderson, Jim. Nevin's History: A Novel of Texas. 2004. (0-89672-518-9) Texas Tech Univ. Pr.
—Safe Delivery. 2000. 224p. 21.95 (0-8263-2191-7) Univ. of New Mexico Pr.
Sands, Marella. Serpent & Storm, No. 2. 1999. (Sky Knife Ser.: Vol. 2). (Illus.). 352p. 24.95 (0-312-86127-3, Forge Bks.) Doherty, Tom Assocs., LLC.
—Sky Knife. 2000. 304p. mass mkt. 6.99 (0-8125-7764-7, Tor Bks.); 1997. 288p. 22.95 (0-312-86126-5, Forge Bks.) Doherty, Tom Assocs., LLC.
Savage, Les, Jr. Phantoms in the Night. 2000. 208p. mass mkt. 3.99 (0-8439-4787-X, Leisure Bks.) Dorchester Publishing Co., Inc.
—Phantoms in the Night. 1998. (Western Ser.). 208p. 19.95 (0-7862-1161-X, Five Star) Gale Group.
—Phantoms in the Night: A Western Story. unabr. ed. 1999. audio 24.99 (0-88646-528-1, DHA-6528) Durkin Hayes Publishing Ltd.
Scofield, Sandra. A Chance to See Egypt: A Novel. 1997. 272p. pap. 13.00 (0-06-092788-7, Perennial) HarperTrade.
—Gringa. 1995. 288p. pap. 10.95 o.p. (0-452-27350-1, Plume) Dutton/Plume.
Scofield, Sandra J. A Chance to See Egypt. 1996. 240p. 22.00 o.p. (0-06-017343-2) HarperCollins Pubs.
—Gringa. 1991. 272p. reprint ed. pap. 5.95 (1-56129-026-2) Knightsbridge Publishing.
—Gringa. 1989. 267p. 28.00 (0-932966-85-3) Permanent Pr., The.
Shaara, Jeff. Gone for Soldiers: A Novel of the Mexican War. 2001. 448p. reprint ed. pap. 15.95 (0-345-42751-3, Ballantine Bks.) Ballantine Bks.
Sharpe, Jon. Mexican Massacre. 1989. (Trailsman Ser.: No. 88). mass mkt. 2.95 o.p. (0-451-15922-5, Signet Bks.) NAL.
Shellabarger, Samuel. Captain from Castile: The Best-Selling Historical Epic. 2002. reprint ed. 640p. 18.95 (1-882593-62-6); 433p. pap. 32.50 (1-882593-63-4) Bridge Works Publishing Co., Inc.
Shorris, Earl. Under the Fifth Sun. 1980. 14.95 o.s.i (0-440-09388-0, Delacorte Pr.) Dell Publishing.
—Under the Fifth Sun. 1993. 624p. pap. 11.95 (0-393-31083-3) Norton, W. W. & Co., Inc.
Simmen, Edward, ed. Gringos in Mexico: One Hundred Years of Mexico in the American Short Story. 1988. 392p. (Orig.). pap. 13.95 (0-87565-029-5) Texas Christian Univ. Pr.
Sipherd, Ray. The Devil's Hawk: A Mystery. 2002. 272p. 23.95 (0-312-24428-2, Saint Martin's Minotaur) St. Martin's Pr.
Skwiot, Rick. Sleeping with Pancho Villa. 1998. 176p. 19.95 (0-87081-506-7) Univ. Pr. of Colorado.
Smith, C. W. Letters from the Horse Latitudes. 1994. 206p. (C). 19.95 (0-87565-131-3) Texas Christian Univ. Pr.
Smith, Michael A. Kingdom River. Singer, Melissa A., ed. 2003. (Snowfall Trilogy: Bk. 2). 400p. 25.95 (0-7653-0008-7, Forge Bks.) Doherty, Tom Assocs., LLC.
Sotelo, Roberto. Anacleto el Esqueleto Inquieto (Anacleto the Restless Skeleton) Un Paseo en el Parque (A Walk in the Park) 2001. (SPA., Illus.). (J). (ps). pap. (950-08-2553-8) Atlantida.
—Anacleto el Esqueleto Inquieto (Anacleto the Restless Skeleton) Una Noche de Insomnia (A Sleepless Night) 2001. (SPA., Illus.). (J). (ps). pap. (950-08-2554-6) Atlantida.
Spalding, Linda. The Paper Wife. 1996. 238p. reprint ed. text 23.00 o.p. (0-88001-453-9) HarperCollins Pubs.
—The Paper Wife. 1997. 248p. pap. 12.00 o.p. (0-88001-524-1, Ecco) HarperTrade.
Steinbeck, John. The Pearl. 1983. mass mkt. 2.50 o.s.i (0-553-26261-0); 224p. mass mkt. 2.95 o.s.i (0-553-27821-5, Bantam Classics); mass mkt. 2.25 o.s.i (0-553-23974-0) Bantam Bks.
—The Pearl. 2002. (Steinbeck's Centennial Ser.). 96p. pap. 11.00 (0-14-200069-8) Penguin Group (USA) Inc.
—The Pearl. l.t. ed. 2003. 121p. 29.95 (0-7862-5891-8) Thorndike Pr.
—The Pearl. (Great Books of the 20th Century Ser.). 1994. (Illus.). 128p. 9.95 (0-14-018738-3, Penguin Classics); abr. ed. 2015. audio 34.95 (0-14-086850-X, Penguin AudioBooks); abr. unabr. ed. 1994. 16.00 (0-453-00875-5); 2nd ed. 1993. 96p. (C). 8.00 (0-14-017737-X) Viking Penguin.
Sundeed, Mark. The Making of Toro: Bullfighting, Broken Hearts, & One Author's Quest for the Acclaim He So Richly Deserves. 2003. (Illus.). 192p. 21.00 (0-7432-3616-5, Simon & Schuster) Simon & Schuster.
Taibo, Paco Ignacio, II. An Easy Thing. 2002. (Missing Mystery Ser.: Vol. 49). 240p. pap. 14.95 o.s.i (1-59058-006-0) Poisoned Pen Pr.
—An Easy Thing. Neuman, William I., tr. 1990. 240p. 16.95 o.p. (0-670-82462-3, Viking) Viking Penguin.
—An Easy Thing. 1990. (Crime Ser.). 240p. reprint ed. pap. 4.50 o.p. (0-14-011523-4, Penguin Bks.) Viking Penguin.
—Four Hands. Dail, Laura C., tr. from SPA. 1995. 384p. pap. 13.00 (0-312-13079-1) Picador.
—Four Hands. Dail, Laura C., tr. 1994. 480p. 22.95 o.p. (0-312-10987-3) St. Martin's Pr.
—Life Itself. Henson, Beth, tr. 1994. 224p. 18.95 o.s.i (0-89296-518-5) Mysterious Pr.
—Life Itself. Henson, Beth, tr. 1995. 208p. mass mkt. 5.99 (0-446-40331-8, Mysterious Pr. Paperback Bks.) Warner Bks., Inc.
—No Happy Ending. Neuman, William I., tr. 1993. 192p. 17.95 (0-89296-517-7) Mysterious Pr.
—No Happy Ending. 2003. 254p. pap. 14.95 o.s.i (1-59058-038-9) Poisoned Pen Pr.
—No Happy Ending. Neuman, William I., tr. 1994. 192p. mass mkt. 5.50 (0-446-40329-6, Mysterious Pr. Paperback Bks.) Warner Bks., Inc.
—Return to the Same City. Dail, Laura, tr. from SPA. 1996. Tr. of Regreso a la Misma Ciudad y Bajo la Lluvia. 192p. 25.00 (0-89296-590-8) Mysterious Pr.
—Return to the Same City. Dail, Laura, tr. 1997. Tr. of Regreso a la Misma Ciudad y Bajo la Lluvia. 176p. mass mkt. 5.99 (0-446-40520-5) Warner Bks., Inc.
—Returning As Shadows: A Novel. Fitz, Ezra E., tr. from SPA. 2003. 352p. 25.95 (0-312-30156-1) St. Martin's Pr.
—The Shadow of a Shadow. Neuman, William I., tr. 1991. 240p. 18.95 o.p. (0-670-83177-8) Viking Penguin.
—Some Clouds. Neuman, William I., tr. 1993. (Crime Ser.). 176p. pap. 9.00 o.p. (0-14-014896-5, Penguin Bks.) Penguin Group (USA) Inc.
—Some Clouds. 2002. 250p. pap. 14.95 o.s.i (1-59058-032-X) Poisoned Pen Pr.
—Some Clouds. Neuman, William I., tr. from SPA. 1992. 176p. 19.00 o.p. (0-670-83825-X, Viking) Viking Penguin.
Theis, David. Rio Ganges. 2002. 272p. pap. 20.00 (0-9701525-6-6) Winedale Publishing.
Thomson, Rupert. Air & Fire. 1995. 320p. pap. 14.00 (0-679-74730-3, Vintage) Knopf Publishing Group.
—Air & Fire. 1994. 309p. 23.00 o.s.i (0-679-42506-3) Knopf, Alfred A. Inc.
Tierney, Richard L. House of the Toad. 1993. (Illus.). 270p. (C). 25.00 (1-878252-03-8); 45.00 (1-878252-09-7) Fedogan & Bremer.
Toma, T. L. Border Dance. 1996. 344p. (Orig.). pap. 12.95 (0-87074-401-1) Southern Methodist Univ. Pr.
—Border Dance: A Novel. 1996. 344p. 22.50 (0-87074-400-3) Southern Methodist Univ. Pr.
Toscana, David. Tula Station. Duncan, Patricia J., tr. from SPA. 2000. 277p. 23.95 (0-312-20538-4) St. Martin's Pr.
—Tula Station: A Novel. Duncan, Patricia J., tr. from SPA. 2001. 288p. pap. 12.95 (0-312-27097-6, Saint Martin's Griffin) St. Martin's Pr.
Tovar, Juan. Creature of a Day: A Novel. Chambers, Leland H., tr. from SPA. 2002. 160p. 20.00 (0-929701-68-2) McPherson & Co.
Traven, B. The Bridge in the Jungle. 2002. Tr. of Brucke in Dschungel. 255p. pap. 14.90 (1-56663-063-0, Elephant Paperbacks) Dee, Ivan R. Pub.
—The Rebellion of the Hanged. 1994. 107p. pap. 16.90 (1-56663-064-9, Elephant Paperbacks) Dee, Ivan R. Pub.
—Trozas. Young, Hugh, tr. from GER. 1998. 304p. 14.95 (1-56663-219-6, Elephant Paperbacks); 1994. 271p. pap. 22.50 (1-56663-044-4) Dee, Ivan R. Pub.
Trolley, Jack. Juarez Justice. 1996. 272p. 22.00 o.p. (0-7867-0356-3, Carroll & Graf Pubs.) Avalon Publishing Group.
Van Alder, Piet. Dropback. 2000. 368p. 24.95 o.p. (0-9643256-7-5) Palancar.
Van Meter, David A. Body of Evidence. 1990. mass mkt. 3.95 o.s.i (0-515-10207-5, Jove) Berkley Publishing Group.
Vicens, Josephina. The False Years. Earle, Peter G., tr. from SPA. & intro. by. 1989. (Discoveries Ser.). 94p. pap. 11.50 (0-935480-40-4) Latin American Literary Review Pr.
Villarreal, Rosa Martha. Chronicles of Air & Dreams. 1999. (Illus.). 235p. 22.00 (0-9662299-2-4) Archer Bks.
Walker, Alice. By the Light of My Father's Smile. 1999. mass mkt. (0-345-43455-2, Ballantine Bks.); 256p. pap. 13.95 (0-345-42606-1) Ballantine Bks.
—By the Light of My Father's Smile. 1998. 222p. 22.95 o.s.i (0-375-50152-5) Random Hse., Inc.
—By the Light of My Father's Smile. 1999. (Illus.). 20.00 (0-606-17985-2) Turtleback Bks.
Waller, Robert James. Puerto Vallarta Squeeze. 1996. 256p. mass mkt. 5.99 o.s.i (0-446-60360-0); 1995. 214p. 18.95 o.p. (0-446-51747-X) Warner Bks., Inc.
Weingardner, Mark. Veracruz Blues. unabr. ed. 1996. audio. audio 70.00 (0-7887-0565-2, 94742E7) Recorded Bks., LLC.
Wells, Rosalie. The Mountains of Tomorrow. l.t. ed. 1994. 19.95 o.p. (0-7927-1830-5); pap. 17.95 o.p. (0-7927-1829-1) BBC Audiobooks America.
Wheeler, Richard S. Going Home: A Barnaby Skye Novel. l.t. ed. 2001. 19.95 o.p. (1-58724-059-9, Wheeler Publishing, Inc.) Gale Group.
Whitman, John. The Mask of Zorro. 1998. (Mighty Chronicles Ser.). (Illus.). 320p. (J). (gr. 3-7). 9.95 o.p. (0-8118-2036-X) Chronicle Bks. LLC.
Wilkerson, Carolyn. Hasta Maanana. 2003. 245p. 25.95 (0-7862-5439-4, Five Star) Gale Group.
Williams, Jeanne. Tame the Wild Stallion. 1985. (Chaparral Bks.). (Illus.). 182p. (YA). (gr. 6 up). 14.95 (0-87565-002-3); (ps up). pap. 8.95 (0-87565-009-0) Texas Christian Univ. Pr.
Wilson, Carter. Green Tree & a Dry Tree. 1995. 291p. reprint ed. pap. 11.95 (0-8263-1655-7) Univ. of New Mexico Pr.
Winegardner, Mark. The Veracruz Blues. 1997. 272p. pap. 11.95 o.s.i (0-14-026028-5) Penguin Group (USA) Inc.
—The Veracruz Blues. 1996. 272p. 22.95 o.p. (0-670-86636-9, Viking) Viking Penguin.
Wright, Rosalind. Veracruz. 1986. 480p. 18.95 o.p. (0-06-015541-8) HarperTrade.
—Veracruz. 1987. (McGraw-Hill Paperbacks). 624p. pap. text 5.95 o.p. (0-07-072077-0) McGraw-Hill Cos., The.
Yacowitz, Caryn. Pumpkin Fiesta. 1998. (Illus.). 32p. (J). (ps-1). 15.99 (0-06-027658-4) HarperCollins Children's Bk. Group.
Zandri, Vincent. Godchild. 2000. 336p. mass mkt. 6.99 (0-440-22622-8) Dell Publishing.
Ziefert, Harriet. Home for Navidad. 2003. (Illus.). 32p. (J). (ps-3). tchr. ed. 15.00 (0-618-34976-6, Lorraine, A. Walter) Houghton Mifflin Co. Trade & Reference Div.
Zollinger, Norman. Chapultepec. 1996. 244p. pap. text 6.99 (0-8125-5541-4); 1995. 384p. 24.95 o.p. (0-312-85530-3) Doherty, Tom Assocs., LLC. (Forge Bks.).
—Not of War Only: A Novel of the Mexican Revolution. 1995. 597p. mass mkt. 5.99 (0-8125-3013-6); 1994. 416p. 22.95 o.p. (0-312-85529-X) Doherty, Tom Assocs., LLC. (Forge Bks.).
Zuckerman, Lilla. Miss Adventures. 2003. 224p. pap. 9.95 (0-7432-3845-1, Fireside) Simon & Schuster.

## MEXICO CITY (MEXICO)—FICTION

Alcala, Kathleen. Treasures in Heaven: A Novel. 2003. (Latino Voices Ser.). 224p. pap. 15.95 (0-8101-2036-4) Northwestern Univ. Pr.
Azuela, Arturo. Shadows of Silence. Murray, Elena C., tr. 1985. 304p. (C). text 26.95 o.p. (0-268-01716-6) Univ. of Notre Dame Pr.
Berman, Sabina. Bubbeh. Labinger, Andrea G., tr. from SPA. 1998. (Discoveries Ser.). 96p. pap. 12.95 (0-935480-93-5) Latin American Literary Review Pr.
Brizzolara, John. Wirecutter. 1987. 240p. 16.95 o.s.i (0-385-23437-6) Doubleday Publishing.
—Wirecutter. 1989. bds. 3.95 o.s.i (0-671-65851-4, Pocket) Simon & Schuster.
Esquivel, Laura. The Law of Love. 1997. Tr. of Ley del Amor. (Illus.). 288p. pap. 18.95 (0-609-80127-9) Random Hse. Value Publishing.
Gilman, Dorothy. The Unexpected Mrs. Pollifax. 1999. pap. 5.99 (0-449-45854-7); 1998. mass mkt. 0.00 (0-449-45884-9); 1986. pap. 2.95 o.p. (0-449-44202-0); 1985. 192p. mass mkt. 6.99 (0-449-20828-1) Ballantine Bks. (Fawcett).
—The Unexpected Mrs. Pollifax. 1991. 300p. reprint ed. lib. bdg. 22.95 (0-89966-873-9) Buccaneer Bks., Inc.
—The Unexpected Mrs. Pollifax. l.t. ed. 1992. (General Ser.). 400p. 18.95 o.p. (0-8161-5352-3, Macmillan Reference USA) Gale Group.
—The Unexpected Mrs. Pollifax. unabr. ed. 2001. audio compact disk 78.00 (0-7887-7162-0, C1415); 1989. (Mrs. Pollifax Mystery Ser.: Vol. 1). audio 51.00 (1-55690-537-8, 89730E7) Recorded Bks., LLC.
Highsmith, Patricia. A Game for the Living. 1988. 288p. pap. 12.00 (0-87113-210-9, Atlantic Monthly Pr.) Grove/Atlantic, Inc.
Ing, Dean. The Nemesis Mission. 1992. 468p. mass mkt. 5.99 (0-8125-1173-5); 1991. 384p. 19.95 o.p. (0-312-85105-7) Doherty, Tom Assocs., LLC. (Tor Bks.).
Neuman, William I., tr. from ITA. The Shadow of the Shadow. 1992. (Crime Ser.).Tr. of Paco Ignacio Taibo Two. 240p. pap. 9.00 o.p. (0-14-013083-7, Penguin Bks.) Penguin Group (USA) Inc.
Peters, Elizabeth, pseud. The Night of Four Hundred Rabbits. l.t. ed. 1992. pap. 15.95 o.p. (0-7927-1000-2); 18.95 o.p. (0-7927-0974-8, E0022) BBC Audiobooks America.
—The Night of Four Hundred Rabbits. unabr. ed. 1997. audio 44.95 (0-7861-1098-8, 1862) Blackstone Audio Bks., Inc.
—The Night of Four Hundred Rabbits. 1996. mass mkt. 5.99 o.s.i (0-8125-6360-3); 1989. 247p. mass mkt. 5.99 (0-8125-0773-8) Doherty, Tom Assocs., LLC. (Tor Bks.).
—The Night of Four Hundred Rabbits. 1992. 18.95 o.p. (0-7278-4306-0); 256p. reprint ed. 18.95 o.p. (0-7278-4303-6) Severn Hse. Pubs., Ltd.
Ruggero, Ed. The Common Defense. McCarthy, Paul, ed. 1992. 352p. 20.00 (0-671-73008-8, Atria); 432p. reprint ed. mass mkt. 5.99 (0-671-73009-6, Pocket) Simon & Schuster.
Taibo, Paco Ignacio, II. An Easy Thing. 2002. (Missing Mystery Ser.: Vol. 49). 240p. pap. 14.95 o.s.i (1-59058-006-0) Poisoned Pen Pr.
—An Easy Thing. Neuman, William I., tr. 1990. 240p. 16.95 o.p. (0-670-82462-3, Viking) Viking Penguin.
—An Easy Thing. 1990. (Crime Ser.). 240p. reprint ed. pap. 4.50 o.p. (0-14-011523-4, Penguin Bks.) Viking Penguin.
—No Happy Ending. Neuman, William I., tr. 1993. 192p. 17.95 (0-89296-517-7) Mysterious Pr.
—No Happy Ending. 2003. 254p. pap. 14.95 o.s.i (1-59058-038-9) Poisoned Pen Pr.
—No Happy Ending. Neuman, William I., tr. 1994. 192p. mass mkt. 5.50 (0-446-40329-6, Mysterious Pr. Paperback Bks.) Warner Bks., Inc.
—Return to the Same City. Dail, Laura, tr. from SPA. 1996. Tr. of Regreso a la Misma Ciudad y Bajo la Lluvia. 192p. 25.00 (0-89296-590-8) Mysterious Pr.
—Return to the Same City. Dail, Laura, tr. 1997. Tr. of Regreso a la Misma Ciudad y Bajo la Lluvia. 176p. mass mkt. 5.99 (0-446-40520-5) Warner Bks., Inc.
—Some Clouds. Neuman, William I., tr. 1993. (Crime Ser.). 176p. pap. 9.00 o.p. (0-14-014896-5, Penguin Bks.) Penguin Group (USA) Inc.
—Some Clouds. 2002. 250p. pap. 14.95 o.s.i (1-59058-032-X) Poisoned Pen Pr.
—Some Clouds. Neuman, William I., tr. from SPA. 1992. 176p. 19.00 o.p. (0-670-83825-X, Viking) Viking Penguin.
Theis, David. Rio Ganges. 2002. 272p. pap. 20.00 (0-9701525-6-6) Winedale Publishing.
Van Meter, David A. Body of Evidence. 1990. mass mkt. 3.95 o.s.i (0-515-10207-5, Jove) Berkley Publishing Group.

## MIAMI (FLA.)—FICTION

Alberro, Elaine. Dance with Me. 2001. (Encanto Ser.). 256p. mass mkt. 4.99 o.s.i (0-7860-1213-7, Encanto) Kensington Publishing Corp.
Asher, Steven. The Undercover Single Man. 1998. 126p. 14.95 o.p. (0-533-12452-2) Vantage Pr., Inc.
Bell, Christine. The Perez Family: A Novel. 1991. 256p. reprint ed. pap. 11.00 o.p. (0-06-097401-X, Perennial) HarperTrade.
—The Perez Family: A Novel. 1990. 19.95 o.p. (0-393-02798-8) Norton, W. W. & Co., Inc.
Booth, Pat. Miami. 1992. mass mkt. 5.99 o.s.i (0-345-38165-3) Ballantine Bks.
—Miami. 1991. 384p. 20.00 o.s.i (0-517-58415-8, Crown) Crown Publishing Group.
—Miami. 1994. 4.99 o.p. (0-517-11672-3) Random Hse. Value Publishing.
Bowman, Eric. Before I Wake. 1998. 336p. reprint ed. mass mkt. 6.99 o.s.i (0-515-12353-6, Jove) Berkley Publishing Group.
—Before I Wake, Set. abr. ed. 1997. 25.00 o.p. (0-7871-1463-4, 695277) NewStar Media, Inc.
—Before I Wake. 1997. 320p. 24.95 o.p. (0-399-14263-0, G. P. Putnam's Sons) Penguin Group (USA) Inc.
Buchanan, Edna. Act of Betrayal. unabr. collector's ed. 1996. (Britt Montero Ser.). audio 56.00 (0-7366-3306-5, 3960) Books on Tape, Inc.
—Act of Betrayal. abr. ed. (Britt Montero Mystery Ser.). 1997. 3p. audio 7.99 o.p. (1-56740-148-1, 617, Paperback Nova Audio Bks.); 1996. audio 17.95 o.p. (1-56100-868-0, 454, Nova Audio Bks.); 1996. 7p. audio 57.25 o.p. (1-56100-296-8, 786, Unabridged Library Editions); 1996. audio 23.95 o.p. (1-56100-671-8, 24, Bookcassette) Brilliance Audio.
—Act of Betrayal, Set. unabr. ed. 1999. audio 57.25 Highsmith Inc.
—Act of Betrayal. 1997. 448p. mass mkt. 5.99 (0-7868-8923-3); 1996. 320p. 21.95 o.p. (0-7868-6098-7) Hyperion Pr.
—Act of Betrayal. unabr. ed. 2000. (Britt Montero Mystery Ser.: Vol. 4). audio 60.00 (0-7887-0488-5, 94681E7) Recorded Bks., LLC.
—Contents under Pressure. unabr. collector's ed. 1993. (Britt Montero Ser.). audio 56.00 (0-7366-2378-7, 3150) Books on Tape, Inc.
—Contents under Pressure. 1992. 304p. (YA). 21.95 o.p. (1-56282-932-7) Hyperion Pr.
—Contents under Pressure. 1994. (Britt Montero Mysteries Ser.). 368p. mass mkt. 6.99 (0-380-72260-7, Avon Bks.) Morrow/Avon.
—Contents under Pressure. l.t. ed. 472p. pap. 2.99 o.s.i (0-7669-1026-1) World Pubns., Inc.
—Garden of Evil. (Britt Montero Mysteries Ser.). 2000. 320p. mass mkt. 6.99 (0-380-79841-7); 1999. 319p. 24.00 (0-380-97654-4) Morrow/Avon. (Avon Bks.).
—Garden of Evil. l.t. ed. 2000. (Mystery Ser.). 437p. 29.95 (0-7862-2331-6) Thorndike Pr.

—The Ice Maiden. l.t. ed. 2003. lib. bdg. 29.95 (*1-58547-309-X*, Platinum) Ctr. Point Large Print.
—The Ice Maiden. 2003. 320p. mass mkt. 7.50 (*0-380-72834-6*, Avon Bks.); 2002. 304p. 23.95 (*0-380-97332-4*, Morrow, William & Co.) Morrow/Avon.
—Margin of Error. unabr. collector's ed. 1997. (Britt Montero Ser.). audio 56.00 (*0-7366-3832-6*, 4552) Books on Tape, Inc.
—Margin of Error. abr. ed. 1998. audio 7.99 o.p. (*1-56740-253-4*, 675, Paperback Nova Audio Bks.); 1997. 8p. audio 57.25 o.p. (*1-56100-822-2*, 937, Unabridged Library Editions); 1997. audio 23.95 (*1-56100-747-1*, 171) Brilliance Audio.
—Margin of Error. l.t. ed. 1998. pap. 24.95 (*1-56895-563-4*, Wheeler Publishing, Inc.) Gale Group.
—Margin of Error. 1997. 304p. 22.95 o.p. (*0-7868-6232-7*); 1998. 384p. reprint ed. mass mkt. 5.99 (*0-7868-8931-4*) Hyperion Pr.
—Margin of Error. unabr. ed. (Britt Montero Mystery Ser.: Vol. 5). 1999. audio compact disk 79.00 (*0-7887-3424-5*, C1030E7); 1997. audio 75.00 (*0-7887-1777-4*, 95251E7) Recorded Bks., LLC.
—Margin of Error. l.t. ed. 2000. (Ulverscroft Large Print Ser.). 488p. (*0-7089-4189-3*, Ulverscroft) Thorpe, F. A. Pubs. GBR. *Dist:* Ulverscroft Large Print Bks., Ltd., Ulverscroft Large Print Canada, Ltd.
—Miami, It's Murder. unabr. collector's ed. 1994. (Britt Montero Ser.). audio 48.00 (*0-7366-2740-5*, 3466) Books on Tape, Inc.
—Miami, It's Murder. unabr. ed. 1994. audio 57.25 o.p. (*1-56100-175-9*, 941, Unabridged Library Editions); audio 21.95 o.p. (*1-56100-548-7*, 175, Bookcassette) Brilliance Audio.
—Miami, It's Murder. abr. ed. audio 17.00 o.p. (*1-55994-794-2*, CPN 2383, HarperAudio) HarperTrade.
—Miami, It's Murder. 1994. 256p. 21.95 o.p. (*1-56282-802-9*) Hyperion Pr.
—Miami, It's Murder. 1995. (Britt Montero Mysteries Ser.). 320p. mass mkt. 6.99 (*0-380-72261-5*, Avon Bks.) Morrow/Avon.
—Suitable for Framing. unabr. collector's ed. 1995. (Britt Montero Ser.). audio 56.00 (*0-7366-3072-4*, 3754) Books on Tape, Inc.
—Suitable for Framing. abr. ed. 1995. audio 16.95 o.p. (*1-56100-401-4*, 1383, Nova Audio Bks.); 9p. audio 57.25 o.p. (*1-56100-234-8*, 1062, Unabridged Library Editions); audio 23.95 o.p. (*1-56100-609-2*, 281, Bookcassette) Brilliance Audio.
—Suitable for Framing. l.t. ed. 1995. 25.95 o.p. (*1-56895-210-4*, Wheeler Publishing, Inc.) Gale Group.
—Suitable for Framing. 1996. 368p. mass mkt. 4.99 (*0-7868-8901-2*); 1995. 256p. 21.95 (*0-7868-6047-2*) Hyperion Pr.
—Suitable for Framing. abr. ed. 2000. audio 7.95 (*1-57815-028-0*, 1033, Media Bks. Audio Publishing) Media Bks., L. L. C.
—Suitable for Framing. unabr. ed. 2000. (Britt Montero Mystery Ser.: Vol. 3). audio 60.00 (*0-7887-0296-3*, 94489E7) Recorded Bks., LLC.
—You Only Die Twice. l.t. ed. 2001. 396p. lib. bdg. 27.95 (*1-58547-124-0*) Ctr. Point Large Print.
—You Only Die Twice. 2002. 368p. mass mkt. 6.99 (*0-380-79842-5*) Morrow/Avon.
Chefitz, Mitchell. The Thirty-Third Hour: A Novel. 2002. 320p. 24.95 (*0-312-27758-X*, Saint Martin's Minotaur); 2003. 288p. reprint ed. pap. 13.95 (*0-312-30323-8*, Saint Martin's Griffin) St. Martin's Pr.
Clark, Mary Jane. Nobody Knows. E-Book 18.95 (*0-312-70752-5*); 2002. 320p. 24.95 (*0-312-28866-2*) St. Martin's Pr.
—Nobody Knows. l.t. ed. 2002. (Core Collection). 338p. 29.95 (*0-7862-4667-7*) Thorndike Pr.
Coffey, Tom. Miami Twilight. 2001. 304p. 23.95 (*0-671-02829-4*, Atria); 2002. 368p. reprint ed. mass mkt. 6.99 (*0-671-02830-8*, Pocket Star) Simon & Schuster.
—The Serpent Club. 1999. 336p. 23.00 o.s.i (*0-671-02827-8*, Atria) Simon & Schuster.
Collins, Max Allan. CSI Miami, Bk. 2. 2004. (CSI Miami Ser.). 288p. pap. 6.99 (*0-7434-8056-2*, Pocket Star) Simon & Schuster.
Cook, Robin. Terminal. 384p. 1996. mass mkt. 7.99 (*0-425-15506-4*); 1994. mass mkt. 6.99 o.s.i (*0-425-14094-6*) Berkley Publishing Group.
—Terminal. 1993. 400p. 21.95 o.p. (*0-399-13771-8*, G. P. Putnam's Sons) Penguin Group (USA) Inc.
—Terminal. pap. 6.98 o.p. (*0-8317-4385-9*) Smithmark Pubs., Inc.
—Terminal. 1994. 14.04 (*0-606-06051-0*) Turtleback Bks.
Cresswell, Jasmine. The Inheritance. 2000. 408p. mass mkt. (*1-55166-511-5*, 1-66511-6, Mira Bks.) Harlequin Enterprises, Ltd.
Crews, Harry. The Mulching of America: A Novel. 1996. 272p. pap. 12.00 (*0-684-82541-4*, Touchstone); 1995. 256p. 22.00 (*0-684-80934-6*, Simon & Schuster) Simon & Schuster.
Curtis, James R. Shango. 1996. 197p. (Orig.). pap. 11.95 (*1-55885-096-1*) Arte Publico Pr.
Delacorta. The Rap Factor: Novel. Texier, Catherine, tr. from FRE. 1993. 208p. pap. 11.00 (*0-87113-617-1*, Atlantic Monthly Pr.); 200p. 18.00 o.p. (*0-87113-529-9*) Grove/Atlantic, Inc.
Dorsey, Tim. Cadillac Beach. 2004. 352p. 24.95 (*0-06-052046-9*, Morrow, William & Co.) Morrow/Avon.
—The Stingray Shuffle. 2004. 400p. mass mkt. 7.50 (*0-06-055693-5*, HarperTorch); 2003. 320p. 24.95 (*0-06-052045-0*, Morrow, William & Co.) Morrow/Avon.
—The Stingray Shuffle. l.t. ed. 2003. 517p. 28.95 (*0-7862-5643-5*) Thorndike Pr.
Due, Tananarive. The Between: A Novel. 288p. 1996. pap. 13.00 (*0-06-092726-7*, Perennial); 1995. 22.00 o.p. (*0-06-017250-9*) HarperTrade.
Elkin, Stanley. Mrs. Ted Bliss. 2002. (American Literature Ser.). 294p. reprint ed. pap. 14.95 (*1-56478-322-7*) Dalkey Archive Pr.
—Mrs. Ted Bliss. l.t. ed. 1996. pap. 22.95 o.p. (*1-56895-314-3*, Wheeler Publishing, Inc.) Gale Group.
—Mrs. Ted Bliss. 1995. 304p. 22.95 (*0-7868-6104-5*) Hyperion Pr.
—Mrs. Ted Bliss. 1996. pap. 12.00 (*0-380-72896-6*, Avon Bks.) Morrow/Avon.
—Mrs. Ted Bliss. unabr. ed. 1997. audio 78.00 (*0-7887-1073-7*, 95086E7) Recorded Bks., LLC.
Frank, Marshall. Dire Straits: A Miami Novel. 2001. 320p. 25.00 (*0-9676528-2-0*) Harlan Publishing Co.
Garcia-Aguilera, Carolina. Bitter Sugar. 2001. (Lupe Solano Mystery Ser.). 336p. 24.00 (*0-380-97781-8*, Morrow, William & Co.) Morrow/Avon.
—Bloody Secrets. 1999. 336p. reprint ed. mass mkt. 6.50 o.s.i (*0-425-16779-8*, Prime Crime) Berkley Publishing Group.
—Bloody Secrets. 1998. 274p. 23.95 o.p. (*0-399-14386-6*, G. P. Putnam's Sons) Penguin Group (USA) Inc.
—Bloody Shame: A Lupe Solano Mystery. 1998. 320p. mass mkt. 6.50 o.s.i (*0-425-16140-4*, Prime Crime) Berkley Publishing Group.
—Bloody Shame: A Lupe Solano Mystery. 1997. 288p. 22.95 o.p. (*0-399-14256-8*, G. P. Putnam's Sons) Penguin Group (USA) Inc.
—Bloody Waters: A Lupe Solano Mystery. 1997. (Lupo Solano Mystery Ser.). 304p. mass mkt. 5.99 o.s.i (*0-425-15670-2*, Prime Crime) Berkley Publishing Group.
—Bloody Waters: A Lupe Solano Mystery. 1996. 256p. 21.95 o.p. (*0-399-14157-X*, G. P. Putnam's Sons) Penguin Group (USA) Inc.
—A Miracle in Paradise. (Lupe Solano Mystery Ser.). 2000. 352p. mass mkt. 5.99 o.s.i (*0-380-80738-6*); 1999. viii, 277p. 23.00 (*0-380-97779-6*) Morrow/Avon. (Avon Bks.).
—One Hot Summer. 2002. 288p. (gr. 5 up). 23.95 (*0-06-000980-2*, Rayo) HarperTrade.
Garcia, Eric. Hot & Sweaty Rex: A Mystery. 2004. 352p. 24.95 (*0-375-50523-7*, Villard Bks.) Random House Adult Trade Publishing Group.
Garcia, Cristina. The Aguero Sisters. 1998. 103.60 o.s.i (*0-345-91389-2*); 103.60 o.s.i (*0-345-91390-6*); 336p. pap. 14.00 (*0-345-40651-6*, Ballantine Bks.) Ballantine Bks.
—Las Hermanas Aguero: Una Novela. 1997. (SPA.). 320p. pap. 13.95 (*0-679-78145-5*, RH9081, Vintage) Knopf Publishing Group.
Graham, Heather. Drop Dead Gorgeous. l.t. ed. 1999. 27.95 (*1-56895-667-3*, Wheeler Publishing, Inc.) Gale Group.
—Drop Dead Gorgeous. 1998. 352p. mass mkt. 6.99 (*0-451-40846-2*, Onyx) NAL.
—Picture Me Dead. 2004. 400p. mass mkt. (*0-7783-2010-3*, Mira Bks.) Harlequin Enterprises, Ltd.
—Slow Burn. l.t. ed. 2002. (Wheeler Large Print Book Ser.). pap. 23.95 (*1-58724-190-0*, Wheeler Publishing, Inc.) Gale Group.
—Slow Burn. 2001. 384p. mass mkt. (*1-55166-864-5*, 1-99/97-9, Mira Bks.) Harlequin Enterprises, Ltd.
—Tall, Dark & Deadly. l.t. ed. (Wheeler Press Paperback Ser.). 2000. pap. 11.95 (*1-56895-971-0*); 1999. 27.95 (*1-56895-799-8*) Gale Group. (Wheeler Publishing, Inc.).
Grippando, James M. Beyond Suspicion. 2002. 336p. 24.95 (*0-06-621344-4*); 592p. pap. 24.95 (*0-06-051742-5*) HarperCollins Pubs.
—Last to Die. 2003. 384p. 23.95 (*0-06-000555-6*) HarperCollins Pubs.
—Last to Die. l.t. ed. 2003. 608p. pap. 23.95 (*0-06-055815-6*, HarperLargePrint) HarperTrade.
Gruber, Michael. Tropic of Night. 2003. 432p. 24.95 (*0-06-050954-6*) HarperCollins Pubs.
—Tropic of Night. 2004. 480p. mass mkt. 7.50 (*0-06-050955-4*, HarperTorch) Morrow/Avon.
Hailey, Arthur. Detective. 1998. 608p. reprint ed. mass mkt. 7.99 (*0-425-16386-5*) Berkley Publishing Group.
—Detective. l.t. ed. 1997. pap. 24.00 o.p. (*0-7838-8132-0*, Macmillan Reference USA) Gale Group.
—Detective. 1999. (SPA.). (*84-08-02910-X*) GeoPlaneta, Editorial, S. A.
Hall, James W. Body Language. abr. ed. 1999. audio 7.99 (*1-56740-310-7*, 1874, Paperback Nova Audio Bks.); 1998. audio 26.95 (*1-56740-073-6*, 1452, Bookcassette); 1998. 10p. audio 73.25 (*1-56740-602-5*, 1455, Unabridged Library Editions); Set. 1998. audio 17.95 o.p. (*1-56740-797-8*, 1453, Nova Audio Bks.) Brilliance Audio.
—Body Language. 1999. E-Book 24.95 o.s.i (*0-312-20761-1*); 1998. 352p. 24.95 (*0-312-19243-6*) St. Martin's Pr.
—Body Language. l.t. ed. 1998. (Americana Ser.). 527p. 28.95 (*0-7862-1686-7*) Thorndike Pr.
—Rough Draft. 2001. 368p. reprint ed. mass mkt. 6.99 (*0-312-97492-2*, St. Martin's Paperbacks) St. Martin's Pr.
Heller, Marion. Paco's Perro. 2001. 163p. (J). (gr. 5-9). pap. 12.95 (*1-56825-080-0*, 080.0) Rainbow Bks., Inc.
Hendricks, Vicki. Miami Purity. 1996. pap. 10.00 o.s.i (*0-679-76800-9*, Vintage) Knopf Publishing Group.
Hiaasen, Carl. Powder Burn. 1998. 288p. pap. 12.00 (*0-375-70068-4*, Vintage) Knopf Publishing Group.
—Tourist Season. l.t. ed. 1996. (G. K. Hall Mystery Ser.). 524p. lib. bdg. 23.95 o.p. (*0-7838-1647-2*, Macmillan Reference USA) Gale Group.
—Tourist Season. 1986. 295p. 15.95 o.p. (*0-399-13145-0*, G. P. Putnam's Sons) Penguin Putnam Bks. for Young Readers.
—Tourist Season. 1989. mass mkt. 3.95 (*0-446-73857-3*); 1987. 384p. reprint ed. mass mkt. 7.99 (*0-446-34345-5*) Warner Bks., Inc.
Hodgman, D. A. The Color of Blood. 1995. (Stakeout Ser.: Vol. 3). per. (*0-373-63412-9*, Harlequin Bks.) Harlequin Enterprises, Ltd.
—Miami Heat. 1995. (Stakeout Ser.). per. (*0-373-63411-0*, 1-63411-2, Harlequin Bks.) Harlequin Enterprises, Ltd.
Hoffman, Jilliane P. Retribution. 2004. 432p. 24.95 (*0-399-15127-3*, Putnam & Grosset); 2003. 224.55 (*0-399-19767-2*) Putnam Publishing Group, The.
Hoyt, Richard. Marimba. 1993. 352p. mass mkt. 4.99 o.p. (*0-8125-1563-3*); 1992. 288p. 18.95 o.p. (*0-312-85193-6*) Doherty, Tom Assocs., LLC. (Tor Bks.).
Jackson, Hialeah. The Alligator's Farewell. 1998. (Annabelle Hardy Mystery Ser.: No. 1). 368p. mass mkt. 5.99 o.s.i (*0-440-22660-0*) Dell Publishing.
Jakubowski, Maxim. It's You That I Want to Kiss. 1997. 222p. pap. 16.95 (*1-899344-15-2*) Do-Not Pr., The GBR. *Dist:* Dufour Editions, Inc.
Katzenbach, John. In the Heat of the Summer. 1982. 13.95 o.p. (*0-689-11269-6*, Scribner) Simon & Schuster.
—The Shadow Man. 1996. mass mkt. 6.99 o.s.i (*0-345-38630-2*); 1995. 480p. 22.00 o.p. (*0-345-38629-9*) Ballantine Bks.
—The Shadow Man. l.t. ed. 1995. 655p. 24.95 o.p. (*0-7838-1357-0*, Macmillan Reference USA) Gale Group.
La Sala, Paula. Lunch Money. 2000. 103p. (Orig.). pap. 13.25 o.p. (*1-929925-26-3*) FirstPublish.
Lamazares, Ivonne. The Sugar Island. 2000. 224p. tchr. ed. 23.00 (*0-395-86040-7*, Mariner Bks.) Houghton Mifflin Co. Trade & Reference Div.
Latour, Jose. Outcast. 1999. 217p. pap. 13.95 o.p. (*1-888451-07-6*, AKB04) Akashic Bks.
—Outcast. 2001. 304p. 24.00 (*0-06-018488-4*, Morrow, William & Co.) Morrow/Avon.
Leonard, Elmore. Cat Chaser. unabr. collector's ed. 1995. audio 48.00 (*0-7366-3117-8*, 3793) Books on Tape, Inc.
—Cat Chaser. abr. ed. (Audio Favorites Ser.). audio 9.99 (*1-55204-011-9*, 390491); 1989. audio 16.99 (*0-88646-239-8*) Durkin Hayes Publishing Ltd.
—Cat Chaser. l.t. ed. 1986. (General Ser.). 364p. 16.95 o.p. (*0-8161-3947-4*, Macmillan Reference USA) Gale Group.
—Cat Chaser. 1998. (Elmore Leonard Library). 288p. pap. 12.00 (*0-688-16341-6*, Perennial) HarperTrade.
—Cat Chaser. 2003. 384p. mass mkt. 7.50 (*0-06-051222-9*, HarperTorch); 1983. 288p. mass mkt. 6.50 (*0-380-64642-0*, Avon Bks.); 1982. 13.50 o.p. (*0-87795-398-8*, Morrow, William & Co.) Morrow/Avon.
—Cat Chaser, unabr. ed. 1995. audio 51.00 (*0-7887-0256-4*, 94465E7) Recorded Bks., LLC.
—LaBrava. l.t. ed. 1984. (General Ser.). 15.95 o.p. (*0-8161-3693-9*, Macmillan Reference USA) Gale Group.
—LaBrava. 2003. 432p. mass mkt. 7.50 (*0-06-051223-7*, HarperTorch); 1984. pap. 4.99 (*0-380-69237-6*, Avon Bks.); 1983. 14.95 o.p. (*0-87795-527-1*, Morrow, William & Co.) Morrow/Avon.
—Stick. unabr. collector's ed. 1996. audio 48.00 (*0-7366-3360-X*, 4010) Books on Tape, Inc.
—Stick. l.t. ed. 1985. (General Ser.). 360p. 15.95 o.p. (*0-8161-3908-3*, Macmillan Reference USA) Gale Group.
—Stick. 1998. (Elmore Leonard Library). 304p. pap. 12.00 (*0-688-16340-8*, Perennial) HarperTrade.
—Stick. 1984. 304p. mass mkt. 6.50 (*0-380-67652-4*, Avon Bks.); 1983. 14.50 o.p. (*0-87795-436-4*, Morrow, William & Co.) Morrow/Avon.
—Stick, unabr. ed. audio 51.00 (*0-7887-0359-5*, 94551E7) Recorded Bks., LLC.
Leonard, Sam. A Difficult Trade: The Baseball Mystery. 2000. 278p. 24.95 (*1-885003-63-3*) Reed, Robert D. Pubs.
Levine, Paul. False Dawn. 1993. 320p. 21.95 o.s.i (*0-553-08995-1*) Bantam Bks.
—False Dawn. 1993. audio 15.99 o.s.i (*0-553-47136-8*, RH Audio) Random Hse. Audio Publishing Group.
—The False Dawn. 1994. 368p. mass mkt. 5.99 o.s.i (*0-553-56504-4*) Bantam Bks.
—Flesh & Bones. 1998. (Jake Lassiter Mystery Ser.). 352p. mass mkt. 5.99 (*0-380-72591-6*, Avon Bks.) Morrow/Avon.
—Flesh & Bones: A Jake Lassiter Novel. l.t. ed. 1997. (G. K. Hall Core Ser.). 468p. 26.95 (*0-7838-8065-0*, Macmillan Reference USA) Gale Group.
—Flesh & Bones: A Jake Lassiter Novel. l.t. ed. 1997. 336p. 23.00 (*0-688-14305-9*, Morrow, William & Co.) Morrow/Avon.
—Fool Me Twice. 1996. 352p. mass mkt. 5.99 (*0-380-72590-8*, Avon Bks.) Morrow/Avon.
—Fool Me Twice: A Jake Lassiter Novel. 1996. 356p. 22.00 o.p. (*0-688-14304-0*, Morrow, William & Co.) Morrow/Avon.
—Mortal Sin. 1995. 352p. mass mkt. 5.50 (*0-380-72161-9*, Avon Bks.); 1994. 20.00 o.p. (*0-688-12717-7*, Morrow, William & Co.) Morrow/Avon.
—Night Vision. 1992. 448p. mass mkt. 5.99 o.s.i (*0-553-29762-7*); 1991. 352p. 20.00 o.s.i (*0-553-07796-1*) Bantam Bks.
—Slashback. abr. ed. 1995. audio 16.95 o.p. (*1-56100-415-4*, 1375, Nova Audio Bks.); audio 57.25 o.p. (*1-56100-246-1*, 1049, Unabridged Library Editions) Brilliance Audio.
—Slashback, abr. ed. 2000. audio 7.95 (*1-57815-144-9*, 1103, Media Bks. Audio Publishing) Media Bks., L. L. C.
—Slashback. 1995. pap. 5.99 o.p. (*0-380-72162-7*, Avon Bks.) Morrow/Avon.
—Slashback: A Jake Lassiter Novel. 1995. 350p. 22.00 o.p. (*0-688-12718-5*, Morrow, William & Co.) Morrow/Avon.
—To Speak for the Dead. 1991. 400p. mass mkt. 5.99 o.s.i (*0-553-29172-6*) Bantam Bks.
Levine, Paul J. To Speak for the Dead. 1990. 304p. 17.95 o.s.i (*0-553-05747-2*) Bantam Bks.
MacGregor, T. J. The Seventh Sense. 1999. 272p. 23.00 o.s.i (*1-57566-411-9*) Kensington Publishing Corp.
—Seventh Sense. 2000. 352p. mass mkt. 6.99 (*0-7860-1083-5*, Pinnacle Bks.) Kensington Publishing Corp.
—Storm Surge. 1993. 336p. (YA). 19.95 o.p. (*1-56282-789-8*) Hyperion Pr.
Mayerson, Evelyn W. Dade County Pine. 1994. 464p. 22.95 o.p. (*0-525-93646-7*, Dutton) Dutton/Plume.
—Miami. 1995. 496p. mass mkt. 5.99 o.s.i (*0-451-18147-6*, Signet Bks.) NAL.
McGuane, Thomas. Ninety-Two in the Shade. 1973. 224p. 8.95 o.p. (*0-374-22259-2*) Farrar, Straus & Giroux.
—Ninety-Two in the Shade. 1980. pap. 4.95 o.p. (*0-14-005319-0*) Penguin Group (USA) Inc.
—Ninety-Two in the Shade. 1995. (Vintage Contemporaries Ser.). 208p. pap. 13.00 (*0-679-75289-7*) Random Hse., Inc.
—Ninety-Two in the Shade. 1987. 208p. pap. 10.00 o.p. (*0-14-009907-7*, Penguin Bks.) Viking Penguin.
Medina, C. C. A Little Love. 2000. 368p. 18.95 (*0-446-52448-4*) Warner Bks., Inc.
Menendez, Ana. In Cuba I Was a German Shepherd. 2001. 229p. 23.00 o.p. (*0-8021-1688-4*); 2002. 240p. reprint ed. pap. 12.00 (*0-8021-3887-X*) Grove/Atlantic, Inc. (Grove Pr.).
Mestre-Reed, Ernesto, tr. The Second Death of Unica Aveyano: A Novel. 2004. 272p. pap. 13.00 (*1-4000-3316-0*, Vintage) Knopf Publishing Group.
Miscione, Lisa. The Darkness Gathers: A Novel. 2003. 304p. 23.95 (*0-312-28359-8*, Saint Martin's Minotaur) St. Martin's Pr.
Mustian, Mark. The Return. 2000. 303p. 18.95 (*1-56164-190-1*) Pineapple Pr., Inc.
Parker, Barbara. Blood Relations. 1996. 384p. 22.95 o.s.i (*0-525-93976-8*) Dutton/Plume.
—Blood Relations. 1997. 448p. mass mkt. 6.99 (*0-451-18473-4*, Signet Bks.) NAL.
—Blood Relations. abr. ed. 1996. audio 16.95 o.p. (*0-14-086285-4*, Penguin AudioBooks) Viking Penguin.
—Criminal Justice. 1997. 320p. 22.95 o.p. (*0-525-93977-6*) Dutton/Plume.
—Criminal Justice. l.t. ed. 1997. 26.95 (*1-56895-498-0*, Wheeler Publishing, Inc.) Gale Group.
—Criminal Justice. 1998. 448p. mass mkt. 6.99 (*0-451-18474-2*, Signet Bks.) NAL.

—Suspicion of Betrayal. 1999. 352p. 23.95 o.s.i (*0-525-94468-0*, Dutton Studio) Dutton/Plume.
—Suspicion of Betrayal. 2000. 432p. mass mkt. 6.99 (*0-451-19838-7*, Signet Bks.) NAL.
—Suspicion of Betrayal. l.t. ed. 1999. (Mystery Ser.). 568p. 29.95 (*0-7862-2000-7*) Thorndike Pr.
—Suspicion of Deceit. 1998. 368p. 23.95 o.p. (*0-525-94401-X*) Dutton/Plume.
—Suspicion of Deceit. 1999. 432p. reprint ed. mass mkt. 6.99 (*0-451-19549-3*, Signet Bks.) NAL.
—Suspicion of Deceit. unabr. ed. 1998. audio 78.00 (*0-7887-3572-1*, 95937E7) Recorded Bks., LLC.
—Suspicion of Deceit. l.t. ed. 1998. (Cloak & Dagger Ser.). 615p. 26.95 o.p. (*0-7862-1460-0*) Thorndike Pr.
—Suspicion of Guilt. 1995. 400p. 22.95 o.p. (*0-525-93769-2*, Dutton) Dutton/Plume.
—Suspicion of Guilt. l.t. ed. 1995. 26.95 (*1-56895-232-5*, Wheeler Publishing, Inc.) Gale Group.
—Suspicion of Guilt. 1996. 432p. mass mkt. 6.99 (*0-451-17703-7*, Signet Bks.) NAL.
—Suspicion of Guilt. unabr. ed. 1995. audio 91.00 (*0-7887-0353-6*, 94545E7) Recorded Bks., LLC.
—Suspicion of Innocence. 1994. 352p. 20.95 o.p. (*0-525-93744-7*); 20.95 (*0-525-93747-1*) Dutton/Plume. (Dutton).
—Suspicion of Innocence. 1994. 448p. mass mkt. 6.99 (*0-451-17340-6*, Signet Bks.) NAL.
—Suspicion of Innocence. unabr. ed. 1994. audio 85.00 (*0-7887-0024-3*, 94223E7) Recorded Bks., LLC.
—Suspicion of Malice. 2000. 352p. 22.95 o.s.i (*0-525-94542-3*) Dutton/Plume.
—Suspicion of Malice. 2001. 432p. reprint ed. mass mkt. 6.99 (*0-451-20125-6*, Signet Bks.) NAL.
—Suspicion of Malice. l.t. ed. 2000. (Mystery Ser.). 565p. 29.95 (*0-7862-2655-2*) Thorndike Pr.
—Suspicion of Vengeance. 2001. 368p. 23.95 o.s.i (*0-525-94601-2*, Dutton) Dutton/Plume.
—Suspicion of Vengeance. l.t. ed. 2002. 30.95 (*0-7862-3751-1*) Gale Group.
—Suspicion of Vengeance. 2003. 448p. reprint ed. mass mkt. 7.50 (*0-451-20451-4*, Signet Bks.) NAL.
Philp, Geoffrey. Benjamin, My Son. 2003. 200p. pap. 14.95 (*1-900715-78-3*) Peepal Tree Pr., Ltd. GBR. *Dist:* Independent Pubs. Group.
Pozzessere, Heather G. If Looks Could Kill. 1997. 48p. mass mkt. (*1-55166-285-X*, 0-66285-8, Mira Bks.) Harlequin Enterprises, Ltd.
Prospero, Ann. Almost Night. 2001. 320p. mass mkt. 6.99 (*0-451-20226-0*, Signet Bks.) NAL.
—Almost Night: A Novel. 2000. 256p. 23.95 o.s.i (*0-525-94532-6*, Dutton) Dutton/Plume.
Puig Zaldivar, Raquel, et al. Women Don't Need to Write. 1998. 352p. pap. 13.95 (*1-55885-257-3*) Arte Publico Pr.
Rivera, Beatriz. Playing with Light. 2000. 245p. pap. 12.95 (*1-55885-310-3*) Arte Publico Pr.
Rosenbaum, Thane. Second Hand Smoke. 320p. 2000. pap. 13.95 (*0-312-25418-0*, Saint Martin's Griffin); 1999. 24.95 (*0-312-19954-6*) St. Martin's Pr.
Rosenfeld, Arthur. Diamond Eye: A Max Diamond Novel. 2001. 320p. 23.95 (*0-312-87871-0*, Forge Bks.) Doherty, Tom Assocs., LLC.
Sayles, John. Los Gusanos. 1999. (SPA.). 536p. (*84-8306-223-2*) Debate, Editorial.
—Los Gusanos. (SPA.). 536p. 30.95 (*84-8306-224-0*, DB11247) Debate, Editorial ESP. *Dist:* Lectorum Pubns., Inc.
—Los Gusanos. 480p. 1992. pap. 12.00 o.p. (*0-06-092159-5*, Perennial); 1991. 22.95 o.p. (*0-06-016653-3*) HarperTrade.
—Los Gusanos. 1992. 4.99 o.p. (*0-517-09228-X*) Random Hse. Value Publishing.
Shulman, Sondra. Moon People. 1994. 353p. 20.00 (*1-880909-18-9*) Baskerville Pubs., Inc.
Standiford, Les. Deal on Ice. 1997. 256p. 23.00 o.p. (*0-06-017620-2*) HarperCollins Pubs.
—Deal on Ice. 1998. 400p. mass mkt. 6.50 o.s.i (*0-06-109338-6*, HarperTorch) Morrow/Avon.
—Deal to Die For. 1995. 352p. 22.00 o.p. (*0-06-017621-0*) HarperTrade.
—Deal to Die For. 1996. 352p. mass mkt. 5.99 o.p. (*0-06-109337-8*, HarperTorch) Morrow/Avon.
—Deal with the Dead. 2001. 336p. 24.95 o.s.i (*0-399-14704-7*) Penguin Group (USA) Inc.
—Done Deal. 1993. 288p. 20.00 o.p. (*0-06-017731-4*) HarperTrade.
—Done Deal. 1994. 336p. mass mkt. 5.50 o.s.i (*0-06-109143-X*, HarperTorch) Morrow/Avon.
—Done Deal. 2002. 299p. pap. 14.95 o.s.i (*1-59058-002-8*) Poisoned Pen Pr.
—Done Deal. unabr. ed. 1998. audio 60.00 (*0-7887-1887-8*, 95309E7) Recorded Bks., LLC.
—Presidential Deal. 1998. 304p. 24.00 o.s.i (*0-06-018655-0*) HarperCollins Pubs.
—Presidential Deal. 1999. 432p. mass mkt. 6.50 o.s.i (*0-06-109553-2*, HarperTorch) Morrow/Avon.
—Presidential Deal. 1998. audio 80.00 (*0-7887-2503-3*, 95575E7) Recorded Bks., LLC.
—Raw Deal. 1994. 288p. 22.00 o.p. (*0-06-017732-2*) HarperCollins Pubs.
—Raw Deal. 1995. 384p. mass mkt. 5.50 o.s.i (*0-06-109144-8*, HarperTorch) Morrow/Avon.
—Raw Deal. 2003. 320p. pap. 14.95 o.s.i (*1-59058-106-7*) Poisoned Pen Pr.
—Raw Deal. unabr. ed. 1998. audio 70.00 (*0-7887-1318-3*, 95176E7) Recorded Bks., LLC.
Suarez, Virgil. Going Under. 1996. 159p. 18.95 (*1-55885-159-3*) Arte Publico Pr.
Sullivan, Winona. Dead South: A Sister Cecile Mystery. 1997. (Sister Cecile Mystery Ser.). 275p. mass mkt. 5.99 o.s.i (*0-8041-1513-3*, Ivy Bks.) Ballantine Bks.
—Dead South: A Sister Cecile Mystery. 1996. 288p. 21.95 o.p. (*0-312-13959-4*, Saint Martin's Minotaur) St. Martin's Pr.
—Death's a Beach: A Sister Cecile Mystery. 1997. (Sister Cecile Mystery Ser.). 276p. mass mkt. 5.99 o.s.i (*0-8041-1568-0*, Ivy Bks.) Ballantine Bks.
—Saving Death: A Sister Cecile Mystery. 2000. 256p. mass mkt. 6.50 (*0-8041-1899-X*, Ivy Bks.) Ballantine Bks.
Veciana-Suarez, Ana. The Chin Kiss King. 1998. 320p. pap. 12.95 o.s.i (*0-452-28009-5*, Plume) Dutton/Plume.
—The Chin Kiss King. 1997. 496p. 24.00 o.p. (*0-374-12130-3*) Farrar, Straus & Giroux.
Wetlaufer, Suzy. Judgement Call: A Novel. 1992. 20.00 o.p. (*0-688-10930-6*, Morrow, William & Co.) Morrow/Avon.
Willeford, Charles. Miami Blues. 1984. 208p. 12.95 o.p. (*0-312-53171-0*) St. Martin's Pr.
—The Shark-Infested Custard. 1993. 272p. 20.95 o.p. (*0-88733-163-7*) Underwood Bks., Inc.
—The Shark Infested Custard. 1996. 320p. mass mkt. 4.99 o.s.i (*0-440-21881-0*) Dell Publishing.
Williams, Lee. Author of Destiny: (Also Known As the Ochoa Case) 2002. (Illus.). 224p. pap. 14.95 (*0-942979-98-2*); lib. bdg. 26.00 (*0-942979-99-0*) Livingston Pr.
Woods, Sherryl. Hot Money. 1993. 288p. mass mkt. 4.99 o.s.i (*0-440-21485-8*) Dell Publishing.
—Hot Money. l.t. ed. 1995. 231p. pap. 19.95 o.p. (*0-7838-1192-6*, Macmillan Reference USA) Gale Group.
—Hot Property. 1992. 272p. mass mkt. 4.50 o.s.i (*0-440-21003-8*) Dell Publishing.
—Hot Schemes. 1994. 288p. mass mkt. 4.99 o.s.i (*0-440-21486-6*) Dell Publishing.
—Hot Schemes. l.t. ed. 1995. 248p. pap. 19.95 (*0-7838-1193-4*, Macmillan Reference USA) Gale Group.
—Hot Secret. 1992. 256p. mass mkt. 4.99 o.s.i (*0-440-21004-6*) Dell Publishing.
Wyle, Dirk. Amazon Gold: A Ben Candidi Mystery. 2003. (The Ben Candidi Mystery Series: 4). 336p. pap. 14.95 (*1-56825-095-9*, 095-9) Rainbow Bks., Inc.
—Biotechnology Is Murder: A Ben Candidi Mystery. 2000. 271p. pap. 14.95 (*1-56825-045-2*, 045-2) Rainbow Bks., Inc.
—Medical School Is Murder: A Ben Candidi Mystery. 2001. (The Ben Candidi Mystery Series). 286p. (C). pap. 14.95 (*1-56825-084-3*) Rainbow Bks., Inc.
—Pharmacology Is Murder: A Novel. 1998. 388p. pap. 16.95 (*1-56825-038-X*, 038X) Rainbow Bks., Inc.

## MICHIGAN—FICTION

Alexander, Carrie. North Country Man. 2002. (Harlequin Superromance Ser.: No. 1102). 304p. mass mkt. (*0-373-71102-6*, Harlequin Bks.) Harlequin Enterprises, Ltd.
Allen, Bobby Jaye. Early's Pride. 2002. 185p. pap. 7.99 (*0-9712082-1-2*) Accolade Bks.
Allyn, Doug. Black Water. 1996. 240p. 21.95 o.p. (*0-312-13932-2*, Saint Martin's Minotaur) St. Martin's Pr.
—The Cheerio Killings. 1989. 256p. 22.95 o.p. (*0-312-03302-8*, Saint Martin's Minotaur) St. Martin's Pr.
—Icewater Mansions. 1995. 247p. 21.00 o.p. (*0-312-11829-5*, Saint Martin's Minotaur) St. Martin's Pr.
—Motown Underground. 1993. 233p. 17.95 o.p. (*0-312-08851-5*, Saint Martin's Minotaur) St. Martin's Pr.
Anderson, Lauri. Children of the Kalevala: Contemporary American Finns Relive the Timeless Tales of the Kalevala. 1997. 128p. pap. 12.95 (*0-87839-119-3*) North Star Pr. of St. Cloud.
—Misery Bay: And Other Stories from Michigan's Upper Peninsula. 2002. 160p. 12.95 (*0-87839-178-9*) North Star Pr. of St. Cloud.
Apple, Max. Zip. 1978. 8.95 o.p. (*0-670-79692-1*) Viking Penguin.
Arnow, Harriette Louisa Simpson. The Dollmaker. 1999. (SPA.). 608p. mass mkt. 6.99 (*0-380-00947-1*, Avon Bks.) Morrow/Avon.
—The Dollmaker. 1985. 560p. 24.00 o.p. (*0-8131-1544-2*) Univ. Pr. of Kentucky.
Barr, Nevada. A Superior Death. 2003. 320p. mass mkt. 6.99 (*0-425-19471-X*) Berkley Publishing Group.
—A Superior Death. 2002. (Anna Pigeon Mysteries Ser.: No. 2). 384p. mass mkt. 7.50 o.s.i (*0-380-72362-X*, Avon Bks.) Morrow/Avon.
—A Superior Death. 1994. 303p. 19.95 o.s.i (*0-399-13916-8*, G. P. Putnam's Sons) Penguin Group (USA) Inc.
—A Superior Death. unabr. ed. 1998. (Anna Pigeon Mystery Ser. : No. 2). audio 72.00 (*0-7887-1896-7*, 95318E7) Recorded Bks., LLC.
—A Superior Death. l.t. ed. 1994. 431p. lib. bdg. 23.95 (*0-8161-7446-6*) Thorndike Pr.
Baxter, Charles. The Feast of Love. E-Book 11.50 (*1-58945-829-X*) Adobe Systems, Inc.
—The Feast of Love. 2001. E-Book 11.50 (*0-375-72782-5*) Random Hse., Inc.
—The Feast of Love: A Novel. 320p. 2000. 24.00 o.s.i (*0-375-41019-8*, Pantheon); 2001. reprint ed. pap. 13.00 (*0-375-70910-X*, Vintage) Knopf Publishing Group.
—A Relative Stranger: Stories. 2001. 224p. reprint ed. pap. 13.00 (*0-393-32220-3*) Norton, W. W. & Co., Inc.
—Saul & Patsy: A Novel. 2003. 336p. 24.00 (*0-375-41029-5*, Pantheon) Knopf Publishing Group.
—Shadow Play: A Novel. 1993. 352p. 21.95 o.p. (*0-393-03437-2*); 2001. 400p. reprint ed. pap. 14.00 (*0-393-32274-2*) Norton, W. W. & Co., Inc.
Beatty, Robert. Sapo. 1996. 285p. 18.95 o.p. (*0-9639705-4-2*) Ecopress.
Benz, Maudy. Oh, Jackie: A Novel. 1999. 208p. (J). reprint ed. pap. 12.95 o.s.i (*0-425-17044-6*) Berkley Publishing Group.
—Oh, Jackie: A Novel. 1998. 224p. 19.95 o.p. (*1-885266-59-6*) Story Line Pr.
Bodoin, Dorothy. Darkness at Foxglove Corners. 2001. (Five Star First Edition Women's Fiction Ser.). 276p. 25.95 (*0-7862-3486-5*, Five Star) Gale Group.
Bouldrey, Brian. The Genius of Desire. 1993. 240p. 17.00 o.s.i (*0-345-38334-6*) Ballantine Bks.
Bowman, Elizabeth A. White Chocolate. 1999. 375p. mass mkt. 6.99 (*0-8125-7181-9*); 1998. 352p. 23.95 o.p. (*0-312-86306-3*) Doherty, Tom Assocs., LLC. (Forge Bks.).
Boyle, T. Coraghessan. The Road to Wellville. 1993. 496p. 22.50 o.p. (*0-670-84334-2*, Viking) Viking Penguin.
Braun, Lilian Jackson. The Cat Who Ate Danish Modern. 1986. (Cat Who Ser.). 192p. mass mkt. 6.99 (*0-515-08712-2*, Jove) Berkley Publishing Group.
—The Cat Who Ate Danish Modern. 1989. (Black Dagger Crime Ser.). 200p. reprint ed. text 12.95 o.p. (*0-86220-755-X*) Chivers Pr. GBR. *Dist:* BBC Audiobooks America.
—The Cat Who Ate Danish Modern. l.t. ed. 1990. (Nightingale Ser.). 274p. 14.95 o.p. (*0-8161-4914-3*, Macmillan Reference USA) Gale Group.
—The Cat Who Ate Danish Modern. unabr. ed. 1990. (Cat Who Ser.). audio 35.00 (*1-55690-090-2*, 90081E7) Recorded Bks., LLC.
—The Cat Who Ate Danish Modern. 1986. 13.04 (*0-606-13246-5*) Turtleback Bks.
—The Cat Who Could Read Backwards. l.t. ed. 1991. 12.95 o.p. (*0-7927-0098-8*, C0139) BBC Audiobooks America.
—The Cat Who Could Read Backwards. 256p. 2003. pap. 10.00 (*0-425-19520-1*); 1986. mass mkt. 6.99 (*0-515-09017-4*, Jove) Berkley Publishing Group.
—The Cat Who Could Read Backwards. l.t. ed. 1997. (Large Print Book Ser.). 25.95 o.p. (*1-56895-470-0*, Wheeler Publishing, Inc.) Gale Group.
—The Cat Who Could Read Backwards. 1997. (Cat Who. . . Ser.). 240p. 19.95 o.p. (*0-399-14286-X*, G. P. Putnam's Sons) Penguin Group (USA) Inc.
—The Cat Who Could Read Backwards. unabr. ed. 1990. (Cat Who Ser.). audio 19.95 (*1-55690-091-0*, 90082) Recorded Bks., LLC.
—The Cat Who Had 14 Tales. unabr. ed. 2000. (Cat Who Ser.). (J). audio 35.00 (*0-7887-0312-9*, 94504E7) Recorded Bks., LLC.
—The Cat Who Had 14 Tales. 1988. 13.04 (*0-606-13247-3*) Turtleback Bks.
—The Cat Who Knew a Cardinal. abr. ed. 1993. 15.95 o.p. (*1-55800-444-0*, 390492) NewStar Media, Inc.
—The Cat Who Knew a Cardinal. 1991. (Cat Who Ser.). 240p. 16.95 o.p. (*0-399-13664-9*, G. P. Putnam's Sons) Penguin Group (USA) Inc.
—The Cat Who Knew a Cardinal; The Cat Who Moved a Mountain; The Cat Who Wasn't There. unabr. ed. 1993. audio 19.95 o.p. (*1-55800-782-2*) NewStar Media, Inc.
—The Cat Who Lived High. l.t. ed. 1991. lib. bdg. 19.95 o.p. (*0-8161-5126-1*, Macmillan Reference USA) Gale Group.
—The Cat Who Lived High. 1990. 240p. 17.95 o.p. (*0-399-13554-5*, G. P. Putnam's Sons) Penguin Putnam Bks. for Young Readers.
—The Cat Who Lived High. unabr. ed. 1994. (Cat Who Ser.: No. 11). audio 32.95 (*1-55690-992-6*, 94131) Recorded Bks., LLC.
—The Cat Who Robbed a Bank, No. 2. abr. ed. 2000. (Cat Who Ser.: Vol. 22). 3p. 17.95 o.s.i (*0-399-14582-6*, Putnam Berkley Audio) Putnam Publishing Group, The.
—The Cat Who Robbed a Bank. unabr. ed. 1999. (Cat Who Ser.). audio 29.95 (*0-7887-4032-6*, 96010 ) Recorded Bks., LLC.
—The Cat Who Saw Red. 1986. (Cat Who Ser.). 256p. mass mkt. 6.99 (*0-515-09016-6*); mass mkt. 2.95 o.s.i (*0-515-08491-3*) Berkley Publishing Group. (Jove).
—The Cat Who Saw Red. l.t. ed. 1989. 13.95 o.p. (*0-8161-4388-9*, Macmillan Reference USA) Gale Group.
—The Cat Who Saw Red. unabr. ed. 1990. (Cat Who Ser.). (YA). (gr. 10 up). audio 35.00 (*1-55690-093-7*, 90083E7) Recorded Bks., LLC.
—The Cat Who Saw Red. 1986. 13.04 (*0-606-13251-1*) Turtleback Bks.
—The Cat Who Smelled a Rat. 2001. (Cat Who. . . Ser.). (Illus.). 256p. 23.95 o.s.i (*0-399-14665-2*, G. P. Putnam's Sons) Penguin Group (USA) Inc.
—The Cat Who Sniffed Glue. 1989. (Cat Who Ser.). 288p. mass mkt. 6.99 (*0-515-09954-6*, Jove) Berkley Publishing Group.
—The Cat Who Sniffed Glue. unabr. ed. 2000. audio 44.00 (*1-55690-837-7*, 93205E7) Recorded Bks., LLC.
—The Cat Who Sniffed Glue. 1989. 13.04 (*0-606-13252-X*) Turtleback Bks.
—The Cat Who Talked to Ghosts. 1990. 224p. 15.95 o.p. (*0-399-13477-8*, G. P. Putnam's Sons) Penguin Putnam Bks. for Young Readers.
—The Cat Who Talked to Ghosts. unabr. ed. 1994. (Cat Who Ser.). audio 32.95 (*0-7887-0050-2*, 94249E7); audio 42.00 Recorded Bks., LLC.
—The Cat Who Talked to Ghosts. 1990. 13.04 (*0-606-13254-6*) Turtleback Bks.
—The Cat Who Wasn't There. l.t. ed. 1993. (General Ser.). 367p. 17.95 o.p. (*0-8161-5694-8*); lib. bdg. 21.95 (*0-8161-5693-X*) Gale Group. (Macmillan Reference USA).
—The Cat Who Wasn't There. abr. ed. (Super Sound Buy, Dove Ser.). 1994. audio 8.99 o.p. (*0-7871-0071-4*, 390494, Dove Audio); 1993. 16.95 o.p. (*1-55800-667-2*) NewStar Media, Inc.
—The Cat Who Wasn't There. 1993. 13.04 (*0-606-12649-X*) Turtleback Bks.
—The Cat Who Wasn't There; The Cat Who Blew the Whistle. abr. ed. 1999. audio 25.00 (*0-7871-1901-6*, Dove Audio) NewStar Media, Inc.
—The Cat Who Went into the Closet. l.t. ed. 1993. 24.95 o.p. (*1-56895-050-0*, Wheeler Publishing, Inc.) Gale Group.
—The Cat Who Went into the Closet. abr. ed. 1993. (Jim Qwilleran Mystery Ser.). audio 16.95 o.p. (*1-55800-785-7*, 390495) NewStar Media, Inc.
—The Cat Who Went into the Closet. 5.98 o.p. (*0-8317-5327-7*) Smithmark Pubs., Inc.
—The Cat Who Went Underground. unabr. ed. 2000. (Cat Who Ser.). audio 32.95 (*1-55690-803-2*, 93112) Recorded Bks., LLC.
—The Cat Who Went Underground. 1989. 13.04 (*0-606-13257-0*) Turtleback Bks.
—The Cat Who Went up the Creek. 2002. 240p. 23.95 o.s.i (*0-399-14675-X*) Penguin Group (USA) Inc.
—The Cat Who Went up the Creek. abr. ed. 2002. audio 17.95 o.s.i (*0-399-14819-1*, Putnam Berkley Audio) Putnam Publishing Group, The.
—El Gato Que Leia del Reves. 1997. Tr. of Cat Who Could Read Backwards. (SPA.). 248p. 14.58 (*84-01-47431-0*) Plaza & Janés Editories, S.A. ESP. *Dist:* Distribooks, Inc., Lectorum Pubns., Inc.
Briskin, Jacqueline. The Onyx. 1983. 512p. mass mkt. 5.99 o.s.i (*0-440-16667-5*); 1982. 448p. 15.95 o.s.i (*0-385-28762-3*, Delacorte Pr.) Dell Publishing.
—The Onyx. l.t. ed. 1995. (G. K. Hall Core Ser.). 739p. 24.95 (*0-7838-1133-0*, Macmillan Reference USA) Gale Group.
Cage, Gully. What? Another Northwoods Reader. 4th ed. 1987. 120p. pap. 10.95 o.p. (*0-932212-51-4*) Avery Color Studios, Inc.
Campbell, Bonnie Jo. Women & Other Animals: Stories. 1999. 208p. 27.50 (*1-55849-219-4*) Univ. of Massachusetts Pr.
Carl, Joanna. The Chocolate Cat Caper. 2002. 240p. mass mkt. 5.99 (*0-451-20556-1*, Signet Bks.) NAL.
—The Chocolate Cat Caper. l.t. ed. 2002. (Mystery Ser.). 328p. 28.95 (*0-7862-4405-4*) Thorndike Pr.
—The Chocolate Frog Frame-Up. 2003. 240p. mass mkt. 5.99 (*0-451-20985-0*, Signet Bks.) NAL.
Carthew, Annick H. Cadillac & the Dawn of Detroit. 2003. (Illus.). 278p. pap. 14.95 (*0-923568-38-7*) Wilderness Adventure Bks.
Cauffiel, Lowell. Marker. 1998. 330p. mass mkt. 6.50 o.p. (*0-312-96497-8*, St. Martin's Paperbacks); 1997. 320p. 23.95 (*0-312-15583-2*) St. Martin's Pr.
Chappel, Bernice M. Bittersweet Trail: An American Saga of the 1800's. 1985. (Illus.). 480p. 12.95 (*0-9606400-1-0*) Great Lakes Bks.
—Reap the Whirlwind. 1987. 408p. (Orig.). pap. 10.95 (*0-9611596-8-5*) Wilderness Adventure Bks.

Clark, Geoffrey. Jackdog Summer. 1996. 240p. pap. 15.00 (*1-57650-083-7*) Hi Jinx Pr.
—Schooling the Spirit: Stories. 1993. 208p. pap. 11.95 (*1-878580-36-1*) Asylum Arts.
Cleage, Pearl. I Wish I Had a Red Dress. l.t. ed. 2001. (Hardcover Ser.). 340p. 30.95 (*1-58724-062-9*, Wheeler Publishing, Inc.) Gale Group.
—I Wish I Had a Red Dress. 2001. 336p. 24.00 (*0-380-97733-8*, Morrow, William & Co.) Morrow/Avon.
—What Looks Like Crazy on an Ordinary Day. 256p. 1998. pap. 13.00 (*0-380-79487-X*, Avon Bks.); 1997. 20.00 (*0-380-97584-X*, Morrow, William & Co.) Morrow/Avon.
—What Looks Like Crazy on an Ordinary Day. l.t. ed. (Americana Ser.). 416p. 2000. pap. 26.95 (*0-7862-1760-X*); 1999. 29.95 (*0-7862-1759-6*) Thorndike Pr.
Coble, Colleen. Without a Trace. 2003. pap. 12.99 (*0-8499-4429-5*) W Publishing Group.
Cogan, Priscilla. Winona's Web. 1996. 280p. 21.00 o.p. (*1-883953-15-4*, Face to Face Bks.) Midwest Traditions, Inc.
Collins, Michael. The Resurrectionists. 2002. 304p. 24.00 (*0-7432-2904-5*, Scribner) Simon & Schuster.
Coughlin, William Jeremiah. Death Penalty. l.t. ed. 1993. pap. 22.95 o.p. (*0-7927-1541-1*); 22.95 o.p. (*0-7927-1542-X*) BBC Audiobooks America.
—Death Penalty. 1992. 304p. 20.00 o.p. (*0-06-017701-2*) HarperTrade.
—Death Penalty. 1993. 432p. mass mkt. 5.99 o.s.i (*0-06-109053-0*, HarperTorch) Morrow/Avon.
—The Judgement. abr. l.t. ed. 1995. 352p. lib. bdg. 27.00 incl. audio (*1-57490-025-0*, Beeler Large Print Bks.) Beeler, Thomas T. Publisher.
—The Judgement. 1999. mass mkt. 223.68 (*0-312-96877-9*); 1997. 352p. 24.95 o.p. (*0-312-15558-1*) St. Martin's Pr.
—The Judgment, Set. abr. ed. 1997. 25.00 o.p. (*0-7871-1505-3*, 695947) NewStar Media, Inc.
—The Judgment. 1999. E-Book 6.99 (*0-312-20724-7*); (Judgement Ser.: Vol. 1). 424p. mass mkt. 6.99 (*0-312-96244-4*, St. Martin's Paperbacks) St. Martin's Pr.
—Shadow of a Doubt. l.t. ed. 1992. (General Ser.). 562p. 18.95 (*0-8161-5346-9*); lib. bdg. 21.95 (*0-8161-5345-0*) Gale Group. (Macmillan Reference USA).
—Shadow of a Doubt. 1993. 407p. mass mkt. 6.99 (*0-312-92745-2*, St. Martin's Paperbacks); 1991. 19.95 o.p. (*0-312-05961-2*) St. Martin's Pr.
Cummings, Jean. Shinglebolt. unabr. ed. 2000. (Illus.). 129p. pap. 8.50 (*0-9679959-2-2*, 005) Rx Ranch Enterprises.
Damrell, Joseph. Billy Maki: A Novel. 1997. 256p. pap. 12.95 (*0-87839-118-5*) North Star Pr. of St. Cloud.
De Angeli, Marguerite. Copper-Toed Boots. 1989. (Great Lakes Bks.). (Illus.). 96p. (J). (gr. 4 up). reprint ed. 14.95 o.p. (*0-8143-1922-X*) Wayne State Univ. Pr.
Dereske, Jo. Cut & Dry. 1997. (Ruby Crane Mystery Ser.). 352p. mass mkt. 5.99 o.s.i (*0-440-22222-2*) Dell Publishing.
—Savage Cut. 1996. (Ruby Crane Mystery Ser.). 320p. mass mkt. 5.50 o.s.i (*0-440-22221-4*) Dell Publishing.
—Short Cut: A Ruby Crane Mystery. 1998. 336p. mass mkt. 5.99 o.s.i (*0-440-22223-0*) Dell Publishing.
Diamond, Rickey G. Second Sight. 2002. pap. 14.95 (*0-934971-80-3*) Calyx Bks.
—Second Sight: A Novel. 1999. 272p. 24.00 o.s.i (*0-06-019203-8*) HarperCollins Pubs.
Dilworth, Sharon. The Long White. 1990. pap. 7.95 o.p. (*0-393-30647-X*) Norton, W. W. & Co., Inc.
—The Long White. 1988. (Iowa Short Fiction Award Ser.). 204p. 10.00 (*0-87745-216-4*); E-Book 20.00 (*1-58729-050-2*) Univ. of Iowa Pr.
Dobyns, Stephen. The House on Alexandrine. 1990. 236p. (C). text 21.95 o.p. (*0-8143-2182-8*); pap. text 15.95 (*0-8143-2183-6*) Wayne State Univ. Pr.
Estleman, Loren D. Angel Eyes. abr. ed. 2001. audio (*1-58807-602-4*); 2000. audio 25.00 (*1-58807-045-X*) Americana Publishing, Inc.
—Angel Eyes. 1986. mass mkt. 3.95 o.s.i (*0-449-21134-7*, Fawcett) Ballantine Bks.
—Angel Eyes. unabr. ed. 1986. (Amos Walker Ser.). audio 19.95 o.p. (*0-930435-19-2*, 369, Bookcassette); audio 57.25 o.p. (*1-56100-014-0*, 551) Brilliance Audio.
—Angel Eyes. 1981. 11.95 o.p. (*0-395-31558-1*) Houghton Mifflin Co.
—Angel Eyes. 1984. 256p. pap. 2.75 o.p. (*0-523-42185-0*, Pinnacle Bks.) Kensington Publishing Corp.
—Angel Eyes. 2000. (Amos Walker Mysteries Ser.). 256p. reprint ed. pap. 14.00 (*0-671-03900-8*) ibooks, Inc.
—Any Man's Death. l.t. ed. 1990. (Magna Large Print Ser.). 310p. 29.99 o.p. (*1-85057-645-9*) Magna Large Print Bks. GBR. *Dist:* Ulverscroft Large Print Bks., Ltd., Ulverscroft Large Print Canada, Ltd.
—Any Man's Death. 1987. 224p. mass mkt. 3.95 o.s.i (*0-445-40588-0*, Mysterious Pr. Paperback Bks.) Warner Bks., Inc.
—Downriver. 1989. mass mkt. 3.95 o.s.i (*0-449-21623-3*, Fawcett) Ballantine Bks.
—Downriver, 001. 1988. 192p. 15.95 o.p. (*0-395-41073-8*) Houghton Mifflin Co.
—Edsel: A Novel of Detroit. 1995. 291p. 21.95 o.p. (*0-89296-552-5*) Mysterious Pr.
—Edsel: A Novel of Detroit. 1999. E-Book 4.95 (*0-446-92306-0*) Time Warner Bk. Group.
—Edsel: A Novel of Detroit. 1999. E-Book 4.95 (*0-446-91298-0*); 1996. 256p. reprint ed. mass mkt. 5.99 o.p. (*0-446-40366-0*) Warner Bks., Inc.
—Every Brilliant Eye. 1987. mass mkt. 4.95 o.s.i (*0-449-21137-1*, Fawcett) Ballantine Bks.
—Every Brilliant Eye. unabr. ed. 1986. (Amos Walker Ser.). audio 19.95 o.p. (*0-930435-26-5*, 378, Bookcassette) Brilliance Audio.
—Every Brilliant Eye. Howe, J. C., ed. unabr. ed. 1986. (Amos Walker Ser.). audio 57.25 o.p. (*1-56100-021-3*, 560) Brilliance Audio.
—Every Brilliant Eye, 001. 1986. 264p. 15.95 o.p. (*0-395-39428-7*) Houghton Mifflin Co.
—General Murders: Ten Amos Walker Mysteries. 1989. 192p. mass mkt. 3.95 o.s.i (*0-449-21696-9*, Fawcett) Ballantine Bks.
—General Murders: Ten Amos Walker Mysteries, 001. 1988. 256p. 16.95 o.p. (*0-395-41071-1*) Houghton Mifflin Co.
—General Murders: Ten Amos Walker Mysteries. l.t. ed. 1992. (Ulverscroft Large Print Ser.). 432p. 29.99 o.p. (*0-7089-2622-3*, Ulverscroft) Thorpe, F. A. Pubs. GBR. *Dist:* Ulverscroft Large Print Bks., Ltd., Ulverscroft Large Print Canada, Ltd.
—The Glass Highway. 1987. mass mkt. 3.95 o.s.i (*0-449-21136-3*, Fawcett) Ballantine Bks.
—The Glass Highway. unabr. ed. 1986. (Amos Walker Ser.). audio 57.25 o.p. (*1-56100-019-1*, 561) Brilliance Audio.
—The Glass Highway, 001. 1983. (Amos Walker Mysteries Ser.). 179p. 13.95 o.p. (*0-395-34636-3*) Houghton Mifflin Co.
—The Glass Highway. 1984. 224p. pap. 2.95 o.p. (*0-523-42263-6*, Pinnacle Bks.) Kensington Publishing Corp.
—The Glass Highway. E-Book 9.99 (*1-58824-389-3*); 2000. 240p. pap. 14.00 (*0-7434-0729-6*) ibooks, Inc.
—The Hours of the Virgin. abr. ed. 1999. (Amos Walker Ser.). audio 17.95 o.p. (*1-56740-847-8*, 1743, Nova Audio Bks.); 7p. audio 24.95 (*1-56740-437-5*, 1741, Bookcassette); audio 57.25 (*1-56740-663-7*, 1742, Unabridged Library Editions) Brilliance Audio.
—The Hours of the Virgin. 1999. (Amos Walker Mysteries Ser.). 288p. 23.00 (*0-89296-683-1*) Mysterious Pr.
—The Hours of the Virgin. 2000. 336p. (gr. 8 up). mass mkt. 6.99 (*0-446-60868-8*) Warner Bks., Inc.
—Jitterbug: A Novel of Detroit. unabr. ed. 1999. audio 69.95 (*0-7927-2264-7*, CSL153, Chivers Sound Library) BBC Audiobooks America.
—Jitterbug: A Novel of Detroit. 304p. 2000. mass mkt. 5.99 (*0-8125-4537-0*); 1998. 22.95 (*0-312-86360-8*) Doherty, Tom Assocs., LLC. (Forge Bks.).
—Jitterbug: A Novel of Detroit. unabr. ed. 1998. audio 60.00 (*0-7887-3120-3*, 95783E7) Recorded Bks., LLC.
—Kill Zone. l.t. ed. 1991. 23.95 o.p. (*0-7927-1027-4*, CH0167); pap. 21.95 o.p. (*0-7927-1028-2*, CS0268) BBC Audiobooks America.
—Kill Zone. 1986. mass mkt. 2.95 o.s.i (*0-449-12839-3*, Fawcett) Ballantine Bks.
—Kill Zone. 1986. 224p. 14.95 o.p. (*0-89296-065-5*) Mysterious Pr.
—King of the Corner. 1992. (Detroit Trilogy Ser.: No. 3). 304p. 20.00 o.s.i (*0-553-08926-9*) Bantam Bks.
—Lady Yesterday. 1988. 224p. mass mkt. 3.95 o.s.i (*0-449-21467-2*, Fawcett) Ballantine Bks.
—Lady Yesterday, 001. 1987. 15.95 o.p. (*0-395-41072-X*) Houghton Mifflin Co.
—The Midnight Man. 1987. mass mkt. 4.95 o.s.i (*0-449-21135-5*, Fawcett) Ballantine Bks.
—The Midnight Man. unabr. ed. 1986. (Amos Walker Ser.). audio 19.95 o.p. (*0-930435-18-4*, 370); audio 57.25 o.p. (*1-56100-013-2*, 552) Brilliance Audio.
—The Midnight Man, 001. 1982. 230p. 12.95 o.p. (*0-395-32204-9*) Houghton Mifflin Co.
—The Midnight Man. 1984. (Amos Walker Mysteries Ser.). 256p. pap. 2.95 o.p. (*0-523-42186-9*, Pinnacle Bks.) Kensington Publishing Corp.
—The Midnight Man. 2000. (Amos Walker Mysteries Ser.). 288p. pap. 14.00 (*0-7434-0002-X*) ibooks, Inc.
—Motor City Blue. 1986. mass mkt. 4.95 o.s.i (*0-449-21133-9*, Fawcett) Ballantine Bks.
—Motor City Blue, 001. 1980. 9.95 o.p. (*0-395-29447-9*) Houghton Mifflin Co.
—Never Street. abr. ed. (Amos Walker Mysteries Ser.). 1998. audio 7.99 o.p. (*1-56740-245-3*, 684, Paperback Nova Audio Bks.); 1997. audio 16.95 o.p. (*1-56100-934-2*, 1311, Nova Audio Bks.); 1997. audio 57.25 o.p. (*1-56100-823-0*, 961, Unabridged Library Editions); 1997. audio 23.95 o.p. (*1-56100-748-X*, 192, Bookcassette) Brilliance Audio.
—Never Street. l.t. ed. 1999. (Magna Large Print Ser.). 432p. (*0-7505-1448-5*) Magna Large Print Bks. GBR. *Dist:* Ulverscroft Large Print Canada, Ltd.
—Never Street. 1998. mass mkt. (*0-446-40483-7*, Mysterious Pr. Paperback Bks.); 1998. 352p. mass mkt. 6.99 (*0-446-60596-4*); 1997. 352p. 23.00 o.p. (*0-89296-633-5*) Warner Bks., Inc.
—Peeper. l.t. ed. 1991. 17.95 o.p. (*0-7451-8203-8*, AH0239); pap. 15.95 o.p. (*0-7927-0751-6*, AS0275) BBC Audiobooks America.
—Peeper. 1990. 224p. reprint ed. mass mkt. 4.99 o.s.i (*0-553-28605-6*) Bantam Bks.
—Poison Blonde: An Amos Walker Novel. 2003. (Amos Walker Ser.). 272p. 24.95 (*0-7653-0447-3*, Forge Bks.) Doherty, Tom Assocs., LLC.
—Roses Are Dead. l.t. ed. 1991. pap. 17.95 o.p. (*0-7927-0589-0*, CS045); 1990. 19.95 o.p. (*0-7927-0588-2*, C0582) BBC Audiobooks America.
—Roses Are Dead. 240p. 1987. pap. 3.95 o.s.i (*0-445-40574-0*); 1986. 15.95 (*0-89296-136-8*) Mysterious Pr.
—Silent Thunder. 1990. 224p. mass mkt. 4.95 o.s.i (*0-449-21854-6*, Fawcett) Ballantine Bks.
—Silent Thunder. l.t. ed. 1990. (Large Print Bks.). 286p. lib. bdg. 18.95 o.p. (*0-8161-4976-3*, Macmillan Reference USA) Gale Group.
—Silent Thunder, 001. 1989. 224p. 16.95 o.p. (*0-395-41074-6*) Houghton Mifflin Co.
—Silent Thunder. 2003. 240p. mass mkt. 6.99 (*0-7434-7480-5*) ibooks, Inc.
—A Smile on the Face of the Tiger. 2000. 304p. E-Book 14.95 (*0-446-92366-4*); 304p. E-Book 14.95 (*0-446-92250-1*); E-Book 14.95 (*0-446-93125-X*); 304p. 24.95 o.p. (*0-89296-706-4*) Mysterious Pr.
—A Smile on the Face of the Tiger. 2000. 304p. E-Book 14.95 (*0-446-92858-5*); E-Book 14.95 (*0-446-96087-X*); E-Book 14.95 (*0-446-91368-5*) Warner Bks., Inc.
—Stress: A Novel of Detroit. 1996. 82p. 21.95 (*0-89296-553-3*) Mysterious Pr.
—Stress: A Novel of Detroit. 1999. E-Book 4.95 (*0-446-92340-0*) Time Warner Bk. Group.
—Stress: A Novel of Detroit. 1999. E-Book 4.95 (*0-446-91299-9*); 1997. 256p. reprint ed. mass mkt. 5.99 o.p. (*0-446-40367-9*) Warner Bks., Inc.
—Sugartown. l.t. ed. 1985. lib. bdg. 16.95 o.p. (*0-89340-931-6*, 159) BBC Audiobooks America.
—Sugartown. l.t. ed. 1985. mass mkt. 4.99 o.s.i (*0-449-20998-9*, Fawcett) Ballantine Bks.
—Sugartown. unabr. ed. 1986. (Amos Walker Ser.). audio 15.95 o.p. (*0-930435-25-7*, 380, Bookcassette); audio 57.25 o.p. (*1-56100-020-5*, 562) Brilliance Audio.
—Sugartown. 1984. 220p. 13.95 o.p. (*0-395-36449-3*) Houghton Mifflin Co.
—Sugartown. 1984. 220p. 25.00 (*0-89366-256-9*) Ultramarine Publishing Co., Inc.
—Sugartown. E-Book 9.99 (*1-58824-394-X*); 2001. 256p. pap. 14.00 (*0-7434-1293-1*) ibooks, Inc.
—Sweet Women Lie. 1991. mass mkt. 4.99 o.s.i (*0-449-21944-5*, Fawcett) Ballantine Bks.
—Sweet Women Lie. 1990. (Amos Walker Mysteries Ser.). 208p. 18.95 o.p. (*0-395-53767-3*) Houghton Mifflin Co.
—Thunder City: A Novel of Detroit. 2001. 245p. mass mkt. 6.99 (*0-8125-4538-9*); 1999. 256p. 22.95 (*0-312-86369-1*) Doherty, Tom Assocs., LLC. (Forge Bks.).
—The Witchfinder. abr. ed. (Amos Walker Mysteries Ser.). 1999. audio 7.99 o.s.i (*1-56740-292-5*, 1753, Paperback Nova Audio Bks.); 1998. audio 24.95 (*1-56740-052-3*, 7, Bookcassette); 1998. audio 57.25 (*1-56740-581-9*, 1101, Unabridged Library Editions); Set. 1998. audio 17.95 o.p. (*1-56740-778-1*, 440, Nova Audio Bks.) Brilliance Audio.
—The Witchfinder. 1998. (Amos Walker Mysteries Ser.). 320p. 23.00 o.p. (*0-89296-663-7*) Mysterious Pr.
—The Witchfinder. l.t. ed. 1998. (Cloak & Dagger Ser.). 408p. 27.95 (*0-7862-1509-7*) Thorndike Pr.
—The Witchfinder. l.t. ed. 2000. (Ulverscroft Large Print Ser.). 416p. 31.99 (*0-7089-4252-0*, Ulverscroft) Thorpe, F. A. Pubs. GBR. *Dist:* Ulverscroft Large Print Bks., Ltd., Ulverscroft Large Print Canada, Ltd.
—The Witchfinder. 1999. E-Book 4.95 (*0-446-92328-1*) Time Warner Bk. Group.
—The Witchfinder. 1999. 320p. mass mkt. 6.50 (*0-446-60760-6*); E-Book 4.95 (*0-446-91300-6*) Warner Bks., Inc.
Ford, Bette. After Dark. 1997. (Arabesque Ser.). 316p. mass mkt. 5.99 (*1-58314-175-8*) Kensington Publishing Corp.
Ford, R. Clyde. A Tale of the Mackinaw Fur Trade: Sandy MacDonald's Man. 3rd ed. 1985. (Illus.). pap. 9.95 o.p. (*0-932212-41-7*) Avery Color Studios, Inc.
Fuller, Iola. Loon Feather. 1967. 468p. pap. 14.00 (*0-15-653200-X*, Harvest Bks.); 1940. 9.50 o.p. (*0-15-153201-X*) Harcourt Trade Pubs.
Gaffer, Willie. No-Count-Charlie. 2002. (Illus.). iv, 234p. text 24.95 (*0-9653732-5-8*) Wesoomi Publishing.
Gaffney, Patricia. Wild at Heart. 1997. 384p. mass mkt. 5.99 o.s.i (*0-451-40536-6*, Onyx) NAL.
Gage, Cully. Heads & Tales. 6th ed. 1982. (Northwoods Reader Ser.). (Illus.). pap. 10.95 o.p. (*0-932212-28-X*) Avery Color Studios, Inc.
—The Northwoods Reader, 3 vols. 2001. 320p. pap. 16.95 (*1-892384-08-6*); 11th ed. 1990. (Illus.). pap. 10.95 o.p. (*0-932212-11-5*) Avery Color Studios, Inc.
—Old Bones & Northern Memories, No. 7. 2nd ed. 1991. (Northwoods Reader Ser.). pap. 10.95 (*0-932212-70-0*) Avery Color Studios, Inc.
—Still Another Northwoods Reader, No. 6. 4th ed. 1990. pap. 10.95 (*0-932212-61-1*) Avery Color Studios, Inc.
—Tales of the Old U. P. A Second Northwoods Reader. 9th ed. 1981. (Illus.). pap. 10.95 (*0-932212-23-9*) Avery Color Studios, Inc.
Gamble, Terry. Water Dancers. 2004. pap. 12.95 (*0-06-054267-5*, Perennial) HarperTrade.
Gerber, Dan. Grass Fires. 1989. (Illus.). 176p. (Orig.). reprint ed. pap. 11.95 o.s.i (*0-944439-09-8*) Clark City Pr.
—Grass Fires. 1987. 232p. (Orig.). pap. 9.95 (*0-916947-09-2*) Winn Bks.
—Grass Fires: Stories. 2nd ed. 2003. 185p. reprint ed. pap. 19.95 (*0-87013-682-8*) Michigan State Univ. Pr.
Gilmore, Monique. The Grass Ain't Greener. l.t. ed. 1996. 320p. mass mkt. 4.99 o.s.i (*0-7860-0318-9*, Pinnacle Bks.) Kensington Publishing Corp.
—The Grass Ain't Greener. l.t. ed. 1999. (Romance Ser.). 360p. 27.95 (*0-7838-8508-3*) Thorndike Pr.
Gosling, Paula. The Body in Blackwater Bay. 1992. 304p. 17.95 (*0-89296-459-6*) Mysterious Pr.
—The Body in Blackwater Bay. 1993. 288p. mass mkt. 4.99 o.s.i (*0-446-40319-9*) Warner Bks., Inc.
—The Dead of Winter. 1997. 316p. mass mkt. o.s.i (*0-7515-1678-3*); 1995. 320p. o.s.i (*0-316-91238-7*) Little Brown & Co.
—The Dead of Winter. 1996. 82p. 21.95 o.p. (*0-89296-511-8*) Mysterious Pr.
—The Dead of Winter. 1997. 304p. mass mkt. 5.99 (*0-446-40499-3*) Warner Bks., Inc.
—A Few Dying Words. l.t. ed. 1994. 460p. pap. 19.95 (*0-8161-7482-2*, Macmillan Reference USA) Gale Group.
—A Few Dying Words. 1994. 352p. 18.95 o.s.i (*0-89296-510-X*) Mysterious Pr.
—A Few Dying Words. 1996. 320p. mass mkt. 5.99 o.s.i (*0-446-40460-8*) Warner Bks., Inc.
Gray, Victoria. Victoria Zane. 2001. 157p. pap. 9.95 (*0-9711675-0-8*) Pro-Q Publishing.
Greene, Jennifer. The Woman Most Likely To... l.t. ed. 2002. (Large Print Ser.). 29.95 (*1-57490-456-6*) Beeler, Thomas T. Publisher.
—The Woman Most Likely To... 2002. 384p. mass mkt. 6.99 (*0-380-81972-4*, Avon Bks.) Morrow/Avon.
Guest, Judith. Errands. 1997. 366p. mass mkt. 7.50 o.s.i (*0-345-40905-1*) Ballantine Bks.
Hall, J. P. Beneath the Surface: A Journal of Life & Love During the Great Copper Strike of 1913. 2001. (Illus.). 102p. 13.95 (*0-9712148-0-8*) P.I.A., Inc., Petticoat Pr.
Hamilton, Steve. Blood Is the Sky: An Alex McKnight Mystery. 2003. 304p. 21.95 (*0-312-30115-4*, Saint Martin's Minotaur) St. Martin's Pr.
—A Cold Day in Paradise. l.t. ed. 2001. 354p. lib. bdg. 28.95 (*1-58547-136-4*) Ctr. Point Large Print.
—A Cold Day in Paradise. (Alex McKnight Mysteries Ser.). 2000. 320p. mass mkt. 6.99 (*0-312-96919-8*, St. Martin's Paperbacks); 1998. 288p. 22.95 (*0-312-19248-7*, Saint Martin's Minotaur) St. Martin's Pr.
—A Cold Day in Paradise: A Mystery, Set. unabr. ed. 1999. (Chivers Sound Library American Collections). audio 54.95 (*0-7927-2326-0*, CSL 215, Chivers Sound Library) BBC Audiobooks America.
—North of Nowhere: An Alex McKnight Mystery. 2003. 352p. mass mkt. 6.99 (*0-312-98381-6*, St. Martin's Paperbacks); 2002. 288p. 23.95 (*0-312-26897-1*, Saint Martin's Minotaur) St. Martin's Pr.
—Southpaw Spring. 2002. 352p. mass mkt. 6.99 (*0-312-98026-4*, St. Martin's Paperbacks); 2001. 306p. 23.95 (*0-312-26894-7*, Saint Martin's Minotaur) St. Martin's Pr.
—Winter of the Wolf Moon. E-Book 6.50 (*0-312-27360-6*) St. Martin's Pr.

—Winter of the Wolf Moon: An Alex McKnight Mystery. 2000. (Alex McKnight Mysteries Ser.). 274p. 23.95 (*0-312-25295-1*, Saint Martin's Minotaur) St. Martin's Pr.

Hardwick, Gary. Cold Medina. 1996. 352p. 22.95 o.p. (*0-525-93919-9*) Dutton/Plume.

—Double Dead. 1997. 368p. 23.95 o.s.i (*0-525-93920-2*) Dutton/Plume.

—Double Dead. 1998. 400p. mass mkt. 6.99 o.s.i (*0-451-18276-6*, Onyx) NAL.

—Supreme Justice: A Novel of Suspense. 1999. 368p. 24.00 (*0-688-16513-3*, Morrow, William & Co.) Morrow/Avon.

Harju, Jerry. Northern D'Lights. 1994. (Illus.). pap. 12.95 o.p. (*0-932212-81-6*) Avery Color Studios, Inc.

—Northern Reflections. 3rd ed. 1993. (Illus.). 128p. pap. 12.95 o.p. (*0-932212-75-1*) Avery Color Studios, Inc.

Harris, Anne. The Nature of Smoke. 1997. 288p. pap. 13.95 (*0-312-86351-9*); 1996. 256p. 22.95 o.p. (*0-312-85286-X*) Doherty, Tom Assocs., LLC. (Tor Bks.).

Harrison, Jim. Wolf: A False Memoir. 1971. 15.00 o.p. (*0-671-21057-2*) Ultramarine Publishing Co., Inc.

Hart, Craig. Street Smart. 2003. 144p. per. 6.95 (*1-59196-220-X*) Instantpublisher.com.

Hartmann, Elizabeth. The Truth about Fire. 2002. 240p. 24.00 (*0-7867-1021-7*, Carroll & Graf Pubs.) Avalon Publishing Group.

Heywood, Joseph. Ice Hunter: A Grady Service Mystery. 2001. 308p. 24.95 (*1-58574-225-2*, Lyons Pr.) Globe Pequot Pr., The.

Hoff, B. J. The Captive Voice. unabr. ed. 1998. (Daybreak Mystery Ser.: Bk. 2). audio 39.95 (*1-55686-835-9*) Books in Motion.

—The Captive Voice. l.t. ed. 1998. (Christian Mystery Ser.). 279p. 23.95 o.p. (*0-7862-1411-2*) Thorndike Pr.

—The Captive Voice. 1996. (Daybreak Mysteries Ser.: Vol. 2). 187p. pap. 8.99 o.p. (*0-8423-7193-1*) Tyndale Hse. Pubs.

Holden, Craig. The River Sorrow. 1995. 432p. mass mkt. 5.99 o.s.i (*0-440-21730-X*) Dell Publishing.

—The River Sorrow. l.t. ed. 1994. 491p. lib. bdg. 24.95 (*0-7838-1168-3*, Macmillan Reference USA) Gale Group.

Holtzer, Susan. Better Than Sex. 240p. 2002. mass mkt. 6.50 (*0-312-98005-1*, St. Martin's Paperbacks); 2001. 22.95 (*0-312-25345-1*, Saint Martin's Minotaur) St. Martin's Pr.

—Black Diamond. 1998. (Dead Letter Mysteries Ser.). 336p. mass mkt. 5.99 (*0-312-96629-6*, St. Martin's Paperbacks) St. Martin's Pr.

—Black Diamond: An Anneke Haagen Mystery. 1997. 272p. text 21.95 o.p. (*0-312-17174-9*, Saint Martin's Minotaur) St. Martin's Pr.

—Bleeding Maize & Blue. 304p. 1996. text 22.95 o.p. (*0-312-14552-7*, Saint Martin's Minotaur); Vol. 1. 1997. mass mkt. 5.99 (*0-312-96284-3*, St. Martin's Paperbacks) St. Martin's Pr.

—Curly Smoke: An Anneke Haagen Mystery. (Anneke Haagen Mystery Ser.). 1996. 213p. mass mkt. 5.99 o.s.i (*0-312-95943-5*, St. Martin's Paperbacks); 1995. 256p. 20.95 o.p. (*0-312-13458-4*, Saint Martin's Minotaur) St. Martin's Pr.

—The Silly Season: A Mystery at the University of Michigan. 2000. 288p. mass mkt. 5.99 (*0-312-97039-0*, St. Martin's Paperbacks) St. Martin's Pr.

—The Silly Season: An Entr'acte. 1998. 272p. 22.95 o.p. (*0-312-20010-2*, Saint Martin's Minotaur) St. Martin's Pr.

—Something to Kill For. 1995. 242p. mass mkt. 5.99 (*0-312-95589-8*, St. Martin's Paperbacks); 1994. 240p. 19.95 o.p. (*0-312-11117-7*, Saint Martin's Minotaur) St. Martin's Pr.

—Wedding Game: A Mystery at the University of Michigan. 2000. ix, 275p. (YA). 23.95 (*0-312-25228-5*, Saint Martin's Minotaur) St. Martin's Pr.

Howard, Ellen. The Log Cabin Church. 2002. (Illus.). (J). (gr. k-3). tchr. ed. 16.95 (*0-8234-1740-9*) Holiday Hse., Inc.

Howard, Linda. Mr. Perfect. l.t. ed. 2000. (Large Print Book Ser.). 401p. 28.95 (*1-56895-929-X*, Wheeler Publishing, Inc.) Gale Group.

—Mr. Perfect. 2000. (Illus.). 352p. 24.95 (*0-671-03406-5*, Atria) Simon & Schuster.

Jackson, Jon A. The Blind Pig. 2001. (Detective Sergeant Mullheisen Mysteries Ser.). 228p. pap. 12.00 (*0-8021-3706-7*) Grove/Atlantic, Inc.

—The Blind Pig. 1988. (Modern Hard-Boiled Detective Ser.). 228p. reprint ed. pap. 7.95 o.p. (*0-939767-07-4*) McMillan, Dennis Pubns.

—The Blind Pig. 1979. 7.95 o.p. (*0-394-42613-4*) Random Hse., Inc.

—The Blind Pig. 1988. 228p. pap. 6.95 (*0-89366-275-5*) Ultramarine Publishing Co., Inc.

—The Blind Pig: A Detective Sergeant Mulheisen Novel. 1995. 288p. mass mkt. 4.99 o.s.i (*0-440-21714-8*) Dell Publishing.

—Dead Folks: A Detective Sergeant Mulheisen Mystery. 1996. 272p. 22.00 o.p. (*0-87113-638-4*, Atlantic Monthly Pr.) Grove/Atlantic, Inc.

—Dead Folks: A Detective Sergeant Mullheisen Mystery. 2001. (Detective Sergeant Mullheisen Mysteries Ser.). 264p. reprint ed. pap. 12.00 (*0-8021-3602-8*) Grove/Atlantic, Inc.

—Deadman. 1994. 272p. 20.00 o.p. (*0-87113-562-0*, Atlantic Monthly Pr.) Grove/Atlantic, Inc.

—Deadman: A Detective Sergeant Mulheisen Novel. 1995. 304p. mass mkt. 4.99 o.s.i (*0-440-22047-5*) Dell Publishing.

—The Die Hard. 2001. (Detective Sergeant Mullheisen Mysteries Ser.). 215p. pap. 12.00 (*0-8021-3707-5*) Grove/Atlantic, Inc.

—The Diehard. 1977. 6.95 o.p. (*0-394-41030-0*) Random Hse., Inc.

—The Diehard: A Detective Sergeant Mulheisen Novel. 1995. 272p. mass mkt. 4.99 o.s.i (*0-440-21717-2*) Dell Publishing.

—Grootka. 1990. 352p. 19.95 o.p. (*0-88150-179-4*) Countryman Pr.

—Grootka. 1992. 352p. mass mkt. 4.99 o.s.i (*0-440-21151-4*) Dell Publishing.

—Hit on the House. 1995. 304p. mass mkt. 4.99 o.s.i (*0-440-21711-3*) Dell Publishing.

—Hit on the House. (Detective Sergeant Mullheisen Mysteries Ser.). 2001. 256p. pap. 12.00 (*0-8021-3705-9*); 1993. 237p. 20.00 o.p. (*0-87113-495-0*) Grove/Atlantic, Inc.

Johnston, Donald. The Echoes of L'Arbre Croche. 2nd ed. 1996. 326p. 24.95 (*0-9647139-0-X*) Lord & Allerton.

Kakonis, Tom. Criss Cross. 336p. 1991. mass mkt. 4.99 o.p. (*0-312-92624-3*, St. Martin's Paperbacks); 1989. 18.95 o.p. (*0-312-03728-7*) St. Martin's Pr.

—Michigan Roll. 1988. 288p. 16.95 o.p. (*0-312-02252-2*) St. Martin's Pr.

Kaminsky, Stuart M. Not Quite Kosher. E-Book 23.95 (*0-312-70934-X*, Tor Bks.); 2003. 256p. mass mkt. 6.99 (*0-8125-6190-2*, Forge Bks.) Doherty, Tom Assocs., LLC.

—Not Quite Kosher. 2003. (Abe Lieberman Mystery Ser.). 327p. 29.95 (*0-7862-5398-3*) Thorndike Pr.

Kienzle, William X. Assault with Intent. 1987. (Father Koesler Mystery Ser.: No. 4). 273p. 9.95 o.p. (*0-8362-6117-8*) Andrews McMeel Publishing.

—Assault with Intent. 1985. (Father Koesler Mystery Ser.: No. 4). 320p. mass mkt. 5.99 o.s.i (*0-345-33283-0*); 1983. mass mkt. 2.95 o.p. (*0-345-30812-3*) Ballantine Bks.

—Assault with Intent. unabr. collector's ed. 1997. (Father Koesler Mystery Ser.). audio 56.00 (*0-7366-3994-2*, 4459) Books on Tape, Inc.

—Bishop As Pawn. 1994. (Father Koesler Mystery Ser.: No. 16). xiii, 266p. 18.95 o.p. (*0-8362-6130-5*) Andrews McMeel Publishing.

—Bishop As Pawn. 1995. (Father Koesler Mystery Ser.: No. 16). mass mkt. 5.99 o.s.i (*0-345-38800-3*) Ballantine Bks.

—Body Count. 1992. (Father Koesler Mystery Ser.: No. 14). viii, 266p. 18.95 o.p. (*0-8362-6128-3*) Andrews McMeel Publishing.

—Body Count. 1993. (Father Koesler Mystery Ser.: No. 14). reprint ed. mass mkt. 5.99 o.s.i (*0-345-37767-2*) Ballantine Bks.

—Call No Man Father. 1995. (Father Koesler Mystery Ser.: No. 17). 272p. 18.95 o.p. (*0-8362-6131-3*) Andrews McMeel Publishing.

—Call No Man Father. 1996. (Father Koesler Mystery Ser.: No. 17). mass mkt. 5.99 o.s.i (*0-345-38801-1*) Ballantine Bks.

—Chameleon. 1991. (Father Koesler Mystery Ser.: No. 13). 289p. pap. 16.95 o.p. (*0-8362-6127-5*) Andrews McMeel Publishing.

—Chameleon. 1992. (Father Koesler Mystery Ser.: No. 13). mass mkt. 5.99 o.s.i (*0-345-36621-2*) Ballantine Bks.

—Dead Wrong. 1993. (Father Koesler Mystery Ser.: No. 15). 269p. 18.95 o.p. (*0-8362-6129-1*) Andrews McMeel Publishing.

—Dead Wrong. 1994. (Father Koesler Mystery Ser.: No. 15). mass mkt. 5.99 o.s.i (*0-345-37766-4*) Ballantine Bks.

—Deadline for a Critic. 1987. (Father Koesler Mystery Ser.: No. 9). 263p. 14.95 o.p. (*0-8362-6123-2*) Andrews McMeel Publishing.

—Deadline for a Critic. 1988. (Father Koesler Mystery Ser.: No. 9). 352p. mass mkt. 5.99 o.s.i (*0-345-33190-7*) Ballantine Bks.

—Deadline for a Critic. 1990. (Father Koesler Mystery Ser.: No. 9). 2.99 o.p. (*0-517-05975-4*) Random Hse. Value Publishing.

—Death Bed. 1987. (Father Koesler Mystery Ser.: No. 8). mass mkt. 5.99 o.s.i (*0-345-33189-3*) Ballantine Bks.

—Death Wears a Red Hat. 1980. (Father Koesler Mystery Ser.: No. 2). 304p. 9.95 o.p. (*0-8362-6111-9*) Andrews McMeel Publishing.

—Death Wears a Red Hat. 1989. (Father Koesler Mystery Ser.: No. 2). mass mkt. 5.99 o.s.i (*0-345-35669-1*) Ballantine Bks.

—Death Wears a Red Hat. 1981. (Father Koesler Mystery Ser.: No. 2). 288p. pap. 3.50 o.p. (*0-553-26524-5*) Bantam Bks.

—Death Wears a Red Hat. unabr. collector's ed. 1997. (Father Koesler Mystery Ser.). audio 56.00 (*0-7366-4063-0*, 4574) Books on Tape, Inc.

—Death Wears a Red Hat. l.t. ed. 1981. (Father Koesler Mystery Ser.: No. 2). 553p. 29.99 o.p. (*0-7089-0647-8*, Ulverscroft) Thorpe, F. A. Pubs. GBR. *Dist:* Ulverscroft Large Print Bks., Ltd., Ulverscroft Large Print Canada, Ltd.

—Deathbed. 1985. (Father Koesler Mystery Ser.: No. 8). 258p. 14.95 o.p. (*0-8362-6122-4*) Andrews McMeel Publishing.

—Eminence. 1989. (Father Koesler Mystery Ser.: No. 11). 312p. 15.95 o.p. (*0-8362-6125-9*) Andrews McMeel Publishing.

—Eminence. 1990. (Father Koesler Mystery Ser.: No. 11). 368p. mass mkt. 5.99 o.s.i (*0-345-35395-1*) Ballantine Bks.

—Eminence. 1990. 3.99 o.p. (*0-517-05976-2*) Random Hse. Value Publishing.

—The Gathering. 2002. 288p. 22.95 (*0-7407-2229-8*) Andrews McMeel Publishing.

—The Gathering. 2003. 304p. mass mkt. 6.99 (*0-345-45794-3*, Fawcett) Ballantine Bks.

—The Greatest Evil. 1998. (Father Koesler Mystery Ser.: No. 20). vii, 278p. 19.95 o.p. (*0-8362-5206-3*) Andrews McMeel Publishing.

—The Greatest Evil. 1999. (Father Koesler Mystery Ser.: No. 20). 294p. mass mkt. 6.99 (*0-345-42638-X*) Ballantine Bks.

—The Greatest Evil. unabr. collector's ed. 1998. (Father Koesler Mystery Ser.). audio 56.00 (*0-7366-4529-2*, 4720) Books on Tape, Inc.

—Kill & Tell. 1984. (Father Koesler Mystery Ser.: No. 6). 250p. 12.95 o.p. (*0-8362-6120-8*) Andrews McMeel Publishing.

—Kill & Tell. 1985. (Father Koesler Mystery Ser.: No. 6). mass mkt. 5.99 o.s.i (*0-345-31856-0*) Ballantine Bks.

—Kill & Tell. l.t. ed. 1984. (Father Koesler Mystery Ser.: No. 6). 378p. 15.95 o.p. (*0-8161-3779-X*, Macmillan Reference USA) Gale Group.

—The Man Who Loved God. 1997. (Father Koesler Mystery Ser.: No. 19). 274p. 19.95 (*0-8362-2754-9*) Andrews McMeel Publishing.

—The Man Who Loved God. 1998. (Father Koesler Mystery Ser.: No. 19). 304p. mass mkt. 6.99 o.s.i (*0-345-40290-1*) Ballantine Bks.

—Marked for Murder. 1988. (Father Koesler Mystery Ser.: No. 10). 281p. 14.95 o.p. (*0-8362-6124-0*) Andrews McMeel Publishing.

—Marked for Murder. 1989. (Father Koesler Mystery Ser.: No. 10). mass mkt. 5.99 o.s.i (*0-345-35397-8*) Ballantine Bks.

—Masquerade. 1990. (Father Koesler Mystery Ser.: No. 12). 267p. 15.95 o.p. (*0-8362-6126-7*) Andrews McMeel Publishing.

—Masquerade. 1991. (Father Koesler Mystery Ser.: No. 12). 384p. mass mkt. 5.99 o.s.i (*0-345-36620-4*) Ballantine Bks.

—Mind over Murder. 1981. (Father Koesler Mystery Ser.: No. 3). v, 296p. 9.95 o.p. (*0-8362-6114-3*) Andrews McMeel Publishing.

—Mind over Murder. 1989. (Father Koesler Mystery Ser.: No. 3). mass mkt. 5.99 o.s.i (*0-345-35667-5*) Ballantine Bks.

—Mind over Murder. 1982. (Father Koesler Mystery Ser.: No. 3). pap. 3.50 o.p. (*0-553-25008-6*) Bantam Bks.

—Mind over Murder. unabr. collector's ed. 1997. (Father Koesler Mystery Ser.). audio 64.00 (*0-7366-4064-9*, 4575) Books on Tape, Inc.

—No Greater Love. 1999. (Father Koesler Mystery Ser.: No. 21). 292p. 19.95 o.p. (*0-8362-7865-8*) Andrews McMeel Publishing.

—No Greater Love. 2000. (Father Koesler Mystery Ser.). 304p. mass mkt. 6.99 (*0-345-42639-8*, Fawcett) Ballantine Bks.

—Requiem for Moses. 1996. (Father Koesler Mystery Ser.: No. 18). 272p. 19.95 o.p. (*0-8362-1042-5*) Andrews McMeel Publishing.

—Requiem for Moses. 1997. (Father Koesler Mystery Ser.: No. 19). 322p. mass mkt. 5.99 o.s.i (*0-345-40291-X*) Ballantine Bks.

—The Rosary Murders. 1979. (Father Koesler Mystery Ser.: No. 1). 257p. 9.95 o.p. (*0-8362-6101-1*) Andrews McMeel Publishing.

—The Rosary Murders. 1989. (Father Koesler Mystery Ser.: No. 1). 304p. mass mkt. 5.99 o.s.i (*0-345-35668-3*) Ballantine Bks.

—The Rosary Murders. 1984. mass mkt. 3.50 o.s.i (*0-553-25084-1*); 1980. (Father Koesler Mystery Ser.: No. 1). 304p. mass mkt. 3.50 o.s.i (*0-553-26406-0*) Bantam Bks.

—Shadow of Death. 1983. (Father Koesler Mystery Ser.: No. 5). 252p. 10.95 o.p. (*0-8362-6119-4*) Andrews McMeel Publishing.

—Shadow of Death. (Father Koesler Mystery Ser.: No. 5). 1985. mass mkt. 5.99 o.s.i (*0-345-33110-9*); 1984. mass mkt. 2.95 o.p. (*0-345-31251-1*) Ballantine Bks.

—Shadow of Death. unabr. collector's ed. 1999. (Father Koesler Mystery Ser.). audio 56.00 (*0-7366-4330-3*, 4824) Books on Tape, Inc.

—Shadow of Death. l.t. ed. 1983. (Father Koesler Mystery Ser.: No. 5). lib. bdg. 16.95 o.p. (*0-8161-3582-7*, Macmillan Reference USA) Gale Group.

—Sudden Death. 1985. (Father Koesler Mystery Ser.: No. 7). 257p. 12.95 o.p. (*0-8362-6121-6*) Andrews McMeel Publishing.

—Sudden Death. 1986. (Father Koesler Mystery Ser.: No. 7). mass mkt. 5.99 o.s.i (*0-345-32851-5*) Ballantine Bks.

—Sudden Death. l.t. ed. 1986. (Father Koesler Mystery Ser.: No. 7). 416p. 16.95 o.p. (*0-8161-3965-2*, Macmillan Reference USA) Gale Group.

—Till Death. 2000. 279p. 19.95 (*0-7407-0489-3*) Andrews McMeel Publishing.

Kinkopf, Eric. Shooter. 1993. 288p. 21.95 o.p. (*0-399-13772-6*, G. P. Putnam's Sons) Penguin Group (USA) Inc.

Kirkland, Caroline M. A New Home, Who'll Follow? Zagarell, Sandra A., ed. 1990. (American Women Writers Ser.). 250p. (C). text 40.00 (*0-8135-1541-6*); pap. text 16.00 (*0-8135-1542-4*) Rutgers Univ. Pr.

Labiner, Norah. Our Sometime Sister. 1998. 452p. 22.95 (*1-56689-072-1*) Coffee Hse. Pr.

Langille, J. H. Snail-Shell Harbor. 2001. (Bigwater Classics Ser.: Vol. 3). (Illus.). 288p. reprint ed. pap. 14.95 (*0-923048-52-9*) Bigwater Publishing.

Lasser, Scott. Battle Creek: A Novel. 2000. 288p. pap. 14.00 (*0-688-17763-8*, Perennial) HarperTrade.

—Battle Creek: A Novel. 1999. 265p. 24.00 o.p. (*0-688-16785-3*, Morrow, William & Co.) Morrow/Avon.

Latreille, Stan. Perjury. 1999. 384p. reprint ed. mass mkt. 6.99 o.s.i (*0-451-19687-2*, Onyx) NAL.

Lenzo, Lisa. Within the Lighted City. 1997. (John Simmons Short Fiction Award Ser.). 112p. 19.95 (*0-87745-611-9*); E-Book 19.95 (*1-58729-134-7*) Univ. of Iowa Pr.

Leonard, Elmore. City Primeval: High Noon in Detroit. l.t. ed. 1986. (General Ser.). 350p. 16.95 o.p. (*0-8161-3948-2*, Macmillan Reference USA) Gale Group.

—City Primeval: High Noon in Detroit. 1980. 10.95 o.p. (*0-87795-282-5*, Morrow, William & Co.) Morrow/Avon.

—Freaky Deaky. unabr. collector's ed. 1997. audio 48.00 (*0-7366-3606-4*, 4260) Books on Tape, Inc.

—Freaky Deaky. unabr. ed. 2000. audio 59.95 (*1-56054-962-9*, SAB 016) Chivers Audio Bks. GBR. *Dist:* BBC Audiobooks America.

—Freaky Deaky. abr. ed. 1988. audio 16.99 (*0-88646-232-0*, LFP 7232) Durkin Hayes Publishing Ltd.

—Freaky Deaky. l.t. ed. 1989. 376p. 20.95 o.p. (*0-8161-4708-6*, Macmillan Reference USA) Gale Group.

—Freaky Deaky. 1998. 320p. pap. 12.00 (*0-688-16096-4*, Quill) HarperTrade.

—Freaky Deaky. 2002. 448p. mass mkt. 7.50 (*0-06-008955-5*); 1988. 18.95 o.p. (*0-87795-975-7*, Morrow, William & Co.) Morrow/Avon.

—Freaky Deaky. 1990. 4.99 o.p. (*0-517-03358-5*) Random Hse. Value Publishing.

—Freaky Deaky, unabr. ed. 1995. audio 51.00 (*0-7887-0324-2*, 94516E7) Recorded Bks., LLC.

—Freaky Deaky. 1989. mass mkt. 5.95 (*0-446-35039-7*) Warner Bks., Inc.

—Out of Sight. 1998. 304p. pap. 9.95 o.s.i (*0-385-33291-2*, 892924Q, Delta); 1997. 352p. mass mkt. 6.99 o.s.i (*0-440-21442-4*) Dell Publishing.

—Out of Sight. l.t. ed. 1996. 27.95 (*1-56895-385-2*, Wheeler Publishing, Inc.) Gale Group.

—Out of Sight: International Edition. 1997. mass mkt. 6.50 (*0-440-29553-X*) Dell Publishing.

—Pagan Babies. abr. ed. 2000. audio 25.95 o.s.i (*0-553-52751-7*, RH Audio) Random Hse. Audio Publishing Group.

—Pagan Babies. l.t. ed. 2000. 352p. 24.95 o.s.i (*0-375-43086-5*) Random Hse. Large Print.

—Swag. unabr. collector's ed. 1996. audio 42.00 (*0-7366-3234-4*, 3895) Books on Tape, Inc.

—Swag. l.t. ed. 2000. 279p. lib. bdg. 28.95 (*1-58547-041-4*) Ctr. Point Large Print.

—Swag. 240p. 1978. mass mkt. 6.99 o.s.i (*0-440-18424-X*); 1976. pap. 7.95 o.s.i (*0-440-08449-0*, Delacorte Pr.) Dell Publishing.

—Swag, Set. abr. ed. 1987. audio 16.99 (*0-88646-221-5*, 7221) Durkin Hayes Publishing Ltd.

—Swag, unabr. ed. 1997. audio 44.00 (*0-7887-0502-4*, 94698E7) Recorded Bks., LLC.

—Unknown Man, No. 89. 1977. 8.95 o.s.i (*0-440-09216-7*, Delacorte Pr.) Dell Publishing.

—Unknown Man. l.t. ed. 1993. (General Ser.: No. 89). 379p. pap. 17.95 (*0-8161-5696-4*, Macmillan Reference USA) Gale Group.

Leslie, Roger. Drowning in Secret: A Novel. 232p. 2004. 24.95 (*1-888842-36-9*); 2002. pap. (*1-888842-37-7*) Absey & Co.

Lewis, Janet. Invasion. 1998. (Illus.). 248p. pap. 21.95 (*0-87013-495-7*) Michigan State Univ. Pr.

—Invasion: A Narrative of Events Concerning the Johnston Family of St. Mary's. 1964. 356p. 15.00 o.p. (*0-8040-0166-9*); pap. 9.00 o.p. (*0-8040-0167-7*) Swallow Pr.

Lewis, Ronald J. Murder in Mackinac. 1994. 238p. pap. 12.95 (*0-9642436-0-1*) Agawa Pr.

—Terror at the Soo Locks: A Novel. 1997. 250p. 12.95 (*0-9642436-1-X*) Agawa Pr.

Ligon, Sam. Safe in Heaven Dead. 2003. 256p. 23.95 (*0-06-009910-0*) HarperCollins Pubs.

Lindsay, Paul. Code Name: Gentkill. 1996. mass mkt. 5.99 o.s.i (*0-449-14902-1*, Fawcett) Ballantine Bks.

—Code Name: Gentkill. l.t. ed. 1996. (Niagara Large Print Ser.). 401p. 29.50 o.p. (*0-7089-5839-7*, Ulverscroft) Thorpe, F. A. Pubs. GBR. *Dist:* Ulverscroft Large Print Bks., Ltd.

—Witness to the Truth. unabr. ed. 1993. audio 21.95 o.p. (*1-56100-491-X*, 320, Bookcassette); audio 57.25 o.p. (*1-56100-125-2*, 1102, Unabridged Library Editions) Brilliance Audio.

Mallon, Thomas. Dewey Defeats Truman. 1997. 368p. pap. 14.00 (*0-312-18086-1*) Picador.

Massie, Larry B. From Frontier Folk to Factory Smoke: Michigan's First Century of Historical Fiction. 1987. 180p. 9.95 o.p. (*0-932212-50-6*) Avery Color Studios, Inc.

McCallum, Dennis. The Summons. 1993. 352p. (Orig.). pap. 11.00 o.p. (*0-89109-768-6*, Discipleship Journal) NavPress Publishing Group.

McGuane, Thomas. The Sporting Club. 1994. lib. bdg. 24.95 (*1-56849-401-7*) Buccaneer Bks., Inc.

—The Sporting Club. 1996. (Vintage Contemporaries Ser.). 224p. pap. 12.00 (*0-679-75290-0*) Random Hse., Inc.

—The Sporting Club. 1987. 224p. pap. 7.95 o.p. (*0-14-009909-3*, Penguin Bks.) Viking Penguin.

McMillan, Rosalyn. Blue Collar Blues, Set. abr. ed. 1998. audio 18.00 (*0-7871-1793-5*, 396117, Dove Audio) NewStar Media, Inc.

—Blue Collar Blues. 2001. 416p. E-Book 4.95 (*0-446-92303-6*); 2000. 400p. mass mkt. 7.50 (*0-446-60764-9*); 1999. E-Book 4.95 (*0-446-91291-3*); 1998. 352p. 30.00 o.p. (*0-446-52243-0*) Warner Bks., Inc.

—Knowing. 2001. 416p. E-Book 4.95 (*0-446-92304-4*); 1997. E-Book 4.95 (*0-446-91290-5*); 1996. 416p. 19.95 o.p. (*0-446-51866-2*); 1997. 416p. reprint ed. mass mkt. 7.50 (*0-446-60376-7*) Warner Bks., Inc.

—One Better. 2001. 384p. E-Book 4.95 (*0-446-92307-9*) Time Warner Bk. Group.

—One Better. 1999. E-Book 4.95 (*0-446-91289-1*); 1998. 400p. mass mkt. 7.99 (*0-446-60599-9*); 1997. 416p. 22.00 o.p. (*0-446-52242-2*) Warner Bks., Inc.

McMillan, Terry. Mama. l.t. ed. 1994. 23.95 o.p. (*0-7927-1777-5*); pap. 21.95 o.p. (*0-7927-1776-7*) BBC Audiobooks America.

—Mama. 1987. 272p. 16.95 o.p. (*0-395-39974-2*) Houghton Mifflin Co.

Meadows, Lee E. Silent Conspiracy. 2002. (Lincoln Keller Mystery Ser.). pap. 16.95 (*1-928623-06-9*) Proctor Pubns.

—Silent Conspiracy: A Lincoln Keller Mystery. 1997. 270p. 24.95 o.p. (*1-882792-38-6*) Proctor Pubns.

—Silent Suspicion: A Lincoln Keller Mystery. 2000. (Lincoln Keller Mystery Ser.). 437p. 24.95 (*1-882792-93-9*) Proctor Pubns.

Meeker, Richard. Better Angel. 1987. 284p. reprint ed. pap. 6.95 o.p. (*1-55583-116-8*) Alyson Pubns.

—Better Angel. 2000. 250p. reprint ed. pap. 14.95 (*1-883938-63-5*) Dry Bones Pr.

Morrison, Toni. Song of Solomon. l.t. ed. 1994. 24.95 o.p. (*0-7927-1936-0*); pap. 22.95 o.p. (*0-7927-1935-2*) BBC Audiobooks America.

—Song of Solomon. 1995. reprint ed. lib. bdg. 24.95 (*1-56849-632-X*) Buccaneer Bks., Inc.

—Song of Solomon. 1987. pap. 8.95 o.p. (*0-452-25244-X*, Plume); 352p. pap. 14.00 (*0-452-26011-6*) Dutton/Plume.

—Song of Solomon. 2004. 352p. pap. 14.00 (*1-4000-3342-X*, Vintage) Knopf Publishing Group.

—Song of Solomon. 1995. (Everyman's Library). 362p. 20.00 (*0-679-44504-8*) Knopf, Alfred A. Inc.

—Song of Solomon. 1993. pap. 5.99 o.s.i (*0-451-18237-5*, Signet Bks.); 1978. mass mkt. 2.50 o.p. (*0-451-08340-7*, Signet Bks.); 1978. mass mkt. 2.75 o.p. (*0-451-09443-3*, Signet Bks.); 1978. mass mkt. 2.95 o.p. (*0-451-11446-9*, Signet Bks.); 1978. mass mkt. 3.50 o.p. (*0-451-12315-8*, Signet Bks.); 1978. 352p. mass mkt. 5.99 o.p. (*0-451-15828-8*, Signet Bks.); 1978. mass mkt. 4.50 o.p. (*0-451-15261-1*); 1978. 352p. mass mkt. 3.95 o.p. (*0-451-12933-4*, AE2933, Signet Bks.) NAL.

—Song of Solomon. 1977. 352p. 27.50 (*0-394-49784-8*) Random Hse. Value Publishing.

—Song of Solomon. (SparkNotes Literature Study Guides). 64-96p. pap., stu. ed. 4.95 (*1-58663-826-2*) Spark Publishing Group.

—Song of Solomon. 1987. (Plume Contemporary Fiction Ser.). 19.00 (*0-606-03092-2*) Turtleback Bks.

—Song of Solomon: Modern Critical Interpretations. Bloom, Harold, ed. 1999. (Bloom's Notes Ser.). 176p. 34.95 (*0-7910-5193-5*) Chelsea Hse. Pubs.

Nelson, Carl. Secret Players. 2003. 336p. per. 16.95 (*1-890035-32-7*, 162) New Century Pr.

Oates, Joyce Carol. Zombie. 1995. 192p. 19.95 o.p. (*0-525-94045-6*, Dutton) Dutton/Plume.

Ohren, Peter. Catch of the Day. 2001. 25.00 (*1-929871-00-7*) Van Neste Bks.

—Catch of the Day. 2003. 223p. pap. 21.99 (*1-4010-9068-0*); E-Book 8.00 (*1-4010-9069-9*) Xlibris Corp.

Panagopoulos, Janie Lynn. North to Iron Country: A Dream-Quest Adventure. 1996. 224p. (J). 14.95 o.p. (*0-938682-40-7*, 682-40-7) River Road Pubns., Inc.

Parrish, P. J. Dead of Winter. 2001. 416p. (Orig.). mass mkt. 6.99 (*0-7860-1189-0*, Pinnacle Bks.) Kensington Publishing Corp.

Pietrzyk, Leslie. Pears on a Willow Tree. 1999. 288p. pap. 13.00 (*0-380-79910-3*, Perennial) HarperTrade.

—Pears on a Willow Tree. 1998. 272p. 23.00 o.p. (*0-380-97667-6*, Avon Bks.) Morrow/Avon.

Polacco, Patricia. Mrs. Mack. 1998. (Illus.). 40p. (J). (ps-3). 16.99 (*0-399-23167-6*, Philomel) Penguin Putnam Bks. for Young Readers.

Prescott, Jerry. Invisible Intrigue. 1999. 354p. per. (*1-882792-90-4*) Proctor Pubns.

Quinn, Tara Taylor. Where the Road Ends. 2003. 384p. mass mkt. (*1-55166-706-1*, Mira Bks.) Harlequin Enterprises, Ltd.

Raphael, Lev. Burning down the House: A Nick Hoffman Novel. 2001. 256p. 23.95 (*0-8027-3365-4*) Walker & Co.

—Death of a Constant Lover. 2000. (Nick Hoffman Mystery Ser.). 288p. pap. 12.95 (*0-312-26496-8*, Saint Martin's Griffin) St. Martin's Pr.

—Death of a Constant Lover. 1999. (Nick Hoffman Mystery Ser.). 288p. 22.95 (*0-8027-3326-3*) Walker & Co.

—The Edith Wharton Murders: A Nick Hoffman Mystery. (Stonewall Inn Editions Ser.). 1998. 240p. pap. 11.95 (*0-312-19863-9*, Saint Martin's Griffin); 1997. 208p. 21.95 o.p. (*0-312-15519-0*, Saint Martin's Minotaur) St. Martin's Pr.

—Let's Get Criminal. 1996. 240p. 20.95 o.p. (*0-312-13999-3*, Saint Martin's Minotaur); 2nd ed. 1997. 244p. pap. 11.95 (*0-312-15160-8*, Saint Martin's Griffin) St. Martin's Pr.

—Little Miss Evil: A Nick Hoffman Mystery. 2000. (Nick Hoffman Mystery Ser.). 184p. 23.95 (*0-8027-3342-5*) Walker & Co.

Rawlings, Marjorie Kinnan. Blood of My Blood. Meriwether, Anne Blythe, ed. 2002. 192p. 24.95 (*0-8130-2443-9*) Univ. Pr. of Florida.

Reardon, Lisa. Billy Dead: A Novel. 1998. 304p. 22.95 o.p. (*0-670-88224-0*) Viking Penguin.

Richards, John. Working Stiff. 1997. 224p. pap. 15.00 (*1-57650-098-5*) Hi Jinx Pr.

Richardson, Arleta. At Home in North Branch. 1988. (Grandma's Attic Ser.). 176p. (J). (gr. 3-7). pap. 3.99 o.p. (*1-55513-312-6*) Cook Communications Ministries.

—New Faces, New Friends. 1989. (Grandma's Attic Ser.). 176p. (J). (gr. 3-7). pap. 3.99 o.p. (*1-55513-985-X*) Cook Communications Ministries.

—Stories from the Growing Years. 1991. (Grandma's Attic Ser.). 128p. (J). (gr. 3-7). pap. 3.99 o.p. (*1-55513-819-5*, 38190) Cook Communications Ministries.

—Wedding Bells Ahead. 1995. (Grandma's Attic Ser.). (Illus.). 156p. (J). (gr. 3-7). pap. 4.99 (*1-55513-668-0*) Cook Communications Ministries.

Roat, Ronald C. Close Softly the Doors. (Stuart Mallory Mystery Ser.). 1993. 148p. pap. 12.95 (*0-934257-96-5*); 2nd ed. 1991. 160p. 18.95 (*0-934257-48-5*) Story Line Pr.

—High Walk. 1996. (Stuart Mallory Mystery Ser.). 288p. 17.95 (*1-885266-16-2*) Story Line Pr.

—A Still & Icy Silence. 1993. (Stuart Mallory Mystery Ser.). 303p. 21.95 (*0-934257-94-9*) Story Line Pr.

Rose, John J. The Marianka Wartz: A True Story. 2001. 192p. pap. 12.95 (*1-58501-066-9*, CeShore) SterlingHouse Pubs., Inc.

Rosewall, Ellen. Sparkle Island: Stories of Life, Love & Walloon Lake. Johnson, Amy, ed. 2000. (Illus.). 171p. pap. 12.95 (*0-9701107-0-7*, 626999) Raven Tree Pr., LLC.

Schreiber, Joseph. Next of Kin. 1994. 256p. 21.95 o.p. (*0-399-13928-1*, G. P. Putnam's Sons) Penguin Group (USA) Inc.

The Sentinel's Dissent. 2001. 200p. (C). pap. 14.95 (*0-9658876-3-4*) She Bear Publishing.

Slezak, Ellen. Last Year's Jesus: A Novella & Nine Stories. 2002. pap. 13.95 (*0-7868-8638-2*); 224p. 22.95 (*0-7868-6741-8*) Hyperion Pr.

Smolens, John. Cold: A Novel. 2001. 320p. 22.00 (*0-609-60794-4*, Harmony) Crown Publishing Group.

Soos, Troy. Hunting a Detroit Tiger. 352p. 1998. (Mickey Rawlings Baseball Mystery Ser.: Vol. 4). mass mkt. 5.99 o.s.i (*1-57566-291-4*); 1997. 18.95 o.s.i (*1-57566-150-0*) Kensington Publishing Corp.

—Hunting a Detroit Tiger. unabr. ed. 1999. (Mickey Rawlings Baseball Ser.: Vol. 4). audio 60.00 (*0-7887-0926-7*, 95066E7) Recorded Bks., LLC.

Stahl, Hilda. The Inheritance Bk. 2: White Pines Chronicles. 1992. 252p. pap. 9.99 o.p. (*0-8407-3216-3*) Nelson, Thomas Inc.

—The White Pines Chronicles. 1996. 792p. 24.99 (*0-7852-7405-7*) Nelson, Thomas Inc.

Stoks, Peggy. Elena's Song. 2002. (HeartQuest Ser.). 288p. pap. 9.99 (*0-8423-1944-1*) Tyndale Hse. Pubs.

Thomas, Newton G. The Long Winter Ends. 1998. (Great Lakes Bks.). 368p. pap. 16.95 (*0-8143-2762-1*) Wayne State Univ. Pr.

Thorne, K. C. Peninsulas. 1997. 80p. (Orig.). pap. 9.95 (*1-56474-204-0*) Fithian Pr.

Traver, Robert. Anatomy of a Murder. lib. bdg. 23.95 (*0-8488-1491-6*) Amereon, Ltd.

—Anatomy of a Murder. 1985. 2.95 o.p. (*0-89559-009-3*) Jameson Bks., Inc.

—Anatomy of a Murder. 2000. (Best Mysteries of All Time Ser.). 527p. (*0-7621-8855-3*) Reader's Digest Assn., Inc., The.

—Anatomy of a Murder. anniv. ed. reprint ed. 1983. 448p. pap. 13.95 (*0-312-03356-7*, NPB 0333, Saint Martin's Griffin); 1991. 300p. lib. bdg. 22.95 (*0-89966-859-3*) St. Martin's Pr.

—Danny & the Boys: Being Some Legends of Hungry Hollow. 1987. (Great Lakes Bks.). reprint ed. 25.00 o.p. (*0-8143-1927-0*); pap. 16.95 (*0-8143-1928-9*) Wayne State Univ. Pr.

Turner, Elizabeth. Wild & Sweet. 2000. 384p. mass mkt. 5.99 (*0-8217-6695-3*, Zebra Bks.) Kensington Publishing Corp.

Turrill, David A. Michilimackinac: A Tale of the Straits. (Orig.). 1989. (Illus.). 490p. pap. 12.95 (*0-923568-04-2*); 2nd ed. 2003. pap. (*0-923568-48-4*) Wilderness Adventure Bks.

Verdelle, A. J. The Good Negress. 1999. 312p. tchr. ed. 19.95 (*1-56512-085-X*, 72085) Algonquin Bks. of Chapel Hill.

—The Good Negress. 1996. 320p. pap. 13.00 (*0-06-097683-7*); pap. 60.00 o.p. (*0-06-097693-4*) HarperTrade. (Perennial).

—The Good Negress. audio o.p. National Humanities Ctr.

—Good Negress. 1996. (Illus.). (J). 19.05 (*0-606-18810-X*) Turtleback Bks.

Walker, Mildred. The Brewers' Big Horses. 1996. 441p. pap. 15.00 (*0-8032-9786-6*, Bison Bks.) Univ. of Nebraska Pr.

—Fireweed. 1994. (Illus.). 314p. pap. 12.95 (*0-8032-9758-0*, Bison Bks.) Univ. of Nebraska Pr.

Weber, Ronald. The Aluminum Hatch: A Michigan Mystery. 1999. (WWL Mystery Ser.: Vol. 324). 256p. pap. (*0-373-26324-4*, Worldwide Library) Harlequin Enterprises, Ltd.

—The Aluminum Hatch: A Michigan Mystery. 1998. 216p. 19.95 o.p. (*1-885173-48-2*) Write Way Publishing.

—Catch & Keep. 2000. 248p. 23.95 (*1-885173-25-3*) Write Way Publishing.

Weiss, Stephen. The Farewell Principle. 1999. 184p. 19.95 o.p. (*1-56315-085-9*) SterlingHouse Pubs., Inc.

Whelan, Gloria. Forgive the River, Forgive the Sky. 1998. 166p. (J). (gr. 4-7). 15.00 o.p. (*0-8028-5155-X*, Eerdmans Bks For Young Readers) Eerdmans, William B. Publishing Co.

Wilson, Robert C. Mysterium. 1994. 288p. pap. 11.95 o.s.i (*0-553-37365-X*) Bantam Bks.

Winters, Donna. Aurora of North Manitou Island. Severance, Anne, ed. 1993. (Great Lakes Romances Ser.). 288p. pap. 9.95 (*0-923048-81-2*) Bigwater Publishing.

—Charlotte of South Manitou Island. Severance, Anne, ed. 1992. (Great Lakes Romances Ser.). (Illus.). 256p. pap. 10.95 (*0-923048-79-0*) Bigwater Publishing.

—Elizabeth of Saginaw Bay. Chambers, Pamela Q., ed. 1995. (Great Lakes Romances Ser.). 232p. (YA). (gr. 7). pap. 8.95 (*0-923048-83-9*) Bigwater Publishing.

—Elizabeth of Saginaw Bay. 1986. (Serenade Saga Ser.: No. 34). pap. 1.49 (*0-310-47272-5*, 15573P) Zondervan.

—Jenny of l'Anse Bay. 1988. (Serenade Saga Ser.). 224p. pap. 5.95 (*0-310-47651-8*, 15617P) Zondervan.

—Jenny of L'Anse Bay. Severance, Anne, ed. 1991. (Great Lakes Romances Ser.). 232p. reprint ed. pap. 9.95 (*0-923048-78-2*) Bigwater Publishing.

—Mackinac. Chambers, Pamela Q., ed. 1993. (Great Lakes Romances Ser.). 208p. pap. 10.95 (*0-923048-75-8*) Bigwater Publishing.

Wolf, William. Whacking Jimmy: A Novel. 1998. 244p. pap. 15.00 (*0-8129-9239-3*, Villard Bks.) Random House Adult Trade Publishing Group.

Woolson, Constance F. Anne. 1977. (Rediscovered Fiction by American Women Ser.). reprint ed. lib. bdg. 33.95 (*0-405-10059-0*) Ayer Co. Pubs., Inc.

—Anne. 1999. (Notable American Authors Ser.). reprint ed. lib. bdg. 125.00 (*0-7812-7791-4*) Reprint Services Corp.

Zadoorian, Michael. Second Hand: A Novel. 2000. 224p. 23.95 (*0-393-04797-0*) Norton, W. W. & Co., Inc.

Zanger, Molleen. Gardenias Where There Are None. 1994. 256p. pap. 9.95 o.p. (*1-56280-056-6*) Naiad Pr., Inc.

Zimmerman, R. D. Blood Trance. 1994. 304p. mass mkt. 4.99 o.s.i (*0-440-21518-8*) Dell Publishing.

—Blood Trance. 1993. 236p. 20.00 o.p. (*0-688-12139-X*, Morrow, William & Co.) Morrow/Avon.

—Death Trance. 1993. 304p. mass mkt. 4.99 o.s.i (*0-440-21326-6*) Dell Publishing.

—Death Trance: A Novel of Hypnotic Detection. 1992. 256p. 20.00 o.p. (*0-688-11451-2*, Morrow, William & Co.) Morrow/Avon.

—Red Trance. 1995. 320p. mass mkt. 4.99 o.s.i (*0-440-21763-6*) Dell Publishing.

—Red Trance. 1994. 237p. 20.00 o.p. (*0-688-13030-5*, Morrow, William & Co.) Morrow/Avon.

## MIDDLE EARTH (IMAGINARY PLACE)—FICTION

Buchholz, Suzanne. The Middle-Earth Quiz Book, 001. 1979. pap. 3.95 o.p. (*0-395-28428-7*) Houghton Mifflin Co.

Fisher, Jude & Tolkien, J. R. R. The Lord of the Rings: The Two Towers Visual Companion. 2002. (Illus.). 72p. 18.95 (*0-618-25802-7*) Houghton Mifflin Co.

Fonstad, Karen Wynn. The Atlas of Middle-Earth. rev. ed. (Illus.). 224p. 2001. pap. 24.00 (*0-618-12699-6*); 1992. pap. 24.00 o.p. (*0-395-53516-6*) Houghton Mifflin Co.

Foster, Robert. The Complete Guide to Middle Earth: Tolkien's World from A to Z. 1985. 592p. mass mkt. 6.99 o.s.i (*0-345-32436-6*, Del Rey) Ballantine Bks.

The Hobbit. 1985. incl. 5.25 hd (*0-201-11157-8*); 32.00 incl. disk (*0-201-11158-6*) Addison-Wesley Longman, Inc.

The Hobbit. (J). audio o.p. HarperTrade.

Sebanc, Mark. Flight to Hollow Mountain. 1996. (Talamadh Ser.). 421p. 25.00 o.p. (*0-8028-3794-8*) Eerdmans, William B. Publishing Co.

Strachey, Barbara. Journeys of Frodo. 1981. 128p. 12.95 o.p. (*0-345-29723-7*) Ballantine Bks.

Tolkien, J. R. R. The Annotated Hobbit. 1988. (Illus.). 352p. 24.95 o.p. (*0-395-47690-9*); 2002. 416p. 28.00 (*0-618-16816-8*); 2002. (Illus.). 416p. 28.00 (*0-618-13470-0*) Houghton Mifflin Co.

—The Annotated Hobbit. 1990. 9.99 o.p. (*0-517-02935-9*) Random Hse. Value Publishing.

—The Book of Lost Tales Vol. 1: The History of Middle-Earth. Tolkien, Christopher, ed. 304p. 1986. pap. 18.00 (*0-395-40927-6*); 1984. 30.00 (*0-395-35439-0*) Houghton Mifflin Co.

—The Book of Lost Tales Vol. 1: The History of Middle-Earth. 1992. 13.04 (*0-606-01297-4*) Turtleback Bks.

—The Book of Lost Tales Vol. 2: The History of Middle-Earth. Tolkien, Christopher, ed. 400p. 1986. pap. 18.00 (*0-395-42640-5*); 1984. 30.00 (*0-395-36614-3*) Houghton Mifflin Co.

—The Book of Lost Tales Vol. 2: The History of Middle-Earth. 1992. 13.04 (*0-606-01299-0*) Turtleback Bks.

—The Book of Lost Tales 1: The History of Middle-Earth. Tolkien, Christopher, ed. 1992. (Illus.). 368p. mass mkt. 7.50 (*0-345-37521-1*, Del Rey) Ballantine Bks.

—The Book of Lost Tales 2: The History of Middle-Earth. Tolkien, Christopher, ed. 1992. 400p. mass mkt. 7.50 (*0-345-37522-X*, Del Rey) Ballantine Bks.

—The Fellowship of the Ring: Being the First Part of the Lord of the Rings. 1999. (Lord of the Rings Ser.: Bk. 1). mass mkt. 2.22 o.s.i (*0-345-91743-X*); 1986. (Lord of the Rings Ser.: Bk. 1). 480p. mass mkt. 7.99 (*0-345-33970-3*, Del Rey); 1985. mass mkt. 3.95 o.p. (*0-345-33208-3*); 1972. mass mkt. 0.95 o.p. (*0-345-21533-8*) Ballantine Bks.

—The Fellowship of the Ring: Being the First Part of the Lord of the Rings. 2002. 19.57 (*1-4046-2528-3*) Book Wholesalers, Inc.

—The Fellowship of the Ring: Being the First Part of the Lord of the Rings. unabr. ed. 2002. (Lord of the Rings Ser.: Bk. 1). audio (*0-00-764608-9*) HarperCollins Pubs. Ltd.

—The Fellowship of the Ring: Being the First Part of the Lord of the Rings. abr. unabr. ed. 2002. (Lord of the Rings Ser.: Bk. 1). audio compact disk 19.95 (*1-56511-667-4*, 89123) HighBridge Co.

—The Fellowship of the Ring: Being the First Part of the Lord of the Rings. (Lord of the Rings Ser.). 2003. pap. 12.00 (*0-618-34625-2*); 2002. (Illus.). xx, 1170p. 27.50 (*0-618-26051-X*); 1999. 432p. pap. 12.00 (*0-618-00222-7*); 1992. (Illus.). 440p.

30.00 o.p. (0-395-64738-X); 1988. (Illus.). 432p. (gr. 7). 22.00 (0-395-48931-8); 2002. 432p. pap. 12.00 o.s.i (0-618-26026-9) Houghton Mifflin Co.

—The Fellowship of the Ring: Being the First Part of the Lord of the Rings. l.t. ed. 1996. (Lord of the Rings Ser.: Bk. 1). (Illus.). 513p. 24.95 (1-85089-414-0) ISIS Large Print Bks. GBR. *Dist:* Transaction Pubs.

—The Fellowship of the Ring: Being the First Part of the Lord of the Rings. abr. ed. 2001. (Lord of the Rings Ser.: Bk. 1). audio 25.95 (0-553-71477-5); audio compact disk 27.50 (0-553-71478-3); audio 25.95 (0-8072-0727-6, RH Audio) Random Hse. Audio Publishing Group.

—The Fellowship of the Ring: Being the First Part of the Lord of the Rings. unabr. ed. (Lord of the Rings Ser.: Bk. 1). 2000. audio 120.00 (1-55690-321-9, 90014E7); 1999. audio compact disk 158.00 Recorded Bks., LLC.

—The Fellowship of the Ring: Being the First Part of the Lord of the Rings. l.t. ed. 2003. (Lord of the Rings Ser.). 855p. pap. 13.95 (1-59413-007-8, Large Print Pr.); 31.95 (0-7862-5178-6) Thorndike Pr.

—The Fellowship of the Ring: Being the First Part of the Lord of the Rings. 50th ed. 1982. (Lord of the Rings Ser.: Bk. 1). 13.04 (0-606-00650-8) Turtleback Bks.

—The Fellowship of the Ring: Radio Dramatization. 2002. audio 39.95 (0-563-53054-5, BBCS 007); audio compact disk 49.95 (0-563-53055-3, BBCD 007) BBC Worldwide Americas.

—The Hobbit. 1977. 35.00 o.p. (0-8109-1060-8) Abrams, Harry N., Inc.

—The Hobbit. 1989. (Illus.). 14.98 (0-88365-746-5, Galahad Bks.) BBS Publishing Corp.

—The Hobbit. 1999. mass mkt. 2.22 o.s.i (0-345-91742-1); 1990. (Illus.). pap. 12.95 (0-345-36858-4); 1988. mass mkt. 4.95 o.p. (0-345-00861-8); 1985. mass mkt. 3.95 o.p. (0-345-33207-5); 1984. mass mkt. 2.95 o.p. (0-345-31858-7); 1981. mass mkt. 2.50 o.p. (0-345-29604-4); 1978. (Illus.). pap. 8.95 o.p. (0-345-27711-2); 1977. mass mkt. 2.50 o.p. (0-345-27257-9); 1976. mass mkt. 1.95 o.p. (0-345-25342-6); 1975. mass mkt. 1.75 o.p. (0-345-24826-0); 1973. mass mkt. 1.25 o.p. (0-345-23512-6); 1972. mass mkt. 0.95 o.p. (0-345-21532-X); 2001. (Illus.). 144p. reprint ed. pap. 15.95 (0-345-44560-0, Del Rey) Ballantine Bks.

—The Hobbit. 1992. pap. 5.95 (0-87129-174-6, H62) Dramatic Publishing Co.

—The Hobbit. abr. ed. 1994. audio 24.99 (0-88646-356-4, LFP 7356) Durkin Hayes Publishing Ltd.

—The Hobbit. abr. ed. 1995. audio 29.95 Filmic Archives.

—The Hobbit. abr. ed. 2001. audio 24.95 (1-56511-551-1); 2001. audio compact disk 29.95 (1-56511-552-X); 2002. audio compact disk 29.95 (1-56511-672-0) HighBridge Co.

—The Hobbit. (Illus.). 1999. 320p. pap. 12.00 (0-618-00221-9); 1988. 312p. pap. 11.95 o.p. (0-395-28265-9) Houghton Mifflin Co.

—The Hobbit. l.t. ed. 1990. (Illus.). 363p. 24.95 (1-85089-805-7) ISIS Large Print Bks. GBR. *Dist:* Transaction Pubs., Ulverscroft Large Print Canada, Ltd.

—The Hobbit. 2001. audio compact disk 39.95 Lodestone Catalog, The.

—The Hobbit. (J). (gr. k up). audio 29.98 Music for Little People, Inc.

—The Hobbit. audio compact disk 39.95. 1992. audio 22.98 o.s.i (0-553-74505-0); 1992. audio 18.39 o.s.i (0-553-70025-1); 1997. audio 25.95 (0-553-47107-4) Random Hse. Audio Publishing Group. (RH Audio).

—The Hobbit. unabr. ed. 2001. audio compact disk 39.99 (0-7887-8982-1); 1999. audio compact disk 87.00; 1991. (J). (gr. 6). audio 70.00 (1-55690-233-6, 91121E7) Recorded Bks., LLC.

—The Hobbit. 2003. 31.95 (0-7862-5177-8); 483p. pap. 13.95 (1-59413-005-1, Large Print Pr.) Thorndike Pr.

—The Hobbit. l.t. ed. 1982. (Classics Ser.). 381p. o.p. (0-7089-8065-1, Charnwood) Thorpe, F. A. Pubs.

—The Hobbit. 1987. 13.04 (0-606-00811-X) Turtleback Bks.

—The Hobbit: BBC Dramatization. abr. ed. 1997. (BBC Radio Presents Ser.). audio compact disk 39.95 (0-553-45562-1, RH Audio) Random Hse. Audio Publishing Group.

—The Hobbit: Fiftieth Anniversary Edition. 1987. (Illus.). 320p. 29.95 o.p. (0-395-45402-6) Houghton Mifflin Co.

—The Hobbit: The Enchanting Prelude to the Lord of the Rings. rev. ed. 1986. (Lord of the Rings Ser.). 320p. mass mkt. 7.99 (0-345-33968-1, Del Rey) Ballantine Bks.

—The Hobbit: 1 Act. 1996. 5.95 (0-87129-589-X, H37) Dramatic Publishing Co.

—The Hobbit & The Fellowship of the Ring. unabr. ed. audio 12.00 Blackstone Audio Bks., Inc.

—The Hobbit & The Fellowship of the Ring. abr. ed. audio 9.95 o.p. (0-89845-222-8, CPN 1477, Caedmon); 1996. audio 12.00 (1-55994-631-8, DCN 1477, HarperAudio) HarperTrade.

—The Hobbit & The Lord of the Rings, 4 vols. 1988. 1540p. 45.95 o.p. (0-395-48907-5); 1979. pap. 24.95 o.p. (0-395-28263-2) Houghton Mifflin Co.

—The Journey Begins. abr. ed. 1996. (Lord of the Rings Ser.: Bk. 1). audio 24.00 o.p. (0-553-47742-0, RH Audio) Random Hse. Audio Publishing Group.

—The Lays of Beleriand. Tolkien, Christopher, ed. (History of Middle-Earth Ser.: Vol. 3). 1988. 400p. pap. 13.95 (0-395-48683-1); 1985. 368p. 30.00 (0-395-39429-5) Houghton Mifflin Co.

—The Lord of the Rings. unabr. ed. (Lord of the Rings Ser.). audio 59.95 Blackstone Audio Bks., Inc.

—The Lord of the Rings. 2003. 35.00 (0-618-34624-4); 2003. (Illus.). 1168p. tchr. ed. 38.00 (0-618-34584-1); 2003. (Illus.). 1168p. pap. 20.00 (0-618-34399-7); 2002. 1168p. 38.00 o.s.i (0-618-26024-2); 2002. (Illus.). 1168p. pap. 20.00 o.s.i (0-618-26025-0); 2001. (Illus.). 1216p. 38.00 o.s.i (0-618-12901-4); 1999. 1216p. pap. 20.00 o.s.i (0-395-97468-2); 1992. (Illus.). 90.00 o.p. (0-395-64741-X); 1991. (Illus.). 1200p. 251.00 o.p. (0-395-60423-0); 1991. (Illus.). 1198p. (gr. 7). 70.00 (0-395-59511-8); 1988. (Illus.). 428p. pap. 11.95 o.p. (0-395-27223-8); 1988. 65.00 (0-395-48932-6); 1978. 1232p. pap. 22.95 o.p. (0-395-27220-3); 1976. 45.85 o.p. (0-395-08257-9); rev. ed. 1954. 423p. 14.95 o.p. (0-395-08254-4); 2nd collector's ed. 1974. (Illus.). 1216p. (gr. 7). 75.00 (0-395-19395-8) Houghton Mifflin Co.

—The Lord of the Rings. 2001. (Lord of the Rings Ser.). (Illus.). xviii, 1137p. pap. 20.00 o.s.i (0-618-12902-2, Mariner Bks.) Houghton Mifflin Co. Trade & Reference Div.

—The Lord of the Rings. 2nd ed. 1968. (Lord of the Rings Ser.). 1077p. o.p. (0-04-823087-1) Independent Pubs. Group.

—The Lord of the Rings. (Lord of the Rings Ser.). (J). (gr. 3 up). audio 59.98 Music for Little People, Inc.

—The Lord of the Rings. (Lord of the Rings Ser.). audio compact disk 64.95. 1993. audio 59.95 (0-553-47228-3, RH Audio); 2000. 1216p. (YA). pap. 80.00 incl. audio (0-8072-8344-4, LL0187, Listening Library); 1999. 69.95 incl. audio compact disk (0-553-45653-9, RH Audio) Random Hse. Audio Publishing Group.

—The Lord of the Rings. unabr. ed. (Lord of the Rings Ser.). audio 49.95 Soundelux Audio Publishing.

—The Lord of the Rings. 1994. 26.05 (0-606-21597-2) Turtleback Bks.

—The Lord of the Rings: Millennium Edition, 7 vols. 1999. (Lord of the Rings Ser.). (Illus.). 70.00 o.p. (0-618-03766-7) Houghton Mifflin Co.

—The Lord of the Rings: The Fellowship of the Ring; The Two Towers; The Return of the King, 3 bks. 2002. (Lord of the Rings Ser.). (Illus.). 1168p. 80.00 (0-618-26058-7); pap. 35.00 o.s.i (0-618-26029-3) Houghton Mifflin Co.

—The Lord of the Rings: The Two Towers & The Return of the King. abr. ed. 1998. audio 12.00 (0-89845-223-6, CPN 1478, Caedmon) HarperTrade.

—The Lord of the Rings & The Hobbit, 3 vols. 1999. (Lord of the Rings Ser.). (Illus.). pap. 45.00 (0-618-00225-1) Houghton Mifflin Co.

—The Lord of the Rings & The Hobbit Trilogy. 1985. (Lord of the Rings Ser.). 138p. (YA). (gr. 10-12). pap. 3.95 (0-8120-3523-2) Barron's Educational Series, Inc.

—The Lord of the Rings & The Hobbit Trilogy. abr. ed. 2002. audio compact disk 89.95 (1-56511-707-7) HighBridge Co.

—The Lost Road & Other Writings: Language & Legend Before The Lord of the Rings. Tolkien, Christopher, ed. & frwd. by. 1987. (Illus.). 464p. 30.00 (0-395-45519-7) Houghton Mifflin Co.

—The Lost Road & Other Writings: Language & Legend Before the Lord of the Rings. Tolkien, Christopher, ed. 1996. 512p. mass mkt. 6.99 (0-345-40685-0) Ballantine Bks.

—Morgoth's Ring. Tolkien, Christopher, ed. 1993. (History of Middle-Earth Ser.: Vol. 10). 488p. 30.00 (0-395-68092-1) Houghton Mifflin Co.

—The Peoples of Middle Earth. Tolkien, Christopher, ed. 1996. (History of Middle-Earth Ser.: Vol. 12). 496p. 30.00 (0-395-82760-4) Houghton Mifflin Co.

—The Return of the King. 1999. (Lord of the Rings Ser.: Bk. 3). mass mkt. 2.22 o.s.i (0-345-91745-6); 1986. (Lord of the Rings Ser.: Bk. 3). 512p. mass mkt. 7.99 (0-345-33973-8, Del Rey); 1985. mass mkt. 3.95 o.p. (0-345-33209-1); 1981. mass mkt. 2.95 o.p. (0-345-29608-7); 1977. mass mkt. 2.50 o.p. (0-345-27260-9); 1976. mass mkt. 1.95 o.p. (0-345-25345-0); 1975. mass mkt. 1.75 o.p. (0-345-24829-5); 1974. mass mkt. 1.50 o.p. (0-345-24034-0) Ballantine Bks.

—The Return of the King. 2002. (J). 16.60 (0-7587-5212-1) Book Wholesalers, Inc.

—The Return of the King. unabr. ed. 2002. (Lord of the Rings Ser.: Bk. 3). audio (0-00-764610-0) HarperCollins Pubs. Ltd.

—The Return of the King. abr. unabr. ed. 2002. (Lord of the Rings Ser.: Bk. 3). audio compact disk 19.95 (1-56511-669-0, 89125) HighBridge Co.

—The Return of the King, 3 vols. (Lord of the Rings Ser.: Bk. 3). 2002. (Illus.). xx, 1170p. 27.50 (0-618-26055-2); 1999. 464p. pap. 12.00 (0-618-00224-3); 1992. (Illus.). 464p. 30.00 o.p. (0-395-64740-1); 1988. (Illus.). 450p. pap. 11.95 o.p. (0-395-27221-1); movie tie-in ed. 2002. 1140p. pap. 12.00 o.s.i (0-618-26028-5); rev. ed. 1967. 14.95 o.p. (0-395-08256-0); 2nd ed. 1988. (Illus.). 448p. (gr. 7). 22.00 (0-395-48930-X) Houghton Mifflin Co.

—The Return of the King. abr. unabr. ed. 2002. (Lord of the Rings Ser.: Bk. 3). (J). audio 25.95 (0-8072-0910-4, Listening Library) Random Hse. Audio Publishing Group.

—The Return of the King. (Lord of the Rings Ser.: Bk. 3). 2001. audio compact disk 49.99 (0-7887-8984-8); 2001. audio 34.99 (0-7887-8955-4); 1997. audio 91.00 (1-55690-320-0, 90016E7) Recorded Bks., LLC.

—The Return of the King. l.t. ed. 2003. (Lord of the Rings Ser.). 864p. pap. 13.95 (1-59413-004-3, Large Print Pr.); 31.95 (0-7862-5176-X) Thorndike Pr.

—The Return of the King. 1983. (Lord of the Rings Ser.: Bk. 3). 13.04 (0-606-01302-4) Turtleback Bks.

—The Return of the King: Being the Third Part of the Lord of the Rings. 2003. (Lord of the Rings Ser.). pap. 12.00 (0-618-34627-9) Houghton Mifflin Co.

—The Shaping of Middle-Earth: The Quenta, The Ambarkanta, & The Annals, Together with the Earliest 'Silmarillion' & the First Map. Tolkien, Christopher, ed. 1986. (History of Middle-Earth Ser.: Vol. 4). (Illus.). 400p. 29.95 (0-395-42501-8) Houghton Mifflin Co.

—The Silmarillion. Tolkien, Christopher, ed. 1977. 365 p. (0-04-823139-8) Allen & Unwin Pty., Ltd. AUS. *Dist:* Independent Pubs. Group.

—The Silmarillion. 1985. (Illus.). 480p. mass mkt. 7.99 (0-345-32581-8, Del Rey); 1982. mass mkt. 3.50 o.p. (0-345-30692-9); 1979. mass mkt. 2.95 o.p. (0-345-27255-2) Ballantine Bks.

—The Silmarillion. (J). audio o.p. 1984. audio 12.95 (0-694-50305-3, SWC 1564); 1978. audio 12.95 o.p. (0-694-50312-6, SWC 1579) HarperTrade. (Caedmon).

—The Silmarillion. Tolkien, Christopher, ed. 1998. (Illus.). 366p. 35.00 (0-395-93946-1) Houghton Mifflin Co.

—The Silmarillion. 1983. 368p. pap. 15.95 o.p. (0-395-34646-0) Houghton Mifflin Co.

—The Silmarillion, 001. Tolkien, Christopher, ed. 1977. 365 p. 10.95 o.p. (0-395-25730-1) Houghton Mifflin Co.

—The Silmarillion. 2nd ed. 2001. (Illus.). 384p. pap. 14.00 (0-618-12698-8) Houghton Mifflin Co.

—The Silmarillion. Tolkien, Christopher, ed. 2nd ed. 2001. (Illus.). 372p. 28.00 (0-618-13504-9) Houghton Mifflin Co.

—The Silmarillion. unabr. ed. (Middle Earth Chronicles ). 2000. 365p. (J). pap. 75.00 incl. audio (0-8072-8295-2, LL0188, Listening Library); 1998. pap. 64.95 incl. audio compact disk (0-553-45606-7, RH Audio); Vol. 1. 1998. audio compact disk 27.00 (0-553-45582-6, RH Audio); Vol. 2. 1998. audio compact disk 27.00 (0-553-45583-4, RH Audio); Vol. 3. 1998. audio compact disk 29.95 (0-553-45584-2, RH Audio) Random Hse. Audio Publishing Group.

—The Silmarillion. 1977. 13.04 (0-606-01371-7) Turtleback Bks.

—The Silmarillion. abr. ed. 1998. audio 65.55 (0-00-105534-8) Ulverscroft Audio (U.S.A.).

—Smith of Wootton Major & Farmer Giles of Ham, 2 vols. in 1. 1986. 160p. mass mkt. 6.99 (0-345-33606-2, Del Rey) Ballantine Bks.

—Tolkien Boxed Set, 4 vols. 1986. 29.96 (0-345-34042-6, Del Rey) Ballantine Bks.

—The Treason of Isengard. Tolkien, Christopher, ed. 1989. (History of Middle-Earth Ser.: Vol. 7). (Illus.). 512p. 29.95 (0-395-51562-9) Houghton Mifflin Co.

—The Treason of Isengard. Tolkien, Christopher, ed. 1989. (History of Middle-Earth Ser.: Vol. 7). 504p. o.p. (0-04-440396-8) Independent Pubs. Group.

—The Two Towers: Being the Second Part of the Lord of the Rings. 1999. (Lord of the Rings Ser.: Bk. 2). mass mkt. 2.22 o.s.i (0-345-91744-8); 1988. (Lord of the Rings Ser.: Bk. 2). mass mkt. 4.95 o.p. (0-345-00863-4); 1986. (Lord of the Rings Ser.: Bk. 2). 416p. mass mkt. 7.99 (0-345-33971-1, Del Rey); 1985. mass mkt. 3.95 o.p. (0-345-33210-5); 1981. mass mkt. 2.95 o.p. (0-345-29606-0); 1977. mass mkt. 2.50 o.p. (0-345-27259-5); 1976. mass mkt. 1.95 o.p. (0-345-25344-2); 1975. mass mkt. 1.75 o.p. (0-345-24828-7); 1974. mass mkt. 1.50 o.p. (0-345-24033-2); 1973. mass mkt. 1.25 o.p. (0-345-23510-X) Ballantine Bks.

—The Two Towers: Being the Second Part of the Lord of the Rings. 2002. 19.57 (1-4046-2531-3) Book Wholesalers, Inc.

—The Two Towers: Being the Second Part of the Lord of the Rings. unabr. ed. 2002. (Lord of the Rings Ser.: Bk. 2). audio (0-00-764609-7) HarperCollins Pubs. Ltd.

—The Two Towers: Being the Second Part of the Lord of the Rings. (Lord of the Rings Ser.). 2003. pap. 12.00 (0-618-34626-0); 2002. (Illus.). xx, 1170p. 27.50 (0-618-26059-5); 1999. 352p. pap. 12.00 (0-618-00223-5); 1992. (Illus.). 368p. 30.00 o.p. (0-395-64739-8); 1988. (Illus.). 356p. pap. 11.95 o.p. (0-395-27222-X); 1967. 14.95 o.p. (0-395-08255-2); movie tie-in ed. 2002. 725p. pap. 12.00 o.s.i (0-618-26027-7); movie tie-in ed. 2001. (Illus.). x, 725p. reprint ed. pap. 12.00 o.s.i (0-618-12908-1); 2nd ed. 1988. (Illus.). 352p. (gr. 7). 22.00 (0-395-48933-4) Houghton Mifflin Co.

—The Two Towers: Being the Second Part of the Lord of the Rings. l.t. ed. 1992. (Lord of the Rings Ser.: Bk. 2). (Illus.). 448p. 24.95 (1-85089-419-1) ISIS Large Print Bks. GBR. *Dist:* Transaction Pubs.

—The Two Towers: Being the Second Part of the Lord of the Rings. unabr. ed. (Lord of the Rings Ser.: Bk. 2). 2001. audio 34.99 (0-7887-8954-6); 1999. audio compact disk 131.00; 1997. (YA). (gr. 8). audio 97.00 (1-55690-322-7, 90015E7) Recorded Bks., LLC.

—The Two Towers: Being the Second Part of the Lord of the Rings. 2003. (Lord of the Rings Ser.: Part II). 746p. 31.95 (0-7862-5175-1); 776p. pap. 13.95 (1-59413-006-X, Large Print Pr.) Thorndike Pr.

—The Two Towers: Being the Second Part of the Lord of the Rings. 50th ed. 1986. (Lord of the Rings Ser.: Bk. 2). 13.04 (0-606-01521-3) Turtleback Bks.

—The Two Towers: Radio Dramatization. 2002. audio 39.95 (0-563-53058-8, BBCS 005); audio compact disk 49.95 (0-563-53059-6, BBCD 005) BBC Worldwide Americas.

—The Two Towers: Reproducible Teaching Unit. 2002. (Lord of the Rings Ser.: Bk. 2). 82p. tchr. ed., ring bd. (1-58049-460-9, TU216) Prestwick Hse., Inc.

—Unfinished Tales. 1988. 512p. mass mkt. 7.50 (0-345-35711-6, Del Rey) Ballantine Bks.

—Unfinished Tales. Tolkien, Christopher, ed. 1982. (Illus.). 368p. pap. 16.00 o.p. (0-395-32441-6) Houghton Mifflin Co.

—Unfinished Tales of Numenor & Middle-Earth. Tolkien, Christopher, ed. & intro. by. 1980. 472p. 14.00 (0-04-823179-7) Allen & Unwin Pty., Ltd. AUS. *Dist:* Paul & Co. Pubs. Consortium, Inc.

—Unfinished Tales of Numenor & Middle-Earth, 001. Tolkien, Christopher, ed. & comment by. 1980. (Illus.). 472 p. 15.00 o.p. (0-395-29917-9) Houghton Mifflin Co.

—The War of the Jewels: The Later Silmarillion, The Legends of Beleriand, Pt. 2. Tolkien, Christopher, ed. 1994. (History of Middle-Earth Ser.: Vol. XI). 488p. 30.00 (0-395-71041-3) Houghton Mifflin Co.

Tolkien, J. R. R. & Gray, Patricia. The Hobbit: A Play. 1967. 5.95 (0-87129-427-3, H22) Dramatic Publishing Co.

Tolkien, J. R. R., et al. The Hobbit: A Musical. 1972. 5.95 (0-87129-393-5, H03) Dramatic Publishing Co.

## MIDDLE EAST—FICTION

Abdul-Baki, Kathryn K. Fields of Fig & Olive: Ameera & Other Stories of the Middle East. 1991. 217p. (YA). (gr. 10 up). 14.00 o.s.i (0-89410-725-9); pap. 14.00 o.p. (0-89410-726-7) Rienner, Lynne Pubs., Inc. (Three Continents).

Abouzeid, Lelia. The Year of the Elephant: A Moroccan Woman's Journey Toward Independence. Parmenter, Barbara M., tr. from ARA. 1989. (Modern Middle Eastern Literature in Translation Ser.). 129p. (Orig.). pap. 10.95 (0-292-79603-X) Univ. of Texas Pr.

Adler, Warren. We Are Holding the President Hostage. 1988. 304p. pap. (0-373-97072-2, Harlequin Bks.) Harlequin Enterprises, Ltd.

Ajemian, Kevork. A Time for Terror. 1997. 200p. 24.95 (1-891078-00-3) Books International, Incorporated.

Al-Atrash, Leila. A Woman of Five Seasons. Halwani, N. & Tingley, C., trs. from ARA. 2002. (Emerging Voices Ser.). 208p. pap. 12.95 (1-56656-416-6) Interlink Publishing Group, Inc.

Al-Khatib, Muhammad Kamil. Just Like a River. Barakat, Maher & Hartman, Michelle, trs. from ARA. 2002. (Emerging Voices Ser.). 120p. pap. 12.95 (1-56656-475-1) Interlink Publishing Group, Inc.

Al-Sa'Dawi, Nawal. Innocence of the Devil. 1998. 278p. pap. text 16.95 (0-520-21652-0) Univ. of California Pr.

Al-Shaykh, Hanan. Women of Sand & Myrrh. Cobham, Catherine, tr. from ARA. 1990. 224p. 19.95 o.p. (0-7043-2736-8) Quartet Bks., Ltd. GBR. *Dist:* Interlink Publishing Group, Inc.

—Women of Sand & Myrrh: A Novel. Cobham, Catherine, tr. 1992. 288p. reprint ed. pap. 11.95 (0-385-42358-6) Doubleday Publishing.

Alameddine, Rabih. Koolaids: The Art of War. 256p. 1999. pap. 13.00 (*0-312-20658-5*); 1998. 23.00 (*0-312-18693-2*) Picador.

—Koolaids: The Art of War, a Novel. 2000. 245p. reprint ed. 23.00 (*0-7881-9338-4*) DIANE Publishing Co.

Alexander, Lloyd. The Jedera Adventure. 1990. 160p. (gr. 4-7). pap. text 4.50 o.s.i (*0-440-40295-6*, Yearling) Random Hse. Children's Bks.

Alshalabi, Firyal M. & Drexler, Sam. The Sky Changed Forever. 2003. 160p. (YA). (gr. 9-12). pap. 8.99 (*0-9669988-3-9*) Aunt Strawberry Bks.

Amirshahi, Mahshid. Suri & Co. Tales of a Persian Teenage Girl. Knorzer, J. E., tr. from IRA. 1995. (Modern Middle Eastern Literature in Translation Ser.). 97p. (Orig.). pap. 9.95 (*0-292-70463-1*) Univ. of Texas Pr.

Archer, Jeffrey. Honor among Thieves. l.t. ed. 1993. 26.95 o.p. (*1-56895-045-4*, Wheeler Publishing, Inc.) Gale Group.

—Honor among Thieves. 1993. 416p. 276.00 o.p. (*0-06-017771-3*); 414.00 o.p. (*0-06-017756-X*) HarperCollins Pubs.

—Honor among Thieves. 1993. 416p. 23.00 o.p. (*0-06-017945-7*) HarperTrade.

—Honor among Thieves. 1994. 480p. mass mkt. 7.99 (*0-06-109204-5*, HarperTorch) Morrow/Avon.

—Honor among Thieves. unabr. ed. 1994. audio 75.00 (*1-55690-968-3*, 94111E7) Recorded Bks., LLC.

Barkhordar-Nahai, Gina. Moonlight on the Avenue of Faith. 2000. 400p. reprint ed. pap. 13.95 (*0-671-04283-1*, Washington Square Pr.) Simon & Schuster.

Bearden, Milton. The Black Tulip. 1998. 336p. 24.95 o.s.i (*0-679-44791-1*) Random Hse., Inc.

Behnam, Mariam. Heirloom: Evening Tales from the East. 2001. (Illus.). 362p. pap. text 19.95 (*0-19-579329-3*) Oxford Univ. Pr., Inc.

Bergren, Lisa Tawn. Chosen. 1996. (Palisades Pure Romance Ser.). 294p. pap. 9.99 o.p. (*0-88070-768-2*, Palisades) Multnomah Pubs., Inc.

—The Chosen. 2001. (Full Circle Ser.). 288p. pap. 9.95 (*1-57856-467-0*) WaterBrook Pr.

Biehl, Michael. Lawyered to Death: A Karen Hayes Mystery. 2003. 320p. 23.95 (*1-882593-76-6*) Bridge Works Publishing Co., Inc.

Blackwood, Grant. The End of Enemies. 2001. 608p. mass mkt. 7.99 (*0-425-17956-7*) Berkley Publishing Group.

Bogary, Hamza. The Sheltered Quarter: A Tale of a Boyhood in Mecca. Jayyusi, Salma K., ed. Reed, Kenny et al, trs. from ARA. 1991. (Modern Middle Eastern Literature in Translation Ser.). 141p. (Orig.). pap. 8.95 (*0-292-72752-6*) Univ. of Texas Pr.

Brand, Moses. Joe's Trial. 2000. 484p. 16.95 (*0-942520-12-2*) Distributors, The.

Brien, Nell. A Veiled Journey. 1999. 408p. per. (*1-55166-528-X*, Mira Bks.) Harlequin Enterprises, Ltd.

Brock, David. Cloning Saddam. E-Book (*1-84045-043-6*) Online Originals.

Bromell, Henry. Little America. 2001. E-Book 19.00 (*1-59061-173-X*) Adobe Systems, Inc.

—Little America. 2002. 416p. pap. 14.00 (*0-375-71891-5*, Vintage) Knopf Publishing Group.

Buchanan, Bill. Virus: A Novel. 1997. 432p. mass mkt. 6.50 o.s.i (*0-515-12011-1*, Jove) Berkley Publishing Group.

—Virus: A Novel. 1998. 415p. pap. text 6.50 (*0-7881-5789-2*) DIANE Publishing Co.

Bunn, T. Davis. Riders of the Pale Horse. 352p. 2002. pap. 12.99 (*0-7642-2759-9*); 1994. pap. 9.99 o.p. (*1-55661-346-6*) Bethany Hse. Pubs.

—Riders of the Pale Horse. l.t. ed. 2002. 533p. pap. 17.95 (*1-4104-0008-5*, Walker Large Print); 26.95 (*0-7862-4010-5*) Gale Group.

Campbell, Claude. Abou & the Angel Cohen: A Novel. 2002. 248p. 23.95 (*1-882593-51-0*); 2003. 184p. reprint ed. pap. 15.95 (*1-882593-71-5*) Bridge Works Publishing Co., Inc.

Chafets, Zev, Jr. Hang Time. 1996. 82p. 21.95 o.s.i (*0-446-52047-0*) Warner Bks., Inc.

Chamberlin, Ann. The Sultan's Daughter. 1998. (Illus.). 348p. pap. text 6.99 (*0-8125-5385-3*, Tor Bks.); 1997. 352p. 24.95 o.p. (*0-312-86203-2*, Forge Bks.) Doherty, Tom Assocs., LLC.

Chopra, Deepak & Greenberg, Martin H. Lords of Light. 1999. 343p. mass mkt. 6.99 (*0-312-96892-2*, St. Martin's Paperbacks) St. Martin's Pr.

Chraibi, Driss. Muhammad. Benabid, Nadia, tr. 1998. (Three Continents Ser.). 90p. lib. bdg. 22.00 (*0-89410-858-1*) Rienner, Lynne Pubs., Inc.

Christie, Agatha. Murder in Mesopotamia. (Hercule Poirot Mystery Ser.). 1987. 272p. mass mkt. 5.99 (*0-425-10363-3*); 1986. mass mkt. 2.95 o.s.i (*0-425-09324-7*); 1984. mass mkt. 2.95 o.s.i (*0-425-06791-2*) Berkley Publishing Group.

—Murder in Mesopotamia. 1976. 192p. pap. 2.50 o.s.i (*0-440-15982-2*) Dell Publishing.

—Murder in Mesopotamia. l.t. ed. (G. K. Hall Large Print Book Ser.). 1992. 348p. 14.95 o.p. (*0-8161-4568-7*); 1991. 384p. 19.95 o.p. (*0-8161-4567-9*) Gale Group. (Macmillan Reference USA).

—Murder in Mesopotamia. l.t. ed. 1969. (Ulverscroft Large Print Ser.). 367p. 12.50 o.p. (*0-85456-667-8*, Ulverscroft) Thorpe, F. A. Pubs. GBR. *Dist:* Ulverscroft Large Print Bks., Ltd., Ulverscroft Large Print Canada, Ltd.

—Murder in Mesopotamia. 1984. 12.04 (*0-606-00965-5*) Turtleback Bks.

—Murder in Mesopotamia: BBC. abr. ed. 1997. (BBC Radio Presents Ser.). audio 18.00 o.s.i (*0-553-47846-X*, RH Audio) Random Hse. Audio Publishing Group.

—Parker Pyne Investigates. 1985. 208p. mass mkt. 5.99 o.s.i (*0-425-08770-0*) Berkley Publishing Group.

—Parker Pyne Investigates. l.t. ed. 1978. (Ulverscroft Large Print Ser.). 299p. 12.00 o.p. (*0-7089-0141-7*, Ulverscroft) Thorpe, F. A. Pubs. GBR. *Dist:* Ulverscroft Large Print Bks., Ltd., Ulverscroft Large Print Canada, Ltd.

—Parker Pyne Investigates. 1992. 12.04 (*0-606-12473-X*) Turtleback Bks.

—They Came to Baghdad. 1984. 240p. mass mkt. 5.99 o.s.i (*0-425-06804-8*) Berkley Publishing Group.

—They Came to Baghdad. 1974. pap. 1.95 o.s.i (*0-440-18700-1*) Dell Publishing.

—They Came to Baghdad. l.t. ed. (Popular Author Ser.). 1991. pap. 12.95 o.p. (*0-8161-4606-3*); 1990. 359p. lib. bdg. 19.95 o.p. (*0-8161-4605-5*) Gale Group. (Macmillan Reference USA).

—They Came to Baghdad. 1987. (Agatha Christie Ser.). 14.95 o.s.i (*0-396-09011-7*, G. P. Putnam's Sons) Penguin Putnam Bks. for Young Readers.

—They Came to Baghdad. l.t. ed. 1978. (Ulverscroft Large Print Ser.). 32.50 (*0-7089-0189-1*, Ulverscroft) Thorpe, F. A. Pubs. GBR. *Dist:* Ulverscroft Large Print Bks., Ltd., Ulverscroft Large Print Canada, Ltd.

—They Came to Baghdad. 1984. 12.04 (*0-606-00960-4*) Turtleback Bks.

Clancy, Tom. The Teeth of the Tiger. 2003. 448p. 27.95 (*0-399-15079-X*); 640p. 150.00 (*0-399-15136-2*) Putnam Publishing Group, The.

Coe, Simon. The Gold Bokhara. 2002. 352p. pap. 21.95 (*0-87714-826-0*) Denlingers Pubs., Ltd.

—The Gold Bokhara. 2000. 387p. pap. 18.00 (*0-7388-1835-6*) Xlibris Corp.

Cook, Nick. Aggressor. 1993. 336p. 19.95 o.p. (*0-312-07623-1*, Saint Martin's Minotaur); 239.40 o.p. (*0-312-07925-7*) St. Martin's Pr.

Coppel, Alfred. Show Me a Hero. 1988. 304p. mass mkt. 3.95 o.s.i (*0-8041-0232-5*, Ivy Bks.) Ballantine Bks.

—Show Me a Hero. 1987. 320p. 16.95 (*0-15-182080-5*) Harcourt Trade Pubs.

Craft, Elisabeth R. In the Court of the Queen: A Novel of Mesopotamia. 2001. 280p. 22.95 (*0-910155-42-9*) Bartleby Pr.

Crawford, F. Marion. Khaled: A Tale of Arabia. 2000. 252p. E-Book 3.95 (*0-594-06403-1*) 1873 Pr.

Cullen, Robert. Heirs of the Fire. 1998. 357p. mass mkt. 6.99 o.s.i (*0-8041-1445-5*, Ivy Bks.); 1997. 368p. 23.00 o.p. (*0-449-00025-7*, Fawcett) Ballantine Bks.

Daoud, Hassan. The House of Mathilde. 2002. (ARA.). 181p. pap. 16.95 (*1-86207-222-1*) Granta.

Dekker, Ted. Blink. 2003. 400p. pap. 14.99 (*0-8499-4371-X*) W Publishing Group.

DeMille, Nelson. By the Rivers of Babylon. 1986. 432p. mass mkt. 3.95 o.s.i (*0-515-08761-0*, Jove) Berkley Publishing Group.

—By the Rivers of Babylon. 1978. 10.00 o.p. (*0-15-115278-0*) Harcourt Trade Pubs.

—By the Rivers of Babylon. l.t. ed. 1983. (Charnwood Large Print Ser.). 624p. 29.99 o.p. (*0-7089-8091-0*, Charnwood) Thorpe, F. A. Pubs. GBR. *Dist:* Ulverscroft Large Print Bks., Ltd., Ulverscroft Large Print Canada, Ltd.

—By the Rivers of Babylon. 432p. 2001. E-Book 6.95 (*0-7595-4257-0*); 2001. E-Book 6.95 (*0-7595-9287-X*); 2001. E-Book 6.95 (*0-7595-6254-7*); 2001. E-Book 6.95 (*0-7595-8260-2*); 2001. E-Book 6.95 (*0-7595-0254-4*); 1990. reprint ed. mass mkt. 7.99 (*0-446-35859-2*) Warner Bks., Inc.

Drummond, Richard H. Life of Jesus the Christ: An Edgar Cayce Guide. 1996. (Edgar Cayce Guides). 222p. mass mkt. 5.99 (*0-312-96057-3*, St. Martin's Paperbacks) St. Martin's Pr.

Dunnett, Dorothy. The Disorderly Knights. 1976. 31.95 (*0-8488-1297-2*) Amereon, Ltd.

—The Disorderly Knights. 1981. 334p. reprint ed. lib. bdg. 47.95 (*0-89966-295-1*) Buccaneer Bks., Inc.

—The Disorderly Knights. 1997. (Legendary Lymond Chronicles: Vol. 3). 528p. pap. 15.00 (*0-679-77745-8*, Vintage) Knopf Publishing Group.

—The Disorderly Knights. 1984. 576p. mass mkt. 3.95 o.s.i (*0-446-31290-8*) Warner Bks., Inc.

—Pawn in Frankincense. 1976. 33.95 (*0-8488-1300-6*) Amereon, Ltd.

—Pawn in Frankincense. 1983. 425p. reprint ed. lib. bdg. 39.95 (*0-89966-321-4*) Buccaneer Bks., Inc.

—Pawn in Frankincense. 1997. (Legendary Lymond Chronicles: Vol. 4). 512p. pap. 15.00 (*0-679-77746-6*, Vintage) Knopf Publishing Group.

—Pawn in Frankincense. 1984. 576p. mass mkt. 3.95 o.s.i (*0-446-31294-0*) Warner Bks., Inc.

Easterman, Daniel. The Seventh Sanctuary. 1987. 456p. 17.95 o.s.i (*0-385-19814-0*) Doubleday Publishing.

—The Seventh Sanctuary. 1988. 608p. mass mkt. 4.50 o.p. (*0-8217-2451-7*, Zebra Bks.) Kensington Publishing Corp.

El Saadawi, Nawal. The Innocence of the Devil. Hetata, Sherif, tr. 1994. (ARA.). 233p. text 23.00 o.p. (*0-520-08889-1*) Univ. of California Pr.

Elray, John. Khalifah: A Novel of Conquest & Personal Triumph. 2002. E-Book 7.95 (*0-9707776-7-1*); 2001. (Illus.). 336p. pap. 14.95 (*0-9707776-2-0*) Aardwolfe Bks.

Ferdowsi, Abolqasem. Fathers & Sons. Davis, Dick, tr. from PER. 2000. (Stories from the Shahnameh of Ferdowsi: Vol. 2). (Illus.). 311p. 75.00 (*0-934211-53-1*) Mage Pubs., Inc.

Fielding, Liz. His Desert Rose. 2000. (Harlequin Romance Ser.: Vol. 3618). mass mkt. (*0-373-03618-3*, 1-03618-5); (Harlequin Large Print Ser.: Vol. 464). mass mkt. (*0-373-15864-5*) Harlequin Enterprises, Ltd. (Harlequin Bks.).

Fisher, David E. Hostage One. 1990. mass mkt. 4.95 o.p. (*0-312-92144-6*, St. Martin's Paperbacks) St. Martin's Pr.

Flynn, Vince. Separation of Power. l.t. ed. 2002. (Wheeler Large Print Book Ser.). 29.95 (*1-58724-196-X*, Wheeler Publishing, Inc.) Gale Group.

—Separation of Power. 2002. 368p. E-Book 25.00 (*0-7434-4922-3*, Atria); 2001. 368p. 25.00 (*0-671-04733-7*, Atria); 2001. 368p. 25.00 (*0-7434-4837-5*, Atria); 2002. (Illus.). 448p. reprint ed. mass mkt. 7.99 (*0-671-04734-5*, Pocket) Simon & Schuster.

—Separation of Power. abr. ed. 2001. audio 26.00 (*0-7435-0930-7*); audio compact disk 32.00 (*0-7435-0931-5*) Simon & Schuster Audio. (Simon & Schuster Audioworks).

Fontaine, Michele. Harem Sister: A Young Woman's Quest for Personal Power in Ancient Persia. 2002. (Sekhmet Ser.: Vol. 1). (Illus.). 192p. pap. 17.99 (*0-615-12146-2*, SEKH-1) Wadjet Publishing.

Forsyth, Frederick. The Fist of God. 1995. 592p. mass mkt. 7.99 (*0-553-57242-3*); 1995. 592p. mass mkt. 9.99 o.s.i (*0-552-13990-4*); 1995. 592p. mass mkt. 6.99 o.s.i (*0-553-84000-2*); 1994. 29.95 o.s.i (*0-593-02798-1*); 1994. 992p. 28.95 o.s.i (*0-553-09662-1*) Bantam Bks.

—The Fist of God. unabr. ed. 1994. audio 120.00 (*0-7366-2762-6*, 3484) Books on Tape, Inc.

—The Fist of God. abr. ed. 1994. audio 23.95 o.s.i (*0-553-47263-1*, RH Audio) Random Hse. Audio Publishing Group.

—The Fist of God. unabr. ed. 1994. audio 64.95 (*0-7887-0027-8*, 94226E7) Recorded Bks., LLC.

Freemantle, Brian. Betrayals. 1991. mass mkt. 4.95 o.p. (*0-8125-8257-8*); 1989. 384p. 18.95 o.p. (*0-312-93138-7*) Doherty, Tom Assocs., LLC. (Tor Bks.).

Gandt, Robert. Acts of Vengeance. 2002. (Illus.). 368p. mass mkt. 6.99 (*0-451-20718-1*, Signet Bks.) NAL.

Gardner, Mary. Milkweed. 1995. 320p. pap. 11.00 (*0-918949-45-9*, Papier-Mache Pr.) Moyer Bell.

Gilman, Dorothy. Mrs. Pollifax & the Innocent Tourist. 1997. 224p. mass mkt. 6.99 (*0-449-18336-X*); 203p. 23.00 o.p. (*0-449-91137-3*) Ballantine Bks. (Fawcett).

—Mrs. Pollifax, Innocent Tourist. l.t. ed. 1997. pap. 23.00 o.s.i (*0-679-77420-3*) Random Hse., Inc.

—Mrs. Pollifax Unveiled. 2001. E-Book 6.99 (*1-58945-767-6*) Adobe Systems, Inc.

—Mrs. Pollifax Unveiled. (Mrs. Pollifax Mystery Ser.). 2001. 224p. mass mkt. 6.99 (*0-449-00670-0*); 2001. E-Book 18.50 (*0-345-44307-1*, Ballantine Bks.); 2000. 208p. 23.00 (*0-345-43652-0*) Ballantine Bks.

—Mrs. Pollifax Unveiled. l.t. ed. 2000. (Wheeler Large Print Book Ser.). 210p. 26.95 o.p. (*1-56895-826-9*, Wheeler Publishing, Inc.) Gale Group.

Goldman, L. C. And the Peace Came Tumbling Down. 2001. pap. 17.10 (*0-7596-1381-8*) 1stBooks Library.

Gordon, Noah. The Physician. 1987. 640p. mass mkt. 6.99 o.s.i (*0-449-21426-5*, Fawcett) Ballantine Bks.

—The Physician. 1986. 624p. 18.45 o.p. (*0-671-47748-X*, Simon & Schuster) Simon & Schuster.

—The Physician. 2002. 720p. pap. 8.95 (*0-7515-0389-4*) Warner Bks. GBR. *Dist:* Trafalgar Square.

Habiby, Emile. The Secret Life of Saeed the Pessoptimist. Jayyusi, Salma K. & LeGassick, T., trs. from ARA. 2001. (Emerging Voices Ser.). 192p. pap. 12.95 (*1-56656-415-8*) Interlink Publishing Group, Inc.

Hagberg, David. Desert Fire. 1993. 384p. 13.99 o.p. (*0-312-85496-X*, Tor Bks.) Doherty, Tom Assocs., LLC.

—Desert Fire. 4.98 o.s.i (*0-8317-5537-7*) Smithmark Pubs., Inc.

Hailstone, David. Six Faces. 1998. 196p. pap. 7.95 (*0-9663490-0-8*) Mother Lode Bks.

Halaby, Laila. West of the Jordan: A Novel. 2003. (Bluestreak Ser.). 240p. pap. 14.00 (*0-8070-8359-3*) Beacon Pr.

Hamilton, Jane. The Book of Ruth. 1996. 336p. tchr. ed. 18.95 o.p. (*0-395-86650-2*); 1988. 265p. 18.95 o.p. (*0-89919-744-2*) Houghton Mifflin Co.

—The Book of Ruth. 1989. 336p. pap. 13.00 (*0-385-26570-0*, Knopf Bks. for Young Readers) Random Hse. Children's Bks.

—The Book of Ruth. unabr. ed. 1997. audio 83.00 (*0-7887-0912-7*, 95052E7) Recorded Bks., LLC.

—The Book of Ruth. abr. ed. 1997. audio 23.00 o.s.i (*0-671-57647-X*, 496001, Simon & Schuster Audioworks) Simon & Schuster Audio.

—A Map of the World. 1992. 400p. pap. 12.95 o.p. (*0-385-47311-7*) Doubleday Publishing.

—A Map of the World. l.t. ed. 1995. (G. K. Hall Core Ser.). 587p. 24.95 o.p. (*0-7838-1189-6*, Macmillan Reference USA) Gale Group.

—A Map of the World. abr. ed. 1999. audio 9.99 o.s.i (*0-553-70206-8*); 1995. audio 18.00 (*0-553-52737-1*) Random Hse. Audio Publishing Group. (RH Audio).

—A Map of the World. 1999. 400p. pap. 12.95 (*0-385-72010-6*, Knopf Bks. for Young Readers) Random Hse. Children's Bks.

—A Map of the World. unabr. ed. 1995. audio 97.00 (*0-7887-0195-9*, 94419K8) Recorded Bks., LLC.

—A Map of the World. 1995. 19.00 (*0-606-18125-3*) Turtleback Bks.

Hamilton, Masha. Staircase of a Thousand Steps: A Novel. 2002. 288p. pap. 13.00 (*0-425-18530-3*) Berkley Publishing Group.

—Staircase of a Thousand Steps: A Novel. 2001. 288p. 23.95 o.s.i (*0-399-14725-X*, BlueHen Bks.) Putnam Publishing Group, The.

Hartov, Steven. The Heat of Ramadan. 1992. 21.95 (*0-15-139858-5*) Harcourt Trade Pubs.

—Heat of Ramadan. 1994. mass mkt. 5.99 o.p. (*0-312-95201-5*, St. Martin's Paperbacks) St. Martin's Pr.

Hays, Tony. The Trouble with Patriots: A Novel. 2002. 184p. 22.95 (*1-882593-52-9*) Bridge Works Publishing Co., Inc.

Herman, Richard. The Last Phoenix. 2003. 496p. mass mkt. 7.99 (*0-06-103181-X*, HarperTorch); 2002. 448p. 25.95 (*0-06-620976-5*, Morrow, William & Co.) Morrow/Avon.

Higgins, Jack. Sheba. 1995. 272p. mass mkt. 7.99 (*0-425-14670-7*) Berkley Publishing Group.

—Sheba. l.t. ed. 1995. (Large Print Bks.). pap. 22.95 o.p. (*1-56895-126-4*, Wheeler Publishing, Inc.) Gale Group.

Hoffman, Andy. Beehive. 1992. 219p. pap. 16.00 (*1-877946-35-4*); 256p. 21.95 o.p. (*1-877946-14-1*) Permanent Pr., The.

—Beehive. 2002. 15.95 (*0-7592-4409-X*) ereads.com.

Huston, James W. Flash Point. 2001. E-Book 7.50 (*0-06-001124-6*) HarperCollins Pubs.

—Flash Point. 2001. 592p. mass mkt. 7.50 (*0-380-73282-3*, Avon Bks.); 2000. 462p. 26.00 (*0-688-17201-6*, Morrow, William & Co.) Morrow/Avon.

Idris, Yusuf. The Cheapest Nights. Wassef, Wadida, tr. from ARA. reprint ed. 1991. 22.00 o.p. (*0-89410-665-1*); 1989. 196p. pap. 13.95 (*0-89410-666-X*) Rienner, Lynne Pubs., Inc. (Three Continents).

Ignatieff, Michael. Scar Tissue. 199p. 2000. pap. 18.00 (*0-374-52769-5*); 1994. 20.00 o.p. (*0-374-25428-1*) Farrar, Straus & Giroux.

Ignatius, David. Agents of Innocence. 1988. 448p. mass mkt. 4.50 (*0-380-70593-1*, Avon Bks.) Morrow/Avon.

—Agents of Innocence. 1997. 448p. pap. 13.95 (*0-393-31738-2*); 1987. 17.95 o.p. (*0-393-02486-5*) Norton, W. W. & Co., Inc.

—Agents of Innocence. 1990. 3.99 o.p. (*0-517-05159-1*) Random Hse. Value Publishing.

—The Bank of Fear. l.t. ed. 1995. (G. K. Hall Core Ser.). 576p. 23.95 (*0-7838-1185-3*, Macmillan Reference USA) Gale Group.

—The Bank of Fear. 1994. 20.00 o.p. (*0-688-13136-0*, Morrow, William & Co.); 1995. 400p. reprint ed. mass mkt. 5.99 (*0-380-72280-1*, Avon Bks.) Morrow/Avon.

—The Bank of Fear, unabr. ed. audio 78.00 (*0-7887-0300-5*, 94493E7) Recorded Bks., LLC.

Irwin, Robert. Prayer-Cushions of the Flesh. 2002. 140p. 22.95 (*1-58567-220-3*) Overlook Pr., The.

Jaco, Charles. Dead Air. 1999. mass mkt. 6.99 o.s.i (*0-345-42184-1*) Ballantine Bks.

—Dead Air. abr. ed. 1998. audio (*1-56876-074-4*) Soundlines Entertainment, Inc.

Johnson-Davies, Denys, tr. Arabic Short Stories. 1987. 208p. 14.95 o.p. (*0-7043-2367-2*) Quartet Bks., Ltd. GBR. *Dist:* Interlink Publishing Group, Inc.

Jones, Harry. Shadow in a Weary Land. 1992. 221p. 24.00 (*1-877946-15-X*) Permanent Pr., The.

Kelly, Fred. The Fourth Generation. 1992. (Orig.). pap. 16.95 (*0-9630986-2-4*) Ribbon Ridge Pr.

Khedairi, Betool. A Sky So Close! A Novel. Jamil, Muhayman, tr. from ARA. 2001. 256p. 23.00 (*0-375-42096-7*, Pantheon) Knopf Publishing Group.

Khoury, Elias. Gates of the City. Haydar, Paula, tr. from ARA. 1993. (Emergent Literatures Ser.: Vol. 12). 112p. (C). 15.95 (*0-8166-2224-8*) Univ. of Minnesota Pr.

—The Kingdom of Strangers. Haydar, Paula, tr. from ARA. 2003. viii, 103p. (C). 24.00 (*1-55728-433-4*); pap. 17.95 (*1-55728-434-2*) Univ. of Arkansas Pr.

Land, Jon. The Pillars of Solomon. 2000. 438p. mass mkt. 6.99 (*0-8125-6672-6*); 1999. (Illus.). 352p. 24.95 (*0-312-86819-7*) Doherty, Tom Assocs., LLC. (Forge Bks.).

—The Walls of Jericho. 1998. 480p. mass mkt. 6.99 (*0-8125-6456-1*, Tor Bks.); 1997. 304p. 23.95 (*0-312-86267-9*, Forge Bks.) Doherty, Tom Assocs., LLC.

—The Walls of Jericho. abr. ed. 1997. audio 17.00 (*1-56876-066-3*) Soundlines Entertainment, Inc.

Larkin, William & Larkin, David. Castles of Paradise. 1997. (*1-901851-00-1*) Dillons Publishing.

Lawhead, Stephen R. The Black Rood. 2000. (Celtic Crusades Ser.: Bk. II). (Illus.). 448p. 25.00 (*0-06-105034-2*) HarperCollins Pubs.

—The Black Rood. 2001. (Celtic Crusades Ser.: Vol. 2). 624p. mass mkt. 7.50 (*0-06-105110-1*, Eos) Morrow/Avon.

—The Black Rood. 2001. (Illus.). 448p. pap. 16.99 (*0-310-21783-0*) Zondervan.

—The Mystic Rose. 2001. (Celtic Crusades Ser.: Bk. III). (Illus.). 432p. 25.00 (*0-06-105031-8*, Eos) Morrow/Avon.

—The Mystic Rose. 2002. (Celtic Crusades Ser.: Bk. III). (Illus.). 432p. pap. 16.99 (*0-310-21784-9*) Zondervan.

Lindisfarne, Nancy. Dancing in Damascus: Stories. 2000. (SUNY Series, The Margins of Literature). vii, 168p. (C). text 16.50 (*0-7914-4635-2*); pap. text 15.95 (*0-7914-4636-0*) State Univ. of New York Pr.

—Dancing in Damascus: Stories. 2000. E-Book 44.50 (*0-585-35045-0*) netLibrary, Inc.

Lyall, Gavin. Uncle Target. l.t. ed. 1989. (Ulverscroft Large Print Ser.). 487p. 29.99 o.p. (*0-7089-1945-6*, Ulverscroft) Thorpe, F. A. Pubs. GBR. *Dist:* Ulverscroft Large Print Bks., Ltd., Ulverscroft Large Print Canada, Ltd.

—Uncle Target. 1988. 256p. 16.95 o.p. (*0-670-82228-0*) Viking Penguin.

Mahfouz, Naguib. The Journey of Ibn Fattouma. 1993. 160p. pap. 12.00 (*0-385-42334-9*) Doubleday Publishing.

—Respected Sir, Wedding Song, The Search. 2001. 464p. pap. 16.00 (*0-385-49836-5*, Knopf Bks. for Young Readers) Random Hse. Children's Bks.

Malone, L. K. Divided Loyalties. 2001. 320p. pap. 9.99 (*0-8254-2796-7*) Kregel Pubns.

Mann, Paul. The Britannia Contract. 1993. 448p. 21.00 o.p. (*0-88184-933-2*, Carroll & Graf Pubs.) Avalon Publishing Group.

Merek, Jack. Target Stealth. 1990. 352p. 18.45 o.s.i (*0-446-51470-5*); mass mkt. 4.95 (*0-446-34843-0*) Warner Bks., Inc.

Mosley, Nicholas. Inventing God. 2003. (British Literature Ser.). 256p. pap. 14.50 (*1-56478-291-3*) Dalkey Archive Pr.

Munif, Abdelrahman. Variations on Night & Day. 1994. 352p. pap. 19.00 (*0-679-75551-9*) Knopf, Alfred A. Inc.

Myers, Bill. The Face of God. E-Book 10.99 (*0-310-25702-6*); 2002. 368p. pap. 12.99 (*0-310-22755-0*) Zondervan.

Nahai, Gina B. Moonlight on the Avenue of Faith. 1999. 384p. 24.00 o.s.i (*0-15-100388-2*) Harcourt Trade Pubs.

Nakhjavani, Bahiyyih. The Saddlebag: A Fable for Doubters & Seekers. 2000. 258p. 22.00 o.p. (*0-8070-8342-9*) Beacon Pr.

Nicole, Christopher. Shadows in the Sun. l.t. ed. 1999. (Magna Large Print Ser.). 448p. 31.99 (*0-7505-1425-6*) Magna Large Print Bks. GBR. *Dist:* Ulverscroft Large Print Bks., Ltd., Ulverscroft Large Print Canada, Ltd.

—Shadows in the Sun. 1998. 288p. 25.00 (*0-7278-5364-3*) Severn Hse. Pubs., Ltd.

North, Oliver. Mission Compromised: A Novel. 2003. 656p. mass mkt. 7.99 (*0-06-055584-X*, HarperTorch) Morrow/Avon.

North, Oliver & Musser, Joe. Mission Compromised: A Novel. 2002. 640p. audio 24.99 (*0-8054-2636-1*); 24.99 (*0-8054-2550-0*) Broadman & Holman Pubs.

—Mission Compromised: A Novel. l.t. ed. 2003. (Compass Ser.). 30.95 (*1-58724-385-7*, Wheeler Publishing, Inc.) Gale Group.

Patterson, Andrew. The Hypocrites: An Epic Novel about the Middle East from 1959-1989. 1994. 19.95 (*0-9641679-0-5*) Patterson, Andrew M. & Assocs.

Peel, Colin D. Dark Armada. 1995. 192p. 19.95 o.p. (*0-312-13460-6*, Saint Martin's Minotaur) St. Martin's Pr.

Petschull, Jurgen. The Martyr. Cappellari, Stephen G., tr. from GER. 1988. 296p. 18.95 o.p. (*0-916515-28-1*) Mercury Hse.

Pezeshkzad, Iraj. My Uncle Napoleon. Davis, Dick, tr. 2000. 712p. pap. 19.95 (*0-934211-62-0*); 1996. 512p. 29.95 o.p. (*0-934211-48-5*) Mage Pubs., Inc.

Pope, Liston, Jr. Redemption: A Novel of War in Lebanon. 294p. 1994. (Works Ser.: Vol. I). 24.95 (*0-9638900-0-X*); 2nd ed. 1997. reprint ed. pap. 15.00 (*0-9638900-2-6*) Mantis Pr.

Poyer, David. Black Storm: A David Lenson Novel. 384p. 2003. (Illus.). mass mkt. 6.99 (*0-312-98385-9*, St. Martin's Paperbacks); 2002. 24.95 (*0-312-26969-2*) St. Martin's Pr.

—The Gulf. 442p. 1991. (Illus.). mass mkt. 7.99 (*0-312-92577-8*, St. Martin's Paperbacks); 1990. 19.95 o.p. (*0-312-05096-8*) St. Martin's Pr.

Randall, John D. The Jihad Ultimatum: A Novel. 1989. mass mkt. 4.50 o.s.i (*1-55817-260-2*, Pinnacle Bks.) Kensington Publishing Corp.

—The Jihad Ultimatum: A Novel. 1988. (*0-933071-23-X*) Saybrook Publishing Co., Inc.

Reiss, Bob. Divine Assassin. 1986. 50p. mass mkt. 3.95 o.p. (*0-425-09721-8*) Berkley Publishing Group.

Reiss, Rob. Divine Assassin. 1985. 224p. 15.95 o.p. (*0-316-73969-3*) Little Brown & Co.

Rizzi, Timothy. The Phalanx Dragon. 2000. 480p. reprint ed. pap. 6.99 (*0-8439-3885-4*, Leisure Bks.) Dorchester Publishing Co., Inc.

—The Phalanx Dragon. 1994. (Illus.). 432p. 21.95 o.p. (*1-55611-391-9*) Fine, Donald I. Bks.

—The Phalanx Dragon. 1995. E-Book 9.95 (*0-585-29807-6*) netLibrary, Inc.

Robinson, Patrick. H. M. S. Unseen. 2000. 528p. mass mkt. 7.50 (*0-06-109801-9*, HarperTorch) Morrow/Avon.

—HMS Unseen. 1999. 448p. 25.00 (*0-06-019315-8*) HarperCollins Pubs.

—HMS Unseen. unabr. ed. 2001. audio compact disk 134.00 (*0-7887-7186-8*, C1436); 1999. audio 96.00 (*0-7887-3463-6*, 95874E7) Recorded Bks., LLC.

Rosenberg, Joel C. The Last Days. Date not set. mass mkt. (*0-7653-4820-9*); 2003. 352p. 24.95 (*0-7653-0928-9*) Doherty, Tom Assocs., LLC. (Forge Bks.).

—The Last Jihad: A Novel. 352p. 2003. mass mkt. 7.99 (*0-7653-4643-5*); 2002. 24.95 (*0-7653-0715-4*) Doherty, Tom Assocs., LLC. (Forge Bks.).

—The Last Jihad: A Novel. l.t. ed. 2003. (Adventure Ser.). 29.95 (*0-7862-5262-6*) Thorndike Pr.

Said, Kurban. Ali & Nino. pap. (*0-385-72838-7*) Knopf Publishing Group.

—Ali & Nino. Graman, Jenia, tr. 1999. (ENG & GER.). 240p. 24.95 (*0-87951-668-2*) Overlook Pr., The.

—Ali & Nino. 1978. mass mkt. 1.95 o.p. (*0-671-82128-8*, Pocket) Simon & Schuster.

Said, Kurban & Graman, Jenia. Ali & Nino. l.t. ed. 2000. (Basic Ser.). 384p. 29.95 (*0-7862-2485-1*) Thorndike Pr.

Said, Kurban, et al. Ali & Nino: A Love Story. 2000. (Illus.). 288p. pap. 13.00 (*0-385-72040-8*, Anchor Bible) Doubleday Publishing.

Sansom, Anthony. Leila & Majnoon. 2003. 624p. 24.95 (*0-9723127-1-4*) Thirsty Horse LLC.

Sasson, Jean. Ester's Child. 448p. 2003. pap. 12.95 (*0-9676737-7-1*); 2nd ed. 2001. (Illus.). 24.95 o.p. (*0-9676737-3-9*) Windsor-Brooke Bks.

Scholder, Henry. The Honorable Correspondent. 2003. 256p. 26.00 (*1-57962-085-X*) Permanent Pr., The.

Seymour, Gerald. Condition Black. 1992. 400p. mass mkt. 5.50 o.p. (*0-06-100435-9*, HarperTorch); 1991. 336p. 20.00 o.p. (*0-688-10631-5*, Morrow, William & Co.) Morrow/Avon.

—Condition Black. l.t. ed. 1992. (Adventure Suspense Ser.). 496p. 29.99 o.p. (*0-7089-8636-6*, Ulverscroft) Thorpe, F. A. Pubs. GBR. *Dist:* Ulverscroft Large Print Bks., Ltd., Ulverscroft Large Print Canada, Ltd.

—The Running Target. 1991. 592p. mass mkt. 4.95 o.p. (*0-06-100143-0*, Perennial) HarperTrade.

—The Running Target. 1990. 19.95 o.p. (*0-688-05201-0*, Morrow, William & Co.) Morrow/Avon.

Silva, Daniel. The Kill Artist. E-Book 20.95 (*1-58945-641-6*) Adobe Systems, Inc.

—The Kill Artist. 2002. 448p. mass mkt. 6.99 o.s.i (*0-449-00212-8*, Fawcett) Ballantine Bks.

—The Kill Artist. 2004. 448p. mass mkt. 7.99 (*0-451-20933-8*, Signet Bks.) NAL.

—The Kill Artist. 2001. E-Book 20.95 (*0-375-50672-1*) Random Hse., Inc.

Simon, Frank. Walls of Terror. 1997. 368p. pap. 12.99 o.p. (*0-89107-952-1*) Crossway Bks.

Stacey, Tom. Deadline. 1989. 128p. 13.95 o.p. (*0-312-03320-6*) St. Martin's Pr.

Stevens, Gordon. Do Not Go Gentle. 1989. 400p. reprint ed. mass mkt. (*0-373-97101-X*, Harlequin Bks.) Harlequin Enterprises, Ltd.

—Do Not Go Gentle. 1988. 384p. 17.95 o.p. (*0-312-01488-0*) St. Martin's Pr.

Tarr, Judith. Devil's Bargain. 2002. 400p. pap. 16.00 (*0-451-45896-6*, ROC) NAL.

Thoene, Jake. Firefly Blue. 2003. 384p. pap. 12.99 (*0-8423-5362-3*) Tyndale Hse. Pubs.

Thoene, Jake & Thoene, Rachel. Shaiton's Fire. 2002. 368p. pap. 12.99 (*0-8423-5361-5*) Tyndale Hse. Pubs.

Traylor, Ellen Gunderson. The Oracle. 2001. 304p. pap. 13.99 o.s.i (*0-8499-3755-8*) W Publishing Group.

Uris, Leon. The Haj. 1984. 566p. 17.95 o.s.i (*0-385-03459-8*) Doubleday Publishing.

—The Haj. l.t. ed. 1985. 12.95 o.p. (*0-8161-3821-4*); 772p. 19.95 o.p. (*0-8161-3788-9*) Gale Group. (Macmillan Reference USA).

Victor, Barbara. Friends, Lovers, Enemies. 1992. mass mkt. 4.99 o.s.i (*0-345-37720-6*) Ballantine Bks.

—Friends, Lovers, Enemies. 1991. 19.95 o.p. (*1-55611-252-1*) Fine, Donald I. Bks.

Walker, Jim. In Search of Eden. 2003. 350p. pap. 12.99 (*1-58229-313-9*) Howard Publishing Co.

West, Morris. The Tower of Babel. l.t. ed. 1986. (Charnwood Large Print Ser.). 512p. 29.99 o.p. (*0-7089-8311-1*, Charnwood) Thorpe, F. A. Pubs. GBR. *Dist:* Ulverscroft Large Print Bks., Ltd., Ulverscroft Large Print Canada, Ltd.

Witham, Larry. The Negev Project. 1994. 301p. 17.95 (*0-9640428-0-0*) Meridian Bks. of Maryland.

Wolf, S. K. MacKinnon's Machine. 1991. 320p. 19.95 o.p. (*0-671-70051-0*, Simon & Schuster) Simon & Schuster.

## MIDDLE WEST—FICTION

Allen, Eadie. Nightmares at Noon. 2001. 383p. pap. 22.99 o.p. (*0-7388-9956-9*) Xlibris Corp.

Becker, Laney K. Dear Stranger, Dearest Friend. 2000. 304p. 24.00 (*0-380-97853-9*, Morrow, William & Co.) Morrow/Avon.

—Dear Stranger, Dearest Friend. l.t. ed. 2001. (G. K. Hall Inspirational Ser.). 381p. 26.95 (*0-7838-9403-1*) Thorndike Pr.

Bellow, Saul. Ravelstein. l.t. ed. 2000. (Compass Press Large Print Book Ser.). 286p. 26.95 (*1-56895-127-2*, Wheeler Publishing, Inc.) Gale Group.

—Ravelstein. unabr. ed. 2000. 29.95 (*1-56511-428-0*) HighBridge Co.

—Ravelstein. 240p. 2000. 24.95 o.p. (*0-670-84134-X*); 50th ed. 2001. reprint ed. 13.00 (*0-14-100176-3*) Viking Penguin.

Bingham, Doris. Send My Roots Rain. 2001. 282p. pap. 21.99 (*0-7388-9941-0*); E-Book 8.00 (*0-7388-9942-9*) Xlibris Corp.

Blake, James Carlos. Handsome Harry. 2004. 320p. 24.95 (*0-06-055478-9*, Morrow, William & Co.) Morrow/Avon.

—Handsome Harry: A Novel. 2004. pap. (*0-06-055479-7*, Morrow, William & Co.) Morrow/Avon.

Brodkey, Harold. The World Is the Home of Love & Death: Stories. 384p. 1998. pap. 15.00 o.s.i (*0-8050-5999-7*, Owl Bks.); 1997. 25.00 o.s.i (*0-8050-5513-4*, Metropolitan Bks.) Holt, Henry & Co.

Clark, Robert. Love among the Ruins. 2001. 352p. text 24.95 (*0-393-02015-0*) Norton, W. W. & Co., Inc.

—Love among the Ruins: A Novel. 2002. 336p. pap. 13.00 (*1-4000-3030-7*) Random Hse., Inc.

Coldsmith, Don. Tallgrass. 1998. 576p. reprint ed. mass mkt. 6.50 o.s.i (*0-553-57776-X*) Bantam Bks.

Collins, Michael. The Keepers of Truth. 2001. 320p. pap. 13.00 (*0-7432-1803-5*, Scribner); E-Book 9.99 (*0-7432-2361-6*, Simon & Schuster) Simon & Schuster.

Cummins, Joseph. The Snow Train. 2001. 285p. pap. 14.95 (*1-888451-23-8*) Akashic Bks.

Daum, Meghan. The Quality of Life Report: A Novel. 2003. 320p. 24.95 (*0-670-03213-1*, Viking) Viking Penguin.

Drury, Tom. Hunts in Dreams. 2000. 208p. tchr. ed. 22.00 o.p. (*0-395-94113-X*) Houghton Mifflin Co.

—Hunts in Dreams: A Novel. 2001. 208p. pap. 13.00 (*0-618-12740-2*, Mariner Bks.) Houghton Mifflin Co. Trade & Reference Div.

Evans, Elizabeth. Rowing In Eden: A Novel. 2000. 352p. 25.00 (*0-06-019550-9*) HarperCollins Pubs.

—Rowing in Eden: A Novel. 2001. 352p. pap. 13.00 (*0-06-095470-1*, Perennial) HarperTrade.

Fay, Christopher. The Arteries of Commerce: A Story of the Great Lakes. 1999. 211p. E-Book 8.00 (*0-7388-8167-8*) Xlibris Corp.

Franzen, Jonathan. The Corrections: A Novel. 2001. 528p. 26.00 o.p. (*0-374-10012-8*); 576p. 26.00 (*0-374-12998-3*); E-Book 26.00 (*0-374-70187-3*); E-Book 26.00 (*0-374-70186-5*); E-Book 26.00 o.p. (*0-374-70185-7*); E-Book 9.00 (*0-374-70184-9*) Farrar, Straus & Giroux.

—The Corrections: A Novel. 2002. pap. (*0-312-42161-3*); 592p. pap. 15.00 (*0-312-42127-3*); mass mkt. 7.99 (*0-312-98429-4*) Picador.

—The Corrections: A Novel. l.t. ed. 2003. (Paperback Bestsellers Ser.). pap. 29.95 (*0-7838-9767-7*) Thorndike Pr.

Gardner, Mary. Milkweed. 1994. 320p. 18.00 (*0-918949-46-7*, Papier-Mache Pr.) Moyer Bell.

Gass, William H. The Tunnel. 1999. (Illus.). 672p. reprint ed. pap. 15.95 (*1-56478-213-1*) Dalkey Archive Pr.

—The Tunnel. 1996. 79p. pap. 17.50 o.p. (*0-06-097686-1*) HarperCollins Pubs.

Guess, Carol. Seeing Dell. 1996. 174p. pap. 12.95 o.p. (*1-57344-023-X*); lib. bdg. 24.95 o.p. (*1-57344-024-8*) Cleis Pr.

Hamilton, Jane. A Map of the World. 1999. (Oprah's Book Club Ser.). 400p. 24.95 o.s.i (*0-385-50076-9*) Doubleday Publishing.

Heppner, Mike. The Egg Code: A Novel. 2003. 512p. pap. 14.95 (*0-375-72725-6*, Vintage) Knopf Publishing Group.

—The Egg Code: A Novel. 2002. 480p. 25.95 (*0-375-41290-5*) Knopf, Alfred A. Inc.

Hynes, James. The Lecturer's Tale. 2001. x, 388p. 25.00 o.s.i (*0-312-20332-2*) Picador.

John, Sally D. A Journey by Chance. 2002. (Other Way Home Ser.: Vol. 1). 400p. pap. 10.99 (*0-7369-0880-3*) Harvest Hse. Pubs.

Johnnie D. 2001. mass mkt. 6.99 (*0-8125-7087-1*, Forge Bks.) Doherty, Tom Assocs., LLC.

Johnson, Denis. The Name of the World. 2000. 144p. 22.00 (*0-06-019248-8*) HarperCollins Pubs.

—The Name of the World: A Novel. 2001. 144p. pap. 12.00 (*0-06-092965-0*, Perennial) HarperTrade.

Just, Ward. Family Trust. 1979. mass mkt. 2.50 o.s.i (*0-345-28093-8*) Ballantine Bks.

—Family Trust. 2001. 336p. pap. text 13.00 (*1-58648-034-0*) PublicAffairs.

Kent, Debra. The Diary of V: The Affair. 2001. 320p. reprint ed. mass mkt. 6.99 (*0-446-61049-6*, Warner Romance) Warner Bks., Inc.

Leithauser, Brad. A Few Corrections: A Novel. 2002. (Vintage Contemporaries Ser.). 288p. pap. 13.00 (*0-375-72558-X*, Vintage) Knopf Publishing Group.

Lentricchia, Frank. Lucchesi & the Whale. Fish, Stanley & Jameson, Fredric, eds. 2003. 128p. pap. 16.95 (*0-8223-3171-3*) Duke Univ. Pr.

—Lucchesi & the Whale. 2001. (Post-Contemporary Interventions Ser.). 104p. pap. 24.95 (*0-8223-2654-X*) Duke Univ. Pr.

Leslie, Naton. Marconi's Dream. 2002. 160p. (Orig.). pap. 18.95 (*1-881515-51-6*) Texas Review Pr.

Lewis, Sinclair. Kingsblood Royal. 2001. (Modern Library Classics). 352p. pap. 12.95 (*0-375-75686-8*, Modern Library) Random House Adult Trade Publishing Group.

Lyons, Richard. Divisible by One. 2001. 152p. 24.00 (*0-9657639-9-4*) Van Neste Bks.

McGugan, Jim. Josepha: A Prairie Boy's Story. ed. 1996. (J). (gr. 2). spiral bd. (*0-616-01722-7*) Canadian National Institute for the Blind/Institut National Canadien pour les Aveugles.

—Josepha: A Prairie Boy's Story. 1994. (Illus.). 32p. (J). (gr. 1-7). 11.95 o.p. (*0-8118-0802-5*) Chronicle Bks. LLC.

—Josepha: A Prairie Boy's Story. (Illus.). 32p. (J). pap. 8.95 (*0-88995-142-X*) Red Deer Pr. CAN. *Dist:* General Distribution Services, Inc.

McSherry, Frank D., et al, eds. Ghosts of the Heartland: Haunting, Spine Chilling Stories from the American Midwest. 1990. (American Ghosts Ser.). 224p. pap. 9.95 (*1-55853-068-1*) Rutledge Hill Pr.

Meyers, Kent. The River Warren: A Novel. 1999. 280p. pap. 13.00 o.s.i (*0-15-601062-3*, Harvest Bks.) Harcourt Trade Pubs.

—The River Warren: A Novel. 1998. 271p. 21.00 o.p. (*1-886913-23-4*) Ruminator Bks.

Nemec, David. Remember Me to My Father. 2001. 279p. 24.95 (*1-885003-70-6*) Reed, Robert D. Pubs.

Peart, Jane. The Heart's Lonely Secret. 1994. (Orphan Train West Ser.). 312p. (gr. 10 up). pap. 9.99 o.p. (*0-8007-5542-1*) Revell, Fleming H. Co.

—The Heart's Lonely Secret. l.t. ed. 2001. (Christian Fiction Ser.). 423p. 27.95 (*0-7862-3286-2*) Thorndike Pr.

Peck, Richard. The Ghost Belonged to Me. l.t. ed. 1989. 230p. (YA). reprint ed. lib. bdg. 16.95 o.s.i (*1-55736-116-9*, Cornerstone Bks.) Pages, Inc.

Powers, J. F. The Stories of J. F. Powers. 2000. (New York Review Books Classics Ser.). xii, 570p. pap. 14.95 (*0-940322-22-6*) New York Review of Bks., Inc., The.

Powers, James F. The Presence of Grace. 1977. (Short Story Index Reprint Ser.). 24.95 (*0-8369-3037-1*) Ayer Co. Pubs., Inc.

Pulver, Mary M. Ashes to Ashes. 1992. 256p. 4.50 o.p. (*1-55773-768-1*, Diamond Bks.) Ace Bks.

—Ashes to Ashes. 1988. 288p. 16.95 o.p. (*0-312-02164-X*, Saint Martin's Minotaur) St. Martin's Pr.

—Knight Fall. 1992. 4.50 o.p. (*1-55773-648-0*, Diamond Bks.) Ace Bks.

—Murder at the War: A Modern-Day Mystery with a Medieval Setting. 1987. 228p. 16.95 o.p. (*0-312-00622-5*) St. Martin's Pr.

—Original Sin. 1993. 256p. 4.50 o.p. (*1-55773-846-7*, Diamond Bks.) Ace Bks.

—Original Sin. 1991. 192p. 18.95 o.s.i (*0-8027-5770-7*) Walker & Co.

—Show Stopper: A Kori & Peter Brichter Mystery. 1993. 240p. 4.50 o.s.i (*1-55773-925-0*, Diamond Bks.) Ace Bks.

—Show Stopper: A Kori & Peter Brichter Mystery. 1993. mass mkt. 4.50 o.p. (*0-425-15828-4*) Berkley Publishing Group.

—Show Stopper: A Kori & Peter Brichter Mystery. 1992. 204p. 19.95 (*0-8027-3210-0*) Walker & Co.

—The Unforgiving Minutes. 1992. 4.50 o.p. (*1-55773-686-3*, Diamond Bks.) Ace Bks.

—The Unforgiving Minutes. 1988. 336p. 17.95 o.p. (*0-312-01528-3*, Saint Martin's Minotaur) St. Martin's Pr.

Robinson, Ronald. Diamond Trump: Events Surrounding the Great Powder-House Blowup by the Man Who Lit the Fuse. Rose, Margaret, ed. 2000. 26p. 19.95 (*0-944287-24-7*) Ex Machina.

Roth, Philip. When She Was Good. 1985. (Fiction Ser.). 320p. pap. 5.95 o.p. (*0-14-007676-X*, Penguin Bks.) Viking Penguin.

Seifert, Elizabeth. The Doctor's Promise. l.t. ed. 2000. (Romance Ser.). 312p. 27.95 (*0-7862-2491-6*) Thorndike Pr.

—Two Doctors & a Girl. 1999. 304p. (*0-7540-3676-6*); (*0-7540-3675-8*) BBC Audiobooks America.

—Two Doctors & a Girl. 1978. mass mkt. 1.50 o.p. (*0-451-08118-8*, W8118, Signet Bks.) NAL.

—Two Doctors & a Girl. l.t. ed. 1999. (Candlelight Romance Ser.). 304p. 21.95 o.p. (*0-7862-1763-4*) Thorndike Pr.

—The Two Faces of Dr. Collier. 23.95 (*0-89190-937-0*) Amereon, Ltd.

—The Two Faces of Dr. Collier. 1974. mass mkt. 1.25 o.p. (*0-451-06534-4*); mass mkt. 0.95 o.p. (*0-451-05799-6*) NAL. (Signet Bks.).

—The Two Faces of Dr. Collier. l.t. ed. 2000. (Candlelight Romance Ser.). 352p. 21.95 (*0-7862-2590-4*); (*0-7540-4197-2*) Thorndike Pr.

—The Two Faces of Dr. Collier: The Doctor's Reputation. 1980. mass mkt. 1.95 o.p. (*0-451-09469-7*, J9469, Signet Bks.) NAL.

Semovitz, Gary. Great American Plain. 2001. 240p. 23.00 o.s.i (*0-8050-6777-9*) Holt, Henry & Co.

—Great American Plain: A Novel. 2002. 240p. pap. 13.00 (*0-312-42107-9*) Picador.

Shepherd, John Scott. Henry's List of Wrongs. 2002. 292p. 24.95 (*1-59071-001-0*) Rugged Land.

Shoemaker, Karen Gettert. Night Sounds & Other Stories. 2002. 159p. pap. 14.95 (*0-8023-1337-X*) Dufour Editions, Inc.

Smith, Mary S. June: A Novel. 2000. (Illus.). 317p. 26.00 (*0-931642-30-2*); pap. 16.00 (*0-931642-29-9*) Lintel.

Snelling, Lauraine. A Dream to Follow: Return to Red River. 2001. (*0-7642-8856-3*); 416p. pap. 16.99 (*0-7642-2611-8*) Bethany Hse. Pubs.

—A Dream to Follow Bk #1. 2001. (Red River of the North Ser.). 320p. pap. 12.99 (*0-7642-2317-8*) Bethany Hse. Pubs.

—A Dream to Follow Bk. 1: Return to Red River. 2002. (Five Star Christian Fiction Ser.). 319p. 24.95 (*0-7862-4441-0*, Five Star) Gale Group.

Tarkington, Booth. Alice Adams. 24.95 (*0-89190-737-8*) Amereon, Ltd.

—Alice Adams. Set. audio 41.95 (*1-55685-398-X*) Audio Bk. Contractors, Inc.

—Alice Adams. 1999. (Works of Booth Tarkington). 434p. reprint ed. lib. bdg. 118.00 (*1-58201-843-X*) Classic Bks.

—Alice Adams. l.t. ed. 1999. (Perennial Bestsellers Ser.). 365p. 25.95 (*0-7838-8561-X*) Thorndike Pr.

Tarkington, Booth & Wells, Angus. Alice Adams. 1997. 288p. mass mkt. 5.95 o.s.i (*0-553-21459-4*, Bantam Classics) Bantam Bks.

Trice, Dawn Turner. An Eighth of August. 2002. 304p. pap. 13.00 (*0-385-72147-1*, Knopf Bks. for Young Readers) Random Hse. Children's Bks.

Walsh, M. M. B. Grass Heart. 2001. 170p. 22.95 (*0-8263-2338-3*) Univ. of New Mexico Pr.

Williams, David. Grandma Essie's Covered Wagon. 1993. (Illus.). 48p. (J). (ps-3). 16.00 o.s.i (*0-679-80253-3*, Knopf Bks. for Young Readers) Random Hse. Children's Bks.

Wilson, Barbara J. Murder & the Mad Hatter: A Brenda Midnight Mystery. 2001. (Brenda Midnight Mysteries Ser.). 256p. mass mkt. 5.99 (*0-380-80357-7*, Avon Bks.) Morrow/Avon.

Winegardner, Mark. That's True of Everybody. 2004. 252p. pap. 13.00 (*0-15-602736-4*) Harcourt Trade Pubs.

—That's True of Everybody: Stories. 2002. 256p. 24.00 (*0-15-100864-7*) Harcourt Trade Pubs.

Wingate, Linda. The Good Hope Road. 2003. (Illus.). 304p. pap. 12.95 (*0-451-20861-7*) NAL.

Woiwode, Larry. So He Says: A Season of Survival in Two Acts. 2001. 336p. pap. text 14.00 (*0-465-07849-4*) Basic Bks.

**MIDKEMIA (IMAGINARY PLACE)—FICTION**

Feist, Raymond E. A Darkness at Sethanon. 1987. 464p. mass mkt. 7.99 (*0-553-26328-5*, Spectra) Bantam Bks.

—Krondor: Tear of the Gods. 2001. (Riftwar Legacy Ser.: Bk. 3). 384p. mass mkt. 7.99 (*0-06-101500-8*) HarperCollins Pubs.

—Krondor: Tear of the Gods. 2001. (Riftwar Legacy Ser.: Bk. 3). (Illus.). 384p. 25.00 (*0-380-97800-8*, Eos) Morrow/Avon.

—Krondor: The Assassins. (Riftwar Legacy Ser.: Bk. 2). 2000. 416p. mass mkt. 7.99 (*0-380-80323-2*, HarperTorch); 1999. 374p. 25.00 (*0-380-97707-9*, Avon Bks.) Morrow/Avon.

—Krondor: The Betrayal. (Riftwar Legacy Ser.: Bk. 1). 1999. 432p. mass mkt. 7.50 (*0-380-79527-2*, Eos); 1998. 384p. 24.00 (*0-380-97715-X*, Avon Bks.) Morrow/Avon.

—Magician. 1992. 22.00 o.s.i (*0-385-42630-5*); 1984. 552p. 8.95 o.s.i (*0-385-19621-0*); 1982. 552p. 19.95 o.p. (*0-385-17580-9*) Doubleday Publishing.

—Magician: Apprentice. 1993. 336p. mass mkt. 5.99 o.s.i (*0-553-26760-4*); (Riftwar Saga Ser.: Vol. 1). 512p. mass mkt. 7.50 (*0-553-56494-3*) Bantam Bks. (Spectra).

—Magician: Master. 1993. 352p. mass mkt. 5.99 o.s.i (*0-553-26761-2*); (Riftwar Saga Ser.: Vol. 2). 528p. mass mkt. 7.50 (*0-553-56493-5*) Bantam Bks. (Spectra).

—Shadow of a Dark Queen. 1994. 22.00 o.p. (*0-688-12408-9*, Morrow, William & Co.) Morrow/Avon.

—Shards of a Broken Crown. (Serpentwar Saga: Vol. IV). 1999. 528p. mass mkt. 6.99 (*0-380-78983-3*, Eos); 1998. 432p. 24.00 (*0-380-97399-5*, Avon Bks.) Morrow/Avon.

—Silverthorn. 1993. (Riftwar Saga Ser.: Vol. 3). 352p. mass mkt. 7.99 (*0-553-27054-0*); 1986. 336p. mass mkt. 3.50 o.s.i (*0-553-25928-8*) Bantam Bks. (Spectra).

**MINNEAPOLIS (MINN.)—FICTION**

Bull, Emma. War for the Oaks. Date not set. mass mkt. (*0-7653-4915-9*, Tor Bks.); 4th ed. 2001. 320p. pap. 13.95 (*0-7653-0034-6*, CPB1150, Orb Bks.) Doherty, Tom Assocs., LLC.

Clark, Mary Higgins. Pretend You Don't See Her. unabr. ed. 1997. audio 48.00 (*0-7366-3711-7*, 4395) Books on Tape, Inc.

—Pretend You Don't See Her. 2000. E-Book 9.95 (*0-7432-0625-8*, Simon & Schuster); 1998. 320p. pap. 7.99 (*0-671-86715-6*, Pocket); 1997. 320p. 25.00 (*0-684-81039-5*, Simon & Schuster); 1997. 480p. 25.00 (*0-684-83416-2*, Simon & Schuster) Simon & Schuster.

—Pretend You Don't See Her. abr. ed. 1997. audio 18.00 (*0-671-57521-X*, 395160); audio compact disk 20.00 (*0-671-55715-7*) Simon & Schuster Audio. (Simon & Schuster Audioworks).

—Pretend You Don't See Her. 1998. 14.04 (*0-606-13721-1*) Turtleback Bks.

Compton, Jodi. The 37th Hour. 2004. 326p. 21.95 (*0-385-33713-2*, Delacorte Pr.) Dell Publishing.

Erdrich, Louise. The Antelope Wife: A Novel. unabr. ed. 1999. audio 48.00 (*0-7366-4277-3*, 4775) Books on Tape, Inc.

—The Antelope Wife: A Novel. 1999. 240p. text 24.00 (*0-7881-6505-4*) DIANE Publishing Co.

—The Antelope Wife: A Novel. l.t. ed. 1998. 27.95 (*1-56895-614-2*, Wheeler Publishing, Inc.) Gale Group.

—The Antelope Wife: A Novel. 1998. 256p. o.s.i (*0-06-018726-3*, HarperFlamingo) HarperCollins Pubs. Canada, Ltd.

—The Antelope Wife: A Novel. 1999. 256p. pap. 13.00 (*0-06-093007-1*, Perennial); 1998. audio 25.00 (*0-694-51922-7*, 695743, Caedmon) HarperTrade.

Erickson, K. J. The Last Witness: A Mystery. 2003. 352p. 24.95 (*0-312-31468-X*, Saint Martin's Minotaur) St. Martin's Pr.

—Third Person Singular. 2001. 309p. 24.95 (*0-312-26666-9*, Saint Martin's Minotaur) St. Martin's Pr.

Giordano, Marie. I Love You Like a Tomato. Date not set. mass mkt. (*0-7653-4588-9*, Forge Bks.); pap. (*0-7653-0669-7*, Forge Bks.); 2003. 477p. 21.95 (*0-7653-0927-0*, Tor Bks.); 2003. 480p. 24.95 (*0-7653-0668-9*, Forge Bks.) Doherty, Tom Assocs., LLC.

Handberg, Ron. Malice Intended. 1997. 608p. mass mkt. 6.50 (*0-06-101246-7*, HarperTorch) Morrow/Avon.

Hart, Ellen. Faint Praise. 1997. (Jane Lawless Mysteries Ser.). 321p. mass mkt. 5.99 o.s.i (*0-345-40493-9*) Ballantine Bks.

—Faint Praise: A Jane Lawless Mystery. 1995. (Jane Lawless Mysteries Ser.). 272p. text 20.95 (*1-878067-67-2*, Seal Pr.) Avalon Publishing Group.

—For Every Evil. 1995. (Jane Lawless Mysteries Ser.). 272p. mass mkt. 5.99 o.s.i (*0-345-38190-4*) Ballantine Bks.

—Hallowed Murder. 1989. 224p. pap. 8.95 o.p. (*0-931188-83-0*, Seal Pr.) Avalon Publishing Group.

—Hallowed Murder. 2003. 256p. pap. 13.95 (*0-312-31931-2*, Saint Martin's Minotaur) St. Martin's Pr.

—A Hallowed Murder. 1993. (Jane Lawless Mysteries Ser.). 256p. reprint ed. mass mkt. 6.99 (*0-345-38140-8*) Ballantine Bks.

—Hallowed Murder. unabr. ed. 1995. (Jane Lawless Mysteries Ser.: No. 1). audio 39.95 (*1-888348-00-3*, HCB101) Hall Closet Bk. Co.

—Hunting the Witch. 1999. 384p. 24.95 (*0-312-20386-1*, Saint Martin's Minotaur) St. Martin's Pr.

—Immaculate Midnight: A Jane Lawless Mystery. E-Book 24.95 (*0-312-70728-2*); 2003. 336p. pap. 13.95 (*0-312-31365-9*, Saint Martin's Griffin); 2002. 384p. 24.95 (*0-312-26676-6*, Saint Martin's Minotaur) St. Martin's Pr.

—A Killing Cure. 1993. 304p. 19.95 (*1-878067-36-2*, Seal Pr.) Avalon Publishing Group.

—A Killing Cure. 1995. (Jane Lawless Mysteries Ser.). 304p. mass mkt. 5.99 o.s.i (*0-345-39112-8*) Ballantine Bks.

—Merchant of Venus. mass mkt. (*0-312-97991-6*, St. Martin's Paperbacks); 2001. 389p. 24.95 (*0-312-26618-9*, Saint Martin's Minotaur) St. Martin's Pr.

—Murder in the Air. 1997. (Culinary Mysteries Ser.). 352p. mass mkt. 6.50 (*0-345-40203-0*, Ballantine Bks.) Ballantine Bks.

—The Oldest Sin. 1996. (Sophie Greenway Mystery Ser.: Bk. 3). 288p. mass mkt. 5.99 (*0-345-40202-2*) Ballantine Bks.

—Robber's Wine: A Jane Lawless Mystery. 1996. (Jane Lawless Mysteries Ser.). 304p. 21.95 (*1-878067-80-X*, Seal Pr.) Avalon Publishing Group.

—Robber's Wine: A Jane Lawless Mystery. 1998. (Jane Lawless Mysteries Ser.). mass mkt. 5.99 o.s.i (*0-345-40494-7*) Ballantine Bks.

—A Small Sacrifice. 1995. (Jane Lawless Mysteries Ser.). mass mkt. 5.99 o.s.i (*0-345-39113-6*) Ballantine Bks.

—Stage Fright. 1992. 261p. 9.95 (*1-878067-21-4*, Seal Pr.) Avalon Publishing Group.

—Stage Fright. 1994. (Midwest Mysteries Ser.). mass mkt. 5.99 o.s.i (*0-345-38142-4*) Ballantine Bks.

—Stage Fright. Date not set. pap. (*0-312-32020-5*); pap. (*0-312-31765-4*) St. Martin's Pr. (St. Martin's Paperbacks).

—This Little Piggy Went to Murder. 1994. (Midwest Mysteries Ser.). 230p. (Orig.). mass mkt. 5.99 o.s.i (*0-345-38189-0*) Ballantine Bks.

—Vital Lies. 1991. 200p. (Orig.). pap. 9.95 o.s.i (*1-878067-02-8*, Seal Pr.) Avalon Publishing Group.

—Vital Lies. 1993. (Jane Lawless Mysteries Ser.). 256p. (Orig.). reprint ed. mass mkt. 5.99 o.s.i (*0-345-38141-6*) Ballantine Bks.

—Vital Lies. Date not set. (Orig.). pap. (*0-312-32046-9*); pap. (*0-312-31766-2*) St. Martin's Pr. (St. Martin's Paperbacks).

—Wicked Games. (Jane Lawless Mysteries Ser.). 368p. 1998. 24.95 (*0-312-18680-0*, Saint Martin's Minotaur); Vol. 1. 3rd ed. 1999. mass mkt. 5.99 (*0-312-96707-1*, St. Martin's Paperbacks) St. Martin's Pr.

Hoag, Tami. Ashes to Ashes. unabr. ed. 2000. 12p. audio 96.95 (*0-7927-2365-1*, CSL 254, Chivers Sound Library) BBC Audiobooks America.

—Ashes to Ashes. 1999. 496p. 24.95 o.s.i (*0-553-10633-3*); 2000. 592p. reprint ed. mass mkt. 7.99 (*0-553-57960-6*) Bantam Bks.

—Ashes to Ashes. l.t. ed. 2000. 12.95 (*1-56895-983-4*); 1999. 26.95 o.p. (*1-56895-713-0*) Gale Group. (Wheeler Publishing, Inc.).

—Ashes to Ashes. abr. ed. 1999. audio 25.00 Highsmith Inc.

—Ashes to Ashes. abr. ed. 1999. audio 25.00 (*0-671-58232-1*, 594124, Simon & Schuster Audioworks) Simon & Schuster Audio.

—Dust to Dust. l.t. ed. 2000. 624p. 25.95 (*0-375-43078-4*) Random Hse. Large Print.

—Dust to Dust. abr. ed. 2000. audio 25.00 (*0-671-58256-9*); audio compact disk 32.00 (*0-7435-0642-1*) Simon & Schuster Audio. (Simon & Schuster Audioworks).

Lake, M. D. Amends for Murder. l.t. ed. 1991. pap. 15.95 o.p. (*0-7927-0801-6*, AS0288) BBC Audiobooks America.

—Amends for Murder. 1989. pap. 4.99 (*0-380-75865-2*, Avon Bks.) Morrow/Avon.

—Cold Comfort. 1990. pap. 5.99 (*0-380-76032-0*, Avon Bks.) Morrow/Avon.

—Flirting with Death. 1996. (Orig.). pap. 5.99 o.p. (*0-380-77522-0*, Avon Bks.) Morrow/Avon.

—A Gift for Murder. 1992. (Peggy O'Neill Mystery Ser.). 256p. mass mkt. 5.50 (*0-380-76855-0*, Avon Bks.) Morrow/Avon.

—Grave Choices: A Peggy O'Neill Mystery. 1995. pap. 5.99 o.p. (*0-380-77521-2*, Avon Bks.) Morrow/Avon.

—Midsummer Malice. 1997. (Peggy O'Neill Mystery Ser.). pap. 5.99 o.p. (*0-380-78759-8*, Avon Bks.) Morrow/Avon.

—Murder by Mail. 1993. (Orig.). pap. 5.99 o.p. (*0-380-76856-9*, Avon Bks.) Morrow/Avon.

—Once upon a Crime. 1995. (Peggy O'Neill Mystery Ser.). (Orig.). pap. 5.50 (*0-380-77520-4*, Avon Bks.) Morrow/Avon.

—Poisoned Ivy. 1992. (Peggy O'Neill Mystery Ser.). 256p. pap. 5.50 (*0-380-76573-X*, Avon Bks.) Morrow/Avon.

Malloy, Brian. Year of Ice. 2003. 272p. pap. 12.95 (*0-312-31369-1*, Saint Martin's Griffin) St. Martin's Pr.

Millett, Larry. Sherlock Holmes & the Ice Palace Murders: From the American Chronicles of John H. Watson, M.D. 1998. 336p. 23.95 o.p. (*0-670-87944-4*) Viking Penguin.

—Sherlock Holmes & the Secret Alliance. 2002. 336p. mass mkt. 6.99 (*0-14-200155-4*) Penguin Group (USA) Inc.

—Sherlock Holmes & the Secret Alliance. 2001. 336p. 24.95 o.s.i (*0-670-03015-5*, Viking) Viking Penguin.

Nelson, Michael J. Mike Nelson's Death Rat! A Novel. 2003. 336p. pap. 14.95 (*0-06-093472-7*, HarperEntertainment) Morrow/Avon.

Sandford, John. Mortal Prey. l.t. ed. 2003. 559p. pap. 14.95 (*0-7862-4367-8*) Thorndike Pr.

Sandford, John, pseud. Certain Prey. 7.99 (*0-425-17521-9*); 2000. 384p. mass mkt. 7.99 (*0-425-17427-1*) Berkley Publishing Group.

—Certain Prey. 1999. 384p. 24.95 o.s.i (*0-399-14496-X*, G. P. Putnam's Sons) Penguin Group (USA) Inc.

—Certain Prey. l.t. ed. (Thorndike/G. K. Hall Paperback Bestsellers Ser.). 2000. 518p. pap. 27.95 (*0-7862-2007-4*); 1999. 512p. 30.95 (*0-7862-2006-6*) Thorndike Pr.

—Chosen Prey. 2002. 400p. mass mkt. 7.99 (*0-425-18287-8*) Berkley Publishing Group.

—Chosen Prey. l.t. ed. 2002. 477p. pap. 13.95 (*0-7838-9589-5*, Wheeler Publishing, Inc.) Gale Group.

—Chosen Prey. 2001. 416p. 26.95 o.s.i (*0-399-14728-4*) Penguin Group (USA) Inc.

—Chosen Prey. l.t. ed. 2001. 480p. 32.95 (*0-7838-9588-7*) Thorndike Pr.

—Easy Prey. 2001. 400p. reprint ed. mass mkt. 7.99 (*0-425-17876-5*) Berkley Publishing Group.

—Easy Prey. 2000. (Prey Ser.). 384p. 25.95 o.s.i (*0-399-14613-X*) Penguin Group (USA) Inc.

—Easy Prey. l.t. ed. (Core Ser.). 519p. 2001. pap. 29.95 (*0-7838-9073-7*); 2000. 31.95 (*0-7838-9074-5*) Thorndike Pr.

—Eyes of Prey. 1992. 368p. mass mkt. 7.99 (*0-425-13204-8*) Berkley Publishing Group.

—Eyes of Prey. abr. ed. audio 15.95 o.p. (*1-55994-420-X*, 326336, HarperAudio) HarperTrade.

—Eyes of Prey. 1991. 320p. 19.95 o.s.i (*0-399-13629-0*, G. P. Putnam's Sons) Penguin Group (USA) Inc.

—Eyes of Prey. 19.95 o.s.i (*0-399-13846-3*) Putnam Publishing Group, The.

—Eyes of Prey. unabr. ed. 1993. (Prey Ser.: No. 3). audio 85.00 (*1-55690-826-1*, 93141K8) Recorded Bks., LLC.

—John Sandford - Three Complete Novels: Mind Prey; Sudden Prey; Secret Prey. 2000. 752p. 14.98 (*0-399-14651-2*) Penguin Group (USA) Inc.

—Mind Prey. 1996. 368p. mass mkt. 7.99 (*0-425-15289-8*) Berkley Publishing Group.

—Mind Prey. l.t. ed. 1995. 25.95 o.p. (*1-56895-233-3*, Wheeler Publishing, Inc.) Gale Group.

—Mind Prey. 1995. o.p. (*0-399-19275-1*); 323p. 23.95 o.p. (*0-399-14009-3*, G. P. Putnam's Sons) Penguin Group (USA) Inc.

—Mind Prey. 23.95 o.s.i (*0-399-14291-6*) Putnam Publishing Group, The.

—Mind Prey. unabr. ed. 1995. (Prey Ser.: No. 7). audio 78.00 (*0-7887-0387-0*, 94578K8) Recorded Bks., LLC.

—Mind Prey. abr. ed. 1995. audio 18.00 o.s.i (*0-671-52290-6*, 392984, Simon & Schuster Audioworks) Simon & Schuster Audio.

—Mortal Prey. 2002. 416p. 26.95 o.s.i (*0-399-14863-9*) Penguin Group (USA) Inc.

—Night Prey. 1995. 416p. mass mkt. 7.99 (*0-425-14641-3*) Berkley Publishing Group.

—Night Prey. l.t. ed. 1994. pap. 21.95 o.p. (*1-56895-075-6*, Wheeler Publishing, Inc.) Gale Group.

—Night Prey. 1994. 320p. 22.95 o.p. (*0-399-13914-1*, G. P. Putnam's Sons) Penguin Group (USA) Inc.

—Night Prey. 22.95 o.s.i (*0-399-14176-6*) Putnam Publishing Group, The.

—Night Prey. unabr. ed. 1995. (Prey Ser.: No. 6). audio 70.00 (*0-7887-0192-4*, 94416E7) Recorded Bks., LLC.

—Night Prey. abr. ed. 1999. audio 17.00 (*0-671-51174-2*, 391266, Simon & Schuster Audioworks) Simon & Schuster Audio.

—Rules of Prey. 1990. 368p. mass mkt. 7.99 (*0-425-12163-1*) Berkley Publishing Group.

—Rules of Prey. 16.95 (*0-399-13635-5*) Penguin Group (USA) Inc.

—Rules of Prey. 1989. 320p. 16.95 o.s.i (*0-399-13465-4*, G. P. Putnam's Sons) Penguin Group Putnam Bks. for Young Readers.

—Secret Prey. 1999. 400p. reprint ed. mass mkt. 7.99 (*0-425-16829-8*) Berkley Publishing Group.
—Secret Prey. l.t. ed. 1998. 27.95 (*1-56895-673-8*, Wheeler Publishing, Inc.) Gale Group.
—Secret Prey. 1998. 384p. 24.95 o.p. (*0-399-14382-3*, G. P. Putnam's Sons) Penguin Group (USA) Inc.
—Shadow Prey. 1991. 368p. mass mkt. 7.99 (*0-425-12606-4*) Berkley Publishing Group.
—Shadow Prey. abr. ed. audio 15.95 o.p. (*1-55994-419-6*, 326323, HarperAudio) HarperTrade.
—Shadow Prey. 1990. 352p. 18.95 o.p. (*0-399-13543-X*, G. P. Putnam's Sons) Penguin Putnam Bks. for Young Readers.
—Shadow Prey. 18.95 o.s.i (*0-399-13750-5*) Putnam Publishing Group, The.
—Silent Prey. 1993. 384p. mass mkt. 7.99 (*0-425-13756-2*) Berkley Publishing Group.
—Silent Prey. 1992. 320p. 21.95 o.p. (*0-399-13742-4*, G. P. Putnam's Sons) Penguin Group (USA) Inc.
—Silent Prey. 21.95 o.s.i (*0-399-13905-2*) Putnam Publishing Group, The.
—Silent Prey, unabr. ed. 1993. (Prey Ser.: No. 4). audio 67.00 (*1-55690-918-7*, 93414K8) Recorded Bks., LLC.
—Sudden Prey. 1997. 400p. mass mkt. 7.99 (*0-425-15753-9*) Berkley Publishing Group.
—Sudden Prey. 23.95 (*0-399-14428-5*); 1996. 320p. 23.95 o.s.i (*0-399-14138-3*, G. P. Putnam's Sons) Penguin Group (USA) Inc.
—Sudden Prey, unabr. ed. 1997. (Prey Ser.: No. 8). audio 80.00 Recorded Bks., LLC.
—Sudden Prey. abr. ed. 1996. audio 18.00 (*0-671-57421-3*, 394521, Simon & Schuster Audioworks) Simon & Schuster Audio.
—Sudden Prey. l.t. ed. 1996. (Core Ser.). 516p. 28.95 (*0-7838-1832-7*) Thorndike Pr.
—Winter Prey. 1994. 352p. mass mkt. 7.99 (*0-425-14123-3*) Berkley Publishing Group.
—Winter Prey. 1994. lib. bdg. 18.95 o.p. (*0-8161-5833-9*); 1993. 464p. lib. bdg. 24.95 (*0-8161-5832-0*) Gale Group. (Macmillan Reference USA).
—Winter Prey. abr. ed. 2000. audio 9.99 (*0-694-52325-9*, HarperAudio) HarperTrade.
—Winter Prey. 1993. 320p. 21.95 o.p. (*0-399-13815-3*, G. P. Putnam's Sons) Penguin Group (USA) Inc.
—Winter Prey. 21.95 o.s.i (*0-399-14071-9*) Putnam Publishing Group, The.
—Winter Prey, unabr. ed. 1995. (Prey Ser.: No. 5). audio 78.00 (*0-7887-0255-6*, 94464E7) Recorded Bks., LLC.
Seeley, Mabel. The Whistling Shadow. 2000. 205p. reprint ed. 24.00 (*1-890434-16-7*) Afton Historical Society Pr.
Sharratt, Mary. Summit Avenue. 2000. ii, 252p. pap. 14.95 (*1-56689-097-7*) Coffee Hse. Pr.
Shott, James R. Bathsheba: People of the Promise, Bk. 8. l.t. ed. 2003. (Christian Fiction Ser.). 26.95 (*0-7862-4534-4*) Thorndike Pr.
Thayer, Steve. Silent Snow. 2000. 416p. reprint ed. mass mkt. 6.99 (*0-451-18664-8*, Signet Bks.) NAL.
—Silent Snow. abr. ed. 2000. audio 18.00 (*0-7871-1980-6*); 1999. audio 30.00 (*0-7871-1979-2*) NewStar Media, Inc. (Dove Audio).
—Silent Snow, unabr. ed. 1999. audio 66.00 (*0-7887-3767-8*, 95984E7) Recorded Bks., LLC.
—Silent Snow. 1999. 416p. 24.95 o.s.i (*0-670-86572-9*, Viking) Viking Penguin.
—The Weatherman. 1996. 416p. mass mkt. 7.99 (*0-451-18438-6*, Signet Bks.) NAL.
—The Weatherman, Set. abr. ed. 1995. audio 16.95 (*1-879371-88-X*, 391877) Publishing Mills, Inc., The.
—The Weatherman, unabr. ed. 1995. audio 91.00 (*0-7887-0267-X*, 94476E7) Recorded Bks., LLC.
—The Weatherman. 1995. 22.95 (*0-670-77309-3*); 464p. 21.95 o.s.i (*0-670-84958-8*, Viking) Viking Penguin.
Tracy, P. J. Live Bait. 2004. 320p. 23.95 (*0-399-15147-8*) Putnam Publishing Group, The.
—Monkeewrench. 2004. 432p. mass mkt. 6.99 (*0-451-21157-X*, Signet Bks.) NAL.
—Monkeewrench. 2003. 384p. 23.95 (*0-399-14978-3*, Putnam & Grosset) Putnam Publishing Group, The.
—Monkeewrench. l.t. ed. 2003. 547p. 28.95 (*0-7862-5645-1*) Thorndike Pr.
Treuer, David. The Hiawatha. 1999. 320p. 24.00 o.p. (*0-312-20313-6*) Picador.
Warren, Susan. Tying the Knot. 2003. (HeartQuest Ser.). 350p. pap. 9.99 (*0-8423-8118-X*) Tyndale Hse. Pubs.
Zimmerman, R. D. Closet: A Todd Mills Mystery. 1995. 320p. mass mkt. 4.99 o.s.i (*0-440-21869-1*) Dell Publishing.
—Closet: A Todd Mills Mystery. 1997. 304p. pap. 10.95 o.s.i (*0-385-32004-3*) Doubleday Publishing.
—Innuendo. 2000. (Todd Mills Mysteries Ser.). 320p. pap. 11.95 (*0-385-31926-6*, Dial Bks.) Dell Publishing.
—Outburst: A Todd Mills Mystery. 1999. (Illus.). 304p. pap. 19.00 (*0-385-31923-1*, Delacorte Pr.) Dell Publishing.
—Tribe. 1996. 288p. mass mkt. 5.50 o.s.i (*0-440-21870-5*) Dell Publishing.
—Tribe: A Todd Mills Mystery. 1997. 272p. pap. 10.95 o.s.i (*0-385-32002-7*) Doubleday Publishing.

**MINNESOTA—FICTION**

Alexander, Kathryn. Twin Wishes. 2000. (Steeple Hill Love Inspired Ser.: Vol. 96). 256p. per. (*0-373-87102-3*, Harlequin Bks.) Harlequin Enterprises, Ltd.
Bausch, Richard. Mr. Field's Daughter. 1989. 18.95 o.p. (*0-671-64051-8*, Simon & Schuster) Simon & Schuster.
Bender, Carrie. Birch Hollow Schoolmarm. 1999. (Dora's Diary Ser.: Bk. 1). (Illus.). 192p. pap. 8.99 (*0-8361-9095-5*) Herald Pr.
—Birch Hollow Schoolmarm. l.t. ed. 2002. (Christian Fiction Ser.). 189p. 27.95 (*0-7862-4584-0*) Thorndike Pr.
—Birch Hollow Schoolmarm. 1999. E-Book 8.99 (*0-585-32381-X*) netLibrary, Inc.
Benitez, Sandra. Night of the Radishes. 2004. 22.95 (*0-7868-6400-1*) Hyperion Pr.
Bergquist, J. Gordon. Minnetaka Indian Boy. 1985. (Illus.). 150p. (Orig.). pap. text 9.75 (*0-9615483-0-4*) Bergquist Publishing.
Bly, Carol. My Lord Bag of Rice: New & Selected Stories. 2000. xi, 361p. pap. 16.95 (*1-57131-031-2*) Milkweed Editions.
—The Tomcat's Wife & Other Stories. 1991. 224p. 19.95 o.p. (*0-06-016504-9*) HarperTrade.
Brenna, Duff. The Altar of the Body. 2001. 336p. 24.00 (*0-312-26865-3*) Picador.
—The Altar of the Body: A Novel. 2002. 336p. pap. 13.00 (*0-312-26914-5*) Picador.
Broker's Open: A Real Estate Murder Mystery in Duluth Minnesota. 2001. 237p. pap. 7.95 (*0-9707111-0-7*) Better Bks. Bureau.
Carter, Emily. Glory Goes & Gets Some. 2000. 239p. 20.95 (*1-56689-101-9*) Coffee Hse. Pr.
—Glory Goes & Gets Some. 2001. 240p. pap. 13.00 (*0-312-28251-6*) Picador.
Casanova, Mary. Wolf Shadows. 1999. 12.04 (*0-606-16667-X*) Turtleback Bks.
Clark, Mary Higgins. Pretend You Don't See Her. unabr. ed. 1997. audio 48.00 (*0-7366-3711-7*, 4395) Books on Tape, Inc.
—Pretend You Don't See Her. 1998. 14.04 (*0-606-13721-1*) Turtleback Bks.
Clark, Robert. In Deep Midwinter. 1996. 288p. 23.00 o.p. (*0-312-15149-7*) Picador.
Cochrane, Mick. Sport. E-Book 22.95 (*1-58945-580-0*) Adobe Systems, Inc.
—Sport. E-Book 22.95 (*0-312-70059-8*); 2001. 246p. 22.95 (*0-312-26994-3*) St. Martin's Pr.
—Sport: A Novel. 2003. 256p. pap. 14.95 (*0-8166-4085-8*) Univ. of Minnesota Pr.
Conner, Michael. Archangel. 1996. 408p. mass mkt. 6.99 (*0-8125-4321-1*); 1995. 352p. 21.95 o.p. (*0-312-85743-8*) Doherty, Tom Assocs., LLC. (Tor Bks.).
—Archangel. 296p. 2002. pap. 19.95 o.p. (*0-7592-0328-8*); 2002. E-Book 6.99 (*0-7592-0324-5*); 2002. E-Book 6.99 (*0-7592-0325-3*); 2001. E-Book 6.99 (*0-7592-1008-X*) ereads.com.
Dean, Pamela. Juniper, Gentian & Rosemary. 1998. 352p. (YA). (gr. 10 up). 24.95 o.p. (*0-312-86004-8*, Tor Bks.) Doherty, Tom Assocs., LLC.
Dennis, Pat. Stand-up & Die. 2000. 208p. pap. 11.95 (*0-9676344-1-5*) Penury Pr.
Disch, Thomas M. The Priest: A Gothic Romance. 1995. 24.00 (*0-679-42880-1*) Knopf, Alfred A. Inc.
Dorner, Marjorie. Seasons of Sun & Rain. 2000. 360p. 23.95 (*1-57131-027-4*); reprint ed. pap. 14.95 (*1-57131-033-9*) Milkweed Editions.
—Seasons of Sun & Rain. l.t. ed. 2000. (Thorndike Senior Lifestyle Ser.). 512p. 26.95 (*0-7862-2414-2*) Thorndike Pr.
Drury, Joan M. Silent Words. 1996. 224p. pap. 10.95 (*1-883523-13-3*) Spinsters Ink Bks.
Eagle, Kathleen. You Never Can Tell. l.t. ed. 2001. 400p. 25.00 o.p. (*0-06-620960-9*) HarperCollins Pubs.
—You Never Can Tell. 2002. 384p. mass mkt. 6.99 (*0-380-81015-8*); 2001. 320p. 24.00 (*0-380-97816-4*) Morrow/Avon. (Morrow, William & Co.).
Edwards, Cassie. Sun Hawk. 2000. 384p. mass mkt. 6.99 o.s.i (*0-451-20014-4*, Signet Bks.) NAL.
Eilola, Patricia. The Fabulous Family Holomolaiset: A Minnesota Finnish Family's Oral Tradition. 1996. (Illus.). 128p. pap. 12.95 (*0-87839-108-8*) North Star Pr. of St. Cloud.
Elkin, Stanley. The Living End. 1979. 7.95 o.p. (*0-525-07020-6*, Dutton) Dutton/Plume.
Enger, L. L. The Sinners' League: A Gun Pedersen Mystery. 1994. 288p. 21.00 (*1-883402-64-6*, Scribner) Simon & Schuster.
Enger, Leif. Peace Like a River. l.t. ed. 2002. (Wheeler Large Print Book Ser.). 28.95 (*1-58724-212-5*, Wheeler Publishing, Inc.) Gale Group.
—Peace Like a River. 320p. 2002. pap. 13.00 (*0-8021-3925-6*, Grove Pr.); 2001. 24.00 (*0-87113-795-X*, Atlantic Monthly Pr.) Grove/Atlantic, Inc.
Feldhake, Susan C. The Darkness & the Dawn. 8th ed. 1996. (Enduring Faith Ser.: Bk. 8). 208p. pap. 9.99 o.p. (*0-310-20262-0*) Zondervan.
—From This Day Forward. 1994. (Enduring Faith Ser.: Bk. 5). 208p. pap. 9.99 o.p. (*0-310-47931-2*) Zondervan.
—Joy in the Morning. 1994. (Enduring Faith Ser.: Vol. 6). 208p. pap. 9.99 o.p. (*0-310-47941-X*) Zondervan.
Ferris, Monica. Framed in Lace. 1999. (Needlecraft Mystery Ser.). 256p. mass mkt. 5.99 (*0-425-17149-3*) Berkley Publishing Group.
—Hanging by a Thread. 2003. 272p. mass mkt. 6.50 (*0-425-18714-4*, Prime Crime) Berkley Publishing Group.
—A Murderous Yarn. 2002. 256p. mass mkt. 5.99 (*0-425-18403-X*) Berkley Publishing Group.
—A Stitch in Time. 2000. (Needlecraft Mysteries Ser.). 256p. mass mkt. 5.99 (*0-425-17511-1*, Prime Crime) Berkley Publishing Group.
—Unraveled Sleeve. 2001. (Needlecraft Mysteries Ser.). (Illus.). 256p. mass mkt. 5.99 (*0-425-18045-X*, Prime Crime) Berkley Publishing Group.
Ferris, Monica & Bookman, Terry. Crewel World. 1999. (Needlecraft Mysteries Ser.). 256p. (Orig.). mass mkt. 5.99 (*0-425-16780-1*, Prime Crime) Berkley Publishing Group.
Fluke, Joanne. Chocolate Chip Cookie Murder. 2001. 336p. mass mkt. 6.50 (*0-7582-0230-X*); 2001. 336p. mass mkt. 5.99 o.s.i (*1-57566-650-2*, Kensington Bks.); 2000. 312p. 20.00 o.s.i (*1-57566-524-7*) Kensington Publishing Corp.
—Strawberry Shortcake Murder. 2002. 32p. mass mkt. 6.50 (*1-57566-721-5*); 2001. 34p. 22.00 o.s.i (*1-57566-644-8*) Kensington Publishing Corp.
Fowler, Karen Joy. The Sweetheart Season: A Novel. 1996. 320p. 23.00 o.s.i (*0-8050-4737-9*) Holt, Henry & Co.
Gilseth, Margaret Chrislock. Julia's Children: A Norwegian Immigrant Family in Minnesota. 1987. 443p. (Orig.). pap. 14.95 (*0-9619327-1-6*) Askeladd Pr.
Gottry, Steven & Jacobsen, Richard. The Spirit of Tocayo. 1995. 16.95 (*1-886158-01-0*) Macalester Park Publishing Co., Inc.
Guest, Judith. Ice Walk. ltd. ed. 2001. (Winter Book Ser.: Vol. 13). (Illus.). 20p. 195.00 (*1-879832-36-4*) Minnesota Ctr. for Bk. Arts.
—Ice Walk: Chapbook. ltd. ed. 2001. (Winter Bks.: Vol. 13). (Illus.). 20p. 20.00 (*1-879832-35-6*) Minnesota Ctr. for Bk. Arts.
Gunn, Elizabeth. Five Card Stud. 2000. (Jake Hines Mysteries Ser.). 195p. (YA). 23.95 (*0-8027-3343-3*) Walker & Co.
—Par Four: A Jake Hines Mystery. 2000. (Jake Hines Mysteries Ser.). 304p. mass mkt. 5.99 o.s.i (*0-440-22636-8*) Dell Publishing.
—Par Four: A Jake Hines Mystery. 1999. (Jake Hines Mysteries Ser.). (Illus.). 291p. pap. 22.95 (*0-8027-3324-7*) Walker & Co.
—Seventh-Inning Stretch: A Jake Hines Mystery. 2002. 228p. 23.95 (*0-8027-3374-3*) Walker & Co.
—Six-Pound Walleye. 2002. (WWL Mystery Ser.). mass mkt. (*0-373-26425-9*, Worldwide Library) Harlequin Enterprises, Ltd.
—Six-Pound Walleye: A Jake Hines Mystery. l.t. ed. 2001. 341p. 27.95 (*0-7862-3616-7*) Thorndike Pr.
—Six-Pound Walleye: A Jake Hines Mystery. 2001. (Jake Hines Mysteries Ser.). 216p. 23.95 (*0-8027-3356-5*) Walker & Co.
—Triple Play: A Jake Hines Mystery. 1998. (Jake Hines Mysteries Ser.). 224p. mass mkt. 5.99 o.s.i (*0-440-22635-X*) Dell Publishing.
—Triple Play: A Jake Hines Mystery. 1997. (Jake Hines Mysteries Ser.). 240p. 21.95 (*0-8027-3307-7*) Walker & Co.
Handberg, Ron. Cry Vengeance. 1995. 464p. mass mkt. 6.50 o.s.i (*0-06-100840-0*, HarperTorch) Morrow/Avon.
—Dead Silence. 1999. 464p. (Orig.). mass mkt. 6.99 (*0-06-101247-5*) HarperCollins Pubs.
Hartwick, Cynthia. Ladies with Options. 2001. 352p. pap. 12.95 (*0-425-17823-4*) Berkley Publishing Group.
—Ladies with Prospects. 2004. 352p. pap. 14.00 (*0-425-19421-3*) Berkley Publishing Group.
Hassler, Jon. The Dean's List. 1999. pap. 0.00 (*0-345-43237-1*); 1998. 432p. mass mkt. 6.99 (*0-345-42473-5*) Ballantine Bks.
—The Dean's List. l.t. ed. 1997. (Niagara Large Print Ser.). 592p. 29.50 o.p. (*0-7089-5887-7*, Ulverscroft) Thorpe, F. A. Pubs. GBR. *Dist:* Ulverscroft Large Print Bks., Ltd.
—Dear James. 1996. pap. 12.95 o.s.i (*0-345-41013-0*); 1994. 432p. mass mkt. 6.99 o.s.i (*0-345-37708-7*) Ballantine Bks.
—Grand Opening. 1987. 368p. 17.95 o.p. (*0-688-06649-6*, Morrow, William & Co.) Morrow/Avon.
—A Green Journey. 1996. 304p. pap. 12.95 (*0-345-41041-6*); 1993. mass mkt. 5.99 o.p. (*0-345-90023-5*); 1986. 304p. mass mkt. 5.99 o.s.i (*0-345-33372-1*) Ballantine Bks.
—A Green Journey. 1985. 320p. 15.95 o.p. (*0-688-03982-0*, Morrow, William & Co.) Morrow/Avon.
—Rookery Blues. 1997. 512p. mass mkt. 6.99 o.s.i (*0-345-42308-9*); 1996. 496p. pap. 12.00 o.s.i (*0-345-40641-9*) Ballantine Bks.
—Rookery Blues. abr. ed. audio 24.95 (*0-9650850-0-7*, PCAB-3500) Pine Curtain Audiobooks.
—Rufus at the Door & Other Stories. 2000. (Illus.). 128p. 29.00 (*1-890434-28-0*); pap. 14.95 (*1-890434-29-9*) Afton Historical Society Pr.
—Staggerford. 1997. pap. 12.00 o.s.i (*0-345-41824-7*); 1986. 304p. mass mkt. 6.99 (*0-345-33375-6*) Ballantine Bks.
—Staggerford. 1977. 8.95 o.p. (*0-689-10793-5*, Atheneum) Simon & Schuster Children's Publishing.
—The Staggerford Flood. 2003. 208p. pap. 13.00 (*0-452-28462-7*, Plume) Dutton/Plume.
—The Staggerford Flood. 2002. 208p. 24.95 (*0-670-03125-9*, Viking) Viking Penguin.
—Staggerford's Indian. ltd. ed. 1988. (Winter Bks.: No. 1). (Illus.). 36p. 60.00 o.s.i (*1-879832-18-6*); pap. 25.00 o.s.i (*1-879832-19-4*) Minnesota Ctr. for Bk. Arts.
Haugland, Cynthia W. Francheska. 1992. 500p. 19.95 (*0-9630340-0-6*); pap. 14.95 (*0-9630340-1-4*) Master Communications Group, Inc.
Hautman, Pete. Drawing Dead. 1997. 320p. pap. 5.99 (*0-671-00302-X*, Pocket); 1993. 285p. 20.50 (*0-671-79374-8*, Simon & Schuster) Simon & Schuster.
—The Mortal Nuts. l.t. ed. 1996. 22.95 o.p. (*0-7838-1925-0*, Macmillan Reference USA) Gale Group.
—The Mortal Nuts. 1997. per. 5.99 (*0-671-00304-6*, Pocket); 1996. 288p. 21.00 o.p. (*0-684-81000-X*, Simon & Schuster) Simon & Schuster.
—Mrs. Million. 288p. 2000. pap. 12.95 (*0-671-03865-6*, Pocket); 1999. 23.00 (*0-684-83243-7*, Simon & Schuster) Simon & Schuster.
—Mrs. Million. l.t. ed. 1999. (Americana Ser.). 424p. 27.95 (*0-7862-1986-6*) Thorndike Pr.
Haynes, David. Heathens. 1996. (Minnesota Voices Project Ser.: No. 72). 182p. 21.95 (*0-89823-166-3*) New Rivers Pr.
Henry, Gordon, Jr. The Light People: A Novel. (American Indian Literature & Critical Studies: Vol. 7). 272p. 1995. pap. 13.95 o.p. (*0-8061-2735-X*); 1994. 22.95 o.p. (*0-8061-2586-1*) Univ. of Oklahoma Pr.
Henry, Gordon. The Light People: A Novel. 2003. x, 226p. 19.95 (*0-87013-664-X*) Michigan State Univ. Pr.
Henschel, Lee, Jr. Deja 'Nam. 2000. 268p. pap. 21.99 (*0-7388-2979-X*) Xlibris Corp.
Hill, Rebecca. Among Birches. 1986. 352p. 17.95 o.p. (*0-688-06165-6*, Morrow, William & Co.) Morrow/Avon.
—Among Birches. 1987. 320p. pap. 6.95 o.p. (*0-14-009852-6*, Penguin Bks.) Viking Penguin.
Hoag, Tami. Ashes to Ashes. unabr. ed. 2000. 12p. audio 96.95 (*0-7927-2365-1*, CSL 254, Chivers Sound Library) BBC Audiobooks America.
—Ashes to Ashes. 1999. 496p. 24.95 o.s.i (*0-553-10633-3*); 2000. 592p. reprint ed. mass mkt. 7.99 (*0-553-57960-6*) Bantam Bks.
—Ashes to Ashes. l.t. ed. 2000. 12.95 (*1-56895-983-4*); 1999. 26.95 o.p. (*1-56895-713-0*) Gale Group. (Wheeler Publishing, Inc.).
—Ashes to Ashes. abr. ed. 1999. audio 25.00 Highsmith Inc.
—Ashes to Ashes. abr. ed. 1999. audio 25.00 (*0-671-58232-1*, 594124, Simon & Schuster Audioworks) Simon & Schuster Audio.
—Dust to Dust. l.t. ed. 2000. 624p. 25.95 (*0-375-43078-4*) Random Hse. Large Print.
—Dust to Dust. abr. ed. 2000. audio 25.00 (*0-671-58256-9*); audio compact disk 32.00 (*0-7435-0642-1*) Simon & Schuster Audio. (Simon & Schuster Audioworks).
—Guilty As Sin. 1997. 624p. mass mkt. 7.99 (*0-553-56452-8*) Bantam Bks.
—Guilty As Sin. l.t. ed. 1996. 825p. 25.95 o.p. (*0-7838-1821-1*, Macmillan Reference USA) Gale Group.
—Guilty As Sin. abr. ed. 1996. 6p. audio 23.00 (*1-56876-057-4*) Soundlines Entertainment, Inc.
—Night Sins. 1995. 576p. mass mkt. 7.99 (*0-553-56451-X*, Fanfare) Bantam Bks.
—Night Sins. l.t. ed. 1995. 821p. 25.95 o.p. (*0-7838-1348-1*, Macmillan Reference USA) Gale Group.
—Night Sins, abr. ed. 1996. audio 17.00 (*1-56876-058-2*, 394501) Soundlines Entertainment, Inc.
—Still Waters. 1992. 464p. mass mkt. 7.99 (*0-553-29272-2*) Bantam Bks.
Hogan, Linda. Solar Storms. 1997. 352p. pap. 13.00 (*0-684-82539-2*); 1995. 320p. 22.00 o.p. (*0-684-81227-4*); 1994. 21.00 o.s.i (*0-689-12190-3*) Simon & Schuster. (Scribner).

Housewright, David. Dearly Departed: A Holland Taylor Mystery. 1999. (Holland Taylor Mystery Ser.). 224p. text 23.95 o.p. (*0-393-04771-7*) Norton, W. W. & Co., Inc.

—Penance. 1997. (Holland Taylor Mystery Ser.). 304p. mass mkt. 6.50 o.s.i (*0-425-15942-6*, Prime Crime) Berkley Publishing Group.

—Penance. 1995. (Holland Taylor Mystery Ser.). 296p. 21.00 (*0-88150-341-X*, Foul Play) Norton, W. W. & Co., Inc.

—Practice to Deceive. 2000. (Holland Taylor Mystery Ser.). 275p. mass mkt. 5.99 o.s.i (*0-425-17312-7*) Berkley Publishing Group.

—Practice to Deceive: A Holland Taylor Mystery. 1997. (Holland Taylor Mystery Ser.). 256p. 22.00 (*0-88150-404-1*, Foul Play) Norton, W. W. & Co., Inc.

Hovey, Dean L. Hooker. 2002. 264p. pap. 14.95 (*1-930922-03-5*) J-Pr. Publishing.

Huber, Harold. South Beulah, Minnesota: Short Stories. 2000. (Illus.). vii, 117p. (Orig.). pap. 14.95 (*0-9675060-0-X*) Stone House Pr., Inc.

Hustvedt, Siri. The Enchantment of Lily Dahl: A Novel. 1996. 288p. 23.00 o.p. (*0-8050-4920-7*) Holt, Henry & Co.

Jacobs, Nancy B. The Silver Scalpel. 1993. (Devon McDonald Ser.). 240p. 21.95 o.p. (*0-399-13834-X*, G. P. Putnam's Sons) Penguin Group (USA) Inc.

—A Slash of Scarlet. 1992. 240p. 19.95 o.p. (*0-399-13733-5*, G. P. Putnam's Sons) Penguin Group (USA) Inc.

—A Slash of Scarlet. Rubenstein, Julie, ed. 1993. 256p. reprint ed. mass mkt. 4.99 (*0-671-86504-8*, Pocket) Simon & Schuster.

—The Turquoise Tattoo. 1992. 256p. reprint ed. mass mkt. 4.99 (*0-671-75535-8*, Pocket) Simon & Schuster.

—The Turquoise Tattoo: A Devon MacDonald Mystery. 1991. 240p. 19.95 o.p. (*0-399-13551-0*, G. P. Putnam's Sons) Penguin Group (USA) Inc.

Johnson, Wayne. Don't Think Twice. 1999. 304p. 23.00 o.s.i (*0-609-60460-0*, Harmony) Crown Publishing Group.

—Don't Think Twice. 2000. 304p. reprint ed. pap. 12.95 (*0-7434-0632-X*, Pocket) Simon & Schuster.

Keillor, Garrison. The Garrison Keillor Box: Lake Wobegon Days, Leaving Home, Happy to Be Here, & We Are Still Married, 4 bks., Set. 1992. reprint ed. 37.50 o.p. (*0-14-095358-2*, Penguin Bks.) Penguin Group (USA) Inc.

—Gospel Birds & Other Stories of Lake Wobegon. audio 14.38. audio compact disk 23.98 NewSound, LLC.

—Lake Wobegon Days. abr. ed. 1999. audio compact disk 36.95 (*1-56511-314-4*); 1991. audio 34.95 (*0-942110-08-0*) HighBridge Co.

—Lake Wobegon Days. 1990. (Illus.). 352p. pap. 14.00 (*0-14-013161-2*, Penguin Bks.); 1989. 432p. pap. 4.95 o.p. (*0-14-012918-9*) Penguin Group (USA) Inc.

—Lake Wobegon Days. 1986. 420p. pap. 3.95 o.p. (*0-14-009232-3*, Penguin Bks.); 1986. 432p. pap. 4.95 o.p. (*0-14-009983-2*, Penguin Bks.); 1985. 384p. 17.95 o.p. (*0-670-80514-9*) Viking Penguin.

—Lake Wobegon Loyalty Days. abr. ed. 1991. (Lake Wobegon Ser.). audio 11.00 (*0-942110-33-1*); audio compact disk 13.95 (*0-942110-34-X*) HighBridge Co.

—Lake Wobegon Sampler. 1986. audio 5.95 (*0-440-85047-9*, RH Audio) Random Hse. Audio Publishing Group.

—Lake Wobegon Summer 1956. l.t. ed. 2001. 341p. pap. 14.00 (*0-7838-9569-0*, Wheeler Publishing, Inc.) Gale Group.

—Lake Wobegon Summer 1956. 2002. 304p. pap. 14.00 (*0-14-200093-0*) Penguin Group (USA) Inc.

—Lake Wobegon Summer 1956. l.t. ed. 2001. 350p. 31.95 (*0-7838-9564-X*) Thorndike Pr.

—Lake Wobegon Summer 1956. 2001. (Illus.). 336p. 24.95 o.s.i (*0-670-03003-1*, Viking) Viking Penguin.

—Lake Wobegon U. S. A. abr. unabr. ed. 1993. (Lake Wobegon Ser.). 23p. audio compact disk 34.95 (*1-56511-001-3*); audio compact disk 36.95 (*1-56511-008-0*) HighBridge Co.

—Lake Wobegon U. S. A. Fertility. abr. unabr. ed. 1995. (Lake Wobegon Ser.). audio 11.00 (*1-56511-110-9*) HighBridge Co.

—Lake Wobegon U. S. A. Patience. abr. unabr. ed. 1995. (Lake Wobegon Ser.). audio 11.00 (*1-56511-109-5*) HighBridge Co.

—Lake Wobegon U. S. A. Rhubarb. abr. unabr. ed. 1995. (Lake Wobegon Ser.). audio 11.00 (*1-56511-112-5*) HighBridge Co.

—Lake Wobegon U. S. A. Youth. abr. unabr. ed. 1995. (Lake Wobegon Ser.). pap. 11.00 incl. audio (*1-56511-111-7*) HighBridge Co.

—Leaving Home. 1989. 288p. mass mkt. 4.95 o.p. (*0-451-82197-1*) NAL.

—Leaving Home. 1990. 288p. pap. 14.00 (*0-14-013160-4*); 1989. (*0-14-770045-0*) Penguin Group (USA) Inc. (Penguin Bks.).

—Leaving Home. 1987. 288p. 18.95 o.p. (*0-670-81976-X*); 19.95 o.p. (*0-670-82011-3*) Viking Penguin. (Viking).

—Life These Days: Stories from Lake Wobegon. abr. unabr. ed. 1998. 3p. audio 18.95 (*1-56511-293-8*); audio 30.00 (*1-56511-307-1*) HighBridge Co.

—Love Me. l.t. ed. 2003. 422p. 32.95 (*0-7862-6076-9*, Large Print Pr.) Thorndike Pr.

—Love Me. 2003. 288p. 24.95 (*0-670-03246-8*) Viking Penguin.

—More News from Lake Wobegon. abr. ed. 1991. (Lake Wobegon Ser.). audio compact disk 36.95 (*0-942110-37-4*); audio 34.95 (*0-942110-30-7*) HighBridge Co.

—More News from Lake Wobegon: Faith. abr. ed. 1991. (More News from Lake Wobegon Ser.). audio 11.00 (*0-942110-75-7*) HighBridge Co.

—More News from Lake Wobegon: Hope. abr. ed. 1991. (More News from Lake Wobegon Ser.). audio 11.00 (*0-942110-76-5*) HighBridge Co.

—More News from Lake Wobegon: Humor. abr. ed. 1991. (More News from Lake Wobegon Ser.). audio 12.95 (*0-942110-78-1*) HighBridge Co.

—More News from Lake Wobegon: Love. abr. ed. 1991. (Lake Wobegon Ser.). audio 11.00 (*0-942110-77-3*) HighBridge Co.

—News from Lake Wobegon: Fall. abr. ed. (News from Lake Wobegon Ser.). 1997. audio compact disk 13.95 (*1-56511-214-8*); 1991. audio 11.00 (*0-942110-22-6*) HighBridge Co.

—News from Lake Wobegon: Spring. abr. ed. 1991. (News from Lake Wobegon Ser.). audio 11.00 (*0-942110-19-6*) HighBridge Co.

—News from Lake Wobegon: Summer. abr. ed. (News from Lake Wobegon Ser.). 1997. audio compact disk 13.95 (*1-56511-209-1*); 1991. audio 11.00 (*0-942110-20-X*) HighBridge Co.

—News from Lake Wobegon: Winter. abr. ed. (News from Lake Wobegon Ser.). 1997. audio compact disk 13.95 (*1-56511-215-6*); 1991. audio 11.00 (*0-942110-21-8*, 25024-10749) HighBridge Co.

—News from Lake Wobegon 1974-1994. 20th abr. ed. 1994. (Prairie Home Companion Ser.). audio 34.95 (*1-56511-105-2*) HighBridge Co.

—Wobegon Boy. l.t. ed. 1998. 426p. 27.95 (*1-56895-560-X*, Wheeler Publishing, Inc.) Gale Group.

—Wobegon Boy. 1998. 288p. pap. 14.00 (*0-14-027478-2*) Penguin Group (USA) Inc.

—Wobegon Boy. abr. ed. 1997. (Lake Wobegon Ser.). audio 29.95 (*0-453-00965-4*, 695573) Penguin/HighBridge.

—Wobegon Boy. 1997. 320p. 24.95 (*0-670-87807-3*) Viking Penguin.

Kim, Walter. She Needed Me. Regan, Judith, ed. 1992. 240p. 20.00 (*0-671-78091-3*, Atria) Simon & Schuster.

Klassen, Duke. The Dance Hall at Spring Hill: Short Stories. Eller, Gary, ed. 1996. (Minnesota Voices Project Ser.: Vol. 75). 134p. pap. 14.95 (*0-89823-169-8*) New Rivers Pr.

Krueger, William Kent. Blood Hollow. 2004. (*0-7434-8867-9*, Atria); pap. (*0-7434-4587-2*, Pocket Star) Simon & Schuster.

—Boundary Waters. (Cork O'Connor Mysteries Ser.). 1999. 336p. 23.00 (*0-671-01698-9*, Atria); 2000. 416p. reprint ed. mass mkt. 6.99 (*0-671-01699-7*, Pocket Star) Simon & Schuster.

—Iron Lake: A Cork O'Connor Mystery. 1999. (Illus.). 464p. mass mkt. 6.99 (*0-671-01697-0*, Pocket Star); 1998. E-Book 23.00 (*0-671-03690-4*, Atria); 1998. (Cork O'Connor Mysteries Ser.: Vol. 1). 320p. 23.00 (*0-671-01696-2*, Atria) Simon & Schuster.

—Iron Lake: A Cork O'Connor Mystery. l.t. ed. 2001. 584p. 29.95 (*0-7862-3174-2*) Thorndike Pr.

—Purgatory Ridge: A Cork O'Connor Mystery. 2001. (Illus.). 368p. 23.95 (*0-671-04753-1*, Atria); 2002. 448p. reprint ed. mass mkt. 6.99 (*0-671-04754-X*, Pocket Star) Simon & Schuster.

—Purgatory Ridge: A Cork O'Connor Mystery. l.t. ed. 2001. (Americana Ser.). 627p. 30.95 (*0-7862-3213-7*) Thorndike Pr.

LaDuke, Winona. Last Standing Woman. 304p. 1999. pap. 14.95 (*0-89658-452-6*); 1997. 22.95 (*0-89658-278-7*) Voyageur Pr., Inc.

LaFavor, Carole. Along the Journey River. 1996. 192p. pap. 10.95 (*1-56341-070-2*); lib. bdg. 22.95 (*1-56341-071-0*) Firebrand Bks.

—Evil Dead Center: A Mystery. 1997. 224p. pap. 11.95 (*1-56341-088-5*); 216p. lib. bdg. 24.95 (*1-56341-089-3*) Firebrand Bks.

Lake, M. D. Amends for Murder. l.t. ed. 1991. pap. 15.95 o.p. (*0-7927-0801-6*, AS0288) BBC Audiobooks America.

—Amends for Murder. 1989. pap. 4.99 (*0-380-75865-2*, Avon Bks.) Morrow/Avon.

—Cold Comfort. 1990. pap. 5.99 (*0-380-76032-0*, Avon Bks.) Morrow/Avon.

—Flirting with Death. 1996. (Orig.). pap. 5.99 o.p. (*0-380-77522-0*, Avon Bks.) Morrow/Avon.

—A Gift for Murder. 1992. (Peggy O'Neill Mystery Ser.). 256p. mass mkt. 5.50 (*0-380-76855-0*, Avon Bks.) Morrow/Avon.

—Grave Choices: A Peggy O'Neill Mystery. 1995. pap. 5.99 o.p. (*0-380-77521-2*, Avon Bks.) Morrow/Avon.

—Midsummer Malice. 1997. (Peggy O'Neill Mystery Ser.). pap. 5.99 o.p. (*0-380-78759-8*, Avon Bks.) Morrow/Avon.

—Murder by Mail. 1993. (Orig.). pap. 5.99 o.p. (*0-380-76856-9*, Avon Bks.) Morrow/Avon.

—Once upon a Crime. 1995. (Peggy O'Neill Mystery Ser.). (Orig.). pap. 5.50 (*0-380-77520-4*, Avon Bks.) Morrow/Avon.

—Poisoned Ivy. 1992. (Peggy O'Neill Mystery Ser.). 256p. pap. 5.50 (*0-380-76573-X*, Avon Bks.) Morrow/Avon.

Landvick, Lorna. Your Oasis on Flame Lake. 2003. 322p. 30.95 (*1-57490-500-7*, Beeler Large Print Bks.) Beeler, Thomas T. Publisher.

Landvik, Lorna. Angry Housewives Eating Bon Bons. 2004. 432p. pap. 13.95 (*0-345-44282-2*) Ballantine Bks.

—Angry Housewives Eating Bon Bons. l.t. ed. 2003. 30.95 (*0-7862-5406-8*) Thorndike Pr.

—Patty Jane's House of Curl. 1999. 304p. (J). mass mkt. 6.99 (*0-8041-1460-9*, Ivy Bks.) Ballantine Bks.

—Patty Jane's House of Curl. l.t. ed. 1998. (Niagara Large Print Ser.). 368p. 29.50 o.p. (*0-7089-5877-X*, Ulverscroft) Thorpe, F. A. Pubs. GBR. *Dist:* Ulverscroft Large Print Bks., Ltd., Ulverscroft Large Print Canada, Ltd.

—Patty Jane's House of Curl: A Novel. 1996. (Reader's Circle Ser.). 320p. pap. 14.00 (*0-449-91100-4*, Ballantine Bks.) Ballantine Bks.

—Patty Jane's House of Curl: A Novel. 1995. 256p. 19.95 o.s.i (*1-882593-12-X*) Bridge Works Publishing Co., Inc.

—The Tall Pine Polka. 2001. (Reader's Circle Ser.). 464p. pap. 14.95 (*0-449-00370-1*, Ballantine Bks.) Ballantine Bks.

—The Tall Pine Polka. l.t. ed. 2000. 21.95 (*1-57490-325-X*) Beeler, Thomas T. Publisher.

—Your Oasis on Flame Lake. (Ballantine Reader's Circle Ser.). 1998. 320p. pap. 12.00 (*0-449-00298-5*); 1997. 256p. 23.00 o.s.i (*0-449-91278-7*) Ballantine Bks. (Fawcett).

Lane, Rose Wilder. Young Pioneers. 1998. (Little House Ser.). (Illus.). 192p. (J). (gr. 3 up). pap. 5.99 (*0-06-440698-9*, Harper Trophy) HarperCollins Children's Bk. Group.

—Young Pioneers. 1998. (Little House Ser.). (YA). (gr. 3 up). 12.00 (*0-606-17778-7*) Turtleback Bks.

Larranaga, Jim. The Dead Farmer's Almanac. 2000. 180p. pap. 20.99 (*0-7388-2117-9*); text 30.99 (*0-7388-2118-7*) Xlibris Corp.

Lee, Robert L. Fever Saga. 1985. (Illus.). 160p. (Orig.). pap. 6.95 (*0-9615377-0-1*) Heirloom Pr.

Lewis, Sinclair. Main Street. E-Book 3.95 (*0-594-05716-7*) 1873 Pr.

—Main Street. 1976. 25.95 (*0-8488-0828-2*) Amereon, Ltd.

—Main Street. 1996. 496p. pap. 10.95 (*0-7867-0325-3*, Carroll & Graf Pubs.) Avalon Publishing Group.

—Main Street. 1996. 544p. mass mkt. 5.95 (*0-553-21451-9*) Bantam Bks.

—Main Street. 1984. 297p. reprint ed. lib. bdg. 31.95 (*0-89966-495-4*) Buccaneer Bks., Inc.

—Main Street. reprint ed. lib. bdg. 48.00 (*0-7426-1369-0*); 2001. 451p. pap. 28.00 (*0-7426-5673-X*); 2001. pap. text 28.00 (*0-7426-6369-8*); 1998. 451p. lib. bdg. 108.00 (*1-58201-673-9*) Classic Bks.

—Main Street. unabr. ed. 1999. (Dover Thrift Editions Ser.). iv, 400p. pap. text 2.50 (*0-486-40655-5*) Dover Pubns., Inc.

—Main Street. 2003. (Barnes & Noble Classics Ser.). 576p. pap. 5.95 (*1-59308-036-0*) Fine Communications.

—Main Street. 1989. (Modern Classic Ser.). 451p. 15.95 o.s.i (*0-15-155547-8*) Harcourt Trade Pubs.

—Main Street. l.t. ed. 1394p. pap. 88.64 (*0-7583-1460-4*); 1714p. pap. 111.80 (*0-7583-1461-2*); 2109p. pap. 127.07 (*0-7583-1462-0*); 1089p. pap. 74.20 (*0-7583-1459-0*); 2446p. pap. 149.71 (*0-7583-1463-9*); 851p. pap. 62.17 (*0-7583-1458-2*); 621p. pap. 44.14 (*0-7583-1457-4*); 497p. pap. 37.12 (*0-7583-1456-6*); 2446p. lib. bdg. 180.60 (*0-7583-1455-8*); 2109p. lib. bdg. 149.57 (*0-7583-1454-X*); 1714p. lib. bdg. 129.80 (*0-7583-1453-1*); 1394p. lib. bdg. 100.64 (*0-7583-1452-3*); 1089p. lib. bdg. 86.20 (*0-7583-1451-5*); 851p. lib. bdg. 74.17 (*0-7583-1450-7*); 621p. lib. bdg. 50.14 (*0-7583-1449-3*); 497p. lib. bdg. 43.12 (*0-7583-1448-5*) Huge Print Pr.

—Main Street. 2002. 472p. 28.99 (*1-4043-1584-5*); per. 23.99 (*1-4043-1585-3*) IndyPublish.com.

—Main Street. 1999. 518p. pap. 9.95 o.p. (*1-930128-08-8*, JNMedia Bks.) JNMedia, Inc.

—Main Street. (*0-451-52742-9*); mass mkt. 0.95 o.p. (*0-451-02005-7*, Signet Bks.); 1970. mass mkt. 1.25 o.p. (*0-451-50500-X*, Signet Classics); 1970. mass mkt. 0.95 o.p. (*0-451-50352-X*, Signet Classics); 1970. mass mkt. 0.75 o.p. (*0-451-50093-8*, Signet Classics); 1961. 440p. mass mkt. 4.50 o.p. (*0-451-52147-1*, Signet Classics); 1961. mass mkt. 3.50 o.p. (*0-451-51831-4*, Signet Classics); 1961. mass mkt. 3.50 o.p. (*0-451-51712-1*, Signet Classics); 1961. mass mkt. 2.95 o.p. (*0-451-51536-6*, Signet Classics); 1961. mass mkt. 2.50 o.p. (*0-451-51392-4*, Signet Classics); 1961. mass mkt. 2.25 o.p. (*0-451-51140-9*, Signet Classics); 1961. mass mkt. 1.50 o.p. (*0-451-50753-3*, Signet Classics); 1961. 448p. mass mkt. 5.95 o.s.i (*0-451-52461-6*, Signet Classics); 1961. mass mkt. 1.75 o.p. (*0-451-50875-0*, Signet Classics); 1961. mass mkt. 3.95 o.p. (*0-451-51898-5*, Signet Classics); 1998. 440p. mass mkt. 5.95 (*0-451-52682-1*, Signet Bks.) NAL.

—Main Street. 2001. 510p. 25.00 (*1-58287-154-X*); 650p. lib. bdg. 26.00 (*1-58287-637-1*) North Bks.

—Main Street. 1996. (Literary Classics). 459p. pap. 10.00 (*1-57392-048-7*) Prometheus Bks., Pubs.

—Main Street. 2000. E-Book 4.95 (*0-679-64167-X*, Modern Library) Random House Adult Trade Publishing Group.

—Main Street. 1999. (Modern Library Ser.). 448p. pap. 9.95 o.s.i (*0-375-75314-1*) Random Hse., Inc.

—Main Street. E-Book 5.00 (*0-7410-0558-1*) SoftBook Pr.

—Main Street. 1920. 12.00 (*0-606-01015-7*) Turtleback Bks.

—Main Street. 1995. (Twentieth Century Classics Ser.). 448p. pap. 11.00 (*0-14-018901-7*, Penguin Classics) Viking Penguin.

—Main Street. 1999. E-Book 5.99 (*0-8220-7126-6*, Cliff Notes) Wiley, John & Sons, Inc.

—Sinclair Lewis: Main Street & Babbitt. Hersey, John, ed. 1992. (Library of America: Vol. 59). 898p. 40.00 (*0-940450-61-5*) Library of America, The.

Lewis, Sinclair & Hersey, John. Main Street & Babbitt. 1992. E-Book 40.00 (*0-585-20170-6*) netLibrary, Inc.

Lindvall, Michael L. The Good News from North Haven. Rubenstein, Julie, ed. 1992. 192p. reprint ed. pap. 10.00 (*0-671-79200-8*, Pocket) Simon & Schuster.

—The Good News from North Haven: A Year in the Life of a Small Town. 2002. 192p. pap. 16.95 (*0-8245-2012-2*) Crossroad Publishing Co.

—The Good News from North Haven: A Year in the Life of a Small Town. 1991. 192p. 15.00 o.s.i (*0-385-41640-7*) Doubleday Publishing.

Logan, Chuck. Absolute Zero. 2002. E-Book 19.95 (*0-06-008539-8*); E-Book 19.95 (*0-06-008538-X*); E-Book 19.95 (*0-06-008537-1*); E-Book 19.95 (*0-06-050460-9*) HarperCollins General Bks. Group. (PerfectBound).

—Absolute Zero. 2002. 400p. 24.95 (*0-06-018572-4*) HarperCollins Pubs.

—Absolute Zero. 2002. audio 25.95 (*0-06-008342-5*, HarperAudio) HarperTrade.

—Absolute Zero. 2003. 464p. mass mkt. 7.99 (*0-06-103156-9*, HarperTorch) Morrow/Avon.

—The Big Law. 1999. 448p. mass mkt. 7.50 (*0-06-109687-3*); 1998. 368p. 24.00 o.s.i (*0-06-019133-3*) HarperCollins Pubs.

—The Big Law. unabr. ed. 1998. audio 87.00 (*0-7887-3244-7*, 95848E7) Recorded Bks., LLC.

—Hunter's Moon: Hunter's Moon. 1996. 416p. mass mkt. 7.50 (*0-06-109384-X*, HarperTorch) Morrow/Avon.

—The Price of Blood. 1997. 400p. 24.00 o.p. (*0-06-017492-7*) HarperCollins Pubs.

—The Price of Blood. 1998. 496p. mass mkt. 7.50 (*0-06-109622-9*, HarperTorch) Morrow/Avon.

Logue, Mary. Still Explosion. 248p. 1994. pap. 9.95 o.p. (*1-878067-48-6*); 1993. text 18.95 o.p. (*1-878067-29-X*) Avalon Publishing Group. (Seal Pr.).

Lovelace, Maud Hart. The Betsy-Tacy Treasury. 1995. (Illus.). (J). (gr. 1-8). 5.50 o.p. (*0-06-024919-6*) HarperCollins Pubs.

—Early Candlelight. 1992. (Borealis Bks.). xix, 322p. reprint ed. pap. 12.95 (*0-87351-269-3*, Borealis Bk.) Minnesota Historical Society Pr.

Macomber, Debbie. Changing Habits. 2004. 384p. mass mkt. (*0-7783-2028-6*); 2003. 352p. (*1-55166-690-1*) Harlequin Enterprises, Ltd. (Mira Bks.).

—Changing Habits. l.t. ed. 2003. 564p. 31.95 (*0-7862-5534-X*) Thorndike Pr.

Manfred, Frederick. Scarlet Plume. 1983. xviii, 365p. reprint ed. pap. 12.95 o.p. (*0-8032-8120-X*, Bison Bks.) Univ. of Nebraska Pr.

Marvin, Isabel R. The Tenth Rifle & the Jesse James Gang. 1994. (Illus.). (J). pap. 5.00 (*0-932433-12-X*) Windswept Hse. Pubs.

McCarthy, Cathy. The Hollow. 2000. 270p. pap. 14.95 (*1-58749-019-6*); 1999. E-Book 4.75 incl. disk (*1-928670-37-7*); 1999. E-Book 4.75 (*1-928670-38-5*) Awe-Struck E-Bks.

McColley, Kevin. Praying to a Laughing God: A Novel. 1998. 352p. 24.00 (*0-684-83761-7*, Simon & Schuster) Simon & Schuster.

Meyers, Kent. Light in the Crossing: Stories. 1999. 226p. 21.95 (*0-312-20337-3*) St. Martin's Pr.

Settings

Murphy, Nora, et al. Twelve Branches: Stories from St. Paul. 2003. 160p. pap. 10.00 (*1-56689-140-X*) Coffee Hse. Pr.

O'Brien, Tim. In the Lake of the Woods. 1994. 320p. tchr. ed. 21.95 o.p. (*0-395-48889-3*) Houghton Mifflin Co.

—In the Lake of the Woods. 1996. o.p. (*0-14-771179-7*); 1995. 320p. pap. 14.00 (*0-14-025094-8*, Penguin Bks.) Penguin Group (USA) Inc.

Olson, Shannon. Children of God Go Bowling. 2004. 304p. 24.95 (*0-670-03281-6*, Viking) Viking Penguin.

Richer, Lois. Daddy on the Way: Brides of the Seasons. 1999. (Steeple Hill Love Inspired Ser.: No. 79). per. (*0-373-87079-5*, 1-87079-9, Harlequin Bks.) Harlequin Enterprises, Ltd.

Ridley, William J. The Summit Sojourners. 2002. 208p. 23.95 (*0-87839-184-3*) North Star Pr. of St. Cloud.

Rose, Howard. The Marrano. 1992. 256p. 20.00 (*1-878352-08-3*); pap. 10.00 (*1-878352-09-1*) Saroff, Raymond Pub.

Roszak, Theodore. The Blizzard. 2001. (*1-58195-107-8*, Zoland Bks., Inc.) Steerforth Pr.

—The Devil & Daniel Silverman. 2003. 348p. pap. 15.95 (*0-9679520-7-7*) Leapfrog Pr.

Roth, Martha. Goodness. 1996. 320p. (Orig.). pap. 10.95 (*1-883523-11-7*) Spinsters Ink Bks.

Sandford, John, pseud. Certain Prey. 7.99 (*0-425-17521-9*); 2000. 384p. mass mkt. 7.99 (*0-425-17427-1*) Berkley Publishing Group.

—Certain Prey. 1999. 384p. 24.95 o.s.i (*0-399-14496-X*, G. P. Putnam's Sons) Penguin Group (USA) Inc.

—Certain Prey. l.t. ed. (Thorndike/G. K. Hall Paperback Bestsellers Ser.). 2000. 518p. pap. 27.95 (*0-7862-2007-4*); 1999. 512p. 30.95 (*0-7862-2006-6*) Thorndike Pr.

—Easy Prey. 2001. 400p. reprint ed. mass mkt. 7.99 (*0-425-17876-5*) Berkley Publishing Group.

—Easy Prey. 2000. (Prey Ser.). 384p. 25.95 o.s.i (*0-399-14613-X*) Penguin Group (USA) Inc.

—Easy Prey. l.t. ed. (Core Ser.). 519p. 2001. pap. 29.95 (*0-7838-9073-7*); 2000. 31.95 (*0-7838-9074-5*) Thorndike Pr.

—Eyes of Prey. 1992. 368p. mass mkt. 7.99 (*0-425-13204-8*) Berkley Publishing Group.

—Eyes of Prey. abr. ed. audio 15.95 o.p. (*1-55994-420-X*, 326336, HarperAudio) HarperTrade.

—Eyes of Prey. 1991. 320p. 19.95 o.s.i (*0-399-13629-0*, G. P. Putnam's Sons) Penguin Group (USA) Inc.

—Eyes of Prey. 19.95 o.s.i (*0-399-13846-3*) Putnam Publishing Group, The.

—Eyes of Prey, unabr. ed. 1993. (Prey Ser.: No. 3). audio 85.00 (*1-55690-826-1*, 93141K8) Recorded Bks., LLC.

—John Sandford - Three Complete Novels: Mind Prey; Sudden Prey; Secret Prey. 2000. 752p. 14.98 (*0-399-14651-2*) Penguin Group (USA) Inc.

—John Sandford - Three Complete Novels: Rules of Prey, Shadows of Prey, Eyes of Prey. 1995. 752p. 11.98 o.p. (*0-399-14007-7*, G. P. Putnam's Sons) Penguin Group (USA) Inc.

—John Sandford - Three Complete Novels: Silent Prey; Winter Prey; Night Prey. 1996. 752p. 12.98 o.p. (*0-399-14191-X*, G. P. Putnam's Sons) Penguin Group (USA) Inc.

—Mind Prey. 1996. 368p. mass mkt. 7.99 (*0-425-15289-8*) Berkley Publishing Group.

—Mind Prey. l.t. ed. 1995. 25.95 o.p. (*1-56895-233-3*, Wheeler Publishing, Inc.) Gale Group.

—Mind Prey. 1995. o.p. (*0-399-19275-1*); 323p. 23.95 o.p. (*0-399-14009-3*, G. P. Putnam's Sons) Penguin Group (USA) Inc.

—Mind Prey. 23.95 o.s.i (*0-399-14291-6*) Putnam Publishing Group, The.

—Mind Prey, unabr. ed. 1995. (Prey Ser.: No. 7). audio 78.00 (*0-7887-0387-0*, 94578K8) Recorded Bks., LLC.

—Mind Prey, abr. ed. 1995. audio 18.00 o.s.i (*0-671-52290-6*, 392984, Simon & Schuster Audioworks) Simon & Schuster Audio.

—Naked Prey. l.t. ed. 2003. 460p. 32.95 (*0-7862-5569-2*) Thorndike Pr.

—Night Prey. 1995. 416p. mass mkt. 7.99 (*0-425-14641-3*) Berkley Publishing Group.

—Night Prey. l.t. ed. 1994. pap. 21.95 o.p. (*1-56895-075-6*, Wheeler Publishing, Inc.) Gale Group.

—Night Prey. 1994. 320p. 22.95 o.p. (*0-399-13914-1*, G. P. Putnam's Sons) Penguin Group (USA) Inc.

—Night Prey. 22.95 o.s.i (*0-399-14176-6*) Putnam Publishing Group, The.

—Night Prey. unabr. ed. 1995. (Prey Ser.: No. 6). audio 70.00 (*0-7887-0192-4*, 94416E7) Recorded Bks., LLC.

—Night Prey, abr. ed. 1999. audio 17.00 (*0-671-51174-2*, 391266, Simon & Schuster Audioworks) Simon & Schuster Audio.

—Rules of Prey. 368p. 2003. pap. 10.00 (*0-425-19519-8*); 1990. mass mkt. 7.99 (*0-425-12163-1*) Berkley Publishing Group.

—Rules of Prey. 16.95 (*0-399-13635-5*) Penguin Group (USA) Inc.

—Rules of Prey. 1989. 320p. 16.95 o.s.i (*0-399-13465-4*, G. P. Putnam's Sons) Penguin Putnam Bks. for Young Readers.

—Rules of Prey. 2002. E-Book 7.99 (*0-7865-2677-7*) Penguin Putnam, Inc E-Books.

—Secret Prey. 1999. 400p. reprint ed. mass mkt. 7.99 (*0-425-16829-8*) Berkley Publishing Group.

—Secret Prey. l.t. ed. 1998. 27.95 (*1-56895-673-8*, Wheeler Publishing, Inc.) Gale Group.

—Secret Prey. 1998. 384p. 24.95 o.p. (*0-399-14382-3*, G. P. Putnam's Sons) Penguin Group (USA) Inc.

—Shadow Prey. 1991. 368p. mass mkt. 7.99 (*0-425-12606-4*) Berkley Publishing Group.

—Shadow Prey. abr. ed. audio 15.95 o.p. (*1-55994-419-6*, 326323, HarperAudio) HarperTrade.

—Shadow Prey. 1990. 352p. 18.95 o.p. (*0-399-13543-X*, G. P. Putnam's Sons) Penguin Putnam Bks. for Young Readers.

—Shadow Prey. 18.95 o.s.i (*0-399-13750-5*) Putnam Publishing Group, The.

—Silent Prey. 1993. 384p. mass mkt. 7.99 (*0-425-13756-2*) Berkley Publishing Group.

—Silent Prey. 1992. 320p. 21.95 o.p. (*0-399-13742-4*, G. P. Putnam's Sons) Penguin Group (USA) Inc.

—Silent Prey. 21.95 o.s.i (*0-399-13905-2*) Putnam Publishing Group, The.

—Silent Prey, unabr. ed. 1993. (Prey Ser.: No. 4). audio 67.00 (*1-55690-918-7*, 93414K8) Recorded Bks., LLC.

—Sudden Prey. 1997. 400p. mass mkt. 7.99 (*0-425-15753-9*) Berkley Publishing Group.

—Sudden Prey. 23.95 (*0-399-14428-5*); 1996. 320p. 23.95 o.s.i (*0-399-14138-3*, G. P. Putnam's Sons) Penguin Group (USA) Inc.

—Sudden Prey, unabr. ed. 1997. (Prey Ser.: No. 8). audio 80.00 Recorded Bks., LLC.

—Sudden Prey. abr. ed. 1996. audio 18.00 (*0-671-57421-3*, 394521, Simon & Schuster Audioworks) Simon & Schuster Audio.

—Sudden Prey. l.t. ed. 1996. (Core Ser.). 516p. 28.95 (*0-7838-1832-7*) Thorndike Pr.

—Winter Prey. 1994. 352p. mass mkt. 7.99 (*0-425-14123-3*) Berkley Publishing Group.

—Winter Prey. 1994. lib. bdg. 18.95 o.p. (*0-8161-5833-9*); 1993. 464p. lib. bdg. 24.95 (*0-8161-5832-0*) Gale Group. (Macmillan Reference USA).

—Winter Prey. abr. ed. 2000. audio 9.99 (*0-694-52325-9*, HarperAudio) HarperTrade.

—Winter Prey. 1993. 320p. 21.95 o.p. (*0-399-13815-3*, G. P. Putnam's Sons) Penguin Group (USA) Inc.

—Winter Prey. 21.95 o.s.i (*0-399-14071-9*) Putnam Publishing Group, The.

—Winter Prey, unabr. ed. 1995. (Prey Ser.: No. 5). audio 78.00 (*0-7887-0255-6*, 94464E7) Recorded Bks., LLC.

Schmitz, Anthony. The Lost Souls. 1988. pap. 15.00 (*0-345-35722-1*) Ballantine Bks.

Seeley, Mabel. The Crying Sisters. 2000. 292p. reprint ed. 24.00 (*1-890434-26-4*) Afton Historical Society Pr.

—The Whistling Shadow. 2000. 205p. reprint ed. 24.00 (*1-890434-16-7*) Afton Historical Society Pr.

Seidel, Kathleen Gilles. Summer's End. 1999. 432p. mass mkt. 6.99 o.s.i (*0-06-101388-9*) HarperCollins Pubs.

Sharpe, Jon. Minnesota Missionary. 1988. (Trailsman Ser.: No. 78). mass mkt. 2.75 o.p. (*0-451-15367-7*, Signet Bks.) NAL.

Sharratt, Mary. Summit Avenue. 2000. ii, 252p. pap. 14.95 (*1-56689-097-7*) Coffee Hse. Pr.

Smith, Taylor. Deadly Grace. 2003. 512p. mass mkt. (*1-55166-945-5*); 2001. 384p. (*1-55166-829-7*) Harlequin Enterprises, Ltd. (Mira Bks.).

Spencer, LaVyrle. Bygones. 1993. 400p. mass mkt. 7.99 (*0-515-11054-X*, Jove) Berkley Publishing Group.

—Bygones. l.t. ed. (General Ser.). 543p. 1993. pap. 16.95 o.p. (*0-8161-5564-X*); 1992. lib. bdg. 23.95 o.p. (*0-8161-5563-1*) Gale Group. (Macmillan Reference USA).

—Bygones. 1992. 384p. 21.95 o.p. (*0-399-13714-9*, G. P. Putnam's Sons) Penguin Group (USA) Inc.

—Home Song. 1999. 432p. pap. 12.95 o.s.i (*0-425-17127-2*); 1996. 400p. mass mkt. 7.50 (*0-515-11823-0*, Jove); 1995. E-Book 7.50 (*0-515-12602-0*, Jove) Berkley Publishing Group.

—Home Song. abr. ed. 1995. 17.95 o.p. (*0-7871-0301-2*); 6p. 24.95 o.p. (*0-7871-0250-4*, 692230); 12p. 39.95 o.p. (*0-7871-0251-2*, 112804) NewStar Media, Inc.

—Home Song. 1995. o.p. (*0-399-19274-3*); 23.95 o.p. (*0-399-14014-X*, G. P. Putnam's Sons) Penguin Group (USA) Inc.

—Home Song. 23.95 o.s.i (*0-399-14290-8*) Putnam Publishing Group, The.

—Home Song. l.t. ed. (Paperback Bestsellers Ser.). 476p. 1996. pap. 25.95 (*0-7838-1251-5*); 1995. lib. bdg. 28.95 (*0-7838-1250-7*) Thorndike Pr.

—November of the Heart. l.t. ed. (General Ser.). 576p. 1994. lib. bdg. 16.95 o.s.i (*0-8161-5701-4*); 1993. 23.95 o.p. (*0-8161-5700-6*) Gale Group. (Macmillan Reference USA).

—November of the Heart. 1993. 384p. 22.95 o.p. (*0-399-13801-3*, G. P. Putnam's Sons) Penguin Group (USA) Inc.

—Then Came Heaven. 368p. 2003. pap. 10.00 (*0-425-19576-7*); 1999. reprint ed. pap. 7.99 (*0-515-12462-1*, Jove) Berkley Publishing Group.

—Then Came Heaven. l.t. ed. 1998. (Large Print Book Ser.). 28.95 (*1-56895-535-9*, Wheeler Publishing, Inc.) Gale Group.

—Then Came Heaven. abr. ed. 1997. 18.00 o.p. (*0-7871-1676-9*, 395617) NewStar Media, Inc.

—Then Came Heaven. 1997. xiii, 332p. 24.95 o.p. (*0-399-14369-6*, G. P. Putnam's Sons); 24.95 o.s.i (*0-399-14699-7*) Penguin Group (USA) Inc.

—Then Came Heaven. l.t. ed. 2000. (Charnwood Large Print Ser.). 376p. (*0-7089-9139-4*, Ulverscroft) Thorpe, F. A. Pubs. GBR. *Dist:* Ulverscroft Large Print Bks., Ltd., Ulverscroft Large Print Canada, Ltd.

Stanton, Maura. The Country I Come From: Stories. 1988. (Illus.). 112p. (Orig.). pap. 9.95 (*0-915943-33-6*) Milkweed Editions.

Sullivan, Faith. The Empress of One. 360p. 1997. pap. 14.95 (*1-57131-016-9*); 1996. 22.95 (*1-57131-011-8*) Milkweed Editions.

Summer, Mark. The Monster of Minnesota. 1997. (News from the Edge Ser.: Vol. 1). 208p. mass mkt. 6.50 o.s.i (*0-441-00459-8*) Ace Bks.

Sutphen, Joyce. Straight Out of View. 1995. (Barnard New Women Poets Ser.). 128p. 22.00 o.p. (*0-8070-6824-1*); pap. 12.95 o.p. (*0-8070-6825-X*) Beacon Pr.

Swanson, Steve. The Mystery of the Killer's Tracks. 1994. (EarthKeepers Ser.: Vol. 4). 128p. (J). (gr. 3-7). pap. 5.99 o.p. (*0-310-39831-2*) Zondervan.

Telemaque, Eleanor. It's Crazy to Stay Chinese in Minnesota: Chasing Bingo Tang. 2000. 104p. E-Book 8.00 (*0-7388-8567-3*) Xlibris Corp.

Thayer, Steve. Moon over Lake Elmo. 2001. 256p. pap. 10.95 o.s.i (*0-451-20373-9*) NAL.

—Silent Snow. 2000. 416p. reprint ed. mass mkt. 6.99 (*0-451-18664-8*, Signet Bks.) NAL.

—Silent Snow. abr. ed. 2000. audio 18.00 (*0-7871-1980-6*); 1999. audio 30.00 (*0-7871-1979-2*) NewStar Media, Inc. (Dove Audio).

—Silent Snow, unabr. ed. 1999. audio 66.00 (*0-7887-3767-8*, 95984E7) Recorded Bks., LLC.

—Silent Snow. 1999. 416p. 24.95 o.s.i (*0-670-86572-9*, Viking) Viking Penguin.

—The Weatherman. 1996. 416p. mass mkt. 7.99 (*0-451-18438-6*, Signet Bks.) NAL.

—The Weatherman, Set. abr. ed. 1995. audio 16.95 (*1-879371-88-X*, 391877) Publishing Mills, Inc., The.

—The Weatherman, unabr. ed. 1995. audio 91.00 (*0-7887-0267-X*, 94476E7) Recorded Bks., LLC.

—The Weatherman. 1995. 22.95 (*0-670-77309-3*); 464p. 21.95 o.s.i (*0-670-84958-8*, Viking) Viking Penguin.

Treuer, David. The Hiawatha. 1999. 320p. 24.00 o.p. (*0-312-20313-6*) Picador.

—Little. 1995. 224p. 22.95 o.s.i (*1-55597-231-4*) Graywolf Pr.

—Little. 1996. 272p. pap. 12.00 (*0-312-15164-0*) Picador.

Ursu, Anne. Spilling Clarence. 2002. (Illus.). 288p. 22.95 (*0-7868-6778-7*) Hyperion Pr.

Waller, Robert James. Border Music. 2001. 304p. E-Book 4.95 (*0-7595-0131-9*); 2001. 304p. E-Book 4.95 (*0-7595-4133-7*); 2001. 304p. E-Book 4.95 (*0-7595-9498-8*); 2001. 304p. E-Book 4.95 (*0-7595-8133-9*); 2001. 304p. E-Book 4.95 (*0-7595-6130-3*); 1995. 248p. 17.95 o.p. (*0-446-51858-1*); 1996. 304p. reprint ed. mass mkt. 5.99 o.s.i (*0-446-60273-6*) Warner Bks., Inc.

Warren, Susan. Happily Ever After. 2003. 384p. pap. 9.99 (*0-8423-8117-1*) Tyndale Hse. Pubs.

Watson, John H. Sherlock Holmes & the Red Demon. Millett, Larry, ed. 1997. 366p. pap. 9.95. 336p. pap. 9.95 o.s.i (*0-14-025882-5*) Penguin Group (USA) Inc.

—Sherlock Holmes & the Red Demon. Millett, Larry, ed. & intro. by. 1996. (Illus.). 336p. 22.95 (*0-670-87039-0*, Viking) Viking Penguin.

Weber, Christin Lore. Altar Music. 256p. 2001. pap. 12.00 o.s.i (*0-684-86865-2*); 2000. (Illus.). 23.00 o.s.i (*0-684-86866-0*) Simon & Schuster. (Scribner).

Whitson, Stephanie Grace. Heart of the Sandhills. 2002. 288p. pap. 13.99 (*0-7852-6824-3*) Nelson, Thomas Inc.

Winter Lake Wobegon. 1986. audio 5.95 (*0-440-85037-1*, RH Audio) Random Hse. Audio Publishing Group.

Wubbels, Lance. In the Shadow of a Secret. 2001. (Christian Fiction Ser.). 347p. 24.95 (*0-7862-3300-1*, Five Star) Gale Group.

—Keeper of the Harvest. 1995. (Gentle Hills Ser.: Bk. 3). 288p. pap. 10.99 o.p. (*1-55661-420-9*); 416p. pap. 15.99 o.p. (*1-55661-685-6*) Bethany Hse. Pubs.

—Whispers in the Valley. 1995. (Gentle Hills Ser.: Bk. 2). 304p. pap. 10.99 o.p. (*1-55661-419-5*); 464p. pap. 15.99 o.p. (*1-55661-630-9*) Bethany Hse. Pubs.

Zimmerman, R. D. Closet: A Todd Mills Mystery. 1995. 320p. mass mkt. 4.99 o.s.i (*0-440-21869-1*) Dell Publishing.

—Closet: A Todd Mills Mystery. 1997. 304p. pap. 10.95 o.s.i (*0-385-32004-3*) Doubleday Publishing.

—Hostage. 1998. 288p. pap. 10.95 o.s.i (*0-385-31892-8*, Delacorte Pr.) Dell Publishing.

—Innuendo. 2000. (Todd Mills Mysteries Ser.). 320p. pap. 11.95 (*0-385-31926-6*, Dial Bks.) Dell Publishing.

—Outburst: A Todd Mills Mystery. 1999. (Illus.). 304p. pap. 19.00 (*0-385-31923-1*, Delacorte Pr.) Dell Publishing.

—Tribe. 1996. 288p. mass mkt. 5.50 o.s.i (*0-440-21870-5*) Dell Publishing.

—Tribe: A Todd Mills Mystery. 1997. 272p. pap. 10.95 o.s.i (*0-385-32002-7*) Doubleday Publishing.

### MIRABEAU (IMAGINARY PLACE: TEX.)—FICTION

Abbott, Jeff. Distant Blood. 1996. 352p. mass mkt. 6.99 (*0-345-39470-4*) Ballantine Bks.

—Do unto Others. 1994. (Southwest Mysteries Ser.). 256p. mass mkt. 6.99 (*0-345-38948-4*) Ballantine Bks.

—The Only Good Yankee. 1995. 256p. mass mkt. 6.50 (*0-345-39438-0*, Del Rey) Ballantine Bks.

—Promises of Home. 1996. 288p. mass mkt. 6.99 (*0-345-39469-0*) Ballantine Bks.

Lattany, Kristin Hunter. Do unto Others. E-Book 19.95 (*1-58945-572-X*) Adobe Systems, Inc.

—Do unto Others. E-Book 19.50 (*0-345-44329-2*, Ballantine Bks.) Ballantine Bks.

### MISSISSIPPI—FICTION

The Adventures of Tom Sawyer. 2001. 8.97 (*0-673-58321-X*) Addison-Wesley Longman, Inc.

The Adventures of Tom Sawyer. 2001. E-Book 2.95 (*1-58853-036-1*) Sensory Publishing, Inc.

Albert, Susan Wittig. Bloodroot. 2003. 320p. reprint ed. mass mkt. 6.99 (*0-425-18814-0*) Berkley Publishing Group.

—Bloodroot. l.t. ed. 2002. (Mystery Ser.). 427p. 30.95 o.p. (*0-7862-3841-0*) Gale Group.

—Bloodroot: A China Bayles Mystery. 2001. 320p. 22.95 (*0-425-18190-1*, Prime Crime) Berkley Publishing Group.

Armistead, John. Cruel as the Grave: A Sheriff Bramlett Mystery. 1998. (Sheriff Bramlett Mystery Ser.). 368p. mass mkt. 5.99 o.s.i (*0-440-22437-3*) Doubleday Publishing.

—Cruel as the Grave: A Sheriff Bramlett Mystery. unabr. ed. 1966. (Sheriff Bramlett Mystery Ser.). audio 78.00 (*0-7887-4053-9*, 96004E7) Recorded Bks., LLC.

—Cruel the Grave: A Sheriff Bramlett Mystery. 1996. 256p. 21.00 (*0-7867-0303-2*, Carroll & Graf Pubs.) Avalon Publishing Group.

—A Homecoming for Murder: A Sheriff Bramlett Mystery. 1995. 272p. 19.95 (*0-7867-0197-8*, Carroll & Graf Pubs.) Avalon Publishing Group.

—A Homecoming for Murder: A Sheriff Bramlett Mystery. 1997. (Sheriff Bramlett Mystery Ser.). 368p. mass mkt. 5.99 o.s.i (*0-440-22435-7*) Dell Publishing.

—A Homecoming for Murder: A Sheriff Bramlett Mystery. unabr. ed. 1999. (Sheriff Bramlett Mystery Ser.). audio 70.00 (*0-7887-3777-5*, 95994E7) Recorded Bks., LLC.

—A Legacy of Vengeance. 1994. 256p. 8.95 (*0-7867-0059-9*, Carroll & Graf Pubs.) Avalon Publishing Group.

—A Legacy of Vengeance. 1997. (Sheriff Brimley Mystery Ser.). 304p. mass mkt. 5.50 o.s.i (*0-440-22384-9*) Dell Publishing.

—A Legacy of Vengeance. unabr. ed. 1994. (Sheriff Bramlett Mystery Ser.). audio 60.00 (*0-7887-3489-X*, 95896E7) Recorded Bks., LLC.

Atkins, Ace. Dirty South. 2004. 304p. 24.95 (*0-06-000462-2*, Morrow, William & Co.) Morrow/Avon.

Atkins, P. W. Crossroad Blues. (Nick Travers Mysteries Ser.). 2000. 256p. mass mkt. 5.99 (*0-312-97192-3*, St. Martin's Paperbacks); 1998. 226p. 21.95 o.p. (*0-312-19254-1*, Saint Martin's Minotaur) St. Martin's Pr.

Bahr, Howard. The Year of Jubilo: A Novel of the Civil War. 2000. 384p. 25.00 o.s.i (*0-8050-5972-5*) Holt, Henry & Co.

Baker, Calvin. Once Two Heroes. 2003. 288p. pap. 14.00 (*0-14-200382-4*) Penguin Group (USA) Inc.

—Once Two Heroes. l.t. ed. 2003. 28.95 (*0-7862-5463-7*) Thorndike Pr.

—Once Two Heroes. 2003. 288p. 23.95 (*0-670-03164-X*, Viking) Viking Penguin.

Ballard, Allen B. Where I'm Bound. 2000. (Illus.). 320p. 24.00 o.s.i (*0-684-87031-2*, Simon & Schuster) Simon & Schuster.
Barr, Nevada. Deep South. 2001. (Anna Pigeon Mysteries Ser.). 384p. mass mkt. 6.99 (*0-425-17895-1*) Berkley Publishing Group.
—Deep South. l.t. ed. 2000. 25.95 o.p. (*1-56895-867-6*, Wheeler Publishing, Inc.) Gale Group.
—Deep South. 2000. (Anna Pigeon Mysteries Ser.). 340p. 23.95 o.s.i (*0-399-14586-9*) Penguin Group (USA) Inc.
—Hunting Season. 2003. 352p. reprint ed. mass mkt. 6.99 (*0-425-18878-7*) Berkley Publishing Group.
—Hunting Season. abr. ed. (Anna Pigeon Ser.). 2004. audio compact disk 16.99 (*1-59355-696-9*, 5314, Brilliance Audio on CD Value Priced); 2003. audio 12.99 (*1-59086-005-5*, 3525, Brilliance Audio Paperback Audiobooks); 2002. audio 24.95 o.p. (*1-59086-003-9*, 3523, Nova Audio Bks.); 2002. audio 53.25 (*1-59086-004-7*, 3524, Library Edition); 2002. audio compact disk 29.95 (*1-59086-001-2*, 3521, CD); 2002. audio compact disk 69.25 (*1-59086-002-0*, 3522, CD Library Edition) Brilliance Audio.
—Hunting Season. l.t. ed. 2002. (Wheeler Large Print Book Ser.). 30.95 (*1-58724-181-1*, Wheeler Publishing, Inc.) Gale Group.
—Hunting Season. 2002. (Illus.). 320p. 24.95 o.s.i (*0-399-14846-9*); 249.50 o.p. (*0-399-19628-5*) Putnam Publishing Group, The.
—Hunting Season, 7 cass. 2002. audio 29.99 (*1-4025-0861-1*, 00974); audio 29.99 (*1-4025-0748-8*, 96913) Recorded Bks., LLC.
—Hunting Season. l.t. ed. 2003. (Paperback Bestsellers Ser.). 12.95 (*1-4104-0088-3*, Large Print Pr.) Thorndike Pr.
Barthelme, Frederick. Bob the Gambler. 1998. 224p. pap. 12.00 o.p. (*0-395-92474-X*); 1997. 256p. tchr. ed. 23.00 o.p. (*0-395-80977-0*) Houghton Mifflin Co.
Baxter, Mary Lynn. Sultry. 2000. 384p. mass mkt. (*1-55166-588-3*, 1-66588-4, Mira Bks.) Harlequin Enterprises, Ltd.
Bowen, Charles. Delta Queen. 2001. 211p. pap. 21.99 (*0-7388-5850-1*); text 31.99 (*0-7388-5849-8*) Xlibris Corp.
Bowen, Michele Andrea. Church Folk. 2001. 368p. 21.95 o.p. (*0-446-52799-8*) Warner Bks., Inc.
Brewer, James D. No Bottom: A Masey Baldridge/Luke Williamson Mystery. 1994. 256p. 19.95 o.p. (*0-8027-3178-3*) Walker & Co.
—No Escape. 1998. (Masey Baldridge/Luke Williamson Mystery Ser.). 264p. 22.95 (*0-8027-3318-2*) Walker & Co.
—No Justice: A Masey Baldridge/Luke Williamson Mystery. 1996. (Masey Baldridge/Luke Williamson Mystery Ser.). 232p. 21.95 (*0-8027-3283-6*) Walker & Co.
—No Remorse: A Masey Baldridge/Luke Williamson Mystery. 1997. (Luke Williamson/Masey Baldridge Mystery Ser.). 224p. 22.95 (*0-8027-3302-6*) Walker & Co.
—No Virtue: A Masey Baldridge/Luke Williamson Mystery. 1995. (Masey Baldridge/Luke Williamson Mystery Ser.). 232p. (YA). 20.95 (*0-8027-3259-3*) Walker & Co.
Brown, Larry. Father & Son. 1996. 360p. tchr. ed. 22.95 (*1-56512-014-0*) Algonquin Bks. of Chapel Hill.
—Father & Son. 1997. 352p. pap. 14.00 (*0-8050-5303-4*, Owl Bks.) Holt, Henry & Co.
—Father & Son. l.t. ed. 1998. (Niagara Large Print Ser.). 422p. 29.50 o.p. (*0-7089-5867-2*, Ulverscroft) Thorpe, F. A. Pubs. GBR. *Dist:* Ulverscroft Large Print Bks., Ltd., Ulverscroft Large Print Canada, Ltd.
—Fay. 2000. 487p. tchr. ed. 24.95 (*1-56512-168-6*, 72168) Algonquin Bks. of Chapel Hill.
—Joe: A Novel. 2003. 345p. pap. 12.95 (*1-56512-413-8*); 1991. 360p. 19.95 (*0-945575-61-0*) Algonquin Bks. of Chapel Hill.
—Joe: A Novel. 1992. 368p. pap. 18.99 (*0-446-39438-6*) Warner Bks., Inc.
Brown, Rosellen. Civil Wars. 1994. 544p. mass mkt. 5.99 o.s.i (*0-440-21695-8*) Dell Publishing.
—Civil Wars. 1985. (Contemporary American Fiction Ser.). 432p. pap. 9.95 o.p. (*0-14-007783-9*, Penguin Bks.) Viking Penguin.
Butler, Luther. Amite County & Mississippi Woman. 1999. (Plata County Ser.: 2). 372p. pap. 15.95 (*1-58348-458-2*) iUniverse, Inc.
Cameron, Angie. The Education of Annie. 2002. 359p. 28.95 (*0-9717610-0-0*) AM & K Publishing.
Campbell, Bebe Moore. Your Blues Ain't Like Mine. 1995. 448p. mass mkt. 7.50 o.s.i (*0-345-40112-3*); 1993. 352p. pap. 14.00 (*0-345-38395-8*, One World/Ballantine) Ballantine Bks.
—Your Blues Ain't Like Mine. l.t. ed. 1995. (Large Print Bks.). 24.95 o.p. (*1-56895-221-X*, Wheeler Publishing, Inc.) Gale Group.
—Your Blues Ain't Like Mine. 1992. 352p. 23.95 o.p. (*0-399-13746-7*) Penguin Group (USA) Inc.
Cantor, Jay. Great Neck: A Novel. 720p. 2004. pap. 15.00 (*0-375-71339-5*); 2003. 27.95 (*0-375-41394-4*) Knopf, Alfred A. Inc.
Chesnut, Mary Boykin Miller. Two Novels by Mary Chesnut. Muhlenfeld, Elisabeth, ed. & intro. by. 2002. (Publications of the Southern Texts Society). xx, 216p. 29.95 (*0-8139-2058-2*) Univ. Pr. of Virginia.
Collier, Louise W. Pilgrimage: A Tale of Old Natchez. 1994. 480p. (J). (gr. 10-12). 6.95 (*1-56554-064-6*) Pelican Publishing Co., Inc.
Craft, Mary Beth. Golden Grove. 1999. 183p. 16.95 (*1-885478-97-6*) Genesis Pr., Inc.
Dailey, Janet. A Tradition of Pride: Mississippi. 1991. (Americana Ser.: No. 874). mass mkt. (*0-373-89874-6*); 1988. pap. (*0-373-21924-5*); 1987. (Americana Ser.: No. 24). pap. (*0-373-89824-X*) Harlequin Enterprises, Ltd. (Harlequin Bks.).
—A Tradition of Pride: Mississippi. l.t. ed. 2001. 224p. (Illus.). 28.95 (*0-7862-2699-4*); (*0-7540-4581-1*); (*0-7540-4582-X*) Thorndike Pr.
—A Tradition of Pride: Mississippi. E-Book 6.99 (*0-7592-0833-6*); 2001. 120p. pap. 12.95 (*0-7592-3798-0*) ereads.com.
Davis, Reuben. Shim. 1995. (Banner Bk.). 288p. pap. 40.00 (*0-87805-773-0*); pap. 20.00 (*0-87805-774-9*) Univ. Pr. of Mississippi.
Dixon, Louisa. Next to Last Chance. 1998. 345p. 24.95 (*1-885478-39-9*) Genesis Pr., Inc.
—Outside Chance. unabr. ed. 1999. 420p. 24.95 (*1-885478-63-1*) Genesis Pr., Inc.
Douglas, Ellen. Black Cloud, White Cloud. ltd. ed. 1989. (Author & Artist Ser.). (Illus.). 260p. reprint ed. 65.00 (*0-87805-397-2*); 26.00 (*0-87805-393-X*) Univ. Pr. of Mississippi.
—A Family's Affairs. 1997. (Voices of the South Ser.). 456p. pap. 14.95 (*0-8071-2163-0*) Louisiana State Univ. Pr.
Douglas, Ellen & Wolfe, Elizabeth. Black Cloud, White Cloud. 1989. E-Book 25.00 (*0-585-31563-9*) netLibrary, Inc.
Dunbar, Wylene. Margaret Cape: A Novel. 1997. 352p. 23.00 o.s.i (*0-15-100248-7*) Harcourt Trade Pubs.
Durkee, Lee. Rides of the Midway. 2001. 316p. text 25.95 (*0-393-04971-X*) Norton, W. W. & Co., Inc.
—Rides of the Midway: A Novel. 2002. 320p. pap. 13.95 (*0-393-32290-4*) Norton, W. W. & Co., Inc.
Faulkner, John. Men Working: A Novel. 1996. (Brown Thrasher Bks.). 320p. (C). pap. 19.95 (*0-8203-1827-2*) Univ. of Georgia Pr.
Faulkner, William. Absalom, Absalom! Date not set. 320p. 24.95 (*0-8488-2606-X*) Amereon, Ltd.
—Absalom, Absalom! 2002. audio 72.00 (*0-7366-8955-9*); 2002. audio compact disk 80.00 (*0-7366-9123-5*); 1993. audio 88.00 (*0-7366-2456-2*, 3220) Books on Tape, Inc.
—Absalom, Absalom! (William Faulkner Annotations to Novels Ser.). 1991. 192p. text 15.00 o.p. (*0-8240-4235-2*); 1987. text 163.00 o.p. (*0-8240-6817-3*) Garland Publishing, Inc.
—Absalom, Absalom! 1991. (Vintage International Ser.). 320p. pap. 12.95 (*0-679-73218-7*, Vintage) Knopf Publishing Group.
—Absalom, Absalom! Polk, Noel, ed. 1987. (Illus.). 384p. pap. 8.95 o.p. (*0-394-74775-5*, Vintage) Knopf Publishing Group.
—Absalom, Absalom! 1972. pap. 3.95 o.p. (*0-394-71780-5*, Vintage) Knopf Publishing Group.
—Absalom, Absalom! 1966. 378p. (C). pap. 7.50 (*0-07-553657-9*, McGraw-Hill Humanities, Social Sciences & World Languages) McGraw-Hill Higher Education.
—Absalom, Absalom! 2002. (Illus.). 392p. 22.00 (*0-375-50872-4*); 1993. (Illus.). 432p. 16.95 (*0-679-60072-8*); 1966. 17.95 o.s.i (*0-394-41400-4*); 1951. 3.95 o.s.i (*0-394-60271-4*) Random Hse., Inc.
—Absalom, Absalom! Polk, Noel, ed. rev. ed. 1986. 320p. 25.00 o.s.i (*0-394-55634-8*) Random Hse., Inc.
—Absalom, Absalom! l.t. ed. 1997. (Perennial Ser.). 496p. 24.95 (*0-7838-8138-X*) Thorndike Pr.
—Absalom, Absalom! 1972. 18.05 (*0-606-00781-4*) Turtleback Bks.
—As I Lay Dying. unabr. ed. 1994. audio 48.00 (*0-7366-2664-6*, 3401) Books on Tape, Inc.
—As I Lay Dying. 1987. (William Faulkner Manuscripts). 504p. text 65.00 o.p. (*0-8240-6809-2*) Garland Publishing, Inc.
—As I Lay Dying. 1991. (Vintage International Ser.). 288p. pap. 11.95 (*0-679-73225-X*, Vintage) Knopf Publishing Group.
—As I Lay Dying. Polk, Noel, ed. 1987. (Illus.). 256p. pap. 7.95 o.p. (*0-394-74745-3*, Vintage) Knopf Publishing Group.
—As I Lay Dying. annuals 2000. 288p. 16.95 (*0-375-50452-4*) Knopf, Alfred A. Inc.
—As I Lay Dying. 1967. 3.95 o.s.i (*0-394-60378-8*) Random Hse., Inc.
—As I Lay Dying. 1964. 17.05 (*0-606-02171-X*) Turtleback Bks.
—Collected Faulkner Stories. 1956. 22.95 o.s.i (*0-394-41967-7*) Random Hse., Inc.
—Go down, Moses. 1991. (Vintage International Ser.). 384p. pap. 12.00 (*0-679-73217-9*, Vintage) Knopf Publishing Group.
—Go down, Moses. 1955. 4.95 o.s.i (*0-394-60175-0*, Modern Library) Random House Adult Trade Publishing Group.
—Go down, Moses. 1995. 364p. 16.95 o.s.i (*0-679-60174-0*); 1942. 17.95 o.s.i (*0-394-42646-0*) Random Hse., Inc.
—Go down, Moses. unabr. ed. 1995. audio 85.00 (*0-7887-0217-3*, 94442E7) Recorded Bks., LLC.
—The Hamlet. 1991. (Vintage International Ser.). 432p. pap. 13.00 (*0-679-73653-0*, Vintage) Knopf Publishing Group.
—The Hamlet. 1956. pap. 8.00 o.p. (*0-394-70139-9*, V139); 1940. 16.95 o.s.i (*0-394-42759-9*) Random Hse., Inc.
—The Hamlet. unabr. ed. 2001. audio 97.00 (*1-55690-916-0*, 93412E7) Recorded Bks., LLC.
—Light in August. unabr. ed. 1994. audio 59.25 o.p. (*1-56100-213-5*, 1269, Unabridged Library Editions); audio 19.95 o.p. (*1-56100-588-6*, 163, Bookcassette) Brilliance Audio.
—Light in August. 1987. (Faulkner Manuscripts). 45.00 o.p. (*0-8240-6813-0*) Garland Publishing, Inc.
—Light in August. Blotner, Joseph Leo, ed. 1987. (Faulkner Manuscripts). 480p. text 60.00 o.p. (*0-8240-6814-9*) Garland Publishing, Inc.
—Light in August. 1985. (Book Notes Ser.). (gr. 10-12). pap. 2.50 o.p. (*0-8120-3521-6*) Library of America, The.
—Light in August. 1965. 480p. (C). pap. 11.25 (*0-07-553648-X*, McGraw-Hill Humanities, Social Sciences & World Languages) McGraw-Hill Higher Education.
—Light in August. 2002. 528p. 19.95 (*0-679-64248-X*); 1931. 3.95 o.s.i (*0-394-60088-6*) Random House Adult Trade Publishing Group. (Modern Library).
—Light in August. 1987. pap. 8.95 o.p. (*0-394-74743-7*); 1967. 16.95 o.s.i (*0-394-43335-1*); Vol. 189. 1972. pap. 4.95 o.p. (*0-394-71189-0*) Random Hse., Inc.
—Light in August, unabr. ed. 1994. audio 97.00 (*0-7887-0037-5*, 94236E7) Recorded Bks., LLC.
—Light in August: The Corrected Text. 1991. (Vintage International Ser.). 528p. pap. 13.95 (*0-679-73226-8*, Vintage) Knopf Publishing Group.
—Light in August: The Corrected Text. 1959. 19.05 (*0-606-01720-8*) Turtleback Bks.
—The Mansion, 2 vols. 1986. 752p. 110.00 o.p. (*0-8240-1833-8*) Garland Publishing, Inc.
—The Mansion. Millgate, Michael, ed. 1986. (William Faulkner Manuscripts). 1088p. text 135.00 (*0-8240-6832-7*) Garland Publishing, Inc.
—The Mansion. 1965. 448p. mass mkt. 12.00 (*0-394-70282-4*); 1959. 10.00 o.s.i (*0-394-43514-1*) Random Hse., Inc.
—Novels, 1930-1935: As I Lay Dying, Sanctuary, Light in August, Pylon. Blotner, Joseph & Polk, Noel, eds. 1985. (Library of America). 1056p. 35.00 (*0-940450-26-7*) Library of America, The.
—Novels, 1936-1940: Absalom, Absalom!; If I Forget Thee, Jerusalem (The Wild Palms); The Unvanquished; The Hamlet. Blotner, Joseph & Polk, Noel, eds. 1990. (Library of America: Vol. 48). 1148p. 37.50 (*0-940450-55-0*) Library of America, The.
—Novels, 1957-1962: The Town; The Mansion; The Reivers. Polk, Noel, ed. 1999. (Library of America: Vol. 112). 1020p. 35.00 (*1-883011-69-8*) Library of America, The.
—The Portable Faulkner. 2003. 688p. pap. 17.00 (*0-14-243728-X*, Penguin Classics) Viking Penguin.
—The Portable Faulkner. Cowley, Malcolm, ed. rev. ed. 1967. 14.95 o.p. (*0-670-31002-6*) Viking Penguin.
—Pylon. 1984. (FRE.). pap. 12.95 (*0-7859-2486-8*, 2070375315) French & European Pubns., Inc.
—Pylon. Polk, Noel, ed. 1987. (William Faulkner Manuscripts). 360p. text 50.00 (*0-8240-6816-5*) Garland Publishing, Inc.
—Pylon. mass mkt. 0.35 o.p. (*0-451-01485-5*, Signet Bks.); mass mkt. 0.25 o.p. (*0-451-00863-4*, Signet Bks.); 1968. mass mkt. 0.95 o.p. (*0-451-50415-1*, Signet Classics) NAL.
—Pylon. 1965. 13.95 o.s.i (*0-394-44156-7*) Random Hse., Inc.
—Pylon: The Corrected Text. Polk, Noel, ed. 1987. (Illus.). 336p. mass mkt. 9.00 (*0-394-74741-0*, Vintage) Knopf Publishing Group.
—Requiem for a Nun, 2 vols. McHaney, Thomas et al, eds. 1987. (William Faulkner Manuscripts). 504p. text 80.00 (*0-8240-6825-4*); 648p. text 85.00 (*0-8240-6827-0*); 464p. text 60.00 (*0-8240-6826-2*) Garland Publishing, Inc.
—Requiem for a Nun. 1975. 256p. pap. 11.00 (*0-394-71412-1*, Vintage) Knopf Publishing Group.
—Requiem for a Nun. 1951. 13.95 o.s.i (*0-394-44274-1*) Random Hse., Inc.
—Requiem for a Nun. 1975. 17.05 (*0-606-19218-2*) Turtleback Bks.
—Sanctuary. unabr. ed. 1995. (Bookcassette Classic Collection). audio 17.95 o.p. (*1-56100-631-9*, 245, Bookcassette); audio 57.25 o.p. (*1-56100-256-9*, 1024, Unabridged Library Editions) Brilliance Audio.
—Sanctuary. 6.95 o.p. (*0-453-00321-4*, Dutton) Dutton/Plume.
—Sanctuary. 1993. 336p. pap. 12.00 (*0-679-74814-8*, Vintage) Knopf Publishing Group.
—Sanctuary. Polk, Noel, ed. 1987. (Illus.). 320p. pap. 7.00 o.p. (*0-394-74744-5*, Vintage) Knopf Publishing Group.
—Sanctuary. mass mkt. 0.25 o.p. (*0-451-00632-1*, Signet Bks.); 1971. mass mkt. 1.25 o.p. (*0-451-04511-4*, Signet Bks.); 1968. mass mkt. 1.25 o.p. (*0-451-50685-5*, Signet Classics); 1968. mass mkt. 0.95 o.p. (*0-451-50413-5*, Signet Classics) NAL.
—Sanctuary. 1966. 10.00 o.s.i (*0-394-44368-3*); Vol. 381. 1967. pap. 4.95 o.p. (*0-394-70381-2*) Random Hse., Inc.
—Sanctuary. 1993. 18.05 (*0-606-19219-0*) Turtleback Bks.
—Sanctuary & Requiem for a Nun. 1976. 25.95 (*0-8488-0999-8*) Amereon, Ltd.
—Sanctuary & Requiem for a Nun. mass mkt. 0.50 o.p. (*0-451-01486-3*); mass mkt. 0.75 o.p. (*0-451-01900-8*); mass mkt. 0.35 o.p. (*0-451-01079-5*) NAL. (Signet Bks.).
—The Sound & the Fury. 1985. (Barron's Book Notes Ser.). 119p. (gr. 10-12). pap. 2.95 (*0-8120-3541-0*) Barron's Educational Series, Inc.
—The Sound & the Fury. Polk, Noel, ed. 1987. (William Faulkner Manuscripts). 464p. text 55.00 (*0-8240-6806-8*); 192p. text 40.00 o.p. (*0-8240-6805-X*) Garland Publishing, Inc.
—The Sound & the Fury. l.t. ed. 1987. (Mainstream Ser.). 377p. reprint ed. 15.95 o.p. (*1-85089-143-5*) ISIS Large Print Bks. GBR. *Dist:* Transaction Pubs.
—The Sound & the Fury. 1991. (Vintage International Ser.). 336p. pap. 10.95 (*0-679-73224-1*, Vintage) Knopf Publishing Group.
—The Sound & the Fury. Polk, Noel, ed. 1987. (Illus.). 448p. pap. 7.95 o.p. (*0-394-74774-7*, Vintage) Knopf Publishing Group.
—The Sound & the Fury. 1967. (Modern Library College Editions Ser.). 427p. (C). pap. 11.25 (*0-07-553666-8*, T94, McGraw-Hill Humanities, Social Sciences & World Languages) McGraw-Hill Higher Education.
—The Sound & the Fury. mass mkt. 0.50 o.p. (*0-451-01628-9*, Signet Bks.) NAL.
—The Sound & the Fury. Minter, David, ed. 2nd ed. 1993. (Critical Editions Ser.). xv, 446p. (C). pap. text 7.50 (*0-393-96481-7*) Norton, W. W. & Co., Inc.
—The Sound & the Fury. (Modern Library of the World's Best Bks.). 1992. 368p. 15.95 (*0-679-60017-5*); 1984. 25.00 o.s.i (*0-394-53241-4*); 1966. 3.95 o.s.i (*0-394-60187-4*); 1966. 14.00 o.s.i (*0-394-44640-2*) Random Hse., Inc.
—The Sound & the Fury. Polk, Noel, ed. rev. ed. 1954. 384p. pap. 3.95 o.p. (*0-394-70005-8*) Random Hse., Inc.
—The Sound & the Fury. 2003. (SparkNotes Literature Study Guides). 72p. pap. 4.95 (*1-58663-436-4*) Spark Publishing Group.
—The Sound & the Fury. 1954. 16.05 (*0-606-04951-7*) Turtleback Bks.
—Three Famous Short Novels. 1958. 16.05 (*0-606-20943-3*) Turtleback Bks.
—Three Famous Short Novels. Bd. with Bear.; Old Man.; Spotted Horses. 320p. 1958. Set mass mkt. 10.00 (*0-394-70149-6*, V-149, Vintage) Knopf Publishing Group.
—The Town. 1961. (ACE.). 384p. mass mkt. 11.00 (*0-394-70184-4*, V184, Vintage) Knopf Publishing Group.
—The Town. 1957. 13.95 o.s.i (*0-394-42452-2*) Random Hse., Inc.
—Uncollected Stories of William Faulkner. Blotner, Joseph L., ed. 1981. 732p. pap. 20.00 o.s.i (*0-394-74656-2*) Knopf, Alfred A. Inc.
—The Unvanquished. (Vintage International Ser.). 1991. 272p. pap. 12.95 (*0-679-73652-2*); Vol. 351. 1966. (Illus.). pap. 8.00 o.p. (*0-394-70351-0*, V351) Knopf Publishing Group. (Vintage).
—The Wild Palms. McHaney, Thomas, ed. 1986. (William Faulkner Manuscripts). 356p. text 50.00 (*0-8240-6818-1*); 408p. text 60.00 (*0-8240-6819-X*) Garland Publishing, Inc.
—The Wild Palms. 1984. 339p. 20.00 o.s.i (*0-394-60513-6*, V262, Vintage) Knopf Publishing Group.
—The Wild Palms. 1964. 352p. pap. 8.00 o.s.i (*0-394-70262-X*) Random Hse., Inc.
Faulkner, William & Blotner, Joseph. Uncollected Stories of William Faulkner. anniv. ed. 1997. 736p. pap. 19.00 (*0-375-70109-5*, Vintage) Knopf Publishing Group.
Faulkner, William & Oatman, Eric F. As I Lay Dying. 1985. (Barron's Book Notes Ser.). (gr. 10-12). pap. 2.50 o.p. (*0-8120-3502-X*) Barron's Educational Series, Inc.

Ferrarella, Marie. Internal Affair. 2003. 304p. mass mkt. (0-373-21836-2, Silhouette) Harlequin Enterprises, Ltd.

Fitzhugh, Bill. Radio Activity. 2004. 352p. 23.95 (0-380-97759-1, Morrow, William & Co.) Morrow/Avon.

Flagg, Fannie. Coming Attractions. l.t. ed. 1983. 14.95 o.p. (0-8161-3294-1, Macmillan Reference USA) Gale Group.

—Daisy Fay & the Miracle Man, Set. abr. ed. 1992. (Illus.). pap. 16.00 o.s.i incl. audio (0-679-41025-2, RH Audio) Random Hse. Audio Publishing Group.

—Daisy Fay & the Miracle Man. l.t. ed. 1993. pap. 18.00 o.s.i (0-679-74947-0) Random Hse. Large Print.

—Daisy Fay & the Miracle Man. 1992. 320p. reprint ed. pap. 13.95 (0-446-39452-1) Warner Bks., Inc.

Foote, Shelby. Follow Me Down. 1993. 288p. pap. 13.00 (0-679-73617-4, Vintage) Knopf Publishing Group.

—Jordan County: A Novel. 1992. 304p. pap. 14.00 (0-679-73616-6, Vintage) Knopf Publishing Group.

—Jordan County: A Novel. 1995. 26.25 (0-8446-6874-5) Smith, Peter Pub., Inc.

—Love in a Dry Season. 1992. 256p. pap. 13.00 (0-679-73618-2, Vintage) Knopf Publishing Group.

—September, September. 1991. 320p. pap. 12.00 o.s.i (0-679-73543-7) Random Hse., Inc.

Forrest, Leon. The Bloodworth Orphans. 2001. 383p. pap. 18.00 (0-226-25722-3) Univ. of Chicago Pr.

—There Is a Tree More Ancient Than Eden. 2001. 213p. pap. 13.00 (0-226-25721-5) Univ. of Chicago Pr.

Foster, Sharon Ewell. Passing by Samaria. 2003. 566p. pap. 16.95 (1-4104-0157-X, Walker Large Print) Gale Group.

—Passing by Samaria. 2003. 384p. pap. 12.99 (1-57673-615-6, Alabaster) Multnomah Pubs., Inc.

—Passing by Samaria. l.t. ed. 2003. 566p. 26.95 (0-7862-5572-2) Thorndike Pr.

French, Albert L. Billy. l.t. ed. 1994. o.p. (0-7927-2074-1) BBC Audiobooks America.

—Billy. l.t. ed. 1994. 256p. lib. bdg. 22.95 (0-8161-7449-0, Macmillan Reference USA) Gale Group.

—Billy. 224p. 1995. 12.95 (0-14-017908-9); 1993. 19.00 o.p. (0-670-85013-6, Viking) Viking Penguin.

Frierson, J. Q. Rocketed into History: NASA Claims a Paradise. 1996. 220p. 18.95 o.p. (0-944957-82-X) Rivercross Publishing, Inc.

Galef, David. Flesh. 1995. 256p. 28.00 (1-877946-55-9) Permanent Pr., The.

Golden, Marita. And Do Remember Me. 1992. 208p. 19.00 o.s.i (0-385-41506-0) Doubleday Publishing.

Goyen, William. In a Farther Country. 1968. 182p. 24.95 (0-7206-4450-X) Dufour Editions, Inc.

Grau, Shirley A. Keepers of the House. 1976. pap. 1.50 o.s.i (0-449-23031-7, Fawcett) Ballantine Bks.

—Keepers of the House. 1985. (Southern Writers Ser.). mass mkt. 4.50 (0-380-70047-6, Avon Bks.) Morrow/Avon.

—Keepers of the House. 1964. 11.95 o.s.i (0-394-43182-0, Knopf Bks. for Young Readers) Random Hse. Children's Bks.

—Keepers of the House: A Novel. 1995. (Voices of the South Ser.). 328p. (C). pap. 16.95 o.p. (0-8071-2031-6) Louisiana State Univ. Pr.

Grisham, John. Camara de Gas. 1998. (Illus.). (J). 15.30 (0-606-18346-9) Turtleback Bks.

—The Chamber. 1995. mass mkt. 8.99 (0-440-91084-6); 688p. mass mkt. 7.99 (0-440-22060-2); mass mkt. (0-440-29533-5) Dell Publishing.

—The Chamber. 1994. 496p. 27.95 (0-385-42472-8); 880p. 29.95 o.s.i (0-385-47439-3); 496p. 250.00 o.s.i (0-385-47440-7) Doubleday Publishing.

—The Chamber, Level 6. 2000. (Penguin Reader Ser.). pap. 7.93 (0-582-36411-6) Longman Publishing Group.

—The Chamber. 1995. 14.04 (0-606-17119-3) Turtleback Bks.

—The Partner. 1998. 480p. pap. 7.99 (0-440-22604-X); 1998. 480p. mass mkt. 7.99 (0-440-22476-4); 1997. mass mkt. 7.99 (0-440-29555-6) Dell Publishing.

—The Partner. 1997. 368p. 27.95 (0-385-47295-1); 528p. 31.95 o.s.i (0-385-48578-6); 368p. 250.00 o.s.i (0-385-48592-1) Doubleday Publishing.

—The Partner, Level 5. 2001. pap. 7.66 (0-582-43406-8) Longman Publishing Group.

—The Partner. abr. ed. 1997. audio 26.95 (0-553-47283-6, 694963); audio compact disk 29.95 (0-553-45553-2) Random Hse. Audio Publishing Group. (RH Audio).

—The Partner. 1998. 14.04 (0-606-15672-0) Turtleback Bks.

—The Runaway Jury. 1997. 560p. mass mkt. 7.99 (0-440-22147-1) Bantam Dell Publishing Group.

—The Runaway Jury. unabr. ed. 1997. audio 80.00 (0-913369-34-9, 4198) Books on Tape, Inc.

—The Runaway Jury. 1997. mass mkt. 10.99 (0-440-22441-1); 1997. 215.73 o.s.i (0-440-78693-2); 1997. 383.52 o.s.i (0-440-78694-0); 1996. mass mkt. 7.99 (0-440-29552-1) Dell Publishing.

—The Runaway Jury. 1996. 416p. 30.00 (0-385-47294-3); 656p. 30.95 o.s.i (0-385-48015-6); 416p. 250.00 o.s.i (0-385-48016-4) Doubleday Publishing.

—The Runaway Jury, Level 6. 2001. pap. 7.93 (0-582-43405-X) Longman Publishing Group.

—The Runaway Jury. abr. ed. 2003. audio 27.95 (0-553-47282-8, 693510); 1996. audio compact disk 29.95 (0-553-45548-6, ) Random Hse. Audio Publishing Group. (RH Audio).

—The Runaway Jury. l.t. ed. 2003. 704p. pap. 15.95 (0-375-43344-9) Random Hse. Large Print.

—The Runaway Jury. unabr. ed. 1997. audio 97.00 (0-7887-0724-8, 94901E7) Recorded Bks., LLC.

—The Runaway Jury. 1997. 14.04 (0-606-18108-3) Turtleback Bks.

—The Summons. 2002. 384p. mass mkt. 7.99 (0-440-24107-3, Delta) Dell Publishing.

—The Summons. 2002. 352p. 27.95 (0-385-50382-2); 250.00 (0-385-50383-0) Doubleday Publishing.

—The Summons. abr. ed. 2002. audio 27.95 (0-553-52890-4); audio 34.95 (0-553-52891-2, RH Audio); audio compact disk 39.95 (0-553-71463-5, RH Audio) Random Hse. Audio Publishing Group.

—The Summons. l.t. ed. 2002. 464p. pap. 15.95 (0-375-43197-7); 27.95 (0-375-43148-9) Random Hse. Large Print.

—A Time to Kill. 1993. audio compact disk 112.00 (0-7366-8912-5); audio 88.00 (0-7366-2362-0, 3136) Books on Tape, Inc.

—A Time to Kill. 1992. 528p. mass mkt. 7.99 (0-440-21172-7) Dell Publishing.

—A Time to Kill. 1993. 496p. 30.00 (0-385-47081-9); 800p. 27.00 o.s.i (0-385-47078-9); 496p. 200.00 o.s.i (0-385-47112-2) Doubleday Publishing.

—A Time to Kill. l.t. ed. 1993. (0-8161-5590-9, Macmillan Reference USA) Gale Group.

—A Time to Kill, Set. unabr. ed. 1999. audio 49.95 Highsmith Inc.

—A Time to Kill, Level 5. 2000. pap. 7.93 (0-582-36410-8) Longman Publishing Group.

—A Time to Kill. 1992. audio 15.95 o.s.i (0-553-74519-0); 1992. audio 12.79 o.s.i (0-553-70018-9); 2001. audio 9.99 (0-553-70220-3); 1992. audio 16.99 (0-553-47069-8, 391785); 1991. audio 13.59 o.s.i (0-553-70067-7); 1998. audio 49.95 (0-553-50222-0, 133760) Random Hse. Audio Publishing Group. (RH Audio).

—A Time to Kill. 1993. 415p. o.s.i (0-7126-5906-4) Random Hse. of Canada, Ltd. CAN. *Dist:* Random Hse., Inc.

—A Time to Kill. 1992. 14.04 (0-606-14351-3) Turtleback Bks.

—A Time to Kill. 1991. 416p. pap. 9.95 o.p. (0-922066-72-8); 1989. 384p. 18.95 o.p. (0-922066-03-5) Wynwood.

Haines, Carolyn. Buried Bones. 2000. 368p. mass mkt. 5.99 (0-553-58172-4) Bantam Bks.

—Buried Bones. l.t. ed. 2003. 588p. 25.95 (0-375-43270-1, Random House Large Print) Random Hse. Large Print.

—Splintered Bones. 2003. 384p. mass mkt. 5.99 (0-440-23721-1); 2002. 320p. 23.95 (0-385-33590-3, Delacorte Pr.) Dell Publishing.

—Splintered Bones. l.t. ed. 2003. 496p. 25.95 (0-375-43248-5) Random Hse. Large Print.

—Summer of the Redeemers. 400p. 1995. pap. 11.95 o.p. (0-452-27402-8, Plume); 1994. 22.95 o.p. (0-525-93787-0, Dutton) Dutton/Plume.

Hannah, Barry. Boomerang & Never Die. 1994. (Banner Bk.). 320p. pap. 20.00 (0-87805-702-1) Univ. Pr. of Mississippi.

—Hey Jack! 1987. 128p. 15.95 o.p. (0-525-24558-8, Seymour Lawrence) NAL.

—Hey Jack! 1988. 144p. pap. 6.95 o.p. (0-14-011185-9, Penguin Bks.) Viking Penguin.

—Yonder Stands Your Orphan. 2001. 288p. 24.00 o.p. (0-87113-811-5, Atlantic Monthly Pr.); 2002. 352p. reprint ed. pap. 13.00 (0-8021-3893-4, Grove Pr.) Grove/Atlantic, Inc.

Hardwick, Phil. Captured in Canton. 1999. (Mississippi Mysteries Ser.: Vol. 3). 112p. pap. 5.00 (1-893062-05-8) Quail Ridge Pr., Inc.

—Conspiracy in Corinth, 8 vols., Vol. 7. 1999. (Mississippi Mysteries Ser.: Vol. 7). (Illus.). 120p. pap. 5.00 (1-893062-11-2) Quail Ridge Pr., Inc.

—Cover-up in Columbus, 8 vols. 2001. (Mississippi Mysteries Ser.: Vol. 8). (Illus.). 128p. pap. 5.00 (1-893062-30-9) Quail Ridge Pr., Inc.

—Found in Flora. 1999. (Mississippi Mysteries Ser.: Vol. 1). (Illus.). 96p. pap. 5.00 (1-893062-03-1) Quail Ridge Pr., Inc.

—Justice in Jackson. 1999. (Mississippi Mysteries Ser.: Vol. 2). 112p. pap. 5.00 (1-893062-04-X) Quail Ridge Pr., Inc.

—Mississippi Mystery Series, 8 vols. 1999. (Mississippi Mysteries Ser.). (Illus.). 936p. pap. 55.00 (1-893062-13-9) Quail Ridge Pr., Inc.

—Newcomer in New Albany. 1999. (Mississippi Mysteries Ser.: Vol. 4). (Illus.). 127p. pap. 5.00 (1-893062-06-6) Quail Ridge Pr., Inc.

Hatch, John. Mississippi Swamp. 2001. (New Africa Chronicles Ser.: Vol. 1). (Illus.). 360p. 27.98 (0-9706854-0-8) 2ndsightbooks.com.

Haynes, Melinda Rucker. Chalktown: A Novel. 2001. 317p. 23.95 (0-7868-6656-X) Hyperion Pr.

—Chalktown: A Novel. 2002. 368p. pap. 14.00 (0-7434-4250-4, Washington Square Pr.) Simon & Schuster.

—Chalktown: A Novel. l.t. ed. 2001. (Americana Ser.). 563p. 31.95 o.p. (0-7862-3356-7) Thorndike Pr.

—Mother of Pearl. l.t. ed. 2000. (Thorndike/G. K. Hall Paperback Bestsellers Ser.). 760p. 30.00 (0-7862-2182-8, Macmillan Reference USA) Gale Group.

—Mother of Pearl. 1999. 445p. 23.95 (0-7868-6485-0); 448p. 23.95 (0-7868-6627-6) Hyperion Pr.

—Mother of Pearl. reprint ed. 2001. 512p. pap. 7.99 (0-7434-3103-0, Pocket); 2000. 496p. pap. 13.95 (0-671-77467-0, Washington Square Pr.) Simon & Schuster.

—Mother of Pearl. l.t. ed. 1999. (Basic Ser.). 760p. 31.95 (0-7862-2181-X) Thorndike Pr.

—Mother of Pearl. 2000. 20.00 (0-606-19128-3) Turtleback Bks.

Heath, William. The Children Bob Moses Led. 350p. 1997. pap. 12.95 (1-57131-012-6); 1995. 21.95 (1-57131-008-8) Milkweed Editions.

Heck, Peter J. A Connecticut Yankee in Criminal Court. 1997. (Mark Twain Mystery Ser.). 320p. mass mkt. 5.99 o.s.i (0-425-16034-3, Prime Crime) Berkley Publishing Group.

—A Connecticut Yankee in Criminal Court: A Mark Twain Mystery. 1996. (Mark Twain Mystery Ser.). 320p. 21.95 o.p. (0-425-15470-X); viii, 311p. pap. o.p. (0-425-15474-2) Berkley Publishing Group. (Prime Crime).

—Death on the Mississippi. 1996. (Mark Twain Mystery Ser.). (Illus.). x, 290p. mass mkt. 5.99 o.s.i (0-425-15512-9) Berkley Publishing Group.

—Death on the Mississippi: A Mark Twain Mystery. 1995. (Mark Twain Mystery Ser.). 304p. 21.95 o.p. (0-425-14938-2); pap. 10.00 o.p. (0-425-14939-0) Berkley Publishing Group. (Prime Crime).

—Guilty Abroad. 1999. (Mark Twain Mystery Ser.). 320p. mass mkt. 6.50 o.s.i (0-425-17122-1) Berkley Publishing Group.

—The Prince & the Prosecutor. (Mark Twain Mystery Ser.: No. 3). 336p. 1998. mass mkt. 5.99 o.s.i (0-425-16567-1); 1997. 21.95 o.s.i (0-425-15970-1) Berkley Publishing Group. (Prime Crime).

Hegwood, Martin. Big Easy Backroad. E-Book 22.95 (0-312-26441-0); 2000. 256p. mass mkt. 5.99 (0-312-97141-9, St. Martin's Paperbacks); 3rd ed. 1999. 247p. 22.95 (0-312-20277-6, Saint Martin's Minotaur) St. Martin's Pr.

—Green-Eyed Hurricane. 2001. 304p. mass mkt. 6.50 (0-312-97975-4, St. Martin's Paperbacks); 2000. 272p. 23.95 (0-312-20919-3, Saint Martin's Minotaur) St. Martin's Pr.

—The Green-Eyed Hurricane. E-Book 23.95 (0-312-27579-X) St. Martin's Pr.

—Jackpot Bay: A Novel. 2002. 272p. 23.95 (0-312-28096-3, Saint Martin's Minotaur) St. Martin's Pr.

Hill, Donna. Rhythms. mass mkt. (0-312-98024-8, St. Martin's Paperbacks); 2001. 352p. 23.95 (0-312-27299-5) St. Martin's Pr.

—Rhythms: A Novel. 2002. 336p. pap. 12.95 (0-312-30069-7, Saint Martin's Griffin) St. Martin's Pr.

Hinze, Vicki. Duplicity. 1999. 370p. mass mkt. 5.99 o.p. (0-312-96894-9, St. Martin's Paperbacks) St. Martin's Pr.

Houghton Mifflin Company Staff & Hannah, Barry. Boomerang. 1989. 160p. 15.95 o.p. (0-395-48882-6) Houghton Mifflin Co. Trade & Reference Div.

Hunter, Stephen. Pale Horse Coming. 2003. 608p. pap. 7.99 (0-671-03546-0, Pocket); 2001. 496p. 25.00 (0-684-86361-8, Simon & Schuster); 2002. 624p. mass mkt. 7.99 (0-7434-4382-9, Pocket) Simon & Schuster.

—Pale Horse Coming. abr. ed. 2001. audio 26.00 (0-7435-1006-2); audio compact disk 32.00 (0-7435-0912-9) Simon & Schuster Audio. (Simon & Schuster Audioworks).

—Pale Horse Coming. l.t. ed. 825p. 2003. 13.95 (0-7862-3949-2); 2002. 28.95 (0-7862-3950-6) Thorndike Pr.

Iles, Greg. The Quiet Game. 1999. 480p. 24.95 o.s.i (0-525-93793-5, Dutton) Dutton/Plume.

—The Quiet Game. l.t. ed. 2000. (G. K. Hall Core Ser.). 720p. 30.95 (0-7838-9299-3, Macmillan Reference USA) Gale Group.

—The Quiet Game. 2000. 576p. mass mkt. 7.99 (0-451-18042-9, Signet Bks.) NAL.

—The Quiet Game. 2001. 720p. 28.95 (0-7838-9300-0) Thorndike Pr.

—24 Hours. abr. ed. 2000. audio 24.95 o.p. (1-56740-929-6, 2196, Nova Audio Bks.); audio 73.25 (1-56740-735-8, 2195, Unabridged Library Editions); audio 32.95 (1-56740-387-5, 2194, Brilliance Audio Unabridged) Brilliance Audio.

—24 Hours. l.t. ed. 2000. (Wheeler Large Print Book Ser.). 448p. 29.95 (1-56895-931-1, Wheeler Publishing, Inc.) Gale Group.

—24 Hours. 2000. 335p. 24.95 o.s.i (0-399-14624-5) Penguin Group (USA) Inc.

James, Dean. Closer Than the Bones. 2001. 208p. pap. 13.95 (1-57072-183-1, Silver Dagger Mysteries) Overmountain Pr.

—Closer Than the Bones: An Ernestine Carpenter Mystery. 2001. 208p. 23.95 (1-57072-182-3, Silver Dagger Mysteries) Overmountain Pr.

Johnson, Sharleen. Whispers in the Mist. 2001. pap. 13.95 (0-7433-0088-2) Clocktower Bks.

Jones, Linda Winstead. Into the Woods. 2001. (Faerie Tale Romance Ser.). 400p. mass mkt. 5.99 (0-505-52428-7, Love Spell) Dorchester Publishing Co., Inc.

Kathryns, G. A. The Borders of Life. 1999. 352p. mass mkt. 6.99 o.s.i (0-451-45574-6, ROC) NAL.

Kean, Jack. Deadly Sacrifice. 1999. 255p. 22.95 (1-885478-78-X) Genesis Pr., Inc.

Kingsbury, Suzanne. The Summer Fletcher Greel Loved Me: A Novel. 2003. 368p. pap. 14.00 (0-7432-2304-7); 2002. 304p. 25.00 (0-7432-2303-9) Simon & Schuster. (Scribner).

Lee, Joseph Thomas. On the Record. 2002. 271p. 19.95 (0-9721611-0-4) Dogwood Pr., LLC.

Lott, Bret. Jewel. 1993. lib. bdg. 14.95 o.p. (1-56054-930-0); 1950. 30.00 (0-7838-8591-1) Gale Group. (Macmillan Reference USA).

—Jewel. (Oprah's Book Club Ser.). 1999. 368p. 23.00 o.s.i (0-671-03823-0, Atria); 1999. 368p. pap. 14.00 (0-671-03818-4, Washington Square Pr.); 1991. 368p. 20.00 (0-671-74038-5, Atria); 1999. (Illus.). 560p. reprint ed. pap. 7.99 (0-671-04257-2, Pocket) Simon & Schuster.

—Jewel. Rosenman, Jane, ed. 1992. 368p. reprint ed. pap. 9.00 (0-671-74039-3, Washington Square Pr.) Simon & Schuster.

—Jewel. 2000. 14.04 (0-606-19056-2) Turtleback Bks.

Lowry, Beverly. Come Back, Lolly Ray. 1977. 7.95 o.p. (0-385-12243-8) Doubleday Publishing.

—Come Back, Lolly Ray: Novel. 2000. (Voices of the South Ser.). 230p. pap. 15.95 (0-8071-2574-1) Louisiana State Univ. Pr.

Marshall, Bev. Walking Through Shadows. 2002. 282p. 25.00 (1-931561-05-2) MacAdam/Cage Publishing, Inc.

Matson, Henrietta. The Mississippi Schoolmaster. 1977. (Black Heritage Library Collection). reprint ed. 25.95 (0-8369-9035-8) Ayer Co. Pubs., Inc.

Melville, Herman. The Confidence Man. l.t. ed. 2000. 339p. 32.95 (1-56000-473-8) Transaction Pubs.

Michaels, Fern. Charming Lily. l.t. ed. 2002. 439p. pap. 12.95 (0-7862-3452-0, Wheeler Publishing, Inc.) Gale Group.

—Charming Lily. 2001. 352p. mass mkt. 7.99 (0-8217-7019-5) Kensington Publishing Corp.

—Charming Lily. l.t. ed. 2001. (Americana Ser.). 509p. 31.95 (0-7862-3451-2) Thorndike Pr.

Morris, Willie. Taps: A Novel. 352p. 2002. pap. 13.00 (0-618-21902-1); 2001. tchr. ed. 26.00 (0-618-09859-3) Houghton Mifflin Co.

Neilson, Melany. The Persia Cafe. 2001. 276p. 23.95 o.p. (0-312-26219-1) St. Martin's Pr.

—The Persia Cafe. l.t. ed. 2001. (Thorndike Press Large Print Americana Ser.). 442p. 28.95 (0-7862-3729-5) Thorndike Pr.

Newberry, Sandra. September's Autumn. 2001. pap. 12.00 (0-8059-5023-0) Dorrance Publishing Co., Inc.

Nordan, Lewis. The All-Girl Football Team. 1989. (Contemporaries Ser.). pap. 5.95 o.s.i (0-394-75701-7, Vintage) Knopf Publishing Group.

—The All-Girl Football Team. Stories. 1986. 125p. text 15.95 o.p. (0-8071-1341-7) Louisiana State Univ. Pr.

—Music of the Swamp. (Front Porch Paperback Ser.). 210p. 1992. pap. 9.95 (1-56512-016-7); 1991. 15.95 (0-945575-76-9) Algonquin Bks. of Chapel Hill.

—The Sharpshooter Blues: A Novel. 1995. 300p. 17.95 (1-56512-083-3, 72083) Algonquin Bks. of Chapel Hill.

—Sugar among the Freaks: Selected Stories. 1996. (Front Porch Paperback Ser.). 312p. (Orig.). pap. 10.95 (1-56512-131-7, 72131) Algonquin Bks. of Chapel Hill.

—Welcome to the Arrow-Catcher Affair. 1989. (Vintage Contemporaries Ser.). pap. 6.95 o.s.i (0-679-72164-9, Vintage) Knopf Publishing Group.

—Welcome to the Arrow-Catcher Fair: Stories. 1983. 127p. text 15.95 o.p. (0-8071-1124-4) Louisiana State Univ. Pr.

—Wolf Whistle: A Novel. 2003. 308p. pap. 12.95 (1-56512-110-4); 1993. 294p. 16.95 (1-56512-028-0) Algonquin Bks. of Chapel Hill.

Octave, Thanet. Otto the Knight. 2000. 252p. E-Book 3.95 (*0-594-06166-0*) 1873 Pr.

Parrish, P. J. Dark of the Moon. 2000. 432p. mass mkt. 6.99 (*0-7860-1054-1*, Pinnacle Bks.); 1999. (Illus.). 384p. 23.00 o.s.i (*1-57566-394-5*) Kensington Publishing Corp.

Phillips, Susan Elizabeth. Ain't She Sweet? l.t. ed. 2004. 544p. pap. 24.95 (*0-06-058977-9*, Harper-LargePrint) HarperTrade.

—Ain't She Sweet? 2004. 400p. 24.95 (*0-06-621124-7*, Morrow, William & Co.) Morrow/Avon.

Phillips, Thomas H. The Bitterweed Path: A Rediscovered Novel. 1996. (Chapel Hill Bks.). 336p. pap. 19.95 (*0-8078-4595-7*) Univ. of North Carolina Pr.

Phillips, Thomas Hal. Red Midnight. 2002. 256p. 28.00 (*1-57806-474-0*) Univ. Pr. of Mississippi.

Prather, Jo Beecher. Mississippi Beau. 1995. (Illus.). 32p. (J). (gr. 4-5). pap. 9.95 (*0-89015-961-0*) Eakin Pr.

Propst, Milam McGraw. Ociee on Her Own: A Novel. 2003. 161p. 23.00 (*0-86554-838-2*) Mercer Univ. Pr.

Rhinock, Sharleen. Whispers in the Mist. E-Book 5.00 o.p. (*0-7433-0032-7*) Clocktower Bks.

Rhythms. 2000. mass mkt. (*0-312-97515-5*, St. Martin's Paperbacks) St. Martin's Pr.

Roberts, Nora. Carnal Innocence. 1999. 400p. 19.95 o.s.i (*0-553-11094-2*); 1991. 512p. mass mkt. 7.99 (*0-553-29597-7*) Bantam Bks.

—Carnal Innocence. l.t. ed. 2000. 13.95 (*1-56895-981-8*); 1999. 659p. 27.95 (*1-56895-810-2*) Gale Group. (Wheeler Publishing, Inc.).

—Carnal Innocence. abr. ed. 1999. audio 25.95 (*0-553-52637-5*, RH Audio) Random Hse. Audio Publishing Group.

—Carnal Innocence. unabr. ed. 1999. audio 109.00 (*0-7887-3766-X*, 95983E7) Recorded Bks., LLC.

Rogers, Rosemary. An Honorable Man. 2002. 400p. mass mkt. (*1-55166-953-6*, Mira Bks.) Harlequin Enterprises, Ltd.

—Return to Me. 2003. 480p. mass mkt. (*1-55166-748-7*, Mira Bks.) Harlequin Enterprises, Ltd.

Ross, Dana Fuller, pseud. Mississippi! l.t. ed. 1986. 360p. 16.95 o.p. (*0-8161-3969-5*, Macmillan Reference USA) Gale Group.

Ruffin, Paul. Islands, Women & God. 2001. 254p. (*0-9651359-8-5*, 005); 247p. pap. (*0-9651359-9-3*) Browder Springs Bks.

—Pompeii Man. 2001. (*0-945083-03-3*) Louisiana Literature Pr.

Ryan, John F. The Redneck Bride. (Illus.). 1986. 176p. pap. 7.95 o.p. (*0-87483-005-2*); 1982. 198p. pap. 8.95 o.p. (*0-935304-54-1*) August Hse. Pubs., Inc.

Sandford, John, pseud. The Empress File. 1991. 288p. 18.95 o.p. (*0-8050-1545-0*) Holt, Henry & Co.

—The Hanged Man's Song. 2003. 336p. 25.95 (*0-399-15139-7*, Putnam & Grosset) Putnam Publishing Group, The.

Savage, Les, Jr. Danger Rides the River: A Frontier Story. 2002. (Five Star First Edition Western Ser.). 398p. 24.95 (*0-7862-3543-8*, Five Star) Gale Group.

Scafidel, James R. Wit's End. 1989. 17.95 o.p. (*0-934601-74-7*) Peachtree Pubs., Ltd.

—Wit's End. 1991. 2.99 o.p. (*0-517-07526-1*) Random Hse. Value Publishing.

Schroder, George L. The Greatest Courage. 1998. 127p. pap. 10.95 o.p. (*0-533-12323-2*) Vantage Pr., Inc.

Schulte, Elaine L. Mercies So Tender. 1995. 312p. pap. 8.99 o.p. (*0-7814-0158-5*) Cook Communications Ministries.

Shankman, Sarah. The King Is Dead. Chelius, Jane, ed. 1992. 288p. 20.00 (*0-671-73459-8*, Atria); 1993. 320p. reprint ed. mass mkt. 5.99 (*0-671-73460-1*, Pocket) Simon & Schuster.

Simms, William Gilmore. Border Beagles: A Tale of Mississippi. rev. ed. reprint ed. 24.50 (*0-404-06007-2*) AMS Pr., Inc.

—Border Beagles: A Tale of Mississippi. 1885. 495p. (YA). reprint ed. pap. text 28.00 (*1-4047-6857-2*) Classic Textbooks.

—Border Beagles: A Tale of Mississippi. 1992. (BCL1-PS American Literature Ser.). 495p. reprint ed. lib. bdg. 99.00 (*0-7812-6857-5*) Reprint Services Corp.

—Border Beagles: A Tale of Mississippi. Guilds, John Caldwell, ed. 1996. 512p. text 55.00 (*1-55728-402-4*); o.p. (*1-55728-403-2*) Univ. of Arkansas Pr.

Singleton, Elyse. This Side of the Sky. 2003. 336p. pap. 14.00 (*0-425-19312-8*); 2002. 304p. 24.95 o.s.i (*0-399-14920-1*) Putnam Publishing Group, The. (BlueHen Bks.).

Smith, Johnny N. Hillcountry Warriors: A Novel That Exposes a Different Side to the Civil War South. Smith, James C., Jr., ed. 1996. 384p. 18.95 (*0-86534-247-4*) Sunstone Pr.

Spencer, Elizabeth. The Voice at the Back Door. 1994. (Voices of the South Ser.). vii, 392p. pap. 17.95 (*0-8071-1927-X*) Louisiana State Univ. Pr.

Stokes, Penelope J. Home Fires Burning. 1996. (Faith on the Home Front Ser.: Vol. 1). 345p. pap. 8.99 o.p. (*0-8423-0851-2*) Tyndale Hse. Pubs.

—Till We Meet Again. 1997. (Faith on the Home Front Ser.: No. 2). 327p. pap. 10.99 o.p. (*0-8423-0852-0*) Tyndale Hse. Pubs.

Sullivan, Clayton. Jesus & the Sweet Pilgrim Baptist Church. 2001. (Muscadine Book Ser.). 112p. reprint ed. pap. 15.00 (*1-57806-332-9*) Univ. Pr. of Mississippi.

—Jesus & the Sweet Pilgrim Baptist Church: A Fable. 1993. 112p. 15.00 o.s.i (*0-385-46876-8*) Doubleday Publishing.

Tartt, Donna. The Little Friend. 2003. 640p. pap. 14.95 (*1-4000-3169-9*); 2002. 576p. 26.00 (*0-679-43938-2*) Knopf Publishing Group. (Vintage).

Tatlock, Ann. All the Way Home: A Friendship That Once Bridged Two Cultural Will It Survive The Span of Time. 2002. 448p. pap. 12.99 (*0-7642-2663-0*) Bethany Hse. Pubs.

Thomason, Cynthia. Stagestruck: A Jubilee Showboat Mystery. 2003. 241p. 25.95 (*1-59414-078-2*, Five Star) Gale Group.

Thompson, Phillip. Enemy Within. 2000. E-Book 7.00 (*1-930486-01-4*); 1999. 160p. pap. 11.00 (*0-9664520-2-X*) Salvo Pr.

Tucker, Judy H. & McCord, Charline R., eds. Christmas Stories from Mississippi. 2001. (Illus.). 208p. 28.00 (*1-57806-381-7*) Univ. Pr. of Mississippi.

Twain, Mark. Huckleberry Finn. 1942. 112p. pap. 5.60 (*0-87129-839-2*, H35) Dramatic Publishing Co.

—Huckleberry Finn. 6th ed. 1997. (FRE., Illus.). (J). (gr. 4-7). pap. 13.95 (*2-07-051625-3*) Gallimard, Editions FRA. *Dist:* Distribooks, Inc.

—Tom Sawyer. 1994. (Illustrated Classics Collection: No. 1). 64p. pap. 3.60 o.p. (*1-56103-441-X*) American Guidance Service, Inc.

Vernon, Olympia. Eden. 288p. 2004. pap. 12.00 (*0-8021-4040-8*); 2003. 23.00 (*0-8021-1728-7*) Grove/Atlantic, Inc. (Grove Pr.).

Ware, Ciji. A Light on the Veranda. 2001. 512p. mass mkt. 6.99 (*0-449-15029-1*, Ivy Bks.) Ballantine Bks.

Watson, Brad. The Heaven of Mercury: A Novel. 2003. (Illus.). 352p. pap. 14.95 (*0-393-32465-6*); 2002. 288p. 23.95 (*0-393-04757-1*) Norton, W. W. & Co., Inc.

Welch, Pat. Moving Targets. 2001. 240p. pap. 11.95 (*0-9677753-6-1*) Bella Bks., Inc.

—Open House. 1995. (Helen Black Mysteries Ser.). 224p. pap. 10.95 (*1-56280-102-3*) Naiad Pr., Inc.

Wells, Ken. Logan's Storm: A Novel. 2003. 304p. pap. 12.95 (*0-375-76067-9*) Random House Adult Trade Publishing Group.

—Logan's Storm: A Novel. 2002. 304p. 21.95 (*0-375-50525-3*) Random Hse., Inc.

Welty, Eudora. Delta Wedding. 22.95 (*0-89190-516-2*) Amereon, Ltd.

—Delta Wedding. (HBJ Book Ser.). 1991. 336p. 17.00 (*0-15-124774-9*); 1979. 336p. (C). pap. 12.00 (*0-15-625280-5*, Harvest Bks.); 1946. 7.95 o.p. (*0-15-124773-0*) Harcourt Trade Pubs.

—Delta Wedding. 1963. mass mkt. 0.75 o.p. (*0-451-02274-2*, Signet Bks.) NAL.

—Delta Wedding. l.t. ed. 2001. (Perennial Bestsellers Ser.). 387p. 28.95 (*0-7838-9379-5*) Thorndike Pr.

—The Optimist's Daughter. 1990. (Paperback Ser.). 190p. 14.95 o.p. (*0-8161-5028-1*, Macmillan Reference USA) Gale Group.

—The Optimist's Daughter. l.t. ed. 1999. pap. 20.00 (*0-375-70688-7*) Random Hse. Large Print.

—The Optimist's Daughter. 2002. 192p. 20.00 o.s.i (*0-375-50835-X*) Random Hse., Inc.

—The Ponder Heart. 18.95 (*0-8488-0661-1*) Amereon, Ltd.

—The Ponder Heart. (Illus.). 1967. 168p. pap. 9.00 (*0-15-672915-6*, Harvest Bks.); 1954. 6.95 o.p. (*0-15-173073-3*) Harcourt Trade Pubs.

—The Robber Bridegroom. 1987. (Illus.). 134p. 19.95 (*0-15-178318-7*); 1948. 6.95 o.p. (*0-15-178317-9*); 1978. 192p. (C). reprint ed. pap. 11.00 (*0-15-676807-0*, Harvest Bks.) Harcourt Trade Pubs.

Whorton, James C. Approximately Heaven. 2004. 224p. pap. 12.00 (*0-7432-4447-8*, Free Pr.) Simon & Schuster.

—Approximately Heaven: A Novel. 2003. 240p. 23.00 (*0-7432-4446-X*, Free Pr.) Simon & Schuster.

Wilson, Charles. The Cassandra Prophecy. 1993. 224p. 18.95 o.p. (*0-88184-951-0*, Carroll & Graf Pubs.) Avalon Publishing Group.

—Donor. 1999. 320p. mass mkt. 6.99 (*0-312-97028-5*, St. Martin's Paperbacks) St. Martin's Pr.

—Nightwatcher. 1992. 272p. pap. 4.95 o.p. (*0-88184-832-8*); 1990. 320p. 17.95 o.p. (*0-88184-638-4*) Avalon Publishing Group. (Carroll & Graf Pubs.).

—Nightwatcher. 1997. 288p. reprint ed. mass mkt. 4.99 (*0-8439-4275-4*, Leisure Bks.) Dorchester Publishing Co., Inc.

—Nightwatcher. 1997. E-Book 9.95 (*0-585-29870-X*) netLibrary, Inc.

—When First We Deceive. 1994. 272p. 19.95 o.p. (*0-7867-0058-0*, Carroll & Graf Pubs.) Avalon Publishing Group.

—When First We Deceive. 1998. 272p. reprint ed. mass mkt. 4.50 (*0-8439-4401-3*, Leisure Bks.) Dorchester Publishing Co., Inc.

—When We First Deceive. 1998. E-Book 9.95 (*0-585-28456-3*) netLibrary, Inc.

Yarbrough, Steve. Mississippi History: Stories. 1994. 176p. (C). pap. 16.95 o.p. (*0-8262-0967-X*) Univ. of Missouri Pr.

—The Oxygen Man: A Novel. 1999. 280p. 20.00 (*1-878448-85-4*) MacMurray & Beck, Inc.

—The Oxygen Man: A Novel. 2000. 288p. pap. 12.00 (*0-7432-0165-5*, Touchstone) Simon & Schuster.

—Prisoners of War: A Novel. 2004. 304p. 23.00 (*0-375-41478-9*) Knopf, Alfred A. Inc.

—Visible Spirits: A Novel. 2002. 288p. pap. 13.00 (*0-375-72577-6*, Vintage) Knopf Publishing Group.

Young, Stark. So Red the Rose. 1992. (Southern Classics Ser.). 453p. reprint ed. pap. 15.95 (*1-879941-12-0*, Sanders, J. S. & Co., Inc.) Dee, Ivan R. Pub.

—So Red the Rose. 1978. reprint ed. 18.00 o.p. (*0-89783-006-7*) Larlin Corp.

**MISSOURI—FICTION**

The Adventures of Tom Sawyer. 2001. 8.97 (*0-673-58321-X*) Addison-Wesley Longman, Inc.

The Adventures of Tom Sawyer. 2001. E-Book 2.95 (*1-58853-036-1*) Sensory Publishing, Inc.

Agee, Jonis. South of Resurrection. 1998. 368p. pap. 12.95 (*0-14-024172-8*) Penguin Group (USA) Inc.

—South of Resurrection. 1997. 360p. 24.95 o.p. (*0-670-85809-9*) Viking Penguin.

Beasley, Conger, Jr., ed. Missouri Short Fiction. 1984. 240p. pap. 8.95 o.p. (*0-933532-44-X*) BkMk Pr. of the Univ. of Missouri-Kansas City.

Berg, Elizabeth. The Joy School. 1998. (Ballantine Reader's Circle Ser.). 240p. pap. 12.95 (*0-345-42309-7*) Ballantine Bks.

—The Joy School. l.t. ed. 1997. (Wheeler Large Print Book Ser.). 25.95 (*1-56895-488-3*, Wheeler Publishing, Inc.) Gale Group.

—The Joy School. 1998. 18.00 (*0-606-17137-1*) Turtleback Bks.

Bowen, Lindsey M. Cicada Grove. 1992. 96p. (Orig.). pap. 7.50 (*1-881048-01-2*) Paladin Contemporaries.

Brodkey, Harold. The Runaway Soul. 1991. 835p. 30.00 o.p. (*0-374-25286-6*) Farrar, Straus & Giroux.

—The Runaway Soul. 1992. 848p. pap. 15.00 o.p. (*0-06-097504-0*, Perennial) HarperTrade.

—The Runaway Soul. 1997. 848p. pap. 17.00 o.s.i (*0-8050-5503-7*, Owl Bks.) Holt, Henry & Co.

—The Runaway Soul. 1991. o.p. (*0-224-03001-9*) Random Hse. UK, Ltd. GBR. *Dist:* Random Hse. of Canada, Ltd.

Brown, Richard E. Fishing for Ghosts: Twelve Short Stories. 1994. 216p. 21.00 (*0-87417-229-2*) Univ. of Nevada Pr.

Buckstaff, Kathryn. No One Dies in Branson. 1994. 224p. 19.95 o.p. (*0-312-11036-7*, Saint Martin's Minotaur) St. Martin's Pr.

Bulock, Lynn. Gifts of Grace. 1999. (Steeple Hill Love Inspired Ser.: No. 80). per. (*0-373-87080-9*, 1-87080-7, Harlequin Bks.) Harlequin Enterprises, Ltd.

—The Prodigal's Return. 2001. (Steeple Hill Love Inspired Ser.: Vol. 144). 256p. mass mkt. (*0-373-87151-1*, Harlequin Bks.) Harlequin Enterprises, Ltd.

Carkeet, David. The Error of Our Ways: A Novel. 288p. 1998. pap. 13.00 o.s.i (*0-8050-5604-1*, Owl Bks.); 1997. per. 15.00 (*0-8050-7114-8*); 1997. 25.00 o.s.i (*0-8050-4502-3*) Holt, Henry & Co.

—The Error of Our Ways: A Novel. l.t. ed. 1997. (Niagara Large Print Ser.). 352p. 29.50 o.p. (*0-7089-5865-6*, Ulverscroft) Thorpe, F. A. Pubs. GBR. *Dist:* Ulverscroft Large Print Bks., Ltd.

Champlin, Tim. Swift Thunder. l.t. ed. 1999. (*0-7540-3763-0*) BBC Audiobooks America.

—Swift Thunder. 2000. 240p. mass mkt. 4.50 (*0-8439-4758-6*, Leisure Bks.) Dorchester Publishing Co., Inc.

—Swift Thunder: A Western Story. l.t. ed. 1999. (Western Ser.). 341p. 21.95 (*0-7862-1172-5*) Thorndike Pr.

Champlin, Tim, contrib. by. Swift Thunder. 1999. pap. (*0-7540-3764-9*) BBC Audiobooks America.

Clark, Carol Higgins. Twanged. abr. ed. 1997. audio 18.00 (*0-7871-1555-X*); audio 30.00 (*0-7871-1556-8*) NewStar Media, Inc. (Dove Audio).

—Twanged. l.t. ed. 1998. (Basic Ser.). 389p. 29.95 (*0-7862-1417-1*) Thorndike Pr.

—Twanged. abr. ed. 1998. (Regan Reilly Mysteries Ser.). audio 17.98 (*1-57042-612-0*, 395934 ) Time Warner AudioBooks.

—Twanged. 1999. 336p. mass mkt. 7.50 (*0-446-60536-0*); 1998. 272p. 28.00 (*0-446-51763-1*) Warner Bks., Inc.

Cook, Olive R. Trails to Poosey. 1986. (Illus.). 200p. (Orig.). (J). (gr. 3-6). pap. 5.95 (*0-930079-01-9*) Misty Hill Pr.

Dailey, Janet. Show Me: Missouri. l.t. ed. 2000. (G. K. Hall Core Ser.). 200p. 28.95 (*0-7838-9111-3*, Macmillan Reference USA) Gale Group.

—Show Me: Missouri. 1992. (Janet Dailey Americana Ser.: No. 875). per. (*0-373-89875-4*, 1-89875-8); 1987. (Americana Ser.: No. 25). pap. (*0-373-89825-8*) Harlequin Enterprises, Ltd. (Harlequin Bks.).

—Show Me: Missouri. l.t. ed. 1976. 188p. (J). (*0-263-72273-2*) Harlequin Mills & Boon, Ltd. GBR. *Dist:* BBC Audiobooks America.

—Show Me: Missouri. 1999. 120p. per. 12.95 (*0-7592-3825-1*) ereads.com.

Deaver, Jeffery. The Lesson of Her Death. 1994. 528p. mass mkt. 7.99 (*0-553-56020-4*) Bantam Bks.

—The Lesson of Her Death. 1993. 432p. 18.50 o.s.i (*0-385-42481-7*) Doubleday Publishing.

Delinsky, Barbara & Roberts, Kelsey. Harlequin Special #1: Father of the Bride; Handsome As Sin, 2 bks. in 1. 2001. 328p. mass mkt. (*0-373-83453-5*, 1-83453-0, Harlequin Bks.) Harlequin Enterprises, Ltd.

Dooling, Richard. Brain Storm. unabr. collector's ed. 1998. audio 104.00 (*0-7366-4335-4*, 4816) Books on Tape, Inc.

—Brain Storm. 1999. 416p. pap. 14.00 (*0-312-20399-3*) Picador.

—Brain Storm. unabr. ed. 1998. audio 97.00 (*0-7887-1988-2*, 95375E7) Recorded Bks., LLC.

Dooly, Paige Winship, et al. Church in the Wildwood: A Missouri Church Stands As a Landmark of Love for Four Generations. 2003. (Historical Collections). 352p. pap. 6.97 (*1-58660-966-1*) Barbour Publishing, Inc.

Dreyer, Eileen. Brain Dead. 1997. 416p. mass mkt. 22.00 o.p. (*0-06-101095-2*) HarperCollins Pubs.

—Brain Dead. 1998. 512p. mass mkt. 6.99 (*0-06-101096-0*, HarperTorch) Morrow/Avon.

Eatock, Marjorie. Over the Rainbow. 1993. 480p. mass mkt. 4.50 o.s.i (*0-8217-4032-6*) Kensington Publishing Corp.

Edwards, Paul M. The Angel Acronym: A Mystery Introducing Toom Taggart. 2003. (Illus.). 250p. pap. 21.95 (*1-56085-166-X*) Signature Bks., Inc.

Essman, Barbara. Night Ride Home. l.t. ed. 2000. 26.95 (*1-57490-303-9*, Beeler Large Print Bks.) Beeler, Thomas T. Publisher.

—Night Ride Home. abr. ed. 1998. audio 7.99 o.s.i (*1-56740-242-9*, 1332, Paperback Nova Audio Bks.); 1997. audio 16.95 o.p. (*1-56100-990-3*, 496, Nova Audio Bks.); 1997. audio 57.25 (*1-56100-839-7*, 963, Unabridged Library Editions); 1997. audio 23.95 (*1-56100-764-1*, 194, Bookcassette) Brilliance Audio.

—Night Ride Home. 1997. 336p. 22.00 o.s.i (*0-15-100288-6*) Harcourt Trade Pubs.

—Night Ride Home: A Novel. 1998. 336p. pap. 13.00 (*0-06-097754-X*, Perennial) HarperTrade.

Estleman, Loren D. Gun Man. 1986. mass mkt. 2.50 o.s.i (*0-449-12862-8*, Fawcett) Ballantine Bks.

—Gun Man. 2000. 224p. mass mkt. 5.99 o.s.i (*0-515-12752-3*, Jove) Berkley Publishing Group.

—Gun Man. 1985. (Double D Western Ser.). 192p. 12.95 o.p. (*0-385-23067-2*) Doubleday Publishing.

—Gun Man. l.t. ed. 2001. (G. K. Hall Western Ser.). 288p. 25.95 (*0-7838-9416-3*, Macmillan Reference USA) Gale Group.

—Gun Man. unabr. ed. 1992. audio 51.00 (*1-55690-675-7*, 92231E7) Recorded Bks., LLC.

Fishkin, Shelley Fisher, ed. The Adventures of Tom Sawyer (1876) 1996. (Oxford Mark Twain Ser.). (Illus.). 368p. 18.95 (*0-19-510136-7*) Oxford Univ. Pr., Inc.

—The Tragedy of Pudd'nhead Wilson & the Comedy Those Extraordinary Twins (1894) 1996. (Oxford Mark Twain Ser.). (Illus.). 512p. 19.95 (*0-19-510147-2*) Oxford Univ. Pr., Inc.

Flagg, Fannie. Standing in the Rainbow: A Novel. 2003. 544p. mass mkt. 7.99 (*0-8041-1935-X*, Ballantine Bks.) Ballantine Bks.

—Standing in the Rainbow: A Novel. 2002. 512p. 25.95 (*0-679-42615-9*); 816p. 27.95 (*0-375-43172-1*) Random Hse., Inc.

—Welcome to the World, Baby Girl! 2001. (Reader's Circle Ser.). 512p. pap. 14.95 (*0-449-00578-X*, Ballantine Bks.) Ballantine Bks.

—Welcome to the World, Baby Girl! abr. ed. 1998. 496p. 25.95 incl. audio (*0-679-42614-0*) Random Hse., Inc.

—Welcome to the World, Baby Girl. abr. ed. 1998. audio 25.00 (*0-375-40377-9*, 596015, RH Audio) Random Hse. Audio Publishing Group.

—Welcome to the World, Baby Girl! unabr. ed. 1999. audio 80.00 (*0-7366-4343-5*, 4820) Books on Tape, Inc.

—Welcome to the World, Baby Girl! A Novel. 1999. 432p. mass mkt. 7.99 (*0-8041-1868-X*, Ivy Bks.) Ballantine Bks.

—Welcome to the World, Baby Girl! A Novel. l.t. ed. 1998. pap. 25.95 o.p. (*0-7838-0258-7*, Macmillan Reference USA) Gale Group.

—Welcome to the World, Baby Girl! A Novel. l.t. ed. 1998. 768p. pap. 25.95 (*0-375-70413-2*) Random Hse. Large Print.

For book reviews, descriptive annotations, tables of contents, cover images, author biographies & additional information, updated daily, subscribe to **www.booksinprint.com** 957

Ford, Aisha. Missouri Gateways: Four Romances Packed with Culture & Grace. 2003. (Contemporary Collection). 464p. pap. 6.97 (1-58660-965-3) Barbour Publishing, Inc.

Garlock, Dorothy. Almost Eden. l.t. ed. 1996. 24.95 o.p. (0-7838-1638-3, Macmillan Reference USA) Gale Group.

—Almost Eden. abr. ed. 1995. audio 5.99 (1-57096-038-0, RAZ 938) Romance Alive Audio.

—Almost Eden. 1995. 336p. reprint ed. mass mkt. 6.99 (0-446-36372-3) Warner Bks., Inc.

—The Edge of Town. l.t. ed. (Americana Ser.). 2002. 563p. pap. 28.95 (0-7862-3165-3); 2001. 370p. 31.95 (0-7862-3164-5) Thorndike Pr.

—The Edge of Town. 2001. 384p. 19.95 o.p. (0-446-52769-6) Warner Bks., Inc.

—High on a Hill. l.t. ed. 2002. lib. bdg. 29.95 (1-58547-221-2, Platinum) Ctr. Point Large Print.

—High on a Hill. 2002. 400p. 21.95 o.p. (0-446-52946-X); 416p. reprint ed. mass mkt. 6.99 (0-446-61209-X) Warner Bks., Inc.

—Wild Sweet Wilderness. 1989. 394p. mass mkt. 5.99 (0-445-20678-0) Warner Bks., Inc.

Garrett, Annie. Angel Flying Too Close to the Ground. l.t. ed. 1996. (Large Print Bks.). pap. 22.95 (1-56895-382-8, Wheeler Publishing, Inc.) Gale Group.

—Angel Flying Too Close to the Ground. 1997. 208p. mass mkt. 5.99 (0-312-96012-3, St. Martin's Paperbacks) St. Martin's Pr.

—Angel Flying Too Close to the Ground: A Love Story. 1996. 192p. 17.95 o.p. (0-312-13920-9) St. Martin's Pr.

Globe-Fearon Staff. Tom Sawyer. 1985. (Globe Ser.). pap. 6.95 o.p. (0-671-55580-4) Alpha Bks.

Grossman, Jeni. Beneath the Surface. 2001. (Illus.). 271p. 14.95 (1-57734-828-1) Covenant Communications.

Grove, Fred. The Spring of Valor: An Historical Story. 2003. 292p. 25.95 (0-7862-3776-7, Five Star) Gale Group.

Grove, Vicki. Reaching Dustin. 1998. 201p. (YA). (gr. 5-9). 16.99 o.p. (0-399-23008-4, G. P. Putnam's Sons) Penguin Group (USA) Inc.

Hager, Jean. Blooming Murder. 1994. (Iris House Mystery Ser.). pap. 5.50 (0-380-77209-4, Avon Bks.) Morrow/Avon.

—Blooming Murder. l.t. ed. 2001. (Illus.). 339p. (0-7862-3215-3) Thorndike Pr.

—Bride & Doom. l.t. ed. 2001. (Beeler Large Print Mystery Ser.). 230p. 25.95 (1-57490-408-6, Beeler Large Print Bks.) Beeler, Thomas T. Publisher.

—Bride & Doom. 2000. (Iris House Mystery Ser.: No. 2). 224p. mass mkt. 5.99 (0-380-80376-3, Avon Bks.) Morrow/Avon.

—Dead & Buried. 1995. (Iris House Mystery Ser.). mass mkt. 5.50 (0-380-77210-8, Avon Bks.) Morrow/Avon.

—Dead & Buried. l.t. ed. 2000. (Mystery Ser.). (Illus.). 339p. 27.95 (0-7862-2928-4) Thorndike Pr.

—Death on the Drunkard's Path. 1996. (Iris House Mystery Ser.: No. 3). pap. 5.50 (0-380-77211-6, Avon Bks.) Morrow/Avon.

—Death on the Drunkard's Path. l.t. ed. 2000. (Mystery Ser.). 328p. 26.95 (0-7862-2353-7) Thorndike Pr.

—The Last Noel. 1997. (Iris House Mystery Ser.). 224p. mass mkt. 5.99 (0-380-78637-0, Avon Bks.) Morrow/Avon.

—Sew Deadly. l.t. ed. 2001. 303p. (0-7838-9498-8); (0-7540-4587-0); (0-7540-4588-9) Gale Group. (Macmillan Reference USA).

—Sew Deadly. 1998. (Iris House Mystery Ser.). 224p. mass mkt. 5.99 (0-380-78638-9, Avon Bks.) Morrow/Avon.

—Weigh Dead. 2003. (Mystery Ser.). 27.95 (1-57490-468-X) Beeler, Thomas T. Publisher.

—Weigh Dead. 1999. (Iris House Mystery Ser.: Vol. 6). 224p. mass mkt. 5.99 (0-380-80375-5, Avon Bks.) Morrow/Avon.

Hamilton, Laurell K. Bloody Bones. 1996. (Anita Blake Vampire Hunter Ser.). 384p. mass mkt. 6.99 o.s.i (0-441-00374-5) Ace Bks.

—Circus of the Damned. 1995. (Anita Blake Vampire Hunter Ser.). 336p. (Orig.). mass mkt. 6.99 o.s.i (0-441-00197-1) Ace Bks.

—Circus of the Damned. (Orig.). 2004. 320p. 22.95 (0-425-19427-2); 2002. 336p. mass mkt. 6.99 (0-515-13448-1) Berkley Publishing Group.

—Guilty Pleasures. 1993. (Anita Blake Vampire Hunter Ser.). 272p. mass mkt. 6.99 o.s.i (0-441-30483-4) Ace Bks.

—Guilty Pleasures. 2004. 368p. pap. 13.00 (0-425-19754-9); 2002. 272p. mass mkt. 6.99 (0-515-13449-X); 2002. 320p. reprint ed. 21.95 (0-425-18756-X) Berkley Publishing Group.

—Guilty Pleasures. 2002. (Anita Blake Vampire Hunter Ser.). E-Book 6.99 (0-7865-2898-2) Penguin Putnam, Inc E-Books.

—The Killing Dance. 1997. (Anita Blake Vampire Hunter Ser.). 400p. mass mkt. 6.99 o.s.i (0-441-00452-0) Ace Bks.

—The Killing Dance. 2002. 400p. mass mkt. 7.99 (0-515-13451-1) Berkley Publishing Group.

Harrison, Janis. Lilies That Fester. l.t. ed. 2002. (Mystery Ser.). 373p. 29.45 (0-7862-4401-1) Thorndike Pr.

—Lilies That Fester: A Gardening Mystery. 2001. 256p. 23.95 (0-312-28406-3, Saint Martin's Minotaur) St. Martin's Pr.

—Murder Sets Seed: A Gardening Mystery. 2001. 256p. mass mkt. 6.50 (0-312-97725-5, St. Martin's Paperbacks); 2000. 248p. 22.95 (0-312-20382-9, Saint Martin's Minotaur) St. Martin's Pr.

—Murder Sets Seed: A Gardening Mystery. l.t. ed. 2001. 347p. (0-7862-3351-6) Thorndike Pr.

—Roots of Murder. l.t. ed. 2002. (Mystery Ser.). 282p. 29.45 (0-7862-3914-X) Gale Group.

—Roots of Murder. 246p. 2000. mass mkt. 5.99 (0-312-97500-7, St. Martin's Paperbacks); 2nd ed. 1999. 21.95 (0-312-20304-7, Saint Martin's Minotaur) St. Martin's Pr.

Hart, Carolyn G. Death in Lovers' Lane. unabr. ed. 1998. (Henrie O Mysteries Ser.). audio 48.00 (0-7366-4168-8, 4670) Books on Tape, Inc.

—Death in Lovers' Lane. l.t. ed. 1997. (Wheeler Large Print Book Ser.). 25.95 (1-56895-467-0, Wheeler Publishing, Inc.) Gale Group.

—Death in Lovers' Lane. 1997. 288p. mass mkt. 20.00 o.p. (0-380-97413-4); 1998. 320p. reprint ed. mass mkt. 6.50 (0-380-79002-5) Morrow/Avon. (Avon Bks.).

—Death in Paradise. unabr. ed. 1998. (Henrie O Mysteries Ser.). audio 48.00 (0-7366-4263-3, 4762) Books on Tape, Inc.

—Death in Paradise. 1999. 304p. mass mkt. 6.50 (0-380-79003-3); 1998. 288p. 20.00 (0-380-97414-2) Morrow/Avon. (Avon Bks.).

—Death in Paradise, Set. abr. ed. 1998. audio 18.00 (0-7871-1704-8, Dove Audio) NewStar Media, Inc.

—Death in Paradise. l.t. ed. 2000. (Mystery Ser.). 415p. 29.95 (0-7862-2679-X) Thorndike Pr.

Hauser, Heinrich. My Farm on the Mississippi: The Story of a German in Missouri, 1945-1948. Poulton, Curt A., tr. from GER. & intro. by. 2001. (Illus.). 192p. 29.95 (0-8262-1332-4) Univ. of Missouri Pr.

Haynes, David. All American Dream Dolls. 1999. (Harvest Book Ser.). 288p. pap. 12.00 (0-15-600572-7, Harvest Bks.) Harcourt Trade Pubs.

—All American Dream Dolls. 1997. 288p. 21.95 (1-57131-015-0) Milkweed Editions.

—Somebody Else's Mama. 1996. (Harvest American Writing Ser.). 360p. (C). pap. 13.00 (0-15-600408-9, Harvest Bks.) Harcourt Trade Pubs.

—Somebody Else's Mama. 1995. 352p. 21.95 (1-57131-003-7) Milkweed Editions.

Heller, Steve. The Automotive History of Lucky Kellerman. 1989. 272p. (Orig.). pap. 7.95 o.s.i (0-385-26351-1) Doubleday Publishing.

Hernon, Peter. The Kindling Effect. 1997. pap. 5.99 (0-380-72634-3, Avon Bks.) Morrow/Avon.

Hoffman, Allen. Big League Dreams. 1997. (Small Worlds Ser.). 296p. 24.95 (0-7892-0191-7) Abbeville Pr., Inc.

Hollingsworth, Gerelyn. Murder at Saint Adelaide's. 1995. 215p. 19.95 o.p. (0-312-11861-9, Saint Martin's Minotaur) St. Martin's Pr.

Hughes, Dean. Lucky, the Detective. 1992. (Lucky Ladd Ser.: Bk. 7). 149p. (Orig.). (J). (gr. 3-7). pap. o.p. (0-87579-654-0, Cinnamon Tree) Deseret Bk. Co.

—Under the Same Stars. 1979. (J). (gr. 7-12). 6.95 o.p. (0-87747-750-7) Trafalgar Square.

Jackson, Jeremy. Life at These Speeds. 2002. 352p. 24.95 (0-312-28808-5) St. Martin's Pr.

—Life at These Speeds: A Novel. 2003. 352p. pap. 14.00 (0-312-31366-7) Picador.

Jackson, Monica. Never Too Late for Love. 2000. 256p. mass mkt. 5.99 (1-58314-107-3) BET Bks.

Jacobs, Kathleen L. Never Forsaken. 1999. (Illus.). 270p. pap. 10.99 (1-58134-110-5) Crossway Bks.

James, Breggie. Sister Secrets. 1997. 432p. (Orig.). pap. 12.95 (0-9659042-0-2) BeeJay Enterprises.

Jeffries, William, pseud. Bloody River Blues. rev. ed. 2000. (Location Scout Mystery Ser.). (Illus.). 368p. mass mkt. 7.99 (0-671-04750-7, Pocket) Simon & Schuster.

—Bloody River Blues: A Location Scout Mystery. l.t. ed. 2002. 400p. pap. 29.95 (0-7838-9310-8, Macmillan Reference USA) Gale Group.

—Bloody River Blues: A Location Scout Mystery. 1993. 256p. mass mkt. 4.50 (0-380-76670-1, Avon Bks.) Morrow/Avon.

—Bloody River Blues: A Location Scout Mystery. l.t. ed. 2001. 400p. 32.95 (0-7838-9309-4) Thorndike Pr.

Jiles, Paulette. Enemy Women. 2003. 336p. pap. 13.95 (0-06-093809-9, Perennial) HarperTrade.

—Enemy Women. l.t. ed. 2002. (Women's Fiction Ser.). 561p. 29.95 (0-7862-4396-1) Thorndike Pr.

—Enemy Women: A Novel. 2002. 336p. 24.95 (0-06-621444-0, Morrow, William & Co.) Morrow/Avon.

Jones, Douglas C. This Savage Race, Set. l.t. ed. 1994. (Studio Ser.). 109.95 o.p. incl. audio (0-7862-9992-4, Macmillan Reference USA) Gale Group.

—This Savage Race. 1994. 512p. mass mkt. 4.50 o.p. (0-06-100770-6) HarperCollins Pubs.

—This Savage Race. 1993. 320p. 23.00 o.p. (0-8050-2243-0) Holt, Henry & Co.

Kagan, Elaine. The Girls. 1995. mass mkt. 6.99 o.s.i (0-345-39351-1) Ballantine Bks.

—The Girls: A Novel. 1994. 307p. 23.00 o.s.i (0-679-43395-3) Knopf, Alfred A. Inc.

Kahn, Michael A. Bearing Witness. 2000. (Rachel Gold Novels Ser.). 316p. 23.95 (0-312-84883-8, Forge Bks.) Doherty, Tom Assocs., LLC.

—Bearing Witness. 1999. pap. 21.95 (0-525-94305-6) NAL.

—Due Diligence. 1996. (Rachel Gold Mystery Ser.). 400p. mass mkt. 5.99 o.s.i (0-451-17970-6, Signet Bks.) NAL.

—Due Dilligence: A Rachel Gold Mystery. 1995. (Rachel Gold Mystery Ser.). 336p. 20.95 o.s.i (0-525-93743-9, Dutton) Dutton/Plume.

—Firm Ambitions. 1995. 320p. mass mkt. 5.99 o.s.i (0-451-17961-7, Onyx) NAL.

—Firm Ambitions: A Rachel Gold Mystery. 1994. (Rachel Gold Mystery Ser.). 320p. 18.95 o.p. (0-525-93742-0, Dutton) Dutton/Plume.

—Sheer Gall. 1996. (Rachel Gold Mystery Ser.). 320p. 23.95 o.s.i (0-525-94188-6) Dutton/Plume.

—Sheer Gall. 1998. (Rachel Gold Mystery Ser.). 368p. mass mkt. 5.99 o.s.i (0-451-40733-4, Onyx) NAL.

Kantor, MacKinlay. The Voice of Bugle Ann. 2003. (Foxhunters' Library). (Illus.). 120p. reprint ed. 18.95 (1-58667-069-7) Derrydale Pr., The.

—The Voice of Bugle Ann & the Daughter of Bugle Ann. 1980. 192p. 1.95 o.s.i (0-515-05458-5, Jove) Berkley Publishing Group.

—The Voice of Bugle Ann & the Romance of Rosy Ridge. 1994. lib. bdg. 21.95 (1-56849-379-7) Buccaneer Bks., Inc.

Keene, John. Annotations. 1995. (Paperbook Ser.: Vol. 809). 96p. (Orig.). pap. 8.95 (0-8112-1304-8, NDP809) New Directions Publishing Corp.

Kennett, Shirley. Chameleon. 1999. 384p. mass mkt. 5.99 (0-7860-0638-2) Kensington Publishing Corp.

—Chameleon: A Novel of Suspense. 1998. 320p. 22.00 o.s.i (1-57566-347-3) Kensington Publishing Corp.

—Fire Cracker. 1997. 320p. pap. 21.95 o.p. (1-57566-181-0) Kensington Publishing Corp.

—Gray Matter. 1996. 224p. 21.95 o.s.i (1-57566-079-2, Kensington Bks.) Kensington Publishing Corp.

Kinder, R. M. Sweet Angel Band: And Other Stories. 1991. (Winner of the 1991 Willa Cather Fiction Prize Ser.). (Orig.). pap. 11.95 (0-9627460-2-9) Helicon 9 Editions.

Kirk, Diana. Murder in Musicland. 1999. E-Book 5.50 (1-58200-224-X) Hard Shell Word Factory.

Kunz, Kathleen. Murder Once Removed. 1995. (WWL Mystery Ser.). 252p. per. (0-373-26175-6, 1-26175-9, Harlequin Bks.) Harlequin Enterprises, Ltd.

—Murder Once Removed. 1993. (Terry Girard Mystery Ser.). 216p. 19.95 o.p. (0-8027-3230-5) Walker & Co.

Lacy, Al. Far above Rubies. 2003. (Angel of Mercy Ser.: Vol. 10). 336p. pap. 10.99 (1-57673-499-4, Multnomah Bks.) Multnomah Pubs., Inc.

Ledbetter, Suzann. East of Peculiar. 2000. 384p. mass mkt. (1-55166-597-2, Mira Bks.) Harlequin Enterprises, Ltd.

—In Hot Pursuit. 2003. 384p. mass mkt. (1-55166-687-1, Mira Bks.) Harlequin Enterprises, Ltd.

—North of Clever. 2001. 384p. mass mkt. (1-55166-848-3, Mira Bks.) Harlequin Enterprises, Ltd.

—West of Bliss. 2002. 384p. mass mkt. (1-55166-925-0, Mira Bks.) Harlequin Enterprises, Ltd.

Lehrer, James. Flying Crows: A Novel. 2004. 256p. 23.95 (1-4000-6197-0) Random Hse., Inc.

Lepsky, Michele. Pathway to Promise. 1993. 250p. (Orig.). pap. 4.99 (1-56722-008-8) Word Aflame Pr.

Lund, Michael. Growing up on Route 66. 2000. (Illus.). viii, 268p. pap. 14.95 (1-888725-31-1, BeachHouse Bks.); 2001. 340p. per. 24.95 (1-888725-45-1, MacroPrintBooks) Science & Humanities Pr.

—Route 66 Kids. 2002. 296p. per. 14.95 (1-888725-70-2, 1-888725-70-2, BeachHouse Bks.); per. 24.95 (1-888725-71-0, 1-888725-71-0, MacroPrint-Books) Science & Humanities Pr.

Lutz, John. Buyer Beware. 1992. (Mystery Scene Bk.). 192p. pap. 3.95 o.p. (0-88184-840-9, Carroll & Graf Pubs.) Avalon Publishing Group.

—Buyer Beware. l.t. ed. 1988. pap. 17.95 o.p. (1-55504-671-1); lib. bdg. 19.95 o.p. (1-55504-690-8) BBC Audiobooks America.

—Buyer Beware. 1976. 6.95 o.p. (0-399-11811-X) Putnam Publishing Group, The.

—Dancer's Debt. 1988. 256p. 16.95 o.p. (0-312-00028-6) St. Martin's Pr.

—Dancing with the Dead. 2001. 208p. reprint ed. pap. 12.95 (1-931755-16-7) Mystery Vault, Inc.

—Dancing with the Dead. 1992. 304p. 18.95 o.p. (0-312-07693-2, Saint Martin's Minotaur) St. Martin's Pr.

—Death by Jury: An Alo Nudger Mystery. 1995. 352p. 23.95 o.p. (0-312-13613-7, Saint Martin's Minotaur) St. Martin's Pr.

—Diamond Eyes. 1990. 224p. 15.95 o.p. (0-312-05074-7, Saint Martin's Minotaur) St. Martin's Pr.

—Nightlines: The First Alo Nudger Mystery. 1987. 352p. pap. 3.95 o.p. (0-8125-0648-0, Tor Bks.) Doherty, Tom Assocs., LLC.

—Nightlines: The First Alo Nudger Mystery. 1984. 13.95 o.p. (0-312-57324-3) St. Martin's Pr.

—Oops! l.t. ed. 1998. (Large Print Book Ser.). pap. 23.95 o.p. (1-56895-653-3, Wheeler Publishing, Inc.) Gale Group.

—Oops! 1997. 304p. 22.95 o.p. (0-312-18152-3, Saint Martin's Minotaur) St. Martin's Pr.

—Ride the Lightning. 1990. mass mkt. 3.95 (0-8125-0642-1, Tor Bks.) Doherty, Tom Assocs., LLC.

—Ride the Lightning. 1987. 256p. 15.95 o.p. (0-312-00182-7) St. Martin's Pr.

—Thicker Than Blood: An Alo Nudger Mystery, Set. unabr. ed. 1999. audio 54.95 (0-7927-2314-7, CSL203, Chivers Sound Library) BBC Audiobooks America.

—Thicker Than Blood: An Alo Nudger Mystery. 1993. 272p. 19.95 o.p. (0-312-09922-3, Saint Martin's Minotaur) St. Martin's Pr.

—Time Exposure. 1990. 2.99 o.p. (0-517-05936-3) Random Hse. Value Publishing.

—Time Exposure. 1989. 16.95 o.p. (0-312-02990-X, Saint Martin's Minotaur) St. Martin's Pr.

MacPherson, Rett. Blood Relations. 2003. 27.95 (1-57490-507-4, Beeler Large Print Bks.) Beeler, Thomas T. Publisher.

—Blood Relations: A Torie O'Shea Mystery. 2003. 288p. 23.95 (0-312-30171-5, Saint Martin's Minotaur) St. Martin's Pr.

—A Comedy of Heirs. 2nd ed. 1999. (Torie O'Shea Mysteries Ser.). 214p. 21.95 (0-312-20513-9, Saint Martin's Minotaur) St. Martin's Pr.

—Family Skeletons. 1998. (Dead Letter Mysteries Ser.: Vol. 1). 224p. mass mkt. 6.50 (0-312-96602-4, St. Martin's Paperbacks); 1997. 208p. 21.95 o.p. (0-312-15236-1, Saint Martin's Minotaur) St. Martin's Pr.

—A Misty Mourning. (Torie O'Shea Mysteries Ser.). 2000. 244p. 22.95 (0-312-26619-7, Saint Martin's Minotaur); 2001. 272p. reprint ed. mass mkt. 6.50 (0-312-97784-0, St. Martin's Paperbacks) St. Martin's Pr.

—Veiled Antiquity. 1999. (Veiled Antiquity Ser.: Vol. 1). 240p. mass mkt. 5.99 (0-312-96701-2, St. Martin's Paperbacks); 1998. 224p. 20.95 (0-312-18677-0, Saint Martin's Minotaur) St. Martin's Pr.

MacPherson, Rett, contrib. by. A Comedy of Heirs: A Novel. l.t. ed. 2000. (Mystery Ser.). 349p. 27.95 o.p. (0-7862-2346-4) Thorndike Pr.

MacPherson, Selina. A Scandalous Bride. 2000. 32p. mass mkt. 5.99 o.s.i (0-8217-6861-1) Kensington Publishing Corp.

Marcy, Jean. Cemetery Murders: A Meg Darcy Mystery. 1997. 200p. pap. 10.95 (0-934678-83-9) New Victoria Pubs., Inc.

McClendon, Lise. Sweet & Lowdown: A Dorie Lennox Mystery. 2002. 288p. 23.95 (0-312-28689-9, Saint Martin's Minotaur) St. Martin's Pr.

McFadden, Bernice L. This Bitter Earth. 2002. 288p. pap. 13.00 (0-452-28381-7, Plume); 23.95 o.s.i (0-525-94636-5, Dutton) Dutton/Plume.

—This Bitter Earth. l.t. ed. 2002. (African American Ser.). 420p. 29.95 (0-7862-3882-8) Thorndike Pr.

McKitterick, Molly. The Medium Is Murder. 1992. 224p. 17.95 o.p. (0-312-07032-2, Saint Martin's Minotaur) St. Martin's Pr.

—Murder in a Mayonnaise Jar. 1993. 224p. 17.95 o.p. (0-312-09346-2, Saint Martin's Minotaur) St. Martin's Pr.

McMurtry, Larry. Sin Killer: A Novel. 2002. (Berrybender Narratives Ser.: Bk. 1). 30.95 (1-58724-301-6, Wheeler Publishing, Inc.) Gale Group.

—Sin Killer: A Novel. (Berrybender Narratives Ser.: Bk. 1). 2003. 368p. mass mkt. 7.99 (0-7434-5141-4, Pocket Star); 2002. (Illus.). 304p. 25.00 (0-7432-3302-6, Simon & Schuster) Simon & Schuster.

McPherson, Rett. A Comedy of Heirs: A Torie O'Shea Mystery. 2000. (Torie O'Shea Mysteries Ser.). 230p. mass mkt. 5.99 (0-312-97133-8, St. Martin's Paperbacks) St. Martin's Pr.

Mounce, Louis. Li'l Charley. 1990. 262p. (Orig.). pap. 9.95 o.p. (0-935069-34-8) White Oak Pr.

Munson, Ronald. Fan Mail. 1993. 320p. 20.00 o.p. (0-525-93624-6, Dutton) Dutton/Plume.

The Mystery on the Mississippi. 1977. (Trixie Belden Ser.: No. 15). (J). (gr. 4 up). pap. o.p. (0-307-21523-7, Golden Bks.) Random Hse. Children's Bks.

Nevins, Francis M. Corrupt & Ensnare. 1978. 8.95 o.p. (0-399-12203-6) Putnam Publishing Group, The.

—Corrupt & Ensnare. 2000. 232p. pap. 14.95 (1-58348-998-3) iUniverse, Inc.

—Publish & Perish. 2000. 192p. pap. 12.95 (*0-595-00059-2*) iUniverse, Inc.

O'Reilly, Jackson, pseud. Cheyenne Raiders. l.t. ed. 2001. (G.K. Hall Large Print Western Ser.). 392p. 25.95 (*0-7838-9538-0*, Macmillan Reference USA) Gale Group.

Palmer, Catherine. Hide & Seek. 2001. (HeartQuest Ser.: Vol. 2). (Illus.). 288p. pap. 9.99 (*0-8423-1165-3*) Tyndale Hse. Pubs.

Porter, Cheryl Anne. Wild Flower. 2001. 320p. mass mkt. 6.50 o.s.i (*0-312-97716-6*, St. Martin's Paperbacks) St. Martin's Pr.

Randisi, Robert J. Blood on the Arch: A Joe Keough Mystery. E-Book 22.95 (*0-312-27407-6*); 2000. 280p. 22.95 (*0-312-24179-8*, Saint Martin's Minotaur) St. Martin's Pr.

—In the Shadow of the Arch. 2000. (Joe Keough Mysteries Ser.). 368p. mass mkt. 4.99 (*0-8439-4761-6*, Leisure Bks.) Dorchester Publishing Co., Inc.

—In the Shadow of the Arch. 1997. (Joe Keough Mysteries Ser.). 368p. 24.95 (*0-312-18115-9*, Saint Martin's Minotaur) St. Martin's Pr.

—The Offer: A Novel of Suspense. 2003. (Five Star First Edition Mystery Ser.). 225p. 25.95 (*0-7862-4865-3*, Five Star) Gale Group.

Rees, Lloyd. The Show-Me State. 1995. 176p. pap. 16.95 (*1-85411-145-0*) Seren Bks. GBR. *Dist:* Dufour Editions, Inc.

Richardson, Boyd C. Knife Thrower. 1996. pap. 8.95 (*1-55503-683-X*, 01111620); Set. audio 11.98 (*1-55503-696-1*, 0700983) Covenant Communications, Inc.

Ripley, W. L. Dreamsicle. unabr. ed. 1993. 57.25 o.p. incl. audio (*1-56100-149-X*, 1189, Unabridged Library Editions); audio 21.95 o.p. (*1-56100-516-9*, 341, Bookcassette) Brilliance Audio.

—Dreamsicle. 1993. 267p. 19.95 o.p. (*0-316-74726-2*) Little Brown & Co.

—Electric Country Roulette: A Wyatt Storme Mystery. 1996. 88p. 25.00 o.p. (*0-8050-3792-6*) Holt, Henry & Co.

—Storme Front. 1995. 340p. 22.50 o.p. (*0-8050-3601-6*) Holt, Henry & Co.

Roberts, J. R. Brothel Inspector, IVol. 219. 2000. (Gunsmith Ser.: Vol. 219). 192p. mass mkt. 4.99 o.s.i (*0-515-12771-X*, Jove) Berkley Publishing Group.

Rollo, Naomi J. Goldy Lark: A Novel. 1992. 224p. (Orig.). pap. 10.95 (*1-56474-018-8*) Fithian Pr.

Savan, Glenn. Goldman's Anatomy. 1993. 336p. 22.00 o.s.i (*0-385-42607-0*) Doubleday Publishing.

Shange, Ntozake. Betsey Brown. 2nd ed. 1995. 208p. pap. 11.00 (*0-312-13434-7*) Picador.

—Betsey Brown. 1985. 208p. 12.95 o.p. (*0-312-07727-0*) St. Martin's Pr.

Simmons, Herbert. Man Walking on Eggshells. 1997. (Old School Bks.). 221p. pap. 11.00 (*0-393-31618-1*) Norton, W. W. & Co., Inc.

Smiley, Jane. The All-True Travels & Adventures of Lidie Newton: A Novel. 1998. 480p. pap. 14.00 (*0-449-91083-0*, Fawcett) Ballantine Bks.

—The All-True Travels & Adventures of Lidie Newton: A Novel. unabr. ed. 1998. audio 104.00 (*0-7366-4142-4*, 4646) Books on Tape, Inc.

—The All-True Travels & Adventures of Lidie Newton: A Novel. l.t. ed. 1998. 736p. 26.00 o.p. (*0-7838-8341-2*, Macmillan Reference USA) Gale Group.

—The All-True Travels & Adventures of Lidie Newton: A Novel. 1998. audio 24.00 o.s.i (*0-679-46119-1*); audio 24.00 o.s.i (*0-375-40173-3*, 593597) Random Hse. Audio Publishing Group. (RH Audio).

—The All-True Travels & Adventures of Lidie Newton: A Novel. 1998. 229.50 (*0-676-54689-7*) Random Hse., Inc.

Spencer, Jon M. Tribes of Benjamin: A Novel. 1999. 199 p. (*1-893562-01-8*) Tubman, Harriet Pr.

Spencer, LaVyrle. Small Town Girl. 2003. 368p. pap. 10.00 (*0-425-19577-5*); 1998. 400p. mass mkt. 7.50 (*0-515-12219-X*, Jove) Berkley Publishing Group.

—Small Town Girl. l.t. ed. 1997. (Core Ser.). 536p. 28.95 o.p. (*0-7838-8048-0*, Macmillan Reference USA) Gale Group.

—Small Town Girl. unabr. ed. 1997. 39.95 o.p. (*0-7871-1201-1*, 104611 );Set. 17.95 o.p. (*0-7871-1200-3*, 685800) NewStar Media, Inc.

—Small Town Girl. 1997. 384p. 23.95 o.p. (*0-399-14249-5*, G. P. Putnam's Sons); 23.95 o.s.i (*0-399-14695-4*) Penguin Group (USA) Inc.

—Small Town Girl. 23.95 o.s.i (*0-399-14548-6*) Putnam Publishing Group, The.

—Small Town Girl. l.t. ed. 1998. (Paperback Bestsellers Ser.). 498p. pap. 28.95 (*0-7838-8049-9*) Thorndike Pr.

Steele, Allen. All American Alien Boy. 1997. 288p. mass mkt. 5.99 o.s.i (*0-441-00460-1*) Ace Bks.

—The Jericho Iteration. 288p. 1995. mass mkt. 5.99 o.s.i (*0-441-00271-4*); 1994. 19.95 o.p. (*0-441-00097-5*) Ace Bks.

Steele, Allen M. All-American Alien Boy: Science Fiction about Missouri, Tennessee, New Hampshire, Massachusetts, North Carolina & the Afterlife. 1996. pap. 15.00 (*1-882968-06-9*) Old Earth Bks.

—All-American Alien Boy: Science Fiction about Missouri, Tennessee, New Hampshire, Massachusetts, North Carolina, & the Afterlife. ltd. ed. 1996. 85.00 (*1-882968-05-0*) Old Earth Bks.

Stolz, Karen. Fanny & Sue. l.t. ed. 2003. 29.95 (*0-7862-5506-4*) Thorndike Pr.

Tate, Eleanora E. The Minstrel's Melody. 2001. (American Girl Collection: Bk. 11). (Illus.). 160p. (J). (gr. 5-9). 9.95 (*1-58485-311-5*, American Girl) Pleasant Co. Pubns.

Taylor, Peter. A Woman of Means. 1983. 140p. 16.95 (*0-913720-44-5*) Beil, Frederic C. Pub., Inc.

—A Woman of Means. 1986. (Southern Writers Ser.). 128p. mass mkt. 3.95 (*0-380-70099-9*, Avon Bks.) Morrow/Avon.

—A Woman of Means. 1996. 144p. pap. 10.00 (*0-312-14448-2*) Picador.

Temple, Lou Jane. Bread on Arrival. l.t. ed. 2003. (Mystery Ser.). 27.95 (*1-57490-486-8*, Beeler Large Print Bks.) Beeler, Thomas T. Publisher.

—Bread on Arrival. (St. Martin's Minotaur Mysteries Ser.). 1999. 288p. mass mkt. 6.50 (*0-312-96942-2*, St. Martin's Paperbacks); 1998. 272p. 22.95 o.p. (*0-312-19244-4*, Saint Martin's Minotaur) St. Martin's Pr.

—The Cornbread Killer. 2000. 272p. mass mkt. 5.99 (*0-312-97427-2*, St. Martin's Paperbacks); 1999. 242p. 22.95 o.p. (*0-312-20605-4*, Saint Martin's Minotaur) St. Martin's Pr.

—The Cornbread Killer: A Heaven Lee Mystery. l.t. ed. 2001. (Beeler Large Print Mystery Ser.). 245p. 25.95 (*1-57490-336-5*, Beeler Large Print Bks.) Beeler, Thomas T. Publisher.

—Death of Rhubarb. 1996. 220p. mass mkt. 6.50 (*0-312-95891-9*, St. Martin's Paperbacks) St. Martin's Pr.

—Revenge of the Barbeque Queens. 1997. (Dead Letter Mysteries Ser.). 217p. mass mkt. 6.50 (*0-312-96074-3*, St. Martin's Paperbacks) St. Martin's Pr.

—Stiff Risotto. 1997. 224p. mass mkt. 6.50 (*0-312-96321-1*, St. Martin's Paperbacks) St. Martin's Pr.

Twain, Mark. The Adventures of Huckleberry Finn. Ogborn, Jane, ed. 1995. (Cambridge Literature Ser.). (Illus.). 352p. pap. text 11.95 (*0-521-48563-0*) Cambridge Univ. Pr.

—The Adventures of Huckleberry Finn. reprint ed. lib. bdg. 48.00 (*0-7426-1051-9*) Classic Bks.

—The Adventures of Huckleberry Finn. 1988. mass mkt. 4.95 (*0-938819-86-0*, Aerie) Doherty, Tom Assocs., LLC.

—The Adventures of Huckleberry Finn. l.t. unabr. ed. 2001. (Large Print Classics). ix, 387p. pap. 14.95 (*0-486-41780-8*) Dover Pubns., Inc.

—The Adventures of Huckleberry Finn. Harris, Susan K., ed. 1999. (Riverside Editions, A125 Ser.). (Illus.). viii, 392p. pap. 6.25 (*0-395-98078-X*) Houghton Mifflin Co.

—The Adventures of Huckleberry Finn. E-Book 2.95 (*1-57799-800-6*) Logos Research Systems, Inc.

—The Adventures of Huckleberry Finn. E-Book 1.95 (*1-58515-201-3*) MesaView, Inc.

—The Adventures of Huckleberry Finn. abr. ed. 1993. audio 19.95 o.p. (*1-55800-670-2*) NewStar Media, Inc.

—The Adventures of Huckleberry Finn. 1985. (Read-Along Ser.). pap. 34.95 incl. audio (*0-88432-961-5*, S23927) Norton Pubs., Inc., Jeffrey /Audio-Forum.

—The Adventures of Huckleberry Finn. (Paperback Classics Ser.). 2001. 304p. pap. 5.95 (*0-375-75737-6*); 1993. 464p. 16.95 (*0-679-42470-9*); 1985. E-Book 4.95 (*0-679-64205-6*) Random House Adult Trade Publishing Group. (Modern Library).

—The Adventures of Huckleberry Finn. 2001. (Literary Classics Ser.). 240p. 6.00 o.p. (*0-7624-0541-4*) Running Pr. Bk. Pubs.

—The Adventures of Huckleberry Finn. 1982. pap. 2.75 (*0-671-46198-2*, Washington Square Pr.) Simon & Schuster.

—The Adventures of Huckleberry Finn. Fischer, Victor et al, eds. 2002. (Illus.). 950p. text 75.00 (*0-520-23771-4*) Univ. of California Pr.

—The Adventures of Huckleberry Finn. 1990. E-Book 5.98 (*0-585-24751-X*) netLibrary, Inc.

—The Adventures of Tom Sawyer. Date not set. lib. bdg. 21.95 (*0-8488-1721-4*) Amereon, Ltd.

—The Adventures of Tom Sawyer. 2001. 7.95 (*0-8010-1217-1*) Baker Bks.

—The Adventures of Tom Sawyer. 274p. reprint ed. lib. bdg. 98.00 (*0-7222-0684-4*) Best Bks.

—The Adventures of Tom Sawyer. 2002. pap. 3.50 (*1-59109-030-X*) Booksurge, LLC.

—The Adventures of Tom Sawyer. 2000. 6.98 (*0-681-99538-6*, 50885589) Borders Pr.

—The Adventures of Tom Sawyer. 1982. reprint ed. lib. bdg. 15.95 (*0-89967-046-6*, Harmony Raine & Co.) Buccaneer Bks., Inc.

—The Adventures of Tom Sawyer. reprint ed. lib. bdg. 48.00 (*0-7426-1052-7*); 2001. (Illus.). pap. text 28.00 (*0-7426-6052-4*) Classic Bks.

—The Adventures of Tom Sawyer. 1994. mass mkt. 2.50 (*1-55902-911-0*, Aerie); 1993. mass mkt. 2.50 (*1-55902-903-X*, Aerie); 1989. 235p. mass mkt. 3.99 (*0-8125-0420-8*, Tor Classics); 1988. mass mkt. 4.95 (*0-938819-91-7*, Aerie) Doherty, Tom Assocs., LLC.

—The Adventures of Tom Sawyer. 1998. (Thrift Editions Ser.). 192p. pap. 2.00 (*0-486-40077-8*) Dover Pubns., Inc.

—The Adventures of Tom Sawyer. abr. ed. 1986. (Read-Along Ser.). audio 29.99 (*0-88646-823-X*, LSR 7143) Durkin Hayes Publishing Ltd.

—The Adventures of Tom Sawyer. E-Book 1.79 (*1-929120-68-0*) Electric Umbrella Publishing.

—The Adventures of Tom Sawyer. (Illus.). 1942. 11.95 o.p. (*0-06-014465-3*); lib. bdg. 7.87 o.p. (*0-06-014427-0*) HarperTrade.

—The Adventures of Tom Sawyer. 1997. text 8.25 (*0-03-051507-6*) Holt, Rinehart & Winston.

—The Adventures of Tom Sawyer. 2001. 228p. 24.99 (*1-58827-454-3*); per. 19.99 (*1-58827-455-1*) IndyPublish.com.

—The Adventures of Tom Sawyer. 1999. 232p. pap. 9.95 o.p. (*1-930128-10-X*, JNMedia Bks.) JNMedia, Inc.

—The Adventures of Tom Sawyer. Stemach, Jerry, ed. l.t. ed. 2002. text 150.00 (*1-58702-056-4*) Johnston, Don Inc.

—The Adventures of Tom Sawyer. 1991. 256p. pap. 8.50 o.s.i (*0-679-73501-1*, Vintage) Knopf Publishing Group.

—The Adventures of Tom Sawyer. E-Book 2.95 (*1-57799-801-4*) Logos Research Systems, Inc.

—The Adventures of Tom Sawyer. (English As a Second Language Bk.). 1990. pap. text 4.62 net. (*0-582-53761-4*); Level 1. 2000. (Illus.). 32p. pap. 7.93 (*0-582-41923-9*) Longman Publishing Group.

—The Adventures of Tom Sawyer. E-Book 1.95 (*1-58515-202-1*) MesaView, Inc.

—The Adventures of Tom Sawyer. (Signet Classics). 1997. 240p. mass mkt. 4.95 (*0-451-52653-8*, Signet Classics); 1959. mass mkt. 1.25 o.p. (*0-451-51165-4*, Signet Classics); 1959. mass mkt. 1.50 o.p. (*0-451-51337-1*, Signet Classics); 1959. mass mkt. 0.95 o.p. (*0-451-50978-1*, Signet Classics); 1959. mass mkt. 1.75 o.p. (*0-451-51962-0*); 1959. mass mkt. 0.75 o.p. (*0-451-50845-9*, Signet Classics); 1959. mass mkt. 0.60 o.p. (*0-451-50747-9*, Signet Classics); 1959. mass mkt. 0.50 o.p. (*0-451-50002-4*, Signet Classics) NAL.

—The Adventures of Tom Sawyer. abr. ed. 1993. (Ultimate Classics Ser.). audio 16.95 o.p. (*1-55800-669-9*) NewStar Media, Inc.

—The Adventures of Tom Sawyer. l.t. ed. 2000. (Large Print Ser.). 350p. lib. bdg. 26.00 (*0-939495-10-4*); 215p. reprint ed. lib. bdg. 25.00 (*1-58287-117-5*) North Bks.

—The Adventures of Tom Sawyer. 1994. (Read-Along Ser.). pap. 34.95 incl. audio (*0-88432-962-3*, S23925) Norton Pubs., Inc., Jeffrey /Audio-Forum.

—The Adventures of Tom Sawyer. 1998. (Illus.). 44p. pap. text 5.75 o.p. (*0-19-422878-9*) Oxford Univ. Pr., Inc.

—The Adventures of Tom Sawyer. Mitchell, Lee C., ed. & intro. by. 1998. (Oxford World's Classics Ser.). 296p. pap. 5.95 (*0-19-283389-8*) Oxford Univ. Pr., Inc.

—The Adventures of Tom Sawyer. Fishkin, Shelley Fisher, ed. 1997. (Oxford Mark Twain Ser.). (Illus.). 368p. text 22.00 o.p. (*0-19-511405-1*) Oxford Univ. Pr., Inc.

—The Adventures of Tom Sawyer. 1993. (Oxford World's Classics Ser.). 292p. (C). pap. 4.95 o.p. (*0-19-282837-1*); 2nd ed. (Illus.). 94p. pap. text 5.95 (*0-19-585333-4*) Oxford Univ. Pr., Inc.

—The Adventures of Tom Sawyer. 1995. (Classic, Ultimate, Dove Ser.). 29.95 o.p. (*0-7871-0231-8*) Penguin Group (USA) Inc.

—The Adventures of Tom Sawyer. 1950. 224p. pap. 1.95 o.p. (*0-14-030062-7*, Puffin Bks.) Penguin Putnam Bks. for Young Readers.

—The Adventures of Tom Sawyer. 2001. (Illus.). pap. (*1-57646-251-X*); 1999. 337p. E-Book 3.99 incl. audio compact disk (*1-57646-151-3*) Quiet Vision Publishing.

—The Adventures of Tom Sawyer. 1983. (Greenwich House Classic Library). (Illus.). 222p. 3.99 o.s.i (*0-517-39991-1*) Random Hse. Value Publishing.

—The Adventures of Tom Sawyer. 1988. (Works of Mark Twain). reprint ed. lib. bdg. 79.00 (*0-7812-1117-4*) Reprint Services Corp.

—The Adventures of Tom Sawyer. (Literary Classics Ser.). 1991. 162p. text 5.98 (*1-56138-023-7*, Courage Bks.); 1987. 160p. (J). (gr. 4 up). pap. 4.95 o.p. (*0-89471-541-0*) Running Pr. Bk. Pubs.

—The Adventures of Tom Sawyer. 1989. pap. 3.95 (*0-671-70137-1*, 44135, Washington Square Pr.); 2000. (Illus.). 320p. reprint ed. mass mkt. 4.99 (*0-7434-0635-4*, Pocket) Simon & Schuster.

—The Adventures of Tom Sawyer. 1983. (Mark Twain Library: No. 1). (Illus.). 292p. text 45.00 (*0-520-04558-0*) Univ. of California Pr.

—The Adventures of Tom Sawyer. 1986. (Classics Ser.). 256p. 7.00 (*0-14-039083-9*); pap. o.s.i (*0-14-039048-0*) Viking Penguin. (Penguin Classics).

—The Adventures of Tom Sawyer. 2000. (New Millennium Library). 212p. pap. 11.95 (*1-58348-341-1*) iUniverse, Inc.

—The Adventures of Tom Sawyer. 1991. E-Book 5.98 (*0-585-23461-2*) netLibrary, Inc.

—Huckleberry Finn. Date not set. pap. text (*0-17-557047-7*) Addison-Wesley Longman, Inc.

—Huckleberry Finn. unabr. ed. 2003. audio 24.95 (*0-563-49687-8*, BBCS 034); audio compact disk 39.95 (*0-563-49688-6*, BBCD 034) BBC Worldwide Americas.

—Huckleberry Finn. 1997. (Cyber Classics Ser.). 317p. pap. 14.95 incl. disk (*1-55701-199-0*); 435p. pap. 19.95 (*1-55701-228-8*) BNI Pubns., Inc.

—Huckleberry Finn. l.t. ed. 1997. 435p. pap. 19.95 (*1-58855-015-X*) Cyber Classics, Inc.

—Huckleberry Finn. 1942. 112p. pap. 5.60 (*0-87129-839-2*, H35) Dramatic Publishing Co.

—Huckleberry Finn. 1998. (SPA.). 384p. (*84-08-00303-8*) GeoPlaneta, Editorial, S. A.

—Huckleberry Finn, Set. abr. ed. 1992. audio 17.00 (*1-55994-630-X*, DCN 2038, HarperAudio) HarperTrade.

—Huckleberry Finn. 1989. audio 44.00 Jimcin Recordings.

—Huckleberry Finn. 1993. audio. audio 47.20 (*1-56544-030-7*, 350039) Literate Ear, Inc.

—Huckleberry Finn. l.t. ed. 1995. 507p. lib. bdg. 26.00 (*0-939495-76-7*); 1998. 320p. reprint ed. lib. bdg. 25.00 (*1-58287-038-1*) North Bks.

—Huckleberry Finn. Teresa Agnes, ed. Heller, Rudolf, tr. 1979. (SPA., Illus.). 64p. pap. text 3.95 (*0-88301-450-5*) Pendulum Pr., Inc.

—Huckleberry Finn. 1985. 366p. 14.50 o.s.i (*0-394-60521-7*) Random Hse., Inc.

—Huckleberry Finn. unabr. ed. 2002. (YA). (gr. 7 up). audio compact disk 88.00 (*1-58472-160-X*, Commuters Library) Sound Room Pubs., Inc.

—Huckleberry Finn: Custom Edition. deluxe ed. 1983. 1000.00 o.p. (*0-8103-1636-6*, 00000512) Gale Group.

—Huckleberry Finn Readalong. 1994. (Illustrated Classics Collection: No. 1). 64p. pap. 14.95 incl. audio (*0-7854-0708-1*, 40348); pap. 13.50 o.p. incl. audio (*1-56103-431-2*) American Guidance Service, Inc.

—Pudd'nhead Wilson. 1997. (Classics Illustrated Notes). (Illus.). pap. text 4.99 (*1-57840-065-1*) Acclaim Bks.

—Pudd'nhead Wilson. 1966. (Airmont Classics Ser.). (Illus.). mass mkt. 2.50 (*0-8049-0124-4*, CL-124) Airmont Publishing Co., Inc.

—Pudd'nhead Wilson. 20.95 (*0-89190-348-8*) Amereon, Ltd.

—Pudd'nhead Wilson. 1984. (Bantam Classics Ser.). 160p. mass mkt. 4.95 (*0-553-21158-7*, Bantam Classics) Bantam Bks.

—Pudd'nhead Wilson. unabr. ed. 1997. audio 39.95 (*1-86015-428-X*) Beeler, Thomas T. Publisher.

—Pudd'nhead Wilson. unabr. ed. 1982. audio 32.95 (*0-7861-0556-9*, 2049) Blackstone Audio Bks., Inc.

—Pudd'nhead Wilson. unabr. collector's ed. 1982. audio 36.00 (*0-7366-3870-9*, 9078) Books on Tape, Inc.

—Pudd'nhead Wilson. 1987. 172p. reprint ed. lib. bdg. 19.95 (*0-89966-577-2*) Buccaneer Bks., Inc.

—Pudd'nhead Wilson. 1999. (Thrift Editions Ser.). 96p. pap. text 1.50 (*0-486-40885-X*) Dover Pubns., Inc.

—Pudd'nhead Wilson. 1989. audio 24.00; 1982. audio 24.00 Jimcin Recordings.

—Pudd'nhead Wilson. E-Book 1.95 (*1-58515-204-8*) MesaView, Inc.

—Pudd'nhead Wilson. 1964. mass mkt. 1.25 o.p. (*0-451-51083-6*); mass mkt. 1.50 o.p. (*0-451-51229-4*); mass mkt. 0.50 o.p. (*0-451-50184-5*); mass mkt. 0.75 o.p. (*0-451-50840-8*); 176p. mass mkt. 4.95 (*0-451-52374-1*); mass mkt. 0.60 o.p. (*0-451-50703-7*) NAL. (Signet Classics).

—Pudd'nhead Wilson. l.t. ed. 2001. 269p. 26.00 (*1-58287-635-5*) North Bks.

—Pudd'nhead Wilson, unabr. ed. 1999. audio 46.00 (*1-55690-687-0*, 92342E7) Recorded Bks., LLC.

—Pudd'nhead Wilson. 1989. (Works of Samuel Clemens). reprint ed. lib. bdg. 79.00 (*0-7812-1119-0*) Reprint Services Corp.

—Pudd'nhead Wilson. 9999. pap. 1.95 o.s.i (*0-590-03437-5*) Scholastic, Inc.

—Pudd'nhead Wilson. 1998. 940p. 22.00 (*0-684-81908-2*, Simon & Schuster) Simon & Schuster.

—Pudd'nhead Wilson. l.t. ed. 2000. (Perennial Bestsellers Ser.). 237p. 27.95 (*0-7838-9147-4*) Thorndike Pr.



For book reviews, descriptive annotations, tables of contents, cover images, author biographies & additional information, updated daily, subscribe to **www.booksinprint.com** 959

Settings

—Pudd'nhead Wilson. Bradbury, Malcolm, ed. & intro. by. 1969. (English Library). 320p. 10.00 (*0-14-043040-7*, Penguin Classics) Viking Penguin.
—Pudd'nhead Wilson. (Classics Library). pap. 3.95 (*1-85326-572-1*, 5721WW) Wordsworth Editions, Ltd. GBR. *Dist:* Combined Publishing.
—Pudd'nhead Wilson & Other Tales. Gooder, R. D., ed. 1992. (Oxford World's Classics Ser.). 312p. pap. 7.95 o.p. (*0-19-281806-6*) Oxford Univ. Pr., Inc.
—Pudd'nhead Wilson & Other Tales: Those Extraordinary Twins, The Man that Corrupted Hadleyburg. Gooder, R. D., ed. 1999. (Oxford World's Classics Ser.). 320p. pap. 8.95 (*0-19-283730-3*) Oxford Univ. Pr., Inc.
—Pudd'nhead Wilson & Those Extraordinary Twins. Berger, Sidney E., ed. 1981. (Critical Editions Ser.). (Illus.). 384p. 22.50 o.p. (*0-393-01337-5*); (C). pap. text 9.00 (*0-393-95027-1*) Norton, W. W. & Co., Inc.
—Pudd'nhead Wilson & Those Extraordinary Twins. 2002. (Modern Library Classics). (Illus.). 288p. pap. 9.95 (*0-8129-6622-8*) Random House Adult Trade Publishing Group.
—Tom Sawyer. 1994. (Illustrated Classics Collection: No. 1). 64p. pap. 3.60 o.p. (*1-56103-441-X*); pap. 4.95 (*0-7854-0671-9*, 40358) American Guidance Service, Inc.
—Tom Sawyer. 2000. (SPA.). per. 14.00 (*1-891355-13-9*); 2001. per. 15.50 (*1-58396-185-2*) Blue Unicorn Editions.
—Tom Sawyer. 1988. (Illustrated Childrens Classics Ser.). 3.99 o.s.i (*0-517-65590-X*, Crown) Crown Publishing Group.
—Tom Sawyer & Friends. 1999. (Workhorse Library Ser.). E-Book 19.99 incl. cd-rom (*1-891595-40-7*) Quiet Vision Publishing.
—Tom Sawyer & Huckleberry Finn. 1972. reprint ed. 2.95 o.p. (*0-460-01976-7*) Biblio Distribution.
—Tom Sawyer & Huckleberry Finn. 1991. (Everyman's Library). 608p. 20.00 (*0-679-40584-4*) Random Hse., Inc.
—Tom Sawyer & Huckleberry Finn. 1943. 448p. pap. 5.95 o.p. (*0-460-87111-0*, Everyman's Classic Library in Paperback) Tuttle Publishing.
—Tom Sawyer & Huckleberry Finn. 1998. (Wordsworth Collection). 400p. pap. 3.95 (*1-85326-011-8*, 0118WW) Wordsworth Editions, Ltd. GBR. *Dist:* Casemate Pubs. & Bk. Distributors, LLC.
—Tom Sawyer, Detective. E-Book 1.95 (*1-58515-207-2*) MesaView, Inc.
—Tom Sawyer, Detective. 2001. pap. (*1-57646-253-6*); 1999. 101p. E-Book 3.99 incl. audio compact disk (*1-57646-153-X*) Quiet Vision Publishing.
Twain, Mark & Mitchell, Lee Clark. The Adventures of Tom Sawyer. 1998. E-Book 5.20 (*0-585-35505-3*) netLibrary, Inc.
Tyree, Omar R. Sweet St. Louis. mass mkt. 6.99 (*0-7434-8242-5*, Pocket); 2000. 368p. pap. 14.00 (*0-684-85611-5*, Simon & Schuster); 1999. (Illus.). 368p. 24.00 (*0-684-85610-7*, Simon & Schuster) Simon & Schuster.
Viets, Elaine. Back Stab: A Francesca Vierling Mystery. 1997. (Francesca Vierling Mystery Ser.). 320p. mass mkt. 5.99 o.s.i (*0-440-22431-4*) Dell Publishing.
—Doc in the Box: A Francesca Vierling Mystery. 2000. (Francesca Vierling Mystery Ser.). 256p. mass mkt. 5.99 o.s.i (*0-440-23620-7*) Bantam Dell Publishing Group.
—The Pink Flamingo Murders: A Francesca Vierling Mystery. 1999. 272p. mass mkt. 5.99 o.s.i (*0-440-22445-4*) Dell Publishing.
—The Pink Flamingo Murders: A Francesca Vierling Mystery. 1999. 272p. pap. 19.00 (*0-440-61351-5*) Random Hse., Inc.
—Rubout: A Francesca Vierling Mystery. 1998. (Francesca Vierling Mystery Ser.). 320p. mass mkt. 5.99 o.s.i (*0-440-22444-6*) Dell Publishing.
—Rubout: A Francesca Vierling Mystery. 1998. 320p. pap. 19.00 (*0-440-61348-5*) Random Hse., Inc.
Vincent, L. M. Pas de Death. 1994. 256p. 20.95 o.p. (*0-312-10521-5*, Saint Martin's Minotaur) St. Martin's Pr.
Walker, Ted. The Twenty Third Psalm: A Novel. 2000. 180p. pap. 8.95 (*0-9660582-1-6*) Rutherford Pr.
Weir, Theresa. Bad Karma. 1999. 352p. mass mkt. 6.50 o.s.i (*0-06-101296-3*, HarperTorch) Morrow/Avon.
Westlake, Donald E. Baby, Would I Lie? unabr. ed. 2000. audio 29.95 (*1-57270-139-0*, N61139u, Audio Editions Mystery Masters) Audio Partners Publishing Corp.
—Baby, Would I Lie? abr. ed. 1994. audio 17.00 o.p. (*1-56100-374-3*, 799, Nova Audio Bks.); audio 57.25 o.p. (*1-56100-197-X*, 1127, Unabridged Library Editions); audio 21.95 o.p. (*1-56100-571-1*, 35, Bookcassette) Brilliance Audio.
—Baby, Would I Lie? unabr. ed. 2000. audio 59.95 (*0-7927-2275-2*, CSL 164) Chivers Audio Bks. GBR. *Dist:* BBC Audiobooks America.
—Baby, Would I Lie? 1994. 304p. 19.95 o.s.i (*0-89296-532-0*) Mysterious Pr.
—Baby, Would I Lie? 1995. 320p. mass mkt. 5.99 (*0-446-40342-3*) Warner Bks., Inc.
Westmoreland, Joe. Tramps Like Us. E-Book 10.95 (*1-891305-85-9*); 2001. 341p. pap. 17.95 (*1-891305-58-1*) Painted Leaf Pr.
—Tramps Like Us: A Novel. 2003. (Illus.). 24.95 (*0-299-19434-5*) Univ. of Wisconsin Pr.
Whitney, P. This Is Graceanne's Book. 1999. 304p. 22.95 (*0-312-20597-X*) St. Martin's Pr.
Wingate, Lisa. Tending Roses. 2001. 304p. pap. 12.95 (*0-451-20307-0*); 2003. 336p. reprint ed. mass mkt. 6.99 (*0-451-20579-0*, Signet Bks.) NAL.
—Tending Roses. l.t. ed. 2001. (Thorndike Press Large Print Women's Fiction Ser.). 447p. 28.95 o.p. (*0-7862-3492-X*) Thorndike Pr.
Wise, Steven W. The Long Train Passing. 1996. 288p. pap. 16.99 o.p. (*0-7852-7705-6*) Nelson, Thomas Inc.
Wolfe, Thomas. The Lost Boy: A Novella. Clark, James W., Jr., ed. 1994. (Chapel Hill Bks.). (Illus.). 95p. (C). pap. 11.95 (*0-8078-4486-1*) Univ. of North Carolina Pr.
—The Lost Boy: A Novella. 1992. (Chapel Hill Bks.). (Illus.). xiv, 82p. (C). 24.95 o.p. (*0-8078-2063-6*) Univ. of North Carolina Pr.
Yoder, James D. Barbara: Sarah's Legacy. 1994. 174p. pap. 4.95 (*0-87303-214-4*) Faith & Life Pr.

## MITFORD (N.C.: IMAGINARY PLACE)—FICTION

Karon, Jan. At Home in Mitford. l.t. ed. (Mitford Ser.: No.1). 21.95 (*1-57490-254-7*); 1996. lib. bdg. 26.95 (*1-57490-071-4*, Beeler Large Print Bks.) Beeler, Thomas T. Publisher.
—At Home in Mitford. 2003. (Radio Theatre Ser.). audio 39.99 (*1-58997-001-2*) Focus on the Family Publishing.
—At Home in Mitford. (Mitford Ser.: No. 1). 448p. pap. 12.99 (*0-7459-2629-0*) Lion Publishing.
—At Home in Mitford. unabr. ed. 2002. audio compact disk 142.00 (*1-4025-2969-4*) Recorded Bks., LLC.
—At Home in Mitford. 2003. (Radio Theatre Ser.). audio compact disk 39.99 (*1-58997-000-4*) Tyndale Hse. Pubs.
—At Home in Mitford. (Mitford Ser.: No. 1). 1998. 432p. 24.95 (*0-670-88225-9*); 1996. 448p. 12.95 (*0-14-025448-X*); 1996. 2p. pap. 16.95 incl. audio (*0-14-086501-2*, Penguin AudioBooks) Viking Penguin.
—A Common Life: The Wedding Story. l.t. ed. 224p. 2002. pap. 12.95 (*0-375-72814-7*); 2001. (Mitford Ser.: Vol. 6). (Illus.). 24.95 (*0-375-43104-7*) Random Hse. Large Print.
—A Common Life: The Wedding Story. 2001. (Mitford Ser.: Vol. 6). (Illus.). 208p. text 24.95 (*0-670-89437-0*, Viking); 2015. audio 16.95 (*0-14-086742-2*, Penguin AudioBooks); 2001. (Mitford Ser.: Vol. 6). 4p. 24.95 incl. audio (*0-14-180274-X*, Penguin AudioBooks); 2002. (Beloved Mitford Ser.: No. 6). (Illus.). 208p. reprint ed. 13.00 (*0-14-200034-5*) Viking Penguin.
—Esther's Gift: A Mitford Christmas Story. 2002. (Illus.). 48p. 10.95 (*0-670-03121-6*, Viking) Viking Penguin.
—In This Mountain. (Mitford Ser.). 2003. 400p. pap. 13.95 (*0-14-200258-5*); 2002. 4p. audio 24.95 (*0-14-280005-8*); 2002. 4p. audio compact disk 29.95 (*0-14-280004-X*); 2002. 12p. audio 49.95 (*0-14-280006-6*) Penguin Group (USA) Inc.
—In This Mountain. l.t. ed. 672p. 2003. pap. 14.95 (*0-375-72820-1*); 2002. 26.95 (*0-375-43166-7*) Random Hse. Large Print.
—In This Mountain. unabr. ed. 2002. audio 49.95 (*1-4025-2389-0*, RG085) Recorded Bks., LLC.
—In This Mountain. 2002. (Illus.). 368p. 25.95 (*0-670-03104-6*, Viking) Viking Penguin.
—A Light in the Window. l.t. ed. (Mitford Ser.: No. 2). 21.95 (*1-57490-255-5*); 1996. (Illus.). 492p. lib. bdg. 26.95 (*1-57490-072-2*, Beeler Large Print Bks.) Beeler, Thomas T. Publisher.
—A Light in the Window. 2003. (Mitford Ser.: No. 2). (Illus.). 413p. pap. 12.99 (*0-7459-2803-X*) Lion Publishing.
—A Light in the Window. unabr. ed. (Mitford Ser.: No. 2). audio. 1999. audio 97.00 (*0-7887-0646-2*, 94823K8) Recorded Bks., LLC.
—A Light in the Window. (Mitford Ser.: No. 2). 1998. 400p. 24.95 (*0-670-88226-7*); 1996. 432p. 12.95 (*0-14-025454-4*); 1997. 2p. audio 16.95 (*0-14-086596-9*, 394980, Penguin AudioBooks) Viking Penguin.
—The Mitford Snowmen: A Christmas Story. l.t. ed. 2001. (Illus.). 45p. 26.95 (*1-58724-120-X*, Wheeler Publishing, Inc.) Gale Group.
—The Mitford Snowmen: A Christmas Story. 2002. (Illus.). 32p. 10.95 (*0-670-03019-8*, Viking) Viking Penguin.
—The Mitford Years: At Home in Mitford; A Light in the Window; These High, Green Hills; Out to Canaan, 4 vols. 1999. (Illus.). pap. 51.80 (*0-14-771256-4*) Penguin Group (USA) Inc.
—The Mitford Years: At Home in Mitford; A Light in the Window; These High, Green Hills; Out to Canaan, 4 vols. abr. ed. 1998. 2p. 49.95 (*0-14-086813-5*, Penguin AudioBooks) Viking Penguin.
—The Mitford Years: At Home in Mitford; A Light in the Window; These High, Green Hills; Out to Canaan; A New Song, 5 vols. 2001. pap. 64.75 o.p. (*0-14-771596-2*); 1997. pap. 38.85 (*0-14-771203-3*); Vols. 4-6. 2002. 38.90 (*0-14-771728-0*) Penguin Group (USA) Inc.
—The Mitford Years Set, Vols. 1-6. 2002. 77.75 (*0-14-771779-5*) Penguin Group (USA) Inc.
—A New Song. l.t. ed. 1999. (Mitford Ser.: No. 5 ). 28.95 (*1-57490-190-7*, Beeler Large Print Bks.) Beeler, Thomas T. Publisher.
—A New Song. abr. ed. 1999. (Mitford Ser.: No. 5). audio 24.95. audio 55.95 Highsmith Inc.
—A New Song. unabr. ed. 1999. (Mitford Ser.: No. 5). audio 102.00 (*0-7887-3098-3*, 95809E7) Recorded Bks., LLC.
—A New Song. (Mitford Ser.: No. 5). 2000. (Illus.). 416p. 12.95 (*0-14-027059-0*); 1999. (Illus.). 368p. 24.95 (*0-670-87810-3*); 1999. 2p. audio 24.95 (*0-14-086901-8*, Penguin AudioBooks); 1999. audio 55.95 (*0-14-180013-5*, Penguin AudioBooks) Viking Penguin.
—Out to Canaan. l.t. ed. (Mitford Ser.: o. 4). 21.95 (*1-57490-257-1*); 1997. (Illus.). 412p. lib. bdg. 26.95 (*1-57490-104-4*, Beeler Large Print Bks.) Beeler, Thomas T. Publisher.
—Out to Canaan. unabr. ed. 1997. (Mitford Ser.: o. 4). audio 83.00 (*0-7887-0973-9*, 95081E7) Recorded Bks., LLC.
—Out to Canaan. (Mitford Ser.: No. 4). 1998. (Illus.). 352p. 12.95 (*0-14-026568-6*); 1997. (Illus.). 368p. 23.95 (*0-670-87485-X*); 1997. 2p. audio 16.95 (*0-14-086597-7*, Penguin AudioBooks) Viking Penguin.
—Shepherds Abiding. l.t. ed. 2003. 486p. 26.95 (*0-375-43287-6*) Random Hse. Large Print.
—Shepherds Abiding. 2003. (Mitford Ser.). 304p. 24.95 (*0-670-03120-8*) Viking Penguin.
—These High, Green Hills. l.t. ed. (Mitford Ser.: No. 3). 21.95 (*1-57490-256-3*); 1997. (Illus.). 414p. lib. bdg. 26.95 (*1-57490-103-6*, Beeler Large Print Bks.) Beeler, Thomas T. Publisher.
—These High, Green Hills. (Mitford Ser.: o. 3). (Illus.). 333p. pap. 12.99 (*0-7459-3741-1*) Cook Communications Ministries.
—These High, Green Hills. unabr. ed. 1999. (Mitford Ser.: No. 3). audio 85.00 (*0-7887-0664-0*, 94841K8) Recorded Bks., LLC.
—These High, Green Hills. (Mitford Ser.: No. 3). 1997. (Illus.). 368p. 12.95 (*0-14-025793-4*); 1996. 352p. 22.95 (*0-670-86934-1*, Viking); 1996. pap. o.s.i (*0-670-87320-9*, Viking); 1997. 2p. pap. 16.95 incl. audio (*0-14-086598-5*, Penguin AudioBooks) Viking Penguin.

## MITHGAR (IMAGINARY PLACE)—FICTION

McKiernan, Dennis L. The Brega Path. 1986. (Science Fiction Ser.). 224p. 12.95 o.p. (*0-385-23352-3*) Doubleday Publishing.
—The Brega Path. 1987. (Silver Call Duology Ser.). 272p. mass mkt. 3.95 o.p. (*0-451-16645-0*, Signet Bks.); 272p. mass mkt. 4.99 o.s.i (*0-451-45241-0*, ROC); mass mkt. 2.95 o.p. (*0-451-14893-2*, ROC); mass mkt. 3.50 o.p. (*0-451-15585-8*, ROC) NAL.
—The Darkest Day. 1984. (Iron Tower Ser.: Vol. 3). 192p. 11.95 o.p. (*0-385-18920-6*) Doubleday Publishing.
—The Darkest Day. 1985. (Iron Tower Ser.). mass mkt. 3.50 o.p. (*0-451-15341-3*); 304p. mass mkt. 4.50 o.s.i (*0-451-45083-3*);Bk. 3. mass mkt. 2.95 o.p. (*0-451-13865-1*) NAL. (ROC).
—The Dragonstone. (Mithgar Ser.). 1997. 576p. mass mkt. 7.50 (*0-451-45456-1*); 1996. 480p. text 24.95 o.s.i (*0-451-45560-6*, ROC) NAL.
—The Eye of the Hunter. (Mithgar Ser.). 1993. 592p. mass mkt. 7.99 (*0-451-45268-2*, ROC); 1992. 624p. pap. 15.00 o.p. (*0-451-45179-1*, ROC); 1992. 624p. text 25.00 o.p. (*0-451-45229-1*) NAL.
—Shadows of Doom. 1984. (Iron Tower Ser.: 2). 192p. 11.95 o.p. (*0-385-18837-4*) Doubleday Publishing.
—Shadows of Doom. (Iron Tower Ser.). 1987. mass mkt. 3.95 o.p. (*0-451-15565-3*, ROC); 1987. 304p. mass mkt. 4.50 o.s.i (*0-451-45103-1*, Signet Bks.); 1985. mass mkt. 2.95 o.p. (*0-451-13815-5*, ROC); 1985. mass mkt. 3.50 o.p. (*0-451-15340-5*, ROC) NAL.
—Silver Wolf, Black Falcon. 2000. 496p. 23.95 o.s.i (*0-451-45786-2*, ROC) NAL.
—Tales of Mithgar. (Mithgar Ser.). 1995. 256p. mass mkt. 4.99 o.s.i (*0-451-45439-1*); 1994. 240p. 19.95 o.p. (*0-451-45410-3*); 1994. 240p. pap. 8.95 o.p. (*0-451-45430-8*) NAL. (ROC).
—Trek to Kraagen-Cor. 1986. (Science Fiction Ser.). 192p. 12.95 o.p. (*0-385-23351-5*) Doubleday Publishing.
—Voyage of the Fox Rider. 1994. 592p. mass mkt. 7.99 (*0-451-45411-1*, ROC); 1993. 576p. pap. 15.00 o.p. (*0-451-45284-4*, ROC); 1993. 576p. text 25.00 o.p. (*0-451-45279-8*) NAL.

## MONTANA—FICTION

Andreae, Christine. Grizzly: A Mystery. 1994. 288p. 19.95 o.p. (*0-312-11433-8*, Saint Martin's Minotaur) St. Martin's Pr.
—A Small Target, Vol. 1. 1996. 272p. 21.95 o.p. (*0-312-14543-8*, Saint Martin's Minotaur) St. Martin's Pr.
—Trail of Murder. 1992. 256p. 17.95 o.p. (*0-312-08327-0*, Saint Martin's Minotaur) St. Martin's Pr.
Barr, Nevada. Blood Lure. abr. ed. 2001. audio 24.95 o.s.i (*1-58788-164-0*, 2423, Nova Audio Bks.) Brilliance Audio.
—Blood Lure. l.t. ed. 2001. (Large Print Book Ser.). 417p. 29.95 (*1-58724-001-7*, Wheeler Publishing, Inc.) Gale Group.
—Blood Lure. 2001. 320p. 24.95 o.p. (*0-399-14702-0*) Penguin Group (USA) Inc.
—Blood Lure. unabr. ed. 2001. audio 29.95 (*0-7887-4974-9*) Recorded Bks., LLC.
Bass, Rick. Fiber. aut. ltd. num. ed. 1998. (Illus.). 57p. text 100.00 (*0-8203-2086-2*) Univ. of Georgia Pr.
—Platte River. 1994. 145p. 19.95 o.p. (*0-395-68080-8*) Houghton Mifflin Co.
—Platte River Tent Card. 1995. pap. 0.00 o.s.i (*0-345-39685-5*, Ballantine Bks.) Ballantine Bks.
Baxter, Stephen. Evolution. 2004. 672p. mass mkt. 7.50 (*0-345-45783-8*, Del Rey); 2003. 592p. 25.95 (*0-345-45782-X*); 2003. E-Book 11.95 (*0-345-45784-6*, Del Rey) Ballantine Bks.
Beer, Ralph. The Blind Corral. 3rd ed. 1996. 275p. reprint ed. 50.00 o.p. (*0-9653336-0-4*) Spring Creek Pubns.
—The Blind Corral. 240p. 1987. pap. 6.95 o.p. (*0-14-010265-5*, Penguin Bks.); 1986. 16.95 o.p. (*0-670-80937-3*) Viking Penguin.
Bell, Ann. Montana. 2000. 480p. pap. 6.97 (*1-57748-794-X*) Barbour Publishing, Inc.
Bergren, Lisa T. Refuge. 1994. 336p. pap. 8.99 o.p. (*0-88070-621-X*, Multnomah Bks.) Multnomah Pubs., Inc.
Bergren, Lisa Tawn. The Bridge. 2002. 256p. pap. 9.99 (*1-57856-536-7*) Random Hse., Inc.
—The Bridge. 2000. 256p. 10.95 (*1-57856-272-4*) WaterBrook Pr.
—Refuge. 1995. 336p. pap. 9.99 o.p. (*0-88070-875-1*, Palisades) Multnomah Pubs., Inc.
—Refuge. 2001. (Full Circle Ser.). 320p. pap. 10.99 (*1-57856-468-9*) WaterBrook Pr.
Bickham, Jack M. Overhead. 1993. (Brad Smith Ser.: No. 3). 352p. mass mkt. 4.50 o.p. (*0-8125-1194-8*); 1991. 18.95 o.p. (*0-312-85143-X*) Doherty, Tom Assocs., LLC. (Tor Bks.).
Blew, Mary C. Runaway. 1990. 201p. pap. 10.00 (*0-917652-77-0*) Confluence Pr., Inc.
Blew, Mary Clearman. Lambing Out & Other Stories. 2001. 97p. reprint ed. pap. 12.95 (*0-8061-3323-6*) Univ. of Oklahoma Pr.
Bly, Stephen A. The Final Chapter of Chance Mccall. 1996. (Austin-Stoner Files Ser.: Bk. 2). 368p. pap. 11.99 o.p. (*0-89107-903-3*) Crossway Bks.
—I'm off to Montana for to Throw the Hoolihan. 1997. (Code of the West Ser.: Vol. 6). 208p. pap. 9.99 (*0-89107-953-X*) Crossway Bks.
—I'm off to Montana for to Throw the Hoolihan. l.t. ed. 1998. (Western Ser.). 271p. 24.95 (*0-7838-0338-9*) Thorndike Pr.
—The Marquesa. 1998. (Heroines of the Golden West Ser.: Vol. 2). 224p. pap. text 10.99 (*1-58134-025-7*) Crossway Bks.
—The Marquesa. l.t. ed. 1999. (G. K. Hall Western Ser.: Vol. 2). 320p. 24.95 (*0-7838-8608-X*) Thorndike Pr.
—Miss Fontenot. 1999. (Heroines of the Golden West Ser.: No. 3). 224p. pap. 10.99 o.p. (*1-58134-074-5*) Crossway Bks.
—Miss Fontenot. l.t. ed. 1999. (Western Ser.). 348p. 25.95 (*0-7838-8729-9*) Thorndike Pr.
Bowen, Asta. Hungry for Home: A Wolf Odyssey. 1998. (Illus.). 224p. pap. 11.00 (*0-684-83660-2*, Touchstone) Simon & Schuster.
Bowen, Asta & Meyer, Jane. Hungry for Home. 1997. 224p. 21.50 (*0-684-82361-6*, Simon & Schuster) Simon & Schuster.
Bowen, Michael. Coyote Wind: A Montana Mystery. 1995. (Montana Mystery Ser.). mass mkt. 4.50 (*0-312-95601-0*, St. Martin's Paperbacks) St. Martin's Pr.
Bowen, Peter. Ash Child: A Montana Mystery Featuring Gabriel Du Pre. 2002. 256p. 23.95 (*0-312-28850-6*, Saint Martin's Minotaur) St. Martin's Pr.
—Badlands: A Montana Mystery Featuring Gabriel Du Pre. 2003. 272p. 23.95 (*0-312-26252-3*, Saint Martin's Minotaur) St. Martin's Pr.
—Coyote Wind. 1994. 160p. 18.95 o.p. (*0-312-10957-1*, Saint Martin's Minotaur) St. Martin's Pr.
—Coyote Wind & Specimen Song: Two Montana Mysteries Featuring Gabriel du Pre. 2000. 368p. pap. 14.95 (*0-312-26514-X*, Saint Martin's Griffin) St. Martin's Pr.

—Cruzatte & Maria: A Montana Mystery Featuring Gabriel Du Pre. 2001. (Montana Mystery Ser.). 256p. 22.95 (*0-312-26253-1*, Saint Martin's Minotaur) St. Martin's Pr.
—Long Son. 1999. (Gabriel Du Pre Mystery Ser.: Vol. 6). 272p. 22.95 o.p. (*0-312-19917-1*, Saint Martin's Minotaur) St. Martin's Pr.
—Long Son: A Montana Mystery Featuring. 2nd ed. 2000. 272p. pap. 13.95 (*0-312-25398-2*, CPB1132, Saint Martin's Griffin) St. Martin's Pr.
—Notches: A Gabriel Du Pre Mystery. (Montana Mystery Ser.). 1998. 224p. mass mkt. 5.50 (*0-312-96492-7*, St. Martin's Paperbacks); 1996. 208p. text 20.95 o.p. (*0-312-15181-0*, Saint Martin's Minotaur) St. Martin's Pr.
—Specimen Song. (Montana Mystery Ser.). 1996. mass mkt. 5.50 (*0-312-95763-7*, St. Martin's Paperbacks); 1995. 201p. 18.95 o.p. (*0-312-11896-1*, Saint Martin's Minotaur) St. Martin's Pr.
—Stick Game: A Montana Mystery Featuring Gabriel Du Pre. 2000. (Montana Mystery Ser.). 282p. 23.95 (*0-312-20297-0*, Saint Martin's Minotaur) St. Martin's Pr.
—Thunder Horse. (Montana Mystery Ser.). 1999. 256p. mass mkt. 5.99 (*0-312-96887-6*, St. Martin's Paperbacks); 1998. 304p. 22.95 o.p. (*0-312-18303-8*, Saint Martin's Minotaur) St. Martin's Pr.
—Thunder Horse: A Montana Mystery Featuring Gabriel Du Pre. 2003. 256p. pap. 13.95 (*0-312-31771-9*, Saint Martin's Griffin) St. Martin's Pr.
—Wolf, No Wolf. l.t. ed. 1997. (Core Ser.). 286p. lib. bdg. 25.95 (*0-7838-8215-7*, Macmillan Reference USA) Gale Group.
—Wolf, No Wolf. 1996. 224p. 20.95 o.p. (*0-312-14078-9*, Saint Martin's Minotaur); 1997. 226p. mass mkt. 5.99 (*0-312-96103-0*, St. Martin's Paperbacks) St. Martin's Pr.
—Wolf, No Wolf & Notches: The Third & Fourth Montana Mysteries Featuring Gabriel Du Pre. 2002. 384p. pap. 15.95 (*0-312-28963-4*, Saint Martin's Griffin) St. Martin's Pr.
Bower, B. M. Lonesome Land. 1975. lib. bdg. 16.95 o.p. (*0-89966-022-3*) Buccaneer Bks., Inc.
—Lonesome Land. 1997. (Illus.). 326p. pap. 13.95 (*0-8032-6134-9*, Bison Bks.) Univ. of Nebraska Pr.
Briggs, Betty. Image of Deception, Set, No. 2. Briggs, Betty, ed. 2000. vi, 202p. (Orig.). pap. 9.95 (*0-9656307-2-2*) Sunrise Selections.
Brinig, Myron. Wide Open Town: A Novel. rev. ed. 1993. (Sweetgrass Bks.). 192p. reprint ed. pap. 12.95 (*1-56037-034-3*) Farcountry Pr.
Brouwer, Sigmund. Blood Ties. 1996. audio 23.00 o.p. (*0-8499-6230-7*); 304p. 19.99 o.s.i (*0-8499-1294-6*) W Publishing Group.
Brown, Harriet. Kit's Railway Adventure. 2003. (American Girls Collection). (YA). 15.95 (*1-58485-575-4*, American Girl) Pleasant Co. Pubns.
Burke, James Lee. Bitterroot: A Novel. unabr. ed. 2001. audio 76.00 (*0-7887-9471-X*) Recorded Bks., LLC.
—Bitterroot: A Novel. 2001. 336p. 25.00 (*0-7432-0483-2*, Simon & Schuster) Simon & Schuster.
—Bitterroot: A Novel. l.t. ed. 2002. 552p. pap. 25.00 (*0-7432-3640-8*); 2001. 560p. 25.00 o.s.i (*0-7432-1402-1*) Simon & Schuster. (Simon & Schuster).
—Bitterroot: A Novel. abr. ed. 2001. audio 26.00 (*0-7435-0480-1*); audio compact disk 32.00 (*0-7435-0481-X*) Simon & Schuster Audio. (Simon & Schuster Audioworks).
—The Lost Get-Back Boogie. Date not set. lib. bdg. 24.95 (*0-8488-1780-X*) Amereon, Ltd.
—The Lost Get-Back Boogie. 1987. 256p. pap. 8.95 o.p. (*0-8050-0541-2*, Owl Bks.) Holt, Henry & Co.
—The Lost Get-Back Boogie. 256p. 1995. pap. 10.95 (*0-7868-8101-1*); 1997. reprint ed. mass mkt. 5.99 (*0-7868-8934-9*) Hyperion Pr.
—The Lost Get-Back Boogie. 1986. 241p. 16.95 (*0-8071-1334-4*) Louisiana State Univ. Pr.
Canty, Kevin. Nine Below Zero. 2000. (Contemporaries Ser.). 384p. pap. 13.00 (*0-375-70799-9*, Vintage) Knopf Publishing Group.
Challenge of Choice. 2002. (YA). per. 11.95 (*0-9656307-3-0*) Sunrise Selections.
Chase, Elaine Raco. Dare the Devil. l.t. ed. 2001. (G. K. Hall Romance Ser.). 239p. 26.95 (*0-7838-9452-X*, Macmillan Reference USA) Gale Group.
Child, Lee. Die Trying. 1999. 448p. reprint ed. mass mkt. 7.99 (*0-515-12502-4*, Jove) Berkley Publishing Group.
—Die Trying. 1998. 384p. 23.95 o.s.i (*0-399-14379-3*, G. P. Putnam's Sons) Penguin Group (USA) Inc.
Christofferson, April. Clinical Trial. 2000. 333p. 24.95 o.p. (*0-312-86899-5*); 2001. 464p. reprint ed. mass mkt. 7.99 (*0-8125-7468-0*) Doherty, Tom Assocs., LLC. (Forge Bks.).
Crumley, James. Bordersnakes. 1997. 288p. mass mkt. 6.50 (*0-446-60448-8*); 1996. 336p. 22.00 o.p. (*0-89296-573-8*) Warner Bks., Inc.
—Dancing Bear. unabr. ed. 1997. audio 48.00 (*0-7366-3819-9*, 4487) Books on Tape, Inc.
—Dancing Bear. 1984. (Vintage Contemporaries Ser.). 240p. pap. 13.00 (*0-394-72576-X*, Vintage) Knopf Publishing Group.
—Dancing Bear. 1983. 256p. 12.95 o.p. (*0-394-52195-1*) Random Hse., Inc.
—The Last Good Kiss. 1992. audio 13.95 (*1-55644-375-7*, 12021) American Audio Prose Library, Inc.
—The Last Good Kiss. 1988. (Vintage Contemporaries Ser.). 256p. pap. 11.95 (*0-394-75989-3*, Vintage) Knopf Publishing Group.
—The Last Good Kiss. 1978. 8.95 o.p. (*0-394-41946-4*) Random Hse., Inc.
—The Last Good Kiss. 1983. mass mkt. 3.50 o.s.i (*0-671-49889-4*, Pocket) Simon & Schuster.
—The Mexican Tree Duck. unabr. ed. 1997. audio 48.00 (*0-7366-3820-2*, 4488) Books on Tape, Inc.
—The Mexican Tree Duck. 1993. 256p. 19.95 (*0-89296-391-3*) Mysterious Pr.
—The Mexican Tree Duck. 1994. 272p. mass mkt. 5.99 (*0-446-40407-1*); 2001. 256p. reprint ed. pap. 11.95 (*0-446-67791-4*) Warner Bks., Inc.
—The Wrong Case. 1985. (Vintage Contemporaries Ser.). 288p. pap. 12.00 (*0-394-73558-7*) Random Hse., Inc.
Cullen, Ann. Emma Parchen: Twelve Years of Her American Dream. 2000. 201p. pap. 9.95 (*0-9670759-1-2*) Book Montana.
—Lilly Cullen: Helena, Montana 1894. 1999. 267p. pap. 9.95 (*0-9670759-0-4*) Book Montana.
—Mary Cruse. 2001. 253p. pap. 9.95 (*0-9670759-2-0*) Book Montana.
Cushman, Dan. Blood on the Saddle: A Western Story. 2003. 336p. mass mkt. 5.50 (*0-8439-5194-X*, Leisure Bks.) Dorchester Publishing Co., Inc.
—Blood on the Saddle: A Western Story. 1998. (Western Ser.). 325p. 19.95 (*0-7862-0993-3*, Five Star) Gale Group.
—Blood on the Saddle: A Western Story. l.t. ed. 1999. (Western Ser.). 576p. 21.95 o.p. (*0-7862-1032-X*) Thorndike Pr.
—Tall Wyoming. l.t. ed. 1994. 285p. lib. bdg. 16.95 (*0-8161-5856-8*, Macmillan Reference USA) Gale Group.
Dailey, Janet. Calder Born, Calder Bred. 2000. 412p. pap. 26.00 (*0-7278-5469-0*) Severn Hse. Pubs., Ltd.
—Calder Born, Calder Bred. 1993. mass mkt. 6.99 (*0-671-87500-0*); 1990. 416p. mass mkt. 5.99 (*0-671-73479-2*); 1989. mass mkt. (*0-671-70072-3*); 1987. mass mkt. (*0-671-63786-X*); 1984. mass mkt. 3.95 (*0-671-50250-6*); Vol. 4. 1999. 416p. reprint ed. mass mkt. 6.99 (*0-671-04049-9*) Simon & Schuster. (Pocket).
—Calder Pride. 1999. 368p. 23.95 (*0-06-017699-7*); 560p. pap. 23.95 (*0-06-093302-X*) HarperCollins Pubs.
—Calder Pride. abr. ed. 1999. audio 25.00 (*0-694-51925-1*, HarperAudio) HarperTrade.
—Calder Pride. abr. ed. 1999. audio 25.00 Highsmith Inc.
—Calder Pride. 2000. 464p. reprint ed. mass mkt. 7.50 (*0-06-109459-5*, HarperTorch) Morrow/Avon.
—Shifting Calder Wind. 2004. 384p. mass mkt. 7.99 (*0-8217-7223-6*); 2003. 304p. 24.00 (*0-7582-0067-6*) Kensington Publishing Corp.
—Shifting Calder Wind. l.t. ed. 2004. 495p. pap. 13.95 (*1-59413-019-1*, Large Print Pr.); 2003. 447p. 32.95 (*0-7862-5652-4*) Thorndike Pr.
—Stands a Calder Man. 1998. (Calder Saga Ser.: Vol. 2). 432p. 25.00 (*0-7278-5383-X*) Severn Hse. Pubs., Ltd.
—Stands a Calder Man. 1993. mass mkt. 6.99 (*0-671-87516-7*); 1990. mass mkt. 5.99 (*0-671-74287-6*); Vol. 2. 1999. 432p. pap. 6.99 (*0-671-04050-2*) Simon & Schuster. (Pocket).
—Stands a Calder Man. 15.80 o.s.i (*0-671-90082-X*, Simon Pulse) Simon & Schuster Children's Publishing.
—This Calder Range. 1998. 448p. pap. 25.00 (*0-7278-5291-4*) Severn Hse. Pubs., Ltd.
—This Calder Range. 1993. mass mkt. 6.99 (*0-671-87517-5*); 1990. mass mkt. 5.99 (*0-671-73210-2*); 1989. mass mkt. 4.95 (*0-671-68586-4*); 1987. mass mkt. 4.50 (*0-671-63385-6*); 1983. mass mkt. 3.95 (*0-671-83608-0*); Vol. 1. 1999. 448p. pap. 7.99 (*0-671-04048-0*) Simon & Schuster. (Pocket).
—This Calder Range & Stands a Calder Man. abr. ed. 1993. 19.95 o.p. (*1-55800-642-7*) NewStar Media, Inc.
—This Calder Sky. l.t. ed. 1999. (Magna Large Print Ser.). 560p. 31.99 (*0-7505-1327-6*) Magna Large Print Bks. GBR. *Dist:* Ulverscroft Large Print Bks., Ltd., Ulverscroft Large Print Canada, Ltd.
—This Calder Sky. Pocket Bks.
—This Calder Sky. 1999. 496p. 26.00 (*0-7278-5401-1*) Severn Hse. Pubs., Ltd.
—This Calder Sky. 1993. mass mkt. 6.99 (*0-671-87518-3*); 1991. mass mkt. 5.99 (*0-671-73969-7*); 1990. mass mkt. 5.50 (*0-671-70881-3*); 1988. mass mkt. (*0-671-68081-1*); 1987. mass mkt. 4.50 (*0-671-63442-9*); 1982. mass mkt. 3.95 o.s.i (*0-671-46478-7*); Vol. 3. 1999. 496p. pap. 7.99 (*0-671-04051-0*) Simon & Schuster. (Pocket).
—This Calder Sky & Calder Born, Calder Bred. abr. ed. 1993. 19.95 o.p. (*1-55800-644-3*) NewStar Media, Inc.
Dallas, Sandra. Buster Midnight's Cafe. l.t. ed. 2004. lib. bdg. 27.95 (*1-58547-381-2*, Premier) Ctr. Point Large Print.
—Buster Midnight's Cafe. 1991. 288p. pap. 8.99 o.s.i (*0-440-50382-5*) Dell Publishing.
—Buster Midnight's Cafe. 1998. 224p. reprint ed. pap. 12.95 (*0-312-18062-4*, NPB 0241, Saint Martin's Griffin) St. Martin's Pr.
Daniels, B. J. Premeditated Marriage. 2002. (Harlequin Intrigue Ser.: No. 691). 256p. mass mkt. o.s.i (*0-373-22687-X*, Harlequin Bks.) Harlequin Enterprises, Ltd.
Davis, Claire. Winter Range. E-Book 23.00 (*0-312-27169-7*); 2001. 272p. pap. 13.00 (*0-312-28425-X*); 2000. 262p. 23.00 o.p. (*0-312-26140-3*) Picador.
Delinsky, Barbara. Montana Man. 1995. 248p. mass mkt. (*1-55166-077-6*, 1-66077-8, Mira Bks.); 1989. (Harlequin Temptation Ser.: No. 280). pap. (*0-373-25380-X*, Harlequin Bks.) Harlequin Enterprises, Ltd.
Doig, Ivan. Bucking the Sun. 1998. 412p. text 23.00 (*0-7881-5700-0*) DIANE Publishing Co.
—Bucking the Sun. 1997. 416p. pap. 13.00 (*0-684-83149-X*, Scribner); 1996. 412p. 23.00 (*0-684-81171-5*, Simon & Schuster) Simon & Schuster.
—Bucking the Sun. 1999. pap. 12.98 (*0-671-04418-4*); Set. 1997. audio 22.00 (*0-671-57382-9*, 595164) Simon & Schuster Audio. (Simon & Schuster Audioworks).
—Dancing at the Rascal Fair. unabr. collector's ed. 1989. audio 104.00 (*0-7366-1490-7*, 2366) Books on Tape, Inc.
—Dancing at the Rascal Fair. l.t. ed. 1988. (General Ser.). 636p. 21.95 o.p. (*0-8161-4519-9*, Macmillan Reference USA) Gale Group.
—Dancing at the Rascal Fair. 1988. pap. 13.00 o.p. (*0-06-097181-9*, PL 7181, Perennial) HarperTrade.
—Dancing at the Rascal Fair. 1996. (Illus.). 416p. pap. 14.00 (*0-684-83105-8*); 1987. 384p. 18.95 o.s.i (*0-689-11764-7*) Simon & Schuster. (Scribner).
—English Creek. audio 16.95 (*0-939643-31-6*) Audio Pr., The.
—English Creek. unabr. collector's ed. 1987. audio 80.00 (*0-7366-1202-5*, 2120) Books on Tape, Inc.
—English Creek, Set. 1994. audio 16.95 Creative Publishing international, Inc.
—English Creek. 1985. (Contemporary American Fiction Ser.). 352p. pap. 13.95 (*0-14-008442-8*, Penguin Bks.) Penguin Group (USA) Inc.
—English Creek. 1984. 352p. 15.95 o.s.i (*0-689-11478-8*, Scribner) Simon & Schuster.
—English Creek. 1992. 24.25 (*0-8446-6608-4*) Smith, Peter Pub., Inc.
—Mountain Time. abr. ed. 1999. 25.00 incl. audio (*0-7871-2016-2*, Dove Audio) NewStar Media, Inc.
—Mountain Time. 320p. 2000. pap. 13.00 (*0-684-86569-6*); 1999. 25.00 o.s.i (*0-684-83295-X*) Simon & Schuster. (Scribner).
—Mountain Time. l.t. ed. 1999. (Americana Ser.). 487p. 29.95 (*0-7862-2216-6*) Thorndike Pr.
—Prairie Nocturne: A Novel. 2003. 384p. 26.00 (*0-7432-0135-3*, Scribner) Simon & Schuster.
—Ride with Me, Mariah Montana. unabr. collector's ed. 1990. audio 80.00 (*0-7366-1868-6*, 2699) Books on Tape, Inc.
—Ride with Me, Mariah Montana. 1991. (Contemporary American Fiction Ser.). 336p. reprint ed. pap. 14.00 (*0-14-015607-0*, Penguin Bks.) Penguin Group (USA) Inc.
—Ride with Me, Mariah Montana. 1990. 384p. text 18.95 (*0-689-12019-2*, Scribner) Simon & Schuster.
Dorris, Michael. A Yellow Raft in Blue Water. 1987. 356p. 16.95 o.p. (*0-8050-0045-3*) Holt, Henry & Co.
—A Yellow Raft in Blue Water. 2001. pap., stu. ed., wbk. ed. (*1-56137-934-4*) Novel Units, Inc.
—A Yellow Raft in Blue Water. 1988. 384p. reprint ed. pap. 14.00 o.p. (*0-446-38787-8*) Warner Bks., Inc.
—A Yellow Raft in Blue Water: A Novel. 2003. 384p. pap. 14.00 (*0-312-42185-0*) Picador.
Douglas, Charlotte. Montana Secrets. 2002. (Harlequin Intrigue Ser.: No. 668). 248p. mass mkt. (*0-373-22668-3*, 1-22668-7, Harlequin Bks.) Harlequin Enterprises, Ltd.
Dunn, J. R. This Side of Judgment. 1994. 320p. 21.95 o.s.i (*0-15-100076-X*) Harcourt Trade Pubs.
—This Side of Judgment. 1995. 368p. mass mkt. 5.99 o.p. (*0-451-45486-3*, ROC) NAL.
Eagle, Tom. White Light: The Lost Vision of Montana. 2000. 216p. pap. 15.00 (*1-930259-12-3*) Anabasis.
Earling, Debra Magpie. Perma Red: A Novel. 2002. 288p. 24.95 (*0-399-14899-X*, BlueHen Bks.) Putnam Publishing Group, The.
Edwards, Cassie. Night Wolf. 2003. 352p. mass mkt. 6.99 (*0-451-21078-6*, Signet Bks.) NAL.
Elliott, Diane. Strength of Stone: The Journal of Electa Bryan Plumer, 1862-1864. 2002. (Illus.). 288p. 19.95 (*0-7627-2464-1*, Falcon Guides) Globe Pequot Pr., The.
Emmons, Jasen. Cowboy Angst. 1996. 272p. pap. 11.00 (*0-684-81897-3*, Scribner Paper Fiction) Simon & Schuster.
—Cowboy Angst. 1995. 240p. 21.00 (*1-56947-021-9*) Soho Pr., Inc.
Estleman, Loren D. High Rocks. 1996. pap. 4.99 (*0-8125-3566-9*, Forge Bks.) Doherty, Tom Assocs., LLC.
—High Rocks. 1979. 7.95 o.p. (*0-385-14696-5*) Doubleday Publishing.
—High Rocks. l.t. ed. 1988. lib. bdg. 14.95 o.p. (*1-85057-425-1*, Macmillan Reference USA) Gale Group.
—High Rocks. 1987. 192p. mass mkt. 2.75 o.s.i (*0-671-63846-7*, Pocket) Simon & Schuster.
—Murdock's Law. 1982. (Double D Western Ser.). 192p. pap. 11.95 o.p. (*0-385-17957-X*) Doubleday Publishing.
—Murdock's Law. 1987. 224p. mass mkt. 2.75 o.s.i (*0-671-44951-6*, Pocket) Simon & Schuster.
Evans, Nicholas. The Horse Whisperer. unabr. ed. 1996. audio 64.00 (*0-7366-3215-8*, 3878) Books on Tape, Inc.
—The Horse Whisperer. 1996. 480p. mass mkt. 7.99 (*0-440-22265-6*); 1995. (Illus.). 416p. 24.95 (*0-385-31523-6*, Delacorte Pr.) Dell Publishing.
—The Horse Whisperer. 1996. 7.50 (*0-440-29545-9*) Doubleday Publishing.
—The Horse Whisperer. unabr. ed. 1999. audio 39.95 Highsmith Inc.
—The Horse Whisperer. 1995. audio 22.98 o.s.i (*0-553-74654-5*); 1998. audio compact disk 29.95 (*0-553-45594-X*); 1995. 360p. pap. 25.95 incl. audio (*0-553-47428-6*, 693169); 1998. 795p. mass mkt. 39.95 incl. audio (*0-553-50220-4*) Random Hse. Audio Publishing Group. (RH Audio).
—The Horse Whisperer. unabr. ed. 1999. audio compact disk 98.00 (*0-7887-3405-9*, C1011E7); 1995. audio 78.00 (*0-7887-0441-9*, 94633E7) Recorded Bks., LLC.
—The Horse Whisperer. l.t. ed. 1995. (Basic Ser.). 618p. 27.95 o.p. (*0-7862-0498-2*) Thorndike Pr.
—The Horse Whisperer. 1996. 14.04 (*0-606-10213-2*) Turtleback Bks.
—The Loop. unabr. ed. 1998. audio 80.00 (*0-7366-4287-0*, 4752); 2001. audio compact disk 96.00 Books on Tape, Inc.
—The Loop. 1999. 560p. mass mkt. 7.99 (*0-440-22462-4*) Dell Publishing.
—The Loop. unabr. ed. 1999. audio 39.95 Highsmith Inc.
—The Loop. abr. ed. 1998. audio 25.95 (*0-553-47880-X*, 692120); audio compact disk 29.95 (*0-553-45564-8*); audio 39.95 (*0-553-50210-7*, 112120) Random Hse. Audio Publishing Group. (RH Audio).
—The Loop. unabr. ed. 1998. audio 90.00 (*0-7887-2281-6*, 95532E7) Recorded Bks., LLC.
—The Loop. l.t. ed. (Thorndike/G. K. Hall Paperback Bestsellers Ser.). 672p. 1999. pap. 27.95 (*0-7862-1634-4*); 1998. 30.95 (*0-7862-1633-6*) Thorndike Pr.
Farris, Jack. Me & Gallagher. 1982. 13.50 o.p. (*0-671-45697-0*, Simon & Schuster) Simon & Schuster.
Fisher, Clay Henry Will. Outcasts of Canyon Creek. 165p. 17.50 o.p. (*0-7451-4686-4*, Gunsmoke) BBC Audiobooks America.
—Outcasts of Canyon Creek. l.t. ed. 2000. (G. K. Hall Nightingale Ser.). 245p. pap. 20.95 (*0-7838-9175-X*); (*0-7540-4309-6*); (*0-7540-4310-X*) Gale Group. (Macmillan Reference USA).
Ford, Richard C. Rock Springs. Fisketjon, Gary, ed. 1987. (Fiction Ser.). 256p. 17.95 o.p. (*0-87113-159-5*) Grove/Atlantic, Inc.
—Rock Springs. 1996. pap. 12.00 (*0-676-51112-0*); 1988. 256p. pap. 13.00 (*0-394-75700-9*) Knopf Publishing Group. (Vintage).
—Wildlife. 1990. 224p. 18.95 o.p. (*0-87113-348-2*) Grove/Atlantic, Inc.
—Wildlife. 1996. pap. 11.00 (*0-676-51109-0*); 1991. 192p. pap. 12.00 (*0-679-73447-3*) Knopf Publishing Group. (Vintage).
Fox, Norman A. Ghostly Hoofbeats. 1989. 192p. bds. 2.95 o.s.i (*0-671-64927-2*, Pocket) Simon & Schuster.
—Ghostly Hoofbeats. l.t. ed. 1996. (Western Ser.). 300p. 19.95 (*0-7862-0807-4*) Thorndike Pr.
—The Phantom Spur. 1992. 192p. mass mkt. 3.50 o.s.i (*0-440-21052-6*) Dell Publishing.
—Silent in the Saddle. 1992. 192p. mass mkt. 3.99 o.s.i (*0-440-21053-4*) Dell Publishing.
—Stranger from Arizona. l.t. ed. 1992. (General Ser.). 254p. pap. 18.95 o.p. (*0-8161-5276-4*, Macmillan Reference USA) Gale Group.
—The Thundering Trail. 1994. 192p. mass mkt. 4.50 o.s.i (*0-440-21058-5*) Dell Publishing.
Fromm, Pete. The Tall Uncut. 1991. 176p. (Orig.). pap. 9.95 o.p. (*0-936784-95-4*) Daniel, John & Co., Pubs.

Gadbow, Kate. Pushed to Shore. 2003. 0290p. pap. 13.95 (*1-889330-81-7*) Sarabande Bks., Inc.

Garlock, Dorothy. Larkspur. 1997. 416p. reprint ed. mass mkt. 7.50 (*0-446-60253-1*) Warner Bks., Inc.

Garwood, Julie. The Clayborne Brides: One Pink Rose, One White Rose, One Red Rose. 1998. (Clayborne Brides Ser.). 464p. pap. 7.99 (*0-671-02177-X*, Pocket) Simon & Schuster.

—The Clayborne Brides: The Rose Trilogy. l.t. ed. 1998. (Large Print Bks.). 26.95 o.p. (*1-56895-515-4*, Wheeler Publishing, Inc.) Gale Group.

—Come the Spring. l.t. ed. 1999. 28.95 (*1-56895-630-4*, Wheeler Publishing, Inc.) Gale Group.

—Come the Spring. 2003. 384p. mass mkt. 5.99 (*0-7434-6712-4*, Pocket); 1998. 384p. per. 6.99 (*0-671-01741-1*, Pocket); 1997. 368p. 24.00 o.s.i (*0-671-00333-X*, Atria); 1998. 384p. reprint ed. pap. 7.99 (*0-671-00334-8*, Pocket) Simon & Schuster.

—For the Roses. 2001. pap. 6.99 (*0-671-00992-3*, Pocket); 1999. per. 3.99 (*0-671-02183-4*, Pocket); 1997. mass mkt. 6.99 (*0-671-01498-6*, Pocket); 1996. 576p. mass mkt. 7.99 (*0-671-87098-X*, Pocket); 1995. 512p. 23.00 o.p. (*0-671-87097-1*, Atria) Simon & Schuster.

—For the Roses, Set. abr. ed. 1995. audio 17.00 o.s.i (*0-671-53447-5*, Simon & Schuster Audioworks) Simon & Schuster Audio.

—For the Roses. l.t. ed. 1996. (Romance Ser.). 808p. lib. bdg. 27.95 (*0-7838-1639-1*) Thorndike Pr.

—One Pink, One White & One Red Rose. abr. ed. 1997. audio 18.00 (*0-671-57690-9*, Simon & Schuster Audioworks) Simon & Schuster Audio.

—One Pink Rose. 1997. per. 2.66 (*0-671-02019-6*); 128p. pap. 2.99 (*0-671-01008-5*) Simon & Schuster. (Pocket).

—One White Rose. 1997. per. 2.66 (*0-671-02020-X*); 128p. mass mkt. 2.99 o.s.i (*0-671-01009-3*) Simon & Schuster. (Pocket).

—Prince Charming. l.t. ed. 1994. 24.95 o.p. (*1-56895-109-4*, Wheeler Publishing, Inc.) Gale Group.

—Prince Charming. Marrow, Linda, ed. 1995. 560p. mass mkt. 7.99 (*0-671-87096-3*, Pocket); 1994. 400p. 22.00 o.s.i (*0-671-87095-5*, Atria) Simon & Schuster.

—Prince Charming. 2001. audio 9.98 (*0-671-04426-5*); Set. 1994. audio 17.00 (*0-671-89174-X*, 391402) Simon & Schuster Audio. (Simon & Schuster Audioworks).

Garza, Pamela. With the Strength to Cry. 2001. 144p. pap. 8.95 (*0-87714-231-9*); 1999. E-Book 6.95 (*0-87714-461-3*) Denlingers Pubs., Ltd.

Gerard, Cindy. Taming the Outlaw. 2002. (Silhouette Desire Ser.). mass mkt. (*0-373-76465-0*, Silhouette) Harlequin Enterprises, Ltd.

Guthrie, A. B., Jr. The Big Sky. 1993. reprint ed. lib. bdg. 24.95 (*1-56849-121-2*) Buccaneer Bks., Inc.

—The Big Sky. abr. ed. audio 12.95 o.p. (*0-694-50259-6*, SWC 1439, Caedmon) HarperTrade.

Guthrie, Alfred B., Jr. Big Sky, 001. 9999. 13.95 o.p. (*0-395-07762-1*, 44); pap. 9.95 o.p. (*0-395-08393-1*) Houghton Mifflin Co. Trade & Reference Div.

Guthrie, Alfred B. Big Sky. 1992. 400p. pap. 14.00 o.p. (*0-395-61153-9*) Houghton Mifflin Co.

Hagberg, David. Eden's Gate. 2002. 384p. mass mkt. 6.99 (*0-8125-4440-4*); 2001. 304p. 24.95 (*0-312-86129-X*) Doherty, Tom Assocs., LLC. (Forge Bks.).

Harrington, Alexis. Montana Born & Bred. 2000. 320p. mass mkt. 5.99 (*0-312-97587-2*, St. Martin's Paperbacks) St. Martin's Pr.

Harrison, Jamie. Blue Deer Thaw: A Mystery. l.t. ed. 2001. (Softcover Ser.). 376p. pap. 23.95 (*1-58724-082-3*, Wheeler Publishing, Inc.) Gale Group.

—Blue Deer Thaw: A Mystery. 2000. 271p. 22.95 (*0-7868-6422-2*) Hyperion Pr.

—Blue Deer Thaw: A Mystery. 2001. 288p. mass mkt. 6.50 (*0-312-97885-5*, St. Martin's Paperbacks) St. Martin's Pr.

—The Edge of the Crazies. 1995. 384p. 20.95 (*0-7868-6085-5*) Hyperion Pr.

—The Edge of the Crazies. 1996. 324p. mass mkt. 6.99 (*0-312-95942-7*, St. Martin's Paperbacks) St. Martin's Pr.

—Going Local. 1996. (Sheriff Jules Clement Ser.: Bk. 2). 323p. 21.95 o.p. (*0-7868-6108-8*) Hyperion Pr.

—Going Local. (Dead Letter Mysteries Ser.). 1998. 336p. mass mkt. 5.99 (*0-312-96484-6*, St. Martin's Paperbacks); Vol. 1. 1997. mass mkt. (*0-312-96271-1*) St. Martin's Pr.

—An Unfortunate Prairie Occurrence. 1998. 304p. 22.95 o.p. (*0-7868-6260-2*) Hyperion Pr.

—An Unfortunate Prairie Occurrence. 1999. (Dead Letter Mysteries Ser.). 400p. mass mkt. 5.99 (*0-312-96829-9*, St. Martin's Paperbacks) St. Martin's Pr.

—An Unfortunate Prairie Occurrence. l.t. ed. 1998. (Americana Ser.). 624p. 28.95 (*0-7862-1459-7*) Thorndike Pr.

Hart, Jillian. Heaven Sent. 2001. (Steeple Hill Love Inspired Ser.: Vol. 143). 256p. mass mkt. (*0-373-87150-3*, Harlequin Bks.) Harlequin Enterprises, Ltd.

—Montana Legend. 2002. (Harlequin Historicals Ser.). 298p. mass mkt. (*0-373-29224-4*, Harlequin Bks.) Harlequin Enterprises, Ltd.

—Montana Man. 2000. (Harlequin Historicals Ser.: Vol. 538). mass mkt. (*0-373-29138-8*, 1-29138-4, Harlequin Bks.) Harlequin Enterprises, Ltd.

Hatcher, Robin Lee. Dear Lady. 1997. 368p. mass mkt. 5.99 o.p. (*0-06-108687-8*) HarperCollins Pubs.

—Dear Lady. 2000. (Coming to America Bk.: No. 1). 304p. pap. 10.99 (*0-310-23083-7*) Zondervan.

Hayes, Penny. Montana Feathers. 1990. 256p. pap. 9.95 o.p. (*0-941483-61-4*) Naiad Pr., Inc.

Hirt, Douglas. Able Gate. 1992. 176p. mass mkt. 3.99 o.s.i (*0-440-21309-6*) Dell Publishing.

Hoag, Tami. Dark Paradise. 1994. 544p. mass mkt. 7.99 (*0-553-56161-8*) Bantam Bks.

Hoffman, Jennifer. A Whisper at Midnight. E-Book 3.50 (*1-58495-057-9*) DiskUs Publishing.

Holm, Stef Ann. Hearts. 2001. 400p. pap. 6.50 (*0-671-77548-0*, Pocket) Simon & Schuster.

—Hooked. 1999. (Brides for All Seasons Ser.: Vol. 2). (Illus.). 432p. pap. 6.50 (*0-671-01941-4*, Pocket) Simon & Schuster.

Honig, Donald. The Ghost of Major Pryor. 1997. 288p. 21.50 (*0-684-80322-4*, Scribner) Simon & Schuster.

Howard, Linda, et al. Finding Home: Duncan's Bride; Chain Lightning; Popcorn & Kisses. 2001. 560p. pap. (*0-373-48443-7*, Harlequin Bks.) Harlequin Enterprises, Ltd.

Hughes, Dean. Lucky's Gold Mine. 1990. (Lucky Ladd Ser.: Bk. 3). 132p. (Orig.). (J). (gr. 3-6). pap. 4.95 (*0-87579-350-9*, Cinnamon Tree) Deseret Bk. Co.

Hugo, Richard. Death & the Good Life. 2002. 231p. 13.95 (*0-89301-261-0*) Univ. of Idaho Pr.

Jackson, Jon A. Badger Games. 2002. (Illus.). 400p. 24.00 (*0-87113-851-4*, Atlantic Monthly Pr.) Grove/Atlantic, Inc.

—Deadman. (Detective Sergeant Mulheisen Mysteries Ser.). 272p. 2001. pap. 11.00 (*0-8021-3771-7*); 1994. 20.00 o.p. (*0-87113-562-0*, Atlantic Monthly Pr.) Grove/Atlantic, Inc.

James, Ellen. My Montana Home. 2001. (Harlequin Superromance Ser.: No. 1014). mass mkt. (*0-373-71014-3*, Harlequin Bks.) Harlequin Enterprises, Ltd.

Jensen, Muriel. Jackpot Baby. 2003. (Harlequin American Romance Ser.: No. 953). 256p. mass mkt. o.s.i (*0-373-16953-1*, Harlequin Bks.) Harlequin Enterprises, Ltd.

Joens, Michael R. The Dawn of Mercy. 1996. pap. 9.99 o.p. (*0-8024-1711-6*) Moody Pr.

Johnson, Dorothy M. Indian Country. 1979. lib. bdg. 10.50 o.p. (*0-8398-2586-2*, Macmillan Reference USA) Gale Group.

—Indian Country. 1995. 199p. pap. 10.00 o.p. (*0-8032-7585-4*, Bison Bks.) Univ. of Nebraska Pr.

Johnston, Joan. Never Tease a Wolf. 2001. 256p. mass mkt. (*1-55166-805-X*, 1-66805-2, Mira Bks.) Harlequin Enterprises, Ltd.

—A Wolf in Sheep's Clothing. 2002. 256p. mass mkt. (*1-55166-913-7*, 1-66913-4, Mira Bks.); 1991. (Silhouette Desire Ser.: No. 658). pap. (*0-373-05658-3*, Harlequin Bks.) Harlequin Enterprises, Ltd.

Johnston, Terry C. Lay the Mountains Low. 2001. (Plainsmen Ser.). (Illus.). 704p. mass mkt. 7.50 (*0-312-97310-1*, 20-3321, St. Martin's Paperbacks) St. Martin's Pr.

Johnstone, William W. Blood of the Mountain Man. l.t. ed. 2001. (G. K. Hall Western Ser.). 297p. 24.95 o.p. (*0-7838-9487-2*, Macmillan Reference USA) Gale Group.

—Blood of the Mountain Man. 1995. 255p. mass mkt. 4.99 o.s.i (*0-8217-5324-X*); 1992. 256p. mass mkt. 3.50 o.s.i (*0-8217-3931-X*) Kensington Publishing Corp. (Zebra Bks.).

—Courage of the Mountain Man. l.t. ed. 2001. (G. K. Hall Western Ser.). 309p. 24.95 (*0-7838-9409-0*, Macmillan Reference USA) Gale Group.

—Courage of the Mountain Man. 2001. 256p. mass mkt. 5.99 (*0-7860-1306-0*); 1995. 256p. mass mkt. 4.99 o.s.i (*0-8217-5366-5*, Zebra Bks.); 1995. 224p. mass mkt. 4.99 (*0-8217-5058-5*); 1992. mass mkt. 3.50 o.s.i (*0-8217-3720-1*, Zebra Bks.) Kensington Publishing Corp.

—Journey of the Mountain Man. l.t. ed. 1999. (Western Ser.). 349p. 24.95 (*0-7838-8808-2*, Macmillan Reference USA) Gale Group.

—Journey of the Mountain Man. 2000. 256p. mass mkt. 5.99 (*0-7860-1302-8*); 1998. 224p. mass mkt. 4.99 o.s.i (*0-8217-5893-4*); 1997. 192p. mass mkt. 4.99 o.s.i (*0-8217-5702-4*); 1995. 224p. mass mkt. 4.99 o.s.i (*0-8217-5771-7*); 1995. mass mkt. 4.50 o.s.i (*0-8217-5015-1*, Zebra Bks.); 1989. mass mkt. 2.95 o.s.i (*0-8217-2602-1*); 1989. mass mkt. 3.50 o.s.i (*0-8217-4244-2*, Zebra Bks.); 1986. mass mkt. 2.25 o.p. (*0-8217-1816-9*, Zebra Bks.) Kensington Publishing Corp.

—War of the Mountain Man. l.t. ed. 2000. (G. K. Hall Western Ser.). 343p. 24.95 (*0-7838-8940-2*, Macmillan Reference USA) Gale Group.

—War of the Mountain Man. 2001. 256p. mass mkt. 5.99 (*0-7860-1303-6*); 1996. 256p. mass mkt. 4.99 o.s.i (*0-8217-5610-9*); 1995. 288p. mass mkt. 4.50 o.s.i (*0-8217-5083-6*); 1990. mass mkt. 3.50 o.p. (*0-8217-3618-3*, Zebra Bks.) Kensington Publishing Corp.

Kauffman, Donna. The Cinderella Rules. 2003. 432p. pap. 11.00 (*0-553-38234-9*) Bantam Bks.

King, Thomas. Truth & Bright Water. 2001. 272p. pap. 13.00 (*0-8021-3840-3*, Grove Pr.); 2000. 266p. 24.00 o.p. (*0-87113-818-2*, Atlantic Monthly Pr.) Grove/Atlantic, Inc.

Lacy, Al. Circle of Fire. 2000. (Journeys of the Stranger Ser.: Bk. 5). 277p. 24.95 (*0-7862-2571-8*, Five Star) Gale Group.

—Snow Ghost. 2001. (Journeys of the Stranger Ser.: Vol. 7). 275p. 24.95 (*0-7862-2949-7*, Five Star) Gale Group.

—Snow Ghost, 7 vols. 2003. (Journeys of the Stranger Ser.: Vol. 7). 300p. pap. 9.99 (*1-57673-047-6*, Multnomah Bks.) Multnomah Pubs., Inc.

Lacy, Al & Lacy, JoAnna. Sincerely Yours. 2003. (Mail Order Bride Ser.: Vol. 7). 277p. pap. 10.99 (*1-57673-572-9*) Multnomah Pubs., Inc.

—Sincerely Yours. l.t. ed. 2001. (Christian Fiction Ser.). 429p. 23.95 (*0-7862-3615-9*) Thorndike Pr.

Langewiesche, William. Devil in Montana. 2004. 256p. 26.00 (*0-86547-581-4*, North Point Pr.) Farrar, Straus & Giroux.

Larsen, Arthur. Next Year Will Be Better. 1983. 175p. 7.95 o.p. (*0-931170-22-2*) Ctr. for Western Studies.

Laskowski, Tim. Every Good Boy Does Fine: A Novel. 2003. 240p. 23.95 (*0-87074-477-1*) Southern Methodist Univ. Pr.

Laundrie, Amy C. Thirty Pieces of Silver: A Kayla Montgomery Mystery. 1996. 156p. (gr. 6 up). pap. 9.99 (*0-88092-364-4*); lib. bdg. o.p. (*0-88092-365-2*) Royal Fireworks Publishing Co.

Lee, Rae Ellen. The Bluebird House. 2002. 277p. pap. 13.95 (*1-4104-0068-9*, Five Star Trade); (Illus.). 276p. 25.95 (*0-7862-4022-9*, Five Star) Gale Group.

Lee, Robert. Guiding Elliott. 1997. 196p. 22.95 (*1-55821-603-0*, Lyons Pr.) Globe Pequot Pr., The.

Lennon, J. Robert. The Light of Falling Stars. 1998. 320p. reprint ed. 13.00 (*1-57322-682-3*, Riverhead Trade (Paperbacks)) Berkley Publishing Group.

—The Light of Falling Stars. 1997. 288p. 23.95 o.s.i (*1-57322-066-3*, Riverhead Bks. (Hardcovers)) Putnam Publishing Group, The.

—On the Night Plain: A Novel. 2001. 256p. 23.00 (*0-8050-6722-1*) Holt, Henry & Co.

—On the Night Plain: A Novel. 2002. 256p. pap. 13.00 (*0-312-42086-2*) Picador.

Lewis, Sherry. L' Homme du Montana. 2000. (Harlequin Amours d'Aujourd'Hui Ser.). mass mkt. (*0-373-38384-3*, 1-38384-3, Harlequin French) Harlequin Enterprises, Ltd.

Linder, Steven. The Measure of Justice. 1992. 194p. 19.95 (*0-8027-4134-7*) Walker & Co.

Linderman, Frank B. The Montana Stories of Frank B. Linderman: The Authorized Edition. 1997. 214p. pap. 9.95 (*0-8032-7970-1*, Bison Bks.) Univ. of Nebraska Pr.

—Wolf & the Winds. 1986. 224p. 21.95 o.p. (*0-8061-2007-X*) Univ. of Oklahoma Pr.

Linderman, Frank Bird. Henry Plummer: A Novel. 2000. (Illus.). 221p. pap. 16.95 (*0-8032-7989-2*, A Bison Original) Univ. of Nebraska Pr.

Long, David. The Falling Boy. 1998. 256p. pap. 12.95 o.s.i (*0-452-27997-6*, Plume) Dutton/Plume.

—The Falling Boy. 1997. 288p. 22.00 o.s.i (*0-684-80034-9*, Scribner) Simon & Schuster.

Long, Elaine. Bittersweet Country. 1991. 19.95 o.p. (*0-312-05971-X*) St. Martin's Pr.

—Bittersweet Country. l.t. ed. 1999. (Romance Ser.). 539p. 28.95 o.p. (*0-7838-8565-2*) Thorndike Pr.

Maclean, Norman F. A River Runs Through It. 1979. 17.05 (*0-606-19234-4*) Turtleback Bks.

—A River Runs Through It. 1989. (Illus.). vi, 168p. 27.50 (*0-226-50060-8*) Univ. of Chicago Pr.

—A River Runs Through It & Other Stories. 1985. audio 13.95 (*1-55644-126-6*, 5031) American Audio Prose Library, Inc.

—A River Runs Through It & Other Stories. 1994. audio 24.95 (*0-939643-41-3*, 3570, NorthWord) Creative Publishing international, Inc.

—A River Runs Through It & Other Stories. 1976. xviii, 422 p. (*0-8161-6398-7*); 1993. 310p. 16.95 o.p. (*0-8161-5735-9*) Gale Group. (Macmillan Reference USA).

—A River Runs Through It & Other Stories. abr. unabr. ed. 2000. audio 24.95 (*1-56511-362-4*) HighBridge Co.

—A River Runs Through It & Other Stories. unabr. ed. 1993. audio 53.00 (*1-55690-822-9*, 93122E7) Recorded Bks., LLC.

—A River Runs Through It & Other Stories. Peters, Sally, ed. 1992. 256p. reprint ed. mass mkt. 6.99 (*0-671-77697-5*, Pocket) Simon & Schuster.

—A River Runs Through It & Other Stories. 2001. 232p. 20.00 o.s.i (*0-226-50055-1*); 1983. (Illus.). 128p. (C). 50.00 o.s.i (*0-226-50059-4*) Univ. of Chicago Pr.

—A River Runs Through It & Other Stories: Anniversity Edition. 25th ed. 2001. 232p. pap. 11.00 o.s.i (*0-226-50057-8*, P821); 1983. (Illus.). 128p. (C). 25.00 o.s.i (*0-226-50058-6*) Univ. of Chicago Pr.

Macomber, Debbie. Montana. abr. ed. 1998. audio 7.99 (*1-55204-141-7*) Durkin Hayes Publishing Ltd.

—Montana. 2003. 384p. mass mkt. (*1-55166-975-7*); 1998. 379p. mass mkt. (*1-55166-434-8*, 1-66434-1); 1997. 299p. pap. (*1-55166-316-3*, 1-66316-0) Harlequin Enterprises, Ltd. (Mira Bks.).

Maki, Alan. A Choice to Cherish. 2000. 184p. 14.99 (*0-8054-2338-9*) Broadman & Holman Pubs.

Mallery, Susan. Christmas in Whitehorn. 2001. (Silhouette Special Edition Ser.). mass mkt. (*0-373-24435-5*, Harlequin Bks.) Harlequin Enterprises, Ltd.

Marshall, Michael. The Straw Men: A Novel. 2002. 400p. mass mkt. 6.99 (*0-515-13427-9*, Jove) Berkley Publishing Group.

Martin, Kat. The Secret. 2001. 512p. mass mkt. 6.99 (*0-8217-6798-4*, Zebra Bks.) Kensington Publishing Corp.

—The Secret. l.t. ed. 2001. (Romance Ser.). 480p. 29.95 o.p. (*0-7838-9534-8*) Thorndike Pr.

Marvine, Dee. Sweet Grass. 2003. (Five Star First Edition Women's Fiction Ser.). 282p. 26.95 (*0-7862-5111-5*, Five Star) Gale Group.

Mason, Connie. To Tame a Renegade. 1998. pap. 5.99 o.p. (*0-380-79341-5*, Avon Bks.) Morrow/Avon.

—To Tame a Renegade. l.t. ed. 2001. 375p. 27.95 (*0-7862-3369-9*) Thorndike Pr.

Mather, Ruth E. & Boswell, Fred E. The Bannack Gallows. 1998. viii, 207p. pap. 15.95 (*0-9625069-3-1*) History West Publishing Co.

McAllister, Anne. The Great Montana Cowboy Auction. 2002. mass mkt. (*0-373-48457-7*, 1-48457-5, Harlequin Bks.) Harlequin Enterprises, Ltd.

McCall, Dinah. White Mountain. l.t. ed. 2002. (Wheeler Romance Ser.). 363p. 28.95 (*1-58724-303-2*, Wheeler Publishing, Inc.) Gale Group.

McClendon, Lise. The Bluejay Shaman. 1996. (Mystery Ser.). per. (*0-373-26213-2*, Worldwide Library) Harlequin Enterprises, Ltd.

McGuane, Thomas. Keep the Change. 1989. 240p. 18.95 o.p. (*0-395-48887-7*) Houghton Mifflin Co. Trade & Reference Div.

—Keep the Change. 1990. (Vintage Contemporaries Ser.). 240p. pap. 12.00 (*0-679-73033-8*, Vintage) Knopf Publishing Group.

—Keep the Change. 1994. pap. 11.00 (*0-394-25889-4*) Random Hse., Inc.

—Nobody's Angel. 1985. 224p. mass mkt. 3.50 o.s.i (*0-345-33087-0*); 1983. mass mkt. 2.95 o.p. (*0-345-30271-0*) Ballantine Bks.

—Nobody's Angel. 1986. (Vintage Contemporaries Ser.). 240p. pap. 14.00 (*0-394-74738-0*, Vintage) Knopf Publishing Group.

—Nobody's Angel. 1994. pap. o.p. (*0-394-25885-1*) Random Hse., Inc.

—Nothing but Blue Skies. 1992. 320p. 21.95 o.s.i (*0-395-54540-4*); 126.00 o.p. (*0-395-64594-8*) Houghton Mifflin Co.

—Nothing but Blue Skies. 1994. (Vintage Contemporaries Ser.). 368p. pap. 14.00 (*0-679-74778-8*) Random Hse., Inc.

—Thomas McGuane: Three Complete Novels. 1994. 13.99 o.s.i (*0-517-10019-3*) Random Hse. Value Publishing.

McMahon, Franci. Staying the Distance: A Novel. 1994. 200p. pap. 9.95 (*1-56341-046-X*); lib. bdg. 20.95 (*1-56341-047-8*) Firebrand Bks.

McNamer, Deirdre. One Sweet Quarrel: A Novel. 1994. 320p. 22.00 o.p. (*0-06-016868-4*) HarperTrade.

—Rima in the Weeds. 1991. 19.95 o.p. (*0-06-016523-5*) HarperTrade.

Mikels, Jennifer. Big Sky Cowboy. 2002. (Silhouette Special Edition Ser.). 256p. mass mkt. (*0-373-24491-6*, Silhouette) Harlequin Enterprises, Ltd.

Miller, Dawn. The Other Side of Jordan. 2003. (Illus.). v, 243p. pap. 12.99 (*1-59145-002-0*) Integrity Pubs.

—Promise Land: The Journal of Callie McGregor. 2002. 288p. pap. 12.99 (*1-59145-001-2*) Integrity Pubs.

Miller, John Ramsey. The Last Family: A Suspense Novel. 1997. 480p. reprint ed. mass mkt. 6.99 (*0-553-57496-5*) Bantam Bks.

Miller, Linda Lael. Jessica. 1999. (Springwater Seasons Ser.: Bk. 4). 151p. pap. 3.99 o.s.i (*0-671-02687-9*, Pocket) Simon & Schuster.

—Jessica. l.t. ed. 1999. (Americana Ser.). 175p. 28.95 (*0-7862-2160-7*) Thorndike Pr.

—Miranda. 1999. (Springwater Seasons Ser.: Bk. 3). 142p. pap. 3.99 o.s.i (*0-671-02686-0*, Pocket) Simon & Schuster.

—Miranda Bk. 3: Springwater Seasons. l.t. ed. 1999. (Americana Ser.). 173p. 27.95 (*0-7862-2159-3*) Thorndike Pr.

—Part of the Bargain. 1999. mass mkt. (*1-55166-512-3*, 1-66512-4, Mira Bks.); 1994. per. (*0-373-45176-8*, 1-45176-4, Harlequin Bks.); 1985. mass mkt. (*0-671-52313-9*, Silhouette); 1985. per. (*0-373-07087-X*, Harlequin Bks.) Harlequin Enterprises, Ltd.

—Part of the Bargain. l.t. ed. 2001. (Romance Ser.). 375p. 27.95 (*0-7862-2621-8*) Thorndike Pr.

—Rachel. 1999. (Springwater Seasons Ser.: Bk. 1). 145p. pap. 3.99 o.s.i (*0-671-02684-4*, Pocket) Simon & Schuster.

—Rachel. l.t. ed. 1999. (Americana Ser.). 189p. 27.95 (*0-7862-2157-7*) Thorndike Pr.

—Savannah. 1999. (Springwater Seasons Ser.: Bk. 2). 144p. mass mkt. 3.99 o.s.i (*0-671-02685-2*, Pocket) Simon & Schuster.

—Savannah. l.t. ed. 1999. (Americana Ser.). 184p. 27.95 (*0-7862-2158-5*) Thorndike Pr.

—Springwater. l.t. ed. 1999. (Wheeler Large Print Book Ser.). 280p. 26.95 (*1-56895-786-6*, Wheeler Publishing, Inc.) Gale Group.

—Springwater. 1998. 304p. mass mkt. 6.99 (*0-671-02751-4*, Pocket) Simon & Schuster.

—A Springwater Christmas. 1999. (Springwater Seasons Ser.). 320p. mass mkt. 6.99 (*0-671-02752-2*, Pocket) Simon & Schuster.

—Springwater Seasons Omnibus. 2000. 592p. mass mkt. 7.99 (*0-7434-0362-2*, Pocket) Simon & Schuster.

—Springwater Wedding. l.t. ed. 2001. (Wheeler Large Print Book Ser.). (Illus.). 378p. 30.95 (*1-58724-056-4*, Wheeler Publishing, Inc.) Gale Group.

—Springwater Wedding. 2001. 288p. 23.95 (*0-671-04248-3*, Atria); 2001. 288p. E-Book 9.99 (*0-7434-4822-7*, Atria); 2002. (Illus.). 384p. reprint ed. mass mkt. 7.99 (*0-671-04249-1*, Pocket) Simon & Schuster.

Mills, Charles. The Secret of Squaw Rock. 1992. (Shadow Creek Ranch Ser.: Vol. 3). 127p. (J). (gr. 4-7). pap. 5.99 (*0-8280-0700-4*) Review & Herald Publishing Assn.

—Stranger in the Shadows. 1998. (Shadow Creek Ranch Ser.: Vol. 11). 151p. (Orig.). (J). (gr. 4-7). pap. 5.99 (*0-8280-1316-0*) Review & Herald Publishing Assn.

—Treasure of the Merrilee. 1993. (Shadow Creek Ranch Ser.: Vol. 4). (J). (gr. 4-7). pap. 5.99 o.p. (*0-8280-0717-9*) Review & Herald Publishing Assn.

Moffat, Gwen. Grizzly Trail. 1984. 208p. o.p. (*0-575-03503-X*) David & Charles Pubs.

—Grizzly Trail. l.t. ed. 1987. (Linford Mystery Library). 334p. pap. 17.99 o.p. (*0-7089-6357-9*, Linford) Thorpe, F. A. Pubs. GBR. *Dist:* Ulverscroft Large Print Bks., Ltd., Ulverscroft Large Print Canada, Ltd.

Moler, Lee. Bone Music. 1999. 320p. 23.00 (*0-684-84355-2*, Simon & Schuster) Simon & Schuster.

Moore, John L. The Breaking of Ezra Riley. rev. ed. 2000. 784p. pap. 14.99 (*0-8054-2331-1*) Broadman & Holman Pubs.

—The Breaking of Ezra Riley. 1986. (Illus.). 226p. pap. 8.50 o.p. (*0-937959-03-0*, Falcon) Globe Pequot Pr., The.

—The Breaking of Ezra Riley. 1990. 287p. pap. 9.99 o.p. (*0-7459-1882-4*) Lion Publishing.

—The Breaking of Ezra Riley. 1994. 10.99 o.p. (*0-8407-6760-9*) Nelson, Thomas Inc.

Morris, Gilbert. Wounded Yankee. 1991. (House of Winslow Ser.: Bk. 10). 304p. pap. 11.99 (*1-55661-116-1*) Bethany Hse. Pubs.

Morrone, Wenda W. No Time for an Everyday Woman. 1997. 320p. 23.95 o.p. (*0-312-15615-4*, Saint Martin's Minotaur) St. Martin's Pr.

Mosher, Jake. The Last Buffalo Hunter. 2002. 256p. 16.95 (*1-56792-226-0*) Godine, David R. Pub.

Mosher, Jake & Godine, David. The Last Buffalo Hunter. 2000. 320p. 24.95 (*1-56792-146-9*) Godine, David R. Pub.

Mourning Dove Staff, ed. Cogewea, the Half Blood. 1981. 302p. 30.00 o.p. (*0-8032-3069-9*) Univ. of Nebraska Pr.

Mourning Dove Staff, intro. Cogewea, the Half Blood. 1981. (Illus.). 302p. pap. text 13.95 (*0-8032-8110-2*, Bison Bks.) Univ. of Nebraska Pr.

Mulford, Clarence E. Buck Peters, Ranchman. 1973. reprint ed. lib. bdg. 26.95 (*0-88411-202-0*) Amereon, Ltd.

—Buck Peters, Ranchman. 1993. 320p. mass mkt. 5.99 (*0-8125-2499-3*, Tor Bks.) Doherty, Tom Assocs., LLC.

Muller, Marcia. Listen to the Silence. l.t. ed. 2000. (Wheeler Large Print Book Ser.). 328p. 28.95 o.p. (*1-56895-908-7*, Wheeler Publishing, Inc.) Gale Group.

Murray, Earl. River at Sundown. 1997. 320p. 22.95 (*0-312-86124-9*, Forge Bks.) Doherty, Tom Assocs., LLC.

—The River of Sundown. 1999. 320p. mass mkt. 5.99 (*0-8125-5144-3*, Forge Bks.) Doherty, Tom Assocs., LLC.

Neilson, Helen P. What the Cow Said to the Calf: Native American Historical Biography. 1993. 200p. (C). pap. text 17.95 o.p. (*1-880222-15-9*) Red Apple Publishing.

Nofziger, Lyn. Tackett. 2000. 214p. pap. text 10.95 (*0-915463-85-7*); 1998. 19.95 (*0-915463-80-6*) Jameson Bks., Inc.

—Tackett. 1993. 192p. 16.95 (*0-89526-495-1*) Regnery Publishing, Inc., An Eagle Publishing Co.

—Tackett & the Indian. 1998. (Tackett Ser.: Vol. 4). 208p. 19.95 (*0-915463-75-X*, Frontier Library, The) Jameson Bks., Inc.

Offutt, Chris. The Good Brother: A Novel. 1998. 320p. pap. 13.00 (*0-684-84619-5*); 1997. 317p. 23.00 o.s.i (*0-684-80983-4*) Simon & Schuster. (Simon & Schuster).

Overholser, Stephen. Molly & the Railroad Tycoon. l.t. ed. 2001. (Thorndike Western Ser.). 269p. 23.95 (*0-7862-3240-4*); (*0-7540-4529-3*); (*0-7540-4530-7*) Thorndike Pr.

Pade, Victoria. The Marriage Bargain. 2000. (Silhouette Special Edition Ser.: No. 4). (Illus.). 256p. mass mkt. (*0-373-65049-3*, 1-65049-8, Harlequin Bks.) Harlequin Enterprises, Ltd.

Paige, Laurie. Cheyenne Bride. 2000. (Silhouette Special Edition Ser.). 256p. per. (*0-373-65047-7*, 1-65047-2, Harlequin Bks.) Harlequin Enterprises, Ltd.

—Her Montana Man. 2002. (Silhouette Special Edition Ser.). mass mkt. (*0-373-24483-5*, Silhouette) Harlequin Enterprises, Ltd.

—Outlaw Marriage. 2001. (Silhouette Special Edition Ser.: No. 11). (Illus.). 256p. mass mkt. (*0-373-65056-6*, Harlequin Bks.) Harlequin Enterprises, Ltd.

Paine, Lauran. The Trail Without End. l.t. ed. 2002. 1973p. lib. bdg. 26.95 (*1-58547-099-6*) Ctr. Point Large Print.

Pfeiffer, Pat. Roughin' It in Montana: Tall Tales of a Pioneer. 2001. pap. 14.95 (*0-595-19941-0*) iUniverse, Inc.

—The Sheriff's Wife: Tangled in Montana's Violent Past. 2001. pap. 18.95 (*0-595-20803-7*, Writers Club Pr.) iUniverse, Inc.

Pronzini, Bill. The Montanans. 1991. 224p. (Orig.). mass mkt. 3.50 o.s.i (*0-449-14643-X*, Fawcett) Ballantine Bks.

Prowell, Sandra West. By Evil Means. 1995. (Phoebe Siegel Mystery Ser.). 384p. mass mkt. 5.99 (*0-553-56966-X*) Bantam Bks.

—By Evil Means. 1993. 216p. 19.95 (*0-8027-1248-7*) Walker & Co.

—The Killing of Monday Brown. unabr. ed. 1994. audio 57.25 o.p. (*1-56100-207-0*, 919, Unabridged Library Editions); audio 21.95 o.p. (*1-56100-582-7*, 349, Bookcassette) Brilliance Audio.

—The Killing of Monday Brown: A Phoebe Siegel Mystery. 1996. 320p. mass mkt. 5.99 (*0-553-56969-4*) Bantam Bks.

—The Killing of Monday Brown: A Phoebe Siegel Mystery. 1994. 240p. 19.95 (*0-8027-3184-8*) Walker & Co.

—When Wallflowers Die. abr. ed. 1996. audio 16.95 o.p. (*1-56100-407-3*, 1406, Nova Audio Bks.); audio 7.99 o.p. (*1-56740-169-4*, 717, Paperback Nova Audio Bks.); audio 57.25 o.p. (*1-56100-239-9*, 1093, Unabridged Library Editions); audio 23.95 o.p. (*1-56100-614-9*, 313, Bookcassette) Brilliance Audio.

—When Wallflowers Die: A Phoebe Siegel Mystery. 1997. (Phoebe Siegel Mystery Ser.). 368p. mass mkt. 5.99 (*0-553-56970-8*, Crimeline) Bantam Bks.

—When Wallflowers Die: A Phoebe Siegel Mystery. 1996. 336p. 22.95 (*0-8027-3254-2*) Walker & Co.

Reid, Robert S. Wild Animals: A Novel of Suspense. 1996. 304p. 22.00 o.p. (*0-7867-0257-5*, Carroll & Graf Pubs.) Avalon Publishing Group.

Rice, Robert. Nature of Midnight. mass mkt. (*0-7653-4260-X*, Forge Bks.) Doherty, Tom Assocs., LLC.

Rimmer, Christine, et al. Big Sky Brides. 2000. 378p. mass mkt. (*0-373-48381-3*, Harlequin Bks.) Harlequin Enterprises, Ltd.

Roberts, Nora. Montana Sky. 1997. 480p. mass mkt. 7.99 (*0-515-12061-8*, Jove) Berkley Publishing Group.

—Montana Sky. unabr. ed. 1997. audio 88.00 (*0-913369-43-8*, 4226) Books on Tape, Inc.

—Montana Sky. abr. ed. 1997. audio 7.99 o.p. (*1-56740-161-9*, 677, Paperback Nova Audio Bks.); 1996. audio 16.95 o.p. (*1-56100-892-3*, 1284, Nova Audio Bks.); 1996. audio 89.25 o.p. (*1-56100-314-X*, 945, Unabridged Library Editions); 1996. audio 25.95 o.p. (*1-56100-689-0*, 179, Bookcassette) Brilliance Audio.

—Montana Sky. 1996. 448p. 23.95 o.s.i (*0-399-14122-7*, G. P. Putnam's Sons) Penguin Group (USA) Inc.

—Montana Sky. 23.95 o.s.i (*0-399-14426-9*) Putnam Publishing Group, The.

—Three Complete Novels. 2001. 852p. 14.98 (*0-399-14731-4*, Putnam & Grosset) Penguin Group (USA) Inc.

Robinson, John A. Rex Barlow, Montana Marshal. 2000. pap. 15.95 (*0-936389-82-6*) Tudor Pubs., Inc.

Rodgers, Joni. Crazy for Trying. 1999. pap. 13.00 (*1-878448-92-7*); 1996. 301p. 24.00 o.p. (*1-878448-73-0*) MacMurray & Beck, Inc.

Rolofson. Man for Maggie Moore. 2001. (Montana Matchmakers Ser.). mass mkt. (*0-373-25958-1*, Harlequin Bks.) Harlequin Enterprises, Ltd.

Rolofson, Kristine. A Bride for Calder Brown. 2001. (Harlequin Temptation Ser.: No. 850). mass mkt. (*0-373-25950-6*, Harlequin Bks.) Harlequin Enterprises, Ltd.

—Brides, Boots & Booties: The Bride Rode West; The Wrong Man in Wyoming; The Right Man in Montana, 3 bks. in 1. 2001. 667p. mass mkt. (*0-373-20186-9*, Harlequin Bks.) Harlequin Enterprises, Ltd.

Rowland, Russell. In Open Spaces: A Novel. 2002. 384p. pap. 13.95 (*0-06-008434-0*, Perennial) HarperTrade.

Savage, Les, Jr. Coffin Gap. 1999. 224p. mass mkt. 4.50 (*0-8439-4632-6*, Leisure Bks.) Dorchester Publishing Co., Inc.

—Coffin Gap. l.t. ed. 1997. (Western Ser.). 212p. 18.95 (*0-7862-0740-X*, Five Star) Gale Group.

—Coffin Gap. l.t. ed. 1998. (Western Ser.). 312p. 20.95 (*0-7862-0763-9*) Thorndike Pr.

—Medicine Wheel. 1998. 224p. mass mkt. 4.50 (*0-8439-4444-7*, Leisure Bks.) Dorchester Publishing Co., Inc.

—Medicine Wheel. (Western Ser.). 1996. 218p. 17.95 (*0-7862-0657-8*, Five Star); 1999. 20.00 (*0-7838-1668-5*, Macmillan Reference USA) Gale Group.

Savage, Thomas. The Corner of Rife & Pacific. 1988. 288p. 16.95 (*0-688-07092-2*, Morrow, William & Co.) Morrow/Avon.

Schaller, Bob. Montana. 1998. (Arlingtons Ser.). (Illus.). 128p. (J). (gr. 8-12). pap. text 7.95 o.p. (*1-887002-78-2*) Cross Training Publishing.

Sharpe, Jon. Montana Maiden. 1982. (Trailsman Ser.: No. 11). mass mkt. 2.50 o.p. (*0-451-11632-1*, AE1632, Signet Bks.) NAL.

Siler, Jenny. Iced. 2001. (John MacRae Bks.). 256p. 24.00 (*0-8050-6438-9*) Holt, Henry & Co.

Smith, Diane. Pictures from an Expedition. 2004. 288p. pap. 14.00 (*0-14-200406-5*) Penguin Group (USA) Inc.

—Pictures from an Expedition. 2002. 288p. 24.95 (*0-670-03129-1*) Viking Penguin.

Smith, Robert F. Never Can Say Good-Bye. 2003. 271p. pap. 13.95 (*1-57008-991-4*) Deseret Bk. Co.

St. John, Cheryl. The Magnificent Seven. 2001. (Silhouette Special Edition Ser.: Vol. 10). (Illus.). 248p. mass mkt. (*0-373-65055-8*, Harlequin Bks.) Harlequin Enterprises, Ltd.

Staley, Ida Jean. Turtle Medicine. 1999. E-Book 4.95 (*1-930364-03-2*, Bookmice) McGraw Publishing, Inc.

Standiford, Les. Spill. 1991. 19.95 o.p. (*0-87113-438-1*) Grove/Atlantic, Inc.

—Spill. 1993. 352p. mass mkt. 4.99 o.s.i (*0-06-100669-6*, HarperTorch) Morrow/Avon.

Stark, Richard. Firebreak. 2001. 304p. 23.45 o.p. (*0-89296-711-0*) Mysterious Pr.

Stroud, Carsten. Lizardskin. 1993. 448p. pap. 23.00 (*0-553-76261-3*) Bantam Bks.

Svee, Gary D. Single Tree. l.t. ed. 1995. 248p. lib. bdg. 19.95 (*0-7838-1220-5*, Macmillan Reference USA) Gale Group.

—Single Tree. 2004. 336p. mass mkt. 4.99 (*0-7434-6353-6*, Pocket) Simon & Schuster.

—Single Tree. 1994. 192p. 19.95 (*0-8027-4142-8*) Walker & Co.

—Spirit Wolf. 2003. 256p. reprint ed. pap. 4.99 (*0-7434-6352-8*, Pocket) Simon & Schuster.

Temple, Lou Jane. Death Is a Semisweet: A Heaven Lee Mystery. 2002. 288p. 23.95 (*0-312-30122-7*, Saint Martin's Minotaur) St. Martin's Pr.

Thon, Melanie Rae. Sweet Hearts. 2001. (Illus.). 256p. tchr. ed. 23.00 (*0-395-78589-8*, Mariner Bks.) Houghton Mifflin Co. Trade & Reference Div.

—Sweet Hearts. 2002. 256p. reprint ed. pap. 13.00 (*0-7434-3679-2*, Washington Square Pr.) Simon & Schuster.

Tilghman, Christopher. The Way People Run: Stories. 2000. 224p. pap. 12.00 o.p. (*0-312-26791-6*) Picador.

—The Way People Run: Stories. l.t. ed. 1999. (Americana Ser.). 254p. 26.95 (*0-7862-2170-4*) Thorndike Pr.

Tronstad, Janet. An Angel for Dry Creek. 1999. (Steeple Hill Love Inspired Ser.: No. 81). 254p. per. (*0-373-87081-7*, 1-87081-5, Harlequin Bks.) Harlequin Enterprises, Ltd.

—A Rich Man for Dry Creek. 2002. (Steeple Hill Love Inspired Ser.: No. 176). mass mkt. (*0-373-87183-X*, 1-87183-9, Steeple Hill) Harlequin Enterprises, Ltd.

Turner, Linda. Nighthawk's Child. 2001. (Silhouette Special Edition Ser.: No. 12). (Illus.). 256p. mass mkt. (*0-373-65057-4*, 1-65057-1, Harlequin Bks.) Harlequin Enterprises, Ltd.

Van Steenwyk, Elizabeth. Three Dog Winter. 1999. 160p. (gr. 4-7). pap. text 3.99 o.s.i (*0-440-41495-4*, Dell Books for Young Readers) Random Hse. Children's Bks.

—Three Dog Winter. 1999. 10.04 (*0-606-16440-5*) Turtleback Bks.

—Three Dog Winter. 1987. (J). (gr. 4-9). 13.95 (*0-8027-6718-4*) Walker & Co.

Volk, Toni. Maybe in Missoula. 1994. 280p. 22.00 o.p. (*1-56947-007-3*) Soho Pr., Inc.

Waldie, Scott. Return to Travers Corners: Stories. 2002. 292p. 22.95 (*1-58574-662-2*, Lyons Pr.) Globe Pequot Pr., The.

—Travers Corners. 1997. 176p. 25.00 o.p. (*1-55821-533-6*, Lyons Pr.) Globe Pequot Pr., The.

—Travers Corners: Classic Stories about Fly Fishing & a Small Montana Town. 2003. 196p. pap. 14.95 (*1-59228-154-0*, Lyons Pr.) Globe Pequot Pr., The.

Walker, Mildred. The Curlew's Cry. 1994. 382p. pap. 15.00 (*0-8032-9757-2*, Bison Bks.) Univ. of Nebraska Pr.

Warren, Pat. The Baby Quest. 2000. (Silhouette Special Edition Ser.: Vol. 6). (Illus.). 241p. mass mkt. (*0-373-65051-5*, 1-65051-4, Harlequin Bks.) Harlequin Enterprises, Ltd.

Watson, Larry. Justice. l.t. ed. 1996. 249p. pap. 20.95 o.p. (*0-7838-1605-7*, Macmillan Reference USA) Gale Group.

—Justice. 1995. 230p. 17.95 (*1-57131-002-9*) Milkweed Editions.

—Justice. 1996. 224p. pap. 10.00 (*0-671-53557-9*, Washington Square Pr.) Simon & Schuster.

—Justice. 1999. pap. 9.98 (*0-671-04466-4*); 1996. audio 17.00 (*0-671-53645-1*) Simon & Schuster Audio. (Simon & Schuster Audioworks).

—Montana, 1948. 1993. (Lakes & Prairies Ser.). 192p. 17.95 (*0-915943-13-1*) Milkweed Editions.

—Montana 1948. Rosenman, Jane, ed. 1995. 182p. pap. 12.95 (*0-671-50703-6*, Washington Square Pr.) Simon & Schuster.

—Montana, 1948. l.t. ed. 1994. 20.95 o.p. (*0-7927-2049-0*) BBC Audiobooks America.

—Montana, 1948. l.t. ed. 1997. (Ulverscroft Large Print Ser.). 256p. 31.50 o.p. (*0-7089-3693-8*, Ulverscroft) Thorpe, F. A. Pubs. GBR. *Dist:* Ulverscroft Large Print Bks., Ltd., Ulverscroft Large Print Canada, Ltd.

—Montana 1948. l.t. ed. 1997. (French Ser.). 251p. pap. 30.99 o.p. (*2-84011-176-4*) Feryane, SA, Editions FRA. *Dist:* Ulverscroft Large Print Bks., Ltd., Ulverscroft Large Print Canada, Ltd.

—Montana, 1948. unabr. ed. 2000. audio compact disk 36.00 (*0-7887-3417-2*, C1023E7); 1999. audio compact disk 36.00 Recorded Bks., LLC.

—Montana, 1948. unabr. ed. 1995. audio 20.00 (*0-671-51992-1*, 492783, Simon & Schuster Audioworks) Simon & Schuster Audio.

—Montana 1948. unabr. ed. 1997. audio 26.00 (*0-7887-0816-3*, 94966E7) Recorded Bks., LLC.

—White Crosses. 384p. 1998. pap. 14.00 (*0-671-56773-X*, Washington Square Pr.); 1997. 23.00 o.s.i (*0-671-56771-3*, Atria) Simon & Schuster.

Welch, James. Fools Crow. 1986. 400p. 18.95 o.p. (*0-670-81121-1*) Viking Penguin.

—The Indian Lawyer. 1990. 19.95 o.p. (*0-393-02896-8*) Norton, W. W. & Co., Inc.

—Winter in the Blood. 1975. reprint ed. lib. bdg. 8.95 o.p. (*0-8161-6299-9*, Macmillan Reference USA) Gale Group.

—Winter in the Blood. 1981. 256p. pap. o.p. (*0-06-080537-4*) HarperCollins Pubs.

—Winter in the Blood. 1986. (Contemporary American Fiction Ser.). 192p. pap. 14.00 (*0-14-008644-7*, Penguin Bks.) Penguin Group (USA) Inc.

West, Charles G. Hero's Hand. 2003. 320p. mass mkt. 5.99 (*0-451-20822-6*, Signet Bks.) NAL.

West, Stanley Gordon. Blind Your Ponies. 2001. (Illus.). 580p. pap. 16.00 (*0-9656247-8-1*) Lexington-Marshall Publishing.

Wheeler, Richard S. The Buffalo Commons. l.t. ed. 1999. (Americana Ser.). 677p. 29.95 (*0-7862-1890-8*) Thorndike Pr.

—Cashbox. 1995. 435p. pap. 5.99 (*0-8125-2143-9*); 1994. 384p. 23.95 o.p. (*0-312-85382-3*) Doherty, Tom Assocs., LLC. (Forge Bks.).

—Cashbox. l.t. ed. 1996. 566p. 23.95 (*0-7838-1566-2*, Macmillan Reference USA) Gale Group.

—Winter Grass. 1983. (Western Ser.). 192p. 12.95 o.p. (*0-8027-4022-7*) Walker & Co.

Wiggs, Susan. The You I Never Knew. l.t. ed. 2001. 667p. 29.95 (*0-7862-3448-2*) Thorndike Pr.

—The You I Never Knew. 2001. 528p. reprint ed. mass mkt. 6.99 (*0-446-60872-6*) Warner Bks., Inc.

Williamson, Penelope. Heart of the West. 1996. 720p. mass mkt. 6.50 o.s.i (*0-440-22211-7*) Dell Publishing.

—Heart of the West. 1995. 591p. 22.50 o.p. (*0-671-50822-9*, Simon & Schuster) Simon & Schuster.

—Heart of the West, Set. abr. ed. 1995. audio 22.00 (*0-671-52458-5*, 592994, Simon & Schuster Audioworks) Simon & Schuster Audio.

Settings

—Heart of the West. 1998. 4.98 o.p. (*0-7651-0776-7*) Smithmark Pubs., Inc.
—The Outsider. 1996. 464p. 23.00 o.p. (*0-684-80759-9*, Simon & Schuster) Simon & Schuster.
—The Outsider. 1997. 560p. mass mkt. 6.50 (*0-446-60477-1*) Warner Bks., Inc.
Windle, Jeanette. Mystery at Death Canyon. 2002. (Parker Twins Ser.: No. 4). 176p. (J). (gr. 3-8). pap. 5.99 (*0-8254-4148-X*) Kregel Pubns.
—Mystery at Death Canyon. 1996. (Twin Pursuits Ser.: No. 1). 128p. pap. 4.99 o.p. (*0-88070-904-9*, Multnomah Bks.) Multnomah Pubs., Inc.
Wings, Mary. Divine Victim. 256p. 1994. pap. 10.95 o.p. (*0-452-27210-6*, Plume); 1993. 20.00 o.p. (*0-525-93626-2*, Dutton) Dutton/Plume.
Wolfe, Swain. The Lake Dreams the Sky: A Love Story. 1999. 352p. pap. 13.00 o.s.i (*0-06-092993-6*, Perennial); 1998. 320p. 23.00 o.s.i (*0-06-017412-9*, HarperCollins) HarperTrade.
Zochert, Donald. Another Weeping Woman. l.t. ed. 1983. lib. bdg. 6.95 o.p. (*0-89340-602-3*, 700) BBC Audiobooks America.
—Another Weeping Woman. 1980. 276p. o.p. (*0-03-046681-4*) Holt, Henry & Co.

### MONTE CARLO—FICTION

Bass, Jules. Headhunters. 2001. mass mkt. 6.99 (*0-425-18006-9*); 336p. mass mkt. 6.99 (*0-515-13133-4*, Jove) Berkley Publishing Group.
Zweig, Stefan. Twenty-Four Hours in the Life of a Woman. 2003. 112p. pap. 12.00 (*1-901285-48-0*) Pushkin Pr., Ltd. GBR. *Dist:* Consortium Bk. Sales & Distribution.

### MONTEREY (CALIF.)—FICTION

Abbott, Keith. Gush: A Comic Novel about Unemployment in California. 1975. 140p. 29.95 (*0-912652-16-0*); pap. 12.95 (*0-912652-17-9*); 49.95 (*0-912652-18-7*) Blue Wind Pr.
Brand, Max, contrib. by. In the Hills of Monterey. (*0-7540-3667-7*) BBC Audiobooks America.
Chamberlain, Diane. Cypress Point. 2003. 416p. mass mkt. (*1-55166-647-2*, Mira Bks.) Harlequin Enterprises, Ltd.
Coates, Lawrence. The Master of Monterey. 2003. (Western Literature Ser.). 288p. pap. 20.00 (*0-87417-529-1*) Univ. of Nevada Pr.
Diakosavvas, Dimitris. Implementation of the Uruguay Round Agreement on Agriculture in OECD Countries: An Evaluation of its Implementation in OECD Countries. 2001. (Agriculture & Food Ser.). 180p. pap. 40.00 (*92-64-18626-3*) Organization for Economic Cooperation & Development FRA. *Dist:* Organization for Economic Cooperation and Development.
DiGirolamo, Vincent. Whispers under the Wharf. 1990. 144p. (J). pap. 8.95 o.p. (*0-931832-52-7*) Fithian Pr.
Gilligan, Roy. Chinese Restaurants Never Serve Breakfast. 1988. 163p. (Orig.). reprint ed. 29.00 o.p. (*0-8095-4203-X*, 19624135) Millefleurs.
—Chinese Restaurants Never Serve Breakfast: Murder in Carmel. 1986. (Pat Riordan Mystery Ser.). 180p. reprint ed. pap. 8.95 (*0-9626136-2-2*) Brendan Bks.
—Happiness Is Often Deadly. 1992. (Pat Riordan Mystery Ser.). pap. 8.95 (*0-9626136-3-0*) Brendan Bks.
—Happiness Is Often Deadly. 1992. (Pat Riordan Mystery Ser.). 180p. reprint ed. lib. bdg. 24.00 o.p. (*0-8095-4211-0*) Millefleurs.
—Live Oaks Also Die. 1990. (Pat Riordan Mystery Ser.). 184p. (Orig.). pap. 8.95 (*0-9626136-0-6*) Brendan Bks.
—Live Oaks Also Die. 1991. (Pat Riordan Mystery Ser.). 188p. (Orig.). (C). reprint ed. pap. text 26.00 o.p. (*0-8095-4209-9*) Millefleurs.
—Playing God . . . & Other Games. 1993. (Pat Riordan Mystery Ser.). 180p. (Orig.). pap. 8.95 (*0-9626136-4-9*) Brendan Bks.
—Poets Never Kill. 1991. (Pat Riordan Mystery Ser.). 200p. pap. 8.95 (*0-9626136-1-4*) Brendan Bks.
—Poets Never Kill. 1991. (Pat Riordan Mystery Ser.). 180p. (C). reprint ed. lib. bdg. 26.00 o.p. (*0-8095-4210-2*) Millefleurs.
Gould, Judith. Time to Say Goodbye. 2000. 291p. 23.95 (*0-525-94548-2*, Dutton) Dutton/Plume.
—Time to Say Goodbye. l.t. ed. 2000. (Wheeler Romance Ser.). 381p. 26.95 (*1-56895-144-2*, Wheeler Publishing, Inc.) Gale Group.
—Time to Say Goodbye. 2001. 416p. reprint ed. mass mkt. 7.50 (*0-451-20407-7*, Signet Bks.) NAL.
Michaels, Fern. Vegas Rich. 2001. 54p. mass mkt. 7.50 (*0-8217-7206-6*) Kensington Publishing Corp.
Roberts, Nora. Daring to Dream. 1996. 384p. mass mkt. 7.99 (*0-515-11920-2*, Jove) Berkley Publishing Group.
—Daring to Dream. abr. ed. (Dream Ser.). 1997. audio 7.99 o.p. (*1-56740-204-6*, 637, Paperback Nova Audio Bks.); 1996. audio 73.25 o.p. (*1-56100-813-3*, 852, Unabridged Library Editions); 1996. audio 23.95 o.p. (*1-56100-738-2*, 81, Bookcassette) Brilliance Audio.
—Daring to Dream. 1998. 384p. 25.00 (*0-7278-5310-4*) Severn Hse. Pubs., Ltd.
—Daring to Dream. l.t. ed. 1997. (Romance Ser.). 528p. lib. bdg. 27.95 (*0-7862-0894-5*) Thorndike Pr.
—Finding the Dream. 1997. 352p. mass mkt. 7.99 (*0-515-12087-1*, Jove) Berkley Publishing Group.
—Finding the Dream. abr. ed. (Dream Ser.). 1998. audio 7.99 o.p. (*1-56740-205-4*, 1303, Paperback Nova Audio Bks.); 1997. audio 16.95 o.p. (*1-56100-929-6*, 469, Nova Audio Bks.); 1997. audio 73.25 o.p. (*1-56100-815-X*, 835, Unabridged Library Editions); 1997. audio 23.95 o.p. (*1-56100-740-4*, 108, Bookcassette) Brilliance Audio.
—Finding the Dream. 1999. 368p. 26.00 (*0-7278-2295-0*) Severn Hse. Pubs., Ltd.
—Finding the Dream. l.t. ed. 1998. (Romance Ser.). 525p. 28.95 (*0-7862-1130-X*) Thorndike Pr.
Scott, Robin. Death by Degrees. 1995. 224p. 20.95 o.p. (*0-312-13462-2*, Saint Martin's Minotaur) St. Martin's Pr.
Steinbeck, John. Cannery Row. 1982. mass mkt. 2.50 o.s.i (*0-553-23416-1*); 128p. mass mkt. 2.75 o.s.i (*0-553-26603-9*); 128p. mass mkt. 2.95 o.s.i (*0-553-27823-1*, Bantam Classics) Bantam Bks.
—Cannery Row. l.t. ed. 2001. 196p. 28.95 (*0-7838-9520-8*, Macmillan Reference USA) Gale Group.
—Cannery Row. l.t. ed. 1989. (Mainstream Ser.). 319p. lib. bdg. 15.95 o.p. (*1-85089-109-5*) ISIS Large Print Bks. GBR. *Dist:* Transaction Pubs.
—Cannery Row. (Steinbeck's Centennial Ser.). 2002. 192p. pap. 12.00 (*0-14-200068-X*); 1963. pap. 1.95 o.p. (*0-670-00131-7*) Penguin Group (USA) Inc.
—Cannery Row. 1992. 12.00 (*0-606-08948-9*) Turtleback Bks.
—Cannery Row. (Great Books of the 20th Century Ser.). 1994. 224p. 11.00 (*0-14-018737-5*, Penguin Classics); 1993. 208p. 8.00 (*0-14-017738-8*); 1945. 20p. 18.95 o.p. (*0-670-20281-9*, Penguin Classics); 1999. 16.95 incl. audio (*0-14-086199-8*, Penguin AudioBooks) Viking Penguin.
—Sweet Thursday. l.t. ed. 2001. (G. K. Hall Perennial Bestsellers Ser. ). 312p. 28.95 (*0-7838-9163-6*) Thorndike Pr.
—Sweet Thursday. (Great Books of the 20th Century Ser.). 1996. 288p. 13.00 (*0-14-018750-2*, Penguin Classics); 1979. 288p. pap. 7.00 o.p. (*0-14-004889-8*, Penguin Bks.); 1954. 3.75 o.p. (*0-670-68686-7*) Viking Penguin.
—To a God Unknown. unabr. collector's ed. 1992. audio 48.00 (*0-7366-2124-5*, 2926) Books on Tape, Inc.
—To a God Unknown. l.t. ed. 1974. (Ulverscroft Large Print Ser.). 29.99 o.p. (*0-85456-304-0*, Ulverscroft) Thorpe, F. A. Pubs. GBR. *Dist:* Ulverscroft Large Print Bks., Ltd., Ulverscroft Large Print Canada, Ltd.
—To a God Unknown. (Great Books of the 20th Century Ser.). 1995. 288p. 12.95 (*0-14-018751-0*, Penguin Classics); 1976. 272p. pap. 6.95 o.p. (*0-14-004233-4*, Penguin Bks.) Viking Penguin.
—Tortilla Flat. mass mkt. 0.25 o.p. (*0-451-00599-6*); mass mkt. 0.25 o.p. (*0-451-00816-2*); mass mkt. 0.25 o.p. (*0-451-01380-8*); mass mkt. 0.35 o.p. (*0-451-01737-4*); mass mkt. 0.60 o.p. (*0-451-02189-4*) NAL. (Signet Bks.).
—Tortilla Flat. (Fiction Ser.). 1977. 224p. pap. 8.00 (*0-14-004240-7*, Penguin Bks.); 1963. pap. 2.25 o.p. (*0-670-00134-1*) Penguin Group (USA) Inc.
—Tortilla Flat, unabr. ed. 1999. audio 44.00 (*0-7887-2928-4*, 95715E7) Recorded Bks., LLC.
—Tortilla Flat. l.t. ed. 1994. 226p. reprint ed. lib. bdg. 21.95 (*0-8161-5901-7*) Thorndike Pr.
—Tortilla Flat. 1986. 13.00 (*0-606-00987-6*) Turtleback Bks.
—Tortilla Flat. 1999. audio; 1997. 192p. 10.00 (*0-14-018740-5*, Penguin Classics); 1935. 16.95 o.s.i (*0-670-72109-3*); 1999. 6p. audio 29.95 (*0-14-086894-1*) Viking Penguin.
Tyler, Lee. The Case of the Missing Links. 1999. 190p. pap. 10.95 (*1-56474-302-0*) Fithian Pr.

### MONTREAL (QUEBEC)—FICTION

Boraks-Nemetz, Lillian. The Old Brown Suitcase: A Teenager's Story of War & Peace. 1994. 210p. (Orig.). (YA). (gr. 8-12). pap. 9.50 (*0-914539-10-8*) Ben-Simon Pubns.
D'Alfonso, Antonio. Fabrizio's Passion. No. 12. 2nd ed. 2000. (Picas Ser.: No. 12). 213p. pap. 10.00 (*1-55071-082-6*); Vol. 1. 1995. (Prose Ser.: No. 34). 214p. pap. 15.00 o.p. (*1-55071-023-0*) Guernica Editions, Inc.
Dandurand, Anne. The Cracks. 1992. pap. 11.95 (*0-920544-93-2*) Mercury Bks. CAN. *Dist:* LPC/InBook.
Druick, Don. Recipe for Murder. 2000. audio (*1-881137-65-1*) Canadian Broadcasting Corp./Societe Radio-Canada.
Epstein, Carole. Perilous Friends. 1996. (Barbara Simons Mystery Ser.). 224p. 21.95 (*0-8027-3287-9*) Walker & Co.
—Perilous Relations: A Barbara Simons Mystery. 1997. (Barbara Simons Mystery Ser.). 276p. 22.95 (*0-8027-3309-3*) Walker & Co.
Farrow, John. City of Ice: A Novel. 1999. 403p. 25.95 o.s.i (*0-375-50140-1*) Random Hse., Inc.
—Ice Lake: A Novel. 2001. 368p. pap. 19.00 (*0-8129-9264-4*) Random House Adult Trade Publishing Group.
—Ice Lake: A Novel. 2001. E-Book 19.95 (*1-58836-016-4*) Random Hse., Inc.
Goliger, Gabriella. Song of Ascent. 2001. 177p. pap. (*1-55192-374-2*) Raincoast Bk. Distribution.
Gostick, Adrian R. Eddy & the Habs. 1994. vii, 157p. (J). (gr. 3-7). pap. o.p. (*0-87579-832-2*) Deseret Bk. Co.
Henderson, Keith. The Restoration: The Referendum Years. 1994. 200p. reprint ed. pap. 12.95 (*0-919688-10-1*) DC Bks. CAN. *Dist:* Literary Pr. Group of Canada.
Hood, Hugh. Around the Mountain. 1994. 160p. pap. (*0-88984-141-1*) Porcupine's Quill, Inc.
Kalman, Judith. The County of Birches. 192p. 2000. pap. 11.95 (*0-312-26724-X*, Saint Martin's Griffin); 1999. 21.95 (*0-312-20886-3*) St. Martin's Pr.
Langan, F. F. The Stringer: A Novel. 2001. 248p. pap. 18.00 (*0-88962-743-6*) Mosaic Pr.
Moore, Jeffrey. Prisoner in a Red-Rose Chain. 2002. 385p. 24.95 o.s.i (*0-399-14864-7*, Putnam & Grosset) Penguin Group (USA) Inc.
Packer, Miriam. Take Me to Coney Island, No. 25. 1993. (Prose Ser.: No. 25). 180p. pap. 15.00 (*0-920717-92-6*) Guernica Editions, Inc.
Patterson, Kevin. Country of Cold: Stories. 2004. 272p. pap. 13.00 (*0-385-72217-6*, Anchor) Knopf Publishing Group.
—Country of Cold: Stories of Sex & Violence. 2003. 272p. 23.95 (*0-385-50627-9*) Doubleday Publishing.
Reichs, Kathy. Deadly Decisions. 2000. 336p. 25.00 (*0-684-85971-8*); E-Book 25.00 (*0-7432-1077-8*); 464p. 25.00 o.s.i (*0-7432-0429-8*) Simon & Schuster. (Scribner).
—Deadly Decisions. abr. ed. 2000. audio 25.00 (*0-7435-0054-7*, Simon & Schuster Audioworks) Simon & Schuster Audio.
—Death du Jour. unabr. ed. 2002. audio compact disk 110.95; 2000. audio 96.95 (*0-7927-2346-5*, CSL235, Chivers Sound Library) BBC Audiobooks America.
—Death du Jour. unabr. ed. 2000. 12p. audio compact disk 110.95 (*0-7540-5330-X*, CCD 021) Chivers Audio Bks. GBR. *Dist:* BBC Audiobooks America.
—Death du Jour. 1999. 384p. mass mkt. 7.99 (*0-671-03472-3*, Pocket); 1999. E-Book 25.00 (*0-7432-0080-2*, Scribner); 1999. 384p. 25.00 (*0-684-84118-5*, Scribner); 1999. 384p. 25.00 (*0-684-86906-3*, Scribner); 2000. (Illus.). 480p. reprint ed. mass mkt. 7.99 (*0-671-01137-5*, Pocket) Simon & Schuster.
—Death du Jour, Set. abr. ed. 1999. audio 24.00 (*0-671-04370-6*, 599126, Simon & Schuster Audioworks) Simon & Schuster Audio.
—Death du Jour. l.t. ed. (Thorndike/G. K. Hall Paperback Bestsellers Ser.). 632p. 2000. (FRE.). pap. 27.95 (*0-7862-1997-1*); 1999. 30.95 (*0-7862-1996-3*) Thorndike Pr.
—Death du Jour. abr. ed. 1999. audio 24.35 (*1-85686-522-3*) Ulverscroft Audio (U.S.A.).
—Deja Dead. 2001. E-Book 9.99 (*1-58945-168-6*) Adobe Systems, Inc.
—Deja Dead. 1998. (Illus.). 411p. (J). o.p. (*0-434-00427-8*) Random Hse. of Canada, Ltd. CAN. *Dist:* Random Hse., Inc.
—Deja Dead, unabr. ed. 1998. audio 96.00 (*0-7887-1750-2*, 95228E7) Recorded Bks., LLC.
—Deja Dead. 2000. E-Book 9.99 (*0-684-83906-7*, Scribner); 1998. (Illus.). 560p. mass mkt. 7.99 (*0-671-01136-7*, Pocket); 1997. 282.00 (*0-684-00611-1*, Scribner); 1997. (Illus.). 416p. 24.00 (*0-684-84117-7*, Scribner) Simon & Schuster.
—Deja Dead. abr. ed. 1997. 5p. audio 24.00 (*0-671-57706-9*, 495419, Simon & Schuster Audioworks) Simon & Schuster Audio.
—Deja Dead. l.t. ed. 1998. (Basic Ser.). 664p. 30.95 (*0-7862-1265-9*) Thorndike Pr.
—Fatal Voyage. 2001. 368p. 25.00 (*0-684-85972-6*); E-Book (*0-7432-1822-1*); 368p. 25.00 o.s.i (*0-7432-2281-4*); 528p. 25.00 (*0-7432-1662-8*) Simon & Schuster. (Scribner).
—Fatal Voyage. abr. ed. 2001. audio 26.00 (*0-7435-0462-3*); audio compact disk 30.00 (*0-7435-0463-1*) Simon & Schuster Audio. (Simon & Schuster Audioworks).
Richler, Mordecai. The Apprenticeship of Duddy Kravitz. 2000. 320p. 24.95 (*0-8488-2769-4*) Amereon, Ltd.
—The Apprenticeship of Duddy Kravitz. Young, George, ed. 1974. (Illus.). 288p. mass mkt. 1.50 o.p. (*0-345-24154-1*) Ballantine Bks.
—The Apprenticeship of Duddy Kravitz. 1981. 304p. pap. 2.95 o.p. (*0-553-14584-3*) Bantam Bks.
—The Apprenticeship of Duddy Kravitz. 1989. (New Canadian Library). 328p. mass mkt. 6.95 (*0-7710-9972-X*) McClelland & Stewart/Tundra Bks.
—The Apprenticeship of Duddy Kravitz. 1991. 384p. pap. 9.95 o.p. (*0-14-015296-2*, Penguin Bks.) Penguin Group (USA) Inc.
—The Apprenticeship of Duddy Kravitz. 1999. 384p. pap. 14.00 (*0-671-02847-2*, Pocket) Simon & Schuster.
—Barney's Version. 1999. 368p. pap. 14.00 (*0-671-02846-4*, Washington Square Pr.) Simon & Schuster.
—Joshua Then & Now. 1997. 384p. mass mkt. 7.95 (*0-7710-9864-2*) McClelland & Stewart/Tundra Bks.
—Joshua Then & Now. 1991. 448p. pap. 9.95 o.p. (*0-14-015280-6*, Penguin Bks.) Penguin Group (USA) Inc.
Ruryk, Jean. Chicken Little Was Right. 1994. 208p. 18.95 o.p. (*0-312-10952-0*, Saint Martin's Minotaur) St. Martin's Pr.
—Next Week Will Be Better. 1998. (Cat Wilde Mystery Ser.). 256p. 21.95 (*0-312-18144-2*, Saint Martin's Minotaur) St. Martin's Pr.
—Next Week Will Be Better: A Cat Wilde Mystery. 1999. (WWL Mystery Ser.: Vol. 333). 256p. per. (*0-373-26333-3*, Harlequin Bks.) Harlequin Enterprises, Ltd.
—Whatever Happened to Jennifer Steele? A Cat Wilde Mystery. 1996. 208p. 20.95 (*0-312-14067-3*, Saint Martin's Minotaur) St. Martin's Pr.
Speare, Elizabeth George. Calico Captive. 1973. 288p. (gr. 4-7). pap. text 4.99 o.s.i (*0-440-41156-4*, Yearling) Random Hse. Children's Bks.
Tremblay, Michel. Hosanna. Van Burek, John & Glassco, Bill, trs. rev. ed. 1991. 126p. pap. 10.95 (*0-88922-296-7*) Talonbooks, Ltd. CAN. *Dist:* General Distribution Services, Inc.
Tucker, Ernest. Underworld Dwellers. 1994. 160p. 15.95 o.p. (*0-944957-22-6*) Rivercross Publishing, Inc.

### MOONLIGHT BAY (CALIF.: IMAGINARY PLACE)—FICTION

Koontz, Dean. Fear Nothing. 1998. mass mkt. 7.99 (*0-553-84021-5*); 448p. mass mkt. 7.99 (*0-553-57975-4*); 400p. 26.95 o.s.i (*0-553-10664-3*) Bantam Bks.
—Fear Nothing. l.t. ed. 1998. (Core Ser.). 577p. 29.95 o.p. (*0-7838-8358-7*, Macmillan Reference USA) Gale Group.
—Fear Nothing. unabr. ed. 1998. (Christopher Snow Stories Ser.). 12p. audio 39.95 (*0-553-47900-8*, 105583, RH Audio) Random Hse. Audio Publishing Group.
—Fear Nothing. 1998. 14.04 (*0-606-16374-3*) Turtleback Bks.
—Seize the Night. 1999. 480p. mass mkt. 7.99 (*0-553-58019-1*); 480p. mass mkt. 7.99 o.s.i (*0-553-58229-1*); mass mkt. 7.99 (*0-553-84020-7*) Bantam Bks.
—Seize the Night, unabr. ed. 1999. audio 39.95 Highsmith Inc.
—Seize the Night. unabr. ed. 1998. (Christopher Snow Stories Ser.). audio 39.95 (*0-553-47901-6*, 116030, RH Audio) Random Hse. Audio Publishing Group.
—Seize the Night. l.t. ed. (Paperback Bestsellers Ser.). 2000. 617p. pap. 27.95 (*0-7838-8529-6*); 1999. 605p. 30.95 (*0-7838-8528-8*) Thorndike Pr.
—Seize the Night. l.t. ed. 2000. (Charnwood Large Print Ser.). 616p. (*0-7089-9144-0*, Ulverscroft) Thorpe, F. A. Pubs. GBR. *Dist:* Ulverscroft Large Print Bks., Ltd., Ulverscroft Large Print Canada, Ltd.
—Seize the Night. 1999. 14.04 (*0-606-18001-X*) Turtleback Bks.

### MOROCCO—FICTION

Anshaw, Carol. Seven Moves. 1996. 220p. tchr. ed. 21.95 o.p. (*0-395-69131-1*) Houghton Mifflin Co.
—Seven Moves. 1997. 240p. pap. 11.00 (*0-395-87756-3*, Mariner Bks.) Houghton Mifflin Co. Trade & Reference Div.
—Seven Moves. 1998. 242p. pap. o.s.i (*1-86049-436-6*) Virago Pr., Ltd. GBR. *Dist:* Little Brown & Co.
Ardizzone, Tony. Larabi's Ox: Stories of Morocco. 1992. (Illus.). 250p. pap. 13.00 (*0-915943-72-7*) Milkweed Editions.
Ben Jelloun, Tahar. This Blinding Absence of Light: A Novel. Coverdale, Linda, tr. from FRE. 2002. 196p. 22.95 (*1-56584-723-7*) New Pr., The.
Binebine, Mahi. Welcome to Paradise. 2002. 192p. 22.00 (*1-86207-517-4*) Granta.
Boulaich, Abdeslam, et al. Five Eyes. Bowles, Paul, ed. 1979. 125p. 14.00 o.p. (*0-87685-409-9*); pap. 5.00 o.p. (*0-87685-408-0*) Godine, David R. Pub. (Black Sparrow Pr.).
Bowles, Paul. Points in Time. 1999. 96p. o.p. (*0-88001-044-4*); pap. o.p. (*0-88001-117-3*) HarperTrade. (Ecco).

—The Sheltering Sky. 2000. 320p. 25.00 (*0-06-019916-4*); 1978. pap. 8.95 o.p. (*0-912946-43-1*); 2nd ed. 1998. 320p. reprint ed. pap. 14.00 (*0-88001-582-9*) HarperTrade. (Ecco).
—The Sheltering Sky. 1990. (Vintage International Ser.). pap. 13.00 o.p. (*0-679-72979-8*, Vintage) Knopf Publishing Group.
—Sheltering Sky Let It Come down the Spiders House. 2002. 938p. 35.00 (*1-931082-19-7*) Library of America, The.
Brackenbury, Rosalind. The House in Morocco. 2003. 286p. 19.95 (*1-902881-76-1*) Toby Pr.
Chraibi, Driss. Inspector Ali. McGlashlan, Lara, tr. from FRE. 1994. 143p. 26.00 (*0-89410-746-1*); pap. 12.95 (*0-89410-747-X*) Rienner, Lynne Pubs., Inc. (Three Continents).
Dale, Virginia. Never Marry in Morocco: A Novel. 1996. 256p. (Orig.). pap. 12.95 (*1-56474-174-5*) Fithian Pr.
Easterman, Daniel. Maroc. 2002. 576p. (*0-00-225862-5*); pap. (*0-00-225864-1*) HarperCollins Pubs.
Gabay, Taity. Bonjour Bijoux. 1992. 350p. pap. text (*0-9632052-0-X*) Cliffrose Pubns.
Gilman, Dorothy. Mrs. Pollifax & the Whirling Dervish. 1991. 224p. mass mkt. 6.99 (*0-449-14760-6*, Fawcett) Ballantine Bks.
—Mrs. Pollifax & the Whirling Dervish. l.t. ed. 1991. (General Ser.). 304p. 21.95 o.p. (*0-8161-5119-9*, Macmillan Reference USA) Gale Group.
—Mrs. Pollifax & the Whirling Dervish. 1991. audio 14.99 o.s.i (*0-553-45275-4*, RH Audio) Random Hse. Audio Publishing Group.
Graham, Winston. Tremor. 2002. 320p. mass mkt. 8.95 (*0-330-34387-4*) Pan Bks. Ltd. GBR. *Dist:* Trafalgar Square.
—Tremor. 1996. 256p. 22.95 o.p. (*0-312-14056-8*) St. Martin's Pr.
Henry, Marguerite. The Sultan's Gift. 1988. (King of the Wind Ser.). (Illus.). 24p. (J). (ps-3). pap. 1.95 o.p. (*0-02-688803-3*) Checkerboard Pr., Inc.
Jackson, Loretta & Britton, Vickie. Nightmare in Morocco. l.t. ed. 2002. (Candlelights Ser.). 234p. 23.95 (*0-7862-4084-9*) Thorndike Pr.
Jelloun, Tahar B. With Downcast Eyes: A Novel. Neugroschel, Joachim, tr. from FRE. 1993. 249p. 19.95 o.p. (*0-316-46059-1*) Little Brown & Co.
Judd, Bob. Spin. 1994. 277p. mass mkt. 4.99 o.p. (*0-425-14179-9*) Berkley Publishing Group.
Kachtick, Keith. Hungry Ghost. 2004. pap. (*0-06-052391-3*, Perennial) HarperTrade.
Layachi, Larbi. A Life Full of Holes. 1982. 128p. pap. 3.50 o.s.i (*0-394-17946-3*, B481) Grove/Atlantic, Inc.
McHugh, Maureen F. Nekropolis. 272p. 2002. pap. 14.95 (*0-380-79123-4*); 2001. 25.00 (*0-380-97457-6*) Morrow/Avon. (Eos).
Mrabet, Mohammed. Big Mirror. Bowles, Paul, tr. 1990. 80p. pap. 10.95 (*0-7206-0730-2*) Owen, Peter Ltd. GBR. *Dist:* Dufour Editions, Inc.
—The Big Mirror. Bowles, Paul, tr. 1977. 90p. 10.00 o.p. (*0-87685-368-8*); pap. 3.50 o.p. (*0-87685-367-X*) Godine, David R. Pub. (Black Sparrow Pr.).
—The Boy Who Set the Fire & Other Stories. Bowles, Paul, tr. 1989. 144p. reprint ed. pap. 8.95 o.p. (*0-87286-230-5*) City Lights Bks.
—The Lemon. Bowles, Paul, tr. 1986. 192p. reprint ed. pap. 8.95 (*0-87286-181-3*) City Lights Bks.
—Love with a Few Hairs. Bowles, Paul, tr. from ARA. 1986. 176p. reprint ed. pap. 8.95 (*0-87286-192-9*) City Lights Bks.
—Marriage with Papers. Bowles, Paul, tr. 1986. 88p. (Orig.). pap. 6.00 (*0-939180-32-4*); 35.00 (*0-939180-29-4*) Tombouctou Bks.
Mutabaruka, Mustafa. Seed. 2002. (Illus.). 275p. pap. 14.95 (*1-888451-31-9*) Akashic Bks.
Myers, Walter Dean. Duel in the Desert. 1986. (Puffin Novels-Arrow Adventure Ser.). 96p. (J). (gr. 5-9). pap. 3.95 o.p. (*0-14-032101-2*, Penguin Bks.) Viking Penguin.
Peets, Leonora. Women of Marrakesh. Taagepera, Rein, tr. from EST. 1988. 200p. text 38.95 (*0-8223-0812-6*) Duke Univ. Pr.
Ruy-Sanchez, Alberto M. Mogador. Schafer, Mark, tr. from SPA. 1992. 124p. pap. 10.95 (*0-87286-271-2*) City Lights Bks.
Setton, Ruth Knafo. Road to Fez: A Novel. 2001. 240p. text 23.00 (*1-58243-082-9*, Counterpoint Pr.) Basic Bks.
Siler, Jenny. Flashback. 2004. 272p. 24.00 (*0-8050-7211-X*) Holt, Henry & Co.
Taylor, Debbie. The Fourth Queen. 2003. 352p. 23.95 (*1-4000-4925-3*) Crown Publishing Group.

**MOSCOW (RUSSIA)—FICTION**

Akunin, Boris. The Winter Queen. 2004. 264p. pap. 12.95 (*0-8129-6877-8*, Random Hse. Trade Paperbacks) Random House Adult Trade Publishing Group.
—The Winter Queen. Bromfield, Andrew, tr. from RUS. 2003. 256p. 19.95 (*1-4000-6049-4*) Random Hse., Inc.
Buckley, William F., Jr. Mongoose R. I. P. A Blackford Oakes Novel. 1998. (Blackford Oakes Novel Ser.). 376p. reprint ed. pap. 12.95 (*1-888952-72-5*) Cumberland Hse. Publishing.
—Mongoose R. I. P. A Blackford Oakes Novel. 1989. 384p. reprint ed. mass mkt. 4.50 o.s.i (*0-440-20231-0*) Dell Publishing.
—Mongoose R. I. P. A Blackford Oakes Novel. 1993. 4.99 o.p. (*0-517-10701-5*) Random Hse. Value Publishing.
Ellis, Scott. The Borzoi Control. 1988. 320p. pap. 3.95 o.p. (*0-8125-0239-6*, Tor Bks.) Doherty, Tom Assocs., LLC.
—The Borzoi Control. 1986. 320p. 16.95 o.p. (*0-312-09309-8*) St. Martin's Pr.
Forsyth, Frederick. Icon. 1997. 576p. mass mkt. (*0-552-13991-2*, Corgi); 1997. 576p. mass mkt. 7.99 (*0-553-57460-4*); 1997. 560p. mass mkt. 7.99 (*0-553-84012-6*); 1996. 400p. 32.95 o.p. (*0-593-02801-5*) Bantam Bks.
—Icon. l.t. ed. (Paperback Bestsellers Ser.). 765p. 1998. pap. 27.95 (*0-7838-1961-7*); 1996. 29.95 (*0-7838-1960-9*) Thorndike Pr.
Francis, Dick. Trial Run. l.t. ed. 1994. 19.95 o.p. (*0-7927-2170-5*); 1994. pap. 18.95 o.p. (*0-7927-2169-1*); 1993. 54.95 incl. audio (*0-7451-5957-5*) BBC Audiobooks America.
—Trial Run. 1987. mass mkt. 5.95 o.s.i (*0-449-21273-4*, Fawcett) Ballantine Bks.
—Trial Run. 2001. 272p. mass mkt. 6.99 (*0-515-12997-6*, Jove) Berkley Publishing Group.
—Trial Run. unabr. ed. 1991. audio 48.00 (*0-7366-2029-X*, 2843) Books on Tape, Inc.
—Trial Run. 1983. mass mkt. 3.50 o.s.i (*0-671-50732-X*); mass mkt. 2.95 (*0-671-47022-1*) Simon & Schuster. (Pocket).
—Trial Run. l.t. ed. 1980. 404p. 12.00 o.p. (*0-7089-0456-4*, Ulverscroft) Thorpe, F. A. Pubs. GBR. *Dist:* Ulverscroft Large Print Bks., Ltd.
Freemantle, Brian. The Button Man. 1993. 400p. 22.95 o.p. (*0-312-08716-0*) St. Martin's Pr.
—Kings of Many Castles. E-Book 24.95 (*0-312-70931-5*) St. Martin's Pr.
—Kings of Many Castles: A Charlie Muffin Thriller. 2002. 352p. 24.95 (*0-312-30412-9*) St. Martin's Pr.
Haig, Brian. The Kingmaker. l.t. ed. 2003. lib. bdg. 29.95 (*1-58547-312-X*, Platinum) Ctr. Point Large Print.
—The Kingmaker. 2003. 496p. mass mkt. 6.99 (*0-446-61290-1*); 400p. 22.95 (*0-446-53055-7*) Warner Bks., Inc.
Holland, William E. Moscow Twilight. Grosse, Bill, ed. 1993. 352p. mass mkt. 5.50 (*0-671-74644-8*, Pocket); 1992. 320p. 20.00 (*0-671-74643-X*, Atria) Simon & Schuster.
James, Donald. Monstrum. 1999. mass mkt. (*0-449-00431-7*, Fawcett); mass mkt. 6.99 o.s.i (*0-8041-1891-4*, Ivy Bks.) Ballantine Bks.
—Monstrum. 1999. (SPA.). 480p. (*84-08-02903-7*) GeoPlaneta, Editorial, S. A.
Kaminsky, Stuart M. Black Knight in Red Square. 1989. (Inspector Porfiry Rostnikov Mystery Ser.). 224p. mass mkt. 5.99 o.s.i (*0-8041-0405-0*, Ivy Bks.) Ballantine Bks.
—Black Knight in Red Square. 1984. (Inspector Porfiry Rostnikov Mystery Ser.). 224p. 2.95 o.s.i (*0-441-06628-3*, Diamond Bks.) Berkley Publishing Group.
—Black Knight in Red Square. unabr. ed. 1993. (Inspector Porfiry Rostnikov Mystery Ser.: Vol. 2). audio 51.00 (*1-55690-943-8*, 93439E7) Recorded Bks., LLC.
—Blood & Rubles. 1996. (Inspector Porfiry Rostnikov Mystery Ser.). 261p. mass mkt. 5.99 o.s.i (*0-8041-1288-6*, Ivy Bks.); 272p. 21.00 o.s.i (*0-449-90949-2*, Fawcett) Ballantine Bks.
—Blood & Rubles. unabr. ed. 1997. audio 44.95 (*0-7861-1119-4*, 1880) Blackstone Audio Bks., Inc.
—Blood & Rubles. unabr. ed. 1997. audio 48.00 (*0-7366-3704-4*, 4388) Books on Tape, Inc.
—Blood & Rubles. l.t. ed. 1996. (Inspector Porfiry Rostnikov Mystery Ser.). 317p. 23.95 o.p. (*1-56895-329-1*, Wheeler Publishing, Inc.) Gale Group.
—Blood & Rubles. unabr. ed. 2000. (Inspector Porfiry Rostnikov Mystery Ser.). audio 60.00 (*0-7887-0511-3*, 94704E7) Recorded Bks., LLC.
—A Cold Red Sunrise. 1989. (Inspector Porfiry Rostnikov Mystery Ser.). mass mkt. 6.99 o.s.i (*0-8041-0428-X*, Ivy Bks.) Ballantine Bks.
—A Cold Red Sunrise. l.t. ed. 2000. 287p. lib. bdg. 27.95 (*1-58547-021-X*) Ctr. Point Large Print.
—A Cold Red Sunrise. 1988. (Inspector Porfiry Rostnikov Mystery Ser.). 224p. 16.95 o.s.i (*0-684-18905-4*, Macmillan Reference USA) Gale Group.
—A Cold Red Sunrise. unabr. ed. 1992. audio 49.00 (*1-55690-677-3*, 92330) Recorded Bks., LLC.
—Death of a Dissident. 1981. (Inspector Porfiry Rostnikov Mystery Ser.). 448p. 2.95 o.s.i (*0-441-14204-4*) Ace Bks.
—Death of a Dissident. 1989. (Inspector Porfiry Rostnikov Mystery Ser.). mass mkt. 5.50 o.s.i (*0-8041-0404-2*, Ivy Bks.) Ballantine Bks.
—Death of a Dissident. unabr. ed. 1993. (Inspector Porfiry Rostnikov Mystery Ser.: Vol. 1). audio 51.00 (*1-55690-898-9*, 93340E7) Recorded Bks., LLC.
—Death of a Russian Priest. (Inspector Porfiry Rostnikov Mystery Ser.). 1993. mass mkt. 5.99 o.s.i (*0-8041-0836-6*, Ivy Bks.); 1992. 256p. 18.00 o.s.i (*0-449-90724-4*, Fawcett) Ballantine Bks.
—Death of a Russian Priest. unabr. ed. 1995. (Inspector Porfiry Rostnikov Mystery Ser.: Vol. 8). audio 51.00 (*0-7887-0104-5*, 94345E7) Recorded Bks., LLC.
—The Dog Who Bit a Policeman. unabr. ed. 2000. audio 59.95 (*0-7927-2255-8*, CSL 144) Chivers Audio Bks. GBR. *Dist:* BBC Audiobooks America.
—The Dog Who Bit a Policeman. 1998. (Inspector Porfiry Rostnikov Mystery Ser.). 275p. (gr. 8 up). 22.00 (*0-89296-667-X*) Mysterious Pr.
—The Dog Who Bit a Policeman. unabr. ed. 2000. (Inspector Porfiry Rostnikov Mystery Ser.: Vol. 12). audio 70.00 (*0-7887-2483-5*, 95558E7) Recorded Bks., LLC.
—The Dog Who Bit a Policeman. l.t. ed. 1999. (Mystery Ser.). 455p. 27.95 (*0-7862-1767-7*) Thorndike Pr.
—Fall of a Cosmonaut. l.t. ed. 2001. (Large Print Bks.). 348p. pap. 23.95 (*1-58724-114-5*, Wheeler Publishing, Inc.) Gale Group.
—Fall of a Cosmonaut. 2000. 288p. 24.95 (*0-89296-668-8*); 288p. E-Book 14.95 (*0-446-92256-0*); 288p. E-Book 14.95 (*0-446-91365-0*); E-Book 14.95 (*0-446-93129-2*); 288p. E-Book 14.95 (*0-446-92860-7*); (Illus.). E-Book 14.95 (*0-446-96089-6*) Mysterious Pr.
—Fall of a Cosmonaut. 2000. 288p. E-Book 14.95 (*0-446-92369-9*) Warner Bks., Inc.
—A Fine Red Rain. 1988. (Inspector Porfiry Rostnikov Mystery Ser.). 208p. mass mkt. 4.99 o.s.i (*0-8041-0279-1*, Ivy Bks.) Ballantine Bks.
—A Fine Red Rain. 1987. (Inspector Porfiry Rostnikov Mystery Ser.). 211p. 14.95 o.p. (*0-684-18666-7*, Macmillan Reference USA) Gale Group.
—A Fine Red Rain. unabr. ed. 1994. (Inspector Porfiry Rostnikov Mystery Ser.: Vol. 4). audio 51.00 (*1-55690-982-9*, 94121E7) Recorded Bks., LLC.
—A Fine Red Rain. 2000. (Inspector Porfiry Rostnikov Mystery Ser.). 224p. pap. 14.95 (*0-7432-1161-8*, Scribner) Simon & Schuster.
—Hard Currency. 1995. (Inspector Porfiry Rostnikov Mystery Ser.). mass mkt. 5.99 o.s.i (*0-8041-0837-4*, Ivy Bks.); 247p. 20.00 o.s.i (*0-449-90725-2*, Fawcett) Ballantine Bks.
—Hard Currency. unabr. ed. 1995. 9p. audio 44.95 (*0-7861-0822-3*, 893333) Blackstone Audio Bks., Inc.
—Hard Currency. unabr. ed. 1995. (Inspector Porfiry Rostnikov Mystery Ser.: Vol. 9). audio 60.00 (*0-7887-0412-5*, 94604E7) Recorded Bks., LLC.
—The Man Who Walked Like a Bear. unabr. ed. 1994. (Inspector Porfiry Rostnikov Mystery Ser.: Vol. 6). audio 44.00 (*0-7887-0049-9*, 94248E7) Recorded Bks., LLC.
—The Man Who Walked Like a Bear: An Inspector Porfiry Rostnikov Novel. 1991. (Inspector Porfiry Rostnikov Mystery Ser.). mass mkt. 4.95 o.s.i (*0-8041-0693-2*, Ivy Bks.) Ballantine Bks.
—Murder on the Trans-Siberian Express. l.t. ed. 2002. (Basic Ser.). 423p. 28.95 (*0-7862-3814-3*) Gale Group.
—Murder on the Trans-Siberian Express. 2001. 288p. 24.95 (*0-89296-747-1*) Mysterious Pr.
—Red Chameleon. 1989. (Inspector Porfiry Rostnikov Mystery Ser.). 208p. mass mkt. 4.99 o.s.i (*0-8041-0465-4*, Ivy Bks.) Ballantine Bks.
—Red Chameleon. 1986. (Inspector Porfiry Rostnikov Mystery Ser.). 240p. 3.50 o.s.i (*0-441-71086-7*, Diamond Bks.) Berkley Publishing Group.
—Red Chameleon. unabr. ed. 1992. (Inspector Porfiry Rostnikov Mystery Ser.: Vol. 3). audio 51.00 (*1-55690-725-7*, 92107E7) Recorded Bks., LLC.
—Red Chameleon. 1985. (Inspector Porfiry Rostnikov Mystery Ser.). 224p. 13.95 o.s.i (*0-684-18424-9*, Scribner) Simon & Schuster.
—Rostnikov's Vacation. 1992. (Inspector Porfiry Rostnikov Mystery Ser.). reprint ed. mass mkt. 5.99 o.s.i (*0-8041-0694-0*, Ivy Bks.) Ballantine Bks.
—Rostnikov's Vacation. unabr. ed. 1993. audio 51.00 (*1-55690-840-7*, 93208E7) Recorded Bks., LLC.
—Rostnikov's Vacation. 1991. (Inspector Porfiry Rostnikov Mystery Ser.). 244p. 19.95 o.s.i (*0-684-19022-2*, Scribner) Simon & Schuster.
—Tarnished Icons. 1997. (Inspector Porfiry Rostnikov Mystery Ser.). 277p. mass mkt. 6.99 o.s.i (*0-8041-1289-4*, Ivy Bks.) Ballantine Bks.
—Tarnished Icons. unabr. ed. 1997. (Inspector Porfiry Rostnikov Mystery Ser.: Vol. 11). audio 70.00 (*0-7887-0930-5*, 95070E7) Recorded Bks., LLC.
Nadelson, Reggie. Red Hot Blues. 1998. Orig. Title: Red Mercury Blues. 272p. 22.95 (*0-312-18166-3*, Saint Martin's Minotaur) St. Martin's Pr.
Page, Myra. Moscow Yankee. 1995. (Radical Novel Reconsidered Ser.). 320p. pap. text 15.95 (*0-252-06499-2*) Univ. of Illinois Pr.
Pelevin, Victor. Homo Zapiens. 2002. 256p. 14.00 (*0-14-200181-3*); 24.95 o.s.i (*0-670-03066-X*, Viking) Viking Penguin.
Perry, A. J. Glas 27: Twelve Stories of Russia. 2001. 283p. 14.95 o.s.i (*1-56663-410-5*) Dee, Ivan R. Pub.
Podrug, Junius. Presumed Guilty. 1998. 576p. mass mkt. 6.99 (*0-8125-5507-4*); 1997. 384p. 24.95 (*0-312-86242-3*) Doherty, Tom Assocs., LLC. (Forge Bks.).
Rovin, Jeff. Starik. 1989. mass mkt. 3.95 o.s.i (*1-55817-270-X*, Pinnacle Bks.) Kensington Publishing Corp.
Rovin, Jeff & Diamond, Sander. Starik. 1988. 288p. 17.95 o.p. (*0-525-24626-6*, Dutton) Dutton/Plume.
Sebastian, Tim. Last Rights. unabr. ed. 1995. audio 69.95 (*0-7451-6495-1*, CAB 1111) BBC Audiobooks America.
—Last Rights. 1995. 272p. mass mkt. 5.50 (*0-380-71864-2*, Avon Bks.) Morrow/Avon.
—Last Rights: A Novel. l.t. ed. 1994. 402p. lib. bdg. 22.95 o.p. (*0-8161-7438-5*, Macmillan Reference USA) Gale Group.
Sebastian, Timothy. Last Rights. 1994. 270p. 22.00 o.p. (*0-688-11448-2*, Morrow, William & Co.) Morrow/Avon.
Smith, Martin Cruz. Gorky Park. 1993. mass mkt. 5.99 o.s.i (*0-345-90112-6*); 1982. 448p. mass mkt. 7.99 (*0-345-29834-9*) Ballantine Bks.
—Havana Bay. l.t. ed. pap. 25.95 o.p. (*0-7838-8547-4*, Macmillan Reference USA) Gale Group.
—Polar Star. 2000. mass mkt. 6.99 (*0-345-91706-5*); 1993. mass mkt. 5.99 o.p. (*0-345-90113-4*); 1990. 384p. mass mkt. 7.99 o.s.i (*0-345-36765-0*) Ballantine Bks.
—Polar Star. 1991. 4.99 o.p. (*0-517-06897-4*) Random Hse. Value Publishing.
—Red Square. 2000. mass mkt. 6.99 (*0-345-91707-3*) Ballantine Bks.
Spang, Michael G. The Spy Who Longed for Home. 1989. 320p. 16.95 o.p. (*0-312-02986-1*, Saint Martin's Minotaur) St. Martin's Pr.
Tolstaya, Tatyana. The Slynx: A Novel. Gambrell, Jamey, tr. from RUS. 2003. 288p. tchr. ed. 24.00 (*0-618-12497-7*) Houghton Mifflin Co.
Womack, Jack. Let's Put the Future Behind Us. 1996. 320p. 23.00 o.p. (*0-87113-627-9*, Atlantic Monthly Pr.) Grove/Atlantic, Inc.

**MOSPHEIRA (IMAGINARY PLACE)—FICTION**

Cherryh, C. J. Defender. 2001. (Foreigner Ser.: No. 5). 448p. 23.95 (*0-88677-911-1*); Vol. 2. 2002. 464p. reprint ed. mass mkt. 6.99 (*0-7564-0020-1*) DAW Bks., Inc.
—Foreigner. 1994. (Daw Book Collectors Ser.: Bk. 1). 432p. mass mkt. 6.99 (*0-88677-637-6*); 320p. 20.00 o.p. (*0-88677-590-6*) DAW Bks., Inc.
—Inheritor. (Foreigner Ser.: Bk. 3). 1997. 464p. mass mkt. 6.99 (*0-88677-728-3*); 1996. 432p. 21.95 o.p. (*0-88677-689-9*) DAW Bks., Inc.
—Invader. (Foreigner Trilogy Ser.: Bk. 2). 1995. 384p. 19.95 o.p. (*0-88677-638-4*); Vol. 2. 1996. 432p. mass mkt. 6.99 (*0-88677-687-2*) DAW Bks., Inc.
—Precursor. (Foreigner Ser.). 1999. (Illus.). 416p. 23.95 o.s.i (*0-88677-836-0*, D A W Fiction); 2000. 464p. reprint ed. mass mkt. 6.99 (*0-88677-910-3*) DAW Bks., Inc.
—Precursor. 2000. 13.04 (*0-606-19369-3*) Turtleback Bks.

**MURPHY'S HARBOR (ONT.: IMAGINARY PLACE)—FICTION**

Wood, Ted. Corkscrew. 1987. (Reid Bennett Mystery Ser.). 240p. 14.95 o.p. (*0-684-18853-8*, Macmillan Reference USA) Gale Group.
—Corkscrew. 1989. 224p. reprint ed. mass mkt. (*0-373-26024-5*, Harlequin Bks.) Harlequin Enterprises, Ltd.
—Corkscrew. 2001. E-Book 6.99 (*0-7592-1043-8*); 1999. 188p. per. 19.95 (*1-58586-863-9*) eread-s.com.
—Dead in the Water. 1984. 160p. mass mkt. 2.95 o.s.i (*0-7704-2006-0*) Bantam Bks.
—Flashback. l.t. ed. 1994. 21.95 o.p. (*0-7927-1819-4*); pap. 19.95 o.p. (*0-7927-1818-6*) BBC Audiobooks America.
—Flashback. 1992. 256p. text 20.00 (*0-684-19414-7*, Macmillan Reference USA) Gale Group.
—Flashback. 1994. (WWL Mystery Ser.). per. (*0-373-26137-3*, 1-26137-9, Harlequin Bks.) Harlequin Enterprises, Ltd.
—Fool's Gold. 1986. 192p. 13.95 o.s.i (*0-684-18568-7*, Macmillan Reference USA) Gale Group.
—Fool's Gold. 1988. 224p. reprint ed. mass mkt. (*0-373-26019-9*, Harlequin Bks.) Harlequin Enterprises, Ltd.
—Live Bait. 1986. (Mystery Ser.). 208p. mass mkt. 2.95 o.s.i (*0-553-25558-4*) Bantam Bks.
—Live Bait. 1985. 192p. 12.95 o.s.i (*0-684-18330-7*, Macmillan Reference USA) Gale Group.

—Live Bait. 2002. 174p. pap. 6.99 (*1-58586-855-8*); E-Book 6.99 (*1-58586-852-3*); E-Book 6.99 (*0-7592-1039-X*); E-Book 6.99 (*0-7592-0395-4*) ereads.com.
—Murder on Ice. 1985. 176p. mass mkt. 2.95 o.s.i (*0-7704-2049-4*) Bantam Bks.
—Murder on Ice. 1984. 160p. 12.95 o.s.i (*0-684-18134-7*, Macmillan Reference USA) Gale Group.
—On the Inside: A Reid Bennett Mystery. 1990. 256p. 18.95 o.s.i (*0-684-19090-7*, Macmillan Reference USA) Gale Group.
—On the Inside: A Reid Bennett Mystery. 1991. 224p. reprint ed. pap. (*0-373-26076-8*, Harlequin Bks.) Harlequin Enterprises, Ltd.
—When the Killing Starts. 1990. mass mkt. (*0-373-26043-1*, Harlequin Bks.) Harlequin Enterprises, Ltd.
—When the Killing Starts. 1989. 224p. 16.95 o.s.i (*0-684-18331-5*, Scribner) Simon & Schuster.

**MYRIAL (IMAGINARY PLACE)—FICTION**

Furey, Maggie. The Heart of Myrial. 2000. (Shadowleague Ser.: Vol. 1). 480p. mass mkt. 7.50 (*0-553-57938-X*) Bantam Bks.

## N

**NANTUCKET ISLAND (MASS.)—FICTION**

Ablow, Keith Russell. Compulsion: A Novel. E-Book 24.95 (*0-312-70706-1*); 2002. 320p. 24.95 (*0-312-26641-3*); 2003. 384p. reprint ed. mass mkt. 6.99 (*0-312-98824-9*, St. Martin's Paperbacks) St. Martin's Pr.
Blanc, Nero. The Crossword Murder. 320p. 2000. mass mkt. 5.99 (*0-425-17701-7*); 1999. pap. 13.00 (*0-425-16977-4*, Prime Crime) Berkley Publishing Group.
—Two Down. 2001. 304p. reprint ed. mass mkt. 5.99 o.s.i (*0-425-18091-3*, Prime Crime) Berkley Publishing Group.
—Two Down: A New Crossword Murder Mystery with Crosswords included. 2000. (Illus.). 304p. pap. 13.00 (*0-425-17510-3*, Prime Crime) Berkley Publishing Group.
Gouge, Louise M. Ahab's Bride. 2004. pap. 12.99 (*1-58919-007-6*) RiverOak Publishing.
Hilderbrand, Elin. The Beach Club. 2000. 357p. 23.95 (*0-312-26125-X*); E-Book 23.95 (*0-312-27424-6*) St. Martin's Pr.
—Nantucket Nights: A Novel. 2002. 288p. 23.95 (*0-312-28335-0*) St. Martin's Pr.
Maness, Larry. Nantucket Revenge. 2001. 241p. pap. 21.99 (*1-4010-0277-3*); E-Book 8.00 (*1-4010-0278-1*) Xlibris Corp.
Mathews, Francine. Death in a Cold Hard Light. 1999. (Indigo Ser.). 352p. reprint ed. mass mkt. 5.99 (*0-553-57625-9*) Bantam Bks.
—Death in a Cold Hard Light. unabr. collector's ed. 1998. (Merry Folger Ser.). audio 64.00 (*0-7366-4262-5*, 4761) Books on Tape, Inc.
—Death in a Mood Indigo. 1998. 352p. mass mkt. 5.99 (*0-553-57624-0*) Bantam Bks.
—Death in a Mood Indigo. unabr. collector's ed. 1997. (Merry Folger Ser.). audio 64.00 (*0-7366-4006-1*, 4504) Books on Tape, Inc.
—Death in Rough Water. unabr. collector's ed. 1997. (Merry Folger Ser.: Vol. 2). audio 56.00 (*0-7366-3631-5*, 4292) Books on Tape, Inc.
—Death in Rough Water: A Merry Folger Mystery. 1995. 320p. 22.00 o.p. (*0-688-13473-4*, Morrow, William & Co.) Morrow/Avon.
—Death in the Off-Season. unabr. collector's ed. 1997. (Merry Folger Ser.: Vol. 1). audio 64.00 (*0-7366-3600-5*, 4255) Books on Tape, Inc.
—Death in the Off-Season. 1995. 352p. mass mkt. 4.99 (*0-380-72334-4*, Avon Bks.); 1994. 318p. 23.00 o.p. (*0-688-13443-2*, Morrow, William & Co.) Morrow/Avon.
Poe, Edgar Allan. The Narrative of Arthur Gordon Pym of Nantucket. 2002. (Paperback Classics Ser.). (Illus.). 224p. pap. 9.95 (*0-375-76007-5*, Modern Library) Random House Adult Trade Publishing Group.
Rich, Virginia. The Baked Bean Supper Murders. l.t. ed. 1983. 499p. reprint ed. 14.95 o.p. (*0-89621-487-7*) Thorndike Pr.
—The Nantucket Diet Murders. (Eugenia Potter Mysteries Ser.). 1986. 288p. mass mkt. 6.99 (*0-440-16264-5*); 1985. 224p. 13.95 o.s.i (*0-385-29386-0*, Delacorte Pr.) Dell Publishing.
—The Nantucket Diet Murders. 1985. 13.95 o.p. (*0-525-24233-3*, Dutton) Dutton/Plume.
Rosenblum, Robert. Afterlove. 2004. 352p. mass mkt. 7.99 (*0-451-41126-9*, Onyx); 2003. 320p. 22.95 (*0-451-20786-6*) NAL.

**NAPA COUNTY (CALIF.)—FICTION**

Gadol, Peter. The Long Rain. 2000. 304p. pap. 13.00 (*0-312-26354-6*); 1998. (Long Rain Ser.: Vol. 1). 295p. mass mkt. 6.99 o.p. (*0-312-96638-5*); 1997. 320p. 23.00 o.p. (*0-312-15571-9*) Picador.
—The Long Rain. unabr. ed. 1997. audio 75.00 (*0-7887-1314-0*, 95172E7) Recorded Bks., LLC.
Koontz, Dean. Intensity. 1997. pap. text 7.99 (*0-345-91189-X*); 1997. pap. 12.95 o.p. (*0-345-41948-0*); 1996. 448p. mass mkt. 7.99 o.s.i (*0-345-38436-9*); 1996. mass mkt. 6.99 (*0-345-40514-5*) Ballantine Bks.
—Intensity. l.t. ed. 1996. 752p. 25.00 o.p. (*0-7838-1678-2*, Macmillan Reference USA) Gale Group.
—Intensity. deluxe ed. 1996. 25.00 o.s.i (*0-676-51387-5*) Random Hse., Inc.
Krentz, Jayne Ann. Witchcraft. 1996. per. (*1-55166-158-6*, 1-66158-6, Mira Bks.); 1985. mass mkt. (*0-373-25174-2*, Harlequin Bks.) Harlequin Enterprises, Ltd.
—Witchcraft. l.t. ed. 2000. (Romance Ser.). (Illus.). 315p. 28.95 (*0-7862-2600-5*) Thorndike Pr.
Krentz, Jayne Ann, et al. Witchcraft: Witchcraft/Last Chance Cafe/Bayou Moon, 3 bks. in 1. 2003. 352p. mass mkt. (*0-373-83542-6*, Harlequin Bks.) Harlequin Enterprises, Ltd.
Peart, Jane. Promise of the Valley. l.t. ed. 2001. (Westward Dreams Ser.). 416p. 24.95 (*0-7862-3129-7*) Thorndike Pr.
—Promise of the Valley. 1995. (Westward Dreams Ser.: Vol. 2). 288p. pap. 18.99 (*0-310-41281-1*) Zondervan.
Roberts, Nora. The Villa. 2002. 496p. reprint ed. mass mkt. 7.99 (*0-515-13218-7*, Jove) Berkley Publishing Group.
—The Villa. 2001. 421p. 25.95 o.s.i (*0-399-14712-8*) Penguin Group (USA) Inc.
—The Villa. 2001. E-Book 25.95 (*0-7865-0269-X*) Penguin Putnam, Inc E-Books.
—The Villa. l.t. ed. 2001. 704p. 25.95 (*0-375-43103-9*) Random Hse. Large Print.

**NASHVILLE (TENN.)—FICTION**

Carew, David M. Voice from the Gutter. 2001. 182p. pap. 20.99 (*0-7388-6367-X*); E-Book 8.00 (*1-4010-1795-9*) Xlibris Corp.
Fitzhugh, Bill. Fender Benders. 2003. 416p. mass mkt. 7.50 (*0-380-80635-5*) Morrow/Avon.
—Fender Benders: A Novel. 2001. 336p. 24.00 (*0-380-97757-5*, Morrow, William & Co.) Morrow/Avon.
Hampton-Jones, Hollis. Vicious Spring. 2004. 192p. pap. 13.00 (*1-57322-385-9*, Riverhead Trade (Paperbacks)) Berkley Publishing Group.
—Vicious Spring. 2003. 176p. 21.95 (*1-57322-243-7*, Riverhead Bks. (Hardcovers)) Putnam Publishing Group, The.
Kijewski, Karen. Honky Tonk Kat. 1997. (Kat Colorado Mysteries Ser.). 368p. mass mkt. 6.99 o.s.i (*0-425-15860-8*) Berkley Publishing Group.
—Honky Tonk Kat. 1996. viii, 323p. 22.95 o.s.i (*0-399-14133-2*, G. P. Putnam's Sons) Penguin Group (USA) Inc.
—Honky Tonk Kat. 22.95 o.s.i (*0-399-14424-2*) Putnam Publishing Group, The.
—Honky Tonk Kat. abr. ed. 1996. (Kat Colorado Mysteries Ser.). 5p. audio 23.00 (*1-56876-059-0*) Soundlines Entertainment, Inc.
Rose, M. L. The Road to Eden's Ridge. 2002. 256p. 21.99 (*1-55853-993-X*) Rutledge Hill Pr.
Shankman, Sarah. I Still Miss My Man, but My Aim Is Getting Better. 1997. 288p. pap. 5.99 (*0-671-89750-0*, Pocket); 1996. 272p. 21.00 o.p. (*0-671-89751-9*, Atria) Simon & Schuster.
Tishy, Cecelia. Cryin' Time. 1998. (Kate Banning Mystery Ser.: No. 2). 336p. 23.95 (*1-891847-01-5*) Dowling Pr., Inc.
—Cryin' Time. 1999. (Kate Banning Mysteries Ser.). 304p. mass mkt. 5.99 o.s.i (*0-451-19832-8*, Signet Bks.) NAL.
—Fall to Pieces. 1999. (Kate Banning Mystery Ser.). 319p. 24.00 (*1-891847-07-4*) Dowling Pr., Inc.
—Fall to Pieces. 2000. (Kate Banning Mysteries Ser.). 304p. mass mkt. 5.99 o.s.i (*0-451-20094-2*, Signet Bks.) NAL.
—Jealous Heart. Sachs, Susan, ed. 1997. 304p. 24.00 o.p. (*0-9646452-5-4*) Dowling Pr., Inc.
—Jealous Heart. 1999. 272p. mass mkt. 5.99 o.s.i (*0-451-19678-3*, Signet Bks.) NAL.
Villatoro, Marcos M. Minos: A Romilia Chacon Mystery. 2003. 320p. 24.95 (*1-932112-13-8*) Justin, Charles & Co. Pubs.
Werthan, Libby Rosenbaum. The Fourth Corner. 2001. (Illus.). 144p. 16.95 (*965-229-275-3*) Gefen Publishing Hse., Ltd ISR. *Dist:* Gefen Bks.
Womack, Steven. Chain of Fools. (Harry James Denton Mysteries Ser.). 320p. 1996. mass mkt. 6.50 (*0-345-39687-1*); 1995. pap. 19.00 (*0-345-46187-8*, Ballantine Bks.) Ballantine Bks.
—Chain of Fools. l.t. ed. 1997. (Ulverscroft Large Print Ser.). 544p. 29.99 (*0-7089-3730-6*, Ulverscroft) Thorpe, F. A. Pubs. GBR. *Dist:* Ulverscroft Large Print Bks., Ltd., Ulverscroft Large Print Canada, Ltd.
—Dead Folks' Blues. 272p. 1995. pap. 19.00 (*0-345-46186-X*, Ballantine Bks.); 1992. mass mkt. 5.99 o.s.i (*0-345-37674-9*) Ballantine Bks.
—Dead Folks' Blues. Haywood, Richard, ed. abr. ed. 1995. (Harry Denton Trilogy Ser.). audio 17.00 (*1-883268-25-7*) Spellbinders, Inc.
—Dirty Money. 2000. 320p. pap. 19.00 (*0-345-46190-8*, Ballantine Bks.); mass mkt. 6.50 (*0-345-41448-9*, Fawcett) Ballantine Bks.
—Murder Manual. 1998. (Harry James Denton Mysteries Ser.). 336p. mass mkt. 5.99 (*0-345-41447-0*); pap. 19.00 (*0-345-46189-4*, Ballantine Bks.) Ballantine Bks.
—Torch Town Boogie. 288p. 1995. pap. 19.00 (*0-345-46317-X*); 1993. mass mkt. 6.50 o.s.i (*0-345-38010-X*) Ballantine Bks.
—Torch Town Boogie. abr. ed. 1997. audio 17.00 (*1-883268-32-X*) Spellbinders, Inc.
—Torch Town Boogie. l.t. ed. 1996. (Ulverscroft Large Print Ser.). 480p. 29.99 o.p. (*0-7089-3600-8*, Ulverscroft) Thorpe, F. A. Pubs. GBR. *Dist:* Ulverscroft Large Print Bks., Ltd., Ulverscroft Large Print Canada, Ltd.
—Way Past Dead. 1995. 352p. pap. 19.00 (*0-345-46188-6*, Ballantine Bks.); 272p. mass mkt. 6.50 (*0-345-39043-1*) Ballantine Bks.
—Way Past Dead. abr. ed. 1997. audio 17.00 (*1-883268-30-3*) Spellbinders, Inc.

**NAVAJO INDIAN RESERVATION—FICTION**

Hillerman, Tony. The Blessing Way. unabr. ed. 1993. audio 36.00 (*0-7366-2510-0*, 3266) Books on Tape, Inc.
—The Blessing Way. l.t. ed. 1992. (General Ser.). 304p. pap. 17.95 o.p. (*0-8161-5431-7*); lib. bdg. 20.95 o.p. (*0-8161-5430-9*) Gale Group. (Macmillan Reference USA).
—The Blessing Way. (Harper Novel of Suspense Ser.). 1970. 10.00 o.p. (*0-06-011896-2*); 1990. 304p. reprint ed. mass mkt. 6.99 (*0-06-100001-9*) HarperCollins Pubs.
—The Blessing Way. abr. ed. 1995. (Joe Leaphorn Mystery Ser.). 3p. audio 18.00 (*1-55994-160-X*, 394151, HarperAudio) HarperTrade.
—The Blessing Way. 1993. audio 39.80 (*1-56544-006-4*, 250020); audio Literate Ear, Inc.
—The Blessing Way. 1978. (gr. 7 up). pap. 2.95 o.p. (*0-380-39941-5*, Avon Bks.) Morrow/Avon.
—The Blessing Way. unabr. ed. 1990. (Joe Leaphorn Mystery Ser.: Vol. 1). audio 44.00 (*1-55690-058-9*, 90080E7) Recorded Bks., LLC.
—The Blessing Way. 1990. 12.55 (*0-606-16174-0*) Turtleback Bks.
—Coyote Waits. unabr. ed. 1990. audio 42.00 (*0-7366-1788-4*, 2625) Books on Tape, Inc.
—Coyote Waits. 1990. 292p. 75.00 o.p. (*0-06-016422-0*); 1990. 292p. 19.95 o.p. (*0-06-016370-4*); 1995. 3p. audio 18.00 o.s.i (*1-55994-198-7*, 390569, HarperAudio); 1990. pap. 19.95 o.p. (*0-06-016423-9*) HarperTrade.
—Coyote Waits. 1992. 368p. mass mkt. 6.99 (*0-06-109932-5*, HarperTorch) Morrow/Avon.
—Coyote Waits. 1990. audio 10.00 New Letters on Air.
—Coyote Waits. 1990. (J). 13.04 (*0-606-01125-0*) Turtleback Bks.
—Dance Hall of the Dead. abr. ed. 1986. audio 15.95 (*0-88690-127-8*, N20024, Audio Editions Bks. on Cassette) Audio Partners Publishing Corp.
—Dance Hall of the Dead. unabr. ed. 1994. audio 36.00 (*0-7366-2610-7*, 3352) Books on Tape, Inc.
—Dance Hall of the Dead. 1997. lib. bdg. 37.95 (*1-56849-695-8*) Buccaneer Bks., Inc.
—Dance Hall of the Dead. 2004. 224p. pap. 11.95 (*0-06-056374-5*); 1990. 272p. reprint ed. mass mkt. 6.99 (*0-06-100002-7*) HarperTrade. (Perennial).
—Dance Hall of the Dead. 1993. audio 37.20 (*1-56544-025-0*, 250021); audio Literate Ear, Inc.
—Dance Hall of the Dead. 1982. (YA). (gr. 9 up). mass mkt. 2.95 o.p. (*0-380-00217-5*, 60093-5, Avon Bks.) Morrow/Avon.
—Dance Hall of the Dead. unabr. ed. 1991. (Joe Leaphorn Mystery Ser.: Vol. 2). (YA). (gr. 10). audio 44.00 (*1-55690-134-8*, 91122E7) Recorded Bks., LLC.
—Dance Hall of the Dead. l.t. ed. (Paperback Bestsellers Ser.). 239p. 1994. pap. 20.95 (*0-8161-5433-3*); 1993. lib. bdg. 25.95 (*0-8161-5432-5*) Thorndike Pr.
—Dance Hall of the Dead. 1990. 12.55 (*0-606-16124-4*) Turtleback Bks.
—The Dark Wind. unabr. ed. 1994. audio 42.00 (*0-7366-2689-1*, 3424) Books on Tape, Inc.
—The Dark Wind. 1982. 224p. o.p. (*0-06-014936-1*) HarperCollins Pubs.
—The Dark Wind. 1990. 320p. reprint ed. mass mkt. 6.99 (*0-06-100003-5*, Perennial); Set. 1993. audio 18.00 (*1-55994-774-8*, CPN 4032, HarperAudio) HarperTrade.
—The Dark Wind. 1993. audio 39.80. audio Literate Ear, Inc.
—The Dark Wind. 1992. 79p. mass mkt. 5.99 o.p. (*0-06-100491-X*, HarperTorch); 1983. 224p. pap. 3.50 o.p. (*0-380-63321-3*, Avon Bks.) Morrow/Avon.
—The Dark Wind. unabr. ed. 1990. (Jim Chee Mystery Ser.: Vol. 2). (YA). (gr. 10 up). audio 51.00 (*1-55690-136-4*, 91101E7) Recorded Bks., LLC.
—The Fallen Man. unabr. ed. 1997. audio 42.00 (*0-913369-37-3*, 4211) Books on Tape, Inc.
—The Fallen Man. 1996. 304p. 24.00 o.p. (*0-06-017773-X*) HarperCollins Pubs.
—The Fallen Man, Set. abr. ed. 1996. (Joe Leaphorn Mystery Ser.). audio 25.00 (*1-55994-978-3*, 694496, HarperAudio) HarperTrade.
—The Fallen Man. 1997. 320p. mass mkt. 6.99 (*0-06-109288-6*, HarperTorch) Morrow/Avon.
—The Fallen Man. unabr. ed. 1997. (Jim Chee Mystery Ser.: Vol. 9). audio 51.00 (*0-7887-0907-0*, 94961E7) Recorded Bks., LLC.
—The Fallen Man. 1998. 5.98 o.p. (*0-7651-0823-2*) Smithmark Pubs., Inc.
—The First Eagle. 1998. 224p. 25.00 (*0-00-224569-8*); 288p. 25.00 o.s.i (*0-06-017581-8*); 25.00 o.s.i (*0-06-099536-X*) HarperCollins Pubs.
—The First Eagle. unabr. ed. 1998. audio 34.95 (*0-694-52051-9*, 896038);Set. audio 25.00 (*0-694-52011-X*, 696034) HarperTrade. (HarperAudio).
—The First Eagle. 1999. 336p. mass mkt. 6.99 (*0-06-109785-3*, HarperTorch) Morrow/Avon.
—The First Eagle. unabr. ed. (Joe Leaphorn Mystery Ser.). 1999. audio compact disk 58.00 (*0-7887-3445-8*, C1051E7); 1998. audio 56.00 (*0-7887-2160-7*, 95456E7) Recorded Bks., LLC.
—The First Eagle. l.t. ed. (Paperback Bestsellers Ser.). 360p. 1999. pap. 28.95 o.p. (*0-7862-1625-5*); 1998. 30.95 (*0-7862-1624-7*) Thorndike Pr.
—The First Eagle. 1999. 13.04 (*0-606-16536-3*) Turtleback Bks.
—The Ghostway. unabr. ed. 1994. audio 42.00 (*0-7366-2748-0*, 3473) Books on Tape, Inc.
—The Ghostway. 1985. 224p. 13.95 o.p. (*0-06-015396-2*); 1992. 3p. audio 18.00 (*1-55994-606-7*, CPN 2301, HarperAudio) HarperTrade.
—The Ghostway. 1993. audio. audio 47.20 (*1-56544-040-4*, 250033) Literate Ear, Inc.
—The Ghostway. 1992. 320p. mass mkt. 6.99 (*0-06-100345-X*, HarperTorch); 1986. 208p. mass mkt. 4.95 (*0-380-70024-7*, Avon Bks.) Morrow/Avon.
—The Ghostway. unabr. ed. 1990. (Jim Chee Mystery Ser.: Vol. 3). audio 44.00 (*1-55690-194-1*, 90098E7) Recorded Bks., LLC.
—The Ghostway. 1984. (J). 12.55 (*0-606-01124-2*) Turtleback Bks.
—Hunting Badger. 1999. 288p. 26.00 (*0-00-224550-7*); 26.00 (*0-06-019289-5*) HarperCollins Pubs.
—Hunting Badger. l.t. ed. 1999. 256p. pap. 26.00 (*0-06-095564-3*, HarperLargePrint); 2000. audio compact disk 29.95 (*0-694-52287-2*, HarperAudio); Set. 2000. 30p. audio 25.00 (*0-694-52057-8*, HarperAudio) HarperTrade.
—Hunting Badger. 2001. 352p. mass mkt. 7.50 (*0-06-109786-1*, HarperTorch) Morrow/Avon.
—Hunting Badger. unabr. ed. 1999. (Joe Leaphorn Mystery Ser.). audio 29.95 (*0-7887-3894-1*, 96076) Recorded Bks., LLC.
—The Jim Chee Mysteries: Three Classic Hillerman Mysteries Featuring Officer Jim Chee: The Dark Wind, People of Darkness & The Ghostway. 1990. 576p. 26.00 (*0-06-016478-6*) HarperTrade.
—The Jim Chee Mysteries: Three Classic Hillerman Mysteries Featuring Officer Jim Chee: The Dark Wind, People of Darkness & The Ghostway. 1993. 576p. 13.99 o.s.i (*0-517-09281-6*) Random Hse. Value Publishing.
—The Joe Leaphorn Mysteries: Three Classic Hillerman Mysteries Featuring Lt. Joe Leaphorn: The Blessing Way, Dance Hall of the Dead, Listening Woman. 1989. 448p. 19.00 o.p. (*0-06-016174-4*) HarperTrade.
—Leaphorn & Chee: Three Classic Mysteries Featuring Lt. Joe Leaphorn & Officer Jim Chee. 1992. 512p. 19.00 o.p. (*0-06-016909-5*) HarperTrade.
—Listening Woman. unabr. ed. 1994. audio 36.00 (*0-7366-2671-9*, 3408) Books on Tape, Inc.
—Listening Woman. l.t. ed. (General Ser.). 303p. 1994. pap. 18.95 o.p. (*0-8161-5435-X*); 1993. lib. bdg. 22.95 (*0-8161-5434-1*) Gale Group. (Macmillan Reference USA).
—Listening Woman. 1978. (Harper Novel of Suspense Ser.). o.p. (*0-06-011901-2*) HarperCollins Pubs.
—Listening Woman. 1993. audio. audio 44.20 (*1-56544-036-6*, 250022) Literate Ear, Inc.
—Listening Woman. 1990. 336p. mass mkt. 6.99 (*0-06-100029-9*, HarperTorch); 1979. pap. 3.95 (*0-380-43554-3*, Avon Bks.) Morrow/Avon.
—Listening Woman. unabr. ed. 1990. (Joe Leaphorn Mystery Ser.: Vol. 3). audio 44.00 (*1-55690-310-3*, 90073E7) Recorded Bks., LLC.
—People of Darkness. unabr. ed. 1994. audio 36.00 (*0-7366-2725-1*, 3455) Books on Tape, Inc.
—People of Darkness. 1988. 196p. reprint ed. mass mkt. 4.95 o.p. (*0-06-080950-7*, P 950, Perennial) HarperTrade.
—People of Darkness. 1993. audio 44.20 (*1-56544-037-4*, 250034); audio Literate Ear, Inc.

—People of Darkness. 1991. 304p. mass mkt. 6.99 (0-06-109915-5, HarperTorch); 1983. 192p. pap. 2.95 o.p. (0-380-57778-X, Avon Bks.) Morrow/Avon.
—People of Darkness. unabr. ed. 1990. (Jim Chee Mystery Ser.: Vol. 1). audio 44.00 (1-55690-405-3, 90087E7) Recorded Bks., LLC.
—Sacred Clowns. unabr. ed. 1994. audio 48.00 (0-7366-2645-X, 3382) Books on Tape, Inc.
—Sacred Clowns. 1994. 368p. mass mkt. 6.99 (0-06-109260-6) HarperCollins Pubs.
—Sacred Clowns. 1993. 304p. 100.00 o.p. (0-06-016830-7); 304p. 23.00 o.p. (0-06-016767-X); audio 17.00 (1-55994-549-4, 391505, HarperAudio) HarperTrade.
—Sacred Clowns. unabr. ed. 1993. (Jim Chee Mystery Ser.: Vol. 8). audio 51.00 (1-55690-910-1, 93406E7) Recorded Bks., LLC.
—Sacred Clowns. 1994. 13.04 (0-606-16175-9) Turtleback Bks.
—Sacred Clowns: A Novel. 2003. 320p. pap. 11.95 (0-06-053805-8, Perennial) HarperTrade.
—Skinwalkers. unabr. ed. 1994. audio 36.00 (0-7366-2795-2, 3510) Books on Tape, Inc.
—Skinwalkers. 1990. 320p. mass mkt. 6.99 (0-06-100017-5); 1987. mass mkt. 4.95 o.p. (0-06-080893-4, P/893) HarperCollins Pubs.
—Skinwalkers. 1990. audio 15.95; 1987. 224p. 19.95 o.p. (0-06-015695-3); 1991. audio 18.00 (1-55994-166-9, CPN 2152, HarperAudio) HarperTrade.
—Skinwalkers. 1993. audio 39.80 (1-56544-007-2, 250032); audio Literate Ear, Inc.
—Skinwalkers. unabr. ed. 1990. (Jim Chee Mystery Ser.: Vol. 4). audio 44.00 (1-55690-480-0, 90074E7) Recorded Bks., LLC.
—Skinwalkers. 1987. 13.04 (0-606-03655-5) Turtleback Bks.
—Talking God. unabr. ed. 1989. audio 42.00 (0-7366-1656-X, 2507) Books on Tape, Inc.
—Talking God. 2003. E-Book 6.99 (0-06-054725-1) HarperCollins Pubs.
—Talking God. 1991. 368p. mass mkt. 6.99 (0-06-109918-X, Perennial); 1989. 17.95 o.p. (0-06-016118-3) HarperTrade.
—Talking God. 1989. 13.04 (0-606-04823-5) Turtleback Bks.
—A Thief of Time. unabr. ed. 1994. audio 36.00 (0-7366-2841-X, 3549) Books on Tape, Inc.
—A Thief of Time. l.t. ed. 1990. 14.95 o.p. (0-8161-5061-3); 1989. 344p. 18.95 o.p. (0-8161-4699-3) Gale Group. (Macmillan Reference USA).
—A Thief of Time. 2002. E-Book 6.99 (0-06-054713-8); E-Book (0-06-054720-0) HarperCollins Pubs.
—A Thief of Time. 1988. 224p. 15.45 o.p. (0-06-015938-3); 2002. 176p. audio 9.99 (0-06-008296-8, HarperAudio); Set. 1995. audio 18.00 (0-89845-794-7, 391761, HarperAudio) HarperTrade.
—A Thief of Time. 1990. 352p. reprint ed. mass mkt. 6.99 (0-06-100004-3, HarperTorch) Morrow/Avon.
—A Thief of Time. 1989. 13.04 (0-606-04346-2) Turtleback Bks.
Hillerman, Tony, reader. Talking God, , abr. ed. 1995. audio 18.00 (0-89845-956-7, CPN 2122, HarperAudio) HarperTrade.

**NEBRASKA—FICTION**

Agee, Jonis. Strange Angels. 1994. 79p. pap. 12.50 o.p. (0-06-097589-X) HarperCollins Pubs.
—Strange Angels. 1993. 384p. 21.95 o.p. (0-395-60835-X) Houghton Mifflin Co.
—Strange Angels. 2000. 416p. pap. 13.95 (0-14-029186-5) Penguin Group (USA) Inc.
Aldrich, Bess S. The Collected Short Works, 1907-1919. Petersen, Carol M., ed. & intro. by. 1995. 246p. text 50.00 (0-8032-1038-8) Univ. of Nebraska Pr.
—A Lantern in Her Hand. Date not set. 278p. reprint ed. lib. bdg. 21.95 (0-88411-260-8) Amereon, Ltd.
—A Lantern in Her Hand. l.t. ed. 1982. 433p. reprint ed. o.p. (0-89621-330-7) Thorndike Pr.
—A Lantern in Her Hand. 1997. (J). 12.04 (0-606-11546-3) Turtleback Bks.
—A Lantern in Her Hand. 1994. 307p. pap. 11.95 (0-8032-5922-0, Bison Bks.) Univ. of Nebraska Pr.
—The Lieutenant's Lady. 1975. 275p. reprint ed. lib. bdg. 24.95 (0-88411-252-7) Amereon, Ltd.
—The Lieutenant's Lady. l.t. ed. 2001. (Romance Ser.). 272p. 28.95 (0-7838-9366-3) Thorndike Pr.
—The Lieutenant's Lady. 1987. 277p. reprint ed. pap. 13.50 o.p. (0-8032-5914-X, Bison Bks.) Univ. of Nebraska Pr.
Allen, Shirley S. Roxanna Britton. 2001. 388p. per. 16.00 (1-884162-08-8) Criterion Hse.
Alter, Judy. Mattie. 1997. 192p. reprint ed. mass mkt. 3.99 (0-8439-4156-1, Leisure Bks.) Dorchester Publishing Co., Inc.
—Mattie. 1988. (Double D Western Ser.). 192p. pap. 12.95 o.s.i (0-385-24167-4) Doubleday Publishing.
Barker, Jane Valentine. Mari: A Novel. 1997. (Women's West Ser.: No. 2). 200p. 19.95 (0-87081-452-4) Univ. Pr. of Colorado.
—Mari: A Novel. 1997. E-Book 19.95 (0-585-02195-3) netLibrary, Inc.
Bly, Stephen. Reason & Riots. 2003. 288p. pap. 11.99 (1-58134-434-1) Crossway Bks.
Bly, Stephen A. Courage & Compromise. 2003. 256p. pap. 11.99 (1-58134-433-3) Crossway Bks.
—Strangers & Pilgrims. 2002. 304p. pap. 11.99 (1-58134-426-0) Crossway Bks.
Cather, Willa. A Lost Lady. 1976. 19.95 (0-8488-0450-3) Amereon, Ltd.
—A Lost Lady. l.t. ed. 1985. 184p. 13.95 o.p. (0-89621-592-X) BBC Audiobooks America.
—A Lost Lady. 1990. reprint ed. lib. bdg. 19.95 (0-89966-650-7) Buccaneer Bks., Inc.
—A Lost Lady. 1998. (Collected Works of Willa Cather). 173p. reprint ed. lib. bdg. 88.00 (1-58201-569-4) Classic Bks.
—A Lost Lady. 1990. (Vintage Bks.). 160p. pap. 9.95 (0-679-72887-2, Vintage) Knopf Publishing Group.
—A Lost Lady. 2015. 160p. mass mkt. 4.95 o.s.i (0-451-52720-8, Signet Classics) NAL.
—A Lost Lady. 1972. pap. 4.95 o.p. (0-394-71705-8) Random Hse., Inc.
—A Lost Lady. Mignon, Charles W. et al, eds. 1997. (Willa Cather Scholarly Edition Ser.). (Illus.). 371p. text 75.00 (0-8032-1427-8) Univ. of Nebraska Pr.
—My Antonia. 2000. 252p. pap. 9.95 (0-594-04185-6); E-Book 3.95 (0-594-04188-0); E-Book 9.95 (0-594-06302-7) 1873 Pr.
—My Antonia. 24.95 (0-88411-287-X) Amereon, Ltd.
—My Antonia, unabr. ed. 1993. audio 41.95 (1-55685-282-7) Audio Bk. Contractors, Inc.
—My Antonia. 1994. (Bantam Classics Ser.). (Illus.). 320p. mass mkt. 4.95 (0-553-21418-7, Bantam Classics) Bantam Bks.
—My Antonia. E-Book (0-7607-1291-3) Barnes & Noble, Inc.
—My Antonia. 1985. (Barron's Book Notes Ser.). (gr. 10-12). pap. 2.50 (0-8120-3528-3) Barron's Educational Series, Inc.
—My Antonia. unabr. ed. 1994. audio 49.95 (0-7861-0495-3, 892570) Blackstone Audio Bks., Inc.
—My Antonia. unabr. ed. 1999. audio 49.95 (1-55686-945-2) Books in Motion.
—My Antonia. unabr. ed. 1997. (Bookcassette Classic Collection). 8p. audio 57.25 (1-56100-819-2, 958, Unabridged Library Editions); (Illus.). audio 17.95 o.p. (1-56100-744-7, 190, Bookcassette) Brilliance Audio.
—My Antonia. 1992. (Illus.). reprint ed. lib. bdg. 25.95 (0-89966-977-8) Buccaneer Bks., Inc.
—My Antonia. (Collected Works of Willa Cather). 418p. reprint ed. 2001. pap. 28.00 (0-7426-5570-9); 1998. lib. bdg. 108.00 (1-58201-570-8) Classic Bks.
—My Antonia. l.t. ed. 2000. 493p. pap. 24.95 (1-58855-003-6) Cyber Classics, Inc.
—My Antonia. unabr. ed. 1994. (Thrift Editions Ser.). 176p. (YA). pap. 2.00 (0-486-28240-6) Dover Pubns., Inc.
—My Antonia. 2002. (EMC Masterpiece Series Access Editions). (Illus.). xxiv, 301p. (YA). 15.93 (0-8219-2509-1) EMC/Paradigm Publishing.
—My Antonia. E-Book 2.49 (1-58744-283-3) Electric Umbrella Publishing.
—My Antonia. l.t. ed. 2000. 352p. pap. 22.00 (0-06-095694-1, HarperCollins) HarperTrade.
—My Antonia, unabr. ed. 1999. audio 49.95 Highsmith Inc.
—My Antonia. 1995. (Illus.). 266p. pap. 5.95 (0-395-75514-X); 1973. 272p. 24.95 o.p. (0-395-07514-9); 1973. 272p. pap. 7.95 o.p. (0-395-08356-7) Houghton Mifflin Co.
—My Antonia. l.t. ed. 1060p. pap. 81.38 (0-7583-1623-2); 913p. pap. 72.13 (0-7583-1622-4); 743p. pap. 55.36 (0-7583-1621-6); 604p. pap. 46.22 (0-7583-1620-8); 472p. pap. 37.52 (0-7583-1619-4); 269p. pap. 24.22 (0-7583-1617-8); 369p. pap. 30.26 (0-7583-1618-6); 215p. pap. 21.18 (0-7583-1616-X); 269p. lib. bdg. 30.22 (0-7583-1609-7); 369p. lib. bdg. 36.26 (0-7583-1610-0); 604p. lib. bdg. 52.22 (0-7583-1612-7); 743p. lib. bdg. 61.36 (0-7583-1613-5); 913p. lib. bdg. 84.56 (0-7583-1614-3); 1060p. lib. bdg. 93.38 (0-7583-1615-1); 215p. lib. bdg. 27.18 (0-7583-1608-9); 472p. lib. bdg. 43.52 (0-7583-1611-9) Huge Print Pr.
—My Antonia, unabr. ed. 1994. audio 35.00 Jimcin Recordings.
—My Antonia. 1994. (Vintage Bks.). (Illus.). 288p. pap. 9.00 (0-679-74187-9, Vintage) 1996) Knopf Publishing Group.
—My Antonia. l.t. ed. 2000. (LRS Large Print Heritage Ser.). 365p. (YA). (gr. 6-12). lib. bdg. 33.95 (1-58118-076-4, 23669) LRS.
—My Antonia. 1994. (Signet Classics). 288p. mass mkt. 4.95 (0-451-52579-5, Signet Classics) NAL.
—My Antonia, Set. 1998. audio 25.00 (0-7871-1756-0, Dove Audio) NewStar Media, Inc.
—My Antonia. l.t. ed. reprint ed. 1996. 400p. lib. bdg. 26.00 (0-939495-05-8); 1998. 240p. lib. bdg. 25.00 (1-58287-051-9) North Bks.
—My Antonia. 1997. (Critical Editions Ser.). (C). pap. text (0-393-96790-5, Norton Paperbacks) Norton, W. W. & Co., Inc.
—My Antonia. (Penguin Great Books of the 20th Century Ser.). 1999. 272p. (C). pap. 12.00 (0-14-028327-7); 1997. (0-14-771198-3) Penguin Group (USA) Inc.
—My Antonia. 1996. (Everyman's Library: Vol. 228). (Illus.). 320p. 16.00 (0-679-44727-X); 1987. 384p. o.s.i (0-86068-125-4) Random Hse., Inc.
—My Antonia, unabr. ed. 1994. audio 51.00 (1-55690-976-4, 94115E7) Recorded Bks., LLC.
—My Antonia. 1981. (Keith Jennison Large Type Bks.). lib. bdg. 9.95 o.p. (0-531-00242-X, Watts, Franklin) Scholastic Library Publishing.
—My Antonia. O'Brien, Sharon, ed. & intro. by. 1994. 336p. reprint ed. mass mkt. 5.50 (0-671-89086-7, Pocket) Simon & Schuster.
—My Antonia. (Ebook Classic Ser.). (YA). E-Book 5.00 (0-7410-1231-6) SoftBook Pr.
—My Antonia. 1994. (Signet Classics Ser.). 11.00 (0-606-05933-4); 10.60 o.p. (0-606-06588-1) Turtleback Bks.
—My Antonia. 1996. (Illus.). 240p. pap. 6.95 (0-460-87723-2, Everyman's Classic Library in Paperback) Tuttle Publishing.
—My Antonia. Mignon, Charles W. & Ronning, Kari, eds. 1995. (Willa Cather Scholary Edition Ser.). (Illus.). 400p. pap. text 19.95 (0-8032-6372-4, Bison Bks.) Univ. of Nebraska Pr.
—My Antonia. Mignon, Charles W. & Ronning, Kari A., eds. 1995. (Willa Cather Scholarly Edition Ser.: Vol. 2). (Illus.). 543p. reprint ed. 70.00 (0-8032-1468-5) Univ. of Nebraska Pr.
—My Antonia. 1999. pap. 16.95 incl. audio (0-14-086313-3); 1994. (Illus.). 320p. pap. 9.95 (0-14-018764-2, Penguin Classics) Viking Penguin.
—My Antonia. 2000. 232p. pap. 10.95 (1-58348-509-0) iUniverse, Inc.
—Novels & Stories, 1905-1918: The Troll Garden; O Pioneers!; The Song of the Lark; My Antonia. 1999. (Library of America College Editions Ser.). 975p. (C). pap. 13.95 (1-883011-74-4) Library of America, The.
—O Pioneers! lib. bdg. 24.95 (0-8488-0454-6) Amereon, Ltd.
—O Pioneers! 1989. (Bantam Classics Ser.). 224p. mass mkt. 4.95 (0-553-21358-X, Bantam Classics) Bantam Bks.
—O Pioneers! 2003. (Barnes & Noble Classics Ser.). 224p. pap. 4.95 (1-59308-019-0) Fine Communications.
—O Pioneers!, 001. 9999. 14.95 o.p. (0-395-07516-5); 1997. 224p. pap. 5.95 (0-395-08365-6) Houghton Mifflin Co.
—O Pioneers! E-Book 2.95 (1-57799-893-6) Logos Research Systems, Inc.
—O Pioneers! 1992. 368p. pap. 4.95 o.p. (0-14-016928-8, Penguin Bks.) Penguin Group (USA) Inc.
—O Pioneers! Rosowski, Susan J. et al, eds. (Willa Cather Scholarly Edition Ser.). (Illus.). 2003. 392p. pap. text 20.00 (0-8032-6437-2); 1992. 295p. pap. text 14.95 (0-8032-6371-6, Bison Bks.) Univ. of Nebraska Pr.
—O Pioneers! 1989. 352p. pap. 6.95 o.p. (0-14-039070-7, Penguin Classics) Viking Penguin.
—O, Pioneers. 2004. 240p. mass mkt. 4.95 (0-451-52919-7, Signet Classics) NAL.
—O Pioneers! l.t. ed. 1981. 279p. lib. bdg. 14.95 o.p. (0-89621-749-3, Bantam Classics) Bantam Bks.
—O Pioneers! 2001. (Collected Works of Willa Cather). 308p. reprint ed. pap. 28.00 (0-7426-5572-5) Classic Bks.
—O Pioneers! l.t. ed. 2002. 28.95 o.p. (0-7862-4108-X) Gale Group.
—O Pioneers! l.t. ed. 1997. (Large Print Heritage Ser.). 259p. lib. bdg. 28.95 (1-58118-018-7, 21493) LRS.
—O Pioneers! l.t. ed. 2001. (Large Print Ser.). 585p. lib. bdg. (1-58287-645-2) North Bks.
—O Pioneers! abr. ed. 1994. (Classics on Cassette). pap. 16.00 incl. audio (0-453-00876-3, 391292) Penguin/HighBridge.
—O Pionniers! 1989. Orig. Title: Oh Pioneers!. (FRE.). 310p. pap. 12.95 (0-7859-2117-6, 2070381382) French & European Pubns., Inc.
—Obscure Destinies. 1974. pap. 8.00 o.p. (0-394-71179-3, V-179, Vintage) Knopf Publishing Group.
Cather, Willa & Dickstein, Morris. A Lost Lady. 1999. (Penguin Twentieth-Century Classics Ser.). 192p. pap. 8.95 (0-14-118131-1) Viking Penguin.
Cather, Willa & Lindemann, Marilee. O Pioneers! 1999. E-Book 8.35 (0-585-36171-1) netLibrary, Inc.
Cather, Willa, et al. Obscure Destinies: Willa Cather Scholarly Edition. 1998. (Willa Cather Scholarly Edition Ser.). (Illus.). 460p. text 75.00 (0-8032-1430-8) Univ. of Nebraska Pr.
Cavanaugh, Kate. Pete Goes to Grand Island. 1992. (Illus.). 24p. (J). pap. 5.95 (0-9622353-3-4) KAC, Inc.
Chehak, Susan T. The Story of Annie D. 1989. 224p. 17.95 o.p. (0-395-51013-9) Houghton Mifflin Co.
Dailey, Janet. Boss Man from Ogallala: Nebraska. 1992. (Janet Dailey Americana Ser.: No. 877). per. (0-373-89877-0, 1-89877-4); 1987. (Americana Ser.: No. 27). pap. (0-373-89827-4) Harlequin Enterprises, Ltd. (Harlequin Bks.).
—Boss Man from Ogallala: Nebraska. l.t. ed. 2001. (Americana Ser.). 216p. 28.95 (0-7862-2693-5); (0-7540-4461-0); (0-7540-4462-9) Thorndike Pr.
—Boss Man from Ogallala: Nebraska. 2001. 104p. pap. 12.99 (0-7592-3804-9); 2001. E-Book 6.99 (0-7592-0098-X); 2001. E-Book 6.99 (0-7592-0843-3); 2001. E-Book 6.99 (1-58586-454-4); 2000. E-Book 6.99 (1-58586-452-8) ereads.com.
Fox, Lyal LeClair. Verdict of Vengeance. 2001. 156p. pap. (1-55212-747-8) Trafford Publishing.
Hansen, Ron. Isn't It Romantic? An Entertainment. 2003. 208p. 17.95 (0-06-051766-2) HarperCollins Pubs.
—Isn't It Romantic? An Entertainment. 2004. 208p. pap. 9.95 (0-06-051767-0, Perennial) HarperTrade.
—Nebraska: Stories. 1990. 208p. pap. 12.00 (0-87113-349-0, Atlantic Monthly Pr.); 1989. 204p. 16.95 o.p. (0-87113-252-4) Grove/Atlantic, Inc.
Harrison, Jim. Dalva. 1988. 18.95 o.p. (0-525-24624-X, Seymour Lawrence) NAL.
—The Road Home. 1998. 464p. 25.00 o.p. (0-87113-724-0, Atlantic Monthly Pr.); 432p. 150.00 o.p. (0-87113-729-1) Grove/Atlantic, Inc.
—The Road Home. 1999. 464p. pap. 14.00 (0-671-77833-1, Washington Square Pr.) Simon & Schuster.
Hayes, Penny. Omaha's Bell. 1999. 197p. pap. 11.95 (1-56280-232-1) Naiad Pr., Inc.
Heath, Jenny, illus. Prairie Meeting. 1998. (Cover-to-Cover Bks.). (J). (0-7891-2160-3); (0-7807-6787-X, Covercraft) Perfection Learning Corp.
Henry, Will. Brass Command. l.t. ed. 1999. (Paperback Ser.). 264p. pap. 22.95 o.p. (0-7838-8532-6) Thorndike Pr.
Kava, Alex. A Perfect Evil. l.t. ed. 2002. 651p. 28.95 (0-7862-3997-2) Gale Group.
—A Perfect Evil. 2001. 408p. mass mkt. (1-55166-824-6, Harlequin Bks.); 2000. 384p. (1-55166-573-5, 1-66573-6, Mira Bks.) Harlequin Enterprises, Ltd.
Kloefkorn, William. A Time to Sink Her Pretty Little Ship. 1999. 67p. pap. 11.95 (0-9674123-0-7) Logan Hse.
Lacy, Al & Lacy, JoAnna. Blessed Are the Merciful, 10 vols. 2003. (Mail Order Bride Ser.: Vol. 4). 288p. pap. 10.99 (1-57673-417-X) Multnomah Pubs., Inc.
—Blessed Are the Merciful. l.t. ed. 2000. (Christian Fiction Ser.). 395p. 26.95 o.p. (0-7862-2520-3) Thorndike Pr.
Ludlum, Robert. The Road to Omaha. 1993. 608p. mass mkt. 7.99 (0-553-56044-1) Bantam Bks.
Mano, D. Keith. Topless. 1992. mass mkt. 4.99 o.s.i (0-449-22165-2, Fawcett) Ballantine Bks.
Moody, Ralph. The Dry Divide. 1963. (Illus.). 8.95 o.p. (0-393-07432-3) Norton, W. W. & Co., Inc.
—The Dry Divide. 1994. (Illus.). 230p. pap. 11.95 (0-8032-8216-8, Bison Bks.) Univ. of Nebraska Pr.
Morris, Wright. Ceremony in Lone Tree. 2001. 304p. pap. 16.00 (0-8032-8276-1); 1973. viii, 304p. reprint ed. pap. 9.95 o.p. (0-8032-5782-1) Univ. of Nebraska Pr. (Bison Bks.).
—Plains Song: For Female Voices. 1991. 232p. reprint ed. pap. 10.95 o.s.i (0-87923-835-6) Godine, David R. Pub.
—Plains Song: For Female Voices. 1980. (Illus.). 12.95 o.p. (0-06-013047-4) HarperTrade.
—Plains Song: For Female Voices. 2000. (Illus.). 229p. pap. 14.00 (0-8032-8267-2, Bison Bks.) Univ. of Nebraska Pr.
—Plains Song: For Female Voices. 1981. (Contemporary American Fiction Ser.). 241p. pap. 6.95 o.p. (0-14-005778-1, Penguin Bks.) Viking Penguin.
Neihardt, John G. The End of the Dream & Other Stories. 1991. 115p. text 25.00 (0-8032-3326-4) Univ. of Nebraska Pr.
Patchett, Ann. The Magician's Assistant. 368p. 1998. pap. 14.00 (0-15-600621-9, Harvest Bks.); 1997. 23.00 (0-15-100263-0) Harcourt Trade Pubs.
Porter, Caryl. A Child Among Us. 1995. 10.99 o.p. (0-7852-8096-0) Nelson, Thomas Inc.
Reynolds, William J. Drive-By: A Nebraska Mystery. Emmel, Gayle, ed. 1995. 329p. pap. 5.95 (0-944287-14-X) Ex Machina.
Ross, Dana Fuller, pseud. Nebraska! 1984. mass mkt. 3.99 o.s.i (0-553-80002-7); 400p. mass mkt. 4.95 o.s.i (0-553-26162-2) Bantam Bks.
—Nebraska! (Reader's Request Ser.). 1982. lib. bdg. 18.95 o.p. (0-8161-3315-8); 1993. 64.95 o.p. incl. audio (0-7838-1105-5) Gale Group. (Macmillan Reference USA).
Ruckman, Ivy. In Care of Cassie Tucker. 1998. 176p. (gr. 5-8). text 14.95 o.s.i (0-385-32514-2, Dell Books for Young Readers) Random Hse. Children's Bks.
—Night of the Twister. 1984. 160p. (J). (gr. 3-6). 14.95 o.p. (0-690-04408-9) HarperCollins Children's Bk. Group.

Settings

—Night of the Twister. 1986. 11.00 (0-606-02536-7) Turtleback Bks.

—Night of the Twisters. 160p. (J). (gr. 4-7). 1984. lib. bdg. 15.89 (0-690-04409-7); 1986. reprint ed. pap. 5.99 (0-06-440176-6, Harper Trophy) HarperCollins Children's Bk. Group.

Saban, Vera. Jennie Barnes: Right Now Forever. 1990. (This Is America Ser.). (Illus.). 130p. (Orig.). (J). (gr. 4-6). pap. 6.95 (0-914565-34-6, Timbertrails) Capstan Pubns.

—The Westering: Joanna. 1994. (This Is America Ser.). (J). 15.95 (0-914565-43-5) Capstan Pubns.

Sandoz, Mari. Miss Morissa: Doctor of the Gold Trail. 1980. 249p. reprint ed. pap. 13.95 (0-8032-9118-3, Bison Bks.) Univ. of Nebraska Pr.

Schaffert, Timothy. The Phantom Limbs of the Rollow Sisters. 2002. 240p. 23.95 o.s.i (0-399-14900-7, BlueHen Bks.) Putnam Publishing Group, The.

Schulte, Elaine L. Voyage. 1996. (Palisades Pure Romance Ser.). 245p. pap. 9.99 o.s.i (1-57673-011-5, Palisades) Multnomah Pubs., Inc.

Sharpe, Jon. Nebraska Nightmare. 1994. (Trailsman Ser.: No. 146). 176p. (Orig.). mass mkt. 3.50 o.s.i (0-451-17876-9, Signet Bks.) NAL.

—Nebraska Slaying Ground. 2000. (Trailsman Ser.: Vol. 226). 176p. mass mkt. 4.99 o.s.i (0-451-20097-7, Signet Bks.) NAL.

Sherwood, Ben. The Man Who Ate the 747. unabr. ed. 2000. audio compact disk 29.95 o.s.i (0-553-71225-X, RH Audio) Random Hse. Audio Publishing Group.

Stark, Richard. The Jugger. 2002. 224p. pap. 12.95 (0-446-67774-4, Mysterious Pr. Paperback Bks.) Warner Bks., Inc.

Thomas, Dorothy. The Getaway & Other Stories. 2002. 120p. pap. 29.95 (0-8032-9448-4, Bison Bks.) Univ. of Nebraska Pr.

—Ma Jeeter's Girls. 1986. (Illus.). 197p. reprint ed. pap. 11.95 (0-8032-9405-0, Bison Bks.); text 17.95 o.p. (0-8032-4414-2) Univ. of Nebraska Pr.

Thompson, Jim. Heed the Thunder. 1994. 320p. pap. 12.00 (0-679-74014-7) Random Hse., Inc.

Walker, Mildred. Light from Arcturus. 1995. 343p. pap. 13.95 (0-8032-9769-6, Bison Bks.) Univ. of Nebraska Pr.

Weir, Theresa. Cool Shade. 1998. 272p. mass mkt. 5.99 o.s.i (0-06-108462-X) HarperCollins Pubs.

Whitson, Stephanie G. Karyn's Memory Box. 1999. (Keepsake Legacies Ser.: Bk. 2). 288p. pap. 12.99 (0-7852-7186-4) Nelson, Thomas Pubs.

Whitson, Stephanie Grace. Secrets on the Wind. 2003. (Pine Ridge Portraits Ser.). (Illus.). 320p. pap. 12.99 (0-7642-2785-8) Bethany Hse. Pubs.

Wiltse, David. The Hangman's Knot. 2003. 336p. reprint ed. mass mkt. 6.99 (0-312-98936-9, St. Martin's Paperbacks) St. Martin's Pr.

—Heartland. 2001. 291p. 24.95 (0-312-26957-9) St. Martin's Pr.

—The Lynching: A Novel. 2002. 352p. 24.95 (0-312-28371-7) St. Martin's Pr.

Winther, Sophus. Take All to Nebraska. 1976. 314p. pap. 97.40 (0-608-05111-X, 206567000005) Bks. on Demand.

Winther, Sophus K. Mortgage Your Heart. Scott, Franklyn D., ed. 1979. (Scandinavians in America Ser.). reprint ed. lib. bdg. 29.95 (0-405-11665-9) Ayer Co. Pubs., Inc.

—Take All to Nebraska. 1976. vi, 306p. reprint ed. pap. 7.50 o.p. (0-8032-5831-3); text 24.95 o.p. (0-8032-0861-8) Univ. of Nebraska Pr.

Wiseman, Stan. Cody's Ride. l.t. ed. 1994. 324p. lib. bdg. 16.95 (0-8161-5929-7, Macmillan Reference USA) Gale Group.

—Cody's Ride. 1993. 182p. 19.95 (0-8027-1266-5) Walker & Co.

## NETHERLANDS—FICTION

Asscher-Pinkhof, Clara. Star Children. Edelstein, Terese & Smidt, Inez, trs. Orig. Title: Sterrekinderen. (Illus.). 267p. reprint ed. pap. 82.80 (0-608-10614-3, 207123600009) Bks. on Demand.

—Star Children. Edelstein, Terese & Smidt, Inez, trs. from DUT. 1987. Orig. Title: Sterrekinderen. (Illus.). 268p. reprint ed. 29.95 o.p. (0-8143-1846-0) Wayne State Univ. Pr.

Baantjer, Albert C. Dekok & Death of a Clown. Smittenaar, H. G., tr. from DUT. 1997. 240p. pap. 8.95 o.p. (1-881164-20-9) Intercontinental Publishing, Inc.

—Dekok & Murder by Melody. Smittenaar, H. G., tr. from DUT. 1997. 240p. pap. 8.95 o.p. (1-881164-19-5) Intercontinental Publishing, Inc.

—Dekok & Murder in Ecstacy. Smittenaar, H. G., tr. from DUT. 1998. (Dekok Ser.: Vol. 16). Tr. of Decock en de Moord in Extase. 196p. pap. 9.95 (1-881164-16-0) Intercontinental Publishing, Inc.

—Dekok & Murder in Seance. Smittenaar, H. G., tr. from DUT. 1996. 205p. pap. 8.95 (1-881164-15-2) Intercontinental Publishing, Inc.

—DeKok & Murder on the Menu. Smittenaar, H. G., tr. from DUT. 1992. (Dekok Ser.: Vol. 31). 180p. pap. 7.95 (1-881164-31-4) Intercontinental Publishing, Inc.

—Dekok & the Begging Death. Smittenaar, H. G., tr. from DUT. 1999. (Dekok Ser.: Vol. 17). 200p. pap. 9.95 (1-881164-17-9) Intercontinental Publishing, Inc.

—DeKok & the Brothers of the Easy Death. Smittenaar, H. G., tr. from DUT. 1995. 196p. pap. 7.95 (1-881164-13-6) Intercontinental Publishing, Inc.

—DeKok & the Careful Killer. Smittenaar, H. G., tr. from DUT. 1993. 245p. pap. 7.95 (1-881164-07-1) Intercontinental Publishing, Inc.

—DeKok & the Corpse at the Church Wall. Smittenaar, H. G., tr. from DUT. 1994. 202p. pap. 7.95 (1-881164-10-1) Intercontinental Publishing, Inc.

—DeKok & the Dancing Death. Smittenaar, H. G., tr. from DUT. 1994. 217p. (Orig.). pap. 7.95 (1-881164-11-X) Intercontinental Publishing, Inc.

—DeKok & the Dead Harlequin. Smittenaar, H. G., tr. from DUT. 1993. 226p. pap. 7.95 (1-881164-04-7) Intercontinental Publishing, Inc.

—Dekok & the Deadly Accord. Smittenaar, H. G., tr. from DUT. 1996. 205p. pap. 8.95 (1-881164-14-4) Intercontinental Publishing, Inc.

—DeKok & the Disillusioned Corpse. Smittenaar, H. G., tr. from DUT. 1993. 246p. (Orig.). pap. 7.95 (1-881164-06-3) Intercontinental Publishing, Inc.

—DeKok & the Dying Stroller. Smittenaar, H. G., tr. from DUT. 1994. 199p. pap. 7.95 (1-881164-09-8) Intercontinental Publishing, Inc.

—Dekok & the Geese of Death. Smittenaar, H. G., tr. from DUT. 2001. 200p. pap. 9.95 (1-881164-18-7) Intercontinental Publishing, Inc.

—DeKok & the Naked Lady. Smittenaar, H. G., tr. from DUT. 1994. (Dekok Ser.: Vol. 12). 205p. pap. 7.95 (1-881164-12-8) Intercontinental Publishing, Inc.

—DeKok & the Romantic Murder. Smittenaar, H. G., tr. from DUT. 1994. 199p. (Orig.). pap. 7.95 (1-881164-08-X) Intercontinental Publishing, Inc.

—DeKok & the Somber Nude. Smittenaar, H. G., tr. from DUT. 1992. 232p. (Orig.). pap. 7.95 (1-881164-01-2) Intercontinental Publishing, Inc.

—DeKok & the Sorrowing Tomcat. Smittenaar, H. G., tr. from DUT. 1993. 240p. pap. 13.95 (1-881164-61-6); pap. 7.95 (1-881164-05-5) Intercontinental Publishing, Inc.

—DeKok & the Sorrowing Tomcat: Mystery. 2001. 256p. 23.95 (0-312-24191-7, Saint Martin's Minotaur) St. Martin's Pr.

—Dekok & Variations on Murder. Smittenaar, H. G., tr. from DUT. 1997. 240p. pap. 8.95 o.p. (1-881164-21-7) Intercontinental Publishing, Inc.

—Murder in Amsterdam: Two "Dekok" Adventures: "Dekok & the Sunday Strangler" & "Dekok & the Corpse on Christmas Eve" Smittenaar, H. G., tr. from DUT. 1996. (Dekok Ser.: Vol. 1). 215p. reprint ed. pap. 9.95 (1-881164-00-4) Intercontinental Publishing, Inc.

Bayley, John. The Red Hat. 1998. 224p. 21.95 (0-312-18658-4) St. Martin's Pr.

—The Red Hat. 2001. 196p. pap. 14.00 (1-56649-194-0) Welcome Rain Pubs.

Bowen, Marjorie. I Will Maintain. 2000. 252p. pap. 9.95 (0-594-00636-8); E-Book 3.95 (0-594-01888-9) 1873 Pr.

—I Will Maintain. 1993. (William & Mary Trilogy Ser.: Vol. 1). 383p. pap. 15.90 (0-921100-42-6) Inheritance Pubns.

Campbell, Will D. Cecelia's Sin. 1986. 93p. 7.95 o.s.i (0-86554-086-1, MUP/H077); pap. 8.95 o.s.i (0-86554-213-9, MUP/P026) Mercer Univ. Pr.

Chevalier, Tracy. Girl with a Pearl Earring. 240p. 2000. 21.95 (0-525-94527-X, Dutton); 2003. pap. 14.00 (0-452-28493-7, Plume); 2001. reprint ed. pap. 14.00 (0-452-28215-2, Plume) Dutton/Plume.

—Girl with a Pearl Earring. l.t. ed. 2001. 12.95 (1-56895-186-8); 2000. 283p. 26.95 o.p. (1-56895-850-1) Gale Group. (Wheeler Publishing, Inc.).

—Girl with a Pearl Earring. 1999. 248p. (0-00-225890-0) HarperCollins Pubs.

—Girl with a Pearl Earring. abr. ed. 2001. audio 24.95 (1-56511-496-5); audio compact disk 26.95 (1-56511-497-3) HighBridge Co.

—Girl with a Pearl Earring. unabr. ed. 2001. audio 25.95 (0-7887-6044-0); 2000. audio 57.00 (0-7887-4355-4) Recorded Bks., LLC.

—Girl with a Pearl Earring. 2001. 18.05 (0-606-20673-6) Turtleback Bks.

—La Joven de la Perla. (SPA., Illus.). 312p. 22.95 (84-204-4236-4) Alfaguara, Ediciones, S.A.- Grupo Santillana ESP. *Dist:* Santillana USA Publishing Co., Inc.

Conover, Chris. Mother Goose & the Sly Fox, RS. (Illus.). 32p. (J). (ps-3). 1991. pap. 4.95 o.p. (0-374-45397-7, Sunburst); 1989. 15.00 o.p. (0-374-35072-8, Farrar, Straus & Giroux (BYR)) Farrar, Straus & Giroux.

Cooperstein, Claire. Johanna: A Novel of Johanna van Gogh-Bonger. 1995. 22.00 (0-684-80234-1, Scribner) Simon & Schuster.

Davenport, Will. The Painter. 2003. 336p. pap. 12.95 (0-553-38206-3) Bantam Bks.

De Jong, Dola. The Tree & the Vine. 1996. 152p. reprint ed. pap. 9.95 (1-55861-141-X); lib. bdg. 27.95 (1-55861-140-1) Feminist Pr. at The City Univ. of New York.

De Vries, Anne. Journey Through the Night. der Nederlanden, Harry, tr. from DUT. 2001. (Illus.). 373p. pap. 14.90 (0-921100-25-6) Inheritance Pubns.

DeJong, Meindert. The Tower by the Sea. 1990. (Illus.). 17.00 (0-8446-6246-1) Smith, Peter Pub., Inc.

Dodge, Mary M. Children's Classics: Hans Brinker, & the Silver Skates. 1989. (Children's Classics Ser.). (Illus.). 352p. (J). 12.99 o.s.i (0-517-68798-4) Random Hse. Value Publishing.

Dodge, Mary Mapes. Hans Brinker or the Silver Skates. 1993. (Classics Ser.). 256p. (gr. 8-12). mass mkt. 3.99 (0-8125-3342-9, Tor Classics) Doherty, Tom Assocs., LLC.

—Hans Brinker or the Silver Skates. 1988. 352p. (J). (gr. 4-6). mass mkt. 3.99 o.p. (0-590-41295-7, Scholastic Paperbacks) Scholastic, Inc.

Dressler, Mylene. The Deadwood Beetle. 2002. 256p. pap. 13.00 (0-425-18760-8) Berkley Publishing Group.

—The Deadwood Beetle. 2001. 208p. 23.95 o.p. (0-399-14805-1, BlueHen Bks.) Putnam Publishing Group, The.

—The Deadwood Beetle. l.t. ed. 2001. 289p. 28.95 (0-7838-9665-4) Thorndike Pr.

Edge, Arabella. The Company. 2002. 384p. E-Book 9.99 (0-7432-1840-X, Simon & Schuster) Simon & Schuster.

—The Company: Story of a Murderer. 2001. (Illus.). 384p. 23.00 (0-7432-1342-4, Simon & Schuster) Simon & Schuster.

—The Company: The Story of a Murderer. 2000. 371p. (0-330-36220-8) Picador.

—The Company: The Story of a Murderer. 2003. 384p. pap. 12.00 (0-7434-1918-9, Simon & Schuster) Simon & Schuster.

Elsink, Henk. Murder by Fax. 1992. 241p. pap. 7.95 (1-881164-52-7) Intercontinental Publishing, Inc.

Elsschot, Willem. Cheese. 2002. 160p. 14.95 (1-86207-481-X) Granta.

Enquist, Anna. The Secret. Ringold, Jennette K., tr. from DUT. 2000. 274p. 29.95 (1-902881-07-9); pap. 15.95 (1-902881-12-5) Toby Pr.

Freeling, Nicolas. Arlette. 1982. pap. 2.95 o.p. (0-394-75260-0, Pantheon) Knopf Publishing Group.

—Aupres de Ma Blonde. 1979. pap. 2.95 o.p. (0-394-74550-7, Vintage) Knopf Publishing Group.

—Because of the Cats. 2000. 190p. pap. (1-900850-36-2) Arcadia Bks.

—Because of the Cats. l.t. ed. 1987. pap. 13.95 o.p. (1-55504-040-3) BBC Audiobooks America.

—Because of the Cats. 1975. (Crime Ser.). 192p. pap. 3.95 o.p. (0-14-002282-1, Penguin Bks.) Viking Penguin.

—Criminal Conversation. 2001. 218p. pap. 9.95 (1-84232-842-5) House of Stratus, Inc. GBR. *Dist:* Midpoint Trade Bks., Inc.

—Criminal Conversation. 1981. (Inspector Van der Valk Suspense Novel Ser.). 213p. pap. 2.50 o.p. (0-394-74692-9, V-692) Random Hse., Inc.

—Double - Barrel. 1981. (Inspector Van der Valk Suspense Novel Ser.). 224p. pap. 2.50 o.p. (0-394-74693-7, V-693) Random Hse., Inc.

—Double - Barrel. 1975. 208p. pap. 1.95 o.p. (0-14-002585-5, Penguin Bks.) Viking Penguin.

—Gun Before Butter. 2001. 216p. pap. 9.95 (1-84232-838-7) House of Stratus, Inc. GBR. *Dist:* Midpoint Trade Bks., Inc.

—The King of the Rainy Country. 2001. 167p. pap. 9.95 (1-84232-843-3) House of Stratus, Inc. GBR. *Dist:* Midpoint Trade Bks., Inc.

—The King of the Rainy Country. 1975. (Crime Ser.). 160p. pap. 3.95 o.p. (0-14-002853-6, Penguin Bks.) Viking Penguin.

—Love in Amsterdam. 1990. 190p. pap. 3.95 o.p. (0-88184-613-9, Carroll & Graf Pubs.) Avalon Publishing Group.

—Love in Amsterdam. 2001. 196p. pap. 9.95 (1-84232-839-5) House of Stratus, Inc. GBR. *Dist:* Midpoint Trade Bks., Inc.

—Love in Amsterdam. 1975. (Crime Ser.). 192p. pap. 3.95 o.p. (0-14-002281-3, Penguin Bks.) Viking Penguin.

—The Lovely Ladies. 1981. (Inspector Van der Valk Suspense Novel Ser.). pap. 3.95 o.p. (0-394-74694-5, V-694) Random Hse., Inc.

—The Lovely Ladies. 1989. 288p. pap. 3.95 o.p. (0-14-011367-3, Penguin Bks.) Viking Penguin.

—Sand Castles. l.t. ed. 1990. 17.95 o.p. (0-7451-9898-8, C0626); pap. 15.95 o.p. (0-7927-0358-8, C0820) BBC Audiobooks America.

—Sand Castles. 2001. 210p. pap. 9.95 (1-84232-864-6) House of Stratus, Inc. GBR. *Dist:* Midpoint Trade Bks., Inc.

—Sand Castles. 1990. 17.95 (0-89296-372-7) Mysterious Pr.

—Sand Castles. 1991. mass mkt. 4.95 o.s.i (0-445-40925-8) Warner Bks., Inc.

—Some Day Tomorrow. 2000. 224p. 22.95 (0-312-26230-2, Saint Martin's Minotaur) St. Martin's Pr.

—Strike Out Where Not Applicable. 2001. 206p. pap. 9.95 (1-84232-845-X) House of Stratus, Inc. GBR. *Dist:* Midpoint Trade Bks., Inc.

—Strike Out Where Not Applicable. 1985. (Crime Ser.). 176p. pap. 3.95 o.p. (0-14-003009-3, Penguin Bks.) Viking Penguin.

—The Widow. 2001. 280p. pap. 9.95 (1-84232-850-6) House of Stratus, Inc. GBR. *Dist:* Midpoint Trade Bks., Inc.

—The Widow. 1980. 256p. pap. 3.95 o.p. (0-394-74467-5, Vintage); 1979. 8.95 o.p. (0-394-50336-8, Pantheon) Knopf Publishing Group.

Friedman, Carl. Nightfather. Pomerans, Arnold J. & Pomerans, Erica, trs. from DUT. 144p. 2002. (C). pap. 7.95 (0-89255-210-7); 1994. 18.50 o.p. (0-89255-193-3) Persea Bks., Inc.

Grunberg, Arnon. Blue Mondays. Pomerans, Arnold J. & Pomerans, Erica, trs. from DUT. 1997. 278p. 22.00 o.p. (0-374-11485-4) Farrar, Straus & Giroux.

—Blue Mondays. 1997. 278p. o.s.i (0-436-20458-4) Random Hse. of Canada, Ltd.

Heller, Joseph. Picture This. 1989. 352p. mass mkt. 5.99 o.s.i (0-345-35886-4) Ballantine Bks.

—Picture This. 1988. 336p. 19.95 o.p. (0-399-13355-0, G. P. Putnam's Sons) Penguin Putnam Bks. for Young Readers.

—Picture This. 2000. 352p. pap. 13.00 (0-684-86819-9, Simon & Schuster) Simon & Schuster.

Henty, G. A. By England's Aid: The Freeing of the Netherlands, 1585-1604. 2000. 20.99 (1-887159-37-1) Preston-Speed Pubns.

Herr, Ethel L. The Dove & the Rose. 1996. (Seekers Ser.: Vol. 1). 336p. pap. 9.99 o.p. (1-55661-746-1) Bethany Hse. Pubs.

Howell, Brian. The Dance of Geometry. 2002. 214p. 24.95 (1-902881-47-8) Toby Pr.

Jaffe, Daniel M. The Limits of Pleasure: A Novel. 2001. 172p. pap. 14.95 (1-56023-373-7); lib. bdg. 24.95 (1-56023-372-9) Haworth Pr., Inc., The. (Harrington Park Pr.).

Kernan, Michael. The Lost Diaries of Frans Hals. 1995. pap. 13.95 (0-312-13117-8, Saint Martin's Griffin); 1994. 336p. 23.95 o.p. (0-312-10946-6) St. Martin's Pr.

Laker, Rosalind, pseud. The Golden Tulip. l.t. ed. 1993. (General Ser.). 896p. 24.95 o.p. (0-8161-5573-9); pap. 19.95 o.p. (0-8161-5574-7) Gale Group. (Macmillan Reference USA).

Lambregtse, Cornelius. He Gathers the Lambs. 1996. (J). 12.90 (0-921100-77-9) Inheritance Pubns.

Liss, David. The Coffee Trader: A Novel. 2004. 416p. pap. 14.95 (0-375-76090-3) Ballantine Bks.

—The Coffee Trader: A Novel. 2003. 400p. 24.95 (0-375-50854-6) Random Hse., Inc.

Maguire, Gregory. Confessions of an Ugly Stepsister. l.t. ed. 2000. 385p. 28.95 (1-56895-884-6, Wheeler Publishing, Inc.) Gale Group.

—Confessions of an Ugly Stepsister. E-Book 12.00 (0-06-051739-5); E-Book 12.00 (0-06-051740-9); E-Book 12.00 (0-06-051741-7); E-Book 12.00 (0-06-051738-7); 2004. audio (0-06-056773-2, ReganBooks); 1999. (Illus.). 384p. 25.00 (0-06-039282-7, ReganBooks); 2000. (Illus.). 400p. reprint ed. pap. 15.00 (0-06-098752-9, ReganBooks) HarperTrade.

—Confessions of an Ugly Stepsister. unabr. ed. 2000. audio 81.00 (0-7887-4321-X, 96227E7) Recorded Bks., LLC.

Mason, Anita. Perfection. 2003. (1-883523-63-X); pap. 14.00 (1-883523-54-0) Spinsters Ink Bks.

McEwan, Ian. Amsterdam: A Novel. unabr. ed. 1999. audio 24.00 (0-7366-4451-2, 4896) Books on Tape, Inc.

—Amsterdam: A Novel. Oeser, Hans-Christian, tr. from ENG. 1999. (GER.). 224p. (3-257-06220-6) Diogenes Verlag AG CHE. *Dist:* International Bk. Import Service, Inc.

—Amsterdam: A Novel. 1998. 208p. 21.00 o.s.i (0-385-49423-8, Talese, Nan A.) Doubleday Publishing.

—Amsterdam: A Novel. unabr. ed. 1999. audio 24.95 (1-57511-060-1) Publishing Mills, Inc., The.

—Amsterdam: A Novel. 1999. 208p. pap. 13.00 (0-385-49424-6, Knopf Bks. for Young Readers) Random Hse. Children's Bks.

—Amsterdam: A Novel. l.t. ed. 1999. (Basic Ser.). 232p. 29.95 (0-7862-1796-0) Thorndike Pr.

—Amsterdam: A Novel. abr. ed. 1999. audio 18.70 (0-00-105566-6) Ulverscroft Audio (U.S.A.).

Minco, Marga, et al. The Other Side. Levitt, Ruth et al, trs. from DUT. 1994. (UNESCO Collection of Representative Works). 118p. 30.00 (0-7206-0908-9) Owen, Peter Ltd. GBR. *Dist:* Dufour Editions, Inc.

Moggach, Deborah. Tulip Fever. l.t. ed. 2000. (General Ser.). 263p. pap. 22.95 (0-7862-2300-6) Thorndike Pr.

Moring, Marcel. The Great Longing. 1995. 211p. 20.00 o.p. (0-06-017243-6) HarperCollins Pubs.

—The Great Longing: A Novel. 1996. 224p. pap. 12.00 o.s.i (*0-06-092739-9*) HarperCollins Pubs.
Morley, John D. The Anatomy Lesson. 1996. 184p. pap. o.s.i (*0-349-10721-1*) Little Brown & Co.
—The Anatomy Lesson: A Novel. 1995. (Illus.). 184p. 21.95 o.p. (*0-312-13426-6*) St. Martin's Pr.
Mulisch, Harry. The Assault. White, Claire, tr. from DUT. 1986. 192p. pap. 13.00 (*0-394-74420-9*, Pantheon) Knopf Publishing Group.
—The Discovery of Heaven: A Novel. 1997. 736p. pap. 17.00 (*0-14-023937-5*) Penguin Group (USA) Inc.
—The Discovery of Heaven: A Novel. Vincent, Paul, tr. from DUT. 1996. 752p. 34.95 o.s.i (*0-670-85668-1*) Viking Penguin.
—Last Call. Dixon, Adrienne, tr. from DUT. 1991. 288p. pap. 18.00 (*0-14-015601-1*, Penguin Bks.) Penguin Group (USA) Inc.
—Last Call. Dixon, Adrienne, tr. 1989. 288p. 18.95 o.p. (*0-670-82549-2*) Viking Penguin.
Neels, Betty. Saturday's Child. l.t. ed. 2001. (Dales Large Print Ser.). 336p. pap. 21.99 o.p. (*1-84262-088-6*) Dales Large Print Bks. GBR. *Dist:* Ulverscroft Large Print Bks., Ltd., Ulverscroft Large Print Canada, Ltd.
—Saturday's Child. 1998. pap. (*0-373-83394-6*, 1-83394-6, Harlequin Bks.) Harlequin Enterprises, Ltd.
Orczy, Baroness Emmuska. The Laughing Cavalier. 1976. lib. bdg. 18.50 (*0-89968-076-3*, Lightyear Pr.) Buccaneer Bks., Inc.
Prins, Piet. Scout: The Secret of the Swamp. 1997. (DUT & ENG.). 176p. (J). pap. 8.90 (*0-921100-50-7*) Inheritance Pubns.
Simenon, Georges. Maigret in Holland. 2003. 180p. pap. 8.00 (*0-15-602852-2*); 2nd ed. 1994. 182p. pap. 5.95 o.s.i (*0-15-600084-9*) Harcourt Trade Pubs. (Harvest Bks.).
—Maigret in Holland. Sainsbury, Geoffrey, tr. 2nd ed. 1993. 165p. 18.95 o.s.i (*0-15-155159-6*) Harcourt Trade Pubs.
Stadler, Matthew. The Dissolution of Nicholas Dee. 1993. (Robert Stewart Bks.). (Illus.). 325p. text 20.00 (*0-684-19352-3*, Macmillan Reference USA) Gale Group.
—The Dissolution of Nicholas Dee. 2000. 352p. reprint ed. pap. 13.00 (*0-8021-3696-6*, Grove Pr.) Grove/Atlantic, Inc.
—The Dissolution of Nicholas Dee: A Novel. 1994. pap. 12.00 o.p. (*0-06-097627-6*, Perennial) HarperTrade.
Stevenson, Jane. The Shadow King. 2003. 320p. 24.00 (*0-618-14913-9*) Houghton Mifflin Co.
—The Winter Queen: A Novel. 2002. 320p. 25.00 (*0-618-14912-0*) Houghton Mifflin Co.
—The Winter Queen: A Novel. 2003. 336p. pap. 13.00 (*0-618-38267-4*, Mariner Bks.) Houghton Mifflin Co. Trade & Reference Div.
Stone, Irving. Lust for Life. 29.95 (*0-89190-127-2*) Amereon, Ltd.
—Lust for Life. 1994. lib. bdg. 29.95 (*1-56849-480-7*) Buccaneer Bks., Inc.
—Lust for Life. 1959. 17.95 o.s.i (*0-385-04270-1*) Doubleday Publishing.
—Lust for Life. 1984. 512p. pap. 15.95 (*0-452-26249-6*, Plume) Dutton/Plume.
—Lust for Life. 1984. pap. 8.95 o.p. (*0-452-25517-1*); 1981. mass mkt. 3.95 o.p. (*0-451-09898-6*, E9898, Signet Bks.) NAL.
Van de Wetering, Janwillem. The Blond Baboon. 1987. 224p. mass mkt. 2.95 o.s.i (*0-345-34497-9*) Ballantine Bks.
—The Blond Baboon. l.t. ed. 1993. 12.50 o.p. (*0-8161-6646-3*, Macmillan Reference USA) Gale Group.
—The Blond Baboon, 001. 1978. 7.95 o.p. (*0-395-26307-7*) Houghton Mifflin Co.
—The Blond Baboon. 1979. (gr. 12). pap. 1.95 o.s.i (*0-671-82318-3*, Pocket) Simon & Schuster.
—The Blond Baboon. 1996. 218p. pap. 12.00 (*1-56947-063-4*) Soho Pr., Inc.
—The Corpse on the Dike. 1987. 224p. mass mkt. 3.50 o.s.i (*0-345-33130-3*) Ballantine Bks.
—The Corpse on the Dike, 001. 1976. 6.95 o.p. (*0-395-24675-X*) Houghton Mifflin Co.
—The Corpse on the Dike. 1982. mass mkt. 2.95 o.s.i (*0-671-43527-2*, Pocket) Simon & Schuster.
—The Corpse on the Dike. 1995. 232p. pap. 12.00 (*1-56947-049-9*) Soho Pr., Inc.
—Death of a Hawker. 1987. 256p. mass mkt. 3.50 o.s.i (*0-345-33131-1*) Ballantine Bks.
—Death of a Hawker. 1977. 6.95 o.p. (*0-395-25171-0*) Houghton Mifflin Co.
—Death of a Hawker. 1980. (gr. 12). pap. 2.25 o.s.i (*0-671-83557-2*, Pocket) Simon & Schuster.
—Hard Rain. 1987. pap. o.s.i (*0-345-00732-8*); mass mkt. 3.95 o.s.i (*0-345-33964-9*) Ballantine Bks.
—Hard Rain. 1986. 288p. 15.95 o.s.i (*0-394-54924-4*, Pantheon) Knopf Publishing Group.
—Hard Rain. 1997. 313p. pap. 12.00 (*1-56947-104-5*) Soho Pr., Inc.
—The Hollow-Eyed Angel. 282p. 1997. pap. 13.00 (*1-56947-091-X*); 1996. 22.00 (*1-56947-056-1*) Soho Pr., Inc.
—The Japanese Corpse. 1987. mass mkt. 3.50 o.s.i (*0-345-33128-1*) Ballantine Bks.
—The Japanese Corpse, 001. 1977. 7.95 o.p. (*0-395-25777-8*) Houghton Mifflin Co.
—The Japanese Corpse. 1982. mass mkt. 2.95 o.s.i (*0-671-43528-0*, Pocket) Simon & Schuster.
—The Japanese Corpse. 1996. 296p. pap. 12.00 (*1-56947-057-X*) Soho Pr., Inc.
—Just a Corpse at Twilight. unabr. ed. 1998. (Grijpstra & De Gier Mystery Ser.). audio 44.00 (*0-7887-2181-X*, 95477E7) Recorded Bks., LLC.
—Just a Corpse at Twilight. 1995. 266p. pap. 12.00 (*1-56947-075-8*); 1994. 265p. 20.00 (*1-56947-016-2*) Soho Pr., Inc.
—The Maine Massacre. 1988. 240p. reprint ed. mass mkt. 3.95 o.s.i (*0-345-34496-0*) Ballantine Bks.
—The Maine Massacre, 001. 1978. 8.95 o.p. (*0-395-27395-1*) Houghton Mifflin Co.
—The Maine Massacre. unabr. ed. 1998. (Grijpstra & De Gier Mystery Ser.). audio 51.00 (*0-7887-2025-2*, 95400E7) Recorded Bks., LLC.
—The Maine Massacre. 1980. pap. 2.50 o.s.i (*0-671-82865-7*, Pocket) Simon & Schuster.
—The Maine Massacre. 1996. 231p. pap. 12.00 (*1-56947-064-2*) Soho Pr., Inc.
—The Mind-Murders. 1988. 208p. mass mkt. 3.95 o.s.i (*0-345-34495-2*) Ballantine Bks.
—The Mind-Murders, 001. 1981. 9.95 o.p. (*0-395-30544-6*) Houghton Mifflin Co.
—The Mind-Murders. 1984. mass mkt. 3.95 o.s.i (*0-671-54065-3*, Pocket) Simon & Schuster.
—The Mind-Murders. 1997. 224p. pap. 12.00 (*1-56947-092-8*) Soho Pr., Inc.
—Outsider in Amsterdam. 1986. mass mkt. 3.50 o.s.i (*0-345-33126-5*) Ballantine Bks.
—Outsider in Amsterdam. 1976. ix, 245p. (*0-434-85920-6*, Butterworth-Heinemann) Elsevier Science & Technology Bks.
—Outsider in Amsterdam, 001. 1975. 256p. 6.95 o.p. (*0-395-20705-3*) Houghton Mifflin Co.
—Outsider in Amsterdam. 1978. pap. 2.50 o.s.i (*0-671-43471-3*, Pocket) Simon & Schuster.
—Outsider in Amsterdam. 1994. 304p. pap. 12.00 (*1-56947-017-0*) Soho Pr., Inc.
—The Perfidious Parrot. 280p. 1998. (Amsterdam Cops Ser.: No. 14). pap. 12.00 (*1-56947-130-4*); 1997. 22.00 (*1-56947-102-9*) Soho Pr., Inc.
—The Rattle-Rat. 1986. mass mkt. 3.50 o.s.i (*0-345-32872-8*) Ballantine Bks.
—The Rattle-Rat. l.t. ed. 1986. 392p. 17.95 o.p. (*0-8161-4121-5*, Macmillan Reference USA) Gale Group.
—The Rattle-Rat. 1985. 14.95 o.s.i (*0-394-54710-1*, Pantheon) Knopf Publishing Group.
—The Rattle-Rat. 1997. 294p. pap. 12.00 (*1-56947-103-7*) Soho Pr., Inc.
—The Sergeant's Cat. l.t. ed. 1991. 8.95 o.p. (*0-7451-9503-2*, 78) BBC Audiobooks America.
—The Streetbird. 1983. 288p. 13.95 o.p. (*0-399-12808-5*, G. P. Putnam's Sons) Penguin Putnam Bks. for Young Readers.
—The Streetbird. 1985. mass mkt. 3.50 o.s.i (*0-671-47521-5*, Pocket) Simon & Schuster.
—The Streetbird. 1997. 288p. pap. 12.00 (*1-56947-093-6*) Soho Pr., Inc.
—Tumbleweed. 1987. mass mkt. 3.50 o.s.i (*0-345-33127-3*) Ballantine Bks.
—Tumbleweed. l.t. ed. 1978. lib. bdg. 11.50 o.p. (*0-8161-6569-6*, Macmillan Reference USA) Gale Group.
—Tumbleweed, 001. 1976. 6.95 o.p. (*0-395-24352-1*) Houghton Mifflin Co.
—Tumbleweed. 1994. (Crime Ser.). 224p. pap. 12.00 (*1-56947-018-9*) Soho Pr., Inc.
Van den Brink, H. M. On the Water. Vincent, Paul, tr. from DUT. 2001. 134p. 22.00 o.p. (*0-8021-1692-2*); 2002. 144p. reprint ed. pap. 11.00 (*0-8021-3895-0*) Grove/Atlantic, Inc. (Grove Pr.).
Van der Velde, Rink. The Trap. Baron, Henry J., tr. from FRI. 1997. 147p. 24.00 (*1-877946-80-X*) Permanent Pr., The.
—The Trap. Baron, Henry J., tr. from FRI. 1995. 144p. pap. 8.95 (*0-9645502-0-2*) Redux Pubns.
Van Steenwyk, Elizabeth. A Traitor among Us. 143p. (J). (gr. 4-7). 1999. pap. 6.00 (*0-8028-5157-6*); 1998. 15.00 (*0-8028-5150-9*) Eerdmans, William B. Publishing Co. (Eerdmans Bks For Young Readers).
—A Traitor among Us. 1999. 12.05 (*0-606-17601-2*) Turtleback Bks.
Weil, Grete. Last Trolley from Beethovenstraat. Barrett, John, tr. from GER. 1997. (Verba Mundi Ser.). 176p. 22.95 (*1-56792-031-4*) Godine, David R. Pub.
Weiss, David. I, Rembrandt. 1979. 10.95 o.p. (*0-312-40261-9*) St. Martin's Pr.

**NEVADA—FICTION**

Adair, Liz. After Goliath: A Spider Latham Mystery. 2003. 240p. pap. 13.95 (*1-59038-156-4*, 5838) Deseret Bk. Co.
—The Lodger: A Spider Latham Mystery. 2003. viii, 275p. pap. 13.95 (*1-57008-950-7*, 5839) Deseret Bk. Co.
Andrews, Sarah. An Eye for Gold. 2000. ix, 387p. 24.95 (*0-312-25349-4*, Saint Martin's Minotaur) St. Martin's Pr.
Arthur, Burt. Gunsmoke in Nevada. l.t. ed. 1990. pap. 16.95 o.p. (*0-7927-0479-7*, C0777); 12.95 o.p. (*0-7927-0478-9*, C0269) BBC Audiobooks America.
—Nevada. l.t. ed. 1993. 20.95 o.p. (*0-7927-1445-8*); pap. 18.95 o.p. (*0-7927-1444-X*) BBC Audiobooks America.
Baker, Elliott. Klynts Law. 1976. 312p. 8.95 o.p. (*0-15-147283-1*) Harcourt Trade Pubs.
Barber, Phyllis. And the Desert Shall Blossom: A Novel. 285p. reprint ed. pap. 88.40 (*0-7837-3965-6*, 204379400011) Bks. on Demand.
—And the Desert Shall Blossom: A Novel. 1993. 288p. reprint ed. pap. 14.95 o.p. (*1-56085-036-1*) Signature Bks., Inc.
—And the Desert Shall Blossom: A Novel. 1991. 340p. 23.95 o.p. (*0-87480-363-2*) Univ. of Utah Pr.
Barton, Dan. Heckler. 2001. 365p. 22.95 (*0-312-27183-2*, Saint Martin's Minotaur) St. Martin's Pr.
Bergon, Frank. Shoshone Mike. 1994. (Western Literature Ser.). 304p. pap. 16.00 (*0-87417-244-6*) Univ. of Nevada Pr.
—Shoshone Mike. 1987. 288p. 17.95 o.p. (*0-670-81563-2*) Viking Penguin.
—The Temptations of St. Ed & Brother S. Frank Bergon. 1993. (Western Literature Ser.). 320p. 22.00 (*0-87417-226-8*) Univ. of Nevada Pr.
—Wild Game. 1995. (Western Literature Ser.). 336p. 22.00 (*0-87417-257-8*) Univ. of Nevada Pr.
Berlin, Adam. Headlock. 2000. 265p. tchr. ed. 21.95 (*1-56512-266-6*, 72266) Algonquin Bks. of Chapel Hill.
Betts, Doris. The Sharp Teeth of Love. 1998. 352p. pap. 12.00 (*0-684-84475-3*, Touchstone) Simon & Schuster.
Bly, Stephen & Bly, Janet. Judith & the Judge. l.t. ed. 2004. 339p. pap. 14.95 (*1-59415-012-5*, Walker Large Print) Gale Group.
—Judith & the Judge. l.t. ed. 2003. (Carson City Chronicles Ser.). 339p. 26.95 (*0-7862-5827-6*) Thorndike Pr.
Bly, Stephen A. Coyote True, No. 2. 1992. (Nathan T. Riggins Western Adventure Ser.: Bk. 2). 128p. (J). (gr. 4-7). pap. 4.99 o.p. (*0-89107-680-8*) Crossway Bks.
—Fool's Gold. l.t. ed. 2001. (G. K. Hall Western Ser.). 352p. 25.95 (*0-7838-9489-9*) Thorndike Pr.
—Hidden Treasure. 2000. (Skinners of Goldfield Ser.: Bk. 2). 250p. pap. 11.99 (*1-58134-199-7*) Crossway Bks.
—Hidden Treasure. l.t. ed. 2001. (G.K. Hall Large Print Western Ser.). 365p. 25.95 (*0-7838-9609-3*, Macmillan Reference USA) Gale Group.
—The Last Stubborn Buffalo in Nevada. 1993. (Nathan T. Riggins Western Adventure Ser.: Vol. 4). 128p. (J). (gr. 4-9). pap. 4.99 o.p. (*0-89107-746-4*) Crossway Bks.
—Picture Rock. 2001. (Skinners of Goldfield Ser.: Vol. 3). 252p. pap. 11.99 (*1-58134-254-3*) Crossway Bks.
Bly, Stephen A. & Bly, Janet. Judith & the Judge. 2000. (Carson City Chronicles Ser.: Vol. 1). 258p. pap. 10.99 (*1-56955-158-8*) Servant Pubns.
—Roberta & the Renegade. 2000. (Carson City Chronicles Ser.: Vol. 3). 251p. pap. 10.99 (*1-56955-123-5*, Vine Bks.) Servant Pubns.
Borg, Todd. Tahoe Blowup: An Owen McKenna Mystery Thriller. 2001. (Illus.). 320p. per. 16.95 (*1-931296-12-X*) Thriller Pr.
Braithwaite, Kent. The Wonderland Murders. 2000. 324p. pap. 14.95 (*1-891929-33-X*) Four Seasons Pubs.
Branon, Bill. Devil's Hole: A Novel. 1995. 336p. 23.00 o.p. (*0-06-017760-8*) HarperCollins Pubs.
Britton, Vickie. The Devil's Gate. 2000. E-Book 3.99 (*1-58608-231-0*); 4.99 (*1-58608-017-2*) New Concepts Publishing.
Byrne, Robert. Mannequin. 1989. mass mkt. 3.95 o.s.i (*1-55817-300-5*, Pinnacle Bks.) Kensington Publishing Corp.
—Mannequin. 1988. 288p. 18.95 o.s.i (*0-689-11836-8*, Scribner) Simon & Schuster.
Cain, James M. Jealous Woman. l.t. ed. 1992. 198p. pap. 14.95 o.p. (*0-8161-5461-9*, Macmillan Reference USA) Gale Group.
Calder, Stephen. The High-Steel Hazard. 1993. (Bonanza Bk.: No. 3). 288p. mass mkt. 3.99 o.s.i (*0-553-29043-6*) Bantam Bks.
—The High-Steel Hazard. l.t. ed. 1995. (Bonanza Ser.: No. III). 380p. 19.95 o.p. (*0-7838-1389-9*, Macmillan Reference USA) Gale Group.
—The Trail to Timberline. l.t. ed. 1996. (Western Ser.: Vol. 6). 340p. 19.95 o.p. (*0-7838-1828-9*, Macmillan Reference USA) Gale Group.
Chaikin, Linda. Desert Star. 2004. pap. 10.99 (*0-7369-1235-5*) Harvest Hse. Pubs.
Chaikin, Linda L. Desert Rose. 2003. (Illus.). 350p. pap. 10.99 (*0-7369-1234-7*) Harvest Hse. Pubs.
Cheever, John. Falconer. 1982. mass mkt. 2.95 o.s.i (*0-345-30792-5*); 1980. mass mkt. 2.75 o.s.i (*0-345-28589-1*); 1978. mass mkt. 2.25 o.s.i (*0-345-27300-1*) Ballantine Bks.
—Falconer. 1977. (Adult Ser.). lib. bdg. 10.95 o.p. (*0-8161-6506-8*, Macmillan Reference USA) Gale Group.
Clark, Walter Van Tilburg. The Ox-Bow Incident. reprint ed. lib. bdg. 24.95 (*0-88411-135-0*) Amereon, Ltd.
—The Ox-Bow Incident. 1970. mass mkt. 0.95 o.p. (*0-451-50496-8*, Signet Classics); 1943. mass mkt. 1.50 o.p. (*0-451-51007-0*, Signet Classics); 1943. mass mkt. 0.60 o.p. (*0-451-50025-3*, Signet Classics); 1943. mass mkt. 0.60 o.p. (*0-451-50124-1*, Signet Classics); 1943. mass mkt. 0.75 o.p. (*0-451-50361-9*, Signet Classics); 1943. mass mkt. 2.50 o.p. (*0-451-51497-1*, Signet Classics); 1943. mass mkt. 1.25 o.p. (*0-451-50667-7*, Signet Classics); 1943. mass mkt. 1.75 o.p. (*0-451-51298-7*, Signet Classics); 1943. mass mkt. 2.95 o.p. (*0-451-51892-6*, Signet Classics); 1943. mass mkt. 0.25 o.p. (*0-451-00521-X*, Signet Bks.); 1943. mass mkt. 0.25 o.p. (*0-451-00745-X*, Signet Bks.); 1943. mass mkt. 0.25 o.p. (*0-451-01160-0*, Signet Bks.); 1943. mass mkt. 0.35 o.p. (*0-451-01470-7*, Signet Bks.) NAL.
—The Ox-Bow Incident. 2001. (Paperback Classics Ser.). (Illus.). 256p. pap. 9.95 (*0-375-75702-3*, Modern Library) Random House Adult Trade Publishing Group.
—The Ox-Bow Incident. 1990. 28.00 (*0-8446-0060-1*) Smith, Peter Pub., Inc.
—The Ox-Bow Incident. 1960. 11.05 (*0-606-01219-2*) Turtleback Bks.
Claus, Hugo. Desire. 1998. 288p. pap. 12.95 o.s.i (*0-14-025538-9*) Penguin Group (USA) Inc.
—Desire. Knecht, Stacey, tr. 1997. 224p. 24.95 o.p. (*0-670-86746-2*) Viking Penguin.
Collins, Jackie. Lethal Seduction. 2003. E-Book 26.00 (*0-7432-1112-X*); 2000. 480p. 26.00 (*0-684-85031-1*) Simon & Schuster. (Simon & Schuster).
—Lethal Seduction. l.t. ed. 2001. 720p. 32.50 o.p. (*0-7432-0425-5*) Thorpe, F. A. Pubs. GBR. *Dist:* Ulverscroft Large Print Bks., Ltd.
Connelly, Michael. Angels Flight. 1999. (Detective Harry Bosch Mysteries Ser.). 400p. (YA). (gr. 8 up). 25.00 o.p. (*0-316-15219-6*) Little Brown & Co.
—Angels Flight. l.t. ed. (Thorndike/G. K. Hall Paperback Bestsellers Ser.). 595p. 2000. pap. 27.95 (*0-7862-1865-7*); 1999. 30.95 (*0-7862-1864-9*) Thorndike Pr.
Connelly, Michael, contrib. by. Angels Flight. 1999. (*0-7540-1281-6*) BBC Audiobooks America.
Crichton, Michael. Prey: A Novel. 2002. 384p. 26.95 (*0-06-621412-2*); E-Book (*0-06-054079-6*); E-Book 14.95 (*0-06-054081-8*) HarperCollins Pubs.
—Prey: A Novel. l.t. ed. 2002. 624p. pap. 26.95 (*0-06-053698-5*, HarperLargePrint) HarperTrade.
—Prey: A Novel. 2003. 528p. mass mkt. 7.99 (*0-06-101572-5*, Avon Bks.) Morrow/Avon.
Dailey, Janet. Notorious. 1996. 368p. 24.00 o.p. (*0-06-017697-0*) HarperCollins Pubs.
Danks, Denise. Wink a Hopeful Eye. 2003. 224p. mass mkt. 7.95 (*0-7528-4397-4*) Orion Publishing Group, Ltd. GBR. *Dist:* Trafalgar Square.
—Wink a Hopeful Eye. 1994. 224p. 19.95 o.p. (*0-312-11355-2*, Saint Martin's Minotaur) St. Martin's Pr.
Daugherty, Tracy. What Falls Away: A Novel. 1996. 256p. 22.50 o.p. (*0-393-03837-8*) Norton, W. W. & Co., Inc.
Davidson, Sara. Cowboy: A Love Story. l.t. ed. 1999. 26.95 (*1-56895-758-0*, Wheeler Publishing, Inc.) Gale Group.
—Cowboy: A Love Story. 288p. 2000. pap. 13.00 (*0-06-093135-3*, Perennial); 1999. 24.00 (*0-06-099582-3*, HarperCollins); 1999. 24.00 o.p. (*0-06-019326-3*, HarperCollins) HarperTrade.
Devereaux, Grant. Nevada Bluff. 2001. 288p. pap. 12.95 (*0-9701466-1-2*); 19.95 (*0-9701466-0-4*) Athenean Pr., Inc.
Dibdin, Michael. Thanksgiving. 2002. 192p. pap. 12.00 (*0-375-72607-1*, Vintage) Knopf Publishing Group.
—Thanksgiving. l.t. ed. 2001. 213p. pap. 24.95 (*0-7862-3308-7*); 190p. (*0-7540-4501-3*); 190p. (*0-7540-4502-1*) Thorndike Pr.
Douglas, Carole Nelson. The Cat & the King of Clubs. 1999. (Mystery Ser.). 227p. 20.95 (*0-7862-1920-3*, Five Star) Gale Group.
—The Cat & the Queen of Hearts. 1999. (Mystery Ser.). 223p. 21.95 (*0-7862-2173-9*, Five Star) Gale Group.

Settings

—Cat in a Crimson Haze: A Midnight Louie Mystery. 1996. mass mkt. 219.68 (*0-8125-6330-1*); 1996. 408p. mass mkt. 6.99 (*0-8125-4414-5*, Forge Bks.); 1995. 352p. 22.95 o.p. (*0-312-85901-5*, Forge Bks.) Doherty, Tom Assocs., LLC.

—Cat in a Crimson Haze: A Midnight Louie Mystery. l.t. ed. 1995. (Midnight Louie Mystery Ser.). 604p. 24.95 o.p. (*0-7838-1390-2*, Macmillan Reference USA) Gale Group.

—Cat in a Crimson Haze: A Midnight Louie Mystery. 1996. mass mkt. 223.68 (*0-8125-6329-8*) Holtzbrinck Pubs.

—Cat in a Diamond Dazzle: A Midnight Louie Mystery. (Midnight Louie Mystery Ser.). 1997. 411p. mass mkt. 6.99 (*0-8125-5506-6*); 1996. 416p. 24.95 o.p. (*0-312-86085-4*) Doherty, Tom Assocs., LLC. (Forge Bks.).

—Cat in a Flamingo Fedora: A Midnight Louie Mystery. (Midnight Louie Mystery Ser.). 1998. 373p. mass mkt. 6.99 (*0-8125-6535-5*); 1997. 384p. 24.95 o.p. (*0-312-86329-2*) Doherty, Tom Assocs., LLC. (Forge Bks.).

—Cat in a Jeweled Jumpsuit: A Midnight Louie Mystery. 2000. 432p. mass mkt. 6.99 (*0-8125-6674-2*); 1999. 384p. 24.95 (*0-312-86817-0*) Doherty, Tom Assocs., LLC. (Forge Bks.).

—Cat in a Jeweled Jumpsuit: A Midnight Louie Mystery. l.t. ed. 2000. (Americana Ser.). 599p. 29.95 (*0-7862-2455-X*) Thorndike Pr.

—Cat in a Kiwi Con: A Midnight Louie Mystery. 2000. (Midnight Louie Mystery Ser.). 384p. 24.95 o.p. (*0-312-86955-X*, Forge Bks.) Doherty, Tom Assocs., LLC.

—Cat in an Indigo Mood: A Midnight Louie Mystery. l.t. ed. 2003. (Large Print Ser.). 29.95 (*1-57490-473-6*, Beeler Large Print Bks.) Beeler, Thomas T. Publisher.

—Cat in an Indigo Mood: A Midnight Louie Mystery. 1999. 384p. mass mkt. 6.99 (*0-8125-6187-2*); (Illus.). 381p. 24.95 (*0-312-86635-6*) Doherty, Tom Assocs., LLC. (Forge Bks.).

—Cat on a Blue Monday: A Midnight Louie Mystery. l.t. ed. 1994. o.p. (*0-7927-2111-X*); pap. o.p. (*0-7927-2110-1*) BBC Audiobooks America.

—Cat on a Blue Monday: A Midnight Louie Mystery. 1994. (Midnight Louie Mystery Ser.). 374p. mass mkt. 6.99 (*0-8125-3441-7*, Forge Bks.) Doherty, Tom Assocs., LLC.

—Cat on a Blue Monday: A Midnight Louie Mystery. l.t. ed. 1994. 540p. pap. 17.95 o.p. (*0-8161-7456-3*, Macmillan Reference USA) Gale Group.

—Cat on a Hyacinth Hunt: A Midnight Louie Mystery. (Midnight Louie Mystery Ser.). 384p. 1999. mass mkt. 6.99 (*0-8125-6186-4*); 1998. 23.95 (*0-312-86634-8*) Doherty, Tom Assocs., LLC. (Forge Bks.).

—Cat on a Hyacinth Hunt: A Midnight Louie Mystery. l.t. ed. 2000. pap. 23.95 (*1-56895-872-2*, Wheeler Publishing, Inc.) Gale Group.

—Cat with an Emerald Eye: A Midnight Louie Mystery. (Midnight Louie Mystery Ser.). 384p. 1997. mass mkt. 6.99 (*0-8125-4012-3*); 1996. 24.95 o.p. (*0-312-86228-8*) Doherty, Tom Assocs., LLC. (Forge Bks.).

—Catnap: A Midnight Louie Mystery. l.t. ed. 1993. (Midnight Louie Mystery Ser.). 23.95 o.p. (*0-7927-1644-2*); pap. 21.95 o.p. (*0-7927-1643-4*) BBC Audiobooks America.

—Catnap: A Midnight Louie Mystery. (Midnight Louie Mystery Ser.). 1993. 241p. mass mkt. 6.99 (*0-8125-1682-6*, Forge Bks.); 1992. 256p. 17.95 o.p. (*0-312-85217-7*, Tor Bks.) Doherty, Tom Assocs., LLC.

—Pussyfoot: A Midnight Louie Mystery. l.t. ed. 1994. (Midnight Louie Mystery Ser.). 24.95 o.p. (*0-7927-1846-1*); pap. 22.95 o.p. (*0-7927-1845-3*) BBC Audiobooks America.

—Pussyfoot: A Midnight Louie Mystery. (Midnight Louie Mystery Ser.). 1994. 304p. mass mkt. 5.99 (*0-8125-1683-4*); 1993. 256p. 19.95 o.p. (*0-312-85218-5*) Doherty, Tom Assocs., LLC. (Tor Bks.).

Edwards, Cassie. Elusive Ecstasy. 2000. 464p. mass mkt. 5.99 (*0-8217-6597-3*) Kensington Publishing Corp.

Edwards, Mary Jane. The Next Best Thing to Paradise. 1998. 337p. pap. 22.99 (*0-7388-0164-X*); text 32.99 (*0-7388-0163-1*) Xlibris Corp.

Fisher, Vardis. City of Illusion. 1983. (Illus.). 400p. mass mkt. 2.50 o.s.i (*0-441-10706-0*); 1982. mass mkt. 3.25 o.s.i (*0-441-10707-9*) Ace Bks.

Freeman, Judith. A Desert of Pure Feeling. 1997. 288p. pap. 19.00 (*0-679-75271-4*) Random Hse., Inc.

—A Desert of Pure Feeling: A Novel. 1996. 288p. 24.00 o.s.i (*0-679-43290-6*, Pantheon) Knopf Publishing Group.

Gibney, Art. Skin of the Earth: Stories from Nevada's Back Country. 2002. (Western Literature Ser.). 132p. pap. 16.00 (*0-87417-513-5*) Univ. of Nevada Pr.

Goldman, Ivan G. Where the Money Is: A Novel of Las Vegas. 1995. 192p. 22.00 (*1-56980-052-9*) Barricade Bks., Inc.

Granger, Bill. Drover. 1992. 272p. mass mkt. 4.99 (*0-380-71210-5*, Avon Bks.) Morrow/Avon.

—Drover & the Designated Hitter. 1995. 240p. mass mkt. 4.99 o.p. (*0-380-71909-6*, Avon Bks.); 1994. 223p. 20.00 o.p. (*0-688-11884-4*, Morrow, William & Co.) Morrow/Avon.

—Drover & the Zebras. 1993. 240p. mass mkt. 4.99 (*0-380-71211-3*, Avon Bks.); 1992. 20.00 o.p. (*0-688-09857-6*, Morrow, William & Co.) Morrow/Avon.

Grey, Zane. Nevada: The Authorized Edition. 1976. 26.95 (*0-8488-1026-0*) Amereon, Ltd.

—Nevada: The Authorized Edition. 1945. 288p. mass mkt. 2.95 o.s.i (*0-553-24343-8*) Bantam Bks.

—Nevada: The Authorized Edition. 1994. 384p. mass mkt. 3.99 o.p. (*0-06-100764-1*) HarperCollins Children's Bk. Group.

—Nevada: The Authorized Edition. l.t. ed. 1979. (Ulverscroft Large Print Ser.). 12.00 o.p. (*0-7089-0301-0*, Ulverscroft) Thorpe, F. A. Pubs. GBR. *Dist:* Ulverscroft Large Print Bks., Ltd., Ulverscroft Large Print Canada, Ltd.

—Nevada: The Authorized Edition. 1995. 367p. (C). pap. 12.00 o.p. (*0-8032-7054-2*, Bison Bks.) Univ. of Nebraska Pr.

Griffin, Shaun T., ed. The River Underground: An Anthology of Nevada Fiction. 2001. (Western Literature Ser.). xxiv, 349p. pap. 22.00 (*0-87417-364-7*) Univ. of Nevada Pr.

Holmes, Perry. Mountains Against the Sun. 1997. 243p. lib. bdg. 17.95 o.p. (*0-7862-0754-X*, Five Star) Gale Group.

—Mountains Against the Sun. l.t. ed. 1998. (Western Ser.). 369p. 21.95 (*0-7862-0778-7*) Thorndike Pr.

Johnston, Joan. The Cowboy. 2000. 400p. mass mkt. 7.50 (*0-440-22380-6*) Dell Publishing.

—The Cowboy. l.t. ed. 2000. (Wheeler Large Print Book Ser.). 425p. 28.95 (*1-56895-903-6*, Wheeler Publishing, Inc.) Gale Group.

Kakonis, Tom. Shadow Counter. 1993. 336p. 21.00 o.p. (*0-525-93633-5*, Dutton) Dutton/Plume.

King, Stephen. Desperation. 1999. 690p. reprint ed. text 28.00 (*0-7881-6597-6*) DIANE Publishing Co.

—Desperation. l.t. ed. 1997. 761p. 28.95 (*1-56895-420-4*, Wheeler Publishing, Inc.) Gale Group.

—Desperation. 1997. 560p. mass mkt. 7.99 (*0-451-18846-2*, Signet Bks.) NAL.

—Desperation, unabr. ed. 1997. audio 125.00 (*0-7887-0950-X*, 95010E7) Recorded Bks., LLC.

—Desperation. 1996. 704p. 27.95 o.s.i (*0-670-86836-1*); audio 29.95 o.p. (*0-14-086318-4*, Penguin AudioBooks) Viking Penguin.

Koontz, Dean. Strangers. 2002. 688p. mass mkt. 7.99 (*0-425-18111-1*); 1989. 704p. mass mkt. 7.99 o.s.i (*0-425-11992-0*); 1986. mass mkt. 4.95 o.s.i (*0-425-09217-8*); 1986. 17.95 o.p. (*0-399-13143-4*) Berkley Publishing Group.

—Strangers. 1986. 14.04 (*0-606-03687-3*) Turtleback Bks.

Kranes, David. Keno Runner: A Dark Romance. 1995. (Western Literature Ser.). 288p. reprint ed. pap. 15.00 (*0-87417-276-4*) Univ. of Nevada Pr.

—Keno Runner: A Romance. 1989. (Fiction Ser.). 17.95 o.p. (*0-87480-320-9*) Univ. of Utah Pr.

Krauss, Nicole. Man Walks into a Room. 2003. 256p. pap. 13.00 (*0-385-72191-9*) Broadway Bks.

—Man Walks into a Room. 2002. 256p. 23.95 (*0-385-50399-7*) Doubleday Publishing.

Lacy, Al. Secrets of the Heart, 10 vols. 2003. (Mail Order Bride Ser.: Vol. 1). 308p. pap. 10.99 (*1-57673-278-9*, Multnomah Fiction) Multnomah Pubs., Inc.

Lacy, Al & Lacy, JoAnna. Secrets of the Heart. l.t. ed. 1999. (Christian Fiction Ser.). 471p. 25.95 (*0-7862-1803-7*) Thorndike Pr.

—A Time to Love, 10 vols. 2003. (Mail Order Bride Ser.: Vol. 2). 312p. pap. 10.99 (*1-57673-284-3*) Multnomah Pubs., Inc.

—A Time to Love. l.t. ed. 1999. (Christian Fiction Ser.). 501p. 25.95 o.p. (*0-7862-2052-X*) Thorndike Pr.

Laxalt, Robert. Dust Devils. 1997. (Western Literature Ser.). 120p. (YA). pap. 16.00 (*0-87417-300-0*) Univ. of Nevada Pr.

—The Governor's Mansion. 1997. (Basque Ser.). 240p. reprint ed. 18.00 (*0-87417-251-9*) Univ. of Nevada Pr.

—A Lean Year & Other Stories. 1994. (Western Literature Ser.). 208p. 21.00 (*0-87417-241-1*) Univ. of Nevada Pr.

—A Man in the Wheatfield. 192p. reprint ed. 2002. pap. 18.00 (*0-87417-521-6*); 1987. 21.00 (*0-87417-130-X*) Univ. of Nevada Pr.

Le Guin, Ursula K. City of Illusions. 1984. mass mkt. 2.75 o.s.i (*0-441-10708-7*); 1980. mass mkt. 2.25 o.s.i (*0-441-10705-2*) Ace Bks.

—City of Illusions. Del Rey, Lester, ed. 1975. (Library of Science Fiction). lib. bdg. 21.00 o.p. (*0-8240-1422-7*) Garland Publishing, Inc.

—City of Illusions. o.p. (*0-06-012569-1*) HarperCollins Pubs.

Lewis, Jim. Real Gone. 1994. (Illus.). 56p. 15.00 (*0-9631095-2-9*) Artspace Bks.

Lowell, Elizabeth. Beautiful Dreamer. 2002. E-Book 7.99 (*0-06-050371-8*); E-Book 7.99 (*0-06-050372-6*); E-Book 7.99 (*0-06-050373-4*); E-Book 7.99 (*0-06-050374-2*) HarperCollins General Bks. Group. (PerfectBound).

—Beautiful Dreamer. l.t. ed. 2001. 400p. pap. 19.95 (*0-06-018804-9*, HarperLargePrint) HarperTrade.

—Beautiful Dreamer. 2001. 400p. mass mkt. 7.99 (*0-380-81876-0*); 2000. 306p. 19.95 (*0-380-78993-0*) Morrow/Avon.

McCord, Howard. The Man Who Walked to the Moon. 1997. 128p. 18.00 (*0-929701-51-8*) McPherson & Co.

McMurtry, Larry. The Desert Rose. 1976. 22.95 (*0-8488-0371-X*) Amereon, Ltd.

—The Desert Rose. unabr. collector's ed. 1985. audio 48.00 (*0-7366-1007-3*, 1940) Books on Tape, Inc.

—The Desert Rose. Grose, Bill, ed. 1990. 288p. mass mkt. 7.50 (*0-671-72763-X*, Pocket) Simon & Schuster.

—The Desert Rose. 1988. mass mkt. 4.50 (*0-671-66016-0*, Pocket); 1987. 256p. pap. 12.00 (*0-671-63721-5*, Simon & Schuster); 1985. pap. 7.95 o.s.i (*0-671-55537-5*, Touchstone); 1983. 254p. 14.50 o.p. (*0-671-46143-5*, Simon & Schuster); 1983. 254p. 75.00 o.p. (*0-671-49423-6*, Simon & Schuster); 2002. 256p. reprint ed. pap. 12.00 (*0-684-85384-1*, Simon & Schuster) Simon & Schuster.

Michaels, Fern. Vegas Heat. abr. ed. 1997. (Vegas Ser.). audio 7.99 o.p. (*1-56740-236-4*, 715, Paperback Nova Audio Bks.); audio 16.95 o.p. (*1-56100-973-3*, 1399, Nova Audio Bks.); 15p. audio 89.25 o.p. (*1-56100-810-9*, 1086, Unabridged Library Editions); audio 29.95 o.p. (*1-56100-735-8*, 308, Bookcassette) Brilliance Audio.

—Vegas Heat. 1997. 480p. mass mkt. 6.99 o.s.i (*0-8217-5758-X*); 400p. 25.00 o.s.i (*1-57566-138-1*) Kensington Publishing Corp.

—Vegas Rich. abr. ed. (Vegas Ser.). 1997. audio 7.99 o.p. (*1-56740-183-X*, 714, Paperback Nova Audio Bks.); 1996. audio 16.95 o.p. (*1-56100-914-8*, 1400, Nova Audio Bks.); 1996. audio 29.95 o.p. (*1-56100-706-4*, 307, Bookcassette); 1996. audio 121.25 o.p. (*1-56100-331-X*, 1087, Unabridged Library Editions) Brilliance Audio.

—Vegas Rich, Vol. 1. l.t. ed. 1996. 26.95 o.p. (*1-56895-370-4*, Wheeler Publishing, Inc.) Gale Group.

—Vegas Rich. 2001. 54p. mass mkt. 7.50 (*0-8217-7206-6*); 1997. 544p. mass mkt. 6.99 o.s.i (*0-8217-5594-3*); 1996. 512p. 25.00 o.s.i (*1-57566-057-1*) Kensington Publishing Corp.

—Vegas Sunrise. abr. ed. (Vegas Ser.). 1998. audio 7.99 o.s.i (*1-56740-259-3*, 1402, Paperback Nova Audio Bks.); 1997. audio 16.95 o.p. (*1-56100-995-4*, 514, Nova Audio Bks.); 1999. audio 17.95 o.p. (*1-56740-844-3*, 1727, Bookcassette); 1997. audio 89.25 (*1-56100-844-3*, 1088, Unabridged Library Editions); 1997. audio 25.95 (*1-56100-769-2*, 309, Bookcassette) Brilliance Audio.

—Vegas Sunrise. l.t. ed. 1998. 28.95 (*1-56895-571-5*, Wheeler Publishing, Inc.) Gale Group.

—Vegas Sunrise. 1998. 48p. mass mkt. 7.50 o.s.i (*0-8217-7208-2*); 1998. 480p. mass mkt. 6.99 o.s.i (*0-8217-5983-3*); 1997. 384p. 25.00 o.s.i (*1-57566-214-0*) Kensington Publishing Corp.

Miller, Linda Lael. Bridget. l.t. ed. 2001. (Softcover Ser.). 142p. pap. 23.95 o.p. (*1-58724-083-1*, Wheeler Publishing, Inc.) Gale Group.

—Bridget. 2000. (Women of Primrose Creek Ser.: Vol. 1). 160p. mass mkt. 3.99 (*0-671-04244-0*, Pocket) Simon & Schuster.

—Christy. l.t. ed. 2001. (Wheeler Large Print Book Ser.). 168p. 28.95 (*1-58724-101-3*, Wheeler Publishing, Inc.) Gale Group.

—Christy. 176p. 2002. E-Book 3.99 (*0-7434-4827-8*); 2000. (Women of Primrose Creek Ser.: Vol. 2). pap. 3.99 o.s.i (*0-671-04245-9*) Simon & Schuster. (Pocket).

—The Last Chance Cafe. 2003. 384p. mass mkt. 7.99 (*0-671-04251-3*, Pocket Star); 2002. 304p. 24.00 (*0-671-04250-5*, Atria); 2002. 288p. 24.00 (*0-7434-4619-4*, Atria) Simon & Schuster.

—Megan. 2000. (Women of Primrose Creek Ser.: No. 4). 256p. mass mkt. 5.99 (*0-671-04247-5*, Pocket) Simon & Schuster.

—Skye. l.t. ed. 2001. (Wheeler Large Print Book Ser.). 162p. pap. 23.95 o.p. (*1-58724-144-7*, Wheeler Publishing, Inc.) Gale Group.

—Skye. 2000. (Women of Primrose Creek Ser.: Vol. 3). 176p. pap. 3.99 o.s.i (*0-671-04246-7*, Pocket) Simon & Schuster.

Moody, Bill. Death of A Tenor Man: An Evan Horne Mystery. 1995. 240p. 21.95 (*0-8027-3269-0*) Walker & Co.

—Death of a Tenor Man: An Evan Horne Mystery. 1997. 288p. mass mkt. 5.50 o.s.i (*0-440-22324-5*) Dell Publishing.

—The Sound of the Trumpet: An Evan Horne Mystery. 1998. (Evan Horne Mysteries Ser.: Vol. 3). 304p. mass mkt. 5.99 o.s.i (*0-440-22194-3*) Dell Publishing.

—The Sound of the Trumpet: An Evan Horne Mystery. 1997. (Evan Horne Mysteries Ser.). 240p. 21.95 (*0-8027-3291-7*) Walker & Co.

Moore, Ruth N. Ghost Town Mystery. 1987. (Sara & Sam Ser.: Vol. 5). (Illus.). 144p. (J). (gr. 4-7). pap. 6.99 o.p. (*0-8361-3445-1*) Herald Pr.

Morris, Gilbert. Boomtown, No. 4. 1992. (Reno Western Saga Ser.). 261p. pap. 7.99 o.p. (*0-8423-7789-1*) Tyndale Hse. Pubs.

Mulvihill, William. Night of the Axe. 1999. 168p. (*0-395-13650-4*) Houghton Mifflin Co.

Murkoff, Bruce. Waterborne. 2004. 416p. 25.00 (*1-4000-4038-8*) Knopf Publishing Group.

Murray, Earl. Midnight Sun & Other Tales of the Unexplained. 2000. (Illus.). 191p. pap. 13.95 (*0-312-87362-X*, Forge Bks.) Doherty, Tom Assocs., LLC.

Names, Larry D. Boomtown. 1981. (Double D Western Ser.). 192p. 10.95 o.p. (*0-385-17429-2*) Doubleday Publishing.

—Boomtown. l.t. ed. 1983. 285p. reprint ed. 11.95 o.p. (*0-89621-429-X*) Thorndike Pr.

Nightingale Staff. Lost Coast. 1997. 272p. pap. 11.95 o.p. (*0-312-15572-7*, Saint Martin's Griffin) St. Martin's Pr.

Nightingale, Steven. Lost Coast. 1996. 208p. 21.95 o.p. (*0-312-14007-X*) St. Martin's Pr.

O'Brien, John. Leaving Las Vegas. 1996. 200p. reprint ed. pap. 11.00 (*0-8021-3445-9*, Grove Pr.) Grove/Atlantic, Inc.

—Leaving Las Vegas. 1991. 206p. 19.50 (*0-922820-12-0*) Watermark Pr., Inc.

O'Shaughnessy, Perri. Writ of Execution. l.t. ed. 2001. 665p. 29.95 o.p. (*0-7862-3511-X*) Thorndike Pr.

Paine, Lauran. Wilderness Road. 1997. (Gunsmoke Western Ser.). 158p. 17.50 o.p. (*0-7451-8716-1*, Gunsmoke) BBC Audiobooks America.

—Wilderness Road. l.t. ed. 2000. (Western Ser.). 244p. 22.95 (*0-7862-2578-5*); (*0-7540-4190-5*); (*0-7540-4191-3*) Thorndike Pr.

Pendleton, Don. Code of Conflict. 1999. (SuperBolan Ser.: Vol. 68). 352p. per. (*0-373-61468-3*, Worldwide Library) Harlequin Enterprises, Ltd.

Pronzini, Bill. Blue Lonesome. l.t. ed. 2002. (Large Print Ser.). 28.95 (*1-57490-453-1*) Beeler, Thomas T. Publisher.

—Blue Lonesome. 240p. 1995. 21.95 o.p. (*0-8027-3268-2*); 1999. reprint ed. pap. 8.95 (*0-8027-7561-6*) Walker & Co.

Rechy, John. The Life & Adventures of Lyle Clemens. 2003. (Illus.). 352p. 24.00 (*0-8021-1746-5*, Grove Pr.) Grove/Atlantic, Inc.

Reilly, Matthew. Area 7. E-Book 18.95 (*0-312-70417-8*); 2003. 512p. mass mkt. 6.99 (*0-312-98322-0*, St. Martin's Paperbacks); 2002. (Illus.). 400p. 24.95 (*0-312-26685-5*) St. Martin's Pr.

—Area 7. l.t. ed. 2002. (Adventure Ser.). 839p. 29.95 (*0-7862-4350-3*) Thorndike Pr.

Ridley, John. Stray Dogs. 2003. (Illus.). 176p. pap. 11.95 (*0-345-41346-6*) Ballantine Bks.

Robbins, Harold. The Raiders. unabr. ed. 1996. audio 80.00 (*0-7366-3232-8*, 3893) Books on Tape, Inc.

—The Raiders. l.t. ed. 1995. 24.95 o.p. (*1-56895-262-7*, Wheeler Publishing, Inc.) Gale Group.

—The Raiders. 1995. 496p. mass mkt. 6.99 o.p. (*0-671-87293-1*, Pocket); 363p. 23.00 (*0-671-87289-3*, Simon & Schuster) Simon & Schuster.

—The Raiders. abr. ed. 1995. audio 17.00 (*0-671-52033-4*, Simon & Schuster Audioworks) Simon & Schuster Audio.

Roberts, J. R. End of the Trail, vol. 220. 2000. (Gunsmith Ser.: Vol. 220). 192p. mass mkt. 4.99 o.s.i (*0-515-12791-4*, Jove) Berkley Publishing Group.

Rock, Peter. This Is the Place. 1997. 256p. pap. 19.00 (*0-385-48598-0*) Doubleday Publishing.

Ross, Dana Fuller, pseud. Nevada! abr. ed. 2003. (Wagon West Ser.: No. 8). audio 25.00 (*1-58807-013-1*) Americana Publishing, Inc.

—Nevada! l.t. ed. 1982. 15.95 o.p. (*0-8161-3396-4*, Macmillan Reference USA) Gale Group.

Schopen, Bernard. The Big Silence. 1994. (Western Literature Ser.). 280p. pap. 18.00 (*0-87417-254-3*) Univ. of Nevada Pr.

—The Desert Look. 1990. 256p. 17.95 (*0-89296-354-9*) Mysterious Pr.

—The Desert Look. 1995. (Western Literature Ser.). 272p. pap. 18.00 (*0-87417-259-4*) Univ. of Nevada Pr.

—The Desert Look. 1991. mass mkt. 4.95 o.s.i (*0-446-40009-2*, Mysterious Pr. Paperback Bks.) Warner Bks., Inc.

—The Iris Deception. 1996. (Western Literature Ser.). 296p. pap. 18.00 (*0-87417-286-1*) Univ. of Nevada Pr.

Schorr, Mark. Ace of Diamonds. 1984. 224p. 13.95 o.p. (*0-312-00260-2*) St. Martin's Pr.

Sharpe, Jon. Nevada Warpath. 1992. (Trailsman Ser.: No. 127). 176p. (Orig.). mass mkt. 3.50 o.p. (*0-451-17303-1*, Signet Bks.) NAL.

Short, Luke. Hard Money. l.t. ed. 1996. 267p. pap. 20.95 (*0-7838-1464-X*, Macmillan Reference USA) Gale Group.

Smith, Rosamond, pseud. Starr Bright Will Be With You Soon. 2000. 272p. pap. 12.95 o.s.i (*0-452-28035-4*, Plume); 1999. 304p. 23.95 o.p. (*0-525-94452-4*, Dutton) Dutton/Plume.
Stookey, Richard. Kinsella's Man. 1994. (Western Literature Ser.). 392p. 25.00 (*0-87417-248-9*) Univ. of Nevada Pr.
Strobridge, Idah M. Sagebrush Trilogy: Idah Meacham Strobridge & Her Works. 1990. (Vintage West Ser.). (Illus.). 452p. reprint ed. pap. 18.95 (*0-87417-164-4*) Univ. of Nevada Pr.
Stuart, Matt. Gun Law at Vermillion. 1994. 17.50 o.p. (*0-7451-4618-X*, Gunsmoke) BBC Audiobooks America.
—Gun Law at Vermillion. l.t. ed. 2001. (G. K. Hall Paperback Ser.). 247p. 23.95 o.p. (*0-7838-9382-5*) Thorndike Pr.
Tarcher, Mallory. Starring Mom. 1994. (Voices Romance Ser.: No. 3). 224p. mass mkt. 15.00 o.s.i (*0-8217-4675-8*) Kensington Publishing Corp.
Thoene, Brock & Thoene, Bodie. Cannons of the Comstock. l.t. ed. 2002. lib. bdg. 27.95 (*1-58547-182-8*, Western) Ctr. Point Large Print.
Ventura, Michael. The Death of Frank Sinatra: A Novel. 1996. 320p. 22.50 o.p. (*0-8050-3738-1*) Holt, Henry & Co.
—The Death of Frank Sinatra: A Novel. 1997. (Dead Letter Mysteries Ser.). 320p. mass mkt. 5.99 (*0-312-96474-9*, St. Martin's Paperbacks) St. Martin's Pr.
Voght, Marty. The Cowboy's Shadow. 2000. 200p. E-Book 4.75 incl. disk (*1-58749-010-2*); E-Book 4.75 (*1-58749-011-0*) Awe-Struck E-Bks.
Watt, Alan. Diamond Dogs. 2000. 256p. 23.95 o.p. (*0-316-92581-0*); 256p. E-Book 14.95 (*0-446-92255-2*); 256p. E-Book 14.95 (*0-446-91361-8*); E-Book 14.95 (*0-446-93128-4*); 256p. E-Book 14.95 (*0-446-92365-6*) Little Brown & Co.
—Diamond Dogs. 2001. 256p. pap. 13.95 (*0-446-67784-1*); 2000. 256p. E-Book 14.95 (*0-446-92857-7*); 2000. E-Book 14.95 (*0-446-96086-1*) Warner Bks., Inc.
Wheeler, Richard S. Goldfield. 1996. 440p. pap. text 5.99 (*0-8125-4803-5*); 1995. 22.95 o.p. (*0-312-85702-0*) Doherty, Tom Assocs., LLC. (Forge Bks.).
—Sun Mountain: A Comstock Memoir. 1999. 304p. 24.95 (*0-312-86725-5*, Forge Bks.) Doherty, Tom Assocs., LLC.
Wheeler, Sessions S. Paiute. 1986. 249p. reprint ed. pap. 71.00 (*0-608-01263-7*, 2062012) Bks. on Demand.
—Paiute. ltd. ed. 1986. 260p. reprint ed. 35.00 o.p. (*0-87417-119-9*); pap. 9.95 o.p. (*0-87417-115-6*) Univ. of Nevada Pr.
Winslow, Don. A Long Walk up the Water Slide. (Neal Carey Mysteries Ser.). 1998. 277p. mass mkt. 5.99 (*0-312-96617-2*, St. Martin's Paperbacks); 1994. 256p. 20.95 o.p. (*0-312-11389-7*, Saint Martin's Minotaur) St. Martin's Pr.
—Way down on the High Lonely. 1998. (Dead Letter Mysteries Ser.). 288p. mass mkt. 5.99 (*0-312-96422-6*, St. Martin's Paperbacks) St. Martin's Pr.
—Way down on the High Lonely: A Neal Carey Mystery. 1993. 288p. 19.95 o.p. (*0-312-09934-7*, Saint Martin's Minotaur) St. Martin's Pr.
—While Drowning in the Desert. 1998. (Neal Carey Mysteries Ser.). 224p. mass mkt. 5.99 (*0-312-96118-9*, St. Martin's Paperbacks) St. Martin's Pr.
—While Drowning in the Desert: A Neal Carey Mystery. 1996. 192p. 20.95 o.p. (*0-312-14446-6*, Saint Martin's Minotaur) St. Martin's Pr.
Yamanaka, Lois-Ann. Father of the Four Passages. 2001. 288p. 23.00 (*0-374-15387-6*) Farrar, Straus & Giroux.

**NEVYA (IMAGINARY PLACE)—FICTION**

Marley, Louise. Receive the Gift. 1997. 304p. mass mkt. 5.99 o.s.i (*0-441-00486-5*) Ace Bks.
—Sing the Light. 1995. 304p. (Orig.). mass mkt. 5.50 o.s.i (*0-441-00272-2*) Ace Bks.
—Sing the Warmth. 1996. mass mkt. 5.99 o.s.i (*0-441-00386-9*) Ace Bks.

**NEW BRUNSWICK (PROVINCE)—FICTION**

Corey, Deborah J. Losing Eddie: A Novel. (Front Porch Paperback Ser.). 238p. 1994. (Illus.). pap. 8.95 (*1-56512-091-4*); 1993. tchr. ed. 15.95 o.p. (*0-945575-67-X*) Algonquin Bks. of Chapel Hill.
Gaston, Bill. The Good Body. 2000. ix, 166p. (*1-896951-21-X*) Cormorant Bks.
—The Good Body. 288p. 2002. pap. 13.95 (*0-06-098887-8*); 2001. 25.00 (*0-06-039411-0*) Harper-Trade. (ReganBooks).
Mooers, Vernon. Briefly a Candle. l.t. ed. 1999. 236p. pap. 14.25 (*0-9684792-0-0*) Fundy Production Assocs. CAN. *Dist:* General Distribution Services, Inc.
Richards, David Adams. Mercy among the Children. 2001. 384p. 24.95 (*1-55970-586-8*) Arcade Publishing, Inc.
—Mercy among the Children. 2001. 432p. pap. (*0-385-25995-6*, Anchor Canada) Doubleday Canada, Ltd. CAN. *Dist:* Random Hse., Inc.

**NEW ENGLAND—FICTION**

Abrahams, Peter. Crying Wolf. 2001. E-Book 6.99 (*1-58945-862-1*) Adobe Systems, Inc.
—Crying Wolf. E-Book 19.95 (*0-345-44260-1*); 2001. 352p. mass mkt. 6.99 (*0-345-43503-6*, Fawcett) Ballantine Bks.
—Crying Wolf. l.t. ed. 2001. 439p. 26.95 (*1-58724-005-X*, Wheeler Publishing, Inc.) Gale Group.
—Crying Wolf. 2000. E-Book 6.99 (*0-345-44261-X*) Random Hse., Inc.
Akst, Daniel. The Webster Chronicle. 2002. 320p. pap. 14.00 (*0-425-18761-6*) Penguin Group (USA) Inc.
—The Webster Chronicle. 2001. 320p. 24.95 o.s.i (*0-399-14812-4*, BlueHen Bks.) Putnam Publishing Group, The.
Alcorn, Alfred. The Long Run of Myles Mayberry. 1999. (Illus.). 240p. pap. 13.00 o.p. (*1-58195-001-2*, Zoland Bks., Inc.) Steerforth Pr.
—Murder in the Museum of Man. 1998. 273p. pap. 13.00 o.p. (*0-944072-78-X*); 1997. 320p. 23.95 o.p. (*0-944072-77-1*) Steerforth Pr. (Zoland Bks., Inc.).
Alcott, Louisa May. The Best of Louisa May Alcott. Booss, Claire, ed. 1993. (Illus.). 800p. (J). 11.99 o.s.i (*0-517-10034-7*) Random Hse. Value Publishing.
—Good Wives. (Classics for Young Readers Ser.). 1995. 368p. (YA). (gr. 5 up). pap. 3.99 o.s.i (*0-14-036695-4*); 1983. 320p. (J). (gr. 3-7). pap. 3.99 o.p. (*0-14-035009-8*) Penguin Putnam Bks. for Young Readers. (Puffin Bks.).
—Jo's Boys. unabr. ed. 1996. audio 41.95 (*1-55685-437-4*) Audio Bk. Contractors, Inc.
—Jo's Boys. unabr. ed. 1999. audio 49.95 (*0-7861-1288-3*, 2188) Blackstone Audio Bks., Inc.
—Little Men: Life at Plumfield with Jo's Boys. unabr. ed. 1996. audio 49.95 (*0-7861-0956-4*, 1733) Blackstone Audio Bks., Inc.
—Little Women. 2000. 252p. E-Book 9.95 (*0-594-05582-2*) 1873 Pr.
—Little Women. 1981. mass mkt. 2.50 o.s.i (*0-441-05466-8*) Ace Bks.
—Little Women. (Early Best Sellers Ser.). reprint ed. lib. bdg. 48.00 (*0-7426-1003-9*) Classic Bks.
—Little Women. 1994. 461p. mass mkt. 3.99 (*0-8125-2333-4*, Tor Classics) Doherty, Tom Assocs., LLC.
—Little Women. 1941. 93p. pap. 5.60 (*0-87129-320-X*, L27) Dramatic Publishing Co.
—Little Women. 1972. 2.95 o.p. (*0-460-01248-7*, Dutton) Dutton/Plume.
—Little Women. E-Book 2.49 (*1-929120-48-6*) Electric Umbrella Publishing.
—Little Women. 1997. pap. 5.50 (*1-57514-326-7*, 1051) Encore Performance Publishing.
—Little Women. 1997. (Classic Collection). 15.99 o.p. (*1-56179-552-6*) Focus on the Family Publishing.
—Little Women, ERS. 1993. (Little Classics Ser.). (Illus.). 308p. (J). (gr. 4-8). 15.95 o.p. (*0-8050-2767-X*, Holt, Henry & Co. Bks. For Young Readers) Holt, Henry & Co.
—Little Women. l.t. ed. 988p. pap. 76.39 (*0-7583-1406-X*); 806p. pap. 64.52 (*0-7583-1405-1*); 659p. pap. 49.05 (*0-7583-1404-3*); 515p. pap. 39.88 (*0-7583-1403-5*); 404p. pap. 32.23 (*0-7583-1402-7*); 298p. pap. 25.86 (*0-7583-1401-9*); 238p. pap. 21.50 (*0-7583-1400-0*); 1145p. pap. 85.69 (*0-7583-1407-8*); 404p. lib. bdg. 38.23 (*0-7583-1394-2*); 515p. lib. bdg. 45.88 (*0-7583-1395-0*); 1145p. lib. bdg. 97.69 (*0-7583-1399-3*); 238p. lib. bdg. 27.50 (*0-7583-1392-6*); 298p. lib. bdg. 31.86 (*0-7583-1393-4*); 659p. lib. bdg. 55.05 (*0-7583-1396-9*); 806p. lib. bdg. 78.69 (*0-7583-1397-7*); 988p. lib. bdg. 88.39 (*0-7583-1398-5*) Huge Print Pr.
—Little Women. E-Book 2.95 (*1-57799-829-4*) Logos Research Systems, Inc.
—Little Women. 1998. (Little Brown Notebooks Ser.). (Illus.). 256p. 9.99 (*1-897954-77-8*) M Q Pubns. GBR. *Dist:* Independent Pubs. Group.
—Little Women. 1983. (Modern Library College Editions Ser.). 603p. (C). pap. 11.25 (*0-07-554389-3*, McGraw-Hill Humanities, Social Sciences & World Languages) McGraw-Hill Higher Education.
—Little Women. 1983. mass mkt. 3.50 o.p. (*0-451-52214-1*) NAL.
—Little Women. l.t. ed. 1998. 665p. lib. bdg. 28.00 (*0-939495-51-1*) North Bks.
—Little Women. Alderson, Valerie, ed. & intro. by. (Oxford World's Classics Ser.). 1998. 530p. pap. 7.95 (*0-19-283434-7*); 1995. 526p. pap. 5.95 o.p. (*0-19-282765-0*) Oxford Univ. Pr., Inc.
—Little Women. 1995. (Literary Classics Giant Ser.). 688p. text 8.98 o.p. (*1-56138-566-2*, Courage Bks.) Running Pr. Bk. Pubs.
—Little Women. 1994. 592p. mass mkt. 5.99 (*0-671-51764-3*, Pocket) Simon & Schuster.
—Little Women. 1995. (Little Brown Notebook Ser.). (Illus.). 256p. 6.95 (*0-8069-3975-3*) Sterling Publishing Co., Inc.
—Little Women. (Bullseye Step into Classics Ser.). 1994. 10.04 (*0-606-09566-7*); 1962. 10.10 o.p. (*0-606-00974-4*) Turtleback Bks.
—Little Women. abr. ed. 1997. 2p. audio 16.95 o.s.i (*0-14-086146-7*) Viking Penguin.
—Louisa May Alcott: Selected Fiction. Shealy, Daniel et al, eds. 1991. 24.95 o.s.i (*0-316-78349-8*) Little Brown & Co.
—Mujercitas. 5th ed. 1997. (SPA., Illus.). 248p. 12.95 (*84-392-8232-X*) Everest Publishing.
—Mujercitas. 1995. (SPA.). 304p. 13.50 (*84-01-00914-6*, PJ9396) Plaza & Janés Editories, S.A. ESP. *Dist:* Distribooks, Inc., Lectorum Pubns., Inc.
—Mujercitas. 2002. (SPA.). 304p. mass mkt. 7.95 (*1-4000-0080-7*) Random Hse., Inc.
—An Old-Fashioned Thanksgiving. 1974. (Illus.). 72p. (J). (gr. 4-6). 12.95 (*0-397-31515-5*) HarperCollins Children's Bk. Group.
—An Old-Fashioned Thanksgiving. 1989. (Illus.). 32p. (J). (gr. 4-7). 14.95 o.p. (*0-8234-0772-1*) Holiday Hse., Inc.
—An Old-Fashioned Thanksgiving. 1993. (Illus.). 40p. (J). (gr. k-3). per. (*1-59093-073-8*, Eager Minds Pr.) Warehousing & Fulfillment Specialists, LLC (WFS, LLC).
—Work: A Story of Experience. Hardwick, Elizabeth, ed. 1977. (Rediscovered Fiction by American Women Ser.). (Illus.). reprint ed. lib. bdg. 29.95 (*0-405-10042-6*) Ayer Co. Pubs., Inc.
—Work: A Story of Experience. 1873. 443p. (YA). reprint ed. pap. text 28.00 (*1-4047-1632-7*) Classic Textbooks.
—Work: A Story of Experience. 1977. (Studies in the Life of Women). (Illus.). (YA). (gr. 10 up). 10.50 o.p. (*0-8052-3656-2*); pap. 14.95 o.s.i (*0-8052-0563-2*) Knopf Publishing Group. (Schocken).
—Work: A Story of Experience. 1989. (Works of Louisa May Alcott). reprint ed. lib. bdg. 79.00 (*0-7812-1632-X*) Reprint Services Corp.
—Work: A Story of Experience. 1976. reprint ed. 39.00 (*0-403-05873-2*, Regency Pr.) Scholarly Pr., Inc.
—Work: A Story of Experience. l.t. ed. 2001. (Perennial Bestsellers Ser.). 483p. 27.95 (*0-7838-9443-0*) Thorndike Pr.
—Work: A Story of Experience. Kasson, Joy S., ed. & intro. by. 139th ed. 1994. (Classics Ser.). 608p. 13.00 (*0-14-039091-X*, Penguin Classics) Viking Penguin.
—The Works of Louisa May Alcott. Booss, Claire, ed. (Avenel Readers Library). (Illus.). 800p. 1988. 7.99 o.s.i (*0-517-37167-7*); 1987. 8.99 o.s.i (*0-517-37146-4*) Random Hse. Value Publishing.
Alcott, Louisa May, photos by. Little Men: Life at Plumfield with Jo's Boys. Date not set. 20.95 (*0-8488-1476-2*) Amereon, Ltd.
—Little Men: Life at Plumfield with Jo's Boys. 1986. 352p. mass mkt. 4.95 (*0-451-52275-3*, Signet Classics) NAL.
Ammerman, Mark. The Rain from God. 1997. (Cross & the Tomahawk Ser.: Vol. I). (Illus.). 320p. (J). pap. 11.99 (*0-88965-134-5*, Horizon Bks.) Christian Pubns., Inc.
Arensberg, Ann. Sister Wolf. 1987. mass mkt. 5.95 o.s.i (*0-671-64507-2*, Pocket) Simon & Schuster.
Auchincloss, Louis. The Rector of Justin. unabr. ed. 1976. audio 56.00 (*0-7366-0039-6*, 1050) Books on Tape, Inc.
—The Rector of Justin. 1964. 4.95 o.p. (*0-395-07361-8*); 1980. reprint ed. pap. 3.95 o.p. (*0-395-29179-8*) Houghton Mifflin Co.
—The Rector of Justin. 1999. pap. (*0-375-75323-0*, Modern Library) Random House Adult Trade Publishing Group.
—The Winthrop Covenant, 001. 1976. 8.95 o.p. (*0-395-24081-6*) Houghton Mifflin Co.
Austin, Phil. On Bethel Ridge: A Christmas Fable. 1998. 128p. 15.00 (*1-890932-03-5*) Sherman Asher Publishing.
Baker, Nicholson. A Box of Matches. 2004. 192p. pap. 12.95 (*0-375-70603-8*, Vintage) Knopf Publishing Group.
—A Box of Matches: A Novel. 2003. 192p. 19.95 (*0-375-50287-4*) Random Hse., Inc.
Baldwin, Faith. The Moon's Our Home. 1976. reprint ed. lib. bdg. 24.95 (*0-88411-602-6*) Amereon, Ltd.
—The Moon's Our Home. l.t. ed. 2001. (Thorndike Candlelight Romance Ser.). 331p. 23.95 (*0-7862-3280-3*); (*0-7540-4519-6*); (*0-7540-4520-X*) Thorndike Pr.
Banks, Russell. Trailerpark. 1986. 288p. mass mkt. 5.95 o.s.i (*0-345-33077-3*) Ballantine Bks.
—Trailerpark. 1996. 288p. pap. 13.00 (*0-06-097706-X*, Perennial) HarperTrade.
—Trailerpark, 001. 1981. 288p. 11.95 o.p. (*0-395-31547-6*) Houghton Mifflin Co.
—Trailerpark. 1996. 240p. 33.00 o.p. (*0-8095-9197-9*) Millefleurs.
Barrett, Andrea. Lucid Stars. 1997. 336p. pap. 19.00 (*0-385-31943-6*); 1988. 340p. pap. 19.00 o.s.i (*0-440-55000-9*) Dell Publishing. (Delta).
Beattie, Ann. Another You. 1996. 336p. pap. 19.00 (*0-679-73464-3*, Vintage) Knopf Publishing Group.
—Another You. audio o.p. National Humanities Ctr.
—My Life, Starring Dara Falcon. 1998. 320p. pap. 13.00 (*0-679-78132-3*, Vintage) Knopf Publishing Group.
Beecher, Henry Ward. Norwood. E-Book 3.95 (*0-594-01865-X*) 1873 Pr.
Begiebing, Robert J. The Adventures of Allegra Fullerton: Or a Memoir of Startling & Amusing Episodes from Itinerant Life - A Novel. 1999. (Illus.). 326p. text 30.00 (*0-87451-947-0*, Hardscrabble Bks.) Univ. Pr. of New England.
Berne, Suzanne. A Perfect Arrangement: A Novel. 2001. 301p. tchr. ed. 23.95 (*1-56512-261-5*, Shannon Ravenel Bks.) Algonquin Bks. of Chapel Hill.
—A Perfect Arrangement: A Novel. 2002. 320p. pap. 13.00 (*0-452-28322-1*, Plume) Dutton/Plume.
Bevan, Gloria. Bachelor Territory. l.t. ed. 1991. 17.95 o.p. (*0-7451-9941-0*, AH001) BBC Audiobooks America.
Binchy, Maeve. Tara Road. l.t. ed. 1999. 743p. (*0-7540-2212-9*) BBC Audiobooks America.
—Tara Road. 2000. 656p. mass mkt. 7.99 (*0-440-23559-6*); 1999. 512p. 24.95 o.s.i (*0-385-33395-1*, Delacorte Pr.) Dell Publishing.
—Tara Road. l.t. ed. (Paperback Bestsellers Ser.). 743p. 2000. pap. 28.95 (*0-7862-1837-1*); 1999. 31.95 (*0-7862-1836-3*) Thorndike Pr.
—Tara Road. 2000. 14.04 (*0-606-18987-4*) Turtleback Bks.
Binchy, Maeve, contrib. by. Tara Road. (*0-7540-1282-4*) BBC Audiobooks America.
Bowman, Elena Dorothy. The House on the Bluff. 2001. 207p. per. (*1-931402-00-0*) Barclay Bks., LLC.
Brockmann, Suzanne. The Unsung Hero. 416p. 2003. mass mkt. 3.99 o.s.i (*0-345-46339-0*); 2003. mass mkt. (*0-345-46561-X*); 2000. mass mkt. 6.99 (*0-8041-1952-X*) Ballantine Bks. (Ivy Bks.).
—The Unsung Hero. l.t. ed. 2001. (Softcover Ser.). 533p. 23.95 (*1-58724-067-X*, Wheeler Publishing, Inc.) Gale Group.
Bromfield, Louis. Early Autumn: A Story of a Lady. 2000. 303p. pap. 14.00 (*1-888683-31-7*) Wooster Bk. Co., The.
Brown, Alice. Meadow-Grass: Tales of New England Life, Vol. 1. 1977. (Short Story Index Reprint Ser.). reprint ed. 25.95 (*0-8369-4172-1*) Ayer Co. Pubs., Inc.
—Meadow-Grass: Tales of New England Life. 1972. reprint ed. lib. bdg. 18.00 (*0-8422-8011-1*) Irvington Pubs.
Brown, Carrie. Rose's Garden. 1998. 252p. tchr. ed. 20.95 (*1-56512-174-0*, 72174) Algonquin Bks. of Chapel Hill.
—Rose's Garden. 1999. 256p. reprint ed. pap. 12.95 (*0-553-38028-1*) Bantam Bks.
—Rose's Garden. l.t. ed. 1998. 273p. 23.95 (*1-57490-141-9*, Beeler Large Print Bks.) Beeler, Thomas T. Publisher.
Brown, Rosellen. Before & After. 1998. 368p. pap. 12.95 (*0-385-33326-9*); 1993. 432p. mass mkt. 6.99 o.s.i (*0-440-21654-0*, Dell Bks.) Dell Publishing.
—Before & After. 1992. 354p. 21.00 o.s.i (*0-374-10999-0*) Farrar, Straus & Giroux.
—Before & After. l.t. ed. 1993. (General Ser.). 518p. pap. 17.95 o.p. (*0-8161-5582-8*); 22.95 o.p. (*0-8161-5583-6*) Gale Group. (Macmillan Reference USA).
—Before & After. unabr. ed. 2000. audio 91.00 (*1-55690-827-X*, 93127E7) Recorded Bks., LLC.
—Before & After. 1999. 9.98 (*0-671-04406-0*); Set. 1996. audio 17.00 (*0-671-56254-1*, 393337) Simon & Schuster Audio. (Simon & Schuster Audioworks).
—Half a Heart. 2000. (*0-374-93384-7*); 2000. 368p. 24.00 o.p. (*0-374-29987-0*); 2000. 402p. (*0-374-44013-1*); 1999. o.p. (*0-374-16772-9*) Farrar, Straus & Giroux.
—Half a Heart. l.t. ed. 2001. (Large Print Book Ser.). 575p. 29.95 (*1-58724-017-3*, Wheeler Publishing, Inc.) Gale Group.
—Half a Heart. 2001. 416p. pap. 14.00 (*0-312-27830-6*) Picador.
—Half a Heart. abr. ed. 2000. audio 25.00 (*0-7435-0579-4*, Simon & Schuster Audioworks) Simon & Schuster Audio.
Bugge, Carole. Who Killed Mona Lisa? 2001. (Claire Rawlings Mysteries Ser.). 256p. mass mkt. 5.99 o.s.i (*0-425-17919-2*, Prime Crime) Berkley Publishing Group.
Burgess, Dean. An Unclean Act. 2002. 288p. 28.00 (*1-57962-046-9*) Permanent Pr., The.
Cadran, Larry. Courage of Conviction: The Story of William Turner. 2002. 268p. per. 29.95 (*1-930586-14-0*, American Univ. & College Pr.) American Bk. Publishing Group.
Center for Learning Network Staff. Tara Road/the Return Journey: Curriculum Unit —Novel Series— Grades 9-12. 1999. (Novel Ser.). 65p. (YA). (gr. 9-12). tchr. ed., spiral bd. 18.95 (*1-56077-636-6*) Ctr. for Learning, The.
Chalfoun, Michelle. The Width of the Sea. 2001. 336p. 25.00 (*0-06-019908-3*, HarperCollins) Harper-Trade.
Chiocchi, Roger. Mean Spirits. 2002. 324p. pap. 17.95 (*0-595-22840-2*, Writers Club Pr.) iUniverse, Inc.

Clark, Nancy. The Hills at Home: A Novel. 496p. 2004. pap. 14.95 (*1-4000-3096-X*, Anchor); 2003. 25.00 (*0-375-42203-X*, Pantheon) Knopf Publishing Group.

Clegg, Douglas. The Hour Before Dark. 2004. mass mkt. 6.99 (*0-8439-5142-7*); 2002. 384p. mass mkt. 24.00 (*0-8439-5044-7*) Dorchester Publishing Co., Inc. (Leisure Bks.).

Cook, Claire. Ready to Fall: A Novel. 2001. 211p. pap. 22.95 (*1-882593-32-4*) Bridge Works Publishing Co., Inc.

Cooke, Elizabeth. Complicity. 1988. 288p. 16.95 (*0-316-15507-1*) Little Brown & Co.

Cooke, Elizabeth & Wharton, Edith. Zeena. 1996. 352p. 23.95 o.p. (*0-312-14775-9*) St. Martin's Pr.

Crawford, F. Marion. Tale of a Lonely Parrish. E-Book 3.95 (*0-594-05678-0*) 1873 Pr.

—Tale of a Lonely Parrish. collector's ed. 2002. (Illus.). im. lthr. 38.85 (*1-4115-1217-0*); pap. 19.95 (*1-4115-0512-3*); 25.95 (*1-4115-0868-8*); pap. 17.95 (*1-4115-0253-1*) Polyglot Pr., Inc.

Daukas, Chuck. A Little Night Fishing. 2003. text (*0-9740176-1-2*) Chuckduck Storytellers.

Deaver, Jeffery. Praying for Sleep, unabr. ed. 1999. audio 72.00 (*0-7366-4310-9*, 4636) Books on Tape, Inc.

—Praying for Sleep. abr. ed. 1994. 16.00 o.p. incl. audio (*0-453-00877-1*, 25024-29318, NAL Bks.) HighBridge Co.

—Praying for Sleep. 1994. 432p. mass mkt. 7.99 o.s.i (*0-451-18146-8*, Signet Bks.) NAL.

—Praying for Sleep. 438p. 4.98 o.p. (*0-8317-4516-9*) Smithmark Pubs., Inc.

—Praying for Sleep. 1994. 448p. 21.95 o.p. (*0-670-85432-8*, Viking) Viking Penguin.

Delinsky, Barbara. Sensuous Burgundy. l.t. ed. 1996. pap. 22.95 o.p. (*1-56895-393-3*, Wheeler Publishing, Inc.) Gale Group.

—Sensuous Burgundy. 1996. 272p. mass mkt. 5.99 (*0-06-101101-0*, HarperTorch) Morrow/Avon.

Dempsey, William. Uniforms, a Love Story (1941-1967) 2000. 414p. 10.00 (*0-9679895-0-7*) Dempsey, William.

Dew, Robb Forman. Dale Loves Sophie to Death. 1981. 217p. 11.95 o.p. (*0-374-13450-2*) Farrar, Straus & Giroux.

—Dale Loves Sophie to Death. 1993. 224p. pap. 12.00 o.s.i (*0-06-097539-3*, Perennial) HarperTrade.

—Dale Loves Sophie to Death. 2001. 256p. reprint ed. pap. 13.95 (*0-316-89066-9*, Back Bay) Little Brown & Co.

—Dale Loves Sophie to Death. 1982. (Contemporary American Fiction Ser.). pap. 6.95 o.p. (*0-14-006183-5*, Penguin Bks.) Viking Penguin.

Dobson, Joanne. The Northbury Papers. 1999. 352p. mass mkt. 6.50 (*0-553-57661-5*) Bantam Bks.

—The Northbury Papers. 1998. 288p. 21.95 o.s.i (*0-385-48693-6*) Doubleday Publishing.

—The Raven & the Nightingale. 2000. 320p. mass mkt. 5.99 (*0-553-57999-1*) Bantam Bks.

—The Raven & the Nightingale: A Modern Mystery of Edgar Allen Poe. 1999. 288p. 21.95 o.s.i (*0-385-49339-8*) Doubleday Publishing.

Drake, Shannon. The Awakening. 2003. 384p. mass mkt. 6.99 (*0-8217-7228-7*, Zebra Bks.) Kensington Publishing Corp.

Earle, Morris. The Cedar in the Morning Sun: Poetry. 1994. 15.00 (*0-87233-111-3*) Bauhan, William L. Inc.

Eberstadt, Fernanda. Isaac & His Devils. 1992. reprint ed. mass mkt. 9.99 (*0-446-39413-0*) Warner Bks., Inc.

Eidson, Bill. The Repo. 2003. 320p. 24.95 (*1-932112-11-1*, Kate's Mystery Bks.) Justin, Charles & Co. Pubs.

Farber, Norma. Mercy Short: A Winter Journal, North Boston, 1692-1693. 1982. 160p. (YA). (gr. 7 up). 11.95 o.p. (*0-525-44014-3*, Dutton) Dutton/Plume.

Field, Rachel. All This & Heaven Too. 1983. 320p. reprint ed. lib. bdg. 35.95 (*0-89966-323-0*) Buccaneer Bks., Inc.

Freeman, Mary E. Wilkins. Best Stories of Mary E. Wilkins Freeman. Lanier, Henry W., ed. 1971. reprint ed. 69.00 (*0-403-00970-7*) Scholarly Pr., Inc.

—Collected Ghost Stories. 1974. 12.95 (*0-87054-065-3*) Arkham Hse. Pubs.

—The Copy-Cat & Other Stories. 1977. (Short Story Index Reprint Ser.). 23.95 (*0-8369-3540-3*) Ayer Co. Pubs., Inc.

—The Copy-Cat & Other Stories. E-Book 5.00 (*0-7410-1245-6*) SoftBook Pr.

—A Humble Romance: And Other Stories. reprint ed. 17.50 o.p. (*0-404-02574-9*) AMS Pr., Inc.

—A Humble Romance: And Other Stories. 436p. reprint ed. 1986. (C). pap. text 19.95 (*0-8290-1874-3*); 1972. 16.00 (*0-8422-8052-9*) Irvington Pubs.

—A Humble Romance: And Other Stories. 11.00 (*0-403-04108-2*) Somerset Pubs., Inc.

—Jane Field. E-Book 3.95 (*0-594-04841-9*) 1873 Pr.

—Jane Field. (Illus.). 273p. reprint ed. lib. bdg. 22.00 (*0-8398-0566-7*); 1986. (C). pap. text 10.95 (*0-8290-1964-2*) Irvington Pubs.

—The Love of Parson Lord & Other Stories. 2000. 252p. E-Book 3.95 (*0-594-05055-3*) 1873 Pr.

—The Love of Parson Lord & Other Stories. 1977. (Short Story Index Reprint Ser.). 19.95 (*0-8369-3001-0*) Ayer Co. Pubs., Inc.

—A Mary Wilkins Freeman Reader. Reichardt, Mary R., ed. & intro. by. 1997. (French Modernist Library Ser.). 428p. text 70.00 (*0-8032-1998-9*); pap. text 27.50 (*0-8032-6894-7*) Univ. of Nebraska Pr.

—A New England Nun: And Other Stories. 1992. (BCL1-PS American Literature Ser.). 468p. reprint ed. lib. bdg. 99.00 (*0-7812-6714-5*) Reprint Services Corp.

—The People of Our Neighborhood. 1977. (Short Story Index Reprint Ser.). 19.95 (*0-8369-3343-5*) Ayer Co. Pubs., Inc.

—Pot of Gold & Other Stories. 1977. (Short Story Index Reprint Ser.). 24.95 (*0-8369-3390-7*) Ayer Co. Pubs., Inc.

—The Revolt of Mother: And Other Stories. 1998. (Thrift Editions Ser.). 128p. pap. 1.50 (*0-486-40428-5*) Dover Pubns., Inc.

—The Revolt of Mother: And Other Stories. 1974. 224p. reprint ed. pap. 3.95 o.p. (*0-912670-18-5*) Feminist Pr. at The City Univ. of New York.

—The Shoulders of Atlas. 1977. (Rediscovered Fiction by American Women Ser.). reprint ed. lib. bdg. 33.95 (*0-405-10044-2*) Ayer Co. Pubs., Inc.

—Silence & Other Stories. 2000. 252p. pap. 9.95 (*0-594-06177-6*); E-Book 9.95 (*0-594-06180-6*) 1873 Pr.

—Silence & Other Stories. 1977. (Short Story Index Reprint Ser.). 24.95 (*0-8369-3200-5*) Ayer Co. Pubs., Inc.

—Six Trees. 1977. (Short Story Index Reprint Ser.). 22.95 (*0-8369-3100-9*) Ayer Co. Pubs., Inc.

—Understudies. 1977. (Short Story Index Reprint Ser.). 23.95 (*0-8369-3045-2*) Ayer Co. Pubs., Inc.

—The Wind in the Rose Bush & Other Stories of the Supernatural. 1986. (Illus.). reprint ed. 237p. 15.95 o.p. (*0-89733-233-4*); 255p. pap. 12.95 (*0-89733-232-6*) Academy Chicago Pubs., Ltd.

—The Winning Lady & Others. 2000. 252p. E-Book 3.95 (*0-594-06431-7*) 1873 Pr.

—Young Lucretia & Other Stories by Mary E. Wilkins Freeman. 1977. (Short Story Index Reprint Ser.). 22.95 (*0-8369-3324-9*) Ayer Co. Pubs., Inc.

Freeman, Mary E. Wilkins & Zagarell, Sandra A. A New England Nun: And Other Stories. 2000. (Classics Ser.). 304p. 12.95 (*0-14-043739-8*, Penguin Classics) Viking Penguin.

French, Allen. The Colonials. E-Book 3.95 (*0-594-02223-1*) 1873 Pr.

Frome, Shelly. Lilac Moon: A Mystery! Gosline, Sheldon, ed. l.t. ed. 2003. (Illus.). 343p. text 22.95 (*0-9719496-5-4*) Shangri-La Pubns.

Gale, Kate. Lake of Fire. 2000. 256p. pap. 16.95 (*0-9701057-9-7*) Winter Street Pr.

Gilman, Samuel. Memoirs of a New England Village Choir. 1984. (Music Reprint Ser.). 150p. reprint ed. pap. text 40.00 o.p. (*0-306-76175-0*) Da Capo Pr., Inc.

Goodger, Jane. Into the Wild Wind. 1999. 320p. mass mkt. 5.99 o.s.i (*0-451-40894-2*, Topaz) NAL.

—Into the Wild Wind. l.t. ed. 2000. (Ulverscroft Large Print Ser.). 496p. 31.99 (*0-7089-4315-2*, Ulverscroft) Thorpe, F. A. Pubs. GBR. *Dist:* Ulverscroft Large Print Bks., Ltd., Ulverscroft Large Print Canada, Ltd.

Gordon, Angela. Love Is a Tempest. l.t. ed. 1997. (Paperback Ser.). 220p. pap. 23.95 (*0-7838-8317-X*) Thorndike Pr.

Gutcheon, Beth Richardson. The New Girls. 1996. 352p. pap. 13.00 (*0-06-097702-7*, Perennial) HarperTrade.

—The New Girls. 1981. 336p. pap. 2.50 o.p. (*0-380-50831-1*, 50831-1, Avon Bks.) Morrow/Avon.

—The New Girls. 1979. 11.95 o.p. (*0-399-12362-8*) Putnam Publishing Group, The.

Hagy, Alyson. Graveyard of the Atlantic. 2000. (Illus.). ix, 186p. pap. 14.00 (*1-55597-301-9*) Graywolf Pr.

Hawley, Richard. The Headmaster's Wife. 2000. 192p. 21.95 (*0-8397-3193-0*) Eriksson, Paul S. Pub.

Hawthorne, Nathaniel. The Best Known Works of Nathaniel Hawthorne. 1977. (Short Story Index Reprint Ser.). reprint ed. 36.95 (*0-8369-4107-1*) Ayer Co. Pubs., Inc.

—The Great Stone Face. (J). audio. (J). audio. audio Audio Bk. Co.

—The Great Stone Face. 48p. (J). (gr. 3-7). 15.99 o.p. (*1-56476-544-X*) Cook Communications Ministries.

—The Great Stone Face. audio 10.00 Estee Audios.

—The Great Stone Face. audio HarperTrade.

—The Great Stone Face. 1984. audio; 1983. audio 7.95 Jimcin Recordings.

—The Great Stone Face. 1992. 50p. reprint ed. pap. 7.00 (*1-56459-059-3*) Kessinger Publishing Co.

—The Great Stone Face. unabr. ed. audio 10.95 (*0-8045-0940-9*, 7028) Spoken Arts, Inc.

—The Great Stone Face & Other Stories, unabr. ed. 1986. audio 18.00 (*1-55690-208-5*, 86120E7) Recorded Bks., LLC.

—The Great Stone Face & Other Tales. 1976. 16.95 (*0-8488-0519-4*) Amereon, Ltd.

—The Scarlet Letter & Other Selected Tales. Harding, Brian, ed. & intro. by. 1998. (Oxford World's Classics Ser.). 352p. pap. 4.95 (*0-19-283371-5*) Oxford Univ. Pr., Inc.

—The Whole History of Grandfather's Chair or True Stories from New England History, 1620-1808. 2000. E-Book 2.49 (*1-58744-159-4*) Electric Umbrella Publishing.

—The Whole History of Grandfather's Chair or True Stories from New England History, 1620-1808. 2002. 216p. per. 316.00 (*1-58963-780-1*) Fredonia Bks.

—The Whole History of Grandfather's Chair or True Stories from New England History, 1620-1808. 2002. 184p. 17.99 (*1-4043-0458-4*); per. 12.99 (*1-4043-0459-2*) IndyPublish.com.

Hayes, Penny. Kathleen O'Donald. 1994. 256p. pap. 9.95 (*1-56280-070-1*) Naiad Pr., Inc.

Hebert, Ernest. The Old American: A Novel. l.t. ed. 2001. (Thorndike Americana Ser.). 496p. 28.95 (*0-7862-3182-3*) Thorndike Pr.

—The Old American: A Novel. 2000. (Hardscrabble Books). 304p. text 26.95 (*1-58465-073-7*, Hardscrabble Bks.) Univ. Pr. of New England.

Hoffman, Alice. At Risk. 1998. 272p. pap. 13.00 (*0-425-16529-9*); 1989. 288p. mass mkt. 7.99 (*0-425-11738-3*) Berkley Publishing Group.

—At Risk. l.t. ed. 1989. (General Ser.). 306p. pap. 13.95 o.p. (*0-8161-4749-3*); lib. bdg. 20.95 o.p. (*0-8161-4748-5*) Gale Group. (Macmillan Reference USA).

—At Risk. 2001. 17.95 (*0-399-13844-7*) Penguin Group (USA) Inc.

—At Risk. 1988. 224p. 17.95 o.s.i (*0-399-13367-4*, G. P. Putnam's Sons) Penguin Putnam Bks. for Young Readers.

—At Risk. 1990. 3.99 o.p. (*0-517-05515-5*) Random Hse. Value Publishing.

—At Risk. abr. ed. 1989. audio 14.95 (*0-671-67696-2*, Simon & Schuster Audioworks) Simon & Schuster Audio.

—The Probable Future. 2003. 336p. 24.95 (*0-385-50760-7*) Doubleday Publishing.

—The Probable Future. l.t. ed. 2003. 512p. 26.95 (*0-375-43216-7*) Random Hse. Large Print.

Holland, Isabelle. Family Trust. 1999. pap. 22.00 (*0-525-93528-2*); 1994. 416p. mass mkt. 5.99 o.s.i (*0-451-18187-5*, Onyx) NAL.

Howells, William Dean. The Landlord at Lion's Head. 2000. 252p. E-Book 3.95 (*0-594-05125-8*) 1873 Pr.

—The Landlord at Lion's Head. (Illus.). reprint ed. 45.00 (*0-404-14778-X*) AMS Pr., Inc.

—The Landlord at Lion's Head. 1897. (YA). reprint ed. 461p. pap. text 28.00 (*1-4047-6925-0*); 318p. pap. text 28.00 (*1-4047-3250-0*) Classic Textbooks.

—The Landlord at Lion's Head. 1983. (Illus.). 512p. reprint ed. pap. 8.95 o.p. (*0-486-24455-5*) Dover Pubns., Inc.

—The Landlord at Lion's Head. 2002. Vol. 1. 152p. 93.99 (*1-4043-1242-0*); Vol. 1. 152p. per. 88.99 (*1-4043-1243-9*); Vol. 2. 196p. 94.99 (*1-4043-1244-7*); Vol. 2. 196p. per. 89.99 (*1-4043-1245-5*) IndyPublish.com.

—The Landlord at Lion's Head. 1992. (Notable American Authors Ser.). reprint ed. lib. bdg. 75.00 (*0-7812-3250-3*) Reprint Services Corp.

Hunt, Angela Elwell. Rehoboth. 1997. (Keepers of the Ring Ser.: No. 4). 356p. pap. 11.99 o.p. (*0-8423-2015-6*) Tyndale Hse. Pubs.

Inness-Brown, Elizabeth. Burning Marguerite. 2003. 256p. pap. 13.00 (*0-375-72622-5*, Vintage) Knopf Publishing Group.

—Burning Marguerite. 2002. 256p. 23.00 (*0-375-41196-8*) Knopf, Alfred A. Inc.

Irving, John. The 158-Pound Marriage. 1997. 176p. pap. 13.95 (*0-345-41796-8*); 1990. 256p. mass mkt. 6.99 (*0-345-36743-X*) Ballantine Bks.

—The 158-Pound Marriage. unabr. ed. audio 48.00 Books on Tape, Inc.

—The 158-Pound Marriage. 1982. mass mkt. 3.95 (*0-671-46811-1*, Pocket) Simon & Schuster.

Irving, Washington. The Legend of Sleepy Hollow. Jones, Michael P., ed. 1985. (Illus.). 60p. pap. text 8.00 (*0-89904-167-1*) Crumb Elbow Publishing.

—The Legend of Sleepy Hollow. 2003. (Spot the Classics Ser.). 192p. (J). 4.99 (*1-4037-0055-9*) Dalmatian Pr.

—The Legend of Sleepy Hollow. 1988. mass mkt. 4.95 (*0-938819-97-6*, Tor Bks.) Doherty, Tom Assocs., LLC.

—The Legend of Sleepy Hollow. 1994. pap. 3.60 (*0-87129-346-3*, L76) Dramatic Publishing Co.

—The Legend of Sleepy Hollow. E-Book 2.49 (*1-58627-964-5*) Electric Umbrella Publishing.

—The Legend of Sleepy Hollow. 32p. 12.95 (*0-8249-5301-0*) Ideals Pubns.

—The Legend of Sleepy Hollow. 2000. (Illustrated Junior Library Ser.). 9.99 o.s.i (*0-448-42450-9*, Grosset & Dunlap) Penguin Putnam Bks. for Young Readers.

—The Legend of Sleepy Hollow. E-Book 2.00 (*0-7410-1441-6*) SoftBook Pr.

—The Legend of Sleepy Hollow. 1990. 9.04 (*0-606-19958-6*) Turtleback Bks.

Jaffe, Rona. The Road Taken. l.t. ed. 2001. 499p. 27.95 (*1-57490-340-3*) Beeler, Thomas T. Publisher.

Jewett, Sarah Orne. Country By-Ways. E-Book 3.95 (*0-594-00071-8*) 1873 Pr.

—Country By-Ways. 1977. (Short Story Index Reprint Ser.). 249p. reprint ed. 19.95 (*0-8369-3115-7*) Ayer Co. Pubs., Inc.

—Country By-Ways. 1988. (Collected Works of Sarah Orne Jewett). reprint ed. lib. bdg. 79.00 (*0-7812-1304-5*) Reprint Services Corp.

—Country By-Ways. reprint ed. 59.00 (*0-403-03183-4*) Somerset Pubs., Inc.

—A Country Doctor, Set. unabr. ed. 1992. audio 41.95 (*1-55685-233-9*) Audio Bk. Contractors, Inc.

—A Country Doctor. 1999. (Bantam Classics Ser.). 288p. mass mkt. 4.95 (*0-553-21498-5*) Bantam Bks.

—A Country Doctor. 1986. 288p. pap. 11.95 o.p. (*0-452-00805-0*, Meridian Bks.) NAL.

—A Country Doctor. 1984. (Illus.). 371p. reprint ed. 25.00 o.p. (*0-89725-048-6*, 1261) Picton Pr.

—A Country Doctor. 1988. (Collected Works of Sarah Orne Jewett). reprint ed. lib. bdg. 59.00 (*0-7812-1306-1*) Reprint Services Corp.

—A Country Doctor. reprint ed. 59.00 (*0-403-03191-5*) Somerset Pubs., Inc.

—The Life of Nancy. 2000. 252p. E-Book 3.95 (*0-594-04803-6*); pap. 9.95 (*0-594-04800-1*) 1873 Pr.

—The Life of Nancy. 1977. (Short Story Index Reprint Ser.). 322p. reprint ed. 23.95 (*0-8369-3153-X*) Ayer Co. Pubs., Inc.

—The Life of Nancy. 1988. (Collected Works of Sarah Orne Jewett). reprint ed. lib. bdg. 59.00 (*0-7812-1312-6*) Reprint Services Corp.

—A Native of Winby & Other Tales. 1977. (Short Story Index Reprint Ser.). 309p. reprint ed. 19.95 (*0-8369-3408-3*) Ayer Co. Pubs., Inc.

—A Native of Winby & Other Tales. 1988. (Collected Works of Sarah Orne Jewett). reprint ed. lib. bdg. 59.00 (*0-7812-1311-8*) Reprint Services Corp.

—Old Friends & New. 1977. (Short Story Index Reprint Ser.). 269p. 18.95 (*0-8369-3067-3*) Ayer Co. Pubs., Inc.

—Old Friends & New. 1988. (Collected Works of Sarah Orne Jewett). reprint ed. lib. bdg. 59.00 (*0-7812-1303-7*) Reprint Services Corp.

—Old Friends & New. reprint ed. 59.00 (*0-403-03182-6*) Somerset Pubs., Inc.

—Tales of New England. 1977. (Short Story Index Reprint Ser.). 276p. reprint ed. 19.95 (*0-8369-3362-1*) Ayer Co. Pubs., Inc.

—Tales of New England. Heller, Terry, ed. 1997. (Sarah Orne Jewett Text Project Ser.). (Illus.). 105p. reprint ed. pap. text (*1-889678-02-3*) Coe Review Pr.

—A White Heron. 1997. (Candlewick Treasures Ser.). (Illus.). 64p. (J). (gr. 3-9). 11.99 o.s.i (*0-7636-0205-1*) Candlewick Pr.

—A White Heron & Other Stories. 1999. (Thrift Editions Ser.). 128p. pap. 1.50 (*0-486-40884-1*) Dover Pubns., Inc.

—A White Heron & Other Stories. 1988. (Collected Works of Sarah Orne Jewett). reprint ed. lib. bdg. 59.00 (*0-7812-1308-8*) Reprint Services Corp.

Jones, Ben. The Rope Eater: A Novel. 2003. 304p. 24.00 (*0-385-50977-4*) Doubleday Publishing.

Kelman, Judith. Fly Away Home. 1997. 336p. mass mkt. 5.99 (*0-553-57210-5*) Bantam Bks.

—Fly Away Home. 1997. 12.04 (*0-606-21631-6*) Turtleback Bks.

Kennedy, Kate. End over End. 2001. 310p. 24.00 (*1-56947-235-1*) Soho Pr., Inc.

King, Stephen. The Dead Zone. 1994. (Collectors' Editions Ser.). 416p. pap. 14.95 o.p. (*0-452-27329-3*, Plume) Dutton/Plume.

—The Dead Zone. l.t. ed. 1993. (General Ser.). 672p. lib. bdg. 23.95 o.p. (*0-8161-5668-9*, Macmillan Reference USA) Gale Group.

—The Dead Zone. 1983. mass mkt. 3.95 o.p. (*0-451-12666-1*); 1983. mass mkt. 4.50 o.p. (*0-451-15068-6*); 1983. mass mkt. 3.95 o.p. (*0-451-12792-7*); 1983. mass mkt. 4.50 o.p. (*0-451-13972-0*); 1980. mass mkt. 3.50 o.p. (*0-451-09338-0*); 1980. mass mkt. 3.95 o.p. (*0-451-11961-4*); 1980. 416p. reprint ed. mass mkt. 7.99 (*0-451-15575-0*) NAL. (Signet Bks.).

—The Dead Zone. l.t. ed. 1983. 656p. 13.95 o.p. (*0-7089-8157-7*, Charnwood) Thorpe, F. A. Pubs. GBR. *Dist:* Ulverscroft Large Print Bks., Ltd.

—The Dead Zone. 1979. 14.04 (*0-606-01917-0*) Turtleback Bks.

—The Dead Zone. 1979. 444p. text 35.00 (*0-670-26077-0*) Viking Penguin.

—The Girl Who Loved Tom Gordon. 2000. (RUS.). pap. 14.95 (*5-237-02949-3*) AST, Izdatel'stvo, OOO, firma RUS. *Dist:* Distribooks, Inc.
—The Girl Who Loved Tom Gordon. 2001. E-Book 16.95 (*1-930161-63-8*) Adobe Systems, Inc.
—The Girl Who Loved Tom Gordon. 1999. (*0-7540-1322-7*); (*0-7540-2239-0*) BBC Audiobooks America.
—The Girl Who Loved Tom Gordon. l.t. ed. (Thorndike/G. K. Hall Paperback Bestsellers Ser.). 261p. 2000. pap. 27.95 (*0-7838-8640-3*); 1999. 30.95 o.p. (*0-7838-8639-X*) Gale Group. (Macmillan Reference USA).
—The Girl Who Loved Tom Gordon. unabr. ed. 1999. audio 29.95 Highsmith Inc.
—The Girl Who Loved Tom Gordon. 1999. 272p. per. 7.99 (*0-671-04213-0*, Pocket); 1999. E-Book 16.95 (*0-684-83583-5*, Scribner); 1999. 224p. 16.95 (*0-684-86762-1*, Scribner); 2000. 272p. reprint ed. pap. 7.99 (*0-671-04285-8*, Pocket) Simon & Schuster.
—The Girl Who Loved Tom Gordon. unabr. ed. 1999. audio 29.95 (*0-671-04585-7*, 758844); audio 32.00 (*0-671-04586-5*) Simon & Schuster Audio. (Simon & Schuster Audioworks).
—The Girl Who Loved Tom Gordon. 2000. (Illus.). (J). 13.04 (*0-606-18369-8*) Turtleback Bks.
—El Misterio de Salem's Lot. 2nd ed. 1999. (SPA., Illus.). 512p. (*84-01-47456-6*) Plaza & Janés Editories, S.A.
—Salem's Lot. 1990. 464p. 35.00 (*0-385-00751-5*) Doubleday Publishing.
—Salem's Lot. 1991. (Stephen King Collectors Editions Ser.). (Illus.). 400p. pap. 14.95 o.p. (*0-452-26721-8*, Plume) Dutton/Plume.
—Salem's Lot. l.t. ed. 1994. 694p. lib. bdg. 23.95 (*0-8161-5686-7*, Macmillan Reference USA) Gale Group.
—Salem's Lot. 1979. mass mkt. 2.75 o.p. (*0-451-09231-7*); 1976. mass mkt. 4.95 o.p. (*0-451-16588-8*); 1976. mass mkt. 4.50 o.p. (*0-451-15065-1*); 1976. mass mkt. 1.95 o.p. (*0-451-07112-3*); 1976. mass mkt. 2.25 o.p. (*0-451-08000-9*); 1976. mass mkt. 2.50 o.p. (*0-451-09000-4*); 1976. mass mkt. 2.95 o.p. (*0-451-09545-6*); 1976. mass mkt. 3.50 o.p. (*0-451-09827-7*); 1976. mass mkt. 3.95 o.p. (*0-451-12158-9*); 1976. mass mkt. 3.95 o.p. (*0-451-12545-2*); 1976. mass mkt. 4.50 o.p. (*0-451-13969-0*); 1976. (Illus.). 448p. (YA). (gr. 10). reprint ed. mass mkt. 7.99 o.s.i (*0-451-16808-9*) NAL. (Signet Bks.).
—Salem's Lot. 1999. 656p. mass mkt. 7.99 (*0-671-03974-1*); 2000. 480p. pap. 13.95 (*0-671-03975-X*) Simon & Schuster. (Pocket).
—Salem's Lot. 1990. 14.04 (*0-606-02434-4*) Turtleback Bks.
—La Zona Muerta. 13th ed. 1999. Tr. of Dead Zone. (SPA., Illus.). 456p. 14.95 (*84-01-49988-7*) Plaza & Janés Editories, S.A. ESP. *Dist:* Distribooks, Inc.
Kinkade, Thomas. A New Leaf No. 4: Cape Light. 2004. 352p. 23.95 (*0-425-19398-5*) Berkley Publishing Group.
Kinkade, Thomas & Spencer, Katherine. The Cape Light. 2002. 368p. 22.95 (*0-425-18337-8*) Berkley Publishing Group.
—A Gathering Place: A Cape Light Novel. 2003. 368p. 23.95 (*0-425-19004-8*) Berkley Publishing Group.
—Home Song: A Cape Light Novel. 384p. 2003. pap. 13.95 (*0-425-19183-4*); 2002. 23.95 (*0-425-18624-5*) Berkley Publishing Group.
Kipling, Rudyard. Captains Courageous. Ormond, Leonee, ed. & intro. by. 1995. (Oxford World's Classics Ser.). 194p. pap. 8.95 o.p. (*0-19-282929-7*) Oxford Univ. Pr., Inc.
Klavan, Andrew. Man & Wife: A Novel of Psychological Suspense. l.t. ed. 2002. lib. bdg. 28.95 (*1-58547-205-0*, Premier) Ctr. Point Large Print.
—Man & Wife: A Novel of Psychological Suspense. 304p. 2001. 24.95 (*0-7653-0215-2*); 2003. reprint ed. mass mkt. 6.99 (*0-7653-4137-9*) Doherty, Tom Assocs., LLC. (Forge Bks.).
Kleinholz, Lisa. Dancing with Mr. D. 2000. 384p. mass mkt. 5.99 o.s.i (*0-06-101412-5*, Avon Bks.) Morrow/Avon.
Korelitz, Jean Hanff. The Sabbathday River. 2001. 528p. mass mkt. 7.99 o.s.i (*0-515-13011-7*, Jove) Berkley Publishing Group.
Kraeger, Linda. Trust & Treachery: An Historical Novel of Early Seventeenth-Century England & New England. 1996. 374p. text 99.95 (*0-7734-4242-1*) Mellen, Edwin Pr., The.
Kramer, Kathryn. A Handbook for Visitors from Outer Space. 1985. (Vintage Contemporaries Ser.). pap. 5.95 o.s.i (*0-394-72989-7*, Vintage) Knopf Publishing Group.
—A Handbook for Visitors from Outer Space. 1984. 336p. 15.95 o.p. (*0-394-52374-1*) Knopf, Alfred A. Inc.
Kraus, Jim & Kraus, Terri. The Price: A Novel. 2000. (Circle of Destiny Ser.). 368p. pap. 8.99 o.p. (*0-8423-1835-6*) Tyndale Hse. Pubs.
Kuong, Richard Stuart. Paradox of the Soul. 2002. 335p. pap. 16.99 (*1-58832-052-9*) Management Advisory Pubns.
Lamb, Wally. I Know This Much Is True. l.t. ed. 1998. 949 p. 29.95 (*1-57490-164-8*) Beeler, Thomas T. Publisher.
—I Know This Much Is True. 2003. 912p. mass mkt. 7.99 (*0-06-109764-0*); 2000. (*0-06-039280-0*); 1998. 912p. pap. 16.00 o.s.i (*0-06-109812-4*) HarperCollins Pubs.
—I Know This Much Is True. 1999. 912p. pap. 16.00 (*0-06-098756-1*, ReganBooks); 1998. 912p. 27.50 (*0-06-039162-6*, ReganBooks); 1998. audio 25.00 (*0-694-51940-5*, 695741, HarperAudio) HarperTrade.
—I Know This Much Is True. unabr. ed. 1999. audio 177.00 (*0-7887-2491-6*, 95566E7) Recorded Bks., LLC.
Laurent, Anne. Victorian House: A New England Ghost Story. enl. ed. 2001. (Illus.). 280p. pap. 17.95 (*1-931144-12-5*, Peace Vision Bks.) Peace Vision Publishing.
LeClaire, Anne D. Grace Point. 1993. 352p. mass mkt. 5.99 o.p. (*0-451-40395-9*, Signet Bks.) NAL.
—Grace Point. 1992. 352p. 22.00 o.p. (*0-670-84327-X*, Viking) Viking Penguin.
Lynch, Patrick. The Policy. abr. ed. 1999. audio 7.99 o.s.i (*1-56740-313-1*, 1871, Paperback Nova Audio Bks.); 1998. audio 17.95 o.p. (*1-56740-803-6*, 1466, Nova Audio Bks.); 1998. audio 26.95 (*1-56740-079-5*, 1464, Bookcassette); 1998. 12p. audio 73.25 (*1-56740-608-4*, 1465, Unabridged Library Editions) Brilliance Audio.
—The Policy. 1998. 384p. 24.95 o.p. (*0-525-94340-4*) Dutton/Plume.
—The Policy. 1999. 416p. reprint ed. mass mkt. 6.99 o.s.i (*0-451-19326-1*, Signet Bks.) NAL.
MacFarlane, Lisa, ed. This World Is Not Conclusion: Faith in Nineteenth-Century New England Fiction. 1998. 301p. per. 22.95 (*0-87451-862-8*, Hardscrabble Bks.) Univ. Pr. of New England.
Mamet, David. The Village. 1998. pap. 11.95 (*0-316-19100-0*, Back Bay) Little Brown & Co.
—The Village: A Novel. 1996. 256p. pap. 11.95 o.p. (*0-316-54338-1*); 1994. 238p. 21.95 o.p. (*0-316-54572-4*) Little Brown & Co.
Maness, Larry. A Once Perfect Place: A Jake Eaton Mystery. 1996. 208p. 19.95 o.s.i (*0-89141-567-X*, Presidio Pr.) Ballantine Bks.
Manson, Cynthia & Ardai, Charles, eds. New England Crime Chowder. 1992. 250p. pap. 11.95 o.p. (*1-55882-127-9*, Library of Crime Classics) International Polygonics, Ltd.
McCaffrey, Anne. The Mark of Merlin. l.t. ed. 1992. 19.95 o.p. (*0-7927-1019-3*); pap. 17.95 o.p. (*0-7927-1020-7*) BBC Audiobooks America.
—The Mark of Merlin. 2002. 196p. 35.00 (*1-59224-013-5*); 196p. per. 15.95 (*1-58715-493-5*); pap. 15.95 (*1-58715-486-2*) Wildside Pr.
McHugh, Frances Y. The Rocking Chair. l.t. ed. 2001. 191p. pap. 23.95 (*0-7838-9463-5*, Macmillan Reference USA) Gale Group.
McSherry, Frank, et al, eds. New England Ghosts. 1990. (American Ghosts Ser.). 214p. (Orig.). pap. 9.95 (*1-55853-090-8*) Rutledge Hill Pr.
Mercier, Ron. Dance the River Whale. 1999. 256p. pap. 13.95 (*0-9668527-0-2*) Deerbridge Bks.
Michelsen, G. F. Hard Bottom: A Novel. (Hardscrabble Bks.). (Illus.). 360p. 2003. pap. 15.95 (*1-58465-082-6*); 2001. text 30.00 (*1-58465-081-8*) Univ. Pr. of New England. (Hardscrabble Bks.).
Miller, Sue. While I Was Gone. 2002. 352p. mass mkt. 7.99 (*0-345-42074-8*); 2000. 304p. pap. 14.00 (*0-345-44328-4*); 2000. 304p. pap. 12.95 o.s.i (*0-345-43500-1*) Ballantine Bks.
—While I Was Gone. l.t. ed. 1999. 30.00 o.p. (*0-7838-8481-8*, Macmillan Reference USA) Gale Group.
—While I Was Gone. l.t. ed. 1999. 448p. 24.00 o.s.i (*0-375-70571-6*) Knopf, Alfred A. Inc.
—While I Was Gone. abr. ed. 2000. audio 25.95 (*0-375-41664-1*); 2000. audio compact disk 29.95 (*0-375-41665-X*); 1999. audio 24.00 o.s.i (*0-375-40563-1*, 691584) Random Hse. Audio Publishing Group. (RH Audio).
—While I Was Gone. l.t. ed. 2000. 448p. pap. 12.95 o.s.i (*0-375-72801-5*) Random Hse. Large Print.
—While I Was Gone. 2000. (Oprah's Book Club Ser.). 288p. 24.00 (*0-375-41178-X*) Random Hse., Inc.
—While I Was Gone. 2000. 19.00 (*0-606-22790-3*) Turtleback Bks.
Minot, George. The Blue Bowl. 2004. 384p. 24.00 (*0-394-57348-X*) Knopf, Alfred A. Inc.
Minshull, Evelyn W. Dune Witch. l.t. ed. 1973. (Illus.). lib. bdg. 8.95 o.p. (*0-8161-6075-9*, Macmillan Reference USA) Gale Group.
—Dune Witch. 1972. (J). (gr. 4-6). 4.95 o.p. (*0-664-32505-X*) Westminster John Knox Pr.
Monahan, William G. Light House. 2000. 208p. 21.95 o.s.i (*1-57322-158-9*, Riverhead Bks. (Hardcovers)) Putnam Publishing Group, The.
Mooney, Chris. Deviant Ways. 2000. 384p. 24.95 (*0-671-04059-6*, Atria) Simon & Schuster.
Morrow, Laurie Bogart. The Hardscrabble Chronicles. 336p. 2003. pap. 14.00 (*0-425-19196-6*); 2002. (Illus.). 21.95 (*0-425-18462-5*) Berkley Publishing Group.
Mosiman, Billie Sue & Greenberg, Martin H., eds. Never Shake a Family Tree: And Other Heart-Stopping Tales of Murder in New England. 1998. 224p. pap. 9.95 o.p. (*1-55853-577-2*) Rutledge Hill Pr.
Munnings, Claire, et al. Overnight Float: A Mystery. 2000. 288p. text 23.95 (*0-393-03849-1*) Norton, W. W. & Co., Inc.
Naslund, Sena Jeter. Ahab's Wife: Or, the Star Gazer. 2000. (Illus.). 688p. pap. 15.00 (*0-688-17785-9*, Perennial) HarperTrade.
—Ahab's Wife: Or, the Star Gazer. 1999. (Illus.). 688p. 28.00 (*0-688-17187-7*, Morrow, William & Co.) Morrow/Avon.
—Ahab's Wife: Or, the Star Gazer. abr. ed. 1999. audio 25.00 o.s.i (*0-671-04644-6*, Simon & Schuster Audioworks) Simon & Schuster Audio.
Navas, Deborah. Things We Lost, Gave Away, Bought High & Sold Low: Stories. 1992. 152p. 16.95 (*0-87074-336-8*) Southern Methodist Univ. Pr.
Navas, Deborah, ed. New Fiction from New England. 1986. 272p. 14.95 o.p. (*0-89909-087-7*) Yankee Bks.
Neggers, Carla. Cold Ridge. l.t. ed. 2003. 438p. 29.95 (*0-7862-5893-4*) Gale Group.
—Cold Ridge. 2003. 384p. mass mkt. (*1-55166-684-7*, Mira Bks.) Harlequin Enterprises, Ltd.
Noon, Jack. Old Sam's Thunder. unabr. ed. 1998. (Illus.). 328p. (YA). pap. 16.00 (*0-9642213-6-5*) Moose Country Pr.
O'Connell, Jack. The Skin Palace. 1996. 82p. 21.95 o.p. (*0-89296-547-9*) Mysterious Pr.
—The Skin Palace. 448p. pap. 16.95 (*1-901982-29-7*) No Exit Pr. GBR. *Dist:* Trafalgar Square.
—The Skin Palace. 1996. 464p. mass mkt. 5.99 (*0-446-40357-1*) Warner Bks., Inc.
O'Nan, Stewart. The Night Country. unabr. ed. 2003. audio 27.95 (*1-59355-232-7*, 4838, Brilliance Audio Unabridged) Brilliance Audio.
—The Night Country: Or, the Darkness on the Edge of Town. 2003. 240p. 22.00 (*0-374-22215-0*) Farrar, Straus & Giroux.
Patton, Robert H. Life Between Wars. 1997. 256p. 24.00 (*1-877946-97-4*) Permanent Pr., The.
Piercy, Marge. Three Women. 2000. 384p. reprint ed. mass mkt. 6.99 (*0-06-101467-2*, HarperTorch) Morrow/Avon.
Plain, Belva. Secrecy. unabr. ed. 1999. audio 69.95 (*0-7540-0145-8*, CAB1568) Chivers Audio Bks. GBR. *Dist:* BBC Audiobooks America.
—Secrecy. 1998. 432p. reprint ed. mass mkt. 7.50 (*0-440-22511-6*, Dell Bks.) Dell Publishing.
—Secrecy. abr. ed. 1997. audio 24.95 (*0-553-47796-X*, 695227, RH Audio) Random Hse. Audio Publishing Group.
—Secrecy. l.t. ed. (Paperback Bestsellers Ser.). 495p. 1998. pap. 28.95 (*0-7862-1220-9*); 1997. lib. bdg. 30.95 (*0-7862-1219-5*) Thorndike Pr.
Proulx, E. Annie. Postcards. l.t. ed. 2001. (Illus.). 470p. lib. bdg. 28.95 (*1-58547-147-X*) Ctr. Point Large Print.
—Postcards. (Scribner Classics). 1996. 352p. 22.00 (*0-684-83368-9*); 1994. 320p. pap. 13.00 (*0-684-80087-X*); 1992. (Illus.). 308p. 22.95 o.s.i (*0-684-18718-3*) Simon & Schuster. (Scribner).
Pryse, Marjorie. Selected Stories of Freeman. 1991. (C). pap. 18.15 (*0-393-30106-0*, Norton Paperbacks) Norton, W. W. & Co., Inc.
Ramsay, Diana. Killing Words. 1994. 192p. 18.95 o.p. (*0-312-11015-4*, Saint Martin's Minotaur) St. Martin's Pr.
Rawlings, Marjorie Kinnan. Sojourner. l.t. ed. 1999. (Perennial Bestsellers Ser.). 519p. 25.95 (*0-7838-8553-9*) Thorndike Pr.
Rice, Luanne. Home Fires. 1996. 320p. mass mkt. 7.50 (*0-553-57322-5*) Bantam Bks.
—Home Fires. unabr. ed. 1996. audio 56.00 (*0-7366-3288-3*, 3943) Books on Tape, Inc.
—Home Fires. l.t. ed. 1996. 24.95 o.p. (*1-56895-299-6*, Wheeler Publishing, Inc.) Gale Group.
—Safe Harbor. 2003. 432p. mass mkt. 7.50 (*0-553-58395-6*, Bantam); 2002. 352p. 22.95 (*0-553-80218-6*) Bantam Bks.
—Safe Harbor. l.t. ed. 2002. (Wheeler Large Print Book Ser.). 28.95 (*1-58724-183-8*, Wheeler Publishing, Inc.) Gale Group.
Riefe, Barbara. Barringer House. 2000. (Five Star Romance Ser.). 202p. 26.95 (*0-7862-2337-5*, Five Star) Gale Group.
Roberts, Nora. Dance upon the Air. 2001. 400p. mass mkt. 7.99 (*0-515-13122-9*, Jove) Berkley Publishing Group.
—Dance upon the Air. l.t. ed. 2001. 414p. 32.95 (*0-7838-9619-0*) Gale Group.
Rudolph, Grace. A Stroke of Good Luck. 2003. 209p. pap. 19.95 (*1-59286-357-4*) PublishAmerica, Inc.
Ruiz de Burton, Maria A. Who Would Have Thought It? Sanchez, Rosaura & Pita, Beatrice, eds. 1995. 298p. pap. 12.95 (*1-55885-081-3*) Arte Publico Pr.
Rule, Rebecca. The Best Revenge: Short Stories. 1995. 208p. text 22.95 (*0-87451-702-8*, Hardscrabble Bks.) Univ. Pr. of New England.
Sadler, William A. Second Growth: The Six Paradoxes of Third Age Renewal. 1998. 256p. 22.95 o.p. (*1-56838-226-X*) Hazelden Publishing & Educational Services.
Santayana, George. The Last Puritan: A Memoir in the Form of a Novel. 1981. 10.00 o.s.i (*0-684-13132-3*); 608p. 60.00 (*0-684-16833-2*) Gale Group. (Macmillan Reference USA).
—The Last Puritan: A Memoir in the Form of a Novel. Saatkamp, Herman J., Jr. & Holsberger, William G., eds. 1995. 680p. pap. text 37.00 (*0-262-69178-7*); 1994. (Works of George Santayana: Vol. 4). (Illus.). 792p. text 85.00 (*0-262-19328-0*) MIT Pr.
Sarton, May. Kinds of Love. 1994. 352p. pap. 13.95 (*0-393-31101-5*); 1970. 12.95 o.p. (*0-393-08620-8*); 1980. 352p. reprint ed. pap. 5.95 o.p. (*0-393-00968-8*) Norton, W. W. & Co., Inc.
Scharnhorst, Gary, ed. The Lost Tales of Horatio Alger: Adventure, Romance & Moral Intrigue, the Best of Alger's Early Tales. 1990. 240p. (YA). (gr. 10 up). 6.95 (*0-934745-11-0*) Acadia Publishing Co.
Schimel, Lawrence & Greenberg, Martin H., eds. Blood Lines: Vampire Stories from New England. 1997. (American Vampire Ser.). (Illus.). 240p. (Orig.). pap. 12.95 (*1-888952-50-4*) Cumberland Hse. Publishing.
Schine, Cathleen. The Evolution of Jane. unabr. ed. 1998. audio 24.95 (*1-56740-087-6*, 1484, Bookcassette); audio 57.25 (*1-56740-616-5*, 1485, Unabridged Library Editions) Brilliance Audio.
—The Evolution of Jane. 1999. 224p. pap. 12.95 (*0-452-28120-2*, Plume) Dutton/Plume.
—The Evolution of Jane. 1998. 256p. tchr. ed. 24.00 o.s.i (*0-395-82657-8*) Houghton Mifflin Co.
—The Love Letter. 1999. pap. 12.95 o.s.i (*0-452-28141-5*); 1998. 272p. pap. 12.95 (*0-452-27948-8*) Dutton/Plume.
—The Love Letter. l.t. ed. 1995. 334p. 23.95 o.p. (*0-7838-1451-8*, Macmillan Reference USA) Gale Group.
—The Love Letter. 1995. 224p. tchr. ed. 19.95 o.p. (*0-395-68996-1*) Houghton Mifflin Co.
—The Love Letter. 1999. 362p. mass mkt. 6.99 o.s.i (*0-451-19867-0*); 1996. 368p. mass mkt. 6.99 o.s.i (*0-451-18847-0*) NAL. (Signet Bks.).
Schmidt, Heidi J. The Rose Thieves. 1990. 192p. 18.95 (*0-15-179013-2*) Harcourt Trade Pubs.
Scott, Angelica. For Love of Sarah. 1995. 272p. 21.50 o.s.i (*1-55611-451-6*) Fine, Donald I. Bks.
Sedgwick, Catharine Maria. A New-England Tale. 2003. (Penguin Classics Ser.). 224p. pap. 13.00 (*0-14-243712-3*, Penguin Classics) Viking Penguin.
—New England Tale. reprint ed. 37.50 (*0-404-17169-9*) AMS Pr., Inc.
—A New-England Tale: Or, Sketches of New-England Character. Clements, Victoria, ed. 1995. (Early American Women Writers Ser.). 208p. pap. 17.95 (*0-19-509327-5*) Oxford Univ. Pr., Inc.
Seymour, Miranda. The Summer of '39: A Novel. l.t. ed. 2000. (G. K. Hall Core Ser.). 312p. 28.95 (*0-7838-8935-6*, Macmillan Reference USA) Gale Group.
Shem, Samuel. Mount Misery. 2003. 576p. pap. 14.95 (*0-345-46334-X*, Ballantine Bks.); 1997. 544p. mass mkt. 7.99 (*0-8041-1555-9*, Ivy Bks.) Ballantine Bks.
Shreve, Anita. Where or When. l.t. ed. 1993. 24.95 o.p. (*0-7927-1807-0*); 293p. pap. 22.95 o.p. (*0-7927-1806-2*) BBC Audiobooks America.
—Where or When. unabr. collector's ed. 1994. audio 42.00 (*0-7366-2759-6*, 3482) Books on Tape, Inc.
—Where or When. (Harvest Book Ser.). 252p. 1999. pap. 13.00 (*0-15-600652-9*, Harvest Bks.); 1993. 13.00 (*0-15-131461-6*) Harcourt Trade Pubs.
—Where or When. 1994. 304p. mass mkt. 5.99 o.s.i (*0-451-40478-5*, Signet Bks.) NAL.
—Where or When. abr. ed. 1994. audio 16.95 (*1-879371-54-5*, 40220) Publishing Mills, Inc., The.
Silber, Diana. Confessions. 1991. 464p. mass mkt. 4.95 o.s.i (*0-553-28681-1*) Bantam Bks.
Simons, Paullina. Red Leaves. abr. ed. 1997. audio 7.99 o.p. (*1-56740-186-4*, 691, Paperback Nova Audio Bks.); 1996. audio 25.95 o.p. (*1-56100-701-3*, 226, Bookcassette); 1996. audio 89.25 o.p. (*1-56100-326-3*, 1003, Unabridged Library Editions) Brilliance Audio.
—Red Leaves. l.t. ed. 1996. 25.95 (*1-56895-387-9*, Wheeler Publishing, Inc.) Gale Group.
—Red Leaves. 1996. 400p. text 24.95 o.p. (*0-312-14715-5*); Vol. 1. 3rd ed. 1997. (Red Leaves Ser.: Vol. 1). 416p. mass mkt. 6.99 (*0-312-96225-8*, St. Martin's Paperbacks) St. Martin's Pr.
Smith, Russell J. Whirligig: A Novel. 1995. pap. 9.95 (*0-910155-29-1*) Bartleby Pr.
Spencer, Katherine & Kinkade, Thomas. Cape Light. 2004. 384p. mass mkt. 6.99 (*0-515-13732-4*, Jove) Berkley Publishing Group.

Settings

For book reviews, descriptive annotations, tables of contents, cover images, author biographies & additional information, updated daily, subscribe to **www.booksinprint.com** 973

St. Edmunds, Anne. Red Right Returning. 1997. (New England Mystery Ser.). per. (*0-373-26258-2*, 1-26258-3, Worldwide Library) Harlequin Enterprises, Ltd.
—Red Right Returning. 1996. 224p. 20.95 o.p. (*0-312-14033-9*, Saint Martin's Minotaur) St. Martin's Pr.
Starnes, Henry G. Summer at the Resort: Remembering the 50s. Epps, Robert, ed. rev. ed. 1997. 250p. pap. 12.00 (*0-9657613-0-4*) Starnes Publishing Co.
Stegner, Lynn. Pipers at the Gates of Dawn: A Triptych. 2000. 270p. pap. (*1-58465-064-8*); 282p. text 27.95 (*1-58465-063-X*) Univ. Pr. of New England. (Hardscrabble Bks.).
Stegner, Wallace. Second Growth. 1985. 240p. text 25.00 o.p. (*0-8032-4162-3*); (Illus.). pap. 12.00 (*0-8032-9157-4*, Bison Bks.) Univ. of Nebraska Pr.
Stein, Michael. The White Life. 1999. 184p. pap. text 16.00 o.s.i (*1-57962-025-6*); 172p. 24.00 o.p. (*1-57962-022-1*) Permanent Pr., The.
Stowe, Harriet Beecher. Betty's Bright Idea. 1977. (Short Story Index Reprint Ser.). reprint ed. 18.95 (*0-8369-4121-7*) Ayer Co. Pubs., Inc.
—The Minister's Wooing. E-Book 3.95 (*0-594-05594-6*) 1873 Pr.
—The Minister's Wooing. (YA). reprint ed. 1887. 417p. pap. text 28.00 (*1-4047-6872-6*); 1859. pap. text 28.00 (*1-4047-8959-6*) Classic Textbooks.
—The Minister's Wooing. 1985. (Americans in Fiction Ser.). reprint ed. lib. bdg. 16.50 o.p. (*0-8398-1875-0*) Irvington Pubs.
—The Minister's Wooing. (Notable American Authors Ser.). reprint ed. 1999. lib. bdg. 125.00 (*0-7812-8959-9*); 1992. 578p. lib. bdg. 99.00 (*0-7812-6872-9*) Reprint Services Corp.
—The Minister's Wooing. 1996. (Harriet Beecher Stowe's New England Novels Ser.). (Illus.). 578p. (C). reprint ed. pap. 17.00 (*0-917482-12-3*) Rutgers Univ. Pr.
—The Minister's Wooing. reprint ed. 14.00 (*0-403-00187-0*) Scholarly Pr., Inc.
—The Minister's Wooing. l.t. ed. 2003. 29.95 (*0-7862-5447-5*) Thorndike Pr.
—The Minister's Wooing. Harris, Susan K., ed. & intro. by. 1999. (Classics Ser.). 480p. 15.00 (*0-14-043702-9*, Penguin Classics) Viking Penguin.
—Oldtown Folks. 2000. 252p. pap. 9.95 (*0-594-01023-3*); E-Book 3.95 (*0-594-05614-4*) 1873 Pr.
—Oldtown Folks. reprint ed. 35.00 (*0-404-06293-8*) AMS Pr., Inc.
—Oldtown Folks. 1992. (BCL1-PS American Literature Ser.). 608p. reprint ed. lib. bdg. 109.00 (*0-7812-6873-7*) Reprint Services Corp.
—Oldtown Folks. Berkson, Dorothy, ed. 1987. (American Women Writers Ser.). 519p. (C). text 45.00 (*0-8135-1219-0*); pap. text 17.00 (*0-8135-1220-4*) Rutgers Univ. Pr.
—Oldtown Folks. 1969. reprint ed. 13.00 (*0-403-00053-X*) Scholarly Pr., Inc.
—Poganuc People. 1999. (Notable American Authors Ser.). reprint ed. lib. bdg. 125.00 (*0-7812-8964-5*) Reprint Services Corp.
—Poganuc People. 1996. (Illus.). 375p. (C). reprint ed. pap. 17.00 (*0-917482-06-9*) Rutgers Univ. Pr.
Strout, Elizabeth. Amy & Isabelle. unabr. ed. 2000. 10p. audio 84.95 (*0-7927-2343-0*, CSL 232, Chivers Sound Library) BBC Audiobooks America.
—Amy & Isabelle. l.t. ed. 1999. 28.95 (*1-56895-728-9*, Wheeler Publishing, Inc.) Gale Group.
—Amy & Isabelle, abr. ed. 1999. audio 24.00 Highsmith Inc.
—Amy & Isabelle. 2000. 320p. pap. 13.00 (*0-375-70519-8*, Vintage) Knopf Publishing Group.
—Amy & Isabelle. abr. ed. 1998. audio 24.00 o.s.i (*0-375-40496-1*, RH Audio) Random Hse. Audio Publishing Group.
Sullivan, Eleanor & Dorbandt, Chris, eds. Murder in New England. l.t. ed. 1992. 19.95 o.p. (*0-7927-1244-7*); pap. 17.95 o.p. (*0-7927-1243-9*) BBC Audiobooks America.
Tartt, Donna. The Secret History. 2004. 576p. pap. 14.95 (*1-4000-3170-2*, Vintage) Knopf Publishing Group.
Tetu, Randeane. Merle's & Marilyn's Mink Ranch. 1992. 216p. 14.00 (*0-918949-17-3*); pap. 9.00 (*0-918949-13-0*) Tetu, Randeane.
Theroux, Alexander. An Adultery. 1997. 388p. pap. 15.00 o.s.i (*0-8050-4460-4*, Owl Bks.) Holt, Henry & Co.
—An Adultery. 1987. 448p. 18.45 o.p. (*0-671-63589-1*, Simon & Schuster) Simon & Schuster.
Towler, Katherine. Snow Island. 2003. 292p. 28.95 (*1-57490-492-2*, Beeler Large Print Bks.) Beeler, Thomas T. Publisher.
—Snow Island: A Novel. 2003. 304p. pap. 13.00 (*0-452-28390-6*) Dutton/Plume.
—Snow Island: A Novel. 2002. 287p. 25.00 (*1-931561-01-X*) MacAdam/Cage Publishing, Inc.
Underwood, Betty. The Forge & the Forest, 001. 1975. (Illus.). 240p. (YA). (gr. 6 up). 6.95 o.p. (*0-395-20492-5*) Houghton Mifflin Co.
Waldron, Robert G. Blue Hope: A Novella. 2002. 128p. pap. 13.95 (*1-55725-290-4*) Paraclete Pr., Inc.
Wallace, Aldora & Provencal, William. Dirty Cops & Small Town Politics: Inspired by a True Story of Arson. Wallace, Aldora, ed. 2000. (Illus.). 196p. reprint ed. per. 8.00 (*0-9706587-0-2*) Wallace, Aldora.
Watkins, Paul. Calm at Sunset, Calm at Dawn. 1989. 304p. 17.95 o.p. (*0-395-50959-9*) Houghton Mifflin Co.
—Calm at Sunset, Calm at Dawn. 1991. pap. 8.95 (*0-380-71222-9*, Avon Bks.) Morrow/Avon.
—Calm at Sunset, Calm at Dawn. 1996. 288p. pap. 12.00 (*0-312-15418-6*) Picador.
—Calm at Sunset, Calm at Dawn. unabr. ed. 1991. audio 60.00 (*1-55690-084-8*, 91107E7) Recorded Bks., LLC.
Waugh, Charles, et al, eds. Yankee Witches: Fifteen Short Stories of Horror & Humor. 1992. (Illus.). 315p. (Orig.). pap. 13.95 (*0-912769-32-7*, 80-451-3) Rodale Pr., Inc.
Waugh, Charles & Greenberg, Martin H., eds. The Best New England Stories. 1990. 328p. (Orig.). pap. 12.95 o.p. (*0-912769-24-6*, 80-551-2) Rodale Pr., Inc.
Waugh, Charles G., et al, eds. Haunted New England. 1988. 288p. 16.95 (*0-89909-156-3*, 80-450-5); pap. 11.95 (*0-89909-339-6*, 80-450-6) Rodale Pr., Inc.
Wetherell, W. D. The Wisest Man in America. 236p. 1996. pap. 15.95 (*0-87451-761-3*); 1995. lib. bdg. 30.00 (*0-87451-700-1*) Univ. Pr. of New England. (Hardscrabble Bks.).
Wharton, Edith. Wharton's New England: Seven Stories & Ethan Frome. White, Barbara A., ed. 1995. 286p. pap. 16.95 (*0-87451-715-X*, Hardscrabble Bks.) Univ. Pr. of New England.
White, Kate. A Body to Die For. l.t. ed. 2003. 460p. 30.95 (*0-7862-5767-9*) Thorndike Pr.
—A Body to Die For. 2004. 400p. mass mkt. 6.99 (*0-446-61385-1*); 2003. 304p. 23.95 (*0-446-53148-0*) Warner Bks., Inc.
Wiggen, Kate D. Rebecca of Sunnybrook Farm. 1991. 272p. (J). mass mkt. 3.95 o.s.i (*0-451-52483-7*, Signet Classics) NAL.
Wiggin, Eric & Wiggin, Kate Douglas. Rebecca of Sunnybrook Farm. 1994. (Rebecca of Sunnybrook Farm Ser.: No. 1). (Illus.). 253p. (J). (gr. 7-12). pap. 6.99 (*0-934998-51-5*) Evangel Publishing Hse.
Wiggin, Kate Douglas. Rebecca of Sunnybrook Farm. unabr. ed. 1993. audio 39.95 (*1-55686-473-6*, 473) Books in Motion.
—Rebecca of Sunnybrook Farm. 1995. (J). 11.04 (*0-606-12495-0*) Turtleback Bks.
—Rebecca of Sunnybrook Farm. 1998. (Children's Classics). 208p. (YA). (ps up). pap. 3.95 (*1-85326-134-3*, 1343WW) Wordsworth Editions, Ltd. GBR. *Dist:* Advanced Global Distribution Services.
Willett, Jincy. Winner of the National Book Award: A Novel of Fame, Honor, & Really Bad Weather. 2003. 336p. 23.95 (*0-312-31181-8*) St. Martin's Pr.
Wilson, Susan. Hawke's Cove. reprint ed. 2003. (Illus.). 320p. pap. 6.99 (*0-671-03574-6*, Pocket); 2001. E-Book 23.95 (*0-7434-1737-2*, Atria) Simon & Schuster.
Winthrop, Elizabeth. Island Justice. 1998. 320p. 25.00 (*0-688-15920-6*, Morrow, William & Co.) Morrow/Avon.
—Island Justice: A Novel. 1999. 368p. reprint ed. pap. 13.00 (*0-688-16968-6*, Quill) HarperTrade.
Wolff, Tobias. Old School: A Novel. 2003. 208p. 22.00 (*0-375-40146-6*) Knopf, Alfred A. Inc.
Woodruff, Nancy. Someone Else's Child. E-Book 23.00 (*1-58945-250-X*) Adobe Systems, Inc.
—Someone Else's Child. 2000. 256p. 23.00 (*0-684-86507-6*, Simon & Schuster) Simon & Schuster.
Ziesk, Edra. A Cold Spring: A Novel. 2002. 288p. tchr. ed. 23.95 (*1-56512-314-X*) Algonquin Bks. of Chapel Hill.

## NEW HAMPSHIRE—FICTION

Abrahams, Peter. A Perfect Crime. 1999. E-Book 6.99 (*0-345-43655-5*) Random Hse., Inc.
Andersen, Jessica S. The Guardian of the Amulets. 2003. 201p. pap. 13.95 (*1-4104-0132-4*, Five Star Trade); 26.95 (*0-7862-4704-5*, Five Star) Gale Group.
Anderson, Susan. Clean Slate. 225p. mass mkt. o.p. (*1-55197-078-3*) Picasso Pubns., Inc.
Babson, Marian. Whiskers & Smoke. 1997. (Dead Letter Mysteries Ser.). 214p. mass mkt. 5.99 (*0-312-96181-2*, St. Martin's Paperbacks) St. Martin's Pr.
—Whiskers & Smoke. abr. ed. 1997. audio 16.96 o.p. (*1-56431-214-3*) Sunset Products.
Banks, Russell. Affliction. 1990. 368p. pap. 13.00 (*0-06-092007-6*, Perennial); 1989. 320p. 18.95 o.p. (*0-06-016142-6*) HarperTrade.
—Hamilton Stark. 1996. 320p. pap. 14.00 (*0-06-097705-1*, Perennial) HarperTrade.
—Hamilton Stark, 001. 1978. 9.95 o.p. (*0-395-26471-5*) Houghton Mifflin Co.
Begiebing, Robert J. Rebecca Wentworth's Distraction: A Novel. 2003. (Hardscrabble Books). 264p. text 24.95 (*1-58465-284-5*) Univ. Pr. of New England.
Binstock, R. C. The Soldier. 1996. 288p. 24.00 o.p. (*1-56947-059-6*) Soho Pr., Inc.
Block, Lawrence. You Could Call It Murder. 1996. 240p. mass mkt. 4.95 o.p. (*0-7867-0342-3*, Carroll & Graf Pubs.) Avalon Publishing Group.
—You Could Call It Murder. 1987. 140p. reprint ed. pap. 4.95 o.p. (*0-88150-086-0*) Countryman Pr.
—You Could Call It Murder. l.t. ed. 1989. 240p. 11.95 o.p. (*0-8161-4628-4*, Macmillan Reference USA) Gale Group.
—You Could Call It Murder. 2002. 176p. pap. 6.99 (*0-7434-4515-5*) ibooks, Inc.
Bunker, Dusty. One Deadly Rhyme: The Number Mysteries. 2000. 304p. pap. 15.95 (*0-595-10063-5*, Writer's Showcase Pr.) iUniverse, Inc.
Campbell, Ann. Wolf Tracks. 2002. 304p. mass mkt. 5.99 o.s.i (*0-451-20585-5*, Signet Bks.) NAL.
Costello, Mark. Big If: A Novel. 2003. 368p. pap. 14.00 (*0-15-602779-8*, Harvest Bks.) Harcourt Trade Pubs.
—Big If: A Novel. 2002. 320p. 24.95 (*0-393-05116-1*) Norton, W. W. & Co., Inc.
—Big If: A Novel. 2002. 29.95 (*0-7862-4795-9*) Thorndike Pr.
Coughlin, Thomas E. Brian Kelly: Route 1. 2001. 332p. pap. 14.95 (*0-9666202-1-6*) Fitzgerald & LaChapelle Publishing.
Dale, Bruce. On Missing Link Road. 1999. 272p. pap. 21.99 (*0-7388-0529-7*); text 31.99 (*0-7388-0528-9*) Xlibris Corp.
Davis, Kathryn. Labrador. 1988. 256p. 17.95 o.s.i (*0-374-18251-5*) Farrar, Straus & Giroux.
—Labrador. 2000. 240p. pap. 13.00 (*0-618-07542-9*, Mariner Bks.) Houghton Mifflin Co. Trade & Reference Div.
Delinsky, Barbara. Lake News. 2002. E-Book 9.99 (*1-59061-637-5*) Adobe Systems, Inc.
—Lake News. 2000. E-Book 9.99 (*0-684-85379-5*, Simon & Schuster); 1999. 384p. mass mkt. 7.99 (*0-671-03711-0*, Pocket); 1999. 384p. 24.00 (*0-684-86432-0*, Simon & Schuster); 2000. 544p. reprint ed. pap. 7.99 (*0-671-03619-X*, Pocket) Simon & Schuster.
—Lake News. l.t. ed. (Paperback Bestsellers Ser.). 584p. 2000. 28.95 (*0-7838-8660-8*); 1999. 31.95 (*0-7838-8659-4*) Thorndike Pr.
—The Passions of Chelsea Kane. 2003. E-Book 14.95 (*0-06-057330-9*); E-Book 14.95 (*0-06-057331-7*); E-Book 14.95 (*0-06-057332-5*); E-Book 14.95 (*0-06-057333-3*) HarperCollins Pubs.
—The Passions of Chelsea Kane. l.t. ed. 2004. 640p. pap. 18.95 (*0-06-057026-1*, HarperLargePrint) HarperTrade.
—The Passions of Chelsea Kane. 2004. 432p. 18.95 (*0-06-621457-2*, Morrow, William & Co.); 1992. 576p. mass mkt. 7.99 (*0-06-104093-2*, HarperTorch) Morrow/Avon.
Dobyns, Stephen. Boy in the Water. 1999. 406p. 25.00 o.s.i (*0-8050-6020-0*, Metropolitan Bks.) Holt, Henry & Co.
—Boy in the Water. 2000. 448p. mass mkt. 6.99 (*0-312-97522-8*, St. Martin's Paperbacks) St. Martin's Pr.
Downes, Anne M. The Pilgrim Soul. unabr. ed. 1997. (Illus.). 288p. (Orig.). pap. 15.00 (*0-9633560-9-7*) Durand Pr., The.
Downing, Kathryn. Horses Don't Have Handlebars. 2003. 211p. pap. 19.95 (*1-59129-830-X*) PublishAmerica, Inc.
Drown, Merle. The Suburbs of Heaven. 2001. 352p. reprint ed. pap. 14.00 o.s.i (*0-425-18156-1*) Berkley Publishing Group.
—The Suburbs of Heaven. 2000. 296p. 24.00 (*1-56947-182-7*) Soho Pr., Inc.
DuBois, Brendan. Black Tide: A Lewis Cole Mystery. 1996. 400p. mass mkt. 5.99 (*0-671-89999-6*, Pocket); 1995. 398p. 21.50 (*1-883402-58-1*, Scribner) Simon & Schuster.
—Dead Sand: A Lewis Cole Mystery. 1996. 320p. mass mkt. 5.99 (*0-671-54521-3*, Pocket) Simon & Schuster.
—Dead Sand: A Lewis Cole Mystery. Grose, Bill, ed. 1995. 336p. mass mkt. 5.50 (*0-671-89998-8*, Pocket) Simon & Schuster.
—Dead Sand: A Lewis Cole Mystery. 1994. 304p. 21.00 (*1-883402-45-X*, Scribner) Simon & Schuster.
—The Killer Waves: A Lewis Cole Mystery. 2002. 352p. 24.95 (*0-312-28487-X*, Saint Martin's Minotaur) St. Martin's Pr.
—Shattered Shell. 2nd ed. 1999. 368p. 24.95 (*0-312-19332-7*, Saint Martin's Minotaur) St. Martin's Pr.
Eslick, Tom. Deadly Kin: A Wil Buchanan Mystery. 2003. 288p. text 22.95 (*0-670-03248-4*, Viking) Viking Penguin.
—Snow Kill. 2000. 304p. 24.95 (*1-885173-18-0*) Write Way Publishing.
—Tracked in the Whites. 1999. (WWL Mystery Ser.: No. 327). 250p. mass mkt. 5.99 (*0-373-26327-9*, Worldwide Library) Harlequin Enterprises, Ltd.
—Tracked in the Whites. 1997. 272p. 21.95 (*1-885173-32-6*) Write Way Publishing.
Farish, Terry. A House in Earnest: A Novel. 2000. 261p. pap. 13.00 (*1-883642-52-3*) Steerforth Pr.
Fender, J. E. Audacity, Privateer out of Portsmouth Vol. II: The Chronicles of Geoffrey Frost. 2003. (Hardscrabble Books). 3634p. text 26.95 (*1-58465-316-7*) Univ. Pr. of New England.
—The Private Revolution of Geoffrey Frost: Being an Account of the Life & Times of Geoffrey Frost, Mariner, of Portsmouth, in New Hampshire, As Faithfully Translated from the Ming Tsun Chronicles, & Diligently Compared with Other Contemporary Histories. 2002. (Hardscrabble Books). 364p. 25.95 (*1-58465-212-8*) Univ. Pr. of New England.
Ferguson, Bruce. Every Day Is Sunday. 1998. 196p. (Orig.). pap. 14.95 (*1-880090-43-0*) Galde Pr., Inc.
Freda, Joseph. Suburban Guerrillas: A Novel. 1995. 192p. 19.95 o.p. (*0-393-03768-1*) Norton, W. W. & Co., Inc.
—Suburban Guerrillas: A Novel. 1996. 224p. reprint ed. pap. 15.95 (*0-87451-763-X*, Hardscrabble Bks.) Univ. Pr. of New England.
Gaines, Charles. Survival Games. 1997. 240p. 23.00 o.p. (*0-87113-684-8*, Atlantic Monthly Pr.) Grove/Atlantic, Inc.
Haddam, Jane. A Stillness in Bethlehem. 1993. (Gregor Demarkian Holiday Mystery Ser.). 368p. mass mkt. 5.50 o.s.i (*0-553-29390-7*) Bantam Bks.
Hall, Donald. Old Home Day. 1996. (Illus.). 48p. 16.00 (*0-15-276896-3*) Harcourt Children's Bks.
Hayes, Carol. Pinkham's Notch: The Daniel Pinkham Story. 1998. (Illus.). 125p. pap. text 14.95 o.p. (*0-914339-74-5*) Randall, Peter E. Pub.
Hebert, Ernest. The Dogs of March. 1980. 272p. pap. 9.00 o.p. (*0-14-005560-6*) Penguin Group (USA) Inc.
—The Dogs of March. 1979. 255p. 25.00 (*0-89366-144-9*) Ultramarine Publishing Co., Inc.
—The Dogs of March. 1995. 272p. pap. 15.95 (*0-87451-719-2*, Hardscrabble Bks.) Univ. Pr. of New England.
—The Dogs of March. 1979. 9.95 o.p. (*0-670-27746-0*) Viking Penguin.
—The Kinship: A Little More Than Kin & the Passion of Estelle Jordan - Two Novels from the Darby Series, with a New Essay. 1993. 472p. pap. 19.95 (*0-87451-630-7*) Univ. Pr. of New England.
—A Little More Than Kin. 1982. 224p. 25.00 (*0-89366-139-2*) Ultramarine Publishing Co., Inc.
—A Little More Than Kin. (Contemporary American Fiction Ser.). 240p. 1984. pap. 6.95 o.p. (*0-14-006889-9*, Penguin Bks.); 1982. 13.95 o.p. (*0-670-43209-1*) Viking Penguin.
—Live Free or Die. 1995. 429p. reprint ed. pap. 17.95 (*0-87451-699-4*, Hardscrabble Bks.) Univ. Pr. of New England.
—Live Free or Die. 1999. pap. 9.00 (*0-14-012978-2*, Viking); 1990. 432p. 19.95 o.p. (*0-670-83133-6*) Viking Penguin.
—The Passion of Estelle Jordan. 1987. 240p. 16.95 o.p. (*0-670-80947-0*) Viking Penguin.
Hershon, Joanna. Swimming. l.t. ed. 2001. 552p. 28.95 (*0-7862-3368-0*) Thorndike Pr.
Hildreth, Mary Anne, ed. 2001 New Hampshire Register. 2000. 900p. 95.00 (*1-881758-79-6*) Tower Publishing.
Hobhouse, Janet. The Furies. 1992. 304p. 22.50 o.s.i (*0-385-24547-5*); 1994. 240p. reprint ed. pap. 12.95 o.s.i (*0-385-47054-1*) Doubleday Publishing.
—The Furies. 2004. (New York Review Books Classics Ser.). 320p. pap. 14.00 (*1-59017-085-7*) New York Review of Bks., Inc., The.
Hynd, Noel. A Room for the Dead. 1994. mass mkt. 18.95 o.s.i (*0-8217-4583-2*) Kensington Publishing Corp.
Irving, John. A Prayer for Owen Meany. 1999. 7.99 (*0-345-91555-0*); 1990. 640p. mass mkt. 7.99 (*0-345-36179-2*, Ballantine Bks.); 1989. mass mkt. 4.95 o.s.i (*0-345-36352-3*); 1997. 560p. reprint ed. pap. 14.95 (*0-345-41797-6*, Ballantine Bks.) Ballantine Bks.
—A Prayer for Owen Meany. 1990. (GER.). 864p. (*3-257-01850-9*) Diogenes Verlag AG CHE. *Dist:* International Bk. Import Service, Inc.
—A Prayer for Owen Meany. 1989. 604p. 25.00 o.p. (*0-688-07708-0*, Morrow, William & Co.) Morrow/Avon.
—A Prayer for Owen Meany. 2002. (Illus.). 672p. 22.95 (*0-679-64259-5*, Modern Library) Random House Adult Trade Publishing Group.
—A Prayer for Owen Meany. 1990. 14.04 (*0-606-16249-6*) Turtleback Bks.
Jennings, Dana Andrew. Women of Granite. 1992. 21.95 (*0-15-198367-4*) Harcourt Trade Pubs.
Knowles, John. Peace Breaks Out. 192p. 1997. mass mkt. 5.99 (*0-553-27574-7*, Bantam Classics); 1982. mass mkt. 3.50 o.s.i (*0-553-25516-9*) Bantam Bks.
—Peace Breaks Out. l.t. ed. 1981. 12.95 o.p. (*0-8161-3270-4*, Macmillan Reference USA) Gale Group.
—Peace Breaks Out. 1981. 192p. o.p. (*0-03-056908-7*) Holt, Henry & Co.
—Peace Breaks Out. 1982. (J). 12.04 (*0-606-02819-6*) Turtleback Bks.

—A Separate Peace. 1990. mass mkt. o.s.i (*0-553-54007-6*); 1984. 208p. mass mkt. 5.99 o.s.i (*0-553-28041-4*) Bantam Bks.

—A Separate Peace. 1988. 52p. (YA). (gr. 10 up). pap. 5.60 (*0-87129-919-4*, S79) Dramatic Publishing Co.

—A Separate Peace. abr. ed. 1987. (J). (gr. 7). audio 18.00 (*0-553-45054-9*, Listening Library) Random Hse. Audio Publishing Group.

—A Separate Peace. (Scribner Classics). 1996. 208p. 20.00 (*0-684-83366-2*); 1987. 192p. bds. 40.00 o.p. (*0-02-564850-0*) Simon & Schuster. (Scribner).

—A Separate Peace. l.t. ed. 1994. 226p. lib. bdg. 22.95 (*0-8161-5895-9*) Thorndike Pr.

—A Separate Peace. 1975. 12.04 (*0-606-01345-8*) Turtleback Bks.

Korelitz, Jean Hanff. The Sabbathday River. 1999. 512p. 25.00 o.p. (*0-374-25323-4*); 1999. E-Book 25.00 (*0-374-70005-2*); 1998. pap. (*0-374-97008-4*) Farrar, Straus & Giroux.

Kumin, Maxine. Women, Animals, & Vegetables: Essays & Stories. 1994. 299p. 25.00 o.p. (*0-393-03655-3*) Norton, W. W. & Co., Inc.

—Women, Animals & Vegetables: Essays & Stories. 1996. 299p. reprint ed. pap. 12.95 (*0-86538-084-8*) Ontario Review Pr.

Lawson, Philip. Muskrat Courage. 2000. 277p. 23.95 (*0-312-26207-8*, Saint Martin's Minotaur) St. Martin's Pr.

Lent, Jeffrey. Lost Nation. 384p. 2003. pap. 14.00 (*0-8021-3985-X*); 2002. 25.00 (*0-87113-843-3*, Atlantic Monthly Pr.) Grove/Atlantic, Inc.

—Lost Nation. 2003. (Adventure Ser.). 29.95 (*0-7862-4981-1*) Thorndike Pr.

Linz, Cathie. One of a Kind Marriage. l.t. ed. 1995. 235p. pap. 19.95 o.p. (*0-7838-1234-5*, Macmillan Reference USA) Gale Group.

Lipman, Elinor. The Dearly Departed. 2001. E-Book 8.95 (*1-58945-947-4*) Adobe Systems, Inc.

—The Dearly Departed. 2002. 288p. pap. 13.00 (*0-375-72458-3*, Vintage) Knopf Publishing Group.

—The Dearly Departed: A Novel. 2001. E-Book 19.00 (*1-58836-013-X*) Random Hse., Inc.

MacDougall, Ruth D. Snowy. 1993. 384p. 21.95 o.p. (*0-312-09913-4*) St. Martin's Pr.

Macomber, Debbie. Can This Be Christmas? 1998. (*1-55166-455-0*, 1-66455-6, Mira Bks.) Harlequin Enterprises, Ltd.

—A Gift to Last: Can This Be Christmas/Shirley, Goodness & Mercy. 2002. 240p. mass mkt. (*1-55166-930-7*, Mira Bks.) Harlequin Enterprises, Ltd.

Mandino, Og. The Twelfth Angel. 1993. 176p. (YA). 17.00 o.s.i (*0-449-90689-2*, Fawcett) Ballantine Bks.

Matthews, Anne M. The Cave. 1997. 288p. 22.50 o.p. (*0-446-52061-6*); 1998. 320p. mass mkt. 6.50 (*0-446-60509-3*) Warner Bks., Inc.

Merrill, Richard. Calls from the Granite State: Stories. 1997. 128p. 17.95 (*1-880284-22-7*) Daniel, John & Co., Pubs.

Monninger, Joe. Incident at Potter's Bridge. 1992. 272p. 21.00 o.p. (*1-55611-307-2*) Fine, Donald I. Bks.

—Razor's Song. 1993. 256p. mass mkt. 4.99 (*0-380-71874-X*, Avon Bks.) Morrow/Avon.

Monninger, Joseph. Mather. 1995. 224p. 20.95 o.p. (*1-55611-447-8*) Fine, Donald I. Bks.

Neggars, Carla. Kiss the Moon. 2003. 384p. mass mkt. (*1-55166-969-2*, Mira Bks.) Harlequin Enterprises, Ltd.

Neggers, Carla. Kiss the Moon. 1999. 384p. (Orig.). mass mkt. (*1-55166-485-2*, 1-66485-3, Mira Bks.) Harlequin Enterprises, Ltd.

Noon, Jack. Up Moosilauke. 2000. (Illus.). 215p. pap. 16.00 (*1-893863-00-X*) Moose Country Pr.

Older, Julia. The Island Queen: Celia Thaxter of the Isles of Shoals. 1998. 206p. (Orig.). reprint ed. pap. 12.00 (*0-9627162-2-7*) Appledore Bks.

Patterson, Richard North. The Final Judgment. 1998. pap. 7.99 (*0-345-91462-7*); 1996. 512p. mass mkt. 7.99 o.s.i (*0-345-40761-X*) Ballantine Bks.

—The Final Judgment. 1996. mass mkt. o.s.i (*0-345-40498-X*) Ballantine Bks. of Canada.

—The Final Judgment. l.t. ed. 1995. 640p. 25.95 o.p. (*0-7838-1581-6*, Macmillan Reference USA) Gale Group.

—The Final Judgment. 1995. 400p. 25.00 o.s.i (*0-679-42989-1*) Knopf, Alfred A. Inc.

—The Final Judgment, Set. abr. ed. 1998. audio 8.99 o.s.i (*0-375-40299-3*); 1995. audio 18.00 o.s.i (*0-679-44765-2*, 393153) Random Hse. Audio Publishing Group. (RH Audio).

—The Final Judgment: A Novel. l.t. ed. 1995. 640p. pap. 25.00 (*0-679-76666-9*) Random Hse. Large Print.

Picoult, Jodi. Keeping Faith: A Novel. 2000. 432p. pap. 13.95 (*0-688-17774-3*, Perennial) HarperTrade.

—Keeping Faith: A Novel. 1999. 422p. 24.00 (*0-688-16825-6*, Morrow, William & Co.) Morrow/Avon.

—Keeping Faith: A Novel. 2000. 19.05 (*0-606-21710-X*) Turtleback Bks.

—Salem Falls. 2001. 448p. 24.95 (*0-7434-1870-0*, Atria); 2001. 704p. 24.95 (*0-7434-2159-0*, Atria); 2002. 464p. reprint ed. pap. 14.00 (*0-7434-1871-9*, Washington Square Pr.); 2001. reprint ed. E-Book 24.95 (*0-7434-2279-1*, Atria) Simon & Schuster.

Pinkham, Peter. The Hidden Mountain. 1998. 233p. pap. 12.95 (*0-9662661-0-2*, MFDC Pr.) Merriman Forest Development Corp.

Rowe, Robert H. Quest for Liberty. 2001. (Illus.). 256p. 23.95 (*0-914339-92-3*) Randall, Peter E. Pub.

Rutter, Joy. A Disturbing Presence. 2003. 232p. pap. 16.95 (*1-4137-0113-2*) PublishAmerica, Inc.

Saul, John. Nightshade. 2000. E-Book 20.95 (*1-930161-85-9*) Adobe Systems, Inc.

—Nightshade. 2001. E-Book 20.95 (*0-345-44238-5*) Ballantine Bks.

—Nightshade. unabr. ed. 2000. 11p. audio 73.25 (*1-56740-726-9*, 2090, Unabridged Library Editions); audio 32.95 (*1-56740-359-X*, 2089, Brilliance Audio Unabridged) Brilliance Audio.

—Nightshade. abr. ed. 2000. audio 25.00 (*0-553-52733-9*, RH Audio) Random Hse. Audio Publishing Group.

—Nightshade. l.t. ed. 2000. (Core Ser.). 477p. pap. 28.95 (*0-7838-9070-2*) Thorndike Pr.

Schilling, Vivian. Quietus: A Novel of Suspense. 2002. 596p. 24.95 (*0-9637846-1-7*, 215, Hannover Hse.) Truman Pr., Inc.

—Quietus: A Novel of Suspense. 2003. 608p. pap. 14.00 (*0-14-200306-9*) Viking Penguin.

Seletz, Jules M. Lincoln Logs. 2002. pap. 16.95 (*0-87714-268-8*) Denlingers Pubs., Ltd.

Shreve, Anita. All He Ever Wanted. 2004. (Illus.). 336p. pap. 14.95 (*0-316-73573-6*, Back Bay); 2003. 320p. 25.95 (*0-316-78226-2*); 2003. 496p. 25.95 (*0-316-71112-8*) Little Brown & Co.

—Eden Close. 1998. 276p. pap. 13.00 (*0-15-600589-1*, Harvest Bks.); 1989. 265p. 17.95 (*0-15-127582-3*) Harcourt Trade Pubs.

—Fortune's Rocks. 1999. 320p. (gr. 8). 24.95 o.p. (*0-316-78101-0*); 2001. 480p. reprint ed. pap. 13.95 (*0-316-67810-4*, Back Bay) Little Brown & Co.

—Fortune's Rocks. l.t. ed. 1999. 688p. 24.95 (*0-375-43052-0*) Random Hse. Large Print.

—Sea Glass. 2002. 416p. mass mkt. 7.99 (*0-316-70782-1*); 2002. 384p. 25.95 (*0-316-78081-2*); 2002. E-Book 14.95 (*0-7595-8693-4*); 2002. 512p. 25.95 (*0-316-73373-3*); 2003. 416p. reprint ed. pap. 14.95 (*0-316-08969-9*, Back Bay) Little Brown & Co.

—The Weight of Water. 2001. 304p. mass mkt. 6.99 (*0-316-78250-5*); 1998. pap. 13.95 (*0-316-19057-8*, Back Bay); 1997. 256p. (gr. 8). 22.95 (*0-316-78997-6*); 1998. 288p. reprint ed. pap. 13.95 (*0-316-78037-5*, Back Bay) Little Brown & Co.

Strong, Jonathan. An Untold Tale. 1993. 240p. 19.95 o.p. (*0-944072-32-1*, Zoland Bks., Inc.) Steerforth Pr.

Ward. The Hunger. Date not set. pap. (*0-312-87753-6*, Forge Bks.) Doherty, Tom Assocs., LLC.

Ward, Jane. Hunger. E-Book 23.95 (*0-312-70130-6*); 2001. 304p. 23.95 (*0-312-87754-4*) Doherty, Tom Assocs., LLC. (Tor Bks.).

Weesner, Theodore. Novemberfest. 1994. 384p. 24.00 o.s.i (*0-679-43099-7*) Knopf, Alfred A. Inc.

—Novemberfest. 1996. 397p. pap. 15.95 (*0-87451-766-4*, Hardscrabble Bks.) Univ. Pr. of New England.

Wesselmann, Debbie Lee. Trutor & the Balloonist. 1997. 259p. 22.95 (*1-878448-74-9*) MacMurray & Beck, Inc.

Williams, Thomas. Leah, New Hampshire: Stories by Thomas Williams. 1993. (Discovery Ser.). 236p. reprint ed. pap. 12.50 o.p. (*1-55597-191-1*) Graywolf Pr.

—Leah, New Hampshire: The Collected Stories of Thomas Williams. 1992. 22.00 o.p. (*0-688-11544-6*, Morrow, William & Co.) Morrow/Avon.

Wilson, Susan. Cameo Lake. l.t. ed. 2001. (Wheeler Large Print Book Ser.). 358p. 29.95 o.p. (*1-58724-086-6*, Wheeler Publishing, Inc.) Gale Group.

—Cameo Lake. 2001. 288p. 24.95 (*0-7434-1276-1*); 272p. reprint ed. E-Book 24.95 (*0-7434-1940-5*) Simon & Schuster. (Atria).

Wood, Jane. Josey Rose. 1998. 288p. 23.00 o.s.i (*0-684-83791-9*, Simon & Schuster) Simon & Schuster.

Wright, Austin. Disciples. unabr. ed. 1997. 300p. 22.00 (*1-880909-55-3*) Baskerville Pubs., Inc.

Yates, Elizabeth. Sarah Whitcher's Story. 1994. (Illus.). 95p. (J). (gr. 2-4). pap. 6.49 (*0-89084-754-1*, 080564) Jones, Bob Univ. Pr.

Yeager, Dorian. Murder Will Out. 1994. (Elizabeth Will Mystery Ser.). 208p. 18.95 o.p. (*0-312-11388-9*, Saint Martin's Minotaur) St. Martin's Pr.

—Summer Will End. 1996. (Elizabeth Will Mystery Ser.). 182p. text 20.95 o.p. (*0-312-14743-0*, Saint Martin's Minotaur) St. Martin's Pr.

**NEW HAVEN (CONN.)—FICTION**

Argiri, Laura. The God in Flight. 1996. 496p. pap. 22.00 o.s.i (*0-14-025413-7*, Penguin Bks.) Penguin Group (USA) Inc.

Bechard, Gorman. The Ninth Square. 2002. 320p. 23.95 (*0-7653-0146-6*, Forge Bks.) Doherty, Tom Assocs., LLC.

Kittredge, Mary. Cadaver. 1993. 250p. mass mkt. 3.99 o.p. (*0-312-95002-0*, St. Martin's Paperbacks) St. Martin's Pr.

—Cadaver: An Edwina Crusoe Medical Mystery. 1992. 208p. 17.95 o.p. (*0-312-06920-0*, Saint Martin's Minotaur) St. Martin's Pr.

—Desperate Remedy. 1997. (Crime Line Ser.). 224p. mass mkt. 5.99 o.s.i (*0-553-57591-0*, Crimeline) Bantam Bks.

—Desperate Remedy, Vol. 1. 1994. (Desperate Remedy Ser.: Vol. 1). mass mkt. 4.50 o.p. (*0-312-95330-5*, St. Martin's Paperbacks) St. Martin's Pr.

—Desperate Remedy: An Edwina Crusoe Medical Mystery. 1993. 208p. 18.95 o.p. (*0-312-09784-0*, Saint Martin's Minotaur) St. Martin's Pr.

—Fatal Diagnosis. 1997. 208p. mass mkt. 5.50 o.s.i (*0-553-57590-2*, Crimeline) Bantam Bks.

—Fatal Diagnosis. 1990. pap. 15.95 o.p. (*0-312-04315-5*, Saint Martin's Minotaur) St. Martin's Pr.

—Kill or Cure. 1996. 288p. mass mkt. 5.50 o.s.i (*0-553-57585-6*, Crimeline) Bantam Bks.

—Kill or Cure: An Edwina Crusoe Medical Mystery. 1995. 216p. 19.95 o.p. (*0-312-13103-8*, Saint Martin's Minotaur) St. Martin's Pr.

—Rigor Mortis. 1991. 14.95 o.p. (*0-312-05504-8*, Saint Martin's Minotaur); 1992. 201p. reprint ed. mass mkt. 3.99 o.p. (*0-312-92865-3*, St. Martin's Paperbacks) St. Martin's Pr.

—Walking Dead Man. 1993. mass mkt. 3.99 o.p. (*0-312-95157-4*, St. Martin's Paperbacks); 1992. 208p. 17.95 o.p. (*0-312-08333-5*, Saint Martin's Minotaur) St. Martin's Pr.

Mattison, Alice. The Wedding of the Two-Headed Woman: A Novel. 2004. (*0-06-621378-9*, Morrow, William & Co.) Morrow/Avon.

Thomas-Graham, Pamela. Blue Blood. (Ivy League Mysteries Ser.). 1999. 288p. 23.00 (*0-684-84527-X*, Simon & Schuster); 2000. 320p. reprint ed. pap. 6.99 (*0-671-01671-7*, Pocket) Simon & Schuster.

Weber, Katharine. The Little Women. 2003. 256p. 23.00 (*0-374-18959-5*) Farrar, Straus & Giroux.

**NEW IBERIA (LA.)—FICTION**

Burke, James Lee. Black Cherry Blues. l.t. ed. 1996. lib. bdg. 24.95 (*1-57490-070-6*, Beeler Large Print Bks.) Beeler, Thomas T. Publisher.

—Black Cherry Blues. 1989. 17.95 o.p. (*0-316-11699-8*) Little Brown & Co.

—Black Cherry Blues. 1990. 384p. reprint ed. mass mkt. 7.99 (*0-380-71204-0*, Avon Bks.) Morrow/Avon.

—Black Cherry Blues. unabr. ed. 2000. audio 78.00 (*1-55690-791-5*, 93106E7) Recorded Bks., LLC.

—Black Cherry Blues. abr. ed. 2001. audio 9.98 (*0-7435-2302-4*); 1991. audio 16.00 (*0-671-73610-8*); Set. 1998. audio 9.98 (*0-671-58255-0*, 390401) Simon & Schuster Audio. (Simon & Schuster Audioworks).

—Burning Angel. l.t. ed. 1995. 502p. 25.95 o.p. (*0-7838-1492-5*, Macmillan Reference USA) Gale Group.

—Burning Angel. 1995. 352p. 22.95 o.p. (*0-7868-6082-0*); 2002. 464p. reprint ed. mass mkt. 7.99 (*0-7868-8904-7*) Hyperion Pr.

—Burning Angel. unabr. ed. 2000. (Dave Robicheaux Ser.: Vol. 8). audio 85.00 (*0-7887-0345-5*, 94537E7) Recorded Bks., LLC.

—Burning Angel. 2001. audio 9.98 (*0-7435-2309-1*); 1998. audio 9.98 (*0-671-58254-2*); 1995. audio 17.00 (*0-671-52927-7*, 393120) Simon & Schuster Audio. (Simon & Schuster Audioworks).

—Burning Angel. deluxe ltd. num. ed. 1995. 340p. 125.00 o.s.i (*0-9631925-3-1*) Trice, B.E. Publishing.

—Cadillac Jukebox. l.t. ed. 1996. (Large Print Bks.). 27.95 o.p. (*1-56895-375-5*, Wheeler Publishing, Inc.) Gale Group.

—Cadillac Jukebox. 1996. 352p. 22.95 (*0-7868-6175-4*); 2002. 464p. reprint ed. mass mkt. 6.99 (*0-7868-8918-7*) Hyperion Pr.

—Cadillac Jukebox. unabr. ed. 1996. (Dave Robicheaux Ser.: Vol. 9). audio 83.00 (*0-7887-0725-6*, 94902E7) Recorded Bks., LLC.

—Cadillac Jukebox. abr. ed. 1998. audio 14.40 (*0-671-57732-8*, 908764); 1996. audio 18.00 (*0-671-57365-9*, 394156) Simon & Schuster Audio. (Simon & Schuster Audioworks).

—Cadillac Jukebox. deluxe ltd. num. ed. 1996. 303p. 150.00 (*0-9631925-5-8*) Trice, B.E. Publishing.

—Dixie City Jam. l.t. ed. 1994. 590p. lib. bdg. 22.95 o.p. (*0-8161-7488-1*, Macmillan Reference USA) Gale Group.

—Dixie City Jam. 1994. 352p. 22.95 (*0-7868-6019-7*); 2002. 512p. reprint ed. mass mkt. 7.99 (*0-7868-8900-4*) Hyperion Pr.

—Dixie City Jam. unabr. ed. 1994. audio. (Dave Robicheaux Ser.: Vol. 7). audio 85.00 (*0-7887-0060-X*, 94316E7) Recorded Bks., LLC.

—Dixie City Jam. 2001. audio 9.98 o.s.i (*0-7435-0476-3*); 1998. audio 9.98 (*0-671-58252-6*); 1994. audio 17.00 o.s.i (*0-671-88761-0*, 390665) Simon & Schuster Audio. (Simon & Schuster Audioworks).

—Heaven's Prisoners. l.t. ed. 1997. lib. bdg. 24.95 (*1-57490-086-2*, Beeler Large Print Bks.) Beeler, Thomas T. Publisher.

—Heaven's Prisoners. 1988. 17.95 o.p. (*0-8050-0665-6*) Holt, Henry & Co.

—Heaven's Prisoners. unabr. ed. 1996. (Dave Robicheaux Ser.: Vol. 2). audio 70.00 (*0-7887-0623-3*, 94797E7) Recorded Bks., LLC.

—Heaven's Prisoners. 288p. 1989. mass mkt. 5.99 o.s.i (*0-671-67629-6*); 1996. pap. 7.99 (*0-671-51741-4*) Simon & Schuster. (Pocket).

—Heaven's Prisoners. abr. ed. 1996. (Dave Robicheaux Mystery Ser.). 3p. audio 17.00 (*0-671-73608-6*, 392196, Simon & Schuster Audioworks) Simon & Schuster Audio.

—In the Electric Mist with Confederate Dead. unabr. collector's ed. 1995. audio 72.00 (*0-7366-2940-8*, 3636) Books on Tape, Inc.

—In the Electric Mist with Confederate Dead. l.t. ed. 1995. 483p. 23.95 o.p. (*0-8161-7487-3*, Macmillan Reference USA) Gale Group.

—In the Electric Mist with Confederate Dead. 1993. 352p. 19.95 o.p. (*1-56282-882-7*) Hyperion Pr.

—In the Electric Mist with Confederate Dead. 1994. 384p. reprint ed. mass mkt. 7.50 (*0-380-72121-X*, Avon Bks.) Morrow/Avon.

—In the Electric Mist with Confederate Dead. abr. ed. 1993. (Dave Robicheaux Mystery Ser.). 3p. audio 17.00 (*0-671-86816-0*, 390972, Simon & Schuster Audioworks) Simon & Schuster Audio.

—The Intruders. abr. ed. 1999. audio 9.98 (*0-671-04407-9*, Simon & Schuster Audioworks) Simon & Schuster Audio.

—A Morning for Flamingos. l.t. ed. 1998. 353p. 24.95 (*1-57490-155-9*, Beeler Large Print Bks.) Beeler, Thomas T. Publisher.

—A Morning for Flamingos. 1990. (Dave Robicheaux Ser.). 18.95 o.p. (*0-316-11721-8*) Little Brown & Co.

—A Morning for Flamingos. 1991. 384p. reprint ed. mass mkt. 7.50 (*0-380-71360-8*, Avon Bks.) Morrow/Avon.

—A Morning for Flamingos. unabr. ed. 1993. (Dave Robicheaux Ser.: Vol. 4). audio 75.00 (*1-55690-940-3*, 93436) Recorded Bks., LLC.

—A Morning for Flamingos. 1999. pap. 9.98 (*0-671-04408-7*); 1991. audio 16.00 (*0-671-73611-6*, 391205) Simon & Schuster Audio. (Simon & Schuster Audioworks).

—The Neon Rain: A Novel. 1987. 16.95 o.p. (*0-8050-0053-4*) Holt, Henry & Co.

—The Neon Rain: A Novel. l.t. ed. 1991. 377p. 21.95 (*1-85089-413-2*) ISIS Large Print Bks. GBR. *Dist:* Transaction Pubs.

—The Neon Rain: A Novel. 288p. reprint ed. 2002. (Illus.). pap. 14.00 (*0-7434-4920-7*); 1992. mass mkt. 6.99 (*0-671-75644-3*) Simon & Schuster. (Pocket).

—Purple Cane Road. l.t. ed. 2000. 512p. 24.95 (*0-375-43055-5*) Random Hse. Large Print.

—A Stained White Radiance. l.t. ed. 1993. (General Ser.). 465p. pap. 16.95 o.p. (*0-8161-5612-3*, Macmillan Reference USA) Gale Group.

—A Stained White Radiance. 1992. 384p. 19.95 o.p. (*1-56282-980-7*) Hyperion Pr.

—A Stained White Radiance. 1993. 384p. reprint ed. mass mkt. 7.50 (*0-380-72047-7*, Avon Bks.) Morrow/Avon.

—A Stained White Radiance. unabr. ed. 1994. (Dave Robicheaux Ser.: No. 5). audio 78.00 (*1-55690-999-3*, 94138E7) Recorded Bks., LLC.

—A Stained White Radiance. 1998. audio 9.98 (*0-671-58249-6*); 1996. audio 17.00 (*0-671-86817-9*, 394196) Simon & Schuster Audio. (Simon & Schuster Audioworks).

—Sunset Limited. 1999. (Dave Robicheaux Mysteries Ser.). 416p. mass mkt. 7.50 (*0-440-22398-9*) Dell Publishing.

—Sunset Limited, Set. abr. ed. 1999. audio 25.00 Highsmith Inc.

—Sunset Limited. (Dave Robicheaux Ser.: Vol. 10). 2001. audio compact disk 99.00 (*0-7887-3399-0*, C1005E7); 1998. audio 83.00 (*0-7887-2592-0*, 95498E7) Recorded Bks., LLC.

—Sunset Limited. abr. ed. 1998. (Dave Robicheaux Mystery Ser.). audio 25.00 (*0-671-58106-6*, 696022, Simon & Schuster Audioworks) Simon & Schuster Audio.

—Sunset Limited. l.t. ed. (Paperback Bestsellers Ser.). 429p. 1999. pap. 27.95 (*0-7838-0332-X*); 1998. 30.95 (*0-7838-0331-1*) Thorndike Pr.

—Sunset Limited. ltd. ed. 1998. 309p. 150.00 o.p. (*1-890885-03-7*) Trice, B.E. Publishing.

**NEW JERSEY—FICTION**

Abresch, Peter. Bloody Bonsai. 1999. (WWL Mystery Ser.: No. 321). per. (*0-373-26321-X*, 1-26321-9, Worldwide Library) Harlequin Enterprises, Ltd.

—Bloody Bonsai. l.t. ed. 1999. (Thorndike Senior Lifestyle Ser.). 360p. 27.95 (*0-7862-1787-1*) Thorndike Pr.

—Bloody Bonsai. 1998. 240p. 21.95 (*1-885173-34-2*) Write Way Publishing.

Alexander, Colin. God's Adamantine Fate. 2000. 491p. pap. 24.99 (*0-7388-0477-0*); text 34.99 (*0-7388-0476-2*) Xlibris Corp.

—God's Adamantine Fate: A Physician's Battle Against Man's Ultimate Evil. 1993. 368p. 22.50 o.p. (*1-55611-371-4*) Fine, Donald I. Bks.

Arnote, Ralph. A Rage in Paradise. 288p. 1999. mass mkt. 5.99 (*0-8125-6263-1*, Tor Bks.); 1997. 23.95 (*0-312-86198-2*, Forge Bks.) Doherty, Tom Assocs., LLC.

Austin, Doris J. After the Garden. 1988. 336p. pap. 11.00 o.p. (*0-452-26079-5*, Plume) Dutton/Plume.

—After the Garden. 1987. 336p. 17.95 o.p. (*0-453-00538-1*) NAL.

Bateman, Robert. Pinelands. 1994. 248p. 21.95 (*0-937548-27-8*); pap. 12.95 (*0-937548-28-6*) Plexus Publishing, Inc.

—Whitman's Tomb: Stories from the Pines. 1997. 215p. 21.95 (*0-937548-32-4*) Plexus Publishing, Inc.

Beim, Norman. Hymie & the Angel. 1999. 198p. pap. 12.95 (*0-931231-09-4*) Newconcept Pr., Inc.

Blauner, Peter. Casino Moon. 1996. 320p. mass mkt. 5.99 o.p. (*0-380-72589-4*, Avon Bks.) Morrow/Avon.

—Casino Moon. 1994. 288p. 21.00 o.p. (*0-671-88177-9*, Simon & Schuster) Simon & Schuster.

Blume, Judy. Then Again, Maybe I Won't. unabr. ed. 1990. (YA). (gr. 7 up). audio 24.00 (*0-8072-7295-7*, YA827CX, Listening Library) Random Hse. Audio Publishing Group.

Bosworth, Beth. Tunneling: A Novel. 304p. 2004. pap. 13.00 (*1-4000-5265-3*, Three Rivers Pr.); 2003. 22.00 (*0-609-61103-8*) Crown Publishing Group.

Bretton, Barbara. The Day We Met. 1999. 320p. mass mkt. 6.99 (*0-425-17190-6*) Berkley Publishing Group.

Bruno, Anthony. Double Espresso. 1998. 256p. 21.95 (*0-312-86650-X*, Forge Bks.) Doherty, Tom Assocs., LLC.

—Double Espresso (A Loretta Kovacs & Frank Marvelli Novel) 1999. 21.95 (*0-312-87077-9*, Tor Bks.) Doherty, Tom Assocs., LLC.

Buechner, Frederick. Love Feast. 1984. (Books of Bebb). 380p. mass mkt. 3.95 o.p. (*0-06-061167-7*, P-5009) HarperSanFrancisco.

—Love Feast. 1974. 7.95 o.p. (*0-689-10612-2*, Atheneum) Simon & Schuster Children's Publishing.

Cantwell, Aston. Double Delight. 1983. 256p. pap. 2.75 o.s.i (*0-446-30298-8*) Warner Bks., Inc.

Choi, Susan. American Woman: A Novel. 2003. 384p. 24.95 (*0-06-054221-7*) HarperCollins Pubs.

Clark, Mary Higgins. On the Street Where You Live. 2001. 320p. 26.00 (*0-7432-0602-9*); 480p. 26.00 o.s.i (*0-7432-1219-3*) Simon & Schuster. (Simon & Schuster).

—On the Street Where You Live. 2001. audio 39.95 (*0-7435-1819-5*); audio 25.00 (*0-7435-1817-9*); audio compact disk 30.00 (*0-7435-1818-7*); audio compact disk 39.95 (*0-7435-0442-9*) Simon & Schuster Audio. (Simon & Schuster Audioworks).

Clark, Mary Jane. Close to You. 2001. 336p. 24.95 (*0-312-26266-3*) St. Martin's Pr.

—Let Me Whisper in Your Ear. l.t. ed. 2000. (G. K. Hall Core Ser.). 347p. 31.95 (*0-7838-9284-5*, Macmillan Reference USA) Gale Group.

—Let Me Whisper in Your Ear. E-Book 22.95 (*0-312-27611-7*); 2000. 304p. 23.95 o.p. (*0-312-26191-8*); 2001. 336p. reprint ed. mass mkt. 6.99 (*0-312-97743-3*, St. Martin's Paperbacks) St. Martin's Pr.

Coben, Harlan. Gone for Good. 2003. 432p. mass mkt. 6.99 (*0-440-23673-8*); 2002. mass mkt. 6.99 (*0-440-29604-8*); 2002. 352p. 23.95 (*0-385-33558-X*, Delacorte Pr.) Dell Publishing.

—Gone for Good. l.t. ed. 2002. (Wheeler Hardcover Ser.). 29.95 (*1-58724-227-3*, Wheeler Publishing, Inc.) Gale Group.

—Gone for Good. abr. ed. 2002. audio compact disk 29.95 (*0-553-71298-5*, RH Audio) Random Hse. Audio Publishing Group.

—Gone for Good. l.t. ed. 2003. (Paperback Bestsellers Ser.). pap. 13.95 (*1-4104-0087-5*) Thorndike Pr.

Cofer, Judith Ortiz. The Line of the Sun: A Novel by Judith Ortiz Cofer. 304p. 1989. 22.95 o.p. (*0-8203-1106-5*); 1991. reprint ed. pap. 14.95 (*0-8203-1335-1*) Univ. of Georgia Pr.

Colicchio, Joseph. High Gate Health & Beauty. 2000. 272p. pap. 14.95 (*0-88739-251-2*) Creative Arts Bk. Co.

Dailey, Janet. One of the Boys: New Jersey. 1992. (Janet Dailey Americana Ser.: No. 880). per. (*0-373-89880-0*, 1-89880-8); 1988. (Janet Dailey Americana Ser.: No. 930). pap. (*0-373-21930-X*); 1987. mass mkt. (*0-373-89830-4*) Harlequin Enterprises, Ltd. (Harlequin Bks.).

—One of the Boys: New Jersey. l.t. ed. 2001. 199p. 28.95 (*0-7862-9119-9*) Thorndike Pr.

—One of the Boys: New Jersey. 124p. 2002. pap. 6.99 (*0-7592-3821-9*); 2002. E-Book 6.99 (*0-7592-0145-5*); 2002. E-Book 6.99 (*1-58586-389-0*); 2001. E-Book 6.99 (*0-7592-0888-3*) ereads.com.

Dandola, John. Dead at the Box Office. 2nd rev. ed. 1993. Orig. Title: West of Orange. (Illus.). 240p. reprint ed. pap. 10.95 o.p. (*1-878452-15-0*, Jersey Yarns) Quincannon Publishing Group.

—Dead at the Box Office: An Edie Koslow - Tony Del Plato Mystery. 2001. (Illus.). 182p. pap. 12.95 (*1-878452-25-8*, Compass Point Mysteries) Quincannon Publishing Group.

—Dead in Their Sights: An Edie Koslow-Tony Del Plato Mystery. 2001. (Illus.). 222p. pap. 12.95 (*1-878452-26-6*, Compass Point Mysteries) Quincannon Publishing Group.

De Haven, Tom. Sunburn Lake. 1988. 304p. 18.95 o.p. (*0-670-80930-6*) Viking Penguin.

—Sunburn Lake: A Trilogy. 1990. 304p. pap. 7.95 o.p. (*0-14-008549-1*, Penguin Bks.) Viking Penguin.

Delaney, Susan. A Star to Sail By. l.t. ed. 2000. (G. K. Hall Core Ser.). (Illus.). 310p. 28.95 (*0-7838-9011-7*, Macmillan Reference USA) Gale Group.

—A Star to Sail By. 1999. 320p. mass mkt. 6.99 o.s.i (*0-451-40899-3*, Onyx) NAL.

DeMille, Nelson. The Gold Coast. l.t. ed. 1995. 828p. lib. bdg. 24.95 o.p. (*0-7838-1225-6*, Macmillan Reference USA) Gale Group.

—The Gold Coast. abr. ed. 1990. audio 16.00 o.p. (*0-394-58633-6*, RH Audio) Random Hse. Audio Publishing Group.

—The Gold Coast. 1992. 5.99 o.p. (*0-517-08860-6*) Random Hse. Value Publishing.

—The Gold Coast. 1990. 19.95 o.p. (*0-446-51504-3*); 1997. 736p. reprint ed. pap. 15.95 (*0-446-67321-8*); 1991. 640p. reprint ed. mass mkt. 7.99 (*0-446-36085-6*) Warner Bks., Inc.

Dickson, Carter, pseud. A Graveyard to Let. 1978. reprint ed. pap. 1.50 o.s.i (*0-505-51222-X*) Dorchester Publishing Co., Inc.

Dulany, Harris. One Kiss Led to Another. 1994. 336p. 20.00 o.p. (*0-06-017737-3*) HarperTrade.

Elkin, Stanley. The Rabbi of Lud. 2001. (American Literature Ser.). 277p. pap. 12.95 (*1-56478-270-0*) Dalkey Archive Pr.

—The Rabbi of Lud. 1989. 256p. pap. 8.95 o.s.i (*0-684-19013-3*, Scribner Paper Fiction); 1987. 222p. 17.95 o.s.i (*0-684-18902-X*, Scribner) Simon & Schuster.

Elwood, Roger. Where Angels Dare: A Novel. 1999. 240p. pap. 9.99 (*0-8054-1877-6*) Broadman & Holman Pubs.

Engelhard, Jack. Deadly Deception. 1997. 288p. 24.00 (*0-914839-43-8*) Gollehon Pr.

Erhart, Margaret. Old Love: A Novel. 246p. 1996. 24.00 o.p. (*1-883642-07-8*); 1998. reprint ed. pap. 13.00 o.p. (*1-883642-73-6*) Steerforth Pr.

Evanovich, Janet. Four to Score. abr. ed. audio (*1-55927-963-X*); 1999. (Stephanie Plum Novel Ser.: No. 4). audio 17.95 (*1-55927-544-8*) Audio Renaissance.

—Four to Score. abr. ed. 2001. audio compact disk 11.99 (*1-57815-544-4*, 1111); audio 7.95 (*1-57815-263-1*) Media Bks., L. L. C.

—Four to Score. (Stephanie Plum Novel Ser.: No. 4). 2000. audio compact disk 89.00 (*0-7887-4749-5*, C1235E7); 1999. audio 66.00 (*0-7887-2593-9*, 95613E7) Recorded Bks., LLC.

—Four to Score. 1999. E-Book 23.95 o.s.i (*0-312-20762-X*); 1998. (Stephanie Plum Novel Ser.: No. 4). 304p. 24.95 (*0-312-18586-3*); 1999. (Stephanie Plum Novel Ser.: No. 4). 352p. reprint ed. mass mkt. 7.99 (*0-312-96697-0*, St. Martin's Paperbacks) St. Martin's Pr.

—Four to Score. abr. ed. 1998. (Stephanie Plum Novel Ser.: No. 4). audio 15.00 (*0-333-74772-0*) Ulverscroft Audio (U.S.A.).

—Hard Eight. abr. ed. 2002. (Illus.). audio 17.95 o.s.i (*1-55927-723-8*); audio 36.95 (*1-55927-725-4*); audio compact disk 40.00 (*1-55927-724-6*) Audio Renaissance.

—Hard Eight. abr. ed. 2001. (Stephanie Plum Ser.: Vol. 7). audio 19.95 o.p. (*1-58788-531-X*, 2802, Nova Audio Bks.); audio compact disk 27.95 o.p. (*1-58788-532-8*, 2803, CD); audio compact disk 61.25 (*1-58788-533-6*, 2804, CD Library Edition); audio 69.25 (*1-58788-530-1*, 2801, Unabridged Library Editions); audio 29.95 (*1-58788-529-8*, 2800, Brilliance Audio Unabridged) Brilliance Audio.

—Hard Eight. l.t. ed. 2002. 432p. 25.95 (*0-375-43170-5*) Random Hse., Inc.

—Hard Eight. unabr. ed. 2002. (Stephanie Plum Ser.: Vol. #8). audio 37.95 (*1-4025-2386-6*, RG083); audio compact disk 89.00 (*1-4025-2965-1*, C1854) Recorded Bks., LLC.

—Hard Eight. 2003. 352p. mass mkt. 7.99 (*0-312-98386-7*, St. Martin's Paperbacks); 2003. mass mkt. 7.99 (*0-312-98894-X*, St. Martin's Paperbacks); 2002. 320p. 25.95 (*0-312-26585-9*); 2002. mass mkt. 7.99 (*0-312-98451-0*, St. Martin's Paperbacks) St. Martin's Pr.

—High Five. abr. ed. audio (*1-55927-964-8*); 1999. (Stephanie Plum Novel Ser.: No. 5). audio 17.95 (*1-55927-545-6*) Audio Renaissance.

—High Five. abr. ed. 2001. audio (*0-333-76587-7*) Macmillan U.K. GBR. *Dist:* Macmillan Publishing Co., Inc.

—High Five. abr. ed. 2002. audio compact disk 11.99 (*1-57815-545-2*); 2001. audio 7.95 (*1-57815-264-X*) Media Bks., L. L. C.

—High Five. unabr. ed. (Stephanie Plum Novel Ser.: No. 5). 2000. audio compact disk 75.00 (*0-7887-4200-0*, C1129E7); 1999. audio 60.00 (*0-7887-3464-4*, 95857E7); 1999. audio 58.00 (*0-7887-3664-7*) Recorded Bks., LLC.

—High Five. (Stephanie Plum Novel Ser.: No. 5). 2000. 340p. mass mkt. 7.99 (*0-312-97134-6*, St. Martin's Paperbacks); 3rd ed. 1999. 292p. 24.95 (*0-312-20303-9*) St. Martin's Pr.

—High Five. l.t. ed. 1999. (Stephanie Plum Novel Ser.: No. 5). 419p. 30.95 (*0-7862-2107-0*) Thorndike Pr.

—Hot Six. abr. ed. audio (*1-55927-965-6*); 2000. (Stephanie Plum Novel Ser.: No. 6). audio 17.95 (*1-55927-605-3*) Audio Renaissance.

—Hot Six. l.t. ed. 2000. (Stephanie Plum Novel Ser.: No. 6). 350p. 31.95 (*0-7838-9083-4*, Macmillan Reference USA) Gale Group.

—Hot Six. abr. ed. 2001. audio (*0-333-78251-8*) Macmillan U.K. GBR. *Dist:* Macmillan Publishing Co., Inc.

—Hot Six. abr. ed. 2002. audio 7.95 (*1-57815-265-8*) Media Bks., L. L. C.

—Hot Six. unabr. ed. 2001. audio compact disk 78.00 (*0-7887-6173-0*); 2000. (Stephanie Plum Novel Ser.: No. 6). audio 67.00 (*0-7887-4848-3*, 96103E7) Recorded Bks., LLC.

—Hot Six. 2001. (Stephanie Plum Novel Ser.: No. 6). 352p. mass mkt. 7.99 (*0-312-97627-5*, St. Martin's Paperbacks); 2000. (Stephanie Plum Novel Ser.: No. 6). x, 294p. 24.95 (*0-312-20540-6*); 2000. 0.01 (*0-312-26526-3*) St. Martin's Pr.

—Hot Six. l.t. ed. 2001. (Stephanie Plum Novel Ser.: No. 6). 350p. pap. 29.95 (*0-7838-9082-6*) Thorndike Pr.

—One for the Money. abr. ed. 2001. audio (*0-333-78015-9*) Macmillan U.K. GBR. *Dist:* Macmillan Publishing Co., Inc.

—One for the Money. 2002. (Stephanie Plum Novel Ser.: No. 1). 304p. mass mkt. 7.99 o.s.i (*0-06-100905-9*, HarperTorch) Morrow/Avon.

—One for the Money. unabr. ed. (Stephanie Plum Novel Ser.: No. 1). 1999. audio compact disk 66.00 (*0-7887-3406-7*, C1012E7); 1995. audio 51.00 (*0-7887-0449-4*, 94639E7) Recorded Bks., LLC.

—One for the Money. (Stephanie Plum Novel Ser.: No. 1). 2000. E-Book 20.00 (*0-684-86731-1*); 1994. 288p. 25.00 (*0-684-19639-5*) Simon & Schuster. (Scribner).

—One for the Money. abr. ed. (Stephanie Plum Novel Ser.: No. 1). 2000. audio compact disk 9.98 (*0-7435-1838-1*); 1996. audio 17.00 o.s.i (*0-671-56255-X*, 393338) Simon & Schuster Audio. (Simon & Schuster Audioworks).

—One for the Money. Date not set. pap. (*0-312-31635-6*); 2003. (Illus.). 352p. reprint ed. mass mkt. 7.99 (*0-312-99045-6*) St. Martin's Pr. (St. Martin's Paperbacks).

—One for the Money. l.t. ed. 1995. (Stephanie Plum Novel Ser.: No. 1). 333p. 23.95 (*0-7838-1186-1*) Thorndike Pr.

—Seven Up. l.t. ed. 2001. (Stephanie Plum Novel Ser.: Bk. 7). 400p. 24.95 (*0-375-43111-X*) Random Hse. Large Print.

—Seven Up. 2001. (Stephanie Plum Novel Ser.: Bk. 7). 309p. 24.95 (*0-312-26584-0*) St. Martin's Pr.

—Three Plums in One: One for the Money, Two for the Dough, Three to Get Deadly. 2001. 800p. 23.00 (*0-7432-1639-3*); E-Book 9.99 (*0-7432-1666-0*) Simon & Schuster. (Scribner).

—Three Plums in One: One for the Money, Two for the Dough, Three to Get Deadly, Set. abr. ed. 2001. audio compact disk 39.95 (*0-7435-0947-1*, Simon & Schuster Audioworks) Simon & Schuster Audio.

—Three to Get Deadly. l.t. ed. 1997. (Stephanie Plum Novel Ser.: No. 3). 25.95 o.p. (*1-56895-429-8*, Wheeler Publishing, Inc.) Gale Group.

—Three to Get Deadly. 2001. audio (*0-333-78011-6*) Macmillan U.K. GBR. *Dist:* Macmillan Publishing Co., Inc.

—Three to Get Deadly. unabr. ed. (Stephanie Plum Novel Ser.: No. 3). 2000. audio compact disk 89.00 (*0-7887-3964-6*, C1119E7); 1997. audio 60.00 (*0-7887-0927-5*, 95067E7) Recorded Bks., LLC.

—Three to Get Deadly. (Stephanie Plum Novel Ser.: No. 3). 1998. E-Book 24.00 (*0-684-86860-1*); 1997. 304p. 25.00 (*0-684-82265-2*); 1997. 24.00 o.s.i (*0-684-84466-4*) Simon & Schuster. (Scribner).

—Three to Get Deadly. abr. ed. (Stephanie Plum Novel Ser.: No. 3). 2000. audio 9.98 (*0-7435-1839-X*); 1994. audio 18.00 (*0-671-57520-1*, 394533) Simon & Schuster Audio. (Simon & Schuster Audioworks).

—Three to Get Deadly. 1998. (Stephanie Plum Novel Ser.: No. 3). 352p. reprint ed. mass mkt. 7.99 (*0-312-96609-1*, St. Martin's Paperbacks) St. Martin's Pr.

—To the Nines. l.t. ed. 2003. 416p. 27.95 (*0-375-43202-7*) Random Hse., Inc.

—To the Nines. Date not set. mass mkt. 7.99 (*0-312-99146-0*, St. Martin's Paperbacks); 2003. 320p. 25.95 (*0-312-26586-7*) St. Martin's Pr.

—Two for the Dough. l.t. ed. 1998. (Stephanie Plum Novel Ser.: No. 2). 25.95 (*1-57490-151-6*, Beeler Large Print Bks.) Beeler, Thomas T. Publisher.

—Two for the Dough. unabr. ed. (Stephanie Plum Novel Ser.: No. 2). 2000. audio 51.00 (*0-7887-0617-9*, 94788E7); 1999. audio compact disk 69.00 (*0-7887-3723-6*, C1080E7) Recorded Bks., LLC.

—Two for the Dough. (Stephanie Plum Novel Ser.: No. 2). 2000. E-Book 22.00 (*0-684-86853-9*, Scribner); 1996. 304p. 22.00 (*0-684-82592-9*, Scribner); 1996. 304p. 25.00 (*0-684-19638-7*, Scribner); 1996. 336p. reprint ed. mass mkt. 7.99 (*0-671-00179-5*, Pocket) Simon & Schuster.

—Two for the Dough. (Stephanie Plum Novel Ser.: No. 2). 1999. audio 9.98 (*0-671-04420-6*); Set. 1996. audio 17.00 (*0-671-56258-4*, 393428) Simon & Schuster Audio. (Simon & Schuster Audioworks).

—Visions of Sugar Plums. l.t. ed. 2002. 256p. 21.99 (*0-375-43188-8*) Random Hse. Large Print.

—Visions of Sugar Plums. 2003. 256p. mass mkt. 6.99 (*0-312-98634-3*, St. Martin's Paperbacks); 2002. 160p. 19.95 (*0-312-30632-6*) St. Martin's Pr.

Faherty, Terence. Deadstick. 1995. (WWL Mystery Ser.). per. (*0-373-26167-5*, 1-26167-6, Harlequin Bks.) Harlequin Enterprises, Ltd.

—Deadstick. 1991. 240p. 11.99 o.p. (*0-312-06332-6*, Saint Martin's Minotaur) St. Martin's Pr.

—Live to Regret. 1995. 251p. per. (*0-373-26180-2*, 1-26180-9, Harlequin Bks.) Harlequin Enterprises, Ltd.

—Live to Regret. 1992. 224p. 17.95 o.p. (*0-312-08255-X*, Saint Martin's Minotaur) St. Martin's Pr.

—Prove the Nameless: An Owen Keane Mystery. 1998. (WWL Mystery Ser.). per. (*0-373-26269-8*, 1-26269-0, Worldwide Library) Harlequin Enterprises, Ltd.

—Prove the Nameless: An Owen Keane Mystery. 1996. (Owen Keane Mysteries Ser.). 304p. 22.95 (*0-312-14706-6*, Saint Martin's Minotaur) St. Martin's Pr.

Finklestein, Barbara. Summer Long-a-Coming. 2000. E-Book 16.95 incl. cd-rom (*1-58444-039-2*) Disc-Us Bks., Inc.

Fleming, Thomas J. Hours of Gladness: A Novel of the Irish in America. 1999. 304p. 24.95 (*0-312-86781-6*, Forge Bks.) Doherty, Tom Assocs., LLC.

—The Wages of Fame. 1999. 688p. mass mkt. 6.99 (*0-8125-7182-7*); 1998. 461p. 26.95 (*0-312-86309-8*) Doherty, Tom Assocs., LLC. (Forge Bks.).

Ford, Richard. Independence Day. 1996. 464p. pap. 14.00 (*0-679-73518-6*, Vintage) Knopf Publishing Group.

—Independence Day. 1995. 464p. 29.95 (*0-679-49265-8*) Knopf, Alfred A. Inc.

—Independence Day. audio o.p. National Humanities Ctr.

—Independence Day. unabr. ed. 1998. audio 112.00 (*0-7887-2601-3*, 95506E7) Recorded Bks., LLC.

—Independence Day. deluxe ltd. num. ed. 1995. 451p. 125.00 (*0-9631925-2-3*) Trice, B.E. Publishing.

Fox, Les & Fox, Sue. Return to Sender: The Secret Son of Elvis Presley. 1996. 350p. 21.95 (*0-9646986-0-9*) West Highland Publishing Co., Inc.

Gallison, Kate. Grave Misgivings: A Mother Lavinia Grey Mystery. 1999. (Mother Lavinia Grey Mysteries Ser.). 256p. mass mkt. 5.99 o.s.i (*0-440-22413-6*) Dell Publishing.

—Hasty Retreat: A Mother Lavinia Grey Mystery. 1998. (Mother Lavinia Grey Mysteries Ser.). 256p. mass mkt. 5.99 o.s.i (*0-440-22410-1*, Dell Bks.) Dell Publishing.

—Jersey Monkey. 1992. 224p. 17.95 o.p. (*0-312-07006-3*, Saint Martin's Minotaur) St. Martin's Pr.

—Unholy Angels: A Mother Lavinia Grey Mystery. 1996. (Mother Lavinia Grey Mysteries Ser.). 272p. mass mkt. 5.99 o.s.i (*0-440-22220-6*) Dell Publishing.

Gilmore, Monique. The Grass Ain't Greener. l.t. ed. 1999. (Romance Ser.). 360p. 27.95 (*0-7838-8508-3*) Thorndike Pr.

Goldstein, Rebecca. Mazel. 1996. 368p. pap. 12.95 o.s.i (*0-14-023905-7*, Penguin Bks.) Penguin Group (USA) Inc.
—Mazel. 2002. (Library of American Fiction). 368p. pap. 19.95 (*0-299-18124-3*) Univ. of Wisconsin Pr.
—Mazel. 1995. 368p. 23.95 o.s.i (*0-670-85648-7*, Viking) Viking Penguin.
Gottlieb, Eli. The Boy Who Went Away. 1998. 224p. reprint ed. pap. 10.95 o.s.i (*0-553-37927-5*) Bantam Bks.
—The Boy Who Went Away. 1996. 208p. 21.95 (*0-312-15070-9*) St. Martin's Pr.
Grames, Selwyn Anne. The Pinecroft Thoroughbreds. 2001. pap. (*1-59109-054-7*, PO 00004) Zumaya Pubns.
Grant, Charles L. Stunts. 1992. mass mkt. 4.99 (*0-8125-0698-7*); 1990. 19.95 o.p. (*0-312-85013-1*) Doherty, Tom Assocs., LLC. (Tor Bks.).
Hanauer, Cathi. My Sister's Bones. 1997. 272p. pap. 14.95 (*0-385-31704-2*) Doubleday Publishing.
Hathaway, Robin. The Doctor & the Dead Man's Chest. 2003. mass mkt. 6.99 (*0-312-98372-7*, St. Martin's Paperbacks); 2001. (Illus.). 352p. 24.95 (*0-312-26956-0*) St. Martin's Pr.
—Scarecrow. l.t. ed. 2003. (Mystery Ser.). 27.95 (*1-57490-510-4*) Beeler, Thomas T. Publisher.
—Scarecrow. Date not set. pap. (*0-312-30852-3*, Saint Martin's Griffin); mass mkt. (*0-312-98656-4*, St. Martin's Paperbacks) St. Martin's Pr.
—Scarecrow: A Mystery. 2003. 224p. 23.95 (*0-312-30851-5*, Saint Martin's Minotaur) St. Martin's Pr.
Hecht, Daniel. Skull Session. 1998. 512p. mass mkt. 6.99 o.s.i (*0-451-19592-2*, Signet Bks.) NAL.
—Skull Session. l.t. ed. 1998. (Core Ser.). 719p. 28.95 (*0-7838-0340-0*) Thorndike Pr.
—Skull Session. 1998. 419p. 23.95 o.p. (*0-670-87661-5*) Viking Penguin.
Homer, Larona. The Shore Ghosts & Other Stories of New Jersey. 1981. (Illus.). 154p. (J). (gr. 4-8). 15.95 (*0-912608-14-5*); pap. 9.95 (*0-912608-82-X*) Middle Atlantic Pr.
Isenberg, Jane. Death in a Hot Flash: A Bel Barrett Mystery. 2000. (Bel Barrett Mysteries Ser.). 224p. mass mkt. 5.99 (*0-380-80281-3*, Avon Bks.) Morrow/Avon.
—Hot & Bothered. 2003. 288p. mass mkt. 6.99 (*0-380-81888-4*, Avon Bks.) Morrow/Avon.
—The "M" Word: A Bel Barrett Mystery. 1999. 224p. mass mkt. 5.99 (*0-380-80280-5*, Avon Bks.) Morrow/Avon.
—Mood Swings to Murder. 2000. (Bel Barrett Mysteries Ser.). 256p. mass mkt. 6.50 (*0-380-80282-1*, Avon Bks.) Morrow/Avon.
—Mood Swings to Murder: A Bel Barrett Mystery. l.t. ed. 2002. 349p. pap. 25.95 (*0-7862-4007-5*) Gale Group.
Jacobs, David. Snake Eyes. 1998. 208p. mass mkt. 6.50 o.s.i (*0-425-16637-6*) Berkley Publishing Group.
Kaplan, James. Two Guys from Verona: A Novel of Suburbia. 1998. 352p. 25.00 o.p. (*0-87113-704-6*, Atlantic Monthly Pr.); 1999. 3521p. reprint ed. pap. 13.00 (*0-8021-3623-0*, Grove Pr.) Grove/ Atlantic, Inc.
Kashner, Sam. Sinatraland: A Novel. 1999. 220p. 22.95 (*0-87951-917-7*) Overlook Pr., The.
—Sinatraland: A Novel. 2000. 192p. pap. 11.00 (*0-684-86907-1*, Scribner Paper Fiction) Simon & Schuster.
Katz, Jon. Death by Station Wagon. 1994. (Suburban Detective Mysteries Ser.). 336p. mass mkt. 5.99 o.s.i (*0-553-29881-X*) Bantam Bks.
—Death Row: A Suburban Detective Mystery. 1999. 288p. mass mkt. 5.99 o.s.i (*0-553-57816-2*) Bantam Bks.
—The Family Stalker. 1995. 336p. mass mkt. 5.50 o.s.i (*0-553-56954-6*) Bantam Bks.
—The Family Stalker: A Suburban Detective Mystery. 1994. 320p. 18.95 o.s.i (*0-385-46903-9*) Doubleday Publishing.
—The Fathers' Club. 1997. (Suburban Detective Mysteries Ser.). 272p. mass mkt. 5.99 o.s.i (*0-553-57536-8*) Bantam Bks.
—The Fathers' Club. l.t. ed. 1997. (Large Print Bks.). 24.95 (*1-56895-406-9*, Wheeler Publishing, Inc.) Gale Group.
—The Last Housewife. 1996. 384p. mass mkt. 5.99 o.s.i (*0-553-56793-4*) Bantam Bks.
—The Last Housewife. 1995. 19.95 (*0-385-47743-0*) Doubleday Publishing.
—The Last Housewife. l.t. ed. 1995. (Niagara Large Print Ser.). 467p. 29.50 o.p. (*0-7089-5811-7*, Ulverscroft) Thorpe, F. A. Pubs. GBR. *Dist:* Ulverscroft Large Print Bks., Ltd.
Kelly, Jane. Wrong Beach Island. 2002. 327p. 22.95 (*0-937548-47-2*) Plexus Publishing, Inc.
Kent, Bill. Down by the Sea. 1993. 320p. 19.95 o.p. (*0-312-09277-6*, Saint Martin's Minotaur) St. Martin's Pr.
—On a Blanket with My Baby. 1995. ix, 275p. 21.00 o.p. (*0-312-11870-8*, Saint Martin's Minotaur) St. Martin's Pr.
—Under the Boardwalk. 1990. mass mkt. 4.50 o.s.i (*1-55817-347-1*, Pinnacle Bks.) Kensington Publishing Corp.
—Under the Boardwalk. 1988. 320p. 18.95 o.p. (*1-55710-019-5*, Morrow, William & Co.) Morrow/ Avon.
King, Kathy Coudle. Wannabe. 2000. (Illus.). 208p. pap. 13.95 (*0-88739-232-6*) Creative Arts Bk. Co.
Klempner, Joseph T. Fogbound. Date not set. mass mkt. (*0-312-99465-6*, St. Martin's Paperbacks); 2003. 224p. 23.95 (*0-312-31067-6*) St. Martin's Pr.
Kramer, Barbara J. The Bud Wilson Dream Book. Smith, Nan, ed. 1997. 281p. (Orig.). pap. 12.95 (*1-882521-05-6*) Stones Point Pr.
Krist, Gary. The Garden State. 1988. 192p. 16.95 (*0-15-134292-X*) Harcourt Trade Pubs.
—The Garden State. 1989. (Vintage Contemporaries Ser.). pap. 7.95 o.s.i (*0-679-72515-6*, Vintage) Knopf Publishing Group.
Lake, Simon. Daughter of Darkness. 1992. (Midnight Place Ser.: No. 3). 160p. (YA). mass mkt. 3.50 o.s.i (*0-553-29442-3*) Bantam Bks.
Lamb, Cynthia. Brigid's Charge, Set. unabr. ed. 2000. audio 32.95 (*1-893530-09-4*) Arania Bks.
—Brigid's Charge. 1997. vi, 296p. 22.00 (*0-9654694-0-9*); pap. 14.00 (*0-9654694-1-7*) Bay Island Bks.
Larson, Ellen. The Hatch & Brood of Time. 1999. (NJ Mysteries Ser.: Vol. 1). 304p. pap. 14.95 (*0-9669877-0-5*) Savvy Pr.
Lennon, J. Robert. The Funnies. 2000. (Illus.). 336p. 13.00 (*1-57322-781-1*, Riverhead Trade (Paperbacks)) Berkley Publishing Group.
—The Funnies. 1999. 320p. 23.95 o.s.i (*1-57322-126-0*, Riverhead Bks. (Hardcovers)) Putnam Publishing Group, The.
Leonard, Elmore. Glitz. l.t. ed. 1985. (General Ser.). 407p. 15.95 o.p. (*0-8161-3834-6*); 9.95 o.p. (*0-8161-3835-4*) Gale Group. (Macmillan Reference USA).
—Glitz. 1998. 432p. pap. 12.00 (*0-688-16095-6*, Quill) HarperTrade.
—Glitz. 2002. 432p. mass mkt. 7.50 (*0-06-008953-9*); 1983. 14.95 o.p. (*0-87795-632-4*, Morrow, William & Co.) Morrow/Avon.
—Glitz. 1987. 368p. mass mkt. 6.99 (*0-446-34343-9*); 1986. mass mkt. 3.95 (*0-446-32920-7*) Warner Bks., Inc.
Leyner, Mark. The Tetherballs of Bougainville. 1997. 224p. 22.00 o.s.i (*0-517-70101-4*, Harmony) Crown Publishing Group.
—The Tetherballs of Bougainville: A Novel. 1998. 240p. pap. 12.00 (*0-679-76349-X*, Vintage) Knopf Publishing Group.
—Tooth Imprints on a Corn Dog. 1996. 240p. pap. 12.00 (*0-679-74521-1*) Random Hse., Inc.
Lin, Edmund C. Waylaid. 2001. 170p. pap. 12.95 (*1-885030-32-0*) Kaya Production.
Lopez. In the Clear. 2004. pap. 14.00 (*0-15-602735-6*, Harvest Bks.) Harcourt Trade Pubs.
Lopez, Steve. In the Clear. 2002. 352p. 25.00 (*0-15-100284-3*) Harcourt Trade Pubs.
Lott, Bret. Reed's Beach. 1999. 352p. pap. 14.00 (*0-671-03819-2*, Washington Square Pr.) Simon & Schuster.
—Reed's Beach. Rosenman, Jane, ed. 352p. 1993. 20.00 (*0-671-79238-5*, Atria); 1994. reprint ed. pap. (*0-671-79239-3*, Washington Square Pr.) Simon & Schuster.
—Reed's Beach. 342p. 4.98 o.p. (*0-8317-2824-8*) Smithmark Pubs., Inc.
Lysaght, Brian. Last Dance of the Viper. 2001. 464p. 27.95 (*0-7653-0062-1*, Forge Bks.) Doherty, Tom Assocs., LLC.
MacDonald, Patricia. Secret Admirer. l.t. ed. 1996. (Large Print Ser.). 456p. lib. bdg. 23.95 (*1-57490-039-0*, Beeler Large Print Bks.) Beeler, Thomas T. Publisher.
—Secret Admirer. abr. ed. 1996. audio 7.99 o.p. (*1-56740-123-6*, 1365, Paperback Nova Audio Bks.); 1995. audio 16.95 o.p. (*1-56100-436-7*, 1364, Nova Audio Bks.); 1995. audio 23.95 o.p. (*1-56100-645-9*, 257, Bookcassette); 1995. audio 73.25 o.p. (*1-56100-270-4*, 1035, Unabridged Library Editions) Brilliance Audio.
—Secret Admirer. 1997. 384p. mass mkt. 6.50 o.s.i (*0-446-60368-6*); 1995. 352p. 30.00 (*0-446-51686-4*) Warner Bks., Inc.
MacDonald, Shari. Stardust. 1997. (Palisades Pure Romance Ser.). 286p. pap. 9.99 o.p. (*1-57673-109-X*, Palisades) Multnomah Pubs., Inc.
—Stardust. l.t. ed. 1999. (Christian Fiction Ser.). 336p. 23.95 (*0-7862-1806-1*) Thorndike Pr.
Major, Marcus. A Man Most Worthy. 2003. 288p. 23.95 (*0-525-94685-3*, Dutton) Dutton/Plume.
—A Man Most Worthy. 2004. 336p. pap. 13.95 (*0-451-21107-3*) NAL.
Markus, Julia. Uncle. 1987. (J). mass mkt. 3.95 o.s.i (*0-440-39187-3*, Laurel) Dell Publishing.
—Uncle, 001. 1978. (Literary Fellowship Award Novel Ser.). 7.95 o.p. (*0-395-27098-7*) Houghton Mifflin Co.
Marshall, Evan. Hanging Hannah. (Jane Stuart & Winky Mystery Ser.). 2001. 32p. mass mkt. 5.99 (*1-57566-663-4*); 2000. (Illus.). 307p. 20.00 o.s.i (*1-57566-550-6*) Kensington Publishing Corp. (Kensington Bks.).
—Missing Marlene. (Jane Stuart & Winky Mystery Ser.). 2000. 336p. mass mkt. 5.99 (*1-57566-555-7*, Kensington Bks.); 1999. 309p. 20.00 o.s.i (*1-57566-420-8*) Kensington Publishing Corp.
Matteson, Stefanie. Murder at the Falls. 1993. 240p. (Orig.). mass mkt. 5.50 o.s.i (*0-425-14008-3*) Berkley Publishing Group.
May, Jesse. Shut up & Deal. 1998. 224p. pap. 15.00 (*0-385-48940-4*) Doubleday Publishing.
McCafferty, Megan. Second Helpings: A Novel. 2003. 368p. pap. 10.95 (*0-609-80791-9*, Three Rivers Pr.) Crown Publishing Group.
—Sloppy Firsts: A Novel. 2001. 304p. pap. 11.95 (*0-609-80790-0*, Crown) Crown Publishing Group.
McPhee, Martha. Gorgeous Lies: A Novel. 2002. 336p. 25.00 (*0-15-100613-X*) Harcourt Trade Pubs.
Melnyczuk, Askold. Ambassador of the Dead. 288p. 2001. text 25.00 o.p. (*1-58243-132-9*); 2002. reprint ed. pap. text 15.00 (*1-58243-251-1*) Basic Bks. (Counterpoint Pr.).
—What Is Told. 1995. 216p. pap. 11.95 o.p. (*0-571-19865-1*) Faber & Faber, Inc.
—What Is Told: A Novel. 1994. 216p. 21.95 o.p. (*0-571-19830-9*) Faber & Faber, Inc.
Mirvis, Tova. The Outside World. 2004. 304p. 24.00 (*1-4000-4161-9*, Knopf) Knopf Publishing Group.
Monahan, Brent. The Book of Common Dread: A Novel of the Infernal. 1993. 336p. 19.95 o.p. (*0-312-09349-7*) St. Martin's Pr.
—The Book of Common Dread Vol. 1. 1994. mass mkt. 4.99 o.p. (*0-312-95359-3*, St. Martin's Paperbacks) St. Martin's Pr.
Moody, Rick. Garden State: A Novel. 1998. pap. 12.95 (*0-316-19007-1*); 1997. 224p. reprint ed. pap. 13.95 (*0-316-55763-3*) Little Brown & Co. (Back Bay).
—Garden State: A Novel. (Editor's Book Award Ser.). 1993. pap. 11.50 (*0-916366-85-5*); 1992. 18.50 (*0-916366-73-1*) Pushcart Pr., The.
Nadelson, Scott. Saving Stanley: The Brickman Stories. 2003. pap. 12.95 (*0-9716915-2-5*) Hawthorne Bks. & Literary Arts, Inc.
Norris, William. Snapshots: A Novel. 2001. 256p. 23.95 o.p. (*1-57322-183-X*, Riverhead Bks. (Hardcovers)) Putnam Publishing Group, The.
O'Brien, Meg. Crashing Down. abr. ed. 1999. audio 7.99 (*1-55204-178-6*, MIR-1178) Durkin Hayes Publishing Ltd.
—Crashing Down. 1999. (Mira Bks.). 408p. mass mkt. (*1-55166-516-6*, 1-66516-5, Mira Bks.) Harlequin Enterprises, Ltd.
Perrotta, Tom. Bad Haircut: Stories of the Seventies. 1995. 256p. mass mkt. 6.99 o.s.i (*0-425-14942-0*); 1997. 240p. reprint ed. pap. 12.95 (*0-425-15954-X*) Berkley Publishing Group.
—Bad Haircut: Stories of the Seventies. 1994. 80p. pap. 18.95 (*1-882593-05-7*) Bridge Works Publishing Co., Inc.
—The Election: A Novel. 1998. 208p. 21.95 o.p. (*0-399-14366-1*, G. P. Putnam's Sons) Penguin Group (USA) Inc.
—Joe College. E-Book 23.95 (*0-312-27167-0*); 2000. 306p. 23.95 (*0-312-26184-5*) St. Martin's Pr.
—The Wishbones, Set. abr. ed. 1997. audio 16.95 (*1-55927-413-1*) Audio Renaissance.
—The Wishbones. 304p. 1998. pap. 12.95 (*0-425-16314-8*); 1999. reprint ed. mass mkt. 6.99 o.s.i (*0-425-16971-5*) Berkley Publishing Group.
—The Wishbones. unabr. ed. 1997. audio 48.00 (*0-7366-3712-5*, 4396) Books on Tape, Inc.
—The Wishbones. 1997. 256p. 22.95 o.p. (*0-399-14267-3*, G. P. Putnam's Sons) Penguin Group (USA) Inc.
Peterson, Charles J. Kate Aylesford: or The Heiress of Sweetwater. 2001. xviii, 276p. reprint ed. 22.95 (*0-937548-46-4*) Plexus Publishing, Inc.
Price, Richard. Clockers. 2001. 608p. pap. 14.95 (*0-06-093498-0*, Perennial) HarperTrade.
—Freedomland. 1999. 736p. mass mkt. 7.99 (*0-440-22644-9*) Dell Publishing.
—Samaritan. 2003. 400p. 25.00 (*0-375-41115-1*) Knopf, Alfred A. Inc.
—Samaritan. l.t. ed. 2003. 30.95 (*0-7862-5428-9*) Thorndike Pr.
Ptacek, Kathryn. The Hunted. 1994. 272p. 4.99 o.p. (*1-55773-982-X*, Diamond Bks.) Ace Bks.
—The Hunted. 1993. 205p. 19.95 o.p. (*0-8027-1227-4*) Walker & Co.
Raeff, Anne. Clara Mondschein's Melancholia: A Novel. 2002. 258p. 25.00 (*1-931561-16-8*) MacAdam/Cage Publishing, Inc.
Ratner, Rochelle. Bobby's Girl. 1986. 128p. (Orig.). pap. 9.95 (*0-918273-22-6*) Coffee Hse. Pr.
Reiken, Frederick. The Lost Legends of New Jersey. 2000. 320p. 24.00 o.s.i (*0-15-100507-9*) Harcourt Trade Pubs.
Reuss, Frederick. Henry of Atlantic City. 1999. 249p. 22.00 (*1-878448-89-7*) MacMurray & Beck, Inc.
—Henry of Atlantic City: A Novel. 2001. (Vintage Contemporaries Ser.). 256p. reprint ed. pap. 12.00 (*0-375-72623-3*, Vintage) Knopf Publishing Group.
Rivera, Beatriz. Midnight Sandwiches at the Mariposa Express. 1997. 118p. pap. 11.95 (*1-55885-216-6*) Arte Publico Pr.
Roberts, Gillian. How I Spent My Summer Vacation. 1995. 256p. mass mkt. 5.99 (*0-345-38594-2*); pap. 19.00 o.s.i (*0-345-46533-4*) Ballantine Bks.
Rockcastle, Mary F. Rainy Lake. 278p. 1996. pap. 14.00 (*1-55597-242-X*); 1994. 22.50 o.s.i (*1-55597-218-7*) Graywolf Pr.
Rosenfeld, Lucinda. Why She Went Home: A Novel. 2004. 320p. 23.95 (*1-4000-6185-7*, Random House) Random House Adult Trade Publishing Group.
Rosenfelt, David. First Degree. 2003. 240p. 23.95 (*0-89296-754-4*) Mysterious Pr.
—First Degree. l.t. ed. 2003. 342p. 28.95 (*0-7862-5859-4*, Large Print Pr.) Thorndike Pr.
—First Degree. 2004. mass mkt. (*0-446-61386-X*) Warner Bks., Inc.
—Open & Shut. 2002. 256p. 23.95 (*0-89296-748-X*) Mysterious Pr.
—Open & Shut. l.t. ed. 2002. (Americana Ser.). 442p. 29.95 (*0-7862-4494-1*) Thorndike Pr.
—Open & Shut. 2003. 320p. reprint ed. mass mkt. 6.99 (*0-446-61253-7*) Warner Bks., Inc.
Rossi, Agnes. The Houseguest. 2000. 304p. reprint ed. 13.00 o.s.i (*0-452-28197-0*, Plume) Dutton/Plume.
—The Houseguest: A Novel. l.t. ed. 2000. (Americana Ser.). 504p. 28.95 (*0-7862-2547-5*) Thorndike Pr.
Rossi, Angnes. Fancy. 2000. (Illus.). 304p. 23.95 o.s.i (*0-525-94365-X*) Dutton/Plume.
Roth, Philip. The Human Stain. tchr. ed. 234.00 o.p. (*0-618-06598-9*); 2000. 368p. tchr. ed. 26.00 (*0-618-05945-8*) Houghton Mifflin Co.
—The Human Stain. 2001. (International Ser.). 384p. pap. 14.95 (*0-375-72634-9*, Vintage) Knopf Publishing Group.
—The Human Stain. l.t. ed. 2000. (Basic Ser.). 614p. 27.95 (*0-7862-2964-0*) Thorndike Pr.
Rozan, S. J. Winter & Night. E-Book 18.95 (*0-312-70434-8*); 2003. 400p. mass mkt. 6.99 (*0-312-98668-8*, St. Martin's Paperbacks); 2002. 304p. 24.95 (*0-312-24555-6*, Saint Martin's Minotaur) St. Martin's Pr.
Rubino, Jane. Cheat the Devil. 1998. 352p. 24.95 (*1-885173-56-3*) Write Way Publishing.
—Death of a DJ. 1997. 224p. mass mkt. 4.99 o.p. (*0-06-104433-4*, HarperTorch) Morrow/Avon.
—Death of a DJ. 1995. 225p. 20.95 (*1-885173-09-1*) Write Way Publishing.
—Fruitcake. 1997. 384p. 24.95 (*1-885173-29-6*) Write Way Publishing.
—Plot Twist. 2000. 400p. 24.95 (*1-885173-80-6*) Write Way Publishing.
Rubino, Jane, et al. Homicide for the Holidays: Fruitcake; Milwaukee Winters Can Be Murder; A Perfect Time for Murder. 2000. (WWL Mystery Ser.: Vol. 362). 512p. mass mkt. (*0-373-26362-7*, 1-26362-3, Worldwide Library) Harlequin Enterprises, Ltd.
Schachter, Esty. Anya's Echoes: A Novel. 2003. 96p. pap. 10.00 (*1-56474-427-2*) Fithian Pr.
Schumacher, Julie. The Body Is Water. 1995. 272p. 21.00 (*1-56947-042-1*) Soho Pr., Inc.
—The Body Is Water: A Novel. 1999. 272p. pap. 12.50 (*0-380-80704-1*); 1997. pap. 6.99 (*0-380-72840-0*, Avon Bks.) Morrow/Avon.
Schwighardt, Joan. Virtual Silence. 1995. 176p. 42.00 (*1-877946-61-3*) Permanent Pr., The.
Scollins-Mantha, Brandi. My Intended. 2000. 240p. 18.00 (*0-688-17404-3*) Morrow/Avon.
Shankman, Sarah. She Walks in Beauty. l.t. ed. 1993. (General Ser.). 484p. 20.95 o.p. (*0-8161-5478-3*, Macmillan Reference USA) Gale Group.
—She Walks in Beauty. 1991. 320p. 20.00 (*0-671-73657-4*, Atria) Simon & Schuster.
—She Walks in Beauty. Chelius, Jane, ed. 1992. 352p. reprint ed. mass mkt. 5.99 (*0-671-73658-2*, Pocket) Simon & Schuster.
Sharp, Paula. Lost in Jersey City. 1993. (Illus.). 304p. 20.00 o.p. (*0-06-016564-2*) HarperTrade.
Sherman, Beth. The Dead Man's Float. l.t. ed. 2003. (Mystery Ser.). 27.95 (*1-57490-489-2*, Beeler Large Print Bks.) Beeler, Thomas T. Publisher.
—The Dead Man's Float. 1998. (Jersey Shore Mysteries Ser.). 288p. mass mkt. 6.50 (*0-380-73107-X*, Avon Bks.) Morrow/Avon.
—Death at High Tide: A Jersey Shore Mystery. 1999. 256p. mass mkt. 6.50 (*0-380-73108-8*, Avon Bks.) Morrow/Avon.
—Death's a Beach. Grader, T. L., ed. 2000. (Jersey Shore Mysteries Ser.). 256p. mass mkt. 5.99 (*0-380-73109-6*, Avon Bks.) Morrow/Avon.
—The Devil & the Deep Blue Sea. 2001. (Jersey Shore Mysteries Ser.). 288p. mass mkt. 5.99 (*0-380-81605-9*, Avon Bks.) Morrow/Avon.
—The Devil & the Deep Blue Sea. l.t. ed. 2002. (Paperback Ser.). 365p. pap. 25.95 (*0-7862-4436-4*) Thorndike Pr.

Settings

—Murder Down the Shore: A Jersey Shore Mystery. 2002. 256p. mass mkt. 6.50 (0-380-81606-7) Morrow/Avon.

Simpson, Thomas W. The Fingerprints of Armless Mike. 1996. 390p. 19.95 o.p. (0-446-51809-3) Warner Bks., Inc.

Smith, F. Hopkinson. The Tides of Barnegat. 2001. (Illus.). 422p. reprint ed. 27.95 (0-945582-83-8); pap. 15.95 (0-945582-82-X) Down The Shore Publishing.

Smith, Rosamond, pseud. Double Delight. 1999. 368p. pap. 12.95 o.s.i (0-452-28041-9, Plume); 1997. 336p. 23.95 o.p. (0-525-94299-8) Dutton/Plume.

—Double Delight. 1999. pap. 6.99 (0-451-40782-2, Signet Bks.) NAL.

—Snake Eyes. 1992. 272p. 20.00 o.p. (0-525-93404-9, Abrahams, William Bks.) Dutton/Plume.

—Snake Eyes. 1993. 352p. reprint ed. mass mkt. 4.99 o.s.i (0-451-40382-7, Onyx) NAL.

Smith, Rosamond, pseud & Oates, Joyce Carol. The Barrens. 2001. 320p. 25.00 (0-7867-0847-6, Carroll & Graf Pubs.) Avalon Publishing Group.

Soehnlein, K. M. The World of Normal Boys. 2000. 256p. 22.00 o.s.i (1-57566-595-6) Kensington Publishing Corp.

Sorrentino, Gilbert. Aberration of Starlight. 1993. 213p. tchr. ed. o.p. (1-56478-052-X); reprint ed. pap. 11.95 (1-56478-028-7) Dalkey Archive Pr.

—Aberration of Starlight. 1981. (Contemporary American Fiction Ser.). 224p. pap. 5.95 o.p. (0-14-005879-6, Penguin Bks.) Viking Penguin.

St. Clare, Katherine. To Tell Me Terrible Lies: First of the Wainwright Chronicles, 1778-1783. 1993. (Wainwright Chronicles Ser.). 348p. 24.95 (0-9632830-1-4) Wainwright Pr.

Stark, Richard. The Man with the Getaway Face. l.t. ed. 1988. pap. 13.95 o.p. (1-55504-393-3) BBC Audiobooks America.

—The Man with the Getaway Face, unabr. collector's ed. 1999. audio 32.00 (0-7366-4410-5, 4871) Books on Tape, Inc.

—The Man with the Getaway Face. 1998. (Parker Novels Ser.). 224p. pap. 12.95 (0-446-67466-4) Warner Bks., Inc.

Stein, Michael. The Lynching Tree. 2000. 196p. 24.00 (1-57962-070-1) Permanent Pr., The.

Stroby, Wallace. Barbed Wire Kiss. 2004. mass mkt. 6.99 (0-312-99547-4, St. Martin's Paperbacks) St. Martin's Pr.

—The Barbed-Wire Kiss: A Novel. 2003. 368p. 24.95 (0-312-30034-4, Saint Martin's Minotaur) St. Martin's Pr.

Sumners, Christina. Crooked Heart. 2003. (Core Ser.). 28.95 (0-7862-5121-2) Thorndike Pr.

Sumners, Cristina. Crooked Heart. 2003. 336p. mass mkt. 6.99 (0-553-58430-8); 2002. 304p. 23.95 (0-553-80303-4); 2002. E-Book 19.50 (0-553-89710-1) Bantam Bks.

Thomas, Abigail. An Actual Life. 1996. 252p. tchr. ed. 17.95 (1-56512-133-3, 72133) Algonquin Bks. of Chapel Hill.

—An Actual Life. 1997. 240p. pap. 14.95 (0-684-83751-X, Touchstone) Simon & Schuster.

Tobin, Greg. Conclave. 2002. 453p. mass mkt. 7.99 (0-8125-7921-6, Tor Bks.); 2001. 432p. 25.95 (0-312-87352-2, Forge Bks.) Doherty, Tom Assocs., LLC.

Waterhouse, Jane. Dead Letter. 2000. 320p. mass mkt. 5.99 o.s.i (0-425-17779-3) Berkley Publishing Group.

—Dead Letter. l.t. ed. 2000. (Large Print Bks.). pap. 25.95 (1-56895-953-2, Wheeler Publishing, Inc.) Gale Group.

—Dead Letter. 1998. 304p. 23.95 o.p. (0-399-14436-6) Penguin Group (USA) Inc.

—Graven Images. 1997. 320p. mass mkt. 5.99 o.s.i (0-425-15673-7, Prime Crime) Berkley Publishing Group.

—Graven Images. 1995. 352p. 23.95 o.s.i (0-399-14080-8, G. P. Putnam's Sons) Penguin Group (USA) Inc.

—Shadow Walk. 1999. (Prime Crime Mysteries Ser.). 320p. reprint ed. mass mkt. 5.99 o.s.i (0-425-16946-4, Prime Crime) Berkley Publishing Group.

—Shadow Walk. 1997. 320p. 23.95 o.p. (0-399-14305-X, G. P. Putnam's Sons) Penguin Group (USA) Inc.

Webster, Brenda S. Paradise Farm. 250p. (C). 2000. pap. text 19.95 (0-7914-4100-8); 1999. text 20.50 (0-7914-4099-0) State Univ. of New York Pr.

Wells, John. Death in a Dry Season. 1997. 352p. 24.95 o.p. (0-312-15509-3, Saint Martin's Minotaur) St. Martin's Pr.

Wesley, Valerie Wilson. The Devil Riding. l.t. ed. 2001. (Softcover Ser.). 240p. pap. 23.95 o.p. (1-58724-084-X, Wheeler Publishing, Inc.) Gale Group.

—The Devil Riding. 2000. 208p. 23.95 o.s.i (0-399-14617-2) Penguin Group (USA) Inc.

—Devil's Gonna Get Him. 1996. (Tamara Hayle Mystery Ser.: Vol. 2). 288p. mass mkt. 6.99 (0-380-72492-8, Avon Bks.) Morrow/Avon.

—Devil's Gonna Get Him. 1995. 212p. 19.95 o.p. (0-399-14027-1, G. P. Putnam's Sons) Penguin Group (USA) Inc.

—Easier to Kill. l.t. ed. 1999. pap. 23.95 o.p. (1-56895-704-1, Wheeler Publishing, Inc.) Gale Group.

—Easier to Kill. 1999. (Tamara Hayle Mystery Ser.). 304p. mass mkt. 6.99 (0-380-72910-5, Avon Bks.) Morrow/Avon.

—Easier to Kill. 1998. (Tamara Hayle Mystery Ser.: Vol. 5). 193p. 23.95 o.p. (0-399-14445-5) Penguin Group (USA) Inc.

—The Hiding Place. 1998. (Tamara Hayle Mystery Ser.). 288p. mass mkt. 6.99 (0-380-72909-1, Avon Bks.) Morrow/Avon.

—No Hiding Place. unabr. ed. 1998. audio 40.00 (0-7366-4214-5, 4712) Books on Tape, Inc.

—No Hiding Place: A Tamara Hayle Mystery. 1997. 207p. 21.95 o.s.i (0-399-14318-1, G. P. Putnam's Sons) Penguin Group (USA) Inc.

—When Death Comes Stealin. 1995. (Tamara Hayle Mystery Ser.: Vol. 1). 320p. reprint ed. mass mkt. 6.99 (0-380-72491-X, Avon Bks.) Morrow/Avon.

—When Death Comes Stealing. 1994. 224p. 19.95 o.p. (0-399-13949-4, G. P. Putnam's Sons) Penguin Group (USA) Inc.

—Where Evil Sleeps. unabr. ed. 1998. audio 40.00 (0-7366-4120-3, 4624) Books on Tape, Inc.

—Where Evil Sleeps. 1997. 288p. mass mkt. 6.50 (0-380-72908-3, Avon Bks.) Morrow/Avon.

—Where Evil Sleeps. 1996. 224p. 21.95 o.p. (0-399-14145-6, G. P. Putnam's Sons) Penguin Group (USA) Inc.

Wharton, William. Pride. l.t. ed. 1986. 445p. 20.95 o.p. (1-55504-132-9); pap. 18.95 o.p. (1-55504-118-3) BBC Audiobooks America.

—Pride. 1987. mass mkt. 4.95 o.s.i (0-440-37118-X, Laurel) Dell Publishing.

—Pride: A Novel. 2004. 288p. pap. 12.95 (1-55704-259-4) Newmarket Pr.

White, Jack M. The Keeper of the Ferris Wheel. 1993. 260p. 10.00 (0-9636031-9-1) Ashleigh-Reid Pubs.

—The Keeper of the Ferris Wheel: A Novel. 1995. 272p. 21.50 o.p. (1-55611-453-2) Fine, Donald I. Bks.

Wilson, F. Paul & Lyon, Steve. Nightkill. 1999. 288p. mass mkt. 6.99 (0-8125-6536-3, Tor Bks.); 1997. 304p. 23.95 (0-312-85910-4, Forge Bks.) Doherty, Tom Assocs., LLC.

Wittenborn, Dirk. Fierce People. 2003. (Illus.). 352p. pap. 14.95 (1-58234-292-X); 2002. 304p. 24.95 (1-58234-242-3) Bloomsbury Publishing.

Ziesk, Edra. Acceptable Losses: A Novel. 1996. 320p. 22.50 (0-87074-412-7); pap. 12.95 (0-87074-413-5) Southern Methodist Univ. Pr.

**NEW KASSEL (MO.: IMAGINARY PLACE)—FICTION**

MacPherson, Rett. A Comedy of Heirs. 2nd ed. 1999. (Torie O'Shea Mysteries Ser.). 214p. 21.95 (0-312-20513-9, Saint Martin's Minotaur) St. Martin's Pr.

—Family Skeletons. 1998. (Dead Letter Mysteries Ser.: Vol. 1). 224p. mass mkt. 6.50 (0-312-96602-4, St. Martin's Paperbacks); 1997. 208p. 21.95 o.p. (0-312-15236-1, Saint Martin's Minotaur) St. Martin's Pr.

—Veiled Antiquity. 1999. (Veiled Antiquity Ser.: Vol. 1). 240p. mass mkt. 5.99 (0-312-96701-2, St. Martin's Paperbacks); 1998. 224p. 20.95 (0-312-18677-0, Saint Martin's Minotaur) St. Martin's Pr.

MacPherson, Rett, contrib. by. A Comedy of Heirs: A Novel. l.t. ed. 2000. (Mystery Ser.). 349p. 27.95 o.p. (0-7862-2346-4) Thorndike Pr.

McPherson, Rett. A Comedy of Heirs: A Torie O'Shea Mystery. 2000. (Torie O'Shea Mysteries Ser.). 230p. mass mkt. 5.99 (0-312-97133-8, St. Martin's Paperbacks) St. Martin's Pr.

**NEW MEXICO—FICTION**

Adler, Dick. The Mozart Code. 1999. 168p. E-Book 6.00 (1-58200-107-3); E-Book 6.00 (1-58200-227-4) Hard Shell Word Factory.

Alers, Rochelle. Just Before Dawn. 2000. (Arabesque Ser.). 256p. mass mkt. 5.99 (1-58314-103-0, Arabesque) BET Bks.

Alico, Stella H. Maria, Mota & the Grandmother: A Novel. Ware, Laura, ed. 1993. (Illus.). 128p. (YA). (gr. 6-10). pap. 12.95 (0-86534-190-7) Sunstone Pr.

Alpert, Cathryn. Rocket City. 1996. (Vintage Contemporaries Ser.). 368p. pap. 13.00 (0-679-77016-X, Vintage) Knopf Publishing Group.

—Rocket City. 1995. 347p. 22.95 o.p. (1-878448-62-5) MacMurray & Beck, Inc.

Anaya, Rudolfo A. Albuquerque. 1992. 13.04 (0-606-06168-1) Turtleback Bks.

—Albuquerque. 1992. 288p. 22.50 o.p. (0-8263-1359-0) Univ. of New Mexico Pr.

—Albuquerque. 1994. 304p. mass mkt. 7.50 (0-446-36544-0); 2000. 336p. reprint ed. pap. 13.95 (0-446-67615-2) Warner Bks., Inc.

—Bless Me, Ultima. 3rd ed. pap. text 14.00 (0-13-800194-4); pap. text, stu. ed. (0-13-772567-1) Prentice Hall (Schl. Div.).

—Bless Me, Ultima. 1976. 249p. pap. 11.95 o.p. (0-89229-002-1) TQS Pubns., Eclectic Chicano Literature.

—Bless Me, Ultima. 1994. 13.04 (0-606-06238-6); 1988. (J). 10.65 (0-606-04174-5) Turtleback Bks.

—Bless Me, Ultima. 1994. (Illus.). 288p. 19.95 o.p. (0-446-51783-6); 1994. (Illus.). 272p. mass mkt. 6.99 (0-446-60025-3); 25th ed. 1999. 304p. reprint ed. pap. 12.95 (0-446-67536-9) Warner Bks., Inc.

—Heart of Aztlan. 1988. 209p. reprint ed. pap. 14.95 (0-8263-1054-0) Univ. of New Mexico Pr.

—Rio Grande Fall. 1997. 352p. mass mkt. 6.99 (0-446-60486-0); 1996. 368p. 23.00 o.p. (0-446-51844-1) Warner Bks., Inc.

—Shaman Winter. 2000. 432p. mass mkt. 7.50 (0-446-60801-7); 1999. (Illus.). 374p. 30.00 o.p. (0-446-52374-7) Warner Bks., Inc.

—Zia Summer. 1996. 13.04 (0-606-17163-0) Turtleback Bks.

—Zia Summer. 1996. 368p. mass mkt. 7.50 (0-446-60316-3); 1995. 400p. (YA). 21.95 o.p. (0-446-51843-3) Warner Bks., Inc.

Anaya, Rudolfo A., ed. Tierra: Contemporary Short Fiction of New Mexico. 1989. 258p. (Orig.). pap. 12.95 o.p. (0-938317-09-1) Cinco Puntos Pr.

Arnold, Elliott. The Time of the Gringo. 626p. reprint ed. lib. bdg. 30.95 (0-88411-180-6) Amereon, Ltd.

Arnold, Marilyn. Fields of Clover: A Novel. 2002. 286p. pap. 16.95 (1-55517-601-1, Salt Pr.) Cedar Fort, Inc./CFI Distribution.

Baker, Laura. Raven. 2001. 320p. mass mkt. 6.50 o.s.i (0-312-97709-3, 20-3426, St. Martin's Paperbacks) St. Martin's Pr.

Barr, Nevada. Blind Descent. l.t. ed. 1998. 25.95 o.p. (1-56895-547-2, Wheeler Publishing, Inc.) Gale Group.

—Blind Descent. 1999. (Anna Pigeon Mysteries Ser.). (Illus.). 384p. mass mkt. 7.99 (0-380-72826-5, Avon Bks.) Morrow/Avon.

—Blind Descent. 1998. 352p. (gr. 5 up). 22.95 o.p. (0-399-14371-8, G. P. Putnam's Sons) Penguin Group (USA) Inc.

—Blind Descent. 1999. audio compact disk 99.00; 1998. audio 83.00 (0-7887-2038-4, 95402E7) Recorded Bks., LLC.

Bechko, Peggy A. Cloud Dancer. 2000. (Five Star Romance Ser.). 278p. 26.95 (0-7862-2332-4, Five Star) Gale Group.

Belle, Judith. The Year We Almost Saved the World: Coming of Age with the Class of 2000. 2001. 612p. pap. 28.99 (0-7388-2861-0); text 38.99 (0-7388-2860-2) Xlibris Corp.

Bergren, Lisa Tawn. Christmas Every Morning. 2002. 240p. 12.99 (1-57856-271-6, Shaw) WaterBrook Pr.

Blackburn, Thomas Wakefield. Compadneros. l.t. ed. 2001. (G. K. Hall Paperback Ser.). 245p. pap. 23.95 (0-7838-9415-5, Macmillan Reference USA) Gale Group.

Bly, Stephen A. The General's Notorious Widow. 2001. (Belles of Lordsburg Ser.: Vol. 2). 240p. pap. 10.99 (1-58134-280-2) Crossway Bks.

—The General's Notorious Widow. l.t. ed. 2002. 397p. (Belles of Lordsburg Ser.: No. 2). pap. 16.95 (1-4104-0033-6, Walker Large Print); 26.95 (0-7862-4023-7) Gale Group.

—The Outlaw's Twin Sister. 2002. (Belles of Lordsburg Ser.: 3). 240p. pap. 10.99 (1-58134-359-0) Crossway Bks.

—The Senator's Other Daughter. 2001. (Belles of Lordsburg Ser.: Vol. 1). 236p. pap. 10.99 (1-58134-236-5) Crossway Bks.

—The Senator's Other Daughter. l.t. ed. 2002. 420p. (Belles of Lordsburg Ser.: No. 1). pap. 16.95 (1-4104-0035-2, Walker Large Print); 26.95 (0-7862-4026-1) Gale Group.

Bock, Dennis. The Ash Garden. 2001. E-Book 18.50 (1-59061-597-2) Adobe Systems, Inc.

—The Ash Garden. 2003. 304p. pap. 13.00 (0-375-72749-3, Vintage) Knopf Publishing Group.

Boggio, Sue. Sunlight & Shadows. 2004. 320p. pap. 12.95 (0-451-21110-3) NAL.

Bohnaker, Joseph J. Of Arms I Sing: A Novel. Smith, James C., Jr., ed. 1989. (Illus.). 260p. pap. 10.95 (0-86534-136-2) Sunstone Pr.

Bonham, Frank. Rawhide Guns. 2003. 176p. 19.00 (0-7540-8211-3) BBC Audiobooks America.

—Rawhide Guns. 1981. mass mkt. 1.95 o.s.i (0-425-04815-2); 1978. mass mkt. 1.50 o.s.i (0-425-03817-3) Berkley Publishing Group.

—Rawhide Guns. l.t. ed. 1997. (Nightingale Ser.). pap. 17.95 o.p. (0-7838-1977-3, Macmillan Reference USA) Gale Group.

Booth, Pat. Marry Me. l.t. ed. 1996. (G. K. Hall Core Ser.). 528p. lib. bdg. 25.95 (0-7838-1865-3, Macmillan Reference USA) Gale Group.

—Marry Me. 1997. 384p. mass mkt. 5.99 o.s.i (1-57566-191-8) Kensington Publishing Corp.

—Marry Me: A Novel. 1996. 343p. 22.95 o.p. (0-316-10256-3) Little Brown & Co.

Boswell, Robert. American Owned Love. 1998. 336p. pap. 13.00 o.s.i (0-06-097746-9) HarperCollins Pubs.

—American Owned Love. 1997. 323p. 24.00 o.s.i (0-679-43251-5) Knopf, Alfred A. Inc.

Boyer, Glenn G. Winchester Affidavit. l.t. ed. 1997. (Western Ser.). 325p. 18.95 (0-7862-0739-6, Five Star) Gale Group.

Bradford, Richard. Red Sky at Morning. 1999. o.s.i (0-06-093210-4) HarperCollins Pubs.

—Red Sky at Morning. 1986. 256p. reprint ed. pap. 13.00 o.p. (0-06-091361-4, PL/1361, Perennial) HarperTrade.

—Red Sky at Morning. 1991. 256p. reprint ed. lib. bdg. 33.00 o.p. (0-8095-9095-6) Millefleurs.

Brewer, Steve. Baby Face. 2000. (Bubba Mabry Mystery Ser.). 256p. mass mkt. 5.95 (1-890768-20-0, Intrigue Pr.) Corvus Publishing.

—Baby Face. 1995. (Illus.). 256p. (J). mass mkt. 5.50 (0-671-74735-5, Pocket) Simon & Schuster.

—Dirty Pool. 2003. (WWL Mystery Ser.: No. 462). 272p. mass mkt. (0-373-26462-3, Worldwide Library) Harlequin Enterprises, Ltd.

—Dirty Pool. 1999. 272p. 23.95 o.p. (0-312-20203-2, Saint Martin's Minotaur) St. Martin's Pr.

—Lonely Street. unabr. ed. 1999. (Bubba Mabry Mystery Ser.). audio 39.95 (1-55686-867-7) Books in Motion.

—Lonely Street. 1999. (Bubba Mabry Mystery Ser.: No. 1). 256p. mass mkt. 5.95 (1-890768-19-7, Intrigue Pr.) Corvus Publishing.

—Lonely Street. Grad, Doug, ed. 1994. 224p. mass mkt. 4.99 (0-671-74734-7, Pocket) Simon & Schuster.

—Shaky Ground. 2003. (WWL Mystery Ser.: No. 454). 256p. mass mkt. (0-373-26454-2, Worldwide Library) Harlequin Enterprises, Ltd.

—Shaky Ground. 1997. 233p. 22.95 o.p. (0-312-15652-9, Saint Martin's Minotaur) St. Martin's Pr.

—Witchy Woman. 1996. 208p. 21.95 o.p. (0-312-14076-2, Saint Martin's Minotaur) St. Martin's Pr.

—Witchy Woman: A Bubba Mabry P. I. Mystery. 1999. (Bubba Mabry Mystery Ser.). 256p. reprint ed. mass mkt. 5.95 (1-890768-13-8, Intrigue Pr.) Corvus Publishing.

Brown, Sam. Devil's Rim. 1997. 224p. 21.95 o.p. (0-8027-4161-4) Walker & Co.

Brown, Sandra. Eloquent Silence. 1997. 272p. 22.00 o.p. (0-7278-4982-4) Severn Hse. Pubs., Ltd.

—Eloquent Silence. 1995. 288p. reprint ed. mass mkt. 6.99 (0-446-36051-1) Warner Bks., Inc.

—The Standoff. l.t. ed. 2000. 336p. 19.95 (0-375-43054-7) Random Hse. Large Print.

—The Standoff. unabr. ed. 2000. audio 25.00 (0-7435-0513-1, Simon & Schuster Audioworks) Simon & Schuster Audio.

—The Standoff. 2001. 272p. E-Book 4.95 (0-446-96028-4); 2000. 224p. 19.95 (0-446-52701-7) Warner Bks., Inc.

Brummett, Curt. Welcome to Querecho Flats. 1995. (Illus.). 112p. pap. 9.95 o.p. (0-87905-697-5) Smith, Gibbs Pub.

Bryant, Grady L. Roswell One. 1999. 232p. pap. 5.99 (0-9671506-0-4) Red River Pr.

Bullis, Don. Bloodville. 2002. 347p. per. 14.95 (1-888725-75-3, BeachHouse Bks.); per. (1-888725-76-1, MacroPrintBooks) Science & Humanities Pr.

Burroughs, Jean M. Bride of the Santa Fe Trail: A Novel. 1984. 160p. pap. 9.95 (0-86534-042-0) Sunstone Pr.

Butler, Robert Olen. Countrymen of Bones. 1985. 256p. mass mkt. 2.95 o.s.i (0-345-32118-9) Ballantine Bks.

—Countrymen of Bones. 1994. 25.00 o.p. (0-8050-3202-9); 224p. pap. 11.00 o.s.i (0-8050-3142-1, Owl Bks.) Holt, Henry & Co.

Camp, Will. Blood Saga. 240p. 1996. mass mkt. 2.50 o.p. (0-06-101118-5); 1994. mass mkt. 3.99 o.p. (0-06-100800-1) Morrow/Avon. (HarperTorch).

Candelaria, Nash. Inheritance of Strangers. 1985. 272p. pap. text 17.00 (0-916950-59-X); lib. bdg. 27.00 (0-916950-58-1) Bilingual Pr./Editorial Bilingüe.

Castillo, Ana. So Far from God: A Novel. 1994. 256p. pap. 14.00 (0-452-27209-2, Plume) Dutton/Plume.

—So Far from God: A Novel. 1993. 256p. 19.95 o.p. (0-393-03490-9) Norton, W. W. & Co., Inc.

—So Far from God: A Novel. 1994. 20.05 (0-606-22208-1) Turtleback Bks.

Cather, Willa. Death Comes for the Archbishop. 1976. 24.95 (0-8488-0448-1) Amereon, Ltd.

—Death Comes for the Archbishop. 1986. 304p. pap. 11.95 o.p. (0-553-06416-9) Bantam Bks.

—Death Comes for the Archbishop. 1992. reprint ed. lib. bdg. 19.95 (0-89966-978-6) Buccaneer Bks., Inc.

—Death Comes for the Archbishop. l.t. ed. 2001. 300p. 28.95 (0-7838-9634-4, Hall, G. K. & Co.) Gale Group.

—Death Comes for the Archbishop. 1990. 304p. pap. 11.00 (0-679-72889-9, Vintage) Knopf Publishing Group.

—Death Comes for the Archbishop. 1992. (Everyman's Library: Vol. 89). 336p. 15.00 (*0-679-41319-7*); 1927. 25.00 o.s.i (*0-394-42154-X*) Knopf, Alfred A. Inc.
—Death Comes for the Archbishop. 1984. 15.00 o.s.i (*0-394-60503-9*); 1971. pap. 6.95 o.p. (*0-394-71679-5*); 19th ed. 1993. 368p. 15.95 (*0-679-60050-7*) Random Hse., Inc.
—Death Comes for the Archbishop. 1971. (Vintage Classics). 16.05 (*0-606-01551-5*) Turtleback Bks.
—Death Comes for the Archbishop. 1999. (Willa Cather Scholarly Edition Ser.). (Illus.). 642p. text 70.00 (*0-8032-1429-4*) Univ. of Nebraska Pr.
Cave, Dorothy. Song on a Blue Guitar: A Novel. 2002. 190p. pap. 18.95 (*0-86534-349-7*) Sunstone Pr.
Chavez, Denise. Loving Pedro Infante. 2001. 325p. 24.00 (*0-374-19411-4*) Farrar, Straus & Giroux.
—Loving Pedro Infante. 2002. 336p. pap. 13.00 (*0-7434-4573-2*, Washington Square Pr.) Simon & Schuster.
Clarke, Richard. The Guns of Peralta. l.t. ed. 1994. 216p. lib. bdg. 18.95 o.p. (*0-8161-5963-7*, Macmillan Reference USA) Gale Group.
—The Guns of Peralta. 1993. 200p. 19.95 (*0-8027-1275-4*) Walker & Co.
—The Peralta Country. 1989. 2.49 o.p. (*0-517-00522-0*) Random Hse. Value Publishing.
—The Peralta Country. 1987. 192p. 15.95 (*0-8027-0949-4*) Walker & Co.
Cohen, Robert. The Organ Builder: A Novel. 1988. 288p. 17.95 o.p. (*0-06-015909-X*) HarperTrade.
Collignon, Rick. A Santo in the Image of Cristobal Garcia. 2003. 288p. pap. 14.00 (*0-425-19313-6*); 2002. 271p. 24.95 (*0-399-14921-X*) Putnam Publishing Group, The. (BlueHen Bks.).
Cooley, Lee. Judgment at Red Creek. 1992. (Novel of the West Ser.). 16.95 o.p. (*0-87131-671-4*) Evans, M. & Co., Inc.
Coolidge, Dane. Under the Sun. l.t. ed. 1995. (Nightingale Ser.). 312p. pap. 16.95 (*0-7838-1147-0*, Macmillan Reference USA) Gale Group.
Cox, Greg. Loose Ends. 2001. (Roswell Ser.: Vol. 1). 288p. (YA). mass mkt. 6.99 (*0-7434-1834-4*, Simon Pulse) Simon & Schuster Children's Publishing.
Dallas, Sandra. The Chili Queen: A Novel. l.t. ed. 2003. lib. bdg. 29.95 (*1-58547-265-4*, Platinum) Ctr. Point Large Print.
—The Chili Queen: A Novel. E-Book 16.95 (*0-312-70782-7*); 2003. 304p. pap. 13.95 (*0-312-32026-4*, Saint Martin's Griffin); 2002. 304p. 22.95 (*0-312-30349-1*) St. Martin's Pr.
Dark Winter. 1991. 208p. 15.00 o.s.i (*0-385-26568-9*) Doubleday Publishing.
David, Kay. Disappear. 2002. (Harlequin Superromance Ser.: No. 1074). 296p. mass mkt. (*0-373-71074-7*, Harlequin Bks.) Harlequin Enterprises, Ltd.
Davis, Val. Track of the Scorpion. 1997. (Nicolette Scott Mystery Ser.). 336p. mass mkt. 5.50 o.s.i (*0-553-57728-X*) Bantam Bks.
—Track of the Scorpion. 1996. 320p. 22.95 (*0-312-14437-7*) St. Martin's Pr.
Davis, Wayne. John Stone & the Choctaw Kid. 1992. 16.95 o.p. (*0-87131-693-5*) Evans, M. & Co., Inc.
—John Stone & the Choctaw Kid. l.t. ed. 1999. (Western Ser.). 404p. 25.95 o.p. (*0-7838-8728-0*) Thorndike Pr.
Dawson, Clarence. Desert Vendetta. 1993. 260p. pap. 12.95 o.p. (*0-86534-205-9*) Sunstone Pr.
Dressman, John. On the Cliffs of Acoma: A Story for Children. Ortega, Pedro R., tr. from SPA. 1984. (Illus.). 32p. (J). (ps-7). pap. 5.95 (*0-86534-021-8*) Sunstone Pr.
Eastlake, William. The Bronc People. 1991. 254p. pap. 11.00 o.p. (*0-9627387-5-1*) Bamberger Bks.
—The Bronc People. 1975. (Zia Bks.). 263p. reprint ed. pap. 8.95 o.p. (*0-8263-0379-X*) Univ. of New Mexico Pr.
—Go in Beauty. 1991. 279p. pap. 11.00 o.p. (*0-9627387-3-5*) Bamberger Bks.
—Go in Beauty. 1980. (Zia Bks.). 286p. pap. 8.95 o.p. (*0-8263-0538-5*) Univ. of New Mexico Pr.
—Lyric of the Circle Heart: The Bowman Family Trilogy. rev. ed. 1996. 518p. pap. 14.95 (*1-56478-136-4*) Dalkey Archive Pr.
—Portrait of an Artist with Twenty-Six Horses. 1991. 221p. pap. 11.00 o.p. (*0-9627387-4-3*) Bamberger Bks.
—Portrait of an Artist with Twenty-Six Horses. 1980. (Zia Bks.). 230p. reprint ed. pap. 8.95 o.p. (*0-8263-0558-X*) Univ. of New Mexico Pr.
Eidson, Tom. The Last Ride. 1995. 352p. mass mkt. 6.99 o.s.i (*0-515-11741-2*, Jove) Berkley Publishing Group.
—The Last Ride. l.t. ed. 1995. (Large Print Bks.). 23.95 (*1-56895-241-4*, Wheeler Publishing, Inc.) Gale Group.
—The Last Ride. 1995. 21.95 o.p. (*0-399-14057-3*, G. P. Putnam's Sons) Penguin Group (USA) Inc.
—St. Agnes' Stand. 1994. 224p. mass mkt. 4.99 o.s.i (*0-425-14396-1*) Berkley Publishing Group.
—St. Agnes' Stand. 1994. 224p. 19.95 o.p. (*0-399-13915-X*) Penguin Group (USA) Inc.
Elkins, Charlotte & Elkins, Aaron. A Golf Mystery. 1924. (*0-688-16495-1*); (*0-688-16496-X*) Morrow/Avon. (Morrow, William & Co.).
—Nasty Breaks. unabr. ed. audio 27.95 (*0-7861-1384-7*); 1999. audio 39.95 (*0-7861-1244-1*, 2153) Blackstone Audio Bks., Inc.
—Nasty Breaks. 1997. 240p. 22.00 o.p. (*0-89296-596-7*) Mysterious Pr.
—Nasty Breaks. unabr. ed. 1998. audio 44.00 (*0-7887-2001-5*, 95388E7) Recorded Bks., LLC.
—Nasty Breaks. l.t. ed. 1998. (Cloak & Dagger Ser.). 335p. 27.95 (*0-7862-1445-7*) Thorndike Pr.
—Rotten Lies. 1995. 82p. 19.95 o.p. (*0-89296-598-3*) Mysterious Pr.
—Rotten Lies. 1997. 224p. mass mkt. 5.99 o.p. (*0-446-40452-7*, Mysterious Pr. Paperback Bks.) Warner Bks., Inc.
—A Wicked Slice. 1990. 192p. mass mkt. 5.50 o.s.i (*0-449-14686-3*, Fawcett) Ballantine Bks.
—A Wicked Slice. 1989. 14.95 o.p. (*0-312-03003-7*, Saint Martin's Minotaur) St. Martin's Pr.
Encinias, M. Two Lives for Onate. 1997. (Paso Por Aqvi Ser.). 231p. 45.00 (*0-8263-1777-4*); pap. 19.95 (*0-8263-1782-0*) Univ. of New Mexico Pr.
Estleman, Loren D. City of Widows. 1995. 254p. pap. text 5.99 (*0-8125-3538-3*); 1994. 256p. 20.95 o.p. (*0-312-85667-9*) Doherty, Tom Assocs., LLC. (Forge Bks.).
Evans, Max. Faraway Blue. 2000. 304p. mass mkt. 6.99 (*0-8125-7076-6*); 1998. (Illus.). 303p. 22.95 (*0-312-86749-2*) Doherty, Tom Assocs., LLC. (Forge Bks.).
—Now & Forever: A Novel of Love & Betrayal Reincarnate. 2003. 176p. 21.95 (*0-8263-3318-4*) Univ. of New Mexico Pr.
Fackler, Elizabeth. Texas Lily. 416p. 2000. pap. 14.95 (*0-312-87380-8*); 2000. pap. 14.95 o.p. (*0-312-57763-X*); 1997. 25.95 o.p. (*0-312-85912-0*) Doherty, Tom Assocs., LLC. (Forge Bks.).
—A Texas Lily. 1999. mass mkt. (*0-8125-7763-9*, Forge Bks.) Doherty, Tom Assocs., LLC.
Farrell, Cliff. Terror in Eagle Basin. 2001. 218p. (*0-7540-4406-8*); (*0-7540-4405-X*) Gale Group. (Macmillan Reference USA).
—Terror in Eagle Basin. l.t. ed. 2001. (G. K. Hall Nightingale Ser.). 218p. 22.95 (*0-7838-9321-3*) Thorndike Pr.
Fink, Jon S. Further Adventures. 1992. 24.95 o.p. (*0-312-08787-X*); pap. 14.95 o.p. (*0-312-09059-5*, Saint Martin's Griffin) St. Martin's Pr.
Fleming, David L. Border Crossings. 1993. 304p. (C). 24.50 (*0-87565-116-X*); pap. 14.95 (*0-87565-117-8*) Texas Christian Univ. Pr.
—Border Crossings. 1993. E-Book 24.50 (*0-585-35547-9*) netLibrary, Inc.
Flynn, T. T. The Man from Nowhere. l.t. ed. 1994. 19.95 o.p. (*0-7927-2162-4*); pap. 18.95 o.p. (*0-7927-2161-6*) BBC Audiobooks America.
—The Man from Nowhere. l.t. ed. 2000. (G. K. Hall Paperback Ser.). 241p. pap. 23.95 (*0-7838-9025-7*, Macmillan Reference USA) Gale Group.
Foster, Barbara Spencer. Girl of the Manzanos. 2002. pap. 16.95 (*0-86534-331-4*); 2001. 176p. 22.95 (*0-86534-313-6*) Sunstone Pr.
Frieder, Patricia. Privileged Communications. 2000. 288p. mass mkt. 5.50 o.s.i (*0-553-57613-5*) Bantam Bks.
Gallegos, Eloy J. Jacona: An Epic Story of the Spanish Southwest. 1996. (Spanish Pioneers Ser.: Vol. I). (Illus.). 377p. pap. 13.50 (*1-882194-22-5*) Tennessee Valley Publishing.
Gallegos, Sally. Stone Horses. 1996. 272p. 16.95 (*0-8263-1666-2*) Univ. of New Mexico Pr.
Garcia, Diana. Aviso Oportuno. 2000. (Encanto Ser.). (SPA.). mass mkt. 3.99 o.s.i (*0-7860-1142-4*) Kensington Publishing Corp.
—Help Wanted. 2000. (Encanto Ser.). 368p. mass mkt. 5.99 o.s.i (*0-7860-1138-6*) Kensington Publishing Corp.
Garcia, Ricardo L. Coal Camp Days: A Boy's Remembrance. 2001. (Illus.). viii, 278p. 24.95 (*0-8263-2304-9*); pap. (*0-8263-2305-7*) Univ. of New Mexico Pr.
Gatewood, Robert Payne. The Sound of the Trees: A Novel. 2002. 304p. 25.00 o.s.i (*0-8050-6802-3*) Holt, Henry & Co.
—The Sound of the Trees: A Novel. 2003. 304p. pap. 14.00 (*0-312-42188-5*) Picador.
Gear, Kathleen O'Neal & Gear, W. Michael. Bone Walker. 2002. (Illus.). 352p. 26.95 (*0-312-87742-0*, Forge Bks.) Doherty, Tom Assocs., LLC.
—The Summoning God. (Illus.). 366p. pap. 15.95 (*0-312-87639-4*, Forge Bks.); 2000. (Anasazia Mysteries Ser.: Vol. 2). (Illus.). 352p. 25.95 (*0-312-86532-5*, Forge Bks.); 2001. (Anasazi Ser.). 576p. reprint ed. mass mkt. 7.99 (*0-8125-4034-4*, Tor Bks.) Doherty, Tom Assocs., LLC.
—The Visitant. (Anasazia Mysteries Ser.: Vol. 1). (Illus.). 2000. 501p. mass mkt. 6.99 (*0-8125-4033-6*, Tor Bks.); 1999. 364p. 19.95 (*0-312-86531-7*, Forge Bks.) Doherty, Tom Assocs., LLC.
Glasco, Michael. Angels in Tesuque: A Novel. 1995. 160p. 24.95 (*0-86534-103-6*); pap. 14.95 (*0-86534-071-4*) Sunstone Pr.
Goldberg, Natalie. The Banana Rose. 1995. 384p. 21.95 o.s.i (*0-553-09527-7*) Bantam Bks.
Gonzalez de Mireles, Jovita. The Woman Who Lost Her Soul: Collected Tales & Short Stories. Reyna, Sergio, ed. 2000. (Recovering the U. S. - Hispanic Literary Heritage Ser.). xxx, 157p. pap. 12.95 (*1-55885-313-8*) Arte Publico Pr.
Grammer, Maurine. The Navajo Brothers & the Stolen Herd. 2004. (Illus.). 120p. (J). (gr. 4-7). pap. 9.95 (*1-878610-23-6*) Red Crane Bks., Inc.
Grey, Zane. Open Range: A Western Story. l.t. ed. 2002. (Five Star First Edition Western Ser.). 179p. 25.95 (*0-7862-3260-9*) Gale Group.
—Open Range: A Western Story. 2003. (Western Ser.). 26.95 (*0-7862-3261-7*) Thorndike Pr.
Grove, Fred. Destiny Valley. 2001. 224p. reprint ed. mass mkt. 4.50 (*0-8439-4924-4*, Leisure Bks.) Dorchester Publishing Co., Inc.
—Destiny Valley. 2000. (Western Ser.). 221p. 21.95 (*0-7862-2116-X*, Five Star) Gale Group.
Haddrill, Marilyn & Holmes, Doris. Sting of the Scorpion. 1994. 216p. (Orig.). pap. 9.95 (*0-9623682-9-6*) Arroyo Pr.
Haley, Michael C. Durango Gold. 2000. 397p. mass mkt. 6.99 (*0-9701862-0-7*) Poncha Pr.
Hall, Sands. Catching Heaven. E-Book 12.50 (*1-930161-77-8*) Adobe Systems, Inc.
—Catching Heaven. 2001. (Reader's Circle Ser.). 400p. pap. 14.00 (*0-345-44000-5*, Ballantine Bks.) Ballantine Bks.
Hamilton, Laurell K. Obsidian Butterfly: An Anita Blake Vampire Hunter Novel. 2000. (Anita Blake Ser.). 400p. 21.95 (*0-441-00684-1*); 608p. reprint ed. mass mkt. 7.50 o.s.i (*0-441-00781-3*) Ace Bks.
—Obsidian Butterfly: An Anita Blake Vampire Hunter Novel. 2002. 608p. mass mkt. 7.99 (*0-515-13450-3*) Berkley Publishing Group.
Harper, Karen. Empty Cradle. l.t. ed. 2000. 342p. 26.95 (*1-57490-282-2*, Beeler Large Print Bks.) Beeler, Thomas T. Publisher.
—Empty Cradle. 1998. 448p. mass mkt. 6.50 o.s.i (*0-451-19482-9*, Signet Bks.) NAL.
Harrigan, Lana M. Acoma: A Novel of Conquest. 383p. 1999. pap. 16.95 (*0-312-87251-8*); 1997. 25.95 (*0-312-85257-6*) Doherty, Tom Assocs., LLC. (Forge Bks.).
Havill, Steven F. Bag Limit. 2002. (WWL Mystery Ser.: No. 441). 256p. mass mkt. (*0-373-26441-0*, Worldwide Library) Harlequin Enterprises, Ltd.
—Bag Limit: A Sheriff Bill Gastner Mystery. 2001. (Illus.). 336p. 24.95 (*0-312-25183-1*, Saint Martin's Minotaur) St. Martin's Pr.
—Before She Dies. 1996. 288p. 21.95 o.p. (*0-312-13927-6*, Saint Martin's Minotaur) St. Martin's Pr.
—Bitter Recoil. 2000. (Missing Mysteries Ser.: Vol. 26). 192p. pap. 14.95 (*1-890208-40-X*) Poisoned Pen Pr.
—Bitter Recoil. 1992. 240p. 17.95 o.p. (*0-312-07656-8*, Saint Martin's Minotaur) St. Martin's Pr.
—Dead Weight. 2000. (Undersheriff Bill Gastner Mysteries Ser.). (Illus.). 280p. 23.95 (*0-312-25203-X*, Saint Martin's Minotaur) St. Martin's Pr.
—Heartshot. 2000. (Missing Mysteries Ser.: Vol. 16). 210p. pap. 14.95 (*1-890208-29-9*) Poisoned Pen Pr.
—Heartshot. 1991. text 16.95 o.p. (*0-312-05442-4*, Saint Martin's Minotaur) St. Martin's Pr.
—Out of Season. 2001. (WWL Mystery Ser.: No. 382). 251p. mass mkt. (*0-373-26382-1*, 1-26382-1, Worldwide Library) Harlequin Enterprises, Ltd.
—Out of Season. 1999. 304p. 23.95 (*0-312-24414-2*, Saint Martin's Minotaur) St. Martin's Pr.
—Privileged to Kill. 1996. 224p. 21.95 o.p. (*0-312-15196-9*, Saint Martin's Minotaur) St. Martin's Pr.
—Prolonged Exposure. 1998. (Undersheriff Bill Gastner Mysteries Ser.). 272p. 21.95 o.p. (*0-312-18158-2*, Saint Martin's Minotaur) St. Martin's Pr.
—The Scavengers: A Posadas County Mystery. 2002. (Illus.). 352p. 24.95 (*0-312-28833-6*, Saint Martin's Minotaur) St. Martin's Pr.
—Twice Buried, Vol. 28. 2000. (Missing Mysteries Ser.: Vol. 28). pap. 14.95 (*1-890208-46-9*) Poisoned Pen Pr.
—Twice Buried. 1994. 224p. 19.95 o.p. (*0-312-10566-5*, Saint Martin's Minotaur) St. Martin's Pr.
Hendricks, Judith R. Isabel's Daughter. 2004. 400p. pap. 13.95 (*0-06-050347-5*, Perennial) HarperTrade.
—Isabel's Daughter. 2003. 400p. 24.95 (*0-06-050346-7*, Morrow, William & Co.) Morrow/Avon.
Hendrie, Laura. Remember Me. 1999. 384p. 24.00 o.s.i (*0-8050-6218-1*) Holt, Henry & Co.
—Remember Me: A Novel. l.t. ed. 2000. (Americana Ser.). 624p. 29.95 (*0-7862-2453-3*) Thorndike Pr.
Hillerman, Tony. Dance Hall of the Dead. abr. ed. 1986. audio 15.95 (*0-88690-127-8*, N20024, Audio Editions Bks. on Cassette) Audio Partners Publishing Corp.
—Dance Hall of the Dead. unabr. ed. 1994. audio 36.00 (*0-7366-2610-7*, 3352) Books on Tape, Inc.
—Dance Hall of the Dead. 1997. lib. bdg. 37.95 (*1-56849-695-8*) Buccaneer Bks., Inc.
—Dance Hall of the Dead. 2004. 224p. pap. 11.95 (*0-06-056374-5*); 1990. 272p. reprint ed. mass mkt. 6.99 (*0-06-100002-7*) HarperTrade. (Perennial).
—Dance Hall of the Dead. 1993. audio 37.20 (*1-56544-025-0*, 250021); audio Literate Ear, Inc.
—Dance Hall of the Dead. 1982. (YA). (gr. 9 up). mass mkt. 2.95 o.p. (*0-380-00217-5*, 60093-5, Avon Bks.) Morrow/Avon.
—Dance Hall of the Dead. unabr. ed. 1991. (Joe Leaphorn Mystery Ser.: Vol. 2). (YA). (gr. 10). audio 44.00 (*1-55690-134-8*, 91122E7) Recorded Bks., LLC.
—Dance Hall of the Dead. l.t. ed. 1994. (Paperback Bestsellers Ser.). 239p. pap. 20.95 (*0-8161-5433-3*) Thorndike Pr.
—Dance Hall of the Dead. 1990. 12.55 (*0-606-16124-4*) Turtleback Bks.
—The Wailing Wind. 2002. (Illus.). 240p. 25.95 (*0-06-019444-8*); E-Book 19.95 (*0-06-054703-0*); E-Book (*0-06-054708-1*) HarperCollins Pubs.
—The Wailing Wind. l.t. ed. 2002. 320p. pap. 25.95 (*0-06-009388-9*, HarperLargePrint) HarperTrade.
—The Wailing Wind. 2003. 368p. mass mkt. 7.99 (*0-06-109879-5*, HarperTorch) Morrow/Avon.
—The Wailing Wind. unabr. ed. 2002. audio 48.00 (*1-4025-2393-9*) Recorded Bks., LLC.
Hodgson, Ken. Surviving Wisdom. 2003. 218p. 25.95 (*0-7862-5437-8*, Five Star) Gale Group.
Hogan, Ray. Bounty Hunter's Moon. l.t. ed. 2000. (Western Ser.). 201p. 22.95 (*0-7862-2421-5*); (*0-7540-4098-4*); (*0-7540-4097-6*) Thorndike Pr.
—A Bullet for Mr. Texas. 1979. mass mkt. 1.95 o.p. (*0-451-08563-9*, J8563); 1971. mass mkt. 0.60 o.p. (*0-451-04583-1*) NAL. (Signet Bks.).
—Day of the Hangman. l.t. ed. 2000. (G. K. Hall Western Ser.). 187p. 24.95 (*0-7838-9023-0*, Macmillan Reference USA) Gale Group.
—Deputy of Violence. 1971. mass mkt. 0.60 o.p. (*0-451-04522-X*, Signet Bks.) NAL.
—Deputy of Violence. l.t. ed. 1999. (Western Ser.). 203p. 25.95 (*0-7838-0438-5*) Thorndike Pr.
—Killer on the Warbucket. l.t. ed. 1995. (G. K. Hall Nightingale Ser.). 132p. pap. 17.95 o.p. (*0-7838-1282-5*, Macmillan Reference USA) Gale Group.
—A Marshal for Lawless. l.t. ed. 1995. 144p. reprint ed. pap. 17.95 o.p. (*0-7838-1281-7*, Macmillan Reference USA) Gale Group.
Holt, A. J. Watch Me. abr. ed. 1995. 24.95 o.p. (*0-7871-0521-X*) NewStar Media, Inc.
—Watch Me. 1996. 370p. mass mkt. 6.99 (*0-312-95997-4*, St. Martin's Paperbacks); 1995. 336p. 22.95 (*0-312-13614-5*) St. Martin's Pr.
Horgan, Paul. The Thin Mountain Air. 1977. 336p. 8.95 o.p. (*0-374-27466-5*) Farrar, Straus & Giroux.
Horsley, Kate. A Killing in New Town. 1995. 286p. pap. 14.00 (*0-9631909-6-2*) La Alameda Pr.
Howard, Linda. A Lady of the West. l.t. ed. 2002. (Thorndike Press Large Print Famous Authors Ser.). 559p. 28.95 (*0-7862-2852-0*) Gale Group.
—A Lady of the West. 1997. 384p. mass mkt. 7.99 (*0-671-01973-2*, Pocket) Simon & Schuster.
—A Lady of the West. Zion, Claire, ed. 1990. 384p. mass mkt. 5.99 (*0-671-66080-2*, Pocket) Simon & Schuster.
Hudson, Janis Reams. Apache Flame. 1996. mass mkt. 4.99 o.s.i (*0-8217-5290-1*, Zebra Bks.) Kensington Publishing Corp.
Hulme, Joy N. The Other Side of the Door. 1990. 168p. (J). (gr. 3-6). pap. 4.95 (*0-87579-412-2*) Deseret Bk. Co.
Jacoby, Kathleen. Vision of the Grail: A Spiritual Adventure at the Dawn of the 21st Century. 2001. 304p. (Orig.). 14.95 (*1-930126-07-7*) Lightlines Publishing Co.
Johnson, Bett Reece. The Woman Who Knew Too Much: A Cordelia Morgan Mystery. 1998. (Cordelia Morgan Mysteries Ser.). 250p. pap. 12.95 (*1-57344-045-0*) Cleis Pr.
Johnson, Willa. Love Denied. 2000. 64p. pap. 6.95 (*1-58597-016-6*) Leathers Publishing.
Johnston, Terry C. A Crack in the Sky. 1997. 496p. 23.95 o.s.i (*0-553-09078-X*); 1998. 672p. reprint ed. mass mkt. 7.50 (*0-553-57284-9*) Bantam Bks.
—Death Rattle. 2000. 592p. mass mkt. 6.99 (*0-553-57286-5*) Bantam Bks.
—Ride the Moon Down: The Plainsmen. 1999. 592p. mass mkt. 6.99 (*0-553-57282-2*) Bantam Bks.
Johnstone, William W. Cunning of the Mountain Man. 320p. 1995. mass mkt. 4.99 o.s.i (*0-8217-5362-2*); 1994. mass mkt. 3.99 o.s.i (*0-8217-4723-1*) Kensington Publishing Corp. (Zebra Bks.).
—Cunning of the Mountain Man. l.t. ed. 2003. 25.95 (*0-7862-4630-8*) Thorndike Pr.
—Triumph of the Mountain Man. abr. ed. 1999. audio 16.95 (*1-882071-92-1*) B&B Audio, Inc.
—Triumph of the Mountain Man. 1997. 288p. mass mkt. 4.99 o.s.i (*0-8217-5551-X*, Zebra Bks.) Kensington Publishing Corp.

Jones, D. J. H. Murder in the New Age. 192p. 2000. pap. 13.95 (0-8263-2236-0); 1997. 19.95 (0-8263-1813-4) Univ. of New Mexico Pr.

Joynes, Monty. Save the Good Seed: A Novel. 1999. (Booker Ser.: Vol. 3). 288p. pap. 12.95 (1-57174-130-5) Hampton Roads Publishing Co., Inc.

Kanon, Joseph. Los Alamos. 1998. 544p. mass mkt. 7.99 (0-440-22407-1) Dell Publishing.

— Los Alamos. l.t. ed. 1997. (Large Print Book Ser.). 26.95 o.p. (1-56895-506-5, Wheeler Publishing, Inc.) Gale Group.

Kauffman, Donna. His Private Pleasure. 2002. (Harlequin Blaze Ser.). mass mkt. (0-373-79050-3, Harlequin Bks.) Harlequin Enterprises, Ltd.

Kelby, N. M. Theatre of the Stars: A Novel of Physics & Memory. Date not set. 23.95 (0-7868-6858-9) Hyperion Pr.

Kingston, Meredith. Longing Unveiled. 2000. (Five Star Romance Ser.). 173p. 26.95 (0-7862-2945-4, Five Star) Gale Group.

Lenard-Cook, Lisa. Dissonance: A Novel. 2003. 186p. 21.95 (0-8263-3090-8) Univ. of New Mexico Pr.

Littell, Robert. Walking Back the Cat. 1997. 224p. 23.95 (0-87951-764-6) Overlook Pr., The.

—Walking Back the Cat. 1997. 21.00 (0-679-43567-0) Random Hse., Inc.

Long, Jeff. Year Zero. 2002. 416p. 25.00 (0-7434-0611-7); E-Book 6.99 (0-7434-8231-X) Simon & Schuster. (Atria).

Lovett, Sarah. Acquired Motives: A Novel. 1997. mass mkt. 5.99 o.s.i (0-8041-1298-3, Ivy Bks.) Ballantine Bks.

—Acquired Motives: A Novel. aut. ed. 1996. 22.95 o.s.i (0-676-51776-5, Villard Bks.) Random House Adult Trade Publishing Group.

—Acquired Motives: A Novel. 2003. (Illus.). 368p. pap. 6.99 (0-7434-6335-8, Pocket) Simon & Schuster.

—Dangerous Attachments. 1996. 344p. mass mkt. 5.99 o.s.i (0-8041-1297-5, Ivy Bks.) Ballantine Bks.

—Dangerous Attachments: A Dr. Sylvia Strange Novel. 2003. 400p. pap. 6.99 (0-7434-6334-X, Pocket) Simon & Schuster.

—Dante's Inferno. 2001. (Dr. Sylvia Strange Novels Ser.: No. 4). 320p. 24.00 (0-684-85598-4, Simon & Schuster) Simon & Schuster.

—A Desperate Silence: A Novel. 1998. mass mkt. 5.99 o.s.i (0-8041-1299-1, Ivy Bks.) Ballantine Bks.

—A Desperate Silence: A Novel. l.t. ed. 1998. 24.95 (1-57490-152-4) Beeler, Thomas T. Publisher.

—A Desperate Silence: A Novel. 2003. (Illus.). 400p. pap. 7.50 (0-7434-6336-6, Pocket) Simon & Schuster.

Lummis, Charles F. King of the Broncos, & Other Stories of New Mexico. 1977. (Short Story Index Reprint Ser.). 19.95 (0-8369-3598-5) Ayer Co. Pubs., Inc.

Lynn, Mary E. The Tavera Legacy. 1993. 448p. 24.95 o.p. (0-312-93136-0, Forge Bks.) Doherty, Tom Assocs., LLC.

MacLean, Amanda. Westward. 1995. 289p. pap. 9.99 o.p. (0-88070-751-8, Palisades) Multnomah Pubs., Inc.

MacLean, Amanda & Noble, Diane. Westward. l.t. ed. 2001. (Christian Romance Ser.). 434p. 25.95 (0-7862-3480-6) Thorndike Pr.

Major, Ann. Inseparable. 1999. 384p. mass mkt. (1-55166-548-4, 1-66548-8, Mira Bks.) Harlequin Enterprises, Ltd.

—Wild Enough for Willa. 2000. 384p. mass mkt. (1-55166-623-5, 1-66623-9, Mira Bks.) Harlequin Enterprises, Ltd.

Mapson, Jo-Ann. Blue Rodeo: A Novel. 1995. 336p. pap. 13.00 (0-06-092635-X, Perennial); 1994. 352p. 22.00 o.p. (0-06-016944-3) HarperTrade.

—The Wilder Sisters: A Novel. l.t. ed. 2000. 26.95 (1-56895-866-8, Wheeler Publishing, Inc.) Gale Group.

—The Wilder Sisters: A Novel. 1999. 384p. (J). 24.00 (0-06-019116-3) HarperCollins Pubs.

—The Wilder Sisters: A Novel. 2000. 384p. pap. 13.00 (0-06-093107-8, Perennial) HarperTrade.

Martinez, Ruben O. CliffsNotes TM Bless Me, Ultima. 1999. E-Book 5.99 (0-8220-7030-8, Cliff Notes) Wiley, John & Sons, Inc.

McCall, Dan. Messenger Bird. (Harvest Book Ser.). 1994. 228p. pap. 15.00 (0-15-600042-3); 1993. 192p. 19.95 o.s.i (0-15-159284-5) Harcourt Trade Pubs.

McCarthy, Cormac. Cities of the Plain. 1999. (Border Trilogy: Vol. 3). 304p. pap. 13.00 (0-679-74719-2, Vintage) Knopf Publishing Group.

—Cities of the Plain. 1998. (Border Trilogy : Vol.3). 304p. 27.50 (0-679-42390-7) Knopf, Alfred A. Inc.

—Cities of the Plain. ltd. ed. 1998. 292p. 195.00 (1-890885-04-5) Trice, B.E. Publishing.

—The Crossing. 1995. (Border Trilogy: Vol. 2). 432p. pap. 14.00 (0-679-76084-9, Vintage) Knopf Publishing Group.

—The Crossing. 1994. (Border Trilogy : Vol. 2). 432p. 27.50 (0-394-57475-3) Knopf, Alfred A. Inc.

McGarrity, Michael. Everyone Dies. l.t. ed. 2004. lib. bdg. 28.95 (1-58547-374-X, Platinum) Ctr. Point Large Print.

—Everyone Dies. 2003. (Kevin Kerney Novel Ser.). 336p. 23.95 (0-525-94761-2, Dutton) Dutton/Plume.

—Everyone Dies. 2004. 352p. mass mkt. 6.99 (0-451-41147-1, Onyx) NAL.

—Hermit's Peak. l.t. ed. 2001. (Illus.). 310p. 27.95 (1-57490-338-1) Beeler, Thomas T. Publisher.

—Hermit's Peak. (Kevin Kerney Novels Ser.). 1999. (Illus.). 320p. 24.00 o.s.i (0-684-85078-8, Scribner); 2000. 368p. reprint ed. mass mkt. 6.99 (0-671-02147-8, Pocket) Simon & Schuster.

—The Judas Judge. abr. ed. 2000. (Kevin Kerney Novels Ser.). audio 25.00 o.s.i (0-7435-0627-8, Simon & Schuster Audioworks) Simon & Schuster Audio.

—The Judas Judge: A Kevin Kerney Novel. 2000. (Kevin Kerney Novels Ser.). 288p. 23.95 o.s.i (0-525-94547-4, Dutton) Dutton/Plume.

—Mexican Hat. l.t. ed. 2001. (Illus.). 302p. 26.95 (1-57490-379-9, Beeler Large Print Bks.) Beeler, Thomas T. Publisher.

—Mexican Hat. unabr. ed. 1998. (Kevin Kerney Mystery Ser.: Vol. 2). audio 51.00 (0-7887-1892-4, 95314E7) Recorded Bks., LLC.

—Mexican Hat. 1998. (Kevin Kerney Novels Ser.). (Illus.). 336p. mass mkt. 6.50 (0-671-00253-8, Pocket Star) Simon & Schuster.

—The Mexican Hat: A Novel. 1997. 304p. 22.95 (0-393-04063-1) Norton, W. W. & Co., Inc.

—Serpent Gate. l.t. ed. 2000. 307p. 27.95 (1-57490-326-8, Beeler Large Print Bks.) Beeler, Thomas T. Publisher.

—Serpent Gate. (Kevin Kerney Novels Ser.). 1999. (Illus.). 368p. mass mkt. 6.99 (0-671-02146-X, Pocket Star); 1998. 320p. 23.00 o.s.i (0-684-85076-1, Scribner); 1998. 22.50 o.p. (0-684-85345-0, Scribner) Simon & Schuster.

—Serpent Gate. 1999. 12.55 (0-606-19062-7) Turtleback Bks.

—Tularosa. l.t. ed. 1996. pap. 23.95 (1-56895-372-0, Wheeler Publishing, Inc.) Gale Group.

—Tularosa. 1996. 304p. 25.00 (0-393-03922-6) Norton, W. W. & Co., Inc.

—Tularosa. unabr. ed. 2000. (Kevin Kerney Mystery Ser.: Vol. 1). audio 51.00 (0-7887-1767-7, 95245E7) Recorded Bks., LLC.

—Tularosa. 1998. 3.99 (0-671-02373-X, Pocket); 1997. (Illus.). 336p. mass mkt. 6.99 (0-671-00252-X, Pocket Star) Simon & Schuster.

—Under the Color of Law: A Kevin Kerney Novel. 2001. 320p. 23.95 o.p. (0-525-94604-7, Dutton) Dutton/Plume.

—Under the Color of Law: A Kevin Kerney Novel. 2002. 400p. mass mkt. 6.99 (0-451-41044-0, Onyx) NAL.

McIlvoy, Kevin. The Fifth Station. 1988. 224p. 12.95 o.p. (0-912697-76-8) Algonquin Bks. of Chapel Hill.

—Hyssop. 1999. 192p. pap. 12.50 (0-380-73271-8, Avon Bks.) Morrow/Avon.

—Hyssop. 1998. 160p. 28.00 (0-8101-5085-9, TriQuarterly Bks.) Northwestern Univ. Pr.

McMahon, Thomas. Principles of American Nuclear Chemistry: A Novel. 1970. 7.95 o.p. (0-316-56221-1) Little Brown & Co.

McMahon, Thomas A. Principles of American Nuclear Chemistry: A Novel. 2003. (Phoenix Fiction Ser.). 256p. pap. 15.00 (0-226-56110-0) Univ. of Chicago Pr.

Mertz, Stephen. Night Wind. 2003. 277p. pap. 13.95 (1-4104-0135-9, Five Star Trade); 2002. 305p. 26.95 (0-7862-4353-8, Five Star) Gale Group.

—Night Wind. l.t. ed. 2003. 406p. pap. 24.95 (0-7862-5503-X) Thorndike Pr.

Meyers, Harold B. Reservations. 1999. 287p. 24.95 (0-87081-524-5) Univ. Pr. of Colorado.

Mixon, Laura J. & Gould, Steven. Greenwar. 1998. 608p. mass mkt. 6.99 (0-8125-7116-9, Tor Bks.); 1997. 384p. 25.95 (0-312-85261-4, Forge Bks.) Doherty, Tom Assocs., LLC.

Moffat, Gwen. Veronica's Sisters. l.t. ed. 1993. 21.95 o.p. (0-7927-1801-1); pap. 19.95 o.p. (0-7927-1800-3) BBC Audiobooks America.

Morrell, David. Extreme Denial. abr. ed. 1996. audio 24.95 o.p. (0-7871-0582-1) NewStar Media, Inc.

—Extreme Denial. 480p. 1996. 32.00 (0-446-51962-6); 1997. reprint ed. mass mkt. 7.50 (0-446-60396-1) Warner Bks., Inc.

Morrow, Bradford. Trinity Fields. 448p. 2002. pap. 14.00 (0-14-200232-1); 1996. pap. 14.00 o.s.i (0-14-024013-6, Viking) Penguin Group (USA) Inc.

—Trinity Fields. 1995. 448p. 22.95 o.p. (0-670-85728-9, Viking) Viking Penguin.

Nagle, P. G. The Guns of Valverde. 2000. (Illus.). 384p. 25.95 o.p. (0-312-86549-X, Forge Bks.) Doherty, Tom Assocs., LLC.

Nesmith, Michael. The Long Sandy Hair of Neftoon Zamora. 1999. E-Book 5.99 (0-312-24615-3); 1998. 256p. 24.95 (0-312-19296-7) St. Martin's Pr.

Nichols, John. The Magic Journey. 1996. 516p. pap. 12.95 o.s.i (0-345-41033-5); 1983. 546p. mass mkt. 5.99 o.s.i (0-345-31049-7, Ballantine Bks.) Ballantine Bks.

—The Magic Journey. 2000. (Illus.). 540p. pap. 15.00 (0-8050-6339-0, Owl Bks.); 1978. o.p. (0-03-015356-5); 1978. pap. o.p. (0-03-042866-1, Owl Bks.) Holt, Henry & Co.

—The Magic Journey. 1979. pap. 2.75 o.p. (0-671-82311-6, Pocket) Simon & Schuster.

—The Milagro Beanfield War. 1996. pap. 12.95 o.s.i (0-345-41016-5); 1987. 640p. mass mkt. 5.95 o.s.i (0-345-34446-4); 1986. mass mkt. 3.95 o.s.i (0-345-33215-6); 1978. mass mkt. 2.95 o.s.i (0-345-28245-0) Ballantine Bks.

—The Milagro Beanfield War. 2000. (Illus.). 464p. pap. 16.00 (0-8050-6374-9, Owl Bks.) Holt, Henry & Co.

—The Milagro Beanfield War: Facsimile Anniversary Edition. 1993. (Illus.). 484p. 27.50 o.p. (0-8050-2805-6) Holt, Henry & Co.

—The Nirvana Blues. 1996. pap. 12.95 o.s.i (0-345-41037-8); 1988. pap. o.p. (0-345-00631-3); 1983. 608p. mass mkt. 5.95 o.s.i (0-345-30465-9) Ballantine Bks.

—The Nirvana Blues. 2000. 528p. pap. 15.00 (0-8050-6340-4, Owl Bks.); 1981. 540p. o.p. (0-03-059256-9) Holt, Henry & Co.

—The Voice of the Butterfly. 2001. 304p. 24.95 o.s.i (0-8118-3201-5) Chronicle Bks. LLC.

Noble, Diane. When the Far Hills Bloom. 1999. (California Chronicles Ser.: Vol. 1). 384p. pap. 11.99 (1-57856-140-X) WaterBrook Pr.

Onley, Glen. Discovery Tree: A Novel of the Old West. 2001. (Illus.). 256p. pap. 18.95 (0-86534-327-6) Sunstone Pr.

Operation Roswell. 2004. mass mkt. (0-7653-4803-9, Forge Bks.) Doherty, Tom Assocs., LLC.

Osborn, Karen. Between Earth & Sky. 1996. 305p. 23.00 o.p. (0-688-14123-4, Morrow, William & Co.) Morrow/Avon.

Owens, Louis. Nightland. 1996. 224p. 22.95 o.s.i (0-525-94073-1) Dutton/Plume.

—Nightland: A Novel. 2001. (American Indian Literature & Critical Studies: Vol. 41). 217p. 14.95 (0-8061-3373-2) Univ. of Oklahoma Pr.

Padilla, Genaro M., ed. The Short Stories of Fray Angelico Chavez. 1987. (Illus.). 159p. 19.95 o.p. (0-8263-0949-6); pap. 14.95 (0-8263-0950-X) Univ. of New Mexico Pr.

Page, Jake. A Certain Malice. 1997. mass mkt. 6.99 (0-345-40539-0) Ballantine Bks.

—The Deadly Canyon. 1994. 240p. 20.00 o.s.i (0-345-37930-6) Ballantine Bks.

—The Deadly Canyon. unabr. ed. 1994. audio 57.25 o.p. (1-56100-168-6, 859, Unabridged Library Editions); audio 21.95 o.p. (1-56100-540-1, 86, Bookcassette) Brilliance Audio.

—The Deadly Canyon. 1995. 272p. mass mkt. 4.99 o.s.i (0-345-37931-4, House of Collectibles) Random Hse. Information Group.

—The Deadly Canyon. 2002. (Illus.). 228p. pap. 13.95 (0-8263-2861-X) Univ. of New Mexico Pr.

—The Knotted Strings. 1995. mass mkt. 5.99 o.s.i (0-345-38783-X); 256p. 20.00 o.s.i (0-345-38782-1) Ballantine Bks.

—The Knotted Strings. abr. ed. 1995. audio 16.95 o.p. (1-56100-406-5, 1318, Nova Audio Bks.); audio 57.25 o.p. (1-56100-238-0, 921, Unabridged Library Editions); audio 23.95 o.p. (1-56100-613-0, 156, Bookcassette) Brilliance Audio.

—The Knotted Strings. abr. ed. 2000. audio 7.95 (1-57815-016-7, 1040, Media Bks. Audio Publishing) Media Bks., L. L. C.

—The Knotted Strings. 2003. 256p. pap. 13.95 (0-8263-2862-8) Univ. of New Mexico Pr.

—The Lethal Partner. 1996. 293p. mass mkt. 5.99 o.s.i (0-345-38785-6); 240p. 21.00 o.s.i (0-345-38784-8) Ballantine Bks.

—The Lethal Partner. unabr. ed. 1997. audio 48.00 (0-913369-64-0, 4305) Books on Tape, Inc.

—The Lethal Partner. 2003. 246p. pap. 13.95 (0-8263-2863-6) Univ. of New Mexico Pr.

Paine, Lauran. The Devil on Horseback. 1995. 224p. 19.95 (0-8027-4148-7) Walker & Co.

—The Grand Ones of San Ildefonso. 1998. 311 p. (0-7540-3458-5, Macmillan Reference USA); 1997. 238p. lib. bdg. 18.95 (0-7862-0744-2, Five Star) Gale Group.

—Spirit Meadow. 1987. 192p. 15.95 o.p. (0-8027-0970-2) Walker & Co.

—Thunder Valley. 1993. 198p. 19.95 o.p. (0-8027-1235-5) Walker & Co.

Patterson, Paul E. Triple Crown: A Novel. 1996. 224p. pap. 14.95 (0-86534-240-7) Sunstone Pr.

Paulsen, Gary & Burks, Brian. Murphy's Ambush. 1995. 118p. 17.95 o.s.i (0-8027-4149-5) Walker & Co.

Peterson, Tracie. Beneath a Harvest Sky. 2003. (Desert Roses Ser.). 384p. pap. 12.99 (0-7642-2519-7) Bethany Hse. Pubs.

—Hidden in a Whisper. 1999. (Westward Chronicles Ser.: Vol. 2). 288p. pap. 11.99 (0-7642-2113-2) Bethany Hse. Pubs.

—Hidden in a Whisper. 2002. 336p. 24.95 (0-7862-3678-7, Five Star) Gale Group.

Pijoan, Teresa. La Cuentista: Traditional Tales in Spanish & English. Zimmerman, Nancy, tr. 1994. (Illus.). 176p. 19.95 o.p. (1-878610-43-0) Red Crane Bks., Inc.

Poling-Kempes, Lesley. The Canyon of Remembering. 1996. 320p. 24.95 (0-89672-363-1) Texas Tech Univ. Pr.

Preston, Douglas J. & Child, Lincoln. Mount Dragon. (J). 1997. 494p. mass mkt. 7.99 (0-8125-6437-5, Tor Bks.); 1996. 349p. 22.95 o.p. (0-312-86042-0, Forge Bks.) Doherty, Tom Assocs., LLC.

Querry, Ronald B. Bad Medicine. 1999. 336p. reprint ed. pap. 10.95 (0-553-37799-X) Bantam Bks.

Quintana, Leroy V. La Promesa & Other Stories. 2002. (Chicana & Chicano Visions of the Americas Ser.: Vol. 1). 192p. 24.95 (0-8061-3449-6) Univ. of Oklahoma Pr.

Rain, Mary Summer. The Seventh Mesa: A Novel. 1997. 272p. reprint ed. pap. 12.95 (1-57174-061-9) Hampton Roads Publishing Co., Inc.

Rain, Mary Summer, ed. The Seventh Mesa: A Novel. 1994. 272p. text 19.95 (1-57174-012-0) Hampton Roads Publishing Co., Inc.

Randi, Robert J. Miracle of the Jacal. 2001. 320p. mass mkt. 4.99 (0-8439-4923-6, Leisure Bks.) Dorchester Publishing Co., Inc.

Randisi, Robert J. Miracle of the Jacal. 2003. (Western Ser.). 25.95 (0-7862-4666-9) Thorndike Pr.

Richter, Conrad. The Lady. 1985. xviii, 191p. reprint ed. pap. 6.50 o.p. (0-8032-8918-9, Bison Bks.) Univ. of Nebraska Pr.

—The Sea of Grass. 1992. 149p. (C). reprint ed. pap. 9.95 (0-8214-1026-1) Ohio Univ. Pr.

Romero, Leo. Rita & Los Angeles. 1994. 144p. (Orig.). pap. 13.00 (0-927534-44-4) Bilingual Pr./Editorial Bilingue.

Root, Eldon, ed. A Star for Benny Peeples. 1999. (Illus.). 383 p. pap. 9.95 (1-929117-01-9) BlueOak Publishing.

Rossner, Judith. Perfidia: A Novel. 1998. 384p. reprint ed. mass mkt. 7.50 o.s.i (0-440-22613-9) Dell Publishing.

Ruiz, Joseph J. Little Juan Learns a Lesson: A Story for Children. Adelo, Samuel, tr. 1997. (ENG & SPA., Illus.). 64p. (J). (ps-3). pap. 8.95 (0-86534-267-9) Sunstone Pr.

Russell, Sharman Apt. The Last Matriarch. 2000. 200p. 19.95 (0-8263-2131-3) Univ. of New Mexico Pr.

Sadler, Jeff. Hangrope Journey. l.t. ed. 1996. (G. K. Hall Nightingale Ser.). 173p. pap. 17.95 o.p. (0-7838-1881-5, Macmillan Reference USA) Gale Group.

Sagel, Jim. Garden of Stories: Jardin de Cuentos. 1996. (Bilingual Ser.).Tr. of Jardin de Cuentos. (SPA., Illus.). 112p. (YA). (gr. 7 up). pap. 12.95 (1-878610-55-4) Red Crane Bks., Inc.

Salmon, M. H. Signal to Depart. 1995. (Illus.). 214p. 21.95 (0-944383-33-5); pap. 12.95 o.p. (0-944383-32-7) High-Lonesome Bks.

Salter, Robert B. Chamisa Dreams: A Novel. 1994. 160p. pap. 12.95 (0-86534-220-2) Sunstone Pr.

Samuel, Barbara. A Piece of Heaven. 2004. 416p. mass mkt. 6.99 (0-345-44568-6); 2003. 336p. 23.95 (0-345-44567-8, Ballantine Bks.) Ballantine Bks.

—A Piece of Heaven. l.t. ed. 2003. (Women's Fiction Ser.). 28.95 (0-7862-5313-4) Thorndike Pr.

Satterthwait, Walter. Accustomed to the Dark. 1998. (WWL Mystery Ser.). per. (0-373-26263-9, 1-26263-3, Worldwide Library) Harlequin Enterprises, Ltd.

—Accustomed to the Dark. 1996. 256p. 21.95 o.p. (0-312-14535-7, Saint Martin's Minotaur) St. Martin's Pr.

—At Ease with the Dead. 1993. per. (0-373-83266-4, 1-83266-6); 1991. mass mkt. (0-373-26072-5) Harlequin Enterprises, Ltd. (Harlequin Bks.).

—At Ease with the Dead. 1990. 16.95 o.p. (0-312-04260-4, Saint Martin's Minotaur) St. Martin's Pr.

—A Flower in the Desert. 1993. (WWL Mystery Ser.). per. (0-373-26134-9, 1-26134-6, Harlequin Bks.) Harlequin Enterprises, Ltd.

—A Flower in the Desert. 1992. 240p. 17.95 o.p. (0-312-07751-3, Saint Martin's Minotaur) St. Martin's Pr.

—The Hanged Man: A Joshua Croft Mystery. 1995. (WWL Mystery Ser.). 250p. per. (0-373-26173-X, 1-26173-4, Harlequin Bks.) Harlequin Enterprises, Ltd.

—The Hanged Man: A Joshua Croft Mystery. 1993. 256p. 19.95 o.p. (0-312-09827-8, Saint Martin's Minotaur) St. Martin's Pr.

—Wall of Glass. 1993. per. (0-373-83265-6, 1-83265-8); 1989. mass mkt. (0-373-26032-6) Harlequin Enterprises, Ltd. (Harlequin Bks.).

—Wall of Glass. 1988. 256p. 16.95 o.p. (0-312-01530-5, Saint Martin's Minotaur) St. Martin's Pr.

Savage, Douglas. The Sons of Grady Rourke. 1996. 320p. reprint ed. pap. 4.99 (*0-8439-4120-0*, Leisure Bks.) Dorchester Publishing Co., Inc.

—The Sons of Grady Rourke. 1995. 210p. 19.95 o.p. (*0-87131-785-0*) Evans, M. & Co., Inc.

Savage, Les, Jr. The Cavan Breed: South-Western Story. 2003. 288p. mass mkt. 4.99 (*0-8439-5197-4*) Dorchester Publishing Co., Inc.

—The Cavan Breed: South-Western Story. l.t. ed. 2001. (Five Star First Edition Western Ser.). 291p. 22.95 (*0-7862-2756-7*) Thorndike Pr.

—The Royal City. Weaver, Richard C., ed. 1988. (Orig.). reprint ed. pap. 0.40 (*0-941108-01-5*) Friends of the Palace Pr.

Schonberg, Leonard A. Deadly Indian Summer: A Novel. 1997. 192p. 24.95 (*0-86534-257-1*) Sunstone Pr.

Sharpe, Jon. New Mexico Nightmare. deluxe ed. 2003. 272p. mass mkt. 5.99 (*0-451-20817-X*, Signet Bks.) NAL.

—New Mexico Nymph. 2004. (Trailsman Ser.). 176p. mass mkt. 4.99 (*0-451-21137-5*) NAL.

—Santa Fe Slaughter. 1988. (Trailsman Ser.: No. 73). 176p. mass mkt. 2.75 o.p. (*0-451-15139-9*, Signet Bks.) NAL.

Shelton, Connie. Deadly Gamble. unabr. ed. 1996. (Charlie Parker Ser.: Bk. 1). audio 39.95 (*1-55686-653-4*) Books in Motion.

—Deadly Gamble: The First Charlie Parker Mystery. Lenz, Leslie, ed. 1995. 216p. 21.95 o.p. (*0-9643161-0-2*, Intrigue Pr.) Corvus Publishing.

—Deadly Gamble: The First Charlie Parker Mystery. 1997. (The Charlie Parker Mystery Ser.: Vol. 1). 288p. reprint ed. mass mkt. 5.50 (*1-890768-00-6*, Intrigue Pr.) Corvus Publishing.

—Honeymoons Can Be Murder. 2002. (WWL Mystery Ser.). 256p. mass mkt. (*0-373-26427-5*, Worldwide Library) Harlequin Enterprises, Ltd.

—Honeymoons Can Be Murder: A Charlie Parker Mystery. 2001. (The Charlie Parker Mystery Ser.: Vol. 6). 268p. 23.95 (*1-890768-30-8*, Intrigue Pr.) Corvus Publishing.

—Memories Can Be Murder. Ellison, Lee, ed. 1999. (The Charlie Parker Mystery Ser.: 5). 224p. 22.95 (*1-890768-18-9*, Intrigue Pr.) Corvus Publishing.

—Partnerships Can Kill. unabr. ed. 1996. (Charlie Parker Ser.: Bk. 3). audio 26.95 (*1-55686-667-4*) Books in Motion.

—Partnerships Can Kill. 1998. (The Charlie Parker Mystery Ser.: No. 3). 240p. mass mkt. 5.50 (*1-890768-02-2*, Intrigue Pr.) Corvus Publishing.

—Partnerships Can Kill. Ellison, Lee, ed. 1997. 208p. 21.95 o.p. (*0-9643161-4-5*, Intrigue Pr.) Corvus Publishing.

—Reunions Can Be Murder: The Seventh Charlie Parker Mystery. 2002. (The Charlie Parker Mystery Ser.: No. 7). 255p. 23.95 (*1-890768-46-4*, Intrigue Pr.) Corvus Publishing.

—Small Towns Can Be Murder. (The Charlie Parker Mystery Ser.: No. 4). 1999. (Illus.). 256p. mass mkt. 5.95 (*1-890768-16-2*); 1998. 224p. 22.95 (*1-890768-05-7*) Corvus Publishing. (Intrigue Pr.).

—Vacations Can Be Murder. unabr. ed. 1996. (Charlie Parker Ser.: Bk. 2). audio 39.95 (*1-55686-660-7*) Books in Motion.

—Vacations Can Be Murder: The Second Charlie Parker Mystery. Lenz, Leslie, ed. 1995. (Charlie Parker Mysteries Ser.). 216p. 21.95 o.p. (*0-9643161-1-0*, Intrigue Pr.) Corvus Publishing.

—Vacations Can Be Murder: The Second Charlie Parker Mystery. 1997. (The Charlie Parker Mystery Ser.: Vol. 2). 272p. reprint ed. mass mkt. 5.50 (*1-890768-01-4*, Intrigue Pr.) Corvus Publishing.

Shigekuni, Julie. Invisible Gardens. Date not set. pap. (*0-312-31184-2*, St. Martin's Paperbacks); Date not set. mass mkt. (*0-312-98849-4*, St. Martin's Paperbacks); 2003. 240p. 23.95 (*0-312-31183-4*) St. Martin's Pr.

Silman, Roberta. Beginning the World Again: A Novel of Los Alamos. 1990. 416p. (J). 19.95 o.p. (*0-670-83062-3*, Viking) Viking Penguin.

Sinclair, John L. In the Time of Harvest. l.t. ed. 1992. 396p. pap. 15.95 o.p. (*0-8161-5485-6*, Macmillan Reference USA) Gale Group.

—In Time of Harvest. 1993. (Illus.). 256p. reprint ed. 24.95 (*0-940666-26-X*) Clear Light Pubs.

—In Time of Harvest. 1989. 236p. reprint ed. 22.95 o.p. (*0-8040-0923-6*) Swallow Pr.

Slater, Susan. The Pumpkin Seed Massacre. Ellison, Lee, ed. 1999. (Ben Pecos Mysteries Ser.: Vol. 1). 240p. 22.95 o.p. (*1-890768-17-0*, Intrigue Pr.) Corvus Publishing.

—Yellow Lies. 2002. (WWL Mystery Ser.: No. 422). mass mkt. (*0-373-26422-4*, 1-26422-5, Worldwide Library) Harlequin Enterprises, Ltd.

—Yellow Lies: A Ben Pecos Mystery. 2000. (Ben Pecos Mysteries Ser.). 297p. 22.95 (*1-890768-26-X*, Intrigue Pr.) Corvus Publishing.

Smith, Taylor. Guilt by Silence. 2000. 408p. mass mkt. (*1-55166-537-9*, 1-66537-1); 1995. 400p. per. (*1-55166-048-2*, 1-66048-9) Harlequin Enterprises, Ltd. (Mira Bks.).

Stephens, Jackie. Apache Angel. 2001. (Zebra Historical Romance Ser.). 384p. mass mkt. 5.99 o.s.i (*0-8217-6763-1*, Zebra Bks.) Kensington Publishing Corp.

Stevens, Jan Romero. Carlos & the Cornfield. 1999. Tr. of Carlos y la Milpa de Maiz. (ENG & SPA., Illus.). 32p. (J). (gr. k-3). pap. 7.95 (*0-87358-735-9*, Rising Moon Bks. for Young Readers) Northland Publishing.

Stovich, Raymond J. Under a Turquoise Sky: Stories from Three Cultures. 1992. 104p. (Orig.). pap. 9.95 o.p. (*0-87358-540-2*) Northland Publishing.

Stuart, Gary L. The Gallup 14: A Novel. 2000. 352p. 24.95 (*0-8263-2133-X*) Univ. of New Mexico Pr.

Stuart, Gary L., et al, contrib. by. The Gallup 14: A Novel. 2000. (*0-8263-2134-8*) Univ. of New Mexico Pr.

Swan, Gladys. Ghost Dance: A Play of Voices. Novel. 1992. 252p. 24.95 (*0-8071-1706-4*) Louisiana State Univ. Pr.

Tallent, Elizabeth. Museum Pieces. 1986. 240p. pap. 7.95 o.p. (*0-03-008003-7*, Owl Bks.) Holt, Henry & Co.

—Museum Pieces. Goerner, Lee, ed. 1985. 206p. 14.95 o.s.i (*0-394-53928-1*) Knopf, Alfred A. Inc.

Tayler, Mark A. Chaco: A Novel. 1993. 288p. pap. 14.95 (*0-86534-203-2*) Sunstone Pr.

Thorne, Alexandra. Past Forgetting. 1992. 336p. 15.00 o.s.i (*0-385-42291-1*) Doubleday Publishing.

Thurlo, Aimee & Thurlo, David. Bad Faith: A Sister Agatha Mystery. 2002. 304p. 23.95 (*0-312-29081-0*, Saint Martin's Minotaur) St. Martin's Pr.

—Bad Faith: A Sister Agatha Mystery. 2003. (Mystery Ser.). 28.95 (*0-7862-5245-6*) Thorndike Pr.

—Bad Medicine. 384p. 1998. mass mkt. 6.99 (*0-8125-6458-8*); 1997. 23.95 (*0-312-86328-4*) Doherty, Tom Assocs., LLC. (Forge Bks.).

—Blackening Song. (Ella Clah Novel Ser.). 1997. 429p. mass mkt. 5.99 (*0-8125-6756-0*); 1995. 384p. 14.99 o.p. (*0-312-85652-0*); 2001. 384p. reprint ed. pap. 14.95 (*0-7653-0256-X*) Doherty, Tom Assocs., LLC. (Forge Bks.).

—Changing Woman. E-Book 24.95 (*0-312-70549-2*, Tor Bks.); 2nd ed. 2002. 384p. 24.95 (*0-312-87059-0*, CPHC0654, Forge Bks.) Doherty, Tom Assocs., LLC.

—Death Walker: An Ella Clah Novel. (Ella Clah Novel Ser.). 1997. 338p. mass mkt. 6.99 (*0-8125-6758-7*); 1996. 352p. 23.95 o.p. (*0-312-85651-2*); 2003. 384p. reprint ed. pap. 14.95 (*0-7653-0651-4*) Doherty, Tom Assocs., LLC. (Forge Bks.).

—Enemy Way. (Ella Clah Novel Ser.: No. 4). 1999. 352p. mass mkt. 6.99 (*0-8125-6459-6*); 1998. 350p. 23.95 (*0-312-85520-6*) Doherty, Tom Assocs., LLC. (Forge Bks.).

—Plant Them Deep. mass mkt. (*0-7653-4398-3*); 2003. 336p. 24.95 (*0-7653-0478-3*) Doherty, Tom Assocs., LLC. (Forge Bks.).

—The Second Shadow. 1993. 384p. 21.95 o.p. (*0-312-85450-1*, Forge Bks.) Doherty, Tom Assocs., LLC.

—Shooting Chant: An Ella Clah Novel. 2000. 349p. 23.95 (*0-312-87061-2*, Forge Bks.) Doherty, Tom Assocs., LLC.

—Tracking Bear. E-Book 24.95 (*0-312-71003-8*, Tor Bks.); 2003. (Ella Clah Novel Ser.: No. 8). 384p. 24.95 (*0-7653-0476-7*, Forge Bks.) Doherty, Tom Assocs., LLC.

Thurlo, David & Thurlo, Aimee. Second Sunrise: A Lee Nez Novel. 2002. (Lee Nez Novel Ser.). 336p. 24.95 (*0-7653-0441-4*, Forge Bks.) Doherty, Tom Assocs., LLC.

Tripp, Valerie. Happy Birthday, Josefina! A Springtime Story. 1998. (American Girls Collection: Bk. 4). (Illus.). (YA). (gr. 2 up). 12.10 (*0-606-13381-X*) Turtleback Bks.

Ulibarri, Sabine R. El Condor & Other Stories. 1989. 180p. (J). (gr. 4-7). pap. 9.50 (*0-934770-92-1*) Arte Publico Pr.

—Tierra Amarilla: Stories of New Mexico, Cuentos de Nuevo Mexico. Nason, Thelma C., tr. 1971. (ENG & SPA., Illus.). 181p. reprint ed. pap. 8.95 o.p. (*0-8263-0212-2*) Univ. of New Mexico Pr.

Ulibarri, Sabine R., et al. Tierra Amarilla: Stories of New Mexico/Cuentos de Nuevo Mexico. 1993. (Paso Por Aqui: Series on the Nuevomexicano Literary Heritage Ser.). (ACE., Illus.). 167p. pap. 14.95 (*0-8263-1438-4*) Univ. of New Mexico Pr.

Ulmer, Mari. Midnight at the Camposanto. 2001. (Taos Mysteries Ser.: No. 1). pap. 14.95 (*1-890208-58-2*) Poisoned Pen Pr.

—Midnight at the Camposanto: A Taos Festival Mystery. 2000. (Taos Mysteries Ser.). 258p. 23.95 (*1-890208-30-2*) Poisoned Pen Pr.

Van Gieson, Judith. Confidence Woman. l.t. ed. 2002. 315p. 27.95 (*0-7862-4217-5*) Gale Group.

—Confidence Woman. 2002. 272p. mass mkt. 5.99 (*0-451-20500-6*, Signet Bks.) NAL.

—Confidence Woman. 2002. (Claire Reynier Mysteries Ser.). 208p. 23.95 (*0-8263-2888-1*) Univ. of New Mexico Pr.

—Ditch Rider: A Neil Hamel Mystery. (Neil Hamel Mystery Ser.). 240p. 1999. mass mkt. 5.99 (*0-06-109515-X*); 1998. 23.00 (*0-06-017513-3*) HarperCollins Pubs.

—Hotshots. 1996. (Neil Hamel Mystery Ser.). 256p. 22.00 o.p. (*0-06-017512-5*) HarperCollins Pubs.

—Land of Burning Heat: A Claire Reynier Mystery. 2003. 272p. mass mkt. 5.99 (*0-451-20800-5*, Signet Bks.) NAL.

—Land of Burning Heat: A Claire Reynier Mystery. l.t. ed. 2003. (Senior Lifestyles Ser.). 28.95 (*0-7862-5470-X*) Thorndike Pr.

—Land of Burning Heat: A Claire Reynier Mystery. 2003. 264p. 24.95 (*0-8263-3172-6*) Univ. of New Mexico Pr.

—The Lies That Bind: A Neil Hamel Mystery. 1994. 304p. mass mkt. 4.99 o.p. (*0-06-109051-4*) HarperCollins Pubs.

—The Lies That Bind: A Neil Hamel Mystery. 1993. 256p. 20.00 o.p. (*0-06-017705-5*) HarperTrade.

—North of the Border: A Neil Hamel Mystery. 1993. 176p. mass mkt. 4.99 (*0-671-76967-7*, Pocket) Simon & Schuster.

—North of the Border: A Neil Hamel Mystery. 1988. 16.95 o.p. (*0-8027-5706-5*) Walker & Co.

—The Other Side of Death. 1991. 224p. 18.95 o.p. (*0-06-016581-2*) HarperTrade.

—The Other Side of Death. 2003. 224p. pap. 13.95 (*0-8263-3207-2*) Univ. of New Mexico Pr.

—Parrot Blues. 1995. 256p. 20.00 o.p. (*0-06-017706-3*) HarperTrade.

—Parrot Blues. 1995. 272p. mass mkt. 4.99 o.p. (*0-06-109048-4*, HarperTorch) Morrow/Avon.

—Raptor. 1990. 17.95 o.p. (*0-06-016167-1*) HarperTrade.

—Raptor. Isaacson, Dana, ed. 1991. 256p. reprint ed. mass mkt. 4.99 (*0-671-73243-9*, Pocket) Simon & Schuster.

—Raptor. 2002. 252p. pap. 13.95 (*0-8263-2974-8*) Univ. of New Mexico Pr.

—Vanishing Point: A Claire Reynier Mystery. 2001. 272p. mass mkt. 5.99 (*0-451-20240-6*) NAL.

—Vanishing Point: A Claire Reynier Mystery. l.t. ed. 2001. (Senior Lifestyles Ser.). 293p. 28.95 (*0-7862-3587-X*) Thorndike Pr.

—Vanishing Point: A Claire Reynier Mystery. 2001. (Claire Reynier Mysteries Ser.). 216p. 24.95 (*0-8263-2383-9*) Univ. of New Mexico Pr.

—The Wolf Path: A Neil Hamel Mystery. 1992. 224p. 19.00 o.p. (*0-06-016804-8*) HarperTrade.

—The Wolf Path: A Neil Hamel Mystery. 1993. 256p. mass mkt. 4.50 o.p. (*0-06-109139-1*, HarperTorch) Morrow/Avon.

Warloe, Constance. The Legend of Olivia Cosmos Montevideo: A Novel. 1994. 320p. 22.00 o.p. (*0-87113-564-7*, Atlantic Monthly Pr.) Grove/Atlantic, Inc.

Wheelas, Jamie. Wild Plum at Night: A Novel. 1996. 192p. pap. 18.95 (*0-86534-049-8*) Sunstone Pr.

Wheeler, Richard S. Flint's Truth. unabr. ed. 1998. audio 56.95 (*0-7861-1373-1*, 2280) Blackstone Audio Bks., Inc.

—Flint's Truth. 1998. (Sam Flint Novels Ser.). 352p. 23.95 o.p. (*0-312-86367-5*, Forge Bks.) Doherty, Tom Assocs., LLC.

—Flint's Truth. l.t. ed. 1998. (Western Ser.). 432p. 25.95 (*0-7838-0333-8*) Thorndike Pr.

Whitlow, Duane & Smith, James C., Jr. Lincoln Country Diary. 1992. 224p. (Orig.). pap. 14.95 o.p. (*0-86534-157-5*) Sunstone Pr.

Whitney, Phyllis A. Secret of the Haunted Mesa. 1975. 144p. (J). (gr. 6 up). 5.75 o.p. (*0-664-32568-8*) Westminster John Knox Pr.

—The Turquoise Mask. l.t. ed. 1989. 21.95 o.p. (*1-55504-789-0*, 158); 1997. audio 69.95 (*0-7451-6782-9*, CAB 1398) BBC Audiobooks America.

—The Turquoise Mask. 1998. mass mkt. 3.99 o.s.i (*0-449-00511-9*); 1981. mass mkt. 5.99 o.s.i (*0-449-23470-3*) Ballantine Bks. (Fawcett).

—The Turquoise Mask. 1974. 336p. 10.95 o.p. (*0-385-08514-1*) Doubleday Publishing.

Williams, Walter J. Days of Atonement. 1992. mass mkt. 4.99 (*0-8125-0180-2*); 1991. 19.95 (*0-312-85118-9*) Doherty, Tom Assocs., LLC. (Tor Bks.).

Wolcott, Jann A. Brujo: Seduced by Evil. 1995. 322p. pap. text 6.95 (*0-9644293-0-6*) Route 66 Publishing, Ltd.

Wolfe, Swain. The Parrot Trainer. (Illus.). mass mkt. (*0-312-98793-5*, St. Martin's Paperbacks); 2003. 288p. 24.95 (*0-312-31091-9*) St. Martin's Pr.

Wood, Summer. Arroyo. 2001. 257p. 22.95 (*0-8118-3094-2*) Chronicle Bks. LLC.

Woodruff, Joan L. Neighbors. 1993. 160p. pap. 11.95 (*0-943219-08-6*) 3rd Woman Pr.

Zimmerman, Nancy, tr. La Cuentista: Traditional Tales in English & Spanish. 1994. (Bilingual Ser.). (ENG & SPA., Illus.). 184p. (YA). (gr. 7 up). pap. 13.95 (*1-878610-42-2*, RC0422) Red Crane Bks., Inc.

Zollinger, Norman. Coyote. 2002. 364p. 25.95 (*0-7653-0005-2*, Forge Bks.) Doherty, Tom Assocs., LLC.

**NEW ORLEANS (LA.)—FICTION**

Abel, Kenneth. The Burying Field. 2003. 352p. reprint ed. mass mkt. 6.99 (*0-451-20853-6*, Signet Bks.) NAL.

—The Burying Field. 2002. 400p. 26.95 o.s.i (*0-399-14796-9*) Penguin Group (USA) Inc.

—The Burying Field. l.t. ed. 2002. (Core Collection). 538p. 29.95 (*0-7862-4672-3*) Thorndike Pr.

—Cold Steel Rain. l.t. ed. 2001. 439p. lib. bdg. 28.95 (*1-58547-077-5*) Ctr. Point Large Print.

—Cold Steel Rain. 2000. 448p. 24.95 o.p. (*0-399-14662-8*) Penguin Group (USA) Inc.

Adams, Pepper. That Old Black Magic. 1991. (Harlequin Romance Ser.: No. 842). pap. (*0-373-08842-6*, 5-08842-2, Silhouette) Harlequin Enterprises, Ltd.

Algren, Nelson. A Walk on the Wild Side. 1990. (Classic Reprint Ser.). 368p. reprint ed. pap. 12.95 (*0-938410-80-6*, Thunder's Mouth Pr.) Avalon Publishing Group.

—A Walk on the Wild Side. 1998. 368p. pap. 14.00 (*0-374-52532-3*) Farrar, Straus & Giroux.

—A Walk on the Wild Side. 1978. 346p. reprint ed. 57.95 (*0-313-20294-X*, ALWW, Greenwood Pr.) Greenwood Publishing Group, Inc.

—A Walk on the Wild Side. 1992. 21.50 o.p. (*0-8446-6532-0*) Smith, Peter Pub., Inc.

—A Walk on the Wild Side. 1977. 352p. pap. 6.95 o.p. (*0-14-003565-6*, Penguin Bks.) Viking Penguin.

Alison, Jane. The Marriage of the Sea: A Novel. 2003. 272p. 24.00 (*0-374-19941-8*) Farrar, Straus & Giroux.

—The Marriage of the Sea: A Novel. 2004. 272p. pap. 13.00 (*0-312-42255-5*) Picador.

Allen, Danice. Arms of a Stranger. 1995. 384p. (Orig.). mass mkt. 4.50 (*0-380-77726-6*, Avon Bks.) Morrow/Avon.

Alvarez, Gloria. Miracle of Love. 2000. 28p. mass mkt. 3.99 o.s.i (*0-7860-1167-X*) Kensington Publishing Corp.

Ambler, Eric. Cause for Alarm. 246p. reprint ed. lib. bdg. 22.95 (*0-89190-466-2*, Rivercity Pr.) Amereon, Ltd.

—Cause for Alarm. 1990. 264p. mass mkt. 3.95 o.p. (*0-88184-664-3*, Carroll & Graf Pubs.) Avalon Publishing Group.

—Cause for Alarm. 1978. mass mkt. 1.95 o.s.i (*0-345-25909-2*) Ballantine Bks.

—Cause for Alarm. 1984. 256p. mass mkt. 2.95 o.s.i (*0-425-07029-8*) Berkley Publishing Group.

—Cause for Alarm. unabr. ed. 1995. audio 44.95 (*0-7861-0772-3*, 1621) Blackstone Audio Bks., Inc.

—Cause for Alarm. unabr. collector's ed. 1987. audio 48.00 (*0-7366-1182-7*, 2102) Books on Tape, Inc.

—Cause for Alarm. 1990. reprint ed. lib. bdg. 22.95 o.p. (*0-89968-470-X*) Buccaneer Bks., Inc.

—Cause for Alarm. 2002. 304p. pap. 12.00 (*0-375-72674-8*, Vintage) Knopf Publishing Group.

—Cause for Alarm. 1942. mass mkt. 0.25 o.p. (*0-451-00511-2*, Signet Bks.) NAL.

Andersen, Susan. Be My Baby. 1999. 384p. mass mkt. 6.99 (*0-380-79512-4*, Avon Bks.) Morrow/Avon.

Andrews, V. C. All That Glitters. l.t. ed. 2000. 26.95 (*1-56895-236-8*, Wheeler Publishing, Inc.) Gale Group.

—All That Glitters. 1995. (Landry Ser.). 352p. mass mkt. 7.99 (*0-671-87319-9*, Pocket) Simon & Schuster.

—All That Glitters. Marrow, Linda, ed. 1995. 352p. 23.00 o.p. (*0-671-87574-4*, Atria) Simon & Schuster.

—Pearl in the Mist. l.t. ed. 1995. 555p. 19.95 o.p. (*0-7838-1165-9*); 514p. 24.95 (*0-7838-1164-0*) Gale Group. (Macmillan Reference USA).

—Pearl in the Mist. Marrow, Linda, ed. 1994. 384p. 23.00 (*0-671-75937-X*, Atria); mass mkt. 7.99 (*0-671-75936-1*, Pocket) Simon & Schuster.

—Pearl in the Mist. 1994. 14.04 (*0-606-07067-2*) Turtleback Bks.

Atkins, Ace. Dirty South. 2004. 304p. 24.95 (*0-06-000462-2*, Morrow, William & Co.) Morrow/Avon.

Atkins, P. W. Crossroad Blues. (Nick Travers Mysteries Ser.). 2000. 256p. mass mkt. 5.99 (*0-312-97192-3*, St. Martin's Paperbacks); 1998. 226p. 21.95 o.p. (*0-312-19254-1*, Saint Martin's Minotaur) St. Martin's Pr.

Barnes, Linda. Cities of the Dead. l.t. ed. 1991. 8.95 o.p. (*0-7451-9581-4*, 5059); pap. 10.95 o.p. (*0-7927-0009-0*, 4616) BBC Audiobooks America.

—Cities of the Dead. 1987. mass mkt. 4.99 o.s.i (*0-449-21188-6*, Fawcett) Ballantine Bks.

—Cities of the Dead. 1996. 272p. mass mkt. 5.99 o.s.i (*0-440-22095-5*) Dell Publishing.

—Cities of the Dead. 1985. 224p. 14.95 o.p. (*0-312-13940-3*) St. Martin's Pr.

Battle, Lois. Storyville. 1993. 496p. mass mkt. 5.99 o.s.i (*0-440-21690-7*) Dell Publishing.

—Storyville. 1997. 448p. pap. 15.00 (*0-14-026769-7*) Penguin Group (USA) Inc.

—Storyville. 1993. 432p. 22.00 o.p. (*0-670-83867-5*, Viking) Viking Penguin.

Bens, Jeff W. Albert, Himself. 2001. 200p. pap. 14.00 (*1-883285-22-4*) Delphinium Bks., Inc.

Bicos, Olga. Wrapped in Wishes. l.t. ed. 1999. 26.95 (*1-56895-759-9*, Wheeler Publishing, Inc.) Gale Group.

—Wrapped in Wishes. 1996. 432p. mass mkt. 5.50 o.s.i (*0-8217-5370-3*, Zebra Bks.) Kensington Publishing Corp.

Blackstock, Terri. Line of Duty. 2003. (Newpointe 911 Ser.: Bk. 5). 384p. pap. 12.99 (*0-310-25064-1*) Zondervan.

Blake, Jennifer. Wildest Dreams. 1995. 341p. pap. 19.00 (*0-449-91264-7*); 1993. mass mkt. 5.99 o.s.i (*0-449-14739-8*, Fawcett) Ballantine Bks.

Bosworth, Sheila. Almost Innocent. 1996. (Voices of the South Ser.). 268p. (C). pap. 16.95 (*0-8071-2066-9*) Louisiana State Univ. Pr.

—Almost Innocent. 1984. 320p. 16.45 o.p. (*0-671-50365-0*, Simon & Schuster) Simon & Schuster.

—Almost Innocent. 1986. (Contemporary American Fiction Ser.). 272p. pap. 6.95 o.p. (*0-14-008443-6*, Penguin Bks.) Viking Penguin.

—Slow Poison. 1993. mass mkt. 4.99 o.s.i (*0-8041-1124-3*, Ivy Bks.) Ballantine Bks.

—Slow Poison. 1998. (Voices of the South Ser.). 336p. pap. 17.95 (*0-8071-2278-5*) Louisiana State Univ. Pr.

Bradley, John Ed. Restoration: A Novel. 2003. 320p. 24.95 (*0-385-50261-3*) Doubleday Publishing.

Breaux, Magdalene. The Family Curse. 2000. 244p. pap. 15.00 (*0-9701709-0-4*) Breaux Bks., LLC.

—The Family Curse. 2000. 248p. pap. 17.95 o.p. (*1-887617-00-0*) St. Barthelemey Pr., Ltd.

Brite, Poppy. Liquor: A Novel. 2004. 352p. pap. 13.95 (*1-4000-5007-3*, Three Rivers Pr.) Crown Publishing Group.

Brite, Poppy Z. The Devil You Know. 2003. 200p. 40.00 (*1-931081-72-7*) Subterranean Pr.

—The Lazarus Heart. 1998. (Crow Ser.). 224p. pap. 13.00 (*0-06-105824-6*, HarperEntertainment) Morrow/Avon.

—The Value of X. 2002. 200p. 35.00 (*1-931081-67-0*) Subterranean Pr.

Brown, John G. The Wrecked, Blessed Body of Shelton Lafleur. l.t. ed. 1997. (Paperback Ser.). 361p. pap. 21.95 (*0-7838-8198-3*, Macmillan Reference USA) Gale Group.

—The Wrecked, Blessed Body of Shelton Lafleur. 1996. 256p. 21.95 o.p. (*0-395-72988-2*) Houghton Mifflin Co.

—The Wrecked, Blessed Body of Shelton Lafleur. 1997. pap. 12.00 (*0-380-72965-2*, Avon Bks.) Morrow/Avon.

Brown, John Gregory. Decorations in a Ruined Cemetery. 2001. 256p. reprint ed. pap. 13.00 (*0-618-15452-3*, Mariner Bks.) Houghton Mifflin Co. Trade & Reference Div.

Brown, Sandra. Fat Tuesday. l.t. ed. 1997. (Wheeler Large Print Book Ser.). 27.95 (*1-56895-465-4*, Wheeler Publishing, Inc.) Gale Group.

—Fat Tuesday. abr. ed. 1997. audio 24.00 (*0-553-47825-7*, 695225); audio compact disk 29.95 o.s.i (*0-553-45557-5*) Random Hse. Audio Publishing Group. (RH Audio).

—Fat Tuesday. 1997. 464p. 23.50 o.p. (*0-446-51632-5*); 1998. 480p. reprint ed. mass mkt. 7.99 (*0-446-60558-1*) Warner Bks., Inc.

—French Silk. l.t. ed. 1993. (General Ser.). 522p. lib. bdg. 17.95 o.p. (*0-8161-5445-7*, Macmillan Reference USA) Gale Group.

—French Silk. 1992. 18.95 o.s.i (*0-446-51654-6*) Warner Bks., Inc.

Bruhns, Nina. Sweet Revenge. 2002. (Silhouette Intimate Moments Ser.). 256p. mass mkt. (*0-373-27233-2*, Silhouette) Harlequin Enterprises, Ltd.

Cable, George W. The Grandissimes. E-Book 3.95 (*0-594-06011-7*) 1873 Pr.

—The Grandissimes. 25.95 (*0-88411-796-0*) Amereon, Ltd.

—The Grandissimes. 1957. pap. 5.95 o.p. (*0-8090-0025-3*, Hill & Wang) Farrar, Straus & Giroux.

—The Grandissimes. 1983. 7.50 o.p. (*0-8446-1791-1*) Smith, Peter Pub., Inc.

—The Grandissimes. 1988. (Classics Ser.). 384p. 14.95 (*0-14-043322-8*, Penguin Classics) Viking Penguin.

—Old Creole Days. E-Book 3.95 (*0-594-04343-3*) 1873 Pr.

—Old Creole Days, Set, Pts. 1 & 2. 1977. (Black Heritage Library Collection). 27.95 (*0-8369-8530-3*) Ayer Co. Pubs., Inc.

—Old Creole Days. 1883. 300p. (YA). reprint ed. pap. text 28.00 (*1-4047-1132-5*) Classic Textbooks.

—Old Creole Days. 1972. reprint ed. lib. bdg. 9.00 o.p. (*0-8422-8184-3*) Irvington Pubs.

—Old Creole Days. 1989. mass mkt. 3.95 o.p. (*0-451-52349-0*, Signet Classics) NAL.

—Old Creole Days. 1990. (Pelican Pouch Ser.). 312p. (YA). (gr. 10-12). reprint ed. pap. 6.99 (*0-88289-780-2*) Pelican Publishing Co., Inc.

—Old Creole Days. 1990. (Works of George Washington Cable). reprint ed. lib. bdg. 79.00 (*0-7812-1132-8*) Reprint Services Corp.

—Old Creole Days. 1974. reprint ed. 10.00 (*0-403-03056-0*) Somerset Pubs., Inc.

Cable, George Washington. The Grandissimes. 2001. (Illus.). 528p. pap. 7.99 (*1-56554-901-5*) Pelican Publishing Co., Inc.

—The Grandissimes. 1990. (Works of George Washington Cable). reprint ed. lib. bdg. 79.00 (*0-7812-1133-6*) Reprint Services Corp.

—The Grandissimes. 1974. reprint ed. 79.00 (*0-403-02979-1*) Somerset Pubs., Inc.

—The Grandissimes. 1988. (Brown Thrasher Bks.). 360p. reprint ed. pap. 15.95 (*0-8203-1020-4*) Univ. of Georgia Pr.

Cameron, Stella. French Quarter. l.t. ed. 1999. 27.95 (*1-56895-643-6*, Wheeler Publishing, Inc.) Gale Group.

—French Quarter. 1999. 445p. mass mkt. 6.99 o.s.i (*0-8217-6251-6*); 1998. (Illus.). 384p. 16.95 o.s.i (*1-57566-312-0*, Kensington Bks.) Kensington Publishing Corp.

Cannon, C. W. Soul Resin. 2002. 304p. pap. 13.95 (*1-57366-099-X*) Fiction Collective Two, Inc.

Catling, Patrick Skene. Jazz, Jazz, Jazz. 1981. 322p. 11.95 o.p. (*0-312-44073-1*) St. Martin's Pr.

Chance, Megan. The Gentleman Caller. l.t. ed. 1999. (Large Print Book Ser.). pap. 23.95 (*1-56895-729-7*, Wheeler Publishing, Inc.) Gale Group.

—The Gentleman Caller. 1998. 432p. mass mkt. 6.99 (*0-06-108704-1*, HarperTorch) Morrow/Avon.

Chesnutt, Charles Waddell. Paul Marchand: Free Man of Color. 1998. 144p. 20.00 (*1-57806-055-9*) Univ. Pr. of Mississippi.

Chesnutt, Charles Waddell & McWilliams, Dean. Paul Marchand, F. M. C. 1999. 223p. text 49.95 (*0-691-05993-4*); pap. text 20.95 o.p. (*0-691-05994-2*) Princeton Univ. Pr.

Chopin, Kate. The Awakening. 2000. 252p. E-Book 9.95 (*0-594-05221-1*) 1873 Pr.

—The Awakening. unabr. ed. 1986. audio 29.95 (*1-55685-000-X*) Audio Bk. Contractors, Inc.

—The Awakening. 1985. mass mkt. 2.95 o.s.i (*0-553-21194-3*) Bantam Bks.

—The Awakening. E-Book (*0-7607-1303-0*); 1997. (Illus.). (*0-7607-0590-9*) Barnes & Noble, Inc.

—The Awakening. 1995. 256p. 9.00 o.s.i (*1-57322-511-8*, Riverhead Trade (Paperbacks)); 1974. pap. 5.95 o.s.i (*0-399-50031-6*, Perigee Bks.) Berkley Publishing Group.

—The Awakening. unabr. ed. 1994. audio 32.95 (*0-7861-0848-7*, 1517) Blackstone Audio Bks., Inc.

—The Awakening. unabr. ed. 1991. audio 39.95 (*1-55686-377-2*, 377) Books in Motion.

—The Awakening. unabr. collector's ed. 1995. audio 30.00 (*0-7366-2968-8*, 3659) Books on Tape, Inc.

—The Awakening. 1992. reprint ed. lib. bdg. 21.95 (*0-89968-270-7*, Lightyear Pr.) Buccaneer Bks., Inc.

—The Awakening. l.t. ed. 2000. 329p. pap. 24.95 (*1-58855-004-4*) Cyber Classics, Inc.

—The Awakening. 1993. 128p. reprint ed. pap. text 1.00 (*0-486-27786-0*) Dover Pubns., Inc.

—The Awakening. l.t. ed. 903p. pap. 71.39 (*0-7583-0319-X*); 777p. pap. 62.47 (*0-7583-0318-1*); 634p. pap. 51.01 (*0-7583-0317-3*); 515p. pap. 42.52 (*0-7583-0316-5*); 231p. pap. 22.08 (*0-7583-0313-0*); 315p. pap. 27.70 (*0-7583-0314-9*); 402p. pap. 34.44 (*0-7583-0315-7*); 185p. lib. bdg. 25.58 (*0-7583-0304-1*); 231p. lib. bdg. 28.08 (*0-7583-0305-X*); 315p. lib. bdg. 33.70 (*0-7583-0306-8*); 402p. lib. bdg. 40.44 (*0-7583-0307-6*); 515p. lib. bdg. 48.52 (*0-7583-0308-4*); 634p. lib. bdg. 57.01 (*0-7583-0309-2*); 777p. lib. bdg. 79.57 (*0-7583-0310-6*); 903p. lib. bdg. 87.76 (*0-7583-0311-4*); 2000. 185p. pap. 19.58 (*0-7583-0312-2*) Huge Print Pr.

—The Awakening. unabr. ed. 1981. audio 26.00 Jimcin Recordings.

—The Awakening. 1992. (Everyman's Library). 272p. 15.00 (*0-679-41721-4*) Knopf, Alfred A. Inc.

—The Awakening. 1982. 192p. mass mkt. 4.50 (*0-380-00245-0*, Avon Bks.) Morrow/Avon.

—The Awakening. abr. ed. 1997. audio 13.98 (*962-634-608-6*, NA210814); audio compact disk 15.98 (*962-634-108-4*, NA210812) Naxos of America, Inc. (Naxos AudioBooks).

—The Awakening. l.t. ed. 1995. 266p. lib. bdg. 25.00 (*0-939495-83-X*); 1998. 172p. reprint ed. lib. bdg. 24.00 (*1-58287-017-9*) North Bks.

—The Awakening. Culley, Margaret, ed. 1977. (Critical Editions Ser.). 256p. (C). pap. o.p. (*0-393-09172-4*) Norton, W. W. & Co., Inc.

—The Awakening. 2nd ed. (Critical Editions Ser.). (C). 1999. pap. text 35.85 (*0-393-99009-5*); 1993. pap. text (*0-393-96057-9*) Norton, W. W. & Co., Inc.

—The Awakening. 1997. (*0-14-771200-9*) Penguin Group (USA) Inc.

—The Awakening. 1996. (Literary Classics). 182p. pap. 10.00 (*1-57392-098-3*) Prometheus Bks., Pubs.

—The Awakening, unabr. ed. 1986. audio 35.00 (*1-55690-583-1*, 86850E7) Recorded Bks., LLC.

—The Awakening. 1988. reprint ed. lib. bdg. 79.00 (*0-7812-1102-6*) Reprint Services Corp.

—The Awakening. 1996. 140p. 21.50 o.p. (*0-684-81912-0*, Simon & Schuster); 1998. (Illus.). 256p. reprint ed. mass mkt. 5.99 (*0-671-01547-8*, Pocket) Simon & Schuster.

—The Awakening. 1996. pap. text 14.95 o.p. (*0-312-13856-3*) St. Martin's Pr.

—The Awakening: And Other Stories. Knights, Pamela, ed. 2000. (Oxford World's Classics Ser.). 480p. pap. 7.95 (*0-19-282300-0*) Oxford Univ. Pr., Inc.

—The Awakening & Other Stories. 1976. 24.95 (*0-8488-0457-0*) Amereon, Ltd.

—The Awakening & Other Stories. Baxter, Judith, ed. 1996. (Cambridge Literature Ser.). (Illus.). 256p. pap. text 11.95 (*0-521-56766-1*) Cambridge Univ. Pr.

—The Awakening & Other Stories. Leary, Lewis Gaston, ed. 1970. (Rinehart Editions Ser.: Vol. 142). (C). pap. text 29.00 o.p. (*0-03-078395-X*) Harcourt College Pubs.

—The Awakening & Other Stories. annuals Baym, Nina, ed. & anno. by. 2000. (Modern Library Classics). 448p. pap. 7.95 (*0-679-78333-4*, Modern Library) Random House Adult Trade Publishing Group.

—The Awakening & Other Stories. 1987. 18.75 o.p. (*0-8446-0544-1*) Smith, Peter Pub., Inc.

—The Awakening & Other Stories. 1998. (Classics Library). pap. 3.95 (*1-85326-556-X*, 556XWW) Wordsworth Editions, Ltd. GBR. *Dist:* Combined Publishing.

—The Awakening & Selected Stories. 1976. mass mkt. 1.50 o.p. (*0-451-50882-3*); mass mkt. 1.95 o.p. (*0-451-51234-0*); mass mkt. 2.75 o.p. (*0-451-51561-7*); mass mkt. 2.95 o.p. (*0-451-51749-0*) NAL. (Signet Classics).

—The Awakening & Selected Stories. 1993. (Modern Library Ser.). 420p. 17.95 o.s.i (*0-679-42469-5*, Modern Library) Random House Adult Trade Publishing Group.

—The Awakening & Selected Stories. 2003. (Penguin Classics Ser.). 288p. pap. 8.00 (*0-14-243732-8*, Penguin Classics) Viking Penguin.

Chopin, Kate & Collier, John, contrib. by. The Awakening. 1997. (Illus.). 88.24 (*0-7607-0815-0*) Barnes & Noble, Inc.

Colbert, James. All I Have Is Blue. unabr. ed. 1994. audio 51.00 (*0-7887-0033-2*, 94232E7) Recorded Bks., LLC.

—No Special Hurry. 1988. 192p. 16.95 o.p. (*0-395-47016-1*) Houghton Mifflin Co.

—No Special Hurry. 1989. 224p. pap. 3.95 o.p. (*0-14-012399-7*, Penguin Bks.) Viking Penguin.

—Skinny Man. unabr. ed. 1993. audio 44.00 (*1-55690-930-6*, 93426E7) Recorded Bks., LLC.

—Skinny Man. 1991. 224p. text 18.95 o.p. (*0-689-12098-2*, Scribner) Simon & Schuster.

Colley, Barbara. Death Tidies Up. 2004. 288p. mass mkt. 6.50 (*1-57566-876-9*, Kensington Bks.) Kensington Publishing Corp.

—Maid for Murder: A Squeaky Clean Charlotte la Rue Mystery. l.t. ed. 2002. 461p. 28.95 o.p. (*0-7862-3947-6*) Gale Group.

—Maid for Murder: A Squeaky Clean Charlotte la Rue Mystery. 288p. 2003. mass mkt. 5.99 (*1-57566-874-2*); 2002. 22.00 (*1-57566-873-4*) Kensington Publishing Corp.

—Polished Off. 2004. 288p. 22.00 (*1-57566-877-7*, Kensington Bks.) Kensington Publishing Corp.

Collins, Nancy A. Tempter. aut. rev. ed. 2001. (Illus.). 232p. 50.00 (*1-887368-51-5*) Gauntlet, Inc.

Coner, Kenyetta. The Mockingbirds. Richards, Lyn, ed. 1988. 250p. pap. 11.00 (*0-9665005-0-4*) 52 Weeks Publishing Hse.

Cushman, Jerome. Tom B. & the Joyful Noise. 1970. (Illus.). (J). (gr. 4-7). 4.25 o.p. (*0-664-32467-3*) Westminster John Knox Pr.

Cuviep, Remi. The Superdome Murders. unabr. ed. 1998. (New Orleans Murder Ser.: No. 1). 100p. pap. 6.95 (*1-892651-05-X*) Columbia Pubns.

Dancer, Rex. Bad Girl Blues. 2001. 304p. pap. 19.95 (*0-7432-3345-X*); 1994. 301p. 20.00 (*0-671-88007-1*) Simon & Schuster. (Simon & Schuster).

—Postcard from Hell. 1995. 297p. 21.00 (*0-671-88009-8*, Simon & Schuster) Simon & Schuster.

—Postcard from Hell: Andy Derain Novel. 1995. 320p. 22.00 (*0-684-80362-3*, Simon & Schuster) Simon & Schuster.

Daniell, Rosemary. The Hurricane Season: A Novel. 1992. 416p. 20.00 o.p. (*0-688-08860-0*, Morrow, William & Co.) Morrow/Avon.

Davis, J. Madison. Red Knight: A Novel. 1992. 232p. 19.95 o.p. (*0-8027-1199-5*) Walker & Co.

Davis, Rod. Corina's Way: A Novel. 2003. 288p. 24.95 (*1-58838-129-3*, NewSouth Bks.) NewSouth, Inc.

De Noux, O'Neil. Big Kiss. 1990. mass mkt. 4.50 o.s.i (*0-8217-3531-4*, Zebra Bks.) Kensington Publishing Corp.

—The Big Show. 1998. 320p. pap. 5.95 (*0-9653145-8-8*, Autumn Bks.) Pontalba Pr.

—Crescent City Kills. 1992. mass mkt. 4.50 o.s.i (*0-8217-3752-X*, Zebra Bks.) Kensington Publishing Corp.

—Lastanza: New Orleans Police Stories. unabr. ed. 1999. 326p. 19.95 (*1-891643-73-8*, Autumn Bks.) Pontalba Pr.

Dewberry, Elizabeth. Sacrament of Lies. 2003. 272p. pap. 13.00 (*0-425-18861-2*) Berkley Publishing Group.

—Sacrament of Lies. l.t. ed. 2002. 380p. 28.95 (*0-7862-4301-5*) Gale Group.

—Sacrament of Lies. 2002. 240p. 23.95 o.s.i (*0-399-14854-X*, BlueHen Bks.) Putnam Publishing Group, The.

Dickson, Athol. They Shall See God: A Novel. 2002. (Moving Fiction Ser.). 464p. pap. 11.99 (*0-8423-5292-9*) Tyndale Hse. Pubs.

Donachie, David. The Scent of Betrayal. 2003. (Privateersman Mysteries Ser.: No. 5). 448p. pap. 17.95 (*1-59013-031-6*) McBooks Pr., Inc.

Donaldson, D. J. Blood on the Bayou. 1991. 16.95 o.p. (*0-312-05387-8*, Saint Martin's Minotaur) St. Martin's Pr.

—Cajun Nights. 1989. pap. 3.95 o.p. (*0-312-91610-8*, St. Martin's Paperbacks); 1988. 256p. 16.95 o.p. (*0-312-02175-5*, Saint Martin's Minotaur) St. Martin's Pr.

—Louisiana Fever. (Andy Broussard/Kit Franklyn Mysteries Ser.). 288p. 1997. mass mkt. 5.99 o.p. (*0-312-96257-6*, St. Martin's Paperbacks); 1996. 21.95 o.p. (*0-312-14362-1*, Saint Martin's Minotaur) St. Martin's Pr.

—New Orleans Requiem. 1995. (Mystery Ser.). 250p. per. (*0-373-26188-8*, 1-26188-2, Worldwide Library) Harlequin Enterprises, Ltd.

—New Orleans Requiem. 1994. 240p. 19.95 o.p. (*0-312-10495-2*, Saint Martin's Minotaur) St. Martin's Pr.

—No Mardi Gras for the Dead. 1995. (WWL Mystery Ser.). mass mkt. (*0-373-26163-2*, 1-26163-5, Harlequin Bks.) Harlequin Enterprises, Ltd.

—No Mardi Gras for the Dead. 1992. (Andy Broussard - Kit Franklyn Mystery Ser.). 216p. 17.95 o.p. (*0-312-08271-1*) St. Martin's Pr.

—Sleeping with the Crawfish: An Andy Broussard & Kit Franklyn Mystery. (Andy Broussard/Kit Franklyn Mysteries Ser.). 272p. 1998. mass mkt. 5.99 (*0-312-96681-4*, St. Martin's Paperbacks); 1997. 21.95 o.p. (*0-312-17025-4*, Saint Martin's Minotaur) St. Martin's Pr.

Donovan, David Michael. Evil Down in the Alley: A Novel. 1999. 438p. 26.00 (*0-9669259-3-9*) J-D Publishing Co.

Drake, Shannon. Beneath a Blood Red Moon. 2000. (Five Star Romance Ser.). 394p. 27.95 (*0-7862-2500-9*, Five Star) Gale Group.

Dunbar, Alice. The Goodness of St. Rocque. 1977. (Black Heritage Library Collection). reprint ed. 22.95 (*0-8369-8817-5*) Ayer Co. Pubs., Inc.

Dunbar, Sophie. A Bad Hair Day: An Eclaire Mystery. 295th ed. 1998. (Eclaire Mysteries Ser.: No. 3). 296p. reprint ed. mass mkt. 5.95 (*1-890768-08-1*, Intrigue Pr.) Corvus Publishing.

—A Bad Hair Day: An Eclaire Mystery. 1996. 272p. 22.95 o.p. (*0-312-13926-8*, Saint Martin's Minotaur) St. Martin's Pr.

—Behind Eclaire's Doors. unabr. ed. 1998. (Claire & Dan Claiborne Eclaire Mystery Ser.: Bk. 1). audio 39.95 (*1-55686-804-9*) Books in Motion.

—Behind Eclaire's Doors. 1994. mass mkt. 4.99 o.p. (*0-312-95259-7*, St. Martin's Paperbacks) St. Martin's Pr.

—Behind Eclaire's Doors: A Tale of Murder & Mayhem in New Orleans. 1993. 224p. 17.95 o.p. (*0-312-09280-6*, Saint Martin's Minotaur) St. Martin's Pr.

—Behind Eclaire's Doors: An Eclaire Mystery. 1998. (Eclaire Mysteries Ser.: No. 1). 296p. reprint ed. mass mkt. 5.95 (*1-890768-10-3*, Intrigue Pr.) Corvus Publishing.

—Shiveree. (Eclaire Mysteries Ser.: 4). 416p. 2000. mass mkt. 5.95 (*1-890768-24-3*); 1999. 22.95 (*1-890768-11-1*) Corvus Publishing. (Intrigue Pr.).

Dunbar, Tony. City of Beads. 1996. 256p. mass mkt. 5.99 o.s.i (*0-425-15578-1*, Prime Crime) Berkley Publishing Group.

—City of Beads. 1996. 256p. 21.95 o.p. (*0-399-14081-6*, G. P. Putnam's Sons) Penguin Group (USA) Inc.

—The Crime Czar: A Tubby Dubonnet Mystery. 1998. (Tubby Dubonnet Mysteries Ser.). 240p. mass mkt. 5.99 o.s.i (*0-440-22658-9*) Dell Publishing.

—Crooked Man. 1996. 208p. mass mkt. 4.99 o.s.i (*0-425-15138-7*) Berkley Publishing Group.

—Crooked Man. 1994. 240p. 21.95 o.p. (*0-399-13973-7*, G. P. Putnam's Sons) Penguin Group (USA) Inc.

—Lucky Man. 1999. (Tubby Dubonnet Mysteries Ser.). 240p. mass mkt. 5.99 o.s.i (*0-440-22662-7*) Dell Publishing.

—Shelter from the Storm. 1998. 224p. mass mkt. 5.99 o.s.i (*0-425-16644-9*) Berkley Publishing Group.

—Shelter from the Storm. l.t. ed. 1998. (Large Print Book Ser.). pap. 23.95 (*1-56895-607-X*, Wheeler Publishing, Inc.) Gale Group.

—Shelter from the Storm. 1997. 256p. 24.95 o.p. (0-399-14301-7, G. P. Putnam's Sons) Penguin Group (USA) Inc.
—Trick Question. l.t. ed. 1997. (Tubby Dubonnet Mysteries Ser.). 224p. mass mkt. 5.99 o.s.i (0-425-16092-0, Prime Crime) Berkley Publishing Group.
—Trick Question. 1997. 256p. 22.95 o.p. (0-399-14184-7, G. P. Putnam's Sons) Penguin Group (USA) Inc.
Eddy, Paul. Flint. l.t. ed. 2001. 520p. 28.95 (1-58724-029-7, Wheeler Publishing, Inc.) Gale Group.
—Flint. 2001. 432p. reprint ed. mass mkt. 6.99 o.s.i (0-451-40995-7, Onyx) NAL.
—Flint. 2000. 320p. 24.95 o.s.i (0-399-14653-9) Penguin Group (USA) Inc.
Edwards, Louis. N: A Romantic Mystery. 240p. 1998. pap. 12.95 o.s.i (0-452-27788-4, Plume); 1997. 22.95 o.p. (0-525-94182-7) Dutton/Plume.
Ellis, Julie. Savage Oaks. 1981. mass mkt. 2.25 o.s.i (0-449-23996-9, Fawcett) Ballantine Bks.
—Savage Oaks. l.t. ed. 2000. (G. K. Hall Romance Ser.). 453p. 26.95 (0-7838-9158-X, Macmillan Reference USA) Gale Group.
Everett, Peter. Bellocq's Women. 2000. 256p. o.p. (0-224-05988-2) Random Hse. UK, Ltd.
Fairbanks, Nancy. Crime Brulee. 2001. (Culinary Mysteries Ser.). 288p. mass mkt. 5.99 (0-425-17918-4) Berkley Publishing Group.
Feather, Jane. Reckless Seduction. 2000. 336p. mass mkt. 6.99 (0-8217-7198-1) Kensington Publishing Corp.
Feehan, Christine. Dark Magic. 2000. 368p. mass mkt. 6.99 (0-505-52389-2) Dorchester Publishing Co., Inc.
—Dark Magic. l.t. ed. 2003. 504p. 28.95 (0-7862-5159-X) Thorndike Pr.
Fennelly, Tony. The Closet Hanging. 1987. (Matt Sinclair Ser.). 224p. 14.95 o.p. (0-88184-306-7); pap. 3.50 o.p. (0-88184-393-8) Avalon Publishing Group. (Carroll & Graf Pubs.).
—The Hippie in the Wall. 1994. 240p. 19.95 o.p. (0-312-10475-8, Saint Martin's Minotaur) St. Martin's Pr.
—Murder with a Twist: The Glory Hole Murders & the Closet Hanging. 1991. 432p. pap. 4.95 o.p. (0-88184-783-6, Carroll & Graf Pubs.) Avalon Publishing Group.
—1 (900) D-E-A-D: A Margo Fortier Mystery. 1996. 240p. 21.95 (0-312-14267-6, Saint Martin's Minotaur) St. Martin's Pr.
Foster, B. J. Bayou Shadows. 2000. 267p. 21.95 (0-9675884-5-6) Cresent Hse. Publishing.
Fox, Frank G. Funky Butt Blues. 1996. 213p. (Orig.). pap. 10.00 (0-9652052-0-7) St. Expedite Pr.
Fox, Paula. The God of Nightmares. 1990. 240p. 18.95 o.p. (0-86547-432-X, North Point Pr.) Farrar, Straus & Giroux.
—The God of Nightmares. 2002. 240p. pap. 13.95 (0-393-32287-4) Norton, W. W. & Co., Inc.
—The God of Nightmares. 1991. mass mkt. 5.95 (0-446-36114-3) Warner Bks., Inc.
Friedmann, Patty. Eleanor Rushing: A Novel. 288p. 2000. pap. text 14.00 (1-58243-077-2); 1999. text 23.00 o.p. (1-58243-003-9) Basic Bks. (Counterpoint Pr.).
—Secondhand Smoke. 2002. 304p. text 25.00 (1-58243-217-1, Counterpoint Pr.) Basic Bks.
Fulmer, David. Chasing the Devil's Tail: A Storyville Mystery. 2003. (Illus.). 348p. pap. 14.00 (0-15-602728-3, Harvest Bks.) Harcourt Trade Pubs.
—Chasing the Devil's Tail: A Storyville Mystery. 2001. 226p. 24.95 (1-890208-84-1); 320p. pap. (1-890208-94-9) Poisoned Pen Pr.
Gifford, Barry. Arise & Walk: A Novel. 1994. 176p. (J). 19.95 (0-7868-6013-8) Hyperion Pr.
—Baby Cat-Face. 1997. 192p. pap. 11.00 (0-15-600525-5, Harvest Bks.) Harcourt Trade Pubs.
Gifford, Barry, ed. Baby Cat-Face: A Novel. 1995. 192p. 20.00 o.s.i (0-15-100183-9) Harcourt Trade Pubs.
Gilchrist, Ellen. The Annunciation. 1985. 14.95 (0-316-31302-5) Little Brown & Co.
—The Annunciation. 2001. (Voices of the South Ser.). 368p. pap. 16.95 (0-8071-2736-1) Louisiana State Univ. Pr.
—Annunciation: A Novel. 1985. 353p. pap. 13.95 (0-316-31308-4) Little Brown & Co.
—In the Land of Dreamy Dreams. unabr. collector's ed. 1989. audio 42.00 (0-7366-1542-3, 2411) Books on Tape, Inc.
—In the Land of Dreamy Dreams. 1985. 14.95 o.s.i (0-316-31304-1); 167p. pap. 11.95 o.p. (0-316-31306-8) Little Brown & Co.
—In the Land of Dreamy Dreams. 1981. 14.95 o.p. (0-938626-02-7); pap. 5.95 o.p. (0-938626-03-5) Univ. of Arkansas Pr.
Girardi, Robert. Madeleine's Ghost: A Novel of New York, New Orleans & the Next World. l.t. ed. 1996. 530p. 24.95 o.p. (0-7838-1507-7, Macmillan Reference USA) Gale Group.
—Madeleine's Ghost: A Novel of New York, New Orleans & the Next World. 1999. E-Book 11.95 (0-440-33399-7) Random Hse., Inc.
—Madeleine's Ghost: A Novel of New York, New Orleans & the Next World. unabr. ed. 1997. audio 85.00 (0-7887-0932-1, 95072E7) Recorded Bks., LLC.
Gores, Joe. Dead Man. set. unabr. ed. 1995. audio 69.95 (0-7862-9974-6, CSL 083) BBC Audiobooks America.
—Dead Man. 1993. 272p. 18.95 (0-89296-541-X) Mysterious Pr.
—Dead Man. 1994. 272p. mass mkt. 5.50 o.s.i (0-446-40391-1) Warner Bks., Inc.
Greenburg, Martin H. & Davis, Russell, eds. Mardi Gras Madness: Stories of Murder & Mayhem in New Orleans. 2000. 239p. pap. 16.95 (1-58182-077-1, Cumberland Hearthside) Cumberland Hse. Publishing.
Grimsley, Jim. Boulevard. 2002. 304p. tchr. ed. 23.95 (1-56512-251-8) Algonquin Bks. of Chapel Hill.
Grisham, John. The Client. l.t. ed. 1993. 432p. 29.95 (0-385-42471-X); (YA). 26.00 o.s.i (0-385-46865-2); 432p. 200.00 o.s.i (0-385-47015-0) Bantam Doubleday Dell Large Print Group, Inc. (Doubleday Large Type).
—The Client. unabr. ed. 1993. audio 80.00 (0-7366-2464-3, 3228) Books on Tape, Inc.
—The Client. 1994. 576p. mass mkt. 7.99 (0-440-21352-5); mass mkt. (0-440-21807-1) Dell Publishing.
—The Client. 1994. audio 27.50 o.s.i (0-553-54152-8); 1993. audio 18.80 o.s.i (0-553-70058-8); 1993. 360p. pap. 23.50 incl. audio (0-553-47139-2, 692172) Random Hse. Audio Publishing Group. (RH Audio).
—The Client. 1994. (Illus.). 14.04 (0-606-18101-6) Turtleback Bks.
—The Client: International Edition. 1993. 512p. mass mkt. 6.99 o.s.i (0-440-29526-2) Dell Publishing.
—El Cliente. 2nd ed. 1998. (SPA.). 424p. (84-08-02141-9) GeoPlaneta, Editorial, S. A.
—El Cliente. 1994. (SPA.). 16.30 (0-606-18347-7) Turtleback Bks.
—Tiempo de Matar. 1995. (SPA., Illus.). 472p. 9.95 (84-08-01475-7, PT9159) GeoPlaneta, Editorial, S. A. ESP. *Dist:* Lectorum Pubns., Inc., Planeta Publishing Corp.
Hall, Barbara. A Summons to New Orleans. E-Book 23.00 (1-58945-114-7) Adobe Systems, Inc.
—A Summons to New Orleans. 2000. 288p. 23.00 (0-684-86319-7, Simon & Schuster) Simon & Schuster.
Hambly, Barbara. Die upon a Kiss. 2002. 480p. mass mkt. 5.99 (0-553-58165-1) Bantam Bks.
—Die upon a Kiss. l.t. ed. 2003. 608p. 25.95 (0-375-43266-3) Random Hse. Large Print.
—A Free Man of Color. 1998. 432p. reprint ed. mass mkt. 6.99 (0-553-57526-0) Bantam Bks.
—Wet Grave. 2003. 384p. mass mkt. 6.50 (0-553-58159-7); 2002. (Illus.). 304p. 23.95 (0-553-10935-9) Bantam Bks.
—Wet Grave. l.t. ed. 2003. 486p. 25.95 (0-375-43274-4, Random House Large Print) Random Hse. Large Print.
Harper, M. A. The Year of Past Things: A New Orleans Ghost Story. 2003. 256p. 24.95 (1-58818-069-7) Hill Street Pr., LLC.
Harris, Thomas. Black Sunday. 1981. mass mkt. 4.50 o.s.i (0-553-28116-X); 1977. pap. 2.25 o.p. (0-553-10940-5) Bantam Bks.
—Black Sunday. 1991. 318p. reprint ed. lib. bdg. 24.95 o.p. (0-89966-876-3) Buccaneer Bks., Inc.
—Black Sunday. 1990. 384p. reprint ed. mass mkt. 7.50 o.s.i (0-440-20614-6) Dell Publishing.
—Black Sunday. 25th anniv. ed. 2000. 320p. 26.95 (0-525-94555-5, Abrahams, William Bks.) Dutton/Plume.
—Black Sunday. 2001. 320p. mass mkt. 7.99 (0-451-20415-8) NAL.
—Black Sunday. 1975. 320p. 7.95 o.p. (0-399-11443-2) Putnam Publishing Group, The.
Haymaker, Lafayette. Nola 46. 1995. (Illus.). 211p. (Orig.). pap. 14.00 (0-9641632-2-5) Mainesburg Pr.
Haynes, Darleen. Dark Face of Light: A Novel. 2003. (1-932303-41-3); (1-932303-42-1) Media Creations, Inc. (Llumina Pr.).
Hebert, Charles J. Swimming to Atlantis. Neil, Winter C., ed. unabr. ed. 1997. 296p. 17.95 (0-9653145-0-2, 97-01, Autumn Bks.) Pontalba Pr.
Hedden, Worth Tuttle. The Other Room. 2002. 274p. pap. 14.95 (0-9624878-1-3, 0-9624878-1-3) Paperback Rack Bks.
Herren, Greg. Murder in the Rue Dauphine. 2002. 227p. pap. 13.95 (1-55583-585-6) Alyson Pubns.
Hicks, Jimmy G. Eight, Skate & Donate. 2001. pap. 21.95 (0-595-16869-8) iUniverse, Inc.
Hill, Sandra. Frankly My Dear. (Timeswept Ser.). 2003. 368p. mass mkt. 5.99 (0-8439-4617-2); 1996. 400p. pap. 5.50 (0-8439-4042-5) Dorchester Publishing Co., Inc. (Leisure Bks.).
—Frankly, My Dear. 1999. E-Book 9.95 (0-585-29855-6) netLibrary, Inc.
Hingle, Metsy. Behind the Mask. 2002. 384p. mass mkt. (1-55166-926-9, Mira Bks.) Harlequin Enterprises, Ltd.
—Flash Point. 2003. 384p. mass mkt. (1-55166-714-2, Mira Bks.) Harlequin Enterprises, Ltd.
Hoag, Tami. A Thin Dark Line. 1998. 608p. reprint ed. mass mkt. 7.99 (0-553-57188-5) Bantam Bks.
—A Thin Dark Line. 2002. pap. incl. audio (0-7435-2754-2) Encore Performance Publishing.
—A Thin Dark Line. l.t. ed. 1997. (Large Print Book Ser.). 26.95 o.p. (1-56895-450-6, Wheeler Publishing, Inc.) Gale Group.
—A Thin Dark Line, unabr. ed. 1997. audio 117.00 (0-7887-1766-9, 95244E7) Recorded Bks., LLC.
—A Thin Dark Line. abr. ed. 1997. audio 23.00 (0-671-57477-9, 495077, Simon & Schuster Audioworks) Simon & Schuster Audio.
Holden, Christine. A Hitch in Time. 2000. (Time Passages Ser.). 336p. mass mkt. 5.99 o.s.i (0-515-12928-3, Jove) Berkley Publishing Group.
Howard, Linda. Kill & Tell. l.t. ed. 1998. pap. 23.95 o.p. (1-56895-554-5, Wheeler Publishing, Inc.) Gale Group.
—Kill & Tell. 1998. 320p. mass mkt. 7.99 (0-671-56883-3, Pocket) Simon & Schuster.
—Tears of the Renegade. 2001. 256p. mass mkt. (1-55166-786-X, 1-66786-4, Mira Bks.); 1985. mass mkt. (0-373-07092-6, Harlequin Bks.) Harlequin Enterprises, Ltd.
Inness-Brown, Elizabeth. Burning Marguerite. 2003. 256p. pap. 13.00 (0-375-72622-5, Vintage) Knopf Publishing Group.
—Burning Marguerite. 2002. 256p. 23.00 (0-375-41196-8) Knopf, Alfred A. Inc.
Jackson, Lisa. Hot Blooded. l.t. ed. 2001. 456p. 28.95 (1-57490-378-0, Beeler Large Print Bks.) Beeler, Thomas T. Publisher.
—Hot Blooded. 2001. 464p. mass mkt. 6.99 (0-8217-6841-7, Zebra Bks.) Kensington Publishing Corp.
Kearney, Susan. Double the Thrill. 2002. (Harlequin Blaze Ser.). mass mkt. (0-373-79054-6, Harlequin Bks.) Harlequin Enterprises, Ltd.
Kelley, William. A Servant of Slaves: The Life of Henriette Delille. 2003. 223p. pap. 21.95 (0-8245-1998-1) Crossroad Publishing Co.
King, Grace E. Tales of a Time & Place. reprint ed. 27.50 (0-404-03690-2) AMS Pr., Inc.
—Tales of a Time & Place. 1972. lib. bdg. 17.00 (0-8422-8086-3); reprint ed. pap. text 6.95 (0-8290-0675-3) Irvington Pubs.
—Tales of a Time & Place. 1992. (BCL1-PS American Literature Ser.). 303p. reprint ed. lib. bdg. 89.00 (0-7812-6778-1) Reprint Services Corp.
—Tales of a Time & Place. 19.00 o.p. (0-403-04304-2) Somerset Pubs., Inc.
King, Peter. Roux the Day: A Gourmet Detective Mystery. 2002. 288p. 23.95 (0-312-28365-2, Saint Martin's Minotaur) St. Martin's Pr.
—Roux the Day: A Gourmet Detective Mystery. 2003. (Mystery Ser.). 28.95 (0-7862-4781-9) Thorndike Pr.
Leonard, Elmore. Bandits. l.t. ed. 1987. 382p. 18.95 o.p. (0-8161-4297-1); 10.95 o.p. (0-8161-4298-X) Gale Group. (Macmillan Reference USA).
—Bandits. 1987. 17.95 o.p. (0-87795-841-6, Morrow, William & Co.) Morrow/Avon.
Lita. Lita. 2003. (Illus.). 352p. 26.00 (0-7434-7398-1, WWE) Simon & Schuster.
Llwellyn, Michael. Twelfth Night. 1997. 384p. (YA). 21.95 o.p. (1-57566-082-2, Kensington Bks.) Kensington Publishing Corp.
Lochte, Dick. Blue Bayou. 1993. (Southern Mysteries Ser.). mass mkt. 4.99 o.s.i (0-8041-1145-6, Ivy Bks.) Ballantine Bks.
—Blue Bayou. 1992. 304p. 20.00 o.p. (0-671-74711-8, Simon & Schuster) Simon & Schuster.
—The Neon Smile. 1996. mass mkt. 5.99 o.s.i (0-8041-1405-6, Ivy Bks.) Ballantine Bks.
—The Neon Smile. 1995. (Illus.). 304p. 21.00 (0-671-74712-6, Simon & Schuster) Simon & Schuster.
Lutz, John. The Right to Sing the Blues. 1988. 256p. pap. 2.95 o.p. (0-8125-0646-4, Tor Bks.) Doherty, Tom Assocs., LLC.
—The Right to Sing the Blues. 1985. 256p. 14.95 o.p. (0-312-68235-2) St. Martin's Pr.
—The Right to Sing the Blues. E-Book 9.99 (1-58824-387-7); 2001. 256p. pap. 14.00 (0-7434-1288-5) ibooks, Inc.
MacBride, Roger Lea. On the Banks of the Bayou. 1998. (Little House Ser.: Vol. 1). (Illus.). 240p. (J). (gr. 3-6). pap. 5.99 (0-06-440582-6) HarperCollins Pubs.
Maiman, Jaye. Old Black Magic: A Robin Miller Mystery. 1997. (Robin Miller Mysteries Ser.: Vol. 6). 288p. pap. 11.95 o.p. (1-56280-175-9) Naiad Pr., Inc.
Martin, David Lozell. Pelikan. 1999. (Illus.). 320p. 23.00 (0-684-85348-5, Simon & Schuster) Simon & Schuster.
Martin, Valerie. Set in Motion. 1978. 224p. 8.95 o.s.i (0-374-26140-7) Farrar, Straus & Giroux.
—Set in Motion. 2001. (Voices of the South Ser.). 224p. pap. 15.95 (0-8071-2735-3) Louisiana State Univ. Pr.
—Set in Motion. 1991. 224p. reprint ed. pap. (0-671-73687-6, Washington Square Pr.) Simon & Schuster.
Mask of Auntie Laveau. Date not set. (0-312-27779-2, Saint Martin's Minotaur) St. Martin's Pr.
Matthews, Christine & Randisi, Robert J. The Masks of Auntie Laveau: A Gil & Claire Hunt Mystery. 2002. 208p. 23.95 (0-312-26898-X, Saint Martin's Minotaur) St. Martin's Pr.
McCloskey, Walter. Risking Elizabeth. 1998. 320p. mass mkt. 6.99 o.s.i (0-425-16413-6) Berkley Publishing Group.
—Risking Elizabeth. 1997. 288p. 21.50 (0-684-82434-5, Simon & Schuster) Simon & Schuster.
McDaniel, Sylvia. Sunlight on Josephine Street. 2002. 32p. mass mkt. 5.99 o.s.i (0-8217-7321-6) Kensington Publishing Corp.
McGaughey, Neil. Otherwise Known As Murder. 1994. 224p. text 20.00 (0-684-19674-3, Macmillan Reference USA) Gale Group.
McKinney, Meagan. A Man to Slay Dragons. l.t. ed. 1996. 440p. lib. bdg. 23.95 (1-57490-063-3, Beeler Large Print Bks.) Beeler, Thomas T. Publisher.
—A Man to Slay Dragons. 1996. 416p. mass mkt. 5.99 o.s.i (0-8217-5345-2, Zebra Bks.); 384p. pap. 21.95 o.p. (1-57566-009-1) Kensington Publishing Corp.
—My Wicked Enchantress. 1988. 416p. mass mkt. 5.50 o.s.i (0-440-20301-5) Dell Publishing.
—My Wicked Enchantress. 1997. (Romance Ser.). 408p. pap. 23.95 (0-7862-1206-3, Five Star) Gale Group.
—My Wicked Enchantress. 1997. 416p. mass mkt. 5.99 o.s.i (0-8217-5661-3) Kensington Publishing Corp.
Michaels, Fern. Listen to Your Heart. abr. ed. 2000. audio 17.95 o.p. (1-56740-907-5, 2120, Nova Audio Bks.); audio 24.95 (1-56740-366-2, 2119, Brilliance Audio Unabridged); 6p. audio 44.25 (1-56740-733-1, 2121, Unabridged Library Editions) Brilliance Audio.
—Listen to Your Heart. l.t. ed. 2000. 27.95 (1-56895-876-5, Wheeler Publishing, Inc.) Gale Group.
—Listen to Your Heart. 2004. 256p. mass mkt. 6.99 (0-8217-7463-8, Zebra Bks.); 2000. 214p. 20.00 o.s.i (1-57566-572-7) Kensington Publishing Corp.
—Listen to Your Heart. l.t. ed. 2004. 229p. pap. 13.95 (1-59413-027-2, Large Print Pr.) Thorndike Pr.
Moores, Amanda. Dream Palace. 1994. 288p. 20.00 o.p. (0-7867-0125-0, Carroll & Graf Pubs.) Avalon Publishing Group.
—Dream Palace. 1993. 288p. 21.00 (0-671-75919-1, Simon & Schuster) Simon & Schuster.
Morris, Gilbert. And Then There Were Two. l.t. ed. 2002. 431p. pap. 16.95 (1-4104-0015-8, Walker Large Print) Gale Group.
—And Then There Were Two. l.t. ed. 2001. (Dani Ross Mysteries Ser.). 463p. 24.95 o.p. (0-7862-3088-6) Thorndike Pr.
—Deadly Deception. 1991. (Danielle Ross Mystery Ser.: No. 3). 320p. (gr. 10). pap. 9.99 o.p. (0-8007-5419-0) Revell, Fleming H. Co.
—Four of a Kind: A Dani Ross Mystery. 2001. (Dani Ross Mysteries Ser.: Vol. 4). 264p. reprint ed. pap. 12.99 (1-58134-244-6) Crossway Bks.
—Four of a Kind: A Dani Ross Mystery. l.t. ed. 2001. (Christian Mystery Ser.). 426p. 24.95 (0-7862-3545-4) Thorndike Pr.
Nance, Kathleen. The Warrior. 2001. 400p. mass mkt. 5.99 (0-505-52417-1) Dorchester Publishing Co., Inc.
Neate, Patrick. Twelve Bar Blues. 416p. 2004. pap. 14.00 (0-8021-4056-4); 2002. 24.00 (0-8021-1727-9) Grove/Atlantic, Inc. (Grove Pr.).
Neihart, Ben. Hey, Joe: A Novel. 1996. 208p. 21.00 o.p. (0-684-81316-5, Simon & Schuster) Simon & Schuster.
North, Hailey. Dear Love Doctor. 2001. 384p. mass mkt. 5.99 o.s.i (0-380-81308-4, Avon Bks.) Morrow/Avon.
Ondaatje, Michael. Coming Through Slaughter. 1996. 160p. pap. 11.00 (0-679-76785-1, Vintage) Knopf Publishing Group.
—Coming Through Slaughter. 1983. pap. 2.25 o.p. (0-380-42911-X, Avon Bks.) Morrow/Avon.
—Coming Through Slaughter. 1977. 9.95 o.p. (0-393-08765-4) Norton, W. W. & Co., Inc.
—Coming Through Slaughter. 1984. 158p. pap. 10.95 o.p. (0-14-007281-0, Penguin Bks.) Viking Penguin.
Orloff, Erica. Diary of a Blues Goddess. 2003. (Red Dress Ink Ser.: No. 21). 304p. pap. (0-373-25032-0, Red Dress Ink) Harlequin Enterprises, Ltd.
Palmer, Karen. All Saints. 272p. 1999. pap. 13.00 (1-56947-138-X); 1997. 24.00 (1-56947-105-3) Soho Pr., Inc.
Parker, F. M. The Assassins. l.t. ed. 1990. (General Ser.). 350p. lib. bdg. 18.95 o.p. (0-8161-4999-2, Macmillan Reference USA) Gale Group.

—The Assassins. 1989. 16.95 o.p. (*0-453-00701-5*); 1990. 256p. reprint ed. mass mkt. 3.95 o.p. (*0-451-16846-1*, Signet Bks.) NAL.

—Distant Thunder. l.t. ed. 2002. (Western Ser.). 415p. pap. 19.95 (*1-58724-269-9*, Wheeler Publishing, Inc.) Gale Group.

—Distant Thunder. 1999. 384p. mass mkt. 5.99 o.s.i (*0-7860-0647-1*, Pinnacle Bks.) Kensington Publishing Corp.

Parkhurst, Carolyn. The Dogs of Babel. 2004. 288p. pap. 15.00 (*0-316-77850-8*, Back Bay); 2003. 272p. (gr. 8 up). 21.95 (*0-316-16868-8*) Little Brown & Co.

—The Dogs of Babel. l.t. ed. 2003. 384p. 32.95 (*0-7862-5913-2*) Thorndike Pr.

Peart, Jane. The House of Haunted Dreams. 1992. 3.99 o.p. (*1-55773-649-9*, Diamond Bks.) Ace Bks.

—The House of Haunted Dreams. l.t. ed. 2001. (Thorndike Candlelight Romance Ser.). 341p. 24.95 o.p. (*0-7862-3112-2*) Thorndike Pr.

Pelikan. 2000. E-Book 23.00 (*0-7432-1353-X*, Simon & Schuster) Simon & Schuster.

Plain, Belva. Crescent City. 1984. 432p. 16.95 o.p. (*0-385-29354-2*, Delacorte Pr.) Dell Publishing.

—Crescent City. l.t. ed. 1985. (General Ser.). 18.95 o.p. (*0-8161-3775-7*, Macmillan Reference USA) Gale Group.

Reaves, Michael. Voodoo Child. 352p. 1999. pap. text 6.99 (*0-8125-1993-0*); 1998. 25.95 o.p. (*0-312-85608-3*) Doherty, Tom Assocs., LLC. (Tor Bks.).

Redmann, J. M. Death by the Riverside. 1990. 256p. (Orig.). pap. 9.95 o.p. (*0-934678-27-8*) New Victoria Pubs., Inc.

—Death of Jocasta. 1992. 288p. (Orig.). pap. 10.95 o.p. (*0-934678-39-1*) New Victoria Pubs., Inc.

—The Intersection of Law & Desire. 1997. mass mkt. 5.99 (*0-380-72819-2*, Avon Bks.) Morrow/Avon.

—The Intersection of Law & Desire. 1995. 336p. 22.00 o.p. (*0-393-03793-2*) Norton, W. W. & Co., Inc.

—Lost Daughters: A Micky Knight Mystery. 1999. (Mickey Knight Mystery Ser.). 320p. text 24.95 o.p. (*0-393-04028-3*) Norton, W. W. & Co., Inc.

Rice, Anne. The Feast of All Saints. 1992. 576p. pap. 15.00 (*0-345-37604-8*); 1986. 640p. mass mkt. 7.99 (*0-345-33453-1*); 1985. mass mkt. 4.95 o.s.i (*0-449-21063-4*, Fawcett); 1981. 640p. mass mkt. 2.95 o.p. (*0-449-24378-8*) Ballantine Bks.

—The Feast of All Saints. abr. ed. 1994. audio 8.99 o.s.i (*0-679-43413-5*, 390765); 1992. audio 16.00 o.p. (*0-394-58812-6*) Random Hse. Audio Publishing Group. (RH Audio).

—The Feast of All Saints. 1980. 14.95 o.p. (*0-671-24755-7*, Simon & Schuster) Simon & Schuster.

—Lasher. (SPA.). 26.95 (*950-08-1316-5*, AA9101) Atlantida ARG. *Dist:* Lectorum Pubns., Inc.

—Lasher. (Lives of the Mayfair Witches Ser.). 1995. 640p. mass mkt. 7.99 (*0-345-39781-9*); 1994. 592p. pap. 14.95 (*0-345-37764-8*) Ballantine Bks.

—Lasher. 1993. 592p. 30.00 (*0-679-41295-6*); 22.00 o.s.i (*0-394-28021-0*) Knopf, Alfred A. Inc.

—Lasher, abr. ed. 1993. audio 17.00 (*0-679-42173-4*, 391044, RH Audio) Random Hse. Audio Publishing Group.

—Merrick. 2001. 400p. reprint ed. mass mkt. 7.99 (*0-345-42240-6*, Ballantine Bks.) Ballantine Bks.

—Merrick. 2000. 320p. o.s.i (*0-676-97331-0*) Knopf Canada CAN. *Dist:* Random Hse. of Canada, Ltd., Random Hse., Inc.

—Merrick. 2000. (Vampire Chronicles). 320p. 26.95 (*0-679-45448-9*) Knopf, Alfred A. Inc.

—Merrick. l.t. ed. 2000. 544p. 26.95 (*0-375-43077-6*) Random Hse. Large Print.

—Taltos. 2000. 12.95 B Ediciones S.A. ESP. *Dist:* Distribooks, Inc.

—Taltos. 1996. 576p. mass mkt. 7.99 (*0-345-40431-9*); 1995. 480p. pap. 14.95 (*0-345-39471-2*); 1995. mass mkt. (*0-345-40006-2*, Ballantine Bks.) Ballantine Bks.

—Taltos. 1994. 467p. 25.00 (*0-679-42573-X*) Knopf, Alfred A. Inc.

—Taltos. (FRE.). pap. 12.95 (*2-266-07477-6*) Presses Pocket FRA. *Dist:* Distribooks, Inc.

—Taltos, Set. abr. ed. 1994. audio 22.50 (*0-679-43654-5*, 492019, RH Audio) Random Hse. Audio Publishing Group.

—Taltos. deluxe ltd. num. ed. 1994. 467p. 150.00 (*0-9631925-1-5*) Trice, B.E. Publishing.

—The Violin. 2002. (SPA.). pap. 17.95 (*950-08-2295-4*, AA11960) Atlantida ARG. *Dist:* Lectorum Pubns., Inc.

—The Violin. 1999. 384p. mass mkt. 7.99 (*0-345-42530-8*); 1998. 304p. pap. 14.00 (*0-345-38942-5*); 1998. 7.50 (*0-345-42446-8*, Del Rey) Ballantine Bks.

—The Violin. unabr. ed. 1997. audio 64.00 (*0-7366-3771-0*, 4444) Books on Tape, Inc.

—The Violin. l.t. ed. 1997. pap. 25.95 o.p. (*0-7838-8247-5*, Macmillan Reference USA) Gale Group.

—The Violin. 1997. 289p. 25.95 (*0-679-43302-3*) Knopf, Alfred A. Inc.

—The Violin. unabr. ed. 1997. audio 39.95 (*0-679-46066-7*, 105975);Set. audio compact disk 27.50 (*0-679-46065-9*) Random Hse. Audio Publishing Group. (RH Audio).

—The Violin. l.t. ed. 1997. (Large Print Ser.). 496p. pap. 25.95 (*0-679-77444-0*) Random Hse. Large Print.

—The Violin. deluxe ltd. ed. 1997. 304p. 150.00 (*1-890885-00-2*) Trice, B.E. Publishing.

—The Witching Hour. (Lives of the Mayfair Witches Ser.). 1993. 1056p. mass mkt. 7.99 (*0-345-38446-6*); 1991. 976p. pap. 15.95 (*0-345-36789-8*) Ballantine Bks.

—The Witching Hour. 1998. pap. o.s.i (*0-394-25663-8*); 1990. 976p. 29.95 (*0-394-58786-3*) Knopf, Alfred A. Inc.

—The Witching Hour. abr. ed. 2002. audio 9.99 (*0-553-71352-3*); Set. 1990. audio 18.00 o.s.i (*0-394-58789-8*) Random Hse. Audio Publishing Group. (RH Audio).

Rice, Christopher. A Density of Souls. abr. ed. 2000. audio 17.95 o.p. (*1-56740-399-9*, 2233, Nova Audio Bks.); 9p. audio 57.25 (*1-56740-398-0*, 2232, Unabridged Library Editions); audio 29.95 (*1-56740-475-8*, 2231, Brilliance Audio Unabridged) Brilliance Audio.

—A Density of Souls. 2001. 288p. pap. 13.00 (*0-7868-8646-3*); 2000. 274p. 23.95 (*0-7868-6646-2*) Talk Miramax Bks.

Rice, James. Gaston Goes to Mardi Gras. 2nd ed. 1999. (Illus.). 40p. (J). (ps-3). 14.95 (*1-56554-286-X*) Pelican Publishing Co., Inc.

Ripley, Alexandra. New Orleans Legacy. 1988. 496p. mass mkt. 6.99 (*0-446-34210-6*) Warner Bks., Inc.

Roberts, Nora. Honest Illusions. 2002. 432p. pap. 13.95 (*0-425-18619-9*); 1993. 512p. mass mkt. 7.99 (*0-515-11097-3*, Jove) Berkley Publishing Group.

—Honest Illusions. abr. ed. 2001. audio 24.95 o.p. (*1-58788-404-6*, 2648, Nova Audio Bks.) Brilliance Audio.

—Honest Illusions. 1992. 384p. 19.95 o.p. (*0-399-13761-0*, G. P. Putnam's Sons) Penguin Group (USA) Inc.

—Honest Illusions. 19.95 o.s.i (*0-399-13958-3*) Putnam Publishing Group, The.

—Midnight Bayou. 2002. 368p. reprint ed. mass mkt. 7.99 (*0-515-13397-3*, Jove) Berkley Publishing Group.

—Midnight Bayou. l.t. ed. 2002. 33.95 (*0-7862-3739-2*) Gale Group.

—Midnight Bayou. 2001. 432p. 25.95 o.s.i (*0-399-14824-8*, Riverhead Bks. (Hardcovers)) Penguin Group (USA) Inc.

—Midnight Bayou. l.t. ed. 2002. 14.95 (*1-4104-0052-2*, Large Print Pr.); 30.95 (*0-7862-3737-6*) Thorndike Pr.

Roberts, Sally-Ann. Angelvision. 2002. 192p. 22.00 (*1-56554-907-4*) Pelican Publishing Co., Inc.

Roberts, Walter A. Royal Street, a Novel of Old New Orleans. reprint ed. 42.50 (*0-404-11415-6*) AMS Pr., Inc.

Ruffin, Paul. Pompeii Man. 2001. (*0-945083-03-3*); (*0-945083-04-1*) Louisiana Literature Pr.

Russell, Josh. Yellow Jack. 1999. 224p. 23.95 o.p. (*0-393-04768-7*) Norton, W. W. & Co., Inc.

Ryan, Nan. The Countess Misbehaves. 2000. 384p. mass mkt. (*1-55166-591-3*, 1-66591-8, Mira Bks.) Harlequin Enterprises, Ltd.

Sallis, James. Black Hornet. 1994. 208p. 18.95 o.p. (*0-7867-0118-8*, Carroll & Graf Pubs.) Avalon Publishing Group.

—Black Hornet. 1996. (New Orleans Mystery Ser.: No. 3). 192p. mass mkt. 5.50 (*0-380-72515-0*, Avon Bks.) Morrow/Avon.

—Black Hornet Bk. 3: A Lew Griffin Novel. 2003. 160p. pap. 8.95 (*0-8027-7643-4*) Walker & Co.

—Bluebottle. (Lew Griffin Mysteries Ser.). 161p. 2000. pap. 8.95 (*0-8027-7595-0*); 1999. (Illus.). pap. 22.95 (*0-8027-3323-9*) Walker & Co.

—Eye of the Cricket. 2000. (Lew Griffin Mysteries Ser.). 196p. reprint ed. pap. 8.95 (*0-8027-7581-0*) Walker & Co.

—Eye of the Cricket: A Lew Griffin Mystery. 1997. (Lew Griffin Mysteries Ser.). 204p. 21.95 (*0-8027-3313-1*) Walker & Co.

—Ghost of a Flea: A Lew Griffin Novel. 2002. 252p. 23.95 (*0-8027-3369-7*) Walker & Co.

—The Long-Legged Fly. 1992. 208p. 17.95 o.p. (*0-88184-810-7*, Carroll & Graf Pubs.) Avalon Publishing Group.

—The Long-Legged Fly. 1994. 192p. mass mkt. 4.99 (*0-380-72242-9*, Avon Bks.) Morrow/Avon.

—The Long-Legged Fly. 183p. pap. 15.00 (*1-901982-41-6*) No Exit Pr. GBR. *Dist:* Trafalgar Square.

—Moth. 1993. 208p. 18.95 o.p. (*0-88184-945-6*, Carroll & Graf Pubs.) Avalon Publishing Group.

—Moth. 1995. (Lew Griffin Ser.). reprint ed. pap. 4.99 o.p. (*0-380-72377-8*, Avon Bks.) Morrow/Avon.

—Moth Bk. 2: A Lew Griffin Novel. 2003. 208p. reprint ed. pap. 8.95 (*0-8027-7642-6*) Walker & Co.

Shaik, Fatima. The Mayor of New Orleans: Just Talking Jazz. 1989. 160p. 9.95 (*0-88739-050-1*); pap. 9.95 (*0-88739-071-4*) Creative Arts Bk. Co.

—On Mardi Gras Day. Kane, Cindy, ed. (Illus.). 32p. (J). (ps-3). 2015. 16.89 o.s.i (*0-8037-1443-2*); 1999. 16.99 o.p. (*0-8037-1442-4*) Penguin Putnam Bks. for Young Readers. (Dial Bks. for Young Readers).

Shankman, Sarah. Now Let's Talk of Graves. Chelius, Jane, ed. 1990. 304p. 18.95 o.p. (*0-671-68456-6*, Atria); 1991. 320p. reprint ed. mass mkt. 5.99 (*0-671-68457-4*, Pocket) Simon & Schuster.

Shoemaker, Bill. Stalking Horse. 1994. (Los Angeles Mysteries Ser.). mass mkt. 5.99 o.s.i (*0-449-14936-6*, Fawcett) Ballantine Bks.

—Stalking Horse. l.t. ed. 1995. 481p. pap. 19.95 o.p. (*0-7838-1296-5*, Macmillan Reference USA) Gale Group.

—Stalking Horse. abr. ed. 1993. 16.95 o.p. (*0-7871-0025-0*) NewStar Media, Inc.

Shuman, M. K. Caesar Clue. 1990. 16.95 o.p. (*0-312-04275-2*, Saint Martin's Minotaur) St. Martin's Pr.

—Deep Kill. 1993. 2.99 o.p. (*0-517-09907-1*) Random Hse. Value Publishing.

—Deep Kill. 1991. 16.95 o.p. (*0-312-05854-3*, Saint Martin's Minotaur) St. Martin's Pr.

—The Last Man to Die: A Micah Dunn Mystery. 1992. 240p. 17.95 o.p. (*0-312-07858-7*, Saint Martin's Minotaur) St. Martin's Pr.

—The Maya Stone Murders. 1989. 256p. 16.95 o.p. (*0-312-02608-0*, Saint Martin's Minotaur) St. Martin's Pr.

Skinner, Robert E. Blood to Drink: A Wesley Farrell Novel. 2001. 251p. pap. 14.95 o.s.i (*1-890208-67-1*) Poisoned Pen Pr.

—Cat-Eyed Trouble. 1999. 256p. mass mkt. 5.99 o.s.i (*1-57566-381-3*); 1998. 288p. 19.95 o.s.i (*1-57566-250-7*) Kensington Publishing Corp.

—Daddy's Gone A-Hunting: A Wesley Farrell Novel. 1999. 256p. 22.00 o.s.i (*1-57566-376-7*) Kensington Publishing Corp.

—Daddy's Gone A-Hunting: A Wesley Farrell Novel. 2000. (Illus.). 306p. 23.95 (*1-890208-17-5*) Poisoned Pen Pr.

—Pale Shadow: A Wesley Farrell Novel. 2003. 226p. pap. 14.95 o.s.i (*1-890208-87-6*); 2001. 300p. 23.95 (*1-890208-66-3*) Poisoned Pen Pr.

—The Righteous Cut: A Wesley Farrell Novel. 2002. 275p. 24.95 o.s.i (*1-59058-029-X*); 253p. pap. (*1-59058-044-3*) Poisoned Pen Pr.

—Skin Deep, Blood Red. 1998. 256p. mass mkt. 5.99 o.s.i (*1-57566-254-X*); 1997. 288p. 19.95 o.s.i (*1-57566-092-X*, Kensington Bks.) Kensington Publishing Corp.

Smith, Julie. The Axeman's Jazz. 1992. (Skip Langdon Novel Ser.). 368p. mass mkt. 6.99 (*0-8041-0954-0*, Ivy Bks.) Ballantine Bks.

—The Axeman's Jazz. 1991. 384p. 19.95 o.p. (*0-312-06295-8*, Saint Martin's Minotaur) St. Martin's Pr.

—Crescent City Kill. (Skip Langdon Novel Ser.). 1998. 368p. mass mkt. 6.50 o.s.i (*0-8041-1397-1*, Ivy Bks.); 1997. 326p. 4.99 o.s.i (*0-449-91000-8*, Fawcett) Ballantine Bks.

—House of Blues. 1996. (Skip Langdon Novel Ser.). 352p. reprint ed. mass mkt. 6.99 o.s.i (*0-8041-1342-4*, Ivy Bks.) Ballantine Bks.

—Jazz Funeral. 1994. (Skip Langdon Novel Ser.). 368p. mass mkt. 5.99 o.s.i (*0-8041-1252-5*, Ivy Bks.) Ballantine Bks.

—The Kindness of Strangers. 1997. (Skip Langdon Novel Ser.). mass mkt. 5.99 o.s.i (*0-8041-1273-8*, Ivy Bks.) Ballantine Bks.

—Louisiana Bigshot. 2002. 304p. 24.95 (*0-7653-0059-1*, Forge Bks.) Doherty, Tom Assocs., LLC.

—Louisiana Hotshot. 2001. 335p. 24.95 (*0-7653-0058-3*, Forge Bks.) Doherty, Tom Assocs., LLC.

—Mean Rooms: A Short Story Collection. 2000. (Five Star Mystery Ser.). 196p. 21.95 (*0-7862-2364-2*, Five Star) Gale Group.

—Mean Woman Blues. E-Book (*0-312-71094-1*, Tor Bks.); 2003. 304p. 24.95 (*0-7653-0552-6*, Forge Bks.) Doherty, Tom Assocs., LLC.

—New Orleans Beat: A Skip Langdon Mystery. 1995. (Skip Langdon Novel Ser.). 368p. mass mkt. 6.50 o.s.i (*0-8041-1336-X*, Ivy Bks.) Ballantine Bks.

—New Orleans Mourning. 1990. (Skip Langdon Novel Ser.). 352p. mass mkt. 6.99 (*0-8041-0738-6*, Ivy Bks.) Ballantine Bks.

—New Orleans Mourning. unabr. ed. 1999. (Skip Langdon Mysteries Ser. ). audio 87.00 (*0-7887-3480-6*, 95775E7) Recorded Bks., LLC.

—New Orleans Mourning. 1990. 384p. 17.95 o.p. (*0-312-03892-5*, Saint Martin's Minotaur) St. Martin's Pr.

—82 Desire. (Skip Langdon Novel Ser.). 1999. 352p. mass mkt. 6.99 (*0-8041-1699-7*, Ivy Bks.); 1998. 320p. 24.00 o.s.i (*0-449-00060-5*, Fawcett) Ballantine Bks.

—82 Desire. l.t. ed. 1999. (Large Print Book Ser.). pap. 24.95 (*1-56895-628-2*, Wheeler Publishing, Inc.) Gale Group.

Speart, Jessica. Bird Brained. l.t. ed. 2002. (Paperback Ser.). 502p. pap. 24.95 (*0-7862-4979-X*) Gale Group.

—Bird Brained. 1999. (Rachel Porter Mysteries Ser.). 288p. mass mkt. 5.99 (*0-380-79290-7*, Avon Bks.) Morrow/Avon.

—Gator Aide. 1997. (Rachel Porter Mysteries Ser.). 304p. mass mkt. 5.99 (*0-380-79288-5*, Avon Bks.) Morrow/Avon.

—Tortoise Soup. 1998. (Rachel Porter Mysteries Ser.). 304p. mass mkt. 5.99 (*0-380-79289-3*, Avon Bks.) Morrow/Avon.

Spencer, Elizabeth. The Snare. 1972. 384p. o.p. (*0-07-060178-X*) McGraw-Hill Cos., The.

—The Snare. 1993. (Banner Bks.). 448p. reprint ed. pap. 20.00 (*0-87805-666-1*) Univ. Pr. of Mississippi.

Spindler, Erica. Bone Cold. l.t. ed. 2002. (Wheeler Large Print Book Ser.). pap. 23.95 (*1-58724-204-4*, Wheeler Publishing, Inc.) Gale Group.

—Bone Cold. 2001. 512p. mass mkt. (*1-55166-794-0*, Mira Bks.) Harlequin Enterprises, Ltd.

—Cause for Alarm. 1999. 512p. per. (*1-55166-497-6*, 1-66497-8, Mira Bks.) Harlequin Enterprises, Ltd.

—Forbidden Fruit. 2003. 512p. mass mkt. (*1-55166-751-7*, 53627253); 1996. 504p. mass mkt. (*1-55166-071-7*, 0-66071-2) Harlequin Enterprises, Ltd. (Mira Bks.).

Stayton, Jeff. Silent Comedians. 2004. 23.00 (*1-893956-45-8*) Context Bks.

Taylor, Mel. The Mitt Man. 1999. 352p. 24.00 (*0-688-16094-8*, Morrow, William & Co.) Morrow/Avon.

Temple, Lou Jane. Red Beans & Vice. mass mkt. o.p. (*0-312-98100-7*, St. Martin's Paperbacks); 2001. 288p. 23.95 (*0-312-28013-0*, Saint Martin's Minotaur) St. Martin's Pr.

Tervalon, Jervey. Dead above Ground. 2001. (Illus.). 240p. pap. 12.95 (*0-671-03469-3*, Washington Square Pr.); 2000. 272p. 23.95 o.s.i (*0-671-03468-5*, Atria) Simon & Schuster.

—Lita. 224p. 2004. pap. 13.00 (*0-7434-4885-5*, Washington Square Pr.); 2003. 24.00 (*0-7434-4884-7*, Atria) Simon & Schuster.

Toole, John Kennedy. A Confederacy of Dunces. 21.95 (*0-8488-1207-7*) Amereon, Ltd.

—A Confederacy of Dunces. unabr. ed. 1997. audio 69.95 (*0-7861-1232-8*, 1978) Blackstone Audio Bks., Inc.

—A Confederacy of Dunces. 416p. 1982. pap. 4.50 o.s.i (*0-394-17969-2*, B-474); 20th anniv. ed. 1987. pap. 14.00 (*0-8021-3020-8*, Grove Pr.) Grove/Atlantic, Inc.

—A Confederacy of Dunces. 1980. 352p. 24.95 (*0-8071-0657-7*); 20th anniv. ed. 2000. 338p. 24.95 (*0-8071-2606-3*); 20th anniv. ltd. ed. 2000. (Illus.). 338p. 75.00 (*0-8071-2607-1*) Louisiana State Univ. Pr.

—A Confederacy of Dunces. abr. ed. 1993. audio 16.95 o.p. (*1-55800-145-X*, 40560); Set. 1998. 3p. audio 18.00 (*0-7871-1766-8*, 390552) NewStar Media, Inc. (Dove Audio).

—A Confederacy of Dunces. 1994. 480p. 10.99 o.s.i (*0-517-12270-7*) Random Hse. Value Publishing.

—A Confederacy of Dunces. 1987. 18.00 (*0-606-20071-1*) Turtleback Bks.

Tyree, Omar R. Leslie. 400p. 2002. (Illus.). 21.00 (*0-7432-2866-9*); 2003. reprint ed. pap. 13.00 (*0-7432-2870-7*) Simon & Schuster. (Simon & Schuster).

Walker, Percy B. The Moviegoer. 1988. 224p. reprint ed. mass mkt. 6.99 o.s.i (*0-8041-0290-2*, Ivy Bks.) Ballantine Bks.

Walker, Percy B., ed. The Moviegoer. 1996. pap. 12.00 o.p. (*0-449-91170-5*, Fawcett) Ballantine Bks.

—The Moviegoer. 1967. 242p. pap. 2.95 o.p. (*0-374-50596-9*) Farrar, Straus & Giroux.

—The Moviegoer. 1998. 256p. pap. 12.95 (*0-375-70196-6*, Vintage) Knopf Publishing Group.

—The Moviegoer. 1961. 256p. 26.95 (*0-394-43703-9*) Knopf, Alfred A. Inc.

—The Moviegoer. 1980. (Southern Writers Ser.). pap. 3.95 o.p. (*0-380-47076-4*, Avon Bks.) Morrow/Avon.

Ware, Ciji. Midnight on Julia Street. 1999. 470p. mass mkt. 6.99 (*0-449-00187-3*, Fawcett) Ballantine Bks.

Warren, Nancy. Whisper. 2002. (Harlequin Blaze Ser.). mass mkt. (*0-373-79051-1*, Harlequin Bks.) Harlequin Enterprises, Ltd.

Williamson, Penelope. Mortal Sins. 2003. 496p. mass mkt. 7.50 (*0-446-60950-1*) Warner Bks., Inc.

—Wages of Sin. 2004. 496p. mass mkt. 7.50 (*0-446-61383-5*); 2003. 416p. 19.95 (*0-446-52841-2*) Warner Bks., Inc.

Williamson, Penn. Mortal Sins. abr. ed. 2000. audio 24.98 (*1-57042-924-3*); audio 24.98 Time Warner AudioBooks.

—Mortal Sins. 2000. 432p. 23.95 o.p. (*0-446-52154-X*) Warner Bks., Inc.

Wiltz, Chris. A Diamond Before You Die. (Neal Rafferty Mystery Ser.). 208p. 1988. mass mkt. 3.95 o.s.i (*0-445-40536-8*); 1987. 15.95 o.p. (*0-89296-192-9*) Mysterious Pr.

—A Diamond Before You Die. l.t. ed. 1990. (Ulverscroft Large Print Ser.). 29.99 o.p. (*0-7089-2194-9*, Ulverscroft) Thorpe, F. A. Pubs. GBR. *Dist:* Ulverscroft Large Print Bks., Ltd., Ulverscroft Large Print Canada, Ltd.

—The Emerald Lizard: A Neal Rafferty Mystery. 1991. 224p. 17.95 o.p. (*0-525-24945-1*, Dutton) Dutton/Plume.

—The Killing Circle. l.t. ed. 1991. 8.95 o.p. (*0-7451-9395-1*, 1599); 1988. pap. 14.95 o.p. (*1-55504-628-2*, 333) BBC Audiobooks America.

—The Killing Circle. 1985. pap. 2.95 o.p. (*0-523-41933-3*, Pinnacle Bks.) Kensington Publishing Corp.

Wiltz, Christine. Glass House: Voices of the South. 1994. 208p. (C). 19.95 (*0-8071-1864-8*) Louisiana State Univ. Pr.

Womack, Steven. Murphy's Fault. 1990. 320p. 17.95 o.p. (*0-312-03896-8*, Saint Martin's Minotaur); Vol. 1. 1991. mass mkt. 3.99 o.p. (*0-312-92539-5*, St. Martin's Paperbacks) St. Martin's Pr.

—Smash Cut. 3.98 o.s.i (*0-8317-4629-7*) Smithmark Pubs., Inc.

—Smash Cut. 1991. 304p. 18.95 o.p. (*0-312-06467-5*, Saint Martin's Minotaur) St. Martin's Pr.

—The Software Bomb. 3.98 o.p. (*0-8317-4632-7*) Smithmark Pubs., Inc.

—The Software Bomb. 1993. 288p. 19.95 o.p. (*0-312-09390-X*, Saint Martin's Minotaur) St. Martin's Pr.

York, Rebecca, et al. Gypsy Magic: Allessandra/Sabina/Andrei, 3 bks. in 1. 2002. (Harlequin Intrigue Ser.). 256p. mass mkt. (*0-373-22684-5*, Harlequin Bks.) Harlequin Enterprises, Ltd.

**NEW YORK (N.Y.)—FICTION**

Abbott, Cameron. An Inexpressible State of Grace. 2003. 17.95 (*1-56023-469-5*, Harrington Park Pr.) Haworth Pr., Inc., The.

—To the Edge. 2001. 247p. pap. 19.95 (*1-56023-223-4*); lib. bdg. 39.95 (*1-56023-222-6*) Haworth Pr., Inc., The. (Alice Street Editions).

Abdoh, Salar. The Poet Game. E-Book 12.00 (*0-312-27357-6*); 2001. 240p. pap. 12.00 (*0-312-20968-1*); 2000. 240p. 23.00 (*0-312-20954-1*) Picador.

Abel, Kenneth. The Blue Wall. 1997. 432p. mass mkt. 5.99 o.s.i (*0-440-21723-7*) Dell Publishing.

Abraham, Pearl. The Romance Reader. 1996. 304p. pap. 13.00 (*1-57322-548-7*, Riverhead Trade (Paperbacks)) Berkley Publishing Group.

—The Romance Reader. 1995. 304p. 21.95 o.s.i (*1-57322-015-9*, Riverhead Bks. (Hardcovers)) Putnam Publishing Group, The.

Adamson, Lydia. A Cat by Any Other Name. unabr. collector's ed. 1997. (Alice Nestleton Ser.). audio 30.00 (*0-7366-3597-1*, 4248) Books on Tape, Inc.

—A Cat by Any Other Name: An Alice Nestleton Mystery. 1992. (Alice Nestleton Mystery Ser.). 208p. mass mkt. 5.50 o.s.i (*0-451-17231-0*, Signet Bks.) NAL.

—A Cat in a Chorus Line. unabr. ed. 1997. (Alice Nestleton Ser.: Vol. 12). audio 24.00 (*0-7366-4052-5*, 4561) Books on Tape, Inc.

—A Cat in a Glass House. unabr. ed. 1997. (Alice Nestleton Ser.). audio 30.00 (*0-7366-3675-7*, 4354) Books on Tape, Inc.

—A Cat in a Glass House. 1993. (Alice Nestleton Mystery Ser.). 208p. mass mkt. 3.99 o.s.i (*0-451-17706-1*, Signet Bks.) NAL.

—A Cat in Fine Style. unabr. ed. 1997. (Alice Nestleton Ser.: Vol. 10). audio 30.00 (*0-7366-3831-8*, 4551) Books on Tape, Inc.

—A Cat in Fine Style: An Alice Nestleton Mystery. 1995. (Alice Nestleton Mystery Ser.). 224p. mass mkt. 5.99 o.s.i (*0-451-18083-6*, Signet Bks.) NAL.

—A Cat in the Manger. unabr. collector's ed. 1997. (Alice Nestleton Ser.: Vol. 1). audio 30.00 (*0-7366-3556-4*, 4201) Books on Tape, Inc.

—A Cat in the Wings. unabr. collector's ed. 1997. (Alice Nestleton Ser.). audio 36.00 (*0-7366-3598-X*, 4249) Books on Tape, Inc.

—A Cat in the Wings: An Alice Nestleton Mystery. l.t. ed. 2001. 301p. 28.95 o.p. (*0-7862-3676-0*) Thorndike Pr.

—A Cat in Wolf's Clothing. unabr. collector's ed. 1997. (Alice Nestleton Ser.: Vol. 3). audio 30.00 (*0-7366-3558-0*, 4203) Books on Tape, Inc.

—A Cat Named Brat. 2002. 208p. mass mkt. 5.99 (*0-451-20664-9*) NAL.

—A Cat Named Brat: An Alice Nestleton Mystery. 2003. (Mystery Ser.). 30.45 (*0-7862-4757-6*) Thorndike Pr.

—A Cat of a Different Color. unabr. collector's ed. 1997. (Alice Nestleton Ser.: Vol. 2). audio 30.00 (*0-7366-3557-2*, 4202) Books on Tape, Inc.

—A Cat of a Different Color. l.t. ed. 1992. (General Ser.). 200p. pap. 14.95 o.p. (*0-8161-5399-X*); lib. bdg. 18.95 o.p. (*0-8161-5398-1*) Gale Group. (Macmillan Reference USA).

—A Cat of a Different Color. 1991. (Alice Nestleton Mystery Ser.). 208p. mass mkt. 5.50 o.s.i (*0-451-16955-7*, Signet Bks.) NAL.

—A Cat of One's Own. 1999. (Alice Nestleton Mysteries Ser.: Bk. 17). 208p. 19.95 (*0-525-94428-1*) Dutton/Plume.

—A Cat of One's Own, 1. 2000. (Alice Nestleton Mysteries Ser.). 208p. mass mkt. 5.99 o.s.i (*0-451-19769-0*) NAL.

—A Cat of One's Own. l.t. ed. 1999. (Mystery Ser.). 216p. 28.95 (*0-7862-1884-3*) Thorndike Pr.

—A Cat on a Beach Blanket. unabr. ed. 1998. (Alice Nestleton Ser.). audio 30.00 (*0-7366-4260-9*, 4759) Books on Tape, Inc.

—A Cat on a Beach Blanket: An Alice Nestleton Mystery. l.t. ed. 2001. 231p. 29.95 (*0-7862-2649-8*); (*0-7540-4552-8*) Thorndike Pr.

—A Cat on a Winning Streak. unabr. ed. 1997. (Alice Nestleton Ser.). audio 24.00 (*0-7366-3746-X*, 4421) Books on Tape, Inc.

—A Cat on Jingle Bell Rock. 1997. (Alice Nestleton Mystery Ser.). 192p. 19.95 o.p. (*0-525-94375-7*) Dutton/Plume.

—A Cat on Jingle Bell Rock. 1998. (Alice Nestleton Mystery Ser.). 340p. mass mkt. 5.99 o.s.i (*0-451-19458-6*, Signet Bks.) NAL.

—A Cat on Jingle Bell Rock: An Alice Nestleton Mystery. l.t. ed. 2000. (Mystery Ser.). 216p. 28.95 (*0-7862-2650-1*) Thorndike Pr.

—A Cat on Stage Left: An Alice Nestleton Mystery. l.t. ed. 1998. (Mystery Ser.). 232p. 27.95 (*0-7862-1559-3*) Thorndike Pr.

—A Cat on the Cutting Edge. unabr. ed. 1997. (Alice Nestleton Ser.: Vol. 9). audio 24.00 (*0-7366-3745-1*, 4420) Books on Tape, Inc.

—A Cat under the Mistletoe. 1997. (Alice Nestleton Mysteries Ser.). 256p. mass mkt. 5.99 o.s.i (*0-451-19105-6*, Signet Bks.) NAL.

—A Cat under the Mistletoe: A Christmas Cat Mystery. 1996. (Alice Nestleton Mystery Ser.). 224p. 18.95 o.p. (*0-525-94226-2*, Dutton) Dutton/Plume.

—A Cat under the Mistletoe: An Alice Nestleton Mystery. l.t. ed. 2000. (Mystery Ser.). 248p. 28.95 (*0-7862-2651-X*) Thorndike Pr.

—A Cat with No Regrets. unabr. ed. 1997. (Alice Nestleton Ser.). audio 30.00 (*0-7366-3744-3*, 4419) Books on Tape, Inc.

—A Cat with the Blues. 2000. (Alice Nestleton Mysteries Ser.: Vol. 10). 208p. mass mkt. 5.99 (*0-451-20196-5*) NAL.

—A Cat with the Blues: An Alice Nestleton Mystery. l.t. ed. 2001. (Thorndike Mystery Ser.). 200p. 29.95 (*0-7862-3076-2*); (*0-7540-4465-3*) Thorndike Pr.

Adcock, Thomas. Dark Maze. Chelius, Jane, ed. 1991. 320p. (Orig.). mass mkt. 5.50 (*0-671-72909-8*, Pocket) Simon & Schuster.

—Devil's Heaven. 1996. 288p. mass mkt. 5.99 (*0-671-77043-8*, Pocket) Simon & Schuster.

—Devil's Heaven. Chelius, Jane, ed. 1995. 336p. 20.00 o.p. (*0-671-89778-0*, Atria) Simon & Schuster.

—Drown All the Dogs. Chelius, Jane, ed. 1995. 368p. mass mkt. 5.99 (*0-671-88329-1*, Pocket) Simon & Schuster.

—Drown All the Dogs: A Neil Hockaday Mystery. 1994. 352p. 20.00 o.p. (*0-671-77041-1*, Atria) Simon & Schuster.

—Grief Street. 1998. (Neil Hockaday Mystery Ser.). 304p. per. 6.50 (*0-671-51987-5*, Pocket) Simon & Schuster.

—Grief Street: A Neil Hockaday Mystery. 1997. (Neil Hockaday Mystery Ser.). 304p. 22.00 (*0-671-51986-7*, Atria) Simon & Schuster.

—Sea of Green. 1989. 17.45 o.p. (*0-89296-384-0*) Mysterious Pr.

—Sea of Green. 1990. 304p. mass mkt. 4.95 o.s.i (*0-445-40918-5*, Mysterious Pr. Paperback Bks.) Warner Bks., Inc.

—Thrown Away Child. (Neil Hockaday Mystery Ser.). 1997. 400p. per. 5.99 (*0-671-51984-0*, Pocket); 1996. 352p. 21.00 o.p. (*0-671-51985-9*, Atria) Simon & Schuster.

Adler, Bill, Jr., et al. Murder in Manhattan. 1986. 320p. 15.95 o.p. (*0-688-06475-2*, Morrow, William & Co.) Morrow/Avon.

Adler, Elizabeth A. In a Heartbeat. l.t. ed. 2000. (Wheeler Large Print Book Ser.). 365p. 28.95 (*1-56895-941-9*, Wheeler Publishing, Inc.) Gale Group.

Adler, Renata. Speedboat. 1988. 192p. reprint ed. pap. 7.95 o.p. (*0-06-097143-6*, PL-7143, Perennial) HarperTrade.

—Speedboat. 1984. pap. 5.95 o.s.i (*0-394-72753-3*); 1976. 7.95 o.p. (*0-394-48876-8*) Random Hse., Inc.

Adrian, Christine. Gob's Grief. 2001. E-Book 19.95 (*0-7679-0936-4*) Broadway Bks.

—Gob's Grief: A Novel. 2002. (Vintage Contemporaries Ser.). 400p. reprint ed. pap. 13.95 (*0-375-72624-1*, Vintage) Knopf Publishing Group.

Akst, Daniel. St. Burl's Obituary. 1997. (Harvest American Writing Ser.). 384p. pap. 12.00 (*0-15-600514-X*, Harvest Bks.) Harcourt Trade Pubs.

—St. Burl's Obituary. 1996. 370p. 22.95 (*1-878448-68-4*) MacMurray & Beck, Inc.

Alexander, David. Brooklynese. 2002. 284p. pap. (*1-58345-628-7*) Domhan Bks.

—Chain Reaction. 2002. 264p. pap. (*1-58345-568-X*) Domhan Bks.

Alexander, Meena. Manhattan Music. 1997. 256p. (Orig.). pap. 14.95 o.p. (*0-562-79092-6*); (Illus.). reprint ed. pap. 14.95 (*1-56279-092-7*) Mercury Hse.

Alfau, Felipe. Chromos. 1990. 348p. 19.95 (*0-916583-52-X*) Dalkey Archive Pr.

—Chromos. 1991. 352p. pap. 11.00 o.s.i (*0-679-73443-0*, Vintage) Knopf Publishing Group.

Alhadeff, Gini. Diary of a Djinn: A Novel. 2004. 224p. pap. 13.00 (*1-4000-3461-2*, Anchor) Knopf Publishing Group.

—Diary of a Djinn: Novel. 2003. 224p. 22.00 (*0-375-40234-9*, Pantheon) Knopf Publishing Group.

Allegretto, Michael. The Night of Reunion. 1990. 256p. 17.95 o.s.i (*0-684-19133-4*, Macmillan Reference USA) Gale Group.

—The Night of Reunion. 1991. 288p. mass mkt. 4.99 (*0-380-71442-6*, Avon Bks.) Morrow/Avon.

Allen, Charlotte Vale. Mood Indigo. l.t. ed. 2000. 408p. lib. bdg. 27.95 (*1-58547-038-4*) Ctr. Point Large Print.

—Mood Indigo. 1997. 288p. 23.95 (*0-9657437-1-3*) Island Nation Pr., LLC.

—Somebody's Baby. 2003. 352p. pap. (*1-55166-754-1*, Mira Bks.) Harlequin Enterprises, Ltd.

Allen, Phillip. Play Money: A Novel. 2003. 304p. 24.00 (*1-56947-338-2*) Soho Pr., Inc.

Allen, Steve. Murder in Manhattan. 1990. mass mkt. 18.95 o.p. (*0-8217-3033-9*, Zebra Bks.) Kensington Publishing Corp.

—Wake up to Murder. 1997. 384p. mass mkt. 5.99 o.s.i (*1-57566-236-1*); 1996. 288p. 18.95 o.s.i (*1-57566-109-8*); 1996. 256p. 19.95 o.s.i (*1-57566-090-3*, Kensington Bks.) Kensington Publishing Corp.

Allingham, Margery, et al. Canine Crimes. Mason, Cynthia, ed. 1993. 240p. (Orig.). mass mkt. 4.50 o.s.i (*0-515-11250-X*, Jove) Berkley Publishing Group.

Allison, Karen H. How I Gave My Heart to the Restaurant Business: A Novel. 1997. 210p. 23.00 o.p. (*0-88001-522-5*) HarperCollins Pubs.

Allman, Paul L. Otis: On the Occasion of His Foray into the Wilderness of Civilization. 1994. (Illus.). 256p. 20.95 o.p. (*0-312-10519-3*) St. Martin's Pr.

Altsheler, Joseph A. A Soldier of Manhattan. Date not set. lib. bdg. 39.95 (*0-8488-1863-6*, 207) Amereon, Ltd.

Alvarez, Julia. Yo! 1999. 350p. tchr. ed. 18.95 (*1-56512-157-0*, 72157) Algonquin Bks. of Chapel Hill.

—Yo! 1999. (SPA.). 416p. pap. 16.95 (*0-452-28140-7*); 1997. 320p. pap. 14.00 (*0-452-27918-6*, Plume) Dutton/Plume.

—Yo! l.t. ed. 2003. (Spanish Language Ser.). (SPA.). 28.95 (*0-7862-5190-5*) Thorndike Pr.

—Yo! 1997. 19.00 (*0-606-22212-X*) Turtleback Bks.

Amato, Angela & Sharkey, Joe. Lady Gold. 1999. 384p. mass mkt. 6.99 (*0-312-96765-9*, St. Martin's Paperbacks); 1999. E-Book 23.95 (*0-312-20726-3*); 1998. 354p. 23.95 (*0-312-18541-3*) St. Martin's Pr.

Ames, Jonathan. I Pass Like Night. 1989. 160p. 15.95 o.p. (*0-688-07804-4*, Morrow, William & Co.) Morrow/Avon.

—I Pass Like Night. 1993. 2.99 o.p. (*0-517-10862-3*) Random Hse. Value Publishing.

—I Pass Like Night. 1999. (Contemporary Classics Ser.). 176p. pap. 12.00 (*0-671-03426-X*, Washington Square Pr.) Simon & Schuster.

Amiel, Joseph. Deeds. 1988. mass mkt. 4.95 o.s.i (*0-449-14522-0*, Fawcett) Ballantine Bks.

—Deeds. 1988. 484p. 19.95 o.s.i (*0-689-11862-7*, Scribner) Simon & Schuster.

Andersen, Kurt. Turn of the Century. 2000. 672p. pap. 14.95 (*0-385-33504-0*, Delta) Dell Publishing.

Anderson, Scott. Triage. 1999. 240p. pap. 12.00 (*0-684-85653-0*, Scribner Paper Fiction) Simon & Schuster.

—Triage: A Novel. 1998. 240p. 23.00 (*0-684-84695-0*, Scribner) Simon & Schuster.

—Triage: A Novel. l.t. ed. 1999. (Ulverscroft Large Print Ser.). 408p. 31.99 o.p. (*0-7089-4117-6*, Ulverscroft) Thorpe, F. A. Pubs. GBR. *Dist:* Ulverscroft Large Print Bks., Ltd., Ulverscroft Large Print Canada, Ltd.

Andrews, V. C. Falling Stars. 2001. 400p. 25.00 (*0-671-03986-5*, Atria); E-Book 7.99 (*0-7434-2168-X*, Pocket); (Illus.). 416p. pap. 7.99 (*0-671-03987-3*, Pocket) Simon & Schuster.

—Falling Stars. l.t. ed. 2002. 403p. 30.95 (*0-7838-9753-7*) Thorndike Pr.

—Midnight Whispers. unabr. ed. 1993. audio 72.00 (*0-7366-2532-1*, 3284) Books on Tape, Inc.

—Midnight Whispers. l.t. ed. 1993. (G. K. Hall Large Print Book Ser.). 515p. 19.95 o.p. (*0-8161-5656-5*); lib. bdg. 23.95 (*0-8161-5655-7*) Gale Group. (Macmillan Reference USA).

—Midnight Whispers. Marrow, Linda, ed. 1992. 448p. (Midnight Whispers Ser.: Vol. 5). mass mkt. 7.99 (*0-671-69516-9*, Pocket);Vol. 5. 22.00 (*0-671-69517-7*, Atria) Simon & Schuster.

—Midnight Whispers. 1992. 14.04 (*0-606-02201-5*) Turtleback Bks.

—Secrets of the Morning. unabr. ed. 1993. (Cutler Ser.). audio 64.00 (*0-7366-2356-6*, 3131) Books on Tape, Inc.

—Secrets of the Morning. l.t. ed. 1992. (General Ser.). 487p. pap. 17.95 (*0-8161-5386-8*); lib. bdg. 20.95 (*0-8161-5385-X*) Gale Group. (Macmillan Reference USA).

—Secrets of the Morning. unabr. ed. 2003. audio 84.95 (*0-7531-1773-8*) ISIS Audio Bks. GBR. *Dist:* Ulverscroft Large Print Bks., Ltd.

—Secrets of the Morning. Marrow, Linda, ed. 1991. (Cutler Ser.). 416p. mass mkt. 7.99 (*0-671-69512-6*, Pocket);Vol. 2. 384p. 21.95 (*0-671-69513-4*, Atria) Simon & Schuster.

—Secrets of the Morning. 1991. 14.04 (*0-606-05012-4*) Turtleback Bks.

Anonymous. The Beautiful Flagellants of New York. 2000. 160p. pap. 7.95 (*1-56201-186-3*, Blue Moon Bks.) Avalon Publishing Group.

Appel, Allan. Club Revelation: A Novel. 2001. 220p. pap. 14.95 (*1-56689-118-3*) Coffee Hse. Pr.

Appel, William. Widowmaker. 1994. 167p. 19.95 (*0-8027-3193-7*) Walker & Co.

Arenas, Reinaldo. The Doorman: A Novel. 1991. 16.95 o.p. (*0-8021-1109-2*) Grove/Atlantic, Inc.

Arensberg, Ann. Group Sex. 1986. 15.95 o.s.i (*0-394-55310-1*) Knopf, Alfred A. Inc.

—Group Sex: A Romantic Comedy. 1987. mass mkt. 5.95 o.s.i (*0-671-64362-2*, Pocket) Simon & Schuster.

Arnold, Emily. Life Drawing. 1986. 288p. 15.95 o.s.i (*0-385-29437-9*, Delacorte Pr.); 1988. reprint ed. mass mkt. 4.95 o.s.i (*0-440-20025-3*, Laurel) Dell Publishing.

Asano, Suchi. In Broken Wigwag. 1997. 21.00 o.p. (*0-8038-9399-X*); 192p. pap. 12.95 o.p. (*0-8038-9404-X*) Hastings Hse. Daytrips Pubs.

Ashley, Leonard R. N. What I Know about You: 100 Lesbian & Gay New York Voices. 2002. 313p. pap. 22.99 (*1-4010-3173-0*) Xlibris Corp.

Ashwood-Collins, Anna. Red Roses for a Dead Trucker. E-Book 5.95 (*0-9712538-2-X*); 2002. 210p. pap. 16.95 (*0-9712538-4-6*) Pendulum Pr.

Astor, Brooke. The Last Blossom on the Plum Tree. l.t. ed. 1987. 8.95 o.p. (*1-55504-239-2*); pap. 18.95 o.p. (*1-55504-317-8*) BBC Audiobooks America.

Auchincloss, Louis. The Book Class, 001. 1984. 224p. 14.95 o.p. (*0-395-36138-9*) Houghton Mifflin Co.

—The Book Class. l.t. ed. 1984. 293p. reprint ed. 14.95 o.p. (*0-89621-558-X*) Thorndike Pr.

—The Dark Lady, 001. 1977. 8.95 o.p. (*0-395-25402-7*) Houghton Mifflin Co.

—The Education of Oscar Fairfax. 1995. 256p. 22.95 o.p. (*0-395-73918-7*) Houghton Mifflin Co.

—The Embezzler. l.t. ed. 1988. 20.95 o.p. (*1-55504-386-0*); pap. 18.95 o.p. (*1-55504-505-7*) BBC Audiobooks America.

—The Embezzler. 1993. reprint ed. lib. bdg. 21.95 (*1-56849-151-4*) Buccaneer Bks., Inc.

—The Embezzler, 001. 1966. 5.95 o.p. (*0-395-07362-6*); 1980. reprint ed. pap. 3.95 o.p. (*0-395-29845-8*) Houghton Mifflin Co.

—The Embezzler. l.t. ed. 2000. 325p. 32.95 (*0-7658-0778-5*) Transaction Pubs.

—The Golden Calves. l.t. ed. 1989. (General Ser.). 315p. lib. bdg. 19.95 o.p. (*0-8161-4682-9*, Macmillan Reference USA) Gale Group.

—The Golden Calves. 1988. 17.95 o.p. (*0-395-47691-7*) Houghton Mifflin Co.

—The Golden Calves. 1990. 2.99 o.p. (*0-517-02946-4*) Random Hse. Value Publishing.

—The Golden Calves. 1990. pap. 3.95 o.p. (*0-312-91487-3*, St. Martin's Paperbacks) St. Martin's Pr.

—Her Infinite Variety. 2000. 224p. tchr. ed. 25.00 (*0-618-02191-4*) Houghton Mifflin Co.

—Her Infinite Variety. l.t. ed. 2001. (Core Ser.). 259p. 29.95 (*0-7838-9341-8*) Thorndike Pr.

—Skinny Island: More Tales of Manhattan. 1987. 17.95 o.p. (*0-395-43295-2*) Houghton Mifflin Co.

Auster, Paul. City of Glass. 1987. (New York Trilogy). 210p. pap. 12.95 (*0-14-009731-7*, Penguin Bks.) Penguin Group (USA) Inc.

—City of Glass. 1985. (New York Trilogy Ser.). 208p. 30.00 o.p. (*0-940650-53-3*); 13.95 o.p. (*0-940650-52-5*) Sun & Moon Pr.

—Ghosts. deluxe ed. 1986. (New York Trilogy Ser.). 110p. 30.00 o.p. (*0-940650-69-X*) Sun & Moon Pr.

—Ghosts. 1987. (New York Trilogy). 96p. pap. 5.95 o.p. (*0-14-009735-X*, Penguin Bks.) Viking Penguin.

—The New York Trilogy: City of Glass; Ghosts; The Locked Room. 2003. (El-e-PHANT Bks.). 360p. 29.95 (*1-931243-57-3*) Green Integer.

Settings

—The New York Trilogy: City of Glass; Ghosts; The Locked Room. deluxe ltd. ed. (New American Fiction Ser.: Nos. 4-6). 472p. 1994. 40.00 o.p. (*1-55713-167-8*); 1995. 21.95 o.p. (*1-55713-166-X*) Sun & Moon Pr.

—The New York Trilogy: City of Glass; Ghosts; The Locked Room. 1990. (American Fiction Ser.). (Illus.). 448p. 14.95 (*0-14-013155-8*) Viking Penguin.

—Timbuktu. 1999. 192p. 22.00 o.s.i (*0-8050-5407-3*) Holt, Henry & Co.

—Timbuktu. 2000. 192p. pap. 11.00 (*0-312-26399-6*); mass mkt. 7.99 o.s.i (*0-312-97528-7*) Picador.

Auster, Paul & Blickle, Frieder. Paul Auster's New York. 1997. 0.01 o.p. (*0-8050-5667-X*) Holt, Henry & Co.

Austin, Virginia. American Jesus. 2002. 280p. 19.95 (*0-940121-72-7*) Cross Cultural Pubns., Inc.

Avignone, June, ed. On Going Home Again. 2002. (Illus.). 32p. pap. (*0-9654628-1-1*) Mill Street Forward, The.

Avrett, Roz. My Turn. 1983. 288p. 14.50 o.p. (*0-87795-476-3*, Morrow, William & Co.) Morrow/Avon.

Baggott, Julianna. Girl Talk. 2001. E-Book 23.95 (*0-7434-2143-4*); (Illus.). 256p. 23.95 (*0-7434-0082-8*) Simon & Schuster. (Atria).

Bagshawe, Louise. The Devil You Know: A Novel. 2003. 384p. 24.95 (*0-312-27305-3*) St. Martin's Pr.

Bahr, Arthur W. Certifiably Insane: A Novel. 1999. 272p. 23.00 (*0-684-80232-5*, Simon & Schuster) Simon & Schuster.

Bain, Donald. Knock 'em Dead: A Murder, She Wrote Mystery. l.t. ed. 2002. 264p. pap. 24.45 (*0-7862-4051-2*) Gale Group.

—Murder, She Wrote: Manhattans & Murder. l.t. ed. 1998. (Murder She Wrote Ser.). 288p. pap. 21.95 (*0-7838-0133-5*) Thorndike Pr.

Baker, Kevin. Dreamland. 2000. (*0-06-099580-7*); 2000. mass mkt. 6.99 (*0-06-103082-1*); 1999. 512p. pap. 15.50 (*0-06-095343-8*); 1999. 528p. 26.00 o.p. (*0-06-019309-3*); 1999. (*0-06-099590-4*) HarperCollins Pubs.

—Dreamland. 2002. 672p. pap. 14.95 (*0-06-093480-8*); 2000. 352p. mass mkt. 6.99 (*0-06-093121-3*) HarperTrade. (Perennial).

—Paradise Alley: A Novel. 2002. 688p. 26.95 (*0-06-019582-7*) HarperCollins Pubs.

—Paradise Alley: A Novel. 2003. 688p. pap. 14.95 (*0-06-095521-X*, Perennial) HarperTrade.

Baker, Kyle. You Are Here. 1998. (Illus.). 160p. pap. 19.95 o.s.i (*1-56389-442-4*) DC Comics.

Baker, Phillip. Blood Posse. 1995. pap. 13.95 o.p. (*0-312-13030-9*, Saint Martin's Griffin) St. Martin's Pr.

Baldwin, Faith. Skyscraper. 1976. reprint ed. lib. bdg. 24.95 (*0-88411-623-9*) Amereon, Ltd.

—Skyscraper. 2003. (Femmes Fatales Ser.). 256p. pap. 14.95 (*1-55861-457-5*); 208p. lib. bdg. 39.00 (*1-55861-463-X*) Feminist Pr. at The City Univ. of New York.

—Skyscraper. l.t. ed. 2002. 24.95 (*0-7862-4086-5*) Thorndike Pr.

Baldwin, Frank. Balling the Jack. 272p. 1998. pap. 11.00 (*0-684-84581-4*, Touchstone); 1997. 22.00 o.s.i (*0-684-83360-3*, Simon & Schuster) Simon & Schuster.

Bandele, Asha. Daughter: A Novel. 2003. 272p. 23.00 (*0-7432-1184-7*, Scribner) Simon & Schuster.

Bandy, Franklin. Athena. 1988. 320p. pap. 3.95 o.p. (*0-8125-8050-8*); 1987. 15.95 o.p. (*0-312-93018-6*) Doherty, Tom Assocs., LLC. (Tor Bks.).

Banks, Russell. Gangsta Bone. 2003. (GER.). 384p. pap. 19.00 (*1-4000-3993-2*) Random Hse. Information Group.

—Rule of the Bone: A Novel. 1996. 400p. pap. 13.00 (*0-06-092724-0*, Perennial); Set. 1999. audio 17.00 o.p. (*1-55994-809-4*, 392857, HarperAudio) HarperTrade.

Barnhardt, Wilton. Emma Who Saved My Life. 1989. 19.95 o.p. (*0-312-02911-X*) St. Martin's Pr.

Barr, Amelia E. The Maid of Maiden Lane. 2000. 252p. E-Book 3.95 (*0-594-01860-9*) 1873 Pr.

—Trinity Bells. 2000. 252p. E-Book 3.95 (*0-594-01861-7*) 1873 Pr.

Barr, Marleen S. Oy Pioneer! 2003. (Library of American Fiction). 19.95 (*0-299-18910-4*) Univ. of Wisconsin Pr.

Barr, Nevada. Liberty Falling. l.t. ed. 1999. (Wheeler Large Print Bks.). 26.95 (*1-56895-711-4*, Wheeler Publishing, Inc.) Gale Group.

—Liberty Falling. 1999. (Anna Pigeon Mysteries Ser.). 321p. 23.95 o.s.i (*0-399-14459-5*) Penguin Group (USA) Inc.

—Liberty Falling. unabr. ed. 1999. (Anna Pigeon Mystery Ser. : No. 7). (Illus.). audio 83.00 (*0-7887-3465-2*, 95649E7) Recorded Bks., LLC.

Barrett, Margaret & Dennis, Charles. Given the Evidence. 1999. 400p. reprint ed. mass mkt. 6.50 o.s.i (*0-671-00154-X*, Pocket) Simon & Schuster.

Barrett, Margaret, et al. Given the Evidence. 1998. 320p. 23.00 (*0-671-00153-1*, Atria) Simon & Schuster.

Barrett, Wilson & Barrett, Barron E. In Old New York. 2000. 252p. E-Book 9.95 (*0-594-01862-5*) 1873 Pr.

Barth, Richard. Blood Doesn't Tell. 1990. (Margaret Binton Mystery Ser.). 192p. mass mkt. 3.95 o.s.i (*0-449-21797-3*, Fawcett) Ballantine Bks.

—Blood Doesn't Tell. 1989. 192p. 15.95 o.p. (*0-312-02547-5*, Saint Martin's Minotaur) St. Martin's Pr.

—The Condo Kill. 1991. (Margaret Binton Mystery Ser.). 160p. mass mkt. 3.95 o.s.i (*0-449-21812-0*, Fawcett) Ballantine Bks.

—The Condo Kill. 1985. (Margaret Binton Mystery Ser.). 192p. 13.95 o.s.i (*0-684-18474-5*, Macmillan Reference USA) Gale Group.

—Deadly Climate. 1989. mass mkt. 3.50 o.s.i (*0-449-21723-X*, Fawcett) Ballantine Bks.

—Deadly Climate. unabr. ed. 2000. (Margaret Binton Mysteries Ser.). audio 44.00 (*1-55690-844-X*, 93211E7) Recorded Bks., LLC.

—Deadly Climate. 1988. 208p. 14.95 o.p. (*0-312-01756-1*, Saint Martin's Minotaur) St. Martin's Pr.

—Deathics: A Margaret Binton Mystery. 1993. 212p. 18.95 o.p. (*0-312-08764-0*, Saint Martin's Minotaur) St. Martin's Pr.

—The Final Shot. 1992. 256p. 17.95 o.p. (*0-312-07748-3*, Saint Martin's Minotaur) St. Martin's Pr.

—Jumper. 2000. 218p. 22.95 (*0-312-26608-1*, Saint Martin's Minotaur); E-Book 22.95 (*0-312-27610-9*) St. Martin's Pr.

—One Dollar Death. 1991. 176p. mass mkt. 3.95 o.s.i (*0-449-21813-9*, Fawcett) Ballantine Bks.

—One Dollar Death. 1982. 228p. 14.95 o.p. (*0-385-27633-8*) Doubleday Publishing.

—One Dollar Death. l.t. ed. 1983. 313p. reprint ed. 11.95 o.p. (*0-89621-419-2*) Thorndike Pr.

—The Rag Bag Clan. 1989. mass mkt. 3.50 o.s.i (*0-449-21814-7*, Fawcett) Ballantine Bks.

—A Ragged Plot. 1990. mass mkt. 3.95 o.s.i (*0-449-21815-5*, Fawcett) Ballantine Bks.

—A Ragged Plot. 1981. 224p. 10.95 o.p. (*0-385-27165-4*) Doubleday Publishing.

—A Ragged Plot. 1982. 176p. pap. 2.25 o.p. (*0-380-59162-6*, 59162-6, Avon Bks.) Morrow/Avon.

—A Ragged Plot. unabr. ed. 1992. (Margaret Binton Mysteries Ser.). audio 44.00 (*1-55690-721-4*, 92417E7) Recorded Bks., LLC.

Barthelme, Donald. Paradise. 1986. 208p. 16.95 o.p. (*0-399-12921-9*) Putnam Publishing Group, The.

—Paradise. 1987. 208p. pap. 8.95 o.p. (*0-14-010358-9*, Penguin Bks.) Viking Penguin.

Bartholemew, John T. He's Dead, She's Dead - Details at Eleven. 1990. 17.95 o.p. (*0-312-04325-2*, Saint Martin's Minotaur) St. Martin's Pr.

Bassett, Marjory. Never Say Stark Naked. 2002. 320p. 25.00 (*1-56649-246-7*) Welcome Rain Pubs.

Baxt, George. A Queer Kind of Death. 1998. 300p. pap. 10.00 o.p. (*1-55583-448-5*) Alyson Pubns.

—A Queer Kind of Death: A Pharoah Love Mystery. 1986. (Library of Crime Classics). pap. 4.95 o.p. (*0-930330-46-3*) International Polygonics, Ltd.

—A Queer Kind of Death: A Pharoah Love Mystery. 1979. pap. 4.95 o.p. (*0-312-66022-7*, Saint Martin's Griffin) St. Martin's Pr.

—A Queer Kind of Love: A Pharoah Love Mystery. 1994. 288p. 20.00 (*1-883402-01-8*, Scribner) Simon & Schuster.

—A Queer Kind of Love: A Pharoah Love Mystery. pap. (*0-312-29217-1*); 1995. pap. 8.95 (*0-312-13152-6*) St. Martin's Pr. (Saint Martin's Griffin).

—A Queer Kind of Umbrella: A Pharoah Love Mystery. 1995. 240p. 20.50 (*0-684-81496-X*, Simon & Schuster); 21.00 (*1-883402-35-2*, Scribner) Simon & Schuster.

—Topsy & Evil. 1987. 232p. reprint ed. pap. 4.95 o.p. (*0-930330-66-8*) International Polygonics, Ltd.

Bayer, William. Switch. l.t. ed. 1986. (General Ser.). 420p. 17.95 o.p. (*0-8161-4037-5*, Macmillan Reference USA) Gale Group.

—Switch. 1985. mass mkt. 3.95 o.p. (*0-451-14333-7*); mass mkt. 3.95 o.p. (*0-451-13603-9*) NAL. (Signet Bks.).

—Switch. 1984. 14.70 o.p. (*0-671-49424-4*, Simon & Schuster) Simon & Schuster.

—Wallflower. 1992. mass mkt. 5.99 o.s.i (*0-515-10843-X*, Jove) Berkley Publishing Group.

—Wallflower. 1993. 3.99 o.p. (*0-517-10959-X*) Random Hse. Value Publishing.

Beasley, David. The Grand Conspiracy: A New York Library Mystery. 1997. 176p. pap. 10.95 (*0-915317-06-0*) Davus Publishing.

—The Jenny: A New York Library Detective Novel. 1994. 120p. pap. 7.95 (*0-915317-03-6*) Davus Publishing.

Beattie, Ann. Falling in Place. 1981. pap. 2.50 o.p. (*0-445-04650-3*, Fawcett) Ballantine Bks.

—Falling in Place. (Vintage Contemporaries Ser.). 1991. 342p. pap. 19.00 (*0-679-73192-X*); 1980. 10.95 o.p. (*0-394-50323-6*) Random Hse., Inc.

—Picturing Will. 1991. (Vintage Contemporaries Ser.). 240p. pap. 15.00 (*0-679-73194-6*, Vintage) Knopf Publishing Group.

—Picturing Will. 1992. 4.99 o.p. (*0-517-08094-X*) Random Hse. Value Publishing.

Beatty, Paul. Tuff: A Novel. 2000. reprint ed. pap. 13.00 o.p. (*0-375-70124-9*, Anchor) Knopf Publishing Group.

Bechard, Gorman. Balls. 1995. 384p. (Orig.). pap. 10.95 o.p. (*0-452-27294-7*, Plume) Dutton/Plume.

Beck, Timothy James. It Had to Be You. 2002. 34p. pap. 14.00 (*1-57566-890-4*); 2001. 352p. 23.00 (*1-57566-889-0*) Kensington Publishing Corp.

Becker, Geoffrey. Bluestown. pap. 15.95 (*0-312-30456-0*, Saint Martin's Griffin); 1997. pap. 11.95 o.p. (*0-312-15481-X*, Saint Martin's Griffin); 1996. 280p. 21.95 o.p. (*0-312-14223-4*) St. Martin's Pr.

Becker, Laney K. Dear Stranger, Dearest Friend. 2000. 304p. 24.00 (*0-380-97853-9*, Morrow, William & Co.) Morrow/Avon.

—Dear Stranger, Dearest Friend. l.t. ed. 2001. (G. K. Hall Inspirational Ser.). 381p. 26.95 (*0-7838-9403-1*) Thorndike Pr.

Beckman, David. Under Pegasus: A Novel. 1997. 200p. 19.95 (*0-9651244-1-X*, Goldengrove Bks.) Derrynane Pr.

Begley, Louis. About Schmidt. 1997. (Ballantine Reader's Circle Ser.). 304p. pap. 13.95 (*0-449-91116-0*, Fawcett) Ballantine Bks.

—About Schmidt, 5 cass. 2002. audio 29.99 (*0-7887-9027-7*, 00494); 1997. audio 51.00 (*0-7887-0876-7*, 95011E7) Recorded Bks., LLC.

—Shipwreck. 2003. 256p. 23.00 (*1-4000-4098-1*) Knopf, Alfred A. Inc.

Beinhart, Larry. Foreign Exchange. 1992. mass mkt. 5.99 o.s.i (*0-345-36665-4*) Ballantine Bks.

—No One Rides for Free. 1993. mass mkt. 4.99 o.s.i (*0-345-37294-8*) Ballantine Bks.

—No One Rides for Free. 1987. 240p. pap. 3.95 (*0-380-70283-5*, Avon Bks.); 1986. 256p. 16.95 o.p. (*0-688-06057-9*, Morrow, William & Co.) Morrow/Avon.

—You Get What You Pay For. 1989. 368p. mass mkt. 4.95 o.s.i (*0-345-36406-6*) Ballantine Bks.

—You Get What You Pay For. 1988. 356p. 18.95 o.p. (*0-688-06613-5*, Morrow, William & Co.) Morrow/Avon.

Bell, Madison Smartt. Waiting for the End of the World. 1985. 16.95 o.p. (*0-89919-377-3*) Houghton Mifflin Co.

—Waiting for the End of the World. 1986. 336p. pap. 9.95 o.p. (*0-14-009330-3*, Penguin Bks.) Viking Penguin.

—The Washington Square Ensemble. 1984. (Penguin Contemporary American Fiction Ser.). 352p. pap. 11.95 o.s.i (*0-14-007025-7*, Penguin Bks.) Penguin Group (USA) Inc.

—The Washington Square Ensemble. 1983. 336p. 15.75 o.p. (*0-670-75005-0*) Viking Penguin.

—The Year of Silence. 1987. 208p. 15.95 o.p. (*0-89919-490-7*) Houghton Mifflin Co.

—The Year of Silence. 1989. (Contemporary American Fiction Ser.). 208p. pap. 12.95 o.s.i (*0-14-011533-1*, Penguin Bks.) Penguin Group (USA) Inc.

Belle, Jennifer. Going Down. 1996. 272p. pap. 13.00 (*1-57322-554-1*, Riverhead Trade (Paperbacks)) Berkley Publishing Group.

—High Maintenance. 2002. 368p. pap. 13.00 (*1-57322-930-X*, Riverhead Trade (Paperbacks)) Berkley Publishing Group.

—High Maintenance. 2001. 416p. 24.95 o.p. (*1-57322-185-6*, Riverhead Bks. (Hardcovers)) Putnam Publishing Group, The.

Beller, Miles. Dream of Venus; or Living Pictures. 1999. (Illus.). 298p. 24.95 (*0-9663480-0-1*) C. M. Publishing.

Beller, Thomas. The Sleep-over Artist. 2000. 256p. 23.95 (*0-393-04925-6*) Norton, W. W. & Co., Inc.

Bellow, Saul. Mr. Sammler's Planet. 1977. pap. 3.95 o.p. (*0-14-004419-1*); 1973. pap. 3.75 o.p. (*0-670-00396-4*) Penguin Group (USA) Inc.

—Mr. Sammler's Planet. (Great Books of the 20th Century Ser.). 1996. 352p. pap. 13.95 (*0-14-018936-X*, Penguin Classics); 1984. 320p. pap. 11.00 o.p. (*0-14-007317-5*, Penguin Bks.); 1970. 12.95 o.p. (*0-670-49322-8*); 1970. 6.95 o.p. (*0-670-49323-6*) Viking Penguin.

—Seize the Day. 1976. pap. 3.95 o.p. (*0-14-004311-X*); 1961. pap. 1.65 o.p. (*0-670-00091-4*) Penguin Group (USA) Inc.

—Seize the Day. 2003. 144p. pap. 12.00 (*0-14-243761-1*, Penguin Classics); 1996. 144p. 12.00 (*0-14-018937-8*, Penguin Classics); 1984. 128p. pap. 10.95 o.p. (*0-14-007285-3*, Penguin Bks.); 1956. 7.95 o.p. (*0-670-63176-0*) Viking Penguin.

—A Theft. 1989. 128p. pap. 7.95 o.p. (*0-14-011969-8*, Penguin Bks.) Viking Penguin.

Belsky, R. G. Loverboy. 1998. mass mkt. 6.50 (*0-380-79068-8*); 1997. 313p. mass mkt. 23.00 (*0-380-97439-8*) Morrow/Avon. (Avon Bks.).

—Playing Dead. 1999. mass mkt. 6.50 (*0-380-79069-6*, Avon Bks.) Morrow/Avon.

Benabib, Kim. Obscene Bodies: A Novel. 1996. 256p. 22.00 o.p. (*0-06-017437-4*) HarperCollins Pubs.

Benderson, Bruce. User. 240p. 1995. pap. 10.95 o.p. (*0-452-27461-3*, Plume); 1994. 19.95 o.p. (*0-525-93722-6*, Dutton) Dutton/Plume.

Benedict, Helen. Bad Angel. 304p. 1997. pap. 12.95 o.p. (*0-452-27586-5*, Plume); 1996. 22.95 o.p. (*0-525-94100-2*, Dutton) Dutton/Plume.

Benioff, David. The 25th Hour. 2001. 192p. 24.00 (*0-7867-0772-0*, Carroll & Graf Pubs.) Avalon Publishing Group.

—The 25th Hour. 2002. 224p. pap. 13.00 (*0-452-28295-0*, Plume) Dutton/Plume.

—25th Hour. movie tie-in ed. 2002. 224p. pap. 13.00 (*0-452-28419-8*, Plume) Dutton/Plume.

Benjamin, Carol Lea. The Dog Who Knew Too Much: A Rachel Alexander & Dash Mystery. 1998. (Rachel Alexander & Dash Mystery Ser.: Vol. 2). 272p. reprint ed. mass mkt. 5.99 o.s.i (*0-440-22637-6*) Dell Publishing.

—The Dog Who Knew Too Much: A Rachel Alexander & Dash Mystery. 1997. (Rachel Alexander & Dash Mystery Ser.). 256p. 21.95 (*0-8027-3312-3*) Walker & Co.

—A Hell of a Dog. 1998. (Rachel Alexander & Dash Mystery Ser.). (Illus.). 276p. 22.95 (*0-8027-3325-5*) Walker & Co.

—A Hell of a Dog: A Rachel Alexander & Dash Mystery. 1999. (Rachel Alexander & Dash Mystery Ser.). 320p. mass mkt. 5.99 (*0-440-22548-5*) Dell Publishing.

—Lady Vanishes. 1999. (Rachel Alexander & Dash Mystery Ser.). 264p. 23.95 (*0-8027-3335-2*) Walker & Co.

—The Long Good Boy: A Rachel Alexander & Dash Mystery. 2001. 240p. 23.95 (*0-8027-3364-6*) Walker & Co.

—This Dog for Hire: A Rachel Alexander & Dash Mystery. 1997. (Rachel Alexander & Dash Mystery Ser.: Vol. 1). 304p. mass mkt. 6.50 (*0-440-22520-5*) Dell Publishing.

—This Dog for Hire: A Rachel Alexander & Dash Mystery. l.t. ed. 2002. 346p. 28.95 o.p. (*0-7862-4191-8*) Thorndike Pr.

—This Dog for Hire: A Rachel Alexander & Dash Mystery. 1996. (Rachel Alexander & Dash Mystery Ser.). 224p. 20.95 (*0-8027-3292-5*) Walker & Co.

Benjamin, Carol Lea & Sallis, James. The Long-Legged Fly: A Lew Griffin Novel. 2001. 200p. pap. 8.95 (*0-8027-7620-5*) Walker & Co.

Bennett, Jay. The Death Ticket. 1985. pap. 2.75 (*0-380-89597-8*, Avon Bks.) Morrow/Avon.

Bergman, Andrew. Tender is Levine: A Jack Levine Mystery. 2001. 289p. 23.95 (*0-312-26205-1*, Saint Martin's Minotaur) St. Martin's Pr.

Berman, Richard. Hostile Witness. 1996. 304p. (Orig.). mass mkt. 5.99 (*0-380-77813-0*, Avon Bks.) Morrow/Avon.

—Unjust Death. 1995. 352p. (Orig.). mass mkt. 5.50 (*0-380-77812-2*, Avon Bks.) Morrow/Avon.

Berne, Betsy. Bad Timing. 2001. E-Book 19.50 (*1-58945-777-3*) Adobe Systems, Inc.

Berry, Bertice. The Haunting of Hip Hop: A Novel. 2002. 240p. pap. 12.00 (*0-7679-1212-8*) Broadway Bks.

Berry, Carole. The Death of a Dancing Fool. 1996. (Orig.). mass mkt. 5.99 o.s.i (*0-425-15513-7*); 272p. 21.95 o.p. (*0-425-15143-3*, Prime Crime); 272p. pap. 9.00 o.p. (*0-425-15142-5*) Berkley Publishing Group.

—The Death of a Difficult Woman. 272p. 1995. mass mkt. 4.99 o.s.i (*0-425-15008-9*); 1994. 18.95 o.p. (*0-425-14356-2*) Berkley Publishing Group. (Prime Crime).

—The Death of a Dimpled Darling. 1997. 272p. mass mkt. 5.99 o.s.i (*0-425-16097-1*, Prime Crime) Berkley Publishing Group.

—Death of a Downsizer. 1999. (Bonnie Indermill Mystery Ser.). 272p. mass mkt. 5.99 o.s.i (*0-425-16614-7*, Prime Crime) Berkley Publishing Group.

—Good Night, Sweet Prince. 1995. 240p. mass mkt. 4.99 o.s.i (*0-425-14773-8*) Berkley Publishing Group.

—Good Night Sweet Prince. 1991. 256p. mass mkt. 3.95 o.s.i (*0-440-20784-3*) Dell Publishing.

—The Letter of the Law. 1990. 224p. mass mkt. 3.95 o.s.i (*0-440-20524-7*) Dell Publishing.

—The Letter of the Law. 1987. 208p. 15.95 o.p. (*0-312-01059-1*, Saint Martin's Minotaur) St. Martin's Pr.

—The Letter of the Law: Bonnie Indermill Mystery. 1995. 224p. mass mkt. 4.99 o.s.i (*0-425-15105-0*) Berkley Publishing Group.

—The Year of the Monkey. 1996. 256p. mass mkt. 5.50 o.s.i (*0-425-15184-0*) Berkley Publishing Group.

—The Year of the Monkey. 1990. 256p. reprint ed. mass mkt. 3.50 o.s.i (*0-440-20672-3*) Dell Publishing.

—The Year of the Monkey. 1988. 288p. 16.95 o.p. (*0-312-01850-9*, Saint Martin's Minotaur) St. Martin's Pr.

Bertematti, Richard. Project Death: A Tito Rico Mystery. 1997. (Tito Rico Mystery Ser.). 200p. 22.95 o.p. (*1-55885-193-3*) Arte Publico Pr.
Betancourt, Marian. Zebra in the Water. 2003. 227p. pap. 19.95 (*1-59129-525-4*) PublishAmerica, Inc.
Birmingham, Stephen. Carriage Trade. 1994. 544p. mass mkt. 5.99 o.s.i (*0-553-56878-7*) Bantam Bks.
—Carriage Trade. l.t. ed. 1993. 25.95 o.p. (*1-56895-027-6*, Wheeler Publishing, Inc.) Gale Group.
—Rothman Scandal, Vol. 1. 1991. 21.95 o.p. (*0-316-09654-7*) Little Brown & Co.
Bishop, Claudia. Marinade for Murder. 2000. (Hemlock Falls Mysteries Ser.). 256p. mass mkt. 5.99 (*0-425-17611-8*, Prime Crime) Berkley Publishing Group.
Black, David. An Impossible Life. 1998. 200p. pap. 18.95 (*1-55921-222-5*) Moyer Bell.
—Impossible Life: A False Family History. 1996. 224p. 22.95 (*1-882206-13-4*) Argonaut Pr.
Black, Ethan. All the Dead Were Strangers. l.t. ed. 2002. (Americana Ser.). 648p. 30.95 (*0-7862-3766-X*) Gale Group.
—All the Dead Were Strangers. 2003. (Illus.). 480p. mass mkt. 7.50 (*0-7434-7104-0*, Pocket) Simon & Schuster.
—The Broken Hearts Club. 2000. 352p. mass mkt. 6.99 (*0-345-42603-7*) Ballantine Bks.
—Dead for Life. 2003. 320p. 24.00 (*0-7432-4400-1*, Simon & Schuster) Simon & Schuster.
Black, Simon. The Book of Frank. Putnam, Jeff, ed. 1994. 228p. pap. 11.00 (*1-880909-28-6*) Baskerville Pubs., Inc.
—The Book of Frank. 2nd ed. 1994. 228p. 19.00 (*1-880909-25-1*) Baskerville Pubs., Inc.
Blake, Lillie D. Fettered for Life. 1997. 432p. pap. 18.95 (*1-55861-155-X*); lib. bdg. 45.00 (*1-55861-159-2*) Feminist Pr. at The City Univ. of New York.
—Fettered for Life or Lord & Master, Set. unabr. ed. 1998. 53.95 incl. audio (*1-55685-539-7*) Audio Bk. Contractors, Inc.
Blanchard, Keith. The Deed: A Novel. 2003. 320p. 24.00 (*0-7432-2387-X*, Simon & Schuster) Simon & Schuster.
Blanchard, Nina. The Look. 1996. 416p. mass mkt. 5.99 o.s.i (*0-451-18034-8*, Signet Bks.) NAL.
Blanchard, Nina & Barsocchini, Peter. The Look. 1995. 368p. 23.95 o.p. (*0-525-93795-1*, Dutton) Dutton/Plume.
Blauner, Peter. The Intruder. l.t. ed. 1996. 26.95 (*1-56895-348-8*, Wheeler Publishing, Inc.) Gale Group.
—The Intruder. unabr. ed. audio 1999. audio 70.00 (*0-7887-0627-6*, 94801E7) Recorded Bks., LLC.
—The Intruder. 1996. 384p. 22.50 o.p. (*0-684-81094-8*, Simon & Schuster) Simon & Schuster.
—The Intruder. abr. ed. 1999. audio; 1996. 192p. pap. 18.00 incl. audio (*0-671-57041-2*, 394045, Simon & Schuster Audioworks) Simon & Schuster Audio.
—The Intruder. 1997. 464p. reprint ed. mass mkt. 6.99 (*0-446-60505-0*) Warner Bks., Inc.
—Man of the Hour. 1999. 432p. 24.00 o.p. (*0-316-03817-2*) Little Brown & Co.
—The Man of the Hour. 2000. 496p. mass mkt. 7.99 o.s.i (*0-446-60541-7*) Warner Bks., Inc.
—Man of the Hour, , unabr. ed. 1999. audio 72.00 (*0-7366-4450-4*, 4895) Books on Tape, Inc.
—Man of the Hour. abr. ed. 2000. audio (*1-57042-878-6*); 1999. audio 24.98 (*1-57042-682-1*, 696584); 2000. audio (*1-57042-879-4*); 1999. audio 39.98 (*1-57042-720-8*, 110113) Time Warner AudioBooks.
—Slow Motion Riot. 1992. 384p. pap. 6.99 (*0-380-71306-3*, Avon Bks.); 1991. 352p. 20.00 o.p. (*0-688-10068-6*, Morrow, William & Co.) Morrow/Avon.
Block, Lawrence. After the First Death. 1994. 268p. mass mkt. 4.50 o.p. (*0-7867-0167-6*, Carroll & Graf Pubs.) Avalon Publishing Group.
—After the First Death. 1984. 192p. reprint ed. pap. 4.95 o.p. (*0-88150-020-8*) Countryman Pr.
—After the First Death. l.t. ed. 1992. (Nightingale Ser.). 291p. pap. 14.95 o.p. (*0-8161-5408-2*, Macmillan Reference USA) Gale Group.
—After the First Death. 2002. 192p. mass mkt. 6.99 (*0-7434-4507-4*) ibooks, Inc.
—The Burglar in the Closet. (Bernie Rhodenbarr Mystery Ser.: No. 2). audio 24.95 (*0-7861-1392-8*); 1997. audio 32.95 (*0-7861-1044-9*, 1816) Blackstone Audio Bks., Inc.
—The Burglar in the Closet. unabr. ed. 2000. (Bernie Rhodenbarr Mystery Ser.: Bk. 2). audio 54.95 (*0-7927-2209-4*, CSL 098) Chivers Audio Bks. GBR. *Dist:* BBC Audiobooks America.
—The Burglar in the Closet. 1995. (Bernie Rhodenbarr Mystery Ser.: No. 2). 256p. 21.95 o.p. (*0-525-93993-8*, Dutton) Dutton/Plume.
—The Burglar in the Closet. 1997. (Bernie Rhodenbarr Mystery Ser.: No. 2). 320p. mass mkt. 6.99 (*0-451-18074-7*, Signet Bks.) NAL.
—The Burglar in the Closet. 1978. (Bernie Rhodenbarr Mystery Ser.: No. 2). 6.95 o.p. (*0-394-42374-7*) Random Hse., Inc.
—The Burglar in the Closet. unabr. ed. 1998. (Bernie Rhodenbarr Mystery Ser.: No. 2). audio 35.00 (*0-7887-0854-6*, 95000E7 ) Recorded Bks., LLC.
—The Burglar in the Closet. 1986. (Bernie Rhodenbarr Mystery Ser.: No. 2). mass mkt. 3.50 o.s.i (*0-671-61704-4*, Pocket) Simon & Schuster.
—The Burglar in the Library. 1997. (Bernie Rhodenbarr Mystery Ser.: No. 8). 320p. 23.95 o.p. (*0-525-94301-3*, Dutton) Dutton/Plume.
—The Burglar in the Library. 1998. (Bernie Rhodenbarr Mystery Ser.: No. 8). 368p. mass mkt. 6.99 (*0-451-40783-0*, Signet Bks.) NAL.
—The Burglar in the Library. l.t. ed. 1998. (Bernie Rhodenbarr Mystery Ser.: No. 8). 464p. 27.95 o.p. (*0-7862-1280-2*) Thorndike Pr.
—The Burglar in the Library. abr. ed. 1997. (Bernie Rhodenbarr Mystery Ser.: No. 8). 2p. audio 16.95 (*0-14-086582-9*, Penguin AudioBooks) Viking Penguin.
—The Burglar in the Rye. 1999. (Bernie Rhodenbarr Mystery Ser.: No. 9). 280p. 23.95 o.p. (*0-525-94500-8*, Dutton) Dutton/Plume.
—The Burglar in the Rye. 2000. (Bernie Rhodenbarr Mystery Ser.: No. 9). 320p. mass mkt. 6.99 (*0-451-19847-6*, Signet Bks.) NAL.
—The Burglar in the Rye. l.t. ed. 1999. (Bernie Rhodenbarr Mystery Ser.: No. 9). 440p. 30.95 (*0-7862-2136-4*) Thorndike Pr.
—The Burglar on the Prowl. l.t. ed. 2004. 416p. pap. 24.95 (*0-06-058979-5*, HarperLargePrint) HarperTrade.
—The Burglar on the Prowl. 2004. 320p. 24.95 (*0-06-019830-3*, Morrow, William & Co.) Morrow/Avon.
—The Burglar Who Liked to Quote Kipling. 1996. (Bernie Rhodenbarr Mystery Ser.: No. 3). 256p. 22.95 o.s.i (*0-525-94159-2*, Dutton) Dutton/Plume.
—The Burglar Who Liked to Quote Kipling. 1997. (Bernie Rhodenbarr Mystery Ser.: No. 3). 320p. mass mkt. 6.99 o.s.i (*0-451-18075-5*, Signet Bks.) NAL.
—The Burglar Who Liked to Quote Kipling. 1979. (Bernie Rhodenbarr Mystery Ser.: No. 3). 7.95 o.p. (*0-394-50417-8*) Random Hse., Inc.
—The Burglar Who Liked to Quote Kipling. 1998. (Bernie Rhodenbarr Mystery Ser.: No. 3). audio 44.00 (*0-7887-0810-4*, 94959E7 ) Recorded Bks., LLC.
—The Burglar Who Liked to Quote Kipling. abr. ed. 1996. (Bernie Rhodenbarr Mystery Ser.: No. 3). audio 16.95 o.s.i (*0-14-086345-1*, Penguin AudioBooks) Viking Penguin.
—The Burglar Who Painted Like Mondrian. 1998. (Bernie Rhodenbarr Mystery Ser.: No. 5). 224p. 23.95 o.p. (*0-525-94382-X*) Dutton/Plume.
—The Burglar Who Painted Like Mondrian. l.t. ed. 1999. (Bernie Rhodenbarr Mystery Ser.: No. 5). 27.95 (*1-56895-726-2*, Wheeler Publishing, Inc.) Gale Group.
—The Burglar Who Painted Like Mondrian. 1983. (Bernie Rhodenbarr Mystery Ser.: No. 5). 217p. 14.50 o.p. (*0-87795-517-4*, Morrow, William & Co.) Morrow/Avon.
—The Burglar Who Painted Like Mondrian. 1999. (Bernie Rhodenbarr Mystery Ser.: No. 5). 320p. reprint ed. mass mkt. 6.99 o.p. (*0-451-18076-3*, Signet Bks.) NAL.
—The Burglar Who Painted Like Mondrian. unabr. ed. 1993. (Bernie Rhodenbarr Mystery Ser.: No. 5). audio 46.00 (*0-7887-3214-5*, 95846E7) Recorded Bks., LLC.
—The Burglar Who Painted Like Mondrian. 1986. (Bernie Rhodenbarr Mystery Ser.: No. 5). mass mkt. 3.50 o.s.i (*0-671-49581-X*, Pocket) Simon & Schuster.
—The Burglar Who Painted Like Mondrian. abr. ed. 1998. (Bernie Rhodenbarr Mystery Ser.: No. 5). 2p. audio 17.95 o.p. (*0-14-086817-8*, Penguin AudioBooks) Viking Penguin.
—The Burglar Who Studied Spinoza. 1997. (Bernie Rhodenbarr Mystery Ser.: No. 4). 240p. 23.95 o.s.i (*0-525-94180-0*, Signet Bks.) Dutton/Plume.
—The Burglar Who Studied Spinoza. l.t. ed. 1998. (Bernie Rhodenbarr Mystery Ser.: No. 4). 26.95 (*1-56895-602-9*, Wheeler Publishing, Inc.) Gale Group.
—The Burglar Who Studied Spinoza. 1998. (Bernie Rhodenbarr Mystery Ser.: No. 4). 320p. mass mkt. 6.99 o.s.i (*0-451-19488-8*, Signet Bks.) NAL.
—The Burglar Who Studied Spinoza. 1981. (Bernie Rhodenbarr Mystery Ser.: No. 4). 8.95 o.p. (*0-394-51065-8*) Random Hse., Inc.
—The Burglar Who Studied Spinoza. 1986. (Bernie Rhodenbarr Mystery Ser.: No. 4). mass mkt. 3.50 o.s.i (*0-671-62485-7*, Pocket) Simon & Schuster.
—The Burglar Who Thought He Was Bogart. unabr. ed. 1997. (Bernie Rhodenbarr Mystery Ser.: No. 7). audio 44.95 (*0-7861-1196-8*, 1957) Blackstone Audio Bks., Inc.
—The Burglar Who Thought He Was Bogart. 1996. (Bernie Rhodenbarr Mystery Ser.: No. 7). 384p. mass mkt. 6.99 o.s.i (*0-451-18634-6*, Onyx) NAL.
—The Burglar Who Thought He Was Bogart. unabr. ed. 1997. (Bernie Rhodenbarr Mystery Ser.: No. 7). audio 51.00 (*0-7887-0476-1*, 94669E7) Recorded Bks., LLC.
—The Burglar Who Thought He Was Bogart. abr. ed. 1995. (Bernie Rhodenbarr Mystery Ser.: No. 7). audio 16.95 o.s.i (*0-14-086190-4*, Penguin AudioBooks) Viking Penguin.
—The Burglar Who Traded Ted Williams. unabr. ed. 1997. (Bernie Rhodenbarr Mystery Ser.: No. 6). audio 44.95 (*0-7861-1166-6*, 1937) Blackstone Audio Bks., Inc.
—The Burglar Who Traded Ted Williams. 1994. (Bernie Rhodenbarr Mystery Ser.: No. 6). 272p. 19.95 o.p. (*0-525-93807-9*, Dutton) Dutton/Plume.
—The Burglar Who Traded Ted Williams. 1995. (Bernie Rhodenbarr Mystery Ser.: No. 6). 384p. mass mkt. 6.99 o.s.i (*0-451-18426-2*, Onyx) NAL.
—The Burglar Who Traded Ted Williams. abr. ed. 1994. (Bernie Rhodenbarr Mystery Ser.: No. 6). pap. 16.00 o.p. incl. audio (*0-453-00890-9*, 25024-31224) Penguin/HighBridge.
—The Burglar Who Traded Ted Williams. unabr. ed. 1994. (Bernie Rhodenbarr Mystery Ser.: No. 6). audio 51.00 (*0-7887-1302-7*, 95138E7) Recorded Bks., LLC.
—Burglars Can't Be Choosers. 1978. (Bernie Rhodenbarr Mystery Ser.: No. 1). pap. 1.75 o.s.i (*0-515-04584-5*, Jove) Berkley Publishing Group.
—Burglars Can't Be Choosers, unabr. ed. 1997. (Bernie Rhodenbarr Mystery Ser.: No. 1). audio 39.95 (*0-7861-1136-4*, 755302) Blackstone Audio Bks., Inc.
—Burglars Can't Be Choosers. 1995. (Bernie Rhodenbarr Mystery Ser.: No. 1). 256p. 19.95 o.p. (*0-525-93943-1*, Dutton) Dutton/Plume.
—Burglars Can't Be Choosers. 2004. 320p. mass mkt. 6.99 (*0-06-058255-3*, HarperTorch) Morrow/Avon.
—Burglars Can't Be Choosers. 1995. (Bernie Rhodenbarr Mystery Ser.: No. 1). 304p. mass mkt. 5.99 o.s.i (*0-451-18073-9*, Signet Bks.) NAL.
—Burglars Can't Be Choosers. abr. ed. 1995. (Bernie Rhodenbarr Mystery Ser.: No. 1). pap. 16.95 o.p. incl. audio (*0-453-00932-8*, 25024-39151) Penguin/HighBridge.
—Burglars Can't Be Choosers. 1977. (Bernie Rhodenbarr Mystery Ser.: No. 1). (Illus.). 6.95 o.p. (*0-394-41183-8*) Random Hse., Inc.
—Burglars Can't Be Choosers. unabr. ed. 1998. (Bernie Rhodenbarr Mystery Ser.: No. 1). audio 44.00 (*0-7887-1990-4*, 95377E7) Recorded Bks., LLC.
—Chip Harrison Scores Again. 1997. (Chip Harrison Mysteries Ser.). 256p. mass mkt. 5.99 o.s.i (*0-451-18797-0*, Signet Bks.) NAL.
—Cinderella Sims. 2002. Orig. Title: Twenty Dollar Lust. 170p. 30.00 (*1-931081-51-4*) Subterranean Pr.
—Coward's Kiss. 1996. 160p. mass mkt. 3.95 (*0-7867-0334-2*, Carroll & Graf Pubs.) Avalon Publishing Group.
—Coward's Kiss. 1987. 160p. reprint ed. pap. 4.95 o.p. (*0-88150-085-2*) Countryman Pr.
—Coward's Kiss. 1999. (Mystery Ser.). 184p. pap. 19.95 (*0-7862-2075-9*, Five Star) Gale Group.
—Coward's Kiss. 2003. 224p. mass mkt. 4.99 (*0-7434-5899-0*) ibooks, Inc.
—A Dance at the Slaughterhouse. (Matthew Scudder Mystery Ser.: No. 9). 2000. 304p. pap. 13.00 (*0-380-81373-4*, Avon Bks.); 1991. 304p. 19.00 o.p. (*0-688-10349-9*, Morrow, William & Co.); 1992. 384p. reprint ed. mass mkt. 7.50 (*0-380-71374-8*, Avon Bks.) Morrow/Avon.
—A Dance at the Slaughterhouse. l.t. ed. 2000. (Matthew Scudder Mystery Ser.: No. 9). 468p. 28.95 (*0-7862-2983-7*) Thorndike Pr.
—The Devil Knows You're Dead. (Matthew Scudder Mystery Ser.: No. 11). 1999. 288p. pap. 12.50 (*0-380-80759-9*, Avon Bks.); 1993. 316p. 20.00 o.p. (*0-688-12192-6*, Morrow, William & Co.); 1994. 384p. reprint ed. mass mkt. 7.50 (*0-380-72023-X*, Avon Bks.) Morrow/Avon.
—The Devil Knows You're Dead. l.t. ed. 2001. (Matthew Scudder Mystery Ser.: No. 11). 503p. 30.95 (*0-7862-3109-2*); (*0-7540-1578-5*); (*0-7540-2440-7*) Thorndike Pr.
—Eight Million Ways to Die. 1986. (Matthew Scudder Mystery Ser.: No. 5). mass mkt. 3.50 o.s.i (*0-515-08840-4*); 1984. (Matthew Scudder Mystery Ser.: No. 5). 304p. mass mkt. 3.95 o.s.i (*0-515-08090-X*); 1983. mass mkt. 3.50 o.s.i (*0-515-07537-X*); 1983. mass mkt. 3.50 o.s.i (*0-515-07257-5*) Berkley Publishing Group. (Jove).
—Eight Million Ways to Die. l.t. ed. 2000. (Matthew Scudder Mystery Ser.: No. 5). 410p. pap. 24.95 (*1-56895-939-7*, Wheeler Publishing, Inc.) Gale Group.
—Eight Million Ways to Die. (Matthew Scudder Mystery Ser.: No. 5). 1982. 13.50 o.p. (*0-87795-405-4*, Morrow, William & Co.); 1993. 384p. reprint ed. mass mkt. 7.50 (*0-380-71573-2*, Avon Bks.) Morrow/Avon.
—Even the Wicked. l.t. ed. 1998. (Matthew Scudder Mystery Ser.: No. 13). 400p. mass mkt. 7.50 (*0-380-72534-7*, Avon Bks.) Morrow/Avon.
—Everybody Dies. (Matthew Scudder Mystery Ser.: No. 14). 1999. 384p. mass mkt. 6.99 (*0-380-72535-5*, Avon Bks.); 1998. 336p. 25.00 o.p. (*0-688-14182-X*, Morrow, William & Co.) Morrow/Avon.
—Everybody Dies. l.t. ed. 1999. (Matthew Scudder Mystery Ser.: No. 14). 461p. 29.95 (*0-7862-1706-5*) Thorndike Pr.
—Hit List. 2002. 384p. E-Book 7.50 (*0-06-103099-6*) HarperCollins Pubs.
—Hit List. 2000. 25.00 (*0-06-018420-5*); 304p. 25.00 (*0-06-019833-8*); 480p. 25.00 (*0-06-019911-3*) Morrow/Avon. (Morrow, William & Co.).
—Hope to Die. l.t. ed. 2001. 480p. pap. 25.00 (*0-06-621400-9*) HarperCollins Pubs.
—Hope to Die. abr. ed. 2001. 32p. (ps-2). audio 25.95 (*0-694-52604-5*, HarperAudio) HarperTrade.
—Hope to Die. 2002. 400p. mass mkt. 7.99 (*0-06-103097-X*); 2001. 336p. 25.00 (*0-06-019832-X*) Morrow/Avon. (Morrow, William & Co.).
—In the Midst of Death. l.t. ed. 1991. (Matthew Scudder Mystery Ser.: No. 2). pap. 15.95 o.p. (*0-7927-0601-3*, AS0192); 17.95 o.p. (*0-7451-8095-7*, AH0156) BBC Audiobooks America.
—In the Midst of Death. 1989. (Matthew Scudder Mystery Ser.: No. 3). 192p. mass mkt. 3.50 o.s.i (*0-515-08684-3*); 1984. mass mkt. 2.95 o.s.i (*0-515-08098-5*); 1983. mass mkt. 2.95 o.s.i (*0-515-07430-6*); 1982. mass mkt. 2.75 o.s.i (*0-515-06731-8*) Berkley Publishing Group. (Jove).
—In the Midst of Death. 1976. (Matthew Scudder Mystery Ser.: No. 3). pap. 1.25 o.p. (*0-440-14037-4*) Dell Publishing.
—In the Midst of Death. 2002. E-Book 7.50 (*0-06-052097-3*); E-Book 7.50 (*0-06-052098-1*); E-Book 7.50 (*0-06-052094-9*); E-Book 7.50 (*0-06-052096-5*) HarperCollins General Bks. Group. (PerfectBound).
—In the Midst of Death. 1992. (Matthew Scudder Mystery Ser.: No. 3). 272p. mass mkt. 7.50 (*0-380-76362-1*, Avon Bks.) Morrow/Avon.
—A Long Line of Dead Men. (Matthew Scudder Mystery Ser.: No. 12). 1999. 304p. pap. 12.50 (*0-380-80604-5*, Avon Bks.); 1996. 368p. mass mkt. 7.50 (*0-380-72024-8*, Avon Bks.); 1994. 20.00 o.p. (*0-688-12193-4*, Morrow, William & Co.) Morrow/Avon.
—Make Out with Murder. unabr. ed. 1999. (Chip Harrison Mystery Ser.). audio 39.95 (*0-7927-2291-4*, CSL180, Chivers Sound Library) BBC Audiobooks America.
—Make Out with Murder. 1997. (Chip Harrison Mystery Ser.). 240p. mass mkt. 5.99 o.s.i (*0-451-18798-9*, Signet Bks.) NAL.
—No Score. 1996. (Chip Harrison Mystery Ser.). 277p. mass mkt. 5.50 o.s.i (*0-451-18796-2*, Signet Bks.) NAL.
—Out on the Cutting Edge. l.t. ed. 1995. (Matthew Scudder Mystery Ser.: No. 7). 330p. pap. 19.95 o.p. (*0-7838-1177-2*, Macmillan Reference USA) Gale Group.
—Out on the Cutting Edge. l.t. ed. 1995. (Magna Large Print Ser.). 348p. o.p. (*0-7505-0761-6*) Magna Large Print Bks. GBR. *Dist:* Ulverscroft Large Print Canada, Ltd.
—Out on the Cutting Edge. (Matthew Scudder Mystery Ser.: No. 7). 1989. 256p. 17.95 o.p. (*0-688-09069-9*, Morrow, William & Co.); 1990. 352p. reprint ed. mass mkt. 6.99 (*0-380-70993-7*, Avon Bks.) Morrow/Avon.
—The Sins of the Fathers. l.t. ed. 1990. (Matthew Scudder Mystery Ser.: No. 1). 17.95 o.p. (*0-7451-9866-X*, C0616); pap. 15.95 o.p. (*0-7927-0317-0*, C0810) BBC Audiobooks America.
—The Sins of the Fathers. mass mkt. 2.95 o.s.i (*0-515-08685-1*); 1988. (Matthew Scudder Mystery Ser.: No. 1). mass mkt. 3.50 o.s.i (*0-515-09831-0*); 1984. mass mkt. 2.95 o.s.i (*0-515-08157-4*); 1983. mass mkt. 2.95 o.s.i (*0-515-07516-7*); 1982. mass mkt. 2.75 o.s.i (*0-515-06729-6*) Berkley Publishing Group. (Jove).
—The Sins of the Fathers. 2002. E-Book 7.50 (*0-06-052103-1*); E-Book 7.50 (*0-06-052108-2*); E-Book 7.50 (*0-06-052104-X*); E-Book 7.50 (*0-06-052105-8*) HarperCollins General Bks. Group. (PerfectBound).
—Small Town. abr. ed. 2003. audio 25.95 (*0-06-053646-2*) HarperCollins Pubs.
—Small Town. l.t. ed. 2003. 688p. pap. 24.95 (*0-06-053744-2*, HarperLargePrint) HarperTrade.
—Small Town. 2003. 576p. mass mkt. 7.99 (*0-06-001191-2*, HarperTorch); mass mkt. 39.90 (*0-06-057957-9*, HarperTorch); 464p. 24.95 (*0-06-001190-4*, Morrow, William & Co.) Morrow/Avon.
—Small Town. unabr. ed. 2003. audio 114.00 (*1-4025-0619-8*) Recorded Bks., LLC.
—A Stab in the Dark. 1989. (Matthew Scudder Mystery Ser.: No. 4). 192p. mass mkt. 3.50 o.s.i (*0-515-09885-X*); 1985. mass mkt. 2.95 o.s.i (*0-515-08635-5*); 1984. mass mkt. 2.95 o.s.i

*(0-515-08158-2)*; 1983. mass mkt. 2.95 o.s.i *(0-515-07399-7)*; 1982. mass mkt. 2.75 o.s.i *(0-515-06717-2)* Berkley Publishing Group. (Jove).

—A Stab in the Dark. 2002. E-Book 7.50 *(0-06-052090-6)*; E-Book 7.50 *(0-06-052093-0)*; E-Book 7.50 *(0-06-052092-2)*; E-Book 7.50 *(0-06-052091-4)* HarperCollins General Bks. Group. (PerfectBound).

—A Stab in the Dark. (Matthew Scudder Mystery Ser.: No. 4). 1981. 192p. 10.95 o.p. *(0-87795-340-6)*, Morrow, William & Co.); 2002. 304p. reprint ed. mass mkt. 7.50 *(0-380-71574-0)*, Avon Bks. Morrow/Avon.

—A Ticket to the Boneyard. l.t. ed. (Matthew Scudder Mystery Ser.: No. 8). 1992. pap. 21.95 o.p. *(0-7927-1089-4)*, CS0293); 1991. 23.95 o.p. *(0-7927-1088-6)*, CH0221) BBC Audiobooks America.

—A Ticket to the Boneyard. l.t. ed. 1995. (Magna Large Print Ser.). 404p. *(0-7505-0911-2)* Magna Large Print Bks. GBR. *Dist:* Ulverscroft Large Print Canada, Ltd.

—A Ticket to the Boneyard. (Matthew Scudder Mystery Ser.: No. 8). 1990. 270p. 18.95 o.p. *(0-688-09070-2)*, Morrow, William & Co.); 1991. 384p. reprint ed. mass mkt. 7.50 *(0-380-70994-5)*, Avon Bks.) Morrow/Avon.

—Time to Murder & Create. 1984. (Matthew Scudder Mystery Ser.: No. 2). 192p. mass mkt. 3.50 o.s.i *(0-515-08159-0)*, Jove) Berkley Publishing Group.

—Time to Murder & Create. l.t. ed. 1985. (Matthew Scudder Mystery Ser.: No. 2). 12.50 o.p. *(0-8166-0137-2)*, Macmillan Reference USA) Gale Group.

—Time to Murder & Create. 1991. (Matthew Scudder Mystery Ser.: No. 2). 304p. mass mkt. 7.50 *(0-380-76365-6)*, Avon Bks.) Morrow/Avon.

—The Topless Tulip Caper: A Chip Harrison Mystery, unabr. ed. 1999. (Chip Harrison Mystery Ser.). audio 39.95 *(0-7927-2303-1)*, CSL192, Chivers Sound Library) BBC Audiobooks America.

—A Walk among the Tombstones. l.t. ed. 1993. (Matthew Scudder Mystery Ser.: No. 10). 431p. lib. bdg. 22.95 o.p. *(0-8161-5759-6)*, Macmillan Reference USA) Gale Group.

—A Walk among the Tombstones. (Matthew Scudder Mystery Ser.: No. 10). 2000. 304p. pap. 12.50 *(0-380-81118-9)*, Avon Bks.); 1992. 309p 17.00 o.p. *(0-688-10350-2)*, Morrow, William & Co.); 1993. 384p. reprint ed. mass mkt. 7.50 *(0-380-71375-6)*, Avon Bks.) Morrow/Avon.

—A Walk among the Tombstones. 4.98 o.p. *(0-8317-8575-6)* Smithmark Pubs., Inc.

—When the Sacred Ginmill Closes. (Matthew Scudder Mystery Ser.: No. 6). 1990. mass mkt. 4.99 o.s.i *(0-515-10278-4)*, Jove); 1987. 272p. 3.95 o.s.i *(0-441-88097-5)*, Diamond Bks.) Berkley Publishing Group.

—When the Sacred Ginmill Closes. l.t. ed. 1987. (Matthew Scudder Mystery Ser.: No. 6). 361p. lib. bdg. 20.95 o.p. *(0-8161-4244-0)*, Macmillan Reference USA) Gale Group.

—When the Sacred Ginmill Closes. 2002. E-Book 7.50 *(0-06-052100-7)*; E-Book 7.50 *(0-06-052102-3)*; E-Book 7.50 *(0-06-052101-5)*; E-Book 7.50 *(0-06-052099-X)* HarperCollins General Bks. Group. (PerfectBound).

—When the Sacred Ginmill Closes. 1997. 384p. mass mkt. 7.50 *(0-380-72825-7)*, Avon Bks.); 1986. 15.95 o.p. *(0-87795-774-6)*, Morrow, William & Co.) Morrow/Avon.

Block, Valerie. Was It Something I Said? 1998. (Ann Rule's Crime Files Ser.). 368p. pap. 14.00 *(0-671-02586-4)*, Washington Square Pr.) Simon & Schuster.

—Was It Something I Said? 1998. 368p. 24.00 *(1-56947-109-6)* Soho Pr., Inc.

Bloom, Amy. Love Invents Us. 1998. 224p. pap. 12.00 *(0-375-75022-3)*, Vintage) Knopf Publishing Group.

Bloom, Matt. Blue Paradise: A Novel. 1998. (New Writers' Ser.). 160p. pap. 12.95 *(1-57826-002-7)*, Red Brick Pr.) Hatherleigh Co., Ltd., The.

—A Death in the Hamptons. 2003. 248p. pap. 14.95 *(1-57826-150-3)*; 2002. 200p. 22.95 *(1-57826-115-5)* Hatherleigh Co., Ltd., The.

Bloom, Steven. No New Jokes: A Novel. 1997. 187p. 23.00 *(0-393-04047-X)* Norton, W. W. & Co., Inc.

Bogart, Stephen Humphrey. Play It Again. 1996. 246p. pap. text 5.99 *(0-8125-5162-1)*; 1995. 240p. 19.95 o.p. *(0-312-85665-2)* Doherty, Tom Assocs., LLC. (Forge Bks.).

—The Remake: As Time Goes By. 288p. 1997. 22.95 o.p. *(0-312-85666-0)*; Vol. 1. 1998. (Remake Ser.: Vol. 1). mass mkt. 6.99 *(0-8125-5164-8)* Doherty, Tom Assocs., LLC. (Forge Bks.).

Bogin, Magda. Natalya, God's Messenger. 1994. 288p. 21.00 o.s.i *(0-684-19624-7)*, Macmillan Reference USA) Gale Group.

Bolton, Isabel. New York Mosaic: Do I Wake or Sleep; The Christmas Tree; Many Mansions. (New York Mosaic Ser.). 401p. 1997. 35.00 *(1-883642-28-0)*; 1998. (Illus.). reprint ed. pap. 18.00 *(1-883642-89-2)* Steerforth Pr.

Bookbinder, Bernie. Out at the Old Ball Game: A Novel. 1995. 347p. 21.95 o.s.i *(1-882593-09-X)*; 2002. 262p. reprint ed. pap. 13.95 *(1-882593-56-1)* Bridge Works Publishing Co., Inc.

Boorstin, Jon. The Newsboys' Lodging-House. 2004. 384p. pap. 14.00 *(0-14-200392-1)* Penguin Group (USA) Inc.

Bourdain, Anthony. Bone in the Throat. 2000. 304p. pap. 14.95 *(1-58234-102-8)* Bloomsbury Publishing.

Bowen, Rhys. For the Love of Mike. Date not set. pap. *(0-312-31301-2*, St. Martin's Paperbacks); Date not set. mass mkt. *(0-312-99466-4*, St. Martin's Paperbacks); 2003. 320p. 23.95 *(0-312-31300-4*, Saint Martin's Minotaur) St. Martin's Pr.

Bowes, Richard. Minions of the Moon. 320p. 2000. pap. 13.95 *(0-312-87228-3)*; 1998. (Illus.). 23.95 *(0-312-86566-X)* Doherty, Tom Assocs., LLC. (Tor Bks.).

Boyle, Thomas. Brooklyn Three. 1992. (Crime Ser.). 256p. pap. 4.95 o.p. *(0-14-012706-2*, Penguin Bks.) Penguin Group (USA) Inc.

—Brooklyn Three. 1991. 256p. 18.95 o.p. *(0-670-83019-4)* Viking Penguin.

—Only the Dead Know Brooklyn. l.t. ed. 1989. 412p. lib. bdg. 11.95 o.p. *(1-85057-479-0*, Macmillan Reference USA) Gale Group.

—Only the Dead Know Brooklyn. 1985. 288p. 15.95 o.p. *(0-87923-565-9)* Godine, David R. Pub.

—Only the Dead Know Brooklyn. mass mkt. 0.25 o.p. *(0-451-00950-9*, Signet Bks.) NAL.

—Only the Dead Know Brooklyn. 1986. (Crime Ser.). pap. 4.95 o.p. *(0-14-017155-X)*; 288p. mass mkt. 3.50 o.p. *(0-14-009257-9)* Viking Penguin. (Penguin Bks.).

—Post-Mortem Effects. 1988. 39.50 o.p. *(0-14-778385-2)* Penguin Group (USA) Inc.

—Post-Mortem Effects. (Crime Ser.). 1988. 288p. pap. 3.95 o.p. *(0-14-009753-8*, Penguin Bks.); 1987. 15.95 o.p. *(0-670-81325-7)* Viking Penguin.

—The Triumph of Katie Byrne. l.t. ed. 2001. 496p. 24.95 o.p. *(0-375-43097-0)* Random Hse. Large Print.

—Voice of the Heart. l.t. ed. 1988. 1096p. 21.95 o.p. *(0-8161-4465-6)*; 13.95 o.p. *(0-8161-4466-4)* Gale Group. (Macmillan Reference USA).

Bradley, Marion Zimmer. Ghostlight. (Light Ser.). 2003. 384p. mass mkt. 6.99 *(0-7653-4666-4)*; 1995. 304p. 22.95 o.p. *(0-312-85881-7)*; 4th ed. 1996. 304p. pap. 15.95 *(0-312-86218-0)* Doherty, Tom Assocs., LLC. (Tor Bks.).

—Gravelight. (Light Ser.). 2003. 416p. mass mkt. 6.99 *(0-7653-4667-2)*; 1998. 352p. pap. 14.95 *(0-312-86507-4)*; 1997. 352p. 24.95 o.p. *(0-312-86503-1)* Doherty, Tom Assocs., LLC. (Tor Bks.).

—Heartlight. 416p. 1999. pap. 15.95 *(0-312-86509-0)*; 1998. 25.95 *(0-312-86508-2)* Doherty, Tom Assocs., LLC. (Tor Bks.).

—Witch Hunt. 1996. 352p. 20.95 *(0-312-85606-7*, Forge Bks.) Doherty, Tom Assocs., LLC. (Tor Bks.).

—Witchlight. 2004. mass mkt. 6.99 *(0-7653-4714-8)*; 1996. 304p 23.95 o.p. *(0-312-86104-4)*; 3rd ed. 1997. 304p. pap. 14.95 *(0-312-85831-0)* Doherty, Tom Assocs., LLC. (Tor Bks.).

—Witchlight. abr. ed. 2000. audio 7.95 *(1-57815-177-5*, 1120, Media Bks. Audio Publishing) Media Bks., L. L.

—Witchlight, Set. abr. ed. 1996. audio 16.95 o.p. *(1-55935-234-5)* Soundelux Audio Publishing.

Bram, Christopher. Lives of the Circus Animals: A Novel. 2003. 352p. 24.95 *(0-06-054253-5)*; pap. 13.95 *(0-06-054254-3)* HarperCollins Pubs.

Brand, Max. Murder Me! l.t. ed. 1996. (G. K. Hall Nightingale Ser.). 304p. pap. 17.95 o.p. *(0-7838-1734-7*, Macmillan Reference USA) Gale Group.

—Murder Me! 1995. 272p. 20.95 o.p. *(0-312-13569-6*, Saint Martin's Minotaur) St. Martin's Pr.

Braudy, Susan. What the Movies Made Me Do. 1985. 234p. 15.95 o.s.i *(0-394-53246-5)* Knopf, Alfred A. Inc.

Brennan, Carol. In the Dark. l.t. ed. 1995. 288p. lib. bdg. 23.95 *(1-57490-029-3*, Beeler Large Print Bks.) Beeler, Thomas T. Publisher.

—In the Dark. 1995. 256p. mass mkt. 4.99 o.p. *(0-425-14579-4*, Prime Crime) Berkley Publishing Group.

—In the Dark. 1994. 288p. 21.95 o.p. *(0-399-13940-0*, G. P. Putnam's Sons) Penguin Group (USA) Inc.

Breslin, Jimmy. The Gang That Couldn't Shoot Straight. 1997. 256p. pap. 12.95 *(0-316-11174-0*, Back Bay) Little Brown & Co.

—The Gang That Couldn't Shoot Straight. l.t. ed. 2001. (G. K. Hall Paperback Ser.). 328p. 24.95 *(0-7838-9391-4)* Thorndike Pr.

—The Gang That Couldn't Shoot Straight. 1987. 256p. mass mkt. 4.50 o.p. *(0-14-010308-2*, Penguin Bks.); 1969. 5.95 o.p. *(0-670-33396-4)* Viking Penguin.

—I Don't Want to Go to Jail: A Good Novel. Clain, Judy, ed. 2001. 320p. 24.95 o.p. *(0-316-11845-1)* Little Brown & Co.

—Table Money. l.t. ed. 1987. 707p. 19.95 o.p. *(0-8161-4260-2*, Macmillan Reference USA) Gale Group.

—Table Money. 1986. 434p. 17.95 *(0-89919-312-9)* Houghton Mifflin Co.

—Table Money. 1990. 4.99 o.p. *(0-517-02971-5)* Random Hse. Value Publishing.

—Table Money. 1987. 608p. mass mkt. 4.95 o.p. *(0-14-010046-6*, Penguin Bks.) Viking Penguin.

—World Without End, Amen. 1976. pap. 1.75 o.p. *(0-380-01628-1*, 19042, Avon Bks.) Morrow/Avon.

—World Without End, Amen. 1987. 384p. pap. 4.95 o.p. *(0-14-010364-3*, Penguin Bks.); 1973. 6.95 o.p. *(0-670-79020-6)* Viking Penguin.

Brewer, Gene. On a Beam of Light. 2001. E-Book 23.95 *(1-58945-743-9)* Adobe Systems, Inc.

—On a Beam of Light. E-Book 23.95 *(0-312-70116-0)*; 2001. 261p. 23.95 *(0-312-26926-9)*; 2002. 320p. reprint ed. mass mkt. 6.99 *(0-312-98208-9*, St. Martin's Paperbacks) St. Martin's Pr.

Bright, Freda. Infidelities. 1986. 384p. 17.95 o.p. *(0-689-11797-3*, Scribner) Simon & Schuster.

—Parting Shots. 1993. 320p. 19.95 o.p. *(0-316-10839-1)* Little Brown & Co.

Brill, Toni. Date with a Dead Doctor. 1992. ber. *(0-373-26109-8*, 1-26109-8, Harlequin Bks.) Harlequin Enterprises, Ltd.

—Date with a Dead Doctor. 1991. 17.95 o.p. *(0-312-05409-2*, Saint Martin's Minotaur) St. Martin's Pr.

—Date with a Plummeting Publisher. 1995. (WWL Mystery Ser.). per. *(0-373-26161-6*, 1-26161-9, Harlequin Bks.) Harlequin Enterprises, Ltd.

—Date with a Plummeting Publisher. 1993. 240p. 17.95 o.p. *(0-312-08753-5*, Saint Martin's Minotaur) St. Martin's Pr.

Brodsky, Michael. Xman. 1987. 540p. 21.95 *(0-941423-01-8)*; pap. 11.95 *(0-941423-02-6)* Four Walls Eight Windows.

Brossard, Chandler. The Double View. 4th rev. ed. 2001. (Classics ). 176p. pap. 13.00 *(1-928746-22-5)* Herodias.

Brown, Sandra. Words of Silk. 1984. mass mkt. *(0-373-45835-5*, Harlequin Bks.) Harlequin Enterprises, Ltd.

Brown, Sandra & St. Claire, Erin. Words of Silk. 2004. 446-53344-0) Warner Bks., Inc.

Browne, Gerald A. Stone 588. 1987. 448p. mass mkt. 4.95 o.p. *(0-425-09884-2)* Berkley Publishing Group.

—Stone 588. l.t. ed. 1986. 640p. 18.95 o.p. *(0-8161-4139-8)*; 10.95 o.p. *(0-8161-4140-1)* Gale Group. (Macmillan Reference USA).

—Stone 588. 1986. 17.95 o.p. *(0-87795-539-5*, Morrow, William & Co.) Morrow/Avon.

—Stone 588. 1996. 448p. mass mkt. 6.50 o.s.i *(0-446-60170-5)* Warner Bks., Inc.

—West 47th. 1997. 416p. mass mkt. 6.99 o.p. *(0-446-60413-5*, Warner Vision); 1996. 82p. 23.95 o.s.i *(0-446-51662-7)* Warner Bks., Inc.

Brownmiller, Susan. Waverly Place. 1989. 302p. 18.95 o.p. *(0-8021-1090-8)* Grove/Atlantic, Inc.

Brownstein, Gabriel. The Curious Case of Benjamin Button, Apt. 3W. 2003. 224p. pap. 13.95 *(0-393-32478-8)*; 2002. 192p. 23.95 *(0-393-05151-X)* Norton, W. W. & Co., Inc.

Brownstein, Michael. Self-Reliance. 1994. 280p. (Orig.). pap. 12.95 *(1-56689-018-7)* Coffee Hse. Pr.

Bruno, Anthony. Bad Apple. 1995. 336p. mass mkt. 4.99 o.s.i *(0-440-21121-2)* Dell Publishing.

—Bad Blood. 1990. 388p. reprint ed. mass mkt. 4.99 o.s.i *(0-440-20705-3)* Dell Publishing.

—Bad Blood. 1989. 256p. 19.95 o.p. *(0-399-13432-8*, G. P. Putnam's Sons) Penguin Putnam Bks. for Young Readers.

—Bad Business. 1992. 304p. mass mkt. 4.99 o.s.i *(0-440-21120-4)* Dell Publishing.

—Bad Guys. 1992. 288p. mass mkt. 4.99 o.s.i *(0-440-21363-0)* Dell Publishing.

—Bad Guys. 1988. 256p. 17.95 o.p. *(0-399-13340-2)* Putnam Publishing Group, The.

—Bad Luck. 1991. 288p. mass mkt. 4.99 o.s.i *(0-440-20924-2)* Dell Publishing.

—Bad Moon. 1993. 336p. mass mkt. 4.99 o.s.i *(0-440-21559-5)* Dell Publishing.

Bryant-Woolridge, Lori. Read Between the Lies. 1999. 464p. 22.95 o.s.i *(0-385-49214-6)* Doubleday Publishing.

Buck, Pearl S. Kinfolk. 3rd ed. 1996. (Oriental Novels of Pearl S. Buck Ser.). 418p. reprint ed. pap. 11.95 *(1-55921-156-3)* Moyer Bell.

Buckley, Kristen. The Parker Grey Show. 2003. 240p. pap. 13.00 *(0-425-19109-5)* Berkley Publishing Group.

Burley, Charlotte & LeFlore, Lyah. Cosmopolitan Girls. 2004. 272p. pap. 11.95 *(0-7679-1567-4)* Broadway Bks.

Burnett, Allison. Christopher: A Tale of Seduction. 2003. 272p. (Orig.). pap. 13.95 *(0-7679-1333-7)* Broadway Bks.

Busch, Charles. Whores of Lost Atlantis. 1995. 304p. 17.00 *(0-14-024391-7)* Viking Penguin.

—Whores of Lost Atlantis: A Novel. 1993. 304p. 21.95 o.p. *(1-56282-780-4)* Hyperion Pr.

Busch, Frederick. A Memory of War. 2004. 368p. pap. 14.95 *(0-345-46051-0)* Ballantine Bks.

—A Memory of War. l.t. ed. 2003. lib. bdg. 28.95 *(1-58547-350-2*, Platinum) Ctr. Point Large Print.

—A Memory of War. 2003. 352p. 25.95 *(0-393-04978-7)* Norton, W. W. & Co., Inc.

—The Night Inspector. E-Book 12.50 *(1-58945-550-9)* Adobe Systems, Inc.

—The Night Inspector. 2000. (Illus.). 304p. pap. 14.00 *(0-449-00615-8*, Ballantine Bks.) Random Hse.

—The Night Inspector. 1999. E-Book 12.50 *(0-609-60768-5*, Harmony) Crown Publishing Group.

—The Night Inspector: A Novel. 1999. 288p. 23.00 o.s.i *(0-609-60235-7*, Harmony) Crown Publishing Group.

Bushnell, Candace. Trading Up. l.t. ed. 2003. 808p. 32.95 *(1-58724-549-3*, Wheeler Publishing, Inc.) Gale Group.

—Trading Up. 2003. pap. 13.95 *(0-7868-8706-0)*; 416p. 24.95 *(0-7868-6818-X)*; pap. 13.95 *(0-7868-8871-7)* Hyperion Pr.

—4 Blondes. 2001. 256p. pap. 12.00 *(0-8021-3825-X*, Grove Pr.); 2000. 245p. 24.00 *(0-87113-819-0*, Atlantic Monthly Pr.) Grove/Atlantic, Inc.

—4 Blondes. 2002. 384p. mass mkt. 7.99 *(0-451-20389-5*, Signet Bks.) NAL.

—4 Blondes. abr. ed. 2000. audio 18.00 *(1-55935-353-8)* Soundelux Audio Publishing.

—4 Blondes. l.t. ed. 445p. 2002. pap. 28.95 *(0-7862-3152-1)*; 2001. 31.95 *(0-7862-3151-3)* Thorndike Pr.

Butler. Fair Warning. 2003. pap. 12.00 *(0-8021-3956-6)* Grove/Atlantic, Inc.

Byrnes, Robert. The Night We Met. 2002. 320p. 23.00 *(0-7582-0193-1)* Kensington Publishing Corp.

Cabot, Meg. Boy Meets Girl. 2004. 400p. pap. 13.95 *(0-06-008545-2*, Avon Bks.) Morrow/Avon.

Cabot, Meggin. The Boy Next Door. 2002. 384p. pap. 13.95 *(0-06-009619-5*, Avon Bks.) Morrow/Avon.

Cahan, Abraham. The Rise of David Levinsky. 2002. 464p. pap. 8.95 *(0-486-42517-7)* Dover Pubns., Inc.

—The Rise of David Levinsky. 2001. (Paperback Classics Ser.). 560p. pap. 13.95 *(0-375-75798-8*, Modern Library) Random House Adult Trade Publishing Group.

Cain, George. Blueschild Baby. 1987. 180p. reprint ed. pap. 7.50 o.p. *(0-88001-133-5)* HarperCollins Pubs.

—Blueschild Baby. 1994. pap. o.p. *(0-88001-349-4*, Ecco) HarperTrade.

Calisher, Hortense. Age: A Love Story. 1996. 124p. reprint ed. pap. 13.95 *(0-7145-3012-3)* Boyars, Marion Pubs., Inc.

—Age: A Love Story. 128p. 1989. pap. 8.95 o.p. *(1-55584-371-9)*; 1987. 14.95 o.p. *(1-55584-132-5)* Grove/Atlantic, Inc.

—In the Slammer with Carol Smith. 204p. 1999. pap. 14.95 *(0-7145-3045-X)*; 1997. 24.95 o.p. *(0-7145-3020-4)* Boyars, Marion Pubs., Inc.

Callahan, Sheila M. Death in a Far Country. 1993. 176p. 17.95 o.p. *(0-312-09892-8*, Saint Martin's Minotaur) St. Martin's Pr.

Cameron, Peter. Leap Year. 1998. 256p. pap. 12.95 *(0-452-27985-2*, Plume) Dutton/Plume.

—Leap Year: A Novel. 256p. 1990. 18.95 o.p. *(0-06-016252-X)*; 1991. reprint ed. pap. 8.95 o.p. *(0-06-092039-4*, Perennial) HarperTrade.

Campbell, R. Wright. Malloy's Subway. 1988. 320p. mass mkt. 3.95 *(0-8125-0116-0*, Tor Bks.) Doherty, Tom Assocs., LLC.

—Malloy's Subway. 1981. 12.95 o.p. *(0-689-11181-9*, Scribner) Simon & Schuster.

Canin, Ethan. For Kings & Planets. unabr. ed. 1999. audio 84.95 *(0-7927-2293-0*, CSL 182, Chivers Sound Library) BBC Audiobooks America.

—For Kings & Planets. 2001. 304p. pap. 14.00 *(0-312-24717-6)*; 2nd ed. 1999. 352p. pap. 14.00 *(0-312-24125-9)* Picador.

Cantrell, Catherine. Constance: A Novel. 2003. 240p. pap. 12.95 *(0-375-75980-8)* Random Hse. Children's Bks.

—Constance: A Novel. 2002. 224p. 22.95 *(0-375-50796-5)* Random Hse., Inc.

Carcaterra, Lorenzo. Gangster. l.t. ed. 2001. 583p. 30.95 *(1-7838-9499-6*, Macmillan Reference USA) Gale Group.

Carillo, Charles. My Ride with Gus. 256p. 1997. pap. 5.99 *(0-671-53569-2*, Pocket Star); 1996. 22.00 *(0-671-53568-4*, Atria) Simon & Schuster.

—Shepherd Avenue. Kroupa, Melanie & Meeker, Amy, eds. 1985. 324p. 15.95 o.p. (*0-87113-043-2*) Grove/Atlantic, Inc.

Carlson, Lori Marie. The Sunday Tertulia. 2000. 224p. 23.00 (*0-06-019536-3*) HarperCollins Pubs.

Carlson, Pat M. Audition for Murder. 1985. 225p. pap. 2.75 o.p. (*0-380-89538-2*, Avon Bks.) Morrow/Avon.

—Bad Blood. 1991. 320p. 15.00 o.s.i (*0-385-42122-2*) Doubleday Publishing.

—Murder in the Dog Days. 1990. 256p. mass mkt. 4.50 o.s.i (*0-553-27778-2*) Bantam Bks.

—Murder Is Academic. 1985. pap. 2.95 o.p. (*0-380-89738-5*, Avon Bks.) Morrow/Avon.

—Murder Is Pathological. 1986. 192p. pap. 2.95 o.p. (*0-380-75071-6*, Avon Bks.) Morrow/Avon.

—Murder Misread. 1991. 256p. mass mkt. 4.50 o.s.i (*0-553-29374-5*) Bantam Bks.

—Murder Misread. 1990. 192p. 14.95 o.s.i (*0-385-41642-3*) Doubleday Publishing.

—Murder Unrenovated. 1990. 240p. mass mkt. 2.25 o.s.i (*0-553-18522-5*); 1987. mass mkt. 3.50 o.s.i (*0-553-26989-5*) Bantam Bks.

—Murder Unrenovated. 1999. (Mystery Ser.). 274p. pap. 19.95 (*0-7862-2077-5*, Five Star) Gale Group.

—Rehearsal for Murder. 1988. 224p. mass mkt. 3.50 o.s.i (*0-553-27234-9*) Bantam Bks.

Carmody, Brian. Fruit Cocktail Diaries. 1994. 15.95 o.p. (*0-312-11796-5*) St. Martin's Pr.

Carr, Caleb. The Alienist. 1995. 608p. mass mkt. 7.99 (*0-553-57299-7*); mass mkt. 6.99 o.s.i (*0-553-84001-0*) Bantam Bks.

—The Alienist. unabr. ed. 1995. audio 104.00 (*0-7366-2898-3*, 3598) Books on Tape, Inc.

—The Alienist. l.t. ed. 1994. pap. 22.95 o.p. (*1-56895-078-0*, Wheeler Publishing, Inc.) Gale Group.

—The Alienist. 1994. 496p. 29.95 o.s.i (*0-679-41779-6*) Random Hse., Inc.

—The Alienist. abr. ed. 1994. audio 22.00 (*0-671-88757-2*, 492028, Simon & Schuster Audioworks) Simon & Schuster Audio.

—The Angel of Darkness. 1998. mass mkt. 7.99 o.s.i (*0-345-42514-6*); 768p. mass mkt. 7.99 (*0-345-42763-7*) Ballantine Bks.

—The Angel of Darkness. unabr. ed. 1998. audio 72.00 (*0-7366-4114-9*, 4619-A); audio 72.00 (*0-7366-4115-7*, 4619-B) Books on Tape, Inc.

—The Angel of Darkness. l.t. ed. 1999. pap. 25.95 o.p. (*0-7838-8242-4*, Macmillan Reference USA) Gale Group.

—The Angel of Darkness. abr. ed. 1997. audio 25.00 (*0-671-57748-4*, 595482, Simon & Schuster Audioworks) Simon & Schuster Audio.

Carr, Jan. Harem Wish. 1994. 256p. 19.95 o.p. (*0-525-93739-0*, Dutton) Dutton/Plume.

Carroll, Leslie. Temporary Insanity. 2004. pap. (*0-06-056337-0*, Avon Bks.) Morrow/Avon.

Carter, Charlotte. Coq Au Vin. 1999. (Nanette Hayes Mystery Ser.). 200p. 22.00 o.s.i (*0-89296-678-5*) Mysterious Pr.

—Coq Au Vin. 2000. (Nanette Hayes Mysteries Ser.). 224p. mass mkt. 6.50 (*0-446-60787-8*) Warner Bks., Inc.

—Drumsticks. 2000. (Nanette Hayes Mystery Ser.). 208p. 22.95 (*0-89296-679-3*) Mysterious Pr.

—Rhode Island Red. (Mask Noir Ser.). 1998. 176p. pap. (*1-85242-591-1*); Vol. 1. 1997. 250p. (*1-85242-564-4*) Serpent's Tail Ltd.

—Rhode Island Red. 1999. (Nanette Hayes Mysteries Ser.). 224p. mass mkt. 5.99 (*0-446-60664-2*) Warner Bks., Inc.

Carter, Emily. Glory Goes & Gets Some. 2000. 239p. 20.95 (*1-56689-101-9*) Coffee Hse. Pr.

—Glory Goes & Gets Some. 2001. 240p. pap. 13.00 (*0-312-28251-6*) Picador.

Carter, Robert A. Casual Slaughters. 1992. 272p. 17.95 o.p. (*0-89296-502-9*) Mysterious Pr.

—Casual Slaughters. 1994. 272p. mass mkt. 5.50 (*0-446-40302-4*, Mysterious Pr. Paperback Bks.) Warner Bks., Inc.

—Final Edit. 1994. 304p. 18.45 o.p. (*0-89296-549-5*) Mysterious Pr.

Caspary, Vera. Laura. 1977. 216p. reprint ed. lib. bdg. 23.95 (*0-89244-066-X*, Queens Hse., Inc.) Amereon, Ltd.

—Laura. 1993. reprint ed. lib. bdg. 29.95 (*1-56849-193-X*) Buccaneer Bks., Inc.

—Laura. 1955. per. 6.50 (*0-8222-0646-3*) Dramatists Play Service, Inc.

—Laura. 1981. 224p. mass mkt. 1.95 o.p. (*0-380-00043-1*, 51565-1, Avon Bks.) Morrow/Avon.

—Laura. 2002. (Best Mysteries of All Time Ser.). 262p. (*0-7621-8876-6*, Impress) Scriptorium Pr., The.

—Laura. E-Book 9.99 (*1-58824-335-4*) ibooks, Inc.

Castaldo, Meg. The Foreigner. 2001. 240p. pap. 12.95 (*0-7434-1264-8*, MTV) Simon & Schuster.

Caunitz, William J. Black Sand. 1994. 20.95 o.p. (*0-7927-1757-0*); pap. 18.95 o.p. (*0-7927-1756-2*) BBC Audiobooks America.

—Black Sand. 1991. mass mkt. 2.99 o.s.i (*0-553-19643-X*); 1990. 384p. mass mkt. 6.50 o.s.i (*0-553-28359-6*); 1989. 384p. mass mkt. 4.95 o.s.i (*0-553-17336-7*) Bantam Bks.

—Black Sand. 1988. 18.95 o.p. (*0-517-57226-5*, Crown) Crown Publishing Group.

—Black Sand. 1991. 3.99 o.p. (*0-517-06438-3*) Random Hse. Value Publishing.

—Cleopatra Gold. 1994. pap. 22.95 o.p. (*0-7927-1897-6*); 23.95 o.p. (*0-7927-1898-4*) BBC Audiobooks America.

—Cleopatra Gold. 1994. 352p. mass mkt. 6.99 o.s.i (*0-425-14394-5*) Berkley Publishing Group.

—Cleopatra Gold. unabr. ed. 2000. audio 59.95 (*0-7927-2228-0*, CSL 117) Chivers Audio Bks. GBR. *Dist:* BBC Audiobooks America.

—Cleopatra Gold. abr. ed. 1994. audio 8.99 o.s.i (*0-679-43788-6*) Knopf, Alfred A. Inc.

—Cleopatra Gold. 1993. audio 16.00 o.p. (*0-679-42799-6*, RH Audio) Random Hse. Audio Publishing Group.

—Exceptional Clearance. l.t. ed. 1993. pap. 16.95 o.p. (*0-7927-1321-4*); 1992. 18.95 o.p. (*0-7927-1322-2*) BBC Audiobooks America.

—Pigtown. 352p. 2002. mass mkt. 6.99 (*0-7860-1484-9*); 1996. mass mkt. 6.99 o.s.i (*0-7860-0293-X*, Pinnacle Bks.) Kensington Publishing Corp.

—Suspects. l.t. ed. 1988. 589p. 19.95 o.p. (*0-8161-4337-4*, Macmillan Reference USA) Gale Group.

—Suspects. 1987. 384p. 3.99 o.p. (*0-517-55864-5*) Random Hse. Value Publishing.

Cavanaugh, Jack. The Pioneers. 2010. (American Family Portrait Ser.). 500p. pap. 13.99 (*1-56476-587-3*) Cook Communications Ministries.

Chabon, Michael. The Amazing Adventures of Kavalier & Clay: A Novel. abr. ed. 2000. audio 29.95 (*1-58788-123-3*, 2378, Nova Audio Bks.) Brilliance Audio.

—The Amazing Adventures of Kavalier & Clay: A Novel. 2001. (Illus.). pap. 180.00 (*0-312-28882-4*); 656p. pap. 15.00 (*0-312-28299-0*) Picador.

—The Amazing Adventures of Kavalier & Clay: A Novel. 2000. 656p. 26.95 (*0-679-45004-1*) Random Hse., Inc.

Chace, Susan. Intimacy. 1990. 180p. pap. 7.95 o.p. (*0-452-26375-1*, Plume) Dutton/Plume.

—Intimacy. 1988. 176p. 14.95 o.s.i (*0-394-57030-8*) Random Hse., Inc.

Channer, Colin. Waiting in Vain. 2003. 416p. mass mkt. 6.99 (*0-345-43012-3*, One World/Ballantine); 1999. 352p. pap. 12.95 (*0-345-42552-9*) Ballantine Bks.

Chanslor, Torrey. Our First Murder. Schantz, Tom & Schantz, Enid, eds. 2002. 191p. reprint ed. pap. 14.95 (*0-915230-50-X*) Rue Morgue Pr.

Charnee, David. To Kill a Clown. 1992. 256p. 18.95 o.p. (*0-312-08324-6*, Saint Martin's Minotaur) St. Martin's Pr.

Charyn, Jerome. El Bronx. l.t. ed. 1997. (Cloak & Dagger Ser.). 292p. 25.95 (*0-7862-1092-3*) Thorndike Pr.

—El Bronx. 1998. mass mkt. (*0-446-40538-8*, Mysterious Pr. Paperback Bks.); 1997. 256p. 21.50 o.p. (*0-89296-604-1*) Warner Bks., Inc.

—Captain Kidd. 1999. 208p. 20.95 (*0-312-20506-6*) St. Martin's Pr.

—Citizen Sidel. 1999. 220p. 23.00 (*0-89296-605-X*) Mysterious Pr.

—The Education of Patrick Silver. 1977. 208p. pap. 2.75 o.p. (*0-380-01698-2*, 53603-X, Avon Bks.); 1976. 7.95 o.p. (*0-87795-142-X*, Morrow, William & Co.) Morrow/Avon.

—The Good Policeman. 1990. 288p. 18.95 o.p. (*0-89296-360-3*) Mysterious Pr.

—The Good Policeman. 1991. mass mkt. 4.99 o.s.i (*0-446-40012-2*, Mysterious Pr. Paperback Bks.) Warner Bks., Inc.

—The Isaac Quartet: Blue Eyes; Marilyn the Wild; The Education of Patrick Silver; Secret Isaac. 2002. 548p. 35.00 (*1-56858-234-X*); reprint ed. pap. 17.95 (*1-56858-228-5*) Four Walls Eight Windows.

—Little Angel Street. 1994. 288p. 19.95 o.s.i (*0-89296-462-6*) Mysterious Pr.

—Maria's Girls. 1992. 25.00 (*0-89296-460-X*) Mysterious Pr.

—Paradise Man. 1987. 17.95 o.s.i (*0-917657-93-4*) Fine, Donald I. Bks.

—Secret Isaac. 1978. 9.95 o.p. (*0-87795-196-9*, Morrow, William & Co.) Morrow/Avon.

—War Cries over Avenue C. 1985. 352p. 17.95 o.s.i (*0-917657-30-6*) Fine, Donald I. Bks.

—War Cries over Avenue C. 1986. (Contemporary American Fiction Ser.). 368p. pap. 7.95 o.p. (*0-14-008796-6*, Penguin Bks.) Viking Penguin.

Chase, Ilka. New York 22. 1971. 308p. reprint ed. lib. bdg. 19.75 o.p. (*0-8371-4710-7*, CHNY, Greenwood Pr.) Greenwood Publishing Group, Inc.

Chase, Linda & St. George, Joyce. Perfect Cover. 1994. 352p. 19.95 (*0-7868-6001-4*) Hyperion Pr.

Chase, Linda, et al. Perfect Cover. 1997. 320p. per. 6.99 (*0-671-52296-5*, Pocket) Simon & Schuster.

Chastain, Thomas. The Prosecutor: A Novel. 1992. 288p. 20.00 o.p. (*0-688-10088-0*, Morrow, William & Co.) Morrow/Avon.

Chastain, Thomas, et al. Justice in Manhattan. 1994. 17.95 o.p. (*0-681-45480-6*) Borders Pr.

Chazin, Suzanne. Fireplay. 2004. 320p. mass mkt. 6.99 (*0-515-13713-8*, Jove) Berkley Publishing Group.

—Fireplay. 2003. 320p. 25.95 (*0-399-15053-6*, Putnam & Grosset) Putnam Publishing Group, The.

—Flashover. 2003. 384p. mass mkt. 6.99 (*0-515-13508-9*, Jove) Berkley Publishing Group.

—Flashover. 2002. 336p. 25.95 (*0-399-14850-7*, Riverhead Bks. (Hardcovers)) Penguin Group (USA) Inc.

—The Fourth Angel. 2002. 400p. reprint ed. mass mkt. 6.99 o.s.i (*0-515-13249-7*, Jove) Berkley Publishing Group.

—The Fourth Angel. 2001. 352p. 24.95 o.s.i (*0-399-14705-5*) Penguin Group (USA) Inc.

Cheever, Benjamin. The Partisan. 1994. 352p. 21.00 o.p. (*0-689-12174-1*, Scribner) Simon & Schuster.

Cheever, John. Bullet Park. 1987. mass mkt. 4.95 o.s.i (*0-345-35006-5*); 1980. mass mkt. 2.75 o.s.i (*0-345-28590-5*); 1978. mass mkt. 2.25 o.s.i (*0-345-27301-X*) Ballantine Bks.

—Bullet Park. unabr. collector's ed. 1986. audio 42.00 (*0-7366-0831-1*, 1781) Books on Tape, Inc.

—Bullet Park. 1992. (Vintage International Ser.). 256p. pap. 13.95 (*0-679-73787-1*, Vintage) Knopf Publishing Group.

Cheever, Susan. The Cage, 001. 1982. 11.45 o.p. (*0-395-32111-5*) Houghton Mifflin Co.

Cherry, Kelly. Augusta Played, 001. 1979. 9.95 o.p. (*0-395-27573-3*) Houghton Mifflin Co.

—Augusta Played. 1998. (Voices of the South Ser.). 320p. pap. 14.95 (*0-8071-2279-3*) Louisiana State Univ. Pr.

Chesbro, George C. An Affair of Sorcerers. 3rd ed. 1999. 352p. reprint ed. pap. 16.99 (*0-9674503-9-X*) Apache Beach Pubns.

—An Affair of Sorcerers. 1988. mass mkt. 3.50 o.s.i (*0-440-20047-4*) Dell Publishing.

—An Affair of Sorcerers. 1980. mass mkt. 2.25 o.p. (*0-451-09243-0*, E9243, Signet Bks.) NAL.

—An Affair of Sorcerers. 1979. 9.95 o.s.i (*0-671-24625-9*, Simon & Schuster) Simon & Schuster.

—The Beasts of Valhalla. 3rd ed. 1999. 336p. reprint ed. pap. 16.99 (*0-9674503-3-0*) Apache Beach Pubns.

—The Beasts of Valhalla. 1987. mass mkt. 3.95 o.s.i (*0-440-10484-X*) Dell Publishing.

—The Beasts of Valhalla. 1985. 352p. 15.95 o.s.i (*0-689-11516-4*, Scribner) Simon & Schuster.

—Bleeding in the Eye of a Brainstorm: A Mongo Mystery. 1995. 224p. 21.00 (*0-684-81495-1*, Simon & Schuster); 21.00 (*1-883402-67-0*, Scribner) Simon & Schuster.

—City of Whispering Stone. 3rd ed. 1999. 236p. reprint ed. pap. 16.99 (*0-9674503-1-4*) Apache Beach Pubns.

—City of Whispering Stone. 1988. pap. 3.50 o.s.i (*0-440-11259-1*) Dell Publishing.

—City of Whispering Stone. 1980. mass mkt. 1.95 o.p. (*0-451-08812-3*, J8812, Signet Bks.) NAL.

—City of Whispering Stone. 1978. 9.95 o.s.i (*0-671-24003-X*, Simon & Schuster) Simon & Schuster.

—The Cold Smell of Sacred Stone. 3rd ed. 1999. 304p. reprint ed. pap. 16.99 (*0-9674503-2-2*) Apache Beach Pubns.

—The Cold Smell of Sacred Stone. 1989. 304p. reprint ed. mass mkt. 4.50 o.s.i (*0-440-20394-5*) Dell Publishing.

—The Cold Smell of Sacred Stone. 1988. 320p. 16.95 o.s.i (*0-689-11913-5*, Scribner) Simon & Schuster.

—Dark Chant in a Crimson Key. 3rd ed. 1999. 224p. reprint ed. pap. 16.99 (*0-9674503-8-1*) Apache Beach Pubns.

—Dark Chant in a Crimson Key. 1992. 224p. 18.95 o.p. (*0-89296-463-4*) Mysterious Pr.

—Dark Chant in a Crimson Key. 1993. 224p. mass mkt. 5.99 o.p. (*0-446-40333-4*, Mysterious Pr. Paperback Bks.) Warner Bks., Inc.

—Dream of a Falling Eagle. 2002. 212p. per. 16.99 (*1-930253-14-1*) Apache Beach Pubns.

—The Fear in Yesterday's Rings. 3rd ed. 1999. 224p. reprint ed. pap. 16.99 (*0-9674503-5-7*) Apache Beach Pubns.

—The Fear in Yesterday's Rings. 1991. 18.95 o.p. (*0-89296-396-4*) Mysterious Pr.

—The Fear in Yesterday's Rings. abr. ed. 1991. audio 16.00 o.s.i Random Hse. Audio Publishing Group.

—The Fear in Yesterday's Rings. 1992. 224p. mass mkt. 4.99 (*0-446-40102-1*, Mysterious Pr. Paperback Bks.) Warner Bks., Inc.

—In the House of Secret Enemies. 1990. 240p. 18.95 o.p. (*0-89296-395-6*) Mysterious Pr.

—In the House of Secret Enemies. 1992. 240p. mass mkt. 4.99 o.p. (*0-446-40043-2*) Warner Bks., Inc.

—An Incident at Bloodtide. 3rd ed. 2000. 208p. reprint ed. 16.99 (*1-930253-00-1*) Apache Beach Pubns.

—An Incident at Bloodtide. 1993. 208p. 18.95 (*0-89296-464-2*) Mysterious Pr.

—An Incident at Bloodtide. 1994. 256p. mass mkt. 5.50 (*0-446-40054-8*, Mysterious Pr. Paperback Bks.) Warner Bks., Inc.

—The Language of Cannibals. 3rd ed. 1999. 208p. reprint ed. pap. 16.99 (*0-9674503-6-5*) Apache Beach Pubns.

—The Language of Cannibals. 1990. 208p. 18.95 o.p. (*0-89296-394-8*) Mysterious Pr.

—The Language of Cannibals. 1991. mass mkt. 4.95 o.p. (*0-446-40003-3*, Mysterious Pr. Paperback Bks.) Warner Bks., Inc.

—Second Horseman Out of Eden. 3rd ed. 1999. 256p. reprint ed. pap. 16.99 (*0-9674503-4-9*) Apache Beach Pubns.

—Second Horseman Out of Eden. 1989. 18.95 o.s.i (*0-689-11979-8*, Scribner) Simon & Schuster.

—Second Horseman Out of Eden. 1990. 256p. reprint ed. mass mkt. 4.95 (*0-445-40862-6*, Mysterious Pr. Paperback Bks.) Warner Bks., Inc.

—Shadow of a Broken Man. 3rd ed. 1999. 260p. reprint ed. pap. 16.99 (*0-9674503-7-3*) Apache Beach Pubns.

—Shadow of a Broken Man. 1987. mass mkt. 3.50 o.s.i (*0-440-17761-8*) Dell Publishing.

—Shadow of a Broken Man. 1983. mass mkt. 2.50 o.p. (*0-451-12013-2*, Signet Bks.) NAL.

—Shadow of a Broken Man. 1977. 7.95 o.p. (*0-671-22696-7*, Simon & Schuster) Simon & Schuster.

—Two Songs This Archangel Sings. 3rd ed. 1999. 256p. reprint ed. pap. 16.99 (*0-9674503-0-6*) Apache Beach Pubns.

—Two Songs This Archangel Sings. 1988. mass mkt. 3.95 o.s.i (*0-440-20105-5*) Dell Publishing.

—Two Songs This Archangel Sings. 1986. 320p. 14.95 o.p. (*0-689-11659-4*, Scribner) Simon & Schuster.

Chesnutt, Charles Waddell & McWilliams, Dean. The Quarry. 1999. 288p. text 42.50 o.p. (*0-691-05995-0*); pap. text 18.95 (*0-691-05996-9*) Princeton Univ. Pr.

Cheuse, Alan. The Grandmother's Club. 1985. 15.95 o.p. (*0-918222-67-2*) Applewood Bks.

—The Grandmother's Club. 1986. 326p. 18.95 o.p. (*0-87905-253-8*) Smith, Gibbs Pub.

—The Grandmother's Club. 1994. 348p. reprint ed. pap. 10.95 (*0-87074-374-0*) Southern Methodist Univ. Pr.

—The Grandmother's Club. 1988. 336p. pap. 6.95 o.p. (*0-14-010484-4*, Penguin Bks.) Viking Penguin.

Chiaverini, Jennifer. Quilter's Legacy. 2004. 320p. pap. 13.00 (*0-452-28467-8*, Plume) Dutton/Plume.

Chopra, Deepak. Soulmate: A Novel of Eternal Love. l.t. ed. 2002. 224p. lib. bdg. 28.95 (*1-58547-170-4*) Ctr. Point Large Print.

—Soulmate: A Novel of Eternal Love. 2002. 304p. reprint ed. pap. 14.00 (*0-451-20704-1*) NAL.

—Soulmate: A Novel of Eternal Love. 2001. 208p. 23.95 o.s.i (*0-399-14798-5*, Putnam & Grosset) Penguin Group (USA) Inc.

Chorao, Ian. Bruiser: A Novel. 2004. 384p. pap. 13.00 (*0-7434-3776-4*, Washington Square Pr.) Simon & Schuster.

Christensen, Kate. In the Drink. 1999. 288p. 22.95 o.s.i (*0-385-49450-5*) Doubleday Publishing.

Christmas, Joyce. A Better Class of Murder: A Lady Margaret Priam/Betty Trenka Mystery. 2000. (Lady Margaret Priam Mysteries Ser.). 272p. mass mkt. 6.50 (*0-449-15013-5*, Fawcett) Ballantine Bks.

—A Better Class of Murder: A Lady Margaret Priam/Betty Trenka Mystery. l.t. ed. 2001. 264p. pap. 24.95 (*0-7838-9472-4*, Macmillan Reference USA) Gale Group.

—Dying Well. 2000. (Lady Margaret Priam Mysteries Ser.). 224p. mass mkt. 6.50 (*0-449-15011-9*, Fawcett) Ballantine Bks.

—Dying Well: A Lady Margaret Priam Mystery. l.t. ed. 2001. (G. K. Hall Paperback Ser.). 253p. pap. 24.95 (*0-7838-9438-4*, Macmillan Reference USA) Gale Group.

—A Fate Worse Than Death. 1990. 208p. mass mkt. 4.99 o.s.i (*0-449-14665-0*, Fawcett) Ballantine Bks.

—Friend or Faux. 1991. mass mkt. 4.99 o.s.i (*0-449-14701-0*, Fawcett) Ballantine Bks.

—Going Out in Style. 1998. (Lady Margaret Priam Mysteries Ser.). 181p. mass mkt. 5.99 o.s.i (*0-449-15010-0*, Fawcett) Ballantine Bks.

—It's Her Funeral, No. 6. 1992. (Orig.). mass mkt. 3.99 o.s.i (*0-449-14702-9*, Fawcett) Ballantine Bks.

—Mourning Gloria. 1996. (Lady Margaret Priam Mysteries Ser.). 232p. mass mkt. 4.99 o.s.i (*0-449-14704-5*, Fawcett) Ballantine Bks.

—Simply to Die For. 1989. 208p. mass mkt. 4.99 o.s.i (*0-449-14539-5*, Fawcett) Ballantine Bks.

—A Stunning Way to Die. 1990. (Lady Margaret Priam Mystery Ser.: No. 4). 192p. mass mkt. 4.99 o.s.i (*0-449-14666-9*, Fawcett) Ballantine Bks.

—A Stunning Way to Die. 1993. 192p. lib. bdg. 18.00 o.p. (*0-7278-4410-5*) Severn Hse. Pubs., Ltd.

—Suddenly in Her Sorbet. 1988. mass mkt. 5.99 o.s.i (*0-449-13311-7*, Fawcett) Ballantine Bks.

Chu, Louis. Eat a Bowl of Tea. 2002. 256p. mass mkt. 12.00 (*0-8184-0395-0*, Stuart, Lyle) Kensington Publishing Corp.

Churchill, Jill. Love for Sale: A Grace & Favor Mystery. l.t. ed. 2003. 280p. 29.95 (0-7862-5919-1) Gale Group.
Cirino, Mark. Name the Baby. 1998. 224p. pap. 12.00 o.s.i (0-385-49159-X) Doubleday Publishing.
Cirni, Jim. The Come On. 1989. (Crime Ser.). 224p. 17.95 o.s.i (0-939149-24-9) Soho Pr., Inc.
Clark, Carol Higgins. Fleeced: A Regan Reilly Mystery. 2001. 272p. 22.00 (0-7432-0581-2); 320p. 22.00 (0-7432-1661-X) Simon & Schuster. (Scribner).
—Fleeced: A Regan Reilly Mystery. 1999. 272p. 22.00 (0-446-52292-9) Warner Bks., Inc.
Clark, Carol Higgins & Clark, Mary Higgins. He Sees You When You're Sleeping. 2001. 208p. E-Book 20.00 (0-7432-3356-5, Scribner) Simon & Schuster.
Clark, Mary Higgins. All Through the Night. 2000. E-Book 9.95 (0-684-86582-3, Simon & Schuster); 1999. (Illus.). 256p. mass mkt. 7.99 (0-671-02712-3, Pocket); 1998. (Illus.). 176p. 17.00 o.s.i (0-684-85660-3, Simon & Schuster); 1998. 192p. pap. 17.00 (0-684-85783-9, Simon & Schuster) Simon & Schuster.
—Deck the Halls. E-Book 24.00 (1-58945-167-8) Adobe Systems, Inc.
—Deck the Halls. E-Book 9.99 (0-7410-0337-6) SoftBook Pr.
—He Sees You When You're Sleeping. 2001. E-Book 20.00 (1-59061-418-6) Adobe Systems, Inc.
—The Lottery Winner. E-Book 9.95 (1-930161-64-6) Adobe Systems, Inc.
—The Lottery Winner. 1997. reprint ed. lib. bdg. 32.95 (1-56849-588-9) Buccaneer Bks., Inc.
—The Lottery Winner. 2000. E-Book 9.95 (0-7432-0626-6, Simon & Schuster); 1995. 304p. mass mkt. 7.99 (0-671-86717-2, Pocket); 1994. 26.00 o.s.i (0-684-80222-8, Simon & Schuster); 1994. (Illus.). 256p. 22.00 (0-671-86716-4, Simon & Schuster) Simon & Schuster.
—The Lottery Winner. abr. ed. 1994. (Willy & Alvirah Mystery Ser.). audio 22.00 (0-671-50136-4, 592256, Simon & Schuster Audioworks) Simon & Schuster Audio.
—The Lottery Winner. 265p. pap. 5.98 o.p. (0-7651-0558-6) Smithmark Pubs., Inc.
—Loves Music, Loves to Dance. unabr. ed. 1992. audio 48.00 (0-7366-2066-4, 2874) Books on Tape, Inc.
—Loves Music, Loves to Dance. 1996. reprint ed. lib. bdg. 35.95 (1-56849-265-0) Buccaneer Bks., Inc.
—Loves Music, Loves to Dance. 2000. E-Book 9.95 (0-7432-0618-5); 1991. 320p. 21.95 o.p. (0-671-67364-5) Simon & Schuster. (Simon & Schuster).
—Loves Music, Loves to Dance. Rubenstein, Julie, ed. 1992. 336p. reprint ed. mass mkt. 7.99 (0-671-75889-6, Pocket) Simon & Schuster.
—Loves Music, Loves to Dance. abr. ed. 1991. audio 17.00 (0-671-72623-4, 391117, Simon & Schuster Audioworks) Simon & Schuster Audio.
—Pretend You Don't See Her. unabr. ed. 1997. audio 48.00 (0-7366-3711-7, 4395) Books on Tape, Inc.
—Pretend You Don't See Her. 2000. E-Book 9.95 (0-7432-0625-8, Simon & Schuster); 1998. 320p. pap. 7.99 (0-671-86715-6, Pocket); 1997. 320p. 25.00 (0-684-81039-5, Simon & Schuster); 1997. 480p. 25.00 (0-684-83416-2, Simon & Schuster) Simon & Schuster.
—Pretend You Don't See Her. abr. ed. 1997. audio 18.00 (0-671-57521-X, 395160); audio compact disk 20.00 (0-671-55715-7) Simon & Schuster Audio. (Simon & Schuster Audioworks).
—Pretend You Don't See Her. 1998. 14.04 (0-606-13721-1) Turtleback Bks.
—Silent Night. E-Book 9.95 (1-930161-30-1) Adobe Systems, Inc.
—Silent Night. 2000. E-Book 9.95 (0-7432-0627-4, Simon & Schuster); 1996. (Illus.). 192p. mass mkt. 6.99 (0-671-00042-X, Pocket); 1995. 160p. 16.00 (0-684-81545-1, Simon & Schuster); 1995. (Illus.). 176p. 18.00 (0-684-81546-X, Simon & Schuster) Simon & Schuster.
—Silent Night. 1998. 2.98 o.p. (0-7651-0774-0) Smithmark Pubs., Inc.
—Silent Night. 1996. 13.04 (0-606-11843-8) Turtleback Bks.
—You Belong to Me. unabr. ed. 1998. audio 56.00 (0-7366-4189-0, 4687) Books on Tape, Inc.
—You Belong to Me. 2000. E-Book 9.95 (0-7432-0629-0, Simon & Schuster); 1999. 384p. mass mkt. 7.99 (0-671-00454-9, Pocket); 1998. 320p. 25.00 (0-684-83595-9, Simon & Schuster); 1998. 496p. 25.00 (0-684-84330-7, Simon & Schuster) Simon & Schuster.
—You Belong to Me. abr. ed. 1998. audio compact disk 22.50 (0-671-58196-1); audio 18.00 (0-671-58066-3, 393596) Simon & Schuster Audio. (Simon & Schuster Audioworks).
Clark, Mary Higgins & Clark, Carol Higgins. Deck the Halls. 2000. 208p. 18.00 (0-7432-1200-2, Simon & Schuster); 2002. 320p. reprint ed. mass mkt. 7.99 (0-7434-1813-1, Pocket) Simon & Schuster.
—He Sees You When You're Sleeping. 2001. 208p. 20.00 (0-7432-3005-1); 288p. 20.00 (0-7432-3323-9) Simon & Schuster. (Scribner).
Clark, Mary Higgins, et al. Missing in Manhattan: The Adams Round Table. 1992. 304p. 17.95 o.p. (0-681-41576-2) Borders Pr.
Clark, Mary Jane. Do You Promise Not to Tell? 2000. 307p. mass mkt. 6.99 (0-312-97424-8, St. Martin's Paperbacks) St. Martin's Pr.
Clarke, Brock. The Ordinary White Boy. 272p. text o.s.i (0-15-100733-0); 2002. pap. 13.00 (0-15-602709-7, Harvest Bks.); 2001. 24.00 o.s.i (0-15-100810-8, Harvest Bks.) Harcourt Trade Pubs.
Clarkson, John. And Justice for One. 1993. 368p. mass mkt. 5.99 o.s.i (0-515-11055-8, Jove) Berkley Publishing Group.
—And Justice for One. 1994. 4.99 o.p. (0-517-12688-5) Random Hse. Value Publishing.
Clegg, Douglas. Naomi. 2001. 368p. mass mkt. 5.99 (0-8439-4857-4) Dorchester Publishing Co., Inc.
—Naomi. 2000. 250p. 28.00 (1-892284-75-8); 150.00 (1-892284-76-6) Subterranean Pr.
Cline, John. The Forever Beat. 1990. 19.95 o.p. (0-525-24855-2, Dutton) Dutton/Plume.
Cline, Rachel. What to Keep: A Novel. 2004. 304p. 23.95 (1-4000-6183-0) Random Hse., Inc.
Coben, Harlan. Darkest Fear. l.t. ed. 2001. 384p. 27.95 (1-58724-016-5, Wheeler Publishing, Inc.) Gale Group.
—Deal Breaker: A Myron Bolitar Mystery. 1995. (Myron Bolitar Mystery Ser.). 368p. mass mkt. 6.99 (0-440-22044-0) Dell Publishing.
—Dropshot. 1996. (Myron Bolitar Mystery Ser.). 368p. mass mkt. 6.99 (0-440-22045-9) Dell Publishing.
—Fade Away. 1996. (Myron Bolitar Mystery Ser.). 368p. mass mkt. 6.99 (0-440-22268-0) Dell Publishing.
—The Final Detail. 2000. 384p. mass mkt. 6.99 (0-440-22545-0) Dell Publishing.
—One False Move. unabr. ed. 2000. audio 48.00 (0-7366-4828-3, 5174) Books on Tape, Inc.
—One False Move: A Myron Bolitar Novel. 1999. (Myron Bolitar Mystery Ser.). 400p. mass mkt. 7.50 (0-440-22544-2) Dell Publishing.
Coe, Tucker. A Jade in Aries. 2001. (Mystery Ser.). 203p. 23.95 (0-7862-3015-0, Five Star) Gale Group.
—Kinds of Love, Kinds of Death. 2000. (Five Star Mystery Ser.). 200p. 22.95 (0-7862-2669-2, Five Star) Gale Group.
—Murder among Children. 2000. (Five Star Mystery Ser.). 194p. 22.95 (0-7862-2893-8, Five Star) Gale Group.
—Wax Apple: A Mitchell Tobin Mystery. l.t. ed. 2000. (Mystery Ser.). 208p. 23.95 (0-7862-3004-5, Five Star) Gale Group.
Cohen, Arthur A. In the Days of Simon Stern. 1987. (Phoenix Fiction Ser.). vi, 466p. reprint ed. pap. 36.00 (0-226-11254-3) Univ. of Chicago Pr.
Cohen, Gabriel. Red Hook. 2001. (Illus.). 304p. 23.95 (0-312-27458-0) St. Martin's Pr.
Cohen, Harlan. Fade Away. unabr. ed. 2001. (Myron Bolitar Mystery Ser.). audio 29.95 (0-7366-4951-4) Books on Tape, Inc.
Cohen, Paula. Gramercy Park: A Novel. 368p. 2002. 24.95 (0-312-27552-8); 2003. reprint ed. pap. 13.95 (0-312-30997-X, Saint Martin's Griffin) St. Martin's Pr.
Cohen, Stanley. Angel Face. 1982. 406p. 13.95 o.p. (0-312-03659-0) St. Martin's Pr.
Cohen, Steven M. Becker's Ring. 1997. 432p. mass mkt. 6.50 o.s.i (0-446-60443-7) Warner Bks., Inc.
Colapinto, John. About the Author. 2001. 272p. 25.00 (0-06-019417-0) HarperCollins Pubs.
—About the Author. 2002. 272p. pap. 12.95 (0-06-093217-1, Perennial) HarperTrade.
Coleman, Reed F. Life Goes Sleeping. 1991. 271p. 28.00 (1-877946-05-2) Permanent Pr., The.
—Little Easter. 1993. 221p. 24.00 (1-877946-23-0) Permanent Pr., The.
—They Don't Play Stickball in Milwaukee. 208p. 1997. 24.00 (1-877946-95-8); 1998. reprint ed. pap. 16.00 (1-57962-016-7) Permanent Pr., The.
Coleman, Reed Farrel. Redemption Street: A Moe Prager Mystery. 2004. 256p. 22.95 (0-670-03291-3, Viking) Viking Penguin.
Coleman, Reed Farrell. Walking the Perfect Square. 2001. 264p. 26.00 (1-57962-039-6) Permanent Pr., The.
Coleman, Val. Beverly & Marigold. 1996. (Illus.). 240p. 23.95 o.p. (0-312-14549-7) St. Martin's Pr.
Coleridge, Nicholas. Streetsmart. 2000. 387p. 26.95 o.p. (0-312-19960-0) St. Martin's Pr.
Collins, Joan. Star Quality. 2003. 368p. mass mkt. 6.99 (0-7868-9048-7) Hyperion Pr.
—Star Quality: A Novel. 2003. mass mkt. 7.99 (0-7868-9060-6); 2002. 368p. 23.95 (1-4013-0000-6); 2002. mass mkt. 7.99 (0-7868-9064-9) Hyperion Pr.
—Star Quality: A Novel. 2003. (Core Ser.). 32.95 (0-7862-4694-4) Thorndike Pr.
Collins, Judy. Shameless: A Novel. 1996. 352p. mass mkt. 6.50 o.s.i (0-671-89234-7, Pocket); 1995. 320p. 23.00 o.p. (0-671-89233-9, Atria) Simon & Schuster.
Collins, Max Allan. Daylight. l.t. ed. 1999. (General Ser.). 248p. pap. 22.95 (0-7862-1725-1) Thorndike Pr.
—NYPD Blue Pt. 1: Blue Beginning. 1998. (Illus.). 48p. pap. 7.00 (0-14-081644-5); 1999. (Penguin Readers Ser.: Level 3). 1p. pap. 7.93 (0-582-40170-4) Longman Publishing Group.
—NYPD Blue Pt. 1: Blue Blood. 1997. (NYPD Blues Ser.). 240p. mass mkt. 5.99 o.s.i (0-451-18392-4, Signet Bks.) NAL.
Collins, Michael. The Blood-Red Dream. l.t. ed. 1991. 17.95 o.p. (0-7451-8144-9, AH0180); pap. 15.95 o.p. (0-7927-0664-1, AS0216) BBC Audiobooks America.
—Castrato. 1991. 416p. reprint ed. pap. 4.99 (0-8439-3131-0) Dorchester Publishing Co., Inc.
—Castrato. 1989. 288p. 17.95 o.p. (1-55611-113-4) Fine, Donald I. Bks.
—Chasing Eights. 1992. 400p. reprint ed. pap. 4.99 (0-8439-3274-0) Dorchester Publishing Co., Inc.
—Chasing Eights. 1990. 18.95 o.p. (1-55611-145-2) Fine, Donald I. Bks.
—Crime, Punishment - & Resurrection. 1992. 272p. 19.95 o.p. (1-55611-295-5) Fine, Donald I. Bks.
—Freak. 1990. mass mkt. (0-373-26050-4, Harlequin Bks.) Harlequin Enterprises, Ltd.
—The Irishman's Horse. 1991. 18.95 o.p. (1-55611-185-1) Fine, Donald I. Bks.
—Minnesota Strip. 1987. 264p. 17.95 o.p. (1-55611-032-4) Fine, Donald I. Bks.
—Minnesota Strip. 1988. pap. (0-373-97093-5, Harlequin Bks.) Harlequin Enterprises, Ltd.
—Red Rosa. 1988. 264p. 17.95 o.p. (1-55611-052-9) Fine, Donald I. Bks.
—Red Rosa. 1989. 304p. reprint ed. mass mkt. (0-373-97099-4, Harlequin Bks.) Harlequin Enterprises, Ltd.
—Silent Scream. 1989. mass mkt. (0-373-28000-9, Harlequin Bks.) Harlequin Enterprises, Ltd.
—The Slasher. 1989. mass mkt. (0-373-27999-X, Harlequin Bks.) Harlequin Enterprises, Ltd.
Collins, Stephen. Double Exposure. 1999. 310p. pap. 6.99 (0-380-73232-7, Avon Bks.) Morrow/Avon.
—Double Exposure: A Novel. 1998. 256p. 24.00 (0-688-15893-5, Morrow, William & Co.) Morrow/Avon.
Colwin, Laurie. Another Marvelous Thing. 1994. 144p. pap. 11.00 (0-06-097650-0) HarperTrade.
—Family Happiness. 1987. mass mkt. 3.50 o.s.i (0-449-21447-8); 1983. mass mkt. 2.95 o.s.i (0-449-20275-5) Ballantine Bks. (Fawcett).
—Family Happiness. 2000. 288p. pap. 13.00 (0-06-095897-9); 1993. 224p. reprint ed. pap. 13.00 (0-06-097272-6) HarperTrade. (Perennial).
—Family Happiness. 1982. 12.95 o.s.i (0-394-52511-6) Knopf, Alfred A. Inc.
—Family Happiness. l.t. ed. 1983. 419p. reprint ed. 13.95 o.p. (0-89621-421-4) Thorndike Pr.
Conde, Nicholas. The Religion. 1982. 384p. 13.95 o.p. (0-453-00412-1, H412) NAL.
Conn, Nicole. Angel Wings. 1997. 208p. 22.50 (0-684-83205-4, Simon & Schuster) Simon & Schuster.
Connell, Evan S. The Connoisseur. 1987. 208p. pap. 8.95 o.p. (0-86547-245-9, North Point Pr.) Farrar, Straus & Giroux.
—The Connoisseur. 1974. 6.95 o.p. (0-394-49203-X, Knopf Bks. for Young Readers) Random Hse. Children's Bks.
Connelly, Joe. Bringing Out the Dead. 1999. 336p. pap. 12.00 (0-676-58971-5); pap. 13.00 (0-375-70029-3) Knopf Publishing Group. (Vintage).
Connolly, John. Dark Hollow: A Novel. 2001. 448p. 25.00 (0-7432-0332-1, Simon & Schuster) Simon & Schuster.
—Every Dead Thing. 1999. 400p. 25.00 (0-684-85714-6, Simon & Schuster) Simon & Schuster.
Conroy, Pat. The Prince of Tides. audio 8.95 American Audio Prose Library, Inc.
—The Prince of Tides. l.t. ed. 1993. pap. 21.95 o.p. (0-7927-1358-3); 1992. 24.95 o.p. (0-7927-1359-1) BBC Audiobooks America.
—The Prince of Tides. 1987. 672p. mass mkt. 7.99 (0-553-26888-0) Bantam Bks.
—The Prince of Tides. unabr. ed. 1988. Pt. A. audio 88.00 (0-7366-1458-3, 2339-A); Pt. B. audio 88.00 (0-7366-1459-1, 2339-B) Books on Tape, Inc.
—The Prince of Tides, 001. 1986. 576p. tchr. ed. 30.00 (0-395-35300-9) Houghton Mifflin Co.
—The Prince of Tides. 1987. audio 12.79 o.s.i (0-553-19969-2); audio 15.95 o.s.i (0-553-74510-7); audio 16.99 (0-553-45096-4, 391403) Random Hse. Audio Publishing Group. (RH Audio).
—The Prince of Tides. unabr. ed. 1988. audio 144.00 (1-55690-425-8, 88020E7) Recorded Bks., LLC.
—The Prince of Tides. 2002. E-Book 8.99 (0-7953-0100-6) RosettaBooks.
—The Prince of Tides. 1991. 14.04 (0-606-03895-7) Turtleback Bks.
Cook, Robin. Three Complete Novels: Contagion, Invasion, Chromosome 6. 1999. 752p. 12.98 o.s.i (0-399-14538-9) Penguin Group (USA) Inc.
—Vector. 1999. mass mkt. 7.99 (0-425-17083-7); 2000. 416p. reprint ed. mass mkt. 7.99 (0-425-17299-6) Berkley Publishing Group.
—Vector. 1999. 416p. 24.95 o.p. (0-399-14471-4) Penguin Group (USA) Inc.
—Vector. l.t. ed. (Thorndike/G. K. Hall Paperback Bestsellers Ser.). 597p. 2000. pap. 27.95 (0-7838-8599-7); 1999. 30.95 (0-7838-8598-9) Thorndike Pr.
Cook, Thomas H. Flesh & Blood. 1989. 336p. 17.95 o.p. (0-399-13409-3, G. P. Putnam's Sons) Penguin Putnam Bks. for Young Readers.
—Night Secrets. 1990. 320p. 19.95 o.p. (0-399-13527-8, G. P. Putnam's Sons) Penguin Putnam Bks. for Young Readers.
Coughlin, T. Glen. The Hero of New York. 1986. 14.95 o.p. (0-393-02262-5) Norton, W. W. & Co., Inc.
Coulter, Catherine. Riptide. 2001. 368p. reprint ed. mass mkt. 7.99 (0-515-13096-6, Jove) Berkley Publishing Group.
—Riptide. 2000. 384p. 23.95 o.s.i (0-399-14616-4) Penguin Group (USA) Inc.
—Riptide. l.t. ed. 560p. 2001. 29.95 (0-7862-2642-0); 2000. 31.95 (0-7862-2641-2) Thorndike Pr.
Courter, Gay. The Midwife's Advice. 1992. 608p. 23.00 o.p. (0-525-93494-4, Dutton) Dutton/Plume.
Crabbe, E. Suspension. 2002. 480p. pap. 14.95 (0-312-28464-0, Saint Martin's Griffin) St. Martin's Pr.
Crane, Stephen. Maggie: A Girl of the Streets. 1999. xvii, 374p. pap. text 10.00 (0-312-15266-3) Bedford/Saint Martin's.
—Maggie: A Girl of the Streets. Gullason, Thomas A., ed. 1979. (Critical Editions Ser.). 258p. (C). pap. text 9.00 net. (0-393-95024-7) Norton, W. W. & Co., Inc.
—Maggie: A Girl of the Streets. Hayes, Kevin J., ed. 1999. (Bedford Cultural Editions Ser.). (Illus.). 396p. 49.95 (0-312-21824-9) Palgrave Macmillan.
—Maggie: A Girl of the Streets. 1995. (Literary Classics). 90p. pap. 9.00 (1-57392-037-1) Prometheus Bks., Pubs.
—Maggie: A Girl of the Streets & Other Tales of New York. 2000. (Penguin Classics Ser.). (Illus.). 272p. pap. 8.95 (0-14-043797-5) Viking Penguin.
Cranny, Robert. Faces along the Bar. 2004. pap. 15.00 (1-56649-279-3) Welcome Rain Pubs.
Cray, David. Keeplock: A Novel of Crime. 1995. 21.00 (1-883402-97-2, Scribner) Simon & Schuster.
—Keeplock: A Novel of Crime. l.t. ed. 1995. (Niagara Large Print Ser.). 411p. 29.50 o.p. (0-7089-5817-6, Ulverscroft) Thorpe, F. A. Pubs. GBR. Dist: Ulverscroft Large Print Bks., Ltd.
—Partners: A Novel of Crime. 2004. 320p. 25.00 (0-7867-1292-9, Carroll & Graf Pubs.) Avalon Publishing Group.
—What You Wish For. 2002. 320p. 24.00 (0-7867-1085-3, Carroll & Graf Pubs.) Avalon Publishing Group.
Crespi, Camilla T. The Trouble with a Bad Fit. 1996. 272p. 21.00 o.p. (0-06-017661-X) HarperCollins Pubs.
—The Trouble with a Bad Fit. 1997. 320p. mass mkt. 4.99 (0-06-109408-0, HarperTorch) Morrow/Avon.
—The Trouble with a Hot Summer: A Simona Griffo Mystery. 1997. 320p. 23.00 o.p. (0-06-017662-8) HarperCollins Pubs.
—The Trouble with a Hot Summer: A Simona Griffo Mystery. mass mkt. o.s.i (0-06-109409-9); 1998. 368p. mass mkt. 5.99 o.s.i (0-06-104464-4) Morrow/Avon. (HarperTorch).
—The Trouble with a Small Raise. 1991. 288p. mass mkt. 3.95 o.s.i (0-8217-3274-9, Zebra Bks.) Kensington Publishing Corp.
—The Trouble with Moonlighting. 1991. 224p. mass mkt. 3.95 o.s.i (0-8217-3452-0, Zebra Bks.) Kensington Publishing Corp.
Criscuolo, C. Clark. Wiseguys in Love. 1993. 240p. 17.95 o.p. (0-312-09413-2, Saint Martin's Minotaur) St. Martin's Pr.
Croft, Barbara. Moon's Crossing. 2003. 208p. pap. 12.00 (0-618-34153-6, Mariner Bks.) Houghton Mifflin Co. Trade & Reference Div.
—Moon's Crossing. l.t. ed. 2003. 336p. 28.95 (0-7862-5958-2) Thorndike Pr.
Cross, Amanda. Amanda Cross: The Collected Stories. l.t. ed. 1997. (Wheeler Large Print Book Ser.). pap. 24.95 (1-56895-453-0, Wheeler Publishing, Inc.) Gale Group.
—Collected Stories of Amanda Cross. 1998. 192p. pap. 12.00 (0-345-42113-2) Ballantine Bks.
—Death in a Tenured Position. (Kate Fansler Novels Ser.). 1986. 208p. mass mkt. 6.99 (0-345-34041-8); 1982. mass mkt. 2.50 o.p. (0-345-30215-X) Ballantine Bks.
—Death in a Tenured Position. 1981. 10.50 o.p. (0-525-08935-7, 01019-310, Dutton) Dutton/Plume.
—Death in a Tenured Position. l.t. ed. 1981. reprint ed. 11.95 o.p. (0-89621-321-8) Thorndike Pr.

—An Imperfect Spy. 1995. (Kate Fansler Novels Ser.). 224p. mass mkt. 6.99 (*0-345-39005-9*); 240p. 20.00 o.p. (*0-345-38917-4*); 224p. pap. 15.00 (*0-345-46493-1*) Ballantine Bks.
—An Imperfect Spy. l.t. ed. 1995. 232p. pap. 18.95 o.p. (*0-7838-1299-X*, Macmillan Reference USA) Gale Group.
—An Imperfect Spy. unabr. ed. 1996. audio 49.95 o.p. (*1-85903-093-9*, 30939) Magna Story Sound GBR. *Dist:* Ulverscroft Large Print Bks., Ltd.
—In the Last Analysis. 2001. (Kate Fansler Novels Ser.: Vol. 1). 224p. mass mkt. 6.50 (*0-449-00711-1*, Fawcett) Ballantine Bks.
—In the Last Analysis. Barzun, Jacques & Taylor, W. H., eds. 1983. (Crime Fiction 1950-1975 Ser.). 187p. lib. bdg. 18.00 o.p. (*0-8240-4960-8*) Garland Publishing, Inc.
—In the Last Analysis. 1981. 176p. mass mkt. 5.50 (*0-380-54510-1*, Avon Bks.) Morrow/Avon.
—In the Last Analysis. l.t. ed. 1982. 305p. reprint ed. 10.95 o.p. (*0-89621-335-8*) Thorndike Pr.
—James Joyce Murder. 1985. mass mkt. 2.95 o.p. (*0-345-33141-9*) Ballantine Bks.
—The James Joyce Murders. 1987. (Kate Fansler Novels Ser.). 208p. mass mkt. 6.50 (*0-345-34686-6*) Ballantine Bks.
—The James Joyce Murders. 1982. 176p. 9.95 o.p. (*0-525-24101-9*, 0995-300, Dutton) Dutton/Plume.
—The James Joyce Murders. l.t. ed. 1993. (Nightingale Ser.). 282p. pap. 16.95 o.p. (*0-8161-5779-0*, Macmillan Reference USA) Gale Group.
—The James Joyce Murders. l.t. ed. 1982. 275p. reprint ed. 9.95 o.p. (*0-89621-373-0*) Thorndike Pr.
—No Word from Winifred. 1988. pap. 3.95 o.p. (*0-345-00728-X*); 1987. 272p. mass mkt. 6.99 (*0-345-33381-0*) Ballantine Bks.
—No Word from Winifred. 1986. 14.95 o.p. (*0-525-24432-8*, Dutton) Dutton/Plume.
—The Players Come Again. 1991. (Kate Fansler Novels Ser.). 240p. mass mkt. 6.99 (*0-345-36998-X*, Ballantine Bks.) Ballantine Bks.
—The Players Come Again. l.t. ed. 1994. 300p. lib. bdg. 15.95 o.p. (*0-8161-5990-4*, Macmillan Reference USA) Gale Group.
—The Players Come Again. 1992. 3.99 o.p. (*0-517-09455-X*) Random Hse. Value Publishing.
—The Players Come Again. l.t. ed. 1991. (Charnwood Large Print Ser.). 29.99 o.p. (*0-7089-8615-3*, Charnwood) Thorpe, F. A. Pubs. GBR. *Dist:* Ulverscroft Large Print Bks., Ltd., Ulverscroft Large Print Canada, Ltd.
—Poetic Justice. 2001. (Kate Fansler Novels Ser.). 224p. mass mkt. 6.50 (*0-449-00703-0*, Fawcett) Ballantine Bks.
—Poetic Justice. 1979. 176p. mass mkt. 4.99 (*0-380-44222-1*, Avon Bks.) Morrow/Avon.
—Poetic Justice. l.t. ed. 1981. 286p. reprint ed. 9.95 o.p. (*0-89621-291-2*) Thorndike Pr.
—The Question of Max. 1987. (Kate Fansler Novels Ser.). 224p. mass mkt. 6.50 (*0-345-35489-3*) Ballantine Bks.
—The Question of Max. 1977. lib. bdg. 10.95 o.p. (*0-8161-6451-7*, Macmillan Reference USA) Gale Group.
—The Question of Max. 1984. 7.95 o.p. (*0-394-48223-9*); mass mkt. 2.50 o.p. (*0-345-31385-2*) Knopf, Alfred A. Inc.
—Sweet Death, Kind Death. 1995. 224p. pap. 15.00 (*0-345-46763-9*); 1987. 244p. mass mkt. 5.99 (*0-345-35254-8*); 1985. mass mkt. 2.95 o.s.i (*0-345-31177-9*) Ballantine Bks.
—Sweet Death, Kind Death. 1984. 192p. 13.95 o.p. (*0-525-24241-4*, 01354-410, Dutton) Dutton/Plume.
—Sweet Death, Kind Death. l.t. ed. 1987. (Nightingale Ser.). 279p. pap. 11.95 o.p. (*0-8161-4222-X*, Macmillan Reference USA) Gale Group.
—The Theban Mysteries. 2001. (Kate Fansler Novels Ser.). 224p. mass mkt. 6.50 (*0-449-00706-5*, Fawcett) Ballantine Bks.
—The Theban Mysteries. 1979. 192p. pap. 4.99 (*0-380-45021-6*, Avon Bks.) Morrow/Avon.
—The Theban Mysteries. l.t. ed. 1982. 275p. reprint ed. 11.95 o.p. (*0-89621-362-5*) Thorndike Pr.
—A Trap for Fools. l.t. ed. 1990. pap. 5.00 (*0-7451-1286-2*) BBC Audiobooks America.
—A Trap for Fools. 1990. (Kate Fansler Novels Ser.). 224p. mass mkt. 5.99 (*0-345-35947-X*) Ballantine Bks.
—A Trap for Fools. 1989. 160p. 16.95 o.p. (*0-525-24754-8*, Dutton) Dutton/Plume.
—A Trap for Fools. l.t. ed. 1990. (Nightingale Ser.). 263p. 14.95 o.p. (*0-8161-4935-6*, Macmillan Reference USA) Gale Group.
Cruz, Angie. Soledad. 240p. 2001. 23.00 (*0-7432-1201-0*); 2002. reprint ed. pap. 13.00 (*0-7432-1202-9*) Simon & Schuster. (Simon & Schuster).
Cunnah, Michelle. 32AA. 2003. 320p. pap. 13.95 (*0-06-056012-6*) HarperCollins Pubs.
Cunningham, Laura Shaine. Beautiful Bodies. 2003. 384p. pap. 14.00 (*0-7434-3402-1*, Washington Square Pr.); 2002. 368p. 24.00 (*0-7434-3401-3*, Atria); 2002. E-Book 9.99 (*0-7434-3664-4*, Atria) Simon & Schuster.
Cunningham, Michael. The Hours. E-Book 13.00 (*0-374-91952-6*); 2003. E-Book 9.00 (*0-374-70468-6*); 1998. 230p. 23.00 (*0-374-17289-7*); 1998. E-Book 23.00 o.p. (*0-374-70011-7*); 1998. E-Book 9.00 o.p. (*0-374-70006-0*); 1998. E-Book 9.00 (*0-374-70009-5*); 1998. E-Book 9.00 (*0-374-70016-8*) Farrar, Straus & Giroux.
—The Hours. 240p. 2000. pap. 13.00 (*0-312-24302-2*); 2002. pap. 13.00 (*0-312-30506-0*) Picador.
—The Hours. l.t. ed. (Paperback Bestsellers Ser.). 2000. 253p. pap. 30.00 (*0-7838-8714-0*); 1999. 250p. pap. 30.95 (*0-7838-8715-9*) Thorndike Pr.
—The Hours. 2000. 19.05 (*0-606-19100-3*) Turtleback Bks.
Curnyn, Lynda. Engaging Men. 2003. 320p. pap. (*0-373-25028-2*, Red Dress Ink) Harlequin Enterprises, Ltd.
Currier, Jameson. Where the Rainbow Ends. 320p. 2000. 14.95 (*1-58567-084-7*); 1998. (Illus.). 24.95 (*0-87951-892-8*) Overlook Pr., The.
Curtis, Jack. Glory. 1988. 352p. 18.95 o.p. (*0-525-24668-1*, Dutton) Dutton/Plume.
—Glory. 1989. mass mkt. 4.50 o.s.i (*0-451-40133-6*, Onyx) NAL.
Czuchlewski, David. The Muse Asylum. 2001. (Illus.). 224p. 23.95 o.p. (*0-399-14745-4*) Putnam Publishing Group, The.
Daley, Robert. A Faint Cold Fear. abr. ed. 1991. audio 15.95 o.p. (*1-55927-142-6*) Audio Renaissance.
—A Faint Cold Fear. 1990. 19.95 o.p. (*0-316-17184-0*) Little Brown & Co.
—A Faint Cold Fear. abr. ed. 1991. audio 7.95 (*1-57815-038-8*, 1010) Media Bks., L. L. C.
—A Faint Cold Fear. 1992. 480p. mass mkt. 5.99 o.s.i (*0-446-36219-0*) Warner Bks., Inc.
—Hands of a Stranger. l.t. ed. 1986. (General Ser.). 615p. 19.95 o.p. (*0-8161-4032-4*); 10.95 o.p. (*0-8161-4071-5*) Gale Group. (Macmillan Reference USA).
—Hands of a Stranger. 1986. mass mkt. 2.95 o.p. (*0-451-15789-3*); mass mkt. 4.95 o.p. (*0-451-16376-1*); mass mkt. 4.50 o.p. (*0-451-15088-0*); mass mkt. 4.50 o.p. (*0-451-14509-7*) NAL. (Signet Bks.).
—Hands of a Stranger. 1985. 418p. 16.45 o.p. (*0-671-49962-9*, Simon & Schuster) Simon & Schuster.
—Night Falls on Manhattan: A Novel. 1993. 391p. 21.95 o.p. (*0-316-17196-4*) Little Brown & Co.
—Tainted Evidence. 1995. pap. 5.99 (*0-446-36083-X*); 1994. 448p. mass mkt. 5.99 o.s.i (*0-446-60083-0*) Warner Bks., Inc.
—To Kill a Cop. 1978. mass mkt. 2.25 o.s.i (*0-345-27644-2*); 1977. mass mkt. 2.25 o.s.i (*0-345-25945-9*) Ballantine Bks.
—To Kill a Cop. 1996. 400p. mass mkt. 6.50 o.s.i (*0-446-36571-8*) Warner Bks., Inc.
—Wall of Brass. 1994. 409p. 22.95 o.p. (*0-316-17206-5*) Little Brown & Co.
—Wall of Brass. 1995. 384p. mass mkt. 6.50 (*0-446-36566-1*) Warner Bks., Inc.
—Year of the Dragon. 1985. mass mkt. 2.95 o.p. (*0-451-15156-9*); 1985. mass mkt. 4.95 o.p. (*0-451-15207-7*); 1982. mass mkt. 3.95 o.p. (*0-451-13786-8*); 1982. mass mkt. 3.95 o.p. (*0-451-11817-0*) NAL. (Signet Bks.).
—Year of the Dragon. 1981. 14.95 o.p. (*0-671-41045-8*, Simon & Schuster) Simon & Schuster.
—Year of the Dragon. 1997. 528p. mass mkt. 6.99 (*0-446-36572-6*) Warner Bks., Inc.
Daly, Carroll J. The Adventures of Race Williams. 1989. 352p. 9.95 (*0-89296-959-8*) Mysterious Pr.
—The Hidden Hand: A Race Williams Mystery. 1992. 320p. reprint ed. pap. 8.00 o.p. (*0-06-097436-2*, Perennial) HarperTrade.
—Murder from the East: A Race Williams Story. 1978. (Library of Crime Classics). 312p. reprint ed. pap. 4.95 o.p. (*0-930330-01-3*) International Polygonics, Ltd.
—The Snarl of the Beast: A Race Williams Mystery. 1992. 320p. reprint ed. pap. 8.00 o.p. (*0-06-097435-4*, Perennial) HarperTrade.
Daly, David J. The Legend of Killer Noon. 2000. 223p. pap. 14.95 (*0-9671411-0-9*) Green Boat Pr.
Daly, Elizabeth. And Dangerous to Know. 1984. 176p. pap. 2.95 o.p. (*0-553-24616-X*) Bantam Bks.
—And Dangerous to Know. 1991. 9.95 o.p. (*0-8050-0805-5*) Holt, Henry & Co.
—Any Shape or Form. 1981. (Murder Ink Mystery Ser.: No. 27). pap. 2.25 o.p. (*0-440-10108-5*) Dell Publishing.
—Arrow Pointing Nowhere. 1983. pap. 3.25 o.p. (*0-440-10021-6*) Dell Publishing.
—The Book of the Lion. 1985. 160p. pap. 2.95 o.p. (*0-553-24883-9*) Bantam Bks.
—The Book of the Lion. 1950. 9.95 o.p. (*0-8050-0806-3*) Holt, Henry & Co.
—Deadly Nightshade. 1993. audio 44.20 (*1-56544-034-X*, 250013); audio Literate Ear, Inc.
—Death & Letters. 1981. pap. 2.25 o.p. (*0-440-11791-7*) Dell Publishing.
—Death & Letters. Barzun, Jacques & Taylor, W. H., eds. 1982. (Crime Fiction 1950-1975 Ser.). 131p. lib. bdg. 18.00 o.p. (*0-8240-4979-9*) Garland Publishing, Inc.
—The House Without the Door. 1984. 192p. pap. 2.95 o.p. (*0-553-24610-0*) Bantam Bks.
—Murders in Volume Two: A Henry Gamadge Mystery. 1993. audio 41.00 (*1-56544-054-4*, 250016); audio Literate Ear, Inc.
—Murders in Volume Two: A Henry Gamadge Mystery. 1994. 320p. reprint ed. pap. 6.95 (*1-883402-52-2*, Scribner) Simon & Schuster.
—Night Walk. 1982. (Murder Ink Mystery Ser.: No. 55). pap. 2.50 o.p. (*0-440-16609-8*) Dell Publishing.
—Nothing Can Rescue Me. 1984. 192p. pap. 2.95 o.p. (*0-553-24605-4*) Bantam Bks.
—Somewhere in the House. 1984. 192p. pap. 2.95 o.p. (*0-553-24267-9*) Bantam Bks.
—Unexpected Night: A Henry Gamadge Mystery. 1986. (Mystery Ser.). 224p. pap. 2.95 o.p. (*0-553-25129-5*) Bantam Bks.
—Unexpected Night: A Henry Gamadge Mystery. 1991. 9.95 o.p. (*0-8050-0807-1*) Holt, Henry & Co.
—Unexpected Night: A Henry Gamadge Mystery. 1993. audio 39.20 (*1-56544-033-1*, 250003); audio Literate Ear, Inc.
—Unexpected Night: A Henry Gamadge Mystery. 1995. pap. 6.95 (*1-883402-14-X*); 1994. 240p. reprint ed. per. 7.00 (*1-883402-51-4*) Simon & Schuster. (Scribner).
—The Wrong Way Down. 1986. mass mkt. 9.95 o.p. (*0-553-06515-7*) Bantam Bks.
Daly, Michael. Under Ground. 1997. 448p. mass mkt. 5.99 o.s.i (*0-451-19154-4*, Signet Bks.) NAL.
—Under Ground: A Novel. 1995. 415p. 21.95 o.p. (*0-316-21709-3*) Little Brown & Co.
Daniel, David & Carpenter, Chris. Murder at the Baseball Hall of Fame. 1996. 224p. 20.95 o.p. (*0-312-14683-3*, Saint Martin's Minotaur) St. Martin's Pr.
Danticat, Edwidge. Breath, Eyes, Memory. 1995. (Vintage Contemporaries Ser.). pap. 11.00 o.p. (*0-679-75661-2*); 2nd ed. 1998. (Breath, Eyes, Memory Ser.: Vol. 16). 256p. pap. 12.00 (*0-375-70504-X*) Knopf Publishing Group. (Vintage).
—Breath, Eyes, Memory. 1994. 230p. 20.00 o.p. (*1-56947-005-7*) Soho Pr., Inc.
—Breath, Eyes, Memory. l.t. ed. (Paperback Bestsellers Ser.). 301p. 1999. pap. 26.95 (*0-7862-1655-7*); 1998. 29.95 (*0-7862-1654-9*) Thorndike Pr.
—The Dew Breaker. 2004. 256p. 22.00 (*1-4000-4114-7*) Knopf Publishing Group.
Danticat, Edwidge, et al. Breath, Eyes, Memory. 2nd ed. 1994. (Breath, Eyes, Memory Ser.: Vol. 16). 230p. 20.00 (*1-56947-142-8*) Soho Pr., Inc.
Dantz, William R. Nine Levels Down. 1999. 312p. mass mkt. 6.99 (*0-8125-2416-0*); 1995. 288p. 21.95 o.p. (*0-312-85483-8*) Doherty, Tom Assocs., LLC. (Forge Bks.).
Darieck, Scott. Traitor to the Race. 1996. 224p. pap. 10.95 o.p. (*0-452-27335-8*, Plume) Dutton/Plume.
Darnton, John. The Experiment. 1999. 416p. 24.95 o.p. (*0-525-94517-2*) Dutton/Plume.
—The Experiment. l.t. ed. 2000. 26.95 (*1-56895-819-6*, Wheeler Publishing, Inc.) Gale Group.
—The Experiment. 2000. 496p. mass mkt. 6.99 (*0-451-20010-1*, Signet Bks.) NAL.
—Mind Catcher. 2002. 416p. 25.95 o.s.i (*0-525-94662-4*) Dutton/Plume.
—Mind Catcher. 2003. 448p. mass mkt. 7.99 (*0-451-41105-6*, Onyx) NAL.
David, Lawrence. Need. 1996. 355p. mass mkt. 6.99 (*0-312-95922-2*, St. Martin's Paperbacks) St. Martin's Pr.
David, Peter. Knight Life. 2003. 352p. mass mkt. 7.99 (*0-441-01077-6*); 2002. 352p. 22.95 (*0-441-00936-0*); 1987. 192p. mass mkt. 2.95 o.s.i (*0-441-45130-6*) Ace Bks.
Davies, Adam. The Frog King: A Love Story. 2002. 336p. pap. 13.00 (*1-57322-938-5*, Riverhead Bks. (Hardcovers)) Putnam Publishing Group, The.
Davies, Valentine. The Miracle on 34th Street. reprint ed. lib. bdg. 17.95 (*0-88411-934-3*) Amereon, Ltd.
—The Miracle on 34th Street. 1994. 160p. pap. 9.95 (*0-15-600198-5*); 1967. pap. 2.50 o.p. (*0-15-660453-1*, Harvest Bks.); 1947. 120p. 13.95 o.s.i (*0-15-160239-5*) Harcourt Trade Pubs.
—Miracle on 34th Street: (Ornament & Book) gif. ed. 2002. (Illus.). 144p. (J). 16.95 (*0-15-204575-9*) Harcourt Children's Bks.
Davis, Jill A. Girls' Poker Night. 2002. 240p. 23.95 o.s.i (*0-375-50514-8*); E-Book 19.00 (*1-58836-225-6*) Random Hse., Inc.
Davis, Lennard J. The Sonnets: A Novel. vi, 163p. (C). 2002. pap. text 16.95 (*0-7914-4978-5*); 2001. E-Book 25.50 (*0-7914-4977-7*) State Univ. of New York Pr.
Davis, Lisa E. Under the Mink. 2001. 267p. pap. 12.95 (*1-55583-556-2*) Alyson Pubns.
Davis, Thulani. Maker of Saints. 1997. 256p. pap. 15.00 (*0-14-026735-2*) Penguin Group (USA) Inc.
—Maker of Saints. 1996. 256p. 22.00 (*0-684-81225-8*, Scribner) Simon & Schuster.
De Felitta, Frank. Funeral March. 1991. 352p. mass mkt. 4.95 o.s.i (*0-553-28927-6*) Bantam Bks.
De Haven, Tom. Funny Papers. (American Fiction Ser.). 384p. 1986. pap. 6.95 o.p. (*0-14-008680-3*, Penguin Bks.); 1985. 15.95 o.p. (*0-670-33251-8*) Viking Penguin.
—Funny Papers: A Novel. 2002. 384p. pap. 14.00 (*0-312-42134-6*) Picador.
De la Cruz, Melissa. Cat's Meow: A Novel. 2001. (Illus.). 224p. pap. 13.00 (*0-7432-0504-9*, Touchstone) Simon & Schuster.
De Vico, Peter J. From the Brooklyn Side. 2000. 724p. pap. 32.95 (*0-595-09677-8*, Writers Club Pr.) iUniverse, Inc.
DeAndrea, William L. Killed in Fringe Time: A Matt Cobb Mystery. 1995. 208p. 21.00 o.p. (*0-684-81498-6*, Simon & Schuster); 21.00 (*1-883402-26-3*, Scribner) Simon & Schuster.
Deaver, Jeffery. The Bone Collector: A Lincoln Rhyme Novel. l.t. ed. 1998. (Large Print Bks.). pap. 23.95 o.p. (*1-56895-524-3*, Wheeler Publishing, Inc.) Gale Group.
—The Bone Collector: A Lincoln Rhyme Novel. 1998. 432p. mass mkt. 7.99 (*0-451-18845-4*, Signet Bks.) NAL.
—The Bone Collector: A Lincoln Rhyme Novel. 1997. 432p. 22.95 o.s.i (*0-670-86871-X*) Viking Penguin.
—The Coffin Dancer: A Lincoln Rhyme Novel. l.t. ed. 1998. 27.95 (*1-56895-698-3*, Wheeler Publishing, Inc.) Gale Group.
—The Coffin Dancer: A Lincoln Rhyme Novel. 1999. E-Book 25.00 (*0-684-86805-9*, Simon & Schuster); 1999. pap. 6.99 (*0-671-02606-2*, Pocket); 1998. 368p. 25.00 o.s.i (*0-684-85285-3*, Simon & Schuster); 1999. (Illus.). 560p. reprint ed. mass mkt. 7.99 (*0-671-02409-4*, Pocket) Simon & Schuster.
—The Coffin Dancer: A Lincoln Rhyme Novel. 2000. audio compact disk 15.99 (*0-7435-0548-4*, Simon & Schuster Audioworks) Simon & Schuster Audio.
—The Devil's Teardrop: A Novel of the Last Night of the Century. E-Book 25.00 (*1-930161-37-9*) Adobe Systems, Inc.
—The Devil's Teardrop: A Novel of the Last Night of the Century. l.t. ed. 2000. pap. 11.95 (*1-56895-982-6*); 1999. 527p. 26.95 o.p. (*1-56895-804-8*) Gale Group. (Wheeler Publishing, Inc.).
—The Devil's Teardrop: A Novel of the Last Night of the Century. 2000. E-Book 9.99 (*0-684-85659-X*, Simon & Schuster); 1999. 400p. mass mkt. 7.99 (*0-671-03712-9*, Pocket); 1999. 400p. 25.00 o.s.i (*0-684-85292-6*, Simon & Schuster); 2000. (Illus.). 480p. reprint ed. pap. 7.99 (*0-671-03844-3*, Pocket) Simon & Schuster.
—The Devil's Teardrop: A Novel of the Last Night of the Century. abr. ed. 1999. 352p. audio 24.00 (*0-671-04569-5*, Simon & Schuster Audioworks) Simon & Schuster Audio.
—The Devil's Teardrop: A Novel of the Last Night of the Century. l.t. ed. 2002. (Charnwood Large Print Ser.). 520p. 32.50 o.p. (*0-7089-9298-6*, Charnwood) Thorpe, F. A. Pubs. GBR. *Dist:* Ulverscroft Large Print Bks., Ltd., Ulverscroft Large Print Canada, Ltd.
—Hard News. 2001. 304p. mass mkt. 7.99 (*0-553-58329-8*); 1992. 256p. mass mkt. 4.99 o.s.i (*0-553-29622-1*) Bantam Bks.
—Hard News. 1991. 320p. 15.00 o.s.i (*0-385-42121-4*) Doubleday Publishing.
—Hard News. l.t. ed. 2001. 438p. 29.95 (*0-7862-3413-X*) Thorndike Pr.
—Manhattan Is My Beat. 2000. 304p. mass mkt. 7.99 (*0-553-58176-7*); 1989. 256p. mass mkt. 3.95 o.s.i (*0-553-28061-9*) Bantam Bks.
—Manhattan Is My Beat. l.t. ed. 2002. (Wheeler Large Print Book Ser.). 329p. 29.95 (*1-58724-154-4*, Wheeler Publishing, Inc.) Gale Group.
DeCarlo, Pamela. Today's Woman. Nixon, Bonnie, ed. E-Book 4.95 (*1-929782-28-4*, e-pulp) Yellow Creek Publishing.
—Today's Woman. 2000. E-Book 4.95 (*1-929782-33-0*) Yellow Creek Publishing.
Dee, Ed. Bronx Angel. 2001. 384p. E-Book 4.95 (*0-7595-0587-X*); 2001. 384p. E-Book 4.95 (*0-7595-4590-1*); 2001. 384p. E-Book 4.95 (*0-7595-8596-2*); 2001. 384p. E-Book 4.95 (*0-7595-6588-0*); 1995. 304p. 21.95 o.p. (*0-446-51774-7*); 1996. 384p. reprint ed. mass mkt. 6.50 (*0-446-60337-6*) Warner Bks., Inc.
—The Con Man's Daughter. 2003. 304p. 23.95 (*0-89296-794-3*) Mysterious Pr.
—Little Boy Blue. l.t. ed. 1997. (Wheeler Large Print Book Ser.). pap. 23.95 (*1-56895-452-2*, Wheeler Publishing, Inc.) Gale Group.
—Little Boy Blue. abr. ed. 2001. audio 7.95 (*1-57815-217-8*, Media Bks. Audio Publishing) Media Bks., L. L. C.

Settings

—Little Boy Blue. abr. ed. 1997. audio 12.98 (*1-57042-475-6*, 394925) Time Warner AudioBooks.

—Little Boy Blue. 1997. 272p. 22.50 o.p. (*0-446-52038-1*); 1998. 320p. reprint ed. mass mkt. 6.99 o.s.i (*0-446-60522-0*) Warner Bks., Inc.

—14 Peck Slip. 1994. 304p. 19.95 o.s.i (*0-446-51770-4*); 1995. 336p. reprint ed. mass mkt. 5.99 (*0-446-60238-8*) Warner Bks., Inc.

Dee, Edward. Nightbird. 2000. 352p. E-Book 4.95 (*0-446-92362-1*) Time Warner Bk. Group.

—Nightbird. 2001. 352p. E-Book 4.95 (*0-446-96023-3*); 2000. 352p. mass mkt. 6.99 (*0-446-60913-7*); 2000. E-Book 4.95 (*0-446-91510-6*); 1999. 304p. 23.95 (*0-446-52039-X*) Warner Bks., Inc.

Dejohn, Jacqueline. Antonio's Wife. 2004. 368p. 24.95 (*0-06-055809-8*, ReganBooks) HarperTrade.

Delamer, John J. The Tarnished Shield. 1995. 208p. (Orig.). pap. 12.95 (*1-56474-156-7*) Fithian Pr.

Delbanco, Francesca. Ask Me Anything. 2004. 256p. 23.95 (*0-393-05170-6*) Norton, W. W. & Co., Inc.

Delbanco, Nicholas. What Remains. 2000. 208p. 24.95 o.p. (*0-446-52416-6*); E-Book 14.95 (*0-7595-4037-3*); E-Book 14.95 (*0-7595-0037-1*); E-Book 14.95 (*0-7595-8038-3*) Warner Bks., Inc.

DeLillo, Don. Cosmopolis: A Novel. 224p. 2004. pap. 13.00 (*0-7432-4425-7*); 2003. 25.00 (*0-7432-4424-9*) Simon & Schuster. (Scribner).

—Great Jones Street. 1994. 272p. pap. 14.00 (*0-14-017917-8*) Penguin Group (USA) Inc.

—Pafko at the Wall. 2001. 96p. 16.00 (*0-7432-3000-0*, Scribner) Simon & Schuster.

—Underworld. 832p. 1998. pap. 16.00 (*0-684-84815-5*); 1997. 27.50 (*0-684-84269-6*) Simon & Schuster. (Scribner).

Delinsky, Barbara. Commitments. l.t. ed. 1995. (Large Print Ser.). 472p. lib. bdg. 23.95 (*1-57490-032-3*, Beeler Large Print Bks.) Beeler, Thomas T. Publisher.

—Commitments. 1996. reprint ed. 19.00 o.p. (*0-7278-4059-2*) Severn Hse. Pubs., Ltd.

—Commitments. 2001. 416p. 16.95 o.p. (*0-446-52725-4*); 1988. 384p. mass mkt. 5.50 o.s.i (*0-445-20600-4*); 1995. 448p. reprint ed. mass mkt. 6.99 (*0-446-60215-9*) Warner Bks., Inc.

Dell, Floyd. Love in Greenwich Village. 1977. (Short Story Index Reprint Ser.). 27.95 (*0-8369-3621-3*) Ayer Co. Pubs., Inc.

Delman, David. Ain't Goin' to Glory. 1991. 224p. 18.95 o.p. (*0-312-06272-9*) St. Martin's Pr.

—The Bluestocking. 1994. 320p. 22.95 o.p. (*0-312-10432-4*) St. Martin's Pr.

DeLynn, Jane. Leash. 2002. (Semiotext(e) / Native Agents Ser.). (Illus.). 255p. pap. 12.95 (*1-58435-014-8*) Semiotexte/Smart Art.

—Real Estate. 1989. 304p. mass mkt. 3.95 o.s.i (*0-345-35978-X*) Ballantine Bks.

—Real Estate. 1998. 316p. pap. 18.00 (*1-891305-10-7*) Painted Leaf Pr.

—Real Estate. 1988. 17.45 o.p. (*0-671-54424-1*, Simon & Schuster) Simon & Schuster.

DeMatteis, J. M. & Barr, Glenn. Brooklyn Dreams. 2003. (Illus.). 384p. pap. 19.95 (*1-4012-0051-6*) DC Comics.

DeMille, Nelson. Cathedral. 1982. 576p. mass mkt. 5.95 o.s.i (*0-440-11620-1*); 1981. 13.95 o.s.i (*0-440-01141-X*, Delacorte Pr.) Dell Publishing.

—Cathedral. Set. abr. ed. 1998. audio 8.99 o.s.i (*0-375-40296-9*, RH Audio) Random Hse. Audio Publishing Group.

—Cathedral. l.t. ed. 1982. (Charnwood Large Print Ser.). 720p. 29.99 o.p. (*0-7089-8079-1*, Charnwood) Thorpe, F. A. Pubs. GBR. *Dist:* Ulverscroft Large Print Bks., Ltd., Ulverscroft Large Print Canada, Ltd.

—Cathedral. 2001. 575p. E-Book 6.95 (*0-7595-4258-9*); 2001. 575p. E-Book 6.95 (*0-7595-9288-8*); 2001. 575p. E-Book 6.95 (*0-7595-6255-5*); 2001. 575p. E-Book 6.95 (*0-7595-8261-0*); 2001. 575p. E-Book 6.95 (*0-7595-0255-2*); 1990. 576p. reprint ed. mass mkt. 7.99 (*0-446-35857-6*) Warner Bks., Inc.

—The Talbot Odyssey. 1985. pap. 3.95 o.p. (*0-440-18488-6*); 1984. 432p. 16.95 o.s.i (*0-385-29322-4*, Delacorte Pr.) Dell Publishing.

—The Talbot Odyssey. l.t. ed. 2000. (Famous Authors Ser.). 853p. 29.95 o.p. (*0-7862-2668-4*) Thorndike Pr.

—The Talbot Odyssey. 1991. 544p. reprint ed. mass mkt. 7.99 (*0-446-35858-4*) Warner Bks., Inc.

Denker, Henry. Doctor on Trial. unabr. ed. 1992. audio 23.95 o.p. (*1-56100-471-5*, 92, Bookcassette); audio 73.25 o.p. (*1-56100-105-8*, 867, Unabridged Library Editions) Brilliance Audio.

—Doctor on Trial: A Novel. 1992. 20.00 o.p. (*0-688-11388-5*, Morrow, William & Co.) Morrow/Avon.

—Labyrinth: A Novel. 1994. 299p. 23.00 o.p. (*0-688-13700-8*, Morrow, William & Co.) Morrow/Avon.

Dennis, Patrick. Auntie Mame: An Irreverent Escapade. 2002. E-Book 10.50 (*1-59061-870-X*) Adobe Systems, Inc.

—Auntie Mame: An Irreverent Escapade. 2001. 320p. reprint ed. pap. 12.95 (*0-7679-0819-8*) Broadway Bks.

Dentinger, Jane. First Hit of the Season. l.t. ed. 1985. lib. bdg. 13.95 o.p. (*0-89340-875-1*, 863) BBC Audiobooks America.

—First Hit of the Season. 1984. (Crime Club Ser.). 192p. 11.95 o.p. (*0-385-19409-9*) Doubleday Publishing.

—First Hit of the Season. 1993. (Jocelyn O'Roarke Mystery Ser.). 192p. pap. 4.95 o.p. (*0-14-015842-1*, Penguin Bks.) Penguin Group (USA) Inc.

Deveraux, Jude. High Tide. l.t. ed. 1999. 25.95 (*1-56895-800-5*, Wheeler Publishing, Inc.) Gale Group.

—High Tide. 2003. (Illus.). 368p. mass mkt. 5.99 (*0-7434-6713-2*, Pocket); 2000. (Illus.). 368p. mass mkt. 7.99 (*0-671-01417-X*, Pocket); 1999. 320p. 24.00 o.s.i (*0-671-01416-1*, Atria) Simon & Schuster.

—Sweet Liar. l.t. ed. 1993. (General Ser.). 586p. pap. 18.95 o.p. (*0-8161-5623-9*); 23.95 o.p. (*0-8161-5622-0*) Gale Group. (Macmillan Reference USA).

—Sweet Liar. Marrow, Linda, ed. 1993. 448p. mass mkt. 7.99 (*0-671-68974-6*, Pocket); 1992. 384p. 22.00 (*0-671-68973-8*, Atria) Simon & Schuster.

—Sweet Liar. abr. ed. 1999. (Angel Ser.). audio 9.98 o.s.i (*0-671-04417-6*, Simon & Schuster Audioworks) Simon & Schuster Audio.

—Sweet Liar. Marrow, Linda, ed. abr. ed. 1992. 384p. pap. 17.00 incl. audio (*0-671-79190-7*, Simon & Schuster Audioworks) Simon & Schuster Audio.

Dewasar, Ahba. MiniPlanner: A Novel. 2000. 250p. pap. 12.95 (*1-57344-115-5*) Cleis Pr.

Di Donato, Pietro. Christ in Concrete. 1977. pap. 1.95 o.p. (*0-671-81183-5*, Pocket) Simon & Schuster.

—Christ in Concrete: A Novel. 1993. 256p. mass mkt. 6.95 (*0-451-52575-2*, Signet Classics) NAL.

Diaz Valcarcel, Emilio. Hot Soles in Harlem. Miller, Yvette E., ed. Fayen, Tanya T., tr. from SPA. 1993. (Discoveries Ser.). 175p. pap. 16.95 (*0-935480-61-7*) Latin American Literary Review Pr.

Dicerto, Joseph. Wall People. 1985. 11.95 o.s.i (*0-689-31090-0*, Atheneum) Simon & Schuster Children's Publishing.

Dickey, Eric Jerome. Milk in My Coffee. 1998. 304p. 23.95 o.s.i (*0-525-94385-4*, Dutton Children's Bks.) Dutton/Plume.

—Milk in My Coffee. 1999. 384p. reprint ed. mass mkt. 7.50 (*0-451-19406-3*, Signet Bks.) NAL.

Dierbeck, Lisa. One Pill Makes You Smaller. 2003. 320p. 24.00 (*0-374-22649-0*) Farrar, Straus & Giroux.

—One Pill Makes You Smaller. 2004. pap. (*0-312-42286-5*) Picador.

Dixon, Melvin. Vanishing Rooms. 224p. 1991. 18.95 o.p. (*0-525-24965-6*, Dutton); 1992. reprint ed. pap. 10.00 o.p. (*0-452-26761-7*, Plume) Dutton/Plume.

—Vanishing Rooms: A Novel. 2001. 211p. pap. 14.95 (*1-57344-123-6*) Cleis Pr.

Doctorow, E. L. Billy Bathgate. 1998. 336p. pap. 14.00 (*0-452-28002-8*, Plume) Dutton/Plume.

—Billy Bathgate. 1991. 496p. mass mkt. 5.99 o.p. (*0-06-100331-X*, HarperTorch) Morrow/Avon.

—City of God. 2001. E-Book 10.00 (*1-59061-401-1*) Adobe Systems, Inc.

—City of God. 2001. 288p. reprint ed. pap. 13.00 (*0-452-28209-8*, Plume) Dutton/Plume.

—City of God. l.t. ed. 2000. (Basic Ser.). 514p. 31.95 (*0-7862-2681-1*); 29.95 (*0-7862-2684-6*) Thorndike Pr.

—Loon Lake. 1980. 35.00 o.p. (*0-394-51176-X*) Random Hse., Inc.

—The Waterworks. 1997. 352p. reprint ed. pap. 14.00 (*0-452-27549-0*, Plume) Dutton/Plume.

—The Waterworks. 1995. 352p. mass mkt. 6.99 o.s.i (*0-451-18563-3*, Signet Bks.) NAL.

—The Waterworks. 1994. audio 22.50 o.s.i (*0-679-43372-4*, RH Audio) Random Hse. Audio Publishing Group.

—The Waterworks. l.t. ed. 1994. 22.00 o.s.i (*0-679-75441-5*) Random Hse. Large Print.

—The Waterworks. deluxe ed. 1994. 100.00 o.s.i (*0-679-43196-9*) Random Hse., Inc.

—World's Fair. 1986. mass mkt. 3.75 o.s.i (*0-449-21231-9*) Ballantine Bks.

—World's Fair. 1996. 304p. pap. 13.95 (*0-452-27572-5*, Plume) Dutton/Plume.

—World's Fair. l.t. ed. 1986. 19.95 o.p. (*0-8161-4085-5*, Macmillan Reference USA) Gale Group.

—World's Fair. 1992. pap. 12.00 o.p. (*0-679-73628-X*, Vintage) Knopf Publishing Group.

—World's Fair. 1993. 24.25 (*0-8446-6696-3*) Smith, Peter Pub., Inc.

Doig, Ivan. Prairie Nocturne: A Novel. 2003. 384p. 26.00 (*0-7432-0135-3*, Scribner) Simon & Schuster.

Dolby, Tom. The Trouble Boy. 2004. 288p. 23.00 (*0-7582-0616-X*) Kensington Publishing Corp.

Donati, Alyssa. Marzipan Pigeon. 1994. 300p. 21.00 (*0-671-86889-6*, Simon & Schuster) Simon & Schuster.

Donleavy, J. P. The Lady Who Liked Clean Restrooms: The Chronicle of One of the Strangest Stories Ever. 1998. 119p. pap. o.s.i (*0-349-10850-1*); 1997. 128p. o.s.i (*0-316-88342-5*) Little Brown & Co.

—The Lady Who Liked Clean Restrooms: The Chronicle of One of the Strangest Stories Ever. 1998. (Illus.). 128p. pap. 9.95 (*0-312-18734-3*, Saint Martin's Griffin); 1997. 132p. 18.95 (*0-312-15563-8*) St. Martin's Pr.

Donnelly, Ignatius. Caesar's Column. 1993. 318p. reprint ed. lib. bdg. 39.00 (*0-8328-3174-3*) Higginson Bk. Co.

—Caesar's Column. Ruddick, Nicholas, ed. & tr. by. 2003. pap. 22.95 (*0-8195-6666-7*); text 65.00 (*0-8195-6665-9*) Univ. Pr. of New England.

Donnelly, Jennifer. The Tea Rose. 2004. mass mkt. 7.99 (*0-312-99356-0*, St. Martin's Paperbacks) St. Martin's Pr.

—The Tea Rose: A Novel. 2002. 560p. 24.95 (*0-312-28835-2*) St. Martin's Pr.

Donner, Rebecca, ed. On the Rocks: The KGB Bar Fiction Anthology. 2002. 288p. pap. 14.95 (*0-312-30152-9*, Saint Martin's Griffin) St. Martin's Pr.

Donohue, John. Sensei: A Thriller. 2003. 288p. 23.95 (*0-312-28812-3*, Saint Martin's Minotaur) St. Martin's Pr.

Dougan, Cameron. Because She Is Beautiful: A Novel. 2001. 888p. E-Book 9.95 (*0-679-64718-X*, AtRandom) Random House Adult Trade Publishing Group.

Douglas, Carole Nelson. Cat in a Golden Garland: A Midnight Louie Mystery. (Midnight Louie Mystery Ser.). 1998. 406p. mass mkt. 6.99 (*0-8125-3036-5*); 1997. 352p. 23.95 (*0-312-86386-1*) Doherty, Tom Assocs., LLC. (Forge Bks.).

—Cat in a Golden Garland: A Midnight Louie Mystery. l.t. ed. 1998. (G. K. Hall Core Ser.). 576p. 25.95 o.p. (*0-7838-8419-2*, Macmillan Reference USA) Gale Group.

Douglas, Kirk. Last Tango in Brooklyn. l.t. ed. 1994. 392p. lib. bdg. 24.95 (*0-8161-7465-2*, Macmillan Reference USA) Gale Group.

—Last Tango in Brooklyn. abr. ed. 1994. audio 21.00 o.s.i (*1-57042-085-8*, 4-520858) Time Warner AudioBooks.

—Last Tango in Brooklyn. 352p. 1995. mass mkt. 6.50 o.s.i (*0-446-60201-9*); 1994. 30.00 (*0-446-51695-3*) Warner Bks., Inc.

Douglass, Thea C. Royal Poinciana. 1988. 448p. 18.95 o.p. (*1-55611-048-0*) Fine, Donald I. Bks.

Downe, Solomon. Confessions of a Social Climber. 2000. E-Book 12.95 incl. cd-rom (*1-58444-034-1*) Disc-Us Bks., Inc.

Drakulic, Slavenka. Taste of a Man. Zoric, Christina P., tr. 1997. 208p. pap. 10.95 o.s.i (*0-14-026622-4*) Penguin Group (USA) Inc.

Dreiser, Theodore. An American Tragedy. 1990. reprint ed. lib. bdg. 54.95 (*0-89966-709-0*) Buccaneer Bks., Inc.

—An American Tragedy. 1964. (Signet Classics). 880p. mass mkt. 9.95 o.s.i (*0-451-52465-9*, Signet Classics) NAL.

—Sister Carrie. (Modern Library Ser.). E-Book 4.95 (*1-931208-42-5*) Adobe Systems, Inc.

—Sister Carrie. 1967. (Airmont Classics Ser.). mass mkt. 2.95 o.p. (*0-8049-0147-3*, CL-147) Airmont Publishing Co., Inc.

—Sister Carrie. 1976. 27.95 (*0-8488-0993-9*) Amereon, Ltd.

—Sister Carrie. 1982. 432p. mass mkt. 2.95 o.s.i (*0-553-21264-8*); mass mkt. 5.99 (*0-553-21374-1*) Bantam Bks. (Bantam Classics).

—Sister Carrie. 1971. 472p. reprint ed. lib. bdg. 20.00 (*0-8376-0401-X*) Bentley Pubs.

—Sister Carrie. 1980. 557p. reprint ed. lib. bdg. 37.95 (*0-89968-207-3*, Lightyear Pr.) Buccaneer Bks., Inc.

—Sister Carrie. (Collected Works of Theodore Dreiser). 382p. reprint ed. 2001. (Illus.). pap. text 28.00 (*0-7426-5625-X*); 1998. lib. bdg. 98.00 (*1-58201-625-9*) Classic Bks.

—Sister Carrie. E-Book 2.49 (*0-7574-0316-6*); E-Book 2.49 (*0-7574-0213-5*) Electric Umbrella Publishing.

—Sister Carrie. 1957. 474p. (C). pap. text 24.00 (*0-03-009075-X*) Harcourt College Pubs.

—Sister Carrie. Simpson, Claude, ed. 1972. pap. 12.36 o.p. (*0-395-05134-7*, Riverside Editions) Houghton Mifflin Co.

—Sister Carrie. l.t. ed. 808p. pap. 60.08 (*0-7583-2330-1*); 1035p. pap. 71.70 (*0-7583-2331-X*); 1324p. pap. 85.64 (*0-7583-2332-8*); 590p. pap. 42.40 (*0-7583-2329-8*); 1629p. pap. 108.27 (*0-7583-2333-6*); 2004p. pap. 123.01 (*0-7583-2334-4*); 2324p. pap. 145.14 (*0-7583-2335-2*); 1035p. lib. bdg. 83.70 (*0-7583-2323-9*); 2324p. lib. bdg. 174.31 (*0-7583-2327-1*); 2004p. lib. bdg. 144.15 (*0-7583-2326-3*); 1629p. lib. bdg. 126.27 (*0-7583-2325-5*); 808p. lib. bdg. 72.08 (*0-7583-2322-0*); 1324p. lib. bdg. 97.64 (*0-7583-2324-7*); 472p. lib. bdg. 41.72 (*0-7583-2320-4*); 590p. lib. bdg. 48.40 (*0-7583-2321-2*) Huge Print Pr.

—Sister Carrie. 1962. mass mkt. 1.75 o.p. (*0-451-51206-5*); 1962. mass mkt. 2.25 o.p. (*0-451-51319-3*); 1962. mass mkt. 2.50 o.p. (*0-451-51462-9*); 1962. mass mkt. 2.25 o.p. (*0-451-51725-3*); 1962. mass mkt. 1.50 o.p. (*0-451-50904-8*); 1962. mass mkt. 0.75 o.p. (*0-451-50086-5*); 1962. mass mkt. 0.95 o.p. (*0-451-50758-4*); 1962. mass mkt. 2.95 o.p. (*0-451-51969-8*); 1962. 480p. mass mkt. 5.95 o.s.i (*0-451-52273-7*); 2000. 512p. mass mkt. 5.95 (*0-451-52760-7*) NAL. (Signet Classics).

—Sister Carrie. l.t. ed. (Large Print Ser.). reprint ed. 1997. 632p. lib. bdg. 28.00 (*0-939495-16-3*); 1998. 453p. lib. bdg. 25.00 (*1-58287-071-3*) North Bks.

—Sister Carrie. 1970. (C). pap. o.p. (*0-393-09949-0*) Norton, W. W. & Co., Inc.

—Sister Carrie. Pizer, Donald, ed. 2nd ed. 1991. (Critical Editions Ser.). 600p. (C). pap. text 12.00 (*0-393-96042-0*, 9949) Norton, W. W. & Co., Inc.

—Sister Carrie. Mitchell, Lee Clark, ed. 1999. (Oxford World's Classics Ser.). 512p. pap. 12.95 (*0-19-283574-2*) Oxford Univ. Pr., Inc.

—Sister Carrie. 1991. (Oxford World's Classics Ser.). 508p. pap. 9.95 o.p. (*0-19-282742-1*, 9673) Oxford Univ. Pr., Inc.

—Sister Carrie. 2000. E-Book 4.95 (*0-679-64138-6*); 1999. 752p. pap. 12.95 (*0-375-75321-4*) Random House Adult Trade Publishing Group. (Modern Library).

—Sister Carrie. 1997. (Modern Library Ser.). 658p. 19.50 o.s.i (*0-679-60250-X*) Random Hse., Inc.

—Sister Carrie. E-Book 5.00 (*0-7410-0562-X*) SoftBook Pr.

—Sister Carrie. 1994. (Penguin Twentieth-Century Classics Ser.). 19.00 (*0-606-04903-7*) Turtleback Bks.

—Sister Carrie. Berkey, John C. et al, eds. 1997. (University of Pennsylvania Dreiser Edition Ser.). 544p. pap. 22.50 (*0-8122-1638-5*) Univ. of Pennsylvania Pr.

—Sister Carrie. West, James L. W., III et al, eds. 1981. (Dreiser Edition Ser.). (Illus.). 704p. 49.95 o.p. (*0-8122-7784-8*); pap. 24.95 o.p. (*0-8122-1110-3*) Univ. of Pennsylvania Pr.

—Sister Carrie. unabr. ed. 1997. 297p. reprint ed. pap. 14.95 o.p. (*1-57002-041-8*) University Publishing Hse., Inc.

—Sister Carrie. 1994. (Twentieth Century Classics Ser.). 496p. 12.95 (*0-14-018828-2*, Penguin Classics) Viking Penguin.

—Sister Carrie. Berkey, John C. et al, eds. 1981. (American Library). 528p. pap. 8.95 o.p. (*0-14-039002-2*, Penguin Classics) Viking Penguin.

—Sister Carrie: An Authoritative Text, Backgrounds & Sources Criticism. 1970. (Critical Editions Ser.). (Illus.). x, 591p. (*0-393-04325-8*) Norton, W. W. & Co., Inc.

—Sister Carrie, Jennie Gerhardt, Twelve Men. Lehan, Richard, ed. 1987. (Library of America). 1168p. 40.00 (*0-940450-41-0*) Library of America, The.

Dressler, Mylene. The Deadwood Beetle. 2002. 256p. pap. 13.00 (*0-425-18760-8*) Berkley Publishing Group.

—The Deadwood Beetle. 2001. 208p. 23.95 o.p. (*0-399-14805-1*, BlueHen Bks.) Putnam Publishing Group, The.

—The Deadwood Beetle. l.t. ed. 2001. 289p. 28.95 (*0-7838-9665-4*) Thorndike Pr.

Ducker, Bruce. Lead Us Not into Penn Station. 1994. 224p. 24.00 (*1-877946-36-2*) Permanent Pr., The.

—Lead Us Not into Penn Station. 1994. 172p. per. 15.95 (*0-7592-4164-3*) ereads.com.

Ducovny, Amram. Coney. 2000. 320p. 26.95 (*1-58567-067-7*) Overlook Pr., The.

Duffy, James. Dog Bites Man: City Shocked. 2001. 304p. 24.00 (*0-7432-1082-4*, Simon & Schuster) Simon & Schuster.

Dunaj, Gregory. Hi, How Are You? 2000. 300p. pap. 22.99 (*0-7388-2182-9*); text 32.99 (*0-7388-2181-0*) Xlibris Corp.

Dunbar, Paul Laurence. The Sport of the Gods. 1991. (American Negro). 262p. (C). reprint ed. pap. 27.95 (*0-88143-136-2*) Ayer Co. Pubs., Inc.

—The Sport of the Gods. 1999. (Signet Classics). 176p. mass mkt. 5.95 (*0-451-52755-0*) NAL.

—The Sport of the Gods. 1992. (Notable American Authors Ser.). reprint ed. lib. bdg. 75.00 (*0-7812-2714-3*) Reprint Services Corp.

Dunker, Marilee. Walker's Point. 1997. (Portraits Ser.). 272p. pap. 8.99 o.p. (*1-55661-997-9*) Bethany Hse. Pubs.

—Walker's Point. l.t. ed. 2001. (Thorndike Press Large Print Christian Romance Ser.). 490p. 25.95 (*0-7862-3659-0*) Thorndike Pr.

Dunn, Carol. The Case of the Murdered Muckaker. 2002. 256p. 23.95 (*0-312-27284-7*, Saint Martin's Minotaur) St. Martin's Pr.

Dunne, Dominick. Dominick Dunne: Three Complete Novels: The Two Mrs. Grenvilles, People Like Us & An Inconvenient Woman. 1994. 896p. 13.99 o.s.i (0-517-11916-1) Random Hse. Value Publishing.
—People Like Us. l.t. ed. 1989. (General Ser.). 602p. 21.95 o.p. (0-8161-4727-2); 13.95 o.p. (0-8161-4806-6) Gale Group. (Macmillan Reference USA).
—The Two Mrs. Grenvilles. 1985. 384p. 4.99 o.p. (0-517-55713-4, Crown) Crown Publishing Group.
—The Two Mrs. Grenvilles. l.t. ed. 1986. (Special Editions Ser.). 552p. 18.95 o.p. (0-8161-4059-6, Macmillan Reference USA) Gale Group.
Dupont, Inge & Mayo, Hope, eds. Morgan Library Ghost Stories. 1990. (Illus.). 108p. 27.50 (0-8232-1283-1) Fordham Univ. Pr.
Dupont, Inge, et al. Morgan Library Ghost Stories. 1990. E-Book 24.95 (0-585-12082-X) netLibrary, Inc.
Duvan, Alexander. Planet New York. 2000. 183p. E-Book 8.00 (0-7388-7790-5) Xlibris Corp.
Early, Jack, pseud. Donato & Daughter. 1987. 320p. 15.95 o.p. (0-553-05208-X) Bantam Bks.
—Donato & Daughter. 1988. 352p. 18.95 o.p. (0-525-24625-8, Dutton) Dutton/Plume.
—Donato & Daughter. 1989. mass mkt. 4.95 o.p. (0-451-40122-0, Onyx) NAL.
Eberhart, Mignon G. Melora. l.t. ed. 2000. (Romance Ser.). 330p. 27.95 (0-7838-9150-4) Thorndike Pr.
—R.S.V.P. Murder. l.t. ed. 2001. (Romance Ser.). 364p. 27.95 o.p. (0-7862-3516-0) Thorndike Pr.
Eberstadt, Fernanda. The Furies: A Novel. 2003. 464p. 26.00 (0-375-41256-5) Knopf, Alfred A. Inc.
Edgerton, Dale. Goneaway Road. 2003. 320p. pap. 17.95 (1-56023-434-2); 39.95 (1-56023-433-4) Haworth Pr., Inc., The. (Southern Tier Editions).
Edghill, Rosemary. Bell, Book & Murder. 3rd ed. 1998. (Bast Novels). 448p. pap. 17.95 (0-312-86768-9, CPB1211, Forge Bks.) Doherty, Tom Assocs., LLC.
—Book of Moons. 1996. mass mkt. 5.99 (0-8125-3439-5, Tor Bks.); 1995. 224p. 20.95 o.p. (0-312-85605-9, Forge Bks.) Doherty, Tom Assocs., LLC.
—Bowl of Night. 1997. mass mkt. 5.99 (0-8125-3440-9, Tor Bks.) Doherty, Tom Assocs., LLC.
—Speak Daggers to Her. 1995. 222p. mass mkt. 5.99 (0-8125-3438-7, Tor Bks.); 1994. 224p. 19.95 o.p. (0-312-85604-0, Forge Bks.) Doherty, Tom Assocs., LLC.
Edmonds, Walter D. Mostly Canallers. 1987. (New York Classics Ser.). 470p. reprint ed. pap. text 16.95 (0-8156-0214-6) Syracuse Univ. Pr.
Edwards, Grace F. Do or Die: A Mali Anderson Mystery. 2000. (Mali Anderson Mystery Ser.). 272p. 22.95 o.s.i (0-385-49248-0) Doubleday Publishing.
—If I Should Die. 1998. (Mali Anderson Mystery Ser.). 320p. reprint ed. mass mkt. 6.50 (0-553-57631-3) Bantam Bks.
—If I Should Die. 1997. 272p. 21.95 o.s.i (0-385-48523-9) Doubleday Publishing.
—No Time to Die. 2000. (Mali Anderson Mystery Ser.). 240p. mass mkt. 5.99 (0-553-57956-8) Bantam Bks.
—No Time to Die. 1999. 272p. 22.95 o.s.i (0-385-49247-2) Doubleday Publishing.
—A Toast Before Dying. 1999. 304p. mass mkt. 5.99 (0-553-57953-3) Bantam Bks.
Edwards-Yearwood, Grace. In the Shadow of the Peacock. 1988. 288p. text 17.95 o.p. (0-07-019037-2) McGraw-Hill Cos., The.
Egan, Jennifer. Look at Me: A Novel. 2001. 432p. 24.95 (0-385-50276-1, Talese, Nan A.) Doubleday Publishing.
—Look at Me: A Novel. 2002. 432p. pap. 14.00 (0-385-72135-8, Anchor) Knopf Publishing Group.
Eichler, Selma. Murder Can Kill Your Social Life. 1994. (Desiree Shapiro Mystery Ser.). 256p. mass mkt. 5.99 (0-451-18139-5, Signet Bks.) NAL.
—Murder Can Kill Your Social Life. l.t. ed. 2001. 388p. 28.95 (0-7862-3473-3) Thorndike Pr.
—Murder Can Rain on Your Shower. 2003. 272p. mass mkt. 5.99 (0-451-20823-4) NAL.
—Murder Can Rain on Your Shower: A Desiree Shapiro Mystery. l.t. ed. 2003. (Mystery Ser.). 28.95 (0-7862-5566-8) Thorndike Pr.
—Murder Can Ruin Your Looks. 1995. (Desiree Shapiro Mystery Ser.: 2). 272p. (Orig.). mass mkt. 5.99 (0-451-18384-3, Signet Bks.) NAL.
—Murder Can Singe Your Old Flame. 1999. (Desiree Shapiro Mystery Ser.). 256p. mass mkt. 5.99 (0-451-19218-4, Signet Bks.) NAL.
—Murder Can Singe Your Old Flame: A Desiree Shapiro Mystery. l.t. ed. 2001. (Thorndike Mystery Ser.). 397p. 28.95 o.p. (0-7862-3191-2) Thorndike Pr.
—Murder Can Spoil Your Appetite. 2000. (Desiree Shapiro Mystery Ser.). 272p. mass mkt. 5.99 (0-451-19958-8, Signet Bks.) NAL.
—Murder Can Spook Your Cat: A Desiree Shapiro Mystery. 1998. (Desiree Shapiro Mystery Ser.). 272p. mass mkt. 5.99 (0-451-19217-6, Signet Bks.) NAL.
—Murder Can Stunt Your Growth. 1996. (Desiree Shapiro Mystery Ser.). 272p. mass mkt. 5.99 (0-451-18514-5, Signet Bks.) NAL.
—Murder Can Wreck a Reunion. 1997. (Desiree Shapiro Mystery Ser.). 272p. mass mkt. 5.99 (0-451-18521-8, Signet Bks.) NAL.
Eidus, Janice. Urban Bliss. 1998. 180p. reprint ed. pap. 9.95 (0-87286-339-5) City Lights Bks.
Eight Mystery Writers. Murder in Manhattan. l.t. ed. 1988. (General Ser.). 360p. 17.95 o.p. (0-8161-4345-5, Macmillan Reference USA) Gale Group.
Eisenberg, Nora. The War at Home. 2002. 217p. pap. 14.95 (0-9679520-4-2) Leapfrog Pr.
Eisner, William. Dropsie Avenue: The Neighborhood. 2000. (Illus.). 176p. pap. 14.95 (1-56389-689-3, Vertigo) DC Comics.
—Dropsie Avenue: The Neighborhood. 1995. 24.95 (0-87816-349-2); pap. 15.95 (0-87816-348-4); 39.95 (0-87816-350-6) Kitchen Sink Pr., Inc.
Elliott, James. Nowhere to Hide. 1998. 400p. mass mkt. 5.99 o.s.i (0-7860-0538-6, Pinnacle Bks.) Kensington Publishing Corp.
—Nowhere to Hide. 1997. 272p. 23.00 (0-684-82362-4, Simon & Schuster) Simon & Schuster.
Ellis, Bret Easton. American Psycho. 1991. (Vintage Contemporaries Ser.). 416p. pap. 14.00 (0-679-73577-1, Vintage) Knopf Publishing Group.
—American Psycho. 1991. 400p. 19.95 (0-671-66397-6, Simon & Schuster) Simon & Schuster.
—Glamorama. 2000. (Vintage Contemporaries Ser.). 560p. pap. 14.95 (0-375-70384-5, Vintage) Knopf Publishing Group.
—Glamorama. abr. ed. 2001. audio (0-333-78165-1) Macmillan U.K. GBR. *Dist:* Macmillan Publishing Co., Inc.
Ellis, Julie. Commitment. 1994. 608p. mass mkt. 5.99 o.s.i (0-8217-4681-2); mass mkt. 18.95 o.p. (0-8217-4422-4, Zebra Bks.) Kensington Publishing Corp.
—Trespassing Hearts. 1992. 384p. 21.95 o.s.i (0-399-13738-6, G. P. Putnam's Sons) Penguin Group (USA) Inc.
Ellison, James W. Finding Forrester: A Novel. 2004. 192p. pap. 9.95 (1-55704-479-1) Newmarket Pr.
Elman, Richard. Tar Beach. 1991. (New American Fiction Ser.: No. 23). 280p. (Orig.). pap. 12.95 o.p. (1-55713-117-1) Sun & Moon Pr.
Elward, James. Monday's Child Is Dead. 1995. 240p. 19.00 o.p. (0-7867-0130-7, Carroll & Graf Pubs.) Avalon Publishing Group.
Ely, Stanley E. Perfect Mondays. E-Book 9.95 (1-891305-87-5); 2002. 271p. pap. 15.95 (1-891305-62-X) Painted Leaf Pr.
Engelhardt, Tom. The Last Days of Publishing: A Novel. 2003. 224p. 24.95 (1-55849-402-2) Univ. of Massachusetts Pr.
Ephron, Amy. A Cup of Tea: A Novel of 1917. 1997. 224p. 20.00 (0-688-14997-9, Morrow, William & Co.) Morrow/Avon.
—White Rose: Una Rosa Blanca. 2000. 288p. pap. 12.00 (0-345-44110-9, Ballantine Bks.) Ballantine Bks.
—White Rose: Una Rosa Blanca. 1999. 259p. 23.00 (0-688-16314-9, Morrow, William & Co.) Morrow/Avon.
Epstein, Leslie. Ice Fire Water. 2000. (Leib Goldkorn Cocktail Ser.). 272p. reprint ed. pap. 13.95 (0-393-32090-1) Norton, W. W. & Co., Inc.
—Ice Fire Water: A Leib Goldkorn Cocktail. 1999. 288p. text 23.95 (0-393-04804-7) Norton, W. W. & Co., Inc.
Epstein, Seymour. A Special Destiny. 1986. 329p. 17.95 o.p. (0-917657-84-5) Fine, Donald I. Bks.
Ermelino, Louisa. The Black Madonna: A Novel. 2002. 272p. pap. 15.00 (0-7582-0190-7) Kensington Publishing Corp.
—The Black Madonna: A Novel. 2001. 256p. 23.00 (0-684-87166-1, Simon & Schuster) Simon & Schuster.
Espinosa, Maria. Dark Plums. 1995. 220p. pap. 9.95 o.p. (1-55885-128-3) Arte Publico Pr.
Estep, Maggie. Gargantuan: A Ruby Murphy Mystery. 2004. 240p. pap. 12.95 (0-609-61033-3, Three Rivers Pr.) Crown Publishing Group.
—Hex: A Ruby Murphy Mystery. 2003. 320p. pap. 14.00 (1-4000-4837-0, Three Rivers Pr.) Crown Publishing Group.
Evans, Lawrence W. Newer York. 1991. (Battletech Ser.). 384p. mass mkt. 4.50 o.p. (0-451-45045-0, ROC) NAL.
Everson, Eva Marie & Chadwick, G. W. Francis. Summon the Shadows. 2002. (Sequel to Shadow of Dreams Ser.). (Illus.). 256p. pap. 10.99 (1-58660-490-2, Promise Pr.) Barbour Publishing, Inc.
Fairey, Wendy W. Full House: A Novel. 2003. 22.50 (0-87074-483-6) Southern Methodist Univ. Pr.
Fairstein, Linda. The Bone Vault: A Novel. 2004. 528p. mass mkt. 7.99 (0-7434-3667-9, Pocket Star); 2003. 400p. 25.00 (0-7432-2354-3, Scribner); 2003. mass mkt. (0-7434-6273-4, Pocket Star); 2003. 592p. 27.00 (0-7432-4091-X, Scribner) Simon & Schuster.
—Cold Hit. l.t. ed. 2000. (Wheeler Large Print Book Ser.). 469p. 27.95 (1-56895-816-1, Wheeler Publishing, Inc.) Gale Group.
—Cold Hit. (Alexandra Cooper Mysteries Ser.). 2003. (Illus.). 464p. pap. 7.99 (0-671-01955-4, Pocket); 2002. 416p. E-Book (0-7432-3006-X, Scribner); 1999. 416p. 25.00 o.s.i (0-684-84846-5, Scribner); 2000. 416p. reprint ed. 7.99 (0-671-04212-2, Pocket) Simon & Schuster.
—Cold Hit. abr. ed. 1999. (Alexandra Cooper Ser.). audio 24.00 (0-671-04550-4, Simon & Schuster Audioworks) Simon & Schuster Audio.
—The Dead-House. 2001. E-Book 25.00 (1-59061-256-6) Adobe Systems, Inc.
—The Dead-House. 2003. 528p. mass mkt. 7.99 (0-671-01954-6, Pocket); 2001. (Illus.). 416p. 25.00 (0-684-84904-6, Scribner); 2001. 416p. E-Book 25.00 (0-7432-3007-8, Scribner); 2001. 560p. 25.00 (0-7432-2403-5, Scribner) Simon & Schuster.
—The Dead-House. abr. ed. 2001. audio 26.00 (0-7435-0902-1); audio compact disk 30.00 (0-7435-0903-X) Simon & Schuster Audio. (Simon & Schuster Audioworks).
—Final Jeopardy. unabr. ed. 1998. audio 64.00 (0-7366-4203-X, 4699) Books on Tape, Inc.
—Final Jeopardy. 1998. 336p. mass mkt. 3.99 (0-671-02487-6, Pocket); 1997. (Illus.). 336p. pap. 7.99 (0-671-01012-3, Pocket); 1996. 23.00 o.p. (0-684-00314-7, Scribner); 1996. 400p. 22.50 o.p. (0-684-81489-7, Scribner) Simon & Schuster.
—The Kills. 2004. 400p. 25.00 (0-7432-2355-1); 2003. 624p. 25.00 (0-7432-5380-9) Simon & Schuster. (Scribner).
—Likely to Die. (Alexandra Cooper Mysteries Ser.). 1998. (Illus.). 448p. mass mkt. 7.99 (0-671-01493-5, Pocket); 1997. 400p. 24.00 (0-684-81488-9, Scribner) Simon & Schuster.
Farell, Anne. Deadly Deception. 1992. 256p. 19.00 o.s.i (0-671-75339-8, Simon & Schuster) Simon & Schuster.
Farrell, Gillian B. Alibi for an Actress. Chelius, Jane, ed. 256p. 1992. 19.00 (0-671-75707-5, Atria); 1993. reprint ed. mass mkt. 5.50 (0-671-75708-3, Pocket) Simon & Schuster.
—Murder & a Muse. 1995. 288p. mass mkt. 5.99 (0-671-75711-3, Pocket); 1994. 256p. 20.00 (0-671-75710-5, Atria) Simon & Schuster.
Farrell, Maud. Skid: A Violet Childes Murder Mystery. 1989. 224p. 16.95 o.p. (0-525-24767-X, Dutton) Dutton/Plume.
Farren, Mick. Time of Feasting. 384p. 1996. 23.95 (0-312-86213-X); Vol. 1. 1998. (Time of Feasting Ser.: Vol. 1). mass mkt. 6.99 (0-8125-3874-9) Doherty, Tom Assocs., LLC. (Tor Bks.).
Farris, John. Soon She Will Be Gone. 1998. 387p. mass mkt. 6.99 (0-8125-0954-4); 1997. 352p. 24.95 (0-312-85375-0) Doherty, Tom Assocs., LLC. (Forge Bks.).
Fast, Howard. Redemption. 2001. 240p. mass mkt. 6.99 o.s.i (0-425-18027-1) Berkley Publishing Group.
—Redemption. 1999. 288p. 24.00 o.s.i (0-15-100455-2) Harcourt Trade Pubs.
Faulks, Sebastian. On Green Dolphin Street: A Novel. 2003. 368p. pap. 14.00 (0-375-70456-6, Vintage) Knopf Publishing Group.
—On Green Dolphin Street: A Novel. 2002. 368p. 24.95 (0-375-50225-4) Random Hse., Inc.
Faust, Irvin. Jim Dandy. 1994. 304p. 21.00 o.p. (0-7867-0062-9, Carroll & Graf Pubs.) Avalon Publishing Group.
Federman, Raymond. Smiles on Washington Square. 1985. 154p. 13.95 o.p. (0-938410-29-6, Thunder's Mouth Pr.) Avalon Publishing Group.
Feldman, Ellen. Rearview Mirror. 1996. 384p. mass mkt. 5.99 o.s.i (0-440-21516-1) Dell Publishing.
Ferrenz, Barbara J. Worse Than Death. 2003. 250p. 25.95 (0-7862-5395-9, Five Star) Gale Group.
Ferriss, Lucy. Against Gravity: A Novel. 1996. 304p. 22.00 (0-684-80091-8, Simon & Schuster) Simon & Schuster.
Fields, Jennie. Crossing Brooklyn Ferry: A Novel. 2002. 384p. pap. 12.95 (0-06-009943-7, Perennial) HarperTrade.
—Crossing Brooklyn Ferry: A Novel. 1998. mass mkt. 6.99 (0-380-73168-1, Avon Bks.); 1997. 288p. 23.00 (0-688-14589-2, Morrow, William & Co.) Morrow/Avon.
—Crossing Brooklyn Ferry: A Novel. l.t. ed. 1998. (Charnwood Large Print Ser.). 512p. 29.99 o.p. (0-7089-9004-5, Ulverscroft) Thorpe, F. A. Pubs. GBR. *Dist:* Ulverscroft Large Print Bks., Ltd., Ulverscroft Large Print Canada, Ltd.
Files, Lolita. Getting to the Good Part. 2000. 352p. pap. 13.95 (0-446-67548-2); 1999. 334p. 24.00 (0-446-52420-4) Warner Bks., Inc.
Filipacchi, Amanda. Vapor. 1999. 320p. 22.95 (0-7867-0617-1, Carroll & Graf Pubs.) Avalon Publishing Group.
—Vapor: A Novel. 2003. 320p. pap. 14.00 (0-7867-1129-9, Carroll & Graf Pubs.) Avalon Publishing Group.
Finder, Joseph. The Zero Hour. abr. ed. 1996. audio 16.95 o.p. (1-56100-888-5, 1119, Nova Audio Bks.); 1996. audio 25.95 o.p. (1-56100-687-4, 326, Bookcassette); 1996. audio 89.25 o.p. (1-56100-312-3, 1118, Unabridged Library Editions); Set. 1997. audio 7.99 o.p. (1-56740-165-1, 721, Nova Audio Bks.) Brilliance Audio.
—The Zero Hour. l.t. ed. 1996. (G. K. Hall Core Ser.). 630p. lib. bdg. 25.95 (0-7838-1825-4, Macmillan Reference USA) Gale Group.
—The Zero Hour. 1997. pap. 6.99 (0-380-72665-3, Avon Bks.); 1996. 432p. 25.00 o.p. (0-688-14450-0, Morrow, William & Co.) Morrow/Avon.
Finney, Jack. From Time to Time: The Sequel to Time & Again. l.t. ed. 1995. (G. K. Hall Core Ser.). 610p. 25.95 o.p. (0-7838-1387-2, Macmillan Reference USA) Gale Group.
—From Time to Time: The Sequel to Time & Again. unabr. ed. 1995. audio 70.00 (0-7887-0338-2, 94530E7) Recorded Bks., LLC.
—From Time to Time: The Sequel to Time & Again. 1996. (Illus.). 304p. pap. 12.00 (0-684-81844-2, Touchstone); 1995. 288p. 22.50 o.p. (0-671-89884-1, Simon & Schuster) Simon & Schuster.
—From Time to Time: The Sequel to Time & Again. abr. ed. 1995. audio 23.00 (0-671-52118-7, 492039, Simon & Schuster Audioworks) Simon & Schuster Audio.
—Time & Again. 1995. reprint ed. lib. bdg. 25.95 (0-89968-403-3, Lightyear Pr.) Buccaneer Bks., Inc.
—Time & Again. l.t. ed. 1995. 512p. 25.95 o.p. (0-7838-1386-4, Macmillan Reference USA) Gale Group.
—Time & Again. unabr. ed. 1996. audio 97.00 (0-7887-0344-7, 94536E7) Recorded Bks., LLC.
—Time & Again. 1995. 25.00 (0-684-80117-5, Simon & Schuster); 1995. (Illus.). 400p. pap. 13.00 (0-684-80105-1, Touchstone); 1986. 400p. pap. 10.95 o.s.i (0-671-24295-4, Fireside) Simon & Schuster.
—Time & Again. abr. ed. 1995. audio 23.00 o.s.i (0-671-52139-X, 492983, Simon & Schuster Audioworks) Simon & Schuster Audio.
—Time & Again: Broadway Edition. 1997. pap. 11.00 (0-684-83594-0, Scribner Paper Fiction) Simon & Schuster.
Fisch, Sholly. Gen 13:3: Version 2.0. 2002. (Ace Science Fiction Ser.). (Illus.). 240p. mass mkt. 5.99 o.s.i (0-441-00946-8) Ace Bks.
Fisher, Mark. The Millionaire's Secrets: Life Lessons in Wisdom & Wealth. 1996. 240p. 18.95 (0-684-80281-3, Simon & Schuster) Simon & Schuster.
Fisher, Rudolph. The Conjure-Man Dies. 320p. reprint ed. 9.00 (0-405-02800-8) Ayer Co. Pubs., Inc.
Fitzgerald, F. Scott. The Beautiful & Damned. 2002. (Dover Thrift Editions Ser.). 288p. pap. 3.00 (0-486-42132-5) Dover Pubns., Inc.
—The Beautiful & Damned. 2003. E-Book 9.99 (0-7432-4730-2, Scribner) Simon & Schuster.
Fitzhugh, Bill. Pest Control. 1997. 304p. mass mkt. 20.00 o.p. (0-380-97348-0, Avon Bks.) Morrow/Avon.
Fleming, Ian. Live & Let Die. mass mkt. 3.50 o.s.i (0-425-08163-X); 1985. mass mkt. 3.50 o.s.i (0-425-08759-X); 1983. mass mkt. 2.95 o.s.i (0-425-06398-4); 1982. mass mkt. 2.75 o.s.i (0-425-05369-5) Berkley Publishing Group.
—Live & Let Die. (James Bond Ser.). mass mkt. 0.50 o.p. (0-451-02051-0); mass mkt. 0.60 o.p. (0-451-02730-2); mass mkt. 0.35 o.p. (0-451-01723-4) NAL. (Signet Bks.).
—Live & Let Die. 2003. 240p. pap. 13.00 (0-14-200323-9) Penguin Group (USA) Inc.
Fletcher, Jessica & Bain, Donald. Manhattans & Murder. 1994. (Murder She Wrote Ser.: Vol. 1). 304p. mass mkt. 6.50 (0-451-18142-5, Signet Bks.) NAL.
—Manhattans & Murder. abr. ed. 1994. (Murder She Wrote Ser.). pap. 16.00 o.p. incl. audio (0-453-00901-8) Penguin/HighBridge.
Foglia, Leonard & Richards, David. Face down in the Park. 1999. 320p. 23.00 (0-671-02728-X, Atria) Simon & Schuster.
Foley, Rae. Sleep Without Morning. l.t. ed. 1997. 21.95 (0-7838-8051-0, Macmillan Reference USA) Gale Group.
—Trust a Woman? l.t. ed. 2000. (Romance Ser.). 315p. 25.95 (0-7862-2867-9); (0-7540-4317-7); (0-7540-4318-5) Thorndike Pr.
Ford, Jeffrey. The Portrait of Mrs. Charbuque. 2003. 320p. pap. 12.95 (0-06-093617-7, Perennial) HarperTrade.
—The Portrait of Mrs. Charbuque. 2002. 320p. 24.95 (0-06-621126-3, Morrow, William & Co.) Morrow/Avon.
Forsyth, Frederick. The Phantom of Manhattan. 2000. 320p. mass mkt. 6.50 (0-312-97585-6, St. Martin's Paperbacks); 1999. 192p. 19.95 o.p. (0-312-24656-0) St. Martin's Pr.

—The Phantom of Manhattan. l.t. ed. (Paperback Bestsellers Ser.). 232p. 2001. 28.95 (0-7862-2203-4); 2000. (0-7540-1395-2); 2000. (0-7540-2297-8); 2000. (Illus.). 30.95 (0-7862-2202-6) Thorndike Pr.

Foster, Ken. The Kind I'm Likely to Get: A Collection. 1999. 208p. pap. 12.00 (0-688-16980-5, Quill) HarperTrade.

Fowler, Nick. A Thing (or Two) about Curtis & Camilla. 2003. 416p. reprint ed. pap. 14.00 (0-375-71323-9, Vintage) Knopf Publishing Group.

Fox, John. The Boys on the Rock. 1985. pap. 6.95 o.p. (0-452-25753-0, Plume) Dutton/Plume.

—The Boys on the Rock. 160p. 1994. pap. 11.95 (0-312-10433-2, Saint Martin's Griffin); 1984. 11.95 o.p. (0-312-09419-1) St. Martin's Pr.

Fox, Paula. Desperate Characters. 1980. 176p. reprint ed. pap. 9.95 o.p. (0-87923-309-5) Godine, David R. Pub.

—Desperate Characters. 1999. 176p. pap. 12.95 (0-393-31894-X) Norton, W. W. & Co., Inc.

—Poor George: A Novel. 2001. 230p. pap. 13.00 (0-393-32151-2, Norton Paperbacks) Norton, W. W. & Co., Inc.

—The Widow's Children. 1999. 224p. pap. 13.00 (0-393-31963-6) Norton, W. W. & Co., Inc.

Frank, Lucy. The Annoyance Bureau. 2002. 176p. (J). (gr. 4-6). 16.95 (0-689-84903-6, Atheneum/Richard Jackson Bks.) Simon & Schuster Children's Publishing.

Frankel, Valerie. A Body to Die For. 1995. 240p. mass mkt. 5.50 (0-671-79520-1, Pocket) Simon & Schuster.

—A Deadline for Murder. Wells, Leslie, ed. 1991. 304p. (Orig.). bds. 3.95 (0-671-73021-5, Pocket) Simon & Schuster.

—Murder on Wheels. Isaacson, Dana, ed. 1992. 224p. (Orig.). mass mkt. 4.50 (0-671-73195-5, Pocket) Simon & Schuster.

—Prime Time for Murder. 1994. 256p. mass mkt. 4.99 (0-671-79519-8, Pocket) Simon & Schuster.

Freeman, Cynthia. Come Pour the Wine. l.t. ed. 1983. 15.95 o.p. (0-8161-3201-1); 1981. 624p. pap. 10.95 o.p. (0-8161-3280-1) Gale Group. (Macmillan Reference USA).

—Come Pour the Wine. 1980. 12.95 o.p. (0-87795-276-0, Morrow, William & Co.) Morrow/Avon.

Freemantle, Brian. The Watchmen. 432p. (0-7278-5915-3) Severn Hse. Pubs., Ltd.

—The Watchmen. 2002. 448p. 25.95 (0-312-24274-3) St. Martin's Pr.

Frey, Stephen. Inner Sanctum. 1997. 336p. 23.95 o.p. (0-525-94206-8) Dutton/Plume.

—Inner Sanctum. 1998. 448p. mass mkt. 7.99 (0-451-19014-9, Signet Bks.) NAL.

—The Inner Sanctum. l.t. ed. 1998. (Large Print Book Ser.). pap. 24.95 (1-56895-533-2, Wheeler Publishing, Inc.) Gale Group.

—The Insider. 2000. 384p. mass mkt. 6.99 (0-345-42828-5, Ballantine Bks.) Ballantine Bks.

—The Insider. unabr. ed. 2000. audio 60.00 (0-7887-4047-4, 96156E7) Recorded Bks., LLC.

—The Insider. l.t. ed. 2000. (Mystery Ser.). 493p. 29.95 (0-7862-2320-0) Thorndike Pr.

—The Vulture Fund. 1996. 384p. 23.95 o.s.i (0-525-93986-5, Dutton) Dutton/Plume.

—The Vulture Fund. l.t. ed. 1996. 26.95 (1-56895-390-9, Wheeler Publishing, Inc.) Gale Group.

—The Vulture Fund. 1997. 416p. mass mkt. 7.99 (0-451-18473-3, Onyx) NAL.

—The Vulture Fund. 1998. 4.98 o.p. (0-7651-0895-X) Smithmark Pubs., Inc.

Freydberg, Margaret H. The Consequences of Loving Syra. 1990. 264p. 18.95 o.p. (0-88150-168-9) Countryman Pr.

Friedman, Bruce Jay. Violencia! A Musical Novel. 2002. 224p. pap. 13.00 (0-8021-3875-6, Grove Pr.) Grove/Atlantic, Inc.

Friedman, Kinky. Blast from the Past. abr. ed. 2002. audio 17.95 (1-56511-593-7) HighBridge Co.

—Blast from the Past. 1999. 256p. pap. 15.00 (0-345-41630-9) Random Hse., Inc.

—Blast from the Past. 1998. 256p. 23.00 (0-684-80379-8, Simon & Schuster) Simon & Schuster.

—Blast from the Past. abr. ed. 1998. audio 17.95 (1-55935-285-5, 282-5BK) Soundelux Audio Publishing.

—A Case of Lone Star. 1988. mass mkt. 3.95 o.p. (0-425-11187-7) Berkley Publishing Group.

—A Case of Lone Star. 1987. 204p. 14.95 o.p. (0-688-06410-8, Morrow, William & Co.) Morrow/Avon.

—Elvis, Jesus & Coca Cola. 1994. 272p. mass mkt. 6.99 (0-553-56891-4) Bantam Bks.

—Elvis, Jesus & Coca Cola. 1993. 304p. 20.00 o.p. (0-671-86921-1, Simon & Schuster) Simon & Schuster.

—Frequent Flyer. 1990. mass mkt. 6.50 o.s.i (0-425-12345-6) Berkley Publishing Group.

—Frequent Flyer. 1989. 204p. 16.95 o.p. (0-688-08166-5, Morrow, William & Co.) Morrow/Avon.

—God Bless John Wayne. 1996. 256p. mass mkt. 6.99 (0-553-57632-X) Bantam Bks.

—God Bless John Wayne. 1995. 253p. 22.00 o.p. (0-684-81051-4, Simon & Schuster) Simon & Schuster.

—Greenwich Killing Time: A Thrilling Murder Mystery. 1987. 240p. mass mkt. 3.95 o.p. (0-425-10497-4) Berkley Publishing Group.

—Greenwich Killing Time: A Thrilling Murder Mystery. 1986. 13.95 o.p. (0-688-06409-4, Morrow, William & Co.) Morrow/Avon.

—Kinky Friedman Mysteries: Greenwich Killing Time - A Case of Lone Star - When the Cat's Away. 1993. 13.99 o.s.i (0-517-09328-6) Random Hse. Value Publishing.

—The Kinky Friedman Crime Club: A Case of Lone Star; Greenwich Killing Time; When the Cat's Away. 1993. 480p. 22.95 o.s.i (0-571-16696-2) Faber & Faber, Inc.

—The Love Song of J. Edgar Hoover. abr. ed. 1996. audio 16.95 (1-55927-412-3) Audio Renaissance.

—The Love Song of J. Edgar Hoover. 1998. mass mkt. o.p. (0-345-41510-8); 1997. 240p. pap. 12.95 (0-345-41509-4) Ballantine Bks.

—The Love Song of J. Edgar Hoover. l.t. ed. 1996. pap. 23.95 (1-56895-394-1, Wheeler Publishing, Inc.) Gale Group.

—The Love Song of J. Edgar Hoover. 1996. 23.00 (0-684-80377-1, Simon & Schuster) Simon & Schuster.

—Musical Chairs. 1991. 288p. 18.95 o.p. (0-688-09148-2, Morrow, William & Co.) Morrow/Avon.

—Musical Chairs. 1993. 3.99 o.p. (0-517-10872-0) Random Hse. Value Publishing.

—Roadkill. abr. ed. 1997. audio 16.95 o.p. (1-55927-456-5) Audio Renaissance.

—Roadkill. 1998. 256p. pap. 12.95 (0-345-41632-5) Ballantine Bks.

—Roadkill. unabr. ed. 1998. audio 32.00 (0-7366-4130-0, 4633) Books on Tape, Inc.

—Roadkill. 1997. 256p. 23.00 o.p. (0-684-80378-X, Simon & Schuster) Simon & Schuster.

—Spanking Watson. 224p. 2000. pap. 12.95 (0-671-04742-6, Pocket); 1999. 23.00 o.s.i (0-684-85061-3, Simon & Schuster); 1999. 23.00 (0-684-86531-9, Simon & Schuster) Simon & Schuster.

—When the Cat's Away. 1989. mass mkt. 3.95 o.p. (0-425-11830-4) Berkley Publishing Group.

—When the Cat's Away. 1988. 224p. 16.95 o.p. (0-688-07555-X, Morrow, William & Co.) Morrow/Avon.

—When the Cat's Away. 1991. 3.99 o.p. (0-517-07564-4) Random Hse. Value Publishing.

Friedman, Philip. Inadmissible Evidence. 1993. 640p. mass mkt. 7.99 (0-8041-0852-8, Ivy Bks.) Ballantine Bks.

—Inadmissible Evidence. unabr. ed. 1993. Pt. 1. audio 64.00; Pt. 2. audio 64.00 Books on Tape, Inc.

—Inadmissible Evidence. 1992. 480p. 23.00 o.p. (1-55611-330-7) Fine, Donald I. Bks.

—Inadmissible Evidence. abr. ed. 1993. audio 25.00 (0-671-86568-4, Simon & Schuster Audioworks) Simon & Schuster Audio.

Frolov, Andrei. The Stories of a Taxi Driver. 1994. 10.95 o.p. (0-533-10747-4) Vantage Pr., Inc.

Fubler, Anson. Genuine Love - The Conspiracy: Bermuda - New York Connection. 1996. 264p. 18.95 o.p. (0-944957-56-0) Rivercross Publishing, Inc.

Fulton, Eileen. Soap Opera. 1999. 320p. 23.95 o.p. (0-312-20365-9) St. Martin's Pr.

Furman, Laura. Tuxedo Park. 1986. 352p. 17.45 o.p. (0-671-49754-5) Summit Bks.

Fusilli, Jim. Closing Time. 2002. 320p. reprint ed. mass mkt. 6.50 (0-425-18712-8) Berkley Publishing Group.

—Closing Time. 2001. 320p. 23.95 o.s.i (0-399-14793-4) Penguin Group (USA) Inc.

—Tribeca Blues. 2003. 288p. 24.95 (0-399-15088-9) Putnam Publishing Group, The.

—A Well-Known Secret. 2003. 320p. mass mkt. 6.99 (0-425-19280-6, Prime Crime) Berkley Publishing Group.

—A Well-Known Secret. 2002. 304p. 23.95 (0-399-14931-7, Putnam & Grosset) Putnam Publishing Group, The.

Gadol, Peter. The Mystery Roast. 1996. 320p. pap. 13.00 o.s.i (0-312-15176-4) Picador.

Gage, Elizabeth. The Hourglass. 1999. 304p. mass mkt. (1-55166-546-8, 1-66546-2); 240p. pap. (1-55166-503-4, 1-66503-3) Harlequin Enterprises, Ltd. (Mira Bks.).

Gale Group Staff, contrib. by. Don't Lie to Me. l.t. ed. 2001. (Five Star Mystery Ser.). 200p. 24.95 (0-7862-3011-8) Thorndike Pr.

Galloway, Steven. Ascension: A Novel. 2003. 280p. 23.00 (0-7867-1208-2, Carroll & Graf Pubs.) Avalon Publishing Group.

Gandal, Keith. Cleveland Anonymous: A Novel. 2002. 265p. pap. 14.95 (1-58394-062-6) Frog, Ltd.

Gantos, Jack. Zip Six: A Novel. 1996. 224p. 21.95 (1-882593-15-4); 2000. 312p. reprint ed. 13.95 (1-882593-39-1) Bridge Works Publishing Co., Inc.

Garber, Joseph R. Vertical Run. 1996. 320p. mass mkt. 6.50 (0-553-57392-6) Bantam Bks.

—Vertical Run. l.t. ed. 1999. 451p. 24.95 o.p. (0-7838-1592-1, Macmillan Reference USA) Gale Group.

Garcia, Cristina. Dreaming in Cuban. 1999. pap. (0-345-91367-1, Ballantine Bks.); 1993. (SPA.). 256p. pap. 14.00 (0-345-38143-2, One World/ Ballantine) Ballantine Bks.

—Dreaming in Cuban. 1992. 20.00 o.s.i (0-679-40883-5) Knopf, Alfred A. Inc.

—Sonar en Cubano. 1994. (SPA.). 336p. pap. 12.95 (0-345-39139-X, RH9018, Ballantine Bks.) Ballantine Bks.

Garrett, Annie. Because I Wanted You. l.t. ed. 1997. lib. bdg. 21.95 (1-57490-105-2, Beeler Large Print Bks.) Beeler, Thomas T. Publisher.

—Because I Wanted You. 1998. (Because I Wanted You Ser.: Vol. 1). 240p. pap. 5.99 (0-312-96659-8, St. Martin's Paperbacks); 1997. 226p. 18.95 (0-312-15427-5); 1997. 18.95 (0-312-15473-9) St. Martin's Pr.

Garrison, Paul. Red Sky at Morning. 2001. 432p. mass mkt. 6.99 (0-380-80220-1, HarperTorch); 2000. 384p. 24.00 (0-380-97693-5) Morrow/Avon.

Geary, Joseph. Spiral: A Novel. 2003. 368p. 24.95 (0-375-42223-4) Random Hse., Inc.

Geary, Nancy Whitman. Misfortune. 2001. 504p. 28.95 (1-58724-066-1, Wheeler Publishing, Inc.) Gale Group.

—Misfortune. 2001. 368p. 23.95 o.p. (0-446-52753-X) Warner Bks., Inc.

Gelb, Alan. Playgrounds. 1987. 304p. 19.95 o.p. (0-399-13277-5, G. P. Putnam's Sons) Penguin Putnam Bks. for Young Readers.

Geller, Michael. Major League Murder. 1988. 224p. 15.95 o.p. (0-312-02247-6, Saint Martin's Minotaur) St. Martin's Pr.

—Three Strikes, You're Dead. 1992. 240p. 17.95 o.p. (0-312-08322-X, Saint Martin's Minotaur) St. Martin's Pr.

Geller, Michael R. Heroes Also Die. 1988. 240p. 15.95 o.p. (0-312-01441-4, Saint Martin's Minotaur) St. Martin's Pr.

Gellin, William. Strangers No More. 1986. 192p. 11.95 o.p. (0-88400-121-0, Shengold Bks.) Schreiber Publishing, Inc.

George, Nelson. Night Work. 2003. 256p. pap. 12.00 (0-7432-3551-7, Touchstone) Simon & Schuster.

—Seduced: The Life & Times of a One-Hit Wonder. 1996. 352p. 23.95 o.p. (0-399-14169-3, G. P. Putnam's Sons) Penguin Group (USA) Inc.

—Show & Tell: A Novel. 2001. 224p. pap. 12.00 (0-7432-0443-3); E-Book 9.99 (0-7432-1225-8) Simon & Schuster. (Touchstone).

—Urban Romance. 1998. mass mkt. 5.99 (0-345-42685-1) Ballantine Bks.

—Urban Romance. 1994. 286p. reprint ed. pap. 12.98 (1-879360-36-5) Noble Pr., Inc., The.

—Urban Romance: A Novel of New York in the '80s. 1994. 288p. 24.95 o.p. (0-399-13865-X, G. P. Putnam's Sons) Penguin Group (USA) Inc.

Gerber, Merrill Joan. The Kingdom of Brooklyn. 1992. 240p. 18.95 o.p. (1-56352-022-2) Longstreet Pr., Inc.

—The Kingdom of Brooklyn. 2000. (Library of Modern Jewish Literature). 239p. pap. 17.95 (0-8156-0661-3) Syracuse Univ. Pr.

Gibbs, Tony. Capitol Offense. 1995. 352p. 19.95 o.p. (0-89296-474-X) Mysterious Pr.

Gilson, Chris. Crazy for Cornelia. 2001. 352p. E-Book 9.95 (0-446-92305-2) Time Warner Bk. Group.

—Crazy for Cornelia. 2000. E-Book 14.95 (0-446-96014-4); 2000. 352p. 23.95 (0-446-52536-7); 2001. 352p. reprint ed. pap. 12.95 o.s.i (0-446-67679-9) Warner Bks., Inc.

Giniger, Henry. Reasons of the Heart. 1989. 2.99 o.p. (0-517-69590-1) Random Hse. Value Publishing.

—Reasons of the Heart. 1987. 16.95 o.p. (0-531-15047-X, Watts, Franklin) Scholastic Library Publishing.

Giovinazzo, Buddy. Life Is Hot in Cracktown. 1993. 256p. 19.95 (1-56025-054-2, Thunder's Mouth Pr.) Avalon Publishing Group.

—Poetry & Purgatory. 1996. 200p. 12.95 o.p. (1-56025-133-6, Thunder's Mouth Pr.) Avalon Publishing Group.

Girardi, Robert. Madeleine's Ghost: A Novel of New York, New Orleans & the Next World. l.t. ed. 1996. 530p. 24.95 o.p. (0-7838-1507-7, Macmillan Reference USA) Gale Group.

—Madeleine's Ghost: A Novel of New York, New Orleans & the Next World. 1999. E-Book 11.95 (0-440-33399-7) Random Hse., Inc.

—Madeleine's Ghost: A Novel of New York, New Orleans & the Next World. unabr. ed. 1997. audio 85.00 (0-7887-0932-1, 95072E7) Recorded Bks., LLC.

Glass, Leslie. Burning Time. 1995. (April Woo Suspense Novels Ser.). 464p. mass mkt. 7.50 (0-553-56172-3) Bantam Bks.

—Hanging Time. 1996. (April Woo Suspense Novels Ser.). 448p. mass mkt. 7.50 (0-553-57191-5) Bantam Bks.

—Judging Time. 1998. (April Woo Suspense Novels Ser.). 320p. 24.95 o.p. (0-525-94404-4) Dutton/ Plume.

—Judging Time. 1999. (April Woo Suspense Novels Ser.). 400p. mass mkt. 6.99 (0-451-19550-7, Signet Bks.) NAL.

—Loving Time. 1997. (April Woo Suspense Novels Ser.). 432p. reprint ed. mass mkt. 6.99 (0-553-57209-1) Bantam Bks.

—Stealing Time. 2000. audio 25.00 (1-58807-055-7); 2003. audio (1-58807-611-3) Americana Publishing, Inc.

—Stealing Time. unabr. ed. 2000. (April Woo Mystery Ser.). audio 69.95 (0-7927-2384-8, CSL273, Chivers Sound Library) BBC Audiobooks America.

—Stealing Time. 1999. (April Woo Suspense Novels Ser.). 320p. 24.95 o.p. (0-525-94460-5) Dutton/ Plume.

—Stealing Time. 2000. (April Woo Suspense Novels Ser.). 400p. reprint ed. mass mkt. 6.99 (0-451-19965-0, Signet Bks.) NAL.

—Tracking Time. l.t. ed. 2001. (Wheeler Large Print Book Ser.). 437p. 28.95 (1-58724-108-0, Wheeler Publishing, Inc.) Gale Group.

—Tracking Time: An April Woo Suspense Novel. 2000. (April Woo Suspense Novels Ser.). 336p. 23.95 o.s.i (0-525-94469-9) Dutton/Plume.

Glatzer, Hal. A Fugue in Hell's Kitchen: A Katy Green Mystery. 2003. 240p. pap. 13.95 (1-880284-70-7) Daniel, John & Co., Pubs.

Glynn, Thomas. The Building. 1985. 416p. 18.95 o.s.i (0-394-54582-6) Knopf, Alfred A. Inc.

Goddard, Robert. Hand in Glove. 1994. mass mkt. o.s.i (0-552-14165-8, Corgi); 528p. mass mkt. 7.99 (0-552-13839-8) Bantam Bks.

—Hand in Glove. unabr. ed. 2000. audio 89.95 (0-7451-4362-8, CAB 1045) Chivers Audio Bks. GBR. *Dist:* BBC Audiobooks America.

—Hand in Glove. 1993. 432p. 22.00 o.p. (0-671-75070-4, Simon & Schuster) Simon & Schuster.

—Hand in Glove. Rosenman, Jane, ed. 1994. 432p. reprint ed. pap. (0-671-89037-9, Washington Square Pr.) Simon & Schuster.

—Hand in Glove. l.t. ed. 1994. (Charnwood Large Print Ser.). 720p. 29.99 o.p. (0-7089-8773-7, Ulverscroft) Thorpe, F. A. Pubs. GBR. *Dist:* Ulverscroft Large Print Bks., Ltd., Ulverscroft Large Print Canada, Ltd.

Godwin, Gail. Violet Clay. 1986. (Contemporary American Fiction Ser.). 336p. pap. 9.95 o.p. (0-14-008220-4, Penguin Bks.) Viking Penguin.

Gold, Michael. Jews Without Money. 1996. 320p. pap. 11.95 (0-7867-0370-9, Carroll & Graf Pubs.) Avalon Publishing Group.

—Jews Without Money. l.t. ed. 1996. 475p. text 27.95 (1-56000-543-2) ISIS Large Print Bks. GBR. *Dist:* Transaction Pubs.

—Jews Without Money. pap. o.p. (0-87140-129-0) Liveright Publishing Corp.

—Jews Without Money. 1981. pap. 0.95 o.p. (0-380-01309-6, 29520-2, Avon Bks.) Morrow/Avon.

Goldberg, Lucianne. People Will Talk. Miller, Tom, ed. 1994. 384p. 22.00 o.p. (0-671-77669-X, Atria) Simon & Schuster.

Goldblatt, Mark. Africa Speaks. 2002. 176p. 24.00 (1-57962-037-X) Permanent Pr., The.

Goldman, Francisco. The Ordinary Seaman. 1997. 387p. 23.00 o.p. (0-87113-671-6, Atlantic Monthly Pr.); 1998. 400p. reprint ed. pap. 13.50 (0-8021-3548-X, Grove Pr.) Grove/Atlantic, Inc.

Goldsborough, Robert. The Bloodied Ivy. 1989. 208p. mass mkt. 4.99 o.s.i (0-553-27816-9) Bantam Bks.

—Death on a Deadline. 1988. mass mkt. 4.95 o.s.i (0-553-27024-9) Bantam Bks.

—Fade to Black. 1991. 256p. mass mkt. 4.99 o.s.i (0-553-29264-1) Bantam Bks.

—The Missing Chapter. 1993. 240p. 19.95 o.s.i (0-553-07241-2) Bantam Bks.

—The Missing Chapter: A Nero Wolfe Mystery. 1994. 272p. mass mkt. 4.99 o.s.i (0-553-56874-4) Bantam Bks.

—Murder in E Minor. 1987. 224p. (Orig.). mass mkt. 3.50 o.s.i (0-553-26120-7); mass mkt. 3.95 o.s.i (0-553-27938-6) Bantam Bks.

—Silver Spire. 1993. (Crime Line Ser.). 256p. mass mkt. 4.99 o.s.i (0-553-56387-4) Bantam Bks.

Goldsmith, Olivia. The Bestseller. unabr. ed. 1997. audio 83.20 (0-7366-3591-2, 4244A/B) Books on Tape, Inc.

—The Bestseller. l.t. ed. 1996. 25.95 o.p. (1-56895-389-5, Wheeler Publishing, Inc.) Gale Group.

—The Bestseller. 1996. 528p. 25.00 o.p. (0-06-017822-1) HarperCollins Pubs.

—The Bestseller. abr. ed. 1996. audio 18.00 o.p. (0-694-51727-5, CPN 2584, HarperAudio) HarperTrade.

—The Bestseller. 1996. 720p. mass mkt. 7.99 (0-06-109608-3, HarperTorch) Morrow/Avon.

—Dumping Billy. 2004. (0-446-53110-3) Warner Bks., Inc.

—Fashionably Late. l.t. ed. 1994. (G. K. Hall Core Ser.). 748p. lib. bdg. 26.95 (*0-8161-7496-2*, Macmillan Reference USA) Gale Group.
—Fashionably Late. 1994. 416p. 24.00 o.p. (*0-06-017611-3*) HarperCollins Pubs.
—Fashionably Late. 1995. 544p. mass mkt. 7.99 (*0-06-109389-0*, HarperTorch) Morrow/Avon.
—Marrying Mom. 1996. 224p. 16.00 o.p. (*0-06-018652-6*) HarperCollins Pubs.
—Marrying Mom. abr. ed. 1996. audio 18.00 o.s.i (*0-694-51746-1*, CPN 2608, Caedmon) HarperTrade.
—Marrying Mom. 1997. 352p. mass mkt. 6.99 (*0-06-109554-0*, HarperTorch) Morrow/Avon.
—Marrying Mom. l.t. ed. 1997. (Basic Ser.). 298p. lib. bdg. 25.95 o.p. (*0-7862-0954-2*) Thorndike Pr.
Goldsmith, Olivia, reader. Marrying Mom. abr. ed. 2000. audio 9.99 (*0-694-52324-0*, HarperAudio) HarperTrade.
Golub, Aaron Richard. The Big Cut: Novel. 2000. 346p. 24.95 (*0-312-24538-6*) St. Martin's Pr.
Gooch, Brad. The Golden Age of Promiscuity. 1996. 303p. 24.00 o.s.i (*0-679-44708-3*) Knopf, Alfred A. Inc.
—The Golden Age of Promiscuity. 1992. mass mkt. 7.95 (*1-56333-550-6*, Hard Candy) Masquerade Bks., Inc.
Goodman, Jo. Forever in My Heart. l.t. ed. 1996. 522p. 23.95 o.p. (*0-7838-1360-0*, Macmillan Reference USA) Gale Group.
—Forever in My Heart. 1994. 480p. mass mkt. 4.99 o.s.i (*0-8217-4618-9*) Kensington Publishing Corp.
—Forever in My Heart. abr. ed. 1995. audio 5.99 (*1-57096-034-8*, RAZ 934) Romance Alive Audio.
—Forever in My Heart. unabr. ed. 1995. audio 5.99 o.p. Time Warner AudioBooks.
Goodman, Lisl Marburg. Light at the End of the Tunnel. 2002. 220p. 25.00 (*0-939713-10-1*) Carriage Hse. Pr.
Goodman, Paul. The Empire City: A Novel of New York City. Stoehr, Taylor, ed. 2001. 600p. pap. 17.50 (*1-57423-177-4*) HarperCollins Pubs.
Gordon, David A. Other High Crimes. 1994. 23.00 (*1-885823-00-2*) Macaulay & Wittenstein Pubs., Inc.
Gotti, Victoria. I'll Be Watching You. l.t. ed. 1999. 26.95 (*1-56895-596-0*, Wheeler Publishing, Inc.) Gale Group.
Goudge, Eileen. Garden of Lies. l.t. ed. 1990. (Magna Large Print Ser.). 820p. o.p. (*1-85057-837-0*) Magna Large Print Bks. GBR. *Dist:* Ulverscroft Large Print Canada, Ltd.
—Garden of Lies. 1989. 544p. 19.95 o.p. (*0-670-82458-5*) Viking Penguin.
—Thorns of Truth. l.t. ed. 1998. 27.95 (*1-56895-659-2*, Wheeler Publishing, Inc.) Gale Group.
—Thorns of Truth. 1999. 416p. reprint ed. mass mkt. 7.99 (*0-451-18527-7*, Signet Bks.) NAL.
—Thorns of Truth. 1998. 448p. 24.95 o.p. (*0-670-87942-8*, Viking) Viking Penguin.
—Trail of Secrets. unabr. ed. 1996. audio 88.00 (*0-7366-3486-X*, 4126) Books on Tape, Inc.
—Trail of Secrets. abr. ed. 1997. audio 7.99 o.p. (*1-56740-162-7*, 710, Paperback Nova Audio Bks.); 1996. audio 16.95 o.p. (*1-56100-882-6*, 1394, Nova Audio Bks.); 1996. audio 105.25 o.p. (*1-56100-306-9*, 1083, Unabridged Library Editions); 1996. audio 27.95 o.p. (*1-56100-681-5*, 295, Bookcassette) Brilliance Audio.
—Trail of Secrets. l.t. ed. 1996. 26.95 o.p. (*1-56895-325-9*, Wheeler Publishing, Inc.) Gale Group.
—Trail of Secrets. 1997. 528p. mass mkt. 7.99 (*0-451-18774-1*, Signet Bks.) NAL.
—Trail of Secrets. 1996. 464p. 23.95 o.p. (*0-670-86191-X*) Viking Penguin.
Goulart, Ron. Groucho Marx & the Broadway Murders. l.t. ed. 2002. (General Ser.). 265p. pap. 24.95 (*0-7862-3692-2*) Gale Group.
—Groucho Marx & the Broadway Murders. 2001. 213p. 22.95 (*0-312-26598-0*, Saint Martin's Minotaur) St. Martin's Pr.
Gould, Heywood. Double Bang. 1990. 2.99 o.p. (*0-517-02338-5*) Random Hse. Value Publishing.
—Double Bang. 1989. mass mkt. 4.50 o.s.i (*0-671-67835-3*, Pocket); 1988. 256p. 16.45 o.p. (*0-671-61886-5*, Simon & Schuster) Simon & Schuster.
Gould, Judith. The Best Is yet to Come. 2003. 448p. mass mkt. 7.99 (*0-451-21016-6*, Signet Bks.) NAL.
—The Best Is Yet to Come: A Novel. 2002. 320p. 24.95 o.s.i (*0-525-94659-4*) NAL.
Gran, Sara. Saturn's Return to New York. 2002. 224p. pap. 12.00 (*1-56947-305-6*); 2001. 208p. 23.00 (*1-56947-252-1*) Soho Pr., Inc.
Granger, Bill. The New York Yanquis. 1995. 288p. 21.95 (*1-55970-289-3*) Arcade Publishing, Inc.
Grant, Michael. Retribution. 1995. 304p. 23.00 o.p. (*0-06-017640-7*) HarperTrade.
—Retribution. 1996. 416p. mass mkt. 5.99 o.p. (*0-06-109377-7*, HarperTorch) Morrow/Avon.
Graubart, Philip. Planet of the Jews. 1999. 206p. pap. 13.95 (*0-88739-186-9*) Creative Arts Bk. Co.
Gray, Gallagher. A Cast of Killers. 1994. (Partners in Crime Ser.). mass mkt. 4.99 o.s.i (*0-8041-1146-4*, Ivy Bks.) Ballantine Bks.
—A Cast of Killers. 1992. 256p. 20.95 o.p. (*1-55611-328-5*) Fine, Donald I. Bks.
—Death of a Dream Maker. 1995. mass mkt. 5.50 o.s.i (*0-8041-1247-9*, Ivy Bks.) Ballantine Bks.
—Hubbert & Lil: Partners in Crime. 1993. mass mkt. 4.99 o.s.i (*0-8041-0948-6*, Ivy Bks.) Ballantine Bks.
—Hubbert & Lil: Partners in Crime. 1991. 256p. 18.95 o.p. (*1-55611-308-0*) Fine, Donald I. Bks.
—A Motive for Murder. 1996. (Partners in Crime Ser.). mass mkt. 5.50 o.s.i (*0-8041-1248-7*, Ivy Bks.) Ballantine Bks.
Graziunas, Daina & Starlin, Jim. Thinning the Predators. 1996. 336p. 22.95 o.s.i (*0-446-51985-5*) Warner Bks., Inc.
Green, George Dawes. The Caveman's Valentine. l.t. ed. 1996. 26.95 (*1-56895-300-3*, Wheeler Publishing, Inc.) Gale Group.
—The Caveman's Valentine. (Fresh Voices Ser.). 336p. 2001. pap. 9.95 (*0-446-51722-4*); 1995. pap. 13.95 (*0-446-67151-7*) Warner Bks., Inc.
Green, Norman. The Angel of Montague Street. 2003. 304p. 24.95 (*0-06-018819-7*) HarperCollins Pubs.
—The Angel of Montague Street: A Novel. 2004. 304p. pap. 13.95 (*0-06-093411-5*, Dark Alley) HarperTrade.
—Shooting Dr. Jack. 2002. 304p. pap. 12.95 (*0-06-093413-1*, Perennial) HarperTrade.
Green, Tim. The Fifth Angel. 384p. 2004. mass mkt. 6.99 (*0-446-61377-0*, Warner Vision); 2003. 24.95 (*0-446-53085-9*) Warner Bks., Inc.
Greenburg, Dan. What Do Women Want? 1982. 465p. 14.50 o.s.i (*0-671-43793-3*, Simon & Schuster) Simon & Schuster.
Griffin, Adele. The Other Shepards. 2000. 224p. (J). pap. o.s.i (*0-7868-1600-7*) Disney Pr.
Griffiths, W. G. Takedown. 2003. 336p. pap. 13.95 (*0-446-67892-9*, Warner Faith) Warner Bks., Inc.
Grimes, Martha. Foul Matter. l.t. ed. 2004. lib. bdg. 29.95 (*1-58547-389-8*, Platinum) Ctr. Point Large Print.
—Foul Matter. 2003. 384p. 25.95 (*0-670-03259-X*, Viking) Viking Penguin.
Grimes, Tom. A Stone of the Heart. 1990. 131p. 15.95 (*0-941423-40-9*) Four Walls Eight Windows.
—A Stone of the Heart: A Novel. 1997. 144p. reprint ed. pap. 12.95 (*0-87074-418-6*) Southern Methodist Univ. Pr.
Gross, Ken. Full Blown Rage. 1995. 288p. 21.00 o.p. (*0-312-85757-8*, Forge Bks.) Doherty, Tom Assocs., LLC.
—A High Pressure System. 1993. 320p. 20.95 o.p. (*0-312-85444-7*, Forge Bks.) Doherty, Tom Assocs., LLC.
—Talk Show Defense. 1997. (Maggie Van Zandt Novels Ser.). 224p. 20.95 o.p. (*0-312-85803-5*, Forge Bks.) Doherty, Tom Assocs., LLC.
—The Talk Show Defense. 2000. (Maggie Van Zandt Novels Ser.). 224p. mass mkt. 6.99 (*0-8125-5025-0*, Tor Bks.) Doherty, Tom Assocs., LLC.
Grossman, Jeni. Behind the Scenes: A Novel. 2002. 248p. (*1-59156-045-4*) Covenant Communications.
Grossman, Patricia. Unexpected Child: A Novel. 2000. 221p. pap. 11.95 o.p. (*1-55583-544-9*, Alyson Bks.) Alyson Pubns.
Guerin, Renee. The Singing Teacher. 1995. 295p. 21.95 o.p. (*0-312-11891-0*) St. Martin's Pr.
Guerra, Erasmo. Between Dances: A Novel. 2000. 224p. pap. 15.00 (*1-891305-23-9*) Painted Leaf Pr.
Guinzburg, Michael. Beam Me up, Scotty. 1997. 256p. pap. 12.95 (*1-55970-388-1*) Arcade Publishing, Inc.
Gunn, James. The Toy Collector: Hilariously Grim Brilliant Ruthless. 2000. 304p. 23.95 o.p. (*1-58234-081-1*) Bloomsbury Publishing.
Gupta, Sunetra. A Sin of Color: A Novel of Obsession. 2001. 288p. pap. 15.00 (*1-57071-856-3*, Sourcebooks Landmark) Sourcebooks, Inc.
Gurganus, Allan. Plays Well with Others. unabr. collector's ed. 1998. audio 96.00 (*0-7366-4206-4*, 4702) Books on Tape, Inc.
—Plays Well with Others. 1999. 368p. pap. 14.00 (*0-375-70203-2*, Vintage) Knopf Publishing Group.
—Plays Well with Others. 1997. 336p. 25.00 o.p. (*0-394-58914-9*) Knopf, Alfred A. Inc.
—Plays Well with Others. abr. ed. 1997. audio 18.00 o.s.i (*0-679-46055-1*, RH Audio) Random Hse. Audio Publishing Group.
Gutcheon, Beth Richardson. Domestic Pleasures. 2001. 368p. pap. 13.00 (*0-06-093476-X*, Perennial) HarperTrade.
Gutman, Amy. Equivocal Death: A Novel. 2001. 368p. 24.95 o.p. (*0-316-38195-0*) Little Brown & Co.
Haber, Leo. The Red Heifer: A Novel. 2001. (New York City History & Culture Ser.). x, 289p. 24.95 (*0-8156-0692-3*) Syracuse Univ. Pr.
Hailey, J. P. The Anonymous Client. 1993. 320p. mass mkt. 4.99 (*0-8125-1388-6*, Tor Bks.) Doherty, Tom Assocs., LLC.
—The Anonymous Client. 1989. 300p. 16.95 o.p. (*1-55611-124-X*) Fine, Donald I. Bks.
—The Baxter Trust. 1988. 256p. 17.95 o.p. (*1-55611-090-1*) Fine, Donald I. Bks.
—The Baxter Trust. 1999. 240p. per. 15.95 (*0-7592-4105-8*) ereads.com.
—The Naked Typist. 1990. 18.95 o.p. (*1-55611-175-4*) Fine, Donald I. Bks.
—The Underground Man. 1994. (C). mass mkt. 4.99 (*0-8125-5011-0*, Forge Bks.) Doherty, Tom Assocs., LLC.
—The Underground Man. 1990. (Steve Winslow Courtroom Drama Ser.). 18.95 o.p. (*1-55611-215-7*) Fine, Donald I. Bks.
—The Wrong Gun. 1992. 288p. 20.95 o.p. (*1-55611-333-1*) Fine, Donald I. Bks.
Hall, James. A Balcony in Brooklyn: And Other Stories. 2000. 184p. E-Book 8.00 (*0-7388-7250-4*) Xlibris Corp.
Hall, Parnell. Actor. 1993. 288p. 19.95 (*0-89296-520-7*) Mysterious Pr.
—Actor. 1994. 304p. mass mkt. 5.50 (*0-446-40364-4*, Mysterious Pr. Paperback Bks.) Warner Bks., Inc.
—Blackmail. 1994. 288p. 19.95 o.p. (*0-89296-521-5*) Mysterious Pr.
—Blackmail. 1995. 304p. mass mkt. 5.99 o.s.i (*0-446-40365-2*) Warner Bks., Inc.
—Client. 1990. 18.95 o.p. (*1-55611-169-X*) Fine, Donald I. Bks.
—Client. 1991. 272p. mass mkt. 4.50 o.p. (*0-451-40249-9*, Onyx) NAL.
—Detective. 1987. 300p. 17.95 o.p. (*1-55611-026-X*) Fine, Donald I. Bks.
—Detective. 1988. 256p. mass mkt. 3.95 o.p. (*0-451-40070-4*, Onyx) NAL.
—Favor. 1988. 17.95 o.p. (*1-55611-096-0*) Fine, Donald I. Bks.
—Favor. 1989. mass mkt. 3.95 o.p. (*0-451-40161-1*, 035, Onyx) NAL.
—Favor. 2002. 186p. pap. 6.99 (*0-7592-1854-4*); E-Book 6.99 (*0-7592-1850-1*); E-Book 6.99 (*0-7592-1851-X*); E-Book 6.99 (*0-7592-1849-8*) ereads.com.
—Juror. 1990. 18.95 o.p. (*1-55611-230-0*) Fine, Donald I. Bks.
—Juror. 1992. 304p. mass mkt. 4.99 o.p. (*0-451-40316-9*, Onyx) NAL.
—Manslaughter: A Stanley Hastings Mystery. 2003. (Otto Penzler Book Ser.). 320p. 25.00 (*0-7867-1127-2*, Carroll & Graf Pubs.) Avalon Publishing Group.
—Movie. 1995. 82p. 19.95 o.p. (*0-89296-569-X*) Mysterious Pr.
—Movie. 1996. 288p. mass mkt. 5.99 (*0-446-40395-4*) Warner Bks., Inc.
—Murder. 1988. 256p. 17.95 o.s.i (*1-55611-058-8*) Fine, Donald I. Bks.
—Murder. 2002. 256p. reprint ed. pap. 13.95 (*1-58754-111-4*, Olmstead Pr.) Moyer Bell.
—Murder. 1989. mass mkt. 3.95 o.p. (*0-451-40110-7*, Onyx) NAL.
—Murder. E-Book 6.99 (*0-7592-1545-6*) ereads.com.
—Scam. 1998. 336p. pap. 6.50 (*0-446-40469-1*, Mysterious Pr. Paperback Bks.) Warner Bks., Inc.
—Scam: A Stanley Hastings Mystery. l.t. ed. 1997. (Americana Ser.). 463p. 26.95 (*0-7862-1210-1*) Thorndike Pr.
—Scam: A Stanley Hastings Mystery. 1997. 320p. 21.50 o.p. (*0-89296-623-8*) Warner Bks., Inc.
—Shot. 1993. 320p. mass mkt. 4.99 o.p. (*0-451-40354-1*, Onyx) NAL.
—Shot: A Stanley Hastings Novel of Suspense. 1991. 18.95 o.p. (*1-55611-239-4*) Fine, Donald I. Bks.
—Strangler. 1989. 304p. 16.95 o.p. (*1-55611-125-8*) Fine, Donald I. Bks.
—Strangler. 1990. mass mkt. 4.50 o.p. (*0-451-40217-0*, Onyx) NAL.
—Suspense: A Stanley Hastings Mystery Novel. 1998. 320p. 23.00 o.p. (*0-89296-624-6*) Mysterious Pr.
—Trial. 1996. 82p. 21.95 o.s.i (*0-89296-570-3*) Mysterious Pr.
—Trial. 1997. 288p. mass mkt. 5.99 (*0-446-40396-2*) Warner Bks., Inc.
Hamill, Denis. A Long Time Gone. 2002. 416p. 25.00 (*0-7434-0709-1*, Atria) Simon & Schuster.
—The Sins of Two Fathers. 2003. 384p. 25.00 (*0-7434-6298-X*, Atria) Simon & Schuster.
—Three Quarters. 1999. 352p. pap. 6.99 (*0-671-00250-3*, Pocket Star); 1998. 320p. 23.00 o.s.i (*0-671-00249-X*, Atria) Simon & Schuster.
—Throwing 7's. 1999. 319p. 24.00 (*0-671-02614-3*, Atria); 2000. (Illus.). 592p. reprint ed. pap. 6.99 (*0-671-02615-1*, Pocket Star) Simon & Schuster.
Hamill, Pete. Forever. 2003. 640p. pap. 14.95 (*0-316-73569-8*, Back Bay); 2002. 624p. 25.95 (*0-316-34111-8*) Little Brown & Co.
—Forever. l.t. ed. 2003. (Americana Ser.). 31.95 (*0-7862-5385-1*) Thorndike Pr.
—Loving Women. 2003. mass mkt. 6.99 o.p. (*0-7582-0678-X*, Kensington Bks.); 2003. mass mkt. 6.99 (*0-7860-1638-8*, Pinnacle Bks.); 1990. mass mkt. 5.50 o.s.i (*1-55817-385-4*, Pinnacle Bks.) Kensington Publishing Corp.
—Snow in August. 2001. 17.95 (*1-56511-626-7*) HighBridge Co.
—Snow in August. 1997. 304p. 23.95 o.p. (*0-316-34094-4*) Little Brown & Co.
—Snow in August. l.t. ed. (Thorndike/G. K. Hall Paperback Bestsellers Ser.). 507p. 1998. pap. 25.95 o.p. (*0-7862-1222-5*); 1997. 28.95 (*0-7862-1221-7*) Thorndike Pr.
—Snow in August. 1999. 20.05 (*0-606-20074-6*) Turtleback Bks.
—Snow in August. reprint ed. 1999. 384p. pap. 14.00 (*0-446-67525-3*); 1998. 400p. mass mkt. 7.99 (*0-446-60625-1*) Warner Bks., Inc.
Hamilton, William. The Lap of Luxury. 1990. 300p. 17.95 o.p. (*0-87113-246-X*); pap. 8.95 (*0-87113-342-3*, Atlantic Monthly Pr.) Grove/Atlantic, Inc.
Hammett, Dashiell. The Thin Man. Date not set. (Thin Man Ser.). 137p. 18.95 (*0-8488-2438-5*) Amereon, Ltd.
—The Thin Man. unabr. ed. 1998. audio 42.00 (*0-7366-4002-9*, 4501) Books on Tape, Inc.
—The Thin Man, , abr. ed. 1987. (Thin Man Ser.). audio 17.00 o.s.i (*0-89845-591-X*, CPN2106, Caedmon) HarperTrade.
—The Thin Man. (Thin Man Ser.). 1992. pap. 9.00 (*0-394-23905-9*); 1989. 208p. pap. 11.00 (*0-679-72263-7*) Knopf Publishing Group. (Vintage).
—The Thin Man. (Thin Man Ser.). 1992. pap. 9.00 (*0-679-74092-9*); 1972. pap. 2.95 o.p. (*0-394-71774-0*) Random Hse., Inc.
—The Thin Man. 1994. (Thin Man Ser.). 272p. 35.00 (*1-883402-70-0*, Scribner) Simon & Schuster.
—The Thin Man. l.t. ed. 2001. (Perennial Bestsellers Ser.). 269p. 28.95 (*0-7838-9460-0*) Thorndike Pr.
Hand, Elizabeth. Glimmering. 1998. 560p. mass mkt. 6.99 o.s.i (*0-06-101216-5*); 1997. 400p. mass mkt. 22.00 o.p. (*0-06-100805-2*) Morrow/Avon. (Eos).
Handler, David. The Man Who Cancelled Himself: A Stewart Hoag Mystery. 1995. 256p. mass mkt. 4.99 o.s.i (*0-553-29397-4*, Crimeline) Bantam Bks.
—The Man Who Cancelled Himself: A Stewart Hoag Mystery. 1995. 416p. 19.95 o.s.i (*0-385-42160-5*) Doubleday Publishing.
—The Man Who Cancelled Himself: A Stewart Hoag Mystery. unabr. ed. 1999. (Stewart Hoag Mystery Ser.: Vol. 6). audio 85.00 (*0-7887-1992-0*, 95379E7) Recorded Bks., LLC.
—The Man Who Died Laughing. 1990. 208p. mass mkt. 2.25 o.s.i (*0-553-18520-9*); 1988. 192p. mass mkt. 3.50 o.s.i (*0-553-27469-4*) Bantam Bks.
—The Man Who Lived by Night. 1989. 181p. mass mkt. 3.50 o.s.i (*0-553-27935-1*) Bantam Bks.
—The Man Who Loved Women to Death. 1997. 304p. 23.95 o.s.i (*0-385-48052-0*) Doubleday Publishing.
—The Man Who Loved Women to Death. unabr. ed. 2001. audio 61.00 (*0-7887-4877-7*, 96453x7) Recorded Bks., LLC.
—The Man Who Would Be F. Scott Fitzgerald. 1995. 224p. mass mkt. 4.99 o.s.i (*0-553-27848-7*) Bantam Bks.
—The Man Who Would Be F. Scott Fitzgerald. 1993. 256p. 17.00 o.s.i (*0-385-46782-6*) Doubleday Publishing.
—The Man Who Would Be F. Scott Fitzgerald. unabr. ed. 1998. (Stewart Hoag Mystery Ser.: Vol. 3). audio 51.00 (*0-7887-0929-1*, 95069E7) Recorded Bks., LLC.
Hardy, James E. B-Boy Blues: A Seriously Sexy, Fiercely Funny, Black-on-Black Love Story. 1994. 240p. pap. 12.95 (*1-55583-268-7*) Alyson Pubns.
—Back 2 Back: An Anthology Featuring the Best-Sellers: B-Boy Blues & 2nd Time Around, 2 vols., Set. 1997. 530p. reprint ed. 22.95 o.p. (*1-55583-420-5*) Alyson Pubns.
—If Only for One Nite. 1998. 208p. pap. 12.95 (*1-55583-467-1*); 1997. 185p. 17.95 (*1-55583-373-X*) Alyson Pubns.
—The 2nd Time Around. 1996. 288p. pap. 12.95 (*1-55583-372-1*) Alyson Pubns.
Harris, Anne. The Nature of Smoke. 1997. 288p. pap. 13.95 (*0-312-86351-9*); 1996. 256p. 22.95 o.p. (*0-312-85286-X*) Doherty, Tom Assocs., LLC. (Tor Bks.).
Harris, Lee. The Christening Day Murder. 1993. (Christine Bennett Mysteries Ser.: Vol. 3). 224p. mass mkt. 6.99 (*0-449-14871-8*, Fawcett) Ballantine Bks.
—The Christmas Night Murder. 1994. (Christine Bennett Mysteries Ser.: Vol. 5). 224p. mass mkt. 6.99 (*0-449-14922-6*, Fawcett) Ballantine Bks.
—The Christmas Night Murder. unabr. ed. 1999. audio 39.95 (*0-7861-1672-2*, 2500) Blackstone Audio Bks., Inc.
—The Father's Day Murder. 1999. (Christine Bennett Mysteries Ser.: Vol. 11). 272p. mass mkt. 6.99 (*0-449-00441-4*, Fawcett) Ballantine Bks.

Settings

—The Good Fri ay Murder. 1992. (Christine Bennett Mysteries S r.: Vol. 1). 208p. mass mkt. 6.99 (0-449-1476 -2, Fawcett) Ballantine Bks.
—The Good Fri ay Murder. abr. ed. 1997. audio 19.95 (0-9658148- -7, SA111) Scheherazade AudioVisions, Inc.
—The Mother's Day Murder. 2000. (Christine Bennett Mysteries S : Vol. 12). 272p. mass mkt. 6.50 (0-449-0044 -2, Fawcett) Ballantine Bks.
—Murder in He 's Kitchen. 2003. 320p. mass mkt. 6.99 (0-449- 0734-0, Fawcett) Ballantine Bks.
—The New Year's Eve Murder. 1997. (Christine Bennett My teries Ser.: Vol. 9). 272p. mass mkt. 6.99 (0-449- 5018-6, Fawcett) Ballantine Bks.
—The Passover Murder. 1996. (Christine Bennett Mysteries S r.: Vol. 7). 288p. mass mkt. 6.99 (0-449-1496 -3, Fawcett) Ballantine Bks.
—The St. Patrick's Day Murder. 1994. (Christine Bennett Mysteries Ser.: Vol. 4). 224p. (Orig.). mass mkt. 6 99 (0-449-14872-6, Fawcett) Ballantine Bks.
—The Thanksgi ng Day Murder. 1995. (Christine Bennett My eries Ser.: Vol. 6). 256p. mass mkt. 6.50 (0-449- 4923-4, Fawcett) Ballantine Bks.
—The Thanksgiving Day Murder. unabr. ed. 1999. (Christine Bennett Mysteries Ser.). audio 39.95 (0-7861-164 -5, 2473) Blackstone Audio Bks., Inc.
—The Valentine Day Murder. 1996. (Christine Bennett Mysteries Ser.: Vol. 8). 272p. mass mkt. 6.99 (0-449-14964-1, Fawcett) Ballantine Bks.
—The Yom Kippur Murder. 1992. (Christine Bennett Mysteries Ser.: Vol. 2). 224p. (Orig.). mass mkt. 6.99 (0-449-14763-0, Fawcett) Ballantine Bks.
Harrison, Colin. Afterburn. pap. (0-374-90064-7); 2000. E-Book 9.00 (0-374-70019-2); 2000. E-Book 9.00 o.p. (0-374-70013-3); 2000. E-Book 9.00 (0-374-70027-3); 2000. (Illus.). 416p. 25.00 o.s.i (0-374-10205-8) Farrar, Straus & Giroux.
—Afterburn. l.t. ed. 2001. (Softcover Ser.). 670p. pap. 23.95 (1-58724-055-6, Wheeler Publishing, Inc.) Gale Group.
—Afterburn. 2001. reprint ed. mass mkt. 6.99 (0-312-97870-7, St. Martin's Paperbacks) St. Martin's Pr.
—Bodies Electric. l.t. ed. 1994. 25.95 o.p. (0-7927-1995-6); pap. 24.95 o.p. (0-7927-1994-8) BBC Audiobooks America.
—Bodies Electric. 1994. pap. 5.99 o.p. (0-380-72310-7, Avon Bks.) Morrow/Avon.
—The Havana Room. 2004. 400p. 24.00 (0-374-29986-2) Farrar, Straus & Giroux.
—Manhattan Nocturne. 1997. o.s.i (0-517-70696-2); 1996. 384p. 5.99 o.s.i (0-517-58492-1) Crown Publishing Group.
—Manhattan Nocturne. 1997. 416p. mass mkt. 6.99 o.s.i (0-440-22433-0) Dell Publishing.
—Manhattan Nocturne. unabr. ed. 1996. 24.95 o.p. (0-7871-1115-5) NewStar Media, Inc.
—Manhattan Nocturne. 2004. 416p. mass mkt. 6.99 (0-312-99303-X, St. Martin's Paperbacks) St. Martin's Pr.
Harrison, Kathryn. Exposure. 1994. 272p. pap. 12.99 o.s.i (0-446-67023-5) Warner Bks., Inc.
Hart, Ellen. Merchant of Venus. mass mkt. (0-312-97991-6, St. Martin's Paperbacks); 2001. 389p. 24.95 (0-312-26618-9, Saint Martin's Minotaur) St. Martin's Pr.
Harvey, James N. By Reason of Insanity. 1991. 346p. pap. 5.99 o.p. (0-312-92533-6, St. Martin's Paperbacks); 1990. 18.95 o.p. (0-312-04295-7) St. Martin's Pr.
—Dead Game. 1997. 304p. text 24.95 o.p. (0-312-15100-4) St. Martin's Pr.
—Flesh & Blood: A Lt. Ben Tolliver Thriller. 1996. 408p. mass mkt. 6.50 o.p. (0-312-95318-6, St. Martin's Paperbacks); 1994. 384p. 22.95 o.p. (0-312-10985-7) St. Martin's Pr.
—Mental Case. 1997. 346p. mass mkt. 6.99 (0-312-95995-8, St. Martin's Paperbacks); 1996. 352p. 23.95 o.p. (0-312-14014-2) St. Martin's Pr.
—Painted Ladies. 1992. 375p. mass mkt. 5.99 (0-312-92895-5, St. Martin's Paperbacks); 448p. 19.95 o.p. (0-312-07056-X) St. Martin's Pr.
Harvey, John. In a True Light. 2002. 256p. 26.00 (0-7867-1053-5, Carroll & Graf Pubs.) Avalon Publishing Group.
Hauser, Marianne. Shootout with Father. 2002. 100p. pap. 11.95 (1-57366-100-7) Fiction Collective Two, Inc.
Hauser, Thomas. Dear Hannah. 256p. 1988. pap. 3.95 o.p. (0-8125-0453-4); 1987. 14.95 o.p. (0-312-93005-4) Doherty, Tom Assocs., LLC. (Tor Bks.).
Hawke, Ethan. The Hottest State. 1996. 208p. 19.95 o.p. (0-316-54083-8) Little Brown & Co.
—The Hottest State. abr. ed. 1996. audio 17.00 (1-57042-399-7) Time Warner AudioBooks.
—The Hottest State: A Novel. 1997. 208p. pap. 12.00 (0-679-78135-8, Vintage) Knopf Publishing Group.
Hay, Elizabeth. A Student of Weather. 2003. 384p. text 24.00 (1-58243-123-X, Counterpoint Pr.) Basic Bks.
—A Student of Weather. 2000. 376p. (0-7710-3789-9) McClelland & Stewart.
Hayes, Hunter. Shoe's on the Otha' Foot. 2000. 320p. mass mkt. 6.99 (0-06-101466-4, HarperTorch) Morrow/Avon.
—Shoe's on the Otha' Foot. Green, Brandi C., ed. 1999. 240p. pap. 12.95 (0-9666435-7-7) Stone Edge Pr.
Hayes, Penny. Kathleen O'Donald. 1994. 256p. pap. 9.95 (1-56280-070-1) Naiad Pr., Inc.
Hayes, Teddy. Dead by Popular Demand. 2003. 240p. pap. 10.95 (1-902934-02-4) X Pr., The GBR. *Dist:* National Bk. Network.
Hays, Clark & McFall, Kathleen. The Cowboy & the Vampire: A Very Unusual Romance. Hill, Connie, ed. 336p. pap. 12.95 (1-56718-451-0, K451) Llewellyn Pubns.
Hayter, Sparkle. The Chelsea Girl Murders. 2000. (Robin Hudson Mysteries Ser.). 240p. 23.00 (0-688-15518-9, Morrow, William & Co.) Morrow/Avon.
—The Last Manly Man. 1999. (Robin Hudson Mysteries Ser.). 256p. reprint ed. pap. 9.95 o.s.i (0-688-16972-4, Quill) HarperTrade.
—The Last Manly Man: A Robin Hudson Mystery. 1998. (Robin Hudson Mysteries Ser.). 256p. 22.00 (0-688-15517-0, Morrow, William & Co.) Morrow/Avon.
—Naked Brunch: A Novel. 2003. 336p. pap. 13.00 (1-4000-4743-9, Three Rivers Pr.) Crown Publishing Group.
—Nice Girls Finish Last. 1997. (Viking Mystery Suspense Ser.). 256p. pap. 5.95 (0-14-024516-2) Penguin Group (USA) Inc.
—Nice Girls Finish Last: A Robin Hudson Mystery. 1996. (Robin Hudson Mystery Ser.). 256p. 20.95 o.p. (0-670-86039-5) Viking Penguin.
—Revenge of the Cootie Girls. 1997. (Robin Hudson Mystery Ser.). 240p. 20.95 o.s.i (0-670-86940-6) Viking Penguin.
—What's a Girl Gotta Do? 1995. (Robin Hudson Mystery Ser.). 288p. pap. 6.99 (0-14-024481-6, Penguin Bks.) Penguin Group (USA) Inc.
—What's a Girl Gotta Do? 1994. 270p. 19.95 o.p. (1-56947-000-6) Soho Pr., Inc.
Heckler, Jonellen. Circumstances Unknown. Grose, Bill, ed. 1993. 288p. 21.00 o.p. (0-671-78056-5, Atria); 1994. 336p. reprint ed. mass mkt. 5.99 (0-671-78059-X, Pocket) Simon & Schuster.
Heffernan, William. Blood Rose. 1991. 320p. 18.95 o.p. (0-525-24962-1, Dutton) Dutton/Plume.
—Blood Rose. 1992. 448p. mass mkt. 6.99 o.s.i (0-451-17163-2, Signet Bks.) NAL.
—Cityside: William Heffernan. 1999. 276p. 24.00 (0-688-16406-4, Morrow, William & Co.) Morrow/Avon.
—Red Angel: A Paul Devlin Mystery. 2000. (Paul Devlin Mysteries Ser.). 273p. 24.00 (0-688-16563-X, Morrow, William & Co.) Morrow/Avon.
—Ritual. 1990. 352p. mass mkt. 5.99 o.s.i (0-451-16397-4, Signet Bks.); 1989. 284p. 18.95 o.p. (0-453-00618-3) NAL.
—Scarred. 1993. 384p. (Orig.). mass mkt. 5.99 o.s.i (0-451-17863-7, Signet Bks.) NAL.
—Tarnished Blue. 1995. 384p. (Orig.). mass mkt. 5.99 o.s.i (0-451-18295-2, Onyx) NAL.
—Time Gone By. 2003. 288p. 24.00 (0-7432-1710-1, Simon & Schuster) Simon & Schuster.
—Unholy Order: A Paul Devlin Mystery. 2002. (Illus.). 288p. 24.95 (0-688-16564-8, Morrow, William & Co.) Morrow/Avon.
—Winter's Gold. 1997. 400p. mass mkt. 6.50 o.s.i (0-451-18865-9, Signet Bks.) NAL.
Heller, Jane. Female Intelligence. 2001. xiii, 335p. 24.95 o.p. (0-312-26159-4); 2002. 352p. reprint ed. mass mkt. 6.99 (0-312-97988-6, St. Martin's Paperbacks) St. Martin's Pr.
—Female Intelligence. l.t. ed. 2001. 541p. 29.95 o.p. (0-7862-3442-3) Thorndike Pr.
—Name Dropping. l.t. ed. 2000. (Basic Ser.). 496p. 29.95 (0-7862-2979-9) Thorndike Pr.
Heller, Ted. Slab Rat. 2001. 336p. pap. 13.00 (0-684-86497-5, Scribner) Simon & Schuster.
—Slab Rat: A Novel. 2000. E-Book 23.00 (0-7432-1361-0); (Illus.). 336p. 23.00 o.s.i (0-684-86496-7) Simon & Schuster. (Scribner).
Hellerstein, David. Stone Babies. 2001. 294p. pap. 21.99 (0-7388-6732-2) Xlibris Corp.
Hellinger, Mark. Moon over Broadway. 1977. (Short Story Index Reprint Ser.). reprint ed. 19.95 (0-8369-4082-2) Ayer Co. Pubs., Inc.
Helprin, Mark. Memoir from Antproof Case. l.t. ed. 1995. 26.95 (1-56895-256-2, Wheeler Publishing, Inc.) Gale Group.
—Memoir from Antproof Case. 1995. 514p. 24.00 o.s.i (0-15-100097-2) Harcourt Trade Pubs.
—Memoir from Antproof Case. 1996. 528p. pap. 15.95 (0-380-72733-1, Avon Bks.) Morrow/Avon.
—Winter's Tale. (Harvest Book Ser.). 688p. 1995. pap. 17.00 (0-15-600194-2, Harvest Bks.); 1983. 35.00 (0-15-197203-6) Harcourt Trade Pubs.
—Winter's Tale. 1985. 704p. mass mkt. 4.95 o.s.i (0-671-62118-1); 1984. mass mkt. 4.50 o.s.i (0-671-50987-X) Simon & Schuster. (Pocket).
—Winter's Tale. Rosenman, Jane, ed. 1990. 704p. reprint ed. pap. (0-671-72707-9, Washington Square Pr.) Simon & Schuster.
Hemmingson, Michael. The Professor: Erotic Fantasy Classics. 2003. (Create Your Own Erotic Fantasy Ser.). 196p. pap. 12.00 (1-59240-031-0) Gothman Bks.
Henderson, Lauren. The Strawberry Tattoo. 2000. (Sam Jones Novel Ser.). (Illus.). 316p. pap. 12.95 (0-609-80685-8, Three Rivers Pr.) Crown Publishing Group.
Hendin, Josephine Gattuso. The Right Thing to Do. 1999. 240p. pap. 13.95 (1-55861-220-3) Feminist Pr. at The City Univ. of New York.
—The Right Thing to Do. 1988. 256p. 16.95 o.p. (0-87923-639-6) Godine, David R. Pub.
Henry, O. The Best of O. Henry. 1978. 160p. lib. bdg. 7.95 o.p. (0-89471-047-8) Running Pr. Bk. Pubs.
—Cabbages & Kings. 320p. 24.95 o.s.i (0-8488-1680-3) Amereon, Ltd.
—Cabbages & Kings. unabr. ed. 1997. audio 39.95 (0-7861-1173-9, 1961) Blackstone Audio Bks., Inc.
—Cabbages & Kings. 2001. per. 12.50 (1-58396-507-6) Blue Unicorn Editions.
—Cabbages & Kings. 2002. 176p. 93.99 (1-58827-225-7); per. 88.99 (1-58827-226-5) IndyPublish.com.
—Cabbages & Kings. mass mkt. 0.25 o.p. (0-451-00595-3, Signet Bks.) NAL.
—Cabbages & Kings. collector's ed. 2002. (Illus.). im. lthr. 38.85 (1-4115-1385-1); pap. 19.95 (1-4115-0667-7); 25.95 (1-4115-1020-8); pap. 17.95 (1-4115-0311-2) Polyglot Pr., Inc.
—Cabbages & Kings. 1993. (Penguin Twentieth-Century Classics Ser.). 256p. pap. 10.95 o.p. (0-14-018689-1, Penguin Classics) Viking Penguin.
—The Four Million: Featuring the Gift of the Magi. Banis, Robert J., ed. l.t. ed. 2001. (1-888725-41-9, MacroPrintBooks) Science & Humanities Pr.
—Strictly Business: More Stories of the Four Million. l.t. ed. 1998. 400p. text 27.95 (1-56000-525-4) Transaction Pubs.
Herlihy, James Leo. Midnight Cowboy. 2002. E-Book 4.99 (0-7953-0812-4) RosettaBooks.
—Midnight Cowboy. 2002. 256p. pap. 14.00 (0-7434-5249-6) ibooks, Inc.
Herrick, Amy. The Happiness Code: A Novel. 2003. 320p. 24.95 (0-670-03197-6, Viking) Viking Penguin.
Hess, Joan. Maggody in Manhattan. 1992. (Arly Hanks Mystery Ser.). 272p. 18.00 o.p. (0-525-93519-3, Dutton) Dutton/Plume.
—Maggody in Manhattan. 1993. (Arly Hanks Mystery Ser.). 256p. reprint ed. mass mkt. 5.50 o.s.i (0-451-40376-2, Onyx) NAL.
Hijuelos, Oscar. The Empress of the Splendid Season. 1999. 352p. mass mkt. 7.99 (0-06-101418-4) HarperCollins Pubs.
—The Empress of the Splendid Season. 1999. 352p. o.s.i (0-06-017570-2, HarperFlamingo) HarperCollins Pubs. Canada, Ltd.
—The Empress of the Splendid Season. 2000. 352p. pap. 13.00 (0-06-092870-0, Perennial) HarperTrade.
—The Mambo Kings Play Songs of Love. 1989. 384p. 18.95 o.s.i (0-374-20125-0) Farrar, Straus & Giroux.
—The Mambo Kings Play Songs of Love. (Perennial Classics Ser.). 2004. 464p. pap. 14.00 (0-06-095545-7); 1994. 416p. pap. 13.00 (0-06-097327-7); 1992. 416p. reprint ed. pap. 12.00 o.p. (0-06-097451-6) HarperTrade. (Perennial).
—Mr. Ives' Christmas. 1996. 256p. pap. 78.00 o.p. (0-06-092774-7); 1995. 272p. 19.00 o.p. (0-06-017131-6) HarperCollins Pubs.
—Mr. Ives' Christmas. 1996. 256p. pap. 13.95 (0-06-092754-2, Perennial) HarperTrade.
—Our House in the Last World. 1991. 236p. reprint ed. pap. 12.00 o.p. (0-89255-165-8); 1989. 236p. reprint ed. 18.95 (0-89255-069-4); 2nd ed. 2002. 256p. pap. 13.00 (0-89255-283-2) Persea Bks., Inc.
—Our House in the Last World. Rosenman, Jane, ed. 1990. 256p. pap. (0-671-72722-2, Washington Square Pr.) Simon & Schuster.
—Our House in the Last World. 1984. reprint ed. pap. 3.95 (0-671-50785-0, Washington Square Pr.) Simon & Schuster.
—Los Reyes del Mambo Tocan Canciones de Amor. 1996. (SPA.). 560p. pap. 14.00 (0-06-095214-8, HC12648, Perennial) HarperTrade.
Hilden, Julie. Three: A Novel. 2003. 224p. pap. 13.00 (0-452-28443-0, Plume) Dutton/Plume.
Himes, Chester B. All Shot up. 1973. 160p. reprint ed. 7.95 o.p. (0-911860-29-0) Chatham Bookseller.
—All Shot Up. 2nd ed. 1996. 170p. reprint ed. pap. 12.95 (1-56025-103-4, Thunder's Mouth Pr.) Avalon Publishing Group.
—The Big Gold Dream. 2nd ed. 1996. 156p. reprint ed. pap. 12.95 (1-56025-104-2, Thunder's Mouth Pr.) Avalon Publishing Group.
—The Big Gold Dream. 1973. 160p. reprint ed. 7.95 o.p. (0-911860-30-4) Chatham Bookseller.
—Blind Man with a Pistol. 1989. (Vintage Crime Ser.). 192p. pap. 11.00 (0-394-75998-2, Vintage) Knopf Publishing Group.
—Cotton Comes to Harlem. 1994. (Illus.). lib. bdg. 11.95 (1-56849-422-X) Buccaneer Bks., Inc.
—Cotton Comes to Harlem. 1975. reprint ed. 8.95 o.p. (0-911860-55-X) Chatham Bookseller.
—Cotton Comes to Harlem. 1988. (Crime Ser.). (Illus.). 160p. pap. 11.00 (0-394-75999-0, Vintage) Knopf Publishing Group.
—The Crazy Kill. 1973. 160p. reprint ed. 7.95 o.p. (0-911860-32-0) Chatham Bookseller.
—The Crazy Kill. 160p. 1995. pap. 25.00 o.s.i (0-8052-8217-3, Schocken); 1989. pap. 11.00 (0-679-72572-5, Vintage) Knopf Publishing Group.
—End of a Primitive. 1997. 220p. pap. 12.00 (0-393-31540-1) Norton, W. W. & Co., Inc.
—For Love of Imabelle. 1973. 192p. reprint ed. 7.95 o.p. (0-911860-33-9) Chatham Bookseller.
—The Heat's On. 1975. 220p. reprint ed. 17.00 (0-911860-57-6) Chatham Bookseller.
—The Heat's On. 1988. (Vintage Crime Ser.). 176p. pap. 15.00 (0-394-75997-4, Vintage) Knopf Publishing Group.
—Pinktoes. 1975. 256p. reprint ed. 8.50 o.p. (0-911860-58-4) Chatham Bookseller.
—Pinktoes. 1996. 264p. (C). 40.00 (0-87805-886-9); pap. 16.95 (0-87805-887-7) Univ. Pr. of Mississippi.
—A Rage in Harlem. 1989. (Vintage Crime Ser.). Orig. Title: For Love of Imabelle. 160p. pap. 10.00 (0-679-72040-5, Vintage) Knopf Publishing Group.
—The Real Cool Killers. 1973. 160p. reprint ed. 7.95 o.p. (0-911860-36-3) Chatham Bookseller.
—The Real Cool Killers. 1988. (Vintage Crime Ser.). 160p. pap. 10.95 (0-679-72039-1, Pantheon) Knopf Publishing Group.
—Run Man Run. 1995. 192p. pap. 8.95 (0-7867-0209-5, Carroll & Graf Pubs.) Avalon Publishing Group.
—Run Man Run. 1975. 192p. reprint ed. 8.50 o.p. (0-911860-56-8) Chatham Bookseller.
Hitchcock, Jane S. The Witches' Hammer. 1994. 352p. 21.95 o.p. (0-525-93641-6) Dutton/Plume.
—The Witches' Hammer. 1995. 464p. mass mkt. 5.99 o.s.i (0-451-18508-0, Signet Bks.) NAL.
Hitchcock, Jane Stanton. Social Crimes. l.t. ed. 2002. 28.95 (1-58724-337-7, Wheeler Publishing, Inc.) Gale Group.
—Social Crimes. 2002. 368p. 22.95 (0-7868-6815-5) Hyperion Pr.
—Social Crimes. Date not set. pap. 12.95 (0-7868-8848-2) Talk Miramax Bks.
Hoff, B. J. Ashes & Lace, Vol. 2. 1999. (Song of Erin Ser.). 432p. pap. 8.99 o.p. (0-8423-1479-2) Tyndale Hse. Pubs.
—Prelude. l.t. ed. 2003. 329p. pap. 15.95 (1-4104-0077-8, Walker Large Print) Gale Group.
—Prelude. 2002. 250p. pap. 12.99 (0-8499-4389-2) W Publishing Group.
Hoffman, Alice. The Drowning Season. 1986. mass mkt. 3.50 o.s.i (0-449-21024-3, Fawcett) Ballantine Bks.
—The Drowning Season. 2002. 240p. pap. 13.00 (0-425-18475-7) Berkley Publishing Group.
—The Drowning Season. (Plume Contemporary Fiction Ser.). 1989. 224p. pap. 12.95 o.s.i (0-452-26302-6, Plume); 1979. 8.95 o.p. (0-525-09577-2, Dutton) Dutton/Plume.
—The Drowning Season. 1993. 224p. mass mkt. 4.99 o.s.i (0-451-17815-7, Signet Bks.) NAL.
—The Drowning Season. l.t. ed. 2000. (Famous Authors Ser.). 307p. 27.95 (0-7862-2626-9) Thorndike Pr.
Holland, Isabelle. Darcourt. 1977. pap. 1.75 o.s.i (0-449-23224-7, Fawcett) Ballantine Bks.
—Darcourt. l.t. ed. 1982. 529p. reprint ed. 13.95 o.p. (0-89621-397-8) Thorndike Pr.
—Death at St. Anselm's. 1984. 240p. 13.95 o.p. (0-385-18332-1) Doubleday Publishing.
—A Fatal Advent: A St. Anselm's Mystery. 1990. (St. Anselm's Mystery Ser.). 256p. mass mkt. 3.95 o.s.i (0-449-21879-1, Fawcett) Ballantine Bks.
—The Long Search. 1992. mass mkt. 3.99 o.s.i (0-449-22009-5, Fawcett) Ballantine Bks.
—The Long Search. 1990. 272p. 16.95 o.s.i (0-385-26545-X) Doubleday Publishing.
—The Long Search. l.t. ed. 1993. (Magna Large Print Ser.). 435p. (0-7505-0444-7) Magna Large Print Bks. GBR. *Dist:* Ulverscroft Large Print Canada, Ltd.
—A Lover Scorned. 1987. 256p. mass mkt. 2.95 o.s.i (0-449-21369-2, Fawcett) Ballantine Bks.
—A Lover Scorned. 1986. 240p. 15.95 o.p. (0-385-23169-5) Doubleday Publishing.
Holmes, Guy. P. E. A. C. E. A Novel of Police Terror. 2000. 320p. 23.00 (0-684-87079-7, Simon & Schuster) Simon & Schuster.
Holmes, Rupert. Where the Truth Lies. 2003. 400p. 24.95 (0-679-45220-6); E-Book 17.50 (1-58836-328-7) Random Hse., Inc.

Holmes, Sharon. Priceless. 2000. 229p. pap. 12.95 (*1-58345-566-3*); 444p. 19.95 (*1-58345-683-X*); 425p. 14.95 (*1-58345-684-8*) Domhan Bks.
Holzer, Erika. Eye for an Eye. 1996. 341p. mass mkt. 5.99 o.p. (*0-8125-4331-9*, Forge Bks.); 1994. 341p. pap. text 4.99 o.p. (*0-8125-1529-3*, Forge Bks.); 1993. 256p. 18.95 o.p. (*0-312-85186-3*, Tor Bks.) Doherty, Tom Assocs., LLC.
—Eye for an Eye. 4.98 o.p. (*0-8317-5561-X*) Smithmark Pubs., Inc.
—Eye for an Eye. 2001. 260p. per. 17.95 (*0-595-19260-2*) iUniverse, Inc.
Honig, Donald. Last Man Out. 1993. 240p. 19.00 o.p. (*0-525-93663-7*, Dutton) Dutton/Plume.
—Last Man Out. 1994. 288p. mass mkt. 3.99 o.p. (*0-451-18300-2*, Signet Bks.) NAL.
—Last Man Out. l.t. ed. 1995. (Niagara Large Print Ser.). 297p. 29.50 o.p. (*0-7089-5804-4*, Ulverscroft) Thorpe, F. A. Pubs. GBR. *Dist:* Ulverscroft Large Print Bks., Ltd.
Honig, Lucy. The Truly Needy: And Other Stories. 2002. 216p. pap. 14.00 (*0-8229-5781-7*) Univ. of Pittsburgh Pr.
Horansky, Ruby. Dead Ahead. 1992. 240p. mass mkt. 4.99 (*0-380-71653-4*, Avon Bks.) Morrow/Avon.
—Dead Ahead: A Mystery Introducing Nikki Trakos. 1990. 256p. 17.95 o.s.i (*0-684-19229-2*, Macmillan Reference USA) Gale Group.
—Dead Center: A Nikki Trakos Mystery. 1994. 224p. 20.00 o.p. (*0-684-19606-9*, Macmillan Reference USA) Gale Group.
Horn, Dara. In the Image. 2003. 288p. (Illus.). 24.95 (*0-393-05106-4*); pap. 13.95 (*0-393-32526-1*) Norton, W. W. & Co., Inc.
Horner, Althea. Chrysalis. 1999. 149p. pap. 21.95 (*0-9668251-0-1*) Monbijou Pr.
Houarner, Gerard. The Beast That Was Max. 2001. 400p. mass mkt. 5.99 (*0-8439-4881-7*, Leisure Bks.) Dorchester Publishing Co., Inc.
Howard, Linda. Now You See Her. 1998. 336p. 23.00 o.s.i (*0-671-56882-5*, Atria); 1999. 368p. reprint ed. mass mkt. 7.99 (*0-671-03405-7*, Pocket) Simon & Schuster.
—Now You See Her. abr. ed. 1998. 18.00 (*0-671-58261-5*, Simon & Schuster Audioworks) Simon & Schuster Audio.
—Now You See Her. l.t. ed. 1999. (Paperback Bestsellers Ser.). 456p. pap. 27.95 (*0-7862-1728-6*); 28.95 o.p. (*0-7862-1727-8*) Thorndike Pr.
Howard, Maureen. A Lover's Almanac. 1999. 288p. pap. 12.95 (*0-14-027512-6*, Penguin Classics) Penguin Group (USA) Inc.
—A Lover's Almanac. 1998. (Illus.). 288p. 24.95 (*0-670-87597-X*) Viking Penguin.
Howard, Tracie. Why Sleeping Dogs Lie. 2003. 288p. pap. 12.95 (*0-451-20977-X*) NAL.
Howard, Tracie & Carter, Danita. Revenge Is Best Served Cold. 2001. 304p. pap. 12.95 (*0-451-20475-1*, Signet Bks.) NAL.
—Talk of the Town. 2002. 304p. pap. 12.95 (*0-451-20703-3*) NAL.
Howells, William Dean. A Hazard of New Fortunes. Lopate, Phillip, ed. & intro. by. 2001. (Classics Ser.). 480p. pap. 14.00 (*0-14-043923-4*, Penguin Classics) Viking Penguin.
Hower, Edward. Night Train Blues. 1996. 221p. 24.00 (*1-877946-71-0*) Permanent Pr., The.
—Shadows & Elephants. 2002. 317p. pap. 14.95 (*0-9679520-3-4*) Leapfrog Pr.
Hruby, Andes. The Trouble with Catherine. 2002. 288p. 23.95 o.s.i (*0-525-94640-3*, Dutton) Dutton/Plume.
Hughes, Susanna. The Slaves of New York. 1999. 256p. pap. 9.95 (*1-901388-45-X*) Chimera Pubns. GBR. *Dist:* Client Distribution Services.
Hunt, Howard. Young Men on Fire. 2003. 256p. pap. 13.00 (*0-7432-4173-8*, Scribner) Simon & Schuster.
Hunter, Evan. Privileged Conversation. unabr. ed. 1996. audio 48.00 (*0-7366-3425-8*, 4070) Books on Tape, Inc.
—Privileged Conversation. Set. abr. ed. 1996. audio 21.95 (*1-55935-195-0*, 693519) Soundelux Audio Publishing.
—Privileged Conversation. 1997. 336p. mass mkt. 6.99 (*0-446-60382-1*); 1996. 82p. 22.95 o.s.i (*0-446-52028-4*) Warner Bks., Inc.
Hunter, Jessie. One Two Buckle My Shoe. 1998. 464p. mass mkt. 6.50 o.s.i (*0-06-101325-0*) HarperCollins Pubs.
—One Two Buckle My Shoe. 1997. 304p. 22.50 (*0-684-83170-8*, Simon & Schuster) Simon & Schuster.
Hunter, M. S. The Final Bell. 1994. 189p. (Orig.). pap. 8.95 o.p. (*1-55583-248-2*) Alyson Pubns.
Hurley, Valerie. St. Ursula's Girls Against the Atomic Bomb. 2003. 19.00 (*1-931561-55-9*) MacAdam/Cage Publishing, Inc.
Hustvedt, Siri. The Blindfold. 1993. (Norton Paperback Fiction Ser.). 220p. pap. 12.00 (*0-393-31013-2*) Norton, W. W. & Co., Inc.
—The Blindfold. 1992. 224p. 20.00 o.s.i (*0-671-75953-1*, Simon & Schuster) Simon & Schuster.
—What I Loved: A Novel. 2003. 384p. 25.00 (*0-8050-7170-9*) Holt, Henry & Co.
—What I Loved: A Novel. 2004. 384p. pap. 14.00 (*0-312-42119-2*); 2003. mass mkt. 7.99 (*0-312-99387-0*) Picador.
Hwang, Caroline. In Full Bloom. 2004. 304p. pap. 13.00 (*0-452-28488-0*, Plume); 2003. 256p. 23.95 (*0-525-94711-6*, Dutton) Dutton/Plume.
Ignacio, Joel R. Honor Thy Brother. 2000. 305p. pap. 17.95 (*1-886225-59-1*) Dageforde Publishing, Inc.
Ignatius, David. A Firing Offense. 1998. mass mkt. 6.99 o.s.i (*0-8041-1802-7*, Ivy Bks.) Ballantine Bks.
—A Firing Offense. unabr. ed. 1998. audio 85.00 (*0-7887-2167-4*, 95463E7) Recorded Bks., LLC.
Indiana, Gary. Rent Boy. 1994. (High Risk Ser.). 128p. (Orig.). pap. (*1-85242-324-2*) Serpent's Tail Ltd.
Irvine, Alexander C. A Scattering of Jades. E-Book 25.95 (*0-312-70730-4*); 2002. 448p. 25.95 (*0-7653-0116-4*) Doherty, Tom Assocs., LLC. (Tor Bks.).
Jackson, Brian Keith. The Queen of Harlem: A Novel. 2003. 256p. pap. 12.95 (*0-7679-0839-2*, Harlem Moon) Broadway Bks.
—The Queen of Harlem: A Novel. 2002. 256p. 22.95 (*0-385-50295-8*) Doubleday Publishing.
Jackson, Faith Reyher. Meadow Fugue & Descant: A Novel. 2002. (*0-931846-66-8*); pap. (*0-931846-64-1*) Washington Writers' Publishing Hse.
Jacobs, Claire R. Mother, May I Sleep with Danger? 1997. 320p. 23.95 o.s.i (*1-55611-515-6*) Fine, Donald I. Bks.
Jacobs, Laura. Women about Town. 2002. 256p. 23.95 o.s.i (*0-670-03088-0*, Viking) Viking Penguin.
—Women about Town: A Novel. 2003. 256p. pap. 14.00 (*0-14-200277-1*) Viking Penguin.
Jacobsen, William. For Hire. 2001. 346p. text 32.99 (*0-7388-6993-7*); E-Book 8.00 (*0-7388-6995-3*) Xlibris Corp.
Jacovsky, Marilyn. Irregulars. 1999. 160p. pap. 16.00 (*1-57962-018-3*) Permanent Pr., The.
Jaffe, Rona. Five Women. l.t. ed. 2000. 560p. 27.95 (*1-57490-263-6*, Beeler Large Print Bks.) Beeler, Thomas T. Publisher.
—Five Women. 1997. 384p. 24.95 (*1-55611-505-9*) Fine, Donald I. Bks.
—Five Women. 1998. (Mira Bks.). 475p. mass mkt. (*1-55166-424-0*, 1-66424-2, Mira Bks.) Harlequin Enterprises, Ltd.
—The Road Taken. 2001. 504p. mass mkt. (*1-55166-825-4*, Mira Bks.) Harlequin Enterprises, Ltd.
—The Room-Mating Season. 2003. 9p. 79.95 (*0-7927-2878-5*); 10p. pap. 94.95 (*0-7927-2879-3*) BBC Audiobooks America.
—The Room-Mating Season. 2003. 384p. 24.95 (*0-525-94713-2*, Dutton) Dutton/Plume.
—The Room-Mating Season. 2004. 448p. mass mkt. (*0-7783-2031-6*, Mira Bks.) Harlequin Enterprises, Ltd.
—The Room-Mating Season. l.t. ed. 2003. (Women's Fiction Ser.). 29.95 (*0-7862-5544-7*) Thorndike Pr.
Jahn, Michael. City of God. 1992. 352p. 21.95 o.p. (*0-312-06927-8*, Saint Martin's Minotaur) St. Martin's Pr.
—Death Games. 1989. mass mkt. 3.95 o.p. (*0-425-11305-1*) Berkley Publishing Group.
—Death Games: A Novel. 1987. 15.95 o.p. (*0-393-02465-2*) Norton, W. W. & Co., Inc.
—Murder at the Museum of Natural History. 2000. (Mystery Ser.: No. 337). per. (*0-373-26337-6*, 1-26337-5, Worldwide Library) Harlequin Enterprises, Ltd.
—Murder at the Museum of Natural History. 1994. (Lt. Bill Donovan Mystery Ser.). 304p. 20.95 o.p. (*0-312-11453-2*, Saint Martin's Minotaur) St. Martin's Pr.
—Murder in Central Park. 2001. (WWL Mystery Ser.: No. 383). 251p. mass mkt. (*0-373-26383-X*, 1-26383-9, Worldwide Library) Harlequin Enterprises, Ltd.
—Murder in Central Park. 2000. (Bill Donovan Mysteries Ser.). 343p. 24.95 (*0-312-24222-0*, Saint Martin's Minotaur) St. Martin's Pr.
—Murder on Coney Island: A Bill Donovan Mystery. 2003. 320p. 24.95 (*0-312-30801-9*, Saint Martin's Minotaur) St. Martin's Pr.
—Murder on Fifth Avenue, Vol. 1. 1998. (Murder on Fifth Avenue Ser.: Vol. 1). 320p. 23.95 (*0-312-18632-0*, Saint Martin's Minotaur) St. Martin's Pr.
—Murder on the Waterfront: A Bill Donovan Mystery. 2001. 304p. 23.95 (*0-312-27857-8*, Saint Martin's Minotaur) St. Martin's Pr.
—Murder on Theater Row. 1997. 304p. text 23.95 o.p. (*0-312-14685-X*, Saint Martin's Minotaur) St. Martin's Pr.
—Murder on Theatre Row. 2000. (Bill Donovan Mysteries Ser.). per. (*0-373-26346-5*, Harlequin Bks.) Harlequin Enterprises, Ltd.
—Night Rituals: A Novel. 1982. 224p. 12.95 o.p. (*0-393-01630-7*) Norton, W. W. & Co., Inc.
James, Henry. Washington Square. 2004. 240p. mass mkt. 4.95 (*0-451-52871-9*); 1964. mass mkt. 0.60 o.p. (*0-451-50222-1*); 1964. mass mkt. 0.75 o.p. (*0-451-50624-3*); 1964. mass mkt. 0.95 o.p. (*0-451-50835-1*); 1964. mass mkt. 1.25 o.p. (*0-451-51023-2*); 1964. mass mkt. 1.50 o.p. (*0-451-51280-4*); 1964. mass mkt. 1.75 o.p. (*0-451-51478-5*); 1964. mass mkt. 2.25 o.p. (*0-451-51766-0*); 1964. 192p. mass mkt. 4.95 (*0-451-52499-3*) NAL. (Signet Classics).
Janowitz, Tama. A Cannibal in Manhattan. 1989. (Illus.). 256p. 3.99 o.p. (*0-517-56624-9*) Random Hse. Value Publishing.
—A Certain Age. 1999. 336p. 23.95 o.s.i (*0-385-49610-9*) Doubleday Publishing.
—The Male Cross-Dresser Support Group. 1994. 320p. pap. 14.00 (*0-671-87150-1*, Washington Square Pr.) Simon & Schuster.
—Slaves of New York. 1986. 288p. 4.99 o.p. (*0-517-56107-7*) Random Hse. Value Publishing.
—Slaves of New York. 1991. 288p. pap. 14.00 (*0-671-74524-7*, Washington Square Pr.); 1989. mass mkt. 3.95 (*0-671-67307-6*, Pocket); 1988. pap. (*0-671-67933-3*, Washington Square Pr.); 1987. mass mkt. (*0-671-63678-2*, Washington Square Pr.) Simon & Schuster.
Janvier, Thomas A. In Old New York. (C). reprint ed. 1986. pap. text 11.95 (*0-8290-2375-5*); 1972. 29.75 (*0-8422-8082-0*) Irvington Pubs.
—In Old New York: A Classic History of New York City. 2000. (Illus.). xx, 285p. 17.95 (*0-312-24282-4*) St. Martin's Pr.
Jedren, Susan. Let 'Em Eat Cake. 1996. pap. 19.00 (*0-679-76805-X*, Vintage) Knopf Publishing Group.
—Let 'em Eat Cake. abr. ed. 1994. 16.96 o.p. (*0-7871-0010-2*) NewStar Media, Inc.
—Let'em Eat Cake: A Novel. 1994. 320p. 22.00 o.s.i (*0-679-43361-9*, Pantheon) Knopf Publishing Group.
Jeffers, H. Paul. Rubout at the Onyx. 1987. mass mkt. 2.95 o.s.i (*0-345-34676-9*) Ballantine Bks.
—Rubout at the Onyx. l.t. ed. 2001. 264p. (*0-7540-4427-0*); (*0-7540-4428-9*) Gale Group. (Macmillan Reference USA).
—Rubout at the Onyx. 1981. (Joan Kahn Bk.). 192p. 10.95 o.p. (*0-89919-046-4*) Houghton Mifflin Co.
—Rubout at the Onyx. l.t. ed. 2001. (Paperback Ser.). 264p. 24.95 (*0-7838-9330-2*) Thorndike Pr.
Jeffrey, Jon. Boyfriend Material. 2002. 240p. 23.00 (*0-7582-0102-8*) Kensington Publishing Corp.
Jeffries, William, pseud. Hell's Kitchen: A Location Scout Mystery. l.t. ed. 2000. (Wheeler Hardcover Ser.). 379p. (Orig.). 26.95 (*1-56895-136-1*, Wheeler Publishing, Inc.) Gale Group.
—Hell's Kitchen: A Location Scout Mystery. 2001. (Orig.). (Illus.). 384p. mass mkt. 7.99 (*0-671-04751-5*); reprint ed. E-Book 6.99 (*0-7434-2403-4*) Simon & Schuster. (Pocket).
Jenkins, Amy. Honeymoon. 2001. 304p. pap. 13.95 (*0-316-65588-0*, Back Bay) Little Brown & Co.
—Honeymoon: A Romantic Rampage. 2000. 288p. 24.95 o.p. (*0-316-65570-8*) Little Brown & Co.
Jenkins, Dan. Rude Behavior: A Novel. 1999. 544p. mass mkt. 7.50 o.s.i (*0-440-23560-X*) Dell Publishing.
Jhabvala, Ruth Prawer. Poet & Dancer. 1994. 208p. pap. 9.00 o.s.i (*0-385-46887-3*); 1993. 19.95 o.s.i (*0-385-46869-5*) Doubleday Publishing.
—Poet & Dancer. 1924. o.s.i (*0-688-11964-6*, Morrow, William & Co.) Morrow/Avon.
—Shards of Memory. 224p. 1996. pap. 11.00 (*0-385-47723-6*); 1995. 22.95 o.s.i (*0-385-47722-8*) Doubleday Publishing.
Johansen, Iris. Dead Aim. 2004. 368p. mass mkt. 7.99 (*0-553-58438-3*); 2003. 352p. 24.95 (*0-553-80246-1*) Bantam Bks.
—Dead Aim. abr. ed. 2003. E-Book 19.95 (*0-553-89727-6*, RH Audio) Random Hse. Audio Publishing Group.
—Dead Aim. l.t. ed. 2003. 448p. 26.95 (*0-375-43192-6*) Random Hse. Large Print.
Johnson-Hodge, Margaret. Some Sunday. 2003. 320p. mass mkt. 6.99 (*0-7582-0026-9*, Kensington Bks.); 2002. 32p. pap. 15.00 (*0-7582-0003-X*); 2001. 32p. 24.00 o.s.i (*1-57566-916-1*, Dafina) Kensington Publishing Corp.
—Some Sunday. l.t. ed. 2002. (African American Ser.). 562p. 29.95 (*0-7862-3870-4*) Thorndike Pr.
Johnson, Joyce. In the Night Cafe. Rosenman, Jane, ed. 1990. 240p. reprint ed. pap. (*0-671-70111-8*, Washington Square Pr.) Simon & Schuster.
Johnson, Mat. Hunting in Harlem. 2003. 300p. 23.95 (*1-58234-272-5*) Bloomsbury Publishing.
Johnston, Brian. With Mallets Aforethought: A Winston Wyc Mystery. 1995. 256p. 20.50 (*1-883402-44-1*, Scribner) Simon & Schuster.
Johnston, Wayne. The Navigator of New York: A Novel. 496p. 2003. pap. 15.95 (*1-4000-3109-5*); 2002. 27.95 (*0-385-50767-4*) Doubleday Publishing.
Jolowicz, Philip. Walls of Silence. 2003. 560p. mass mkt. (*0-552-14901-2*, Corgi) Bantam Bks.
—Walls of Silence. 2003. 528p. mass mkt. 7.50 (*0-7434-2845-5*, Pocket Star); 2002. 448p. 25.00 (*0-7434-2844-7*, Atria) Simon & Schuster.
Jong-Fast, Molly. Normal Girl: A Novel. 208p. 2001. pap. 11.95 (*0-375-75759-7*); 2000. 21.95 o.s.i (*0-375-50281-5*) Random House Adult Trade Publishing Group. (Villard Bks.).
Joseph, Mark. Deadline Y2K. 1999. 304p. mass mkt. 6.50 (*0-312-97187-7*, St. Martin's Paperbacks) St. Martin's Pr.
—Deadline Y2K: A Thriller. 1999. 294p. 24.95 o.p. (*0-312-20202-4*) St. Martin's Pr.
Joyce, B. D. Deadly Love: A Francesca Cahill Novel. 2001. 352p. mass mkt. 6.99 (*0-312-97767-0*, St. Martin's Paperbacks) St. Martin's Pr.
Joyce, Brenda. Deadly Caress. 2003. 384p. mass mkt. 6.99 (*0-312-98943-1*, St. Martin's Paperbacks) St. Martin's Pr.
—Deadly Desire, Vol. 4. 2002. 352p. mass mkt. 6.99 (*0-312-98263-1*, St. Martin's Paperbacks) St. Martin's Pr.
Kaplow, Robert. Me & Orson Welles: A Novel. 2003. 278p. 18.50 (*1-931561-49-4*) MacAdam/Cage Publishing, Inc.
Katchor, Ben. The Jew of New York: A Historical Romance. 1998. (Illus.). 104p. 20.00 o.s.i (*0-375-40104-0*) Random Hse., Inc.
Katz, William. Facemaker. 1988. 256p. text 16.95 o.p. (*0-07-033553-2*) McGraw-Hill Cos., The.
—Facemaker. 1989. 256p. mass mkt. 4.50 (*0-380-70685-7*, Avon Bks.) Morrow/Avon.
Keating, Susannah. The Picture Book. 2000. 244p. 20.00 (*0-688-17888-X*, Morrow, William & Co.) Morrow/Avon.
Keenan, Joe. Putting on the Ritz. 1991. 336p. 19.95 o.p. (*0-670-83877-2*, Viking) Viking Penguin.
Kelland, Horace K. An Almost Perfect Gent. E-Book 20.00 (*0-941711-48-X*); 1999. 350p. 24.95 (*0-941711-43-9*) Wyrick & Co.
Kellerman, Faye. Stone Kiss. 2003. 528p. mass mkt. 7.99 (*0-446-61147-6*, Warner Vision); 2002. 400p. 25.95 (*0-446-53038-7*); 2002. 668p. 25.95 (*0-446-53078-6*) Warner Bks., Inc.
Kelly, Mary A. Foxglove. 1992. 240p. 18.95 o.p. (*0-312-08195-2*, Saint Martin's Minotaur) St. Martin's Pr.
Kelly, Mary Anne. The Cordelia Squad: A Novel of Queens, New York. 2003. 336p. 24.95 (*0-312-31065-X*, Saint Martin's Minotaur) St. Martin's Pr.
Kelly, Thomas. Payback. unabr. ed. 1997. audio 78.00 (*0-7887-1594-1*, 95213E7) Recorded Bks., LLC.
—Payback: A Novel. 1997. mass mkt. 6.99 o.s.i (*0-449-00223-3*, Fawcett) Ballantine Bks.
—The Rackets: A Novel. 2002. 384p. pap. 14.00 (*0-452-28326-4*, Plume) Dutton/Plume.
—The Rackets: A Novel. 2001. 320p. 24.00 (*0-374-17720-1*) Farrar, Straus & Giroux.
Kennedy, Douglas. The Job. (*0-7540-1238-7*); 1999. 652p. pap. (*0-7540-2173-4*) BBC Audiobooks America.
—The Job. 1998. 387p. 23.95 o.p. (*0-7868-6370-6*); 1999. 496p. reprint ed. mass mkt. 6.99 (*0-7868-8954-3*) Hyperion Pr.
—The Job. l.t. ed. 1998. (Mystery Ser.). 653p. 29.95 (*0-7862-1613-1*) Thorndike Pr.
Kennedy, William. The Albany Trilogy. 795th ed. 1996. 624p. pap. 20.00 (*0-14-025786-1*, Penguin Bks.) Penguin Group (USA) Inc.
—Ironweed. 1983. 256p. 16.95 o.p. (*0-670-40176-5*) Viking Penguin.
—Quinn's Book. l.t. ed. 1991. pap. 8.95 o.p. (*1-55504-805-6*, 524) BBC Audiobooks America.
Kernan, Michael. The Lost Diaries of Frans Hals. 1995. pap. 13.95 (*0-312-13117-8*, Saint Martin's Griffin); 1994. 336p. 23.95 o.p. (*0-312-10946-6*) St. Martin's Pr.
Kerr, Peg. The Wild Swans. 1999. 400p. pap. 13.99 (*0-446-67366-8*) Warner Bks., Inc.
Kessler, Alfred. The Eighth Day of the Week. 2000. 185p. pap. 16.00 (*1-929355-00-9*) Pleasure Boat Studio: A Literary Pr.
Kessler, Brad. The Woodcutter's Christmas. 2001. (Illus.). 54p. 14.95 (*1-57178-105-6*) Council Oak Bks.
Keyes, Marian. Rachel's Holiday. 2002. 592p. pap. 13.95 (*0-06-009038-3*, Perennial) HarperTrade.
—Rachel's Holiday. 2001. 528p. mass mkt. 6.99 (*0-380-81768-3*, Avon Bks.); 2000. 576p. 25.00 (*0-688-18071-X*, Morrow, William & Co.) Morrow/Avon.
—Rachel's Holiday. 1998. (*1-85371-896-3*) Poolbeg Pr. IRL. *Dist:* Dufour Editions, Inc.
Kihn, Greg. Shade of Pale. 256p. 1998. pap. 5.99 (*0-8125-5109-5*, Tor Bks.); 1997. 21.95 (*0-312-86046-3*, Forge Bks.) Doherty, Tom Assocs., LLC.
Kilian, Michael. Looker. 1990. 19.95 o.p. (*0-312-05123-9*) St. Martin's Pr.
Kim, Suki. The Interpreter. 2003. 304p. 24.00 o.s.i (*0-374-17713-9*) Farrar, Straus & Giroux.
Kincaid, Jamaica. Lucy. 1991. (Plume Contemporary Fiction Ser.). 176p. pap. 11.95 o.s.i (*0-452-26677-7*, Plume) Dutton/Plume.
—Lucy. 2002. 176p. pap. 12.00 (*0-374-52735-0*); 1990. 163p. 17.95 o.s.i (*0-374-19434-3*) Farrar, Straus & Giroux.

Settings

—Lucy. l.t. ed. 1991. (General Ser.). 169p. lib. bdg. 19.95 (*0-8161-5201-2*, Macmillan Reference USA) Gale Group.
—Lucy. Schaffer-De Vries, Stefanie, tr. from ENG. 1991. (GER.). 152p. (*3-8105-1043-2*) Kruger, Wolfgang Verlag, GmbH DEU. *Dist:* International Bk. Import Service, Inc.
Kincaid, Nell. Turn Back the Dawn. 1983. (Candlelight Regency Romance Ser.: No. 185). 192p. (Orig.). pap. 1.95 o.s.i (*0-440-19098-3*) Dell Publishing.
—Turn Back the Dawn. l.t. ed. 2002. 179p. (Orig.). pap. 23.95 (*0-7838-9774-X*) Gale Group.
King, Frank. Take the D Train. 1990. 16.95 o.p. (*0-525-24836-6*, Dutton) Dutton/Plume.
King, Peter. Spiced to Death. (Culinary Mysteries Ser.). 1998. 304p. mass mkt. 5.99 (*0-312-96500-1*, St. Martin's Paperbacks); 1997. 352p. text 23.95 o.p. (*0-312-15661-8*, Saint Martin's Minotaur) St. Martin's Pr.
Kingsbury, Karen. One Tuesday Morning. l.t. ed. 2004. 689p. 27.95 (*0-7862-6111-0*) Thorndike Pr.
—One Tuesday Morning. 2003. 352p. pap. 12.99 (*0-310-24752-7*) Zondervan.
Kingsbury, Karen & Smalley, Gary. Return. 2003. (Redemption Ser.). 250p. pap. 12.99 (*0-8423-8289-5*) Tyndale Hse. Pubs.
Kinsella, Sophie. Shopaholic Takes Manhattan. Orig. Title: Shopaholic Abroad. 2004. 416p. mass mkt. 6.99 (*0-440-24181-2*); 2002. 336p. pap. 11.95 (*0-385-33588-1*, Delta) Dell Publishing.
—Shopaholic Takes Manhattan. Orig. Title: Shopaholic Abroad. audio 29.99 (*1-4025-3624-0*) Recorded Bks., LLC.
—Shopaholic Ties the Knot. 2003. 352p. pap. 10.95 (*0-385-33617-9*, Delta) Dell Publishing.
—Shopaholic Ties the Knot. audio 29.99 (*1-4025-3625-9*) Recorded Bks., LLC.
Kirby, Robert. Curbside Boys. 2002. (Illus.). 150p. pap. 10.95 (*1-57344-154-6*) Cleis Pr.
Kirshenbaum, Binnie. An Almost Perfect Moment: A Novel. 2004. 288p. 23.95 (*0-06-052086-8*, Ecco) HarperTrade.
Kitt, Sandra. Family Affairs. l.t. ed. 2003. (Large Print Ser.). 29.95 (*1-57490-470-1*, Beeler Large Print Bks.) Beeler, Thomas T. Publisher.
—Family Affairs. 1999. (Signet Book Ser.). 368p. mass mkt. 6.99 (*0-451-19185-4*, Signet Bks.) NAL.
—Significant Others. 1996. 400p. mass mkt. 6.99 (*0-451-18824-1*, Signet Bks.) NAL.
Klavan, Andrew. The Animal Hour. Rosenman, Jane, ed. 1993. reprint ed. 352p. mass mkt. 5.50 (*0-671-74011-3*, Pocket); 368p. 20.00 o.p. (*0-671-74010-5*, Atria) Simon & Schuster.
—Don't Say a Word. Rubenstein, Julie, ed. 1991. 19.95 o.p. (*0-671-74008-3*, Atria) Simon & Schuster.
Klempner, Joseph T. Felony Murder. 368p. 1996. (Felony Murder Ser.: Vol. 1). mass mkt. 6.99 (*0-312-96037-9*, St. Martin's Paperbacks); 1995. 23.95 o.p. (*0-312-13494-0*) St. Martin's Pr.
—Shoot the Moon. 1998. (Shoot Moon Ser.: Vol. 1). 376p. pap. 6.99 (*0-312-96446-3*, St. Martin's Paperbacks); 1997. 24.95 o.p. (*0-312-15424-0*) St. Martin's Pr.
Kluger, Steve. Last Days of Summer. 1998. 348p. 21.00 (*0-380-97645-5*, Avon Bks.) Morrow/Avon.
—Last Days of Summer. 1999. 18.05 (*0-606-19266-2*) Turtleback Bks.
—The Last Days of Summer. 1999. 368p. reprint ed. pap. 13.00 (*0-380-79763-1*, Avon Bks.) Morrow/ Avon.
Koch, Edward I. Murder at City Hall. 1995. 208p. mass mkt. 19.95 o.p. (*0-8217-5087-9*, Zebra Bks.) Kensington Publishing Corp.
—Murder on Broadway. 1997. 320p. mass mkt. 5.99 o.s.i (*1-57566-186-1*) Kensington Publishing Corp.
—Murder on 34th Street. 1998. 288p. mass mkt. 5.99 o.s.i (*1-57566-355-4*); 1997. 192p. 19.95 o.s.i (*1-57566-232-9*) Kensington Publishing Corp.
—The Senator Must Die. 1998. 224p. 22.00 o.s.i (*1-57566-325-2*, Kensington Bks.) Kensington Publishing Corp.
Koch, Edward I. & Resnicow, Herbert. Murder at City Hall. 1996. 224p. mass mkt. 5.99 o.s.i (*1-57566-053-9*) Kensington Publishing Corp.
Koch, Edward I. & Staub, Wendy Corsi. Murder on Broadway. 1996. 192p. 19.95 o.s.i (*1-57566-049-0*) Kensington Publishing Corp.
Koch, Stephen. The Bachelor's Bride. 1986. 224p. 18.95 o.p. (*0-7145-2856-0*) Boyars, Marion Pubs., Inc.
Komarnicki, Todd. Famine. 1997. 256p. 22.95 (*1-55970-365-2*) Arcade Publishing, Inc.
—Famine. 1998. 288p. pap. 12.95 o.s.i (*0-452-27932-1*, Plume) Dutton/Plume.
Kondoleon, Harry. Diary of a Lost Boy. 1995. 224p. 10.00 o.s.i (*1-57322-504-5*, Riverhead Trade (Paperbacks)) Berkley Publishing Group.
Konecky, Edith. Allegra Maud Goldman. 1990. (Illus.). 160p. pap. 12.95 o.p. (*1-55861-022-7*); 2nd ed. 2001. 187p. pap. 14.95 (*1-55861-281-5*) Feminist Pr. at The City Univ. of New York.
—Allegra Maud Goldman. 1976. 160p. 7.95 o.p. (*0-06-012452-0*) HarperCollins Pubs.
—Allegra Maud Goldman. 1987. (Gems of American Jewish Literature Ser.). 150p. pap. 7.95 o.p. (*0-8276-0282-0*) Jewish Pubn. Society.
—A Place at the Table. 1989. 16.95 o.s.i (*0-394-57522-9*) Random Hse., Inc.
Koning, Hans. Pursuit of a Woman on the Hinge of History. 1997. 220p. (Orig.). pap. 15.95 (*1-57129-045-1*, Lumen Editions) Brookline Bks., Inc.
Korelitz, Jean H. A Jury of Her Peers. l.t. ed. 1996. 25.95 (*1-56895-386-0*, Wheeler Publishing, Inc.) Gale Group.
—A Jury of Her Peers. 1997. 448p. mass mkt. 5.99 o.s.i (*0-451-18871-3*, Signet Bks.) NAL.
Kotzwinkle, William. The Fan Man. 1994. (Vintage Contemporaries Ser.). 208p. pap. 12.00 (*0-679-75245-5*, Vintage) Knopf Publishing Group.
—Game of Thirty. 1994. 262p. 21.95 o.p. (*0-395-53270-1*) Houghton Mifflin Co.
—The Game of Thirty. 1995. 304p. mass mkt. 5.99 o.s.i (*0-553-57385-3*) Bantam Bks.
—The Midnight Examiner. 1989. 256p. 17.95 o.p. (*0-395-49859-7*) Houghton Mifflin Co.
Krahn, Betina. Sweet Talkin' Man. 2000. 384p. mass mkt. 6.50 (*0-553-57619-4*) Bantam Bks.
Krantz, Judith. I'll Take Manhattan. 1986. 443p. 4.99 o.p. (*0-517-56110-7*) Random Hse. Value Publishing.
Krantz, Sherrie. Vivian Lives. 2003. 208p. pap. 11.95 (*0-345-45355-7*, Ballantine Bks.) Ballantine Bks.
Kranz, Rachel. Leaps of Faith. 2000. 565p. 25.00 o.p. (*0-374-18444-5*) Farrar, Straus & Giroux.
Kriegel, Mark. Bless Me, Father. 1996. 352p. reprint ed. mass mkt. 6.99 o.s.i (*0-425-15574-9*) Berkley Publishing Group.
Kroll, Morton. Old Caper, Youngblood. 292p. E-Book 5.00 (*1-929939-05-1*) PublishingOnline.
Kruger, Mary. Masterpiece of Murder: A Gilded Age Mystery. 1997. (Gilded Age Mystery Ser.). 272p. mass mkt. 5.50 o.s.i (*1-57566-229-9*) Kensington Publishing Corp.
—No Honeymoon for Death: A Gilded Age Mystery. 1996. 304p. mass mkt. 5.50 o.s.i (*1-57566-110-1*); 1995. 288p. mass mkt. 18.95 o.s.i (*0-8217-5159-X*) Kensington Publishing Corp.
Kunstler, James Howard. Maggie Darling: A Modern Romance. 2004. 336p. 23.00 (*0-87113-910-3*, Atlantic Monthly Pr.) Grove/Atlantic, Inc.
Kurland, Michael. Girls in High Heeled Shoes. 1998. (Alexander Brass Mysteries Ser.). 256p. 22.95 (*0-312-18104-3*, 874694, Saint Martin's Minotaur) St. Martin's Pr.
—Too Soon Dead. 1997. 288p. 22.95 o.p. (*0-312-15228-0*, Saint Martin's Minotaur) St. Martin's Pr.
Kwitney, Alisa. Till the Fat Lady Sings. 1992. 224p. 19.00 o.p. (*0-06-019021-3*); 1993. 240p. reprint ed. pap. 10.00 o.p. (*0-06-099511-4*, HarperCollins) HarperTrade.
La Puma, Salvatore. The Boys of Bensonhurst. 1987. (Flannery O'Connor Award for Short Fiction Ser.). 136p. 15.95 o.p. (*0-8203-0891-9*) Univ. of Georgia Pr.
Lackey, Mercedes. Spirits White as Lightning. 2003. 512p. pap. 7.99 (*0-7434-3608-3*) Baen Bks.
Lackey, Mercedes & Edghill, Rosemary. Beyond World's End. 2001. 352p. 24.00 (*0-671-31955-8*) Baen Bks.
—Mad Maudlin. 2003. 448p. 25.00 (*0-7434-7143-1*) Baen Bks.
—Spirits White as Lightning. 2001. 448p. 24.00 (*0-671-31853-5*) Baen Bks.
Lacy, Al & Lacy, JoAnna. All My Tomorrows. 2003. (Orphan Train Trilogy, Book Two Ser.). 400p. pap. 11.99 (*1-59052-130-7*) Multnomah Pubs., Inc.
—The Little Sparrows. 2003. (Orphan Train Trilogy Ser.). 368p. pap. 7.99 (*1-59052-063-7*) Multnomah Pubs., Inc.
Lamalle, Cecile. Prepared for Murder: A Culinary Mystery with Recipes. 2001. (Illus.). 304p. mass mkt. 6.50 (*0-446-61028-3*) Warner Bks., Inc.
Lance, Peter. First Degree Burn. 1997. 384p. mass mkt. 5.99 o.s.i (*0-425-15698-2*, Prime Crime) Berkley Publishing Group.
Land, Jon. Dead Simple. 1999. 404p. mass mkt. 6.99 (*0-8125-4001-8*); 1998. 320p. 23.95 (*0-312-86489-2*) Doherty, Tom Assocs., LLC. (Forge Bks.).
Landesman, Peter. Blood Acre. 2000. 272p. pap. 12.95 o.s.i (*0-14-028236-X*) Penguin Group (USA) Inc.
—Blood Acre. 1999. 272p. 23.95 o.p. (*0-670-88207-0*); 262p. 23.95 (*0-670-78181-9*) Viking Penguin.
Larsen, Nella. The Complete Fiction of Nella Larsen: Passing, Quicksand & Three Stories. 2001. 304p. pap. 13.00 (*0-385-72100-5*, Knopf Bks. for Young Readers) Random Hse. Children's Bks.
—Passing. 1970. (American Negro: His History & Literature, Ser. No. 3). reprint ed. 27.95 (*0-405-01930-0*) Ayer Co. Pubs., Inc.
—Passing. 2002. (Modern Library Classics). 304p. pap. 9.95 (*0-375-75813-5*, Modern Library) Random House Adult Trade Publishing Group.
—Passing. 2003. 160p. pap. 10.00 (*0-14-243727-1*, Penguin Classics) Viking Penguin.
Larsgaard, Chris. The Heir Hunter. 2001. 448p. mass mkt. 6.99 (*0-440-23462-X*) Dell Publishing.
Lasdun, James. The Horned Man: A Novel. 2002. 208p. 24.95 (*0-393-00336-1*) Norton, W. W. & Co., Inc.
Laser, Michael. Old Buddy, Old Pal. 1999. 160p. 24.00 (*1-57962-021-3*) Permanent Pr., The.
Lasser, Scott. All I Could Get: A Novel. 2003. 256p. pap. 12.00 (*0-375-72787-6*, Vintage) Knopf Publishing Group.
Lathen, Emma. Accounting for Murder. 1995. pap. 7.00 (*0-684-80103-5*); pap. 7.00 (*0-684-80245-7*) Simon & Schuster. (Scribner).
—Accounting for Murder: A John Putnam Thatcher Mystery. 1995. 192p. per. 7.00 o.p. (*1-57283-000-X*, Scribner); 1987. mass mkt. 3.50 (*0-671-64550-1*, Pocket) Simon & Schuster.
—Banking on Death: A John Putnam Thatcher Mystery. 1993. 168p. reprint ed. pap. 6.95 o.s.i (*1-883402-06-9*, Scribner) Simon & Schuster.
—Brewing up a Storm. l.t. ed. 1998. 368p. mass mkt. 5.99 o.s.i (*0-06-104434-2*, HarperTorch) Morrow/ Avon.
—Brewing up a Storm. l.t. ed. 1996. (John Thatcher Mystery Ser.). 272p. 21.95 o.p. (*0-312-14554-3*, Saint Martin's Minotaur) St. Martin's Pr.
—Brewing up a Storm: A John Thatcher Mystery. l.t. ed. 1997. (G. K. Hall Mystery Ser.). 400p. 23.95 o.p. (*0-7838-8096-0*, Macmillan Reference USA) Gale Group.
—By Hook or by Crook. l.t. ed. 1993. (Nightingale Ser.). 313p. lib. bdg. 15.95 o.p. (*0-8161-5707-3*, Macmillan Reference USA) Gale Group.
—Come to Dust. 1997. (Black Dagger Crime Ser.). 256p. 18.50 o.p. (*0-7451-8940-7*, Black Dagger) BBC Audiobooks America.
—Double, Double Oil & Trouble. 1983. mass mkt. 2.95 o.s.i (*0-671-49990-4*, Pocket); 1978. 8.95 o.s.i (*0-671-24215-6*, Simon & Schuster) Simon & Schuster.
—East Is East. 1994. 336p. mass mkt. 5.99 o.s.i (*0-06-104296-X*) HarperCollins Children's Bk. Group.
—East Is East. 1994. 79p. mass mkt. 5.99 o.p. (*0-06-104297-8*, HarperTorch) Morrow/Avon.
—East Is East: A John Putnam Thatcher Mystery. 1991. 224p. 19.00 o.p. (*0-671-73707-4*, Simon & Schuster) Simon & Schuster.
—Going for the Gold. 1981. (General Ser.). lib. bdg. 12.95 o.p. (*0-8161-3200-3*, Macmillan Reference USA) Gale Group.
—Going for the Gold. 1981. 12.95 o.p. (*0-671-41407-0*, Simon & Schuster) Simon & Schuster.
—Green Grow the Dollars. 1982. (General Ser.). lib. bdg. 14.95 o.p. (*0-8161-3397-2*, Macmillan Reference USA) Gale Group.
—Green Grow the Dollars. 1984. mass mkt. 3.95 o.s.i (*0-671-52767-3*, Pocket); 1983. mass mkt. 2.95 o.s.i (*0-671-45049-2*, Pocket); 1982. 12.95 o.p. (*0-671-44130-2*, Simon & Schuster) Simon & Schuster.
—The Longer the Thread. l.t. ed. 1984. (Nightingale Ser.). 328p. pap. 9.95 o.p. (*0-8161-3668-8*, Macmillan Reference USA) Gale Group.
—The Longer the Thread. 1988. 192p. mass mkt. 3.50 (*0-671-65053-X*, Pocket) Simon & Schuster.
—Murder Against the Grain. 1987. 192p. mass mkt. 3.95 o.s.i (*0-671-63973-0*, Pocket) Simon & Schuster.
—Murder Makes the Wheels Go 'Round. Barzun, Jacques & Taylor, W. H., eds. 1983. (Crime Fiction 1950-1975 Ser.). 183p. lib. bdg. 18.00 o.p. (*0-8240-4985-3*) Garland Publishing, Inc.
—Murder Makes the Wheels Go 'Round. 1987. 192p. mass mkt. 3.50 o.s.i (*0-671-45528-1*, Pocket) Simon & Schuster.
—Murder to Go. 1983. mass mkt. 2.95 o.s.i (*0-671-45529-X*, Pocket) Simon & Schuster.
—Murder Without Icing. l.t. ed. 1989. lib. bdg. 22.95 o.p. (*0-7451-7186-9*, Macmillan Reference USA) Gale Group.
—Murder Without Icing. 1983. mass mkt. 2.95 o.s.i (*0-671-49202-0*, Pocket); 1972. 5.95 o.s.i (*0-671-21207-9*, Simon & Schuster) Simon & Schuster.
—Pick-Up Sticks. 1984. 240p. mass mkt. 2.95 o.s.i (*0-671-50997-7*, Pocket) Simon & Schuster.
—A Place for Murder. 1983. mass mkt. 2.95 o.s.i (*0-671-47760-9*, Pocket) Simon & Schuster.
—Right on the Money: A John Putman Thatcher Mystery. 1995. (John Putnam Thatcher Mystery Ser.). 288p. mass mkt. 4.99 o.s.i (*0-06-104295-1*, HarperTorch) Morrow/Avon.
—Right on the Money: A John Putman Thatcher Mystery. 1993. 256p. 20.00 o.p. (*0-671-73708-2*, Simon & Schuster) Simon & Schuster.
—A Shark out of Water. 1998. (John Putnam Thatcher Mystery Ser.). 336p. reprint ed. mass mkt. 5.99 o.s.i (*0-06-104460-1*, HarperTorch) Morrow/Avon.
—A Shark Out of Water: A John Putnam Thatcher Mystery. 1997. 293p. 22.95 (*0-312-17018-1*, Saint Martin's Minotaur) St. Martin's Pr.
—A Shark Out of Water: A John Thatcher Mystery. l.t. ed. 1997. (G. K. Hall Mystery Ser.). 372p. 25.95 o.p. (*0-7838-8357-9*, Macmillan Reference USA) Gale Group.
—Something in the Air. 1989. 256p. mass mkt. 3.95 o.s.i (*0-671-68356-X*, Pocket); 1988. 240p. 16.95 o.p. (*0-671-66599-5*, Simon & Schuster) Simon & Schuster.
—Stitch in Time. 1983. mass mkt. 2.95 o.s.i (*0-671-45526-5*, Pocket) Simon & Schuster.
—Sweet & Low. 1983. mass mkt. 2.95 o.s.i (*0-671-45527-3*, Pocket); 1974. 6.95 o.s.i (*0-671-21785-2*, Simon & Schuster) Simon & Schuster.
LaValle, Victor D. Slapboxing with Jesus. 1999. 224p. pap. 11.00 (*0-375-70590-2*) Knopf, Alfred A. Inc.
Lawrence, Jerome. A Golden Circle: A Tale of the Stage & the Screen & Music of Yesterday & Now & Tomorrow & Maybe the Day after Tomorrow. 1993. 170p. 19.95 o.p. (*1-55713-086-8*) Sun & Moon Pr.
Leahey, Michael. Broken Machines. 2000. 294p. 23.95 (*0-312-26130-6*, Saint Martin's Minotaur) St. Martin's Pr.
Leahey, Michael I. The Pale Green Horse: A J. J. Donovan Mystery. 2002. 272p. 23.95 (*0-312-27813-6*, Saint Martin's Minotaur) St. Martin's Pr.
Ledwidge, Michael. Bad Connection. 2001. 272p. 23.95 (*0-7434-0593-5*, Atria) Simon & Schuster.
—The Narrowback. 2001. (Illus.). 352p. reprint ed. mass mkt. 6.99 (*0-7434-0354-1*, Pocket) Simon & Schuster.
Lee, Anthony. Martin Quinn. 2004. pap. (*0-06-059534-5*, Dark Alley) HarperTrade.
—Martin Quinn. 2003. 384p. 24.95 (*0-06-009042-1*, Morrow, William & Co.) Morrow/Avon.
Lee, Chang-Rae. A Gesture Life. 1999. 356p. 23.95 o.s.i (*1-57322-146-5*, Riverhead Bks. (Hardcovers)) Putnam Publishing Group, The.
—Native Speaker. 1995. 324p. 22.95 o.p. (*1-57322-001-9*, Riverhead Bks. (Hardcovers)) Putnam Publishing Group, The.
Lehman, Ernest. Sweet Smell of Success: Short Fiction of Ernest Lehman. 2000. 272p. 15.95 (*1-58567-047-2*) Overlook Pr., The.
Lehrer, Kate. Confessions of a Bigamist: A Novel. 2004. 288p. 24.00 (*1-4000-5025-1*) Crown Publishing Group.
Leigh, Robert. The Turner Journals. 1996. 288p. 22.95 (*0-8027-3260-7*) Walker & Co.
Lemann, Nancy. Malaise. l.t. ed. 2002. 28.95 (*1-58724-338-5*, Wheeler Publishing, Inc.) Gale Group.
—Malaise. 256p. 2003. pap. 13.00 (*0-7432-1549-4*); 2002. 24.00 (*0-7432-1548-6*) Simon & Schuster. (Scribner).
Leontief, Estelle. Sellie & Dee: A Friendship. 1993. (Crimson Edge Chapbook Ser.). pap. 7.95 (*0-9619111-6-6*) Chicory Blue Pr., Inc.
Lethem, Jonathan. The Fortress of Solitude: A Novel. 2003. 528p. 26.00 (*0-385-50069-6*) Doubleday Publishing.
—The Fortress of Solitude: A Novel. l.t. ed. 2003. 824p. 31.95 (*0-7862-5996-5*) Gale Group.
—Motherless Brooklyn. 1999. 320p. 23.95 o.s.i (*0-385-49183-2*) Doubleday Publishing.
—Motherless Brooklyn. l.t. ed. 2000. (Basic Ser.). 492p. 30.95 (*0-7862-2695-1*) Thorndike Pr.
—Motherless Brooklyn. 2000. 19.05 (*0-606-21849-1*) Turtleback Bks.
—Motherless Brooklyn: A Novel. 2000. (Vintage Contemporaries Ser.). 336p. pap. 13.00 (*0-375-72483-4*, Vintage) Knopf Publishing Group.
Leuci, Robert. Fence Jumpers: A Novel. 1996. 403p. pap. 5.99 o.p. (*0-312-95937-0*, St. Martin's Paperbacks); 1995. 338p. 22.95 o.p. (*0-312-13073-2*) St. Martin's Pr.
—Odessa Beach. 1985. 240p. 15.95 (*0-88191-029-5*) Freundlich Bks.
—Odessa Beach. 2000. 288p. pap. 10.95 (*1-55921-242-X*) Moyer Bell.
—Odessa Beach. 1986. 288p. mass mkt. 3.95 o.p. (*0-451-14603-4*, Signet Bks.) NAL.
—Snitch. 1998. (Snitch Ser.: Vol. 1). 352p. pap. 6.99 (*0-312-96510-9*, St. Martin's Paperbacks); 1997. 384p. 24.95 (*0-312-14739-2*) St. Martin's Pr.
Leventhal, Stan. Skydiving on Christopher Street. 1995. 225p. (Orig.). mass mkt. 6.95 (*1-56333-287-6*, Hard Candy) Masquerade Bks., Inc.
Levien, D. J. Swagbelly. 2003. 240p. pap. 13.00 (*0-452-28454-6*, Plume) Dutton/Plume.
Levin, Ira. Sliver. 1991. 288p. mass mkt. 5.99 o.s.i (*0-553-29507-1*) Bantam Bks.
—Sliver. l.t. ed. 1991. 288p. 21.95 o.s.i (*0-385-41826-4*, Bantam Large Type) Bantam Doubleday Dell Large Print Group, Inc.
Levinson, Paul. The Pixel Eye. E-Book (*0-312-71086-0*);Vol. 3. 2003. 336p. 24.95 (*0-7653-0556-9*) Doherty, Tom Assocs., LLC. (Tor Bks.).
Levy, Elizabeth. Cold As Ice. 1989. 176p. pap. 2.95 (*0-380-70315-7*, Avon Bks.) Morrow/Avon.
Lewis, R. W. B., ed. The Collected Short Stories of Edith Wharton, Vol. 2. 1989. (Hudson River Editions Ser.). 908p. 50.00 o.s.i (*0-02-626161-8*, Macmillan Reference USA) Gale Group.

Lewis, Sara. Heart Conditions. 1994. x, 276p. 21.95 o.p. (*0-15-139805-4*); 2nd ed. 1997. 288p. pap. 12.00 (*0-15-600499-2*, Harvest Bks.) Harcourt Trade Pubs.

Lewis, Sinclair. The Job. (Collected Works of Sinclair Lewis). 326p. reprint ed. 2001. pap. 28.00 (*0-7426-5672-1*); 1998. lib. bdg. 98.00 (*1-58201-672-0*) Classic Bks.

—The Job. 1994. 327p. pap. 15.00 (*0-8032-7948-5*, Bison Bks.) Univ. of Nebraska Pr.

Lewis, Stephen. And Baby Makes None. 1991. 208p. 18.95 (*0-8027-5789-8*) Walker & Co.

Liddy, G. Gordon. The Monkey Handlers. abr. ed. 1990. audio 15.95 o.p. (*1-55927-100-0*) Audio Renaissance.

—The Monkey Handlers. 1991. 352p. mass mkt. 5.99 (*0-312-92613-8*, St. Martin's Paperbacks); 1990. 19.95 o.p. (*0-312-05127-1*) St. Martin's Pr.

Lieberman, Herbert. The Girl with the Botticelli Eyes. 1996. 308p. 22.95 o.p. (*0-312-11815-5*) St. Martin's Pr.

Lieberman, Robert H. The Last Boy. 512p. 2003. pap. 14.00 (*1-4022-0057-9*); 2002. 22.00 (*1-57071-943-8*) Sourcebooks, Inc. (Sourcebooks Landmark).

Lish, Gordon. Dear Mr. Capote. 3rd ed. 1996. 264p. reprint ed. pap. 12.95 (*1-56858-079-7*) Four Walls Eight Windows.

—Dear Mr. Capote. 1983. 264p. o.p. (*0-03-061477-5*) Holt, Henry & Co.

—Zimzum. 2nd ed. 1997. 98p. reprint ed. pap. 12.95 (*1-56858-109-2*) Four Walls Eight Windows.

Lissner, Caren. Carrie Pilby. 2003. 336p. pap. (*0-373-25029-0*, Red Dress Ink) Harlequin Enterprises, Ltd.

Listfield, Emily. The Last Good Night. l.t. ed. 1997. 24.95 (*1-57490-128-1*, Beeler Large Print Bks.) Beeler, Thomas T. Publisher.

—The Last Good Night. 1998. 352p. mass mkt. 5.99 o.s.i (*1-57566-354-6*) Kensington Publishing Corp.

—The Last Good Night. 1997. 320p. 22.95 o.p. (*0-316-54091-9*) Little Brown & Co.

Little, Benilde. Good Hair. 1996. 240p. 22.00 (*0-684-80176-0*, Simon & Schuster) Simon & Schuster.

—Good Hair: A Novel. 2003. 240p. pap. 12.00 (*0-684-83557-6*, Free Pr.) Simon & Schuster.

Liu, Aimee E. The Face. 1994. 368p. 21.95 o.s.i (*0-446-51829-8*) Warner Bks., Inc.

Livingston, Harold. Ride a Tiger. 1987. 648p. 18.95 o.p. (*0-688-04291-0*, Morrow, William & Co.) Morrow/Avon.

Lloyd, Joan Elizabeth. Slow Dancing. 1997. 224p. pap. 9.95 (*0-7867-0436-5*, Carroll & Graf Pubs.) Avalon Publishing Group.

Lockridge, Richard. Plate of Red Herrings. l.t. ed. 1985. (Nightingale Ser.). 304p. 10.95 o.p. (*0-8161-3832-X*, Macmillan Reference USA) Gale Group.

Lopate, Phillip. The Rug Merchant. 1987. 224p. 16.95 o.p. (*0-670-81434-2*) Viking Penguin.

—Writing New York: A Literary Anthology. 2000. 1088p. reprint ed. pap. 22.95 (*0-671-04235-1*, Washington Square Pr.) Simon & Schuster.

Lord, Shirley. The Crasher. 1999. 464p. mass mkt. 6.99 (*0-446-60663-4*); 1998. 400p. 24.00 o.p. (*0-446-52027-6*) Warner Bks., Inc.

—My Sister's Keeper. 1994. (Super Sound Buy, Dove Ser.). 8.99 o.p. (*0-7871-0148-6*) Penguin Group (USA) Inc.

Lordon, Randye. Brotherly Love. 272p. 1994. pap. 9.95 (*0-312-10947-4*, Saint Martin's Griffin); 1993. 18.95 o.p. (*0-312-09254-7*, Saint Martin's Minotaur) St. Martin's Pr.

—Sister's Keeper. 1994. 272p. 20.95 o.p. (*0-312-11336-6*, Saint Martin's Minotaur) St. Martin's Pr.

—Sisters Keeper. 1996. (Stonewall Inn Editions Ser.). 320p. pap. 11.95 (*0-312-14134-3*, Saint Martin's Griffin) St. Martin's Pr.

Love, William F. Bishop's Revenge: A Bishop Regan & Davey Goldman Myster. 1993. 276p. 20.00 o.p. (*1-55611-351-X*) Fine, Donald I. Bks.

—Bloody Ten. 1992. 19.95 o.p. (*1-55611-275-0*) Fine, Donald I. Bks.

—Bloody Ten. 1994. mass mkt. (*0-373-26140-3*, Harlequin Bks.) Harlequin Enterprises, Ltd.

—The Chartreuse Clue. 1990. 18.95 o.p. (*1-55611-211-4*) Fine, Donald I. Bks.

—The Chartreuse Clue. 1991. 352p. reprint ed. mass mkt. 5.50 o.p. (*0-451-40273-1*, Onyx) NAL.

—The Fundamentals of Murder. 1991. 18.95 o.p. (*1-55611-233-5*) Fine, Donald I. Bks.

—The Ruby-Red Clue. 1992. Orig. Title: The Fundamentals of Murder. 288p. mass mkt. 4.99 o.s.i (*0-451-40329-0*, Onyx) NAL.

Lovell, Glenville. Too Beautiful to Die. 2004. 320p. mass mkt. 6.99 (*0-425-19702-6*) Berkley Publishing Group.

—Too Beautiful to Die. 2003. 304p. 23.95 (*0-399-15048-X*) Putnam Publishing Group, The.

Lowell, Jax P. Mothers. 336p. 1996. pap. 13.95 (*0-312-14373-7*, Saint Martin's Griffin); 1995. 22.95 o.p. (*0-312-13126-7*) St. Martin's Pr.

Ludlum, Robert & Shelby, Philip. The Cassandra Compact. 2002. 448p. mass mkt. 7.99 (*0-312-98158-9*, St. Martin's Paperbacks) St. Martin's Pr.

Lundy, Mike. Baby Farm. 1988. mass mkt. 3.95 o.p. (*0-425-10896-1*) Berkley Publishing Group.

Lupica, Mike. Jump. 384p. 2002. mass mkt. 6.99 (*0-7860-1522-5*); 1996. mass mkt. 5.99 o.s.i (*0-7860-0303-0*); 1996. mass mkt. 5.99 o.s.i (*1-57566-112-8*) Kensington Publishing Corp.

—Red Zone. 2003. 352p. 24.95 (*0-399-15082-X*) Putnam Publishing Group, The.

Lupoff, Richard A. The Silver Chariot Killer. 1996. 192p. text 21.95 o.p. (*0-312-14736-8*, Saint Martin's Minotaur) St. Martin's Pr.

Luttrell, Steve. Home Movies: A Collection of Poems by Steve Luttrell. 1998. 61p. 9.95 (*1-878471-05-8*) Big Bridge Pr.

Lutz, John. The Ex. 1999. 320p. mass mkt. 4.99 o.s.i (*0-7860-0186-0*); 1997. 304p. mass mkt. 5.50 o.s.i (*1-57566-178-0*); 1996. 256p. 21.00 o.s.i (*1-57566-078-4*, Kensington Bks.) Kensington Publishing Corp.

—Night Watcher. 2002. 400p. mass mkt. 6.99 (*0-7860-1515-2*) Kensington Publishing Corp.

Lynn, Alison. One Man Missing. 2004. 224p. pap. 13.00 (*0-7432-5026-5*, Touchstone) Simon & Schuster.

Maas, Peter. China White. l.t. ed. 1995. (Large Print Bks.). pap. 23.95 (*1-56895-096-9*, Wheeler Publishing, Inc.) Gale Group.

—China White. 1994. 272p. 23.00 o.s.i (*0-671-69417-0*, Simon & Schuster) Simon & Schuster.

MacDonald, Ann-Marie. Fall on Your Knees: A Novel. 512p. 2002. pap. 14.00 (*0-7432-3718-8*, Touchstone); 1998. pap. 14.00 (*0-684-83868-0*, Touchstone); 1997. 23.00 (*0-684-83320-4*, Simon & Schuster) Simon & Schuster.

MacDonnell, Julia. A Year of Favor: A Novel. 1994. 330p. 25.00 o.p. (*0-688-12546-8*, Morrow, William & Co.) Morrow/Avon.

Machado de Assis, Joaquim Maria. The Alienist. MacAdam, Alfred, tr. from POR. ltd. ed. 1998. Orig. Title: O Alienista. (Illus.). 58p. 450.00 (*0-910457-38-7*) Arion Pr.

Mackie, John. Manhattan North. 2003. 384p. mass mkt. 6.99 (*0-451-41095-5*, Onyx) NAL.

Macomber, Debbie. Between Friends: A Novel. l.t. ed. 2002. (Wheeler Hardcover Ser.). 489p. 28.95 (*1-58724-363-6*, Wheeler Publishing, Inc.) Gale Group.

—Between Friends: A Novel. 2002. 384p. (*1-55166-905-6*, 1-66905-0, Mira Bks.) Harlequin Enterprises, Ltd.

Macy, Caitlin. The Fundamentals of Play. 2001. 304p. pap. 13.00 (*0-385-72112-9*, Knopf Bks. for Young Readers) Random Hse. Children's Bks.

Maguire, Elizabeth. Thinner, Blonder, Whiter. 2004. 336p. pap. 14.00 (*0-7867-1299-6*); 2002. 320p. 25.00 (*0-7867-1019-5*) Avalon Publishing Group. (Carroll & Graf Pubs.).

Mahoney, Dan. Black & White. E-Book 24.95 (*0-312-26442-9*); 2000. 528p. mass mkt. 6.99 (*0-312-97149-4*, St. Martin's Paperbacks); 1999. 356p. 24.95 o.p. (*0-312-20278-4*) St. Martin's Pr.

—Detective First Grade. 1994. 443p. mass mkt. 6.99 (*0-312-95313-5*, St. Martin's Paperbacks); 1993. 384p. 21.95 o.p. (*0-312-09288-1*) St. Martin's Pr.

—The Edge of the City. 1996. 514p. mass mkt. 6.99 (*0-312-95788-2*, St. Martin's Paperbacks); 1995. 22.95 (*0-312-11812-0*); 1995. 464p. 14.99 o.p. (*0-312-13058-9*) St. Martin's Pr.

—Hyde. unabr. ed. 2000. audio 83.95 (*0-7861-1755-9*, 2559) Blackstone Audio Bks., Inc.

—Hyde. 1999. E-Book 6.99 (*0-312-20723-9*); 1997. 560p. mass mkt. 6.99 (*0-312-96392-0*, St. Martin's Paperbacks); 1996. 384p. 24.95 (*0-312-15146-2*) St. Martin's Pr.

—Justice: A Novel of the NYPD. 2003. 352p. 24.95 (*0-312-30957-0*) St. Martin's Pr.

—Once in, Never Out. unabr. ed. 1999. audio 76.95 (*0-7861-1509-2*, 2359) Blackstone Audio Bks., Inc.

—Once in, Never Out. 1999. 480p. mass mkt. 6.99 (*0-312-96676-8*, St. Martin's Paperbacks); 1998. 352p. 24.95 (*0-312-18228-7*) St. Martin's Pr.

—The Protectors. E-Book 18.95 (*0-312-70763-0*); 2002. 352p. 24.95 (*0-312-28450-0*) St. Martin's Pr.

—The Two Chinatowns. 2001. E-Book 24.95 (*1-59061-043-1*) Adobe Systems, Inc.

—The Two Chinatowns. 2002. 432p. mass mkt. 6.99 (*0-312-98361-1*, St. Martin's Paperbacks); 2001. 342p. 24.95 (*0-312-26134-9*) St. Martin's Pr.

Maiman, Jaye. Baby, It's Cold: A Robin Miller Mystery. 1997. (Robin Miller Mysteries Ser.: Vol. 5). 256p. pap. 10.95 o.p. (*1-56280-156-2*); 1996. 288p. 19.95 (*1-56280-141-4*) Naiad Pr., Inc.

—Crazy for Loving. 1992. (Robin Miller Mysteries Ser.: No. 2). 320p. pap. 11.95 (*1-56280-025-6*) Naiad Pr., Inc.

—Every Time We Say Goodbye. 1999. (Robin Miller Mysteries Ser.: No. 7). 250p. pap. 11.95 (*1-56280-248-8*) Naiad Pr., Inc.

—Someone to Watch. 1995. (Robin Miller Mysteries Ser.: Vol. 4). 288p. pap. 10.95 (*1-56280-095-7*) Naiad Pr., Inc.

Maiorana, Sal. A Lifetime of Yankee Octobers. 2002. 352p. 24.95 (*1-58536-039-2*) Clock Tower Pr. LLC.

Major, Clarence. All-Night Visitors. unexpurg. ed. 1998. (Library of Black Literature). 288p. text 37.50 (*1-55553-367-1*) Northeastern Univ. Pr.

Malamud, Bernard. The Assistant. 2003. (Illus.). 264p. pap. 13.00 (*0-374-50484-9*); 1957. 246p. 12.95 o.p. (*0-374-10644-4*) Farrar, Straus & Giroux.

—The Assistant. 2000. (Perennial Classics Ser.). 256p. reprint ed. pap. 13.00 o.s.i (*0-06-095830-8*, Perennial) HarperTrade.

—The Assistant. 1993. 304p. pap. 10.00 (*0-380-72085-X*); 1980. mass mkt. 4.95 o.p. (*0-380-68338-5*); 1980. 272p. mass mkt. 6.99 o.s.i (*0-380-51474-5*) Morrow/Avon. (Avon Bks.).

—The Assistant. 1967. mass mkt. 0.50 o.p. (*0-451-01514-2*); mass mkt. 0.60 o.p. (*0-451-02215-7*); mass mkt. 0.75 o.p. (*0-451-03398-1*) NAL. (Signet Bks.).

—The Assistant. l.t. ed. 1998. (Perennial Bestsellers Ser.). 339p. 25.95 (*0-7838-0364-8*) Thorndike Pr.

—The Assistant. 1957. 11.09 o.p. (*0-606-03718-7*) Turtleback Bks.

Mancini, Anthony. Godmother. 1993. 272p. 21.95 o.p. (*1-55611-376-5*) Fine, Donald I. Bks.

—Godmother. 264p. 4.98 o.p. (*0-8317-5539-3*) Smithmark Pubs., Inc.

Mandel, Sally. Heart & Soul. 2003. 304p. mass mkt. 6.99 (*0-345-42893-5*, Ivy Bks.); 2002. 288p. 23.95 (*0-345-42892-7*, Ballantine Bks.) Ballantine Bks.

—Out of the Blue. 2002. 304p. mass mkt. 6.99 (*0-345-42891-9*, Ballantine Bks.) Ballantine Bks.

—Out of the Blue. l.t. ed. 2000. (Americana Ser.). 420p. 26.95 o.p. (*0-7862-2551-3*) Thorndike Pr.

Manrique, Jaime. Latin Moon in Manhattan. 1992. 224p. 17.95 o.p. (*0-312-07100-0*) St. Martin's Pr.

—Latin Moon in Manhattan: A Novel. 2003. 212p. pap. 15.95 (*0-299-18754-3*) Univ. of Wisconsin Pr.

—Twilight at the Equator: A Novel. 1997. 224p. 23.95 o.s.i (*0-571-19901-1*) Faber & Faber, Inc.

—Twilight at the Equator: A Novel. 1997. pap. 18.00 (*1-891305-18-2*) Painted Leaf Pr.

—Twilight at the Equator: A Novel. 2003. 198p. pap. 15.95 (*0-299-18774-8*) Univ. of Wisconsin Pr.

Mansbach, Adam. Shackling Water. 2002. 240p. 22.95 (*0-385-50205-2*) Doubleday Publishing.

—Shackling Water. 2003. 240p. reprint ed. pap. 12.00 (*1-4000-3159-1*, Anchor) Knopf Publishing Group.

Marciano, Francesca. Casa Rossa. 352p. 2003. pap. 14.00 (*0-375-72637-3*, Vintage); 2002. 25.00 (*0-375-42123-8*, Pantheon) Knopf Publishing Group.

Marcuse, Irene. Consider the Alternative. 2003. (WWL Mystery Ser.: No. 464). 272p. mass mkt. (*0-373-26464-X*, Worldwide Library) Harlequin Enterprises, Ltd.

—Consider the Alternatives. 2002. 264p. 23.95 (*0-8027-3377-8*) Walker & Co.

—The Death of an Amiable Child. 2002. (WWL Mystery Ser.: No. 433). 256p. mass mkt. (*0-373-26433-X*, Worldwide Library) Harlequin Enterprises, Ltd.

—The Death of an Amiable Child: An Anita Servi Novel. 2000. (Anita Servi Novels Ser.). 227p. 23.95 (*0-8027-3346-8*) Walker & Co.

—Guilty Mind: An Anita Servi Novel. 2001. (Anita Servi Novels Ser.). 256p. 23.95 (*0-8027-3354-9*) Walker & Co.

Margolis, David. The Stepman. 1996. 192p. 24.00 (*1-877946-76-1*) Permanent Pr., The.

Margolis, Seth. Vanishing Act. 1993. 233p. 17.95 o.p. (*0-312-08770-5*, Saint Martin's Minotaur) St. Martin's Pr.

Margolis, Seth J. Losing Isaiah. 1994. 400p. reprint ed. mass mkt. 5.99 o.s.i (*0-515-11539-8*, Jove) Berkley Publishing Group.

—Losing Isaiah. 1993. 384p. 22.95 o.p. (*1-56282-807-X*) Hyperion Pr.

—Perfect Angel. unabr. collector's ed. 1997. audio 56.00 (*0-913369-90-X*, 4390) Books on Tape, Inc.

—Perfect Angel. 1997. 352p. mass mkt. 23.00 o.p. (*0-380-97311-1*); 1998. reprint ed. mass mkt. 6.99 (*0-380-78748-2*) Morrow/Avon. (Avon Bks.).

Mark, Jan. Zeno Was Here. 1988. 284p. 19.95 o.s.i (*0-374-29664-2*) Farrar, Straus & Giroux.

Markham, Wendy. Slightly Single. 2002. 288p. pap. (*0-373-25013-4*, 1-25013-3, Red Dress Ink) Harlequin Enterprises, Ltd.

Markson, David. Going Down. 2002. 278p. pap. 15.00 (*1-928746-27-6*) Herodias.

Maron, Margaret. Baby Doll Games. 1988. 224p. mass mkt. 3.50 o.s.i (*0-553-27281-0*) Bantam Bks.

—Baby Doll Games. 1995. (Sigrid Harald Mystery Ser.). 224p. mass mkt. 5.99 o.s.i (*0-446-40418-7*) Warner Bks., Inc.

—Bloody Kin. 1992. 224p. mass mkt. 4.50 o.s.i (*0-553-29514-4*) Bantam Bks.

—Bloody Kin. 1985. (Crime Club Ser.). 192p. 12.95 o.p. (*0-385-23231-4*) Doubleday Publishing.

—Bloody Kin. 1995. 224p. mass mkt. 5.99 (*0-446-40416-0*) Warner Bks., Inc.

—Corpus Christmas. 1990. 224p. mass mkt. 3.95 o.s.i (*0-553-27410-4*) Bantam Bks.

—Corpus Christmas. 2001. 288p. reprint ed. pap. 12.95 (*0-446-67766-3*) Warner Bks., Inc.

—Death in Blue Folders. 1992. (Crime Line Ser.). 224p. mass mkt. 4.50 o.s.i (*0-553-29498-9*) Bantam Bks.

—Death in Blue Folders. l.t. ed. 1992. (Mystery Ser.). 400p. 29.99 o.p. (*0-7089-2665-7*, Ulverscroft) Thorpe, F. A. Pubs. GBR. *Dist:* Ulverscroft Large Print Bks., Ltd., Ulverscroft Large Print Canada, Ltd.

—Death of a Butterfly. 1991. 192p. mass mkt. 3.99 o.s.i (*0-553-29121-1*) Bantam Bks.

—Death of a Butterfly. 1984. (Crime Club Ser.). 192p. 11.95 o.p. (*0-385-19554-0*) Doubleday Publishing.

—Death of a Butterfly. l.t. ed. 1991. (Ulverscroft Large Print Ser.). 29.99 o.p. (*0-7089-2465-4*, Ulverscroft) Thorpe, F. A. Pubs. GBR. *Dist:* Ulverscroft Large Print Bks., Ltd., Ulverscroft Large Print Canada, Ltd.

—Fugitive Colors. 1995. 272p. 18.95 o.s.i (*0-89296-567-3*) Mysterious Pr.

—Fugitive Colors. 260p. pap. 3.98 o.p. (*0-7651-0363-X*) Smithmark Pubs., Inc.

—Fugitive Colors. 1996. (Sigrid Harald Mystery Ser.). 256p. mass mkt. 5.99 (*0-446-40393-8*) Warner Bks., Inc.

—One Coffee With. 1988. mass mkt. 3.50 o.s.i (*0-553-27479-1*) Bantam Bks.

—One Coffee With. l.t. ed. 1991. (Ulverscroft Large Print Ser.). 29.99 o.p. (*0-7089-2433-6*, Ulverscroft) Thorpe, F. A. Pubs. GBR. *Dist:* Ulverscroft Large Print Bks., Ltd., Ulverscroft Large Print Canada, Ltd.

—One Coffee With. 1995. (Sigrid Harald Mystery Ser.). 192p. mass mkt. 5.99 o.s.i (*0-446-40415-2*) Warner Bks., Inc.

—Past Imperfect. 1992. 256p. mass mkt. 4.99 o.s.i (*0-553-29546-2*) Bantam Bks.

—Past Imperfect. 1991. 192p. 14.95 o.s.i (*0-385-41364-5*) Doubleday Publishing.

—The Right Jack. 1987. 224p. mass mkt. 3.50 o.s.i (*0-553-26859-7*) Bantam Bks.

—The Right Jack. l.t. ed. 1992. (Mystery Ser.). 480p. 29.99 o.p. (*0-7089-2730-0*, Ulverscroft) Thorpe, F. A. Pubs. GBR. *Dist:* Ulverscroft Large Print Bks., Ltd., Ulverscroft Large Print Canada, Ltd.

—The Right Jack. 1995. (Sigrid Harald Mystery Ser.). 224p. mass mkt. 5.99 o.s.i (*0-446-40417-9*) Warner Bks., Inc.

Marquis, Traci. I Can't Cry: A Journey from Shame to Redemption. 2002. ii, 190p. 25.00 (*0-9720310-0-6*); pap. 14.95 (*0-9720310-1-4*) Sterling Pubs.

Marshall, Paule. The Fisher King: A Novel. l.t. ed. 2001. 256p. lib. bdg. 27.95 (*1-58547-074-0*) Ctr. Point Large Print.

—The Fisher King: A Novel. 224p. 2000. 23.00 o.s.i (*0-684-87283-8*); 2001. reprint ed. pap. 12.00 (*0-684-86970-5*) Simon & Schuster. (Scribner).

Martinac, Paula. Home Movies. 1993. 222p. (Orig.). pap. 10.95 (*1-878067-32-X*, Seal Pr.) Avalon Publishing Group.

Marx, Pearson. On the Way to the Venus de Milo. 1995. 270p. 21.00 (*0-671-88335-6*, Simon & Schuster) Simon & Schuster.

Masini, Donna. About Yvonne: A Novel. 1997. 288p. 23.00 o.p. (*0-393-04091-7*) Norton, W. W. & Co., Inc.

Mathes, Charles. Girl in the Face of the Clock. 2001. x, 239p. 23.95 (*0-312-26895-5*, Saint Martin's Minotaur) St. Martin's Pr.

Matheson, Richard. Come Fygures, Come Shadowes. 2003. 144p. 40.00 (*1-887368-60-4*) Gauntlet, Inc.

Mathews, Harry. Cigarettes. 1998. (American Literature Ser.). 304p. reprint ed. pap. 13.50 (*1-56478-203-4*) Dalkey Archive Pr.

—Cigarettes. 1987. 288p. 17.95 o.p. (*1-55584-092-2*) Grove/Atlantic, Inc.

Matthews, Brander. Vignettes of Manhattan. 1977. (Short Story Index Reprint Ser.). 22.95 (*0-8369-3070-3*) Ayer Co. Pubs., Inc.

Matthews, Carole. For Better, for Worse. 2002. 352p. pap. 14.95 (*0-380-82044-7*, Avon Bks.) Morrow/Avon.

Maxim, John R. The Shadow Box. 1997. mass mkt. 6.99 (*0-380-78668-0*); 1996. 384p. mass mkt. 23.00 o.p. (*0-380-97300-6*) Morrow/Avon. (Avon Bks.).

—Time Out of Mind. 1994. 624p. mass mkt. 5.99 o.s.i (*0-553-56039-5*) Bantam Bks.

—Time Out of Mind. 1987. mass mkt. 4.50 (*0-8125-8569-0*, Tor Bks.) Doherty, Tom Assocs., LLC.

—Time Out of Mind, 1986. 502p. 17.95 o.p. (*0-395-36801-4*) Houghton Mifflin Co.

—Time Out of Mind. 1999. 528p. mass mkt. 6.99 (*0-380-73006-5*, Avon Bks.) Morrow/Avon.

Maxwell, William. All the Days & Nights: The Collected Stories of William Maxwell. 1995. 432p. pap. 15.00 (*0-679-76102-0*, Vintage) Knopf Publishing Group.

Mayfield, Julian. The Hit & the Long Night. 1989. (Library of Black Literature). 310p. reprint ed. pap. text 17.95 (*1-55553-065-6*) Northeastern Univ. Pr.

Maynard, Joyce. The Usual Rules. E-Book 24.95 (*0-312-70971-4*) St. Martin's Pr.

—The Usual Rules. l.t. ed. 2003. 542p. 29.95 (*0-7862-5548-X*) Thorndike Pr.

—The Usual Rules: A Novel. 2004. 400p. pap. 13.95 (*0-312-28369-5*) St. Martin's Pr.

Mayor, Archer. The Sniper's Wife. l.t. ed. 2003. 30.95 (*1-58724-392-X*, Wheeler Publishing, Inc.) Gale Group.

—The Sniper's Wife. 2002. 320p. 23.95 (*0-89296-767-6*) Mysterious Pr.

—The Sniper's Wife. 2003. 352p. mass mkt. 6.99 (*0-446-61321-5*) Warner Bks., Inc.

Mazel, Henry F. Murderously Incorrect. 1999. 208p. pap. 12.95 (*0-9665899-0-4*) Crime & Again Pr.

McAllister, Anne. Gibson's Girl. 1999. (Harlequin Presents Ser.: No. 2060). mass mkt. (*0-373-12060-5*, 1-12060-9, Harlequin Bks.) Harlequin Enterprises, Ltd.

McBain, Ed, pseud. Another Part of the City. l.t. ed. 1989. (General Ser.). 407p. 20.95 o.p. (*0-8161-4520-2*, Macmillan Reference USA) Gale Group.

—Another Part of the City. 1987. 45.00 o.p. (*0-89296-157-0*); 1986. 15.45 o.p. (*0-89296-153-8*) Mysterious Pr.

—Another Part of the City. 1989. mass mkt. 4.50 o.s.i (*0-445-40896-0*); 1987. mass mkt. 3.95 (*0-445-40584-8*) Warner Bks., Inc.

—Downtown. l.t. ed. 1992. pap. 17.95 o.p. (*0-7927-1111-4*); 18.95 o.p. (*0-7927-1112-2*, E0032) BBC Audiobooks America.

—Downtown. unabr. ed. 1992. (Eighty-Seventh Precinct Ser.). audio 48.00 (*0-7366-2142-3*, 2940) Books on Tape, Inc.

—Downtown. unabr. ed. 1991. audio 57.25 o.p. (*1-56100-083-3*, 870, Unabridged Library Editions); audio 22.95 o.p. (*0-930435-89-3*, 94, Bookcassette) Brilliance Audio.

—Downtown. 1991. 302p. 20.00 o.p. (*0-688-08736-1*, Morrow, William & Co.); 1993. 352p. reprint ed. mass mkt. 5.99 (*0-380-70761-6*, Avon Bks.) Morrow/Avon.

—Downtown. 1993. 15.95 o.p. (*1-55800-454-8*) NewStar Media, Inc.

—Downtown. unabr. ed. 1991. audio 70.00 (*1-55690-153-4*, 91405E7) Recorded Bks., LLC.

McBain, Ed, pseud & Hunter, Evan. Candyland: A Novel in Two Parts. l.t. ed. 2001. (Wheeler Large Print Book Ser.). 374p. 30.95 (*1-58724-094-7*, Wheeler Publishing, Inc.) Gale Group.

—Candyland: A Novel in Two Parts. 2001. 304p. 25.00 (*0-7432-1316-5*, Simon & Schuster); (Illus.). 368p. reprint ed. pap. 7.99 (*0-7434-1904-9*, Pocket) Simon & Schuster.

McCabe, Peter. City of Lies: A Novel. 1993. 271p. 20.00 o.p. (*0-688-12118-7*, Morrow, William & Co.) Morrow/Avon.

McCafferty, Jeanne. Star Gazer. 1994. 208p. 19.95 o.p. (*0-312-11074-X*, Saint Martin's Minotaur) St. Martin's Pr.

McCahery, James R. What Evil Lurks. 1996. 256p. mass mkt. 4.99 o.s.i (*1-57566-001-6*); 1995. 304p. mass mkt. 16.95 o.p. (*0-8217-4797-5*) Kensington Publishing Corp.

McCann, Colum. This Side of Brightness: A Novel. l.t. ed. 1998. (Large Print Book Ser.). 26.95 (*1-56895-587-1*, Wheeler Publishing, Inc.) Gale Group.

—This Side of Brightness: A Novel. 1999. 288p. pap. 13.00 o.s.i (*0-8050-5453-7*, Owl Bks.); 1998. 292p. 23.00 o.s.i (*0-8050-5452-9*, Metropolitan Bks.) Holt, Henry & Co.

—This Side of Brightness: A Novel. 2003. (Illus.). 304p. pap. 13.00 (*0-312-42197-4*) Picador.

McCarthy, Mary. The Company She Keeps. 2003. 324p. pap. 13.00 (*0-15-602786-0*, Harvest Bks.) Harcourt Trade Pubs.

McCloy, Kristin. Some Girls. 272p. 1995. pap. 12.95 o.s.i (*0-452-27273-4*, Plume); 1994. 20.95 o.s.i (*0-525-93837-0*) Dutton/Plume.

McCouch, Hannah. Girl Cook: A Novel. 2003. 224p. 22.95 (*1-4000-6042-7*, Villard Bks.) Random House Adult Trade Publishing Group.

McCourt, James. Mawrdew Czgowchwz. 1976. 230p. pap. 6.95 o.p. (*0-374-51361-9*); 1970. 8.95 o.p. (*0-374-20461-6*) Farrar, Straus & Giroux.

—Mawrdew Czgowchwz. 2002. (New York Review Books Classics Ser.). 205p. pap. 12.95 (*0-940322-97-8*) New York Review of Bks., Inc., The.

McCown, Clint. The Member-Guest: A Novel in Stories. 1995. 256p. 20.00 o.s.i (*0-385-47655-8*) Doubleday Publishing.

McCrae, Jackson Tippett. The Bark of the Dogwood: A Tour of Southern Homes & Gardens. 2002. 563p. 28.00 (*0-9715536-0-2*) Enolam Group, Inc., The.

McDermott, Alice. Charming Billy. 1999. 256p. pap. 12.95 (*0-385-33334-X*, Delta) Dell Publishing.

—Charming Billy. 1997. 280p. 22.00 (*0-374-12080-3*); (*0-374-91390-0*) Farrar, Straus & Giroux.

—Charming Billy. l.t. ed. 1998. 26.95 (*1-56895-685-1*, Wheeler Publishing, Inc.) Gale Group.

McDonell, J. M. Half Crazy. abr. ed. 1995. 17.95 o.p. (*0-7871-0377-2*) NewStar Media, Inc.

—Half Crazy: A Novel, Vol. 1. 1995. 258p. 19.95 (*0-316-55560-6*) Little Brown & Co.

—Half Crazy: A Novel. 2000. 310p. pap. 12.95 (*1-893224-04-X*, New Millennium Pr.) New Millennium Entertainment.

McDonell, Nick. Twelve. 2003. 256p. pap. 12.00 (*0-8021-4012-2*) Grove/Atlantic, Inc.

—Twelve: A Novel. 2002. 256p. 23.00 (*0-8021-1717-1*, Grove Pr.) Grove/Atlantic, Inc.

McDonough, Yona Zeldis. The Four Temperaments. 2002. 320p. 23.95 (*0-385-50361-X*) Doubleday Publishing.

McElroy, Joseph. Actress in the House: A Novel. 2003. 445p. 26.95 (*1-58567-350-1*) Overlook Pr., The.

—A Smuggler's Bible. 2003. 435p. pap. 15.95 (*1-58567-351-X*) Overlook Pr., The.

—Women & Men. 1993. 1192p. reprint ed. pap. 15.95 o.p. (*1-56478-023-6*) Dalkey Archive Pr.

—Women & Men. 1987. 27.50 o.s.i (*0-394-50344-9*) Knopf, Alfred A. Inc.

McEvoy, Dermot. Terrible Angel: Michael Collins in New York, 1992: A Novel. 2002. 304p. 22.95 (*1-58574-742-4*, Lyons Pr.) Globe Pequot Pr., The.

McFadden, Bernice L. The Warmest December. 2001. 256p. 22.95 o.s.i (*0-525-94564-4*) Dutton/Plume.

—The Warmest December. l.t. ed. 2001. 208p. 29.95 (*0-7862-3439-3*) Thorndike Pr.

McFarland, Philip. Seasons of Fear. 1987. 288p. 15.95 o.s.i (*0-8052-3850-6*, Schocken) Knopf Publishing Group.

McGarry, Jean. The Courage of Girls. 1992. (Rutgers Press Fiction Ser.). 250p. 22.95 (*0-8135-1771-0*) Rutgers Univ. Pr.

McGonigle, Thomas. Going to Patchogue. 1992. (Illus.). 220p. 19.95 (*0-916583-87-2*) Dalkey Archive Pr.

McHugh, Frances Y. The Dropped Living Room. l.t. ed. 2001. (Candlelight Ser.). 192p. 22.95 o.p. (*0-7862-3468-7*) Thorndike Pr.

McHugh, Vincent. I Am Thinking of My Darling. 1991. 308p. reprint ed. pap. 9.95 (*1-878274-05-8*) Yarrow Pr.

—I Am Thinking of My Darling: An Adventure Story. Reginald, R. & Melville, Douglas, eds. 1978. (Lost Race & Adult Fantasy Ser.). reprint ed. lib. bdg. 28.95 (*0-405-10998-9*) Ayer Co. Pubs., Inc.

McInerney, Jay. Bright Lights, Big City. 1984. (Vintage Contemporaries Ser.). 208p. pap. 12.00 (*0-394-72641-3*, Vintage) Knopf Publishing Group.

McInerney, Merry. Burning down the House. 1995. 337p. pap. 5.99 o.p. (*0-8125-3651-7*); 1994. 256p. 17.95 o.p. (*0-312-85698-9*) Doherty, Tom Assocs., LLC. (Forge Bks.).

McKay, Deborah. Eve's Longing: The Infinite Possibilities in All Things. 1992. 139p. 18.95 o.s.i (*0-932511-64-3*); pap. 11.95 (*0-932511-65-1*) Fiction Collective Two, Inc.

McKinney, Meagan. The Merry Widow. l.t. ed. 2000. (Wheeler Large Print Book Ser.). 392p. 26.95 (*1-56895-863-3*, Wheeler Publishing, Inc.) Gale Group.

—The Merry Widow. 2000. 352p. mass mkt. 6.50 o.s.i (*0-8217-6707-0*, Zebra Bks.); 1999. 294p. 23.00 o.s.i (*1-57566-487-9*, Kensington Bks.) Kensington Publishing Corp.

—Moonlight Becomes Her. 2002. (Americana Ser.). 658p. 30.95 o.p. (*0-7862-3757-0*) Gale Group.

—Moonlight Becomes Her. 2002. 352p. mass mkt. 6.50 o.s.i (*0-8217-7050-0*); 2001. 32p. 23.00 o.s.i (*1-57566-787-8*) Kensington Publishing Corp.

McKinnon, Karen. Narcissus Ascending. 2002. 224p. 21.00 (*0-312-29058-6*) Picador.

—Narcissus Ascending: A Novel. 2003. 224p. pap. 13.00 (*0-312-31218-0*) Picador.

McKinty, A. G. Dead I Well May Be. 2004. 288p. mass mkt. 6.99 (*0-7434-7056-7*, Pocket); 2003. 320p. 24.00 (*0-7432-4699-3*, Scribner) Simon & Schuster.

McLaughlin, Emma & Kraus, Nicola. The Nanny Diaries: A Novel. l.t. ed. 2002. (Wheeler Hardcover Ser.). 443p. 30.95 (*1-58724-275-3*, Wheeler Publishing, Inc.) Gale Group.

—The Nanny Diaries: A Novel. abr. ed. 2002. audio 25.00 (*0-553-71475-9*); audio compact disk 29.95 (*0-553-71476-7*) Random Hse. Audio Publishing Group.

—The Nanny Diaries: A Novel. 352p. 2002. 24.95 (*0-312-27858-6*); 2003. reprint ed. pap. 13.95 (*0-312-29163-9*, Saint Martin's Griffin) St. Martin's Pr.

McLoughlin, Tim. Heart of the Old Country. 2001. (Illus.). 230p. pap. 14.95 (*1-888451-15-7*) Akashic Bks.

McMullan, Margaret. When Warhol Was Still Alive: A Novel. 1994. 199p. 18.95 o.p. (*0-89594-651-3*) Crossing Pr., Inc., The.

McNulty, John. This Place on Third Avenue: The New York Stories of John McNulty. 2001. 240p. text 23.00 o.p. (*1-58243-117-5*, Counterpoint Pr.) Basic Bks.

McPhee, Jenny. The Center of Things. 2002. 272p. pap. 13.95 (*0-345-44765-4*, Ballantine Bks.) Ballantine Bks.

—The Center of Things. 2001. 256p. 22.95 (*0-385-50077-7*) Doubleday Publishing.

Medina, Pablo. The Marks of Birth. 1994. 224p. 22.00 o.p. (*0-374-20296-6*) Farrar, Straus & Giroux.

Meeker, Richard. Better Angel. 1987. 284p. reprint ed. pap. 6.95 o.p. (*1-55583-116-8*) Alyson Pubns.

—Better Angel. 2000. 250p. reprint ed. pap. 14.95 (*1-883938-63-5*) Dry Bones Pr.

Meltzer, Brad. Dead Even. 2003. audio 14.95 (*0-06-053571-7*); 1998. 6p. pap. 25.00 o.s.i incl. audio (*0-694-51991-X*) HarperTrade. (HarperAudio).

—Dead Even. 1998. 368p. 25.00 o.p. (*0-688-15090-X*, Morrow, William & Co.) Morrow/Avon.

—Dead Even. 1999. 544p. reprint ed. mass mkt. 7.99 (*0-446-60733-9*) Warner Bks., Inc.

Melville, Herman. Bartleby the Scrivener. 1997. 77p. 21.50 o.p. (*0-684-81910-4*, Simon & Schuster) Simon & Schuster.

—Bartleby the Scrivener & Benito Cereno. 1990. 112p. pap. 1.00 (*0-486-26473-4*) Dover Pubns., Inc.

Menaker, Daniel. The Treatment. 1999. 288p. pap. 18.95 (*0-671-03263-1*, Pocket) Simon & Schuster.

Mendelsohn, Jane. Innocence. 2001. 208p. reprint ed. pap. 12.00 (*1-57322-874-5*, Riverhead Trade (Paperbacks)) Berkley Publishing Group.

Mendelson, Cheryl. Morningside Heights: A Novel. 2003. 336p. 24.95 (*0-375-50836-8*) Random Hse., Inc.

Meredith, Don. Home Movies. 1982. 176p. pap. 2.25 o.p. (*0-380-79855-7*, 79855-7, Avon Bks.) Morrow/Avon.

Meriwether, Louise. Daddy Was a Number Runner. 1970. 8.95 o.p. (*0-13-197103-4*) Prentice Hall PTR.

Merrick, Gordon. An Idol for Others. 1998. 400p. pap. 14.95 o.p. (*1-55583-295-4*) Alyson Pubns.

—An Idol for Others. 1977. pap. 3.95 o.p. (*0-380-00971-4*, 84756-6, Avon Bks.) Morrow/Avon.

Merrick, Gordon & Hulse, Charles. The Good Life. 1997. 350p. (Orig.). pap. 14.95 o.p. (*1-55583-298-9*) Alyson Pubns.

Merrill, Robin. Sex & the City. deluxe ed. 2004. (Illus.). 184p. pap. 20.00 (*0-7434-5730-7*, Pocket) Simon & Schuster.

Messina, Lynn. Fashionistas. 2003. 288p. pap. (*0-373-25025-8*, Red Dress Ink) Harlequin Enterprises, Ltd.

Mestre-Reed, Ernesto, tr. The Second Death of Unica Aveyano: A Novel. 2004. 272p. pap. 13.00 (*1-4000-3316-0*, Vintage) Knopf Publishing Group.

Metzger, R. S. A Master of the Century Past. 1996. 288p. 17.95 (*0-913720-87-9*) Beil, Frederic C. Pub., Inc.

Meyers, Annette. The Big Killing. 1990. (Smith & Wetzon Ser.). 384p. mass mkt. 4.50 o.s.i (*0-553-28418-5*) Bantam Bks.

—The Big Killing. 1998. 270p. pap. 15.95 (*0-7351-0405-0*); reprint ed. lib. bdg. 29.95 (*0-7351-0035-7*) Replica Bks.

—Blood on the Street. 1993. (Smith & Wetzon Ser.). 400p. mass mkt. 4.99 o.s.i (*0-553-29731-7*) Bantam Bks.

—The Deadliest Option. 1992. (Smith & Wetzon Ser.). 416p. mass mkt. 4.99 o.s.i (*0-553-29530-6*) Bantam Bks.

—The Deadliest Option. 1998. 354p. pap. 15.95 (*0-7351-0404-2*); reprint ed. lib. bdg. 29.95 (*0-7351-0036-5*) Replica Bks.

—Free Love. 1999. (Olivia Brown Mysteries Ser.). 256p. 23.95 (*0-89296-694-7*) Mysterious Pr.

—Free Love. 2001. 336p. mass mkt. 6.99 (*0-446-60921-8*) Warner Bks., Inc.

—The Groaning Board: A Smith & Wetzon Mystery. 1998. 368p. mass mkt. 5.99 o.s.i (*0-553-56977-5*) Bantam Bks.

—The Groaning Board: A Smith & Wetzon Mystery. 1997. 336p. 21.95 o.s.i (*0-385-47654-X*) Doubleday Publishing.

—Murder: The Musical. 1994. (Smith & Wetzon Ser.). 496p. mass mkt. 5.50 o.s.i (*0-553-56785-3*) Bantam Bks.

—Murder: The Musical. 1998. 370p. pap. 15.95 (*0-7351-0403-4*); reprint ed. lib. bdg. 29.95 (*0-7351-0034-9*) Replica Bks.

—Murder Me Now. 2001. 290p. 23.95 o.p. (*0-89296-695-5*) Mysterious Pr.

—Murder Me Now. l.t. ed. 2001. 427p. 29.95 (*0-7862-3079-7*) Thorndike Pr.

—Tender Death. 1991. (Smith & Wetzon Ser.). 336p. mass mkt. 4.50 o.s.i (*0-553-28719-2*) Bantam Bks.

—Tender Death. 1998. 288p. pap. 15.95 (*0-7351-0406-9*); reprint ed. lib. bdg. 29.95 (*0-7351-0037-3*) Replica Bks.

—These Bones Were Made for Dancin' A Smith & Wetzon Mystery. 1996. 336p. reprint ed. mass mkt. 5.50 o.s.i (*0-553-56976-7*, Crimeline) Bantam Bks.

Meyers, Maan. The Dutchman. 2000. (Illus.). 318p. 29.95 (*0-7351-0437-9*); 316p. pap. 15.95 (*0-7351-0438-7*) Replica Bks.

—The Dutchman's Dilemma. 1996. 304p. mass mkt. 5.99 o.s.i (*0-553-57201-6*, Crimeline) Bantam Bks.

—The Dutchman's Dilemma. 2000. (Illus.). 270p. 29.95 (*0-7351-0435-2*); pap. 15.95 (*0-7351-0436-0*) Replica Bks.

—The High Constable. 2000. (Illus.). 318p. 29.95 (*0-7351-0441-7*); pap. 15.95 (*0-7351-0442-5*) Replica Bks.

—The Kingsbridge Plot. 2000. (Illus.). 332p. 29.95 (*0-7351-0439-5*); pap. 15.95 (*0-7351-0440-9*) Replica Bks.

Miano, Mark. Flesh & Stone: A Michael Carpo Mystery. (Michael Carpo Mystery Ser.). 288p. 1998. mass mkt. 5.99 o.s.i (*1-57566-273-6*); 1997. 18.95 o.p. (*1-57566-128-4*, Kensington Bks.) Kensington Publishing Corp.

—The Street Where She Lived: A Michael Carpo Mystery. 1998. (Michael Carpo Mystery Ser.). 320p. 20.00 o.s.i (*1-57566-270-1*, Kensington Bks.) Kensington Publishing Corp.

Michael, Judith, pseud. Acts of Love. l.t. ed. 1997. 480p. mass mkt. 7.99 (*0-8041-1787-X*, Ivy Bks.) Ballantine Bks.

—Acts of Love. abr. ed. 1997. (Civil War Ser.). 3p. audio 7.99 o.p. (*1-56740-225-9*, 618, Paperback Nova Audio Bks.); audio 16.95 o.p. (*1-56100-968-7*, 1128, Nova Audio Bks.); audio 105.25 o.p. (*1-56100-809-5*, 787, Unabridged Library Editions); audio 27.95 o.p. (*1-56100-731-5*, 25, Bookcassette) Brilliance Audio.

—Acts of Love. l.t. ed. 1997. 6624p. pap. 24.00 o.s.i (*0-679-77418-1*) Random Hse., Inc.

Michaels, Fern. The Future Scrolls. l.t. ed. 2003. 320p. pap. 25.95 (*1-58724-525-6*, Wheeler Publishing, Inc.) Gale Group.

—The Future Scrolls. 2003. 288p. mass mkt. 6.99 (*0-8217-7586-3*, Zebra Bks.) Kensington Publishing Corp.

—The Future Scrolls. 2002. 28.99 (*0-7278-7145-5*); 2001. 288p. 25.99 (*0-7278-5721-5*) Severn Hse. Pubs., Ltd.

Michaels, Kasey. Maggie by the Book. 2003. 288p. 20.00 (*1-57566-881-5*) Kensington Publishing Corp.

—Maggie by the Book. l.t. ed. 2003. 496p. 28.95 (*0-7862-5788-1*) Thorndike Pr.

—Maggie Needs an Alibi. 2003. 333p. mass mkt. 6.99 (*1-57566-880-7*); 2002. 320p. 20.00 (*1-57566-879-3*) Kensington Publishing Corp.

—Maggie Needs an Alibi. l.t. ed. 2002. (Americana 5 Ser.). 560p. 28.95 (*0-7862-4765-7*) Thorndike Pr.

Michaels, Leonard. Sylvia. 1992. 144p. 10.00 (*1-56279-029-3*) Mercury Hse.

Miller, Denene & Chiles, Nick. Love Don't Live Here Anymore. 2003. 320p. reprint ed. pap. 13.95 (*0-451-20778-5*) NAL.

Miller, Elise Abrams. Star Craving Mad. 2004. (*0-446-69284-0*) Warner Bks., Inc.

Miller, Ellen. Like Being Killed. 352p. 1999. pap. 12.95 o.s.i (*0-452-27929-1*, Plume); 1998. 24.95 o.p. (*0-525-94372-2*) Dutton/Plume.

Miller, Karen E. Quinones. I'm Telling. 240p. 2002. 21.00 (*0-7432-1435-8*); 2003. reprint ed. pap. 12.00 (*0-7432-1436-6*) Simon & Schuster. (Simon & Schuster).

Millhauser, Steven. Martin Dressler: The Tale of an American Dreamer. 1997. 304p. pap. 13.00 (*0-679-78127-7*, Vintage) Knopf Publishing Group.

—Martin Dressler: The Tale of an American Dreamer. unabr. ed. 1997. audio 56.00 (*0-7887-1757-X*, 95235E7) Recorded Bks., LLC.

Millner, Denene & Chiles, Nick. Love Don't Live Here Anymore. 2002. 324p. 23.95 o.s.i (*0-525-94641-1*, Dutton) Dutton/Plume.

Mills, James. Haywire. 1995. 416p. 23.95 o.s.i (*0-446-51619-8*) Warner Bks., Inc.

Minot, Susan. Lust & Other Stories. 2000. (Contemporaries Ser.). 160p. pap. 11.00 (*0-375-70925-8*, Vintage) Knopf Publishing Group.

Minter, Alex. Killing Cousins. 2nd ed. 2003. 240p. pap. 9.95 (*0-7434-6332-3*, Pocket) Simon & Schuster.

—Little Sister's Last Dose. 2003. 272p. pap. 9.95 (*0-7434-6331-5*, Pocket) Simon & Schuster.

Mitchell, David. Ghostwritten: A Novel. 2001. 448p. reprint ed. pap. 14.00 (*0-375-72450-8*, Vintage) Knopf Publishing Group.

Mitchell, Joseph. Up in the Old Hotel. 1993. 736p. pap. 16.00 (*0-679-74631-5*) Random Hse., Inc.

Mohr, Nicholasa. A Matter of Pride & Other Stories. 1997. 164p. 19.95 (*1-55885-163-1*); pap. 11.95 (*1-55885-177-1*) Arte Publico Pr.

—Rituals of Survival: A Woman's Portfolio. 1985. 158p. (C). pap. 11.95 (*0-934770-39-5*) Arte Publico Pr.

Monahan, Brent. The Manhattan Island Clubs: A Novel. 2003. 320p. 24.95 (*0-312-30413-7*, Saint Martin's Minotaur) St. Martin's Pr.

Montemarano, Nicholas. A Fine Place. 226p. 2002. 21.95 (*1-893956-21-0*); 2003. reprint ed. pap. 14.00 (*1-893956-43-1*) Context Bks.

Mooney, Ted. Singing into the Piano. 1999. 368p. pap. 19.00 (*0-679-74306-5*) Knopf, Alfred A. Inc.

Moore, Christopher & Johnson, Pamela. Santa & Pete: A Novel of Christmas Present & Past. 1998. (Illus.). 176p. 14.95 (*0-684-85495-3*, Simon & Schuster) Simon & Schuster.

Moore, Harker. A Cruel Season for Dying. 2003. 336p. 24.95 (*0-89296-774-9*) Mysterious Pr.

—A Cruel Season for Dying. 2004. mass mkt. (*0-446-61373-8*) Warner Bks., Inc.

Moore, Robin. The Moscow Connection. 1994. 500p. 20.00 (*1-879915-11-1*) Alexander & Fraser, Inc.

Moore, Susanna. In the Cut: A Novel. 1999. 192p. pap. 12.95 (*0-452-28129-6*, Plume) Dutton/Plume.

—In the Cut: A Novel. 1995. 177p. 21.00 o.s.i (*0-679-42258-7*) Knopf, Alfred A. Inc.

Moran, Thomas. The World I Made for Her. 1999. 288p. reprint ed. 12.00 (*1-57322-731-5*, Riverhead Trade (Paperbacks)) Berkley Publishing Group.

—The World I Made for Her. 1998. 267p. 23.95 o.p. (*1-57322-084-1*, Riverhead Bks. (Hardcovers)) Putnam Publishing Group, The.

Mordden, Ethan. Buddies. (Stonewall Inn Editions Ser.). 1987. 256p. pap. 9.95 (*0-312-01005-2*, Saint Martin's Griffin); 1986. 304p. 6.50 o.p. (*0-312-10686-6*) St. Martin's Pr.

—Everybody Loves You. 1989. (Stonewall Inn Editions Ser.). 308p. pap. 10.95 (*0-312-03334-6*, Saint Martin's Griffin) St. Martin's Pr.

—Everybody Loves You: Further Adventures in Gay Manhattan. 1988. 288p. 16.95 o.p. (*0-312-02201-8*) St. Martin's Pr.

—I've a Feeling We're Not in Kansas Anymore. 1987. 208p. pap. 11.95 o.p. (*0-452-25929-0*, Plume) Dutton/Plume.

—I've a Feeling We're Not in Kansas Anymore. 1996. (Stonewall Inn Editions Ser.: Vol. 1). 208p. pap. 9.95 (*0-312-14112-2*, Saint Martin's Griffin) St. Martin's Pr.

—I've a Feeling We're Not in Kansas Anymore: Tales from Manhattan. 1985. 170p. 12.95 o.p. (*0-312-40291-0*) St. Martin's Pr.

—Some Men Are Lookers. 1997. 352p. 23.95 (*0-312-15660-X*) St. Martin's Pr.

—Some Men Are Lookers: New Stories in the Buddies Cycle. 1999. E-Book 13.95 (*0-312-20743-3*) St. Martin's Pr.

Moriarty, Michael. The Voyeur. 1997. 223p. 22.00 o.p. (*0-684-80425-5*, Simon & Schuster) Simon & Schuster.

Morrell, David. The Covenant of the Flame. unabr. ed. 1991. audio 25.95 o.p. (*0-930435-81-8*, 70, Bookcassette); audio 89.25 o.p. (*1-56100-075-2*, 542) Brilliance Audio.

—The Covenant of the Flame. 1992. 480p. mass mkt. 7.50 (*0-446-36292-1*); 1991. 19.95 o.p. (*0-446-51563-9*); 1999. reprint ed. mass mkt. 3.99 (*0-446-60752-5*) Warner Bks., Inc.

—Desperate Measures. 1994. 416p. 22.95 o.s.i (*0-446-51791-7*); 1999. reprint ed. mass mkt. 3.99 (*0-446-60750-9*); 1995. 512p. reprint ed. mass mkt. 7.50 (*0-446-60239-6*) Warner Bks., Inc.

Morris, Gilbert. The Beloved Enemy. 2003. (House of Winslow Ser.). 320p. pap. 11.99 (*0-7642-2704-1*) Bethany Hse. Pubs.

—The End of Act Three. 2001. (Dani Ross Mysteries Ser.: Vol. 3). Orig. Title: The Final Curtain. 266p. reprint ed. pap. 12.99 (*1-58134-245-4*) Crossway Bks.

—The End of Act Three. l.t. ed. 2002. Orig. Title: The Final Curtain. 436p. pap. 16.95 (*1-4104-0032-8*, Walker Large Print) Gale Group.

—The End of Act Three. l.t. ed. 2001. Orig. Title: The Final Curtain. 423p. 24.95 (*0-7862-3406-7*) Thorndike Pr.

—The Final Adversary. 1992. (House of Winslow Ser.: Bk. 12). 304p. pap. 11.99 (*1-55661-261-3*) Bethany Hse. Pubs.

—The Heavenly Fugitive. 2002. (House of Winslow Ser.: 27). (Illus.). 320p. pap. 11.99 (*0-7642-2599-5*) Bethany Hse. Pubs.

—The Iron Lady. 1996. (House of Winslow Ser.: Vol. 19). 320p. pap. 11.99 (*1-55661-687-2*) Bethany Hse. Pubs.

—The Iron Lady. l.t. ed. 1997. (Inspirational Ser.). 522p. lib. bdg. 23.95 (*0-7838-8221-1*, Macmillan Reference USA) Gale Group.

—The Shadow Portrait. 1998. (House of Winslow Ser.: Vol. 21). 320p. pap. 11.99 (*1-55661-689-9*) Bethany Hse. Pubs.

Morris, Lynn & Morris, Gilbert. A City Not Forsaken. 1995. (Cheney Duvall, M. D. Ser.: Bk. 3). 336p. pap. 11.99 (*1-55661-424-1*) Bethany Hse. Pubs.

—A City Not Forsaken. 2000. (Christian Fiction Ser.: Bk. 3). 312p. 23.95 (*0-7862-2227-1*, Five Star); 1997. (Inspirational Ser.). 498p. lib. bdg. 23.95 (*0-7838-2025-9*, Macmillan Reference USA) Gale Group.

Morrison, Toni. Jazz. 1993. (Contemporary Fiction Ser.). 240p. pap. 12.95 (*0-452-26965-2*, Plume) Dutton/Plume.

—Jazz. l.t. ed. 1993. (General Ser.). 312p. lib. bdg. 22.95 (*0-8161-5624-7*, Macmillan Reference USA) Gale Group.

—Jazz. 2004. 240p. pap. 13.00 (*1-4000-7621-8*, Vintage) Knopf Publishing Group.

—Jazz. 1992. o.s.i (*0-394-22282-2*); audio o.s.i (*0-679-41353-7*) Knopf, Alfred A. Inc.

—Jazz. 1992. 240p. 26.95 (*0-679-41167-4*) McKay, David Co., Inc.

—Jazz. 1993. pap. 5.99 (*0-451-17780-0*, Signet Bks.) NAL.

—Jazz. 1993. 19.04 (*0-606-19196-8*) Turtleback Bks.

Morrone, Wenda Wardell. Year 2000 Killers: Terrorism by Computer. 1999. 352p. 23.95 o.p. (*0-312-20622-4*, Saint Martin's Minotaur) St. Martin's Pr.

Mortman, Doris. Out of Nowhere, 1. 1999. 544p. mass mkt. 6.99 (*0-8217-6253-2*); 1998. 480p. 23.95 o.s.i (*1-57566-301-5*, Kensington Bks.) Kensington Publishing Corp.

—Rightfully Mine. 1990. 736p. mass mkt. 6.99 o.s.i (*0-553-28416-9*); 700p. mass mkt. 5.50 o.s.i (*0-553-17341-3*) Bantam Bks.

—Rightfully Mine, Pt. 1. unabr. ed. 1996. audio 88.00 (*0-7366-3397-9*, 4045A) Books on Tape, Inc.

Mosby, Katherine. The Season of Lillian Dawes. 2002. E-Book 10.50 (*0-06-008500-2*) HarperCollins Pubs.

—The Season of Lillian Dawes. 288p. 2003. pap. 12.95 (*0-06-093695-9*, Perennial); 2002. 24.95 (*0-06-621272-3*, HarperCollins) HarperTrade.

—The Season of Lillian Dawes: A Novel. unabr. ed. 2002. 256p. audio 34.95 (*0-06-008297-6*, Harper-Audio) HarperTrade.

Mosley, Walter. RL's Dream. abr. ed. 1995. audio 16.95 (*1-55927-345-3*, 392939) Audio Renaissance.

—RL's Dream. unabr. ed. 1996. audio 48.00 Books on Tape, Inc.

—RL's Dream. 1995. 288p. 22.00 (*0-393-03802-5*) Norton, W. W. & Co., Inc.

—RL's Dream. 1996. 272p. pap. 14.00 (*0-671-88428-X*, Washington Square Pr.) Simon & Schuster.

Moynihan, Danny. Boogie-Woogie. 2001. 256p. 22.95 (*0-312-27281-2*) St. Martin's Pr.

—Boogie Woogie. 2002. 256p. pap. 12.95 (*0-312-28851-4*, Saint Martin's Griffin) St. Martin's Pr.

Murano, Vincent & Hammer, Richard. The Thursday Club: A Novel. 1992. 304p. 21.00 o.p. (*0-671-73448-2*, Simon & Schuster) Simon & Schuster.

—The Thursday Club: A Novel. Rubenstein, Julie, ed. 1994. 304p. reprint ed. mass mkt. 5.50 (*0-671-73864-X*, Pocket) Simon & Schuster.

Murdoch, Anna. Coming to Terms: A Novel. 1991. 240p. 19.95 o.p. (*0-06-018303-9*) HarperTrade.

Murphy, Dallas. Don't Explain. 1997. 288p. mass mkt. 5.99 (*0-671-86688-5*, Pocket) Simon & Schuster.

—Don't Explain. Grose, Bill, ed. 1996. 304p. 22.00 o.p. (*0-671-86687-7*, Atria) Simon & Schuster.

—Lover Man. 1988. mass mkt. 5.50 (*0-671-66188-4*, Pocket) Simon & Schuster.

—Lover Man: A Mystery Introducing Artie Deemer. 1987. 14.95 o.p. (*0-684-18757-4*, Macmillan Reference USA) Gale Group.

—Lush Life. 1993. 288p. (Orig.). mass mkt. 4.99 (*0-671-68556-2*, Pocket) Simon & Schuster.

—Lush Life. Chelius, Jane, ed. 1992. 288p. (Orig.). pap. 20.00 (*0-671-68555-4*, Atria) Simon & Schuster.

Murphy, Haughton. Murder for Lunch. 1987. mass mkt. 2.95 o.s.i (*0-449-21276-9*, Fawcett) Ballantine Bks.

—Murder for Lunch. 1986. 240p. 14.70 o.p. (*0-671-60628-X*, Simon & Schuster) Simon & Schuster.

—Murder for Lunch. l.t. ed. 1990. (Ulverscroft Large Print Ser.). 29.99 o.p. (*0-7089-2225-2*, Ulverscroft) Thorpe, F. A. Pubs. GBR. *Dist:* Ulverscroft Large Print Bks., Ltd., Ulverscroft Large Print Canada, Ltd.

—Murder Keeps a Secret. 1990. 240p. mass mkt. 4.99 o.s.i (*0-449-21788-4*, Fawcett) Ballantine Bks.

—Murder Keeps a Secret. 1989. 16.95 o.p. (*0-671-66981-8*, Simon & Schuster) Simon & Schuster.

—Murder Saves Face. 1992. reprint ed. mass mkt. 3.99 o.s.i (*0-449-22065-6*, Fawcett) Ballantine Bks.

—Murder Saves Face. 1991. 288p. 18.95 o.p. (*0-671-70663-2*, Simon & Schuster) Simon & Schuster.

—Murder Takes a Partner. 1987. 288p. reprint ed. mass mkt. 3.50 o.s.i (*0-449-21434-6*, Fawcett) Ballantine Bks.

—Murder Takes a Partner. 1987. 240p. 15.45 o.p. (*0-671-63422-4*, Simon & Schuster) Simon & Schuster.

—Murder Takes a Partner. l.t. ed. 1990. (Ulverscroft Large Print Ser.). 29.99 o.p. (*0-7089-2158-2*, Ulverscroft) Thorpe, F. A. Pubs. GBR. *Dist:* Ulverscroft Large Print Bks., Ltd., Ulverscroft Large Print Canada, Ltd.

—Murder Times Two. 1990. 17.95 o.p. (*0-671-66982-6*, Simon & Schuster) Simon & Schuster.

—Murder Times Two: A Ruben Frost Mystery. 1991. 256p. mass mkt. 3.95 o.s.i (*0-449-21947-X*, Fawcett) Ballantine Bks.

—Murders & Acquisitions. 1989. mass mkt. 3.95 o.s.i (*0-449-21643-8*, Fawcett) Ballantine Bks.

—Murders & Acquisitions. 1988. 224p. 16.45 o.p. (*0-671-63735-5*, Simon & Schuster) Simon & Schuster.

Murphy, Warren & Sapir, Richard. Unnatural Selection. 2003. (Destroyer Ser.: No. 131). 352p. mass mkt. (*0-373-63246-0*, Gold Eagle) Harlequin Enterprises, Ltd.

Musto, Michael. Manhattan on the Rocks. 1989. 298p. 18.95 o.p. (*0-8050-1032-7*) Holt, Henry & Co.

Myles, Eileen. Chelsea Girls. 276p. 1997. 25.00 (*0-87685-933-3*); 1994. 35.00 o.p. (*0-87685-934-1*) Godine, David R. Pub. (Black Sparrow Pr.).

—Chelsea Girls. 1997. 276p. pap. 14.00 (*0-87685-932-5*) HarperCollins Pubs.

Nadelson, Reggie. Hot Poppies. l.t. ed. 1999. (Ulverscroft Large Print Ser.). 384p. 31.99 (*0-7089-4077-3*, Ulverscroft) Thorpe, F. A. Pubs. GBR. *Dist:* Ulverscroft Large Print Bks., Ltd., Ulverscroft Large Print Canada, Ltd.

—Hot Poppies: An Artie Cohen Mystery. 1998. 256p. 22.95 o.p. (*0-312-19986-4*, Saint Martin's Minotaur) St. Martin's Pr.

—Red Hot Blues. 1998. Orig. Title: Red Mercury Blues. 272p. 22.95 (*0-312-18166-3*, Saint Martin's Minotaur) St. Martin's Pr.

Nash, Sibylla. Savage Rhythms. 2001. 300p. pap. 15.95 (*0-9701706-2-9*) Tribeca Hse.

Nathan, Paul. Count Your Enemies: A Bert Swain Mystery. 2000. (Bert Swain Mystery Ser.). per. (*0-373-26348-1*, Harlequin Bks.) Harlequin Enterprises, Ltd.

—Count Your Enemies: A Bert Swain Mystery. 1997. (Bert Swain Mystery Ser.). 224p. 21.95 (*0-8027-3296-8*) Walker & Co.

—No Good Deed. 1995. (Bert Swain Mystery Ser.). 202p. 24.00 (*1-877946-56-7*) Permanent Pr., The.

—Protocol for Murder. 1994. (Bert Swain Mystery Ser.). 176p. 24.00 (*1-877946-46-X*); pap. 16.00 (*1-877946-64-8*) Permanent Pr., The.

Neihart, Ben. Rough Amusements: The True Story of A'Lelia Walker, Patroness of the Harlem Renaissance's Down-Low Culture: An Urban Historical. 2003. 160p. 21.95 (*1-58234-285-7*) Bloomsbury Publishing.

Neimark, Jill. Bloodsong. 1994. 288p. pap. 9.95 o.p. (*0-452-27296-3*, Plume) Dutton/Plume.

—Bloodsong. 1924. o.s.i (*0-688-09132-6*, Morrow, William & Co.) Morrow/Avon.

Nelson, Blake. Exile. 1997. 288p. pap. 18.00 (*0-684-83838-9*, Scribner) Simon & Schuster.

Nelson, James L. By Force of Arms. Wolverton, Peter, ed. 1996. (Revolution at Sea Trilogy Ser.: Vol. 1). 336p. pap. 14.00 (*0-671-51924-7*, Pocket) Simon & Schuster.

—By Force of Arms. l.t. ed. 1999. (Sea Trilogy Ser.: Vol. 1). 469p. 28.95 (*0-7838-8526-1*) Thorndike Pr.

Nelson, Lee J. The Boy in the Box: A Novel. 2003. 256p. 23.95 (*1-882593-66-9*); 2004. 222p. reprint ed. pap. 15.95 (*1-882593-80-4*) Bridge Works Publishing Co., Inc.

Nersesian, Arthur. Dogrun. 2000. (Illus.). 272p. pap. 12.95 (*0-671-77542-1*, MTV) Simon & Schuster.

—The Fuck-Up. 1997. 274p. pap. 13.00 (*1-888451-03-3*) Akashic Bks.

—The Fuck-Up. 1999. (Ann Rule's Crime Files Ser.). 304p. pap. 12.95 (*0-671-02763-8*, MTV) Simon & Schuster.

—Suicide Casanova. 2002. 370p. 25.00 (*1-888451-30-0*) Akashic Bks.

Neugeboren, Jay. The Stolen Jew. 1981. 336p. o.p. (*0-03-056223-6*) Holt, Henry & Co.

—The Stolen Jew. 1998. (Library of Modern Jewish Literature). 320p. pap. 21.95 (*0-8156-0536-6*) Syracuse Univ. Pr.

Nevins, Francis M. Into the Same River Twice. 1996. 224p. 21.00 o.p. (*0-7867-0314-8*, Carroll & Graf Pubs.) Avalon Publishing Group.

—Into the Same River Twice. 2000. 228p. pap. 14.95 (*0-595-00001-0*, Authors Choice Pr.) iUniverse, Inc.

Newman, Christopher. Dead End Game. 1995. 320p. mass mkt. 5.99 o.s.i (*0-425-14564-6*) Berkley Publishing Group.

—Dead End Game. 1994. 256p. 21.95 o.p. (*0-399-13952-4*, G. P. Putnam's Sons) Penguin Group (USA) Inc.

—Hit & Run. 1997. (Lt. Joe Dante Novels Ser.). 352p. mass mkt. 5.99 o.s.i (*0-440-22263-X*) Dell Publishing.

—Killer. 1996. (Lt. Joe Dante Novels Ser.). 320p. mass mkt. 5.99 o.s.i (*0-440-22262-1*) Dell Publishing.

—Killer. 1997. 21.95 (*0-399-14044-1*, G. P. Putnam's Sons) Penguin Putnam Bks. for Young Readers.

—Knock-Off. 1989. mass mkt. 5.99 o.s.i (*0-449-13294-3*, Fawcett) Ballantine Bks.

—Midtown North. 1991. mass mkt. 5.95 o.s.i (*0-449-14689-8*, Fawcett) Ballantine Bks.

—Midtown South. 1986. mass mkt. 5.99 o.s.i (*0-449-13064-9*, Fawcett) Ballantine Bks.

—Nineteenth Precinct. 1992. mass mkt. 5.99 o.s.i (*0-449-14732-0*, Fawcett) Ballantine Bks.

—Precinct Command. 1993. mass mkt. 5.99 o.s.i (*0-449-14795-9*, Fawcett) Ballantine Bks.

—Sixth Precinct. 1987. 320p. mass mkt. 5.99 o.s.i (*0-449-13174-2*, Fawcett) Ballantine Bks.

Newman, Nancy. Disturbing the Peace. 2002. 320p. pap. 13.95 (*0-380-79839-5*, Avon Bks.) Morrow/Avon.

Ng, Mei. Eating Chinese Food Naked. 1998. 256p. mass mkt. 14.00 (*0-671-01145-6*, Scribner) Simon & Schuster.

—Eating Chinese Food Naked. l.t. ed. 1998. (Core Ser.). 344p. 26.95 (*0-7838-0240-4*) Thorndike Pr.

—Eating Chinese Food Naked: A Novel. 1998. 224p. 20.50 (*0-684-81416-1*, Scribner) Simon & Schuster.

Nicolaysen, Bruce. Beekman Place. 1982. (Novel of New York Ser.: Vol. 3). 576p. pap. 3.50 o.p. (*0-380-79673-2*, 79673-2, Avon Bks.) Morrow/Avon.

Niederman, Derrick. A Killing on Wall Street: An Investment Mystery. 2000. 208p. 21.95 (*0-471-37458-X*) Wiley, John & Sons, Inc.

Nigam, Sanjay. The Transplanted Man. 2003. 368p. pap. 13.95 (*0-06-051215-6*, Perennial) HarperTrade.

—The Transplanted Man. 2002. 368p. 24.95 (*0-688-16819-1*, Morrow, William & Co.) Morrow/Avon.

Niles, Chris. Hell's Kitchen. 2001. 280p. pap. 15.95 (*1-888451-21-1*) Akashic Bks.

Nishiyama, Yuriko. Harlem Beat. Vol. 6. 6th ed. 2000. (Illus.). 190p. pap. 9.95 (*1-892213-57-5*); Vol. 8. 2001. 184p. pap. 9.95 (*1-931514-00-3*) TOKYOPOP, Inc.

Nissen, Thisbe. The Good People of New York. 2001. E-Book 18.00 (*1-58945-897-4*) Adobe Systems, Inc.

—The Good People of New York. pap. (*0-375-72878-3*) Knopf Publishing Group.

—The Good People of New York. 2002. 304p. pap. 13.00 (*0-385-72061-0*, Knopf Bks. for Young Readers) Random Hse. Children's Bks.

Noble, Diane. At Play in the Promised Land. 2001. (California Chronicles Ser.: Vol. 3). 384p. pap. 11.95 (*1-57856-091-8*) WaterBrook Pr.

North, Darian. Criminal Seduction. 1993. 544p. 22.00 o.p. (*0-525-93740-4*, Dutton) Dutton/Plume.

—Criminal Seduction. 1994. 560p. mass mkt. 6.99 (*0-451-18022-4*, Signet Bks.) NAL.

—Criminal Seduction. 536p. 4.98 o.p. (*0-8317-9389-9*) Smithmark Pubs., Inc.

Nunez, Sigrid. A Feather on the Breath of God: A Novel. 1994. 224p. 18.00 o.p. (*0-06-017151-0*) HarperCollins Pubs.

Oates, Joyce Carol. Bellefleur. 1991. 592p. pap. 17.95 (*0-452-26794-3*, Plume); 1990. pap. 11.95 o.p. (*0-525-48567-8*); 1980. (C). 13.95 o.p. (*0-525-06302-1*, Dutton) Dutton/Plume.

—Bellefleur. 1987. pap. 9.95 o.p. (*0-525-48347-0*, Obelisk) NAL.

—Bellefleur. 1981. 688p. mass mkt. 4.50 o.s.i (*0-446-30732-7*) Warner Bks., Inc.

O'Brien, Judith. To Marry a British Lord. 1997. 320p. mass mkt. 5.99 o.s.i (*0-671-00039-X*, Pocket) Simon & Schuster.

O'Connell, Carol. Crime School. 2003. 416p. mass mkt. 7.99 (*0-515-13535-6*, Jove) Berkley Publishing Group.

—Crime School. l.t. ed. 2003. 30.95 (*1-58724-376-8*, Wheeler Publishing, Inc.) Gale Group.

—Crime School. 2002. 352p. 24.95 o.s.i (*0-399-14928-7*, Putnam & Grosset) Putnam Publishing Group, The.

—Dead Famous. 2003. 304p. 24.95 (*0-399-15084-6*) Putnam Publishing Group, The.

—Killing Critics. 1997. (Kathleen Mallory Novels Ser.). 400p. mass mkt. 7.99 (*0-515-12086-3*, Jove) Berkley Publishing Group.

—Killing Critics. abr. ed. (Kathleen Mallory Mystery Ser.). 1997. audio 7.99 o.p. (*1-56740-170-8*, 667, Paperback Nova Audio Bks.); 1996. audio 16.95 o.p. (*1-56100-894-X*, 1260, Nova Audio Bks.); 1996. 11p. audio 73.25 o.p. (*1-56100-316-6*, 917); 1996. audio 23.95 o.p. (*1-56100-691-2*, 152, Bookcassette) Brilliance Audio.

—Killing Critics. l.t. ed. 1996. (G. K. Hall Mystery Ser.). 534p. 25.95 o.p. (*0-7838-1903-X*, Macmillan Reference USA) Gale Group.

—Killing Critics. 1996. 304p. 23.95 o.s.i (*0-399-14168-5*, G. P. Putnam's Sons) Penguin Group (USA) Inc.

—Mallory's Oracle. l.t. ed. 1995. (Large Print Ser.). 330p. lib. bdg. 25.95 (1-57490-024-2, Beeler Large Print Bks.) Beeler, Thomas T. Publisher.
—Mallory's Oracle. 1995. (Kathleen Mallory Novels Ser.). 336p. mass mkt. 7.99 (0-515-11647-5, Jove) Berkley Publishing Group.
—Mallory's Oracle. 1994. 288p. 21.95 o.p. (0-399-13975-3, G. P. Putnam's Sons) Penguin Group (USA) Inc.
—Mallory's Oracle. abr. ed. 1996. audio 8.99 o.s.i (0-679-45593-0, RH Audio) Random Hse. Audio Publishing Group.
—Mallory's Oracle. 4.98 o.p. (0-7651-0181-5) Smithmark Pubs., Inc.
—The Man Who Cast Two Shadows. 1996. (Kathleen Mallory Novels Ser.). 336p. mass mkt. 7.99 (0-515-11890-7, Jove) Berkley Publishing Group.
—The Man Who Cast Two Shadows. l.t. ed. 1995. pap. 20.95 o.p. (1-56895-258-9, Wheeler Publishing, Inc.) Gale Group.
—The Man Who Cast Two Shadows. abr. ed. 1998. 8.99 o.s.i incl. audio (0-375-40328-0) Knopf, Alfred A. Inc.
—The Man Who Cast Two Shadows. 1995. 23.95 o.p. (0-399-14064-6, G. P. Putnam's Sons) Penguin Group (USA) Inc.
—Shell Game. 1999. (James Bond Adventure Ser.). 374p. 24.95 o.p. (0-399-14495-1, G. P. Putnam's Sons) Penguin Group (USA) Inc.
—The Shell Game. 2000. (Kathleen Mallory Novels Ser.). 416p. mass mkt. 7.50 (0-425-17603-7) Berkley Publishing Group.
—Shell Game, unabr. ed. 1999. (Chivers Sound Library American Collections). audio 96.95 (0-7927-2347-3, CSL 236, Chivers Sound Library) BBC Audiobooks America.
—Shell Game. l.t. ed. 2001. (Wheeler Large Print Book Ser.). 547p. pap. 23.95 (1-58724-008-4, Wheeler Publishing, Inc.) Gale Group.
—Stone Angel. 1998. (Kathleen Mallory Novels Ser.). 400p. mass mkt. 7.99 (0-515-12298-X, Jove) Berkley Publishing Group.
—Stone Angel. abr. ed. (Kathleen Mallory Mystery Ser.). 1998. audio 7.99 o.p. (1-56740-255-0, 705, Paperback Nova Audio Bks.); 1997. audio 16.95 o.p. (1-56100-935-0, 1382, Nova Audio Bks.); 1997. audio 73.25 o.p. (1-56100-824-9, 1059, Unabridged Library Editions); 1997. audio 23.95 (1-56100-749-8, 278, Bookcassette) Brilliance Audio.
—Stone Angel. l.t. ed. 1997. 24.95 o.p. (1-56895-507-3, Wheeler Publishing, Inc.) Gale Group.
—Stone Angel. 1997. 341p. 24.95 o.s.i (0-399-14234-7, G. P. Putnam's Sons) Penguin Group (USA) Inc.
O'Connell, Catherine. Skins. 1993. 215p. 20.00 o.p. (1-55611-343-9) Fine, Donald I. Bks.
O'Conner, Varley. A Company of Three. 2003. 320p. 24.95 (1-56512-373-5) Algonquin Bks. of Chapel Hill.
O'Cork, Shannon. End of the Line. 1983. (A.T.T. Baldwin Mystery Ser.). mass mkt. 2.95 o.s.i (0-671-44488-3, Pocket) Simon & Schuster.
—End of the Line. 1981. 224p. 10.95 o.p. (0-312-25102-5) St. Martin's Pr.
—Hell Bent for Heaven. 1983. 224p. 12.95 o.p. (0-312-36698-1) St. Martin's Pr.
—Sports Freak. 1980. 8.95 o.p. (0-312-75331-4) St. Martin's Pr.
O'Donnell, Lillian. Aftershock. 1982. mass mkt. 2.50 o.s.i (0-449-24479-2, Fawcett) Ballantine Bks.
—Aftershock. 1977. 7.95 o.p. (0-399-11951-5) Putnam Publishing Group, The.
—Blue Death. 1998. 224p. 22.95 o.p. (0-399-14367-X) Penguin Group (USA) Inc.
—Casual Affairs. 1987. mass mkt. 2.95 o.s.i (0-449-21064-2, Fawcett) Ballantine Bks.
—Casual Affairs. 1985. 240p. 16.95 o.p. (0-399-13100-0) Putnam Publishing Group, The.
—The Children's Zoo. 1982. mass mkt. 3.50 o.s.i (0-449-24498-9, Fawcett) Ballantine Bks.
—Cop Without a Shield. 1984. 256p. mass mkt. 2.95 o.s.i (0-449-20534-7, Fawcett) Ballantine Bks.
—Cop Without a Shield. 1983. 256p. 13.95 o.p. (0-399-12872-7, G. P. Putnam's Sons) Penguin Putnam Bks. for Young Readers.
—Falling Star. 1987. 224p. mass mkt. 2.95 o.s.i (0-449-21395-1, Fawcett); 1980. mass mkt. 1.95 o.s.i (0-449-24347-8) Ballantine Bks.
—Falling Star. 1979. 9.95 o.p. (0-399-12407-1) Putnam Publishing Group, The.
—A Good Night to Kill. 1989. 224p. mass mkt. 4.99 o.s.i (0-449-21706-X, Fawcett) Ballantine Bks.
—A Good Night to Kill. 1989. 256p. 17.95 o.p. (0-399-13403-4, G. P. Putnam's Sons) Penguin Putnam Bks. for Young Readers.
—Ladykiller. 1985. 240p. mass mkt. 2.95 o.s.i (0-449-20744-7, Fawcett) Ballantine Bks.
—Leisure Dying. 1976. 6.95 o.p. (0-399-11741-5) Putnam Publishing Group, The.
—Lockout. 1995. (Norah Mulcahaney Ser.). mass mkt. 5.99 o.s.i (0-449-22329-9, Fawcett) Ballantine Bks.
—Lockout. 1994. 240p. 19.95 o.p. (0-399-13921-4, G. P. Putnam's Sons) Penguin Group (USA) Inc.
—No Business Being a Cop. 1987. mass mkt. 2.95 o.s.i (0-449-21322-6); 1980. mass mkt. 1.95 o.p. (0-449-24219-6) Ballantine Bks. (Fawcett).
—No Business Being a Cop. 1979. 8.95 o.p. (0-399-12276-1) Putnam Publishing Group, The.
—The Other Side of the Door. 1988. mass mkt. 2.95 o.s.i (0-449-21598-9, Fawcett) Ballantine Bks.
—The Other Side of the Door. 1988. 240p. 17.95 o.p. (0-399-13316-X, G. P. Putnam's Sons) Penguin Putnam Bks. for Young Readers.
—A Private Crime. 1992. mass mkt. 3.99 o.s.i (0-449-21989-5, Fawcett) Ballantine Bks.
—A Private Crime. l.t. ed. 1992. (General Ser.). 333p. lib. bdg. 21.95 o.p. (0-8161-5277-2, Macmillan Reference USA) Gale Group.
—A Private Crime. 1991. 240p. 19.95 o.p. (0-399-13585-5, G. P. Putnam's Sons) Penguin Group (USA) Inc.
—Pushover. 1993. mass mkt. 4.99 o.s.i (0-449-22152-0, Fawcett) Ballantine Bks.
—Pushover. 1992. 240p. 19.95 o.p. (0-399-13674-6, G. P. Putnam's Sons) Penguin Group (USA) Inc.
—The Raggedy Man. 1997. (Norah Mulcahaney Ser.). mass mkt. 5.99 o.s.i (0-449-22428-7, Fawcett) Ballantine Bks.
—The Raggedy Man. 1995. 240p. 19.95 o.p. (0-399-14019-0, G. P. Putnam's Sons) Penguin Group (USA) Inc.
—Used to Kill. 1994. mass mkt. 4.99 o.s.i (0-449-22249-7, Fawcett) Ballantine Bks.
—Used to Kill. 1993. 240p. 19.95 o.p. (0-399-13782-3, G. P. Putnam's Sons) Penguin Group (USA) Inc.
—Wicked Designs. 1987. 224p. mass mkt. 2.95 o.s.i (0-449-21532-6, Fawcett); 1981. mass mkt. 2.25 o.s.i (0-449-24437-7) Ballantine Bks.
—Wicked Designs. 1980. 228p. 9.95 o.p. (0-399-12523-X) Putnam Publishing Group, The.
—A Wreath for the Bride. 1991. 224p. mass mkt. 4.99 o.s.i (0-449-21867-8, Fawcett) Ballantine Bks.
—A Wreath for the Bride. 1990. 240p. 18.95 o.p. (0-399-13478-6, G. P. Putnam's Sons) Penguin Putnam Bks. for Young Readers.
—A Wreath for the Bride. 1992. 2.99 o.p. (0-517-07978-X) Random Hse. Value Publishing.
O'Donnell, Mark. Getting over Homer. 1997. 208p. pap. 11.00 (0-679-78122-6, Vintage) Knopf Publishing Group.
—Let Nothing You Dismay. 1998. 224p. 22.00 o.s.i (0-375-40103-2) Knopf, Alfred A. Inc.
O'Donnelly, Kristina. Ride the Eagle. 2000. 304p. pap. 13.95 (1-930574-17-7) Rose International Publishing Hse., Inc.
—The Scorpion Child. 2000. pap. 15.95 (1-930574-01-0); (Illus.). 320p. 27.95 (1-930574-11-8) Rose International Publishing Hse., Inc.
O'Hagan, Christine. Benediction at the Savoia. 1992. 21.95 o.s.i (0-15-111810-8) Harcourt Trade Pubs.
O'Hara, John. Butterfield 8. 2003. 256p. pap. 12.95 (0-8129-6698-8, Modern Library) Random House Adult Trade Publishing Group.
Olden, Marc. Fear's Justice. 1998. 352p. pap. 6.99 (0-671-00379-8, Pocket) Simon & Schuster.
Ong, Han. Fixer Chao. 2001. 377p. 25.00 (0-374-15575-5) Farrar, Straus & Giroux.
—Fixer Chao. 2002. 384p. pap. 14.00 (0-312-42053-6) Picador.
Orlando, Jordon. The Object Lesson: A Novel. 1993. 560p. 23.00 o.p. (0-671-66978-8, Simon & Schuster) Simon & Schuster.
Ortleb, Charles. Iron Peter: A Year in the Mythopoetic Life of New York City. 1998. 150p. pap. 13.00 (0-9663454-0-1) Rubicon Media.
Osborne, John J., Jr. The Man Who Owned New York, 001. 1981. 10.95 o.p. (0-395-30511-X) Houghton Mifflin Co.
—The Man Who Owned New York. 1984. 288p. mass mkt. 3.50 o.s.i (0-446-31260-6) Warner Bks., Inc.
Oster, Jerry. Fixin' to Die. 1992. 320p. mass mkt. 4.99 o.s.i (0-553-29908-5) Bantam Bks.
—Internal Affairs. 1990. 320p. reprint ed. mass mkt. 4.50 o.s.i (0-553-28676-5) Bantam Bks.
O'Sullivan, Bill. Precious Blood. 1992. 202p. 18.95 o.p. (0-939149-67-2) Soho Pr., Inc.
Ozick, Cynthia. The Puttermesser Papers. 1998. 256p. pap. 13.00 (0-679-77739-3, Vintage) Knopf Publishing Group.
—The Puttermesser Papers. 1997. 236p. 23.00 o.s.i (0-679-45476-4) Knopf, Alfred A. Inc.
Page, Katherine Hall. The Body in the Big Apple. l.t. ed. 2001. (Beeler Large Print Mystery Ser.). 272p. 26.95 (1-57490-367-5, Beeler Large Print Bks.) Beeler, Thomas T. Publisher.
—The Body in the Big Apple. (Faith Fairchild Mysteries Ser.). 2001. 304p. mass mkt. 6.50 (0-380-73130-4, Avon Bks.); 1999. 239p. 22.00 (0-688-15748-3, Morrow, William & Co.) Morrow/Avon.
Pall, Ellen. Among the Ginzburgs: A Novel. 1996. 256p. 22.95 o.p. (0-944072-61-5, Zoland Bks., Inc.) Steerforth Pr.
—Corpse de Ballet: A Nine Muses Mystery:Terpsichore. 2001. 288p. 23.95 (0-312-28033-5, Saint Martin's Minotaur) St. Martin's Pr.
—Slightly Abridged: A Nine Muses Mystery: Erato. 2003. 288p. 23.95 (0-312-28185-4, Saint Martin's Minotaur) St. Martin's Pr.
—Slightly Abridged: A Nine Muses Mystery: Erato. l.t. ed. 2003. (Nine Muses Mystery: Erato Ser.). 420p. 28.95 (0-7862-5817-9) Thorndike Pr.
Palmer, Frank. Bent Grasses: An Inspector "Jacko" Jackson Mystery. 1994. 191p. 18.95 o.p. (0-312-11752-3, Saint Martin's Minotaur) St. Martin's Pr.
Palmer, Michael. Silent Treatment. 1996. 480p. reprint ed. mass mkt. 7.50 (0-553-57221-0) Bantam Bks.
—Silent Treatment. l.t. ed. (Core Collection). 632p. 1996. 23.95 (0-7838-1405-4); 1995. 26.95 o.p. (0-7838-1406-2) Gale Group. (Macmillan Reference USA).
—Silent Treatment. abr. ed. 1995. audio 16.99 o.s.i (0-553-47345-X, RH Audio) Random Hse. Audio Publishing Group.
—Silent Treatment, unabr. ed. audio 85.00 (0-7887-0268-8, 94477E7) Recorded Bks., LLC.
Palmer, Stuart. Hildegarde Withers: Uncollected Riddles. 2002. (Lost Classics Ser.). 196p. 29.00 (1-885941-84-6); pap. 19.00 (1-885941-85-4) Crippen & Landru, Pubs.
—A Murder on the Blackboard. 1988. (Mystery Ser.). 224p. mass mkt. 3.50 o.s.i (0-553-26796-5) Bantam Bks.
—Murder on the Blackboard. 1992. 186p. reprint ed. pap. 5.95 (1-55882-124-4, Library of Crime Classics) International Polygonics, Ltd.
—Murder on Wheels. 1992. 307p. pap. 6.95 o.p. (1-55882-113-9) International Polygonics, Ltd.
—The Penguin Pool Murder. 1987. 224p. mass mkt. 2.95 o.s.i (0-553-26334-X) Bantam Bks.
—The Penguin Pool Murder. 1990. 182p. reprint ed. pap. 7.95 (1-55882-076-0) International Polygonics, Ltd.
Palmer, Stuart & Rice, Craig. People vs. Withers & Malone. 1990. 254p. reprint ed. pap. 7.95 o.p. (1-55882-077-9) International Polygonics, Ltd.
Papa, Ariella. On the Verge. 2002. 304p. pap. (0-373-25017-7, Red Dress Ink) Harlequin Enterprises, Ltd.
—Up & Out. 2003. 320p. pap. (0-373-25042-8, Red Dress Ink) Harlequin Enterprises, Ltd.
Parker, Una-Mary. Enticements. 1991. 320p. 18.95 o.p. (0-525-24949-4, Dutton) Dutton/Plume.
Pashman, Susan. The Speed of Light. 1997. 207p. 24.00 (1-877946-86-9) Permanent Pr., The.
Patrick, Robert. Temple Slave. 1998. mass mkt. 7.95 (1-56333-635-9, Hard Candy); 1994. 464p. pap. 12.95 o.s.i (1-56333-191-8, Kasak, Richard Bks.) Masquerade Bks., Inc.
Patterson, James. Cat & Mouse. unabr. ed. 1998. audio 56.00 (0-7366-4138-6, 4643) Books on Tape, Inc.
—Cat & Mouse. 1997. 400p. 24.95 o.p. (0-316-69329-4) Little Brown & Co.
—Cat & Mouse. unabr. ed. 1999. audio compact disk 69.00 (0-7887-3411-3, C1017E7); 1998. audio 70.00 (0-7887-2022-8, 95395E7) Recorded Bks., LLC.
—Cat & Mouse. l.t. ed. (Paperback Bestsellers Ser.). 472p. 1999. pap. 27.95 (0-7838-8345-5); 1998. 30.95 (0-7838-8344-7) Thorndike Pr.
—Cat & Mouse. abr. ed. 1999. audio (1-57042-737-2); 1997. audio 24.00 (1-57042-577-9, 695410) Time Warner AudioBooks.
—Cat & Mouse. 1998. 480p. reprint ed. mass mkt. 7.99 (0-446-60618-9) Warner Bks., Inc.
—The Midnight Club. 1993. pap. 5.99 o.p. (0-8041-9803-9); 1990. 256p. mass mkt. 5.99 o.s.i (0-8041-0597-9) Ballantine Bks. (Ivy Bks.).
—The Midnight Club. l.t. ed. 1999. (Large Print Book Ser.). pap. 24.95 o.p. (1-56895-716-5, Wheeler Publishing, Inc.) Gale Group.
—The Midnight Club. 1989. 320p. 17.95 o.p. (0-316-69363-4) Little Brown & Co.
—The Midnight Club. 1999. 368p. reprint ed. mass mkt. 7.99 (0-446-60638-3) Warner Bks., Inc.
Paul, Barbara. The Apostrophe Thief. 1994. mass mkt. (0-373-26155-1, 1-26155-1, Harlequin Bks.) Harlequin Enterprises, Ltd.
—The Apostrophe Thief: A Mystery with Marian Larch. 1993. 256p. 20.00 o.p. (0-684-19553-4, Macmillan Reference USA) Gale Group.
—Fare Play. 1995. 256p. 20.00 (0-684-19715-4, Scribner) Simon & Schuster.
—Fare Play. l.t. ed. 1997. (Ulverscroft Large Print Ser.). 400p. 31.50 o.p. (0-7089-3690-3, Ulverscroft) Thorpe, F. A. Pubs. GBR. Dist: Ulverscroft Large Print Bks., Ltd., Ulverscroft Large Print Canada, Ltd.
—Fare Play: A Mystery with Marian Larch. l.t. ed. 1995. 314p. pap. 20.95 o.p. (0-7838-1413-5, Macmillan Reference USA) Gale Group.
—Full Frontal Murder. 1998. (WWL Mystery Ser.). per. (0-373-26284-1, 1-26284-1, Worldwide Library) Harlequin Enterprises, Ltd.
—Full Frontal Murder, Bk. 2. 1997. (Full Frontal Murder Ser.: Vol. 2). 256p. 20.50 (0-684-19716-2, Scribner) Simon & Schuster.
—Full Frontal Murder: A Mystery with Marian Larch. l.t. ed. 1998. (Mystery Ser.). 319p. 27.95 (0-7838-8363-3) Thorndike Pr.
—The Renewable Virgin. 1986. (Mystery Ser.). 192p. mass mkt. 2.95 o.s.i (0-553-26234-3) Bantam Bks.
—Renewable Virgin. l.t. ed. 1985. (Nightingale Ser.). 360p. 9.95 o.p. (0-8161-3888-5, Macmillan Reference USA) Gale Group.
—Renewable Virgin. 1985. 12.95 o.p. (0-684-18300-5, Scribner) Simon & Schuster.
—You Have the Right to Remain Silent. 1993. (Mystery Ser.). mass mkt. 3.99 (0-373-26132-2, 1-26132-0, Harlequin Bks.) Harlequin Enterprises, Ltd.
—You Have the Right to Remain Silent, unabr. ed. 1993. audio 51.00 (1-55690-836-9, 93204E7) Recorded Bks., LLC.
—You Have the Right to Remain Silent: A Mystery with Marian Larch. 1992. 256p. 20.00 o.s.i (0-684-19380-9, Scribner) Simon & Schuster.
Paul, Raymond. The Bond Street Burlesque. 1987. 16.95 o.p. (0-393-02402-4) Norton, W. W. & Co., Inc.
Paula, Cohen. Gramercy Park. mass mkt. (0-312-98323-9, St. Martin's Paperbacks) St. Martin's Pr.
Pekarkova, Iva. Gimme the Money. 2000. 224p. pap. (1-85242-658-6) Serpent's Tail Ltd.
Pentecost, Hugh. Bargain with Death. 1989. 224p. reprint ed. mass mkt. (0-373-26018-0, Harlequin Bks.) Harlequin Enterprises, Ltd.
—Beware Young Lovers. 1982. (Nightingale Ser.). pap. 9.95 o.p. (0-8161-3458-8, Macmillan Reference USA) Gale Group.
—Beware Young Lovers. 1990. 224p. mass mkt. (0-373-26057-1, Harlequin Bks.) Harlequin Enterprises, Ltd.
—The Cannibal Who Overate. 1990. 191p. mass mkt. 3.95 (0-88184-614-7, Carroll & Graf Pubs.) Avalon Publishing Group.
—The Cannibal Who Overate. l.t. ed. 1986. (Nightingale Ser.). 283p. 10.95 o.p. (0-8161-3998-9, Macmillan Reference USA) Gale Group.
—The Copycat Killers. l.t. ed. 1984. (Nightingale Ser.). pap. 9.95 o.p. (0-8161-3662-9, Macmillan Reference USA) Gale Group.
—Deadly Trap. l.t. ed. 1997. (Linford Mystery Library). 368p. pap. 17.99 o.p. (0-7089-5170-8, Ulverscroft) Thorpe, F. A. Pubs. GBR. Dist: Ulverscroft Large Print Bks., Ltd., Ulverscroft Large Print Canada, Ltd.
—Death After Breakfast. 1980. pap. 2.25 o.p. (0-440-11687-2) Dell Publishing.
—Death Mask. 1983. (Nightingale Ser.). pap. 9.95 o.p. (0-8161-3500-2, Macmillan Reference USA) Gale Group.
—Fourteen Dilemma. 1990. mass mkt. (0-373-26045-8, Harlequin Bks.) Harlequin Enterprises, Ltd.
—Murder As Usual. l.t. ed. 1997. (Linford Mystery Library). 368p. pap. 17.99 o.p. (0-7089-5103-1, Linford) Thorpe, F. A. Pubs. GBR. Dist: Ulverscroft Large Print Bks., Ltd., Ulverscroft Large Print Canada, Ltd.
—Murder Goes Round & Round. l.t. ed. 1998. (Linford Mystery Library). 272p. pap. 17.99 o.p. (0-7089-5218-6, Linford) Thorpe, F. A. Pubs. GBR. Dist: Ulverscroft Large Print Bks., Ltd., Ulverscroft Large Print Canada, Ltd.
—Murder in High Places. 1992. (WWL Mystery Ser.: No. 94). mass mkt. (0-373-26094-6, 1-26094-2, Harlequin Bks.) Harlequin Enterprises, Ltd.
—Murder in Luxury. 1991. 224p. mass mkt. (0-373-26069-5, Harlequin Bks.) Harlequin Enterprises, Ltd.
—Nightmare Time: A Pierre Chambrun Mystery Novel. 1988. 224p. mass mkt. (0-373-26001-6, Harlequin Bks.) Harlequin Enterprises, Ltd.
—Nightmare Time: A Pierre Chambrun Mystery Novel. l.t. ed. 1988. (Linford Mystery Library). 304p. pap. 17.99 o.p. (0-7089-6563-6, Linford) Thorpe, F. A. Pubs. GBR. Dist: Ulverscroft Large Print Bks., Ltd., Ulverscroft Large Print Canada, Ltd.
—The Party Killer. l.t. ed. 1997. (Linford Mystery Library). 368p. pap. 17.99 o.p. (0-7089-5099-X, Linford) Thorpe, F. A. Pubs. GBR. Dist: Ulverscroft Large Print Bks., Ltd., Ulverscroft Large Print Canada, Ltd.
—Pattern for Terror. 1990. 15.95 o.p. (0-88184-519-1, Carroll & Graf Pubs.) Avalon Publishing Group.
—Pattern for Terror. l.t. ed. 1993. (Nightingale Ser.). 208p. pap. 14.95 o.p. (0-8161-5637-9, Macmillan Reference USA) Gale Group.
—Random Killer. 1981. pap. 2.25 o.p. (0-440-17210-1) Dell Publishing.
—Remember to Kill Me. l.t. ed. 1985. (Nightingale Ser.). 299p. 10.95 o.p. (0-8161-3848-6, Macmillan Reference USA) Gale Group.
—Remember to Kill Me. 1988. 224p. reprint ed. pap. (0-373-26010-5, Harlequin Bks.) Harlequin Enterprises, Ltd.

—Time of Terror. 1989. mass mkt. (*0-373-26033-4*, Harlequin Bks.) Harlequin Enterprises, Ltd.
—Walking Dead Man. l.t. ed. 1997. (Linford Mystery Library). 368p. pap. 17.99 o.p. (*0-7089-5158-9*, Ulverscroft) Thorpe, F. A. Pubs. GBR. *Dist:* Ulverscroft Large Print Bks., Ltd., Ulverscroft Large Print Canada, Ltd.
—With Intent to Kill: A Pierre Chambrun Mystery Movel. 1991. reprint ed. mass mkt. (*0-373-26081-4*, Harlequin Bks.) Harlequin Enterprises, Ltd.
Percy, Walker. The Last Gentleman. 1989. 336p. mass mkt. 5.99 o.s.i (*0-8041-0379-8*, Ivy Bks.) Ballantine Bks.
—The Last Gentleman. unabr. ed. 1994. audio 76.95 (*0-7861-0420-1*, 1372) Blackstone Audio Bks., Inc.
—The Last Gentleman. 409p. 1982. pap. 10.95 o.p. (*0-374-50916-6*); 1966. 22.95 o.s.i (*0-374-18372-4*) Farrar, Straus & Giroux.
—The Last Gentleman. 1999. 416p. pap. 15.00 (*0-312-24308-1*) Picador.
Pereira, J. Gordon. Cocktails in a Churchyard. 2001. 417p. pap. 24.99 (*0-7388-5345-3*) Xlibris Corp.
Perry, Charles. Portrait of a Young Man Drowning. 1996. (Old School Bks.). 296p. pap. 11.00 o.p. (*0-393-31462-6*) Norton, W. W. & Co., Inc.
Petry, Ann. The Street. 1985. (Black Women Writers Ser.). 258p. reprint ed. pap. 11.95 o.p. (*0-8070-6357-6*, BP699) Beacon Pr.
—The Street. 448p. 1998. pap. 12.00 (*0-395-90149-9*); 1992. pap. 12.00 o.p. (*0-395-57380-7*) Houghton Mifflin Co.
—The Street. unabr. ed. 1998. audio 85.00 (*0-7887-0851-1*, 94997E7) Recorded Bks., LLC.
Phillips, Max. Snakebite Sonnet: A Novel. 1996. 320p. 22.95 o.p. (*0-316-70620-5*) Little Brown & Co.
Phillips, Mike. Point of Darkness: A Sam Dean Mystery. 1995. 310p. 21.95 o.p. (*0-312-11875-9*, Saint Martin's Minotaur) St. Martin's Pr.
Phillips, T. J. Woman in the Dark. 1997. (Joe Wilder Mysteries Ser.). 208p. reprint ed. mass mkt. 5.99 o.s.i (*0-425-16110-2*, Prime Crime) Berkley Publishing Group.
—Woman in the Dark: A Joe Wilder Mystery. 1997. (Joe Wilder Mysteries Ser.). 288p. 21.95 o.p. (*0-425-15312-6*, Prime Crime) Berkley Publishing Group.
Picano, Felice. The Lure: A Novel. 2002. 344p. pap. 14.95 (*1-55583-699-2*) Alyson Pubns.
—Men Who Loved Me. 2003. 303p. 19.95 (*1-56023-442-3*, Southern Tier Editions) Haworth Pr., Inc., The.
—The New York Years: Stories. 2000. 223p. pap. 12.95 (*1-55583-522-8*, Alyson Bks.) Alyson Pubns.
Pickard, Nancy. But I Wouldn't Want to Die There. 1993. (Jenny Cain Mystery Ser.). 256p. 20.00 (*0-671-72330-8*, Atria) Simon & Schuster.
—But I Wouldn't Want to Die There. Marrow, Linda, ed. 1994. (Jenny Cain Mystery Ser.). 272p. reprint ed. mass mkt. 5.50 (*0-671-72331-6*, Pocket) Simon & Schuster.
Piesman, Marissa. Alternate Sides. 1996. 304p. mass mkt. 5.50 o.s.i (*0-440-22240-0*) Dell Publishing.
—Close Quarters. 1995. 304p. mass mkt. 4.99 o.s.i (*0-440-21162-X*) Dell Publishing.
—Heading Uptown: A Nina Fischman Mystery. l.t. ed. 1993. 21.95 o.p. (*0-7927-1658-2*); pap. 19.95 o.p. (*0-7927-1657-4*) BBC Audiobooks America.
—Heading Uptown: A Nina Fischman Mystery. 1994. 320p. mass mkt. 5.50 o.s.i (*0-440-21161-1*) Dell Publishing.
—Personal Effects. Chelius, Jane, ed. 1991. 224p. (Orig.). mass mkt. 4.50 (*0-671-74275-2*, Pocket) Simon & Schuster.
—Survival Instincts. 1997. (Nina Fischman Mystery Ser.). 224p. mass mkt. 5.99 o.s.i (*0-440-22453-5*, Dell Bks.) Dell Publishing.
—Unorthodox Practices. 1989. 224p. mass mkt. 4.99 (*0-671-67315-7*, Pocket) Simon & Schuster.
Pilcer, Robin. An Ocean Apart. unabr. ed. 1999. audio 44.00 (*0-7871-1868-0*, Dove Audio) NewStar Media, Inc.
Pilcer, Sonia. The Holocaust Kid. 2001. 176p. 23.95 (*0-89255-261-1*) Persea Bks., Inc.
—I-Land: Manhattan in Monologue. 1987. (Orig.). pap. 6.95 o.s.i (*0-345-34551-7*) Ballantine Bks.
Pilgrim, Millie W. All Kneel down & Pray. 1998. 186p. pap. 10.95 (*0-9613184-3-0*) H&M Enterprises.
Pinard, Nancy. Shadow Dancing. 2000. E-Book 12.95 incl. cd-rom (*1-58444-028-7*); 224p. pap. 17.95 (*1-58444-074-0*) Disc-Us Bks., Inc.
Plain, Belva. Evergreen. 1991. 598p. reprint ed. lib. bdg. 38.95 (*0-89966-813-5*) Buccaneer Bks., Inc.
—Evergreen. 1980. 704p. mass mkt. 7.99 (*0-440-13278-9*); 1979. 19.95 o.s.i (*0-385-28299-0*, Delacorte Pr.) Dell Publishing.
—Evergreen. 1910. mass mkt. o.s.i (*0-385-31997-5*) Doubleday Publishing.
—Evergreen. 1980. (General Ser.). lib. bdg. 23.95 o.p. (*0-8161-3114-7*, Macmillan Reference USA) Gale Group.
—Her Father's House. 2002. 352p. 25.95 (*0-385-33472-9*, Delacorte Pr.) Dell Publishing.
Pollock, J. C. Payback. 1992. 400p. reprint ed. mass mkt. 5.99 o.s.i (*0-440-20518-2*) Dell Publishing.
—Threat Case. 1992. 368p. mass mkt. 5.99 o.s.i (*0-440-21204-9*) Dell Publishing.
Postupack, Kevin. The Serial Killer's Diet Book. 2002. 275p. pap. 15.95 (*1-930754-06-X*, Durban Hse.) Durban Hse. Publishing Co., Inc.
Potok, Chaim. The Chosen. (Ballantine Reader's Circle Ser.). 1996. 304p. pap. 13.95 (*0-449-91154-3*); 1987. 304p. mass mkt. 6.99 (*0-449-21344-7*); 1985. mass mkt. 3.50 o.p. (*0-449-20962-8*); 1982. mass mkt. 2.95 o.p. (*0-449-20334-4*) Ballantine Bks. (Fawcett).
—The Chosen. 1994. reprint ed. lib. bdg. 35.95 (*1-56849-319-3*) Buccaneer Bks., Inc.
—The Chosen. 25th anniv. ed. 1992. 30.00 o.s.i (*0-679-40222-5*) Knopf, Alfred A. Inc.
—The Chosen. 1967. 9.95 o.p. (*0-671-13674-7*, Simon & Schuster) Simon & Schuster.
—The Chosen. l.t. ed. 1998. (Perennial Bestsellers Ser.). 413p. 27.95 (*0-7838-8450-8*) Thorndike Pr.
—The Chosen. 1976. 13.04 (*0-606-00469-6*) Turtleback Bks.
—In the Beginning. 1975. 13.95 o.s.i (*0-394-49960-3*) Knopf, Alfred A. Inc.
—My Name Is Asher Lev. 1996. 384p. pap. 13.95 o.s.i (*0-449-91168-3*); 1983. mass mkt. 3.50 o.s.i (*0-449-20406-5*) Ballantine Bks. (Fawcett).
—My Name Is Asher Lev. 2003. 384p. reprint ed. pap. 14.00 (*1-4000-3104-4*, Anchor) Knopf Publishing Group.
—The Promise. 1997. 384p. pap. 12.95 (*0-449-00116-4*); 1985. 384p. mass mkt. 7.99 (*0-449-20910-5*); 1982. mass mkt. 3.25 o.p. (*0-449-20076-0*) Ballantine Bks. (Fawcett).
—The Promise. l.t. ed. 1998. (Perennial Bestsellers Ser.). 512p. 26.95 (*0-7838-0256-0*) Thorndike Pr.
Powell, Dawn. Angels on Toast. 1990. pap. 8.95 o.s.i (*0-679-72686-1*, Vintage) Knopf Publishing Group.
—Angels on Toast. 1996. 273p. pap. 14.00 (*1-883642-40-X*) Steerforth Pr.
—Dawn Powell at Her Best: Including the Novels "Dance Night" & "Turn Magic Wheel" & Selected Stories. 1994. 452p. 28.00 (*1-883642-16-7*) Steerforth Pr.
—The Locusts Have No King. 1996. 286p. pap. 14.00 (*1-883642-42-6*) Steerforth Pr.
—The Locusts Have No King. 1990. 304p. reprint ed. pap. 9.95 o.s.i (*1-878274-00-7*) Yarrow Pr.
—Novels, 1930-1942, Vol. 1. Page, Tim, ed. 2001. (Library of America: Vol. 126). 1075p. 35.00 (*1-931082-01-4*) Library of America, The.
—Novels, 1944-1962, Vol. 2. Page, Tim, ed. 2001. (Library of America: Vol. 127). 985p. 35.00 (*1-931082-02-2*) Library of America, The.
—A Time to Be Born. reprint ed. 30.00 (*0-404-20206-3*, PS3531) AMS Pr., Inc.
—A Time to Be Born. 1996. 334p. pap. 14.00 (*1-883642-41-8*) Steerforth Pr.
—A Time to Be Born. 1991. 352p. reprint ed. pap. 9.95 o.p. (*1-878274-06-6*) Yarrow Pr.
Power, Nani. Crawling at Night. 2001. 234p. 24.00 o.p. (*0-87113-784-4*, Atlantic Monthly Pr.); 2002. 240p. reprint ed. pap. 13.00 (*0-8021-3884-5*, Grove Pr.) Grove/Atlantic, Inc.
Preston, Douglas J. Relic. 1996. 13.04 (*0-606-11786-5*) Turtleback Bks.
—Reliquary: Sequel to the Relic! 1998. 464p. mass mkt. 7.99 (*0-8125-4283-5*, Tor Bks.) Doherty, Tom Assocs., LLC.
—Reliquary: Sequel to the Relic! 1998. 5.98 o.p. (*0-7651-1480-1*) Smithmark Pubs., Inc.
Preston, Douglas J. & Child, Lincoln. The Cabinet of Curiosities. 2003. 656p. mass mkt. 7.99 (*0-446-61123-9*); 2002. 480p. 25.95 (*0-446-53022-0*) Warner Bks., Inc.
—Relic. 1996. mass mkt. 6.99 o.s.i (*0-8125-6358-1*, Tor Bks.); 1996. 474p. pap. text 7.99 (*0-8125-4326-2*, Tor Bks.); 1995. 384p. 22.95 o.p. (*0-312-85630-X*, Forge Bks.) Doherty, Tom Assocs., LLC.
—Reliquary: Sequel to the Relic! abr. ed. 1998. audio 7.99 o.p. (*1-56740-246-1*, 693, Paperback Nova Audio Bks.); 1997. audio 16.95 o.p. (*1-56100-982-2*, 1353, Nova Audio Bks.); 1997. audio 89.25 o.p. (*1-56100-831-1*, 1007, Unabridged Library Editions); 1997. audio 25.95 o.p. (*1-56100-756-0*, 230, Bookcassette) Brilliance Audio.
—Reliquary: Sequel to the Relic! 1997. 384p. 24.95 o.p. (*0-312-86095-1*, Forge Bks.) Doherty, Tom Assocs., LLC.
Prete, David. Say That to My Face. 2003. 192p. text 23.95 (*0-393-05798-4*) Norton, W. W. & Co., Inc.
Price, Bruce D. Too Easy. 1994. 21.00 (*0-671-88673-8*, Simon & Schuster) Simon & Schuster.
Price-Thompson, Tracy. Chocolate Sangria: A Novel. 2004. 304p. pap. 13.95 (*0-375-75779-1*, Random House); 2003. 288p. 21.95 (*0-375-50651-9*, Villard Bks.) Random House Adult Trade Publishing Group.
Pronzini, Bill, et al, eds. Manhattan Mysteries. 1987. 1.99 o.s.i (*0-517-63179-2*) Random Hse. Value Publishing.
Prose, Francine. Bigfoot Dreams. 1998. 288p. pap. 12.00 (*0-8050-4860-X*, Owl Bks.) Holt, Henry & Co.
—Bigfoot Dreams. 1986. 16.95 o.p. (*0-394-54976-7*, Pantheon) Knopf Publishing Group.
—Bigfoot Dreams. 1987. 288p. pap. 6.95 o.p. (*0-14-009837-2*, Penguin Bks.) Viking Penguin.
Provinzano, A. M. The Secret Spring of Edith Cooley. 2000. 138p. pap. 11.95 (*1-930185-00-6*, 101) Joan of Arc Publishing.
Pulaski, Jack. The St. Veronica Gig Stories. 1986. 178p. (Orig.). 15.95 (*0-939010-10-0*); pap. 8.95 (*0-939010-09-7*) Zephyr Pr.
Purdy, James. Out with the Stars. 1993. 192p. 19.95 o.p. (*0-87286-287-9*); pap. 9.95 o.p. (*0-87286-284-4*) City Lights Bks.
—Out with the Stars. 1993. 192p. 30.00 (*0-7206-0861-9*) Owen, Peter Ltd. GBR. *Dist:* Dufour Editions, Inc.
Puzo, Mario. The Fortunate Pilgrim. 1998. 304p. pap. 13.95 (*0-449-00358-2*); 1982. mass mkt. 2.50 o.s.i (*0-449-23456-8*) Ballantine Bks. (Fawcett).
—The Fortunate Pilgrim. 1985. 256p. mass mkt. 3.95 o.s.i (*0-553-24859-6*) Bantam Bks.
—The Fortunate Pilgrim. abr. ed. 1998. audio 7.99 o.p. (*1-56740-239-9*, 651, Paperback Nova Audio Bks.); 1997. audio 16.95 o.p. (*1-56100-986-5*, 1201, Nova Audio Bks.); 1997. audio 23.95 o.p. (*1-56100-760-9*, 113, Bookcassette); 1997. audio 73.25 o.p. (*1-56100-835-4*, 841, Unabridged Library Editions) Brilliance Audio.
—The Fortunate Pilgrim. abr. ed. 2000. audio 7.95 (*1-57815-171-6*, 1114, Media Bks. Audio Publishing) Media Bks., L. L. C.
—The Fortunate Pilgrim. 1997. 304p. 23.00 o.s.i (*0-679-45778-X*) Random Hse., Inc.
—The Godfather. abr. ed. 1998. audio 24.95 (*1-882071-84-0*) B&B Audio, Inc.
—The Godfather. 1977. mass mkt. 2.25 o.p. (*0-449-23408-8*, Fawcett) Ballantine Bks.
—The Godfather. unabr. collector's ed. 1993. audio 88.00 (*0-7366-2386-8*, 3157) Books on Tape, Inc.
—The Godfather. unabr. ed. 1986. audio 89.25 (*1-56100-016-7*, 1220, Unabridged Library Editions); audio 23.95 o.p. (*0-930435-21-4*, 122, Bookcassette) Brilliance Audio.
—The Godfather. l.t. ed. 1985. (Special Editions Ser.). 688p. 19.95 o.p. (*0-8161-3875-3*, Macmillan Reference USA) Gale Group.
—The Godfather. 2002. 9.99 (*0-451-20844-7*); 2002. 464p. pap. 14.00 (*0-451-20576-6*); 1983. mass mkt. 1.95 o.p. (*0-451-12891-5*, Signet Bks.); 1983. mass mkt. 3.95 o.p. (*0-451-13644-6*, Signet Bks.); 1983. mass mkt. 4.95 o.p. (*0-451-15736-2*, Signet Bks.); 1983. 448p. mass mkt. 7.99 (*0-451-16771-6*, Signet Bks.); 1983. mass mkt. 4.50 o.p. (*0-451-14506-2*, Signet Bks.); 1978. mass mkt. 3.50 o.p. (*0-451-12580-0*, Signet Bks.); 1978. mass mkt. 2.95 o.p. (*0-451-09438-7*, Signet Bks.); 1978. mass mkt. 2.75 o.p. (*0-451-08970-7*, Signet Bks.); 1978. mass mkt. 2.50 o.p. (*0-451-08508-6*, Signet Bks.) NAL.
—The Godfather. 1969. 448p. 24.95 (*0-399-10342-2*, G. P. Putnam's Sons) Penguin Group (USA) Inc.
—The Godfather. l.t. ed. 1986. (Charnwood Large Print Ser.). 752p. 29.99 o.p. (*0-7089-8351-0*, Charnwood) Thorpe, F. A. Pubs. GBR. *Dist:* Ulverscroft Large Print Bks., Ltd., Ulverscroft Large Print Canada, Ltd.
—The Godfather Papers & Other Confessions. 1972. 224p. 6.95 o.p. (*0-399-10935-8*) Putnam Publishing Group, The.
Puzo, Mario & Sinatra, Nancy. The Godfather Pack: The Godfather & Frank Sinatra: An American Legend. abr. unabr. ed. 2001. audio 34.95 (*0-929071-26-3*) B&B Audio, Inc.
Pye, Michael. The Drowning Room: A Novel of New Amsterdam. 1997. 256p. 12.95 (*0-14-014149-9*); 1997. 252p. pap. 11.95 (*0-14-014122-7*); 1996. 256p. 22.95 (*0-670-86598-2*, Viking) Viking Penguin.
Quan, Tracy. The Diary of a Manhattan Call Girl: A Novel. 2003. 288p. pap. 13.00 (*0-609-81010-3*, Three Rivers Pr.) Crown Publishing Group.
Queen, Ellery. A Fine & Private Place. l.t. ed. 2002. (Paperback Ser.). 257p. 24.95 o.p. (*0-7838-9759-6*) Gale Group.
—A Fine & Private Place. 1976. mass mkt. 1.25 o.p. (*0-451-07183-2*); 1972. mass mkt. 0.95 o.p. (*0-451-04978-0*) NAL. (Signet Bks.).
—French Powder Mystery. lib. bdg. 21.95 (*0-8488-1870-9*) Amereon, Ltd.
—French Powder Mystery. 1995. pap. 7.00 o.s.i (*1-883402-90-5*, Scribner) Simon & Schuster.
—The King Is Dead. l.t. ed. 2000. (G. K. Hall Paperback Ser.). 328p. pap. 23.95 (*0-7838-9282-9*, Macmillan Reference USA) Gale Group.
—The King Is Dead. 1994. (Ellery Queen Mystery Ser.). 224p. reprint ed. pap. 8.00 o.p. (*0-06-097605-5*, Perennial) HarperTrade.
—The King Is Dead. mass mkt. 0.25 o.p. (*0-451-00629-1*); 1977. mass mkt. 1.25 o.p. (*0-451-07361-4*); 1972. mass mkt. 0.95 o.p. (*0-451-05290-0*) NAL. (Signet Bks.).
—The Siamese Twin Mystery. unabr. ed. 1998. audio 49.95 (*0-7861-1266-2*, 2203) Blackstone Audio Bks., Inc.
—The Siamese Twin Mystery. unabr. collector's ed. 1978. audio 48.00 (*0-7366-0136-8*, 1140) Books on Tape, Inc.
—The Siamese Twin Mystery. 1970. mass mkt. 0.75 o.p. (*0-451-04086-4*, Signet Bks.) NAL.
—The Siamese Twin Mystery. 1993. pap. 6.95 (*1-883402-11-5*, Scribner) Simon & Schuster.
—The Siamese Twin Mystery: Kill As Directed. 1983. mass mkt. 2.95 o.p. (*0-451-12271-2*, Signet Bks.) NAL.
—The Siamese Twin Mystery: Special 50th Anniversary Edition. 1979. mass mkt. 1.75 o.p. (*0-451-08664-3*, E8664, Signet Bks.) NAL.
Quesada, Roberto. The Big Banana. Krochmal, Walter, tr. 1999. 304p. pap. 12.95 (*1-55885-255-7*) Arte Publico Pr.
Quinn, Peter. Banished Children of Eve. 1995. 624p. pap. 14.00 (*0-14-023003-3*, Penguin Bks.) Penguin Group (USA) Inc.
—Banished Children of Eve. 1994. 624p. 22.95 o.p. (*0-670-85076-4*, Viking) Viking Penguin.
Quinones Miller, Karen E. Satin Doll. 2002. 320p. pap. 13.00 (*0-7432-1434-X*, Simon & Schuster) Simon & Schuster.
—Satin Doll: A Novel. 2000. 288p. pap. 12.95 (*0-9676028-0-7*) Oshun Publishing Co., Inc.
—Satin Doll: A Novel. 2001. 320p. 21.00 (*0-7432-1433-1*, Simon & Schuster) Simon & Schuster.
Quinonez, Ernesto. Bodega Dreams. 2000. (Illus.). 224p. pap. 12.00 (*0-375-70589-9*, Vintage) Knopf Publishing Group.
Quittner, Joshua & Slatalla, Michelle. Shoo-Fly Pie to Die. 1992. 224p. 17.95 o.p. (*0-312-06943-X*, Saint Martin's Minotaur) St. Martin's Pr.
Rae, Catherine M. Afterward. 1992. 192p. 16.95 o.p. (*0-312-06894-8*) St. Martin's Pr.
—Brownstone Facade. 1987. 192p. 13.95 o.p. (*0-312-01004-4*) St. Martin's Pr.
—Flight from Fifth Avenue. 1995. 18.95 o.p. (*0-312-11788-4*) St. Martin's Pr.
—The Hidden Cove. l.t. ed. 2000. 268p. lib. bdg. 27.95 (*1-58547-035-X*) Ctr. Point Large Print.
—The Hidden Cove. 1999. 183p. reprint ed. text 20.00 (*0-7881-6634-4*) DIANE Publishing Co.
—The Hidden Cove. 1995. 192p. 19.95 o.p. (*0-312-13511-4*) St. Martin's Pr.
—Marike's World. E-Book 21.95 (*0-312-27585-4*); 2000. 186p. 21.95 (*0-312-26199-3*) St. Martin's Pr.
—The Ship's Clock. 1993. 192p. 17.95 o.p. (*0-312-09386-1*) St. Martin's Pr.
—Sunlight on a Broken Column. 1997. 192p. 20.95 o.p. (*0-312-17039-4*) St. Martin's Pr.
—Sunlight on a Broken Column. l.t. ed. 1998. (Basic Ser.). 269p. 27.95 (*0-7862-1316-7*) Thorndike Pr.
Raeff, Anne. Clara Mondschein's Melancholia: A Novel. 2002. 258p. 25.00 (*1-931561-16-8*) MacAdam/Cage Publishing, Inc.
Ragen, Naomi. Chains Around the Grass. 2003. pap. 12.95 (*1-902881-82-6*); 2002. (Illus.). 256p. 26.95 (*1-902881-53-2*); 2003. 394p. 24.95 (*1-902881-72-9*) Toby Pr.
—The Ghost of Hannah Mendes. 5th ed. 2001. (Illus.). 384p. reprint ed. pap. 14.95 (*0-312-28125-0*, CPB1198, Saint Martin's Griffin) St. Martin's Pr.
—The Ghost of Hannah Mendes: A Novel. 1998. 384p. 25.00 o.s.i (*0-684-83393-X*, Simon & Schuster) Simon & Schuster.
—The Sacrifice of Tamar. 1994. 448p. 24.00 o.s.i (*0-517-59561-3*, Crown) Crown Publishing Group.
Raillard, Matthieu P. Castles in the Sky. 2000. 520p. pap. 26.99 (*0-7388-2220-5*); text 36.99 (*0-7388-2219-1*) Xlibris Corp.
Raines, Jeff. Unbalanced Acts. 1990. 272p. mass mkt. 4.50 (*0-380-76008-8*, Avon Bks.) Morrow/Avon.
Ramone, Dee Dee. Chelsea Horror Hotel. 2001. (Illus.). 244p. pap. 13.95 (*1-56025-304-5*, Thunder's Mouth Pr.) Avalon Publishing Group.
Ramsay, Diana. Four Steps to Death. 1990. 192p. 14.95 o.p. (*0-312-03835-6*, Saint Martin's Minotaur) St. Martin's Pr.
Ramus, David. Thief of Light. l.t. ed. 1996. pap. 23.95 (*1-56895-304-6*, Wheeler Publishing, Inc.) Gale Group.
—Thief of Light. 1995. 352p. 23.00 o.p. (*0-06-017664-4*); 184.00 o.p. (*0-06-017685-7*) HarperCollins Pubs.
—Thief of Light. 1997. 384p. mass mkt. 6.50 o.s.i (*0-06-109420-X*, HarperTorch) Morrow/Avon.
Rand, Naomi R. The One That Got Away: An Emma Price Mystery. 2001. 320p. 24.00 (*0-06-019938-5*) HarperCollins Pubs.
—Stealing for a Living. 2003. 256p. 23.95 (*0-06-019936-9*) HarperCollins Pubs.

Randisi, Robert J. Alone with the Dead. unabr. ed. 1999. audio 69.95 (*0-7927-2267-1*, CSL156, Chivers Sound Library) BBC Audiobooks America.

—Alone with the Dead. (Joe Keough Mysteries Ser.). 368p. reprint ed. 1999. mass mkt. 6.99 (*0-8439-4641-5*); 1998. pap. 5.50 (*0-8439-4435-8*) Dorchester Publishing Co., Inc. (Leisure Bks.).

—Alone with the Dead. 1995. 262p. 21.95 o.p. (*0-312-13022-8*, Saint Martin's Minotaur) St. Martin's Pr.

—Alone with the Dead. 1999. E-Book 9.95 (*0-585-29635-9*) netLibrary, Inc.

—The Dead of Brooklyn: A Nick Delvecchio Mystery. 1991. 272p. 18.95 o.p. (*0-312-06330-X*, Saint Martin's Minotaur) St. Martin's Pr.

—Delvecchio's Brooklyn: A Short Story Collection. l.t. ed. 2001. 207p. 23.95 (*0-7862-3044-4*, Five Star) Gale Group.

—Eye in the Ring. 1986. 256p. pap. 2.75 o.p. (*0-380-81455-2*, 81455-2, Avon Bks.) Morrow/Avon.

—Full Contact: A Miles Jacoby Mystery. l.t. ed. 1988. pap. 14.95 o.p. (*1-55504-699-1*, 827) BBC Audiobooks America.

—Full Contact: A Miles Jacoby Mystery. 2000. mass mkt. 2.95 (*0-380-69984-2*, Avon Bks.) Morrow/Avon.

—Full Contact: A Miles Jacoby Mystery. 1984. 256p. 13.95 o.p. (*0-312-30966-X*) St. Martin's Pr.

—Hard Look: A Miles Jacoby Mystery. 1993. (Miles Jacoby Mystery Ser.). 252p. 21.00 o.s.i (*0-8027-1251-7*) Walker & Co.

—No Exit from Brooklyn: A Nick Delvecchio Mystery. 1989. mass mkt. 3.95 (*0-8125-0825-4*, Tor Bks.) Doherty, Tom Assocs., LLC.

—No Exit from Brooklyn: A Nick Delvecchio Mystery. l.t. ed. 2002. (Mystery Ser.). 408p. 28.95 o.p. (*0-7862-3886-0*) Gale Group.

—No Exit from Brooklyn: A Nick Delvecchio Mystery. 2001. 277p. reprint ed. pap. 12.95 (*1-931755-13-2*) Mystery Vault, Inc.

—No Exit from Brooklyn: A Nick Delvecchio Mystery. 1987. 288p. 16.95 o.p. (*0-312-00169-X*) St. Martin's Pr.

—Separate Cases. 1990. 192p. 18.95 (*0-8027-5723-5*) Walker & Co.

—Stand-Up: A Miles Jacoby Mystery. 1994. 246p. 20.95 o.p. (*0-8027-3196-1*) Walker & Co.

—The Steinway Collection. 1986. 272p. pap. 2.75 o.p. (*0-380-85175-X*, 85175, Avon Bks.) Morrow/Avon.

Ransom, Jane. Bye-Bye. 1997. 150p. 19.00 (*0-8147-7490-3*) New York Univ. Pr.

—Bye-Bye. 1999. 208p. reprint ed. pap. 12.00 (*0-671-02708-5*, Washington Square Pr.) Simon & Schuster.

Raphael, Lev. The German Money: A Novel. 2003. 212p. pap. 14.95 (*0-9679520-0-X*) Leapfrog Pr.

Ratner, Rochelle. Bobby's Girl. 1986. 128p. (Orig.). pap. 9.95 (*0-918273-22-6*) Coffee Hse. Pr.

Rayner, Richard. The Cloud Sketcher. 2001. 448p. 25.00 (*0-06-019634-3*) HarperCollins Pubs.

—The Cloud Sketcher. 2002. 432p. pap. 14.95 (*0-06-095613-5*, Perennial) HarperTrade.

Redwood, John H. The Old Settler. 1998. per. 6.50 (*0-8222-1642-6*) Dramatists Play Service, Inc.

Reich, Tova. Mara: A Novel. 2001. (Library of Modern Jewish Literature). 256p. pap. 18.95 (*0-8156-0659-1*) Syracuse Univ. Pr.

Reilly, Matthew. Contest. E-Book 24.95 (*0-312-70986-2*); 2004. mass mkt. (*0-312-99004-9*, St. Martin's Paperbacks); 2003. (Illus.). 336p. 24.95 (*0-312-28625-2*) St. Martin's Pr.

—Contest. 2004. (*0-7862-6117-X*) Thorndike Pr.

Remnick, David. Wonderful Town: New York Stories from The New Yorker. 2000. 496p. 26.95 o.s.i (*0-375-50356-0*) Random Hse., Inc.

Renek, Morris. Bread & Circus. 1987. 352p. 18.95 o.s.i (*1-55584-070-1*) Grove/Atlantic, Inc.

Renino, Christopher. Way Home Is Longer. 1997. 352p. 23.95 o.p. (*0-312-15686-3*) St. Martin's Pr.

Rettenmund, Matthew. Blind Items. 288p. 2000. pap. 13.95 (*0-312-26295-7*, Saint Martin's Griffin); 1998. 22.95 (*0-312-19242-8*) St. Martin's Pr.

Reuben, Shelly. Origin & Cause. 1996. 384p. mass mkt. 5.50 o.p. (*0-06-104392-3*, HarperTorch) Morrow/Avon.

—Origin & Cause: A Crime Novel. 1994. 352p. 20.00 (*0-684-19702-2*, Macmillan Reference USA) Gale Group.

—Spent Matches. 1996. 320p. 21.00 (*0-684-80107-8*, Scribner) Simon & Schuster.

Reuland, Rob. Hollowpoint. abr. ed. 2001. audio 19.95 o.s.i (*1-58788-468-2*, 2737, Nova Audio Bks.); audio 27.95 (*1-58788-466-6*, 2735, Brilliance Audio Unabridged); audio 61.25 (*1-58788-467-4*, 2736, Unabridged Library Editions) Brilliance Audio.

—Hollowpoint. 2001. E-Book 19.95 (*0-375-50698-5*) Random Hse., Inc.

Reznikoff, Charles. By the Waters of Manhattan. 1986. (Masterworks of Modern Jewish Writings). (Illus.). 264p. (C). reprint ed. pap. 9.95 (*0-910129-55-X*) Wiener, Markus Pubs., Inc.

Rice, Anne. Memnoch, the Devil. (Vampire Chronicles: Bk. 5). 1997. pap. 14.00 o.s.i (*0-345-91273-X*); 1996. mass mkt. 7.50 o.s.i (*0-345-40499-8*); 1996. 464p. pap. 14.95 (*0-345-38940-9*) Ballantine Bks.

—Memnoch, the Devil. 1995. (Vampire Chronicles: Bk. 5). 368p. 29.95 (*0-679-44101-8*) Knopf, Alfred A. Inc.

—Memnoch, the Devil. abr. ed. 1995. (Vampire Chronicles). audio 23.50 (*0-679-43832-7*, 493006, RH Audio) Random Hse. Audio Publishing Group.

—Memnoch, the Devil. deluxe ltd. num. ed. 1995. (Vampire Chronicles: Vol. 5). 354p. 195.00 (*0-9631925-4-X*) Trice, B.E. Publishing.

Richards, Elizabeth. Every Day: A Novel. 240p. 1999. pap. 12.00 (*0-671-00156-6*); 1997. 22.00 (*0-671-00155-8*) Simon & Schuster. (Atria).

—Rescue. 1999. 276p. 22.00 (*0-671-02397-7*); 2000. 288p. reprint ed. pap. 12.95 o.s.i (*0-671-02398-5*) Simon & Schuster. (Atria).

—Rescue. 2000. 19.00 (*0-606-19502-5*) Turtleback Bks.

Ridley, John. A Conversation with the Mann. 448p. 2003. pap. 14.95 (*0-446-69075-9*); 2002. 24.95 (*0-446-52836-6*) Warner Bks., Inc.

Riley, Len. Harlem. 1998. (Berkeley Signature Edition Ser.). 304p. mass mkt. 6.99 o.s.i (*0-425-16343-1*) Berkley Publishing Group.

—Harlem. 1997. 384p. 21.95 o.s.i (*0-385-48508-5*) Doubleday Publishing.

Rinaldi, Nicholas. Between Two Rivers. 2004. 448p. 24.95 (*0-06-057876-9*) HarperCollins Pubs.

Ritz, David. Take It Off, Take It All Off! 1993. 224p. 21.00 o.p. (*1-55611-366-8*) Fine, Donald I. Bks.

Ro, Ronin. Street Sweeper. 2000. (Illus.). 156p. pap. 16.98 incl. audio compact disk (*1-930306-00-8*) Syndicate Media Group, The.

Robb, J. D., pseud. Betrayal in Death. l.t. ed. 2001. 536p. (*0-7862-3397-4*) Thorndike Pr.

—Ceremony in Death. 1997. 336p. mass mkt. 7.99 (*0-425-15762-8*) Berkley Publishing Group.

—Conspiracy in Death. 1999. 400p. mass mkt. 7.99 (*0-425-16813-1*) Berkley Publishing Group.

—Divided in Death. 2004. 448p. 23.95 (*0-399-15154-0*, Putnam & Grosset) Putnam Publishing Group, The.

—Glory in Death. 1995. 320p. mass mkt. 7.99 (*0-425-15098-4*) Berkley Publishing Group.

—Glory in Death. 2004. 320p. reprint ed. 19.95 (*0-399-15158-3*) Putnam Publishing Group, The.

—Holiday in Death. 1998. 336p. mass mkt. 7.99 (*0-425-16371-7*) Berkley Publishing Group.

—Imitation in Death. 2003. 352p. mass mkt. 7.99 (*0-425-19158-3*) Berkley Publishing Group.

—Imitation in Death. abr. ed. 2005. (In Death Ser.). audio 12.99 (*1-59086-726-2*, 4317, Brilliance Audio Paperback Audiobooks); 2003. (In Death Series: Vol. 17). audio 24.95 (*1-59086-725-4*, 4316); 2003. (In Death Series: Vol. 17). audio 30.95 (*1-59086-723-8*, 4314, Brilliance Audio Unabridged); 2003. (In Death Series: Vol. 17). audio 87.25 (*1-59086-724-6*, 4315) Brilliance Audio.

—Immortal in Death. 1996. 320p. mass mkt. 7.99 (*0-425-15378-9*) Berkley Publishing Group.

—Immortal in Death. 2004. 288p. reprint ed. 19.95 (*0-399-15159-1*) Putnam Publishing Group, The.

—Judgment in Death. 2000. 368p. mass mkt. 7.99 (*0-425-17630-4*) Berkley Publishing Group.

—Judgment in Death. abr. ed. (In Death Ser.). 2005. audio 12.99 (*1-58788-323-6*, 2902, Brilliance Audio Paperback Audiobooks); 2000. audio 24.95 (*1-58788-079-2*, 2327, Nova Audio Bks.); 2000. audio 44.25 (*1-58788-174-8*, 2447, Unabridged Library Editions) Brilliance Audio.

—Judgment in Death. l.t. ed. 2002. (Core Ser.). 472p. pap. 30.95 (*0-7838-9335-3*) Gale Group.

—Judgment in Death. l.t. ed. 2001. (Core Ser.). 472p. 32.95 (*0-7838-9334-5*) Thorndike Pr.

—Loyalty in Death. 1999. 368p. mass mkt. 7.99 (*0-425-17140-X*) Berkley Publishing Group.

—Loyalty in Death. l.t. ed. 2000. (Americana Ser.). 539p. 30.95 (*0-7862-2443-6*) Thorndike Pr.

—Una Muerte Desnuda. 1999. (SPA.). 368p. 19.95 (*84-01-46800-0*) Lectorum Pubns., Inc.

—Naked in Death. 1995. 320p. mass mkt. 7.99 (*0-425-14829-7*) Berkley Publishing Group.

—Naked in Death. 2004. 304p. reprint ed. 19.95 (*0-399-15157-5*) Putnam Publishing Group, The.

—Naked in Death. l.t. ed. 2000. (Americana Ser.). 445p. 29.95 (*0-7862-2415-0*) Thorndike Pr.

—Rapture in Death. 1996. 320p. mass mkt. 7.99 (*0-425-15518-8*) Berkley Publishing Group.

—Reunion in Death. 2002. 384p. mass mkt. 7.99 (*0-425-18397-1*) Berkley Publishing Group.

—Reunion in Death. abr. ed. (In Death Ser.). 2005. audio 12.99 (*1-58788-688-X*, 2983, Brilliance Audio Paperback Audiobooks); 2002. audio 24.95 (*1-58788-687-1*, 2982, Nova Audio Bks.); 2002. audio 30.95 (*1-58788-685-5*, 2980, Brilliance Audio Unabridged) Brilliance Audio.

—Reunion in Death. abr. ed. 2003. (In Death Ser.). audio 19.99 (*1-59335-140-2*, 30236) Soulmate Audio Bks., Inc.

—Vengeance in Death. 1997. 384p. mass mkt. 7.99 (*0-425-16039-4*) Berkley Publishing Group.

—Witness in Death. 2000. 368p. mass mkt. 7.99 (*0-425-17363-1*) Berkley Publishing Group.

—Witness in Death. l.t. ed. 2001. 28.95 (*0-7862-2716-8*); 2000. 547p. 30.95 (*0-7862-2715-X*) Thorndike Pr.

Robb, J. D., pseud, et al. Silent Night. 1998. 352p. mass mkt. 7.50 (*0-515-12385-4*, Jove) Berkley Publishing Group.

Robbe-Grillet, Alain. Project for a Revolution in New York. Howard, Richard, tr. from FRE. 1989. pap. 3.95 o.p. (*0-394-17768-1*, E685) Grove/Atlantic, Inc.

Robbins, Harold. Never Enough. 2001. 336p. 25.95 (*0-7653-0000-1*); 2002. reprint ed. mass mkt. 7.99 (*0-7653-4050-X*) Doherty, Tom Assocs., LLC. (Forge Bks.).

—The Predators. 1999. 407p. mass mkt. 7.99 (*0-8125-7178-9*); 1998. 348p. 24.95 o.p. (*0-312-85294-0*) Doherty, Tom Assocs., LLC. (Forge Bks.).

—The Predators, Set. unabr. ed. 1998. audio 40.00 (*0-7871-1734-X*, 896017) NewStar Media, Inc.

—The Secret. 2000. 364p. 25.95 (*0-312-86608-9*, Forge Bks.) Doherty, Tom Assocs., LLC.

Robbins, Jerry. For Love & Liberty. 1998. 224p. (*1-892358-00-X*) Medea Publishing, Inc.

Roberts, Nora. Divine Evil. 1992. 512p. mass mkt. 7.50 (*0-553-29490-3*) Bantam Bks.

—Divine Evil. l.t. ed. 24.95 o.p. (*1-56895-118-3*, Wheeler Publishing, Inc.) Gale Group.

—Divine Evil. l.t. ed. 2004. 800p. 24.00 (*0-375-43377-5*) Random Hse. Large Print.

—Remember When. 2004. 512p. mass mkt. 7.99 (*0-425-19547-3*) Berkley Publishing Group.

—Truly, Madly, Manhattan: Local Hero & Dual Image. 2003. 480p. mass mkt. (*0-373-21803-6*, Silhouette) Harlequin Enterprises, Ltd.

Roberts, Nora & Robb, J. D. Remember When. 2003. 448p. 25.95 (*0-399-15106-0*, Putnam & Grosset) Putnam Publishing Group, The.

—Remember When. l.t. ed. 2004. 544p. pap. 14.95 (*1-59413-022-1*); 2003. 729p. 32.95 (*0-7862-5695-8*) Thorndike Pr. (Large Print Pr.).

Roberts, Tatheena. MacDougal Alley: A Novel. 2001. 289p. pap. 11.95 o.p. (*1-55583-540-6*, Alyson Bks.) Alyson Pubns.

Roberts, Walter A. Mayor Harding of New York. reprint ed. 42.50 (*0-404-11412-1*) AMS Pr., Inc.

Robertson, Ray. Home Movies: A Novel. 1997. 228p. pap. text (*1-896951-02-3*) Cormorant Bks.

Robins, Madeleine. The Stone War. 1999. 320p. 23.95 (*0-312-85486-2*, Tor Bks.) Doherty, Tom Assocs., LLC.

Robins, Madeleine E. The Stone War. 2000. 342p. mass mkt. 6.99 (*0-8125-2431-4*, Tor Bks.) Doherty, Tom Assocs., LLC.

Robinson, Leah Ruth. Blood Run. 1999. 352p. mass mkt. 6.99 (*0-380-79113-7*, Avon Bks.) Morrow/Avon.

—Blood Run. 1989. mass mkt. 4.50 o.p. (*0-451-40143-3*, Onyx); 1988. 17.95 o.p. (*0-453-00611-6*) NAL.

—Unnatural Causes. 1999. 384p. 24.00 (*0-380-97459-2*, Avon Bks.) Morrow/Avon.

Robinson, Leah Ruth, photos by. First Cut. 1997. 368p. mass mkt. 24.00 o.p. (*0-380-97458-4*); 1998. reprint ed. mass mkt. 6.99 (*0-380-79124-2*) Morrow/Avon. (Avon Bks.).

Robson, Ruthann. A/K/A: A Novel. (Stonewall Inn Editions Ser.). 1998. pap. 13.95 (*0-312-19825-6*, Saint Martin's Griffin); 1997. 277p. 23.95 (*0-312-15469-0*) St. Martin's Pr.

Rodriguez, Abraham, Jr. The Boy Without a Flag: Tales of the South Bronx. (Illus.). 120p. 1992. pap. 12.95 o.p. (*0-915943-74-3*); 2nd ed. 1999. pap. 13.95 (*1-57131-028-2*) Milkweed Editions.

Rodriguez, Abraham. The Buddha Book. 2001. 304p. pap. 14.00 (*0-312-26299-X*) Picador.

Rodriguez, Abraham, Jr. Spidertown. 1998. (Vintage Espanol Ser.). (SPA.). 406p. pap. 14.00 o.s.i (*0-375-70178-8*, Vintage) Knopf Publishing Group.

—Spidertown. 1994. 336p. reprint ed. pap. 11.95 o.s.i (*0-14-023838-7*, Penguin Bks.) Penguin Group (USA) Inc.

—Spidertown: A Novel. 1993. 336p. 19.95 o.p. (*1-56282-845-2*) Hyperion Pr.

Roiphe, Anne. Secrets of the City. 2003. 320p. 24.00 (*1-4000-4945-8*, Shaye Areheart Bks.) Crown Publishing Group.

Roper, Martin. Gone: A Novel. 2002. 256p. 23.00 o.s.i (*0-8050-6775-2*) Holt, Henry & Co.

—Gone: A Novel. 2003. 240p. pap. 13.00 (*0-312-42125-7*) Picador.

Rose, Jackie. Slim Chance. 2003. 336p. pap. (*0-373-25031-2*, Red Dress Ink) Harlequin Enterprises, Ltd.

Rose, M. J. Lip Service. E-Book 18.00 (*1-930161-19-0*) Adobe Systems, Inc.

—Lip Service. 1998. 285p. pap. 12.95 o.p. (*0-9664332-0-3*) Pigeonhole Pr.

—Lip Service. 2000. E-Book 18.00 (*0-7434-1253-2*, Pocket); 1999. 320p. 18.00 o.s.i (*0-671-04131-2*, Atria); 2000. 320p. reprint ed. pap. 13.00 (*0-671-04132-0*, Atria) Simon & Schuster.

Rosenbaum, David. Sasha's Trick. 1995. 82p. 21.95 o.p. (*0-89296-591-6*) Mysterious Pr.

—Sasha's Trick. 1996. 384p. mass mkt. 5.99 o.s.i (*0-446-40441-1*) Warner Bks., Inc.

—Zaddik. 2002. 448p. pap. 14.95 (*1-931229-20-1*) Invisible Cities Pr.

—Zaddik. 1993. 448p. 19.95 (*0-89296-540-1*) Mysterious Pr.

—Zaddik. 1994. 464p. mass mkt. 5.99 o.s.i (*0-446-40322-9*) Warner Bks., Inc.

Rosenbaum, Thane. The Golems of Gotham. 2002. 384p. 25.95 (*0-06-018490-6*) HarperCollins Pubs.

—The Golems of Gotham. 2003. 384p. pap. 13.95 (*0-06-095945-2*, Perennial) HarperTrade.

Rosenberg, Philip. House of Lords. 2002. 480p. 24.95 (*0-06-019415-4*) HarperCollins Pubs.

—The House of Lords. 2003. 496p. mass mkt. 7.50 (*0-06-109861-2*) HarperCollins Pubs.

Rosenfelt, David. First Degree. 2003. 240p. 23.95 (*0-89296-754-4*) Mysterious Pr.

—First Degree. l.t. ed. 2003. 342p. 28.95 (*0-7862-5859-4*, Large Print Pr.) Thorndike Pr.

—First Degree. 2004. mass mkt. (*0-446-61386-X*) Warner Bks., Inc.

Ross, Fran. Oreo. 1974. 10.95 o.p. (*0-914870-00-9*) Greyfalcon Hse.

—Oreo. 2000. (Library of Black Literature). 212p. pap. 16.95 (*1-55553-464-3*) Northeastern Univ. Pr.

Ross, L. M. The Long Blue Moan. 2002. 300p. pap. 13.95 (*1-55583-621-6*) Alyson Pubns.

Ross, Leone. Orange Laughter. 2000. 225p. 23.00 o.p. (*0-374-22676-8*) Farrar, Straus & Giroux.

—Orange Laughter. 2001. 240p. pap. 13.00 (*0-312-42016-1*) Picador.

Rossner, Judith. Olivia: Or The Weight of the Past. 1995. mass mkt. 6.99 o.s.i (*0-8041-1246-0*, Ivy Bks.) Ballantine Bks.

—Olivia: Or The Weight of the Past. l.t. ed. 1995. (Large Print Bks.). 24.95 (*1-56895-166-3*, Wheeler Publishing, Inc.) Gale Group.

Roth, Henry. Call It Sleep. ltd. ed. 1995. (Illus.). 482p. 700.00 (*0-910457-30-1*) Arion Pr.

—Call It Sleep. 1995. reprint ed. lib. bdg. 29.95 (*1-56849-634-6*) Buccaneer Bks., Inc.

—Call It Sleep. reprint ed. 20.00 o.p. (*0-8154-0198-1*) Cooper Square Pubs., Inc.

—Call It Sleep. 1992. 30.00 o.s.i (*0-374-11819-1*); 448p. pap. 16.00 (*0-374-52292-8*) Farrar, Straus & Giroux.

—Call It Sleep. 1976. mass mkt. 4.95 o.p. (*0-380-01002-X*, Avon Bks.) Morrow/Avon.

—Call It Sleep. l.t. ed. 1995. 655p. 24.95 (*0-7838-1564-6*) Thorndike Pr.

—China Superpower Vol. 1: Requisites for High Growth. 1997. (Illus.). 248p. 55.00 (*0-312-16499-8*) Palgrave Macmillan.

—A Diving Rock on the Hudson. 1996. (Mercy of a Rude Stream Ser.: Vol. 2). 432p. pap. 14.00 o.s.i (*0-312-14085-1*) Picador.

—A Diving Rock on the Hudson: Mercy of a Rude Stream, Vol. II. 1995. (Mercy of a Rude Stream Ser.). 1p. 23.95 o.p. (*0-312-11777-9*) St. Martin's Pr.

—From Bondage. 1997. (Mercy of a Rude Stream Ser.: Vol. 3). 416p. pap. 15.00 (*0-312-15532-8*) Picador.

—From Bondage. 1996. (Mercy of a Rude Stream Ser.: Vol. 3). 432p. 25.95 o.p. (*0-312-14341-9*) St. Martin's Pr.

—Mercy of a Rude Stream. 1994. 304p. 250.00 (*0-312-10501-0*); 1993. 1p. 23.00 o.p. (*0-312-10499-5*) St. Martin's Pr.

—Mercy of a Rude Stream: A Star Shines over Mt. Morris Park. 1994. (Mercy of a Rude Stream Ser.: Vol. 1). pap. 13.00 o.s.i (*0-312-11929-1*) Picador.

—Requiem for Harlem. 1998. (Mercy of a Rude Stream Ser.: Vol. 4). 304p. pap. 14.00 (*0-312-20205-9*); 24.95 o.s.i (*0-312-16980-9*) Picador.

Roth, Philip. The Dying Animal. 2001. 176p. 22.00 (*0-618-15272-5*); 156p. tchr. ed. 23.00 (*0-618-13587-1*) Houghton Mifflin Co.

—The Dying Animal. 2002. 176p. pap. 12.00 (*0-375-71412-X*) Knopf, Alfred A. Inc.

Roughan, Howard. The Up & Comer. abr. ed. 2001. audio 24.98 (*1-58621-052-1*) Time Warner AudioBooks.

—The Up & Comer. 2001. 336p. 23.95 o.p. (*0-446-52666-5*) Warner Bks., Inc.

Rovin, Jeff. Vespers. 1999. 304p. mass mkt. 6.99 (*0-312-96993-7*, St. Martin's Paperbacks); 1999. E-Book 6.99 (*0-312-24619-6*); 1998. 320p. 23.95 o.p. (*0-312-19351-3*) St. Martin's Pr.

Rozan, S. J. A Bitter Feast. 1998. 320p. 23.95 o.p. (*0-312-19259-2*, Saint Martin's Minotaur); 1999. 336p. reprint ed. mass mkt. 5.99 (*0-312-97011-0*, St. Martin's Paperbacks) St. Martin's Pr.

—A Bitter Feast. l.t. ed. 1999. (Mystery Ser.). 519p. 27.95 (*0-7862-1773-1*) Thorndike Pr.

—A Bitter Feast: A Bill Smith-Lydia Chin Mystery. unabr. ed. 1999. audio 69.95 (*0-7927-2280-9*, CSL169, Chivers Sound Library) BBC Audiobooks America.
—China Trade. 1994. 263 p. 20.95 o.p. (*0-312-11254-8*, Saint Martin's Minotaur); 1995. (Lydia Chin, Bill Smith Mystery Ser.: Vol. 1). 275p. reprint ed. mass mkt. 6.50 (*0-312-95590-1*, St. Martin's Paperbacks) St. Martin's Pr.
—Concourse: A Bill Smith-Lydia Chin Mystery. unabr. ed. 1998. audio 69.95 (*0-7927-2245-0*, CSL134, Chivers Sound Library) BBC Audiobooks America.
—Concourse: A Bill Smith-Lydia Chin Mystery. 1995. 288p. 21.95 o.p. (*0-312-13453-3*, Saint Martin's Minotaur) St. Martin's Pr.
—Mandarin Plaid. (Lydia Chin, Bill Smith Mystery Ser.: Vol. 3). 288p. 1996. 22.95 o.p. (*0-312-14674-4*, Saint Martin's Minotaur); Vol. 1. 1997. mass mkt. 6.50 (*0-312-96283-5*, St. Martin's Paperbacks) St. Martin's Pr.
—No Colder Place. 1998. (No Colder Place Ser.: Vol. 1). 304p. pap. 6.99 (*0-312-96664-4*, St. Martin's Paperbacks); 1997. (Lydia Chin, Bill Smith Mystery Ser.). 288p. 23.95 (*0-312-16811-X*, Saint Martin's Minotaur) St. Martin's Pr.
—No Colder Place. l.t. ed. 1997. (Cloak & Dagger Ser.). 473p. lib. bdg. 28.95 (*0-7862-1251-9*) Thorndike Pr.
—Reflecting the Sky. 2001. 312p. 24.95 (*0-312-24427-4*, Saint Martin's Minotaur); 2002. 384p. reprint ed. mass mkt. 6.50 (*0-312-98134-1*, St. Martin's Paperbacks) St. Martin's Pr.
—Stone Quarry. 1999. 288p. 23.95 o.p. (*0-312-20912-6*, Saint Martin's Minotaur) St. Martin's Pr.
—Winter & Night. E-Book 18.95 (*0-312-70434-8*); 2003. 400p. mass mkt. 6.99 (*0-312-98668-8*, St. Martin's Paperbacks); 2002. 304p. 24.95 (*0-312-24555-6*, Saint Martin's Minotaur) St. Martin's Pr.
Rucka, Greg. Keeper. 1997. 368p. mass mkt. 6.99 (*0-553-57428-0*, Crimeline) Bantam Bks.
—Keeper: An Atticus Kodiac Novel, unabr. ed. 1998. audio 60.00 (*0-7887-1876-2*, 95298E7) Recorded Bks., LLC.
—Shooting at Midnight. 2000. 400p. mass mkt. 6.99 (*0-553-57827-8*) Bantam Bks.
—Smoker. 1999. 432p. mass mkt. 6.99 (*0-553-57829-4*) Bantam Bks.
Rucka, Gregory. Finder. 1999. audio 60.00 Recorded Bks., LLC.
—Finder: An Atticus Kodiac Novel. 1998. 352p. mass mkt. 6.99 (*0-553-57429-9*) Bantam Bks.
—Finder: An Atticus Kodiac Novel, unabr. ed. 1999. audio 62.00 (*0-7887-3994-8*, 96082E7) Recorded Bks., LLC.
Rudman, Anne Beane, et al. Given the Crime. 1998. 336p. pap. 6.50 (*0-671-00152-3*, Pocket); 320p. 22.00 (*0-671-00151-5*, Atria) Simon & Schuster.
Rudner, Rita. Tickled Pink. abr. ed. 2004. audio compact disk 14.99 (*1-59355-666-7*, 5285) Brilliance Audio.
—Tickled Pink. 2001. 320p. 25.00 (*0-7434-4261-X*); E-Book 25.00 (*0-7434-5135-X*) Simon & Schuster. (Atria).
—Tickled Pink: A Comic Novel. l.t. ed. 2002. 486p. 29.95 (*0-7862-4074-1*) Gale Group.
—Tickled Pink: A Comic Novel. 2002. 320p. reprint ed. pap. 14.00 (*0-7434-4262-8*, Washington Square Pr.) Simon & Schuster.
Rudnick, Paul. Social Disease. 1997. 208p. pap. 11.95 o.p. (*0-312-15659-6*, Saint Martin's Griffin) St. Martin's Pr.
Ruff, Matt. Sewer, Gas & Electric: The Public Works Trilogy. 1996. 384p. 23.00 o.p. (*0-87113-641-4*, Atlantic Monthly Pr.) Grove/Atlantic, Inc.
Ruffner, Sara S. A Liberal Education. 1991. 256p. (Orig.). pap. 10.95 o.p. (*0-931832-74-8*) Fithian Pr.
Rumaker, Michael. To Kill a Cardinal. 1992. 160p. text 11.95 (*0-9632962-2-1*) Arthur Mann Kaye.
Runyon, Damon. The Bloodhounds of Broadway & Other Stories. 1981. 320p. pap. 10.95 o.p. (*0-688-00625-6*, Quill) HarperTrade.
—Damon Runyon Omnibus. 1976. reprint ed. lib. bdg. 32.95 (*0-89190-441-7*, Rivercity Pr.) Amereon, Ltd.
—Damon Runyon Omnibus. 1993. reprint ed. lib. bdg. 28.95 (*1-56849-217-0*) Buccaneer Bks., Inc.
—Guys & Dolls. reprint ed. lib. bdg. 20.95 (*0-89190-438-7*, Rivercity Pr.) Amereon, Ltd.
—Guys & Dolls. 2015. 320p. pap. 10.95 (*0-14-118046-3*, Penguin Classics); 1993. 704p. 27.50 o.p. (*0-670-84868-9*, Viking) Viking Penguin.
—Guys & Dolls: The Stories of Damon Runyon. 1992. 480p. 14.95 (*0-14-017659-4*) Viking Penguin.
—Romance in the Roaring Forties & Other Stories. 1986. 324p. (Orig.). pap. 9.95 o.p. (*0-688-06148-6*, Quill) HarperTrade.
—Romance in the Roaring Forties & Other Stories. 1986. 324p. (Orig.). 19.95 o.p. (*0-688-05421-8*, Morrow, William & Co.) Morrow/Avon.
—Treasury of Damon Runyn. Kinnaird, Clark, ed. 1978. 6.95 o.p. (*0-394-60444-X*) Random Hse., Inc.
Rushdie, Salman. Fury: A Novel. 2002. 272p. pap. 12.95 (*0-679-78350-4*, Modern Library) Random House Adult Trade Publishing Group.
—Fury: A Novel. 2001. 272p. 24.95 (*0-679-46333-X*); E-Book 19.95 (*1-58836-058-X*) Random Hse., Inc.
—Fury: A Novel, 6 cass. 2002. audio 29.99 (*1-4025-0176-5*, 00614) Recorded Bks., LLC.
Russo, Richard. Mohawk. 1994. 432p. pap. 14.00 (*0-679-75382-6*, Vintage) Knopf Publishing Group.
Rutman, Leo. Thy Father's Son: A Novel. 2002. 352p. 24.95 (*0-312-29061-6*) St. Martin's Pr.
Ryan, Patricia. Twice the Spice. 1997. per. (*0-373-25731-7*, 1-25731-0, Harlequin Bks.) Harlequin Enterprises, Ltd.
Sala, Sharon. Snowball. l.t. ed. 2002. 403p. 29.95 (*0-7862-4039-3*) Gale Group.
Salamon, Julie. The Christmas Tree. 2002. 128p. pap. 9.95 (*0-375-76108-X*) Random House Adult Trade Publishing Group.
Salinger, J. D. The Catcher in the Rye. l.t. ed. 1993. pap. 19.95 o.p. (*0-7927-1516-0*) BBC Audiobooks America.
—The Catcher in the Rye. 1984. 224p. mass mkt. 3.95 o.s.i (*0-553-25025-6*) Bantam Bks.
—The Catcher in the Rye. 2002. 13.19 (*0-7587-7857-0*) Book Wholesalers, Inc.
—The Catcher in the Rye. 1991. 300p. reprint ed. lib. bdg. 23.95 o.p. (*0-89966-782-1*) Buccaneer Bks., Inc.
—The Catcher in the Rye. 2000. (RUS.). pap. 12.95 (*966-03-0586-9*) Folio, Editions UKR. *Dist:* Distribooks, Inc.
—The Catcher in the Rye. 2001. (Illus.). 288p. pap. 13.95 (*0-316-76917-7*, Back Bay); 1951. 277p. 25.95 (*0-316-76953-3*); 1991. 224p. reprint ed. mass mkt. 5.99 (*0-316-76948-7*) Little Brown & Co.
—The Catcher in the Rye. 1959. mass mkt. 0.50 o.p. (*0-451-01001-9*); mass mkt. 0.50 o.p. (*0-451-01667-X*) NAL. (Signet Bks.).
—The Catcher in the Rye, 2 vols., Set. l.t. ed. reprint ed. 10.00 (*0-89064-019-X*) National Assn. for Visually Handicapped.
—The Catcher in the Rye. 1991. 12.04 (*0-606-04887-1*) Turtleback Bks.
—The Catcher in the Rye. 2000. text 6.00 (*0-8220-7038-3*, Cliff Notes) Wiley, John & Sons, Inc.
—Franny & Zooey. 1981. mass mkt. 2.95 o.s.i (*0-553-20348-7*); 208p. mass mkt. 3.95 o.s.i (*0-553-26973-9*, Bantam Classics) Bantam Bks.
—Franny & Zooey. (FRE.). pap. 15.50 (*2-02-013327-X*) Editions du Seuil FRA. *Dist:* Distribooks, Inc.
—Franny & Zooey. 2001. (Illus.). 208p. pap. 13.95 (*0-316-76902-9*, Back Bay); 1961. 201p. 24.95 (*0-316-76954-1*); 1991. 208p. reprint ed. mass mkt. 5.99 (*0-316-76949-5*) Little Brown & Co.
—El Guardian Entre el Centeno.Tr. of Catcher in the Rye. (SPA.). 232p. 11.95 (*84-206-1689-3*); 2001. (Illus.). 236p. 11.95 (*84-206-3409-3*, AZ9200) Alianza Editorial, S. A. ESP. *Dist:* AIMS International Bks., Inc., Distribooks, Inc., AIMS International Bks., Inc., Lectorum Pubns., Inc.
—El Guardian Entre el Centeno. 1978. Tr. of Catcher in the Rye. 16.00 (*0-606-13453-0*) Turtleback Bks.
Salinger, Steven D. White Darkness. 2001. 368p. 24.00 o.s.i (*0-609-60728-6*, Crown) Crown Publishing Group.
—White Darkness. 2003. 368p. reprint ed. pap. 13.95 (*0-451-20784-X*) NAL.
Sampson, John. Up at Lighthouse Hill. 1999. (Illus.). 203p. 8.95 (*0-9613075-7-9*) Thornfield Pr.
Sanders, Lawrence. The Anderson Tapes. 22.95 (*0-89190-854-4*) Amereon, Ltd.
—The Anderson Tapes. unabr. ed. 1986. audio 41.65 Audio Bk. Co.
—The Anderson Tapes. 1987. 336p. mass mkt. 7.50 (*0-425-10364-1*) Berkley Publishing Group.
—The Anderson Tapes. 1994. reprint ed. lib. bdg. 32.95 o.p. (*1-56849-331-2*) Buccaneer Bks., Inc.
—The Anderson Tapes. l.t. ed. 2000. 319p. lib. bdg. 25.95 (*1-58547-023-6*) Ctr. Point Large Print.
—The Anderson Tapes. 1971. pap. 2.50 o.p. (*0-440-10217-0*) Dell Publishing.
—Lawrence Sanders - Three Complete Novels: The Anderson Tapes; The Tenth Commandment; The Fourth Deadly Sin. 1996. 752p. 12.98 o.p. (*0-399-14182-0*) Penguin Group (USA) Inc.
—The Seventh Commandment. 1992. 368p. mass mkt. 7.50 (*0-425-13329-X*) Berkley Publishing Group.
—The Seventh Commandment. l.t. ed. 1992. (General Ser.: Vol. 6). 303p. pap. 16.95 (*0-8161-5342-6*);Vol. 6. lib. bdg. 22.95 o.p. (*0-8161-5341-8*) Gale Group. (Macmillan Reference USA).
—The Seventh Commandment. 1991. 352p. 21.95 o.s.i (*0-399-13611-8*, G. P. Putnam's Sons) Penguin Group (USA) Inc.
—The Seventh Commandment. 1999. audio 9.98 (*0-671-04458-3*); 1991. audio 15.95 (*0-671-73382-6*) Simon & Schuster Audio. (Simon & Schuster Audioworks).
—Three Complete Novels: The Timothy Files, Timothy's Game, Sullivan's Sting. 1999. 784p. 12.98 o.s.i (*0-399-14531-1*) Penguin Group (USA) Inc.
—The Timothy Files. 1988. mass mkt. 7.50 (*0-425-10924-0*) Berkley Publishing Group.
—The Timothy Files. l.t. ed. 1988. (General Ser.). 508p. 19.95 o.p. (*0-8161-4479-6*, Macmillan Reference USA) Gale Group.
—The Timothy Files. 1987. 384p. 18.95 o.p. (*0-399-13261-9*, G. P. Putnam's Sons) Penguin Putnam Bks. for Young Readers.
—Timothy's Game. 1989. 352p. mass mkt. 7.50 (*0-425-11641-7*) Berkley Publishing Group.
—Timothy's Game. l.t. ed. 1989. (General Ser.). 468p. lib. bdg. 19.95 o.p. (*0-8161-4757-4*, Macmillan Reference USA) Gale Group.
—Timothy's Game. 1988. 384p. 18.95 o.p. (*0-399-13368-2*, G. P. Putnam's Sons) Penguin Putnam Bks. for Young Readers.
—Timothy's Game. abr. ed. 1988. audio 14.95 (*0-671-67015-8*, Simon & Schuster Audioworks) Simon & Schuster Audio.
—The 1st Deadly Sin. audio 95.20 Audio Bk. Co.
—The 1st Deadly Sin. 1987. 640p. mass mkt. 7.99 (*0-425-10427-3*); 1986. mass mkt. 4.50 o.s.i (*0-425-10061-8*); 1986. mass mkt. 4.50 o.s.i (*0-425-09310-7*); 1985. mass mkt. 4.50 o.s.i (*0-425-08169-9*); 1983. mass mkt. 3.95 o.s.i (*0-425-07154-5*); 1983. mass mkt. 4.95 o.s.i (*0-425-07039-5*); 1983. mass mkt. 3.95 o.s.i (*0-425-06299-6*); 1982. mass mkt. 3.75 o.s.i (*0-425-05604-X*); 1980. mass mkt. 2.95 o.s.i (*0-425-04692-3*); 1978. mass mkt. 2.50 o.s.i (*0-425-03904-8*); 1976. mass mkt. 2.25 o.s.i (*0-425-03424-0*); 1974. mass mkt. 1.95 o.s.i (*0-425-02506-3*) Berkley Publishing Group.
—The 1st Deadly Sin, Pt. 2. unabr. collector's ed. 1999. audio 64.00 (*0-7366-4365-6*, 4818-B) Books on Tape, Inc.
—The 1st Deadly Sin. 1994. reprint ed. lib. bdg. 35.95 o.p. (*1-56849-330-4*) Buccaneer Bks., Inc.
—The 1st Deadly Sin. 1989. audio 16.00 o.s.i (*0-394-29961-2*, RH Audio) Random Hse. Audio Publishing Group.
—The 2nd Deadly Sin. abr. ed. audio 59.50 Audio Bk. Co.
—The 2nd Deadly Sin. mass mkt. 4.50 o.s.i (*0-425-08170-2*); 1990. 448p. mass mkt. 7.99 (*0-425-12519-X*); 1987. mass mkt. 4.95 o.s.i (*0-425-10428-1*); 1985. mass mkt. 4.50 o.s.i (*0-425-08801-4*); 1983. mass mkt. 3.95 o.s.i (*0-425-07155-3*); 1983. mass mkt. 3.95 o.s.i (*0-425-06300-3*); 1983. mass mkt. 4.95 o.s.i (*0-425-06993-1*); 1982. mass mkt. 3.75 o.s.i (*0-425-05992-8*); 1982. mass mkt. 3.50 o.s.i (*0-425-05545-0*); 1981. mass mkt. 2.95 o.s.i (*0-425-04806-3*); 1978. mass mkt. 2.50 o.s.i (*0-425-03923-4*); 1978. mass mkt. 2.25 o.s.i (*0-425-03802-5*) Berkley Publishing Group.
—The 2nd Deadly Sin. unabr. collector's ed. 1999. audio 80.00 (*0-7366-4492-X*, 4930) Books on Tape, Inc.
—The 2nd Deadly Sin. 1977. 9.95 o.s.i (*0-399-12023-8*) Putnam Publishing Group, The.
—The 3rd Deadly Sin. 1985. mass mkt. 4.50 o.s.i (*0-425-09151-1*); 1985. mass mkt. 4.50 o.s.i (*0-425-08171-0*); 1984. mass mkt. 3.95 o.s.i (*0-425-07172-3*); 1982. mass mkt. 3.95 o.s.i (*0-425-05465-9*); 1982. mass mkt. 4.50 o.s.i (*0-425-05507-8*); 1987. 416p. mass mkt. 7.99 (*0-425-10429-X*) Berkley Publishing Group.
—The 3rd Deadly Sin. unabr. collector's ed. 1999. audio 88.00 (*0-7366-4513-6*, 4944) Books on Tape, Inc.
—The 3rd Deadly Sin. l.t. ed. 1982. 17.95 o.p. (*0-8161-3405-7*, Macmillan Reference USA) Gale Group.
—The 3rd Deadly Sin. 1981. 480p. 13.95 o.s.i (*0-399-12614-7*) Putnam Publishing Group, The.
—The 4th Deadly Sin. 1986. 352p. mass mkt. 7.99 (*0-425-09078-7*) Berkley Publishing Group.
—The 4th Deadly Sin. l.t. ed. 1986. (Special Editions Ser.). 512p. 18.95 o.p. (*0-8161-3989-X*); 10.95 o.p. (*0-8161-3990-3*) Gale Group. (Macmillan Reference USA).
—The 4th Deadly Sin. 1985. 384p. 17.95 o.p. (*0-399-13062-4*, G. P. Putnam's Sons) Penguin Putnam Bks. for Young Readers.
Sandom, J. G. The Hunting Club. 1993. 18.50 o.s.i (*0-385-46778-8*) Doubleday Publishing.
Santiago, Esmeralda. America's Dream. 336p. 2002. pap. 12.95 (*0-06-050884-1*, Rayo); 1997. pap. 14.00 (*0-06-092826-3*, Perennial) HarperTrade.
—America's Dream: El Sueno de America. 1996. 79p. 23.00 o.p. (*0-06-017279-7*) HarperCollins Pubs.
Santiago, Silviano. Stella Manhattan. Yudice, George, tr. 1994. 224p. pap. 19.95 (*0-8223-1498-3*); text 64.95 (*0-8223-1486-X*) Duke Univ. Pr.
Santiago, Soledad. Nightside. 1995. 304p. mass mkt. 5.50 o.s.i (*0-553-56250-9*) Bantam Bks.
—Streets of Fire. 1999. 342p. reprint ed. text 24.00 (*0-7881-6605-0*) DIANE Publishing Co.
—Streets of Fire. 1996. 352p. 23.95 o.s.i (*0-525-94078-2*) Dutton/Plume.
—Streets of Fire. 1997. 416p. mass mkt. 5.99 o.s.i (*0-451-18855-1*, Signet Bks.) NAL.
Santlofer, Jonathan. The Death Artist: A Novel of Suspense. 2003. 448p. mass mkt. 7.50 (*0-06-000442-8*, HarperTorch); 2002. 352p. 24.95 (*0-06-000441-X*, Morrow, William & Co.) Morrow/Avon.
Santmyer, Helen Hooven. Herbs & Apples. 1985. 352p. 16.95 o.p. (*0-06-015486-1*) HarperTrade.
—Herbs & Apples. 1987. mass mkt. 4.95 o.p. (*0-312-90601-3*, St. Martin's Paperbacks) St. Martin's Pr.
Sapphire. Push: A Novel. 1997. 192p. pap. 11.95 (*0-679-76675-8*, Vintage) Knopf Publishing Group.
Sargent, Patricia. Black Valentine. 1991. mass mkt. 4.50 o.p. (*1-55817-548-2*, Pinnacle Bks.) Kensington Publishing Corp.
—Black Valentine. l.t. ed. 1990. (Ulverscroft Large Print Ser.). 29.99 o.p. (*0-7089-2257-0*, Ulverscroft) Thorpe, F. A. Pubs. GBR. *Dist:* Ulverscroft Large Print Bks., Ltd., Ulverscroft Large Print Canada, Ltd.
Saroyan, Aram. Artists in Trouble: New Stories. 2001. 200p. 30.00 (*1-57423-172-3*); 35.00 (*1-57423-173-1*) Godine, David R. Pub. (Black Sparrow Pr.).
—Artists in Trouble: New Stories. 2001. 200p. pap. 16.50 (*1-57423-171-5*) HarperCollins Pubs.
Sarrantonio, Al. Orangefield. 2002. 180p. 35.00 (*1-58767-064-X*) Cemetery Dance Pubns.
Saul, John. The Manhattan Hunt Club. abr. ed. 2001. audio 25.95 (*0-553-52806-8*, RH Audio) Random Hse. Audio Publishing Group.
—The Manhattan Hunt Club. l.t. ed. 2002. 28.95 o.p. (*0-7862-3738-4*) Thorndike Pr.
—Midnight Voices. l.t. ed. 2002. (Basic Ser.). 685p. 30.95 (*0-7862-4629-4*) Thorndike Pr.
Savage, Marc. Paradise. 1994. 320p. mass mkt. 4.99 o.s.i (*0-553-56018-2*) Bantam Bks.
—Paradise. 1993. 17.00 o.s.i (*0-385-46770-2*); 368p. 17.00 o.s.i (*0-385-46779-6*) Doubleday Publishing.
Savage, Tom. Valentine. l.t. ed. 1999. 321p. 25.95 (*1-57490-243-1*) Beeler, Thomas T. Publisher.
—Valentine. 1996. 336p. 20.95 o.p. (*0-316-77164-3*) Little Brown & Co.
—Valentine. 1997. 448p. mass mkt. 6.99 o.s.i (*0-451-40719-9*, Onyx) NAL.
Sawikin, Harvey. The Education of Rick Green, Esquire. 1995. 320p. 23.00 (*0-684-80363-1*, Simon & Schuster) Simon & Schuster.
Scanlan, Dick. Does Freddy Dance. 1995. 207p. 19.95 o.p. (*1-55583-287-3*) Alyson Pubns.
Schaffner, Val. Algonquin Cat. 1980. (Illus.). 9.95 o.s.i (*0-440-00073-4*, Delacorte Pr.) Dell Publishing.
—Algonquin Cat. 1995. (Illus.). 144p. 7.99 o.s.i (*0-517-14711-4*) Random Hse. Value Publishing.
—The Algonquin Cat. 2001. (Illus.). 146p. reprint ed. pap. 12.00 (*0-8065-1030-7*, Citadel Pr.) Kensington Publishing Corp.
Schechter, Harold. The Hum Bug. 2001. 400p. 25.00 (*0-671-04115-0*, Atria); 2002. 512p. reprint ed. mass mkt. 6.99 o.s.i (*0-671-04116-9*, Pocket) Simon & Schuster.
Schindler, Steven. From the Block. 2001. 345p. pap. 12.95 (*0-9662408-7-1*) Elevated Pr., The.
Schine, Cathleen. Alice in Bed. 1984. mass mkt. 3.50 o.p. (*0-425-07189-8*) Berkley Publishing Group.
—Alice in Bed. 1996. 240p. pap. 12.95 o.s.i (*0-452-27675-6*, Plume) Dutton/Plume.
—Rameau's Niece. 1994. 288p. pap. 14.00 o.s.i (*0-452-27161-4*, Plume) Dutton/Plume.
—Rameau's Niece. 1993. 256p. tchr. ed. 19.95 o.p. (*0-395-65490-4*) Houghton Mifflin Co.
Schmais, Libby. The Perfect Elizabeth: A Tale of Two Sisters. E-Book 22.95 (*0-312-27589-7*); 2001. 240p. pap. 12.95 (*0-312-27080-1*, CPB1125, Saint Martin's Griffin); 2000. 228p. 22.95 o.p. (*0-312-25225-0*) St. Martin's Pr.
Schorr, Mark. Red Diamond: Private Eye. 1983. 256p. 12.95 o.p. (*0-312-66645-4*) St. Martin's Pr.
—Red Diamond, Private Eye. 1987. pap. 3.95 o.p. (*0-312-90657-9*, St. Martin's Paperbacks) St. Martin's Pr.
Schreiner, Samuel A., Jr. Van Alews: First Family of a Nation's First City. 1981. 448p. 13.95 o.p. (*0-87795-311-2*, Morrow, William & Co.) Morrow/Avon.
Schulman, Sarah. After Delores. 1989. 160p. pap. 10.95 o.p. (*0-452-26228-3*, Plume); 1988. 176p. 16.95 o.p. (*0-525-24641-X*, Dutton) Dutton/Plume.
—Empathy. 192p. 1993. pap. 10.00 o.p. (*0-452-27049-9*, Plume); 1992. 18.00 o.p. (*0-525-93521-5*, Dutton) Dutton/Plume.
—Rat Bohemia. 240p. 1996. pap. 10.95 o.p. (*0-452-27182-7*, Plume); 1995. 19.95 o.p. (*0-525-93790-0*, Dutton) Dutton/Plume.
Schwartz, Alvin. The Blowtop. 2nd ed. 2001. xiii, 211p. (gr. 4-7). reprint ed. pap. (*1-58754-007-X*, Olmstead Pr.) Moyer Bell.
Scoppettone, Sandra. Everything You Have Is Mine. 1992. (Lauren Laurano Mystery Ser.). 320p. mass mkt. 6.99 o.s.i (*0-345-37682-X*) Ballantine Bks.

Settings

For book reviews, descriptive annotations, tables of contents, cover images, author biographies & additional information, updated daily, subscribe to **www.booksinprint.com** 1005

—I'll Be Leaving You Always: A Lauren Laurano Mystery. 1994. 288p. mass mkt. 6.50 (0-345-38269-2) Ballantine Bks.
—I'll Be Leaving You Always: A Lauren Laurano Mystery. 1993. 251p. 19.95 o.p. (0-316-77647-5) Little Brown & Co.
—Let's Face the Music & Die: A Lauren Laurano Mystery. 1997. (Lauren Laurano Mystery Ser.). 320p. mass mkt. 6.50 (0-345-41225-7) Ballantine Bks.
—Let's Face the Music & Die: A Lauren Laurano Mystery. 1996. 249p. 21.95 o.p. (0-316-77664-5) Little Brown & Co.
—My Sweet Untraceable You. 1995. 320p. mass mkt. 6.50 o.s.i (0-345-39162-4) Ballantine Bks.
—My Sweet Untraceable You. 1994. 275p. 19.95 o.p. (0-316-77648-3) Little Brown & Co.
Scott, Darieck. Traitor to the Race. 1995. 224p. 20.95 o.p. (0-525-93912-1) Dutton/Plume.
Selby, Hubert, Jr. Requiem for a Dream. 2000. viii, 279p. pap. 14.95 (1-56025-248-0); 1988. 280p. (C). reprint ed. pap. 12.95 (0-938410-56-3); 1988. 304p. (C). reprint ed. lib. bdg. 20.00 o.p. (0-938410-57-1) Avalon Publishing Group. (Thunder's Mouth Pr.).
Senate, Melissa. See Jane Date. 2003. 352p. mass mkt. (0-373-25027-4); 2001. 283p. pap. (0-373-25011-8, 1-25011-7) Harlequin Enterprises, Ltd. (Red Dress Ink).
—The Solomon Sisters Wise Up. 2003. 320p. pap. (0-373-25041-X, Red Dress Ink) Harlequin Enterprises, Ltd.
Sepia, Riva. The Queens of New York City. 2000. 124p. pap. 9.95 (0-595-00154-8, Writers Club Pr.) iUniverse, Inc.
Sethi, Robbie Clipper. Fifty-Fifty: A Novel in Many Voices. 2003. (Illus.). 217p. 24.95 (0-929306-24-4) Silicon Pr.
Shaffer, Louise. All My Suspects: A Daytime Crime Mystery. 1995. 224p. mass mkt. 4.99 o.s.i (0-425-14770-3, Prime Crime) Berkley Publishing Group.
—All My Suspects: A Daytime Crime Mystery. 1994. 224p. 19.95 o.p. (0-399-13965-6, G. P. Putnam's Sons) Penguin Group (USA) Inc.
—Talked to Death. 1996. mass mkt. 5.99 o.s.i (0-425-15407-6) Berkley Publishing Group.
—Talked to Death. 1995. 256p. 22.95 o.p. (0-399-14095-6, G. P. Putnam's Sons) Penguin Group (USA) Inc.
Shange, Ntozake. Liliane: Resurrection of the Daughter. 1995. 304p. pap. 12.00 (0-312-13559-9) Picador.
—Liliane: Resurrection of the Daughter. 1994. 224p. 18.95 o.p. (0-312-11310-2) St. Martin's Pr.
Shapiro, Anna. Life & Love, Such As They Are. 1994. 240p. 21.00 (0-671-87114-5, Simon & Schuster) Simon & Schuster.
Sharp, Adrienne. White Swan, Black Swan. 2002. 256p. pap. 13.95 (0-345-43868-X) Ballantine Bks.
Sheckley, Robert. Draconian New York. 224p. 1997. pap. 12.95 (0-312-86359-4); 1996. 20.95 o.p. (0-312-85130-8) Doherty, Tom Assocs., LLC. (Forge Bks.).
Sheed, Wilfrid. Max Jamison. 2001. 280p. pap. 18.95 (1-58579-039-7) Akadine Pr., The.
—Max Jamison. 1970. 260p. 6.50 o.p. (0-374-20476-4) Farrar, Straus & Giroux.
—Max Jamison. 1986. 260p. pap. 5.95 o.p. (0-87795-836-X, Morrow, William & Co.) Morrow/Avon.
Sheldon, Dyan. Dreams of an Average Man. 1986. 320p. 1.99 o.p. (0-517-56139-5) Random Hse. Value Publishing.
Sheldon, Mary. Reflection. 2004. 30p. mass mkt. 6.99 (0-7582-0311-X, Kensington Bks.); 2003. 320p. 23.00 (0-7582-0308-X) Kensington Publishing Corp.
Sheldon, Sidney. Rage of Angels. 1980. 504p. 18.95 (0-688-03687-2, Morrow, William & Co.) Morrow/Avon.
Shimada, Masahiko. Dream Messenger. Luke, Elmer, ed. Gabriel, Philip, tr. from JPN. 1992. 304p. 22.00 (4-7700-1535-6) Kodansha America, Inc.
—Dream Messenger. 1994. pap. (0-446-60062-8); 293p. pap. 10.99 o.s.i (0-446-67010-3) Warner Bks., Inc.
Shteyngart, Gary. The Russian Debutante's Handbook. 2003. 496p. pap. 14.00 (1-57322-988-1, Riverhead Trade (Paperbacks)) Berkley Publishing Group.
—The Russian Debutante's Handbook. 2002. 464p. 24.95 o.s.i (1-57322-213-5, Riverhead Bks. (Hardcovers)) Putnam Publishing Group, The.
Shulman, Irving. West Side Story: A Novelization. novel ed. 17.95 (0-8488-0847-9) Amereon, Ltd.
—West Side Story: A Novelization. novel ed. 1967. (Kangaroo Bks.). 12.04 (0-606-01566-3) Turtleback Bks.
Siebert, Steven. Cleopatras Needle. 2000. 426p. mass mkt. 6.99 (0-8125-7071-5, Tor Bks.) Doherty, Tom Assocs., LLC.
—Cleopatra's Needle. 2nd ed. 1999. 352p. 23.95 (0-312-86748-4, Forge Bks.) Doherty, Tom Assocs., LLC.
Siegel, James. Derailed: A Novel. 2003. 304p. 23.95 (0-89296-761-7) Mysterious Pr.
—Epitaph. l.t. ed. 2003. (Large Print Ser.). 29.95 (1-57490-484-1, Beeler Large Print Bks.) Beeler, Thomas T. Publisher.
—Epitaph. 2001. 320p. 23.95 (0-89296-712-9) Mysterious Pr.
—Epitaph. 2003. 320p. pap. 12.95 (0-446-67870-8, Mysterious Pr. Paperback Bks.) Warner Bks., Inc.
Sigerson, Davitt. Faithful: A Novel. 2004. 224p. 23.95 (0-385-51050-0, Talese, Nan A.) Doubleday Publishing.
Silber, Diana. Confessions. 1991. 464p. mass mkt. 4.95 o.s.i (0-553-28681-1) Bantam Bks.
Silber, Joan. In My Other Life: Stories. 2000. 223p. 21.95 (1-889330-42-6); pap. 13.95 (1-889330-43-4) Sarabande Bks., Inc.
—In the City. 1987. 256p. 16.95 o.p. (0-670-81479-2) Viking Penguin.
—Lucky Us. 2001. 288p. tchr. ed. 22.95 (1-56512-320-4, Shannon Ravenel Bks.) Algonquin Bks. of Chapel Hill.
Silvis, Randall. Mary Rogers. Date not set. (0-312-28617-1) St. Martin's Pr.
—On Night's Shore. E-Book 24.95 (1-58945-579-7) Adobe Systems, Inc.
—On Night's Shore. 2001. 352p. 24.95 o.s.i (0-312-26201-9, Saint Martin's Minotaur); 2002. 384p. reprint ed. mass mkt. 6.99 (0-312-98210-0, St. Martin's Paperbacks) St. Martin's Pr.
Simenon, Georges. Three Bedrooms in Manhattan. Romano, Marc, tr. from FRE. 2003. (New York Review Books Classics Ser.). pap. 12.95 (1-59017-044-X) New York Review of Bks., Inc., The.
Simmons, Dan. Hardcase. 2001. 256p. 23.95 (0-312-27497-1, Saint Martin's Minotaur) St. Martin's Pr.
Simmons, William. Rolling Thunder. 1999. 275p. 28.00 (1-57962-019-1) Permanent Pr., The.
Simone, Carol. The Goddess of 5th Avenue: A Novel. 2001. 232p. 22.00 (1-930880-00-6) HAYDEN Publishing.
Singer, Isaac Bashevis. Meshugah. Singer, Isaac Bashevis & Wachtel, Nili, trs. 1995. 240p. pap. 12.95 o.s.i (0-452-27384-6, Plume) Dutton/Plume.
—Meshugah. 2003. pap. 20.00 (0-374-52909-4) Farrar, Straus & Giroux.
—Meshugah. Singer, Isaac Bashevis & Wachtel, Nili, trs. 1994. (ENG & YID.). 240p. 22.00 o.p. (0-374-20847-6) Farrar, Straus & Giroux.
—Meshugah. 1999. 240p. pap. (0-14-018877-0) Penguin Group (USA) Inc.
—Shadows on the Hudson. Sherman, Joseph, tr. from YID. 1999. 560p. pap. 16.00 (0-452-28003-6, Plume) Dutton/Plume.
—Shadows on the Hudson. Sherman, Joseph, tr. from YID. 1998. 548p. 28.00 (0-374-26186-5) Farrar, Straus & Giroux.
Singer, Katie. The Wholeness of a Broken Heart. 1999. 336p. 24.95 o.p. (1-57322-147-3, Riverhead Bks. (Hardcovers)) Putnam Publishing Group, The.
Sister Souljah. The Coldest Winter Ever: A Novel. (Ann Rule's Crime Files Ser.). 1999. 352p. 23.00 o.s.i (0-671-02578-3, Atria); 2000. 432p. reprint ed. mass mkt. 7.99 (0-671-02536-8, Pocket) Simon & Schuster.
Skloot, Floyd. Open Door. 2004. 230p. pap. text 14.95 (1-885266-48-0) Story Line Pr.
Slate, Caroline. A Fractured Truth: A Novel. 2003. 352p. 25.00 (0-7434-1890-5, Atria) Simon & Schuster.
Slesar, Henry. Murder at Heartbreak Hospital. 247p. reprint ed. 2000. pap. 14.00 (0-89733-486-8); 1998. 21.00 (0-89733-463-9) Academy Chicago Pubs., Ltd.
Slesinger, Tess. The Unpossessed: A Novel of the Thirties. 2002. (New York Review Books Classics Ser.). (Illus.). 328p. reprint ed. pap. 14.95 (1-59017-014-8) New York Review of Bks., Inc., The.
Sloan, Bob. Bliss. 1996. 192p. 21.00 (0-684-82250-4, Scribner) Simon & Schuster.
—Bliss Jumps the Gun: A Lenny Bliss Mystery. (Lenny Bliss Mysteries Ser.). 2000. 288p. pap. 7.95 (0-393-32114-2, Norton Paperbacks); 1999. 224p. text 22.95 o.p. (0-393-04750-4) Norton, W. W. & Co., Inc.
—The Middle of Nowhere: A Lenny Bliss Mystery. 2003. 224p. 23.00 (0-87113-872-7, Atlantic Monthly Pr.) Grove/Atlantic, Inc.
Slouka, Mark. Lost Lake: Stories. 2002. 192p. reprint ed. pap. 13.00 (0-375-70208-3, Vintage) Knopf Publishing Group.
—Lost Lake: Stories. 1998. 192p. 21.00 o.s.i (0-375-40215-2) Random Hse., Inc.
Slyke, L. V. Murder on the Rocks. 1995. 256p. (Orig.). mass mkt. 4.99 (0-380-76798-8, Avon Bks.) Morrow/Avon.
—Murder with a Twist. 1994. 256p. (Orig.). mass mkt. 4.99 (0-380-76797-X, Avon Bks.) Morrow/Avon.
Smiley, Jane. Duplicate Keys. 1993. 320p. pap. 13.95 (0-449-90879-8, Fawcett) Ballantine Bks.
—Duplicate Keys. unabr. ed. 2000. audio compact disk 90.00 (0-7887-3961-1, C1116E7); 1998. audio 70.00 (0-7887-2177-1, 95473E7) Recorded Bks., LLC.
—Duplicate Keys. 1985. mass mkt. 3.95 o.s.i (0-671-55172-8, Pocket) Simon & Schuster.
Smith, Andrea. Friday Night at Honeybee's. 2004. 400p. pap. 12.00 (0-385-33698-5, Delta) Dell Publishing.
—Friday Nights at Honeybee's. 2003. 320p. 22.95 (0-385-33428-1, Dial Bks.) Dell Publishing.
Smith, Betty. Maggie-Now. l.t. ed. 1982. 18.95 o.p. (0-8161-3303-4, Macmillan Reference USA) Gale Group.
—Maggie-Now. 1966. pap. 2.25 o.p. (0-06-080098-4, P98, Perennial) HarperTrade.
—A Tree Grows in Brooklyn. Date not set. 424p. 28.95 (0-8488-2392-3) Amereon, Ltd.
—A Tree Grows in Brooklyn. 1981. 321p. reprint ed. lib. bdg. 21.95 (0-89966-303-6) Buccaneer Bks., Inc.
—A Tree Grows in Brooklyn. l.t. ed. 1982. lib. bdg. 21.95 o.p. (0-8161-3301-8, Macmillan Reference USA) Gale Group.
—A Tree Grows in Brooklyn. 2001. 512p. 23.95 (0-06-000194-1); 1998. (0-06-099528-9); 1947. (Illus.). o.p. (0-06-013935-8) HarperCollins Pubs.
—A Tree Grows in Brooklyn. (Perennial Classics Ser.). 1998. 496p. pap. 13.00 (0-06-092988-X, Perennial); 1993. 432p. mass mkt. 5.95 o.p. (0-06-080126-3, P126, Perennial); 2001. audio 39.95 (0-694-52582-0, HarperAudio) HarperTrade.
—A Tree Grows in Brooklyn. l.t. ed. 1993. 615p. lib. bdg. 22.95 (0-8161-5813-4) Thorndike Pr.
—A Tree Grows in Brooklyn. 1968. 18.05 (0-606-05072-8) Turtleback Bks.
Smith, Evelyn E. Miss Melville Regrets. 1987. mass mkt. 5.99 o.s.i (0-449-21259-9, Fawcett) Ballantine Bks.
—Miss Melville Regrets. 1986. 288p. 17.95 o.p. (0-917657-45-4) Fine, Donald I. Bks.
—Miss Melville Regrets. l.t. ed. 1989. (Ulverscroft Large Print Ser.). 29.99 o.p. (0-7089-2110-8, Ulverscroft) Thorpe, F. A. Pubs. GBR. *Dist:* Ulverscroft Large Print Bks., Ltd., Ulverscroft Large Print Canada, Ltd.
—Miss Melville Returns. 1988. mass mkt. 4.99 o.s.i (0-449-21499-0, Fawcett) Ballantine Bks.
—Miss Melville Returns. 1987. 272p. 17.95 o.s.i (1-55611-015-4) Fine, Donald I. Bks.
—Miss Melville Rides a Tiger. 1992. mass mkt. 4.99 o.s.i (0-449-22105-9, Fawcett) Ballantine Bks.
—Miss Melville Rides a Tiger. 1991. 18.95 o.p. (1-55611-219-X) Fine, Donald I. Bks.
—Miss Melville Rides a Tiger. l.t. ed. 1993. (General Ser.). 334p. 20.95 o.p. (0-8161-5559-3); pap. o.p. (0-8161-5560-7) Gale Group. (Macmillan Reference USA).
—Miss Melville's Revenge. 1990. 224p. mass mkt. 5.99 o.s.i (0-449-21794-9, Fawcett) Ballantine Bks.
—Miss Melville's Revenge. 1989. 288p. 17.95 o.p. (1-55611-076-6) Fine, Donald I. Bks.
Smith, J. C. Nightcap: A Quentin Jacoby Mystery. 1984. 192p. 13.95 o.s.i (0-689-11411-7, Scribner) Simon & Schuster.
Smith, Joan. Full Stop. (Loretta Lawson Mystery Ser.). 1997. 262p. mass mkt. 5.99 o.s.i (0-449-22300-0); 1996. 288p. 21.00 o.s.i (0-449-91048-2) Ballantine Bks. (Fawcett).
Smith, Justin. Forsyth Street: Eye of a Fly. 2000. 204p. pap. 21.99 (0-7388-2458-5) Xlibris Corp.
Smith, Martin Cruz. Canto for a Gypsy. 1982. 176p. mass mkt. 2.50 o.s.i (0-345-30615-5) Ballantine Bks.
—Gypsy in Amber. 1982. 192p. mass mkt. 2.50 o.s.i (0-345-30614-7) Ballantine Bks.
Smith, Mitchell. Daydreams. 1987. 464p. 17.95 o.p. (0-07-059082-6) McGraw-Hill Cos., The.
—Daydreams. 1988. 448p. mass mkt. 5.99 o.s.i (0-451-40089-5, Onyx) NAL.
—Karma. 1994. 352p. 22.95 o.p. (0-525-93773-0) Dutton/Plume.
Smith, Peter Moore. Raveling: A Novel. abr. ed. 2000. audio 24.98 (1-57042-910-3) Time Warner AudioBooks.
—Raveling: A Novel of Suspense. 2000. 400p. 23.95 o.p. (0-316-44217-8) Little Brown & Co.
Snyder, Keith. The Night Men: A Jason Keltner Mystery. 2001. 312p. 23.95 (0-8027-3370-0) Walker & Co.
Sohn, Amy. Run Catch Kiss: A Gratifying Novel. 256p. 2000. pap. 12.00 (0-684-86753-2); 1999. 23.00 (0-684-85302-7) Simon & Schuster. (Simon & Schuster).
—Sex & the City: Kiss & Tell. 160p. 2005. 50.00 (0-7434-6370-6); 2002. (Illus.). 40.00 (0-7434-5681-5) Simon & Schuster. (Pocket).
Solomita, Stephen. Bad to the Bone. 1992. 352p. mass mkt. 4.99 (0-380-71760-3, Avon Bks.) Morrow/Avon.
—Bad to the Bone. 1991. 256p. 21.95 o.p. (0-399-13593-6, G. P. Putnam's Sons) Penguin Group (USA) Inc.
—Damaged Goods: A Stanley Moodrow Novel. 1996. 384p. 22.00 o.p. (0-684-81584-2, Scribner) Simon & Schuster.
—Force of Nature. 1990. 352p. pap. 4.95 (0-380-70949-X, Avon Bks.) Morrow/Avon.
—Force of Nature. 1989. 288p. 19.95 o.s.i (0-399-13491-3, G. P. Putnam's Sons) Penguin Putnam Bks. for Young Readers.
—Forced Entry. 1991. 384p. pap. 4.99 (0-380-71361-6, Avon Bks.) Morrow/Avon.
—Forced Entry. 1990. 320p. 19.95 o.p. (0-399-13559-6, G. P. Putnam's Sons) Penguin Putnam Bks. for Young Readers.
—A Good Day to Die. l.t. ed. 1994. 420p. pap. 18.95 (0-8161-5976-9, Macmillan Reference USA) Gale Group.
—A Good Day to Die. 1993. 300p. 21.00 o.p. (1-883402-03-4, Scribner) Simon & Schuster.
—A Piece of the Action. 1994. 352p. mass mkt. 4.99 (0-380-72103-1, Avon Bks.) Morrow/Avon.
—A Piece of the Action. 1992. 256p. 22.95 o.p. (0-399-13730-0, G. P. Putnam's Sons) Penguin Group (USA) Inc.
—A Twist of the Knife. 1990. 336p. pap. 4.95 (0-380-70997-X, Avon Bks.) Morrow/Avon.
—A Twist of the Knife. 1988. 288p. 17.95 o.p. (0-399-13401-8, G. P. Putnam's Sons) Penguin Putnam Bks. for Young Readers.
Solomon, Barbara Probst. The Beat of Life, Vol. 1. 1999. pap. 16.00 (1-928863-00-0) Great Marsh Pr.
Solomon, Nina. Single Wife: A Novel. 2003. 336p. tchr. ed. 23.95 (1-56512-382-4, 72382) Algonquin Bks. of Chapel Hill.
Sommer, Scott. Still Lives. 1989. 304p. 18.95 o.p. (0-670-82581-6) Viking Penguin.
Soos, Troy. The Gilded Cage. 2003. 384p. mass mkt. 6.99 (1-57566-770-3); 2002. 288p. 23.00 (1-57566-769-X) Kensington Publishing Corp.
—Murder at Ebbets Field. 1996. mass mkt. 4.99 o.s.i (1-57566-027-X); 1995. 240p. mass mkt. 16.95 o.s.i (0-8217-4889-0) Kensington Publishing Corp.
Sorrentino, Christopher. Sound on Sound. 1995. 200p. 19.95 (1-56478-073-2) Dalkey Archive Pr.
Sorrentino, Gilbert. Imaginative Qualities of Actual Things. 1991. 243p. reprint ed. pap. 12.95 (0-916583-86-4) Dalkey Archive Pr.
—Imaginative Qualities of Actual Things. 1972. 30.00 (0-394-47108-3) SPD-Small Pr. Distribution.
—Little Casino. 2002. 220p. pap. 14.95 (1-56689-126-4) Coffee Hse. Pr.
Soto, Pedro Juan. Spiks. Ortiz, Victoria, tr. from SPA. & intro. by. 1974. 96p. 22.00 o.p. (0-85345-299-7, CL-2997); pap. 10.00 (0-85345-331-4, PB3314) Monthly Review Pr.
Spanbauer, Tom. In the City of Shy Hunters: A Novel. 2001. viii, 504p. 26.00 o.p. (0-8021-1691-4); 2002. 512p. reprint ed. pap. 14.00 (0-8021-3898-5) Grove/Atlantic, Inc. (Grove Pr.).
Spencer-Fleming, Julia. A Fountain Filled with Blood. E-Book 23.95 (0-312-71002-X); 2004. mass mkt. 6.99 (0-312-99543-1, St. Martin's Paperbacks); 2003. 304p. 23.95 (0-312-30410-2, Saint Martin's Minotaur) St. Martin's Pr.
—Out of the Deep I Cry. 2004. 304p. 23.95 (0-312-31262-8) St. Martin's Pr.
Spencer, Nelsie. The Playgroup: A Novel. 2003. 352p. 24.95 (0-312-31172-9) St. Martin's Pr.
Spencer, Scott. The Rich Man's Table. 1999. 272p. reprint ed. pap. 12.95 o.s.i (0-425-16945-6) Berkley Publishing Group.
Spiegelman, Ian. Everyone's Burning: A Novel. 2003. 176p. 18.95 (1-4000-6056-7, Villard Bks.) Random House Adult Trade Publishing Group.
Spiegelman, Katia. Peculiar Politics: A Romantic Comedy. 1993. 240p. 21.95 o.p. (0-7145-2952-4) Boyars, Marion Pubs., Inc.
Spiegelman, Peter. Black Maps. 2003. 304p. 22.95 (1-4000-4075-2) Knopf Publishing Group.
Spillane, Mickey. Survival— Zero! l.t. ed. 1999. (Mike Hammer Ser.). 264p. (0-7540-3955-2, Macmillan Reference USA) Gale Group.
—Survival-Zero. 1971. (Mike Hammer Ser.). 160p. mass mkt. 4.50 o.p. (0-451-13704-3, Signet Bks.) NAL.
—Survival Zero! l.t. ed. 1999. (Mike Hammer Ser.). 264p. pap. 24.95 (0-7838-8735-3) Wiley, John & Sons, Inc.
Spirit of the Flying Lady: The Novel. 2000. E-Book 21.95 (0-9713623-5-1) EBOOKSITES.ORG.
Sprague, Gretchen. Death in Good Company. 1999. (WWL Mystery Ser.: No. 303). mass mkt. (0-373-26303-1, 1-26303-7, Worldwide Library) Harlequin Enterprises, Ltd.
—Maquette for Murder. 2001. (WWL Mystery Ser.: No. 378). 251p. mass mkt. (0-373-26378-3, Worldwide Library) Harlequin Enterprises, Ltd.
—Maquette for Murder. E-Book 5.99 (0-312-27355-X); 2000. 240p. 22.95 (0-312-19920-1, Saint Martin's Minotaur) St. Martin's Pr.
—Murder in a Heat Wave. 2004. (WWL Mystery Ser.: No. 489). 256p. mass mkt. (0-373-26489-5, Worldwide Library) Harlequin Enterprises, Ltd.

—Murder in a Heat Wave. 2003. (Martha Patterson Mysteries Ser.). 224p. 22.95 (*0-312-27662-1*, Saint Martin's Minotaur) St. Martin's Pr.

Star, Nancy. Up Next. (May Morrison Mysteries Ser.). 1999. 368p. mass mkt. 6.50 (*0-671-00894-3*, Pocket Star); 1998. 352p. 23.00 (*0-671-00893-5*, Atria) Simon & Schuster.

Starr, Jason. Tough Luck. 2003. 256p. pap. 12.00 (*0-375-72711-6*) Knopf, Alfred A. Inc.

Steel, Danielle. Irresistible Forces. 2000. 384p. mass mkt. 7.99 (*0-440-22486-1*); 2000. 18.87 (*0-385-33461-3*, Delacorte Pr.); 1999. 384p. 26.95 (*0-385-31960-6*, Delacorte Pr.); 1999. 384p. 200.00 (*0-385-33476-1*, Delacorte Pr.) Dell Publishing.

—Irresistible Forces, Set. abr. ed. 1999. audio 26.95 Highsmith Inc.

—Irresistible Forces. abr. ed. 1999. audio 26.95 (*0-553-47935-0*); audio compact disk 29.95 (*0-553-45574-5*); audio 39.95 (*0-553-50215-8*) Random Hse. Audio Publishing Group. (RH Audio).

—Irresistible Forces. l.t. ed. 528p. 2000. pap. 13.95 (*0-375-70787-5*); 1999. 26.95 (*0-375-40863-0*) Random Hse. Large Print.

—Lightning. 1996. 464p. pap. 7.99 (*0-440-22150-1*); 1995. 408p. 24.95 (*0-385-31192-3*, Delacorte Pr.); 1995. 408p. 200.00 (*0-385-31488-4*, Delacorte Pr.) Dell Publishing.

—Lightning. 1996. mass mkt. 8.99 o.s.i (*0-440-22292-3*) Doubleday Publishing.

—Lightning. 1995. audio 24.98 o.s.i (*0-553-74681-2*); audio 24.95 (*0-553-47364-6*, 692955) Random Hse. Audio Publishing Group. (RH Audio).

—The Long Road Home. 1999. 448p. mass mkt. 7.99 (*0-440-22483-7*); 1998. 397p. 25.95 (*0-385-33285-8*, Delacorte Pr.); 1998. 408p. 25.95 (*0-385-31956-8*, Delacorte Pr.); 1998. 408p. 200.00 (*0-385-32410-3*, Delacorte Pr.); 1998. 397p. 29.95 (*0-385-31992-4*, Delacorte Pr.) Dell Publishing.

—Vanished. 1994. 400p. mass mkt. 7.50 (*0-440-21746-6*); 1993. 312p. 23.95 (*0-385-30603-2*, Delacorte Pr.) Dell Publishing.

—Vanished. ltd. ed. 1993. 312p. 200.00 o.s.i (*0-385-31046-3*) Doubleday Publishing.

—Vanished. 1993. audio 13.59 o.s.i (*0-553-70073-1*); audio 18.00 o.s.i (*0-553-47180-5*, 391848) Random Hse. Audio Publishing Group. (RH Audio).

—Vanished. 1993. 13.04 (*0-606-07130-X*) Turtleback Bks.

Steiker, Valerie. The Leopard Hat: A Daughter's Story. 2003. 336p. pap. 13.00 (*0-375-72620-9*, Vintage) Knopf Publishing Group.

Stein, Eugene. Straitjacket & Tie. 1996. 278p. reprint ed. pap. text 9.95 o.p. (*1-55583-358-6*) Alyson Pubns.

—Straitjacket & Tie. 1994. 277p. 19.95 o.p. (*0-395-67031-4*) World Pubns., Inc.

Stein, Scott. Lost. 2000. 207p. 22.95 (*0-9701554-0-9*, 1) Free Reign Pr.

Stein, Triss. Digging up Death: A Kay Engles Mystery. 1999. (WWL Mystery Ser.: Bk. 310). per. (*0-373-26310-4*, 1-26310-2, Harlequin Bks.) Harlequin Enterprises, Ltd.

—Digging up Death: A Kay Engles Mystery. 1998. (Kay Engles Mystery Ser.). 204p. 22.95 (*0-8027-3319-0*) Walker & Co.

Steinke, Rene. Holy Skirts. 2003. 23.95 (*0-688-17694-1*, Morrow, William & Co.) Morrow/Avon.

Stephen, Solomita. Force of Nature. 1991. 4.99 o.p. (*0-517-07422-2*) Random Hse. Value Publishing.

Stephens, Michael. The Brooklyn Book of the Dead. 1994. 228p. 19.95 o.p. (*1-56478-037-6*) Dalkey Archive Pr.

Stern, Daniel. After the War. 1994. (First Rediscovered Modern Masterpieces Edition Ser.). 243p. (C). pap. 11.95 (*0-89263-332-8*); 22.50 (*0-89263-331-X*) Texas A&M Univ. Pr.

—Who Shall Live, Who Shall Die. 1994. 328p. pap. 11.95 (*0-89263-330-1*) Rice Univ. Pr.

—Who Shall Live, Who Shall Die. 1994. (First Rediscovered Modern Masterpieces Edition Ser.). 319p. 22.50 (*0-89263-329-8*) Texas A&M Univ. Pr.

Stewart, Edward. Deadly Rich. 1992. 640p. mass mkt. 5.99 o.s.i (*0-440-21288-X*) Dell Publishing.

—Jury Double. 1996. 512p. mass mkt. 6.50 o.s.i (*0-440-22278-8*) Dell Publishing.

—Mortal Grace. 1995. 560p. mass mkt. 6.50 o.s.i (*0-440-21697-4*) Dell Publishing.

—Privileged Lives. 1989. 528p. mass mkt. 6.99 o.s.i (*0-440-20230-2*) Dell Publishing.

Stewart, Fred Mustard. The Young Savages. 1999. 320p. mass mkt. 6.99 (*0-8125-7194-0*, Tor Bks.); 1998. 304p. 23.95 (*0-312-86412-4*, Forge Bks.); 1997. 500p. mass mkt. 6.99 o.p. (*0-8125-6794-3*, Forge Bks.) Doherty, Tom Assocs., LLC.

Stewart, Michael. Compulsion. 1994. 384p. 23.00 o.p. (*0-06-017767-5*) HarperTrade.

Stillman, Whit. The Last Days of Disco: With Cocktails at Petrossian Afterwards. 2000. 339p. 24.00 o.p. (*0-374-18339-2*) Farrar, Straus & Giroux.

Stout, Rex. And Be a Villain. 1994. 256p. mass mkt. 5.99 (*0-553-23931-7*) Bantam Bks.

—And Four to Go. 1992. 240p. mass mkt. 5.99 (*0-553-24985-1*) Bantam Bks.

—And Four to Go. unabr. collector's ed. 1997. (Nero Wolfe Ser.). audio 42.00 (*0-7366-4059-2*, 4570) Books on Tape, Inc.

—And Four to Go. 1958. 2.95 o.p. (*0-670-12285-8*) Viking Penguin.

—Before Midnight. 1995. 224p. pap. 15.00 (*0-553-76304-0*); 1981. 160p. pap. 2.25 o.p. (*0-553-14797-8*) Bantam Bks.

—Before Midnight. unabr. collector's ed. 1995. (Nero Wolfe Ser.). audio 36.00 (*0-7366-3166-6*, 3836) Books on Tape, Inc.

—Before Midnight. l.t. ed. 1994. 267p. lib. bdg. 15.95 o.p. (*0-8161-5985-8*, Macmillan Reference USA) Gale Group.

—Before Midnight. 1955. 2.75 o.p. (*0-670-15525-X*) Viking Penguin.

—Bitter End: A Nero Wolfe Mystery. unabr. ed. 1997. audio 4.99 (*0-88646-941-4*, 7941) Durkin Hayes Publishing Ltd.

—The Black Mountain. unabr. ed. 2001. (Nero Wolfe Mystery Ser.). audio 29.95 (*1-57270-039-4*, N61039u, Audio Editions Bks. on Cassette) Audio Partners Publishing Corp.

—The Black Mountain. 1988. 224p. mass mkt. 3.50 o.s.i (*0-553-27291-8*) Bantam Bks.

—The Black Mountain. unabr. collector's ed. 1995. (Nero Wolfe Ser.). audio 42.00 (*0-7366-3167-4*, 3837) Books on Tape, Inc.

—The Black Mountain. 1954. 2.75 o.p. (*0-670-17258-8*) Viking Penguin.

—Black Orchids. 1992. 208p. mass mkt. 5.99 (*0-553-25719-6*) Bantam Bks.

—Black Orchids. unabr. collector's ed. 1994. (Nero Wolfe Ser.). audio 42.00 (*0-7366-2797-9*, 3512) Books on Tape, Inc.

—Black Orchids. abr. ed. 1996. (Paperback Audio Ser.). audio 9.99 (*0-88646-889-2*, 7889) Durkin Hayes Publishing Ltd.

—Black Orchids. 1982. (Reader's Request Ser.). lib. bdg. 13.95 o.p. (*0-8161-3289-5*, Macmillan Reference USA) Gale Group.

—Champagne for One: A Nero Wolfe Mystery. 1995. 224p. mass mkt. 5.99 (*0-553-24438-8*); 1980. 160p. pap. 1.95 o.p. (*0-553-13657-7*) Bantam Bks.

—Champagne for One: A Nero Wolfe Mystery. unabr. collector's ed. 1996. (Nero Wolfe Ser.). audio 36.00 (*0-7366-3345-6*, 3995) Books on Tape, Inc.

—Champagne for One: A Nero Wolfe Mystery. abr. ed. 1998. (Nero Wolfe Mysteries Ser.). audio 16.99 (*0-88646-456-0*, 7456) Durkin Hayes Publishing Ltd.

—Champagne for One: A Nero Wolfe Mystery. l.t. ed. 1987. (Nightingale Ser.). 302p. 11.95 o.p. (*0-8161-4282-3*, Macmillan Reference USA) Gale Group.

—The Cop-Killer: A Nero Wolfe Mystery. unabr. ed. 1994. audio 4.99 (*0-88646-705-5*) Durkin Hayes Publishing Ltd.

—Curtains for Three. 240p. 1995. pap. 15.00 (*0-553-76294-X*); 1994. mass mkt. 4.99 (*0-553-24498-1*) Bantam Bks.

—Curtains for Three. unabr. collector's ed. 1997. (Nero Wolfe Ser.). audio 42.00 (*0-7366-3747-8*, 4422) Books on Tape, Inc.

—Death of a Doxy. unabr. collector's ed. 1998. (Nero Wolfe Ser.). audio 36.00 (*0-7366-4044-4*, 4543) Books on Tape, Inc.

—Death of a Doxy. l.t. ed. 1996. (Nightingale Ser.). 208p. pap. 17.95 o.p. (*0-7838-1573-5*, Macmillan Reference USA) Gale Group.

—Death of a Doxy. 1966. 3.75 o.p. (*0-670-26126-2*) Viking Penguin.

—Death of a Dude: A Nero Wolfe Novel. 1990. 160p. pap. 3.95 o.s.i (*0-553-27422-8*); Vol. 1. 1994. (Death of a Dude Ser.: Vol. 1). 208p. mass mkt. 4.99 (*0-553-24730-1*) Bantam Bks.

—Death of a Dude: A Nero Wolfe Novel, Set. unabr. ed. 1994. audio 32.95 (*0-7861-0793-6*, 1533) Blackstone Audio Bks., Inc.

—Death of a Dude: A Nero Wolfe Novel. l.t. ed. 1999. (Mystery Ser.). 271p. 27.95 (*0-7862-1904-1*) Thorndike Pr.

—Death Times Three. 1995. 254p. pap. 15.00 (*0-553-76305-9*); 1994. 256p. mass mkt. 4.99 o.s.i (*0-553-27828-2*); 1991. mass mkt. 2.99 o.s.i (*0-553-19646-4*); 1985. 240p. mass mkt. 3.50 (*0-553-25425-1*) Bantam Bks.

—Death Times Three, Set. unabr. ed. 1995. audio 32.95 (*0-7861-0701-4*, 1578) Blackstone Audio Bks., Inc.

—The Doorbell Rang. 1992. 192p. mass mkt. 5.99 (*0-553-23721-7*) Bantam Bks.

—The Doorbell Rang. audio 19.95 (*0-7861-1394-4*); 1994. audio 23.95 (*0-7861-0775-8*, 1503) Blackstone Audio Bks., Inc.

—The Doorbell Rang. abr. ed. (Nero Wolfe Mystery Ser.). 2000. audio 19.99 (*0-88646-561-3*, DHA-6561); 1997. audio (*0-88646-443-9*, 7443) Durkin Hayes Publishing Ltd.

—The Doorbell Rang. l.t. ed. 1985. (Nightingale Ser.). 227p. 9.95 o.p. (*0-8161-3795-1*, Macmillan Reference USA) Gale Group.

—The Doorbell Rang. 2000. (Best Mysteries of All Time Ser.). 207p. (*0-7621-8857-X*) Reader's Digest Assn., Inc., The.

—The Doorbell Rang. 1968. 9.95 o.p. (*0-670-28021-6*, LT4); 1965. 3.50 o.p. (*0-670-27993-5*) Viking Penguin.

—Eeny Meeny Murder Mo: A Nero Wolfe Mystery. unabr. ed. 1999. audio 5.99 (*0-88646-992-9*, PAC-7992) Durkin Hayes Publishing Ltd.

—A Family Affair. 1993. 208p. mass mkt. 4.99 o.s.i (*0-553-24122-2*) Bantam Bks.

—A Family Affair. l.t. ed. 1978. lib. bdg. 9.95 o.p. (*0-8161-6561-0*, Macmillan Reference USA) Gale Group.

—A Family Affair. 1975. 152p. 9.95 o.p. (*0-670-30611-8*) Viking Penguin.

—The Father Hunt. 208p. 1995. pap. 15.00 (*0-553-76297-4*); Vol. 1. 1991. mass mkt. 3.95 (*0-553-24728-X*) Bantam Bks.

—The Father Hunt. 1983. (Nightingale Ser.). 240p. pap. 9.95 o.p. (*0-8161-3548-7*, Macmillan Reference USA) Gale Group.

—The Father Hunt. 1968. 4.50 o.p. (*0-670-30945-1*) Viking Penguin.

—Fer-de-Lance. Date not set. 304p. 23.95 (*0-8488-2403-2*) Amereon, Ltd.

—Fer-de-Lance, unabr. ed. 1997. (Nero Wolfe Mystery Ser.). audio 29.95 (*1-57270-035-1*, N61035u, Audio Editions Mystery Masters) Audio Partners Publishing Corp.

—Fer-de-Lance. 1997. 304p. mass mkt. 5.99 (*0-553-27819-3*); 1992. pap. 2.50 o.s.i (*0-553-23033-6*); 1984. mass mkt. 2.95 o.s.i (*0-553-24918-5*) Bantam Bks.

—Fer-de-Lance. unabr. collector's ed. 1994. (Nero Wolfe Ser.). audio 48.00 (*0-7366-2621-2*, 3361) Books on Tape, Inc.

—Fer-de-Lance. 1994. 320p. reprint ed. 35.00 (*1-883402-17-4*, Scribner) Simon & Schuster.

—The Final Deduction: A Nero Wolfe Novel. 1999. 261p. (*0-7540-3706-1*) BBC Audiobooks America.

—The Final Deduction: A Nero Wolfe Novel. 1992. 144p. mass mkt. 4.99 (*0-553-25254-2*) Bantam Bks.

—The Final Deduction: A Nero Wolfe Novel. unabr. collector's ed. 1996. (Nero Wolfe Ser.). audio 36.00 (*0-7366-3413-4*, 4059) Books on Tape, Inc.

—The Final Deduction: A Nero Wolfe Novel. l.t. ed. 1999. (Mystery Ser.). 261p. 26.95 (*0-7862-1771-5*) Thorndike Pr.

—Five of a Kind: The Third Nero Wolfe Omnibus. 1980. (Short Story Index Reprint Ser.). reprint ed. 37.95 (*0-8369-4136-5*) Ayer Co. Pubs., Inc.

—Frame-up for Murder. unabr. ed. 1997. audio 4.99 (*0-88646-931-7*, 7931) Durkin Hayes Publishing Ltd.

—Gambit. 1985. 160p. mass mkt. 2.95 o.s.i (*0-553-25172-4*) Bantam Bks.

—Gambit. unabr. collector's ed. 1996. (Nero Wolfe Ser.). audio 36.00 (*0-7366-3415-0*, 4061) Books on Tape, Inc.

—Gambit. l.t. ed. 1997. (Nightingale Ser.). 18.95 o.p. (*0-7838-1571-9*, Macmillan Reference USA) Gale Group.

—Gambit. 1962. 3.50 o.p. (*0-670-33376-X*) Viking Penguin.

—The Golden Spiders, unabr. ed. 1997. (Nero Wolfe Mystery Ser.). audio 29.95 (*1-57270-038-6*, N61038u, Audio Editions Mystery Masters) Audio Partners Publishing Corp.

—The Golden Spiders. 1984. 160p. pap. 2.50 o.p. (*0-553-23995-3*) Bantam Bks.

—The Golden Spiders. unabr. collector's ed. 1995. (Nero Wolfe Ser.). audio 42.00 (*0-7366-3132-1*, 3807) Books on Tape, Inc.

—The Golden Spiders. l.t. ed. 1996. (Nightingale Ser.). pap. 17.95 (*0-7838-1572-7*, Macmillan Reference USA) Gale Group.

—The Golden Spiders. 1953. 2.50 o.p. (*0-670-34452-4*) Viking Penguin.

—The Great Legend. 1997. 288p. mass mkt. 4.95 (*0-7867-0443-8*, Carroll & Graf Pubs.) Avalon Publishing Group.

—The Hand in the Glove. 1992. 256p. mass mkt. 4.99 o.s.i (*0-553-22857-9*) Bantam Bks.

—Hand in the Glove. l.t. ed. 1986. (Nightingale Ser.). 384p. 10.95 o.p. (*0-8161-3964-4*, Macmillan Reference USA) Gale Group.

—Her Forbidden Knight. 256p. 2000. mass mkt. 5.95 (*0-7867-0729-1*); 1997. mass mkt. 4.95 o.p. (*0-7867-0444-6*) Avalon Publishing Group. (Carroll & Graf Pubs.).

—Her Forbidden Knight. 1998. 256p. 24.00 o.p. (*0-7278-5369-4*) Severn Hse. Pubs., Ltd.

—Homicide Trinity. 1993. 224p. mass mkt. 5.99 (*0-553-23446-3*) Bantam Bks.

—Homicide Trinity. unabr. collector's ed. 1999. (Nero Wolfe Ser.). audio 64.00 (*0-7366-4062-2*, 4573) Books on Tape, Inc.

—Homicide Trinity. 1962. 2.95 o.p. (*0-670-37758-9*) Viking Penguin.

—If Death Ever Slept. unabr. ed. 2002. (Nero Wolfe Mystery Ser.). audio 24.95 (*1-57270-252-4*, Audio Editions Bks. on Cassette) Audio Partners Publishing Corp.

—If Death Ever Slept. 208p. 1995. pap. 15.00 (*0-553-76296-6*); 1992. mass mkt. 4.99 (*0-553-23649-0*) Bantam Bks.

—If Death Ever Slept. abr. l.t. ed. 1989. 274p. 13.95 o.p. (*0-8161-4794-9*, Macmillan Reference USA) Gale Group.

—In the Best of Families. 1995. 272p. mass mkt. 5.99 (*0-553-27776-6*); 1980. pap. 2.50 o.p. (*0-553-24375-6*) Bantam Bks.

—In the Best of Families. l.t. ed. 1991. (Nightingale Series Large Print Bks.). 322p. pap. 13.95 o.p. (*0-8161-5203-9*, Macmillan Reference USA) Gale Group.

—Invitation to Murder. unabr. ed. 1996. (Paperback Audio Ser.). audio 9.99 (*0-88646-883-3*, 7883) Durkin Hayes Publishing Ltd.

—Justice Ends at Home & Other Stories. 1977. 8.95 o.p. (*0-670-41105-1*) Viking Penguin.

—The League of Frightened Men, unabr. ed. 1999. (Nero Wolfe Mystery Ser.). audio 29.95 (*1-57270-037-8*, N61037u) Audio Partners Publishing Corp.

—The League of Frightened Men. 320p. 1995. pap. 19.00 (*0-553-76298-2*); 1992. mass mkt. 4.99 (*0-553-25933-4*) Bantam Bks.

—The League of Frightened Men. 1979. 1.75 o.p. (*0-515-05116-0*, Jove) Berkley Publishing Group.

—The League of Frightened Men. unabr. collector's ed. 1994. (Nero Wolfe Ser.). audio 56.00 (*0-7366-2631-X*, 3370) Books on Tape, Inc.

—The League of Frightened Men. abr. ed. 1996. audio 16.99 (*0-88646-418-8*) Durkin Hayes Publishing Ltd.

—The League of Frightened Men. 1981. (Reader's Request Ser.). lib. bdg. 14.50 o.p. (*0-8161-3225-9*, Macmillan Reference USA) Gale Group.

—Might As Well Be Dead. 1980. 160p. pap. 1.95 o.p. (*0-553-14447-2*) Bantam Bks.

—Might as Well Be Dead. 1995. 224p. pap. 15.00 (*0-553-76303-2*) Bantam Bks.

—Might As Well Be Dead, Vol. 1. 1992. 224p. mass mkt. 4.99 (*0-553-24729-8*) Bantam Bks.

—Might As Well Be Dead. unabr. collector's ed. 1996. (Nero Wolfe Ser.). audio 42.00 (*0-7366-3225-5*, 3886) Books on Tape, Inc.

—Might As Well Be Dead. l.t. ed. 1997. (Nightingale Ser.). 262p. lib. bdg. 18.95 (*0-7838-1570-0*) Thorndike Pr.

—More Deaths Than One: A Nero Wolfe Mystery. l.t. ed. 1993. (Nightingale Ser.). 304p. reprint ed. pap. 16.95 o.p. (*0-8161-5757-X*, Macmillan Reference USA) Gale Group.

—The Mother Hunt. 1993. 224p. mass mkt. 5.99 (*0-553-24737-9*) Bantam Bks.

—The Mother Hunt. unabr. collector's ed. 1996. (Nero Wolfe Ser.). audio 36.00 (*0-7366-3523-8*, 4160) Books on Tape, Inc.

—The Mother Hunt. 1963. 3.50 o.p. (*0-670-49015-6*) Viking Penguin.

—The Mountain Cat Murders. 1993. 272p. mass mkt. 4.99 o.s.i (*0-553-25879-6*); 1982. 176p. pap. 2.50 o.p. (*0-553-20826-8*) Bantam Bks.

—Murder by the Book. 1995. 256p. pap. 19.00 (*0-553-76311-3*); 1985. mass mkt. 2.95 o.s.i (*0-553-24884-7*) Bantam Bks.

—Murder by the Book. unabr. collector's ed. 1995. (Nero Wolfe Ser.). audio 48.00 (*0-7366-3103-8*, 3779) Books on Tape, Inc.

—Murder by the Book. l.t. ed. 1996. 301p. 21.95 o.p. (*0-7838-1568-9*, Macmillan Reference USA) Gale Group.

—Murder by the Book. 1951. 2.50 o.p. (*0-670-49547-6*) Viking Penguin.

—Nero Wolfe: And Be a Villain. l.t. ed. 1988. 19.95 o.p. (*1-55504-643-6*); pap. 17.95 o.p. (*1-55504-644-4*) BBC Audiobooks America.

—Nero Wolfe Omnibus. lib. bdg. 26.95 (*0-8488-1893-8*) Amereon, Ltd.

—Not Quite Dead Enough. 1992. 208p. mass mkt. 5.99 (*0-553-26109-6*) Bantam Bks.

—Not Quite Dead Enough. unabr. collector's ed. 1994. (Nero Wolfe Ser.). audio 36.00 (*0-7366-2828-2*, 3536) Books on Tape, Inc.

—Not Quite Dead Enough. 1994. reprint ed. lib. bdg. 27.95 (*1-56849-341-X*) Buccaneer Bks., Inc.

—Not Quite Dead Enough. unabr. ed. 1994. audio 4.99 (*0-88646-727-6*) Durkin Hayes Publishing Ltd.

—An Officer & a Lady & Other Stories. 2000. 192p. mass mkt. 5.95 (*0-7867-0764-X*, Carroll & Graf Pubs.) Avalon Publishing Group.

—Over My Dead Body. 20.95 (*0-89190-341-0*) Amereon, Ltd.

—Over My Dead Body, unabr. ed. 2001. (Nero Wolfe Mystery Ser.). audio 29.95 (*1-57270-062-9*, N61062u, Audio Editions Bks. on Cassette) Audio Partners Publishing Corp.

—Over My Dead Body. 1993. (Crime Line Ser.). 272p. mass mkt. 5.99 (*0-553-23116-2*) Bantam Bks.

—Over My Dead Body. unabr. collector's ed. 1994. (Nero Wolfe Ser.). audio 48.00 (*0-7366-2747-2*, 3472) Books on Tape, Inc.
—Over My Dead Body. l.t. ed. 1982. lib. bdg. 13.95 o.p. (*0-8161-3288-7*, Macmillan Reference USA) Gale Group.
—Please Pass the Guilt. 1995. 176p. pap. 15.00 (*0-553-76308-3*); 1993. 192p. mass mkt. 4.99 (*0-553-23854-X*) Bantam Bks.
—Please Pass the Guilt. unabr. collector's ed. 1999. (Nero Wolfe Ser.). audio 32.00 (*0-7366-4456-3*, 4901) Books on Tape, Inc.
—Please Pass the Guilt. 1979. pap. 10.95 o.p. (*0-8161-6737-0*, Macmillan Reference USA) Gale Group.
—Plot It Yourself. unabr. ed. 2002. audio 24.95 (*1-57270-301-6*) Audio Partners Publishing Corp.
—Plot It Yourself. 1989. pap. 3.50 o.s.i (*0-553-27849-5*); 1985. 176p. mass mkt. 4.99 o.s.i (*0-553-25363-8*) Bantam Bks.
—Plot It Yourself. unabr. collector's ed. 1996. (Nero Wolfe Ser.). audio 36.00 (*0-7366-3354-5*, 4005) Books on Tape, Inc.
—Plot It Yourself. l.t. ed. 1984. (Nightingale Ser.). 248p. 8.95 o.p. (*0-8161-3547-9*, Macmillan Reference USA) Gale Group.
—Plot It Yourself. 1959. 2.95 o.p. (*0-670-56144-4*) Viking Penguin.
—The President Vanishes. 1982. 272p. pap. 2.50 o.p. (*0-553-22665-7*) Bantam Bks.
—Prisoner's Base. unabr. ed. 2001. (Nero Wolfe Mystery Ser.). audio 29.95 (*1-57270-191-9*, N61191u, Audio Editions Mystery Masters) Audio Partners Publishing Corp.
—Prisoner's Base. 1992. 224p. mass mkt. 5.99 (*0-553-24269-5*) Bantam Bks.
—Prisoner's Base. unabr. collector's ed. 1995. (Nero Wolfe Ser.). audio 42.00 (*0-7366-3137-2*, 3812) Books on Tape, Inc.
—Prisoner's Base. 1952. 2.50 o.p. (*0-670-57839-8*) Viking Penguin.
—A Prize for Princes. 1994. 256p. mass mkt. 4.95 o.p. (*0-7867-0104-8*, Carroll & Graf Pubs.) Avalon Publishing Group.
—A Prize for Princes. 1999. 312p. 26.00 (*0-7278-2277-2*) Severn Hse. Pubs., Ltd.
—The Red Box. unabr. ed. 1997. audio 29.95 (*1-57270-053-X*, N61053u, Audio Editions Bks. on Cassette) Audio Partners Publishing Corp.
—The Red Box. 1992. (Crime Line Ser.). 272p. mass mkt. 4.99 o.s.i (*0-553-24919-3*) Bantam Bks.
—The Red Box. 1979. 1.75 o.s.i (*0-515-05117-9*, Jove) Berkley Publishing Group.
—The Red Box. unabr. collector's ed. 1994. (Nero Wolfe Ser.). audio 48.00 (*0-7366-2697-2*, 3431) Books on Tape, Inc.
—The Red Box. abr. ed. 1995. audio 16.99 (*0-88646-377-7*, LFP 7377) Durkin Hayes Publishing Ltd.
—The Red Box. 1981. (Reader's Request Ser.). lib. bdg. 13.50 o.p. (*0-8161-3223-2*, Macmillan Reference USA) Gale Group.
—Red Threads. 1995. 272p. pap. 19.00 (*0-553-76299-0*); mass mkt. 4.99 (*0-553-22530-8*, Crimeline) Bantam Bks.
—A Right to Die? 1991. 208p. mass mkt. 5.99 (*0-553-24032-3*) Bantam Bks.
—A Right to Die? l.t. ed. 1996. (G. K. Hall Mystery Ser.). 224p. lib. bdg. 21.95 o.p. (*0-7838-1569-7*, Macmillan Reference USA) Gale Group.
—A Right to Die. unabr. collector's ed. 1997. (Nero Wolfe Ser.). audio 36.00 (*0-7366-3531-9*, 4170) Books on Tape, Inc.
—Royal Flush. 1965. 3.95 o.p. (*0-670-60934-X*) Viking Penguin.
—The Rubber Band. unabr. ed. 1997. (Nero Wolfe Mystery Ser.). audio 29.95 (*1-57270-052-1*, N61052u, Audio Editions Mystery Masters) Audio Partners Publishing Corp.
—The Rubber Band. 1995. 208p. pap. 15.00 (*0-553-76309-1*); 1982. 192p. mass mkt. 2.95 (*0-553-25550-9*) Bantam Bks.
—The Rubber Band. 1979. 1.75 o.s.i (*0-515-04867-4*, Jove) Berkley Publishing Group.
—The Rubber Band. unabr. collector's ed. 1994. (Nero Wolfe Ser.). audio 48.00 (*0-7366-2695-6*, 3429) Books on Tape, Inc.
—The Rubber Band. 1981. (Reader's Request Ser.). lib. bdg. 12.95 o.p. (*0-8161-3224-0*, Macmillan Reference USA) Gale Group.
—The Second Confession. unabr. ed. 2000. (Nero Wolfe Mystery Ser.). audio 29.95 (*1-57270-132-3*, N61132u, Audio Editions Mystery Masters) Audio Partners Publishing Corp.
—The Second Confession. 1995. 256p. mass mkt. 5.99 (*0-553-24594-5*) Bantam Bks.
—The Second Confession. unabr. collector's ed. 1995. (Nero Wolfe Ser.). audio 48.00 (*0-7366-3070-8*, 3752) Books on Tape, Inc.
—The Second Confession. l.t. ed. 1992. (Nightingale Series Large Print Bks.). 311p. pap. 15.95 (*0-8161-5202-0*, Macmillan Reference USA) Gale Group.
—The Silent Speaker. 1994. (Crime Line Ser.). 288p. mass mkt. 5.99 (*0-553-23497-8*) Bantam Bks.
—The Silent Speaker. unabr. collector's ed. 1994. (Nero Wolfe Ser.). audio 48.00 (*0-7366-2837-1*, 3545) Books on Tape, Inc.
—The Silent Speaker. l.t. ed. 2002. 350p. 29.45 (*0-7862-4195-0*) Thorndike Pr.
—Some Buried Caesar. 20.95 (*0-89190-340-2*) Amereon, Ltd.
—Some Buried Caesar. 1990. (Nero Wolfe Ser.). 288p. mass mkt. 5.99 (*0-553-25464-2*) Bantam Bks.
—Some Buried Caesar. 1982. (Reader's Request Ser.). 13.95 o.p. (*0-8161-3286-0*, Macmillan Reference USA) Gale Group.
—Some Buried Caeser. 1979. 1.75 o.s.i (*0-515-05118-7*, Jove) Berkley Publishing Group.
—The Sound of Murder. 1986. (Mystery Ser.). 192p. pap. 2.95 o.p. (*0-553-26148-7*) Bantam Bks.
—The Sound of Murder. 1979. 1.75 o.s.i (*0-515-05281-7*, Jove) Berkley Publishing Group.
—Target Practice. 1998. 320p. mass mkt. 5.95 (*0-7867-0496-9*, Carroll & Graf Pubs.) Avalon Publishing Group.
—Target Practice. l.t. ed. 1998. (Mystery Ser.). 424p. 28.95 (*0-7838-0178-5*) Thorndike Pr.
—This Won't Kill You. unabr. ed. 1998. audio 5.99 (*0-88646-865-5*, PAC-7865) Durkin Hayes Publishing Ltd.
—Three Aces. 1971. 8.95 o.p. (*0-670-70622-1*) Viking Penguin.
—Three at Wolfe's Door. 1995. 240p. mass mkt. 5.99 (*0-553-23803-5*, Crimeline) Bantam Bks.
—Three at Wolfe's Door. unabr. collector's ed. 1997. (Nero Wolfe Ser.). audio 48.00 (*0-7366-4060-6*, 4571) Books on Tape, Inc.
—Three for the Chair. 1985. 240p. mass mkt. 5.99 (*0-553-24813-8*) Bantam Bks.
—Three for the Chair. unabr. collector's ed. 1997. (Nero Wolfe Ser.). audio 42.00 (*0-7366-3750-8*, 4425) Books on Tape, Inc.
—Three for the Chair. 1957. 2.95 o.p. (*0-670-70779-1*) Viking Penguin.
—Three Men Out. 1991. 224p. mass mkt. 3.99 o.s.i (*0-553-24547-3*) Bantam Bks.
—Three Men Out. l.t. ed. 1990. (Nightingale Ser.). 296p. lib. bdg. 13.95 o.p. (*0-8161-4793-0*, Macmillan Reference USA) Gale Group.
—Three Men Out. 1954. 2.50 o.p. (*0-670-70846-1*) Viking Penguin.
—Three Trumps. 1973. 6.95 o.p. (*0-670-71031-8*) Viking Penguin.
—Three Witnesses. 1981. 224p. mass mkt. 5.99 (*0-553-24959-2*) Bantam Bks.
—Three Witnesses. unabr. collector's ed. 1997. (Nero Wolfe Ser.). audio 42.00 (*0-7366-3751-6*, 4426) Books on Tape, Inc.
—Three Witnesses. 1956. 2.75 o.p. (*0-670-71080-6*) Viking Penguin.
—Too Many Clients. 1955. 192p. mass mkt. 2.95 o.s.i (*0-553-25423-5*) Bantam Bks.
—Too Many Clients. unabr. collector's ed. 1996. (Nero Wolfe Ser.). audio 36.00 (*0-7366-3400-2*, 4047) Books on Tape, Inc.
—Too Many Clients. 1983. (Nightingale Ser.). 241p. pap. 9.95 o.p. (*0-8161-3549-5*, Macmillan Reference USA) Gale Group.
—Too Many Clients. 1960. 2.95 o.p. (*0-670-72010-0*) Viking Penguin.
—Too Many Cooks. 1995. 208p. pap. 15.00 (*0-553-76306-7*); 1988. 256p. mass mkt. 3.50 (*0-553-27290-X*) Bantam Bks.
—Too Many Cooks, Set. unabr. ed. 1995. 5p. audio 39.95 (*0-7861-0660-3*, 1561) Blackstone Audio Bks., Inc.
—Too Many Cooks. l.t. ed. 1985. (Nightingale Ser.). 397p. 10.95 o.p. (*0-8161-3868-0*, Macmillan Reference USA) Gale Group.
—Too Many Cooks. 1976. (Crime Fiction Ser.). reprint ed. lib. bdg. 21.00 o.p. (*0-8240-2394-3*) Garland Publishing, Inc.
—Too Many Women: A Nero Wolfe Mystery. unabr. ed. 1999. audio 29.95 (*1-57270-104-8*, N61104u, Audio Editions Mystery Masters) Audio Partners Publishing Corp.
—Too Many Women: A Nero Wolfe Mystery. l.t. ed. 1999. 355p. (*0-7540-3882-3*); pap. (*0-7540-3883-1*) BBC Audiobooks America.
—Too Many Women: A Nero Wolfe Mystery. unabr. collector's ed. 1995. (Nero Wolfe Ser.). audio 48.00 (*0-7366-3045-7*, 3727) Books on Tape, Inc.
—Too Many Women: A Nero Wolfe Mystery. l.t. ed. 1999. (Mystery Ser.). 355p. 26.95 o.p. (*0-7862-2049-X*) Thorndike Pr.
—Trio for Blunt Instruments. 1979. pap. 1.75 o.p. (*0-553-13232-6*) Bantam Bks.
—Trio for Blunt Instruments. unabr. collector's ed. 1997. (Nero Wolfe Ser.). audio 48.00 (*0-7366-4061-4*, 4572) Books on Tape, Inc.
—Triple Jeopardy. 1995. 192p. pap. 15.00 (*0-553-76307-5*); 1993. 256p. mass mkt. 4.99 (*0-553-23591-5*) Bantam Bks.
—Triple Jeopardy. 1952. 2.50 o.p. (*0-670-73109-9*) Viking Penguin.
—Trouble in Triplicate. unabr. collector's ed. 1996. (Nero Wolfe Ser.). audio 48.00 (*0-7366-3268-9*, 3925) Books on Tape, Inc.
—Trouble in Triplicate. 1949. 2.50 o.p. (*0-670-73241-9*) Viking Penguin.
—Under the Andes. 1994. 290p. mass mkt. 4.95 (*0-7867-0179-X*, Carroll & Graf Pubs.) Avalon Publishing Group.
—Under the Andes. unabr. ed. 1997. audio 49.95 (*0-7861-1187-9*, 1947) Blackstone Audio Bks., Inc.
—Under the Andes. E-Book 2.95 (*1-57799-901-0*) Logos Research Systems, Inc.
—Under the Andes. 1985. 15.95 o.p. (*0-89296-119-8*) Mysterious Pr.
—Under the Andes. 1986. 312p. reprint ed. mass mkt. 3.50 (*0-445-40507-4*, Mysterious Pr. Paperback Bks.) Warner Bks., Inc.
—Where There's a Will. unabr. ed. 1999. (Nero Wolfe Mystery Ser.). audio 29.95 (*1-57270-096-3*, N61096u, Audio Editions Mystery Masters) Audio Partners Publishing Corp.
—Where There's a Will. l.t. ed. (Nero Wolfe Mystery Ser.). 1992. pap. 20.95 o.p. (*0-7927-1138-6*, CS0304); 1991. 22.95 o.p. (*0-7927-1137-8*, CH0233) BBC Audiobooks America.
—Where There's a Will. 256p. 1995. pap. 15.00 (*0-553-76301-6*); 1992. mass mkt. 4.99 (*0-553-29591-8*) Bantam Bks.
—Where There's a Will. unabr. collector's ed. 1994. (Nero Wolfe Ser.). audio 42.00 (*0-7366-2766-9*, 3487) Books on Tape, Inc.
—Where There's a Will. 1982. (Reader's Request Ser.). 13.95 o.p. (*0-8161-3287-9*, Macmillan Reference USA) Gale Group.
—Where There's a Will. 1941. pap. 1.50 o.p. (*0-380-01620-6*, 39529, Avon Bks.) Morrow/Avon.
Stout, Rex, contrib. by. Death of a Dude: A Nero Wolfe Novel. 1999. (*0-7540-3797-5*); (*0-7540-3798-3*) BBC Audiobooks America.
—The Final Deduction: A Nero Wolfe Novel. (*0-7540-3705-3*) BBC Audiobooks America.
Stover, Laren. Pluto, Animal Lover. 1995. 176p. pap. 10.00 o.p. (*0-06-092627-9*, Perennial); 1994. 160p. 15.00 o.p. (*0-06-017111-1*) HarperTrade.
Stowe, Rebecca. The Shadow of Desire. 1997. (Illus.). 240p. pap. 12.00 o.p. (*0-393-31658-0*) Norton, W. W. & Co., Inc.
Straub, Peter. Koko. 1988. 19.95 o.p. (*0-525-24660-6*, Dutton) Dutton/Plume.
—Koko. 1989. 608p. mass mkt. 7.99 (*0-451-16214-5*, 001, Signet Bks.) NAL.
—Koko. 1990. 4.99 o.p. (*0-517-05233-4*) Random Hse. Value Publishing.
—Koko. 1999. pap. 9.98 (*0-671-04461-3*); 1988. audio 14.95 (*0-671-65239-7*) Simon & Schuster Audio. (Simon & Schuster Audioworks).
Strieber, Whitley. The Forbidden Zone. 1993. 320p. 21.00 o.p. (*0-525-93683-1*, Dutton) Dutton/Plume.
—The Night Church. 1983. 320p. 15.50 o.p. (*0-671-46955-X*, Simon & Schuster) Simon & Schuster.
Stryker, Dev. End Game. 1994. 320p. 22.95 o.p. (*0-312-85195-2*, Forge Bks.); Vol. 1. 1998. (End Game Ser.: Vol. 1). (Illus.). 344p. mass mkt. 5.99 o.p. (*0-8125-1597-8*, Tor Bks.) Doherty, Tom Assocs., LLC.
Styron, William. Sophie's Choice. l.t. ed. 1993. (General Ser.). 886p. lib. bdg. 23.95 o.p. (*0-8161-5650-6*, Macmillan Reference USA) Gale Group.
—Sophie's Choice. (Modern Library Ser.). 1998. 608p. 22.00 (*0-679-60289-5*); 1992. 576p. pap. 14.95 (*0-679-73637-9*) Random Hse., Inc.
Summers, Cara. Short, Sweet & Sexy. 2002. (Harlequin Temptation Ser.). 216p. mass mkt. (*0-373-69100-9*, Harlequin Bks.) Harlequin Enterprises, Ltd.
Swados, Elizabeth. Fabulous. 1998. 244p. 22.00 o.p. (*0-312-19547-8*) Picador.
—The Myth Man. 1994. 336p. 21.95 o.p. (*0-670-84202-8*, Viking) Viking Penguin.
Swados, Harvey. Nights in the Gardens of Brooklyn: The Collected Stories of Harvey Swados. 1977. (Short Story Index Reprint Ser.). 19.95 (*0-8369-3642-6*) Ayer Co. Pubs., Inc.
—Nights in the Gardens of Brooklyn: The Collected Stories of Harvey Swados. 2004. (New York Review Books Classics Ser.). 400p. pap. 14.95 (*1-59017-084-9*) New York Review of Bks., Inc., The.
Swerling, Beverly. City of Dreams: A Novel of Nieuw Amsterdam & Early Manhattan. 2001. (Illus.). 592p. 26.95 (*0-684-87172-6*, Simon & Schuster) Simon & Schuster.
Sykes, Plum. Bergdorf Blondes. 2004. 24.95 (*1-4013-5196-4*) Hyperion Pr.
Tamar, Erika. Good-Bye Glamour Girl. 1985. mass mkt. 2.50 o.p. (*0-451-14019-2*, Signet Vista) NAL.
Tanenbaum, Robert K. Act of Revenge. l.t. ed. 2001. (Large Print Book Ser.). 575p. 28.95 (*1-58724-025-4*, Wheeler Publishing, Inc.) Gale Group.
—Act of Revenge. 1999. 416p. o.p. (*0-06-019218-6*, HarperFlamingo) HarperCollins Pubs. Canada, Ltd.
—Act of Revenge. 2000. 544p. mass mkt. 7.50 (*0-06-109730-6*, HarperTorch) Morrow/Avon.
—Corruption of Blood. unabr. ed. 1998. (Butch Karp Mystery Ser.). audio 80.00 (*0-7366-4045-2*, 4544) Books on Tape, Inc.
—Corruption of Blood. 1995. 368p. 22.95 o.p. (*0-525-93870-2*, Dutton) Dutton/Plume.
—Depraved Indifference. 1989. 18.95 o.p. (*0-453-00679-5*); 1990. 400p. reprint ed. mass mkt. 7.99 (*0-451-16842-9*, Signet Bks.) NAL.
—Enemy Within. 2001. (Illus.). 368p. 24.95 (*0-7434-0342-8*, Atria) Simon & Schuster.
—Falsely Accused. unabr. ed. 1998. (Butch Karp Mystery Ser.). audio 56.00 (*0-7366-4026-6*, 452511.95) Books on Tape, Inc.
—Falsely Accused. 1996. 320p. 23.95 o.s.i (*0-525-94168-1*) Dutton/Plume.
—Falsely Accused. 1997. 448p. mass mkt. 7.99 (*0-451-19000-9*, Signet Bks.) NAL.
—Immoral Certainty. unabr. ed. 1997. (Butch Karp Mystery Ser.). audio 64.00 (*0-7366-3689-7*, 4368) Books on Tape, Inc.
—Immoral Certainty. 1991. 304p. 18.95 o.p. (*0-525-24941-9*, Dutton) Dutton/Plume.
—Immoral Certainty. 1992. 400p. reprint ed. mass mkt. 7.99 (*0-451-17186-1*, Signet Bks.) NAL.
—Irresistible Impulse. unabr. ed. 1998. (Butch Karp Mystery Ser.). audio 64.00 (*0-7366-4134-3*, 4639) Books on Tape, Inc.
—Irresistible Impulse. 1997. 352p. 24.95 o.p. (*0-525-94310-2*) Dutton/Plume.
—Irresistible Impulse. 1998. 445p. mass mkt. 6.99 (*0-451-19261-3*, Signet Bks.) NAL.
—Justice Denied. unabr. ed. 1997. (Butch Karp Mystery Ser.). audio 64.00 (*0-7366-3688-9*, 4367) Books on Tape, Inc.
—Justice Denied. 1994. 320p. 18.95 o.p. (*0-525-93814-1*) Dutton/Plume.
—Justice Denied. abr. ed. 1994. pap. 16.00 o.p. incl. audio (*0-453-00903-4*, 25024-33894) Penguin/HighBridge.
—Material Witness. unabr. ed. 1997. (Butch Karp Mystery Ser.). audio 64.00 (*0-7366-3687-0*, 4366) Books on Tape, Inc.
—Material Witness. 1993. 320p. 20.00 o.p. (*0-525-93579-7*, Dutton) Dutton/Plume.
—Material Witness. 1994. 416p. mass mkt. 7.99 (*0-451-18020-8*, Signet Bks.) NAL.
—No Lesser Plea. 1988. 368p. reprint ed. mass mkt. 7.99 (*0-451-15496-7*, Signet Bks.) NAL.
—No Lesser Plea. 1987. 17.95 o.p. (*0-531-09783-8*, Watts, Franklin) Scholastic Library Publishing.
—Reckless Endangerment. unabr. ed. 1999. (Butch Karp Mystery Ser.). audio 88.00 (*0-7366-4351-6*, 4828) Books on Tape, Inc.
—Reckless Endangerment. abr. ed. 1998. audio 17.95 o.p. (*1-56740-784-6*, 443, Nova Audio Bks.); audio 26.95 (*1-56740-059-0*, 10, Bookcassette); audio 73.25 o.p. (*1-56740-588-6*, 1001) Brilliance Audio.
—Reckless Endangerment. 1998. 352p. 23.95 o.p. (*0-525-94347-1*) Dutton/Plume.
—Reckless Endangerment. 1999. 448p. reprint ed. mass mkt. 7.99 (*0-451-19328-8*, Signet Bks.) NAL.
—Reversible Error. unabr. ed. 1997. (Butch Karp Mystery Ser.). audio 56.00 (*0-7366-3686-2*, 4365) Books on Tape, Inc.
—Reversible Error. 1992. 288p. 20.00 o.p. (*0-525-93423-5*, Dutton) Dutton/Plume.
—Reversible Error. 1993. 448p. reprint ed. mass mkt. 7.99 (*0-451-17519-0*, Signet Bks.) NAL.
Tannen, Mary. Loving Edith. l.t. ed. 1995. 272p. lib. bdg. 24.95 (*1-57490-026-9*, Beeler Large Print Bks.) Beeler, Thomas T. Publisher.
—Loving Edith. 1996. 12.00 o.s.i (*1-57322-544-4*, Riverhead Trade (Paperbacks)) Berkley Publishing Group.
—Loving Edith. 1995. 275p. 22.95 o.p. (*1-57322-008-6*, Riverhead Bks. (Hardcovers)) Putnam Publishing Group, The.
Tanner, Janet. Folly's Child. 1992. 400p. 21.95 o.p. (*0-312-06976-6*) St. Martin's Pr.
Tax, Meredith. Union Square. 1988. 473p. 18.95 o.p. (*0-688-05069-7*, Morrow, William & Co.) Morrow/Avon.
Tax, Meredith, ed. Rivington Street: A Novel. 2002. 437p. pap. 18.95 (*0-252-07032-1*) Univ. of Illinois Pr.
—Union Square: A Novel. 2002. 440p. pap. 19.95 (*0-252-07031-3*) Univ. of Illinois Pr.
Taylor, Karen E. Bitter Blood. (Vampire Legacy). 352p. 1998. mass mkt. 4.99 o.s.i (*0-8217-6021-1*); 1994. mass mkt. 4.50 o.s.i (*0-8217-4722-3*, Zebra Bks.) Kensington Publishing Corp.
—Blood Secrets. (Vampire Legacy). 304p. 1998. mass mkt. 4.99 o.s.i (*0-8217-6022-X*); 1994. mass mkt. 4.50 o.s.i (*0-8217-4437-2*, Zebra Bks.) Kensington Publishing Corp.
—Blood Ties. (Vampire Legacy). 1998. 352p. mass mkt. 4.99 o.s.i (*0-8217-6023-8*); 1996. 352p. mass mkt. 2.99 o.p. (*0-8217-5496-3*); 1995. mass mkt. 4.99 o.s.i (*0-8217-5114-X*) Kensington Publishing Corp.

Settings

Taylor, Mel. The Mitt Man. 1999. 352p. 24.00 (*0-688-16094-8*, Morrow, William & Co.) Morrow/Avon.

Taylor, Phoebe Atwood. Murder at the New York World's Fair. 1987. 265p. reprint ed. pap. 8.95 o.p. (*0-88150-095-X*) Countryman Pr.

Templeton, Karen. Loose Screws. 2002. 336p. pap. (*0-373-25019-3*, Red Dress Ink) Harlequin Enterprises, Ltd.

Thayer, James. White Star. 1996. 368p. mass mkt. 6.99 (*0-671-52817-3*, Pocket); 1995. 303p. 22.00 (*0-671-79814-6*, Simon & Schuster) Simon & Schuster.

Thirault, Philippe. Miss: Better Living Through Crime. 2002. (Illus.). 192p. pap. 24.95 (*1-930652-81-X*) Humanoids, Inc.

Thomas, Abigail. Herb's Pajamas. 1998. 210p. tchr. ed. 17.95 (*1-56512-189-9*, 72189) Algonquin Bks. of Chapel Hill.

Thomas, Rosanne D. The Angel Carver. 1995. 272p. pap. 16.99 o.p. (*0-446-67054-5*) Warner Bks., Inc.

Thompson, Victoria. Murder on Astor Place. 1999. (Gaslight Mysteries Ser.). 288p. mass mkt. 6.99 (*0-425-16896-4*, Prime Crime) Berkley Publishing Group.

—Murder on Gramercy Park. 2001. 336p. mass mkt. 6.99 (*0-425-17886-2*) Berkley Publishing Group.

—Murder on Mulberry Bend. 2003. 352p. (Orig.). mass mkt. 6.99 (*0-425-18910-4*, Prime Crime) Berkley Publishing Group.

—Murder on St. Mark's Place. 2000. (Gaslight Mysteries Ser.). 288p. mass mkt. 6.99 (*0-425-17361-5*, Prime Crime) Berkley Publishing Group.

Thorp, Roderick. Devlin. 1992. (Orig.). mass mkt. 5.99 o.s.i (*0-449-14793-2*, Fawcett) Ballantine Bks.

Thurman, Wallace. The Blacker the Berry. reprint ed. 27.50 (*0-404-00217-X*) AMS Pr., Inc.

—The Blacker the Berry. 1978. (American Negro). reprint ed. 34.06 (*0-405-01897-5*) Ayer Co. Pubs., Inc.

—The Blacker the Berry. 1996. 224p. pap. 12.00 (*0-684-81580-X*, Touchstone) Simon & Schuster.

—The Blacker the Berry. 1996. (X Press Black Classics Ser.). 215p. pap. 9.95 (*1-874509-13-1*) X Pr., The GBR. *Dist:* LPC Group.

—Infants of the Spring. reprint ed. 29.50 (*0-404-11418-0*) AMS Pr., Inc.

—Infants of the Spring. 1977. (Black Heritage Library Collection). reprint ed. 28.95 (*0-8369-9129-X*) Ayer Co. Pubs., Inc.

—Infants of the Spring. 1999. (Harlem Renaissance Ser.: Vol. 2). xii, 175p. pap. 11.95 o.s.i (*0-375-75232-3*) Random Hse., Inc.

—Infants of the Spring. 2003. (Black Classics Ser.). 186p. pap. (*1-874509-61-1*) X Pr., The GBR. *Dist:* National Bk. Network.

—Infants of the Spring. A Novel. 1979. (Lost American Fiction Ser.). 314p. reprint ed. 13.95 o.p. (*0-8093-0864-9*) Southern Illinois Univ. Pr.

Tiffin, Patricia M. Watching Vanessa. unabr. ed. 1997. 320p. 22.00 (*1-880909-54-5*) Baskerville Pubs., Inc.

—Watching Vanessa. 2000. 340p. mass mkt. 6.99 (*0-312-97415-9*, St. Martin's Paperbacks) St. Martin's Pr.

Tifft, Ellen. Moon, Moon, Tell Me True. 1996. 25.00 o.p. (*1-879378-26-4*) Xenos Bks.

Tillman, Lynne. No Lease on Life: A Novel. 1998. 192p. 21.00 o.s.i (*0-15-100272-X*) Harcourt Trade Pubs.

Tinsley, Kevin. The Festering Season: A Tale of Urban Vodou. Creighton, Deborah, ed. 2002. (Illus.). 240p. 38.95 (*0-9675423-1-6*); pap. 19.95 (*0-9675423-2-4*) Stickman Graphics.

Tippens, Elizabeth. Winging It: A Tale of Turning Thirty. 1996. 224p. 10.00 o.s.i (*1-57322-528-2*, Riverhead Trade (Paperbacks)) Berkley Publishing Group.

Tocher, Timothy. Playing for Pride. 2002. 110p. (J). (*0-88166-424-3*) Meadowbrook Pr.

Tosches, Nick. In the Hand of Dante. 384p. 2002. 24.95 (*0-316-89524-5*); 2003. reprint ed. pap. 13.95 (*0-316-73564-7*, Back Bay) Little Brown & Co.

—Trinities. 1996. mass mkt. 6.50 (*0-312-95689-4*, St. Martin's Paperbacks) St. Martin's Pr.

Trevor, Elleston. Flycatcher. 1994. 288p. 21.95 o.p. (*0-312-85647-4*, Forge Bks.) Doherty, Tom Assocs., LLC.

Trigiani, Adriana. Lucia, Lucia: A Novel. 2004. 288p. pap. 13.95 (*0-8129-6779-8*) Ballantine Bks.

—Lucia, Lucia: A Novel. abr. ed. 2003. audio compact disk 29.95 (*0-7393-0364-3*, RH Audio) Random Hse. Audio Publishing Group.

—Lucia, Lucia: A Novel. 2003. 272p. 24.95 (*1-4000-6005-2*) Random Hse., Inc.

—Lucia, Lucia: A Novel. l.t. ed. 2003. 440p. 31.95 (*0-7862-5863-2*, Large Print Pr.) Thorndike Pr.

Trigoboff, Joseph. The Bone Orchard: A Detective Yablonsky Mystery. 2004. 288p. pap. 12.95 (*1-59228-046-3*, Lyons Pr.) Globe Pequot Pr., The.

—The Shooting Gallery: A Detective Yablonsky Mystery. 320p. 2004. pap. 14.95 (*1-59228-143-5*); 2002. 19.95 (*1-58574-547-2*) Globe Pequot Pr., The. (Lyons Pr.).

Trillin, Calvin. Tepper Isn't Going Out: A Novel. 2003. 224p. pap. 12.95 (*0-375-75851-8*) Random House Adult Trade Publishing Group.

—Tepper Isn't Going Out: A Novel. 2002. E-Book 18.00 (*1-58836-046-6*) Random Hse., Inc.

Trump, Ivana. For Love Alone. 1992. 22.00 o.p. (*0-671-74368-6*, Atria) Simon & Schuster.

Tucker, Kerry. Cold Feet: A Libby Kincaid Mystery. 1992. 208p. 19.00 o.p. (*0-06-016530-8*) HarperTrade.

—Cold Feet: A Libby Kincaid Mystery. 1993. 304p. mass mkt. 4.50 o.p. (*0-06-109985-6*, HarperTorch) Morrow/Avon.

—Death Echo: A Libby Kincaid Mystery. 1993. 224p. 19.00 o.p. (*0-06-017700-4*) HarperTrade.

—Death Echo: A Libby Kincaid Mystery. 1994. 288p. mass mkt. 4.50 o.p. (*0-06-109986-4*, HarperTorch) Morrow/Avon.

Turnipseed, Erica Simone. A Love Noire: A Novel. 2003. 320p. 19.95 (*0-06-053679-9*, Amistad Pr.) HarperTrade.

Tuten, Frederic. Tallien: A Brief Romance. 1994. 152p. pap. 13.95 o.p. (*0-7145-2990-7*) Boyars, Marion Pubs., Inc.

—Tallien: A Brief Romance. 1988. 230p. 17.95 o.p. (*0-374-27249-2*) Farrar, Straus & Giroux.

Tyre, Peg. In the Midnight Hour. 1996. 272p. mass mkt. 5.99 (*0-380-72811-7*, Avon Bks.) Morrow/Avon.

Uhnak, Dorothy. The Bait. 1976. pap. 1.95 o.s.i (*0-671-82326-4*, Pocket) Simon & Schuster.

—Codes of Betrayal. 1999. 320p. pap. 6.99 o.p. (*0-312-96531-1*, St. Martin's Paperbacks); 1997. 293p. 23.95 (*0-312-15582-4*) St. Martin's Pr.

—The Ledger. 1977. pap. 1.95 o.s.i (*0-671-82328-0*, Pocket) Simon & Schuster.

—The Ryer Avenue Story. 1994. mass mkt. 5.99 o.p. (*0-312-95222-8*, St. Martin's Paperbacks); 1993. 406p. 22.95 o.p. (*0-312-08888-4*) St. Martin's Pr.

—Secrets & Mysteries. 1993. 21.95 (*0-312-08289-4*) St. Martin's Pr.

Ullmann, Linn. Before You Sleep. Nunnally, Tiina, tr. 2001. 304p. pap. 13.00 o.s.i (*0-14-029833-9*) Penguin Group (USA) Inc.

—Before You Sleep. Nunnally, Tiina, tr. from ENG. 1999. (ENG & NOR.). 256p. 23.95 o.s.i (*0-670-88698-X*, Viking) Viking Penguin.

Urquhart, Jane. The Underpainter. 256p. 1998. 14.00 (*0-14-026973-8*); 1997. 22.95 o.s.i (*0-670-87726-3*) Viking Penguin.

Vachss, Andrew. Blossom. 2001. E-Book 11.50 (*1-59061-234-5*) Adobe Systems, Inc.

—Blossom. 1991. 320p. mass mkt. 5.95 o.s.i (*0-8041-0751-3*, Ivy Bks.) Ballantine Bks.

—Blossom. 1996. 272p. pap. 13.00 (*0-679-77261-8*) McKay, David Co., Inc.

—Blue Belle. 2001. E-Book 11.00 (*1-59061-228-0*) Adobe Systems, Inc.

—Blue Belle. 1994. lib. bdg. 24.95 o.p. (*1-56849-463-7*) Buccaneer Bks., Inc.

—Blue Belle. 1990. 336p. mass mkt. 4.95 o.p. (*0-451-16290-0*, Signet Bks.) NAL.

—Blue Belle. 1995. 352p. pap. 13.00 (*0-679-76168-3*) Random Hse., Inc.

—Choice of Evil: A Burke Novel. 2001. E-Book 11.50 (*1-59061-222-1*) Adobe Systems, Inc.

—Choice of Evil: A Burke Novel. 2000. (Crime - Black Lizard Ser.). 336p. pap. 13.00 (*0-375-70662-3*, Vintage) Knopf Publishing Group.

—Choice of Evil: A Burke Novel. 1999. (Burke Novels Ser.). 305p. 23.00 o.s.i (*0-375-40647-6*) Knopf, Alfred A. Inc.

—Choice of Evil: A Burke Novel. 2001. E-Book 7.99 (*0-375-71913-X*) Random Hse., Inc.

—Down in the Zero. 2001. E-Book 11.00 (*1-59061-229-9*) Adobe Systems, Inc.

—Down in the Zero. 1995. pap. 7.00 o.s.i (*0-679-76087-3*); 272p. pap. 12.00 (*0-679-76066-0*) Random Hse., Inc.

—False Allegations: A Burke Novel. 2001. E-Book 11.00 (*1-59061-235-3*) Adobe Systems, Inc.

—False Allegations: A Burke Novel. 1997. 240p. pap. 12.00 (*0-679-77293-6*, Vintage) Knopf Publishing Group.

—False Allegations: A Burke Novel. 1996. 229p. 23.00 (*0-679-45109-9*) Knopf, Alfred A. Inc.

—Flood: A Burke Novel. 2002. E-Book 11.50 (*1-59061-886-6*) Adobe Systems, Inc.

—Flood: A Burke Novel. 1994. lib. bdg. 24.95 o.p. (*1-56849-465-3*) Buccaneer Bks., Inc.

—Flood: A Burke Novel. 1985. 341p. 17.95 o.s.i (*0-917657-43-8*) Fine, Donald I. Bks.

—Flood: A Burke Novel. 1986. mass mkt. 5.99 (*0-671-61905-5*, Pocket) Simon & Schuster.

—Footsteps of the Hawk. 2001. E-Book 11.00 (*1-59061-233-7*) Adobe Systems, Inc.

—Footsteps of the Hawk. 1996. 256p. pap. 12.00 (*0-679-76663-4*) Random Hse., Inc.

—Hard Candy. 2001. E-Book 11.00 (*1-59061-230-2*) Adobe Systems, Inc.

—Hard Candy. 1994. lib. bdg. 24.95 o.p. (*1-56849-464-5*) Buccaneer Bks., Inc.

—Hard Candy. 1990. mass mkt. 4.95 o.p. (*0-451-16690-6*, Signet Bks.) NAL.

—Hard Candy. 1990. 4.99 o.p. (*0-517-05629-1*) Random Hse. Value Publishing.

—Hard Candy. 1995. 256p. pap. 12.00 (*0-679-76169-1*) Random Hse., Inc.

—Only Child: A Burke Novel. 2002. 288p. 24.00 (*0-375-41487-8*) Knopf, Alfred A. Inc.

—Sacrifice. 2001. E-Book 11.00 (*1-59061-231-0*) Adobe Systems, Inc.

—Sacrifice. 1992. mass mkt. 5.99 o.s.i (*0-8041-0919-2*, Ivy Bks.) Ballantine Bks.

—Sacrifice. 1992. 4.99 o.p. (*0-517-09513-0*) Random Hse. Value Publishing.

—Sacrifice. 1996. 288p. pap. 12.00 (*0-679-76410-0*) Random Hse., Inc.

—Safe House: A Burke Novel. 2001. E-Book 11.00 (*1-59061-225-6*) Adobe Systems, Inc.

—Safe House: A Burke Novel. 1999. 320p. pap. 12.00 (*0-375-70074-9*, Vintage) Knopf Publishing Group.

—Safe House: A Burke Novel. 2001. E-Book 7.99 (*0-375-71912-1*) Random Hse., Inc.

—Strega. 2001. E-Book 11.00 (*1-59061-232-9*) Adobe Systems, Inc.

—Strega. 1991. mass mkt. 5.99 o.s.i (*0-8041-0925-7*, Ivy Bks.) Ballantine Bks.

—Strega. 1987. 293p. 18.95 o.s.i (*0-394-55937-1*) Knopf, Alfred A. Inc.

—Strega. 1988. mass mkt. 4.50 o.p. (*0-451-15179-8*, Signet Bks.) NAL.

—Strega. 1988. 3.99 o.p. (*0-517-68183-8*) Random Hse. Value Publishing.

—Strega. 1996. 304p. pap. 12.00 (*0-679-76409-7*) Random Hse., Inc.

Van Dine, S. S. The Benson Murder Case. reprint ed. lib. bdg. 24.95 (*0-89190-511-1*, Rivercity Pr.) Amereon, Ltd.

—The Benson Murder Case. 1983. 256p. pap. 3.95 o.s.i (*0-684-17976-8*, Macmillan Reference USA) Gale Group.

—The Bishop Murder Case. reprint ed. lib. bdg. 25.95 (*0-89190-512-X*, Rivercity Pr.) Amereon, Ltd.

—The Bishop Murder Case. 1983. 256p. pap. 3.95 o.s.i (*0-684-17977-6*, Macmillan Reference USA) Gale Group.

—The Bishop Murder Case. l.t. ed. 1984. (Philo Vance Mystery Ser.). 453p. reprint ed. 14.95 o.p. (*0-89621-501-6*) Thorndike Pr.

—The Canary Murder Case. reprint ed. lib. bdg. 25.95 (*0-89190-513-8*, Rivercity Pr.) Amereon, Ltd.

—The Canary Murder Case. 1979. pap. 2.25 o.s.i (*0-684-16404-3*, Macmillan Reference USA) Gale Group.

—The Casino Murder Case. 1985. 312p. pap. 3.95 o.p. (*0-684-18503-2*, Macmillan Reference USA) Gale Group.

—The Dragon Murder Case: A Philo Vance Mystery. 1994. 336p. 35.00 (*1-883402-21-2*, Scribner) Simon & Schuster.

—Gracie Allen Murder Case: A Philo Vance Story. 21.95 (*0-8488-0850-9*) Amereon, Ltd.

—Gracie Allen Murder Case: A Philo Vance Story. 1994. 336p. reprint ed. pap. 6.95 (*1-883402-09-3*, Scribner) Simon & Schuster.

—The Greene Murder Case. reprint ed. lib. bdg. 27.95 (*0-89190-514-6*, Rivercity Pr.) Amereon, Ltd.

—The Greene Murder Case. 1980. pap. 2.95 o.s.i (*0-684-16734-4*, Scribner Paper Fiction) Simon & Schuster.

—The Kennel Murder Case: A Philo Vance Mystery. 1984. 312p. pap. 3.95 o.s.i (*0-684-18248-3*, Macmillan Reference USA) Gale Group.

—The Kidnap Murder Case: A Philo Vance Story. 1994. 320p. reprint ed. pap. 7.95 o.s.i (*1-883402-93-X*, Scribner) Simon & Schuster.

—The Scarab Murder Case. 1984. (Philo Vance Mystery Ser.). pap. 4.50 o.s.i (*0-684-18159-2*, Scribner Paper Fiction) Simon & Schuster.

—The Winter Murder Case: A Philo Vance Story. 1993. 196p. pap. 6.95 o.s.i (*1-883402-08-5*, Scribner) Simon & Schuster.

Van Dyke, Henry Jackson. Dead Piano. 1971. 182p. 5.95 o.p. (*0-374-13550-9*) Farrar, Straus & Giroux.

—Dead Piano. 1997. (Old School Bks.). 200p. pap. 10.00 (*0-393-31542-8*) Norton, W. W. & Co., Inc.

Van Horne, Hollie. Speak of the Dead. 2000. 218p. (Orig.). pap. 12.95 (*0-9674552-5-1*) Time Travelers.

Van Lustbader, Eric. Black Blade. 1995. 558p. pap. 27.00 (*0-345-46684-5*, Fawcett) Ballantine Bks.

—Black Blade. abr. ed. 1993. 16.95 o.p. (*1-55800-643-5*) NewStar Media, Inc.

Van Vechten, Carl. Parties. 1977. (Select Bibliographies Reprint Ser.). 25.95 (*0-8369-5758-X*) Ayer Co. Pubs., Inc.

Van Wormer, Laura. Expose. 1999. 384p. (*1-55166-526-3*, Mira Bks.) Harlequin Enterprises, Ltd.

—The Kill Fee. 2003. 352p. (*1-55166-744-4*, Mira Bks.) Harlequin Enterprises, Ltd.

—Riverside Drive. 1997. mass mkt. (*1-55166-303-1*, 1-66303-8, Mira Bks.) Harlequin Enterprises, Ltd.

—Riverside Drive. 1989. mass mkt. 5.95 o.p. (*0-312-91572-1*, St. Martin's Paperbacks) St. Martin's Pr.

—Trouble Becomes Her. 2002. 384p. mass mkt. (*1-55166-947-1*); 2001. 304p. (*1-55166-847-5*) Harlequin Enterprises, Ltd. (Mira Bks.).

—West End. 1998. 603p. mass mkt. (*1-55166-448-8*, 1-66448-1, Mira Bks.) Harlequin Enterprises, Ltd.

Vanderbilt, Gloria. The Memory Book of Starr Faithfull. 1994. 336p. 24.00 o.s.i (*0-394-58775-8*) Knopf, Alfred A. Inc.

Vega Yunqué, Edgardo. No Matter How Much You Promise to Cook or Pay the Rent You Blew It Cauze Bill Bailey Ain't Never Coming Home Again. 2003. 656p. 25.00 (*0-374-22311-4*); pap. (*0-374-96112-3*) Farrar, Straus & Giroux.

Veltri, George. Nice Boy. 1995. 186p. pap. 9.95 (*0-87286-302-6*) City Lights Bks.

Victor, Barbara. Coriander. 1994. mass mkt. 5.99 o.s.i (*0-345-38454-7*) Ballantine Bks.

—Coriander. 1993. 22.00 o.p. (*1-55611-353-6*) Fine, Donald I. Bks.

—Coriander. l.t. ed. 1996. 24.95 o.p. (*1-56895-281-3*, Wheeler Publishing, Inc.) Gale Group.

—Misplaced Lives. 1990. 320p. 19.95 o.p. (*0-06-016373-9*) HarperTrade.

Victor, Cynthia. Only You. l.t. ed. 2000. 463p. 28.95 (*1-57490-322-5*, Beeler Large Print Bks.) Beeler, Thomas T. Publisher.

—Only You. 1995. 416p. mass mkt. 5.99 o.s.i (*0-451-40606-0*, Onyx) NAL.

—Only You. 1994. 416p. 19.95 o.p. (*0-670-84981-2*, Viking) Viking Penguin.

Vida, Vendela. And Now You Can Go. 2003. 208p. 19.95 (*1-4000-4027-2*) Knopf, Alfred A. Inc.

Vinge, Joan D. Catspaw. 2002. (Cat Ser.). 416p. reprint ed. pap. 15.95 (*0-7653-0341-8*, Orb Bks.) Doherty, Tom Assocs., LLC.

Virga, Vincent. Vadriel Vail. 2001. 382p. pap. 14.95 (*1-55583-583-X*) Alyson Pubns.

Wachtel, Chuck. The Gates: A Novel. 1994. 416p. 23.95 o.p. (*0-670-83886-1*, Viking) Viking Penguin.

Wager, Walter. Fifty-Eight Minutes. 1989. mass mkt. 4.95 (*0-8125-1036-4*, Tor Bks.) Doherty, Tom Assocs., LLC.

—Fifty-Eight Minutes: Die Hard II. 1990. mass mkt. 4.95 o.p. (*0-8125-1003-8*, Tor Bks.) Doherty, Tom Assocs., LLC.

—Tunnel. 2000. 317p. 23.95 (*0-312-86488-4*, Forge Bks.) Doherty, Tom Assocs., LLC.

—The Tunnel. 2001. 304p. mass mkt. 6.99 (*0-8125-6467-7*, Forge Bks.) Doherty, Tom Assocs., LLC.

Wald, Noreen. Death Comes for the Critic. 2000. (Ghostwriter Ser.). 240p. mass mkt. 5.99 o.s.i (*0-425-17344-5*) Berkley Publishing Group.

—Death Never Takes a Holiday. 2000. (Ghostwriter Mystery Ser.). 240p. mass mkt. 5.99 o.s.i (*0-425-17744-0*) Berkley Publishing Group.

Walker, Persia. Harlem Redux. 2003. 352p. reprint ed. pap. 12.95 (*0-451-20874-9*) NAL.

—Harlem Redux. 2002. 320p. 23.00 (*0-7432-2497-3*, Simon & Schuster) Simon & Schuster.

—Harlem Redux. 2000. 319p. pap. 16.95 o.p. (*0-595-12921-8*) iUniverse, Inc.

Wallace, Marilyn. Current Danger. 1999. 320p. mass mkt. 5.99 o.s.i (*0-553-58072-8*) Bantam Bks.

—Current Danger. l.t. ed. 1998. 317p. 24.95 (*1-57490-140-0*, Beeler Large Print Bks.) Beeler, Thomas T. Publisher.

Wallach, Anne T. Trials. 1996. 382p. 24.95 o.s.i (*0-525-94091-X*) Dutton/Plume.

—Trials. 1998. 416p. mass mkt. 6.99 o.s.i (*0-451-18741-5*, Signet Bks.) NAL.

Walsh, Michael. Exchange Alley. abr. ed. 1997. audio 19.00 o.p. Beeler, Thomas T. Publisher.

—Exchange Alley. abr. ed. 1997. audio 17.98 (*1-57042-529-9*, 390019) Time Warner AudioBooks.

—Exchange Alley. 1998. 480p. mass mkt. 6.99 (*0-446-60563-8*); 1997. 400p. 23.50 o.p. (*0-446-52069-1*) Warner Bks., Inc.

Warhol, Andy. A: A Novel. 1998. o.p. (*0-8021-3538-2*, Grove Pr.) Grove/Atlantic, Inc.

Warren, John, II. The Torquemada Killer. 1997. 296p. (Orig.). mass mkt. 7.95 o.s.i (*1-56333-367-8*, Rhinoceros) Masquerade Bks., Inc.

Webb, Cynthia. Incidental Darkness. 2002. pap. 12.95 (*0-9705049-9-3*) Avocet Pr., Inc.

Weikart, James. Casualty Loss. 1991. 208p. 18.95 o.s.i (*0-8027-5790-1*) Walker & Co.

Weiner, Ellis. Drop Dead, My Lovely. 2004. 288p. 23.95 (*0-451-21117-0*) NAL.

Weinfeld, Chaya B. New Beginnings. 1999. 288p. 13.95 (*1-880582-46-5*) Judaica Pr., Inc., The.

Weinstein, Debra. Apprentice to the Flower Poet Z: A Novel. 2004. (Illus.). 256p. 23.95 (*1-4000-6155-5*) Random Hse., Inc.

Weinstock, Nicholas. As Long as She Needs Me. 2001. 256p. 22.00 (*0-06-019824-9*, Morrow, William & Co.) Morrow/Avon.

Weisberger, Lauren. The Devil Wears Prada: A Novel. 2004. 368p. pap. 13.95 (*0-7679-1476-7*) Broadway Bks.

—The Devil Wears Prada: A Novel. 2003. 368p. 21.95 (*0-385-50926-X*) Doubleday Publishing.

—The Devil Wears Prada: A Novel. abr. ed. 2003. audio 25.95 (*0-7393-0732-0*, Listening Library) Random Hse. Audio Publishing Group.

—The Devil Wears Prada: A Novel. l.t. ed. 2003. 712p. 29.95 (*0-7862-5575-7*) Thorndike Pr.

Weiss, Daniel Evan. Honk If You Love Aphrodite. 1999. (Illus.). 192p. pap. 13.99 (*1-85242-453-2*) Serpent's Tail Ltd. GBR. *Dist:* Consortium Bk. Sales & Distribution.

Weiss, Phillip. Cock-a-Doodle-Doo. 1995. 256p. 21.00 o.p. (*0-374-12515-5*) Farrar, Straus & Giroux.

—Cock-A-Doodle-Doo. 1996. 304p. pap. 12.95 o.p. (*0-312-14100-9*, Saint Martin's Griffin) St. Martin's Pr.

West, Nathanael. Miss Lonelyhearts & the Day of the Locust. 1962. pap. 9.95 (*0-8112-0215-1*, NDP125) New Directions Publishing Corp.

—Miss Lonelyhearts & the Day of the Locust. 1998. (Modern Library Ser.). 308p. 15.50 o.s.i (*0-679-60278-X*) Random Hse., Inc.

—Novels & Other Writings: The Dream Life of Balso Snell; Miss Lonelyhearts; A Cool Million; The Day of the Locust; Other Writings; Letters. Bercovitch, Sacvan, ed. 1997. (Library of America: Vol. 93). 840p. 35.00 (*1-883011-28-0*) Library of America, The.

Westlake, Donald E. Bad News. l.t. ed. 2001. 344p. lib. bdg. 28.95 (*1-58547-123-2*) Ctr. Point Large Print.

—Bad News. 2001. 352p. 23.95 (*0-89296-717-X*) Mysterious Pr.

—Bad News. 2002. 384p. mass mkt. 7.50 (*0-446-61084-4*) Warner Bks., Inc.

—Bank Shot. unabr. collector's ed. 1996. (Dortmunder Ser.). audio 36.00 (*0-7366-3455-X*, 4099) Books on Tape, Inc.

—Bank Shot. 1987. mass mkt. 3.95 o.s.i (*0-445-40610-0*); 1989. 192p. reprint ed. mass mkt. 5.50 o.s.i (*0-445-40883-9*) Warner Bks., Inc.

—Don't Ask. unabr. collector's ed. 1997. (Dortmunder Ser.). audio 64.00 (*0-7366-3491-6*, 4131) Books on Tape, Inc.

—Don't Ask. 1993. 336p. 18.95 (*0-89296-469-3*) Mysterious Pr.

—Don't Ask. 1994. (Dortmunder Novel Ser.). 352p. reprint ed. mass mkt. 7.50 (*0-446-40095-5*) Warner Bks., Inc.

—Drowned Hopes. unabr. collector's ed. 1997. (Dortmunder Ser.). audio 88.00 (*0-7366-3677-3*, 4357) Books on Tape, Inc.

—Drowned Hopes. 1990. 75.00 (*0-89296-421-9*); 18.95 o.p. (*0-89296-178-3*) Mysterious Pr.

—Drowned Hopes. abr. ed. 1993. 15.95 o.p. (*1-55800-316-9*) NewStar Media, Inc.

—Drowned Hopes. 1991. 464p. mass mkt. 5.99 o.s.i (*0-446-40006-8*) Warner Bks., Inc.

—Good Behavior. unabr. collector's ed. 1997. (Dortmunder Ser.). audio 48.00 (*0-7366-3673-0*, 4350) Books on Tape, Inc.

—Good Behavior. 1988. mass mkt. 3.95 (*0-8125-1060-7*, Tor Bks.) Doherty, Tom Assocs., LLC.

—Good Behavior. l.t. ed. 1987. (General Ser.). 383p. 17.95 o.p. (*0-8161-4275-0*, Macmillan Reference USA) Gale Group.

—Good Behavior. 1986. 256p. 15.45 o.p. (*0-89296-240-2*) Mysterious Pr.

—Good Behavior. 1990. 2.99 o.p. (*0-517-68035-1*) Random Hse. Value Publishing.

—The Hook. 2000. 288p. 23.95 (*0-89296-588-6*) Mysterious Pr.

—The Hook. l.t. ed. 2000. (Americana Ser.). 392p. 29.95 (*0-7862-2466-5*) Thorndike Pr.

—The Hot Rock. unabr. collector's ed. 1996. (Dortmunder Ser.). audio 42.00 (*0-7366-3417-7*, 4063) Books on Tape, Inc.

—The Hot Rock. (Dortmunder Novel Ser.). 2001. 304p. pap. 12.95 (*0-446-67703-5*); 1987. 256p. reprint ed. mass mkt. 5.50 o.s.i (*0-445-40608-9*) Warner Bks., Inc.

—Jimmy the Kid. 1975. mass mkt. 1.50 o.p. (*0-345-24650-0*) Ballantine Bks.

—Jimmy the Kid. unabr. collector's ed. 1996. audio 36.00 (*0-7366-3517-3*, 4154) Books on Tape, Inc.

—Jimmy the Kid. 1974. 192p. 6.95 o.p. (*0-87131-157-7*) Holt, Henry & Co.

—Jimmy the Kid. 192p. 1994. mass mkt. 5.50 (*0-446-40409-8*, Mysterious Pr. Paperback Bks.); 1989. mass mkt. 5.50 o.s.i (*0-445-40747-6*) Warner Bks., Inc.

—Money for Nothing. 2003. 304p. 24.95 (*0-89296-787-0*) Mysterious Pr.

—Nobody's Perfect. 1979. mass mkt. 1.95 o.s.i (*0-449-23909-8*, Fawcett) Ballantine Bks.

—Nobody's Perfect. unabr. collector's ed. 1996. (Dortmunder Ser.: Vol. 4). audio 42.00 (*0-7366-3542-4*, 4189) Books on Tape, Inc.

—Nobody's Perfect. 1977. 228p. 7.95 o.p. (*0-87131-249-2*) Holt, Henry & Co.

—Nobody's Perfect. 1994. pap. (*0-446-40715-1*, Mysterious Pr. Paperback Bks.); 1989. 240p. mass mkt. 5.50 o.s.i (*0-445-40715-8*) Warner Bks., Inc.

—What's the Worst That Could Happen? unabr. collector's ed. 1997. (Dortmunder Ser.). audio 56.00 (*0-7366-3773-7*, 4446) Books on Tape, Inc.

—What's the Worst That Could Happen? 1996. 384p. 22.00 o.p. (*0-89296-586-X*) Mysterious Pr.

—What's the Worst That Could Happen? movie tie-in ed. 1997. (Dortmunder Novel Ser.). 336p. reprint ed. mass mkt. 6.50 (*0-446-60471-2*) Warner Bks., Inc.

—Why Me? unabr. collector's ed. 1997. (Dortmunder Ser.). audio 42.00 (*0-7366-3653-6*, 4318) Books on Tape, Inc.

—Why Me? 1985. 288p. reprint ed. mass mkt. 3.50 (*0-8125-1052-6*, Tor Bks.) Doherty, Tom Assocs., LLC.

—Why Me? 1983. 204p. 13.50 o.p. (*0-670-76569-4*) Viking Penguin.

—Why Me? 1994. 240p. mass mkt. 5.50 (*0-446-40346-6*) Warner Bks., Inc.

Westlake, Donald E., ed. Money for Nothing. 2004. 336p. mass mkt. 7.50 (*0-446-61378-9*) Warner Bks., Inc.

Wharton, Edith. The Buccaneers, Set. 1996. audio 41.95 (*1-55685-427-7*) Audio Bk. Contractors, Inc.

—The Buccaneers. unabr. ed. 1994. audio 72.00 (*0-7366-2717-0*, 3447) Books on Tape, Inc.

—The Buccaneers. 2000. (Illus.). 414p. reprint ed. 16.00 (*0-7881-9371-6*) DIANE Publishing Co.

—The Buccaneers. Mainwaring, Marion, ed. l.t. ed. 1994. 26.95 (*1-56895-062-4*, Wheeler Publishing, Inc.) Gale Group.

—The Buccaneers. 1995. (Illus.). 448p. 15.95 o.p. (*0-670-86645-8*, Viking); 1969. pap. 3.50 o.p. (*0-14-044212-X*, Penguin Classics); 1994. 384p. reprint ed. 13.00 (*0-14-023202-8*) Viking Penguin.

—The Collected Short Stories of Edith Wharton, Vol. 1. Lewis, R. W. B., ed. 1987. (Hudson River Editions Ser.). 752p. 60.00 (*0-02-570600-4*, Macmillan Reference USA) Gale Group.

—The Custom of the Country. 608p. 1976. 55.00 (*0-684-14655-X*); 1910. pap. 12.95 o.s.i (*0-684-71926-6*) Gale Group. (Macmillan Reference USA).

—The Custom of the Country. 1994. (Everyman's Library). 448p. 17.00 (*0-679-42301-X*) Knopf, Alfred A. Inc.

—The Custom of the Country. 1989. mass mkt. 4.95 o.p. (*0-451-52367-9*, Signet Classics) NAL.

—The Custom of the Country. Orgel, Stephen, ed. 1995. (Oxford World's Classics Ser.). 406p. pap. 9.95 o.p. (*0-19-282288-8*) Oxford Univ. Pr., Inc.

—Edith Wharton: Three Complete Novels, 3 bks. in 1. 1994. 672p. 11.99 o.s.i (*0-517-11828-9*) Random Hse. Value Publishing.

—Four Novels: The House of Mirth; Ethan Frome; The Custom of the Country; The Age of Innocence. 1996. (Library of America). 1168p. (C). pap. 13.95 (*1-883011-37-X*) Library of America, The.

—The Greater Inclination. reprint ed. 29.50 (*0-404-06913-4*) AMS Pr., Inc.

—The Greater Inclination. 1914. reprint ed. 15.00 (*0-403-00188-9*) Scholarly Pr., Inc.

—The House of Mirth. 2000. 252p. E-Book 3.95 (*0-594-06337-X*) 1873 Pr.

—The House of Mirth. Benstock, Shari, ed. 1993. (Case Studies in Contemporary Criticism). 498p. pap. text 9.50 (*0-312-06234-6*) Bedford/Saint Martin's.

—The House of Mirth. 1990. (Vintage-Library of America ). 384p. pap. 11.50 o.s.i (*0-679-72539-3*, Vintage) Knopf Publishing Group.

—The House of Mirth. 1998. 380p. reprint ed. lib. bdg. 25.00 (*1-58287-090-X*) North Bks.

—The House of Mirth. Ammons, Elizabeth, ed. 1990. (Critical Editions Ser.). 374p. (C). pap. text 9.00 net. (*0-393-95901-5*) Norton, W. W. & Co., Inc.

—The House of Mirth. Banta, Martha, ed. 1994. (Oxford World's Classics Ser.). 366p. pap. 6.95 o.p. (*0-19-282944-0*) Oxford Univ. Pr., Inc.

—The Mother's Recompense. (Collected Works of Edith Wharton). 341p. reprint ed. 2001. (Illus.). pap. text 28.00 (*0-7426-5988-7*); 1998. lib. bdg. 98.00 (*1-58201-988-6*) Classic Bks.

—The Mother's Recompense. 1986. 342p. 15.95 o.s.i (*0-684-18771-X*); pap. 12.00 (*0-684-18737-X*) Gale Group. (Macmillan Reference USA).

—The Mother's Recompense. 1996. 288p. pap. 13.00 (*0-684-82531-7*, Scribner) Simon & Schuster.

—Novels: The House of Mirth; The Reef; The Custom of the Country; The Age of Innocence. Lewis, R. W. B., ed. 1986. 1328p. 40.00 (*0-940450-31-3*) Library of America, The.

—The Old Maid: The 'Fifties. 2003. 144p. pap. 10.95 (*0-8129-7002-0*, Modern Library) Random House Adult Trade Publishing Group.

—Old New York. 1981. mass mkt. 2.95 o.p. (*0-425-04612-5*) Berkley Publishing Group.

—Old New York. (Collected Works of Edith Wharton). reprint ed. 2001. pap. text 112.00 (*0-7426-5990-9*); 1998. lib. bdg. 480.00 (*1-58201-990-8*) Classic Bks.

—Old New York. 1987. xiv, 306p. o.s.i (*0-86068-490-3*) Random Hse., Inc.

—Old New York. (Enriched Classics Ser.). 2002. 320p. mass mkt. 6.99 (*0-7434-5149-X*); 1998. 336p. pap. 6.99 (*0-671-02336-5*) Simon & Schuster. (Pocket).

—Short Stories. unabr. ed. 1994. (Thrift Editions Ser.). (Illus.). 128p. pap. 2.00 (*0-486-28235-X*) Dover Pubns., Inc.

—Three Novels of Old New York: The House of Mirth; The Custom of the the Country; The Age of Innocence. 1997. (Penguin Twentieth-Century Classics Ser.). 992p. pap. 16.95 o.p. (*0-14-018984-X*) Viking Penguin.

Wharton, Edith & Mainwaring, Marion. The Buccaneers. abr. ed. 1993. (Classics on Cassette). 16.00 o.p. incl. audio (*0-453-00854-2*, 390454) Penguin/HighBridge.

—The Buccaneers. 1993. 416p. 22.00 o.p. (*0-670-85219-8*, Viking) Viking Penguin.

Wharton, Edith & Wharton, Tom. The House of Mirth. 1991. 370p. 17.00 o.s.i (*0-679-40667-0*) Random Hse., Inc.

Wheat, Carolyn. Dead Man's Thoughts. 1995. 240p. mass mkt. 4.99 o.p. (*0-425-14933-1*) Berkley Publishing Group.

—Dead Man's Thoughts. 1983. 256p. 14.95 o.p. (*0-312-18501-4*) St. Martin's Pr.

—Fresh Kills. 240p. (Orig.). 1996. mass mkt. 5.50 o.s.i (*0-425-15276-6*); 1995. 19.95 o.p. (*0-425-14785-1*, Prime Crime); 1995. pap. 9.00 o.p. (*0-425-14920-X*, Prime Crime) Berkley Publishing Group.

—Mean Streak. (Cass Jameson Legal Mysteries Ser.). 240p. 1997. mass mkt. 5.99 o.s.i (*0-425-15577-3*); 1996. 19.95 o.p. (*0-425-15317-7*) Berkley Publishing Group. (Prime Crime).

—Sworn to Defend. (Cass Jameson Legal Mysteries Ser.). 320p. 1998. 22.95 o.s.i (*0-425-16303-2*); 1999. reprint ed. mass mkt. 5.99 o.s.i (*0-425-16932-4*) Berkley Publishing Group. (Prime Crime).

—Troubled Waters. (Cass Jameson Legal Mysteries Ser.). 1998. 256p. mass mkt. 5.99 o.s.i (*0-425-16380-6*); 1997. 240p. 21.95 o.s.i (*0-425-15784-9*) Berkley Publishing Group. (Prime Crime).

—Troubled Waters. 1998. 12.04 (*0-606-15743-3*) Turtleback Bks.

—Where Nobody Dies. 1988. 240p. mass mkt. 3.50 o.s.i (*0-553-27369-8*) Bantam Bks.

—Where Nobody Dies. 1996. (Cass Jameson Legal Mysteries Ser.). 272p. mass mkt. 5.99 o.s.i (*0-425-15408-4*, Prime Crime) Berkley Publishing Group.

—Where Nobody Dies. 1986. 288p. 15.95 o.p. (*0-312-86700-X*) St. Martin's Pr.

White, Ellen E. All Emergencies, Ring Super. (Dead Letter Mysteries Ser.). 300p. 1998. pap. 5.99 (*0-312-96601-6*, St. Martin's Paperbacks); 1997. 22.95 o.p. (*0-312-15651-0*, Saint Martin's Minotaur) St. Martin's Pr.

White, Kate. A Body to Die For. l.t. ed. 2003. 460p. 30.95 (*0-7862-5767-9*) Thorndike Pr.

—A Body to Die For. 2004. 400p. mass mkt. 6.99 (*0-446-61385-1*); 2003. 304p. 23.95 (*0-446-53148-0*) Warner Bks., Inc.

—If Looks Could Kill. l.t. ed. 2002. (Core Collection). 470p. 28.95 o.p. (*0-7862-4497-6*) Thorndike Pr.

—If Looks Could Kill. (Bailey Wiggins Mystery Ser.). 2002. 336p. 22.95 o.p. (*0-446-53023-9*); 2003. 416p. reprint ed. mass mkt. 6.99 (*0-446-61257-X*) Warner Bks., Inc.

Whitman, Stephen F. Predestined: A Novel of New York Life. 1974. (Lost American Fiction Ser.). 486p. reprint ed. 8.95 o.p. (*0-8093-0701-4*) Southern Illinois Univ. Pr.

Whitney, Polly. Until Death. 1996. per. (*0-373-26219-1*, 1-26219-5, Worldwide Library) Harlequin Enterprises, Ltd.

—Until Death. 1994. 320p. 21.95 o.p. (*0-312-11089-8*, Saint Martin's Minotaur) St. Martin's Pr.

—Until It Hurts. 1998. (Worldwide Library Mysteries: Vol. 272). per. (*0-373-26272-8*, 0-26272-5, Worldwide Library) Harlequin Enterprises, Ltd.

—Until It Hurts: An Ike & Abby Mystery. 1997. 304p. 22.95 (*0-312-15237-X*, Saint Martin's Minotaur) St. Martin's Pr.

—Until the End of Time. 1997. per. (*0-373-26233-7*, 1-26233-6, Worldwide Library) Harlequin Enterprises, Ltd.

—Until the End of Time. 1995. 272p. 21.95 o.p. (*0-312-13199-2*, Saint Martin's Minotaur) St. Martin's Pr.

Whyte, Anthony J. Ghetto Falsehoods. 2001. 244p. pap. 19.95 (*1-58721-772-4*) 1stBooks Library.

Wibberley, Leonard. The Mouse That Roared. 20.95 (*0-8488-0190-3*) Amereon, Ltd.

—The Mouse That Roared. 1992. 288p. reprint ed. lib. bdg. 27.95 (*0-89966-887-9*) Buccaneer Bks., Inc.

—The Mouse That Roared. 1963. 5.95 (*0-87129-455-9*, M36) Dramatic Publishing Co.

—The Mouse That Roared. 2003. 288p. pap. 13.95 (*1-56858-249-8*) Four Walls Eight Windows.

—The Mouse That Roared. l.t. ed. 1997. (Perennial Ser.). 242p. 22.95 (*0-7838-8189-4*) Thorndike Pr.

Wilbee, Brenda. Shipwreck! 1991. (Classic Women of Faith Ser.). 256p. pap. 7.99 o.p. (*0-89081-858-4*) Harvest Hse. Pubs.

Wilcox, James. Guest of a Sinner: A Novel. 1993. 288p. 20.00 o.p. (*0-06-016875-7*) HarperTrade.

—Guest of a Sinner: A Novel. 2004. (Voices of the South Ser.). 288p. pap. (*0-8071-2969-0*) Louisiana State Univ. Pr.

—Polite Sex: A Novel. 1991. 228p. 19.95 o.p. (*0-06-016356-9*); 1993. 288p. reprint ed. pap. 12.00 o.p. (*0-06-092165-X*, Perennial) HarperTrade.

—Polite Sex: A Novel. 1999. pap. (*0-316-94010-0*); 288p. pap. 13.00 (*0-316-94134-4*, Back Bay) Little Brown & Co.

Wilhelm, Kate. The Casebook of Constance & Charlie. Vol. 1. 1999. 614p. pap. 18.95 (*0-312-24501-7*); Vol. 2. 2000. 595p. pap. 16.95 (*0-312-25378-8*) St. Martin's Pr. (Saint Martin's Griffin).

—The Dark Door. 1993. 352p. pap. 4.50 (*0-8439-3416-6*) Dorchester Publishing Co., Inc.

—The Dark Door. 1988. 256p. 16.95 o.p. (*0-312-02182-8*) St. Martin's Pr.

—A Flush of Shadows: Five Short Novels. 1996. mass mkt. 5.99 o.s.i (*0-449-22434-1*, Fawcett) Ballantine Bks.

—A Flush of Shadows: Five Short Novels. 1995. 352p. 22.95 o.p. (*0-312-13075-9*, Saint Martin's Minotaur) St. Martin's Pr.

—Hamlet Trap: A Charlie Meiklejohn & Constance Leidl Mystery. 1988. mass mkt. 4.50 (*0-312-91125-4*, St. Martin's Paperbacks) St. Martin's Pr.

—The Hamlet Trap: A Constance & Charlie Micklejohn Mystery. 1987. 240p. 15.95 o.p. (*0-312-94000-9*, Saint Martin's Minotaur) St. Martin's Pr.

—Seven Kinds of Death. 1994. 256p. reprint ed. pap. 4.50 (*0-8439-3570-7*) Dorchester Publishing Co., Inc.

—Seven Kinds of Death. 1992. 256p. 18.95 o.p. (*0-312-08290-8*, Saint Martin's Minotaur) St. Martin's Pr.

—Smart House. l.t. ed. 1991. 16.95 o.p. (*0-7451-9790-6*, C0300); pap. 15.95 o.p. (*0-7927-0255-7*, C0434) BBC Audiobooks America.

—Smart House. 1991. 272p. reprint ed. pap. 3.95 (*0-8439-3043-8*) Dorchester Publishing Co., Inc.

—Smart House: A Charlie Meiklejohn-Constance Leidl Mystery. 1989. 272p. 16.95 o.p. (*0-312-02642-0*, Saint Martin's Minotaur) St. Martin's Pr.

—Sweet, Sweet Poison. 1991. 272p. reprint ed. pap. 3.99 (*0-8439-3163-9*) Dorchester Publishing Co., Inc.

—Sweet, Sweet Poison. 1990. 16.95 o.p. (*0-312-04433-X*, Saint Martin's Minotaur) St. Martin's Pr.

Wilkinson, Lee. Ruthless! 2002. mass mkt. (*0-373-80519-5*, 1-805191, Harlequin Bks.) Harlequin Enterprises, Ltd.

Willis, Sarah. Some Things That Stay: Novel. 2001. 288p. reprint ed. pap. 14.00 (*0-425-17960-5*) Berkley Publishing Group.

Wilson, A. N. Hearing Voices. 1997. 224p. pap. 12.00 (*0-393-31633-5*) Norton, W. W. & Co., Inc.

Wilson, Barbara J. Accessory to Murder. 1998. (Brenda Midnight Mysteries Ser.). mass mkt. 5.50 (*0-380-78821-7*, Avon Bks.) Morrow/Avon.

—Capped Off. 1999. (Brenda Midnight Mysteries Ser.). 256p. mass mkt. 5.99 (*0-380-80355-0*, Avon Bks.) Morrow/Avon.

—Death Brims Over. 1997. (Brenda Midnight Mysteries Ser.). mass mkt. 5.50 (*0-380-78820-9*, Avon Bks.) Morrow/Avon.

—Death Flips It's Lid. 1998. (Brenda Midnight Mysteries Ser.). mass mkt. 5.99 (*0-380-78822-5*, Avon Bks.) Morrow/Avon.

Wilson, Edmund. The Higher Jazz. Reinitz, Neale, ed. 1998. 224p. pap. 17.95 (*0-87745-655-0*); text 34.95 (*0-87745-653-4*) Univ. of Iowa Pr.

—I Thought of Daisy. 2001. vii, 278p. 12.95 (*0-87745-769-7*) Univ. of Iowa Pr.

Wilson, F. Paul. The Haunted Air: A Repairman Jack Novel. 2002. (Repairman Jack Ser.). 416p. 24.95 (*0-312-87868-0*, Tor Bks.) Doherty, Tom Assocs., LLC.

—The Haunted Air: A Repairman Jack Novel. 2002. (Repairman Jack Ser.). 50.00 (*1-887368-57-4*) Gauntlet, Inc.

—Legacies. 2000. 440p. mass mkt. 6.99 (*0-8125-7199-1*); 1998. 352p. 24.95 o.p. (*0-312-86414-0*) Doherty, Tom Assocs., LLC. (Forge Bks.).

—The Tomb. 1986. 410p. mass mkt. 5.99 o.s.i (*0-515-08876-5*, Jove); 1984. 416p. mass mkt. 3.95 o.s.i (*0-425-07295-9*) Berkley Publishing Group.

—The Tomb. 1998. (Repairman Jack Ser.). 448p. mass mkt. 7.99 (*0-8125-8037-0*, Tor Bks.) Doherty, Tom Assocs., LLC.

—The Tomb. 1984. 19.95 o.p. (*0-918372-11-9*); 41.00 o.p. (*0-918372-12-7*) Whispers Pr.

Wilson, F. Paul & Lyon, Steve. Nightkill. 1999. 288p. mass mkt. 6.99 (*0-8125-6536-3*, Tor Bks.); 1997. 304p. 23.95 (*0-312-85910-4*, Forge Bks.) Doherty, Tom Assocs., LLC.

Wiltse, David. Blown Away. l.t. ed. 1997. 368p. mass mkt. 6.50 o.s.i (*0-425-15971-X*) Berkley Publishing Group.

—Blown Away. l.t. ed. 1997. (G. K. Hall Core Ser.). 469p. lib. bdg. 26.95 (*0-7838-2009-7*, Macmillan Reference USA) Gale Group.

—Blown Away. 1996. 352p. 24.95 o.s.i (*0-399-14208-8*, G. P. Putnam's Sons) Penguin Group (USA) Inc.

—Blown Away: A John Becker Thriller. abr. ed. 1997. audio 17.00 (*1-56876-063-9*) Soundlines Entertainment, Inc.

—Close to the Bone. 1993. 352p. mass mkt. 6.50 o.s.i (*0-425-13976-X*) Berkley Publishing Group.

—Close to the Bone. 1992. 304p. 21.95 o.p. (*0-399-13718-1*, G. P. Putnam's Sons) Penguin Group (USA) Inc.

—The Edge of Sleep. 1994. 368p. reprint ed. mass mkt. 5.99 o.s.i (*0-425-14333-3*) Berkley Publishing Group.

—The Edge of Sleep. 1993. 320p. 22.95 o.p. (*0-399-13880-3*, G. P. Putnam's Sons) Penguin Group (USA) Inc.

—Into the Fire. 1995. 384p. mass mkt. 6.99 o.s.i (*0-425-15012-7*) Berkley Publishing Group.

—Into the Fire. 1994. 320p. 22.95 o.p. (*0-399-13969-9*, G. P. Putnam's Sons) Penguin Group (USA) Inc.

Wimmer, Dick. The Irish Wine Trilogy. 2001. 320p. 13.00 (*0-14-100059-7*) Viking Penguin.

Winslow, Don. Cool Breeze on the Underground. 1991. 17.95 o.p. (*0-312-05407-6*, Saint Martin's Minotaur) St. Martin's Pr.

Winslow, Pauline G. Cry in the City. 1990. 16.95 o.p. (*0-312-04289-2*, Saint Martin's Minotaur) St. Martin's Pr.

Winthrop, Elizabeth. In My Mother's House. 1989. mass mkt. 4.95 o.p. (*0-451-16657-4*); mass mkt. 4.50 o.p. (*0-451-16260-9*) NAL. (Signet Bks.).

Wishnia, K. J. A. Flat Rate & Other Tales. 1997. vi, 106p. (Orig.). pap. 4.95 (*0-9656814-0-8*) Imaginary Pr., The.

—Red House. 2002. E-Book 23.95 (*1-59061-727-4*) Adobe Systems, Inc.

—Red House. 2002. 288p. mass mkt. 6.50 (*0-312-98500-2*, St. Martin's Paperbacks) St. Martin's Pr.

—Red House: A Filomena Buscarsela Mystery. 2001. 288p. 23.95 (*0-312-28182-X*, Saint Martin's Minotaur) St. Martin's Pr.

—Soft Money. 1999. (Filomena Se La Busca Misteriosamente Ser.). 226p. 23.95 o.p. (*0-525-94501-6*) Dutton/Plume.

—23 Shades of Black. 1997. pap. text 7.95 o.p. (*0-9656814-1-6*) Imaginary Pr., The.

—23 Shades of Black. 1998. (Filomena Buscarsela Mysteries Ser.). 304p. mass mkt. 6.99 o.s.i (*0-451-19748-8*, Signet Bks.) NAL.

—23 Shades of Black. 1998. 13.04 (*0-606-15828-6*) Turtleback Bks.

Witchel, Alex. Me Times Three: A Novel. 2003. 320p. reprint ed. pap. 13.00 (*0-7432-4085-5*, Touchstone) Simon & Schuster.

Wolf, Laura. Diary of a Mad Bride. 2002. 304p. pap. 10.95 (*0-385-33583-0*, Delta) Dell Publishing.

Wolfe, Thomas. The Party at Jack's: A Novella. Stutman, Suzanne & Idol, John L., Jr., eds. 1995. 290p. pap. 24.95 o.p. (*0-8078-2206-X*) Univ. of North Carolina Pr.

—The Web & the Rock. 1939. lib. bdg. o.p. (*0-06-014706-7*); 1973. 640p. reprint ed. mass mkt. o.p. (*0-06-080313-4*, P313) HarperCollins Pubs.

—The Web & the Rock. 1986. 704p. pap. 10.95 o.p. (*0-06-091320-7*, PL 1320, Perennial) HarperTrade.

—The Web & the Rock. 1999. (Voices of the South Ser.). 712p. pap. 19.95 (*0-8071-2389-7*) Louisiana State Univ. Pr.

Wolfe, Tom. The Bonfire of the Vanities. 2001. 656p. pap. 14.95 (*0-553-38134-2*) Bantam Bks.

—The Bonfire of the Vanities. 552p. 1989. 75.00 o.p. (*0-374-11535-4*); 1990. 25.00 (*0-374-11537-0*) Farrar, Straus & Giroux.

—The Bonfire of the Vanities. l.t. ed. 1989. 992p. 21.95 o.p. (*0-8161-4742-6*); pap. 13.95 o.p. (*0-8161-4745-0*) Gale Group. (Macmillan Reference USA).

—Two Complete Books. 1994. 784p. 13.99 o.s.i (*0-517-11998-6*) Random Hse., Inc.

Wolitzer, Hilma. Silver. 1989. mass mkt. 4.95 o.s.i (*0-8041-0485-9*, Ivy Bks.) Ballantine Bks.

—Silver. 1988. 352p. 18.95 o.s.i (*0-374-26422-8*) Farrar, Straus & Giroux.

—Silver. l.t. ed. 1989. (General Ser.). 384p. pap. 13.95 o.p. (*0-8161-4933-X*); lib. bdg. 20.95 o.p. (*0-8161-4743-4*) Gale Group. (Macmillan Reference USA).

Wolitzer, Meg. Surrender, Dorothy. 1999. 224p. 22.00 (*0-684-84844-9*); 2000. 240p. reprint ed. pap. 12.95 (*0-671-04254-8*) Simon & Schuster. (Scribner).

Womack, Jack. Going, Going, Gone. 224p. 2002. pap. 13.00 (*0-8021-3866-7*, Grove Pr.); 2001. 24.00 o.p. (*0-8021-1685-X*) Grove/Atlantic, Inc.

—Random Acts of Senseless Violence. 256p. 1995. pap. 13.50 (*0-8021-3424-6*, Grove Pr.); 1994. 21.00 o.p. (*0-87113-577-9*, Atlantic Monthly Pr.) Grove/Atlantic, Inc.

Wood, Valerie. Far from Home. 2004. 560p. mass mkt. (*0-552-15032-0*, Corgi) Bantam Bks.

Woods, Stuart. Cold Paradise. l.t. ed. 2001. 523p. 32.95 (*0-7838-9470-8*, Macmillan Reference USA) Gale Group.

—Cold Paradise. 2002. 432p. reprint ed. mass mkt. 7.99 (*0-451-20562-6*, Signet Bks.) NAL.

—Cold Paradise. 2001. 352p. 24.95 o.p. (*0-399-14736-5*) Penguin Group (USA) Inc.

—Cold Paradise. l.t. ed. 2002. (Paperback Bestsellers Ser.). 440p. pap. 29.95 (*0-7838-9471-6*) Thorndike Pr.

—Dead in the Water. unabr. ed. 1997. audio 56.00 (*0-7366-3753-2*, 4428) Books on Tape, Inc.

—Dead in the Water. l.t. ed. 1997. 26.95 o.p. (*1-56895-508-1*, Wheeler Publishing, Inc.) Gale Group.

—Dead in the Water. 1998. 432p. mass mkt. 7.99 (*0-06-109349-1*) HarperCollins Pubs.

—Dead in the Water. 1997. 336p. 25.00 o.p. (*0-06-018368-3*, HarperCollins);Set. 5p. audio 19.95 (*0-694-51849-2*, 495369, HarperAudio) HarperTrade.

—Dead in the Water. unabr. ed. 1999. audio compact disk 79.00 (*0-7887-3423-7*, C1029E7); 1997. audio 70.00 (*0-7887-1776-6*, 95250E7) Recorded Bks., LLC.

—Dirt. unabr. ed. 1996. audio 48.00 (*0-913369-26-8*, 4177) Books on Tape, Inc.

—Dirt. l.t. ed. 1997. (Large Print Bks.). 26.95 o.p. (*1-56895-398-4*, Wheeler Publishing, Inc.) Gale Group.

—Dirt. 1996. 288p. 24.00 o.p. (*0-06-017666-0*) HarperCollins Pubs.

—Dirt, Set. abr. ed. 1996. audio 18.00 o.s.i (*0-694-51723-2*, 394233, HarperAudio) HarperTrade.

—Dirt. 1997. 448p. mass mkt. 7.99 (*0-06-109423-4*, HarperTorch) Morrow/Avon.

—Dirt, unabr. ed. audio 51.00 (*0-7887-0630-6*, 94805E7) Recorded Bks., LLC.

—Dirty Work. l.t. ed. (Stone Barrington Ser.). 436p. 28.95 (*1-58724-440-3*, Wheeler Publishing, Inc.) Gale Group.

—Dirty Work. 2003. 368p. mass mkt. 7.99 (*0-451-21015-8*, Signet Bks.) NAL.

—Dirty Work. 2003. (Stone Barrington Ser.). 336p. 25.95 (*0-399-14982-1*) Penguin Group (USA) Inc.

—Dirty Work. abr. ed. 2003. (Stone Barrington Ser.). audio 25.95 (*0-399-14994-5*, Putnam Berkley Audio) Putnam Publishing Group, The.

—L. A. Dead. l.t. ed. 2000. (Hardcover Ser.). 409p. 29.95 (*1-56895-999-0*, Wheeler Publishing, Inc.) Gale Group.

—L. A. Dead. 2000. (Stone Barrington Ser.). 352p. 24.95 o.s.i (*0-399-14664-4*) Penguin Group (USA) Inc.

—New York Dead. l.t. ed. 1993. pap. 17.95 o.p. (*0-7927-1368-0*); 1992. 19.95 o.p. (*0-7927-1369-9*) BBC Audiobooks America.

—New York Dead. 1991. 320p. 20.00 o.p. (*0-06-017925-2*) HarperTrade.

—New York Dead, abr. ed. 1999. audio 25.00 Highsmith Inc.

—New York Dead. 1995. 79p. mass mkt. 3.99 o.p. (*0-06-109478-1*); 1992. 352p. mass mkt. 7.99 (*0-06-109080-8*) Morrow/Avon. (HarperTorch).

—Reckless Abandon. 2004. 336p. 25.95 (*0-399-15151-6*) Putnam Publishing Group, The.

—The Short Forever. l.t. ed. 2002. (Wheeler Large Print Book Ser.). 29.95 (*1-58724-215-X*, Wheeler Publishing, Inc.) Gale Group.

—The Short Forever. 2003. 368p. reprint ed. mass mkt. 7.99 (*0-451-20808-0*, Signet Bks.) NAL.

—The Short Forever. 2002. 336p. 24.95 o.s.i (*0-399-14868-X*) Putnam Publishing Group, The.

—Swimming to Catalina. unabr. ed. 1998. audio 64.00 (*0-7366-4188-2*, 4686) Books on Tape, Inc.

—Swimming to Catalina. l.t. ed. 1998. (Wheeler Large Print Book Ser.). 27.95 (*1-56895-620-7*, Wheeler Publishing, Inc.) Gale Group.

—Swimming to Catalina. 1998. 320p. 25.00 o.s.i (*0-06-018369-1*) HarperCollins Pubs.

—Swimming to Catalina. abr. ed. 2004. audio 14.95 (*0-06-072533-8*); Set. 1998. audio 25.00 (*0-694-51938-3*, 693583) HarperTrade. (HarperAudio).

—Swimming to Catalina. 1998. 416p. mass mkt. 7.99 (*0-06-109980-5*, HarperTorch) Morrow/Avon.

—Swimming to Catalina, unabr. ed. 1998. audio 60.00 (*0-7887-1973-4*, 95360E7) Recorded Bks., LLC.

—Worst Fears Realized. 2000. 416p. mass mkt. 7.99 (*0-06-101342-0*); Set. 1999. 336p. 25.00 o.p. (*0-06-019182-1*) HarperCollins Pubs.

—Worst Fears Realized, Set. abr. ed. 1999. audio 25.00 (*0-694-52150-7*, HarperAudio) HarperTrade.

—Worst Fears Realized, Set. abr. ed. 1999. audio 25.00 Highsmith Inc.

Woodson, Jacqueline. Autobiography of a Family Photo: A Novel. 1995. 128p. 17.95 o.s.i (*0-525-93721-8*) Dutton/Plume.

Woolf, Douglas. Fade Out. 1996. 275p. (C). 30.00 (*0-87685-989-9*, Black Sparrow Pr.) Godine, David R. Pub.

—Fade Out. 1996. (C). 275p. 25.00 (*0-87685-988-0*); 273p. pap. 14.00 (*0-87685-987-2*) HarperCollins Pubs.

Woolridge, Lori Bryant. Read Between the Lies. 2000. 528p. mass mkt. 6.99 (*0-446-60911-0*) Warner Bks., Inc.

Wouk, Herman. The Caine Mutiny. 1992. 560p. reprint ed. pap. 14.95 (*0-316-95510-8*, Back Bay) Little Brown & Co.

—City Boy: The Adventures of Herbie Bookbinder. 1968. 12.95 o.s.i (*0-385-04072-5*) Doubleday Publishing.

—City Boy: The Adventures of Herbie Bookbinder. 1992. 352p. pap. 15.95 (*0-316-95511-6*) Little Brown & Co.

—City Boy: The Adventures of Herbie Bookbinder. 1983. mass mkt. 4.95 o.s.i (*0-671-46013-7*, Pocket) Simon & Schuster.

Wright, Charles. Absolutely Nothing to Get Alarmed About: The Complete Novels of Charles Wright. 1993. 624p. pap. 13.00 o.p. (*0-06-096958-X*, Perennial) HarperTrade.

—The Wig. 2003. (NEA Heritage & Preservation Ser.: Vol. 2). 192p. pap. 14.95 (*1-56279-127-3*) Mercury Hse.

Wright, Richard. Savage Holiday. 1975. 220p. reprint ed. 8.50 o.p. (*0-911860-54-1*) Chatham Bookseller.

—Savage Holiday. 1995. (Banner Bks.). 220p. reprint ed. pap. 20.00 (*0-87805-750-1*); lib. bdg. 40.00 (*0-87805-749-8*) Univ. Pr. of Mississippi.

Wright, Richard B. Clara Callan: A Novel. 2002. 432p. 25.95 (*0-06-050606-7*) HarperCollins Pubs.

—Clara Callan: A Novel. 2003. 432p. pap. 13.95 (*0-06-050607-5*, Perennial) HarperTrade.

Yablonsky, Linda. The Story of Junk: A Novel. 1997. 325p. 23.00 o.p. (*0-374-27024-4*) Farrar, Straus & Giroux.

—Story of Junk: A Novel. 1998. 336p. pap. 12.95 (*0-316-96808-0*) Little Brown & Co.

Yaffe, James. My Mother, the Detective: The Complete "Mom" Short Stories. 1996. 175p. pap. 15.00 (*1-885941-11-0*); 40.00 o.p. (*1-885941-10-2*) Crippen & Landru, Pubs.

Yager, Fred & Yager, Jan. Untimely Death: A Novel. 1998. 308p. 24.95 (*1-889262-01-3*) Hannacroix Creek Bks., Inc.

Yamada, Amy. Trash: A Novel. Noma, Chikako & Bell, Susan, eds. Johnson, Sonya L., tr. 1995. 384p. 18.00 (*1-56836-018-5*) Kodansha America, Inc.

Yapalater, Karin. An Hour to Kill. 2003. 288p. 23.95 (*0-688-16599-0*, Morrow, William & Co.) Morrow/Avon.

Yates, Richard. Cold Spring Harbor. 1986. 192p. 16.95 o.s.i (*0-385-29502-2*, Delacorte Pr.) Dell Publishing.

Yau, John. Hawaiian Cowboys. 1995. 169p. (C). 25.00 (*0-87685-957-0*);signed ed. 35.00 o.p. (*0-87685-958-9*) Godine, David R. Pub. (Black Sparrow Pr.).

—Hawaiian Cowboys. 1995. 169p. (C). pap. 13.50 (*0-87685-956-2*) HarperCollins Pubs.

Yeager, Dorian. Cancellation by Death. 1994. (WWL Mystery Ser.). per. (*0-373-26159-4*, 1-26159-3, Harlequin Bks.) Harlequin Enterprises, Ltd.

—Cancellation by Death. 1992. 240p. 17.95 o.p. (*0-312-08152-9*, Saint Martin's Minotaur) St. Martin's Pr.

—Eviction by Death. 1995. per. (*0-373-26176-4*, Harlequin Bks.) Harlequin Enterprises, Ltd.

—Eviction by Death: A Victoria Bowering Mystery. 1993. 192p. 17.95 o.p. (*0-312-09803-0*, Saint Martin's Minotaur) St. Martin's Pr.

—Libation by Death. 1998. (Vic Bowering Mystery Ser.). 240p. 21.95 (*0-312-18128-0*, 874692, Saint Martin's Minotaur) St. Martin's Pr.

—Ovation by Death. 1996. 208p. 20.95 o.p. (*0-312-14022-3*, Saint Martin's Minotaur) St. Martin's Pr.

Yezierska, Anzia. Arrogant Beggar. 1996. 192p. pap. 18.95 (*0-8223-1749-4*); text 59.95 (*0-8223-1752-4*) Duke Univ. Pr.

—How I Found America: Collected Stories of Anzia Yezierska. 1995. 272p. (C). pap. 11.95 (*0-89255-211-5*); 1980. 352p. 24.95 o.p. (*0-89255-160-7*) Persea Bks., Inc.

—Hungry Hearts. 1975. (Modern Jewish Experience Ser.). reprint ed. 26.95 (*0-405-06754-2*) Ayer Co. Pubs., Inc.

—Hungry Hearts & Other Stories. 1985. 364p. (Orig.). (C). pap. 9.95 o.p. (*0-89255-093-7*) Persea Bks., Inc.

Yglesias, Rafael. Only Children. 1988. 420p. 19.95 o.p. (*0-688-07219-4*, Morrow, William & Co.) Morrow/Avon.

Young, Jim. Armed Memory. 1996. 246p. pap. text 5.99 (*0-8125-5027-7*); 1995. 256p. 21.95 o.p. (*0-312-85766-7*) Doherty, Tom Assocs., LLC. (Tor Bks.).

Young, L. M. Michael's Journal Bk. 1: Being the Journals of Michael Cooke Holt, 1917-1925. 2001. 148p. pap. 17.95 (*0-7596-4694-5*) 1stBooks Library.

Yurick, Sol. The Warriors. 2003. 224p. pap. 12.00 (*0-8021-3992-2*, Grove Pr.) Grove/Atlantic, Inc.

Zabor, Rafi. The Bear Comes Home: A Novel. 480p. 1998. pap. 15.00 (*0-393-31863-X*); 1997. 25.00 o.p. (*0-393-04037-2*) Norton, W. W. & Co., Inc.

Zicree, Marc S. Magic Time. 2002. 448p. mass mkt. 7.50 (*0-06-105957-9*, Eos) Morrow/Avon.

Zigman, Laura. Animal Husbandry. abr. ed. 1997. audio 16.95 (*1-55927-489-1*) Audio Renaissance.

—Animal Husbandry. unabr. ed. 2000. audio 69.95 (*0-7927-2368-6*, CSL257, Chivers Sound Library) BBC Audiobooks America.

—Animal Husbandry. 1998. 320p. pap. 13.95 (*0-385-31903-7*, Delta) Dell Publishing.

—Animal Husbandry. l.t. ed. 1998. (Americana Ser.). 389p. 27.95 (*0-7862-1434-1*) Thorndike Pr.

—Dating Big Bird. 2001. 67.75 o.s.i (*0-385-33088-X*); 256p. pap. 13.95 (*0-385-33341-2*) Dell Publishing. (Delta).

—Dating Big Bird. unabr. ed. 2001. audio 24.95 (*1-57511-068-7*) Publishing Mills, Inc., The.

Zinn, Howard. Marx in Soho: A Play on History. 1999. 60p. 23.00 (*0-89608-594-5*); 88p. pap. 12.00 (*0-89608-593-7*) South End Pr.

Zucker, Benjamin. Blue. 2001. 248p. pap. 29.95 (*1-58567-181-9*); 2000. (Illus.). 224p. 40.00 (*1-58567-000-6*) Overlook Pr., The.

—Green. 2001. (Illus.). 288p. 40.00 (*1-58567-174-6*) Overlook Pr., The.

Zukowski, Sharon. Dancing in the Dark. 1994. (Mystery Ser.). mass mkt. (*0-373-26148-9*, 1-26148-6, Harlequin Bks.) Harlequin Enterprises, Ltd.

—Dancing in the Dark. 1992. 224p. 17.95 o.p. (*0-312-08174-X*, Saint Martin's Minotaur) St. Martin's Pr.

—The Hour of the Knife. 1993. (Mystery Ser.). mass mkt. (*0-373-26123-3*, 1-26123-9, Harlequin Bks.) Harlequin Enterprises, Ltd.

—The Hour of the Knife. 1991. 208p. 17.95 o.p. (*0-312-06372-5*, Saint Martin's Minotaur) St. Martin's Pr.

—Jungleland. 1999. pap. 22.95 (*0-525-93917-2*); 1997. 384p. mass mkt. 5.99 o.s.i (*0-451-19253-2*, Signet Bks.) NAL.

—Leap of Faith. 240p. pap. 3.98 o.p. (*0-7651-0402-4*) Smithmark Pubs., Inc.

—Leap of Faith: A Blaine Stewart Mystery. 1994. (Blaine Stewart Mystery Ser.). 256p. 18.95 o.p. (*0-525-93897-4*, Dutton) Dutton/Plume.

—Leap of Faith: A Blaine Stewart Mystery. 1995. (Blaine Stewart Mystery Ser.). 256p. mass mkt. 4.99 o.s.i (*0-451-18273-1*, Signet Bks.) NAL.

—Prelude to Death: A Blaine Stewart Mystery. 1996. (Blaine Stewart Mystery Ser.). 256p. 20.95 o.p. (*0-525-94079-0*, Dutton) Dutton/Plume.

—Prelude to Death: A Blaine Stewart Mystery. 1997. (Blaine Stewart Mystery Ser.). 272p. mass mkt. 5.50 o.s.i (*0-451-18272-3*) NAL.

**NEW YORK (STATE)—FICTION**

Abel, Kenneth. The Blue Wall. 1997. 432p. mass mkt. 5.99 o.s.i (*0-440-21723-7*) Dell Publishing.

Abu-Jaber, Diana. Arabian Jazz. (Harvest Book Ser.). 1994. 392p. pap. 19.00 (*0-15-600048-2*, Harvest Bks.); 1993. 374p. 21.95 o.s.i (*0-15-107862-9*) Harcourt Trade Pubs.

—Arabian Jazz: A Novel. 2003. 384p. pap. 14.95 (*0-393-32422-2*) Norton, W. W. & Co., Inc.

Acker, Kathy. Rip-Off Red, Girl Detective & the Burning Bombing of America. 2002. 208p. pap. 14.00 (*0-8021-3920-5*, Grove Pr.) Grove/Atlantic, Inc.

Adams, Samuel Hopkins. Canal Town. Bergmann, Frank, ed. 1988. (New York Classics Ser.). 476p. pap. 17.95 (*0-8156-0228-6*) Syracuse Univ. Pr.

—Grandfather Stories. lib. bdg. 24.95 (*0-8488-1950-0*) Amereon, Ltd.

—Grandfather Stories. 1989. (New York Classics Ser.). 336p. reprint ed. pap. text 17.95 (*0-8156-0232-4*) Syracuse Univ. Pr.

Adamson, Lydia. A Cat by Any Other Name. unabr. collector's ed. 1997. (Alice Nestleton Ser.). audio 30.00 (*0-7366-3597-1*, 4248) Books on Tape, Inc.

—A Cat by Any Other Name: An Alice Nestleton Mystery. 1992. (Alice Nestleton Mystery Ser.). 208p. mass mkt. 5.50 o.s.i (*0-451-17231-0*, Signet Bks.) NAL.

—A Cat in a Chorus Line. unabr. ed. 1997. (Alice Nestleton Ser.: Vol. 12). audio 24.00 (*0-7366-4052-5*, 4561) Books on Tape, Inc.

—A Cat in a Chorus Line. 1996. (Alice Nestleton Mystery Ser.). 256p. mass mkt. 5.50 o.s.i (*0-451-18084-4*, Signet Bks.) NAL.

—A Cat in a Glass House. unabr. ed. 1997. (Alice Nestleton Ser.). audio 30.00 (*0-7366-3675-7*, 4354) Books on Tape, Inc.

—A Cat in a Glass House. 1993. (Alice Nestleton Mystery Ser.). 208p. mass mkt. 3.99 o.s.i (*0-451-17706-1*, Signet Bks.) NAL.

Settings

—A Cat in Fine Style. unabr. ed. 1997. (Alice Nestleton Ser.: Vol. 10). audio 30.00 (*0-7366-3831-8*, 4551) Books on Tape, Inc.

—A Cat in Fine Style: An Alice Nestleton Mystery. 1995. (Alice Nestleton Mystery Ser.). 224p. mass mkt. 5.99 o.s.i (*0-451-18083-6*, Signet Bks.) NAL.

—A Cat in the Manger. l.t. ed. 1991. 17.95 o.p. (*0-7451-8142-2*, AH0179); pap. 15.95 o.p. (*0-7927-0663-3*, AS0215) BBC Audiobooks America.

—A Cat in the Manger. unabr. collector's ed. 1997. (Alice Nestleton Ser.: Vol. 1). audio 30.00 (*0-7366-3556-4*, 4201) Books on Tape, Inc.

—A Cat in the Manger. 1990. (Alice Nestleton Mystery Ser.). 208p. mass mkt. 5.50 o.s.i (*0-451-16787-2*, Signet Bks.) NAL.

—A Cat in the Wings. unabr. collector's ed. 1997. (Alice Nestleton Ser.). audio 36.00 (*0-7366-3598-X*, 4249) Books on Tape, Inc.

—A Cat in the Wings. 1992. (Alice Nestleton Mystery Ser.: No. 5). 208p. mass mkt. 5.99 o.s.i (*0-451-17336-8*, Signet Bks.) NAL.

—A Cat in Wolf's Clothing. unabr. collector's ed. 1997. (Alice Nestleton Ser.: Vol. 3). audio 30.00 (*0-7366-3558-0*, 4203) Books on Tape, Inc.

—A Cat in Wolf's Clothing. 1991. (Alice Nestleton Mystery Ser.). 208p. mass mkt. 4.99 o.s.i (*0-451-17085-7*, Signet Bks.) NAL.

—A Cat in Wolf's Clothing: An Alice Nestleton Mystery. l.t. ed. 1993. (General Ser.). 223p. pap. 16.95 (*0-8161-5401-5*); lib. bdg. 18.95 o.p. (*0-8161-5400-7*) Gale Group. (Macmillan Reference USA).

—A Cat of a Different Color. unabr. collector's ed. 1997. (Alice Nestleton Ser.: Vol. 2). audio 30.00 (*0-7366-3557-2*, 4202) Books on Tape, Inc.

—A Cat of a Different Color. l.t. ed. 1992. (General Ser.). 200p. pap. 14.95 o.p. (*0-8161-5399-X*); lib. bdg. 18.95 o.p. (*0-8161-5398-1*) Gale Group. (Macmillan Reference USA).

—A Cat of a Different Color. 1991. (Alice Nestleton Mystery Ser.). 208p. mass mkt. 5.50 o.s.i (*0-451-16955-7*, Signet Bks.) NAL.

—A Cat of One's Own. 1999. (Alice Nestleton Mysteries Ser.: Bk. 17). 208p. 19.95 (*0-525-94428-1*) Dutton/Plume.

—A Cat of One's Own, 1. 2000. (Alice Nestleton Mysteries Ser.). 208p. mass mkt. 5.99 o.s.i (*0-451-19769-0*) NAL.

—A Cat of One's Own. l.t. ed. 1999. (Mystery Ser.). 216p. 28.95 (*0-7862-1884-3*) Thorndike Pr.

—A Cat on a Beach Blanket. unabr. ed. 1998. (Alice Nestleton Ser.). audio 30.00 (*0-7366-4260-9*, 4759) Books on Tape, Inc.

—A Cat on a Beach Blanket. 1997. (Alice Nestleton Mystery Ser.). (Illus.). 192p. 18.95 o.p. (*0-525-94304-8*) Dutton/Plume.

—A Cat on a Beach Blanket. 1998. (Alice Nestleton Mysteries Ser.). 256p. mass mkt. 5.99 o.s.i (*0-451-19259-1*, Signet Bks.) NAL.

—A Cat on a Beach Blanket: An Alice Nestleton Mystery. l.t. ed. 2001. 231p. (*0-7540-4552-8*) Thorndike Pr.

—A Cat on a Winning Streak. unabr. ed. 1997. (Alice Nestleton Ser.). audio 24.00 (*0-7366-3746-X*, 4421) Books on Tape, Inc.

—A Cat on a Winning Streak. 1995. (Alice Nestleton Mystery Ser.). 240p. mass mkt. 4.50 o.s.i (*0-451-18082-8*, Signet Bks.) NAL.

—A Cat on Stage Left. 1998. (Alice Nestleton Mysteries Ser.: Vol. 16). (Illus.). 176p. 19.95 o.p. (*0-525-94419-2*) Dutton/Plume.

—A Cat on Stage Left: An Alice Nestleton Mystery, 1 vol., Vol. 16. 1999. (Alice Nestleton Mysteries Ser.: Vol. 16). 256p. mass mkt. 5.99 o.s.i (*0-451-19734-8*) NAL.

—A Cat on Stage Left: An Alice Nestleton Mystery. l.t. ed. 1998. (Mystery Ser.). 232p. 27.95 (*0-7862-1559-3*) Thorndike Pr.

—A Cat on the Cutting Edge. unabr. ed. 1997. (Alice Nestleton Ser.: Vol. 9). audio 24.00 (*0-7366-3745-1*, 4420) Books on Tape, Inc.

—A Cat on the Cutting Edge. l.t. ed. 1995. (Alice Nestleton Mystery Ser.). 178p. lib. bdg. 21.95 o.p. (*0-7838-1243-4*, Macmillan Reference USA) Gale Group.

—A Cat on the Cutting Edge. 1994. (Alice Nestleton Mystery Ser.). 224p. mass mkt. 4.50 o.s.i (*0-451-18080-1*, Signet Bks.) NAL.

—A Cat with No Regrets. unabr. ed. 1997. (Alice Nestleton Ser.). audio 30.00 (*0-7366-3744-3*, 4419) Books on Tape, Inc.

—A Cat with No Regrets. 1994. (Alice Nestleton Mystery Ser.: No. 8). 208p. mass mkt. 3.99 o.s.i (*0-451-18055-0*, Signet Bks.) NAL.

—A Cat with No Regrets. 1999. pap. (*0-525-93811-7*) Viking Penguin.

—A Cat with the Blues. 2000. (Alice Nestleton Mysteries Ser.: Vol. 10). 208p. mass mkt. 5.99 (*0-451-20196-5*) NAL.

—A Cat with the Blues: An Alice Nestleton Mystery. l.t. ed. 2001. (Thorndike Mystery Ser.). 200p. 29.95 (*0-7862-3076-2*); (*0-7540-4465-3*) Thorndike Pr.

—Dr. Nightingale Follows a Canine Clue. l.t. ed. 2001. (Beeler Large Print Mystery Ser.). 141p. 25.95 (*1-57490-409-4*, Beeler Large Print Bks.) Beeler, Thomas T. Publisher.

—Dr. Nightingale Follows a Canine Clue. 2001. (Dr. Nightingale Mystery Ser.). 208p. mass mkt. 5.99 o.s.i (*0-451-20366-6*, Signet Bks.) NAL.

—Dr. Nightingale Races the Outlaw Colt. 1998. (Deirdre Quinn Nightingale Mystery Ser.). 224p. mass mkt. 5.99 o.s.i (*0-451-18815-2*, Signet Bks.) NAL.

—Dr. Nightingale Races the Outlaw Colt: A Deirdre Quinn Nightingale Mystery. l.t. ed. 2000. (Mystery Ser.). 235p. 27.95 (*0-7862-2486-X*) Thorndike Pr.

Adcock, Thomas. Dark Maze. Chelius, Jane, ed. 1991. 320p. (Orig.). mass mkt. 5.50 (*0-671-72909-8*, Pocket) Simon & Schuster.

—Devil's Heaven. 1996. 288p. mass mkt. 5.99 (*0-671-77043-8*, Pocket) Simon & Schuster.

—Devil's Heaven. Chelius, Jane, ed. 1995. 336p. 20.00 o.p. (*0-671-89778-0*, Atria) Simon & Schuster.

—Drown All the Dogs. Chelius, Jane, ed. 1995. 368p. mass mkt. 5.99 (*0-671-88329-1*, Pocket) Simon & Schuster.

—Drown All the Dogs: A Neil Hockaday Mystery. 1994. 352p. 20.00 o.p. (*0-671-77041-1*, Atria) Simon & Schuster.

—Grief Street. 1998. (Neil Hockaday Mystery Ser.). 304p. per. 6.50 (*0-671-51987-5*, Pocket) Simon & Schuster.

—Grief Street: A Neil Hockaday Mystery. 1997. (Neil Hockaday Mystery Ser.). 304p. 22.00 (*0-671-51986-7*, Atria) Simon & Schuster.

—Sea of Green. 1989. 17.45 o.p. (*0-89296-384-0*) Mysterious Pr.

—Sea of Green. 1990. 304p. mass mkt. 4.95 o.s.i (*0-445-40918-5*, Mysterious Pr. Paperback Bks.) Warner Bks., Inc.

—Thrown Away Child. (Neil Hockaday Mystery Ser.). 1997. 400p. per. 5.99 (*0-671-51984-0*, Pocket); 1996. 352p. 21.00 o.p. (*0-671-51985-9*, Atria) Simon & Schuster.

Adler, Bill, Jr., et al. Murder in Manhattan. 1986. 320p. 15.95 o.p. (*0-688-06475-2*, Morrow, William & Co.) Morrow/Avon.

Adler, Elizabeth A. In a Heartbeat. l.t. ed. 2000. (Wheeler Large Print Book Ser.). 365p. 28.95 (*1-56895-941-9*, Wheeler Publishing, Inc.) Gale Group.

Adler, Renata. Speedboat. 1988. 192p. reprint ed. pap. 7.95 o.p. (*0-06-097143-6*, PL-7143, Perennial) HarperTrade.

—Speedboat. 1984. pap. 5.95 o.s.i (*0-394-72753-3*); 1976. 7.95 o.p. (*0-394-48876-8*) Random Hse., Inc.

Akst, Daniel. St. Burl's Obituary. 1997. (Harvest American Writing Ser.). 384p. pap. 12.00 (*0-15-600514-X*, Harvest Bks.) Harcourt Trade Pubs.

—St. Burl's Obituary. 1996. 370p. 22.95 (*1-878448-68-4*) MacMurray & Beck, Inc.

Alexander, Meena. Manhattan Music. 1997. 256p. (Orig.). pap. 14.95 o.p. (*0-562-79092-6*); (Illus.). reprint ed. pap. 14.95 (*1-56279-092-7*) Mercury Hse.

Alfau, Felipe. Chromos. 1990. 348p. 19.95 (*0-916583-52-X*) Dalkey Archive Pr.

—Chromos. 1991. 352p. pap. 11.00 o.s.i (*0-679-73443-0*, Vintage) Knopf Publishing Group.

Allegretto, Michael. The Night of Reunion. 1990. 256p. 17.95 o.s.i (*0-684-19133-4*, Macmillan Reference USA) Gale Group.

—The Night of Reunion. 1991. 288p. mass mkt. 4.99 (*0-380-71442-6*, Avon Bks.) Morrow/Avon.

Allen, Charlotte Vale. Mood Indigo. l.t. ed. 2000. 408p. lib. bdg. 27.95 (*1-58547-038-4*) Ctr. Point Large Print.

—Mood Indigo. 1997. 288p. 23.95 (*0-9657437-1-3*) Island Nation Pr., LLC.

Allen, Steve. Murder in Manhattan. 1990. mass mkt. 18.95 o.p. (*0-8217-3033-9*, Zebra Bks.) Kensington Publishing Corp.

—Wake up to Murder. 1997. 384p. mass mkt. 5.99 o.s.i (*1-57566-236-1*); 1996. 288p. 18.95 o.s.i (*1-57566-109-8*); 1996. 256p. 19.95 o.s.i (*1-57566-090-3*, Kensington Bks.) Kensington Publishing Corp.

Allingham, Margery, et al. Canine Crimes. Mason, Cynthia, ed. 1993. 240p. (Orig.). mass mkt. 4.50 o.s.i (*0-515-11250-X*, Jove) Berkley Publishing Group.

Allison, Karen H. How I Gave My Heart to the Restaurant Business: A Novel. 1997. 210p. 23.00 o.p. (*0-88001-522-5*) HarperCollins Pubs.

Allman, Paul L. Otis: On the Occasion of His Foray into the Wilderness of Civilization. 1994. (Illus.). 256p. 20.95 o.p. (*0-312-10519-3*) St. Martin's Pr.

Altsheler, Joseph A. The Lords of the Wild. 2000. 252p. E-Book 3.95 (*0-594-01820-X*) 1873 Pr.

—The Lords of the Wild. 24.95 (*0-8488-0905-X*) Amereon, Ltd.

—The Lords of the Wild. 1993. reprint ed. lib. bdg. 21.95 (*0-89968-563-3*) Buccaneer Bks., Inc.

—The Shadow of the North. 2000. 252p. E-Book 3.95 (*0-594-01821-8*) 1873 Pr.

Amato, Angela & Sharkey, Joe. Lady Gold. 1999. 384p. mass mkt. 6.99 (*0-312-96765-9*, St. Martin's Paperbacks); E-Book 23.95 (*0-312-20726-3*) St. Martin's Pr.

Ambrose, David. Superstition. 1998. 368p. 30.00 o.p. (*0-446-52344-5*); 1999. 432p. reprint ed. mass mkt. 6.99 (*0-446-60782-7*) Warner Bks., Inc.

Ames, Jonathan. I Pass Like Night. 1989. 160p. 15.95 o.p. (*0-688-07804-4*, Morrow, William & Co.) Morrow/Avon.

—I Pass Like Night. 1993. 2.99 o.p. (*0-517-10862-3*) Random Hse. Value Publishing.

—I Pass Like Night. 1999. (Contemporary Classics Ser.). 176p. pap. 12.00 (*0-671-03426-X*, Washington Square Pr.) Simon & Schuster.

Amiel, Joseph. Deeds. 1988. mass mkt. 4.95 o.s.i (*0-449-14522-0*, Fawcett) Ballantine Bks.

—Deeds. 1988. 484p. 19.95 o.s.i (*0-689-11862-7*, Scribner) Simon & Schuster.

Anderson, Douglas. First & Ten: A Novel. 1993. 22.00 o.s.i (*0-517-58859-5*, Crown) Crown Publishing Group.

Anderson, Scott. Triage. 1999. 240p. pap. 12.00 (*0-684-85653-0*, Scribner Paper Fiction) Simon & Schuster.

—Triage: A Novel. 1998. 240p. 23.00 (*0-684-84695-0*, Scribner) Simon & Schuster.

—Triage: A Novel. l.t. ed. 1999. (Ulverscroft Large Print Ser.). 408p. 31.99 o.p. (*0-7089-4117-6*, Ulverscroft) Thorpe, F. A. Pubs. GBR. *Dist:* Ulverscroft Large Print Bks., Ltd., Ulverscroft Large Print Canada, Ltd.

Ansay, A. Manette. Sister. 1997. 240p. pap. 13.00 (*0-380-72976-8*, Perennial) HarperTrade.

—Sister. 1996. 224p. 24.00 o.p. (*0-688-14449-7*, Morrow, William & Co.) Morrow/Avon.

Appel, William. Widowmaker. 1994. 167p. 19.95 (*0-8027-3193-7*) Walker & Co.

Arenas, Reinaldo. The Doorman: A Novel. 1991. 16.95 o.p. (*0-8021-1109-2*) Grove/Atlantic, Inc.

Arensberg, Ann. Group Sex. 1986. 15.95 o.s.i (*0-394-55310-1*) Knopf, Alfred A. Inc.

—Group Sex: A Romantic Comedy. 1987. mass mkt. 5.95 o.s.i (*0-671-64362-2*, Pocket) Simon & Schuster.

Armstrong, Kelley. Bitten. unabr. ed. 2001. audio 34.95 (*1-56740-383-2*, 2182, Brilliance Audio Unabridged) Brilliance Audio.

—Bitten. 2002. 384p. pap. 13.00 (*0-452-28348-5*, Plume) Dutton/Plume.

—Bitten. 2001. 400p. 24.95 o.s.i (*0-670-89471-0*, Viking) Viking Penguin.

Arnold, Emily. Life Drawing. 1986. 288p. 15.95 o.s.i (*0-385-29437-9*, Delacorte Pr.); 1988. reprint ed. mass mkt. 4.95 o.s.i (*0-440-20025-3*, Laurel) Dell Publishing.

Ashbery, John & Schuyler, James. A Nest of Ninnies. 1997. 192p. 21.00 o.p. (*0-88001-523-3*) HarperCollins Pubs.

Ashwood-Collins, Anna. Deadly Resolutions. 1995. (*4-06-184902-6*) Kodansha, Ltd. JPN. *Dist:* Kodansha America, Inc.

—Deadly Resolutions. 1989. 18.95 (*0-8027-5739-1*) Walker & Co.

Astor, Brooke. The Last Blossom on the Plum Tree. l.t. ed. 1987. 8.95 o.p. (*1-55504-239-2*); pap. 18.95 o.p. (*1-55504-317-8*) BBC Audiobooks America.

Atwood, Margaret. Oryx & Crake. 2003. 400p. 26.00 (*0-385-50385-7*, Talese, Nan A.); E-Book 12.00 (*0-385-51088-8*) Doubleday Publishing.

—Oryx & Crake. 2004. 400p. pap. 14.00 (*0-385-72167-6*, Anchor) Knopf Publishing Group.

—Oryx & Crake. 2003. 392p. (*0-7710-0868-6*) McClelland & Stewart/Tundra Bks.

—Oryx & Crake. l.t. ed. 2003. 592p. 28.00 (*0-375-43212-4*) Random Hse. Large Print.

Atwood, Russell. East of A. 2000. 256p. mass mkt. 6.50 o.s.i (*0-345-42778-5*, Fawcett) Ballantine Bks.

Auchincloss, Louis. The Book Class, 001. 1984. 224p. 14.95 o.p. (*0-395-36138-9*) Houghton Mifflin Co.

—The Book Class. l.t. ed. 1984. 293p. reprint ed. 14.95 o.p. (*0-89621-558-X*) Thorndike Pr.

—The Dark Lady, 001. 1977. 8.95 o.p. (*0-395-25402-7*) Houghton Mifflin Co.

—The Education of Oscar Fairfax. 1995. 256p. 22.95 o.p. (*0-395-73918-7*) Houghton Mifflin Co.

—The Embezzler. l.t. ed. 1988. 20.95 o.p. (*1-55504-386-0*); pap. 18.95 o.p. (*1-55504-505-7*) BBC Audiobooks America.

—The Embezzler. 1993. reprint ed. lib. bdg. 21.95 (*1-56849-151-4*) Buccaneer Bks., Inc.

—The Embezzler, 001. 1966. 5.95 o.p. (*0-395-07362-6*); 1980. reprint ed. pap. 3.95 o.p. (*0-395-29845-8*) Houghton Mifflin Co.

—The Embezzler. l.t. ed. 2000. 325p. 32.95 (*0-7658-0778-5*) Transaction Pubs.

—The Golden Calves. l.t. ed. 1989. (General Ser.). 315p. lib. bdg. 19.95 o.p. (*0-8161-4682-9*, Macmillan Reference USA) Gale Group.

—The Golden Calves. 1988. 17.95 o.p. (*0-395-47691-7*) Houghton Mifflin Co.

—The Golden Calves. 1990. 2.99 o.p. (*0-517-02946-4*) Random Hse. Value Publishing.

—The Golden Calves. 1990. pap. 3.95 o.p. (*0-312-91487-3*, St. Martin's Paperbacks) St. Martin's Pr.

—Her Infinite Variety. 2000. 224p. tchr. ed. 25.00 (*0-618-02191-4*) Houghton Mifflin Co.

—Her Infinite Variety. l.t. ed. 2001. (Core Ser.). 259p. 29.95 (*0-7838-9341-8*) Thorndike Pr.

—Skinny Island: More Tales of Manhattan. 1987. 17.95 o.p. (*0-395-43295-2*) Houghton Mifflin Co.

Auster, Paul. City of Glass. 1987. (New York Trilogy). 210p. pap. 12.95 (*0-14-009731-7*, Penguin Bks.) Penguin Group (USA) Inc.

—City of Glass. 1985. (New York Trilogy Ser.). 208p. 30.00 o.p. (*0-940650-53-3*); 13.95 o.p. (*0-940650-52-5*) Sun & Moon Pr.

—Ghosts. deluxe ed. 1986. (New York Trilogy Ser.). 110p. 30.00 o.p. (*0-940650-69-X*) Sun & Moon Pr.

—Ghosts. 1987. (New York Trilogy). 96p. pap. 5.95 o.p. (*0-14-009735-X*, Penguin Bks.) Viking Penguin.

—The New York Trilogy: City of Glass; Ghosts; The Locked Room. deluxe ltd. ed. (New American Fiction Ser.: Nos. 4-6). 472p. 1994. 40.00 o.p. (*1-55713-167-8*); 1995. 21.95 o.p. (*1-55713-166-X*) Sun & Moon Pr.

—The New York Trilogy: City of Glass; Ghosts; The Locked Room. 1990. (American Fiction Ser.). (Illus.). 448p. 14.95 (*0-14-013155-8*) Viking Penguin.

Avrett, Roz. My Turn. 1983. 288p. 14.50 o.p. (*0-87795-476-3*, Morrow, William & Co.) Morrow/Avon.

Bacheller, Irving. Eben Holden: A Tale of the North Country. 1974. (BCL Ser.: No. I). 27.50 (*0-404-00439-3*) AMS Pr., Inc.

—Eben Holden: A Tale of the North Country. reprint ed. lib. bdg. 48.00 (*0-7426-1108-6*) Classic Bks.

—Eben Holden: A Tale of the North Country. 1903. 432p. (YA). reprint ed. pap. text 28.00 (*1-4047-6671-5*) Classic Textbooks.

—Eben Holden: A Tale of the North Country. 1992. (BCL1-PS American Literature Ser.). 432p. reprint ed. lib. bdg. 99.00 (*0-7812-6671-8*) Reprint Services Corp.

—Eben Holden: A Tale of the North Country. 1969. reprint ed. 16.00 (*0-403-00142-0*) Scholarly Pr., Inc.

—Eben Holden: A Tale of the North Country. 1998. (Classics Library). pap. 3.95 (*1-85326-573-X*, 573XWW) Wordsworth Editions, Ltd. GBR. *Dist:* Combined Publishing.

Baldwin, Frank. Balling the Jack. 272p. 1998. pap. 11.00 (*0-684-84581-4*, Touchstone); 1997. 22.00 o.s.i (*0-684-83360-3*, Simon & Schuster) Simon & Schuster.

Banks, Russell. Rule of the Bone: A Novel. 1996. 400p. pap. 60.00 o.p. (*0-06-092743-7*); 1995. 390p. 22.00 o.p. (*0-06-017275-4*) HarperCollins Pubs.

—Rule of the Bone: A Novel. 1996. 400p. pap. 13.00 (*0-06-092724-0*, Perennial); Set. 1999. audio 17.00 o.p. (*1-55994-809-4*, 392857, HarperAudio) HarperTrade.

—The Sweet Hereafter: A Novel. 1991. 272p. 20.00 o.p. (*0-06-016703-3*) HarperTrade.

Barbash, Tom. The Last Good Chance: A Novel. 448p. 2003. pap. 15.00 (*0-312-42267-9*); 2002. 24.00 (*0-312-28796-8*) Picador.

Barnhardt, Wilton. Emma Who Saved My Life. 1989. 19.95 o.p. (*0-312-02911-X*) St. Martin's Pr.

Barr, Nevada. Liberty Falling. 2000. (Anna Pigeon Mysteries Ser.). (Illus.). 384p. mass mkt. 7.99 (*0-380-72827-3*, Avon Bks.) Morrow/Avon.

Barrett, Margaret & Dennis, Charles. Given the Evidence. 1999. 400p. reprint ed. mass mkt. 6.50 o.s.i (*0-671-00154-X*, Pocket) Simon & Schuster.

Barrett, Margaret, et al. Given the Evidence. 1998. 320p. 23.00 (*0-671-00153-1*, Atria) Simon & Schuster.

Barth, Richard. Blood Doesn't Tell. 1990. (Margaret Binton Mystery Ser.). 192p. mass mkt. 3.95 o.s.i (*0-449-21797-3*, Fawcett) Ballantine Bks.

—Blood Doesn't Tell. 1989. 192p. 15.95 o.p. (*0-312-02547-5*, Saint Martin's Minotaur) St. Martin's Pr.

—The Condo Kill. 1991. (Margaret Binton Mystery Ser.). 160p. mass mkt. 3.95 o.s.i (*0-449-21812-0*, Fawcett) Ballantine Bks.

—The Condo Kill. 1985. (Margaret Binton Mystery Ser.). 192p. 13.95 o.s.i (*0-684-18474-5*, Macmillan Reference USA) Gale Group.

—Deadly Climate. 1989. mass mkt. 3.50 o.s.i (*0-449-21723-X*, Fawcett) Ballantine Bks.

—Deadly Climate. unabr. ed. 2000. (Margaret Binton Mysteries Ser.). audio 44.00 (*1-55690-844-X*, 93211E7) Recorded Bks., LLC.

—Deadly Climate. 1988. 208p. 14.95 o.p. (*0-312-01756-1*, Saint Martin's Minotaur) St. Martin's Pr.

—Deathics: A Margaret Binton Mystery. 1993. 212p. 18.95 o.p. (*0-312-08764-0*, Saint Martin's Minotaur) St. Martin's Pr.
—The Final Shot. 1992. 256p. 17.95 o.p. (*0-312-07748-3*, Saint Martin's Minotaur) St. Martin's Pr.
—Jumper. l.t. ed. 2001. 240p. 25.95 (*1-57490-343-8*) Beeler, Thomas T. Publisher.
—One Dollar Death. 1991. 176p. mass mkt. 3.95 o.s.i (*0-449-21813-9*, Fawcett) Ballantine Bks.
—One Dollar Death. 1982. 228p. 14.95 o.p. (*0-385-27633-8*) Doubleday Publishing.
—One Dollar Death. l.t. ed. 1983. 313p. reprint ed. 11.95 o.p. (*0-89621-419-2*) Thorndike Pr.
—A Ragged Plot. 1990. mass mkt. 3.95 o.s.i (*0-449-21815-5*, Fawcett) Ballantine Bks.
—A Ragged Plot. 1981. 224p. 10.95 o.p. (*0-385-27165-4*) Doubleday Publishing.
—A Ragged Plot. 1982. 176p. pap. 2.25 o.p. (*0-380-59162-6*, 59162-6, Avon Bks.) Morrow/Avon.
—A Ragged Plot. unabr. ed. 1992. (Margaret Binton Mysteries Ser.). audio 44.00 (*1-55690-721-4*, 92417E7) Recorded Bks., LLC.
Barthelme, Donald. Paradise. 1986. 208p. 16.95 o.p. (*0-399-12921-9*) Putnam Publishing Group, The.
—Paradise. 1987. 208p. pap. 8.95 o.p. (*0-14-010358-9*, Penguin Bks.) Viking Penguin.
Bartholemew, John T. He's Dead, She's Dead - Details at Eleven. 1990. 17.95 o.p. (*0-312-04325-2*, Saint Martin's Minotaur) St. Martin's Pr.
Baxt, George. A Queer Kind of Death. 1998. 300p. pap. 10.00 o.p. (*1-55583-448-5*) Alyson Pubns.
—A Queer Kind of Death: A Pharoah Love Mystery. 1986. (Library of Crime Classics). pap. 4.95 o.p. (*0-930330-46-3*) International Polygonics, Ltd.
—A Queer Kind of Death: A Pharoah Love Mystery. 1979. pap. 4.95 o.p. (*0-312-66022-7*, Saint Martin's Griffin) St. Martin's Pr.
—A Queer Kind of Love: A Pharoah Love Mystery. 1994. 288p. 20.00 (*1-883402-01-8*, Scribner) Simon & Schuster.
—A Queer Kind of Love: A Pharoah Love Mystery. pap. (*0-312-29217-1*); 1995. pap. 8.95 (*0-312-13152-6*) St. Martin's Pr. (Saint Martin's Griffin).
—A Queer Kind of Umbrella: A Pharoah Love Mystery. 1995. 240p. 20.50 (*0-684-81496-X*, Simon & Schuster); 21.00 (*1-883402-35-2*, Scribner) Simon & Schuster.
—Topsy & Evil. 1987. 232p. reprint ed. pap. 4.95 o.p. (*0-930330-66-8*) International Polygonics, Ltd.
Bayer, William. Switch. l.t. ed. 1986. (General Ser.). 420p. 17.95 o.p. (*0-8161-4037-5*, Macmillan Reference USA) Gale Group.
—Switch. 1985. mass mkt. 3.95 o.p. (*0-451-14333-7*); mass mkt. 3.95 o.p. (*0-451-13603-9*) NAL. (Signet Bks.).
—Switch. 1984. 14.70 o.p. (*0-671-49424-4*, Simon & Schuster) Simon & Schuster.
Beasley, David. The Jenny: A New York Library Detective Novel. 1994. 120p. pap. 7.95 (*0-915317-03-6*) Davus Publishing.
Beattie, Ann. Falling in Place. 1981. pap. 2.50 o.p. (*0-445-04650-3*, Fawcett) Ballantine Bks.
—Falling in Place. (Vintage Contemporaries Ser.). 1991. 342p. pap. 19.00 (*0-679-73192-X*); 1980. 10.95 o.p. (*0-394-50323-6*) Random Hse., Inc.
—Picturing Will. 1991. (Vintage Contemporaries Ser.). 240p. pap. 15.00 (*0-679-73194-6*, Vintage) Knopf Publishing Group.
—Picturing Will. 1992. 4.99 o.p. (*0-517-08094-X*) Random Hse. Value Publishing.
Beatty, Paul. Tuff: A Novel. 2000. reprint ed. pap. 13.00 o.p. (*0-375-70124-9*, Anchor) Knopf Publishing Group.
Bechard, Gorman. Balls. 1995. 384p. (Orig.). pap. 10.95 o.p. (*0-452-27294-7*, Plume) Dutton/Plume.
Becker, Geoffrey. Bluestown. pap. 15.95 (*0-312-30456-0*, Saint Martin's Griffin); 1997. pap. 11.95 o.p. (*0-312-15481-X*, Saint Martin's Griffin); 1996. 280p. 21.95 o.p. (*0-312-14223-4*) St. Martin's Pr.
Becker, Laney K. Dear Stranger, Dearest Friend. 2000. 304p. 24.00 (*0-380-97853-9*, Morrow, William & Co.) Morrow/Avon.
—Dear Stranger, Dearest Friend. l.t. ed. 2001. (G. K. Hall Inspirational Ser.). 381p. 26.95 (*0-7838-9403-1*) Thorndike Pr.
Beckman, David. Under Pegasus: A Novel. 1997. 200p. 19.95 (*0-9651244-1-X*, Goldengrove Bks.) Derrynane Pr.
Begley, Louis. About Schmidt. 1997. (Ballantine Reader's Circle Ser.). 304p. pap. 13.95 (*0-449-91116-0*, Fawcett) Ballantine Bks.
—About Schmidt, 5 cass. 2002. audio 29.99 (*0-7887-9027-7*, 00494); 1997. audio 51.00 (*0-7887-0876-7*, 95011E7) Recorded Bks., LLC.
Beinhart, Larry. Foreign Exchange. 1992. mass mkt. 5.99 o.s.i (*0-345-36665-4*) Ballantine Bks.
—No One Rides for Free. 1993. mass mkt. 4.99 o.s.i (*0-345-37294-8*) Ballantine Bks.
—No One Rides for Free. 1987. 240p. pap. 3.95 (*0-380-70283-5*, Avon Bks.); 1986. 256p. 16.95 o.p. (*0-688-06057-9*, Morrow, William & Co.) Morrow/Avon.
—You Get What You Pay For. 1989. 368p. mass mkt. 4.95 o.s.i (*0-345-36406-6*) Ballantine Bks.
—You Get What You Pay For. 1988. 356p. 18.95 o.p. (*0-688-06613-5*, Morrow, William & Co.) Morrow/Avon.
Belfer, Lauren. City of Light. 2003. 512p. pap. 12.95 (*0-385-33764-7*, Delta); 2000. 704p. mass mkt. 6.99 (*0-440-23512-X*); 1999. 518p. pap. 24.95 (*0-385-22401-X*, Delacorte Pr.) Dell Publishing.
—The City of Light. abr. ed. 1999. audio 25.00 (*0-553-52625-1*, RH Audio) Random Hse. Audio Publishing Group.
—City of Light. l.t. ed. 1999. (Basic Ser.). 851p. 29.95 (*0-7862-1991-2*) Thorndike Pr.
Bell, Madison Smartt. Waiting for the End of the World. 1985. 16.95 o.p. (*0-89919-377-3*) Houghton Mifflin Co.
—Waiting for the End of the World. 1986. 336p. pap. 9.95 o.p. (*0-14-009330-3*, Penguin Bks.) Viking Penguin.
—The Washington Square Ensemble. 1984. (Penguin Contemporary American Fiction Ser.). 352p. pap. 11.95 o.s.i (*0-14-007025-7*, Penguin Bks.) Penguin Group (USA) Inc.
—The Washington Square Ensemble. 1983. 336p. 15.75 o.p. (*0-670-75005-0*) Viking Penguin.
—The Year of Silence. 1987. 208p. 15.95 o.p. (*0-89919-490-7*) Houghton Mifflin Co.
—The Year of Silence. 1989. (Contemporary American Fiction Ser.). 208p. pap. 12.95 o.s.i (*0-14-011533-1*, Penguin Bks.) Penguin Group (USA) Inc.
Belle, Jennifer. Going Down. 1996. 272p. pap. 13.00 (*1-57322-554-1*, Riverhead Trade (Paperbacks)) Berkley Publishing Group.
Beller, Thomas. The Sleep-over Artist. 2000. 256p. 23.95 (*0-393-04925-6*) Norton, W. W. & Co., Inc.
Bellow, Saul. Seize the Day. 1976. pap. 3.95 o.p. (*0-14-004311-X*); 1961. pap. 1.65 o.p. (*0-670-00091-4*) Penguin Group (USA) Inc.
—Seize the Day. 2003. 144p. pap. 12.00 (*0-14-243761-1*, Penguin Classics); 1996. 144p. 12.00 (*0-14-018937-8*, Penguin Classics); 1984. 128p. pap. 10.95 o.p. (*0-14-007285-3*, Penguin Bks.); 1956. 7.95 o.p. (*0-670-63176-0*) Viking Penguin.
—A Theft. 1989. 128p. pap. 7.95 o.p. (*0-14-011969-8*, Penguin Bks.) Viking Penguin.
Benabib, Kim. Obscene Bodies: A Novel. 1996. 256p. 22.00 o.p. (*0-06-017437-4*) HarperCollins Pubs.
Benderson, Bruce. User. 240p. 1995. pap. 10.95 o.p. (*0-452-27461-3*, Plume); 1994. 19.95 o.p. (*0-525-93722-6*, Dutton) Dutton/Plume.
Benedict, Helen. Bad Angel. 1996. 304p. 22.95 o.p. (*0-525-94100-2*, Dutton) Dutton/Plume.
Berman, Richard. Hostile Witness. 1996. 304p. (Orig.). mass mkt. 5.99 (*0-380-77813-0*, Avon Bks.) Morrow/Avon.
—Unjust Death. 1995. 352p. (Orig.). mass mkt. 5.50 (*0-380-77812-2*, Avon Bks.) Morrow/Avon.
Bertematti, Richard. Project Death: A Tito Rico Mystery. 1997. (Tito Rico Mystery Ser.). 200p. 22.95 o.p. (*1-55885-193-3*) Arte Publico Pr.
Birmingham, Stephen. Rothman Scandal, Vol. 1. 1991. 21.95 o.p. (*0-316-09654-7*) Little Brown & Co.
Bishop, Claudia. A Dash of Death. 1995. 240p. (Orig.). mass mkt. 5.99 (*0-425-14638-3*, Prime Crime) Berkley Publishing Group.
—Death Dines Out. 1997. (Hemlock Falls Mysteries Ser.). 256p. mass mkt. 5.99 (*0-425-16111-0*, Prime Crime) Berkley Publishing Group.
—Murder Well-Done. 1996. (Hemlock Falls Mysteries Ser.). 272p. mass mkt. 5.99 o.s.i (*0-425-15336-3*) Berkley Publishing Group.
—A Pinch of Poison. 1995. (Hemlock Falls Mysteries Ser.). 256p. mass mkt. 5.99 (*0-425-15104-2*) Berkley Publishing Group.
—A Steak in Murder. 1999. (Hemlock Falls Mysteries Ser.). 272p. mass mkt. 5.99 o.s.i (*0-425-16966-9*, Prime Crime) Berkley Publishing Group.
—A Taste for Murder. 1994. 240p. mass mkt. 5.99 (*0-425-14350-3*, Prime Crime) Berkley Publishing Group.
—A Touch of the Grape. 1998. (Hemlock Falls Mysteries Ser.). 256p. mass mkt. 5.99 (*0-425-16397-0*, Prime Crime) Berkley Publishing Group.
Black, Simon. The Book of Frank. Putnam, Jeff, ed. 1994. 228p. pap. 11.00 (*1-880909-28-6*) Baskerville Pubs., Inc.
—The Book of Frank. 2nd ed. 1994. 228p. 19.00 (*1-880909-25-1*) Baskerville Pubs., Inc.
Blake, Lillie D. Fettered for Life. 1997. 432p. pap. 18.95 (*1-55861-155-X*); lib. bdg. 45.00 (*1-55861-159-2*) Feminist Pr. at The City Univ. of New York.
—Fettered for Life or Lord & Master, Set. unabr. ed. 1998. 53.95 incl. audio (*1-55685-539-7*) Audio Bk. Contractors, Inc.
Blakeslee, Mermer. Same Blood. 1989. 16.95 o.p. (*0-395-48601-7*) Houghton Mifflin Co.
Blanchard, Nina. The Look. 1996. 416p. mass mkt. 5.99 o.s.i (*0-451-18034-8*, Signet Bks.) NAL.
Blanchard, Nina & Barsocchini, Peter. The Look. 1995. 368p. 23.95 o.p. (*0-525-93795-1*, Dutton) Dutton/Plume.
Blauner, Peter. The Intruder. l.t. ed. 1996. 26.95 (*1-56895-348-8*, Wheeler Publishing, Inc.) Gale Group.
—The Intruder. unabr. ed. audio 1999. audio 70.00 (*0-7887-0627-6*, 94801E7) Recorded Bks., LLC.
—The Intruder. 1996. 384p. 22.50 o.p. (*0-684-81094-8*, Simon & Schuster) Simon & Schuster.
—The Intruder. abr. ed. 1999. audio; 1996. 192p. pap. 18.00 incl. audio (*0-671-57041-2*, 394045, Simon & Schuster Audioworks) Simon & Schuster Audio.
—The Intruder. 1997. 464p. reprint ed. mass mkt. 6.99 (*0-446-60505-0*) Warner Bks., Inc.
—The Last Good Day. 2003. 432p. 24.95 (*0-316-09873-6*) Little Brown & Co.
—Slow Motion Riot. 1992. 384p. pap. 6.99 (*0-380-71306-3*, Avon Bks.); 1991. 352p. 20.00 o.p. (*0-688-10068-6*, Morrow, William & Co.) Morrow/Avon.
Block, Barbara. Chutes & Adders. 1995. mass mkt. 4.99 o.s.i (*0-8217-4997-8*) Kensington Publishing Corp.
—Chutes & Adders: A Robin Light Mystery. 1994. 320p. mass mkt. 16.95 o.s.i (*0-8217-4533-6*) Kensington Publishing Corp.
—Endangered Species: A Robin Light Mystery. 1999. (Robin Light Mystery Ser.). 320p. 20.00 o.s.i (*1-57566-449-6*, Kensington Bks.) Kensington Publishing Corp.
—In Plain Sight: A Robin Light Mystery. (Robin Light Mystery Ser.). 1997. 336p. mass mkt. 5.50 o.s.i (*1-57566-199-3*); 1996. 321p. 18.95 o.p. (*1-57566-059-8*, Kensington Bks.) Kensington Publishing Corp.
—Rubbed Out. 2003. 304p. mass mkt. 5.99 (*1-57566-724-X*, Kensington Bks.) Kensington Publishing Corp.
—Rubbed Out: A Robin Light Thriller. 2002. (Robin Light Thriller Ser.). 368p. 22.00 (*1-57566-709-6*, Kensington Bks.) Kensington Publishing Corp.
—The Scent of Murder. 336p. 1999. mass mkt. 5.99 o.s.i (*1-57566-331-7*); 1997. 18.95 o.s.i (*1-57566-195-0*) Kensington Publishing Corp.
—Twister. 1996. (Robin Light Mystery Ser.). 304p. mass mkt. 4.99 (*1-57566-062-8*, Kensington Bks.) Kensington Publishing Corp.
—Twister: A Robin Light Mystery. 1995. mass mkt. 16.95 o.p. (*0-8217-4989-7*, Zebra Bks.) Kensington Publishing Corp.
—Vanishing Act. 1998. (Robin Light Mystery Ser.). 352p. 20.00 o.s.i (*1-57566-326-0*, Kensington Bks.) Kensington Publishing Corp.
—Vanishing Act: A Robin Light Mystery. 1999. (Robin Light Mystery Ser.). 320p. mass mkt. 5.99 (*1-57566-442-9*) Kensington Publishing Corp.
Block, Lawrence. After the First Death. 1994. 268p. mass mkt. 4.50 o.p. (*0-7867-0167-6*, Carroll & Graf Pubs.) Avalon Publishing Group.
—After the First Death. 1984. 192p. reprint ed. pap. 4.95 o.p. (*0-88150-020-8*) Countryman Pr.
—After the First Death. l.t. ed. 1992. (Nightingale Ser.). 291p. pap. 14.95 o.p. (*0-8161-5408-2*, Macmillan Reference USA) Gale Group.
—After the First Death. 2002. 192p. mass mkt. 6.99 (*0-7434-4507-4*) ibooks, Inc.
—The Burglar in the Closet. 1995. (Bernie Rhodenbarr Mystery Ser.: No. 2). 256p. 21.95 o.p. (*0-525-93993-8*, Dutton) Dutton/Plume.
—The Burglar in the Closet. l.t. ed. 1996. (Bernie Rhodenbarr Mystery Ser.: No. 2). 277p. 25.95 o.p. (*0-7862-0548-2*) Thorndike Pr.
—The Burglar in the Library. 1997. (Bernie Rhodenbarr Mystery Ser.: No. 8). 320p. 23.95 o.p. (*0-525-94301-3*, Dutton) Dutton/Plume.
—The Burglar in the Library. l.t. ed. 1998. (Bernie Rhodenbarr Mystery Ser.: No. 8). 464p. 27.95 o.p. (*0-7862-1280-2*) Thorndike Pr.
—The Burglar Who Liked to Quote Kipling. 1996. (Bernie Rhodenbarr Mystery Ser.: No. 3). 256p. 22.95 o.s.i (*0-525-94159-2*, Dutton) Dutton/Plume.
—The Burglar Who Liked to Quote Kipling. 1979. (Bernie Rhodenbarr Mystery Ser.: No. 3). 7.95 o.p. (*0-394-50417-8*) Random Hse., Inc.
—The Burglar Who Painted Like Mondrian. 1983. (Bernie Rhodenbarr Mystery Ser.: No. 5). 217p. 14.50 o.p. (*0-87795-517-4*, Morrow, William & Co.) Morrow/Avon.
—The Burglar Who Traded Ted Williams. 1994. (Bernie Rhodenbarr Mystery Ser.: No. 6). 272p. 19.95 o.p. (*0-525-93807-9*, Dutton) Dutton/Plume.
—Burglars Can't Be Choosers. 1995. (Bernie Rhodenbarr Mystery Ser.: No. 1). 256p. 19.95 o.p. (*0-525-93943-1*, Dutton) Dutton/Plume.
—Coward's Kiss. 1996. 160p. mass mkt. 3.95 (*0-7867-0334-2*, Carroll & Graf Pubs.) Avalon Publishing Group.
—Coward's Kiss. 1987. 160p. reprint ed. pap. 4.95 o.p. (*0-88150-085-2*) Countryman Pr.
—Coward's Kiss. 1999. (Mystery Ser.). 184p. pap. 19.95 (*0-7862-2075-9*, Five Star) Gale Group.
—Coward's Kiss. 2003. 224p. mass mkt. 4.99 (*0-7434-5899-0*) ibooks, Inc.
—A Dance at the Slaughterhouse. (Matthew Scudder Mystery Ser.: No. 9). 2000. 304p. pap. 13.00 (*0-380-81373-4*, Avon Bks.); 1991. 304p. 19.00 o.p. (*0-688-10349-9*, Morrow, William & Co.); 1992. 384p. reprint ed. mass mkt. 7.50 (*0-380-71374-8*, Avon Bks.) Morrow/Avon.
—A Dance at the Slaughterhouse. l.t. ed. 2000. (Matthew Scudder Mystery Ser.: No. 9). 468p. 28.95 (*0-7862-2983-7*) Thorndike Pr.
—The Devil Knows You're Dead. (Matthew Scudder Mystery Ser.: No. 11). 1999. 288p. pap. 12.50 (*0-380-80759-9*, Avon Bks.); 1993. 316p. 20.00 o.p. (*0-688-12192-6*, Morrow, William & Co.); 1994. 384p. reprint ed. mass mkt. 7.50 (*0-380-72023-X*, Avon Bks.) Morrow/Avon.
—The Devil Knows You're Dead. l.t. ed. 2001. (Matthew Scudder Mystery Ser.: No. 11). 503p. 30.95 (*0-7862-3109-2*); (*0-7540-1578-5*); (*0-7540-2440-7*) Thorndike Pr.
—Eight Million Ways to Die. 1986. (Matthew Scudder Mystery Ser.: No. 5). mass mkt. 3.50 o.s.i (*0-515-08840-4*); 1984. (Matthew Scudder Mystery Ser.: No. 5). 304p. mass mkt. 3.95 o.s.i (*0-515-08090-X*); 1983. mass mkt. 3.50 o.s.i (*0-515-07537-X*); 1983. mass mkt. 3.50 o.s.i (*0-515-07257-5*) Berkley Publishing Group. (Jove).
—Eight Million Ways to Die. l.t. ed. 2000. (Matthew Scudder Ser.: No. 5). 410p. pap. 24.95 (*1-56895-939-7*, Wheeler Publishing, Inc.) Gale Group.
—Eight Million Ways to Die. (Matthew Scudder Mystery Ser.: No. 5). 1982. 13.50 o.p. (*0-87795-405-4*, Morrow, William & Co.); 1993. 384p. reprint ed. mass mkt. 7.50 (*0-380-71573-2*, Avon Bks.) Morrow/Avon.
—Even the Wicked. 1997. (Matthew Scudder Mystery Ser.: No. 13). 328p. 23.00 (*0-688-14181-1*, Morrow, William & Co.) Morrow/Avon.
—Everybody Dies. (Matthew Scudder Mystery Ser.: No. 14). 1999. 384p. mass mkt. 6.99 (*0-380-72535-5*, Avon Bks.); 1998. 336p. 25.00 o.p. (*0-688-14182-X*, Morrow, William & Co.) Morrow/Avon.
—Everybody Dies. l.t. ed. 1999. (Matthew Scudder Mystery Ser.: No. 14). 461p. 29.95 (*0-7862-1706-5*) Thorndike Pr.
—In the Midst of Death. l.t. ed. 1991. (Matthew Scudder Mystery Ser.: No. 2). pap. 15.95 o.p. (*0-7927-0601-3*, AS0192); 17.95 o.p. (*0-7451-8095-7*, AH0156) BBC Audiobooks America.
—In the Midst of Death. 1989. (Matthew Scudder Mystery Ser.: No. 3). 192p. mass mkt. 3.50 o.s.i (*0-515-08684-3*); 1984. mass mkt. 2.95 o.s.i (*0-515-08098-5*); 1983. mass mkt. 2.95 o.s.i (*0-515-07430-6*); 1982. mass mkt. 2.75 o.s.i (*0-515-06731-8*) Berkley Publishing Group. (Jove).
—In the Midst of Death. 1976. (Matthew Scudder Mystery Ser.: No. 3). pap. 1.25 o.p. (*0-440-14037-4*) Dell Publishing.
—In the Midst of Death. 2002. E-Book 7.50 (*0-06-052097-3*); E-Book 7.50 (*0-06-052098-1*); E-Book 7.50 (*0-06-052094-9*); E-Book 7.50 (*0-06-052096-5*) HarperCollins General Bks. Group. (PerfectBound).
—In the Midst of Death. 1992. (Matthew Scudder Mystery Ser.: No. 3). 272p. mass mkt. 7.50 (*0-380-76362-1*, Avon Bks.) Morrow/Avon.
—A Long Line of Dead Men. (Matthew Scudder Mystery Ser.: No. 12). 1999. 304p. pap. 12.50 (*0-380-80604-5*, Avon Bks.); 1996. 368p. mass mkt. 7.50 (*0-380-72024-8*, Avon Bks.); 1994. 20.00 o.p. (*0-688-12193-4*, Morrow, William & Co.) Morrow/Avon.
—Out on the Cutting Edge. l.t. ed. 1995. (Matthew Scudder Mystery Ser.: No. 7). 330p. pap. 19.95 o.p. (*0-7838-1177-2*, Macmillan Reference USA) Gale Group.
—Out on the Cutting Edge. l.t. ed. 1995. (Magna Large Print Ser.). 348p. o.p. (*0-7505-0761-6*) Magna Large Print Bks. GBR. *Dist:* Ulverscroft Large Print Canada, Ltd.
—Out on the Cutting Edge. (Matthew Scudder Mystery Ser.: No. 7). 1989. 256p. 17.95 o.p. (*0-688-09069-9*, Morrow, William & Co.); 1990. 352p. reprint ed. mass mkt. 6.99 (*0-380-70993-7*, Avon Bks.) Morrow/Avon.
—The Sins of the Fathers. l.t. ed. 1990. (Matthew Scudder Mystery Ser.: No. 1). 17.95 o.p. (*0-7451-9866-X*, C0616); pap. 15.95 o.p. (*0-7927-0317-0*, C0810) BBC Audiobooks America.
—The Sins of the Fathers. mass mkt. 2.95 o.s.i (*0-515-08685-1*); 1988. (Matthew Scudder Mystery Ser.: No. 1). mass mkt. 3.50 o.s.i (*0-515-09831-0*); 1984. mass mkt. 2.95 o.s.i (*0-515-08157-4*); 1983. mass mkt. 2.95 o.s.i (*0-515-07516-7*); 1982. mass mkt. 2.75 o.s.i (*0-515-06729-6*) Berkley Publishing Group. (Jove).
—The Sins of the Fathers. 2002. E-Book 7.50 (*0-06-052103-1*); E-Book 7.50 (*0-06-052108-2*); E-Book 7.50 (*0-06-052104-X*); E-Book 7.50 (*0-06-052105-8*) HarperCollins General Bks. Group. (PerfectBound).

Settings

Settings

—A Stab in the Dark. 1989. (Matthew Scudder Mystery Ser.: No. 4). 192p. mass mkt. 3.50 o.s.i (0-515-09885-X); 1985. mass mkt. 2.95 o.s.i (0-515-08635-5); 1984. mass mkt. 2.95 o.s.i (0-515-08158-2); 1983. mass mkt. 2.95 o.s.i (0-515-07399-7); 1982. mass mkt. 2.75 o.s.i (0-515-06717-2) Berkley Publishing Group. (Jove).

—A Stab in the Dark. 2002. E-Book 7.50 (0-06-052090-6); E-Book 7.50 (0-06-052093-0); E-Book 7.50 (0-06-052092-2); E-Book 7.50 (0-06-052091-4) HarperCollins General Bks. Group. (PerfectBound).

—A Stab in the Dark. (Matthew Scudder Mystery Ser.: No. 4). 1981. 192p. 10.95 o.p. (0-87795-340-6), Morrow, William & Co.); 2002. 304p. reprint ed. mass mkt. 7.50 (0-380-71574-0, Avon Bks.) Morrow/Avon.

—A Ticket to the Boneyard. l.t. ed. (Matthew Scudder Mystery Ser.: No. 8). 1992. pap. 21.95 o.p. (0-7927-1089-4, CS0293); 1991. 23.95 o.p. (0-7927-1088-6, CH0221) BBC Audiobooks America.

—A Ticket to the Boneyard. l.t. ed. 1995. (Magna Large Print Ser.). 404p. (0-7505-0911-2) Magna Large Print Bks. GBR. Dist: Ulverscroft Large Print Canada, Ltd.

—A Ticket to the Boneyard. (Matthew Scudder Mystery Ser.: No. 8). 1990. 270p. 18.95 o.p. (0-688-09070-2, Morrow, William & Co.); 1991. 384p. reprint ed. mass mkt. 7.50 (0-380-70994-5, Avon Bks.) Morrow/Avon.

—Time to Murder & Create. 1984. (Matthew Scudder Mystery Ser.: No. 2). 192p. mass mkt. 3.50 o.s.i (0-515-08159-0, Jove) Berkley Publishing Group.

—Time to Murder & Create. l.t. ed. 1985. (Matthew Scudder Mystery Ser.: No. 2). 12.50 o.p. (0-8166-0137-2, Macmillan Reference USA) Gale Group.

—Time to Murder & Create. 1991. (Matthew Scudder Mystery Ser.: No. 2). 304p. mass mkt. 7.50 (0-380-76365-6, Avon Bks.) Morrow/Avon.

—A Walk among the Tombstones. l.t. ed. 1993. (Matthew Scudder Mystery Ser.: No. 10). 431p. lib. bdg. 22.95 (0-8161-5759-6, Macmillan Reference USA) Gale Group.

—A Walk among the Tombstones. (Matthew Scudder Mystery Ser.: No. 10). 2000. 304p. pap. 12.50 (0-380-81118-9, Avon Bks.); 1992. 309p. 17.00 o.p. (0-688-10350-2, Morrow, William & Co.); 1993. 384p. reprint ed. mass mkt. 7.50 (0-380-71375-6, Avon Bks.) Morrow/Avon.

—A Walk among the Tombstones. 4.98 o.p. (0-8317-8575-6) Smithmark Pubs., Inc.

—When the Sacred Ginmill Closes. (Matthew Scudder Mystery Ser.: No. 6). 1990. mass mkt. 4.99 o.s.i (0-515-10278-4, Jove); 1987. 272p. 3.95 o.s.i (0-441-88097-5, Diamond Bks.) Berkley Publishing Group.

—When the Sacred Ginmill Closes. l.t. ed. 1987. (Matthew Scudder Mystery Ser.: No. 6). 361p. lib. bdg. 20.95 o.p. (0-8161-4244-0, Macmillan Reference USA) Gale Group.

—When the Sacred Ginmill Closes. 2002. E-Book 7.50 (0-06-052100-7); E-Book 7.50 (0-06-052102-3); E-Book 7.50 (0-06-052101-5); E-Book 7.50 (0-06-052099-X) HarperCollins General Bks. Group. (PerfectBound).

—When the Sacred Ginmill Closes. (Matthew Scudder Mystery Ser.: No. 6). 1997. 384p. mass mkt. 7.50 (0-380-72825-7, Avon Bks.); 1986. 15.95 o.p. (0-87795-774-6, Morrow, William & Co.) Morrow/Avon.

Block, Valerie. Was It Something I Said? 1998. (Ann Rule's Crime Files Ser.). 368p. pap. 14.00 (0-671-02586-4, Washington Square Pr.) Simon & Schuster.

—Was It Something I Said? 1998. 368p. 24.00 (1-56947-109-6) Soho Pr., Inc.

Bloom, Steven. No New Jokes: A Novel. 1997. 187p. 23.00 (0-393-04047-X) Norton, W. W. & Co., Inc.

Bogin, Magda. Natalya, God's Messenger. 1994. 288p. 21.00 o.s.i (0-684-19624-7, Macmillan Reference USA) Gale Group.

Bolton, Isabel. New York Mosaic: Do I Wake or Sleep; The Christmas Tree; Many Mansions. (New York Mosaic Ser.). 401p. 1997. 35.00 (1-883642-28-0); 1998. (Illus.). reprint ed. pap. 18.00 (1-883642-89-2) Steerforth Pr.

Bourdain, Anthony. Bone in the Throat. 2000. 304p. pap. 14.95 (1-58234-102-8) Bloomsbury Publishing.

Bowen, Rhys. For the Love of Mike. Date not set. pap. (0-312-31301-2, St. Martin's Paperbacks); Date not set. mass mkt. 5.99 (0-312-99466-4, St. Martin's Paperbacks); 2003. 320p. 23.95 (0-312-31300-4, Saint Martin's Minotaur) St. Martin's Pr.

—Murphy's Law: A Molly Murphy Mystery. 2001. 242p. 22.95 (0-312-28206-0) St. Martin's Pr.

Bowman, Eric. Before I Wake. 1998. 336p. reprint ed. mass mkt. 6.99 o.s.i (0-515-12353-6, Jove) Berkley Publishing Group.

—Before I Wake, Set. abr. ed. 1997. 25.00 o.p. (0-7871-1463-4, 695277) NewStar Media, Inc.

—Before I Wake. 1997. 320p. 24.95 o.p. (0-399-14263-0, G. P. Putnam's Sons) Penguin Group (USA) Inc.

Boyle, Gerry. Cover Story. 2000. (Jack McMorrow Mystery Ser.: No. 7). 371p. 22.95 o.s.i (0-425-16893-X, Prime Crime) Berkley Publishing Group.

—The Cover Story. 2001. (Jack McMorrow Mystery Ser.: No. 7). 384p. 6.99 (0-425-17852-8, Prime Crime) Berkley Publishing Group.

Boyle, Thomas. Brooklyn Three. 1992. (Crime Ser.). 256p. pap. 4.95 o.p. (0-14-012706-2, Penguin Bks.) Penguin Group (USA) Inc.

—Brooklyn Three. 1991. 256p. 18.95 o.p. (0-670-83019-4) Viking Penguin.

—Only the Dead Know Brooklyn. l.t. ed. 1989. 412p. lib. bdg. 11.95 o.p. (1-85057-479-0, Macmillan Reference USA) Gale Group.

—Only the Dead Know Brooklyn. 1985. 288p. 15.95 o.p. (0-87923-565-9) Godine, David R. Pub.

—Only the Dead Know Brooklyn. mass mkt. 0.25 o.p. (0-451-00950-9, Signet Bks.) NAL.

—Only the Dead Know Brooklyn. 1986. (Crime Ser.). pap. 4.95 o.p. (0-14-017155-X); 288p. mass mkt. 3.50 o.p. (0-14-009257-9) Viking Penguin. (Penguin Bks.).

—Post-Mortem Effects. 1988. 39.50 o.p. (0-14-778385-2) Penguin Group (USA) Inc.

—Post-Mortem Effects. (Crime Ser.). 1988. 288p. pap. 3.95 o.p. (0-14-009753-8, Penguin Bks.); 1987. 15.95 o.p. (0-670-81325-7) Viking Penguin.

Bradford, Barbara Taylor. Dangerous to Know. unabr. ed. 1996. audio 56.00 (0-7366-3209-3, 3872) Books on Tape, Inc.

—Dangerous to Know. 1995. 514p. 24.00 o.p. (0-06-017722-5); audio 22.50 o.p. (0-694-51554-X, HarperAudio) HarperTrade.

—Dangerous to Know. 1996. 400p. mass mkt. 7.99 o.p. (0-06-109208-8, HarperTorch) Morrow/Avon.

—Dangerous to Know. l.t. ed. (Paperback Bestsellers Ser.). 431p. 1996. pap. 25.95 (0-7838-1364-3); 1995. 28.95 (0-7838-1363-5) Thorndike Pr.

—The Triumph of Katie Byrne. l.t. ed. 2001. 496p. 24.95 (0-375-43097-0) Random Hse. Large Print.

—Voice of the Heart. l.t. ed. 1988. 1096p. 21.95 o.p. (0-8161-4465-6); 13.95 o.p. (0-8161-4466-4) Gale Group. (Macmillan Reference USA).

Bradley, Marion Zimmer. Ghostlight. (Light Ser.). 2003. 384p. mass mkt. 6.99 (0-7653-4666-4); 1995. 384p. 22.95 o.p. (0-312-85881-7); 4th ed. 1996. 304p. pap. 15.95 (0-312-86218-0) Doherty, Tom Assocs., LLC. (Tor Bks.).

—Gravelight. (Light Ser.). 2003. 416p. mass mkt. 6.99 (0-7653-4667-2); 1998. 352p. pap. 14.95 (0-312-86507-4); 1997. 352p. 24.95 o.p. (0-312-86503-1) Doherty, Tom Assocs., LLC. (Tor Bks.).

—Heartlight. 416p. 1999. pap. 15.95 (0-312-86509-0); 1998. 25.95 o.p. (0-312-86508-2) Doherty, Tom Assocs., LLC. (Tor Bks.).

—Witch Hunt. 1996. 352p. 20.95 (0-312-85606-7, Forge Bks.) Doherty, Tom Assocs., LLC.

—Witchlight. 2004. mass mkt. 6.99 (0-7653-4714-8); 1996. 304p. 23.95 o.p. (0-312-86104-4); 3rd ed. 1997. 304p. mass mkt. 6.99 o.p. (0-312-85831-0) Doherty, Tom Assocs., LLC. (Tor Bks.).

—Witchlight. abr. ed. 2000. audio 7.95 (1-57815-177-5, 1120, Media Bks. Audio Publishing) Media Bks., L. L. C.

—Witchlight, Set. abr. ed. 1996. audio 16.95 o.p. (1-55935-234-5) Soundelux Audio Publishing.

Brady, James. Further Lane. 1999. E-Book 6.50 o.s.i (0-312-20716-6); 1998. (Further Lane Ser.: Vol. 1). 304p. pap. 6.50 (0-312-96598-2, St. Martin's Paperbacks); 1997. 224p. 22.95 (0-312-15533-6) St. Martin's Pr.

—A Hampton's Christmas. 2000. (Illus.). 211p. 23.95 (0-312-26604-9) St. Martin's Pr.

Brand, Max. Murder Me! l.t. ed. 1996. (G. K. Hall Nightingale Ser.). 304p. pap. 17.95 o.p. (0-7838-1734-7, Macmillan Reference USA) Thorndike Pr.

—Murder Me! 1995. 272p. 20.95 o.p. (0-312-13569-6, Saint Martin's Minotaur) St. Martin's Pr.

Braudy, Susan. What the Movies Made Me Do. 1985. 234p. 15.95 o.s.i (0-394-53246-5) Knopf, Alfred A. Inc.

Breed, Nancy L. The Van Wies of Nine Mile Creek: A Story of the Erie Canal. 1995. (J). pap. 12.50 (0-925168-12-2) North Country Bks., Inc.

Brennan, Carol. Full Commission: A Liz Wareham Mystery. 1993. 224p. 18.95 o.p. (0-88184-911-1, Carroll & Graf Pubs.) Avalon Publishing Group.

—Full Commission: A Liz Wareham Mystery. 1994. 256p. mass mkt. 4.50 o.s.i (0-425-14467-4, Prime Crime) Berkley Publishing Group.

—In the Dark. l.t. ed. 1995. 288p. lib. bdg. 23.95 (1-57490-029-3, Beeler Large Print Bks.) Beeler, Thomas T. Publisher.

—In the Dark. 1995. 256p. mass mkt. 4.99 o.p. (0-425-14579-4, Prime Crime) Berkley Publishing Group.

—In the Dark. 1994. 288p. 21.95 o.p. (0-399-13940-0, G. P. Putnam's Sons) Penguin Group (USA) Inc.

Breslin, Jimmy. The Gang That Couldn't Shoot Straight. 1996. 256p. pap. 12.95 (0-316-11174-0, Back Bay) Little Brown & Co.

—The Gang That Couldn't Shoot Straight. l.t. ed. 2001. (G. K. Hall Paperback Ser.). 328p. 24.95 (0-7838-9391-4) Thorndike Pr.

—The Gang That Couldn't Shoot Straight. 1987. 256p. mass mkt. 4.50 o.p. (0-14-010308-2, Penguin Bks.); 1969. 5.95 o.p. (0-670-33396-4) Viking Penguin.

Bright, Freda. Infidelities. 1986. 384p. 17.95 o.p. (0-689-11797-3, Scribner) Simon & Schuster.

—Parting Shots. 1993. 320p. 19.95 o.p. (0-316-10839-1) Little Brown & Co.

Brodsky, Michael. Xman. 1987. 540p. 21.95 (0-941423-01-8); pap. 11.95 (0-941423-02-6) Four Walls Eight Windows.

Browne, Gerald A. West 47th. 1997. 416p. mass mkt. 6.99 o.p. (0-446-60413-5, Warner Vision); 1996. 82p. 23.95 o.s.i (0-446-51662-7) Warner Bks., Inc.

Brownmiller, Susan. Waverly Place. 1989. 302p. 18.95 o.p. (0-8021-1090-8) Grove/Atlantic, Inc.

Brownstein, Michael. Self-Reliance. 1994. 280p. (Orig.). pap. 12.95 (1-56689-018-7) Coffee Hse. Pr.

Bruchac, Joseph. Long River: A Novel. 1995. 312p. 19.95 (1-55591-213-3) Fulcrum Publishing.

—Turtle Meat & Other Stories. 1992. (Orig.). 144p. 18.95 o.p. (0-930100-48-4); 119p. pap. 12.95 (0-930100-49-2) Holy Cow! Pr.

—The Waters Between: A Novel of the Dawn Land. 1998. 310p. pap. 14.95 (1-58465-015-X); text 26.00 o.p. (0-87451-881-4) Univ. Pr. of New England. (Hardscrabble Bks.).

Buck, Pearl S. Kinfolk. 3rd ed. 1996. (Oriental Novels of Pearl S. Buck Ser.). 418p. reprint ed. pap. 11.95 (1-55921-156-3) Moyer Bell.

Bunting, Josiah, III. All Loves Excelling. 2002. 320p. reprint ed. pap. 14.00 (0-425-18612-1) Berkley Publishing Group.

—All Loves Excelling: A Novel. 2001. 224p. 22.95 (1-882593-40-5) Bridge Works Publishing Co., Inc.

Burton, Gabrielle. Heartbreak Hotel. 1999. 320p. reprint ed. pap. 13.50 (1-56478-167-4) Dalkey Archive Pr.

—Heartbreak Hotel. 1988. pap. 6.95 o.p. (0-14-010819-X, Penguin Bks.) Viking Penguin.

—Heartbreak Hotel: A Novel. 1986. 304p. 15.95 o.p. (0-684-18594-6, Macmillan Reference USA) Gale Group.

Busch, Charles. Whores of Lost Atlantis. 1995. 304p. 17.00 (0-14-024391-7) Viking Penguin.

Busch, Frederick. Harry & Catherine. 1991. 304p. pap. 10.00 o.s.i (0-679-73076-1, Vintage) Knopf Publishing Group.

—Harry & Catherine: A Love Story. 2000. 304p. pap. 14.00 (0-393-32076-6) Norton, W. W. & Co., Inc.

Busia, Akosua. The Seasons of Beento Blackbird: A Novel. 1996. 368p. 22.95 o.p. (0-316-11495-2) Little Brown & Co.

Cain, George. Blueschild Baby. 1987. 180p. reprint ed. pap. 7.50 o.p. (0-88001-133-5) HarperCollins Pubs.

—Blueschild Baby. 1994. pap. o.p. (0-88001-349-4, Ecco) HarperTrade.

Calisher, Hortense. Age: A Love Story. 1996. 124p. reprint ed. pap. 13.95 (0-7145-3012-3) Boyars, Marion Pubs., Inc.

—Age: A Love Story. 128p. 1989. pap. 8.95 o.p. (1-55584-371-9); 1987. 14.95 o.p. (1-55584-132-5) Grove/Atlantic, Inc.

—In the Slammer with Carol Smith. 204p. 1999. pap. 14.95 (0-7145-3045-X); 1997. 24.95 o.p. (0-7145-3020-4) Boyars, Marion Pubs., Inc.

Callahan, Sheila M. Death in a Far Country. 1993. 176p. 17.95 o.p. (0-312-09892-8, Saint Martin's Minotaur) St. Martin's Pr.

Cameron, Peter. Leap Year. 1998. 256p. pap. 12.95 (0-452-27985-2, Plume) Dutton/Plume.

—Leap Year: A Novel. 256p. 1990. 18.95 o.p. (0-06-016252-X); 1991. reprint ed. pap. 8.95 o.p. (0-06-092039-4, Perennial) HarperTrade.

—The Weekend. 1995. 256p. pap. 13.00 o.p. (0-452-27411-7) Dutton/Plume.

—The Weekend. 1994. 184p. 17.00 o.p. (0-374-28739-2) Farrar, Straus & Giroux.

Cameron, Stella. Glass Houses. 2000. 356p. 24.00 o.p. (1-57566-586-7) Kensington Publishing Corp.

Campbell, R. Wright. Malloy's Subway. 1988. 320p. mass mkt. 3.95 (0-8125-0116-0, Tor Bks.) Doherty, Tom Assocs., LLC.

—Malloy's Subway. 1981. 12.95 o.p. (0-689-11181-9, Scribner) Simon & Schuster.

Card, Orson Scott. Treasure Box. abr. ed. 1997. audio 7.99 o.p. (1-56740-182-1, 711, Paperback Nova Audio Bks.); audio 23.95 (1-56100-717-X, 297, Bookcassette); 5p. audio 57.25 o.p. (1-56100-342-5, 1085, Unabridged Library Editions) Brilliance Audio.

—Treasure Box. 1996. 320p. 24.00 o.p. (0-06-017654-7) HarperCollins Pubs.

—Treasure Box. 1998. 384p. mass mkt. 6.99 o.p. (0-06-109398-X, MorrowTorch) Morrow/Avon.

—Treasure Box. 1997. 13.04 (0-606-22211-1) Turtleback Bks.

Carillo, Charles. My Ride with Gus. 256p. 1997. pap. 5.99 (0-671-53569-2, Pocket Star); 1996. 22.00 (0-671-53568-4, Atria) Simon & Schuster.

Carmody, Brian. Fruit Cocktail Diaries. 1994. 15.95 o.p. (0-312-11796-5) St. Martin's Pr.

Carr, Caleb. Killing Time: A Novel of the Future. E-Book 20.95 (1-58945-534-7) Adobe Systems, Inc.

—Killing Time: A Novel of the Future. l.t. ed. 2000. 368p. 25.95 (0-375-43076-8) Random Hse. Large Print.

—Killing Time: A Novel of the Future. 2001. E-Book 20.95 (0-375-50648-9) Random Hse., Inc.

Carr, Jan. Harem Wish. 1994. 256p. 19.95 o.p. (0-525-93739-0, Dutton) Dutton/Plume.

Carroll, Jonathan. The Wooden Sea. 2001. 304p. 23.95 (0-312-87823-0); 2002. reprint ed. pap. 13.95 (0-7653-0013-3) Doherty, Tom Assocs., LLC. (Tor Bks.).

Carter, Robert A. Casual Slaughters. 1992. 272p. 17.95 o.p. (0-89296-502-9) Mysterious Pr.

—Casual Slaughters. 1994. 272p. mass mkt. 5.50 (0-446-40302-4, Mysterious Pr. Paperback Bks.) Warner Bks., Inc.

—Final Edit. 1994. 304p. 18.45 o.p. (0-89296-549-5) Mysterious Pr.

Caunitz, William J. Cleopatra Gold. 1994. pap. 22.95 o.p. (0-7927-1897-6); 23.95 o.p. (0-7927-1898-4) BBC Audiobooks America.

—Cleopatra Gold. 1994. 352p. mass mkt. 6.99 o.s.i (0-425-14394-5) Berkley Publishing Group.

—Cleopatra Gold. unabr. ed. 2000. audio 59.95 o.p. (0-7927-2228-0, CSL 117) Chivers Audio Bks. GBR. Dist: BBC Audiobooks America.

—Cleopatra Gold. abr. ed. 1994. audio 8.99 o.s.i (0-679-43788-6) Knopf, Alfred A. Inc.

—Cleopatra Gold. 1993. audio 16.00 o.p. (0-679-42799-6, RH Audio) Random Hse. Audio Publishing Group.

—Exceptional Clearance. l.t. ed. 1993. pap. 16.95 o.p. (0-7927-1321-4); 1992. 18.95 o.p. (0-7927-1322-2) BBC Audiobooks America.

—Suspects. l.t. ed. 1988. 589p. 19.95 o.p. (0-8161-4337-4, Macmillan Reference USA) Gale Group.

—Suspects. 1987. 384p. 3.99 o.p. (0-517-55864-5) Random Hse. Value Publishing.

Cavanaugh, Jack. The Pioneers. 2010. (American Family Portrait Ser.). 500p. pap. 13.99 (1-56476-587-3) Cook Communications Ministries.

Chace, Rebecca. Capture the Flag. 1999. (Illus.). 288p. 23.00 (0-684-85758-8, Simon & Schuster) Simon & Schuster.

Chace, Susan. Intimacy. 1990. 180p. pap. 7.95 o.p. (0-452-26375-1, Plume) Dutton/Plume.

—Intimacy. 1988. 176p. 14.95 o.p. (0-394-57030-8) Random Hse., Inc.

Charbonneau, Eileen. Honor to the Hills. 1996. 192p. (J). (gr. 7-12). 18.95 (0-312-86094-3, Tor Bks.) Doherty, Tom Assocs., LLC.

Charnee, David. To Kill a Clown. 1992. 256p. 18.95 o.p. (0-312-08324-6, Saint Martin's Minotaur) St. Martin's Pr.

Charyn, Jerome. El Bronx. l.t. ed. 1997. (Cloak & Dagger Ser.). 292p. 25.95 (0-7862-1092-3) Thorndike Pr.

—El Bronx. 1998. mass mkt. (0-446-40538-8, Mysterious Pr. Paperback Bks.); 1997. 256p. 21.50 o.p. (0-89296-604-1) Warner Bks., Inc.

—The Education of Patrick Silver. 1976. 7.95 o.p. (0-87795-142-X, Morrow, William & Co.) Morrow/Avon.

—The Good Policeman. 1990. 288p. 18.95 o.p. (0-89296-360-3) Mysterious Pr.

—The Good Policeman. 1991. mass mkt. 4.99 o.s.i (0-446-40012-2, Mysterious Pr. Paperback Bks.) Warner Bks., Inc.

—The Isaac Quartet: Blue Eyes; Marilyn the Wild; The Education of Patrick Silver; Secret Isaac. 2002. 548p. 35.00 (1-56858-234-X); reprint ed. pap. 17.95 (1-56858-228-5) Four Walls Eight Windows.

—Little Angel Street. 1994. 288p. 19.95 o.s.i (0-89296-462-6) Mysterious Pr.

—Maria's Girls. 1992. 25.00 (0-89296-460-X) Mysterious Pr.

—Marilyn the Wild. 1976. 8.95 o.p. (0-87795-129-2, Morrow, William & Co.) Morrow/Avon.

—Paradise Man. 1987. 17.95 o.s.i (0-917657-93-4) Fine, Donald I. Bks.

Settings

—Secret Isaac. 1978. 9.95 o.p. (0-87795-196-9, Morrow, William & Co.) Morrow/Avon.
—War Cries over Avenue C. 1985. 352p. 17.95 o.s.i (0-917657-30-6) Fine, Donald I. Bks.
—War Cries over Avenue C. 1986. (Contemporary American Fiction Ser.). 368p. pap. 7.95 o.p. (0-14-008796-6, Penguin Bks.) Viking Penguin.
Chase, Ilka. New York 22. 1971. 308p. reprint ed. lib. bdg. 19.75 o.p. (0-8371-4710-7, CHNY, Greenwood Pr.) Greenwood Publishing Group, Inc.
Chase, Linda, et al. Perfect Cover. 1997. 320p. per. 6.99 (0-671-52296-5, Pocket) Simon & Schuster.
Chastain, Thomas. The Prosecutor: A Novel. 1992. 288p. 20.00 o.p. (0-688-10088-0, Morrow, William & Co.) Morrow/Avon.
Chastain, Thomas, et al. Justice in Manhattan. 1994. 17.95 o.p. (0-681-45480-6) Borders Pr.
Cheever, Benjamin. The Partisan. 1994. 352p. 21.00 o.p. (0-689-12174-1, Scribner) Simon & Schuster.
Cheever, John. Bullet Park. 1987. mass mkt. 4.95 o.s.i (0-345-35006-5); 1980. mass mkt. 2.75 o.s.i (0-345-28590-5); 1978. mass mkt. 2.25 o.s.i (0-345-27301-X) Ballantine Bks.
—Bullet Park. unabr. collector's ed. 1986. audio 42.00 (0-7366-0831-1, 1781) Books on Tape, Inc.
—Bullet Park. 1992. (Vintage International Ser.). 256p. pap. 13.95 (0-679-73787-1, Vintage) Knopf Publishing Group.
Cheever, Susan. The Cage, 001. 1982. 11.45 o.p. (0-395-32111-5) Houghton Mifflin Co.
Chepaitis, Barbara. These Dreams. 2003. 320p. pap. 13.00 (0-7434-3751-9, Washington Square Pr.); 2002. 320p. 24.00 (0-7434-3750-0, Atria); 2002. E-Book 9.99 (0-7434-3793-4, Atria) Simon & Schuster.
Cherry, Kelly. Augusta Played, 001. 1979. 9.95 o.p. (0-395-27573-3) Houghton Mifflin Co.
—Augusta Played. 1998. (Voices of the South Ser.). 320p. pap. 14.95 (0-8071-2279-3) Louisiana State Univ. Pr.
Cheuse, Alan. The Grandmother's Club. 1994. 348p. reprint ed. pap. 10.95 (0-87074-374-0) Southern Methodist Univ. Pr.
Child, Lee. Tripwire. 1999. 343p. 23.95 o.p. (0-399-14467-6, G. P. Putnam's Sons) Penguin Group (USA) Inc.
Choi, Susan. American Woman: A Novel. 2003. 384p. 24.95 (0-06-054221-7) HarperCollins Pubs.
Chowder, Ken. Jadis. 1985. 224p. 14.95 o.p. (0-06-015388-1) HarperTrade.
—Jadis. 1986. (Contemporary American Fiction Ser.). 240p. pap. 6.95 o.p. (0-14-008797-4, Penguin Bks.) Viking Penguin.
Christilian, J. D. Scarlet Women. 1996. 304p. 22.95 o.s.i (1-55611-475-3) Fine, Donald I. Bks.
—Scarlet Women. l.t. ed. 1996. 26.95 (1-56895-349-6, Wheeler Publishing, Inc.) Gale Group.
—Scarlet Women. 1997. 384p. mass mkt. 5.99 o.s.i (0-451-19096-3) NAL.
Chu, Louis. Eat a Bowl of Tea. 2002. 256p. mass mkt. 12.00 (0-8184-0395-0, Stuart, Lyle) Kensington Publishing Corp.
Churchill, Jill. Anything Goes: A Grace & Favor Mystery. 1999. 272p. mass mkt. 6.99 (0-380-80244-9, Avon Bks.) Morrow/Avon.
—Love for Sale: A Grace & Favor Mystery. 2004. 272p. mass mkt. 6.99 (0-06-103122-4, Avon Bks.); 2003. 224p. 23.95 (0-06-019942-3, Morrow, William & Co.) Morrow/Avon.
—Someone to Watch over Me: A Grace & Favor Mystery. l.t. ed. 2002. 309p. 28.95 (0-7862-4356-2) Gale Group.
—Someone to Watch over Me: A Grace & Favor Mystery. 2002. 272p. mass mkt. 6.99 (0-06-103123-2, Avon Bks.); 2001. 240p. 24.00 (0-06-019941-5, Morrow, William & Co.) Morrow/Avon.
Ciresi, Rita. Pink Slip. 1999. 416p. pap. 12.95 (0-385-32363-8, Delta) Dell Publishing.
Cimi, Jim. The Come On. 1989. (Crime Ser.). 224p. 17.95 o.s.i (0-939149-24-9) Soho Pr., Inc.
Clark, Jean. The Marriage Bed. 1986. 320p. 3.95 o.s.i (0-441-51994-6, Diamond Bks.) Berkley Publishing Group.
—The Marriage Bed. 1983. 320p. 16.95 o.p. (0-399-12746-1, G. P. Putnam's Sons) Penguin Putnam Bks. for Young Readers.
Clark, Mary Higgins. Loves Music, Loves to Dance. unabr. ed. 1992. audio 48.00 (0-7366-2066-4, 2874) Books on Tape, Inc.
—Loves Music, Loves to Dance. 1996. reprint ed. lib. bdg. 35.95 (1-56849-265-0) Buccaneer Bks., Inc.
—Loves Music, Loves to Dance. 2000. E-Book 9.95 (0-7432-0618-5); 1991. 320p. 21.95 o.p. (0-671-67364-5) Simon & Schuster. (Simon & Schuster).
—Loves Music, Loves to Dance. Rubenstein, Julie, ed. 1992. 336p. reprint ed. mass mkt. 7.99 (0-671-75889-6, Pocket) Simon & Schuster.
—Loves Music, Loves to Dance. abr. ed. 1991. audio 17.00 (0-671-72623-4, 391117, Simon & Schuster Audioworks) Simon & Schuster Audio.
—Pretend You Don't See Her. unabr. ed. 1997. audio 48.00 (0-7366-3711-7, 4395) Books on Tape, Inc.
—Pretend You Don't See Her. 1998. 14.04 (0-606-13721-1) Turtleback Bks.
—You Belong to Me. unabr. ed. 1998. audio 56.00 (0-7366-4189-0, 4687) Books on Tape, Inc.
Clark, Mary Higgins, et al. Missing in Manhattan: The Adams Round Table. 1992. 304p. 17.95 o.p. (0-681-41576-2) Borders Pr.
Clement, Mickey. The Irish Princess. 1995. 304p. mass mkt. 6.99 o.s.i (0-425-14830-0) Berkley Publishing Group.
—The Irish Princess. 1994. 272p. 19.95 o.p. (0-399-13951-6, G. P. Putnam's Sons) Penguin Group (USA) Inc.
Clement, Peter. Death Rounds. 1999. 345p. mass mkt. 6.99 (0-449-00450-3, Fawcett) Ballantine Bks.
—Lethal Practice. 1998. mass mkt. 6.99 (0-8041-1781-0, Ivy Bks.); 1998. 352p. mass mkt. 7.99 (0-449-00281-0, Fawcett); 1997. mass mkt. 6.99 (0-345-40776-8) Ballantine Bks.
Cline, John. The Forever Beat. 1990. 19.95 o.p. (0-525-24855-2, Dutton) Dutton/Plume.
Coben, Harlan. The Final Detail. 2000. 384p. mass mkt. 6.99 (0-440-22545-0) Dell Publishing.
Cohen, Arthur A. In the Days of Simon Stern. 1987. (Phoenix Fiction Ser.). vi, 466p. reprint ed. pap. 36.00 (0-226-11254-3) Univ. of Chicago Pr.
Cohen, Stanley. Angel Face. 1982. 406p. 13.95 o.p. (0-312-03659-0) St. Martin's Pr.
Cohen, Steven M. Becker's Ring. 1997. 432p. mass mkt. 6.50 o.s.i (0-446-60443-7) Warner Bks., Inc.
Coleman, Reed Farrell. Walking the Perfect Square. 2001. 264p. 26.00 (1-57962-039-6) Permanent Pr., The.
Coleman, Val. Beverly & Marigold. 1996. (Illus.). 240p. 23.95 o.p. (0-312-14549-7) St. Martin's Pr.
Collins, Judy. Shameless: A Novel. 1996. 352p. mass mkt. 6.50 o.s.i (0-671-89234-7, Pocket); 1995. 320p. 23.00 o.p. (0-671-89233-9, Atria) Simon & Schuster.
Collins, Michael. The Blood-Red Dream. l.t. ed. 1991. 17.95 o.p. (0-7451-8144-9, AH0180); pap. 15.95 o.p. (0-7927-0664-1, AS0216) BBC Audiobooks America.
—Castrato. 1991. 416p. reprint ed. pap. 4.99 (0-8439-3131-0) Dorchester Publishing Co., Inc.
—Castrato. 1989. 288p. 17.95 o.p. (1-55611-113-4) Fine, Donald I. Bks.
—Chasing Eights. 1992. 400p. reprint ed. pap. 4.99 (0-8439-3274-0) Dorchester Publishing Co., Inc.
—Chasing Eights. 1990. 18.95 o.p. (1-55611-145-2) Fine, Donald I. Bks.
—Crime, Punishment - & Resurrection. 1992. 272p. 19.95 o.p. (1-55611-295-5) Fine, Donald I. Bks.
—Freak. 1990. mass mkt. (0-373-26050-4, Harlequin Bks.) Harlequin Enterprises, Ltd.
—The Irishman's Horse. 1991. 18.95 o.p. (1-55611-185-1) Fine, Donald I. Bks.
—Minnesota Strip. 1987. 264p. 17.95 o.p. (1-55611-032-4) Fine, Donald I. Bks.
—Minnesota Strip. 1988. pap. (0-373-97093-5, Harlequin Bks.) Harlequin Enterprises, Ltd.
—Red Rosa. 1988. 264p. 17.95 o.p. (1-55611-052-9) Fine, Donald I. Bks.
—Red Rosa. 1989. 304p. reprint ed. mass mkt. (0-373-97099-4, Harlequin Bks.) Harlequin Enterprises, Ltd.
—Silent Scream. 1989. mass mkt. (0-373-28000-9, Harlequin Bks.) Harlequin Enterprises, Ltd.
—The Slasher. 1989. mass mkt. (0-373-27999-X, Harlequin Bks.) Harlequin Enterprises, Ltd.
Colter, Gordon. Artist's Proof. 1999. per. (0-373-26300-7, Harlequin Bks.) Harlequin Enterprises, Ltd.
Colwin, Laurie. Another Marvelous Thing. 1994. 144p. pap. 11.00 (0-06-097650-0) HarperTrade.
—Family Happiness. 1987. mass mkt. 3.50 o.s.i (0-449-21447-8); 1983. mass mkt. 2.95 o.s.i (0-449-20275-5) Ballantine Bks. (Fawcett).
—Family Happiness. 2000. 288p. pap. 13.00 (0-06-095897-9); 1993. 224p. reprint ed. pap. 13.00 (0-06-097272-6) HarperTrade. (Perennial).
—Family Happiness. 1982. 12.95 o.s.i (0-394-52511-6) Knopf, Alfred A. Inc.
—Family Happiness. l.t. ed. 1983. 419p. reprint ed. 13.95 o.p. (0-89621-421-4) Thorndike Pr.
Conde, Nicholas. The Religion. 1982. 384p. 13.95 o.p. (0-453-00412-1, H412) NAL.
Connell, Evan S. The Connoisseur. 1987. 208p. pap. 8.95 o.p. (0-86547-245-9, North Point Pr.) Farrar, Straus & Giroux.
—The Connoisseur. 1974. 6.95 o.p. (0-394-49203-X, Knopf Bks. for Young Readers) Random Hse. Children's Bks.
Conroy, Pat. The Prince of Tides. audio 8.95 American Audio Prose Library, Inc.
—The Prince of Tides. l.t. ed. 1993. pap. 21.95 o.p. (0-7927-1358-3); 1992. 24.95 o.p. (0-7927-1359-1) BBC Audiobooks America.
—The Prince of Tides. 1987. 672p. mass mkt. 7.99 (0-553-26888-0) Bantam Bks.
—The Prince of Tides. unabr. ed. 1988. Pt. A. audio 88.00 (0-7366-1458-3, 2339-A); Pt. B. audio 88.00 (0-7366-1459-1, 2339-B) Books on Tape, Inc.
—The Prince of Tides, 001. 1986. 576p. tchr. ed. 30.00 (0-395-35300-9) Houghton Mifflin Co.
—The Prince of Tides. 1987. audio 12.79 o.s.i (0-553-19969-2); audio 15.95 o.s.i (0-553-74510-7); audio 16.99 (0-553-45096-4, 391403) Random Hse. Audio Publishing Group. (RH Audio).
—The Prince of Tides. unabr. ed. 1988. audio 144.00 (1-55690-425-8, 88020E7) Recorded Bks., LLC.
—The Prince of Tides. 2002. E-Book 8.99 (0-7953-0100-6) RosettaBooks.
—The Prince of Tides. 1991. 14.04 (0-606-03895-7) Turtleback Bks.
Cook, Thomas H. Flesh & Blood. 1989. 336p. 17.95 o.p. (0-399-13409-3, G. P. Putnam's Sons) Penguin Putnam Bks. for Young Readers.
—Night Secrets. 1990. 320p. 19.95 o.p. (0-399-13527-8, G. P. Putnam's Sons) Penguin Putnam Bks. for Young Readers.
Cooper, James Fenimore. The Deerslayer. 1964. (YA). (gr. 6 up). pap. 2.95 o.p. (0-8049-0031-0, CL31) Airmont Publishing Co., Inc.
—The Deerslayer. Date not set. 410p. 27.95 (0-8488-2517-9) Amereon, Ltd.
—The Deerslayer. 1991. (States & Their Symbols Ser.). 528p. (gr. 9-12). mass mkt. 5.95 (0-553-21085-8, Bantam Classics) Bantam Bks.
—The Deerslayer. unabr. collector's ed. 1983. Pt. A. (J). audio 64.00 (0-7366-3981-0, 9529A); Pt. B. audio 64.00 (0-7366-3982-9, 9529-B) Books on Tape, Inc.
—The Deerslayer. 1984. 517p. lib. bdg. 27.95 o.p. (0-89966-490-3); 1976. lib. bdg. 21.95 (0-89968-162-X, Lightyear Pr.) Buccaneer Bks., Inc.
—The Deerslayer. 1841. 572p. (YA). reprint ed. pap. text 34.00 (1-4047-2387-0) Classic Textbooks.
—The Deerslayer. 1963. 544p. (J). (gr. 7). mass mkt. 5.95 (0-451-52484-5, CE1645); mass mkt. 2.95 o.p. (0-451-51645-1) NAL. (Signet Classics).
—The Deerslayer. Peck, Daniel H., ed. 2000. (Oxford World's Classics Ser.). (Illus.). 592p. pap. 10.95 (0-19-283725-7) Oxford Univ. Pr., Inc.
—The Deerslayer. 1993. (Oxford World's Classics Ser.). (Illus.). 588p. pap. 7.95 o.p. (0-19-282811-8) Oxford Univ. Pr., Inc.
—The Deerslayer. 1990. (Works of James Fenimore Cooper). reprint ed. lib. bdg. 79.00 (0-7812-2387-3) Reprint Services Corp.
—The Deerslayer. Pease, Donald, ed. & intro. by. 1996. (Classics Ser.). 576p. pap. 10.95 (0-14-039061-8, Penguin Classics) Viking Penguin.
—The Deerslayer. 1998. (Classics Library). pap. 3.95 (1-85326-552-7, 5527WW) Wordsworth Editions, Ltd. GBR. Dist: Combined Publishing.
—The Deerslayer, or the First Warpath. 1990. (Scribner Illustrated Classics Ser.). (Illus.). 480p. (YA). (gr. 7 up). 27.00 (0-684-19224-1, Atheneum) Simon & Schuster Children's Publishing.
—The Deerslayer, or the First Warpath. 1987. 12.00 (0-606-00553-6) Turtleback Bks.
—The Deerslayer or the First Warpath. Schachterle, Lance, ed. & intro. by. 1987. (Writings of James Fenimore Cooper Ser.). 682p. (C). pap. text 19.95 (0-87395-790-3); text 59.50 (0-87395-361-4) State Univ. of New York Pr.
—The Deerslayer, or the First Warpath. deluxe ed. 1990. (Illustrated Classics Ser.). (Illus.). 480p. (YA). 75.00 o.s.i (0-684-19234-9, Atheneum) Simon & Schuster Children's Publishing.
—The Pioneers. Date not set. 346p. 25.95 (0-8488-2544-6) Amereon, Ltd.
—The Pioneers. 1993. 608p. mass mkt. 4.50 o.s.i (0-553-21417-9, Bantam Classics) Bantam Bks.
—The Pioneers. unabr. ed. 1986. audio 85.95 (0-7861-0543-7, 2038) Blackstone Audio Bks., Inc.
—The Pioneers. 1976. lib. bdg. 26.95 (0-89968-157-3, Lightyear Pr.); 1984. 493p. reprint ed. lib. bdg. 26.95 o.p. (0-89966-492-X) Buccaneer Bks., Inc.
—The Pioneers. Set. unabr. ed. 1999. audio 85.95 Highsmith Inc.
—The Pioneers. 1989. audio 69.00 Jimcin Recordings.
—The Pioneers. 1969. mass mkt. 0.60 o.p. (0-451-50214-0, Signet Classics); 1969. mass mkt. 0.75 o.p. (0-451-50480-1, Signet Classics); 1964. mass mkt. 1.25 o.p. (0-451-50746-0, Signet Classics); 1964. mass mkt. 3.95 o.p. (0-451-52145-5); 1964. mass mkt. 1.50 o.p. (0-451-50921-8, Signet Classics); 1964. mass mkt. 1.95 o.p. (0-451-51156-5, Signet Classics); 1964. mass mkt. 2.50 o.p. (0-451-51416-5, Signet Classics); 1964. mass mkt. 3.50 o.p. (0-451-51621-4, Signet Classics) NAL.
—The Pioneers. unabr. ed. 2001. audio 68.95 NorthStar Audio Bks.
—The Pioneers. Wallace, James D., ed. & intro. by. 2000. (Oxford World's Classics Ser.). (Illus.). 496p. pap. 10.95 (0-19-283667-6) Oxford Univ. Pr., Inc.
—The Pioneers. Wallace, James D., ed. 1992. (Oxford World's Classics Ser.). (Illus.). 484p. pap. 7.95 o.p. (0-19-282802-9, 4581) Oxford Univ. Pr., Inc.
—The Pioneers. 1990. (Works of James Fenimore Cooper). reprint ed. lib. bdg. 79.00 (0-7812-2371-7) Reprint Services Corp.
—The Pioneers. Clark, Robert, ed. 1993. (Illus.). 444p. pap. 6.95 o.p. (0-460-87187-0, Everyman's Classic Library in Paperback) Tuttle Publishing.
—The Pioneers. Ringe, Donald A., ed. & intro. by. 1988. (Classics Ser.). 480p. pap. 11.00 (0-14-039007-3, Penguin Classics) Viking Penguin.
—The Pioneers or the Sources of the Susquehanna: A Descriptive Tale. 1980. (Writings of James Fenimore Cooper Ser.). 460p. (C). pap. text 31.95 (0-87395-423-8) State Univ. of New York Pr.
—The Pioneers or the Susquehanna: A Descriptive Tale. 1980. (Writings of James Fenimore Cooper Ser.). 460p. (C). text 18.50 o.p. (0-87395-359-2) State Univ. of New York Pr.
—Satanstoe, or the Littlepage Manuscripts: A Tale of the Colony. 1990. (Writings of James Fenimore Cooper Ser.). 500p. (C). text 26.50 (0-88706-903-7); pap. text 24.95 (0-88706-904-5) State Univ. of New York Pr.
—The Spy: A Tale of the Neutral Ground. 2000. (Writings of James Fenimore Cooper Ser.: No. 24). xxxv, 551p. 115.00 (0-404-64454-6) AMS Pr., Inc.
—The Spy: A Tale of the Neutral Ground. 1970. (Library of Classics: No. 18). (Illus.). pap. text 5.95 o.p. (0-02-843130-8) Hafner Pr.
—The Spy: A Tale of the Neutral Ground. 1997. (Practical Resources for the Mental Health Professionals Ser.). 448p. pap. 15.00 (0-14-043628-6, Penguin Classics) Viking Penguin.
Corbin, Steven. No Easy Place to Be. 1989. 19.95 o.p. (0-671-65884-0, Simon & Schuster) Simon & Schuster.
Cotler, Gordon. Artist's Proof. unabr. ed. 1998. audio 51.00 (0-7887-1307-8, 95149E7) Recorded Bks., LLC.
—Artist's Proof: A Mystery. 1997. 272p. 21.95 o.p. (0-312-16831-4, Saint Martin's Minotaur) St. Martin's Pr.
Coughlin, T. Glen. The Hero of New York. 1986. 14.95 o.p. (0-393-02262-5) Norton, W. W. & Co., Inc.
Courter, Gay. The Midwife's Advice. 1992. 608p. 23.00 o.p. (0-525-93494-4, Dutton) Dutton/Plume.
Craddock, Charles Egbert. The Despot of Broomsedge Cove. E-Book 3.95 (0-594-04707-2) 1873 Pr.
Crane, Stephen. Maggie: A Girl of the Streets. 1999. xvii, 374p. pap. text 10.00 (0-312-15266-3) Bedford/Saint Martin's.
—Maggie: A Girl of the Streets. Gullason, Thomas A., ed. 1979. (Critical Editions Ser.). 258p. (C). pap. text 9.00 net. (0-393-95024-7) Norton, W. W. & Co., Inc.
—Maggie: A Girl of the Streets. 1995. (Literary Classics). 90p. pap. 9.00 (1-57392-037-1) Prometheus Bks., Pubs.
Crawford, Claudia. Bliss. 1994. 432p. (Orig.). mass mkt. 5.50 o.s.i (0-451-17937-4, Signet Bks.) NAL.
Cray, David. Keeplock: A Novel of Crime. 1995. 21.00 (1-883402-97-2, Scribner) Simon & Schuster.
—Keeplock: A Novel of Crime. l.t. ed. 1995. (Niagara Large Print Ser.). 411p. 29.50 o.p. (0-7089-5817-6, Ulverscroft) Thorpe, F. A. Pubs. GBR. Dist: Ulverscroft Large Print Bks., Ltd.
Crespi, Camilla T. The Trouble with a Bad Fit. 1996. 272p. 21.00 o.p. (0-06-017661-X) HarperCollins Pubs.
—The Trouble with a Bad Fit. 1997. 320p. mass mkt. 4.99 (0-06-109408-0, HarperTorch) Morrow/Avon.
—The Trouble with a Hot Summer: A Simona Griffo Mystery. 1997. 320p. 23.00 o.p. (0-06-017662-8) HarperCollins Pubs.
—The Trouble with a Hot Summer: A Simona Griffo Mystery. mass mkt. o.s.i (0-06-109409-9); 1998. 368p. mass mkt. 5.99 o.s.i (0-06-104464-4) Morrow/Avon. (HarperTorch).
—The Trouble with a Small Raise. 1991. 288p. mass mkt. 3.95 o.s.i (0-8217-3274-9, Zebra Bks.) Kensington Publishing Corp.
—The Trouble with Moonlighting. 1991. 224p. mass mkt. 3.95 o.s.i (0-8217-3452-0, Zebra Bks.) Kensington Publishing Corp.
Criscuolo, C. Clark. Wiseguys in Love. 1993. 240p. 17.95 o.p. (0-312-09413-2, Saint Martin's Minotaur) St. Martin's Pr.
Cross, Amanda. The Puzzled Heart. 1998. (Kate Fansler Novels Ser.). 256p. mass mkt. 6.99 (0-345-41884-0) Ballantine Bks.
—The Puzzled Heart. l.t. ed. 1998. (0-7540-3401-1); (0-7540-3402-X) Thorndike Pr.
Crowley, John. AEgypt. 1994. 400p. pap. 13.95 o.s.i (0-553-37430-3) Bantam Bks.
—Love & Sleep. 1995. 512p. pap. 12.95 o.s.i (0-553-37468-0) Bantam Bks.
Cunningham, Elizabeth. Return of the Goddess. 1993. 388p. pap. 12.95 (0-88268-157-5) Station Hill Pr.
—The Return of the Goddess: A Divine Comedy. 1992. 384p. 22.50 (0-88268-115-X) Station Hill Pr.
Cunningham, Michael. A Home at the End of the World. 352p. audio compact disk 39.95 (1-55927-990-7) Audio Renaissance.

—A Home at the End of the World. l.t. ed. 2003. 536p. 29.95 (*0-7862-5745-8*, Large Print Pr.) Thorndike Pr.

—A Home at the End of the World: A Novel. 1995. mass mkt. 6.99 o.s.i (*0-553-57550-3*); 1992. 480p. pap. 6.99 o.s.i (*0-553-55002-0*) Bantam Bks.

—A Home at the End of the World: A Novel. 1990. 18.95 o.s.i (*0-374-17250-1*) Farrar, Straus & Giroux.

—A Home at the End of the World: A Novel. 1998. 352p. pap. 14.00 (*0-312-20231-8*) Picador.

Dailey, Janet. Beware of the Stranger: New York. 1992. (Janet Dailey Americana Ser.: No. 882). per. (*0-373-89882-7*, 1-89882-4); 1987. (Americana Ser.: No. 32). pap. (*0-373-89832-0*) Harlequin Enterprises, Ltd. (Harlequin Bks.).

—Beware of the Stranger: New York. 2002. pap. 6.99 (*0-7592-3801-4*); E-Book 6.99 (*0-7592-0094-7*); E-Book 6.99 (*1-58586-458-7*); E-Book 6.99 (*0-7592-0839-5*) ereads.com.

Daley, Robert. A Faint Cold Fear. abr. ed. 1991. audio 15.95 o.p. (*1-55927-142-6*) Audio Renaissance.

—A Faint Cold Fear. 1990. 19.95 o.p. (*0-316-17184-0*) Little Brown & Co.

—A Faint Cold Fear. abr. ed. 1991. audio 7.95 (*1-57815-038-8*, 1010) Media Bks., L. L. C.

—A Faint Cold Fear. 1992. 480p. mass mkt. 5.99 o.s.i (*0-446-36219-0*) Warner Bks., Inc.

—Hands of a Stranger. l.t. ed. 1986. (General Ser.). 615p. 19.95 o.p. (*0-8161-4032-4*); 10.95 o.p. (*0-8161-4071-5*) Gale Group. (Macmillan Reference USA).

—Hands of a Stranger. 1986. mass mkt. 2.95 o.p. (*0-451-15789-3*); mass mkt. 4.50 o.p. (*0-451-14509-7*) NAL. (Signet Bks.).

—Hands of a Stranger. 1985. 418p. 16.45 o.p. (*0-671-49962-9*, Simon & Schuster) Simon & Schuster.

—Night Falls on Manhattan: A Novel. 1993. 391p. 21.95 o.p. (*0-316-17196-4*) Little Brown & Co.

—To Kill a Cop. 1978. mass mkt. 2.25 o.s.i (*0-345-27644-2*); 1977. mass mkt. 2.25 o.s.i (*0-345-25945-9*) Ballantine Bks.

—To Kill a Cop. 1996. 400p. mass mkt. 6.50 o.s.i (*0-446-36571-8*) Warner Bks., Inc.

Daly, Carroll J. The Adventures of Race Williams. 1989. 352p. 9.95 (*0-89296-959-8*) Mysterious Pr.

—The Hidden Hand: A Race Williams Mystery. 1992. 320p. reprint ed. pap. 8.00 o.p. (*0-06-097436-2*, Perennial) HarperTrade.

—Murder from the East: A Race Williams Story. 1978. (Library of Crime Classics). 312p. reprint ed. pap. 4.95 o.p. (*0-930330-01-3*) International Polygonics, Ltd.

—The Snarl of the Beast: A Race Williams Mystery. 1992. 320p. reprint ed. pap. 8.00 o.p. (*0-06-097435-4*, Perennial) HarperTrade.

Daly, Conor. Buried Lies. (Kieran Lenahan Mystery Ser.). 1997. 304p. mass mkt. 5.50 o.s.i (*1-57566-168-3*); 1996. 320p. 18.95 o.p. (*1-57566-033-4*) Kensington Publishing Corp.

Daly, David J. The Legend of Killer Noon. 2000. 223p. pap. 14.95 (*0-9671411-0-9*) Green Boat Pr.

Daly, Elizabeth. And Dangerous to Know. 1984. 176p. pap. 2.95 o.p. (*0-553-24616-X*) Bantam Bks.

—And Dangerous to Know. 1991. 9.95 o.p. (*0-8050-0805-5*) Holt, Henry & Co.

—Any Shape or Form. 1981. (Murder Ink Mystery Ser.: No. 27). pap. 2.25 o.p. (*0-440-10108-5*) Dell Publishing.

—Arrow Pointing Nowhere. 1983. pap. 3.25 o.p. (*0-440-10021-6*) Dell Publishing.

—The Book of the Lion. 1985. 160p. pap. 2.95 o.p. (*0-553-24883-9*) Bantam Bks.

—The Book of the Lion. 1950. 9.95 o.p. (*0-8050-0806-3*) Holt, Henry & Co.

—Deadly Nightshade. 1993. audio 44.20 (*1-56544-034-X*, 250013); audio Literate Ear, Inc.

—Death & Letters. 1981. pap. 2.25 o.p. (*0-440-11791-7*) Dell Publishing.

—Death & Letters. Barzun, Jacques & Taylor, W. H., eds. 1982. (Crime Fiction 1950-1975 Ser.). 131p. lib. bdg. 18.00 o.p. (*0-8240-4979-9*) Garland Publishing, Inc.

—The House Without the Door. 1984. 192p. pap. 2.95 o.p. (*0-553-24610-0*) Bantam Bks.

—Murders in Volume Two: A Henry Gamadge Mystery. 1993. audio 41.00 (*1-56544-054-4*, 250016); audio Literate Ear, Inc.

—Murders in Volume Two: A Henry Gamadge Mystery. 1994. 320p. reprint ed. pap. 6.95 (*1-883402-52-2*, Scribner) Simon & Schuster.

—Night Walk. 1982. (Murder Ink Mystery Ser.: No. 55). pap. 2.50 o.p. (*0-440-16609-8*) Dell Publishing.

—Nothing Can Rescue Me. 1984. 192p. pap. 2.95 o.p. (*0-553-24605-4*) Bantam Bks.

—Somewhere in the House. 1984. 192p. pap. 2.95 o.p. (*0-553-24267-9*) Bantam Bks.

—Unexpected Night: A Henry Gamadge Mystery. 1986. (Mystery Ser.). 224p. pap. 2.95 o.p. (*0-553-25129-5*) Bantam Bks.

—Unexpected Night: A Henry Gamadge Mystery. 1991. 9.95 o.p. (*0-8050-0807-1*) Holt, Henry & Co.

—Unexpected Night: A Henry Gamadge Mystery. 1993. audio 39.20 (*1-56544-033-1*, 250003); audio Literate Ear, Inc.

—Unexpected Night: A Henry Gamadge Mystery. 1995. pap. 6.95 (*1-883402-14-X*); 1994. 240p. reprint ed. per. 7.00 (*1-883402-51-4*) Simon & Schuster. (Scribner).

—The Wrong Way Down. 1986. mass mkt. 9.95 o.p. (*0-553-06515-7*) Bantam Bks.

Daly, Michael. Under Ground. 1997. 448p. mass mkt. 5.99 o.s.i (*0-451-19154-4*, Signet Bks.) NAL.

—Under Ground: A Novel. 1995. 415p. 21.95 o.p. (*0-316-21709-3*) Little Brown & Co.

Darieck, Scott. Traitor to the Race. 1996. 224p. pap. 10.95 o.p. (*0-452-27335-8*, Plume) Dutton/Plume.

David, Lawrence. Need. 1996. 355p. mass mkt. 6.99 (*0-312-95922-2*, St. Martin's Paperbacks) St. Martin's Pr.

Davies, June W. Storm Before Sunrise. 1993. 574p. 24.95 o.p. (*0-312-10552-5*) St. Martin's Pr.

Davies, Valentine. The Miracle on 34th Street. reprint ed. lib. bdg. 17.95 (*0-88411-934-3*) Amereon, Ltd.

—The Miracle on 34th Street. 1994. 160p. pap. 9.95 (*0-15-600198-5*); 1967. pap. 2.50 o.p. (*0-15-660453-1*, Harvest Bks.); 1947. 120p. 13.95 o.s.i (*0-15-160239-5*) Harcourt Trade Pubs.

Davis, Kathryn. The Girl Who Trod on a Loaf. 2003. 416p. pap. 14.95 (*0-316-73503-5*, Back Bay) Little Brown & Co.

Davis, Thulani. Maker of Saints. 1997. 256p. pap. 15.00 (*0-14-026735-2*) Penguin Group (USA) Inc.

—Maker of Saints. 1996. 256p. 22.00 (*0-684-81225-8*, Scribner) Simon & Schuster.

Dawe, Margaret. Nissequott. 1994. 304p. pap. 10.95 (*0-8112-1260-2*, NDP775); 1992. 288p. 19.95 o.p. (*0-8112-1202-5*) New Directions Publishing Corp.

De Haven, Tom. Funny Papers. (American Fiction Ser.). 384p. 1986. pap. 6.95 o.p. (*0-14-008680-3*, Penguin Bks.); 1985. 15.95 o.p. (*0-670-33251-8*) Viking Penguin.

—Funny Papers: A Novel. 2002. 384p. pap. 14.00 (*0-312-42134-6*) Picador.

DeAndrea, William L. The Hog Murders. 1999. (*0-7862-1942-4*, Five Star) Gale Group.

—The Hog Murders. 1999. 210p. pap. 8.95 o.p. (*1-55882-030-2*, Library of Crime Classics) International Polygonics, Ltd.

—The Hog Murders. 1985. pap. 1.95 o.p. (*0-380-47548-0*, 47548-0, Avon Bks.) Morrow/Avon.

—Killed on the Rocks. 1990. 240p. 17.95 o.p. (*0-89296-210-0*) Mysterious Pr.

—Killed on the Rocks. 1992. 2.99 o.p. (*0-517-08869-X*) Random Hse. Value Publishing.

—Killed on the Rocks. 1991. 240p. mass mkt. 4.99 (*0-446-40060-2*, Mysterious Pr. Paperback Bks.) Warner Bks., Inc.

—The Manx Murders: A Professor Niccolo Benedetti Mystery. 1994. 17.00 o.s.i (*0-385-42500-7*) Doubleday Publishing.

—The Manx Murders: A Professor Niccolo Benedetti Mystery. 1994. 256p. 20.00 (*1-883402-66-2*, Scribner) Simon & Schuster.

Deaner, Janice. Where Blue Begins. 1993. 432p. 22.00 o.p. (*0-525-93580-0*, Dutton) Dutton/Plume.

Deaver, Jeffery. The Devil's Teardrop: A Novel of the Last Night of the Century. E-Book 25.00 (*1-930161-37-9*) Adobe Systems, Inc.

—The Devil's Teardrop: A Novel of the Last Night of the Century. l.t. ed. 2000. pap. 11.95 (*1-56895-982-6*); 1999. 527p. 26.95 o.p. (*1-56895-804-8*) Gale Group. (Wheeler Publishing, Inc.).

—The Devil's Teardrop: A Novel of the Last Night of the Century. 2000. E-Book 9.99 (*0-684-85659-X*, Simon & Schuster); 1999. 400p. mass mkt. 7.99 (*0-671-03712-9*, Pocket); 1999. 400p. 25.00 o.s.i (*0-684-85292-6*, Simon & Schuster); 2000. (Illus.). 480p. reprint ed. pap. 7.99 (*0-671-03844-3*, Pocket) Simon & Schuster.

—The Devil's Teardrop: A Novel of the Last Night of the Century. abr. ed. 1999. 352p. audio 24.00 (*0-671-04569-5*, Simon & Schuster Audioworks) Simon & Schuster Audio.

—The Devil's Teardrop: A Novel of the Last Night of the Century. l.t. ed. 2002. (Charnwood Large Print Ser.). 520p. 32.50 o.p. (*0-7089-9298-6*, Charnwood) Thorpe, F. A. Pubs. GBR. *Dist:* Ulverscroft Large Print Bks., Ltd., Ulverscroft Large Print Canada, Ltd.

—Hard News. 1992. 256p. mass mkt. 4.99 o.s.i (*0-553-29622-1*) Bantam Bks.

—Hard News. 1991. 320p. 15.00 o.s.i (*0-385-42121-4*) Doubleday Publishing.

—Shallow Graves. 2001. E-Book 6.99 (*0-7434-2401-8*, Pocket) Simon & Schuster.

Dee, Jonathan. The Liberty Campaign. l.t. ed. 1994. 22.95 o.p. (*0-7927-1946-8*); 1994. pap. 21.95 o.p. (*0-7927-1945-X*); 1995. audio 69.95 (*0-7862-9978-9*, CSL 082) BBC Audiobooks America.

—The Liberty Campaign. 1995. 288p. pap. 17.95 (*0-671-89085-9*, Pocket) Simon & Schuster.

DeFilippi, Jim. Blood Sugar: A Novel. 1992. 352p. 20.00 o.p. (*0-06-016879-X*) HarperTrade.

Delamer, John J. The Tarnished Shield. 1995. 208p. (Orig.). pap. 12.95 (*1-56474-156-7*) Fithian Pr.

Deleva, John. Hours Like Diamonds. 2000. 169p. (Orig.). pap. 11.77 (*0-9701668-0-X*) Johnsbook-.com.

DeLillo, Don. Great Jones Street. 1994. 272p. pap. 14.00 (*0-14-017917-8*) Penguin Group (USA) Inc.

Delinsky, Barbara. T. L. C. 2001. 250p. mass mkt. (*1-55166-822-X*, 1-66822-7, Mira Bks.); 1994. 256p. per. (*1-55166-010-5*, 1-66010-9, Mira Bks.); 1988. pap. (*0-373-25299-4*, Harlequin Bks.) Harlequin Enterprises, Ltd.

Dell, Floyd. Love in Greenwich Village. 1977. (Short Story Index Reprint Ser.). 27.95 (*0-8369-3621-3*) Ayer Co. Pubs., Inc.

Delman, David. Ain't Goin' to Glory. 1991. 224p. 18.95 o.p. (*0-312-06272-9*) St. Martin's Pr.

DeLynn, Jane. Real Estate. 1989. 304p. mass mkt. 3.95 o.s.i (*0-345-35978-X*) Ballantine Bks.

—Real Estate. 1998. 316p. pap. 18.00 (*1-891305-10-7*) Painted Leaf Pr.

—Real Estate. 1988. 17.45 o.p. (*0-671-54424-1*, Simon & Schuster) Simon & Schuster.

Deming, Philander. The Best Adirondack Stories of Philander Deming. 1997. (Ne York Classics Ser.). (Illus.). 221p. 24.95 (*0-8156-0442-4*) Syracuse Univ. Pr.

Denker, Henry. Doctor on Trial. unabr. ed. 1992. audio 23.95 o.p. (*1-56100-471-5*, 92, Bookcassette); audio 73.25 o.p. (*1-56100-105-8*, 867, Unabridged Library Editions) Brilliance Audio.

—Doctor on Trial: A Novel. 1992. 20.00 o.p. (*0-688-11388-5*, Morrow, William & Co.) Morrow/Avon.

—Labyrinth: A Novel. 1994. 299p. 23.00 o.p. (*0-688-13700-8*, Morrow, William & Co.) Morrow/Avon.

Dentinger, Jane. First Hit of the Season. l.t. ed. 1985. lib. bdg. 13.95 o.p. (*0-89340-875-1*, 863) BBC Audiobooks America.

—First Hit of the Season. 1984. (Crime Club Ser.). 192p. 11.95 o.p. (*0-385-19409-9*) Doubleday Publishing.

—First Hit of the Season. 1993. (Jocelyn O'Roarke Mystery Ser.). 192p. pap. 4.95 o.p. (*0-14-015842-1*, Penguin Bks.) Penguin Group (USA) Inc.

Deveraux, Jude. Sweet Liar. l.t. ed. 1993. (General Ser.). 586p. pap. 18.95 o.p. (*0-8161-5623-9*); 23.95 o.p. (*0-8161-5622-0*) Gale Group. (Macmillan Reference USA).

—Sweet Liar. Marrow, Linda, ed. 1993. 448p. mass mkt. 7.99 (*0-671-68974-6*, Pocket); 1992. 384p. 22.00 (*0-671-68973-8*, Atria) Simon & Schuster.

—Sweet Liar. abr. ed. 1999. (Angel Ser.). audio 9.98 o.s.i (*0-671-04417-6*, Simon & Schuster Audioworks) Simon & Schuster Audio.

—Sweet Liar. Marrow, Linda, ed. abr. ed. 1992. 384p. pap. 17.00 incl. audio (*0-671-79190-7*, Simon & Schuster Audioworks) Simon & Schuster Audio.

Di Donato, Pietro. Christ in Concrete. 1977. pap. 1.95 o.p. (*0-671-81183-5*, Pocket) Simon & Schuster.

—Christ in Concrete: A Novel. 1993. 256p. mass mkt. 6.95 (*0-451-52575-2*, Signet Classics) NAL.

Diaz Valcarcel, Emilio. Hot Soles in Harlem. Miller, Yvette E., ed. Fayen, Tanya T., tr. from SPA. 1993. (Discoveries Ser.). 175p. pap. 16.95 (*0-935480-61-7*) Latin American Literary Review Pr.

Dicerto, Joseph. Wall People. 1985. 11.95 o.s.i (*0-689-31090-0*, Atheneum) Simon & Schuster Children's Publishing.

Dickson, Carter, pseud. A Graveyard to Let. 1978. reprint ed. pap. 1.50 o.s.i (*0-505-51222-X*) Dorchester Publishing Co., Inc.

Dixon, Melvin. Vanishing Rooms. 224p. 1991. 18.95 o.p. (*0-525-24965-6*, Dutton); 1992. reprint ed. pap. 10.00 o.p. (*0-452-26761-7*, Plume) Dutton/Plume.

Dobyns, Stephen. The Church of Dead Girls. l.t. ed. 1997. (Large Print Book Ser.). 26.95 (*1-56895-478-6*, Wheeler Publishing, Inc.) Gale Group.

—The Church of Dead Girls. 400p. 1998. pap. 14.00 o.s.i (*0-8050-5104-X*, Owl Bks.); 1997. 23.00 o.s.i (*0-8050-5103-1*, Metropolitan Bks.) Holt, Henry & Co.

—The Church of Dead Girls. 2001. 432p. reprint ed. mass mkt. 6.99 (*0-312-97736-0*, St. Martin's Paperbacks) St. Martin's Pr.

—Saratoga Backtalk. unabr. collector's ed. 1995. audio 36.00 (*0-7366-2969-6*, 3660) Books on Tape, Inc.

—Saratoga Backtalk. l.t. ed. 1995. (Large Print Bks.). pap. 21.95 o.p. (*1-56895-089-6*, Wheeler Publishing, Inc.) Gale Group.

—Saratoga Backtalk. 1994. 221p. 19.95 o.p. (*0-393-03659-6*) Norton, W. W. & Co., Inc.

—Saratoga Backtalk. 1995. (Charlie Bradshaw Mystery Ser.). 224p. pap. 5.99 o.s.i (*0-14-024708-4*, Penguin Bks.) Penguin Group (USA) Inc.

—Saratoga Bestiary. unabr. collector's ed. 1994. audio 42.00 (*0-7366-2792-8*, 3507) Books on Tape, Inc.

—Saratoga Bestiary. (Charlie Bradshaw Mystery Ser.). 1990. 304p. pap. 4.50 o.p. (*0-14-010613-8*, Penguin Bks.); 1988. 272p. 16.95 o.p. (*0-670-82024-5*) Viking Penguin.

—Saratoga Fleshpot. unabr. collector's ed. 1996. audio 36.00 (*0-7366-3356-1*, 4007) Books on Tape, Inc.

—Saratoga Fleshpot. 1995. 220p. 21.00 (*0-393-03805-X*) Norton, W. W. & Co., Inc.

—Saratoga Fleshpot. 1996. (Charlie Bradshaw Mystery Ser.). 224p. pap. 5.95 o.p. (*0-14-025535-4*, Penguin Bks.) Penguin Group (USA) Inc.

—Saratoga Haunting. unabr. collector's ed. 1994. audio 36.00 (*0-7366-2836-3*, 3544) Books on Tape, Inc.

—Saratoga Haunting. 1994. (Charlie Bradshaw Mystery Ser.). 224p. pap. 6.95 o.p. (*0-14-017162-2*, Penguin Bks.) Penguin Group (USA) Inc.

—Saratoga Haunting. 1993. (Charlie Bradshaw Mystery Ser.). 224p. 19.00 o.p. (*0-670-84581-7*, Viking) Viking Penguin.

—Saratoga Headhunter. unabr. collector's ed. 1994. audio 36.00 (*0-7366-2754-5*, 3477) Books on Tape, Inc.

—Saratoga Headhunter. 1991. (Charlie Bradshaw Mystery Ser.). 224p. pap. 4.95 o.p. (*0-14-015606-2*, Penguin Bks.) Penguin Group (USA) Inc.

—Saratoga Headhunter. (Crime Monthly Ser.). 1986. pap. 3.50 o.p. (*0-14-007772-3*, Penguin Bks.); 1985. 13.95 o.p. (*0-670-80488-6*) Viking Penguin.

—Saratoga Hexameter. unabr. collector's ed. 1994. audio 48.00 (*0-7366-2890-8*, 3590) Books on Tape, Inc.

—Saratoga Hexameter. l.t. ed. 1991. (General Ser.). 391p. lib. bdg. 20.95 (*0-8161-5133-4*, Macmillan Reference USA) Gale Group.

—Saratoga Hexameter. 1991. (Crime Monthly Ser.). 256p. pap. 4.95 o.p. (*0-14-011691-5*, Penguin Bks.) Penguin Group (USA) Inc.

—Saratoga Hexameter. 1990. (Charlie Bradshaw Mystery Ser.). 256p. 16.95 o.p. (*0-670-82568-9*, Viking) Viking Penguin.

—Saratoga Longshot. unabr. collector's ed. 1994. audio 36.00 (*0-7366-2698-0*, 3432) Books on Tape, Inc.

—Saratoga Longshot. 1987. (Charlie Bradshaw Mystery Ser.). 256p. pap. 3.95 o.p. (*0-14-009627-2*, Penguin Bks.) Viking Penguin.

—Saratoga Snapper. unabr. collector's ed. 1994. audio 42.00 (*0-7366-2793-6*, 3508) Books on Tape, Inc.

—Saratoga Snapper. l.t. ed. 1988. 329p. 17.95 o.p. (*0-8161-4348-X*, Macmillan Reference USA) Gale Group.

—Saratoga Snapper. (Charlie Bradshaw Mystery Ser.). 1987. 272p. pap. 3.95 o.p. (*0-14-008812-1*, Penguin Bks.); 1986. 288p. 15.95 o.p. (*0-670-81059-2*) Viking Penguin.

—Saratoga Strongbox. l.t. ed. 2000. pap. 23.95 (*1-56895-848-X*, Wheeler Publishing, Inc.) Gale Group.

—Saratoga Strongbox. 1999. (Charlie Bradshaw Mysteries Ser.). 224p. pap. 5.99 o.s.i (*0-14-028012-X*) Penguin Group (USA) Inc.

—Saratoga Strongbox. 1998. (Charlie Bradshaw Mysteries Ser.). 208p. 21.95 o.p. (*0-670-87692-5*) Viking Penguin.

—Saratoga Swimmer. unabr. collector's ed. 1994. audio 36.00 (*0-7366-2753-7*, 3476) Books on Tape, Inc.

—Saratoga Swimmer. 1981. 12.95 o.p. (*0-689-11193-2*, Scribner) Simon & Schuster.

—Saratoga Swimmer. 1983. (Charlie Bradshaw Mystery Ser.). 224p. pap. 5.95 o.p. (*0-14-006357-9*, Penguin Bks.) Viking Penguin.

—Saratoga Trifecta. 1995. (Charlie Bradshaw Mystery Ser.). 544p. pap. 24.00 o.s.i (*0-14-025196-0*, Penguin Bks.) Penguin Group (USA) Inc.

Doctorow, E. L. Billy Bathgate. l.t. ed. 1990. (General Ser.). 448p. lib. bdg. 13.95 o.p. (*0-8161-4899-6*, Macmillan Reference USA) Gale Group.

—Billy Bathgate. 1994. 576p. reprint ed. pap. 12.00 o.p. (*0-06-097595-4*, Perennial) HarperTrade.

—E. L. Doctorow: Three Complete Novels. 1994. 672p. 4.99 o.s.i (*0-517-10078-9*) Random Hse. Value Publishing.

—Loon Lake. 1988. 320p. mass mkt. 5.95 o.s.i (*0-449-21603-9*, Fawcett) Ballantine Bks.

—Loon Lake. 1981. 304p. pap. 3.50 o.s.i (*0-553-20027-5*) Bantam Bks.

—Loon Lake. 1996. 272p. reprint ed. pap. 14.00 (*0-452-27568-7*, Plume) Dutton/Plume.

—Loon Lake. 1992. pap. 11.00 o.s.i (*0-679-73625-5*, Vintage) Knopf Publishing Group.

—Loon Lake. 1980. 35.00 o.p. (*0-394-51176-X*) Random Hse., Inc.

—Ragtime. 1987. 352p. mass mkt. 5.95 o.s.i (*0-449-21428-1*, Fawcett) Ballantine Bks.

—Ragtime. 1984. mass mkt. 4.95 o.s.i (*0-553-25736-6*) Bantam Bks.

—Ragtime. (Modern Critical Interpretations Ser.). 176p. pap. 19.95 (*0-7910-7119-7*) Chelsea Hse. Pubs.

—Ragtime. 288p. 1997. pap. 14.00 (*0-452-27907-0*); 1996. pap. 9.95 o.s.i (*0-452-27570-9*, Plume) Dutton/Plume.

—Ragtime. 1975. reprint ed. lib. bdg. 13.50 o.p. (*0-8161-6306-5*, Macmillan Reference USA) Gale Group.

—Ragtime. Praesent, Angela, tr. (GER.). 565p. pap. (*3-462-02901-0*) Kiepenheuer & Witsch GmbH & Company KG DEU. *Dist:* International Bk. Import Service, Inc.

—Ragtime. 1991. (Vintage International Ser.). 288p. pap. 12.00 o.s.i (*0-679-73626-3*, Vintage) Knopf Publishing Group.

—Ragtime. (Modern Library Ser.). 336p. 1997. 17.95 (*0-679-60297-6*); 1994. 15.50 o.s.i (*0-679-60088-4*) Random Hse., Inc.

—World's Fair. 1986. mass mkt. 3.75 o.s.i (*0-449-21231-9*) Ballantine Bks.

—World's Fair. 1996. 304p. pap. 13.95 (*0-452-27572-5*, Plume) Dutton/Plume.

—World's Fair. l.t. ed. 1986. 19.95 o.p. (*0-8161-4085-5*, Macmillan Reference USA) Gale Group.

—World's Fair. 1992. pap. 12.00 o.p. (*0-679-73628-X*, Vintage) Knopf Publishing Group.

—World's Fair. 1993. 24.25 (*0-8446-6696-3*) Smith, Peter Pub., Inc.

Donati, Alyssa. Marzipan Pigeon. 1994. 300p. 21.00 (*0-671-86889-6*, Simon & Schuster) Simon & Schuster.

Donati, Sara. Into the Wilderness. 1999. 912p. mass mkt. 6.50 (*0-553-57852-9*) Bantam Bks.

—Into the Wilderness. 1999. audio 88.00 (*0-7366-4397-4*); 1999. audio 88.00 (*0-7366-4396-6*); Pt. 2. 1998. audio 88.00 Books on Tape, Inc.

Donleavy, J. P. The Lady Who Liked Clean Restrooms: The Chronicle of One of the Strangest Stories Ever. 1998. 119p. pap. o.s.i (*0-349-10850-1*); 1997. 128p. o.s.i (*0-316-88342-5*) Little Brown & Co.

—The Lady Who Liked Clean Restrooms: The Chronicle of One of the Strangest Stories Ever. 1998. (Illus.). 128p. pap. 9.95 (*0-312-18734-3*, Saint Martin's Griffin); 1997. 132p. 18.95 (*0-312-15563-8*) St. Martin's Pr.

Dougan, Cameron. Because She Is Beautiful: A Novel. E-Book 9.95 (*1-58945-509-6*) Adobe Systems, Inc.

Douglas, Carole Nelson. Femme Fatale. Date not set. mass mkt. (*0-7653-4595-1*); 2003. 554p. 25.95 (*0-7653-0682-4*) Doherty, Tom Assocs., LLC. (Forge Bks.).

Douglas, Kirk. Last Tango in Brooklyn. l.t. ed. 1994. 392p. lib. bdg. 24.95 (*0-8161-7465-2*, Macmillan Reference USA) Gale Group.

—Last Tango in Brooklyn. abr. ed. 1994. audio 21.00 o.s.i (*1-57042-085-8*, 4-520858) Time Warner AudioBooks.

—Last Tango in Brooklyn. 352p. 1995. mass mkt. 6.50 o.s.i (*0-446-60201-9*); 1994. 30.00 (*0-446-51695-3*) Warner Bks., Inc.

Douglass, Thea C. Royal Poinciana. 1988. 448p. 18.95 o.p. (*1-55611-048-0*) Fine, Donald I. Bks.

Drakulic, Slavenka. Taste of a Man. Zoric, Christina P., tr. 1997. 208p. pap. 10.95 o.s.i (*0-14-026622-4*) Penguin Group (USA) Inc.

Dreiser, Theodore. An American Tragedy. Date not set. pap. text (*0-17-557044-2*) Addison-Wesley Longman, Inc.

—An American Tragedy. Date not set. 832p. 38.95 (*0-8488-2253-6*) Amereon, Ltd.

—An American Tragedy. 1978. 874 p. reprint ed. lib. bdg. 32.00 (*0-8376-0424-9*) Bentley Pubs.

—An American Tragedy. 1990. reprint ed. lib. bdg. 54.95 (*0-89966-709-0*) Buccaneer Bks., Inc.

—An American Tragedy. (Collected Works of Theodore Dreiser). 349p. reprint ed. 2001. (Illus.). pap. text 28.00 (*0-7426-5614-4*); 1998. lib. bdg. 98.00 (*1-58201-614-3*) Classic Bks.

—An American Tragedy. 1999. 17.95 (*0-8085-0951-9*) Econo-Clad Bks.

—An American Tragedy. 2003. (Library of America: Vol. 140). 972p. 40.00 (*1-931082-31-6*) Library of America, The.

—An American Tragedy. mass mkt. 0.25 o.p. (*0-451-00755-7*, Signet Bks.); 2000. 880p. mass mkt. 9.95 (*0-451-52770-4*, Signet Classics); 1964. mass mkt. 1.50 o.p. (*0-451-50619-7*, Signet Classics); 1964. mass mkt. 1.95 o.p. (*0-451-50938-2*, Signet Classics); 1964. mass mkt. 1.25 o.p. (*0-451-50365-1*, Signet Classics); 1964. mass mkt. 3.50 o.p. (*0-451-51563-3*, Signet Classics); 1964. mass mkt. 3.95 o.p. (*0-451-51696-6*, Signet Classics); 1964. mass mkt. 4.50 o.p. (*0-451-52043-2*, Signet Classics); 1964. mass mkt. 0.95 o.p. (*0-451-50235-3*, Signet Classics); 1964. 880p. mass mkt. 9.95 o.s.i (*0-451-52465-9*, Signet Classics); 1964. 832p. mass mkt. 4.95 o.p. (*0-451-52204-4*, Signet Classics); 1964. mass mkt. 2.50 o.p. (*0-451-51276-6*, Signet Classics) NAL.

—An American Tragedy. 2002. E-Book 5.24 (*0-7953-0792-6*) RosettaBooks.

—An American Tragedy. 1964. 16.00 (*0-606-00332-0*) Turtleback Bks.

Ducker, Bruce. Lead Us Not into Penn Station. 1994. 224p. 24.00 (*1-877946-36-2*) Permanent Pr., The.

—Lead Us Not into Penn Station. 1994. 172p. per. 15.95 (*0-7592-4164-3*) ereads.com.

Ducovny, Amram. Coney. 2000. 320p. 26.95 (*1-58567-067-7*) Overlook Pr., The.

Duffy, James. Dog Bites Man: City Shocked. 2001. 304p. 24.00 (*0-7432-1082-4*, Simon & Schuster) Simon & Schuster.

Dunker, Marilee. Walker's Point. 1997. (Portraits Ser.). 272p. pap. 8.99 o.p. (*1-55661-997-9*) Bethany Hse. Pubs.

—Walker's Point. l.t. ed. 2001. (Thorndike Press Large Print Christian Romance Ser.). 490p. 25.95 (*0-7862-3659-0*) Thorndike Pr.

Dunne, Dominick. Dominick Dunne: Three Complete Novels: The Two Mrs. Grenvilles, People Like Us & An Inconvenient Woman. 1994. 896p. 13.99 o.s.i (*0-517-11916-1*) Random Hse. Value Publishing.

—People Like Us. l.t. ed. 1989. (General Ser.). 602p. 21.95 o.p. (*0-8161-4727-2*); 13.95 o.p. (*0-8161-4806-6*) Gale Group. (Macmillan Reference USA).

—The Two Mrs. Grenvilles. 1985. 384p. 4.99 o.p. (*0-517-55713-4*, Crown) Crown Publishing Group.

—The Two Mrs. Grenvilles. l.t. ed. 1986. (Special Editions Ser.). 552p. 18.95 o.p. (*0-8161-4059-6*, Macmillan Reference USA) Gale Group.

Dupont, Inge & Mayo, Hope, eds. Morgan Library Ghost Stories. 1990. (Illus.). 108p. 27.50 (*0-8232-1283-1*) Fordham Univ. Pr.

Dupont, Inge, et al. Morgan Library Ghost Stories. 1990. E-Book 24.95 (*0-585-12082-X*) netLibrary, Inc.

Dworkin, Susan. The Book of Candy. 1996. 360p. 20.00 (*1-56858-078-9*) Four Walls Eight Windows.

Dykewoman, Elana. Beyond the Pale. 1997. 404p. pap. (*0-88974-074-7*, Press Gang Pubs.) Raincoast Bk. Distribution.

Eastburn, Joseph. Kiss Them Goodbye: A Mystery Thriller. 1993. 300p. 20.00 o.p. (*0-688-04598-7*, Morrow, William & Co.) Morrow/Avon.

Eastby, Allen G. The Tenth Men. 1990. 384p. 17.95 (*0-912526-41-6*) Library Research Assocs., Inc.

Edmonds, Walter D. The Boyds of Black River: A Family Chronicle. 1988. (New York Classics Ser.). 264p. pap. 16.95 (*0-8156-2454-9*) Syracuse Univ. Pr.

—Drums along the Mohawk. Date not set. 374p. 26.95 (*0-8488-2519-5*) Amereon, Ltd.

—Drums along the Mohawk. 1981. 320p. reprint ed. lib. bdg. 35.95 (*0-89966-291-9*) Buccaneer Bks., Inc.

—Drums along the Mohawk. 1936. 19.95 o.p. (*0-316-21142-7*) Little Brown & Co.

—Drums along the Mohawk. 1997. (New York Classics Ser.). 608p. pap. 19.95 (*0-8156-0457-2*) Syracuse Univ. Pr.

—Drums along the Mohawk. 1997. 26.00 (*0-606-12592-2*) Turtleback Bks.

—In the Hands of the Senecas. 1995. (New York Classics Ser.). 214p. pap. 15.95 (*0-8156-0326-6*) Syracuse Univ. Pr.

—Mostly Canallers. 1987. (New York Classics Ser.). 470p. reprint ed. pap. text 16.95 (*0-8156-0214-6*) Syracuse Univ. Pr.

—Rome Haul. Bergmann, Frank, ed. 1987. (New York Classics Ser.). 362p. pap. 16.95 (*0-8156-0213-8*) Syracuse Univ. Pr.

—The South African Quirt. 1985. 192p. 14.95 o.s.i (*0-316-21153-2*) Little Brown & Co.

Edwards, Grace F. Do or Die: A Mali Anderson Mystery. 2000. (Mali Anderson Mystery Ser.). 272p. 22.95 o.s.i (*0-385-49248-0*) Doubleday Publishing.

—If I Should Die. 1998. (Mali Anderson Mystery Ser.). 320p. reprint ed. mass mkt. 6.50 (*0-553-57631-3*) Bantam Bks.

—If I Should Die. 1997. 272p. 21.95 o.s.i (*0-385-48523-9*) Doubleday Publishing.

—No Time to Die. 2000. (Mali Anderson Mystery Ser.). 240p. mass mkt. 5.99 (*0-553-57956-8*) Bantam Bks.

—No Time to Die. 1999. 272p. 22.95 o.s.i (*0-385-49247-2*) Doubleday Publishing.

—A Toast Before Dying. 1999. 304p. mass mkt. 5.99 (*0-553-57953-3*) Bantam Bks.

Edwards-Yearwood, Grace. In the Shadow of the Peacock. 1988. 288p. text 17.95 o.p. (*0-07-019037-2*) McGraw-Hill Cos., The.

Eidus, Janice. Urban Bliss. 1998. 180p. reprint ed. pap. 9.95 (*0-87286-339-5*) City Lights Bks.

Eight Mystery Writers. Murder in Manhattan. l.t. ed. 1988. (General Ser.). 360p. 17.95 o.p. (*0-8161-4345-5*, Macmillan Reference USA) Gale Group.

Eisner, William. Dropsie Avenue: The Neighborhood. 2000. (Illus.). 176p. pap. 14.95 (*1-56389-689-3*, Vertigo) DC Comics.

—Dropsie Avenue: The Neighborhood. 1995. 24.95 (*0-87816-349-2*); pap. 15.95 (*0-87816-348-4*); 39.95 (*0-87816-350-6*) Kitchen Sink Pr., Inc.

Elliott, James. Nowhere to Hide. 1998. 400p. mass mkt. 5.99 o.s.i (*0-7860-0538-6*, Pinnacle Bks.) Kensington Publishing Corp.

—Nowhere to Hide. 1997. 272p. 23.00 (*0-684-82362-4*, Simon & Schuster) Simon & Schuster.

Ellis, Bret Easton. American Psycho. 1991. (Vintage Contemporaries Ser.). 416p. pap. 14.00 (*0-679-73577-1*, Vintage) Knopf Publishing Group.

—American Psycho. 1991. 400p. 19.95 (*0-671-66397-6*, Simon & Schuster) Simon & Schuster.

Ellis, Julie. Commitment. 1994. 608p. mass mkt. 5.99 o.s.i (*0-8217-4681-2*); mass mkt. 18.95 o.p. (*0-8217-4422-4*, Zebra Bks.) Kensington Publishing Corp.

—Trespassing Hearts. 1992. 384p. 21.95 o.s.i (*0-399-13738-6*, G. P. Putnam's Sons) Penguin Group (USA) Inc.

Ellis, Rhian. After Life. 2000. 288p. 23.95 o.p. (*0-670-89242-4*, Viking) Viking Penguin.

Elward, James. Monday's Child Is Dead. 1995. 240p. 19.00 o.p. (*0-7867-0130-7*, Carroll & Graf Pubs.) Avalon Publishing Group.

Ephron, Amy. A Cup of Tea: A Novel of 1917. 1997. 224p. 20.00 (*0-688-14997-9*, Morrow, William & Co.) Morrow/Avon.

Epstein, Leslie. Goldkorn Tales. 1986. 256p. pap. 8.95 o.p. (*0-452-25822-7*, Plume); 252p. 16.95 o.p. (*0-525-24286-4*, Dutton) Dutton/Plume.

—Goldkorn Tales: Three Novellas. 1998. 264p. reprint ed. pap. 12.95 (*0-87074-435-6*) Southern Methodist Univ. Pr.

Epstein, Seymour. A Special Destiny. 1986. 329p. 17.95 o.p. (*0-917657-84-5*) Fine, Donald I. Bks.

Esaki-Smith, Anna. Meeting Luciano. 1999. 252p. tchr. ed. 18.95 (*1-56512-215-1*, 72215) Algonquin Bks. of Chapel Hill.

—Meeting Luciano. 2000. 272p. pap. 12.00 (*0-345-43682-2*, Ballantine Bks.) Ballantine Bks.

Espinosa, Maria. Dark Plums. 1995. 220p. pap. 9.95 o.p. (*1-55885-128-3*) Arte Publico Pr.

Estabrook, Barry. Whirlpool. 1995. 336p. 14.30 o.p. (*0-312-13622-6*, Saint Martin's Minotaur) St. Martin's Pr.

Evans, Lawrence W. Newer York. 1991. (Battletech Ser.). 384p. mass mkt. 4.50 o.p. (*0-451-45045-0*, ROC) NAL.

Fagan, Louis J. New Boots. 1999. 192p. (Orig.). pap. 11.95 (*0-9667407-7-7*) A-Peak Publishing.

Fairstein, Linda. Cold Hit. l.t. ed. 2000. (Wheeler Large Print Book Ser.). 469p. 27.95 (*1-56895-816-1*, Wheeler Publishing, Inc.) Gale Group.

Farell, Anne. Deadly Deception. 1992. 256p. 19.00 o.s.i (*0-671-75339-8*, Simon & Schuster) Simon & Schuster.

Farrelly, Rita. Not in Bronxville. 1999. 400p. pap. 6.99 (*1-886094-83-7*) Chicago Spectrum Pr.

Farris, John. Soon She Will Be Gone. 1998. 387p. mass mkt. 6.99 (*0-8125-0954-4*); 1997. 352p. 24.95 (*0-312-85375-0*) Doherty, Tom Assocs., LLC. (Forge Bks.).

Faust, Irvin. Jim Dandy. 1994. 304p. 21.00 o.p. (*0-7867-0062-9*, Carroll & Graf Pubs.) Avalon Publishing Group.

Federman, Raymond. Smiles on Washington Square. 1985. 154p. 13.95 o.p. (*0-938410-29-6*, Thunder's Mouth Pr.) Avalon Publishing Group.

Feldman, Ellen. God Bless the Child. 1999. 384p. mass mkt. (*1-55166-540-9*, 1-66540-5, Mira Bks.) Harlequin Enterprises, Ltd.

—God Bless the Child. 1998. 256p. 23.00 (*0-684-83121-X*, Simon & Schuster) Simon & Schuster.

Ferriss, Lucy. Against Gravity: A Novel. 1996. 304p. 22.00 (*0-684-80091-8*, Simon & Schuster) Simon & Schuster.

Fields, Jennie. The Middle Ages. 2002. 288p. 24.95 (*0-688-14590-6*, Morrow, William & Co.) Morrow/Avon.

—The Middle Ages: A Novel. 2003. 288p. pap. 12.95 (*0-06-051746-8*, Perennial) HarperTrade.

Files, Lolita. Getting to the Good Part. 2000. 352p. pap. 13.95 (*0-446-67548-2*); 1999. 334p. 24.00 (*0-446-52420-4*) Warner Bks., Inc.

Finder, Joseph. The Zero Hour. abr. ed. 1996. audio 16.95 o.p. (*1-56100-888-5*, 1119, Nova Audio Bks.); 1996. audio 25.95 o.p. (*1-56100-687-4*, 326, Bookcassette); 1996. audio 89.25 o.p. (*1-56100-312-3*, 1118, Unabridged Library Editions); Set. 1997. audio 7.99 o.p. (*1-56740-165-1*, 721, Nova Audio Bks.) Brilliance Audio.

—The Zero Hour. l.t. ed. 1996. (G. K. Hall Core Ser.). 630p. lib. bdg. 25.95 (*0-7838-1825-4*, Macmillan Reference USA) Gale Group.

—The Zero Hour. 1997. pap. 6.99 (*0-380-72665-3*, Avon Bks.); 1996. 432p. 25.00 o.p. (*0-688-14450-0*, Morrow, William & Co.) Morrow/Avon.

Fisher, Mark. The Millionaire's Secrets: Life Lessons in Wisdom & Wealth. 1996. 240p. 18.95 (*0-684-80281-3*, Simon & Schuster) Simon & Schuster.

Fisher, Rudolph. The Conjure-Man Dies. 320p. reprint ed. 9.00 (*0-405-02800-8*) Ayer Co. Pubs., Inc.

Fitzgerald, F. Scott. The Great Gatsby. (Scribner Classics). 1996. 176p. 25.00 (*0-684-83042-6*, Scribner); 1992. pap. 6.00 o.s.i (*0-02-019882-5*, Scribner Paper Fiction) Simon & Schuster.

—The Great Gatsby. l.t. ed. 1995. 203p. 21.95 (*0-7838-1222-1*) Thorndike Pr.

—The Great Gatsby. l.t. ed. 1999. 240p. 24.95 (*1-56000-490-8*) Transaction Pubs.

Fitzhugh, Bill. Pest Control. 1997. 304p. mass mkt. 20.00 o.p. (*0-380-97348-0*, Avon Bks.) Morrow/Avon.

Flock, Elizabeth. But Inside I'm Screaming. 2003. 320p. pap. (*1-55166-727-4*, Mira Bks.) Harlequin Enterprises, Ltd.

Foley, Mick. Tietam Brown. 2003. 256p. 23.95 (*0-375-41550-5*) Knopf, Alfred A. Inc.

Foley, Rae. Sleep Without Morning. l.t. ed. 1997. 21.95 (*0-7838-8051-0*, Macmillan Reference USA) Gale Group.

Ford, Michael Thomas. Looking for It: A Novel. 2004. 23.00 (*0-7582-0407-8*) Kensington Publishing Corp.

Fox, John. The Boys on the Rock. 1985. pap. 6.95 o.p. (*0-452-25753-0*, Plume) Dutton/Plume.

—The Boys on the Rock. 160p. 1994. pap. 11.95 (*0-312-10433-2*, Saint Martin's Griffin); 1984. 11.95 o.p. (*0-312-09419-1*) St. Martin's Pr.

Freda, Joseph. The Patience of Rivers. 2003. 320p. 24.95 (*0-393-05176-5*) Norton, W. W. & Co., Inc.

Frederic, Harold. The Civil War Stories of Harold Frederic. O'Donnell, Thomas F., ed. 1992. (New York Classics Ser.). 360p. reprint ed. pap. 19.95 (*0-8156-2572-3*) Syracuse Univ. Pr.

—The Damnation of Theron Ware. unabr. ed. 1993. audio 53.95 (*1-55685-272-X*) Audio Bk. Contractors, Inc.

—The Damnation of Theron Ware. Raleigh, John H., ed. 1960. (Rinehart Editions Ser.). 378p. (C). pap. text 26.50 o.s.i (*0-03-010200-6*) Harcourt College Pubs.

—The Damnation of Theron Ware. Carter, Everett, ed. 1996. (John Harvard Library). (Illus.). 384p. pap. 14.95 (*0-674-19001-7*, Belknap Pr.) Harvard Univ. Pr.

—The Damnation of Theron Ware. 1987. audio 39.00 Jimcin Recordings.

—The Damnation of Theron Ware. 1997. (Literary Classics). 315p. pap. 11.00 (*1-57392-169-6*) Prometheus Bks., Pubs.

—The Damnation of Theron Ware. 1988. (Collected Works of Harold Frederic). reprint ed. lib. bdg. 79.00 (*0-7812-1192-1*) Reprint Services Corp.

—The Damnation of Theron Ware. 1984. 6.50 o.p. (*0-8446-2090-4*) Smith, Peter Pub., Inc.

—The Damnation of Theron Ware. reprint ed. 69.00 Somerset Pubs., Inc.

—The Damnation of Theron Ware. l.t. ed. 1999. 530p. text 32.95 (*1-56000-488-6*) Transaction Pubs.

—The Damnation of Theron Ware. 1986. (Classics Ser.). 512p. 13.95 (*0-14-039025-1*, Penguin Classics) Viking Penguin.

—The Damnation of Theron Ware: or Illumination. 1985. (Harold Frederic Edition Ser.: Vol. 3). 515p. reprint ed. pap. 159.70 (*0-608-07071-8*, 206728500009) Bks. on Demand.

—The Damnation of Theron Ware: or Illumination. Dodge, Charlyne & Garner, Stanton, eds. 1985. (Harold Frederic Edition Ser.: Vol. 3). 506p. text 40.00 o.p. (*0-8032-1967-9*) Univ. of Nebraska Pr.

Freeman, Cynthia. Come Pour the Wine. l.t. ed. 1983. 15.95 o.p. (*0-8161-3201-1*); 1981. 624p. pap. 10.95 o.p. (*0-8161-3280-1*) Gale Group. (Macmillan Reference USA).

—Come Pour the Wine. 1980. 12.95 o.p. (*0-87795-276-0*, Morrow, William & Co.) Morrow/Avon.

Freemantle, Brian. The Watchmen. 432p. (*0-7278-5915-3*) Severn Hse. Pubs., Ltd.

—The Watchmen. 2002. 448p. 25.95 (*0-312-24274-3*) St. Martin's Pr.

Frey, James N. Winter of the Wolves. 1992. 288p. 19.95 o.p. (*0-8050-1764-X*) Holt, Henry & Co.

—Winter of the Wolves. 1993. 320p. mass mkt. 4.50 o.p. (*0-06-104274-9*, HarperTorch) Morrow/Avon.

Frey, Stephen. Inner Sanctum. 1997. 336p. 23.95 o.p. (*0-525-94206-8*) Dutton/Plume.

—Inner Sanctum. 1998. 448p. mass mkt. 7.99 (*0-451-19014-9*, Signet Bks.) NAL.

—The Inner Sanctum. l.t. ed. 1998. (Large Print Book Ser.). pap. 24.95 (*1-56895-533-2*, Wheeler Publishing, Inc.) Gale Group.

—The Vulture Fund. 1996. 384p. 23.95 o.s.i (*0-525-93986-5*, Dutton) Dutton/Plume.

—The Vulture Fund. l.t. ed. 1996. 26.95 (*1-56895-390-9*, Wheeler Publishing, Inc.) Gale Group.

Freydberg, Margaret H. The Consequences of Loving Syra. 1990. 264p. 18.95 o.p. (*0-88150-168-9*) Countryman Pr.

Freydont, Shelley. Midsummer Murder. 2002. 34p. mass mkt. 5.99 o.s.i (*1-57566-730-4*); 2001. 288p. 22.00 (*1-57566-674-X*) Kensington Publishing Corp. (Kensington Bks.).

Friedman, Kinky. Kinky Friedman Mysteries: Greenwich Killing Time - A Case of Lone Star - When the Cat's Away. 1993. 13.99 o.s.i (*0-517-09328-6*) Random Hse. Value Publishing.

—The Kinky Friedman Crime Club: A Case of Lone Star; Greenwich Killing Time; When the Cat's Away. 1993. 480p. 22.95 o.s.i (*0-571-16696-2*) Faber & Faber, Inc.

Friedman, Philip. Inadmissible Evidence. 1993. 640p. mass mkt. 7.99 (*0-8041-0852-8*, Ivy Bks.) Ballantine Bks.

—Inadmissible Evidence. unabr. ed. 1993. Pt. 1. audio 64.00; Pt. 2. audio 64.00 Books on Tape, Inc.

—Inadmissible Evidence. 1992. 480p. 23.00 o.p. (*1-55611-330-7*) Fine, Donald I. Bks.

—Inadmissible Evidence. abr. ed. 1993. audio 25.00 (*0-671-86568-4*, Simon & Schuster Audioworks) Simon & Schuster Audio.

Frolov, Andrei. The Stories of a Taxi Driver. 1994. 10.95 o.p. (*0-533-10747-4*) Vantage Pr., Inc.

Froshcer, Jonathan. The Woodstock Murders: (Or Happiness Is a Naked Policeman) 1998. 228p. pap. 23.95 (*0-87951-858-8*, Elephant's Eye) Overlook Pr., The.

Frost, Gregory. Fitcher's Brides. (Fairy Tales Ser.). 400p. 2003. pap. 15.95 (*0-7653-0195-4*); 2002. 25.95 (*0-7653-0194-6*) Doherty, Tom Assocs., LLC. (Tor Bks.).

Fubler, Anson. Genuine Love - The Conspiracy: Bermuda - New York Connection. 1996. 264p. 18.95 o.p. (*0-944957-56-0*) Rivercross Publishing, Inc.

Furman, Laura. Tuxedo Park. 1986. 352p. 17.45 o.p. (*0-671-49754-5*) Summit Bks.

Gadol, Peter. The Mystery Roast. 1996. 320p. pap. 13.00 o.s.i (*0-312-15176-4*) Picador.

Gantos, Jack. Zip Six: A Novel. 1996. 224p. 21.95 (*1-882593-15-4*); 2000. 312p. reprint ed. 13.95 (*1-882593-39-1*) Bridge Works Publishing Co., Inc.

Gardner, John. The Sunlight Dialogues. 1982. mass mkt. 4.95 o.s.i (*0-345-30492-6*) Ballantine Bks.

—The Sunlight Dialogues. 1987. 758p. pap. 16.00 o.s.i (*0-394-74394-6*, Vintage) Knopf Publishing Group.

—The Sunlight Dialogues. 1972. 15.00 o.p. (*0-394-47144-X*, Knopf Bks. for Young Readers) Random Hse. Children's Bks.

Garrett, Annie. Because I Wanted You. l.t. ed. 1997. lib. bdg. 21.95 (*1-57490-105-2*, Beeler Large Print Bks.) Beeler, Thomas T. Publisher.

—Because I Wanted You. 1998. (Because I Wanted You Ser.: Vol. 1). 240p. pap. 5.99 (*0-312-96659-8*, St. Martin's Paperbacks); 1997. 226p. 18.95 (*0-312-15427-5*); 1997. 18.95 (*0-312-15473-9*) St. Martin's Pr.

Garrison, Paul. Red Sky at Morning. 2001. 432p. mass mkt. 6.99 (*0-380-80220-1*, HarperTorch); 2000. 384p. 24.00 (*0-380-97693-5*) Morrow/Avon.

Gates, David. Preston Falls. 1999. (Vintage Contemporaries Ser.). 352p. pap. 13.00 (*0-679-75643-4*) Random Hse., Inc.

Gear, Kathleen O'Neal & Gear, W. Michael. People of the Masks. 1999. mass mkt. 125.82 (*0-8125-7624-1*); 1999. (Illus.). 552p. mass mkt. 6.99 (*0-8125-1561-7*, Tor Bks.); 1998. (Illus.). 416p. 25.95 (*0-312-85857-4*, Forge Bks.) Doherty, Tom Assocs., LLC.

Gelb, Alan. Playgrounds. 1987. 304p. 19.95 o.p. (*0-399-13277-5*, G. P. Putnam's Sons) Penguin Putnam Bks. for Young Readers.

Geller, Michael. Major League Murder. 1988. 224p. 15.95 o.p. (*0-312-02247-6*, Saint Martin's Minotaur) St. Martin's Pr.

—Three Strikes, You're Dead. 1992. 240p. 17.95 o.p. (*0-312-08322-X*, Saint Martin's Minotaur) St. Martin's Pr.

Geller, Michael R. Heroes Also Die. 1988. 240p. 15.95 o.p. (*0-312-01441-4*, Saint Martin's Minotaur) St. Martin's Pr.

Gellin, William. Strangers No More. 1986. 192p. 11.95 o.p. (*0-88400-121-0*, Shengold Bks.) Schreiber Publishing, Inc.

George, Nelson. Seduced: The Life & Times of a One-Hit Wonder. 1996. 352p. 23.95 o.p. (*0-399-14169-3*, G. P. Putnam's Sons) Penguin Group (USA) Inc.

—Urban Romance. 1998. mass mkt. 5.99 (*0-345-42685-1*) Ballantine Bks.

—Urban Romance. 1994. 286p. reprint ed. pap. 12.98 (*1-879360-36-5*) Noble Pr., Inc., The.

—Urban Romance: A Novel of New York in the '80s. 1994. 288p. 24.95 o.p. (*0-399-13865-X*, G. P. Putnam's Sons) Penguin Group (USA) Inc.

Gerber, Merrill Joan. The Kingdom of Brooklyn. 1992. 240p. 18.95 o.p. (*1-56352-022-2*) Longstreet Pr., Inc.

—The Kingdom of Brooklyn. 2000. (Library of Modern Jewish Literature). 239p. pap. 17.95 (*0-8156-0661-3*) Syracuse Univ. Pr.

Gertler, Stephanie. The Puzzle Bark Tree. 2002. 336p. 23.95 o.s.i (*0-525-94639-X*, Dutton) Dutton/Plume.

—The Puzzle Bark Tree. l.t. ed. 2002. (Women's Fiction Ser.). 511p. 28.95 (*0-7862-4699-5*) Thorndike Pr.

Gibbs, Tony. Capitol Offense. 1995. 352p. 19.95 o.p. (*0-89296-474-X*) Mysterious Pr.

Gilman, Dorothy. A Nun in the Closet. 1986. 224p. mass mkt. 6.50 (*0-449-21167-3*); 1984. mass mkt. 2.50 o.p. (*0-449-20662-9*) Ballantine Bks. (Fawcett).

—A Nun in the Closet. 1975. 192p. 5.95 o.p. (*0-385-05635-4*) Doubleday Publishing.

—A Nun in the Closet. 1975. lib. bdg. 10.95 o.p. (*0-8161-6296-4*); 1993. 296p. pap. 16.95 o.p. (*0-8161-5719-7*) Gale Group. (Macmillan Reference USA).

Gilroy, Jack. The Wisdom Box. 2002. 277p. pap. 14.00 (*1-58684-234-X*) Global Academic Publishing.

Giniger, Henry. Reasons of the Heart. 1989. 2.99 o.p. (*0-517-69590-1*) Random Hse. Value Publishing.

—Reasons of the Heart. 1987. 16.95 o.p. (*0-531-15047-X*, Watts, Franklin) Scholastic Library Publishing.

Giovinazzo, Buddy. Life Is Hot in Cracktown. 1993. 256p. 19.95 (*1-56025-054-2*, Thunder's Mouth Pr.) Avalon Publishing Group.

—Poetry & Purgatory. 1996. 200p. 12.95 o.p. (*1-56025-133-6*, Thunder's Mouth Pr.) Avalon Publishing Group.

Girardi, Robert. Madeleine's Ghost: A Novel of New York, New Orleans & the Next World. l.t. ed. 1996. 530p. 24.95 o.p. (*0-7838-1507-7*, Macmillan Reference USA) Gale Group.

—Madeleine's Ghost: A Novel of New York, New Orleans & the Next World. 1999. E-Book 11.95 (*0-440-33399-7*) Random Hse., Inc.

—Madeleine's Ghost: A Novel of New York, New Orleans & the Next World. unabr. ed. 1997. audio 85.00 (*0-7887-0932-1*, 95072E7) Recorded Bks., LLC.

Glass, Leslie. Loving Time. 1997. (April Woo Suspense Novels Ser.). 432p. reprint ed. mass mkt. 6.99 (*0-553-57209-1*) Bantam Bks.

—To Do No Harm. 1992. 320p. 17.00 o.s.i (*0-385-42602-X*) Doubleday Publishing.

Glynn, Thomas. The Building. 1985. 416p. 18.95 o.s.i (*0-394-54582-6*) Knopf, Alfred A. Inc.

Goddard, Robert. Hand in Glove. 1994. mass mkt. o.s.i (*0-552-14165-8*, Corgi); 528p. mass mkt. 7.99 (*0-552-13839-8*) Bantam Bks.

—Hand in Glove. unabr. ed. 2000. audio 89.95 (*0-7451-4362-8*, CAB 1045) Chivers Audio Bks. GBR. *Dist:* BBC Audiobooks America.

—Hand in Glove. 1993. 432p. 22.00 o.p. (*0-671-75070-4*, Simon & Schuster) Simon & Schuster.

—Hand in Glove. Rosenman, Jane, ed. 1994. 432p. reprint ed. pap. (*0-671-89037-9*, Washington Square Pr.) Simon & Schuster.

—Hand in Glove. l.t. ed. 1994. (Charnwood Large Print Ser.). 720p. 29.99 o.p. (*0-7089-8773-7*, Ulverscroft) Thorpe, F. A. Pubs. GBR. *Dist:* Ulverscroft Large Print Bks., Ltd., Ulverscroft Large Print Canada, Ltd.

Godfrey, Fred G. Fugitive Deckhand: A Novel of the Canalways of New York State. 1990. 190p. 18.95 (*0-912526-49-1*) Library Research Assocs., Inc.

Godwin, Gail. The Good Husband. 1995. 496p. pap. 13.95 (*0-345-39645-6*) Ballantine Bks.

—The Good Husband. l.t. ed. 1994. (Large Print Bks.). 620p. pap. 24.95 (*1-56895-086-1*, Wheeler Publishing, Inc.) Gale Group.

—Violet Clay. 1986. (Contemporary American Fiction Ser.). 336p. pap. 9.95 o.p. (*0-14-008220-4*, Penguin Bks.) Viking Penguin.

Gold, Michael. Jews Without Money. 1996. 320p. pap. 11.95 (*0-7867-0370-9*, Carroll & Graf Pubs.) Avalon Publishing Group.

—Jews Without Money. l.t. ed. 1996. 475p. text 27.95 (*1-56000-543-2*) ISIS Large Print Bks. GBR. *Dist:* Transaction Pubs.

—Jews Without Money. pap. o.p. (*0-87140-129-0*) Liveright Publishing Corp.

—Jews Without Money. 1981. pap. 0.95 o.p. (*0-380-01309-6*, 29520-2, Avon Bks.) Morrow/Avon.

Goldberg, Lucianne. People Will Talk. Miller, Tom, ed. 1994. 384p. 22.00 o.p. (*0-671-77669-X*, Atria) Simon & Schuster.

Goldberg, Philip. This Is Next Year. 1992. 320p. pap. 9.00 o.s.i (*0-345-36647-6*) Ballantine Bks.

—This Is Next Year. 2000. 316p. pap. 18.95 (*0-595-08923-2*, Backinprint.com) iUniverse, Inc.

Goldman, William. Marathon Man. 22.95 (*0-88411-653-0*) Amereon, Ltd.

—Marathon Man. 2001. 336p. reprint ed. pap. 14.00 (*0-345-43972-4*, Ballantine Bks.) Ballantine Bks.

—Marathon Man. 1993. reprint ed. lib. bdg. 27.95 (*1-56849-201-4*) Buccaneer Bks., Inc.

—Marathon Man. 1975. 272p. mass mkt. 4.95 o.s.i (*0-440-15502-9*); 1974. (J). 7.95 o.p. (*0-440-05327-7*, Delacorte Pr.) Dell Publishing.

Goldreich, Gloria. That Year of Our War. l.t. ed. 1994. pap. 21.95 (*1-56895-081-0*, Wheeler Publishing, Inc.) Gale Group.

—That Year of Our War. 1994. 356p. 22.95 o.p. (*0-316-31943-0*) Little Brown & Co.

Goldsborough, Robert. The Bloodied Ivy. 1989. 208p. mass mkt. 4.99 o.s.i (*0-553-27816-9*) Bantam Bks.

—Death on a Deadline. 1988. mass mkt. 4.95 o.s.i (*0-553-27024-9*) Bantam Bks.

—Fade to Black. 1991. 256p. mass mkt. 4.99 o.s.i (*0-553-29264-1*) Bantam Bks.

—The Missing Chapter. 1993. 240p. 19.95 o.s.i (*0-553-07241-2*) Bantam Bks.

—The Missing Chapter: A Nero Wolfe Mystery. 1994. 272p. mass mkt. 4.99 o.s.i (*0-553-56874-4*) Bantam Bks.

—Murder in E Minor. 1987. 224p. (Orig.). mass mkt. 3.50 o.s.i (*0-553-26120-7*); mass mkt. 3.95 o.s.i (*0-553-27938-6*) Bantam Bks.

—Silver Spire. 1993. (Crime Line Ser.). 256p. mass mkt. 4.99 o.s.i (*0-553-56387-4*) Bantam Bks.

Goldsmith, Olivia. The Bestseller. unabr. ed. 1997. audio 83.20 (*0-7366-3591-2*, 4244A/B) Books on Tape, Inc.

—The Bestseller. l.t. ed. 1996. 25.95 o.p. (*1-56895-389-5*, Wheeler Publishing, Inc.) Gale Group.

—The Bestseller. 1996. 528p. 25.00 o.p. (*0-06-017822-1*) HarperCollins Pubs.

—The Bestseller. abr. ed. 1996. audio 18.00 o.p. (*0-694-51727-5*, CPN 2584, HarperAudio) HarperTrade.

—The Bestseller. 1996. 720p. mass mkt. 7.99 (*0-06-109608-3*, HarperTorch) Morrow/Avon.

—Fashionably Late. l.t. ed. 1994. (G. K. Hall Core Ser.). 748p. lib. bdg. 26.95 (*0-8161-7496-2*, Macmillan Reference USA) Gale Group.

—Fashionably Late. 1994. 416p. 24.00 o.p. (*0-06-017611-3*) HarperCollins Pubs.

—Fashionably Late. 1995. 544p. mass mkt. 7.99 (*0-06-109389-0*, HarperTorch) Morrow/Avon.

—Marrying Mom. 1996. 224p. 16.00 o.p. (*0-06-018652-6*) HarperCollins Pubs.

—Marrying Mom. abr. ed. 1996. audio 18.00 o.s.i (*0-694-51746-1*, CPN 2608, Caedmon) HarperTrade.

—Marrying Mom. 1997. 352p. mass mkt. 6.99 (*0-06-109554-0*, HarperTorch) Morrow/Avon.

—Marrying Mom. l.t. ed. 1997. (Basic Ser.). 298p. lib. bdg. 25.95 o.p. (*0-7862-0954-2*) Thorndike Pr.

Goldsmith, Olivia, reader. Marrying Mom. abr. ed. 2000. audio 9.99 (*0-694-52324-0*, HarperAudio) HarperTrade.

Gooch, Brad. The Golden Age of Promiscuity. 1996. 303p. 24.00 o.s.i (*0-679-44708-3*) Knopf, Alfred A. Inc.

—The Golden Age of Promiscuity. 1992. mass mkt. 7.95 (*1-56333-550-6*, Hard Candy) Masquerade Bks., Inc.

Goodman, Allegra. Kaaterskill Falls. 1999. 336p. pap. 13.95 (*0-385-32390-5*, Delta) Dell Publishing.

—Kaaterskill Falls. unabr. ed. 1999. audio 83.00 (*0-7887-2919-5*, 95711E7) Recorded Bks., LLC.

—Kaaterskills Falls. l.t. ed. 1999. (Americana Ser.). 576p. 29.95 (*0-7862-1863-0*) Thorndike Pr.

Goodman, Jo. Forever in My Heart. l.t. ed. 1996. 522p. 23.95 o.p. (*0-7838-1360-0*, Macmillan Reference USA) Gale Group.

—Forever in My Heart. 1994. 480p. mass mkt. 4.99 o.s.i (*0-8217-4618-9*) Kensington Publishing Corp.

—Forever in My Heart. abr. ed. 1995. audio 5.99 (*1-57096-034-8*, RAZ 934) Romance Alive Audio.

—Forever in My Heart. unabr. ed. 1995. audio 5.99 o.p. Time Warner AudioBooks.

Gordon, David A. Other High Crimes. 1994. 23.00 (*1-885823-00-2*) Macaulay & Wittenstein Pubs., Inc.

Goudge, Eileen. Garden of Lies. l.t. ed. 1990. (Magna Large Print Ser.). 820p. o.p. (*1-85057-837-0*) Magna Large Print Bks. GBR. *Dist:* Ulverscroft Large Print Canada, Ltd.

—Garden of Lies. 1989. 544p. 19.95 o.p. (*0-670-82458-5*) Viking Penguin.

—The Second Silence. l.t. ed. 2000. (Wheeler Large Print Book Ser.). 544p. 30.95 (*1-56895-902-8*, Wheeler Publishing, Inc.) Gale Group.

—The Second Silence. 2000. 384p. 24.95 o.s.i (*0-670-89159-2*, Viking) Viking Penguin.

—Trail of Secrets. unabr. ed. 1996. audio 88.00 (*0-7366-3486-X*, 4126) Books on Tape, Inc.

—Trail of Secrets. abr. ed. 1997. audio 7.99 o.p. (*1-56740-162-7*, 710, Paperback Nova Audio Bks.); 1996. audio 16.95 o.p. (*1-56100-882-6*, 1394, Nova Audio Bks.); 1996. audio 105.25 o.p. (*1-56100-306-9*, 1083, Unabridged Library Editions); 1996. audio 27.95 o.p. (*1-56100-681-5*, 295, Bookcassette) Brilliance Audio.

—Trail of Secrets. l.t. ed. 1996. 26.95 o.p. (*1-56895-325-9*, Wheeler Publishing, Inc.) Gale Group.

—Trail of Secrets. 1997. 528p. mass mkt. 7.99 (*0-451-18774-1*, Signet Bks.) NAL.

—Trail of Secrets. 1996. 464p. 23.95 o.p. (*0-670-86191-X*) Viking Penguin.

Granger, Bill. The New York Yanquis. 1995. 288p. 21.95 (*1-55970-289-3*) Arcade Publishing, Inc.

Grant, Michael. Retribution. 1995. 304p. 23.00 o.p. (*0-06-017640-7*) HarperTrade.

—Retribution. 1996. 416p. mass mkt. 5.99 o.p. (*0-06-109377-7*, HarperTorch) Morrow/Avon.

Graver, Elizabeth. The Honey Thief: A Novel. 2000. 272p. pap. 13.00 (*0-15-601390-8*, Harvest Bks.) Harcourt Trade Pubs.

—The Honey Thief: A Novel. 1999. 263p. 22.95 (*0-7868-6282-3*) Hyperion Pr.

—The Honey Thief: A Novel. l.t. ed. 1999. (Basic Ser.). 400p. 28.95 (*0-7862-2256-5*) Thorndike Pr.

Gray, Gallagher. A Cast of Killers. 1994. (Partners in Crime Ser.). mass mkt. 4.99 o.s.i (*0-8041-1146-4*, Ivy Bks.) Ballantine Bks.

—A Cast of Killers. 1992. 256p. 20.95 o.p. (*1-55611-328-5*) Fine, Donald I. Bks.

—Death of a Dream Maker. 1995. mass mkt. 5.50 o.s.i (*0-8041-1247-9*, Ivy Bks.) Ballantine Bks.

—Hubbert & Lil: Partners in Crime. 1993. mass mkt. 4.99 o.s.i (*0-8041-0948-6*, Ivy Bks.) Ballantine Bks.

—Hubbert & Lil: Partners in Crime. 1991. 256p. 18.95 o.p. (*1-55611-308-0*) Fine, Donald I. Bks.

—A Motive for Murder. 1996. (Partners in Crime Ser.). mass mkt. 5.50 o.s.i (*0-8041-1248-7*, Ivy Bks.) Ballantine Bks.

Grayson, Emily. The Gazebo. l.t. ed. 1999. (G. K. Hall Core Ser.). 189p. 28.95 (*0-7838-8634-9*, Macmillan Reference USA) Gale Group.

—The Gazebo. 2000. audio 48.00 (*0-7887-4406-2*, 96187E7) Recorded Bks., LLC.

—The Gazebo: A Novel. 2000. 320p. mass mkt. 6.99 (*0-380-73320-X*, Avon Bks.); 1999. 210p. 20.00 (*0-688-16753-5*, Morrow, William & Co.) Morrow/Avon.

Graziunas, Daina & Starlin, Jim. Thinning the Predators. 1996. 336p. 22.95 o.s.i (*0-446-51985-5*) Warner Bks., Inc.

Green, George Dawes. The Juror. l.t. ed. 1995. 27.95 (*1-56895-220-1*, Wheeler Publishing, Inc.) Gale Group.

—The Juror. 415p. pap. 5.98 o.p. (*0-7651-0302-8*) Smithmark Pubs., Inc.

—The Juror. 1995. 432p. 21.95 o.s.i (*0-446-51885-9*); 464p. reprint ed. mass mkt. 6.99 o.s.i (*0-446-60269-8*) Warner Bks., Inc.

Green, Tim. Titans. 1995. 469p. mass mkt. 5.99 (*0-312-95678-9*, St. Martin's Paperbacks) St. Martin's Pr.

—Titans. 1999. 544p. mass mkt. 6.99 (*0-446-60636-7*) Warner Bks., Inc.

Greenburg, Dan. What Do Women Want? 1982. 465p. 14.50 o.s.i (*0-671-43793-3*, Simon & Schuster) Simon & Schuster.

Griffin, Frank James. Till the Tide Comes In. 2003. (*0-945582-90-0*) Down The Shore Publishing.

Grimes, Tom. A Stone of the Heart. 1990. 131p. 15.95 (*0-941423-40-9*) Four Walls Eight Windows.

—A Stone of the Heart: A Novel. 1997. 144p. reprint ed. pap. 12.95 (*0-87074-418-6*) Southern Methodist Univ. Pr.

Gross, Ken. Full Blown Rage. 1995. 288p. 21.00 o.p. (*0-312-85757-8*, Forge Bks.) Doherty, Tom Assocs., LLC.

—A High Pressure System. 1993. 320p. 20.95 o.p. (*0-312-85444-7*, Forge Bks.) Doherty, Tom Assocs., LLC.

—Talk Show Defense. 1997. (Maggie Van Zandt Novels Ser.). 224p. 20.95 o.p. (*0-312-85803-5*, Forge Bks.) Doherty, Tom Assocs., LLC.

—The Talk Show Defense. 2000. (Maggie Van Zandt Novels Ser.). 224p. mass mkt. 6.99 (*0-8125-5025-0*, Tor Bks.) Doherty, Tom Assocs., LLC.

Guerin, Renee. The Singing Teacher. 1995. 295p. 21.95 o.p. (*0-312-11891-0*) St. Martin's Pr.

Guinzburg, Michael. Beam Me up, Scotty. 1997. 256p. pap. 12.95 (*1-55970-388-1*) Arcade Publishing, Inc.

Gurganus, Allan. Plays Well with Others. unabr. collector's ed. 1998. audio 96.00 (*0-7366-4206-4*, 4702) Books on Tape, Inc.

—Plays Well with Others. 1999. 368p. pap. 14.00 (*0-375-70203-2*, Vintage) Knopf Publishing Group.

—Plays Well with Others. 1997. 336p. 25.00 o.p. (*0-394-58914-9*) Knopf, Alfred A. Inc.

—Plays Well with Others. abr. ed. 1997. audio 18.00 o.s.i (*0-679-46055-1*, RH Audio) Random Hse. Audio Publishing Group.

Gurney, A. R. Snow Ball. 1985. 15.95 o.p. (*0-87795-621-9*, Morrow, William & Co.) Morrow/Avon.

Hall, Parnell. Actor. 1993. 288p. 19.95 (*0-89296-520-7*) Mysterious Pr.

—Actor. 1994. 304p. mass mkt. 5.50 (*0-446-40364-4*, Mysterious Pr. Paperback Bks.) Warner Bks., Inc.

—Blackmail. 1994. 288p. 19.95 o.p. (*0-89296-521-5*) Mysterious Pr.

—Blackmail. 1995. 304p. mass mkt. 5.99 o.s.i (*0-446-40365-2*) Warner Bks., Inc.

—Client. 1990. 18.95 o.p. (*1-55611-169-X*) Fine, Donald I. Bks.

—Client. 1991. 272p. mass mkt. 4.50 o.p. (*0-451-40249-9*, Onyx) NAL.

—Detective. 1987. 300p. 17.95 o.p. (*1-55611-026-X*) Fine, Donald I. Bks.

—Detective. 1988. 256p. mass mkt. 3.95 o.p. (*0-451-40070-4*, Onyx) NAL.

—Favor. 1988. 17.95 o.p. (*1-55611-096-0*) Fine, Donald I. Bks.
—Favor. 1989. mass mkt. 3.95 o.p. (*0-451-40161-1*, 035, Onyx) NAL.
—Favor. 2002. 186p. pap. 6.99 (*0-7592-1854-4*); E-Book 6.99 (*0-7592-1850-1*); E-Book 6.99 (*0-7592-1851-X*); E-Book 6.99 (*0-7592-1849-8*) ereads.com.
—Juror. 1990. 18.95 o.p. (*1-55611-230-0*) Fine, Donald I. Bks.
—Juror. 1992. 304p. mass mkt. 4.99 o.p. (*0-451-40316-9*, Onyx) NAL.
—Movie. 1995. 82p. 19.95 o.p. (*0-89296-569-X*) Mysterious Pr.
—Movie. 1996. 288p. mass mkt. 5.99 (*0-446-40395-4*) Warner Bks., Inc.
—Murder. 1988. 256p. 17.95 o.s.i (*1-55611-058-8*) Fine, Donald I. Bks.
—Murder. 2002. 256p. reprint ed. pap. 13.95 (*1-58754-111-4*, Olmstead Pr.) Moyer Bell.
—Murder. 1989. mass mkt. 3.95 o.p. (*0-451-40110-7*, Onyx) NAL.
—Murder. E-Book 6.99 (*0-7592-1545-6*) ereads.com.
—Scam. 1998. 336p. pap. 6.50 (*0-446-40469-1*, Mysterious Pr. Paperback Bks.) Warner Bks., Inc.
—Scam: A Stanley Hastings Mystery. l.t. ed. 1997. (Americana Ser.). 463p. 26.95 (*0-7862-1210-1*) Thorndike Pr.
—Scam: A Stanley Hastings Mystery. 1997. 320p. 21.50 o.p. (*0-89296-623-8*) Warner Bks., Inc.
—Shot. 1993. 320p. mass mkt. 4.99 o.p. (*0-451-40354-1*, Onyx) NAL.
—Shot: A Stanley Hastings Novel of Suspense. 1991. 18.95 o.p. (*1-55611-239-4*) Fine, Donald I. Bks.
—Strangler. 1989. 304p. 16.95 o.p. (*1-55611-125-8*) Fine, Donald I. Bks.
—Strangler. 1990. mass mkt. 4.50 o.p. (*0-451-40217-0*, Onyx) NAL.
—Suspense: A Stanley Hastings Mystery Novel. 1998. 320p. 23.00 o.p. (*0-89296-624-6*) Mysterious Pr.
—Trial. 1996. 82p. 21.95 o.s.i (*0-89296-570-3*) Mysterious Pr.
—Trial. 1997. 288p. mass mkt. 5.99 (*0-446-40396-2*) Warner Bks., Inc.
Hamill, Denis. Three Quarters. 1999. 352p. pap. 6.99 (*0-671-00250-3*, Pocket Star); 1998. 320p. 23.00 o.s.i (*0-671-00249-X*, Atria) Simon & Schuster.
—Throwing 7's. 1999. 319p. 24.00 (*0-671-02614-3*, Atria); 2000. (Illus.). 592p. reprint ed. pap. 6.99 (*0-671-02615-1*, Pocket Star) Simon & Schuster.
Hamill, Pete. Loving Women. 2003. mass mkt. 6.99 o.p. (*0-7582-0678-X*, Kensington Bks.); 2003. mass mkt. 6.99 (*0-7860-1638-8*, Pinnacle Bks.); 1990. mass mkt. 5.50 o.s.i (*1-55817-385-4*, Pinnacle Bks.) Kensington Publishing Corp.
Hamilton, William. The Lap of Luxury. 1990. 300p. 17.95 o.p. (*0-87113-246-X*); pap. 8.95 (*0-87113-342-3*, Atlantic Monthly Pr.) Grove/Atlantic, Inc.
Hammett, Dashiell. The Thin Man. Date not set. (Thin Man Ser.). 137p. 18.95 (*0-8488-2438-5*) Amereon, Ltd.
—The Thin Man. unabr. ed. 1998. audio 42.00 (*0-7366-4002-9*, 4501) Books on Tape, Inc.
—The Thin Man, , abr. ed. 1987. (Thin Man Ser.). audio 17.00 o.s.i (*0-89845-591-X*, CPN2106, Caedmon) HarperTrade.
—The Thin Man. (Thin Man Ser.). 1992. pap. 9.00 (*0-394-23905-9*); 1989. 208p. pap. 11.00 (*0-679-72263-7*) Knopf Publishing Group. (Vintage).
—The Thin Man. (Thin Man Ser.). 1992. pap. 9.00 (*0-679-74092-9*); 1972. pap. 2.95 o.p. (*0-394-71774-0*) Random Hse., Inc.
—The Thin Man. 1994. (Thin Man Ser.). 272p. 35.00 (*1-883402-70-0*, Scribner) Simon & Schuster.
—The Thin Man. l.t. ed. 2001. (Perennial Bestsellers Ser.). 269p. 28.95 (*0-7838-9460-0*) Thorndike Pr.
Hand, Elizabeth. Black Light. 1999. 288p. 25.00 o.p. (*0-06-105266-3*) HarperCollins Pubs.
—Black Light. 2000. 400p. mass mkt. 5.99 (*0-06-105732-0*, Eos) Morrow/Avon.
—Black Light. 2000. 12.04 (*0-606-19415-0*) Turtleback Bks.
—Glimmering. 1998. 560p. mass mkt. 6.99 o.s.i (*0-06-101216-5*); 1997. 400p. mass mkt. 22.00 o.p. (*0-06-100805-2*) Morrow/Avon. (Eos).
Handler, David. The Man Who Cancelled Himself: A Stewart Hoag Mystery. 1995. 256p. mass mkt. 4.99 o.s.i (*0-553-29397-4*, Crimeline) Bantam Bks.
—The Man Who Cancelled Himself: A Stewart Hoag Mystery. 1995. 416p. 19.95 o.s.i (*0-385-42160-5*) Doubleday Publishing.
—The Man Who Cancelled Himself: A Stewart Hoag Mystery. unabr. ed. 1999. (Stewart Hoag Mystery Ser.: Vol. 6). audio 85.00 (*0-7887-1992-0*, 95379E7) Recorded Bks., LLC.
—The Man Who Died Laughing. 1990. 208p. mass mkt. 2.25 o.s.i (*0-553-18520-9*); 1988. 192p. mass mkt. 3.50 o.s.i (*0-553-27469-4*) Bantam Bks.
—The Man Who Lived by Night. 1989. 181p. mass mkt. 3.50 o.s.i (*0-553-27935-1*) Bantam Bks.
—The Man Who Loved Women to Death. 1997. 304p. 23.95 o.s.i (*0-385-48052-0*) Doubleday Publishing.
—The Man Who Loved Women to Death. unabr. ed. 2001. audio 61.00 (*0-7887-4877-7*, 96453x7) Recorded Bks., LLC.
—The Man Who Would Be F. Scott Fitzgerald. 1995. 224p. mass mkt. 4.99 o.s.i (*0-553-27848-7*) Bantam Bks.
—The Man Who Would Be F. Scott Fitzgerald. 1993. 256p. 17.00 o.s.i (*0-385-46782-6*) Doubleday Publishing.
—The Man Who Would Be F. Scott Fitzgerald. unabr. ed. 1998. (Stewart Hoag Mystery Ser.: Vol. 3). audio 51.00 (*0-7887-0929-1*, 95069E7) Recorded Bks., LLC.
Hansen, Ron. Mariette in Ecstasy: A Novel. 1991. 192p. 20.00 o.p. (*0-06-018214-8*, HarperCollins) HarperTrade.
Hanyen, Jim. All the Way Home. 1995. 230p. 10.75 o.p. (*1-880664-06-2*) E. M. Productions.
Hardy, James E. B-Boy Blues: A Seriously Sexy, Fiercely Funny, Black-on-Black Love Story. 1994. 240p. pap. 12.95 (*1-55583-268-7*) Alyson Pubns.
—If Only for One Nite. 1998. 208p. pap. 12.95 (*1-55583-467-1*); 1997. 185p. 17.95 (*1-55583-373-X*) Alyson Pubns.
—The 2nd Time Around. 1996. 288p. pap. 12.95 (*1-55583-372-1*) Alyson Pubns.
Hardy, Robin. Padre: A Novel. 1994. 288p. (Orig.). pap. 10.00 o.p. (*0-89109-799-6*) NavPress Publishing Group.
Harris, Anne. The Nature of Smoke. 1997. 288p. pap. 13.95 (*0-312-86351-9*); 1996. 256p. 22.95 o.p. (*0-312-85286-X*) Doherty, Tom Assocs., LLC. (Tor Bks.).
Harris, Lee. The Christening Day Murder. 1993. (Christine Bennett Mysteries Ser.: Vol. 3). 224p. mass mkt. 6.99 (*0-449-14871-8*, Fawcett) Ballantine Bks.
—The Christmas Night Murder. 1994. (Christine Bennett Mysteries Ser.: Vol. 5). 224p. mass mkt. 6.99 (*0-449-14922-6*, Fawcett) Ballantine Bks.
—The Christmas Night Murder. unabr. ed. 1999. audio 39.95 (*0-7861-1672-2*, 2500) Blackstone Audio Bks., Inc.
—The Good Friday Murder. 1992. (Christine Bennett Mysteries Ser.: Vol. 1). 208p. mass mkt. 6.99 (*0-449-14762-2*, Fawcett) Ballantine Bks.
—The Good Friday Murder. abr. ed. 1997. audio 19.95 (*0-9658148-0-7*, SA111) Scheherazade AudioVisions, Inc.
—The Labor Day Murder. 1998. 272p. (Christine Bennett Mysteries Ser.: Vol. 10). mass mkt. 5.99 (*0-449-15017-8*); pap. 19.00 (*0-345-46760-4*) Ballantine Bks. (Fawcett).
—The Mother's Day Murder. 2000. (Christine Bennett Mysteries Ser.: Vol. 12). 272p. mass mkt. 6.50 (*0-449-00442-2*, Fawcett) Ballantine Bks.
—The New Year's Eve Murder. 1997. (Christine Bennett Mysteries Ser.: Vol. 9). 272p. mass mkt. 6.99 (*0-449-15018-6*, Fawcett) Ballantine Bks.
—The Passover Murder. 1996. (Christine Bennett Mysteries Ser.: Vol. 7). 288p. mass mkt. 6.99 (*0-449-14963-3*, Fawcett) Ballantine Bks.
—The St. Patrick's Day Murder. 1994. (Christine Bennett Mysteries Ser.: Vol. 4). 224p. (Orig.). mass mkt. 6.99 (*0-449-14872-6*, Fawcett) Ballantine Bks.
—The Thanksgiving Day Murder. 1995. (Christine Bennett Mysteries Ser.: Vol. 6). 256p. mass mkt. 6.50 (*0-449-14923-4*, Fawcett) Ballantine Bks.
—The Thanksgiving Day Murder. unabr. ed. 1999. (Christine Bennett Mysteries Ser.). audio 39.95 (*0-7861-1645-5*, 2473) Blackstone Audio Bks., Inc.
—The Valentine's Day Murder. 1996. (Christine Bennett Mysteries Ser.: Vol. 8). 272p. mass mkt. 6.99 (*0-449-14964-1*, Fawcett) Ballantine Bks.
—The Yom Kippur Murder. 1992. (Christine Bennett Mysteries Ser.: Vol. 2). 224p. (Orig.). mass mkt. 6.99 (*0-449-14763-0*, Fawcett) Ballantine Bks.
Harrison, Colin. Manhattan Nocturne. 1997. o.s.i (*0-517-70696-2*); 1996. 384p. 5.99 o.s.i (*0-517-58492-1*) Crown Publishing Group.
—Manhattan Nocturne. 1997. 416p. mass mkt. 6.99 o.s.i (*0-440-22433-0*) Dell Publishing.
—Manhattan Nocturne. unabr. ed. 1996. 24.95 o.p. (*0-7871-1115-5*) NewStar Media, Inc.
—Manhattan Nocturne. 2004. 416p. mass mkt. 6.99 (*0-312-99303-X*, St. Martin's Paperbacks) St. Martin's Pr.
Harrison, Kathryn. Exposure. 1994. 272p. pap. 12.99 o.s.i (*0-446-67023-5*) Warner Bks., Inc.
Harte, Amanda. North Star. 2000. 320p. mass mkt. 4.99 (*0-8439-4764-0*, Leisure Bks.) Dorchester Publishing Co., Inc.
Hartov, Steven. The Nylon Hand of God. 1996. 512p. 23.00 o.p. (*0-688-14120-X*, Morrow, William & Co.) Morrow/Avon.
Harvey, James N. By Reason of Insanity. 1991. 346p. pap. 5.99 o.p. (*0-312-92533-6*, St. Martin's Paperbacks); 1990. 18.95 o.p. (*0-312-04295-7*) St. Martin's Pr.
—Dead Game. 1997. 304p. text 24.95 o.p. (*0-312-15100-4*) St. Martin's Pr.
—Flesh & Blood: A Lt. Ben Tolliver Thriller. 1996. 408p. mass mkt. 6.50 o.p. (*0-312-95318-6*, St. Martin's Paperbacks); 1994. 384p. 22.95 o.p. (*0-312-10985-7*) St. Martin's Pr.
—The Headsman. 1993. mass mkt. 4.99 o.s.i (*0-515-11209-7*, Jove) Berkley Publishing Group.
—The Headsman. 1991. 19.95 o.p. (*1-55611-263-7*) Fine, Donald I. Bks.
—Mental Case. 1997. 346p. mass mkt. 6.99 (*0-312-95995-8*, St. Martin's Paperbacks); 1996. 352p. 23.95 o.p. (*0-312-14014-2*) St. Martin's Pr.
—Painted Ladies. 1992. 375p. mass mkt. 5.99 (*0-312-92895-5*, St. Martin's Paperbacks); 448p. 19.95 o.p. (*0-312-07056-X*) St. Martin's Pr.
Haviland, Diana. Fortune's Daughter. 2000. (Five Star Romance Ser.). 393p. 26.95 (*0-7862-2340-5*, Five Star) Gale Group.
Hawke, Ethan. The Hottest State. 1996. 208p. 19.95 o.p. (*0-316-54083-8*) Little Brown & Co.
—The Hottest State. abr. ed. 1996. audio 17.00 (*1-57042-399-7*) Time Warner AudioBooks.
—The Hottest State: A Novel. 1997. 208p. pap. 12.00 (*0-679-78135-8*, Vintage) Knopf Publishing Group.
Hayes, Hunter. Shoe's on the Otha' Foot. 2000. 320p. mass mkt. 6.99 (*0-06-101466-4*, HarperTorch) Morrow/Avon.
—Shoe's on the Otha' Foot. Green, Brandi C., ed. 1999. 240p. pap. 12.95 (*0-9666435-7-7*) Stone Edge Pr.
Hayes, Penny. Kathleen O'Donald. 1994. 256p. pap. 9.95 (*1-56280-070-1*) Naiad Pr., Inc.
Healy, R. Austin. The Ninth Race. 224p. 1995. pap. 12.95 o.p. (*0-8338-0217-8*); 1994. 21.95 o.p. (*0-8338-0211-9*) Marshall Jones Co.
—Sweetfeed: A Mike Flint Murder Mystery. 1996. 256p. 24.95 o.p. (*0-8338-0230-5*) Marshall Jones Co.
Hecht, Daniel. Skull Session. 1998. 512p. mass mkt. 6.99 o.s.i (*0-451-19592-2*, Signet Bks.) NAL.
—Skull Session. l.t. ed. 1998. (Core Ser.). 719p. 28.95 (*0-7838-0340-0*) Thorndike Pr.
—Skull Session. 1998. 419p. 23.95 o.p. (*0-670-87661-5*) Viking Penguin.
Heffernan, William. Blood Rose. 1991. 320p. 18.95 o.p. (*0-525-24962-1*, Dutton) Dutton/Plume.
—Blood Rose. 1992. 448p. mass mkt. 6.99 o.s.i (*0-451-17163-2*, Signet Bks.) NAL.
—Red Angel: A Paul Devlin Mystery. 2000. (Paul Devlin Mysteries Ser.). 273p. 24.00 (*0-688-16563-X*, Morrow, William & Co.) Morrow/Avon.
—Ritual. 1990. 352p. mass mkt. 5.99 o.s.i (*0-451-16397-4*, Signet Bks.); 1989. 284p. 18.95 o.p. (*0-453-00618-3*) NAL.
—Scarred. 1993. 384p. (Orig.). mass mkt. 5.99 o.s.i (*0-451-17863-7*, Signet Bks.) NAL.
—Tarnished Blue. 1995. 384p. (Orig.). mass mkt. 5.99 o.s.i (*0-451-18295-2*, Onyx) NAL.
—Unholy Order: A Paul Devlin Mystery. 2002. (Illus.). 288p. 24.95 (*0-688-16564-8*, Morrow, William & Co.) Morrow/Avon.
—Winter's Gold. 1997. 400p. mass mkt. 6.50 o.s.i (*0-451-18865-9*, Signet Bks.) NAL.
Heller, Murray. Placid's View: A Mike Diamond Mystery. 1997. 196p. 22.50 (*0-935796-81-9*) Purple Mountain Pr., Ltd.
Hellinger, Mark. Moon over Broadway. 1977. (Short Story Index Reprint Ser.). reprint ed. 19.95 (*0-8369-4082-2*) Ayer Co. Pubs., Inc.
Helprin, Mark. Memoir from Antproof Case. l.t. ed. 1995. 26.95 (*1-56895-256-2*, Wheeler Publishing, Inc.) Gale Group.
—Memoir from Antproof Case. 1995. 514p. 24.00 o.s.i (*0-15-100097-2*) Harcourt Trade Pubs.
—Memoir from Antproof Case. 1996. 528p. pap. 15.95 (*0-380-72733-1*, Avon Bks.) Morrow/Avon.
—Winter's Tale. (Harvest Book Ser.). 688p. 1995. pap. 17.00 (*0-15-600194-2*, Harvest Bks.); 1983. 35.00 (*0-15-197203-6*) Harcourt Trade Pubs.
—Winter's Tale. 1985. 704p. mass mkt. 4.95 o.s.i (*0-671-62118-1*); 1984. mass mkt. 4.50 o.s.i (*0-671-50987-X*) Simon & Schuster. (Pocket).
—Winter's Tale. Rosenman, Jane, ed. 1990. 704p. reprint ed. pap. (*0-671-72707-9*, Washington Square Pr.) Simon & Schuster.
Hendin, Josephine Gattuso. The Right Thing to Do. 1999. 240p. pap. 13.95 (*1-55861-220-3*) Feminist Pr. at The City Univ. of New York.
—The Right Thing to Do. 1988. 256p. 16.95 o.p. (*0-87923-639-6*) Godine, David R. Pub.
Henke, Jack. Tales of Oneida Lake. 1993. 250p. 25.00 (*0-925168-14-9*) North Country Bks., Inc.
Henry, O. The Best of O. Henry. 1978. 160p. lib. bdg. 7.95 o.p. (*0-89471-047-8*) Running Pr. Bk. Pubs.
—Cabbages & Kings. 320p. 24.95 o.s.i (*0-8488-1680-3*) Amereon, Ltd.
—Cabbages & Kings. unabr. ed. 1997. audio 39.95 (*0-7861-1173-9*, 1961) Blackstone Audio Bks., Inc.
—Cabbages & Kings. 2001. per. 12.50 (*1-58396-507-6*) Blue Unicorn Editions.
—Cabbages & Kings. 2002. 176p. 93.99 (*1-58827-225-7*); per. 88.99 (*1-58827-226-5*) IndyPublish.com.
—Cabbages & Kings. mass mkt. 0.25 o.p. (*0-451-00595-3*, Signet Bks.) NAL.
—Cabbages & Kings. collector's ed. 2002. (Illus.). im. lthr. 38.85 (*1-4115-1385-1*); pap. 19.95 (*1-4115-0667-7*); 25.95 (*1-4115-1020-8*); pap. 17.95 (*1-4115-0311-2*) Polyglot Pr., Inc.
—Cabbages & Kings. 1993. (Penguin Twentieth-Century Classics Ser.). 256p. pap. 10.95 o.p. (*0-14-018689-1*, Penguin Classics) Viking Penguin.
—Strictly Business: More Stories of the Four Million. l.t. ed. 1998. 400p. text 27.95 (*1-56000-525-4*) Transaction Pubs.
Higgins, Alton. The B. A. M. B. I. Syndrome. 2000. 240p. pap. 21.99 (*0-7388-1604-3*); text 31.99 (*0-7388-1603-5*); E-Book 8.00 (*0-7388-8519-3*) Xlibris Corp.
Himes, Chester B. All Shot up. 1973. 160p. reprint ed. 7.95 o.p. (*0-911860-29-0*) Chatham Bookseller.
—All Shot Up. 2nd ed. 1996. 170p. reprint ed. pap. 12.95 (*1-56025-103-4*, Thunder's Mouth Pr.) Avalon Publishing Group.
—The Big Gold Dream. 2nd ed. 1996. 156p. reprint ed. pap. 12.95 (*1-56025-104-2*, Thunder's Mouth Pr.) Avalon Publishing Group.
—The Big Gold Dream. 1973. 160p. reprint ed. 7.95 o.p. (*0-911860-30-4*) Chatham Bookseller.
—Blind Man with a Pistol. 1989. (Vintage Crime Ser.). 192p. pap. 11.00 (*0-394-75998-2*, Vintage) Knopf Publishing Group.
—Cotton Comes to Harlem. 1994. (Illus.). lib. bdg. 11.95 (*1-56849-422-X*) Buccaneer Bks., Inc.
—Cotton Comes to Harlem. 1975. reprint ed. 8.95 o.p. (*0-911860-55-X*) Chatham Bookseller.
—Cotton Comes to Harlem. 1988. (Crime Ser.). (Illus.). 160p. pap. 11.00 (*0-394-75999-0*, Vintage) Knopf Publishing Group.
—The Crazy Kill. 1973. 160p. reprint ed. 7.95 o.p. (*0-911860-32-0*) Chatham Bookseller.
—The Crazy Kill. 160p. 1995. pap. 25.00 o.s.i (*0-8052-8217-3*, Schocken); 1989. pap. 11.00 (*0-679-72572-5*, Vintage) Knopf Publishing Group.
—End of a Primitive. 1997. 220p. pap. 12.00 (*0-393-31540-1*) Norton, W. W. & Co., Inc.
—For Love of Imabelle. 1973. 192p. reprint ed. 7.95 o.p. (*0-911860-33-9*) Chatham Bookseller.
—The Heat's On. 1975. 220p. reprint ed. 17.00 (*0-911860-57-6*) Chatham Bookseller.
—The Heat's On. 1988. (Vintage Crime Ser.). 176p. pap. 15.00 (*0-394-75997-4*, Vintage) Knopf Publishing Group.
—Pinktoes. 1975. 256p. reprint ed. 8.50 o.p. (*0-911860-58-4*) Chatham Bookseller.
—Pinktoes. 1996. 264p. (C). 40.00 (*0-87805-886-9*); pap. 16.95 (*0-87805-887-7*) Univ. Pr. of Mississippi.
—A Rage in Harlem. 1989. (Vintage Crime Ser.). Orig. Title: For Love of Imabelle. 160p. pap. 10.00 (*0-679-72040-5*, Vintage) Knopf Publishing Group.
—The Real Cool Killers. 1973. 160p. reprint ed. 7.95 o.p. (*0-911860-36-3*) Chatham Bookseller.
—The Real Cool Killers. 1988. (Vintage Crime Ser.). 160p. pap. 10.95 (*0-679-72039-1*, Pantheon) Knopf Publishing Group.
—Run Man Run. 1995. 192p. pap. 8.95 (*0-7867-0209-5*, Carroll & Graf Pubs.) Avalon Publishing Group.
—Run Man Run. 1975. 192p. reprint ed. 8.50 o.p. (*0-911860-56-8*) Chatham Bookseller.
Hitchcock, Jane S. Trick of the Eye. l.t. ed. 1993. 23.95 o.p. (*0-7927-1482-2*); pap. 21.95 o.p. (*0-7927-1481-4*) BBC Audiobooks America.
—Trick of the Eye. 1992. 288p. 19.00 o.p. (*0-525-93529-0*, Dutton) Dutton/Plume.
—Trick of the Eye. 1993. 256p. pap. o.p. (*0-451-17480-1*); 368p. mass mkt. 5.50 o.s.i (*0-451-17673-1*) NAL. (Signet Bks.).
—The Witches' Hammer. 1994. 352p. 21.95 o.p. (*0-525-93641-6*) Dutton/Plume.
—The Witches' Hammer. 1995. 464p. mass mkt. 5.99 o.s.i (*0-451-18508-0*, Signet Bks.) NAL.
Hobhouse, Janet. The Furies. 1992. 304p. 22.50 o.s.i (*0-385-24547-5*); 1994. 240p. reprint ed. pap. 12.95 o.s.i (*0-385-47054-1*) Doubleday Publishing.
—The Furies. 2004. (New York Review Books Classics Ser.). 320p. pap. 14.00 (*1-59017-085-7*) New York Review of Bks., Inc., The.
Hoff, B. J. The Winds of Graystone Manor. 1995. (St Clare Trilogy Ser.: No. 1). pap. 15.99 o.p. incl. audio (*1-55661-827-1*); 320p. pap. 10.99 o.p. (*1-55661-435-7*) Bethany Hse. Pubs.
—The Winds of Graystone Manor. l.t. ed. 1996. 504p. 22.95 o.s.i (*0-7838-1703-7*, Macmillan Reference USA) Gale Group.
Hoffman, Alice. The Drowning Season. 1986. mass mkt. 3.50 o.s.i (*0-449-21024-3*, Fawcett) Ballantine Bks.
—The Drowning Season. 2002. 240p. pap. 13.00 (*0-425-18475-7*) Berkley Publishing Group.
—The Drowning Season. (Plume Contemporary Fiction Ser.). 1989. 224p. pap. 12.95 o.s.i (*0-452-26302-6*, Plume); 1979. 8.95 o.p. (*0-525-09577-2*, Dutton) Dutton/Plume.

—The Drowning Season. 1993. 224p. mass mkt. 4.99 o.s.i (0-451-17815-7, Signet Bks.) NAL.

—The Drowning Season. l.t. ed. 2000. (Famous Authors Ser.). 307p. 27.95 (0-7862-2626-9) Thorndike Pr.

—Local Girls. 2000. 208p. pap. 12.95 (0-425-17434-4) Berkley Publishing Group.

—Local Girls. l.t. ed. (Thorndike/G. K. Hall Paperback Bestsellers Ser.). 208p. 2000. pap. 28.95 (0-7862-2010-4); 1999. 29.95 (0-7862-2009-0) Thorndike Pr.

—Local Girls. 2000. 19.00 (0-606-20422-9) Turtleback Bks.

—Seventh Heaven. 1990. 256p. 19.95 o.p. (0-399-13535-9, G. P. Putnam's Sons) Penguin Putnam Bks. for Young Readers.

Holland, Isabelle. Darcourt. 1977. pap. 1.75 o.s.i (0-449-23224-7, Fawcett) Ballantine Bks.

—Darcourt. l.t. ed. 1982. 529p. reprint ed. 13.95 o.p. (0-89621-397-8) Thorndike Pr.

—Death at St. Anselm's. 1984. 240p. 13.95 o.p. (0-385-18332-1) Doubleday Publishing.

—A Fatal Advent: A St. Anselm's Mystery. 1990. (St. Anselm's Mystery Ser.). 256p. mass mkt. 3.95 o.s.i (0-449-21879-1, Fawcett) Ballantine Bks.

—The Long Search. 1992. mass mkt. 3.99 o.s.i (0-449-22009-5, Fawcett) Ballantine Bks.

—The Long Search. 1990. 272p. 16.95 o.s.i (0-385-26545-X) Doubleday Publishing.

—The Long Search. l.t. ed. 1993. (Magna Large Print Ser.). 435p. (0-7505-0444-7) Magna Large Print Bks. GBR. Dist: Ulverscroft Large Print Canada, Ltd.

—A Lover Scorned. 1987. 256p. mass mkt. 2.95 o.s.i (0-449-21369-2, Fawcett) Ballantine Bks.

—A Lover Scorned. 1986. 240p. 15.95 o.p. (0-385-23169-5) Doubleday Publishing.

Holzer, Erika. Eye for an Eye. 1996. 341p. mass mkt. 5.99 o.p. (0-8125-4331-9, Forge Bks.); 1994. 341p. pap. text 4.99 o.p. (0-8125-1529-3, Forge Bks.); 1993. 256p. 18.95 o.p. (0-312-85186-3, Tor Bks.) Doherty, Tom Assocs., LLC.

—Eye for an Eye. 4.98 o.p. (0-8317-5561-X) Smithmark Pubs., Inc.

—Eye for an Eye. 2001. 260p. per. 17.95 (0-595-19260-2) iUniverse, Inc.

Howard, Linda. Now You See Her. 1998. 336p. 23.00 o.s.i (0-671-56882-5, Atria); 1999. 368p. reprint ed. mass mkt. 7.99 (0-671-03405-7, Pocket) Simon & Schuster.

—Now You See Her. abr. ed. 1998. 18.00 (0-671-58261-5, Simon & Schuster Audioworks) Simon & Schuster Audio.

—Now You See Her. l.t. ed. 1999. (Paperback Bestsellers Ser.). 456p. pap. 27.95 (0-7862-1728-6); 28.95 o.p. (0-7862-1727-8) Thorndike Pr.

Howard, Maureen. A Lover's Almanac. 1999. 288p. pap. 12.95 (0-14-027512-6, Penguin Classics) Penguin Group (USA) Inc.

—A Lover's Almanac. 1998. (Illus.). 288p. 24.95 (0-670-87597-X) Viking Penguin.

Howells, William Dean. A Hazard of New Fortunes. Lopate, Phillip, ed. & intro. by. 2001. (Classics Ser.). 480p. pap. 14.00 (0-14-043923-4, Penguin Classics) Viking Penguin.

Hower, Edward. Night Train Blues. 1996. 221p. 24.00 (1-877946-71-0) Permanent Pr., The.

Hruby, Andes. The Trouble with Catherine. 2002. 288p. 23.95 o.s.i (0-525-94640-3, Dutton) Dutton/Plume.

Hunter, Evan. Privileged Conversation. unabr. ed. 1996. audio 48.00 (0-7366-3425-8, 4070) Books on Tape, Inc.

—Privileged Conversation, Set. abr. ed. 1996. audio 21.95 (1-55935-195-0, 693519) Soundelux Audio Publishing.

—Privileged Conversation. 1997. 336p. mass mkt. 6.99 (0-446-60382-1); 1996. 82p. 22.95 o.s.i (0-446-52028-4) Warner Bks., Inc.

Hunter, Jessie. One Two Buckle My Shoe. 1998. 464p. mass mkt. 6.50 o.s.i (0-06-101325-0) HarperCollins Pubs.

—One Two Buckle My Shoe. 1997. 304p. 22.50 (0-684-83170-8, Simon & Schuster) Simon & Schuster.

Hunter, M. S. The Final Bell. 1994. 189p. (Orig.). pap. 8.95 o.p. (1-55583-248-2) Alyson Pubns.

Hustvedt, Siri. The Blindfold. 1993. (Norton Paperback Fiction Ser.). 220p. pap. 12.00 (0-393-31013-2) Norton, W. W. & Co., Inc.

—The Blindfold. 1992. 224p. 20.00 o.s.i (0-671-75953-1, Simon & Schuster) Simon & Schuster.

Ignatius, David. A Firing Offense. 1998. mass mkt. 6.99 o.s.i (0-8041-1802-7, Ivy Bks.) Ballantine Bks.

—A Firing Offense. unabr. ed. 1998. audio 85.00 (0-7887-2167-4, 95463E7) Recorded Bks., LLC.

Indiana, Gary. Rent Boy. 1994. (High Risk Ser.). 128p. (Orig.). pap. (1-85242-324-2) Serpent's Tail Ltd.

Irving, Washington. The Headless Horseman: A Retelling of The Legend of Sleepy Hollow, ERS. 1995. (Illus.). 88p. (J). (gr. k-3). 15.95 o.p. (0-8050-3584-2, Holt, Henry & Co. Bks. For Young Readers) Holt, Henry & Co.

—Rip Van Winkle. 1976. 17.95 (0-8488-1382-0) Amereon, Ltd.

—Rip Van Winkle. 2002. (Read-Along Radio Dramas Ser.). ring bd. 38.00 (1-878298-38-0) Balance Publishing Co.

—Rip Van Winkle. l.t. ed. 2000. (Illus.). 110p. text 14.95 (1-883789-40-0) Black Dome Pr. Corp.

—Rip Van Winkle. 1983. 73p. reprint ed. lib. bdg. 16.95 (0-89966-411-3) Buccaneer Bks., Inc.

—Rip Van Winkle & the Legend of Sleepy Hollow. 2002. pap. 3.95 (1-59109-079-2) Booksurge, LLC.

—Rip Van Winkle & the Legend of Sleepy Hollow. 2002. pap. text 5.95 (0-19-424337-0) Oxford Univ. Pr., Inc.

—Rip Van Winkle & the Legend of Sleepy Hollow. 1995. 96p. pap. 0.95 o.p. (0-14-600071-4) Penguin Group (USA) Inc.

—Rip Van Winkle & the Legend of Sleepy Hollow. 1987. (Radiobook Ser.). audio 4.98 (0-929541-25-1) Radiola Co.

—Rip Van Winkle & the Legend of Sleepy Hollow. (Illus.). 152p. 1974. (J). 9.95 o.p. (0-912882-09-3); 2nd ed. 1980. 19.95 (0-912882-42-5) Sleepy Hollow Pr.

—Rip Van Winkle & the Legend of Sleepy Hollow. 1980. (Facsimile Classics Ser.). xi, 218 p. o.p. (0-8317-7410-X) Smithmark Pubs., Inc.

—Rip Van Winkle & the Legend of Sleepy Hollow. 1998. (Children's Library). (J). pap. 3.95 (1-85326-169-6, 1696WW) Wordsworth Editions, Ltd. GBR. Dist: Casemate Pubs. & Bk. Distributors, LLC.

—Stories of the Hudson. 1984. 320p. 16.95 o.p. (0-916346-52-8) Harbor Hill Bks.

Isaacs, Susan. After All These Years: A Novel. l.t. ed. 1993. 25.95 o.p. (1-56895-035-7, Wheeler Publishing, Inc.) Gale Group.

—After All These Years: A Novel. 1993. 400p. 23.00 o.p. (0-06-016768-8) HarperTrade.

—Compromising Positions. 1987. 352p. mass mkt. 7.99 (0-515-09302-5, Jove) Berkley Publishing Group.

—Compromising Positions. 1978. 8.95 o.p. (0-8129-0736-1, Crown) Crown Publishing Group.

—Compromising Positions. l.t. ed. 2001. 359p. lib. bdg. 27.95 (1-58547-086-4) Ctr. Point Large Print.

—Lily White. 1996. 480p. 25.00 o.p. (0-06-017607-5) HarperCollins Pubs.

—Lily White. l.t. ed. 1997. 656p. mass mkt. 7.99 (0-06-109309-2, HarperTorch) Morrow/Avon.

—Lily White. l.t. ed. (Paperback Bestsellers Ser.). 738p. 1997. pap. 27.95 (0-7862-0829-5); 1996. 28.95 o.p. (0-7862-0828-7) Thorndike Pr.

Jackson, Charles. The Sunnier Side: Arcadian Tales. 1996. 320p. pap. 17.95 (0-8156-0327-4) Syracuse Univ. Pr.

Jackson, Charles R. Sunnier Side: Twelve Arcadian Tales. 1977. (Short Story Index Reprint Ser.). reprint ed. 23.95 (0-8369-3891-7) Ayer Co. Pubs., Inc.

Jacobs, Claire R. Mother, May I Sleep with Danger? 1997. 320p. 23.95 o.s.i (1-55611-515-6) Fine, Donald I. Bks.

Jacobs, Harvey. American Goliath. 352p. 1998. pap. 14.95 (0-312-19438-2, Saint Martin's Griffin); 1997. 24.95 o.p. (0-312-16771-7) St. Martin's Pr.

Jacobs, Laura. Women about Town. 2002. 256p. 23.95 o.s.i (0-670-03088-0, Viking) Viking Penguin.

—Women about Town: A Novel. 2003. 256p. pap. 14.00 (0-14-200277-1) Viking Penguin.

Jaffe, Rona. Five Women. l.t. ed. 2000. 560p. 27.95 (1-57490-263-6, Beeler Large Print Bks.) Beeler, Thomas T. Publisher.

—Five Women. 1997. 384p. 24.95 (1-55611-505-9) Fine, Donald I. Bks.

—Five Women. 1998. (Mira Bks.). 475p. mass mkt. (1-55166-424-0, 1-66424-2, Mira Bks.) Harlequin Enterprises, Ltd.

Jahn, Michael. City of God. 1992. 352p. 21.95 o.p. (0-312-06927-8, Saint Martin's Minotaur) St. Martin's Pr.

—Death Games: A Novel. 1987. 15.95 o.p. (0-393-02465-2) Norton, W. W. & Co., Inc.

—Murder at the Museum of Natural History. 1994. (Lt. Bill Donovan Mystery Ser.). 304p. 20.95 o.p. (0-312-11453-2, Saint Martin's Minotaur) St. Martin's Pr.

—Murder on the Waterfront: A Bill Donovan Mystery. 2001. 304p. 23.95 (0-312-27857-8, Saint Martin's Minotaur) St. Martin's Pr.

Janowitz, Tama. A Cannibal in Manhattan. 1989. (Illus.). 256p. 3.99 o.p. (0-517-56624-9) Random Hse. Value Publishing.

Jedren, Susan. Let 'Em Eat Cake. 1996. pap. 19.00 (0-679-76805-X, Vintage) Knopf Publishing Group.

—Let 'em Eat Cake. abr. ed. 1994. 16.96 o.p. (0-7871-0010-2) NewStar Media, Inc.

—Let'em Eat Cake: A Novel. 1994. 320p. 22.00 o.s.i (0-679-43361-9, Pantheon) Knopf Publishing Group.

Jeffers, H. Paul. A Grand Night for Murder. 1995. 224p. 20.95 o.p. (0-312-13084-8, Saint Martin's Minotaur) St. Martin's Pr.

—Rubout at the Onyx. 1987. mass mkt. 2.95 o.s.i (0-345-34676-9) Ballantine Bks.

—Rubout at the Onyx. l.t. ed. 2001. 264p. (0-7540-4427-0); (0-7540-4428-9) Gale Group. (Macmillan Reference USA).

—Rubout at the Onyx. 1981. (Joan Kahn Bk.). 192p. 10.95 o.p. (0-89919-046-4) Houghton Mifflin Co.

—Rubout at the Onyx. l.t. ed. 2001. (Paperback Ser.). 264p. 24.95 (0-7838-9330-2) Thorndike Pr.

Jeffries, William, pseud. Shallow Graves. E-Book 6.99 (1-59061-257-4) Adobe Systems, Inc.

—Shallow Graves: A Location Scout Mystery. l.t. ed. 2000. (G. K. Hall Core Ser.). 380p. 31.95 (0-7838-9296-9, Macmillan Reference USA) Gale Group.

—Shallow Graves: A Location Scout Mystery. 1992. (Location Scout Mystery Ser.). 272p. mass mkt. 4.50 (0-380-76669-8, Avon Bks.) Morrow/Avon.

—Shallow Graves: A Location Scout Mystery. 2000. (Illus.). 368p. pap. 6.99 (0-671-04748-5, Pocket) Simon & Schuster.

—Shallow Graves: A Location Scout Mystery. l.t. ed. 2001. pap. 29.95 o.p. (0-7838-9297-7) Thorndike Pr.

Jen, Gish. Mona in the Promised Land: A Novel. 1997. 320p. pap. 14.00 (0-679-77650-8, Vintage) Knopf Publishing Group.

Jhabvala, Ruth Prawer. Poet & Dancer. 1994. 208p. pap. 9.00 o.s.i (0-385-46887-3); 1993. 19.95 o.s.i (0-385-46869-5) Doubleday Publishing.

—Poet & Dancer. 1924. o.s.i (0-688-11964-6, Morrow, William & Co.) Morrow/Avon.

Johnson, Joyce. In the Night Cafe. Rosenman, Jane, ed. 1990. 240p. reprint ed. pap. (0-671-70111-8, Washington Square Pr.) Simon & Schuster.

Johnston, Brian. Dutch Treat Murders. 1991. mass mkt. 3.99 o.s.i (1-55817-570-9, Pinnacle Bks.) Kensington Publishing Corp.

—The Gift Horse Murders: A Wynston Wyc Mystery. 1992. 288p. mass mkt. 3.99 o.s.i (1-55817-652-7, Pinnacle Bks.) Kensington Publishing Corp.

—Good Luck Murders. 1991. mass mkt. 3.95 o.s.i (1-55817-479-6, Pinnacle Bks.) Kensington Publishing Corp.

—With Mallets Aforethought: A Winston Wyc Mystery. 1995. 256p. 20.50 (1-883402-44-1, Scribner) Simon & Schuster.

Jones, Matthew F. The Cooter Farm. 1991. 320p. 19.95 o.p. (1-56282-991-2) Hyperion Pr.

—The Cooter Farm. 306p. 3.98 o.p. (0-8317-6708-1) Smithmark Pubs., Inc.

Joyce, B. D. Deadly Love: A Francesca Cahill Novel. 2001. 352p. mass mkt. 6.99 (0-312-97767-0, St. Martin's Paperbacks) St. Martin's Pr.

Joyce, Michael. Liam's Going. 2002. 208p. 22.00 (0-929701-66-6) McPherson & Co.

Kane, Andrea. Run for Your Life. 480p. 2003. mass mkt. 5.99 o.s.i (0-7434-6740-X); 2000. pap. 6.99 (0-671-03656-4) Simon & Schuster. (Pocket).

Kaufelt, David A. The Fat Boy Murders. 1993. 240p. 20.00 (0-671-76092-0, Atria) Simon & Schuster.

—The Fat Boy Murders. Grose, Bill, ed. 1994. 256p. reprint ed. mass mkt. 5.50 (0-671-76093-9, Pocket) Simon & Schuster.

—The Fat Boy Murders. 230p. 3.98 o.p. (0-8317-2355-6) Smithmark Pubs., Inc.

—The Ruthless Realtor Murders: A Wyn Lewis Mystery. 1998. per. 6.50 (0-671-51148-3, Pocket); 1997. 240p. 22.00 o.s.i (0-671-51147-5, Atria) Simon & Schuster.

—The Winter Women Murders. 1995. 256p. mass mkt. 5.50 (0-671-76095-5, Pocket) Simon & Schuster.

—The Winter Women Murders: A Wyn Lewis Mystery. Grose, Bill, ed. 1994. 224p. 20.00 o.p. (0-671-76094-7, Atria) Simon & Schuster.

Kay, Terry. Shadow Song. l.t. ed. 1994. (Wheeler Large Print Book Ser.). 473p. 25.95 (1-56895-157-4, Wheeler Publishing, Inc.) Gale Group.

—Shadow Song. Rosenman, Jane, ed. 1994. 400p. 20.00 o.p. (0-671-89261-4, Atria) Simon & Schuster.

—Shadow Song. Ng, Donna, ed. 1995. 400p. reprint ed. pap. 14.00 (0-671-89260-6, Washington Square Pr.) Simon & Schuster.

—Shadow Song. 388p. pap. 4.98 o.s.i (0-7651-0607-8) Smithmark Pubs., Inc.

Keenan, Joe. Putting on the Ritz. 1991. 336p. 19.95 o.p. (0-670-83877-2, Viking) Viking Penguin.

Kelly, Jack. Line of Sight. 2000. 324p. 23.95 (0-7868-6614-4) Disney Pr.

—Mobtown. 2003. 320p. mass mkt. 7.99 (0-7868-8981-0); 2002. pap. 13.95 (0-7868-8532-7); 2002. 288p. 23.95 (0-7868-6615-2) Hyperion Pr.

Kelly, Jeffrey G. Adirondack Heist. 2002. (Illus.). 257p. pap. 14.95 (0-9663423-2-1, Creative Bloc Pr.) Adirondack Empire, Inc.

Kelly, Mary A. Foxglove. 1992. 240p. 18.95 o.p. (0-312-08195-2, Saint Martin's Minotaur) St. Martin's Pr.

Kelly, Nora. Old Wounds. l.t. ed. 1999. (Magna Large Print Ser.). 464p. (0-7505-1410-8) Magna Large Print Bks. GBR. Dist: Ulverscroft Large Print Canada, Ltd.

—Old Wounds. 2000. 300p. pap. 12.95 (1-890208-25-6) Poisoned Pen Pr.

Kelly, Thomas. Payback. unabr. ed. 1997. audio 78.00 (0-7887-1594-1, 95213E7) Recorded Bks., LLC.

—Payback: A Novel. 1997. mass mkt. 6.99 o.s.i (0-449-00223-3, Fawcett) Ballantine Bks.

Kennedy, William. The Albany Trilogy. 795th ed. 1996. 624p. pap. 20.00 (0-14-025786-1, Penguin Bks.) Penguin Group (USA) Inc.

—Billy Phelan's Greatest Game. 1983. 288p. 14.00 (0-14-006340-4); 1978. 9.95 o.p. (0-670-16667-7) Viking Penguin.

—The Flaming Corsage. unabr. collector's ed. 1996. audio 48.00 (0-7366-3405-3, 4051) Books on Tape, Inc.

—The Flaming Corsage. l.t. ed. 1997. (Large Print Bks.). 24.95 (1-56895-397-6, Wheeler Publishing, Inc.) Gale Group.

—The Flaming Corsage. 1997. 224p. pap. 11.95 (0-14-024270-8) Penguin Group (USA) Inc.

—The Flaming Corsage. 1996. 224p. 23.95 o.s.i (0-670-85872-2, Viking) Viking Penguin.

—The Flaming Corsage: Selections from the Novel. abr. ed. 1996. audio 18.95 o.p. (0-14-086342-7, Penguin AudioBooks) Viking Penguin.

—Ironweed. 1984. (Contemporay American Fiction Ser.). 240p. pap. 13.00 (0-14-007020-6, Penguin Bks.) Penguin Group (USA) Inc.

—Ironweed. 1983. 256p. 16.95 o.p. (0-670-40176-5) Viking Penguin.

—Legs. abr. ed. 2000. audio 7.95 (1-57815-188-0, 1128); audio compact disk 11.99 (1-57815-514-2, 1128 CD3) Media Bks., L. L. C. (Media Bks. Audio Publishing).

—Quinn's Book. l.t. ed. 1991. pap. 8.95 o.p. (1-55504-805-6, 524) BBC Audiobooks America.

—Quinn's Book. 1989. 304p. pap. 13.95 (0-14-007737-5, Penguin Bks.) Penguin Group (USA) Inc.

—Quinn's Book. 1988. 304p. 75.00 o.p. (0-670-82213-2); 18.95 o.p. (0-670-80437-1) Viking Penguin.

—Very Old Bones. 1992. 304p. 22.00 o.p. (0-670-83457-2, Viking) Viking Penguin.

Kernan, Michael. The Lost Diaries of Frans Hals. 1995. pap. 13.95 (0-312-13117-8, Saint Martin's Griffin); 1994. 336p. 23.95 o.p. (0-312-10946-6) St. Martin's Pr.

Keyes, Marian. Rachel's Holiday. 2002. 592p. pap. 13.95 (0-06-009038-3, Perennial) HarperTrade.

—Rachel's Holiday. 2001. 528p. mass mkt. 6.99 (0-380-81768-3, Avon Bks.); 2000. 576p. 25.00 (0-688-18071-X, Morrow, William & Co.) Morrow/Avon.

—Rachel's Holiday. 1998. (1-85371-896-3) Poolbeg Pr. IRL. Dist: Dufour Editions, Inc.

Kihn, Greg. Shade of Pale. 256p. 1998. pap. 5.99 (0-8125-5109-5, Tor Bks.); 1997. 21.95 (0-312-86046-3, Forge Bks.) Doherty, Tom Assocs., LLC.

Kilian, Michael. Looker. 1990. 19.95 o.p. (0-312-05123-9) St. Martin's Pr.

Kincaid, Jamaica. Lucy. 1991. (Plume Contemporary Fiction Ser.). 176p. pap. 11.95 o.s.i (0-452-26677-7, Plume) Dutton/Plume.

—Lucy. 2002. 176p. pap. 12.00 (0-374-52735-0); 1990. 163p. 17.95 o.s.i (0-374-19434-3) Farrar, Straus & Giroux.

—Lucy. l.t. ed. 1991. (General Ser.). 169p. lib. bdg. 19.95 (0-8161-5201-2, Macmillan Reference USA) Gale Group.

—Lucy. Schaffer-De Vries, Stefanie, tr. from ENG. 1991. (GER.). 152p. (3-8105-1043-2) Kruger, Wolfgang Verlag, GmbH DEU. Dist: International Bk. Import Service, Inc.

—Untitled Novel on Early Life in New York. 2004. (0-374-28171-8) Farrar, Straus & Giroux.

Kitt, Sandra. Significant Others. 1996. 400p. mass mkt. 6.99 (0-451-18824-1, Signet Bks.) NAL.

Klavan, Andrew. The Animal Hour. Rosenman, Jane, ed. 1993. reprint ed. 352p. mass mkt. 5.50 (0-671-74011-3, Pocket); 368p. 20.00 o.p. (0-671-74010-5, Atria) Simon & Schuster.

—Corruption. 1994. 332p. 23.00 o.p. (0-688-11816-X, Morrow, William & Co.) Morrow/Avon.

—Corruption. 1995. 374p. pap. 6.50 o.p. (0-312-95681-9, St. Martin's Paperbacks) St. Martin's Pr.

—Don't Say a Word. Rubenstein, Julie, ed. 1991. 19.95 o.p. (0-671-74008-3, Atria) Simon & Schuster.

Klempner, Joseph T. Felony Murder. 368p. 1996. (Felony Murder Ser.: Vol. 1). mass mkt. 6.99 (0-312-96037-9, St. Martin's Paperbacks); 1995. 23.95 o.p. (0-312-13494-0) St. Martin's Pr.

—Shoot the Moon. 1998. (Shoot Moon Ser.: Vol. 1). 376p. pap. 6.99 (0-312-96446-3, St. Martin's Paperbacks); 1997. 24.95 o.p. (0-312-15424-0) St. Martin's Pr.

Koch, Edward I. Murder at City Hall. 1995. 208p. mass mkt. 19.95 o.p. (0-8217-5087-9, Zebra Bks.) Kensington Publishing Corp.

—Murder on Broadway. 1997. 320p. mass mkt. 5.99 o.s.i (1-57566-186-1) Kensington Publishing Corp.

—Murder on 34th Street. 1998. 288p. mass mkt. 5.99 o.s.i (*1-57566-355-4*); 1997. 192p. 19.95 o.s.i (*1-57566-232-9*) Kensington Publishing Corp.

—The Senator Must Die. 1998. 224p. 22.00 o.s.i (*1-57566-325-2*, Kensington Bks.) Kensington Publishing Corp.

Koch, Edward I. & Resnicow, Herbert. Murder at City Hall. 1996. 224p. mass mkt. 5.99 o.s.i (*1-57566-053-9*) Kensington Publishing Corp.

Koch, Edward I. & Staub, Wendy Corsi. Murder on Broadway. 1996. 192p. 19.95 o.s.i (*1-57566-049-0*) Kensington Publishing Corp.

Koch, Stephen. The Bachelor's Bride. 1986. 224p. 18.95 o.p. (*0-7145-2856-0*) Boyars, Marion Pubs., Inc.

Kondoleon, Harry. Diary of a Lost Boy. 1995. 224p. 10.00 o.s.i (*1-57322-504-5*, Riverhead Trade (Paperbacks)) Berkley Publishing Group.

Konecky, Edith. A Place at the Table. 1989. 16.95 o.s.i (*0-394-57522-9*) Random Hse., Inc.

Koning, Hans. Pursuit of a Woman on the Hinge of History. 1997. 220p. (Orig.). pap. 15.95 (*1-57129-045-1*, Lumen Editions) Brookline Bks., Inc.

Korelitz, Jean H. A Jury of Her Peers. l.t. ed. 1996. 25.95 (*1-56895-386-0*, Wheeler Publishing, Inc.) Gale Group.

—A Jury of Her Peers. 1997. 448p. mass mkt. 5.99 o.s.i (*0-451-18871-3*, Signet Bks.) NAL.

Kotzwinkle, William. The Fan Man. 1994. (Vintage Contemporaries Ser.). 208p. pap. 12.00 (*0-679-75245-5*, Vintage) Knopf Publishing Group.

—Game of Thirty. 1994. 262p. 21.95 o.p. (*0-395-53270-1*) Houghton Mifflin Co.

—The Game of Thirty. 1995. 304p. mass mkt. 5.99 o.s.i (*0-553-57385-3*) Bantam Bks.

—The Midnight Examiner. 1989. 256p. 17.95 o.p. (*0-395-49859-7*) Houghton Mifflin Co.

Kowalski, William. The Adventures of Flash Jackson: A Novel. 2003. 320p. 24.95 (*0-06-621136-0*) HarperCollins Pubs.

—The Adventures of Flash Jackson: A Novel. 2004. 336p. pap. 13.95 (*0-06-093624-X*, Perennial) HarperTrade.

Kraft, Eric. At Home with the Glynns: The Personal History, Experiences & Observations of Peter Leroy (Continued) 1996. pap. 11.00 (*0-312-14279-X*) Picador.

—Do Clams Bite? 1982. (Peter Leroy Ser.: Vol. 1, No. 2). (Illus.). 96p. pap. 4.95 o.p. (*0-918222-45-1*) Applewood Bks.

—Do Clams Bite? 1986. 96p. mass mkt. 4.95 o.p. (*0-446-38353-8*) Warner Bks., Inc.

—The Fox & the Clam. 1984. (Personal History, Adventures, Experiences & Observations of Peter Leroy Ser.). pap. 4.95 o.p. (*0-918222-53-2*) Applewood Bks.

—Leaving Small's Hotel. 1999. 352p. pap. 14.00 (*0-312-20660-7*); 1998. 336p. 23.00 o.p. (*0-312-18689-4*) Picador.

—Life on the Bolotomy. 1983. (Peter Leroy Ser.: Vol. 1, No. 3). (Illus.). 96p. pap. 4.95 o.p. (*0-918222-48-6*) Applewood Bks.

—Life on the Bolotomy. 1986. 96p. mass mkt. 4.95 o.p. (*0-446-38354-6*) Warner Bks., Inc.

—The Little Follies: The Personal History, Adventure, Experiences & Observations of Peter Leroy (So Far) 1995. pap. 13.00 (*0-312-11928-3*) Picador.

—Mutiny!, No. 10. 1985. 96p. pap. 4.95 o.p. (*0-918222-76-1*) Applewood Bks.

—My Mother Takes a Tumble. 1982. (Portable Peter Leroy Ser.: Vol. 1 No. 1). 96p. pap. 4.95 o.p. (*0-918222-40-0*) Applewood Bks.

—My Mother Takes a Tumble. 1986. 96p. mass mkt. 4.95 o.p. (*0-446-38350-3*) Warner Bks., Inc.

—The Personal History, Adventures, Experiences, & Observations of Peter Leroy, Vol. 1. 1983. (Peter Leroy Ser.). 400p. 17.95 o.p. (*0-918222-50-8*) Applewood Bks.

—Peter Leroy: Take the Long Way Home. 1984. (Peter Leroy Ser.: No. 7). pap. 4.95 o.p. (*0-918222-61-3*) Applewood Bks.

—The Static of the Spheres. 1983. (Peter Leroy Ser.: Vol. 1, No. 4). pap. 4.95 o.p. (*0-918222-49-4*) Applewood Bks.

—The Static of the Spheres. 1986. 96p. mass mkt. 4.95 o.p. (*0-446-38356-2*) Warner Bks., Inc.

—What a Piece of Work I Am. 3rd ed. 1995. 288p. pap. 11.00 (*0-312-13211-5*) Picador.

—What a Piece of Work I Am: A Novel. 1994. 275p. 22.00 o.s.i (*0-517-59612-1*, Crown) Crown Publishing Group.

—Where Do You Stop? The Personal History, Adventures, Experiences, & Observations of Peter Leroy. 1992. (Illus.). 192p. 15.00 o.s.i (*0-517-58544-8*, Crown) Crown Publishing Group.

—Where Do You Stop? The Personal History, Adventures, Experiences & Observations of Peter Leroy. 1995. pap. 10.00 (*0-312-11932-1*) Picador.

—The Young Tars, No. 9. 1985. 96p. pap. 4.95 o.p. (*0-918222-68-0*) Applewood Bks.

Krantz, Judith. I'll Take Manhattan. 1986. 443p. 4.99 o.p. (*0-517-56110-7*) Random Hse. Value Publishing.

Kriegel, Mark. Bless Me, Father. 1996. 352p. reprint ed. mass mkt. 6.99 o.s.i (*0-425-15574-9*) Berkley Publishing Group.

Kruger, Mary. Masterpiece of Murder: A Gilded Age Mystery. 1997. (Gilded Age Mystery Ser.). 272p. mass mkt. 5.50 o.s.i (*1-57566-229-9*) Kensington Publishing Corp.

—No Honeymoon for Death: A Gilded Age Mystery. 1996. 304p. mass mkt. 5.50 o.s.i (*1-57566-110-1*); 1995. 288p. mass mkt. 18.95 o.s.i (*0-8217-5159-X*) Kensington Publishing Corp.

Krupat, Arnold. Woodsmen: or Thoreau & the Indians: A Novel. 1994. (American Indian Literature & Critical Studies Ser.: Vol. 11). 140p. reprint ed. pap. 10.95 (*0-8061-2671-X*) Univ. of Oklahoma Pr.

Kurland, Michael. Girls in High Heeled Shoes. 1998. (Alexander Brass Mysteries Ser.). 256p. 22.95 (*0-312-18104-3*, 874694, Saint Martin's Minotaur) St. Martin's Pr.

—Too Soon Dead. 1997. 288p. 22.95 o.p. (*0-312-15228-0*, Saint Martin's Minotaur) St. Martin's Pr.

Kurlansky, Mark. The White Man in the Tree: And Other Stories. 2000. (Illus.). 320p. 23.95 o.s.i (*0-671-03605-X*); 2001. 336p. reprint ed. pap. 13.00 (*0-671-03606-8*) Simon & Schuster. (Washington Square Pr.).

Kwitney, Alisa. Till the Fat Lady Sings. 1992. 224p. 19.00 o.p. (*0-06-019021-3*); 1993. 240p. reprint ed. pap. 10.00 o.p. (*0-06-099511-4*, HarperCollins) HarperTrade.

La Puma, Salvatore. The Boys of Bensonhurst. 1987. (Flannery O'Connor Award for Short Fiction Ser.). 136p. 15.95 o.p. (*0-8203-0891-9*) Univ. of Georgia Pr.

LaForge, Emily. Beneath the Raven's Moon. 2003. 400p. pap. 6.99 (*0-7434-5613-0*, Pocket) Simon & Schuster.

Lamalle, Cecile. Glutton for Punishment: A Culinary Mystery. 2000. 304p. mass mkt. 6.50 (*0-446-60937-4*); E-Book 4.95 (*0-7595-4046-2*); E-Book 4.95 (*0-7595-6045-5*); E-Book 4.95 (*0-7595-8047-2*); E-Book 4.95 (*0-7595-9052-4*); E-Book 4.95 (*0-7595-0045-2*) Warner Bks., Inc.

Lance, Peter. First Degree Burn. 1997. 384p. mass mkt. 5.99 o.s.i (*0-425-15698-2*, Prime Crime) Berkley Publishing Group.

Larrabee, Kathryn. An Everyday Savior. 2002. 288p. 24.95 (*1-56858-225-0*) Four Walls Eight Windows.

Larsen, Nella. Passing. 1970. (American Negro: His History & Literature, Ser. No. 3). reprint ed. 27.95 (*0-405-01930-0*) Ayer Co. Pubs., Inc.

—Passing. 2002. (Modern Library Classics). 304p. pap. 9.95 (*0-375-75813-5*, Modern Library) Random House Adult Trade Publishing Group.

—Passing. 2003. 160p. pap. 10.00 (*0-14-243727-1*, Penguin Classics) Viking Penguin.

Larsgaard, Chris. The Heir Hunter. 2001. 448p. mass mkt. 6.99 (*0-440-23462-X*) Dell Publishing.

Larson, Doran. Marginalia. 1997. 176p. 24.00 (*1-877946-90-7*) Permanent Pr., The.

Lasdun, James. The Horned Man: A Novel. 2003. 204p. pap. 13.95 (*0-393-32438-9*) Norton, W. W. & Co., Inc.

Lathen, Emma. Accounting for Murder: A John Putnam Thatcher Mystery. 1995. 192p. per. 7.00 o.p. (*1-57283-000-X*, Scribner) Simon & Schuster.

—Banking on Death: A John Putnam Thatcher Mystery. 1993. 168p. reprint ed. pap. 6.95 o.s.i (*1-883402-06-9*, Scribner) Simon & Schuster.

—Brewing up a Storm. l.t. ed. 1996. (John Thatcher Mystery Ser.). 272p. 21.95 o.p. (*0-312-14554-3*, Saint Martin's Minotaur) St. Martin's Pr.

—Brewing up a Storm: A John Thatcher Mystery. l.t. ed. 1997. (G. K. Hall Mystery Ser.). 400p. 23.95 o.p. (*0-7838-8096-0*, Macmillan Reference USA) Gale Group.

—By Hook or by Crook. l.t. ed. 1993. (Nightingale Ser.). 313p. lib. bdg. 15.95 o.p. (*0-8161-5707-3*, Macmillan Reference USA) Gale Group.

—Green Grow the Dollars. 1982. 12.95 o.p. (*0-671-44130-2*, Simon & Schuster) Simon & Schuster.

—The Longer the Thread. l.t. ed. 1984. (Nightingale Ser.). 328p. pap. 9.95 o.p. (*0-8161-3668-8*, Macmillan Reference USA) Gale Group.

—Right on the Money: A John Putman Thatcher Mystery. 1993. 256p. 20.00 o.p. (*0-671-73708-2*, Simon & Schuster) Simon & Schuster.

—A Shark out of Water. 1998. (John Putnam Thatcher Mystery Ser.). 336p. reprint ed. mass mkt. 5.99 o.s.i (*0-06-104460-1*, HarperTorch) Morrow/Avon.

—A Shark Out of Water: A John Putnam Thatcher Mystery. 1997. 293p. 22.95 (*0-312-17018-1*, Saint Martin's Minotaur) St. Martin's Pr.

—A Shark Out of Water: A John Thatcher Mystery. l.t. ed. 1997. (G. K. Hall Mystery Ser.). 372p. 25.95 o.p. (*0-7838-8357-9*, Macmillan Reference USA) Gale Group.

—Something in the Air. 1988. 240p. 16.95 o.p. (*0-671-66599-5*, Simon & Schuster) Simon & Schuster.

—Sweet & Low. 1983. mass mkt. 2.95 o.s.i (*0-671-45527-3*, Pocket); 1974. 6.95 o.s.i (*0-671-21785-2*, Simon & Schuster) Simon & Schuster.

Lawrence, Jerome. A Golden Circle: A Tale of the Stage & the Screen & Music of Yesterday & Now & Tomorrow & Maybe the Day after Tomorrow. 1993. 170p. 19.95 o.p. (*1-55713-086-8*) Sun & Moon Pr.

Leavitt, David. Martin Bauman: Or, A Sure Thing. 2000. 352p. tchr. ed. 26.00 (*0-395-90243-6*); 2001. 387p. reprint ed. pap. 14.00 (*0-618-15451-5*) Houghton Mifflin Co. Trade & Reference Div. (Mariner Bks.).

Lee, Chang-Rae. A Gesture Life. 2000. 368p. pap. 14.00 (*1-57322-828-1*, Riverhead Trade (Paperbacks)) Berkley Publishing Group.

—A Gesture Life. 1999. 356p. 23.95 o.s.i (*1-57322-146-5*, Riverhead Bks. (Hardcovers)) Putnam Publishing Group, The.

—Native Speaker. 1995. 324p. 22.95 o.p. (*1-57322-001-9*, Riverhead Bks. (Hardcovers)) Putnam Publishing Group, The.

Lehman, Eric Gabriel. Quaspeck: A Novel. 1993. 352p. 20.00 o.p. (*1-56279-036-6*) Mercury Hse.

Leigh, Robert. The Turner Journals. 1996. 288p. 22.95 (*0-8027-3260-7*) Walker & Co.

Lemann, Nancy. Sportsman's Paradise. 1993. 2.99 o.p. (*0-517-10900-X*) Random Hse. Value Publishing.

Lennon, J. Robert. Mailman. 2003. 448p. text 24.95 (*0-393-05731-3*) Norton, W. W. & Co., Inc.

Lentricchia, Frank. The Music of the Inferno. (Suny Series, Italian/American Culture Ser.). 220p. (C). 2000. pap. text 20.95 (*0-7914-4348-5*); 1999. text 21.50 (*0-7914-4347-7*) State Univ. of New York Pr.

Leontief, Estelle. Sellie & Dee: A Friendship. 1993. (Crimson Edge Chapbook Ser.). pap. 7.95 (*0-9619111-6-6*) Chicory Blue Pr., Inc.

Lethem, Jonathan. Motherless Brooklyn. 1999. 320p. 23.95 o.s.i (*0-385-49183-2*) Doubleday Publishing.

—Motherless Brooklyn. l.t. ed. 2000. (Basic Ser.). 492p. 30.95 (*0-7862-2695-1*) Thorndike Pr.

—Motherless Brooklyn. 2000. 19.05 (*0-606-21849-1*) Turtleback Bks.

—Motherless Brooklyn: A Novel. 2000. (Vintage Contemporaries Ser.). 336p. pap. 13.00 (*0-375-72483-4*, Vintage) Knopf Publishing Group.

Leuci, Robert. Fence Jumpers: A Novel. 1996. 403p. pap. 5.99 o.p. (*0-312-95937-0*, St. Martin's Paperbacks); 1995. 338p. 22.95 o.p. (*0-312-13073-2*) St. Martin's Pr.

—Snitch. 1998. (Snitch Ser.: Vol. 1). 352p. pap. 6.99 (*0-312-96510-9*, St. Martin's Paperbacks); 1997. 384p. 24.95 (*0-312-14739-2*) St. Martin's Pr.

Leventhal, Stan. Skydiving on Christopher Street. 1995. 225p. (Orig.). mass mkt. 6.95 (*1-56333-287-6*, Hard Candy) Masquerade Bks., Inc.

Levy, Elizabeth. Cold As Ice. 1989. 176p. pap. 2.95 (*0-380-70315-7*, Avon Bks.) Morrow/Avon.

Lewis, Alfred H. Apaches of New York. 1977. (Short Story Index Reprint Ser.). reprint ed. 25.95 (*0-8369-4088-1*) Ayer Co. Pubs., Inc.

Lewis, Beverly. The Confession. (Heritage of Lancaster County Ser.). 288p. 2000. pap. 6.99 (*0-7642-2474-3*); 1997. (J). pap. 12.99 (*1-55661-867-0*) Bethany Hse. Pubs.

—The Confession. l.t. ed. 1998. (Christian Fiction Ser.). 400p. 25.95 (*0-7862-1522-4*) Thorndike Pr.

Lewis, R. W. B., ed. The Collected Short Stories of Edith Wharton, Vol. 2. 1989. (Hudson River Editions Ser.). 908p. 50.00 o.s.i (*0-02-626161-8*, Macmillan Reference USA) Gale Group.

Lewis, Sara. Heart Conditions. 1994. x, 276p. 21.95 o.p. (*0-15-139805-4*); 2nd ed. 1997. 288p. pap. 12.00 (*0-15-600499-2*, Harvest Bks.) Harcourt Trade Pubs.

Lewis, Sinclair. The Job. (Collected Works of Sinclair Lewis). 326p. reprint ed. 2001. pap. 28.00 (*0-7426-5672-1*); 1998. lib. bdg. 98.00 (*1-58201-672-0*) Classic Bks.

—The Job. 1994. 327p. pap. 15.00 (*0-8032-7948-5*, Bison Bks.) Univ. of Nebraska Pr.

Lewis, Stephen. And Baby Makes None. 1991. 208p. 18.95 (*0-8027-5789-8*) Walker & Co.

Liddy, G. Gordon. The Monkey Handlers. abr. ed. 1990. audio 15.95 o.p. (*1-55927-100-0*) Audio Renaissance.

—The Monkey Handlers. 1991. 352p. mass mkt. 5.99 (*0-312-92613-8*, St. Martin's Paperbacks); 1990. 19.95 o.p. (*0-312-05127-1*) St. Martin's Pr.

Lieberman, Herbert. The Girl with the Botticelli Eyes. 1996. 308p. 22.95 o.p. (*0-312-11815-5*) St. Martin's Pr.

Lipp, David. 38 Adults, 45 Children, a Life Preserver & a Fire Axe. 2001. 189p. pap. 20.99 (*0-7388-6306-8*) Xlibris Corp.

Lish, Gordon. Dear Mr. Capote. 3rd ed. 1996. 264p. reprint ed. pap. 12.95 (*1-56858-079-7*) Four Walls Eight Windows.

—Dear Mr. Capote. 1983. 264p. o.p. (*0-03-061477-5*) Holt, Henry & Co.

—Zimzum. 2nd ed. 1997. 98p. reprint ed. pap. 12.95 (*1-56858-109-2*) Four Walls Eight Windows.

Listfield, Emily. Acts of Love. 1995. 384p. pap. 10.95 o.p. (*0-14-023281-8*, Penguin Bks.) Penguin Group (USA) Inc.

—Acts of Love. 370p. pap. 3.98 o.p. (*0-7651-0409-1*) Smithmark Pubs., Inc.

—Acts of Love. 1994. 384p. 21.95 o.p. (*0-670-85278-3*, Viking) Viking Penguin.

—The Last Good Night. l.t. ed. 1997. 24.95 (*1-57490-128-1*, Beeler Large Print Bks.) Beeler, Thomas T. Publisher.

—The Last Good Night. 1998. 352p. mass mkt. 5.99 o.s.i (*1-57566-354-6*) Kensington Publishing Corp.

—The Last Good Night. 1997. 320p. 22.95 o.p. (*0-316-54091-9*) Little Brown & Co.

Litman, Robert B. Allergy Shots. 1993. 254p. (Orig.). pap. text 9.95 (*0-918921-04-X*) Ivy League Pr., Inc.

Little, Benilde. Good Hair. 1996. 240p. 22.00 (*0-684-80176-0*, Simon & Schuster) Simon & Schuster.

—Good Hair: A Novel. 2003. 240p. pap. 12.00 (*0-684-83557-6*, Free Pr.) Simon & Schuster.

Little, Constance & Little, Gwenyth. The Black Shrouds. 2002. 155p. reprint ed. pap. 14.00 (*0-915230-52-6*) Rue Morgue Pr.

Liu, Aimee E. The Face. 1994. 368p. 21.95 o.s.i (*0-446-51829-8*) Warner Bks., Inc.

Livingston, Harold. Ride a Tiger. 1987. 648p. 18.95 o.p. (*0-688-04291-0*, Morrow, William & Co.) Morrow/Avon.

Lloyd, Joan Elizabeth. Slow Dancing. 1997. 224p. pap. 9.95 (*0-7867-0436-5*, Carroll & Graf Pubs.) Avalon Publishing Group.

Lockridge, Frances & Lockeridge, Richard. The Norths Meet Murder. 19.95 (*0-89190-916-8*) Amereon, Ltd.

Lockridge, Frances. Death Has a Small Voice. Date not set. 272p. pap. 8.00 (*0-06-092523-X*) HarperCollins Pubs.

—Death of an Angel. Date not set. 464p. pap. 8.00 (*0-06-092524-8*) HarperCollins Pubs.

—A Key to Death. Date not set. pap. 8.00 (*0-06-092522-1*) HarperCollins Pubs.

—Murder Comes First. Date not set. pap. 8.00 (*0-06-092521-3*) HarperCollins Pubs.

—Murder in a Hurry. Date not set. 352p. pap. 8.00 (*0-06-092520-5*) HarperCollins Pubs.

—Murder Is Served. 1987. mass mkt. 3.50 o.s.i (*0-671-63988-9*, Pocket) Simon & Schuster.

Lockridge, Frances & Lockridge, R. Death Takes a Bow. (Mr. & Mrs. North Mystery Ser.). 21.95 (*0-89190-918-4*) Amereon, Ltd.

Lockridge, Frances & Lockridge, Richard. Curtain for a Jester. 1975. (Mr. & Mrs. North Ser.). 222p. reprint ed. lib. bdg. 21.95 (*0-89190-904-4*, Rivercity Pr.) Amereon, Ltd.

—Dead As a Dinosaur. 1975. (Mr. & Mrs. North Ser.). 185p. reprint ed. lib. bdg. 21.95 (*0-89190-903-6*, Rivercity Pr.) Amereon, Ltd.

—Dead As a Dinosaur. 1993. reprint ed. lib. bdg. 17.95 (*1-56849-208-1*) Buccaneer Bks., Inc.

—Dead As a Dinosaur. 1994. (Mr. & Mrs. North Mystery Ser.). 192p. reprint ed. pap. 8.00 o.p. (*0-06-092510-8*) HarperCollins Pubs.

—Death Has a Small Voice. 1993. reprint ed. lib. bdg. 17.95 (*1-56849-209-X*) Buccaneer Bks., Inc.

—Death of a Tall Man. 1994. 256p. reprint ed. pap. 8.00 o.p. (*0-06-092513-2*, Perennial) HarperTrade.

—Death of an Angel. 1975. (Mr. & Mrs. North Ser.). reprint ed. lib. bdg. 21.95 (*0-89190-907-9*, Rivercity Pr.) Amereon, Ltd.

—Death Takes a Bow. 1994. 288p. reprint ed. pap. 8.00 o.p. (*0-06-092516-7*, Perennial) HarperTrade.

—The Dishonest Murderer. 1975. 223p. reprint ed. lib. bdg. 21.95 (*0-89190-901-X*) Amereon, Ltd.

—The Dishonest Murderer. 1994. (Mr. & Mrs. North Mystery Ser.). 224p. reprint ed. pap. 8.00 o.p. (*0-06-092509-4*) HarperCollins Pubs.

—Hanged for a Sheep. 1994. (Mr. & Mrs. North Mystery). 304p. reprint ed. pap. 8.00 o.p. (*0-06-092488-8*, Perennial) HarperTrade.

—The Judge Is Reversed. 1975. reprint ed. lib. bdg. 21.95 (*0-89190-910-9*, Rivercity Pr.) Amereon, Ltd.

—A Key to Death. 1975. 224p. reprint ed. lib. bdg. 21.95 (*0-89190-906-0*, Rivercity Pr.) Amereon, Ltd.

—Killing the Goose. 1994. 256p. reprint ed. pap. 8.00 o.p. (*0-06-092515-9*, Perennial) HarperTrade.

—Long Skeleton. 1975. reprint ed. lib. bdg. 21.95 (*0-89190-909-5*, Rivercity Pr.) Amereon, Ltd.

—Murder by the Book. 1983. mass mkt. 2.95 o.s.i (*0-671-47333-6*, Pocket) Simon & Schuster.

—Murder Comes First. 1975. 192p. reprint ed. lib. bdg. 22.95 (*0-89190-902-8*, Rivercity Pr.) Amereon, Ltd.

—Murder Is Served. 1994. (Mr. & Mrs. North Mystery Ser.). 240p. reprint ed. pap. 8.00 o.p. (*0-06-092511-6*, Perennial) HarperTrade.

—Murder Is Suggested. 1987. (Mr.and Mrs. North Mystery Ser.: No. 11). 224p. mass mkt. 3.50 o.s.i (*0-671-65728-3*, Pocket) Simon & Schuster.

—Murder Out of Turn. 18.95 (*0-89190-914-1*) Amereon, Ltd.

—Murder Out of Turn. 1994. (Mr. & Mrs. North Mystery). 304p. reprint ed. pap. 8.00 o.p. (0-06-092489-6, HarperTorch) Morrow/Avon.

—Murder Within a Murder. 1994. (Mr. & Mrs. North Mystery Ser.). 240p. reprint ed. pap. 8.00 o.p. (0-06-092512-4, Perennial) HarperTrade.

—The Norths Meet Murder. 1994. (Mr. & Mrs. North Mystery Ser.). 320p. reprint ed. pap. 8.00 o.p. (0-06-092490-X, Perennial) HarperTrade.

—Payoff for the Banker. 1994. 224p. reprint ed. pap. 8.00 o.p. (0-06-092514-0, Perennial) HarperTrade.

—A Pinch of Poison. 18.95 (0-89190-917-6) Amereon, Ltd.

—A Pinch of Poison. 1994. (Mr. & Mrs. North Mystery). 320p. reprint ed. pap. 8.00 o.p. (0-06-092491-8, Perennial) HarperTrade.

—Voyage into Violence: A Mr. & Mrs. North Mystery. 1975. reprint ed. lib. bdg. 21.95 (0-89190-908-7, Rivercity Pr.) Amereon, Ltd.

Lockridge, Richard. Plate of Red Herrings. l.t. ed. 1985. (Nightingale Ser.). 304p. 10.95 o.p. (0-8161-3832-X, Macmillan Reference USA) Gale Group.

Lockridge, Richard & Lockridge, Frances. Death of an Angel. 1988. (Mr.and Mrs. North Mystery Ser.). 224p. mass mkt. 3.50 o.s.i (0-671-65665-1, Pocket) Simon & Schuster.

—Death on an Aisle. 1986. pap. 9.95 o.p. (0-553-06512-2) Bantam Bks.

—Death Takes a Bow. 1982. (Mr. & Mrs. North Ser.: No. 4). 240p. mass mkt. 2.95 o.s.i (0-671-44337-2, Pocket) Simon & Schuster.

—The Judge Is Reversed. 1983. mass mkt. 2.95 o.s.i (0-671-44338-0, Pocket) Simon & Schuster.

—Killing the Goose. 22.95 (0-89190-911-7) Amereon, Ltd.

—Let Dead Enough Alone: A Captain Heimrich Mystery. l.t. ed. 1995. 232p. pap. 18.95 (0-7838-1159-4, Macmillan Reference USA) Gale Group.

—Murder Comes First. 1982. (Mr.and Mrs. North Mystery Ser.). mass mkt. 2.95 o.s.i (0-671-44335-6, Pocket) Simon & Schuster.

—Murder Has Its Points. 1984. (Mr.and Mrs. North Mystery Ser.). 224p. mass mkt. 2.95 o.s.i (0-671-47331-X, Pocket) Simon & Schuster.

—Murder in a Hurry. 1983. mass mkt. 2.95 o.s.i (0-671-44436-0, Pocket) Simon & Schuster.

—Voyage into Violence: A Mr. & Mrs. North Mystery. 1983. (Mr.and Mrs. North Mystery Ser.). 224p. mass mkt. 2.95 o.s.i (0-671-47329-8, Pocket) Simon & Schuster.

Lockridge, Richard & Lockridge, Francis Louis Davis. Death Has a Small Voice. 1976. 20.95 (0-89190-905-2) Amereon, Ltd.

Logan, J. W. Hardscrabble: A Country Story. 1987. 166p. 13.95 o.p. (1-878151-01-0) J&J Bks.

Lopate, Phillip. The Rug Merchant. 1987. 224p. 16.95 o.p. (0-670-81434-2) Viking Penguin.

Lord, Shirley. My Sister's Keeper. 1994. (Super Sound Buy, Dove Ser.). 8.99 o.p. (0-7871-0148-6) Penguin Group (USA) Inc.

Lordon, Randye. Brotherly Love. 272p. 1994. pap. 9.95 (0-312-10947-4, Saint Martin's Griffin); 1993. 18.95 o.p. (0-312-09254-7, Saint Martin's Minotaur) St. Martin's Pr.

—Sister's Keeper. 1994. 272p. 20.95 o.p. (0-312-11336-6, Saint Martin's Minotaur) St. Martin's Pr.

—Sisters Keeper. 1996. (Stonewall Inn Editions Ser.). 320p. pap. 11.95 (0-312-14134-3, Saint Martin's Griffin) St. Martin's Pr.

Lorens, M. K. Deception Island. 1990. 240p. mass mkt. 3.95 o.s.i (0-553-28793-1) Bantam Bks.

—Dreamland. 1993. 320p. mass mkt. 4.99 o.s.i (0-553-29437-7) Bantam Bks.

—Dreamland. 1992. 304p. 16.50 o.s.i (0-385-42237-7) Doubleday Publishing.

—Ropedancer's Fall. 1990. 288p. mass mkt. 3.95 o.s.i (0-553-28312-X) Bantam Bks.

—Sorrowheart. 1994. (Winston Marlowe Sherman Mystery Ser.). 416p. mass mkt. 4.99 o.s.i (0-553-29441-5) Bantam Bks.

—Sorrowheart: A Winston Marlowe Sherman Mystery. 1993. 384p. 17.00 o.s.i (0-385-46781-8) Doubleday Publishing.

—Sweet Narcissus. 1989. 288p. mass mkt. 3.95 o.s.i (0-553-28005-8) Bantam Bks.

Loring, Emilie Baker. As Long As I Live. 1976. 21.95 (0-88411-366-3) Amereon, Ltd.

—As Long As I Live. l.t. ed. 2000. (Candlelight Romance Ser.). 359p. 22.95 o.p. (0-7862-2459-2) Thorndike Pr.

Love, William F. Bishop's Revenge: A Bishop Regan & Davey Goldman Myster. 1993. 276p. 20.00 o.p. (1-55611-351-X) Fine, Donald I. Bks.

—Bloody Ten. 1992. 19.95 o.p. (1-55611-275-0) Fine, Donald I. Bks.

—Bloody Ten. 1994. mass mkt. (0-373-26140-3, Harlequin Bks.) Harlequin Enterprises, Ltd.

—The Chartreuse Clue. 1990. 18.95 o.p. (1-55611-211-4) Fine, Donald I. Bks.

—The Chartreuse Clue. 1991. 352p. reprint ed. mass mkt. 5.50 o.p. (0-451-40273-1, Onyx) NAL.

—The Fundamentals of Murder. 1991. 18.95 o.p. (1-55611-233-5) Fine, Donald I. Bks.

—The Ruby-Red Clue. 1992. Orig. Title: The Fundamentals of Murder. 288p. mass mkt. 4.99 o.s.i (0-451-40329-0, Onyx) NAL.

Lowell, Jax P. Mothers. 336p. 1996. pap. 13.95 (0-312-14373-7, Saint Martin's Griffin); 1995. 22.95 o.p. (0-312-13126-7) St. Martin's Pr.

Lundy, Mike. Baby Farm. 1988. mass mkt. 3.95 o.p. (0-425-10896-1) Berkley Publishing Group.

Lupica, Mike. Jump. 384p. 2002. mass mkt. 6.99 (0-7860-1522-5); 1996. mass mkt. 5.99 o.s.i (0-7860-0303-0); 1996. mass mkt. 5.99 o.s.i (1-57566-112-8) Kensington Publishing Corp.

Lupoff, Richard A. The Silver Chariot Killer. 1996. 192p. text 21.95 o.p. (0-312-14736-8, Saint Martin's Minotaur) St. Martin's Pr.

Lurie, Alison. Only Children. 1979. 9.95 o.p. (0-394-50471-2) Random Hse., Inc.

Luttrell, Steve. Home Movies: A Collection of Poems by Steve Luttrell. 1998. 61p. 9.95 (1-878471-05-8) Big Bridge Pr.

Lutz, John. The Ex. 1999. 320p. mass mkt. 4.99 o.s.i (0-7860-0186-0); 1997. 304p. mass mkt. 5.50 o.s.i (1-57566-178-0); 1996. 256p. 21.00 o.s.i (1-57566-078-4, Kensington Bks.) Kensington Publishing Corp.

MacDonnell, Julia. A Year of Favor: A Novel. 1994. 330p. 25.00 o.p. (0-688-12546-8, Morrow, William & Co.) Morrow/Avon.

Mackin, Jeanne. The Sweet By & By. 2001. 293p. 24.95 o.p. (0-312-26997-8) St. Martin's Pr.

Mancini, Anthony. Godmother. 1993. 272p. 21.95 o.p. (1-55611-376-5) Fine, Donald I. Bks.

—Godmother. 264p. 4.98 o.p. (0-8317-5539-3) Smithmark Pubs., Inc.

Mandava, Bhargavi C. Where the Oceans Meet. 1996. 272p. (Orig.). 22.95 o.p. (1-878067-86-9, Seal Pr.) Avalon Publishing Group.

Mandel, Sally. Out of the Blue. 2002. 304p. mass mkt. 6.99 (0-345-42891-9, Ballantine Bks.) Ballantine Bks.

—Out of the Blue. l.t. ed. 2000. (Americana Ser.). 420p. 26.95 o.p. (0-7862-2551-3) Thorndike Pr.

Manos, James, Jr. Little Ellie Claus. 2000. (Illus.). 256p. 15.95 o.s.i (0-7434-0624-9, Atria) Simon & Schuster.

Manrique, Jaime. Latin Moon in Manhattan. 1992. 224p. 17.95 o.p. (0-312-07100-0) St. Martin's Pr.

—Twilight at the Equator: A Novel. 1997. 224p. 23.95 o.s.i (0-571-19901-1) Faber & Faber, Inc.

—Twilight at the Equator: A Novel. 1997. pap. 18.00 (1-891305-18-2) Painted Leaf Pr.

—Twilight at the Equator: A Novel. 2003. 198p. pap. 15.95 (0-299-18774-8) Univ. of Wisconsin Pr.

Marcuse, Irene. The Death of an Amiable Child: An Anita Servi Novel. 2000. (Anita Servi Novels Ser.). 227p. 23.95 (0-8027-3346-8) Walker & Co.

Margolis, David. The Stepman. 1996. 192p. 24.00 (1-877946-76-1) Permanent Pr., The.

Margolis, Seth. Vanishing Act. 1993. 233p. 17.95 o.p. (0-312-08770-5, Saint Martin's Minotaur) St. Martin's Pr.

Margolis, Seth J. Perfect Angel. unabr. collector's ed. 1997. audio 56.00 (0-913369-90-X, 4390) Books on Tape, Inc.

—Perfect Angel. 1997. 352p. mass mkt. 23.00 o.p. (0-380-97311-1); 1998. reprint ed. mass mkt. 6.99 (0-380-78748-2) Morrow/Avon. (Avon Bks.).

Marks, Walter. Dangerous Behavior. Penzler, Otto, ed. 2002. 288p. 24.00 (0-7867-1043-8, Carroll & Graf Pubs.) Avalon Publishing Group.

Maron, Margaret. Fugitive Colors. 1995. 272p. 18.95 o.s.i (0-89296-567-3) Mysterious Pr.

Martin, Larry J. Sounding Drum. 1999. 345p. 23.00 o.s.i (1-57566-368-6) Kensington Publishing Corp.

Martinac, Paula. Home Movies. 1993. 222p. (Orig.). pap. 10.95 (1-878067-32-X, Seal Pr.) Avalon Publishing Group.

Martino, Terry DeFranco. A Town in a Home. 1999. 188p. pap. 11.95 (1-56315-192-8) SterlingHouse Pubs., Inc.

Marx, Pearson. On the Way to the Venus de Milo. 1995. 270p. 21.00 (0-671-88335-6, Simon & Schuster) Simon & Schuster.

Masini, Donna. About Yvonne: A Novel. 1997. 288p. 23.00 o.p. (0-393-04091-7) Norton, W. W. & Co., Inc.

Masterton, Graham. The House That Jack Built. 1996. 384p. 24.00 o.p. (0-7867-0353-9, Carroll & Graf Pubs.) Avalon Publishing Group.

—The House That Jack Built. 2000. 400p. pap. 5.50 (0-8439-4746-2, Leisure Bks.) Dorchester Publishing Co., Inc.

Matranga, Frances C. The Mysterious Prowler. 1984. 120p. pap. 4.50 o.p. (0-88207-616-7) Cook Communications Ministries.

Matteson, Stefanie. Murder among the Angels. 1996. 256p. mass mkt. 5.99 o.s.i (0-425-15548-X); 19.95 o.p. (0-425-15149-2) Berkley Publishing Group. (Prime Crime).

Maxim, John R. The Shadow Box. 1997. mass mkt. 6.99 (0-380-78668-0); 1996. 384p. mass mkt. 23.00 o.p. (0-380-97300-6) Morrow/Avon. (Avon Bks.).

Maxwell, William. All the Days & Nights: The Collected Stories of William Maxwell. 1995. 432p. pap. 15.00 (0-679-76102-0, Vintage) Knopf Publishing Group.

Mayfield, Julian. The Hit & the Long Night. 1989. (Library of Black Literature). 310p. reprint ed. pap. text 17.95 (1-55553-065-6) Northeastern Univ. Pr.

Mazzaro, Jerome. War Games. 2001. 201p. pap. 21.99 (0-7388-6769-1); text 31.99 (0-7388-6768-3); E-Book 8.00 (0-7388-6770-5) Xlibris Corp.

McBain, Ed, pseud. And All Through the House. 1994. 48p. 12.45 o.p. (0-446-51845-X) Warner Bks., Inc.

—Ax. unabr. ed. 1996. (Eighty-Seventh Precinct Ser.). audio 30.00 (0-7366-3506-8, 4145) Books on Tape, Inc.

—Ax. 1977. (87th Precinct Mystery Ser.). mass mkt. 2.95 o.p. (0-451-14599-2); mass mkt. 1.25 o.p. (0-451-07654-0, Signet Bks.); 160p. mass mkt. 4.50 o.s.i (0-451-16407-5, Signet Bks.) NAL.

—Ax. 1964. 3.50 o.p. (0-671-06283-2) Simon & Schuster.

—Blood Relatives. 1977. pap. 1.50 o.p. (0-394-25462-7) Ballantine Bks.

—Blood Relatives. 1978. (Eighty-Seventh Precinct Ser.). pap. 1.75 o.p. (0-553-11759-9) Bantam Bks.

—Blood Relatives. unabr. ed. 1987. (Eighty-Seventh Precinct Ser.). audio 36.00 (0-7366-1147-9, 2071) Books on Tape, Inc.

—Blood Relatives. 1987. mass mkt. 3.50 o.p. (0-451-15084-8, Signet Bks.) NAL.

—Bread. unabr. ed. 1987. (Eighty-Seventh Precinct Ser.). audio 42.00 (0-7366-1198-3, 2116) Books on Tape, Inc.

—Bread. 1987. 176p. mass mkt. 4.50 (0-380-70368-8, Avon Bks.) Morrow/Avon.

—Bread. 1982. mass mkt. 2.25 o.p. (0-451-11279-2, AE1279); 1975. mass mkt. 1.25 o.p. (0-451-06754-1) NAL. (Signet Bks.).

—Bread. 1974. 213p. (J). o.p. (0-394-48580-7) Random Hse., Inc.

—Bread. 1997. (Eighty Seventh Precinct Ser.). 224p. reprint ed. mass mkt. 6.50 (0-446-60425-9) Warner Bks., Inc.

—Calypso. 1980. 208p. pap. 1.95 o.s.i (0-553-13399-3) Bantam Bks.

—Calypso. unabr. ed. 1998. (Eighty-Seventh Precinct Ser.). audio 42.00 (0-7366-3775-3, 4448) Books on Tape, Inc.

—Calypso. 1988. 208p. mass mkt. 4.99 (0-380-70591-5, Avon Bks.) Morrow/Avon.

—Calypso. 1979. 10.95 o.p. (0-670-20030-1) Viking Penguin.

—The Con Man. unabr. ed. 1993. audio 54.95 (0-7451-4157-9, CAB 840) BBC Audiobooks America.

—The Con Man. unabr. ed. 1990. (Eighty-Seventh Precinct Ser.). audio 36.00 (0-7366-1787-6, 2624) Books on Tape, Inc.

—The Con Man. l.t. ed. 1986. (Nightingale Ser.). 296p. 10.95 o.p. (0-8161-3982-2, Macmillan Reference USA) Gale Group.

—The Con Man. (Eighty-Seventh Precinct Mysteries Ser.). 1987. 160p. mass mkt. 3.99 o.s.i (0-451-15085-6); 1980. mass mkt. 1.75 o.p. (0-451-09351-8); 1974. mass mkt. 0.95 o.p. (0-451-05863-1) NAL. (Signet Bks.).

—Cop Hater. unabr. ed. 1992. (Eighty-Seventh Precinct Novels Ser.). audio 54.95 (0-7451-6153-7, CAB 674) BBC Audiobooks America.

—Cop Hater. unabr. ed. 1990. (Eighty-Seventh Precinct Ser.). audio 36.00 (0-7366-1710-8, 2552) Books on Tape, Inc.

—Cop Hater. l.t. ed. 1989. (Nightingale Ser.). 316p. 13.95 o.p. (0-8161-4517-2, Macmillan Reference USA) Gale Group.

—Cop Hater. (Eighty-Seventh Precinct Mysteries Ser.). 9999. 160p. mass mkt. 3.95 o.p. (0-451-16441-5); 1987. 160p. mass mkt. 3.99 o.p. (0-451-15079-1); 1980. mass mkt. 1.75 o.p. (0-451-09170-1); 1973. mass mkt. 0.95 o.p. (0-451-05617-5) NAL. (Signet Bks.).

—Cop Hater. 1999. (Eighty-Seventh Precinct Ser.). (Illus.). 272p. pap. 7.99 (0-671-77547-2, Pocket) Simon & Schuster.

—Doll. 1981. mass mkt. 2.25 o.s.i (0-345-29289-8) Ballantine Bks.

—Doll. unabr. ed. 1996. (Eighty-Seventh Precinct Ser.). audio 30.00 (0-7366-3512-2, 4151) Books on Tape, Inc.

—Doll. 1986. (Eighty-Seventh Precinct Novel Ser.). 160p. mass mkt. 4.50 (0-380-70082-4, Avon Bks.) Morrow/Avon.

—Doll. 1997. (Eighty Seventh Precinct Ser.). 208p. reprint ed. mass mkt. 5.99 (0-446-60146-2) Warner Bks., Inc.

—Downtown. l.t. ed. 1992. pap. 17.95 o.p. (0-7927-1111-4); 18.95 o.p. (0-7927-1112-2, E0032) BBC Audiobooks America.

—Downtown. unabr. ed. 1992. (Eighty-Seventh Precinct Ser.). audio 48.00 (0-7366-2142-3, 2940) Books on Tape, Inc.

—Downtown. unabr. ed. 1991. audio 57.25 o.p. (1-56100-083-3, 870, Unabridged Library Editions); audio 22.95 o.p. (0-930435-89-3, 94, Bookcassette) Brilliance Audio.

—Downtown. 1991. 302p. 20.00 o.p. (0-688-08736-1, Morrow, William & Co.); 1993. 352p. reprint ed. mass mkt. 5.99 (0-380-70761-6, Avon Bks.) Morrow/Avon.

—Downtown. 1993. 15.95 o.p. (1-55800-454-8) NewStar Media, Inc.

—Downtown. unabr. ed. 1991. audio 70.00 (1-55690-153-4, 91405E7) Recorded Bks., LLC.

—Eight Black Horses. l.t. ed. 1986. (General Ser.). 350p. 15.95 o.p. (0-8161-4022-7, Macmillan Reference USA) Gale Group.

—Eight Black Horses. (Eighty-Seventh Precinct Novel Ser.). 1986. 256p. mass mkt. 4.99 (0-380-70029-8, Avon Bks.); 1985. 15.95 o.p. (0-87795-681-2, Morrow, William & Co.) Morrow/Avon.

—Eight Black Horses. 2003. (Illus.). 336p. pap. 7.99 (0-7434-6308-0, Pocket) Simon & Schuster.

—Eighty Million Eyes. 1983. 192p. mass mkt. 2.25 o.s.i (0-345-29292-8); 1975. mass mkt. 1.25 o.s.i (0-345-24604-7) Ballantine Bks.

—Eighty Million Eyes. unabr. ed. 1997. (Eighty-Seventh Precinct Ser.). audio 30.00 (0-7366-3565-3, 4209) Books on Tape, Inc.

—Eighty Million Eyes. l.t. ed. 2000. 229p. lib. bdg. 25.95 (1-58547-011-2) Ctr. Point Large Print.

—Eighty Million Eyes. 1987. 176p. mass mkt. 4.50 (0-380-70367-X, Avon Bks.) Morrow/Avon.

—Eighty Million Eyes. 1997. (Eighty Seventh Precinct Ser.). 208p. reprint ed. mass mkt. 5.99 (0-446-60386-4) Warner Bks., Inc.

—The Empty Hours. unabr. ed. 1996. (Eighty-Seventh Precinct Ser.). audio 36.00 (0-7366-3409-6, 4056) Books on Tape, Inc.

—The Empty Hours. (87th Precinct Mystery Ser.). 1982. mass mkt. 2.25 o.p. (0-451-11835-9); 1982. 256p. mass mkt. 4.50 o.p. (0-451-14601-8); 1977. mass mkt. 1.25 o.p. (0-451-07287-1) NAL. (Signet Bks.).

—Fuzz. unabr. ed. 1995. (87th Precinct Mystery Ser.). audio 54.95 (0-7451-6157-X, CAB 133) BBC Audiobooks America.

—Fuzz. unabr. ed. 1997. (Eighty-Seventh Precinct Ser.). audio 42.00 (0-7366-3637-4, 4298) Books on Tape, Inc.

—Fuzz. 1978. mass mkt. 1.75 o.p. (0-451-08399-7); 1978. 192p. mass mkt. 3.99 o.p. (0-451-15554-8, E8399); 1972. mass mkt. 0.75 o.p. (0-451-05151-3); 1969. mass mkt. 0.60 o.p. (0-451-04001-5) NAL. (Signet Bks.).

—Fuzz. E-Book 6.99 (0-7953-0320-3); E-Book 6.99 (0-7953-0322-X) RosettaBooks.

—Fuzz. 2000. (Eighty Seventh Precinct Ser.). 288p. mass mkt. 6.50 o.s.i (0-446-60971-4) Warner Bks., Inc.

—Ghosts. 1981. 176p. pap. 2.50 o.p. (0-553-23240-1) Bantam Bks.

—Ghosts. unabr. ed. 1998. (Eighty-Seventh Precinct Ser.). audio 36.00 (0-7366-4109-2, 4614) Books on Tape, Inc.

—Ghosts. 1980. 212p. 9.95 o.p. (0-670-33806-0) Viking Penguin.

—Give the Boys a Great Big Hand. unabr. ed. 1992. (Eighty-Seventh Precinct Ser.). audio 36.00 (0-7366-2251-9, 3040) Books on Tape, Inc.

—Give the Boys a Great Big Hand. l.t. ed. 1988. (Nightingale Ser.). 307p. 12.95 o.p. (0-8161-4516-4, Macmillan Reference USA) Gale Group.

—Give the Boys a Great Big Hand. (87th Precinct Mystery Ser.). 1981. mass mkt. 2.25 o.p. (0-451-11081-1); 1981. 240p. mass mkt. 4.50 o.p. (0-451-15921-7); 1981. mass mkt. 2.95 o.p. (0-451-13900-3); 1975. mass mkt. 1.25 o.p. (0-451-06683-9) NAL. (Signet Bks.).

—Hail, Hail, the Gang's All Here. unabr. ed. 1997. (Eighty-Seventh Precinct Ser.). audio 36.00 (0-7366-3752-4, 4427) Books on Tape, Inc.

—Hail, Hail, the Gang's All Here. 1972. 307p. (J). (0-8161-6025-2, Macmillan Reference USA) Gale Group.

—Hail, Hail, the Gang's All Here. 1972. 160p. mass mkt. 3.99 o.s.i (0-451-15609-9, Signet Bks.) NAL.

—Hail to the Chief. unabr. ed. 1995. audio 36.00 o.p. audio o.p. audio 30.00 (0-7366-3199-2, 3863) Books on Tape, Inc.

—Hail to the Chief. l.t. ed. 2003. lib. bdg. 28.95 (1-58547-307-3, Premier) Ctr. Point Large Print.

—Hail to the Chief. 1987. (Eighty-Seventh Precinct Novel Ser.). 160p. mass mkt. 4.50 (0-380-70370-X, Avon Bks.) Morrow/Avon.

—Hail to the Chief. 1981. mass mkt. 2.25 o.p. (0-451-11214-8); 1975. mass mkt. 1.25 o.p. (0-451-06548-4) NAL. (Signet Bks.).

—Hail to the Chief. 1973. 182p. o.p. (0-394-48581-5) Random Hse., Inc.

—Hail to the Chief. 1997. 192p. reprint ed. mass mkt. 5.99 (0-446-60405-4) Warner Bks., Inc.

—He Who Hesitates. 1981. 160p. mass mkt. 2.25 o.s.i (*0-345-29291-X*); 1975. mass mkt. 1.25 o.s.i (*0-345-24757-4*) Ballantine Bks.
—He Who Hesitates. l.t. ed. 1990. (Nightingale Ser.). 248p. 13.95 o.p. (*0-8161-4769-8*, Macmillan Reference USA) Gale Group.
—He Who Hesitates. 2000. mass mkt. 3.50 (*0-380-64198-4*); 1986. 160p. mass mkt. 4.50 (*0-380-70084-0*, Avon Bks.) Morrow/Avon.
—He Who Hesitates. 1996. 160p. reprint ed. mass mkt. 5.99 (*0-446-60147-0*) Warner Bks., Inc.
—Heat. 1987. 208p. mass mkt. 3.95 o.s.i (*0-345-34597-5*); 1983. mass mkt. 2.95 o.s.i (*0-345-30673-2*) Ballantine Bks.
—Heat. unabr. ed. 1998. (Eighty-Seventh Precinct Ser.). audio 42.00 (*0-7366-4110-6*, 4615) Books on Tape, Inc.
—Heat. 1992. (Eighty-Seventh Precinct Mysteries Ser.). 208p. mass mkt. 4.99 o.s.i (*0-451-17078-4*, Signet Bks.) NAL.
—Heat. 1981. 288p. 12.95 o.p. (*0-670-36479-7*) Viking Penguin.
—The Heckler. unabr. ed. 1996. (Eighty-Seventh Precinct Ser.). audio 36.00 (*0-7366-3254-9*, 3911) Books on Tape, Inc.
—The Heckler. 1982. mass mkt. 2.25 o.p. (*0-451-11421-3*); 1982. 176p. mass mkt. 4.50 o.p. (*0-451-15970-5*); 1982. mass mkt. 2.95 o.p. (*0-451-13901-1*); 1976. mass mkt. 1.25 o.p. (*0-451-06839-4*) NAL. (Signet Bks.).
—The Heckler. 2003. (Illus.). 288p. pap. 7.99 (*0-7434-6307-2*, Pocket) Simon & Schuster.
—Ice. unabr. ed. 1995. (Eighty-Seventh Precinct Ser.). audio 56.00 (*0-7366-3180-1*, 3849) Books on Tape, Inc.
—Ice. l.t. ed. 1983. 510p. lib. bdg. 17.95 o.p. (*0-8161-3568-1*, Macmillan Reference USA) Gale Group.
—Ice. 1984. 320p. pap. 5.99 (*0-380-67108-5*, Avon Bks.); 1983. 305p. 15.50 o.p. (*0-87795-468-2*, Morrow, William & Co.) Morrow/Avon.
—Ice. 2003. (Best Mysteries of All Time Ser.). 360p. (*0-7621-8889-8*, Impress) Scriptorium Pr., The.
—Ice. 1996. 336p. reprint ed. mass mkt. 5.99 o.p. (*0-446-60390-2*) Warner Bks., Inc.
—Jigsaw. unabr. ed. 1997. (Eighty-Seventh Precinct Ser.). audio 30.00 (*0-7366-3641-2*, 4303) Books on Tape, Inc.
—Jigsaw. 1970. (Eighty-Seventh Precinct Mysteries Ser.). 160p. mass mkt. 4.50 o.p. (*0-451-15480-0*, Signet Bks.) NAL.
—Killer's Choice. 1981. mass mkt. 2.25 o.s.i (*0-345-29288-X*) Ballantine Bks.
—Killer's Choice. unabr. ed. 1991. (Eighty-Seventh Precinct Ser.). audio 36.00 (*0-7366-2064-8*, 2872) Books on Tape, Inc.
—Killer's Choice. 1986. (Eighty-Seventh Precinct Novel Ser.). pap. 4.50 (*0-380-70083-2*, Avon Bks.) Morrow/Avon.
—Killer's Choice. 1996. 160p. mass mkt. 5.99 o.s.i (*0-446-60144-6*) Warner Bks., Inc.
—Killer's Payoff. unabr. ed. 1991. (Eighty-Seventh Precinct Ser.). audio 36.00 (*0-7366-2065-6*, 2873) Books on Tape, Inc.
—Killer's Payoff. l.t. ed. 1987. (Nightingale Ser.). 295p. 11.95 o.p. (*0-8161-4257-2*, Macmillan Reference USA) Gale Group.
—Killer's Payoff. (Eighty-Seventh Precinct Mysteries Ser.). 1987. 160p. mass mkt. 3.99 o.p. (*0-451-15081-3*); 1980. mass mkt. 1.75 o.p. (*0-451-09464-6*); 1974. mass mkt. 0.95 o.p. (*0-451-05939-5*) NAL. (Signet Bks.).
—Killer's Payoff. 2003. (Illus.). 272p. pap. 6.99 (*0-7434-6306-4*, Pocket) Simon & Schuster.
—Killer's Wedge. unabr. ed. 1992. (Eighty-Seventh Precinct Ser.). audio 36.00 (*0-7366-2105-9*, 2909) Books on Tape, Inc.
—Killer's Wedge. l.t. ed. 2000. 198p. lib. bdg. 27.95 o.p. (*1-58547-032-5*) Ctr. Point Large Print.
—Killer's Wedge. 1981. mass mkt. 1.75 o.p. (*0-451-09614-2*); 1981. 160p. mass mkt. 3.99 o.p. (*0-451-16336-2*); 1981. mass mkt. 2.95 o.p. (*0-451-14597-6*); 1974. mass mkt. 0.95 o.p. (*0-451-06219-1*) NAL. (Signet Bks.).
—King's Ransom. unabr. ed. 1991. (Eighty-Seventh Precinct Ser.). audio 42.00 (*0-7366-1894-5*, 2721) Books on Tape, Inc.
—King's Ransom. l.t. ed. 1986. (Nightingale Ser.). 327p. 11.95 o.p. (*0-8161-4127-4*, Macmillan Reference USA) Gale Group.
—King's Ransom. (87th Precinct Mystery Ser.). 1981. mass mkt. 2.25 o.p. (*0-451-09815-3*, Signet Bks.); 1981. 176p. mass mkt. 4.50 o.p. (*0-451-15933-0*); 1981. mass mkt. 2.95 o.p. (*0-451-13898-8*, Signet Bks.); 1975. mass mkt. 1.25 o.p. (*0-451-06467-4*, Signet Bks.) NAL.
—Kiss. unabr. ed. 1992. (Eighty-Seventh Precinct Ser.). audio 64.00 (*0-7366-2286-1*, 3072) Books on Tape, Inc.
—Kiss. unabr. ed. 1992. audio 22.95 o.p. (*1-56100-461-8*, 155, Bookcassette); audio 57.25 o.p. (*1-56100-095-7*, 543, Unabridged Library Editions) Brilliance Audio.
—Kiss. l.t. ed. 1993. (General Ser.). 458p. 16.95 o.p. (*0-8161-5589-5*); 21.95 o.p. (*0-8161-5588-7*) Gale Group. (Macmillan Reference USA).
—Kiss. 2002. 400p. audio 9.99 (*0-06-008392-1*); 1992. audio 16.00 o.p. (*1-55994-461-7*) HarperTrade. (HarperAudio).
—Kiss. abr. ed. 2000. (Eighty Seventh Precinct Novels Ser.). audio 7.95 (*1-57815-052-3*, 1013, Media Bks. Audio Publishing) Media Bks., L. L. C.
—Kiss. 1992. 384p. pap. 5.99 (*0-380-71382-9*, Avon Bks.); 330p. 17.00 o.p. (*0-688-10220-4*, Morrow, William & Co.) Morrow/Avon.
—Kiss. 1993. 4.99 o.p. (*0-517-11033-4*) Random Hse. Value Publishing.
—Lady Killer. unabr. ed. 1995. (Eighty-Seventh Precinct Novels Ser.). audio 39.95 BBC Audiobooks America.
—Lady Killer. unabr. ed. 1996. (Eighty-Seventh Precinct Ser.). audio 30.00 (*0-7366-3219-0*, 3882) Books on Tape, Inc.
—Lady Killer. l.t. ed. 1984. (General Ser.). lib. bdg. 12.95 o.p. (*0-8161-3665-3*, Macmillan Reference USA) Gale Group.
—Lady Killer. (Eighty-Seventh Precinct Mysteries Ser.). 1987. 160p. mass mkt. 4.50 o.s.i (*0-451-15082-1*); 1980. mass mkt. 1.75 o.p. (*0-451-09532-4*); 1974. mass mkt. 0.95 o.p. (*0-451-06067-9*) NAL. (Signet Bks.).
—Lady, Lady, I Did It! unabr. ed. 1996. (Eighty-Seventh Precinct Ser.). audio 30.00 (*0-7366-3495-9*, 4135) Books on Tape, Inc.
—Lady, Lady, I Did It! (87th Precinct Mystery Ser.). 1982. mass mkt. 2.25 o.p. (*0-451-11779-4*); 1982. 256p. mass mkt. 4.50 o.p. (*0-451-15841-5*); 1982. mass mkt. 2.95 o.p. (*0-451-13899-6*); 1976. mass mkt. 1.25 o.p. (*0-451-07151-4*) NAL. (Signet Bks.).
—Lady, Lady, I Did It! 1961. 3.50 o.p. (*0-671-40555-1*) Simon & Schuster.
—The Last Dance. l.t. ed. 2000. (Wheeler Large Print Book Ser.). 27.95 (*1-56895-814-5*, Wheeler Publishing, Inc.) Gale Group.
—The Last Dance. 2000. (Illus.). 272p. 25.00 o.s.i (*0-684-85513-5*, Simon & Schuster); 1999. E-Book 25.00 (*0-7432-0047-0*, Simon & Schuster); 2000. (Illus.). 336p. reprint ed. mass mkt. 7.99 (*0-671-02570-8*, Pocket) Simon & Schuster.
—Let's Hear It for the Deaf Man. unabr. ed. 1998. (Eighty-Seventh Precinct Ser.). audio 36.00 (*0-7366-3776-1*, 4449) Books on Tape, Inc.
—Let's Hear It for the Deaf Man. 1973. 231p. (J). o.p. (*0-385-01600-X*) Doubleday Publishing.
—Let's Hear It for the Deaf Man. 1974. (87th Precinct Mystery Ser.). 160p. mass mkt. 3.99 o.p. (*0-451-15403-7*, Signet Bks.) NAL.
—Lightning. 1999. (Eighty-Seventh Precinct Ser.). audio 56.00 (*0-7366-4624-8*, 5009) Books on Tape, Inc.
—Lightning. abr. ed. audio 17.00 o.p. (*0-694-51547-7*, CPN 2489, HarperAudio) HarperTrade.
—Lightning. (Eighty-Seventh Precinct Novel Ser.). 1985. 304p. mass mkt. 4.95 (*0-380-69974-5*, Avon Bks.); 1984. 15.95 o.p. (*0-87795-581-6*, Morrow, William & Co.) Morrow/Avon.
—Like Love. unabr. ed. 1996. (Eighty-Seventh Precinct Ser.). audio 36.00 (*0-7366-3496-7*, 4136) Books on Tape, Inc.
—Like Love. l.t. ed. 1993. (Nightingale Ser.). 304p. lib. bdg. 15.95 o.p. (*0-8161-5705-7*, Macmillan Reference USA) Gale Group.
—Like Love. (87th Precinct Mystery Ser.). 1982. mass mkt. 2.25 o.p. (*0-451-11628-3*); 1982. 176p. mass mkt. 2.95 o.p. (*0-451-13903-8*); 1982. 160p. mass mkt. 4.50 o.s.i (*0-451-16383-4*); 1976. mass mkt. 1.25 o.p. (*0-451-07221-9*) NAL. (Signet Bks.).
—Long Time No See. 1982. pap. 2.50 o.p. (*0-553-23130-8*) Bantam Bks.
—Long Time No See. unabr. ed. 1986. (Eighty-Seventh Precinct Ser.). audio 40.00 (*0-7366-0823-0*, 1773) Books on Tape, Inc.
—Long Time No See. abr. ed. audio 17.00 o.p. (*0-694-51546-9*, CPN 2488, HarperAudio) HarperTrade.
—Long Time No See. 1987. 272p. mass mkt. 4.99 (*0-380-70369-6*, Avon Bks.) Morrow/Avon.
—Long Time No See. 1997. 304p. mass mkt. 5.99 (*0-446-60449-6*) Warner Bks., Inc.
—Lullaby. unabr. ed. 1992. (Audio Bks.). audio 69.95 (*0-7451-6154-5*, CAB 549) BBC Audiobooks America.
—Lullaby. 1999. audio 48.00 (*0-7366-4872-0*); 1989. audio 48.00 Books on Tape, Inc.
—Lullaby. l.t. ed. 1990. (General Ser.). 437p. 20.95 o.p. (*0-8161-4923-2*, Macmillan Reference USA) Gale Group.
—Lullaby. abr. ed. audio 16.00 o.p. (*1-55994-819-1*, CPN 2392, HarperAudio) HarperTrade.
—Lullaby. 1990. 352p. mass mkt. 5.99 (*0-380-70384-X*, Avon Bks.); 1989. 17.95 o.p. (*0-87795-994-3*, Morrow, William & Co.) Morrow/Avon.
—Mischief. l.t. ed. 1995. pap. 23.95 o.p. (*0-7927-2014-8*); 1994. 25.95 o.p. (*0-7927-2015-6*) BBC Audiobooks America.
—Mischief. unabr. ed. 1993. (Eighty-Seventh Precinct Ser.). audio 64.00 (*0-7366-2591-7*, 3336) Books on Tape, Inc.
—Mischief. unabr. ed. 1993. 57.25 o.p. incl. audio (*1-56100-147-3*, 942, Unabridged Library Editions); audio 21.95 o.p. (*1-56100-514-2*, 176, Bookcassette) Brilliance Audio.
—Mischief. abr. ed. 2000. audio 9.99 (*0-694-52329-1*, HarperAudio) HarperTrade.
—Mischief. abr. ed. 2000. (Eighty Seventh Precinct Novels Ser.). audio 7.95 (*1-57815-051-5*, 1043, Media Bks. Audio Publishing) Media Bks., L. L. C.
—Mischief. 1994. 352p. pap. 5.99 o.p. (*0-380-71384-5*, Avon Bks.); 1993. 346p. 20.00 o.p. (*0-688-10221-2*, Morrow, William & Co.) Morrow/Avon.
—The Mugger. unabr. ed. 1995. (Eighty-Seventh Precinct Novels Ser.). audio 39.95 (*0-7451-6855-8*, CAB 321) BBC Audiobooks America.
—The Mugger. 1981. 160p. mass mkt. 2.25 o.s.i (*0-345-29290-1*) Ballantine Bks.
—The Mugger. unabr. ed. 1990. (Eighty-Seventh Precinct Ser.). audio 36.00 (*0-7366-1721-3*, 2562) Books on Tape, Inc.
—The Mugger. 1996. 192p. mass mkt. 5.99 (*0-446-60143-8*) Warner Bks., Inc.
—Nocturne. abr. ed. 1997. (Eighty Seventh Precinct Ser.). audio 24.95 (*1-55927-439-5*, 695087) Audio Renaissance.
—Nocturne. unabr. ed. 1997. (Eighty-Seventh Precinct Ser.). audio 48.00 (*0-7366-3777-X*, 4450) Books on Tape, Inc.
—Nocturne. (Eighty Seventh Precinct Ser.). 1998. mass mkt. 188.73 (*0-446-16558-1*); 1997. 320p. 23.50 o.p. (*0-446-51805-0*); 1998. 352p. reprint ed. mass mkt. 6.99 (*0-446-60538-7*) Warner Bks., Inc.
—Poison. 2001. audio 64.00 (*0-7366-5935-8*) Books on Tape, Inc.
—Poison. l.t. ed. 1988. 352p. 19.95 o.p. (*0-8161-4299-8*, Macmillan Reference USA) Gale Group.
—Poison. 1988. 256p. mass mkt. 4.99 (*0-380-70030-1*, Avon Bks.); 1987. 242p. 16.95 o.p. (*0-87795-787-8*, Morrow, William & Co.) Morrow/Avon.
—Poison. abr. ed. 1987. audio 14.95 (*0-671-64160-3*, Simon & Schuster Audioworks) Simon & Schuster Audio.
—The Pusher. unabr. ed. 1994. (Eighty-Seventh Precinct Novels Ser.). audio 54.95 (*0-7451-4228-1*, CAB 911) BBC Audiobooks America.
—The Pusher. unabr. ed. 1992. (Eighty-Seventh Precinct Ser.). audio 36.00 (*0-7366-2155-5*, 2954) Books on Tape, Inc.
—The Pusher. l.t. ed. 1987. (Large Print Books, Nightingale Ser.). 266p. 11.95 o.p. (*0-8161-4258-0*, Macmillan Reference USA) Gale Group.
—The Pusher. 9999. pap. 3.95 o.p. (*0-451-16480-6*); 1987. 160p. mass mkt. 3.99 o.p. (*0-451-15080-5*, Signet Bks.); 1980. mass mkt. 1.75 o.p. (*0-451-09256-2*, Signet Bks.); 1973. mass mkt. 0.95 o.p. (*0-451-05705-8*, Signet Bks.) NAL.
—The Pusher. 2002. 256p. pap. 6.99 (*0-7434-6305-6*, Pocket) Simon & Schuster.
—Romance. unabr. ed. 1995. (Eighty-Seventh Precinct Ser.). audio 48.00 (*0-7366-3122-4*, 3798) Books on Tape, Inc.
—Romance. abr. ed. audio 17.00 o.p. (*1-55994-995-3*, CPN 2484, HarperAudio) HarperTrade.
—Romance. 338p. pap. 5.98 o.p. (*0-7651-0365-6*) Smithmark Pubs., Inc.
—Romance. 1995. 336p. 22.95 o.s.i (*0-446-51804-2*); 1996. 352p. reprint ed. mass mkt. 6.50 o.s.i (*0-446-60280-9*) Warner Bks., Inc.
—Sadie When She Died. unabr. ed. 1998. (Eighty-Seventh Precinct Ser.). audio 30.00 (*0-7366-3993-4*, 4356) Books on Tape, Inc.
—Sadie When She Died. 1973. (87th Precinct Mystery Ser.). 160p. mass mkt. 3.99 o.s.i (*0-451-15366-9*, Signet Bks.) NAL.
—See Them Die. unabr. ed. 1996. (Eighty-Seventh Precinct Ser.). audio 36.00 (*0-7366-3359-6*, 4009) Books on Tape, Inc.
—See Them Die. (87th Precinct Mystery Ser.). 1982. mass mkt. 2.25 o.p. (*0-451-11561-9*, Signet Bks.); 1982. mass mkt. 2.95 o.p. (*0-451-14596-8*); 1976. mass mkt. 1.25 o.p. (*0-451-07030-5*, Signet Bks.); 1982. 160p. reprint ed. mass mkt. 4.50 o.p. (*0-451-16426-1*, Signet Bks.) NAL.
—Shotgun. unabr. ed. 1997. (Eighty-Seventh Precinct Ser.). audio 30.00 (*0-7366-3578-5*, 4230) Books on Tape, Inc.
—Shotgun. 1970. (87th Precinct Mystery Ser.). 176p. mass mkt. 4.50 o.p. (*0-451-15674-9*); mass mkt. 2.50 o.p. (*0-451-11971-1*) NAL. (Signet Bks.).
—So Long As You Both Shall Live. unabr. ed. 1998. (Eighty-Seventh Precinct Ser.). audio 30.00 (*0-7366-3778-8*, 4451) Books on Tape, Inc.
—So Long As You Both Shall Live. 1977. mass mkt. 3.50 o.p. (*0-451-15718-4*); mass mkt. 1.50 o.p. (*0-451-07749-0*) NAL. (Signet Bks.).
—Ten Plus One. unabr. ed. 1997. (Eighty-Seventh Precinct Ser.). audio 36.00 (*0-7366-3532-7*, 4171) Books on Tape, Inc.
—Ten Plus One. (87th Precinct Mystery Ser.). 1982. mass mkt. 2.25 o.p. (*0-451-11923-1*, Signet Bks.); 1982. 176p. mass mkt. 4.50 o.s.i (*0-451-16367-2*, Signet Bks.); 1982. mass mkt. 2.95 o.p. (*0-451-14598-4*); 1977. mass mkt. 1.25 o.p. (*0-451-07463-7*, Signet Bks.) NAL.
—'Til Death. unabr. ed. 1992. (Eighty-Seventh Precinct Ser.). audio 36.00 (*0-7366-2123-7*, 2925) Books on Tape, Inc.
—'Til Death. (Eighty-Seventh Precinct Mysteries Ser.). 1989. 176p. mass mkt. 4.50 o.s.i (*0-451-15891-1*); 1981. mass mkt. 2.25 o.p. (*0-451-09734-3*); 1981. mass mkt. 2.95 o.p. (*0-451-13896-1*) NAL. (Signet Bks.).
—Till Death Us Do Part. 1975. mass mkt. 1.25 o.p. (*0-451-06320-1*, Signet Bks.) NAL.
—Tricks. unabr. ed. 1992. (Eighty-Seventh Precinct Novels Ser.). audio 54.95 (*0-7451-6156-1*, CAB 616) BBC Audiobooks America.
—Tricks. 2001. audio 56.00 (*0-7366-6021-6*) Books on Tape, Inc.
—Tricks. 256p. 1987. 16.95 o.p. (*0-87795-927-7*, Morrow, William & Co.); 1989. reprint ed. mass mkt. 5.99 (*0-380-70383-1*, Avon Bks.) Morrow/Avon.
—Tricks. 1989. 3.99 o.p. (*0-517-69431-X*) Random Hse. Value Publishing.
—Tricks. abr. ed. 1988. audio 14.95 Simon & Schuster Audio.
—Vespers. unabr. ed. 1990. (Eighty-Seventh Precinct Ser.). audio 64.00 (*0-7366-1807-4*, 2644) Books on Tape, Inc.
—Vespers. l.t. ed. 1991. 470p. 24.95 o.p. (*1-85089-498-1*) ISIS Large Print Bks. GBR. *Dist:* Transaction Pubs.
—Vespers. 1991. 352p. mass mkt. 5.99 (*0-380-70385-8*, Avon Bks.); 1990. 350p. 18.95 o.p. (*0-87795-987-0*, Morrow, William & Co.) Morrow/Avon.
—Widows. unabr. ed. 1991. (Eighty-Seventh Precinct Ser.). audio 64.00 (*0-7366-1965-8*, 2786) Books on Tape, Inc.
—Widows. l.t. ed. 1992. (General Ser.). 454p. lib. bdg. 21.95 o.p. (*0-8161-5311-6*, Macmillan Reference USA) Gale Group.
—Widows. abr. ed. 2000. (Eighty Seventh Precinct Novels Ser.). audio 7.95 (*1-57815-056-6*, 1054, Media Bks. Audio Publishing) Media Bks., L. L. C.
—Widows. 1991. 330p. 19.00 o.p. (*0-688-10219-0*, Morrow, William & Co.); 1992. 336p. reprint ed. mass mkt. 6.50 (*0-380-71383-7*, Avon Bks.) Morrow/Avon.
McBride, Jule. The Seducer. 2002. (Harlequin Temptation Ser.: No. 833). 217p. mass mkt. (*0-373-25983-2*, 1-25983-7, Harlequin Bks.) Harlequin Enterprises, Ltd.
McCabe, Peter. City of Lies: A Novel. 1993. 271p. 20.00 o.p. (*0-688-12118-7*, Morrow, William & Co.) Morrow/Avon.
McCafferty, Jeanne. Star Gazer. 1994. 208p. 19.95 o.p. (*0-312-11074-X*, Saint Martin's Minotaur) St. Martin's Pr.
McCahery, James R. What Evil Lurks. 1996. 256p. mass mkt. 4.99 o.s.i (*1-57566-001-6*); 1995. 304p. mass mkt. 16.95 o.p. (*0-8217-4797-5*) Kensington Publishing Corp.
McCall, Dan. Triphammer. 1990. 18.95 o.p. (*0-87113-333-4*) Grove/Atlantic, Inc.
McCloy, Kristin. Some Girls. 272p. 1995. pap. 12.95 o.s.i (*0-452-27273-4*, Plume); 1994. 20.95 o.s.i (*0-525-93837-0*) Dutton/Plume.
McDermott, Alice. At Weddings & Wakes. 1998. 224p. pap. 12.95 (*0-385-31985-1*, Delacorte Pr.); 1993. 320p. mass mkt. 6.50 o.s.i (*0-440-21523-4*) Dell Publishing.
—At Weddings & Wakes. 1992. 213p. 19.00 o.p. (*0-374-10674-6*) Farrar, Straus & Giroux.
—At Weddings & Wakes. l.t. ed. 1993. (General Ser.). 320p. 20.95 (*0-8161-5570-4*); lib. bdg. 16.95 o.p. (*0-8161-5571-2*) Gale Group. (Macmillan Reference USA).
—At Weddings & Wakes. abr. ed. 1993. audio 8.99 o.p. (*1-55800-829-2*); 16.95 o.p. (*1-55800-693-1*) NewStar Media, Inc.
McDonell, J. M. Half Crazy. abr. ed. 1995. 17.95 o.p. (*0-7871-0377-2*) NewStar Media, Inc.
—Half Crazy: A Novel, Vol. 1. 1995. 258p. 19.95 (*0-316-55560-6*) Little Brown & Co.
—Half Crazy: A Novel. 2000. 310p. pap. 12.95 (*1-893224-04-X*, New Millennium Pr.) New Millennium Entertainment.
McElroy, Joseph. Women & Men. 1987. 27.50 o.s.i (*0-394-50344-9*) Knopf, Alfred A. Inc.
McFarland, Philip. Seasons of Fear. 1987. 288p. 15.95 o.s.i (*0-8052-3850-6*, Schocken) Knopf Publishing Group.
McGarry, Jean. The Courage of Girls. 1992. (Rutgers Press Fiction Ser.). 250p. 22.95 (*0-8135-1771-0*) Rutgers Univ. Pr.
McGhee, Alison. Shadow Baby: Today Show Book Club Edition. 2003. 256p. pap. 14.00 (*0-312-42377-2*) Picador.

McGonigle, Thomas. Going to Patchogue. 1992. (Illus.). 220p. 19.95 (0-916583-87-2) Dalkey Archive Pr.

McHugh, Frances Y. The Hyacinth Spell. l.t. ed. 2000. (Candlelight Romance Ser.). 206p. 21.95 (0-7862-2797-4) Thorndike Pr.

McHugh, Vincent. I Am Thinking of My Darling. 1991. 308p. reprint ed. pap. 9.95 (1-878274-05-8) Yarrow Pr.

—I Am Thinking of My Darling: An Adventure Story. Reginald, R. & Melville, Douglas, eds. 1978. (Lost Race & Adult Fantasy Ser.). reprint ed. lib. bdg. 28.95 (0-405-10998-9) Ayer Co. Pubs., Inc.

McInerney, Jay. Bright Lights, Big City. 1984. (Vintage Contemporaries Ser.). 208p. pap. 12.00 (0-394-72641-3, Vintage) Knopf Publishing Group.

McInerney, Merry. Burning down the House. 1995. 337p. pap. 5.99 o.p. (0-8125-3651-7); 1994. 256p. 17.95 o.p. (0-312-85698-9) Doherty, Tom Assocs., LLC. (Forge Bks.).

McKay, Deborah. Eve's Longing: The Infinite Possibilities in All Things. 1992. 139p. 18.95 o.s.i (0-932511-64-3); pap. 11.95 (0-932511-65-1) Fiction Collective Two, Inc.

McMillan, Terry. Disappearing Acts. Rosenman, Jane, ed. 1993. 384p. mass mkt. 7.99 (0-671-87200-1, Pocket); 1990. 400p. reprint ed. pap. (0-671-70843-0, Washington Square Pr.) Simon & Schuster.

—Disappearing Acts. 1989. 448p. 26.95 (0-670-82461-5) Viking Penguin.

McMullan, Margaret. When Warhol Was Still Alive: A Novel. 1994. 199p. 18.95 o.p. (0-89594-651-3) Crossing Pr., Inc., The.

McNeal, Laura. Zipped. 2003. 288p. (J). (gr. 7-12). lib. bdg. 17.99 (0-375-91491-9, Knopf Bks. for Young Readers) Random Hse. Children's Bks.

McNeal, Laura & McNeal, Tom. Zipped. 2003. 288p. (J). (gr. 7). 15.95 (0-375-81491-4, Knopf Bks. for Young Readers) Random Hse. Children's Bks.

Medina, Pablo. The Marks of Birth. 1994. 224p. 22.00 o.p. (0-374-20296-6) Farrar, Straus & Giroux.

Medoff, Jillian. Hunger Point. 1998. 544p. mass mkt. 6.99 o.s.i (0-06-101227-0, HarperTorch) Morrow/Avon.

—Hunger Point: A Novel. 2002. 384p. pap. 13.95 (0-06-098923-8) HarperCollins Pubs.

—Hunger Point: A Novel. 1997. 384p. 24.00 o.p. (0-06-039189-8, ReganBooks) HarperTrade.

Melville, Herman. Bartleby the Scrivener. 1997. 77p. 21.50 o.p. (0-684-81910-4, Simon & Schuster) Simon & Schuster.

—Bartleby the Scrivener & Benito Cereno. 1990. 112p. pap. 1.00 (0-486-26473-4) Dover Pubns., Inc.

Meredith, Don. Home Movies. 1982. 176p. pap. 2.25 o.p. (0-380-79855-7, 79855-7, Avon Bks.) Morrow/Avon.

Meriwether, Louise. Daddy Was a Number Runner. 1970. 8.95 o.p. (0-13-197103-4) Prentice Hall PTR.

Merrick, Gordon & Hulse, Charles. The Good Life. 1997. 350p. (Orig.). pap. 14.95 o.p. (1-55583-298-9) Alyson Pubns.

Metzger, R. S. A Master of the Century Past. 1996. 288p. 17.95 (0-913720-87-9) Beil, Frederic C. Pub., Inc.

Meyers, Maan. The Dutchman. 1993. mass mkt. 5.50 o.s.i (0-553-56285-1) Bantam Bks.

—The Dutchman. 1992. 18.50 o.s.i (0-385-42603-8) Doubleday Publishing.

—The Dutchman's Dilemma. 1996. 304p. mass mkt. 5.99 o.s.i (0-553-57201-6, Crimeline) Bantam Bks.

—The House on Mulberry Street. 1997. 352p. reprint ed. mass mkt. 5.99 o.s.i (0-553-57212-1, Crimeline) Bantam Bks.

—The House on Mulberry Street. 2000. 312p. 27.95 (0-7351-0433-6); pap. 17.95 (0-7351-0434-4) Replica Bks.

—The Kingsbridge Plot. 1994. (Dutchman Historical Ser.). 432p. mass mkt. 4.99 o.s.i (0-553-56380-7) Bantam Bks.

—The Lucifer Contract: A Civil War Thriller. 1999. 320p. reprint ed. mass mkt. 6.50 o.s.i (0-553-57199-0) Bantam Bks.

Miano, Mark. Flesh & Stone: A Michael Carpo Mystery. (Michael Carpo Mystery Ser.). 288p. 1998. mass mkt. 5.99 o.s.i (1-57566-273-6); 1997. 18.95 o.p. (1-57566-128-4, Kensington Bks.) Kensington Publishing Corp.

—The Street Where She Lived: A Michael Carpo Mystery. 1998. (Michael Carpo Mystery Ser.). 320p. 20.00 o.s.i (1-57566-270-1, Kensington Bks.) Kensington Publishing Corp.

Michael, Judith, pseud. Acts of Love. l.t. ed. 1997. 480p. mass mkt. 7.99 (0-8041-1787-X, Ivy Bks.) Ballantine Bks.

—Acts of Love. abr. ed. 1997. (Civil War Ser.). 3p. audio 7.99 o.p. (1-56740-225-9, 618, Paperback Nova Audio Bks.); audio 16.95 o.p. (1-56100-968-7, 1128, Nova Audio Bks.); audio 105.25 o.p. (1-56100-809-5, 787, Unabridged Library Editions); audio 27.95 o.p. (1-56100-731-5, 25, Bookcassette) Brilliance Audio.

—Acts of Love. l.t. ed. 1997. 6624p. pap. 24.00 o.s.i (0-679-77418-1) Random Hse., Inc.

Michaels, Joanne. Nun in the Closet. 1994. 200p. (Orig.). pap. 9.95 (0-934678-43-X) New Victoria Pubs., Inc.

Michaels, Leonard. Sylvia. 1992. 144p. 10.00 (1-56279-029-3) Mercury Hse.

Millership, Richard, contrib. by. Dagger Dark. 1997. (1-86330-618-8) Mandarin Australia.

Millhauser, Steven. Martin Dressler: The Tale of an American Dreamer. 1997. 304p. pap. 13.00 (0-679-78127-7, Vintage) Knopf Publishing Group.

—Martin Dressler: The Tale of an American Dreamer. unabr. ed. 1997. audio 56.00 (0-7887-1757-X, 95235E7) Recorded Bks., LLC.

Mills, James. Haywire. 1995. 416p. 23.95 o.s.i (0-446-51619-8) Warner Bks., Inc.

Mirabelli, Eugene. The Language Nobody Speaks. 1999. 144p. 20.00 (0-935891-02-1) Spring Harbor Pr.

—The Language Nobody Speaks: A Novel. 1999. 139p. pap. 13.00 (0-935891-03-X) Spring Harbor Pr.

Mitchell, Joseph. Up in the Old Hotel. 1993. 736p. pap. 16.00 (0-679-74631-5) Random Hse., Inc.

Mitchell, Kirk. Sky Woman Falling. 2003. 352p. 22.95 (0-425-19191-5, Prime Crime) Berkley Publishing Group.

Mohin, Ann. The Farm She Was: A Novel. 1998. 245p. 22.95 (1-882593-21-9); 2000. 262p. reprint ed. 13.95 o.s.i (1-882593-34-0) Bridge Works Publishing Co., Inc.

Mohr, Nicholasa. A Matter of Pride & Other Stories. 1997. 164p. 19.95 (1-55885-163-1); pap. 11.95 (1-55885-177-1) Arte Publico Pr.

—Rituals of Survival: A Woman's Portfolio. 1985. 158p. (C). pap. 11.95 (0-934770-39-5) Arte Publico Pr.

Monfredo, Miriam G. Blackwater Spirits. 1996. 368p. reprint ed. mass mkt. 6.99 o.s.i (0-425-15266-9) Berkley Publishing Group.

—Blackwater Spirits. 1995. vii, 328p. 21.95 o.p. (0-312-11754-X, Saint Martin's Minotaur) St. Martin's Pr.

—Must the Maiden Die? 1999. (Seneca Falls Historical Mysteries Ser.: No. 6). 384p. 21.95 o.s.i (0-425-16699-6, Prime Crime) Berkley Publishing Group.

—Must the Maiden Die: A Seneca Falls Historical Mystery. 2000. (Seneca Falls Historical Mysteries Ser.). 384p. mass mkt. 6.99 o.s.i (0-425-17610-X) Berkley Publishing Group.

—North Star Conspiracy. 1993. 256p. 21.95 o.p. (0-312-09355-1, Saint Martin's Minotaur) St. Martin's Pr.

—The North Star Conspiracy. 1995. 368p. mass mkt. 6.99 (0-425-14720-7, Prime Crime) Berkley Publishing Group.

—Seneca Falls Inheritance. 1994. 304p. mass mkt. 6.99 (0-425-14465-8, Prime Crime) Berkley Publishing Group.

—Seneca Falls Inheritance. 1992. 320p. 19.95 o.p. (0-312-07082-9, Saint Martin's Minotaur) St. Martin's Pr.

—Sisters of Cain: A Seneca Falls Civil War Mystery. 2000. (Illus.). 384p. 21.95 o.s.i (0-425-17672-X, Prime Crime) Berkley Publishing Group.

—The Stalking Horse. 1999. (Historical Mystery Ser.: Vol. 5). 352p. reprint ed. mass mkt. 6.99 o.s.i (0-425-16695-3, Prime Crime) Berkley Publishing Group.

—The Stalking Horse: A Seneca Falls Historical Mystery. 1998. (Glynis Tryon Historical Mysteries Ser.). 352p. 21.95 o.s.i (0-425-15783-0, Prime Crime) Berkley Publishing Group.

—Through a Gold Eagle: A Glynis Tryon Mystery. 1997. 384p. mass mkt. 6.50 o.s.i (0-425-15898-5); 1996. 400p. 21.95 o.p. (0-425-15318-5) Berkley Publishing Group. (Prime Crime).

Moore, Lorrie. Who Will Run the Frog Hospital? 2004. 160p. pap. 12.95 (1-4000-3382-9, Vintage) Knopf Publishing Group.

—Who Will Run the Frog Hospital? 1994. 20.00 (0-679-43484-4) Knopf, Alfred A. Inc.

—Who Will Run the Frog Hospital? 1995. 160p. pap. 12.99 (0-446-67191-6) Warner Bks., Inc.

Moore, Robin. The Moscow Connection. 1994. 500p. 20.00 (1-879915-11-1) Alexander & Fraser, Inc.

Moore, Susanna. In the Cut: A Novel. 1999. 192p. pap. 12.95 (0-452-28129-6, Plume) Dutton/Plume.

—In the Cut: A Novel. 1995. 177p. 21.00 o.s.i (0-679-42258-7) Knopf, Alfred A. Inc.

Moran, Thomas. The World I Made for Her. 1999. 288p. reprint ed. 12.00 (1-57322-731-5, Riverhead Trade (Paperbacks)) Berkley Publishing Group.

—The World I Made for Her. 1998. 267p. 23.95 o.p. (1-57322-084-1, Riverhead Bks. (Hardcovers)) Putnam Publishing Group, The.

Mordden, Ethan. Buddies. (Stonewall Inn Editions Ser.). 1987. 256p. pap. 9.95 (0-312-01005-2, Saint Martin's Griffin); 1986. 304p. 6.50 o.p. (0-312-10686-6) St. Martin's Pr.

—Everybody Loves You. 1989. (Stonewall Inn Editions Ser.). 308p. pap. 10.95 (0-312-03334-6, Saint Martin's Griffin) St. Martin's Pr.

—Everybody Loves You: Further Adventures in Gay Manhattan. 1988. 288p. 16.95 o.p. (0-312-02201-8) St. Martin's Pr.

—I've a Feeling We're Not in Kansas Anymore. 1987. 208p. pap. 11.95 o.p. (0-452-25929-0, Plume) Dutton/Plume.

—I've a Feeling We're Not in Kansas Anymore. 1996. (Stonewall Inn Editions Ser.: Vol. 1). 208p. pap. 9.95 (0-312-14112-2, Saint Martin's Griffin) St. Martin's Pr.

—I've a Feeling We're Not in Kansas Anymore: Tales from Manhattan. 1985. 170p. 12.95 o.p. (0-312-40291-0) St. Martin's Pr.

—Some Men Are Lookers. 1997. 352p. 23.95 (0-312-15660-X) St. Martin's Pr.

—Some Men Are Lookers: New Stories in the Buddies Cycle. 1999. E-Book 13.95 (0-312-20743-3) St. Martin's Pr.

Moriarty, Michael. The Voyeur. 1997. 223p. 22.00 o.p. (0-684-80425-5, Simon & Schuster) Simon & Schuster.

Morrell, David. The Covenant of the Flame. unabr. ed. 1991. audio 25.95 o.p. (0-930435-81-8, 70, Bookcassette); audio 89.25 o.p. (1-56100-075-2, 542) Brilliance Audio.

—The Covenant of the Flame. 1992. 480p. mass mkt. 7.50 (0-446-36292-1); 1991. 19.95 o.p. (0-446-51563-9); 1999. reprint ed. mass mkt. 3.99 (0-446-60752-5) Warner Bks., Inc.

Morris, Betty. Falling, I Find Wings. 1998. 464p. (Orig.). pap. 12.95 (0-9666055-1-9) Mayflower Pr.

Morris, Gilbert. The Final Adversary. 1992. (House of Winslow Ser.: Bk. 12). 304p. pap. 11.99 (1-55661-261-3) Bethany Hse. Pubs.

—The Iron Lady. 1996. (House of Winslow Ser.: Vol. 19). 320p. pap. 11.99 (1-55661-687-2) Bethany Hse. Pubs.

—The Iron Lady. l.t. ed. 1997. (Inspirational Ser.). 522p. lib. bdg. 23.95 (0-7838-8221-1, Macmillan Reference USA) Gale Group.

—The Shadow Portrait. 1998. (House of Winslow Ser.: Vol. 21). 320p. pap. 11.99 (1-55661-689-9) Bethany Hse. Pubs.

Morris, Lynn & Morris, Gilbert. A City Not Forsaken. 1995. (Cheney Duvall, M. D. Ser.: Bk. 3). 336p. pap. 11.99 (1-55661-424-1) Bethany Hse. Pubs.

—A City Not Forsaken. 2000. (Christian Fiction Ser.: Bk. 3). 312p. 23.95 (0-7862-2227-1, Five Star) Gale Group.

Mosley, Walter. RL's Dream. abr. ed. 1995. audio 16.95 (1-55927-345-3, 392939) Audio Renaissance.

—RL's Dream. unabr. ed. 1996. audio 48.00 Books on Tape, Inc.

—RL's Dream. 1995. 288p. 22.00 (0-393-03802-5) Norton, W. W. & Co., Inc.

—RL's Dream. 1996. 272p. pap. 14.00 (0-671-88428-X, Washington Square Pr.) Simon & Schuster.

Mr. & Mrs. North: Case of the Missing Sparkler. audio National Recording Co.

Murano, Vincent & Hammer, Richard. The Thursday Club: A Novel. 1992. 304p. 21.00 o.p. (0-671-73448-2, Simon & Schuster) Simon & Schuster.

—The Thursday Club: A Novel. Rubenstein, Julie, ed. 1994. 304p. reprint ed. mass mkt. 5.50 (0-671-73864-X, Pocket) Simon & Schuster.

Murdoch, Anna. Coming to Terms: A Novel. 1991. 240p. 19.95 o.p. (0-06-018303-9) HarperTrade.

Murphy, Dallas. Lush Life. Chelius, Jane, ed. 1992. 288p. (Orig.). pap. 20.00 (0-671-68555-4, Atria) Simon & Schuster.

Musto, Michael. Manhattan on the Rocks. 1989. 298p. 18.95 o.p. (0-8050-1032-7) Holt, Henry & Co.

Myles, Eileen. Chelsea Girls. 276p. 1997. 25.00 (0-87685-933-3); 1994. 35.00 o.p. (0-87685-934-1) Godine, David R. Pub. (Black Sparrow Pr.).

—Chelsea Girls. 1997. 276p. pap. 14.00 (0-87685-932-5) HarperCollins Pubs.

Nathan, Paul. No Good Deed. 1995. (Bert Swain Mystery Ser.). 202p. 24.00 (1-877946-56-7) Permanent Pr., The.

—Protocol for Murder. 1994. (Bert Swain Mystery Ser.). 176p. 24.00 (1-877946-46-X) Permanent Pr., The.

Neimark, Jill. Bloodsong. 1994. 288p. pap. 9.95 o.p. (0-452-27296-3, Plume) Dutton/Plume.

—Bloodsong. 1924. o.s.i (0-688-09132-6, Morrow, William & Co.) Morrow/Avon.

Nelson, Blake. Exile. 1997. 288p. pap. 18.00 (0-684-83838-9, Scribner) Simon & Schuster.

Nelson, James L. By Force of Arms. Wolverton, Peter, ed. 1996. (Revolution at Sea Trilogy Ser.: Vol. 1). 336p. pap. 14.00 (0-671-51924-7, Pocket) Simon & Schuster.

Nevins, Francis M. Into the Same River Twice. 1996. 224p. 21.00 o.p. (0-7867-0314-8, Carroll & Graf Pubs.) Avalon Publishing Group.

—Into the Same River Twice. 2000. 228p. pap. 14.95 (0-595-00001-0, Authors Choice Pr.) iUniverse, Inc.

Ng, Mei. Eating Chinese Food Naked. 1998. 256p. mass mkt. 14.00 (0-671-01145-6, Scribner) Simon & Schuster.

—Eating Chinese Food Naked: A Novel. 1998. 224p. 20.50 (0-684-81416-1, Scribner) Simon & Schuster.

Nicolaysen, Bruce. Beekman Place. 1982. (Novel of New York Ser.: Vol. 3). 576p. pap. 3.50 o.p. (0-380-79673-2, 79673-2, Avon Bks.) Morrow/Avon.

Nigam, Sanjay. The Transplanted Man. 2003. 368p. pap. 13.95 (0-06-051215-6, Perennial) HarperTrade.

—The Transplanted Man. 2002. 368p. 24.95 (0-688-16819-1, Morrow, William & Co.) Morrow/Avon.

North, Darian. Criminal Seduction. 1993. 544p. 22.00 o.p. (0-525-93740-4, Dutton) Dutton/Plume.

—Criminal Seduction. 1994. 560p. mass mkt. 6.99 (0-451-18022-4, Signet Bks.) NAL.

—Criminal Seduction. 536p. 4.98 o.p. (0-8317-9389-9) Smithmark Pubs., Inc.

Nunez, Sigrid. A Feather on the Breath of God: A Novel. 1994. 224p. 18.00 o.p. (0-06-017151-0) HarperCollins Pubs.

Oates, Joyce Carol. Bellefleur. 1991. 592p. pap. 17.95 (0-452-26794-3, Plume); 1990. pap. 11.95 o.p. (0-525-48567-8); 1980. (C). 13.95 o.p. (0-525-06302-1, Dutton) Dutton/Plume.

—Bellefleur. 1987. pap. 9.95 o.p. (0-525-48347-0, Obelisk) NAL.

—Bellefleur. 1981. 688p. mass mkt. 4.50 o.s.i (0-446-30732-7) Warner Bks., Inc.

—Broke Heart Blues. 384p. 2000. pap. 13.95 (0-452-28034-6, Plume); 1999. 24.95 o.p. (0-525-94451-6) Dutton/Plume.

—First Love: A Gothic Tale. (Illus.). 1997. 144p. pap. 9.00 o.p. (0-88001-508-X); 1996. 288p. 18.00 (0-88001-457-1) HarperTrade. (Ecco).

—Foxfire: Confessions of a Girl Gang. 1993. 336p. 21.00 o.p. (0-525-93632-7, Abrahams, William Bks.) Dutton/Plume.

—I Lock My Door upon Myself. 1991. 112p. pap. 9.95 o.p. (0-452-26708-0, Plume) Dutton/Plume.

—Man Crazy: A Novel. 288p. 1998. pap. 14.00 (0-452-27724-8, Plume); 1997. 23.95 o.p. (0-525-94232-7, Abrahams, William Bks.) Dutton/Plume.

—Man Crazy: A Novel. l.t. ed. 1998. (Basic Ser.). 307p. 28.95 (0-7862-1273-X) Thorndike Pr.

—Middle Age: A Romance. 2002. E-Book 10.00 (0-06-008725-0) HarperCollins Pubs.

—Middle Age: A Romance. 480p. 2002. pap. 15.00 (0-06-093490-5); 2001. 28.00 (0-06-620946-3) HarperTrade. (Ecco).

—Mysteries of Winterthurn. 1984. 482p. 16.95 o.p. (0-525-24208-2, Dutton) Dutton/Plume.

—We Were the Mulvaneys. 464p. 2001. pap. 13.95 (0-452-28282-9, Plume); 1997. pap. 13.95 (0-452-27720-5, Plume); 1996. 24.95 o.s.i (0-525-94223-8) Dutton/Plume.

—We Were the Mulvaneys. l.t. ed. 2001. (Hardcover Ser.). 730p. 31.95 o.p. (1-58724-043-2, Wheeler Publishing, Inc.) Gale Group.

—We Were the Mulvaneys. abr. ed. 2001. audio compact disk 34.95 (1-56511-495-7) HighBridge Co.

—We Were the Mulvaneys. 2001. 20.00 (0-606-20982-4) Turtleback Bks.

—What I Lived For. 1994. 624p. 23.95 o.p. (0-525-93836-2, Dutton) Dutton/Plume.

O'Brien, Judith. To Marry a British Lord. 1997. 320p. mass mkt. 5.99 o.s.i (0-671-00039-X, Pocket) Simon & Schuster.

O'Brien, Meg. Eagles Die Too: A Jessica James Mystery. 1992. 256p. 16.50 o.s.i (0-385-42265-2) Doubleday Publishing.

—Salmon in the Soup. 1990. 256p. (Orig.). mass mkt. 3.95 o.s.i (0-553-28617-X) Bantam Bks.

—Thin Ice. 1994. 416p. mass mkt. 4.99 o.s.i (0-553-56962-7) Bantam Bks.

O'Connell, Carol. Judas Child. 1999. 432p. reprint ed. mass mkt. 7.99 (0-515-12549-0, Jove) Berkley Publishing Group.

—Judas Child. abr. ed. 1999. audio 7.99 o.s.i (1-56740-294-1, 1863, Paperback Nova Audio Bks.); 1998. audio 28.95 (1-56100-797-8, 16, Bookcassette); 1998. audio 89.25 (1-56740-576-2, 913, Unabridged Library Editions); Set. 1998. audio 17.95 o.p. (1-56740-771-4, 447, Nova Audio Bks.) Brilliance Audio.

—Judas Child. 1998. 340p. 24.95 o.p. (0-399-14380-7, G. P. Putnam's Sons) Penguin Group (USA) Inc.

—Killing Critics. l.t. ed. 1996. (G. K. Hall Mystery Ser.). 534p. 25.95 o.p. (0-7838-1903-X, Macmillan Reference USA) Gale Group.

—Killing Critics. 1996. 304p. 23.95 o.s.i (0-399-14168-5, G. P. Putnam's Sons) Penguin Group (USA) Inc.

—Mallory's Oracle. l.t. ed. 1995. (Large Print Ser.). 330p. lib. bdg. 25.95 (1-57490-024-2, Beeler Large Print Bks.) Beeler, Thomas T. Publisher.

—Mallory's Oracle. 1994. 288p. 21.95 o.p. (0-399-13975-3, G. P. Putnam's Sons) Penguin Group (USA) Inc.

—The Man Who Cast Two Shadows. 1996. (Kathleen Mallory Novels Ser.). 336p. mass mkt. 7.99 *(0-515-11890-7*, Jove) Berkley Publishing Group.
—The Man Who Cast Two Shadows. l.t. ed. 1995. pap. 20.95 o.p. *(1-56895-258-9*, Wheeler Publishing, Inc.) Gale Group.
—The Man Who Cast Two Shadows. abr. ed. 1998. 8.99 o.s.i incl. audio *(0-375-40328-0)* Knopf, Alfred A. Inc.
—The Man Who Cast Two Shadows. 1995. 23.95 o.p. *(0-399-14064-6*, G. P. Putnam's Sons) Penguin Group (USA) Inc.
—Stone Angel. l.t. ed. 1997. 24.95 o.p. *(1-56895-507-3*, Wheeler Publishing, Inc.) Gale Group.
—Stone Angel. 1997. 341p. 24.95 o.s.i *(0-399-14234-7*, G. P. Putnam's Sons) Penguin Group (USA) Inc.
O'Connell, Catherine. Skins. 1993. 215p. 20.00 o.p. *(1-55611-343-9)* Fine, Donald I. Bks.
O'Cork, Shannon. End of the Line. 1981. 224p. 10.95 o.p. *(0-312-25102-5)* St. Martin's Pr.
O'Donnell, Lillian. Aftershock. 1982. mass mkt. 2.50 o.s.i *(0-449-24479-2*, Fawcett) Ballantine Bks.
—Aftershock. 1977. 7.95 o.p. *(0-399-11951-5)* Putnam Publishing Group, The.
—Blue Death. 1998. 224p. 22.95 o.p. *(0-399-14367-X)* Penguin Group (USA) Inc.
—Casual Affairs. 1987. mass mkt. 2.95 o.s.i *(0-449-21064-2*, Fawcett) Ballantine Bks.
—Casual Affairs. 1985. 240p. 16.95 o.p. *(0-399-13100-0)* Putnam Publishing Group, The.
—The Children's Zoo. 1982. mass mkt. 3.50 o.s.i *(0-449-24498-9*, Fawcett) Ballantine Bks.
—Cop Without a Shield. 1984. 256p. mass mkt. 2.95 o.s.i *(0-449-20534-7*, Fawcett) Ballantine Bks.
—Cop Without a Shield. 1983. 256p. 13.95 o.p. *(0-399-12872-7*, G. P. Putnam's Sons) Penguin Putnam Bks. for Young Readers.
—Falling Star. 1987. 224p. mass mkt. 2.95 o.s.i *(0-449-21395-1*, Fawcett); 1980. mass mkt. 1.95 o.s.i *(0-449-24347-8)* Ballantine Bks.
—Falling Star. 1979. 9.95 o.p. *(0-399-12407-1)* Putnam Publishing Group, The.
—A Good Night to Kill. 1989. 224p. mass mkt. 4.99 o.s.i *(0-449-21706-X*, Fawcett) Ballantine Bks.
—A Good Night to Kill. 1989. 256p. 17.95 o.p. *(0-399-13403-4*, G. P. Putnam's Sons) Penguin Putnam Bks. for Young Readers.
—Ladykiller. 1985. 240p. mass mkt. 2.95 o.s.i *(0-449-20744-7*, Fawcett) Ballantine Bks.
—Leisure Dying. 1976. 6.95 o.p. *(0-399-11741-5)* Putnam Publishing Group, The.
—Lockout. 1995. (Norah Mulcahaney Ser.). mass mkt. 5.99 o.s.i *(0-449-22329-9*, Fawcett) Ballantine Bks.
—Lockout. 1994. 240p. 19.95 o.p. *(0-399-13921-4*, G. P. Putnam's Sons) Penguin Group (USA) Inc.
—No Business Being a Cop. 1987. mass mkt. 2.95 o.s.i *(0-449-21322-6)*; 1980. mass mkt. 1.95 o.p. *(0-449-24219-6)* Ballantine Bks. (Fawcett).
—No Business Being a Cop. 1979. 8.95 o.p. *(0-399-12276-1)* Putnam Publishing Group, The.
—The Other Side of the Door. 1988. mass mkt. 2.95 o.s.i *(0-449-21598-9*, Fawcett) Ballantine Bks.
—The Other Side of the Door. 1988. 240p. 17.95 o.p. *(0-399-13316-X*, G. P. Putnam's Sons) Penguin Putnam Bks. for Young Readers.
—A Private Crime. 1992. mass mkt. 3.99 o.s.i *(0-449-21989-5*, Fawcett) Ballantine Bks.
—A Private Crime. l.t. ed. 1992. (General Ser.). 333p. lib. bdg. 21.95 o.p. *(0-8161-5277-2*, Macmillan Reference USA) Gale Group.
—A Private Crime. 1991. 240p. 19.95 o.p. *(0-399-13585-5*, G. P. Putnam's Sons) Penguin Group (USA) Inc.
—Pushover. 1993. mass mkt. 4.99 o.s.i *(0-449-22152-0*, Fawcett) Ballantine Bks.
—Pushover. 1992. 240p. 19.95 o.p. *(0-399-13674-6*, G. P. Putnam's Sons) Penguin Group (USA) Inc.
—Wicked Designs. 1987. 224p. mass mkt. 2.95 o.s.i *(0-449-21532-6*, Fawcett); 1981. mass mkt. 2.25 o.s.i *(0-449-24437-7)* Ballantine Bks.
—Wicked Designs. 1980. 228p. 9.95 o.p. *(0-399-12523-X)* Putnam Publishing Group, The.
O'Donnell, Mark. Getting over Homer. 1997. 208p. pap. 11.00 *(0-679-78122-6*, Vintage) Knopf Publishing Group.
Oeste, Bob. The Last Pumpkin Paper. 1996. 224p. 23.00 o.s.i *(0-679-44837-3)* Random Hse., Inc.
O'Hagan, Christine. Benediction at the Savoia. 1992. 21.95 o.s.i *(0-15-111810-8)* Harcourt Trade Pubs.
O'Kane, Leslie. The Cold, Hard Fax: A Molly Masters Mystery. 1998. (Molly Masters Mysteries Ser.). 288p. mass mkt. 5.99 o.s.i *(0-449-00158-X*, Fawcett) Ballantine Bks.
—The Cold, Hard Fax: A Molly Masters Mystery. l.t. ed. 2000. (Mystery Ser.). 381p. 26.95 *(0-7862-2833-4)* Thorndike Pr.
—Death & Faxes. 1997. per. *(0-373-26248-5*, 1-26248-4, Worldwide Library) Harlequin Enterprises, Ltd.
—Death & Faxes. 1996. 240p. 19.95 o.p. *(0-312-13960-8*, Saint Martin's Minotaur) St. Martin's Pr.
—Just the Fax, Ma'am. 1997. per. *(0-373-26254-X*, 1-26254-2, Worldwide Library) Harlequin Enterprises, Ltd.
—Just the Fax, Ma'am. 1996. 256p. 21.95 o.p. *(0-312-14637-X*, Saint Martin's Minotaur) St. Martin's Pr.
—The School Board Murder. 2000. (Molly Masters Mysteries Ser.). 240p. mass mkt. 6.50 o.s.i *(0-449-00567-4*, Fawcett) Ballantine Bks.
Olden, Marc. Fear's Justice. 1998. 352p. pap. 6.99 *(0-671-00379-8*, Pocket) Simon & Schuster.
—The Ghost. 2000. 400p. pap. 6.99 *(0-671-00418-2*, Pocket) Simon & Schuster.
O'Nan, Stewart. The Names of the Dead. 1997. 416p. pap. 11.95 o.s.i *(0-14-026309-8)* Penguin Group (USA) Inc.
—Wish You Were Here. 528p. 2003. pap. 14.00 *(0-8021-3989-2)*; 2002. 25.00 *(0-8021-1715-5*, Grove Pr.) Grove/Atlantic, Inc.
—A World Away: A Novel. 352p. 1999. pap. 13.00 o.s.i *(0-8050-5775-7*, Owl Bks.); 1998. 23.00 o.s.i *(0-8050-5774-9)* Holt, Henry & Co.
—A World Away: A Novel. 2003. 352p. pap. 14.00 *(0-312-42277-6)* Picador.
Ong, Han. Fixer Chao. 2001. 377p. 25.00 *(0-374-15575-5)* Farrar, Straus & Giroux.
—Fixer Chao. 2002. 384p. pap. 14.00 *(0-312-42053-6)* Picador.
O'Reilly, Bill. Those Who Trespass: A Novel of Television & Murder. 2004. 320p. pap. 14.00 *(0-7679-1381-7)* Broadway Bks.
Orlando, Jordon. The Object Lesson: A Novel. 1993. 560p. 23.00 o.p. *(0-671-66978-8*, Simon & Schuster) Simon & Schuster.
Osborne, John J., Jr. The Man Who Owned New York, 001. 1981. 10.95 o.p. *(0-395-30511-X)* Houghton Mifflin Co.
—The Man Who Owned New York. 1984. 288p. mass mkt. 3.50 o.s.i *(0-446-31260-6)* Warner Bks., Inc.
Oster, Jerry. Fixin' to Die. 1992. 320p. mass mkt. 4.99 o.s.i *(0-553-29908-5)* Bantam Bks.
—Internal Affairs. 1990. 320p. reprint ed. mass mkt. 4.50 o.s.i *(0-553-28676-5)* Bantam Bks.
O'Sullivan, Bill. Precious Blood. 1992. 202p. 18.95 o.p. *(0-939149-67-2)* Soho Pr., Inc.
Page, Katherine Hall. The Body in the Big Apple. 1999. 239p. 22.00 *(0-688-15748-3*, Morrow, William & Co.) Morrow/Avon.
Pall, Ellen. Among the Ginzburgs: A Novel. 1996. 256p. 22.95 o.p. *(0-944072-61-5*, Zoland Bks., Inc.) Steerforth Pr.
Palmer, Frank. Bent Grasses: An Inspector "Jacko" Jackson Mystery. 1994. 191p. 18.95 o.p. *(0-312-11752-3*, Saint Martin's Minotaur) St. Martin's Pr.
Palmer, Michael. Silent Treatment. 1996. 480p. reprint ed. mass mkt. 7.50 *(0-553-57221-0)* Bantam Bks.
—Silent Treatment. l.t. ed. (Core Collection). 632p. 1996. 23.95 *(0-7838-1405-4)*; 1995. 26.95 o.p. *(0-7838-1406-2)* Gale Group. (Macmillan Reference USA).
—Silent Treatment. abr. ed. 1995. audio 16.99 o.s.i *(0-553-47345-X*, RH Audio) Random Hse. Audio Publishing Group.
—Silent Treatment, unabr. ed. audio 85.00 *(0-7887-0268-8*, 94477E7) Recorded Bks., LLC.
Palmer, Stuart. A Murder on the Blackboard. 1988. (Mystery Ser.). 224p. mass mkt. 3.50 o.s.i *(0-553-26796-5)* Bantam Bks.
—Murder on the Blackboard. 1992. 186p. reprint ed. pap. 5.95 *(1-55882-124-4*, Library of Crime Classics) International Polygonics, Ltd.
—Murder on Wheels. 1992. 307p. pap. 6.95 o.p. *(1-55882-113-9)* International Polygonics, Ltd.
—The Penguin Pool Murder. 1987. 224p. mass mkt. 2.95 o.s.i *(0-553-26334-X)* Bantam Bks.
—The Penguin Pool Murder. 1990. 182p. reprint ed. pap. 7.95 *(1-55882-076-0)* International Polygonics, Ltd.
Palmer, Stuart & Rice, Craig. People vs. Withers & Malone. 1990. 254p. reprint ed. pap. 7.95 o.p. *(1-55882-077-9)* International Polygonics, Ltd.
Pappano, Marilyn. Father to Be. 1999. 384p. mass mkt. 5.99 *(0-553-57985-1)* Bantam Bks.
—First Kiss. 2000. 368p. mass mkt. 5.99 *(0-553-58231-3)* Bantam Bks.
—Getting Lucky. 2001. 384p. mass mkt. 6.50 *(0-553-58232-1*, Spectra) Bantam Bks.
Parker, Una-Mary. Enticements. 1991. 320p. 18.95 o.p. *(0-525-24949-4*, Dutton) Dutton/Plume.
Patrick, Robert. Temple Slave. 1998. mass mkt. 7.95 *(1-56333-635-9*, Hard Candy); 1994. 464p. pap. 12.95 o.s.i *(1-56333-191-8*, Kasak, Richard Bks.) Masquerade Bks., Inc.
Patrick, William B. Roxa: Voices of the Culver Family. 1989. (American Poets Continuum Ser.: No. 16). 181p. pap. 12.50 *(0-918526-69-8)*; 20.00 *(0-918526-68-X)* BOA Editions, Ltd.
Patterson, James. The Beach House. 2002. 368p. pap. 16.00 *(0-446-67938-0)* Warner Bks., Inc.
Patterson, James & de Jonge, Peter. The Beach House. 2002. 368p. 26.95 *(0-316-96968-0)*; 464p. 26.95 o.p. *(0-316-73374-1)* Little Brown & Co.
—The Beach House. 2003. 384p. reprint ed. mass mkt. 7.99 *(0-446-61254-5)* Warner Bks., Inc.
Paul, Barbara. The Apostrophe Thief. 1994. mass mkt. *(0-373-26155-1*, 1-26155-1, Harlequin Bks.) Harlequin Enterprises, Ltd.
—The Apostrophe Thief: A Mystery with Marian Larch. 1993. 256p. 20.00 o.p. *(0-684-19553-4*, Macmillan Reference USA) Gale Group.
—Fare Play. l.t. ed. 1997. (Ulverscroft Large Print Ser.). 400p. 31.50 o.p. *(0-7089-3690-3*, Ulverscroft) Thorpe, F. A. Pubs. GBR. *Dist:* Ulverscroft Large Print Bks., Ltd., Ulverscroft Large Print Canada, Ltd.
—Fare Play: A Mystery with Marian Larch. l.t. ed. 1995. 314p. pap. 20.95 o.p. *(0-7838-1413-5*, Macmillan Reference USA) Gale Group.
—Full Frontal Murder. 1998. (WWL Mystery Ser.). per. *(0-373-26284-1*, 1-26284-9, Worldwide Library) Harlequin Enterprises, Ltd.
—Full Frontal Murder, Bk. 2. 1997. (Full Frontal Murder Ser.: Vol. 2). 256p. 20.50 *(0-684-19716-2*, Scribner) Simon & Schuster.
—Full Frontal Murder: A Mystery with Marian Larch. l.t. ed. 1998. (Mystery Ser.). 319p. 27.95 *(0-7838-8363-3)* Thorndike Pr.
—The Renewable Virgin. 1986. (Mystery Ser.). 192p. mass mkt. 2.95 o.s.i *(0-553-26234-3)* Bantam Bks.
—Renewable Virgin. l.t. ed. 1985. (Nightingale Ser.). 360p. 9.95 o.p. *(0-8161-3888-5*, Macmillan Reference USA) Gale Group.
—Renewable Virgin. 1985. 12.95 o.p. *(0-684-18300-5*, Scribner) Simon & Schuster.
—You Have the Right to Remain Silent. 1993. (Mystery Ser.). mass mkt. *(0-373-26132-2*, 1-26132-0, Harlequin Bks.) Harlequin Enterprises, Ltd.
—You Have the Right to Remain Silent, unabr. ed. 1993. audio 51.00 *(1-55690-836-9*, 93204E7) Recorded Bks., LLC.
—You Have the Right to Remain Silent: A Mystery with Marian Larch. 1992. 256p. 20.00 o.s.i *(0-684-19380-9*, Scribner) Simon & Schuster.
Paul, Raymond. The Bond Street Burlesque. 1987. 16.95 o.p. *(0-393-02402-4)* Norton, W. W. & Co., Inc.
Paulding, James K. Stories of St. Nicholas. 1995. (New York Classics Ser.). Orig. Title: Book of Saint Nicholas. 152p. 19.95 *(0-8156-0325-8)* Syracuse Univ. Pr.
Peck, Dale. What We Lost: Based on a True Story. 2003. 240p. 23.00 *(0-618-25128-6)* Houghton Mifflin Co.
Pekarkova, Iva. Gimme the Money. 2000. 224p. pap. *(1-85242-658-6)* Serpent's Tail Ltd.
Pentecost, Hugh. Beware Young Lovers. 1982. (Nightingale Ser.). pap. 9.95 o.p. *(0-8161-3458-8*, Macmillan Reference USA) Gale Group.
—Beware Young Lovers. 1990. 224p. mass mkt. *(0-373-26057-1*, Harlequin Bks.) Harlequin Enterprises, Ltd.
—Deadly Trap. l.t. ed. 1997. (Linford Mystery Library). 368p. pap. 17.99 o.p. *(0-7089-5170-8*, Ulverscroft) Thorpe, F. A. Pubs. GBR. *Dist:* Ulverscroft Large Print Bks., Ltd., Ulverscroft Large Print Canada, Ltd.
—Death Mask. 1983. (Nightingale Ser.). pap. 9.95 o.p. *(0-8161-3500-2*, Macmillan Reference USA) Gale Group.
—The Party Killer. l.t. ed. 1997. (Linford Mystery Library). 368p. pap. 17.99 o.p. *(0-7089-5099-X*, Linford) Thorpe, F. A. Pubs. GBR. *Dist:* Ulverscroft Large Print Bks., Ltd., Ulverscroft Large Print Canada, Ltd.
Percy, Walker. The Last Gentleman. 1989. 336p. mass mkt. 5.99 o.s.i *(0-8041-0379-8*, Ivy Bks.) Ballantine Bks.
—The Last Gentleman. unabr. ed. 1994. audio 76.95 *(0-7861-0420-1*, 1372) Blackstone Audio Bks., Inc.
—The Last Gentleman. 409p. 1982. pap. 10.95 o.p. *(0-374-50916-6)*; 1966. 22.95 o.s.i *(0-374-18372-4)* Farrar, Straus & Giroux.
—The Last Gentleman. 1999. 416p. pap. 15.00 *(0-312-24308-1)* Picador.
Perez, Loida Maritza. Geographies of Home. 2000. 336p. 12.95 *(0-14-025371-8)*; 1999. 288p. 23.95 o.p. *(0-670-86889-2)* Viking Penguin.
Perez, N. A. One Special Year. 1987. 212p. (J). (gr. 5-12). pap. 3.95 o.p. *(0-14-032202-7*, Puffin Bks.) Penguin Putnam Bks. for Young Readers.
Perks, Micah. We Are Gathered Here: A Novel. 1995. 336p. 22.95 *(0-312-14065-7)* St. Martin's Pr.
Perry, Charles. Portrait of a Young Man Drowning. 1996. (Old School Bks.). 296p. pap. 11.00 o.p. *(0-393-31462-6)* Norton, W. W. & Co., Inc.
Perry, Marta. Always in Her Heart. 2003. (Steeple Hill Love Inspired Ser.: No. 220). 256p. mass mkt. *(0-373-87227-5*, Steeple Hill) Harlequin Enterprises, Ltd.
Perry, Richard. No Other Tale to Tell: A Novel. 1994. 313p. 25.00 o.p. *(0-688-11595-0*, Morrow, William & Co.) Morrow/Avon.
Perry, Thomas. Blood Money. l.t. ed. 2000. (Large Print Book Ser.). 513p. pap. 26.95 *(1-56895-925-7*, Wheeler Publishing, Inc.) Gale Group.
—Blood Money. 2000. audio 30.00 *(0-7871-2284-X)* NewStar Media, Inc.
—Blood Money: A Novel. 1999. (Illus.). 368p. 24.95 o.s.i *(0-679-45304-0)* Random Hse., Inc.
—Dance for the Dead. 1997. (Jane Whitefield Novels Ser.). 416p. mass mkt. 6.99 *(0-8041-1425-0*, Ivy Bks.) Ballantine Bks.
—Dance for the Dead. l.t. ed. 1996. 416p. lib. bdg. 24.95 *(1-57490-065-X*, Beeler Large Print Bks.) Beeler, Thomas T. Publisher.
—Dance for the Dead, Set. abr. ed. 1998. (Jane Whitefield Mystery Ser.). audio 8.99 o.s.i *(0-375-40298-5*, 393900, RH Audio) Random Hse. Audio Publishing Group.
—Dance for the Dead. l.t. ed. 1997. (Charnwood Large Print Ser.). 464p. 34.50 o.p. *(0-7089-8938-1*, Ulverscroft) Thorpe, F. A. Pubs. GBR. *Dist:* Ulverscroft Large Print Bks., Ltd., Ulverscroft Large Print Canada, Ltd.
—Dance for the Dead: A Jane Whitefield Novel. abr. ed. 1996. audio 18.00 o.s.i *(0-679-45169-2*, 393900, RH Audio) Random Hse. Audio Publishing Group.
—The Face-Changers. 1999. (Jane Whitefield Novels Ser.). 432p. mass mkt. 7.50 *(0-8041-1540-0*, Ivy Bks.) Ballantine Bks.
—The Face-Changers. l.t. ed. 1998. (Americana Ser.). 640p. 28.95 *(0-7862-1611-5)* Thorndike Pr.
—The Face-Changers: A Novel. aut. ed. 1998. 372p. 24.00 o.s.i *(0-676-57765-2)* Random Hse., Inc.
—Shadow Woman. 1998. (Jane Whitefield Novels Ser.). 432p. mass mkt. 6.99 *(0-8041-1539-7*, Ivy Bks.) Ballantine Bks.
—Shadow Woman. l.t. ed. 1997. (Large Print Book Ser.). pap. 24.95 *(1-56895-513-8*, Wheeler Publishing, Inc.) Gale Group.
—Shadow Woman. l.t. ed. 1999. (Charnwood Large Print Ser.). 480p. 31.99 *(0-7089-9098-3*, Ulverscroft) Thorpe, F. A. Pubs. GBR. *Dist:* Ulverscroft Large Print Bks., Ltd., Ulverscroft Large Print Canada, Ltd.
—Vanishing Act. 1997. mass mkt. 2.99 o.s.i *(0-8041-1648-2)*; 1996. 368p. mass mkt. 6.99 *(0-8041-1387-4)* Ballantine Bks. (Ivy Bks.).
—Vanishing Act. l.t. ed. 1995. (Large Print Bks.). pap. 22.95 *(1-56895-234-1*, Wheeler Publishing, Inc.) Gale Group.
Petry, Ann. The Street. 1985. (Black Women Writers Ser.). 258p. reprint ed. pap. 11.95 o.p. *(0-8070-6357-6*, BP699) Beacon Pr.
—The Street. 448p. 1998. pap. 12.00 *(0-395-90149-9)*; 1992. pap. 12.00 o.p. *(0-395-57380-7)* Houghton Mifflin Co.
—The Street, unabr. ed. 1998. audio 85.00 *(0-7887-0851-1*, 94997E7) Recorded Bks., LLC.
Phillips, Carly. The Heartbreaker. l.t. ed. 2003. 385p. 31.95 *(1-58724-517-5*, Wheeler Publishing, Inc.) Gale Group.
—The Heartbreaker. 2004. mass mkt. 6.99 *(0-446-61056-9)*; 2003. 288p. 16.95 *(0-446-51152-8)* Warner Bks., Inc.
Phillips, Max. Snakebite Sonnet: A Novel. 1996. 320p. 22.95 o.p. *(0-316-70620-5)* Little Brown & Co.
Phillips, T. J. Woman in the Dark. 1997. (Joe Wilder Mysteries Ser.). 208p. reprint ed. mass mkt. 5.99 o.s.i *(0-425-16110-2*, Prime Crime) Berkley Publishing Group.
—Woman in the Dark: A Joe Wilder Mystery. 1997. (Joe Wilder Mysteries Ser.). 288p. 21.95 o.p. *(0-425-15312-6*, Prime Crime) Berkley Publishing Group.
Picano, Felice. A House on the Ocean, a House on the Bay. 2003. 270p. 17.95 *(1-56023-440-7*, Southern Tier Editions) Haworth Pr., Inc., The.
Piccirilli, Tom. The Dead Past, Vol. 1. 1999. (Felicity Grove Mysteries Ser.). 208p. reprint ed. mass mkt. 5.99 o.s.i *(0-425-16696-1*, Prime Crime) Berkley Publishing Group.
—The Dead Past. l.t. ed. 1999. (Thorndike Senior Lifestyle Ser.). 285p. 26.95 *(0-7862-1833-9)* Thorndike Pr.
—The Dead Past. 1997. (Felicity Grove Mysteries Ser.). 212p. 21.95 o.p. *(1-885173-28-8)* Write Way Publishing.
—The Deceased. 2000. 352p. mass mkt. 5.50 *(0-8439-4752-7*, Leisure Bks.) Dorchester Publishing Co., Inc.
—Sorrow's Crown. 1999. (Felicity Grove Mysteries Ser.). 208p. mass mkt. 5.99 o.s.i *(0-425-17028-4*, Prime Crime) Berkley Publishing Group.
—Sorrow's Crown. 1999. 240p. 21.95 o.p. *(1-885173-53-9)* Write Way Publishing.
Pickard, Nancy. But I Wouldn't Want to Die There. 1993. (Jenny Cain Mystery Ser.). 256p. 20.00 *(0-671-72330-8*, Atria) Simon & Schuster.
—But I Wouldn't Want to Die There. Marrow, Linda, ed. 1994. (Jenny Cain Mystery Ser.). 272p. reprint ed. mass mkt. 5.50 *(0-671-72331-6*, Pocket) Simon & Schuster.

Piesman, Marissa. Alternate Sides. 1996. 304p. mass mkt. 5.50 o.s.i (*0-440-22240-0*) Dell Publishing.
—Close Quarters. 1995. 304p. mass mkt. 4.99 o.s.i (*0-440-21162-X*) Dell Publishing.
—Heading Uptown: A Nina Fischman Mystery. l.t. ed. 1993. 21.95 o.p. (*0-7927-1658-2*); pap. 19.95 o.p. (*0-7927-1657-4*) BBC Audiobooks America.
—Heading Uptown: A Nina Fischman Mystery. 1994. 320p. mass mkt. 5.50 o.s.i (*0-440-21161-1*) Dell Publishing.
—Personal Effects. Chelius, Jane, ed. 1991. 224p. (Orig.). mass mkt. 4.50 (*0-671-74275-2*, Pocket) Simon & Schuster.
—Survival Instincts. 1997. (Nina Fischman Mystery Ser.). 224p. mass mkt. 5.99 o.s.i (*0-440-22453-5*, Dell Bks.) Dell Publishing.
—Unorthodox Practices. 1989. 224p. mass mkt. 4.99 (*0-671-67315-7*, Pocket) Simon & Schuster.
Pilcer, Sonia. I-Land: Manhattan in Monologue. 1987. (Orig.). pap. 6.95 o.s.i (*0-345-34551-7*) Ballantine Bks.
Pilcher, Robin. An Ocean Apart. abr. ed. 1999. audio 25.00 (*0-7871-1867-2*, 698452, Dove Audio) NewStar Media, Inc.
—An Ocean Apart. 1999. 512p. mass mkt. 6.99 (*0-312-97184-2*, St. Martin's Paperbacks); 1998. 470p. 24.95 o.p. (*0-312-19995-3*) St. Martin's Pr.
—An Ocean Apart. l.t. ed. 1999. (Basic Ser.). 699p. 30.95 (*0-7862-1911-4*) Thorndike Pr.
Pollack, Eileen. Paradise, New York: A Novel. 2000. 288p. 49.50 (*1-56639-657-3*); pap. 17.95 (*1-56639-789-8*) Temple Univ. Pr.
Pollock, J. C. Payback. 1992. 400p. reprint ed. mass mkt. 5.99 o.s.i (*0-440-20518-2*) Dell Publishing.
Porter, Connie Rose. All-Bright Court. 1991. 256p. 19.95 o.p. (*0-395-53271-X*) Houghton Mifflin Co.
—All-Bright Court: A Novel. 1992. 240p. pap. 10.00 o.p. (*0-06-097498-2*, Perennial) HarperTrade.
Potok, Chaim. In the Beginning. 1975. 13.95 o.s.i (*0-394-49960-3*) Knopf, Alfred A. Inc.
—My Name Is Asher Lev. 1996. 384p. pap. 13.95 o.s.i (*0-449-91168-3*); 1983. mass mkt. 3.50 o.s.i (*0-449-20406-5*) Ballantine Bks. (Fawcett).
—My Name Is Asher Lev. 2003. 384p. reprint ed. pap. 14.00 (*1-4000-3104-4*, Anchor) Knopf Publishing Group.
Powell, Dawn. Angels on Toast. 1990. pap. 8.95 o.s.i (*0-679-72686-1*, Vintage) Knopf Publishing Group.
—Angels on Toast. 1996. 273p. pap. 14.00 (*1-883642-40-X*) Steerforth Pr.
—Dawn Powell at Her Best: Including the Novels "Dance Night" & "Turn Magic Wheel" & Selected Stories. 1994. 452p. 28.00 (*1-883642-16-7*) Steerforth Pr.
—The Locusts Have No King. 1996. 286p. pap. 14.00 (*1-883642-42-6*) Steerforth Pr.
—The Locusts Have No King. 1990. 304p. reprint ed. pap. 9.95 o.s.i (*1-878274-00-7*) Yarrow Pr.
—A Time to Be Born. reprint ed. 30.00 (*0-404-20206-3*, PS3531) AMS Pr., Inc.
—A Time to Be Born. 1996. 334p. pap. 14.00 (*1-883642-41-8*) Steerforth Pr.
—A Time to Be Born. 1991. 352p. reprint ed. pap. 9.95 o.p. (*1-878274-06-6*) Yarrow Pr.
Preston, Douglas J. Reliquary: Sequel to the Relic! 1998. 464p. mass mkt. 7.99 (*0-8125-4283-5*, Tor Bks.) Doherty, Tom Assocs., LLC.
—Reliquary: Sequel to the Relic! 1998. 5.98 o.p. (*0-7651-1480-1*) Smithmark Pubs., Inc.
Preston, Douglas J. & Child, Lincoln. The Cabinet of Curiosities. 2003. 656p. mass mkt. 7.99 (*0-446-61123-9*); 2002. 480p. 25.95 (*0-446-53022-0*) Warner Bks., Inc.
—Reliquary: Sequel to the Relic! abr. ed. 1998. audio 7.99 o.p. (*1-56740-246-1*, 693, Paperback Nova Audio Bks.); 1997. audio 16.95 o.p. (*1-56100-982-2*, 1353, Nova Audio Bks.); 1997. audio 89.25 o.p. (*1-56100-831-1*, 1007, Unabridged Library Editions); 1997. audio 25.95 o.p. (*1-56100-756-0*, 230, Bookcassette) Brilliance Audio.
—Reliquary: Sequel to the Relic! 1997. 384p. 24.95 o.p. (*0-312-86095-1*, Forge Bks.) Doherty, Tom Assocs., LLC.
Preston, Richard. The Cobra Event. 1998. 448p. mass mkt. 7.99 (*0-345-40997-3*) Ballantine Bks.
Price, Bruce D. Too Easy. 1994. 21.00 (*0-671-88673-8*, Simon & Schuster) Simon & Schuster.
Price, Richard. Blood Brothers. 1999. 272p. pap. 12.00 (*0-395-97773-8*) Houghton Mifflin Co.
—Bloodbrothers. 1993. pap. 9.00 (*0-380-77476-3*, Avon Bks.) Morrow/Avon.
Pronzini, Bill, et al, eds. Manhattan Mysteries. 1987. 1.99 o.s.i (*0-517-63179-2*) Random Hse. Value Publishing.
Prose, Francine. Bigfoot Dreams. 1998. 288p. pap. 12.00 (*0-8050-4860-X*, Owl Bks.) Holt, Henry & Co.
—Bigfoot Dreams. 1986. 16.95 o.p. (*0-394-54976-7*, Pantheon) Knopf Publishing Group.
—Bigfoot Dreams. 1987. 288p. pap. 6.95 o.p. (*0-14-009837-2*, Penguin Bks.) Viking Penguin.
—Primitive People. 1993. 240p. mass mkt. 4.99 o.s.i (*0-8041-1110-3*, Ivy Bks.) Ballantine Bks.
—Primitive People. 1992. 250p. 20.00 o.p. (*0-374-23722-0*) Farrar, Straus & Giroux.
—Primitive People. 2001. 240p. pap. 13.00 (*0-06-093469-7*, Perennial) HarperTrade.
Pulaski, Jack. The St. Veronica Gig Stories. 1986. 178p. (Orig.). 15.95 (*0-939010-10-0*); pap. 8.95 (*0-939010-09-7*) Zephyr Pr.
Purdy, James. Out with the Stars. 1993. 192p. 19.95 o.p. (*0-87286-287-9*); pap. 9.95 o.p. (*0-87286-284-4*) City Lights Bks.
—Out with the Stars. 1993. 192p. 30.00 (*0-7206-0861-9*) Owen, Peter Ltd. GBR. *Dist:* Dufour Editions, Inc.
Puzo, Mario. The Fortunate Pilgrim. 1998. 304p. pap. 13.95 (*0-449-00358-2*); 1982. mass mkt. 2.50 o.s.i (*0-449-23456-8*) Ballantine Bks. (Fawcett).
—The Fortunate Pilgrim. 1985. 256p. mass mkt. 3.95 o.s.i (*0-553-24859-6*) Bantam Bks.
—The Fortunate Pilgrim. abr. ed. 1998. audio 7.99 o.p. (*1-56740-239-9*, 651, Paperback Nova Audio Bks.); 1997. audio 16.95 o.p. (*1-56100-986-5*, 1201, Nova Audio Bks.); 1997. audio 23.95 o.p. (*1-56100-760-9*, 113, Bookcassette); 1997. audio 73.25 o.p. (*1-56100-835-4*, 841, Unabridged Library Editions) Brilliance Audio.
—The Fortunate Pilgrim. abr. ed. 2000. audio 7.95 (*1-57815-171-6*, 1114, Media Bks. Audio Publishing) Media Bks., L. L. C.
—The Fortunate Pilgrim. 1997. 304p. 23.00 o.s.i (*0-679-45778-X*) Random Hse., Inc.
Pye, Michael. The Drowning Room: A Novel of New Amsterdam. 1997. 256p. 12.95 (*0-14-014149-9*); 1997. 252p. pap. 11.95 (*0-14-014122-7*); 1996. 256p. 22.95 (*0-670-86598-2*, Viking) Viking Penguin.
Queen, Ellery. French Powder Mystery. lib. bdg. 21.95 (*0-8488-1870-9*) Amereon, Ltd.
—French Powder Mystery. 1995. pap. 7.00 o.s.i (*1-883402-90-5*, Scribner) Simon & Schuster.
—The House of Brass. l.t. ed. 2001. 278p. pap. 24.95 (*0-7838-9598-4*, Macmillan Reference USA) Gale Group.
—The King Is Dead. l.t. ed. 2000. (G. K. Hall Paperback Ser.). 328p. pap. 23.95 (*0-7838-9282-9*, Macmillan Reference USA) Gale Group.
—The King Is Dead. 1994. (Ellery Queen Mystery Ser.). 224p. reprint ed. pap. 8.00 o.p. (*0-06-097605-5*, Perennial) HarperTrade.
—The King Is Dead. mass mkt. 0.25 o.p. (*0-451-00629-1*); 1977. mass mkt. 1.25 o.p. (*0-451-07361-4*); 1972. mass mkt. 0.95 o.p. (*0-451-05290-0*) NAL. (Signet Bks.).
—The Siamese Twin Mystery. unabr. ed. 1998. audio 49.95 (*0-7861-1266-2*, 2203) Blackstone Audio Bks., Inc.
—The Siamese Twin Mystery. unabr. collector's ed. 1978. audio 48.00 (*0-7366-0136-8*, 1140) Books on Tape, Inc.
—The Siamese Twin Mystery. 1970. mass mkt. 0.75 o.p. (*0-451-04086-4*, Signet Bks.) NAL.
—The Siamese Twin Mystery. 1993. pap. 6.95 (*1-883402-11-5*, Scribner) Simon & Schuster.
—The Siamese Twin Mystery: Kill As Directed. 1983. mass mkt. 2.95 o.p. (*0-451-12271-2*, Signet Bks.) NAL.
—The Siamese Twin Mystery: Special 50th Anniversary Edition. 1979. mass mkt. 1.75 o.p. (*0-451-08664-3*, E8664, Signet Bks.) NAL.
Quinn, Peter. Banished Children of Eve. 1995. 624p. pap. 14.00 (*0-14-023003-3*, Penguin Bks.) Penguin Group (USA) Inc.
—Banished Children of Eve. 1994. 624p. 22.95 o.p. (*0-670-85076-4*, Viking) Viking Penguin.
Quinones Miller, Karen E. Satin Doll: A Novel. 2001. 320p. 21.00 (*0-7432-1433-1*, Simon & Schuster) Simon & Schuster.
Quittner, Joshua & Slatalla, Michelle. Shoo-Fly Pie to Die. 1992. 224p. 17.95 o.p. (*0-312-06943-X*, Saint Martin's Minotaur) St. Martin's Pr.
Rae, Catherine M. Afterward. 1992. 192p. 16.95 o.p. (*0-312-06894-8*) St. Martin's Pr.
—Brownstone Facade. 1987. 192p. 13.95 o.p. (*0-312-01004-4*) St. Martin's Pr.
—Flight from Fifth Avenue. 1995. 18.95 o.p. (*0-312-11788-4*) St. Martin's Pr.
—The Hidden Cove. l.t. ed. 2000. 268p. lib. bdg. 27.95 (*1-58547-035-X*) Ctr. Point Large Print.
—The Hidden Cove. 1999. 183p. reprint ed. text 20.00 (*0-7881-6634-4*) DIANE Publishing Co.
—The Hidden Cove. 1995. 192p. 19.95 o.p. (*0-312-13511-4*) St. Martin's Pr.
—The Ship's Clock. 1993. 192p. 17.95 o.p. (*0-312-09386-1*) St. Martin's Pr.
Ragen, Naomi. The Ghost of Hannah Mendes. 5th ed. 2001. (Illus.). 384p. reprint ed. pap. 14.95 (*0-312-28125-0*, CPB1198, Saint Martin's Griffin) St. Martin's Pr.
—The Ghost of Hannah Mendes: A Novel. 1998. 384p. 25.00 o.s.i (*0-684-83393-X*, Simon & Schuster) Simon & Schuster.
—The Sacrifice of Tamar. 1994. 448p. 24.00 o.s.i (*0-517-59561-3*, Crown) Crown Publishing Group.
Ramsay, Diana. Four Steps to Death. 1990. 192p. 14.95 o.p. (*0-312-03835-6*, Saint Martin's Minotaur) St. Martin's Pr.
Ramus, David. Thief of Light. l.t. ed. 1996. pap. 23.95 (*1-56895-304-6*, Wheeler Publishing, Inc.) Gale Group.
—Thief of Light. 1995. 352p. 23.00 o.p. (*0-06-017664-4*); 184.00 o.p. (*0-06-017685-7*) HarperCollins Pubs.
—Thief of Light. 1997. 384p. mass mkt. 6.50 o.s.i (*0-06-109420-X*, HarperTorch) Morrow/Avon.
Randisi, Robert J. The Dead of Brooklyn: A Nick Delvecchio Mystery. pap. 12.95 (*1-931755-19-1*) Mystery Vault, Inc.
—The Dead of Brooklyn: A Nick Delvecchio Mystery. l.t. ed. 2002. (Mystery Ser.). 341p. 28.95 (*0-7862-4399-6*) Thorndike Pr.
—Ham Reporter. 1987. (Double D Western Ser.). 384p. 16.95 o.p. (*0-385-23991-2*) Doubleday Publishing.
Random House Value Publishing Staff & Irving, Washington. The Legend of Sleepy Hollow. 1998. (Illustrated Stories for Children Ser.). (Illus.). 112p. (J). (gr. 4-7). 7.99 (*0-517-20303-0*) Random Hse. Value Publishing.
Ransom, Jane. Bye-Bye. 1997. 150p. 19.00 (*0-8147-7490-3*) New York Univ. Pr.
—Bye-Bye. 1999. 208p. reprint ed. pap. 12.00 (*0-671-02708-5*, Washington Square Pr.) Simon & Schuster.
Ratner, Rochelle. Bobby's Girl. 1986. 128p. (Orig.). pap. 9.95 (*0-918273-22-6*) Coffee Hse. Pr.
Ray, Mary Lyn. Basket Moon. 1999. (Illus.). 32p. (J). (ps-3). 15.95 (*0-316-73521-3*) Little Brown & Co.
Renek, Morris. Bread & Circus. 1987. 352p. 18.95 o.s.i (*1-55584-070-1*) Grove/Atlantic, Inc.
Renino, Christopher. Way Home Is Longer. 1997. 352p. 23.95 o.p. (*0-312-15686-3*) St. Martin's Pr.
Reuben, Shelly. Origin & Cause. 1996. 384p. mass mkt. 5.50 o.p. (*0-06-104392-3*, HarperTorch) Morrow/Avon.
—Origin & Cause: A Crime Novel. 1994. 352p. 20.00 (*0-684-19702-2*, Macmillan Reference USA) Gale Group.
—Spent Matches. 1996. 320p. 21.00 (*0-684-80107-8*, Scribner) Simon & Schuster.
Reznikoff, Charles. By the Waters of Manhattan. 1986. (Masterworks of Modern Jewish Writings). (Illus.). 264p. (C). reprint ed. pap. 9.95 (*0-910129-55-X*) Wiener, Markus Pubs., Inc.
Rice, Anne. Memnoch, the Devil. (Vampire Chronicles: Bk. 5). 1997. pap. 14.00 o.s.i (*0-345-91273-X*); 1996. mass mkt. 7.50 o.s.i (*0-345-40499-8*); 1996. 464p. pap. 14.95 (*0-345-38940-9*) Ballantine Bks.
—Memnoch, the Devil. 1995. (Vampire Chronicles: Bk. 5). 368p. 29.95 (*0-679-44101-8*) Knopf, Alfred A. Inc.
—Memnoch, the Devil. abr. ed. 1995. (Vampire Chronicles). audio 23.50 (*0-679-43832-7*, 493006, RH Audio) Random Hse. Audio Publishing Group.
—Memnoch, the Devil. deluxe ltd. num. ed. 1995. (Vampire Chronicles: Vol. 5). 354p. 195.00 (*0-9631925-4-X*) Trice, B.E. Publishing.
Rice, Luanne. Cloud Nine. 2000. 400p. mass mkt. 7.50 (*0-553-58099-X*); 1999. 21.95 (*0-553-09729-6*) Bantam Bks.
—Cloud Nine. abr. ed. 2000. audio 7.99 o.s.i (*1-56740-326-3*, 1886, Paperback Nova Audio Bks.) Brilliance Audio.
—Cloud Nine. l.t. ed. 1999. 26.95 o.p. (*1-56895-708-4*, Wheeler Publishing, Inc.) Gale Group.
Riley, Len. Harlem. 1998. (Berkeley Signature Edition Ser.). 304p. mass mkt. 6.99 o.s.i (*0-425-16343-1*) Berkley Publishing Group.
—Harlem. 1997. 384p. 21.95 o.s.i (*0-385-48508-5*) Doubleday Publishing.
Rinehart, Mary Roberts. The Circular Staircase. Date not set. lib. bdg. 20.95 (*0-8488-2159-9*) Amereon, Ltd.
—The Circular Staircase. 1976. lib. bdg. 19.95 (*0-89968-181-6*, Lightyear Pr.) Buccaneer Bks., Inc.
—The Circular Staircase. 1997. (Dover Mystery Classics Ser.). (Illus.). 160p. reprint ed. pap. text 2.00 (*0-486-29713-6*) Dover Pubns., Inc.
—The Circular Staircase. E-Book 2.49 (*1-58627-657-3*) Electric Umbrella Publishing.
—The Circular Staircase. 1997. 288p. mass mkt. 5.50 o.s.i (*1-57566-180-2*); 1985. mass mkt. 3.50 o.p. (*0-8217-1723-5*, Zebra Bks.); 1985. mass mkt. 3.95 o.s.i (*0-8217-3528-4*, Zebra Bks.) Kensington Publishing Corp.
Ritz, David. Take It Off, Take It All Off! 1993. 224p. 21.00 o.p. (*1-55611-366-8*) Fine, Donald I. Bks.
Robb, J. D., pseud. Judgment in Death. 2000. 368p. mass mkt. 7.99 (*0-425-17630-4*) Berkley Publishing Group.
—Judgment in Death. abr. ed. (In Death Ser.). 2005. audio 12.99 (*1-58788-323-6*, 2902, Brilliance Audio Paperback Audiobooks); 2000. audio 24.95 (*1-58788-079-2*, 2327, Nova Audio Bks.); 2000. audio 44.25 (*1-58788-174-8*, 2447, Unabridged Library Editions) Brilliance Audio.
—Judgment in Death. l.t. ed. 2002. (Core Ser.). 472p. pap. 30.95 (*0-7838-9335-3*) Gale Group.
—Judgment in Death. l.t. ed. 2001. (Core Ser.). 472p. 32.95 (*0-7838-9334-5*) Thorndike Pr.
—Loyalty in Death. l.t. ed. 2000. (Americana Ser.). 539p. 30.95 (*0-7862-2443-6*) Thorndike Pr.
Robbe-Grillet, Alain. Project for a Revolution in New York. Howard, Richard, tr. from FRE. 1989. pap. 3.95 o.p. (*0-394-17768-1*, E685) Grove/Atlantic, Inc.
Robbins, Harold. Never Leave Me. Date not set. pap. (*0-312-87911-3*); mass mkt. (*0-7653-4057-7*); 2001. 352p. 25.95 (*0-312-86610-0*) Doherty, Tom Assocs., LLC. (Forge Bks.).
—Never Leave Me. 1978. 224p. pap. 4.99 (*0-380-00179-9*, Avon Bks.) Morrow/Avon.
—Never Leave Me. l.t. ed. 1982. (Charnwood Large Print Ser.). 13.00 o.p. (*0-7089-8023-6*, Charnwood) Thorpe, F. A. Pubs. GBR. *Dist:* Ulverscroft Large Print Bks., Ltd., Ulverscroft Large Print Canada, Ltd.
Roberts, Walter A. Mayor Harding of New York. reprint ed. 42.50 (*0-404-11412-1*) AMS Pr., Inc.
Robertson, Ray. Home Movies: A Novel. 1997. 228p. pap. text (*1-896951-02-3*) Cormorant Bks.
Robinson, Leah Ruth. Unnatural Causes. 2000. 384p. mass mkt. 6.99 (*0-380-79125-0*, HarperTorch) Morrow/Avon.
Robinson, Roxana. Sweetwater: A Novel. 2003. 336p. 24.95 (*0-375-50916-X*) Random Hse., Inc.
—Sweetwater: A Novel. l.t. ed. 2003. 565p. 29.95 (*0-7862-5648-6*) Thorndike Pr.
Robson, Ruthann. A/K/A: A Novel. (Stonewall Inn Editions Ser.). 1998. pap. 13.95 (*0-312-19825-6*, Saint Martin's Griffin); 1997. 277p. 23.95 (*0-312-15469-0*) St. Martin's Pr.
Rodriguez, Abraham, Jr. The Boy Without a Flag: Tales of the South Bronx. (Illus.). 120p. 1992. pap. 12.95 o.p. (*0-915943-74-3*); 2nd ed. 1999. pap. 13.95 (*1-57131-028-2*) Milkweed Editions.
—Spidertown. 1994. 336p. reprint ed. pap. 11.95 o.s.i (*0-14-023838-7*, Penguin Bks.) Penguin Group (USA) Inc.
Rodriguez, Victor. Eldorado in East Harlem. 1992. 156p. 9.50 (*1-55885-054-6*) Arte Publico Pr.
Roper, Martin. Gone: A Novel. 2002. 256p. 23.00 o.s.i (*0-8050-6775-2*) Holt, Henry & Co.
—Gone: A Novel. 2003. 240p. pap. 13.00 (*0-312-42125-7*) Picador.
Rosenbaum, David. Sasha's Trick. 1995. 82p. 21.95 o.p. (*0-89296-591-6*) Mysterious Pr.
—Sasha's Trick. 1996. 384p. mass mkt. 5.99 o.s.i (*0-446-40441-1*) Warner Bks., Inc.
Rosenbaum, Thane. The Golems of Gotham. 2002. 384p. 25.95 (*0-06-018490-6*) HarperCollins Pubs.
—The Golems of Gotham. 2003. 384p. pap. 13.95 (*0-06-095945-2*, Perennial) HarperTrade.
Rosenberg, Philip. House of Lords. 2002. 480p. 24.95 (*0-06-019415-4*) HarperCollins Pubs.
Ross, Clarissa. Beware the Kindly Stranger. l.t. ed. 2000. (G. K. Hall Romance Ser.). 246p. 27.95 (*0-7838-8980-1*, Macmillan Reference USA) Gale Group.
Ross, Leone. Orange Laughter. 2000. 225p. 23.00 o.p. (*0-374-22676-8*) Farrar, Straus & Giroux.
—Orange Laughter. 2001. 240p. pap. 13.00 (*0-312-42016-1*) Picador.
Rossner, Judith. Olivia: Or The Weight of the Past. 1995. mass mkt. 6.99 o.s.i (*0-8041-1246-0*, Ivy Bks.) Ballantine Bks.
—Olivia: Or The Weight of the Past. l.t. ed. 1995. (Large Print Bks.). 24.95 (*1-56895-166-3*, Wheeler Publishing, Inc.) Gale Group.
Roth, Henry. China Superpower Vol. 1: Requisites for High Growth. 1997. (Illus.). 248p. 55.00 (*0-312-16499-8*) Palgrave Macmillan.
—A Diving Rock on the Hudson. 1996. (Mercy of a Rude Stream Ser.: Vol. 2). 432p. pap. 14.00 o.s.i (*0-312-14085-1*) Picador.
—A Diving Rock on the Hudson: Mercy of a Rude Stream, Vol. II. 1995. (Mercy of a Rude Stream Ser.). 1p. 23.95 o.p. (*0-312-11777-9*) St. Martin's Pr.
—From Bondage. 1997. (Mercy of a Rude Stream Ser.: Vol. 3). 416p. pap. 15.00 (*0-312-15532-8*) Picador.
—From Bondage. 1996. (Mercy of a Rude Stream Ser.: Vol. 3). 432p. 25.95 o.p. (*0-312-14341-9*) St. Martin's Pr.
—Mercy of a Rude Stream. 1994. 304p. 250.00 (*0-312-10501-0*); 1993. 1p. 23.00 o.p. (*0-312-10499-5*) St. Martin's Pr.
—Mercy of a Rude Stream: A Star Shines over Mt. Morris Park. 1994. (Mercy of a Rude Stream Ser.: Vol. 1). pap. 13.00 o.s.i (*0-312-11929-1*) Picador.
—Requiem for Harlem. 1998. (Mercy of a Rude Stream Ser.: Vol. 4). 304p. pap. 14.00 (*0-312-20205-9*); 24.95 o.s.i (*0-312-16980-9*) Picador.

Settings

Rozan, S. J. China Trade. 1994. 263 p. 20.95 o.p. (0-312-11254-8, Saint Martin's Minotaur); 1995. (Lydia Chin, Bill Smith Mystery Ser.: Vol. 1). 275p. reprint ed. mass mkt. 6.50 (0-312-95590-1, St. Martin's Paperbacks) St. Martin's Pr.
—Concourse: A Bill Smith-Lydia Chin Mystery. 1995. 288p. 21.95 o.p. (0-312-13453-3, Saint Martin's Minotaur); 3rd ed. 1996. (Lydia Chin, Bill Smith Mystery Ser.: Vol. 2). 291p. mass mkt. 6.50 (0-312-95944-3, St. Martin's Paperbacks) St. Martin's Pr.
—Mandarin Plaid. (Lydia Chin, Bill Smith Mystery Ser.: Vol. 3). 288p. 1996. 22.95 o.p. (0-312-14674-4, Saint Martin's Minotaur); Vol. 1. 1997. mass mkt. 6.50 (0-312-96283-5, St. Martin's Paperbacks) St. Martin's Pr.
—No Colder Place. 1998. (No Colder Place Ser.: Vol. 1). 304p. pap. 6.99 (0-312-96664-4, St. Martin's Paperbacks); 1997. (Lydia Chin, Bill Smith Mystery Ser.). 288p. 23.95 (0-312-16811-X, Saint Martin's Minotaur) St. Martin's Pr.
—No Colder Place. l.t. ed. 1997. (Cloak & Dagger Ser.). 473p. lib. bdg. 28.95 (0-7862-1251-9) Thorndike Pr.
—Reflecting the Sky. 2001. 312p. 24.95 (0-312-24427-4, Saint Martin's Minotaur); 2002. 384p. reprint ed. mass mkt. 6.50 (0-312-98134-1, St. Martin's Paperbacks) St. Martin's Pr.
—Stone Quarry. 1999. 288p. 23.95 o.p. (0-312-20912-6, Saint Martin's Minotaur) St. Martin's Pr.
Rubino, Diana. It Was Like This. 2002. 280p. pap. 14.95 (1-58345-611-2) Domhan Bks.
Rucka, Gregory. Finder. 1999. audio 60.00 Recorded Bks., LLC.
—Finder: An Atticus Kodiac Novel. 1998. 352p. mass mkt. 6.99 (0-553-57429-9) Bantam Bks.
—Finder: An Atticus Kodiac Novel, unabr. ed. 1999. audio 62.00 (0-7887-3994-8, 96082E7) Recorded Bks., LLC.
Rudman, Anne Beane, et al. Given the Crime. 1998. 336p. pap. 6.50 (0-671-00152-3, Pocket); 320p. 22.00 (0-671-00151-5, Atria) Simon & Schuster.
Rudnick, Paul. Social Disease. 1997. 208p. pap. 11.95 o.p. (0-312-15659-6, Saint Martin's Griffin) St. Martin's Pr.
Ruff, Matt. Sewer, Gas & Electric: The Public Works Trilogy. 1996. 384p. 23.00 o.p. (0-87113-641-4, Atlantic Monthly Pr.) Grove/Atlantic, Inc.
Ruffner, Sara S. A Liberal Education. 1991. 256p. (Orig.). pap. 10.95 o.p. (0-931832-74-8) Fithian Pr.
Rumaker, Michael. To Kill a Cardinal. 1992. 160p. text 11.95 (0-9632962-2-1) Arthur Mann Kaye.
Runyon, Damon. The Bloodhounds of Broadway & Other Stories. 1981. 320p. pap. 10.95 o.p. (0-688-00625-6, Quill) HarperTrade.
—Damon Runyon Omnibus. 1976. reprint ed. lib. bdg. 32.95 (0-89190-441-7, Rivercity Pr.) Amereon, Ltd.
—Damon Runyon Omnibus. 1993. reprint ed. lib. bdg. 28.95 (1-56849-217-0) Buccaneer Bks., Inc.
—Guys & Dolls. reprint ed. lib. bdg. 20.95 (0-89190-438-7, Rivercity Pr.) Amereon, Ltd.
—Guys & Dolls. 2015. 320p. pap. 10.95 (0-14-118046-3, Penguin Classics); 1993. 704p. 27.50 o.p. (0-670-84868-9, Viking) Viking Penguin.
—Guys & Dolls: The Stories of Damon Runyon. 1992. 480p. 14.95 (0-14-017659-4) Viking Penguin.
—Romance in the Roaring Forties & Other Stories. 1986. 324p. (Orig.). pap. 9.95 o.p. (0-688-06148-6, Quill) HarperTrade.
—Romance in the Roaring Forties & Other Stories. 1986. 324p. (Orig.). 19.95 o.p. (0-688-05421-8, Morrow, William & Co.) Morrow/Avon.
—Treasury of Damon Runyn. Kinnaird, Clark, ed. 1978. 6.95 o.p. (0-394-60444-X) Random Hse., Inc.
Rushdie, Salman. The Ground Beneath Her Feet: A Novel. l.t. ed. 2000. (Thorndike/G. K. Hall Paperback Bestsellers Ser.). 816p. pap. 30.95 (0-7838-8712-4, Macmillan Reference USA) Gale Group.
—The Ground Beneath Her Feet: A Novel. 1999. 592p. 27.50 o.s.i (0-8050-5308-5) Holt, Henry & Co.
—The Ground Beneath Her Feet: A Novel. abr. ed. 1999. audio 25.00 (0-7871-1917-2, Dove Audio) NewStar Media, Inc.
—The Ground Beneath Her Feet: A Novel. 2000. 592p. pap. 16.00 (0-312-25499-7) Picador.
—The Ground Beneath Her Feet: A Novel. unabr. ed. 1999. audio 104.00 (0-7887-3747-3, 95939E5); audio 163.00 (0-7887-4350-3, 95939E7) Recorded Bks., LLC.
—The Ground Beneath Her Feet: A Novel. l.t. ed. 1999. (G. K. Hall Core Ser.). 816p. 31.95 (0-7838-8713-2) Thorndike Pr.
Russell, Paul. War Against the Animals: A Novel. 2003. 320p. 24.95 (0-312-20935-5) St. Martin's Pr.
Russo, Richard. Mohawk. 432p. 1994. pap. 14.00 (0-679-75382-6); 1989. pap. 12.00 o.p. (0-679-72577-6) Knopf Publishing Group. (Vintage).
—Mohawk. Fisketjon, Gary, ed. 2001. 304p. 25.95 (0-375-41286-7) Knopf, Alfred A. Inc.
—Nobody's Fool. 1994. 560p. pap. 14.95 (0-679-75333-8, Vintage) Knopf Publishing Group.
—The Risk Pool. 1994. 496p. pap. 15.00 (0-679-75383-4); 1989. pap. 12.00 o.p. (0-679-72334-X) Knopf Publishing Group. (Vintage).
Sanders, Lawrence. The Anderson Tapes. 22.95 (0-89190-854-4) Amereon, Ltd.
—The Anderson Tapes. unabr. ed. 1986. audio 41.65 Audio Bk. Co.
—The Anderson Tapes. 1987. 336p. mass mkt. 7.50 (0-425-10364-1) Berkley Publishing Group.
—The Anderson Tapes. 1994. reprint ed. lib. bdg. 32.95 o.p. (1-56849-331-2) Buccaneer Bks., Inc.
—The Anderson Tapes. l.t. ed. 2000. 319p. lib. bdg. 25.95 (1-58547-023-6) Ctr. Point Large Print.
—The Anderson Tapes. 1971. pap. 2.50 o.p. (0-440-10217-0) Dell Publishing.
—Lawrence Sanders - Three Complete Novels: The Anderson Tapes; The Tenth Commandment; The Fourth Deadly Sin. 1996. 752p. 12.98 o.p. (0-399-14182-0) Penguin Group (USA) Inc.
—The Seventh Commandment. 1992. 368p. mass mkt. 7.50 (0-425-13329-X) Berkley Publishing Group.
—The Seventh Commandment. l.t. ed. 1992. (General Ser.: Vol. 6). 303p. pap. 16.95 (0-8161-5342-6);Vol. 6. lib. bdg. 22.95 o.p. (0-8161-5341-8) Gale Group. (Macmillan Reference USA).
—The Seventh Commandment. 1991. 352p. 21.95 o.s.i (0-399-13611-8, G. P. Putnam's Sons) Penguin Group (USA) Inc.
—The Seventh Commandment. 1999. audio 9.98 (0-671-04458-3); 1991. audio 15.95 (0-671-73382-6) Simon & Schuster Audio. (Simon & Schuster Audioworks).
—Three Complete Novels: The Timothy Files, Timothy's Game, Sullivan's Sting. 1999. 784p. 12.98 o.s.i (0-399-14531-1) Penguin Group (USA) Inc.
Sandom, J. G. The Hunting Club. 1993. 18.50 o.s.i (0-385-46778-8) Doubleday Publishing.
Sanford, John B. The People from Heaven. 1995. (Radical Novel Reconsidered Ser.). 264p. pap. text 14.95 (0-252-06491-7) Univ. of Illinois Pr.
Santiago, Esmeralda. America's Dream. 336p. 2002. pap. 12.95 (0-06-050884-1, Rayo); 1997. pap. 14.00 (0-06-092826-3, Perennial) HarperTrade.
—America's Dream: El Sueno de America. 1996. 79p. 23.00 o.p. (0-06-017279-7) HarperCollins Pubs.
Santiago, Silviano. Stella Manhattan. Yudice, George, tr. 1994. 224p. pap. 19.95 (0-8223-1498-3); text 64.95 (0-8223-1486-X) Duke Univ. Pr.
Santiago, Soledad. Nightside. 1995. 304p. mass mkt. 5.50 o.s.i (0-553-56250-9) Bantam Bks.
—Streets of Fire. 1999. 342p. reprint ed. text 24.00 (0-7881-6605-0) DIANE Publishing Co.
—Streets of Fire. 1996. 352p. 23.95 o.s.i (0-525-94078-2) Dutton/Plume.
—Streets of Fire. 1997. 416p. mass mkt. 5.99 o.s.i (0-451-18855-1, Signet Bks.) NAL.
Santmyer, Helen Hooven. Herbs & Apples. 1985. 352p. 16.95 o.p. (0-06-015486-1) HarperTrade.
—Herbs & Apples. 1987. mass mkt. 4.95 o.p. (0-312-90601-3, St. Martin's Paperbacks) St. Martin's Pr.
Saulnier, Beth. Distemper. 2000. (Alex Bernier Mysteries Ser.). 400p. reprint ed. mass mkt. 6.50 (0-446-60861-0) Warner Bks., Inc.
—The Fourth Wall. 2001. 432p. reprint ed. mass mkt. 6.99 (0-446-60998-6) Warner Bks., Inc.
—Reliable Sources. 1999. 352p. reprint ed. mass mkt. 6.50 (0-446-60781-9) Warner Bks., Inc.
Savage, Tom. Valentine. l.t. ed. 1999. 321p. 25.95 (1-57490-243-1) Beeler, Thomas T. Publisher.
—Valentine. 1996. 336p. 20.95 o.p. (0-316-77164-3) Little Brown & Co.
—Valentine. 1997. 448p. mass mkt. 6.99 o.s.i (0-451-40719-9, Onyx) NAL.
Sawikin, Harvey. The Education of Rick Green, Esquire. 1995. 320p. 23.00 (0-684-80363-1, Simon & Schuster) Simon & Schuster.
Scanlan, Dick. Does Freddy Dance. 1995. 207p. 19.95 o.p. (1-55583-287-3) Alyson Pubns.
Schaffner, Val. Algonquin Cat. 1980. (Illus.). 9.95 o.s.i (0-440-00073-4, Delacorte Pr.) Dell Publishing.
—Algonquin Cat. 1995. (Illus.). 144p. 7.99 o.s.i (0-517-14711-4) Random Hse. Value Publishing.
—The Algonquin Cat. 2001. (Illus.). 146p. reprint ed. pap. 12.00 (0-8065-1030-7, Citadel Pr.) Kensington Publishing Corp.
Schine, Cathleen. Alice in Bed. 1984. mass mkt. 3.50 o.p. (0-425-07189-8) Berkley Publishing Group.
—Alice in Bed. 1996. 240p. pap. 12.95 o.s.i (0-452-27675-6, Plume) Dutton/Plume.
—Rameau's Niece. 1994. 288p. pap. 14.00 o.s.i (0-452-27161-4, Plume) Dutton/Plume.
—Rameau's Niece. 1993. 256p. tchr. ed. 19.95 o.p. (0-395-65490-4) Houghton Mifflin Co.
Schorr, Mark. Red Diamond: Private Eye. 1983. 256p. 12.95 o.p. (0-312-66645-4) St. Martin's Pr.
—Red Diamond, Private Eye. 1987. pap. 3.95 o.p. (0-312-90657-9, St. Martin's Paperbacks) St. Martin's Pr.
Schreiner, Samuel A., Jr. The Possessors & the Possessed. 1980. 12.95 o.p. (0-87795-229-9, Morrow, William & Co.) Morrow/Avon.
—Van Alews: First Family of a Nation's First City. 1981. 448p. 13.95 o.p. (0-87795-311-2, Morrow, William & Co.) Morrow/Avon.
Schulman, Sarah. After Delores. 1989. 160p. pap. 10.95 o.p. (0-452-26228-3, Plume); 1988. 176p. 16.95 o.p. (0-525-24641-X, Dutton) Dutton/Plume.
—Empathy. 192p. 1993. pap. 10.00 o.p. (0-452-27049-9, Plume); 1992. 18.00 o.p. (0-525-93521-5, Dutton) Dutton/Plume.
—Rat Bohemia. 240p. 1996. pap. 10.95 o.p. (0-452-27182-7, Plume); 1995. 19.95 o.p. (0-525-93790-0, Dutton) Dutton/Plume.
Scoppettone, Sandra. Everything You Have Is Mine. 1991. 261p. 19.95 o.p. (0-316-77646-7) Little Brown & Co.
—Gonna Take a Homicidal Journey: A Lauren Laurano Mystery. 1999. (Lauren Laurano Mystery Ser.). 288p. mass mkt. 6.99 (0-345-43118-9) Ballantine Bks.
—Gonna Take a Homicidal Journey: A Lauren Laurano Mystery. 1998. 240p. (gr. 8). 22.95 o.p. (0-316-77665-3) Little Brown & Co.
Scott, Darieck. Traitor to the Race. 1995. 224p. 20.95 o.p. (0-525-93912-1) Dutton/Plume.
Scott, Joanna. The Manikin: A Novel. 288p. 1998. pap. 12.00 o.s.i (0-8050-5591-6, Owl Bks.); 1996. 22.50 o.s.i (0-8050-3974-0) Holt, Henry & Co.
—The Manikin: A Novel. 2002. 288p. pap. 13.00 (0-312-42138-9) Picador.
Scott, Justin. Treasure Island. 1994. 240p. 19.95 o.p. (0-312-11368-4) St. Martin's Pr.
Scribner, Keith. Miracle Girl. 2004. 304p. pap. 14.00 (1-59448-013-3, Riverhead Trade (Paperbacks)) Berkley Publishing Group.
—Miracle Girl. 2003. 272p. 23.95 (1-57322-250-X, Riverhead Bks. (Hardcovers)) Putnam Publishing Group, The.
Segal, Susan. Aria: Novel. 2001. 23.95 (1-882593-45-6) Bridge Works Publishing Co., Inc.
Senator, Mel. Catskill Summers. 2000. 224p. E-Book 8.00 (0-7388-9360-9) Xlibris Corp.
Sepia, Riva. The Queens of New York City. 2000. 124p. pap. 9.95 (0-595-00154-8, Writers Club Pr.) iUniverse, Inc.
Seton, Anya. Dragonwyck. 1977. mass mkt. 1.95 o.s.i (0-449-23341-3, Fawcett) Ballantine Bks.
—Dragonwyck. 1994. lib. bdg. 37.95 (1-56849-484-X) Buccaneer Bks., Inc.
—Dragonwyck. 1968. 9.95 o.p. (0-395-08175-0) Houghton Mifflin Co.
—Dragonwyck. l.t. ed. 1973. (Ulverscroft Large Print Ser.). 12.00 o.p. (0-85456-171-4, Ulverscroft) Thorpe, F. A. Pubs. GBR. *Dist:* Ulverscroft Large Print Bks., Ltd., Ulverscroft Large Print Canada, Ltd.
Shaffer, Louise. All My Suspects: A Daytime Crime Mystery. 1995. 224p. mass mkt. 4.99 o.s.i (0-425-14770-3, Prime Crime) Berkley Publishing Group.
—All My Suspects: A Daytime Crime Mystery. 1994. 224p. 19.95 o.p. (0-399-13965-6, G. P. Putnam's Sons) Penguin Group (USA) Inc.
—Talked to Death. 1996. mass mkt. 5.99 o.s.i (0-425-15407-6) Berkley Publishing Group.
—Talked to Death. 1995. 256p. 22.95 o.p. (0-399-14095-6, G. P. Putnam's Sons) Penguin Group (USA) Inc.
Shange, Ntozake. Liliane: Resurrection of the Daughter. 1995. 304p. pap. 12.00 (0-312-13559-9) Picador.
—Liliane: Resurrection of the Daughter. 1994. 224p. 18.95 o.p. (0-312-11310-2) St. Martin's Pr.
Shapiro, Anna. Life & Love, Such As They Are. 1994. 240p. 21.00 (0-671-87114-5, Simon & Schuster) Simon & Schuster.
Sharp, Paula. I Loved You All. 2000. 370p. 23.95 (0-7868-6266-1) Hyperion Pr.
Shayne, Magie. The Gingerbread Man. 2001. 336p. mass mkt. 6.99 (0-515-13167-9, Jove) Berkley Publishing Group.
Sheckley, Robert. Draconian New York. 224p. 1997. pap. 12.95 (0-312-86359-4); 1996. 20.95 o.p. (0-312-85130-8) Doherty, Tom Assocs., LLC. (Forge Bks.).
Sheffer, Roger. Lost River. 1988. (Illus.). 144p. (Orig.). pap. 14.95 (0-935939-02-4) Night Tree Pr.
Sheldon, Sidney. Rage of Angels. 1980. 504p. 18.95 (0-688-03687-2, Morrow, William & Co.) Morrow/Avon.
Sherburne, James. Death's Pale Horse, 001. 1980. 8.95 o.p. (0-395-29087-2) Houghton Mifflin Co.
Shimada, Masahiko. Dream Messenger. Luke, Elmer, ed. Gabriel, Philip, tr. from JPN. 1992. 304p. 22.00 (4-7700-1535-6) Kodansha America, Inc.
—Dream Messenger. 1994. pap. (0-446-60062-8); 293p. pap. 10.99 o.s.i (0-446-67010-3) Warner Bks., Inc.
Shimko, Bonnie. Letters in the Attic. 2002. 227p. 23.50 (0-89733-511-2) Academy Chicago Pubs., Ltd.
Shriver, Lionel. We Need to Talk about Kevin: A Novel. 416p. 2004. pap. 14.95 (1-58243-268-6); 2003. text 25.00 (1-58243-267-8) Basic Bks. (Counterpoint Pr.).
—We Need to Talk about Kevin: A Novel. 2004. 416p. pap. 13.95 (0-06-072448-X, Perennial) HarperTrade.
Shulman, Irving. West Side Story: A Novelization. novel ed. 17.95 (0-8488-0847-9) Amereon, Ltd.
—West Side Story: A Novelization. novel ed. 1967. (Kangaroo Bks.). 12.04 (0-606-01566-3) Turtleback Bks.
Siegel, James. Derailed: A Novel. l.t. ed. 2003. 31.95 (1-58724-405-5, Wheeler Publishing, Inc.) Gale Group.
—Derailed: A Novel. 2004. pap. (0-446-69165-8) Mysterious Pr.
—Derailed: A Novel. 2003. E-Book 15.95 (0-7595-4747-5) Time Warner Bk. Group.
—Derailed: A Novel. 2003. 352p. 23.95 (0-446-53158-8) Warner Bks., Inc.
Silber, Joan. In My Other Life: Stories. 2000. 223p. 21.95 (1-889330-42-6) Sarabande Bks., Inc.
—In the City. 1987. 256p. 16.95 o.p. (0-670-81479-2) Viking Penguin.
Sinclair, Alison. Legacies. 1996. 448p. mass mkt. 5.50 o.s.i (0-06-105699-5, Eos) Morrow/Avon.
Singer, Isaac Bashevis. Meshugah. Singer, Isaac Bashevis & Wachtel, Nili, trs. 1995. 240p. pap. 12.95 o.s.i (0-452-27384-6, Plume) Dutton/Plume.
—Meshugah. 2003. pap. 20.00 (0-374-52909-4) Farrar, Straus & Giroux.
—Meshugah. Singer, Isaac Bashevis & Wachtel, Nili, trs. 1994. (ENG & YID.). 240p. 22.00 o.p. (0-374-20847-6) Farrar, Straus & Giroux.
—Meshugah. 1999. 240p. pap. (0-14-018877-0) Penguin Group (USA) Inc.
Singer, Katie. The Wholeness of a Broken Heart. 1999. 336p. 24.95 o.p. (1-57322-147-3, Riverhead Bks. (Hardcovers)) Putnam Publishing Group, The.
Skloot, Floyd. Open Door. 2004. 230p. pap. text 14.95 (1-885266-48-0) Story Line Pr.
Sloan, Bob. Bliss. 1996. 192p. 21.00 (0-684-82250-4, Scribner) Simon & Schuster.
—Bliss Jumps the Gun: A Lenny Bliss Mystery. (Lenny Bliss Mysteries Ser.). 2000. 288p. pap. 7.95 (0-393-32114-2, Norton Paperbacks); 1999. 224p. text 22.95 o.p. (0-393-04750-4) Norton, W. W. & Co., Inc.
Sloan, Susan R. Guilt by Association. 1995. 512p. 22.95 o.s.i (0-446-51857-3); 1996. 544p. reprint ed. mass mkt. 7.99 (0-446-60306-6) Warner Bks., Inc.
Slouka, Mark. Lost Lake: Stories. 2002. 192p. reprint ed. pap. 13.00 (0-375-70208-3, Vintage) Knopf Publishing Group.
—Lost Lake: Stories. 1998. 192p. 21.00 o.s.i (0-375-40215-2) Random Hse., Inc.
Slyke, L. V. Murder on the Rocks. 1995. 256p. (Orig.). mass mkt. 4.99 (0-380-76798-8, Avon Bks.) Morrow/Avon.
—Murder with a Twist. 1994. 256p. (Orig.). mass mkt. 4.99 (0-380-76797-X, Avon Bks.) Morrow/Avon.
Smiley, Jane. Duplicate Keys. 1993. 320p. pap. 13.95 (0-449-90879-8, Fawcett) Ballantine Bks.
—Duplicate Keys. 1985. mass mkt. 3.95 o.s.i (0-671-55172-8, Pocket) Simon & Schuster.
Smith, Betty. Maggie-Now. l.t. ed. 1982. 18.95 o.p. (0-8161-3303-4, Macmillan Reference USA) Gale Group.
—Maggie-Now. 1966. pap. 2.25 o.p. (0-06-080098-4, P98, Perennial) HarperTrade.
Smith, Dinitia. The Illusionist: A Novel. 256p. 1999. pap. 12.00 (0-684-84819-8); 1997. 22.00 o.s.i (0-684-84329-3) Simon & Schuster. (Scribner).
Smith, Evelyn E. Miss Melville Rides a Tiger. 1991. 18.95 o.p. (1-55611-219-X) Fine, Donald I. Bks.
—Miss Melville Rides a Tiger. l.t. ed. 1993. (General Ser.). 334p. 20.95 o.p. (0-8161-5559-3, Macmillan Reference USA) Gale Group.
—Miss Melville's Revenge. 1989. 288p. 17.95 o.p. (1-55611-076-6) Fine, Donald I. Bks.
Smith, J. C. Nightcap: A Quentin Jacoby Mystery. 1984. 192p. 13.95 o.s.i (0-689-11411-7, Scribner) Simon & Schuster.
Smith, Mitchell. Karma. 1994. 352p. 22.95 o.p. (0-525-93773-0) Dutton/Plume.
Smith, Peter Moore. Raveling: A Novel. abr. ed. 2000. audio 24.98 (1-57042-910-3) Time Warner AudioBooks.
—Raveling: A Novel of Suspense. 2000. 400p. 23.95 o.p. (0-316-44217-8) Little Brown & Co.
Smith, Rosamond, pseud. Starr Bright Will Be With You Soon. 2000. 272p. pap. 12.95 o.s.i (0-452-28035-4, Plume); 1999. 304p. 23.95 o.p. (0-525-94452-4, Dutton) Dutton/Plume.
Soehnlein, K. M. The World of Normal Boys. 2000. 256p. 22.00 o.s.i (1-57566-595-6) Kensington Publishing Corp.
Solomita, Stephen. A Good Day to Die. l.t. ed. 1994. 420p. pap. 18.95 (0-8161-5976-9, Macmillan Reference USA) Gale Group.
—A Good Day to Die. 1993. 300p. 21.00 o.p. (1-883402-03-4, Scribner) Simon & Schuster.
Sommer, Scott. Still Lives. 1989. 304p. 18.95 o.p. (0-670-82581-6) Viking Penguin.

For book reviews, descriptive annotations, tables of contents, cover images, author biographies & additional information, updated daily, subscribe to **www.booksinprint.com** 1027

Soos, Troy. Murder at Ebbets Field. 1996. mass mkt. 4.99 o.s.i (*1-57566-027-X*); 1995. 240p. mass mkt. 16.95 o.s.i (*0-8217-4889-0*) Kensington Publishing Corp.

Sorrentino, Christopher. Sound on Sound. 1995. 200p. 19.95 (*1-56478-073-2*) Dalkey Archive Pr.

Soto, Pedro Juan. Spiks. Ortiz, Victoria, tr. from SPA. & intro. by. 1974. 96p. 22.00 o.p. (*0-85345-299-7*, CL-2997); pap. 10.00 (*0-85345-331-4*, PB3314) Monthly Review Pr.

Spencer-Fleming, Julia. In the Bleak Midwinter. E-Book 17.95 (*0-312-70446-1*); 2003. 384p. mass mkt. 6.99 (*0-312-98676-9*, St. Martin's Paperbacks); 2002. 272p. 23.95 (*0-312-28847-6*, Saint Martin's Minotaur) St. Martin's Pr.

Spencer, Scott. A Ship Made of Paper: A Novel. l.t. ed. 2003. 550p. 30.95 (*1-58724-488-8*, Wheeler Publishing, Inc.) Gale Group.

—A Ship Made of Paper: A Novel. 368p. 2004. pap. 13.95 (*0-06-093342-9*); 2003. 25.95 (*0-06-018534-1*) HarperTrade. (Ecco).

Spiegelman, Katia. Peculiar Politics: A Romantic Comedy. 1993. 240p. 21.95 o.p. (*0-7145-2952-4*) Boyars, Marion Pubs., Inc.

Spillane, Mickey. Body Lovers. l.t. ed. 1999. (Mike Hammer Ser.). 248p. pap. 24.95 (*0-7838-8540-7*) Thorndike Pr.

—The Mike Hammer Collection, 2 vols. 2001. 448p. pap. 15.00 (*0-451-20352-6*) NAL.

—Survival— Zero! l.t. ed. 1999. (Mike Hammer Ser.). 264p. (*0-7540-3955-2*, Macmillan Reference USA) Gale Group.

—Survival-Zero. 1971. (Mike Hammer Ser.). 160p. mass mkt. 4.50 o.p. (*0-451-13704-3*, Signet Bks.) NAL.

—Survival Zero! l.t. ed. 1999. (Mike Hammer Ser.). 264p. pap. 24.95 (*0-7838-8735-3*) Wiley, John & Sons, Inc.

Sprague, Gretchen. Death in Good Company. 1997. 224p. 21.95 o.p. (*0-312-16813-6*, Saint Martin's Minotaur) St. Martin's Pr.

—Death in Good Company. l.t. ed. 1998. (Basic Ser.). 335p. 28.95 (*0-7862-1345-0*) Thorndike Pr.

Staffel, Megan. The Notebook of Lost Things. 2001. 224p. reprint ed. pap. 13.00 (*1-56947-230-0*) Soho Pr., Inc.

—The Notebook of Lost Things: A Novel. 1999. 240p. 23.00 (*1-56947-160-6*) Soho Pr., Inc.

Stark, Richard. Backflash. 1998. 292p. 20.00 o.p. (*0-89296-662-9*) Mysterious Pr.

—Backflash. 1999. 304p. pap. 12.95 (*0-446-67526-1*) Warner Bks., Inc.

Steel, Danielle. Irresistible Forces. 2000. 384p. mass mkt. 7.99 (*0-440-22486-1*); 2000. 18.87 (*0-385-33461-3*, Delacorte Pr.); 1999. 384p. 26.95 (*0-385-31960-6*, Delacorte Pr.); 1999. 384p. 200.00 (*0-385-33476-1*, Delacorte Pr.) Dell Publishing.

—Irresistible Forces, Set. abr. ed. 1999. audio 26.95 Highsmith Inc.

—Irresistible Forces. abr. ed. 1999. audio 26.95 (*0-553-47935-0*); audio compact disk 29.95 (*0-553-45574-5*); audio 39.95 (*0-553-50215-8*) Random Hse. Audio Publishing Group. (RH Audio).

—Irresistible Forces. l.t. ed. 528p. 2000. pap. 13.95 (*0-375-70787-5*); 1999. 26.95 (*0-375-40863-0*) Random Hse. Large Print.

—Lightning. 1996. 464p. pap. 7.99 (*0-440-22150-1*); 1995. 408p. 24.95 (*0-385-31192-3*, Delacorte Pr.); 1995. 408p. 200.00 (*0-385-31488-4*, Delacorte Pr.) Dell Publishing.

—Lightning. 1996. mass mkt. 8.99 o.s.i (*0-440-22292-3*) Doubleday Publishing.

—Lightning. 1995. audio 24.98 o.s.i (*0-553-74681-2*); audio 24.95 (*0-553-47364-6*, 692955) Random Hse. Audio Publishing Group. (RH Audio).

—Mirror Image. 1999. 560p. mass mkt. 7.99 (*0-440-22477-2*); 1998. 432p. 200.00 (*0-385-33343-9*, Delacorte Pr.); 1998. 752p. 31.95 o.s.i (*0-385-33331-5*, Delacorte Pr.) Dell Publishing.

—Mirror Image. l.t. ed. 1998. 432p. 26.95 (*0-385-31509-0*) Doubleday Publishing.

—Mirror Image. unabr. ed. 1999. audio 39.95 Highsmith Inc.

—Mirror Image. abr. ed. 1998. audio 26.95 (*0-553-47932-6*, 693758); audio compact disk 29.95 (*0-553-45572-9*); audio 39.95 (*0-553-50221-2*, 113706) Random Hse. Audio Publishing Group. (RH Audio).

—Vanished. 1994. 400p. mass mkt. 7.50 (*0-440-21746-6*); 1993. 312p. 23.95 (*0-385-30603-2*, Delacorte Pr.) Dell Publishing.

—Vanished. ltd. ed. 1993. 312p. 200.00 o.s.i (*0-385-31046-3*) Doubleday Publishing.

—Vanished. 1993. audio 13.59 o.s.i (*0-553-70073-1*); audio 18.00 o.s.i (*0-553-47180-5*, 391848) Random Hse. Audio Publishing Group. (RH Audio).

—Vanished. 1993. 13.04 (*0-606-07130-X*) Turtleback Bks.

Stein, Eugene. Straitjacket & Tie. 1996. 278p. reprint ed. pap. text 9.95 o.p. (*1-55583-358-6*) Alyson Pubns.

—Straitjacket & Tie. 1994. 277p. 19.95 o.p. (*0-395-67031-4*) World Pubns., Inc.

Stein, Triss. Digging up Death: A Kay Engles Mystery. 1999. (WWL Mystery Ser.: Bk. 310). per. (*0-373-26310-4*, 1-26310-2, Harlequin Bks.) Harlequin Enterprises, Ltd.

—Digging up Death: A Kay Engles Mystery. 1998. (Kay Engles Mystery Ser.). 204p. 22.95 (*0-8027-3319-0*) Walker & Co.

—Murder at the Class Reunion. 1995. 253p. per. (*0-373-26181-0*, 1-26181-7, Harlequin Bks.) Harlequin Enterprises, Ltd.

—Murder at the Class Reunion. 1993. 205p. 19.95 (*0-8027-3232-1*) Walker & Co.

Stephens, Michael. The Brooklyn Book of the Dead. 1994. 228p. 19.95 o.p. (*1-56478-037-6*) Dalkey Archive Pr.

Sterman, Betsy. Saratoga Secret. 1998. 176p. (YA). (gr. 5-9). 16.99 (*0-8037-2332-6*, Dial Bks. for Young Readers) Penguin Putnam Bks. for Young Readers.

Stern, Daniel. After the War. 1994. (First Rediscovered Modern Masterpieces Edition Ser.). 243p. (C). pap. 11.95 (*0-89263-332-8*); 22.50 (*0-89263-331-X*) Texas A&M Univ. Pr.

—Who Shall Live, Who Shall Die. 1994. 328p. pap. 11.95 (*0-89263-330-1*) Rice Univ. Pr.

—Who Shall Live, Who Shall Die. 1994. (First Rediscovered Modern Masterpieces Edition Ser.). 319p. 22.50 (*0-89263-329-8*) Texas A&M Univ. Pr.

Stevenson, Richard. Chain of Fools. 1996. 208p. 20.95 o.p. (*0-312-14563-2*, Saint Martin's Minotaur) St. Martin's Pr.

—Chain of Fools: A Donald Strachey Mystery. 1997. (Donald Strachey Mystery Ser.). 192p. pap. 11.95 (*0-312-16796-2*, Saint Martin's Griffin) St. Martin's Pr.

—Death Trick. 190p. reprint ed. 1983. pap. 6.95 o.p. (*0-932870-27-9*); 2nd ed. 1996. pap. 9.95 o.p. (*1-55583-387-X*) Alyson Pubns.

—Death Trick. 1981. 224p. 10.95 o.p. (*0-312-18876-5*) St. Martin's Pr.

—Ice Blues. 1987. 224p. mass mkt. 3.95 o.p. (*0-14-009403-2*, Penguin Bks.) Viking Penguin.

—Ice Blues: A Donald Strachey Mystery. 1995. 224p. pap. 8.95 (*0-312-13517-3*, Saint Martin's Griffin); 1986. 256p. 15.95 o.p. (*0-312-40379-8*) St. Martin's Pr.

—On the Other Hand, Death. 1995. 216p. 8.95 (*0-312-11871-6*, Saint Martin's Griffin) St. Martin's Pr.

—On the Other Hand, Death. 1985. (Crime Monthly Ser.). 224p. pap. 3.95 o.p. (*0-14-008319-7*, Penguin Bks.) Viking Penguin.

—On the Other Hand, Death: A Donald Strachey Mystery. 1984. 224p. 12.95 o.p. (*0-312-58458-X*) St. Martin's Pr.

—A Shock to the System: A Donald Strachey Mystery. 192p. 1996. pap. 9.95 (*0-312-14732-5*, Saint Martin's Griffin); 1995. 19.95 o.p. (*0-312-13610-2*, Saint Martin's Minotaur) St. Martin's Pr.

—Strachey's Folly. (Donald Strachey Mystery Ser.). 1999. 224p. pap. 11.95 (*0-312-24328-6*, Saint Martin's Griffin); 1998. 216p. 22.95 o.p. (*0-312-18669-X*, Saint Martin's Minotaur) St. Martin's Pr.

—Third Man Out: A Donald Strachey Mystery. pap. 15.95 (*0-312-30214-2*, Saint Martin's Griffin); 1993. pap. 8.95 (*0-312-08906-6*, Saint Martin's Griffin); 1992. 224p. 17.95 o.p. (*0-312-07110-8*, Saint Martin's Minotaur) St. Martin's Pr.

Stewart, Edward. Deadly Rich. 1992. 640p. mass mkt. 5.99 o.s.i (*0-440-21288-X*) Dell Publishing.

—Jury Double. 1996. 512p. mass mkt. 6.50 o.s.i (*0-440-22278-8*) Dell Publishing.

—Mortal Grace. 1995. 560p. mass mkt. 6.50 o.s.i (*0-440-21697-4*) Dell Publishing.

—Privileged Lives. 1989. 528p. mass mkt. 6.99 o.s.i (*0-440-20230-2*) Dell Publishing.

Stewart, Michael. Compulsion. 1994. 384p. 23.00 o.p. (*0-06-017767-5*) HarperTrade.

Stone, Jonathan. The Cold Truth. E-Book 23.95 (*0-312-26450-X*); 1999. 276p. 23.95 o.p. (*0-312-19942-2*); 2000. 352p. reprint ed. mass mkt. 6.50 (*0-312-97143-5*, St. Martin's Paperbacks) St. Martin's Pr.

—The Heat of Lies. E-Book 23.95 (*1-58945-578-9*) Adobe Systems, Inc.

—The Heat of Lies. 2001. 295p. pap. 23.95 o.p. (*0-312-20604-6*, Saint Martin's Minotaur); 320p. reprint ed. mass mkt. 6.99 (*0-312-97786-7*, St. Martin's Paperbacks) St. Martin's Pr.

Stout, David. The Dog Hermit. 1993. 320p. 18.95 o.p. (*0-89296-503-7*) Mysterious Pr.

—The Dog Hermit. 1995. 272p. mass mkt. 5.50 (*0-446-40406-3*, Mysterious Pr. Paperback Bks.) Warner Bks., Inc.

Stout, Rex. And Be a Villain. 1994. 256p. mass mkt. 5.99 (*0-553-23931-7*) Bantam Bks.

—And Four to Go. 1992. 240p. mass mkt. 5.99 (*0-553-24985-1*) Bantam Bks.

—And Four to Go. unabr. collector's ed. 1997. (Nero Wolfe Ser.). audio 42.00 (*0-7366-4059-2*, 4570) Books on Tape, Inc.

—And Four to Go. 1958. 2.95 o.p. (*0-670-12285-8*) Viking Penguin.

—Bad for Business. 1995. (Orig.). 240p. pap. 15.00 (*0-553-76302-4*); 176p. reprint ed. mass mkt. 4.99 (*0-553-25810-9*) Bantam Bks.

—Before Midnight. 1995. 224p. pap. 15.00 (*0-553-76304-0*); 1981. 160p. pap. 2.25 o.p. (*0-553-14797-8*) Bantam Bks.

—Before Midnight. unabr. collector's ed. 1995. (Nero Wolfe Ser.). audio 36.00 (*0-7366-3166-6*, 3836) Books on Tape, Inc.

—Before Midnight. l.t. ed. 1994. 267p. lib. bdg. 15.95 o.p. (*0-8161-5985-8*, Macmillan Reference USA) Gale Group.

—Before Midnight. 1955. 2.75 o.p. (*0-670-15525-X*) Viking Penguin.

—Bitter End: A Nero Wolfe Mystery. unabr. ed. 1997. audio 4.99 (*0-88646-941-4*, 7941) Durkin Hayes Publishing Ltd.

—The Black Mountain. unabr. ed. 2001. (Nero Wolfe Mystery Ser.). audio 29.95 (*1-57270-039-4*, N61039u, Audio Editions Bks. on Cassette) Audio Partners Publishing Corp.

—The Black Mountain. 1988. 224p. mass mkt. 3.50 o.s.i (*0-553-27291-8*) Bantam Bks.

—The Black Mountain. unabr. collector's ed. 1995. (Nero Wolfe Ser.). audio 42.00 (*0-7366-3167-4*, 3837) Books on Tape, Inc.

—The Black Mountain. 1954. 2.75 o.p. (*0-670-17258-8*) Viking Penguin.

—Black Orchids. 1992. 208p. mass mkt. 5.99 (*0-553-25719-6*) Bantam Bks.

—Black Orchids. unabr. collector's ed. 1994. (Nero Wolfe Ser.). audio 42.00 (*0-7366-2797-9*, 3512) Books on Tape, Inc.

—Black Orchids. abr. ed. 1996. (Paperback Audio Ser.). audio 9.99 (*0-88646-889-2*, 7889) Durkin Hayes Publishing Ltd.

—Black Orchids. 1982. (Reader's Request Ser.). lib. bdg. 13.95 o.p. (*0-8161-3289-5*, Macmillan Reference USA) Gale Group.

—The Broken Vase. 1995. (Mystery Ser.). 160p. (Orig.). mass mkt. 4.99 o.s.i (*0-553-25632-7*) Bantam Bks.

—The Broken Vase. 1976. (Orig.). pap. 1.25 o.s.i (*0-515-04065-7*, Jove) Berkley Publishing Group.

—The Broken Vase. l.t. ed. 1988. (Nightingale Ser.). 284p. (Orig.). pap. 11.95 o.p. (*0-8161-4392-7*, Macmillan Reference USA) Gale Group.

—Champagne for One: A Nero Wolfe Mystery. 1995. 224p. mass mkt. 5.99 (*0-553-24438-8*); 1980. 160p. pap. 1.95 o.p. (*0-553-13657-7*) Bantam Bks.

—Champagne for One: A Nero Wolfe Mystery. unabr. collector's ed. 1996. (Nero Wolfe Ser.). audio 36.00 (*0-7366-3345-6*, 3995) Books on Tape, Inc.

—Champagne for One: A Nero Wolfe Mystery. abr. ed. 1998. (Nero Wolfe Mysteries Ser.). audio 16.99 (*0-88646-456-0*, 7456) Durkin Hayes Publishing Ltd.

—Champagne for One: A Nero Wolfe Mystery. l.t. ed. 1987. (Nightingale Ser.). 302p. 11.95 o.p. (*0-8161-4282-3*, Macmillan Reference USA) Gale Group.

—The Cop-Killer: A Nero Wolfe Mystery. unabr. ed. 1994. audio 4.99 (*0-88646-705-5*) Durkin Hayes Publishing Ltd.

—Curtains for Three. 240p. 1995. pap. 15.00 (*0-553-76294-X*); 1994. mass mkt. 4.99 (*0-553-24498-1*) Bantam Bks.

—Curtains for Three. unabr. collector's ed. 1997. (Nero Wolfe Ser.). audio 42.00 (*0-7366-3747-8*, 4422) Books on Tape, Inc.

—Death of a Doxy. unabr. collector's ed. 1998. (Nero Wolfe Ser.). audio 36.00 (*0-7366-4044-4*, 4543) Books on Tape, Inc.

—Death of a Doxy. l.t. ed. 1996. (Nightingale Ser.). 208p. pap. 17.95 o.p. (*0-7838-1573-5*, Macmillan Reference USA) Gale Group.

—Death of a Doxy. 1966. 3.75 o.p. (*0-670-26126-2*) Viking Penguin.

—Death of a Dude: A Nero Wolfe Novel. 1990. 160p. pap. 3.95 o.s.i (*0-553-27422-8*); Vol. 1. 1994. (Death of a Dude Ser.: Vol. 1). 208p. mass mkt. 4.99 (*0-553-24730-1*) Bantam Bks.

—Death of a Dude: A Nero Wolfe Novel, Set. unabr. ed. 1994. audio 32.95 (*0-7861-0793-6*, 1533) Blackstone Audio Bks., Inc.

—Death of a Dude: A Nero Wolfe Novel. l.t. ed. 1999. (Mystery Ser.). 271p. 27.95 (*0-7862-1904-1*) Thorndike Pr.

—Death Times Three. 1995. 254p. pap. 15.00 (*0-553-76305-9*); 1994. 256p. mass mkt. 4.99 o.s.i (*0-553-27828-2*); 1991. mass mkt. 2.99 o.s.i (*0-553-19646-4*); 1985. 240p. mass mkt. 3.50 (*0-553-25425-1*) Bantam Bks.

—Death Times Three, Set. unabr. ed. 1995. audio 32.95 (*0-7861-0701-4*, 1578) Blackstone Audio Bks., Inc.

—The Doorbell Rang. 1992. 192p. mass mkt. 5.99 (*0-553-23721-7*) Bantam Bks.

—The Doorbell Rang. audio 19.95 (*0-7861-1394-4*); 1994. audio 23.95 (*0-7861-0775-8*, 1503) Blackstone Audio Bks., Inc.

—The Doorbell Rang. abr. ed. (Nero Wolfe Mystery Ser.). 2000. audio 19.99 (*0-88646-561-3*, DHA-6561); 1997. audio (*0-88646-443-9*, 7443) Durkin Hayes Publishing Ltd.

—The Doorbell Rang. l.t. ed. 1985. (Nightingale Ser.). 227p. 9.95 o.p. (*0-8161-3795-1*, Macmillan Reference USA) Gale Group.

—The Doorbell Rang. 2000. (Best Mysteries of All Time Ser.). 207p. (*0-7621-8857-X*) Reader's Digest Assn., Inc., The.

—The Doorbell Rang. 1968. 9.95 o.p. (*0-670-28021-6*, LT4); 1965. 3.50 o.p. (*0-670-27993-5*) Viking Penguin.

—Double for Death. 1995. (Orig.). 272p. pap. 19.00 (*0-553-76300-8*); 192p. mass mkt. 4.99 (*0-553-26059-6*) Bantam Bks.

—Eeny Meeny Murder Mo: A Nero Wolfe Mystery. abr. ed. 1999. (Nero Wolfe Ser.). audio 5.99 o.p. Brilliance Audio.

—Eeny Meeny Murder Mo: A Nero Wolfe Mystery. unabr. ed. 1999. audio 5.99 (*0-88646-992-9*, PAC-7992) Durkin Hayes Publishing Ltd.

—A Family Affair. 1993. 208p. mass mkt. 4.99 o.s.i (*0-553-24122-2*) Bantam Bks.

—A Family Affair. l.t. ed. 1978. lib. bdg. 9.95 o.p. (*0-8161-6561-0*, Macmillan Reference USA) Gale Group.

—A Family Affair. 1975. 152p. 9.95 o.p. (*0-670-30611-8*) Viking Penguin.

—The Father Hunt. 208p. 1995. pap. 15.00 (*0-553-76297-4*); Vol. 1. 1991. mass mkt. 3.95 (*0-553-24728-X*) Bantam Bks.

—The Father Hunt. 1983. (Nightingale Ser.). 240p. pap. 9.95 o.p. (*0-8161-3548-7*, Macmillan Reference USA) Gale Group.

—The Father Hunt. 1968. 4.50 o.p. (*0-670-30945-1*) Viking Penguin.

—Fer-de-Lance. Date not set. 304p. 23.95 (*0-8488-2403-2*) Amereon, Ltd.

—Fer-de-Lance. unabr. ed. 1997. (Nero Wolfe Mystery Ser.). audio 29.95 (*1-57270-035-1*, N61035u, Audio Editions Mystery Masters) Audio Partners Publishing Corp.

—Fer-de-Lance. 1997. 304p. mass mkt. 5.99 (*0-553-27819-3*); 1992. pap. 2.50 o.s.i (*0-553-23033-6*); 1984. mass mkt. 2.95 o.s.i (*0-553-24918-5*) Bantam Bks.

—Fer-de-Lance. unabr. collector's ed. 1994. (Nero Wolfe Ser.). audio 48.00 (*0-7366-2621-2*, 3361) Books on Tape, Inc.

—Fer-de-Lance. 1994. 320p. reprint ed. 35.00 (*1-883402-17-4*, Scribner) Simon & Schuster.

—The Final Deduction: A Nero Wolfe Novel. 1999. 261p. (*0-7540-3706-1*) BBC Audiobooks America.

—The Final Deduction: A Nero Wolfe Novel. 1992. 144p. mass mkt. 4.99 (*0-553-25254-2*) Bantam Bks.

—The Final Deduction: A Nero Wolfe Novel. unabr. collector's ed. 1996. (Nero Wolfe Ser.). audio 36.00 (*0-7366-3413-4*, 4059) Books on Tape, Inc.

—Five of a Kind: The Third Nero Wolfe Omnibus. 1980. (Short Story Index Reprint Ser.). reprint ed. 37.95 (*0-8369-4136-5*) Ayer Co. Pubs., Inc.

—Frame-up for Murder. unabr. ed. 1997. audio 4.99 (*0-88646-931-7*, 7931) Durkin Hayes Publishing Ltd.

—Gambit. 1985. 160p. mass mkt. 2.95 o.s.i (*0-553-25172-4*) Bantam Bks.

—Gambit. unabr. collector's ed. 1996. (Nero Wolfe Ser.). audio 36.00 (*0-7366-3415-0*, 4061) Books on Tape, Inc.

—Gambit. l.t. ed. 1997. (Nightingale Ser.). 18.95 o.p. (*0-7838-1571-9*, Macmillan Reference USA) Gale Group.

—Gambit. 1962. 3.50 o.p. (*0-670-33376-X*) Viking Penguin.

—The Golden Spiders. unabr. ed. 1997. (Nero Wolfe Mystery Ser.). audio 29.95 (*1-57270-038-6*, N61038u, Audio Editions Mystery Masters) Audio Partners Publishing Corp.

—The Golden Spiders. 1984. 160p. pap. 2.50 o.p. (*0-553-23995-3*) Bantam Bks.

—The Golden Spiders. unabr. collector's ed. 1995. (Nero Wolfe Ser.). audio 42.00 (*0-7366-3132-1*, 3807) Books on Tape, Inc.

—The Golden Spiders. l.t. ed. 1996. (Nightingale Ser.). pap. 17.95 (*0-7838-1572-7*, Macmillan Reference USA) Gale Group.

—The Golden Spiders. 1953. 2.50 o.p. (*0-670-34452-4*) Viking Penguin.

—The Great Legend. 1997. 288p. mass mkt. 4.95 (*0-7867-0443-8*, Carroll & Graf Pubs.) Avalon Publishing Group.

—The Hand in the Glove. 1992. 256p. mass mkt. 4.99 o.s.i (*0-553-22857-9*) Bantam Bks.

—Hand in the Glove. l.t. ed. 1986. (Nightingale Ser.). 384p. 10.95 o.p. (*0-8161-3964-4*, Macmillan Reference USA) Gale Group.

—Her Forbidden Knight. 256p. 2000. mass mkt. 5.95 (*0-7867-0729-1*); 1997. mass mkt. 4.95 o.p. (*0-7867-0444-6*) Avalon Publishing Group. (Carroll & Graf Pubs.).

—Her Forbidden Knight. 1998. 256p. 24.00 o.p. (0-7278-5369-4) Severn Hse. Pubs., Ltd.
—Homicide Trinity. 1993. 224p. mass mkt. 5.99 (0-553-23446-3) Bantam Bks.
—Homicide Trinity. unabr. collector's ed. 1999. (Nero Wolfe Ser.). audio 64.00 (0-7366-4062-2, 4573) Books on Tape, Inc.
—Homicide Trinity. 1962. 2.95 o.p. (0-670-37758-9) Viking Penguin.
—If Death Ever Slept. unabr. collector's ed. 1996. (Nero Wolfe Ser.). audio 42.00 (0-7366-3323-5, 3975) Books on Tape, Inc.
—In the Best of Families. 1995. 272p. mass mkt. 5.99 (0-553-27776-6); 1980. pap. 2.50 o.p. (0-553-24375-6) Bantam Bks.
—In the Best of Families. l.t. ed. 1991. (Nightingale Series Large Print Bks.). 322p. pap. 13.95 o.p. (0-8161-5203-9, Macmillan Reference USA) Gale Group.
—Invitation to Murder. unabr. ed. 1996. (Paperback Audio Ser.). audio 9.99 (0-88646-883-3, 7883) Durkin Hayes Publishing Ltd.
—Justice Ends at Home & Other Stories. 1977. 8.95 o.p. (0-670-41105-1) Viking Penguin.
—The League of Frightened Men. unabr. ed. 1999. (Nero Wolfe Mystery Ser.). audio 29.95 (1-57270-037-8, N61037u) Audio Partners Publishing Corp.
—The League of Frightened Men. 320p. 1995. pap. 19.00 (0-553-76298-2); 1992. mass mkt. 4.99 (0-553-25933-4) Bantam Bks.
—The League of Frightened Men. 1979. 1.75 o.p. (0-515-05116-0, Jove) Berkley Publishing Group.
—The League of Frightened Men. unabr. collector's ed. 1994. (Nero Wolfe Ser.). audio 56.00 (0-7366-2631-X, 3370) Books on Tape, Inc.
—The League of Frightened Men. abr. ed. 1996. audio 16.99 (0-88646-418-8) Durkin Hayes Publishing Ltd.
—The League of Frightened Men. 1981. (Reader's Request Ser.). lib. bdg. 14.50 o.p. (0-8161-3225-9, Macmillan Reference USA) Gale Group.
—Might As Well Be Dead. 1980. 160p. pap. 1.95 o.p. (0-553-14447-2) Bantam Bks.
—Might as Well Be Dead. 1995. 224p. pap. 15.00 (0-553-76303-2) Bantam Bks.
—Might As Well Be Dead, Vol. 1. 1992. 224p. mass mkt. 4.99 (0-553-24729-8) Bantam Bks.
—Might As Well Be Dead. unabr. collector's ed. 1996. (Nero Wolfe Ser.). audio 42.00 (0-7366-3225-5, 3886) Books on Tape, Inc.
—Might As Well Be Dead. l.t. ed. 1997. (Nightingale Ser.). 262p. lib. bdg. 18.95 (0-7838-1570-0) Thorndike Pr.
—More Deaths Than One: A Nero Wolfe Mystery. l.t. ed. 1993. (Nightingale Ser.). 304p. reprint ed. pap. 16.95 o.p. (0-8161-5757-X, Macmillan Reference USA) Gale Group.
—The Mother Hunt. 1993. 224p. mass mkt. 5.99 (0-553-24737-9) Bantam Bks.
—The Mother Hunt. unabr. collector's ed. 1996. (Nero Wolfe Ser.). audio 36.00 (0-7366-3523-8, 4160) Books on Tape, Inc.
—The Mother Hunt. 1963. 3.50 o.p. (0-670-49015-6) Viking Penguin.
—The Mountain Cat Murders. 1993. 272p. mass mkt. 4.99 o.s.i (0-553-25879-6); 1982. 176p. pap. 2.50 o.p. (0-553-20826-8) Bantam Bks.
—Murder by the Book. 1995. 256p. pap. 19.00 (0-553-76311-3); 1985. mass mkt. 2.95 o.s.i (0-553-24884-7) Bantam Bks.
—Murder by the Book. unabr. collector's ed. 1995. (Nero Wolfe Ser.). audio 48.00 (0-7366-3103-8, 3779) Books on Tape, Inc.
—Murder by the Book. l.t. ed. 1996. 301p. 21.95 o.p. (0-7838-1568-9, Macmillan Reference USA) Gale Group.
—Murder by the Book. 1951. 2.50 o.p. (0-670-49547-6) Viking Penguin.
—Nero Wolfe: And Be a Villain. l.t. ed. 1988. 19.95 o.p. (1-55504-643-6); pap. 17.95 o.p. (1-55504-644-4) BBC Audiobooks America.
—Nero Wolfe Omnibus. lib. bdg. 26.95 (0-8488-1893-8) Amereon, Ltd.
—Not Quite Dead Enough. 1992. 208p. mass mkt. 5.99 (0-553-26109-6) Bantam Bks.
—Not Quite Dead Enough. unabr. collector's ed. 1994. (Nero Wolfe Ser.). audio 36.00 (0-7366-2828-2, 3536) Books on Tape, Inc.
—Not Quite Dead Enough. 1994. reprint ed. lib. bdg. 27.95 (1-56849-341-X) Buccaneer Bks., Inc.
—Not Quite Dead Enough. unabr. ed. 1994. audio 4.99 (0-88646-727-6) Durkin Hayes Publishing Ltd.
—An Officer & a Lady & Other Stories. 2000. 192p. mass mkt. 5.95 (0-7867-0764-X, Carroll & Graf Pubs.) Avalon Publishing Group.
—Over My Dead Body. 20.95 (0-89190-341-0) Amereon, Ltd.
—Over My Dead Body. unabr. ed. 2001. (Nero Wolfe Mystery Ser.). audio 29.95 (1-57270-062-9, N61062u, Audio Editions Bks. on Cassette) Audio Partners Publishing Corp.
—Over My Dead Body. 1993. (Crime Line Ser.). 272p. mass mkt. 5.99 (0-553-23116-2) Bantam Bks.
—Over My Dead Body. unabr. collector's ed. 1994. (Nero Wolfe Ser.). audio 48.00 (0-7366-2747-2, 3472) Books on Tape, Inc.
—Over My Dead Body. l.t. ed. 1982. lib. bdg. 13.95 o.p. (0-8161-3288-7, Macmillan Reference USA) Gale Group.
—Please Pass the Guilt. 1995. 176p. pap. 15.00 (0-553-76308-3); 1993. 192p. mass mkt. 4.99 (0-553-23854-X) Bantam Bks.
—Please Pass the Guilt. unabr. collector's ed. 1999. (Nero Wolfe Ser.). audio 32.00 (0-7366-4456-3, 4901) Books on Tape, Inc.
—Please Pass the Guilt. 1979. pap. 10.95 o.p. (0-8161-6737-0, Macmillan Reference USA) Gale Group.
—Plot It Yourself. unabr. ed. 2002. audio 24.95 (1-57270-301-6) Audio Partners Publishing Corp.
—Plot It Yourself. 1989. pap. 3.50 o.s.i (0-553-27849-5); 1985. 176p. mass mkt. 4.99 o.s.i (0-553-25363-8) Bantam Bks.
—Plot It Yourself. unabr. collector's ed. 1996. (Nero Wolfe Ser.). audio 36.00 (0-7366-3354-5, 4005) Books on Tape, Inc.
—Plot It Yourself. l.t. ed. 1984. (Nightingale Ser.). 248p. 8.95 o.p. (0-8161-3547-9, Macmillan Reference USA) Gale Group.
—Plot It Yourself. 1959. 2.95 o.p. (0-670-56144-4) Viking Penguin.
—The President Vanishes. 1982. 272p. pap. 2.50 o.p. (0-553-22665-7) Bantam Bks.
—Prisoner's Base. unabr. ed. 2001. (Nero Wolfe Mystery Ser.). audio 29.95 (1-57270-191-9, N61191u, Audio Editions Mystery Masters) Audio Partners Publishing Corp.
—Prisoner's Base. 1992. 224p. mass mkt. 5.99 (0-553-24269-5) Bantam Bks.
—Prisoner's Base. unabr. collector's ed. 1995. (Nero Wolfe Ser.). audio 42.00 (0-7366-3137-2, 3812) Books on Tape, Inc.
—Prisoner's Base. 1952. 2.50 o.p. (0-670-57839-8) Viking Penguin.
—A Prize for Princes. 1994. 256p. mass mkt. 4.95 o.p. (0-7867-0104-8, Carroll & Graf Pubs.) Avalon Publishing Group.
—A Prize for Princes. 1999. 312p. 26.00 (0-7278-2277-2) Severn Hse. Pubs., Ltd.
—The Red Box. unabr. ed. 1997. audio 29.95 (1-57270-053-X, N61053u, Audio Editions Bks. on Cassette) Audio Partners Publishing Corp.
—The Red Box. 1992. (Crime Line Ser.). 272p. mass mkt. 4.99 o.s.i (0-553-24919-3) Bantam Bks.
—The Red Box. 1979. 1.75 o.s.i (0-515-05117-9, Jove) Berkley Publishing Group.
—The Red Box. unabr. collector's ed. 1994. (Nero Wolfe Ser.). audio 48.00 (0-7366-2697-2, 3431) Books on Tape, Inc.
—The Red Box. abr. ed. 1995. audio 16.99 (0-88646-377-7, LFP 7377) Durkin Hayes Publishing Ltd.
—The Red Box. 1981. (Reader's Request Ser.). lib. bdg. 13.50 o.p. (0-8161-3223-2, Macmillan Reference USA) Gale Group.
—Red Threads. 1995. 272p. pap. 19.00 (0-553-76299-0); mass mkt. 4.99 (0-553-22530-8, Crimeline) Bantam Bks.
—A Right to Die? 1991. 208p. mass mkt. 5.99 (0-553-24032-3) Bantam Bks.
—A Right to Die? l.t. ed. 1996. (G. K. Hall Mystery Ser.). 224p. lib. bdg. 21.95 o.p. (0-7838-1569-7, Macmillan Reference USA) Gale Group.
—A Right to Die. unabr. collector's ed. 1997. (Nero Wolfe Ser.). audio 36.00 (0-7366-3531-9, 4170) Books on Tape, Inc.
—Royal Flush. 1965. 3.95 o.p. (0-670-60934-X) Viking Penguin.
—The Rubber Band. unabr. ed. 1997. (Nero Wolfe Mystery Ser.). audio 29.95 (1-57270-052-1, N61052u, Audio Editions Mystery Masters) Audio Partners Publishing Corp.
—The Rubber Band. 1995. 208p. pap. 15.00 (0-553-76309-1); 1982. 192p. mass mkt. 2.95 (0-553-25550-9) Bantam Bks.
—The Rubber Band. 1979. 1.75 o.s.i (0-515-04867-4, Jove) Berkley Publishing Group.
—The Rubber Band. unabr. collector's ed. 1994. (Nero Wolfe Ser.). audio 48.00 (0-7366-2695-6, 3429) Books on Tape, Inc.
—The Rubber Band. 1981. (Reader's Request Ser.). lib. bdg. 12.95 o.p. (0-8161-3224-0, Macmillan Reference USA) Gale Group.
—The Second Confession. unabr. ed. 2000. (Nero Wolfe Mystery Ser.). audio 29.95 (1-57270-132-3, N61132u, Audio Editions Mystery Masters) Audio Partners Publishing Corp.
—The Second Confession. 1995. 256p. mass mkt. 5.99 (0-553-24594-5) Bantam Bks.
—The Second Confession. unabr. collector's ed. 1995. (Nero Wolfe Ser.). audio 48.00 (0-7366-3070-8, 3752) Books on Tape, Inc.
—The Second Confession. l.t. ed. 1992. (Nightingale Series Large Print Bks.). 311p. pap. 15.95 (0-8161-5202-0, Macmillan Reference USA) Gale Group.
—Some Buried Caeser. 1979. 1.75 o.s.i (0-515-05118-7, Jove) Berkley Publishing Group.
—The Sound of Murder. 1986. (Mystery Ser.). 192p. pap. 2.95 o.p. (0-553-26148-7) Bantam Bks.
—The Sound of Murder. 1979. 1.75 o.s.i (0-515-05281-7, Jove) Berkley Publishing Group.
—Target Practice. 1998. 320p. mass mkt. 5.95 (0-7867-0496-9, Carroll & Graf Pubs.) Avalon Publishing Group.
—Target Practice. l.t. ed. 1998. (Mystery Ser.). 424p. 28.95 (0-7838-0178-5) Thorndike Pr.
—This Won't Kill You. unabr. ed. 1998. audio 5.99 (0-88646-865-5, PAC-7865) Durkin Hayes Publishing Ltd.
—Three Aces. 1971. 8.95 o.p. (0-670-70622-1) Viking Penguin.
—Three at Wolfe's Door. 1995. 240p. mass mkt. 5.99 (0-553-23803-5, Crimeline) Bantam Bks.
—Three at Wolfe's Door. unabr. collector's ed. 1997. (Nero Wolfe Ser.). audio 48.00 (0-7366-4060-6, 4571) Books on Tape, Inc.
—Three for the Chair. 1985. 240p. mass mkt. 5.99 (0-553-24813-8) Bantam Bks.
—Three for the Chair. unabr. collector's ed. 1997. (Nero Wolfe Ser.). audio 42.00 (0-7366-3750-8, 4425) Books on Tape, Inc.
—Three for the Chair. 1957. 2.95 o.p. (0-670-70779-1) Viking Penguin.
—Three Men Out. 1991. 224p. mass mkt. 3.99 o.s.i (0-553-24547-3) Bantam Bks.
—Three Men Out. l.t. ed. 1990. (Nightingale Ser.). 296p. lib. bdg. 13.95 o.p. (0-8161-4793-0, Macmillan Reference USA) Gale Group.
—Three Men Out. 1954. 2.50 o.p. (0-670-70846-1) Viking Penguin.
—Three Trumps. 1973. 6.95 o.p. (0-670-71031-8) Viking Penguin.
—Three Witnesses. 1981. 224p. mass mkt. 5.99 (0-553-24959-2) Bantam Bks.
—Three Witnesses. unabr. collector's ed. 1997. (Nero Wolfe Ser.). audio 42.00 (0-7366-3751-6, 4426) Books on Tape, Inc.
—Three Witnesses. 1956. 2.75 o.p. (0-670-71080-6) Viking Penguin.
—Too Many Clients. 1955. 192p. mass mkt. 2.95 o.s.i (0-553-25423-5) Bantam Bks.
—Too Many Clients. unabr. collector's ed. 1996. (Nero Wolfe Ser.). audio 36.00 (0-7366-3400-2, 4047) Books on Tape, Inc.
—Too Many Clients. 1983. (Nightingale Ser.). 241p. pap. 9.95 o.p. (0-8161-3549-5, Macmillan Reference USA) Gale Group.
—Too Many Clients. 1960. 2.95 o.p. (0-670-72010-0) Viking Penguin.
—Too Many Cooks. 1995. 208p. pap. 15.00 (0-553-76306-7); 1988. 256p. mass mkt. 3.50 (0-553-27290-X) Bantam Bks.
—Too Many Cooks, Set. unabr. ed. 1995. 5p. audio 39.95 (0-7861-0660-3, 1561) Blackstone Audio Bks., Inc.
—Too Many Cooks. l.t. ed. 1985. (Nightingale Ser.). 397p. 10.95 o.p. (0-8161-3868-0, Macmillan Reference USA) Gale Group.
—Too Many Cooks. 1976. (Crime Fiction Ser.). reprint ed. lib. bdg. 21.00 o.p. (0-8240-2394-3) Garland Publishing, Inc.
—Too Many Women: A Nero Wolfe Mystery. unabr. ed. 1999. audio 29.95 (1-57270-104-8, N61104u, Audio Editions Mystery Masters) Audio Partners Publishing Corp.
—Too Many Women: A Nero Wolfe Mystery. l.t. ed. 1999. 355p. (0-7540-3882-3); pap. (0-7540-3883-1) BBC Audiobooks America.
—Too Many Women: A Nero Wolfe Mystery. unabr. collector's ed. 1995. (Nero Wolfe Ser.). audio 48.00 (0-7366-3045-7, 3727) Books on Tape, Inc.
—Too Many Women: A Nero Wolfe Mystery. l.t. ed. 1999. (Mystery Ser.). 355p. 26.95 o.p. (0-7862-2049-X) Thorndike Pr.
—Trio for Blunt Instruments. 1979. pap. 1.75 o.p. (0-553-13232-6) Bantam Bks.
—Trio for Blunt Instruments. unabr. collector's ed. 1997. (Nero Wolfe Ser.). audio 48.00 (0-7366-4061-4, 4572) Books on Tape, Inc.
—Triple Jeopardy. 1995. 192p. pap. 15.00 (0-553-76307-5); 1993. 256p. mass mkt. 4.99 (0-553-23591-5) Bantam Bks.
—Triple Jeopardy. 1952. 2.50 o.p. (0-670-73109-9) Viking Penguin.
—Trouble in Triplicate. unabr. collector's ed. 1996. (Nero Wolfe Ser.). audio 48.00 (0-7366-3268-9, 3925) Books on Tape, Inc.
—Trouble in Triplicate. 1949. 2.50 o.p. (0-670-73241-9) Viking Penguin.
—Under the Andes. 1994. 290p. mass mkt. 4.95 (0-7867-0179-X, Carroll & Graf Pubs.) Avalon Publishing Group.
—Under the Andes. unabr. ed. 1997. audio 49.95 (0-7861-1187-9, 1947) Blackstone Audio Bks., Inc.
—Under the Andes. E-Book 2.95 (1-57799-901-0) Logos Research Systems, Inc.
—Under the Andes. 1985. 15.95 o.p. (0-89296-119-8) Mysterious Pr.
—Under the Andes. 1986. 312p. reprint ed. mass mkt. 3.50 (0-445-40507-4, Mysterious Pr. Paperback Bks.) Warner Bks., Inc.
—Where There's a Will. unabr. ed. 1999. (Nero Wolfe Mystery Ser.). audio 29.95 (1-57270-096-3, N61096u, Audio Editions Mystery Masters) Audio Partners Publishing Corp.
—Where There's a Will. l.t. ed. (Nero Wolfe Mystery Ser.). 1992. pap. 20.95 o.p. (0-7927-1138-6, CS0304); 1991. 22.95 o.p. (0-7927-1137-8, CH0233) BBC Audiobooks America.
—Where There's a Will. 256p. 1995. pap. 15.00 (0-553-76301-6); 1992. mass mkt. 4.99 (0-553-29591-8) Bantam Bks.
—Where There's a Will. unabr. collector's ed. 1994. (Nero Wolfe Ser.). audio 42.00 (0-7366-2766-9, 3487) Books on Tape, Inc.
—Where There's a Will. 1982. (Reader's Request Ser.). 13.95 o.p. (0-8161-3287-9, Macmillan Reference USA) Gale Group.
—Where There's a Will. 1941. pap. 1.50 o.p. (0-380-01620-6, 39529, Avon Bks.) Morrow/Avon.
Stout, Rex, contrib. by. The Final Deduction: A Nero Wolfe Novel. (0-7540-3705-3) BBC Audiobooks America.
Stover, Laren. Pluto, Animal Lover. 1995. 176p. pap. 10.00 o.p. (0-06-092627-9, Perennial); 1994. 160p. 15.00 o.p. (0-06-017111-1) HarperTrade.
Stowe, Rebecca. The Shadow of Desire. 1997. (Illus.). 240p. pap. 12.00 o.p. (0-393-31658-0) Norton, W. W. & Co., Inc.
Strieber, Whitley. The Forbidden Zone. 1993. 320p. 21.00 o.p. (0-525-93683-1, Dutton) Dutton/Plume.
—The Night Church. 1983. 320p. 15.50 o.p. (0-671-46955-X, Simon & Schuster) Simon & Schuster.
Stryker, Dev. End Game. 1994. 320p. 22.95 o.p. (0-312-85195-2, Forge Bks.); Vol. 1. 1998. (End Game Ser.: Vol. 1). (Illus.). 344p. mass mkt. 5.99 o.p. (0-8125-1597-8, Tor Bks.) Doherty, Tom Assocs., LLC.
Stuart, Sebastian. The Mentor. 2000. 288p. mass mkt. 5.99 o.s.i (0-553-58031-0) Bantam Bks.
Styron, William. Sophie's Choice. l.t. ed. 1993. (General Ser.). 886p. lib. bdg. 23.95 o.p. (0-8161-5650-6, Macmillan Reference USA) Gale Group.
—Sophie's Choice. (Modern Library Ser.). 1998. 608p. 22.00 (0-679-60289-5); 1992. 576p. pap. 14.95 (0-679-73637-9) Random Hse., Inc.
Swados, Elizabeth. The Myth Man. 1994. 336p. 21.95 o.p. (0-670-84202-8, Viking) Viking Penguin.
Swados, Harvey. Nights in the Gardens of Brooklyn: The Collected Stories of Harvey Swados. 1977. (Short Story Index Reprint Ser.). 19.95 (0-8369-3642-6) Ayer Co. Pubs., Inc.
—Nights in the Gardens of Brooklyn: The Collected Stories of Harvey Swados. 2004. (New York Review Books Classics Ser.). 400p. pap. 14.95 (1-59017-084-9) New York Review of Bks., Inc., The.
Tamar, Erika. Good-Bye Glamour Girl. 1985. mass mkt. 2.50 o.p. (0-451-14019-2, Signet Vista) NAL.
Tanenbaum, Robert K. Corruption of Blood. 1995. 368p. 22.95 o.p. (0-525-93870-2, Dutton) Dutton/Plume.
—Corruption of Blood. 1996. 416p. mass mkt. 7.99 (0-451-18196-4, Signet Bks.) NAL.
—Depraved Indifference. 1989. 18.95 o.p. (0-453-00679-5) NAL.
—Falsely Accused. 1996. 320p. 23.95 o.s.i (0-525-94168-1) Dutton/Plume.
—Falsely Accused. 1997. 448p. mass mkt. 7.99 (0-451-19000-9, Signet Bks.) NAL.
—Immoral Certainty. 1991. 304p. 18.95 o.p. (0-525-24941-9, Dutton) Dutton/Plume.
—Irresistible Impulse. 1997. 352p. 24.95 o.p. (0-525-94310-2) Dutton/Plume.
—Justice Denied. 1994. 320p. 18.95 o.p. (0-525-93814-1) Dutton/Plume.
—Material Witness. 1993. 320p. 20.00 o.p. (0-525-93579-7, Dutton) Dutton/Plume.
—No Lesser Plea. 1987. 17.95 o.p. (0-531-09783-8, Watts, Franklin) Scholastic Library Publishing.
—Reversible Error. 1992. 288p. 20.00 o.p. (0-525-93423-5, Dutton) Dutton/Plume.
Tannen, Mary. Loving Edith. l.t. ed. 1995. 272p. lib. bdg. 24.95 (1-57490-026-9, Beeler Large Print Bks.) Beeler, Thomas T. Publisher.
—Loving Edith. 1996. 12.00 o.s.i (1-57322-544-4, Riverhead Trade (Paperbacks)) Berkley Publishing Group.
—Loving Edith. 1995. 275p. 22.95 o.p. (1-57322-008-6, Riverhead Bks. (Hardcovers)) Putnam Publishing Group, The.
Tanner, Janet. Folly's Child. 1992. 400p. 21.95 o.p. (0-312-06976-6) St. Martin's Pr.
Tax, Meredith. Union Square. 1988. 473p. 18.95 o.p. (0-688-05069-7, Morrow, William & Co.) Morrow/Avon.
Tax, Meredith, ed. Rivington Street: A Novel. 2002. 437p. pap. 18.95 (0-252-07032-1) Univ. of Illinois Pr.



 

Taylor, Phoebe Atwood. Murder at the New York World's Fair. 1987. 265p. reprint ed. pap. 8.95 o.p. (*0-88150-095-X*) Countryman Pr.

Thomas, Abigail. Herb's Pajamas. 1998. 210p. tchr. ed. 17.95 (*1-56512-189-9*, 72189) Algonquin Bks. of Chapel Hill.

Thomas, Rosanne D. The Angel Carver. 1995. 272p. pap. 16.99 o.p. (*0-446-67054-5*) Warner Bks., Inc.

Thompson, Victoria. Murder on St. Mark's Place. 2000. (Gaslight Mysteries Ser.). 288p. mass mkt. 6.99 (*0-425-17361-5*, Prime Crime) Berkley Publishing Group.

Thurman, Wallace. Infants of the Spring. 1992. (Library of Black Literature). 284p. pap. text 15.95 (*1-55553-128-8*) Northeastern Univ. Pr.

Tiffin, Patricia M. Watching Vanessa. unabr. ed. 1997. 320p. 22.00 (*1-880909-54-5*) Baskerville Pubs., Inc.

—Watching Vanessa. 2000. 340p. mass mkt. 6.99 (*0-312-97415-9*, St. Martin's Paperbacks) St. Martin's Pr.

Tippens, Elizabeth. Winging It: A Tale of Turning Thirty. 1996. 224p. 10.00 o.s.i (*1-57322-528-2*, Riverhead Trade (Paperbacks)) Berkley Publishing Group.

Toby-Potter, Ellen. The Average Human. 2003. 270p. 24.00 (*1-931561-33-8*) MacAdam/Cage Publishing, Inc.

Tosches, Nick. Cut Numbers. 2001. 240p. reprint ed. pap. 13.95 (*0-316-89658-6*, Back Bay) Little Brown & Co.

—Cut Numbers. 1990. 2.99 o.p. (*0-517-02903-0*) Random Hse. Value Publishing.

Trevor, Elleston. Flycatcher. 1994. 288p. 21.95 o.p. (*0-312-85647-4*, Forge Bks.) Doherty, Tom Assocs., LLC.

Trump, Ivana. For Love Alone. 1992. 22.00 o.p. (*0-671-74368-6*, Atria) Simon & Schuster.

Truscott, Lucian K., IV. Dress Gray. 1980. mass mkt. 2.75 o.p. (*0-449-24158-0*, Fawcett) Ballantine Bks.

—Dress Gray. 1979. 10.95 o.p. (*0-385-13475-4*) Doubleday Publishing.

—Dress Gray. 1997. 464p. mass mkt. 6.99 o.s.i (*0-451-19047-5*, Signet Bks.) NAL.

Truscott, Lucian K., Jr. Dress Gray. 1986. mass mkt. 3.95 o.s.i (*0-449-21163-0*, Fawcett) Ballantine Bks.

Truscott, Lucian K., IV. Full Dress Gray. abr. ed. 1998. audio 7.99 o.s.i (*1-56740-297-6*, 1801, Paperback Nova Audio Bks.); audio 26.95 (*1-56740-069-8*, 8, Bookcassette); audio 73.25 (*1-56740-598-3*, 848, Unabridged Library Editions);Set. audio 17.95 o.p. (*1-56740-794-3*, 441, Nova Audio Bks.) Brilliance Audio.

—Full Dress Gray, Pt. 2. 1998. (Full Dress Gray Ser.: Vol. 2). 320p. 25.00 (*0-688-15993-1*, Morrow, William & Co.) Morrow/Avon.

—Full Dress Gray. 1999. 464p. reprint ed. mass mkt. 6.99 o.s.i (*0-451-19933-2*) NAL.

Tucker, Kerry. Cold Feet: A Libby Kincaid Mystery. 1992. 208p. 19.00 o.p. (*0-06-016530-8*) HarperTrade.

—Cold Feet: A Libby Kincaid Mystery. 1993. 304p. mass mkt. 4.50 o.p. (*0-06-109985-6*, HarperTorch) Morrow/Avon.

—Death Echo: A Libby Kincaid Mystery. 1993. 224p. 19.00 o.p. (*0-06-017700-4*) HarperTrade.

—Death Echo: A Libby Kincaid Mystery. 1994. 288p. mass mkt. 4.50 o.p. (*0-06-109986-4*, HarperTorch) Morrow/Avon.

Turbek, Joan. The Little River & the Big, Big Bridge. 1993. 48p. (J). pap. 7.50 o.p. (*0-925168-18-1*) North Country Bks., Inc.

Tuten, Frederic. Tallien: A Brief Romance. 1994. 152p. pap. 13.95 o.p. (*0-7145-2990-7*) Boyars, Marion Pubs., Inc.

—Tallien: A Brief Romance. 1988. 230p. 17.95 o.p. (*0-374-27249-2*) Farrar, Straus & Giroux.

Tyre, Peg. In the Midnight Hour. 1996. 272p. mass mkt. 5.99 (*0-380-72811-7*, Avon Bks.) Morrow/Avon.

Upcher, Caroline. Boathouse. 2003. 352p. pap. 14.00 (*0-7582-0320-9*) Kensington Publishing Corp.

Urquhart, Jane. The Underpainter. 256p. 1998. 14.00 (*0-14-026973-8*); 1997. 22.95 o.s.i (*0-670-87726-3*) Viking Penguin.

Vachss, Andrew. Blossom. 2001. E-Book 11.50 (*1-59061-234-5*) Adobe Systems, Inc.

—Blossom. 1991. 320p. mass mkt. 5.95 o.s.i (*0-8041-0751-3*, Ivy Bks.) Ballantine Bks.

—Blossom. 1996. 272p. pap. 13.00 (*0-679-77261-8*) McKay, David Co., Inc.

—Blue Belle. 2001. E-Book 11.00 (*1-59061-228-0*) Adobe Systems, Inc.

—Blue Belle. 1994. lib. bdg. 24.95 o.p. (*1-56849-463-7*) Buccaneer Bks., Inc.

—Blue Belle. 1990. 336p. mass mkt. 4.95 o.p. (*0-451-16290-0*, Signet Bks.) NAL.

—Blue Belle. 1995. 352p. pap. 13.00 (*0-679-76168-3*) Random Hse., Inc.

—Choice of Evil: A Burke Novel. 2001. E-Book 11.50 (*1-59061-222-1*) Adobe Systems, Inc.

—Choice of Evil: A Burke Novel. 2000. (Crime - Black Lizard Ser.). 336p. pap. 13.00 (*0-375-70662-3*, Vintage) Knopf Publishing Group.

—Choice of Evil: A Burke Novel. 1999. (Burke Novels Ser.). 305p. 23.00 o.s.i (*0-375-40647-6*) Knopf, Alfred A. Inc.

—Choice of Evil: A Burke Novel. 2001. E-Book 7.99 (*0-375-71913-X*) Random Hse., Inc.

—Down Here: A Burke Novel. 2004. 304p. 19.95 (*1-4000-4173-2*, Knopf) Knopf Publishing Group.

—Down in the Zero. 2001. E-Book 11.00 (*1-59061-229-9*) Adobe Systems, Inc.

—Down in the Zero. 1995. pap. 7.00 o.s.i (*0-679-76087-3*); 272p. pap. 12.00 (*0-679-76066-0*) Random Hse., Inc.

—False Allegations: A Burke Novel. 2001. E-Book 11.00 (*1-59061-235-3*) Adobe Systems, Inc.

—False Allegations: A Burke Novel. 1997. 240p. pap. 12.00 (*0-679-77293-6*, Vintage) Knopf Publishing Group.

—False Allegations: A Burke Novel. 1996. 229p. 23.00 (*0-679-45109-9*) Knopf, Alfred A. Inc.

—Flood: A Burke Novel. 2002. E-Book 11.50 (*1-59061-886-6*) Adobe Systems, Inc.

—Flood: A Burke Novel. 1994. lib. bdg. 24.95 o.p. (*1-56849-465-3*) Buccaneer Bks., Inc.

—Flood: A Burke Novel. 1985. 341p. 17.95 o.s.i (*0-917657-43-8*) Fine, Donald I. Bks.

—Flood: A Burke Novel. 1986. mass mkt. 5.99 (*0-671-61905-5*, Pocket) Simon & Schuster.

—Footsteps of the Hawk. 2001. E-Book 11.00 (*1-59061-233-7*) Adobe Systems, Inc.

—Footsteps of the Hawk. 1996. 256p. pap. 12.00 (*0-679-76663-4*) Random Hse., Inc.

—Hard Candy. 2001. E-Book 11.00 (*1-59061-230-2*) Adobe Systems, Inc.

—Hard Candy. 1994. lib. bdg. 24.95 o.p. (*1-56849-464-5*) Buccaneer Bks., Inc.

—Hard Candy. 1990. mass mkt. 4.95 o.p. (*0-451-16690-6*, Signet Bks.) NAL.

—Hard Candy. 1990. 4.99 o.p. (*0-517-05629-1*) Random Hse. Value Publishing.

—Hard Candy. 1995. 256p. pap. 12.00 (*0-679-76169-1*) Random Hse., Inc.

—Sacrifice. 2001. E-Book 11.00 (*1-59061-231-0*) Adobe Systems, Inc.

—Sacrifice. 1992. mass mkt. 5.99 o.s.i (*0-8041-0919-2*, Ivy Bks.) Ballantine Bks.

—Sacrifice. 1992. 4.99 o.p. (*0-517-09513-0*) Random Hse. Value Publishing.

—Sacrifice. 1996. 288p. pap. 12.00 (*0-679-76410-0*) Random Hse., Inc.

—Safe House: A Burke Novel. 2001. E-Book 11.00 (*1-59061-225-6*) Adobe Systems, Inc.

—Safe House: A Burke Novel. 1999. 320p. pap. 12.00 (*0-375-70074-9*, Vintage) Knopf Publishing Group.

—Safe House: A Burke Novel. 2001. E-Book 7.99 (*0-375-71912-1*) Random Hse., Inc.

—Strega. 2001. E-Book 11.00 (*1-59061-232-9*) Adobe Systems, Inc.

—Strega. 1991. mass mkt. 5.99 o.s.i (*0-8041-0925-7*, Ivy Bks.) Ballantine Bks.

—Strega. 1987. 293p. 18.95 o.s.i (*0-394-55937-1*) Knopf, Alfred A. Inc.

—Strega. 1988. mass mkt. 4.50 o.p. (*0-451-15179-8*, Signet Bks.) NAL.

—Strega. 1988. 3.99 o.p. (*0-517-68183-8*) Random Hse. Value Publishing.

—Strega. 1996. 304p. pap. 12.00 (*0-679-76409-7*) Random Hse., Inc.

Valtorta, Laura. Family Meal. 1993. 127p. (Orig.). pap. 9.95 (*0-932112-33-1*) Carolina Wren Pr.

Van Dine, S. S. The Benson Murder Case. reprint ed. lib. bdg. 24.95 (*0-89190-511-1*, Rivercity Pr.) Amereon, Ltd.

—The Benson Murder Case. 1983. 256p. pap. 3.95 o.s.i (*0-684-17976-8*, Macmillan Reference USA) Gale Group.

—The Bishop Murder Case. reprint ed. lib. bdg. 25.95 (*0-89190-512-X*, Rivercity Pr.) Amereon, Ltd.

—The Bishop Murder Case. 1983. 256p. pap. 3.95 o.s.i (*0-684-17977-6*, Macmillan Reference USA) Gale Group.

—The Bishop Murder Case. l.t. ed. 1984. (Philo Vance Mystery Ser.). 453p. reprint ed. 14.95 o.p. (*0-89621-501-6*) Thorndike Pr.

—The Canary Murder Case. reprint ed. lib. bdg. 25.95 (*0-89190-513-8*, Rivercity Pr.) Amereon, Ltd.

—The Canary Murder Case. 1979. pap. 2.25 o.s.i (*0-684-16404-3*, Macmillan Reference USA) Gale Group.

—The Casino Murder Case. 1985. 312p. pap. 3.95 o.p. (*0-684-18503-2*, Macmillan Reference USA) Gale Group.

—The Dragon Murder Case: A Philo Vance Mystery. 1994. 336p. 35.00 (*1-883402-21-2*, Scribner) Simon & Schuster.

—Gracie Allen Murder Case: A Philo Vance Story. 21.95 (*0-8488-0850-9*) Amereon, Ltd.

—Gracie Allen Murder Case: A Philo Vance Story. 1994. 336p. reprint ed. pap. 6.95 (*1-883402-09-3*, Scribner) Simon & Schuster.

—The Greene Murder Case. 1980. pap. 2.95 o.s.i (*0-684-16734-4*, Scribner Paper Fiction) Simon & Schuster.

—The Kennel Murder Case: A Philo Vance Mystery. 1984. 312p. pap. 3.95 o.s.i (*0-684-18248-3*, Macmillan Reference USA) Gale Group.

—The Kidnap Murder Case: A Philo Vance Story. 1994. 320p. reprint ed. pap. 7.95 o.s.i (*1-883402-93-X*, Scribner) Simon & Schuster.

—The Scarab Murder Case. 1984. (Philo Vance Mystery Ser.). pap. 4.50 o.s.i (*0-684-18159-2*, Scribner Paper Fiction) Simon & Schuster.

—The Winter Murder Case: A Philo Vance Story. 1993. 196p. pap. 6.95 o.s.i (*1-883402-08-5*, Scribner) Simon & Schuster.

Van Dyke, Henry Jackson. Dead Piano. 1971. 182p. 5.95 o.p. (*0-374-13550-9*) Farrar, Straus & Giroux.

—Dead Piano. 1997. (Old School Bks.). 200p. pap. 10.00 (*0-393-31542-8*) Norton, W. W. & Co., Inc.

Van Lustbader, Eric. Black Blade. 1995. 558p. pap. 27.00 (*0-345-46684-5*, Fawcett) Ballantine Bks.

—Black Blade. abr. ed. 1993. 16.95 o.p. (*1-55800-643-5*) NewStar Media, Inc.

Van Valkenburgh, Norman J. Mayhem in the Catskills. 1994. 158p. 25.00 o.p. (*0-935796-60-6*); 2nd ed. pap. 12.50 (*0-935796-59-2*) Purple Mountain Pr., Ltd.

—Mischief in the Catskills: A Ward Eastman Mystery with Five Short Stories. 2001. 159p. pap. 12.50 (*0-935796-94-0*, 94) Purple Mountain Pr., Ltd.

Van Vechten, Carl. Parties. 1977. (Select Bibliographies Reprint Ser.). 25.95 (*0-8369-5758-X*) Ayer Co. Pubs., Inc.

Van Wormer, Laura. Jury Duty. 1996. 364p. 24.00 o.s.i (*0-517-70065-4*); 1995. o.s.i (*0-517-70674-1*) Crown Publishing Group.

—Jury Duty. 1996. 410p. mass mkt. (*1-55166-169-1*, 1-66169-3, Mira Bks.) Harlequin Enterprises, Ltd.

Vanderbilt, Gloria. The Memory Book of Starr Faithfull. 1994. 336p. 24.00 o.s.i (*0-394-58775-8*) Knopf, Alfred A. Inc.

Veltri, George. Nice Boy. 1995. 186p. pap. 9.95 (*0-87286-302-6*) City Lights Bks.

Victor, Barbara. Coriander. 1994. mass mkt. 5.99 o.s.i (*0-345-38454-7*) Ballantine Bks.

—Coriander. 1993. 22.00 o.p. (*1-55611-353-6*) Fine, Donald I. Bks.

—Coriander. l.t. ed. 1996. 24.95 o.p. (*1-56895-281-3*, Wheeler Publishing, Inc.) Gale Group.

—Misplaced Lives. 1990. 320p. 19.95 o.p. (*0-06-016373-9*) HarperTrade.

Victor, Cynthia. Only You. l.t. ed. 2000. 463p. 28.95 (*1-57490-322-5*, Beeler Large Print Bks.) Beeler, Thomas T. Publisher.

—Only You. 1995. 416p. mass mkt. 5.99 o.s.i (*0-451-40606-0*, Onyx) NAL.

—Only You. 1994. 416p. 19.95 o.p. (*0-670-84981-2*, Viking) Viking Penguin.

Vinton, John. A Treasury of Great Adirondack Stories. 1991. (Illus.). 155p. 35.00 o.s.i (*0-932052-34-7*); pap. 19.95 o.s.i (*0-932052-35-5*) North Country Bks., Inc.

Vogel, Joseph. Man's Courage. 1989. (New York Classics Ser.). 336p. reprint ed. pap. text 16.95 (*0-8156-0233-2*) Syracuse Univ. Pr.

Wachtel, Chuck. The Gates: A Novel. 1994. 416p. 23.95 o.p. (*0-670-83886-1*, Viking) Viking Penguin.

Wallace, Marilyn. Current Danger. 1999. 320p. mass mkt. 5.99 o.s.i (*0-553-58072-8*) Bantam Bks.

—Current Danger. l.t. ed. 1998. 317p. 24.95 (*1-57490-140-0*, Beeler Large Print Bks.) Beeler, Thomas T. Publisher.

Wallach, Anne T. Trials. 1996. 382p. 24.95 o.s.i (*0-525-94091-X*) Dutton/Plume.

—Trials. 1998. 416p. mass mkt. 6.99 o.s.i (*0-451-18741-5*, Signet Bks.) NAL.

Walsh, Michael. Exchange Alley. abr. ed. 1997. audio 19.00 o.p. Beeler, Thomas T. Publisher.

—Exchange Alley. abr. ed. 1997. audio 17.98 (*1-57042-529-9*, 390019) Time Warner AudioBooks.

—Exchange Alley. 1998. 480p. mass mkt. 6.99 (*0-446-60563-8*); 1997. 400p. 23.50 o.p. (*0-446-52069-1*) Warner Bks., Inc.

Walter, George W. Sinners & Saints: Stories of Upstate New York. 1983. 7.95 o.s.i (*0-932052-31-2*) North Country Bks., Inc.

Warhol, Andy. A: A Novel. 1998. o.p. (*0-8021-3538-2*, Grove Pr.) Grove/Atlantic, Inc.

Watson, Clarissa. The Bishop in the Back Seat. 1986. 256p. mass mkt. 2.95 o.s.i (*0-345-33084-6*) Ballantine Bks.

—The Bishop in the Back Seat. 1979. 9.95 o.p. (*0-689-11012-X*, Scribner) Simon & Schuster.

—The Fourth Stage of Gainsborough Brown. 1986. 224p. mass mkt. 2.95 o.s.i (*0-345-33531-7*) Ballantine Bks.

—The Fourth Stage of Gainsborough Brown. 1977. 7.95 o.p. (*0-679-50667-5*) McKay, David Co., Inc.

—The Fourth Stage of Gainsborough Brown. 1978. (Crime Ser.). pap. 1.95 o.p. (*0-14-004789-1*, Penguin Bks.) Viking Penguin.

—Last Plane from Nice. 1988. (Persis Willum Mystery Ser.). 224p. 16.95 o.s.i (*0-689-11835-X*, Scribner) Simon & Schuster.

—Runaway. l.t. ed. 1989. (Atlantic Mystery Ser.). pap. 14.95 o.p. (*1-55504-739-4*, 838) BBC Audiobooks America.

—Runaway. 1986. 208p. mass mkt. 2.95 o.s.i (*0-345-33114-1*) Ballantine Bks.

—Runaway. 1985. 250p. 12.95 o.p. (*0-689-11521-0*, Scribner) Simon & Schuster.

—Somebody Killed the Messenger. 1988. 224p. 16.95 o.s.i (*0-689-11963-1*, Scribner) Simon & Schuster.

Watson, Richard. Niagara. 1993. 192p. 19.95 (*1-56689-006-3*) Coffee Hse. Pr.

Weikart, James. Casualty Loss. 1991. 208p. 18.95 o.s.i (*0-8027-5790-1*) Walker & Co.

Weiss, Phillip. Cock-a-Doodle-Doo. 1995. 256p. 21.00 o.p. (*0-374-12515-5*) Farrar, Straus & Giroux.

—Cock-A-Doodle-Doo. 1996. 304p. pap. 12.95 o.p. (*0-312-14100-9*, Saint Martin's Griffin) St. Martin's Pr.

Welles, Edward R., 3rd, et al. The Forgotten Legend of Sleepy Hollow. 1984. pap. 4.00 (*0-913692-12-3*) Learning, Inc.

Wersba, Barbara. Beautiful Losers. 1988. (Charlotte Zolotow Bk.). 192p. (YA). (gr. 7 up). 11.95 (*0-06-026363-6*) HarperCollins Children's Bk. Group.

West, Nathanael. Miss Lonelyhearts & the Day of the Locust. 1962. pap. 9.95 (*0-8112-0215-1*, NDP125) New Directions Publishing Corp.

—Miss Lonelyhearts & the Day of the Locust. 1998. (Modern Library Ser.). 308p. 15.50 o.s.i (*0-679-60278-X*) Random Hse., Inc.

—Novels & Other Writings: The Dream Life of Balso Snell; Miss Lonelyhearts; A Cool Million; The Day of the Locust; Other Writings; Letters. Bercovitch, Sacvan, ed. 1997. (Library of America: Vol. 93). 840p. 35.00 (*1-883011-28-0*) Library of America, The.

Westermann, John. The Honor Farm. 2000. 320p. pap. 6.99 (*0-671-87126-9*, Pocket Star); 1997. (Illus.). 368p. pap. 6.99 (*0-671-87123-4*, Pocket); 1996. 320p. 22.00 o.p. (*0-671-87122-6*, Atria) Simon & Schuster.

—Ladies of the Night. 1998. 288p. 23.00 (*0-671-87124-2*, Atria) Simon & Schuster.

—Sweet Deal. 1992. 224p. 18.95 (*0-939149-56-7*) Soho Pr., Inc.

Westlake, Donald E. The Hook. 2000. 288p. 23.95 (*0-89296-588-6*) Mysterious Pr.

—The Hook. l.t. ed. 2000. (Americana Ser.). 392p. 29.95 (*0-7862-2466-5*) Thorndike Pr.

Wharton, Edith. The Buccaneers, Set. 1996. audio 41.95 (*1-55685-427-7*) Audio Bk. Contractors, Inc.

—The Buccaneers. unabr. ed. 1994. audio 72.00 (*0-7366-2717-0*, 3447) Books on Tape, Inc.

—The Buccaneers. 2000. (Illus.). 414p. reprint ed. 16.00 (*0-7881-9371-6*) DIANE Publishing Co.

—The Buccaneers. Mainwaring, Marion, ed. l.t. ed. 1994. 26.95 (*1-56895-062-4*, Wheeler Publishing, Inc.) Gale Group.

—The Buccaneers. 1995. (Illus.). 448p. 15.95 o.p. (*0-670-86645-8*, Viking); 1969. pap. 3.50 o.p. (*0-14-044212-X*, Penguin Classics); 1994. 384p. reprint ed. 13.00 (*0-14-023202-8*) Viking Penguin.

—The Collected Short Stories of Edith Wharton, Vol. 1. Lewis, R. W. B., ed. 1987. (Hudson River Editions Ser.). 752p. 60.00 (*0-02-570600-4*, Macmillan Reference USA) Gale Group.

—The Custom of the Country. 608p. 1976. 55.00 (*0-684-14655-X*); 1910. pap. 12.95 o.s.i (*0-684-71926-6*) Gale Group. (Macmillan Reference USA).

—The Custom of the Country. 1994. (Everyman's Library). 448p. 17.00 (*0-679-42301-X*) Knopf, Alfred A. Inc.

—The Custom of the Country. 1989. mass mkt. 4.95 o.p. (*0-451-52367-9*, Signet Classics) NAL.

—The Custom of the Country. Orgel, Stephen, ed. 1995. (Oxford World's Classics Ser.). 406p. pap. 9.95 o.p. (*0-19-282288-8*) Oxford Univ. Pr., Inc.

—Edith Wharton: Three Complete Novels, 3 bks. in 1. 1994. 672p. 11.99 o.s.i (*0-517-11828-9*) Random Hse. Value Publishing.

—Four Novels: The House of Mirth; Ethan Frome; The Custom of the Country; The Age of Innocence. 1996. (Library of America). 1168p. (C). pap. 13.95 (*1-883011-37-X*) Library of America, The.

—The Greater Inclination. reprint ed. 29.50 (*0-404-06913-4*) AMS Pr., Inc.

—The Greater Inclination. 1914. reprint ed. 15.00 (*0-403-00188-9*) Scholarly Pr., Inc.

—The House of Mirth. Benstock, Shari, ed. 1993. (Case Studies in Contemporary Criticism). 498p. pap. text 9.50 (*0-312-06234-6*) Bedford/Saint Martin's.

—The House of Mirth. 1990. (Vintage-Library of America ). 384p. pap. 11.50 o.s.i (*0-679-72539-3*, Vintage) Knopf Publishing Group.

—The House of Mirth. 1998. 380p. reprint ed. lib. bdg. 25.00 (*1-58287-090-X*) North Bks.
—The House of Mirth. Ammons, Elizabeth, ed. 1990. (Critical Editions Ser.). 374p. (C). pap. text 9.00 net. (*0-393-95901-5*) Norton, W. W. & Co., Inc.
—The House of Mirth. Banta, Martha, ed. 1994. (Oxford World's Classics Ser.). 366p. pap. 6.95 o.p. (*0-19-282944-0*) Oxford Univ. Pr., Inc.
—The Mother's Recompense. (Collected Works of Edith Wharton). 341p. reprint ed. 2001. (Illus.). pap. text 28.00 (*0-7426-5988-7*); 1998. lib. bdg. 98.00 (*1-58201-988-6*) Classic Bks.
—The Mother's Recompense. 1986. 342p. 15.95 o.s.i (*0-684-18771-X*); pap. 12.00 (*0-684-18737-X*) Gale Group. (Macmillan Reference USA).
—The Mother's Recompense. 1996. 288p. pap. 13.00 (*0-684-82531-7*, Scribner) Simon & Schuster.
—Novels: The House of Mirth; The Reef; The Custom of the Country; The Age of Innocence. Lewis, R. W. B., ed. 1986. 1328p. 40.00 (*0-940450-31-3*) Library of America, The.
—Three Novels of Old New York: The House of Mirth; The Custom of the the Country; The Age of Innocence. 1997. (Penguin Twentieth-Century Classics Ser.). 992p. pap. 16.95 o.p. (*0-14-018984-X*) Viking Penguin.
Wharton, Edith & Mainwaring, Marion. The Buccaneers. abr. ed. 1993. (Classics on Cassette). 16.00 o.p. incl. audio (*0-453-00854-2*, 390454) Penguin/HighBridge.
—The Buccaneers. 1993. 416p. 22.00 o.p. (*0-670-85219-8*, Viking) Viking Penguin.
Wharton, Edith & Wharton, Tom. The House of Mirth. 1991. 370p. 17.00 o.s.i (*0-679-40667-0*) Random Hse., Inc.
Wheat, Carolyn. Dead Man's Thoughts. 1983. 256p. 14.95 o.p. (*0-312-18501-4*) St. Martin's Pr.
—Fresh Kills. 1995. 240p. (Orig.). 19.95 o.p. (*0-425-14785-1*); pap. 9.00 o.p. (*0-425-14920-X*) Berkley Publishing Group. (Prime Crime).
—Mean Streak. 1996. (Cass Jameson Legal Mysteries Ser.). 240p. 19.95 o.p. (*0-425-15317-7*, Prime Crime) Berkley Publishing Group.
—Troubled Waters. 1997. (Cass Jameson Legal Mysteries Ser.). 240p. 21.95 o.s.i (*0-425-15784-9*, Prime Crime) Berkley Publishing Group.
—Where Nobody Dies. 1986. 288p. 15.95 o.p. (*0-312-86700-X*) St. Martin's Pr.
White, Ellen E. All Emergencies, Ring Super. (Dead Letter Mysteries Ser.). 300p. 1998. pap. 5.99 (*0-312-96601-6*, St. Martin's Paperbacks); 1997. 22.95 o.p. (*0-312-15651-0*, Saint Martin's Minotaur) St. Martin's Pr.
Whiteford, Merry. If Wishes Were Horses: A Novel. 2003. 256p. 23.95 (*0-312-30188-X*) St. Martin's Pr.
Whitman, Stephen F. Predestined: A Novel of New York Life. 1974. (Lost American Fiction Ser.). 486p. reprint ed. 8.95 o.p. (*0-8093-0701-4*) Southern Illinois Univ. Pr.
Whitney, Polly. Until It Hurts: An Ike & Abby Mystery. 1997. 304p. 22.95 (*0-312-15237-X*, Saint Martin's Minotaur) St. Martin's Pr.
Wiesel, Elie. Twilight. Wiesel, Marion, tr. from FRE. 1995. 224p. pap. 12.00 (*0-8052-1058-X*, Schocken) Knopf Publishing Group.
—Twilight. 1988. 17.95 o.p. (*0-671-64407-6*); 75.00 o.s.i (*0-671-66435-2*) Summit Bks.
—Twilight. Wiesel, Marion, tr. 1989. 224p. pap. 9.95 (*0-446-39066-6*) Warner Bks., Inc.
Wilbee, Brenda. Shipwreck! 1991. (Classic Women of Faith Ser.). 256p. pap. 7.99 o.p. (*0-89081-858-4*) Harvest Hse. Pubs.
Wilcox, James. Guest of a Sinner: A Novel. 1993. 288p. 20.00 o.p. (*0-06-016875-7*) HarperTrade.
—Guest of a Sinner: A Novel. 2004. (Voices of the South Ser.). 288p. pap. (*0-8071-2969-0*) Louisiana State Univ. Pr.
—Polite Sex: A Novel. 1991. 228p. 19.95 o.p. (*0-06-016356-9*); 1993. 288p. reprint ed. pap. 12.00 o.p. (*0-06-092165-X*, Perennial) HarperTrade.
—Polite Sex: A Novel. 1999. pap. (*0-316-94010-0*); 288p. pap. 13.00 (*0-316-94134-4*, Back Bay) Little Brown & Co.
Wilcox, Stephen F. All the Dead Heroes. 1992. 224p. 18.95 o.p. (*0-312-06896-4*, Saint Martin's Minotaur) St. Martin's Pr.
—The Nimby Factor. 1992. 256p. 18.95 o.p. (*0-312-08270-3*, Saint Martin's Minotaur) St. Martin's Pr.
—The Painted Lady. 1993. 272p. 21.95 o.p. (*0-312-10520-7*, Saint Martin's Minotaur) St. Martin's Pr.
—The Twenty-Acre Plot. 1991. 16.95 o.p. (*0-312-05846-2*, Saint Martin's Minotaur) St. Martin's Pr.
Wilder, Patrick A. Battle of Sackett's Harbour. 1994. (Illus.). 300p. 29.95 (*1-877853-27-5*) Nautical & Aviation Publishing Co. of America, Inc., The.
Williams, John A. Sons of Darkness, Sons of Light: A Novel of Some Probability. 1999. (Library of Black Literature). 279p. pap. text 16.95 (*1-55553-396-5*) Northeastern Univ. Pr.
Wilson, Edmund. The Higher Jazz. Reinitz, Neale, ed. 1998. 224p. pap. 17.95 (*0-87745-655-0*); text 34.95 (*0-87745-653-4*) Univ. of Iowa Pr.
Wilson, F. Paul & Lyon, Steve. Nightkill. 1999. 288p. mass mkt. 6.99 (*0-8125-6536-3*, Tor Bks.); 1997. 304p. 23.95 (*0-312-85910-4*, Forge Bks.) Doherty, Tom Assocs., LLC.
Wilson, Leigh A. Wind: Stories. 1989. 288p. 17.95 o.p. (*0-688-08111-8*, Morrow, William & Co.) Morrow/Avon.
Wilson, Sloan. Small Town. 1978. 10.95 o.p. (*0-87795-172-1*, Morrow, William & Co.) Morrow/Avon.
Wiltse, David. Blown Away. l.t. ed. 1997. 368p. mass mkt. 6.50 o.s.i (*0-425-15971-X*) Berkley Publishing Group.
—Blown Away. 1996. 352p. 24.95 o.s.i (*0-399-14208-8*, G. P. Putnam's Sons) Penguin Group (USA) Inc.
Winslow, Pauline G. Cry in the City. 1990. 16.95 o.p. (*0-312-04289-2*, Saint Martin's Minotaur) St. Martin's Pr.
Winthrop, Elizabeth. In My Mother's House. 1989. mass mkt. 4.95 o.p. (*0-451-16657-4*, Signet Bks.) NAL.
Wishnia, K. J. A. The Glass Factory: A Filomena Buscarsela Mystery. 2000. (Filomena Buscarsela Mysteries Ser.). 224p. 23.95 o.s.i (*0-525-94545-8*, Dutton) Dutton/Plume.
—The Glass Factory: A Filomena Buscarsela Mystery. 2001. 256p. reprint ed. mass mkt. 5.99 o.s.i (*0-451-19751-8*, Signet Bks.) NAL.
—The Glass Factory: A Filomena Buscarsela Mystery. l.t. ed. 2000. (Mystery Ser.). 375p. 27.95 (*0-7862-2841-5*) Thorndike Pr.
—23 Shades of Black. 1997. pap. text 7.95 o.p. (*0-9656814-1-6*) Imaginary Pr., The.
—23 Shades of Black. 1998. (Filomena Buscarsela Mysteries Ser.). 304p. mass mkt. 6.99 o.s.i (*0-451-19748-8*, Signet Bks.) NAL.
—23 Shades of Black. 1998. 13.04 (*0-606-15828-6*) Turtleback Bks.
Witten, Matt. Breakfast at Madeline's. 1999. (Signet Book Ser.). 256p. mass mkt. 5.99 o.s.i (*0-451-19681-3*) NAL.
—Grand Illusion. 2000. (Jacob Burns Mysteries Ser.). 256p. mass mkt. 5.99 o.s.i (*0-451-19897-2*, Signet Bks.) NAL.
—Strange Bedfellows: A Jacob Burns Mystery. 2000. (Jacob Burns Mysteries Ser.). 240p. mass mkt. 6.50 o.s.i (*0-451-20159-0*) NAL.
—Strange Bedfellows: A Jacob Burns Mystery. l.t. ed. 2001. (Thorndike Mystery Ser.). 352p. 27.95 (*0-7862-3214-5*) Thorndike Pr.
Wolfe, Thomas. The Party at Jack's: A Novella. Stutman, Suzanne & Idol, John L., Jr., eds. 1995. 290p. pap. 24.95 o.p. (*0-8078-2206-X*) Univ. of North Carolina Pr.
Wolfe, Tom. The Bonfire of the Vanities. 552p. 1989. 75.00 o.p. (*0-374-11535-4*); 1990. 25.00 (*0-374-11537-0*) Farrar, Straus & Giroux.
—The Bonfire of the Vanities. l.t. ed. 1989. 992p. 21.95 o.p. (*0-8161-4742-6*); pap. 13.95 o.p. (*0-8161-4745-0*) Gale Group. (Macmillan Reference USA).
—Two Complete Books. 1994. 784p. 13.99 o.s.i (*0-517-11998-6*) Random Hse., Inc.
Wolff, Geoffrey. The Age of Consent. 1996. 240p. pap. 12.00 (*0-312-14081-9*) Picador.
Womack, Jack. Going, Going, Gone. 224p. 2002. pap. 13.00 (*0-8021-3866-7*, Grove Pr.); 2001. 24.00 o.p. (*0-8021-1685-X*) Grove/Atlantic, Inc.
—Random Acts of Senseless Violence. 256p. 1995. pap. 13.50 (*0-8021-3424-6*, Grove Pr.); 1994. 21.00 o.p. (*0-87113-577-9*, Atlantic Monthly Pr.) Grove/Atlantic, Inc.
Wood, Bari. Doll's Eyes. 1994. 384p. mass mkt. 5.50 (*0-380-72097-3*, Avon Bks.); 1993. 303p. 20.00 o.p. (*0-688-12440-2*, Morrow, William & Co.) Morrow/Avon.
Woods, Stuart. Imperfect Strangers. l.t. ed. 1995. 26.95 o.p. (*1-56895-203-1*, Wheeler Publishing, Inc.) Gale Group.
—Imperfect Strangers. 1994. 320p. 23.00 o.p. (*0-06-017775-6*) HarperCollins Pubs.
—Imperfect Strangers. abr. ed. audio 17.00 o.p. (*1-55994-673-3*, CPN 2472, HarperAudio) HarperTrade.
—Imperfect Strangers. 1995. 368p. mass mkt. 7.99 (*0-06-109404-8*, HarperTorch) Morrow/Avon.
Woodson, Jacqueline. Autobiography of a Family Photo: A Novel. 1995. 128p. 17.95 o.s.i (*0-525-93721-8*) Dutton/Plume.
Woolf, Douglas. Fade Out. 1996. 275p. (C). 30.00 (*0-87685-989-9*, Black Sparrow Pr.) Godine, David R. Pub.
—Fade Out. 1996. (C). 275p. 25.00 (*0-87685-988-0*); 273p. pap. 14.00 (*0-87685-987-2*) HarperCollins Pubs.
Wouk, Herman. The Caine Mutiny. 1992. 560p. reprint ed. pap. 14.95 (*0-316-95510-8*, Back Bay) Little Brown & Co.
—City Boy: The Adventures of Herbie Bookbinder. 1968. 12.95 o.s.i (*0-385-04072-5*) Doubleday Publishing.
—City Boy: The Adventures of Herbie Bookbinder. 1992. 352p. pap. 15.95 (*0-316-95511-6*) Little Brown & Co.
—City Boy: The Adventures of Herbie Bookbinder. 1983. mass mkt. 4.95 o.s.i (*0-671-46013-7*, Pocket) Simon & Schuster.
—Marjorie Morningstar. l.t. ed. 1996. (Core Ser.). 836p. 28.95 (*0-7838-1993-5*) Thorndike Pr.
Wright, Charles. Absolutely Nothing to Get Alarmed About: The Complete Novels of Charles Wright. 1993. 624p. pap. 13.00 o.p. (*0-06-096958-X*, Perennial) HarperTrade.
Wright, Richard. Savage Holiday. 1975. 220p. reprint ed. 8.50 o.p. (*0-911860-54-1*) Chatham Bookseller.
—Savage Holiday. 1995. (Banner Bks.). 220p. reprint ed. pap. 20.00 (*0-87805-750-1*); lib. bdg. 40.00 (*0-87805-749-8*) Univ. Pr. of Mississippi.
Yablonsky, Linda. The Story of Junk: A Novel. 1997. 325p. 23.00 o.p. (*0-374-27024-4*) Farrar, Straus & Giroux.
—Story of Junk: A Novel. 1998. 336p. pap. 12.95 (*0-316-96808-0*) Little Brown & Co.
Yaffe, James. My Mother, the Detective: The Complete "Mom" Short Stories. 1996. 175p. pap. 15.00 (*1-885941-11-0*); 40.00 o.p. (*1-885941-10-2*) Crippen & Landru, Pubs.
Yamada, Amy. Trash: A Novel. Noma, Chikako & Bell, Susan, eds. Johnson, Sonya L., tr. 1995. 384p. 18.00 (*1-56836-018-5*) Kodansha America, Inc.
Yates, Richard. Cold Spring Harbor. 1986. 192p. 16.95 o.s.i (*0-385-29502-2*, Delacorte Pr.) Dell Publishing.
Yau, John. Hawaiian Cowboys. 1995. 169p. (C). 25.00 (*0-87685-957-0*);signed ed. 35.00 o.p. (*0-87685-958-9*) Godine, David R. Pub. (Black Sparrow Pr.).
—Hawaiian Cowboys. 1995. 169p. (C). pap. 13.50 (*0-87685-956-2*) HarperCollins Pubs.
Yezierska, Anzia. Arrogant Beggar. 1996. 192p. pap. 18.95 (*0-8223-1749-4*); text 59.95 (*0-8223-1752-4*) Duke Univ. Pr.
—How I Found America: Collected Stories of Anzia Yezierska. 1995. 272p. (C). pap. 11.95 (*0-89255-211-5*); 1980. 352p. 24.95 o.p. (*0-89255-160-7*) Persea Bks., Inc.
—Hungry Hearts. lib. bdg. 21.95 (*0-8488-2086-X*) Amereon, Ltd.
—Hungry Hearts. 1975. (Modern Jewish Experience Ser.). reprint ed. 26.95 (*0-405-06754-2*) Ayer Co. Pubs., Inc.
—Hungry Hearts. 1996. (Signet Classics). 256p. mass mkt. 4.95 (*0-451-52641-4*) NAL.
—Hungry Hearts. 1997. (Twentieth Century Classics Ser.). 288p. pap. 12.00 (*0-14-118005-6*, Penguin Classics) Viking Penguin.
—Hungry Hearts & Other Stories. 1985. 364p. (Orig.). (C). pap. 9.95 o.p. (*0-89255-093-7*) Persea Bks., Inc.
—Salome of the Tenements. l.t. ed. 1998. 235p. text 27.95 (*1-56000-478-9*) Transaction Pubs.
—Salome of the Tenements. 1995. (Radical Novel Reconsidered Ser.). 160p. pap. text 15.95 (*0-252-06435-6*) Univ. of Illinois Pr.
Yglesias, Rafael. Only Children. 1989. 512p. mass mkt. 4.95 o.s.i (*0-345-36031-1*) Ballantine Bks.
—Only Children. 1988. 420p. 19.95 o.p. (*0-688-07219-4*, Morrow, William & Co.) Morrow/Avon.
Youmans, Marly. Catherwood. 1996. 20.00 o.p. (*0-374-11972-4*) Farrar, Straus & Giroux.
—Catherwood. 1997. reprint ed. pap. 10.00 (*0-380-72988-1*, Avon Bks.) Morrow/Avon.
Young, Jim. Armed Memory. 1996. 246p. pap. text 5.99 (*0-8125-5027-7*); 1995. 256p. 21.95 o.p. (*0-312-85766-7*) Doherty, Tom Assocs., LLC. (Tor Bks.).
Zabor, Rafi. The Bear Comes Home: A Novel. 480p. 1998. pap. 15.00 (*0-393-31863-X*); 1997. 25.00 o.p. (*0-393-04037-2*) Norton, W. W. & Co., Inc.
Zigman, Laura. Dating Big Bird. unabr. ed. 2001. audio 24.95 (*1-57511-068-7*) Publishing Mills, Inc., The.

**NEW ZEALAND—FICTION**

Anderson, Barbara. Portrait of the Artist's Wife. 1993. 320p. 21.95 o.p. (*0-393-03489-5*) Norton, W. W. & Co., Inc.
Bacon, Ron. Home of the Winds. 1989. (Illus.). 36p. (J). (ps-3). 11.99 (*0-85953-302-6*) Child's Play of England GBR. *Dist:* Child's Play-International.
—House of the People. 1989. (Illus.). 36p. (J). (ps-3). 11.99 (*0-85953-300-X*) Child's Play of England GBR. *Dist:* Child's Play-International.
Ballantyne, David. The Cunninghams. 1987. (New Zealand Classics Ser.). 240p. pap. 9.95 o.p. (*0-19-558158-X*) Oxford Univ. Pr., Inc.
Beecham, Rose. Fair Play: An Amanda Valentine Mystery. 1995. (Amanda Valentine Mysteries Ser.: Vol. 3). 256p. pap. 10.95 o.p. (*1-56280-081-7*) Naiad Pr., Inc.
—Introducing Amanda Valentine. 1992. (Amanda Valentine Mystery Ser.: No. 1). 256p. pap. 10.95 o.p. (*1-56280-021-3*) Naiad Pr., Inc.
—Second Guess: Second Amanda Valentine Mystery. 1994. (Amanda Valentine Mysteries Ser.: Vol. 2). 208p. pap. 9.95 o.p. (*1-56280-069-8*) Naiad Pr., Inc.
Bevan, Gloria. Bachelor Territory. l.t. ed. 1991. pap. 15.95 o.p. (*0-7927-0404-5*, AS037) BBC Audiobooks America.
—Kowhai Country. l.t. ed. 1992. 18.95 o.p. (*0-7451-8399-9*); pap. 16.95 o.p. (*0-7927-1156-4*) BBC Audiobooks America.
Billing, Graham. Slipway. 1973. 6.95 o.p. (*0-670-65206-7*) Viking Penguin.
Burgess, Linda. Between Friends. 1994. 184p. pap. 24.95 (*0-908569-88-2*) Univ. of Otago Pr. NZL. *Dist:* International Specialized Bk. Services.
—On the Grapevine. 1996. 200p. pap. 24.95 (*1-877133-12-4*) International Specialized Bk. Services.
Campion, Jane & Pullinger, Kate. The Piano: A Novel. 218p. 1995. pap. 12.95 (*0-7868-8096-1*); 1994. (J). 17.95 o.p. (*0-7868-6121-5*) Hyperion Pr.
Cooper, Matthew & Rodman, Margaret C. New Neighbours: A Case Study of Cooperative Housing in Toronto. 1992. (Orig.). 650p. text (*0-8020-5992-9*); 520p. pap. text (*0-8020-6925-8*) Univ. of Toronto Pr.
Dallas, Ruth. The Black Horse & Other Stories. 2000. 111p. pap. 24.95 (*1-877133-85-X*) Univ. of Otago Pr. NZL. *Dist:* International Specialized Bk. Services.
Davin, Dan. The Salamander & the Fire. 1987. (New Zealand Classics Ser.). 240p. pap. 8.95 o.p. (*0-19-558147-4*) Oxford Univ. Pr., Inc.
Du Fresne, Yvonne. Frederique. 1987. 224p. pap. 6.95 o.p. (*0-14-008962-4*, Penguin Bks.) Viking Penguin.
Duffy, Stella. Beneath the Blonde. 5th ed. 2000. 249p. pap. (*1-85242-711-6*) Serpent's Tail Ltd.
Eden, Dorothy. The House on Hay Hill. 1980. 224p. mass mkt. 2.25 o.s.i (*0-449-23789-3*, Fawcett); 1976. mass mkt. 1.75 o.s.i (*0-449-22839-8*) Ballantine Bks.
Eldred-Grigg, Stevan. Oracles & Miracles. 1988. 272p. pap. 6.95 o.p. (*0-14-009927-1*, Penguin Bks.) Viking Penguin.
Else, Chris. Endangered Species. 1997. 80p. (*0-908790-95-3*) Hazard Pr.
Farrell, Fiona. The Hopeful Traveller. 2002. (Illus.). 152p. pap. o.s.i (*1-86941-517-5*, Vintage) Knopf Publishing Group.
Faville, Barry. The Return. 1989. 164p. (YA). (gr. 11 up). 14.95 o.p. (*0-19-558166-0*) Oxford Univ. Pr., Inc.
Fisher, Michael. The Nightmare Man. 1991. 304p. 21.95 (*1-56129-110-2*) Knightsbridge Publishing.
—The Nightmare Man. 1993. 352p. pap. 5.50 (*1-56171-223-X*) SPI Bks.
—The Nightmare Man. l.t. ed. 1998. (Niagara Large Print Ser.). 443p. 29.50 o.p. (*0-7089-5854-0*, Ulverscroft) Thorpe, F. A. Pubs. GBR. *Dist:* Ulverscroft Large Print Bks., Ltd., Ulverscroft Large Print Canada, Ltd.
Frame, Janet. The Carpathians. 1993. pap. 11.95 (*0-8076-1298-7*); 1988. 196p. 17.50 o.p. (*0-8076-1205-7*) Braziller, George Inc.
Fulton, Jennifer. True Love. 1994. 240p. pap. 11.95 (*1-56280-035-3*) Naiad Pr., Inc.
Gee, Maurice. Live Bodies. 1998. 264p. (*0-14-027380-8*) Penguin Bks. Canada, Ltd.
—Meg. 1981. 266p. 12.95 o.p. (*0-312-52861-2*) St. Martin's Pr.
Grace, Patricia. Baby No-Eyes. 1999. (Talanoa Ser.). 294p. pap. 19.95 (*0-8248-2161-0*) Univ. of Hawaii Pr.
—Baby No-eyes. 1998. 294p. (*0-14-027993-8*) Penguin Bks. Canada, Ltd.
—Dogside Story. 2001. 301p. (*0-14-100419-3*) Penguin Group (USA) Inc.
—Dogside Story. 2002. (Contemporary Pacific Literature Ser.). 302p. (C). pap. 14.95 (*0-8248-2584-5*) Univ. of Hawaii Pr.
—Electric City: And Other Stories. 1988. 112p. pap. 5.95 o.p. (*0-14-010151-9*, Penguin Bks.) Viking Penguin.
Greenwood, Kerry. Flying Too High. 1992. mass mkt. 3.99 o.s.i (*0-449-14777-0*, Fawcett) Ballantine Bks.
Hansen, Derek. Sole Survivor. 1999. (Illus.). 432p. 25.00 o.s.i (*0-684-85407-4*, Simon & Schuster) Simon & Schuster.
Hargreaves, Raymond Philip & Holland, Peter. The Duel on the Creek & Other Tales of Victorian New Zealand. 1995. 208p. pap. 24.95 (*0-908569-91-2*) Univ. of Otago Pr. NZL. *Dist:* International Specialized Bk. Services.
Hearst, W. P. Inca Girls Aren't Easy: Thirteen Stories, Twelve of Which Are True. 1999. 182p. (*1-86941-374-1*, Vintage) Knopf Publishing Group.
Henaghan, Rosalie. For Ever & a Day. l.t. ed. 1991. pap. 15.95 o.p. (*0-7927-0767-2*, AS0279) BBC Audiobooks America.
Henaghan, Rosalie. For Ever & a Day. l.t. ed. 1991. 17.95 o.p. (*0-7451-8219-4*, AH0243) BBC Audiobooks America.

Hulme, Keri. The Bone People: A Masterful Story of Myth & Emotional Healing. 1986. 464p. 13.95 (*0-14-008922-5*) Viking Penguin.
—Bone People. Novel. 1985. 450p. 19.95 o.p. (*0-8071-1284-4*) Louisiana State Univ. Pr.
Hyde, Robin. Nor the Years Condemn. 1994. 272p. pap. 29.95 (*0-908569-83-1*) Univ. of Otago Pr. NZL. *Dist:* International Specialized Bk. Services.
Ihimaera, Witi. The Dream Swimmer. 1997. 423p. (*0-14-027240-2*) Penguin Bks. Canada, Ltd.
Illsley, Amber Jo. A Bountiful Lot. 2001. E-Book 6.95 (*0-87714-587-3*) Denlingers Pubs., Ltd.
Ireland, Kevin. The Craymore Affair: A Novel. 2000. (Illus.). 223p. (*1-86941-426-8*, Vintage) Knopf Publishing Group.
Kalman, Yvonne. After the Rainbow. 1990. 352p. 18.95 o.p. (*0-312-04957-9*) St. Martin's Pr.
—Mists of Heaven. 1988. 448p. 19.95 o.p. (*0-312-01793-6*) St. Martin's Pr.
Kidman, Fiona, ed. New Zealand Love Stories: An Oxford Anthology. 2000. 344p. 35.00 (*0-19-558399-X*) Oxford Univ. Pr., Inc.
Lasenby, Jack. The Mangrove Summer. 1989. 184p. (YA). (gr. 12 up). 15.00 o.p. (*0-19-558194-6*) Oxford Univ. Pr., Inc.
Lindsey, Olive. Never Go Back. l.t. ed. 1992. 18.95 o.p. (*0-7451-8400-6*); pap. 16.96 o.p. (*0-7927-1160-2*) BBC Audiobooks America.
Mackay, Shena. Dunedin. 1993. 296p. reprint ed. 21.95 o.p. (*1-55921-093-1*) Moyer Bell.
Mackay, Shena. Dunedin. 1994. pap. 5.95 o.p. (*1-55921-119-9*) Moyer Bell.
Mansfield, Katherine. The Short Stories of Katherine Mansfield. 1947. (YA). (gr. 7-12). 22.95 o.s.i (*0-394-44532-5*, Knopf Bks. for Young Readers) Random Hse. Children's Bks.
McCarten, Anthony. Spinners: A Novel. 1999. 288p. 24.00 (*0-688-16303-3*, Morrow, William & Co.) Morrow/Avon.
McCauley, Sue, contrib. by. It Could Be You. 1997. 208p. (*1-86941-317-2*) Random Hse. New Zealand.
McLeod, Marion & Wevers, Lydia. Women's Work. 1986. 240p. pap. 9.95 o.p. (*0-19-558136-9*) Oxford Univ. Pr., Inc.
Morgan, Clay. The Boy Who Spoke Dog. 2003. 192p. (J). 15.99 (*0-525-47159-6*, Dutton Children's Bks.) Penguin Putnam Bks. for Young Readers.
Morrissey, Michael. Flamingo Anthology of New Zealand Short Stories. 2000. 501p. pap. 29.95 (*1-86950-335-X*) HarperCollins NZL. *Dist:* Antipodes Bks. & Beyond.
Orio, Miguel. The Feather Chest: Te Waka Huia. 1997. 797p. 32.00 o.p. (*1-85756-259-3*) Janus Publishing Co. GBR. *Dist:* Paul & Co. Pubs. Consortium, Inc.
O'Sullivan, Vincent. Believers to the Bright Coast. 1998. 274p. (*0-14-028027-8*) Penguin Bks. New Zealand, Ltd.
O'Sullivan, Vincent, selected by. The Oxford Book of New Zealand Short Stories. 464p. 1994. pap. text 19.95 (*0-19-558291-8*); 1993. pap. text 16.95 o.p. (*0-19-558251-9*) Oxford Univ. Pr., Inc.
Quigley, Sarah. After Robert. 1999. 315p. (*0-14-028437-0*) Viking Penguin.
Reid, Pamela. Something Familiar: A Novel. 2003. (Illus.). 214p. 14.95 (*1-59156-161-2*) Covenant Communications.
Reidy, Sue. The Visitation. 1997. (Illus.). 272p. pap. 16.00 (*0-684-83954-7*, Scribner Paper Fiction) Simon & Schuster.
Savage, Deborah. The Flight of the Albatross. 1989. (YA). (gr. 7 up). 14.95 o.p. (*0-395-45711-4*) Houghton Mifflin Co.
Shadbolt, Maurice. Monday's Warriors. 1992. 320p. 21.95 (*0-87923-915-8*) Godine, David R. Pub.
—Season of the Jew. 1989. 384p. pap. 12.95 (*0-87923-753-8*) Godine, David R. Pub.
—Season of the Jew: A Novel. 1987. 16.95 o.p. (*0-393-02431-8*) Norton, W. W. & Co., Inc.
—A Touch of Clay. 1988. (New Zealand Classics Ser.). 192p. pap. 9.95 o.p. (*0-19-558173-3*) Oxford Univ. Pr., Inc.
Shadbolt, Maurice, et al, contrib. by. Selected Stories Maurice Shadbolt. 1998. 368p. (*0-908990-56-1*) Ling, David Publishing.
Sharp, Helen. Ward Nurse. l.t. ed. 2001. (Dales Large Print Ser.). 256p. pap. 21.99 (*1-84262-110-6*) Dales Large Print Bks. GBR. *Dist:* Ulverscroft Large Print Bks., Ltd., Ulverscroft Large Print Canada, Ltd.
Sherwood, John. A Botanist at Bay. 1986. mass mkt. 2.95 o.s.i (*0-345-33023-4*) Ballantine Bks.
—A Botanist at Bay. 1985. 176p. 13.95 o.s.i (*0-684-18432-X*); 1989. lib. bdg. 11.95 o.p. (*1-85057-559-2*) Gale Group. (Macmillan Reference USA).
Stewart, Robin. Moonbird. 1995. (Storybridge Ser.). (Illus.). 80p. (J). (gr. 3-7). pap. 10.95 (*0-7022-2695-5*) Univ. of Queensland Pr. AUS. *Dist:* International Specialized Bk. Services.
Sutherland, Margaret. Dark Places, Deep Regions & Other Stories. 1980. 196p. 9.95 o.p. (*0-916144-53-4*) Stemmer Hse. Pubs., Inc.
Taylor, Apirana. Ki Te Ao: New Stories. 1991. 176p. (Orig.). pap. 7.95 o.p. (*0-14-013140-X*) Penguin Group (USA) Inc.
Taylor, Chad. Shirker: A Novel. 2000. 234p. reprint ed. 23.95 (*0-8027-3350-6*) Walker & Co.
Taylor, William. The Blue Lawn. 2004. 120p. (YA). (gr. 7-12). pap. 10.95 (*1-55583-493-0*) Alyson Pubns.
—Paradise Lane. 176p. (gr. 7-9). 1989. (J). pap. 2.75 o.p. (*0-590-41014-8*); 1987. (YA). reprint ed. pap. 12.95 o.p. (*0-590-41013-X*) Scholastic, Inc.
Te Awekotuku, Ngahuia. Tahuri. 1993. 104p. pap. 12.95 (*0-88961-183-1*) Women's Pr. CAN. *Dist:* Univ. of Toronto Pr.
Tremain, Rose. The Colour. 2003. (Illus.). 352p. 25.00 (*0-374-12605-4*); pap. (*0-374-91874-0*) Farrar, Straus & Giroux.
Uris, Leon. Redemption. 1995. 827p. 25.00 o.p. (*0-06-018333-0*) HarperTrade.
—Redemption. l.t. ed. 1995. (Core Collection). 1054p. 28.95 (*0-7838-1453-4*) Thorndike Pr.
Wells, Peter. Dangerous Desires. 1994. 224p. 20.95 o.p. (*0-670-85012-8*, Viking) Viking Penguin.
Wells, Peter & Pilgrim, Rex, contrib. by. Best Mates: Gay Writing in Aotearoa, New Zealand. 1997. (Illus.). 240p. (*0-7900-0527-1*) Reed Publishing (NZ), Ltd.
Wilkins, Damien. Chemistry. 2003. 302p. pap. 14.00 (*1-86207-549-2*) Granta.
—Veteran Perils. 1990. (Pacific Writers Ser.). 166p. (C). pap. o.p. (*0-7900-0124-1*, A0481) Reed Publishing (NZ), Ltd.
Worboys, Anne. Aurora Rose. 1988. 512p. 19.95 o.p. (*0-525-24578-2*, Dutton) Dutton/Plume.
—Aurora Rose. 1989. 592p. mass mkt. 4.95 o.p. (*0-451-16211-0*, Signet Bks.) NAL.

**NEWFORD (IMAGINARY PLACE)—FICTION**

De Lint, Charles. Dreams Underfoot. 1994. 480p. mass mkt. 6.99 (*0-8125-1621-4*, Tor Bks.) Doherty, Tom Assocs., LLC.
—The Ivory & the Horn. (Tor Fantasy Ser.). 1996. mass mkt. 6.99 (*0-8125-3408-5*); 1995. 320p. 21.95 o.p. (*0-312-85573-7*) Doherty, Tom Assocs., LLC. (Tor Bks.).
—Memory & Dream. 1995. 448p. mass mkt. 6.99 (*0-8125-3407-7*); 1994. 400p. 22.95 o.p. (*0-312-85572-9*) Doherty, Tom Assocs., LLC. (Tor Bks.).
—Moonlight & Vines. 1999. 461p. mass mkt. 6.99 o.s.i (*0-8125-6549-5*); 1998. (Illus.). 384p. 24.95 (*0-312-86518-X*) Doherty, Tom Assocs., LLC. (Tor Bks.).
—Paperjack. 1992. (Illus.). 72p. 190.00 (*0-941826-21-X*) Cheap Street.
—Someplace to Be Flying. 1999. 544p. mass mkt. 6.99 o.s.i (*0-8125-5158-3*); 1998. 380p. 24.95 o.p. (*0-312-85849-3*) Doherty, Tom Assocs., LLC. (Tor Bks.).
—Tapping the Dream Tree. (Newford Ser.). 2003. 542p. pap. 15.95 (*0-312-86840-5*); 2002. 544p. 26.95 (*0-312-87401-4*) Doherty, Tom Assocs., LLC. (Tor Bks.).

**NEWFOUNDLAND AND LABRADOR—FICTION**

Assiniwi, Bernard. The Beothuk Saga. Grady, Wayne, tr. from FRE. (Illus.). 352p. 2001. pap. (*0-7710-0799-X*); 2000. (*0-7710-0798-1*) McClelland & Stewart/Tundra Bks.
—The Beothuk Saga. Grady, Wayne, tr. from FRE. 2002. (Illus.). 352p. 25.95 (*0-312-28390-3*) St. Martin's Pr.
Clark, Joan. Latitudes of Melt. 2002. 295p. pap. 14.00 o.s.i (*1-56947-318-8*); 332p. 24.00 (*1-56947-267-X*) Soho Pr., Inc.
Crummey, Michael. Flesh & Blood. 2000. 198p. pap. 12.95 (*0-88878-387-6*, Porcepic Bks.) Beach Holme Pubs., Ltd. CAN. *Dist:* Strauss Consultants.
—Flesh & Blood. 2003. 288p. pap. (*0-385-65927-X*, Anchor Canada) Doubleday Canada, Ltd. CAN. *Dist:* Random Hse., Inc.
—River Thieves: A Novel. 2002. 432p. pap. (*0-385-65817-6*, Anchor Canada) Doubleday Canada, Ltd. CAN. *Dist:* Random Hse., Inc.
—River Thieves: A Novel. 2002. (Illus.). 352p. 24.00 (*0-618-14531-1*) Houghton Mifflin Co.
—River Thieves: A Novel. 2003. 352p. pap. 13.00 (*0-618-34071-8*, Mariner Bks.) Houghton Mifflin Co. Trade & Reference Div.
Johnston, Wayne. The Colony of Unrequited Dreams. 1999. (Illus.). 576p. 24.95 o.s.i (*0-385-49542-0*) Doubleday Publishing.
—The Divine Ryans. 1999. 224p. pap. 12.95 o.s.i (*0-385-49544-7*) Doubleday Publishing.
—The Divine Ryans. 1996. mass mkt. 6.99 o.p. (*0-7710-4436-4*); 1990. 0.00 o.p. (*0-7710-4447-X*) McClelland & Stewart/Tundra Bks.
Major, Kevin. Gaffer. 1998. 208p. pap. 14.95 (*0-385-25729-5*) Bantam Bks.
—Thirty-Six Exposures. 1988. 160p. (J). (gr. k-12). mass mkt. 3.25 o.s.i (*0-440-20163-2*, Laurel Leaf) Random Hse. Children's Bks.
Morgan, Bernice. Cape Random: A Novel. 2002. 384p. pap. 12.95 (*1-57062-953-6*) Shambhala Pubns., Inc.
Morrissey, Donna. Downhill Chance. 2003. (Illus.). 448p. pap. 14.00 (*0-618-18927-0*) Houghton Mifflin Co.
—Kit's Law. 2001. (Illus.). 384p. pap. 13.00 (*0-618-10927-7*, Mariner Bks.) Houghton Mifflin Co. Trade & Reference Div.
—Kit's Law. 1999. 383p. pap. (*0-670-88601-7*) Viking.
Mowat, Claire. The Girl from Away. 1993. 96p. pap. 4.99 o.s.i (*0-7704-2571-2*) Bantam Bks.
Proulx, E. Annie. The Shipping News: A Novel. l.t. ed. 1994. 443p. 24.95 o.p. (*1-56895-069-1*, Wheeler Publishing, Inc.) Gale Group.
—The Shipping News: A Novel. 2001. 368p. pap. 7.99 (*0-7432-2540-6*); 1999. 352p. 25.00 (*0-684-85791-X*); 1994. (Illus.). 352p. pap. 14.00 (*0-671-51005-3*) Simon & Schuster. (Scribner).
—The Shipping News: A Novel. Grossman, B., ed. 1993. 320p. 25.00 o.s.i (*0-684-19337-X*, Scribner) Simon & Schuster.
—The Shipping News: A Novel. movie tie-in ed. 2001. 352p. pap. 14.00 (*0-7432-2542-2*, Scribner) Simon & Schuster.
—The Shipping News: A Novel. 1994. 20.05 (*0-606-21896-3*) Turtleback Bks.
Spinka, Penina Keen. Dream Weaver. 2003. (Illus.). 464p. 26.95 (*0-525-94684-5*, Dutton) Dutton/Plume.
—Dream Weaver. 2004. 512p. mass mkt. 7.99 (*0-451-41111-0*, Onyx) NAL.
Winter, Michael. One Last Good Look. 2001. 234p. pap. 12.95 (*0-88784-667-X*) House of Anansi Pr. CAN. *Dist:* General Distribution Services, Inc.

**NEWPORT BEACH (CALIF.)—FICTION**

Tiller, Denise. Calculated Risk. 2000. 250p. pap. 14.95 (*1-58752-015-X*); 2000. E-Book 14.95 (*1-58752-031-1*); 1999. E-Book 14.95 (*1-58752-035-4*) Timberwolf Pr., Inc.
—Calculated Risk. unabr. ed. 2000. lib. bdg. 29.95 incl. audio (*1-58752-016-8*); lib. bdg. 34.95 incl. audio compact disk (*1-58752-017-6*) Timberwolf Pr., Inc.
Wambaugh, Joseph. The Golden Orange. l.t. ed. 1992. 16.95 o.p. (*0-7927-0621-8*); 1991. 363p. 20.95 o.p. (*0-7927-0620-X*, E0005) BBC Audiobooks America.
—The Golden Orange. 1991. 416p. mass mkt. 7.50 (*0-553-29026-6*) Bantam Bks.
—The Golden Orange. unabr. ed. 1991. audio 73.25 o.p. (*1-56100-070-1*, 596); audio 23.95 o.p. (*0-930435-75-3*, 414, Bookcassette) Brilliance Audio.
—The Golden Orange. 1990. 317p. 19.95 o.p. (*0-688-09408-2*, Morrow, William & Co.) Morrow/Avon.

**NEWTON LAUDER (SCOTLAND: IMAGINARY PLACE)—FICTION**

Hammond, Gerald. Adverse Report. 1990. 2.99 o.p. (*0-517-05806-5*) Random Hse. Value Publishing.
—Adverse Report. 1989. 14.95 o.p. (*0-312-02858-X*, Saint Martin's Minotaur) St. Martin's Pr.
—Adverse Report. l.t. ed. 1990. (Ulverscroft Large Print Ser.). 29.99 o.p. (*0-7089-2119-1*, Ulverscroft) Thorpe, F. A. Pubs. GBR. *Dist:* Ulverscroft Large Print Bks., Ltd., Ulverscroft Large Print Canada, Ltd.
—A Brace of Skeet. 1990. 192p. 15.95 o.p. (*0-312-04688-X*, Saint Martin's Minotaur) St. Martin's Pr.
—A Brace of Skeet. l.t. ed. 1991. (Ulverscroft Large Print Ser.). 29.99 o.p. (*0-7089-2480-8*, Ulverscroft) Thorpe, F. A. Pubs. GBR. *Dist:* Ulverscroft Large Print Bks., Ltd., Ulverscroft Large Print Canada, Ltd.
—Carriage of Justice. l.t. ed. 1996. 221p. pap. 20.95 (*0-7838-1633-2*, Macmillan Reference USA) Gale Group.
—Carriage of Justice. 1995. 192p. 19.95 o.p. (*0-312-13941-1*, Saint Martin's Minotaur) St. Martin's Pr.
—Cousin Once Removed. 1984. 192p. 10.95 o.p. (*0-312-17055-6*) St. Martin's Pr.
—Cousin Once Removed. l.t. ed. 1988. (Linford Mystery Library). 256p. pap. 17.99 o.p. (*0-7089-6616-0*, Linford) Thorpe, F. A. Pubs. GBR. *Dist:* Ulverscroft Large Print Bks., Ltd., Ulverscroft Large Print Canada, Ltd.
—The Executor. 1987. 176p. 12.95 o.p. (*0-312-00593-8*) St. Martin's Pr.
—The Executor. l.t. ed. 1997. (Linford Mystery Library). 320p. pap. 17.99 o.p. (*0-7089-5155-4*, Ulverscroft) Thorpe, F. A. Pubs. GBR. *Dist:* Ulverscroft Large Print Bks., Ltd., Ulverscroft Large Print Canada, Ltd.
—Fair Game. 1982. 224p. 9.95 o.p. (*0-312-27961-2*) St. Martin's Pr.
—Fair Game. l.t. ed. 1983. (Ulverscroft Large Print Ser.). 336p. 29.99 o.p. (*0-7089-1014-9*, Ulverscroft) Thorpe, F. A. Pubs. GBR. *Dist:* Ulverscroft Large Print Bks., Ltd., Ulverscroft Large Print Canada, Ltd.
—The Game. 1982. 176p. 10.95 o.p. (*0-312-31590-2*) St. Martin's Pr.
—Home to Roost. 1991. 160p. 16.95 o.p. (*0-312-06369-5*, Saint Martin's Minotaur) St. Martin's Pr.
—Hook or Crook. l.t. ed. 1995. 209p. pap. 19.95 o.p. (*0-7838-1174-8*, Macmillan Reference USA) Gale Group.
—Hook or Crook. 1995. 154p. 17.95 o.p. (*0-312-11825-2*, Saint Martin's Minotaur) St. Martin's Pr.
—In Camera. l.t. ed. 1993. (Dales Large Print Ser.). 247p. pap. 19.99 o.p. (*1-85389-390-0*) Dales Large Print Bks. GBR. *Dist:* Ulverscroft Large Print Bks., Ltd., Ulverscroft Large Print Canada, Ltd.
—In Camera. 1992. 192p. 16.95 o.p. (*0-312-06997-9*, Saint Martin's Minotaur) St. Martin's Pr.
—Let Us Prey. 1991. 15.95 o.p. (*0-312-05891-8*, Saint Martin's Minotaur) St. Martin's Pr.
—Let Us Prey. l.t. ed. 1993. (Mystery Ser.). 256p. 29.99 o.p. (*0-7089-2893-5*, Ulverscroft) Thorpe, F. A. Pubs. GBR. *Dist:* Ulverscroft Large Print Bks., Ltd., Ulverscroft Large Print Canada, Ltd.
—Pursuit of Arms. 1985. 192p. 12.95 o.p. (*0-312-65697-1*) St. Martin's Pr.
—Pursuit of Arms. l.t. ed. 1998. (Linford Mystery Library). 320p. pap. 17.99 o.p. (*0-7089-5215-1*, Linford) Thorpe, F. A. Pubs. GBR. *Dist:* Ulverscroft Large Print Bks., Ltd., Ulverscroft Large Print Canada, Ltd.
—The Revenge Game. 1981. 192p. 9.95 o.p. (*0-312-67930-0*) St. Martin's Pr.
—The Reward Game. 1980. 224p. 9.95 o.p. (*0-312-68078-3*) St. Martin's Pr.
—The Reward Game. l.t. ed. 1981. (Ulverscroft Large Print Ser.). 326p. 29.99 o.p. (*0-7089-0717-2*, Ulverscroft) Thorpe, F. A. Pubs. GBR. *Dist:* Ulverscroft Large Print Bks., Ltd., Ulverscroft Large Print Canada, Ltd.
—Sauce for the Pigeon. 1985. 192p. 12.95 o.p. (*0-312-69977-8*) St. Martin's Pr.
—Sauce for the Pigeon. l.t. ed. 1989. (Linford Mystery Library). 305p. pap. 17.99 o.p. (*0-7089-6631-4*, Linford) Thorpe, F. A. Pubs. GBR. *Dist:* Ulverscroft Large Print Bks., Ltd., Ulverscroft Large Print Canada, Ltd.
—Silver City Scandal. 1986. 12.95 o.p. (*0-312-72588-4*) St. Martin's Pr.
—Silver City Scandal. l.t. ed. 1987. (Ulverscroft Large Print Ser.). 272p. 29.99 o.p. (*0-7089-1639-2*, Ulverscroft) Thorpe, F. A. Pubs. GBR. *Dist:* Ulverscroft Large Print Bks., Ltd., Ulverscroft Large Print Canada, Ltd.
—Sink or Swim. 1997. 176p. 19.95 o.p. (*0-312-15657-X*, Saint Martin's Minotaur) St. Martin's Pr.
—Sink or Swim. l.t. ed. 1997. (General Ser.). 224p. pap. 24.95 (*0-7862-1071-0*) Thorndike Pr.
—Stray Shot. 1989. 192p. 14.95 o.p. (*0-312-03435-0*, Saint Martin's Minotaur) St. Martin's Pr.
—Stray Shot. l.t. ed. 1990. (Ulverscroft Large Print Ser.). 29.99 o.p. (*0-7089-2211-2*, Ulverscroft) Thorpe, F. A. Pubs. GBR. *Dist:* Ulverscroft Large Print Bks., Ltd., Ulverscroft Large Print Canada, Ltd.
—Thin Air. 1994. 144p. 17.95 o.p. (*0-312-11339-0*, Saint Martin's Minotaur) St. Martin's Pr.

**NEXIS (IMAGINARY PLACE: FUREY)—FICTION**

Furey, Maggie. Aurian. 1994. 608p. mass mkt. 6.99 (*0-553-56525-7*) Bantam Bks.
—Harp of Winds. 1995. 464p. mass mkt. 6.99 (*0-553-56526-5*, Spectra) Bantam Bks.
—Sword of the Flame. 1996. (Bantam Spectra Book Ser.). 464p. mass mkt. 7.50 (*0-553-56527-3*, Spectra) Bantam Bks.

**NICARAGUA—FICTION**

Cussler, Clive. Trojan Odyssey: A Dirk Pitt Novel. 2003. (Dirk Pitt Adventure Ser.: No. 17). 496p. 27.95 (*0-399-15080-3*) Putnam Publishing Group, The.
Elman, Richard. Disco Frito. 1988. 224p. 15.95 o.p. (*0-87905-289-9*) Smith, Gibbs Pub.
Henley, Patricia. The Hummingbird House. 2000. pap. 13.00 (*1-878448-98-6*); 1999. 399p. 22.00 (*1-878448-87-0*) MacMurray & Beck, Inc.
Land, Jon. Valhalla Testament. 1990. 352p. mass mkt. 5.95 o.s.i (*0-449-14634-0*, Fawcett) Ballantine Bks.
Martin, Ian K. Billions. 1980. 192p. 8.95 o.p. (*0-689-11050-2*, Scribner) Simon & Schuster.
Ramirez, Sergio. Margarita, How Beautiful the Sea. Miller, Michael B., tr. from SPA. 2004. 24.95 (*1-880684-84-5*) Curbstone Pr.
—Stories from Nicaragua. Caistor, Nick, tr. from SPA. 1987. (Readers International Ser.). (Illus.). (C). 130p. 14.95 o.p. (*0-930523-28-8*); 120p. pap. 7.95 (*0-930523-29-6*) Readers International.
—To Bury Our Fathers: A Novel of Nicaragua. Caistor, Nick, tr. from SPA. 1985. (Illus.). (C). 250p. 14.95 o.p. (*0-930523-02-4*); 257p. pap. 11.95 (*0-930523-03-2*) Readers International.
Wilcox, John C. El Aliento de la Vida: Cuentos Nicaraguenses. 1981. (Coleccion Caniqui). (SPA.). 214p. (Orig.). pap. 9.95 (*0-89729-244-8*) Ediciones Universal.

**NIGERIA—FICTION**

Abani, Chris. GraceLand. 2004. 336p. 24.00 (*0-374-16589-0*) Farrar, Straus & Giroux.

Achebe, Chinua. Arrow of God. 1989. (Anchor Literary Library). 240p. pap. 11.95 (*0-385-01480-5*) Doubleday Publishing.
—Girls at War: And Other Stories. 1986. mass mkt. 3.50 o.s.i (*0-449-30046-3*, Fawcett) Ballantine Bks.
—Girls at War: And Other Stories. 1991. 128p. pap. 12.00 (*0-385-41896-5*) Doubleday Publishing.
—A Man of the People. 1981. 160p. pap. 10.95 (*0-385-08616-4*) Doubleday Publishing.
—No Longer at Ease. 1961. (C). 12.95 (*0-8392-1077-9*); pap. 12.95 (*0-8392-5008-8*) Astor-Honor, Inc.
—No Longer at Ease. 1982. mass mkt. 2.50 o.s.i (*0-449-30847-2*); 2nd ed. 1985. 160p. mass mkt. 4.95 o.s.i (*0-449-30023-4*) Ballantine Bks. (Fawcett).
—No Longer at Ease. 1994. 208p. pap. 9.95 (*0-385-47455-5*) Doubleday Publishing.
—No Longer at Ease. (African Writers Ser.). 1987. 160p. (C). pap. 9.95 o.p. (*0-435-90528-7*); 1985. pap. 4.00 o.p. (*0-435-90003-X*) Heinemann.
—No Longer at Ease. 1994. 14.00 (*0-606-20072-X*) Turtleback Bks.
—Things Fall Apart. 1959. (C). 15.95 (*0-8392-1113-9*); pap. 12.95 o.p. (*0-8392-5006-1*) Astor-Honor, Inc.
—Things Fall Apart. 1994. 4.95 o.s.i (*0-449-45327-8*); 1985. 192p. mass mkt. 4.95 o.s.i (*0-449-20810-9*, Fawcett); 1983. mass mkt. 2.50 o.s.i (*0-449-20538-X*, Fawcett); 1982. mass mkt. 2.50 o.s.i (*0-449-24142-4*, Fawcett); 1975. mass mkt. 1.50 o.s.i (*0-449-22637-9*, Fawcett) Ballantine Bks.
—Things Fall Apart. (Modern Critical Interpretations Ser.). 176p. pap. 19.95 (*0-7910-7171-5*) Chelsea Hse. Pubs.
—Things Fall Apart. 2002. (EMC Masterpiece Series Access Editions). (Illus.). xxvii, 232p. 10.95 (*0-8219-2412-5*, 35368) EMC/Paradigm Publishing.
—Things Fall Apart. (African Writers Ser.). 1995. (Illus.). 160p. pap. 9.95 o.p. (*0-435-90988-6*); 1987. (Illus.). 150p. (C). pap. 5.95 o.p. (*0-435-90526-0*); 1985. pap. 3.00 o.p. (*0-435-90001-3*); 1996. (Illus.). 206p. pap. 13.95 (*0-435-90525-2*, African Writers Series) Heinemann.
—Things Fall Apart. 1995. 272p. 15.00 (*0-679-44623-0*); 1992. 15.00 o.s.i (*0-679-41714-1*) Knopf, Alfred A. Inc.
—Things Fall Apart. 1994. 224p. pap. 9.95 (*0-385-47454-7*, Knopf Bks. for Young Readers) Random Hse. Children's Bks.
—Things Fall Apart, unabr. ed. 1997. audio 44.00 (*0-7887-0815-5*, 94965E7) Recorded Bks., LLC.
—Things Fall Apart. 1994. 15.00 (*0-606-11979-5*) Turtleback Bks.
Achebe, Chinua & Dabey, John. Things Fall Apart. 1981. (Heinemann Guided Readers Ser.). (C). pap. text 2.00 o.p. (*0-435-27010-9*) Heinemann.
Adichie, Chimamanda Ngozi. Purple Hibiscus: A Novel. 2003. 320p. 23.95 (*1-56512-387-5*) Algonquin Bks. of Chapel Hill.
Akwanga, Amechi. Orimili: One Man's Struggle for Power in Pre-Colonial Nigeria. 1991. (African Writers Ser.). 186p. (C). pap. 8.95 (*0-435-90670-4*, 90670, African Writers Series) Heinemann.
Aluko, T. M. Kinsman & Foreman. 1968. (African Writers Ser.). pap. text 6.00 o.p. (*0-435-90032-3*) Heinemann.
—Wrong Ones in the Dock. 1982. (African Writers Ser.). 195p. pap. text 6.50 o.p. (*0-435-90242-3*) Heinemann.
Amadi, Elechi. Estrangement. 1986. (African Writers Ser.). 244p. (Orig.). (C). pap. 7.95 (*0-435-90564-3*, 90564) Heinemann.
Aniebo, I. N. The Anonymity of Sacrifice. 1974. (African Writers Ser.). pap. text 6.00 o.p. (*0-435-90148-6*) Heinemann.
—The Journey Within. 1978. (African Writers Ser.). pap. 7.95 o.p. (*0-435-90206-7*) Heinemann.
—Of Wives, Talismans & the Dead. 1984. (African Writers Ser.). 154p. (C). pap. text 7.50 o.p. (*0-435-90253-9*) Heinemann.
Balogun, F. Odun. Adjusted Lives: Stories of Structural Adjustments. 1995. 125p. pap. 12.95 (*0-86543-487-5*); 49.95 (*0-86543-486-7*) Africa World Pr.
Beier, Ulli. The Stolen Images. 1976. 55p. pap. text 3.95 o.p. (*0-521-20901-3*) Cambridge Univ. Pr.
Dale, Barbara. The Joys of Motherhood. 1993. pap. 3.50 o.p. (*0-8362-8931-5*) Andrews McMeel Publishing.
Dale, Barbara & Dale, Jim. The Joys of Motherhood. (Cartoon Bks.). (Illus.). 1993. 48p. 4.95 (*0-8362-3047-7*); 1987. 128p. pap. 7.95 (*0-8362-2097-8*) Andrews McMeel Publishing.
Echewa, O. T. I Saw the Sky Catch Fire. 336p. 1993. pap. 12.95 o.p. (*0-452-26949-0*, Plume); 1992. 20.00 o.p. (*0-525-93398-0*, Dutton) Dutton/Plume.
Emecheta, Buchi. The Bride Price. 1980. 168p. pap. 12.95 (*0-8076-0951-X*) Braziller, George Inc.
—The Joys of Motherhood. 244p. 1980. pap. 10.95 (*0-8076-0950-1*); 1979. reprint ed. 7.95 o.p. (*0-8076-0914-5*) Braziller, George Inc.
—The Joys of Motherhood. (African Writers Ser.). 224p. 1994. pap. 12.95 (*0-435-90972-X*, 90972); 1989. pap. 8.95 o.p. (*0-435-90684-4*, 90684) Heinemann.
—Kehinde. 1994. (African Writers Ser.). 160p. pap. 13.95 (*0-435-90985-1*, 90985) Heinemann.
—The Slave Girl. 179p. 1980. pap. 9.95 (*0-8076-0952-8*); 1977. 7.95 o.p. (*0-8076-0872-6*) Braziller, George Inc.
Habila, Helon. Waiting for an Angel: A Novel. 2004. 236p. pap. 13.95 (*0-393-32511-3*); 2003. 256p. 23.95 (*0-393-05193-5*) Norton, W. W. & Co., Inc.
Hill, Kathleen. Still Waters in Niger. 2002. 205p. pap. 15.95 (*0-8101-5134-0*); 1999. 207p. 24.95 (*0-8101-5089-1*) Northwestern Univ. Pr. (TriQuarterly Bks.).
Iroh, Eddie. Forty-Eight Guns for the General. 1976. (African Writers Ser.). 218p. (Orig.). pap. 8.95 o.p. (*0-435-90189-3*) Heinemann.
—The Siren in the Night. 1982. (African Writers Ser.). 207p. pap. text 7.50 o.p. (*0-435-90255-5*) Heinemann.
—Toads of War. 1979. (African Writers Ser.). 144p. (C). pap. 8.95 (*0-435-90213-X*, 90213) Heinemann.
Kalu, Anthonia C. Broken Lives & Other Stories. 2003. (Research in International Studies Ser.: 79). 212p. (C). pap. text 19.95 (*0-89680-229-9*) Ohio Univ. Pr.
Kotun, Debo. Abiku: A Novel of Heart-Stopping Suspense. 1999. xviii, 419p. 26.95 (*0-9668772-7-6*); pap. 14.95 (*0-9668772-8-4*) Nepotist Bks.
Mezu, S. Okechukwu. Behind the Rising Sun. 1972. (African Writers Ser.). 241p. (C). pap. 8.95 o.p. (*0-435-90113-3*) Heinemann.
Mitton, Jennifer. Fadimatu. 1993. 261p. pap. (*0-86492-121-7*) Goose Lane Editions.
Moore, Gerald, et al. Things Fall Apart. 1974. (Books in focus Ser). 10 p. (*0-435-28091-0*) Heinemann.
Njoku, John E. Short Stories of the Traditional People of Nigeria: African Folks, Back Home. 1992. (Studies in African Literature: Vol. 7). 172p. lib. bdg. 79.95 (*0-7734-9631-9*) Mellen, Edwin Pr., The.
Nwapa, Flora. Idu. 1981. (African Writers Ser.). 218p. (C). pap. 8.95 o.p. (*0-435-90056-0*) Heinemann.
—Never Again. 1992. 90p. 24.95 (*0-86543-318-6*); pap. 9.95 (*0-86543-319-4*) Africa World Pr.
—One Is Enough. 1992. 157p. 24.95 (*0-86543-322-4*); pap. 9.95 (*0-86543-323-2*) Africa World Pr.
—This Is Lagos & Other Stories. 1992. 140p. 24.95 (*0-86543-320-8*); pap. 9.95 (*0-86543-321-6*) Africa World Pr.
—Wives at War & Other Stories. 1992. 125p. 24.95 (*0-86543-327-5*); pap. 9.95 (*0-86543-328-3*) Africa World Pr.
Okpewho, Isidore. Call Me by My Rightful Name. 2004. (*1-59221-191-7*); pap. (*1-59221-190-9*) Africa World Pr.
Okri, Ben. The Famished Road. 1992. 512p. 22.50 o.s.i (*0-385-42476-0*) Doubleday Publishing.
—The Famished Road. 1993. 512p. pap. 15.00 (*0-385-42513-9*, Knopf Bks. for Young Readers) Random Hse. Children's Bks.
—Stars of the New Curfew. 208p. 1990. pap. 10.00 o.p. (*0-14-011602-8*, Penguin Bks.); 1989. 17.95 o.p. (*0-670-82520-4*) Viking Penguin.
Onyefulu, Ifeoma. Grandfather's Work: A Traditional Healer in Nigeria. 1998. (Around the World Ser.). (Illus.). 32p. (gr. 2-4). lib. bdg. 22.90 o.p. (*0-7613-0412-6*) Millbrook Pr., Inc.
Saro-Wiwa, Ken. Sozaboy. 1995. (Longman African Writers Ser.). 188p. (C). pap. 16.00 (*0-582-23699-1*) Longman Publishing Group.
Tutuola, Amos. Palm-Wine Drinkard & His Dead Palm-Wine Tapster in the Dead's Town. 1970. 130p. reprint ed. 38.50 o.s.i (*0-8371-4044-7*, TUPD, Greenwood Pr.) Greenwood Publishing Group, Inc.
—Palm-Wine Drinkard & My Life in the Bush of Ghosts. 1988. 320p. pap. 13.50 (*0-8021-3363-0*, Grove Pr.) Grove/Atlantic, Inc.
Van Wert, William F. Stool Wives. 1996. (Nivola Ser.). 190p. 20.00 (*0-917635-20-5*) Plover Pr.
Wiley, Richard. Indigo. 272p. 1993. pap. 10.00 o.p. (*0-452-27044-8*, Plume); 1992. 19.00 o.p. (*0-525-93547-9*, Dutton) Dutton/Plume.

**NODD'S RIDGE (ME.: IMAGINARY PLACE)—FICTION**

King, Tabitha. Caretakers. 1984. mass mkt. 3.95 o.p. (*0-451-13156-8*); 352p. mass mkt. 5.99 o.s.i (*0-451-16169-6*) NAL. (Signet Bks.).

**NORTH CAROLINA—FICTION**

Adams, Alice. After the War. l.t. ed. 2001. (G. K. Hall Core Ser.). 367p. 31.95 (*0-7838-9392-2*, Macmillan Reference USA) Gale Group.
—After the War. 2001. 320p. reprint ed. pap. 14.00 (*0-7434-2222-8*, Washington Square Pr.) Simon & Schuster.
—A Southern Exposure. 1996. mass mkt. (*0-449-14949-8*, Fawcett) Ballantine Bks.
—A Southern Exposure. l.t. ed. 1996. pap. 23.95 (*1-56895-324-0*, Wheeler Publishing, Inc.) Gale Group.
—A Southern Exposure. 1995. 304p. 23.00 o.s.i (*0-679-44452-1*) Knopf, Alfred A. Inc.
Alers, Rochelle. Summer Magic. 1999. (Arabesque Ser.). 252p. mass mkt. 4.99 (*1-58314-012-3*) Kensington Publishing Corp.
Alley, Howard Eugene. Presumed Dead: A Civil War Mystery. 2002. (Illus.). 256p. pap. 16.00 (*0-914875-36-1*, Historical Images) Bright Mountain Bks., Inc.
Amidon, Stephen. The Primitive. 1995. 272p. 23.00 o.p. (*0-88001-411-3*) HarperCollins Pubs.
Anderson, Linda. When Night Falls. 2000. 448p. pap. 6.99 (*0-7434-1147-1*, Pocket) Simon & Schuster.
Autry, Curt. The Reunion. 2002. 279p. pap. (*1-59058-019-2*) Poisoned Pen Pr.
Bache, Ellyn. The Activist's Daughter. 1997. (Coming of Age Ser.). 264p. (Orig.). pap. 10.95 (*1-883523-18-4*) Spinsters Ink Bks.
Ballard, Mignon F. Angel at Troublesome Creek. l.t. ed. 2000. (Beeler Large Print Mystery Ser.). 209p. 25.95 (*1-57490-275-X*, Beeler Large Print Bks.) Beeler, Thomas T. Publisher.
—Angel at Troublesome Creek. 2001. 224p. mass mkt. 5.99 (*0-425-17854-4*, Prime Crime) Berkley Publishing Group.
—Angel at Troublesome Creek. 1999. (Augusta Goodnight Mysteries Ser.). 213p. 22.95 (*0-312-24175-5*, Saint Martin's Minotaur) St. Martin's Pr.
—Angel at Troublesome Creek. 2001. 12.04 (*0-606-20547-0*) Turtleback Bks.
—Final Curtain. 1992. 192p. 18.95 o.p. (*0-88184-799-2*, Carroll & Graf Pubs.) Avalon Publishing Group.
Bardi, Abby. The Book of Fred: A Novel. 2001. 304p. 24.00 (*0-7434-1193-5*, Washington Square Pr.) Simon & Schuster.
Barkley, Brad. Money Love. 2000. 320p. 24.95 (*0-393-04929-9*) Norton, W. W. & Co., Inc.
Bartholomew, Nancy. Stand by Your Man. 2001. 240p. mass mkt. 6.50 (*0-06-101410-9*) Morrow/Avon.
Betts, Doris. The Astronomer & Other Stories. 1995. (Voices of the South Ser.). 242p. pap. 11.95 (*0-8071-2010-3*) Louisiana State Univ. Pr.
Bishop, Maggie. Appalachian Paradise. 2003. 172p. 9.95 (*0-9713045-6-4*) High Country Pubs., Ltd.
Bledsoe, Jerry. The Angel Doll: A Christmas Story. 1996. (Illus.). 125p. 14.95 (*1-878086-54-5*) Down Home Pr.
—The Angel Doll: A Christmas Story. 1999. 112p. 13.95 (*0-312-17104-8*) St. Martin's Pr.
—A Gift of Angels. 1999. (Illus.). 149p. 16.95 (*1-878086-80-4*) Down Home Pr.
Bone, Patrick. The Aliens of Transylvania County. 2002. 160p. pap. 13.95 (*1-57072-175-0*); 23.95 (*1-57072-174-2*) Overmountain Pr. (Silver Dagger Mysteries).
Booth, Carolyn R. Between the Rivers. 2001. 430p. 13.95 (*1-928556-29-9*) Coastal Carolina Pr.
Boyne, Walter J. Dawn over Kitty Hawk: A Novel of the Wright Brothers. 2003. 400p. 24.95 (*0-7653-0471-6*, 52996964, Forge Bks.) Doherty, Tom Assocs., LLC.
Brady, Maureen. Folly. 1994. 224p. reprint ed. 35.00 (*1-55861-078-2*); pap. 12.95 (*1-55861-079-0*) Feminist Pr. at The City Univ. of New York.
—Folly: A Novel. 1982. 198p. 23.95 o.p. (*0-89594-091-4*); pap. 8.95 o.p. (*0-89594-090-6*) Crossing Pr., Inc., The.
Brand, Irene. Summer's Promise. 2001. (Steeple Hill Love Inspired Ser.: No. 148). mass mkt. (*0-373-87155-4*, 1-87155-7, Steeple Hill) Harlequin Enterprises, Ltd.
Brandt, Ann. Crowfoot Ridge. 1997. 224p. 22.95 (*1-57090-053-1*) Alexander Bks.
—Crowfoot Ridge. 1999. 288p. 20.00 (*0-06-019215-1*) HarperCollins Pubs.
—Crowfoot Ridge. 2000. 368p. mass mkt. 6.50 (*0-06-109709-8*, HarperTorch) Morrow/Avon.
Brooks, Skip. Monteith's Mountains: Death Stalks the Southern Appalachians. 2002. (Illus.). 288p. 21.95 (*0-9713045-4-8*) High Country Pubs., Ltd.
Brown, Sandra. Seduction by Design. 2001. (Illus.). 192p. 19.95 o.p. (*0-446-52767-X*) Warner Bks., Inc.
Bryant, Henry E. Tar Heel Tales. 1977. (Black Heritage Library Collection). reprint ed. 23.95 (*0-8369-9162-1*) Ayer Co. Pubs., Inc.
Burford, Miles. Days of a Fledgling. 1998. 256p. 24.95 (*1-56474-262-8*) Fithian Pr.
Byrd, Martha. A Shoebox of Violets. 1995. (Illus.). 129p. pap. 12.00 (*0-9623388-5-0*) Laney-Smith, Inc.
Canada, Wanda. Cape Fear Murders: A Carroll Davenport Mystery. 2003. 248p. 19.95 (*1-928556-41-8*); 280p. pap. 6.99 (*1-928556-42-6*) Coastal Carolina Pr.
—Island Murders. 2001. (Illus.). 327p. pap. 6.99 (*1-928556-26-4*) Coastal Carolina Pr.
Cantrell, Lisa W. Boneman. 256p. 1995. mass mkt. 4.99 (*0-8125-1970-1*); 1992. 18.95 o.p. (*0-312-85307-6*) Doherty, Tom Assocs., LLC. (Tor Bks.).
Card, Orson Scott. Lost Boys: A Novel. abr. ed. audio 16.95 o.p. (*1-55927-218-X*) Audio Renaissance.
—Lost Boys: A Novel. 1992. 320p. 20.00 o.p. (*0-06-016693-2*) HarperTrade.
—Lost Boys: A Novel. 1993. 544p. mass mkt. 7.99 (*0-06-109131-6*, HarperTorch) Morrow/Avon.
—Lost Boys: A Novel. 1994. 5.99 o.p. (*0-517-12577-3*) Random Hse. Value Publishing.
Carmichael, G. Wade. Jack's Resolve: A True Patriot's Tale. 2000. 249p. (*1-883103-12-6*) United, Inc.
Chadwick, Cynn. Cat Rising: A Novel. 2002. 244p. 27.95 (*1-56023-407-5*); pap. 17.95 (*1-56023-408-3*) Haworth Pr., Inc., The. (Alice Street Editions).
Chamberlain, Diane. Keeper of the Light: A Novel. 1992. 448p. 22.00 o.p. (*0-06-017964-3*) HarperTrade.
—Kiss River. 384p. 2004. mass mkt. (*0-7783-2002-2*); 2003. (*1-55166-664-2*) Harlequin Enterprises, Ltd. (Mira Bks.).
—Summer's Child. 2000. 416p. mass mkt. (*1-55166-509-3*, 1-66509-0, Mira Bks.) Harlequin Enterprises, Ltd.
Chappell, Fred. Brighten the Corner Where You Are. 1989. 15.95 o.p. (*0-312-03297-8*); 8th ed. 1990. 212p. reprint ed. pap. 11.95 (*0-312-05057-7*, CPB1110, Saint Martin's Griffin) St. Martin's Pr.
—Dagon. E-Book 7.50 (*1-886420-63-7*); 1996. E-Book 7.50 (*1-886420-29-7*) C&M Online Media, Inc. (Boson Bks.).
—Dagon. 2002. (Voices of the South Ser.). 192p. pap. 15.95 (*0-8071-2791-4*) Louisiana State Univ. Pr.
—Dagon. 1986. pap. 3.50 o.p. (*0-312-90676-5*, St. Martin's Paperbacks) St. Martin's Pr.
—I Am One of You Forever. 1987. 184p. pap. 12.95 (*0-8071-1410-3*); 1985. 192p. 14.95 o.p. (*0-8071-1216-X*) Louisiana State Univ. Pr.
—Look Back All the Green Valley. 288p. 2000. pap. 13.00 (*0-312-24310-3*); 1999. 24.00 o.p. (*0-312-24215-8*) Picador.
Chesnutt, Charles Waddell. The Marrow of Tradition. reprint ed. 42.50 (*0-404-00014-2*) AMS Pr., Inc.
—The Marrow of Tradition. 1976. 25.95 (*0-8488-0962-9*) Amereon, Ltd.
—The Marrow of Tradition. 1977. (Black Heritage Library Collection). 17.95 (*0-8369-8539-7*) Ayer Co. Pubs., Inc.
—The Marrow of Tradition. 1986. (Muckrakers Ser.). reprint ed. pap. 6.95 o.p. (*0-89197-836-4*); lib. bdg. 13.00 o.p. (*0-8398-0260-9*) Irvington Pubs.
—The Marrow of Tradition. 2001. 352p. pap. 12.95 (*0-375-75690-6*, Modern Library) Random House Adult Trade Publishing Group.
—The Marrow of Tradition. l.t. ed. 1999. 310p. text 29.95 (*1-56000-493-2*) Transaction Pubs.
—The Marrow of Tradition. 2nd ed. 1969. (Ann Arbor Paperbacks Ser.). (Illus.). 352p. (C). pap. text 14.95 (*0-472-06147-X*, 06147) Univ. of Michigan Pr.
—The Marrow of Tradition. Sundquist, Eric J., ed. & intro. by. 1993. (Penguin Twentieth-Century Classics Ser.). 400p. pap. 13.95 (*0-14-018686-7*, Penguin Classics) Viking Penguin.
—The Marrow of Tradition: American Negro. 1968. (His History & Literature Ser.: No. 2). reprint ed. 17.95 (*0-405-01855-X*) Ayer Co. Pubs., Inc.
Clark, Martin. The Many Aspects of Mobile Home Living: A Novel. 2001. 352p. pap. 13.00 (*0-375-70709-3*, Vintage) Knopf Publishing Group.
Coe, Marian. Eve's Mountain: A Novel of Passion & Mystery in the Blue Ridge. 1998. (Illus.). 384p. pap. 14.98 o.p. (*0-9633341-5-8*) SouthLore Pr.
Combe, Louis. Watching the Watcher. 2000. (Illus.). 174p. pap. 12.95 (*1-880849-24-0*) Chapel Hill Pr.
Cornwell, Patricia. The Body Farm. l.t. ed. 1994. 403p. lib. bdg. 26.95 o.p. (*0-7838-1122-5*, Macmillan Reference USA) Gale Group.
—The Body Farm. 1999. audio 9.98 (*0-671-04687-X*, Simon & Schuster Audioworks) Simon & Schuster Audio.
—The Body Farm. l.t. ed. 1996. (Paperback Bestsellers Ser.). pap. 20.95 (*0-7838-1123-3*) Thorndike Pr.
—Hornet's Nest. l.t. ed. 1998. 384p. mass mkt. 7.99 (*0-425-16098-X*) Berkley Publishing Group.
—Hornet's Nest. unabr. ed. 1997. (Judy Hammer Mystery Ser.). audio 72.00 (*0-913369-52-7*, 4264) Books on Tape, Inc.
—Hornet's Nest. l.t. ed. 1997. 523p. lib. bdg. 27.95 o.p. (*0-7838-8085-5*, Macmillan Reference USA) Gale Group.
—Hornet's Nest. 2000. 25.95 o.s.i (*0-399-14554-0*); 1997. 384p. 25.95 o.s.i (*0-399-14228-2*, G. P. Putnam's Sons); Set. 1997. audio 24.95 (*0-399-14282-7*, 694558) Penguin Group (USA) Inc.
—Hornet's Nest. l.t. ed. 1998. (Paperback Bestsellers Ser.). 490p. pap. 27.95 (*0-7838-8086-3*) Thorndike Pr.
Correa, Raul. I Don't Know but I've Been Told. 2002. 272p. 24.95 (*0-06-019611-4*) HarperCollins Pubs.

Dailey, Janet. That Carolina Summer. l.t. ed. 2001. 200p. (0-7540-4537-4); (0-7540-4538-2) Gale Group. (Macmillan Reference USA).

—That Carolina Summer. 1992. (Janet Dailey Americana Ser.: No. 883). per. (0-373-89883-5, 1-89883-2); 1987. pap. (0-373-89833-9) Harlequin Enterprises, Ltd. (Harlequin Bks.).

—That Carolina Summer. l.t. ed. 2001. (Romance Ser.). 200p. 28.95 (0-7838-9123-7) Thorndike Pr.

—That Carolina Summer. E-Book 6.99 (0-7592-0917-0); 1999. 120p. per. 12.95 (0-7592-3832-4) ereads.com.

Darty, Peggy. Spirits. 1998. (Palisades Pure Romance Ser.). 252p. pap. 9.99 o.s.i (1-57673-460-9) Multnomah Pubs., Inc.

Davidson, Donald. The Big Ballad Jamboree. Ellison, Curtis W. & Pratt, William, eds. 295p. 1996. 27.00 (0-87805-853-2); 2nd ed. 1998. reprint ed. pap. 17.00 (1-57806-098-2) Univ. Pr. of Mississippi.

Davis, Donald. Barking at a Fox-Fur Coat. 1991. 206p. 19.95 (0-87483-141-5); pap. 12.95 (0-87483-140-7) August Hse. Pubs., Inc.

—Listening for the Crack of Dawn. (American Storytelling Ser.). unabr. ed. 1991. audio 18.00 (0-87483-147-4); 10th ed. 2000. 224p. reprint ed. pap. 11.95 (0-87483-605-0) August Hse. Pubs., Inc.

—See Rock City: A Story Journey Through Appalachia. 1996. (American Storytelling Ser.). 247p. 22.95 (0-87483-448-1); (YA). (gr. 6 up). pap. text 12.95 (0-87483-456-2); (YA). (gr. 6 up). audio 12.00 (0-87483-452-X) August Hse. Pubs., Inc.

—Thirteen Miles from Suncrest: A Novel. 1996. pap. text 14.95 (0-87483-455-4); 1994. 256p. 22.95 (0-87483-379-5) August Hse. Pubs., Inc.

Davis, Donald D. Listening for the Crack of Dawn. 1990. 224p. 19.95 o.p. (0-87483-153-9) August Hse. Pubs., Inc.

—Listening for the Crack of Dawn: A Master Storyteller Recalls the Appalachia of the 1950's & 60's. 1991. 220p. pap. 12.95 o.p. (0-87483-130-X) August Hse. Pubs., Inc.

Davis-Gardner, Angela. Forms of Shelter. l.t. ed. 1993. (General Ser.). 346p. 16.95 o.p. (0-8161-5423-6, Macmillan Reference USA) Gale Group.

—Forms of Shelter. 1991. 256p. 19.95 o.p. (0-395-59312-3) Houghton Mifflin Co.

Deaver, Jeffery. The Empty Chair: A Lincoln Rhyme Novel. 2000. E-Book 25.00 (0-7432-1165-0); (Illus.). 416p. 25.00 o.s.i (0-684-85563-1); 416p. 25.00 (0-7432-0162-0); 624p. 25.00 o.s.i (0-7432-0424-7) Simon & Schuster. (Simon & Schuster).

—The Empty Chair: A Lincoln Rhyme Novel. abr. ed. 2000. audio 25.00 (0-7435-0052-0, Simon & Schuster Audioworks) Simon & Schuster Audio.

—Speaking in Tongues: A Novel. 2000. 336p. 25.00 o.s.i (0-684-87126-2, Simon & Schuster) Simon & Schuster.

—Speaking in Tongues: A Novel. 1999. 21.95 (0-670-86073-5, Viking) Viking Penguin.

Dierbeck, Lisa. One Pill Makes You Smaller. 2003. 320p. 24.00 (0-374-22649-0) Farrar, Straus & Giroux.

—One Pill Makes You Smaller. 2004. pap. (0-312-42286-5) Picador.

Dodd, Susan. The Mourners' Bench: A Novel. l.t. ed. 1999. 26.95 (1-56895-599-5, Wheeler Publishing, Inc.) Gale Group.

—The Mourners' Bench: A Novel. 1999. 288p. reprint ed. pap. 13.00 (0-688-16973-2, Perennial) HarperTrade.

—The Mourners' Bench: A Novel. 1998. 288p. 24.00 (0-688-15799-8, Morrow, William & Co.) Morrow/Avon.

Duncan, Pamela. Moon Women. 2002. 336p. pap. 12.95 (0-385-33521-0, Delta) Dell Publishing.

Earley, Tony. Here We Are in Paradise: Stories. 1998. pap. 11.95 (0-316-19089-6, Back Bay); 1997. 208p. pap. 13.95 (0-316-19949-4); 1994. 198p. 19.45 (0-316-19962-1) Little Brown & Co.

—Jim the Boy: A Novel. l.t. ed. 2000. (Wheeler Large Print Book Ser.). 227p. 27.95 (1-56895-990-7, Wheeler Publishing, Inc.) Gale Group.

—Jim the Boy: A Novel. Adams, Terry, ed. 2001. (Illus.). 256p. pap. 12.95 (0-316-19895-1, Back Bay); 2000. 240p. 23.95 (0-316-19964-8) Little Brown & Co.

Edelson, Julie. Bad Housekeeping. 1995. 258p. 21.00 (1-880909-31-6) Baskerville Pubs., Inc.

Edgerton, Clyde. In Memory of Junior. 1992. 224p. 16.95 (1-56512-010-8) Algonquin Bks. of Chapel Hill.

—In Memory of Junior. 1996. 228p. pap. 15.00 (0-345-41029-7); 1993. 256p. reprint ed. mass mkt. 5.99 o.s.i (0-345-38360-5) Ballantine Bks.

—In Memory of Junior. audio o.p. National Humanities Ctr.

—In Memory of Junior. unabr. ed. 1993. audio 51.00 (1-55690-789-3, 93101E7) Recorded Bks., LLC.

—Killer Diller. 1991. 264p. 17.95 (0-945575-53-X) Algonquin Bks. of Chapel Hill.

—Killer Diller. 1996. 272p. pap. 12.95 (0-345-41030-0); 1992. 288p. mass mkt. 5.99 o.s.i (0-345-37072-4, Ballantine Bks.) Ballantine Bks.

—Killer Diller. l.t. ed. 1991. 288p. lib. bdg. 19.95 (0-8161-5254-3, Macmillan Reference USA) Gale Group.

—Killer Diller. audio o.p. National Humanities Ctr.

—Killer Diller, unabr. ed. audio 51.00 (1-55690-682-X, 92112E7) Recorded Bks., LLC.

—Where Trouble Sleeps. 1997. 380p. tchr. ed. 18.95 (1-56512-061-2) Algonquin Bks. of Chapel Hill.

—Where Trouble Sleeps. 1998. 288p. pap. 12.95 (0-345-42632-0) Ballantine Bks.

Edgerton, Dale. Goneaway Road. 2003. 320p. pap. 17.95 (1-56023-434-2); 39.95 (1-56023-433-4) Haworth Pr., Inc., The. (Southern Tier Editions).

Ehle, John. The Road. 1998. (Appalachian Echoes Ser.). 416p. reprint ed. pap. 19.95 (1-57233-016-3) Univ. of Tennessee Pr.

—The Winter People. 1982. pap. 3.95 o.p. (0-440-39770-7) Dell Publishing.

—The Winter People. 4th ed. 1999. 272p. reprint ed. pap. 14.95 (1-878086-74-X) Down Home Pr.

—The Winter People. 1982. 256p. 13.95 o.p. (0-06-014930-2); 1989. 320p. reprint ed. mass mkt. 4.95 o.p. (0-06-080939-6, P 939, Perennial) HarperTrade.

Ferrell, Anderson. Where She Was. 1985. 141p. 13.95 o.s.i (0-394-53521-9) Knopf, Alfred A. Inc.

—Where She Was. 1986. mass mkt. 6.95 o.s.i (0-671-62438-5, Pocket) Simon & Schuster.

—Women Too Much. 2004. 288p. 23.95 (1-58234-189-3) Bloomsbury Publishing.

Fine, Africa. Becoming Maren. 2003. 26.95 (1-59414-081-2, Five Star) Gale Group.

Fleming, Julie Elaine. Moving Lila. E-Book 22.95 (0-312-27533-1); 2000. 212p. 22.95 (0-312-24409-6) St. Martin's Pr.

Fletcher, Inglis. Bennett's Welcome. (Albemarle Ser.). 451p. reprint ed. lib. bdg. 29.95 (0-89244-001-5, Queens Hse., Inc.) Amereon, Ltd.

—Bennett's Welcome. 1990. reprint ed. lib. bdg. 25.95 (0-89968-503-X) Buccaneer Bks., Inc.

—Lusty Wind for Carolina. 1976. reprint ed. lib. bdg. 33.95 (0-89244-003-1, Queens Hse., Inc.) Amereon, Ltd.

—Lusty Wind for Carolina. 1970. 576p. mass mkt. 4.50 o.s.i (0-553-25657-2) Bantam Bks.

—Lusty Wind for Carolina. 1990. reprint ed. lib. bdg. 39.95 (0-89968-504-8) Buccaneer Bks., Inc.

—Lusty Wind for Carolina. 1995. 512p. reprint ed. 38.00 (0-87797-225-7) Cherokee Publishing Co.

—Men of Albemarle. 1976. 500p. reprint ed. lib. bdg. 31.95 (0-89244-004-X, Queens Hse., Inc.) Amereon, Ltd.

—Men of Albemarle. 1990. reprint ed. lib. bdg. 27.95 (0-89968-505-6) Buccaneer Bks., Inc.

—Men of Albemarle. 1986. 512p. mass mkt. 4.50 o.s.i (0-553-25670-X) Bantam Bks.

—Queen's Gift. (Albemarle Ser.). 448p. reprint ed. lib. bdg. 29.95 (0-89244-005-8, Queens Hse., Inc.) Amereon, Ltd.

—Queen's Gift. 1990. reprint ed. lib. bdg. 25.95 (0-89968-506-4) Buccaneer Bks., Inc.

—Raleigh's Eden. 1976. (Albemarle Ser.). reprint ed. lib. bdg. 34.95 (0-89244-006-6, Queens Hse., Inc.) Amereon, Ltd.

—Raleigh's Eden. 1980. 608p. mass mkt. 4.50 o.s.i (0-553-25950-4) Bantam Bks.

—Roanoke Hundred. (Albemarle Ser.). 501p. reprint ed. lib. bdg. 30.95 (0-89244-007-4, Queens Hse., Inc.) Amereon, Ltd.

—Roanoke Hundred. 1990. reprint ed. lib. bdg. 26.95 (0-89968-507-2) Buccaneer Bks., Inc.

—Wind in the Forest. 1976. 28.95 (0-89244-011-2, Queens Hse., Inc.) Amereon, Ltd.

Flynt, Candace. Mother Love. 1988. 352p. pap. 7.95 o.p. (0-452-26076-0, Plume) Dutton/Plume.

—Mother Love. 1987. 84p. 17.95 o.s.i (0-374-21374-7) Farrar, Straus & Giroux.

—Mother Love. 2003. (Voices of the South Ser.). 360p. pap. 17.95 (0-8071-2697-7) Louisiana State Univ. Pr.

Forster, Gwynne. Blues from down Deep. 2004. 304p. pap. 14.00 (0-7582-0010-2, Kensington Bks.) Kensington Publishing Corp.

Freeble, Charles R. Toscape Death: A Novelized Version of the Life of Herman Husband, a Forgotton Early American Original, Vol. 1. 1996. 69p. per. 7.95 (1-55856-224-9, 275) Closson Pr.

Gaskill, Cathy. Ruth's Gift: A Family Legend. exp. ed. 1998. (Illus.). 160p. per. 15.00 (1-887774-03-3) Canmore Pr.

Gibbons, Kaye. Charms for the Easy Life. unabr. ed. 2000. audio 54.95 (0-7927-2352-X, CSL 241, Chivers Sound Library) BBC Audiobooks America.

—Charms for the Easy Life. l.t. ed. 1993. 23.95 o.p. (1-56895-030-6, Wheeler Publishing, Inc.) Gale Group.

—Charms for the Easy Life. 1995. 256p. pap. 12.95 (0-380-72557-6); 1994. 304p. mass mkt. 7.99 (0-380-72270-4) Morrow/Avon. (Avon Bks.).

—Charms for the Easy Life. 1993. 256p. 19.95 o.s.i (0-399-13791-2) Penguin Group (USA) Inc.

—Charms for the Easy Life, Set. abr. ed. 1999. audio 17.00 (0-671-88535-9, 390510, Simon & Schuster Audioworks) Simon & Schuster Audio.

—Charms for the Easy Life. 1993. 13.04 (0-606-07154-7) Turtleback Bks.

—Divining Women: A Novel. 2004. (0-399-15076-5, Putnam & Grosset) Putnam Publishing Group, The.

—Sights Unseen. l.t. ed. 1995. 191p. 23.95 o.p. (0-7838-1485-2, Macmillan Reference USA) Gale Group.

—Sights Unseen. 1996. mass mkt. o.s.i (0-349-10759-9) Little Brown & Co.

—Sights Unseen. 1997. 224p. pap. 12.00 (0-380-72972-5); 1996. 240p. mass mkt. 6.99 (0-380-72681-5) Morrow/Avon. (Avon Bks.).

—Sights Unseen. 1995. 256p. 19.95 o.p. (0-399-13986-9, G. P. Putnam's Sons) Penguin Group (USA) Inc.

—Sights Unseen. abr. ed. 1995. audio 17.00 (0-671-88568-5, 393158, Simon & Schuster Audioworks) Simon & Schuster Audio.

Gilchrist, Ellen. I Cannot Get You Close Enough. unabr. collector's ed. 1993. audio 64.00 (0-7366-2432-5, 3197) Books on Tape, Inc.

—I Cannot Get You Close Enough. 1991. 391p. pap. 12.95 (0-316-31423-4); Vol. 1. 1990. 19.95 o.p. (0-316-31313-0) Little Brown & Co.

Gingher, Robert, intro. The Rough Road Home: Stories by North Carolina Writers. 1992. xviii, 332p. (C). 29.95 (0-8078-2064-4); pap. 16.95 (0-8078-4397-0) Univ. of North Carolina Pr.

Gire, Ken. Kim's Diary. 97p. (J). (gr. 3-7). pap. 4.99 (0-7814-3427-0) Cook Communications Ministries.

Godwin, Gail. A Mother & Two Daughters. 1982. 576p. 16.95 o.p. (0-670-49021-0) Viking Penguin.

—The Odd Woman. 1995. 436p. pap. 19.00 (0-345-38991-3) Ballantine Bks.

—The Odd Woman. 1976. 1.95 o.p. (0-425-03167-5) Berkley Publishing Group.

—The Odd Woman. 1985. (Contemporary American Fiction Ser.). 432p. pap. 8.95 o.p. (0-14-008221-2, Penguin Bks.) Viking Penguin.

—The Odd Woman. 1983. 432p. mass mkt. 3.95 o.p. (0-446-30569-3, 305693) Warner Bks., Inc.

Green, Carmen. Commitments. 2001. 256p. mass mkt. 5.99 (1-58314-226-6) BET Bks.

Greer, Ben. Slammer. 2002. (Voices of the South Ser.). 280p. pap. 16.95 (0-8071-2789-2) Louisiana State Univ. Pr.

Gurley-Highgate, Hilda. Sapphire's Grave: A Novel. 2002. 256p. 23.95 (0-385-50323-7) Doubleday Publishing.

Haddam, Jane. Baptism in Blood. 1996. 352p. mass mkt. 5.99 o.s.i (0-553-57464-7, Crimeline) Bantam Bks.

Harvey, Clay. A Whisper of Black. 1997. 240p. 23.95 o.s.i (0-399-14232-0, G. P. Putnam's Sons) Penguin Group (USA) Inc.

—Whisper of Black. 1998. 320p. mass mkt. 6.99 o.s.i (0-425-16450-0) Berkley Publishing Group.

—A Whisper of Black. l.t. ed. 1998. (Charnwood Large Print Ser.). 336p. 29.99 o.p. (0-7089-9016-9, Ulverscroft) Thorpe, F. A. Pubs. GBR. *Dist:* Ulverscroft Large Print Bks., Ltd., Ulverscroft Large Print Canada, Ltd.

Henderson, Walter. Death by Suicidal Means. 1994. 227p. 19.95 (0-9638086-0-5); pap. 8.95 (0-9638086-1-3) Inheritance Pr., Inc.

Herrick, Rick. An Uncommon Woman. 2001. ii, 182p. 14.95 (1-887905-45-6) Parkway Pubs., Inc.

—A Week in October. 2002. xii, 195p. 14.95 (1-887905-65-0) Parkway Pubs., Inc.

Hill, Richard. What Rough Beast? 1992. 216p. 20.00 o.p. (0-88150-238-3) Countryman Pr.

Hinton, J. Lynne. Forever Friends. 2004. 213p. pap. 12.95 (0-06-251749-X) HarperSanFrancisco.

—Forever Friends: A Novel. 2003. 224p. 21.95 (0-06-251748-1) HarperSanFrancisco.

Hinton, Lynne. Friendship Cake. l.t. ed. 2001. lib. bdg. 27.95 (1-58547-153-4) Ctr. Point Large Print.

—Friendship Cake. 2000. 224p. 20.00 (0-688-17147-8) HarperCollins Pubs.

—Friendship Cake. 2001. 336p. mass mkt. 7.50 o.s.i (0-380-82014-5) Morrow/Avon.

—Friendship Cake: A Novel. 2002. 240p. pap. 11.95 (0-06-251731-7) HarperSanFrancisco.

—Last Odd Day. 2004. (0-06-056338-9) HarperSanFrancisco.

Hoffman, Margaret. Blackbeard: A Tale of Villainy & Murder in Colonial America. 2000. (Illus.). 330p. 24.00 (0-9607300-1-X) Coastal Plains Publishing Co.

Hooper, Kay. Stealing Shadows. 2000. (Shadows Trilogy Ser.). 384p. mass mkt. 7.50 (0-553-57553-8) Bantam Bks.

—Stealing Shadows. l.t. ed. 2002. (Basic Ser.). 495p. pap. 28.95 (0-7862-3062-2) Gale Group.

—Stealing Shadows. l.t. ed. 2001. (Basic Ser.). 495p. 30.95 (0-7862-3061-4) Thorndike Pr.

Hopkiins, Lila. Strike a Golden Chord. 2003. (Illus.). 236p. 23.95 (1-932158-51-0) High Country Pubs., Ltd.

Hopkins, Lila. Weave Me a Song: A Novel: a Chronicle of Family Devotion, a Story of Love, Betrayal, Forgiveness & Reunion. 2002. 229p. 19.95 (0-9713045-7-2) High Country Pubs., Ltd.

Horne, J. S. Willard Jerhom. 2003. 139p. pap. 8.00 (0-9740335-0-2) Smith, Kenneth.

Humphreys, Josephine. Nowhere Else on Earth. l.t. ed. 2000. (Large Print Bks.). 460p. 28.95 (1-56895-957-5, Wheeler Publishing, Inc.) Gale Group.

—Nowhere Else on Earth. 2000. (0-670-78270-X); (Illus.). 288p. 24.95 o.p. (0-670-89176-2, Viking) Viking Penguin.

—Nowhere Else on Earth: A Novel. 2001. 368p. reprint ed. pap. 14.00 (0-14-100206-9) Penguin Group (USA) Inc.

Hunt, Angela Elwell. Roanoke: The Lost Colony. 1996. (Keepers of the Ring Ser.: Vol. 1). 512p. pap. 8.99 o.p. (0-8423-2012-1) Tyndale Hse. Pubs.

Hyman, John H. The Relationship. 1995. (Illus.). 251p. (YA). (gr. 7 up). 16.95 (1-880664-14-3) E. M. Productions.

Inman, Robert. Captain Saturday: A Novel. 464p. 2002. 24.95 o.p. (0-316-41502-2); 2003. reprint ed. pap. 13.95 (0-316-08973-7, Back Bay) Little Brown & Co.

Jackson, Muriel R. The Garden Club. l.t. ed. 1993. 307p. lib. bdg. 22.95 (0-8161-5758-8, Macmillan Reference USA) Gale Group.

—The Garden Club. 1992. 224p. 17.95 o.p. (0-312-08196-0, Saint Martin's Minotaur) St. Martin's Pr.

Jaffe, Jody. Chestnut Mare, Beware. 1997. mass mkt. 5.99 o.s.i (0-8041-1552-4, Ivy Bks.); 1996. 288p. 21.00 o.s.i (0-449-90998-0, Fawcett) Ballantine Bks.

—Chestnut Mare, Beware. unabr. collector's ed. 1997. audio 64.00 (0-7366-3599-8, 4250) Books on Tape, Inc.

—Horse of a Different Killer. 1996. mass mkt. 5.99 o.s.i (0-8041-1472-2, Ivy Bks.); 1995. 288p. 21.00 o.s.i (0-449-90997-2) Ballantine Bks.

—Horse of a Different Killer. unabr. collector's ed. 1997. audio 48.00 (0-913369-53-5, 4265) Books on Tape, Inc.

—In Colt Blood. 1999. mass mkt. 5.99 o.s.i (0-8041-1711-X, Ivy Bks.) Ballantine Bks.

—In Colt Blood. collector's ed. 1999. audio 56.00 (0-7366-4787-2, 5134) Books on Tape, Inc.

Jekel, Pamela. Deepwater. 1995. 576p. mass mkt. 5.99 o.s.i (0-8217-4828-9); 1994. mass mkt. 20.00 o.s.i (0-8217-4485-2, Zebra Bks.) Kensington Publishing Corp.

Jelliffe, Belinda Dobson. For Dear Life & Selected Short Stories. Pruitt, Virginia D. & Faulkner, Howard J., eds. 2002. (Illus.). xxxiii, 293p. pap. 34.00 (0-87338-747-3) Kent State Univ. Pr.

John, Charlotte S. Showdown. 1987. 160p. mass mkt. 2.50 o.s.i (0-449-70200-6, Fawcett) Ballantine Bks.

Johnson, Cherry L. Half Moon Pocosin. 1997. 175p. 20.00 (0-89733-438-8) Academy Chicago Pubs., Ltd.

Johnson-Coleman, Lorraine. Just Plain Folks: Original Tales of Living, Loving, & Learning, as Told by a Perfectly Ordinary, Quite Commonly Sensible & Absolutely Awe-Inspiring Colored Woman. 2000. 256p. pap. 12.95 (0-316-46007-9, Back Bay) Little Brown & Co.

—Just Plain Folks: Original Tales of Living, Loving, Longing & Learning, As Told by a Perfectly Ordinary, Quite Commonly Sensible & Absolutely Awe-Inspiring Colored Woman. 1998. 256p. 22.00 o.p. (0-316-46084-2) Little Brown & Co.

—Just Plain Folks: Original Tales of Living, Loving, Longing & Learning as Told by a Perfectly Ordinary, Quite Commonly Sensible & Absolutely Awe-Inspiring Colored Woman. 2001. 192p. E-Book 9.95 (0-446-91468-1) Little Brown & Co.

—Just Plain Folks: Original Tales of Living, Loving, Longing, & Learning as Told by a Perfectly Ordinary, Quite Commonly Sensible & Absolutely Awe-Inspiring Colored Woman. 2001. 192p. E-Book 9.95 (0-446-92360-5) Warner Bks., Inc.

—Talking Mules & Other Folks: A Fable. 2003. 128p. 16.95 (1-58818-045-X) Hill Street Pr., LLC.

Jones, Elizabeth McDavid. The Night Flyers. 1999. (American Girl Collection: Bk. 3). (Illus.). 160p. (J). (gr. 5-9). 9.95 (1-56247-815-X, American Girl) Pleasant Co. Pubns.

Jones, Simmons. Show Me the Way to Go Home. 1991. 336p. 19.95 o.p. (0-945575-41-6) Algonquin Bks. of Chapel Hill.

—Show Me the Way to Go Home. 1993. (Stonewall Inn Editions Ser.). 336p. pap. 9.95 (0-312-09387-X, Saint Martin's Griffin) St. Martin's Pr.

Judson, Suzanne. Harper's Moon. 2000. 336p. mass mkt. 6.99 o.s.i (0-425-17542-1) Berkley Publishing Group.

—Harper's Moon. l.t. ed. 2001. (G. K. Hall Core Ser.). 424p. 28.95 (*0-7838-9390-6*, Macmillan Reference USA) Gale Group.

Julie & Ro: A Jewish-Christian Love Story for the Young at Heart Age 10-90. 1996. 233p. pap. 9.50 (*1-889361-05-4*) Ruroanik Pubs.

Kaiper, Gina V. I Shall Never Speak. 1995. 184p. pap. 11.95 (*0-9645206-2-1*) Days & Years Pr., The.

—The Story of Lina Holt. 1996. 207p. (Orig.). pap. 12.95 (*0-9645206-3-X*) Days & Years Pr., The.

Karon, Jan. At Home in Mitford. l.t. ed. (Mitford Ser.: No.1). 21.95 (*1-57490-254-7*); 1996. lib. bdg. 26.95 (*1-57490-071-4*, Beeler Large Print Bks.) Beeler, Thomas T. Publisher.

—At Home in Mitford. 2003. (Radio Theatre Ser.). audio 39.99 (*1-58997-001-2*) Focus on the Family Publishing.

—At Home in Mitford. (Mitford Ser.: No. 1). 448p. pap. 12.99 (*0-7459-2629-0*) Lion Publishing.

—At Home in Mitford. unabr. ed. 2002. audio compact disk 142.00 (*1-4025-2969-4*) Recorded Bks., LLC.

—At Home in Mitford. 2003. (Radio Theatre Ser.). audio compact disk 39.99 (*1-58997-000-4*) Tyndale Hse. Pubs.

—At Home in Mitford. (Mitford Ser.: No. 1). 1998. 432p. 24.95 (*0-670-88225-9*); 1996. 448p. 12.95 (*0-14-025448-X*); 1996. 2p. pap. 16.95 incl. audio (*0-14-086501-2*, Penguin AudioBooks) Viking Penguin.

—A Common Life: The Wedding Story. l.t. ed. 224p. 2002. pap. 12.95 (*0-375-72814-7*); 2001. (Mitford Ser.: Vol. 6). (Illus.). 24.95 (*0-375-43104-7*) Random Hse. Large Print.

—A Common Life: The Wedding Story. 2001. (Mitford Ser.: Vol. 6). (Illus.). 208p. text 24.95 (*0-670-89437-0*, Viking); 2015. audio 16.95 (*0-14-086742-2*, Penguin AudioBooks); 2001. (Mitford Ser.: Vol. 6). 4p. 24.95 incl. audio (*0-14-180274-X*, Penguin AudioBooks); 2002. (Beloved Mitford Ser.: No. 6). (Illus.). 208p. reprint ed. 13.00 (*0-14-200034-5*) Viking Penguin.

—Esther's Gift: A Mitford Christmas Story. 2002. (Illus.). 48p. 10.95 (*0-670-03121-6*, Viking) Viking Penguin.

—In This Mountain. 2003. (Mitford Ser.). 400p. pap. 13.95 (*0-14-200258-5*) Penguin Group (USA) Inc.

—In This Mountain. l.t. ed. 672p. 2003. pap. 14.95 (*0-375-72820-1*); 2002. 26.95 (*0-375-43166-7*) Random Hse. Large Print.

—In This Mountain. 2002. (Illus.). 368p. 25.95 (*0-670-03104-6*, Viking) Viking Penguin.

—A Light in the Window. l.t. ed. (Mitford Ser.: No. 2). 21.95 (*1-57490-255-5*); 1996. (Illus.). 492p. lib. bdg. 26.95 (*1-57490-072-2*, Beeler Large Print Bks.) Beeler, Thomas T. Publisher.

—A Light in the Window. 2003. (Mitford Ser.: No. 2). (Illus.). 413p. pap. 12.99 (*0-7459-2803-X*) Lion Publishing.

—A Light in the Window. unabr. ed. (Mitford Ser.: No. 2). audio. 1999. audio 97.00 (*0-7887-0646-2*, 94823K8) Recorded Bks., LLC.

—A Light in the Window. (Mitford Ser.: No. 2). 1998. 400p. 24.95 (*0-670-88226-7*); 1996. 432p. 12.95 (*0-14-025454-4*); 1997. 2p. audio 16.95 (*0-14-086596-9*, 394980, Penguin AudioBooks) Viking Penguin.

—The Mitford Years: At Home in Mitford; A Light in the Window; These High, Green Hills; Out to Canaan, 4 vols. 1999. (Illus.). pap. 51.80 (*0-14-771256-4*) Penguin Group (USA) Inc.

—The Mitford Years: At Home in Mitford; A Light in the Window; These High, Green Hills; Out to Canaan, 4 vols. abr. ed. 1998. 2p. 49.95 (*0-14-086813-5*, Penguin AudioBooks) Viking Penguin.

—The Mitford Years: At Home in Mitford; A Light in the Window; These High, Green Hills; Out to Canaan; A New Song, 5 vols. 2001. pap. 64.75 o.p. (*0-14-771596-2*); 1997. pap. 38.85 (*0-14-771203-3*) Penguin Group (USA) Inc.

—A New Song. l.t. ed. 1999. (Mitford Ser.: No. 5 ). 28.95 (*1-57490-190-7*, Beeler Large Print Bks.) Beeler, Thomas T. Publisher.

—A New Song, abr. ed. 1999. (Mitford Ser.: No. 5). audio 24.95. audio 55.95 Highsmith Inc.

—A New Song. unabr. ed. 1999. (Mitford Ser.: No. 5). audio 102.00 (*0-7887-3098-3*, 95809E7) Recorded Bks., LLC.

—A New Song. (Mitford Ser.: No. 5). 2000. (Illus.). 416p. 12.95 (*0-14-027059-0*); 1999. (Illus.). 368p. 24.95 (*0-670-87810-3*); 1999. 2p. audio 24.95 (*0-14-086901-8*, Penguin AudioBooks); 1999. audio 55.95 (*0-14-180013-5*, Penguin AudioBooks) Viking Penguin.

—Out to Canaan. l.t. ed. (Mitford Ser.: o. 4). 21.95 (*1-57490-257-1*); 1997. (Illus.). 412p. lib. bdg. 26.95 (*1-57490-104-4*, Beeler Large Print Bks.) Beeler, Thomas T. Publisher.

—Out to Canaan. unabr. ed. 1997. (Mitford Ser.: o. 4). audio 83.00 (*0-7887-0973-9*, 95081E7) Recorded Bks., LLC.

—Out to Canaan. (Mitford Ser.: No. 4). 1998. (Illus.). 352p. 12.95 (*0-14-026568-6*); 1997. (Illus.). 368p. 23.95 (*0-670-87485-X*); 1997. 2p. audio 16.95 (*0-14-086597-7*, Penguin AudioBooks) Viking Penguin.

—These High, Green Hills. l.t. ed. (Mitford Ser.: No. 3). 21.95 (*1-57490-256-3*); 1997. (Illus.). 414p. lib. bdg. 26.95 (*1-57490-103-6*, Beeler Large Print Bks.) Beeler, Thomas T. Publisher.

—These High, Green Hills. (Mitford Ser.: o. 3). (Illus.). 333p. pap. 12.99 (*0-7459-3741-1*) Cook Communications Ministries.

—These High, Green Hills. unabr. ed. 1999. (Mitford Ser.: No. 3). audio 85.00 (*0-7887-0664-0*, 94841K8) Recorded Bks., LLC.

—These High, Green Hills. (Mitford Ser.: No. 3). 1997. (Illus.). 368p. 12.95 (*0-14-025793-4*); 1996. 352p. 22.95 (*0-670-86934-1*, Viking); 1996. pap. o.s.i (*0-670-87320-9*, Viking); 1997. 2p. pap. 16.95 incl. audio (*0-14-086598-5*, Penguin AudioBooks) Viking Penguin.

Katkov, Norman. Millionaires Row. 1996. 384p. 23.95 o.p. (*0-525-93843-5*, Dutton) Dutton/Plume.

Kay, Terry. The Valley of Light. abr. ed. 2004. audio 9.99 (*1-59355-082-0*, 4662, Brilliance Audio Paperback Audiobooks); 2003. audio 19.95 (*1-59355-081-2*, 4661); 2003. audio 29.95 (*1-59355-079-0*, 4659, Brilliance Audio Unabridged); 2003. audio 74.25 (*1-59355-080-4*, 4660, Brilliance Audio Unabridged Lib Ed) Brilliance Audio.

—The Valley of Light. 2004. pap. (*0-7434-7595-X*, Washington Square Pr.); 2003. (Illus.). 256p. 24.00 (*0-7434-7594-1*, Atria) Simon & Schuster.

Kelly, Susan S. Even Now. l.t. ed. 2001. (Thorndike Press Large Print Women's Fiction Ser.). 358p. 28.95 (*0-7862-3677-9*) Thorndike Pr.

—Even Now. 2001. 288p. 22.95 o.p. (*0-446-52762-9*) Warner Bks., Inc.

Kelner, Toni L. P. Country Comes to Town: A Laura Fleming Mystery. (Laura Fleming Mystery Ser.). 336p. 1998. mass mkt. 5.99 (*1-57566-244-2*); 1996. 18.95 o.s.i (*1-57566-083-0*, Kensington Bks.) Kensington Publishing Corp.

—Dead Ringer. 1994. 304p. mass mkt. 3.99 o.s.i (*0-8217-4469-0*, Zebra Bks.) Kensington Publishing Corp.

—Death of a Damn Yankee. 2001. 32p. mass mkt. 5.99 o.s.i (*1-57566-686-3*); 1999. 295p. 20.00 o.s.i (*1-57566-431-3*, Kensington Bks.) Kensington Publishing Corp.

—Down Home Murder. 304p. 1999. mass mkt. 5.99 (*1-57566-429-1*); 1993. mass mkt. 3.99 o.s.i (*0-8217-4196-9*, Zebra Bks.) Kensington Publishing Corp.

—Tight As a Tick. 1998. (Laura Fleming Mystery Ser.). 320p. 18.95 o.s.i (*1-57566-242-6*) Kensington Publishing Corp.

—Tight as a Tick, 1. 1999. (Laura Fleming Mystery Ser.). 320p. mass mkt. 5.99 o.s.i (*1-57566-434-8*) Kensington Publishing Corp.

—Tight As a Tick. unabr. ed. 1999. audio 69.95 (*0-7927-2274-4*, CSL163, Chivers Sound Library) BBC Audiobooks America.

—Trouble Looking for a Place to Happen: A Laura Fleming Mystery. 1996. 352p. mass mkt. 4.99 o.s.i (*1-57566-007-5*); 1995. 336p. mass mkt. 16.95 o.p. (*0-8217-4855-6*) Kensington Publishing Corp.

—Wed & Buried: A Laura Fleming Mystery. 2003. (Laura Fleming Mystery Ser.). 272p. 22.00 (*1-57566-840-8*) Kensington Publishing Corp.

Kenan, Randall. Let the Dead Bury Their Dead & Other Stories. 1993. 348p. pap. 13.00 (*0-15-650515-0*, Harvest Bks.); 1992. (C). 19.95 o.s.i (*0-15-149886-5*) Harcourt Trade Pubs.

—A Visitation of Spirits. 1989. 272p. 17.95 o.p. (*0-8021-1118-1*) Grove/Atlantic, Inc.

Kinston Dean, Sheila. Full Circle. Bodnarchuk, Kari J., ed. unabr. ed. 2003. 372p. 24.95 (*0-9729392-0-2*) Joseph, Beatrice Publishing.

Kraus, Joanna H. Sunday Gold. 2003. 110p. 9.95 (*1-932162-19-4*) Benoy Publishing.

—Sunday Gold. 1998. 53p. pap. 5.60 (*0-87129-867-8*, SC6) Dramatic Publishing Co.

Krawiec, Richard, ed. Voices from Home: The North Carolina Prose Anthology. 1997. 376p. pap. 18.00 (*1-888105-30-5*); lib. bdg. 42.00 (*1-888105-29-1*) Avisson Pr., Inc.

Landis, Catherine E. Some Days There's Pie. 2002. (Illus.). 304p. 23.95 (*0-312-28384-9*) St. Martin's Pr.

—Some Days There's Pie. l.t. ed. 2002. 28.95 (*0-7862-4598-0*) Thorndike Pr.

—Some Days There's Pie: A Novel. 2003. 304p. reprint ed. pap. 12.95 (*0-312-30929-5*, Saint Martin's Griffin) St. Martin's Pr.

Layng, Ruth D. Letters from James. 2000. ii, 348p. pap. 19.95 (*1-887905-23-5*) Parkway Pubs., Inc.

Leebron, Fred G. Six Figures. 2000. 240p. 22.00 o.s.i (*0-375-40640-9*) Knopf, Alfred A. Inc.

Levitin, Sonia. Rohnoke Novel of Lost. 1973. 7.95 o.p. (*0-689-30114-6*, Atheneum) Simon & Schuster Children's Publishing.

A Long & Happy Life. Incl. Names & Faces of Heroes. audio Permanent Errors. audio Source of Light. audio Surface of Earth. audio Set audio 13.95 (*1-55644-051-0*, 2101) American Audio Prose Library, Inc.

Loring, Emilie Baker. Rainbow at Dusk. 1976. reprint ed. lib. bdg. 24.95 (*0-88411-360-4*) Amereon, Ltd.

—Rainbow at Dusk. l.t. ed. 2000. (Romance Ser.). 424p. 26.95 (*0-7862-2333-2*) Thorndike Pr.

Malone, Michael. First Lady. l.t. ed. 2003. (Magna Large Print Ser.). 545p. (*0-7505-1985-1*) Magna Large Print Bks. GBR. *Dist:* Ulverscroft Large Print Canada, Ltd.

—First Lady. 448p. 2002. pap. 15.00 (*1-57071-971-3*); 2001. 24.00 (*1-57071-743-5*) Sourcebooks, Inc. (Sourcebooks Landmark).

—Time's Witness. Rosenman, Jane, ed. 1994. 592p. pap. (*0-671-87527-2*, Washington Square Pr.) Simon & Schuster.

—Times Witness. Peters, Sally, ed. 1991. 592p. reprint ed. mass mkt. 5.95 (*0-671-70318-8*, Pocket) Simon & Schuster.

—Time's Witness: A Justin & Cuddy Novel. 2002. 576p. pap. 15.00 (*1-57071-754-0*, Sourcebooks Landmark) Sourcebooks, Inc.

—Time's Witness: A Novel. 1989. 540p. 19.95 o.s.i (*0-316-54480-9*) Little Brown & Co.

—Uncivil Seasons. 1988. 336p. pap. 3.95 o.p. (*0-440-19244-7*); 1983. 288p. 13.95 o.s.i (*0-385-29267-8*, Delacorte Pr.) Dell Publishing.

—Uncivil Seasons. Rosenman, Jane, ed. 1993. 320p. pap. 12.00 (*0-671-87528-0*, Pocket) Simon & Schuster.

—Uncivil Seasons. 1988. 336p. bds. 3.95 (*0-671-65838-7*, Pocket) Simon & Schuster.

—Uncivil Seasons. 2001. 368p. pap. 15.00 (*1-57071-755-9*, Sourcebooks Landmark) Sourcebooks, Inc.

March, Stephen. Armadillo. 2003. 96p. (Orig.). pap. 12.95 (*1-881515-54-0*) Texas Review Pr.

Marlette, Doug. The Bridge. 2001. 400p. 26.00 (*0-06-018630-5*) HarperCollins Pubs.

—The Bridge. 2002. 400p. pap. 13.95 (*0-06-050521-4*, Perennial) HarperTrade.

Maron, Margaret. Bootlegger's Daughter. 1992. 272p. 18.95 (*0-89296-445-6*) Mysterious Pr.

—Bootlegger's Daughter. audio o.p. National Humanities Ctr.

—Bootlegger's Daughter. unabr. ed. 1994. (Deborah Knott Mystery Ser.: Vol. 1). audio 60.00 (*0-7887-0086-3*, 94326E7) Recorded Bks., LLC.

—Bootlegger's Daughter. l.t. ed. 2000. (Mystery Ser.). 426p. 29.95 o.p. (*0-7862-2327-8*) Thorndike Pr.

—Bootlegger's Daughter. 1993. 272p. reprint ed. mass mkt. 6.99 (*0-446-40323-7*) Warner Bks., Inc.

—Home Fires: A Deborah Knott Mystery. 1998. (Deborah Knott Mysteries Ser.: Vol. 6). 245p. 22.00 o.p. (*0-89296-655-6*) Mysterious Pr.

—Home Fires: A Deborah Knott Mystery. unabr. ed. 1999. (Deborah Knott Mystery Ser.: Vol. 6). audio 46.00 (*0-7887-3212-9*, 95726E7) Recorded Bks., LLC.

—Home Fires: A Deborah Knott Mystery. l.t. ed. 1999. (Mystery Ser.). 325p. 29.95 (*0-7862-1620-4*) Thorndike Pr.

—Home Fires: A Deborah Knott Mystery. 2000. 288p. reprint ed. mass mkt. 6.50 (*0-446-60810-6*) Warner Bks., Inc.

—Killer Market. 1997. 288p. 22.00 o.p. (*0-89296-654-8*) Mysterious Pr.

—Killer Market. unabr. ed. 2000. (Deborah Knott Ser.: Vol. 5). audio 51.00 (*0-7887-2944-6*, 95724E7) Recorded Bks., LLC.

—Killer Market. l.t. ed. 1998. (*0-7540-3329-5*); (*0-7540-3330-9*) Thorndike Pr.

—Killer Market. 1999. 304p. reprint ed. mass mkt. 6.99 (*0-446-60619-7*) Warner Bks., Inc.

—Last Lessons of Summer. 2003. 288p. 23.95 (*0-89296-780-3*, 53360614) Mysterious Pr.

—Last Lessons of Summer. l.t. ed. 2003. 478p. 30.95 (*0-7862-5849-7*) Thorndike Pr.

—Shooting at Loons. l.t. ed. 1994. pap. 19.95 o.p. (*1-56895-083-7*, Wheeler Publishing, Inc.) Gale Group.

—Shooting at Loons. 1994. 240p. 18.95 (*0-89296-447-2*) Mysterious Pr.

—Shooting at Loons. 1995. 256p. reprint ed. mass mkt. 6.99 (*0-446-40424-1*) Warner Bks., Inc.

—Slow Dollar. l.t. ed. 2002. (Basic Ser.). 344p. 29.95 o.p. (*0-7862-4670-7*) Thorndike Pr.

—Southern Discomfort, Bk. II. 1993. 256p. 17.95 (*0-89296-446-4*) Mysterious Pr.

—Southern Discomfort. unabr. ed. 1994. (Deborah Knott Mystery Ser.: Vol. 2). audio 51.00 (*0-7887-0032-4*, 94231E7) Recorded Bks., LLC.

—Southern Discomfort. l.t. ed. 2000. (Mystery Ser.). 351p. 29.95 (*0-7862-2330-8*) Thorndike Pr.

—Southern Discomfort. 1994. 224p. reprint ed. mass mkt. 6.99 (*0-446-40080-7*) Warner Bks., Inc.

—Storm Track. 2000. (Deborah Knott Mysteries Ser.). 272p. 22.95 (*0-89296-656-4*) Mysterious Pr.

—Storm Track. l.t. ed. 2000. (Mystery Ser.). 349p. 29.95 (*0-7862-2465-7*) Thorndike Pr.

—Storm Track. 2001. 304p. reprint ed. mass mkt. 6.99 (*0-446-60939-0*) Warner Bks., Inc.

—Uncommon Clay. 2001. (Deborah Knott Mysteries Ser.). 304p. 23.95 o.p. (*0-89296-720-X*) Mysterious Pr.

—Uncommon Clay. l.t. ed. 2001. 371p. 30.95 o.p. (*0-7862-3370-2*) Thorndike Pr.

—Uncommon Clay. 2002. 336p. mass mkt. 6.99 (*0-446-61087-9*) Warner Bks., Inc.

—Up Jumps the Devil. unabr. ed. 2000. (Deborah Knott Mystery Ser.: Vol. 4). audio 51.00 (*0-7887-1310-8*, 95152E7) Recorded Bks., LLC.

—Up Jumps the Devil. 1996. 256p. 20.00 o.s.i (*0-89296-568-1*); 1997. 304p. reprint ed. mass mkt. 6.99 (*0-446-60406-2*) Warner Bks., Inc.

Martin, Eric. Luck. 2000. 288p. 23.95 (*0-393-04912-4*) Norton, W. W. & Co., Inc.

Mathes, Charles. The Girl at the End of the Line. 2000. (WWL Mystery Ser.: Vol. 341). 256p. per. (*0-373-26341-4*, Harlequin Bks.) Harlequin Enterprises, Ltd.

—The Girl at the End of the Line. 17.95 (*0-312-33171-1*); 1999. 288p. 22.95 o.p. (*0-312-19887-6*, Saint Martin's Minotaur) St. Martin's Pr.

McCall, Eva. Edge of Heaven. 1997. 256p. pap. 14.95 (*0-914875-27-2*, Historical Images) Bright Mountain Bks., Inc.

McCammon, Robert R. Speaks the Nightbird. 2002. 700p. 29.95 (*1-880216-62-0*) River City Publishing.

—Speaks the Nightbird. 2003. 496p. mass mkt. 7.99 (*0-7434-7432-5*, Pocket) Simon & Schuster.

McCorkle, Jill. Carolina Moon. 1996. 276p. tchr. ed. 18.95 (*1-56512-136-8*) Algonquin Bks. of Chapel Hill.

—Carolina Moon. 1997. (Ballantine Reader's Circle Ser.). 288p. pap. 13.95 (*0-449-91280-9*, Fawcett) Ballantine Bks.

—Carolina Moon. unabr. collector's ed. 1997. audio 48.00 (*0-7366-3723-0*, 4404) Books on Tape, Inc.

—Creatures of Habit: Stories. 2001. 256p. tchr. ed. 22.95 (*1-56512-256-9*, Shannon Ravenel Bks.) Algonquin Bks. of Chapel Hill.

McCrumb, Sharyn. Ghost Riders: A Novel. 2003. 336p. 24.95 (*0-525-94718-3*, Dutton) Dutton/Plume.

—The Songcatcher. 2001. 368p. 24.95 o.p. (*0-525-94488-5*, Dutton) Dutton/Plume.

—The Songcatcher. l.t. ed. 2001. (Hardcover Ser.). 431p. 29.95 (*1-58724-047-5*, Wheeler Publishing, Inc.) Gale Group.

—The Songcatcher. 2002. 416p. reprint ed. mass mkt. 7.99 (*0-451-20250-3*) NAL.

McEachin, James. Tell Me a Tale. 1996. 224p. 18.95 (*0-89141-584-X*, Presidio Pr.) Ballantine Bks.

McFee, Michael, ed. This Is Where We Live: Short Stories by 25 Contemporary North Carolina Writers. 2000. 0296p. pap. 16.95 (*0-8078-4895-6*) Univ. of North Carolina Pr.

McGuinn, Doug. The Apple Indians: A Novel. 2000. 315p. 19.95 (*1-887905-46-4*) Parkway Pubs., Inc.

McLaurin, Tim. Cured by Fire. 1995. 240p. 22.95 o.p. (*0-399-14003-4*, G. P. Putnam's Sons) Penguin Group (USA) Inc.

McNab, Andy. Crisis Four. 2001. 416p. reprint ed. mass mkt. 6.99 (*0-345-42808-0*, Ballantine Bks.) Ballantine Bks.

—Crisis Four. 2001. 416p. mass mkt. (*0-7704-2866-5*, Random Hse. Bks. for Young Readers) Random Hse. Children's Bks.

Medlicott, Joan. From the Heart of Covington. l.t. ed. 2002. 533p. 28.95 (*1-58724-257-5*, Wheeler Publishing, Inc.) Gale Group.

—From the Heart of Covington. 2003. 352p. mass mkt. 6.99 (*0-312-98825-7*, St. Martin's Paperbacks); 2002. (Illus.). 320p. 24.95 (*0-312-28555-8*) St. Martin's Pr.

—The Gardens of Covington. 2001. E-Book 23.95 (*1-58945-793-5*) Adobe Systems, Inc.

—The Gardens of Covington. l.t. ed. 2001. (Illus.). 451p. 28.95 o.p. (*1-58724-081-5*, Wheeler Publishing, Inc.) Gale Group.

—The Gardens of Covington. 2001. (Illus.). 326p. 23.95 (*0-312-27555-2*) St. Martin's Pr.

—Ladies of Covington Send Their Love. 2000. 326p. 24.95 (*0-312-25329-X*) St. Martin's Pr.

—The Ladies of Covington Send Their Love. 2000. E-Book 6.99 (*0-312-27387-8*) St. Martin's Pr.

—The Ladies of Covington Send Their Love. l.t. ed. 2000. (Americana Ser.). 624p. 26.95 (*0-7862-2976-4*) Thorndike Pr.

Michaels, Fern. Sea Gypsy. abr. ed. 2000. (Mira Bks.). audio 9.99 (*1-55204-219-7*, MIR-1219) Durkin Hayes Publishing Ltd.

—Sea Gypsy. 1981. (General Ser.). lib. bdg. 10.95 o.p. (*0-8161-3204-6*, Macmillan Reference USA) Gale Group.

—Sea Gypsy. 2000. per. (*1-55166-605-7*, Mira Bks.); 1993. (C). per. (*0-373-48275-2*, 5-48275-7, Silhouette) Harlequin Enterprises, Ltd.

Miller, Stephen E. The Woman in the Yard. 304p. 2000. pap. 13.00 (*0-312-26414-3*); 1999. 23.00 o.p. (*0-312-19962-7*) Picador.

Settings

Mills, Wendy Howell. Callie & the Dealer & a Dog Named Jake. 2001. (Dark Oak Mysteries Ser.). 204p. pap. 11.95 (*1-892343-15-0*, Dark Oak Mysteries) Oak Tree Publishing.
—Death of a Mermaid: A Callie McKinley Outer Banks Mystery. 2002. 336p. pap. 7.99 (*1-928556-38-8*) Coastal Carolina Pr.
Moose, Ruth. Dreaming in Color. 1989. 192p. 15.95 o.p. (*0-87483-078-8*) August Hse. Pubs., Inc.
Morgan, Robert. The Blue Valley: A Collection of Stories. 2000. 176p. pap. 11.00 (*0-7432-0422-0*, Touchstone) Simon & Schuster.
—The Blue Valleys: A Collection of Stories. 1989. 176p. 15.95 (*0-934601-71-2*) Peachtree Pubs., Ltd.
—Gap Creek: The Story of a Marriage. 2000. (Oprah's Book Club Ser.). 324p. tchr. ed. 22.95 (*1-56512-296-8*) Algonquin Bks. of Chapel Hill.
—Gap Creek: The Story of a Marriage. abr. ed. 2000. 24.95 (*1-56511-386-1*) HighBridge Co.
—Gap Creek: The Story of a Marriage. unabr. ed. 2000. audio 76.00 Recorded Bks., LLC.
—Gap Creek: The Story of a Marriage. 2000. 336p. pap. 14.00 (*0-7432-0363-1*); pap. 7.99 (*0-7432-0334-8*) Simon & Schuster. (Touchstone).
—Gap Creek: The Story of a Marriage. l.t. ed. 2000. (Basic Ser.). 488p. 30.95 (*0-7862-2545-9*) Thorndike Pr.
—The Mountains Won't Remember Us: And Other Stories. 2000. 256p. pap. 12.00 (*0-7432-0421-2*, Touchstone) Simon & Schuster.
—The Mountains Won't Remember Us & Other Stories. 1992. 256p. 15.95 (*1-56145-049-9*) Peachtree Pubs., Ltd.
—The Truest Pleasure. 1998. 334p. pap. 12.95 (*1-56512-222-4*); 1995. 336p. tchr. ed. 18.95 o.p. (*1-56512-105-8*, 72105) Algonquin Bks. of Chapel Hill.
—The Truest Pleasure. unabr. ed. 1999. audio 69.95 (*0-7927-2298-1*, CSL187, Chivers Sound Library) BBC Audiobooks America.
—The Truest Pleasure. abr. ed. 2000. 18.95 (*1-56511-389-6*) HighBridge Co.
Mountford, B. J. Sea-Born Women. 2002. (Illus.). 306p. pap. 14.95 (*0-89587-265-X*) Blair, John F. Pub.
Munger, Katy. Bad to the Bone. 2000. (Casey Jones Mysteries Ser.). 288p. mass mkt. 6.50 (*0-380-80064-0*, Avon Bks.) Morrow/Avon.
—Better off Dead: A Casey Jones Mystery. 2001. 304p. mass mkt. 5.99 (*0-380-80065-9*, Avon Bks.) Morrow/Avon.
—Legwork. 1997. (Casey Jones Mysteries Ser.). 224p. mass mkt. 5.99 (*0-380-79136-6*, Avon Bks.) Morrow/Avon.
—Money to Burn. 1999. (Casey Jones Mysteries Ser.). 320p. mass mkt. 6.50 (*0-380-80063-2*, Avon Bks.) Morrow/Avon.
—Out of Time. 1998. (Casey Jones Mysteries Ser.). 272p. mass mkt. 6.50 (*0-380-79138-2*, Avon Bks.) Morrow/Avon.
Myers, Tamar. Baroque & Desperate. 1999. (Den of Antiquity Ser.). 256p. mass mkt. 6.99 (*0-380-80225-2*, Avon Bks.) Morrow/Avon.
—Estate of Mind. 1999. 320p. mass mkt. 6.50 (*0-380-80227-9*, Avon Bks.) Morrow/Avon.
—Guilt by Association. 1996. (Den of Antiquity Ser.). 256p. mass mkt. 6.50 (*0-380-78237-5*, Avon Bks.) Morrow/Avon.
—Larceny & Old Lace. 1996. (Den of Antiquity Ser.). 224p. (Orig.). mass mkt. 6.99 (*0-380-78239-1*, Avon Bks.) Morrow/Avon.
—Ming & I. 1997. (Den of Antiquity Ser.). 256p. mass mkt. 6.99 (*0-380-79255-9*, Avon Bks.) Morrow/Avon.
—So Faux, So Good. 1998. (Den of Antiquity Ser.). 256p. mass mkt. 6.50 (*0-380-79254-0*, Avon Bks.) Morrow/Avon.
Myers, Tim. Innkeeping with Murder. 2001. 208p. mass mkt. 5.99 (*0-425-18002-6*, Prime Crime) Berkley Publishing Group.
—Reservations for Murder. 2002. 192p. mass mkt. 5.99 (*0-425-18525-7*) Berkley Publishing Group.
Naumoff, Lawrence. The Night of the Weeping Women. 1989. 240p. mass mkt. 3.95 o.s.i (*0-8041-0488-3*, Ivy Bks.) Ballantine Bks.
—The Night of the Weeping Women. 1988. 252p. 16.95 o.p. (*0-87113-187-0*) Grove/Atlantic, Inc.
—The Night of the Weeping Women. 1997. (Harvest Book Ser.). 256p. pap. 11.00 (*0-15-600364-3*, Harvest Bks.) Harcourt Trade Pubs.
—Silk Hope, N. C. 368p. 1995. pap. 12.00 (*0-15-600207-8*, Harvest Bks.); 1994. 21.95 o.s.i (*0-15-188900-7*) Harcourt Trade Pubs.
Neely, Barbara. Blanche on the Lam. 1993. (Crime Ser.). 224p. pap. 5.99 (*0-14-017439-7*, Penguin Bks.) Penguin Group (USA) Inc.
—Blanche on the Lam. 1991. 192p. 16.95 o.p. (*0-312-06908-1*, Saint Martin's Minotaur) St. Martin's Pr.
—Blanche Passes Go. 2001. 288p. 5.99 (*0-14-100197-6*); 2000. 272p. 22.95 o.s.i (*0-670-89165-7*, Viking) Viking Penguin.
Oke, Janette & Bunn, T. Davis. Return to Harmony. 1996. 224p. text 15.99 o.p. (*1-55661-901-4*); 288p. pap. 12.99 o.p. (*1-55661-902-2*); 224p. pap. 10.99 o.p. (*1-55661-878-6*) Bethany Hse. Pubs.
—Return to Harmony. l.t. ed. 1997. (Inspirational Ser.). 273p. lib. bdg. 24.95 (*0-7838-8220-3*, Macmillan Reference USA) Gale Group.
Owen, Howard. Answers to Lucky. 1996. 224p. 22.00 o.p. (*0-06-017312-2*) HarperCollins Pubs.
—Answers to Lucky: A Novel. 1997. 224p. pap. 12.00 (*0-06-092809-3*, Perennial) HarperTrade.
—Littlejohn. 1994. 240p. pap. 15.00 (*0-679-75001-0*, Vintage) Knopf Publishing Group.
—Littlejohn. 1992. 209p. pap. 16.00 (*1-877946-37-0*) Permanent Pr., The.
—Littlejohn. abr. ed. 1994. audio 16.95 (*1-879371-79-0*, 391080) Publishing Mills, Inc., The.
—Littlejohn. 1993. 18.00 o.s.i (*0-679-42769-4*, Villard Bks.) Random House Adult Trade Publishing Group.
Parker, Gary E. Highland Hopes. 2001. (Blue Ridge Legacy Ser.). 400p. pap. 12.99 (*0-7642-2452-2*) Bethany Hse. Pubs.
—Highland Mercies. 2002. (Blue Ridge Legacy Ser.). 400p. pap. 12.99 (*0-7642-2453-0*) Bethany Hse. Pubs.
Parker, Gwendolyn M. These Same Long Bones. 1995. 272p. pap. 10.95 o.p. (*0-452-27428-1*, Plume) Dutton/Plume.
—These Same Long Bones. 1994. 260p. 21.95 o.s.i (*0-395-67172-8*) Houghton Mifflin Co.
Parker, Michael. Hello down There. 1994. (Contemporary American Fiction Ser.). 288p. pap. 9.95 o.p. (*0-14-023424-1*, Penguin Bks.) Penguin Group (USA) Inc.
—Hello down There: A Novel. 1993. 288p. 20.00 o.p. (*0-684-19424-4*, Macmillan Reference USA) Gale Group.
—Towns Without Rivers. 2001. 368p. 25.00 (*0-380-97860-1*, Morrow, William & Co.) Morrow/Avon.
Pate, Jeff. Winner Take All: A Novel of Suspense. 2000. 358p. 25.00 (*0-9676528-0-4*) Harlan Publishing Co.
Payne, David. Ruin Creek. 2002. 384p. pap. 13.00 (*0-452-28281-0*, Plume) Dutton/Plume.
—Ruin Creek. l.t. ed. 1994. 576p. lib. bdg. 23.95 (*0-8161-5948-3*, Macmillan Reference USA) Gale Group.
—Ruin Creek, Vol. 1. 1994. mass mkt. 5.50 o.p. (*0-312-95389-5*, St. Martin's Paperbacks) St. Martin's Pr.
Pearson, T. R. The Last of How It Was. 1988. 368p. mass mkt. 4.95 o.s.i (*0-345-35640-3*) Ballantine Bks.
—The Last of How It Was. 1987. 352p. 17.45 o.p. (*0-671-61738-9*, Simon & Schuster) Simon & Schuster.
—The Last of How It Was: A Novel. 1996. 352p. pap. 15.00 o.s.i (*0-8050-3757-8*, Owl Bks.) Holt, Henry & Co.
—Off for the Sweet Hereafter. 1987. 352p. mass mkt. 4.50 o.s.i (*0-345-34369-7*) Ballantine Bks.
—Off for the Sweet Hereafter. 1986. 283p. 17.45 o.p. (*0-671-61437-1*, Simon & Schuster) Simon & Schuster.
—Off for the Sweet Hereafter: A Novel. 1995. 384p. pap. 12.00 o.s.i (*0-8050-3756-X*, Owl Bks.) Holt, Henry & Co.
—A Short History of a Small Place. 1986. 408p. mass mkt. 6.99 o.s.i (*0-345-33263-6*) Ballantine Bks.
—A Short History of a Small Place. 1994. 384p. pap. 15.00 o.s.i (*0-8050-3320-3*, Owl Bks.) Holt, Henry & Co.
—A Short History of a Small Place. 2003. 384p. pap. 14.00 (*0-14-200362-X*) Penguin Group (USA) Inc.
—A Short History of a Small Place: A Novel. 1986. 17.45 o.s.i (*0-671-54352-0*, Simon & Schuster) Simon & Schuster.
Peart, Jane. The Pattern. 1996. (American Quilt Ser.: Bk. 1). 240p. pap. 16.99 (*0-310-20166-7*) Zondervan.
Pettigrew, Dawn Karima. The Way We Make Sense: A Novel. 2002. 136p. pap. 11.95 (*1-879960-66-4*) Aunt Lute Bks.
Phillips, Michael. Angels Watching over Me. 2002. (Shenandoah Sisters Ser.: Bk. 1). 320p. 16.99 (*0-7642-2705-X*); pap. 12.99 (*0-7642-2700-9*) Bethany Hse. Pubs.
—A Day to Pick Your Own Cotton. 2003. (Shenandoah Sisters Ser.). 320p. 17.99 (*0-7642-2706-8*); pap. 12.99 (*0-7642-2701-7*) Bethany Hse. Pubs.
Phillips, Susan Elizabeth. Dream a Little Dream, , unabr. collector's ed. 1999. audio 64.00 (*0-7366-4280-3*, 4778) Books on Tape, Inc.
—Dream a Little Dream. 2002. E-Book 6.99 (*0-06-621211-1*); E-Book 6.99 (*0-06-621212-X*); E-Book 6.99 (*0-06-009847-3*); E-Book 6.99 (*0-06-621214-6*) HarperCollins General Bks. Group. (PerfectBound).
—Dream a Little Dream. 1998. 400p. mass mkt. 7.99 (*0-380-79447-0*, Avon Bks.) Morrow/Avon.
Powell, Mark. Prodigals: A Novel. 2002. 193p. 26.95 (*1-57233-189-5*) Univ. of Tennessee Pr.
Poyer, David. Hatteras Blue: A Tiller Gallaway Underwater Thriller. 1992. 288p. mass mkt. 5.99 (*0-312-92749-5*, St. Martin's Paperbacks); 1989. 16.95 o.p. (*0-312-02926-8*) St. Martin's Pr.
Price, Charles F. Freedom's Altar. 1999. (Salem Selections Ser.). (Illus.). 291p. 19.95 (*0-89587-177-7*) Blair, John F. Pub.
—Hiwassee: A Novel of the Civil War. 1996. 193p. 20.00 (*0-89733-429-9*) Academy Chicago Pubs., Ltd.
—Where the Water-Dogs Laughed: Or the Sacred Dream of the Great Bear. 2003. 24.95 (*1-932158-50-2*) High Country Pubs., Ltd.
Price, Reynolds. The Collected Stories. 1994. 640p. pap. 15.00 (*0-452-27218-1*, Plume) Dutton/Plume.
—The Collected Stories. 2004. 640p. pap. 18.00 (*0-7432-4499-0*, Scribner) Simon & Schuster.
—Home Made. 1990. (Illus.). 64p. 150.00 o.p. (*0-933598-24-6*); 30.00 o.p. (*0-933598-22-X*); 55.00 (*0-933598-23-8*) North Carolina Wesleyan College Pr.
—Kate Vaiden. 1987. 384p. mass mkt. 5.99 o.s.i (*0-345-34358-1*) Ballantine Bks.
—Kate Vaiden. l.t. ed. 1987. 491p. 18.95 o.p. (*0-8161-4238-6*, Macmillan Reference USA) Gale Group.
—Kate Vaiden. 1998. 320p. pap. 13.00 (*0-684-84694-2*); 1986. 352p. 17.00 (*0-689-11787-6*) Simon & Schuster. (Scribner).
—A Long & Happy Life. 1983. pap. 2.25 o.p. (*0-380-01399-1*, 59279-7, Avon Bks.) Morrow/Avon.
—A Long & Happy Life. 1987. 208p. 20.00 (*0-689-11947-X*, Scribner) Simon & Schuster.
—A Long & Happy Life. 1987. 208p. pap. 4.95 (*0-689-10224-0*, Atheneum) Simon & Schuster Children's Publishing.
—The Promise of Rest. 1996. 368p. pap. 13.00 (*0-684-82510-4*); 1995. 353p. 24.00 o.p. (*0-684-80149-3*) Simon & Schuster. (Scribner).
—The Promise of Rest. abr. ed. 1995. audio 23.00 (*0-671-52895-5*, Simon & Schuster Audioworks) Simon & Schuster Audio.
—Roxanna Slade. 304p. 1999. pap. 13.00 (*0-684-85373-6*); 1998. 25.00 (*0-684-83292-5*) Simon & Schuster. (Scribner).
—Roxanna Slade. l.t. ed. 1998. (Basic Ser.). 589p. 29.95 (*0-7862-1518-6*) Thorndike Pr.
—The Source of Light. 1988. mass mkt. 4.95 o.s.i (*0-345-34993-8*) Ballantine Bks.
—The Source of Light. 1995. 336p. pap. 14.00 (*0-684-81338-6*); 1981. 13.95 o.p. (*0-689-11136-3*) Simon & Schuster. (Scribner).
Pritchard, Sara. Crackpots: A Novel. 2003. 208p. pap. 12.00 (*0-618-30245-X*, Mariner Bks.) Houghton Mifflin Co. Trade & Reference Div.
Propst, Milam McGraw. Ociee on Her Own: A Novel. 2003. 161p. 23.00 (*0-86554-838-2*) Mercer Univ. Pr.
Purcell, Trip. Sunset Beach. 1996. 320p. (Orig.). pap. 12.95 (*1-884570-47-X*) Research Triangle Publishing.
Rash, Ron. The Night the New Jesus Fell to Earth & Other Stories from Cliffside, North Carolina. 1994. pap. 14.95 o.p. (*0-930769-11-2*) Bench Pr., The.
Ray, Clyde. Across the Dark River: The Odyssey of the 56th N. C. Infantry in the American Civil War. 1996. 260p. pap. 18.95 (*1-887905-04-9*) Parkway Pubs., Inc.
Ray, Jeanne. Step-Ball-Change. 2004. 320p. pap. 13.95 (*0-451-21116-2*) NAL.
—Step-Ball-Change: A Novel. unabr. ed. 2002. audio 62.25 (*1-59086-083-7*, 3632, Unabridged Library Editions) Brilliance Audio.
—Step-Ball-Change: A Novel. 2002. 240p. 22.95 (*0-609-61003-1*, Shaye Areheart Bks.) Crown Publishing Group.
Reavis, Cheryl. The Forbidden Bride. 2003. (Harlequin Historicals Ser.: No. 640). 304p. mass mkt. (*0-373-29240-6*, Harlequin Bks.) Harlequin Enterprises, Ltd.
Reichs, Kathy. Bare Bones. 2003. (Illus.). 320p. 25.00 (*0-7432-3346-8*); E-Book 19.99 (*0-7432-6008-2*); 448p. 25.00 o.s.i (*0-7432-4675-6*) Simon & Schuster. (Scribner).
Riggs, Jack. When the Finch Rises. 2003. 256p. 23.95 (*0-345-46794-9*) Ballantine Bks.
Ripley, Alexandra. From Fields of Gold. l.t. ed. 1995. 577p. lib. bdg. 24.95 o.p. (*0-7838-1237-X*, Macmillan Reference USA) Gale Group.
—From Fields of Gold. 1996. 464p. mass mkt. 6.50 (*0-446-60249-3*); 1994. 480p. 24.95 o.s.i (*0-446-51406-3*) Warner Bks., Inc.
Robards, Karen. To Trust a Stranger. 2001. E-Book 25.00 (*0-7434-2456-5*, Atria) Simon & Schuster.
Robertson, Brewster Milton. The Grail Mystique: A Novel of the New South. 2003. 494p. 24.95 (*0-941711-64-1*) Wyrick & Co.
Robinson, Fay. Christmas on Snowbird Mountain. 2002. (Harlequin Superromance Ser.). 304p. mass mkt. (*0-373-71094-1*, Harlequin Bks.) Harlequin Enterprises, Ltd.
Robinson, Patrick. U.S.S. Seawolf. 2001. 496p. mass mkt. 7.99 (*0-06-101498-2*) HarperCollins Pubs.
—U.S.S. Seawolf. 2001. (Illus.). 496p. mass mkt. 7.50 (*0-06-103065-1*) Morrow/Avon.
Ross, Ann B. Miss Julia Hits the Road. 2003. 7p. 59.95 (*0-7927-2872-6*); 9p. 89.95 (*0-7927-2873-4*) BBC Audiobooks America.
—Miss Julia Hits the Road. 2004. 352p. pap. 14.00 (*0-14-200404-9*) Penguin Group (USA) Inc.
—Miss Julia Hits the Road. l.t. ed. 2003. (Basic Ser.). 30.95 (*0-7862-5497-1*) Thorndike Pr.
—Miss Julia Hits the Road. 2003. 320p. 24.95 (*0-670-03207-7*, Viking) Viking Penguin.
—Miss Julia Speaks Her Mind: A Novel. 2000. 288p. pap. 13.00 (*0-688-17775-1*); 1999. 273p. 23.00 (*0-688-16788-8*, Morrow, William & Co.) Morrow/Avon.
—Miss Julia Speaks Her Mind: A Novel. l.t. ed. 1999. (Thorndike Senior Lifestyle Ser.). 393p. 27.95 (*0-7862-2255-7*) Thorndike Pr.
—Miss Julia Takes Over. 2002. 336p. reprint ed. pap. 14.00 (*0-14-200089-2*) Penguin Group (USA) Inc.
—Miss Julia Takes Over. l.t. ed. 2001. (Thorndike Press Large Print Senior Lifestyles Ser.). 482p. 28.95 (*0-7862-3515-2*) Thorndike Pr.
—Miss Julia Takes Over. 2001. 352p. 24.95 o.s.i (*0-670-91026-0*, Viking) Viking Penguin.
—Miss Julia Throws a Wedding. 2003. 336p. pap. 14.00 (*0-14-200271-2*) Penguin Group (USA) Inc.
—Miss Julia Throws a Wedding. l.t. ed. 2002. (Basic Ser.). 453p. 28.95 o.p. (*0-7862-4561-1*) Thorndike Pr.
—Miss Julia Throws a Wedding. 2002. 304p. text 24.95 (*0-670-03105-4*, Viking) Viking Penguin.
Ross, Leone. Orange Laughter. 2000. 225p. 23.00 o.p. (*0-374-22676-8*) Farrar, Straus & Giroux.
—Orange Laughter. 2001. 240p. pap. 13.00 (*0-312-42016-1*) Picador.
Rowan, William. Incident at Roan High Bluff. 2003. 273p. (YA). pap. 15.95 (*0-7414-1695-6*) Buy Bks. on the Web.Com.
—Incident at Roan High Bluff. 2000. 272p. pap. 14.50 (*0-9662860-2-2*) Cenografix.
Rowley, Jane. Back to the Wind & Waves. 1994. 250p. 19.95 o.p. (*0-944957-19-6*) Rivercross Publishing, Inc.
Ruark, Robert. The Old Man & the Boy. 320p. 1993. pap. 16.00 (*0-8050-2669-X*, Owl Bks.); 1990. 27.50 (*0-8050-0239-1*) Holt, Henry & Co.
—Old Man & the Boy. 1976. mass mkt. 1.95 o.s.i (*0-449-23151-8*, Fawcett) Ballantine Bks.
—Old Man & the Boy. 1957. o.p. (*0-03-027910-0*) Holt, Henry & Co.
—The Old Man & the Boy. unabr. collector's ed. 1990. audio 56.00 (*0-7366-1864-3*, 2695) Books on Tape, Inc.
—The Old Man & the Boy. 1991. (Illus.). 316p. reprint ed. lib. bdg. 24.95 o.p. (*0-89966-818-6*) Buccaneer Bks., Inc.
—The Old Man & the Boy. l.t. ed. 1994. 417p. reprint ed. lib. bdg. 22.95 (*0-8161-5966-1*) Thorndike Pr.
—The Old Man & the Boy & the Old Man's Boy Grows Older. 1988. 620p. reprint ed. pap. 17.95 o.p. (*0-8117-2297-X*) Stackpole Bks.
Saunders, Ray. Blood Tells: A Thriller. 1996. 382p. 21.95 o.p. (*0-89141-588-2*, Presidio Pr.) Ballantine Bks.
Sawyer, David J. My Great-Grandfather Was Stonewall Jackson: The Story of a Negro Boy Growing up in the Segregated South. 1994. (Illus.). 288p. pap. 14.00 (*0-9635159-1-8*) Publishing Concepts.
—My Great-Grandfather Was Stonewall Jackson Vol. 1: The Story of a Negro Boy Growing up in the Segregated South. Evans, Paul, ed. 2nd rev. ed. 1994. (Illus.). 304p. reprint ed. pap. 16.00 (*0-9634206-1-5*) Jonathan Publishing Co.
—My Great-Grandfather Was Stonewall Jackson Vol. 2: Stonewalling in the Shadow of a Legend. Evans, Paul, ed. rev. ed. 1994. 317p. (Orig.). reprint ed. pap. 16.00 (*0-9634206-9-0*) Jonathan Publishing Co.
Secreast, Donald. The Rat Becomes Light. 1990. 18.95 o.p. (*0-06-016440-9*) HarperTrade.
—White Trash, Red Velvet: Stories. 1993. 256p. 20.00 o.p. (*0-06-016441-7*) HarperTrade.
Shaber, Sarah R. The Fugitive King: A Professor Simon Shaw Mystery. 2002. (Illus.). 240p. 22.95 (*0-312-29046-2*, Saint Martin's Minotaur) St. Martin's Pr.
—Simon Said. (Simon Shaw Mysteries Ser.). 224p. 1998. pap. 5.99 (*0-312-96555-9*, St. Martin's Paperbacks); 1997. 20.95 o.p. (*0-312-15207-8*, Saint Martin's Minotaur) St. Martin's Pr.
—Snipe Hunt. 2000. (Professor Simon Shaw Mysteries Ser.). 288p. 23.95 (*0-312-25337-0*, Saint Martin's Minotaur) St. Martin's Pr.
—Snipe Hunt: A Professor Simon Shaw Mystery. E-Book 6.50 (*0-312-27376-2*); 2001. 304p. reprint ed. mass mkt. 6.50 (*0-312-97470-1*, 20-3260, St. Martin's Paperbacks) St. Martin's Pr.

Siddons, Anne Rivers. Outer Banks. 2003. audio 9.99 (*0-06-055666-8*, HarperAudio); 2003. 416p. pap. 11.95 (*0-06-053806-6*, Perennial); 1991. 416p. 19.95 o.p. (*0-06-016249-X*); audio 16.00 o.s.i (*1-55994-477-3*, 391330, HarperAudio) Harper-Trade.

—Outer Banks. abr. ed. 2000. audio 7.95 (*1-57815-044-2*, 1035, Media Bks. Audio Publishing) Media Bks., L. L. C.

—Outer Banks. 1992. 576p. mass mkt. 7.99 (*0-06-109973-2*, HarperTorch) Morrow/Avon.

—Outer Banks. unabr. ed. 1994. audio 91.00 (*1-55690-974-8*, 94113E7) Recorded Bks., LLC.

Sleem, Patty. Back in Time: Women in Ministry in the Twentieth Century (Fictional Depiction) 160p. 2001. 22.00 (*1-885288-01-8*); 1997. pap. 18.00 (*1-885288-03-4*, 914-011) PREP Publishing.

—Back in Time: Women in Ministry in the Twentieth Century (Fictional Depiction) l.t. ed. 1998. (Christian Mystery Ser.). 271p. 23.95 (*0-7862-1567-4*) Thorndike Pr.

Slouka, Mark. God's Fool: A Novel. 2002. 288p. 24.00 (*0-375-40216-0*) Knopf, Alfred A. Inc.

Smith, Deborah. The Stone Flower Garden: A Novel. l.t. ed. 2002. (Wheeler Large Print Book Ser.). 28.95 (*1-58724-161-7*, Wheeler Publishing, Inc.) Gale Group.

—The Stone Flower Garden: A Novel. 2002. 320p. 23.95 o.p. (*0-316-80094-5*) Little Brown & Co.

Sparks, Nicholas. The Guardian. 2003. E-Book 15.95 (*0-7595-4749-1*) Time Warner Bk. Group.

—The Guardian. 2004. 528p. mass mkt. 7.50 (*0-446-61343-6*); 2003. 400p. 24.95 (*0-446-52779-3*); 2003. 720p. 24.95 (*0-446-53231-2*) Warner Bks., Inc.

—Nights in Rodanthe. l.t. ed. 352p. 2003. pap. 13.95 (*0-375-72822-8*); 2002. 24.95 (*0-375-43088-1*) Random Hse., Inc.

—Nights in Rodanthe. 2004. 240p. mass mkt. 7.99 (*0-446-61270-7*); 2003. (Illus.). 256p. pap. 12.00 (*0-446-69179-8*); 2002. 224p. 22.95 (*0-446-53133-2*) Warner Bks., Inc.

—The Notebook. l.t. ed. 1996. (Basic Ser.). 268p. 27.95 o.p. (*0-7862-0821-X*) Thorndike Pr.

—The Notebook. 2000. 13.04 (*0-606-19126-7*) Turtleback Bks.

—The Notebook. 2000. 214p. E-Book 5.95 (*0-446-96105-1*); 2000. E-Book 5.95 (*0-446-93064-4*); 1999. 214p. E-Book 4.95 (*0-446-91459-2*); 1996. 224p. 20.00 (*0-446-52080-2*); 1999. 240p. reprint ed. pap. 12.95 (*0-446-67609-8*); 1998. 256p. reprint ed. mass mkt. 7.50 (*0-446-60523-9*) Warner Bks., Inc.

—The Notebook: Reading Group Guide. 2000. pap. (*0-446-79043-5*) Warner Bks., Inc.

—The Rescue. l.t. ed. 2000. 576p. 22.95 (*0-375-43075-X*) Random Hse. Large Print.

—The Rescue. 464p. 26.99 (*0-7278-5822-X*) Severn Hse. Pubs., Ltd.

—The Rescue. 2000. 352p. E-Book 14.95 (*0-446-92371-0*) Time Warner Bk. Group.

—The Rescue. 2001. 13.55 (*0-606-21855-6*) Turtleback Bks.

—The Rescue. 2000. 352p. 22.95 o.p. (*0-446-52550-2*); 2000. 352p. E-Book 14.95 (*0-446-92863-1*); 2000. 352p. E-Book 14.95 (*0-446-96091-8*); 2000. 352p. E-Book 14.95 (*0-446-92266-8*); 2000. 352p. E-Book 14.95 (*0-446-91354-5*); 2000. E-Book 14.95 (*0-446-93139-X*); 2001. 432p. reprint ed. mass mkt. 7.50 (*0-446-61039-9*) Warner Bks., Inc.

—A Walk to Remember. l.t. ed. 1999. pap. 20.00 o.p. (*0-7838-8699-3*, Macmillan Reference USA) Gale Group.

—A Walk to Remember. 1999. 20.00 (*0-375-70763-8*); 2000. 320p. pap. 13.95 (*0-375-72800-7*); 1999. 320p. 19.95 (*0-375-40872-X*) Random Hse. Large Print.

—A Walk to Remember. 2000. 256p. E-Book 6.95 (*0-446-92350-8*) Time Warner Bk. Group.

—A Walk to Remember. 2000. E-Book 6.95 (*0-446-92869-0*); 2000. 256p. E-Book 6.95 (*0-446-92006-1*); 2000. E-Book 6.95 (*0-446-93040-7*); 2000. 256p. E-Book 9.95 (*0-446-91475-4*); 1999. E-Book 6.95 (*0-446-96003-9*); 1999. 256p. (gr. 10-12). 19.95 (*0-446-52553-7*); 2000. 256p. reprint ed. mass mkt. 6.99 (*0-446-60895-5*) Warner Bks., Inc.

Spindler, Erica. All Fall Down. abr. ed. 2000. (Mira Bks.). audio 9.99 (*1-55204-208-1*, MIR-1208) Durkin Hayes Publishing Ltd.

—All Fall Down. 2000. 512p. per. (*1-55166-551-4*, Mira Bks.) Harlequin Enterprises, Ltd.

Sprinkle, Patricia. The Remember Box. 2000. (Illus.). 416p. pap. 11.99 (*0-310-22992-8*) Zondervan.

Squire, Elizabeth Daniels. Forget about Murder. 2000. (Peaches Dan Mysteries Ser.). 268p. mass mkt. 5.99 o.s.i (*0-425-17343-7*, Prime Crime) Berkley Publishing Group.

—Is There a Dead Man in the House? 1998. 256p. mass mkt. 5.99 o.s.i (*0-425-16142-0*, Prime Crime) Berkley Publishing Group.

—Is There a Dead Man in the House? l.t. ed. 2004. 333p. pap. 23.95 (*1-58724-606-6*, Wheeler Publishing, Inc.) Gale Group.

—Is There a Dead Man in the House? 1998. 12.04 (*0-606-19297-2*) Turtleback Bks.

—Kill the Messenger. l.t. ed. 2000. (G. K. Hall Paperback Ser.). 313p. pap. 23.95 (*0-7838-8856-2*, Macmillan Reference USA) Gale Group.

—Kill the Messenger. 1991. mass mkt. 3.95 (*0-312-92436-4*, St. Martin's Paperbacks); 1989. 240p. 16.95 o.p. (*0-312-03854-2*, Saint Martin's Minotaur) St. Martin's Pr.

—Memory Can Be Murder. 1995. 256p. mass mkt. 5.99 o.s.i (*0-425-14772-X*) Berkley Publishing Group.

—Memory Can Be Murder. l.t. ed. 2001. (G. K. Hall Paperback Ser.). 335p. pap. 24.95 (*0-7838-9408-2*, Macmillan Reference USA) Gale Group.

—Remember the Alibi. 1994. 272p. mass mkt. 4.99 o.s.i (*0-425-14351-1*, Prime Crime) Berkley Publishing Group.

—Remember the Alibi. l.t. ed. 2000. (G. K. Hall Paperback Ser.). 397p. pap. 23.95 o.p. (*0-7838-8858-9*, Macmillan Reference USA) Gale Group.

—Where There's a Will. 1999. (Peaches Dan Mysteries Ser.). 256p. mass mkt. 5.99 o.s.i (*0-425-16984-7*, Prime Crime) Berkley Publishing Group.

—Where There's a Will. 2003. (Paperback Ser.). lib. bdg. 25.95 (*0-7862-5246-4*) Thorndike Pr.

—Who Killed What's-Her-Name? 1994. mass mkt. 4.99 o.s.i (*0-425-14208-6*) Berkley Publishing Group.

—Who Killed What's-Her-Name? l.t. ed. 1999. (Paperback Ser.). 429p. pap. 23.95 (*0-7838-8497-4*) Thorndike Pr.

—Who Killed What's-Her-Name? A Peaches Dann Mystery. 2000. 240p. pap. 14.95 (*1-57090-092-2*) aBOOKS Distributing.

—Whose Death Is It, Anyway? 1997. 256p. mass mkt. 5.99 o.s.i (*0-425-15627-3*, Prime Crime) Berkley Publishing Group.

—Whose Death Is It, Anyway? 2001. pap. 13.95 (*1-57072-193-9*, Silver Dagger Mysteries) Overmountain Pr.

Stanley, Maurice. The Legend of Nance Dude. 1991. (Illus.). 253p. 17.95 o.p. (*0-89587-081-9*) Blair, John F. Pub.

—The Legend of Nance Dude. 1999. 264p. pap. 9.95 (*0-943335-16-7*) Marblehead Publishing.

Stanton, Judith. His Stolen Bride. 1999. 448p. mass mkt. 5.99 (*0-06-109787-X*) HarperCollins Pubs.

Steinke, Darcey. Up Through the Water. 2000. 176p. reprint ed. pap. 12.00 (*0-8021-3734-2*, Grove Pr.) Grove/Atlantic, Inc.

—Up Through the Water. Rosenman, Jane, ed. 1991. 176p. reprint ed. pap. (*0-671-70647-0*, Washington Square Pr.) Simon & Schuster.

Stewart, Gaither. To Be a Stranger. 2003. (*0-9721513-6-2*); 314p. pap. 15.00 (*0-9721513-5-4*) Wind River Pr.

Stokes, Penelope J. The Amber Photograph. 2001. 400p. 21.99 (*0-8499-4283-7*); vi, 358p. pap. 12.99 (*0-8499-3722-1*) W Publishing Group.

Strauss, Darin. Chang & Eng. 336p. 2001. pap. 13.00 (*0-452-28109-1*, Plume); 2000. 23.95 o.s.i (*0-525-94512-1*) Dutton/Plume.

—Chang & Eng. l.t. ed. 2000. (Hardcover Ser.). 478p. 25.95 (*1-56895-135-3*, Wheeler Publishing, Inc.) Gale Group.

—Chang & Eng. 2000. o.p. (*0-525-94551-2*) NAL.

—Chang & Eng. 2001. 19.05 (*0-606-22779-2*) Turtleback Bks.

Sumner, Tracy. Tides of Love. 2000. 32p. mass mkt. 5.99 o.s.i (*0-8217-6696-1*, Zebra Bks.) Kensington Publishing Corp.

Szittya, Ruth O. That's My Brother. 1982. (Illus.). 32p. (Orig.). (J). (gr. 3). pap. 3.95 o.p. (*0-913408-74-3*) Friends United Pr.

Terrell, Bob. Grandpa's Town: Asheville at the Turn of the Century... rev. ed. 1997. (Illus.). 192p. pap. 14.95 (*1-56664-119-5*) WorldComm.

Thomasson, Clarissa. Lorinda's Legacy. 2000. 288p. 12.95 (*1-929202-02-4*) Salt Marsh Pubns.

—Reconstructing Hillsborough. 1999. 304p. pap. 12.95 (*1-929202-01-6*) Salt Marsh Pubns.

Thompson, Jim. Pop. 1280. 1984. 224p. reprint ed. pap. 4.95 o.p. (*0-916870-76-6*, Black Mask) Creative Arts Bk. Co.

—Pop. 1280. 1990. (Vintage Crime Ser.). 224p. pap. 11.00 (*0-679-73249-7*, Vintage) Knopf Publishing Group.

Trotter, William R. The Sands of Pride. 2003. 768p. reprint ed. pap. 15.00 (*0-452-28442-2*, Plume) Dutton/Plume.

Warner, Gertrude Chandler. The Mystery of the Wild Ponies. 2000. (Boxcar Children Ser.: Vol. 77). (Illus.). (J). (gr. 2-5). 10.00 (*0-606-18908-4*) Turtleback Bks.

Wechter, Nell W. Taffy of Torpedo Junction. 1996. 160p. (C). pap. 9.95 (*0-8078-4619-8*) Univ. of North Carolina Pr.

Weinstein, Fannie & Schumann, Ruth. Please Don't Kill Mommy! 2001. (True Crime Library). (Illus.). 304p. mass mkt. 6.50 (*0-312-97720-4*, St. Martin's Paperbacks) St. Martin's Pr.

West, John Foster. The Summer People. 1989. 243p. 14.95 o.p. (*0-913239-65-8*) Appalachian Consortium Pr.

—The Summer People. 2000. iv, 243p. pap. 14.95 (*1-887905-27-8*) Parkway Pubs., Inc.

Whitney, Phyllis A. Amethyst Dreams. unabr. ed. 1998. audio 69.95 (*0-7540-0160-1*, CAB 1583) BBC Audiobooks America.

—Amethyst Dreams. 1998. 304p. mass mkt. 6.99 (*0-449-22618-2*, Fawcett) Ballantine Bks.

—Amethyst Dreams. unabr. ed. 1999. audio 29.95 (*0-7861-1542-4*); 1997. audio 44.95 (*0-7861-1170-4*, 1954) Blackstone Audio Bks., Inc.

—Amethyst Dreams. unabr. ed. 1997. audio 21.95 o.p. (*1-56100-762-5*, 327, Bookcassette); 9p. audio 57.25 o.p. (*1-56100-837-0*, 797, Unabridged Library Editions) Brilliance Audio.

—Amethyst Dreams. l.t. ed. 1997. pap. 24.00 o.p. (*0-7838-8130-4*, Macmillan Reference USA) Gale Group.

—Amethyst Dreams. l.t. ed. 1997. (Large Print Ser.). pap. 25.00 o.s.i (*0-679-77436-X*) Random Hse., Inc.

—Amethyst Dreams. 1998. 13.04 (*0-606-14150-2*) Turtleback Bks.

—Star Flight. 1994. mass mkt. 5.99 o.s.i (*0-449-22258-6*, Fawcett) Ballantine Bks.

—Star Flight. unabr. ed. 1997. audio 44.95 (*0-7861-1211-5*) Blackstone Audio Bks., Inc.

—Star Flight. l.t. ed. 1993. 19.00 o.s.i (*0-679-74949-7*) McKay, David Co., Inc.

Wilkinson, Sylvia. On the 7th Day God Created the Chevrolet. 1993. 424p. 18.95 o.p. (*0-945575-13-0*) Algonquin Bks. of Chapel Hill.

Williams, Bronwyn. Beckett's Birthright. 2002. (Harlequin Historicals Ser.). 304p. mass mkt. (*0-373-29233-3*, Harlequin Bks.) Harlequin Enterprises, Ltd.

Williams, Theresa. The Secret of Hurricanes. 2002. 209p. 17.50 (*1-931561-10-9*) MacAdam/Cage Publishing, Inc.

Wilson, P. B. Night Comes Swiftly. 1997. 350p. (Orig.). pap. 9.99 o.p. (*1-56507-718-0*) Harvest Hse. Pubs.

Winslow, Vicki. Follow the Leader. 1998. (Illus.). 224p. (gr. 2-6). pap. text 3.99 o.s.i (*0-440-41296-X*) Dell Publishing.

—Follow the Leader. 1998. 10.04 (*0-606-15531-7*) Turtleback Bks.

Winters, Donna. Rosalie of Grand Traverse Bay. Chambers, Pamela Q., ed. 1996. (Great Lakes Romances Ser.). 352p. (Orig.). pap. 10.95 (*0-923048-84-7*) Bigwater Publishing.

Wofford, Ben. Uncle Henry's Ghost. 2002. iv, 212p. 14.95 (*1-887905-58-8*) Parkway Pubs., Inc.

Wolfe, Thomas. Look Homeward, Angel. 1997. (Scribner Classics). 528p. 30.00 (*0-684-84221-1*, Scribner) Simon & Schuster.

York, Lynn. The Piano Teacher: A Novel of Swan's Knob. 2004. 304p. pap. 13.00 (*0-452-28477-5*, Plume) Dutton/Plume.

Zachary, Hugh. Munday. 2003. 288p. pap. 13.95 (*1-4104-0134-0*, Five Star Trade); 318p. 25.95 (*0-7862-4323-6*, Five Star) Gale Group.

Zuber, Isbael. Salt. 2002. 352p. 25.00 (*0-312-28133-1*) Picador.

**NORTH DAKOTA—FICTION**

Adams, Harold. A Way with Widows. l.t. ed. 1995. (Nightingale Ser.). 219p. pap. 17.95 (*0-7838-1144-6*, Macmillan Reference USA) Gale Group.

—A Way with Widows. (Carl Wilcox Mystery Ser.). 1999. 156p. pap. 7.95 (*0-8027-7574-8*); 1994. 142p. 18.95 (*0-8027-3190-2*) Walker & Co.

The Beet Queen. 1986. audio American Audio Prose Library, Inc.

Doctorow, E. L. Welcome to Hard Times. 1988. mass mkt. 5.99 o.s.i (*0-449-21602-0*, Fawcett) Ballantine Bks.

—Welcome to Hard Times. 1976. 224p. pap. 2.95 o.s.i (*0-553-14189-9*, 14189-9) Bantam Bks.

—Welcome to Hard Times. 1994. lib. bdg. 24.95 (*1-56849-393-2*) Buccaneer Bks., Inc.

—Welcome to Hard Times. 1996. 224p. pap. 12.95 (*0-452-27571-7*, Plume) Dutton/Plume.

—Welcome to Hard Times. 1992. pap. 10.00 o.p. (*0-679-73627-1*, Vintage) Knopf Publishing Group.

—Welcome to Hard Times. mass mkt. 0.50 o.p. (*0-451-01959-8*, Signet Bks.) NAL.

—Welcome to Hard Times. 1975. 224p. 8.95 o.p. (*0-394-49833-X*) Random Hse., Inc.

Erdrich, Louise. The Beet Queen. 1989. 360p. pap. 13.95 o.s.i (*0-553-34723-3*); 1987. 320p. mass mkt. 4.50 o.s.i (*0-553-26807-4*, Bantam Classics) Bantam Bks.

—The Beet Queen. l.t. ed. 1987. 455p. 18.95 o.p. (*0-8161-4300-5*, Macmillan Reference USA) Gale Group.

—The Beet Queen. 1986. 338p. 16.45 o.p. (*0-03-070612-2*) Harcourt College Pubs.

—The Beet Queen. 1998. 352p. pap. 14.00 (*0-06-097750-7*, Perennial); 1991. audio 15.95 (*1-55994-211-8*, CPN 2170, HarperAudio) HarperTrade.

—The Beet Queen. 1986. 352p. 16.95 o.p. (*0-8050-0058-5*) Holt, Henry & Co.

—The Bingo Palace. l.t. ed. 1994. 25.95 o.p. (*1-56895-073-X*, Wheeler Publishing, Inc.) Gale Group.

—The Bingo Palace. 288p. 1995. pap. 78.00 o.p. (*0-06-092614-7*); 1994. 207.00 o.p. (*0-06-017102-2*) HarperCollins Pubs.

—The Bingo Palace. 288p. 1995. pap. 13.00 (*0-06-092585-X*, Perennial); 1994. 23.00 o.p. (*0-06-017080-8*) HarperTrade.

—Love Medicine. 1986. (American Audio Prose Library: Series VI). audio 13.95 (*1-55644-149-5*, 6021) American Audio Prose Library, Inc.

—Love Medicine. 288p. 1989. pap. 11.00 o.s.i (*0-553-34423-4*); 1987. mass mkt. 4.50 o.s.i (*0-553-26808-2*) Bantam Bks.

—Love Medicine. l.t. ed. 1986. (General Ser.). 360p. 17.95 o.p. (*0-8161-3957-1*, Macmillan Reference USA) Gale Group.

—Love Medicine. 1993. 288p. pap. 10.00 o.p. (*0-06-097581-4*, Perennial); audio 15.95 o.p. (*1-55994-145-6*, CPN 2142, HarperAudio); 1993. 304p. pap. 72.00 o.p. (*0-06-097571-7*, Perennial); 1993. 384p. pap. 14.00 (*0-06-097554-7*, Perennial) HarperTrade.

—Love Medicine. 1984. 88p. 19.95 o.p. (*0-8050-1716-X*); 1984. 288p. 13.95 o.p. (*0-03-070611-4*); 1993. 352p. 24.00 o.p. (*0-8050-2798-X*) Holt, Henry & Co.

—The Master Butchers Singing Club. 2003. 400p. 25.95 (*0-06-620977-3*) HarperCollins Pubs.

—The Master Butchers Singing Club. 2004. 416p. pap. 13.95 (*0-06-093533-2*, Perennial); 2003. 704p. pap. 25.95 (*0-06-053327-7*, HarperLargePrint) HarperTrade.

—Tales of Burning Love: A Novel. l.t. ed. 1996. 25.95 o.p. (*1-56895-328-3*, Wheeler Publishing, Inc.) Gale Group.

—Tales of Burning Love: A Novel. 1996. 448p. 225.00 o.p. (*0-06-017523-0*); 79p. 25.00 o.p. (*0-06-017605-9*) HarperCollins Pubs.

—Tales of Burning Love: A Novel. 1997. 464p. pap. 14.00 (*0-06-092836-0*, Perennial) HarperTrade.

Estleman, Loren D. Stamping Ground. 1997. 213p. pap. 5.99 (*0-8125-3569-3*, Forge Bks.) Doherty, Tom Assocs., LLC.

—Stamping Ground. 1980. (Double D Western Ser.). 10.95 o.p. (*0-385-15563-8*) Doubleday Publishing.

Greiman, Lois. Counterfeit Cowgirl. 1998. (Love & Laughter Ser.: Vol. 48). per. (*0-373-44048-0*, 1-44048-6, Harlequin Bks.) Harlequin Enterprises, Ltd.

Henke, Roxanne. Becoming Olivia. 2004. (Coming Home to Brewster Ser.). pap. 11.99 (*0-7369-1149-9*) Harvest Hse. Pubs.

Henke, Roxanne Sayler. Finding Ruth. 2003. (Coming Home to Brewster Ser.). 450p. pap. 10.99 (*0-7369-0968-0*, 6909680) Harvest Hse. Pubs.

Macomber, Debbie. Always Dakota. 2001. 384p. mass mkt. (*1-55166-800-9*, 1-66800-3, Mira Bks.) Harlequin Enterprises, Ltd.

—Buffalo Valley. 2001. 256p. (*1-55166-841-6*, Mira Bks.) Harlequin Enterprises, Ltd.

—Dakota Born. l.t. ed. 2004. lib. bdg. 28.95 (*1-58547-397-9*, Premier) Ctr. Point Large Print.

—Dakota Born. 2000. (*1-55166-560-3*, 1-66560-3); 384p. mass mkt. (*1-55166-576-X*) Harlequin Enterprises, Ltd. (Mira Bks.).

—Dakota Home. 2000. 384p. mass mkt. (*1-55166-602-2*, 1-66602-3, Mira Bks.) Harlequin Enterprises, Ltd.

Marshall, Brenda K. Mavis. 1997. 323p. mass mkt. 5.99 o.s.i (*0-449-22571-2*); 1996. 320p. 4.99 o.s.i (*0-449-91041-5*) Ballantine Bks. (Fawcett).

Moloney, Susie. A Dry Spell. 1998. 448p. mass mkt. 6.99 o.s.i (*0-440-22345-8*) Doubleday Publishing.

Nelson, Rodney. Villy Sadness: A Novella. 1987. 114p. pap. 7.95 (*0-89823-093-4*) New Rivers Pr.

Snelling, Lauraine. An Untamed Land. 1996. (Red River of the North Ser.: Vol. 1). 352p. pap. 11.99 (*1-55661-576-0*) Bethany Hse. Pubs.

—An Untamed Land. l.t. ed. 2002. (Red River of the North Ser.: No. 1). 352p. pap. 17.95 (*1-4104-0014-X*, Walker Large Print); 26.95 (*0-7862-4019-9*) Gale Group.

—Untamed Land, a New Day Rising & Land to Call Home, 3 vols. 1997. (Red River of the North Ser.). pap. 35.99 (*0-7642-8150-X*) Bethany Hse. Pubs.

Spencer, LaVyrle. Years. 496p. 2003. pap. 10.00 (*0-425-19578-3*); 1986. mass mkt. 7.99 (*0-515-08489-1*, Jove) Berkley Publishing Group.

—Years. l.t. ed. 1994. (General Ser.). 18.95 (*0-8161-5763-4*); 669p. lib. bdg. 21.95 o.p. (*0-8161-5762-6*) Gale Group. (Macmillan Reference USA).

Stone, Joel. A Town Called Jericho. 1992. 320p. 21.95 o.p. (*1-55611-319-6*) Fine, Donald I. Bks.

Woiwode, Larry. Beyond the Bedroom Wall. 1984. audio 13.95 (*1-55644-117-7*, 4141) American Audio Prose Library, Inc.

—Beyond the Bedroom Wall. 1975. 620p. 17.95 o.p. (*0-374-11237-1*) Farrar, Straus & Giroux.

—Beyond the Bedroom Wall. 1997. (Rediscovery Ser.). 625p. reprint ed. pap. 16.00 (1-55597-258-6) Graywolf Pr.

—Beyond the Bedroom Wall. 1976. pap. 1.95 o.p. (0-380-00684-7, 47670-3, Avon Bks.) Morrow/Avon.

—Beyond the Bedroom Wall. 1989. 640p. pap. 8.95 o.p. (0-14-012186-2, Penguin Bks.) Viking Penguin.

Young, Carrie. The Wedding Dress: Stories from the Dakota Plains. 1993. 176p. pap. 8.95 o.s.i (0-440-50524-0, Laurel) Dell Publishing.

—The Wedding Dress: Stories from the Dakota Plains. (Bur Oak Original Ser.). 1992. 135p. 17.95 (0-87745-386-1); 1992. E-Book 16.95 (1-58729-258-0); 2000. 135p. reprint ed. pap. 12.95 (0-87745-718-2) Univ. of Iowa Pr.

—The Wedding Dress & Other Short Stories. 1996. 176p. pap. 9.95 o.s.i (0-385-31899-5, Delta) Dell Publishing.

### NORTH HOMAGE (KY.: IMAGINARY PLACE)—FICTION

Woodworth, Deborah. Deadly Shaker Spring. 1998. (Sister Rose Callahan Mystery Ser.). 304p. mass mkt. 5.99 (0-380-79203-6, Avon Bks.) Morrow/Avon.

—The Death of a Winter Shaker. 1997. (Sister Rose Callahan Mystery Ser.). 224p. mass mkt. 5.50 (0-380-79201-X, Avon Bks.) Morrow/Avon.

—A Simple Shaker Murder. 2000. (Sister Rose Callahan Mystery Ser.). 256p. mass mkt. 5.99 (0-380-80425-5, Avon Bks.) Morrow/Avon.

—The Sins of a Shaker Summer: A Sister Rose Callahan Mystery. 1999. 272p. mass mkt. 5.99 (0-380-79204-4, Avon Bks.) Morrow/Avon.

### NORTHERN IRELAND—FICTION

Baker, Jeanette. The Delaney Woman. l.t. ed. 2003. 392p. 30.95 (1-58724-552-3, Wheeler Publishing, Inc.) Gale Group.

—The Delaney Woman. 2003. 384p. mass mkt. (1-55166-696-0, Mira Bks.) Harlequin Enterprises, Ltd.

Baker, Keith. Inheritance. l.t. ed. 1998. (Ulverscroft Large Print Ser.). 608p. 29.99 (0-7089-3890-6, Ulverscroft) Thorpe, F. A. Pubs. GBR. Dist: Ulverscroft Large Print Bks., Ltd., Ulverscroft Large Print Canada, Ltd.

—Inheritance: A Novel. 1998. 288p. 24.00 (0-688-15321-6, Morrow, William & Co.) Morrow/Avon.

Bannister, Jo. Echoes of Lies. 2001. 320p. 23.95 (0-312-28432-2, Saint Martin's Minotaur) St. Martin's Pr.

—True Witness. l.t. ed. 2003. (Magna Large Print Ser.). 416p. (0-7505-2013-2) Magna Large Print Bks. GBR. Dist: Ulverscroft Large Print Canada, Ltd.

—True Witness. Date not set. pap. (0-312-30818-3, Saint Martin's Griffin); mass mkt. (0-312-98645-9, St. Martin's Paperbacks); E-Book 23.95 (0-312-70924-2); 2002. 304p. 23.95 (0-312-30817-5, Saint Martin's Minotaur) St. Martin's Pr.

Beckett, Mary. A Belfast Woman. 1996. 112p. pap. 10.95 (0-905169-85-9) Poolbeg Pr. IRL. Dist: Dufour Editions, Inc.

Bellacera, Carole. The Spotlight. 352p. 2000. 25.95 o.s.i (0-312-87451-0); 2001. reprint ed. mass mkt. 6.99 (0-8125-6158-9) Doherty, Tom Assocs., LLC. (Forge Bks.).

Carr, Hugh. Voices from a Far Country. 1996. 304p. pap. 18.95 (0-85640-545-0) Blackstaff Pr., The IRL. Dist: Dufour Editions, Inc.

Crow, Donna Fletcher. The Banks of the Boyne: A Quest for a Christian Ireland. 1998. 750p. pap. 19.99 (0-8024-7737-2) Moody Pr.

Deane, Seamus. Reading in the Dark. unabr. ed. 2000. audio 54.95 (0-7540-0080-X, CAB 1503) Chivers Audio Bks. GBR. Dist: BBC Audiobooks America.

—Reading in the Dark. 1998. 256p. pap. 12.95 (0-375-70023-4, Vintage) Knopf Publishing Group.

—Reading in the Dark, unabr. ed. 1999. audio 60.00 (0-7887-2934-9, 95539E7) Recorded Bks., LLC.

—Reading in the Dark: A Novel. 1997. 246p. 23.00 o.s.i (0-394-57440-0) Knopf, Alfred A. Inc.

Eickhoff, Lee. Fallons Wake. E-Book 23.95 (0-312-87708-0, Tor Bks.) Doherty, Tom Assocs., LLC.

Eickhoff, Randy Lee. Fallon's Wake. 2000. 347p. 23.95 (0-312-86762-X, Forge Bks.) Doherty, Tom Assocs., LLC.

—The Gombeen Man. 1992. 252p. 19.95 o.p. (0-8027-1197-9) Walker & Co.

Foley, Michael. The Road to Notown. 1997. 342p. pap. 16.95 (0-85640-576-0) Blackstaff Pr., The IRL. Dist: Dufour Editions, Inc.

Gibson, Elizabeth. The Water Is Wide: A Novel of Northern Ireland. 304p. 1990. pap. 8.99 (0-310-31821-1); 1984. 8.95 o.p. (0-310-31820-3, 12327) Zondervan.

Gould, Lois. No Brakes: A Novel. 1997. 22.00 o.p. (0-8050-4117-6) Holt, Henry & Co.

Higgins, Jack. A Prayer for the Dying. 1978. 224p. pap. 1.75 o.s.i (0-449-23755-9, Fawcett) Ballantine Bks.

—A Prayer for the Dying. 1985. mass mkt. 3.95 o.p. (0-451-14994-7); 288p. mass mkt. 4.99 o.p. (0-451-16672-8); mass mkt. 3.50 o.p. (0-451-13801-5); mass mkt. 3.95 o.p. (0-451-14873-8) NAL. (Signet Bks.).

—A Prayer for the Dying. abr. ed. 1987. audio 14.95 (0-671-64636-2, Simon & Schuster Audioworks) Simon & Schuster Audio.

MacLaverty, Bernard. The Anatomy School. 368p. 2003. 14.95 (0-393-32457-5); 2002. 25.95 (0-393-05052-1) Norton, W. W. & Co., Inc.

—The Anatomy School. 2002. 368p. pap. (0-676-97445-7, Vintage) Random Hse. of Canada, Ltd. CAN. Dist: Random Hse., Inc.

McCabe, Patrick. Call Me the Breeze. 2003. 352p. 24.95 (0-06-052388-3, HarperCollins) HarperTrade.

O'Reilly, Sean. Love & Sleep: A Romance. 2003. 13.00 (0-7867-1235-X, Carroll & Graf Pubs.) Avalon Publishing Group.

—Love & Sleep: A Romance. 2002. 208p. pap. (0-571-20545-3) Faber & Faber, Inc.

Park, David. The Big Snow. 2002. 278p. (0-7475-5726-8) Bloomsbury Pr.

—The Big Snow. 288p. 2003. (Illus.). pap. 13.95 (1-58234-293-8); 2002. 24.95 (1-58234-249-0) Bloomsbury Publishing.

### NORTHWEST, PACIFIC—FICTION

Adams, Hazard. Many Pretty Toys. (SUNY Series in Postmodern Culture). viii, 245p. (C). 2000. pap. text 20.95 (0-7914-4086-9); 1999. text 32.50 (0-7914-4085-0) State Univ. of New York Pr.

Byers, Michael. The Coast of Good Intentions. 1998. 176p. pap. 12.00 (0-395-89170-1, Mariner Bks.) Houghton Mifflin Co. Trade & Reference Div.

Champlin, Tim. Great Timber Race. l.t. ed. 2001. (G.K. Hall Large Print Western Ser.). 324p. 24.95 (0-7838-9491-0, Macmillan Reference USA) Gale Group.

Daheim, Mary R. Hocus Croakus. 2003. 314p. 6.99 (0-380-81564-8); 320p. 23.95 (0-380-97868-7) Morrow/Avon. (Morrow, William & Co.).

—Silver Scream. 2002. 320p. 23.95 (0-380-97867-9, Morrow, William & Co.) Morrow/Avon.

—Silver Scream. l.t. ed. 2002. 28.95 (0-7862-4612-X) Thorndike Pr.

Dillon, Grace L., ed. Hive of Dreams: Contemporary Science Fiction from the Pacific Northwest. 2003. (Northwest Readers Ser.). 288p. pap. 19.95 (0-87071-555-0) Oregon State Univ. Pr.

Duncan, Sharon. Death on a Casual Friday. 2001. 288p. mass mkt. 5.99 o.p. (0-451-20398-4, Signet Bks.) NAL.

Fairweather, Lori. Blood & Water: A Pacific Northwest Mystery. 1999. 321p. 24.00 (0-688-16118-9, Morrow, William & Co.) Morrow/Avon.

Goddard, Ken. Double Blind. 1998. (Henry Lightstone Ser.: 3). 460p. mass mkt. 6.99 (0-8125-5061-7); 1997. 384p. 24.95 o.p. (0-312-85796-9) Doherty, Tom Assocs., LLC. (Forge Bks.).

—Prey. 1993. 398p. mass mkt. 5.99 (0-8125-1198-0); 1992. 336p. 21.95 o.p. (0-312-85112-X) Doherty, Tom Assocs., LLC. (Tor Bks.).

Harrison, Stuart. The Snow Falcon. abr. ed. 2000. audio 7.99 o.s.i (1-56740-330-1, 1955, Paperback Nova Audio Bks.); 1999. audio 17.95 o.p. (1-56740-821-4, 1597, Nova Audio Bks.); 1999. 12p. audio 73.25 (1-56740-629-7, 1633, Unabridged Library Editions); 1999. audio 39.95 (1-56740-400-6, 1594, Brilliance Audio Unabridged) Brilliance Audio.

—The Snow Falcon, abr. ed. 1999. audio 17.95 Highsmith Inc.

—The Snow Falcon. 352p. 2000. pap. 13.95 (0-312-25420-2, Saint Martin's Griffin); 1999. 23.95 o.p. (0-312-20166-4) St. Martin's Pr.

—The Snow Falcon. l.t. ed. 1999. (Americana Ser.). 645p. 29.95 (0-7862-1974-2) Thorndike Pr.

Harrison, Stuart J. The Snow Falcon. E-Book 13.95 (0-312-26470-4) St. Martin's Pr.

James, Sibyl. The Adventures of Stout Mama. 1993. 140p. 14.00 (0-918949-34-3); pap. 9.00 (0-918949-33-5) Moyer Bell. (Papier-Mache Pr.).

Kirkpatrick, Jane. A Name of Her Own. 2002. (Tender Ties Historical Ser.: Vol. 1). (Illus.). 400p. pap. 13.99 (1-57856-499-9) WaterBrook Pr.

Koho, Sharon Lewis. The Painting on the Pond. 2003. 198p. pap. 13.95 (1-55517-703-4, 77034, Bonneville Bks.) Cedar Fort, Inc./CFI Distribution.

La Pierre, Betty Sullivan. The Enemy Stalks. 2002. pap. 14.00 (1-59109-204-3) Booksurge, LLC.

—The Enemy Stalks. 2000. 247p. E-Book 8.95 (0-9679076-3-2) E-Pub2000.

Lebowitz, Paul. Breaking Balls: A Novel of Baseball. 2001. 232p. per. 24.95 (0-7864-1065-5) McFarland & Co., Inc. Pubs.

Lowell, Elizabeth. Amber Beach. abr. ed. 1998. audio 7.99 o.s.i (1-56740-261-5, 1561, Paperback Nova Audio Bks.); 1997. audio 17.95 o.p. (1-56100-993-8, 456, Nova Audio Bks.); 1997. audio 23.95 o.p. (1-56100-767-6, 33, Bookcassette); 1997. 11p. audio 73.25 o.p. (1-56100-842-7, 796, Unabridged Library Editions) Brilliance Audio.

—Amber Beach. l.t. ed. 1998. (Romance Ser.). 27.95 (1-56895-577-4, Wheeler Publishing, Inc.) Gale Group.

—Amber Beach. 2002. E-Book 7.50 (0-06-050368-8); E-Book 7.50 (0-06-050370-X); E-Book 7.50 (0-06-050369-6); E-Book 7.50 (0-06-050367-X) HarperCollins General Bks. Group. (PerfectBound).

—Amber Beach. 2001. 384p. mass mkt. 7.50 (0-380-77584-0); 1997. 400p. 22.00 (0-380-97317-0) Morrow/Avon. (Avon Bks.).

—Pearl Cove. abr. ed. 2000. audio 7.99 o.s.i (1-56740-348-4, 2109, Paperback Nova Audio Bks.); 1999. audio 17.95 o.p. (1-56740-835-4, 1670, Nova Audio Bks.); 1999. audio 39.95 (1-56740-422-7, 1668, Brilliance Audio Unabridged); 1999. audio 73.25 (1-56740-648-3, 1669, Unabridged Library Editions) Brilliance Audio.

—Pearl Cove. l.t. ed. 1999. (Wheeler Press Paperback Ser.). pap. 11.95 (1-56895-964-8); 28.95 o.p. (1-56895-746-7) Gale Group. (Wheeler Publishing, Inc.).

—Pearl Cove. 2002. E-Book 7.50 (0-06-050383-1); E-Book 7.50 (0-06-050384-X); E-Book 7.50 (0-06-050385-8); E-Book 7.50 (0-06-050382-3) HarperCollins General Bks. Group. (PerfectBound).

—Pearl Cove. 2000. 432p. mass mkt. 7.50 (0-380-78988-4); 1999. 376p. 24.00 (0-380-97404-5) Morrow/Avon. (Avon Bks.).

McNamer, Deirdre. My Russian. 2000. 304p. pap. 14.00 (0-345-43951-1) Ballantine Bks.

—My Russian. 1999. 278p. tchr. ed. 24.00 o.p. (0-395-95637-4) Houghton Mifflin Co.

Moody, Skye Kathleen. K Falls. 2001. E-Book 23.95 (1-59061-040-7) Adobe Systems, Inc.

—K Falls. 2002. (WWL Mystery Ser.). 256p. mass mkt. (0-373-26426-7, Worldwide Library) Harlequin Enterprises, Ltd.

—Medusa: A Pacific Northwest Mystery. 2003. (Pacific Northwest Mystery Ser.). 336p. 24.95 (0-312-26678-2) St. Martin's Pr.

Morgan, Deborah. The Weedless Widow. 2002. 208p. mass mkt. 5.99 (0-425-18689-X, Prime Crime) Berkley Publishing Group.

—The Weedless Widow. l.t. ed. 2003. 324p. 25.95 (0-7862-5599-4) Thorndike Pr.

Platt, Randall Beth. The Cornerstone. 1998. 244p. 21.95 (0-945774-40-0) Catbird Pr.

Robinson, Eden. Monkey Beach. 2000. 384p. 24.00 (0-618-07327-2, Mariner Bks.) Houghton Mifflin Co. Trade & Reference Div.

Ross, Dana Fuller, pseud. Carolina Courage! 1990. (Holts: An American Dynasty Ser.: No. 3). 368p. mass mkt. 5.99 o.s.i (0-553-28756-7) Bantam Bks.

—Carolina Courage! l.t. ed. 1991. (Holts, an American Dynasty Ser.: Vol. 3). 400p. 21.95 (0-8161-5309-4, Macmillan Reference USA) Gale Group.

—Homecoming! 1994. (Holts: An American Dynasty Ser.: Bk. 9). 384p. mass mkt. 5.99 o.s.i (0-553-56150-2) Bantam Bks.

—Homecoming! l.t. ed. 1995. (G. K. Hall Core Ser.). 455p. 23.95 (0-7838-1173-X, Macmillan Reference USA) Gale Group.

—Pacific Destiny. 1994. 368p. mass mkt. 5.99 o.s.i (0-553-56149-9) Bantam Bks.

—Pacific Destiny. l.t. ed. 1994. 507p. lib. bdg. 23.95 (0-8161-7466-0, Macmillan Reference USA) Gale Group.

—Yukon Justice. 1992. (Holts: An American Dynasty Ser.: No. 7). 368p. mass mkt. 5.99 o.s.i (0-553-29763-5) Bantam Bks.

—Yukon Justice. l.t. ed. 1992. (General Ser.). 18.95 o.p. (0-8161-5488-0); lib. bdg. 21.95 o.p. (0-8161-5487-2) Gale Group. (Macmillan Reference USA).

### NORTHWEST TERRITORIES—FICTION

Paine, Lauran. Trail of the Sioux. l.t. ed. 2001. 155p. 21.95 (1-57490-345-4, Sagebrush Large Print Westerns) Beeler, Thomas T. Publisher.

Young, Scott. Murder in a Cold Climate. 1989. mass mkt. o.s.i (0-449-21746-9) Ballantine Bks.

—Murder in a Cold Climate. (Crime Ser.). 1990. 240p. pap. 4.50 o.p. (0-14-012336-9, Penguin Bks.); 1989. 256p. 16.95 o.p. (0-670-82889-0) Viking Penguin.

—The Shaman's Knife. 1994. (Crime Ser.). 288p. pap. 5.95 o.p. (0-14-014353-X, Penguin Bks.) Penguin Group (USA) Inc.

—The Shaman's Knife. 1993. 288p. 20.00 o.p. (0-670-83555-2, Viking) Viking Penguin.

### NORWAY—FICTION

Afeltra, Louise R. Lovisa: Angel from Norway. 1997. (Illus.). 96p. (Orig.). pap. 9.95 (1-56474-206-7) Fithian Pr.

Bjorneboe, Jens. Moment of Freedom. 1975. 217p. 9.95 o.p. (0-393-08719-0) Norton, W. W. & Co., Inc.

—Moment of Freedom: The Heiligenberg Manuscript. 2000. 220p. pap. 15.95 (0-8023-1328-0) Dufour Editions, Inc.

Bjornson, Bjornstjerne. Bridal March & Other Stories. Anderson, Rasmos B., tr. 1977. (Short Story Index Reprint Ser.). 19.95 (0-8369-3136-X) Ayer Co. Pubs., Inc.

Borgen, Johan. The Scapegoat. Rokkan, Elizabeth, tr. from NOR. 1994. 187p. pap. 23.00 (1-870041-21-6) Norvik Pr. GBR. Dist: Dufour Editions, Inc.

Brett, Jan. Who's That Knocking on Christmas Eve? 2002. (Illus.). 32p. (J). (gr. k-3). 16.99 (0-399-23873-5) Putnam Publishing Group, The.

Brooks, Betty. Warrior's Destiny. 1995. mass mkt. 4.99 o.s.i (0-8217-4934-X); 384p. mass mkt. 4.99 o.s.i (0-8217-4999-4) Kensington Publishing Corp.

Christensen, Lars S. Herman. Nordby, Steven, tr. 1992. 186p. pap. 12.00 (1-877727-24-5) White Pine Pr.

Christiansen, Sigurd. Two Living & One Dead. Bjorkman, Edwin August, tr. from NOR. 1975. 288p. reprint ed. 76.95 (0-8371-7348-5, CHTL, Greenwood Pr.) Greenwood Publishing Group, Inc.

Ekman, Kerstin. The Spring. 2001. 400p. pap. 16.95 (1-870041-47-X) Norvik Pr. GBR. Dist: Dufour Editions, Inc.

Francis, Dick. Slay Ride. l.t. ed. 1993. 19.95 o.p. (0-7927-1431-8); pap. o.p. (0-7927-1430-X); 54.95 incl. audio (0-7451-5956-7) BBC Audiobooks America.

—Slay Ride. 1987. 272p. reprint ed. mass mkt. 5.95 o.s.i (0-449-21271-8, Fawcett) Ballantine Bks.

—Slay Ride. unabr. ed. 1991. audio 42.00 (0-7366-2081-8, 2886) Books on Tape, Inc.

—Slay Ride. 1984. mass mkt. 3.50 (0-671-50731-1); 1983. mass mkt. 2.95 (0-671-47021-3) Simon & Schuster. (Pocket).

—Slay Ride. l.t. ed. 1975. o.p. (0-85456-337-7, Ulverscroft) Thorpe, F. A. Pubs.

Gaarder, Jostein. The Solitaire Mystery. 1997. 368p. reprint ed. 6.99 (0-425-16047-5) Berkley Publishing Group.

—The Solitaire Mystery. 2003. pap. (0-374-52943-4); 1996. 356p. 22.00 o.p. (0-374-26651-4) Farrar, Straus & Giroux.

—The Solitaire Mystery: A Novel about Family & Destiny. 1997. 336p. reprint ed. pap. 14.00 (0-425-15999-X) Berkley Publishing Group.

Gaup, Ailo. In Search of the Drum. Sjordal, Bente K., tr. from NOR. 1993. 251p. pap. 11.95 (0-9631750-1-7) Muse Pubns.

Griffith, Nicola. The Blue Place: A Novel of Suspense. 1999. 320p. pap. 13.00 (0-380-79088-2, Perennial) HarperTrade.

—The Blue Place: A Novel of Suspense. 1998. 320p. pap. 23.00 (0-380-97446-0, Avon Bks.) Morrow/Avon.

Hamsun, Knut. Dreamers. Geddes, Tom, tr. from NOR. 1996. (Classics Ser.).Tr. of Svaermere. 128p. pap. 9.95 (0-8112-1321-8, NDP821) New Directions Publishing Corp.

—Growth of the Soil. 1972. 448p. pap. 12.00 (0-394-71781-3, Vintage) Knopf Publishing Group.

—Growth of the Soil. 1980. (YA). (gr. 7-12). 16.95 o.s.i (0-394-42743-2) Knopf, Alfred A. Inc.

—Hunger. 2001. 224p. pap. 9.83 (1-84195-206-0) Canongate Bks. GBR. Dist: Grove/Atlantic, Inc.

—Hunger. reprint ed. 2001. pap. text 28.00 (0-7426-9475-5); 1923. 118.00 (0-7426-4475-8) Classic Bks.

—Hunger. Egerton, George, tr. from NOR. 2003. 144p. pap. 5.95 (0-486-43168-1) Dover Pubns., Inc.

—Hunger. Bly, Robert, tr. & afterword by by. 1998. 240p. pap. 14.00 (0-374-52528-5) Farrar, Straus & Giroux.

—Hunger. Bly, Robert, tr. from NOR. 1967. 256p. pap. 10.00 o.s.i (0-374-50520-9) Farrar, Straus & Giroux.

—Hunger. Bly, Robert, tr. 1980. pap. 1.75 o.p. (0-380-00556-5, 42028, Avon Bks.) Morrow/Avon.

—Hunger. 2002. (YID.). (C). reprint ed. pap. 29.00 (0-657-03477-0); pap. 29.00 (0-657-07065-3); pap. 29.00 (0-657-07069-6) National Yiddish Bk. Ctr.

—Hunger. Lyngstad, Sverre, tr. from NOR. 1996. 194p. reprint ed. pap. 14.95 (0-86241-625-6) Rebel, Inc. GBR. Dist: AK Pr. Distribution.

—Hunger. Lyngstad, Sverre, ed. & tr. by. 1998. (Twentieth Century Classics Ser.). 224p. 13.00 (0-14-118064-1, Penguin Classics) Viking Penguin.

—Mysteries. 1984. 340p. pap. 8.95 o.p. (0-88184-031-9, Carroll & Graf Pubs.) Avalon Publishing Group.

—Mysteries. Bothmer, Gerry, tr. 1971. 8.95 o.p. (0-374-21764-5) Farrar, Straus & Giroux.

—Mysteries. 1980. pap. 1.95 o.p. (0-380-00504-2, 25221, Avon Bks.) Morrow/Avon.

—Mysteries. Lyngstad, Sverre, tr. from NOR. & intro. by. 2001. (Twentieth Century Classics Ser.). 352p. 14.00 (0-14-118618-6, Penguin Classics) Viking Penguin.

Haslund, Ebba. Nothing Happened. Wilson, Barbara, tr. from NOR. 1987. (Women in Translation Ser.).Tr. of Det/Hendte Ingenting. 134p. 14.95 o.p. (0-931188-48-2); pap. 8.95 o.p. (0-931188-47-4) Avalon Publishing Group. (Seal Pr.).

Haslund, Ebba & Wilson, Barbara. Nothing Happened. 1999. Tr. of Det/Hendte Ingenting. (Illus.). 200p. 12.95 (1-879679-13-2) Women In Translation.

Hoel, Sigurd. Meeting at the Milestone. Lyngstad, Sverre, tr. from NOR. 2002. 284p. pap. 15.95 (1-892295-31-8) Green Integer.

—The Troll Circle. 1991. (Modern Scandinavian Literature in Translation Ser.). 326p. reprint ed. pap. 101.10 (*0-608-07998-7*, 206796300012) Bks. on Demand.

—The Troll Circle. Lyngstad, Sverre, tr. from NOR. 1992. (Modern Scandinavian Literature in Translation Ser.). 313p. text 35.00 o.p. (*0-8032-2359-5*) Univ. of Nebraska Pr.

Laker, Rosalind, pseud. The Fragile Hour. 1996. 320p. 24.00 o.p. (*0-7278-5181-0*) Severn Hse. Pubs., Ltd.

Larsen, Hanna A., ed. Norway's Best Stories: An Introduction to Modern Norwegian Fiction. Orbeck, Anders, tr. from NOR. 1977. (Short Story Index Reprint Ser.). reprint ed. 25.95 (*0-8369-4019-9*) Ayer Co. Pubs., Inc.

Lie, Jonas. The Seer & Other Norwegian Tales. Morton, Brian & Trevor, Richard, trs. from NOR. 1990. 160p. (Orig.). pap. 19.95 (*0-948259-65-5*) Forest Bks. GBR. *Dist:* Dufour Editions, Inc.

Litton, Josie. Dream of Me/Believe in Me. 2001. 816p. mass mkt. 5.99 (*0-553-58436-7*) Bantam Bks.

Marshall, Jonathan. Reunion in Norway. 2004. 200p. pap. 14.95 (*0-9720119-9-4*) Ruder Finn Pr.

McFarlane, James, ed. Slaves of Love & Other Norwegian Short Stories. 1982. 27.95 o.p. (*0-19-212601-6*) Oxford Univ. Pr., Inc.

Nedreaas, Torborg. Music from a Blue Well. Lee, Bibbi, tr. 1988. (European Women Writers Ser.). 244p. reprint ed. pap. 75.70 (*0-608-02669-7*, 206332200004) Bks. on Demand.

—Music from a Blue Well. Lee, Bibbi, tr. 1988. (European Women Writers Ser.). vi, 238p. text 21.00 o.p. (*0-8032-3315-9*) Univ. of Nebraska Pr.

—Nothing Grows by Moonlight. Lee, Bibbi, tr. from NOR. 1987. (European Women Writers Ser.).Tr. of Av Maneskinn Gror det Ingenting. 198p. text 40.00 (*0-8032-3313-2*) Univ. of Nebraska Pr.

Oystein, Lonn. The Necessary Rituals of Maren Gripe. 2003. 160p. pap. 13.00 (*0-00-711334-X*) Collins Willow GBR. *Dist:* Trafalgar Square.

Page, Katherine Hall. The Body in the Fjord. l.t. ed. 1998. pap. 24.95 (*1-56895-562-6*, Wheeler Publishing, Inc.) Gale Group.

—The Body in the Fjord. 1998. 304p. mass mkt. 6.99 (*0-380-73129-0*, Avon Bks.); 1997. 272p. 22.00 (*0-688-14574-4*, Morrow, William & Co.) Morrow/Avon.

Sandemose, Aksel. The Werewolf. Lannestock, Gustaf, tr. from NOR. 2nd ed. 2002. (Library of World Fiction). 394p. pap. 24.95 (*0-299-03744-4*) Univ. of Wisconsin Pr.

Senje, Sigurd. Escape! Ramsden, Evelyn, tr. 1966. (YA). (gr. 7 up). pap. 1.25 o.p. (*0-15-629041-3*, Voyager Bks./Libros Viajeros) Harcourt Children's Bks.

Senstad, Susan Schwartz. Music for the Third Ear. 256p. 2002. pap. 13.00 (*0-312-28776-3*); 2001. 22.00 (*0-312-26621-9*) Picador.

Skram, Amalie. Lucie. Hanson, Katherine & Messick, Judith, trs. 2002. 168p. pap. 16.95 (*1-870041-48-8*) Norvik Pr. GBR. *Dist:* Dufour Editions, Inc.

Spang, Michael G. The Spy Who Longed for Home. 1989. 320p. 16.95 o.p. (*0-312-02986-1*, Saint Martin's Minotaur) St. Martin's Pr.

Stigen, Terge. An Interrupted Passage. Langomo, Amando, tr. from NOR. 1974. (Library of Scandinavian Literature). lib. bdg. 10.50 (*0-8057-3322-1*) Irvington Pubs.

Thorpe, Kay. A Reckless Attraction. 2002. (Harlequin Presents Ser.). 192p. mass mkt. (*0-373-80522-5*, Harlequin Bks.) Harlequin Enterprises, Ltd.

Ullmann, Linn. Before You Sleep. Nunnally, Tiina, tr. 2001. 304p. pap. 13.00 o.s.i (*0-14-029833-9*) Penguin Group (USA) Inc.

—Before You Sleep. Nunnally, Tiina, tr. from ENG. 1999. (ENG & NOR.). 256p. 23.95 o.s.i (*0-670-88698-X*, Viking) Viking Penguin.

—Stella Descending. A Novel. 2004. 256p. pap. 13.00 (*1-4000-3094-3*, Anchor) Knopf Publishing Group.

—Stella Descending: A Novel. Haveland, Barbara, tr. from NOR. 2003. 256p. 23.00 (*0-375-41499-1*) Knopf, Alfred A. Inc.

Undset, Sigrid. The Axe: The Master of Hestviken, Vol. 1. 1994. (Master of Hestviken Ser.: Vol. 1). 304p. pap. 13.00 (*0-679-75273-0*) Random Hse., Inc.

—Gunnar's Daughter. Harbison, Sherrill, ed. Chater, Arthur G., tr. 1998. (Twentieth Century Classics Ser.). 240p. pap. 11.95 (*0-14-118020-X*, Penguin Classics) Viking Penguin.

—In the Wilderness. 1995. (Master of Hestviken Ser.: Vol. 3). 208p. pap. 13.00 (*0-679-75553-5*, Vintage) Knopf Publishing Group.

—Kristin Lavransdatter. 1951. 1088p. 50.00 (*0-394-43262-2*) Knopf, Alfred A. Inc.

—The Master of Hestviken. 1978. 998p. pap. 15.95 o.p. (*0-452-26034-5*, Z5630); pap. 8.95 o.p. (*0-452-25179-6*); pap. 9.95 o.p. (*0-452-25383-7*); pap. 11.95 o.p. (*0-452-25630-5*) Dutton/Plume. (Plume).

—Master of Hestviken. 1934. 15.00 o.p. (*0-394-43555-9*, Knopf Bks. for Young Readers) Random Hse. Children's Bks.

—The Snake Pit. 1994. (Master of Hestviken / Sigrid Undset Ser.: Vol. 2). 240p. pap. 13.00 (*0-679-75554-3*, Vintage) Knopf Publishing Group.

—The Son Avenger. 1995. (Master of Hestviken Ser.: Vol. 4). 288p. pap. 13.00 (*0-679-75552-7*, Vintage) Knopf Publishing Group.

Vesaas, Tarjei. Birds. Stoverud, Torbjorn & Barnes, Michael, trs. 1996. 28.00 (*0-7206-0701-9*) Owen, Peter Ltd. GBR. *Dist:* Dufour Editions, Inc.

—The Birds. Barnes, Michael & Stoverud, Torbjorn, trs. from NOR. 2002. (Peter Owen Modern Classics Ser.). 234p. pap. 18.95 (*0-7206-1143-1*) Owen, Peter Ltd. GBR. *Dist:* Dufour Editions, Inc.

—The Birds. Stoverud, Torbjorn & Barnes, Michael, trs. from NOR. 1995. 224p. pap. 24.00 (*0-7206-0952-6*) Owen, Peter Ltd. GBR. *Dist:* Dufour Editions, Inc.

Wassmo, Herbjorg. Dina's Book. Christensen, Nadia, tr. from NOR. 1994. 448p. 22.95 (*1-55970-243-5*) Arcade Publishing, Inc.

—Dina's Book: A Novel. Christensen, Nadia M., tr. 1996. 464p. pap. 13.95 (*1-55970-348-2*) Arcade Publishing, Inc.

—House with the Blind Glass Windows. Lloyd, Roseann & Simpson, Allen, trs. from NOR. 1995. 232p. (Orig.). pap. 10.95 (*1-878067-59-1*, Seal Pr.) Avalon Publishing Group.

—The House with the Blind Glass Windows. Lloyd, Roseann & Simpson, Allen, trs. from NOR. 1987. (Women in Translation Ser.). 223p. 16.95 o.p. (*0-931188-51-2*); pap. 9.95 o.p. (*0-931188-50-4*) Avalon Publishing Group. (Seal Pr.).

Watson, Ian. Mockymen. 2003. 300p. 26.95 (*1-930846-21-5*) Golden Gryphon Pr.

Whitney, Phyllis A. Listen for the Whisperer. 23.95 (*0-8488-1222-0*) Amereon, Ltd.

—Listen for the Whisperer. 9999. pap. 5.99 o.p. (*0-449-45244-1*); 1995. 256p. pap. 19.00 (*0-345-46622-5*); 1982. mass mkt. 2.95 o.p. (*0-449-23156-9*) Ballantine Bks. (Fawcett).

—Listen for the Whisperer. 1972. 5.95 o.p. (*0-385-03354-0*) Doubleday Publishing.

—Listen for the Whisperer. l.t. ed. 2001. 400p. 29.95 (*0-7838-9546-1*, Macmillan Reference USA) Gale Group.

Wikstrom, Karl S. North of Skarv Island: A Trading Adventure Between Norwegians & Lapps. Carlson, Signe M., ed. 1985. (Illus.). 148p. 9.95 (*0-9615948-0-2*) Midgard Pr.

Woodman, Richard. Beneath the Aurora: A Nathaniel Drinkwater Novel. 2001. (Mariner's Library Fiction Classics: Vol. 12). 256p. pap. 14.95 (*1-57409-102-6*) Sheridan Hse., Inc.

**NOVA SCOTIA—FICTION**

Bruneau, Carol. Purple for Sky. 2000. 407p. (*1-896951-24-4*) Cormorant Bks.

—A Purple Thread for Sky: A Novel of Intertwined Lives. 2001. 416p. 26.00 (*0-7867-0860-3*, Carroll & Graf Pubs.) Avalon Publishing Group.

Coady, Lynn. Saints of Big Harbour. 2003. 432p. pap. (*0-385-65900-8*, Anchor Canada) Doubleday Canada, Ltd. CAN. *Dist:* Random Hse., Inc.

—Saints of Big Harbour. 2002. 336p. 24.00 (*0-618-11976-0*) Houghton Mifflin Co.

—Saints of Big Harbour. 2003. 336p. pap. 13.00 (*0-618-38045-0*, Mariner Bks.) Houghton Mifflin Co. Trade & Reference Div.

Conlin, Christy Ann. Heave. 2002. 336p. pap. (*0-385-65808-7*, Anchor Canada) Doubleday Canada, Ltd. CAN. *Dist:* Random Hse. of Canada, Ltd., Random Hse., Inc.

Eaton, Evelyn. Quietly My Captain Waits. Davies, Gwendolyn, ed. 2001. (Fiction Treasures Ser.). 392p. pap. (*0-88780-544-2*) Formac Publishing Co., Ltd.

Haliburton, Thomas Chandler. The Clockmaker. 1979. (American Humorists Ser.). reprint ed. lib. bdg. 46.75 o.p. (*0-8398-0754-6*) Irvington Pubs.

—The Clockmaker. (New Canadian Library). 1993. 224p. mass mkt. 6.95 (*0-7710-9888-X*); 1965. mass mkt. o.p. (*0-7710-9106-0*) McClelland & Stewart/Tundra Bks.

Hickman, W. Albert. The Sacrifice of the Shannon. Davies, Gwendolyn, ed. 2001 (Fiction Treasures Ser.). 352p. pap. (*0-88780-542-6*) Formac Publishing Co., Ltd.

MacDonald, Ann-Marie. Fall on Your Knees: A Novel. 512p. 2002. 27.50 (*0-7432-3719-6*, Simon & Schuster); 2002. pap. 14.00 (*0-7432-3718-8*, Touchstone); 1998. pap. 14.00 (*0-684-83868-0*, Touchstone); 1997. 23.00 (*0-684-83320-4*, Simon & Schuster) Simon & Schuster.

MacLennan, Hugh. Barometer Rising. 1996. (New Canadian Library: Vol. 8). 240p. mass mkt. 6.95 (*0-7710-9991-6*) McClelland & Stewart/Tundra Bks.

MacLeod, Alistair. Island: The Collected Stories. 2002. 448p. pap. 14.00 (*0-375-71304-2*, Vintage) Knopf Publishing Group.

—Island: The Collected Stories. 2001. v, 434p. 25.95 (*0-393-05035-1*) Norton, W. W. & Co., Inc.

—The Lost Salt Gift of Blood. 1996. 168p. mass mkt. 6.95 (*0-7710-9969-X*) McClelland & Stewart/Tundra Bks.

—The Lost Salt Gift of Blood. 1988. 227p. pap. 11.95 o.p. (*0-86538-063-5*) Ontario Review Pr.

—No Great Mischief. 2000. (Illus.). 283p. 23.95 o.p. (*0-393-04970-1*) Norton, W. W. & Co., Inc.

MacNeil, Robert. Burden of Desire. 1993. 576p. mass mkt. 5.99 o.s.i (*0-440-21509-9*) Dell Publishing.

—Burden of Desire. l.t. ed. 1996. pap. 23.95 o.p. (*1-56895-303-8*, Wheeler Publishing, Inc.) Gale Group.

Magruder, Owen. The Strange Case of Mr. Nobody. 2000. 212p. pap. 7.95 (*1-892059-01-0*) Edmonston Publishing, Inc.

McNeil, Jean. Hunting down Home. 1999. 240p. 16.00 (*1-57131-026-6*) Milkweed Editions.

Norman, Howard. The Museum Guard. 1998. 310p. 24.00 o.p. (*0-374-21649-5*); 1994. E-Book 13.00 (*0-374-70237-3*); 1994. E-Book 13.00 (*0-374-70236-5*); 1994. E-Book 13.00 (*0-374-70235-7*); 1994. E-Book 13.00 (*0-374-70234-9*) Farrar, Straus & Giroux.

—The Museum Guard. 1999. pap. (*0-312-24716-8*); 320p. pap. 14.00 (*0-312-20427-2*) Picador.

O'Callahan, Jay. The Herring Shed. 1983. (YA). (gr. 9 up). 10.00 incl. audio (*1-877954-01-2*) Artana Productions.

—The Herring Shed. 1990. audio 9.98 o.p. National Storytelling Network.

—The Herring Shed. 1983. (J). (gr. 6 up). audio 9.95 Yellow Moon Pr.

Smythe, Karen E. Stubborn Bones. 2001. (Illus.). 177p. pap. (*1-55192-364-5*, Polestar Book Pubs.) Raincoast Bk. Distribution.

Williams, Mrs. Neutral French: The Exiles of Nova Scotia. 1999. (Illus.). 416p. pap. 7.95 (*1-56554-473-0*) Pelican Publishing Co., Inc.

## O

**OAKALLA (WISC.: IMAGINARY PLACE)—FICTION**

Riggs, John R. Cold Hearts & Gentle People. 1994. 272p. 17.95 (*1-56980-021-9*) Barricade Bks., Inc.

—Dead Letter. 1992. 15.95 (*0-942637-40-2*) Barricade Bks., Inc.

—Dead Letter. 1994. 208p. mass mkt. 4.50 o.s.i (*0-515-11280-1*, Jove) Berkley Publishing Group.

—A Dragon Lives Forever. 1992. (Garth Ryland Mystery Ser.). 344p. 17.95 (*0-942637-78-X*) Barricade Bks., Inc.

—A Dragon Lives Forever. 1994. 224p. reprint ed. mass mkt. 4.50 o.p. (*0-425-14301-5*, Prime Crime) Berkley Publishing Group.

—Glory Hound. 1986. (Garth Ryland Mystery Ser.). 14.95 o.p. (*0-934878-78-1*, Dembner Bks.) Barricade Bks., Inc.

—Haunt of the Nightingale. (Garth Ryland Mystery Ser.). 224p. 15.95 o.p. (*0-934878-97-8*, Dembner Bks.) Barricade Bks., Inc.

—Haunt of the Nightingale. 1992. 192p. mass mkt. 3.99 o.s.i (*0-515-10953-3*, Jove) Berkley Publishing Group.

—He Who Waits: A Garth Ryland Mystery. 1997. (Garth Ryland Mystery Ser.). 288p. 17.95 (*1-56980-096-0*) Barricade Bks., Inc.

—Killing Frost: A Garth Ryland Mystery. 1995. 304p. 17.95 (*1-56980-053-7*) Barricade Bks., Inc.

—The Last Laugh. l.t. ed. 1992. 19.95 o.p. (*0-7927-1394-X*); pap. 17.95 o.p. (*0-7927-1393-1*) BBC Audiobooks America.

—The Last Laugh. 1984. (Garth Ryland Mystery Ser.). 191p. 13.95 o.p. (*0-934878-37-4*, Dembner Bks.) Barricade Bks., Inc.

—The Last Laugh. 1993. 192p. mass mkt. 3.99 o.s.i (*0-515-11134-1*, Jove) Berkley Publishing Group.

—The Last Laugh. 1988. mass mkt. 2.95 (*0-312-91131-9*, St. Martin's Paperbacks) St. Martin's Pr.

—Let Sleeping Dogs Lie. 1986. (Garth Ryland Mystery Ser.). 14.95 o.p. (*0-934878-67-6*, Dembner Bks.) Barricade Bks., Inc.

—Let Sleeping Dogs Lie. 1993. mass mkt. 4.50 o.s.i (*0-515-11211-9*, Jove) Berkley Publishing Group.

—Let Sleeping Dogs Lie. 1988. mass mkt. 3.50 (*0-312-91140-8*, St. Martin's Paperbacks) St. Martin's Pr.

—The Lost Scout: A Garth Ryland Mystery. 1998. 352p. 17.95 (*1-56980-121-5*) Barricade Bks., Inc.

—One Man's Poison. 1991. (Garth Ryland Mystery Ser.). 17.95 o.p. (*0-942637-31-3*, Dembner Bks.) Barricade Bks., Inc.

—One Man's Poison, No. 4. 1993. 208p. mass mkt. 3.99 o.s.i (*0-515-11078-7*, Jove) Berkley Publishing Group.

—Snow on the Roses: A Garth Ryland Mystery. 1996. 272p. 17.95 (*1-56980-072-3*) Barricade Bks., Inc.

—Wolf in Sheep's Clothing. 1993. 192p. (Orig.). mass mkt. 3.99 o.s.i (*0-515-11016-7*, Jove) Berkley Publishing Group.

—Wolf in Sheep's Clothing: A Garth Ryland Mystery. 1989. 16.95 o.p. (*0-942637-16-X*, Dembner Bks.) Barricade Bks., Inc.

**OAKLAND (CALIF.)—FICTION**

Apollo. Concrete Candy: Stories. 1996. 144p. pap. 15.00 (*0-385-47780-5*) Doubleday Publishing.

Byrne, Robert. Mannequin. 1989. mass mkt. 3.95 o.s.i (*1-55817-300-5*, Pinnacle Bks.) Kensington Publishing Corp.

—Mannequin. 1988. 288p. 18.95 o.s.i (*0-689-11836-8*, Scribner) Simon & Schuster.

Dry, Richard. Leaving: A Novel. 2003. 464p. pap. 14.95 (*0-312-30287-8*, Saint Martin's Griffin); 2002. 448p. 24.95 (*0-312-28331-8*) St. Martin's Pr.

Gores, Joe. Dead Skip. 1981. mass mkt. 2.25 o.s.i (*0-345-29206-5*); 1974. mass mkt. 1.25 o.p. (*0-345-24129-0*) Ballantine Bks.

—Dead Skip. 1992. 208p. reprint ed. mass mkt. 4.99 o.s.i (*0-446-40312-1*, Mysterious Pr. Paperback Bks.) Warner Bks., Inc.

Johnson, Guy. Echoes of a Distant Summer: A Novel. 2002. 688p. 24.95 (*0-375-50567-9*) Random Hse., Inc.

Lethem, Jonathan. Gun with Occasional Music. 2003. 288p. pap. 14.00 (*0-15-602897-2*, 53586160) Harcourt Trade Pubs.

Mittman, Stephanie. The Courtship. 1997. 400p. mass mkt. 5.99 o.s.i (*0-440-22181-1*) Dell Publishing.

Morris, Monique W. Too Beautiful for Words. 288p. 2002. pap. 11.95 (*0-06-093594-4*); 2001. 24.00 (*0-06-621105-0*) HarperTrade. (Amistad Pr.).

Smith, Danyel. More Like Wrestling: A Novel. 304p. 2004. pap. 12.95 (*0-609-80993-8*, Three Rivers Pr.); 2003. 23.95 (*1-4000-4644-0*, Crown) Crown Publishing Group.

Soto, Gary. Nickel & Dime. 2000. 189p. 29.95 (*0-8263-2185-2*); pap. 16.95 (*0-8263-2186-0*) Univ. of New Mexico Pr.

Tramble, Nichelle D. The Dying Ground: A Hip-Hop Noir Novel. E-Book 11.00 (*1-58945-588-6*) Adobe Systems, Inc.

—The Dying Ground: A Hip-Hop Noir Novel. 2001. 336p. pap. 13.95 (*0-375-75653-1*, Villard Bks.) Random House Adult Trade Publishing Group.

**OHIO—FICTION**

Abbott, Patricia. Goodbye Dear, I'll Be Back in a Year. 2003. 295p. pap. 13.95 (*1-4104-0108-1*, Five Star Trade); 2002. 320p. 26.95 (*0-7862-4077-6*, Five Star) Gale Group.

Alexander, Kathryn. The Forever Husband. 1999. 256p. per. (*0-373-87078-7*, Steeple Hill) Harlequin Enterprises, Ltd.

Altsheler, Joseph A. The Rifleman of the Ohio. 2000. 252p. pap. 9.95 (*0-594-06414-7*); E-Book 3.95 (*0-594-06415-5*) 1873 Pr.

—The Rifleman of the Ohio. 25.95 (*0-8488-1239-5*) Amereon, Ltd.

—The Rifleman of the Ohio. (Young Trailer Ser.). reprint ed. 1984. 319p. lib. bdg. 35.95 o.p. (*0-89966-483-0*); 1981. 432p. lib. bdg. 35.95 (*0-89968-226-X*, Lightyear Pr.) Buccaneer Bks., Inc.

Anderson, Sherwood. Certain Things Last: The Selected Stories of Sherwood Anderson. 1995. 384p. pap. 14.95 o.p. (*1-56858-022-3*) Four Walls Eight Windows.

—Certain Things Last: The Selected Stories of Sherwood Anderson. Modlin, Charles E., ed. & intro. by. 1992. 388p. 24.95 (*0-941423-85-9*) Four Walls Eight Windows.

—Death in the Woods & Other Stories. Date not set. lib. bdg. 23.95 (*0-8488-1952-7*) Amereon, Ltd.

—Death in the Woods & Other Stories. 1986. (Shoreline Bks.). 298p. pap. 7.95 (*0-87140-140-1*) Norton, W. W. & Co., Inc.

—The Egg & Other Stories. 2000. (Thrift Editions Ser.). vii, 133p. pap. 1.50 (*0-486-41411-6*) Dover Pubns., Inc.

—Winesburg, Ohio. 1988. 22.95 (*0-8488-0417-1*) Amereon, Ltd.

—Winesburg, Ohio. 1995. 256p. mass mkt. 5.95 (*0-553-21439-X*) Bantam Bks.

—Winesburg, Ohio. E-Book 5.00 (*0-7607-1296-4*) Barnes & Noble, Inc.

—Winesburg, Ohio. (Collected Works of Sherwood Anderson). 303p. reprint ed. 2001. (Illus.). pap. text 28.00 (*0-7426-5509-1*); 1998. lib. bdg. 98.00 (*1-58201-509-0*) Classic Bks.

—Winesburg, Ohio. E-Book 2.49 (*0-7574-0493-6*) Electric Umbrella Publishing.

—Winesburg, Ohio. unabr. ed. 2002. audio 34.95 (*0-06-001025-8*, HarperAudio) HarperTrade.

—Winesburg, Ohio. mass mkt. 0.25 o.p. (*0-451-01304-2*, Signet Bks.); 1993. 272p. mass mkt. 5.95 (*0-451-52569-8*, Signet Classics); 1976. mass mkt. 0.25 o.p. (*0-451-00585-6*, Signet Bks.) NAL.

Settings

—Winesburg, Ohio. l.t. ed. (Large Print Ser.). reprint ed. 1993. 330p. lib. bdg. 26.00 (*0-939495-45-7*); 1998. 210p. lib. bdg. 25.00 (*1-58287-081-0*) North Bks.

—Winesburg, Ohio. Love, Glen A., ed. (Oxford World's Classics Ser.). 1999. 240p. pap. 8.95 (*0-19-283977-2*); 1997. 238p. pap. 7.95 o.p. (*0-19-282405-8*) Oxford Univ. Pr., Inc.

—Winesburg, Ohio. 1967. pap. 2.45 o.p. (*0-670-01801-5*); 1958. pap. 1.75 o.p. (*0-670-00039-6*) Penguin Group (USA) Inc.

—Winesburg, Ohio. 1995. (Modern Library Ser.). 252p. 14.95 o.s.i (*0-679-60146-5*, Modern Library) Random House Adult Trade Publishing Group.

—Winesburg, Ohio. 1993. reprint ed. lib. bdg. 89.00 (*0-7812-5336-5*) Reprint Services Corp.

—Winesburg, Ohio. l.t. ed. 1999. (Perennial Bestsellers Ser.). 308p. pap. 26.95 (*0-7838-8625-X*) Thorndike Pr.

—Winesburg, Ohio. (Twentieth Century Classics Ser.). 1992. 256p. pap. 8.95 (*0-14-018655-7*, Penguin Classics); 1988. 256p. pap. 3.95 (*0-14-043304-X*, Penguin Bks.); 1987. 256p. pap. 4.95 o.p. (*0-14-039059-6*, Penguin Classics); 1976. pap. 3.95 o.p. (*0-14-000609-5*, Penguin Bks.); 2nd ed. 1960. 15.00 o.p. (*0-670-77236-4*) Viking Penguin.

—Winesburg, Ohio: An Authoritative Text, Backgrounds & Contexts, Criticism. Modlin, Charles E. & Norton, W. W., eds. 1995. (Critical Editions Ser.). 224p. (C). pap. text 7.00 (*0-393-96795-6*) Norton, W. W. & Co., Inc.

Armington, Raymond Q. & Ellis, William D. Boomerang. 348p. (Orig.). 1989. 14.95 o.p. (*0-9621126-0-7*); 1988. pap. 9.95 o.p. (*0-9621126-1-5*) Ward & Ward.

Bachman, Richard, pseud. The Regulators. 1996. 480p. 24.95 o.s.i (*0-525-94190-8*); 325.00 o.s.i (*0-525-94224-6*) Dutton/Plume.

—The Regulators. 1997. (Illus.). 512p. mass mkt. 7.99 (*0-451-19101-3*, Signet Bks.) NAL.

—The Regulators, unabr. ed. 1997. audio 80.00 (*0-7887-1163-6*, 95006E7) Recorded Bks., LLC.

—The Regulators. l.t. ed. 1997. (Thorndike/G. K. Hall Paperback Bestsellers Ser.). 598p. pap. 26.95 (*0-7862-0845-7*) Thorndike Pr.

—The Regulators. 1996. (Illus.). 466p. text 24.95 (*0-670-87281-4*); 6p. pap. 29.95 o.p. incl. audio (*0-14-086322-2*, Penguin AudioBooks) Viking Penguin.

Bialosky, Jill. House under Snow. 2003. 264p. pap. 14.00 (*0-15-602746-1*, Harvest Bks.); 2002. 256p. 24.00 (*0-15-100685-7*) Harcourt Trade Pubs.

Borntrager, Mary Christner. Reuben. l.t. ed. 2001. (Christian Fiction Ser.). 193p. 23.95 (*0-7862-3596-9*) Thorndike Pr.

Borton, D. B. Five Alarm Fire. 1996. 240p. mass mkt. 5.99 o.s.i (*0-425-15338-X*, Prime Crime) Berkley Publishing Group.

—Four Elements of Murder. 1995. 256p. (Orig.). mass mkt. 5.99 o.s.i (*0-425-14722-3*, Prime Crime) Berkley Publishing Group.

—One for the Money. 1993. 208p. 4.50 o.s.i (*1-55773-869-6*) Ace Bks.

—One for the Money. 1993. 208p. mass mkt. 4.99 o.s.i (*0-425-15328-2*) Berkley Publishing Group.

—Six Feet Under. 1997. 240p. mass mkt. 5.99 o.s.i (*0-425-15700-8*, Prime Crime) Berkley Publishing Group.

—Three Is a Crowd. 1994. 240p. (Orig.). mass mkt. 4.99 o.s.i (*0-425-14327-9*, Prime Crime) Berkley Publishing Group.

—Two Points for Murder. 1993. mass mkt. 4.99 o.s.i (*0-425-13947-6*) Berkley Publishing Group.

Borton, Della. Fade to Black. 1999. (Movie Lover's Mysteries Ser.). 288p. mass mkt. 5.99 o.s.i (*0-449-00407-4*, Fawcett) Ballantine Bks.

Brasfield, Lynette. Nature Lessons: A Novel. 2003. 288p. 23.95 (*0-312-31034-X*) St. Martin's Pr.

Brock, Darryl. If I Never Get Back. 1991. 480p. mass mkt. 5.99 o.s.i (*0-345-37055-4*, Ballantine Bks.) Ballantine Bks.

—If I Never Get Back. 2002. 400p. pap. 14.00 (*0-452-28372-8*, Plume) Dutton/Plume.

—If I Never Get Back. 1992. 3.99 o.p. (*0-517-08634-4*) Random Hse. Value Publishing.

—If I Never Get Back. 2001. reprint ed. pap. 14.95 o.p. (*1-892129-96-5*) Total Sports Publishing.

Brodine, Virginia W. Seed of the Fire. 1996. 310p. 18.95 (*0-7178-0721-5*); pap. 9.95 (*0-7178-0722-3*) International Publishers Co., Inc.

Bromfield, Louis. The Green Bay Tree. 2002. 390p. pap. 14.00 (*1-888683-64-3*) Wooster Bk. Co., The.

Brookhouse, Christopher. Dear Otto. 1995. 160p. 24.00 (*1-877946-63-X*) Permanent Pr., The.

Busch, Jim. Trials in Youngstown, Ohio. 2000. 121p. E-Book 8.00 (*0-7388-8574-6*) Xlibris Corp.

Cary, Alice. Clovernook Sketches & Other Stories. Fetterly, Judith, ed. 1987. (American Women Writers Ser.). 314p. (C). text 35.00 o.p. (*0-8135-1250-6*); pap. text 15.00 o.p. (*0-8135-1251-4*) Rutgers Univ. Pr.

Chase, Joan. During the Reign of the Queen of Persia. 1996. 275p. pap. 11.00 o.s.i (*0-345-41046-7*); 1984. 288p. mass mkt. 5.99 o.s.i (*0-345-31525-1*, Ballantine Bks.) Ballantine Bks.

—During the Reign of the Queen of Persia. l.t. ed. 1983. 16.95 o.p. (*0-8161-3611-4*, Macmillan Reference USA) Gale Group.

—During the Reign of the Queen of Persia. 1983. 144p. 13.95 o.p. (*0-06-015136-6*) HarperTrade.

Chessman, Harriet Scott. Ohio Angels. 1999. 144p. 24.00 (*1-57962-020-5*) Permanent Pr., The.

—Ohio Angels: A Novel. 2002. 144p. 24.00 (*1-58322-519-6*) Seven Stories Pr.

Chessman, Harriet Scott, ed. Ohio Angels. 1999. 144p. pap. 16.00 (*1-57962-071-X*) Permanent Pr., The.

Christopher, Debbonnaire. The Day the Ohio Canal Turned Eerie. 1993. (Illus.). (J). 3.00 (*1-880443-10-4*) Roscoe Village Foundation, Inc.

Cline, Rachel. What to Keep: A Novel. 2004. 304p. 23.95 (*1-4000-6183-0*) Random Hse., Inc.

Corwin, C. R. The Cross Kisses Back: A Morgue Mama Mystery. 2003. 327p. 24.95 o.s.i (*1-59058-074-5*) Poisoned Pen Pr.

Crusie, Jennifer. Crazy for You. l.t. ed. 2000. (Wheeler Large Print Book Ser.). 408p. 26.95 (*1-56895-853-6*, Wheeler Publishing, Inc.) Gale Group.

—Crazy for You. 2004. mass mkt. 3.99 (*0-312-93281-2*); 2000. 336p. mass mkt. 7.50 (*0-312-97112-5*, St. Martin's Paperbacks); 1999. 336p. 24.95 o.p. (*0-312-19849-3*) St. Martin's Pr.

—Fast Women. l.t. ed. 2001. (Romance Ser.). 536p. 29.95 (*1-58724-072-6*, Wheeler Publishing, Inc.) Gale Group.

—Fast Women. 2004. mass mkt. 3.99 (*0-312-93279-0*); 2002. mass mkt. 7.50 (*0-312-98015-9*, St. Martin's Paperbacks); 2001. 358p. 24.95 (*0-312-25261-7*) St. Martin's Pr.

—Tell Me Lies. l.t. ed. 1998. 26.95 o.p. (*1-56895-568-5*, Wheeler Publishing, Inc.) Gale Group.

—Tell Me Lies. 2004. mass mkt. 3.99 (*0-312-93282-0*); 1999. (Tell Me Lies Ser.: Vol. 1). 368p. mass mkt. 7.50 (*0-312-96680-6*, St. Martin's Paperbacks); 1998. 322p. 24.95 o.p. (*0-312-17940-5*) St. Martin's Pr.

—Welcome to Temptation. l.t. ed. 2000. (Wheeler Large Print Book Ser.). 479p. 28.95 (*1-56895-906-0*, Wheeler Publishing, Inc.) Gale Group.

—Welcome to Temptation. 2004. mass mkt. 3.99 (*0-312-93280-4*); 2000. 352p. 24.95 (*0-312-25294-3*); 2001. 416p. reprint ed. mass mkt. 7.50 (*0-312-97425-6*, St. Martin's Paperbacks) St. Martin's Pr.

Daheim, Mary R. Silver Scream/Death of a Domestic Diva. 2003. mass mkt. 121.41 (*0-06-058004-6*) HarperCollins Pubs.

Dailey, Janet. The Widow & the Wastrel: Ohio. 1992. (Americana Ser.: No. 885). mass mkt. (*0-373-89885-1*); 1988. pap. (*0-373-21935-0*) Harlequin Enterprises, Ltd. (Harlequin Bks.).

—The Widow & the Wastrel: Ohio. l.t. ed. 2001. 231p. 29.95 (*0-7862-2746-X*); (*0-7540-4675-3*); (*0-7540-4676-1*) Thorndike Pr.

—The Widow & the Wastrel: Ohio. 124p. 2002. pap. 6.99 (*0-7592-3840-5*); 2002. E-Book 6.99 (*0-7592-0191-9*); 2002. E-Book 6.99 (*1-58586-473-0*); 2001. E-Book 6.99 (*0-7592-0934-0*) ereads.com.

Danielewski, Mark Z. The Whalestoe Letters. 2000. 86p. pap. 8.95 (*0-375-71441-3*, Pantheon) Knopf Publishing Group.

Dann, Patty. Sweet & Crazy. Date not set. pap. (*0-312-31667-4*, St. Martin's Paperbacks); mass mkt. (*0-312-99049-9*, St. Martin's Paperbacks); 2003. 208p. 22.95 (*0-312-31666-6*) St. Martin's Pr.

Date, S. V. Speed Week. 2001. 288p. reprint ed. mass mkt. 5.99 o.s.i (*0-425-18222-3*, Prime Crime) Berkley Publishing Group.

DeBrosse, Jim. Hidden City: A Rick Decker Mystery. 1991. 304p. 18.95 o.p. (*0-312-06368-7*, Saint Martin's Minotaur) St. Martin's Pr.

—The Serpentine Wall. 1988. 336p. 17.95 o.p. (*0-312-02278-6*, Saint Martin's Minotaur) St. Martin's Pr.

DeLancey, Kiki. Coal Miner's Holiday. 2002. (Illus.). 240p. pap. 13.95 (*1-889330-70-1*) Sarabande Bks., Inc.

Deleva, John. Hours Like Diamonds. 2000. 169p. (Orig.). pap. 11.77 (*0-9701668-0-X*) Johnsbook.com.

Dell, George. Dance unto the Lord. 2001. 400p. 54.95 (*0-8142-0886-X*); (Illus.). pap. 21.95 (*0-8142-5084-X*) Ohio State Univ. Pr.

Dell, George F. The Earth Abideth. 1986. 314p. 30.00 o.p. (*0-8142-0411-2*) Ohio State Univ. Pr.

DeMille, Nelson. Spencerville. 1994. 464p. 23.95 o.p. (*0-446-51505-1*); 1995. 656p. reprint ed. mass mkt. 7.99 (*0-446-60245-0*) Warner Bks., Inc.

Dew, Robb Forman. Dale Loves Sophie to Death. 1981. 217p. 11.95 o.p. (*0-374-13450-2*) Farrar, Straus & Giroux.

—Dale Loves Sophie to Death. 1993. 224p. pap. 12.00 o.s.i (*0-06-097539-3*, Perennial) HarperTrade.

—Dale Loves Sophie to Death. 2001. 256p. reprint ed. pap. 13.95 (*0-316-89066-9*, Back Bay) Little Brown & Co.

—Dale Loves Sophie to Death. 1982. (Contemporary American Fiction Ser.). pap. 6.95 o.p. (*0-14-006183-5*, Penguin Bks.) Viking Penguin.

—The Evidence Against Her: A Novel. l.t. ed. 2002. (Basic Ser.). 451p. 29.95 (*0-7862-3742-2*) Gale Group.

—The Evidence Against Her: A Novel. 2001. 336p. 24.95 (*0-316-89019-7*); E-Book 14.95 (*0-7595-4576-6*); E-Book 14.95 (*0-7595-6574-0*) Little Brown & Co.

Dominic, R. B. The Attending Physician. 1980. (Harper Novel of Suspense Ser.). o.p. (*0-06-011073-2*) HarperCollins Pubs.

—Unexpected Developments. 1983. 225p. 11.95 o.p. (*0-312-83278-8*) St. Martin's Pr.

Durstin, Larry. Still Looking: A Novel Concerning Single Men. 1996. (Illus.). 249p. (Orig.). pap. 11.95 (*1-877978-14-0*, FLF Pr.) Florida Literary Foundation.

Eitzen, Ruth. The White Feather. 1987. (Illus.). 64p. (J). (gr. 3-4). 14.95 o.p. (*0-8361-3439-7*) Herald Pr.

Ellis, William D. Jonathan Blair: Bounty Lands Lawyer. 1999. (Bounty Land Trilogy Ser.). 462p. pap. 14.95 (*1-888683-03-1*) Wooster Bk. Co., The.

Gass, William H. Omensetter's Luck. 1972. pap. 6.95 o.p. (*0-452-25785-9*, Z5349, Plume); 1972. pap. 1.95 o.p. (*0-452-25068-4*, Plume); 1972. pap. 2.95 o.p. (*0-452-25105-2*, Plume); 1972. pap. 3.95 o.p. (*0-452-25197-4*, Plume); 1972. pap. 5.95 o.p. (*0-452-25349-7*, Plume); 1966. 5.95 o.p. (*0-453-00059-2*, Dutton) Dutton/Plume.

—Omensetter's Luck. mass mkt. 0.95 o.p. (*0-451-03121-0*, Signet Bks.) NAL.

—Omensetter's Luck. 1997. (Twentieth Century Classics Ser.). 320p. 14.00 (*0-14-118010-2*, Penguin Classics) Viking Penguin.

Gaus, P. L. Blood of the Prodigal: An Ohio Amish Mystery. 1999. (Ohio Amish Mysteries Ser.). 230p. pap. 12.95 (*0-8214-1277-9*); 24.95 (*0-8214-1276-0*) Ohio Univ. Pr.

—Broken English: An Ohio Amish Mystery. 2000. (Ohio Amish Mysteries Ser.). 200p. 24.95 (*0-8214-1325-2*); pap. 12.95 (*0-8214-1326-0*) Ohio Univ. Pr. (Ohio Univ. Ctr. for International Studies).

—Cast a Blue Shadow: An Ohio Amish Mystery. 2003. (Ohio Amish Mysteries Ser.). 24.95 (*0-8214-1529-8*); pap. 12.95 (*0-8214-1530-1*) Ohio Univ. Pr.

—Clouds Without Rain: An Ohio Amish Mystery. 2001. (Ohio Amish Mysteries Ser.). vii, 196p. 24.95 (*0-8214-1379-1*); pap. 12.95 (*0-8214-1380-5*) Ohio Univ. Pr.

Geha, Joseph. Through & Through: Toledo Stories. 1990. (Graywolf Short Fiction Ser.). 180p. (Orig.). (C). pap. 7.95 (*1-55597-135-0*) Graywolf Pr.

Glen, Alison. Showcase: A Charlotte Sams Mystery. 1992. 206p. 19.00 o.s.i (*0-671-74573-5*, Simon & Schuster) Simon & Schuster.

—Trunk Show. 1995. 238p. 20.00 (*0-671-79115-X*, Simon & Schuster) Simon & Schuster.

Goldsmith, Olivia. Switcheroo. unabr. ed. 1998. audio 56.00 (*0-7366-4190-4*, 896064) Books on Tape, Inc.

—Switcheroo. l.t. ed. 1998. (Large Print Book Ser.). 26.95 (*1-56895-680-0*, Wheeler Publishing, Inc.) Gale Group.

—Switcheroo. 1998. 272p. 23.00 (*0-06-017568-0*) HarperCollins Pubs.

—Switcheroo, Set. abr. ed. 1998. audio 22.00 o.s.i (*0-694-51868-9*, 695730, HarperAudio) HarperTrade.

—Switcheroo. unabr. ed. 1998. audio 60.00 (*0-7887-1977-7*, 95364E7) Recorded Bks., LLC.

—Switcheroo: A Novel. 1999. 400p. mass mkt. 6.99 (*0-06-109765-9*, HarperTorch) Morrow/Avon.

Goonan, Kathleen A. Queen City Jazz. 1996. 465p. pap. text 5.99 o.s.i (*0-8125-3626-6*); 1994. 416p. 23.95 o.p. (*0-312-85678-4*) Doherty, Tom Assocs., LLC. (Tor Bks.).

Grey, Zane. The Spirit of the Border. E-Book 2.49 (*1-58744-192-6*) Electric Umbrella Publishing.

Hansen, Brooks. The Chess Garden: Or, the Twilight Letters of Gustav Uyterhoeven. 1996. (Illus.). 480p. reprint ed. 16.00 (*1-57322-563-0*, Riverhead Trade (Paperbacks)) Berkley Publishing Group.

—The Chess Garden: Or, the Twilight Letters of Gustav Uyterhoeven. 1995. (Illus.). 496p. 23.00 o.p. (*0-374-16015-5*) Farrar, Straus & Giroux.

—Chess Garden Readers. 1995. pap. (*0-374-99817-5*) Farrar, Straus & Giroux.

Harayda, Janice. The Accidental Bride. 304p. 2000. pap. 13.95 (*0-312-26281-7*, Saint Martin's Griffin); 3rd ed. 1999. 22.95 o.p. (*0-312-20357-8*) St. Martin's Pr.

Harper, Karen. The Dark Road Home. l.t. ed. 1998. 26.95 (*1-57490-135-4*, Beeler Large Print Bks.) Beeler, Thomas T. Publisher.

—The Dark Road Home. 1996. 448p. mass mkt. 5.99 o.s.i (*0-451-18725-3*) NAL.

Harris, Charlaine. A Fool & His Honey. 2001. (WWL Mystery Ser.: No. 384). 253p. mass mkt. (*0-373-26384-8*, 1-26384-7, Worldwide Library) Harlequin Enterprises, Ltd.

—A Fool & His Honey. 1999. 224p. 22.95 (*0-312-20306-3*, Saint Martin's Minotaur) St. Martin's Pr.

—A Fool & His Honey. l.t. ed. 2000. (Mystery Ser.). 304p. 28.95 (*0-7862-2467-3*) Thorndike Pr.

Hightower, Lynn S. Eyeshot. 1996. 368p. 23.00 o.p. (*0-06-017649-0*) HarperCollins Pubs.

—Eyeshot. 1997. 368p. mass mkt. 6.50 o.p. (*0-06-109609-1*, HarperTorch) Morrow/Avon.

—Flashpoint. 1995. 352p. 22.00 o.p. (*0-06-017648-2*) HarperTrade.

—Flashpoint. 1996. 448p. mass mkt. 6.50 o.s.i (*0-06-109456-0*, HarperTorch) Morrow/Avon.

—No Good Deed. unabr. ed. 1998. audio 44.95 (*0-7861-1438-X*, 2324) Blackstone Audio Bks., Inc.

—No Good Deed. 1998. (Sonora Blair Mysteries Ser.). 400p. mass mkt. 6.50 (*0-440-22531-0*); 336p. 22.95 o.s.i (*0-385-32359-X*, Delacorte Pr.) Dell Publishing.

James, Lily. High Drama in Fabulous Toledo. 2001. 223p. pap. 12.95 (*1-57366-094-9*) Fiction Collective Two, Inc.

John, Cathie, et al. Add One Dead Critic: Journals of Kate Cavanaugh. 1997. 249p. pap. 12.95 (*0-9634183-4-3*, Journey Bk. Pr.) C C Publishing.

—Beat a Rotten Egg to the Punch: Journals of Kate Cavanaugh. 1998. (Journals of Kate Cavanaugh Ser.). 287p. pap. 12.95 (*0-9634183-5-1*) C C Publishing.

—Carve a Witness to Shreds: A Kate Cavanaugh Mystery. 1999. (Journals of Kate Cavanaugh Ser.). 260p. (Orig.). pap. 12.95 (*0-9634183-6-X*, Journey Bk. Pr.) C C Publishing.

Johnson, Shawne. Eden, Ohio. 2004. 288p. 23.95 (*0-525-94810-4*, Dutton) Dutton/Plume.

Jones, Annie. Irish Eyes. 1997. (Palisades Pure Romance Ser.). 238p. pap. 9.99 o.s.i (*1-57673-108-1*, Palisades) Multnomah Pubs., Inc.

Kinsey, Kathryne Ann. Edelweiss: A Historical Novel. 2001. (Illus.). 154p. per. 15.95 (*1-880849-41-0*) Chapel Hill Pr.

Kitchen, Judith. The House on Eccles Road. 2002. 200p. 22.00 (*1-55597-368-X*) Graywolf Pr.

—The House on Eccles Road. 2003. 240p. pap. 14.00 (*0-14-200330-1*) Penguin Group (USA) Inc.

Kittle, Katrina. Traveling Light. l.t. ed. 2000. (G. K. Hall Core Ser.). 407p. 27.95 (*0-7838-9173-3*) Thorndike Pr.

—Traveling Light. 2000. 320p. 18.95 (*0-446-52480-8*); 2001. 336p. reprint ed. pap. 13.95 (*0-446-67694-2*) Warner Bks., Inc.

—Two Truths & a Lie. l.t. ed. 2001. 559p. 27.95 (*0-7838-9578-X*, Macmillan Reference USA) Gale Group.

—Two Truths & a Lie. 2001. 368p. 22.95 o.p. (*0-446-52487-5*) Warner Bks., Inc.

Klauprecht, Emil. Cincinnati, or The Mysteries of the West: Emil Klauprecht's German-American Novel. Rowan, Steven & Tolzmann, Don H., trs. from GER. 1996. (New German-American Studies: Vol. 10). XXV, 657p. (C). text 79.95 (*0-8204-2681-4*) Lang, Peter Publishing, Inc.

Lamb, John L. The End of Summer. 1996. 168p. pap. 10.00 (*0-671-53616-8*); 1900. mass mkt. (*0-671-53617-6*) Simon & Schuster. (Pocket).

—The End of Summer. abr. ed. 1996. audio 17.00 (*0-671-88660-6*, 393083, Simon & Schuster Audioworks) Simon & Schuster Audio.

Latham, Dennis. Michael in Hell. l.t. ed. 1999. E-Book 14.99 incl. cd-rom (*1-929077-61-0*, Books OnScreen) PageFree Publishing, Inc.

Lauber, Lynn. Twenty-One Sugar Street. 1993. 196p. 19.95 o.p. (*0-393-03449-6*) Norton, W. W. & Co., Inc.

—White Girls. 1991. (Vintage Contemporaries Ser.). 192p. pap. 9.00 o.s.i (*0-679-73411-2*, Vintage) Knopf Publishing Group.

—White Girls. 1990. 17.95 o.p. (*0-393-02717-1*) Norton, W. W. & Co., Inc.

—White Girls. 1993. 2.99 o.p. (*0-517-10381-8*) Random Hse. Value Publishing.

—White Girls. 2002. 175p. pap. 20.99 (*1-4010-4208-2*); E-Book 8.00 (*1-4010-4209-0*) Xlibris Corp.

—21 Sugar Street. 1994. 240p. pap. 10.00 o.p. (*0-393-31235-6*) Norton, W. W. & Co., Inc.

Lax, Scott. The Year That Trembled: A Novel. 1998. 192p. 21.95 (*0-8397-8660-3*) Eriksson, Paul S. Pub.

Logsdon, Gene. The Man Who Created Paradise: A Fable. 2001. (Illus.). 72p. 20.00 (*0-8214-1407-0*, Ohio Univ. Ctr. for International Studies) Ohio Univ. Pr.

Louie, Andrea. Moon Cakes. 1995. 341.10 (*0-345-39622-7*); o.s.i (*0-345-39674-X*); 288p. 21.00 o.s.i (*0-345-38554-3*) Ballantine Bks.

Marsh, Rebecca. Always in Her Heart. l.t. ed. 1993. 18.95 o.p. (*0-7927-1619-1*); pap. 16.95 o.p. (*0-7927-1618-3*) BBC Audiobooks America.

Matthews, Jack. Tales of the Ohio Land. 1978. (Illus.). 186p. 11.95 (*0-87758-011-1*) Ohio Historical Society.

McConnell, David. The Firebrat. 2003. 246p. 22.00 (*0-929435-71-0*) AttaGirl Pr.

McInerny, Ralph. Still Life: A Novel. 2000. (First Edition Mystery Ser.). 255p. 21.95 (*0-7862-2895-4*, Five Star) Gale Group.
—Sub Rosa: An Egidio Manfredi Mystery. 2001. (Five Star First Edition Mystery Ser.). 200p. 24.95 (*0-7862-3559-4*, Five Star) Gale Group.
McKenney, Ruth. Industrial Valley. 1939. (YA). reprint ed. pap. text 28.00 (*1-4047-5389-3*) Classic Textbooks.
—Industrial Valley. 1992. (Literature of American Labor Ser.). 408p. reprint ed. pap. 19.95 (*0-87546-183-2*, ILR Pr.) Cornell Univ. Pr.
—Industrial Valley. 1986. reprint ed. lib. bdg. 18.75 o.p. (*0-8371-0585-4*, MCIV) Greenwood Publishing Group, Inc.
—Industrial Valley. 1993. reprint ed. lib. bdg. 89.00 (*0-7812-5389-6*) Reprint Services Corp.
McMillen, William. Sticks. 2000. (Illus.). 351p. (ps up). pap. 22.95 (*1-58536-010-4*) Clock Tower Pr. LLC.
Mockler, Karen. After Moses. 2003. 212p. 23.00 (*1-931561-37-0*) MacAdam/Cage Publishing, Inc.
Morrison, Toni. Beloved. 2002. (SPA., Illus.). 445p. pap. 12.50 (*84-406-5695-5*, EB9055) B Ediciones S.A. ESP. *Dist:* Lectorum Pubns., Inc.
—Beloved. unabr. ed. 2000. audio 39.95 Blackstone Audio Bks., Inc.
—Beloved. Bloom, Harold, ed. 1999. (Modern Critical Interpretations Ser.). 223p. 34.95 (*0-7910-5132-3*) Chelsea Hse. Pubs.
—Beloved. 1996. (*0-452-26897-4*, Plume); 1988. pap. 9.95 o.p. (*0-452-25230-X*, Plume); 1988. (Illus.). 288p. pap. 12.95 (*0-452-26446-4*); 1998. 512p. reprint ed. pap. 12.95 (*0-452-28062-1*) Dutton/Plume.
—Beloved. l.t. ed. 1998. pap. 16.95 o.p. (*0-7838-0262-5*); 1991. lib. bdg. 10.95 o.p. (*0-89621-207-6*) Gale Group. (Macmillan Reference USA).
—Beloved. 2004. 288p. pap. 13.00 (*1-4000-3341-1*, Vintage) Knopf Publishing Group.
—Beloved. 1987. 275p. 27.50 (*0-394-53597-9*); 1998. 16.95 o.s.i (*0-375-40562-3*); 1998. 322p. 16.95 (*0-375-40273-X*) Knopf, Alfred A. Inc.
—Beloved. 1997. (C). pap. text (*0-8013-3148-X*) Longman Publishing Group.
—Beloved. 1991. 352p. mass mkt. 5.95 o.p. (*0-451-16139-4*); 1991. mass mkt. 5.99 (*0-451-15659-5*); 1988. pap. 8.95 o.p. (*0-452-26136-8*) NAL.
—Beloved. 2000. (Penguin Great Books of the 20th Century Ser.). (Illus.). 272p. pap. 14.95 (*0-14-028340-4*) Penguin Group (USA) Inc.
—Beloved. abr. ed. 1998. audio 18.00 o.s.i (*0-375-40432-5*, 395999); audio 39.95 (*0-375-40487-2*, 104512) Random Hse. Audio Publishing Group. (RH Audio).
—Beloved. l.t. ed. 1998. 379p. pap. 19.95 (*0-375-70414-0*) Random Hse. Large Print.
—Beloved. 1989. 4.99 o.p. (*0-517-01744-X*); 4.99 o.p. (*0-517-01209-X*) Random Hse. Value Publishing.
—Beloved. 1987. 19.00 (*0-606-04046-3*) Turtleback Bks.
—Beloved. abr. ed. 1999. audio 16.85 (*1-85686-751-X*) Ulverscroft Audio (U.S.A.).
—The Bluest Eye. Bloom, Harold, ed. 1999. (Bloom's Notes Ser.). viii, 270p. 34.95 (*0-7910-5191-9*) Chelsea Hse. Pubs.
—The Bluest Eye. 224p. 2000. pap. 12.95 (*0-452-28219-5*, Plume); 1994. pap. 12.95 (*0-452-27305-6*) Dutton/Plume.
—The Bluest Eye. 1993. 224p. 24.00 o.s.i (*0-679-43373-2*) Knopf, Alfred A. Inc.
—The Bluest Eye. 1994. mass mkt. 5.99 o.s.i (*0-451-18367-3*) NAL.
—The Bluest Eye. abr. ed. 2000. audio 18.00 (*0-375-41652-8*); 2000. audio compact disk 22.95 (*0-375-41653-6*); Set. 1994. audio 17.00 o.s.i (*0-679-43474-7*, 390426) Random Hse. Audio Publishing Group, (RH Audio).
—The Bluest Eye. 1993. (Oprah's Book Club Ser.). 224p. 15.00 (*0-375-41155-0*) Random Hse., Inc.
—The Bluest Eye. 2001. audio compact disk 58.00 (*0-7887-5158-1*, C1321E7); 1970. audio 53.00 (*0-7887-4354-6*, 96306K8) Recorded Bks., LLC. (Griot Audio).
—The Bluest Eye. 1991. mass mkt. 5.50 (*0-671-74292-2*, Pocket); 1984. 160p. pap. 3.95 (*0-671-53146-8*, Washington Square Pr.) Simon & Schuster.
—The Bluest Eye. l.t. ed. 1999. (Core Ser.). 253p. 29.95 (*0-7838-8815-5*) Thorndike Pr.
—The Bluest Eye. 1994. 215p. 19.00 (*0-606-06940-2*) Turtleback Bks.
—Sula. Bloom, Harold, ed. 1999. (Modern Critical Interpretations Ser.). 176p. 34.95 (*0-7910-5194-3*) Chelsea Hse. Pubs.
—Sula. 1987. pap. 7.95 o.p. (*0-452-25227-X*, Plume); 1987. 176p. pap. 6.95 o.p. (*0-452-26010-8*, Z5476, Plume); 1987. 192p. pap. 13.00 (*0-452-26349-2*); 1982. pap. 5.95 o.p. (*0-452-25333-0*, Plume); 1982. pap. 5.95 o.p. (*0-452-25476-0*, Plume) Dutton/Plume.
—Sula. 2004. 192p. pap. 13.00 (*1-4000-3343-8*, Vintage) Knopf Publishing Group.
—Sula. 192p. 2002. 15.00 (*0-375-41535-1*); 1973. 26.00 (*0-394-48044-9*) Knopf, Alfred A. Inc.
—Sula. 1993. mass mkt. 5.99 o.s.i (*0-451-18240-5*, Signet Bks.) NAL.
—Sula. l.t. ed. 2002. (Basic Ser.). 214p. 30.95 (*0-7862-4653-7*) Thorndike Pr.
Mortman, Doris. Rightfully Mine. 1990. 736p. mass mkt. 6.99 o.s.i (*0-553-28416-9*); 700p. mass mkt. 5.50 o.s.i (*0-553-17341-3*) Bantam Bks.
—Rightfully Mine, Pt. 1. unabr. ed. 1996. audio 88.00 (*0-7366-3397-9*, 4045A) Books on Tape, Inc.
Nissenson, Hugh. The Tree of Life. 2000. (Illus.). 189p. reprint ed. pap. 14.95 (*0-9664913-2-7*) Dry, Paul Bks., Inc.
—The Tree of Life. 1985. (Illus.). 224p. 15.95 o.p. (*0-06-015143-9*) HarperTrade.
Parker, Sandra. Home Material: Ohio's Nineteenth-Century Regional Women's Fiction. 1998. 240p. 49.95 (*0-87972-765-9*); pap. 24.95 (*0-87972-766-7*) Univ. of Wisconsin Pr. (Popular Pr.).
Patterson, Richard North. Silent Witness. 1997. 512p. mass mkt. 7.99 (*0-345-40476-9*) Ballantine Bks.
—Silent Witness. unabr. ed. 1997. audio 104.00 (*0-913369-44-6*, 4231) Books on Tape, Inc.
—Silent Witness. l.t. ed. 1996. 494p. pap. 25.95 (*0-679-77416-5*) Random Hse. Large Print.
Porter, Lorle. Sara's Table: Keeping House in Ohio: 1800-1950. Leland, Toni M., ed. 2001. (Illus.). 176p. pap. 16.95 (*1-887932-80-1*, New Concord Pr.) Equine Graphics Publishing.
Powell, Dawn. Come Back to Sorrento. 1997. Orig. Title: The Tenth Moon. 185p. pap. 14.00 (*1-883642-26-4*) Steerforth Pr.
—Dawn Powell at Her Best: Including the Novels "Dance Night" & "Turn Magic Wheel" & Selected Stories. 1994. 452p. 28.00 (*1-883642-16-7*) Steerforth Pr.
—My Home Is Far Away. 1995. 295p. pap. 14.00 (*1-883642-43-4*) Steerforth Pr.
—Novels, 1930-1942, Vol. 1. Page, Tim, ed. 2001. (Library of America: Vol. 126). 1075p. 35.00 (*1-931082-01-4*) Library of America, The.
—Novels, 1944-1962, Vol. 2. Page, Tim, ed. 2001. (Library of America: Vol. 127). 985p. 35.00 (*1-931082-02-2*) Library of America, The.
Pride, Regina. Small Sacrifices. 2000. 382p. pap. 18.95 (*0-595-14315-6*) iUniverse, Inc.
—Toughest Battle. 2001. pap. 14.95 (*0-595-18590-8*) iUniverse, Inc.
Pyle, A. M. Murder Moves In. 1987. 256p. mass mkt. 3.50 o.p. (*0-451-14889-4*, Signet Bks.) NAL.
—Murder Moves In. 1986. 216p. 14.95 o.s.i (*0-8027-5635-2*) Walker & Co.
—Pure Murder. 1990. 256p. 16.95 o.p. (*0-312-03917-4*, Saint Martin's Minotaur) St. Martin's Pr.
—Trouble Making Toys. 1986. 256p. mass mkt. 2.95 o.p. (*0-451-14570-4*, Signet Bks.) NAL.
—Trouble Making Toys. 1985. 192p. 13.95 (*0-8027-5610-7*) Walker & Co.
Raymond, Linda. Rocking the Babies. 1994. 272p. 21.95 o.p. (*0-670-85263-5*, Viking) Viking Penguin.
Resnick, Mike. Dog in the Manger. Bolkey, Lorna et al, eds. 1995. (Illus.). 160p. pap. 12.95 (*1-57090-021-3*) Alexander Bks.
Richards, Emilie. Whiskey Island. 2000. 512p. mass mkt. (*1-55166-570-0*, 1-66570-2, Mira Bks.) Harlequin Enterprises, Ltd.
Richter, Conrad. Awakening Land. 1966. 29.95 o.p. (*0-394-41703-8*) Knopf, Alfred A. Inc.
—The Trees. 1984. 208p. pap. 2.95 o.p. (*0-553-23802-7*) Bantam Bks.
—The Trees. 1991. 167p. reprint ed. pap. 12.95 (*0-8214-0978-6*) Ohio Univ. Pr.
Robards, Karen. The Midnight Hour. 2001. E-Book 6.99 (*1-58945-937-7*) Adobe Systems, Inc.
—The Midnight Hour. 1999. 464p. mass mkt. 7.99 (*0-440-22504-3*) Dell Publishing.
—The Midnight Hour. l.t. ed. 1999. (Wheeler Large Print Book Ser.). 26.95 o.p. (*1-56895-719-X*, Wheeler Publishing, Inc.) Gale Group.
—The Midnight Hour. 1999. E-Book 6.99 (*0-440-33420-9*) Random Hse., Inc.
Roberts, John Maddox. Desperate Highways. 1997. 304p. 23.95 o.p. (*0-312-17176-5*, Saint Martin's Minotaur) St. Martin's Pr.
—Ghosts of Saigon. 1996. 288p. 21.95 o.p. (*0-312-14345-1*, Saint Martin's Minotaur) St. Martin's Pr.
—A Typical American Town. 1994. 256p. 20.95 o.p. (*0-312-11359-5*, Saint Martin's Minotaur) St. Martin's Pr.
—A Typical American Town. l.t. ed. 1996. (Ulverscroft Large Print Ser.). 480p. 29.99 o.p. (*0-7089-3507-9*, Ulverscroft) Thorpe, F. A. Pubs. GBR. *Dist:* Ulverscroft Large Print Bks., Ltd., Ulverscroft Large Print Canada, Ltd.
Roberts, Les. Irish Sports Pages. mass mkt. (*0-312-98380-8*, St. Martin's Paperbacks); 2002. 304p. 23.95 (*0-312-28661-9*, Saint Martin's Minotaur) St. Martin's Pr.
Ross, Dana Fuller, pseud. Honor! 1998. (Wagons West: The Empire Trilogy : Bk. 1). (Illus.). 400p. mass mkt. 5.99 o.s.i (*0-553-57764-6*) Bantam Bks.
—Honor! l.t. ed. 2001. (Thorndike Western Ser.). (Illus.). 576p. (J). 26.95 (*0-7862-3116-5*) Thorndike Pr.
Santmyer, Helen Hooven. And Ladies of the Club. 2000. 1184p. pap. 19.95 (*0-425-17440-9*); 1986. 1440p. mass mkt. 8.99 o.s.i (*0-425-10243-2*); 1985. mass mkt. 5.95 o.s.i (*0-425-07704-7*) Berkley Publishing Group.
—And Ladies of the Club. 1982. 1344p. 69.00 o.s.i (*0-8142-0323-X*) Ohio State Univ. Pr.
—And Ladies of the Club. 1984. 1216p. 19.95 o.p. (*0-399-12965-0*, G. P. Putnam's Sons) Penguin Putnam Bks. for Young Readers.
—Farewell, Summer. 1988. (Illus.). 128p. 12.95 o.p. (*0-06-015889-1*) HarperTrade.
—Farewell, Summer. 2001. 144p. 42.95 (*0-8142-0868-1*); pap. 17.95 (*0-8142-5069-6*) Ohio State Univ. Pr.
—Farewell, Summer. 1989. pap. 3.95 o.p. (*0-312-91595-0*, St. Martin's Paperbacks) St. Martin's Pr.
—The Fierce Dispute. l.t. ed. 1989. 265p. lib. bdg. 18.95 o.p. (*0-8161-4645-4*, Macmillan Reference USA) Gale Group.
—The Fierce Dispute. 1999. xiv, 214p. reprint ed. pap. 16.95 (*0-8142-5035-1*); text 36.95 (*0-8142-0834-7*) Ohio State Univ. Pr.
—The Fierce Dispute. 1988. 340p. mass mkt. 4.50 o.p. (*0-312-91028-2*, St. Martin's Paperbacks); 1987. 288p. 16.95 o.p. (*0-312-01152-0*) St. Martin's Pr.
Seguin, Marilyn Weymouth. Silver Ribbon Skinny. Caso, Adolph, ed. 1996. (Illus.). 96p. (J). (gr. 4-10). pap. 12.95 (*0-8283-2020-9*) Branden Bks.
Short, Sharon G. The Death We Share. 1995. mass mkt. 5.99 o.s.i (*0-449-14916-1*, Fawcett) Ballantine Bks.
—Past Pretense. 1994. (Orig.). mass mkt. 4.99 o.s.i (*0-449-14915-3*, Fawcett) Ballantine Bks.
Short, Sharon Gwyn. Angel's Bidding. 1993. (Midwest Mysteries Ser.). mass mkt. 4.99 o.s.i (*0-449-14873-4*, Fawcett) Ballantine Bks.
Shreve, Susan Richards. The Visiting Physician. l.t. ed. 1996. (Large Print Bks.). 25.95 o.p. (*1-56895-369-0*, Wheeler Publishing, Inc.) Gale Group.
Sites, James N. America: The Search & the Secret. 1998. (Illus.). 252p. 22.00 (*0-945084-71-4*) Stuart, Jesse Foundation, The.
Smith, Scott B. A Simple Plan. 1994. 25.95 o.p. (*0-7927-1952-2*); pap. o.p. (*0-7927-1951-4*) BBC Audiobooks America.
—A Simple Plan. unabr. ed. 1994. audio 64.00 (*0-7366-2757-X*, 3480) Books on Tape, Inc.
—A Simple Plan. 1994. 4.99 o.p. (*0-517-13635-X*) Random Hse. Value Publishing.
—A Simple Plan. abr. ed. 1993. 17.00 incl. audio (*0-671-87180-3*); Set. 1998. pap. 18.00 incl. audio (*0-671-04331-5*, 391580) Simon & Schuster Audio. (Simon & Schuster Audioworks).
—A Simple Plan. 1994. 416p. mass mkt. 6.99 (*0-312-95271-6*, St. Martin's Paperbacks) St. Martin's Pr.
Soos, Troy. Cincinnati Red Stalkings. 1999. 336p. mass mkt. 5.99 o.s.i (*1-57566-408-9*) Kensington Publishing Corp.
—Cincinnati Red Stalkings. unabr. ed. 1998. (Mickey Rawlings Baseball Ser.: Vol. 5). audio 52.00 (*0-7887-2478-9*, 95553E7) Recorded Bks., LLC.
—The Cincinnati Red Stalkings: A Mickey Rawlings Baseball Mystery. 1998. (Mickey Rawlings Baseball Mystery Ser.). 352p. 20.00 o.s.i (*1-57566-286-8*, Kensington Bks.) Kensington Publishing Corp.
Stevens, Brooke. Tattoo Girl. 2001. 322p. pap. 13.95 (*0-312-26910-2*, Saint Martin's Griffin) St. Martin's Pr.
Stone, Beatrice. Entwined: A Novel. 1995. 224p. pap. 10.95 o.p. (*1-879427-21-4*) 3rd Side Pr., Inc.
Swann, S. Andrew. The Dragons of the Cuyahoga. 2001. 320p. mass mkt. 6.99 (*0-7564-0009-0*) DAW Bks., Inc.
Swanson, Eric. The Boy in the Lake. 2000. 204p. pap. 11.95 (*0-312-26297-3*, Saint Martin's Griffin); 1999. 197p. 21.95 (*0-312-20281-4*) St. Martin's Pr.
Taylor, Phyllis. Joshua, the Word & the Light. Taylor, Phyllis & Minner, Rose, eds. 2004. 280p. pap. 13.95 (*0-9742233-1-X*) Daybreak Publishing.
Thomas, Annabel. Stone Man Mountain. 2002. 471p. 45.00 (*1-57233-149-6*); pap. 19.95 (*1-57233-150-X*) Univ. of Tennessee Pr.
Tucker, Kerry. Death Echo: A Libby Kincaid Mystery. 1993. 224p. 19.00 o.p. (*0-06-017700-4*) HarperTrade.
—Death Echo: A Libby Kincaid Mystery. 1994. 288p. mass mkt. 4.50 o.p. (*0-06-109986-4*, HarperTorch) Morrow/Avon.
—Still Waters. l.t. ed. 1992. 18.95 o.p. (*0-7451-8356-5*); pap. 16.95 o.p. (*0-7927-1104-1*) BBC Audiobooks America.
—Still Waters. 1991. 208p. 18.95 o.p. (*0-06-016529-4*) HarperTrade.
—Still Waters. 1992. 272p. mass mkt. 3.99 o.p. (*0-06-109095-6*, HarperTorch) Morrow/Avon.
Valin, Jonathan. Day of Wrath. 1994. 320p. mass mkt. 4.99 o.s.i (*0-440-21041-0*) Dell Publishing.
—Day of Wrath. 1983. (Harry Stoner Mystery Ser.). 256p. pap. 3.50 (*0-380-63917-3*, Avon Bks.) Morrow/Avon.
—Dead Letter. 1994. 320p. mass mkt. 4.99 o.s.i (*0-440-21038-0*) Dell Publishing.
—Dead Letter. 1983. (Harry Stoner Mystery Ser.). 224p. pap. 3.50 (*0-380-61366-2*, Avon Bks.) Morrow/Avon.
—Extenuating Circumstances. 1989. 15.95 o.s.i (*0-440-50110-5*, Delacorte Pr.); 1989. 240p. 15.95 o.s.i (*0-385-29683-5*, Delacorte Pr.); 1990. 256p. reprint ed. mass mkt. 3.95 o.s.i (*0-440-20630-8*) Dell Publishing.
—Final Notice. 1994. 320p. mass mkt. 4.99 o.s.i (*0-440-21032-1*) Dell Publishing.
—Final Notice. 1982. (Harry Stoner Mystery Ser.). 192p. pap. 3.50 (*0-380-57893-X*, Avon Bks.) Morrow/Avon.
—Fire Lake. 1989. 272p. (YA). reprint ed. mass mkt. 4.99 o.s.i (*0-440-20145-4*) Dell Publishing.
—Fire Lake: A Harry Stoner Novel. 1987. 264p. 14.95 o.s.i (*0-385-29589-8*, Delacorte Pr.) Dell Publishing.
—Life's Work. 1987. 256p. reprint ed. mass mkt. 4.99 o.s.i (*0-440-14790-5*) Dell Publishing.
—Life's Work: A Harry Stoner Novel. 1986. 240p. 14.95 o.s.i (*0-385-29503-0*, Delacorte Pr.) Dell Publishing.
—The Lime Pit. 1994. 320p. mass mkt. 4.99 o.s.i (*0-440-21029-1*) Dell Publishing.
—The Lime Pit. 1983. (Harry Stoner Mystery Ser.). 208p. pap. 3.50 (*0-380-55442-9*, Avon Bks.) Morrow/Avon.
—The Music Lovers: A Harry Stoner Mystery. 1994. 304p. mass mkt. 4.99 o.s.i (*0-440-21686-9*) Dell Publishing.
—Natural Causes. 1994. 384p. mass mkt. 4.99 o.s.i (*0-440-21035-6*) Dell Publishing.
—Natural Causes. 1984. (Harry Stoner Mystery Ser.). 304p. pap. 2.95 o.p. (*0-380-68247-8*, 68247, Avon Bks.) Morrow/Avon.
—Second Chance: A Harry Stoner Mystery. 288p. 1992. mass mkt. 4.99 o.s.i (*0-440-21222-7*); 1991. 18.00 o.s.i (*0-385-29912-5*, Delacorte Pr.) Dell Publishing.
Van Leeuwen, Jean. Nothing Here but Trees. 1998. (Illus.). 32p. (J). (ps-3). 15.89 o.p. (*0-8037-2180-3*); 15.99 o.p. (*0-8037-2178-1*) Penguin Putnam Bks. for Young Readers. (Dial Bks. for Young Readers).
Wellman, Mac. Annie Salem: An American Tale. 1995. (New American Fiction Ser.: No. 34). 240p. pap. 12.95 (*1-55713-207-0*) Sun & Moon Pr.
Westfall, Patricia T. Fowl Play. 1998. (Worldwide Library Mysteries: Vol. 273). per. (*0-373-26273-6*, 0-26273-3, Worldwide Library) Harlequin Enterprises, Ltd.
—Fowl Play. 1996. 208p. 21.95 (*0-312-14604-3*, Saint Martin's Minotaur) St. Martin's Pr.
—Mother of the Bride. 1999. (WWL Mystery Ser.: No. 312). per. (*0-373-26312-0*, 1-26312-8, Worldwide Library) Harlequin Enterprises, Ltd.
—Mother of the Bride. pap. 15.95 (*0-312-30103-0*, Saint Martin's Griffin);Vol. 1. 1998. 224p. 21.95 (*0-312-18631-2*, Saint Martin's Minotaur) St. Martin's Pr.
Wieland, Mitch. Willy Slater's Lane. 1996. 176p. pap. 12.95 (*0-87074-409-7*) Southern Methodist Univ. Pr.
—Willy Slater's Lane: A Novel. 1996. 176p. 22.50 o.p. (*0-87074-408-9*) Southern Methodist Univ. Pr.
Willoughby, Lee D. Americana - The Making of the Cities: Cincinnati. 1990. (Making of the Cities Ser.). 384p. (Orig.). pap. 4.95 (*1-877961-04-3*) Knightsbridge Publishing.
Wright, Sally S. Publish & Perish. 1999. 224p. mass mkt. 5.99 (*0-345-42588-X*) Ballantine Bks.
—Publish & Perish, 3 vols. 2003. (Ben Reese Mysteries Ser.: Vol. 1 ). 238p. pap. 9.99 (*1-57673-067-0*, Multnomah Bks.) Multnomah Pubs., Inc.
—Publish & Perish. l.t. ed. 1998. (Christian Mystery Ser.). 307p. 24.95 (*0-7862-1566-6*) Thorndike Pr.
Zafris, Nancy. The Metal Shredders. 2002. 320p. 24.95 o.s.i (*0-399-14922-8*, BlueHen Bks.) Putnam Publishing Group, The.
Zoller, James S. Beyond the Bridge. 2001. 423p. pap. 20.95 (*0-595-17016-1*) iUniverse, Inc.

### OKLAHOMA—FICTION

Albright, Letha. Daredevil's Apprentice. 2002. (Viv Powers Mystery Ser.). 255p. pap. 12.95 (*0-9705049-4-2*) Avocet Pr., Inc.
—Tulsa Time. 2000. (Dark Oak Mysteries Ser.). 220p. pap. 11.95 (*1-892343-12-6*) Oak Tree Publishing.
Ashour, Linda P. Joy Baby: A Novel. 1992. 512p. 22.00 o.p. (*0-671-68331-4*) Summit Bks.
Askew, Rilla. Fire in Beulah. 2001. 352p. 25.95 o.p. (*0-670-88843-5*, Viking) Viking Penguin.
—The Mercy Seat. 1998. 448p. pap. 13.95 (*0-14-026515-5*) Penguin Group (USA) Inc.

Settings

—The Mercy Seat. 1997. 448p. 23.95 o.p. (0-670-87467-1) Viking Penguin.

Askey, Rilla. Strange Business. 1992. 208p. 20.00 o.p. (0-670-84259-1, Viking) Viking Penguin.

Babb, Sanora. Whose Names Are Unknown: A Novel. 2004. (0-8061-3579-4) Univ. of Oklahoma Pr.

Bagwell, Stella. White Dove's Promise. 2002. (Silhouette Special Edition Ser.). (Illus.). 248p. mass mkt. (0-373-24478-9, Silhouette) Harlequin Enterprises, Ltd.

Bell, Betty L. Faces in the Moon. (American Indian Literature & Critical Studies Ser.: Vol. 9). 1995. 200p. pap. 14.95 (0-8061-2774-0); 1994. 192p. 19.95 o.p. (0-8061-2601-9) Univ. of Oklahoma Pr.

Berkey, Brian F. The Keys to Tulsa. 1989. 18.95 o.p. (0-87113-314-8) Grove/Atlantic, Inc.

—The Keys to Tulsa. Rosenman, Jane, ed. 1991. 416p. reprint ed. pap. 12.00 (0-671-70727-2, Washington Square Pr.) Simon & Schuster.

Berney, Louis. The Road to Bobby Joe: And Other Stories. 1991. 18.95 (0-15-177870-1) Harcourt Trade Pubs.

Bernhardt, William. Blind Justice. 1997. mass mkt. 3.50 o.s.i (0-345-41806-9); 1992. 320p. mass mkt. 6.99 (0-345-37483-5) Ballantine Bks.

—Blind Justice. unabr. ed. 1998. (Justice Ser.: Vol. 2). audio 48.00 (0-7366-4106-8, 4611) Books on Tape, Inc.

—Blind Justice. unabr. ed. 2001. (Attorney Ben Kincaid Mystery Ser.). audio Chivers Audio Bks. GBR. *Dist:* BBC Audiobooks America.

—Blind Justice. l.t. ed. 1993. 80.95 o.p. (0-7862-9989-4, Macmillan Reference USA) Gale Group.

—Criminal Intent. 2003. 416p. mass mkt. 7.50 (0-345-44175-3, Fawcett); 2002. E-Book 16.95 (0-345-45862-1, Ballantine Bks.); 2002. 368p. 23.95 (0-345-44173-7, Ballantine Bks.) Ballantine Bks.

—Criminal Intent. l.t. ed. 2004. 592p. 25.95 (0-375-43262-0) Random Hse. Large Print.

—Cruel Justice. 1997. mass mkt. 3.50 o.s.i (0-345-41807-7); 1996. 480p. mass mkt. 7.50 (0-345-40803-9) Ballantine Bks.

—Cruel Justice. unabr. ed. 1998. (Justice Ser.). audio 72.00 (0-7366-4180-7, 4678) Books on Tape, Inc.

—Cruel Justice. l.t. ed. 1996. pap. 23.95 (1-56895-323-2, Wheeler Publishing, Inc.) Gale Group.

—Dark Justice. 1999. 448p. mass mkt. 6.99 (0-345-43476-5) Ballantine Bks.

—Deadly Justice. 1997. mass mkt. 3.50 o.s.i (0-345-41808-5); 1993. 320p. mass mkt. 7.50 (0-345-38027-4) Ballantine Bks.

—Deadly Justice. unabr. ed. 1998. (Justice Ser.: Vol. 3). audio 48.00 (0-7366-4107-6, 4612) Books on Tape, Inc.

—Deadly Justice. l.t. ed. 1994. 65.95 o.p. (0-7862-9988-6, Macmillan Reference USA) Gale Group.

—Double Jeopardy. 1996. 416p. mass mkt. 7.99 (0-345-39784-3) Ballantine Bks.

—Double Jeopardy. l.t. ed. 1996. (Niagara Large Print Ser.). 431p. 29.50 o.p. (0-7089-5828-1, Ulverscroft) Thorpe, F. A. Pubs. GBR. *Dist:* Ulverscroft Large Print Bks., Ltd.

—Extreme Justice. 1998. (Ben Kincaid Ser.). 384p. mass mkt. 6.99 (0-345-42481-6) Ballantine Bks.

—Naked Justice. 1997. 448p. mass mkt. 6.99 (0-449-00087-7, Fawcett) Ballantine Bks.

—Naked Justice. unabr. ed. 1997. (Justice Ser.). audio 88.00 (0-7366-3789-3, 4463) Books on Tape, Inc.

—Naked Justice. l.t. ed. 1997. (Niagara Large Print Ser.). 688p. 29.50 o.p. (0-7089-5879-6, Ulverscroft) Thorpe, F. A. Pubs. GBR. *Dist:* Ulverscroft Large Print Bks., Ltd.

—Perfect Justice. 1997. mass mkt. 3.50 o.s.i (0-345-41809-3) Ballantine Bks.

—Perfect Justice. unabr. ed. 1998. (Justice Ser.: Vol. 4). audio 56.00 (0-7366-4108-4, 4613) Books on Tape, Inc.

—Perfect Justice, Set. l.t. ed. 1994. (Studio Ser.). 64.95 o.p. incl. audio (0-7862-9987-8, Macmillan Reference USA) Gale Group.

—Perfect Justice. 1995. 416p. mass mkt. 6.99 (0-345-39133-0, House of Collectibles) Random Hse. Information Group.

—Primary Justice. 1997. mass mkt. 3.50 o.s.i (0-345-41810-7); 1991. 320p. mass mkt. 6.99 (0-345-37479-7) Ballantine Bks.

—Primary Justice. unabr. ed. 1998. (Justice Ser.: Vol. 1). audio 48.00 (0-7366-4105-X, 4610) Books on Tape, Inc.

—Primary Justice. (Mystery Ser.). 1998. 309p. 22.95 (0-7862-1659-X, Five Star); Set. 1993. 79.95 o.p. incl. audio (0-7862-9991-6, Macmillan Reference USA) Gale Group.

Black, Baxter. Hey, Cowboy, Wanna Get Lucky. 1995. 240p. pap. 13.00 (0-14-025093-X, Penguin Bks.) Penguin Group (USA) Inc.

—Hey Cowboy, Wanna Get Lucky? 1994. 240p. 21.00 o.s.i (0-517-59377-7, Crown) Crown Publishing Group.

—Hey Cowboy, Wanna Get Lucky? A Rodeo Novel. Set. abr. ed. 1996. 180p. audio 16.99 o.s.i (0-553-47693-9, 393414, RH Audio) Random Hse. Audio Publishing Group.

Blair, Clifford. Gunman's Odds. 1989. 192p. 13.95 o.p. (0-8034-8789-4) Bouregy, Thomas & Co., Inc.

—Gunman's Odds. l.t. ed. 1995. 213p. pap. 18.95 o.p. (0-7838-1232-9, Macmillan Reference USA) Gale Group.

—Showdown at Viking Cave. l.t. ed. 1994. 255p. pap. 18.95 (0-8161-7473-3, Macmillan Reference USA) Gale Group.

—Showdown at Viking Cave. 1994. 198p. 19.95 (0-8027-4136-3) Walker & Co.

Blanchard, Alice. The Breathtaker. 2003. 400p. 24.95 (0-446-53139-1) Warner Bks., Inc.

Bonham, Frank. Trago. 1984. 192p. 2.25 o.s.i (0-441-82096-4) Ace Bks.

—Trago. 186p. 19.00 (0-7540-8113-3, Gunsmoke) BBC Audiobooks America.

—Trago. 1981. 192p. mass mkt. 1.95 o.s.i (0-425-05041-6); 1979. mass mkt. 1.75 o.s.i (0-425-03895-5) Berkley Publishing Group.

Brody, Jean. Cleo. 1997. 368p. pap. 14.95 (0-312-15078-4, Saint Martin's Griffin); 1995. 361p. 21.95 o.p. (0-312-11761-2) St. Martin's Pr.

Carlile, Clancy. Children of the Dust. 1995. mass mkt. 6.99 o.s.i (0-8041-1416-1, Ivy Bks.) Ballantine Bks.

—Children of the Dust. unabr. ed. 1995. audio 104.00 (0-7366-3168-2, 3838) Books on Tape, Inc.

—Children of the Dust, Set. abr. ed. 1999. 3p. audio 16.95 (1-879371-91-X, 392832) Publishing Mills, Inc., The.

Carr, Pat M. If We Must Die: A Novel. 2002. (Chaparral Book for Young Readers Ser.). 168p. (J). 15.95 (0-87565-262-X) Texas Christian Univ. Pr.

Charbonneau, Eileen. Rachel Lemoyne. (Women of the West Novels Ser.). 320p. 1999. pap. 5.99 (0-8125-7114-2); 1998. (YA). (gr. 8 up). 22.95 o.p. (0-312-86448-5) Doherty, Tom Assocs., LLC. (Forge Bks.).

Clement, Rosemary. Christopher Park. 1993. 212p. 20.00 (1-883285-00-3) Delphinium Bks., Inc.

—Christopher Park: A Novel. 1993. 20.00 o.p. (0-671-86758-X) Delphinium Bks., Inc.

Cole, Jameson. A Killing in Quail County. 1996. 320p. 22.95 o.p. (0-312-13996-9, Saint Martin's Minotaur) St. Martin's Pr.

Conley, Robert J. Go-Ahead Rider. 1990. (Novel of the West Ser.). 192p. 15.95 o.p. (0-87131-612-9) Evans, M. & Co., Inc.

—Go-Ahead Rider. l.t. ed. 1994. (Evans Novel of the West Ser.). 16.95 (0-8161-5853-3, Macmillan Reference USA) Gale Group.

—Go-Ahead Rider. Grad, Doug, ed. 1992. 192p. reprint ed. mass mkt. 3.50 (0-671-74365-1, Pocket) Simon & Schuster.

Cooper, Susan Rogers. Chasing Away the Devil. 1993. (Mystery Ser.). per. (0-373-26129-2, 1-26129-6, Harlequin Bks.) Harlequin Enterprises, Ltd.

—Chasing Away the Devil. 1991. 192p. 16.95 o.p. (0-312-06316-4, Saint Martin's Minotaur) St. Martin's Pr.

—Doctors & Lawyers & Such. 1995. 256p. 21.95 o.p. (0-312-13468-1, Saint Martin's Minotaur) St. Martin's Pr.

—Houston in the Rearview Mirror. 1992. (WWL Mystery Ser.: No. 95). per. (0-373-26095-4, 1-26095-9, Harlequin Bks.) Harlequin Enterprises, Ltd.

—Houston in the Rearview Mirror. 1990. 160p. 14.95 o.p. (0-312-03843-7, Saint Martin's Minotaur) St. Martin's Pr.

—Lying Wonders: A Sheriff Milt Kovak Mystery. 2003. 224p. 22.95 (0-312-29056-X, Saint Martin's Minotaur) St. Martin's Pr.

—The Man in the Green Chevy. 1991. reprint ed. per. (0-373-26071-7, Harlequin Bks.) Harlequin Enterprises, Ltd.

—The Man in the Green Chevy. abr. ed. 1997. audio 17.00 (1-883268-46-X) Spellbinders, Inc.

—The Man in the Green Chevy. 1989. 208p. 15.95 o.p. (0-312-02604-8, Saint Martin's Minotaur) St. Martin's Pr.

—Other People's Houses. 1992. per. (0-373-26112-8, 1-26112-2, Harlequin Bks.) Harlequin Enterprises, Ltd.

—Other People's Houses. pap. 3.99 (0-373-05139-5); 1990. 176p. 14.95 o.p. (0-312-05139-5, Saint Martin's Minotaur) St. Martin's Pr.

Dillen, Frederick G. Fool. 1999. 302p. tchr. ed. 23.95 (1-56512-234-8) Algonquin Bks. of Chapel Hill.

Earle, Ralph. Come Here - Go Away. Zion, Claire, ed. 1991. 288p. (Orig.). pap. text 19.95 (0-671-68435-3, Atria) Simon & Schuster.

Earle, Ralph & Mettzner, Susan. Come Here, Go Away: Stop Running from the Love You Want. Zion, Claire, ed. 1992. 272p. reprint ed. pap. 9.00 (0-671-75968-X, Pocket) Simon & Schuster.

Earle, Ralph H. Come Here/Go Away. Meltsner, Susan & Zion, Claire, eds. 2nd ed. 1996. 257p. reprint ed. pap. 14.00 (0-9652879-0-4) Psychological Counseling Services, Inc.

Eighner, Lars. Pawn to Queen Four. 1997. 288p. pap. 11.95 (0-312-15188-8, Saint Martin's Griffin) St. Martin's Pr.

—Pawn to Queen 4. 1995. 288p. 21.95 o.p. (0-312-13581-5) St. Martin's Pr.

Fall, Thomas. The Ordeal of Running Standing. 1993. 312p. 15.95 (0-8061-2571-3) Univ. of Oklahoma Pr.

—The Ordeal of Running Standing. 1993. E-Book 15.95 (0-585-10056-X) netLibrary, Inc.

Furgerson, Celesta. Sculptured in Twilight. 1999. 202p. pap. 12.00 (0-9679875-0-4) River Bend Pr., Inc.

Garlock, Dorothy. After the Parade. l.t. ed. 2000. (Wheeler Large Print Book Ser.). 439p. 27.95 (1-56895-890-0, Wheeler Publishing, Inc.) Gale Group.

—After the Parade. 2000. 416p. reprint ed. mass mkt. 6.99 (0-446-60811-4) Warner Bks., Inc.

—Mother Road. l.t. ed. 2003. 516p. 32.95 (0-7862-5801-2) Thorndike Pr.

—Mother Road. 2003. 448p. mass mkt. 6.99 (0-446-61168-9); 448p. pap. 12.00 (0-446-69273-5); 400p. 22.95 (0-446-53062-X) Warner Bks., Inc.

—A Place Called Rainwater. 2003. 32.95 (0-7862-5172-7) Thorndike Pr.

—A Place Called Rainwater. 2003. 480p. mass mkt. 6.99 (0-446-61146-8); 2003. 416p. 22.95 (0-446-52950-8); 2002. 192p. 19.95 (0-446-53037-9) Warner Bks., Inc.

—With Heart. l.t. ed. 1999. (Basic Ser.). 551p. 30.95 (0-7862-2265-4) Thorndike Pr.

—With Heart. 1999. 464p. reprint ed. mass mkt. 6.99 (0-446-60589-1) Warner Bks., Inc.

—With Hope. l.t. ed. 1998. (Basic Ser.). 599p. 29.95 (0-7862-1694-8) Thorndike Pr.

Gentry, Georgina. Warrior's Honor. 2002. (Five Star Romance Ser.). (Illus.). 340p. 26.95 (0-7862-3920-4, Five Star) Gale Group.

—Warrior's Honor. 2000. mass mkt. 3.99 (0-8217-7728-9); 32p. mass mkt. 5.99 o.s.i (0-8217-6726-7) Kensington Publishing Corp. (Zebra Bks.).

Gischler, Victor. The Pistol Poets. 2004. 336p. 22.95 (0-385-33724-8, Delacorte Pr.) Dell Publishing.

Glancy, Diane. Designs of the Night Sky. 2002. (Series of American Narratives). 152p. 24.95 (0-8032-2190-8) Univ. of Nebraska Pr.

—The Mask Maker: A Novel. 2002. (American Indian Literature & Critical Studies: Vol. 42). 141p. 24.95 (0-8061-3400-3) Univ. of Oklahoma Pr.

Graham, Darlene. Dreamless. 2002. (Harlequin Superromance Ser.). mass mkt. (0-373-71091-7, Harlequin Bks.) Harlequin Enterprises, Ltd.

Graham, Janice. Sarah's Window. 2002. 320p. reprint ed. mass mkt. 6.99 (0-515-13412-0, Jove) Berkley Publishing Group.

—Sarah's Window. l.t. ed. 2002. 458p. 29.95 (0-7862-3891-7) Gale Group.

—Sarah's Window. 2001. 304p. 23.95 o.s.i (0-399-14629-6) Penguin Group (USA) Inc.

Graham, Virginia L. Daughter of Oklahoma. 2001. (Harlequin Superromance Ser.). mass mkt. (0-373-71028-3, Harlequin Bks.) Harlequin Enterprises, Ltd.

Grove, Fred. The Years of Fear. 2002. 241p. pap. 13.95 (1-4104-0069-7, Five Star Trade); 24.95 (0-7862-3272-2) Gale Group.

Haddock, Lisa. Edited Out. 1994. (Carmen Ramirez Mystery Ser.: Vol. 1). 224p. pap. 9.95 (1-56280-077-9) Naiad Pr., Inc.

—Final Cut. 1995. (Carmen Ramirez Mystery Ser.: Vol. 2). 224p. pap. 10.95 o.p. (1-56280-088-4) Naiad Pr., Inc.

Hager, Jean. The Fire Carrier. 1996. 82p. 21.95 o.s.i (0-89296-566-5) Mysterious Pr.

—The Fire Carrier. 1997. 224p. reprint ed. mass mkt. 5.99 o.s.i (0-446-40387-3) Warner Bks., Inc.

—Ghostland. 1993. mass mkt. (0-373-26117-9, 1-26117-1, Harlequin Bks.) Harlequin Enterprises, Ltd.

—Ghostland. 1991. 272p. 18.95 o.p. (0-312-06982-0, Saint Martin's Minotaur) St. Martin's Pr.

—The Grandfather Medicine. 1993. per. (0-373-83303-2, 1-83303-7); 1990. 224p. mass mkt. (0-373-26059-8) Harlequin Enterprises, Ltd. (Harlequin Bks.).

—The Grandfather Medicine. 1998. 248p. pap. 11.95 (0-9662145-2-8) Southmont Publishing.

—The Grandfather Medicine. 1989. 16.95 o.p. (0-312-02923-3, Saint Martin's Minotaur) St. Martin's Pr.

—Masked Dancers. 1998. 288p. 23.00 o.p. (0-89296-641-6) Mysterious Pr.

—Masked Dancers. l.t. ed. 1998. (Cloak & Dagger Ser.). 376p. 25.95 (0-7862-1485-6) Thorndike Pr.

—Night Walker. 1991. reprint ed. mass mkt. (0-373-26085-7, Harlequin Bks.) Harlequin Enterprises, Ltd.

—Night Walker. 1990. 15.95 o.p. (0-312-05138-7, Saint Martin's Minotaur) St. Martin's Pr.

—Ravenmocker. 1992. 272p. 17.95 (0-89296-493-6) Mysterious Pr.

—Ravenmocker. 1994. 256p. reprint ed. mass mkt. 5.99 o.s.i (0-446-40107-2) Warner Bks., Inc.

—The Redbird's Cry. l.t. ed. 1994. 357p. pap. 18.95 (0-8161-7402-4, Macmillan Reference USA) Gale Group.

—The Redbird's Cry. 1994. 288p. 18.95 (0-89296-494-4) Mysterious Pr.

—The Redbird's Cry. 1995. 256p. reprint ed. mass mkt. 5.50 (0-446-40106-4) Warner Bks., Inc.

—Seven Black Stones. 1995. (Molly Bearpaw Ser.). 304p. 18.95 o.s.i (0-89296-565-7) Mysterious Pr.

—Seven Black Stones. 1996. 256p. reprint ed. mass mkt. 5.99 (0-446-40386-5) Warner Bks., Inc.

—The Spirit Caller. 1997. 272p. 21.50 o.p. (0-89296-640-8) Mysterious Pr.

—The Spirit Caller. 1998. mass mkt. (0-446-40488-8, Mysterious Pr. Paperback Bks.); 320p. mass mkt. 6.99 (0-446-60595-6) Warner Bks., Inc.

Harper, B. H. B. The Highest Bidder. 2001. (Five Star First Edition Romance Ser.). ***p. 25.95 (0-7862-3341-9, Five Star) Gale Group.

Harris, Fred. Coyote Revenge. 1999. 208p. 24.00 (0-06-018396-9) HarperCollins Pubs.

—Coyote Revenge. 2000. 224p. mass mkt. 5.99 (0-06-098503-8, Avon Bks.) Morrow/Avon.

—Easy Pickin's. 2000. 288p. pap. 25.00 (0-06-018399-3) HarperCollins Pubs.

Hart, Carolyn G. Letter from Home. 2003. 272p. 22.95 (0-425-19179-6, Prime Crime) Berkley Publishing Group.

Hollingsworth, A. B. Flatbellies. 2001. 344p. 22.95 (1-58536-038-4) Clock Tower Pr. LLC.

—Flatbellies. 2003. 344p. pap. 13.95 (0-393-32420-6) Norton, W. W. & Co., Inc.

Hunter, Stephen. Dirty White Boys. 1995. 496p. mass mkt. 7.99 (0-440-22179-X) Dell Publishing.

—Dirty White Boys. abr. ed. 1994. audio 17.00 (1-57042-192-7, 4-521927) Time Warner AudioBooks.

Ishcomer, Kathy L. That Ole Pastel Magic. 2000. (First Edition Romance Ser.). 163p. 25.95 (0-7862-2765-6, Five Star) Gale Group.

Jerman, Jerry. The Secret of Whispering Woods: The Journeys of Jessie Land. 1996. 132p. (J). (gr. 3-7). mass mkt. 5.99 (1-56476-552-0) Cook Communications Ministries.

Johansen, Iris. Long after Midnight. 1997. 464p. reprint ed. mass mkt. 7.50 (0-553-57181-8) Bantam Bks.

—Long after Midnight. l.t. ed. 1997. (G. K. Hall Romance Ser.). 560p. 29.95 (0-7838-2040-2) Thorndike Pr.

Johnson, Guy. Standing at the Scratch Line. 2001. E-Book 11.95 (1-58945-866-4) Adobe Systems, Inc.

—Standing at the Scratch Line. 2001. E-Book 11.95 (0-375-50656-X) Random Hse., Inc.

—Standing at the Scratch Line: A Novel. 2001. 576p. pap. 14.95 o.s.i (0-375-75667-1, Villard Bks.) Random House Adult Trade Publishing Group.

—Standing at the Scratch Line: A Novel. 1998. 432p. 24.95 o.s.i (0-375-50158-4) Random Hse. Information Group.

Johnstone, William W. Blood of Eagles. 2000. 304p. mass mkt. 5.99 (0-7860-1106-8, Pinnacle Bks.) Kensington Publishing Corp.

Kimball, Philip. Harvesting Ballads. 1984. 448p. 17.95 o.p. (0-525-24228-7, 01743-520, Dutton) Dutton/Plume.

—Harvesting Ballads. 1994. 400p. reprint ed. pap. 14.95 (0-8061-2632-9) Univ. of Oklahoma Pr.

—Harvesting Ballads. 1984. E-Book 14.95 (0-585-14537-7) netLibrary, Inc.

Lackey, Mercedes. Sacred Ground. 1995. 375p. mass mkt. 5.99 (0-8125-1965-5); 1994. 384p. 22.95 o.p. (0-312-85281-9) Doherty, Tom Assocs., LLC. (Tor Bks.).

Lanham, Edwin. The Stricklands: A Novel. 2nd ed. 2002. 336p. 19.95 (0-8061-3419-4) Univ. of Oklahoma Pr.

Larsen, Jodie. Deadly Silence. 1997. 416p. mass mkt. 5.99 o.s.i (0-451-40786-5, Onyx) NAL.

Lehrer, Jim. Crown Oklahoma. 1991. 208p. mass mkt. 3.95 o.s.i (0-345-36124-5) Ballantine Bks.

—Crown Oklahoma. 1997. (One-Eyed Mack Mystery Ser.). 324p. pap. 12.95 (1-57178-040-8) Council Oak Bks.

—Crown Oklahoma. 1989. 224p. 18.95 o.p. (0-399-13434-4, G. P. Putnam's Sons) Penguin Putnam Bks. for Young Readers.

—Kick the Can. 1997. 420p. (C). reprint ed. pap. 12.95 (1-57178-059-9) Council Oak Bks.

—Kick the Can. 1988. 256p. 17.95 o.p. (0-399-13350-X, G. P. Putnam's Sons) Penguin Putnam Bks. for Young Readers.

—Kick the Can. 1992. 3.99 o.p. (0-517-09580-7) Random Hse. Value Publishing.

—Lost & Found. abr. ed. audio 16.99 (0-88646-293-2, 7293) Durkin Hayes Publishing Ltd.

—Lost & Found. 1991. 224p. 19.95 o.p. (0-399-13601-0, G. P. Putnam's Sons) Penguin Group (USA) Inc.

—Lost & Found. 1992. 3.99 o.p. (0-517-09582-3) Random Hse. Value Publishing.

—Short List. abr. ed. 1992. (One-Eyed Mack Ser.: No. 2). audio 16.99 (0-88646-314-9, 7314) Durkin Hayes Publishing Ltd.

—Short List. 1992. 224p. 19.95 o.p. (0-399-13665-7, G. P. Putnam's Sons) Penguin Group (USA) Inc.
—The Sooner Spy. 1997. (One-Eyed Mack Mystery Ser.). 328p. pap. 12.95 (1-57178-041-6) Council Oak Bks.
—The Sooner Spy. 1990. 224p. 19.95 o.p. (0-399-13536-7, G. P. Putnam's Sons) Penguin Putnam Bks. for Young Readers.
Letts, Billie. The Honk & Holler Opening Soon. l.t. ed. 2000. 318p. 28.95 (1-57490-283-0, Beeler Large Print Bks.) Beeler, Thomas T. Publisher.
—The Honk & Holler Opening Soon. abr. ed. 1998. audio 17.95 o.p. (1-56740-781-1, 442, Nova Audio Bks.); audio 7.99 o.s.i (1-56740-295-X, 1802, Paperback Nova Audio Bks.); audio 24.95 (1-56740-056-6, 9, Bookcassette); 9p. audio 57.25 (1-56740-585-1, 900, Unabridged Library Editions) Brilliance Audio.
—The Honk & Holler Opening Soon. unabr. ed. 1999. audio 72.25 Highsmith Inc.
—The Honk & Holler Opening Soon. 1999. 320p. pap. 13.99 (0-446-67505-9); 1998. 304p. (YA). 22.00 o.p. (0-446-52158-2) Warner Bks., Inc.
—Where the Heart Is. abr. ed. 1999. audio 7.99 o.s.i (1-56740-120-1, 718, Paperback Nova Audio Bks.); 1999. audio 17.95 o.p. (1-56740-664-5, 1744, Nova Audio Bks.); 1995. audio 16.95 (1-56100-435-9, Nova Audio Bks.); 1999. audio 35.95 (1-56740-438-3, 1745, Brilliance Audio Unabridged); 1995. audio 23.95 o.s.i (1-56100-644-0, 314, Bookcassette); 1995. audio 57.25 (1-56100-269-0, 1094, Unabridged Library Editions) Brilliance Audio.
—Where the Heart Is. l.t. ed. 1995. 427p. 23.95 o.p. (0-7838-1478-X, Macmillan Reference USA) Gale Group.
—Where the Heart Is. unabr. ed. 1999. audio 57.25 Highsmith Inc.
—Where the Heart Is. 2000. pap. 12.00 (0-446-78770-1); 1998. 17.95 (0-446-78928-3); 1998. pap. 12.00 (0-446-78929-1); 1995. 368p. 17.95 o.p. (0-446-51972-3); 1998. 384p. reprint ed. pap. 13.95 (0-446-67221-1); 1996. 336p. reprint ed. mass mkt. 5.99 (0-446-60365-1) Warner Bks., Inc.
Lovelace, Merline. A Savage Beauty. 2003. 384p. mass mkt. (1-55166-707-X, Mira Bks.) Harlequin Enterprises, Ltd.
—A Savage Beauty. l.t. ed. 2003. 444p. 28.95 (0-7862-6072-6, Large Print Pr.) Thorndike Pr.
Maine, Priscilla. Angels Unaware. E-Book 3.50 o.p. (1-58495-011-0) DiskUs Publishing.
—Angels Unaware. 2002. 258p. pap. 16.95 (1-59105-042-1); E-Book 5.50 (1-59105-017-0) NovelBooks, Inc.
Maine, Priscilla A. Angels Unaware. Rowell, Skip, ed. 1999. 192p. E-Book 6.50 o.p. incl. disk (0-9667995-6-9) DiskUs Publishing.
Matlock, Curtiss Ann. At the Corner of Love & Heartache. 2002. 448p. mass mkt. (1-55166-917-X, Mira Bks.) Harlequin Enterprises, Ltd.
—Lost Highways. 1999. mass mkt. (1-55166-499-2, 1-66499-4, Mira Bks.) Harlequin Enterprises, Ltd.
McCourtney, Lorena. Escape. 1996. (Palisades Pure Romance Ser.). 266p. pap. 9.99 o.p. (1-57673-012-3, Palisades) Multnomah Pubs., Inc.
McReynolds, Mary. Wells of Glory. 1996. (Legacy of the Land Ser.: Bk. 1). 320p. pap. 9.99 o.p. (0-89107-889-4) Crossway Bks.
Medawar, Mardi Oakley. The Fort Larned Incident. 2000. (Tay-Bodal Mystery Ser.). 270p. 23.95 (0-312-20878-2, Saint Martin's Minotaur) St. Martin's Pr.
—The Ft. Larned Incident. E-Book 23.95 (0-312-27592-7) St. Martin's Pr.
Milburn, George. Catalogue. 1987. 312p. reprint ed. lib. bdg. 18.95 (0-940827-00-X) Davenport Pr.
—Catalogue. 1986. pap. 1.95 o.p. (0-380-01650-8, 33084, Avon Bks.) Morrow/Avon.
—No More Trumpets & Other Stories. 1977. (Short Story Index Reprint Ser.). 22.95 (0-8369-3699-X) Ayer Co. Pubs., Inc.
—Oklahoma Town. 1977. (Short Story Index Reprint Ser.). 16.95 (0-8369-3700-7) Ayer Co. Pubs., Inc.
Miles, John. A Most Deadly Retirement. 1997. per. (0-373-26252-3, 1-26252-6, Worldwide Library) Harlequin Enterprises, Ltd.
—A Most Deadly Retirement: A Laura Michaels Mystery. 1995. 246p. 22.95 (0-8027-3258-5) Walker & Co.
—Murder in Retirement. 1997. (WWL Mystery Ser.: No. 243). per. (0-373-26243-4, 1-26243-5, Worldwide Library) Harlequin Enterprises, Ltd.
—Murder in Retirement: A Laura Michaels Mystery. 1994. 246p. 19.95 (0-8027-3246-1) Walker & Co.
—A Permanent Retirement. 1997. (Laura Michaels Mystery Ser.). 256p. per. (0-373-26228-0, 1-26228-6, Worldwide Library) Harlequin Enterprises, Ltd.
—A Permanent Retirement. 1992. 230p. 19.95 (0-8027-1243-6) Walker & Co.
Mitchell, Alvan. Little Tom & Fats. Arrington, Veneta B., ed. 1987. (Illus.). 272p. reprint ed. 14.95 (0-9615098-2-1) Prairie Imprints.
Mitchell, Robert H. Ride the Lightning: A Novel. 1997. 304p. 26.95 (0-8061-2917-4) Univ. of Oklahoma Pr.
Morgan, Speer. The Freshour Cylinders. 2000. 345p. pap. 13.00 (1-878448-99-4); 1998. 245p. 23.00 (1-878448-84-6) MacMurray & Beck, Inc.
—The Whipping Boy. 1994. 326p. 21.95 o.p. (0-395-67725-4) Houghton Mifflin Co.
Morris, Gilbert. The Gallant Outlaw. 1994. (House of Winslow Ser.: No. 15). 288p. pap. 11.99 o.s.i (1-55661-311-3) Bethany Hse. Pubs.
Morrison, Toni. Paradise. 1999. 340p. pap. 13.95 (0-452-28039-7, Plume) Dutton/Plume.
—Paradise. l.t. ed. 1998. 26.95 o.p. (0-7838-8336-6, Macmillan Reference USA) Gale Group.
—Paradise. 1997. 320p. 25.00 (0-679-43374-0) Knopf, Alfred A. Inc.
—Paradise, Set. unabr. ed. 1997. audio 25.95 (0-375-40179-2, 690038, RH Audio) Random Hse. Audio Publishing Group.
—Paradise. enl. l.t. ed. 1997. 453p. pap. 25.00 (0-375-70217-2) Random Hse. Large Print.
—Paradise. unabr. ed. 1999. audio 90.00 (0-7887-3094-0, 95805E7) Recorded Bks., LLC.
—Paradise. 1999. 20.00 (0-606-15852-9) Turtleback Bks.
Moseley, Margaret. Bonita Faye. 1997. 240p. mass mkt. 5.99 o.s.i (0-06-101189-4, HarperTorch) Morrow/Avon.
—Bonita Faye. l.t. ed. 2001. (G. K. Hall Paperback Ser.). 307p. 24.95 (0-7838-9378-7) Thorndike Pr.
—Bonita Faye. 1996. 178p. 20.00 (0-9637629-4-X) Three Forks Pr.
Moss, Basil. Tales of the Wichitas. 1998. 224p. 25.95 (0-89672-390-9) Texas Tech Univ. Pr.
Myers, Anna. Captain's Command. 2001. 144p. (gr. 4-7). pap. text 4.50 (0-440-41699-X, Yearling) Random Hse. Children's Bks.
—When the Bough Breaks. 2000. 170p. (J). 16.95 (0-8027-8725-8) Walker & Co.
O'Nan, Stewart. The Speed Queen. 1997. 256p. 21.95 o.s.i (0-385-48701-0) Doubleday Publishing.
—The Speed Queen. 2001. 224p. 13.00 (0-8021-3853-5, Grove Pr.) Grove/Atlantic, Inc.
Orwig, Sara. Cowboy's Special Woman. 2002. (Silhouette Desire Ser.). 192p. mass mkt. (0-373-76449-9, Silhouette) Harlequin Enterprises, Ltd.
Palmer, Diana. Fit for a King. abr. ed. 2000. (Mira Bks.). audio 9.99 (1-55204-210-3) Durkin Hayes Publishing Ltd.
—Fit for a King. 2000. 256p. mass mkt. (1-55166-585-9, Mira Bks.); 1987. per. (0-373-05349-5, Harlequin Bks.) Harlequin Enterprises, Ltd.
Park, June. The Bingo Queens of Paradise. 1999. 288p. 24.00 (0-06-019312-3) HarperCollins Pubs.
—Bingo Queens of Paradise: A Novel. 2000. 288p. pap. 13.00 (0-06-093128-0, Perennial) HarperTrade.
Pointon, Bill. "Turn over a Rain Barrel" 2000. 444p. 24.95 (0-9704351-1-8) Epic OKC Pr. & Trust Co.
Pratt, James Michael. Ticket Home. l.t. ed. 2001. (Large Print Book Ser.). 399p. 28.95 (1-58724-004-1, Wheeler Publishing, Inc.) Gale Group.
—Ticket Home. 2002. 352p. mass mkt. 6.99 (0-312-97989-4, St. Martin's Paperbacks); 2001. 356p. 23.95 (0-312-26633-2) St. Martin's Pr.
Preston, M. K. Perhaps She'll Die. 2001. 218p. 23.95 (1-890768-33-2, Intrigue Pr.) Corvus Publishing.
—Perhaps She'll Die. 2002. (WWL Mystery Ser.). 256p. mass mkt. o.s.i (0-373-26430-5, Harlequin Bks.) Harlequin Enterprises, Ltd.
—Song of the Bones: A Chantalene Mystery. 2003. 300p. 24.95 (1-890768-54-5, Intrigue Pr.) Corvus Publishing.
Proulx, E. Annie. That Old Ace in the Hole: A Novel. 2003. 352p. pap. 12.00 (0-7432-4147-9); 2003. mass mkt. 7.99 (0-7432-4148-7); 2002. 384p. 26.00 (0-684-81307-6); 2002. 560p. 26.00 (0-7432-4092-8) Simon & Schuster. (Scribner).
Rawls, Wilson. Summer of the Monkeys. 1989. (J). lib. bdg. o.s.i (0-385-13004-X) Doubleday Publishing.
Red Corn, Charles H. A Pipe for February: A Novel. 2002. (American Indian Literature & Critical Studies: Vol. 44). (Illus.). 272p. 29.95 (0-8061-3454-2) Univ. of Oklahoma Pr.
Reed, Gary. Pryor Rendering. 288p. 1997. pap. 11.95 o.p. (0-452-27797-3, Plume); 1996. 20.95 o.s.i (0-525-94102-9, Dutton) Dutton/Plume.
Reiswig, Gary. Water Boy. 1993. 304p. 20.00 (0-671-79506-6, Simon & Schuster) Simon & Schuster.
Rhodes, Jewell P. Magic City. 1997. 288p. 23.00 o.p. (0-06-018732-8) HarperCollins Pubs.
Ross, Dana Fuller, pseud. Oklahoma Pride. 1990. (Holts: An American Dynasty Ser.: No. 2). 336p. mass mkt. 5.50 o.s.i (0-553-28446-0) Bantam Bks.
—Oklahoma Pride. l.t. ed. 1991. (General Ser.). lib. bdg. 20.95 o.p. (0-8161-5101-6, Macmillan Reference USA) Gale Group.
Russell, Helen D. Come in This House. 1982. 230p. (J). (gr. 6-12). lib. bdg. 15.95 (0-934188-07-6) Evans Pubns.
Russell, Sheldon. Requiem at Dawn. 2000. (Illus.). 416p. mass mkt. 5.99 o.s.i (0-7860-1103-3, Pinnacle Bks.) Kensington Publishing Corp.
Sabbeleu. Witch or Prophet? 1997. (Illus.). 100p. 20.00 (0-9653990-1-X) Whispering Willows, Ltd., Co.
Sanders, Leonard. Light on the Mountain. 1986. 376p. (Orig.). mass mkt. 3.95 o.s.i (0-553-25817-6) Bantam Bks.
Sanders, William. Blood Autumn. 1995. 272p. 21.00 o.p. (0-312-11755-8, Saint Martin's Minotaur) St. Martin's Pr.
—A Death on 66: A Taggart Roper Mystery. 1993. 256p. 20.95 o.p. (0-312-10452-9, Saint Martin's Minotaur) St. Martin's Pr.
—The Next Victim. 1993. 240p. 17.95 o.p. (0-312-08861-2, Saint Martin's Minotaur) St. Martin's Pr.
Sandstrom, Eve K. Death Down Home. 1990. 256p. 18.95 o.s.i (0-684-19244-6, Macmillan Reference USA) Gale Group.
—Death down Home. 1993. per. (0-373-26125-X, 1-26125-4, Harlequin Bks.) Harlequin Enterprises, Ltd.
—The Devil down Home. 1991. (Sam & Nicky Titus Mystery Ser.: No. 2). 256p. 19.95 o.s.i (0-684-19268-3, Macmillan Reference USA) Gale Group.
—The Devil down Home. 1994. per. (0-373-26139-X, Harlequin Bks.) Harlequin Enterprises, Ltd.
—Down Home Heifer Heist. 1994. per. (0-373-26153-5, 1-26153-6, Harlequin Bks.) Harlequin Enterprises, Ltd.
—Down Home Heifer Heist: A Sam & Nicky Titus Mystery. 1993. 256p. 20.00 o.p. (0-684-19428-7, Macmillan Reference USA) Gale Group.
—Homicide Report. 1998. 368p. mass mkt. 5.99 o.s.i (0-451-19034-3, Onyx) NAL.
—The Smoking Gun: A Nell Matthews Mystery. 2000. (Neil Matthews Mysteries Ser.). 240p. mass mkt. 5.99 o.s.i (0-451-19976-6, Signet Bks.) NAL.
—The Smoking Gun: A Nell Matthews Mystery. l.t. ed. 2000. (Mystery Ser.). 365p. 26.95 (0-7862-2977-2) Thorndike Pr.
—Violence Beat. 1997. 384p. mass mkt. 5.99 o.s.i (0-451-19033-5, Signet Bks.) NAL.
Sharpe, Jon. Oklahoma Ordeal. 1994. (Trailsman Ser.: No. 155). 176p. (Orig.). mass mkt. 3.99 o.s.i (0-451-17891-2) NAL.
Shaw, P. B. The Seraphim Kill: A Lt. Abe Rainfinch Mystery. 1994. 224p. 21.95 (0-8027-3181-3) Walker & Co.
Shayne. Brand New Heartache. 2001. (Oklahoma All Girl Brands Ser.). mass mkt. (0-373-27187-5, Harlequin Bks.) Harlequin Enterprises, Ltd.
Smythe, Sheridon. A Perfect Fit. 2000. (Time of Your Life Ser.). 400p. mass mkt. 5.99 (0-505-52402-3, Love Spell) Dorchester Publishing Co., Inc.
Taylor, Robert L. The Lost Sister. 1989. 288p. 17.95 o.p. (0-945575-10-6) Algonquin Bks. of Chapel Hill.
Tharp, Tim. Falling Dark. 1999. 256p. 21.95 (1-57131-030-4) Milkweed Editions.
—Falling Dark: A Novel. 2001. 256p. reprint ed. pap. 13.95 (1-57131-034-7) Milkweed Editions.
Thomas, Joyce Carol. House of Light: A Novel. 2001. 273p. 22.95 (0-7868-6606-3) Hyperion Pr.
Thompson, Jim. Cropper's Cabin. 1992. 160p. pap. 15.00 (0-679-73315-9, Vintage) Knopf Publishing Group.
Whitworth, Artie. Turkey John. 1996. (Illus.). 175p. (J). 25.25 (1-56763-190-8); pap. 4.95 o.p. (1-56763-191-6) Ozark Publishing.
Williams, Jeanne. Home Station. 1995. 336p. 22.95 o.p. (0-312-13512-2) St. Martin's Pr.
—Home Station. 2000. 336p. pap. 19.95 (0-595-00447-4, Backinprint.com) iUniverse, Inc.

### OKLAHOMA CITY (OKLA.)—FICTION

Dillen, Frederick G. Fool. 1999. 302p. tchr. ed. 23.95 (1-56512-234-8) Algonquin Bks. of Chapel Hill.
Larsen, Jodie. Deadly Silence. 1997. 416p. mass mkt. 5.99 o.s.i (0-451-40786-5, Onyx) NAL.

### OLIVER (IND.: IMAGINARY PLACE)—FICTION

Frommer, Sara H. Buried in Quilts. 1996. (WWL Mystery Ser.). per. (0-373-26204-3, 1-26204-7, Worldwide Library) Harlequin Enterprises, Ltd.
—Buried in Quilts. 1994. (Joan Spencer Mystery Ser.). 224p. 19.95 o.p. (0-312-11472-9, Saint Martin's Minotaur) St. Martin's Pr.
—Murder & Sullivan: A Joan Spencer Mystery. 1998. (WWL Mystery Ser.). per. (0-373-26285-X, 1-26285-6, Worldwide Library) Harlequin Enterprises, Ltd.
—Murder & Sullivan: A Joan Spencer Mystery. 1997. 256p. 21.95 o.p. (0-312-15595-6, Saint Martin's Minotaur) St. Martin's Pr.
—Murder in C Major. 1988. 224p. reprint ed. spiral bd. (0-373-26017-2, Harlequin Bks.) Harlequin Enterprises, Ltd.
—Murder in C Major. 2000. (Missing Mysteries Ser.: Vol. 17). 183p. pap. 14.95 (1-890208-31-0) Poisoned Pen Pr.
—Murder in C Major. 1986. 240p. 14.95 o.p. (0-312-55299-8) St. Martin's Pr.
—Murder in C Major. l.t. ed. 2003. 331p. 24.95 (0-7862-5987-6) Thorndike Pr.
—The Vanishing Violinist. 2000. (WWL Mystery Ser.: No. 359). 256p. mass mkt. (0-373-26359-7, 1-26359-9, Worldwide Library) Harlequin Enterprises, Ltd.
—The Vanishing Violinist: A Joan Spencer Mystery. 2nd ed. 1999. 272p. 23.95 (0-312-24104-6, Saint Martin's Minotaur) St. Martin's Pr.
Outlet Book Company Staff. Murder in C Major. 1987. 1.99 o.p. (0-517-65735-X) Random Hse. Value Publishing.

### OMAHA (NEB.)—FICTION

Dooling, Richard. Bet Your Life. 2002. 352p. 25.95 (0-06-050539-7) HarperCollins Pubs.
—Bet Your Life. 2003. 352p. pap. 13.95 (0-06-050540-0, Perennial) HarperTrade.
Kirk, Diana. A Caduceus Is for Killing. 1998. E-Book 5.50 (1-58200-183-9) Hard Shell Word Factory.
Ludlum, Robert. The Road to Omaha. 1993. 608p. mass mkt. 7.99 (0-553-56044-1) Bantam Bks.
Reynolds, William J. Drive-By: A Nebraska Mystery. Emmel, Gayle, ed. 1995. 329p. pap. 5.95 (0-944287-14-X) Ex Machina.
Sherwood, Ben. The Man Who Ate the 747. unabr. ed. 2000. audio compact disk 29.95 o.s.i (0-553-71225-X, RH Audio) Random Hse. Audio Publishing Group.

### ONTARIO—FICTION

Alexis, Andre. Childhood. 1997. 256p. pap. 13.95 o.p. (0-88910-505-7) Consortium Bk. Sales & Distribution.
—Childhood. 2000. 272p. pap. 14.00 o.s.i (0-8050-5982-2, Owl Bks.); 1998. 256p. 23.00 o.s.i (0-8050-5981-4) Holt, Henry & Co.
—Despair: And Other Stories of Ottawa. 2000. 212p. 23.00 o.s.i (0-8050-5979-2) Holt, Henry & Co.
Aubert, Rosemary. The Feast of Stephen. 2001. 272p. mass mkt. 6.99 o.s.i (0-425-17799-8, Prime Crime) Berkley Publishing Group.
—The Feast of Stephen: An Ellis Portal Mystery. 1999. (Ellis Portal Mystery Ser.). 224p. 22.95 (1-882593-27-8) Bridge Works Publishing Co., Inc.
—Free Reign. 1998. 304p. mass mkt. 6.99 o.s.i (0-425-16427-6) Berkley Publishing Group.
—Free Reign: A Suspense Novel. 1997. (Ellis Portal Mystery Ser.). 240p. 21.95 o.s.i (1-882593-18-9) Bridge Works Publishing Co., Inc.
Bemrose, John. The Island Walkers. 2004. 464p. 25.00 (0-8050-7411-2, Metropolitan Bks.) Holt, Henry & Co.
—The Island Walkers. 2003. 504p. (0-7710-1111-3) McClelland & Stewart.
Blunt, Giles. The Delicate Storm. 2003. 320p. 24.95 (0-399-14865-5, G. P. Putnam's Sons) Penguin Putnam Bks. for Young Readers.
—Forty Words for Sorrow. 2002. 368p. mass mkt. 6.99 o.s.i (0-425-18516-8) Berkley Publishing Group.
—Forty Words for Sorrow. 2001. 384p. 24.95 o.p. (0-399-14752-7, Wood, Marian Bks.) Penguin Group (USA) Inc.
Burgess, Tony. Caesarea. 1999. 246p. pap. (1-55022-381-X) ECW Pr.
Cohen, Matt. Elizabeth & After. 2000. 384p. 25.00 o.s.i (0-312-26151-9) Picador.
Craig, Alisa, pseud. The Grub & Stakers House a Haunt. l.t. ed. 1994. 21.95 o.p. (0-7927-1919-0); pap. 19.95 o.p. (0-7927-1918-2) BBC Audiobooks America.
—The Grub & Stakers House a Haunt. 224p. 1994. pap. 4.99 (0-380-71044-7, Avon Bks.); 1993. 18.00 o.p. (0-688-08644-6, Morrow, William & Co.) Morrow/Avon.
—The Grub-&-Stakers Move a Mountain. 1981. (Crime Club Ser.). 192p. 10.95 o.p. (0-385-17411-X) Doubleday Publishing.
—The Grub-&-Stakers Move a Mountain. 1987. 192p. pap. 3.50 o.p. (0-380-70331-9, Avon Bks.) Morrow/Avon.
—The Grub-&-Stakers Move a Mountain. l.t. ed. 1981. 332p. reprint ed. 9.95 o.p. (0-89621-288-2) Thorndike Pr.
—The Grub-&-Stakers Pinch a Poke. 1988. (Illus.). 208p. (Orig.). pap. 3.50 (0-380-75538-6, Avon Bks.) Morrow/Avon.
—The Grub-&-Stakers Quilt a Bee. 1985. (Crime Club Ser.). 192p. 11.95 o.p. (0-385-19767-5) Doubleday Publishing.
—The Grub-&-Stakers Quilt a Bee. 1987. 192p. pap. 3.50 (0-380-70337-8, Avon Bks.) Morrow/Avon.
—The Grub-&-Stakers Spin a Yarn. 1990. 224p. pap. 3.50 (0-380-75540-8, Avon Bks.) Morrow/Avon.
Den Hartog, Kristen. Water Wings. 2001. 240p. o.s.i (0-676-97289-6) Knopf, Alfred A. Inc.
—Water Wings. 2004. 23.00 (1-931561-61-3) MacAdam/Cage Publishing, Inc.
Drew, Wayland. The Wabeno Feast: A Novel. 2001. 296p. pap. 15.95 (0-88784-663-7) House of Anansi Pr. CAN. *Dist:* General Distribution Services, Inc.
Echlin, Kim. Elephant Winter. 1999. 206p. 22.00 (0-7867-0610-4, Carroll & Graf Pubs.) Avalon Publishing Group.

Engel, Howard. A City Called July. 1988. 39.50 o.p. (*0-14-778233-3*) Penguin Group (USA) Inc.

—A City Called July. 1986. 256p. 15.95 o.p. (*0-312-13986-1*) St. Martin's Pr.

—A City Called July. l.t. ed. 1989. (Ulverscroft Large Print Ser.). 481p. 29.99 o.p. (*0-7089-1957-X*, Ulverscroft) Thorpe, F. A. Pubs. GBR. *Dist:* Ulverscroft Large Print Bks., Ltd., Ulverscroft Large Print Canada, Ltd.

—A City Called July. 1988. 228p. pap. 3.95 o.p. (*0-14-010454-2*, Penguin Bks.) Viking Penguin.

—Dead & Buried. 290p. 2003. pap. 14.95 (*1-58567-281-5*); 2001. 24.95 (*1-58567-155-X*) Overlook Pr., The.

—Dead & Buried. l.t. ed. 2001. (Core Ser.). 394p. 28.95 (*0-7838-9659-X*) Thorndike Pr.

—Getting Away with Murder. 1998. (Benny Cooperman Mystery Ser.). 248p. 22.95 (*0-87951-829-4*) Overlook Pr., The.

—Murder on Location. 1986. 35.00 o.p. (*0-14-779206-1*) Penguin Group (USA) Inc.

—Murder on Location. 1985. 222p. 12.95 o.p. (*0-312-55314-5*) St. Martin's Pr.

—Murder on Location. 1986. (Crime Monthly Ser.). 222p. pap. 3.50 o.p. (*0-14-007742-1*, Penguin Bks.) Viking Penguin.

—Murder Sees the Light: A Benny Cooperman Mystery. 1985. 256p. 13.95 o.p. (*0-312-55324-2*) St. Martin's Pr.

—Murder Sees the Light: A Benny Cooperman Mystery. l.t. ed. 1988. (Ulverscroft Large Print Ser.). 432p. 29.99 o.p. (*0-7089-1911-1*, Ulverscroft) Thorpe, F. A. Pubs. GBR. *Dist:* Ulverscroft Large Print Bks., Ltd., Ulverscroft Large Print Canada, Ltd.

—Murder Sees the Light: A Benny Cooperman Mystery. 1986. 240p. pap. 3.50 o.p. (*0-14-008975-6*, Penguin Bks.) Viking Penguin.

—The Ransom Game. 1984. 218p. 11.95 o.p. (*0-312-66383-8*) St. Martin's Pr.

—The Ransom Game. l.t. ed. 1989. (Ulverscroft Large Print Ser.). 29.99 o.p. (*0-7089-2052-7*, Ulverscroft) Thorpe, F. A. Pubs. GBR. *Dist:* Ulverscroft Large Print Bks., Ltd., Ulverscroft Large Print Canada, Ltd.

—The Ransom Game. 1986. (Crime Monthly Ser.). 224p. pap. 3.95 o.p. (*0-14-007741-3*, Penguin Bks.) Viking Penguin.

—The Suicide Murders. l.t. ed. 1987. pap. 13.95 o.p. (*1-55504-257-0*) BBC Audiobooks America.

—The Suicide Murders. 1984. 200p. 11.95 o.p. (*0-312-77527-X*) St. Martin's Pr.

—The Suicide Murders. 1985. (Crime Ser.). 208p. pap. 3.95 o.p. (*0-14-007740-5*, Penguin Bks.) Viking Penguin.

—There Was an Old Woman. 2000. (Benny Cooperman Mystery Ser.). 262p. 24.95 (*1-58567-044-8*) Overlook Pr., The.

—A Victim Must Be Found: A Benny Cooperman Mystery. l.t. ed. 1989. 383p. lib. bdg. 17.95 o.p. (*1-85057-734-X*, Macmillan Reference USA) Gale Group.

—A Victim Must Be Found: A Benny Cooperman Mystery. 1988. 288p. 16.95 o.p. (*0-312-02315-4*, Saint Martin's Minotaur) St. Martin's Pr.

—A Victim Must Be Found: A Benny Cooperman Mystery. 1990. 288p. pap. 3.95 o.p. (*0-14-011205-7*, Penguin Bks.) Viking Penguin.

Findley, Timothy. The Piano Man's Daughter. 1996. 480p. 26.00 o.s.i (*0-517-70307-6*, Crown) Crown Publishing Group.

—The Piano Man's Daughter. 2002. 512p. pap. 14.95 (*0-06-093643-6*, Perennial) HarperTrade.

—Spadework: A Novel. 416p. 2003. pap. 13.95 (*0-06-093262-7*); 2002. 24.95 (*0-06-019472-3*) HarperCollins Pubs.

Gear, Kathleen O'Neal & Gear, W. Michael. People of the Masks. 1999. mass mkt. 125.82 (*0-8125-7624-1*); 1999. (Illus.). 552p. mass mkt. 6.99 (*0-8125-1561-7*, Tor Bks.); 1998. (Illus.). 416p. 25.95 (*0-312-85857-4*, Forge Bks.) Doherty, Tom Assocs., LLC.

Gibson, Graeme. Gentleman Death. 1995. 256p. pap. 12.95 (*0-7710-3312-5*) McClelland & Stewart/Tundra Bks.

—Perpetual Motion. 1998. (New Canadian Library). 272p. mass mkt. 8.95 (*0-7710-3462-8*) McClelland & Stewart/Tundra Bks.

—Perpetual Motion. 1983. 283p. 12.95 o.p. (*0-312-60132-8*) St. Martin's Pr.

—Perpetual Motion. 1988. 288p. pap. 6.95 o.p. (*0-14-010382-1*, Penguin Bks.) Viking Penguin.

Giroux, E. X. The Dying Room. 1993. 288p. 19.95 o.p. (*0-312-09791-3*, Saint Martin's Minotaur) St. Martin's Pr.

Hamilton, Steve. Blood Is the Sky: An Alex McKnight Mystery. 2003. 304p. 21.95 (*0-312-30115-4*, Saint Martin's Minotaur) St. Martin's Pr.

Huff, Tanya. Blood Pact. 1993. (Daw Book Collectors Ser.: Vol. 931). 336p. mass mkt. 5.99 o.s.i (*0-88677-582-5*) DAW Bks., Inc.

—Blood Price. 1991. (Daw Book Collectors Ser.: Vol. 850). 272p. (Orig.). mass mkt. 6.99 (*0-88677-471-3*) DAW Bks., Inc.

Itani, Frances. Deafening: A Novel. l.t. ed. 2003. 639p. 29.95 (*0-7862-6010-6*) Gale Group.

—Deafening: A Novel. 2003. 368p. 24.00 (*0-87113-902-2*, Atlantic Monthly Pr.) Grove/Atlantic, Inc.

Jennings, Maureen. Let Loose the Dogs: A Mystery. Date not set. pap. (*0-312-30752-7*, Saint Martin's Griffin); E-Book (*0-312-70575-1*); 2003. 320p. 24.95 (*0-312-30751-9*, Saint Martin's Minotaur) St. Martin's Pr.

—Poor Tom Is Cold. E-Book 23.95 (*1-58945-671-8*) Adobe Systems, Inc.

—Poor Tom Is Cold. E-Book 23.95 (*0-312-70097-0*); 2001. vii, 278p. 23.95 (*0-312-26892-0*, Saint Martin's Minotaur) St. Martin's Pr.

Knowles, G. North with Doc. 1993. pap. 11.95 (*0-929384-40-7*) In-Fisherman, Inc.

Kosar, Richelle. The Drum King. 1998. 416p. pap. 15.95 (*0-88801-220-9*) Turnstone Pr. CAN. *Dist:* General Distribution Services, Inc.

Lansens, Lori. Rush Home Road. 2002. 400p. 23.95 o.p. (*0-316-06902-7*) Little Brown & Co.

Lawson, Mary. Crow Lake: A Novel. 304p. 2003. pap. 12.95 (*0-385-33613-6*, Delta); 2002. 23.95 o.s.i (*0-385-33611-X*, Dial Bks.) Dell Publishing.

MacDonald, Ann-Marie. The Way the Crow Flies. 2003. 736p. 26.95 (*0-06-057895-5*); pap. (*0-06-058637-0*); 242.55 (*0-06-057902-1*); 322.45 (*0-06-057903-X*); audio 39.95 (*0-06-057896-3*) HarperCollins Pubs.

Mestern, Pat Mattaini. Magdalena's Song. 2003. (Illus.). 270p. 16.95 (*0-9713045-8-0*) High Country Pubs., Ltd.

Munro, Alice. Friend of My Youth. unabr. ed. 1990. 16.00 o.s.i incl. audio (*0-394-58486-4*, RH Audio) Random Hse. Audio Publishing Group.

—Friend of My Youth. 1991. (Vintage Contemporaries Ser.). 288p. pap. 13.00 (*0-679-72957-7*) Random Hse., Inc.

Prince, Althea. Loving This Man. 2002. 200p. pap. 15.95 (*1-894663-06-3*) Insomniac Pr. CAN. *Dist:* Strauss Consultants.

Reaney, James. The Box Social & Other Stories. 1996. 160p. pap. (*0-88984-173-X*) Porcupine's Quill, Inc.

Ricci, Nino. Where She Has Gone. 336p. 1999. pap. 13.00 o.s.i (*0-312-20681-X*); 1998. 25.00 o.p. (*0-312-18700-9*) Picador.

Ross, Veronica. The Anastasia Connection. 204p. pap. 15.95 (*1-55128-038-8*) Mercury Bks. CAN. *Dist:* LPC/InBook.

—Millicent: A Mystery. 2001. 256p. pap. 7.99 (*1-55128-042-6*) Mercury Bks. CAN. *Dist:* LPC/InBook.

Sale, Medora. Murder in a Good Cause. 1990. 224p. 18.95 o.s.i (*0-684-19216-0*) Macmillan Information.

—Murder in Focus. 1989. 288p. 17.95 o.s.i (*0-684-19082-6*, Macmillan Reference USA) Gale Group.

—Murder on the Run. unabr. ed. 1998. (Inspector John Sanders Mystery Ser.). audio 39.95 (*1-55686-825-1*) Books in Motion.

—Pursued by Shadows. 1992. (Inspector John Sanders Mystery Ser.). 256p. text 20.00 (*0-684-19505-4*, Scribner) Simon & Schuster.

—Shortcut to Santa Fe. 1994. 256p. 20.00 (*0-684-19680-8*, Scribner) Simon & Schuster.

—Sleep of the Innocent. unabr. ed. 1999. (Inspector John Sanders Mystery Ser.). audio 49.95 (*1-55686-906-1*) Books in Motion.

—Sleep of the Innocent. 1991. 256p. 18.95 o.s.i (*0-684-19305-1*, Scribner) Simon & Schuster.

Schoemperlen, Diane. In the Language of Love: A Novel in 100 Chapters. 1996. 368p. 23.95 o.p. (*0-670-86517-6*, Viking) Viking Penguin.

Schulman, Audrey. A House Named Brazil. 2001. 320p. pap. 13.95 (*0-380-80880-3*, Perennial) HarperTrade.

—A House Named Brazil. 2000. (Illus.). 301p. 23.00 (*0-380-97799-0*, Morrow, William & Co.) Morrow/Avon.

Shields, Carol. Small Ceremonies. l.t. ed. 1996. (G. K. Hall Core Ser.). 241p. lib. bdg. 24.95 (*0-7838-1830-0*, Macmillan Reference USA) Gale Group.

—Small Ceremonies. 1976. text 7.95 o.p. (*0-07-082340-5*) McGraw-Hill Cos., The.

—Small Ceremonies. 1996. 194p. pap. 12.00 (*0-14-025145-6*, Penguin Bks.) Penguin Group (USA) Inc.

—Unless: A Novel. 2003. 336p. pap. 13.95 (*0-00-715461-5*); 2002. (Illus.). 224p. 24.95 (*0-00-714107-6*) HarperTrade. (Fourth Estate).

—Unless: A Novel. l.t. ed. 2002. (Basic Ser.). 29.95 (*0-7862-4599-9*) Thorndike Pr.

Sileika, Antanas. Buying on Time. 1997. 240p. pap. (*0-88984-186-1*) Porcupine's Quill, Inc.

Slipperjack, Ruby. Weesquachak & the Lost Ones. 2000. 203p. (C). pap. 15.95 (*0-919441-88-2*) Theytus Bks., Ltd. CAN. *Dist:* Orca Bk. Pubs.

Stollman, Aryeh L. Far Euphrates: A Novel. 1998. 224p. 14.00 (*1-57322-697-1*, Riverhead Trade (Paperbacks)) Berkley Publishing Group.

Stollman, Aryeh Lev. Far Euphrates: A Novel. 1997. 224p. 21.95 o.s.i (*1-57322-075-2*, Riverhead Bks. (Hardcovers)) Putnam Publishing Group, The.

Urquhart, Jane. The Stone Carvers. 2003. 400p. pap. 14.00 (*0-14-200358-1*) Penguin Group (USA) Inc.

—The Stone Carvers. 2002. 400p. 25.95 (*0-670-03044-9*, Viking) Viking Penguin.

Ward, Gregory. Water Damage. 1992. 320p. (*0-316-92233-1*) Little Brown & Co.

Watt, Kelly. Mad Dog. 208p. 2002. pap. (*0-385-25768-6*, Anchor Canada); 2001. o.s.i (*0-385-25761-9*) Doubleday Canada, Ltd. CAN. *Dist:* Random Hse., Inc., Random Hse. of Canada, Ltd., Random Hse., Inc.

Wood, Ted. Corkscrew. 1987. (Reid Bennett Mystery Ser.). 240p. 14.95 o.p. (*0-684-18853-8*, Macmillan Reference USA) Gale Group.

—Corkscrew. 1989. 224p. reprint ed. mass mkt. (*0-373-26024-5*, Harlequin Bks.) Harlequin Enterprises, Ltd.

—Corkscrew. 2001. E-Book 6.99 (*0-7592-1043-8*); 1999. 188p. per. 19.95 (*1-58586-863-9*) ereads.com.

—Dead in the Water. 1984. 160p. mass mkt. 2.95 o.s.i (*0-7704-2006-0*) Bantam Bks.

—Flashback. l.t. ed. 1994. 21.95 o.p. (*0-7927-1819-4*); pap. 19.95 o.p. (*0-7927-1818-6*) BBC Audiobooks America.

—Flashback. 1992. 256p. text 20.00 (*0-684-19414-7*, Macmillan Reference USA) Gale Group.

—Flashback. 1994. (WWL Mystery Ser.). per. (*0-373-26137-3*, 1-26137-9, Harlequin Bks.) Harlequin Enterprises, Ltd.

—Fool's Gold. 1986. 192p. 13.95 o.s.i (*0-684-18568-7*, Macmillan Reference USA) Gale Group.

—Fool's Gold. 1988. 224p. reprint ed. mass mkt. (*0-373-26019-9*, Harlequin Bks.) Harlequin Enterprises, Ltd.

—Live Bait. 1986. (Mystery Ser.). 208p. mass mkt. 2.95 o.s.i (*0-553-25558-4*) Bantam Bks.

—Live Bait. 1985. 192p. 12.95 o.s.i (*0-684-18330-7*, Macmillan Reference USA) Gale Group.

—Live Bait. 2002. 174p. pap. 6.99 (*1-58586-855-8*); E-Book 6.99 (*1-58586-852-3*); E-Book 6.99 (*0-7592-1039-X*); E-Book 6.99 (*0-7592-0395-4*) ereads.com.

—Murder on Ice. 1985. 176p. mass mkt. 2.95 o.s.i (*0-7704-2049-4*) Bantam Bks.

—Murder on Ice. 1984. 160p. 12.95 o.s.i (*0-684-18134-7*, Macmillan Reference USA) Gale Group.

—On the Inside: A Reid Bennett Mystery. 1990. 256p. 18.95 o.s.i (*0-684-19090-7*, Macmillan Reference USA) Gale Group.

—On the Inside: A Reid Bennett Mystery. 1991. 224p. reprint ed. pap. (*0-373-26076-8*, Harlequin Bks.) Harlequin Enterprises, Ltd.

—When the Killing Starts. 1990. mass mkt. (*0-373-26043-1*, Harlequin Bks.) Harlequin Enterprises, Ltd.

—When the Killing Starts. 1989. 224p. 16.95 o.s.i (*0-684-18331-5*, Scribner) Simon & Schuster.

Wright, Eric. Buried in Stone: A Mel Pickett Mystery. 1997. 256p. mass mkt. 7.99 (*0-7704-2741-3*) Bantam Bks.

—Buried in Stone: A Mel Pickett Mystery. 1996. 256p. 24.95 o.p. (*0-385-25518-7*) Doubleday Publishing.

—Buried in Stone: A Mel Pickett Mystery. 1998. (WWL Mystery Ser.). per. (*0-373-26286-8*, 1-26286-4, Worldwide Library) Harlequin Enterprises, Ltd.

—Buried in Stone: A Mel Pickett Mystery. 1996. 256p. 20.00 (*0-684-81304-1*, Scribner) Simon & Schuster.

—Death of a Hired Man. 2001. E-Book 22.95 (*1-58945-725-0*) Adobe Systems, Inc.

—Death of a Hired Man. l.t. ed. 24.95 (*1-58724-250-8*) Gale Group.

—Death of a Hired Man. E-Book 22.95 (*0-312-70110-1*); 2001. 197p. 22.95 (*0-312-26876-9*, Saint Martin's Minotaur) St. Martin's Pr.

Wright, Richard B. Clara Callan: A Novel. 2002. 432p. 25.95 (*0-06-050606-7*) HarperCollins Pubs.

—Clara Callan: A Novel. 2003. 432p. pap. 13.95 (*0-06-050607-5*, Perennial) HarperTrade.

## OOLSMOUTH (IMAGINARY PLACE)—FICTION

Brenner, Mayer A. Catastrophe's Spell. 1989. (Dance of Gods Ser.: 1). 320p. mass mkt. 4.99 o.p. (*0-88677-357-1*) DAW Bks., Inc.

—Spell of Apocalypse. 1994. (Dance of Gods Ser.: 4). 320p. (Orig.). mass mkt. 4.99 o.p. (*0-88677-602-3*) DAW Bks., Inc.

—Spell of Fate. 1992. (Dance of Gods Ser.: 3). 432p. (Orig.). mass mkt. 4.99 o.p. (*0-88677-508-6*) DAW Bks., Inc.

—Spell of Intrigue. 1990. (Dance of Gods Ser.: 2). 336p. mass mkt. 4.50 o.p. (*0-88677-453-5*) DAW Bks., Inc.

## ORAN (IMAGINARY PLACE)—FICTION

Snyder, Midori. Beldan's Fire. 1993. 378p. mass mkt. 4.99 (*0-8125-0913-7*, Tor Bks.) Doherty, Tom Assocs., LLC.

—New Moon. 1989. mass mkt. 3.95 o.s.i (*0-441-57179-4*) Ace Bks.

—Sadar's Keep. 1991. pap. 3.95 o.p. (*0-8125-0912-9*, Tor Bks.) Doherty, Tom Assocs., LLC.

## ORANGE COUNTY (CALIF.)—FICTION

Ayres, Noreen. Carcass Trade. unabr. ed. 1995. audio 56.00 (*0-7366-2934-3*, 3630) Books on Tape, Inc.

—Carcass Trade. 1994. 285p. 20.00 o.p. (*0-688-10875-X*, Morrow, William & Co.); 1995. 352p. reprint ed. mass mkt. 4.99 o.p. (*0-380-71572-4*, Avon Bks.) Morrow/Avon.

—A World the Color of Salt. unabr. ed. 1992. audio 32.00 (*0-7366-2321-3*, 3101) Books on Tape, Inc.

—A World the Color of Salt. 1993. 304p. mass mkt. 4.99 (*0-380-71571-6*, Avon Bks.); 1992. 352p. 19.00 o.p. (*0-688-10824-5*, Morrow, William & Co.) Morrow/Avon.

Board, Sherri L. Angels of Anguish. 1999. (Katlin Lamar Mystery Ser.). 304p. pap. 11.95 (*0-9634767-5-0*) Crime-Zone Bks.

—Blind Belief. 2002. ("A Katlin LaMar Mystery" —Cover Ser.). 284p. pap. 12.95 (*0-9705049-6-9*) Avocet Pr., Inc.

O'Callaghan, Maxine. Death Is Forever. l.t. ed. 1999. (Five Star Mystery Ser.). 205p. 19.95 o.p. (*0-7862-1729-4*, Five Star) Gale Group.

—Down for the Count: A Delilah West Novel. 1998. (WWL Mystery Ser.: No. 294). per. (*0-373-26294-9*, 0-26294-9, Worldwide Library) Harlequin Enterprises, Ltd.

—Down for the Count: A Delilah West Novel. 1997. (Delilah West Mystery Ser.: Vol. 60). 240p. 20.95 (*0-312-16820-9*, Saint Martin's Minotaur) St. Martin's Pr.

—Down for the Count: A Delilah West Novel. l.t. ed. 1998. (Mystery Ser.). 307p. 26.95 (*0-7838-8404-4*) Thorndike Pr.

—Hit & Run. 1991. pap. 3.95 o.p. (*0-312-92440-2*, St. Martin's Paperbacks); 1989. 192p. 14.95 o.p. (*0-312-02584-X*, Saint Martin's Minotaur) St. Martin's Pr.

—Set-Up: A Delilah West Mystery. 1994. mass mkt. (*0-373-26144-6*, Harlequin Bks.) Harlequin Enterprises, Ltd.

—Set-Up: A Delilah West Mystery. 1991. 208p. 18.95 o.p. (*0-312-06462-4*, Saint Martin's Minotaur) St. Martin's Pr.

—Trade-Off. 1996. (Mystery Ser.). per. (*0-373-26191-8*, 1-26191-6, Worldwide Library) Harlequin Enterprises, Ltd.

—Trade-Off. 1994. 224p. 19.95 o.p. (*0-312-11081-2*, Saint Martin's Minotaur) St. Martin's Pr.

Parker, T. Jefferson. The Blue Hour. unabr. ed. 1999. audio 64.00 (*0-7366-4563-2*, 4970) Books on Tape, Inc.

—The Blue Hour. aut. ltd. ed. 1999. 384p. 23.95 (*0-7868-6559-8*) Disney Pr.

—The Blue Hour, Set. abr. ed. 1999. audio 25.00 Highsmith Inc.

—The Blue Hour. 1999. 359p. 23.95 (*0-7868-6288-2*); 2003. 480p. reprint ed. mass mkt. 7.99 (*0-7868-8969-1*) Hyperion Pr.

—The Blue Hour. abr. ed. 1999. audio 26.95 (*0-7871-1935-0*); audio 39.95 (*0-7871-1938-5*) NewStar Media, Inc. (Dove Audio).

—The Blue Hour. l.t. ed. 1999. (Americana Ser.). 597p. 29.95 (*0-7862-2164-X*) Thorndike Pr.

—Where Serpents Lie. 1999. mass mkt. 6.99 (*0-7868-8949-7*); 2003. 576p. reprint ed. mass mkt. 7.50 (*0-7868-8944-6*) Hyperion Pr.

—Where Serpents Lie. l.t. ed. 1998. (Cloak & Dagger Ser.). 655p. 28.95 (*0-7862-1526-7*) Thorndike Pr.

Winslow, Don. California Fire & Life. unabr. ed. 1999. audio 80.00 (*0-7887-3770-8*, 95987E7, Clipper Audio) Recorded Bks., LLC.

## ORCHARD VALLEY (IMAGINARY PLACE)—FICTION

Macomber, Debbie. Norah. 1992. pap. (*0-373-03244-7*, 1-03244-0, Harlequin Bks.) Harlequin Enterprises, Ltd.

—Stephanie. 1992. per. (*0-373-03239-0*, 1-03239-0, Harlequin Bks.) Harlequin Enterprises, Ltd.

—Valerie. 1992. (Harlequin Romance Ser.). pap. (*0-373-03232-3*, 1-03232-5, Harlequin Bks.) Harlequin Enterprises, Ltd.

## OREGON—FICTION

Adleman, Robert H. Sweetwater Fever. 1984. 500p. text 16.95 o.p. (*0-07-000354-8*) McGraw-Hill Cos., The.

Alcorn, Randy. Dominion. 2003. 612p. pap. 14.99 (*1-57673-661-X*, Multnomah Bks.); 2003. audio 24.99 (*1-57673-682-2*); 1986. 612p. pap. 14.99 o.p. (*0-88070-939-1*, Multnomah Bks.) Multnomah Pubs., Inc.

Anderson, Kent. Night Dogs. 1999. 544p. reprint ed. mass mkt. 6.99 (*0-553-57877-4*) Bantam Bks.

—Night Dogs. 1996. (Illus.). 544p. 35.00 o.p. (*0-939767-27-9*); 150.00 o.p. (*0-939767-28-7*) McMillan, Dennis Pubns.

Settings

Angus, John. The Monster Squad. 1994. 304p. 20.95 o.p. (*0-312-11319-6*, Saint Martin's Minotaur) St. Martin's Pr.

Bacher, June M. Love Follows the Heart. l.t. ed. 1991. 352p. (Orig.). pap. 14.95 o.p. (*0-8027-2662-3*, Walker Large Print) Gale Group.

—Love Follows the Heart. 1990. (Orig.). pap. 6.99 o.p. (*0-89081-748-0*) Harvest Hse. Pubs.

Bailey, Margaret J. The Grains or Passages in the Life of Ruth Rover, with Occasional Pictures of Oregon, Natural & Moral. Leasher, Evelyn & Frank, Robert J., eds. 1986. (Illus.). 352p. reprint ed. 29.95 (*0-87071-346-9*) Oregon State Univ. Pr.

Ball, Karen. The Breaking Point. 2003. 400p. pap. 12.99 (*1-59052-033-5*) Multnomah Pubs., Inc.

Beck, K. K. Death in a Deck Chair. 1987. 176p. mass mkt. 4.99 o.s.i (*0-8041-0118-3*, Ivy Bks.) Ballantine Bks.

—Death in a Deck Chair. 1984. 12.95 (*0-8027-5601-8*) Walker & Co.

—Murder in a Mummy Case. l.t. ed. 1989. 8.95 o.p. (*0-7451-9460-5*, 352); pap. 8.95 o.p. (*1-55504-841-2*) BBC Audiobooks America.

—Peril under the Palms. 1990. 176p. mass mkt. 4.99 o.s.i (*0-8041-0594-4*, Ivy Bks.) Ballantine Bks.

—Peril under the Palms. 1989. 208p. 18.95 (*0-8027-5715-4*) Walker & Co.

Bickmore, Barbara. Beyond the Promise. l.t. ed. 1997. 25.95 (*1-57490-129-X*, Beeler Large Print Bks.) Beeler, Thomas T. Publisher.

—Beyond the Promise. 1998. 480p. mass mkt. 6.99 o.s.i (*1-57566-329-5*); 1997. 384p. 23.00 o.s.i (*1-57566-220-5*) Kensington Publishing Corp.

Billings, Andrew. Tainted Blood. 1997. 544p. mass mkt. 6.99 o.s.i (*0-515-12046-4*, Jove) Berkley Publishing Group.

Biondello, Sal. A Pebble Cast. 2002. (Five Star First Edition Women's Fiction Ser.). (Illus.). 347p. 25.95 (*0-7862-4521-2*, Five Star) Gale Group.

Blake, Michelle. The Tentmaker. 2000. (Lily Connor Mysteries Ser.). 304p. reprint ed. mass mkt. 5.99 (*0-425-17668-1*) Berkley Publishing Group.

Block, Lawrence. Hit Man. 2003. E-Book 7.50 (*0-06-058167-0*) HarperCollins Pubs.

—Hit Man. 1999. 352p. mass mkt. 7.50 (*0-380-72541-X*, Avon Bks.); 1998. 256p. 22.00 (*0-688-14179-X*, Morrow, William & Co.) Morrow/Avon.

—Hit Man. l.t. ed. 1998. (Americana Ser.). 423p. 28.95 (*0-7862-1618-2*) Thorndike Pr.

Blood, Marje. A Song Heard in a Strange Land: Narcissa Her Story, Bk. 1. 1985. 220p. pap. 9.95 (*0-9615233-1-X*) Image Imprints.

Bonham, Frank. Sound of Gunfire. 1984. 192p. 2.25 o.s.i (*0-441-77596-9*) Ace Bks.

—Sound of Gunfire. 1981. mass mkt. 1.95 o.s.i (*0-425-05090-4*); 1979. mass mkt. 1.75 o.s.i (*0-425-04097-6*) Berkley Publishing Group.

—Sound of Gunfire. l.t. ed. 1995. (Nightingale Ser.). 232p. pap. 16.95 (*0-7838-1150-0*, Macmillan Reference USA) Gale Group.

Bookman, Jay. Caught in the Current. Date not set. pap. (*0-312-30942-2*, Saint Martin's Griffin) St. Martin's Pr.

Borofka, David. The Island. 1997. 218p. 19.50 (*1-878448-78-1*) MacMurray & Beck, Inc.

Bruyer, Kris. Whispers. 1995. 224p. pap. 10.95 o.p. (*1-56280-082-5*) Naiad Pr., Inc.

Buffa, D. W. The Prosecution: A Legal Thriller. 1999. 274p. 25.00 o.s.i (*0-8050-6107-X*) Holt, Henry & Co.

Byers, Roland O. The Linchpin: The Oregon Trail in 1843. 1984. (Illus.). 300p. (Orig.). pap. 12.95 o.p. (*0-89301-094-4*) Univ. of Idaho Pr.

Calloway, Kate. Fifth Wheel: A Cassidy James Mystery. 1998. (Cassidy James Mysteries Ser.: No. 5). 256p. pap. 11.95 (*1-56280-218-6*) Naiad Pr., Inc.

—First Impressions: A Cassidy James Mystery. 1996. (Cassidy James Mysteries Ser.). 208p. (Orig.). pap. 11.95 (*1-56280-133-3*) Naiad Pr., Inc.

—Fourth Down: A Cassidy James Mystery. 1998. (Cassidy James Mysteries Ser.). 240p. (Orig.). pap. 11.95 (*1-56280-193-7*) Naiad Pr., Inc.

—Second Fiddle: A Cassidy James Mystery. 1996. (Cassidy James Mysteries Ser.). 224p. (Orig.). pap. 11.95 (*1-56280-161-9*) Naiad Pr., Inc.

—Seventh Heaven: A Cassidy James Mystery. 1999. (Cassidy James Mysteries Ser.). 230p. pap. 11.95 (*1-56280-262-3*) Naiad Pr., Inc.

—Sixth Sense: A Cassidy James Mystery. 1999. (Cassidy James Mysteries Ser.). 215p. pap. 11.95 (*1-56280-228-3*) Naiad Pr., Inc.

—Third Degree: A Cassidy James Mystery. 1997. (Cassidy James Mysteries Ser.). 256p. (Orig.). pap. 11.95 (*1-56280-185-6*) Naiad Pr., Inc.

Carlson, Melody. Someone to Belong To. 2001. (Whispering Pines Ser.: Vol. 3). (Illus.). 311p. pap. 9.99 o.p. (*0-7369-0064-0*) Harvest Hse. Pubs.

Cleary, Beverly. Emily's Runaway Imagination. 1988. mass mkt. o.s.i (*0-440-80049-8*) Dell Publishing.

—Emily's Runaway Imagination. unabr. ed. 1986. (Soundways to Reading Ser.). (J). (gr. 2-4). audio 15.98 (*0-8072-1140-0*, SWR48SP, Listening Library) Random Hse. Audio Publishing Group.

—Emily's Runaway Imagination. unabr. ed. 1992. (J). (gr. 4). audio 35.00 (*1-55690-609-9*, 92302E7) Recorded Bks., LLC.

Corbin, William. A Dog Worth Stealing. 1987. 176p. (gr. 5 up). (J). 12.95 o.p. (*0-531-05712-7*); (YA). mass mkt. 12.99 o.p. (*0-531-08312-8*) Scholastic, Inc. (Orchard Bks.).

Corey, Ryanne. The Secret Millionaire. 2002. (Silhouette Desire Ser.). 192p. mass mkt. (*0-373-76450-2*, Silhouette) Harlequin Enterprises, Ltd.

Coulter, Catherine. The Cove. l.t. ed. 1996. 384p. mass mkt. 7.99 (*0-515-11865-6*, Jove) Berkley Publishing Group.

—The Cove. unabr. ed. 1996. audio 32.00 (*0-7366-2564-X*, 4253) Books on Tape, Inc.

—The Cove: An FBI Thriller. 2003. 336p. 19.95 (*0-399-15086-2*, Putnam & Grosset) Putnam Publishing Group, The.

—The Edge. 2000. 352p. mass mkt. 7.99 (*0-515-12860-0*, Jove) Berkley Publishing Group.

—The Edge. unabr. ed. 1999. audio 39.95 (*1-56740-430-8*, 1708, Brilliance Audio Unabridged); audio 73.25 (*1-56740-653-X*, 1709, Unabridged Library Editions) Brilliance Audio.

—The Edge, Set. unabr. ed. 1999. audio 39.95 Highsmith Inc.

—The Edge. 1999. 388p. 22.95 o.p. (*0-399-14506-0*); 24.95 o.p. (*0-399-14519-2*, Putnam Berkley Audio) Penguin Group (USA) Inc.

—The Edge. l.t. ed. 1999. (Basic Ser.). 493p. 31.95 o.p. (*0-7862-2240-9*) Thorndike Pr.

Crew, Linda. Ordinary Miracles. 1993. 299p. 20.00 o.p. (*0-688-11409-1*, Morrow, William & Co.) Morrow/Avon.

Crow, Donna Fletcher. All Things New. 1997. (Virtuous Heart Ser.: Vol. 1). 208p. pap. 11.99 (*0-8341-1674-X*) Beacon Hill Pr. of Kansas City.

—All Things New. 2003. 204p. 25.95 (*1-59414-084-7*, Five Star) Gale Group.

David, James F. Before the Cradle Falls. Date not set. pap. (*0-7653-0320-5*, Forge Bks.); E-Book 25.95 (*0-312-70660-X*, Tor Bks.); 2002. 336p. 25.95 (*0-7653-0319-1*, Forge Bks.) Doherty, Tom Assocs., LLC.

Dighton, Stephen D. Locked In. 2000. 296p. pap. 21.99 (*0-7388-3302-9*) Xlibris Corp.

Doolittle, Jerome. Half Nelson. Grose, Bill, ed. 1994. 288p. 20.00 o.p. (*0-671-50289-1*, Atria) Simon & Schuster.

—Half Nelson: A Tom Bethany Mystery. 1995. 288p. mass mkt. 5.50 (*0-671-79979-7*, Pocket) Simon & Schuster.

Duplex, Mary H. The Rockhound Mystery. 1993. pap. 1.97 o.p. (*0-8163-1130-7*) Pacific Pr. Publishing Assn.

Elkins, Aaron. Make No Bones. l.t. ed. 1993. 22.95 o.p. (*0-7927-1505-5*); pap. 20.95 o.p. (*0-7927-1504-7*) BBC Audiobooks America.

—Make No Bones. 1991. (Gideon Oliver Mystery Ser.). 304p. 17.95 o.p. (*0-89296-378-6*) Mysterious Pr.

—Make No Bones. 1993. 240p. mass mkt. 5.99 o.p. (*0-446-40308-3*, Mysterious Pr. Paperback Bks.) Warner Bks., Inc.

Elwood, Roger. Survival in the Wilderness. 2000. (Angelwalk Bks.). 238p. pap. o.s.i (*0-373-87090-6*, Harlequin Bks.) Harlequin Enterprises, Ltd.

Evans, Shirlee. Tree Tall to the Rescue. 1987. (Tree Tall Ser.: Vol. 3). (Illus.). 144p. (Orig.). (J). (gr. 4-9). pap. 4.50 o.p. (*0-8361-3444-3*) Herald Pr.

Fine, Arthur L. The Bitter Seed: A Fictional History of Shaniko, Oregon. Clemens, Paul M., ed. 1986. (Illus.). 180p. (Orig.). pap. 7.95 o.p. (*0-931892-06-6*) Blue Dolphin Publishing, Inc.

Freeman, Mary. Bleeding Heart. 2000. (Gardening Mysteries Ser.). 288p. mass mkt. 5.99 o.s.i (*0-425-17669-X*) Berkley Publishing Group.

—Devil's Trumpet. 1999. (Gardening Mysteries Ser.). 272p. (Orig.). mass mkt. 5.99 o.s.i (*0-425-16821-2*, Prime Crime) Berkley Publishing Group.

Freeman, Mary E. Wilkins. Deadly Nightshade. 1999. (Gardening Mysteries Ser.). 224p. mass mkt. 5.99 o.s.i (*0-425-17196-5*, Prime Crime) Berkley Publishing Group.

Gaffney, Patricia. Outlaw in Paradise. 1998. (Five Star Romance Ser.). 25.95 (*0-7862-1492-9*, Five Star); pap. 23.95 o.p. (*1-56895-544-8*, Wheeler Publishing, Inc.) Gale Group.

—Outlaw in Paradise. (Topaz Historical Romance Ser.). 384p. 1997. mass mkt. 5.99 o.s.i (*0-451-40793-8*, Onyx); 2002. reprint ed. pap. 13.00 (*0-451-20643-6*) NAL.

Gerritsen, Tess. Keeper of the Bride. 1996. (Harlequin Intrigue Ser.). (Illus.). 249p. per. (*0-373-22359-5*, 1-22359-3, Harlequin Bks.) Harlequin Enterprises, Ltd.

—Keeper of the Bride. l.t. ed. 2002. 29.95 o.p. (*0-7862-3974-3*) Thorndike Pr.

Gloss, Molly. The Jump-Off Creek. 192p. 1990. pap. 12.00 (*0-395-56001-2*); 1989. (J). 16.95 o.p. (*0-395-51086-4*) Houghton Mifflin Co.

Goddard, Ken. First Evidence. 2000. (Illus.). 464p. reprint ed. mass mkt. 7.50 (*0-553-57913-4*) Bantam Bks.

—Outer Perimeter. 2001. 496p. mass mkt. 6.99 (*0-553-57916-9*) Bantam Bks.

Griffitts, Eleanor Weber. Firestorm: A Love Story of the Spirit. 2001. iv, 205p. pap. 17.95 (*0-9678801-9-X*) Acorn Publishing.

Hammond, Diane Coplin. Going to Bend: A Novel. 2004. 304p. 23.95 (*0-385-50943-X*) Doubleday Publishing.

Hanson, Rick. Extreme Odds. 1998. 240p. 22.00 o.s.i (*1-57566-333-3*) Kensington Publishing Corp.

—Mortal Remains. 1996. mass mkt. 4.99 o.s.i (*0-7860-0284-0*, Pinnacle Bks.); 1995. 256p. mass mkt. 18.95 o.p. (*0-8217-4955-2*, Zebra Bks.) Kensington Publishing Corp.

—Spare Parts. 1995. 256p. mass mkt. 4.99 (*0-8217-0156-8*, Zebra Bks.); 1995. 256p. mass mkt. 4.99 o.s.i (*0-7860-0156-9*, Pinnacle Bks.); 1994. 288p. mass mkt. 20.00 o.s.i (*0-8217-4738-X*, Zebra Bks.) Kensington Publishing Corp.

—Splitting Heirs. (Adam McCleet Mysteries Ser. ). 1998. 256p. mass mkt. 5.99 o.s.i (*1-57566-365-1*); 1997. 240p. 21.95 o.p. (*1-57566-194-2*, Kensington Bks.) Kensington Publishing Corp.

—Still Life. (Adam McCleet Mysteries Ser. ). 1997. 256p. mass mkt. 5.50 o.s.i (*1-57566-200-0*); 1996. 204p. 19.95 o.s.i (*1-57566-041-5*) Kensington Publishing Corp.

Henry, April. Circles of Confusion. 1998. (Claire Montrose Mysteries Ser.). 288p. 23.00 (*0-06-019204-6*) HarperCollins Pubs.

—Circles of Confusion. 1999. (Claire Montrose Mysteries Ser.). 368p. mass mkt. 5.99 (*0-06-109715-2*, HarperTorch) Morrow/Avon.

—The Heart-Shaped Box: A Claire Montrose Mystery. 2001. 272p. 24.00 (*0-06-019655-6*) HarperCollins Pubs.

—Learning to Fly. E-Book 23.95 (*0-312-70633-2*); 2002. 288p. 23.95 (*0-312-29052-7*, Saint Martin's Minotaur) St. Martin's Pr.

—Square in the Face. 2000. (Claire Montrose Mysteries Ser.). 272p. 24.00 (*0-06-019205-4*) HarperCollins Pubs.

Herter, David. Evening's Empire. 352p. 2003. pap. 15.95 (*0-7653-0297-7*); 2002. 24.95 (*0-312-87034-5*) Doherty, Tom Assocs., LLC. (Tor Bks.).

Hicks, Barbara Jean. China Doll. l.t. ed. 1999. (Christian Fiction Ser.). 332p. 23.95 o.p. (*0-7862-2155-0*) Thorndike Pr.

Hicks, Barbara Jean, et al. China Doll. 1998. (Palisades Pure Romance Ser.). 266p. pap. 9.99 o.p. (*1-57673-262-2*, Palisades) Multnomah Pubs., Inc.

Hodgson, Ken. Fool's Gold: A Western Story. 2003. 240p. 25.95 (*0-7862-3275-7*, Five Star) Gale Group.

Hooper, Kay. After Caroline. unabr. ed. 2000. audio 69.95 (*0-7927-2358-9*, CSL 247, Chivers Sound Library) BBC Audiobooks America.

—After Caroline. l.t. ed. 1997. 368p. mass mkt. 6.99 (*0-553-57184-2*) Bantam Bks.

—After Caroline. l.t. ed. 1997. 471p. lib. bdg. 25.95 (*0-7838-1965-X*, Macmillan Reference USA) Gale Group.

Jackson, Lisa. Intimacies. 1998. mass mkt. 5.99 (*0-8217-7054-3*) Kensington Publishing Corp.

Jessett, Thomas E. The Indian Side of the Whitman Massacre. 1993. 45p. reprint ed. pap. 5.95 (*0-87770-374-4*) Ye Galleon Pr.

Jones, Nard. Oregon Detour. 1990. (Northwest Reprints Ser.). 320p. pap. 13.95 (*0-87071-501-1*); text 24.95 (*0-87071-500-3*) Oregon State Univ. Pr.

Karr, Kathleen. Oregon Sweet Oregon. (Petticoat Party Ser.: Vol. 3). 160p. (gr. 5 up). 1998. (J). pap. 4.95 o.p. (*0-06-440497-8*, Harper Trophy); 1997. (YA). lib. bdg. 14.89 (*0-06-027234-1*) HarperCollins Children's Bk. Group.

Keeble, John. Broken Ground. 1987. 416p. 17.95 o.p. (*0-06-015811-5*); 1989. 336p. reprint ed. pap. 8.95 o.p. (*0-06-091523-4*, PL 1523, Perennial) HarperTrade.

Kesey, Ken & Babbs, Ken. Last Go Round: A Dime Western. 1995. (Illus.). 256p. pap. 13.00 (*0-14-017667-5*, Penguin Bks.) Penguin Group (USA) Inc.

—Last Go Round: A Dime Western. 1994. (Illus.). 256p. 21.95 o.p. (*0-670-84883-2*, Viking) Viking Penguin.

Killingsworth, Monte. Eli's Songs. 1991. 144p. (YA). (gr. 5 up). 13.95 o.s.i (*0-689-50527-2*, McElderry, Margaret K.) Simon & Schuster Children's Publishing.

Kirkpatrick, Jane. Love to Water My Soul, 3 vols. 2003. (Dreamcatcher Ser.: Vol. 2). 368p. pap. 12.99 (*0-88070-938-3*, Multnomah Bks.) Multnomah Pubs., Inc.

—What Once We Loved. 2001. 400p. pap. 13.99 (*1-57856-234-1*) WaterBrook Pr.

Kleiner, Gregg. Where River Turns to Sky. l.t. ed. 1997. (Wheeler Large Print Book Ser.). 25.95 (*1-56895-458-1*, Wheeler Publishing, Inc.) Gale Group.

—Where River Turns to Sky. 1999. 400p. pap. 13.95 (*0-380-80559-6*); 1997. pap. 6.99 (*0-380-78866-7*); 1996. 400p. 23.00 o.p. (*0-380-97347-2*) Morrow/Avon. (Avon Bks.).

Kohler, Vincent. Banjo Boy. 1994. 226p. 19.95 o.p. (*0-312-11475-3*, Saint Martin's Minotaur) St. Martin's Pr.

—Rainy North Woods. Isaacson, Dana, ed. 1990. 320p. reprint ed. mass mkt. 3.95 (*0-671-72971-3*, Pocket) Simon & Schuster.

—Rainy North Woods. 1990. 256p. 16.95 o.p. (*0-312-03918-2*, Saint Martin's Minotaur) St. Martin's Pr.

—Raven's Widows. 1997. 256p. text 22.95 o.p. (*0-312-14714-7*, Saint Martin's Minotaur) St. Martin's Pr.

—Rising Dog. 1992. 288p. 18.95 o.p. (*0-312-07075-6*, Saint Martin's Minotaur) St. Martin's Pr.

Koontz, Dean. Cold Fire. 1991. 432p. mass mkt. 7.99 (*0-425-13071-1*) Berkley Publishing Group.

—Cold Fire. 1991. 14.04 (*0-606-00937-X*) Turtleback Bks.

Krentz, Jayne Ann. Eclipse Bay. 2000. 352p. mass mkt. 7.50 (*0-515-12801-5*, Jove) Berkley Publishing Group.

—Eclipse Bay. l.t. ed. 471p. 2001. pap. 29.95 (*0-7862-2963-2*); 2000. 31.95 o.p. (*0-7862-2960-8*) Thorndike Pr.

—Together in Eclipse Bay. 2003. 544p. pap. 15.00 (*0-425-19250-4*) Berkley Publishing Group.

—Uneasy Alliance. 2002. 256p. mass mkt. (*1-55166-958-7*, Mira Bks.) Harlequin Enterprises, Ltd.

—Uneasy Alliance. l.t. ed. 2003. 309p. 29.95 (*0-7862-5167-0*) Thorndike Pr.

Larson, Elsie J. Dawn's Early Light. 1996. (Tides of War Ser.: Bk. 1). 240p. pap. 10.99 o.p. (*0-7852-7688-2*) Nelson, Thomas Inc.

Le Guin, Ursula K. Searoad. 2004. 224p. pap. 13.95 (*1-59030-084-X*) Shambhala Pubns., Inc.

Love, Glen A., ed. The World Begins Here: An Anthology of Oregon Short Fiction. 1993. (Oregon Literature Ser.: Vol. 1). (Illus.). 320p. (Orig.). (YA). pap. 21.95 (*0-87071-370-1*); pap. text 35.95 (*0-87071-369-8*) Oregon State Univ. Pr.

Lovell, Ron. Dead Whales Tell No Tales: A Thomas Martindale Mystery. 2003. 184p. pap. 18.95 (*0-86534-383-7*) Sunstone Pr.

—Murder at Yaquina Head: A Thomas Martindale Mystery. 2002. 184p. pap. 18.95 (*0-86534-369-1*); 256p. 22.95 (*0-86534-345-4*) Sunstone Pr.

Macomber, Debbie. Country Brides. 2000. 280p. pap. o.s.i (*1-55166-626-X*, 1-66626-2, Mira Bks.) Harlequin Enterprises, Ltd.

Madden, Mickee L. & Baird, Glennora. Haunting Rose. l.t. ed. 1999. E-Book 14.99 incl. cd-rom (*1-929077-10-6*, Books OnScreen) PageFree Publishing, Inc.

Margolin, Phillip. After Dark. 1996. 384p. mass mkt. 7.99 (*0-553-56908-2*) Bantam Bks.

—After Dark. l.t. ed. 1995. (Large Print Bks.). 24.95 o.p. (*1-56895-240-6*, Wheeler Publishing, Inc.) Gale Group.

—The Associate. 2001. 304p. 26.00 (*0-06-019625-4*) HarperCollins Pubs.

—The Burning Man. 1997. 384p. mass mkt. 7.99 (*0-553-57495-7*) Bantam Bks.

—The Burning Man. l.t. ed. 1997. (Wheeler Large Print Book Ser.). 27.95 (*1-56895-415-8*, Wheeler Publishing, Inc.) Gale Group.

—Ties That Bind. 2003. 352p. 25.95 (*0-06-008324-7*) HarperCollins Pubs.

—Ties That Bind. l.t. ed. 2003. 544p. pap. 25.95 (*0-06-053326-9*, HarperLargePrint) HarperTrade.

—Ties That Bind. 2004. 416p. mass mkt. 7.99 (*0-06-008325-5*, HarperTorch) Morrow/Avon.

—The Undertaker's Widow. 1999. 336p. reprint ed. mass mkt. 7.99 (*0-553-58088-4*) Bantam Bks.

—The Undertaker's Widow. unabr. ed. 1998. audio 48.00 (*0-7366-4219-6*, 4717) Books on Tape, Inc.

—The Undertaker's Widow. unabr. ed. 1998. audio 29.95 o.s.i (*0-553-50218-2*, 751090, RH Audio) Random Hse. Audio Publishing Group.

—The Undertaker's Widow. l.t. ed. 2000. (Charnwood Large Print Ser.). 392p. (*0-7089-9146-7*, Ulverscroft) Thorpe, F. A. Pubs. GBR. *Dist:* Ulverscroft Large Print Bks., Ltd., Ulverscroft Large Print Canada, Ltd.

—Wild Justice. 2002. E-Book 7.99 (*0-06-621025-9*); 2002. E-Book 7.99 (*0-06-621026-7*); 2001. mass mkt. 186.37 o.s.i (*0-06-008372-7*); 2001. E-Book 7.99 (*0-06-018919-3*); 2000. 464p. pap. 26.00 (*0-06-019913-X*) HarperCollins Pubs.

—Wild Justice. 2000. 384p. 26.00 (*0-06-019624-6*, HarperCollins) HarperTrade.

Margolin, Phillip, ed. Gone, but Not Forgotten. l.t. ed. 2001. (Hardcover Ser.). 465p. 29.95 o.p. (*1-58724-078-5*, Wheeler Publishing, Inc.) Gale Group.

Margolis, David. Change of Partners. 1997. 231p. 24.00 (*1-877946-87-7*) Permanent Pr., The.

McClain, Florence W. & Wagner, Mcclain. Visions of Murder. 1995. 336p. pap. 5.99 (*1-56718-452-9*) Llewellyn Pubns.

McConnell, Vicki P. The Burnton Widows: A Nyla Wade Mystery. 1984. (Nyla Wade Mystery Ser.). (Illus.). 240p. pap. 7.95 o.p. (*0-930044-52-5*) Naiad Pr., Inc.

—Double Daughter. 1988. 216p. pap. 8.95 o.p. (*0-941483-26-6*) Naiad Pr., Inc.

—Mrs. Porter's Letter. 1982. (Nyla Wade Ser.). 224p. pap. 7.95 o.p. (*0-930044-29-0*) Naiad Pr., Inc.

McCourtney, Lorena. Betrayed. 1996. 290p. pap. 9.99 o.p. (*0-88070-756-9*, Palisades) Multnomah Pubs., Inc.

—Riptide: A Novel. 2002. (Julesburg Mysteries Ser.: Vol. 2). 336p. (gr. 13 up). pap. 12.99 (*0-8007-5777-7*) Revell, Fleming H. Co.

—Undertow: A Novel. 2003. 320p. pap. 12.99 (*0-8007-5778-5*) Revell, Fleming H. Co.

McIlwraith, Hiro. Shahnaz. 2000. 365p. pap. (*0-88982-188-7*) Oolichan Bks.

Millhiser, Marlys. Murder at Moot Point. 2001. 272p. pap. 19.00 (*0-385-50405-5*) Doubleday Publishing.

Mitcheltree, Tom. Katie's Gold: A Paul Fischer Mystery. 2003. 24.95 (*1-890768-48-0*, Intrigue Pr.) Corvus Publishing.

—Katie's Will. 1999. (WWL Mystery Ser.: No. 328). mass mkt. (*0-373-26328-7*, Worldwide Library) Harlequin Enterprises, Ltd.

—Katie's Will. 1997. 288p. 22.95 o.p. (*1-885173-20-2*) Write Way Publishing.

Monroe, Anne S. Happy Valley. 1991. (Northwest Reprints Ser.). 392p. reprint ed. pap. 13.95 (*0-87071-507-0*); text 24.95 (*0-87071-506-2*) Oregon State Univ. Pr.

Mortenson, Denis. Cinema Verite. 2003. 216p. pap. 19.95 (*1-59129-794-X*) PublishAmerica, Inc.

Myers, Katherine. Codebreaker. 2000. 289p. pap. 16.95 (*0-9664520-9-7*) Salvo Pr.

Nelson, Blake. Girl: A Novel. 1994. 256p. pap. 12.00 (*0-671-89707-1*, Touchstone) Simon & Schuster.

Nykanen, Mark. Hush. 1999. E-Book 23.95 (*0-312-20722-0*); 1999. 336p. mass mkt. 6.99 (*0-312-96852-3*, St. Martin's Paperbacks); 1998. 304p. 23.95 (*0-312-18051-9*) St. Martin's Pr.

O'Brien, Kevin. Only Son. 1998. 352p. mass mkt. 5.99 (*1-57566-211-6*) Kensington Publishing Corp.

Oetinger, Annis. Elk for Sale. 1999. (Brant Grayson Mystery Ser.: Vol. 2). 224p. pap. 11.00 (*0-9634757-2-X*) Oetinger, Annis.

Ohio, Denise. End of the Empire. 160p. 1994. pap. 8.95 o.p. (*0-312-10975-X*, Saint Martin's Griffin); 1993. 10.99 o.p. (*0-312-09282-2*) St. Martin's Pr.

Overholser, Wayne D. The Violent Land. 1992. 224p. reprint ed. pap. 3.50 (*0-8439-3233-3*) Dorchester Publishing Co., Inc.

—The Violent Land. l.t. ed. 1995. (Nightingale Ser.). 365p. pap. 17.95 (*0-7838-1385-6*, Macmillan Reference USA) Gale Group.

—The Violent Land: The Judas Gun, 2 bks. in 1. 1995. 400p. pap. 4.99 (*0-8439-3802-1*) Dorchester Publishing Co., Inc.

Peart, Jane. Runaway Heart. l.t. ed. 2001. (Westward Dreams Ser.). 429p. 24.95 (*0-7862-3124-6*) Thorndike Pr.

—Runaway Heart. 1994. (Westward Dreams Ser.: Vol. 1). 256p. pap. 18.99 (*0-310-41271-4*) Zondervan.

Pronzini, Bill. Sentinels: A "Nameless Detective" Mystery. 2002. 224p. reprint ed. pap. 11.00 (*0-7867-1014-4*, Carroll & Graf Pubs.) Avalon Publishing Group.

Pronzini, Bill & Muller. The Lighthouse: A Novel of Terror. 1987. pap. 3.95 o.p. (*0-312-90876-8*, St. Martin's Paperbacks) St. Martin's Pr.

Pronzini, Bill & Muller, Marcia. The Lighthouse: A Novel of Terror. 1992. (Mystery Scene Bk.). 304p. mass mkt. 4.50 (*0-88184-885-9*, Carroll & Graf Pubs.) Avalon Publishing Group.

—The Lighthouse: A Novel of Terror. l.t. ed. 2001. 390p. pap. 24.95 (*0-7838-9616-6*, Hall, G. K. & Co.) Gale Group.

—The Lighthouse: A Novel of Terror. 1986. 336p. 16.95 o.p. (*0-312-00150-9*) St. Martin's Pr.

Redon, Joel. The Road to Zena: A Novel. 1992. 320p. 19.95 o.p. (*0-312-07791-2*) St. Martin's Pr.

Roberts, J. R. The Spirit Box, Vol. 238. 2001. (Gunsmith Ser.: No. 238). 192p. mass mkt. 4.99 o.s.i (*0-515-13172-5*, Jove) Berkley Publishing Group.

Rose, Christie. The Hunt. 2003. 280p. pap. 11.95 (*1-892343-21-5*, Oak Tree Pr.) Oak Tree Publishing.

Ross, Dana Fuller, pseud. Oregon! 1983. mass mkt. 3.99 o.s.i (*0-553-80004-3*); 384p. mass mkt. 4.99 o.s.i (*0-553-26072-3*) Bantam Bks.

—Oregon! l.t. ed. 1982. (Reader's Request Ser.). lib. bdg. 16.95 o.p. (*0-8161-3317-4*, Macmillan Reference USA) Gale Group.

Rushford, Patricia H. Now I Lay Me down to Sleep. 1997. (Helen Bradley Mysteries Ser.: No. 1). 240p. pap. 9.99 o.p. (*1-55661-730-5*) Bethany Hse. Pubs.

Rushford, Patricia H. & James, Harrison. Secrets, Lies, & Alibis. 2003. 320p. 13.99 (*1-59145-081-0*) Integrity Pubs.

Scofield, Sandra J. More Than Allies. 1994. 192p. pap. 9.95 o.p. (*0-452-27306-4*, Plume) Dutton/Plume.

—More Than Allies. 1993. 176p. 24.00 (*1-877946-32-X*) Permanent Pr., The.

Scroggin, Martel. The Moonlighters: A Fictionalized Account of Central Oregon's Vigilant Years 1882-1884. 1992. (Illus.). 200p. (Orig.). pap. 9.95 (*0-8323-0496-4*) Binford & Mort Publishing.

—WASCO: An Epic Novel of Early San Francisco & the Untamed Oregon Frontier. 1987. 264p. pap. 8.95 (*0-8323-0457-3*) Binford & Mort Publishing.

Sharpe, Jon. Oregon Outrider, 206. 1999. (Trailsman Ser.: Vol. 206). 176p. mass mkt. 4.99 o.s.i (*0-451-19581-7*, Signet Bks.) NAL.

Sherburne, Zoa. Almost April. 1956. (J). (gr. 7 up). lib. bdg. 12.88 o.p. (*0-688-31013-3*, Morrow, William & Co.) Morrow/Avon.

Smith, Stephanie A. Other Nature. 256p. 1997. pap. 13.95 (*0-312-86352-7*); 1995. 21.95 o.p. (*0-312-85638-5*) Doherty, Tom Assocs., LLC. (Tor Bks.).

Sullivan, William L. A Deeper Wild. 2000. 464p. 26.95 (*0-9618152-9-9*); pap. 18.95 (*0-9677830-0-3*) Navillus Pr.

Terpening, Ron. The Turning: Novel. 2001. 168p. (YA). (gr. 7 up). pap. 10.95 (*0-9621452-1-1*) Desert Bloom Pr.

Thompson, Jean. Up-Hill All the Way. 2000. (First Edition Romance Ser.). 368p. 25.95 (*0-7862-2714-1*, Five Star) Gale Group.

Thompson, Thomas. Trouble Rider. l.t. ed. 1993. (Nightingale Ser.). pap. 15.95 (*0-8161-5480-5*, Macmillan Reference USA) Gale Group.

Thrasher, L. L. Cat's Paw, Incorporated. 1995. (Brown Bag Mystery Line Ser.). 616p. 3.00 o.p. (*0-933031-41-6*) Council Oak Bks.

—Dogsbody, Inc. 1999. 288p. 22.95 o.p. (*1-885173-65-2*) Write Way Publishing.

Towslee, Thomas. Prince of Snakes. 2003. 231p. pap. 19.95 (*1-59286-286-1*) PublishAmerica, Inc.

Troyer, Kit. Roseburg. 2001. 268p. pap. 21.99 (*0-7388-6287-8*) Xlibris Corp.

Van Pelt, Nicholas. Stomp. 1999. 288p. 24.95 (*0-312-86525-2*, Forge Bks.) Doherty, Tom Assocs., LLC.

Van Sant, Gus. Pink: A Novel. (Illus.). 272p. 1998. pap. 13.95 (*0-385-49353-3*); 1997. 21.95 o.s.i (*0-385-48828-9*) Doubleday Publishing.

Victor, Frances F. Women of the Gold Rush: "The New Penelope" & Other Stories. Egli, Ida R., ed. 1998. 192p. reprint ed. pap. 12.95 (*1-890771-03-1*) Heyday Bks.

Vukcevich, Ray. Man of Maybe Half-a-Dozen Faces. 2000. 245p. 22.95 (*0-312-24652-8*, Saint Martin's Minotaur) St. Martin's Pr.

Wallingford, Lee. Clear-Cut Murder: A Frank Carver - Ginny Trask Mystery. 1995. (WWL Mystery Ser.). mass mkt. (*0-373-26165-9*, 1-26165-0, Harlequin Bks.) Harlequin Enterprises, Ltd.

—Clear-Cut Murder: A Frank Carver - Ginny Trask Mystery. 1993. 212p. 19.95 o.s.i (*0-8027-3231-3*) Walker & Co.

—Cold Tracks. 1993. (Mystery Ser.). mass mkt. (*0-373-26114-4*, 1-26114-8, Harlequin Bks.) Harlequin Enterprises, Ltd.

—Cold Tracks. 1991. 192p. 18.95 (*0-8027-5783-9*) Walker & Co.

Warburton, Carol. Before the Dawn: A Novel. 2003. (Illus.). 282p. 14.95 (*1-59156-173-6*) Covenant Communications.

White, Patricia Lucas. Edwina Parkhurst, Spinster. 2003. pap. 13.99 (*1-58124-378-2*) Fiction Works, The.

—Edwina Parkhurst, Spinster. 2000. (First Edition Romance Ser.). 229p. 25.95 (*0-7862-2584-X*, Five Star) Gale Group.

—Edwina Parkhurst, Spinster. l.t. ed. 2002. (Ulverscroft Large Print Ser.). 320p. 32.50 (*0-7089-4767-0*, Ulverscroft) Thorpe, F. A. Pubs. GBR. *Dist:* Ulverscroft Large Print Bks., Ltd., Ulverscroft Large Print Canada, Ltd.

Whitney, Diana. The Raven Master. 2002. 256p. mass mkt. o.s.i (*0-373-51196-5*, 1-51196-3, Harlequin Bks.); 1994. (*0-373-27031-3*, Silhouette) Harlequin Enterprises, Ltd.

Wilhelm, Kate. Best Defense. 1995. mass mkt. 6.99 o.s.i (*0-449-22314-0*, Fawcett) Ballantine Bks.

—Best Defense. 1994. 352p. 21.95 o.p. (*0-312-10937-7*) St. Martin's Pr.

—Clear & Convincing Proof. l.t. ed. 2003. 417p. 28.95 (*0-7862-6011-4*) Gale Group.

—Clear & Convincing Proof. 2003. 352p. (*1-55166-697-9*, Mira Bks.) Harlequin Enterprises, Ltd.

—Death Qualified. 1992. (Northwest Mysteries Ser.). mass mkt. 5.99 o.s.i (*0-449-22155-5*, Fawcett) Ballantine Bks.

—Death Qualified. 1991. 22.95 o.p. (*0-312-05853-5*) St. Martin's Pr.

—Defense for the Devil. 2000. 448p. mass mkt. (*1-55166-628-6*, 1-66628-8, Mira Bks.) Harlequin Enterprises, Ltd.

—Defense for the Devil. E-Book 24.95 (*0-312-26451-8*); 1999. 400p. 24.95 o.p. (*0-312-19854-X*) St. Martin's Pr.

—The Good Children. 1999. 272p. mass mkt. 6.99 o.s.i (*0-449-00455-4*, Fawcett) Ballantine Bks.

—The Good Children. 1998. 224p. (YA). 22.95 o.p. (*0-312-17914-6*) St. Martin's Pr.

—The Good Children. l.t. ed. 1998. (Core Ser.). 301p. 29.95 (*0-7838-0167-X*) Thorndike Pr.

—The Good Children. l.t. ed. 2000. (Ulverscroft Large Print Ser.). 360p. 31.99 (*0-7089-4261-X*, Ulverscroft) Thorpe, F. A. Pubs. GBR. *Dist:* Ulverscroft Large Print Bks., Ltd., Ulverscroft Large Print Canada, Ltd.

—Justice for Some. 1994. (Northwest Mysteries Ser.). mass mkt. 5.99 o.s.i (*0-449-22247-0*, Fawcett) Ballantine Bks.

—Justice for Some. 1993. 272p. 18.95 o.p. (*0-312-09319-5*, Saint Martin's Minotaur) St. Martin's Pr.

—Malice Prepense. 1996. 368p. text 24.95 o.p. (*0-312-14364-8*) St. Martin's Pr.

—No Defense. l.t. ed. 2003. (Large Print Ser.). 29.95 (*1-57490-503-1*) Beeler, Thomas T. Publisher.

—No Defense. 2001. 448p. mass mkt. (*1-55166-785-1*, 1-66785-6, Mira Bks.) Harlequin Enterprises, Ltd.

—No Defense. 2000. 376p. 24.95 (*0-312-20953-3*) St. Martin's Pr.

—Skeletons. 2003. 384p. mass mkt. (*1-55166-749-5*, Mira Bks.) Harlequin Enterprises, Ltd.

—Skeletons. E-Book 17.95 (*0-312-70777-0*) St. Martin's Pr.

Wilson, Nancy. A Woman's Diary on the Barlow Road: The Final Segment of the Oregon Trail. Webber, Bert, ed. 1996. (Illus.). pap. 9.95 (*0-936738-05-7*) Webb Research Group Pubs.

Winther, Sophus K. Beyond the Garden Gate. 1991. (Northwest Reprints Ser.). 320p. reprint ed. pap. 13.95 (*0-87071-511-9*); text 24.95 (*0-87071-510-0*) Oregon State Univ. Pr.

Wren, M. K. Curiosity Didn't Kill the Cat. 1988. 272p. mass mkt. 4.95 o.s.i (*0-345-35002-2*) Ballantine Bks.

—Dead Matter. 1993. (Northwest Mysteries Ser.). 283p. mass mkt. 4.99 o.s.i (*0-345-37821-0*) Ballantine Bks.

—King of the Mountain. 1994. mass mkt. 4.99 o.s.i (*0-345-39019-9*) Ballantine Bks.

—A Multitude of Sins. 1989. mass mkt. 3.50 o.s.i (*0-345-35001-4*) Ballantine Bks.

—Neely Jones: The Medusa Pool. 1999. 313p. 24.95 (*0-312-24223-9*, Saint Martin's Minotaur) St. Martin's Pr.

—Nothing's Certain but Death. 1989. 256p. mass mkt. 3.95 o.s.i (*0-345-35000-6*) Ballantine Bks.

—Nothing's Certain but Death. 1978. 6.95 o.p. (*0-385-13283-2*) Doubleday Publishing.

—Oh, Bury Me Not! 1989. 256p. mass mkt. 4.99 o.s.i (*0-345-35004-9*) Ballantine Bks.

—Seasons of Death. 1989. 192p. mass mkt. 4.99 o.s.i (*0-345-35003-0*) Ballantine Bks.

—Seasons of Death. 1981. (Crime Club Ser.). 192p. 9.95 o.p. (*0-385-17413-6*) Doubleday Publishing.

—Wake up, Darlin' Corey. 1990. 224p. mass mkt. 4.95 o.s.i (*0-345-35071-5*) Ballantine Bks.

—Wake up, Darlin' Corey. 1984. (Crime Club Ser.). 192p. 11.95 o.p. (*0-385-19292-4*) Doubleday Publishing.

## ORISSA (IMAGINARY PLACE)—FICTION

Cole, Alan & Bunch, Chris. The Far Kingdoms: A Mythic Tale. 1994. 448p. mass mkt. 5.99 o.s.i (*0-345-38056-8*) Ballantine Bks.

Cole, Allan. The Warrior Returns: An Epic Fantasy of the Anteros. 1997. (Anteros Ser.). 440p. mass mkt. 6.99 o.s.i (*0-345-41312-1*, Del Rey) Ballantine Bks.

Cole, Allan & Bunch, Chris. The Far Kingdoms: A Mythic Tale. 1993. 432p. 20.00 o.p. (*0-345-38055-X*, Del Rey) Ballantine Bks.

—Kingdoms of the Night. 1996. mass mkt. 5.99 o.s.i (*0-345-38732-5*, Del Rey); 1995. 528p. 23.00 o.s.i (*0-345-38731-7*) Ballantine Bks.

—The Warrior's Tale. 1995. (Wizards of Fantasy Promotion Ser.). mass mkt. 5.99 o.s.i (*0-345-38734-1*, Del Rey) Ballantine Bks.

## OTHERLAND (IMAGINARY PLACE)—FICTION

Mensch, James R. Ethics & Selfhood: Alterity & the Phenomenology of Obligation. 2003. ix, 256p. (C). text 62.50 (*0-7914-5751-6*) State Univ. of New York Pr.

Williams, Tad. City of Golden Shadow. (Otherland Ser.: Vol. 1). 1998. 792p. mass mkt. 7.99 (*0-88677-763-1*); 1997. 784p. 24.95 o.s.i (*0-88677-710-0*, D A W Fiction) DAW Bks., Inc.

—Mountain of Black Glass. (Otherland Ser.: Vol. 3). 1999. 720p. 24.95 o.s.i (*0-88677-849-2*); 2000. 784p. reprint ed. mass mkt. 7.99 (*0-88677-906-5*) DAW Bks., Inc.

—The River of Blue Fire, Vol. 2. (Otherland Ser.: Vol. 2). 1999. 704p. mass mkt. 7.99 (*0-88677-844-1*); 1998. 576p. 24.95 o.s.i (*0-88677-777-1*) DAW Bks., Inc.

## OZ (IMAGINARY PLACE)—FICTION

Abbott, Donald & Baum, L. Frank. How the Wizard Saved Oz. 1996. (Oz Ser.). (Illus.). 112p. (YA). (gr. 5-8). 34.95 o.p. (*0-929605-59-4*) Books of Wonder.

Baum, L. Frank. Adventures in Oz: Ozma of Oz & Marvelous Land of Oz. unabr. ed. 1985. (Juvenile Classics). 575p. (J). (gr. 2 up). pap. 11.90 o.p. (*0-486-24880-1*) Dover Pubns., Inc.

—Adventures in Oz: Ozma of Oz & Marvelous Land of Oz. 1991. (Wonderful Wizard of Oz Pop-Ups Ser.). (J). 2.99 o.s.i (*0-517-05267-9*) Random Hse. Value Publishing.

—Aerie's Dorothy & the Wizard of Oz. 1995. mass mkt. 2.50 (*1-55902-925-0*, Aerie) Doherty, Tom Assocs., LLC.

—Aerie's Ozma of Oz. 1995. mass mkt. 2.50 (*1-55902-928-5*, Aerie) Doherty, Tom Assocs., LLC.

—Aerie's Rinkitink in Oz. 1995. mass mkt. 2.50 (*1-55902-926-9*, Aerie) Doherty, Tom Assocs., LLC.

—Aerie's The Emerald City of Oz. 1995. mass mkt. 2.50 (*1-55902-931-5*, Aerie) Doherty, Tom Assocs., LLC.

—Aerie's The Land of Oz. 1995. mass mkt. 2.50 (*1-55902-930-7*, Aerie) Doherty, Tom Assocs., LLC.

—Aerie's The Lost Princess of Oz. 1995. mass mkt. 2.50 (*1-55902-929-3*, Aerie) Doherty, Tom Assocs., LLC.

—Aerie's The Road to Oz. 1995. mass mkt. 2.50 (*1-55902-927-7*, Aerie) Doherty, Tom Assocs., LLC.

—Aerie's Tik Tok of Oz. 1995. mass mkt. 2.50 (*1-55902-989-7*, Aerie) Doherty, Tom Assocs., LLC.

—The Annotated Wizard of Oz. Hearn, Michael Patrick, ed. annot. ed. 2003. (Oz Ser.). (Illus.). 432p. (YA). (gr. 5-8). 39.95 (*0-393-04992-2*) Norton, W. W. & Co., Inc.

—The Classical Wizard: Magus Mirabilis in Oz. Hinke, C. J. & Van Buren, George, trs. from ENG. 1987. (Oz Ser.). (LAT., Illus.). (YA). (gr. 5-8). 19.95 o.p. (*0-85967-723-0*) Ashgate Publishing Co.

—The Critical Heritage Edition of the Wizard of Oz. Hearn, Michael Patrick, ed. 1986. (Illus.). 320p. reprint ed. pap. 8.95 o.s.i (*0-8052-0803-8*, Schocken) Knopf Publishing Group.

—Cyclone. 1991. (Wonderful Wizard of Oz Pop-Ups Ser.). 6p. (J). 2.99 o.p. (*0-517-05269-5*) Random Hse. Value Publishing.

—Dorothy & the Wizard in Oz. (Oz Ser.). (YA). (gr. 5 up). 20.95 (*0-8488-0704-9*) Amereon, Ltd.

—Dorothy & the Wizard in Oz. 1986. (Wonderful Oz Bks.: Vol. 4). 240p. (YA). (gr. 4-7). mass mkt. 5.99 o.s.i (*0-345-34168-6*, Del Rey) Ballantine Bks.

—The Emerald City of Oz. (Oz Ser.). (YA). (gr. 5-8). 21.95 (*0-8488-0733-2*) Amereon, Ltd.

—The Emerald City of Oz. 1985. (Wonderful Oz Bks.). 320p. (gr. 5-8). mass mkt. 5.99 (*0-345-33464-7*, Del Rey) Ballantine Bks.

—The Emerald City of Oz. 1988. (Oz Ser.). (Illus.). 336p. (YA). (gr. 5-8). reprint ed. pap. 8.95 (*0-486-25681-2*) Dover Pubns., Inc.

—The Emerald City of Oz. 1993. (Books of Wonder). (Illus.). 304p. (J). (gr. 5-8). 24.99 (*0-688-11558-6*) HarperCollins Children's Bk. Group.

—The Emerald City of Oz. l.t. ed. (Oz Ser.). (YA). (gr. 5). 666p. lib. bdg. 62.73 (*0-7583-0790-X*); 157p. pap. 17.88 (*0-7583-0792-6*); 196p. pap. 20.87 (*0-7583-0793-4*); 269p. pap. 26.24 (*0-7583-0794-2*); 344p. pap. 31.82 (*0-7583-0795-0*); 440p. pap. 38.63 (*0-7583-0796-9*); 541p. pap. 45.78 (*0-7583-0797-7*); 666p. pap. 54.59 (*0-7583-0798-5*); 772p. pap. 62.12 (*0-7583-0799-3*); 440p. lib. bdg. 46.42 (*0-7583-0788-8*); 541p. lib. bdg. 54.55 (*0-7583-0789-6*); 772p. lib. bdg. 84.57 (*0-7583-0791-8*); 196p. lib. bdg. 26.87 (*0-7583-0785-3*); 269p. lib. bdg. 32.24 (*0-7583-0786-1*); 344p. lib. bdg. 38.69 (*0-7583-0787-X*); 157p. lib. bdg. 23.88 (*0-7583-0784-5*) Huge Print Pr.

—The Emerald City of Oz. 1990. (Oz Ser.). (YA). (gr. 5-8). 24.50 (*0-8446-6399-9*) Smith, Peter Pub., Inc.

—Glinda of Oz. (Oz Ser.). (YA). (gr. 5-8). E-Book 4.95 (*1-58824-056-8*) ibooks, Inc.

—The Land of Oz. 1968. (Oz Ser.). (Illus.). (YA). (gr. 5-8). mass mkt. 1.25 o.p. (*0-8049-0181-3*, CL-181) Airmont Publishing Co., Inc.

—The Land of Oz. (Oz Ser.). (YA). (gr. 5-8). 21.95 (*0-8488-0785-5*) Amereon, Ltd.

—Le Magicien d'Oz. 2001. Tr. of Wizard of Oz. 7.95 (*2-277-21652-6*) 84, Editions FRA. *Dist:* Distribooks, Inc.

—The Marvelous Land of Oz. (Oz Ser.). (YA). (gr. 5-8). 22.95 (*0-88411-773-1*) Amereon, Ltd.

—The Marvelous Land of Oz. (Oz Ser.). (Illus.). (YA). (gr. 5-8). 1985. 287p. pap. 7.95 (*0-486-20692-0*); 1997. 144p. reprint ed. pap. text 1.50 (*0-486-29686-5*) Dover Pubns., Inc.

—The Marvelous Land of Oz. 1985. (Books of Wonder). (Illus.). 294p. (J). (gr. 5-8). 24.99 (*0-688-05439-0*) HarperCollins Children's Bk. Group.

—The Marvelous Land of Oz. 1985. (Oz Ser.). (Illus.). 192p. (YA). (gr. 5-8). pap. 2.25 o.p. (*0-14-035041-1*, Puffin Bks.) Penguin Putnam Bks. for Young Readers.

—The Marvelous Land of Oz. 1999. (Wizard of Oz Ser.). (Illus.). 276p. (YA). (gr. 5-8). E-Book 5.99 incl. cd-rom (*1-891595-15-6*) Quiet Vision Publishing.

—The Marvelous Land of Oz. 1990. (Oz Ser.). (YA). (gr. 5-8). 25.25 (*0-8446-6231-3*) Smith, Peter Pub., Inc.

—Oz-Story. Maxine, David, ed. 1995. (Oz Ser.). (Illus.). 128p. (Orig.). (YA). (gr. 5-8). pap. 14.95 o.p. (*0-9644988-1-2*) Hungry Tiger Pr.

—The Patchwork Girl of Oz. 1985. (Oz Ser.). 384p. (YA). (gr. 5-8). mass mkt. 5.99 o.s.i (*0-345-33290-3*) Ballantine Bks.

—The Pop-Up Wizard of Oz. 1982. (Windmill Pop-up-Bks.). (Illus.). 12p. (J). (ps-2). 7.75 o.s.i (*0-671-44433-6*, Simon & Schuster Children's Publishing) Simon & Schuster Children's Publishing.

—The Scarecrow of Oz, No. 9. 1985. (Oz Ser.). 288p. (YA). (gr. 5-8). mass mkt. 5.99 o.s.i (*0-345-33396-9*, Del Rey) Ballantine Bks.

—Tik-Tok of Oz. 1994. (Oz Ser.). (Illus.). 304p. (YA). (gr. 5-8). reprint ed. pap. 6.95 (*0-486-28002-0*) Dover Pubns., Inc.

—The Tin Woodman of Oz. 1985. (Oz Ser.). (Illus.). 272p. (gr. 5-8). mass mkt. 5.99 (*0-345-33436-1*, Del Rey) Ballantine Bks.

—The Tin Woodman of Oz, No. 12. (Oz Ser.). (YA). (gr. 5-8). E-Book 2.49 (*1-58744-077-6*) Electric Umbrella Publishing.

—The Tin Woodman of Oz. (Oz Ser.). E-Book (*1-58824-136-X*) ipicturebooks, LLC.

—The Witch Is Dead: The Complete Books of Oz Volume One. 2003. (Creation Classic Portable Ser.: 4). 512p. pap. 14.95 (*1-84068-084-9*) Creation Bks.

—The Wizard of Oz. 1982. (Tempo Classics Ser.). 1.95 o.s.i (*0-448-16941-X*) Ace Bks.

—The Wizard of Oz. 1979. mass mkt. 1.95 o.p. (*0-345-28223-X*, Del Rey) Ballantine Bks.

—The Wizard of Oz. unabr. ed. 2002. audio 23.95 (*0-7861-2156-4*) Blackstone Audio Bks., Inc.

—The Wizard of Oz. 1993. 171p. mass mkt. 2.99 (*0-8125-2335-0*, Tor Classics) Doherty, Tom Assocs., LLC.

—The Wizard of Oz. 1963. 3.60 (*0-87129-402-8*, W39) Dramatic Publishing Co.

—The Wizard of Oz. l.t. ed. 2001. (Large Print Ser.). 201p. lib. bdg. 26.00 (*1-58287-621-5*) North Bks.

—The Wizard of Oz. 2000. (Illustrated Junior Library Ser.). 9.99 o.p. (*0-448-42452-5*, Grosset & Dunlap) Penguin Putnam Bks. for Young Readers.

—The Wizard of Oz. 1991. 5.99 o.p. (*0-517-06169-4*) Random Hse. Value Publishing.

—The Wizard of Oz. 1985. 7.95 o.p. (*0-671-60504-6*, Atheneum) Simon & Schuster Children's Publishing.

—The Wizard of Oz. 2003. (Perennial Bestseller Ser.). lib. bdg. 28.95 (*0-7862-5105-0*) Thorndike Pr.

—The Wizard of Oz. 1985. 18.95 o.p. (*0-88101-018-9*) Unicorn Publishing Hse., Inc., The.

—The Wizard of Oz: Collectors Edition. 1992. 6.98 (*0-88365-797-X*, Galahad Bks.) BBS Publishing Corp.

—The Wizard of Oz: Includes Necklace. 1999. (Charming Classics Ser.). (Illus.). 208p. (J). (gr. 3-7). pap. 6.99 (*0-694-01319-6*) HarperCollins Children's Bk. Group.

—The Wizard of Oz Waddle Book. 1993. (Illus.). 160p. (J). reprint ed. 24.95 (*1-55709-205-2*) Applewood Bks.

—The Wonderful Wizard of Oz: The Kansas Centennial Edition. 1999. (Oz Ser.). (Illus.). (YA). (gr. 5-8). xviii, 194p. 24.95 (*0-7006-0985-7*); 216p. 100.00 (*0-7006-0986-5*) Univ. Pr. of Kansas.

—The Wonderful World of Oz: The Wizard of Oz, The Emerald City of Oz & Glinda of Oz. Zipes, Jack D., ed. 1998. (Illus.). 389p. (YA). pap. 14.00 (*0-7567-6039-9*) DIANE Publishing Co.

—The Wonderful World of Oz: The Wizard of Oz, The Emerald City of Oz & Glinda of Oz. Zipes, Jack D., ed. & intro. by. 1998. (Twentieth Century Classics Ser.). (Illus.). 368p. (J). 13.95 (*0-14-118085-4*, Penguin Classics) Viking Penguin.

—Yellow Brick Road. 1991. (Wonderful Wizard of Oz Pop-Ups Ser.). (Illus.). 6p. (J). 2.99 o.s.i (*0-517-05268-7*) Random Hse. Value Publishing.

Baum, L. Frank & McGraw, Eloise Jarvis. Oz-Story 2. Maxine, David, ed. 1996. (Oz Ser.). (Illus.). 128p. (Orig.). (YA). (gr. 5-8). pap. 14.95 o.p. (*0-9644988-2-0*) Hungry Tiger Pr.

Baum, L. Frank & Payes, Rachel C. Oz-Story 3. Maxine, David, ed. & illus. by. Shanower, Eric, illus. 1997. (Oz Ser.). 128p. (Orig.). (YA). (gr. 5-8). pap. 14.95 o.p. (*0-9644988-4-7*) Hungry Tiger Pr.

Baum, L. Frank & Shanahan, Patrick. Oz. 1996. (Oz Ser.). 53p. (YA). (gr. 5-8). pap. 5.60 (*0-87129-713-2*, O55) Dramatic Publishing Co.

Classic Wizard of Oz: The Wizard of Oz, the Land of Oz. unabr. ed. 2002. audio 19.95 (*1-931953-12-0*, AA103) Listen & Live Audio, Inc.

Dulabone, Christopher. Vampires & Oz. 2000. 148p. E-Book 8.00 (*0-7388-9239-4*) Xlibris Corp.

Evans, Robert. Dorothy's Mystical Adventures in Oz. 2000. 240p. E-Book 8.00 (*0-7388-8594-0*) Xlibris Corp.

Fricke, John, et al. The Wizard of Oz: The Official 50th Anniversary Pictorial History. 1989. (Illus.). x, 245 p. (*0-340-50848-5*) St. Martin's Pr.

Gardner, Martin. Visitors from Oz: Wild Adventures of Dorothy, the Scarecrow, & the Tin Woodman. 2000. (Illus.). 208p. pap. 12.95 (*0-312-25437-7*, Saint Martin's Griffin) St. Martin's Pr.

Gardner, Martin & Baum, L. Frank. Visitors from Oz: The Wild Adventures of Dorothy, the Scarecrow, & the Tin Woodman in the United States. 1998. 208p. 22.95 o.p. (*0-312-19353-X*) St. Martin's Pr.

Hardenbrook, David. The Unknown Witches of Oz: Locasta & the Three Adepts. 2001. (Illus.). 240p. pap. 19.95 (*1-880090-23-6*) Galde Pr., Inc.

Hearn, Michael Patrick, intro. The Annotated Wizard of Oz. 1973. (Oz Ser.). (Illus.). 384p. (YA). (gr. 5-8). 20.00 o.s.i (*0-517-50086-8*, Crown) Crown Publishing Group.

Koste, Virginia G. The Wonderful Wizard of Oz. 1982. (Oz Ser.). 70p. (YA). (gr. 5-8). pap. 5.60 (*0-87129-009-X*, W67) Dramatic Publishing Co.

Koste, Virginia G. & Baum, L. Frank. Scraps! The Ragtime Girl of Oz. 1984. 54p. reprint ed. pap. 5.60 (*0-87129-033-2*, S88) Dramatic Publishing Co.

Langley, Noel, et al. The Wizard of Oz: The Screenplay. 1989. (Illus.). 160p. pap. 9.95 o.s.i (*0-385-29760-2*, Delta) Dell Publishing.

Maguire, Gregory. Wicked: The Life & Times of the Wicked Witch of the West. Date not set. (*0-06-099603-X*); E-Book 11.95 (*0-06-053891-0*); E-Book 11.95 (*0-06-053892-9*); E-Book 11.95 (*0-06-053890-2*); 1996. (Illus.). 448p. pap. 15.00 (*0-06-098710-3*) HarperCollins Pubs.

—Wicked: The Life & Times of the Wicked Witch of the West. E-Book 11.95 (*0-06-053889-9*); 1995. (Illus.). 448p. 24.00 o.p. (*0-06-039144-8*) HarperTrade.

Smalls, Charlie. The Wiz. 1979. pap. 6.00 (*0-573-68091-4*) French, Samuel Inc.

Thompson, Ruth P. Kabumpo in Oz. 1998. (Oz Ser.). (Illus.). 312p. (YA). (gr. 5-8). 22.95 o.p. (*0-929605-78-0*) Books of Wonder.

—Ojo in Oz. 1986. (Oz Ser.). (YA). (gr. 5-8). pap. 19.00 (*0-345-33704-2*) Ballantine Bks.

—The Royal Book of Oz. 1985. (Oz Ser.). 272p. (YA). (gr. 5-8). pap. 19.00 (*0-345-31585-5*, Ballantine Bks.) Ballantine Bks.

—The Wishing Horse of Oz. 1986. (Oz Ser.). (YA). (gr. 5 up). pap. 19.00 (*0-345-33706-9*) Ballantine Bks.

Thompson, Ruth Plumly. The Cowardly Lion of Oz. 1985. (Wonderful Oz Bks.: No. 17). (YA). (gr. 5-8). pap. 19.00 (*0-345-31586-3*, Ballantine Bks.) Ballantine Bks.

—The Giant Horse of Oz. 1985. (Wonderful Oz Bks.: No. 22). (YA). (gr. 5-8). pap. 19.00 (*0-345-32359-9*, Del Rey) Ballantine Bks.

—The Gnome King of Oz. 1985. (Wonderful Oz Bks.: No. 21). (YA). (gr. 5-8). pap. 19.00 (*0-345-32358-0*, Del Rey) Ballantine Bks.

—Grampa in Oz. 1985. (Wonderful Oz Bks.: No. 18). (YA). (gr. 5-8). pap. 15.00 (*0-345-31587-1*, Del Rey) Ballantine Bks.

—The Hungry Tiger of Oz. 1985. (Wonderful Oz Bks.: No. 20). (YA). (gr. 5-8). pap. 15.00 (*0-345-31589-8*, Ballantine Bks.) Ballantine Bks.

—Jack Pumpkinhead of Oz. 1985. (Wonderful Oz Bks.: No. 23). (YA). (gr. 5-8). pap. 15.00 (*0-345-32360-2*, Del Rey) Ballantine Bks.

—The Lost King of Oz. 1985. (Wonderful Oz Bks.: No. 19). (YA). (gr. 5-8). pap. 19.00 (*0-345-31588-X*, Ballantine Bks.) Ballantine Bks.

—Pirates in Oz. 1986. (Wonderful Oz Bks.: No. 25). (YA). (gr. 5-8). pap. 15.00 (*0-345-33099-4*) Ballantine Bks.

—The Purple Prince of Oz. 1986. (Wonderful Oz Bks.: No. 26). (YA). (gr. 5-8). pap. 15.00 (*0-345-32869-8*) Ballantine Bks.

—The Yellow Knight of Oz. 1986. (Wonderful Oz Bks.: No. 24). (YA). (gr. 5-8). pap. 15.00 (*0-345-32867-1*) Ballantine Bks.

**OZARK MOUNTAINS REGION—FICTION**

Agee, Jonis. South of Resurrection. 1998. 368p. pap. 12.95 (*0-14-024172-8*) Penguin Group (USA) Inc.

—South of Resurrection. 1997. 360p. 24.95 o.p. (*0-670-85809-9*) Viking Penguin.

Cart, Dorothy. Jail Bait: A Novel. 1994. 128p. pap. 10.95 (*0-86534-197-4*) Sunstone Pr.

Estes, Martha Hogan. Whitest Wash: A Collection of Short Fiction by Ozark Women. 1996. 117 p. ;p. (*1-57087-298-8*) Professional Pr.

Gray, Judson. Caywood Valley Feud. 2002. 288p. mass mkt. 5.99 o.s.i (*0-451-20656-8*) NAL.

Harington, Donald. The Architecture of the Arkansas Ozarks. 1987. (Illus.). 384p. pap. 20.00 o.p. (*0-15-607880-5*, Harvest Bks.) Harcourt Trade Pubs.

—The Architecture of the Arkansas Ozarks. 2004. pap. 14.95 (*1-59264-073-7*) Toby Pr.

—When Angels Rest. 1998. 256p. 24.00 (*1-887178-07-4*, Counterpoint Pr.) Basic Bks.

Hefley, Howard J. Way Back in the Ozarks. 1992. 280p. pap. 5.95 (*0-929292-26-X*) Hannibal Bks.

—Way Back in the Ozarks: The Tale of Danny Boy, Bk. 2. 1993. 260p. pap. 5.95 (*0-929292-38-3*) Hannibal Bks.

Hess, Joan. Malice in Maggody. 1991. (Arly Hanks Mystery Ser.). 240p. mass mkt. 5.99 o.s.i (*0-451-40236-7*, Onyx) NAL.

—Mischief in Maggody. 1991. (Arly Hanks Mystery Ser.). 256p. mass mkt. 5.99 o.s.i (*0-451-40253-7*, Onyx) NAL.

—Mischief in Maggody. 1988. 176p. 14.95 o.p. (*0-312-01792-8*, Saint Martin's Minotaur) St. Martin's Pr.

McMurtry, Larry & Ossana, Diana. Zeke & Ned. l.t. ed. (Paperback Bestsellers Ser.). 657p. 1998. pap. 28.95 (*0-7838-8095-2*); 1997. lib. bdg. 30.95 (*0-7838-8094-4*) Thorndike Pr.

Morris, Lynn & Morris, Gilbert. Shadow of the Mountains. (Christian Fiction Ser.). 1999. 23.95 (*0-7862-2089-9*, Five Star); 1995. 481p. 21.95 (*0-7838-1489-5*, Macmillan Reference USA) Gale Group.

Morsi, Pamela. Marrying Stone. l.t. ed. 1995. 423p. pap. 20.95 o.p. (*0-7838-1415-1*, Macmillan Reference USA) Gale Group.

Nehring, Radine Trees. A Valley to Die For. 2002. (Something to Die for Ser.). 284p. pap. 14.00 (*0-9661879-9-7*) St Kitts Pr.

Woodrell, Daniel. Give Us a Kiss: A Country Noir. 1996. 237p. 22.50 o.p. (*0-8050-2298-8*) Holt, Henry & Co.

—Tomato Red: A Country Noir. 1998. 240p. 20.00 o.s.i (*0-8050-5577-0*) Holt, Henry & Co.

Wright, Harold Bell. The Calling of Dan Matthews. Date not set. 370p. 26.95 (*0-8488-2509-8*) Amereon, Ltd.

—The Calling of Dan Matthews. 363p. reprint ed. lib. bdg. 98.00 (*0-7222-0745-X*) Best Bks.

—The Calling of Dan Matthews. (Collected Works of Harold Bell Wright). 363p. 2001. pap. text 28.00 (*0-7426-5888-0*); 1999. reprint ed. lib. bdg. 98.00 (*1-58201-888-X*) Classic Bks.

—The Calling of Dan Matthews. 1995. 368p. pap. 5.99 (*1-56554-048-4*) Pelican Publishing Co., Inc.

—A Higher Call. Phillips, Michael R., ed. 1990. 304p. reprint ed. pap. 8.99 o.p. (*1-55661-136-6*) Bethany Hse. Pubs.

—The Shepherd of the Hills. 347p. reprint ed. lib. bdg. 98.00 (*0-7222-0733-6*) Best Bks.

—The Shepherd of the Hills. Phillips, Michael R., ed. rev. ed. 1988. 256p. pap. 9.99 (*0-87123-916-7*) Bethany Hse. Pubs.

—The Shepherd of the Hills. 1975. lib. bdg. 27.95 (*0-89966-206-4*) Buccaneer Bks., Inc.

—The Shepherd of the Hills. (Collected Works of Harold Bell Wright). 347p. 2001. pap. text 28.00 (*0-7426-5893-7*); 1999. reprint ed. lib. bdg. 98.00 (*1-58201-893-6*) Classic Bks.

—The Shepherd of the Hills. 1987. 269p. reprint ed. (*0-911978-04-6*) McCormick-Armstrong Co., Inc.

—The Shepherd of the Hills. 7th ed. 1992. 304p. pap. 5.99 (*0-88289-884-1*) Pelican Publishing Co., Inc.

—The Shepherd of the Hills. 1958. 9.95 o.s.i (*0-448-01056-9*, Grosset & Dunlap) Penguin Putnam Bks. for Young Readers.

Wright, Harold Bell & Phillips, Michael R. The Shepherd of the Hills. l.t. ed. 2000. (G. K. Hall Inspirational Ser.). 326p. 27.95 (*0-7838-8941-0*, Macmillan Reference USA) Gale Group.

# P

**PACIFIC AREA—FICTION**

Alten, Steven. Meg: A Novel of Deep Terror. 352p. 1997. mass mkt. 6.99 (*0-553-84016-9*); 1998. reprint ed. mass mkt. 6.99 (*0-553-57910-X*) Bantam Bks.

Baly, Lindsay. Ironbottom Sound. l.t. ed. 1991. (Magna Large Print Ser.). 361p. o.p. (*1-85057-994-6*) Magna Large Print Bks. GBR. *Dist:* Ulverscroft Large Print Canada, Ltd.

—Ironbottom Sound. 1989. 240p. 18.95 o.p. (*0-8027-1063-8*) Walker & Co.

Becke, Louis. Pacific Tales. 1977. (Short Story Index Reprint Ser.). 23.95 (*0-8369-3135-1*) Ayer Co. Pubs., Inc.

—Pacific Tales. 1998. (Pacific Basin Ser.). pap. 31.00 (*0-7103-0254-1*) Kegan Paul International Ltd. GBR. *Dist:* Columbia Univ. Pr.

Cobb, James H. Sea Strike. 1999. 368p. reprint ed. mass mkt. 6.99 (*0-425-16616-3*) Berkley Publishing Group.

—Sea Strike. 1997. 480p. 24.95 o.p. (*0-399-14324-6*, G. P. Putnam's Sons) Penguin Group (USA) Inc.

Cresse, Gina. A Deadly Bargain: Plan C. 2000. 207p. 19.95 (*0-8034-9409-2*, Avalon Bks.) Bouregy, Thomas & Co., Inc.

Dunsford, Cathie. Manawa Toa Heart Warrior. 2001. 146p. pap. 14.95 (*1-875559-69-8*) Spinifex Pr. AUS. *Dist:* Strauss Consultants.

Garrison, Paul. Fire & Ice. 1999. 384p. mass mkt. 6.99 (*0-380-79436-5*, Eos); 1998. 400p. mass mkt. 15.95 (*0-380-97566-1*, Avon Bks.) Morrow/Avon.

—Fire & Ice. abr. ed. 1998. 25.00 incl. audio (*0-7871-1015-9*, Dove Audio) NewStar Media, Inc.

Gillison, Samantha. The King of America: A Novel. 2004. (Illus.). 240p. 21.95 (*0-375-50819-8*) Random Hse., Inc.

Innes, Hammond. The Strode Venturer. 1979. mass mkt. 1.95 o.s.i (*0-345-27845-3*) Ballantine Bks.

—The Strode Venturer. l.t. ed. 1998. (General Ser.). 448p. pap. 23.95 (*0-7862-1484-8*) Thorndike Pr.

Mitchell, Margaret. Lost Laysen. Freer, Debra, ed. 1997. (Illus.). 128p. pap. 8.95 (*0-684-83768-4*, Scribner Paper Fiction) Simon & Schuster.

—Lost Laysen. 1996. (Illus.). 128p. 18.00 (*0-684-82428-0*, Scribner) Simon & Schuster.

—Lost Laysen. abr. ed. 192p. pap. 14.00 o.s.i incl. audio (*0-671-57059-5*, Simon & Schuster Audioworks) Simon & Schuster Audio.

—Lost Laysen. 1998. 3.98 o.p. (*0-7651-0767-8*) Smithmark Pubs., Inc.

Murray, Sabina. The Caprices: Stories of the Pacific Campaign. 2002. 208p. pap. 13.00 (*0-618-09525-X*) Houghton Mifflin Co.

Reasoner, James. Trial by Fire Bk. 2: The Last Good War. 2002. (Illus.). 448p. 25.95 (*0-312-87346-8*, Forge Bks.) Doherty, Tom Assocs., LLC.

Reynolds, George A. M'aidez. 2000. (Illus.). 169p. pap. 13.95 o.p. (*1-57197-196-3*) Pentland Pr., Inc.

Rogers, Irv C. Motoo Eetee: Shipwrecked at the Edge of the World. 2002. (Illus.). 464p. 24.95 (*1-59013-018-9*) McBooks Pr., Inc.

Schonberg, Leonard A. Fish Heads: A Novel. 1999. 176p. 26.95 (*0-86534-290-3*) Sunstone Pr.

Spencer, James. Pilots. 2003. 288p. 23.95 (*0-399-14973-2*, Putnam & Grosset) Putnam Publishing Group, The.

Wendt, Albert. Pouliuli. 1977. 147p. (*0-582-71754-X*) Longman, Paul (NZ).

—Pouliuli. 1980. (Pacific Classics Ser.: Vol. 8). 147p. pap. text 10.00 (*0-8248-0728-6*) Univ. of Hawaii Pr.

Wenzel, Lawrence A. Turnip Patch Infield & a Navajo. 1999. 256p. 22.95 (*0-918606-13-6*) Heidelberg Graphics.

Zimmermann, Frank W. Not by Arms Alone: A Novel of a U. S. Navy Destroyer in the Pacific Theater, 1941-1945. 1994. (Illus.). 626p. pap. 22.50 (*0-9644793-0-3*) Zimmermann Publishing.

**PAKISTAN—FICTION**

Benard, Cheryl. Moghul Buffet. 2000. (Soho Crime Ser.). 263p. pap. 12.00 (*1-56947-179-7*) Soho Pr., Inc.

Bernard, Cheryl. Moghul Buffet. o.p. (*0-374-23830-8*); 1998. 208p. 22.00 o.p. (*0-374-21179-5*) Farrar, Straus & Giroux.

DeFelice, Jim. War Breaker. 1999. 448p. reprint ed. mass mkt. 6.99 (*0-8439-4601-6*, Leisure Bks.) Dorchester Publishing Co., Inc.

—War Breaker. 1993. 320p. 19.95 o.p. (*0-312-09404-3*) St. Martin's Pr.

—The War Breaker. 1996. 400p. reprint ed. pap. 6.99 (*0-8439-4043-3*, Leisure Bks.) Dorchester Publishing Co., Inc.

Fullilove, Eric James. Blowback. 2001. 304p. 24.00 (*0-06-621250-2*, Amistad Pr.) HarperTrade.

Hagberg, David. By Dawn's Early Light. E-Book (*0-312-71083-6*, Tor Bks.);Vol. 1. 2003. 336p. 25.95 (*0-7653-0454-6*, Forge Bks.) Doherty, Tom Assocs., LLC.

Hamid, Mohsin. Moth Smoke. 2000. 244p. 23.00 o.p. (*0-374-21354-2*) Farrar, Straus & Giroux.

Haq, Hina. Sadika's Way: A Novel of Pakistan & America. 2003. 300p. 23.95 (*0-89733-518-X*) Academy Chicago Pubs., Ltd.

Naqvi, Tahira, tr. from URD. Attar of Roses & Other Stories from Pakistan. 1997. 145p. 25.00 (*0-89410-808-5*); pap. 15.95 (*0-89410-809-3*) Rienner, Lynne Pubs., Inc. (Three Continents).

Roper, Robert. Victory to the Moth. 2002. 288p. 23.00 (*1-893956-31-8*) Context Bks.

Rovin, Jeff. Line of Control, Vol. 8. 2001. (Tom Clancy's Op Center Ser.: Vol. 8). 384p. mass mkt. 7.99 (*0-425-18005-0*) Berkley Publishing Group.

Shamsie, Kamila. Kartography. 2002. (Illus.). 352p. pap. (*0-7475-5730-6*) Bloomsbury Pr.

—Kartography. 320p. 2004. pap. (*0-15-602973-1*, Harvest Bks.); 2003. 24.00 (*0-15-101010-2*) Harcourt Trade Pubs.

—Kartography. 2002. 343p. (*0-19-579833-3*) Oxford Univ. Pr., Inc.

Singh, Khushwant. Train to Pakistan. 1975. Orig. Title: Mano Majra. 181p. reprint ed. 62.95 (*0-8371-8226-3*, SIMM, Greenwood Pr.) Greenwood Publishing Group, Inc.

—Train to Pakistan. Orig. Title: Mano Majra. 192p. 1990. pap. 13.00 (*0-8021-3221-9*, Grove Pr.); 1988. (YA). (gr. 9 up). pap. 5.95 o.p. (*0-394-17887-4*) Grove/Atlantic, Inc.

—Train to Pakistan. 1988. Orig. Title: Mano Majra. (C). 8.50 (*0-86131-985-0*) South Asia Bks.

## PALENOC (IMAGINARY PLACE)—FICTION

Bailey, Robin W. Brothers of the Dragon. 1993. (Brothers of the Dragon Ser.). 320p. (Orig.). mass mkt. 4.99 o.s.i (*0-451-45251-8*, ROC) NAL.

—Flames of the Dragon. 1994. (Brothers of the Dragon Ser.). 352p. (Orig.). mass mkt. 4.99 o.s.i (*0-451-45289-5*, ROC) NAL.

—Triumph of the Dragon. 1995. (Brothers of the Dragon Ser.). 320p. (Orig.). mass mkt. 4.99 o.s.i (*0-451-45437-5*, ROC) NAL.

## PALESTINE—FICTION

Antaki, Myriam. Verses of Forgiveness. de Jager, Marjolijn, tr. from FRE. 2002. 174p. 22.00 (*1-59051-038-0*) Other Pr., LLC.

Badr, Liyana. A Balcony over the Fakihani. Clark, Peter & Tingley, Christopher, trs. 2002. (Emerging Voices Ser.). 144p. pap. 12.95 (*1-56656-464-6*) Interlink Publishing Group, Inc.

—A Balcony over the Fakihani. Clark, P. & Tingley, Christopher, trs. from ARA. 1993. (Emerging Voices Ser.). 128p. 19.95 (*1-56656-104-3*); pap. 9.95 (*1-56656-107-8*) Interlink Publishing Group, Inc.

Benning, Barry. The Unspoken Power of Rome. 2002. (Illus.). 436p. 23.95 (*0-9715676-0-3*) Wellspring Bks.

Cooke, Miriam. Hayati, My Life: A Novel. 2000. (Arab American Writings). x, 152p. 22.95 (*0-8156-0671-0*) Syracuse Univ. Pr.

Dallal, Shaw J. Scattered Like Seeds: A Novel. 1998. 192p. 26.95 (*0-8156-0553-6*) Syracuse Univ. Pr.

Dorr, Roberta Kells. Honored. 2003. 96p. 10.99 (*0-8007-1817-8*) Revell, Fleming H. Co.

Elmer, Robert. Freedom Trap. 2002. (Promise of Zion Ser.: Vol. 5). (Illus.). 160p. (J). pap. 5.99 (*0-7642-2313-5*) Bethany Hse. Pubs.

—Refugee Treasure. 2001. (Promise of Zion Ser.: Vol. 3). 176p. (J). (gr. 3-7). pap. 5.99 (*0-7642-2299-6*) Bethany Hse. Pubs.

Fawal, Ibrahim. On the Hills of God. 1998. 450p. 27.95 o.p. (*1-57966-002-9*); pap. text 17.95 o.p. (*1-57966-016-9*) River City Publishing. (Black Belt Pr.).

Gavron, Daniel. Pilgrims' 2000. 272p. pap. 15.95 (*0-88739-255-5*) Creative Arts Bk. Co.

George, Margaret. Mary Called Magdalene: A Novel. 2003. 656p. pap. 16.00 (*0-14-200279-8*); 2002. 528p. 27.95 o.s.i (*0-670-03096-1*, Viking) Viking Penguin.

Grant, Linda. When I Lived in Modern Times. 2001. (Illus.). 288p. 23.95 o.s.i (*0-525-94594-6*) Dutton/Plume.

—When I Lived in Modern Times. l.t. ed. 2001. (Women's Fiction Ser.). 399p. 28.95 (*0-7862-3396-6*) Thorndike Pr.

Hoffmann, Yoel. Katschen & The Book of Joseph. Kriss, David et al, trs. from HEB. 1998. 160p. 17.95 (*0-8112-1373-0*); 1999. 161p. reprint ed. pap. 11.95 (*0-8112-1405-2*, NDP875) New Directions Publishing Corp.

Holman, Sheri. A Stolen Tongue. 1998. 352p. pap. 13.00 (*0-385-49124-7*, Delacorte Pr.) Dell Publishing.

—A Stolen Tongue. 1997. 320p. 23.00 o.p. (*0-87113-669-4*, Atlantic Monthly Pr.) Grove/Atlantic, Inc.

Maier, Paul L. Pontius Pilate: A Biographical Novel. 384p. 1995. pap. 13.99 (*0-8254-3296-0*); 1990. 19.99 (*0-8254-3261-8*) Kregel Pubns.

—Pontius Pilate: A Biographical Novel. 1981. pap. 4.95 o.p. (*0-8423-4852-2*) Tyndale Hse. Pubs.

Shalev, Meir. The Loves of Judith. Harshav, Barbara, tr. from HEB. 1999. 320p. o.p. (*0-88001-635-3*, Ecco) HarperTrade.

Shammas, Anton. Arabesques. Eden, Vivian, tr. from ENG. 1988. 256p. 16.95 o.p. (*0-06-015744-5*) HarperTrade.

—Arabesques. 2001. 264p. pap. text 15.95 (*0-520-22832-4*) Univ. of California Pr.

Thoene, Bodie & Thoene, Brock. Jerusalem Vigil. 2001. (Zion Legacy Ser.: No. 1). 336p. pap. 13.00 (*0-14-029856-8*) Penguin Group (USA) Inc.

—Jerusalem Vigil. 2000. (Zion Legacy Ser.: No. 1). (Illus.). 352p. 19.95 o.p. (*0-670-88911-3*) Viking Penguin.

—Thunder from Jerusalem. 2000. (Zion Legacy Ser.: No. 2). (Illus.). 352p. 19.95 o.s.i (*0-670-89206-8*, Viking); 4p. 25.95 o.s.i (*0-14-180237-5*, Penguin AudioBooks) Viking Penguin.

Thoene, Brock. The Jerusalem Scrolls: A Novel of Struggle for Jerusalem. 2002. 288p. pap. 13.00 (*0-14-200151-1*) Penguin Group (USA) Inc.

Thoene, Brock & Thoene, Bodie. Jerusalem Vigil. l.t. ed. 2001. (Illus.). 413p. lib. bdg. 27.95 (*1-58547-132-1*) Ctr. Point Large Print.

—Thunder in Jerusalem. 16th l.t. ed. 2002. 408p. lib. bdg. 27.95 (*1-58547-133-X*) Ctr. Point Large Print.

Tugwell, Maurice. Herzl Street. 1997. 200p. pap. 21.99 (*0-7388-0036-8*); text 31.99 (*0-7388-0007-4*) Xlibris Corp.

Uris, Leon. Exodus. 1983. (Illus.). 608p. mass mkt. 7.99 (*0-553-25847-8*) Bantam Bks.

—Exodus. 1994. reprint ed. lib. bdg. 35.95 (*1-56849-353-3*) Buccaneer Bks., Inc.

—Exodus. 2000. (Modern Classics Ser.). (Illus.). 640p. 10.99 (*0-517-20798-2*) Random Hse., Inc.

—Exodus. 1959. 14.04 (*0-606-00621-4*) Turtleback Bks.

Wallace, Lew. Ben Hur: A Tale of the Christ. 2000. (Radio Theatre Ser.). audio compact disk 18.97 (*1-56179-840-1*); (J). (gr. 4 up). audio compact disk 16.97 (*1-56179-841-X*) Focus on the Family Publishing.

—Ben Hur: A Tale of the Christ. 2003. 576p. mass mkt. 7.95 (*0-451-52874-3*, Signet Classics) NAL.

—Ben-Hur: A Tale of the Christ. 2000. (Classics Library). 496p. pap. 4.97 (*1-57748-776-1*) Barbour Publishing, Inc.

—Ben-Hur: A Tale of the Christ. 2002. 596p. per. 25.99 (*1-58827-783-6*); 30.99 (*1-58827-782-8*) IndyPublish.com.

—Ben-Hur: A Tale of the Christ. 2002. 480p. pap. 24.95 (*1-58715-538-9*); lib. bdg. 39.95 (*1-58715-539-7*) Wildside Pr.

—Ben Hur: A Tale of the Christ. 1999. (Notable American Authors Ser.). reprint ed. lib. bdg. 125.00 (*0-7812-9866-0*) Reprint Services Corp.

—Ben-Hur: A Tale of the Christ. 1993. (Illus.). 450p. reprint ed. 29.95 o.p. (*1-877767-85-9*) University Publishing Hse., Inc.

—Ben Hur: A Tale of the Christ. unabr. ed. 1992. 400p. reprint ed. pap. 14.95 (*1-57002-067-1*) University Publishing Hse., Inc.

Wilson, Jonathan. A Palestine Affair. 272p. 2004. pap. 13.00 (*1-4000-3122-2*, Anchor); 2003. 23.00 (*0-375-42209-9*, Pantheon) Knopf Publishing Group.

Zelitch, Simone. Louisa. 2001. 400p. reprint ed. pap. 14.00 (*0-425-18195-2*) Berkley Publishing Group.

—Louisa. 2000. 384p. 24.95 o.s.i (*0-399-14659-8*) Penguin Group (USA) Inc.

## PALM SPRINGS (CALIF.)—FICTION

Craft, Michael. Desert Winter: A Claire Gray Mystery. 2003. 288p. 23.95 (*0-312-30501-X*, Saint Martin's Minotaur) St. Martin's Pr.

Hinton, Gregory. Cathedral City. 2002. 352p. pap. 15.00 (*1-57566-850-5*); 2001. 32p. 23.00 (*1-57566-849-1*) Kensington Publishing Corp.

Lowell, Elizabeth. Moving Target. 2002. E-Book 19.95 (*0-06-001063-0*); 2001. E-Book 19.95 (*0-06-001065-7*); 2001. 592p. pap. 24.00 (*0-06-620962-5*) HarperCollins Pubs.

—Moving Target. abr. ed. 2001. audio 25.95 (*0-694-52562-6*, HarperAudio) HarperTrade.

—Moving Target. 464p. 2002. mass mkt. 7.99 (*0-06-103107-0*, Avon Bks.); 2001. 24.00 (*0-06-019875-3*, Morrow, William & Co.) Morrow/Avon.

Roberts, Lillian. Almost Human. 1998. mass mkt. 5.99 o.s.i (*0-449-00228-4*, Fawcett) Ballantine Bks.

—The Hand That Feeds You. 1997. mass mkt. 5.50 o.s.i (*0-449-14986-2*, Fawcett) Ballantine Bks.

—Riding for a Fall. 1996. (Veterinarian Mystery Ser.). mass mkt. 5.50 o.s.i (*0-449-14985-4*, Fawcett) Ballantine Bks.

Sanders, Lawrence. McNally's Caper. 1995. (Archy McNally Mystery Ser.). 352p. mass mkt. 7.99 (*0-425-14530-1*) Berkley Publishing Group.

—McNally's Caper. l.t. ed. 384p. reprint ed. 1995. pap. 18.95 o.p. (*0-8161-5975-0*); 1994. lib. bdg. 24.95 (*0-8161-5974-2*) Gale Group. (Macmillan Reference USA).

—McNally's Caper. l.t. ed. 1995. (Magna Large Print Ser.). 403p. o.p. (*0-7505-0837-X*) Magna Large Print Bks. GBR. *Dist:* Ulverscroft Large Print Canada, Ltd.

—McNally's Caper. 1994. 320p. 22.95 o.p. (*0-399-13919-2*, G. P. Putnam's Sons) Penguin Group (USA) Inc.

—McNally's Caper. abr. ed. 1994. (Archy McNally Mystery Ser.). audio 17.00 (*0-671-87164-1*, 391157, Simon & Schuster Audioworks) Simon & Schuster Audio.

—McNally's Dilemma. 2000. (Archy McNally Mystery Ser.). 336p. mass mkt. 7.99 (*0-425-17536-7*) Berkley Publishing Group.

—McNally's Dilemma. 1999. 320p. 24.95 o.s.i (*0-399-14490-0*) Penguin Group (USA) Inc.

—McNally's Dilemma. l.t. ed. (Thorndike/G. K. Hall Paperback Bestsellers Ser.). 2000. 407p. 28.95 (*0-7862-2247-6*); 1999. 432p. 31.95 (*0-7862-2246-8*) Thorndike Pr.

—McNally's Gamble. 1998. (Archy McNally Mystery Ser.). 368p. mass mkt. 7.50 (*0-425-16259-1*) Berkley Publishing Group.

—McNally's Gamble. l.t. ed. 1997. 26.95 o.p. (*1-56895-487-5*, Wheeler Publishing, Inc.) Gale Group.

—McNally's Gamble. 1997. 307p. 24.95 o.s.i (*0-399-14248-7*, G. P. Putnam's Sons) Penguin Group (USA) Inc.

—McNally's Gamble. 24.95 o.s.i (*0-399-14560-5*) Putnam Publishing Group, The.

—McNally's Gamble. 1998. audio 9.98 (*0-671-58153-8*); 1997. audio 18.00 (*0-671-53793-8*, 394532) Simon & Schuster Audio. (Simon & Schuster Audioworks).

—McNally's Luck. 1993. (Archy McNally Mystery Ser.). 336p. mass mkt. 7.99 (*0-425-13745-7*) Berkley Publishing Group.

—McNally's Luck. l.t. ed. (G. K. Hall Large Print Book Ser.). 350p. 1994. pap. 19.95 o.p. (*0-8161-5678-6*); 1993. 24.95 (*0-8161-5677-8*) Gale Group. (Macmillan Reference USA).

—McNally's Luck. l.t. ed. 1994. (Magna Large Print Ser.). 406p. o.p. (*0-7505-0679-2*) Magna Large Print Bks. GBR. *Dist:* Ulverscroft Large Print Canada, Ltd.

—McNally's Luck. 1992. 320p. 22.95 o.p. (*0-399-13762-9*, G. P. Putnam's Sons) Penguin Group (USA) Inc.

—McNally's Luck. 1994. 5.99 o.p. (*0-517-12590-0*) Random Hse. Value Publishing.

—McNally's Luck, abr. ed. 1992. (Archy McNally Mystery Ser.). audio 17.00 (*0-671-76989-8*, Simon & Schuster Audioworks) Simon & Schuster Audio.

—McNally's Puzzle. l.t. ed. 1997. (Archy McNally Mystery Ser.). 352p. mass mkt. 7.99 (*0-425-15746-6*) Berkley Publishing Group.

—McNally's Puzzle. l.t. ed. 1996. 26.95 o.p. (*0-7838-1712-6*, Macmillan Reference USA) Gale Group.

—McNally's Puzzle. 1996. 320p. 24.95 o.p. (*0-399-14135-9*, G. P. Putnam's Sons) Penguin Group (USA) Inc.

—McNally's Puzzle, abr. ed. 1996. (Archy McNally Mystery Ser.). audio 18.00 (*0-671-53792-X*, 393484, Simon & Schuster Audioworks) Simon & Schuster Audio.

—McNally's Puzzle. l.t. ed. 1997. (Paperback Bestsellers Ser.). pap. 26.95 (*0-7838-1713-4*) Thorndike Pr.

—McNally's Risk. 1994. (Archy McNally Mystery Ser.). 336p. reprint ed. pap. 7.99 (*0-425-14286-8*) Berkley Publishing Group.

—McNally's Risk. l.t. ed. 1993. 322p. 26.95 o.p. (*1-56895-042-X*, Wheeler Publishing, Inc.) Gale Group.

—McNally's Risk. l.t. ed. 1994. (Magna Large Print Ser.). 420p. (*0-7505-0680-6*) Magna Large Print Bks. GBR. *Dist:* Ulverscroft Large Print Canada, Ltd.

—McNally's Risk. 1993. 320p. 22.95 o.p. (*0-399-13816-1*, G. P. Putnam's Sons) Penguin Group (USA) Inc.

—McNally's Risk, abr. ed. 1993. (Archy McNally Mystery Ser.). audio 17.00 (*0-671-79743-3*, 391159, Simon & Schuster Audioworks) Simon & Schuster Audio.

—McNally's Secret. 1993. (Archy McNally Mystery Ser.). 352p. pap. 7.99 (*0-425-13572-1*) Berkley Publishing Group.

—McNally's Secret. l.t. ed. 1993. (General Ser.). 381p. pap. 17.95 o.p. (*0-8161-5540-2*); lib. bdg. 22.95 o.p. (*0-8161-5539-9*) Gale Group. (Macmillan Reference USA).

—McNally's Secret. 1992. 320p. 21.95 o.p. (*0-399-13675-4*, G. P. Putnam's Sons) Penguin Group (USA) Inc.

—McNally's Secret. abr. ed. 1992. (Archy McNally Mystery Ser.). audio 17.00 (*0-671-74472-0*, 391160, Simon & Schuster Audioworks) Simon & Schuster Audio.

—McNally's Trial. 1996. (Archy McNally Mystery Ser.). 352p. pap. 7.99 (*0-425-14755-X*) Berkley Publishing Group.

—McNally's Trial. l.t. ed. 1995. (Large Print Bks.). 26.95 o.p. (*1-56895-208-2*, Wheeler Publishing, Inc.) Gale Group.

—McNally's Trial. 1995. 309p. 23.95 o.p. (*0-399-14006-9*) Penguin Group (USA) Inc.

—McNally's Trial. 1999. pap. 12.98 (*0-671-04455-9*, Simon & Schuster Audioworks) Simon & Schuster Audio.

Sims, Elizabeth. Damn Straight. 2003. (Lillian Byrd Crime Story Ser.). 280p. pap. 13.95 (*1-55583-786-7*) Alyson Pubns.

Wambaugh, Joseph. Fugitive Nights. 1992. 384p. mass mkt. 7.50 (*0-553-29578-0*) Bantam Bks.

—Fugitive Nights. unabr. ed. 1992. audio 22.95 o.p. (*1-56100-455-3*, 431, Bookcassette); audio 57.25 o.p. (*1-56100-088-4*, 613, Unabridged Library Editions) Brilliance Audio.

—Fugitive Nights. 1992. 336p. 22.00 o.p. (*0-688-11128-9*, Morrow, William & Co.) Morrow/Avon.

—The Secrets of Harry Bright. 1986. 320p. mass mkt. 4.50 o.s.i (*0-553-26021-9*); 352p. mass mkt. 6.99 (*0-553-27430-9*) Bantam Bks.

## PALO ALTO (CALIF.)—FICTION

Roberts, Lora. Murder Bone by Bone. 1997. (Liz Sullivan Mysteries Ser.). mass mkt. 5.50 o.s.i (*0-449-14946-3*, Fawcett) Ballantine Bks.

—Murder Crops Up. 1998. (Liz Sullivan Mysteries Ser.). 240p. mass mkt. 5.99 o.s.i (*0-449-15048-8*, Fawcett) Ballantine Bks.

—Murder in a Nice Neighborhood. 1994. (Liz Sullivan Mysteries Ser.). (Orig.). mass mkt. 4.99 o.s.i (*0-449-14891-2*, Fawcett) Ballantine Bks.

—Murder in the Marketplace. 1995. mass mkt. 5.50 o.s.i (*0-449-14890-4*, Fawcett) Ballantine Bks.

## PANAMA—FICTION

Boyd, William Y. Panama. 1999. 192p. 21.95 (*1-892123-15-0*) Capital Bks., Inc.

Chambers, John W. Marisol y Magdelena, Bk. 1. 1998. (J). 15.00 (*0-689-81024-5*, Simon & Schuster Children's Publishing) Simon & Schuster Children's Publishing.

Correa, Raul. I Don't Know but I've Been Told. 2002. 272p. 24.95 (*0-06-019611-4*) HarperCollins Pubs.

Du Brul, Jack. River of Ruin. 2002. 544p. mass mkt. 6.99 (*0-451-41054-8*, Onyx) NAL.

Galbraith, Douglas. The Rising Sun. 2002. 544p. pap. 13.00 (*0-8021-3864-0*, Grove Pr.) Grove/Atlantic, Inc.

—The Rising Sun. 2000. 520p. (*0-330-37297-1*) Picador.

—The Rising Sun: A Novel. 2001. 544p. 25.00 o.p. (*0-87113-781-X*, Atlantic Monthly Pr.) Grove/Atlantic, Inc.

Griffin, Adele. Rainy Season. 1998. 12.00 (*0-606-13726-2*) Turtleback Bks.

Hughes, Richard. Isla Grande. 1994. 215p. (Orig.). pap. 12.50 (*1-883721-10-5*) Silver Mountain Pr.

Le Carré, John. The Tailor of Panama. 1997. (George Smiley Novels Ser.). mass mkt. 6.99 o.p. (*0-449-22739-1*, Fawcett); 416p. mass mkt. 7.99 (*0-345-42043-8*, Ballantine Bks.) Ballantine Bks.

—The Tailor of Panama, unabr. collector's ed. 1997. (George Smiley Novels Ser.). audio 80.00 (*0-913369-86-1*, 4382) Books on Tape, Inc.

—The Tailor of Panama. 1996. (George Smiley Novels Ser.). 320p. 25.00 (*0-679-45480-2*); 25.00 o.s.i (*0-679-45446-2*); pap. 25.00 o.p. (*0-679-77413-0*) Knopf, Alfred A. Inc.

—The Tailor of Panama. abr. ed. 1996. (George Smiley Ser.). audio 25.95 (*0-679-45813-1*, 694392, RH Audio) Random Hse. Audio Publishing Group.

—The Tailor of Panama. l.t. ed. 1996. (George Smiley Ser.). 512p. pap. 25.00 o.p. (*0-7838-1933-1*) Random Hse. Large Print.

Levi, Enrique J., ed. When New Flowers Bloomed: Short Stories by Women Writers from Costa Rica & Panama. 1988. (Discoveries Ser.). 208p. pap. 14.95 (*0-935480-47-1*) Latin American Literary Review Pr.

Markun, Patricia M. Mystery on Taboga Island. 1995. 160p. (J). (gr. 5-8). pap. 2.99 o.p. (*0-87406-727-8*) Darby Creek Publishing.

Miller, Carlos. Panama: A Novel. 1999. 326p. E-Book 8.00 (*0-7388-8252-6*) Xlibris Corp.

Saunders, Raymond M. Fenwick Travers & the Panama Canal: An Entertainment. 336p. 1996. pap. 12.95 o.p. (*0-89141-607-2*); 1995. (Illus.). 21.95 o.p. (*0-89141-481-9*) Ballantine Bks. (Presidio Pr.).

White, Randy Wayne. The Mangrove Coast. 1999. (Prime Crime Mysteries Ser.). 336p. reprint ed. mass mkt. 6.99 (*0-425-17194-9*, Prime Crime) Berkley Publishing Group.

—The Mangrove Coast. 1998. 256p. 22.95 o.p. (*0-399-14372-6*, G. P. Putnam's Sons) Penguin Group (USA) Inc.

## PAPUA NEW GUINEA—FICTION

Braver, Gary. Elixir. 2000. 352p. 25.95 (*0-312-87308-5*, Forge Bks.); 2001. 448p. reprint ed. mass mkt. 7.99 (*0-8125-7591-1*, Tor Bks.) Doherty, Tom Assocs., LLC.

Carlson, Melody. Awakening Heart. 1998. (Portraits Ser.). 288p. pap. 8.99 o.p. (*1-55661-998-7*) Bethany Hse. Pubs.

—Awakening Heart. l.t. ed. 2001. (Thorndike Press Large Print Christian Romance Ser.). 487p. 24.95 (*0-7862-3660-4*) Thorndike Pr.

Gillison, Samantha. The Undiscovered Country. 1998. 224p. (YA). (gr. 11 up). 23.00 o.p. (*0-8021-1627-2*, Grove Pr.) Grove/Atlantic, Inc.

—The Undiscovered Country: A Novel. 1999. 240p. pap. 13.00 o.s.i (*0-8050-6198-3*, Owl Bks.) Holt, Henry & Co.

Jay, Charlotte. Beat Not the Bones. 1995. 232p. pap. 11.00 (*1-56947-047-2*) Soho Pr., Inc.

Malouf, David & Jay, Charlotte. Beat Not the Bones. l.t. unabr. ed. 1997. pap. incl. audio (*1-86340-726-X*, 570725) Bolinda Publishing Pty, Ltd.
Shearston, Trevor. Something in the Blood. 1989. 255p. pap. 10.95 (*0-7022-1336-5*) International Specialized Bk. Services.
—Something in the Blood. 1979. 255p. 14.95 o.p. (*0-7022-1335-7*) Univ. of Queensland Pr. AUS. *Dist:* International Specialized Bk. Services.

**PARADISE COURT (LONDON, ENGLAND: IMAGINARY PLACE)—FICTION**

Oldfield, Jenny. All Fall Down. 1998. 551 p. (*0-7540-2120-3*, Macmillan Reference USA) Gale Group.
—All Fall Down. 2003. 392p. pap. (*0-330-34843-4*) Pan Macmillan.
—All Fall Down. l.t. ed. 1998. (Romance Ser.). 552p. 26.95 (*0-7862-1393-0*) Thorndike Pr.
—Paradise Court. l.t. ed. 1997. 603 p. (*0-7540-2011-8*, Galaxy Children's Large Print) BBC Audiobooks America.
—Paradise Court. 2003. 421p. pap. (*0-330-33886-2*) Macmillan Children's Bks.

**PARADYS (IMAGINARY PLACE)—FICTION**

Lee, Tanith. The Book of the Beast. (Secret Books of Paradys: Vol. 2). 1991. 240p. 19.95 (*0-87951-417-5*); 1997. 196p. reprint ed. pap. 13.95 o.p. (*0-87951-761-1*); Vol. 2. 1997. 240p. reprint ed. pap. 13.95 (*0-87951-698-4*) Overlook Pr., The.
—The Book of the Damned. 240p. 1990. (Secret Books of Paradys: Vol. 2). 19.95 o.s.i (*0-87951-408-6*); 1997. (Secret Books of Paradys: Vol. 1). reprint ed. pap. 13.95 (*0-87951-697-6*) Overlook Pr., The.
—The Book of the Dead. 1997. (Secret Books of Paradys: Vol. III). 208p. pap. 13.95 (*0-87951-798-0*) Overlook Pr., The.
—The Book of the Dead: The Secret Books of Paradys III. 1991. (Secret Books of Paradys Ser.). 196p. 19.95 (*0-87951-440-X*) Overlook Pr., The.
—The Book of the Mad. 1997. (Secret Books of Paradys: Vol. IV). 216p. pap. 13.95 (*0-87951-799-9*) Overlook Pr., The.
—The Book of the Mad: The Secret Books of Paradys IV. 1993. (Secret Books of Paradys Ser.). 216p. 19.95 (*0-87951-481-7*) Overlook Pr., The.

**PARAGUAY—FICTION**

Enright, Anne. The Pleasure of Eliza Lynch. 2003. 256p. 23.00 (*0-87113-868-9*, Atlantic Monthly Pr.) Grove/Atlantic, Inc.
Jacobs, Mark. The Liberation of Little Heaven: And Other Stories. 1999. 254p. 23.00 (*1-56947-135-5*) Soho Pr., Inc.
Lieberman, Herbert. The Climate of Hell. 1978. 9.95 o.s.i (*0-671-24363-2*, Simon & Schuster) Simon & Schuster.
Roa Bastos, Augusto. Son of Man. 1988. (Voices of Resistance Ser.). 288p. 30.00 (*0-85345-767-0*); pap. 13.00 (*0-85345-733-6*) Monthly Review Pr.
Upton, Peter. Green Hill Far Away. 1978. mass mkt. 2.25 o.s.i (*0-345-27208-0*) Ballantine Bks.
—Green Hill Far Away. 1977. 10.95 o.s.i (*0-671-22344-5*, Simon & Schuster) Simon & Schuster.

**PARIS (FRANCE)—FICTION**

Adler, Elizabeth A. The Last Time I Saw Paris. E-Book 23.95 (*0-312-70197-7*); 2002. 352p. mass mkt. 6.99 (*0-312-98030-2*, St. Martin's Paperbacks); 2001. (Illus.). 304p. 23.95 (*0-312-26982-X*) St. Martin's Pr.
—The Last Time I Saw Paris. (Illus.). 2001. 423p. (*0-7540-1684-6*); 2002. 423p. 28.95 (*0-7862-3437-7*); 2001. 390p. 31.95 (*0-7862-3436-9*); 2001. 423p. (*0-7540-9084-1*) Thorndike Pr.
Adnan, Etel. Paris, When It's Naked. 1993. 115p. (Orig.). pap. 13.50 (*0-942996-20-8*) Post-Apollo Pr., The.
Allain, Marcel. The Silent Executioner: Being the Second in the Series of Fantomas Adventures. 1987. (Fantomas Ser.: No. 2). (Illus.). 288p. 15.95 o.p. (*0-688-07265-8*, Morrow, William & Co.) Morrow/Avon.
Allbeury, Ted. The Lantern Network. 1989. 208p. 17.95 (*0-89296-185-6*) Mysterious Pr.
—The Lantern Network. l.t. ed. 1982. (Ulverscroft Large Print Ser.). 352p. 29.99 o.p. (*0-7089-0864-0*, Ulverscroft) Thorpe, F. A. Pubs. GBR. *Dist:* Ulverscroft Large Print Bks., Ltd., Ulverscroft Large Print Canada, Ltd.
—The Lantern Network. 1990. mass mkt. 4.95 o.s.i (*0-445-40875-8*, Mysterious Pr. Paperback Bks.) Warner Bks., Inc.
—The Stalking Angel. 208p. 1989. mass mkt. 3.95 o.s.i (*0-445-40834-0*); 1988. 17.95 (*0-89296-184-8*) Mysterious Pr.
Angelica, J. Fermentation. 1997. 128p. 20.00 o.p. (*0-8021-1614-0*, Grove Pr.) Grove/Atlantic, Inc.
Anonymous. Parisian Frolics. 2000. 144p. pap. 7.95 (*1-56201-210-X*, Blue Moon Bks.) Avalon Publishing Group.
Appignanesi, Lisa. Paris Requiem. 2004. 430p. pap. 7.99 (*1-55278-298-0*) McArthur & Co. CAN. *Dist:* National Bk. Network.
Baker, Leslie A. Paris Cat. 1999. (Illus.). 32p. (J). (ps-3). 15.95 o.p. (*0-316-07309-1*) Little Brown & Co.
—Paris Cat. 1999. E-Book (*1-58824-663-9*); E-Book (*1-58824-888-7*); E-Book (*1-58824-662-0*) ipicturebooks, LLC.
Baldwin, James. Giovanni's Room. 1985. 7.95 o.p. (*0-385-27465-3*) Doubleday Publishing.
—Giovanni's Room. 2001. 208p. 16.95 (*0-679-64219-6*, Modern Library) Random House Adult Trade Publishing Group.
Ball, Terence. Rousseau's Ghost: A Novel. (C). 1999. 206p. pap. text 19.95 (*0-7914-3934-8*); 1998. 224p. text 31.50 (*0-7914-3933-X*) State Univ. of New York Pr.
—Rousseau's Ghost: A Novel. 1998. E-Book 31.50 (*0-585-28283-8*) netLibrary, Inc.
Balzac, Honoré de. La Cousine Bette. Allem, Maurice, ed. 1984. (Coll. Prestige). (FRE.). pap. 10.95 (*0-7859-3466-9*, 2070361381) French & European Pubns., Inc.
—La Cousine Bette. 8.95 (*2-253-01067-7*, LO0009E) Librairie Generale Francaise, LGF FRA. *Dist:* Continental Bk. Co., Inc.
—La Cousine Bette. Raphael, Sylvia & Bellos, David, eds. 1992. (Illus.). 518p. pap. 7.95 o.p. (*0-19-282606-9*) Oxford Univ. Pr., Inc.
—La Cousine Bette. 1955. (Folio Ser.: No. 138). (FRE.). pap. 10.95 (*2-07-036138-1*, 952) Schoenhof's Foreign Bks., Inc.
—La Cousine Bette. Crawford, Marion A., tr. 1965. (Classics Ser.). 448p. 10.95 (*0-14-044160-3*, Penguin Classics) Viking Penguin.
—La Cousine Bette. unabr. ed. (FRE.). pap. 7.95 (*2-87714-154-3*) Bookking International FRA. *Dist:* Distribooks, Inc.
Balzac, Honoré de & Everyman's Library Staff. Cousin Bette. 1991. 496p. 20.00 (*0-679-40671-9*) Random Hse., Inc.
Barclay, Steven, ed. A Place in the World Called Paris. 2002. (Illus.). 176p. pap. 16.95 (*0-8118-3318-6*) Chronicle Bks. LLC.
Bassett, Jennifer. The Phantom of the Opera. 1993. (Illus.). 48p. pap. text 5.95 o.p. (*0-19-422707-3*) Oxford Univ. Pr., Inc.
Begley, Louis. Shipwreck. 2003. 256p. 23.00 (*1-4000-4098-1*) Knopf, Alfred A. Inc.
Belletto, Rene. Machine: A Novel. 1993. 368p. 21.00 o.p. (*0-8021-1437-7*, Grove Pr.) Grove/Atlantic, Inc.
Bellow, Saul. Ravelstein. l.t. ed. 2000. (Compass Press Large Print Book Ser.). 286p. 26.95 (*1-56895-127-2*, Wheeler Publishing, Inc.) Gale Group.
—Ravelstein. unabr. ed. 2000. 29.95 (*1-56511-428-0*) HighBridge Co.
—Ravelstein. 240p. 2000. 24.95 o.p. (*0-670-84134-X*); 50th ed. 2001. reprint ed. 13.00 (*0-14-100176-3*) Viking Penguin.
Bernanos, Georges. The Impostor. Whitehouse, J. C., tr. from FRE. 1999. 250p. pap. 20.00 (*0-8032-6153-5*); text 50.00 (*0-8032-1290-9*) Univ. of Nebraska Pr.
Black, Cara. Murder in Belleville: An Aimee Leduc Investigation. 2000. (Aimee Leduc Investigation Ser.). (Illus.). 341p. 23.00 (*1-56947-211-4*) Soho Pr., Inc.
—Murder in the Bastille. 2003. 304p. 24.00 (*1-56947-324-2*) Soho Pr., Inc.
—Murder in the Marais. 1999. (Aimee Leduc Investigation Ser.). 354p. 22.00 (*1-56947-159-2*) Soho Pr., Inc.
—Murder in the Marais: An Aimee Leduc Investigation. 2000. (Illus.). 360p. pap. 13.00 (*1-56947-212-2*) Soho Pr., Inc.
—Murder in the Sentier. (Illus.). 2003. 336p. pap. 13.00 (*1-56947-331-5*); 2002. 304p. 24.00 (*1-56947-278-5*) Soho Pr., Inc.
Blake, Jennifer. Royal Passion. 384p. 1991. mass mkt. 5.99 o.s.i (*0-449-14790-8*); 1986. pap. 8.95 o.p. (*0-449-90101-7*) Ballantine Bks. (Fawcett).
—Royal Passion. 1993. 20.00 o.p. (*0-7278-4419-9*) Severn Hse. Pubs., Ltd.
Blank, Hannah. Brave Man Dead: An Alphonse Dantan. 2000. (Alphonse Dantan Mystery Ser.: No. 2). 300p. (*0-9652778-3-6*, Hightrees Bks.) Prism Corp.
—A Murder of Convenience. 1999. 24.95 (*0-9652778-1-X*, Hightrees Bks.) Prism Corp.
Bonner, Cindy. Right from Wrong: A Novel. 1999. 336p. tchr. ed. 19.95 (*1-56512-104-X*, 72104) Algonquin Bks. of Chapel Hill.
—Right from Wrong: A Novel. l.t. ed. 1999. (Basic Ser.). 472p. 28.95 (*0-7862-1990-4*) Thorndike Pr.
Bowen, Elizabeth. The House in Paris. 2002. 288p. pap. 13.00 (*0-385-72125-0*, Knopf Bks. for Young Readers) Random Hse. Children's Bks.
Braddon, M. E. The Trail of the Serpent. Willis, Chris, ed. 2003. (Modern Library Classics). (Illus.). 496p. pap. 13.95 (*0-8129-6678-3*, Modern Library) Random House Adult Trade Publishing Group.
Bradford, Barbara Taylor. A Sudden Change of Heart. 1999. mass mkt. (*0-440-29567-X*); 400p. mass mkt. 7.99 (*0-440-23514-6*) Dell Publishing.
—A Sudden Change of Heart. l.t. ed. 1999. 11.95 (*1-56895-965-6*); 29.95 o.p. (*1-56895-735-1*) Gale Group. (Wheeler Publishing, Inc.).
—A Sudden Change of Heart. l.t. ed. 2000. (Charnwood Large Print Ser.). 440p. o.p. (*0-7089-9134-3*, Ulverscroft) Thorpe, F. A. Pubs. GBR. *Dist:* Ulverscroft Large Print Bks., Ltd., Ulverscroft Large Print Canada, Ltd.
—Three Weeks in Paris: A Novel. 2002. 352p. mass mkt. 7.99 (*0-440-23730-0*, Delta) Dell Publishing.
—Three Weeks in Paris: A Novel. 2002. 336p. 24.95 (*0-385-50141-2*) Doubleday Publishing.
—Three Weeks in Paris: A Novel. abr. ed. 2002. audio compact disk 29.95 (*0-553-71464-3*); audio 25.95 (*0-553-52892-0*) Random Hse. Audio Publishing Group.
—Three Weeks in Paris: A Novel. l.t. ed. 2002. 464p. 24.95 (*0-375-43149-7*) Random Hse. Large Print.
Brian, Bex. Promiscuous Unbound: A Novel. 2003. 190p. 23.00 (*0-87113-873-5*) Grove/Atlantic, Inc.
Brodrick, William. The 6th Lamentation: A Novel. 2003. 400p. 24.95 (*0-670-03191-7*, Viking) Viking Penguin.
Brown, Dan. The Da Vinci Code: A Novel. 2004. 512p. mass mkt. 7.99 (*0-345-45151-1*, Fawcett) Ballantine Bks.
—The Da Vinci Code: A Novel. 2003. 464p. 24.95 (*0-385-50420-9*); E-Book 12.00 (*0-385-50421-7*) Doubleday Publishing.
—The Da Vinci Code: A Novel. l.t. ed. 2003. 752p. 26.95 (*0-375-43230-2*) Random Hse. Large Print.
Carlile, Clancy. The Paris Pilgrims. 2000. 464p. pap. 14.00 (*0-7867-0753-4*); 1999. 496p. 25.00 o.p. (*0-7867-0615-5*) Avalon Publishing Group. (Carroll & Graf Pubs.).
Carr, John Dickson. The Corpse in the Waxworks: A Monsieur Bencolin Mystery. 1990. 192p. reprint ed. mass mkt. 4.95 o.p. (*0-06-081039-4*, Perennial) HarperTrade.
—The Corpse in the Waxworks: A Monsieur Bencolin Mystery. 1990. 192p. (C). reprint ed. lib. bdg. 20.00 o.p. (*0-8095-9026-3*) Millefleurs.
—It Walks by Night. 1997. 19.50 o.p. (*0-7451-8698-X*, Black Dagger) BBC Audiobooks America.
—It Walks by Night. 1986. 256p. mass mkt. 3.50 o.p. (*0-8217-1931-9*, Zebra Bks.) Kensington Publishing Corp.
Carroll, Lewis, pseud, ed. The Works of Charles Dickens, 21 vols. reprint ed. lib. bdg. 2058.00 (*0-7426-2349-1*) Classic Bks.
Carter, Charlotte. Coq Au Vin. 1999. (Nanette Hayes Mystery Ser.). 200p. 22.00 o.s.i (*0-89296-678-5*) Mysterious Pr.
—Coq Au Vin. 2000. (Nanette Hayes Mysteries Ser.). 224p. mass mkt. 6.50 (*0-446-60787-8*) Warner Bks., Inc.
Cerasini, Marc A. The Hunchback of Notre Dame. 1995. (Bullseye Step into Classics Ser.). 9.09 o.p. (*0-606-09442-3*) Turtleback Bks.
Chambers, Robert W. In the Quarter. 2003. 146p. pap. 12.95 (*0-9718305-4-1*) Sattre Pr.
—In the Quarter. 2003. pap. 18.95 (*1-59224-471-8*) Wildside Pr.
Charney, Ann. Rousseau's Garden: A Novel. 2001. 207p. 24.00 (*1-57962-033-7*) Permanent Pr., The.
Chessman, Harriet Scott. Lydia Cassatt Reading the Morning Paper. 2002. 176p. pap. 13.00 (*0-452-28350-7*) Dutton/Plume.
—Lydia Cassatt Reading the Morning Paper. 2001. (Illus.). 176p. 24.00 (*1-58322-272-3*) Seven Stories Pr.
Chevalier, Tracy. The Lady & the Unicorn. 2003. 256p. 23.95 (*0-525-94767-1*, Dutton) Dutton/Plume.
Coffman, Virginia. Veronique. 1975. 8.95 o.p. (*0-87795-107-1*, Morrow, William & Co.) Morrow/Avon.
Colter, Cyrus. City of Light: A Novel. 1993. 352p. 22.95 o.p. (*1-56025-059-3*); pap. 12.95 o.p. (*1-56025-061-5*) Avalon Publishing Group. (Thunder's Mouth Pr.).
—City of Light: A Novel. 1998. 432p. pap. 22.00 (*0-8101-5080-8*, TriQuarterly Bks.) Northwestern Univ. Pr.
Cornwell, Patricia. Black Notice. 2000. 464p. mass mkt. 7.99 (*0-425-17540-5*) Berkley Publishing Group.
—Black Notice. unabr. ed. 1999. audio 72.00 (*0-7366-4581-0*, 4988) Books on Tape, Inc.
—Black Notice. l.t. ed. 1999. 25.95 o.p. (*0-7838-8688-8*, Macmillan Reference USA) Gale Group.
—Black Notice, Set. abr. ed. 1999. audio 24.95. audio 39.95 Highsmith Inc.
—Black Notice. abr. ed. 1999. 24.95 o.s.i (*0-399-14515-X*); 368p. 150.00 (*0-399-14522-2*, G. P. Putnam's Sons);Set. 5p. 39.95 o.s.i (*0-399-14516-8*, Putnam Berkley Audio) Penguin Group (USA) Inc.
—Black Notice. 2002. 25.95 o.s.i (*0-399-15031-5*); 1999. 415p. 25.95 o.p. (*0-399-14508-7*) Putnam Publishing Group, The.
—Black Notice. l.t. ed. 2000. 544p. pap. 13.95 (*0-375-70771-9*); 1999. 576p. 25.95 (*0-375-40845-2*) Random Hse. Large Print.
—Black Notice. unabr. ed. 2000. (Kay Scarpetta Mystery Ser. : Vol. 5). audio compact disk 112.00 (*0-7887-3975-1*, C1094E7); 1999. audio compact disk 112.00; 1999. (Kay Scarpetta Mystery Ser. : Vol. 5). audio 85.00 (*0-7887-3458-X*, 95881E7) Recorded Bks., LLC.
—Black Notice. 2000. 14.04 (*0-606-19510-6*) Turtleback Bks.
Courtine, Robert J. Madame Maigret's Recipes. Manheim, Mary, tr. 1987. pap. 5.95 o.p. (*0-15-650172-4*, Harvest Bks.) Harcourt Trade Pubs.
Croutier, Alev Lytle. The Palace of Tears. 2002. 192p. pap. 12.95 (*0-385-33491-5*, Delta) Dell Publishing.
Dadie, Bernard B. An African in Paris. Hatch, Karen C., tr. from FRE. 1994. Tr. of Negre a Paris. 184p. text 32.50 (*0-252-02040-5*); 136p. pap. text 16.95 (*0-252-06407-0*) Univ. of Illinois Pr.
Daudet, Alphonse. The Nabob. E-Book 3.95 (*0-594-02079-4*) 1873 Pr.
—The Nabob. Trent, William P., tr. from FRE. 1976. reprint ed. 40.00 o.p. (*0-86527-282-4*) Fertig, Howard Inc.
—The Nabob. 2002. 368p. 96.99 (*1-4043-2134-9*); per. 92.99 (*1-4043-2135-7*) IndyPublish.com.
Davies, Luke. Isabelle the Navigator. 2002. 272p. pap. 12.95 (*0-425-18604-0*) Berkley Publishing Group.
De Witt, Abigail. Lili: A Novel. 2002. 320p. pap. 13.95 (*0-393-32318-8*) Norton, W. W. & Co., Inc.
Debreczeny, Paul. Temptations of the Past. 1982. 110p. (C). pap. 6.50 o.p. (*0-938920-17-0*) Hermitage Pubs.
Delacorta. Alba. 1990. 208p. pap. 7.95 o.p. (*0-87113-387-3*, Atlantic Monthly Pr.) Grove/Atlantic, Inc.
—Alba. Texier, Catherine, tr. 1989. 288p. 17.95 o.p. (*0-87113-324-5*) Grove/Atlantic, Inc.
Delelis, Philippe. The Last Cantata. 2000. 352p. pap. 15.95 (*1-902881-31-1*); (*1-902881-30-3*) Toby Pr.
DeMaria, Robert. The White Road. 2000. 272p. 25.00 (*1-57962-073-6*) Permanent Pr., The.
Desplechin, Marie. Taking It to Heart. Hobson, Will, tr. from FRE. 2002. 224p. pap. 11.95 (*1-86207-407-0*) Granta.
Dickens, Charles. Charles Dickens. 1993. 864p. 13.99 (*0-517-09339-1*) Random Hse. Value Publishing.
—Charles Dickens. unabr. ed. 1995. (Classic Author Ser.). (J). audio 16.95 (*1-55935-169-1*) Soundelux Audio Publishing.
—Charles Dickens: Three Great Novels: Hard Times; A Tale of Two Cities; Great Expectations. 1994. 836p. pap. 15.95 o.p. (*0-19-282332-9*) Oxford Univ. Pr., Inc.
—A Tale of Two Cities. 1994. (Illustrated Classics Collection). 64p. pap. 3.60 o.p. (*1-56103-506-8*) American Guidance Service, Inc.
—A Tale of Two Cities. l.t. unabr. ed. (Large Print Classics Ser.). 2001. viii, 528p. 14.95 (*0-486-41776-X*); 1999. 304p. pap. 2.50 (*0-486-40651-2*) Dover Pubns., Inc.
—A Tale of Two Cities. 1993. (Everyman's Library). 480p. 20.00 (*0-679-42073-8*) Knopf, Alfred A. Inc.
—A Tale of Two Cities. Sanders, Andrew, ed. & intro. by. 1998. (Oxford World's Classics Ser.). 560p. pap. 5.95 (*0-19-283390-1*) Oxford Univ. Pr., Inc.
—A Tale of Two Cities. 1996. (Modern Library Ser.). 512p. 19.95 (*0-679-60208-9*) Random Hse., Inc.
—A Tale of Two Cities. 1984. (Illus.). 400p. 12.95 o.p. (*0-89577-179-9*) Reader's Digest Assn., Inc., The.
—A Tale of Two Cities. 1992. (Literary Classics Ser.). 272p. text 5.98 o.p. (*1-56138-114-4*, Courage Bks.) Running Pr. Bk. Pubs.
—A Tale of Two Cities. 2000. (Signature Classics Ser.). iv, 358p. 24.95 (*1-58279-078-7*); (*1-58279-079-5*) Trident Pr. International.
—A Tale of Two Cities. 2000. (Penguin Classics Ser.). (Illus.). 528p. 6.95 o.s.i (*0-14-043730-4*, Penguin Classics) Viking Penguin.
—A Tale of Two Cities. Woodcock, George, ed. 1970. (English Library). (Illus.). 416p. pap. 6.95 o.s.i (*0-14-043054-7*, Penguin Classics) Viking Penguin.
—The Works of Charles Dickens. 2001. (Collected Works of Charles Dickens). reprint ed. pap. text 588.00 (*0-7426-7349-9*) Classic Bks.
—The Works of Charles Dickens. 1988. 11.99 o.s.i (*0-517-61831-1*); 1990. 864p. 19.99 (*0-517-05360-8*) Random Hse. Value Publishing.
—The Works of Charles Dickens. 1989. 9.98 o.p. (*0-8317-9504-2*) Smithmark Pubs., Inc.
—The Works of Charles Dickens. 1995. 797p. pap. o.p. (*1-57215-128-5*) World Pubns., Inc.
—The Works of Charles Dickens. unabr. ed. Incl. Great Expectations. audio Pickwick Papers. audio Tale of Two Cities. audio Set audio 29.75 Audio Bk. Co.
Diliberto, Gioia. I Am Madame X. 2003. (Illus.). 272p. 24.00 (*0-7432-1155-3*, Scribner) Simon & Schuster.
Doane, Michael. City of Light. 1992. 323 p. 22.00 o.s.i (*0-394-58107-5*) Knopf, Alfred A. Inc.
Dougan, Cameron. Because She Is Beautiful: A Novel. E-Book 9.95 (*1-58945-509-6*) Adobe Systems, Inc.
—Because She Is Beautiful: A Novel. 2001. 888p. E-Book 9.95 (*0-679-64718-X*, AtRandom) Random House Adult Trade Publishing Group.

Douglas, Carole Nelson. Castle Rouge: A Novel of Suspense Featuring Sherlock Holmes, Irene Adler, & Jack the Ripper. 2002. (Irene Adler Novel Ser.). (Illus.). 544p. 25.95 (*0-312-86941-X*, Forge Bks.) Doherty, Tom Assocs., LLC.

—Chapel Noir. 2001. 480p. 25.95 (*0-312-85493-5*, Forge Bks.) Doherty, Tom Assocs., LLC.

—Irene's Last Waltz. 1994. (Irene Adler Adventure Ser.). 480p. mass mkt. 4.99 (*0-8125-1703-2*, Forge Bks.) Doherty, Tom Assocs., LLC.

—Irene's Last Waltz. unabr. ed. 2000. audio 97.00 (*0-7887-2493-2*, 95568E7) Recorded Bks., LLC.

Dryansky, Joanne & Dryansky, Gerry. Fatima's Good Fortune. 2003. 22.95 (*1-4013-5199-9*) Hyperion Pr.

Du Maurier, George Louis Palmella Busson. Trilby. 1976. 26.95 (*0-8488-0265-9*) Amereon, Ltd.

—Trilby. unabr. ed. 1998. (YA). (gr. 9 up). audio 47.95 (*1-55685-567-2*) Audio Bk. Contractors, Inc.

—Trilby. unabr. ed. 1998. audio 56.95 (*0-7861-1298-0*, 2194) Blackstone Audio Bks., Inc.

—Trilby. 1994. reprint ed. lib. bdg. 32.95 (*1-56849-527-7*) Buccaneer Bks., Inc.

—Trilby. (Early Best Sellers Ser.). reprint ed. lib. bdg. 48.00 (*0-7426-1020-9*); 2001. (Illus.). pap. text 28.00 (*0-7426-6020-6*) Classic Bks.

—Trilby. unabr. ed. 1994. (Illus.). 384p. pap. text 9.95 (*0-486-28319-4*) Dover Pubns., Inc.

—Trilby. 1956. 7.50 o.p. (*0-460-00863-3*, Dutton) Dutton/Plume.

—Trilby. Showalter, Elaine, ed. 1999. (Oxford World's Classics Ser.). (Illus.). 368p. pap. 7.95 (*0-19-283351-0*) Oxford Univ. Pr., Inc.

—Trilby. Showalter, Elaine & Trotter, David, eds. 1995. (Oxford Popular Fiction Ser.). (Illus.). 316p. pap. 8.95 o.p. (*0-19-282323-X*) Oxford Univ. Pr., Inc.

—Trilby. 1998. 447p. reprint ed. lib. bdg. 75.00 (*0-7812-7712-4*) Reprint Services Corp.

—Trilby. 1994. 390p. pap. 7.50 (*0-460-87447-0*, Everyman's Classic Library in Paperback) Tuttle Publishing.

—Trilby. Pick, Daniel, ed. & intro. by. 1995. (Penguin Classics Ser.). 336p. pap. 7.95 o.p. (*0-14-043403-8*, Penguin Classics) Viking Penguin.

—Trilby. 368p. pap. 4.00 o.p. (*1-85326-233-1*) Wordsworth Editions, Ltd. GBR. *Dist:* Casemate Pubs. & Bk. Distributors, LLC.

Duffy, James. The Christmas Gang. 1989. (Illus.). 80p. (J). (gr. 3-6). 12.95 o.s.i (*0-684-19008-7*, Atheneum) Simon & Schuster Children's Publishing.

—The Revolt of the Teddy Bears: A May Gray Mystery. 1985. (Illus.). 80p. (J). (gr. 5 up). 1.00 o.p. (*0-517-55533-6*) Random Hse. Value Publishing.

Dukthas, Ann. The Prince Lost to Time. 1996. 229p. mass mkt. 5.99 (*0-312-95843-9*, St. Martin's Paperbacks); 1995. 240p. 21.95 o.p. (*0-312-13592-0*, Saint Martin's Minotaur) St. Martin's Pr.

Dunn, Samantha. Failing Paris. 2000. 169p. pap. 12.95 (*1-902881-17-6*); 1999. 146p. 19.95 (*1-902881-01-X*) Toby Pr.

Duras, Marguerite. Summer Rain. Bray, Barbara, tr. from FRE. 1992. 128p. 18.00 o.s.i (*0-684-19403-1*, Scribner) Simon & Schuster.

Durham, Lyn. Marie No. 2: Mystery at the Paris Ballet. 1997. (Girlhood Journeys Ser.: Bk. 2). (J). 12.95 (*0-689-81205-1*, Simon & Schuster Children's Publishing) Simon & Schuster Children's Publishing.

Dyer, Geoff. Paris Trance: A Romance. 272p. 2000. pap. 13.00 (*0-86547-600-4*, North Point Pr.); 1999. 23.00 o.p. (*0-374-22981-3*) Farrar, Straus & Giroux.

—Paris Trance: A Romance. 1998. 274p. o.s.i (*0-349-11020-4*) Little Brown & Co.

Edgeworth, Maria. Ormond. 1972. reprint ed. 13.00 o.p. (*0-7165-1799-X*) Biblio Distribution.

—Ormond. 2001. (Tales & Novels Ser.). reprint ed. pap. text 28.00 (*0-7426-8398-2*) Classic Bks.

—Ormond. 2001. (Penguin Classics Ser.). 352p. 12.00 (*0-14-043644-8*) Viking Penguin.

Eisner, William. The Sevigne Letters. Putnam, Jeff, ed. 1994. 201p. 18.00 (*1-880909-27-8*) Baskerville Pubs., Inc.

Ellis, Bret Easton. Glamorama. 2000. (Vintage Contemporaries Ser.). 560p. pap. 14.95 (*0-375-70384-5*, Vintage) Knopf Publishing Group.

—Glamorama. abr. ed. 2001. audio (*0-333-78165-1*) Macmillan U.K. GBR. *Dist:* Macmillan Publishing Co., Inc.

Endore, Guy. The Werewolf of Paris. 1993. reprint ed. lib. bdg. 18.95 (*0-89968-425-4*, Lightyear Pr.) Buccaneer Bks., Inc.

—The Werewolf of Paris. 1976. pap. 1.95 o.s.i (*0-671-80584-3*, Pocket) Simon & Schuster.

Engel, Howard. Murder in Montparnasse. 304p. 2000. 14.95 (*1-58567-094-4*); 1999. 23.95 (*0-87951-701-8*) Overlook Pr., The.

Espinosa, Maria. Longing. 1995. 298p. pap. 9.95 (*1-55885-145-3*) Arte Publico Pr.

Federman, Raymond. The Voice in the Closet. 2001. (ENG & FRE.). pap. 9.00 (*0-9703165-8-5*) Starcherone Bks.

—The Voice in the Closet. 1986. 80p. pap. 30.00 o.p. (*0-930956-05-2*) Station Hill Pr.

Fell, Doris Elaine. Always in September. 1993. (Seasons of Intrigue Ser.: Vol. 1). 288p. pap. 9.99 o.p. (*0-89107-760-X*) Crossway Bks.

—Betrayal in Paris. 2003. 350p. pap. 12.99 (*1-58229-314-7*) Howard Publishing Co.

Ferlinghetti, Lawrence. Love in the Days of Rage. 2001. 116p. 13.95 (*1-58567-202-5*) Overlook Pr., The.

Fiechter, J. J. A Masterpiece of Revenge: A Novel. 1998. 192p. 21.95 (*1-55970-430-6*) Arcade Publishing, Inc.

Flanagan, Mary. Adele. 1997. 245p. (*0-7475-3332-6*) Bloomsbury Publishing, Ltd.

—Adele: A Novel. 1997. 304p. 22.00 (*0-393-04547-1*) Norton, W. W. & Co., Inc.

Flokos, Nicholas. Nike: A Romance. 2000. (Illus.). 192p. pap. 10.00 (*0-618-00207-3*); 1998. 179p. tchr. ed. 20.00 o.s.i (*0-395-88396-2*) Houghton Mifflin Co.

Four on Maigret. unabr. ed. Incl. Drowned Men's Inn. audio o.s.i Maigret's Mistake. audio o.s.i Maigret's Pipe. audio o.s.i Mr. Monday. audio o.s.i 1985. 1985. Set audio 16.95 o.s.i (*1-55656-002-8*) Dercum Audio.

Friedman, Mickey. Magic Mirror. l.t. ed. 1990. (General Ser.). 354p. lib. bdg. 18.95 o.p. (*0-8161-4823-6*, Macmillan Reference USA) Gale Group.

—Magic Mirror. 256p. 1989. pap. 3.95 o.p. (*0-14-010847-5*, Penguin Bks.); 1988. 16.95 o.p. (*0-670-82132-2*) Viking Penguin.

Fuller, Dean. A Death in Paris: An Alex Grismolet Mystery. 1992. 352p. 19.95 o.p. (*0-316-29603-1*) Little Brown & Co.

—Death of a Critic: An Alex Grismolet Mystery. 1996. 304p. 21.95 o.p. (*0-316-29601-5*) Little Brown & Co.

—Death of a Critic Vol. 1: An Alex Grismolet Mystery. 1996. 21.95 (*0-316-92601-9*) Little Brown & Co.

Furst, Alan. Red Gold. 2000. 283p. reprint ed. pap. 13.00 (*0-00-649903-1*) HarperCollins Pubs. Ltd. GBR. *Dist:* Trafalgar Square.

—Red Gold. l.t. ed. 2000. (Ulverscroft Large Print Ser.). 432p. 31.99 (*0-7089-4253-9*, Ulverscroft) Thorpe, F. A. Pubs. GBR. *Dist:* Ulverscroft Large Print Bks., Ltd., Ulverscroft Large Print Canada, Ltd.

—Red Gold: A Novel. 1999. (Illus.). 288p. 23.95 o.s.i (*0-679-45186-2*) Random Hse., Inc.

—The World at Night. 2000. 320p. pap. 13.00 (*0-00-651097-3*) HarperCollins Pubs. Ltd. GBR. *Dist:* Trafalgar Square.

—The World at Night, abr. ed. 2000. audio compact disk 79.95 (*0-7531-0704-X*, 10704X); 1998. audio 69.95 (*0-7531-0383-4*, 980508) ISIS Audio Bks. GBR. *Dist:* Ulverscroft Large Print Bks., Ltd.

—The World at Night. l.t. ed. 1999. (Ulverscroft Large Print Ser.). 448p. 31.99 o.p. (*0-7089-4024-2*, Ulverscroft) Thorpe, F. A. Pubs. GBR. *Dist:* Ulverscroft Large Print Bks., Ltd., Ulverscroft Large Print Canada, Ltd.

Gadol, Peter. Light at Dusk. 2000. 288p. 24.00 (*0-312-20336-5*) Picador.

Gale, Barbara. The Ambassador's Vow. 2002. (Silhouette Special Edition Ser.). mass mkt. (*0-373-24500-9*, Silhouette) Harlequin Enterprises, Ltd.

Gallant, Mavis. Paris Stories. 2002. (New York Review Books Classics Ser.). 350p. pap. 14.95 (*1-59017-022-9*) New York Review of Bks., Inc., The.

Gerritsen, Tess. In Their Footsteps. 1999. mass mkt. (*1-55166-532-8*, Mira Bks.); 1994. (Illus.). 251p. mass mkt. (*0-373-22278-5*, 1-22278-5, Harlequin Bks.) Harlequin Enterprises, Ltd.

—In Their Footsteps. l.t. ed. 2001. (Thorndike Famous Authors Ser.). 344p. 29.95 (*0-7862-3154-8*) Thorndike Pr.

Geudj, Denis. The Parrot's Theorem: A Novel. Wynne, Frank, tr. from FRE. 2001. (Illus.). 352p. 24.95 (*0-312-28055-6*) St. Martin's Pr.

Gilbar, Steven, selected by. Americans in Paris: Great Short Stories of the City of Light. 2003. (Illus.). 228p. pap. 17.99 (*0-9722503-0-1*) Capra Pr.

Gilman, Dorothy. Mrs. Pollifax Pursued. 1995. 198p. 20.00 o.p. (*0-449-90954-9*, Fawcett) Ballantine Bks.

—Mrs. Pollifax Pursued. l.t. ed. 1995. (Large Print Bks.). pap. 22.95 o.p. (*1-56895-088-8*, Wheeler Publishing, Inc.) Gale Group.

Goddard, Robert. Hand in Glove. 1994. mass mkt. o.s.i (*0-552-14165-8*, Corgi); 528p. mass mkt. 7.99 (*0-552-13839-8*) Bantam Bks.

—Hand in Glove. unabr. ed. 2000. audio 89.95 (*0-7451-4362-8*, CAB 1045) Chivers Audio Bks. GBR. *Dist:* BBC Audiobooks America.

—Hand in Glove. 1993. 432p. 22.00 o.p. (*0-671-75070-4*, Simon & Schuster) Simon & Schuster.

—Hand in Glove. Rosenman, Jane, ed. 1994. 432p. reprint ed. pap. (*0-671-89037-9*, Washington Square Pr.) Simon & Schuster.

—Hand in Glove. l.t. ed. 1994. (Charnwood Large Print Ser.). 720p. 29.99 o.p. (*0-7089-8773-7*, Ulverscroft) Thorpe, F. A. Pubs. GBR. *Dist:* Ulverscroft Large Print Bks., Ltd., Ulverscroft Large Print Canada, Ltd.

Goldberg, Lucianne. Madame Cleo's Girls. Zion, Claire, ed. 1992. 416p. 21.00 (*0-671-69524-X*, Atria) Simon & Schuster.

Grayson, Richard. Death au Gratin. 1995. 192p. 19.95 o.p. (*0-312-13047-3*, Saint Martin's Minotaur) St. Martin's Pr.

—Death off Stage. 1992. 192p. 16.95 o.p. (*0-312-06951-0*, Saint Martin's Minotaur) St. Martin's Pr.

—Death on the Cards. 2001. audio 54.95 (*1-85496-746-0*, 67460) Soundings, Ltd. GBR. *Dist:* Ulverscroft Large Print Bks., Ltd.

—Death on the Cards. 1988. 176p. 13.95 o.p. (*0-312-01758-8*, Saint Martin's Minotaur) St. Martin's Pr.

—Death on the Cards. l.t. ed. 1990. (Ulverscroft Large Print Ser.). 29.99 (*0-7089-2190-6*, Ulverscroft) Thorpe, F. A. Pubs. GBR. *Dist:* Ulverscroft Large Print Bks., Ltd., Ulverscroft Large Print Canada, Ltd.

Greeley, Andrew M. The Bishop & the Beggar Girl of St. Germain: A Blackie Ryan Mystery. 2001. 304p. 24.95 (*0-312-86874-X*); 2002. 259p. reprint ed. mass mkt. 6.99 (*0-8125-7597-0*) Doherty, Tom Assocs., LLC. (Forge Bks.).

Green, Julian. The Other Sleep. Cameron, Euan, tr. 2002. 128p. pap. 14.00 (*1-901285-28-6*) Pushkin Pr., Ltd. GBR. *Dist:* Consortium Bk. Sales & Distribution.

—The Other Sleep. Cameron, Evan W., tr. from FRE. 1999. 160p. pap. 12.95 o.p. (*1-885586-08-6*) Turtle Point Pr.

Greene, Sheldon. Burnt Umber. 2001. 300p. pap. 14.95 o.p. (*0-9679520-1-8*) Leapfrog Pr.

Guedj, Dennis. The Parrot's Theorem: A Novel. 2001. (Illus.). 344p. (*0-297-64578-1*, Dunne, Thomas Bks.) St. Martin's Pr.

Guerard, Albert. Gabrielle. 1992. 224p. 20.00 o.p. (*1-55611-288-2*) Fine, Donald I. Bks.

Hall, Jessica. The Deepest Edge. 2003. 352p. mass mkt. 6.99 (*0-451-20796-3*, Signet Bks.) NAL.

Hall, John. Sherlock Holmes & the Boulevard Assassin. 1998. 174p. pap. 14.95 (*0-947533-52-4*) Breese Bks., Ltd. GBR. *Dist:* Midpoint Trade Bks., Inc.

Halligan, Marion. The Golden Dress. 1999. 380p. (*0-14-027302-6*) Penguin Group (USA) Inc.

Henty, G. A. At Agincourt: A Story of the White Hoods of Paris. 2000. 252p. pap. 9.95 (*0-594-02851-5*); E-Book 3.95 (*0-594-02854-X*) 1873 Pr.

—At Agincourt: A Story of the White Hoods of Paris. 2002. 400p. 29.95 (*1-59087-027-1*, GAH027); per. 19.95 (*1-59087-026-3*, GAH026) Althouse Pr.

—At Agincourt: A Story of the White Hoods of Paris. collector's ed. 2002. (Illus.). im. lthr. 38.85 (*1-4115-1326-6*); pap. 19.95 (*1-4115-0627-8*); 25.95 (*1-4115-0904-8*); pap. 17.95 (*1-4115-0119-5*) Polyglot Pr., Inc.

Hijuelos, Oscar. A Simple Habana Melody: From When the World Was Good. l.t. ed. 2003. lib. bdg. 29.95 (*1-58547-298-0*, Platinum) Ctr. Point Large Print.

Hijuelos, Oscar. A Simple Habana Melody: From When the World Was Good. 2002. 352p. 24.95 (*0-06-017569-9*) HarperCollins Pubs.

—A Simple Habana Melody: From When the World Was Good. 2003. 368p. pap. 13.95 (*0-06-092869-7*, Perennial) HarperTrade.

Hoffmann, Kate, et al. Paris or Bust! Romancing Roxanne?/Daddy Come Lately/Love Is in the Air, 3 bks. in 1. 2003. 384p. mass mkt. (*0-373-83573-6*, Harlequin Bks.) Harlequin Enterprises, Ltd.

Holland, Sharon. The Hunchback of Notre Dame. 1996. 96p. mass mkt. 3.50 o.p. (*0-06-106434-3*, HarperTorch) Morrow/Avon.

Hughes, Judith E. Betty & Rita Go to Paris. 1999. (Illus.). 82p. (YA). 12.95 (*0-8118-2370-9*) Chronicle Bks. LLC.

Hugo, Victor. The Hunchback of Notre-Dame. E-Book 5.00 (*0-7607-1310-3*) Barnes & Noble, Inc.

—The Hunchback of Notre-Dame. Cobb, Walter J., tr. from FRE. 2001. (Signet Classics). 512p. mass mkt. 5.95 (*0-451-52788-7*) NAL.

—The Hunchback of Notre-Dame. 1995. (Literary Classics Giant Ser.). 696p. text 8.98 o.p. (*1-56138-602-2*, Courage Bks.) Running Pr. Bk. Pubs.

—The Hunchback of Notre Dame. 1997. (Classics Illustrated Notes). pap. text 4.99 (*1-57840-067-8*) Acclaim Bks.

—The Hunchback of Notre Dame. 1976. 24.95 (*0-8488-0534-8*) Amereon, Ltd.

—The Hunchback of Notre Dame, Set. 1995. audio 71.95 (*1-55685-390-4*) Audio Bk. Contractors, Inc.

—The Hunchback of Notre Dame. 1981. mass mkt. 2.50 o.s.i (*0-553-21224-9*) Bantam Bks.

—The Hunchback of Notre Dame. Bair, Lowell, tr. 1981. 320p. mass mkt. 5.95 (*0-553-21370-9*, Bantam Classics) Bantam Bks.

—The Hunchback of Notre Dame. 1991. 3.95 (*0-425-12667-6*) Berkley Publishing Group.

—The Hunchback of Notre Dame. 1991. audio 73.95 (*0-7861-0570-4*); 1996. audio 85.95 (*0-7861-0988-2*, 1765) Blackstone Audio Bks., Inc.

—The Hunchback of Notre Dame. unabr. collector's ed. 1992. (J). audio 104.00 (*0-7366-2281-0*, 3068) Books on Tape, Inc.

—The Hunchback of Notre Dame. 1981. reprint ed. lib. bdg. 31.95 (*0-89966-382-6*) Buccaneer Bks., Inc.

—The Hunchback of Notre Dame. 1996. 458p. mass mkt. 3.99 (*0-8125-6312-3*, Tor Classics) Doherty, Tom Assocs., LLC.

—The Hunchback of Notre Dame. 1995. (Illus.). 96p. pap. text 1.00 (*0-486-28564-2*) Dover Pubns., Inc.

—The Hunchback of Notre Dame. abr. ed. audio 15.95 o.p. (*0-88646-139-1*, 7140); 1986. (YA). (gr. 7-9). audio 29.95 o.p. (*0-88646-808-6*, R 7140);Set. 1996. audio 9.99 (*1-55204-005-4*, 9005) Durkin Hayes Publishing Ltd.

—The Hunchback of Notre Dame. 1996. (Illus.). 584p. reprint ed. 17.95 (*0-7868-6235-1*) Hyperion Pr.

—The Hunchback of Notre Dame. 1986. (Illus.). (J). pap. 8.95 o.p. (*0-86685-142-9*) International Bk. Ctr., Inc.

—The Hunchback of Notre Dame. unabr. ed. 1991. audio 89.00 Jimcin Recordings.

—The Hunchback of Notre Dame. 1989. (English As a Second Language Bk.). pap. text 4.46 net. o.p. (*0-582-53494-1*, 74095) Longman Publishing Group.

—The Hunchback of Notre Dame. Cobb, Walter J., tr. 1965. 512p. mass mkt. 5.95 o.s.i (*0-451-52222-2*, Signet Classics) NAL.

—The Hunchback of Notre Dame. abr. ed. 1996. 37p. audio 13.98 (*962-634-506-3*, NA200614); 1994. audio compact disk 15.98 o.p. (*962-634-006-1*, NA200612) Naxos of America, Inc. (Naxos AudioBooks).

—The Hunchback of Notre Dame. abr. ed. 1996. (Ultimate Classics Ser.). 19.95 o.p. (*0-7871-0526-0*, 628385) NewStar Media, Inc.

—The Hunchback of Notre Dame. unabr. ed. 34.95 incl. audio Norton Pubs., Inc., Jeffrey /Audio-Forum.

—The Hunchback of Notre Dame. 1991. pap. 4.95 o.p. (*0-8114-6827-5*) Raintree Pubs.

—The Hunchback of Notre Dame. 1996. (Modern Library Ser.). 416p. 15.00 o.s.i (*0-679-60255-0*) Random Hse., Inc.

—The Hunchback of Notre Dame, unabr. ed. 1991. audio 128.00 (*1-55690-241-7*, 91224E7) Recorded Bks., LLC.

—The Hunchback of Notre Dame. 1989. 5.98 o.p. (*0-86136-602-6*) Smithmark Pubs., Inc.

—The Hunchback of Notre Dame. 1996. 9.60 o.p. (*0-606-09443-1*); 1956. 12.00 (*0-606-00835-7*) Turtleback Bks.

—The Hunchback of Notre Dame. 1998. (Classics Library). 448p. pap. 3.95 (*1-85326-068-1*, 0681WW) Wordsworth Editions, Ltd. GBR. *Dist:* Casemate Pubs. & Bk. Distributors, LLC.

—Les Miserables. Wilbour, Charles E., tr. 1996. 336p. pap. 12.95 (*0-449-91167-5*, Fawcett) Ballantine Bks.

—Les Miserables. abr. ed. 1997. (Penguin Classics Ser.). 4p. (J). pap. 18.95 o.p. incl. audio (*0-14-086261-7*, Penguin AudioBooks) Viking Penguin.

—Notre-Dame of Paris. Sturrock, John, tr. from FRE. & intro. by. 1978. (Classics Ser.). 496p. 11.95 (*0-14-044353-3*, Penguin Classics) Viking Penguin.

Hull, Jonathan. Losing Julia. 2001. 400p. mass mkt. 6.99 (*0-440-23485-9*, Delta) Dell Publishing.

—Losing Julia. l.t. ed. 2000. 26.95 o.p. (*1-56895-827-7*, Wheeler Publishing, Inc.) Gale Group.

Hunt, E. Howard. The Paris Edge. 1995. 329p. 22.95 o.p. (*0-312-13138-0*, Saint Martin's Minotaur) St. Martin's Pr.

Jack, W. Two Flappers in Paris. 2000. 128p. pap. 7.95 (*1-56201-209-6*, Blue Moon Bks.) Avalon Publishing Group.

James, Henry. The Ambassadors. E-Book 3.95 (*0-594-05586-5*) 1873 Pr.

—The Ambassadors. 1965. (Airmont Classics Ser.). mass mkt. 2.50 o.p. (*0-8049-0095-7*, CL 95) Airmont Publishing Co., Inc.

—The Ambassadors. 1976. 30.95 (*0-8488-1384-7*) Amereon, Ltd.

—The Ambassadors. 2000. per. 14.00 (*1-891355-30-9*); 2001. per. 15.50 (*1-58396-198-4*) Blue Unicorn Editions.

—The Ambassadors. 1987. 382p. reprint ed. lib. bdg. 29.95 (*0-89966-606-X*) Buccaneer Bks., Inc.

—The Ambassadors. 2002. (Thrift Editions Ser.). 320p. 3.50 (*0-486-42457-X*) Dover Pubns., Inc.

—The Ambassadors. 1972. 2.95 o.p. (*0-460-01987-2*, Dutton) Dutton/Plume.

—The Ambassadors. 1999. E-Book 2.49 (*1-58627-979-3*) Electric Umbrella Publishing.

—The Ambassadors. 1903. o.p. (*0-06-012170-X*) HarperCollins Pubs.

—The Ambassadors. Edel, Leon, ed. 1972. (C). pap. 12.36 o.p. (*0-395-05137-1*, Riverside Editions) Houghton Mifflin Co.
—The Ambassadors. l.t. ed. 1936p. pap. 120.35 (*0-7583-0158-8*); 2245p. pap. 134.14 (*0-7583-0159-6*); 1574p. pap. 105.96 (*0-7583-0157-X*); 1279p. pap. 83.67 (*0-7583-0156-1*); 1000p. pap. 70.05 (*0-7583-0155-3*); 781p. pap. 58.71 (*0-7583-0154-5*); 570p. pap. 41.26 (*0-7583-0153-7*); 456p. pap. 34.80 (*0-7583-0152-9*); 2245p. lib. bdg. 156.60 (*0-7583-0151-0*); 1936p. lib. bdg. 140.65 (*0-7583-0150-2*); 1574p. lib. bdg. 123.96 (*0-7583-0149-9*); 1279p. lib. bdg. 95.67 (*0-7583-0148-0*); 1000p. lib. bdg. 82.05 (*0-7583-0147-2*); 781p. lib. bdg. 70.71 (*0-7583-0146-4*); 570p. lib. bdg. 47.26 (*0-7583-0145-6*); 456p. lib. bdg. 40.80 (*0-7583-0144-8*) Huge Print Pr.
—The Ambassadors. 2001. 444p. 28.99 (*1-58827-518-3*); per. 23.99 (*1-58827-519-1*) IndyPublish.com.
—The Ambassadors. 1971. (Novels & Tales of Henry James Ser.: Vol. 21). reprint ed. xxii, 286p. lib. bdg. 37.50 (*0-678-02821-4*);Vol. 2. 326p. lib. bdg. 32.50 o.p. (*0-678-02822-2*) Kelley, Augustus M. Pubs.
—The Ambassadors. 1998. (Cloth Bound Pocket Ser.). 240p. 7.95 (*3-89508-203-1*); 463p. 7.95 (*3-89508-230-9*, 520022) Konemann.
—The Ambassadors. 1960. mass mkt. 1.50 o.p. (*0-451-51205-7*); mass mkt. 1.25 o.p. (*0-451-50896-3*); mass mkt. 0.95 o.p. (*0-451-50716-9*); mass mkt. 0.75 o.p. (*0-451-50571-9*); mass mkt. 0.60 o.p. (*0-451-50117-9*); mass mkt. 0.50 o.p. (*0-451-50012-1*); mass mkt. 2.50 o.p. (*0-451-51512-9*); mass mkt. 3.50 o.p. (*0-451-51746-6*); mass mkt. 3.95 o.p. (*0-451-51989-2*, CE1746) NAL. (Signet Classics).
—The Ambassadors. Butler, Christopher, ed. & intro. by. (Oxford World's Classics Ser.). 1998. 512p. pap. 4.95 (*0-19-283647-1*); 1985. 496p. pap. 4.95 o.p. (*0-19-281703-5*) Oxford Univ. Pr., Inc.
—The Ambassadors, 2 vols., Set. 2000. (Notable American Authors Ser.). reprint ed. lib. bdg. 99.00 (*0-7812-3431-X*) Reprint Services Corp.
—The Ambassadors. 1998. 11.00 (*0-606-19199-2*) Turtleback Bks.
—The Ambassadors. 1998. (Everyman Paperback Classics Ser.). 464p. pap. 5.95 (*0-460-87160-9*) Tuttle Publishing.
—The Ambassadors. Levin, Harry, ed. & intro. by. 1987. (Classics Ser.). 520p. 5.95 (*0-14-043233-7*, Penguin Classics) Viking Penguin.
—The Ambassadors. 1975. (Modern Classics Ser.). 400p. pap. 3.95 o.p. (*0-14-003499-4*, Penguin Bks.) Viking Penguin.
—The Ambassadors. 1998. (Classics Library). 345p. pap. 3.95 (*1-85326-034-7*, 0347WW) Wordsworth Editions, Ltd. GBR. *Dist:* Casemate Pubs. & Bk. Distributors, LLC.
—The Ambassadors: An Authoritative Text, the Author on the Novel, Criticism. 1964. (C). pap. o.p. (*0-393-09613-0*) Norton, W. W. & Co., Inc.
—The Ambassadors: An Authoritative Text, the Author on the Novel, Criticism. Rosenbaum, S. P., ed. 2nd ed. 1994. (Critical Editions Ser.). 543p. (C). pap. text 9.00 (*0-393-96314-4*) Norton, W. W. & Co., Inc.
—The American. 1968. (Airmont Classics Ser.). mass mkt. 2.95 o.p. (*0-8049-0176-7*, CL 176) Airmont Publishing Co., Inc.
—The American. 1976. 22.95 (*0-8488-0756-1*) Amereon, Ltd.
—The American. 2001. per. 14.00 (*1-891355-32-5*) Blue Unicorn Editions.
—The American. 1990. 336p. reprint ed. lib. bdg. 28.95 (*0-89966-697-3*) Buccaneer Bks., Inc.
—The American. reprint ed. pap. 75.00 (*1-4047-3446-5*); 1877. pap. text 28.00 (*1-4047-3370-1*) Classic Textbooks.
—The American. 1999. E-Book 2.49 (*1-58627-978-5*) Electric Umbrella Publishing.
—The American. Bruccoli, Matthew J. & Pearce, R. H., eds. 1962. (C). pap. 16.36 (*0-395-05163-0*, Riverside Editions) Houghton Mifflin Co.
—The American. l.t. ed. 1875p. pap. 120.17 (*0-7583-0175-8*); 1616p. pap. 107.93 (*0-7583-0174-X*); 1314p. pap. 87.15 (*0-7583-0173-1*); 1068p. pap. 74.47 (*0-7583-0172-3*); 835p. pap. 62.39 (*0-7583-0171-5*); 652p. pap. 44.33 (*0-7583-0170-7*); 476p. pap. 35.94 (*0-7583-0169-3*); 381p. pap. 30.56 (*0-7583-0168-5*); 1068p. lib. bdg. 86.47 (*0-7583-0164-2*); 652p. lib. bdg. 50.33 (*0-7583-0162-6*); 381p. lib. bdg. 36.56 (*0-7583-0160-X*); 476p. lib. bdg. 41.94 (*0-7583-0161-8*); 835p. lib. bdg. 74.39 (*0-7583-0163-4*); 1314p. lib. bdg. 99.15 (*0-7583-0165-0*); 1616p. lib. bdg. 125.93 (*0-7583-0166-9*); 1875p. lib. bdg. 138.17 (*0-7583-0167-7*) Huge Print Pr.
—The American. 1976. (Novels & Tales of Henry James Ser.: Vol. 2). xxii, 539p. reprint ed. lib. bdg. 45.00 (*0-678-02802-8*) Kelley, Augustus M. Pubs.
—The American. 2000. (Vintage Bks.). 384p. pap. 13.00 (*0-375-72611-X*, Vintage) Knopf Publishing Group.
—The American. 1965. 336p. mass mkt. 7.95 (*0-451-52517-5*); mass mkt. 4.50 o.p. (*0-451-52241-9*, Signet Classics) NAL.
—The American. 2001. (Twelve-Point Ser.). 402p. lib. bdg. 25.00 (*1-58287-148-5*); 508p. 26.00 (*1-58287-631-2*) North Bks.
—The American. Tuttleton, James W., ed. 1978. (Critical Editions Ser.). 14.95 o.p. (*0-393-04476-9*); 496p. (C). pap. text 10.50 (*0-393-09091-4*) Norton, W. W. & Co., Inc.
—The American. Poole, Adrian, ed. & intro. by. 1999. (Oxford World's Classics Ser.). 448p. pap. 10.95 (*0-19-283322-7*) Oxford Univ. Pr., Inc.
—The American. 2001. E-Book 2.95 (*1-58882-619-8*) PublishingOnline.
—The American. 1999. 544p. pap. 22.95 (*0-7351-0195-7*); lib. bdg. 32.95 (*0-7351-0174-4*) Replica Bks.
—The American. 1992. (Notable American Authors Ser.). reprint ed. lib. bdg. 75.00 (*0-7812-3370-4*); lib. bdg. 75.00 (*0-7812-3446-8*) Reprint Services Corp.
—The American. (Ebook Classic Ser.). E-Book 5.00 (*0-7410-0466-6*) SoftBook Pr.
—The American. Bradbury, Malcolm, ed. 1989. (Everyman Paperback Classics Ser.). 416p. pap. 8.95 (*0-460-87657-0*, Everyman's Classic Library in Paperback) Tuttle Publishing.
—The American. Spengemann, William C., ed. 1981. (American Library). 480p. pap. 4.95 o.p. (*0-14-039009-X*, Penguin Classics) Viking Penguin.
—The American. Spengemann, William C., ed. & intro. by. 1981. (Classics Ser.). 480p. pap. 11.95 (*0-14-039082-0*, Penguin Classics) Viking Penguin.
James, Henry & Poole, Adrian. The American. 1999. E-Book 11.50 (*0-585-38492-4*) netLibrary, Inc.
Janes, J. Robert. Carousel. 1993. 20.00 o.p. (*1-55611-357-9*) Fine, Donald I. Bks.
—Carousel. 1999. (St-Cyr & Kohler Ser.). 288p. pap. 12.00 (*1-56947-175-4*) Soho Pr., Inc.
—Mannequin. (St-Cyr & Kohler Ser.). 1999. 272p. pap. 12.00 (*1-56947-176-2*); 1998. 266p. 22.00 (*1-56947-129-0*) Soho Pr., Inc.
—Sandman. (St-Cyr & Kohler Ser.). 272p. 1998. pap. 12.00 (*1-56947-120-7*); 1997. 22.00 (*1-56947-106-1*) Soho Pr., Inc.
Jha, Radhika. Smell. 307p. 2002. pap. 14.00 (*1-56947-288-2*); 2001. 24.00 (*1-56947-241-6*) Soho Pr., Inc.
—Smell. 1999. 290p. (*0-670-89188-6*, Viking) Viking Penguin.
Johnson, Diane. Le Divorce. (William Abrahams Book Ser.). 320p. 1998. pap. 14.00 (*0-452-27733-7*, Plume); 1997. 23.95 (*0-525-94238-6*); 2003. pap. 12.95 (*0-452-28448-1*, Plume) Dutton/Plume.
—Le Divorce. l.t. ed. 2004. 482p. pap. 25.95 (*1-58724-591-4*, Wheeler Publishing, Inc.) Gale Group.
—Le Mariage. 2001. 336p. pap. 13.00 (*0-452-28226-8*, Plume); 2000. 320p. 23.95 o.s.i (*0-525-94518-0*, Dutton) Dutton/Plume.
—Le Mariage. l.t. ed. 2000. 457p. 27.95 (*1-56895-936-2*, Wheeler Publishing, Inc.) Gale Group.
Johnston, Velda. House of Illusion. 2001. (Five Star First Edition Women's Fiction Ser.). 355p. 25.95 (*0-7862-3086-X*, Five Star) Gale Group.
Jonath, Leslie. Postmark Paris: A Little Album of Memories. 1995. (Illus.). 108p. 12.95 o.p. (*0-8118-0555-7*) Chronicle Bks. LLC.
Jones, Kaylie. A Soldier's Daughter Never Cries. 2003. 190p. pap. 13.95 (*1-888451-46-7*) Akashic Bks.
—A Soldier's Daughter Never Cries. 1998. 208p. pap. 12.00 o.s.i (*0-06-097755-8*) HarperCollins Pubs.
Just, Ward. The Translator. 1991. 313p. 21.95 o.p. (*0-395-57168-5*) Houghton Mifflin Co.
Kafka, Paul. Love Enter. 1993. 288p. 19.95 o.p. (*0-395-60478-8*) Houghton Mifflin Co.
Kelby, N. M. Theatre of the Stars: A Novel of Physics & Memory. Date not set. 23.95 (*0-7868-6858-9*) Hyperion Pr.
Kincaid, Nell. Fateful Embrace. 2002. (Five Star Romance Ser.). 248p. 26.95 (*0-7862-4609-X*, Five Star) Gale Group.
King, Lily. The Pleasing Hour. 1999. 237p. (YA). 24.00 o.p. (*0-87113-754-2*, Atlantic Monthly Pr.) Grove/Atlantic, Inc.
—The Pleasing Hour. 2000. 256p. pap. 12.00 (*0-7432-0164-7*, Touchstone) Simon & Schuster.
Kotzwinkle, William. Fata Morgana. 1996. (Illus.). 209p. pap. 12.95 (*1-56924-787-0*, Marlowe & Co.) Avalon Publishing Group.
—Fata Morgana. 1980. 208p. pap. 2.95 o.p. (*0-553-11736-X*) Bantam Bks.
—Fata Morgana. 1983. 208p. pap. 3.50 o.p. (*0-380-64691-9*, 64691, Avon Bks.) Morrow/Avon.
—Fata Morgana. 1977. 7.95 o.p. (*0-394-40905-1*, Knopf Bks. for Young Readers) Random Hse. Children's Bks.
Kricorian, Nancy. Dreams of Bread & Fire: A Novel. 2003. 240p. 24.00 (*0-8021-1743-0*, Grove Pr.) Grove/Atlantic, Inc.
Kristeva, Julia. The Samurai: A Novel. Bray, Barbara, tr. from FRE. 1992. 341p. (C). 40.50 (*0-231-07542-1*) Columbia Univ. Pr.
Kurlansky, Mark. The White Man in the Tree: And Other Stories. 2000. (Illus.). 320p. 23.95 o.s.i (*0-671-03605-X*); 2001. 336p. reprint ed. pap. 13.00 (*0-671-03606-8*) Simon & Schuster. (Washington Square Pr.).
LaFarge, Paul. Haussman, or the Distinction. 2001. (Illus.). 384p. 24.00 (*0-374-16833-4*) Farrar, Straus & Giroux.
—Haussmann, or the Distinction: A Novel. 2002. (Illus.). 400p. pap. 13.00 (*0-312-42092-7*) Picador.
Lamorisse, Albert. The Red Balloon. 1990. (Short Story Library). (Illus.). 32p. (YA). (gr. 5 up). lib. bdg. 13.95 o.p. (*0-88682-304-8*, Creative Education) Creative Co., The.
Lane, Simon. Fear. A Novel. 2002. 192p. reprint ed. 13.00 (*1-882593-53-7*) Bridge Works Publishing Co., Inc.
—Still Life with Books: A Novel. 1993. 176p. 17.95 (*1-882593-02-2*) Bridge Works Publishing Co., Inc.
Leroux, Gaston. Le Fantome de l'Opera. 1992. (FRE., Illus.). 152p. pap. 14.64 (*0-8442-1233-4*, 12334) Glencoe/McGraw-Hill.
—The Phantom of the Opera. 2002. (World Digital Library). E-Book 3.95 (*0-594-08398-2*) 1873 Pr.
—The Phantom of the Opera. Date not set. lib. bdg. 26.95 (*0-8488-1652-8*) Amereon, Ltd.
—The Phantom of the Opera, Set. unabr. ed. 1988. (Classic Books on Cassettes Ser.). audio 41.95 (*1-55685-118-9*) Audio Bk. Contractors, Inc.
—The Phantom of the Opera. 1986. 269p. reprint ed. pap. 3.95 o.p. (*0-88184-249-4*, Carroll & Graf Pubs.) Avalon Publishing Group.
—The Phantom of the Opera. 1990. (Bantam Classics Ser.). 288p. mass mkt. 4.95 (*0-553-21376-8*) Bantam Bks.
—The Phantom of the Opera. E-Book 5.00 (*0-7607-1322-7*) Barnes & Noble, Inc.
—The Phantom of the Opera. unabr. ed. 1988. audio 49.95 (*0-7861-0565-8*, 2057) Blackstone Audio Bks., Inc.
—The Phantom of the Opera. unabr. collector's ed. 2000. audio 56.00 (*0-7366-5139-X*, 9188); 1998. audio 48.00 (*0-7366-4154-8*, 4657) Books on Tape, Inc.
—The Phantom of the Opera. 2002. pap. 3.95 (*1-59109-403-8*) Booksurge, LLC.
—The Phantom of the Opera. 1975. lib. bdg. 28.95 (*0-89966-136-X*) Buccaneer Bks., Inc.
—The Phantom of the Opera. abr. ed. audio 15.95 o.p. (*0-88646-216-9*, 7216) Durkin Hayes Publishing Ltd.
—The Phantom of the Opera. E-Book 2.49 (*1-58627-839-8*) Electric Umbrella Publishing.
—The Phantom of the Opera, Set. abr. ed. 1998. audio 18.00 (*0-89845-776-9*, CPN 2108, HarperAudio) HarperTrade.
—The Phantom of the Opera. 1990. 300p. pap. 9.95 o.s.i (*0-87052-937-4*) Hippocrene Bks., Inc.
—The Phantom of the Opera. l.t. ed. 1075p. pap. 83.07 (*0-7583-1806-5*); 874p. pap. 69.34 (*0-7583-1805-7*); 710p. pap. 54.00 (*0-7583-1804-9*); 249p. pap. 23.80 (*0-7583-1800-6*); 313p. pap. 28.72 (*0-7583-1801-4*); 1262p. pap. 93.20 (*0-7583-1807-3*); 429p. pap. 35.66 (*0-7583-1802-2*); 551p. pap. 44.00 (*0-7583-1803-0*); 249p. lib. bdg. 29.80 (*0-7583-1792-1*); 313p. lib. bdg. 34.72 (*0-7583-1793-X*); 429p. lib. bdg. 41.66 (*0-7583-1794-8*); 710p. lib. bdg. 60.00 (*0-7583-1796-4*); 874p. lib. bdg. 84.50 (*0-7583-1797-2*); 1075p. lib. bdg. 95.07 (*0-7583-1798-0*); 1262p. lib. bdg. 105.20 (*0-7583-1799-9*); 551p. lib. bdg. 50.00 (*0-7583-1795-6*) Huge Print Pr.
—The Phantom of the Opera. l.t. ed. 1988. (Mainstream Ser.). 432p. reprint ed. lib. bdg. 18.95 o.p. (*1-85089-234-2*) ISIS Large Print Bks. GBR. *Dist:* Transaction Pubs.
—The Phantom of the Opera. 1989. audio 36.00 Jimcin Recordings.
—The Phantom of the Opera, Level 5. 2002. pap. 7.67 (*0-582-50502-X*) Longman Publishing Group.
—The Phantom of the Opera. 1988. (Illus.). 25.00 o.p. (*0-89296-279-8*) Mysterious Pr.
—The Phantom of the Opera. 2001. 288p. mass mkt. 4.95 (*0-451-52815-8*, Signet Classics); 1989. 288p. mass mkt. 4.95 o.s.i (*0-451-52482-9*, Signet Classics); 1987. mass mkt. 4.50 o.p. (*0-451-52432-2*, Signet Classics); 1987. mass mkt. 3.95 o.p. (*0-451-52173-0*) NAL.
—The Phantom of the Opera. abr. ed. 1997. audio 13.98 (*962-634-618-3*, NA211814); audio compact disk 15.98 o.p. (*962-634-118-1*, NA211812) Naxos of America, Inc. (Naxos AudioBooks).
—The Phantom of the Opera. abr. ed. 1993. (Classic, Ultimate, Dove Ser.). audio 29.95 o.p. (*0-7871-0110-9*);Set. audio 15.95 o.p. (*1-55800-007-0*, 390236, Dove Audio) NewStar Media, Inc.
—The Phantom of the Opera. 2002. (Modern Library Classics). 320p. pap. 8.95 (*0-375-76113-6*) Random Hse., Inc.
—The Phantom of the Opera, unabr. ed. 1988. audio 60.00 (*1-55690-410-X*, 88991E7) Recorded Bks., LLC.
—The Phantom of the Opera. 1938. 10.60 o.p. (*0-606-03258-4*) Turtleback Bks.
—The Phantom of the Opera. 1995. mass mkt. 5.95 (*0-352-31716-7*) Virgin Bks. GBR. *Dist:* London Bridge.
—The Phantom of the Opera. 1986. 272p. mass mkt. 5.99 (*0-446-30120-5*) Warner Bks., Inc.
—The Phantom of the Opera. 1998. (Classics Library). 224p. pap. 3.95 (*1-85326-273-0*, 2730WW) Wordsworth Editions, Ltd. GBR. *Dist:* Combined Publishing.
—The Phantom of the Opera: The Original Novel. 1988. 368p. reprint ed. mass mkt. 7.00 (*0-06-080924-8*, PL-7140, Perennial) HarperTrade.
—The Phantom of the Opera: The Play. 1979. pap. 5.60 (*0-87129-363-3*, P45) Dramatic Publishing Co.
Ludlum, Robert. The Tristan Betrayal: A Novel. Date not set. mass mkt. (*0-312-99774-4*, St. Martin's Paperbacks); 2003. 528p. 27.95 (*0-312-31669-0*); 2003. E-Book 27.95 (*0-312-71133-6*) St. Martin's Pr.
Lytton, Edward Bulwer. The Parisians. E-Book 3.95 (*0-594-02585-0*) 1873 Pr.
—The Parisians. 2001. (Works of Edward George Bulwer-Lytton ). reprint ed. pap. text 28.00 (*0-7426-8357-5*) Classic Bks.
MacLeod, Robert. The Money Mountain. l.t. ed. 1988. (Ulverscroft Large Print Ser.). 400p. 29.99 o.p. (*0-7089-1838-7*, Ulverscroft) Thorpe, F. A. Pubs. GBR. *Dist:* Ulverscroft Large Print Bks., Ltd., Ulverscroft Large Print Canada, Ltd.
Marley, Louise. The Maquisarde. 2002. 400p. 23.95 (*0-441-00976-X*) Ace Bks.
Marshall, Paule. The Fisher King: A Novel. l.t. ed. 2001. 256p. lib. bdg. 27.95 (*1-58547-074-0*) Ctr. Point Large Print.
—The Fisher King: A Novel. 224p. 2000. 23.00 o.s.i (*0-684-87283-8*); 2001. reprint ed. pap. 12.00 (*0-684-86970-5*) Simon & Schuster. (Scribner).
Marton, Sandra. Until You. 1997. 416p. mass mkt. 5.50 o.s.i (*0-7860-0372-3*, Pinnacle Bks.) Kensington Publishing Corp.
Maugham, W. Somerset. Christmas Holiday. 2000. (Vintage International Ser.). 320p. pap. 13.00 (*0-375-72461-3*, Vintage) Knopf Publishing Group.
Maughon, Robert M. Elvis Is Alive. Maughon, Donna, ed. 1997. 24.95 (*0-9650366-1-8*); 2nd ed. 1999. 254p. pap. 19.95 (*0-9650366-2-6*) Cinnamon Moon.
McCarver, Sam. The Case of the Uninvited Guest. 2002. 256p. mass mkt. 6.50 o.s.i (*0-451-20715-7*) NAL.
McHugh, Frances Y. Window on the Seine. l.t. ed. 2001. (Paperback Ser.). 191p. 23.95 (*0-7838-9345-0*) Thorndike Pr.
Meade, Marion. Stealing Heaven. 1985. 448p. pap. 2.95 o.p. (*0-380-50674-2*, 50674-2, Avon Bks.) Morrow/Avon.
—Stealing Heaven. 1994. (Hera Ser.). 415p. pap. 16.00 (*1-56947-011-1*) Soho Pr., Inc.
Mehdi, Charef. Tea in the Harem. Emery, Ed, tr. from FRE. 1991. 160p. (Orig.). (*1-85242-151-7*) Serpent's Tail Ltd.
Mendoza, George. Henri Mouse. 1986. (Picture Puffin Ser.). (Illus.). 32p. (J). (ps-3). pap. 3.95 o.p. (*0-14-050636-5*, Puffin Bks.) Penguin Putnam Bks. for Young Readers.
Meyer, Nicholas. Canary Trainer: From the Memoirs of John H. Watson. 1995. 224p. pap. 10.95 (*0-393-31241-0*) Norton, W. W. & Co., Inc.
Meyer, Nicholas, ed. The Canary Trainer: From the Memoirs of John H. Watson. 1993. 224p. 19.95 o.p. (*0-393-03608-1*) Norton, W. W. & Co., Inc.
Miller, Andrew. Oxygen. 2003. 352p. pap. 14.00 (*0-15-602740-2*, Harvest Bks.); 2002. 336p. 24.00 (*0-15-100721-7*) Harcourt Trade Pubs.
Miller, Denene & Chiles, Nick. Love Don't Live Here Anymore. 2003. 320p. reprint ed. pap. 13.95 (*0-451-20778-5*) NAL.
Milne, John. Daddy's Girl. 201p. pap. 13.00 (*1-874061-90-4*) No Exit Pr. GBR. *Dist:* Trafalgar Square.
—Daddy's Girl. 1989. 15.95 o.p. (*0-312-02893-8*, Saint Martin's Minotaur) St. Martin's Pr.
Mitchell, Judith Claire. The Last Day of the War. 2004. 400p. 24.95 (*0-375-42166-1*, Pantheon) Knopf Publishing Group.
Modiano, Patrick. Honeymoon. Wright, Barbara, tr. from FRE. 1995. (Verba Mundi Ser.). 128p. 19.95 (*0-87923-947-6*) Godine, David R. Pub.
—Out of the Dark. Stump, Jordan, tr. from FRE. 1998. Orig. Title: Du Plus Loin de L'Oubli. 139p. text 50.00 (*0-8032-3196-2*) Univ. of Nebraska Pr.
Moore, Madeline. As You Desire. 1993. 180p. (Orig.). pap. 9.95 (*0-933216-95-5*) Spinsters Ink Bks.
Morgenstern, Susie. Secret Letters from 0 to 10. Rosner, Gill, tr. 1998. 208p. (J). (gr. 4-7). 16.99 (*0-670-88007-8*, Viking) Penguin Putnam Bks. for Young Readers.
Moseley, Margaret. Bonita Faye. 1997. 240p. mass mkt. 5.99 o.s.i (*0-06-101189-4*, HarperTorch) Morrow/Avon.

Settings

—Bonita Faye. l.t. ed. 2001. (G. K. Hall Paperback Ser.). 307p. 24.95 (*0-7838-9378-7*) Thorndike Pr.
—Bonita Faye. 1996. 178p. 20.00 (*0-9637629-4-X*) Three Forks Pr.
Navratilova, Martina & Nickles, Liz. Breaking Point: A Novel of Suspense. 1997. 200p. mass mkt. 5.99 o.s.i (*0-345-38868-2*) Ballantine Bks.
Noah, Robert. The Man Who Stole the Mona Lisa. 1998. 256p. 22.95 o.p. (*0-312-16916-7*) St. Martin's Pr.
Page, Patricia Margaret. Clean Start. 2002. 322p. 24.95 (*0-89733-506-6*) Academy Chicago Pubs., Ltd.
Palmer, Diana. Once in Paris. unabr. ed. 1998. audio 7.99 (*1-55204-159-X*, MIR-1159) Durkin Hayes Publishing Ltd.
—Once in Paris. l.t. ed. 2002. pap. 24.95 (*1-58724-233-8*, Wheeler Publishing, Inc.) Gale Group.
—Once in Paris. 1998. 377p. mass mkt. o.s.i (*1-55166-470-4*, 1-66470-5, Mira Bks.) Harlequin Enterprises, Ltd.
Patterson, Kevin. Country of Cold: Stories. 2004. 272p. pap. 13.00 (*0-385-72217-6*, Anchor) Knopf Publishing Group.
—Country of Cold: Stories of Sex & Violence. 2003. 272p. 23.95 (*0-385-50627-9*) Doubleday Publishing.
Paul, Elliot. Hugger-Mugger in the Louvre: A Homer Evans Murder Mystery. 1986. viii, 328p. reprint ed. pap. 5.95 o.p. (*0-486-25185-3*) Dover Pubns., Inc.
—Mayhem in B-Flat: A Homer Evans Murder Mystery. 1988. 320p. reprint ed. pap. 6.95 (*0-486-25621-9*) Dover Pubns., Inc.
—The Mysterious Mickey Finn. 1984. 256p. reprint ed. pap. 5.95 o.p. (*0-486-24751-1*) Dover Pubns., Inc.
Pelham, Jackie. Under the Rose. 2002. 269p. pap. 21.95 (*1-57168-652-5*, Eakin Pr.) Eakin Pr.
Pennac, Daniel. Monsieur Malaussene. l.t. ed. 1996. (French Ser.). (FRE.). Vol. 1. 450p. pap. 30.99 o.p. (*2-84011-150-0*); Vol. 2. 419p. pap. 30.99 o.p. (*2-84011-151-9*) Feryane, SA, Editions FRA. *Dist:* Ulverscroft Large Print Bks., Ltd., Ulverscroft Large Print Canada, Ltd.
—Monsieur Malaussene. 2003. 368p. pap. (*1-84343-020-7*) Harvill Pr., The GBR. *Dist:* Trafalgar Square.
Perec, Georges. A Void. Adair, Gilbert, tr. 1994. 256p. 25.00 o.p. (*0-00-271119-2*) HarperTrade.
The Phantom of the Opera. 1998. 16p. pap. 6.95 (*0-7935-9664-5*) Leonard, Hal Corp.
Piercy, Marge. City of Darkness, City of Light. 1997. 496p. pap. 14.95 (*0-449-91275-2*, Fawcett) Ballantine Bks.
Poe, Edgar Allan. The Murders in the Rue Morgue. 1985. audio Dercum Audio.
—The Murders in the Rue Morgue. 1984. audio; 1977. audio 7.95 Jimcin Recordings.
—The Murders in the Rue Morgue. 1998. (Cloth Bound Pocket Ser.). 240p. 7.95 (*3-89508-090-X*, 520019) Konemann.
—The Murders in the Rue Morgue. 1977. (American Classics). (gr. 9-12). pap. 9.08 o.p. (*0-88343-404-0*) McDougal Littell Inc.
—The Murders in the Rue Morgue. 1996. (Classic Ser.). 64p. pap. 0.95 o.p. (*0-14-600191-5*) Penguin Group (USA) Inc.
—The Murders in the Rue Morgue. 1981. audio Recorded Bks., LLC.
—The Murders in the Rue Morgue. (Radio Ser.). audio 7.95 o.p. (*0-88142-430-7*, 126) Soundelux Audio Publishing.
—The Murders in the Rue Morgue & Other Stories. unabr. collector's ed. 1992. audio 30.00 (*0-7366-2189-X*, 2984) Books on Tape, Inc.
—The Murders in the Rue Morgue & Other Stories. 1999. 322p. pap. 7.95 (*1-902058-02-X*) Pulp Fictions GBR. *Dist:* 7 Hills Bk. Distributors.
—The Murders in the Rue Morgue & Other Tales. l.t. ed. 1997. (Murders in the Rue Morgue & Other Tales Ser.: Vol. 2). 240p. text 22.95 (*1-56000-535-1*) Transaction Pubs.
—The Purloined Letter. 1985. audio Dercum Audio.
—The Purloined Letter. 1984. audio; 1977. audio Jimcin Recordings.
—The Purloined Letter. 1980. audio Random Hse. Audio Publishing Group.
The Purloined Letter & Other Works. abr. ed. Incl. Dream Within a Dream. audio Ulalume. audio Valley of Unrest. audio 1984. Set audio 9.95 (*1-55994-101-4*, CPN 1288, Caedmon) HarperTrade.
Radiguet, Raymond. Count d'Orgel. 1970. pap. 1.25 o.p. (*0-394-17448-8*, B214, Grove Pr.) Grove/Atlantic, Inc.
—Count D'Orgel's Ball. Cancogni, Annapaola, tr. from FRE. 1989. 174p. reprint ed. 20.00 o.p. (*0-941419-31-2*); pap. 11.00 (*0-941419-30-4*) Marsilio Pubs. (Eridanos Library).
—Count D'Orgel's Ball. Schiff, Violet, tr. from FRE. 2001. 160p. pap. 14.00 (*1-901285-03-0*) Pushkin Pr., Ltd. GBR. *Dist:* Consortium Bk. Sales & Distribution.
Radiquet, Raymond. Count d'Orgel. Schiff, Violet, tr. from FRE. 2000. 160p. pap. 12.95 (*1-885586-02-7*) Turtle Point Pr.
Rhys, Jean. Good Morning, Midnight. 1982. 192p. pap. o.p. (*0-06-080580-3*, P 580) HarperCollins Pubs.
—Good Morning, Midnight. 1999. (Shoreline Bks.). 192p. pap. 12.00 (*0-393-30394-2*) Norton, W. W. & Co., Inc.
—Good Morning, Midnight. 1974. pap. 2.95 o.p. (*0-394-71042-8*) Random Hse., Inc.
—Quartet. l.t. ed. 1994. reprint ed. 19.95 o.p. (*0-7927-2101-2*); pap. 18.95 o.p. (*0-7927-2100-4*) BBC Audiobooks America.
Rice, Luanne. Secrets of Paris. l.t. ed. 1992. (General Ser.). 393p. 20.95 o.p. (*0-8161-5329-9*, Macmillan Reference USA) Gale Group.
—Secrets of Paris. 1991. 336p. 19.95 o.p. (*0-670-82773-8*) Viking Penguin.
Richardson, Bill. Waiting for Gertrude. 2001. (Illus.). 240p. pap. (*1-55054-892-1*) Douglas & McIntyre, Ltd.
—Waiting for Gertrude. Date not set. mass mkt. (*0-312-99198-3*, St. Martin's Paperbacks) St. Martin's Pr.
Riley, Judith M. The Oracle Glass. 1995. 528p. pap. 14.00 (*0-449-91006-7*, Fawcett) Ballantine Bks.
—The Oracle Glass. 1994. 544p. 22.95 o.p. (*0-670-85054-3*, Penguin Bks.) Viking Penguin.
Riley, Philip J. The Phantom of the Opera: The Original Shooting Script. Conforti, John, ed. 1999. (Universal Filmscript Series: Classic Silents: 1). (Illus.). pap. text 24.95 (*1-882127-33-1*) Magicimage Filmbooks.
Robbins, Adreana. Paris Never Leaves You. unabr. ed. 1999. audio 83.95 (*0-7861-1630-7*, 2458) Blackstone Audio Bks., Inc.
—Paris Never Leaves You. 2000. 468p. mass mkt. 6.99 (*0-8125-7078-2*); 2nd ed. 1999. 384p. 25.95 (*0-312-86755-7*) Doherty, Tom Assocs., LLC. (Forge Bks.).
Robinette, Joseph & Chauls, Robert. The Phantom of the Opera: Musical. 1992. pap. 5.95 (*0-87129-173-8*, P08) Dramatic Publishing Co.
Ross, JoAnn. Legacy of Lies. 2001. 384p. mass mkt. (*1-55166-821-1*, Harlequin Bks.) Harlequin Enterprises, Ltd.
Sand, George. Horace. Rogow, Zack, tr. from FRE. 1995. (Illus.). 352p. pap. 15.95 (*1-56279-082-X*) Mercury Hse.
Satterthwait, Walter. Masquerade. 1999. 336p. mass mkt. 5.99 (*0-312-96989-9*, St. Martin's Paperbacks); Vol. 1. 1998. (Masquerade Ser.: Vol. 1). 272p. 22.95 (*0-312-18629-0*, Saint Martin's Minotaur) St. Martin's Pr.
Sayers, Dorothy L. & Paton Walsh, Jill. Thrones, Dominations. unabr. ed. 2001. (Lord Peter Wimsey Mystery Ser.). audio 34.95 (*1-57270-129-3*, N81129u, Audio Editions Mystery Masters) Audio Partners Publishing Corp.
—Thrones, Dominations. unabr. ed. 1998. (Lord Peter Wimsey Mysteries Ser.: Bk. 15). audio 59.95 (*0-7540-0203-9*, CAB 1626) Chivers Audio Bks. GBR. *Dist:* BBC Audiobooks America.
Sayers, Dorothy L. & Walsh, J. P. Thrones, Dominations, unabr. collector's ed. 1999. (Lord Peter Wimsey Mystery Ser.). audio 56.00 (*0-7366-4299-4*, 4791) Books on Tape, Inc.
Sayers, Dorothy L., et al. Thrones, Dominations. 1999. 322p. mass mkt. 6.50 (*0-312-96830-2*, St. Martin's Paperbacks); 1998. 312p. (gr. 5-6). 23.95 o.p. (*0-312-18196-5*, Saint Martin's Minotaur) St. Martin's Pr.
—Thrones, Dominations. l.t. ed. 1998. (Lord Peter Wimsey Mystery Ser.). 439p. 29.95 (*0-7838-8438-9*) Thorndike Pr.
Scott, Gail. My Paris. 2003. 136p. per. 12.95 (*1-56478-297-2*) Dalkey Archive Pr.
—My Paris: A Novel. 1999. 180p. pap. 14.50 (*1-55128-068-X*) Mercury Pr., The CAN. *Dist:* SPD-Small Pr. Distribution.
Settle, Mary Lee. Charley Bland. 1991. 208p. pap. 8.95 o.p. (*0-88184-709-7*, Carroll & Graf Pubs.) Avalon Publishing Group.
—Charley Bland. 1989. 18.95 o.p. (*0-374-12078-1*) Farrar, Straus & Giroux.
—Charley Bland. 1996. (Mary Lee Settle Collection). 208p. pap. 12.95 (*1-57003-149-5*) Univ. of South Carolina Pr.
Sheckley, Robert. Soma Blues. 224p. 1998. pap. 13.95 (*0-312-86579-1*); 1997. 20.95 o.p. (*0-312-86273-3*) Doherty, Tom Assocs., LLC. (Forge Bks.).
Shelby, Philip. Gatekeeper. l.t. ed. 1997. 27.95 o.p. (*1-56895-660-6*, Wheeler Publishing, Inc.) Gale Group.
—Gatekeeper. 2000. E-Book 25.00 (*0-684-86476-2*, Simon & Schuster); 1999. 448p. pap. 7.50 (*0-671-01392-0*, Pocket); 1998. 336p. 25.00 (*0-684-84260-2*, Simon & Schuster) Simon & Schuster.
Siciliano, Sam. The Angel of the Opera: Sherlock Holmes Meets the Phantom of the Opera. 1994. 272p. 21.95 (*1-883402-46-8*, Scribner) Simon & Schuster.
Simenon. Maigret & the Wine Merchant. 2003. pap. 8.00 (*0-15-602844-1*) Harcourt Trade Pubs.
Simenon, Georges. The Accomplices. Frechtman, Bernard, tr. 1977. pap. 2.25 o.p. (*0-15-602670-8*, Harvest Bks.) Harcourt Trade Pubs.
—The Accomplices. mass mkt. 0.50 o.p. (*0-451-02751-5*, Signet Bks.) NAL.
—Across the Street. 1992. 18.95 (*0-15-103266-1*) Harcourt Trade Pubs.
—African Trio: Talatala, Tropic Moon, Aboard the Aquitaine. 1979. 9.95 o.p. (*0-15-103955-0*) Harcourt Trade Pubs.
—Aine des Ferchaux. 1985. (Folio Ser.: No. 930). (FRE.). 4332p. (Orig.). pap. 10.95 o.p. (*2-07-036930-7*) Schoenhof's Foreign Bks., Inc.
—L' Aine des Ferchaux. 1977. (FRE.). pap. 13.95 (*0-7859-4076-6*) French & European Pubns., Inc.
—L' Ami d'Enfance de Maigret. pap. 10.95 (*0-8288-6099-8*, F126480) French & European Pubns., Inc.
—L' Ami d'Enfance de Maigret. 2000. (Maigret Mystery Ser.). (FRE.). pap. 12.95 (*2-253-14213-1*) Librairie Generale Francaise, LGF FRA. *Dist:* Distribooks, Inc.
—L' Amie de Madame Maigret. (FRE.). pap. 10.95 (*0-8288-6156-0*, F126404) French & European Pubns., Inc.
—L' Amie de Madame Maigret. 2000. (Maigret Mystery Ser.). (FRE.). pap. 12.95 (*2-253-14225-5*) Librairie Generale Francaise, LGF FRA. *Dist:* Distribooks, Inc.
—Aunt Jeanne. Sainsbury, Geoffrey, tr. from FRE. 1983. 160p. 13.95 o.p. (*0-15-109792-5*) Harcourt Trade Pubs.
—Les Autres. 1992. (FRE.). pap. 11.95 (*0-7859-3261-5*, 2266053019) French & European Pubns., Inc.
—Betty. 1992. (FRE.). pap. 11.95 (*0-7859-3255-0*, 2266049801) French & European Pubns., Inc.
—Big Bob. Lowe, Eileen M., tr. 1981. 180p. 11.95 o.p. (*0-15-112075-7*) Harcourt Trade Pubs.
—Le Blanc a Lunettes. 1978. (FRE.). pap. 10.95 (*0-7859-4093-6*) French & European Pubns., Inc.
—The Blue Room. Ellenbogen, Eileen, tr. 1978. 141p. reprint ed. pap. 2.95 o.s.i (*0-15-613267-2*, Harvest Bks.) Harcourt Trade Pubs.
—Le Bourgmestre de Fumes, Malempin, les Inconnus Dans la Masion. 1992. (FRE.). 1148p. 49.95 (*0-7859-0494-8*, 2258035279) French & European Pubns., Inc.
—Le Bourgmestre de Furnes. 1977. (FRE.). pap. 10.95 (*0-7859-4077-4*) French & European Pubns., Inc.
—The Cat. Frechtman, Bernard, tr. from FRE. 1976. (Helen & Kurt Wolff Bk.). 182p. pap. 2.95 o.s.i (*0-15-615549-4*, Harvest Bks.) Harcourt Trade Pubs.
—Le Cercle des Mahe. 1981. (FRE.). pap. 10.95 (*0-7859-4161-4*) French & European Pubns., Inc.
—Ceux de la Soif. 1978. (FRE.). pap. 10.95 (*0-7859-4098-7*) French & European Pubns., Inc.
—Le Chat. 1992. (FRE.). pap. 11.95 (*0-7859-3254-2*, 2266049798) French & European Pubns., Inc.
—Chemin sans Issue. 1979. (FRE.). pap. 10.95 (*0-7859-4118-5*) French & European Pubns., Inc.
—Le Chien Jaune. Katz, Eve & Hall, Donald R., eds. 1967. (FRE.). (C). pap. text 18.12 o.p. (*0-06-046163-2*) Addison-Wesley Educational Pubs., Inc.
—Le Chien Jaune. 1967. (College French Ser.). (FRE.). pap. 21.95 o.p. (*0-8384-3771-0*) Heinle.
—Choix De Simenon. Lindsay, Frank W. & Nazzaro, Anthony M., eds. 1972. (Illus.). pap. o.p. (*0-13-133033-0*) Prentice-Hall.
—Les Clients d'Avrenos. 1966. (FRE.). pap. 11.95 (*0-7859-3962-8*) French & European Pubns., Inc.
—The Clockmaker. Benny, Norman, tr. 1977. 124p. pap. 2.95 o.s.i (*0-15-618170-3*, Harvest Bks.) Harcourt Trade Pubs.
—Colere de Maigret. 1963. (FRE.). 192p. pap. 11.95 (*0-7859-1472-2*, 2258001730) French & European Pubns., Inc.
—Confidence de Maigret. 1992. (FRE.). 192p. pap. 11.95 (*0-7859-1605-9*, 226604978X) French & European Pubns., Inc.
—Le Coup de Vague. 1978. (FRE.). pap. 10.95 (*0-7859-4100-2*) French & European Pubns., Inc.
—The Couple from Poitiers. Ellenbogen, Eileen, tr. 1986. 144p. 13.95 (*0-15-122700-4*) Harcourt Trade Pubs.
—La Dansuese Du Gai-Moulin, la Guinguette a Deux Sous, l'Ombre Chinoise. 1991. (FRE.). 928p. 49.95 (*0-7859-0486-7*, 2258032725) French & European Pubns., Inc.
—The Delivery. Ellenbogen, Eileen, ed. 1981. (Helen & Kurt Wolff Bk.). 10.95 o.p. (*0-15-124655-6*) Harcourt Trade Pubs.
—Demoiselles de Concarneau. 1936. (Folio Ser.: No. 933). (FRE.). 148p. pap. 6.95 (*2-07-036933-1*) Schoenhof's Foreign Bks., Inc.
—Les Demoiselles de Concarneau. 1977. (FRE.). pap. 10.95 (*0-7859-4078-2*) French & European Pubns., Inc.
—The Disappearance of Odile. 1972. (Helen & Kurt Wolff Bk.). 6.95 o.p. (*0-15-125720-5*) Harcourt Trade Pubs.
—Donadieu's Will. Gilbert, Stuart, tr. 2nd ed. 1991. 343p. 22.95 (*0-15-126310-8*) Harcourt Trade Pubs.
—The Door. Woodward, Daphne, tr. 1990. 138p. 18.95 o.s.i (*0-15-126370-1*) Harcourt Trade Pubs.
—Echec de Maigret. 1990. (FRE.). 192p. pap. 11.95 (*0-7859-1494-3*, 2285002475) French & European Pubns., Inc.
—Enigmes, Level B. (FRE.). text 8.95 (*0-88436-058-X*, 40269) EMC/Paradigm Publishing.
—The Family Lie. Hillier, Caroline & Quigly, Isabel, trs. 1978. (Helen & Kurt Wolff Bk.). 7.95 o.p. (*0-15-156247-4*) Harcourt Trade Pubs.
—Les Fantomes du Chapelier. 1992. (FRE.). pap. 11.95 (*0-7859-3256-9*, 2266050877) French & European Pubns., Inc.
—Faubourg. 1978. (FRE.). pap. 8.95 (*0-7859-4094-4*) French & European Pubns., Inc.
—Fils Cardinaud. 1943. (Folio Ser.: No. 1047). (FRE.). 148p. pap. 6.95 (*2-07-037047-X*) Schoenhof's Foreign Bks., Inc.
—Le Fils, le Negre, Maigret Voyage, Strip-Tease, les Scruples de Maigret, le President, le Passage de la Ligne, 23 vols., Set. 1989. (FRE.). 832p. 49.95 (*0-7859-0555-3*, 225803003X) French & European Pubns., Inc.
—La Folle de Maigret. 1990. (FRE.). 186p. pap. 11.95 (*0-7859-1495-1*, 2285003846) French & European Pubns., Inc.
—Four on Maigret. unabr. ed. (Inspector Maigret Mystery Ser.). audio 21.95 o.p. (*1-55656-077-X*, DAB056) BBC Audiobooks America.
—Four on Maigret. unabr. ed. 1997. (Mystery Library). pap. 16.95 o.p. incl. audio (*1-55656-254-3*) Dercum Audio.
—The Girl with a Squint. Thomson, Helen, tr. 1978. 7.95 o.p. (*0-15-135692-0*) Harcourt Trade Pubs.
—The Glass Cage. 1973. (Helen & Kurt Wolff Bk.). 5.50 o.p. (*0-15-135800-1*) Harcourt Trade Pubs.
—The Grandmother. Stewart, Jean, tr. 1980. (Helen & Kurt Wolff Bk.). 192p. reprint ed. 8.95 o.p. (*0-15-136738-8*) Harcourt Trade Pubs.
—The Hatter's Phantoms. 19.95 (*0-89190-428-X*) Amereon, Ltd.
—The Hatter's Phantoms. Trask, Willard R., tr. (Helen & Kurt Wolff Bk.). 1981. 176p. pap. 3.95 o.s.i (*0-15-639342-5*, Harvest Bks.); 1976. 6.95 o.p. (*0-15-139270-6*) Harcourt Trade Pubs.
—L' Homme Qui Regardait Passer les Trains. 1967. (FRE.). pap. 15.95 (*0-7859-3963-6*) French & European Pubns., Inc.
—L' Horloger d'Everton. 1992. (FRE.). pap. 16.95 (*0-7859-3304-2*, 2804007790) French & European Pubns., Inc.
—The House on the Quai Notre-Dame. Hamilton, Alastair, tr. 1975. (Helen & Kurt Wolff Bk.). 160p. 6.95 o.p. (*0-15-142181-1*) Harcourt Trade Pubs.
—Inconnus Dans la Maison. 1975. (Folio Ser.: No. 664). (FRE.). pap. 8.95 (*2-07-036664-2*) Schoenhof's Foreign Bks., Inc.
—Les Inconnus dans la Maison. 1975. (FRE.). pap. 10.95 (*0-7859-4041-3*) French & European Pubns., Inc.
—The Innocents. 1974. (Helen & Kurt Wolff Bk.). 6.50 o.p. (*0-15-144430-7*) Harcourt Trade Pubs.
—Inspector Maigret & the Strangled Stripper. unabr. collector's ed. 1983. audio 30.00 (*0-7366-0533-9*, 1507) Books on Tape, Inc.
—Inspector Maigret's Case Files: Murder a la Carte. 1992. 9.98 (*0-88365-810-0*, Galahad Bks.) BBS Publishing Corp.
—Intimate Memoirs: Including Marie-Jo's Book. Salemson, Harold J., tr. 1984. 800p. 22.95 o.s.i (*0-15-144892-2*) Harcourt Trade Pubs.
—Intimate Memoirs: Including Marie-Jo's Book. Salemson, Harold J., tr. 1984. 815 p. o.p. (*0-241-11219-2*, Hamilton, Hamish) Viking Penguin.
—The Iron Staircase. Date not set. lib. bdg. 18.95 (*0-8488-2161-0*) Amereon, Ltd.
—The Iron Staircase. Ellenbogen, Eileen, tr. 1981. 192p. pap. 2.95 o.s.i (*0-15-645484-X*, Harvest Bks.) Harcourt Trade Pubs.
—Justice. Sainsbury, Geoffrey, tr. from FRE. 1985. (Helen & Kurt Wolff Bk.). 176p. reprint ed. 13.95 (*0-15-146585-1*) Harcourt Trade Pubs.
—Letter to My Mother. Manheim, Ralph, tr. 1976. (Helen & Kurt Wolff Bk.). 96p. 5.95 o.p. (*0-15-150445-8*) Harcourt Trade Pubs.
—The Little Doctor. Stewart, Jean, tr. from FRE. 1981. (Helen & Kurt Wolff Bk.). 10.95 o.p. (*0-15-152768-7*) Harcourt Trade Pubs.
—Le Locataire. 1978. (FRE.). pap. 10.95 (*0-7859-4091-X*, 2070369986) French & European Pubns., Inc.
—Le Locataire. 1934. (Folio Ser.: No. 998). (FRE.). 181p. pap. 6.95 (*2-07-036998-6*) Schoenhof's Foreign Bks., Inc.
—Le Locataire, les Suicides, les Pitard. 1992. (FRE.). 990p. 49.95 (*0-7859-0491-3*, 2258035244) French & European Pubns., Inc.
—The Lodger. Gilbert, Stuart, tr. from FRE. 1983. (Helen & Kurt Wolff Bk.). 176p. reprint ed. 12.95 o.p. (*0-15-152960-4*) Harcourt Trade Pubs.

—The Long Exile. Ellenbogen, Eileen, tr. 1983. (Helen & Kurt Wolff Bk.). 372p. 15.95 o.s.i (*0-15-152997-3*) Harcourt Trade Pubs.

—Madame Maigret's Own Case. 2003. 180p. pap. 8.00 (*0-15-602849-2*); 2nd ed. 1991. 182p. (C). pap. 6.00 o.s.i (*0-15-655106-3*, Harvest Bks.); 2nd ed. 1990. 192p. 17.95 o.s.i (*0-15-154968-0*) Harcourt Trade Pubs.

—Maigret a New York. 1996. (FRE.). audio 21.95 Olivia & Hill Pr., The.

—Maigret a Vichy. 2000. (Maigret Mystery Ser.). (FRE.). pap. 12.95 (*2-253-14216-6*) Librairie Generale Francaise, LGF FRA. *Dist:* Distribooks, Inc.

—Maigret a Vichy. 1992. (FRE.). audio 32.95 Olivia & Hill Pr., The.

—Maigret Afraid. Duff, Margaret, tr. (Helen & Kurt Wolff Bk.). 1996. 170p. pap. 6.00 o.s.i (*0-15-655142-X*, Harvest Bks.); 1983. 176p. 13.95 o.s.i (*0-15-155560-5*) Harcourt Trade Pubs.

—Maigret among the Rich. 1978. mass mkt. 5.95 o.p. (*0-671-79051-X*, Pocket) Simon & Schuster.

—Maigret & the Apparition. Ellenbogen, Eileen, tr. 1978. (Adult Ser.). lib. bdg. 9.95 o.p. (*0-8161-6503-3*, Macmillan Reference USA) Gale Group.

—Maigret & the Apparition. 168p. 2003. pap. 8.00 (*0-15-602838-7*); 1991. pap. 6.00 o.s.i (*0-15-655127-6*) Harcourt Trade Pubs. (Harvest Bks.).

—Maigret & the Apparition. Ellenbogen, Eileen, tr. 1976. (Helen & Kurt Wolff Bk.). 6.95 o.p. (*0-15-155125-1*) Harcourt Trade Pubs.

—Maigret & the Black Sheep. l.t. ed. 2001. (Dales Large Print Ser.). 208p. pap. 21.99 (*1-84262-061-4*) Dales Large Print Bks. GBR. *Dist:* Ulverscroft Large Print Bks., Ltd., Ulverscroft Large Print Canada, Ltd.

—Maigret & the Black Sheep. Thompson, Helen, tr. 1976. (Helen & Kurt Wolff Bk.). 168p. 6.95 o.p. (*0-15-155146-4*) Harcourt Trade Pubs.

—Maigret & the Black Sheep. Thomson, Helen, tr. 1983. 168p. reprint ed. pap. 3.95 o.s.i (*0-15-655138-1*, Harvest Bks.) Harcourt Trade Pubs.

—Maigret & the Bum. unabr. collector's ed. 1984. audio 24.00 (*0-7366-0540-1*, 1514) Books on Tape, Inc.

—Maigret & the Bum. 2003. 160p. pap. 8.00 (*0-15-602839-5*, Harvest Bks.) Harcourt Trade Pubs.

—Maigret & the Bum. Stewart, Jean, tr. 1996. 156p. (C). pap. 3.95 o.s.i (*0-15-655130-6*, Harvest Bks.) Harcourt Trade Pubs.

—Maigret & the Bum. 1995. pap. 6.00 (*0-15-600249-3*) Harcourt Trade Pubs.

—Maigret & the Burglar's Wife. 2003. 176p. pap. 8.00 (*0-15-602840-9*); 1992. 167p. pap. 5.95 o.s.i (*0-15-655167-5*, Harvest Bks.) Harcourt Trade Pubs.

—Maigret & the Burglar's Wife. Maclaren-Ross, J., tr. 1990. 18.95 o.s.i (*0-15-155572-9*) Harcourt Trade Pubs.

—Maigret & the Calame Report. Budberg, Moura, tr. 1996. 192p. pap. 6.00 (*0-15-655153-5*, Harvest Bks.) Harcourt Trade Pubs.

—Maigret & the Calame Report. 1995. pap. o.s.i (*0-15-600248-5*) Harcourt Trade Pubs.

—Maigret & the Death of a Harbor-Master. Gilbert, Stuart, tr. 1989. 182p. pap. 6.00 (*0-15-655161-6*, Harvest Bks.) Harcourt Trade Pubs.

—Maigret & the Enigmatic Letter. 1964. pap. 2.95 o.p. (*0-14-002023-3*, Penguin Bks.) Viking Penguin.

—Maigret & the Flemish Shop. Sainsbury, Geoffrey, tr. 1990. 182p. pap. 5.95 o.p. (*0-15-655118-7*) Harcourt Trade Pubs.

—Maigret & the Fortuneteller. 1990. 140p. pap. 5.95 o.s.i (*0-15-655163-2*) Harcourt Trade Pubs.

—Maigret & the Fortuneteller. Sainsbury, Geoffrey, tr. 1989. 144p. 16.95 o.s.i (*0-15-155571-0*) Harcourt Trade Pubs.

—Maigret & the Gangsters. Varese, Louise, tr. from FRE. 1986. 162p. 14.95 (*0-15-155565-6*) Harcourt Trade Pubs.

—Maigret & the Gangsters. Varese, Louise, tr. 1988. 160p. pap. 3.50 (*0-380-70414-5*, Avon Bks.) Morrow/Avon.

—Maigret & the Headless Corpse. Ellenbogen, Eileen, tr. l.t. ed. 1989. (Nightingale Ser.). 274p. 13.95 o.p. (*0-8161-4664-0*, Macmillan Reference USA) Gale Group.

—Maigret & the Headless Corpse. Ellenbogen, Eileen, tr. 1985. (Helen & Kurt Wolff Bk.). 196p. (C). pap. 6.00 (*0-15-655144-6*, Harvest Bks.) Harcourt Trade Pubs.

—Maigret & the Hotel Majestic. Hillier, Caroline, tr. 1991. 182p. pap. 6.00 o.s.i (*0-15-655133-0*, Harvest Bks.) Harcourt Trade Pubs.

—Maigret & the Hundred Gibbets. 1963. pap. 2.95 o.p. (*0-14-002025-X*, Penguin Bks.) Viking Penguin.

—Maigret & the Informer. lib. bdg. 18.95 (*0-8488-2033-9*) Amereon, Ltd.

—Maigret & the Informer. 1973. 5.95 o.p. (*0-15-155140-5*) Harcourt Trade Pubs.

—Maigret & the Killer. lib. bdg. 19.95 (*0-8488-2034-7*) Amereon, Ltd.

—Maigret & the Killer, unabr. ed. 1993. (Inspector Maigret Mystery Ser.). audio 39.95 (*0-7451-6284-3*, CAB 600) BBC Audiobooks America.

—Maigret & the Killer. unabr. ed. 2000. (Inspector Maigret Mystery Ser.). audio 34.95 Chivers Audio Bks. GBR. *Dist:* BBC Audiobooks America.

—Maigret & the Killer. abr. ed. 1997. (Maigret Ser.). audio 16.99 (*0-88646-452-8*, 7452) Durkin Hayes Publishing Ltd.

—Maigret & the Killer. Moir, Lyn, tr. l.t. ed. 1991. (Nightingale Ser.). 239p. pap. 14.95 o.p. (*0-8161-5117-2*, Macmillan Reference USA) Gale Group.

—Maigret & the Killer. 2003. 168p. pap. 8.00 (*0-15-602841-7*, Harvest Bks.) Harcourt Trade Pubs.

—Maigret & the Killer. Moir, Lyn, tr. 1991. (Helen & Kurt Wolff Bk.). 165p. pap. 5.95 o.s.i (*0-15-655124-1*, Harvest Bks.) Harcourt Trade Pubs.

—Maigret & the Loner. 166p. 19.95 (*0-89190-429-8*) Amereon, Ltd.

—Maigret & the Loner. 1983. 168p. pap. 3.95 o.s.i (*0-15-655139-X*, Harvest Bks.) Harcourt Trade Pubs.

—Maigret & the Madwoman. unabr. ed. 1999. audio 21.95 (*1-57270-125-0*, N31125u, Audio Editions Mystery Masters) Audio Partners Publishing Corp.

—Maigret & the Madwoman. unabr. ed. 1995. (Inspector Maigret Mystery Ser.). audio 31.95 (*0-7451-6520-6*, CAB 1136) BBC Audiobooks America.

—Maigret & the Madwoman. 2003. 180p. pap. 8.00 (*0-15-602850-6*, Harvest Bks.) Harcourt Trade Pubs.

—Maigret & the Madwoman. Ellenbogen, Eileen, tr. 1992. (Helen & Kurt Wolff Bk.). 176p. pap. 5.95 o.s.i (*0-15-655122-5*, Harvest Bks.) Harcourt Trade Pubs.

—Maigret & the Man on the Bench. 2003. 192p. pap. 8.00 (*0-15-602837-9*, Harvest Bks.) Harcourt Trade Pubs.

—Maigret & the Man on the Bench. Ellenbogen, Eileen, tr. from FRE. (Helen & Kurt Wolff Bk.). 1993. 181p. pap. 5.95 o.s.i (*0-15-655123-3*, Harvest Bks.); 1975. 9.95 o.p. (*0-15-155145-6*) Harcourt Trade Pubs.

—Maigret & the Millionaires. l.t. ed. 2002. (Dales Large Print Ser.). 224p. pap. 21.99 (*1-84262-097-5*) Dales Large Print Bks. GBR. *Dist:* Ulverscroft Large Print Bks., Ltd., Ulverscroft Large Print Canada, Ltd.

—Maigret & the Millionaires. Stewart, Jean, tr. 1992. 182p. pap. 5.95 o.s.i (*0-15-655150-0*, Harvest Bks.); 1974. 168p. 5.95 o.p. (*0-15-155143-X*) Harcourt Trade Pubs.

—Maigret & the Nahour Case. Hamilton, Alastair, tr. l.t. ed. 1992. (Nightingale Ser.). 229p. pap. 14.95 o.p. (*0-8161-5274-8*, Macmillan Reference USA) Gale Group.

—Maigret & the Nahour Case. Hamilton, Alastair, tr. 1993. 168p. pap. 5.95 (*0-15-655149-7*, Harvest Bks.) Harcourt Trade Pubs.

—Maigret & the Nahour Case. 1983. (Helen & Kurt Wolff Bk.). 168p. 10.95 o.p. (*0-15-155559-1*) Harcourt Trade Pubs.

—Maigret & the Pickpocket. unabr. ed. 1992. (Inspector Maigret Mystery Ser.). 39.95 incl. audio (*0-7451-4030-0*, CAB 727) BBC Audiobooks America.

—Maigret & the Pickpocket. unabr. ed. 2000. (Inspector Maigret Mystery Ser.). audio 34.95 Chivers Audio Bks. GBR. *Dist:* BBC Audiobooks America.

—Maigret & the Pickpocket. Ryan, Nigel, tr. l.t. ed. 1990. (Nightingale Ser.). 13.95 o.p. (*0-8161-4666-7*, Macmillan Reference USA) Gale Group.

—Maigret & the Pickpocket. Ryan, Nigel, tr. from FRE. 1995. (Helen & Kurt Wolff Bk.). 156p. pap. 6.00 (*0-15-655145-4*, Harvest Bks.) Harcourt Trade Pubs.

—Maigret & the Reluctant Witness. abr. ed. 1998. audio 16.99 (*0-88646-458-7*, 7458) Durkin Hayes Publishing Ltd.

—Maigret & the Saturday Caller. 2003. 128p. pap. 8.00 (*0-15-602842-5*); 1992. 132p. pap. 6.00 o.s.i (*0-15-655175-6*, Harvest Bks.) Harcourt Trade Pubs.

—Maigret & the Saturday Caller. White, Tony, tr. 1991. 124p. 17.95 (*0-15-155566-4*) Harcourt Trade Pubs.

—Maigret & the Spinster. 2003. 168p. pap. 8.00 (*0-15-602843-3*, Harvest Bks.) Harcourt Trade Pubs.

—Maigret & the Spinster. Ellenbogen, Eileen, tr. 1996. 168p. (C). pap. 6.00 o.s.i (*0-15-655129-2*, Harvest Bks.); 1977. reprint ed. 6.95 o.p. (*0-15-155550-8*) Harcourt Trade Pubs.

—Maigret & the Tavern by the Seine. Sainsbury, Geoffrey, tr. 1990. 182p. pap. 6.00 (*0-15-655164-0*, Harvest Bks.) Harcourt Trade Pubs.

—Maigret & the Toy Village. unabr. ed. 1992. (Inspector Maigret Mystery Ser.). audio 39.95 (*0-7451-6283-5*, CAB 666) BBC Audiobooks America.

—Maigret & the Toy Village. Ellenbogen, Eileen, tr. l.t. ed. 1989. 216p. pap. 12.95 o.p. (*0-8161-4427-3*, Macmillan Reference USA) Gale Group.

—Maigret & the Toy Village. Ellenbogen, Eileen, tr. 1994. pap. 5.95 (*0-15-655154-3*, Harvest Bks.); 1979. 7.95 o.p. (*0-15-155554-0*) Harcourt Trade Pubs.

—Maigret & the Wine Merchant. unabr. collector's ed. 1984. audio 30.00 (*0-7366-0544-4*, 1518) Books on Tape, Inc.

—Maigret & the Wine Merchant. Ellenbogen, Eileen, tr. 1993. 187p. pap. 6.00 o.s.i (*0-15-655125-X*, Harvest Bks.) Harcourt Trade Pubs.

—Maigret & the Yellow Dog. 1995. (Helen & Kurt Wolff Bk.). 140p. pap. 6.00 (*0-15-655157-8*) Harcourt Trade Pubs.

—Maigret & the Yellow Dog. Asher, Linda, tr. 1987. 15.95 o.s.i (*0-15-155564-8*) Harcourt Trade Pubs.

—Maigret at the Coroner's. Keene, Frances, tr. (Helen & Kurt Wolff Bk.). 1992. 176p. (C). pap. 5.95 o.s.i (*0-15-655143-8*, Harvest Bks.); 1980. 180p. reprint ed. 8.95 o.p. (*0-15-155556-7*) Harcourt Trade Pubs.

—Maigret at the Crossroads. 1963. pap. 2.95 o.p. (*0-14-002028-4*, Penguin Bks.) Viking Penguin.

—Maigret at the Crossroads (Omnibus) 1984. (Crime Ser.). 320p. pap. 6.95 o.p. (*0-14-006652-7*, Penguin Bks.) Viking Penguin.

—Maigret at the Gai-Moulin.Tr. of Danseuse du Gai-Moulin. 2003. 176p. pap. 8.00 (*0-15-602845-X*); 1993. 182p. pap. 6.00 (*0-15-655176-4*) Harcourt Trade Pubs.

—Maigret at the Gai-Moulin. Sainsbury, Geoffrey, tr. 2nd ed. 1991. Tr. of Danseuse du Gai-Moulin. 166p. 17.95 o.s.i (*0-15-155568-0*) Harcourt Trade Pubs.

—Maigret au Picratt's. 2000. (Maigret Mystery Ser.). (FRE.). pap. 12.95 (*2-253-14219-0*) Librairie Generale Francaise, LGF FRA. *Dist:* Distribooks, Inc.

—Maigret Bides His Time. Hamilton, Alastair, tr. 160p. 1992. pap. 5.95 (*0-15-655151-9*, Harvest Bks.); 1985. 12.95 o.p. (*0-15-155563-X*) Harcourt Trade Pubs.

—Maigret et la Grande Perche. 2000. (Maigret Mystery Ser.). (FRE.). pap. 12.95 (*2-253-14223-9*) Librairie Generale Francaise, LGF FRA. *Dist:* Distribooks, Inc.

—Maigret et l'Affaire Nahour. 2000. (Maigret Mystery Ser.). (FRE.). pap. 12.95 (*2-253-14220-4*) Librairie Generale Francaise, LGF FRA. *Dist:* Distribooks, Inc.

—Maigret et le Clochard, Level B. (FRE.). text 8.95 (*0-88436-047-4*, 40270) EMC/Paradigm Publishing.

—Maigret et le Clochard. l.t. ed. 1997. (French Ser.). (FRE.). 236p. pap. 30.99 o.p. (*2-84011-186-1*) Feryane, SA, Editions FRA. *Dist:* Ulverscroft Large Print Bks., Ltd., Ulverscroft Large Print Canada, Ltd.

—Maigret et le Clochard. 2000. (Maigret Mystery Ser.). (FRE.). pap. 12.95 (*2-253-14228-X*) Librairie Generale Francaise, LGF FRA. *Dist:* Distribooks, Inc.

—Maigret et le Clochard. 1995. (FRE.). audio 28.95 Olivia & Hill Pr., The.

—Maigret et le Corps Sans Tete. 1992. (FRE.). pap. 11.95 (*0-7859-3257-7*, 2266051032) French & European Pubns., Inc.

—Maigret et le Corps Sans Tete, La Boule Noire, Maigret Tend un Piege, Les Complices, En Cas de Malheur, Un Echec de Maigret, Le Petit Homme d'Arkhangelsh, Maigret S'Amuse. 1989. (FRE.). 49.95 (*0-7859-0482-4*, 2258027977) French & European Pubns., Inc.

—Maigret et le Fantome, Level B. 2000. (FRE.). text 8.95 (*0-8219-1470-7*, 40271) EMC/Paradigm Publishing.

—Maigret et le Fantome. l.t. ed. 1996. (French Ser.). (FRE.). 224p. pap. 30.99 o.p. (*2-84011-152-7*) Feryane, SA, Editions FRA. *Dist:* Ulverscroft Large Print Bks., Ltd., Ulverscroft Large Print Canada, Ltd.

—Maigret et les Braves Gens. l.t. ed. 2002. (French Ser.). 221p. pap. 30.99 o.p. (*2-84011-459-3*) Feryane, SA, Editions FRA. *Dist:* Ulverscroft Large Print Bks., Ltd., Ulverscroft Large Print Canada, Ltd.

—Maigret et les Braves Gens: Student Edition. Daudon, Rene, ed. 1969. (FRE.). (Orig.). (C). pap. text, stu. ed. 4.95 o.p. (*0-15-551287-0*) Harcourt College Pubs.

—Maigret et les Temoins Recalcitrants, La Vielle, L'Ours en Peluche, Une Confidence de Maigret, Le Veuf, Maigret aux Assises, Maigret et les Viellards, Betty. 1990. (FRE.). 830p. 49.95 (*0-7859-0483-2*, 2258031532) French & European Pubns., Inc.

—Maigret et l'Inspecteur Maigrecieux, la Passager Clandestin, le Temoignage de l'Enfant Du Choeur, le Client le Plus Obstine Du Monde, On Ne Tue Pas les Pauvres Types, la Jument Perdue, Maigret et Son Mort, Pedigree. 1988. (FRE.). 49.95 (*0-7859-0477-8*, 2258021154) French & European Pubns., Inc.

—Maigret Goes Home. Baldick, Robert, tr. 1992. 144p. pap. 5.95 o.s.i (*0-15-655165-9*, Harvest Bks.); 1989. 16.95 (*0-15-155150-2*) Harcourt Trade Pubs.

—Maigret Goes Home. Baldick, Robert, tr. 1967. 139p. pap. 1.95 o.p. (*0-14-001901-4*, Penguin Bks.) Viking Penguin.

—Maigret Goes to School. Woodward, Daphne, tr. 1992. Tr. of Maigret a l'Ecole. 196p. pap. 5.95 o.s.i (*0-15-655156-X*) Harcourt Trade Pubs.

—Maigret Has Doubts. Moir, Lyn, tr. 1982. 144p. 10.95 o.p. (*0-15-155558-3*) Harcourt Trade Pubs.

—Maigret Has Doubts. 1988. 160p. pap. 3.50 (*0-380-70410-2*, Avon Bks.) Morrow/Avon.

—Maigret Has Scruples. Eglesfield, Robert, tr. 1996. (Helen & Kurt Wolff Bk.). 192p. pap. 6.00 (*0-15-655160-8*) Harcourt Trade Pubs.

—Maigret Has Scruples. 1995. pap. 6.00 (*0-15-600247-7*) Harcourt Trade Pubs.

—Maigret Hesitates. Moir, Lyn, tr. 1993. 182p. pap. 5.95 (*0-15-655152-7*, Harvest Bks.) Harcourt Trade Pubs.

—Maigret in Court. Brain, Robert, tr. 1983. (Helen & Kurt Wolff Bk.). 160p. reprint ed. 11.95 o.s.i (*0-15-155561-3*) Harcourt Trade Pubs.

—Maigret in Court. Brain, Robert, tr. 1988. 160p. pap. 3.50 (*0-380-70411-0*, Avon Bks.) Morrow/Avon.

—Maigret in Exile. Ellenbogen, Eileen, tr. from FRE. (Harvest Book Ser.). 1994. 168p. pap. 5.95 (*0-15-655136-5*, Harvest Bks.); 1979. 7.95 o.p. (*0-15-155147-2*) Harcourt Trade Pubs.

—Maigret in Holland. 2003. 180p. pap. 8.00 (*0-15-602852-2*); 2nd ed. 1994. 182p. pap. 5.95 o.s.i (*0-15-600084-9*) Harcourt Trade Pubs. (Harvest Bks.).

—Maigret in Holland. Sainsbury, Geoffrey, tr. 2nd ed. 1993. 165p. 18.95 o.s.i (*0-15-155159-6*) Harcourt Trade Pubs.

—Maigret in Montmartre. Woodward, Daphne, tr. 1989. 202p. pap. 6.00 (*0-15-655162-4*) Harcourt Trade Pubs.

—Maigret in Vichy. Ellenbogen, Eileen, tr. 1995. (Harvest Book Ser.). 182p. pap. 6.00 o.s.i (*0-15-655140-3*, Harvest Bks.) Harcourt Trade Pubs.

—Maigret Loses His Temper. 2003. 144p. pap. 8.00 (*0-15-602847-6*, Harvest Bks.) Harcourt Trade Pubs.

—Maigret Loses His Temper. Eglesfield, Robert, tr. 1993. (Helen & Kurt Wolff Bk.). 144p. pap. 5.95 o.s.i (*0-15-655128-4*, Harvest Bks.) Harcourt Trade Pubs.

—Maigret Meets a Milord. 1963. pap. 2.95 o.p. (*0-14-002027-6*, Penguin Bks.) Viking Penguin.

—Maigret Meets a Milord (Omnibus) 1983. pap. 6.95 o.p. (*0-14-006651-9*, Penguin Bks.) Viking Penguin.

—Maigret Mystified. 1964. Orig. Title: Shadow in the Courtyard. pap. 1.95 o.p. (*0-14-002024-1*, Penguin Bks.) Viking Penguin.

—Maigret on the Defensive. Hamilton, Alastair, tr. 1981. (Helen & Kurt Wolff Bk.). 144p. 10.95 o.p. (*0-15-155557-5*) Harcourt Trade Pubs.

—Maigret on the Defensive. 1987. 160p. pap. 3.50 (*0-380-70409-9*, Avon Bks.) Morrow/Avon.

—Maigret on the Riviera. 1989. 140p. pap. 6.00 o.s.i (*0-15-655158-6*, Harvest Bks.) Harcourt Trade Pubs.

—Maigret on the Riviera. Sainsbury, Geoffrey, tr. 1988. 144p. 14.95 o.s.i (*0-15-155149-9*) Harcourt Trade Pubs.

—Maigret S'Amuse. l.t. ed. 1999. (French Ser.). (FRE.). 275p. pap. 30.99 (*2-84011-329-5*) Feryane, SA, Editions FRA. *Dist:* Ulverscroft Large Print Bks., Ltd., Ulverscroft Large Print Canada, Ltd.

—Maigret Se Trompe. 2000. (Maigret Mystery Ser.). (FRE.). pap. 12.95 (*2-253-14227-1*) Librairie Generale Francaise, LGF FRA. *Dist:* Distribooks, Inc.

—Maigret Se Trompe, Crime Impuni, Maigret a l'Ecole, Maigret et la Jeun Morte. 1990. (FRE.). 860p. 49.95 (*0-7859-0480-8*, 2258025966) French & European Pubns., Inc.

—Maigret Sets a Trap. 20.95 (*0-89190-427-1*) Amereon, Ltd.

—Maigret Sets a Trap. unabr. ed. 2000. audio 21.95 (*1-57270-152-8*, N31152u, Audio Editions Mystery Masters) Audio Partners Publishing Corp.

—Maigret Sets a Trap. (Black Dagger Crime Ser.). 16.50 o.p. (*0-86220-825-4*, BD024, Black Dagger) BBC Audiobooks America.

—Maigret Sets a Trap. unabr. collector's ed. 1983. audio 30.00 (*0-7366-0534-7*, 1508) Books on Tape, Inc.

—Maigret Sets a Trap. unabr. ed. 2000. (Inspector Maigret Mystery Ser.). audio 34.95 (*0-7451-4118-8*, CAB 801) Chivers Audio Bks. GBR. *Dist:* BBC Audiobooks America.

—Maigret Sets a Trap. Woodward, Daphne, tr. l.t. ed. 1990. (Nightingale Ser.). 230p. pap. 13.95 o.p. (*0-8161-4665-9*, Macmillan Reference USA) Gale Group.

—Maigret Sets a Trap. 2003. 192p. pap. 8.00 (*0-15-602848-4*, Harvest Bks.) Harcourt Trade Pubs.

—Maigret Sets a Trap. Woodward, Daphne, tr. 1992. (Helen & Kurt Wolff Bk.). 182p. pap. 5.95 o.s.i (*0-15-655126-8*, Harvest Bks.) Harcourt Trade Pubs.

—Maigret Stonewalled. 1963. pap. 2.95 o.p. (*0-14-002026-8*, Penguin Bks.) Viking Penguin.

—Maigret Tend un Piege. l.t. ed. 1994. (French Ser.). (FRE.). pap. 30.99 o.p. (*2-84011-095-4*) Feryane, SA, Editions FRA. *Dist:* Ulverscroft Large Print Bks., Ltd., Ulverscroft Large Print Canada, Ltd.

—A Maigret Trio: Maigret's Failure, Maigret in Society, & Maigret & the Lazy Burglar. 23.95 (*0-89190-425-5*) Amereon, Ltd.

—A Maigret Trio: Maigret's Failure, Maigret in Society, & Maigret & the Lazy Burglar. Woodward, Daphne & Eglesfield, Robert, trs. 1994. (Harvest Book Ser.). 288p. pap. 10.00 o.s.i (*0-15-655137-3*, Harvest Bks.) Harcourt Trade Pubs.

—Maigret's Boyhood Friend. 19.95 (*0-89190-426-3*) Amereon, Ltd.

—Maigret's Boyhood Friend. unabr. collector's ed. 1984. audio 36.00 (*0-7366-0543-6*, 1517) Books on Tape, Inc.

—Maigret's Boyhood Friend. Ellenbogen, Eileen, tr. l.t. ed. 1991. (Nightingale Ser.). 260p. pap. 14.95 o.p. (*0-8161-5116-4*, Macmillan Reference USA) Gale Group.

—Maigret's Boyhood Friend. 2003. 192p. pap. 8.00 (*0-15-602851-4*, Harvest Bks.) Harcourt Trade Pubs.

—Maigret's Boyhood Friend. Ellenbogen, Eileen, tr. (Harvest Book Ser.). 1996. 196p. pap. 6.00 o.s.i (*0-15-655131-4*, Harvest Bks.); 1970. 4.95 o.p. (*0-15-155135-9*) Harcourt Trade Pubs.

—Maigret's Christmas. unabr. collector's ed. 1979. audio 80.00 (*0-7366-0226-7*, 1223) Books on Tape, Inc.

—Maigret's Christmas: 9 Stories. Stewart, Jean, tr. (Helen & Kurt Wolff Bk.). 1992. 336p. pap. 12.00 o.s.i (*0-15-655132-2*, Harvest Bks.); 1977. 8.95 o.p. (*0-15-155551-6*) Harcourt Trade Pubs.

—Maigret's Memoirs. Stewart, Jean, tr. from FRE. 1985. (Helen & Kurt Wolff Bk.). 160p. reprint ed. 13.95 (*0-15-155148-0*) Harcourt Trade Pubs.

—Maigret's Memoirs. Stewart, Jean, tr. 1989. 144p. reprint ed. pap. 3.50 (*0-380-70412-9*, Avon Bks.) Morrow/Avon.

—Maigret's Mistake. Hodge, Alan, tr. 1988. 188p. pap. 6.00 (*0-15-655155-1*) Harcourt Trade Pubs.

—Maigret's Pipe. Stewart, Jean, tr. from FRE. (Harvest Book Ser.). 1994. 336p. pap. 11.00 (*0-15-655146-2*, Harvest Bks.); 1978. 8.95 o.p. (*0-15-155553-2*) Harcourt Trade Pubs.

—Maigret's Revolver. Ryan, Nigel, tr. from FRE. l.t. ed. 1992. (Nightingale Ser.). 241p. pap. 14.95 o.p. (*0-8161-5316-7*, Macmillan Reference USA) Gale Group.

—Maigret's Revolver. Ryan, Nigel, tr. from FRE. (Helen & Kurt Wolff Bk.). 1991. 182p. (C). pap. 5.95 o.s.i (*0-15-659556-7*, Harvest Bks.); 1984. (FRE.). 176p. 12.95 o.s.i (*0-15-155562-1*) Harcourt Trade Pubs.

—Maigret's Rival. Thomson, Helen, tr. l.t. ed. 1988. (Nightingale Ser.). 244p. 12.95 o.p. (*0-8161-4426-5*, Macmillan Reference USA) Gale Group.

—Maigret's Rival. Thomson, Helen, tr. 1994. 182p. pap. 5.95 (*0-15-655141-1*, Harvest Bks.); 1980. 180p. reprint ed. 7.95 o.p. (*0-15-155555-9*) Harcourt Trade Pubs.

—Maigret's War of Nerves. Sainsbury, Geoffrey, tr. l.t. ed. 1987. (Nightingale Ser.). 280p. 10.95 o.p. (*0-8161-4309-9*, Macmillan Reference USA) Gale Group.

—Maigret's War of Nerves. Sainsbury, Geoffrey, tr. 1986. (Helen & Kurt Wolff Bk.). 180p. 13.95 (*0-15-155570-2*) Harcourt Trade Pubs.

—Maigret's War of Nerves. Sainsbury, Geoffrey, tr. 1989. 160p. pap. 3.50 (*0-380-70413-7*, Avon Bks.) Morrow/Avon.

—The Man on the Bench in the Barn. Budberg, Moura, tr. 1970. (Helen & Kurt Wolff Bk.). 188p. 5.95 o.p. (*0-15-156928-2*) Harcourt Trade Pubs.

—The Man with the Little Dog. Stewart, Jean, tr. 1989. 176p. 16.95 (*0-15-156933-9*) Harcourt Trade Pubs.

—Mon Ami Maigret. 1996. (FRE.). audio 28.95 Olivia & Hill Pr., The.

—Monsieur Gallet, Decede, le Pendu De Saint-Pholien, le Charretier De la Providence. 1991. (FRE.). 924p. 49.95 (*0-7859-0485-9*, 2258032458) French & European Pubns., Inc.

—Monsieur Monde Vanishes. Stewart, Jean, tr. 1977. (Helen & Kurt Wolff Bk.). 6.95 o.p. (*0-15-162098-9*) Harcourt Trade Pubs.

—Monsieur Monde Vanishes. 2004. 144p. pap. 12.95 (*1-59017-096-2*) New York Review of Bks., Inc., The.

—La Mort de Belle, le Revolver de Maigret, les Freres Rico, Maigret et l'Homme du Banc, Antoine et Julie, Maigret a Peur, l'Escalier de Fer, Feux Rouges. 1989. (FRE.). 49.95 (*0-7859-0481-6*, 2258027098) French & European Pubns., Inc.

—La Morte d'August. 1991. (FRE.). pap. 11.95 (*0-7859-3249-6*, 2266045911) French & European Pubns., Inc.

—The Murderer. Sainsbury, Geoffrey, tr. 1986. 144p. 15.95 (*0-15-163270-7*) Harcourt Trade Pubs.

—Mystery: Four Great Inspector Maigret Novels. 1996. 12.98 o.p. (*0-88365-948-4*, Galahad Bks.) BBS Publishing Corp.

—The Nightclub. Stewart, Jean, tr. 1979. (Helen & Kurt Wolff Bk.). 7.95 o.p. (*0-15-165589-8*) Harcourt Trade Pubs.

—None of Maigret's Business. unabr. collector's ed. 1983. audio 30.00 (*0-7366-0535-5*, 1509) Books on Tape, Inc.

—Un Nouveau Dans la Ville, Maigret et la Vielle Dame, l'Amie de Madame Maigret, l'Enterrement de Monsieur Bouvet, Maigret et les Petits Cochons Sans Queue, les Voles Verts, Tante Jeanne, les Memoires de Maigret, 23 vols., Set. 1988. (FRE.). 860p. 49.95 (*0-7859-0554-5*, 225802353X) French & European Pubns., Inc.

—November. Stewart, Jean, tr. 1978. 185p. pap. 2.95 o.s.i (*0-15-667582-X*, Harvest Bks.); 1970. 9.95 o.p. (*0-15-167560-0*) Harcourt Trade Pubs.

—Oncle Charles S'est Enferme, la Veuve Couderc, Cecile Est Morte. 1992. (FRE.). 1018p. 49.95 (*0-7859-0495-6*, 2258035287) French & European Pubns., Inc.

—The Outlaw. Curtis, Howard, tr. 1987. 15.95 (*0-15-170509-7*) Harcourt Trade Pubs.

—La Patience de Maigret. 2000. (Maigret Mystery Ser.). (FRE.). pap. 12.95 (*2-253-14221-2*) Librairie Generale Francaise, LGF FRA. *Dist:* Distribooks, Inc.

—La Patience de Maigret, le Confessional, la Morte d'Auguste. 1990. (FRE.). 896p. 49.95 (*0-7859-0488-3*, 2258033039) French & European Pubns., Inc.

—The Patience of Maigret. unabr. ed. 1996. (Inspector Maigret Mystery Ser.). audio 31.95 (*0-7451-6564-8*, CAB1180) BBC Audiobooks America.

—Il Peut Bergere. 1966. (FRE.). pap. 11.95 (*0-7859-3964-4*) French & European Pubns., Inc.

—La Pipe de Maigret. Goodall, Geoffrey, ed. 1969. (FRE.). 70p. pap. text 6.95 o.p. (*0-312-46235-2*) St. Martin's Pr.

—La Pipe de Maigret, Maigret Se Fache, Maigret a New York, Lettre a Mon Juge, le Destin Des Malou. 1988. (FRE.). 49.95 (*0-7859-0476-X*, 2258020980) French & European Pubns., Inc.

—La Porte. 1993. (FRE.). pap. 11.95 (*0-7859-3258-5*, 2266052683) French & European Pubns., Inc.

—La Premiere Enquete de Maigret, Les Fantomes du Chapelier, Mon Ami Maigret, Les Quatres Jours du Pauvre Homme, Maigret Chez le Corormer, Un Nouveau dans la Ville, La Neige Etait Sale, Le Fond de la Bouteille. (FRE.). 49.95 (*0-7859-0478-6*, 2258021421) French & European Pubns., Inc.

—La Prison, Maigret Hesite, la Main. 1991. (FRE.). 896p. 49.95 (*0-7859-0489-1*, 2258033047) French & European Pubns., Inc.

—The Reckoning. Read, Emily, tr. 1984. (Helen & Kurt Wolff Bk.). 128p. 12.95 o.p. (*0-15-175980-4*) Harcourt Trade Pubs.

—The Rich Man. Stewart, Jean, tr. from FRE. 1971. (Helen & Kurt Wolff Bk.). 5.95 o.p. (*0-15-177162-6*) Harcourt Trade Pubs.

—Le Riche Homme, la Folie de Maigret, la Disparition D'Odile. 1991. (FRE.). 864p. 49.95 (*0-7859-0490-5*, 2258033055) French & European Pubns., Inc.

—La Rue aux Trois Poussins. 1992. (FRE.). pap. 11.95 (*0-7859-3260-7*, 2266052993) French & European Pubns., Inc.

—La Rue aux Trois Poussins: Le Mari de Melie, Level A. (FRE.). text 7.95 (*0-88436-985-4*, 40301) EMC/Paradigm Publishing.

—The Rules of the Game. l.t. ed. 1991. 212p. reprint ed. lib. bdg. 11.95 o.p. (*1-85057-869-9*, Macmillan Reference USA) Gale Group.

—The Rules of the Game. Curtis, Howard, tr. 1988. (Helen & Kurt Wolff Bk.). 160p. 18.95 o.p. (*0-15-169475-3*) Harcourt Trade Pubs.

—The Rules of the Game. l.t. ed. 1991. (Magna Large Print Ser.). 212p. o.p. (*1-85057-868-0*) Magna Large Print Bks. GBR. *Dist:* Ulverscroft Large Print Canada, Ltd.

—Sailors' Rendezvous. 1970. pap. 1.95 o.p. (*0-14-003136-7*, Penguin Bks.) Viking Penguin.

—Soeurs Lacroix. (Folio Ser.: No. 1209). (FRE.). pap. 8.95 (*2-07-037209-X*) Schoenhof's Foreign Bks., Inc.

—Striptease. 1993. (FRE.). pap. 11.95 (*0-7859-3259-3*, 2266052691) French & European Pubns., Inc.

—Striptease. Brain, Robert, tr. 1989. 17.95 (*0-15-185910-8*) Harcourt Trade Pubs.

—Sunday. Ryan, Nigel, tr. 1976. (Helen & Kurt Wolff Bk.). pap. 2.50 o.p. (*0-15-686301-4*, Harvest Bks.) Harcourt Trade Pubs.

—The Survivors. Gilbert, Stuart, tr. from FRE. 1985. (Helen & Kurt Wolff Bk.). 180p. 14.95 o.s.i (*0-15-187047-0*) Harcourt Trade Pubs.

—The Suspect. Gilbert, Stuart, tr. 1991. 17.95 o.s.i (*0-15-137057-5*) Harcourt Trade Pubs.

—Tante Jeanne. 1991. (FRE.). pap. 11.95 (*0-7859-3244-5*, 2266045202) French & European Pubns., Inc.

—Le Temps de Anais, un Noel de Maigret, Maigret Au Picratt's, Maigret en Meuble, une Vie Comme Neuve, Maigret et la Grande Perche, Marie Qui Louche, Miagret Lognon et les Gangsters. 1988. (FRE.). 49.95 (*0-7859-0479-4*, 2258023564) French & European Pubns., Inc.

—Le Testament Donadieu, l'Assassin, le Blanc a Lunettes. 1992. (FRE.). 1000p. 49.95 (*0-7859-0492-1*, 2258035252) French & European Pubns., Inc.

—Le Train. 1991. (FRE.). pap. 11.95 (*0-7859-3248-8*, 2266045849) French & European Pubns., Inc.

—Les Treize Enigmes, la Folle d'Itteville, les Treize Mysteres. 1992. (FRE.). 1047p. 49.95 (*0-7859-0487-5*, 2258032733) French & European Pubns., Inc.

—Trois Crimes de Mes Amis. (Folio Ser.: No. 1112). (FRE.). pap. 8.95 (*2-07-037112-3*) Schoenhof's Foreign Bks., Inc.

—Les Trois Crimes de Mes Amis, le Suspect, les Soeurs Lacroix. 1992. (FRE.). 1021p. 49.95 (*0-7859-0493-X*, 2258035260) French & European Pubns., Inc.

—Trois Nouvelles de Georges Simenon. Lindsay, Frank W. & Nazzaro, Anthony M., eds. 1966. (gr. 10-12). pap. text o.p. (*0-13-930917-9*) Prentice-Hall.

—The Truth about Bebe Donge. Varese, Louise, tr. 2nd ed. 1992. 176p. 18.95 (*0-15-191319-6*) Harcourt Trade Pubs.

—Uncle Charles. l.t. unabr. ed. 1998. (Keating's Choice Ser.). 202p. 22.95 (*1-85089-418-3*, 894183) ISIS Large Print Bks. GBR. *Dist:* Transaction Pubs.

—Uncle Charles Has Locked Himself In. Curtis, Howard, tr. 1987. 19.95 o.s.i (*0-15-192685-9*) Harcourt Trade Pubs.

—The Venice Train. Hamilton, Alastair, tr. (Helen & Kurt Wolff Bk.). 1983. 160p. pap. 3.95 o.s.i (*0-15-693523-6*, Harvest Bks.); 1974. 168p. 6.50 o.p. (*0-15-193506-8*) Harcourt Trade Pubs.

—La Vieille. 1991. (FRE.). pap. 11.95 (*0-7859-3245-3*, 2266045210) French & European Pubns., Inc.

—Le Voleur de Maigret. 2000. (Maigret Mystery Ser.). (FRE.). pap. 12.95 (*2-253-14218-2*) Librairie Generale Francaise, LGF FRA. *Dist:* Distribooks, Inc.

—Voyageur de la Toussaint. 1941. (Folio Ser.: No. 932). (FRE.). 360p. pap. 9.95 (*2-07-036932-3*) Schoenhof's Foreign Bks., Inc.

—When I Was Old. 1971. (Helen & Kurt Wolff Bk.). (Illus.). 343p. 8.50 o.p. (*0-15-195950-1*) Harcourt Trade Pubs.

—The White Horse Inn. Denny, Norman, tr. 1980. (Helen & Kurt Wolff Bk.). 144p. 7.95 o.p. (*0-15-196240-5*) Harcourt Trade Pubs.

—The Widower. Baldick, Robert, tr. from FRE. 1982. 10.95 o.p. (*0-15-196644-3*) Harcourt Trade Pubs.

Sisman, Robyn. Weekend in Paris. 2004. pap. 13.00 (*0-452-28490-2*, Plume) Dutton/Plume.

Smith, Sarah. The Knowledge of Water. 2000. 416p. mass mkt. 6.99 (*0-345-43946-5*, Ballantine Bks.); 1997. 496p. pap. 12.00 (*0-345-40963-9*) Ballantine Bks.

Sohmers, Barbara. The Fox & the Puma. 1997. 148p. pap. 10.00 (*1-58345-486-1*) Domhan Bks.

—The Fox & the Pussycat. 2000. 163p. pap. 10.00 (*1-58345-491-8*) Domhan Bks.

Steel, Danielle. Five Days in Paris. 1997. 304p. mass mkt. 7.50 (*0-440-22284-2*); 1995. 288p. 15.95 (*0-385-31530-9*, Delacorte Pr.) Dell Publishing.

—Five Days in Paris. 1996. pap. 6.50 (*0-440-29548-3*) Doubleday Publishing.

—Five Days in Paris. unabr. ed. 1995. audio 25.95 (*0-553-47429-4*, 693303, RH Audio) Random Hse. Audio Publishing Group.

—Five Days in Paris. l.t. ed. 1998. (Core Ser.). 288p. 29.95 (*0-7838-0181-5*) Thorndike Pr.

—The Kiss. 2002. 448p. mass mkt. 7.99 (*0-440-23669-X*); 2001. 360p. 200.00 (*0-385-33589-X*, Delacorte Pr.); 2001. 360p. 26.95 (*0-385-33540-7*, Delacorte Pr.) Dell Publishing.

—The Kiss. abr. ed. 2001. audio 26.95 (*0-553-52786-X*); audio compact disk 29.95 (*0-553-71229-2*) Random Hse. Audio Publishing Group. (RH Audio).

—The Kiss. l.t. ed. 544p. 2002. pap. 14.95 (*0-375-72817-1*); 2001. 26.95 (*0-375-43132-2*) Random Hse. Large Print.

Sullivan, Jean. Eternity, My Beloved (Car Jet'aime, O Eternite) Riordan, Francis Ellen, tr. from FRE. 1998. 160p. pap. 15.00 (*0-9654756-2-X*) River Boat Bks.

Tapon, Philippe. The Mistress: A Novel. 192p. 2000. pap. 12.95 o.s.i (*0-452-28058-3*, Plume); 1999. 23.95 o.p. (*0-525-94461-3*, Abrahams, William Bks.) Dutton/Plume.

—The Mistress: A Novel. l.t. ed. 1999. (Wheeler Large Print Book Ser.). 213p. 26.95 (*1-56895-725-4*, Wheeler Publishing, Inc.) Gale Group.

—Parisian from Kansas. (William Abrahams Book Ser.). 336p. 1998. pap. 13.95 o.s.i (*0-452-27735-3*, Plume); 1997. 23.95 o.s.i (*0-525-94239-4*) Dutton/Plume.

Tennant, Emma. Adele: Jane Eyre's Hidden Story. 2003. 240p. pap. 12.95 (*0-06-000455-X*, Perennial) HarperTrade.

Thompson, Kay. Eloise in Paris. ltd. ed. 1999. (Eloise In Paris Ser.). 64p. (J). 100.00 o.s.i (*0-689-82960-4*, Simon & Schuster Children's Publishing) Simon & Schuster Children's Publishing.

Tindall, Gillian. Fly Away Home. 1971. 222p. (*0-340-15039-4*) St. Martin's Pr.

Tremain, Rose. The Way I Found Her, Set. unabr. ed. 1999. audio 84.95 (*0-7540-0343-4*, CAB1766, Sterling Audio Bks.) BBC Audiobooks America.

—The Way I Found Her. l.t. ed. 1998. 24.95 (*1-57490-165-6*, Beeler Large Print Bks.) Beeler, Thomas T. Publisher.

—The Way I Found Her. 1998. 368p. 25.00 o.s.i (*0-374-28666-3*) Farrar, Straus & Giroux.

—The Way I Found Her. 1999. 368p. pap. 14.00 (*0-671-03570-3*, Washington Square Pr.) Simon & Schuster.

Trott, Susan. Sightings. 1988. 224p. reprint ed. pap. 6.95 o.p. (*0-06-097158-4*, PL-7158, Perennial) HarperTrade.

—Sightings. 1987. 16.45 o.p. (*0-671-63804-1*, Simon & Schuster) Simon & Schuster.

Truong, Monique. The Book of Salt. 2003. 272p. tchr. ed. 24.00 (*0-618-30400-2*) Houghton Mifflin Co.

Van Horne, Hollie. The Diary of Jean-Jacques Coupier. 2002. (Time Travelers Ser.: No. 5). 336p. mass mkt. 16.50 (*0-9674552-1-9*) Time Travelers.

Van Lustbader, Eric. The Kaisho. abr. ed. 1993. audio 16.95 o.p. (*1-55800-889-6*) NewStar Media, Inc.

—The Kaisho. 1998. 3.99 (*0-671-02329-2*, Pocket) Simon & Schuster.

—The Kaisho. Zion, Claire, ed. 1993. 496p. 22.00 (*0-671-86806-3*, Atria); 1994. 592p. reprint ed. mass mkt. 6.99 (*0-671-86807-1*, Pocket Star) Simon & Schuster.

Vandenberg, Margaret. An American in Paris: A Novel. 2000. (Illus.). 300p. pap. 14.95 (*1-57344-107-4*) Cleis Pr.

Verne, Jules. Paris in the Twentieth Century. Howard, Richard, tr. from FRE. 1997. (Illus.). 256p. pap. 12.95 (*0-345-42039-X*, Del Rey) Ballantine Bks.

Villefranche, Anne-Marie. Plaisir D'Amour: An Erotic Memoir of Paris in the 1920s. 1984. 252p. 12.95 o.p. (*0-88184-022-X*, Carroll & Graf Pubs.) Avalon Publishing Group.

Wainwright, John. The Forest. 1984. 192p. 11.95 o.p. (*0-312-29871-4*) St. Martin's Pr.

Walter, Victor. The Craftsmen. 2001. (Destiny Suite Ser.: Vol. 2). 176p. pap. 12.00 (*1-877800-06-6*) Lyric Pr.

Ward, Just S. Ambition & Love. 1994. 277p. 22.95 o.p. (*0-395-68196-0*) Houghton Mifflin Co.

Webster, Noah. Flight from Paris. 1987. (Crime Club Ser.). 192p. 12.95 o.s.i (*0-385-23560-7*) Doubleday Publishing.

Werber, Bernard. An Empire of the Ants. 1999. 320p. reprint ed. mass mkt. 5.99 (*0-553-57352-7*) Bantam Bks.

Wharton, Edith. A Son at the Front. (Collected Works of Edith Wharton). 426p. reprint ed. 2001. (Illus.). pap. text 28.00 (*0-7426-5993-3*); 1998. lib. bdg. 98.00 (*1-58201-993-2*) Classic Bks.

—A Son at the Front. rev. ed. 2003. 280p. (C). pap. 16.00 (*0-87580-568-X*); lib. bdg. 38.00 (*0-87580-203-6*) Northern Illinois Univ. Pr.

Wharton, William. Last Lovers. unabr. ed. 1991. 23.95 o.p. incl. audio (*0-930435-87-7*, 158, Bookcassette); audio 73.25 o.p. (*1-56100-081-7*, 923, Unabridged Library Editions) Brilliance Audio.

—Last Lovers. 1991. 288p. 22.00 o.s.i (*0-374-18389-9*) Farrar, Straus & Giroux.

—Scumbler. 1985. 288p. pap. 3.95 o.p. (*0-88184-135-8*, Carroll & Graf Pubs.) Avalon Publishing Group.

—Scumbler. 1984. 288p. 14.95 o.p. (*0-394-53574-X*) Knopf, Alfred A. Inc.

—Scumbler. 2004. 288p. pap. 12.95 (*1-55704-258-6*) Newmarket Pr.

Williams, Elmer A. Au Revoir Parisienne. 1999. 112p. pap. 11.00 o.p. (*0-8059-4542-3*) Dorrance Publishing Co., Inc.

Yates, Dornford. Adele & Co. 1986. 272p. 14.95 o.p. (*0-8253-0308-7*) Beaufort Bks., Inc.

Youngblood, Shay. Black Girl in Paris. 2001. (Illus.). 256p. pap. 12.00 (*1-57322-851-6*, Riverhead Trade (Paperbacks)) Berkley Publishing Group.

—Black Girl in Paris. 2000. (Illus.). 300p. 23.95 o.p. (*1-57322-151-1*, Riverhead Bks. (Hardcovers)) Putnam Publishing Group, The.

Zencey, Eric. Panama. 1997. 400p. reprint ed. mass mkt. 6.99 o.s.i (*0-425-15602-8*) Berkley Publishing Group.

—Panama. 1995. 384p. 24.00 o.p. (*0-374-22943-0*) Farrar, Straus & Giroux.
—Panama. unabr. ed. 1995. audio 91.00 (*0-7887-0454-0*, 94646E7) Recorded Bks., LLC.
—Panama. abr. ed. 1995. audio 23.00 (*0-671-54922-7*, 494361, Simon & Schuster Audioworks) Simon & Schuster Audio.
—Panama. l.t. ed. 1996. (Niagara Large Print Ser.). 514p. 29.50 o.p. (*0-7089-5833-8*, Ulverscroft) Thorpe, F. A. Pubs. GBR. *Dist:* Ulverscroft Large Print Bks., Ltd.
—Panama: A Novel. 2001. 400p. pap. 14.00 (*0-425-17833-1*) Berkley Publishing Group.
Zola, Emile. L' Assommoir. unabr. ed. 1999. (FRE.). pap. 5.95 (*2-87714-127-6*) Bookking International FRA. *Dist:* Distribooks, Inc.
—L' Assommoir. Dubois, Jacques, ed. 1990. (FRE.). 568p. pap. 11.95 (*0-7859-1486-2*, 2266033646) French & European Pubns., Inc.
—L' Assommoir. 1983. (FRE.). (C). pap. 11.95 (*0-8442-1748-4*, VF1748-4) McGraw-Hill/Contemporary.
—L' Assommoir. Tancock, Leonard, tr. & intro. by. mass mkt. 0.75 o.p. (*0-451-50128-4*, Signet Classics) NAL.
—L' Assommoir. Lethbridge, Robert, ed. Mauldon, Margaret, tr. from FRE. 1999. (Oxford World's Classics Ser.). (Illus.). 528p. pap. 10.95 (*0-19-283813-X*) Oxford Univ. Pr., Inc.
—L' Assommoir. Mauldon, Margaret, tr. 1995. (Oxford World's Classics Ser.). (Illus.). 514p. pap. 6.95 o.p. (*0-19-282983-1*) Oxford Univ. Pr., Inc.
—L' Assommoir. 1955. (Folio Ser.: No. 1051). pap. 12.95 (*2-07-037051-8*) Schoenhof's Foreign Bks., Inc.
—L' Assommoir. audio Spoken Arts, Inc.
—L' Assommoir. White, Nicholas, ed. rev. ed. 1995. (Everyman Paperback Classics Ser.). 288p. pap. 7.50 (*0-460-87576-0*, Everyman's Classic Library in Paperback) Tuttle Publishing.
—L' Assommoir. 2001. (Classics Ser.). (Illus.). 480p. pap. 11.00 (*0-14-044753-9*, Penguin Classics) Viking Penguin.
—L' Assommoir. Tancock, Leonard W., tr. 1970. (Penguin Classics Ser.). 432p. pap. 10.95 o.s.i (*0-14-044231-6*, Penguin Classics) Viking Penguin.
—The Belly of Paris. unabr. ed. 1999. audio 62.95 Blackstone Audio Bks., Inc.
—The Belly of Paris. Vizetelly, Ernest A., tr. 2003. (Green Integer Bks.: Vol. 57). 400p. pap. 15.95 (*1-892295-99-7*) Green Integer.
—The Belly of Paris. Vizetelly, Ernest Alfred, tr. from FRE. 1995. (Sun & Moon Classics Ser.: No. 70). 397p. pap. 14.95 o.p. (*1-55713-066-3*) Sun & Moon Pr.
—The Belly of Paris. Vizetelly, Ernest Alfred, tr. from FRE. 1993. (Pocket Classics Ser.). pap. 10.95 (*0-7509-0449-6*) Sutton Publishing, Ltd. GBR. *Dist:* International Publishers Marketing.
—Paris. Vizetelly, Ernest Alfred, tr. 1993. (Pocket Classics Ser.). pap. text 10.95 (*0-7509-0450-X*) Sutton Publishing.

### PASADENA (CALIF.)—FICTION

Ball, John. The Cool Cottontail. 1985. 176p. (Orig.). mass mkt. 3.50 o.p. (*0-06-080734-2*, P734, Perennial) HarperTrade.
—The Eyes of Buddha: A Virgil Tibbs Mystery. 1985. 256p. reprint ed. mass mkt. 3.50 o.p. (*0-06-080751-2*, P751, Perennial) HarperTrade.
—Five Pieces of Jade. l.t. ed. 1983. (Ulverscroft Large Print Ser.). 352p. 29.99 o.p. (*0-7089-0997-3*, Ulverscroft) Thorpe, F. A. Pubs. GBR. *Dist:* Ulverscroft Large Print Bks., Ltd., Ulverscroft Large Print Canada, Ltd.
—In the Heat of the Night. l.t. ed. 2001. 248p. lib. bdg. 25.95 (*1-58547-115-1*) Ctr. Point Large Print.
—Then Came Violence. 1980. (Crime Club Ser.). 8.95 o.p. (*0-385-15726-6*) Doubleday Publishing.
—Then Came Violence. l.t. ed. 1982. (Ulverscroft Large Print Ser.). 352p. 29.99 o.p. (*0-7089-0870-5*, Ulverscroft) Thorpe, F. A. Pubs. GBR. *Dist:* Ulverscroft Large Print Bks., Ltd., Ulverscroft Large Print Canada, Ltd.
—Then Came Violence: A Virgil Tibbs Mystery. 1988. 208p. reprint ed. mass mkt. 3.95 o.p. (*0-06-080883-7*, P-883, Perennial) HarperTrade.
Beardwood, Roger. The Winner's Share. 1980. 10.00 o.p. (*0-385-14426-1*) Doubleday Publishing.
Blankenship, William D. Brotherly Love. 1981. 12.95 o.p. (*0-87795-301-5*, Morrow, William & Co.) Morrow/Avon.
—Brotherly Love. 1983. mass mkt. 3.50 o.s.i (*0-671-44765-3*, Pocket) Simon & Schuster.
Bugliosi, Vincent T. & Hurwitz, Ken. Shadow of Cain. 1982. 304p. 3.95 o.p. (*0-553-20922-1*) Bantam Bks.
—Shadow of Cain. 1981. 12.95 o.p. (*0-393-01466-5*) Norton, W. W. & Co., Inc.
Dick, Philip K. A Scanner Darkly. 1979. (Del Rey Bk.). mass mkt. 1.95 o.s.i (*0-345-26064-3*) Ballantine Bks.
—A Scanner Darkly. 1984. 224p. mass mkt. 2.50 o.p. (*0-87997-923-2*) DAW Bks., Inc.
—A Scanner Darkly. 1991. 288p. pap. 12.00 (*0-679-73665-4*, Vintage) Knopf Publishing Group.
Duncan, Alice. Strong Spirits. 2003. 32p. mass mkt. 5.99 (*0-8217-7517-0*) Kensington Publishing Corp.
Stinson, Jim. Double Exposure. 1988. (Illus.). 160p. mass mkt. 3.50 o.s.i (*0-553-26665-9*) Bantam Bks.
—Double Exposure. 1986. (Stoney Winston Mystery Ser.). 224p. 13.95 o.s.i (*0-684-18458-3*, Macmillan Reference USA) Gale Group.
—Low Angles: A Stoney Winston Mystery. 1986. 240p. 13.95 o.s.i (*0-684-18626-8*, Macmillan Reference USA) Gale Group.
—Truck Shot: A Stoney Winston Mystery. 1989. 256p. 17.95 o.p. (*0-684-18876-7*, Scribner) Simon & Schuster.
—TV Safe. 1991. 256p. 19.95 o.p. (*0-684-19225-X*, Scribner) Simon & Schuster.

### PEBBLE BEACH (CALIF.)—FICTION

Clark, Mary Higgins. Weep No More, My Lady. E-Book 9.95 (*1-930161-66-2*) Adobe Systems, Inc.
—Weep No More, My Lady. 1993. reprint ed. lib. bdg. 37.95 (*0-89968-446-7*, Lightyear Pr.) Buccaneer Bks., Inc.
—Weep No More, My Lady. 1993. 384p. mass mkt. 3.99 o.s.i (*0-440-21473-4*); reprint ed. mass mkt. 6.99 o.s.i (*0-440-20098-9*) Dell Publishing.
—Weep No More, My Lady. 1997. 384p. pap. 11.95 o.s.i (*0-385-31921-5*) Doubleday Publishing.
—Weep No More, My Lady. l.t. ed. 1988. (General Ser.). 441p. 19.95 o.p. (*0-8161-4367-6*, Macmillan Reference USA) Gale Group.
—Weep No More, My Lady. 2000. E-Book 9.95 (*0-7432-0616-9*, Simon & Schuster); 1998. (Illus.). 336p. mass mkt. 7.99 (*0-671-02558-9*, Pocket); 1987. (Illus.). 320p. bds. 17.45 o.p. (*0-671-55664-9*, Simon & Schuster) Simon & Schuster.
—Weep No More, My Lady. 1987. 12.09 o.p. (*0-606-04108-7*) Turtleback Bks.
Logue, John. A Rain of Death. 1998. (Morris & Sullivan Mystery Ser.). 304p. mass mkt. 5.99 o.s.i (*0-440-22397-0*) Dell Publishing.

### PECAN SPRINGS (TEX.: IMAGINARY PLACE)—FICTION

Albert, Susan Wittig. Chile Death. 1999. (West Coast Crime Ser.: No. 7). 320p. reprint ed. mass mkt. 6.99 (*0-425-17147-7*, Prime Crime) Berkley Publishing Group.
—Chile Death. abr. ed. 1999. (China Bayles Mystery Ser.). audio 17.95 (*1-56511-323-3*) HighBridge Co.
—Chile Death: A China Bayles Mystery. 1998. (China Bayles Mystery Ser.). 320p. 21.95 o.s.i (*0-425-16539-6*, Prime Crime) Berkley Publishing Group.
—Chile Death: A China Bayles Mystery. l.t. ed. 2001. 435p. 29.95 (*0-7862-3161-0*) Thorndike Pr.
—Hangman's Root: A China Bayles Mystery. 1995. 272p. mass mkt. 6.99 (*0-425-14898-X*) Berkley Publishing Group.
—Hangman's Root: A China Bayles Mystery. 1994. 256p. 20.00 (*0-684-19677-8*); 1995. 319p. pap. 19.95 (*0-7838-1246-9*) Gale Group. (Macmillan Reference USA).
—Lavender Lies. 2000. (Prime Crime Mysteries Ser.). 320p. reprint ed. mass mkt. 6.99 (*0-425-17700-9*) Berkley Publishing Group.
—Lavender Lies. abr. ed. 1999. (China Bayles Mystery Ser.). audio 17.95 (*1-56511-332-2*) HighBridge Co.
—Lavender Lies: A China Bayles Mystery. 1999. (China Bayles Mystery Ser.: No. 8). 320p. 21.95 o.s.i (*0-425-17032-2*, Prime Crime) Berkley Publishing Group.
—Lavender Lies: A China Bayles Mystery. l.t. ed. 2001. 437p. o.p. (*0-7862-3162-9*) Thorndike Pr.
—Love Lies Bleeding: A China Bayles Mystery. (China Bayles Mystery Ser.). 1997. 320p. 21.95 o.s.i (*0-425-15969-8*); 1998. 336p. reprint ed. mass mkt. 6.99 (*0-425-16611-2*) Berkley Publishing Group. (Prime Crime).
—Mistletoe Man: A China Bayles Mystery. 2000. (China Bayles Ser.). 304p. 21.95 o.s.i (*0-425-17673-8*) Berkley Publishing Group.
—Mistletoe Man: A China Bayles Mystery. l.t. ed. 2001. (Thorndike Mystery Ser.). 408p. 29.95 (*0-7862-3163-7*) Thorndike Pr.
—Rosemary Remembered: A China Bayles Mystery. 304p. 1996. mass mkt. 6.99 (*0-425-15405-X*); 1995. 19.95 o.p. (*0-425-14937-4*, Prime Crime) Berkley Publishing Group.
—Rueful Death: A China Bayles Mystery. 1996. 320p. 21.95 o.p. (*0-425-15469-6*); 1997. 304p. reprint ed. mass mkt. 6.99 (*0-425-15941-8*, Prime Crime) Berkley Publishing Group.
—Thyme of Death: A Mystery Introducing China Bayles. 1994. (West Coast Crime Ser.). 320p. mass mkt. 6.99 (*0-425-14098-9*) Berkley Publishing Group.
—Thyme of Death: A Mystery Introducing China Bayles. 1992. 256p. bds. 20.00 o.s.i (*0-684-19522-4*, Scribner) Simon & Schuster.
—Witches' Bane: A China Bayles Mystery. 1994. 272p. reprint ed. mass mkt. 6.99 (*0-425-14406-2*, Prime Crime) Berkley Publishing Group.
—Witches' Bane: A China Bayles Mystery. 1993. 256p. bds. 20.00 o.p. (*0-684-19636-0*, Scribner) Simon & Schuster.

### PEGANA (IMAGINARY PLACE)—FICTION

Dunsany, Lord. Complete Pegana: All the Tales Pertaining to the Fabulous Realm of Pegana. Joshi, S. T., ed. & intro. by. 1997. (Call of Cthulhu Fiction Ser.). 240p. pap. text 12.95 o.p. (*1-56882-116-6*, Chaosium Fiction Series) Chaosium, Inc.
—Time & the Gods. 1977. (Short Story Index Reprint Ser.). 16.00 (*0-8369-3388-5*) Ayer Co. Pubs., Inc.
—Time & the Gods. 15.00 (*1-58715-719-5*) Wildside Pr.

### PENNSYLVANIA—FICTION

Albert, Neil. An Appointment in May: A Dave Garrett Mystery. 1996. (Dave Garrett Mystery Ser.). 288p. 20.95 (*0-8027-3279-8*) Walker & Co.
—Burning March. 1994. (Dave Garrett Mystery Ser.). 256p. 18.95 o.p. (*0-525-93718-8*, Dutton) Dutton/Plume.
—Burning March. 1995. (Dave Garrett Mystery Ser.). 256p. mass mkt. 4.50 o.s.i (*0-451-17860-2*, Signet Bks.) NAL.
—Cruel April: A Dave Garrett Mystery. 1995. (Dave Garrett Mystery Ser.). 272p. 19.95 o.s.i (*0-525-93719-6*, Dutton) Dutton/Plume.
—Cruel April: A Dave Garrett Mystery. 1996. (Dave Garrett Mystery Ser.). 272p. mass mkt. 5.50 o.s.i (*0-451-17861-0*, Signet Bks.) NAL.
—Cruel April: A Dave Garrett Mystery. l.t. ed. 1996. (Niagara Large Print Ser.). 336p. 29.50 o.p. (*0-7089-5826-5*, Ulverscroft) Thorpe, F. A. Pubs. GBR. *Dist:* Ulverscroft Large Print Bks., Ltd.
—The February Trouble: A Dave Garrett Mystery. 1994. (Dave Garrett Mystery Ser.). 256p. mass mkt. 3.99 o.s.i (*0-451-40417-3*, Signet Bks.) NAL.
—The February Trouble: A Dave Garrett Mystery. 1992. 235p. 19.95 (*0-8027-1244-4*) Walker & Co.
—The January Corpse. 1993. (Dave Garrett Mystery Ser.). 256p. mass mkt. 3.99 o.s.i (*0-451-40377-0*) NAL.
—The January Corpse. 1991. 192p. 18.95 (*0-8027-3206-2*) Walker & Co.
—Tangled June: A Dave Garrett Mystery. 1997. (Dave Garrett Mystery Ser.). 246p. 20.95 (*0-8027-3305-0*) Walker & Co.
Albright, Harry. Gettysburg: Crisis of Command. 1991. 320p. (Orig.). pap. 8.95 o.p. (*0-87052-972-2*) Hippocrene Bks., Inc.
Anderson, Launi K. Hannah's Treasure. 1996. (Latter-Day Daughters Ser.). (J). pap. 4.95 (*1-57345-297-1*, Cinnamon Tree) Deseret Bk. Co.
Appollo, Annette. The Last One Home. 2000. 400p. mass mkt. 6.99 o.s.i (*0-06-109721-7*); 1999. 288p. 24.00 o.s.i (*0-06-019208-9*) HarperCollins Pubs.
—The Last One Home. l.t. ed. 1999. (Thorndike Senior Lifestyle Ser.). 464p. pap. 26.95 (*0-7862-2069-4*) Thorndike Pr.
Attaway, William. Blood on the Forge. 1969. 279p. reprint ed. 8.95 o.p. (*0-911860-00-2*) Chatham Bookseller.
—Blood on the Forge. 1992. 304p. pap. 9.00 o.s.i (*0-385-42542-2*) Doubleday Publishing.
Ayres, Diane. Other Girls. 2003. 416p. pap. 15.00 (*0-7582-0112-5*, Kensington Bks.); 2002. 432p. 23.00 (*0-7582-0111-7*) Kensington Publishing Corp.
Bailey-Williams, Nicole. A Little Piece of Sky. 2002. 176p. reprint ed. pap. 9.95 (*0-7679-1216-0*, Harlem Moon) Broadway Bks.
Bell, Thomas. Out of This Furnace. 1976. (C). reprint ed. 432p. 9.95 o.p. (*0-8229-3321-7*); (Illus.). 424p. (gr. 9-12). pap. 14.95 (*0-8229-5273-4*) Univ. of Pittsburgh Pr.
—Out of This Furnace: Fiftieth Anniversary Edition. 1991. (Social & Labor History Ser.). (Illus.). 424p. (C). (gr. 9-12). text 29.95 (*0-8229-3690-9*) Univ. of Pittsburgh Pr.
Bender, Carrie. A Joyous Heart. 2003. (Miriam's Journal Ser.). 151p. (Orig.). 24.95 (*0-7862-4427-5*, Five Star) Gale Group.
—A Joyous Heart. 1996. (Miriam's Journal Ser.: Vol. 3). 168p. (Orig.). pap. 8.99 (*0-8361-3668-3*) Herald Pr.
—A Joyous Heart. 1994. (Orig.). E-Book 7.99 (*0-585-29213-2*) netLibrary, Inc.
—Lilac Blossom Time. 2001. (Dora's Diary Ser.: Bk. 2). (Illus.). 176p. pap. 8.99 (*0-8361-9137-4*) Herald Pr.
—A Treasured Friendship. 2003. (Miriam's Journal Ser.). 128p. 24.95 (*0-7862-4428-3*, Five Star) Gale Group.
—A Treasured Friendship. 1996. (Miriam's Journal Ser.: Vol. 4). 160p. (gr. 8-12). pap. 8.99 (*0-8361-9033-5*) Herald Pr.
—A Treasured Friendship. 1996. E-Book 7.99 (*0-585-29207-8*) netLibrary, Inc.
—Whispering Brook Farm. 1995. (Whispering Brook Ser.: Vol. 1). (Illus.). 184p. (J). (gr. 4-7). pap. 8.99 (*0-8361-9011-4*) Herald Pr.
—A Winding Path. 2002. (Five Star Christian Fiction Ser.). (Illus.). 152p. (Orig.). 24.95 (*0-7862-4429-1*, Five Star) Gale Group.
—A Winding Path. 1996. (Miriam's Journal Ser.: Vol. 2). 160p. (Orig.). pap. 8.99 (*0-8361-3656-X*) Herald Pr.
—A Winding Path. 1994. (Orig.). E-Book 7.99 (*0-585-28211-0*) netLibrary, Inc.
—Woodland Dell's Secret. 2002. (Whispering Brook Ser.: Bk. 5). (Illus.). 176p. pap. 8.99 (*0-8361-9169-2*) Herald Pr.
Block, Brett Ellen. The Grave of God's Daughter. 2004. 304p. 23.95 (*0-06-052504-5*, Morrow, William & Co.) Morrow/Avon.
Bradberry, James. Eakins' Mistress: A Jamie Ramsgill Mystery. 1997. 169p. text 19.95 o.p. (*0-312-15518-2*, Saint Martin's Minotaur) St. Martin's Pr.
Bradley, David. The Chaneysville Incident. 1981. 480p. 14.95 o.p. (*0-06-010491-0*) HarperTrade.
—South Street. 1988. 16.25 o.p. (*0-8446-6323-9*) Smith, Peter Pub., Inc.
Brown, Rita Mae. Bingo. 1989. 384p. mass mkt. 6.50 o.s.i (*0-553-28220-4*); 1999. 288p. reprint ed. pap. 19.00 (*0-553-38040-0*) Bantam Bks.
—Six of One. 1983. mass mkt. 3.95 o.s.i (*0-553-23768-3*); 1983. mass mkt. 4.50 o.s.i (*0-553-26974-7*); 1979. 352p. mass mkt. 6.99 o.s.i (*0-553-27887-8*, Bantam Classics); 1999. 288p. reprint ed. pap. 12.95 (*0-553-38037-0*) Bantam Bks.
—Six of One. 1978. 9.95 o.p. (*0-06-010524-0*) HarperTrade.
Burkholder, Mabel. The Herrs: And Lancaster County's Other First Mennonite Pioneers. 2003. pap. 9.00 (*1-930353-69-3*) Masthof Pr.
Callaghan, Mary R. I Met a Man Who Was Not There. 1997. 280p. 24.95 o.p. (*0-7145-3019-0*) Boyars, Marion Pubs., Inc.
Cambor, Kathleen. In Sunlight, in a Beautiful Garden. 2001. 256p. 23.00 (*0-374-16537-8*); 2000. pap. o.p. (*0-374-94124-6*) Farrar, Straus & Giroux.
—In Sunlight, in a Beautiful Garden. l.t. ed. 2001. (Wheeler Large Print Book Ser.). 425p. 29.95 (*1-58724-070-X*, Wheeler Publishing, Inc.) Gale Group.
Campbell, Bebe Moore. Singing in the Comeback Choir. 1999. 400p. reprint ed. mass mkt. 7.99 (*0-425-16662-7*) Berkley Publishing Group.
—Singing in the Comeback Choir. l.t. ed. 1998. (Large Print Book Ser.). 27.95 (*1-56895-613-4*, Wheeler Publishing, Inc.) Gale Group.
—Singing in the Comeback Choir. 1998. 320p. 24.95 o.p. (*0-399-14298-3*, G. P. Putnam's Sons) Penguin Group (USA) Inc.
—Singing in the Comeback Choir. 1999. 13.55 (*0-606-19302-2*) Turtleback Bks.
Cary, Lorene. The Price of a Child. 1996. 336p. pap. 14.00 (*0-679-74467-3*) Random Hse., Inc.
Cassel, Virginia. The Juniata Valley. 1981. 336p. 14.95 o.p. (*0-670-41085-3*) Viking Penguin.
Cercone, Karen R. Blood Tracks. 1998. (American Historical Mysteries Ser.). 256p. mass mkt. 5.99 o.s.i (*0-425-16241-9*, Prime Crime) Berkley Publishing Group.
—Coal Bones. 1999. 288p. mass mkt. 5.99 o.s.i (*0-425-16698-8*, Prime Crime) Berkley Publishing Group.
—Steel Ashes. 1997. 272p. mass mkt. 5.99 o.s.i (*0-425-15856-X*, Prime Crime) Berkley Publishing Group.
Chabon, Michael. The Mysteries of Pittsburgh. 1988. 256p. 16.95 o.p. (*0-688-07632-7*, Morrow, William & Co.) Morrow/Avon.
Chamberlain, Diane. Reflection. 1996. 384p. 24.00 o.p. (*0-06-017652-0*) HarperCollins Pubs.
—Reflection. 1997. 416p. mass mkt. 5.99 o.s.i (*0-06-109396-3*, HarperTorch) Morrow/Avon.
Chase-Riboud, Barbara. The President's Daughter. 1995. 480p. pap. 12.00 o.s.i (*0-345-38970-0*) Ballantine Bks.
Chiaverini, Jennifer. The Cross-Country Quilters: An Elm Creek Quilts Novel. 2002. 368p. pap. 13.00 (*0-452-28308-6*, Plume) Dutton/Plume.
—The Cross-Country Quilters: An Elm Creek Quilts Novel. l.t. ed. 2001. 495p. 29.95 (*0-7838-9559-3*, Macmillan Reference USA) Gale Group.
—The Cross-Country Quilters: An Elm Creek Quilts Novel. 2001. 368p. 21.00 (*0-7432-0257-0*, Simon & Schuster) Simon & Schuster.
—The Quilter's Apprentice. l.t. ed. 2003. 426p. 28.95 (*0-7862-5740-7*) Thorndike Pr.
—The Quilter's Apprentice: A Novel. 2000. 272p. pap. 13.00 (*0-452-28172-5*, Plume) Dutton/Plume.
—The Quilter's Apprentice: A Novel. 1999. 272p. 18.00 (*0-684-84972-0*, Simon & Schuster) Simon & Schuster.
—Quilter's Legacy. 2004. 320p. pap. 13.00 (*0-452-28467-8*, Plume) Dutton/Plume.
—Round Robin: An Elm Creek Quilts Novel. 2001. 304p. pap. 13.00 (*0-452-28227-6*, Plume) Dutton/Plume.

—Round Robin: An Elm Creek Quilts Novel. l.t. ed. 2000. (Large Print Bks.). 420p. pap. 24.95 (*1-56895-952-4*, Wheeler Publishing, Inc.) Gale Group.

—Round Robin: An Elm Creek Quilts Novel. 2000. 336p. 20.00 (*0-684-86892-X*, Simon & Schuster) Simon & Schuster.

—The Runaway Quilt: An Elm Creek Quilts Novel. 2003. 336p. reprint ed. pap. 13.00 (*0-452-28398-1*, Plume) Dutton/Plume.

—The Runaway Quilt: An Elm Creek Quilts Novel. 2002. (Illus.). 336p. 21.00 (*0-7432-2226-1*, Simon & Schuster) Simon & Schuster.

—The Runaway Quilt: An Elm Creek Quilts Novel. l.t. ed. 2002. (Core Ser.). 29.95 (*0-7862-4472-0*) Thorndike Pr.

Clark, Beverly. Yesterday Is Gone. 1997. 293p. mass mkt. 10.95 (*1-885478-12-7*, Indigo) Genesis Pr., Inc.

Constable, George. Where You Are. 1996. 336p. 21.95 o.s.i (*0-385-48438-0*) Doubleday Publishing.

Constantine, K. C. Always a Body to Trade. unabr. ed. 1997. (Mario Balzic Ser.). audio 48.00 (*0-7366-3685-4*, 4364) Books on Tape, Inc.

—Always a Body to Trade. 2001. 256p. pap. 10.95 (*1-56792-191-4*) Godine, David R. Pub.

—Always a Body to Trade: A Mario Balzic Mystery. 1983. 256p. 13.95 o.p. (*0-87923-458-X*); 1993. 248p. reprint ed. pap. 5.95 (*0-87923-952-2*) Godine, David R. Pub.

—Always a Body to Trade: A Mario Balzic Mystery. 1984. (Crime Monthly Ser.). 256p. pap. 3.95 o.p. (*0-14-007059-1*, Penguin Bks.) Viking Penguin.

—Blank Page. 11th ed. 1989. pap. 3.95 o.p. (*0-87923-707-4*) Godine, David R. Pub.

—Blood Mud. 1999. 384p. 23.00 o.s.i (*0-89296-647-5*) Mysterious Pr.

—Blood Mud. l.t. ed. 1999. (Mystery Ser.). 615p. 28.95 (*0-7862-2031-7*) Thorndike Pr.

—Blood Mud. 2000. 384p. pap. 13.95 (*0-446-67640-3*) Warner Bks., Inc.

—Bottom Liner Blues. unabr. ed. 1997. (Mario Balzic Ser.). audio 56.00 (*0-7366-3691-9*, 4370) Books on Tape, Inc.

—Bottom Liner Blues. 1993. 256p. 18.95 (*0-89296-289-5*) Mysterious Pr.

—Bottom Liner Blues. 1994. 272p. mass mkt. 5.99 o.s.i (*0-446-40372-5*) Warner Bks., Inc.

—Brushback. unabr. collector's ed. 1998. (Mario Balzic Ser.). audio 64.00 (*0-7366-4216-1*, 4714) Books on Tape, Inc.

—Brushback. 1998. (Mario Balzic Novel Ser.). 288p. 22.00 (*0-89296-646-7*) Mysterious Pr.

—Brushback. 1999. mass mkt. (*0-446-60675-8*) Warner Bks., Inc.

—Cranks & Shadows. unabr. ed. 1997. (Mario Balzic Ser.). audio 72.00 (*0-7366-3692-7*, 4371) Books on Tape, Inc.

—Cranks & Shadows. 1995. 314p. 19.95 o.p. (*0-89296-543-6*) Mysterious Pr.

—Cranks & Shadows. 1996. 320p. mass mkt. 5.99 o.s.i (*0-446-40353-9*) Warner Bks., Inc.

—Family Values. unabr. ed. 1998. (Mario Balzic Ser.: Vol. 13). audio 48.00 (*0-7366-4035-5*, 4534) Books on Tape, Inc.

—Family Values. l.t. ed. 1997. (G. K. Hall Mystery Ser.). 290p. lib. bdg. 26.95 o.p. (*0-7838-8232-7*, Macmillan Reference USA) Gale Group.

—Family Values. 1998. mass mkt. (*0-446-40355-5*, Mysterious Pr. Paperback Bks.); 1997. 224p. 22.00 o.p. (*0-89296-545-2*); 1998. 256p. mass mkt. 5.99 (*0-446-60594-8*) Warner Bks., Inc.

—A Fix Like This. unabr. ed. 1997. (Mario Balzic Ser.). audio 64.00 (*0-7366-3693-5*, 4372) Books on Tape, Inc.

—A Fix Like This. 1988. 3.95 o.p. (*0-87923-718-X*) Godine, David R. Pub.

—Good Sons. unabr. ed. 1998. (Mario Balzic Ser.). audio 56.00 (*0-7366-4015-0*, 4513) Books on Tape, Inc.

—Good Sons. 1996. 304p. 21.95 o.p. (*0-89296-544-4*) Mysterious Pr.

—Good Sons. 1997. (Rocksburg Novels Ser.). 304p. mass mkt. 5.99 o.s.i (*0-446-40354-7*) Warner Bks., Inc.

—Grievance. l.t. ed. 2001. (Large Print Bks.). 399p. pap. 23.95 o.p. (*1-56895-946-X*, Wheeler Publishing, Inc.) Gale Group.

—Grievance: A Rugs Carlucci Novel. 2000. 288p. 23.95 o.p. (*0-89296-648-3*) Mysterious Pr.

—Joey's Case. unabr. ed. 1997. (Mario Balzic Ser.). audio 56.00 (*0-7366-3783-4*, 4455) Books on Tape, Inc.

—Joey's Case. 1989. 224p. mass mkt. 4.50 (*0-445-40786-7*, Mysterious Pr. Paperback Bks.) Warner Bks., Inc.

—Joey's Case: A Mario Balzic Novel. 1988. 15.95 (*0-89296-347-6*) Mysterious Pr.

—The Man Who Liked Slow Tomatoes. 2001. 192p. pap. 10.95 (*1-56792-192-2*); 1993. (Mario Balzic Detective Novel Ser.). 192p. pap. 5.95 (*0-87923-953-0*); 1982. (Mario Balzic Mystery Ser.: No. 5). 256p. 13.95 o.p. (*0-87923-407-5*) Godine, David R. Pub.

—The Man Who Liked Slow Tomatoes. 1983. 224p. pap. 2.95 o.p. (*0-14-006621-7*, Penguin Bks.) Viking Penguin.

—The Man Who Liked to Look at Himself. l.t. ed. 1987. (Nightingale Ser.). 249p. 11.95 o.p. (*0-8161-4373-0*, Macmillan Reference USA) Gale Group.

—The Man Who Liked to Look at Himself. Barzun, Jacques & Taylor, W. H., eds. 1983. (Crime Fiction 1950-1975 Ser.). 151p. lib. bdg. 18.00 o.p. (*0-8240-4955-1*) Garland Publishing, Inc.

—The Man Who Liked to Look at Himself. 1987. (Double Detective Ser.: No. 3). 160p. pap. 8.95 o.p. (*0-87923-468-7*); pap. 3.95 o.p. (*0-87923-663-9*) Godine, David R. Pub.

—Man Who Liked to Look at Himself & The Blank Page. unabr. ed. 1997. (Mario Balzic Ser.: Vol. 2 & 3). audio 64.00 (*0-7366-3612-9*, 4271) Books on Tape, Inc.

—The Rocksburg Railroad Murders. unabr. ed. 1997. (Mario Balzic Ser.: Vol. 1). audio 40.00 (*0-7366-3622-6*, 4281) Books on Tape, Inc.

—Saving Room for Dessert. 2002. 304p. 23.95 (*0-89296-763-3*) Mysterious Pr.

—Sunshine Enemies. unabr. ed. 1997. (Mario Balzic Ser.). audio 42.00 (*0-7366-3784-2*, 4456) Books on Tape, Inc.

—Sunshine Enemies. 1990. 176p. 18.95 o.p. (*0-89296-288-7*) Mysterious Pr.

—Sunshine Enemies. 1991. mass mkt. 4.95 o.s.i (*0-446-40008-4*, Mysterious Pr. Paperback Bks.) Warner Bks., Inc.

—Upon Some Midnights Clear. unabr. ed. 1997. (Mario Balzic Ser.). audio 48.00 (*0-7366-3694-3*, 4373) Books on Tape, Inc.

—Upon Some Midnights Clear. 1985. (Mario Balzic Mystery Ser.). 256p. 15.95 o.p. (*0-87923-570-5*) Godine, David R. Pub.

—Upon Some Midnights Clear. 1987. 24p. mass mkt. 3.50 o.p. (*0-14-009404-0*, Penguin Bks.) Viking Penguin.

Coover, Robert. The Origin of the Brunists. 2000. 512p. reprint ed. pap. 12.00 (*0-8021-3743-1*, Grove Pr.) Grove/Atlantic, Inc.

—The Origin of the Brunists. 1989. pap. 10.95 o.p. (*0-393-30600-3*) Norton, W. W. & Co., Inc.

—The Origin of the Brunists. 1978. (Richard Seaver Bks.). 12.50 o.p. (*0-670-52863-3*) Viking Penguin.

Cozzens, James Gould. By Love Possessed. 1998. 570p. pap. 13.95 (*0-7867-0503-5*, Carroll & Graf Pubs.) Avalon Publishing Group.

—By Love Possessed. 1977. mass mkt. 2.25 o.s.i (*0-449-22954-8*, Fawcett) Ballantine Bks.

—By Love Possessed. 1994. reprint ed. lib. bdg. 21.95 (*1-56849-549-8*) Buccaneer Bks., Inc.

—By Love Possessed. 1957. 8.50 o.s.i (*0-15-115113-X*); 1901. pap. 2.95 o.p. (*0-15-614870-6*, Harvest Bks.) Harcourt Trade Pubs.

Dark, Alice Elliott. In the Gloaming: Stories. 288p. 2001. pap. 13.00 (*0-684-87005-3*); 2000. (Illus.). 23.00 o.s.i (*0-684-86521-1*) Simon & Schuster. (Simon & Schuster).

De Angeli, Marguerite. Yonie Wondernose. 1997. (Illus.). 48p. (J). (gr. 2-6). pap. 14.99 (*0-8361-9083-1*) Herald Pr.

Deland, Margaret W. Old Chester Days. 1977. (Short Story Index Reprint Ser.). 25.95 (*0-8369-3386-9*) Ayer Co. Pubs., Inc.

—Old Chester Tales. E-Book 3.95 (*0-594-00587-6*) 1873 Pr.

—Old Chester Tales. (BCL Ser. I). reprint ed. 32.50 (*0-404-02075-5*) AMS Pr., Inc.

—Old Chester Tales. reprint ed. 1986. (C). pap. text 7.95 (*0-8290-1940-5*); 1972. lib. bdg. 20.00 (*0-8422-8037-5*) Irvington Pubs.

Demarest, David, Jr., ed. From These Hills, from These Valleys: Selected Fiction about Western Pennsylvania. 1976. 256p. text 19.95 o.p. (*0-8229-1123-X*) Univ. of Pittsburgh Pr.

DiBartolomeo, Albert. Fool's Gold. 1993. vii, 279p. 18.95 o.p. (*0-312-09058-7*, Saint Martin's Minotaur) St. Martin's Pr.

Dimmick, Barbara. In the Presence of Horses: A Novel. l.t. ed. 2000. (Wheeler Large Print Bks.). 398p. pap. 23.95 (*1-56895-860-9*, Wheeler Publishing, Inc.) Gale Group.

—In the Presence of Horses: A Novel. 1999. 352p. pap. 14.00 (*0-312-24567-X*); 1958. pap. o.s.i (*0-312-24527-0*) Picador.

Drayer, David. Strip Cuts. 2000. 292p. pap. 13.95 (*0-9675215-6-4*) Rowdy Hse. Publishing.

Dunphy, Jack. The Murderous McLaughlins. 1988. 256p. text 16.95 o.p. (*0-07-018316-3*) McGraw-Hill Cos., The.

Dye, Kitty. Maconaquah's Story: The Saga of Frances Slocum. 1996. (Illus.). 110p. pap. 8.95 (*0-9642058-2-3*) InChem Publishing Div.

—Maconaquah's Story: The Saga of Frances Slocum. 2nd rev. ed. 2000. (Illus.). 172p. pap. 17.95 (*0-9702501-0-X*) LeClere Publishing Co.

Elm, Joanna. Delusion. 1999. 374p. mass mkt. 6.99 (*0-8125-6480-4*, Tor Bks.); 1997. 384p. 23.95 (*0-312-86064-1*, Forge Bks.) Doherty, Tom Assocs., LLC.

Fauset, Jessie Redmon. There Is Confusion. reprint ed. 23.50 (*0-404-11386-9*) AMS Pr., Inc.

—There Is Confusion. 1989. (Library of Black Literature). 304p. reprint ed. pap. text 17.95 (*1-55553-066-4*) Northeastern Univ. Pr.

Fenton, Edward. Duffy's Rocks. 1988. (J). (gr. k-12). mass mkt. 3.25 o.s.i (*0-440-20242-6*, Laurel Leaf) Random Hse. Children's Bks.

Flory, Jane. It Was a Pretty Good Year, 001. 1977. (Illus.). (J). (gr. 3-7). 6.95 o.p. (*0-395-25835-9*) Houghton Mifflin Co.

Foglia, Leonard. 1 Ragged Ridge Road. 1998. per. 6.50 (*0-671-00355-0*, Pocket) Simon & Schuster.

Foglia, Leonard & Richards, David. 1 Ragged Ridge Road. 1997. 352p. 22.00 (*0-671-00354-2*, Atria) Simon & Schuster.

Freeble, Charles R. Toscape Death: A Novelized Version of the Life of Herman Husband, a Forgotten Early American Original, Vol. 1. 1996. 69p. per. 7.95 (*1-55856-224-9*, 275) Closson Pr.

French, Albert L. I Can't Wait on God: A Novel. 1999. 256p. pap. 19.00 o.s.i (*0-385-48367-8*) Doubleday Publishing.

Fritz, Jean. The Cabin Faced West. 1987. (Classics for Young Readers Ser.). (Illus.). 128p. (J). (gr. 3-7). pap. 5.99 o.s.i (*0-14-032256-6*, Puffin Bks.) Penguin Putnam Bks. for Young Readers.

Gaffney, Patricia. Sweet Everlasting. 384p. 2001. mass mkt. 6.99 (*0-451-20290-2*); 1993. mass mkt. 4.99 o.s.i (*0-451-40375-4*, Topaz) NAL.

—Sweet Everlasting. l.t. ed. 2001. (Americana Ser.). 608p. 30.95 (*0-7862-3319-2*); 581p. (*0-7862-3318-4*) Thorndike Pr.

Gallagher, Stephen. Red, Red Robin. 1996. mass mkt. 5.99 o.s.i (*0-345-40649-4*) Ballantine Bks.

—Red, Red Robin. l.t. ed. 1996. (Charnwood Large Print Ser.). 544p. 29.99 o.p. (*0-7089-8880-6*, Ulverscroft) Thorpe, F. A. Pubs. GBR. *Dist:* Ulverscroft Large Print Bks., Ltd., Ulverscroft Large Print Canada, Ltd.

Gardner, John. Mickelsson's Ghosts. 1985. pap. 6.95 o.s.i (*0-394-72938-2*) Random Hse., Inc.

—Mickelsson's Ghosts. 1989. pap. 9.95 o.s.i (*0-679-72308-0*, Vintage) Knopf Publishing Group.

Gautreaux, Tim. The Clearing. 2003. 320p. 23.00 (*0-375-41474-6*) Knopf, Alfred A. Inc.

Gibbon, Maureen. Swimming Sweet Arrow: A Novel. 2000. 352p. (YA). (gr. 8). 21.95 o.p. (*0-316-30599-5*) Little Brown & Co.

Gilman, Julia M. William Wells & Maconaquah, White Rose of the Miamis. 1985. 317p. (Orig.). pap. 16.95 (*0-9614890-2-2*) Jewel Publishing Co.

Gilroy, Jack. Absolute Flanigan. 2002. 320p. pap. 14.00 (*1-58684-233-1*) Global Academic Publishing.

Gleiter, Jan. A House by the Side of the Road. (Dead Letter Mysteries Ser.: Vol. 1). 1999. 272p. mass mkt. 5.99 (*0-312-96693-8*, St. Martin's Paperbacks); Vol. 1. 1998. 288p. 22.95 (*0-312-18596-0*, Saint Martin's Minotaur) St. Martin's Pr.

Glodek, Geraldine. Nine Bells at the Breaker: An Immigrant's Story. 1998. viii, 248p. 24.00 (*0-9665943-0-4*); pap. 15.00 (*0-9665943-1-2*) Barn Peg Pr., The.

Goldberg, Marshall. A Deadly Operation: A Novel of Medical Espionage. 1996. 240p. pap. 14.95 (*0-8023-1310-8*) Dufour Editions, Inc.

—The Family Scalpel. 1995. 384p. 25.00 (*0-8023-1307-8*); pap. 13.95 (*0-8023-1308-6*) Dufour Editions, Inc.

—Intelligence. 1996. 240p. pap. 14.95 (*0-8023-1311-6*) Dufour Editions, Inc.

Goran, Lester. Outlaws of the Purple Cow & Other Stories. 1999. 358p. pap. 35.00 (*0-87338-639-6*) Kent State Univ. Pr.

—She Loved Me Once: And Other Stories. 1997. 306p. (gr. 11-12). 26.00 (*0-87338-576-4*) Kent State Univ. Pr.

—Tales from the Irish Club: A Collection of Short Stories. 1996. 144p. (Orig.). (gr. 9-12). pap. 12.00 (*0-87338-539-X*) Kent State Univ. Pr.

Graham, Mark. The Black Maria. 2000. (Mysteries of Old Philadelphia Ser.). 384p. mass mkt. 6.50 (*0-380-80068-3*, Avon Bks.) Morrow/Avon.

—The Killing Breed. 1998. (Mysteries of Old Philadelphia Ser.). 272p. mass mkt. 5.99 (*0-380-80066-7*, Avon Bks.) Morrow/Avon.

—The Resurrectionist. 1999. (Mysteries of Old Philadelphia Ser.). 320p. mass mkt. 5.99 (*0-380-80067-5*, Avon Bks.) Morrow/Avon.

Griffin, Adele. Witch Twins. 2001. (Illus.). 160p. (J). (gr. 2-5). 14.99 (*0-7868-0739-3*, Volo) Hyperion Bks. for Children.

Griffin, W. E. B. The Assassin: A Badge of Honor Novel. 5th ed. 1993. (Badge of Honor Ser.). 464p. mass mkt. 7.99 (*0-515-11113-9*, Jove) Berkley Publishing Group.

—The Assassin: A Badge of Honor Novel. unabr. collector's ed. 1994. audio 96.00 (*0-7366-2851-7*, 133263) Books on Tape, Inc.

—Badge of Honor Boxed Set. (Badge of Honor Ser.). 1993. 23.96 o.s.i (*0-515-11301-8*); 1992. 19.84 o.s.i (*0-515-11030-2*); 1991. 14.85 o.s.i (*0-515-10777-8*) Berkley Publishing Group. (Jove).

—Badge of Honor Boxed Set: Men in Blue, Special Operations, the Victim. 1996. 12.98 o.s.i (*0-399-14152-9*) Penguin Group (USA) Inc.

—Badge of Honor Boxed Set: The Witness; the Assassin; the Murderers. 1997. 816p. 12.98 o.s.i (*0-399-14238-X*) Penguin Group (USA) Inc.

—The Corps: Semper Fi, Call to Arms, Counterattack. 1994. 816p. 11.98 o.p. (*0-399-13913-3*, G. P. Putnam's Sons) Penguin Group (USA) Inc.

—In the Line of Duty. 352p. 17.99 (*0-7278-5450-X*) Severn Hse. Pubs., Ltd.

—The Investigators: A Badge of Honor Novel. 1998. 592p. reprint ed. mass mkt. 7.99 (*0-515-12406-0*, Jove) Berkley Publishing Group.

—The Investigators: A Badge of Honor Novel. unabr. ed. 1998. audio 104.00 (*0-7366-4084-3*, 4593) Books on Tape, Inc.

—The Investigators: A Badge of Honor Novel. l.t. ed. 1999. 735p. pap. 20.00 o.p. (*0-7838-0140-8*, Macmillan Reference USA) Gale Group.

—The Investigators: A Badge of Honor Novel. 1998. 448p. 24.95 o.p. (*0-399-14308-4*); 24.95 (*0-399-14349-1*, 695430) Penguin Group (USA) Inc.

—The Investigators: A Badge of Honor Novel. 416p. (*0-7278-5476-3*) Severn Hse. Pubs., Ltd.

—The Investigators: A Badge of Honor Novel. l.t. ed. 1998. 735p. 30.94 (*0-7838-0139-4*) Thorndike Pr.

—Men in Blue: A Badge of Honor Novel. 1988. (Badge of Honor Ser.). 352p. mass mkt. 7.99 (*0-515-09750-0*, Jove) Berkley Publishing Group.

—Men in Blue: A Badge of Honor Novel. unabr. collector's ed. 1993. audio 64.00 (*0-7366-2482-1*, 3244) Books on Tape, Inc.

—The Murderers: A Badge of Honor Novel. 1995. (Badge of Honor Ser.). 544p. mass mkt. 7.99 (*0-515-11742-0*, Jove) Berkley Publishing Group.

—The Murderers: A Badge of Honor Novel. unabr. ed. 1995. audio 96.00 (*0-7366-2949-1*, 3643) Books on Tape, Inc.

—The Murderers: A Badge of Honor Novel. unabr. ed. 1995. audio 25.95 (*1-56100-586-X*, 189, Bookcassette); audio 89.25 (*1-56100-211-9*, 957, Unabridged Library Editions) Brilliance Audio.

—The Murderers: A Badge of Honor Novel. l.t. ed. 1995. 24.95 o.p. (*1-56895-209-0*, Wheeler Publishing, Inc.) Gale Group.

—The Murderers: A Badge of Honor Novel. abr. ed. 2000. audio 7.95 (*1-57815-001-9*, 1017, Media Bks. Audio Publishing) Media Bks., L. L. C.

—The Murderers: A Badge of Honor Novel. 1995. 384p. 23.95 o.p. (*0-399-13976-1*) Putnam Publishing Group, The.

—The Murderers: A Badge of Honor Novel. 396p. pap. 5.98 o.p. (*0-7651-0428-8*) Smithmark Pubs., Inc.

—Special Operations: A Badge of Honor Novel. 1989. (Badge of Honor Ser.). (Illus.). 368p. mass mkt. 7.99 (*0-515-10148-6*, Jove) Berkley Publishing Group.

—Special Operations: A Badge of Honor Novel. unabr. collector's ed. 1993. audio 64.00 (*0-7366-2492-9*, 3251) Books on Tape, Inc.

—The Victim: A Badge of Honor Novel. 1991. (Badge of Honor Ser.). 352p. mass mkt. 7.99 (*0-515-10397-7*, Jove) Berkley Publishing Group.

—The Victim: A Badge of Honor Novel. unabr. collector's ed. 1993. audio 72.00 (*0-7366-2498-8*, 3256) Books on Tape, Inc.

—The Witness: A Badge of Honor Novel. 1992. (Badge of Honor Ser.). 432p. mass mkt. 7.99 (*0-515-10747-6*, Jove) Berkley Publishing Group.

—The Witness: A Badge of Honor Novel. unabr. collector's ed. 1993. audio 88.00 (*0-7366-2553-4*, 3304) Books on Tape, Inc.

Guy, David. Second Brother. 1986. pap. 6.95 o.p. (*0-452-25887-1*, Plume) Dutton/Plume.

—Second Brother. 1985. 264p. 14.95 o.p. (*0-453-00497-0*) NAL.

Haddam, Jane. True Believers: A Gregor Demarkian Mystery. 2001. (Gregor Demarkian Mystery Ser.). 328p. 24.95 (*0-312-20929-0*, Saint Martin's Minotaur) St. Martin's Pr.

Harper, Philip. Final Fear. 2001. 219p. reprint ed. pap. 12.95 (*1-931755-03-5*) Mystery Vault, Inc.

—Final Fear. 1993. 224p. 20.00 o.p. (*0-671-74532-8*, Simon & Schuster) Simon & Schuster.

Harris, Lisa. Boxes. 2000. (Bright Hill Press Chapbook Award Ser.). 32p. pap. 6.00 (*1-892471-03-5*) Bright Hill Pr.

Harrison, Colin. Break & Enter. 1991. 400p. reprint ed. pap. 4.95 (*0-380-71526-0*, Avon Bks.) Morrow/Avon.

—Break & Enter. unabr. ed. 1990. audio 85.00 (*1-55690-071-6*, 90092E7) Recorded Bks., LLC.

Hendershot, Eric. Jimmy Stillman, I Will Always Love You. 1994. o.p. (*0-88494-949-4*, Bookcraft, Inc.) Deseret Bk. Co.

Highsmith, Patricia. Cry of the Owl. 1989. 276p. pap. 12.00 (*0-87113-290-7*, Atlantic Monthly Pr.) Grove/Atlantic, Inc.

Hill, Grace Livingston. The Red Signal. reprint ed. lib. bdg. 23.95 (*0-89190-047-0*, Rivercity Pr.) Amereon, Ltd.

—The Red Signal, No. 51. 1978. pap. 1.75 o.p. (*0-553-13939-8*, X13939-8) Bantam Bks.

—The Red Signal. 1999. 295 p. (*0-7540-3616-2*, Macmillan Reference USA) Gale Group.

—The Red Signal. l.t. ed. 1999. 296p. pap. 23.95 (*0-7838-0420-2*) Thorndike Pr.

—The Red Signal. 1993. (Grace Livingston Hill Ser.: Vol. 51). pap. 4.99 o.p. (*0-8423-5402-6*) Tyndale Hse. Pubs.

Hill, Grace Livingston, contrib. by. The Red Signal. (*0-7540-3615-4*) BBC Audiobooks America.

Hogan, James Patrick. Realtime Interrupt. 1995. 336p. pap. 12.95 o.s.i (*0-553-37454-0*) Bantam Bks.

Hohl, Joan. Ever After. l.t. ed. 2000. (Americana Ser.). 371p. 26.95 (*0-7862-2410-X*) Thorndike Pr.

Holt, Hazel. Mrs. Malory: Detective in Residence. 1994. (Mrs. Malory Mystery Ser.). 192p. 18.95 o.p. (*0-525-93903-2*) Dutton/Plume.

—Mrs. Malory: Detective in Residence. 1995. (Sheila Malory Mysteries Ser.). 256p. mass mkt. 4.99 o.s.i (*0-451-18017-8*, Signet Bks.) NAL.

Horgan, Paul. Everything to Live For. 1968. 224p. 8.95 o.p. (*0-374-15040-0*) Farrar, Straus & Giroux.

Hunt, Marsha. Free. 288p. 1994. pap. 9.95 o.p. (*0-452-27061-8*, Plume); 1993. 20.00 o.p. (*0-525-93575-4*) Dutton/Plume.

Jefferson, Blanche. So Strong This Bond. 1995. pap. 11.95 (*0-935016-35-X*) Zinn Publishing Group.

Joyce, William. First Born of an Ass. 1989. 300p. pap. 10.50 (*0-922820-04-X*) Watermark Pr., Inc.

Kauffman, Janet. Collaborators. 1993. 144p. reprint ed. pap. 11.00 o.p. (*1-55597-185-7*) Graywolf Pr.

—Collaborators. 1987. 136p. pap. 5.95 o.p. (*0-14-009342-7*, Penguin Bks.) Viking Penguin.

Kernek, Clyde. Field Surgeon at Gettysburg. 1993. 120p. 20.95 (*1-878208-32-2*); pap. 14.95 (*1-57860-014-6*) Emmis Bks.

King, Stephen. From a Buick 8: A Novel. 2002. 368p. 28.00 (*0-7432-1137-5*, Scribner) Simon & Schuster.

Kope, Spencer. When the Drummer Falls. 1995. 191p. pap. 17.95 (*0-9647183-0-8*) Lion's Gate Publishing.

Kubicki, Jan. Breaker Boys. Brady, Upton B., ed. 1987. 390p. 17.95 o.p. (*0-87113-112-9*) Grove/Atlantic, Inc.

Lacy, Al. Season of Valor: Gettysburg, 8 vols., Vol. 6. 2003. (Battles of Destiny Ser.: No. 6). 294p. pap. 9.99 (*0-88070-865-4*, Multnomah Bks.) Multnomah Pubs., Inc.

LaPlante, Richard. Mantis. 1993. 352p. 19.95 o.p. (*0-312-85531-1*, Tor Bks.) Doherty, Tom Assocs., LLC.

Lashner, William. Hostile Witness. l.t. ed. 1995. (Large Print Bks.). 25.95 o.p. (*1-56895-248-1*, Wheeler Publishing, Inc.) Gale Group.

—Hostile Witness. 1995. 501p. 23.00 o.p. (*0-06-039146-4*) HarperCollins Pubs.

—Hostile Witness. 1996. 608p. mass mkt. 7.50 (*0-06-100988-1*, ReganBooks); 1995. audio 17.00 o.p. (*0-694-51559-0*, HarperAudio) HarperTrade.

—Hostile Witness. unabr. ed. 1998. audio 112.00 (*0-7887-1954-8*, 95352E7) Recorded Bks., LLC.

—Veritas. 1997. 464p. 25.00 o.p. (*0-06-039147-2*, ReganBooks);Set. audio 18.00 (*0-694-51789-5*, 392878, HarperAudio) HarperTrade.

—Veritas. 1997. 592p. mass mkt. 6.50 o.s.i (*0-06-101023-5*, HarperTorch) Morrow/Avon.

—Veritas, unabr. ed. 1997. audio 112.00 (*0-7887-1768-5*, 95246E5) Recorded Bks., LLC.

Leavitt, Caroline. Living Other Lives. 1995. 336p. 21.95 o.p. (*0-446-51705-4*) Warner Bks., Inc.

Leebron, Fred G. In the Middle of All This. 264p. 2004. pap. 13.00 (*0-15-602742-9*, Harvest Bks.); 2002. 24.00 (*0-15-100834-5*) Harcourt Trade Pubs.

Leonard, Ann Georgi. Hoops of Steel: A Civil War Novel. 2001. (Illus.). 352p. 22.00 (*0-9708053-0-6*) Authors & Artists Publishers of New York.

Lewis, Beverly. The Betrayal. 2003. (Abram's Daughters Ser.). 320p. 17.99 (*0-7642-2807-2*); 432p. pap. 16.99 (*0-7642-2806-4*); 320p. pap. 12.99 (*0-7642-2331-3*); audio 16.99 (*0-7642-2808-0*) Bethany Hse. Pubs.

—The Confession. (Heritage of Lancaster County Ser.). 288p. 2000. pap. 6.99 (*0-7642-2474-3*); 1997. (J). pap. 12.99 (*1-55661-867-0*) Bethany Hse. Pubs.

—The Confession. l.t. ed. 1998. (Christian Fiction Ser.). 400p. 25.95 (*0-7862-1522-4*) Thorndike Pr.

—The Covenant. 2002. (Abram's Daughters Ser.: No. 1). 320p. 16.99 (*0-7642-2717-3*); 320p. pap. 12.99 (*0-7642-2330-5*); pap. 16.99 (*0-7642-2719-X*); 400p. pap. 16.99 (*0-7642-2718-1*) Bethany Hse. Pubs.

—The Crossroad. 1999. 320p. pap. 12.99 (*0-7642-2212-0*); 320p. text 15.99 o.p. (*0-7642-2239-2*); 1p. audio 15.99 o.p. (*0-7642-2238-4*); 352p. pap. 16.99 o.p. (*0-7642-2240-6*) Bethany Hse. Pubs.

—The Crossroad. l.t. ed. 2000. 369p. 25.95 (*0-7862-2712-5*) Thorndike Pr.

—October Song: Lancaster County is Cloaked in Autumn Splendor, & a Reunion is in the Air... 2001. (Heritage of Lancaster County Ser.). 256p. pap. 12.99 (*0-7642-2332-1*); 258p. text 16.99 o.p. (*0-7642-2588-X*); pap. 15.99 (*0-7642-2589-8*); 320p. pap. 16.99 (*0-7642-2590-1*) Bethany Hse. Pubs.

—October Song: Lancaster County is Cloaked in Autumn Splendor, & a Reunion is in the Air... l.t. ed. 2002. 317p. 28.95 (*0-7862-4028-8*) Gale Group.

—The Postcard. 1999. 1p. audio 15.99 o.p. (*0-7642-2223-6*); 320p. pap. 12.99 (*0-7642-2211-2*) Bethany Hse. Pubs.

—Postcard. l.t. ed. 1999. 384p. pap. 16.99 o.p. (*0-7642-2225-2*) Bethany Hse. Pubs.

—The Postcard. l.t. ed. 2000. (Christian Romance Ser.). 408p. 25.95 (*0-7862-2713-3*) Thorndike Pr.

—The Reckoning. (Heritage of Lancaster County Ser.). 288p. 2000. pap. 6.99 (*0-7642-2475-1*); 1998. pap. 12.99 (*1-55661-868-9*) Bethany Hse. Pubs.

—The Reckoning. l.t. ed. 1999. (Christian Fiction Ser.). 383p. 25.95 (*0-7862-1691-3*) Thorndike Pr.

—The Redemption of Sarah Cain. 2000. (Heritage of Lancaster County Ser.). 320p. 16.99 (*0-7642-2388-7*); 320p. pap. 12.99 (*0-7642-2329-1*); 1p. pap. 15.99 o.p. (*0-7642-2389-5*); 384p. pap. 15.99 o.p. (*0-7642-2390-9*) Bethany Hse. Pubs.

—The Redemption of Sarah Cain. l.t. ed. 2001. (Thorndike Press Large Print Christian Romance Ser.). 384p. 25.95 (*0-7862-3113-0*) Thorndike Pr.

—The Shunning. 1997. (Heritage of Lancaster County Ser.: Vol. 1). 288p. pap. 12.99 (*1-55661-866-2*) Bethany Hse. Pubs.

—Shunning. 2000. (Heritage of Lancaster County Ser.). 288p. pap. 6.99 (*0-7642-2473-5*) Bethany Hse. Pubs.

—The Shunning. unabr. ed. 1998. audio 51.00 (*0-7887-2192-5*, 95488E7) Recorded Bks., LLC.

—The Sunroom. 1998. 144p. 12.99 (*0-7642-2076-4*) Bethany Hse. Pubs.

Lewis, Beverly & Lewis, David. Sanctuary. 2001. 320p. 16.99 o.p. (*0-7642-2511-1*); 320p. pap. 12.99 (*0-7642-2510-3*); 400p. pap. 16.99 (*0-7642-2513-8*) Bethany Hse. Pubs.

—Sanctuary. l.t. ed. 2001. (Thorndike Press Large Print Christian Fiction Ser.). 399p. 28.95 (*0-7862-3706-6*) Thorndike Pr.

Lewis, John. Godfather of the Brandywine. 1996. (Illus.). 298p. 24.95 (*1-878970-04-6*); pap. 7.95 (*1-878970-05-4*) Dyne-American Pubns., Inc.

Lipinski, Thomas. Death in the Steel City. 2000. (Carroll Dorsey Mystery Ser.: Vol. 4). 224p. mass mkt. 5.99 (*0-380-79432-2*, Avon Bks.) Morrow/Avon.

—The Fall-Down Artist. 1994. (Carroll Dorsey Mystery Ser.). 304p. 20.95 o.p. (*0-312-10461-8*, Saint Martin's Minotaur) St. Martin's Pr.

—Picture of Her Tombstone. 1998. (Carroll Dorsey Mystery Ser.: 2). mass mkt. 5.99 (*0-380-73024-3*, Avon Bks.) Morrow/Avon.

—Picture of Her Tombstone. 1996. 240p. 21.95 (*0-312-14390-7*, Saint Martin's Minotaur) St. Martin's Pr.

—Steel City Confessions. 1999. (Carroll Dorsey Mystery Ser.: Vol. 3). 224p. mass mkt. 5.99 (*0-380-79431-4*, Avon Bks.) Morrow/Avon.

Lippard, George. The Quaker City: or The Monks of Monk Hall: A Romance of Philadelphia Life, Mystery, & Crime. Reynolds, David S., ed. & intro. by. 1995. 632p. pap. 24.95 (*0-87023-971-6*) Univ. of Massachusetts Pr.

Lissfelt, J. Fred. The Dutchman Died & Other Tales of Pittsburgh's Southside. 1992. (Illus.). 152p. (C). (gr. 9-12). pap. 10.95 o.p. (*0-8229-5483-4*); text 29.95 o.p. (*0-8229-3726-3*) Univ. of Pittsburgh Pr.

Lopez, Steve. The Sunday Macaroni Club. 1999. 384p. pap. 12.95 (*0-452-28138-5*, Plume) Dutton/Plume.

—The Sunday Macaroni Club. 1997. 384p. 24.00 (*0-15-100264-9*) Harcourt Trade Pubs.

—The Sunday Macaroni Club. 1998. 368p. mass mkt. 6.99 o.s.i (*0-451-19723-2*, Signet Bks.) NAL.

—The Sunday Macaroni Club, Set. abr. ed. 1997. audio 24.95 (*1-57511-025-3*, 695317) Publishing Mills, Inc., The.

—The Sunday Macaroni Club. 1999. pap. 23.95 (*0-670-86311-4*) Viking Penguin.

—Third & Indiana: A Novel. 1994. 336p. (J). 21.95 o.p. (*0-670-85676-2*, Viking) Viking Penguin.

Lorin, Amii, pseud. Come Home to Love. 2000. 320p. mass mkt. 5.50 (*0-505-52426-0*, Love Spell) Dorchester Publishing Co., Inc.

Lowenthal, Michael. Avoidance: A Novel. 2002. 272p. pap. 16.00 (*1-55597-367-1*) Graywolf Pr.

MacDougal, Bonnie. Angle of Impact. 1998. mass mkt. 6.99 o.s.i (*0-345-41446-2*) Ballantine Bks.

—Angle of Impact. abr. ed. 1999. audio 7.99 o.s.i (*1-56740-290-9*, 1747, Nova Audio Bks.); 1998. audio 17.95 o.p. (*1-56740-773-0*, 458, Nova Audio Bks.); 1998. audio 26.95 (*1-56100-799-4*, 34, Bookcassette); 1998. audio 73.25 (*1-56740-833-8*, 798, Unabridged Library Editions) Brilliance Audio.

—Breach of Trust. 384p. 2002. pap. 21.95 (*0-7434-6514-8*, Pocket); 1998. per. 6.99 o.s.i (*0-671-53719-9*, Pocket); 1996. 23.00 o.p. (*0-671-53720-2*, Atria) Simon & Schuster.

Maiman, Jaye. Under My Skin. 1993. (Robin Miller Mysteries Ser.: No. 3). 336p. pap. 11.95 (*1-56280-049-3*) Naiad Pr., Inc.

Major, Marcus. Good Peoples: A Novel. 2000. 272p. 22.95 o.s.i (*0-525-94535-0*, Dutton) Dutton/Plume.

Malmont, Valerie S. Death, Bones & Stately Homes: A Tori Miracle Pennsylvania Dutch Mystery. 2003. 286p. pap. 13.95 (*1-880284-65-0*) Daniel, John & Co., Pubs.

—Death, Guns & Sticky Buns. 2000. (Tori Miracle Mysteries Ser.). 320p. mass mkt. 6.50 (*0-440-23598-7*) Bantam Dell Publishing Group.

—Death, Lies & Apple Pies. 1998. (Tori Miracle Mysteries Ser.). 288p. mass mkt. 5.99 (*0-440-22634-1*) Dell Publishing.

—Death, Lies & Apple Pies. l.t. ed. 1997. (Core Ser.). 326p. lib. bdg. 25.95 o.p. (*0-7838-8333-1*, Macmillan Reference USA) Gale Group.

—Death, Lies & Apple Pies. 1997. (Illus.). 224p. 22.00 o.s.i (*0-684-80189-2*, Simon & Schuster) Simon & Schuster.

—Death Pays the Rose Rent: A Tori Miracle Mystery. (Tori Miracle Mysteries Ser.). 1999. 304p. mass mkt. 6.50 (*0-440-22633-3*); 1998. 352p. mass mkt. 5.99 o.s.i (*0-440-22628-7*) Dell Publishing.

—Death Pays the Rose Rent: A Tori Miracle Mystery. 1994. 286p. 20.00 (*0-671-86967-1*, Simon & Schuster) Simon & Schuster.

—Death, Snow & Mistletoe. 2000. (Tori Miracle Mysteries Ser.). 320p. mass mkt. 5.99 (*0-440-23601-0*) Dell Publishing.

Manfredi, Renee. Where Love Leaves Us. 1994. (Iowa Short Fiction Award Ser.). 158p. 11.50 (*0-87745-444-2*); E-Book 20.00 (*1-58729-138-X*) Univ. of Iowa Pr.

Marshall, Catherine. Julie. l.t. ed. 1985. (General Ser.). 19.95 o.p. (*0-8161-3813-3*, Macmillan Reference USA) Gale Group.

—Julie. 1984. text 15.95 o.p. (*0-07-040608-1*) McGraw-Hill Cos., The.

—Julie. 1985. 384p. reprint ed. pap. 4.50 o.p. (*0-8007-8585-1*) Revell, Fleming H. Co.

—Julie. 2002. (Illus.). 384p. pap. 12.99 (*0-310-24620-2*) Zondervan.

Martin, Kat. The Duchess of Carbon County. 1997. (Romance Ser.). 264p. lib. bdg. 23.95 (*0-7862-1105-9*, Five Star) Gale Group.

Masters, Hilary. Home Is the Exile. 1996. 288p. 28.00 (*1-877946-73-7*) Permanent Pr., The.

McGrath, Kristina. House Work: A Novel. 1994. 192p. 19.95 (*1-882593-07-3*) Bridge Works Publishing Co., Inc.

McKinney-Whetstone, Diane. Tempest Rising. 1998. 288p. 24.00 (*0-688-14994-4*, Morrow, William & Co.) Morrow/Avon.

—Tempest Rising: A Novel. 1999. (Illus.). 288p. pap. 12.00 (*0-688-16640-7*, Quill) HarperTrade.

Medlicott, Joan. Untitled Ladies of Covington. 320p. No. 1. 2004. mass mkt. 6.99 (*0-7434-7037-0*, Pocket Star); No. 2. 2005. mass mkt. (*0-7434-7041-9*, Pocket); No. 3. 2006. mass mkt. (*0-7434-7045-1*, Pocket); Vol. 2. 2004. 24.00 (*0-7434-7039-7*, Atria); Vol. 3. 2005. 24.00 (*0-7434-7043-5*, Atria) Simon & Schuster.

Menkin, Arthur H. Different Times. 2000. 216p. pap. 21.99 (*0-7388-2235-3*); text 31.99 (*0-7388-2474-7*) Xlibris Corp.

Meyer, Carolyn. Brown Eyes Blue: A Novel. 2003. 352p. 23.95 (*1-882593-68-5*); 2004. 240p. reprint ed. pap. 15.95 (*1-882593-83-9*) Bridge Works Publishing Co., Inc.

Michaels, Fern. Serendipity. 9999. mass mkt. o.p. (*0-345-37328-6*); 1997. 384p. mass mkt. 6.99 (*0-449-14982-X*, Fawcett) Ballantine Bks.

Michaels, Kasey. Can't Take My Eyes Off of You. l.t. ed. 2000. 323p. 25.95 (*1-57490-265-2*, Beeler Large Print Bks.) Beeler, Thomas T. Publisher.

—Can't Take My Eyes off You. 2000. 352p. mass mkt. 6.50 (*0-8217-6522-1*) Kensington Publishing Corp.

Miller, Calvin. Frost. 2002. 160p. 12.99 (*0-7642-2364-X*) Bethany Hse. Pubs.

—Shade. 2001. 160p. 12.99 (*0-7642-2363-1*) Bethany Hse. Pubs.

—Shade. l.t. ed. 2002. (Inspirational Ser.). 168p. 27.95 (*0-7862-4420-8*) Thorndike Pr.

—Wind. 2000. (Illus.). 160p. 12.99 (*0-7642-2362-3*) Bethany Hse. Pubs.

Moore, Ruth N. Mystery of the Lost Heirloom. 1985. (Sara & Sam Mysteries Ser.: Vol. 3). (Illus.). 152p. (J). (gr. 6-9). pap. 6.99 o.p. (*0-8361-3408-7*) Herald Pr.

Moss, Robert. The Interpreter: A Story of Two Worlds. 1997. 346p. 24.95 o.p. (*0-312-85739-X*, Forge Bks.) Doherty, Tom Assocs., LLC.

Murray, Donna Huston. Farewell Performance: A Ginger Barnes Main Line Mystery. 2000. (Ginger Barnes Main Line Mysteries Ser.). 272p. mass mkt. 5.99 (*0-312-97456-6*, St. Martin's Paperbacks) St. Martin's Pr.

—Final Arrangements. 1996. (Ginger Barnes Main Line Mysteries Ser.). 290p. pap. text 5.99 (*0-312-95765-3*, St. Martin's Paperbacks) St. Martin's Pr.

—The Main Line Is Murder. 1995. (Ginger Barnes Main Line Mysteries Ser.). 294p. mass mkt. 5.99 (*0-312-95637-1*, St. Martin's Paperbacks) St. Martin's Pr.

—School of Hard Knocks: A Dead Letter Mystery. 1997. (Ginger Barnes Main Line Mysteries Ser.). 288p. mass mkt. 5.99 (*0-312-96104-9*, St. Martin's Paperbacks) St. Martin's Pr.

—A Score to Settle. 1999. (Ginger Barnes Main Line Mysteries Ser.). 288p. mass mkt. 5.99 (*0-312-96951-1*, St. Martin's Paperbacks) St. Martin's Pr.

Myers, Dody. Echoes of the Falling Spring. 2001. iii, 220p. 24.95 (*1-57249-231-7*, 1572492317, Burd Street Pr.) White Mane Publishing Co., Inc.

Myers, Tamar. Between a Wok & a Hard Place. 1998. (Magdalena Yoda Ser.: Vol. 5). 272p. mass mkt. 5.99 (*0-451-19230-3*, Signet Bks.) NAL.

—Between a Wok & a Hard Place. l.t. ed. 2002. (Mystery Ser.). 373p. 29.45 (*0-7862-4640-5*) Thorndike Pr.

—The Crepes of Wrath: A Pennsylvania Dutch Mystery with Recipes. 2001. (Pennsylvania Dutch Mystery with Recipes Ser.). 240p. 19.99 o.s.i (*0-451-20225-2*) NAL.

—The Crepes of Wrath: A Pennsylvania Dutch Mystery with Recipes. l.t. ed. 2001. 415p. 28.95 (*0-7862-3673-6*) Thorndike Pr.

—Custard's Last Stand. 2004. 240p. mass mkt. 5.99 (*0-451-20848-X*, Signet Bks.) NAL.

—Custard's Last Stand: A Pennsylvania Dutch Mystery with Recipes. 2003. 240p. 19.95 (*0-451-20782-3*) NAL.

—Eat, Drink & Be Wary: A Pennsylvania Dutch Mystery with Recipes. 1998. (PennDutch Mysteries Ser.). 272p. mass mkt. 5.99 (*0-451-19231-1*, Signet Bks.) NAL.

—Eat, Drink, & Be Wary: A Pennsylvania Dutch Mystery with Recipes. l.t. ed. 2001. 384p. 28.95 o.p. (*0-7862-3455-5*) Thorndike Pr.

—Gruel & Unusual Punishment. 2002. 240p. 19.99 (*0-451-20508-1*); 2003. 272p. reprint ed. mass mkt. 5.99 (*0-451-20568-5*, Signet Bks.) NAL.

—Hand That Rocks the Ladle. 2000. (Pennsylvania Dutch Mystery with Recipes Ser.). 272p. mass mkt. 5.99 (*0-451-19755-0*, Signet Bks.) NAL.

—The Hand That Rocks the Ladle: A Pennsylvania Dutch Mystery with Recipes. l.t. ed. 2000. (Mystery Ser.). 347p. 26.95 (*0-7862-2987-X*) Thorndike Pr.

—Just Plain Pickled. 1997. 272p. mass mkt. 5.99 (*0-451-19293-1*, Signet Bks.) NAL.

—No Use Dying over Spilled Milk: A Pennsylvania-Dutch Mystery with Recipes. 1996. 272p. 20.95 o.p. (*0-525-94099-5*, Dutton) Dutton/Plume.

—No Use Dying over Spilled Milk: A Pennsylvania-Dutch Mystery with Recipes. 1997. 272p. mass mkt. 5.99 (*0-451-18854-3*, Signet Bks.) NAL.

—Parsley, Sage, Rosemary & Crime. 1996. (PennDutch Inn Mystery Ser.). 272p. mass mkt. 5.99 (*0-451-18297-9*, Signet Bks.) NAL.

—Play It Again Spam. 1999. (Pennsylvania Dutch Mystery with Recipes Ser.). 272p. mass mkt. 5.99 (*0-451-19754-2*, Signet Bks.) NAL.

—Thou Shalt Not Grill. 2004. 240p. 19.95 (*0-451-21113-8*) NAL.

—Too Many Crooks Spoil the Broth. 1995. (PennDutch Inn Mystery Ser.). 256p. mass mkt. 5.99 (*0-451-18296-0*, Signet Bks.) NAL.

—Too Many Crooks Spoil the Broth: A Pennsylvania-Dutch Mystery with Recipes. 1993. 256p. 17.00 o.s.i (*0-385-47139-4*) Doubleday Publishing.

Myers, Tamar & Myers, Les. Parsley, Sage, Rosemary & Crime. 1995. 256p. 21.95 o.s.i (*0-385-47140-8*) Doubleday Publishing.

Oakley, Don. The Adventure of Christian Fast. 1989. (Illus.). 279p. (Orig.). (YA). (gr. 9 up). 12.95 (*0-9619465-1-2*); pap. 8.95 (*0-9619465-2-0*) Eyrie Pr.

Oates, Joyce Carol. Solstice. 2000. 223p. reprint ed. pap. 14.95 (*0-86538-100-3*) Ontario Review Pr.

O'Dell, Tawni. Back Roads. abr. ed. 2000. 6p. audio 25.00 (*0-694-52291-0*, HarperAudio) HarperTrade.

—Back Roads. 2004. 432p. pap. 14.00 (*0-451-21245-2*); 2001. 416p. mass mkt. 7.99 (*0-451-20234-1*, Signet Bks.) NAL.

—Back Roads. unabr. ed. 2000. audio 61.00 (*0-7887-4629-4*, 96340K8) Recorded Bks., LLC.

—Back Roads. l.t. ed. 511p. 2001. 28.95 o.p. (*0-7862-2762-1*); 2000. 30.95 (*0-7862-2754-0*) Thorndike Pr.

For book reviews, descriptive annotations, tables of contents, cover images, author biographies & additional information, updated daily, subscribe to **www.booksinprint.com** 1057

—Back Roads. 2000. 338p. 24.95 o.s.i (*0-670-89418-4*, Penguin Bks.); 1999. 352p. 24.95 o.s.i (*0-670-88760-9*) Viking Penguin.

Ohannessian, Griselda Jackson. Once - As It Was. 2001. 176p. pap. 14.95 (*0-87233-131-8*) Bauhan, William L. Inc.

O'Hara, John. Appointment in Samarra. (Modern Library Ser.). 1994. 364p. 14.95 o.s.i (*0-679-60110-4*); 1982. 256p. mass mkt. 10.00 o.s.i (*0-394-71192-0*); 1934. 3.00 o.p. (*0-394-41542-6*) Random Hse., Inc.

—Appointment in Samarra. 1993. reprint ed. lib. bdg. 89.00 (*0-7812-5481-7*) Reprint Services Corp.

—Appointment in Samarra. l.t. ed. 1998. (Perennial Bestsellers Ser.). 331p. 25.95 (*0-7838-0376-1*) Thorndike Pr.

—A Rage to Live. 1986. 542p. reprint ed. mass mkt. 4.95 (*0-88184-216-8*, Carroll & Graf Pubs.) Avalon Publishing Group.

—A Rage to Live. 2004. 752p. pap. 14.95 (*0-8129-7135-3*, Modern Library) Random House Adult Trade Publishing Group.

—A Rage to Live. (Modern Library Ser.). 1997. 608p. 22.00 o.s.i (*0-679-60266-6*); 1949. 10.00 o.s.i (*0-394-44214-8*) Random Hse., Inc.

Oliver, Jim. Wings in the Snow. 1998. 288p. pap. 12.95 (*1-55583-462-0*, Alyson Bks.) Alyson Pubns.

O'Nan, Stewart. Snow Angels: A Novel. 1994. 240p. 20.00 o.s.i (*0-385-47574-8*) Doubleday Publishing.

Otto, Carolyn B. Pioneer Church, ERS. 1999. (Illus.). 32p. (J). (ps-3). 16.95 o.s.i (*0-8050-2554-5*, Holt, Henry & Co. Bks. For Young Readers) Holt, Henry & Co.

Parini, Jay. The Patch Boys. l.t. ed. 1987. pap. 17.95 o.p. (*1-55504-458-1*) BBC Audiobooks America.

—The Patch Boys. 1988. pap. 8.95 o.s.i (*0-8050-0770-9*, Owl Bks.); 1986. 15.95 o.p. (*0-8050-0047-X*) Holt, Henry & Co.

—Patch Boys. l.t. ed. 1987. 19.95 o.p. (*1-55504-298-8*) BBC Audiobooks America.

Parr, Delia. Home to Trinity: A Novel. 2003. 352p. 25.95 (*0-312-27098-4*) St. Martin's Pr.

—A Place Called Trinity. 2002. (Illus.). 304p. 24.95 (*0-312-28288-5*) St. Martin's Pr.

—A Place Called Trinity. l.t. ed. 2002. (Americana Ser.). 491p. 28.95 (*0-7862-4443-7*) Thorndike Pr.

—A Place Called Trinity: A Novel. 2003. 320p. reprint ed. pap. 12.95 (*0-312-31005-6*, Saint Martin's Griffin) St. Martin's Pr.

—The Promise of Flowers. 2000. 256p. mass mkt. 5.99 (*0-312-97505-8*, St. Martin's Paperbacks) St. Martin's Pr.

Perry, Marta. Since You've Been Gone. 1999. (Steeple Hill Love Inspired Ser.: Vol. 75). mass mkt. (*0-373-87075-2*, 1-87075-7, Harlequin Bks.) Harlequin Enterprises, Ltd.

Peterson, Tracie. Silent Star. 2003. 208p. pap. 10.99 (*0-7642-2824-2*) Bethany Hse. Pubs.

Poyer, David. As the Wolf Loves Winter. 1997. 432p. mass mkt. 6.99 (*0-8125-3433-6*); 1996. 352p. 23.95 o.p. (*0-312-85601-6*) Doherty, Tom Assocs., LLC. (Forge Bks.).

—As the Wolf Loves Winter. l.t. ed. 1996. 25.95 (*1-56895-379-8*, Wheeler Publishing, Inc.) Gale Group.

—The Dead of Winter. 1988. 320p. pap. 5.99 (*0-8125-0787-8*, Tor Bks.) Doherty, Tom Assocs., LLC.

—Thunder on the Mountain: A Novel of 1936, Set. unabr. ed. 2000. audio 84.95 (*0-7927-2323-6*, CSL 212, Chivers Sound Library) BBC Audiobooks America.

—Thunder on the Mountain: A Novel of 1936. (Hemlock County Ser.). 2000. 419p. mass mkt. 6.99 (*0-8125-4004-2*); 1999. (Illus.). 384p. 25.95 (*0-312-86494-9*) Doherty, Tom Assocs., LLC. (Forge Bks.).

—Winter in the Heart. 1994. 416p. mass mkt. 5.99 o.p. (*0-8125-2298-2*); 1993. 352p. 21.95 o.p. (*0-312-85421-8*) Doherty, Tom Assocs., LLC. (Tor Bks.).

—Winter in the Heart. 4.98 o.s.i (*0-8317-4649-1*) Smithmark Pubs., Inc.

Prescott, Michael. Comes the Dark. 1999. 400p. mass mkt. 6.99 (*0-451-19250-8*, Signet Bks.) NAL.

Pritchard, Sara. Crackpots: A Novel. 2003. 208p. pap. 12.00 (*0-618-30245-X*, Mariner Bks.) Houghton Mifflin Co. Trade & Reference Div.

Pynchon, Thomas. Mason & Dixon, Pt. 2. unabr. collector's ed. 1997. audio 80.00 (*0-7366-3782-6*, 4454-B) Books on Tape, Inc.

—Mason & Dixon. 1998. 0.01 o.s.i (*0-8050-5850-8*, Owl Bks.); 1998. 773p. pap. 17.00 (*0-8050-5837-0*, Owl Bks.); 1997. 784p. 27.50 o.s.i (*0-8050-3758-6*) Holt, Henry & Co.

—Mason & Dixon. 2004. 784p. pap. 15.00 (*0-312-42320-9*) Picador.

Quinones Miller, Karen E. Satin Doll: A Novel. 2001. 320p. 21.00 (*0-7432-1433-1*, Simon & Schuster) Simon & Schuster.

RavenWolf, Silver & Thorsen, Jes, eds. Beneath a Mountain Moon. 1995. (Illus.). 360p. pap. 14.95 (*1-56718-722-6*) Llewellyn Pubns.

Robbins, Harold. The Stallion. 1996. 368p. 23.00 o.p. (*0-684-81067-0*, Simon & Schuster) Simon & Schuster.

Roberts, Gillian. Adam & Evil. 2000. (Amanda Pepper Mysteries Ser.). 240p. mass mkt. 6.50 (*0-345-42935-4*, Ballantine Bks.) Ballantine Bks.

—Adam & Evil. l.t. ed. 2000. (Beeler Large Print Mystery Ser.). 260p. 26.95 (*1-57490-292-X*, Beeler Large Print Bks.) Beeler, Thomas T. Publisher.

—Adam & Evil. unabr. ed. 2000. (Amanda Pepper Mysteries Ser.: No. 9). audio 54.00 (*0-7887-4311-2*, 96107E7) Recorded Bks., LLC.

—The Bluest Blood: An Amanda Pepper Mystery. (Amanda Pepper Mysteries Ser.). 1999. 304p. mass mkt. 6.50 (*0-345-42315-1*); Vol. 8. 1998. 240p. 22.00 o.s.i (*0-345-40326-6*, Ballantine Bks.) Ballantine Bks.

—The Bluest Blood: An Amanda Pepper Mystery. l.t. ed. 2000. (Beeler Large Print Mystery Ser.). (Illus.). 261p. 25.95 (*1-57490-321-7*, Beeler Large Print Bks.) Beeler, Thomas T. Publisher.

—Caught Dead in Philadelphia. 1988. 208p. mass mkt. 6.50 (*0-345-35340-4*) Ballantine Bks.

—Caught Dead in Philadelphia. unabr. ed. 1993. (Amanda Pepper Mysteries Ser.: Vol. 1). audio 44.00 (*1-55690-900-4*, 93342E7) Recorded Bks., LLC.

—Caught Dead in Philadelphia: A Mystery Introducing Amanda Pepper. 1987. 224p. 16.95 o.s.i (*0-684-18809-0*, Macmillan Reference USA) Gale Group.

—I'd Rather Be in Philadelphia. 1993. 240p. mass mkt. 5.99 (*0-345-37782-6*) Ballantine Bks.

—In the Dead of Summer. 288p. 1996. mass mkt. 5.99 (*0-345-40650-8*); 1995. pap. 19.00 o.s.i (*0-345-46534-2*, Ballantine Bks.) Ballantine Bks.

—The Mummer's Curse. unabr. ed. 1996. (Amanda Pepper Mysteries Ser.: Vol. 7). audio 51.00 (*0-7887-0667-5*, 94844E7) Recorded Bks., LLC.

—The Mummers' Curse, Vol. 7. 1997. (Amanda Pepper Mysteries Ser.). 288p. mass mkt. 5.99 (*0-345-40324-X*, Ballantine Bks.) Ballantine Bks.

—Philly Stakes. 1990. 208p. mass mkt. 5.99 (*0-345-36266-7*) Ballantine Bks.

—Philly Stakes. unabr. ed. 1994. (Amanda Pepper Mysteries Ser.: Vol. 2). audio 51.00 (*1-55690-994-2*, 94133E7) Recorded Bks., LLC.

—Philly Stakes. 1989. 240p. 17.95 o.s.i (*0-684-19071-0*, Scribner) Simon & Schuster.

—With Friends Like These... 1995. 272p. pap. 19.00 o.s.i (*0-345-46535-0*) Ballantine Bks.

Roberts, Gillian & Foster, Alan Dean. With Friends Like These... 1994. 272p. mass mkt. 5.99 (*0-345-37784-2*); 1993. 256p. 18.00 o.s.i (*0-345-37783-4*) Ballantine Bks.

Roberts, Nora. Hidden Riches. 2004. 400p. pap. 13.95 (*0-425-19722-0*); 1995. 480p. mass mkt. 7.99 (*0-515-11606-8*, Jove) Berkley Publishing Group.

—Hidden Riches. abr. ed. 1994. audio 17.00 o.p. (*1-56100-362-X*, 895, Nova Audio Bks.); audio 89.25 (*1-56100-180-5*, 1228, Unabridged Library Editions); audio 25.95 (*1-56100-554-1*, 330, Bookcassette) Brilliance Audio.

—Hidden Riches. l.t. ed. 1995. (Magna Large Print Ser.). 685p. o.p. (*0-7505-0843-4*) Magna Large Print Bks. GBR. *Dist:* Ulverscroft Large Print Canada, Ltd.

—Hidden Riches. abr. ed. 2000. audio 7.95 (*1-57815-011-6*, 1004, Media Bks. Audio Publishing) Media Bks., L. L. C.

—Hidden Riches. (*0-399-19232-8*, Perigee Bks.); 1994. 400p. 21.95 o.p. (*0-399-13948-6*, G. P. Putnam's Sons) Penguin Group (USA) Inc.

—Hidden Riches. 21.95 o.s.i (*0-399-14175-8*) Putnam Publishing Group, The.

—Three Complete Novels. (Dream Ser.). 1999. 757p. 14.98 (*0-399-14480-3*); 1998. 768p. 14.98 (*0-399-14388-2*, G. P. Putnam's Sons) Penguin Group (USA) Inc.

—Three Complete Novels: Honest Illusions, Private Scandals & Hidden Riches. 2000. 864p. 14.98 (*0-399-14627-X*, G. P. Putnam's Sons) Penguin Group (USA) Inc.

Rock, Peter. The Ambidextrist: A Novel. 2002. 224p. 21.95 (*1-893956-22-9*) Context Bks.

Roper, Gayle G. Caught in a Bind. 2000. (Amhearst Mystery Ser.). 320p. pap. 10.99 (*0-310-21850-0*) Zondervan.

—Caught in the Act. 2000. (Five Star Christian Fiction Ser.). 311p. 24.95 (*0-7862-2776-1*, Five Star) Gale Group.

—Caught in the Act? 1998. (Amhearst Mystery Ser.: 2). 272p. pap. 10.99 (*0-310-21909-4*) Zondervan.

—Caught in the Middle. 1997. (Amhearst Mystery Ser.: Vol. 1). 240p. pap. 10.99 (*0-310-20995-1*) Zondervan.

—The Document, Vol. 2. 1998. (Key Ser.: Vol. 2). 256p. pap. 9.99 o.s.i (*1-57673-295-9*, Palisades) Multnomah Pubs., Inc.

Rosenthal, Chuck. Loop's End. 1992. 21.95 o.p. (*0-87905-478-6*) Smith, Gibbs Pub.

Scheid, Mary Jean. Firewater. 2001. pap. 19.95 (*0-7596-6773-X*) 1stBooks Library.

Schroeder, Joan Vannorsdall. The Hearts of Soldiers: A Novel. 1999. (Illus.). 336p. (J). pap. 24.95 o.p. (*0-7894-2553-X*, D K Ink) Dorling Kindersley Publishing, Inc.

Schwartz, Steven. A Good Doctor's Son. 1998. 256p. 24.00 (*0-688-15401-8*, Morrow, William & Co.) Morrow/Avon.

Shade, Eric. Eyesores: Stories. 2002. 205p. 24.95 (*0-8203-2432-9*) Univ. of Georgia Pr.

Sharp, Priscilla Stone. Langhorn & Mary: A Nineteenth Century American Love Story. Rose, Tony & Rose, Yvonne, eds. 2003. 528p. 25.99 (*0-9727519-0-4*) Amber Bks.

Shuster, Bud. Secret Harvest. 2001. vi, 381p. 24.95 (*1-57249-230-9*, 1572492309, Burd Street Pr.) White Mane Publishing Co., Inc.

Singmaster, Elsie. Gettysburg: Stories of Memory, Grief, & Greatness. 2003. (Classics of Civil War Fiction Ser.). (Illus.). 232p. reprint ed. pap. 19.95 (*0-8173-1279-X*) Univ. of Alabama Pr.

Smith, Larry. Working It Out. unabr. ed. 1998. 104p. pap. 9.95 (*1-56439-071-3*) Ridgeway Pr.

Smith, Martin J. Time Release. 1997. 352p. mass mkt. 5.99 o.s.i (*0-515-12028-6*, Jove) Berkley Publishing Group.

Snyder, John. The Golden Ring: A Christmas Story. 2001. 192p. (J). 15.95 (*0-446-53006-9*) Warner Bks., Inc.

Spencer, Brent. The Lost Son. 1995. 288p. 19.95 (*1-55970-266-4*) Arcade Publishing, Inc.

Stambaugh, Sara. I Hear the Reaper's Song. 1984. 221p. 12.95 (*0-934672-24-5*); reprint ed. pap. 8.95 (*0-934672-41-5*) Good Bks.

—The Sign of the Fox. 1991. 182p. 16.95 (*1-56148-011-8*) Good Bks.

Stanton, Judith. His Stolen Bride. 1999. 448p. mass mkt. 5.99 (*0-06-109787-X*) HarperCollins Pubs.

Stine, R. L. Superstitious. 1995. (*0-446-51925-1*); 390p. 21.95 o.p. (*0-446-51953-7*) Warner Bks., Inc.

Strohmeyer, Sarah. Bubbles Ablaze: A Mystery. 2003. 256p. 23.95 (*0-525-94738-8*, Dutton) Dutton/Plume.

—Bubbles in Trouble. 2002. 288p. 22.95 o.s.i (*0-525-94649-7*, Dutton) Dutton/Plume.

—Bubbles Unbound. 2001. (Illus.). 288p. 22.95 o.s.i (*0-525-94580-6*, Dutton) Dutton/Plume.

—Bubbles Unbound. 2002. 352p. reprint ed. mass mkt. 6.99 (*0-451-20544-8*) NAL.

Tarvin, Al. Chelsea & Sally. Haycox, Bobbi & Wordsmiths Unlimited Staff, eds. 1997. (Chelsea Ser.: No. 4). 280p. pap. 12.95 (*0-9643250-4-7*) CJH Enterprises.

—Chelsea & the Lords. 1999. (Chelsea Ser.: No. 5). 300p. pap. 12.95 (*0-9643250-5-5*) CJH Enterprises.

—Chelsea, Chelsea. Ausley, Lisa, ed. rev. ed. (Chelsea Ser.: No. 1). 233p. 1996. reprint ed. pap. 12.95 (*0-9643250-6-3*); Vol. 1. 1994. (Illus.). pap. 12.95 o.p. (*0-9643250-0-4*) CJH Enterprises.

—Chelsea, the Final Chapter. 2nd rev. ed. 1997. (Chelsea Ser.: No. 5). 305p. reprint ed. pap. 12.95 o.p. (*0-9643250-7-1*); (Illus.). pap. 12.95 (*0-9643250-1-2*) CJH Enterprises.

—Run, Chelsea, Run, Vol. 3. Haycox, Bobbi & CJH Enterprises Staff, eds. 1996. (Chelsea Ser.: Vol. 5). 260p. pap. 12.95 (*0-9643250-3-9*) CJH Enterprises.

Thorp, A. D. Volunteers for Glory. 1999. 560p. (Orig.). pap. 18.95 (*1-56167-477-X*) American Literary Pr., Inc.

Tyree, Omar R. Flyy Girl. 1996. 416p. 22.50 o.s.i (*0-684-82928-2*, Simon & Schuster) Simon & Schuster.

—One Crazy-A** Night. 2003. pap. 12.00 (*0-9710397-3-9*) Mars Productions.

Updike, John. The Centaur. 1996. 320p. pap. 14.00 (*0-449-91216-7*); 1987. 224p. mass mkt. 5.95 o.s.i (*0-449-21522-9*); 1983. mass mkt. 2.95 o.p. (*0-449-20371-9*); 1981. mass mkt. 2.75 o.p. (*0-449-23974-8*) Ballantine Bks. (Fawcett).

—The Centaur. unabr. collector's ed. 1984. audio 54.00 (*0-7366-0692-0*, 1655) Books on Tape, Inc.

—The Centaur. 1963. 320p. 32.50 (*0-394-41881-6*) Knopf, Alfred A. Inc.

—Rabbit, Run. 1996. 272p. pap. 14.95 (*0-449-91165-9*); 1992. mass mkt. 5.99 o.p. (*0-449-44943-2*); 1983. 288p. mass mkt. 5.99 o.s.i (*0-449-20506-1*) Ballantine Bks. (Fawcett).

—Rabbit, Run. unabr. collector's ed. 1980. (Rabbit Quartet). audio 64.00 (*0-7366-0292-5*, 1280) Books on Tape, Inc.

—Rabbit, Run. 1960. 320p. 27.50 (*0-394-44206-7*) Knopf, Alfred A. Inc.

—Rabbit, Run. l.t. ed. 1996. 448p. lib. bdg. 25.95 (*0-7838-1823-8*) Thorndike Pr.

—Rabbit, Run. 1996. 20.05 (*0-606-20873-9*) Turtleback Bks.

Van Adler, T. C. The Evil That Boys Do: A Novel. 2003. 304p. pap. 13.95 (*1-55583-660-7*) Alyson Pubns.

Walker, Jim. Murder at Gettysburg. 1999. (Mysteries in Time Ser.: Vol. 3). 480p. pap. 13.99 (*0-8054-1970-5*) Broadman & Holman Pubs.

Welsh, Kate. Never Lie to an Angel. 1999. (Steeple Hill Love Inspired Ser.: Bk. 69). 256p. per. (*0-373-87069-8*, 1-87069-0, Harlequin Bks.) Harlequin Enterprises, Ltd.

West, Laurel. Beloved Dissident. 1999. 256p. pap. 12.99 (*1-880226-76-6*) Messianic Jewish Pubs.

Wideman, John Edgar. The Homewood Books. 1992. 536p. text 24.95 (*0-8229-3831-6*) Univ. of Pittsburgh Pr.

—Sent for You Yesterday. 1998. 208p. pap. 14.00 (*0-395-87729-6*) Houghton Mifflin Co.

—Sent for You Yesterday. 1988. pap. 11.00 o.s.i (*0-679-72029-4*, Vintage) Knopf Publishing Group.

—Sent for You Yesterday. 1983. 208p. pap. 3.50 o.p. (*0-380-82644-5*, 82644-5, Avon Bks.) Morrow/Avon.

—Two Cities: A Love Story. 1998. 256p. tchr. ed. 24.00 (*0-395-85730-9*) Houghton Mifflin Co.

—Two Cities: A Love Story. 1999. 256p. pap. 13.00 (*0-618-00185-9*, Mariner Bks.) Houghton Mifflin Co. Trade & Reference Div.

Williams, William G. The Coal King Slaves: A Coal Miner's Story. 2002. (Illus.). 208p. pap. 14.95 (*1-57249-319-4*, Burd Street Pr.) White Mane Publishing Co., Inc.

—Days of Darkness: The Gettysburg Civilians. 1990. mass mkt. 6.99 o.s.i (*0-425-12353-7*) Berkley Publishing Group.

—Days of Darkness: The Gettysburg Civilians. (Illus.). 1994. 254p. 19.95 o.p. (*0-932751-05-9*); rev. ed. 2001. 268p. lib. bdg. 24.95 (*1-57249-262-7*); 2nd ed. 1994. 254p. 19.95 (*0-942597-59-1*) White Mane Publishing Co., Inc.

Williamson, Denise. When Stars Begin to Fall. 2000. (Roots of Faith Ser.: Vol. 2). 448p. pap. 12.99 (*1-55661-883-2*) Bethany Hse. Pubs.

Wojtasik, Ted. No Strange Fire. 1996. 400p. (Orig.). pap. 14.99 (*0-8361-9041-6*) Herald Pr.

—No Strange Fire. 1996. (Orig.). E-Book 14.99 (*0-585-18192-6*) netLibrary, Inc.

Yarnall, Sophia. The Clark Inheritance: A Coal Country Saga. 1981. 224p. 11.95 o.s.i (*0-8027-0679-7*) Walker & Co.

**PENNYFOOT HOTEL (ENGLAND: IMAGINARY PLACE)—FICTION**

Kingsbury, Kate. Check-Out Time. 1995. 224p. (Orig.). mass mkt. 5.50 o.s.i (*0-425-14640-5*, Prime Crime) Berkley Publishing Group.

—Chivalry Is Dead. 1996. mass mkt. 5.50 o.s.i (*0-425-15515-3*) Berkley Publishing Group.

—Death with Reservations: A Pennyfoot Hotel Mystery. 1998. (Pennyfoot Hotel Mystery Ser.). 224p. mass mkt. 5.99 o.s.i (*0-425-16144-7*, Prime Crime) Berkley Publishing Group.

—Do Not Disturb. 1994. (Orig.). mass mkt. 4.99 o.s.i (*0-425-14914-5*); 208p. mass mkt. 4.50 o.s.i (*0-515-11282-8*) Berkley Publishing Group. (Jove).

—Dying Room Only. 1998. (Pennyfoot Hotel Mystery Ser.). 224p. mass mkt. 5.99 o.s.i (*0-425-16568-X*, Prime Crime) Berkley Publishing Group.

—Eat, Drink, & Be Buried. 1994. 208p. mass mkt. 4.50 o.p. (*0-425-14352-X*, Prime Crime) Berkley Publishing Group.

—Grounds for Murder. 1995. (Pennyfoot Hotel Mystery Ser.). 240p. (Orig.). mass mkt. 5.50 o.s.i (*0-425-14901-3*) Berkley Publishing Group.

—Maid to Murder, 1 vol. 1999. (Pennyfoot Hotel Mystery Ser.: Vol.12). 224p. mass mkt. 5.99 o.s.i (*0-425-16967-7*) Berkley Publishing Group.

—Pay the Piper. 1996. 224p. (Orig.). mass mkt. 5.50 o.s.i (*0-425-15231-6*) Berkley Publishing Group.

—Ring for Tomb Service: In Edwardian England Murder Rings a Bell. 1997. 240p. mass mkt. 5.99 o.s.i (*0-425-15857-8*, Prime Crime) Berkley Publishing Group.

—Room with a Clue. 1993. 208p. (Orig.). mass mkt. 3.99 o.s.i (*0-515-11188-0*, Jove) Berkley Publishing Group.

—A Room with a Clue. 1993. 208p. (Orig.). mass mkt. 5.50 o.s.i (*0-425-14326-0*) Berkley Publishing Group.

—Service for Two. 1994. 208p. (Orig.). mass mkt. 4.99 o.s.i (*0-425-14223-X*, Prime Crime) Berkley Publishing Group.

**PERN (IMAGINARY PLACE)—FICTION**

McCaffrey, Anne. All the Weyrs of Pern. 2002. (Dragonriders of Pern Ser.: No. 11). E-Book 6.99 (*1-59061-890-4*) Adobe Systems, Inc.

—All the Weyrs of Pern. 1997. pap. 12.95 o.s.i (*0-345-41935-9*); 1992. 448p. mass mkt. 7.99 (*0-345-36893-2*) Ballantine Bks. (Del Rey).

—The Chronicles of Pern: First Fall. 2002. (Dragonriders of Pern Ser.: No. 12). E-Book 6.99 (*1-59061-875-0*) Adobe Systems, Inc.

—The Chronicles of Pern: First Fall. 1997. pap. 12.95 o.s.i (*0-345-41959-6*); 1994. 336p. mass mkt. 6.99 (*0-345-36899-1*) Ballantine Bks. (Del Rey).

—The Dolphins of Pern. 2002. E-Book 6.99 (*1-59061-883-1*) Adobe Systems, Inc.

—The Dolphins of Pern. (Pern Ser.). 1997. pap. 12.95 o.s.i (*0-345-41938-3*); 1995. 384p. mass mkt. 7.50 (*0-345-36895-9*) Ballantine Bks. (Del Rey).

—Dragondrums. 1997. (Harper Hall Trilogy Ser.: Vol. 3). 208p. mass mkt. 7.50 o.s.i (*0-553-25855-9*, Spectra) Bantam Bks.

—Dragondrums. 1993. (Dragon Ser.: Vol. 3). audio 44.20 (*1-56544-041-2*, 550012); audio Literate Ear, Inc.

—Dragondrums. 1993. (Super Sound Buy, Dove Ser.). 8.99 o.p. (*0-7871-0067-6*) Penguin Group (USA) Inc.

—Dragondrums, unabr. ed. 1992. (YA). (gr. 7). audio 53.00 (*1-55690-618-8*, 92311E7) Recorded Bks., LLC.

—Dragondrums. (Illus.). 256p. 2003. (J). pap. 5.99 (*0-689-86006-4*, Aladdin); 2003. (YA). mass mkt. 6.99 (*0-689-86025-0*, Simon Pulse); 1979. (YA). (gr. 6 up). lib. bdg. 16.95 o.s.i (*0-689-30685-7*, Atheneum) Simon & Schuster Children's Publishing.

—Dragondrums. l.t. ed. 1999. (Science Fiction Ser.). 304p. 24.95 o.p. (*0-7838-8506-7*) Thorndike Pr.

—Dragondrums. 1980. (Harper Hall Trilogy Ser.). (J). 13.04 (*0-606-01413-6*) Turtleback Bks.

—Dragondrums & the White Dragon. abr. ed. 1993. 19.95 o.p. (*1-55800-640-0*) NewStar Media, Inc.

—Dragonflight. 2002. (Dragonriders of Pern Ser.). E-Book 6.99 (*1-59061-876-9*) Adobe Systems, Inc.

—Dragonflight. 9999. mass mkt. o.s.i (*0-345-43112-X*); 1999. mass mkt. 2.22 o.s.i (*0-345-91747-2*); 1997. 320p. pap. 19.00 o.s.i (*0-345-41936-7*, Del Rey); 1986. 320p. mass mkt. 6.99 (*0-345-33546-5*, Del Rey); 1983. mass mkt. 2.95 o.p. (*0-345-31447-6*, Del Rey); 1980. mass mkt. 2.50 o.p. (*0-345-29568-4*, Del Rey); 1979. mass mkt. 2.25 o.p. (*0-345-28426-7*, Del Rey); 1978. 8.95 o.s.i (*0-345-27749-X*, Del Rey); 1978. mass mkt. 1.95 o.p. (*0-345-27694-9*, Del Rey); 1975. mass mkt. 1.50 o.p. (*0-345-24776-0*); 1973. mass mkt. 1.25 o.p. (*0-345-23443-X*) Ballantine Bks.

—Dragonflight. 1993. 79p. mass mkt. 12.99 o.p. (*0-06-105003-2*, Perennial) HarperTrade.

—Dragonflight. 1994. (Select Sound, Dove Ser.). 8.99 o.p. (*0-7871-0072-2*) Penguin Group (USA) Inc.

—Dragonflight. 2002. 320p. pap. 6.99 (*0-345-45633-5*) Random Hse., Inc.

—Dragonflight. 1978. (Dragonriders of Pern Ser.). 13.04 (*0-606-01414-4*) Turtleback Bks.

—Dragonquest. 2002. (Dragonriders of Pern Ser.: No. 2). E-Book 6.99 (*1-59061-877-7*) Adobe Systems, Inc.

—Dragonquest. 1997. pap. 12.95 o.s.i (*0-345-41937-5*, Del Rey); 1986. (Dragonriders of Pern Ser.: Vol. 2). 352p. mass mkt. 6.99 (*0-345-33508-2*, Del Rey); 1983. mass mkt. 2.95 o.p. (*0-345-31448-4*, Del Rey); 1980. mass mkt. 2.50 o.p. (*0-345-29666-4*, Del Rey); 1979. mass mkt. 2.25 o.p. (*0-345-28425-9*, Del Rey); 1978. mass mkt. 1.95 o.p. (*0-345-27695-7*, Del Rey); 1975. mass mkt. 1.50 o.p. (*0-345-24777-9*); 1973. mass mkt. 1.25 o.p. (*0-345-23444-8*); Vol. 2. 1979. 8.95 o.s.i (*0-345-28030-X*, Del Rey) Ballantine Bks.

—Dragonquest. 1994. (Super Sound Buy, Dove Ser.). 8.99 o.p. (*0-7871-0111-7*) Penguin Group (USA) Inc.

—Dragonquest. 1978. (Dragonriders of Pern Ser.). 13.04 (*0-606-01416-0*) Turtleback Bks.

—The Dragonriders of Pern. (Pern Ser.). 1988. 832p. pap. 17.95 (*0-345-34024-8*); Set. 1986. 27.96 o.s.i (*0-345-34045-0*) Ballantine Bks. (Del Rey).

—Dragonsdawn. 2002. (Dragonriders of Pern Ser.: No. 9). E-Book 6.99 (*1-59061-878-5*) Adobe Systems, Inc.

—Dragonsdawn. 1997. pap. 12.95 o.s.i (*0-345-41956-1*, Del Rey); 1989. 384p. mass mkt. 6.99 (*0-345-36286-1*, Del Rey); 1989. mass mkt. 4.95 o.s.i (*0-345-36255-1*); 1988. 448p. 18.45 o.s.i (*0-345-33160-5*, Del Rey) Ballantine Bks.

—Dragonsdawn. 1988. 431p. 25.00 (*0-89366-213-5*) Ultramarine Publishing Co., Inc.

—Dragonseye. 2002. (Dragonriders of Pern Ser.: No. 15). E-Book 6.99 (*1-59061-879-3*) Adobe Systems, Inc.

—Dragonseye. 2002. E-Book 6.99 (*0-345-45400-6*); 1997. 416p. mass mkt. 7.99 (*0-345-41879-4*) Ballantine Bks. (Del Rey).

—Dragonsinger. 1997. (Harper Hall Trilogy Ser.: Vol. 2). 256p. mass mkt. 7.50 o.s.i (*0-553-25854-0*, Spectra) Bantam Bks.

—Dragonsinger. 1994. (Super Sound Buy, Dove Ser.). 8.99 o.p. (*0-7871-0080-3*) Penguin Group (USA) Inc.

—Dragonsinger, unabr. ed. 1992. (Harper Hall Trilogy: Vol. 2). (YA). (gr. 7 up). audio 60.00 (*1-55690-617-X*, 92310) Recorded Bks., LLC.

—Dragonsinger. 2003. (Illus.). 288p. (J). pap. 5.99 (*0-689-86007-2*, Aladdin); 2003. (Illus.). 288p. (YA). mass mkt. 6.99 (*0-689-86024-2*, Simon Pulse); 1977. (Dragon Singer Ser.: Vol. 1). 276p. (J). 18.00 (*0-689-30570-2*, Atheneum) Simon & Schuster Children's Publishing.

—Dragonsinger. l.t. ed. 1999. (Science Fiction Ser.). 347p. 24.95 (*0-7838-8499-0*) Thorndike Pr.

—Dragonsinger. 1977. (Harper Hall Trilogy Ser.). (J). 13.04 (*0-606-01501-9*) Turtleback Bks.

—Dragonsong. 1994. mass mkt. 6.99 (*0-553-54176-5*); 1986. 192p. pap. 3.50 o.s.i (*0-553-23460-9*, Spectra); 1977. (Harper Hall Trilogy Ser.: Vol. 1). 192p. mass mkt. 7.50 o.s.i (*0-553-25852-4*, Bantam Classics) Bantam Bks.

—Dragonsong. 1993. (Dragon Ser.: Vol. 1). audio 41.00 (*1-56544-029-3*, 550010); audio Literate Ear, Inc.

—Dragonsong, Set. abr. ed. 1994. (Super Sound Buy, Dove Ser.). audio 8.99 o.p. (*0-7871-0075-7*, Dove Audio) NewStar Media, Inc.

—Dragonsong, unabr. ed. 1992. (Harper Hall Trilogy: Vol. 1). (YA). (gr. 7). audio 46.00 (*1-55690-588-2*, 92125E7) Recorded Bks., LLC.

—Dragonsong. (Illus.). 2003. 208p. (J). pap. 5.99 (*0-689-86008-0*, Aladdin); 2003. 208p. (YA). mass mkt. 6.99 (*0-689-86023-4*, Simon Pulse); 1976. 224p. (gr. 5-9). text 16.95 o.s.i (*0-689-30507-9*, Atheneum) Simon & Schuster Children's Publishing.

—Dragonsong. l.t. ed. 1998. (Science Fiction Ser.). 255p. 24.95 (*0-7838-8422-2*) Thorndike Pr.

—Dragonsong. 1977. (Harper Hall Trilogy Ser.). 13.04 (*0-606-01138-2*) Turtleback Bks.

—Dragonsong & Dragonsinger. abr. ed. 1993. 22.95 o.p. (*1-55800-638-9*) NewStar Media, Inc.

—The Girl Who Heard Dragons. deluxe ltd. ed. 1986. (Illus.). 96p. ring bd. 90.00 o.p. (*0-941826-16-3*); ring bd. 350.00 o.p. (*0-941826-17-1*) Cheap Street.

—The Girl Who Heard Dragons. 1995. 402p. mass mkt. 7.99 (*0-8125-1099-2*); 1994. 352p. 22.95 o.p. (*0-312-93173-5*) Doherty, Tom Assocs., LLC. (Tor Bks.).

—The Girl Who Heard Dragons. 1995. 13.04 (*0-606-19654-4*) Turtleback Bks.

—The Masterharper of Pern. 2002. E-Book 6.99 (*1-59061-880-7*) Adobe Systems, Inc.

—The Masterharper of Pern. 1998. (Dragonriders of Pern Ser.). 432p. mass mkt. 6.99 (*0-345-42460-3*, Del Rey) Ballantine Bks.

—The Masterharper of Pern. abr. ed. 1998. (Dragonriders of Pern Ser.). audio 7.99 (*1-56740-275-5*, 1683, Paperback Nova Audio Bks.); audio 17.95 o.p. (*1-56740-762-5*, 479, Nova Audio Bks.); audio 28.95 (*1-56100-787-0*, 174, Bookcassette); 13p. audio 89.25 (*1-56740-566-5*, 939, Unabridged Library Editions) Brilliance Audio.

—The Masterharper of Pern, unabr. ed. 1999. audio 89.25 Highsmith Inc.

—Moreta: Dragonlady of Pern. 2002. E-Book 6.99 (*1-59061-881-5*) Adobe Systems, Inc.

—Moreta: Dragonlady of Pern. 1997. pap. 12.95 o.s.i (*0-345-41957-X*); 1984. (Illus.). 384p. mass mkt. 7.99 (*0-345-29873-X*); 1983. 14.95 o.s.i (*0-345-29874-8*) Ballantine Bks. (Del Rey).

—Moreta: Dragonlady of Pern. 1983. 13.04 (*0-606-03412-9*) Turtleback Bks.

—Moreta: Dragonlady of Pern. 1983. 286p. 25.00 (*0-89366-251-8*) Ultramarine Publishing Co., Inc.

—Nerilka's Story. 2002. (Dragonriders of Pern Ser.: No. 8). E-Book 5.99 (*1-59061-882-3*) Adobe Systems, Inc.

—Nerilka's Story. (Dragonriders of Pern Ser.). 1987. 208p. mass mkt. 6.99 (*0-345-33949-5*); 1986. 12.95 o.p. (*0-345-33159-1*) Ballantine Bks. (Del Rey).

—Nerilka's Story. 1986. 188p. 20.00 o.p. (*0-89366-188-0*) Ultramarine Publishing Co., Inc.

—The Pern Saga: Nerilka's Story, Dragonsdawn, All the Weyrs of Pern, & The Renegades of Pern, Set. 1993. 26.96 o.s.i (*0-345-38535-7*, Del Rey) Ballantine Bks.

—The Renegades of Pern. 2002. E-Book 6.99 (*1-59061-884-X*) Adobe Systems, Inc.

—The Renegades of Pern. 1997. pap. 12.95 o.s.i (*0-345-41939-1*); 1990. 352p. mass mkt. 6.99 (*0-345-36933-5*) Ballantine Bks. (Del Rey).

—The Renegades of Pern. abr. ed. 1993. (Dragonsdawn Ser.). 19.95 o.p. (*1-55800-641-9*) NewStar Media, Inc.

—The Renegades of Pern. 1994. (Super Sound Buy, Dove Ser.). 8.99 o.p. (*0-7871-0081-1*) Penguin Group (USA) Inc.

—The Renegades of Pern. 1991. 4.99 o.p. (*0-517-06790-0*) Random Hse. Value Publishing.

—The Renegades of Pern. 1989. 384p. text 25.00 (*0-89366-284-4*) Ultramarine Publishing Co., Inc.

—The Skies of Pern. 2001. E-Book 7.99 (*1-58945-680-7*) Adobe Systems, Inc.

—The Skies of Pern. 2001. (Illus.). 448p. 25.00 (*0-345-43468-4*, Del Rey); 2002. 480p. reprint ed. mass mkt. 7.99 (*0-345-43469-2*, Ballantine Bks.) Ballantine Bks.

—The Skies of Pern. 2001. E-Book 19.95 (*0-345-44713-1*) Random Hse., Inc.

—The White Dragon. 2002. (Dragonriders of Pern Ser.: No. 3). E-Book 6.99 (*1-59061-891-2*) Adobe Systems, Inc.

—The White Dragon. 1999. mass mkt. 2.22 o.s.i (*0-345-91749-9*); 1997. pap. 12.95 o.s.i (*0-345-41940-5*, Del Rey); 1986. (Dragonriders of Pern Ser.: Vol. 3). 480p. mass mkt. 7.50 (*0-345-34167-8*, Del Rey); 1983. mass mkt. 2.95 o.p. (*0-345-31336-4*, Del Rey); 1980. mass mkt. 2.50 o.p. (*0-345-29525-0*, Del Rey); 1979. mass mkt. 2.25 o.p. (*0-345-25373-6*, Del Rey) Ballantine Bks.

—The White Dragon. 1994. (Super Sound Buy, Dove Ser.). 8.99 o.p. (*0-7871-0130-3*) Penguin Group (USA) Inc.

—The White Dragon. 1978. (Dragonriders of Pern Ser.). 13.04 (*0-606-01881-6*) Turtleback Bks.

—The White Dragon. 1981. 15.00 o.p. (*0-345-27567-5*) Ultramarine Publishing Co., Inc.

McCaffrey, Anne & McCaffrey, Todd. Dragon's Kin. 2003. (Pern Ser.). 304p. 24.95 (*0-345-46198-3*, Del Rey) Ballantine Bks.

—Dragon's Kin. abr. ed. (Dragonriders of Pern Ser.). 2004. audio 9.99 (*1-59355-183-5*, 4793, Brilliance Audio Paperback Audiobooks); 2003. audio 19.95 (*1-59355-182-7*, 4792); 2003. audio 29.95 (*1-59355-180-0*, 4790, Brilliance Audio Unabridged); 2003. audio 74.25 (*1-59355-181-9*, 4791, Brilliance Audio Unabridged Lib Ed); 2003. audio compact disk 31.95 (*1-59355-480-X*, 5104, Brilliance Audio on CD Unabridged); 2003. audio compact disk 87.25 (*1-59355-481-8*, 5105, Brilliance Audio on CD Unabridged Lib Ed) Brilliance Audio.

**PETAYBEE (IMAGINARY PLACE)—FICTION**

McCaffrey, Anne & Scarborough, Elizabeth. Power Play. 1992. 5.99 o.s.i (*0-345-38175-0*) Ballantine Bks.

McCaffrey, Anne & Scarborough, Elizabeth Ann. Power Lines. 1995. 336p. mass mkt. 6.99 (*0-345-38780-5*, Del Rey) Ballantine Bks.

—Power Play. 1996. 352p. mass mkt. 6.99 (*0-345-38781-3*, Del Rey) Ballantine Bks.

—The Powers That Be. 2002. E-Book 6.99 (*0-345-45755-2*); 1994. 384p. mass mkt. 6.99 (*0-345-38779-1*, Del Rey) Ballantine Bks.

—The Powers That Be. abr. ed. 1993. audio 16.95 o.p. (*1-55800-855-1*) NewStar Media, Inc.

**PHAZE (IMAGINARY PLACE)—FICTION**

Anthony, Piers. Blue Adept. 1987. (Apprentice Adept Ser.: Vol. 2). 336p. mass mkt. 7.50 (*0-345-35245-9*); 1986. mass mkt. 3.50 o.p. (*0-345-33632-1*); 1983. mass mkt. 2.95 o.p. (*0-345-31424-7*); 1982. mass mkt. 2.75 o.p. (*0-345-28214-0*); 1981. 368p. 10.95 o.s.i (*0-345-29384-3*) Ballantine Bks. (Del Rey).

—Juxtaposition. 1987. (Apprentice Adept Ser.: Vol. 3). 368p. mass mkt. 6.99 (*0-345-34934-2*); 1986. mass mkt. 3.50 o.p. (*0-345-33637-2*); 1983. mass mkt. 2.95 o.p. (*0-345-28215-9*); 1982. 13.50 o.p. (*0-345-30196-X*) Ballantine Bks. (Del Rey).

—Out of Phaze. 1988. (Apprentice Adept Ser.: Vol. 4). 320p. mass mkt. 6.50 o.s.i (*0-441-64465-1*) Ace Bks.

—Out of Phaze. 1987. (Apprentice Adept Ser.: Bk. 4). 288p. 17.95 o.p. (*0-399-13272-4*) Putnam Publishing Group, The.

—Robot Adept. 1989. mass mkt. 5.99 o.s.i (*0-441-73118-X*) Ace Bks.

—Robot Adept. 1988. (Apprentice Adept Ser.: Bk. 5). 288p. 16.95 o.p. (*0-399-13359-3*, G. P. Putnam's Sons) Penguin Putnam Bks. for Young Readers.

—Split Infinity. 1987. (Apprentice Adept Ser.: Vol. 1). 368p. mass mkt. 7.50 (*0-345-35491-5*); 1986. mass mkt. 3.50 o.p. (*0-345-33600-3*); 1982. mass mkt. 2.95 o.p. (*0-345-30761-5*); 1980. mass mkt. 2.50 o.p. (*0-345-28213-2*); 1980. 9.95 o.s.i (*0-345-28645-6*) Ballantine Bks. (Del Rey).

—Unicorn Point. 1990. (Apprentice Adept Ser.: No. 6). 352p. mass mkt. 6.99 o.s.i (*0-441-84563-0*) Ace Bks.

—Unicorn Point. 1989. (Apprentice Adept Ser.). 15.95 o.p. (*0-399-13433-6*, G. P. Putnam's Sons) Penguin Putnam Bks. for Young Readers.

**PHILADELPHIA (PA.)—FICTION**

Attaway, William. Blood on the Forge. 1969. 279p. reprint ed. 8.95 o.p. (*0-911860-00-2*) Chatham Bookseller.

—Blood on the Forge. 1992. 304p. pap. 9.00 o.s.i (*0-385-42542-2*) Doubleday Publishing.

Bailey-Williams, Nicole. A Little Piece of Sky. 2002. 176p. reprint ed. pap. 9.95 (*0-7679-1216-0*, Harlem Moon) Broadway Bks.

Bradberry, James. Eakins' Mistress: A Jamie Ramsgill Mystery. 1997. 169p. text 19.95 o.p. (*0-312-15518-2*, Saint Martin's Minotaur) St. Martin's Pr.

Bradley, David. The Chaneysville Incident. 1981. 480p. 14.95 o.p. (*0-06-010491-0*) HarperTrade.

—South Street. 1988. 16.25 o.p. (*0-8446-6323-9*) Smith, Peter Pub., Inc.

Brown, Charles Brockden. Arthur Mervyn: Or, Memoirs of the Year 1793. (Novels & Related Works of Charles Brockden Brown: Vol. 3). 557p. reprint ed. pap. 172.70 (*0-608-08076-4*, 206903500002) Bks. on Demand.

—Arthur Mervyn: Or, Memoirs of the Year 1793. (Works of Charles Brockden Brown). reprint ed. 1989. lib. bdg. 79.00 (*0-7812-2069-6*); Set. 1993. lib. bdg. 150.00 (*0-7812-5436-1*) Reprint Services Corp.

—Arthur Mervyn: Or, Memoirs of the Year 1793. 1984. 6.75 o.p. (*0-8446-1751-2*) Smith, Peter Pub., Inc.

—Arthur Mervyn, or Memoirs of the Year 1793. Gabo, Frank, ed. 1991. pap. 22.95 (*0-8084-0446-6*) Rowman & Littlefield Pubs., Inc.

—Arthur Mervyn, or, Memoirs of the Year 1793: First & Second Parts. Krause, Sydney J. & Reid, S. W., eds. 2002. (Illus.). 479p. 20.00 (*0-87338-738-4*) Kent State Univ. Pr.

Campbell, Bebe Moore. Singing in the Comeback Choir. 1999. 400p. reprint ed. mass mkt. 7.99 (*0-425-16662-7*) Berkley Publishing Group.

—Singing in the Comeback Choir. l.t. ed. 1998. (Large Print Book Ser.). 27.95 (*1-56895-613-4*, Wheeler Publishing, Inc.) Gale Group.

—Singing in the Comeback Choir. 1998. 320p. 24.95 o.p. (*0-399-14298-3*, G. P. Putnam's Sons) Penguin Group (USA) Inc.

—Singing in the Comeback Choir. 1999. 13.55 (*0-606-19302-2*) Turtleback Bks.

Carl, Lee. The Cherry Tree. 2003. 312p. 26.95 (*0-9704143-4-X*, Northern Liberties Pr.) Old City Publishing, Inc.

Carr, Josephine. The Dewey Decimal System of Love. 2003. 272p. pap. 12.95 (*0-451-20971-0*) NAL.

—The Dewey Decimal System of Love. l.t. ed. 2004. 330p. 28.95 (*0-7862-6226-5*) Thorndike Pr.

Cary, Lorene. The Price of a Child. 1996. 336p. pap. 14.00 (*0-679-74467-3*) Random Hse., Inc.

—Pride: A Novel. 1999. 336p. pap. 14.00 (*0-385-48183-7*) Doubleday Publishing.

Chabon, Michael. The Mysteries of Pittsburgh. 1988. 256p. 16.95 o.p. (*0-688-07632-7*, Morrow, William & Co.) Morrow/Avon.

Chase-Riboud, Barbara. The President's Daughter. 1995. 480p. pap. 12.00 o.s.i (*0-345-38970-0*) Ballantine Bks.

Clark, Beverly. Yesterday Is Gone. 1997. 293p. mass mkt. 10.95 (*1-885478-12-7*, Indigo) Genesis Pr., Inc.

Coffey, Jan. Triple Threat. 2003. 400p. mass mkt. (*1-55166-703-7*, Mira Bks.) Harlequin Enterprises, Ltd.

Conard, Mark T. Dark As Night. 2003. 24.95 (*0-9724412-3-9*); (*0-9724412-6-3*); (*0-9724412-7-1*) UglyTown.

Constable, George. Where You Are. 1996. 336p. 21.95 o.s.i (*0-385-48438-0*) Doubleday Publishing.

Cooper, Armin A. Tribes: A Novel. 2001. pap. 16.95 (*0-595-18046-9*) iUniverse, Inc.

Cronin, Justin. Mary & O'Neil. 2002. 256p. pap. 11.95 (*0-385-33359-5*, Delta) Dell Publishing.

Danica, John & Freeman, Lucy. Lerza's Lives. 1991. 352p. 18.95 o.p. (*0-312-05976-0*) St. Martin's Pr.

Dexter, Pete. Train. 2003. 288p. 26.00 (*0-385-50591-4*) Doubleday Publishing.

DiBartolomeo, Albert. Fool's Gold. 1993. vii, 279p. 18.95 o.p. (*0-312-09058-7*, Saint Martin's Minotaur) St. Martin's Pr.

Dunphy, Jack. The Murderous McLaughlins. 1988. 256p. text 16.95 o.p. (*0-07-018316-3*) McGraw-Hill Cos., The.

Elm, Joanna. Delusion. 1999. 374p. mass mkt. 6.99 (*0-8125-6480-4*, Tor Bks.); 1997. 384p. 23.95 (*0-312-86064-1*, Forge Bks.) Doherty, Tom Assocs., LLC.

Fauset, Jessie Redmon. There Is Confusion. reprint ed. 23.50 (*0-404-11386-9*) AMS Pr., Inc.

—There Is Confusion. 1989. (Library of Black Literature). 304p. reprint ed. pap. text 17.95 (*1-55553-066-4*) Northeastern Univ. Pr.

Fenton, Edward. Duffy's Rocks. 1988. (J). (gr. k-12). mass mkt. 3.25 o.s.i (*0-440-20242-6*, Laurel Leaf) Random Hse. Children's Bks.

Flander, Scott. Four to Midnight. 2004. 368p. mass mkt. 7.50 (*0-06-103170-4*, Avon Bks.) Morrow/Avon.

Flanders, Scott. Sons of the City. 1999. 308p. 24.00 (*0-688-16429-3*, Morrow, William & Co.) Morrow/Avon.

Flory, Jane. It Was a Pretty Good Year, 001. 1977. (Illus.). (J). (gr. 3-7). 6.95 o.p. (*0-395-25835-9*) Houghton Mifflin Co.

Gallagher, Stephen. Red, Red Robin. 1996. mass mkt. 5.99 o.s.i (*0-345-40649-4*) Ballantine Bks.

—Red, Red Robin. l.t. ed. 1996. (Charnwood Large Print Ser.). 544p. 29.99 o.p. (*0-7089-8880-6*, Ulverscroft) Thorpe, F. A. Pubs. GBR. *Dist:* Ulverscroft Large Print Bks., Ltd., Ulverscroft Large Print Canada, Ltd.

Gangemi, Joseph. Inamorata: A Novel. 2004. 336p. 24.95 (*0-670-03279-4*, Viking) Viking Penguin.

Goldberg, Marshall. A Deadly Operation: A Novel of Medical Espionage. 1996. 240p. pap. 14.95 (*0-8023-1310-8*) Dufour Editions, Inc.



For book reviews, descriptive annotations, tables of contents, cover images, author biographies & additional information, updated daily, subscribe to **www.booksinprint.com** 1059

—The Family Scalpel. 1995. 384p. 25.00 (*0-8023-1307-8*); pap. 13.95 (*0-8023-1308-6*) Dufour Editions, Inc.

—Intelligence. 1996. 240p. pap. 14.95 (*0-8023-1311-6*) Dufour Editions, Inc.

Goodis, David. Of Tender Sin. 2001. (Midnight Classics Ser.). 224p. pap. (*1-85242-674-8*) Serpent's Tail Ltd.

Graham, Mark. The Black Maria. 2000. (Mysteries of Old Philadelphia Ser.). 384p. mass mkt. 6.50 (*0-380-80068-3*, Avon Bks.) Morrow/Avon.

—The Killing Breed. 1998. (Mysteries of Old Philadelphia Ser.). 272p. mass mkt. 5.99 (*0-380-80066-7*, Avon Bks.) Morrow/Avon.

—The Resurrectionist. 1999. (Mysteries of Old Philadelphia Ser.). 320p. mass mkt. 5.99 (*0-380-80067-5*, Avon Bks.) Morrow/Avon.

Grayson, George. The Revolutionary's Confession. 2000. 331p. 24.95 (*1-890768-21-9*, Intrigue Pr.) Corvus Publishing.

Griffin, W. E. B. The Assassin: A Badge of Honor Novel. 5th ed. 1993. (Badge of Honor Ser.). 464p. mass mkt. 7.99 (*0-515-11113-9*, Jove) Berkley Publishing Group.

—The Assassin: A Badge of Honor Novel. unabr. collector's ed. 1994. audio 96.00 (*0-7366-2851-7*, 133263) Books on Tape, Inc.

—Badge of Honor Boxed Set. (Badge of Honor Ser.). 1993. 23.96 o.s.i (*0-515-11301-8*); 1992. 19.84 o.s.i (*0-515-11030-2*); 1991. 14.85 o.s.i (*0-515-10777-8*) Berkley Publishing Group. (Jove).

—Badge of Honor Boxed Set: Men in Blue, Special Operations, the Victim. 1996. 12.98 o.s.i (*0-399-14152-9*) Penguin Group (USA) Inc.

—Badge of Honor Boxed Set: The Witness; the Assassin; the Murderers. 1997. 816p. 12.98 o.s.i (*0-399-14238-X*) Penguin Group (USA) Inc.

—Badge of Honor VIII: Final Justice. 2003. 528p. mass mkt. 7.99 (*0-515-13656-5*, Jove) Berkley Publishing Group.

—The Corps: Semper Fi, Call to Arms, Counterattack. 1994. 816p. 11.98 o.p. (*0-399-13913-3*, G. P. Putnam's Sons) Penguin Group (USA) Inc.

—Final Justice: A Badge of Honor Novel. 2003. 480p. 26.95 (*0-399-14926-0*) Putnam Publishing Group, The.

—Final Justice: A Badge of Honor Novel. 512p. (*0-7278-5917-X*) Severn Hse. Pubs., Ltd.

—Final Justice: A Badge of Honor Novel. l.t. ed. 2003. (Core Ser.). 32.95 (*0-7862-5571-4*) Thorndike Pr.

—In the Line of Duty. 352p. 17.99 (*0-7278-5450-X*) Severn Hse. Pubs., Ltd.

—The Investigators: A Badge of Honor Novel. 1998. 592p. reprint ed. mass mkt. 7.99 (*0-515-12406-0*, Jove) Berkley Publishing Group.

—The Investigators: A Badge of Honor Novel. unabr. ed. 1998. audio 104.00 (*0-7366-4084-3*, 4593) Books on Tape, Inc.

—The Investigators: A Badge of Honor Novel. l.t. ed. 1999. 735p. pap. 20.00 o.p. (*0-7838-0140-8*, Macmillan Reference USA) Gale Group.

—The Investigators: A Badge of Honor Novel. 1998. 448p. 24.95 o.p. (*0-399-14308-4*); 24.95 (*0-399-14349-1*, 695430) Penguin Group (USA) Inc.

—The Investigators: A Badge of Honor Novel. 416p. (*0-7278-5476-3*) Severn Hse. Pubs., Ltd.

—The Investigators: A Badge of Honor Novel. l.t. ed. 1998. 735p. 30.94 (*0-7838-0139-4*) Thorndike Pr.

—Men in Blue: A Badge of Honor Novel. 1988. (Badge of Honor Ser.). 352p. mass mkt. 7.99 (*0-515-09750-0*, Jove) Berkley Publishing Group.

—Men in Blue: A Badge of Honor Novel. unabr. collector's ed. 1993. audio 64.00 (*0-7366-2482-1*, 3244) Books on Tape, Inc.

—The Murderers: A Badge of Honor Novel. 1995. (Badge of Honor Ser.). 544p. mass mkt. 7.99 (*0-515-11742-0*, Jove) Berkley Publishing Group.

—The Murderers: A Badge of Honor Novel. unabr. ed. 1995. audio 96.00 (*0-7366-2949-1*, 3643) Books on Tape, Inc.

—The Murderers: A Badge of Honor Novel. unabr. ed. 1995. audio 25.95 (*1-56100-586-X*, 189, Bookcassette); audio 89.25 (*1-56100-211-9*, 957, Unabridged Library Editions) Brilliance Audio.

—The Murderers: A Badge of Honor Novel. l.t. ed. 1995. 24.95 o.p. (*1-56895-209-0*, Wheeler Publishing, Inc.) Gale Group.

—The Murderers: A Badge of Honor Novel. abr. ed. 2000. audio 7.95 (*1-57815-001-9*, 1017, Media Bks. Audio Publishing) Media Bks., L. L. C.

—The Murderers: A Badge of Honor Novel. 1995. 384p. 23.95 o.p. (*0-399-13976-1*) Putnam Publishing Group, The.

—The Murderers: A Badge of Honor Novel. 396p. pap. 5.98 o.p. (*0-7651-0428-8*) Smithmark Pubs., Inc.

—Special Operations: A Badge of Honor Novel. 1989. (Badge of Honor Ser.). (Illus.). 368p. mass mkt. 7.99 (*0-515-10148-6*, Jove) Berkley Publishing Group.

—Special Operations: A Badge of Honor Novel. unabr. collector's ed. 1993. audio 64.00 (*0-7366-2492-9*, 3251) Books on Tape, Inc.

—The Victim: A Badge of Honor Novel. 1991. (Badge of Honor Ser.). 352p. mass mkt. 7.99 (*0-515-10397-7*, Jove) Berkley Publishing Group.

—The Victim: A Badge of Honor Novel. unabr. collector's ed. 1993. audio 72.00 (*0-7366-2498-8*, 3256) Books on Tape, Inc.

—The Witness: A Badge of Honor Novel. 1992. (Badge of Honor Ser.). 432p. mass mkt. 7.99 (*0-515-10747-6*, Jove) Berkley Publishing Group.

—The Witness: A Badge of Honor Novel. unabr. collector's ed. 1993. audio 88.00 (*0-7366-2553-4*, 3304) Books on Tape, Inc.

Grindle, Lucretia W. The Nightspinners: A Novel. 2003. 304p. 23.95 (*0-375-50776-0*) Random Hse., Inc.

Haddam, Jane. Act of Darkness. 1991. 288p. mass mkt. 4.50 o.s.i (*0-553-29086-X*) Bantam Bks.

—Bleeding Hearts. 1995. 368p. mass mkt. 5.50 o.s.i (*0-553-56936-8*) Bantam Bks.

—Conspiracy Theory: A Gregor Demarkian Novel. 2003. 288p. 24.95 (*0-312-27188-3*) St. Martin's Pr.

—Deadly Beloved. 1998. 336p. mass mkt. 5.99 o.s.i (*0-553-57200-8*) Bantam Bks.

—Feast of Murder. 1992. 336p. mass mkt. 5.50 o.s.i (*0-553-29389-3*) Bantam Bks.

—A Festival of Deaths. 1994. 384p. mass mkt. 5.99 o.s.i (*0-553-56085-9*) Bantam Bks.

—The Fountain of Death. 1995. 352p. (Orig.). mass mkt. 5.50 o.s.i (*0-553-56449-8*, Crimeline) Bantam Bks.

—A Great Day for the Deadly. 1992. 288p. mass mkt. 5.50 o.s.i (*0-553-29388-5*) Bantam Bks.

—Murder Superior. 1993. 304p. mass mkt. 5.99 o.s.i (*0-553-56084-0*) Bantam Bks.

—Not a Creature Was Stirring: A Gregor Demarkian Holiday Mystery. 1990. 320p. mass mkt. 5.99 o.s.i (*0-553-28792-3*) Bantam Bks.

—Precious Blood. 1991. 336p. mass mkt. 5.99 o.s.i (*0-553-28913-6*) Bantam Bks.

—Quoth the Raven. 1991. 288p. mass mkt. 5.99 o.s.i (*0-553-29255-2*) Bantam Bks.

Harper, Philip. Final Fear. 2001. 219p. reprint ed. pap. 12.95 (*1-931755-03-5*) Mystery Vault, Inc.

—Final Fear. 1993. 224p. 20.00 o.p. (*0-671-74532-8*, Simon & Schuster) Simon & Schuster.

Harrison, Colin. Break & Enter. 1991. 400p. reprint ed. pap. 4.95 (*0-380-71526-0*, Avon Bks.) Morrow/Avon.

—Break & Enter. unabr. ed. 1990. audio 85.00 (*1-55690-071-6*, 90092E7) Recorded Bks., LLC.

Hathaway, Robin. The Doctor & the Dead Man's Chest. 2003. mass mkt. 6.99 (*0-312-98372-7*, St. Martin's Paperbacks); 2001. (Illus.). 352p. 24.95 (*0-312-26956-0*) St. Martin's Pr.

—The Doctor Digs a Grave. 272p. 1998. 22.95 (*0-312-18568-5*, Saint Martin's Minotaur); Vol. 1. 2nd ed. 1999. mass mkt. 5.99 (*0-312-96703-9*, St. Martin's Paperbacks) St. Martin's Pr.

—Doctor Makes a Dollhouse Call: Doctor Fenimore Mystery. 2000. (Doctor Fenimore Mysteries Ser.). 272p. 23.95 (*0-312-24192-5*, Saint Martin's Minotaur) St. Martin's Pr.

Heggan, Christiane. Blind Faith. 2001. 408p. mass mkt. (*1-55166-783-5*, 1-66783-1, Mira Bks.) Harlequin Enterprises, Ltd.

Henry, DeWitt. The Marriage of Anna Maye Potts: A Novel. 2001. 232p. 24.95 (*1-57233-139-9*) Univ. of Tennessee Pr.

Hoffman, Barry. Born Bad. ltd. ed. 2000. 400p. 40.00 o.p. (*1-881475-99-9*) Cemetery Dance Pubns.

Howell, Hannah. Wild Roses. l.t. ed. 2001. (Five Star Romance Ser.). 336p. 26.95 (*0-7862-3702-3*, Five Star) Gale Group.

Hunt, Marsha. Free. 288p. 1994. pap. 9.95 o.p. (*0-452-27061-8*, Plume); 1993. 20.00 o.p. (*0-525-93575-4*) Dutton/Plume.

Hunter, Travis E. Trouble Man: A Novel. 2003. (Strivers Row Ser.). 240p. 22.95 (*0-375-50895-3*, Villard Bks.) Random House Adult Trade Publishing Group.

Jones, Antonne M. The Family: A Philadelphia Mob Story. 1998. 160p. pap. 12.95 (*0-9662541-0-4*) Eldon Pubs.

Jones, Solomon. Pipe Dream: A Novel. 2001. 368p. pap. 13.95 (*0-375-75660-4*, Villard Bks.) Random House Adult Trade Publishing Group.

Kent, Bill. Street Money: A Mystery. 2002. 304p. 23.95 (*0-312-28585-X*, Saint Martin's Minotaur) St. Martin's Pr.

LaPlante, Richard. Mantis. 1993. 352p. 19.95 o.p. (*0-312-85531-1*, Tor Bks.) Doherty, Tom Assocs., LLC.

Lashner, William. Fatal Flaw. 2004. 576p. mass mkt. 7.50 (*0-06-050818-3*, HarperTorch); 2003. 448p. 24.95 (*0-06-050816-7*, Morrow, William & Co.) Morrow/Avon.

—Hostile Witness. l.t. ed. 1995. (Large Print Bks.). 25.95 o.p. (*1-56895-248-1*, Wheeler Publishing, Inc.) Gale Group.

—Hostile Witness. 1995. 501p. 23.00 o.p. (*0-06-039146-4*) HarperCollins Pubs.

—Hostile Witness. 1996. 608p. mass mkt. 7.50 (*0-06-100988-1*, ReganBooks); 1995. audio 17.00 o.p. (*0-694-51559-0*, HarperAudio) HarperTrade.

—Hostile Witness. unabr. ed. 1998. audio 112.00 (*0-7887-1954-8*, 95352E7) Recorded Bks., LLC.

—Veritas. 1997. 464p. 25.00 o.p. (*0-06-039147-2*, ReganBooks);Set. audio 18.00 (*0-694-51789-5*, 392878, HarperAudio) HarperTrade.

—Veritas. 1997. 592p. mass mkt. 6.50 o.s.i (*0-06-101023-5*, HarperTorch) Morrow/Avon.

—Veritas. unabr. ed. 1997. audio 112.00 (*0-7887-1768-5*, 95246E5) Recorded Bks., LLC.

LeMaitre, Corene. April Rising. 2001. 288p. reprint ed. pap. 12.00 (*0-7867-0872-7*, Carroll & Graf Pubs.) Avalon Publishing Group.

Lippard, George. The Quaker City: or The Monks of Monk Hall: A Romance of Philadelphia Life, Mystery, & Crime. Reynolds, David S., ed. & intro. by. 1995. 632p. pap. 24.95 (*0-87023-971-6*) Univ. of Massachusetts Pr.

Lopez, Steve. The Sunday Macaroni Club. 1999. 384p. pap. 12.95 (*0-452-28138-5*, Plume) Dutton/Plume.

—The Sunday Macaroni Club. 1997. 384p. 24.00 (*0-15-100264-9*) Harcourt Trade Pubs.

—The Sunday Macaroni Club. 1998. 368p. mass mkt. 6.99 o.s.i (*0-451-19723-2*, Signet Bks.) NAL.

—The Sunday Macaroni Club, Set. abr. ed. 1997. audio 24.95 (*1-57511-025-3*, 695317) Publishing Mills, Inc., The.

—The Sunday Macaroni Club. 1999. pap. 23.95 (*0-670-86311-4*) Viking Penguin.

—Third & Indiana: A Novel. 1994. 336p. (J). 21.95 o.p. (*0-670-85676-2*, Viking) Viking Penguin.

MacDougal, Bonnie. Angle of Impact. 1998. mass mkt. 6.99 o.s.i (*0-345-41446-2*) Ballantine Bks.

—Angle of Impact. abr. ed. 1999. audio 7.99 o.s.i (*1-56740-290-9*, 1747, Nova Audio Bks.); 1998. audio 17.95 o.p. (*1-56740-773-0*, 458, Nova Audio Bks.); 1998. audio 26.95 (*1-56100-799-4*, 34, Bookcassette); 1998. audio 73.25 (*1-56740-833-8*, 798, Unabridged Library Editions) Brilliance Audio.

—Breach of Trust. 384p. 2002. pap. 21.95 (*0-7434-6514-8*, Pocket); 1998. per. 6.99 o.s.i (*0-671-53719-9*, Pocket); 1996. 23.00 o.p. (*0-671-53720-2*, Atria) Simon & Schuster.

Major, Marcus. A Family Affair. 2003. 304p. 24.95 (*0-525-94768-X*, Dutton) Dutton/Plume.

—Good Peoples. 2001. 384p. reprint ed. mass mkt. 6.99 (*0-451-40979-5*, Onyx) NAL.

—Good Peoples: A Novel. 2000. 272p. 22.95 o.s.i (*0-525-94535-0*, Dutton) Dutton/Plume.

Martin, Nancy. How to Murder a Millionaire. 2002. 272p. mass mkt. 6.50 (*0-451-20724-6*, Signet Bks.) NAL.

—How to Murder a Millionaire. 2003. (Mystery Ser.). 359p. 28.95 (*0-7862-5391-6*) Thorndike Pr.

McKinney-Whetstone, Diane. Leaving Cecil Street. 2004. 320p. 24.95 (*0-688-16385-8*, Morrow, William & Co.) Morrow/Avon.

—Tempest Rising. 1998. 288p. 24.00 (*0-688-14994-4*, Morrow, William & Co.) Morrow/Avon.

—Tempest Rising: A Novel. 1999. (Illus.). 288p. pap. 12.00 (*0-688-16640-7*, Quill) HarperTrade.

—Tumbling. 1996. 288p. 24.00 (*0-688-14487-X*, Morrow, William & Co.) Morrow/Avon.

—Tumbling. 1997. 352p. pap. 12.00 (*0-684-83724-2*, Touchstone) Simon & Schuster.

Michaels, Fern. Serendipity. 9999. mass mkt. o.p. (*0-345-37328-6*); 1997. 384p. mass mkt. 6.99 (*0-449-14982-X*, Fawcett) Ballantine Bks.

Michaels, Kasey. Can't Take My Eyes Off of You. l.t. ed. 2000. 323p. 25.95 (*1-57490-265-2*, Beeler Large Print Bks.) Beeler, Thomas T. Publisher.

—Can't Take My Eyes off You. 2000. 352p. mass mkt. 6.50 (*0-8217-6522-1*) Kensington Publishing Corp.

Murray, Donna Huston. Farewell Performance: A Ginger Barnes Main Line Mystery. 2000. (Ginger Barnes Main Line Mysteries Ser.). 272p. mass mkt. 5.99 (*0-312-97456-6*, St. Martin's Paperbacks) St. Martin's Pr.

—Final Arrangements. 1996. (Ginger Barnes Main Line Mysteries Ser.). 290p. pap. text 5.99 (*0-312-95765-3*, St. Martin's Paperbacks) St. Martin's Pr.

—Lie Like a Rug. 2001. 256p. mass mkt. 6.50 (*0-312-97897-9*, St. Martin's Paperbacks) St. Martin's Pr.

—The Main Line Is Murder. 1995. (Ginger Barnes Main Line Mysteries Ser.). 294p. mass mkt. 5.99 (*0-312-95637-1*, St. Martin's Paperbacks) St. Martin's Pr.

—School of Hard Knocks: A Dead Letter Mystery. 1997. (Ginger Barnes Main Line Mysteries Ser.). 288p. mass mkt. 5.99 (*0-312-96104-9*, St. Martin's Paperbacks) St. Martin's Pr.

—A Score to Settle. 1999. (Ginger Barnes Main Line Mysteries Ser.). 288p. mass mkt. 5.99 (*0-312-96951-1*, St. Martin's Paperbacks) St. Martin's Pr.

Oliver, Jim. Wings in the Snow. 1998. 288p. pap. 12.95 (*1-55583-462-0*, Alyson Bks.) Alyson Pubns.

Parr, Delia. The Promise of Flowers. 2000. 256p. mass mkt. 5.99 (*0-312-97505-8*, St. Martin's Paperbacks) St. Martin's Pr.

Pastan, Rachel. This Side of Married. 2004. 272p. 23.95 (*0-670-03306-5*) Viking Penguin.

Quinones Miller, Karen E. Satin Doll. 2002. 320p. pap. 13.00 (*0-7432-1434-X*, Simon & Schuster) Simon & Schuster.

—Satin Doll: A Novel. 2000. 288p. pap. 12.95 (*0-9676028-0-7*) Oshun Publishing Co., Inc.

—Satin Doll: A Novel. 2001. 320p. 21.00 (*0-7432-1433-1*, Simon & Schuster) Simon & Schuster.

Roberts, Gillian. Adam & Evil. 2000. (Amanda Pepper Mysteries Ser.). 240p. mass mkt. 6.50 (*0-345-42935-4*, Ballantine Bks.) Ballantine Bks.

—Adam & Evil. l.t. ed. 2000. (Beeler Large Print Mystery Ser.). 260p. 26.95 (*1-57490-292-X*, Beeler Large Print Bks.) Beeler, Thomas T. Publisher.

—Adam & Evil. unabr. ed. 2000. (Amanda Pepper Mysteries Ser.: No. 9). audio 54.00 (*0-7887-4311-2*, 96107E7) Recorded Bks., LLC.

—The Bluest Blood: An Amanda Pepper Mystery. (Amanda Pepper Mysteries Ser.). 1999. 304p. mass mkt. 6.50 (*0-345-42315-1*); Vol. 8. 1998. 240p. 22.00 o.s.i (*0-345-40326-6*, Ballantine Bks.) Ballantine Bks.

—The Bluest Blood: An Amanda Pepper Mystery. l.t. ed. 2000. (Beeler Large Print Mystery Ser.). (Illus.). 261p. 25.95 (*1-57490-321-7*, Beeler Large Print Bks.) Beeler, Thomas T. Publisher.

—Caught Dead in Philadelphia. 1988. 208p. mass mkt. 6.50 (*0-345-35340-4*) Ballantine Bks.

—Caught Dead in Philadelphia. unabr. ed. 1993. (Amanda Pepper Mysteries Ser.: Vol. 1). audio 44.00 (*1-55690-900-4*, 93342E7) Recorded Bks., LLC.

—Caught Dead in Philadelphia: A Mystery Introducing Amanda Pepper. 1987. 224p. 16.95 o.s.i (*0-684-18809-0*, Macmillan Reference USA) Gale Group.

—Claire & Present Danger. 2003. 256p. 22.95 (*0-345-45490-1*, Ballantine Bks.) Ballantine Bks.

—Claire & Present Danger. l.t. ed. 2003. (Mystery Ser.). 28.95 (*1-57490-527-9*) Beeler, Thomas T. Publisher.

—Helen Hath No Fury: An Amanda Pepper Mystery. 2001. 256p. reprint ed. mass mkt. 6.99 (*0-345-42932-X*, Fawcett) Ballantine Bks.

—Helen Hath No Fury: An Amanda Pepper Mystery. l.t. ed. 2001. (Beeler Large Print Mystery Ser.). 240p. 25.95 (*1-57490-334-9*, Beeler Large Print Bks.) Beeler, Thomas T. Publisher.

—How I Spent My Summer Vacation. 1995. 256p. mass mkt. 5.99 (*0-345-38594-2*); pap. 19.00 o.s.i (*0-345-46533-4*) Ballantine Bks.

—I'd Rather Be in Philadelphia. 1993. 240p. mass mkt. 5.99 (*0-345-37782-6*) Ballantine Bks.

—In the Dead of Summer. 288p. 1996. mass mkt. 5.99 (*0-345-40650-8*); 1995. pap. 19.00 o.s.i (*0-345-46534-2*, Ballantine Bks.) Ballantine Bks.

—The Mummer's Curse. unabr. ed. 1996. (Amanda Pepper Mysteries Ser.: Vol. 7). audio 51.00 (*0-7887-0667-5*, 94844E7) Recorded Bks., LLC.

—The Mummers' Curse, Vol. 7. 1997. (Amanda Pepper Mysteries Ser.). 288p. mass mkt. 5.99 (*0-345-40324-X*, Ballantine Bks.) Ballantine Bks.

—Philly Stakes. 1990. 208p. mass mkt. 5.99 (*0-345-36266-7*) Ballantine Bks.

—Philly Stakes. unabr. ed. 1994. (Amanda Pepper Mysteries Ser.: Vol. 2). audio 51.00 (*1-55690-994-2*, 94133E7) Recorded Bks., LLC.

—Philly Stakes. 1989. 240p. 17.95 o.s.i (*0-684-19071-0*, Scribner) Simon & Schuster.

—With Friends Like These... 1995. 272p. pap. 19.00 o.s.i (*0-345-46535-0*) Ballantine Bks.

Roberts, Gillian & Foster, Alan Dean. With Friends Like These... 1994. 272p. mass mkt. 5.99 (*0-345-37784-2*); 1993. 256p. 18.00 o.s.i (*0-345-37783-4*) Ballantine Bks.

Roberts, Nora. Hidden Riches. 2004. 400p. pap. 13.95 (*0-425-19722-0*); 1995. 480p. mass mkt. 7.99 (*0-515-11606-8*, Jove) Berkley Publishing Group.

—Hidden Riches. abr. ed. 1994. audio 17.00 o.p. (*1-56100-362-X*, 895, Nova Audio Bks.); audio 89.25 (*1-56100-180-5*, 1228, Unabridged Library Editions); audio 25.95 (*1-56100-554-1*, 330, Bookcassette) Brilliance Audio.

—Hidden Riches. l.t. ed. 1995. (Magna Large Print Ser.). 685p. o.p. (*0-7505-0843-4*) Magna Large Print Bks. GBR. *Dist:* Ulverscroft Large Print Canada, Ltd.

—Hidden Riches. abr. ed. 2000. audio 7.95 (*1-57815-011-6*, 1004, Media Bks. Audio Publishing) Media Bks., L. L. C.

—Hidden Riches. (*0-399-19232-8*, Perigee Bks.); 1994. 400p. 21.95 o.p. (*0-399-13948-6*, G. P. Putnam's Sons) Penguin Group (USA) Inc.

—Hidden Riches. 21.95 o.s.i (*0-399-14175-8*) Putnam Publishing Group, The.

—Three Complete Novels. (Dream Ser.). 1999. 757p. 14.98 (*0-399-14480-3*); 1998. 768p. 14.98 (*0-399-14388-2*, G. P. Putnam's Sons) Penguin Group (USA) Inc.

—Three Complete Novels: Honest Illusions, Private Scandals & Hidden Riches. 2000. 864p. 14.98 (*0-399-14627-X*, G. P. Putnam's Sons) Penguin Group (USA) Inc.

Robotham, Rosemarie. Zachary's Wings. 288p. mass mkt. 6.99 (*0-7434-8255-7*); 1999. pap. 12.00 (*0-684-85736-7*); 1998. 22.00 (*0-684-84726-4*) Simon & Schuster. (Scribner).

Rock, Peter. The Ambidextrist: A Novel. 2002. 224p. 21.95 (*1-893956-22-9*) Context Bks.

Sarkessian, Juliet, ed. Trio Sonata: A Novel. 2002. (Gay Men's Fiction Ser.). 200p. 24.95 (*1-56023-401-6*); pap. 14.95 (*1-56023-402-4*) Haworth Pr., Inc., The. (Harrington Park Pr.).

Scott, Anne. Calpurnia. 2003. 304p. 24.00 (*0-375-41380-4*) Knopf, Alfred A. Inc.

Scottoline, Lisa. Courting Trouble. 2002. 320p. 25.95 (*0-06-018514-7*) HarperCollins Pubs.

—Courting Trouble. l.t. ed. 2002. 496p. 25.95 (*0-06-008193-7*, HarperLargePrint) HarperTrade.

—Courting Trouble. 2003. 432p. mass mkt. 7.99 (*0-06-103141-0*, HarperTorch) Morrow/Avon.

—Dead Ringer. 2003. 352p. 25.95 (*0-06-051493-0*, HarperCollins) HarperTrade.

—Everywhere That Mary Went. l.t. ed. 2000. (Wheeler Large Print Book Ser.). 350p. 25.95 o.p. (*1-56895-854-4*, Wheeler Publishing, Inc.) Gale Group.

—Everywhere That Mary Went. 2003. 352p. pap. 11.95 (*0-06-054047-8*, Perennial) HarperTrade.

—Everywhere That Mary Went. 1993. 368p. mass mkt. 7.99 (*0-06-104293-5*, HarperTorch) Morrow/Avon.

—Final Appeal. l.t. ed. 1997. (Large Print Book Ser.). 25.95 (*1-56895-489-1*, Wheeler Publishing, Inc.) Gale Group.

—Final Appeal. 2003. 336p. pap. 11.95 (*0-06-053955-0*, Perennial) HarperTrade.

—Legal Tender. l.t. ed. 1997. (Large Print Bks.). pap. 24.95 (*1-56895-413-1*, Wheeler Publishing, Inc.) Gale Group.

—Legal Tender. 1997. 464p. mass mkt. 7.99 (*0-06-109412-9*); 1996. 304p. 23.00 o.p. (*0-06-017658-X*) HarperCollins Pubs.

—Mistaken Identity. 1999. 496p. 24.00 o.s.i (*0-06-018747-6*); 608p. mass mkt. 7.99 o.p. (*0-06-101419-2*) HarperCollins Pubs.

—Mistaken Identity. abr. ed. 1999. audio 18.00 (*0-694-52110-8*, 394823, HarperAudio) HarperTrade.

—Mistaken Identity. 2000. 592p. mass mkt. 7.99 (*0-06-109611-3*, HarperTorch) Morrow/Avon.

—Mistaken Identity. l.t. ed. (Thorndike/G. K. Hall Paperback Bestsellers Ser.). 704p. 2000. pap. 27.95 (*0-7862-1976-9*); 1999. 30.95 (*0-7862-1975-0*) Thorndike Pr.

—Mistaken Identity. 2000. 13.55 (*0-606-17714-0*) Turtleback Bks.

—Moment of Truth. 2000. 358p. 25.00 (*0-06-019609-2*); 544p. pap. 25.00 (*0-06-095611-9*) HarperCollins Pubs.

—Moment of Truth. abr. ed. 2000. audio 25.00 (*0-694-52310-0*); audio 39.95 (*0-694-52305-4*) HarperTrade. (HarperAudio).

—Moment of Truth. 2001. 448p. mass mkt. 7.50 (*0-06-103059-7*, HarperTorch) Morrow/Avon.

—Moment of Truth. unabr. ed. 1999. audio 75.00 (*0-7887-4152-7*, 96182E7) Recorded Bks., LLC.

—Rough Justice. l.t. ed. 1998. (Large Print Book Ser.). 26.95 o.p. (*1-56895-521-9*, Wheeler Publishing, Inc.) Gale Group.

—Rough Justice. 1998. 480p. mass mkt. 7.99 (*0-06-109610-5*); 1997. 352p. 24.00 o.s.i (*0-06-018746-8*) HarperCollins Pubs.

—Running from the Law. l.t. ed. 1996. 24.95 o.p. (*1-56895-319-4*, Wheeler Publishing, Inc.) Gale Group.

—Running from the Law. 1996. 464p. mass mkt. 7.99 (*0-06-109411-0*) HarperCollins Pubs.

—The Vendetta Defense. 2001. 403p. E-Book 19.95 (*0-06-621323-1*); 400p. 25.00 (*0-06-018507-4*) HarperCollins Pubs.

—The Vendetta Defense. l.t. ed. 2001. 608p. pap. 25.00 (*0-06-018559-7*, HarperLargePrint) HarperTrade.

Sheard, Timothy. Some Cuts Never Heal: A Lenny Moss Mystery. 2003. 352p. 25.00 (*0-7867-1126-4*, Carroll & Graf Pubs.) Avalon Publishing Group.

The Spirited Philadelphia Adventure. 2000. (Illus.). 32p. (J). (gr. k-2). (*0-9626959-1-2*) Junior League of Philadelphia, Inc.

Stern, Ellen Norman. The French Physician's Boy: A Story of Philadelphia's 1793 Yellow Fever Epidemic. 2001. 126p. pap. 20.99 (*0-7388-5877-3*) Xlibris Corp.

Tyree, Omar R. Flyy Girl. 1996. 416p. 22.50 o.s.i (*0-684-82928-2*, Simon & Schuster) Simon & Schuster.

—For the Love of Money. 2001. 416p. reprint ed. pap. 14.00 (*0-684-87292-7*, Simon & Schuster) Simon & Schuster.

—For the Love of Money: A Novel. E-Book 24.00 (*1-58945-187-2*) Adobe Systems, Inc.

—For the Love of Money: A Novel. 2000. E-Book 24.00 (*0-7432-1207-X*); (Illus.). 416p. 24.00 o.s.i (*0-684-87291-9*) Simon & Schuster. (Simon & Schuster).

—For the Love of Money: A Novel. l.t. ed. 2001. (Basic Ser.). 729p. 31.95 (*0-7862-3077-0*) Thorndike Pr.

Walker, Robert W. Bitter Instinct. 400p. 2003. mass mkt. 6.99 (*0-515-13569-0*, Jove); 2001. 21.95 o.s.i (*0-425-17963-X*) Berkley Publishing Group.

Watts, Timothy. Steal Away. 1996. 272p. 22.00 (*1-56947-067-7*) Soho Pr., Inc.

Weiner, Jennifer. Good in Bed. 2006. 432p. mass mkt. (*0-7434-7549-6*, Pocket Star); 2002. 400p. pap. 14.00 (*0-7434-1817-4*, Washington Square Pr.); 2001. 384p. 24.95 (*0-7434-1816-6*, Atria); 2001. reprint ed. E-Book 24.95 (*0-7434-1818-2*, Atria) Simon & Schuster.

—Good in Bed. l.t. ed. 2001. (Large Print Women's Fiction Ser.). 689p. 29.95 (*0-7862-3644-2*) Thorndike Pr.

—In Her Shoes. 2003. 448p. pap. 14.00 (*0-7434-1820-4*, Washington Square Pr.); 2002. 432p. 25.00 (*0-7434-1819-0*, Atria) Simon & Schuster.

—In Her Shoes. 2002. audio compact disk 30.00 (*0-7435-2828-X*); audio 26.00 (*0-7435-2827-1*) Simon & Schuster Audio. (Simon & Schuster Audioworks).

—In Her Shoes. 2003. (Women's Fiction Ser.). 29.95 (*0-7862-4942-0*) Thorndike Pr.

Wideman, John Edgar. Two Cities: A Love Story. 1998. 256p. tchr. ed. 24.00 (*0-395-85730-9*) Houghton Mifflin Co.

—Two Cities: A Love Story. 1999. 256p. pap. 13.00 (*0-618-00185-9*, Mariner Bks.) Houghton Mifflin Co. Trade & Reference Div.

Williamson, Denise. When Stars Begin to Fall. 2000. (Roots of Faith Ser.: Vol. 2). 448p. pap. 12.99 (*1-55661-883-2*) Bethany Hse. Pubs.

The Window Pain: Steve Perry. 2001. (Window Pain: Vol. 1). 180p. pap. 14.00 (*0-9708929-0-X*) Renegade Bks.

**PHILIPPINES—FICTION**

Bacho, Peter. Cebu. E-Book 14.95 (*0-295-97989-5*); 1991. 212p. pap. 16.95 (*0-295-97132-0*); 1991. 212p. text 25.00 (*0-295-97113-4*) Univ. of Washington Pr.

—Nelson's Run. 2002. 145p. pap. 12.95 (*1-930008-02-3*) Willowgate Pr.

Bobis, Merlinda. The Kissing: A Collection of Short Stories. 2001. (Illus.). 183p. pap. 11.95 (*1-879960-60-5*) Aunt Lute Bks.

Brainard, Cecilia M. When the Rainbow Goddess Wept. Orig. Title: Song of Yvonne. 224p. 1995. pap. 10.95 o.p. (*0-452-27471-0*, Plume); 1994. 19.95 o.p. (*0-525-93821-4*, Dutton) Dutton/Plume.

Garland, Alex. The Tesseract. abr. ed. 1999. audio 17.95 (*1-56740-818-4*, Nova Audio Bks.); audio 24.95 (*1-56740-097-3*, 1470, Brilliance Audio Unabridged); audio 41.25 (*1-56740-626-2*, 1471, Unabridged Library Editions) Brilliance Audio.

—The Tesseract. 2000. 288p. 13.00 (*1-57322-774-9*); 1999. 273p. 24.95 o.p. (*1-57322-109-0*) Putnam Publishing Group, The. (Riverhead Bks. (Hardcovers)).

Gobbell, John J. A Code for Tomorrow. E-Book 24.95 (*0-312-26449-6*); 2002. 496p. mass mkt. 7.50 (*0-312-97142-7*, St. Martin's Paperbacks); 2000. pap. (*0-312-97385-3*, St. Martin's Paperbacks); 1999. (Illus.). 316p. 24.95 (*0-312-20511-2*) St. Martin's Pr.

Hagedorn, Jessica. Dream Jungle. 2003. 320p. 23.95 (*0-670-88458-8*, Viking) Viking Penguin.

Holthe, Tess Uriza. When the Elephants Dance: A Novel. 2002. (Illus.). 384p. 24.95 (*0-609-60952-1*, Crown) Crown Publishing Group.

—When the Elephants Dance: A Novel. 2003. 384p. pap. 14.00 (*0-14-200288-7*) Penguin Group (USA) Inc.

Hoyt, Richard. Old Soldiers Sometimes Lie. E-Book 19.95 (*0-312-70863-7*, Tor Bks.); 2002. 432p. 25.95 (*0-7653-0331-0*, Forge Bks.) Doherty, Tom Assocs., LLC.

Jones, James. The Thin Red Line. 1998. 528p. pap. 11.95 (*0-385-32408-1*, Delacorte Pr.); 1985. 480p. mass mkt. 5.95 o.s.i (*0-440-38876-7*, Laurel) Dell Publishing.

—The Thin Red Line. 1975. mass mkt. 1.95 o.p. (*0-380-00309-0*, 41095, Avon Bks.) Morrow/Avon.

Kluge, P. F. Biggest Elvis. 1997. 352p. pap. 11.95 o.p. (*0-14-025811-6*) Penguin Group (USA) Inc.

—Biggest Elvis. 1996. 320p. 22.95 o.s.i (*0-670-86974-0*, Viking) Viking Penguin.

Lim, Paulino, Jr. Sparrows Don't Sing in the Philippines. 1994. 133p. pap. 20.50 (*971-10-0527-1*) New Day Pubs., Philippines PHL. *Dist:* Book Bin - Pacifica, The.

Marshall, William. Whisper. 1991. 3.99 o.p. (*0-517-06314-X*) Random Hse. Value Publishing.

—Whisper. 1989. 288p. pap. 3.95 o.p. (*0-14-010531-X*, Penguin Bks.); 1989. 39.50 o.p. (*0-14-778437-9*); 1988. 15.95 o.p. (*0-670-81959-X*) Viking Penguin.

Nimmo, H. Arlo. The Songs of Salanda: And Other Stories of Sulu. E-Book 19.95 (*0-295-98005-2*); 1994. 248p. 22.50 o.p. (*0-295-97334-X*); 1994. x, 237p. pap. (*0-295-97335-8*) Univ. of Washington Pr.

Saunders, Raymond M. Fenwick Travers & the Forbidden Kingdom: An Entertainment. 352p. 1995. pap. 9.95 o.p. (*0-89141-587-4*); 1994. 21.95 o.p. (*0-89141-480-0*) Ballantine Bks. (Presidio Pr.).

—Fenwick Travers & the Years of Empire: An Entertainment. 1995. 368p. pap. 9.95 o.p. (*0-89141-571-8*); 1993. 400p. 21.95 o.p. (*0-89141-479-7*) Ballantine Bks. (Presidio Pr.).

Sionil, Jose F. Don Vicente: Two Novels. 1999. (Modern Library Ser.). 448p. pap. 23.00 (*0-375-75243-9*) Random Hse., Inc.

Stern, Tom. Gold Fever. 2000. 296p. 21.95 (*0-9703056-0-5*) A E I/TITAN.

Vida, Vendela. And Now You Can Go. 2003. 208p. 19.95 (*1-4000-4027-2*) Knopf, Alfred A. Inc.

Wagner, Philip. Marlowe in the South Seas. 2001. 120p. 11.95 (*0-931896-20-7*) Cove View Pr.

Webb, James H. The Emperor's General. 2000. 480p. mass mkt. 6.99 (*0-553-57854-5*) Bantam Bks.

—The Emperor's General: A Novel. l.t. ed. 1999. (Basic Ser.). 712p. 29.95 (*0-7862-2037-6*) Thorndike Pr.

**PHOENIX (ARIZ.)—FICTION**

Duarte, Stella Pope. Let Their Spirits Dance. 2003. 336p. pap. 12.95 (*0-06-008948-2*, Rayo) HarperTrade.

—Let Their Spirits Dance: A Novel. 2002. 336p. 24.95 (*0-06-018637-2*, Rayo) HarperTrade.

Howard, Linda. Come Lie with Me. 1999. 248p. mass mkt. (*1-55166-549-2*, Mira Bks.); 1993. mass mkt. (*0-373-48271-X*, Silhouette); 1984. mass mkt. (*0-373-53677-1*, Harlequin Bks.) Harlequin Enterprises, Ltd.

Jones, Rennie. Behind the Scenes. 1997. 255p. 22.50 (*0-684-80751-3*, Simon & Schuster) Simon & Schuster.

Judd, Bob. Burn. 1993. 290p. mass mkt. 4.99 o.p. (*0-425-13946-8*) Berkley Publishing Group.

Kostoff, Lynn. The Long Fall. 2003. (Otto Penzler Book Ser.). 208p. 24.00 (*0-7867-1165-5*, Carroll & Graf Pubs.) Avalon Publishing Group.

McMillan, Terry. Waiting to Exhale. unabr. ed. 1992. audio 80.00 (*0-7366-2320-5*, 3100) Books on Tape, Inc.

—Waiting to Exhale. l.t. ed. 1993. (General Ser.). 600p. pap. 17.95 (*0-8161-5618-2*); lib. bdg. 23.95 o.p. (*0-8161-5617-4*) Gale Group. (Macmillan Reference USA).

—Waiting to Exhale. abr. ed. 1995. pap. 16.95 incl. audio (*0-453-00960-3*, 391864); 1992. 15.95 o.p. incl. audio (*0-453-00777-5*, 51855-01595) Penguin/HighBridge.

—Waiting to Exhale. 1996. 155p. per. 20.97 (*0-671-85153-5*); 1993. 416p. mass mkt. 6.50 (*0-671-86417-3*); 1992. 264.00 o.p. (*0-670-77972-5*); 1995. 416p. reprint ed. mass mkt. 7.99 (*0-671-53745-8*) Simon & Schuster. (Pocket).

—Waiting to Exhale. Rosenman, Jane, ed. 1994. 416p. reprint ed. pap. 14.00 (*0-671-50148-8*, Washington Square Pr.) Simon & Schuster.

—Waiting to Exhale. 1992. 416p. 22.95 (*0-670-83980-9*, Viking) Viking Penguin.

O'Callaghan, Maxine. Only in the Ashes. 1997. 320p. mass mkt. 5.99 o.s.i (*0-515-12077-4*, Jove) Berkley Publishing Group.

—Shadow of the Child. 1996. 336p. mass mkt. 5.99 o.s.i (*0-515-11822-2*, Jove) Berkley Publishing Group.

Padilla, Joe. Eliminating the Stress Factor: Definitely NOT a Self-Help Book! 2002. 160p. per. 9.95 (*0-9671187-4-3*) Acacia Publishing, Inc.

Rainey, Yvonne. Dear Lover. Taylor, Chandra Sparks, ed. 2001. 306p. pap. 19.99 (*0-9706847-2-X*) Beginning II End Publishing, Inc.

Rawley, Donald. The Night Bird Cantata. 256p. 1998. 23.00 (*0-380-97609-9*, Avon Bks.); 1999. reprint ed. pap. 12.00 (*0-380-79584-1*) Morrow/Avon.

Talton, Jon. Camelback Falls: A David Mapstone Mystery. 2003. 224p. 22.95 (*0-312-30404-8*, Saint Martin's Minotaur) St. Martin's Pr.

—Concrete Desert: David Mapstone Mystery. 2001. 212p. 22.95 (*0-312-26953-6*, Saint Martin's Minotaur) St. Martin's Pr.

**PICKAX CITY (MICH.: IMAGINARY PLACE)—FICTION**

Braun, Lilian Jackson. The Cat Who Blew the Whistle. 1996. (Cat Who Ser.). 320p. mass mkt. 6.99 (*0-515-11824-9*, Jove) Berkley Publishing Group.

—The Cat Who Blew the Whistle. abr. ed. 1995. (J). audio 17.95 o.p. (*0-7871-0229-6*, 393238) NewStar Media, Inc.

—The Cat Who Blew the Whistle. 1995. 240p. 21.95 o.p. (*0-399-13981-8*, G. P. Putnam's Sons) Penguin Group (USA) Inc.

—The Cat Who Blew the Whistle. l.t. ed. (Paperback Bestsellers Ser.). 270p. 1996. lib. bdg. 18.95 (*0-7838-1253-1*); 1995. lib. bdg. 24.95 (*0-7838-1252-3*) Thorndike Pr.

—The Cat Who Blew the Whistle. 1996. 13.04 (*0-606-12643-0*) Turtleback Bks.

—The Cat Who Came to Breakfast. 1995. (Cat Who Ser.). 272p. (J). pap. 6.99 (*0-515-11564-9*, Jove) Berkley Publishing Group.

—The Cat Who Came to Breakfast. l.t. ed. 296p. 1995. 17.95 o.p. (*0-8161-5935-1*); 1994. lib. bdg. 23.95 o.p. (*0-8161-5934-3*) Gale Group. (Macmillan Reference USA).

—The Cat Who Came to Breakfast. abr. ed. 1993. audio 16.95 o.p. (*1-55800-937-X*, 393255, Dove Audio) NewStar Media, Inc.

—The Cat Who Came to Breakfast. 1994. 240p. 19.95 o.p. (*0-399-13868-4*, G. P. Putnam's Sons) Penguin Group (USA) Inc.

—The Cat Who Came to Breakfast. 1995. 13.04 (*0-606-12644-9*) Turtleback Bks.

—The Cat Who Had 14 Tales. 1988. (Cat Who Ser.). 256p. mass mkt. 6.99 (*0-515-09497-8*, Jove) Berkley Publishing Group.

—The Cat Who Had 14 Tales. unabr. ed. 2000. (Cat Who Ser.). (J). audio 35.00 (*0-7887-0312-9*, 94504E7) Recorded Bks., LLC.

—The Cat Who Had 14 Tales. 1988. 13.04 (*0-606-13247-3*) Turtleback Bks.

—The Cat Who Knew a Cardinal. 1992. (Cat Who Ser.). 288p. mass mkt. 6.99 (*0-515-10786-7*, Jove) Berkley Publishing Group.

—The Cat Who Knew a Cardinal. l.t. ed. 1992. (General Ser.). 316p. 18.95 (*0-8161-5279-9*); lib. bdg. 19.95 o.p. (*0-8161-5278-0*) Gale Group. (Macmillan Reference USA).

—The Cat Who Knew a Cardinal. 1991. (Cat Who Ser.). 240p. 16.95 o.p. (*0-399-13664-9*, G. P. Putnam's Sons) Penguin Group (USA) Inc.

—The Cat Who Knew a Cardinal. 1992. 13.04 (*0-606-12645-7*) Turtleback Bks.

—The Cat Who Knew Shakespeare. 1988. (Cat Who Ser.). 256p. mass mkt. 6.99 (*0-515-09582-6*, Jove) Berkley Publishing Group.

—The Cat Who Knew Shakespeare. l.t. ed. 1989. 284p. 12.95 o.p. (*0-8161-4790-6*, Macmillan Reference USA) Gale Group.

—The Cat Who Knew Shakespeare. unabr. ed. 1991. (Cat Who Ser.). (YA). (gr. 10 up). audio 24.95 (*1-55690-092-9*, 91115E7) Recorded Bks., LLC.

—The Cat Who Knew Shakespeare. 1991. 13.04 (*0-606-13248-1*) Turtleback Bks.

—The Cat Who Lived High. 1991. (Cat Who Ser.). 304p. mass mkt. 6.99 (*0-515-10566-X*, Jove) Berkley Publishing Group.

—The Cat Who Lived High. 1991. 13.04 (*0-606-12646-5*) Turtleback Bks.

—The Cat Who Moved a Mountain. 1992. (Cat Who Ser.). 272p. mass mkt. 6.99 (*0-515-10950-9*, Jove) Berkley Publishing Group.

—The Cat Who Moved a Mountain. l.t. ed. 1993. (General Ser.). 379p. 18.95 o.p. (*0-8161-5551-8*); 20.95 o.p. (*0-8161-5550-X*) Gale Group. (Macmillan Reference USA).

—The Cat Who Moved a Mountain. abr. ed. 1993. 15.95 o.p. (*1-55800-470-X*, 390493) NewStar Media, Inc.

—The Cat Who Moved a Mountain. 1992. (Cat Who Ser.). 240p. 18.95 o.p. (*0-399-13646-0*, G. P. Putnam's Sons) Penguin Group (USA) Inc.

—The Cat Who Moved a Mountain. 1992. 13.04 (*0-606-12647-3*) Turtleback Bks.

—The Cat Who Played Brahms. l.t. ed. 1990. 18.95 o.p. (*0-7927-0335-9*, C0029); pap. 16.95 o.p. (*0-7927-0345-6*) BBC Audiobooks America.

—The Cat Who Played Brahms. 1987. (Cat Who Ser.). 256p. mass mkt. 6.99 (*0-515-09050-6*, Jove) Berkley Publishing Group.

—The Cat Who Played Brahms. unabr. ed. 1992. (Cat Who Ser.). audio 24.95 (*1-55690-651-X*, 92133) Recorded Bks., LLC.

—The Cat Who Played Brahms. 1990. 13.04 (*0-606-13249-X*) Turtleback Bks.

—The Cat Who Played Post Office. 1987. (Cat Who Ser.). 272p. pap. 6.99 (*0-515-09320-3*, Jove) Berkley Publishing Group.

—The Cat Who Played Post Office. l.t. ed. 2000. (Wheeler Large Print Book Ser.). (Illus.). 230p. 27.95 o.p. (*1-56895-840-4*, Wheeler Publishing, Inc.) Gale Group.

—The Cat Who Played Post Office. unabr. ed. 2001. audio 24.95 (*0-7887-5432-7*); 2000. audio 24.95 (*1-55690-689-7*, 92343) Recorded Bks., LLC.

—The Cat Who Played Post Office. 1987. 13.04 (*0-606-13250-3*) Turtleback Bks.

—The Cat Who Robbed a Bank. 2001. (Cat Who Ser.). 304p. mass mkt. 6.99 (*0-515-12994-1*, Jove) Berkley Publishing Group.

—The Cat Who Said Cheese. 1997. (Cat Who Ser.). 272p. reprint ed. pap. 6.99 (*0-515-12027-8*, Jove) Berkley Publishing Group.

—The Cat Who Said Cheese. l.t. ed. 1997. pap. 23.95 o.p. (*0-7838-1632-4*, Macmillan Reference USA) Gale Group.

—The Cat Who Said Cheese. abr. ed. 1996. 17.95 o.p. (*0-7871-0610-0*) NewStar Media, Inc.

—The Cat Who Said Cheese. 1996. (Cat Who Ser.). (*0-399-19300-6*); 256p. 22.95 o.p. (*0-399-14075-1*, G. P. Putnam's Sons) Penguin Group (USA) Inc.

—The Cat Who Said Cheese. l.t. ed. 1996. (Core Collection). 303p. 27.95 (*0-7838-1631-6*) Thorndike Pr.

—The Cat Who Said Cheese. 1997. 13.04 (*0-606-12648-1*) Turtleback Bks.

—The Cat Who Sang for the Birds. 1999. (Cat Who Ser.). (Illus.). 272p. reprint ed. mass mkt. 6.99 (*0-515-12463-X*, Jove) Berkley Publishing Group.

—The Cat Who Sang for the Birds. l.t. ed. 1998. 26.95 o.p. (*1-56895-555-3*, Wheeler Publishing, Inc.) Gale Group.

—The Cat Who Sang for the Birds. 1998. (Cat Who. . . Ser.). 256p. (YA). 22.95 o.p. (*0-399-14333-5*, G. P. Putnam's Sons) Penguin Group (USA) Inc.

—The Cat Who Saw Stars. 2000. (Cat Who Ser.). 304p. reprint ed. mass mkt. 6.99 (*0-515-12739-6*, Jove) Berkley Publishing Group.

—The Cat Who Saw Stars. l.t. ed. 2000. 11.95 (*1-56895-980-X*); 1999. 27.95 (*1-56895-595-2*) Gale Group. (Wheeler Publishing, Inc.).

—The Cat Who Saw Stars. 1999. (Cat Who. . . Ser.). 240p. 22.95 o.p. (*0-399-14431-5*) Penguin Group (USA) Inc.

—The Cat Who Smelled a Rat. 2001. (Cat Who. . . Ser.). (Illus.). 256p. 23.95 o.s.i (*0-399-14665-2*, G. P. Putnam's Sons) Penguin Group (USA) Inc.

—The Cat Who Smelled a Rat. abr. ed. 2001. (Cat Who Ser.). audio 17.95 o.s.i (*0-399-14681-4*, Putnam Berkley Audio) Putnam Publishing Group, The.

—The Cat Who Smelled a Rat. unabr. ed. 2001. audio 29.95 (*0-7887-4977-3*, 964417); audio compact disk 48.00 Recorded Bks., LLC.

—The Cat Who Smelled a Rat. l.t. ed. 293p. 2002. pap. 29.95 (*0-7862-2823-7*); 2001. 32.95 (*0-7862-2822-9*) Thorndike Pr.

—The Cat Who Sniffed Glue. 1989. (Cat Who Ser.). 288p. mass mkt. 6.99 (*0-515-09954-6*, Jove) Berkley Publishing Group.

—The Cat Who Sniffed Glue. l.t. ed. 1990. (Nightingale Ser.). 312p. 13.95 o.p. (*0-8161-4864-3*, Macmillan Reference USA) Gale Group.

—The Cat Who Sniffed Glue. 1988. (Cat Who. . . Ser.). 192p. 14.95 o.p. (*0-399-13381-X*, G. P. Putnam's Sons) Penguin Putnam Bks. for Young Readers.

—The Cat Who Sniffed Glue. unabr. ed. 2000. audio 44.00 (*1-55690-837-7*, 93205E7) Recorded Bks., LLC.

—The Cat Who Tailed a Thief. 1998. (Cat Who. . . Ser.). 272p. mass mkt. 6.99 (*0-515-12240-8*, Jove) Berkley Publishing Group.

—The Cat Who Tailed a Thief. l.t. ed. 1997. 293p. 27.95 o.p. (*0-7838-8046-4*, Macmillan Reference USA) Gale Group.

—The Cat Who Tailed a Thief. abr. ed. 1997. 17.95 o.p. (*0-7871-1352-2*, 394616) NewStar Media, Inc.

—The Cat Who Tailed a Thief. 1997. (Cat Who. . . Ser.). 256p. 22.95 o.p. (*0-399-14210-X*, G. P. Putnam's Sons) Penguin Group (USA) Inc.

—The Cat Who Tailed a Thief. l.t. ed. 1998. (Paperback Bestsellers Ser.). 293p. pap. 27.95 (*0-7838-8047-2*) Thorndike Pr.

—The Cat Who Tailed a Thief. 1998. 13.04 (*0-606-13253-8*) Turtleback Bks.

—The Cat Who Talked to Ghosts. 1990. (Cat Who Ser.). 288p. pap. 6.99 (*0-515-10265-2*, Jove) Berkley Publishing Group.

—The Cat Who Talked to Ghosts. l.t. ed. 1991. (General Ser.). 300p. 21.95 (*0-8161-5081-8*, Macmillan Reference USA) Gale Group.

—The Cat Who Talked to Ghosts. unabr. ed. 1994. (Cat Who Ser.). audio 32.95 (*0-7887-0050-2*, 94249E7); audio 42.00 Recorded Bks., LLC.

—The Cat Who Wasn't There. 1993. (Cat Who Ser.). 288p. mass mkt. 6.99 (*0-515-11127-9*, Jove) Berkley Publishing Group.

—The Cat Who Wasn't There. l.t. ed. 1993. (General Ser.). 367p. lib. bdg. 21.95 (*0-8161-5693-X*, Macmillan Reference USA) Gale Group.

—The Cat Who Wasn't There. abr. ed. 1994. (Super Sound Buy, Dove Ser.). audio 8.99 o.p. (*0-7871-0071-4*, 390494, Dove Audio) NewStar Media, Inc.

—The Cat Who Wasn't There. 1992. 240p. 18.95 o.p. (*0-399-13780-7*, G. P. Putnam's Sons) Penguin Group (USA) Inc.

—The Cat Who Wasn't There; The Cat Who Blew the Whistle. abr. ed. 1999. audio 25.00 (*0-7871-1901-6*, Dove Audio) NewStar Media, Inc.

—The Cat Who Went into the Closet. 1994. (Cat Who Ser.). 288p. mass mkt. 6.99 (*0-515-11332-8*, Jove) Berkley Publishing Group.

—The Cat Who Went into the Closet. 1993. (Cat Who Ser.). 240p. 19.95 o.p. (*0-399-13830-7*, G. P. Putnam's Sons) Penguin Group (USA) Inc.

—The Cat Who Went into the Closet. 1994. 13.04 (*0-606-13256-2*) Turtleback Bks.

—The Cat Who Went Underground. 1989. (Cat Who Ser.). 288p. mass mkt. 6.99 (*0-515-10123-0*, Jove) Berkley Publishing Group.

—The Cat Who Went Underground. l.t. ed. 1990. (General Ser.). 324p. 19.95 o.p. (*0-8161-4941-0*, Macmillan Reference USA) Gale Group.

—The Cat Who Went Underground. 1989. (Cat Who. . . Ser.). 224p. 14.95 o.p. (*0-399-13431-X*, G. P. Putnam's Sons) Penguin Putnam Bks. for Young Readers.

—The Cat Who Went Underground. unabr. ed. 2000. (Cat Who Ser.). audio 32.95 (*1-55690-803-2*, 93112) Recorded Bks., LLC.

—The Cat Who Went Underground. 1989. 13.04 (*0-606-13257-0*) Turtleback Bks.

—The Cat Who Went up the Creek. 2002. 240p. 23.95 o.s.i (*0-399-14675-X*) Penguin Group (USA) Inc.

—The Cat Who Went up the Creek. abr. ed. 2002. audio 17.95 o.s.i (*0-399-14819-1*, Putnam Berkley Audio) Putnam Publishing Group, The.

**PIGEON FORK (KY.: IMAGINARY PLACE)—FICTION**

McCafferty, Taylor. Bed Bugs. Chelius, Jane, ed. 1993. 256p. (Orig.). mass mkt. 5.50 (*0-671-75468-8*, Pocket) Simon & Schuster.

—Hanky Panky. 1995. 256p. mass mkt. 5.50 (*0-671-51049-5*, Pocket) Simon & Schuster.

—Pet Peeves. Chelius, Jane, ed. 1990. 224p. (Orig.). mass mkt. 4.99 (*0-671-72802-4*, Pocket) Simon & Schuster.

—Ruffled Feathers. Chelius, Jane, ed. 1992. 224p. (Orig.). mass mkt. 4.50 (*0-671-72803-2*, Pocket) Simon & Schuster.

—Thin Skins. 1994. 256p. mass mkt. 4.99 (*0-671-79977-0*, Pocket) Simon & Schuster.

**PITTSBURGH (PA.)—FICTION**

Aiello, Robert J. The Deceivers. 2001. 250p. pap. 14.95 (*0-88739-187-7*) Creative Arts Bk. Co.

Bathanti, Joseph. East Liberty. 2001. 208p. 21.95 (*1-889199-08-7*) Banks Channel Bks.

Canin, Ethan. Carry Me Across the Water: A Novel. 2001. E-Book 19.00 (*1-58945-887-7*) Adobe Systems, Inc.

—Carry Me Across the Water: A Novel. 2002. 240p. pap. 12.95 (*0-375-75993-X*); 2001. E-Book 19.00 (*1-58836-007-5*) Random Hse., Inc.

Claire, Edie. Never Preach Past Noon. 2000. (Leigh Koslow Mysteries Ser.). 272p. mass mkt. 5.99 (*0-451-20144-2*, Signet Bks.) NAL.

—Never Preach Past Noon: A Leigh Koslow Mystery. l.t. ed. 2001. (Thorndike Mystery Ser.). 392p. 28.95 (*0-7862-3177-7*) Thorndike Pr.

French, Albert L. I Can't Wait on God: A Novel. 1999. 256p. pap. 19.00 o.s.i (*0-385-48367-8*) Doubleday Publishing.

Goran, Lester. Outlaws of the Purple Cow & Other Stories. 1999. 358p. pap. 35.00 (*0-87338-639-6*) Kent State Univ. Pr.

—She Loved Me Once: And Other Stories. 1997. 306p. (gr. 11-12). 26.00 (*0-87338-576-4*) Kent State Univ. Pr.

—Tales from the Irish Club: A Collection of Short Stories. 1996. 144p. (Orig.). (gr. 9-12). pap. 12.00 (*0-87338-539-X*) Kent State Univ. Pr.

Guy, David. Second Brother. 1986. pap. 6.95 o.p. (*0-452-25887-1*, Plume) Dutton/Plume.

—Second Brother. 1985. 264p. 14.95 o.p. (*0-453-00497-0*) NAL.

Handler, Daniel. Watch Your Mouth. 2000. 232p. 23.95 (*0-312-20940-1*) St. Martin's Pr.

Hogan, James Patrick. Realtime Interrupt. 1995. 336p. pap. 12.95 o.s.i (*0-553-37454-0*) Bantam Bks.

Leavitt, Caroline. Living Other Lives. 1995. 336p. 21.95 o.p. (*0-446-51705-4*) Warner Bks., Inc.

Lipinski, Thomas. Death in the Steel City. 2000. (Carroll Dorsey Mystery Ser.: Vol. 4). 224p. mass mkt. 5.99 (*0-380-79432-2*, Avon Bks.) Morrow/Avon.

—The Fall-Down Artist. 1994. (Carroll Dorsey Mystery Ser.). 304p. 20.95 o.p. (*0-312-10461-8*, Saint Martin's Minotaur) St. Martin's Pr.

—Picture of Her Tombstone. 1998. (Carroll Dorsey Mystery Ser.: 2). mass mkt. 5.99 (*0-380-73024-3*, Avon Bks.) Morrow/Avon.

—Picture of Her Tombstone. 1996. 240p. 21.95 (*0-312-14390-7*, Saint Martin's Minotaur) St. Martin's Pr.

—Steel City Confessions. 1999. (Carroll Dorsey Mystery Ser.: Vol. 3). 224p. mass mkt. 5.99 (*0-380-79431-4*, Avon Bks.) Morrow/Avon.

Lissfelt, J. Fred. The Dutchman Died & Other Tales of Pittsburgh's Southside. 1992. (Illus.). 152p. (C). (gr. 9-12). pap. 10.95 o.p. (*0-8229-5483-4*); text 29.95 o.p. (*0-8229-3726-3*) Univ. of Pittsburgh Pr.

Manfredi, Renee. Where Love Leaves Us. 1994. (Iowa Short Fiction Award Ser.). 158p. 11.50 (*0-87745-444-2*); E-Book 20.00 (*1-58729-138-X*) Univ. of Iowa Pr.

Masters, Hilary. Home Is the Exile. 1996. 288p. 28.00 (*1-877946-73-7*) Permanent Pr., The.

McGrath, Kristina. House Work: A Novel. 1994. 192p. 19.95 (*1-882593-07-3*) Bridge Works Publishing Co., Inc.

Michaels, Fern. Serendipity. 9999. mass mkt. o.p. (*0-345-37328-6*); 1997. 384p. mass mkt. 6.99 (*0-449-14982-X*, Fawcett) Ballantine Bks.

Patterson, Richard North. Dark Lady. 448p. 2003. pap. 12.95 (*0-345-46748-5*); 2000. mass mkt. 7.99 (*0-345-40478-5*, Ballantine Bks.) Ballantine Bks.

—Dark Lady. 1999. audio 44.95 (*0-7366-4674-4*, 5056) Books on Tape, Inc.

—Dark Lady. l.t. ed. 1999. pap. 25.95 o.p. (*0-7838-8687-X*, Macmillan Reference USA) Gale Group.

—Dark Lady, Set. abr. ed. 1999. audio 25.95. audio 39.95 Highsmith Inc.

—Dark Lady. unabr. ed. 1999. audio 39.95 audio 39.95 (*0-375-40831-2*);Set. audio compact disk 29.95 (*0-375-40830-4*) Random Hse. Audio Publishing Group. (RH Audio).

—Dark Lady. l.t. ed. 2000. 560p. pap. 14.95 (*0-375-72789-2*); 1999. 608p. 25.95 (*0-375-40844-4*) Random Hse. Large Print.

Scottoline, Lisa. Final Appeal. 1994. 352p. mass mkt. 7.99 (*0-06-104294-3*, HarperTorch) Morrow/Avon.

Silvis, Randall. Disquiet Heart. E-Book 24.95 (*0-312-70623-5*); 2002. 336p. 24.95 (*0-312-26248-5*, Saint Martin's Minotaur) St. Martin's Pr.

Smith, Helene. The Parade Vol. I: A Novel History of Pittsburgh. 2000. 40p. ring bd. 14.95 (*0-945437-47-1*) MacDonald Sward Publishing Co.

Smith, Martin J. Time Release. 1997. 352p. mass mkt. 5.99 o.s.i (*0-515-12028-6*, Jove) Berkley Publishing Group.

Stahl, Jerry. Plainclothes Naked. 2002. 336p. pap. 13.95 (*0-06-093353-4*, Perennial) HarperTrade.

—Plainclothes Naked. 2001. 336p. 25.00 (*0-06-018556-2*, Morrow, William & Co.) Morrow/Avon.

Tucker, James. Tragic Wand. 2000. 416p. mass mkt. 6.99 o.s.i (*0-451-40946-9*, Onyx) NAL.

Walton, David. Ride. 2002. 200p. pap. 15.95 (*0-88748-377-1*) Carnegie-Mellon Univ. Pr.

—Ride. 2004. 192p. pap. 10.00 (*0-14-200407-3*) Penguin Group (USA) Inc.

Wideman, John Edgar. All Stories Are True. 1993. pap. 12.00 o.s.i (*0-679-73752-9*, Vintage) Knopf Publishing Group.

—Damballah. 1998. (Illus.). 205p. pap. 14.00 (*0-395-89797-1*) Houghton Mifflin Co.

—Damballah. 1988. pap. 11.00 o.s.i (*0-679-72028-6*, Vintage) Knopf Publishing Group.

—Damballah. 1988. 6.95 (*0-07-541813-4*) McGraw-Hill Cos., The.

—Damballah. 1981. pap. 2.95 o.p. (*0-380-78519-6*, 78519-6, Avon Bks.) Morrow/Avon.

—Hiding Place. 1998. 158p. pap. 12.00 (*0-395-89798-X*, Mariner Bks.) Houghton Mifflin Co. Trade & Reference Div.

—Hiding Place. 1988. pap. 10.00 o.s.i (*0-679-72027-8*, Vintage) Knopf Publishing Group.

—Hiding Place. 1981. pap. 2.95 o.p. (*0-380-78501-3*, 78501-3, Avon Bks.) Morrow/Avon.

—The Homewood Books. 1992. 536p. text 24.95 (*0-8229-3831-6*) Univ. of Pittsburgh Pr.

—Sent for You Yesterday. 1998. 208p. pap. 14.00 (*0-395-87729-6*) Houghton Mifflin Co.

—Sent for You Yesterday. 1988. pap. 11.00 o.s.i (*0-679-72029-4*, Vintage) Knopf Publishing Group.

—Sent for You Yesterday. 1983. 208p. pap. 3.50 o.p. (*0-380-82644-5*, 82644-5, Avon Bks.) Morrow/Avon.

**POICTESME (IMAGINARY PLACE)—FICTION**

Cabell, James Branch. Beyond Life. (Collected Works of James Branch Cabell). 358p. reprint ed. 2001. (Illus.). pap. text 28.00 (*0-7426-5550-4*); 1998. lib. bdg. 98.00 (*1-58201-550-3*) Classic Bks.

—The Certain Hour. 1998. (Collected Works of James Branch Cabell). 253p. reprint ed. lib. bdg. 88.00 (*1-58201-551-1*) Classic Bks.

—Chivalry. 1977. (Short Story Index Reprint Ser.). 17.95 (*0-8369-3718-X*) Ayer Co. Pubs., Inc.

—Chivalry. (Collected Works of James Branch Cabell). reprint ed. 2001. (Illus.). 223p. pap. text 28.00 (*0-7426-5552-0*); 1999. (*1-58201-552-X*) Classic Bks.

—Chivalry. 2001. 296p. per. 17.50 (*1-58715-352-1*) Wildside Pr.

—Cords of Vanity. 1998. (Collected Works of James Branch Cabell). 341p. reprint ed. lib. bdg. 98.00 (*1-58201-553-8*) Classic Bks.

—The Cream of the Jest. 1979. mass mkt. 2.25 o.s.i (*0-345-28358-9*) Ballantine Bks.

—The Cream of the Jest. (Collected Works of James Branch Cabell). 280p. reprint ed. 2001. (Illus.). pap. text 28.00 (*0-7426-5554-7*); 1998. lib. bdg. 90.00 (*1-58201-554-6*) Classic Bks.

—The Cream of the Jest. Flora, Joseph M., ed. 1973. pap. 24.95 (*0-8084-0396-6*) Rowman & Littlefield Pubs., Inc.

—The Eagle's Shadow. E-Book 3.95 (*0-594-03608-9*) 1873 Pr.

—The Eagle's Shadow. (Collected Works of James Branch Cabell). 256p. reprint ed. 2001. (Illus.). pap. text 28.00 (*0-7426-5555-5*); 1998. lib. bdg. 88.00 (*1-58201-555-4*) Classic Bks.

—Figures of Earth. 1979. mass mkt. 2.25 o.s.i (*0-345-28170-5*) Ballantine Bks.

—Figures of Earth. (Collected Works of James Branch Cabell). 356p. reprint ed. 2001. (Illus.). pap. text 28.00 (*0-7426-5556-3*); 1998. lib. bdg. 99.00 (*1-58201-556-2*) Classic Bks.

—Figures of Earth. 1923. (Wildside Fantasy Ser.). 356p. pap. 17.50 (*1-58715-221-5*) Wildside Pr.

—From the Hidden Way. (Collected Works of James Branch Cabell). 187p. 1998. 88.00 (*1-58201-557-0*); 2001. (Illus.). reprint ed. pap. text 28.00 (*0-7426-5557-1*) Classic Bks.

—The High Place. 24.95 (*0-88411-795-2*) Amereon, Ltd.

—The High Place. 1979. mass mkt. 2.25 o.s.i (*0-345-28284-1*) Ballantine Bks.

—The High Place. 1998. (Collected Works of James Branch Cabell). 234p. reprint ed. lib. bdg. 88.00 (*1-58201-558-9*) Classic Bks.

—The High Place. 1978. (Illus.). pap. 5.95 o.p. (*0-486-23670-6*) Dover Pubns., Inc.

—Jewel Merchants. 1998. (Collected Works of James Branch Cabell). 63p. reprint ed. lib. bdg. 88.00 (*1-58201-559-7*) Classic Bks.

—Jurgen. E-Book 3.95 (*0-594-06603-4*) 1873 Pr.

—Jurgen. 1990. reprint ed. lib. bdg. 21.95 (*0-89966-708-2*) Buccaneer Bks., Inc.

—Jurgen. (Collected Works of James Branch Cabell). 325p. reprint ed. 2001. (Illus.). pap. text 28.00 (*0-7426-5561-X*); 1998. lib. bdg. 98.00 (*1-58201-561-9*) Classic Bks.

—Jurgen. 1990. (Illus.). 25.50 (*0-8446-5561-9*) Smith, Peter Pub., Inc.

—Jurgen: A Comedy of Justice. 287p. reprint ed. lib. bdg. 25.95 (*0-88411-794-4*) Amereon, Ltd.

—Jurgen: A Comedy of Justice. 1977. (Illus.). 346p. reprint ed. pap. 7.95 (*0-486-23507-6*) Dover Pubns., Inc.

—The Line of Love. 1998. (Collected Works of James Branch Cabell). 368p. reprint ed. lib. bdg. 98.00 (*1-58201-562-7*) Classic Bks.

—Line of Love, Dizain des Mariages. 1977. (Select Bibliographies Reprint Ser.). 28.95 (*0-8369-5106-9*) Ayer Co. Pubs., Inc.

—Rivet in Grandfather's Neck. (Collected Works of James Branch Cabell). 368p. reprint ed. 2001. (Illus.). pap. 28.00 (*0-7426-5563-6*); 1998. lib. bdg. 98.00 (*1-58201-563-5*) Classic Bks.

—The Rivet in Grandfather's Neck, a Comedy of Limitations. reprint ed. 39.00 o.p. (*0-403-00892-1*) Scholarly Pr., Inc.

—The Silver Stallion. 1979. mass mkt. 2.25 o.s.i (*0-345-28072-5*) Ballantine Bks.

—Something about Eve. 1979. mass mkt. 2.25 o.s.i (*0-345-28352-X*) Ballantine Bks.

—Soul of Melicent. (Collected Works of James Branch Cabell). 216p. reprint ed. 2001. (Illus.). pap. 28.00 (*0-7426-5564-4*); 1998. lib. bdg. 88.00 (*1-58201-564-3*) Classic Bks.

—Straws & Prayer Books. (Collected Works of James Branch Cabell). reprint ed. 2001. 302p. pap. 28.00 (*0-7426-5565-2*); 1999. 98.00 (*1-58201-565-1*) Classic Bks.

Cable, George W. Bylow Hill. 2000. 252p. E-Book 3.95 (*0-594-03618-6*) 1873 Pr.

—Bylow Hill. (Illus.). 228p. pap. 15.95 (*1-56554-972-4*, Firebird Pr.) Pelican Publishing Co., Inc.

**POLAND—FICTION**

Agnon, Shmuel Yosef. A Simple Story. Halkin, Hillel, tr. from HEB. 1999. (Library of Modern Jewish Literature). 252p. pap. text 17.95 (*0-8156-0618-4*) Syracuse Univ. Pr.

Anthony, Evelyn. Valentina. l.t. ed. 1993. pap. 18.95 o.p. (*0-7927-1586-1*); 20.95 o.p. (*0-7927-1587-X*) BBC Audiobooks America.

—Valentina. 1979. mass mkt. 2.25 o.p. (*0-451-08598-1*, E8598, Signet Bks.) NAL.

Basu, Jay. The Stars Can Wait: A Novel. 2002. 192p. 21.00 o.s.i (*0-8050-6887-2*) Holt, Henry & Co.

—The Stars Can Wait: A Novel. 2003. 192p. pap. 12.00 (*0-312-42115-X*) Picador.

Beckman, John. The Winter Zoo: A Novel. 2002. 368p. 25.00 (*0-8050-6904-6*) Holt, Henry & Co.

Braun, Kazimierz. Day of Witness. unabr. ed. 2002. Orig. Title: Dzien Swiadectwa. 403p. (*0-9716771-0-7*) Omnibus Printers Ltd.

Brett, Lily. Too Many Men. 2002. 544p. pap. 14.95 (*0-06-008444-8*, Perennial) HarperTrade.

—Too Many Men. 2001. 544p. 26.00 (*0-688-17755-7*, Morrow, William & Co.) Morrow/Avon.

Bukiet, Melvin Jules. Stories of an Imaginary Childhood. 2002. (Library of American Fiction). 201p. pap. 17.95 (*0-299-18074-3*) Univ. of Wisconsin Pr.

De Graaf, Anne. Bread upon the Waters. 1995. (Hidden Harvest Ser.: Bk. 1). 352p. pap. 10.99 o.p. (*1-55661-618-X*) Bethany Hse. Pubs.

—Bread upon the Waters. 1999. 17.04 (*0-606-18971-8*) Turtleback Bks.

—Out of the Red Shadow. 1999. (Hidden Harvest Ser.: Vol. 3). 352p. pap. 10.99 o.p. (*1-55661-620-1*) Bethany Hse. Pubs.

—Out of the Red Shadow. 1999. 17.04 (*0-606-18972-6*) Turtleback Bks.

Egleton, Clive. A Double Deception. 1992. 288p. 18.95 o.p. (*0-312-07736-X*, Saint Martin's Minotaur) St. Martin's Pr.

—A Double Deception. l.t. ed. 1994. (Charnwood Large Print Ser.). 496p. 29.99 o.p. (*0-7089-8769-9*, Ulverscroft) Thorpe, F. A. Pubs. GBR. *Dist:* Ulverscroft Large Print Bks., Ltd., Ulverscroft Large Print Canada, Ltd.

Elberg, Yehuda, tr. from YID. Ship of the Hunted. 1997. (Library of Modern Jewish Literature). 400p. reprint ed. 28.95 (*0-8156-0449-1*) Syracuse Univ. Pr.

Fox, John. The Thunderbird Covenant. Dageforde, Linda J., ed. 1999. 448p. pap. 19.95 (*1-886225-46-X*, 5000) Dageforde Publishing, Inc.

Furst, Alan. The Polish Officer: A Novel. 2000. 352p. pap. 13.00 (*0-00-651129-5*) HarperCollins Pubs. Ltd. GBR. *Dist:* Trafalgar Square.

—The Polish Officer: A Novel. 2001. 304p. pap. 12.95 (*0-375-75827-5*) Random House Adult Trade Publishing Group.

Goldstein, Rebecca. Mazel. 1996. 368p. pap. 12.95 o.s.i (*0-14-023905-7*, Penguin Bks.) Penguin Group (USA) Inc.

—Mazel. 2002. (Library of American Fiction). 368p. pap. 19.95 (*0-299-18124-3*) Univ. of Wisconsin Pr.

—Mazel. 1995. 368p. 23.95 o.s.i (*0-670-85648-7*, Viking) Viking Penguin.

Grass, Gunter. The Call of the Toad. Manheim, Ralph, tr. from GER. (Harvest Book Ser.).Tr. of Unkenrufe. 1993. 256p. pap. 14.00 (*0-15-615340-8*, Harvest Bks.); 1992. (Illus.). 248p. (C). 19.95 o.s.i (*0-15-125743-4*) Harcourt Trade Pubs.

—The Call of the Toad. 1997. Tr. of Unkenrufe. pap. o.s.i (*0-7493-9878-7*) Random Hse. of Canada, Ltd.

Grynberg, Henryk. The Jewish War & the Victory. Lourie, Richard & Wieniewska, Celina, trs. from POL. 2001. (Jewish Lives Ser.). 152p. text 49.95 (*0-8101-1901-3*) Northwestern Univ. Pr.

—The Jewish War & the Victory. Wieniewska, Celina & Lourie, Richard, trs. from POL. 2001. (Jewish Lives Ser.). 152p. reprint ed. pap. 15.95 (*0-8101-1785-1*) Northwestern Univ. Pr.

Helmreich, Helaine. The Chimney Tree. 2003. 506p. 19.95 (*1-59264-031-1*) Toby Pr.

—The Chimney Tree. 2000. 296p. 24.95 (*0-87081-562-8*) Univ. Pr. of Colorado.

Hirsch, Harvey. Grandma's Lost Gift: A Christmas Story. 1994. Orig. Title: The Creche of Krakow. (Illus.). 56p. pap. 7.95 (*0-929613-00-7*, 100GLG) Cobblestone Pr.

Hirsch, Harvey & Hirsch, Audrey. Grandma's Lost Gift: A Christmas Story. rev. ed. 1994. Orig. Title: The Creche of Krakow. (Illus.). 46p. pap. 6.95 o.p. (*1-879094-14-2*) Momentum Bks., LLC.

Huelle, Pawel. Moving House & Other Stories. Lloyd-Jones, Antonia, tr. 1995. 248p. 18.95 (*0-15-162731-2*) Harcourt Trade Pubs.

Kubert, Joe. April 19, 1943: A Story of the Warsaw Ghetto Uprising. 2003. 128p. 24.95 (*0-7434-7516-X*) ibooks, Inc.

Libera, Antoni. Madame. Kolakowska, Agniewska, tr. from POL. 2000. vi, 439p. 26.00 o.p. (*0-374-20006-8*) Farrar, Straus & Giroux.

MacMillan, Ian. Village of a Million Spirits: A Novel of the Treblinka Uprising. 1999. 257p. 24.00 o.p. (*1-883642-84-1*) Steerforth Pr.

—Village of a Million Spirits: A Novel of the Treblinka Uprising. 2000. 272p. 12.95 o.s.i (*0-14-029033-8*) Viking Penguin.

Masterson, Graham. The Chosen Child. 2000. 320p. 23.95 o.p. (*0-312-87382-4*, Tor Bks.) Doherty, Tom Assocs., LLC.

McDivitt, Carl B. Flowers for Kasia. 2001. 256p. pap. 21.99 (*0-7388-1827-5*); text 31.99 (*0-7388-1826-7*) Xlibris Corp.

Michener, James A. Poland. 1984. 640p. mass mkt. 7.99 (*0-449-20587-8*, Fawcett) Ballantine Bks.

—Poland. l.t. ed. 1984. pap. 10.95 o.p. (*0-8161-3728-5*); lib. bdg. 18.95 o.p. (*0-8161-3689-0*) Gale Group. (Macmillan Reference USA).

Nattel, Lilian. The River Midnight: A Novel. 1999. 416p. pap. 14.00 (*0-684-85304-3*); (Illus.). 25.00 o.s.i (*0-684-85303-5*) Simon & Schuster. (Scribner).

Plain, Belva. Evergreen. 1991. 598p. reprint ed. lib. bdg. 38.95 (*0-89966-813-5*) Buccaneer Bks., Inc.

—Evergreen. 1980. 704p. mass mkt. 7.99 (*0-440-13278-9*); 1979. 19.95 o.s.i (*0-385-28299-0*, Delacorte Pr.) Dell Publishing.

—Evergreen. 1910. mass mkt. o.s.i (*0-385-31997-5*) Doubleday Publishing.

—Evergreen. 1980. (General Ser.). lib. bdg. 23.95 o.p. (*0-8161-3114-7*, Macmillan Reference USA) Gale Group.

Powers, Charles T. In the Memory of the Forest. 1997. 384p. 22.50 (*0-684-83030-2*, Scribner) Simon & Schuster.

—In the Memory of the Forest. 1998. 384p. 14.00 (*0-14-027281-X*) Viking Penguin.

Rosenbaum, Thane. Second Hand Smoke. 320p. 2000. pap. 13.95 (*0-312-25418-0*, Saint Martin's Griffin); 1999. 24.95 (*0-312-19954-6*) St. Martin's Pr.

Sachs, Herb. The Fifth Notebook. 2002. 342p. text 32.99 (*0-7388-6420-X*); E-Book 8.00 (*0-7388-6422-6*) Xlibris Corp.

Sasson, Jean. Ester's Child. 448p. 2003. pap. 12.95 (*0-9676737-7-1*); 2nd ed. 2001. (Illus.). 24.95 o.p. (*0-9676737-3-9*) Windsor-Brooke Bks.

Schulz, Bruno. The Complete Fiction of Bruno Schulz: The Street of Crocodiles & Sanatorium Under the Sign of the Hourglass. 1989. 320p. 22.95 (*0-8027-1091-3*) Walker & Co.

Sienkiewicz, Henryk. On the Field of Glory. Lipinski, Miroslav, tr. from POL. 1999. vi, 257p. 24.95 (*0-7818-0762-X*) Hippocrene Bks., Inc.

—On the Field of Glory. 2002. per. 29.95 (*1-932080-17-1*) Ross & Perry, Inc.

Skibell, Joseph. A Blessing on the Moon. 1997. 276p. tchr. ed. 21.95 (*1-56512-179-1*) Algonquin Bks. of Chapel Hill.

—A Blessing on the Moon. 1999. 288p. reprint ed. pap. 12.00 o.s.i (*0-425-16713-5*) Berkley Publishing Group.

Spiegel, Isaiah. Ghetto Kingdom: Tales of the Lodz Ghetto. Hirsch, David H. & Hirsch, Roslyn, trs. from YID. 1998. (Jewish Lives Ser.). 184p. 44.00 o.p. (*0-8101-1624-3*) Northwestern Univ. Pr.

Stark, Marisa K. Bring Us the Old People: A Novel. 1998. 208p. 22.95 (*1-56689-074-8*) Coffee Hse. Pr.

Stasiuk, Andrzej. White Raven. 2001. 256p. pap. 18.00 (*1-85242-667-5*) Serpent's Tail Ltd. GBR. *Dist:* Consortium Bk. Sales & Distribution.

Szczypiorski, Andrzej. The Beautiful Mrs. Seidenman. Glowczewska, Klara, tr. from POL. 208p. 1997. pap. 12.00 (*0-8021-3502-1*, Grove Pr.); 1990. 16.95 o.p. (*0-8021-1140-8*) Grove/Atlantic, Inc.

—The Beautiful Mrs. Seidenman. 1991. (Vintage International Ser.). 208p. pap. 9.95 o.s.i (*0-679-73214-4*, Vintage) Knopf Publishing Group.

—The Beautiful Mrs. Seidenman. 1993. 3.49 o.p. (*0-517-11006-7*) Random Hse. Value Publishing.

Szewc, Piotr. Annihilation. Hryniewicz-Yarbrough, Ewa, tr. from POL. (Coleman Dowell Ser.). 107p. 1993. 16.95 (*1-56478-034-1*); 1999. reprint ed. pap. 10.95 (*1-56478-205-0*) Dalkey Archive Pr.

Uris, Leon. Mila 18. 1983. 576p. mass mkt. 7.99 (*0-553-24160-5*) Bantam Bks.

Vogler, Peter Z. The Broken Cross. 1997. 220p. 24.95 (*0-9656650-3-8*) Danville Creek Publishing.

Wallace, Christopher. The Pied Piper's Poison. 2000. 298p. 25.95 (*1-58567-013-8*) Overlook Pr., The.

Wiechecki, Stefan. Bitwa W Tramwaju: Cayli Opowiadania Warszawski. 2001. (POL.). 276p. (*83-911378-4-8*) Etiuda, Wydawnictwo, Atanaziewicz, Igor.

Wojdowski, Bogdan. Bread for the Departed. Levine, Madeline G., tr. from ENG. 1997. (Jewish Lives Ser.). 304p. 59.95 (*0-8101-1455-0*); pap. 24.00 (*0-8101-1456-9*) Northwestern Univ. Pr.

Zeromski, Stefan. The Faithful River. Johnston, Bill, tr. from POL. 1999. (European Classics Ser.). 216p. pap. 19.00 (*0-8101-1596-4*) Northwestern Univ. Pr.

## POLYNESIA—FICTION

Finau, Louise L. Toki. Weine, Ruth, ed. 1999. (Illus.). xx, 450p. 29.95 (*0-9667463-0-9*); pap. 19.95 (*0-9667463-1-7*) Simmons Publishing Co.

Garnett, Griffin T. Taboo Avenged. 1997. 320p. pap. 14.95 (*1-883911-16-8*) Brandylane Pubs., Inc.

Melville, Herman. Mardi: And a Voyage Thither. 1983. (FRE.). pap. 20.95 (*0-7859-4190-8*) French & European Pubns., Inc.

—Mardi: And a Voyage Thither. Wright, Nathalia, ed. annot. ed. 1990. (Complete Works of Herman Melville Ser.). 29.95 (*0-87532-015-5*) Hendricks Hse., Inc.

—Mardi: And a Voyage Thither. 1998. (Northwestern-Newberry Edition of the Writings of Herman Melville). 704p. pap. 22.00 (*0-8101-1690-1*) Northwestern Univ. Pr.

—Mardi: And a Voyage Thither. Hayford, Harrison et al, eds. 1970. (Northwestern-Newberry Edition of the Writings of Herman Melville: Vol. 3). 96.00 (*0-8101-0015-0*); pap. 38.00 (*0-8101-0014-2*) Northwestern Univ. Pr.

—Mardi: And a Voyage Thither, 2 vols., Set. 1992. (BCL1-PS American Literature Ser.). reprint ed. lib. bdg. 150.00 (*0-7812-6795-1*) Reprint Services Corp.

—Mardi: And a Voyage Thither. Hillway, Tyrus, ed. 1973. (Masterworks of Literature Ser.). 128p. pap. 22.95 (*0-8084-0017-7*); 544p. pap. 26.95 (*0-8084-0016-9*) Rowman & Littlefield Pubs., Inc.

—Omoo. E-Book 3.95 (*0-594-05648-9*) 1873 Pr.

—Omoo. 1976. 23.95 (*0-8488-1098-8*) Amereon, Ltd.

—Omoo. 2000. per. 12.50 (*1-58396-533-5*) Blue Unicorn Editions.

—Omoo. 1924. 375p. (YA). reprint ed. pap. text 28.00 (*1-4047-6796-7*) Classic Textbooks.

—Omoo. 2000. 320p. text 8.95 (*0-486-40873-6*) Dover Pubns., Inc.

—Omoo. Hayford, Harrison & Blair, Walter, eds. 1969. (Complete Works of Herman Melville Ser.). 494p. reprint ed. 19.00 o.p. (*0-87532-013-9*) Hendricks Hse., Inc.

—Omoo. 2002. 316p. 96.99 (*1-4043-2262-0*); per. 91.99 (*1-4043-2263-9*) IndyPublish.com.

—Omoo. l.t. ed. 2003. (Large Print Ser.). lib. bdg. 26.00 (*1-58287-697-5*) North Bks.

—Omoo. 1999. 336p. pap. 16.95 (*0-8101-1765-7*) Northwestern Univ. Pr.

—Omoo. Hayford, Harrison et al, eds. 1968. (Northwestern-Newberry Edition of the Writings of Herman Melville: Vol. 2). 380p. 75.00 o.s.i (*0-8101-0162-9*); pap. 27.00 (*0-8101-0160-2*) Northwestern Univ. Pr.

—Omoo. 1992. (BCL1-PS American Literature Ser.). 299p. reprint ed. lib. bdg. 79.00 (*0-7812-6796-X*) Reprint Services Corp.

—Omoo. 1985. (Pacific Basin Ser.). 220p. pap. 14.95 (*0-7103-0133-2*) Routledge.

—Typee: A Peep at Polynesian Life. 1976. 26.95 (*0-8488-0581-X*) Amereon, Ltd.

—Typee: A Peep at Polynesian Life. 1846. 425p. (YA). reprint ed. pap. text 28.00 (*1-4047-3991-2*) Classic Textbooks.

—Typee: A Peep at Polynesian Life. 2001. (Illus.). 336p. pap. 12.95 (*0-375-75745-7*, Modern Library) Random House Adult Trade Publishing Group.

—Typee: A Peep at Polynesian Life. 1999. (Notable American Authors Ser.). reprint ed. lib. bdg. 125.00 (*0-7812-3991-5*) Reprint Services Corp.

—Typee: A Peep at Polynesian Life. l.t. ed. 2003. 552p. 29.95 (*0-7862-6105-6*, Large Print Pr.) Thorndike Pr.

Melville, Herman, et al. Omoo. 1968. E-Book 64.95 (*0-585-37995-5*) netLibrary, Inc.

—Typee: A Peep at Polynesian Life. 1968. E-Book 64.95 (*0-585-38172-0*) netLibrary, Inc.

Wright, Ronald. Henderson's Spear: A Novel. 2002. 368p. 25.00 (*0-8050-6996-8*) Holt, Henry & Co.

## POMONA (CALIF.)—FICTION

Nunn, Kem. The Dogs of Winter. 1998. 368p. pap. 14.00 o.s.i (*0-671-79334-9*); 1997. 400p. 23.50 (*0-684-82647-X*) Simon & Schuster. (Scribner).

## POOR RELATION HOTEL (LONDON, ENGLAND: IMAGINARY PLACE)—FICTION

Chesney, Marion. Back in Society. l.t. ed. 1995. (G. K. Hall Nightingale Ser.: Vol. 6). pap. 18.95 o.p. (*0-7838-1454-2*, Macmillan Reference USA) Gale Group.

—Back in Society. (Poor Relation Ser.: Vol. 6). 1995. mass mkt. 4.50 (*0-312-95338-0*, St. Martin's Paperbacks); 1994. 160p. 12.99 o.p. (*0-312-10932-6*) St. Martin's Pr.

—Colonel Sandhurst to the Rescue. l.t. ed. 1995. (G. K. Hall Nightingale Ser.: Vol. 5). 208p. pap. 18.95 o.p. (*0-8161-7415-6*, Macmillan Reference USA) Gale Group.

—Colonel Sandhurst to the Rescue. (Poor Relation Ser.: Vol. 5). 1995. 152p. mass mkt. 4.50 (*0-312-95337-2*, St. Martin's Paperbacks); 1994. 160p. 17.95 o.p. (*0-312-10444-8*) St. Martin's Pr.

—Lady Fortescue Steps Out. (Poor Relation Ser.: Vol. 1). 1993. 152p. mass mkt. 3.99 (*0-312-95129-9*, St. Martin's Paperbacks); 1992. 160p. 17.95 o.p. (*0-312-08231-2*) St. Martin's Pr.

—Miss Tonks Takes a Risk. 1994. (Poor Relation Ser.: Vol. 2). 152p. mass mkt. 3.99 (*0-312-95219-8*, St. Martin's Paperbacks) St. Martin's Pr.

—Miss Tonks Turns to Crime. l.t. ed. 1994. (Poor Relation Ser.: Vol. 2). 251p. lib. bdg. 17.95 (*0-8161-5898-3*, Macmillan Reference USA) Gale Group.

—Miss Tonks Turns to Crime. 1993. (Poor Relation Ser.: Vol. 2). 16.95 o.p. (*0-312-08846-9*) St. Martin's Pr.

—Mrs. Budley Falls from Grace. l.t. ed. 1994. (Poor Relation Ser.: Vol. 3). 274p. lib. bdg. 15.95 o.p. (*0-8161-5980-7*, Macmillan Reference USA) Gale Group.

—Mrs. Budley Falls from Grace. (Poor Relation Ser.: Vol. 3). 160p. 1994. mass mkt. 3.99 (*0-312-95275-9*, St. Martin's Paperbacks); 1993. 16.95 o.p. (*0-312-09342-X*) St. Martin's Pr.

## PORT SILVA (CALIF.: IMAGINARY PLACE)—FICTION

Lapierre, Janet. Baby Mine: A Port Silva Mystery. 1999. (Port Silva Mysteries Ser.). (Illus.). 255p. pap. 12.95 (*1-880284-32-4*) Daniel, John & Co., Pubs.

—Children's Games. 1989. 16.95 o.s.i (*0-684-19064-8*, Macmillan Reference USA) Gale Group.

—Children's Games. 1990. mass mkt. (*0-373-26052-0*, Harlequin Bks.) Harlequin Enterprises, Ltd.

—Children's Games. 1990. pap. o.s.i (*1-85381-112-2*) Virago Pr., Ltd. GBR. *Dist:* Little Brown & Co.

—The Cruel Mother. 1991. reprint ed. per. (*0-373-26078-4*, Harlequin Bks.) Harlequin Enterprises, Ltd.

—The Cruel Mother: A Meg Halloran Mystery. 1990. 224p. 18.95 o.s.i (*0-684-19170-9*, Macmillan Reference USA) Gale Group.

—Grandmother's House. 1991. 288p. 19.95 o.s.i (*0-684-19382-5*, Macmillan Reference USA) Gale Group.

—Grandmother's House. 1993. (Mystery Ser.). per. (*0-373-26120-9*, 1-26120-5, Harlequin Bks.) Harlequin Enterprises, Ltd.

—The Unquiet Grave. 1987. 240p. 15.95 o.p. (*0-312-01102-4*, Saint Martin's Minotaur) St. Martin's Pr.

## PORT WILLIAM (KY.: IMAGINARY PLACE)—FICTION

Berry, Wendell. Jayber Crow: The Life Story of Jayber Crow, Barber, of the Port William Membership, as Written by Himself. 384p. 2001. pap. text 15.00 (*1-58243-160-4*); 2000. text 25.00 o.p. (*1-58243-029-2*) Basic Bks. (Counterpoint Pr.).

—A Place on Earth. 1982. pap. 12.95 o.p. (*0-86547-083-9*); 352p. reprint ed. pap. 13.00 o.p. (*0-86547-044-8*) Farrar, Straus & Giroux. (North Point Pr.).

—Place on Earth. rev. ed. 2001. 336p. pap. text 15.00 (*1-58243-124-8*, Counterpoint Pr.) Basic Bks.

—Remembering. 1990. 124p. pap. 11.00 o.p. (*0-86547-331-5*); 1988. 144p. 14.95 o.p. (*0-86547-330-7*) Farrar, Straus & Giroux. (North Point Pr.).

—Two More Stories of the Port William Membership. 1997. (Chapbook Ser.: Vol. 4). 64p. 15.00 o.p. (*0-917788-64-8*); 1997. (Chapbook Ser.: Vol. 4). 64p. 35.00 o.p. (*0-917788-67-2*); 1999. 62p. reprint ed. pap. 10.50 (*0-917788-71-0*) Gnomon Pr.

—The Wild Birds: Six Stories of the Port William Membership. 160p. 1989. pap. 11.00 o.p. (*0-86547-217-3*); 1986. 13.95 o.p. (*0-86547-216-5*) Farrar, Straus & Giroux. (North Point Pr.).

—A World Lost. 160p. 1997. pap. text 12.50 (*1-887178-54-6*); 1996. text 20.00 o.p. (*1-887178-22-8*) Basic Bks. (Counterpoint Pr.).

Berry, Wendell, ed. Jayber Crow: The Life Story of Jayber Crow, Barber, of the Port William Membership, as Written by Himself. l.t. ed. 2001. (Thorndike Press Large Print Americana Ser.). 687p. 28.95 o.p. (*0-7862-3222-6*) Thorndike Pr.

## PORTLAND (OR.)—FICTION

Anderson, Kent. Night Dogs. 1999. 544p. reprint ed. mass mkt. 6.99 (*0-553-57877-4*) Bantam Bks.

—Night Dogs. 1996. (Illus.). 544p. 35.00 o.p. (*0-939767-27-9*); 150.00 o.p. (*0-939767-28-7*) McMillan, Dennis Pubns.

Beck, K. K. Death in a Deck Chair. 1987. 176p. mass mkt. 4.99 o.s.i (*0-8041-0118-3*, Ivy Bks.) Ballantine Bks.

—Death in a Deck Chair. 1984. 12.95 (*0-8027-5601-8*) Walker & Co.

—Murder in a Mummy Case. l.t. ed. 1989. 8.95 o.p. (*0-7451-9460-5*, 352); pap. 8.95 o.p. (*1-55504-841-2*) BBC Audiobooks America.

—Peril under the Palms. 1990. 176p. mass mkt. 4.99 o.s.i (*0-8041-0594-4*, Ivy Bks.) Ballantine Bks.

—Peril under the Palms. 1989. 208p. 18.95 (*0-8027-5715-4*) Walker & Co.

Buffa, D. W. The Prosecution: A Legal Thriller. 1999. 274p. 25.00 o.s.i (*0-8050-6107-X*) Holt, Henry & Co.

Burke, Alafair. Judgment Calls: A Mystery. 2003. 352p. 23.00 (*0-8050-7386-8*) Holt, Henry & Co.

Calloway, Kate. Fifth Wheel: A Cassidy James Mystery. 1998. (Cassidy James Mysteries Ser.: No. 5). 256p. pap. 11.95 (*1-56280-218-6*) Naiad Pr., Inc.

—First Impressions: A Cassidy James Mystery. 1996. (Cassidy James Mysteries Ser.). 208p. (Orig.). pap. 11.95 (*1-56280-133-3*) Naiad Pr., Inc.

—Fourth Down: A Cassidy James Mystery. 1998. (Cassidy James Mysteries Ser.). 240p. (Orig.). pap. 11.95 (*1-56280-193-7*) Naiad Pr., Inc.

—Second Fiddle: A Cassidy James Mystery. 1996. (Cassidy James Mysteries Ser.). 224p. (Orig.). pap. 11.95 (*1-56280-161-9*) Naiad Pr., Inc.

—Seventh Heaven: A Cassidy James Mystery. 1999. (Cassidy James Mysteries Ser.). 230p. pap. 11.95 (*1-56280-262-3*) Naiad Pr., Inc.

—Sixth Sense: A Cassidy James Mystery. 1999. (Cassidy James Mysteries Ser.). 215p. pap. 11.95 (*1-56280-228-3*) Naiad Pr., Inc.

—Third Degree: A Cassidy James Mystery. 1997. (Cassidy James Mysteries Ser.). 256p. (Orig.). pap. 11.95 (*1-56280-185-6*) Naiad Pr., Inc.

David, James F. Before the Cradle Falls. Date not set. pap. (*0-7653-0320-5*, Forge Bks.); E-Book 25.95 (*0-312-70660-X*, Tor Bks.); 2002. 336p. 25.95 (*0-7653-0319-1*, Forge Bks.) Doherty, Tom Assocs., LLC.

French, Wendy. Smothering. Date not set. mass mkt. (*0-7653-4703-2*); 2003. 304p. 23.95 (*0-7653-0793-6*) Doherty, Tom Assocs., LLC. (Forge Bks.).

Gerritsen, Tess. Keeper of the Bride. 1996. (Harlequin Intrigue Ser.). (Illus.). 249p. per. (*0-373-22359-5*, 1-22359-3, Harlequin Bks.) Harlequin Enterprises, Ltd.

—Keeper of the Bride. l.t. ed. 2002. 29.95 o.p. (*0-7862-3974-3*) Thorndike Pr.

For book reviews, descriptive annotations, tables of contents, cover images, author biographies & additional information, updated daily, subscribe to **www.booksinprint.com** 1063

Hanson, Dirk. The Incursion. 1987. 16.95 o.p. (*0-316-34374-9*) Little Brown & Co.

—The Incursion. 1988. 272p. mass mkt. 3.95 (*0-380-70554-0*, Avon Bks.) Morrow/Avon.

Hanson, Rick. Extreme Odds. 1998. 240p. 22.00 o.s.i (*1-57566-333-3*) Kensington Publishing Corp.

—Mortal Remains. 1996. mass mkt. 4.99 o.s.i (*0-7860-0284-0*, Pinnacle Bks.); 1995. 256p. mass mkt. 18.95 o.p. (*0-8217-4955-2*, Zebra Bks.) Kensington Publishing Corp.

—Spare Parts. 1995. 256p. mass mkt. 4.99 (*0-8217-0156-8*, Zebra Bks.); 1995. 256p. mass mkt. 4.99 o.s.i (*0-7860-0156-9*, Pinnacle Bks.); 1994. 288p. mass mkt. 20.00 o.s.i (*0-8217-4738-X*, Zebra Bks.) Kensington Publishing Corp.

—Splitting Heirs. (Adam McCleet Mysteries Ser. ). 1998. 256p. mass mkt. 5.99 o.s.i (*1-57566-365-1*); 1997. 240p. 21.95 o.p. (*1-57566-194-2*, Kensington Bks.) Kensington Publishing Corp.

—Still Life. (Adam McCleet Mysteries Ser. ). 1997. 256p. mass mkt. 5.50 o.s.i (*1-57566-200-0*); 1996. 204p. 19.95 o.s.i (*1-57566-041-5*) Kensington Publishing Corp.

Hartman, Cherry. The Well-Heeled Murders. 1996. 224p. pap. 10.95 (*1-883523-10-9*) Spinsters Ink Bks.

Henry, April. Learning to Fly. E-Book 23.95 (*0-312-70633-2*); 2002. 288p. 23.95 (*0-312-29052-7*, Saint Martin's Minotaur) St. Martin's Pr.

Margolin, Phillip. After Dark. 1996. 384p. mass mkt. 7.99 (*0-553-56908-2*) Bantam Bks.

—After Dark. unabr. ed. 1996. audio 64.00 (*0-7366-3200-X*, 3864) Books on Tape, Inc.

—After Dark. l.t. ed. 1995. (Large Print Bks.). 24.95 o.p. (*1-56895-240-6*, Wheeler Publishing, Inc.) Gale Group.

—After Dark. 1995. audio 23.98 o.s.i (*0-553-74587-5*, RH Audio) Random Hse. Audio Publishing Group.

—The Undertaker's Widow. 1999. 336p. reprint ed. mass mkt. 7.99 (*0-553-58088-4*) Bantam Bks.

—The Undertaker's Widow. unabr. ed. 1998. audio 48.00 (*0-7366-4219-6*, 4717) Books on Tape, Inc.

—The Undertaker's Widow. unabr. ed. 1998. audio 29.95 o.s.i (*0-553-50218-2*, 751090, RH Audio) Random Hse. Audio Publishing Group.

—The Undertaker's Widow. l.t. ed. 2000. (Charnwood Large Print Ser.). 392p. (*0-7089-9146-7*, Ulverscroft) Thorpe, F. A. Pubs. GBR. *Dist:* Ulverscroft Large Print Bks., Ltd., Ulverscroft Large Print Canada, Ltd.

Miller, Linda Lael. Mixed Messages. 2003. 256p. mass mkt. (*1-55166-652-9*, Mira Bks.) Harlequin Enterprises, Ltd.

—Mixed Messages. l.t. ed. 2003. 238p. 29.95 (*0-7862-5860-8*) Thorndike Pr.

Mitcheltree, Tom. Dataman. 1998. 240p. 22.95 o.p. (*1-885173-52-0*) Write Way Publishing.

O'Brien, Kevin. Only Son. 1998. 352p. mass mkt. 5.99 (*1-57566-211-6*); 1997. 304p. 21.95 o.p. (*1-57566-091-1*, Kensington Bks.) Kensington Publishing Corp.

Rushford, Patricia H. Now I Lay Me down to Sleep. 1997. (Helen Bradley Mysteries Ser.: No. 1). 240p. pap. 9.99 o.p. (*1-55661-730-5*) Bethany Hse. Pubs.

Vachss, Andrew. Pain Management: A Burke Novel. 2001. E-Book 19.00 (*1-59061-376-7*) Adobe Systems, Inc.

—Pain Management: A Burke Novel. 2002. 336p. pap. 13.00 (*0-375-72647-0*) Random Hse., Inc.

Waiwaiole, Lono. Wiley's Lament: A Novel. 2003. 320p. 24.95 (*0-312-30383-1*, Saint Martin's Minotaur) St. Martin's Pr.

## PORTUGAL—FICTION

Agualusa, Jose Eduardo. Creole Nation. 2002. 288p. pap. 16.00 (*1-900850-61-3*) Arcadia Bks. GBR. *Dist:* Consortium Bk. Sales & Distribution.

Amis, Kingsley. I Like It Here. l.t. ed. 1993. 23.95 o.p. (*0-7927-1682-5*); pap. 21.95 o.p. (*0-7927-1681-7*) BBC Audiobooks America.

—I Like It Here. 1958. 4.50 o.p. (*0-15-152097-6*) Harcourt Trade Pubs.

Anthony, Patricia. God's Fires. 384p. 1998. mass mkt. 6.50 o.s.i (*0-441-00537-3*); 1997. 22.95 o.s.i (*0-441-00407-5*) Ace Bks.

Antunes. Return of the Caravels. 2003. pap. 13.00 (*0-8021-3955-8*) Grove/Atlantic, Inc.

Antunes, Antonio Lobo. The Inquisitors' Manual. Zenith, Richard, tr. from POR. 2003. 448p. 25.00 (*0-8021-1732-5*, Grove Pr.) Grove/Atlantic, Inc.

Berti, Eduardo. Agua. Cameron, Alexander, tr. 2002. 256p. pap. 14.00 (*1-901285-42-1*) Pushkin Pr., Ltd. GBR. *Dist:* Consortium Bk. Sales & Distribution.

Cartland, Barbara. Lovers in Lisbon. 1988. (Camfield Romance Ser.: No. 57). mass mkt. 2.75 o.s.i (*0-515-09545-1*, Jove) Berkley Publishing Group.

—Lovers in Lisbon. l.t. ed. 2000. (G. K. Hall Paperback Ser.). 183p. pap. 23.95 (*0-7838-8929-1*, Macmillan Reference USA) Gale Group.

Cornwell, Bernard. Sharpe's Havoc: Richard Sharpe & the Campaign in Northern Portugal, Spring 1809. 2003. (Richard Sharpe Adventure Ser.). 320p. 25.95 (*0-06-053046-4*) HarperCollins Pubs.

—Sharpe's Havoc: Richard Sharpe & the Campaign in Northern Portugal, Spring 1809. 2004. 336p. pap. 12.95 (*0-06-056670-1*, Perennial) HarperTrade.

—Sharpe's Havoc: Richard Sharpe & the Campaign in Northern Portugal, Spring 1809. l.t. ed. 2003. (Sharpe Novels Ser.). 498p. 29.95 (*0-7862-5601-X*) Thorndike Pr.

De Carvalho, Mario. A God Strolling in the Cool of the Evening. Rabassa, Gregory, tr. from POR. 2001. (Pegasus Prize for Literature Ser.). 288p. pap. 12.00 (*0-8021-3774-1*) Grove/Atlantic, Inc.

—A God Strolling in the Cool of the Evening. Rabassa, Gregory, tr. from POR. 1997. (Pegasus Prize for Literature Ser.). xiv, 266p. 26.95 (*0-8071-2235-1*) Louisiana State Univ. Pr.

De Sena, Jorge. By the Rivers of Babylon & Other Stories. Patai, Daphne, ed. (Fiction Ser.). 155p. 1991. pap. 10.95 (*0-8135-1688-9*); 1989. 19.95 o.p. (*0-8135-1388-X*) Rutgers Univ. Pr.

Eca de Queiros, Jose Maria. The Illustrious House of Ramires. Stevens, Anne, tr. from POR. 1994. (Revived Modern Classic Ser.). 320p. (Orig.). pap. 14.95 (*0-8112-1264-5*, NDP785) New Directions Publishing Corp.

—The Illustrious House of Ramires. Stevens, Ann, tr. 1969. 310p. (Orig.). 15.00 o.p. (*0-8214-0044-4*, 82-80489) Ohio Univ. Pr.

Ericson, Donald E. The Portuguese Letters: Love Letters of a Nun to a French Officer. 2nd ed. 1986. 78p. pap. 9.95 (*0-9617271-0-1*) Bennett-Edwards.

Forbath, Peter. Lord of the Kongo. 1996. 510p. 27.00 o.p. (*0-684-80951-6*, Simon & Schuster) Simon & Schuster.

George, Catherine. The Marriage Bed. l.t. ed. 1995. (Nightingale Ser.). 268p. pap. 17.95 (*0-7838-1191-8*, Macmillan Reference USA) Gale Group.

—The Marriage Bed. 1987. mass mkt. (*0-373-10992-X*, Harlequin Bks.) Harlequin Enterprises, Ltd.

Hodge, Jane Aiken. Whispering. unabr. ed. 1996. audio 54.95 (*0-7451-6604-0*, CAB1220) BBC Audiobooks America.

—Whispering. 1995. 224p. 20.95 (*0-312-13213-1*) St. Martin's Pr.

Jorge, Lidia & Costa, Margaret Jull. The Painter of Birds. 2001. 240p. 24.00 o.s.i (*0-15-100658-X*) Harcourt Trade Pubs.

Knox, Bill. A Burial in Portugal. l.t. ed. 1997. (Ulverscroft Large Print Ser.). 352p. 29.99 (*0-7089-3704-7*, Ulverscroft) Thorpe, F. A. Pubs. GBR. *Dist:* Ulverscroft Large Print Bks., Ltd., Ulverscroft Large Print Canada, Ltd.

Langley, Lee. Distant Music. 2003. 322p. 22.00 (*1-57131-040-1*) Milkweed Editions.

L'Engle, Madeleine. The Love Letters. 1983. (Epiphany Bks.). 384p. mass mkt. 4.95 o.s.i (*0-345-30617-1*) Ballantine Bks.

Lobo Antunes, Antonio. The Natural Order of Things. Zenith, Richard, tr. 2000. 320p. 25.00 o.p. (*0-8021-1658-2*, Grove Pr.) Grove/Atlantic, Inc.

Nooteboom, Cees. Following Story. 1994. 128p. 14.95 (*0-15-100098-0*) Harcourt Trade Pubs.

—The Following Story. Rilke, Ina, tr. from DUT. 1996. (Harvest Book Ser.). 128p. reprint ed. pap. 11.00 (*0-15-600254-X*, Harvest Bks.) Harcourt Trade Pubs.

Norfolk, Lawrence. The Pope's Rhinoceros. 1996. 574p. 25.00 o.s.i (*0-517-59532-X*, Harmony) Crown Publishing Group.

—The Pope's Rhinoceros. 1997. 592p. pap. 16.00 o.s.i (*0-8050-5475-8*, Owl Bks.) Holt, Henry & Co.

—The Pope's Rhinoceros: A Novel. 2003. 592p. pap. 16.00 (*0-8021-3988-4*, Grove Pr.) Grove/Atlantic, Inc.

Nunes, Rachel. A Greater Love. 2000. 192p. pap. 12.95 (*0-9675174-6-X*) Truebekon Bks.

Pires, Jose C. Ballad of Dogs' Beach: Dossier of a Crime. Fitton, Mary, tr. from POR. 1987. Tr. of Balada da Praia dos Caes. 192p. 15.95 o.p. (*0-8253-0416-4*) Beaufort Bks., Inc.

Saramago, José. All the Names. Costa, Margaret Jull, tr. from POR. 2000. 256p. 24.00 (*0-15-100421-8*) Harcourt Trade Pubs.

—Baltasar & Blimunda. 1988. (Illus.). mass mkt. 4.95 o.s.i (*0-345-35676-4*) Ballantine Bks.

—Baltasar & Blimunda. 1998. pap. 13.00 (*0-15-600625-1*); 360p. pap. 13.00 (*0-15-600520-4*, Harvest Bks.) Harcourt Trade Pubs.

—Baltasar & Blimunda. Pontiero, Giovanni, tr. from POR. 1987. 336p. 17.95 (*0-15-110555-3*) Harcourt Trade Pubs.

—The Cave. Costa, Margaret Jull, tr. from POR. 2002. 320p. 25.00 (*0-15-100414-5*) Harcourt Trade Pubs.

—La Caverna. (SPA., Illus.). 456p. 24.95 (*84-204-4228-3*) Alfaguara, Ediciones, S.A.- Grupo Santillana ESP. *Dist:* Santillana USA Publishing Co., Inc.

—The History of the Siege of Lisbon: A Novel. Pontiero, Giovanni, tr. from POR. & afterword by by. 1998. 324p. pap. 14.00 (*0-15-600624-3*, Harvest Bks.) Harcourt Trade Pubs.

—The History of the Siege of Lisbon: A Novel. Pontiero, Giovanni, tr. from POR. 1997. 320p. 24.00 (*0-15-100238-X*) Harcourt Trade Pubs.

—The Year of the Death of Ricardo Reis. Pontiero, Giovanni, tr. from POR. (Harvest in Translation Ser.). 1992. 368p. pap. 14.00 (*0-15-699693-6*, Harvest Bks.); 1991. 416p. (C). 21.95 o.s.i (*0-15-199735-7*) Harcourt Trade Pubs.

Slavitt, David R. Salazar Blinks. 1988. 176p. 16.95 o.p. (*0-689-12030-3*, Scribner) Simon & Schuster.

Tabucchi, Antonio. The Missing Head of Damasceno Monteiro. 2003. 181p. pap. 16.95 (*1-86046-770-9*) Harvill Pr., The GBR. *Dist:* Trafalgar Square.

—The Missing Head of Damasceno Monteiro. Creagh, Patrick, tr. 2000. (ITA.). 192p. 23.95 (*0-8112-1393-5*) New Directions Publishing Corp.

—Pereira Declares: A Testimony. Creagh, Patrick, tr. from ITA. 1997. 136p. pap. 9.95 (*0-8112-1358-7*, NDP848); 1996. 144p. 19.95 (*0-8112-1319-6*) New Directions Publishing Corp.

—Requiem: A Hallucination. Costa, Jull, tr. 2002. 112p. pap. 12.95 (*0-8112-1517-2*, NDP944) New Directions Publishing Corp.

—Requiem: A Hallucination. Costa, Margaret Jull, tr. from POR. 1994. 128p. 15.95 (*0-8112-1270-X*) New Directions Publishing Corp.

Zimler, Richard. Hunting Midnight: A Novel. 2003. 512p. 24.95 (*0-385-33644-6*); E-Book 19.95 (*0-440-33428-4*) Dell Publishing. (Delacorte Pr.).

—The Last Kabbalist of Lisbon. 2000. 318p. 15.95 (*1-58567-022-7*); 1998. 272p. 24.95 (*0-87951-834-0*) Overlook Pr., The.

## POSSILTUM (IMAGINARY PLACE)—FICTION

Asprin, Robert L. Another Fine Myth. 1986. 208p. mass mkt. 5.50 o.s.i (*0-441-02362-2*); 1985. mass mkt. 2.95 o.s.i (*0-441-02361-4*); 1984. mass mkt. 2.95 o.s.i (*0-441-02360-6*); 1984. mass mkt. 2.75 o.s.i (*0-441-02359-2*) Ace Bks.

—Another Fine Myth. 1984. pap. 7.95 o.p. (*0-915442-54-X*) Donning Co. Pubs.

—Another Fine Myth. Freas, Polly & Freas, Kelly, eds. 1978. (Myth Adventures Ser.: No. 1). (Illus.). 12.95 o.p. (*0-89865-383-5*); 35.00 o.p. (*0-89865-382-7*) Donning Co. Pubs. (Starblaze).

—Another Fine Myth. abr. ed. 1992. (Myth Ser.). audio 16.99 (*0-88646-329-7*, 7329) Durkin Hayes Publishing Ltd.

—Another Fine Myth. l.t. ed. 2001. 200p. 27.95 (*0-7838-9505-4*); 256p. (*0-7540-4638-9*); 256p. (*0-7540-4637-0*) Gale Group. (Macmillan Reference USA).

—Another Fine Myth. unabr. ed. 1997. audio 44.00 (*0-7887-0924-0*, 95064E7) Recorded Bks., LLC.

—Hit or Myth. 1985. mass mkt. 2.95 o.s.i (*0-441-33853-4*); mass mkt. 2.95 o.s.i (*0-441-33850-X*); 176p. mass mkt. 5.50 o.s.i (*0-441-33851-8*) Ace Bks.

—Hit or Myth. Reynolds, Kay, ed. 1983. (Myth Adventures Ser.: No. 4). (Illus.). 172p. pap. 7.95 o.p. (*0-89865-331-2*); lib. bdg. 12.95 o.p. (*0-89865-339-8*) Donning Co. Pubs. (Starblaze).

—Little Myth Marker. 1987. (Myth Ser.). mass mkt. 5.99 o.s.i (*0-441-48499-9*) Ace Bks.

—Little Myth Marker. Reynolds, Kay, ed. 1985. (Myth Adventures Ser.). (Illus.). 172p. pap. 7.95 o.p. (*0-89865-413-0*); lib. bdg. 12.95 o.p. (*0-89865-411-4*); 35.00 o.p. (*0-89865-418-1*) Donning Co. Pubs. (Starblaze).

—M. Y. T. H. Inc. in Action. 1991. 256p. mass mkt. 5.99 o.s.i (*0-441-55282-X*) Ace Bks.

—M. Y. T. H. Inc. in Action. Hainer, Beverley B., ed. 1990. (Myth Adventures Ser.). (Illus.). 180p. pap. 8.95 o.p. (*0-89865-803-9*, Starblaze) Donning Co. Pubs.

—M. Y. T. H. Inc. in Action. 1989. pap. 7.95 o.p. (*0-89865-787-3*) Donning Co. Pubs.

—M. Y. T. H. Inc. in Action. Hainer, Beverley B., ed. ltd. ed. 1990. (Myth Adventures Ser.). (Illus.). 180p. 40.00 o.p. (*0-89865-788-1*, Starblaze) Donning Co. Pubs.

—M. Y. T. H. Inc. Link. 1988. (Myth Ser.: No. 7). 176p. (Orig.). mass mkt. 5.50 o.s.i (*0-441-55277-3*) Ace Bks.

—M. Y. T. H. Inc. Link. 1986. (Myth Adventures Ser.). (Illus.). 160p. (Orig.). pap. 7.95 o.p. (*0-89865-472-6*); pap. 12.95 o.p. (*0-89865-471-8*); pap. 35.00 o.p. (*0-89865-470-X*) Donning Co. Pubs. (Starblaze).

—Myth Adventures One. 2001. 16.00 (*1-892065-36-3*); 30.00 (*1-892065-35-5*) Meisha Merlin Publishing, Inc.

—Myth Conceptions. (Myth Bks.). 1986. 224p. mass mkt. 5.99 o.s.i (*0-441-55521-7*); 1985. mass mkt. 2.95 o.s.i (*0-441-55520-9*); 1985. mass mkt. 2.95 o.s.i (*0-441-55519-5*) Ace Bks.

—Myth Conceptions. Freas, Polly & Freas, Kelly, eds. 1980. (Illus.). pap. 7.95 o.p. (*0-915442-94-9*, Starblaze) Donning Co. Pubs.

—Myth Conceptions. l.t. ed. 2001. 273p. 27.95 (*0-7838-9550-X*) Thorndike Pr.

—Myth Directions. (Myth Ser.). 1986. mass mkt. 5.99 o.s.i (*0-441-55529-2*); 1985. mass mkt. 2.95 o.s.i (*0-441-55527-6*); 1985. mass mkt. 2.95 o.s.i (*0-441-55525-X*) Ace Bks.

—Myth Directions. Stine, Hank, ed. 1982. (Myth Adventures Ser.: No. 3). (Illus.). 176p. pap. 7.95 o.p. (*0-89865-250-2*, Starblaze) Donning Co. Pubs.

—Myth Directions. l.t. ed. 2002. 261p. 27.95 (*0-7838-9551-8*, Macmillan Reference USA) Gale Group.

—M.Y.T.H. Inc. in Action. l.t. ed. 2003. 27.95 (*0-7838-9563-1*) Thorndike Pr.

—Myth-ing Persons. 1986. 176p. mass mkt. 5.50 o.s.i (*0-441-55276-5*) Ace Bks.

—Myth-ing Persons. Reynolds, Kay, ed. 1984. (Myth Adventures Ser.: No. 5). (Illus.). 170p. 12.95 o.p. (*0-89865-380-0*); pap. 7.95 o.p. (*0-89865-379-7*); 35.00 o.p. (*0-89865-381-9*) Donning Co. Pubs. (Starblaze).

—Myth-Nomers & Im-Pervections, No. 8. 1988. (Myth-Nomers & Im-Pervections Ser.: Vol. 8). mass mkt. 5.99 o.s.i (*0-441-55279-X*) Ace Bks.

—Myth-Nomers & Im-Pervections. Gray, Mary E., ed. 1987. (Myth Adventures Ser.). (Illus.). 180p. 12.95 o.p. (*0-89865-540-4*); pap. 7.95 o.p. (*0-89865-529-3*); 35.00 o.p. (*0-89865-530-7*) Donning Co. Pubs. (Starblaze).

—Myth-Nomers & Im-Pervections. 2003. (Science Fiction Ser.). 27.95 (*0-7838-9549-6*) Thorndike Pr.

—Sweet Myth-tery of Life. 1995. 240p. mass mkt. 5.99 o.s.i (*0-441-00194-7*) Ace Bks.

—Sweet Myth-tery of Life. 1994. (Illus.). 29.95 o.p. (*0-89865-891-8*); o.p. (*0-89865-892-6*) Donning Co. Pubs.

Asprin, Robert L. & Foglio, Phil. Myth Adventures One. Reynolds, Kay & Pini, Richard, eds. 1985. (Myth Adventures Ser.). (Illus.). 108p. pap. 12.95 o.p. (*0-89865-414-9*); 40.00 o.p. (*0-89865-419-X*) Donning Co. Pubs. (Starblaze).

Asprin, Robert L., et al. Myth Adventures Two. Pini, Richard, ed. 1986. (Myth Adventures Ser.). (Illus.). 110p. (Orig.). pap. 12.95 o.p. (*0-89865-473-4*); pap. 40.00 o.p. (*0-89865-474-2*) Donning Co. Pubs. (Starblaze).

## PRAGUE (CZECH REPUBLIC)—FICTION

Bryers, Paul. In a Pig's Ear. 2000. 277p. pap. 23.00 (*0-374-52768-7*); 1996. 288p. 23.00 o.p. (*0-374-17564-0*) Farrar, Straus & Giroux.

Chatwin, Bruce. Utz. l.t. ed. 1990. 130p. 17.95 (*1-85089-328-4*) ISIS Large Print Bks. GBR. *Dist:* Transaction Pubs.

—Utz. 1989. 160p. pap. 11.95 (*0-14-011576-5*, Penguin Bks.) Penguin Group (USA) Inc.

—Utz. 1989. 160p. 16.95 o.p. (*0-670-82497-6*) Viking Penguin.

Eversz, Robert M. Gypsy Hearts. 1997. 272p. 23.00 o.p. (*0-8021-1609-4*, Grove Pr.) Grove/Atlantic, Inc.

Goldstein, Lisa. The Alchemist's Door. 2003. 288p. pap. 14.95 (*0-7653-0151-2*); 2002. 256p. 23.95 (*0-7653-0150-4*) Doherty, Tom Assocs., LLC. (Tor Bks.).

Hamburger, Aaron. The View from Stalin's Head: Stories. 2004. 272p. pap. 12.95 (*0-8129-7093-4*, Random Hse. Trade Paperbacks) Random House Adult Trade Publishing Group.

Klima, Ivan. My Merry Mornings: Stories from Prague. Theiner, George, tr. from CZE. 1985. (Illus.). (C). 160p. 14.95 o.p. (*0-930523-04-0*); 156p. pap. 14.95 (*0-930523-05-9*) Readers International.

—No Saints or Angels. Turner, Gerald, tr. Tr. of Ani svati, ani andeele. 272p. 2002. pap. 13.00 (*0-8021-3923-X*); 2001. 24.00 o.p. (*0-8021-1695-7*) Grove/Atlantic, Inc. (Grove Pr.).

Knox, Bill. A Problem in Prague. l.t. ed. 1998. (Ulverscroft Large Print Ser.). 320p. 29.99 (*0-7089-3968-6*, Ulverscroft) Thorpe, F. A. Pubs. GBR. *Dist:* Ulverscroft Large Print Bks., Ltd., Ulverscroft Large Print Canada, Ltd.

Kohout, Pavel. I Am Snowing: The Confessions of a Woman of Prague. Bermel, Neil, tr. 1994. 308p. 27.50 o.p. (*0-374-17400-8*) Farrar, Straus & Giroux.

—I Am Snowing: The Confessions of a Woman of Prague. Bermel, Neil, tr. 1995. (Harvest in Translation Ser.). 320p. pap. 13.00 o.s.i (*0-15-600187-X*, Harvest Bks.) Harcourt Trade Pubs.

—The Widow Killer. 2000. 400p. pap. 14.00 (*0-312-25289-7*) Picador.

—The Widow Killer: A Novel. Bermel, Neil, tr. 1998. (Illus.). 391p. 24.95 o.p. (*0-312-19363-7*) Picador.

—The Widow Killer: A Novel. 1999. mass mkt. (*0-312-96920-1*, St. Martin's Paperbacks) St. Martin's Pr.

—The Widow Killer: A Novel. Bermel, Neil, tr. 1999. E-Book 24.95 (*0-312-24620-X*) St. Martin's Pr.

Kundera, Milan. Ignorance. 2003. 208p. pap. 12.95 (*0-06-000210-7*, Morrow Cookbooks, William) HarperInformation.

—Ignorance. Asher, Linda, tr. l.t. ed. 2003. (General Ser.). lib. bdg. 24.95 (*0-7862-5164-6*) Thorndike Pr.

—Ignorance: A Novel. Asher, Linda, tr. from FRE. 2002. 208p. 23.95 (*0-06-000209-3*) HarperCollins Pubs.

—The Unbearable Lightness of Being. Heim, Michael Henry, tr. 1994. 314p. reprint ed. pap. 13.50 o.p. (*0-06-091465-3*, PL/1465, Perennial) HarperTrade.

MacKenzie, Donald. The Eyes of the Goat. 1993. 16.95 o.p. (*0-312-09056-0*, Saint Martin's Minotaur) St. Martin's Pr.

Molinard, Ursule. Fat Skeletons. 2001. 144p. pap. 11.95 (*1-897959-02-8*) Serif GBR. *Dist:* Interlink Publishing Group, Inc.

Perutz, Leo. By Night under the Stone Bridge. Mosbacher, Eric, tr. from GER. 1990. 208p. lib. bdg. 18.95 o.s.i (*1-55970-055-6*) Arcade Publishing, Inc.

Polacek, Karel. What Ownership's All About. Kussi, Peter, tr. from CZE. & intro. by. 1993. 238p. 21.95 o.p. (*0-945774-19-2*, PG5038.P64D813) Catbird Pr.

Rilke, Rainer Maria. Two Stories of Prague: King Bohush & The Siblings. Esterhammer, Angela, tr. from GER. & intro. by. (Illus.). 151p. 1996. pap. 13.95 (*0-87451-789-3*); 1994. (C). lib. bdg. 18.95 o.p. (*0-87451-661-7*) Univ. Pr. of New England.

Rudel, Anthony J. Imagining Don Giovanni. 2001. 288p. 24.00 (*0-87113-827-1*, Atlantic Monthly Pr.) Grove/Atlantic, Inc.

Sargent, Patricia. Black Valentine. 1991. mass mkt. 4.50 o.p. (*1-55817-548-2*, Pinnacle Bks.) Kensington Publishing Corp.

—Black Valentine. l.t. ed. 1990. (Ulverscroft Large Print Ser.). 29.99 o.p. (*0-7089-2257-0*, Ulverscroft) Thorpe, F. A. Pubs. GBR. *Dist:* Ulverscroft Large Print Bks., Ltd., Ulverscroft Large Print Canada, Ltd.

Sherwood, Frances. The Book of Splendor. 2002. (Illus.). 352p. 25.95 (*0-393-02138-6*) Norton, W. W. & Co., Inc.

—The Book of Splendor: A Novel. 2003. (Illus.). 352p. pap. 14.95 (*0-393-32458-3*) Norton, W. W. & Co., Inc.

Skeggs, Douglas. The Phoenix of Prague. 1996. 320p. 23.95 (*0-312-15189-6*, Saint Martin's Minotaur) St. Martin's Pr.

Skvorecky, Josef. The Miracle Game. 1992. Orig. Title: Mirakl. 435p. pap. 10.95 (*0-393-30849-9*) Norton, W. W. & Co., Inc.

Thoene, Bodie. Prague Counterpoint: The Zion Covenant. (Zion Covenant Ser.: No. 2). 2000. 416p. pap. 7.99 (*0-7642-2428-X*); 1989. 384p. pap. 12.99 (*1-55661-078-5*) Bethany Hse. Pubs.

Viewegh, Michal. Bringing up Girls in Bohemia. Brain, A. G., tr. from CZE. 1997. 200p. pap. text 12.95 (*1-887378-05-7*) Readers International.

Webster, Noah. A Problem in Prague. 1982. (Crime Club Ser.). 192p. 10.95 o.p. (*0-385-17944-8*) Doubleday Publishing.

Weil, Jiri. Life with a Star. Schloss, Roslyn, tr. 1989. 280p. 22.95 o.s.i (*0-374-18737-1*) Farrar, Straus & Giroux.

—Life with a Star. 1991. 224p. pap. 8.95 o.p. (*0-14-013171-X*, Penguin Bks.) Penguin Group (USA) Inc.

—Life with a Star. Klimova, Rita & Schloss, Roslyn, trs. 1993. 224p. pap. 10.95 o.p. (*0-14-018766-9*, Penguin Classics) Viking Penguin.

—Life with a Star: A Novel. Klimova, Rita & Schloss, Roslyn, trs. 1998. (Jewish Lives Ser.). 224p. pap. 19.00 (*0-8101-1685-5*) Northwestern Univ. Pr.

—Mendelssohn Is on the Roof. Winn, Marie, tr. 1991. 228p. 23.95 (*0-374-20810-7*) Farrar, Straus & Giroux.

—Mendelssohn Is on the Roof. Winn, Marie, tr. 1998. (Jewish Lives Ser.). 240p. pap. 19.00 (*0-8101-1686-3*) Northwestern Univ. Pr.

—Mendelssohn Is on the Roof: A Novel. 1992. 240p. pap. 10.00 o.p. (*0-14-016776-5*, Penguin Bks.) Penguin Group (USA) Inc.

**PRAIRIE PROVINCES—FICTION**

Klebeck, William. Down Milligan Creek Way. 1995. 128p. pap. 12.95 (*1-55050-088-0*) Coteau Bks. CAN. *Dist:* General Distribution Services, Inc.

**PRIMROSE CREEK (NEV.: IMAGINARY PLACE)—FICTION**

Miller, Linda Lael. Bridget. 2000. (Women of Primrose Creek Ser.: Vol. 1). 160p. mass mkt. 3.99 (*0-671-04244-0*, Pocket) Simon & Schuster.

—Christy. l.t. ed. 2001. (Wheeler Large Print Book Ser.). 168p. 28.95 (*1-58724-101-3*, Wheeler Publishing, Inc.) Gale Group.

—Christy. 176p. 2002. E-Book 3.99 (*0-7434-4827-8*); 2000. (Women of Primrose Creek Ser.: Vol. 2). pap. 3.99 o.s.i (*0-671-04245-9*) Simon & Schuster. (Pocket).

—The Last Chance Cafe. 2003. 384p. mass mkt. 7.99 (*0-671-04251-3*, Pocket Star); 2002. 304p. 24.00 (*0-671-04250-5*, Atria); 2002. 288p. 24.00 (*0-7434-4619-4*, Atria) Simon & Schuster.

—Megan. 2000. (Women of Primrose Creek Ser.: No. 4). 256p. mass mkt. 5.99 (*0-671-04247-5*, Pocket) Simon & Schuster.

—Skye. l.t. ed. 2001. (Wheeler Large Print Book Ser.). 162p. pap. 23.95 o.p. (*1-58724-144-7*, Wheeler Publishing, Inc.) Gale Group.

—Skye. 2000. (Women of Primrose Creek Ser.: Vol. 3). 176p. pap. 3.99 o.s.i (*0-671-04246-7*, Pocket) Simon & Schuster.

**PROMISE (TEX.: IMAGINARY PLACE)—FICTION**

Macomber, Debbie. Caroline's Child. abr. ed. 1999. (Harlequin Romance Ser.). audio 7.99 o.p. (*1-56740-530-4*, 1824, Harlequin Romance Audio) Brilliance Audio.

—Caroline's Child. 1998. (Promo Ser.). 217p. per. (*0-373-83344-X*, 1-83344-1, Harlequin Bks.) Harlequin Enterprises, Ltd.

—Caroline's Child. l.t. ed. 1999. (Mills & Boon Large Print Ser.). 288p. 25.99 o.p. (*0-263-16104-8*) Harlequin Mills & Boon, Ltd. GBR. *Dist:* Ulverscroft Large Print Bks., Ltd., Ulverscroft Large Print Canada, Ltd.

—Dr. Texas. abr. ed. 1999. (Heart of Texas Ser.). audio 7.99 o.p. (*1-56740-534-7*, 1831, Harlequin Romance Audio) Brilliance Audio.

—Dr. Texas. 1998. (Promo Ser.). 216p. per. (*0-373-83345-8*, 1-83345-8, Harlequin Bks.) Harlequin Enterprises, Ltd.

—Dr. Texas. l.t. ed. (Mills & Boon Large Print Ser.). 1999. 288p. 25.99 o.p. (*0-263-16141-2*); 1998. 187p. 6.25 (*0-263-16130-7*) Harlequin Mills & Boon, Ltd. GBR. *Dist:* Ulverscroft Large Print Bks., Ltd., Ulverscroft Large Print Canada, Ltd., Ulverscroft Large Print Bks., Ltd.

—Lone Star Baby. abr. ed. 2000. (Harlequin Romance Ser.). audio 7.99 o.p. (*1-56740-545-2*, 1846, Harlequin Romance Audio) Brilliance Audio.

—Lone Star Baby. 1998. (Harlequin Ser.). per. (*0-373-83347-4*, Harlequin Bks.) Harlequin Enterprises, Ltd.

—Lone Star Baby. l.t. ed. 1999. (Mills & Boon Large Print Ser.). 288p. 25.99 o.p. (*0-263-16208-7*) Harlequin Mills & Boon, Ltd. GBR. *Dist:* Ulverscroft Large Print Bks., Ltd., Ulverscroft Large Print Canada, Ltd.

—Lonesome Cowboy. abr. ed. 1998. (Harlequin Romance Ser.: Vol. 2). audio 7.99 o.p. (*1-56740-032-9*, 779, Harlequin Romance Audio) Brilliance Audio.

—Lonesome Cowboy. 1998. (Promo Ser.). per. (*0-373-83342-3*, 1-83342-5, Harlequin Bks.) Harlequin Enterprises, Ltd.

—Lonesome Cowboy. l.t. ed. 1999. (Mills & Boon Large Print Ser.). 25.99 o.p. (*0-263-16058-0*) Harlequin Mills & Boon, Ltd. GBR. *Dist:* Ulverscroft Large Print Bks., Ltd., Ulverscroft Large Print Canada, Ltd.

—Nell's Cowboy. abr. ed. 2000. (Harlequin Romance Ser.). audio 7.99 o.p. (*1-56740-539-8*, 1839, Harlequin Romance Audio) Brilliance Audio.

—Nell's Cowboy. 1998. (Harlequin Ser.: No. 5). per. (*0-373-83346-6*, 1-83346-6, Harlequin Bks.) Harlequin Enterprises, Ltd.

—Nell's Cowboy. l.t. ed. 1999. (Mills & Boon Large Print Ser.). 288p. 25.99 o.p. (*0-263-16173-0*) Harlequin Mills & Boon, Ltd. GBR. *Dist:* Ulverscroft Large Print Bks., Ltd., Ulverscroft Large Print Canada, Ltd.

—Promise, Texas. unabr. ed. 1999. audio 7.99 (*1-55204-187-5*, MIR-1187) Durkin Hayes Publishing Ltd.

—Promise, Texas. 384p. 2003. mass mkt. (*1-55166-976-5*); 1999. mass mkt. (*1-55166-502-6*) Harlequin Enterprises, Ltd. (Mira Bks.).

—Texas Two-Step. abr. ed. 1998. (Harlequin Romance Ser.: Vol. 2). audio 7.99 o.p. (*1-56740-039-6*, 1543, Harlequin Romance Audio) Brilliance Audio.

—Texas Two-Step. 1998. (Promo Ser.: Vol. 2). 219p. per. (*0-373-83343-1*, 1-83343-3, Harlequin Bks.) Harlequin Enterprises, Ltd.

—Texas Two-Step. l.t. ed. 1999. (Mills & Boon Large Print Ser.). 288p. 25.99 o.p. (*0-263-16081-5*) Harlequin Mills & Boon, Ltd. GBR. *Dist:* Ulverscroft Large Print Bks., Ltd., Ulverscroft Large Print Canada, Ltd.

**PROPHESY COUNTY (OKLA.: IMAGINARY PLACE)—FICTION**

Cooper, Susan Rogers. Chasing Away the Devil. 1993. (Mystery Ser.). per. (*0-373-26129-2*, 1-26129-6, Harlequin Bks.) Harlequin Enterprises, Ltd.

—Chasing Away the Devil. 1991. 192p. 16.95 o.p. (*0-312-06316-4*, Saint Martin's Minotaur) St. Martin's Pr.

—Doctors & Lawyers & Such. 1995. 256p. 21.95 o.p. (*0-312-13468-1*, Saint Martin's Minotaur) St. Martin's Pr.

—Houston in the Rearview Mirror. 1992. (WWL Mystery Ser.: No. 95). per. (*0-373-26095-4*, 1-26095-9, Harlequin Bks.) Harlequin Enterprises, Ltd.

—Houston in the Rearview Mirror. 1990. 160p. 14.95 o.p. (*0-312-03843-7*, Saint Martin's Minotaur) St. Martin's Pr.

—The Man in the Green Chevy. 1991. reprint ed. per. (*0-373-26071-7*, Harlequin Bks.) Harlequin Enterprises, Ltd.

—The Man in the Green Chevy. abr. ed. 1997. audio 17.00 (*1-883268-46-X*) Spellbinders, Inc.

—The Man in the Green Chevy. 1989. 208p. 15.95 o.p. (*0-312-02604-8*, Saint Martin's Minotaur) St. Martin's Pr.

—Other People's Houses. 1992. per. (*0-373-26112-8*, 1-26112-2, Harlequin Bks.) Harlequin Enterprises, Ltd.

—Other People's Houses. pap. 3.99 (*0-373-05139-5*); 1990. 176p. 14.95 o.p. (*0-312-05139-5*, Saint Martin's Minotaur) St. Martin's Pr.

**PROTON (IMAGINARY PLACE)—FICTION**

Anthony, Piers. Blue Adept. 1987. (Apprentice Adept Ser.: Vol. 2). 336p. mass mkt. 7.50 (*0-345-35245-9*); 1986. mass mkt. 3.50 o.p. (*0-345-33632-1*); 1983. mass mkt. 2.95 o.p. (*0-345-31424-7*); 1982. mass mkt. 2.75 o.p. (*0-345-28214-0*); 1981. 368p. 10.95 o.s.i (*0-345-29384-3*) Ballantine Bks. (Del Rey).

—Juxtaposition. 1987. (Apprentice Adept Ser.: Vol. 3). 368p. mass mkt. 6.99 (*0-345-34934-2*); 1986. mass mkt. 3.50 o.p. (*0-345-33637-2*); 1983. mass mkt. 2.95 o.p. (*0-345-28215-9*); 1982. 13.50 o.p. (*0-345-30196-X*) Ballantine Bks. (Del Rey).

—Out of Phaze. 1988. (Apprentice Adept Ser.: Vol. 4). 320p. mass mkt. 6.50 o.s.i (*0-441-64465-1*) Ace Bks.

—Out of Phaze. 1987. (Apprentice Adept Ser.: Bk. 4). 288p. 17.95 o.p. (*0-399-13272-4*) Putnam Publishing Group, The.

—Robot Adept. 1989. mass mkt. 5.99 o.s.i (*0-441-73118-X*) Ace Bks.

—Robot Adept. 1988. (Apprentice Adept Ser.: Bk. 5). 288p. 16.95 o.p. (*0-399-13359-3*, G. P. Putnam's Sons) Penguin Putnam Bks. for Young Readers.

—Split Infinity. 1987. (Apprentice Adept Ser.: Vol. 1). 368p. mass mkt. 7.50 (*0-345-35491-5*); 1986. mass mkt. 3.50 o.p. (*0-345-33600-3*); 1982. mass mkt. 2.95 o.p. (*0-345-30761-5*); 1980. mass mkt. 2.50 o.p. (*0-345-28213-2*); 1980. 9.95 o.s.i (*0-345-28645-6*) Ballantine Bks. (Del Rey).

—Unicorn Point. 1990. (Apprentice Adept Ser.: No. 6). 352p. mass mkt. 6.99 o.s.i (*0-441-84563-0*) Ace Bks.

—Unicorn Point. 1989. (Apprentice Adept Ser.). 15.95 o.p. (*0-399-13433-6*, G. P. Putnam's Sons) Penguin Putnam Bks. for Young Readers.

**PROVINCETOWN (MASS.)—FICTION**

Berry, Carole. Nightmare Point. 1993. 264p. 18.95 o.p. (*0-312-08889-2*, Saint Martin's Minotaur) St. Martin's Pr.

Gordon, Mary. Spending: A Utopian Divertimento. 304p. 1999. pap. 13.00 (*0-684-85204-7*); 1998. 24.00 (*0-684-83945-8*) Simon & Schuster. (Scribner).

—Spending: A Utopian Divertimento. 1999. 18.00 (*0-671-57994-0*, Simon & Schuster Audioworks) Simon & Schuster Audio.

Preston, John. Franny, the Queen of Provincetown. 1983. 96p. pap. 4.95 o.p. (*0-932870-31-7*) Alyson Pubns.

—Franny, the Queen of Provincetown. 1995. 112p. pap. 8.95 o.p. (*0-312-14106-8*, Saint Martin's Griffin) St. Martin's Pr.

Skillings, R. D. How Many Die. 2001. (Hardscrabble Bks.). 330p. 24.95 (*1-58465-065-6*, Hardscrabble Bks.) Univ. Pr. of New England.

**PUERTO RICO—FICTION**

Andreu Iglesias, Cesar. The Vanquished: A Novel. Mintz, Sidney Wilfred, tr. from SPA. 2002. (Latin America in Translation Ser.). 0232p. pap. 19.95 (*0-8078-5412-3*); lib. bdg. 49.95 (*0-8078-2746-0*) Univ. of North Carolina Pr.

Carlson, Lori. The Flamboyant. 2002. (Illus.). 256p. 24.95 (*0-06-621068-2*) HarperCollins Pubs.

Cofer, Judith. The Meaning of Consuelo. 2003. 200p. 20.00 (*0-374-20509-4*) Farrar, Straus & Giroux.

Cope, Todd F. So Much for Christmas. 2003. 140p. pap. 10.95 (*1-55517-710-7*, 77107, Bonneville Bks.) Cedar Fort, Inc./CFI Distribution.

Derouin, R. E. San Juan Solution. 2000. 283p. pap. 16.95 (*1-890437-52-2*) Western Reflections Publishing Co.

Ferré, Rosario. Flight of the Swan. 2002. 272p. pap. 14.00 (*0-452-28331-0*, Plume) Dutton/Plume.

—Flight of the Swan. 2001. 256p. 24.00 o.s.i (*0-374-15648-4*) Farrar, Straus & Giroux.

—The House on the Lagoon. 1996. 416p. pap. 13.95 (*0-452-27707-8*, Plume) Dutton/Plume.

—The House on the Lagoon. 1995. 320p. 23.00 o.p. (*0-374-17311-7*) Farrar, Straus & Giroux.

—Vuelo del Cisne. 2002. (ENG & SPA.). 304p. pap. 13.00 (*0-375-71385-9*, Vintage) Knopf Publishing Group.

—Vuelo del Cisne. 2002. (Spanish Language Ser.). (SPA.). 409p. 28.95 (*0-7862-4804-1*) Thorndike Pr.

Hoyt, Garry. Isla Verde. 2001. xii, 209p. (*0-9712696-0-2*) Newport R&D, Inc.

Jordan, B. B. Secondary Immunization: A Scientific Mystery. 1999. (Scientific Mysteries Ser.). 272p. (YA). mass mkt. 5.99 o.s.i (*0-425-17118-3*, Prime Crime) Berkley Publishing Group.

Julia, Edgardo R. The Renunciation. Hurley, Andrew, tr. from SPA. 1997. 144p. (C). 18.00 (*1-56858-057-6*) Four Walls Eight Windows.

Marx Weinraub, Ricard. Wonder Bread Hill. 2001. xiv, 90p. (*0-8477-0134-4*) Univ. of Puerto Rico Pr.

Merced De Mendez, Ana T. Tales from the Island: Puerto Rican Stories. 1995. (Illus.). 60p. (J). (gr. 6-10). 20.00 (*0-9627442-1-2*) Merced de Mendez, Ana T.

Montero, Mayra. Deep Purple. Grossman, Edith, tr. from SPA. 2003. 192p. 22.95 (*0-06-621420-3*); pap. 11.95 (*0-06-093821-8*) HarperTrade. (Ecco).

Morris, Lynn. The Balcony. 1997. (Portraits Ser.). 256p. pap. 8.99 o.p. (*1-55661-981-2*) Bethany Hse. Pubs.

—The Balcony. l.t. ed. 1999. (Christian Fiction Ser.). 376p. 24.95 (*0-7862-2146-1*) Thorndike Pr.

Rodriguez, Julia E. & Hurley, Andrew. The Renunciation: A Novel. 1997. 135p. pap. 27.50 (*92-3-103162-7*) United Nations Educational, Scientific & Cultural Organization FRA. *Dist:* Bernan Assocs., Renouf Publishing Co., Ltd.

Roman, Hebby. To Dance Again. 2002. 256p. mass mkt. 4.99 o.s.i (*0-7860-1348-6*) Kensington Publishing Corp.

Stevens-Arce, James. Soulsaver. 2000. 272p. 24.00 (*0-15-100472-2*) Harcourt Trade Pubs.

Thompson, Hunter S. The Rum Diary: A Novel. 1999. (Illus.). 224p. pap. 12.00 (*0-684-85647-6*); 1998. (Illus.). 224p. 24.00 o.s.i (*0-684-85521-6*); 1998. pap. 15.99 (*0-684-85224-1*) Simon & Schuster. (Simon & Schuster).

—The Rum Diary: A Novel. abr. ed. 1998. 5p. audio 25.00 (*0-671-58277-1*, Simon & Schuster Audioworks) Simon & Schuster Audio.

—The Rum Diary: A Novel. abr. ed. 1999. audio 24.35 (*0-671-03352-2*) Ulverscroft Audio (U.S.A.).

Torres, Steven. Death in Precinct Puerto Rico Bk. 2: A Luis Gonzalo Novel. 2003. 256p. 23.95 (*0-312-28989-8*, Saint Martin's Minotaur) St. Martin's Pr.

—Precinct Puerto Rico. 2002. (Luis Gonzalo Novel Ser.). 224p. 23.95 (*0-312-28580-9*, Saint Martin's Minotaur) St. Martin's Pr.

# Q

**QUEBEC (PROVINCE)—FICTION**

Atwood, Margaret. Surfacing. 1987. 240p. mass mkt. 5.99 o.s.i (*0-449-21375-7*, Fawcett) Ballantine Bks.

—Surfacing. 1995. 208p. pap. 10.95 o.s.i (*0-553-37780-9*) Bantam Bks.

—Surfacing. 1998. 208p. pap. 12.95 (*0-385-49105-0*) Doubleday Publishing.

—Surfacing. 1997. 200p. mass mkt. 6.95 (*0-7710-9899-5*) McClelland & Stewart/Tundra Bks.

—Surfacing. 1983. 224p. pap. 3.50 o.p. (*0-446-31107-3*) Warner Bks., Inc.

Bock, Dennis. The Ash Garden. 2001. E-Book 18.50 (*1-59061-597-2*) Adobe Systems, Inc.

—The Ash Garden. 2003. 304p. pap. 13.00 (*0-375-72749-3*, Vintage) Knopf Publishing Group.

Boswell, Hazel. Town House, Country House: Recollections of a Quebec Childhood. 1990. (Illus.). 152p. (C). 29.95 (*0-7735-0721-3*) McGill-Queen's Univ. Pr. CAN. *Dist:* CUP Services.

Chaput, Sylvie. Isabelle's Notebooks. Sloate, Daniel & Vranckx, Peter, trs. from FRE. 2002. (Prose Ser.: 61). 200p. pap. 13.00 (*1-55071-142-3*) Guernica Editions, Inc.

Farrow, John. City of Ice: A Novel. 1999. 403p. 25.95 o.s.i (*0-375-50140-1*) Random Hse., Inc.

—Ice Lake: A Novel. 2001. 368p. pap. 19.00 (*0-8129-9264-4*) Random House Adult Trade Publishing Group.

—Ice Lake: A Novel. 2001. E-Book 19.95 (*1-58836-016-4*) Random Hse., Inc.

Goliger, Gabriella. Song of Ascent. 2001. 177p. pap. (*1-55192-374-2*) Raincoast Bk. Distribution.

Hancock, Geoff, intro. Invisible Fictions: Contemporary Stories from Quebec. 1987. 352p. pap. 16.95 (*0-88784-153-8*) House of Anansi Pr. CAN. *Dist:* General Distribution Services, Inc.

Mars, Peter. A Taste for Money: A Novel Based on the True Story of a Dirty Boston Cop. 1999. (Illus.). 320p. pap. 14.95 (*0-9664475-1-4*) Commonwealth Publishing.

Moore, Brian. Black Robe. 1991. mass mkt. 4.99 o.p. (*0-449-45066-X*, Fawcett); 1986. mass mkt. 5.99 o.s.i (*0-449-20947-4*) Ballantine Bks.

—Black Robe. 1997. 256p. pap. 14.00 (*0-452-27865-1*, Plume); 1985. 15.95 o.p. (*0-525-24311-9*, Dutton) Dutton/Plume.

—Black Robe. 1995. 80p. pap. 10.00 o.p. (*0-586-08615-3*) HarperCollins Pubs. Ltd. GBR. *Dist:* HarperCollins Pubs.

Moore, Jeffrey. Prisoner in a Red-Rose Chain. 2002. 385p. 24.95 o.s.i (*0-399-14864-7*, Putnam & Grosset) Penguin Group (USA) Inc.

Settings

Piat, Colette. Les Filles du Roi. 1999. (FRE.). 264p. reprint ed. pap. 13.95 (*1-58348-163-X*) iUniverse, Inc.

Reichs, Kathy. Death du Jour. unabr. ed. 2002. audio compact disk 110.95; 2000. audio 96.95 (*0-7927-2346-5*, CSL235, Chivers Sound Library) BBC Audiobooks America.

—Death du Jour. unabr. ed. 2000. 12p. audio compact disk 110.95 (*0-7540-5330-X*, CCD 021) Chivers Audio Bks. GBR. *Dist:* BBC Audiobooks America.

—Death du Jour. 1999. 384p. mass mkt. 7.99 (*0-671-03472-3*, Pocket); 1999. E-Book 25.00 (*0-7432-0080-2*, Scribner); 1999. 384p. 25.00 (*0-684-84118-5*, Scribner); 1999. 384p. 25.00 (*0-684-86906-3*, Scribner); 2000. (Illus.). 480p. reprint ed. mass mkt. 7.99 (*0-671-01137-5*, Pocket) Simon & Schuster.

—Death du Jour, Set. abr. ed. 1999. audio 24.00 (*0-671-04370-6*, 599126, Simon & Schuster Audioworks) Simon & Schuster Audio.

—Death du Jour. l.t. ed. (Thorndike/G. K. Hall Paperback Bestsellers Ser.). 632p. 2000. (FRE.). pap. 27.95 (*0-7862-1997-1*); 1999. 30.95 (*0-7862-1996-3*) Thorndike Pr.

—Death du Jour. abr. ed. 1999. audio 24.35 (*1-85686-522-3*) Ulverscroft Audio (U.S.A.).

Rogal, Stan. The Long Drive Home. 1999. 176p. pap. 14.99 (*1-895837-56-1*) Insomniac Pr. CAN. *Dist:* Stackpole Bks.

Soucy, Gaetan. The Little Girl Who Was Too Fond of Matches: A Novel. Fischman, Sheila, tr. from FRE. 2000. Tr. of Petite Fille Qui Aimait Trop les Allumettes. 138p. pap. 19.95 (*0-88784-655-6*) House of Anansi Pr. CAN. *Dist:* General Distribution Services, Inc.

Tefs, Wayne. The Cartier Street Contract. 1997. pap. 7.95 (*0-88801-098-2*) Turnstone Pr. CAN. *Dist:* General Distribution Services, Inc.

Tremblay, Michel. News from Edouard. Fischman, Sheila, tr. from FRE. 2000. (FRE.). 300p. pap. 15.95 (*0-88922-435-8*) Talonbooks, Ltd. CAN. *Dist:* General Distribution Services, Inc.

### QUIVIRA (LEGENDARY PLACE)—FICTION

Preston, Douglas J. Thunderhead, Set. abr. ed. 1999. audio 24.98 Highsmith Inc.

Preston, Douglas J. & Child, Lincoln. Thunderhead. 2001. audio 24.98 (*1-57042-899-9*); 1999. audio 24.98 (*1-57042-667-8*) Time Warner AudioBooks.

—Thunderhead. 1999. 496p. 32.00 (*0-446-52337-2*); 2000. 560p. reprint ed. mass mkt. 7.50 (*0-446-60837-8*) Warner Bks., Inc.

## R

### RAINBOW ROCK (IMAGINARY PLACE)—FICTION

Aylworth, Susan. At the Rainbow's End. 1996. (Rainbow Rock Ser.: Bk. 2). 192p. 18.95 (*0-8034-9172-7*, Avalon Bks.) Bouregy, Thomas & Co., Inc.

—Don't Promise Me Rainbows. 1996. 192p. 18.95 (*0-8034-9208-1*, Avalon Bks.) Bouregy, Thomas & Co., Inc.

—A Little Night Rainbow. 1999. 192p. lib. bdg. 18.95 (*0-8034-9333-9*, Avalon Bks.) Bouregy, Thomas & Co., Inc.

—A Rainbow in Paradise. 1997. 192p. lib. bdg. 18.95 (*0-8034-9354-1*, Avalon Bks.) Bouregy, Thomas & Co., Inc.

—Ride the Rainbow Home. 1995. (Rainbow Rock Ser.: Bk. 1). 192p. 18.95 (*0-8034-9143-3*, Avalon Bks.) Bouregy, Thomas & Co., Inc.

### RALEIGH (N.C.)—FICTION

Grant, Anne U. Multiple Listing. 1998. (Sydney Teague Mysteries Ser.: Vol. 1). 336p. mass mkt. 5.99 o.s.i (*0-440-22551-5*) Dell Publishing.

Munger, Katy. Legwork. 1997. (Casey Jones Mysteries Ser.). 224p. mass mkt. 5.99 (*0-380-79136-6*, Avon Bks.) Morrow/Avon.

Ray, Jeanne. Step-Ball-Change: A Novel. unabr. ed. 2002. audio 62.25 (*1-59086-083-7*, 3632, Unabridged Library Editions) Brilliance Audio.

—Step-Ball-Change: A Novel. 2002. 240p. 22.95 (*0-609-61003-1*, Shaye Areheart Bks.) Crown Publishing Group.

—Step-Ball-Change: A Novel. l.t. ed. 2002. (Core Collection). 284p. 31.95 (*0-7862-4371-6*) Thorndike Pr.

Shaber, Sarah R. Simon Said. (Simon Shaw Mysteries Ser.). 224p. 1998. pap. 5.99 (*0-312-96555-9*, St. Martin's Paperbacks); 1997. 20.95 o.p. (*0-312-15207-8*, Saint Martin's Minotaur) St. Martin's Pr.

### RAPSTONE VALLEY (ENGLAND: IMAGINARY PLACE)—FICTION

Mortimer, John. Paradise Postponed. unabr. ed. 2000. (Leslie Titmuss Trilogy Ser.: Bk. 1). audio 69.95 (*0-7451-6175-8*, CAB 504) Chivers Audio Bks. GBR. *Dist:* BBC Audiobooks America.

—Paradise Postponed. abr. ed. audio 15.95 o.p. (*0-88646-209-6*, 7209) Durkin Hayes Publishing Ltd.

—Paradise Postponed. l.t. ed. 1987. 555p. 18.95 o.p. (*0-8161-4247-5*, Macmillan Reference USA) Gale Group.

—Paradise Postponed. 1986. 384p. pap. 12.95 (*0-14-009864-X*, Penguin Bks.) Penguin Group (USA) Inc.

—Paradise Postponed. 1986. 400p. 17.95 o.p. (*0-670-80094-5*); 448p. reprint ed. pap. 11.95 o.s.i (*0-14-006928-3*) Viking Penguin.

—The Rapstone Chronicles: Paradise Postponed & Titmuss Regained. 1993. 704p. pap. 14.00 o.p. (*0-14-017595-4*, Penguin Bks.) Penguin Group (USA) Inc.

—The Sound of Trumpets. unabr. ed. 2000. (Leslie Titmuss Trilogy Ser.: Bk. 3). audio 59.95 (*0-7540-0315-9*, CAB 1738) Chivers Audio Bks. GBR. *Dist:* BBC Audiobooks America.

—The Sound of Trumpets. l.t. ed. 1999. (Core Ser.). 359p. 27.95 (*0-7838-8716-7*, Macmillan Reference USA) Gale Group.

—The Sound of Trumpets. 1999. 288p. pap. 12.95 o.s.i (*0-14-028851-1*) Penguin Group (USA) Inc.

—The Sound of Trumpets. 1999. (Rapstone Chronicles Ser.). 256p. 23.95 o.p. (*0-670-87861-8*) Viking Penguin.

—Titmuss Regained. l.t. ed. 1992. pap. 15.95 o.p. (*0-7927-0666-8*); 1991. 17.95 o.p. (*0-7927-0665-X*, E0007) BBC Audiobooks America.

—Titmuss Regained. l.t. ed. 1992. 70.95 o.p. (*0-8161-3213-5*, Macmillan Reference USA) Gale Group.

—Titmuss Regained. 1991. 288p. pap. 12.95 o.s.i (*0-14-014921-X*, Penguin Bks.) Penguin Group (USA) Inc.

—Titmuss Regained. 1990. 288p. 19.95 o.p. (*0-670-82333-3*, Viking) Viking Penguin.

—Titmuss Regained: Movie-TV Tie-In. 1992. 272p. pap. 10.00 o.p. (*0-14-017185-1*, Penguin Bks.) Penguin Group (USA) Inc.

### RAVENLOFT (IMAGINARY PLACE)—FICTION

Baren, Nick. Castle of the Undead. 1994. (Endless Quest, Ravenloft Ser.: No. 2). 192p. (Orig.). pap. 3.95 (*1-56076-836-3*) Wizards of the Coast.

Bergstrom, Elaine. Baroness of Blood. 1995. (Ravenloft Ser.). 320p. (Orig.). pap. 4.95 o.p. (*0-7869-0146-2*) Wizards of the Coast.

—Ravenloft: Tapestry of Dark Souls. 1993. 310p. (Orig.). pap. 4.95 o.p. (*1-56076-571-2*) Wizards of the Coast.

Bittner, Drew. Circle of Darkness: Ravenloft Adventure. 1995. (Advanced Dungeons & Dragons, 2nd Edition). (Illus.). 9.95 o.p. (*0-7869-0128-4*) Wizards of the Coast.

Connors & Denning, Troy. Hour of the Knife. 1994. (Advanced Dungeons & Dragons, 2nd Edition). 9.95 o.p. (*1-56076-892-4*) TSR, Inc.

Connors, William W., et al. Masque of the Red Death & Other Tales. 1994. (Advanced Dungeons & Dragons, 2nd Edition). 25.00 (*1-56076-877-0*) TSR, Inc.

Deweese, Eugene. Lord of the Necropolis. 1997. (Ravenloft Ser.). 303p. pap. 5.99 o.p. (*0-7869-0660-X*) Wizards of the Coast.

Elrod, P. N. I, Strahd. 1995. (Ravenloft Ser.). 310p. (Orig.). pap. 6.99 (*0-7869-0175-6*) Wizards of the Coast.

—I, Strahd: Ravenloft. 1993. (Ravenloft Bks.). pap. 16.95 o.p. (*1-56076-670-0*) Wizards of the Coast.

—I, Strahd: The War Against Azalin. 1998. (Ravenloft Ser.). 310p. mass mkt. 5.99 (*0-7869-0754-1*) Wizards of the Coast.

Golden, Christie. The Enemy Within. 1994. (Ravenloft Ser.: No. 7). 320p. (Orig.). pap. 4.95 o.p. (*1-56076-887-8*) Wizards of the Coast.

—Ravenloft: Dance of the Dead. 1992. 320p. (Orig.). pap. 4.95 o.p. (*1-56076-352-3*) Wizards of the Coast.

—Ravenloft: Vampire of the Mists. 1999. 341p. (Orig.). pap. 5.99 o.p. (*1-56076-155-5*) Wizards of the Coast.

Hickman, Tracy. Advanced Dungeons & Dragons Standard Module 10 Ravenloft: The House on Gryphone Hill. 1986. pap. 8.00 o.p. (*0-88038-322-4*) TSR, Inc.

Huff, Tanya. Scholar of Decay. 1995. (Ravenloft Ser.). 320p. (Orig.). pap. 4.95 o.p. (*0-7869-0206-X*) Wizards of the Coast.

King, J. Robert. Ravenloft: Carnival of Fear. 1993. 320p. (Orig.). pap. 4.95 o.p. (*1-56076-628-X*) Wizards of the Coast.

—Ravenloft: Heart of Midnight. 1992. 313p. (Orig.). pap. 4.95 o.p. (*1-56076-355-8*) Wizards of the Coast.

Lafountain, James. Van Richten's Guide to Vampires: Ravenloft Accessory. 1992. (Advanced Dungeons & Dragons, 2nd Edition). (Illus.). 10.95 o.p. (*1-56076-151-2*, RR3) TSR, Inc.

Lowder, James. Ravenloft: Knight of the Black Rose. 1991. 313p. (Orig.). pap. 5.99 (*1-56076-156-3*) Wizards of the Coast.

McComb, Colin. Howls in the Night: Ravenloft Adventure. 1995. (Advanced Dungeons & Dragons Ser.). 6.95 o.p. (*1-56076-927-0*) TSR, Inc.

Slavicsek, Bill. Night of the Walking Dead. 1992. (Advanced Dungeons & Dragons, 2nd Edition). (Illus.). 6.95 o.p. (*1-56076-350-7*) TSR, Inc.

Smedman, Lisa. Awakening. 1994. (Advanced Dungeons & Dragons, 2nd Edition). 9.95 o.p. (*1-56076-883-5*) TSR, Inc.

—Chilling Tales: Ravenloft Adventure. 1995. 9.95 o.p. (*0-7869-0142-X*) TSR, Inc.

Thomspon, Brian & TSR Inc. Staff. Tales of Ravenloft. 1994. 316p. (Orig.). pap. 4.95 o.p. (*1-56076-931-9*) Wizards of the Coast.

TRS Staff. A Light in the Belfry. 1995. (Advanced Dungeons & Dragons, 2nd Edition). 15.00 o.p. (*0-7869-0133-0*) TSR, Inc.

TSR Inc. Staff. Evil Eye: A Ravenloft Adventure. 1995. 9.95 o.p. (*0-7869-0167-5*) Wizards of the Coast.

—Monstrous Compendium: Ravenloft. (Advanced Dungeons & Dragons). (Illus.). Vol. 2. 1993. pap. 10.95 (*1-56076-586-0*); Vol. 3. 1994. pap. 18.00 o.p. (*1-56076-914-9*) Wizards of the Coast.

—Neither Man nor Beast. 1996. (Advanced Dungeons & Dragons, 2nd Edition). 9.95 o.p. (*0-7869-0205-1*) TSR, Inc.

—The Nightmare Lands. 1995. (Advanced Dungeons & Dragons, 2nd Edition). 20.00 (*0-7869-0174-8*) Wizards of the Coast.

—Ravenloft. 1990. 18.00 o.p. (*0-88038-853-6*) TSR, Inc.

—Ravenloft Campaign Setting. 1994. (Advanced Dungeons & Dragons Ser.). (Illus.). 30.00 o.p. (*1-56076-942-4*) TSR, Inc.

—Ravenloft Monstrous Compendium: Appendix 1 & 2, 1 & 2. 1996. 20.00 (*0-7869-0392-9*) Wizards of the Coast.

—Spectre of the Black Rose. 1999. (Ravenloft Ser.). 312p. pap. 5.99 (*0-7869-1333-9*) Wizards of the Coast.

Williams, Skip. Van Richten's Guide to the Ancient Dead. 1994. (Ravenloft Ser.: RR9). 12.95 (*1-56076-873-8*) TSR, Inc.

Williamson, Chet. Mordenheim. 1994. (Ravenloft Ser.: No. 8). 320p. (Orig.). pap. 4.95 o.p. (*1-56076-852-5*) Wizards of the Coast.

### RECLUCE (IMAGINARY PLACE)—FICTION

Modesitt, L. E., Jr. The Chaos Balance. (Saga of Recluce Ser.: No. 7). 1998. 596p. mass mkt. 7.99 (*0-8125-7130-4*); 1997. 448p. (YA). (gr. 5-12). 25.95 o.p. (*0-312-86389-6*) Doherty, Tom Assocs., LLC. (Tor Bks.).

—The Chaos Balance. 1997. (Saga of Recluse Ser.). 13.04 (*0-606-19649-8*) Turtleback Bks.

—Colors of Chaos. (Saga of Recluce Ser.: No. 9). 2000. 798p. mass mkt. 7.99 (*0-8125-7093-6*); 1998. (Illus.). 634p. 27.95 (*0-312-86767-0*) Doherty, Tom Assocs., LLC. (Tor Bks.).

—Colors of Chaos. 2000. (Saga of Recluse Ser.). 14.04 (*0-606-19651-X*) Turtleback Bks.

—The Death of Chaos. (Saga of Recluce Ser.: No. 5). 1996. 629p. mass mkt. 7.99 (*0-8125-4824-8*); 1995. 480p. 24.95 o.p. (*0-312-85721-7*) Doherty, Tom Assocs., LLC. (Tor Bks.).

—The Death of Chaos. 1996. (Saga of Recluse Ser.). 13.04 (*0-606-19652-8*) Turtleback Bks.

—Fall of Angels. (Saga of Recluce Ser.: No. 6). 1997. 592p. mass mkt. 7.99 (*0-8125-3895-1*); 1996. 448p. 25.95 o.p. (*0-312-85905-8*) Doherty, Tom Assocs., LLC. (Tor Bks.).

—The Magic Engineer. (Saga of Recluce Ser.: No. 3). 1995. 617p. mass mkt. 7.99 (*0-8125-3405-0*); 1994. 512p. 23.95 o.p. (*0-312-85570-2*) Doherty, Tom Assocs., LLC. (Tor Bks.).

—The Magic of Recluce. (Saga of Recluce Ser.). 1992. 501p. mass mkt. 7.99 (*0-8125-0518-2*); 1991. 21.95 o.p. (*0-312-85116-2*) Doherty, Tom Assocs., LLC. (Tor Bks.).

—Magi'i of Cyador. 2000. (Saga of Recluce Ser.: No. 10). 444p. 27.95 (*0-312-87226-7*, Tor Bks.) Doherty, Tom Assocs., LLC.

—The Order War. (Saga of Recluce Ser.: No. 4). 1996. 597p. mass mkt. 7.99 (*0-8125-3404-2*); 1995. 480p. 23.95 o.p. (*0-312-85569-9*) Doherty, Tom Assocs., LLC. (Tor Bks.).

—The Order War. 1996. (Saga of Recluse Ser.). 14.04 (*0-606-19666-8*) Turtleback Bks.

—Scion of Cyador. 2000. (Saga of Recluce Ser.: No. 11). (Illus.). 541p. reprint ed. 27.95 (*0-312-87379-4*, NHC 0135, Tor Bks.) Doherty, Tom Assocs., LLC.

—The Towers of the Sunset. (Saga of Recluce Ser.: No. 2). 1993. 536p. mass mkt. 7.99 (*0-8125-1967-1*); 1992. 368p. 21.95 (*0-312-85297-5*) Doherty, Tom Assocs., LLC. (Tor Bks.).

—The Towers of the Sunset. 1996. (Saga of Recluse Ser.). 13.04 (*0-606-19671-4*) Turtleback Bks.

—The White Order. (Saga of Recluce Ser.: No. 8). 1999. 480p. mass mkt. 7.99 (*0-8125-4171-5*); 1998. 384p. 24.95 o.s.i (*0-312-86645-3*) Doherty, Tom Assocs., LLC. (Tor Bks.).

—The White Order. 1998. (Saga of Recluse Ser.). 13.04 (*0-606-19672-2*) Turtleback Bks.

### RELIAN KRU (IMAGINARY PLACE)—FICTION

Volsky, Paula. The Luck of Relian Kru. 1987. 304p. mass mkt. 3.50 o.s.i (*0-441-83816-2*) Ace Bks.

—Sorcerer's Curse. 1989. mass mkt. 3.95 o.s.i (*0-441-44458-X*) Ace Bks.

—The Sorcerer's Heir. 1988. mass mkt. 3.50 o.s.i (*0-441-77231-5*) Ace Bks.

—The Sorcerer's Lady. 1986. 256p. mass mkt. 2.95 o.s.i (*0-441-77533-0*) Ace Bks.

### RHODE ISLAND—FICTION

Allen, Charlotte Vale. Somebody's Baby. 2003. 352p. pap. (*1-55166-754-1*, Mira Bks.) Harlequin Enterprises, Ltd.

Barnes, Peter W. & Barnes, Cheryl Shaw. Cornelius Vandermouse: The Pride of Newport. 1997. (Illus.). 32p. (J). 15.95 (*0-9637688-5-9*) Vacation Spot Publishing.

Bennett, James W. & Raycraft, Donald R. Old Hoss: A Fictional Baseball Biography of Charles Radbourn. 2002. (Illus.). 201p. per. 24.95 (*0-7864-1321-2*) McFarland & Co., Inc. Pubs.

Bischoff, David. The H. P. Lovecraft Institute. 2002. 388p. 34.95 (*1-59224-962-0*) Wildside Pr.

Briody, Thomas G. Rogue's Isles. 1995. 273p. 21.95 o.p. (*0-312-13157-7*, Saint Martin's Minotaur) St. Martin's Pr.

—Rogue's Justice: A Michael Carolina Mystery. 1996. 288p. 22.95 o.p. (*0-312-14402-4*, Saint Martin's Minotaur) St. Martin's Pr.

—Rogues Regatta. 1999. 272p. 23.95 (*0-312-24235-2*, Saint Martin's Minotaur) St. Martin's Pr.

—Rogue's Wager: A Michael Carolina Mystery. 1997. (Michael Carolina Mystery Ser.). 160p. 21.95 (*0-312-16990-6*, Saint Martin's Minotaur) St. Martin's Pr.

Cannell, Stephen J. The Plan. 1996. 464p. mass mkt. 7.99 (*0-380-72754-4*, Avon Bks.); 1995. 420p. 23.00 (*0-688-14046-7*, Morrow, William & Co.) Morrow/Avon.

—The Plan. abr. ed. 1995. 24.95 o.p. (*0-7871-0444-2*, 692957) NewStar Media, Inc.

Clark, Mary Higgins. Moonlight Becomes You. E-Book 9.95 (*1-930161-21-2*) Adobe Systems, Inc.

—Moonlight Becomes You. 2000. E-Book 9.95 (*0-7432-0624-X*, Simon & Schuster); 1997. 352p. pap. 7.99 (*0-671-86711-3*, Pocket); 1996. 336p. 24.00 (*0-684-81038-7*, Simon & Schuster); 2005. 496p. pap. 12.00 (*0-7432-6136-4*, Simon & Schuster); 1996. 496p. pap. 24.00 (*0-684-83127-9*, Simon & Schuster) Simon & Schuster.

—Moonlight Becomes You. 1998. 5.98 o.p. (*0-7651-0912-3*) Smithmark Pubs., Inc.

—Moonlight Becomes You. 1996. 14.04 (*0-606-11638-9*) Turtleback Bks.

Coffey, Jan. Trust Me Once. 2001. 408p. mass mkt. (*1-55166-859-9*, Mira Bks.) Harlequin Enterprises, Ltd.

Dailey, Janet. Strange Bedfellows: Rhode Island. 1992. per. (*0-373-89889-4*, 1-89889-9); 1987. (Americana Ser.: No. 39). pap. (*0-373-89839-8*) Harlequin Enterprises, Ltd. (Harlequin Bks.).

—Strange Bedfellows: Rhode Island. l.t. ed. 2000. (Romance Ser.). 243p. 28.95 (*0-7862-2745-1*) Thorndike Pr.

—Strange Bedfellows: Rhode Island. 2002. 128p. pap. 6.99 (*0-7592-3829-4*); E-Book 6.99 (*0-7592-0167-6*); E-Book 6.99 (*1-58586-404-8*); E-Book 6.99 (*0-7592-0911-1*) ereads.com.

Delinsky, Barbara. Heart of the Night. l.t. ed. 1996. lib. bdg. 24.95 (*1-57490-073-0*, Beeler Large Print Bks.) Beeler, Thomas T. Publisher.

—Heart of the Night. abr. ed. 2003. audio 12.99 (*1-58788-827-0*, 3789, Brilliance Audio Paperback Audiobooks); audio 24.95 (*1-58788-826-2*, 3788); audio 34.95 (*1-58788-824-6*, 3786) Brilliance Audio.

—Heart of the Night. 1991. reprint ed. 19.95 o.p. (*0-7278-4130-0*) Severn Hse. Pubs., Ltd.

—Heart of the Night. unabr. ed. 2003. audio 19.99 (*1-59335-089-9*, 30181) Soulmate Audio Bks., Inc.

—Heart of the Night. 2003. 432p. 18.95 (*0-446-53096-4*); 1989. 512p. mass mkt. 6.99 (*0-446-35477-5*) Warner Bks., Inc.

—The Vineyard: A Novel. 2000. E-Book 25.00 (*0-7432-1111-1*); (Illus.). 368p. 25.00 (*0-684-86484-3*) Simon & Schuster. (Simon & Schuster).

—The Vineyard: A Novel. l.t. ed. 2001. 592p. 32.50 o.p. (*0-7432-0426-3*) Thorpe, F. A. Pubs. GBR. *Dist:* Ulverscroft Large Print Bks., Ltd.

Florence, Ronald. The Last Season. 2000. 348p. 24.95 (*0-312-84873-0*, Forge Bks.) Doherty, Tom Assocs., LLC.

Gardner, Lisa. The Survivor's Club. l.t. ed. 2002. (Basic Ser.). 651p. 30.95 (*0-7862-4715-0*) Thorndike Pr.

Goodger, Jane. The Perfect Wife. 2000. 320p. mass mkt. 5.99 o.s.i (*0-451-20130-2*, Signet Bks.) NAL.

—The Perfect Wife. l.t. ed. 2002. (Ulverscroft Large Print Ser.). 472p. 32.50 o.p. (*0-7089-4608-9*) Thorpe, F. A. Pubs. GBR. *Dist:* Ulverscroft Large Print Bks., Ltd., Ulverscroft Large Print Canada, Ltd.

Grant, Richard. In the Land of Winter. 1998. mass mkt. 6.99 o.s.i (*0-380-79140-4*); 1997. 352p. 24.00 (*0-380-97465-7*) Morrow/Avon. (Avon Bks.).

Hood, Ann. The Properties of Water. 1996. 288p. reprint ed. pap. 9.95 o.s.i (*0-553-37565-2*) Bantam Bks.

Kennedy, William P. Siren's Lullaby. 1997. 256p. text 22.95 o.p. (*0-312-15658-8*) St. Martin's Pr.

—Sirens Lullaby. 1998. (Sirens Lullaby Ser.: Vol. 1). 288p. mass mkt. 5.99 (*0-312-96736-5*, St. Martin's Paperbacks) St. Martin's Pr.

Kruger, Mary. Death on the Cliff Walk. 1995. mass mkt. 4.99 o.s.i (*0-8217-5164-6*); 1994. mass mkt. 16.95 o.s.i (*0-8217-4769-X*, Zebra Bks.) Kensington Publishing Corp.

Mazur, Grace Dane. Trespass. 2002. 300p. pap. 14.95 (*1-55597-364-7*) Graywolf Pr.

Rice, Luanne. Blue Moon. 1994. 352p. mass mkt. 7.50 (*0-553-56818-3*) Bantam Bks.

—Blue Moon. 1993. 320p. 21.00 o.p. (*0-670-84301-6*, Viking) Viking Penguin.

—Dance with Me. 2004. 352p. 22.95 (*0-553-80227-5*) Bantam Bks.

Settle, Mary Lee. I, Roger Williams: A Fragment of Autobiography. 2001. (Illus.). 320p. 24.95 (*0-393-04905-1*) Norton, W. W. & Co., Inc.

Smith, Mary-Ann Tirone. She's Not There: A Poppy Rice Novel. 2003. (Illus.). 336p. 25.00 (*0-8050-7223-3*) Holt, Henry & Co.

Staub, Wendy Corsi. Fade to Black. 320p. 1999. mass mkt. 5.99 (*0-7860-0652-8*); 1998. 23.00 o.s.i (*1-57566-285-X*, Kensington Bks.) Kensington Publishing Corp.

Storandt, William. The Summer They Came: A Novel. 2002. 272p. pap. 12.95 (*0-375-75909-3*, Villard Bks.) Random House Adult Trade Publishing Group.

Updike, John. The Witches of Eastwick. 1996. 320p. pap. 14.00 (*0-449-91210-8*); 1985. 352p. mass mkt. 6.99 o.s.i (*0-449-20647-5*) Ballantine Bks. (Fawcett).

—The Witches of Eastwick. l.t. ed. 1985. (General Ser.). 421p. 17.95 o.p. (*0-8161-3777-3*, Macmillan Reference USA) Gale Group.

—The Witches of Eastwick. 1984. 320p. 27.95 (*0-394-53760-2*); 336p. 65.00 o.p. (*0-394-53765-3*) Knopf, Alfred A. Inc.

Watkins, Paul. The Story of My Disappearance. 224p. 1999. pap. 11.00 (*0-312-20026-9*); 1998. 21.00 o.p. (*0-312-17995-2*) Picador.

—Story of My Disappearance. unabr. ed. 1998. audio 51.00 (*0-7887-2179-8*, 95475E7 ) Recorded Bks., LLC.

Weldon, Fay. Rhode Island Blues. l.t. ed. 2001. 501p. (*0-7540-1543-2*); (*0-7540-2411-3*) Gale Group. (Macmillan Reference USA).

—Rhode Island Blues. 2000. 325p. 24.00 o.p. (*0-87113-775-5*, Atlantic Monthly Pr.) Grove/Atlantic, Inc.

—Rhode Island Blues. l.t. ed. 2001. (Core Ser.). 501p. 28.95 (*0-7838-9343-4*) Thorndike Pr.

Wetherell, W. D. The Man Who Loved Levittown. 1987. 128p. pap. 3.95 (*0-380-70112-X*, Avon Bks.) Morrow/Avon.

—The Man Who Loved Levittown. 1985. (Drue Heinz Literature Prize Ser.). 145p. 22.50 (*0-8229-3520-1*) Univ. of Pittsburgh Pr.

Williamson, Penelope. The Passions of Emma. l.t. ed. 1998. (Large Print Book Ser.). 26.95 (*1-56895-526-X*, Wheeler Publishing, Inc.) Gale Group.

—The Passions of Emma. 1997. 432p. 19.50 o.p. (*0-446-52153-1*); 1998. 464p. reprint ed. mass mkt. 6.99 (*0-446-60597-2*) Warner Bks., Inc.

**RIGANTE (IMAGINARY PLACE)—FICTION**

Gemmell, David. Midnight Falcon. 2001. (Rigante Ser.: Bk. 2). 448p. mass mkt. 7.50 (*0-345-43236-3*, Del Rey) Ballantine Bks.

—The Midnight Falcon, Bk. 2. 2000. 404p. mass mkt. (*0-552-14257-3*, Corgi) Bantam Bks.

—The Sword in the Storm. 2001. (Rigante Ser.: Bk. 1). 448p. mass mkt. 7.50 (*0-345-43234-7*, Del Rey) Ballantine Bks.

—Sword in the Storm. 1999. (Illus.). 352p. o.s.i (*0-593-03718-9*, Corgi) Bantam Bks.

—A Sword in the Storm: Book One in The Rigante Series. 1999. (Illus.). 480p. mass mkt. (*0-552-14256-5*, Corgi) Bantam Bks.

**RINGWORLD (IMAGINARY PLACE)—FICTION**

Niven, Larry. Ringworld. 1997. pap. 11.00 o.s.i (*0-345-41840-9*, Del Rey); 1985. 352p. mass mkt. 6.99 (*0-345-33392-6*, Del Rey); 1983. mass mkt. 2.95 o.p. (*0-345-31675-4*, Del Rey); 1982. mass mkt. 2.75 o.p. (*0-345-30634-1*, Del Rey); 1981. mass mkt. 2.50 o.p. (*0-345-29301-0*, Del Rey); 1979. mass mkt. 2.25 o.p. (*0-345-28866-1*, Del Rey); 1977. mass mkt. 1.95 o.p. (*0-345-27550-0*, Del Rey); 1977. mass mkt. 1.75 o.p. (*0-345-25776-6*); 1975. mass mkt. 1.50 o.p. (*0-345-24795-7*); 1972. mass mkt. 1.25 o.p. (*0-345-22759-X*); 1971. mass mkt. 0.95 o.p. (*0-345-22046-3*) Ballantine Bks.

—Ringworld. unabr. ed. 1996. audio 56.95 (*0-7861-0977-7*, 1754) Blackstone Audio Bks., Inc.

—Ringworld. unabr. collector's ed. 1997. audio 64.00 (*0-7366-3770-2*, 4443) Books on Tape, Inc.

—The Ringworld Engineers. 1997. pap. 11.00 o.p. (*0-345-41841-7*); 1985. 368p. mass mkt. 6.99 (*0-345-33430-2*) Ballantine Bks. (Del Rey).

—The Ringworld Engineers. unabr. collector's ed. 1998. audio 64.00 (*0-7366-3992-6*, 4280) Books on Tape, Inc.

—The Ringworld Engineers. 1980. 372p. o.p. (*0-03-021376-2*) Holt, Henry & Co.

—The Ringworld Engineers. 1979. (Illus.). 356p. 30.00 o.p. (*0-932096-03-4*) Phantasia Pr.

—The Ringworld Throne. 1997. 368p. mass mkt. 6.99 (*0-345-41296-6*, Del Rey) Ballantine Bks.

—The Ringworld Throne. unabr. collector's ed. 1996. audio 72.00 (*0-7366-4321-4*, 4800) Books on Tape, Inc.

**RIO DE JANEIRO (BRAZIL)—FICTION**

Garcia-Roza, Luiz Alfredo. The Silence of the Rain: A Detective Espinosa Mystery. 2003. Tr. of Silencio da Chuva. 272p. pap. 14.00 (*0-312-42118-4*) Picador.

—The Silence of the Rain: A Novel. Moser, Benjamin, tr. from POR. 2002. Tr. of Silencio da Chuva. 272p. 24.00 (*0-8050-6889-9*) Holt, Henry & Co.

Kaiser, Janice. Last Night in Rio. 1996. 441p. per. (*1-55166-174-8*, 1-66174-3, Mira Bks.) Harlequin Enterprises, Ltd.

L'Abbe, Pierre. Ten Days in Rio: A Novella in Verse. 1998. 194p. pap. (*1-894205-07-3*) Watershed Bks.

Lispector, Clarice. The Hour of the Star. Pontiero, Giovanni, tr. from POR. & afterword by by. 1992. (Paperbook Ser.: Vol. 733). 96p. reprint ed. pap. 8.95 (*0-8112-1190-8*, NDP733) New Directions Publishing Corp.

Mullenax, Foster. Red Rose of Rio. 2001. 132p. E-Book 8.00 (*0-7388-7848-0*) Xlibris Corp.

Ripley, J. R. The Body from Ipanema: A Tony Kozol Mystery. 2002. (Tony Kozol Mystery Ser.: Vol. 4). 244p. (YA). kivar 22.95 (*1-892695-08-1*) Long Wind Publishing.

Soares, Jo. A Samba for Sherlock. Landers, Clifford E., tr. from POR. 1997. 288p. 3.99 o.s.i (*0-375-40065-6*, Pantheon) Knopf Publishing Group.

—A Samba for Sherlock: A Novel. 1998. 288p. pap. 19.00 (*0-375-70066-8*, Vintage) Knopf Publishing Group.

**RIVER CITY (MO.: IMAGINARY PLACE)—FICTION**

Harrison, Janis. Murder Sets Seed: A Gardening Mystery. 2001. 256p. mass mkt. 6.50 (*0-312-97725-5*, St. Martin's Paperbacks); 2000. 248p. 22.95 (*0-312-20382-9*, Saint Martin's Minotaur) St. Martin's Pr.

—Murder Sets Seed: A Gardening Mystery. l.t. ed. 2001. 347p. (*0-7862-3351-6*) Thorndike Pr.

—Roots of Murder. l.t. ed. 2002. (Mystery Ser.). 282p. 29.45 (*0-7862-3914-X*) Gale Group.

—Roots of Murder. 246p. 2000. mass mkt. 5.99 (*0-312-97500-7*, St. Martin's Paperbacks); 2nd ed. 1999. 21.95 (*0-312-20304-7*, Saint Martin's Minotaur) St. Martin's Pr.

**RIVERWORLD (IMAGINARY PLACE)—FICTION**

Farmer, Philip Jose. The Dark Design. 1998. (Riverworld Saga Ser.: Vol. 3). 464p. pap. 13.95 (*0-345-41969-3*, Del Rey) Ballantine Bks.

—The Dark Design. 1986. 3.95 o.s.i (*0-425-09842-7*); 1984. 2.95 o.s.i (*0-425-07284-3*); 1984. (YA). 3.50 o.s.i (*0-425-08678-X*); 1983. 2.95 o.s.i (*0-425-06584-7*); 1983. 2.75 o.s.i (*0-425-05546-9*); 1981. 2.50 o.s.i (*0-425-05027-0*); 1978. 2.25 o.s.i (*0-425-03831-9*) Berkley Publishing Group.

—The Fabulous Riverboat. 1998. (Riverworld Saga Ser.: Vol. 2). 240p. pap. 14.00 (*0-345-41968-5*, Del Rey) Ballantine Bks.

—The Fabulous Riverboat. 1986. 416p. 3.50 o.s.i (*0-425-09958-X*); 1984. (Riverworld Ser.: No. 2). 2.95 o.s.i (*0-425-07756-X*) Berkley Publishing Group.

—The Magic Labyrinth. 1998. (Riverworld Saga Ser.: Vol. 4). 416p. pap. 13.95 (*0-345-41970-7*, Del Rey) Ballantine Bks.

—The Magic Labyrinth. 1986. 416p. 3.50 o.s.i (*0-425-09550-9*) Berkley Publishing Group.

—River of Eternity. 1983. 17.00 (*0-932096-28-X*) Phantasia Pr.

—Riverworld & Other Stories. 1984. 272p. 2.75 o.s.i (*0-425-06487-5*) Berkley Publishing Group.

—Riverworld War: The suppressed fiction of Philip Jose Farmer. 1980. 112p. 25.00 o.p. (*0-933180-13-6*) Ellis Pr., The.

—To Your Scattered Bodies Go. 1988. (Riverworld Ser.: Vol. 1). mass mkt. 4.50 o.s.i (*0-441-82069-7*) Ace Bks.

—To Your Scattered Bodies Go. 1998. (Riverworld Saga Ser.: Vol. 1). 224p. pap. 13.95 (*0-345-41967-7*, Del Rey) Ballantine Bks.

—To Your Scattered Bodies Go. 1987. 224p. 2.95 o.s.i (*0-425-10334-X*); 1982. Berkley Publishing Group.

—To Your Scattered Bodies Go, unabr. ed. 2000. audio 57.00 (*0-7887-4318-X*, 96123E7) Recorded Bks., LLC.

**ROCKSBURG (PA.: IMAGINARY PLACE)—FICTION**

Constantine, K. C. Always a Body to Trade. unabr. ed. 1997. (Mario Balzic Ser.). audio 48.00 (*0-7366-3685-4*, 4364) Books on Tape, Inc.

—Always a Body to Trade: A Mario Balzic Mystery. 1983. 256p. 13.95 o.p. (*0-87923-458-X*); 1993. 248p. reprint ed. pap. 5.95 (*0-87923-952-2*) Godine, David R. Pub.

—Always a Body to Trade: A Mario Balzic Mystery. 1984. (Crime Monthly Ser.). 256p. pap. 3.95 o.p. (*0-14-007059-1*, Penguin Bks.) Viking Penguin.

—Blank Page. 11th ed. 1989. pap. 3.95 o.p. (*0-87923-707-4*) Godine, David R. Pub.

—Bottom Liner Blues. unabr. ed. 1997. (Mario Balzic Ser.). audio 56.00 (*0-7366-3691-9*, 4370) Books on Tape, Inc.

—Bottom Liner Blues. 1993. 256p. 18.95 (*0-89296-289-5*) Mysterious Pr.

—Bottom Liner Blues. 1994. 272p. mass mkt. 5.99 o.s.i (*0-446-40372-5*) Warner Bks., Inc.

—Brushback. unabr. collector's ed. 1998. (Mario Balzic Ser.). audio 64.00 (*0-7366-4216-1*, 4714) Books on Tape, Inc.

—Brushback. 1998. (Mario Balzic Novel Ser.). 288p. 22.00 (*0-89296-646-7*) Mysterious Pr.

—Brushback. 1999. mass mkt. (*0-446-60675-8*) Warner Bks., Inc.

—Cranks & Shadows. unabr. ed. 1997. (Mario Balzic Ser.). audio 72.00 (*0-7366-3692-7*, 4371) Books on Tape, Inc.

—Cranks & Shadows. 1995. 314p. 19.95 o.p. (*0-89296-543-6*) Mysterious Pr.

—Cranks & Shadows. 1996. 320p. mass mkt. 5.99 o.s.i (*0-446-40353-9*) Warner Bks., Inc.

—Family Values. unabr. ed. 1998. (Mario Balzic Ser.: Vol. 13). audio 48.00 (*0-7366-4035-5*, 4534) Books on Tape, Inc.

—Family Values. l.t. ed. 1997. (G. K. Hall Mystery Ser.). 290p. lib. bdg. 26.95 o.p. (*0-7838-8232-7*, Macmillan Reference USA) Gale Group.

—Family Values. 1998. mass mkt. (*0-446-40355-5*, Mysterious Pr. Paperback Bks.); 1997. 224p. 22.00 o.p. (*0-89296-545-2*); 1998. 256p. mass mkt. 5.99 (*0-446-60594-8*) Warner Bks., Inc.

—A Fix Like This. unabr. ed. 1997. (Mario Balzic Ser.). audio 64.00 (*0-7366-3693-5*, 4372) Books on Tape, Inc.

—A Fix Like This. 1988. 3.95 o.p. (*0-87923-718-X*) Godine, David R. Pub.

—Good Sons. unabr. ed. 1998. (Mario Balzic Ser.). audio 56.00 (*0-7366-4015-0*, 4513) Books on Tape, Inc.

—Good Sons. 1996. 304p. 21.95 o.p. (*0-89296-544-4*) Mysterious Pr.

—Good Sons. 1997. (Rocksburg Novels Ser.). 304p. mass mkt. 5.99 o.s.i (*0-446-40354-7*) Warner Bks., Inc.

—Joey's Case. unabr. ed. 1997. (Mario Balzic Ser.). audio 56.00 (*0-7366-3783-4*, 4455) Books on Tape, Inc.

—Joey's Case. 1989. 224p. mass mkt. 4.50 (*0-445-40786-7*, Mysterious Pr. Paperback Bks.) Warner Bks., Inc.

—Joey's Case: A Mario Balzic Novel. 1988. 15.95 (*0-89296-347-6*) Mysterious Pr.

—The Man Who Liked Slow Tomatoes. 1993. (Mario Balzic Detective Novel Ser.). 192p. pap. 5.95 (*0-87923-953-0*); 1982. (Mario Balzic Mystery Ser.: No. 5). 256p. 13.95 o.p. (*0-87923-407-5*) Godine, David R. Pub.

—The Man Who Liked Slow Tomatoes. 1983. 224p. pap. 2.95 o.p. (*0-14-006621-7*, Penguin Bks.) Viking Penguin.

—The Man Who Liked to Look at Himself. l.t. ed. 1987. (Nightingale Ser.). 249p. 11.95 o.p. (*0-8161-4373-0*, Macmillan Reference USA) Gale Group.

—The Man Who Liked to Look at Himself. Barzun, Jacques & Taylor, W. H., eds. 1983. (Crime Fiction 1950-1975 Ser.). 151p. lib. bdg. 18.00 o.p. (*0-8240-4955-1*) Garland Publishing, Inc.

—The Man Who Liked to Look at Himself. 1987. (Double Detective Ser.: No. 3). 160p. pap. 8.95 o.p. (*0-87923-468-7*); pap. 3.95 o.p. (*0-87923-663-9*) Godine, David R. Pub.

—Man Who Liked to Look at Himself & The Blank Page. unabr. ed. 1997. (Mario Balzic Ser.: Vol. 2 & 3). audio 64.00 (*0-7366-3612-9*, 4271) Books on Tape, Inc.

—The Rocksburg Railroad Murders. unabr. ed. 1997. (Mario Balzic Ser.: Vol. 1). audio 40.00 (*0-7366-3622-6*, 4281) Books on Tape, Inc.

—Sunshine Enemies. unabr. ed. 1997. (Mario Balzic Ser.). audio 42.00 (*0-7366-3784-2*, 4456) Books on Tape, Inc.

—Sunshine Enemies. 1990. 176p. 18.95 o.p. (*0-89296-288-7*) Mysterious Pr.

—Sunshine Enemies. 1991. mass mkt. 4.95 o.s.i (*0-446-40008-4*, Mysterious Pr. Paperback Bks.) Warner Bks., Inc.

—Upon Some Midnights Clear. unabr. ed. 1997. (Mario Balzic Ser.). audio 48.00 (*0-7366-3694-3*, 4373) Books on Tape, Inc.

—Upon Some Midnights Clear. 1985. (Mario Balzic Mystery Ser.). 256p. 15.95 o.p. (*0-87923-570-5*) Godine, David R. Pub.

—Upon Some Midnights Clear. 1987. 24p. mass mkt. 3.50 o.p. (*0-14-009404-0*, Penguin Bks.) Viking Penguin.

**ROCKY MOUNTAINS—FICTION**

Blevins, Win. So Wild a Dream. 2003. (Rendezvous Ser.). 400p. 24.95 (*0-7653-0573-9*, Forge Bks.) Doherty, Tom Assocs., LLC.

Castillo, Linda. A Cry in the Night. 2002. (Silhouette Intimate Moments Ser.: No. 1186). 256p. mass mkt. (*0-373-27256-1*, Silhouette) Harlequin Enterprises, Ltd.

Champlin, Tim. Iron Trail. l.t. ed. 2001. 252p. 24.95 (*0-7838-9492-9*, Macmillan Reference USA) Gale Group.

Chaudet, Annette. Hard Ground 2000: Writing the Rockies. 2001. 272p. E-Book 8.00 (*0-7388-9708-6*) Xlibris Corp.

Doucet, Sharon Arms. Back Before Dark. 2004. 272p. pap. 12.95 (*0-451-21104-9*) NAL.

Gustafson, Sid. Prisoners of Flight. 2003. 256p. pap. 16.00 (*1-57962-088-4*) Permanent Pr., The.

Heitzmann, Kristen. Honor's Disguise, 4. 1999. (Rocky Mountain Legacy Ser.: Vol. 4). 288p. pap. 11.99 (*0-7642-2203-1*) Bethany Hse. Pubs.

—Honor's Disguise. 2002. 275p. 24.95 (*0-7862-3568-3*, Five Star) Gale Group.

—Honor's Price. 1998. (Rocky Mountain Legacy Ser.: Vol. 2). 304p. pap. 11.99 (*0-7642-2032-2*) Bethany Hse. Pubs.

—Honor's Price. 2001. 333p. 23.95 (*0-7862-3569-1*, Five Star) Gale Group.

—Honor's Quest. 1999. (Rocky Mountain Legacy Ser.: Bk. 3). 288p. pap. 11.99 (*0-7642-2033-0*) Bethany Hse. Pubs.

—Honor's Quest. 2002. 307p. 23.95 (*0-7862-3570-5*, Five Star) Gale Group.

—Honor's Reward. 2000. (Rocky Mountain Legacy Ser.: Vol. 5). 320p. pap. 11.99 (*0-7642-2204-X*) Bethany Hse. Pubs.

—Honor's Reward. 2002. (Five Star Christian Fiction Ser.). 380p. 24.95 (*0-7862-3571-3*, Five Star) Gale Group.

—A Rush of Wings. 2003. 384p. pap. 12.99 (*0-7642-2606-1*) Bethany Hse. Pubs.

Johnstone, William W. Blood of the Mountain Man. l.t. ed. 2001. (G. K. Hall Western Ser.). 297p. 24.95 o.p. (*0-7838-9487-2*, Macmillan Reference USA) Gale Group.

—Blood on the Divide. 1996. (First Mountain Man Ser.). 320p. mass mkt. 4.99 o.s.i (*0-8217-5511-0*, Zebra Bks.) Kensington Publishing Corp.

—Code of the Mountain Man. 2001. 288p. mass mkt. 5.99 (*0-7860-1304-4*); 1998. 288p. mass mkt. 4.99 (*0-8217-5944-2*); 1995. mass mkt. 4.99 o.s.i (*0-8217-5365-7*, Zebra Bks.); 1991. 288p. mass mkt. 3.50 o.s.i (*0-8217-3342-7*, Zebra Bks.) Kensington Publishing Corp.

—Code of the Mountain Man. l.t. ed. 2000. (G. K. Hall Western Ser.). (Illus.). 328p. 24.95 o.p. (*0-7838-9130-X*) Thorndike Pr.

—Valor of the Mountain Man. l.t. ed. 2001. (G.K. Hall Large Print Western Ser.). 325p. 25.95 (*0-7838-9539-9*, Macmillan Reference USA) Gale Group.

—Valor of the Mountain Man. 2001. 256p. mass mkt. 5.99 (*0-7860-1299-4*, Pinnacle Bks.) Kensington Publishing Corp.

—War of the Mountain Man. l.t. ed. 2000. (G. K. Hall Western Ser.). 343p. 24.95 (*0-7838-8940-2*, Macmillan Reference USA) Gale Group.

—War of the Mountain Man. 2001. 256p. mass mkt. 5.99 (*0-7860-1303-6*); 1996. 256p. mass mkt. 4.99 o.s.i (*0-8217-5610-9*); 1995. 288p. mass mkt. 4.50 o.s.i (*0-8217-5083-6*); 1990. mass mkt. 3.50 o.p. (*0-8217-3618-3*, Zebra Bks.) Kensington Publishing Corp.

Jones, Pauline Baird. Missing You. 2002. (Five Star First Edition Romance Ser.). 335p. 26.95 (*0-7862-3748-1*, Five Star) Gale Group.

—Missing You. 2002. (Lonesome Lawman Ser.: Bk. 3). 240p. pap. 12.95 (*0-7599-0526-6*) Hard Shell Word Factory.

McDaniel, Whitt. Addie Fay & Old Yellow Streak. 1999. E-Book 6.95 (*0-87714-361-7*) Denlingers Pubs., Ltd.

Osborne, Maggie. Silver Lining. 2000. 352p. mass mkt. 6.99 (*0-449-00516-X*, Ivy Bks.) Ballantine Bks.

—Silver Lining. l.t. ed. 2001. 358p. 28.95 (*1-57490-375-6*, Beeler Large Print Bks.) Beeler, Thomas T. Publisher.

Robinson, Eden. Monkey Beach. 2000. 384p. 24.00 (*0-618-07327-2*, Mariner Bks.) Houghton Mifflin Co. Trade & Reference Div.

—Monkey Beach. 2000. 384p. (*0-676-97075-3*) Knopf, Alfred A. Inc.

—Monkey Beach: A Novel. 2002. (Illus.). 384p. pap. 13.00 (*0-618-21905-6*, Mariner Bks.) Houghton Mifflin Co. Trade & Reference Div.

Whipple, Dan. Click: A Novel. 2001. 258p. 35.00 (*0-87081-632-2*) Univ. Pr. of Colorado.

White, Stewart Edward. The Long Rifle. reprint ed. lib. bdg. 25.95 (*0-88411-885-1*) Amereon, Ltd.

—The Long Rifle. 1990. (Classics of the Fur Trade). 384p. 24.95 (*0-87842-254-4*) Scurlock Publishing Co., Inc.

—The Long Rifle. 1987. (Illus.). 544p. reprint ed. 25.00 (*0-935632-54-9*) Wolfe Publishing Co.

### ROMANIA—FICTION

Astrachan, Samuel. Malaparte in Jassy. 155p. reprint ed. pap. 48.10 (*0-608-10587-2*, 2071208) Bks. on Demand.

—Malaparte in Jassy. 1989. 156p. (C). 24.95 (*0-8143-2162-3*) Wayne State Univ. Pr.

Aycliffe, Jonathan. Lost. 1997. 272p. mass mkt. 5.50 o.p. (*0-06-105483-6*); 1996. 144p. mass mkt. 16.00 o.p. (*0-06-105225-6*) Morrow/Avon. (Eos).

Berecz, Sophie & Soo, Arpad. In His Hands. 2002. 159p. 12.99 (*0-8163-1903-0*) Pacific Pr. Publishing Assn.

Brownjohn, Alan, contrib. by. The Long Shadows. 1997. 382p. (*1-899235-21-3*) Lewis, Dewi Publishing GBR. *Dist:* Distributed Art Pubs./D.A.P.

Byng, Lucy M., tr. from RUM. Roumanian Stories. 1977. (Short Story Index Reprint Ser.). reprint ed. 22.95 (*0-8369-4004-0*) Ayer Co. Pubs., Inc.

Furst, Alan. Blood of Victory: A Novel. 2003. (Illus.). 272p. pap. 12.95 (*0-8129-6872-7*, Modern Library) Random House Adult Trade Publishing Group.

—Blood of Victory: A Novel. 2002. (Illus.). 256p. 24.95 (*0-375-50574-1*) Random Hse., Inc.

—Blood of Victory: A Novel. 2002. (Core Ser.). 29.95 (*0-7862-4915-3*) Thorndike Pr.

Galloway, Steven. Ascension: A Novel. 2003. 280p. 23.00 (*0-7867-1208-2*, Carroll & Graf Pubs.) Avalon Publishing Group.

Istrati, Panait. Kyra Kyralina. Whitall, James, tr. from FRE. 1977. (Short Story Index Reprint Ser.). reprint ed. 19.95 (*0-8369-3889-5*) Ayer Co. Pubs., Inc.

Kalogridis, Jeanne. Children of the Vampire. abr. ed. 1996. audio 7.99 o.p. (*1-56740-135-X*, 633, Paperback Nova Audio Bks.); 1995. audio 17.95 o.p. (*1-56100-444-8*, 1637, Nova Audio Bks.); 1995. audio 57.25 o.p. (*1-56100-276-3*, 1150, Unabridged Library Editions); 1995. audio 23.95 o.p. (*1-56100-651-3*, 62, Bookcassette) Brilliance Audio.

—Children of the Vampire. 1996. (Diaries of the Family Dracula: Vol. 2). 368p. mass mkt. 6.99 (*0-440-22269-9*) Dell Publishing.

—Covenant with the Vampire: The Diaries of the Family Dracula. abr. ed. 1994. audio 16.95 o.p. (*1-56100-393-X*, 1552, Nova Audio Bks.); audio 73.25 o.p. (*1-56100-227-5*, 849, Unabridged Library Editions); audio 23.95 o.p. (*1-56100-602-5*, 71, Bookcassette) Brilliance Audio.

—Covenant with the Vampire: The Diaries of the Family Dracula. 1995. (Diaries of the Family Dracula: Vol. 1). 384p. mass mkt. 6.99 (*0-440-21543-9*) Dell Publishing.

—Covenant with the Vampire: The Diaries of the Family Dracula. l.t. ed. 1995. (Charnwood Large Print Ser.). 448p. 29.99 o.p. (*0-7089-8872-5*, Charnwood) Thorpe, F. A. Pubs. GBR. *Dist:* Ulverscroft Large Print Bks., Ltd., Ulverscroft Large Print Canada, Ltd.

—Lord of the Vampires: The Diaries of the Family Dracul. 1997. (Diaries of the Family Dracula: Vol. 3). 384p. mass mkt. 6.50 (*0-440-22442-X*); 1996. 336p. 22.95 o.s.i (*0-385-31414-0*, Delacorte Pr.) Dell Publishing.

Lee, Earl. Drakulya: The Lost Journal of Mircea Drakulya, Lord of the Undead. 1994. 224p. pap. 10.95 o.p. (*1-884365-02-7*) See Sharp Pr.

Malouf, David. An Imaginary Life. 1978. 7.95 o.s.i (*0-8076-0884-X*) Braziller, George Inc.

—An Imaginary Life. 1996. 160p. pap. 12.00 (*0-679-76793-2*) Random Hse., Inc.

Manea, Norman. The Black Envelope. 2004. Tr. of Plicul Negru. pap. (*0-374-52947-7*) Farrar, Straus & Giroux.

—The Black Envelope. Camiller, Patrick, tr. 1995. Tr. of Plicul Negru. (ENG & RUM.). 336p. 25.00 o.p. (*0-374-11397-1*) Farrar, Straus & Giroux.

—The Black Envelope. Camiller, Patrick, tr. 1996. Tr. of Plicul Negru. 329p. pap. 16.95 (*0-8101-1377-5*, Hydra Bks.) Northwestern Univ. Pr.

Muller, Herta. The Appointment: A Novel. Hulse, Michael & Boehm, Philip, trs. from GER. 2001. 224p. 23.00 o.s.i (*0-8050-6012-X*, Metropolitan Bks.) Holt, Henry & Co.

—The Land of Green Plums: A Novel. Hofmann, Michael, tr. 1996. 256p. 23.00 o.s.i (*0-8050-4295-4*, Metropolitan Bks.) Holt, Henry & Co.

—The Land of Green Plums: A Novel. Hofmann, Michael, tr. from GER. 1998. 256p. pap. 17.00 (*0-8101-1597-2*, Hydra Bks.) Northwestern Univ. Pr.

Quint, Bert. Transylvania Red. 2002. 280p. pap. 15.95 (*0-595-22507-1*, Writers Club Pr.) iUniverse, Inc.

Rhodes, Kristopher. Fall of the Tyrant: A Novel of the 1989 Romanian Revolution. 2001. 209p. pap. 21.99 (*1-4010-1414-3*) Xlibris Corp.

Saberhagen, Fred & Hart, James V. Bram Stoker's Dracula. 1992. 304p. mass mkt. 4.99 o.p. (*0-451-17575-1*, Signet Bks.) NAL.

Simmons, Dan. Children of the Night. unabr. ed. 1992. audio 23.95 o.p. (*1-56100-470-7*, 61, Bookcassette);Set. audio 73.25 o.p. (*1-56100-104-X*, 825, Unabridged Library Editions) Brilliance Audio.

—Children of the Night. deluxe ed. 1992. 450p. (J). 125.00 (*0-935716-63-7*) Lord John Pr.

—Children of the Night. 320p. (J). 2015. 100.00 (*0-399-13757-2*); 1992. 21.95 o.p. (*0-399-13717-3*) Penguin Group (USA) Inc. (G. P. Putnam's Sons).

—Children of the Night. 1993. 464p. reprint ed. mass mkt. 6.99 (*0-446-36475-4*) Warner Bks., Inc.

Stoker, Bram. Dracula. Date not set. pap. text (*0-17-557040-X*) Addison-Wesley Longman, Inc.

—Dracula. Date not set. reprint ed. lib. bdg. 27.95 (*0-88411-131-8*, Aeonian Pr.) Amereon, Ltd.

—Dracula. 2000. (SPA.). 496p. 10.95 (*84-406-5500-2*) B Ediciones S.A. ESP. *Dist:* Distribooks, Inc.

—Dracula. abr. ed. 1995. audio 19.95 (*1-882071-36-0*) B&B Audio, Inc.

—Dracula. 1983. mass mkt. 1.95 o.s.i (*0-553-21148-X*, Bantam Classics) Bantam Bks.

—Dracula. E-Book 5.00 (*0-7607-1358-8*) Barnes & Noble, Inc.

—Dracula. Bennett, S. A., ed. 1992. (Illus.). 64p. pap. (*0-944099-20-3*) Bill Barry's Compass Bks.

—Dracula. 2002. pap. 4.50 (*1-59109-321-X*) Booksurge, LLC.

—Dracula. 1992. 320p. reprint ed. pap. 9.95 (*0-86322-143-2*) Brandon Bk. Pubs., Ltd. IRL. *Dist:* Irish Bks. & Media, Inc.

—Dracula. Byron, Glennis, ed. 1997. (Literary Texts Ser.). 400p. (C). pap. (*1-55111-136-5*) Broadview Pr.

—Dracula. 1990. reprint ed. lib. bdg. 26.95 (*0-89966-692-2*) Buccaneer Bks., Inc.

—Dracula. ed. 1999. (J). (gr. 2). spiral bd. (*0-616-01788-X*) Canadian National Institute for the Blind/Institut National Canadien pour les Aveugles.

—Dracula. reprint ed. lib. bdg. 98.00 (*0-7426-2890-6*); 2001. pap. text 28.00 (*0-7426-7890-3*) Classic Bks.

—Dracula. 1997. 384p. 21.95 (*0-312-86358-6*, Tor Bks.); 1992. 384p. mass mkt. 4.99 (*0-8125-2301-6*, Tor Classics); 1988. mass mkt. 4.95 (*1-55902-006-7*, Aerie) Doherty, Tom Assocs., LLC.

—Dracula. 1959. 7.95 o.p. (*0-385-00383-8*) Doubleday Publishing.

—Dracula. 2000. 320p. pap. 2.00 (*0-486-41109-5*) Dover Pubns., Inc.

—Dracula. 1980. 82p. (YA). (gr. 7 up). pap. 5.60 (*0-87129-308-0*, D35) Dramatic Publishing Co.

—Dracula. l.t. ed. 2079p. pap. 123.00 (*0-7583-3191-6*); 1792p. pap. 110.00 (*0-7583-3190-8*); 406p. pap. 32.00 (*0-7583-3184-3*); 528p. pap. 37.00 (*0-7583-3185-1*); 723p. pap. 45.00 (*0-7583-3186-X*); 926p. pap. 64.00 (*0-7583-3187-8*); 1185p. pap. 76.00 (*0-7583-3188-6*); 528p. lib. bdg. 43.00 (*0-7583-3177-0*); 1792p. lib. bdg. 133.00 (*0-7583-3182-7*); 406p. lib. bdg. 38.00 (*0-7583-3176-2*); 1185p. lib. bdg. 88.00 (*0-7583-3180-0*); 723p. lib. bdg. 51.00 (*0-7583-3178-9*); 926p. lib. bdg. 76.00 (*0-7583-3179-7*); 2079p. lib. bdg. 148.00 (*0-7583-3183-5*); 1457p. lib. bdg. 102.00 (*0-7583-3181-9*) Huge Print Pr.

—Dracula. 1998. (Cloth Bound Pocket Ser.). 240p. 7.95 (*3-89508-096-9*, 520018) Konemann.

—Dracula. 2002. (Classics for Young Readers Ser.). (SPA.). (YA). 14.95 (*84-392-0934-7*, EV30652) Lectorum Pubns., Inc.

—Dracula. 2000. (English As a Second Language Bk.). pap. text 5.95 o.p. (*0-582-53523-9*) Longman Publishing Group.

—Dracula. 1989. 368p. 19.95 o.p. (*0-87226-189-1*, Bedrick, Peter Bks.) McGraw-Hill Children's Publishing.

—Dracula. 1992. 392p. mass mkt. 3.99 o.p. (*0-451-17581-6*, Signet Classics); 1986. mass mkt. 2.50 o.p. (*0-451-52097-1*); 1973. mass mkt. 0.95 o.p. (*0-451-05438-5*, Signet Bks.); 1973. mass mkt. 0.60 o.p. (*0-451-02793-0*, Signet Bks.); 1965. mass mkt. 2.50 o.p. (*0-451-51670-2*, Signet Classics); 1965. mass mkt. 1.25 o.p. (*0-451-50717-7*, Signet Classics); 1965. mass mkt. 1.95 o.p. (*0-451-51889-6*, Signet Classics); 1965. mass mkt. 1.50 o.p. (*0-451-51030-5*, Signet Classics); 1965. mass mkt. 1.75 o.p. (*0-451-51129-8*, Signet Classics) NAL.

—Dracula. l.t. ed. (Large Print Ser.). 1993. 558p. lib. bdg. 26.00 (*0-939495-43-0*); 1998. 435p. reprint ed. lib. bdg. 25.00 (*1-58287-024-1*) North Bks.

—Dracula. l.t. ed. 2003. 448p. E-Book 2.99 (*1-932681-17-5*) NuVision Pubns.

—Dracula. Ellmann, Maud, ed. & intro. by. 1998. (Oxford World's Classics Ser.). 432p. pap. 9.95 (*0-19-283386-3*) Oxford Univ. Pr., Inc.

—Dracula. 1995. (Illus.). 126p. pap. text 5.95 (*0-19-586322-4*); 1984. 408p. pap. 4.95 o.p. (*0-19-281598-9*) Oxford Univ. Pr., Inc.

—Dracula. Ellman, Maud, ed. & intro. by. 2nd ed. 1996. (Oxford World's Classics Ser.). 428p. pap. 6.95 o.p. (*0-19-282462-7*) Oxford Univ. Pr., Inc.

—Dracula. Teresa Agnes, ed. Heller, Rudolf, tr. 1979. (SPA., Illus.). 64p. stu. ed. 1.50 (*0-88301-566-8*); pap. text 3.95 (*0-88301-446-7*) Pendulum Pr., Inc.

—Dracula. abr. ed. 1992. (Classics on Cassette). 15.95 o.p. incl. audio (*0-453-00786-4*) Penguin/HighBridge.

—Dracula. 1993. (SPA.). 464p. (*84-01-49200-9*) Plaza & Janés Editories, S.A.

—Dracula. (Paperback Classics Ser.). 2001. 432p. pap. 10.95 (*0-375-75670-1*); 2000. E-Book 4.95 (*0-679-64197-1*) Random House Adult Trade Publishing Group. (Modern Library).

—Dracula. (Modern Library Ser.). 1996. 448p. 17.95 o.s.i (*0-679-60229-1*); 1978. 6.95 o.s.i (*0-394-60447-4*) Random Hse., Inc.

—Dracula. 2002. E-Book 4.95 (*0-9712207-1-9*) Riverdale Electronic Bks.

—Dracula. unabr. ed. 1995. 528p. text 8.98 o.p. (*1-56138-515-8*, Courage Bks.) Running Pr. Bk. Pubs.

—Dracula. 2003. 528p. mass mkt. 5.99 (*0-7434-7736-7*, Pocket) Simon & Schuster.

—Dracula. l.t. ed. 1993. 592p. lib. bdg. 22.95 (*0-8161-5692-1*) Thorndike Pr.

—Dracula. Johnson, Beth, ed. & afterword by by. 2003. 428p. mass mkt. 2.00 (*1-59194-003-6*) Townsend Pr.

—Dracula. 2001. (Classics of Mystery & Suspense Ser.). 334p. (*1-58279-187-2*) Trident Pr. International.

—Dracula. 1965. (Signet Classics Ser.). 11.00 (*0-606-00578-1*) Turtleback Bks.

—Dracula. 1993. 432p. pap. 5.95 o.p. (*0-460-87189-7*, Everyman's Classic Library in Paperback) Tuttle Publishing.

—Dracula. Howes, Marjorie, ed. rev. ed. 1995. 400p. pap. 5.95 (*0-460-87598-1*, Everyman's Classic Library in Paperback) Tuttle Publishing.

—Dracula. (Penguin Classics Ser.). 560p. 2003. pap. 11.00 (*0-14-143984-X*, Penguin Classics); 1999. pap. (*0-14-043381-3*) Viking Penguin.

—Dracula. annuals Hindle, Maurice, ed. & intro. by. 1993. (Classics Ser.). 560p. 10.95 (*0-14-043406-2*, Penguin Classics) Viking Penguin.

—Dracula. 1979. 448p. pap. 4.95 o.p. (*0-14-005280-1*, Penguin Bks.) Viking Penguin.

—Dracula. 2002. 324p. pap. 18.95 (*1-58715-588-5*); lib. bdg. 29.95 (*1-58715-589-3*) Wildside Pr.

—Dracula. 1997. (Classics Library). 336p. pap. 3.95 (*1-85326-086-X*, 086XWW) Wordsworth Editions, Ltd. GBR. *Dist:* Casemate Pubs. & Bk. Distributors, LLC.

—Dracula. l.t. ed. 1994. 592p. pap. 14.95 o.p. (*0-8161-5817-7*) World Pubns., Inc.

Stoker, Bram & Byron, Glennis. Dracula. 1998. E-Book 9.95 (*0-585-29380-5*) netLibrary, Inc.

Stoker, Bram & Outlet Book Company Staff. Dracula. 1992. 9.99 o.s.i (*0-517-06973-3*) Random Hse. Value Publishing.

Wilson, Barbara. Trouble in Transylvania. 288p. 1993. 18.95 o.p. (*1-878067-34-6*); 3rd ed. 1994. pap. 10.95 (*1-878067-49-4*) Avalon Publishing Group. (Seal Pr.).

Wolf, Leonard & Stoker, Bram. The Essential Dracula. 1993. (Essentials Ser.). (Illus.). 512p. pap. 16.95 o.p. (*0-452-26943-1*, Plume) Dutton/Plume.

### ROME—FICTION

Alison, Jane. The Love-Artist. 2001. 242p. 23.00 o.p. (*0-374-23179-6*) Farrar, Straus & Giroux.

—The Love-Artist. 2002. 256p. pap. 13.00 (*0-312-42006-4*) Picador.

Ashley, Mike, ed. The Mammoth Book of Roman Whodunnits. 2003. 544p. pap. 11.95 (*0-7867-1241-4*) Avalon Publishing Group.

Benning, Barry. The Unspoken Power of Rome. 2002. (Illus.). 436p. 23.95 (*0-9715676-0-3*) Wellspring Bks.

Borchardt, Alice. Night of the Wolf. 2000. 512p. mass mkt. 6.99 (*0-345-42363-1*) Ballantine Bks.

Bradshaw, Gillian. The Beacon at Alexandria, 001. 1986. 17.95 o.p. (*0-395-41159-9*) Houghton Mifflin Co.

—Cleopatra's Heir. 2003. 448p. reprint ed. pap. 15.95 (*0-7653-0229-2*, Forge Bks.) Doherty, Tom Assocs., LLC.

Broughton, T. Alan. Winter Journey. 1985. 10.95 o.p. (*0-525-23515-9*, Dutton) Dutton/Plume.

Clifton, Barry. Ben-Hur: The Odyssey. 2000. 392p. pap. 18.95 (*0-595-08857-0*, Writers Club Pr.) iUniverse, Inc.

Conroy, Pat. Beach Music, 2 Pts. unabr. ed. 1995. audio 152.00 (*0-7366-3080-5*, 3761A/B); audio 72.00. audio 80.00 Books on Tape, Inc.

—Beach Music. 1995. 640p. 32.50 (*0-385-41304-1*, Talese, Nan A.); 628p. 200.00 o.s.i (*0-385-47590-X*) Doubleday Publishing.

—Beach Music. abr. ed. 1995. audio 29.95 (*0-553-47270-4*, 892989); audio 27.50 o.s.i (*0-553-74619-7*) Random Hse. Audio Publishing Group. (RH Audio).

—Beach Music. unabr. ed. audio 158.00 (*0-7887-0335-8*, 94527E7) Recorded Bks., LLC.

Crawford, F. Marion. Roman Singer. 2000. 252p. E-Book 9.95 (*0-594-06287-X*) 1873 Pr.

—Roman Singer. collector's ed. 2002. (Illus.). im. lthr. 38.85 (*1-4115-1200-6*); pap. 19.95 (*1-4115-0504-2*); 25.95 (*1-4115-0858-0*); pap. 17.95 (*1-4115-0244-2*) Polyglot Pr., Inc.

Davis, Lindsey. The Accusers. 2004. (*0-89296-811-7*) Mysterious Pr.

—A Body in the Bath House. 2002. 368p. 24.95 (*0-89296-771-4*) Mysterious Pr.

—A Body in the Bath House. 2003. 368p. pap. 12.95 (*0-446-69170-4*, Mysterious Pr. Paperback Bks.) Warner Bks., Inc.

—The Course of Honor. 2000. 336p. 22.00 o.p. (*0-89296-674-2*); E-Book 14.95 (*0-7595-6042-0*); 336p. E-Book 14.95 (*0-7595-8044-8*); 336p. E-Book 14.95 (*0-7595-9048-6*); 336p. E-Book 14.95 (*0-7595-4043-8*); 336p. E-Book 14.95 (*0-7595-0042-8*) Mysterious Pr.

—The Course of Honor. 2003. 336p. pap. 12.95 (*0-446-67966-6*, Mysterious Pr. Paperback Bks.) Warner Bks., Inc.

—A Dying Light in Corduba. l.t. ed. 1997. (G. K. Hall Mystery Ser.). 589p. 26.95 o.p. (*0-7838-8347-1*, Macmillan Reference USA) Gale Group.

—A Dying Light in Corduba. 1998. 400p. 23.00 o.p. (*0-89296-664-5*) Mysterious Pr.

—A Dying Light in Corduba. unabr. ed. 1996. audio 97.00 (*0-7887-3108-4*, 95819E7) Recorded Bks., LLC.

—A Dying Light in Corduba. 1999. (Marcus Didius Falco Mystery Ser.). 464p. mass mkt. 6.99 (*0-446-60680-4*) Warner Bks., Inc.

—The Iron Hand of Mars. 1994. 320p. mass mkt. 6.50 o.s.i (*0-345-38024-X*) Ballantine Bks.

—The Iron Hand of Mars. unabr. ed. 2000. (Marcus Didius Falco Ser.: Vol. 4). audio 85.00 (*0-7887-0226-2*, 94451E7) Recorded Bks., LLC.

—The Jupiter Myth. 2003. (Illus.). 336p. 24.95 (*0-89296-777-3*) Mysterious Pr.

—The Jupiter Myth. 2004. (*0-446-69297-2*) Warner Bks., Inc.

—Last Act in Palmyra. l.t. ed. 1995. (Magna Large Print Ser.). 693p. o.p. (*0-7505-0839-6*) Magna Large Print Bks. GBR. *Dist:* Ulverscroft Large Print Canada, Ltd.

—Last Act in Palmyra. 1996. 82p. 22.95 o.p. (*0-89296-625-4*) Mysterious Pr.

—Last Act in Palmyra. unabr. ed. 1997. (Marcus Didius Falco Ser.: Vol. 6). audio 104.00 (*0-7887-1306-X*, 95144E7) Recorded Bks., LLC.

—Last Act in Palmyra. 1997. 432p. reprint ed. mass mkt. 6.99 (*0-446-40474-8*) Warner Bks., Inc.

—Ode to a Banker. 2001. (Marcus Didius Falco Mystery Ser.). (Illus.). 368p. 23.45 o.p. (*0-89296-740-4*) Mysterious Pr.

—One Virgin Too Many. 2000. E-Book 14.95 (*0-7595-6032-3*); 368p. E-Book 14.95 (*0-7595-8033-2*); 368p. E-Book 14.95 (*0-7595-9037-0*); E-Book 14.95 (*0-7595-4032-2*); 368p. E-Book 14.95 (*0-7595-0032-0*); (Illus.). 356p. 23.95 (*0-89296-716-1*) Mysterious Pr.

—One Virgin Too Many. 2001. 368p. reprint ed. pap. 12.95 (*0-446-67769-8*) Warner Bks., Inc.

—Poseidon's Gold. 1995. 352p. mass mkt. 5.99 o.s.i (*0-345-38025-8*) Ballantine Bks.

—Poseidon's Gold. 1994. 288p. 22.00 o.s.i (*0-517-59241-X*, Crown) Crown Publishing Group.

—Poseidon's Gold. l.t. ed. 1994. (Magna Large Print Ser.). 560p. (*0-7505-0733-0*) Magna Large Print Bks. GBR. *Dist:* Ulverscroft Large Print Canada, Ltd.

—Poseidon's Gold. unabr. ed. 1995. (Marcus Didius Falco Ser.: Vol. 5). audio 97.00 (*0-7887-0391-9*, 94583E7) Recorded Bks., LLC.

—Shadows in Bronze. 1992. 384p. mass mkt. 6.50 o.s.i (*0-345-37426-6*) Ballantine Bks.

—Shadows in Bronze. 1993. 3.99 o.p. (*0-517-09846-6*) Random Hse. Value Publishing.

—Shadows in Bronze. unabr. ed. 1992. (Marcus Didius Falco Ser.: Vol. 2). audio 97.00 (*1-55690-728-1*, 92223E7) Recorded Bks., LLC.

—Silver Pigs. 1991. 256p. mass mkt. 5.99 o.s.i (*0-345-36907-6*) Ballantine Bks.
—Silver Pigs. 1989. 18.95 o.s.i (*0-517-57363-6*, Crown) Crown Publishing Group.
—Silver Pigs. unabr. ed. 1992. (Marcus Didius Falco Ser.: Vol. 1). audio 70.00 (*1-55690-635-8*, 92103E7) Recorded Bks., LLC.
—Three Hands in the Fountain. 1999. (Marcus Didius Falco Mystery Ser.). 368p. 30.00 o.p. (*0-89296-691-2*) Mysterious Pr.
—Three Hands in the Fountain. 2000. 432p. mass mkt. 6.99 (*0-446-60774-6*) Warner Bks., Inc.
—Time to Depart. unabr. ed. 1998. (Marcus Didius Falco Ser.: Vol. 7). audio 97.00 (*0-7887-1922-X*, 95343E7) Recorded Bks., LLC.
—Time to Depart. l.t. ed. 1998. (Marcus Didius Falco Mystery Ser.). 432p. mass mkt. 6.99 (*0-446-60591-3*) Warner Bks., Inc.
—Time to Depart: A Marcus Didius Falco Mystery Novel. 1998. 432p. pap. 6.50 (*0-446-40528-0*, Mysterious Pr. Paperback Bks.); 1997. 416p. 22.50 o.p. (*0-89296-626-2*) Warner Bks., Inc.
—Two for the Lions. 2000. 464p. 23.95 (*0-89296-693-9*); 464p. E-Book 4.95 (*0-7595-9035-4*); 464p. E-Book 4.95 (*0-7595-4030-6*); 464p. E-Book 4.95 (*0-7595-0030-4*); E-Book 4.95 (*0-7595-6030-7*) Mysterious Pr.
—Two for the Lions. 2000. (Marcus Didius Falco Mystery Ser.). 464p. mass mkt. 6.99 (*0-446-60902-1*); E-Book 4.95 (*0-7595-8031-6*) Warner Bks., Inc.
—Venus in Copper. 1993. 288p. mass mkt. 5.99 o.s.i (*0-345-37390-1*) Ballantine Bks.
—Venus in Copper. unabr. ed. 1992. (Marcus Didius Falco Ser.: Vol. 3). audio 78.00 (*1-55690-738-9*, 92334E7) Recorded Bks., LLC.
De Carvalho, Mario. A God Strolling in the Cool of the Evening. Rabassa, Gregory, tr. from POR. 2001. (Pegasus Prize for Literature Ser.). 288p. pap. 12.00 (*0-8021-3774-1*) Grove/Atlantic, Inc.
Douglas, Lloyd Cassel. The Robe. Date not set. 476p. 30.95 (*0-8488-2252-8*) Amereon, Ltd.
—The Robe. 1985. 544p. 11.95 o.p. (*0-553-06400-2*) Bantam Bks.
—The Robe. unabr. ed. 1984. Pt. 1. audio 64.00 (*0-7366-0377-8*, 1356-A); Pt. 2. audio 64.00 Books on Tape, Inc.
—The Robe. 1952. 77p. pap. 5.60 (*0-87129-941-0*, R19) Dramatic Publishing Co.
—The Robe. 1999. 520p. pap. 14.00 (*0-395-95775-3*); 1986. 528p. pap. 14.95 o.p. (*0-395-40799-0*); 1986. pap. 9.95 (*0-395-40299-9*); 1942. 528p. 24.95 o.p. (*0-395-07635-8*) Houghton Mifflin Co.
—The Robe. l.t. ed. 1995. 889p. lib. bdg. 22.95 (*0-7838-1362-7*) Thorndike Pr.
Edwards, Gene. The Gaius Diary. 2002. (First-Century Diaries Ser.). (Illus.). 176p. pap. 10.99 (*0-8423-3871-3*) Tyndale Hse. Pubs.
—The Priscilla Diary. 2001. (First Century Diaries). (Illus.). 224p. pap. 9.99 (*0-8423-3870-5*) Tyndale Hse. Pubs.
Elliott, Ben. The Slave King. 2002. pap. 13.95 (*1-873741-68-5*) Millivres Bks. GBR. *Dist:* Consortium Bk. Sales & Distribution.
Fisk, Alan. Lord of Silver. 2000. 316p. pap. 22.99 (*0-7388-3416-5*) Xlibris Corp.
Flaubert, Gustave. Salammbo. unabr. ed. 1999. (World Classics Ser.). (FRE.). pap. 7.95 (*2-87714-151-9*) Bookking International FRA. *Dist:* Distribooks, Inc.
—Salammbo. 1961. (Coll. GF). (FRE.). pap. 10.95 (*0-8288-9981-9*, F62313) French & European Pubns., Inc.
—Salammbo. 1999. (Twelve-Point Ser.). 320p. lib. bdg. 25.00 (*1-58287-104-3*) North Bks.
—Salammbo. (Folio Ser.: No. 608). (FRE.). pap. 12.95 (*2-07-036608-1*) Schoenhof's Foreign Bks., Inc.
—Salammbo. Krailsheimer, Alban J., tr. 1977. (Penguin Classics Ser.). 288p. 12.95 (*0-14-044328-2*, Penguin Classics) Viking Penguin.
Graham, John W. Neaera. E-Book 3.95 (*0-594-02285-1*) 1873 Pr.
Graves, Robert. I, Claudius. 2002. 468p. 23.05 (*0-613-17297-3*) Econo-Clad Bks.
Hagee, John. Devil's Island: A Novel. 2002. 352p. pap. 14.99 (*0-7852-6401-9*) Nelson, Thomas Inc.
—Devil's Island: A Novel. 2001. (Apocalypse Diaries: Bk. 1). 320p. 19.99 (*0-7852-6787-5*) Nelson, Thomas Pubs.
Hamilton, Lyn. The Etruscan Chimera. 2003. 304p. mass mkt. 6.50 (*0-425-18908-2*, Prime Crime) Berkley Publishing Group.
Harlan, Thomas. The Dark Lord. E-Book 27.95 (*0-312-70725-8*); 2002. (Oath of Empire Ser.: Bk. 4). (Illus.). 512p. 27.95 (*0-312-86560-0*) Doherty, Tom Assocs., LLC. (Tor Bks.).
—The Gate of Fire Bk. 2: Oath of Empire. 2000. (Book Two of the Oath of Empire Ser.). (Illus.). 477p. 27.95 (*0-312-86544-9*, Tor Bks.) Doherty, Tom Assocs., LLC.
—The Shadow of Ararat. E-Book 6.99 (*0-312-70727-4*); 2000. (Illus.). 816p. mass mkt. 6.99 (*0-8125-9009-0*); 1999. (Illus.). 510p. 26.95 (*0-312-86543-0*) Doherty, Tom Assocs., LLC. (Tor Bks.).
Hewson, David. A Season for the Dead. 2004. 400p. 21.95 (*0-385-33722-1*, Delacorte Pr.) Dell Publishing.
Hill, Reginald. Traitor's Blood. 1986. 256p. 16.95 o.p. (*0-88150-076-3*) Countryman Pr.
—Traitor's Blood. l.t. ed. 1985. (Ulverscroft Large Print Ser.). 504p. 29.99 o.p. (*0-7089-1297-4*, Ulverscroft) Thorpe, F. A. Pubs. GBR. *Dist:* Ulverscroft Large Print Bks., Ltd., Ulverscroft Large Print Canada, Ltd.
—Traitor's Blood. 1987. 256p. mass mkt. 3.95 (*0-446-34719-1*) Warner Bks., Inc.
Holman, S. R. Domitian the Younger: A Novel. 1999. 225p. pap. 16.95 o.p. (*1-889298-96-4*) Rhwymbooks.
Iggulden, Conn. Emperor: The Death of Kings. 2004. 480p. 24.95 (*0-385-33662-4*, Delacorte Pr.) Dell Publishing.
—Emperor: The Gates of Rome. 2004. 480p. mass mkt. 6.99 (*0-440-24094-8*); 2003. 368p. 24.95 (*0-385-33660-8*, Delacorte Pr.); 2003. E-Book 19.95 (*0-440-33421-7*, Delacorte Pr.) Dell Publishing.
Jaro, Benita Kane. The Door in the Wall. 2002. (Illus.). xi, 207p. pap. 19.95 (*0-86516-534-3*) Bolchazy-Carducci Pubs.
—The Lock. 2002. (Illus.). xxii, 280p. pap. 19.95 (*0-86516-535-1*) Bolchazy-Carducci Pubs.
Jaro, Benita Kane, contrib. by. The Door in the Wall. 2002. (Illus.). pap. 19.95 (*0-86516-533-5*) Bolchazy-Carducci Pubs.
LaPierre, Alexandra. Artemisia: A Novel. Heron, Liz, tr. from FRE. 2000. (Illus.). xvi, 427p. 27.00 (*0-8021-1672-8*, Grove Pr.) Grove/Atlantic, Inc.
Larkin, Patrick. The Tribune: A Novel of Ancient Rome. l.t. ed. 2003. 478p. pap. 24.95 (*1-58724-546-9*, Wheeler Publishing, Inc.) Gale Group.
—The Tribune: A Novel of Ancient Rome. 2003. 400p. mass mkt. 7.99 (*0-451-20904-4*) NAL.
Leckie, Ross. Carthage. 2001. (Illus.). 240p. 24.00 (*0-86241-944-1*) Canongate Bks. GBR. *Dist:* Grove/Atlantic, Inc.
Llywelyn, Morgan & Scott, Michael. Etruscans. 2001. 368p. reprint ed. mass mkt. 6.99 (*0-8125-8012-5*, Tor Bks.) Doherty, Tom Assocs., LLC.
—Etruscans: Beloved of the Gods. 2000. (Beloved of the Gods Ser.: Vol. 1). 334p. 24.95 (*0-312-86627-5*, Tor Bks.) Doherty, Tom Assocs., LLC.
Maier, Paul L. The Flames of Rome: A Novel. 456p. 1995. pap. 13.99 (*0-8254-3297-9*); 1991. reprint ed. 20.99 (*0-8254-3262-6*) Kregel Pubns.
—The Flames of Rome: A Novel. 1987. (Living Bks.). 640p. pap. 4.95 o.p. (*0-8423-0903-9*) Tyndale Hse. Pubs.
Maier, Paul L. The Flames of Rome. 1982. mass mkt. 3.95 o.p. (*0-451-11737-9*, AE1737, Signet Bks.) NAL.
Malouf, David. An Imaginary Life. 1978. 7.95 o.s.i (*0-8076-0884-X*) Braziller, George Inc.
—An Imaginary Life. 1996. 160p. pap. 12.00 (*0-679-76793-2*) Random Hse., Inc.
McCullough, Colleen. Caesar. (Masters of Rome Ser.: No. 5). (Illus.). 1999. 672p. pap. 16.50 (*0-380-71085-4*, Avon Bks.); 1997. 752p. 27.50 (*0-688-09372-8*, Morrow, William & Co.) Morrow/Avon.
—Caesar's Women. unabr. ed. 1996. (Masters of Rome Ser.: No. 4). Pt. 1. audio 88.00 (*0-7366-3311-1*, 3964-A); Pt. 2. audio 80.00 Books on Tape, Inc.
—Caesar's Women. (Masters of Rome Ser.: No. 4). 1997. 960p. mass mkt. 7.99 (*0-380-71084-6*, Avon Bks.); 1996. (Illus.). 878p. 25.00 o.p. (*0-688-09371-X*, Morrow, William & Co.) Morrow/Avon.
—Caesar's Women. 1996. (Masters of Rome Ser.: No. 4). audio 25.00 (*0-671-73154-8*, 693426, Simon & Schuster Audioworks) Simon & Schuster Audio.
—Caesar's Women. 1998. (Masters of Rome Ser.: No. 4). 3.98 o.p. (*0-7651-0910-7*) Smithmark Pubs., Inc.
—The First Man in Rome. unabr. ed. 1990. (Masters of Rome Ser.: No. 1). audio 96.00 (*0-7366-1856-2*, 2688A) Books on Tape, Inc.
—The First Man in Rome. (Masters of Rome Ser.: No. 1). 1991. 1104p. mass mkt. 7.99 (*0-380-71081-1*, Avon Bks.); 1990. 22.95 o.p. (*0-688-09368-X*, Morrow, William & Co.) Morrow/Avon.
—The First Man in Rome. (Masters of Rome Ser.: No. 1). 2000. audio 15.99 (*0-7435-0547-6*); 1990. audio 22.95 (*0-671-72628-5*) Simon & Schuster Audio. (Simon & Schuster Audioworks).
—Fortune's Favorites, Pt. 1. unabr. ed. 1994. (Masters of Rome Ser.: No. 3). audio 112.00 (*0-7366-2677-8*, 3414A) Books on Tape, Inc.
—Fortune's Favorites. (Masters of Rome Ser.: No. 3). 1994. 1072p. mass mkt. 7.99 (*0-380-71083-8*, Avon Bks.); 1993. 25.00 o.p. (*0-688-09370-1*, Morrow, William & Co.) Morrow/Avon.
—Fortune's Favorites. (Masters of Rome Ser.: No. 3). 5.98 o.p. (*0-8317-8689-2*) Smithmark Pubs., Inc.
—The Grass Crown. unabr. ed. 1992. (Masters of Rome Ser.: No. 2). audio 96.00 (*0-7366-2103-2*, 2908A); audio 104.00 Books on Tape, Inc.
—The Grass Crown. (Masters of Rome Ser.: No. 2). 1992. 1104p. mass mkt. 7.99 (*0-380-71082-X*, Avon Bks.); 1991. (Illus.). 756p. 23.00 o.p. (*0-688-09369-8*, Morrow, William & Co.) Morrow/Avon.
—The Grass Crown, Set. abr. ed. 1991. (Masters of Rome Ser.: No. 2). audio 24.00 (*0-671-73151-3*, 692218, Simon & Schuster Audioworks) Simon & Schuster Audio.
—The October Horse. 2003. 1120p. mass mkt. 7.99 (*0-671-02420-5*, Pocket); 2003. E-Book (*0-7432-1469-2*, Simon & Schuster); 2002. (Illus.). 800p. 28.00 (*0-684-85331-0*, Simon & Schuster) Simon & Schuster.
Minick, H. Henry. The Corinthian: The Poignant Story of an Unwanted & Abandoned Imperial Roman Infant. 2001. 292p. E-Book 8.00 (*0-7388-7660-7*) Xlibris Corp.
Morante, Elsa. History. 1983. pap. 2.95 o.p. (*0-380-41889-4*, Avon Bks.) Morrow/Avon.
—History: A Novel. Weaver, William, tr. from ITA. 2nd ed. 2000. (Steerforth Italia Ser.). 740p. pap. 19.50 (*1-58642-004-6*, Steerforth Italia) Steerforth Pr.
Moravia, Alberto. The Woman of Rome. 1982. 448p. 3.50 (*0-86721-100-8*) Berkley Publishing Group.
—The Woman of Rome: A Novel. 1999. (Steerforth Italia Ser.). 408p. reprint ed. pap. 16.00 (*1-883642-80-9*) Steerforth Pr.
Norton, Andre & Shwartz, Susan. Empire of the Eagle. 416p. 1995. pap. text 5.99 (*0-8125-1393-2*); 1993. 22.95 o.p. (*0-312-85169-3*) Doherty, Tom Assocs., LLC. (Tor Bks.).
Panella, Vincent. Cutter's Island: Caesar in Captivity. 2000. 192p. 23.00 (*0-89733-484-1*) Academy Chicago Pubs., Ltd.
Pears, Iain. Death & Restoration: A Jonathan Argyll Mystery. 2000. (Art History Mysteries Ser.). 288p. mass mkt. 6.50 (*0-425-17742-4*, Prime Crime); 223p. mass mkt. 6.50 (*0-00-649875-2*) Berkley Publishing Group.
Petronius. Satyricon. Ruden, Sarah, tr. from LAT. & comment by. 2000. 256p. (C). pap. 9.95 (*0-87220-510-X*); lib. bdg. 34.95 (*0-87220-511-8*) Hackett Publishing Co., Inc.
—Satyricon. (World Literature Ser.). 176p. pap. 5.95 (*1-84022-110-0*) Wordsworth Editions, Ltd. GBR. *Dist:* Combined Publishing.
Pilpel, Robert H. Between Eternities. 1985. (Illus.). 576p. 19.95 o.p. (*0-15-111928-7*) Harcourt Trade Pubs.
Reed, Mary & Mayer, Eric. Three for a Letter. 2001. (Illus.). 242p. 24.95 (*1-890208-82-5*) Poisoned Pen Pr.
—Two for Joy. 2001. 335p. pap. 13.95 (*1-890208-76-0*) Poisoned Pen Pr.
Revely, Edith. In Good Faith. 1985. 272p. 22.95 (*0-87951-992-4*) Overlook Pr., The.
Roberts, John M. Nobody Loves a Centurion. 2001. (Illus.). 224p. 23.95 (*0-312-27257-X*) St. Martin's Pr.
—SPQR. 1990. 224p. mass mkt. 3.99 (*0-380-75993-4*, Avon Bks.) Morrow/Avon.
Roberts, John Maddox. The Catiline Conspiracy. 1991. (SPQR Ser. : No. 2). 224p. mass mkt. 3.50 (*0-380-75995-0*, Avon Bks.) Morrow/Avon.
—Hannibal's Children. 2002. 368p. 22.95 o.s.i (*0-441-00933-6*) Ace Bks.
—Hannibal's Children: A Novel of Alternate History. 2003. 368p. mass mkt. 6.99 (*0-441-01038-5*) Ace Bks.
—The King's Gambit. 2001. (SPQR Ser.: Vol. I). 240p. pap. 13.95 (*0-312-27705-9*, Saint Martin's Griffin) St. Martin's Pr.
—The Tribune's Curse. 2003. (SPQR Ser.: No. VII). (Illus.). 224p. 22.95 o.s.i (*0-312-30488-9*, Saint Martin's Minotaur) St. Martin's Pr.
Roberts, Keith. The Boat of Fate. 2002. pap. 19.95 (*1-58715-356-4*) Wildside Pr.
Saylor, Steven. Arms of Nemesis. 1993. 336p. reprint ed. mass mkt. 5.99 o.s.i (*0-8041-1127-8*, Ivy Bks.) Ballantine Bks.
—Arms of Nemesis. unabr. ed. 1997. audio 56.95 Blackstone Audio Bks., Inc.
—Arms of Nemesis. 1992. 320p. 19.95 o.p. (*0-312-08135-9*, Saint Martin's Minotaur); 2001. 336p. reprint ed. mass mkt. 6.50 (*0-312-97832-4*, 20-3388, St. Martin's Paperbacks) St. Martin's Pr.
—Catilina's Riddle. unabr. ed. 1997. audio 85.95 (*0-7861-1177-1*, 1920) Blackstone Audio Bks., Inc.
—Catilina's Riddle. 1993. 22.95 o.p. (*0-312-09763-8*) St. Martin's Pr.
—The House of the Vestals: The Investigations of Gordianus the Finder. 1998. mass mkt. (*0-312-96628-8*, St. Martin's Paperbacks); 1998. (House of Vestals Ser.: Vol. 1). 272p. mass mkt. 6.99 (*0-312-96452-8*, St. Martin's Paperbacks); 1997. 288p. 22.95 (*0-312-15444-5*, Saint Martin's Minotaur) St. Martin's Pr.
—Last Seen in Massilia. 2000. 277p. 23.95 (*0-312-20928-2*, Saint Martin's Minotaur); 2001. 288p. reprint ed. mass mkt. 6.50 (*0-312-97787-5*, St. Martin's Paperbacks) St. Martin's Pr.
—A Murder on the Appian Way. unabr. ed. 1996. audio 83.95 (*0-7861-0983-1*, 1760) Blackstone Audio Bks., Inc.
—A Murder on the Appian Way. 1996. 384p. 23.95 o.p. (*0-312-14377-X*, Saint Martin's Minotaur); 1997. 432p. reprint ed. mass mkt. 6.99 (*0-312-96173-1*, St. Martin's Paperbacks) St. Martin's Pr.
—Roman Blood. 1992. 416p. mass mkt. 6.50 o.s.i (*0-8041-1039-5*, Ivy Bks.) Ballantine Bks.
—Roman Blood. unabr. ed. 1996. audio 76.95 (*0-7861-1058-9*, 1829) Blackstone Audio Bks., Inc.
—Roman Blood. (St. Martin's Minotaur Mysteries Ser.). 2000. 416p. mass mkt. 6.99 (*0-312-97296-2*, St. Martin's Paperbacks); 1991. 288p. 19.95 (*0-312-06454-3*, Saint Martin's Minotaur) St. Martin's Pr.
—Rubicon. 2000. 301p. mass mkt. 6.50 (*0-312-97118-4*, St. Martin's Paperbacks); 1999. 288p. 23.95 o.p. (*0-312-20576-7*, Saint Martin's Minotaur) St. Martin's Pr.
—The Venus Throw. unabr. ed. 1997. audio 62.95 (*0-7861-1218-2*, 1998) Blackstone Audio Bks., Inc.
—The Venus Throw. l.t. ed. 1995. 587p. 25.95 o.p. (*0-7838-1443-7*, Macmillan Reference USA) Gale Group.
—The Venus Throw. 1995. x, 308p. 22.95 o.p. (*0-312-11912-7*, Saint Martin's Minotaur); 1996. 400p. reprint ed. pap. text 6.99 (*0-312-95778-5*, St. Martin's Paperbacks) St. Martin's Pr.
Serao, Mathilde. The Conquest of Rome. Caesar, Ann, ed. (Women's Classics Ser.). 250p. (C). 1993. pap. text 20.00 (*0-8147-7964-6*); 1992. text 55.00 (*0-8147-7955-7*) New York Univ. Pr.
Sienkiewicz, Henryk. Quo Vadis. 2000. (Classics Library). 496p. pap. 4.97 (*1-57748-777-X*) Barbour Publishing, Inc.
—Quo Vadis. Kuniczak, W. S., tr. from POL. 1999. 589p. 29.95 (*0-7818-0763-8*) Hippocrene Bks., Inc.
Silone, Ignazio, et al. Open City: Seven Writers in Postwar Rome. Weaver, William, ed. 1999. (Steerforth Italia Ser.). 462p. pap. 19.00 (*1-883642-82-5*) Steerforth Pr.
Silverberg, Robert. Roma Eterna. 2003. 416p. 25.95 (*0-380-97859-8*, Eos) Morrow/Avon.
Snyder, James D. All God's Children: How the First Christians Challenged the Roman World & Shaped the Next 2000 Years. 2000. (Illus.). xv, 679p. pap. 19.95 (*0-9675200-0-2*) Pharos Bks.
Spark, Muriel. The Public Image. 1993. (Revived Modern Classic Ser.: Vol. 767). 160p. pap. 9.95 (*0-8112-1246-7*, NDP767) New Directions Publishing Corp.
Tepper, Sheri S. Gibbon's Decline & Fall. 1997. 480p. mass mkt. 7.50 (*0-553-57398-5*) Bantam Bks.
Tine, Robert. Black Market. 1992. 320p. 21.95 o.p. (*0-312-06907-3*) St. Martin's Pr.
Todd, Marilyn. Dream Boat. 2002. 256p. 26.99 (*0-7278-5818-1*) Severn Hse. Pubs., Ltd.
—Man Eater. 2002. 384p. mass mkt. 11.95 (*0-330-35407-8*) Pan Bks. Ltd. GBR. *Dist:* Trafalgar Square.
—Virgin Territory. l.t. unabr. ed. 1997. 351p. 32.50 o.p. (*0-7531-5529-X*, 15529X) ISIS Large Print Bks. GBR. *Dist:* Ulverscroft Large Print Bks., Ltd., Ulverscroft Large Print Canada, Ltd.
—Wolf Whistle. 2002. 356p. mass mkt. 11.95 (*0-330-37199-1*) Pan Bks. Ltd. GBR. *Dist:* Trafalgar Square.
Turtledove, Harry. Gunpowder Empire. Date not set. mass mkt. (*0-7653-4609-5*); 2003. 288p. 24.95 (*0-7653-0693-X*) Doherty, Tom Assocs., LLC. (Tor Bks.).
Van Adler, T. C. St. Agatha's Breast. 2001. 292p. pap. 13.95 (*1-55583-708-5*, Alyson Bks.) Alyson Pubns.
—St. Agatha's Breast. 1998. 292p. 22.95 (*0-312-20019-6*) St. Martin's Pr.
Wallace, Lew. Ben Hur: A Tale of the Christ. 2000. (Radio Theatre Ser.). audio compact disk 18.97 (*1-56179-840-1*); (J). (gr. 4 up). audio compact disk 16.97 (*1-56179-841-X*) Focus on the Family Publishing.
—Ben Hur: A Tale of the Christ. 2003. 576p. mass mkt. 7.95 (*0-451-52874-3*, Signet Classics) NAL.
—Ben-Hur: A Tale of the Christ. 2000. (Classics Library). 496p. pap. 4.97 (*1-57748-776-1*) Barbour Publishing, Inc.
—Ben-Hur: A Tale of the Christ. 2002. 596p. per. 25.99 (*1-58827-783-6*); 30.99 (*1-58827-782-8*) IndyPublish.com.
—Ben-Hur: A Tale of the Christ. 2002. 480p. pap. 24.95 (*1-58715-538-9*); lib. bdg. 39.95 (*1-58715-539-7*) Wildside Pr.
—Ben Hur: A Tale of the Christ. 1999. (Notable American Authors Ser.). reprint ed. lib. bdg. 125.00 (*0-7812-9866-0*) Reprint Services Corp.
—Ben-Hur: A Tale of the Christ. 1993. (Illus.). 450p. reprint ed. 29.95 o.p. (*1-877767-85-9*) University Publishing Hse., Inc.

—Ben Hur: A Tale of the Christ. unabr. ed. 1992. 400p. reprint ed. pap. 14.95 (*1-57002-067-1*) University Publishing Hse., Inc.

Weldon, Virginia. Bound by Honor: A Novel. 2003. xii, 284p. 14.95 (*1-59156-156-6*) Covenant Communications.

Wishart, David. Last Rites. 2002. (Illus.). 317p. (*0-340-76885-1*) Coronet GBR. *Dist:* Trafalgar Square.

—A Vote for Murder. 2003. 368p. 24.95 (*0-340-77129-1*) Hodder & Stoughton, Ltd. GBR. *Dist:* Trafalgar Square.

—A Vote for Murder. 2003. 368p. pap. 8.95 (*0-340-77130-5*) New English Library, Ltd. GBR. *Dist:* Trafalgar Square.

—White Murder. 2002. (Illus.). 624p. mass mkt. (*0-340-77128-3*) New English Library, Ltd.

Wolf, Sarah. The Harbinger Effect. 1989. 18.95 o.p. (*0-671-68324-1*, Simon & Schuster) Simon & Schuster.

Yourcenar, Marguerite. The Memoirs of Hadrian. 1963. (Illus.). 347p. 22.95 o.s.i (*0-374-20728-3*); 408p. pap. 15.00 (*0-374-50348-6*) Farrar, Straus & Giroux.

—The Memoirs of Hadrian. 1995. 18.00 o.s.i (*0-679-60160-0*) Random Hse., Inc.

—The Memoirs of Hadrian. Frick, Grace, tr. 1984. (Illus.). 368p. 20.00 o.s.i (*0-394-60505-5*) Random Hse., Inc.

—The Memoirs of Hadrian. 1977. mass mkt. 3.50 o.p. (*0-671-43748-8*, Pocket) Simon & Schuster.

### ROME (ITALY)—FICTION

Adamoli, Vida. Sons, Lovers, Etcetera. 1997. 250p. pap. 13.95 o.p. (*0-7472-5501-6*) Headline Bk. Publishing, Ltd. GBR. *Dist:* Trafalgar Square.

Arnold, Margot, pseud. The Catacomb Conspiracy. 1992. (Penny Spring & Sir Toby Glendower Mystery Ser.). 260p. 18.95 o.p. (*0-88150-208-1*) Countryman Pr.

—The Catacomb Conspiracy. 1993. (Penny Spring & Sir Toby Glendower Mystery Ser.). 240p. pap. 7.95 (*0-88150-255-3*, Foul Play) Norton, W. W. & Co., Inc.

Bowen, Marjorie. Viper of Milan. 2000. 252p. pap. 9.95 (*0-594-00198-6*) 1873 Pr.

Cartland, Barbara. A Kiss in Rome. l.t. ed. 2001. (G. K. Hall Paperback Ser.). 163p. pap. 23.95 (*0-7838-9442-2*, Macmillan Reference USA) Gale Group.

Case, John. The Eighth Day. E-Book (*0-345-45872-9*); 2002. 384p. 25.95 (*0-345-43309-2*) Ballantine Bks.

—The Eighth Day. 2003. (Basic Ser.). 29.95 (*0-7862-5130-1*) Thorndike Pr.

Chamberlin, Mary. The Palazzo. Harding, John, ed. 2nd ed. 2002. 260p. pap. 12.50 (*0-9710929-5-8*) IDKPr.

Christmas, Joyce. Forged in Blood. l.t. ed. 2002. 277p. (*0-7862-4829-7*) Thorndike Pr.

—Forged in Blood: A Lady Margaret Priam/Betty Trenka Mystery. 2002. 277p. (*0-7540-8849-9*) Thorndike Pr.

Conroy, Pat. Beach Music. 1996. (Illus.). 816p. reprint ed. mass mkt. 7.99 (*0-553-57457-4*) Bantam Bks.

—Beach Music, 2 Pts. unabr. ed. 1995. audio 152.00 (*0-7366-3080-5*, 3761A/B); audio 72.00. audio 80.00 Books on Tape, Inc.

—Beach Music. 1995. 640p. 32.50 (*0-385-41304-1*, Talese, Nan A.); 628p. 200.00 o.s.i (*0-385-47590-X*) Doubleday Publishing.

—Beach Music. abr. ed. 1995. audio 29.95 (*0-553-47270-4*, 892989); audio 27.50 o.s.i (*0-553-74619-7*) Random Hse. Audio Publishing Group. (RH Audio).

—Beach Music. unabr. ed. audio 158.00 (*0-7887-0335-8*, 94527E7) Recorded Bks., LLC.

—Beach Music. 628p. pap. 8.98 o.p. (*0-7651-0633-7*) Smithmark Pubs., Inc.

—Beach Music. 1996. 14.04 (*0-606-11096-8*) Turtleback Bks.

Crawford, F. Marion. Heart of Rome. 2000. 252p. E-Book 3.95 (*0-594-03503-1*) 1873 Pr.

—Heart of Rome. collector's ed. 2002. (Illus.). im. lthr. 38.85 (*1-4115-1201-4*); pap. 19.95 (*1-4115-0503-4*); 25.95 (*1-4115-0842-4*); pap. 17.95 (*1-4115-0243-4*) Polyglot Pr., Inc.

Crespi, Camilla T. The Trouble with Going Home. 1996. 224p. mass mkt. 4.99 o.s.i (*0-06-109153-7*) HarperCollins Pubs.

—The Trouble with Going Home. 1994. 288p. 20.00 o.p. (*0-06-017725-X*) HarperTrade.

Davis, Lindsey. Ode to a Banker. 2002. 384p. pap. 12.95 (*0-446-67906-2*, Mysterious Pr. Paperback Bks.) Warner Bks., Inc.

Feinstein, Elaine. Dark Inheritance. l.t. ed. 2001. 258p. pap. 22.95 (*0-7862-3566-7*); 274p. (*0-7540-4623-0*); 274p. (*0-7540-4624-9*) Thorndike Pr.

—Dark Inheritance. 2001. 154p. pap. 13.95 (*0-7043-4725-3*); 234p. pap. 16.95 (*0-7043-4671-0*) Women's Pr., Ltd., The GBR. *Dist:* Trafalgar Square.

Fruttero, Carl & Lucentini, Franco. The D. Case: The Truth about the Mystery of Edwin Drood. Dowling, Gregory, tr. 1992. 587p. 23.95 (*0-15-113732-3*) Harcourt Trade Pubs.

Fruttero, Carlo, et al. The D. Case: The Truth about the Mystery of Edwin Drood. Dowling, Gregory, tr. from ITA. 1993. 608p. pap. 12.95 o.s.i (*0-15-623600-1*, Harvest Bks.) Harcourt Trade Pubs.

Gallizier, Nathan. The Sorceress of Rome. 2000. 252p. E-Book 3.95 (*0-594-02237-1*) 1873 Pr.

Hawthorne, Nathaniel. The Marble Faun. 1966. (Airmont Classics Ser.). mass mkt. 1.95 o.p. (*0-8049-0104-X*, CL-104) Airmont Publishing Co., Inc.

—The Marble Faun. 2004. 288p. pap. 3.50 (*0-486-43411-7*) Dover Pubns., Inc.

—The Marble Faun. 2002. Vol. 1. 168p. 93.99 (*1-4043-1676-0*); Vol. 1. 168p. per. 88.99 (*1-4043-1677-9*); Vol. 2. 204p. 94.99 (*1-4043-1678-7*); Vol. 2. 204p. per. 89.99 (*1-4043-1679-5*) IndyPublish.com.

—The Marble Faun. 1968. mass mkt. 0.50 o.p. (*0-451-50112-8*, Signet Classics); 1968. mass mkt. 0.60 o.p. (*0-451-50321-X*, Signet Classics); 1968. mass mkt. 0.75 o.p. (*0-451-50423-2*, Signet Classics); 1961. pap. 3.95 o.p. (*0-452-00903-0*, Meridian Bks.); 1961. 352p. pap. 4.95 o.p. (*0-452-01012-8*); 1961. mass mkt. 1.95 o.p. (*0-451-51316-9*, Signet Classics); 1961. mass mkt. 1.25 o.p. (*0-451-50851-3*, Signet Classics); 1961. mass mkt. 1.50 o.p. (*0-451-51084-4*, Signet Classics); 1961. mass mkt. 2.95 o.p. (*0-451-51771-7*, Signet Classics); 1961. mass mkt. 3.50 o.p. (*0-451-51991-4*, CE1771, Signet Classics) NAL.

—The Marble Faun. 2001. (Twelve-Point Ser.). 450p. lib. bdg. 25.00 (*1-58287-159-0*); 570p. lib. bdg. 26.00 (*1-58287-642-8*) North Bks.

—The Marble Faun. Charvat, William et al, eds. 1969. (Centenary Edition of the Works of Nathaniel Hawthorne: Vol. 4). (Illus.). 610p. text 83.95 (*0-8142-0062-1*) Ohio State Univ. Pr.

—The Marble Faun. Manning, Susan, ed. 2002. (Oxford World's Classics Ser.). (Illus.). 432p. pap. 9.95 (*0-19-283976-4*) Oxford Univ. Pr., Inc.

—The Marble Faun. 1992. (Notable American Authors Ser.). reprint ed. lib. bdg. 75.00 (*0-7812-3041-1*) Reprint Services Corp.

—The Marble Faun. (Ebook Classic Ser.). E-Book 5.00 (*0-7410-1275-8*); E-Book 5.00 (*0-7410-1449-1*) SoftBook Pr.

—The Marble Faun. l.t. ed. 2003. 652p. 28.95 (*0-7862-6106-4*, Large Print Pr.) Thorndike Pr.

—The Marble Faun. 1990. 16.00 (*0-606-20784-8*) Turtleback Bks.

—The Marble Faun. Bradbury, Malcolm, ed. 1995. 424p. pap. 6.95 (*0-460-87532-9*, Everyman's Classic Library in Paperback) Tuttle Publishing.

—The Marble Faun. 1990. (Classics Ser.). 480p. 9.95 (*0-14-039077-4*, Penguin Classics) Viking Penguin.

—The Marble Faun: Or the Romance of Monte Beni. 2001. E-Book 2.95 (*1-58882-564-7*) PublishingOnline.

—The Marble Faun: or The Romance of Monte Beni. 2002. (Modern Library Classics). 496p. pap. 9.95 (*0-375-75928-X*, Modern Library) Random House Adult Trade Publishing Group.

Joyce, Graham. Indigo. 272p. 2001. pap. 14.00 (*0-671-03938-5*, Washington Square Pr.); 2000. 23.95 (*0-671-03937-7*, Atria) Simon & Schuster.

Mawer, Simon. The Gospel of Judas. Clain, Judy, ed. 2001. (Illus.). 336p. 24.95 o.p. (*0-316-09750-0*) Little Brown & Co.

Mitchell, Michele. The Latest Bombshell: A Novel. 2003. 288p. 23.00 (*0-8050-7321-3*) Holt, Henry & Co.

Moon, Lawrence D. God's Fool. 1981. 12.95 o.p. (*0-531-09946-6*, Watts, Franklin) Scholastic Library Publishing.

Newman, Kim. Judgement of Tears: Anno Dracula 1959. 1998. 240p. 22.95 o.p. (*0-7867-0558-2*, Carroll & Graf Pubs.) Avalon Publishing Group.

Paci, F. G. Italian Shoes. 2002. (Prose Ser.: 64). 64p. pap. (*1-55071-170-9*) Guernica Editions, Inc.

Pears, Iain. Death & Restoration: A Jonathan Argyll Mystery. 2003. 320p. reprint ed. pap. 13.00 (*0-425-19042-0*, Prime Crime) Berkley Publishing Group.

—Death & Restoration: A Jonathan Argyll Mystery. 1998. (Jonathan Argyll Mysteries Ser.: Vol. 6). 224p. 22.00 o.s.i (*0-684-81461-7*, Scribner) Simon & Schuster.

—Giotto's Hand. (Art History Mysteries Ser.). 2000. 288p. mass mkt. 6.50 (*0-425-17358-5*); 2003. 304p. reprint ed. pap. 13.00 (*0-425-18854-X*) Berkley Publishing Group. (Prime Crime).

—Giotto's Hand. l.t. ed. 1997. (G. K. Hall Mystery Ser.). 305p. 25.95 o.p. (*0-7838-8362-5*, Macmillan Reference USA) Gale Group.

—Giotto's Hand. 1997. 224p. 20.50 (*0-684-81460-9*, Scribner) Simon & Schuster.

—The Immaculate Deception. 2000. 224p. 25.00 o.s.i (*0-7432-1257-6*, Scribner); 2001. 272p. reprint ed. mass mkt. 7.99 (*0-7434-2208-2*, Pocket) Simon & Schuster.

—The Immaculate Deception. l.t. ed. 2001. (Thorndike Basic Ser.). 333p. 28.95 (*0-7862-3257-9*) Thorndike Pr.

—The Last Judgement. 2002. 336p. pap. 13.00 (*0-425-18647-4*) Berkley Publishing Group.

—The Last Judgement: A Jonathan Argyll Mystery. 1999. (Art History Mysteries Ser.). 288p. mass mkt. 6.50 (*0-425-17148-5*, Prime Crime) Berkley Publishing Group.

—The Last Judgement: A Jonathan Argyll Mystery. 1996. 224p. 20.50 (*0-684-81459-5*); 1995. 21.00 (*1-57283-001-8*) Simon & Schuster. (Scribner).

—The Raphael Affair. 1998. (Prime Crime Mysteries Ser.: Bk. 1). 240p. reprint ed. mass mkt. 6.50 (*0-425-16613-9*, Prime Crime) Berkley Publishing Group.

—The Raphael Affair. 1992. 191p. 18.95 (*0-15-178912-6*) Harcourt Trade Pubs.

—The Raphael Affair. l.t. ed. 1991. (Linford Mystery Library). pap. 17.99 o.p. (*0-7089-7155-5*, Ulverscroft) Thorpe, F. A. Pubs. GBR. *Dist:* Ulverscroft Large Print Bks., Ltd., Ulverscroft Large Print Canada, Ltd.

—The Titian Committee. 2002. 272p. pap. 12.00 (*0-425-18500-1*); 1999. 240p. reprint ed. pap. 6.50 (*0-425-16895-6*, Prime Crime) Berkley Publishing Group.

—The Titian Committee. 1993. 189p. 19.95 (*0-15-190472-3*) Harcourt Trade Pubs.

Peters, Elizabeth, pseud. The Seventh Sinner. unabr. ed. 2001. audio compact disk 19.95; 2000. audio compact disk 40.00 (*0-7861-9942-3*, z2249); 1998. audio 32.95 (*0-7861-1467-3*, 2249); 1998. audio 32.95 (*0-7861-1324-3*, 696025) Blackstone Audio Bks., Inc.

—The Seventh Sinner. l.t. ed. 2002. lib. bdg. 27.95 (*1-58547-188-7*, Premier) Ctr. Point Large Print.

—The Seventh Sinner. 1991. reprint ed. 18.95 o.p. (*0-7278-4195-5*) Severn Hse. Pubs., Ltd.

—The Seventh Sinner. 1990. mass mkt. 3.95 (*0-445-77323-5*); 1989. 256p. mass mkt. 6.99 (*0-445-40778-6*); 1986. mass mkt. 3.95 o.s.i (*0-445-40225-3*) Warner Bks., Inc.

Picano, Felice. Men Who Loved Me. 2003. 303p. 19.95 (*1-56023-442-3*, Southern Tier Editions) Haworth Pr., Inc., The.

Roberts, John M. Saturnalia. 1999. (SPQR Ser.: Vol. 5). (Illus.). 275p. 23.95 (*0-312-20582-1*, Saint Martin's Minotaur) St. Martin's Pr.

Roberts, John Maddox. Saturnalia. 2000. (SPQR Ser.: Vol. V). E-Book 23.95 (*0-312-26844-0*) St. Martin's Pr.

Rucker, Rudolf V. B. As above, So Below: A Novel of Peter Bruegel. 2002. (Illus.). 320p. 23.95 (*0-7653-0403-1*, Forge Bks.) Doherty, Tom Assocs., LLC.

Saylor, Steven. A Mist of Prophecies: A Novel of Ancient Rome. 2002. 288p. 24.95 (*0-312-27121-2*, Saint Martin's Minotaur) St. Martin's Pr.

Schiefelbein, Michael. Vampire Thrall: A Novel. 2003. 224p. pap. 13.95 (*1-55583-728-X*) Alyson Pubns.

Sienkiewicz, Henryk. Quo Vadis? E-Book 3.95 (*0-594-02781-0*) 1873 Pr.

—Quo Vadis? Hogarth, C. J., tr. 1980. reprint ed. 11.95 o.p. (*0-460-00970-2*) Biblio Distribution.

—Quo Vadis? Conrad, Stanley F., tr. from POL. 1992. 500p. 22.50 o.p. (*0-7818-0100-1*) Hippocrene Bks., Inc.

—Quo Vadis? Kuniczak, W. S., tr. from POL. 1997. 589p. reprint ed. pap. 19.95 (*0-7818-0550-3*) Hippocrene Bks., Inc.

—Quo Vadis? Conrad, Stanley P., tr. 1993. 500p. 14.95 o.p. (*0-89870-475-8*) Ignatius Pr.

Townley, Gemma. When in Rome... 2004. 352p. pap. 12.95 (*0-345-46756-6*) Ballantine Bks.

Veronesi, Sandro. The Force of the Past. 2004. pap. (*0-06-093661-4*, Ecco) HarperTrade.

—The Force of the Past: A Novel. McEwen, Alastair, tr. from ITA. 2003. 240p. 23.95 (*0-06-621245-6*, Ecco) HarperTrade.

Vidal, Gore. Julian. 1985. 480p. mass mkt. 6.99 o.s.i (*0-345-32908-2*) Ballantine Bks.

—Julian. 2003. (Illus.). 528p. pap. 16.00 (*0-375-72706-X*) Knopf, Alfred A. Inc.

—Julian. 1974. mass mkt. 1.25 o.p. (*0-451-05923-9*); mass mkt. 0.95 o.p. (*0-451-02563-6*) NAL. (Signet Bks.).

—Julian. 1977. pap. 5.95 o.p. (*0-394-72101-2*); 1970. reprint ed. 3.95 o.s.i (*0-394-60395-8*, M395) Random Hse., Inc.

West, Morris. Eminence. l.t. ed. 2000. 424p. lib. bdg. 27.95 (*1-58547-044-9*) Ctr. Point Large Print.

—Eminence. 1998. 336p. 25.00 o.s.i (*0-15-100439-0*) Harcourt Trade Pubs.

—Eminence. 1998. (*0-7322-6704-8*) HarperCollins Pubs.

—Eminence. unabr. ed. 1999. audio 71.00 (*1-84197-007-7*, H1007E7);Set. audio 71.00 Recorded Bks., LLC.

—Eminence. 2003. 328p. pap. 14.95 (*1-902881-69-9*) Toby Pr.

Wheatcroft, John. The Education of Malcolm Palmer. 1997. 160p. 18.95 (*0-8453-4863-9*, Cornwall Bks.) Associated Univ. Presses.

Willman, Marianne. The Mistress of Rossmor. 2002. 320p. mass mkt. 6.50 (*0-312-98132-5*, St. Martin's Paperbacks) St. Martin's Pr.

### ROTH (LONDON, ENGLAND: IMAGINARY PLACE)—FICTION

Taylor, Andrew. The Four Last Things. 1997. (Roth Trilogy Ser.: Vol. 1). 304p. 22.95 (*0-312-16845-4*, Saint Martin's Minotaur) St. Martin's Pr.

—Judgement of Strangers. pap. 14.95 (*0-312-28730-5*, Saint Martin's Griffin); 1998. (Roth Trilogy Ser.: Vol. 2). 304p. 22.95 o.p. (*0-312-19292-4*, Saint Martin's Minotaur) St. Martin's Pr.

—The Office of the Dead. 2000. (Roth Trilogy Ser.: Vol. 3). 352p. 24.95 (*0-312-20348-9*, Saint Martin's Minotaur) St. Martin's Pr.

### RUFFORD (ME.: IMAGINARY PLACE)—FICTION

Lawrence, Margaret. Blood Red Roses: A Novel of Historical Suspense. 1998. 416p. mass mkt. 6.50 (*0-380-78880-2*); 1997. 368p. 23.00 (*0-380-97352-9*) Morrow/Avon. (Avon Bks.).

—The Burning Bride. 400p. 1999. mass mkt. 6.99 (*0-380-79612-0*); 1998. 23.00 (*0-380-97620-X*) Morrow/Avon. (Avon Bks.).

—Hearts & Bones. 1997. 352p. mass mkt. 6.50 (*0-380-78879-9*); 1996. 304p. 23.00 (*0-380-97351-0*) Morrow/Avon. (Avon Bks.).

### RUSSIA (FEDERATION)—FICTION

Adler, Warren. The Trans-Siberian Express. 2001. 0412p. 26.95 (*1-59006-003-2*) Stonehouse Pubns.

Alexander, Robert. The Kitchen Boy: A Novel of the Last Tsar. 2003. 240p. 23.95 (*0-670-03178-X*, Viking) Viking Penguin.

Archer, Jeffrey. The Eleventh Commandment. 1999. 448p. mass mkt. 7.99 (*0-06-101331-5*); 1998. 368p. 26.00 o.s.i (*0-06-019150-3*) HarperCollins Pubs.

—The Eleventh Commandment, Set. abr. ed. 1998. audio 25.00 (*0-694-51973-1*, 696013, HarperAudio) HarperTrade.

—The Eleventh Commandment. unabr. ed. 1999. audio compact disk 83.00 (*0-7887-3440-7*, C1046E7); 1998. audio 75.00 (*0-7887-1968-8*, 95355E7) Recorded Bks., LLC.

—The Eleventh Commandment. l.t. ed. (Paperback Bestsellers Ser.). 567p. 1999. pap. 28.95 (*0-7862-1593-3*); 1998. 30.95 (*0-7862-1592-5*) Thorndike Pr.

Bakin, Dmitry. Reasons for Living. Bromfield, Andrew, tr. from RUS. 2002. 150p. pap. 14.95 (*1-86207-526-3*) Granta.

Baxter, Stephen. Silverhair. 1999. (Mammoth Trilogy). 212p. 24.00 (*0-06-105132-2*) HarperCollins Pubs.

Bond, Larry. Day of Wrath. unabr. ed. 1998. audio 96.00 (*0-7366-4187-4*, 4685) Books on Tape, Inc.

—Day of Wrath. abr. ed. 1998. 5p. audio 25.00 (*0-671-58224-0*, 495728, Simon & Schuster Audioworks) Simon & Schuster Audio.

—Day of Wrath. l.t. ed. 1999. (Mystery Ser.). 725p. 30.95 o.p. (*0-7862-1616-6*) Thorndike Pr.

—Day of Wrath. 1999. 528p. mass mkt. 7.99 (*0-446-60705-3*); 1998. 496p. 25.00 (*0-446-51677-5*) Warner Bks., Inc.

Brahms, Libby. Siberian Exile: A Novel of My Mother. 2001. 162p. E-Book 8.00 (*0-7388-9650-0*) Xlibris Corp.

Brown, Dale. Warrior Class. 2001. 448p. 25.95 o.s.i (*0-399-14714-4*) Penguin Group (USA) Inc.

Card, Orson Scott. Enchantment. 2000. 432p. mass mkt. 6.99 (*0-345-41688-0*); 1999. 400p. 25.00 o.s.i (*0-345-41687-2*) Ballantine Bks. (Del Rey).

—Enchantment, Set. abr. ed. 1999. audio 25.00 Highsmith Inc.

—Enchantment. abr. ed. 1999. audio 25.00 (*0-7871-1942-3*, 694163, Dove Audio) NewStar Media, Inc.

—Enchantment. 2000. (Illus.). (J). 13.04 (*0-606-18096-6*) Turtleback Bks.

Cartland, Barbara. An Innocent in Russia, No. 148. 1981. pap. 1.95 o.p. (*0-553-20126-3*) Bantam Bks.

—An Innocent in Russia. l.t. ed. 2000. (Candlelight Romance Ser.). 226p. 22.95 o.p. (*0-7862-2579-3*) Thorndike Pr.

Christmas, Sylvia. One Way Ticket to Moscow. 2000. 284p. pap. 14.95 (*0-595-09549-6*, Writers Club Pr.) iUniverse, Inc.

Clancy, Tom. The Bear & the Dragon. 2000. 752p. 28.95 (*0-399-14563-X*) Penguin Group (USA) Inc.

—The Bear & the Dragon. l.t. ed. 2000. 1504p. 28.95 (*0-375-43069-5*) Random Hse. Large Print.

Coonts, Stephen. The Red Horseman. unabr. ed. 1993. audio 80.00 (*0-7366-2541-0*, 3292) Books on Tape, Inc.

—The Red Horseman. l.t. ed. 1993. 25.95 o.p. (*1-56895-032-2*, Wheeler Publishing, Inc.) Gale Group.

—The Red Horseman. 1994. mass mkt. 6.50 (*0-671-89489-7*); 1993. pap. 6.50 (*0-671-88413-1*) Simon & Schuster. (Pocket).

—The Red Horseman. McCarthy, Paul, ed. 1993. 352p. 23.00 (*0-671-74887-4*, Atria); 1994. 432p. reprint ed. mass mkt. 7.99 (*0-671-74888-2*, Pocket) Simon & Schuster.

—The Red Horseman. abr. ed. 1993. audio 17.00 (*0-671-79067-6*, 391458, Simon & Schuster Audioworks) Simon & Schuster Audio.

Couch, Dick. Silent Descent. 1994. 400p. mass mkt. 5.99 o.s.i (*0-425-14335-X*) Berkley Publishing Group.

—Silent Descent. 1993. 288p. 21.95 o.p. (*0-399-13897-8*, G. P. Putnam's Sons) Penguin Group (USA) Inc.

Coyle, Harold. Dead Hand. 2001. 304p. 24.95 (*0-312-87919-9*); 2002. reprint ed. mass mkt. 7.99 (*0-8125-7539-3*) Doherty, Tom Assocs., LLC. (Forge Bks.).

Davidson, Lionel. Kolymsky Heights. l.t. ed. 1994. 26.95 (*1-56895-158-2*, Wheeler Publishing, Inc.) Gale Group.

—Kolymsky Heights. 1995. 436p. mass mkt. 6.50 (*0-312-95661-4*, St. Martin's Paperbacks); 1994. 368p. 22.95 o.p. (*0-312-11407-9*) St. Martin's Pr.

—The Night of Wenceslas. (Black Dagger Crime Ser.). 16.50 o.p. (*0-86220-725-8*, C0853, Black Dagger) BBC Audiobooks America.

—The Night of Wenceslas. 1982. 224p. pap. 2.95 o.p. (*0-06-080595-1*, P595) HarperCollins Pubs.

—The Night of Wenceslas. 1996. 313p. pap. text 6.99 o.p. (*0-312-95876-5*, St. Martin's Paperbacks) St. Martin's Pr.

—The Night of Wenceslas. 1977. pap. 1.95 o.p. (*0-14-001758-5*, Penguin Bks.) Viking Penguin.

DeFelice, Jim. Brother's Keeper. 2000. 400p. mass mkt. 6.99 (*0-8439-4740-3*, Leisure Bks.) Dorchester Publishing Co., Inc.

Dick, Janice L. Calm Before the Storm. 2002. (Crossings of Promise Ser.: Bk. 1). (Illus.). 368p. pap. 14.99 (*0-8361-9201-X*) Herald Pr.

—Eye of the Storm, 3 vols. 2003. (Crossings of Promise Ser.). 360p. pap. 14.99 (*0-8361-9253-2*) Herald Pr.

Dostoyevsky, Fyodor. The Brothers Karamazov. 2001. (Critical Editions Ser.). (C). pap. text 28.75 (*0-393-94526-X*) Norton, W. W. & Co., Inc.

—Demons. Pevear, Richard, tr. from RUS. 2000. 784p. 23.00 (*0-375-41122-4*) Knopf, Alfred A. Inc.

—Notes from Underground. 2nd ed. 2000. (Critical Editions Ser.). xiv, 258p. (C). pap. 8.00 (*0-393-97612-2*, Norton Paperbacks) Norton, W. W. & Co., Inc.

Dunnett, Dorothy. The Ringed Castle. 1976. 32.95 (*0-8488-1302-2*) Amereon, Ltd.

—The Ringed Castle. 1983. 425p. reprint ed. lib. bdg. 39.95 (*0-89966-322-2*) Buccaneer Bks., Inc.

—The Ringed Castle. 1997. (Legendary Lymond Chronicles: Vol. 5). 544p. pap. 15.00 (*0-679-77747-4*, Vintage) Knopf Publishing Group.

—The Ringed Castle. 1984. 640p. mass mkt. 4.95 o.s.i (*0-446-31296-7*) Warner Bks., Inc.

Epp, Margaret. The Earth Is Round. 1974. 228p. (Orig.). pap. 4.50 o.p. (*0-919797-00-8*) Kindred Productions.

Epp, Margaret A. The Earth Is Round. 1998. 228 p. (Orig.). mass mkt. 4.95 (*0-87813-575-8*) Christian Light Pubns., Inc.

Fitzgerald, Penelope. The Beginning of Spring. 1988. 187p. (*0-00-223261-8*) HarperSanFrancisco.

—The Beginning of Spring. 1989. 192p. 18.95 o.p. (*0-8050-0981-7*) Holt, Henry & Co.

—The Beginning of Spring. 1998. 192p. pap. 12.00 (*0-395-90871-X*) Houghton Mifflin Co.

—The Beginning of Spring. l.t. ed. 1990. 240p. 19.95 o.p. (*1-85089-353-5*) ISIS Large Print Bks. GBR. *Dist:* Transaction Pubs.

—Offshore, Human Voices: The Beginning of Spring. 2003. 480p. 23.00 (*1-4000-4125-2*, Everyman's Library) Knopf Publishing Group.

Fletcher, Jessica & Bain, Donald. Murder in Moscow. 1998. (Murder She Wrote Ser.: Vol. 9). 304p. mass mkt. 6.50 (*0-451-19474-8*, Signet Bks.) NAL.

Forsyth, Frederick. Icon. 1997. 576p. mass mkt. (*0-552-13991-2*, Corgi); 1997. 576p. mass mkt. 7.99 (*0-553-57460-4*); 1997. 560p. mass mkt. 7.99 (*0-553-84012-6*); 1996. 400p. 32.95 o.p. (*0-593-02801-5*) Bantam Bks.

—Icon. l.t. ed. (Paperback Bestsellers Ser.). 765p. 1998. pap. 27.95 (*0-7838-1961-7*); 1996. 29.95 (*0-7838-1960-9*) Thorndike Pr.

—El Manifiesto Negro. 1997. (SPA.). pap. 18.95 o.s.i (*0-553-06056-2*) Bantam Bks.

—El Manifiesto Negro. 1999. (SPA.). (*84-01-24269-X*) Plaza & Janés Editories, S.A.

Francis, Dick. Trial Run. l.t. ed. 1994. 19.95 o.p. (*0-7927-2170-5*); 1994. pap. 18.95 o.p. (*0-7927-2169-1*); 1993. 54.95 incl. audio (*0-7451-5957-5*) BBC Audiobooks America.

—Trial Run. 1987. mass mkt. 5.95 o.s.i (*0-449-21273-4*, Fawcett) Ballantine Bks.

—Trial Run. 2001. 272p. mass mkt. 6.99 (*0-515-12997-6*, Jove) Berkley Publishing Group.

—Trial Run. unabr. ed. 1991. audio 48.00 (*0-7366-2029-X*, 2843) Books on Tape, Inc.

—Trial Run. 1983. mass mkt. 3.50 o.s.i (*0-671-50732-X*); mass mkt. 2.95 (*0-671-47022-1*) Simon & Schuster. (Pocket).

—Trial Run. l.t. ed. 1980. 404p. 12.00 o.p. (*0-7089-0456-4*, Ulverscroft) Thorpe, F. A. Pubs. GBR. *Dist:* Ulverscroft Large Print Bks., Ltd.

Freemantle, Brian. Bomb Grade. 1997. 416p. 25.95 (*0-312-14565-9*) St. Martin's Pr.

—The Button Man. 1993. 400p. 22.95 o.p. (*0-312-08716-0*) St. Martin's Pr.

—Dead Men Living. 352p. 26.00 (*0-7278-5660-X*); 2001. 608p. 26.00 (*0-7278-7071-8*) Severn Hse. Pubs., Ltd.

—Dead Men Living. 2000. (Charlie Muffin Thrillers Ser.). 345p. 24.95 (*0-312-24379-0*) St. Martin's Pr.

Hagberg, David. Assassin. 1997. 384p. 24.95 o.p. (*0-312-85028-X*, Forge Bks.) Doherty, Tom Assocs., LLC.

—The Assassin. 1998. (Kirk McGarvey Novels Ser.). 530p. mass mkt. 7.99 (*0-8125-0848-3*, Forge Bks.) Doherty, Tom Assocs., LLC.

—Assassin. abr. ed. 2003. audio 25.00 (*1-58807-213-4*); audio (*1-58807-680-6*) Americana Publishing, Inc.

Hall, Adam. Quiller Balalaika. 2003. 288p. 24.00 (*0-7867-1265-1*) Avalon Publishing Group.

Harris, Robert. Archangel. 2000. 432p. reprint ed. mass mkt. 7.99 (*0-515-12748-5*, Jove) Berkley Publishing Group.

—Archangel. unabr. ed. 2000. 10p. audio compact disk 94.95 (*0-7540-5356-3*, CCD 047); audio 84.95 (*0-7540-0295-0*, CAB 1718) Chivers Audio Bks. GBR. *Dist:* BBC Audiobooks America.

—Archangel. 1999. 30.00 o.p. (*0-7838-8480-X*, Macmillan Reference USA) Gale Group.

—Archangel. 1998. 421p. (*0-09-177924-3*); audio (*1-85686-390-5*) Random Hse. of Canada, Ltd. CAN. *Dist:* Random Hse., Inc.

Harrod-Eagles, Cynthia. Emily. 1993. 528p. 24.95 o.p. (*0-312-09794-8*) St. Martin's Pr.

Heaven, Constance. Heir to Kuragin. 1979. (General Ser.). lib. bdg. 14.95 o.p. (*0-8161-6703-6*, Macmillan Reference USA) Gale Group.

—Heir to Kuragin. 1979. 8.95 o.p. (*0-698-10943-0*) Putnam Publishing Group, The.

High, John A. The Desire Notebooks: A Trilogy of Novellas. 1999. (Illus.). 287p. 29.95 (*1-881471-34-9*); pap. 14.95 (*1-881471-33-0*) Spuyten Duyvil.

Holland, William E. Moscow Twilight. Grosse, Bill, ed. 1993. 352p. mass mkt. 5.50 (*0-671-74644-8*, Pocket); 1992. 320p. 20.00 (*0-671-74643-X*, Atria) Simon & Schuster.

Hyman, Tom. Seven Days to Petrograd. 1989. mass mkt. 4.50 o.s.i (*0-553-27996-3*) Bantam Bks.

—Seven Days to Petrograd. 1988. 18.95 o.p. (*0-670-80865-2*) Viking Penguin.

James, Donald. Monstrum. 1999. mass mkt. (*0-449-00431-7*, Fawcett); mass mkt. 6.99 o.s.i (*0-8041-1891-4*, Ivy Bks.) Ballantine Bks.

—Monstrum. 1999. (SPA.). 480p. (*84-08-02903-7*) GeoPlaneta, Editorial, S. A.

Johnson, Susan. Golden Paradise. 2001. 352p. mass mkt. (*1-55166-854-8*, 1-66854-0, Mira Bks.) Harlequin Enterprises, Ltd.

Kalfus, Ken. PU-239 & Other Russian Fantasies. 1999. 272p. 22.00 (*1-57131-029-0*) Milkweed Editions.

—PU-239 & Other Russian Fantasies. 2000. 304p. reprint ed. pap. 13.95 (*0-7434-0075-5*, Washington Square Pr.) Simon & Schuster.

Kaminsky, Stuart M. Black Knight in Red Square. 1989. (Inspector Porfiry Rostnikov Mystery Ser.). 224p. mass mkt. 5.99 o.s.i (*0-8041-0405-0*, Ivy Bks.) Ballantine Bks.

—Black Knight in Red Square. 1984. (Inspector Porfiry Rostnikov Mystery Ser.). 224p. 2.95 o.s.i (*0-441-06628-3*, Diamond Bks.) Berkley Publishing Group.

—Black Knight in Red Square. unabr. ed. 1993. (Inspector Porfiry Rostnikov Mystery Ser.: Vol. 2). audio 51.00 (*1-55690-943-8*, 93439E7) Recorded Bks., LLC.

—Blood & Rubles. 1996. (Inspector Porfiry Rostnikov Mystery Ser.). 261p. mass mkt. 5.99 o.s.i (*0-8041-1288-6*, Ivy Bks.); 272p. 21.00 o.s.i (*0-449-90949-2*, Fawcett) Ballantine Bks.

—Blood & Rubles, unabr. ed. 1997. audio 44.95 (*0-7861-1119-4*, 1880) Blackstone Audio Bks., Inc.

—Blood & Rubles. unabr. ed. 1997. audio 48.00 (*0-7366-3704-4*, 4388) Books on Tape, Inc.

—Blood & Rubles. l.t. ed. 1996. (Inspector Porfiry Rostnikov Mystery Ser.). 317p. 23.95 o.p. (*1-56895-329-1*, Wheeler Publishing, Inc.) Gale Group.

—Blood & Rubles. unabr. ed. 2000. (Inspector Porfiry Rostnikov Mystery Ser.). audio 60.00 (*0-7887-0511-3*, 94704E7) Recorded Bks., LLC.

—A Cold Red Sunrise. 1989. (Inspector Porfiry Rostnikov Mystery Ser.). mass mkt. 6.99 o.s.i (*0-8041-0428-X*, Ivy Bks.) Ballantine Bks.

—A Cold Red Sunrise. l.t. ed. 2000. 287p. lib. bdg. 27.95 (*1-58547-021-X*) Ctr. Point Large Print.

—A Cold Red Sunrise. 1988. (Inspector Porfiry Rostnikov Mystery Ser.). 224p. 16.95 o.s.i (*0-684-18905-4*, Macmillan Reference USA) Gale Group.

—A Cold Red Sunrise. unabr. ed. 1992. audio 49.00 (*1-55690-677-3*, 92330) Recorded Bks., LLC.

—Death of a Dissident. 1981. (Inspector Porfiry Rostnikov Mystery Ser.). 448p. 2.95 o.s.i (*0-441-14204-4*) Ace Bks.

—Death of a Dissident. 1989. (Inspector Porfiry Rostnikov Mystery Ser.). mass mkt. 5.50 o.s.i (*0-8041-0404-2*, Ivy Bks.) Ballantine Bks.

—Death of a Dissident. unabr. ed. 1993. (Inspector Porfiry Rostnikov Mystery Ser.: Vol. 1). audio 51.00 (*1-55690-898-9*, 93340E7) Recorded Bks., LLC.

—Death of a Russian Priest. (Inspector Porfiry Rostnikov Mystery Ser.). 1993. mass mkt. 5.99 o.s.i (*0-8041-0836-6*, Ivy Bks.); 1992. 256p. 18.00 o.s.i (*0-449-90724-4*, Fawcett) Ballantine Bks.

—Death of a Russian Priest. unabr. ed. 1995. (Inspector Porfiry Rostnikov Mystery Ser.: Vol. 8). audio 51.00 (*0-7887-0104-5*, 94345E7) Recorded Bks., LLC.

—The Dog Who Bit a Policeman. unabr. ed. 2000. audio 59.95 (*0-7927-2255-8*, CSL 144) Chivers Audio Bks. GBR. *Dist:* BBC Audiobooks America.

—The Dog Who Bit a Policeman. 1998. (Inspector Porfiry Rostnikov Mystery Ser.). 275p. (gr. 8 up). 22.00 (*0-89296-667-X*) Mysterious Pr.

—The Dog Who Bit a Policeman. unabr. ed. 2000. (Inspector Porfiry Rostnikov Mystery Ser.: Vol. 12). audio 70.00 (*0-7887-2483-5*, 95558E7) Recorded Bks., LLC.

—The Dog Who Bit a Policeman. l.t. ed. 1999. (Mystery Ser.). 455p. 27.95 (*0-7862-1767-7*) Thorndike Pr.

—Fall of a Cosmonaut. l.t. ed. 2001. (Large Print Bks.). 348p. pap. 23.95 (*1-58724-114-5*, Wheeler Publishing, Inc.) Gale Group.

—Fall of a Cosmonaut. 2000. 288p. 24.95 (*0-89296-668-8*); 288p. E-Book 14.95 (*0-446-92256-0*); 288p. E-Book 14.95 (*0-446-91365-0*); E-Book 14.95 (*0-446-93129-2*); 288p. E-Book 14.95 (*0-446-92860-7*); (Illus.). E-Book 14.95 (*0-446-96089-6*) Mysterious Pr.

—Fall of a Cosmonaut. 2000. 288p. E-Book 14.95 (*0-446-92369-9*) Warner Bks., Inc.

—A Fine Red Rain. 1988. (Inspector Porfiry Rostnikov Mystery Ser.). 208p. mass mkt. 4.99 o.s.i (*0-8041-0279-1*, Ivy Bks.) Ballantine Bks.

—A Fine Red Rain. 1987. (Inspector Porfiry Rostnikov Mystery Ser.). 211p. 14.95 o.p. (*0-684-18666-7*, Macmillan Reference USA) Gale Group.

—A Fine Red Rain. unabr. ed. 1994. (Inspector Porfiry Rostnikov Mystery Ser.: Vol. 4). audio 51.00 (*1-55690-982-9*, 94121E7) Recorded Bks., LLC.

—A Fine Red Rain. 2000. (Inspector Porfiry Rostnikov Mystery Ser.). 224p. pap. 14.95 (*0-7432-1161-8*, Scribner) Simon & Schuster.

—Hard Currency. 1995. (Inspector Porfiry Rostnikov Mystery Ser.). mass mkt. 5.99 o.s.i (*0-8041-0837-4*, Ivy Bks.); 247p. 20.00 o.s.i (*0-449-90725-2*, Fawcett) Ballantine Bks.

—Hard Currency, unabr. ed. 1995. 9p. audio 44.95 (*0-7861-0822-3*, 893333) Blackstone Audio Bks., Inc.

—Hard Currency. unabr. ed. 1995. (Inspector Porfiry Rostnikov Mystery Ser.: Vol. 9). audio 60.00 (*0-7887-0412-5*, 94604E7) Recorded Bks., LLC.

—The Man Who Walked Like a Bear. unabr. ed. 1994. (Inspector Porfiry Rostnikov Mystery Ser.: Vol. 6). audio 44.00 (*0-7887-0049-9*, 94248E7) Recorded Bks., LLC.

—The Man Who Walked Like a Bear: An Inspector Porfiry Rostnikov Novel. 1991. (Inspector Porfiry Rostnikov Mystery Ser.). mass mkt. 4.95 o.s.i (*0-8041-0693-2*, Ivy Bks.) Ballantine Bks.

—Murder on the Trans-Siberian Express. 2001. 288p. 24.95 (*0-89296-747-1*) Mysterious Pr.

—Red Chameleon. 1989. (Inspector Porfiry Rostnikov Mystery Ser.). 208p. mass mkt. 4.99 o.s.i (*0-8041-0465-4*, Ivy Bks.) Ballantine Bks.

—Red Chameleon. 1986. (Inspector Porfiry Rostnikov Mystery Ser.). 240p. 3.50 o.s.i (*0-441-71086-7*, Diamond Bks.) Berkley Publishing Group.

—Red Chameleon. unabr. ed. 1992. (Inspector Porfiry Rostnikov Mystery Ser.: Vol. 3). audio 51.00 (*1-55690-725-7*, 92107E7) Recorded Bks., LLC.

—Red Chameleon. 1985. (Inspector Porfiry Rostnikov Mystery Ser.). 224p. 13.95 o.s.i (*0-684-18424-9*, Scribner) Simon & Schuster.

—Rostnikov's Vacation. 1992. (Inspector Porfiry Rostnikov Mystery Ser.). reprint ed. mass mkt. 5.99 o.s.i (*0-8041-0694-0*, Ivy Bks.) Ballantine Bks.

—Rostnikov's Vacation. unabr. ed. 1993. audio 51.00 (*1-55690-840-7*, 93208E7) Recorded Bks., LLC.

—Rostnikov's Vacation. 1991. (Inspector Porfiry Rostnikov Mystery Ser.). 244p. 19.95 o.s.i (*0-684-19022-2*, Scribner) Simon & Schuster.

—Tarnished Icons. 1997. (Inspector Porfiry Rostnikov Mystery Ser.). 277p. mass mkt. 6.99 o.s.i (*0-8041-1289-4*, Ivy Bks.) Ballantine Bks.

—Tarnished Icons. unabr. ed. 1997. (Inspector Porfiry Rostnikov Mystery Ser.: Vol. 11). audio 70.00 (*0-7887-0930-5*, 95070E7) Recorded Bks., LLC.

Kerschner, Nolan K. Welcome to Moscow. 2001. 168p. pap. 20.99 (*0-7388-2687-1*); E-Book 8.00 (*0-7388-8901-6*) Xlibris Corp.

Kravetz, Nathan. Moscow, Farewell! A Russian Boys Adventure in Times Past. 2000. 164p. E-Book 8.00 (*0-7388-9371-4*) Xlibris Corp.

Krepismann, Charlotte. Inheritance: A Mixed Blessing. 1999. 192p. (Orig.). pap. 12.95 (*1-891571-04-4*) Easy Break, First Time Publishing.

Lacy, Al & Lacy, JoAnna. Let Freedom Ring, 4 vols. 2003. (Shadow of Liberty Ser.). 352p. pap. 10.99 (*1-57673-756-X*) Multnomah Pubs., Inc.

Le Carré, John. La Casa Rusia.Tr. of Rusia House. (SPA.). 1993. 384p. (*84-01-32304-5*); 5th ed. 1999. (Illus.). 509p. (*84-01-49981-X*) Plaza & Janés Editories, S.A.

—Our Game. (George Smiley Ser.). 1997. 320p. pap. 19.00 (*0-345-41831-X*); 1996. 352p. mass mkt. 7.99 (*0-345-40000-3*) Ballantine Bks.

—Our Game. unabr. ed. 1996. (George Smiley Ser.). audio 56.95 (*0-7861-1085-6*, 1853) Blackstone Audio Bks., Inc.

—Our Game. unabr. ed. 2000. (George Smiley Novels Ser.). audio 84.95 (*0-7451-6592-3*, CAB 1208) Chivers Audio Bks. GBR. *Dist:* BBC Audiobooks America.

—Our Game, unabr. ed. 1997. (George Smiley Novels Ser.). audio 42.95 (*0-7887-0809-0*, RD802) Recorded Bks., LLC.

—Single & Single. l.t. ed. (Wheeler Press Paperback Ser.). 2000. 11.95 (*1-56895-969-9*); 1999. 28.95 (*1-56895-748-3*) Gale Group. (Wheeler Publishing, Inc.).

—Single & Single. 1999. (SPA.). 352p. (*84-01-01220-1*) Plaza & Janés Editories, S.A.

—Single & Single. 2000. (SPA.). pap. 13.95 (*84-01-01350-X*) Plaza & Janés Editories, S.A. ESP. *Dist:* Distribooks, Inc.

—Single & Single. 1999. 352p. 26.00 o.s.i (*0-684-86305-7*, Scribner); 1999. (Illus.). 352p. 26.00 o.s.i (*0-684-85926-2*, Scribner); 2003. 368p. reprint ed. pap. 14.00 (*0-7434-5806-0*, Scribner); 2000. 400p. reprint ed. mass mkt. 7.99 (*0-671-02797-2*, Pocket) Simon & Schuster.

le Roy, Patricia. The Angels of Russia. E-Book (*1-84045-027-4*) Online Originals.

Lermontov, Mikhail. A Hero of Our Time. Nabokov, Vladimir & Nabokov, Dmitri, trs. from RUS. 1988. 210p. reprint ed. pap. 12.95 (*0-87501-049-0*) Ardis Pubs.

—A Hero of Our Time. unabr. ed. 1999. (World Classic Literature Ser.). (RUS.). pap. 8.95 (*2-87714-259-0*) Bookking International FRA. *Dist:* Distribooks, Inc.

—A Hero of Our Time. Nabokov, Vladimir & Nabokov, Dmitri, trs. from RUS. 1982. (Anchor Literary Library). mass mkt. 4.95 o.p. (*0-385-09344-6*) Doubleday Publishing.

—A Hero of Our Time. E-Book 2.49 (*1-58627-842-8*) Electric Umbrella Publishing.

—A Hero of Our Time. 1992. (Everyman's Library). 224p. 15.00 (*0-679-41327-8*, Everyman's Library) Knopf Publishing Group.

—A Hero of Our Time. Nabokov, Vladimir & Nabokov, Dmitri, trs. 1984. (Oxford World's Classics Ser.). 200p. pap. (*0-19-281401-X*) Oxford Univ. Pr., Inc.

—A Hero of Our Time. Cornwell, Neil, ed. 1995. 208p. pap. 8.50 (*0-460-87566-3*, Everyman's Classic Library in Paperback) Tuttle Publishing.

—A Hero of Our Time. Foote, Paul, tr. 1966. (Penguin Classics Ser.). 192p. pap. 12.00 o.s.i (*0-14-044176-X*, Penguin Classics) Viking Penguin.

Ludlum, Robert. The Tristan Betrayal: A Novel. Date not set. mass mkt. (*0-312-99774-4*, St. Martin's Paperbacks); 2003. 528p. 27.95 (*0-312-31669-0*); 2003. E-Book 27.95 (*0-312-71133-6*) St. Martin's Pr.

Ludlum, Robert & Shelby, Philip. The Cassandra Compact. l.t. ed. 2001. (Wheeler Large Print Book Ser.). 454p. 30.95 o.p. (*1-58724-075-0*, Wheeler Publishing, Inc.) Gale Group.

—The Cassandra Compact. 2001. (Covert-One Ser.). 400p. pap. 15.95 (*0-312-25343-5*, Saint Martin's Griffin) St. Martin's Pr.

Mackay, Colin. Fires in the Night. E-Book (*1-84045-041-X*) Online Originals.

Makine, Andrei. Dreams of My Russian Summers. Strachan, Geoffrey, tr. from FRE. 1997. 320p. 23.95 (*1-55970-383-0*) Arcade Publishing, Inc.

—Dreams of My Russian Summers. 1998. audio 48.00 (*0-7366-4437-7*, 4690); audio 48.00 (*0-7366-4192-0*, 896053) Books on Tape, Inc.

—Dreams of My Russian Summers. 1998. 256p. pap. 7.99 (*0-684-85650-6*, Touchstone) Simon & Schuster.

—Dreams of My Russian Summers. Strachan, Geoffrey, tr. from FRE. 1998. 256p. pap. 13.00 (*0-684-85268-3*, Touchstone) Simon & Schuster.

—Dreams of My Russian Summers. abr. ed. 1998. audio 17.95 (*1-55935-301-5*) Soundelux Audio Publishing.

Settings

Settings

—The Music of a Life: Novel. Strachan, Geoffrey, tr. from FRE. 2002. 144p. pap. 21.95 (*1-55970-637-6*) Arcade Publishing, Inc.

Marcinko, Richard & Weisman, John. Designation Gold. 1997. (Rogue Warrior Ser.). 368p. 24.00 (*0-671-89673-3*, Atria) Simon & Schuster.

May, Daryl & Bansemer, Roger. Rachael's Splendifilous Adventure. Little, Carl, ed. 1992. (Illus.). 40p. (Orig.). (J). (ps-4). 10.95 (*0-932433-83-9*) Windswept Hse. Pubs.

McConkey, James. To a Distant Island. 2000. (Illus.). 203p. reprint ed. pap. 14.95 (*0-9664913-5-1*) Dry, Paul Bks., Inc.

Michaels, Fern. Whitefire. 1997. (Romance Ser.). 369p. lib. bdg. 27.95 (*0-7862-1208-X*, Five Star); pap. 23.95 o.p. (*1-56895-493-X*, Wheeler Publishing, Inc.) Gale Group.

—Whitefire. 1997. 352p. mass mkt. 6.99 o.s.i (*0-8217-5638-9*, Zebra Bks.) Kensington Publishing Corp.

Modesitt, L. E., Jr. Ghost of the White Nights. 2001. 400p. 25.95 (*0-7653-0025-7*); (Illus.). 24.95 (*0-7653-0095-8*) Doherty, Tom Assocs., LLC. (Tor Bks.).

Page, Myra. Moscow Yankee. 1995. (Radical Novel Reconsidered Ser.). 320p. pap. text 15.95 (*0-252-06499-2*) Univ. of Illinois Pr.

Pavlova, Karolina. A Double Life. Monter, Barbara H., tr. 1978. (ENG & RUS.). 12.00 o.p. (*0-88233-223-6*); pap. 3.95 o.p. (*0-88233-224-4*) Ardis Pubs.

—A Double Life. Heldt, Barbara, tr. from RUS. & intro. by. (Illus.). 2nd ed. 1986. xxii, 111p. reprint ed. pap. 8.95 o.p. (*0-936041-01-3*); 3rd rev. ed. 1996. 133p. (C). pap. text 8.95 (*0-936041-09-9*) Barbary Coast Bks.

Pelevin, Victor. Buddha's Little Finger. Bromfield, Andrew, tr. from RUS. 2000. 336p. 25.95 o.s.i (*0-670-89168-1*, Viking) Viking Penguin.

—Buddha's Little Finger. 2001. 352p. reprint ed. 13.00 (*0-14-100232-8*) Viking Penguin.

Pella, Judith. Dawning of Deliverance. 1995. (Russians Ser.: Bk. 5). 432p. pap. 12.99 (*1-55661-359-8*) Bethany Hse. Pubs.

—Heirs of the Motherland. 1993. (Russians Ser.: Vol. 4). 384p. pap. 12.99 (*1-55661-358-X*) Bethany Hse. Pubs.

—Passage into Light. 1998. (Russians Ser.: Vol. 7). 304p. pap. 11.99 (*1-55661-869-7*) Bethany Hse. Pubs.

—Russians, 5 vols., Vol. 1-5, set. 1995. (Russians Ser.: Vol. 1-5). pap. 64.99 (*1-55661-795-X*) Bethany Hse. Pubs.

—White Nights, Red Morning. 1996. (Russians Ser.: Bk. 6). 416p. pap. 12.99 (*1-55661-360-1*) Bethany Hse. Pubs.

Petrushevskaya, Ludmilla. Time: Night. 1995. pap. 11.00 o.s.i (*0-679-75768-6*) Random Hse., Inc.

—Time: Night. Laird, Sally, tr. 1994. 96p. o.s.i (*1-85381-701-5*) Random Hse., Inc.

—The Time: Night. 2000. 155p. pap. 14.95 (*0-8101-1800-9*) Northwestern Univ. Pr.

Phillips, Michael & Pella, Judith. The Crown & the Crucible. 1991. (Russians Ser.: Bk. 1). 416p. pap. 12.99 (*1-55661-172-2*) Bethany Hse. Pubs.

—A House Divided. 1992. (Russians Ser.: Vol. 2). 352p. pap. 12.99 (*1-55661-173-0*) Bethany Hse. Pubs.

—The Russians Series, Vols. 1-3. 1992. (Russians Ser.). pap. 32.99 o.p. (*1-55661-770-4*, 252770) Bethany Hse. Pubs.

—Travail & Triumph Vol. 3: The Russians. 1992. (Russians Ser.: Vol. 3). 400p. pap. 12.99 (*1-55661-174-9*) Bethany Hse. Pubs.

Podrug, Junius. Presumed Guilty. 1998. 576p. mass mkt. 6.99 (*0-8125-5507-4*); 1997. 384p. 24.95 (*0-312-86242-3*) Doherty, Tom Assocs., LLC. (Forge Bks.).

Prieto, Jose Manuel. Nocturnal Butterflies of the Russian Empire: A Novel. Christensen, Thomas & Christensen, Carol, trs. from SPA. 2000. 322p. 24.00 o.p. (*0-8021-1665-5*, Grove Pr.) Grove/Atlantic, Inc.

Richler, Nancy. Your Mouth Is Lovely: A Novel. 368p. 2003. pap. 13.95 (*0-06-009678-0*); 2002. 25.95 (*0-06-009677-2*, Ecco) HarperTrade.

Robbins, David L. The Last Citadel: A Novel of the Battle of Kursk. 2003. (Illus.). 432p. 24.95 (*0-553-80177-5*) Bantam Bks.

Rothenberg, Michael. Punk Rockwell. 2000. (Illus.). 186p. pap. 19.95 (*0-9666173-2-0*) Tropical Pr., Inc.

Sebastian, Tim. Last Rights. unabr. ed. 1995. audio 69.95 (*0-7451-6495-1*, CAB 1111) BBC Audiobooks America.

—Last Rights. 1995. 272p. mass mkt. 5.50 (*0-380-71864-2*, Avon Bks.) Morrow/Avon.

—Last Rights: A Novel. l.t. ed. 1994. 402p. lib. bdg. 22.95 o.p. (*0-8161-7438-5*, Macmillan Reference USA) Gale Group.

Sebastian, Timothy. Last Rights. 1994. 270p. 22.00 o.p. (*0-688-11448-2*, Morrow, William & Co.) Morrow/Avon.

Simons, Paullina. The Bronze Horseman. Date not set. E-Book 7.99 (*0-06-000610-2*); 2002. 658p. E-Book 7.99 (*0-06-000608-0*) HarperCollins Pubs.

—The Bronze Horseman. 2002. 912p. mass mkt. 7.99 (*0-06-103112-7*, Avon Bks.); 2001. (Illus.). 656p. 26.95 (*0-06-019926-1*, Morrow, William & Co.) Morrow/Avon.

—The Bronze Horseman: A Novel. unabr. ed. 2001. audio 29.95 (*0-694-52553-7*, HarperAudio) HarperTrade.

Skeggs, Douglas. The Talinin Madonna. 1991. 272p. 18.95 o.p. (*0-312-07092-6*, Saint Martin's Minotaur) St. Martin's Pr.

Smith, Cynthia. Royals & Rogues. 1998. (Royals & Rogues Ser.: Vol. 4). 288p. mass mkt. 5.99 o.s.i (*0-425-16643-0*, Prime Crime) Berkley Publishing Group.

Smith, Martin Cruz. Gorky Park. 2000. mass mkt. 6.99 (*0-345-91704-9*); 1981. mass mkt. 2.95 o.s.i (*0-345-30392-X*) Ballantine Bks.

—Gorky Park. l.t. ed. 1981. 18.95 o.p. (*0-8161-3295-X*, Macmillan Reference USA) Gale Group.

—Gorky Park. 1993. 4.99 o.p. (*0-517-10699-X*) Random Hse. Value Publishing.

—Polar Star. 1993. mass mkt. 3.99 o.p. (*0-345-38550-0*) Ballantine Bks.

—Red Square. 2000. mass mkt. 6.99 (*0-345-91707-3*) Ballantine Bks.

Sologub, Fedor. The Created Legend, Vol. 3. Cioran, Samuel, tr. 1979. (ENG & RUS.). pap. 5.00 o.p. (*0-88233-145-0*) Ardis Pubs.

—The Created Legend. Cournos, J., tr. from RUS. 1975. 318p. reprint ed. 40.00 o.p. (*0-86527-232-8*) Fertig, Howard Inc.

—The Created Legend. 1975. (ENG & RUS.). 318p. reprint ed. lib. bdg. 35.00 o.p. (*0-8371-7714-6*, TECL) Greenwood Publishing Group, Inc.

Stewart, Chris. Shattered Bone. 1997. 384p. 21.95 (*0-87131-831-8*) Evans, M. & Co., Inc.

—Shattered Bone. 1998. 432p. mass mkt. 6.99 o.s.i (*0-451-40857-8*, Onyx) NAL.

Stewart, Sally. Travelling Girl. 2002. 192p. 25.99 (*0-7278-5909-9*) Severn Hse. Pubs., Ltd.

Stonov, Dmitry. In the Past Night: The Siberian Stories. Darrell, Kathryn & Stonov, Natasha S., trs. 1995. (Illus.). 236p. (C). 27.95 (*0-89672-358-5*) Texas Tech Univ. Pr.

Thomas, Craig. A Wild Justice. 1995. 368p. 24.00 o.p. (*0-06-017956-2*) HarperTrade.

Tolstoy, Leo. Anna Karenina. 2000. (Modern Library Classics). 976p. pap. 9.95 (*0-679-78330-X*, Modern Library) Random House Adult Trade Publishing Group.

Tur, Evgeniia & Katz, Michael R. Antonina. 1996. (European Classics Ser.). 192p. pap. 15.95 (*0-8101-1407-0*) Northwestern Univ. Pr.

Turgenev, Ivan. The Torrents of Spring. Garnett, Constance, tr. from RUS. 1977. (Short Story Index Reprint Ser.). 405p. reprint ed. 25.95 (*0-8369-3830-5*) Ayer Co. Pubs., Inc.

—The Torrents of Spring. 1999. 188p. pap. 18.00 (*0-374-52662-1*) Farrar, Straus & Giroux.

—The Torrents of Spring. Litvinov, Ivy & Litvinov, Tatiana, trs. from RUS. 1996. (Illus.). 174p. 25.00 (*0-8021-1594-2*, Grove Pr.) Grove/Atlantic, Inc.

Volos, Andrei. Hurramabad No. 26: A Novel as a Dotted Line. 2001. (Glas Ser.: Vol. 26). 320p. pap. 14.95 (*1-56663-373-7*) Dee, Ivan R. Pub.

Wallace, Randall. Love & Honor. 2004. 24.95 (*1-4013-0109-6*) Hyperion Pr.

White, Robin. Siberian Light. 1998. 528p. mass mkt. 6.99 (*0-440-22460-8*) Dell Publishing.

Womack, Jack. Let's Put the Future Behind Us. 1996. 320p. 23.00 o.p. (*0-87113-627-9*, Atlantic Monthly Pr.) Grove/Atlantic, Inc.

Woodiwiss, Kathleen E. Forever in Your Embrace. unabr. ed. 1999. 19p. audio 121.25 (*1-56740-696-3*, 1941, Unabridged Library Editions) Brilliance Audio.

—Forever in Your Embrace. l.t. ed. 1993. (General Ser.). 669p. pap. 19.95 (*0-8161-5749-9*); lib. bdg. 21.95 (*0-8161-5748-0*) Gale Group. (Macmillan Reference USA).

—Forever in Your Embrace. 2000. 592p. mass mkt. 7.99 (*0-380-81644-X*); 1999. 608p. 25.00 (*0-380-97831-8*); 1993. pap. 6.99 (*0-380-77246-9*); 1992. 560p. pap. 12.50 (*0-380-89818-7*) Morrow/Avon. (Avon Bks.).

Yarbro, Chelsea Quinn. Writ in Blood: A Novel of Saint-Germain. 1997. 544p. 26.95 o.p. (*0-312-86318-7*, Tor Bks.) Doherty, Tom Assocs., LLC.

**RUWENDA (IMAGINARY PLACE)—FICTION**

Bradley, Marion Zimmer. Black Trillium. 1991. (Trillium Ser.). 512p. mass mkt. 5.99 o.s.i (*0-553-29079-7*, Spectra) Bantam Bks.

—Lady of the Trillium. 1996. 320p. mass mkt. 5.99 o.s.i (*0-553-57263-6*, Spectra); 1995. 304p. 22.95 o.s.i (*0-553-09299-5*) Bantam Bks.

May, Julian. Blood Trillium. 1993. 480p. mass mkt. 5.99 o.s.i (*0-553-56198-7*) Bantam Bks.

Norton, Andre. The Golden Trillium. 1994. 352p. mass mkt. 5.99 o.s.i (*0-553-56095-6*) Bantam Bks.

**RYHOPE WOOD (IMAGINARY PLACE)—FICTION**

Holdstock, Robert. The Bone Forest. 1992. 256p. mass mkt. 4.50 (*0-380-76781-3*, Avon Bks.) Morrow/Avon.

—Gate of Ivory, Gate of Horn. (Mythago Wood Ser.). 2015. pap. 12.00 (*0-451-45646-7*); 1997. 320p. 24.95 o.p. (*0-451-45570-3*) NAL. (ROC).

—The Hollowing. Date not set. pap. (*0-7653-1110-0*, Tor Bks.) Doherty, Tom Assocs., LLC.

—The Hollowing. 1995. 336p. mass mkt. 4.99 o.s.i (*0-451-45356-5*, ROC); 1994. 384p. 17.95 o.p. (*0-451-45355-7*, Penguin Bks.) NAL.

—The Hollowing. pap. 3.98 o.p. (*0-7651-0416-4*) Smithmark Pubs., Inc.

—Lavondyss. Date not set. (*0-7653-0730-8*); pap. (*0-7653-0731-6*) Doherty, Tom Assocs., LLC. (Tor Bks.).

—Lavondyss. 1991. 400p. mass mkt. 4.50 (*0-380-71184-2*, Avon Bks.); 1989. 384p. 18.95 o.p. (*0-688-09185-7*, Morrow, William & Co.) Morrow/Avon.

—Mythago Wood. 1986. 2.95 o.s.i (*0-425-08785-9*) Berkley Publishing Group.

—Mythago Wood. Date not set. (*0-7653-0728-6*, Tor Bks.); 2003. 336p. pap. 14.95 (*0-7653-0729-4*, Orb Bks.) Doherty, Tom Assocs., LLC.

—Mythago Wood. 1991. pap. 3.95 (*0-380-76276-5*, Avon Bks.); 1985. 256p. 14.95 o.p. (*0-87795-761-4*, Morrow, William & Co.) Morrow/Avon.

—Mythago Wood. 1984. 252p. pap. 25.00 (*0-89366-283-6*) Ultramarine Publishing Co., Inc.

## S

**SACRAMENTO COUNTY (CALIF.)—FICTION**

Alwyn, Cynthia G. Scent of Murder. 2001. E-Book 23.95 (*1-59061-037-7*) Adobe Systems, Inc.

—Scent of Murder. 2001. 294p. 23.95 (*0-312-26559-X*, Saint Martin's Minotaur) St. Martin's Pr.

Barton, Wayne. Lockhart's Nightmare. 2000. 350p. mass mkt. 6.99 (*0-8125-7196-7*, Forge Bks.) Doherty, Tom Assocs., LLC.

Barton, Wayne & Williams, Stan. Lockharts Nightmare. 1998. 384p. 24.95 o.p. (*0-312-86142-7*, Forge Bks.) Doherty, Tom Assocs., LLC.

Bly, Stephen A. The Last Swan in Sacramento. 1999. (Old California Ser.: Vol. 2). 224p. pap. 10.99 o.p. (*1-58134-109-1*) Crossway Bks.

—The Last Swan in Sacramento. l.t. ed. 2000. (G. K. Hall Western Ser.). 326p. 25.95 (*0-7838-9127-X*) Thorndike Pr.

Grimes, Terris M. Somebody Else's Child. 1996. 272p. mass mkt. 5.99 o.s.i (*0-451-18672-9*, Signet Bks.) NAL.

Hall, Mary B. Emma Chizzit & the Mother Lode Marauder. 1995. per. (*0-373-26178-0*, Harlequin Bks.) Harlequin Enterprises, Ltd.

—Emma Chizzit & the Mother Lode Marauder. 1993. 19.95 (*0-8027-3225-9*) Walker & Co.

—Emma Chizzit & the Napa Nemesis. 1992. 202p. 19.95 (*0-8027-3211-9*) Walker & Co.

—Emma Chizzit & the Queen Anne Killer. 1989. 224p. 17.95 o.s.i (*0-8027-5751-0*) Walker & Co.

—Emma Chizzit & the Sacramento Stalker. 1995. (WWL Mystery Ser.). pap. (*0-373-28023-8*, 1-28023-9, Harlequin Bks.) Harlequin Enterprises, Ltd.

—Emma Chizzit & the Sacramento Stalker. 1991. 192p. 17.95 o.s.i (*0-8027-5777-4*) Walker & Co.

Hanson, Jacquelyn. Susan's Quest. 1998. (Illus.). 280p. pap. 5.95 (*0-9637265-2-8*, 9802); 268p. (*0-9637265-7-9*) Glenhaven Pr.

Hill, Bonnie Hearn. Intern: A Novel. 2003. 320p. (*1-55166-691-X*, Mira Bks.) Harlequin Enterprises, Ltd.

Jacobson, Alan. False Accusations. 1999. 407p. 23.00 (*0-671-02678-X*, Atria); 2000. (Illus.). 448p. reprint ed. pap. 6.99 (*0-671-02679-8*, Pocket) Simon & Schuster.

Kaiser, R. J. Fruitcake. 2000. 448p. mass mkt. (*1-55166-625-1*, Harlequin Bks.) Harlequin Enterprises, Ltd.

Kijewski, Karen. Alley Kat Blues. 1996. (Kat Colorado Mysteries Ser.). 384p. mass mkt. 6.99 (*0-553-57315-2*, Crimeline) Bantam Bks.

—Kat Scratch Fever. 1998. (Kat Colorado Mysteries Ser.). 368p. mass mkt. 6.99 o.s.i (*0-425-16339-3*) Berkley Publishing Group.

—Kat Scratch Fever. 1997. 323p. 22.95 o.p. (*0-399-14245-2*) Penguin Group (USA) Inc.

—Katapult. 1992. (Kat Colorado Mysteries Ser.). 288p. reprint ed. mass mkt. 6.99 (*0-380-71486-8*, Avon Bks.) Morrow/Avon.

—Katapult. 1990. 244p. 16.95 o.p. (*0-312-04679-0*, Saint Martin's Minotaur) St. Martin's Pr.

—Kat's Cradle. 1997. (Kat Colorado Mysteries Ser.). 320p. mass mkt. 6.99 (*0-553-29391-5*) Bantam Bks.

—Katwalk. 1990. (Kat Colorado Mysteries Ser.). 240p. reprint ed. mass mkt. 6.99 (*0-380-71187-7*, Avon Bks.) Morrow/Avon.

—Katwalk. 1989. 232p. 16.95 o.p. (*0-312-02969-1*, Saint Martin's Minotaur) St. Martin's Pr.

—Stray Kat Waltz. 1999. (Kat Colorado Mysteries Ser.). 352p. reprint ed. pap. 6.99 o.s.i (*0-425-16988-X*) Berkley Publishing Group.

—Stray Kat Waltz. 1998. (Kat Colorado Mysteries Ser. ). 311p. 22.95 o.s.i (*0-399-14368-8*, G. P. Putnam's Sons) Penguin Group (USA) Inc.

—Wild Kat. 1994. (Kat Colorado Mysteries Ser.). 400p. mass mkt. 6.99 (*0-553-56877-9*) Bantam Bks.

Krieg, Joyce. Murder off Mike: A Talk Radio Mystery. l.t. ed. 2003. (Talk Radio Mystery Ser.). 464p. 28.95 (*1-58724-485-3*, Wheeler Publishing, Inc.) Gale Group.

—Murder off Mike: A Talk Radio Mystery. 2003. 288p. 23.95 (*0-312-31026-9*, Saint Martin's Minotaur) St. Martin's Pr.

Lee, Gus. No Physical Evidence. 1998. 400p. 24.95 o.s.i (*0-449-91139-X*, Fawcett) Ballantine Bks.

—No Physical Evidence. abr. ed. 1998. audio 17.95 o.p. (*1-56740-785-4*, 1462, Nova Audio Bks.); audio 28.95 (*1-56740-060-4*, 1460, Bookcassette); audio 89.25 (*1-56740-589-4*, 1461, Unabridged Library Editions) Brilliance Audio.

—No Physical Evidence: A Courtroom Novel. 2000. 384p. mass mkt. 6.99 o.s.i (*0-8041-1779-9*, Ivy Bks.) Ballantine Bks.

**SAINT ANSELM'S EPISCOPAL CHURCH (NEW YORK, N.Y.: IMAGINARY PLACE)—FICTION**

Holland, Isabelle. Flight of the Archangel. 1986. mass mkt. 2.95 o.s.i (*0-449-20977-6*, Fawcett) Ballantine Bks.

**SAINT BRUNO (LA.: IMAGINARY PLACE)—FICTION**

Woodrell, Daniel. Muscle for the Wing: A Rene Shade Mystery. 1988. 16.95 o.p. (*0-8050-0788-1*) Holt, Henry & Co.

—Muscle for the Wing: A Rene Shade Mystery. 1990. 224p. mass mkt. 4.50 o.p. (*0-451-16569-1*, Signet Bks.) NAL.

—Muscle for the Wing: A Rene Shade Mystery. 1998. 224p. pap. 14.00 (*0-671-00137-X*, Pocket) Simon & Schuster.

—The Ones You Do. 1992. 224p. 19.95 o.p. (*0-8050-0972-8*) Holt, Henry & Co.

—The Ones You Do. 1993. 256p. mass mkt. 4.99 o.p. (*0-451-40385-1*, Onyx) NAL.

—The Ones You Do. 1998. 224p. pap. 17.95 (*0-671-00135-3*, Pocket) Simon & Schuster.

—Under the Bright Lights. 1986. o.p. (*0-03-008514-4*) Holt, Henry & Co.

—Under the Bright Lights. 1988. 192p. pap. 3.50 (*0-380-70456-0*, Avon Bks.) Morrow/Avon.

**SAINT HILAIRE (ME.: IMAGINARY PLACE)—FICTION**

Shreve, Anita. Strange Fits of Passion. unabr. collector's ed. 1999. audio 48.00 (*0-7366-4497-0*, 4933) Books on Tape, Inc.

—Strange Fits of Passion. l.t. ed. 2000. 350p. lib. bdg. 25.95 (*1-58547-045-7*) Ctr. Point Large Print.

—Strange Fits of Passion. (Harvest Book Ser.). 1999. 352p. pap. 13.00 (*0-15-600710-X*, Harvest Bks.); 1991. 336p. 18.95 (*0-15-185760-1*) Harcourt Trade Pubs.

—Strange Fits of Passion. 1992. 384p. mass mkt. 5.99 o.s.i (*0-451-40300-2*, Onyx) NAL.

**SAINT LOUIS (MO.)—FICTION**

Brodkey, Harold. The Runaway Soul. 1991. 835p. 30.00 o.p. (*0-374-25286-6*) Farrar, Straus & Giroux.

—The Runaway Soul. 1992. 848p. pap. 15.00 o.p. (*0-06-097504-0*, Perennial) HarperTrade.

—The Runaway Soul. 1997. 848p. pap. 17.00 o.s.i (*0-8050-5503-7*, Owl Bks.) Holt, Henry & Co.

—The Runaway Soul. 1991. o.p. (*0-224-03001-9*) Random Hse. UK, Ltd. GBR. *Dist:* Random Hse. of Canada, Ltd.

Carkeet, David. The Error of Our Ways: A Novel. 288p. 1998. pap. 13.00 o.s.i (*0-8050-5604-1*, Owl Bks.); 1997. per. 15.00 (*0-8050-7114-8*); 1997. 25.00 o.s.i (*0-8050-4502-3*) Holt, Henry & Co.

—The Error of Our Ways: A Novel. l.t. ed. 1997. (Niagara Large Print Ser.). 352p. 29.50 o.p. (*0-7089-5865-6*, Ulverscroft) Thorpe, F. A. Pubs. GBR. *Dist:* Ulverscroft Large Print Bks., Ltd.

Dooling, Richard. Brain Storm. unabr. collector's ed. 1998. audio 104.00 (*0-7366-4335-4*, 4816) Books on Tape, Inc.

—Brain Storm. 1999. 416p. pap. 14.00 (*0-312-20399-3*) Picador.

—Brain Storm. unabr. ed. 1998. audio 97.00 (*0-7887-1988-2*, 95375E7) Recorded Bks., LLC.

Franzen, Jonathan. The Twenty-Seventh City. 1997. 528p. pap. 15.00 o.s.i (*0-374-52505-6*); 1988. 544p. 19.95 o.s.i (*0-374-27972-1*) Farrar, Straus & Giroux.
—The Twenty-Seventh City. 1990. pap. 8.95 (*0-380-70840-X*, Avon Bks.) Morrow/Avon.
—The Twenty-Seventh City. 2001. 528p. pap. 14.00 (*0-312-42014-5*) Picador.
—The Twenty-Seventh City. 1992. 1.99 o.p. (*0-517-08590-9*); 1991. 2.99 o.p. (*0-517-06299-2*) Random Hse. Value Publishing.
Greiman, Lois. The Gambler. 1995. mass mkt. 5.99 o.s.i (*0-515-11787-0*, Jove) Berkley Publishing Group.
Hamilton, Laurell K. Circus of the Damned. 1995. (Anita Blake Vampire Hunter Ser.). 336p. (Orig.). mass mkt. 6.99 o.s.i (*0-441-00197-1*) Ace Bks.
—Circus of the Damned. (Orig.). 2004. 320p. 22.95 (*0-425-19427-2*); 2002. 336p. mass mkt. 6.99 (*0-515-13448-1*) Berkley Publishing Group.
—Guilty Pleasures. 1993. (Anita Blake Vampire Hunter Ser.). 272p. mass mkt. 6.99 o.s.i (*0-441-30483-4*) Ace Bks.
—Guilty Pleasures. 2004. 368p. pap. 13.00 (*0-425-19754-9*); 2002. 272p. mass mkt. 6.99 (*0-515-13449-X*); 2002. 320p. reprint ed. 21.95 (*0-425-18756-X*) Berkley Publishing Group.
—Guilty Pleasures. 2002. (Anita Blake Vampire Hunter Ser.). E-Book 6.99 (*0-7865-2898-2*) Penguin Putnam, Inc E-Books.
—The Killing Dance. 1997. (Anita Blake Vampire Hunter Ser.). 400p. mass mkt. 6.99 o.s.i (*0-441-00452-0*) Ace Bks.
—The Killing Dance. 2002. 400p. mass mkt. 7.99 (*0-515-13451-1*) Berkley Publishing Group.
Haynes, David. All American Dream Dolls. 1999. (Harvest Book Ser.). 288p. pap. 12.00 (*0-15-600572-7*, Harvest Bks.) Harcourt Trade Pubs.
—All American Dream Dolls. 1997. 288p. 21.95 (*1-57131-015-0*) Milkweed Editions.
Hemon, Peter. The Kindling Effect. 1997. pap. 5.99 (*0-380-72634-3*, Avon Bks.) Morrow/Avon.
Hoffman, Allen. Big League Dreams. 1997. (Small Worlds Ser.). 296p. 24.95 (*0-7892-0191-7*) Abbeville Pr., Inc.
Hunter, Liz. Beyond the Shadow. 2000. E-Book 5.50 (*1-58200-549-4*) Hard Shell Word Factory.
Jackson, Monica. Never Too Late for Love. 2000. 256p. mass mkt. 5.99 (*1-58314-107-3*) BET Bks.
Jacobs, Kathleen L. Never Forsaken. 1999. (Illus.). 270p. pap. 10.99 (*1-58134-110-5*) Crossway Bks.
Jones, Douglas C. This Savage Race, Set. l.t. ed. 1994. (Studio Ser.). 109.95 o.p. incl. audio (*0-7862-9992-4*, Macmillan Reference USA) Gale Group.
—This Savage Race. 1994. 512p. mass mkt. 4.50 o.p. (*0-06-100770-6*) HarperCollins Pubs.
—This Savage Race. 1993. 320p. 23.00 o.p. (*0-8050-2243-0*) Holt, Henry & Co.
Kahn, Michael A. Bearing Witness. 2000. (Rachel Gold Novels Ser.). 316p. 23.95 (*0-312-84883-8*, Forge Bks.) Doherty, Tom Assocs., LLC.
—Bearing Witness. 1999. pap. 21.95 (*0-525-94305-6*) NAL.
—Due Diligence. 1996. (Rachel Gold Mystery Ser.). 400p. mass mkt. 5.99 o.s.i (*0-451-17970-6*, Signet Bks.) NAL.
—Due Dilligence: A Rachel Gold Mystery. 1995. (Rachel Gold Mystery Ser.). 336p. 20.95 o.s.i (*0-525-93743-9*, Dutton) Dutton/Plume.
—Firm Ambitions. 1995. 320p. mass mkt. 5.99 o.s.i (*0-451-17961-7*, Onyx) NAL.
—Firm Ambitions: A Rachel Gold Mystery. 1994. (Rachel Gold Mystery Ser.). 320p. 18.95 o.p. (*0-525-93742-0*, Dutton) Dutton/Plume.
—Sheer Gall. 1996. (Rachel Gold Mystery Ser.). 320p. 23.95 o.s.i (*0-525-94188-6*) Dutton/Plume.
—Sheer Gall. 1998. (Rachel Gold Mystery Ser.). 368p. mass mkt. 5.99 o.s.i (*0-451-40733-4*, Onyx) NAL.
—Trophy Widow. E-Book 25.95 (*0-312-70732-0*, Tor Bks.); 2002. 432p. 25.95 (*0-7653-0218-7*, Forge Bks.) Doherty, Tom Assocs., LLC.
Keene, John. Annotations. 1995. (Paperbook Ser.: Vol. 809). 96p. (Orig.). pap. 8.95 (*0-8112-1304-8*, NDP809) New Directions Publishing Corp.
Kennett, Shirley. Firecracker. 1998. 320p. mass mkt. 5.99 o.s.i (*0-7860-0525-4*, Pinnacle Bks.) Kensington Publishing Corp.
Kennett, Shirley. Chameleon. 1999. 384p. mass mkt. 5.99 (*0-7860-0638-2*) Kensington Publishing Corp.
—Chameleon: A Novel of Suspense. 1998. 320p. 22.00 o.s.i (*1-57566-347-3*) Kensington Publishing Corp.
—Fire Cracker. 1997. 320p. pap. 21.95 o.p. (*1-57566-181-0*) Kensington Publishing Corp.
—Gray Matter. 1997. 320p. mass mkt. 5.99 o.s.i (*0-7860-0389-8*, Pinnacle Bks.); 1996. 224p. 21.95 o.s.i (*1-57566-079-2*, Kensington Bks.) Kensington Publishing Corp.
Kunz, Kathleen. Murder Once Removed. 1995. (WWL Mystery Ser.). 252p. per. (*0-373-26175-6*, 1-26175-9, Harlequin Bks.) Harlequin Enterprises, Ltd.
—Murder Once Removed. 1993. (Terry Girard Mystery Ser.). 216p. 19.95 o.p. (*0-8027-3230-5*) Walker & Co.
Lutz, John. Buyer Beware. 1992. (Mystery Scene Bk.). 192p. pap. 3.95 o.p. (*0-88184-840-9*, Carroll & Graf Pubs.) Avalon Publishing Group.
—Buyer Beware. l.t. ed. 1988. pap. 17.95 o.p. (*1-55504-671-1*); lib. bdg. 19.95 o.p. (*1-55504-690-8*) BBC Audiobooks America.
—Buyer Beware. 1976. 6.95 o.p. (*0-399-11811-X*) Putnam Publishing Group, The.
—Dancer's Debt. 1988. 256p. 16.95 o.p. (*0-312-00028-6*) St. Martin's Pr.
—Dancing with the Dead. 2001. 208p. reprint ed. pap. 12.95 (*1-931755-16-7*) Mystery Vault, Inc.
—Dancing with the Dead. 1992. 304p. 18.95 o.p. (*0-312-07693-2*, Saint Martin's Minotaur) St. Martin's Pr.
—Death by Jury: An Alo Nudger Mystery. 1995. 352p. 23.95 o.p. (*0-312-13613-7*, Saint Martin's Minotaur) St. Martin's Pr.
—Diamond Eyes. 1990. 224p. 15.95 o.p. (*0-312-05074-7*, Saint Martin's Minotaur) St. Martin's Pr.
—Nightlines: The First Alo Nudger Mystery. 1987. 352p. pap. 3.95 o.p. (*0-8125-0648-0*, Tor Bks.) Doherty, Tom Assocs., LLC.
—Nightlines: The First Alo Nudger Mystery. 1984. 13.95 o.p. (*0-312-57324-3*) St. Martin's Pr.
—Oops! l.t. ed. 1998. (Large Print Book Ser.). pap. 23.95 o.p. (*1-56895-653-3*, Wheeler Publishing, Inc.) Gale Group.
—Oops! 1997. 304p. 22.95 o.p. (*0-312-18152-3*, Saint Martin's Minotaur) St. Martin's Pr.
—Ride the Lightning. 1990. mass mkt. 3.95 (*0-8125-0642-1*, Tor Bks.) Doherty, Tom Assocs., LLC.
—Ride the Lightning. 1987. 256p. 15.95 o.p. (*0-312-00182-7*) St. Martin's Pr.
—Thicker Than Blood: An Alo Nudger Mystery, Set. unabr. ed. 1999. audio 54.95 (*0-7927-2314-7*, CSL203, Chivers Sound Library) BBC Audiobooks America.
—Thicker Than Blood: An Alo Nudger Mystery. 1993. 272p. 19.95 o.p. (*0-312-09922-3*, Saint Martin's Minotaur) St. Martin's Pr.
—Time Exposure. 1990. 2.99 o.p. (*0-517-05936-3*) Random Hse. Value Publishing.
—Time Exposure. 1989. 16.95 o.p. (*0-312-02990-X*, Saint Martin's Minotaur) St. Martin's Pr.
Lyons, Andrew. Darkness in Him: A Novel. 2003. 304p. 24.95 (*0-312-30146-4*) St. Martin's Pr.
Marcy, Jean. Cemetery Murders: A Meg Darcy Mystery. 1997. 200p. pap. 10.95 (*0-934678-83-9*) New Victoria Pubs., Inc.
Matthews, Christine & Randisi, Robert J. Murder Is the Deal of the Day. 2003. (WWL Mystery Ser.: No. 472). 256p. mass mkt. (*0-373-26472-0*, Worldwide Library) Harlequin Enterprises, Ltd.
—Murder Is the Deal of the Day. 1998. 240p. 22.95 o.p. (*0-312-19928-7*, Saint Martin's Minotaur) St. Martin's Pr.
McFadden, Bernice L. This Bitter Earth. 2002. 288p. pap. 13.00 (*0-452-28381-7*, Plume); 23.95 o.s.i (*0-525-94636-5*, Dutton) Dutton/Plume.
—This Bitter Earth. l.t. ed. 2002. (African American Ser.). 420p. 29.95 (*0-7862-3882-8*) Thorndike Pr.
McKitterick, Molly. The Medium Is Murder. 1992. 224p. 17.95 o.p. (*0-312-07032-2*, Saint Martin's Minotaur) St. Martin's Pr.
—Murder in a Mayonnaise Jar. 1993. 224p. 17.95 o.p. (*0-312-09346-2*, Saint Martin's Minotaur) St. Martin's Pr.
Munson, Ronald. Fan Mail. 1993. 320p. 20.00 o.p. (*0-525-93624-6*, Dutton) Dutton/Plume.
Nevins, Francis M. Corrupt & Ensnare. 1978. 8.95 o.p. (*0-399-12203-6*) Putnam Publishing Group, The.
—Corrupt & Ensnare. 2000. 232p. pap. 14.95 (*1-58348-998-3*) iUniverse, Inc.
—Publish & Perish. 2000. 192p. pap. 12.95 (*0-595-00059-2*) iUniverse, Inc.
Powell, Jacqueline. Anyone Who Has a Heart. 2003. 352p. 23.95 (*0-446-53174-X*) Warner Bks., Inc.
Randisi, Robert J. Blood on the Arch: A Joe Keough Mystery. E-Book 22.95 (*0-312-27407-6*); 2000. 280p. 22.95 (*0-312-24179-8*, Saint Martin's Minotaur) St. Martin's Pr.
—In the Shadow of the Arch. 2000. (Joe Keough Mysteries Ser.). 368p. mass mkt. 4.99 (*0-8439-4761-6*, Leisure Bks.) Dorchester Publishing Co., Inc.
—In the Shadow of the Arch. 1997. (Joe Keough Mysteries Ser.). 368p. 24.95 (*0-312-18115-9*, Saint Martin's Minotaur) St. Martin's Pr.
Savan, Glenn. Goldman's Anatomy. 1993. 336p. 22.00 o.s.i (*0-385-42607-0*) Doubleday Publishing.
Shange, Ntozake. Betsey Brown. 2nd ed. 1995. 208p. pap. 11.00 (*0-312-13434-7*) Picador.
—Betsey Brown. 1985. 208p. 12.95 o.p. (*0-312-07727-0*) St. Martin's Pr.
Simmons, Herbert. Man Walking on Eggshells. 1997. (Old School Bks.). 221p. pap. 11.00 (*0-393-31618-1*) Norton, W. W. & Co., Inc.
Spencer, Jon M. Tribes of Benjamin: A Novel. 1999. 199 p. (*1-893562-01-8*) Tubman, Harriet Pr.
Steele, Allen. The Jericho Iteration. 288p. 1995. mass mkt. 5.99 o.s.i (*0-441-00271-4*); 1994. 19.95 o.p. (*0-441-00097-5*) Ace Bks.
Stolz, Karen. Fanny & Sue: A Novel. 2004. 256p. pap. 13.00 (*0-7868-8605-6*) Hyperion Pr.
Taylor, Peter. A Woman of Means. 1983. 140p. 16.95 (*0-913720-44-5*) Beil, Frederic C. Pub., Inc.
—A Woman of Means. 1986. (Southern Writers Ser.). 128p. mass mkt. 3.95 (*0-380-70099-9*, Avon Bks.) Morrow/Avon.
—A Woman of Means. 1996. 144p. pap. 10.00 (*0-312-14448-2*) Picador.
Tyree, Omar R. Sweet St. Louis. mass mkt. 6.99 (*0-7434-8242-5*, Pocket); 2000. 368p. pap. 14.00 (*0-684-85611-5*, Simon & Schuster); 1999. (Illus.). 368p. 24.00 (*0-684-85610-7*, Simon & Schuster) Simon & Schuster.
Viets, Elaine. Back Stab: A Francesca Vierling Mystery. 1997. (Francesca Vierling Mystery Ser.). 320p. mass mkt. 5.99 o.s.i (*0-440-22431-4*) Dell Publishing.
—Doc in the Box: A Francesca Vierling Mystery. 2000. (Francesca Vierling Mystery Ser.). 256p. mass mkt. 5.99 o.s.i (*0-440-23620-7*) Bantam Dell Publishing Group.
—The Pink Flamingo Murders: A Francesca Vierling Mystery. 1999. 272p. mass mkt. 5.99 o.s.i (*0-440-22445-4*) Dell Publishing.
—The Pink Flamingo Murders: A Francesca Vierling Mystery. 1999. 272p. pap. 19.00 (*0-440-61351-5*) Random Hse., Inc.
—Rubout: A Francesca Vierling Mystery. 1998. (Francesca Vierling Mystery Ser.). 320p. mass mkt. 5.99 o.s.i (*0-440-22444-6*) Dell Publishing.
—Rubout: A Francesca Vierling Mystery. 1998. 320p. pap. 19.00 (*0-440-61348-5*) Random Hse., Inc.
Wolfe, Thomas. The Lost Boy: A Novella. Clark, James W., Jr., ed. 1994. (Chapel Hill Bks.). (Illus.). 95p. (C). pap. 11.95 (*0-8078-4486-1*) Univ. of North Carolina Pr.
—The Lost Boy: A Novella. 1992. (Chapel Hill Bks.). (Illus.). xiv, 82p. (C). 24.95 o.p. (*0-8078-2063-6*) Univ. of North Carolina Pr.

**SAINT PAUL (MINN.)—FICTION**

Clark, Robert. Mr. White's Confession. 2001. pap. (*0-312-24719-2*); 1999. 352p. pap. 14.00 (*0-312-20426-4*); 1998. 341p. 24.00 o.p. (*0-312-19217-7*) Picador.
—Mr. White's Confession. unabr. ed. audio 70.00 (*0-7887-2498-3*, 95573E7) Recorded Bks., LLC.
—Mr. White's Confession. l.t. ed. 1999. (Basic Ser.). 436p. 28.95 (*0-7862-1733-2*) Thorndike Pr.
Housewright, David. Dearly Departed: A Holland Taylor Mystery. 1999. (Holland Taylor Mystery Ser.). 224p. text 23.95 o.p. (*0-393-04771-7*) Norton, W. W. & Co., Inc.
—Penance. 1997. (Holland Taylor Mystery Ser.). 304p. mass mkt. 6.50 o.s.i (*0-425-15942-6*, Prime Crime) Berkley Publishing Group.
—Penance. 1995. (Holland Taylor Mystery Ser.). 296p. 21.00 (*0-88150-341-X*, Foul Play) Norton, W. W. & Co., Inc.
—Practice to Deceive. 2000. (Holland Taylor Mystery Ser.). 275p. mass mkt. 5.99 o.s.i (*0-425-17312-7*) Berkley Publishing Group.
—Practice to Deceive: A Holland Taylor Mystery. 1997. (Holland Taylor Mystery Ser.). 256p. 22.00 (*0-88150-404-1*, Foul Play) Norton, W. W. & Co., Inc.
Jacobs, Nancy B. The Silver Scalpel. 1993. (Devon McDonald Ser.). 240p. 21.95 o.p. (*0-399-13834-X*, G. P. Putnam's Sons) Penguin Group (USA) Inc.
—A Slash of Scarlet. 1992. 240p. 19.95 o.p. (*0-399-13733-5*, G. P. Putnam's Sons) Penguin Group (USA) Inc.
—A Slash of Scarlet. Rubenstein, Julie, ed. 1993. 256p. reprint ed. mass mkt. 4.99 (*0-671-86504-8*, Pocket) Simon & Schuster.
—The Turquoise Tattoo. 1992. 256p. reprint ed. mass mkt. 4.99 (*0-671-75535-8*, Pocket) Simon & Schuster.
—The Turquoise Tattoo: A Devon MacDonald Mystery. 1991. 240p. 19.95 o.p. (*0-399-13551-0*, G. P. Putnam's Sons) Penguin Group (USA) Inc.
Monsour, Theresa. Clean Cut. 2004. 368p. mass mkt. 7.99 (*0-515-13705-7*, Jove) Berkley Publishing Group.
—Clean Cut. 2003. 304p. 23.95 (*0-399-14968-6*) Putnam Publishing Group, The.
—Road Kill. 2004. 320p. 24.95 (*0-399-15156-7*) Putnam Publishing Group, The.
Sandford, John, pseud. The Hanged Man's Song. 2003. 336p. 25.95 (*0-399-15139-7*, Putnam & Grosset) Putnam Publishing Group, The.
Sharratt, Mary. Summit Avenue. 2000. ii, 252p. pap. 14.95 (*1-56689-097-7*) Coffee Hse. Pr.

**SAINT PETERSBURG (RUSSIA)—FICTION**

Bankoff, Peter N. A Soviet Assignment. 1988. 192p. 14.75 (*0-930950-19-4*); pap. 8.75 (*0-930950-20-8*) Nopoly Pr., Inc.
Bely, Andrei. Petersburg. unabr. ed. 1999. (World Classic Literature Ser.). (RUS.). pap. 10.95 (*2-87714-266-3*) Bookking International FRA. *Dist:* Distribooks, Inc.
—Petersburg. Maguire, Robert A. & Malmstad, John E., trs. from RUS. 384p. 1979. pap. 15.95 (*0-253-20219-1*, MB 219); 1978. 27.50 o.p. (*0-253-34410-7*) Indiana Univ. Pr.
—Petersburg. McDuff, David, tr. from RUS. 1996. (Penguin Twentieth-Century Classics Ser.). 624p. pap. 15.95 o.s.i (*0-14-018696-4*, Penguin Classics) Viking Penguin.
Berman, Leonard H. Consider My Servant. 2001. 437p. pap. 24.99 (*0-7388-1680-9*); text 34.99 (*0-7388-1679-5*); E-Book 8.00 (*0-7388-8569-X*) Xlibris Corp.
Bradby, Tom. The White Russian. 2004. 560p. mass mkt. (*0-552-14900-4*, Corgi) Bantam Bks.
—The White Russian: A Novel. 2003. (Illus.). 464p. 25.00 (*0-385-50840-9*) Doubleday Publishing.
—The White Russian: A Novel. 2004. 464p. pap. 14.95 (*1-4000-3200-8*, Anchor) Knopf Publishing Group.
Bunn, T. Davis. Winter Palace. 1993. (Priceless Collection: No. 3). 352p. pap. 9.99 o.p. (*1-55661-324-5*) Bethany Hse. Pubs.
—Winter Palace. l.t. ed. 2001. (Thorndike Christian Mystery Ser.). (Illus.). 512p. 24.95 (*0-7862-3179-3*) Thorndike Pr.
Conrad, Joseph. Under Western Eyes. 1976. (Orig.). 17.95 (*0-8488-0749-9*) Amereon, Ltd.
—Under Western Eyes. (Collected Works of Joseph Conrad). (Orig.). 2001. pap. text 28.00 (*0-7426-7663-3*); reprint ed. lib. bdg. 98.00 (*0-7426-2663-6*) Classic Bks.
—Under Western Eyes. 1963. (Orig.). pap. 1.95 o.p. (*0-385-03001-0*) Doubleday Publishing.
—Under Western Eyes. 2003. (Dover Thrift Editions Ser.). 224p. (Orig.). 3.00 (*0-486-43164-9*) Dover Pubns., Inc.
—Under Western Eyes. 1987. (Orig.). mass mkt. 3.50 o.p. (*0-451-52114-5*, Signet Classics) NAL.
—Under Western Eyes. Hawthorn, Jeremy, ed. (Oxford World's Classics Ser.). (Orig.). 1996. 416p. (C). pap. 7.95 o.p. (*0-19-281619-5*); 2nd ed. 2003. 368p. pap. 10.95 (*0-19-280171-6*) Oxford Univ. Pr., Inc.
—Under Western Eyes. 2001. (Modern Library Classics). 336p. (Orig.). pap. 9.95 (*0-375-75735-X*, Modern Library) Random House Adult Trade Publishing Group.
—Under Western Eyes. 1991. (Everyman's Library). 512p. (Orig.). 20.00 (*0-679-40554-2*) Random Hse., Inc.
—Under Western Eyes. 1997. (Great Books of the 20th Century Ser.). 400p. (Orig.). 11.00 (*0-14-018849-5*, Penguin Classics) Viking Penguin.
—Under Western Eyes. Ford, Boris, ed. & intro. by. 1990. 352p. (Orig.). pap. 9.95 o.p. (*0-14-018287-X*, 158, Penguin Classics) Viking Penguin.
—Under Western Eyes. (Orig.). 1986. pap. 4.95 o.p. (*0-14-043243-4*, Penguin Classics); 1979. pap. 3.95 o.p. (*0-14-001254-0*, Penguin Bks.) Viking Penguin.
Cullen, Robert. Dispatch from a Cold Country. 1997. 407p. mass mkt. 6.99 o.s.i (*0-8041-1444-7*, Ivy Bks.) Ballantine Bks.
Dostoyevsky, Fyodor. Crime & Punishment. 2002. (World Digital Library). E-Book 3.95 (*0-594-08378-8*) 1873 Pr.
—Crime & Punishment. 1967. (Airmont Classics Ser.). (Illus.). mass mkt. 3.95 (*0-8049-0145-7*, CL-145) Airmont Publishing Co., Inc.
—Crime & Punishment. Date not set. 522p. 31.95 (*0-8488-2516-0*) Amereon, Ltd.
—Crime & Punishment. l.t. ed. 1998. 760p. pap. 24.95 (*1-55701-214-8*) BNI Pubns., Inc.
—Crime & Punishment. 1994. mass mkt. 4.95 (*0-553-85015-6*); 1982. 496p. mass mkt. 2.25 o.s.i (*0-553-21093-9*, Bantam Classics) Bantam Bks.
—Crime & Punishment. Garnett, Constance, tr. 1996. (Bantam Classics Ser.). 576p. reprint ed. mass mkt. 6.99 (*0-553-21175-7*) Bantam Dell Publishing Group.
—Crime & Punishment. 2002. per. 14.50 (*1-58396-571-8*) Blue Unicorn Editions.
—Crime & Punishment. unabr. ed. 1999. (World Classic Literature Ser.). (RUS.). pap. 10.95 (*2-87714-263-9*) Bookking International FRA. *Dist:* Distribooks, Inc.
—Crime & Punishment. 1982. reprint ed. lib. bdg. 37.95 (*0-89966-397-4*) Buccaneer Bks., Inc.
—Crime & Punishment. l.t. ed. 1998. 760p. pap. 24.95 (*1-58855-027-3*) Cyber Classics, Inc.
—Crime & Punishment. Garnett, Constance, tr. 1984. 576p. pap. 2.50 o.p. (*0-440-31555-7*) Dell Publishing.
—Crime & Punishment. Garnett, Constance Black, tr. from RUS. 2001. (Dover Thrift Editions Ser.). 480p. mass mkt. 3.00 (*0-486-41587-2*) Dover Pubns., Inc.
—Crime & Punishment. 1972. 4.50 o.p. (*0-460-01501-X*); 1955. 12.95 o.p. (*0-460-00501-4*) Dutton/Plume. (Dutton).

Settings

—Crime & Punishment. E-Book 2.49 (*0-7574-2947-5*) Electric Umbrella Publishing.

—Crime & Punishment. 1991. pap. text, stu. ed. 19.95 (*0-8224-9445-0*) Globe Fearon Educational Publishing.

—Crime & Punishment. 2003. pap. 6.95 (*1-59456-790-5*) GreatUNpublished.com.

—Crime & Punishment. abr. ed. 1994. audio 24.95 (*1-56511-643-7*) HighBridge Co.

—Crime & Punishment. l.t. ed. 2627p. pap. 156.59 (*0-7583-0671-7*); 2265p. pap. 141.19 (*0-7583-0670-9*); 1497p. pap. 93.17 (*0-7583-0668-7*); 1170p. pap. 77.97 (*0-7583-0667-9*); 914p. pap. 65.31 (*0-7583-0666-0*); 667p. pap. 46.76 (*0-7583-0665-2*); 534p. pap. 39.20 (*0-7583-0664-4*); 1841p. pap. 117.12 (*0-7583-0669-5*); 914p. lib. bdg. 77.31 (*0-7583-0658-X*); 2265p. lib. bdg. 171.26 (*0-7583-0662-8*); 1841p. lib. bdg. 135.80 (*0-7583-0661-X*); 2627p. lib. bdg. 189.93 (*0-7583-0663-6*); 667p. lib. bdg. 52.76 (*0-7583-0657-1*); 534p. lib. bdg. 45.20 (*0-7583-0656-3*); 1497p. lib. bdg. 105.17 (*0-7583-0660-1*) Huge Print Pr.

—Crime & Punishment. Pevear, Richard & Volokhonsky, Larissa, trs. from RUS. 1993. (Everyman's Library). 608p. 20.00 (*0-679-42029-0*) Knopf, Alfred A. Inc.

—Crime & Punishment, 2 vols. 1999. (Cloth Bound Pocket Ser.). 1000p. 7.95 (*3-8290-0904-6*, 520666) Konemann.

—Crime & Punishment. 1950. 492p. (C). 11.25 (*0-07-553574-2*, McGraw-Hill Humanities, Social Sciences & World Languages) McGraw-Hill Higher Education.

—Crime & Punishment. mass mkt. 0.25 o.p. (*0-451-00733-6*, Signet Bks.); 1968. mass mkt. 1.95 o.p. (*0-451-51287-1*, Signet Classics); 1968. mass mkt. 2.25 o.p. (*0-451-51745-8*, Signet Classics); 1968. mass mkt. 1.50 o.p. (*0-451-51088-7*, Signet Classics); 1968. mass mkt. 1.25 o.p. (*0-451-50924-2*, Signet Classics); 1968. mass mkt. 0.95 o.p. (*0-451-50762-2*, Signet Classics); 1968. mass mkt. 0.75 o.p. (*0-451-50362-7*, Signet Classics); 1968. mass mkt. 2.50 o.p. (*0-451-51995-7*); 1968. mass mkt. 2.75 o.p. (*0-451-51479-3*, Signet Classics) NAL.

—Crime & Punishment. Monas, Sidney, tr. 1968. 544p. mass mkt. 7.95 o.s.i (*0-451-52335-0*, Signet Classics) NAL.

—Crime & Punishment. Monas, Sidney, tr. from RUS. & afterword by by. rev. ed. 1999. (Signet Classics). 560p. mass mkt. 7.95 (*0-451-52723-2*, Signet Classics) NAL.

—Crime & Punishment. 1998. (Twelve-Point Ser.). 605p. reprint ed. lib. bdg. 27.00 (*1-58287-087-X*) North Bks.

—Crime & Punishment. 1975. (C). pap. o.p. (*0-393-09292-5*) Norton, W. W. & Co., Inc.

—Crime & Punishment. Gibian, George, ed. 3rd annot. ed. 1989. (Critical Editions Ser.). (C). pap. text (*0-393-95623-7*, 95623) Norton, W. W. & Co., Inc.

—Crime & Punishment. Coulson, Jessie & Peace, Richard, eds. 2nd ed. 1995. (Oxford World's Classics Ser.). (Illus.). 564p. pap. 7.95 o.p. (*0-19-282358-2*) Oxford Univ. Pr., Inc.

—Crime & Punishment. McDuff, David, tr. abr. ed. 1994. (Classics on Cassette). pap. 24.00 o.s.i incl. audio (*0-453-00915-8*) Penguin/HighBridge.

—Crime & Punishment. 2000. E-Book 4.95 (*0-679-64003-7*, Modern Library) Random House Adult Trade Publishing Group.

—Crime & Punishment. 1988. 4.99 o.s.i (*0-517-39588-6*) Random Hse. Value Publishing.

—Crime & Punishment. Garnett, Constance, tr. (Modern Library Ser.). 1994. 656p. 19.95 (*0-679-60100-7*); 1978. 15.00 o.s.i (*0-394-60450-4*) Random Hse., Inc.

—Crime & Punishment. 1959. 3.95 o.s.i (*0-394-60199-8*) Random Hse., Inc.

—Crime & Punishment. Garnett, Constance, tr. 1955. (Modern Library College Editions Ser.). pap. 6.95 o.p. (*0-394-70721-4*) Random Hse., Inc.

—Crime & Punishment. 2001. E-Book 2.95 (*1-58853-029-9*) Sensory Publishing, Inc.

—Crime & Punishment. 1981. pap. (*0-02-917680-8*, Free Pr.) Simon & Schuster.

—Crime & Punishment. Scammel, ed. 1972. (Enriched Classics Ser.). 614p. mass mkt. 3.50 o.p. (*0-671-48956-9*, Pocket) Simon & Schuster.

—Crime & Punishment. 1972. (Washington Square Press Enriched Classic Ser.). 14.00 (*0-606-00502-1*) Turtleback Bks.

—Crime & Punishment. (Classics Ser.). 2002. 718p. pap. 13.00 (*0-14-044913-2*); 1998. (*0-14-771372-2*) Viking Penguin. (Penguin Classics).

—Crime & Punishment. McDuff, David, tr. & intro. by. 1996. (Penguin Classics Ser.). 656p. pap. 13.00 o.s.i (*0-14-044528-5*, Penguin Classics) Viking Penguin.

—Crime & Punishment. McDuff, David, tr. from RUS. 1991. 656p. 30.00 o.p. (*0-670-83640-0*, Viking) Viking Penguin.

—Crime & Punishment. Magarshack, David, tr. 1952. (Penguin Classics Ser.). 560p. pap. 7.95 o.p. (*0-14-044023-2*, Penguin Classics) Viking Penguin.

—Crime & Punishment. 1999. E-Book 4.99 (*0-8220-7043-X*, Cliff Notes) Wiley, John & Sons, Inc.

—Crime & Punishment. 1997. (Classics Library). 416p. pap. 3.95 (*1-85326-200-5*, 2005WW) Wordsworth Editions, Ltd. GBR. *Dist:* Casemate Pubs. & Bk. Distributors, LLC.

—Crime & Punishment: A Novel in Six Parts & an Epilogue. Coulson, Jessie, tr. from RUS. 1981. (Oxford World's Classics Ser.). 560p. pap. 7.95 o.p. (*0-19-281549-0*) Oxford Univ. Pr., Inc.

—Crime & Punishment: A Novel in Six Parts with Epilogue. Pevear, Richard & Volokhonsky, Larissa, trs. 1993. (Vintage Bks.). 592p. pap. 15.00 (*0-679-73450-3*, Vintage) Knopf Publishing Group.

Dostoyevsky, Fyodor & Everyman's Library Staff. Crime & Punishment. Pevear, Richard & Volokhonsky, Larissa, trs. 1992. 25.00 o.p. (*0-679-40557-7*) Knopf, Alfred A. Inc.

Dostoyevsky, Fyodor & Rahv, Philip. Crime & Punishment. 1996. (Literary Classics Giant Ser.). 528p. text 8.98 o.p. (*1-56138-714-2*, Courage Bks.) Running Pr. Bk. Pubs.

Dunmore. Siege. 2003. pap. 13.00 (*0-8021-3958-2*) Grove/Atlantic, Inc.

Dunmore, Helen. The Siege: A Novel. 2002. 304p. 24.00 o.p. (*0-8021-1700-7*, Grove Pr.) Grove/Atlantic, Inc.

Hanlon, Emily. Petersburg. 1989. 640p. mass mkt. 4.95 o.s.i (*0-8041-0484-0*, Ivy Bks.) Ballantine Bks.

—Petersburg. 1988. 544p. 19.95 o.p. (*0-399-13374-7*, G. P. Putnam's Sons) Penguin Putnam Bks. for Young Readers.

Harrod-Eagles, Cynthia. Fleur. 1992. 22.95 o.p. (*0-312-08782-9*) St. Martin's Pr.

Iossel, Mikhail. Every Hunter Wants to Know: A Leningrad Life. 1991. 288p. 21.95 o.p. (*0-393-02985-9*) Norton, W. W. & Co., Inc.

Kerr, Philip. Dead Meat. 1996. 228p. mass mkt. 7.99 o.s.i (*0-7704-2704-9*) Bantam Bks.

—Dead Meat. 1994. 256p. pap. 13.95 o.p. (*0-385-25466-0*) Doubleday Publishing.

—Dead Meat. 1994. 256p. 18.95 o.s.i (*0-89296-562-2*) Mysterious Pr.

—Dead Meat. 1995. 272p. mass mkt. 5.99 o.s.i (*0-446-40379-2*) Warner Bks., Inc.

Makine, Andrei. Confessions of a Fallen Standard-Bearer. Strachan, Geoffrey, tr. from FRE. 2000. viii, 130p. 21.95 (*1-55970-529-9*) Arcade Publishing, Inc.

—Confessions of a Fallen Standard-Bearer. 2001. 144p. reprint ed. pap. 12.00 (*0-14-200001-9*) Penguin Group (USA) Inc.

Pickens, Andrea. The Storybook Hero. 2002. (Signet Regency Romance Ser.). 224p. mass mkt. 4.99 (*0-451-20731-9*, Signet Bks.) NAL.

Templeton, Natasha. Winter in the Summer Garden. 1999. 320p. pap. (*1-86941-369-5*, Vintage) Knopf Publishing Group.

Walton, C. S. The Voice of Leningrad: The Story of a Siege. 2003. 170p. per. 14.95 (*1-891053-82-5*) Garrett County Pr.

## SAINT SIMONS ISLAND (GA.: ISLAND)—FICTION

Price, Eugenia. The Beloved Invader. 1999. mass mkt. (*0-553-22798-X*); 1999. mass mkt. (*0-553-23898-1*); 1984. mass mkt. 3.95 o.s.i (*0-553-25618-1*); 1977. 288p. mass mkt. 6.99 o.s.i (*0-553-26909-7*) Bantam Bks.

—The Beloved Invader. 1965. 12.95 o.p. (*0-397-10013-2*) HarperCollins Pubs.

—The Beloved Invader. 2000. (St. Simons Trilogy Ser.). viii, 312p. pap. 14.95 (*1-57736-204-7*) Providence Hse. Pubs.

—The Beloved Invader. 1977. 12.09 o.p. (*0-606-00608-7*) Turtleback Bks.

—Lighthouse. 1999. mass mkt. (*0-553-23158-8*); 1985. 352p. mass mkt. 3.95 o.s.i (*0-553-24137-0*); 1972. 352p. mass mkt. 6.99 o.s.i (*0-553-26910-0*) Bantam Bks.

—Lighthouse. 1999. (St. Simons Trilogy Ser.: Vol. 1). 344p. pap. 14.95 (*1-57736-154-7*) Providence Hse. Pubs.

—Lighthouse. 1985. (St. Simons Island Trilogy Ser.). 356p. reprint ed. 14.95 o.p. (*0-934395-08-X*); 39.95 o.p. (*0-934395-09-8*) Rutledge Hill Pr.

—New Moon Rising. 1999. mass mkt. (*0-553-20970-1*); 1999. mass mkt. (*0-553-23478-1*); 1999. mass mkt. (*0-553-24232-6*); 1985. 320p. mass mkt. 6.99 o.s.i (*0-553-26848-1*); 1984. 320p. mass mkt. 3.95 o.s.i (*0-553-25017-5*) Bantam Bks.

—New Moon Rising. 2000. (Illus.). viii, 344p. pap. 14.95 (*1-57736-181-4*) Providence Hse. Pubs.

—New Moon Rising. 1972. (Spire Bk). pap. 1.95 o.p. (*0-8007-8083-3*) Revell, Fleming H. Co.

—New Moon Rising. 1985. (St. Simons Island Trilogy Ser.). 288p. reprint ed. 14.95 o.p. (*0-934395-10-1*); 39.95 o.p. (*0-934395-11-X*) Rutledge Hill Pr.

—New Moon Rising. pap. 12.95 (*0-8027-2607-0*) Walker & Co.

Price, Eugenia & Stone, Lawrence M. The Beloved Invader. 1985. (St. Simons Island Trilogy Ser.). 288p. reprint ed. 14.95 o.p. (*0-934395-12-8*); ring bd. 39.95 o.p. (*0-934395-13-6*) Rutledge Hill Pr.

## SALEM (MASS.)—FICTION

Bloom, Harold, ed. & intro. Arthur Miller's The Crucible. (YA). (gr. 8 up). 1996. pap. 4.95 (*0-7910-3688-X*); 1995. 77p. lib. bdg. 21.95 (*0-7910-3663-4*) Chelsea Hse. Pubs.

Chance, Megan. Susannah Morrow. 2003. 480p. mass mkt. 7.50 (*0-446-61323-1*); 2002. 416p. 24.95 (*0-446-52953-2*) Warner Bks., Inc.

Earhart, Rose. Dorcas Good: The Diary of a Salem Witch. 2000. 374p. pap. 12.95 (*1-893221-02-4*) Pendleton Bks.

Elliott, Edward E. The Devil & the Mathers: An Historical Novel. 1989. 376p. 16.95 (*0-89407-142-4*); pap. 9.95 (*0-89407-095-9*) Strawberry Hill Pr.

Hawthorne, Nathaniel. The House of the Seven Gables. 2002. (World Digital Library). E-Book 3.95 (*0-594-09090-3*) 1873 Pr.

—The House of the Seven Gables. 1964. (Airmont Classics Ser.). mass mkt. 2.95 (*0-8049-0016-7*, CL-16) Airmont Publishing Co., Inc.

—The House of the Seven Gables. Date not set. 318p. 24.95 (*0-8488-2290-0*) Amereon, Ltd.

—The House of the Seven Gables. 1981. 256p. mass mkt. 5.95 (*0-553-21270-2*, Bantam Classics) Bantam Bks.

—The House of the Seven Gables. E-Book 5.00 (*0-7607-1501-7*) Barnes & Noble, Inc.

—The House of the Seven Gables. 1982. reprint ed. 4.95 o.p. (*0-460-01176-6*) Biblio Distribution.

—The House of the Seven Gables. 2002. pap. 4.50 (*1-59109-461-5*) Booksurge, LLC.

—The House of the Seven Gables. 1982. reprint ed. lib. bdg. 25.95 (*0-89966-379-6*) Buccaneer Bks., Inc.

—The House of the Seven Gables. 1986. 3.99 o.s.i (*0-517-62633-0*) Crown Publishing Group.

—The House of the Seven Gables. 1989. mass mkt. 3.25 o.s.i (*0-8125-0460-7*, Tor Classics); 1989. 330p. mass mkt. 3.99 (*0-8125-0459-3*, Tor Classics); 1988. mass mkt. 4.95 (*0-938819-82-8*, Aerie); 1988. mass mkt. 2.25 (*0-938819-66-6*, Aerie) Doherty, Tom Assocs., LLC.

—The House of the Seven Gables. 1999. (Thrift Editions Ser.). 240p. pap. 2.50 (*0-486-40882-5*) Dover Pubns., Inc.

—The House of the Seven Gables. E-Book 2.49 (*1-58627-448-1*); E-Book 2.49 (*1-58744-049-0*) Electric Umbrella Publishing.

—The House of the Seven Gables. l.t. ed. 1994. 419p. pap. 15.95 (*0-8161-5945-9*, Macmillan Reference USA) Gale Group.

—The House of the Seven Gables, 001. 1952. (Riverside Bookshelf Ser.). (Illus.). 7.95 o.p. (*0-395-07072-4*) Houghton Mifflin Co.

—The House of the Seven Gables. l.t. ed. 666p. pap. 46.53 (*0-7583-1091-9*); 380p. pap. 30.48 (*0-7583-1089-7*); 292p. pap. 25.62 (*0-7583-1088-9*); 852p. pap. 65.04 (*0-7583-1092-7*); 1048p. pap. 76.07 (*0-7583-1093-5*); 520p. pap. 37.78 (*0-7583-1090-0*); 1495p. pap. 97.83 (*0-7583-1095-1*); 1289p. pap. 87.18 (*0-7583-1094-3*); 1289p. lib. bdg. 99.18 (*0-7583-1086-2*); 1048p. lib. bdg. 88.07 (*0-7583-1085-4*); 852p. lib. bdg. 77.04 (*0-7583-1084-6*); 666p. lib. bdg. 52.53 (*0-7583-1083-8*); 520p. lib. bdg. 43.78 (*0-7583-1082-X*); 1495p. lib. bdg. 109.83 (*0-7583-1087-0*); 380p. lib. bdg. 36.48 (*0-7583-1081-1*); 292p. lib. bdg. 31.62 (*0-7583-1080-3*) Huge Print Pr.

—The House of the Seven Gables. 2002. 248p. 94.99 (*1-4043-0778-8*); per. 90.99 (*1-4043-0779-6*) IndyPublish.com.

—The House of the Seven Gables. E-Book 2.95 (*1-57799-890-1*) Logos Research Systems, Inc.

—The House of the Seven Gables, Level 1. 2000. (C). pap. 7.93 (*0-582-42657-X*) Longman Publishing Group.

—The House of the Seven Gables. 1977. (American Classics). pap. text 4.62 o.p. (*0-88343-400-8*) McDougal Littell Inc.

—The House of the Seven Gables. 1975. (Merrill Standard Ser.). 6.00 (*0-675-09471-2*); pap. 4.00 (*0-675-09470-4*) Merrill College.

—The House of the Seven Gables. (Signet Classics). 2001. 288p. mass mkt. 5.95 (*0-451-52791-7*, Signet Classics); 1998. pap. 2.95 o.p. (*0-89375-998-8*); 1961. 288p. mass mkt. 5.95 o.s.i (*0-451-52436-5*, Signet Bks.); 1961. mass mkt. 0.60 o.p. (*0-451-50556-5*, Signet Classics); 1961. mass mkt. 2.25 o.p. (*0-451-52171-4*); 1961. mass mkt. 1.95 o.p. (*0-451-51934-5*, Signet Classics); 1961. mass mkt. 1.50 o.p. (*0-451-51262-6*, Signet Classics); 1961. mass mkt. 1.25 o.p. (*0-451-51043-7*, Signet Classics); 1961. mass mkt. 0.95 o.p. (*0-451-50834-3*, Signet Classics); 1961. mass mkt. 0.75 o.p. (*0-451-50621-9*, Signet Classics); 1961. mass mkt. 0.50 o.p. (*0-451-50058-X*, Signet Classics); 1961. 288p. mass mkt. 2.50 o.p. (*0-451-52309-1*, Signet Classics) NAL.

—The House of the Seven Gables. l.t. ed. reprint ed. 1997. 520p. lib. bdg. 26.00 (*0-939495-12-0*); 1998. 318p. lib. bdg. 25.00 (*1-58287-037-3*) North Bks.

—The House of the Seven Gables. annot. ed. 1967. (Critical Editions Ser.). (C). pap. text 10.50 (*0-393-09705-6*, 9705) Norton, W. W. & Co., Inc.

—The House of the Seven Gables. Charvat, William et al, eds. 1965. (Centenary Edition of the Works of Nathaniel Hawthorne: Vol. 2). (Illus.). 420p. text 62.95 (*0-8142-0060-5*) Ohio State Univ. Pr.

—The House of the Seven Gables. Bell, Michael D., ed. (Oxford World's Classics Ser.). 1998. 360p. pap. 8.95 (*0-19-283645-5*); 1992. 356p. pap. 6.95 o.p. (*0-19-282678-6*) Oxford Univ. Pr., Inc.

—The House of the Seven Gables. 2001. E-Book 2.95 (*1-58882-563-9*) PublishingOnline.

—The House of the Seven Gables. 2001. (Paperback Classics Ser.). 336p. pap. 8.95 (*0-375-75687-6*, Modern Library) Random House Adult Trade Publishing Group.

—The House of the Seven Gables. 1988. 21.99 o.p. (*0-517-14110-8*) Random Hse. Value Publishing.

—The House of the Seven Gables. 1985. (Illus.). 304p. 12.95 o.p. (*0-89577-219-1*) Reader's Digest Assn., Inc., The.

—The House of the Seven Gables. 1992. (Notable American Authors Ser.). reprint ed. lib. bdg. 75.00 (*0-7812-3039-X*) Reprint Services Corp.

—The House of the Seven Gables. (Ebook Classic Ser.). E-Book 5.00 (*0-7410-0441-0*) SoftBook Pr.

—The House of the Seven Gables. l.t. ed. 1994. 419p. lib. bdg. 22.95 (*0-8161-5944-0*) Thorndike Pr.

—The House of the Seven Gables. 1981. 12.00 (*0-606-01867-0*); 15.00 (*0-606-00821-7*) Turtleback Bks.

—The House of the Seven Gables. Smith, Allan L., ed. 1995. 304p. pap. 5.95 (*0-460-87464-0*, Everyman's Classic Library in Paperback) Tuttle Publishing.

—The House of the Seven Gables. 1992. reprint ed. (Illus.). 309p. 29.95 o.p. (*1-877767-63-8*); 315p. pap. 14.95 (*1-57002-073-6*) University Publishing Hse., Inc.

—The House of the Seven Gables. Stern, Milton R., ed. & intro. by. 1981. (Penguin American Library). 368p. pap. 8.95 (*0-14-039005-7*, Penguin Classics) Viking Penguin.

—The House of the Seven Gables. 1998. (Classics Library). pap. 3.95 (*1-85326-557-8*, 5578WW) Wordsworth Editions, Ltd. GBR. *Dist:* Casemate Pubs. & Bk. Distributors, LLC.

Hawthorne, Nathaniel & Young, P. The House of the Seven Gables. 1957. (C). pap. text 3.00 o.p. (*0-03-009975-7*) Harcourt College Pubs.

Marcoux, Alex, ed. Back to Salem. (C). 2003. 323p. 27.95 (*1-56023-224-2*); 2001. 324p. pap. 17.95 (*1-56023-225-0*) Haworth Pr., Inc., The. (Alice Street Editions).

McInerney, Merry. Dog People. 287p. 2000. pap. 14.95 (*0-312-87292-5*); 1998. 22.95 (*0-312-85699-7*) Doherty, Tom Assocs., LLC. (Forge Bks.).

## SALT LAKE CITY (UTAH)—FICTION

Andrews, Sarah. Bone Hunter. 2nd ed. 1999. 320p. 24.95 (*0-312-20381-0*, Saint Martin's Minotaur) St. Martin's Pr.

—Bone Hunter: An Em Hansen Mystery. 2000. (Em Hansen Mysteries Ser.). 353p. mass mkt. 6.50 (*0-312-97317-9*, St. Martin's Paperbacks) St. Martin's Pr.

—An Eye for Gold. E-Book 24.95 (*0-312-27607-9*) St. Martin's Pr.

—Fault Line. 2003. 336p. mass mkt. 6.50 (*0-312-98445-6*, St. Martin's Paperbacks); 2002. 304p. 23.95 (*0-312-25350-8*, Saint Martin's Minotaur) St. Martin's Pr.

Black, Angela K. Bitterbrush. 1994. 274p. (Orig.). pap. 9.95 (*0-9642571-0-6*) ABCDE Publishing.

Fulton, John. More Than Enough. 2002. 192p. pap. 13.00 (*0-312-27675-3*) Picador.

Gardner, Willard Boyd. Race Against Time: A Novel. 2001. (Illus.). 198p. 14.95 (*1-57734-805-2*) Covenant Communications.

Hill, Theresa S. Life & Times of Erastus Snow. l.t. ed. 1997. (Life & Times Ser.: Vol. I). (Illus.). 285p. 29.95 o.p. (*1-888106-18-2*) Agreka Bks., LLC.

Irvine, Robert. The Angels' Share. Isaacson, Dana, ed. 1990. 224p. reprint ed. bds. 3.95 (*0-671-69494-4*, Pocket) Simon & Schuster.

—The Angels' Share. 1989. 15.95 o.p. (*0-312-02862-8*, Saint Martin's Minotaur) St. Martin's Pr.

—Baptism for the Dead. 1990. 256p. mass mkt. 3.95 (*0-671-69495-2*, Pocket) Simon & Schuster.

—Called Home. 1991. 17.95 o.p. (*0-312-05829-2*, Saint Martin's Minotaur) St. Martin's Pr.

—Gone to Glory. Isaacson, Dana, ed. 1991. 224p. reprint ed. mass mkt. 3.95 (*0-671-72799-0*, Pocket) Simon & Schuster.

—Gone to Glory. 1990. 16.95 o.p. (*0-312-04321-X*, Saint Martin's Minotaur) St. Martin's Pr.

—The Great Reminder. 1993. 224p. 17.95 o.p. (*0-312-09302-0*, Saint Martin's Minotaur) St. Martin's Pr.

—The Hosanna Shout. 1994. 240p. 19.95 o.p. (*0-312-11418-4*, Saint Martin's Minotaur) St. Martin's Pr.

—Pillar of Fire: A Moroni Traveler Mystery. 1995. 272p. 21.95 o.p. (*0-312-13588-2*, Saint Martin's Minotaur) St. Martin's Pr.
—The Spoken Word. 1992. 224p. 17.95 o.p. (*0-312-07841-2*, Saint Martin's Minotaur) St. Martin's Pr.
Johnson. Belief. Date not set. pap. (*0-312-29112-4*, Saint Martin's Griffin) St. Martin's Pr.
Johnson, Stephanie. Belief. 2002. 496p. 26.95 (*0-312-29110-8*) St. Martin's Pr.

**SAMOAN ISLANDS—FICTION**

Perkins, Leialoha A. The Firemakers & Other Stories about Hawaii, the Samoas, & Tonga. 1987. 107p. (*1-892174-05-7*) Kamalu'uluolele Pubs.
Wendt, Albert. Flying Fox in a Freedom Tree. 1974. 149 p. (*0-582-71733-7*) Longman, Paul (NZ).
—Flying Fox in a Freedom Tree. 1999. 149p. pap. 16.95 (*0-8248-1823-7*) Univ. of Hawaii Pr.
—Flying Fox in a Freedom Tree. 1988. 160p. pap. 4.95 o.p. (*0-14-010221-3*, Penguin Bks.) Viking Penguin.
—Leaves of the Banyan Tree. 1979. 416p. (*0-582-71770-1*) Longman, Paul (NZ).
—Leaves of the Banyan Tree. 1994. (Talanoa Ser.). 424p. pap. 19.00 (*0-8248-1584-X*) Univ. of Hawaii Pr.

**SAN ANTONIO (TEX.)—FICTION**

Brandon, Jay. Afterimage. 2000. 373p. mass mkt. 6.99 (*0-8125-4044-1*, Tor Bks.) Doherty, Tom Assocs., LLC.
—Angel of Death. 1999. 383p. mass mkt. 6.99 (*0-8125-4043-3*); 1998. 384p. 24.95 (*0-312-86541-4*) Doherty, Tom Assocs., LLC. (Forge Bks.).
—Executive Privilege. (Chris Sinclair Ser.). 2003. mass mkt. 6.99 (*0-8125-7545-8*, Tor Bks.); 2001. 464p. 25.95 (*0-312-87425-1*, Forge Bks.) Doherty, Tom Assocs., LLC.
—Fade the Heat. 1991. 368p. mass mkt. 6.99 (*0-671-70261-0*, Pocket) Simon & Schuster.
—Fade the Heat. Gross, Bill, ed. 1990. 352p. 18.95 o.p. (*0-671-70260-2*, Atria) Simon & Schuster.
—Fade the Heat. abr. ed. 1990. audio 14.95 (*0-671-70893-7*, Simon & Schuster Audioworks) Simon & Schuster Audio.
—Loose among the Lambs. Grose, Bill, ed. 1993. 384p. 22.00 (*0-671-76032-7*, Atria); 1994. 400p. reprint ed. mass mkt. 5.99 (*0-671-76033-5*, Pocket); 1994. reprint ed. pap. 6.50 (*0-671-88315-1*, Pocket) Simon & Schuster.
Chase, Elaine Raco. A Dream Come True. 2003. 26.95 (*0-7862-5622-2*, Five Star) Gale Group.
Davenport, Bill. Love Song Blue. 2001. 320p. lib. bdg. 22.95 (*0-9707390-2-8*) Daugherty, Royce Publishing.
Estleman, Loren D. Something Borrowed, Something Black. E-Book 24.95 (*0-312-70606-5*, Tor Bks.); 2003. 224p. mass mkt. 6.99 (*0-8125-4546-X*, Tor Bks.); 2002. 236p. 24.95 (*0-312-87863-X*, CPHC0630, Forge Bks.) Doherty, Tom Assocs., LLC.
Garza, Pamela. Turning of the Shadow. 2002. pap. 6.95 (*0-87714-524-5*); 2001. 136p. pap. 8.95 (*0-87714-256-4*) Denlingers Pubs., Ltd.
Harrigan, Stephen. The Gates of the Alamo. 2000. (Illus.). 592p. 25.00 (*0-679-44717-2*) Knopf, Alfred A. Inc.
—The Gates of the Alamo, Set. abr. ed. 2000. audio compact disk 29.95 (*0-375-41560-2*, RH Audio) Random Hse. Audio Publishing Group.
—The Gates of the Alamo: A Novel. abr. ed. 2000. audio 25.95 o.s.i (*0-375-41559-9*, RH Audio) Random Hse. Audio Publishing Group.
Hart, Carolyn G. Death on the River Walk. l.t. ed. 2000. (Large Print Book Ser.). pap. 23.95 (*1-56895-822-6*, Wheeler Publishing, Inc.) Gale Group.
—Death on the River Walk. 2000. 336p. mass mkt. 6.99 (*0-380-79005-X*); 1999. 256p. 22.00 (*0-380-97415-0*) Morrow/Avon. (Avon Bks.).
Lindsey, David L. Black Gold, Red Death. 1986. 256p. mass mkt. 5.99 o.s.i (*0-449-13121-1*, Fawcett) Ballantine Bks.
Matinez, Manuel Luis. Drift. 2003. 256p. pap. 14.00 o.s.i (*0-312-30995-3*) Picador.
Morris, M. E. Sword of the Shaheen. 1990. 320p. 18.95 o.p. (*0-89141-328-6*, Presidio Pr.) Ballantine Bks.
Riordan, Rick. Big Red Tequilla. 1997. 400p. mass mkt. 6.50 (*0-553-57644-5*) Bantam Bks.
Sanderson, Jim. Safe Delivery. 2000. 224p. 21.95 (*0-8263-2191-7*) Univ. of New Mexico Pr.

**SAN DIEGO (CALIF.)—FICTION**

Benke, Patricia D. False Witness. 1996. mass mkt. 5.99 (*0-380-78184-0*, Avon Bks.) Morrow/Avon.
Boggio, Sue. Sunlight & Shadows. 2004. 320p. pap. 12.95 (*0-451-21110-3*) NAL.
Brandeis, Gayle. The Book of Dead Birds: A Novel. 2003. 256p. 23.95 (*0-06-052803-6*, HarperCollins) HarperTrade.
Brizzolara, John. Wirecutter. 1987. 240p. 16.95 o.s.i (*0-385-23437-6*) Doubleday Publishing.
—Wirecutter. 1989. bds. 3.95 o.s.i (*0-671-65851-4*, Pocket) Simon & Schuster.
Brockmann, Suzanne. Into the Night. 2002. 480p. mass mkt. 6.99 (*0-8041-1972-4*, Ballantine Bks.) Ballantine Bks.
—Into the Night. 2002. 480p. 26.00 (*0-345-45885-0*) Random Hse., Inc.
—Into the Night. 2003. (Core Ser.). 28.95 (*0-7862-5149-2*) Thorndike Pr.
Crosby, Harry W. Portrait of Paloma: A Novel. 2001. (Illus.). 320p. pap. 14.95 (*0-916251-56-X*) Sunbelt Pubns., Inc.
Dunlap, Susan. High Fall. 1995. (Kiernan O'Shaugnessy Mystery Ser.). 320p. mass mkt. 5.99 o.s.i (*0-440-21560-9*) Dell Publishing.
—High Fall. l.t. ed. 1995. (Large Print Bks.). pap. 20.95 (*1-56895-093-4*, Wheeler Publishing, Inc.) Gale Group.
—No Immunity: A Kiernan O'Shaughnessy Mystery. 1999. (Kiernan O'Shaugnessy Mystery Ser.). 352p. mass mkt. 5.99 o.s.i (*0-440-22480-2*) Dell Publishing.
—No Immunity: A Kiernan O'Shaughnessy Mystery. l.t. ed. 1999. pap. 23.95 (*1-56895-782-3*, Wheeler Publishing, Inc.) Gale Group.
—Pious Deception. 1990. 256p. mass mkt. 5.99 o.s.i (*0-440-20746-0*) Dell Publishing.
—Rogue Wave. 1992. 272p. mass mkt. 5.99 o.s.i (*0-440-21197-2*) Dell Publishing.
—Rogue Wave. 1994. 3.99 o.p. (*0-517-13047-5*) Random Hse. Value Publishing.
Jackson, Edwardo. Neva Hafta: A Novel. 368p. 2003. pap. 13.95 (*0-375-75774-0*); 2002. 22.95 (*0-375-50637-3*, Villard Bks.) Random House Adult Trade Publishing Group.
John, Sally D. To Dream Again. 2000. 256p. pap. 10.99 o.p. (*1-58134-186-5*) Crossway Bks.
—To Dream Again. l.t. ed. 2002. 431p. 24.95 (*0-7862-4088-1*) Gale Group.
Landreth, Marsha. The Holiday Murders. l.t. ed. 1999. (Paperback Ser.). 328p. 24.95 (*0-7838-8827-9*) Thorndike Pr.
—The Holiday Murders. 1992. 243p. 19.95 o.s.i (*0-8027-1246-0*) Walker & Co.
Lawrence, Martha C. Ashes of Aries. 2001. 256p. 23.95 (*0-312-20299-7*, Saint Martin's Minotaur) St. Martin's Pr.
—The Cold Heart of Capricorn. 240p. 1996. text 21.95 o.p. (*0-312-14569-1*, Saint Martin's Minotaur); Vol. 1. 1998. mass mkt. 5.99 o.s.i (*0-312-96294-0*, St. Martin's Paperbacks) St. Martin's Pr.
Le Thi Diem Thuy. The Gangster We Are All Looking For: A Novel. 2003. 176p. 18.00 (*0-375-40018-4*) Knopf, Alfred A. Inc.
Lewis, Sara. The Answer Is Yes. 1998. 288p. (C). 23.00 o.s.i (*0-15-100326-2*) Harcourt Trade Pubs.
—The Answer Is Yes. l.t. ed. 1998. (Inspirational Ser.). 407p. 26.95 o.p. (*0-7838-0392-3*) Thorndike Pr.
—The Answer Is Yes: A Novel. 1999. (Harvest Book Ser.). 272p. pap. 13.00 (*0-15-600564-6*, Harvest Bks.) Harcourt Trade Pubs.
Mazza, Cris. Your Name Here. 1995. 280p. (Orig.). pap. 12.95 (*1-56689-031-4*) Coffee Hse. Pr.
Mullen, Jack. Behind the Shield. 1996. 352p. (Orig.). mass mkt. 5.99 (*0-380-78236-7*, Avon Bks.) Morrow/Avon.
—In the Line of Duty. 1995. 320p. (Orig.). mass mkt. 5.50 o.p. (*0-380-77614-6*, Avon Bks.) Morrow/Avon.
Murray, Lynne. At Large. 2002. 288p. mass mkt. 6.50 (*0-312-98004-3*, St. Martin's Paperbacks); 2001. 260p. 23.95 (*0-312-28029-7*, Saint Martin's Minotaur); 2001. 287.40 (*0-312-28026-2*, Saint Martin's Minotaur) St. Martin's Pr.
—Large Target: A Josephine Fuller Mystery. E-Book 6.50 (*0-312-27388-6*); 2001. 304p. mass mkt. 6.50 (*0-312-97537-6*, St. Martin's Paperbacks); 2000. viii, 258p. 23.95 (*0-312-25456-3*, Saint Martin's Minotaur) St. Martin's Pr.
—Larger Than Death: A Josephine Fuller Mystery. 1997. 300p. 23.00 (*0-9642949-0-7*) Orloff Pr.
—Larger Than Death: A Josephine Fuller Mystery. 2000. (Josephine Fuller Mystery Ser.). 304p. mass mkt. 5.99 (*0-312-97277-6*, St. Martin's Paperbacks) St. Martin's Pr.
Padgett, Abigail. Child of Silence. 1993. 208p. 17.95 (*0-89296-488-X*) Mysterious Pr.
—Child of Silence. 1994. 208p. mass mkt. 5.99 o.p. (*0-446-40184-6*, Mysterious Pr. Paperback Bks.) Warner Bks., Inc.
—The Dollmaker's Daughters. (Bo Bradley Mystery Ser.). 1998. 320p. mass mkt. 6.50 (*0-446-40536-1*); 1997. 288p. 22.00 o.p. (*0-89296-614-9*) Warner Bks., Inc.
—The Last Blue Plate Special. 2001. 304p. 23.95 o.p. (*0-89296-731-5*) Mysterious Pr.
—Moonbird Boy. 1996. 82p. 21.95 o.s.i (*0-89296-613-0*) Mysterious Pr.
—Moonbird Boy. 1997. 256p. mass mkt. 5.99 o.p. (*0-446-40513-2*, Mysterious Pr. Paperback Bks.) Warner Bks., Inc.
—Strawgirl. 1994. 256p. 18.95 o.s.i (*0-89296-489-8*) Mysterious Pr.
—Strawgirl. 1995. 240p. mass mkt. 5.50 o.p. (*0-446-40199-4*, Mysterious Pr. Paperback Bks.) Warner Bks., Inc.
—Turtle Baby. 1995. 288p. 19.95 o.s.i (*0-89296-580-0*) Mysterious Pr.
—Turtle Baby. l.t. ed. 1996. (Large Print Ser.). 496p. 29.99 o.p. (*0-7089-3560-5*, Ulverscroft) Thorpe, F. A. Pubs. GBR. *Dist:* Ulverscroft Large Print Bks., Ltd., Ulverscroft Large Print Canada, Ltd.
—Turtle Baby. 1996. 256p. mass mkt. 5.99 o.p. (*0-446-40478-0*, Mysterious Pr. Paperback Bks.) Warner Bks., Inc.
Parker, T. Jefferson. Cold Pursuit. 2003. 384p. 23.95 (*0-7868-6805-8*) Hyperion Pr.
—Cold Pursuit. 2004. mass mkt. (*0-06-059327-X*, Avon Bks.) Morrow/Avon.
—Cold Pursuit. 2003. (Thorndike Press Large Print Basic Ser.). 544p. (*0-7540-1970-5*); 544p. (*0-7540-9325-5*); 559p. 31.95 (*0-7862-5464-5*) Thorndike Pr.
Steinberg, Janice. The Dead Man & the Sea. 1997. 256p. mass mkt. 5.99 o.s.i (*0-425-16037-8*, Prime Crime) Berkley Publishing Group.
—Death Crosses the Border. 1995. 240p. mass mkt. 4.99 o.s.i (*0-425-15052-6*) Berkley Publishing Group.
—Death-Fires Dance. 1996. 272p. (Orig.). mass mkt. 5.99 o.s.i (*0-425-15551-X*, Prime Crime) Berkley Publishing Group.
—Death of a Postmodernist. 1995. 256p. (Orig.). mass mkt. 5.99 o.s.i (*0-425-14546-8*, Prime Crime) Berkley Publishing Group.
Tarrant, Newell. Shadow War. 2002. 356p. 29.95 (*1-932047-81-6*); pap. 19.95 (*1-932047-80-8*) Media Creations, Inc. (Llumina Pr.).
Trapp, E. Philip. The Red-Ribboned Letters. 2003. (*0-9713470-3-4*) Phoenix International, Inc.
Trolley, Jack. Juarez Justice. 1996. 272p. 22.00 o.p. (*0-7867-0356-3*, Carroll & Graf Pubs.) Avalon Publishing Group.
— La Jolla Spindrift. 1998. 208p. 22.00 o.p. (*0-7867-0513-2*, Carroll & Graf Pubs.) Avalon Publishing Group.
—Manila Time: A Novel. 1995. 304p. 21.00 o.p. (*0-7867-0255-9*, Carroll & Graf Pubs.) Avalon Publishing Group.
Van der Veer, Judy. November Grass. 2001. (California Legacy Ser.). 208p. pap. 13.95 (*1-890771-39-2*) Heyday Bks.
Wallace, Patricia. August Nights. (Five Star First Edition Mystery Ser.). 2002. 274p. 25.95 (*0-7862-4180-2*, Five Star); 2003. 259p. pap. 13.95 (*1-4104-0125-1*, Five Star Trade) Gale Group.
Wambaugh, Joseph. Floaters. 1997. 304p. mass mkt. 6.99 (*0-553-57595-3*) Bantam Bks.
—Floaters. l.t. ed. 1996. 375p. 26.95 o.p. (*1-56895-365-8*, Wheeler Publishing, Inc.) Gale Group.
—Lines & Shadows. 1984. 384p. mass mkt. 4.50 o.s.i (*0-553-24607-0*); 416p. mass mkt. 6.99 (*0-553-27148-2*) Bantam Bks.
—Lines & Shadows. unabr. ed. 1985. lib. bdg. 73.25 o.p. incl. audio (*1-56100-002-7*, 926, Unabridged Library Editions); audio 19.95 o.p. (*0-930435-03-6*, 350, Bookcassette) Brilliance Audio.
—Lines & Shadows. 1984. 383p. 15.95 o.p. (*0-688-02619-2*, Morrow, William & Co.) Morrow/Avon.
Wellington, Janet. Forever Rose. 2000. (Time Passages Romance Ser.). 272p. mass mkt. 5.99 o.s.i (*0-515-12782-5*, Jove) Berkley Publishing Group.

**SAN FRANCISCO (CALIF.)—FICTION**

Abramo, J. L. Catching Water in a Net. l.t. ed. 2002. 367p. 28.95 (*0-7862-3996-4*) Gale Group.
—Catching Water in a Net: A Mystery. 2001. 224p. 22.95 (*0-312-28232-X*, Saint Martin's Minotaur) St. Martin's Pr.
—Clutching at Straws. mass mkt. (*0-312-98655-6*, St. Martin's Paperbacks); 2003. 240p. 22.95 (*0-312-30849-3*, Saint Martin's Minotaur) St. Martin's Pr.
—Clutching at Straws. l.t. ed. 2003. 400p. 28.95 (*0-7862-5824-1*) Thorndike Pr.
Adams, Alice. Caroline's Daughters. l.t. ed. 1991. 432p. lib. bdg. 23.95 o.p. (*0-8161-5302-7*, Macmillan Reference USA) Gale Group.
Adams, Clint. Just Say Mikey. 2002. 204p. pap. 14.95 (*1-59113-097-2*) Booklocker.com, Inc.
Alef, Daniel. Pale Truth. 2000. (California Chronicles: Vol. 1). (Illus.). 588p. 27.00 (*0-9700174-1-3*) Maxit Publishing, Inc.
—Pale Truth: The California Chronicles. 2001. 588p. E-Book 8.95 (*0-9700174-7-2*);Vol. 1. E-Book 12.00 (*0-9700174-8-0*) Maxit Publishing, Inc.
Allende, Isabel. Daughter of Fortune. 1999. audio 44.95 (*0-7366-4811-9*, 5127) Books on Tape, Inc.
—Daughter of Fortune. 2001. 464p. mass mkt. 7.99 (*0-380-82101-X*) HarperCollins Pubs.
—Daughter of Fortune. Peden, Margaret Sayers, tr. from SPA. 1999. (Oprah's Book Club Ser.). (Illus.). 416p. 26.00 (*0-06-019491-X*) HarperCollins Pubs.
—Daughter of Fortune. Peden, Margaret Sayers, tr. from SPA. 2000. 416p. pap. 14.00 (*0-06-093275-9*, Perennial) HarperTrade.
—Daughter of Fortune. 2000. 20.05 (*0-606-20501-2*) Turtleback Bks.
Andersen, Susan. Baby, Don't Go. 2000. 384p. mass mkt. 6.50 (*0-380-80712-2*, Avon Bks.) Morrow/Avon.
Andrews, Brian. Knife under Fire. 1993. (*1-881529-01-0*) Custom & Limited Editions.
Armstrong, Campbell. A Concert of Ghosts: A Novel. 1993. 256p. 20.00 o.p. (*0-06-017946-5*) HarperTrade.
Atherton, Gertrude Franklin Horn. The Californians. 2000. 252p. E-Book 3.95 (*0-594-03823-5*) 1873 Pr.
Atkins, Peter. Morningstar. 1992. 304p. mass mkt. 4.50 o.p. (*0-06-100512-6*, HarperTorch) Morrow/Avon.
Babula, William. According to St. John. 2000. (Jeremiah St. John Detective Ser.: Vol. 2). 240p. pap. 12.95 (*1-58345-501-9*) Domhan Bks.
—St. John & the Seven Veils. 2000. (Jeremiah St. John Detective Ser.: Vol. 3). 208p. pap. 12.95 (*1-58345-506-X*) Domhan Bks.
—St. John's Baptism. 2000. (Jeremiah St. John Detective Ser.: Vol. 1). 260p. pap. 12.95 (*1-58345-496-9*) Domhan Bks.
—St. John's Bestiary. 2000. (Jeremiah St. John Detective Ser.: Vol. 4). 264p. pap. 12.95 (*1-58345-511-6*) Domhan Bks.
—St. John's Bestiary. 1994. 264p. 19.95 o.p. (*1-885173-01-6*) Write Way Publishing.
Barker, Clive. Sacrament. 1996. 79p. 25.00 o.p. (*0-06-017949-X*) HarperCollins Pubs.
—Sacrament. 1997. 624p. mass mkt. 7.99 (*0-06-109199-5*, HarperTorch) Morrow/Avon.
Barone, Michael. Bruce Lee: Ghost of the Dragon. 2001. 320p. pap. 14.00 (*0-7434-1323-7*) ibooks, Inc.
Beale, Elaine. Murder in the Castro. 1997. 192p. pap. 10.95 (*0-934678-87-1*) New Victoria Pubs., Inc.
Beck, K. K. Murder in a Mummy Case. l.t. ed. 1989. 8.95 o.p. (*0-7451-9460-5*, 352) BBC Audiobooks America.
—Murder in a Mummy Case. 1987. 176p. mass mkt. 3.95 o.s.i (*0-8041-0117-5*, Ivy Bks.) Ballantine Bks.
—Murder in a Mummy Case. 1986. 176p. 15.95 o.s.i (*0-8027-5655-7*) Walker & Co.
Berlinski, David. The Body Shop: An Aaron Asherfeld Mystery. 1996. 208p. text 20.95 o.p. (*0-312-13935-7*, Saint Martin's Minotaur) St. Martin's Pr.
—A Clean Sweep. 1992. 240p. 17.95 o.p. (*0-312-08744-6*, Saint Martin's Minotaur) St. Martin's Pr.
—Less than Meets the Eye: An Aaron Asherfield Mystery. 1994. (Aaron Asherfeld Mystery Ser.). 208p. 18.95 o.p. (*0-312-11298-X*, Saint Martin's Minotaur) St. Martin's Pr.
—Less Than Meets the Eye: An Aaron Asherfield Mystery. 1994. 240p. 19.95 (*0-312-10611-4*, Saint Martin's Minotaur) St. Martin's Pr.
Berriault, Gina. The Lights of Earth. 2nd ed. 1997. 156p. pap. text 12.50 (*1-887178-53-8*, Counterpoint Pr.) Basic Bks.
—The Lights of Earth: A Novel. 1982. 176p. (Orig.). 12.50 o.p. (*0-86547-141-X*, North Point Pr.) Farrar, Straus & Giroux.
Boray, Paul. Cash Out. 2002. 320p. mass mkt. 6.99 o.s.i (*0-451-41016-5*, Onyx) NAL.
Bowman, Robert J. The Screaming Buddha. 1994. 256p. 20.95 o.p. (*0-312-11056-1*, Saint Martin's Minotaur) St. Martin's Pr.
Boyer, G. G. Morgette on the Barbay Coast. 2001. 288p. reprint ed. mass mkt. 4.50 (*0-8439-4925-2*, Leisure Bks.) Dorchester Publishing Co., Inc.
Bradley, Marion Zimmer. The Inheritor. (Orig.). 1997. 25.95 o.p. (*0-312-85996-1*); 1997. 352p. pap. 15.95 (*0-312-86293-8*); 1984. 448p. mass mkt. 3.50 (*0-8125-1600-1*) Doherty, Tom Assocs., LLC. (Tor Bks.).
—The Inheritor. 1992. 416p. (Orig.). reprint ed. pap. 22.00 o.p. (*0-7278-4298-6*) Severn Hse. Pubs., Ltd.
Brown, Sandra. Breakfast in Bed. 1991. 192p. mass mkt. 2.75 o.s.i (*0-553-21623-6*); 1996. 240p. mass mkt. 7.50 (*0-553-57158-3*) Bantam Bks.
—Breakfast in Bed. l.t. ed. 1996. (Large Print Bks.). 25.95 o.p. (*1-56895-307-0*, Wheeler Publishing, Inc.) Gale Group.
—Breakfast in Bed. abr. ed. 1995. audio 16.99 o.s.i (*0-553-47432-4*, RH Audio) Random Hse. Audio Publishing Group.
—Breakfast in Bed. unabr. ed. 1997. audio 35.00 (*0-7887-0845-7*, 94991E7) Recorded Bks., LLC.
—A Treasure Worth Seeking. 288p. reprint ed. 1997. mass mkt. 3.99 (*0-446-60567-0*); 1992. mass mkt. 6.99 (*0-446-36073-2*) Warner Bks., Inc.
Bruno, Anthony. Hot Fudge. (Loretta Kovac Mystery Ser.). 288p. 2000. (Illus.). (J). 23.95 (*0-312-86651-8*); 2001. reprint ed. pap. 14.95 (*0-312-87590-8*) Doherty, Tom Assocs., LLC. (Forge Bks.).
Bryan, Kate. Murder at Bent Elbow. 1998. (Maggie Maguire Mysteries Ser.: Vol. 1). 224p. mass mkt. 5.99 o.s.i (*0-425-16194-3*, Prime Crime) Berkley Publishing Group.

—A Record of Death. 1998. (Maggie Maguire Mysteries Ser.: Vol. 2). 224p. mass mkt. 5.99 o.s.i (*0-425-16537-X*) Berkley Publishing Group.

Bryant, Dorothy. Miss Giardino. 1978. 160p. pap. 11.95 (*0-931688-01-9*); 1997. 192p. reprint ed. pap. 11.95 (*1-55861-174-6*); 1997. 192p. reprint ed. lib. bdg. 32.00 (*1-55861-180-0*) Feminist Pr. at The City Univ. of New York.

Buffa, D. W. The Legacy. l.t. ed. 2002. (Americana Ser.). 656p. 29.95 (*0-7862-4655-3*) Thorndike Pr.

—The Legacy. 2003. 496p. mass mkt. 7.99 (*0-446-61368-1*); 2002. 448p. 25.95 (*0-446-52738-6*) Warner Bks., Inc.

—The Star Witness: A Joseph Antonelli Novel. abr. ed. 2004. (Joseph Antonelli Ser.). audio 12.99 (*1-59086-795-5*, 4392, Brilliance Audio Paperback Audiobooks); 2003. (Joseph Antonelli Ser.). audio 24.95 (*1-59086-794-7*, 4391); 2003. (The Joseph Antonelli Series: Vol. 5). audio 34.95 (*1-59086-792-0*, 4389, Brilliance Audio Unabridged); 2003. (The Joseph Antonelli Series: Vol. 5). audio 97.25 (*1-59086-793-9*, 4390, Unabridged Library Editions) Brilliance Audio.

—The Star Witness: A Joseph Antonelli Novel. 2004. 432p. mass mkt. 6.99 (*0-451-41133-1*, Onyx) NAL.

—The Star Witness: A Joseph Antonelli Novel. 2003. 400p. 24.95 (*0-399-15034-X*, Putnam & Grosset) Putnam Publishing Group, The.

—The Star Witness: A Joseph Antonelli Novel. unabr. ed. 2003. (Joseph Antonelli Ser.). audio 19.99 (*1-59335-170-4*, 30266) Soulmate Audio Bks., Inc.

Burrows, Geraldine. Chinatown Mission. 2002. (Five Star First Edition Women's Fiction Ser.). 381p. 25.95 (*0-7862-3613-2*, Five Star) Gale Group.

Byrne, Robert. Thrill. 1995. 224p. 19.95 o.p. (*0-7867-0199-4*, Carroll & Graf Pubs.) Avalon Publishing Group.

Byrnes, W. P. The Marvelous Crucifixion on Twin Peaks. 2000. 232p. pap. 21.99 (*0-7388-1207-2*); text 31.99 (*0-7388-1206-4*) Xlibris Corp.

Cadnum, Michael. Ghostwright. 1993. 320p. mass mkt. 5.95 (*0-7867-0048-3*); 1992. 288p. 19.95 o.p. (*0-88184-801-8*) Avalon Publishing Group. (Carroll & Graf Pubs.).

—The Horses of the Night. 1993. 320p. 19.95 o.p. (*0-88184-930-8*, Carroll & Graf Pubs.) Avalon Publishing Group.

Cameron, Sue. Love, Sex & Murder. 1996. 368p. 23.95 o.s.i (*0-446-51852-2*) Warner Bks., Inc.

Chambers, Rick. Anything but Free. 1993. (Open Door Bks.). pap. 4.75 (*1-56212-033-6*, 350700, Faith Alive Christian Resources) CRC Pubns.

Champlin, Tim. Deadly Season. 2003. 256p. mass mkt. 4.99 (*0-8439-5131-1*) Dorchester Publishing Co., Inc.

—Deadly Season. 1997. (Western Ser.). 256p. lib. bdg. 18.95 o.p. (*0-7862-0783-3*, Five Star) Gale Group.

—Deadly Season. l.t. ed. 1998. (Western Ser.). 360p. 21.95 (*0-7862-0777-9*) Thorndike Pr.

—King of the Highbinders. 1989. 192p. mass mkt. 2.95 o.s.i (*0-345-36320-5*) Ballantine Bks.

—King of the Highbinders. l.t. ed. 1997. (Western Ser.). 284p. 20.95 (*0-7862-0898-8*) Thorndike Pr.

Charbonneau, Eileen. Waltzing in Ragtime. 1997. 399p. mass mkt. 6.99 (*0-8125-4468-4*); 1996. 480p. 26.95 o.p. (*0-312-86180-X*) Doherty, Tom Assocs., LLC. (Forge Bks.).

Chittenden, Margaret. Dead Beat & Deadly, 1. (Charlie Plato Mysteries Ser.). 1999. 320p. mass mkt. 5.99 o.s.i (*1-57566-436-4*); 1998. 304p. 20.00 o.s.i (*1-57566-314-7*, Kensington Bks.) Kensington Publishing Corp.

—Dead Men Don't Dance. 1998. (Charlie Plato Mysteries Ser.: Vol. 2). 304p. mass mkt. 5.99 o.s.i (*1-57566-318-X*); 1997. 320p. pap. 18.95 o.p. (*1-57566-184-5*, Kensington Bks.) Kensington Publishing Corp.

—Don't Forget to Die. 2000. 320p. mass mkt. 5.99 o.s.i (*1-57566-566-2*); 1999. 293p. 20.00 o.s.i (*1-57566-435-6*) Kensington Publishing Corp.

—Dying to See You: A Charlie Plato Mystery. 2000. (Charlie Plato Mysteries Ser.). 311p. 20.00 o.s.i (*1-57566-561-1*) Kensington Publishing Corp.

—Dying to Sing. 288p. 1997. (Charlie Plato Mysteries Ser.: Vol. 1). mass mkt. 5.50 o.s.i (*1-57566-189-6*); 1996. 18.95 o.s.i (*1-57566-052-0*) Kensington Publishing Corp.

Clarke, Marion. The Jade Pagoda. 1992. 272p. mass mkt. 4.99 o.s.i (*0-440-21182-4*) Dell Publishing.

Coffman, Virginia. The Lombard Cavalcade. l.t. ed. 2001. 597p. 28.95 (*0-7838-9400-7*, Macmillan Reference USA) Gale Group.

—The Lombard Cavalcade. 1982. 464p. 15.50 o.p. (*0-87795-355-4*, Morrow, William & Co.) Morrow/Avon.

—Pacific Cavalcade. 1982. 560p. mass mkt. 3.50 o.s.i (*0-449-20002-7*, Fawcett) Ballantine Bks.

—Pacific Cavalcade. l.t. ed. 2001. 728p. (*0-7540-1584-X*, Macmillan Reference USA) Gale Group.

—Pacific Cavalcade. 1981. 12.95 o.p. (*0-87795-277-9*, Morrow, William & Co.) Morrow/Avon.

—Pacific Cavalcade. l.t. ed. 2001. (G. K. Hall Core Ser.). 728p. 29.95 (*0-7838-9397-3*) Thorndike Pr.

Coggins, Mark. The Immortal Game. 1999. (Illus.). 310p. 25.00 (*0-918395-17-8*) Poltroon Pr.

Conway, Martha. 12 Bliss Street: A Novel. 2003. 224p. 23.95 (*0-312-31543-0*, Saint Martin's Minotaur) St. Martin's Pr.

Cossairt II, Joseph A. Third Mate on a Tramp. Diaz, Arthur S., ed. 2001. IX,487p. 26.00 (*0-9705259-3-1*); pap. 7.99 (*0-9705259-0-7*) St. Aztec Publishing.

Cote, Lyn. Lost in His Love. 2000. (Blessed Assurance Ser.: No. 2). 256p. pap. 12.99 (*0-8054-1968-3*) Broadman & Holman Pubs.

Coulter, Catherine. Beyond Eden. 1992. 368p. 20.00 o.p. (*0-525-93397-2*, Dutton) Dutton/Plume.

—Beyond Eden. l.t. ed. 1998. 25.95 o.p. (*1-56895-658-4*, Wheeler Publishing, Inc.) Gale Group.

—Beyond Eden. 448p. 1993. mass mkt. 7.50 o.s.i (*0-451-40339-8*, Onyx); 2000. reprint ed. mass mkt. 7.99 (*0-451-20231-7*, Signet Bks.) NAL.

—Eleventh Hour: An FBI Thriller. 2003. 368p. mass mkt. 7.99 (*0-515-13573-9*, Jove) Berkley Publishing Group.

—Jade Star. l.t. ed. 2000. (Large Print Bks.). 441p. 27.95 o.p. (*1-56895-954-0*, Wheeler Publishing, Inc.) Gale Group.

—Jade Star. 1987. mass mkt. 4.50 o.p. (*0-451-40086-0*); 416p. mass mkt. 7.99 o.s.i (*0-451-40448-3*, Onyx); 416p. mass mkt. 4.99 o.p. (*0-451-40157-3*, Onyx); mass mkt. 3.95 o.p. (*0-451-40034-8*) NAL.

—Jade Star. 1999. 416p. 26.00 (*0-7278-2291-8*) Severn Hse. Pubs., Ltd.

—Midnight Star. l.t. ed. 2000. (Wheeler Large Print Book Ser.). 465p. 26.95 o.p. (*1-56895-862-5*, Wheeler Publishing, Inc.) Gale Group.

—Midnight Star. 1986. 464p. mass mkt. 5.99 o.p. (*0-451-16254-4*, Onyx); 464p. mass mkt. 7.99 (*0-451-40446-7*, Onyx); mass mkt. 3.95 o.p. (*0-451-14297-7*, Signet Bks.); mass mkt. 4.50 o.p. (*0-451-15379-0*, Signet Bks.) NAL.

—Midnight Star. 2001. 464p. 26.00 (*0-7278-5625-1*) Severn Hse. Pubs., Ltd.

Craft, Melanie. Trust Me. 2003. 384p. mass mkt. 5.99 (*0-446-61285-5*, Warner Romance) Warner Bks., Inc.

Craft, Michael. Body Language. 2000. (Mark Manning Mystery Ser.). 288p. pap. 13.00 (*1-57566-554-9*, Kensington Bks.) Kensington Publishing Corp.

Cramer, Cahroul. Twisted. 1998. 196p. pap. 9.95 (*1-881164-82-9*) Intercontinental Publishing, Inc.

Dalessandro, James. Bohemian Heart. 1993. 256p. 19.95 o.p. (*0-312-09756-5*, Saint Martin's Minotaur) St. Martin's Pr.

Daniel, David. White Rabbit: A Mystery. 2003. 368p. 25.95 (*0-312-30429-3*, Saint Martin's Minotaur) St. Martin's Pr.

Davis, Kenn. Acts of Homicide. 1989. 224p. mass mkt. 3.50 o.s.i (*0-449-13351-6*, Fawcett) Ballantine Bks.

—As October Dies. 1987. 240p. mass mkt. 2.95 o.s.i (*0-449-13097-5*, Fawcett) Ballantine Bks.

—Blood of Poets. 1990. 208p. (Orig.). mass mkt. 3.95 o.s.i (*0-449-13352-4*, Fawcett) Ballantine Bks.

—Melting Point. 1986. 256p. (Orig.). mass mkt. 2.95 o.s.i (*0-449-12901-2*, Fawcett) Ballantine Bks.

—Nijinsky Is Dead. 1987. 240p. mass mkt. 2.95 o.s.i (*0-449-13096-7*, Fawcett) Ballantine Bks.

—Words Can Kill. 1984. (Orig.). mass mkt. 2.50 o.s.i (*0-449-12667-6*, Fawcett) Ballantine Bks.

Dawson, Janet. A Credible Threat. 1996. 256p. 21.00 o.p. (*0-449-90977-8*, Fawcett) Ballantine Bks.

Day, Dianne. The Bohemian Murders. 1998. (Fremont Jones Mystery Ser.). 288p. reprint ed. mass mkt. 6.50 (*0-553-57412-4*, Crimeline) Bantam Bks.

—The Bohemian Murders: A Fremont Jones Mystery. l.t. ed. 1999. 25.95 (*1-57490-217-2*) Beeler, Thomas T. Publisher.

—The Bohemian Murders: A Fremont Jones Mystery. 1997. 256p. 21.95 o.s.i (*0-385-47923-9*) Doubleday Publishing.

—Emperor Norton's Ghost. 1999. (Fremont Jones Mystery Ser.). 336p. mass mkt. 6.50 (*0-553-58078-7*) Bantam Bks.

—Emperor Norton's Ghost, , unabr. ed. 1999. (Fremont Jones Mystery Ser.). audio 56.00 (*0-7366-4505-5*, 4920) Books on Tape, Inc.

—Fire & Fog. 1997. 288p. mass mkt. 6.50 (*0-553-56922-8*, Crimeline) Bantam Bks.

—Fire & Fog. 2000. audio 48.00 (*0-7366-4839-9*); (Fremont Jones Mystery Ser.: 2). audio 36.00 Books on Tape, Inc.

—Fire & Fog. 1996. 320p. 21.00 o.s.i (*0-385-47550-0*) Doubleday Publishing.

—The Strange Files of Fremont Jones. 1996. (Fremont Jones Mystery Ser.: Vol. 1). 272p. mass mkt. 5.99 (*0-553-56921-X*, Crimeline) Bantam Bks.

—The Strange Files of Fremont Jones. 1999. audio 48.00 (*0-7366-4788-0*); Set. 2000. audio 48.00 Books on Tape, Inc.

—The Strange Files of Fremont Jones. 1995. 240p. 19.95 o.s.i (*0-385-47549-7*) Doubleday Publishing.

—The Strange Files of Fremont Jones. l.t. ed. 1996. (Niagara Large Print Ser.). 336p. 29.50 o.p. (*0-7089-5824-9*, Ulverscroft) Thorpe, F. A. Pubs. GBR. *Dist:* Ulverscroft Large Print Bks., Ltd.

De Haven, Tom. Dugan under Ground. 2001. (Illus.). 296p. 25.00 o.s.i (*0-8050-5741-2*, Metropolitan Bks.) Holt, Henry & Co.

—Dugan under Ground: A Novel. 2002. 304p. pap. 14.00 (*0-312-42101-X*) Picador.

Dedman, Stephen. Foreign Bodies. 286p. 2000. pap. 14.95 (*0-312-87259-3*); 1999. 23.95 (*0-312-86864-2*) Doherty, Tom Assocs., LLC. (Tor Bks.).

Dickey, Eric Jerome. Between Lovers. 2002. 400p. mass mkt. 7.50 (*0-451-20467-0*, Signet Bks.) NAL.

—Between Lovers: A Novel. 2001. 320p. 23.95 o.p. (*0-525-94603-9*, Dutton) Dutton/Plume.

Dickey, Jerome Eric. Between Lovers. 2003. 384p. reprint ed. pap. 13.95 (*0-451-20468-9*) NAL.

Dold, Gaylord. The Devil to Pay. 1999. 384p. 24.95 o.p. (*0-312-19257-6*) St. Martin's Pr.

—Schedule 2, Vol. 1. 1996. 256p. text 21.95 o.p. (*0-312-14730-9*, Saint Martin's Minotaur) St. Martin's Pr.

Donnelly, Nisa. The Love Songs of Phoenix Bay. (Stonewall Inn Editions Ser.). 1995. 320p. pap. 12.95 o.p. (*0-312-13561-0*, Saint Martin's Griffin); 1994. 304p. 13.99 o.p. (*0-312-11391-9*) St. Martin's Pr.

Douglas, John E. Man Down: A Broken Wings Thriller. 2002. 336p. 24.00 (*0-671-02392-6*, Atria) Simon & Schuster.

Douglas, John E. & Olshaker, Mark. Broken Wings. l.t. ed. 2000. (G. K. Hall Core Ser.). 570p. 29.95 (*0-7838-9027-3*, Macmillan Reference USA) Gale Group.

—Broken Wings. 1999. 336p. 24.00 o.s.i (*0-671-02391-8*, Atria); 2001. 384p. reprint ed. pap. 7.99 (*0-671-00395-X*, Pocket) Simon & Schuster.

Drury, Joan M. The Other Side of Silence. 1993. 256p. pap. 9.95 (*0-933216-92-0*) Spinsters Ink Bks.

Duchin, Peter. Blue Moon. 2003. 320p. mass mkt. 6.99 (*0-425-19306-3*) Berkley Publishing Group.

Duchin, Peter & Wilson, John Morgan. Blue Moon: A Philip Damon Mystery. 2002. 320p. 22.95 (*0-425-18645-8*, Prime Crime) Berkley Publishing Group.

Due, Linnea. Life Savings. 1992. 250p. (Orig.). pap. 10.95 o.p. (*0-933216-89-0*) Spinsters Ink Bks.

Duffy, Stella. Wavewalker. 1996. (Mask Noir Ser.). 272p. pap. o.p. (*1-85242-508-3*) Serpent's Tail Ltd.

—Wavewalker. 2001. 272p. pap. 6.99 (*1-85242-713-2*) Serpent's Tail Ltd. GBR. *Dist:* Consortium Bk. Sales & Distribution.

Edwards, Jane. Believe No Evil. l.t. ed. 2000. (Candlelight Romance Ser.). 247p. 22.95 o.p. (*0-7862-2843-1*) Thorndike Pr.

—A Whisper of Suspicion. 2002. (Five Star First Edition Romance Ser.). 249p. 26.95 (*0-7862-3747-3*, Five Star) Gale Group.

Ellroy, James. Killer on the Road. 1999. 272p. pap. 13.00 (*0-380-80896-X*, Perennial) HarperTrade.

—Killer on the Road. 1986. 288p. mass mkt. 5.99 (*0-380-89934-5*, Avon Bks.) Morrow/Avon.

Emerson, Scott, ed. The Case of the Cat with the Missing Ear: From the Notebooks of Dr. Edward R. Smithfield, D.V.M. 2003. (Adventures of Samuel Blackthorne Ser.). (Illus.). 240p. (J). 15.95 (*0-689-85861-2*, Simon & Schuster Children's Publishing) Simon & Schuster Children's Publishing.

Farrington, Tim. The California Book of the Dead. 1998. (Illus.). 352p. pap. 21.95 (*0-671-51959-X*, Pocket) Simon & Schuster.

—The California Book of the Dead: A Novel. 1997. 352p. 23.00 o.p. (*0-671-51960-3*, Atria) Simon & Schuster.

—The Monk Downstairs: A Novel. 2002. 288p. 22.95 (*0-06-251785-6*) HarperSanFrancisco.

—The Monk Downstairs: A Novel. l.t. ed. 2003. (Americana Ser.). 384p. 28.95 (*0-7862-4926-9*) Thorndike Pr.

Fast, Howard. The Establishment, 001. 1979. 11.95 o.p. (*0-395-28160-1*) Houghton Mifflin Co.

—The Immigrants, 001. 1977. 12.95 o.p. (*0-395-25699-2*) Houghton Mifflin Co.

—An Independent Woman. 1997. 340p. 25.00 (*0-15-100271-1*) Harcourt Trade Pubs.

—The Second Generation, 001. 1978. 10.95 o.p. (*0-395-26683-1*) Houghton Mifflin Co.

Finch, Phillip. F2F. 1997. 320p. mass mkt. 6.50 o.s.i (*0-553-57216-4*) Bantam Bks.

—F2F: The Ultimate Thriller of High Tech Terror. abr. ed. 1996. audio 17.00 (*0-671-52282-5*, 393930, Simon & Schuster Audioworks) Simon & Schuster Audio.

Fischer-Dixon, Eva. The Third Cloud: A Novel. 1900. 552p. pap. 26.99 (*0-7388-0751-6*); text 36.99 (*0-7388-0750-8*) Xlibris Corp.

Fisher, David E. Hostage One. 1990. mass mkt. 4.95 o.p. (*0-312-92144-6*, St. Martin's Paperbacks) St. Martin's Pr.

Fitch, Marian. The Seventh Heart. 1997. 320p. mass mkt. 5.99 o.s.i (*0-441-00451-2*) Ace Bks.

Fletcher, Jessica & Bain, Donald. Murder, She Wrote: Martinis & Mayhem. 1995. (Murder She Wrote Ser.: Vol. 4). 304p. mass mkt. 6.50 (*0-451-18512-9*, Signet Bks.) NAL.

Forman, Bruce. Trust Me: A Novel. 2003. 285p. pap. (*1-882897-75-7*) Lost Coast Pr.

Fowler, Karen Joy. Sister Noon. 2002. 336p. pap. 14.00 (*0-452-28328-0*, Plume) Dutton/Plume.

—Sister Noon. 2001. 288p. 24.95 o.p. (*0-399-14750-0*, Wood, Marian Bks.) Penguin Group (USA) Inc.

—Sister Noon. l.t. ed. 2001. (Women's Fiction Ser.). 423p. 28.95 (*0-7862-3549-7*) Thorndike Pr.

Freethy, Barbara. Some Kind of Wonderful. 2001. (Avon Romance Ser.). 384p. mass mkt. 6.50 (*0-380-81553-2*, Avon Bks.) Morrow/Avon.

—The Sweetest Thing. 2002. 376p. reprint ed. pap. 6.00 (*0-7881-9389-9*) DIANE Publishing Co.

—The Sweetest Thing. 1999. 384p. mass mkt. 6.50 (*0-380-79481-0*, Avon Bks.) Morrow/Avon.

Frey, James. Came a Dead Cat. 1991. 256p. 18.95 o.p. (*0-312-06314-8*, Saint Martin's Minotaur) St. Martin's Pr.

Frost, Frank J. Bay to Breakers: A Novel. 2002. 220p. pap. 14.95 (*1-56474-395-0*) Fithian Pr.

Gaffney, Patricia. Crooked Hearts. l.t. ed. 2002. (Wheeler Large Print Book Ser.). 28.95 (*1-58724-198-6*, Wheeler Publishing, Inc.) Gale Group.

—Crooked Hearts. 384p. 2001. mass mkt. 6.99 o.s.i (*0-451-20479-4*); 1994. mass mkt. 4.99 o.p. (*0-451-40459-9*, Topaz) NAL.

Garlic. 2000. 109p. pap. 12.95 (*1-891021-08-7*) Radical Romantic Pr., The.

Gibson, William. All Tomorrow's Parties. 2000. 288p. pap. 13.95 (*0-441-00755-4*) Ace Bks.

—All Tomorrow's Parties. 1999. 304p. 24.95 o.p. (*0-399-14579-6*, G. P. Putnam's Sons) Penguin Group (USA) Inc.

Gold, Herbert. Daughter Mine. E-Book 23.95 (*0-312-27576-5*) St. Martin's Pr.

—Dreaming. 1988. 288p. 17.95 o.s.i (*1-55611-071-5*) Fine, Donald I. Bks.

—She Took My Arm As If She Loved Me. 1997. 256p. 21.95 (*0-312-15653-7*) St. Martin's Pr.

—Travels in San Francisco. 1991. pap. 8.95 o.p. (*1-55970-086-6*) Arcade Publishing, Inc.

Goldmark, Kathi Kamen. And My Shoes Keep Walking Back: A Novel. pap. 13.95 (*0-8118-4315-7*); 2002. 288p. 22.95 (*0-8118-3495-6*) Chronicle Bks. LLC.

Goldstein, Lisa. Walking the Labyrinth. 256p. 1998. pap. 12.95 (*0-312-85968-6*, Forge Bks.); 1996. 21.95 o.p. (*0-312-86175-3*, Tor Bks.) Doherty, Tom Assocs., LLC.

Goodger, Jane. Into the Wild Wind. l.t. ed. 2000. (Ulverscroft Large Print Ser.). 496p. 31.99 (*0-7089-4315-2*, Ulverscroft) Thorpe, F. A. Pubs. GBR. *Dist:* Ulverscroft Large Print Bks., Ltd., Ulverscroft Large Print Canada, Ltd.

Goodman, Jo. With All My Heart. 2001. (Thorne Brothers Trilogy Ser.). (Illus.). 473p. (J). 26.95 (*0-7862-2959-4*, Five Star) Gale Group.

—With All My Heart, 1. 1999. 429p. mass mkt. 5.99 o.s.i (*0-8217-6145-5*) Kensington Publishing Corp.

Gores, Joe. Cases. 1999. 354p. 23.00 (*0-89296-593-2*) Mysterious Pr.

—Cases. l.t. ed. 1999. (Mystery Ser.). 555p. 27.95 (*0-7862-1882-7*) Thorndike Pr.

—Cases. 1999. mass mkt. (*0-446-60703-7*) Warner Bks., Inc.

—Cons, Scams & Grifts. 2001. 336p. 24.95 (*0-89296-594-0*) Mysterious Pr.

—Contract Null & Void. 1996. 82p. 21.95 o.s.i (*0-89296-592-4*) Mysterious Pr.

—Contract Null & Void. 1997. (Dka File Novel Ser.). 336p. mass mkt. 6.50 o.s.i (*0-446-40447-0*) Warner Bks., Inc.

—Dead Skip. 1981. mass mkt. 2.25 o.s.i (*0-345-29206-5*); 1974. mass mkt. 1.25 o.p. (*0-345-24129-0*) Ballantine Bks.

—Dead Skip. 1992. 208p. reprint ed. mass mkt. 4.99 o.s.i (*0-446-40312-1*, Mysterious Pr. Paperback Bks.) Warner Bks., Inc.

—Final Notice. 1992. 208p. reprint ed. mass mkt. 4.99 (*0-446-40314-8*, Mysterious Pr. Paperback Bks.) Warner Bks., Inc.

—Gone, No Forwarding. 1981. mass mkt. 2.25 o.s.i (*0-345-29208-1*) Ballantine Bks.

—Gone, No Forwarding. 1993. 224p. mass mkt. 5.50 o.s.i (*0-446-40315-6*) Warner Bks., Inc.

—Menaced Assassin. 1994. 336p. 19.95 o.s.i (*0-89296-542-8*) Mysterious Pr.

—Menaced Assassin. 1995. 384p. mass mkt. 5.50 (*0-446-40390-3*) Warner Bks., Inc.

—32 Cadillacs. 1992. 352p. 18.95 (*0-89296-298-4*) Mysterious Pr.

—32 Cadillacs. 1993. 352p. mass mkt. 5.99 o.s.i (*0-446-40360-1*) Warner Bks., Inc.

Gould, Judith. My Second Love. 1997. 464p. 25.95 o.p. (*0-525-93930-X*) Dutton/Plume.

Grant, Jean. The Promise of Victory: A Novel, No. 3. 1995. (Salinas Valley Saga Ser.: Vol. 3). 9.99 o.p. (*0-7852-8103-7*) Nelson, Thomas Inc.

Grant, Linda. Blind Trust. 1991. (Catherine Sayler Mystery Ser.). mass mkt. 5.99 o.s.i (*0-8041-0791-2*, Ivy Bks.) Ballantine Bks.
—Blind Trust. 1990. 224p. 18.95 o.s.i (*0-684-19165-2*, Macmillan Reference USA) Gale Group.
—Lethal Genes. 1997. mass mkt. 5.99 o.s.i (*0-8041-1558-3*, Ivy Bks.) Ballantine Bks.
—Lethal Genes. 1996. 256p. 21.00 (*0-684-82653-4*, Scribner) Simon & Schuster.
—Love nor Money: An Inspector Catherine Sayler. 1992. (Northern California Mysteries Ser.). mass mkt. 4.50 o.s.i (*0-8041-0947-8*, Ivy Bks.) Ballantine Bks.
—Love nor Money: An Inspector Catherine Sayler. 1991. 288p. 19.95 o.s.i (*0-684-19379-5*, Macmillan Reference USA) Gale Group.
—Random Access Murder: The First Catherine Sayler Mystery. 1998. (Catherine Sayler Mystery Ser.: No. 1). 192p. reprint ed. mass mkt. 5.50 o.p. (*1-890768-09-X*, Intrigue Pr.) Corvus Publishing.
—Random Access Murder: The First Catherine Sayler Mystery. 1988. 192p. pap. 2.95 (*0-380-75534-3*, Avon Bks.) Morrow/Avon.
—Vampire Bytes: A Crime Novel with Catherine Sayler. 1999. mass mkt. 5.99 o.s.i (*0-8041-1862-0*, Ivy Bks.) Ballantine Bks.
—Vampire Bytes: A Crime Novel with Catherine Sayler. 1998. (Crime Novels Ser.). 288p. 22.00 (*0-684-82675-5*, Scribner) Simon & Schuster.
—A Woman's Place. 1995. (Catherine Sayler Mystery Ser.). mass mkt. 5.50 o.s.i (*0-8041-1327-0*, Ivy Bks.) Ballantine Bks.
—A Woman's Place. 1994. 288p. 20.00 o.p. (*0-684-19631-X*, Scribner) Simon & Schuster.
Graysmith, Robert. Zodiac. 1987. 384p. mass mkt. 7.99 (*0-425-09808-7*) Berkley Publishing Group.
—Zodiac. 1985. (Illus.). 384p. 16.95 o.p. (*0-312-89895-9*) St. Martin's Pr.
Green, David A. The Beginning of Sorrow. 1996. 176p. pap. (*1-57502-302-4*, P01036) Morris Publishing.
Greenleaf, Stephen. Beyond Blame. 1986. pap. o.s.i (*0-345-00733-6*); mass mkt. 4.99 o.s.i (*0-345-33670-4*) Ballantine Bks.
—Blood Type: The New John Marshall Tanner Mystery. 1993. 304p. mass mkt. 4.99 o.s.i (*0-553-56106-5*) Bantam Bks.
—Blood Type: The New John Marshall Tanner Mystery. 1992. 304p. 20.00 o.p. (*0-688-11268-4*, Morrow, William & Co.) Morrow/Avon.
—Book Case: A John Marshall Tanner Mystery. 1991. 352p. mass mkt. 4.99 o.s.i (*0-553-29061-4*) Bantam Bks.
—Book Case: A John Marshall Tanner Mystery. 1991. 19.95 o.p. (*0-688-07669-6*, Morrow, William & Co.) Morrow/Avon.
—Death Bed. 1982. mass mkt. 2.50 o.s.i (*0-345-30189-7*) Ballantine Bks.
—Death Bed. 1991. 304p. mass mkt. 4.99 o.s.i (*0-553-29348-6*) Bantam Bks.
—Death Bed. 1980. 320p. 10.95 o.p. (*0-385-27139-5*) Doubleday Publishing.
—Death Bed. 1980. 306p. (J). o.p. (*0-8037-1701-6*, Dial Bks. for Young Readers) Penguin Putnam Bks. for Young Readers.
—The Death Bed. 1985. mass mkt. 2.95 o.s.i (*0-345-32742-X*) Ballantine Bks.
—Ellipsis: A John Marshall Tanner Novel. 2001. E-Book 24.00 (*1-58945-174-0*) Adobe Systems, Inc.
—Ellipsis: A John Marshall Tanner Novel. 2000. (John Marshall Tanner Mysteries Ser.). 272p. 24.00 o.s.i (*0-684-84955-0*); E-Book 24.00 (*0-7432-1075-1*) Simon & Schuster. (Scribner).
—False Conception: A John Marshall Tanner Novel. (John Marshall Tanner Mysteries Ser.). 1997. 336p. pap. 5.99 (*0-671-00794-7*, Pocket); 1994. 320p. 22.00 (*1-883402-87-5*, Scribner) Simon & Schuster.
—Fatal Obsession. 1985. mass mkt. 2.95 o.s.i (*0-345-33287-3*); 1984. mass mkt. 2.50 o.s.i (*0-345-31485-9*) Ballantine Bks.
—Fatal Obsession. 1991. 256p. mass mkt. 4.99 o.s.i (*0-553-29350-8*) Bantam Bks.
—Fatal Obsession. 1983. 264p. 14.95 o.p. (*0-385-27886-1*) Doubleday Publishing.
—Flesh Wounds: A John Marshall Tanner Mystery. (John Marshall Tanner Mysteries Ser.). 1997. 288p. per. 5.99 (*0-671-00795-5*, Pocket); 1996. 318p. 22.00 (*0-684-81583-4*, Scribner) Simon & Schuster.
—Grave Error. 1982. 240p. mass mkt. 2.50 o.s.i (*0-345-30188-9*) Ballantine Bks.
—Grave Error. 1991. 272p. mass mkt. 4.99 o.s.i (*0-553-29347-8*) Bantam Bks.
—Grave Error. 1985. 8.95 o.p. (*0-385-27058-5*) Doubleday Publishing.
—Past Tense. 1997. (John Marshall Tanner Mysteries Ser.). 352p. 22.00 (*0-684-83249-6*, Scribner) Simon & Schuster.
—Southern Cross: A John Marshall Tanner Novel. 1995. 320p. mass mkt. 4.99 o.s.i (*0-553-56817-5*) Bantam Bks.
—Southern Cross: A John Marshall Tanner Novel. 1993. 320p. 20.00 o.p. (*0-688-12772-X*, Morrow, William & Co.) Morrow/Avon.
—State's Evidence. 1985. 288p. mass mkt. 2.95 o.s.i (*0-345-32534-6*); 1983. mass mkt. 2.50 o.s.i (*0-345-30869-7*) Ballantine Bks.
—State's Evidence. 1991. 320p. mass mkt. 4.99 o.s.i (*0-553-29349-4*) Bantam Bks.
—State's Evidence. 1982. 320p. 15.95 o.p. (*0-385-27236-7*) Doubleday Publishing.
—Strawberry Sunday: A John Marshall Tanner Novel, 2000. audio 44.95 (*0-7861-1574-2*, P2403) Blackstone Audio Bks., Inc.
—Strawberry Sunday: A John Marshall Tanner Novel. 1999. 288p. 23.00 o.p. (*0-684-84954-2*, Scribner) Simon & Schuster.
—Strawberry Sunday: A John Marshall Tanner Novel. l.t. ed. 1999. (Americana Ser.). 439p. 27.95 (*0-7862-1951-3*) Thorndike Pr.
—Toll Call. 1988. mass mkt. 4.99 o.s.i (*0-345-35349-8*) Ballantine Bks.
Hagberg, David. Critical Mass. unabr. ed. 1992. audio 23.95 o.p. (*1-56100-466-9*, 73, Bookcassette); audio 73.25 o.p. (*1-56100-100-7*, 1158, Unabridged Library Editions) Brilliance Audio.
—Critical Mass. 1999. 472p. mass mkt. 6.99 (*0-8125-2497-7*); 1992. 384p. 4.99 o.p. (*0-312-85255-X*) Doherty, Tom Assocs., LLC. (Tor Bks.).
Hailey, Arthur. Hotel. 2000. 480p. mass mkt. 7.99 (*0-425-17636-3*) Berkley Publishing Group.
—Hotel. 1964. 14.95 o.s.i (*0-385-03222-6*) Doubleday Publishing.
—Hotel. l.t. ed. 1977. (Ulverscroft Large Print Ser.). 12.00 o.p. (*0-85456-557-4*, Ulverscroft) Thorpe, F. A. Pubs. GBR. *Dist:* Ulverscroft Large Print Bks., Ltd., Ulverscroft Large Print Canada, Ltd.
Hall, Oakley M. Ambrose Bierce & the Queen of Spades: A Novel. 2000. 288p. pap. 5.99 (*0-14-028860-0*, Penguin Bks.) Penguin Group (USA) Inc.
—Ambrose Bierce & the Queen of Spades: A Novel. 1998. 321p. text 22.95 (*0-520-21555-9*) Univ. of California Pr.
—Ambrose Bierce & the Trey of Pearls. 2004. 224p. 24.95 (*0-670-03270-0*, Viking) Viking Penguin.
Hammett, Dashiell. The Maltese Falcon. 1983. (Illus.). 300p. 325.00 o.p. (*0-910457-01-8*) Arion Pr.
—The Maltese Falcon. 1985. (Mystery Ser.). mass mkt. 9.95 o.p. (*0-553-06509-2*) Bantam Bks.
—The Maltese Falcon. 1982. (Illus.). 352p. reprint ed. 20.00 o.p. (*0-86547-156-8*, North Point Pr.) Farrar, Straus & Giroux.
—The Maltese Falcon. l.t. ed. 2001. 217p. 28.95 (*0-7838-9459-7*, Macmillan Reference USA) Gale Group.
—The Maltese Falcon. 1992. pap. 9.00 (*0-394-23903-2*); 1989. 224p. pap. 11.00 (*0-679-72264-5*) Knopf Publishing Group. (Vintage).
—The Maltese Falcon, Set. l.t. ed. (YA). (gr. 10 up). reprint ed. 10.00 (*0-89064-044-0*) National Assn. for Visually Handicapped.
—The Maltese Falcon. 1992. pap. 9.00 (*0-679-74094-5*); 1972. pap. 4.95 o.p. (*0-394-71772-4*) Random Hse., Inc.
—The Maltese Falcon. 2001. (Best Mysteries of All Time Ser.). 271p. (*0-7621-8867-7*, IM Pr.) Reader's Digest Assn., Inc., The.
—The Maltese Falcon. 1993. 284p. reprint ed. 35.00 o.p. (*1-883402-15-8*, Scribner) Simon & Schuster.
Handler, Daniel. The Basic Eight. E-Book 13.95 (*0-312-26440-2*); 2000. 352p. pap. 13.95 (*0-312-25373-7*, Saint Martin's Griffin); 1999. 352p. 23.95 (*0-312-19833-7*) St. Martin's Pr.
Hanson, Dirk. The Incursion. 1987. 16.95 o.p. (*0-316-34374-9*) Little Brown & Co.
—The Incursion. 1988. 272p. mass mkt. 3.95 (*0-380-70554-0*, Avon Bks.) Morrow/Avon.
Hart, Carolyn G. Skulduggery. 2000. (Five Star Mystery Ser.). 190p. 22.95 (*0-7862-2672-2*, Five Star) Gale Group.
Harte, Bret. Under the Redwoods. 2000. 252p. E-Book 3.95 (*0-594-05574-1*) 1873 Pr.
—Under the Redwoods. 1977. (Short Story Index Reprint Ser.). 23.95 (*0-8369-3403-2*) Ayer Co. Pubs., Inc.
—Under the Redwoods. 1896. (YA). reprint ed. pap. text 38.00 (*1-4047-7842-X*) Classic Textbooks.
—Under the Redwoods. 1999. (Works of Bret Harte: Vol. 10). 340p. reprint ed. lib. bdg. 90.00 (*0-7812-7842-2*) Reprint Services Corp.
Hartman, Claire. Sherlock Holmes' Granddaughter—Shirlee Holmes: The Sutro Murder Case. 2001. vi, 247p. pap. 12.95 (*0-9711586-0-6*) Hartman, Claire.
Hausman, Pamela. The Golden Gate Park Murder. Feinen, Cynthia, ed. 2000. 190p. per. 14.95 (*1-880254-66-2*) Vista Publishing, Inc.
Headmess, m. j. r. Zero Is the Hero. 1999. (Pseudonymous Ser.: 4). (Illus.). 176p. pap. 7.00 (*0-915090-99-6*) Firefall.
Hoffman, Blair. Murder for the Prosecution. 1993. 208p. 18.95 o.p. (*0-88184-995-2*, Carroll & Graf Pubs.) Avalon Publishing Group.
Holland, Cecelia. Pacific Street. 1991. 21.95 o.p. (*0-395-56144-2*) Houghton Mifflin Co.
Hollis, Tom. Honky Tonk Logic: A Novel. 1996. 352p. 23.95 o.p. (*0-312-13981-0*) St. Martin's Pr.
Holtzer, Susan. Better Than Sex. 240p. 2002. mass mkt. 6.50 (*0-312-98005-1*, St. Martin's Paperbacks); 2001. 22.95 (*0-312-25345-1*, Saint Martin's Minotaur) St. Martin's Pr.
Hrbek, Greg. The Hindenburg Crashes Nightly. 2000. 368p. pap. 13.00 (*0-380-80543-X*, Perennial) HarperTrade.
—The Hindenburg Crashes Nightly. 1999. 368p. 23.00 (*0-380-97741-9*, Avon Bks.) Morrow/Avon.
Hunt, David, pseud. The Magician's Tale. 1998. 416p. reprint ed. mass mkt. 7.50 o.s.i (*0-425-16482-9*) Berkley Publishing Group.
—The Magician's Tale. 1997. 416p. 24.95 o.s.i (*0-399-14260-6*, G. P. Putnam's Sons) Penguin Group (USA) Inc.
—Trick of Light. 1999. 416p. reprint ed. mass mkt. 7.50 o.s.i (*0-425-17035-7*) Berkley Publishing Group.
—Trick of Light. 1998. 400p. 24.95 o.p. (*0-399-14393-9*, G. P. Putnam's Sons) Penguin Group (USA) Inc.
Hurst, Jim. Fatal Image. 1998. 200p. (Orig.). pap. 14.50 (*0-88739-120-6*) Creative Arts Bk. Co.
Hurwitz, Gregg. The Tower. 2001. (Illus.). 432p. mass mkt. 6.99 (*0-671-02321-7*, Pocket) Simon & Schuster.
—The Tower: A Novel. 2000. E-Book 23.00 (*0-684-87189-0*, Simon & Schuster) Simon & Schuster.
Hurwitz, Gregg, et al. The Tower: A Novel. 1999. 384p. 23.00 (*0-684-85191-1*, Simon & Schuster) Simon & Schuster.
Inclan, Jessica Barksdale. The Matter of Grace. 2004. 320p. mass mkt. 6.99 (*0-451-21185-5*, Signet Bks.) NAL.
—The Matter of Grace. 2002. 272p. pap. 12.95 (*0-451-20575-8*) Penguin Group (USA) Inc.
Islas, Arturo. La Mollie & the King of Tears. 1996. 200p. (C). pap. 14.95 (*0-8263-1732-4*) Univ. of New Mexico Pr.
Jacobs, Jonnie. Evidence of Guilt. 1997. 368p. 18.95 o.p. (*1-57566-141-1*, Kensington Bks.) Kensington Publishing Corp.
—Shadow of Doubt. (Kali O'Brien Mystery Ser.). 1997. 308p. mass mkt. 5.50 o.s.i (*1-57566-146-2*, Kensington Bks.); 1996. 304p. pap. 18.95 o.p. (*1-57566-017-2*); 1996. mass mkt. 18.95 o.s.i (*0-8217-5254-5*) Kensington Publishing Corp.
—Witness for the Defense. 2002. 432p. mass mkt. 6.99 (*1-57566-828-9*, Kensington Bks.); 2001. 336p. 23.00 o.s.i (*1-57566-643-X*) Kensington Publishing Corp.
Jacobs, Nancy Baker. Double or Nothing. l.t. ed. 2001. (Five Star First Edition Mystery Ser.). 156p. 23.95 o.p. (*0-7862-3010-X*) Thorndike Pr.
—Flash Point: A Susan Kim Delancey Mystery. 2002. 216p. pap. 13.95 (*1-880284-56-1*, Perseverance Pr.) Daniel, John & Co., Pubs.
Jacoby, Kathleen. Vision of the Grail: A Spiritual Adventure at the Dawn of the 21st Century. 2001. 304p. (Orig.). 14.95 (*1-930126-07-7*) Lightlines Publishing Co.
Jaramillo, Stephan. Going Postal: A Novel. 1997. 256p. pap. 12.00 o.s.i (*0-425-15768-7*) Berkley Publishing Group.
Jefferson, Jemiah. Voice of Blood. 2001. 288p. mass mkt. 5.99 (*0-8439-4830-2*, Leisure Bks.) Dorchester Publishing Co., Inc.
Jenkins, James. Crazy Cruising in a Chinese Restaurant: A San Francisco Comedy. 2000. 190p. pap. 16.00 (*0-7388-3204-9*) Xlibris Corp.
Jennings, Patrick. Faith & the Rocket Cat. 1998. (Illus.). 224p. (J). (gr. 3-6). pap. 15.95 (*0-590-11004-7*) Scholastic, Inc.
Johnson, Claire M. Beat until Stiff. 2002. 300p. 24.95 o.s.i (*1-59058-040-0*) Poisoned Pen Pr.
—Beat until Stiff. 2003. 224p. mass mkt. 6.99 (*0-7434-7512-7*) ibooks, Inc.
Johnson, Diane. Health & Happiness. 1991. mass mkt. 5.99 o.s.i (*0-449-21841-4*, Fawcett) Ballantine Bks.
—Health & Happiness. 1998. 272p. pap. 14.00 (*0-452-28000-1*, Plume) Dutton/Plume.
Johnstone, William W. Power of the Mountain Man. 1995. (Zebra Bks.). mass mkt. 4.99 o.s.i (*0-8217-5363-0*, Zebra Bks.); 256p. mass mkt. 3.99 o.s.i (*0-8217-4871-8*) Kensington Publishing Corp.
Kaiser, R. J. Black Sheep. 2003. 464p. (*1-55166-726-6*, Mira Bks.) Harlequin Enterprises, Ltd.
Kaiser, R. J., as told by. Squeeze Play. 2002. 464p. (*1-55166-936-6*, Mira Bks.) Harlequin Enterprises, Ltd.
Katz, Lieselotte & von Schalow, Ottilia Louise. Going Away. 2001. 300p. pap. 14.95 (*0-595-16001-8*) iUniverse, Inc.
Kaufman, Lynne. Slow Hands. 2004. mass mkt. (*0-7783-2039-1*); 2003. 288p. (*1-55166-718-5*) Harlequin Enterprises, Ltd. (Mira Bks.).
Keannealy, Jerry. Vintage Polo. 1993. 256p. 19.95 o.p. (*0-312-09932-0*, Saint Martin's Minotaur) St. Martin's Pr.
Keats, Jonathan. The Pathology of Lies. 1999. 288p. pap. 14.00 (*0-446-67445-1*) Warner Bks., Inc.
Kelleher, Michael. The Mission District Murders. 2000. E-Book 10.99 (*1-929429-57-6*) Dead End Street, LLC.
Kelleher, Michael D. The Mission District Murders. 2000. E-Book 10.99 (*1-929429-58-4*) Dead End Street, LLC.
Keltner, Kim Wong. The Dim Sum of All Things. 2004. 352p. pap. 13.95 (*0-06-056075-4*, Avon Bks.) Morrow/Avon.
Kennealy, Jerry. All That Glitters: A Nick Polo Mystery. 1996. 240p. 21.95 o.p. (*0-312-15049-0*, Saint Martin's Minotaur) St. Martin's Pr.
—Beggar's Choice. 1994. 256p. 20.95 o.p. (*0-312-11478-8*, Saint Martin's Minotaur) St. Martin's Pr.
—Green with Envy: A Nick Polo Mystery. 1991. 240p. 17.95 o.p. (*0-312-06572-8*, Saint Martin's Minotaur) St. Martin's Pr.
—The Hunted. 1999. 320p. mass mkt. 5.99 o.s.i (*0-451-19776-3*) NAL.
—Polo, Anyone? 1988. 224p. 15.95 o.p. (*0-312-01491-0*, Saint Martin's Minotaur) St. Martin's Pr.
—Polo in the Rough. 1989. 14.95 o.p. (*0-312-02964-0*, Saint Martin's Minotaur) St. Martin's Pr.
—Polo Solo. 1988. pap. 2.95 o.p. (*0-312-91074-6*, St. Martin's Paperbacks); 1987. 192p. 13.95 o.p. (*0-312-00671-3*) St. Martin's Pr.
—Polo's Ponies. 1988. 176p. 14.95 o.p. (*0-312-02267-0*, Saint Martin's Minotaur) St. Martin's Pr.
—Polo's Wild Card. 1992. 1.99 o.p. (*0-517-08490-2*) Random Hse. Value Publishing.
—Polo's Wild Card. 1990. 15.95 o.p. (*0-312-04437-2*, Saint Martin's Minotaur) St. Martin's Pr.
—Special Delivery: A Case for Nick Polo. 1992. 224p. 17.95 o.p. (*0-312-08304-1*, Saint Martin's Minotaur) St. Martin's Pr.
Kent, Stan. The City of One-Night Stands. 2001. 256p. pap. 7.95 (*1-56201-241-X*, Blue Moon Bks.) Avalon Publishing Group.
Kilworth, Garry D. Angel. 1996. 320p. 22.95 o.p. (*0-312-86107-9*, Forge Bks.) Doherty, Tom Assocs., LLC.
Kim, Willyce. Dancer Dawkins & the California Kid. 1985. 133p. (Orig.). pap. 5.95 o.p. (*0-932870-59-7*) Alyson Pubns.
King, Laurie R. A Grave Talent. 1995. 368p. mass mkt. 6.99 (*0-553-57399-3*, Crimeline) Bantam Bks.
—A Grave Talent. unabr. ed. 1996. (Kate Martinelli Mystery Ser.: Vol. 1). audio 85.00 (*0-7887-0395-1*, 94587E7) Recorded Bks., LLC.
—A Grave Talent. 1993. 310p. 19.95 (*0-312-08804-3*, Saint Martin's Minotaur) St. Martin's Pr.
—Night Work. 2000. (Kate Martinelli Mysteries Ser.). 416p. mass mkt. 6.99 (*0-553-57825-1*) Bantam Bks.
—To Play the Fool. 1996. 320p. mass mkt. 6.99 (*0-553-57455-8*, Crimeline) Bantam Bks.
—To Play the Fool. unabr. ed. 1996. (Kate Martinelli Mystery Ser.: Vol. 2). audio 60.00 (*0-7887-0406-0*, 94598E7); audio Recorded Bks., LLC.
—To Play the Fool. 1995. 260p. 21.00 o.p. (*0-312-11907-0*, Saint Martin's Minotaur) St. Martin's Pr.
—With Child. 1997. 320p. mass mkt. 6.99 (*0-553-57458-2*) Bantam Bks.
—With Child. unabr. ed. 1996. (Kate Martinelli Mystery Ser.: Vol. 3). audio 70.00 (*0-7887-0579-2*, 94757E7) Recorded Bks., LLC.
—With Child. 1996. 275p. 21.95 o.p. (*0-312-14077-0*, Saint Martin's Minotaur) St. Martin's Pr.
—With Child. l.t. ed. 1998. (Ulverscroft Large Print Ser.). 528p. 29.99 (*0-7089-3904-X*, Ulverscroft) Thorpe, F. A. Pubs. GBR. *Dist:* Ulverscroft Large Print Bks., Ltd., Ulverscroft Large Print Canada, Ltd.
King, Peter. Dead Man's Coast. 2002. 272p. (YA). mass mkt. 5.99 o.s.i (*0-451-20584-7*, Signet Bks.) NAL.
Kirchner, Bharti. Shiva Dancing. 336p. 1999. pap. 12.95 o.s.i (*0-452-27882-1*, Plume); 1998. 23.95 o.p. (*0-525-94367-6*) Dutton/Plume.
Klavan, Andrew. Dynamite Road. Date not set. mass mkt. (*0-7653-4694-X*); 2003. 320p. 25.95 (*0-7653-0785-5*) Doherty, Tom Assocs., LLC. (Forge Bks.).
Lackey, Mercedes. The Fire Rose. 1996. 448p. pap. 6.99 (*0-671-87750-X*); 1995. 22.00 (*0-671-87687-2*); 2001. 448p. reprint ed. 6.99 (*0-671-31967-1*) Baen Bks.
Lacy, Al. A Dream Fulfilled, 10 vols. 2003. (Angel of Mercy Ser.: Vol. 4). 270p. pap. 10.99 (*0-88070-940-5*, Multnomah Bks.) Multnomah Pubs., Inc.
—Faithful Heart, 10 vols. 2003. (Angel of Mercy Ser.: Vol. 2). 308p. pap. 10.99 (*0-88070-835-2*, Multnomah Bks.) Multnomah Pubs., Inc.
Lamott, Anne. Blue Shoe. 2003. 336p. pap. 14.00 (*1-57322-342-5*, Riverhead Trade (Paperbacks)) Berkley Publishing Group.
—Blue Shoe. l.t. ed. 2002. (Wheeler Hardcover Ser.). 430p. 31.95 (*1-58724-362-8*, Wheeler Publishing, Inc.) Gale Group.
—Blue Shoe. 2002. 304p. 24.95 (*1-57322-226-7*, Riverhead Bks. (Hardcovers)) Putnam Publishing Group, The.

Larsgaard, Chris. The Heir Hunter. 2001. 448p. mass mkt. 6.99 (*0-440-23462-X*) Dell Publishing.

Laws, Jay B. The Unfinished. 1993. 283p. pap. 9.95 o.p. (*1-55583-217-2*) Alyson Pubns.

Lee, Gus. China Boy. 336p. 1994. pap. 14.00 (*0-452-27158-4*, Plume); 1991. 19.95 o.p. (*0-525-24994-X*) Dutton/Plume.

—China Boy. 1992. 400p. mass mkt. 5.99 o.p. (*0-451-17434-8*, Signet Bks.) NAL.

—China Boy. 1994. 19.00 (*0-606-16250-X*) Turtleback Bks.

Lee, Y. C. The Flower Drum Song. 2002. 272p. 14.00 (*0-14-200218-6*) Viking Penguin.

Leebron, Fred G. Out West. 1997. (Harvest Book Ser.). 256p. pap. 12.00 o.s.i (*0-15-600546-8*, Harvest Bks.) Harcourt Trade Pubs.

—Out West: A Novel. 1996. 256p. 21.95 o.s.i (*0-385-48420-8*) Doubleday Publishing.

Lescroart, John. A Certain Justice. 1996. pap. 6.99 (*0-440-29547-5*) Bantam Bks.

—A Certain Justice. 1996. 544p. mass mkt. 7.99 (*0-440-22104-8*) Dell Publishing.

—A Certain Justice. 1995. 448p. 22.95 o.p. (*1-55611-445-1*) Fine, Donald I. Bks.

—A Certain Justice. l.t. ed. 1996. 756p. 25.95 (*0-7838-1565-4*, Macmillan Reference USA) Gale Group.

—Dead Irish. l.t. ed. 2001. 359p. 28.95 (*1-57490-358-6*, Beeler Large Print Bks.) Beeler, Thomas T. Publisher.

—Dead Irish. 1996. 416p. mass mkt. 7.99 (*0-440-20783-5*) Dell Publishing.

—Dead Irish. 1990. 18.95 o.p. (*1-55611-159-2*) Fine, Donald I. Bks.

—Dead Irish. 1996. audio 16.98 o.s.i (*0-553-74643-X*); 2000. audio 9.99 o.s.i (*0-553-52702-9*) Random Hse. Audio Publishing Group. (RH Audio).

—The First Law. abr. ed. 2003. (Dismas Hardy Ser.: Vol. 11). audio 24.95 (*1-59086-371-2*, 3959); audio 12.99 (*1-59086-374-7*, 3962, Brilliance Audio Paperback Audiobooks); audio 92.25 (*1-59086-370-4*, 3958); audio 34.95 (*1-59086-369-0*, 3957); audio compact disk 107.25 (*1-59086-373-9*, 3961); audio compact disk 42.95 (*1-59086-372-0*, 3960) Brilliance Audio.

—The First Law. 2003. 384p. 25.95 (*0-525-94705-1*) Dutton/Plume.

—The First Law. 2004. 757p. pap. 13.95 (*1-4104-0171-5*, Wheeler Publishing, Inc.) Gale Group.

—The First Law. 2004. 448p. mass mkt. 7.99 (*0-451-21022-0*, Signet Bks.) NAL.

—The First Law. 2003. 31.95 (*0-7862-5187-5*) Thorndike Pr.

—Guilt. 1998. 656p. mass mkt. 7.99 (*0-440-22281-8*) Doubleday Publishing.

—Guilt. l.t. ed. 1997. (Large Print Book Ser.). 26.95 (*1-56895-477-8*, Wheeler Publishing, Inc.) Gale Group.

—Hard Evidence. 1994. (Northern California Mysteries Ser.). 512p. mass mkt. 6.99 o.s.i (*0-8041-1275-4*, Ivy Bks.) Ballantine Bks.

—Hard Evidence. 1993. 478p. 21.95 o.p. (*1-55611-344-7*) Fine, Donald I. Bks.

—The Hearing. 2001. (Illus.). 464p. 25.95 o.s.i (*0-525-94575-X*, Dutton) Dutton/Plume.

—The Hearing. l.t. ed. 2002. 655p. pap. 29.95 (*0-7838-9394-9*, Macmillan Reference USA); 2001. 480p. 32.95 (*0-7838-9393-0*, Hall, G. K. & Co.) Gale Group.

—The Hearing. 2001. 544p. pap. 7.99 (*0-451-20450-6*); 2002. 560p. reprint ed. mass mkt. 7.99 (*0-451-20489-1*) NAL. (Signet Bks.).

—The Mercy Rule. 1999. 640p. mass mkt. 7.99 (*0-440-22282-6*) Dell Publishing.

—The Mercy Rule. l.t. ed. (Paperback Bestsellers Ser.). 684p. 1999. pap. 27.95 (*0-7838-0394-X*); 1998. 30.95 (*0-7838-0344-3*) Thorndike Pr.

—Nothing but the Truth. 1999. mass mkt. 7.99 (*0-440-29574-2*) Bantam Dell Publishing Group.

—Nothing but the Truth. 2000. mass mkt. 7.99 (*0-440-22664-3*); 448p. 24.95 o.s.i (*0-385-33353-6*, Delacorte Pr.) Dell Publishing.

—Nothing but the Truth. l.t. ed. 2000. 27.95 (*1-56895-813-7*, Wheeler Publishing, Inc.) Gale Group.

—Nothing but the Truth. 2001. 464p. mass mkt. 7.99 (*0-451-20285-6*) NAL.

—Nothing but the Truth. abr. ed. 2000. audio 25.95 (*0-553-52662-6*, RH Audio) Random Hse. Audio Publishing Group.

—The Oath. unabr. ed. 2002. (Dismas Hardy Ser.: Vol. 10). audio 34.95 (*1-58788-981-1*, 3501, Brilliance Audio Unabridged); audio 87.25 (*1-58788-982-X*, 3502, Unabridged Library Editions) Brilliance Audio.

—The Oath. 2002. 480p. 25.95 o.s.i (*0-525-94576-8*, Dutton) Dutton/Plume.

—The Oath. l.t. ed. 2002. 653p. 32.95 (*0-7862-4193-4*) Gale Group.

—The Oath. l.t. ed. 2002. 598p. pap. 13.95 (*0-7862-4194-2*) Thorndike Pr.

—The Second Chair. 2004. 400p. 25.95 (*0-525-94775-2*, Dutton) Dutton/Plume.

—The Vig. 1998. 384p. mass mkt. 7.99 (*0-440-20986-2*) Dell Publishing.

—The Vig. 1991. 18.95 o.p. (*1-55611-221-1*) Fine, Donald I. Bks.

—The Vig. abr. ed. 1998. audio 16.99 o.p. Random Hse. Audio Publishing Group.

—The 13th Juror. 1995. 560p. mass mkt. 7.99 (*0-440-22079-3*) Dell Publishing.

—The 13th Juror. 1994. 480p. 22.95 o.s.i (*1-55611-402-8*) Fine, Donald I. Bks.

—The 13th Juror. l.t. ed. 1994. 803p. lib. bdg. 24.95 o.p. (*0-8161-7448-2*, Macmillan Reference USA) Gale Group.

Levin, Donna. California Street. 1992. 336p. mass mkt. 4.50 o.s.i (*0-451-40303-7*, Onyx) NAL.

—California Street. 1990. 18.95 o.p. (*0-671-69300-X*, Simon & Schuster) Simon & Schuster.

Levy, JoAnn. Daughter of Joy. 1997. (Women of the West Novels Ser.). 320p. 23.95 (*0-312-86502-3*, Tor Bks.) Doherty, Tom Assocs., LLC.

—The Daughter of Joy. 1999. (Women of the West Novels Ser.). 320p. pap. 6.99 (*0-8125-4029-8*, Forge Bks.) Doherty, Tom Assocs., LLC.

Levy, Marc. If Only It Were True. Leggatt, Jeremy, tr. from FRE. 2000. 224p. 22.95 o.s.i (*0-7434-0617-6*, Atria) Simon & Schuster.

Liu, Aimee. Cloud Mountain. abr. ed. 1997. audio 17.98 (*1-57042-480-2*) Time Warner AudioBooks.

Liu, Aimee E. Cloud Mountain. abr. ed. 1997. audio 19.00 o.p. Beeler, Thomas T. Publisher.

—Cloud Mountain. 1998. mass mkt. (*0-446-60544-1*); 1997. 368p. 24.00 o.p. (*0-446-51987-1*); 1998. 672p. reprint ed. pap. 14.99 (*0-446-67434-6*) Warner Bks., Inc.

Livia, Anna. Bruised Fruit: A Novel. 1999. 256p. 26.95 (*1-56341-107-5*); pap. 13.95 (*1-56341-106-7*) Firebrand Bks.

London, Mary. Look Fatter in Jeans: An Adventure in Growing Older & Wiser. 1997. (Illus.). vi, 306p. (Orig.). pap. 12.95 (*0-9656648-0-5*) Boomer Pubns.

Longhi, Jon. Wake up & Smell the Beer. 2003. 160p. pap. 13.95 (*0-916397-83-1*) Manic D Pr.

Lopez, Erika. Hoochie Mama. 2001. (Illus.). 272p. 30.00 o.s.i (*0-684-86974-8*, Simon & Schuster) Simon & Schuster.

Lucke, Margaret. A Relative Stranger. 1991. 320p. 19.95 o.p. (*0-312-06307-5*, Saint Martin's Minotaur) St. Martin's Pr.

Macomber, Debbie. A Gift to Last: Can This Be Christmas/Shirley, Goodness & Mercy. 2002. 240p. mass mkt. (*1-55166-930-7*, Mira Bks.) Harlequin Enterprises, Ltd.

—Shirley, Goodness & Mercy. unabr. ed. 1999. 3p. audio 7.99 (*1-55204-194-8*, MIR-1194) Durkin Hayes Publishing Ltd.

—Shirley, Goodness & Mercy. 1999. 136p. (*1-55166-529-8*, 1-66529-8); mass mkt. (*1-55166-562-X*, 1-66562-9) Harlequin Enterprises, Ltd. (Mira Bks.).

—Someday Soon. l.t. ed. 2000. (Wheeler Large Print Book Ser.). 353p. pap. 24.95 (*1-56895-900-1*, Wheeler Publishing, Inc.) Gale Group.

—Someday Soon. 1998. 352p. mass mkt. 3.99 o.p. (*0-06-104478-4*, HarperBusiness) HarperInformation.

—Someday Soon. 1995. 352p. mass mkt. 6.99 (*0-06-108309-7*, HarperTorch) Morrow/Avon.

MacPherson, Malcolm C. Deadlock. 1998. 320p. 23.00 (*0-684-83157-0*, Simon & Schuster) Simon & Schuster.

Maiman, Jaye. I Left My Heart. 1991. (Robin Miller Mysteries Ser.: Vol. 1). 320p. pap. 11.95 o.p. (*0-941483-72-X*) Naiad Pr., Inc.

Major, Devorah. Brown Glass Windows. 2002. 194p. pap. 15.95 (*1-880684-87-X*) Curbstone Pr.

Marino, Anne N. The Collapsible World. 2000. 171p. 22.95 (*0-393-04909-4*) Norton, W. W. & Co., Inc.

Martel, John. The Alternate. 1999. 480p. 24.95 o.p. (*0-525-94487-7*) Dutton/Plume.

—Conflicts of Interest. 2002. 480p. mass mkt. 6.99 (*0-451-41040-8*, Onyx) NAL.

—Conflicts of Interest. 1996. 480p. mass mkt. 6.99 (*0-671-89095-6*, Pocket); 1995. 448p. 23.00 (*0-671-89094-8*, Atria) Simon & Schuster.

Mason. Cyberweb. 2000. 20.00 (*0-380-97248-4*) Morrow/Avon.

Mason, Lisa. Cyberweb. 1998. 272p. pap. 12.00 (*0-380-79917-0*, Eos); 1996. 272p. mass mkt. 4.99 (*0-380-77486-0*, Avon Bks.); 1995. 256p. 20.00 (*0-688-13987-6*, Avon Bks.) Morrow/Avon.

—Summer of Love. 1994. (Illus.). 400p. pap. 12.95 o.s.i (*0-553-37330-7*) Bantam Bks.

Masterton, Graham. Master of Lies. 1995. 336p. mass mkt. 4.99 (*0-8125-1166-2*); 1991. 320p. 19.95 o.p. (*0-312-85102-2*) Doherty, Tom Assocs., LLC. (Tor Bks.).

Matera, Lia. Designer Crimes: A Laura Di Palma Mystery. (Laura Di Palma Mystery Ser.). 1996. 288p. pap. 6.50 (*0-671-00196-5*, Pocket); 1995. 240p. 21.00 o.s.i (*0-684-80312-7*, Simon & Schuster) Simon & Schuster.

—Face Value: A Laura Di Palma Mystery. (Laura Di Palma Ser.). 1995. o.s.i (*0-684-88840-8*, Pocket); 1995. (Illus.). 272p. mass mkt. 5.99 (*0-671-88840-4*, Pocket); 1994. 221p. 20.00 (*0-671-74197-7*, Simon & Schuster) Simon & Schuster.

—The Good Fight. 1991. (Laura Di Palma Ser.). mass mkt. 5.99 o.s.i (*0-345-37107-0*, Ballantine Bks.) Ballantine Bks.

—The Good Fight. 1990. 17.95 o.p. (*0-671-68561-9*, Simon & Schuster) Simon & Schuster.

—A Hard Bargain. 1993. (Laura Di Palma Ser.). mass mkt. 5.99 o.s.i (*0-345-38059-2*) Ballantine Bks.

—A Hard Bargain. 1992. 224p. 19.00 o.p. (*0-671-74196-9*, Simon & Schuster) Simon & Schuster.

—Havana Twist: A Willa Jansson Mystery. abr. ed. 1998. (Willa Jansson Mystery Ser.). 3p. audio 18.00 (*0-7871-1735-8*, Dove Audio) NewStar Media, Inc.

—Havana Twist: A Willa Jansson Mystery. (Willa Jansson Mystery Ser.). 1999. 352p. pap. 6.99 o.s.i (*0-671-00421-2*, Pocket); 1998. 256p. 22.00 (*0-684-83470-7*, Simon & Schuster) Simon & Schuster.

—Hidden Agenda. 1992. (Willa Jansson Ser.). mass mkt. 5.99 o.s.i (*0-345-37128-3*, Ballantine Bks.) Ballantine Bks.

—Hidden Agenda. 1988. mass mkt. 3.50 o.s.i (*0-553-27721-9*) Bantam Bks.

—Last Chants. (Willa Jansson Mystery Ser.). 1997. 320p. pap. 5.99 (*0-671-88096-9*, Pocket); 1996. 240p. 21.00 (*0-684-81085-9*, Simon & Schuster) Simon & Schuster.

—Prior Convictions. 1992. (Northern California Mysteries Ser.). mass mkt. 5.99 o.s.i (*0-345-37445-2*) Ballantine Bks.

—Prior Convictions. 1991. 224p. 17.95 o.p. (*0-671-68560-0*, Simon & Schuster) Simon & Schuster.

—Radical Departure. 1991. (Laura Di Palma Ser.). 224p. (Orig.). mass mkt. 5.99 o.s.i (*0-345-37126-7*) Ballantine Bks.

—A Radical Departure. 1988. mass mkt. 3.50 o.s.i (*0-553-27072-9*) Bantam Bks.

—The Smart Money. 1991. 192p. (Orig.). mass mkt. 5.99 o.s.i (*0-345-37127-5*) Ballantine Bks.

—The Smart Money. 1988. 208p. (Orig.). mass mkt. 3.50 o.s.i (*0-553-27268-3*) Bantam Bks.

—Star Witness. (Willa Jansson Mystery Ser.). 1998. 336p. pap. 6.50 (*0-671-00420-4*, Pocket); 1997. 240p. 21.50 (*0-684-83469-3*, Simon & Schuster) Simon & Schuster.

—Where Lawyers Fear to Tread. 1991. (Willa Jansson Ser.). mass mkt. 5.99 o.s.i (*0-345-37125-9*) Ballantine Bks.

—Where Lawyers Fear to Tread. 1987. mass mkt. 3.50 o.s.i (*0-553-27588-7*) Bantam Bks.

—Where Lawyers Fear to Tread. 1999. (Mystery Ser.). 209p. 20.95 o.p. (*0-7862-1814-2*, Five Star) Gale Group.

Mathes, Charles. The Girl Who Remembered the Snow. 1996. 304p. 23.95 (*0-312-13977-2*, Saint Martin's Minotaur) St. Martin's Pr.

Maupin, Armistead. Babycakes. 1994. (Tales of the City Ser.: Vol. 4). 336p. pap. 14.00 (*0-06-092483-7*, Perennial); 1984. 254p. 15.95 o.p. (*0-06-015262-1*); 1984. 254p. pap. 9.95 o.p. (*0-06-091099-2*, CN 1099, Perennial); 1990. audio 17.00 o.s.i (*1-55994-276-2*, CPN 2179, HarperAudio) HarperTrade.

—Babycakes Reiss. 1989. 336p. reprint ed. pap. 12.00 o.p. (*0-06-096407-3*, Perennial) HarperTrade.

—Back to Barbary Lane: The Final Tales of the City Omnibus. 1991. 720p. 34.95 (*0-06-016649-5*) HarperTrade.

—The Complete Tales of the City, 6 vols. 1991. pap. 66.00 o.p. (*0-06-092098-X*); 1989. 125.00 o.p. (*0-06-016433-6*) HarperTrade.

—Further Tales of the City. 1982. 176p. o.p. (*0-06-014991-4*); pap. 9.95 o.p. (*0-06-090916-1*) HarperCollins Pubs.

—Further Tales of the City. 1994. (Tales of the City Ser.: Vol. 3). 384p. pap. 14.00 (*0-06-092492-6*, Perennial); 1989. 368p. reprint ed. pap. 12.00 o.p. (*0-06-096406-5*, Perennial); Set. 1990. audio 16.00 o.s.i (*1-55994-301-7*, CPN 2186, HarperAudio) HarperTrade.

—Further Tales of the City. unabr. ed. 1995. (Tales of the City Ser.: Vol. 3). audio 70.00 (*0-7887-0254-8*, 94463E7) Recorded Bks., LLC.

—More Tales of the City. 1980. pap. 10.95 o.p. (*0-06-090726-6*); 1989. 320p. reprint ed. pap. 12.00 o.p. (*0-06-096405-7*) HarperCollins Pubs.

—More Tales of the City. 352p. 1998. (Tales of the City Ser.: Vol. 2). (Illus.). pap. 14.00 (*0-06-092938-3*); 1994. pap. 13.00 o.p. (*0-06-092479-9*) HarperTrade. (Perennial).

—The Night Listener: A Novel. 2000. (Illus.). 352p. 26.00 (*0-06-017143-X*, HarperCollins); audio 34.95 (*0-694-52144-2*, HarperAudio) HarperTrade.

—The Night Listener: A Novel. l.t. ed. 2001. (Thorndike Americana Ser.). 451p. 31.95 (*0-7862-3180-7*); pap. 28.95 (*0-7862-3181-5*) Thorndike Pr.

—Significant Others. 1987. pap. 9.95 o.p. (*0-06-096126-0*) HarperCollins Pubs.

—Significant Others. 1994. (Tales of the City Ser.: Vol. 5). 336p. pap. 14.00 (*0-06-092481-0*, Perennial); 1987. 19.95 o.p. (*0-06-055086-4*, Perennial); 1999. audio 18.00 o.s.i (*1-55994-300-9*, CPN 2185, HarperAudio); 1989. 384p. reprint ed. pap. 12.00 o.p. (*0-06-096408-1*, Perennial) HarperTrade.

—Sure of You. 1990. pap. 65.70 o.p. (*0-06-092034-3*) HarperCollins Pubs.

—Sure of You. 1994. (Tales of the City Ser.: Vol. 6). 272p. pap. 14.00 (*0-06-092484-5*, Perennial); 1989. 288p. 18.95 o.p. (*0-06-016164-7*, Perennial); 1990. (Tales of the City Ser.). 272p. reprint ed. 11.00 o.p. (*0-06-092033-5*, Perennial); Set. 1991. audio 15.95 o.s.i (*1-55994-299-1*, CPN 2184, HarperAudio) HarperTrade.

—Tales of the City. 1987. mass mkt. 3.50 o.s.i (*0-345-35190-8*); 1984. mass mkt. 2.95 o.s.i (*0-345-32037-9*); 1983. mass mkt. 2.75 o.s.i (*0-345-31170-1*); 1979. mass mkt. 2.50 o.s.i (*0-345-28422-4*) Ballantine Bks.

—Tales of the City. 1994. 384p. pap. 72.00 o.p. (*0-06-092493-4*); 1978. pap. 10.95 o.p. (*0-06-090654-5*); 1996. 384p. 18.00 o.p. (*0-06-018669-0*) HarperCollins Pubs.

—Tales of the City. 1990. audio 15.95; 1989. (Tales of the City Ser.: Vol. 1). 384p. pap. 14.00 (*0-06-096404-9*, Perennial); 1991. audio 18.00 o.s.i (*1-55994-203-7*, CPN 2162, HarperAudio); 1994. 384p. reprint ed. pap. 12.00 o.p. (*0-06-092480-2*, Perennial) HarperTrade.

—Tales of the City. 1994. 371p. lib. bdg. 33.00 o.p. (*0-8095-9139-1*) Millefleurs.

—Tales of the City. unabr. ed. 1994. audio 60.00 (*0-7887-0066-9*, 94322E7) Recorded Bks., LLC.

—28 Barbary Lane: A "Tales of the City" Omnibus. 2000. pap. 19.95 (*0-06-093771-8*); 1990. 768p. 34.95 (*0-06-016466-2*) HarperTrade.

McDougall, Ruth B. Tell Me a Story. 1985. (Illus.). 152p. (Orig.). pap. 7.95 (*0-89407-070-3*) Strawberry Hill Pr.

McGee, Marcus. Legal Thriller. 2000. 430p. 28.95 (*0-9673123-2-9*) McGee, Marcus Media.

McGoogan, Ken. Kerouac's Ghost. rev. ed. 1996. 192p. pap. text 12.99 (*1-895854-54-7*) Davies, Robert Publishing CAN. *Dist:* General Distribution Services, Inc.

McMahon, Neil. Blood Double. 2003. 336p. mass mkt. 6.99 (*0-06-103090-2*); 2002. 240p. 22.95 (*0-06-019766-8*) HarperCollins Pubs.

—Twice Dying. 2000. 288p. mass mkt. 6.99 (*0-06-109835-3*, HarperTorch) Morrow/Avon.

—Twice Dying: A Novel. 2000. xiii, 205p. 24.00 (*0-06-019364-6*) HarperCollins Pubs.

McMurtry, Larry. Somebody's Darling. unabr. collector's ed. 1986. audio 64.00 (*0-7366-0791-9*, 1743) Books on Tape, Inc.

—Somebody's Darling. 2002. 352p. pap. 14.00 (*0-684-85389-2*, Simon & Schuster) Simon & Schuster.

—Somebody's Darling. Grose, Bill, ed. 1991. 352p. mass mkt. 5.99 o.s.i (*0-671-74585-9*, Pocket) Simon & Schuster.

—Somebody's Darling. 1990. 416p. mass mkt. 5.50 (*0-671-72777-X*, Pocket); 1987. 352p. pap. 10.00 (*0-671-63319-8*, Simon & Schuster); 1978. 10.00 o.s.i (*0-671-24394-2*, Simon & Schuster) Simon & Schuster.

McNamara, Joseph D. Code 211 Blue. 1996. mass mkt. 5.99 o.s.i (*0-449-14894-7*, Fawcett) Ballantine Bks.

Meno, Joe. Tender As Hellfire. E-Book 22.95 (*0-312-26852-1*); 1999. 244p. 22.95 (*0-312-20051-X*) St. Martin's Pr.

Michaels, Melisa C. Through the Eyes of the Dead. 2000. (WWL Mystery Ser.: Vol. 370). 256p. mass mkt. (*0-373-26370-8*, 1-26370-6, Worldwide Library) Harlequin Enterprises, Ltd.

—Through the Eyes of the Dead. 1989. 192p. 17.95 o.p. (*0-8027-5718-9*) Walker & Co.

Miller, John & Smith, Tim, eds. San Francisco Thrillers: True Crimes & Dark Mysteries from the City by the Bay. 1995. (Illus.). 272p. pap. 14.95 o.p. (*0-8118-1043-7*) Chronicle Bks. LLC.

Miner, Valerie. Winter's Edge. 1997. 216p. (gr. 11-12). reprint ed. pap. 10.95 (*1-55861-150-9*) Feminist Pr. at The City Univ. of New York.

—Winter's Edge: A Novel. 1985. (Feminist Ser.). 184p. (Orig.). (C). 20.95 o.p. (*0-89594-176-7*) Crossing Pr., Inc., The.

Miss Giardino. 1987. pap. 7.95 o.p. (*0-931688-26-4*) Ata Bks.

Mohanraj, Mary Anne. Kathryn in the City. 2003. (Create Your Own Erotic Fantasy Ser.). 196p. pap. 12.00 (*1-59240-030-2*) Gothman Bks.

Moore, Christopher. Bloodsucking Friends: A Love Story. 1995. 300p. 23.00 o.p. (*0-684-81097-2*, Simon & Schuster) Simon & Schuster.

Moore, Elaine. Retribution: Madonna of the Dark, Book II. 2002. 248p. pap. 12.95 (*1-928704-19-0*, Authorlink Pr.) Authorlink.

Morris, Lynn & Morris, Gilbert. In the Twilight, in the Evening, 6. 1997. (Cheney Duvall, M. D. Ser.: Vol. 6). 320p. pap. 11.99 (*1-55661-427-6*) Bethany Hse. Pubs.

—In the Twilight, in the Evening. 1998. 23.95 (0-7862-1365-5, Five Star) Gale Group.

Mosley, Walter. Blue Light. l.t. ed. 1999. 27.95 (1-56895-639-8, Wheeler Publishing, Inc.) Gale Group.

—Blue Light. 1998. 304p. (YA). (gr. 8 up). 24.00 o.p. (0-316-57098-2) Little Brown & Co.

—Blue Light. 1999. 400p. reprint ed. mass mkt. 6.99 (0-446-60692-8, Aspect) Warner Bks., Inc.

Muller, Eddie. The Distance: A Crime Novel Introducing Billy Nichols. 2002. 304p. 25.00 (0-7432-1762-4); (Illus.). 25.00 (0-7432-1443-9) Simon & Schuster. (Scribner).

—Shadow Boxer. l.t. ed. 2003. 28.95 (1-58724-418-7, Wheeler Publishing, Inc.) Gale Group.

—Shadow Boxer: A Crime Novel Featuring Billy Nichols. 2003. (Illus.). 272p. 24.00 (0-7432-1444-7, Scribner) Simon & Schuster.

Muller, Marcia. Ask the Cards a Question. unabr. ed. 1996. (Sharon McCone Ser.). audio 36.00 (0-7366-3454-1, 4098) Books on Tape, Inc.

—Ask the Cards a Question: A Sharon McCone Mystery. l.t. ed. 1996. 239p. pap. 19.95 o.p. (0-7838-1480-1, Macmillan Reference USA) Gale Group.

—Ask the Cards a Question: A Sharon McCone Mystery. 1982. 168p. 10.95 o.p. (0-312-05653-2) St. Martin's Pr.

—Ask the Cards a Question: A Sharon McCone Mystery. 1990. 224p. reprint ed. mass mkt. 6.99 (0-445-40849-9) Warner Bks., Inc.

—Both Ends of the Night. unabr. ed. 1997. (Sharon McCone Ser.). audio 48.00 (0-7366-3802-4, 4473) Books on Tape, Inc.

—Both Ends of the Night. abr. ed. (Sharon Mccone Ser.). 1998. audio 7.99 o.p. (1-56740-250-X, 629, Paperback Nova Audio Bks.); 1997. audio 16.95 o.p. (1-56100-985-7, 1137); 1997. audio 73.25 o.p. (1-56100-834-6, 814, Unabridged Library Editions); 1997. audio 23.95 (1-56100-759-5, 51, Bookcassette) Brilliance Audio.

—Both Ends of the Night. l.t. ed. 1997. (Wheeler Large Print Book Ser.). pap. 24.95 (1-56895-463-8, Wheeler Publishing, Inc.) Gale Group.

—Both Ends of the Night. 1997. 368p. 22.50 o.p. (0-89296-622-X) Mysterious Pr.

—Both Ends of the Night. 1998. (Sharon McCone Mysteries Ser.). 384p. reprint ed. mass mkt. 6.99 (0-446-60550-6) Warner Bks., Inc.

—The Broken Promise Land. unabr. ed. 1996. (Sharon McCone Ser.). audio 64.00 (0-7366-3383-9, 4033) Books on Tape, Inc.

—The Broken Promise Land. abr. ed. (Sharon Mccone Ser.). 1997. audio 7.99 o.p. (1-56740-177-5, 630, Paperback Nova Audio Bks.); 1996. audio 16.95 o.p. (1-56100-956-3, 817, Nova Audio Bks.); 1996. audio 23.95 o.p. (1-56100-718-8, 53, Bookcassette); 1996. audio 73.25 o.p. (1-56100-343-3, 816, Unabridged Library Editions) Brilliance Audio.

—The Broken Promise Land. 1996. 82p. 22.95 o.s.i (0-89296-621-1) Mysterious Pr.

—The Broken Promise Land. 1997. (Sharon McCone Mysteries Ser.). 400p. reprint ed. mass mkt. 6.50 (0-446-60410-0) Warner Bks., Inc.

—The Cavalier in White. l.t. ed. 1990. 19.95 o.p. (0-7927-0633-1, C0594); pap. 17.95 o.p. (0-7927-0634-X) BBC Audiobooks America.

—The Cavalier in White. 1993. per. (0-373-83304-0, 1-83304-5); 1988. 224p. reprint ed. pap. (0-373-26008-3) Harlequin Enterprises, Ltd. (Harlequin Bks.).

—The Cavalier in White. 1986. 256p. 15.95 o.p. (0-312-12539-9) St. Martin's Pr.

—The Cheshire Cat's Eye: A Sharon McCone Mystery. unabr. ed. 1996. (Sharon McCone Ser.). audio 36.00 (0-7366-3490-8, 4130) Books on Tape, Inc.

—The Cheshire Cat's Eye: A Sharon McCone Mystery. l.t. ed. 1988. (Nightingale Ser.). 278p. pap. 12.95 o.p. (0-8161-4396-X, Macmillan Reference USA) Gale Group.

—The Cheshire Cat's Eye: A Sharon McCone Mystery. 1983. 160p. 10.95 o.p. (0-312-13175-5) St. Martin's Pr.

—The Cheshire Cat's Eye: A Sharon McCone Mystery. 1990. 224p. reprint ed. mass mkt. 6.99 (0-445-40850-2) Warner Bks., Inc.

—Dark Star. l.t. ed. 2000. 218p. 27.95 (1-57490-327-6, Beeler Large Print Bks.) Beeler, Thomas T. Publisher.

—Dark Star. 1993. per. (0-373-83308-3, 1-83308-6); 1990. 224p. mass mkt. (0-373-26058-X) Harlequin Enterprises, Ltd. (Harlequin Bks.).

—Dark Star. 1989. 15.95 o.p. (0-312-02897-0, Saint Martin's Minotaur) St. Martin's Pr.

—Edwin of the Iron Shoes. 1993. (Black Dagger Crime Ser.). 184p. 16.50 o.p. (0-7451-8617-3, Black Dagger) BBC Audiobooks America.

—Edwin of the Iron Shoes. unabr. ed. 1996. (Sharon McCone Ser.). audio 36.00 (0-7366-3408-8, 4054) Books on Tape, Inc.

—Edwin of the Iron Shoes. 1977. (McKay-Washburn Mystery Ser.). 7.95 o.p. (0-679-50782-5) McKay, David Co., Inc.

—Edwin of the Iron Shoes. 1978. (Crime Ser.). pap. 1.95 o.p. (0-14-004915-0, Penguin Bks.) Viking Penguin.

—Edwin of the Iron Shoes. 1990. 224p. reprint ed. mass mkt. 6.99 (0-445-40902-9) Warner Bks., Inc.

—Eye of the Storm. unabr. ed. 1998. (Sharon McCone Ser.). audio 56.00 (0-7366-4135-1, 4640) Books on Tape, Inc.

—Eye of the Storm. 1988. 15.95 o.p. (0-89296-269-0) Mysterious Pr.

—Eye of the Storm. 1989. 256p. reprint ed. mass mkt. 6.99 o.s.i (0-445-40625-9) Warner Bks., Inc.

—Games to Keep the Dark Away: A Sharon McCone Mystery. unabr. ed. 1997. (Sharon McCone Ser.). audio 36.00 (0-7366-3566-1, 4212) Books on Tape, Inc.

—Games to Keep the Dark Away: A Sharon McCone Mystery. l.t. ed. 1986. (Nightingale Ser.). 278p. 11.95 o.p. (0-8161-3903-2, Macmillan Reference USA) Gale Group.

—Games to Keep the Dark Away: A Sharon McCone Mystery. 2003. 320p. pap. 14.95 (0-312-31620-8, L. A. Weekly Bks.) St. Martin's Pr.

—Games to Keep the Dark Away: A Sharon McCone Mystery. 1990. reprint ed. mass mkt. 6.99 (0-445-40851-0) Warner Bks., Inc.

—Leave a Message for Willie: A Sharon McCone Mystery. unabr. ed. 1997. (Sharon McCone Ser.). audio 42.00 (0-7366-3779-6, 4452) Books on Tape, Inc.

—Leave a Message for Willie: A Sharon McCone Mystery. l.t. ed. 1995. 266p. pap. 20.95 o.p. (0-7838-1481-X, Macmillan Reference USA) Gale Group.

—Leave a Message for Willie: A Sharon McCone Mystery. 1984. 192p. 11.95 o.p. (0-312-47728-7) St. Martin's Pr.

—Leave a Message for Willie: A Sharon McCone Mystery. 1990. 224p. reprint ed. mass mkt. 6.99 (0-445-40900-2) Warner Bks., Inc.

—Listen to the Silence. 2000. 304p. 23.95 (0-89296-689-0) Mysterious Pr.

—McCone & Friends. 2000. 202p. (Illus.). (J). pap. 16.00 (1-885941-38-2); 40.00 o.p. (1-885941-37-4) Crippen & Landru, Pubs.

—Pennies on a Dead Woman's Eyes. 1992. 304p. 18.95 (0-89296-454-5) Mysterious Pr.

—Pennies on a Dead Woman's Eyes. 1993. 366p. reprint ed. mass mkt. 6.99 (0-446-40033-5) Warner Bks., Inc.

—The Shape of Dread. unabr. ed. 1999. audio 48.00 (0-7366-4455-5, 4900) Books on Tape, Inc.

—The Shape of Dread. 1989. 16.95 o.p. (0-89296-271-2) Mysterious Pr.

—The Shape of Dread. 1990. 288p. reprint ed. mass mkt. 6.99 (0-445-40916-9) Warner Bks., Inc.

—There Hangs the Knife. 1993. per. (0-373-83307-5, 1-83307-8); 1989. mass mkt. (0-373-26034-2) Harlequin Enterprises, Ltd. (Harlequin Bks.).

—There Hangs the Knife. 1990. 2.99 o.p. (0-517-05927-4) Random Hse. Value Publishing.

—There Hangs the Knife. 1988. 240p. 15.95 o.p. (0-312-01833-9, Saint Martin's Minotaur) St. Martin's Pr.

—There's Nothing to Be Afraid Of. unabr. ed. 1997. (Sharon McCone Ser.). audio 48.00 (0-7366-3780-X, 4453) Books on Tape, Inc.

—There's Nothing to Be Afraid Of. 1985. 256p. 14.95 o.p. (0-312-79955-1) St. Martin's Pr.

—There's Nothing to Be Afraid Of. 1990. 224p. reprint ed. mass mkt. 6.99 o.s.i (0-445-40901-0) Warner Bks., Inc.

—There's Something in a Sunday: A Sharon McCone Mystery. unabr. ed. 1998. (Sharon McCone Ser.). audio 48.00 (0-7366-4136-X, 4641) Books on Tape, Inc.

—There's Something in a Sunday: A Sharon McCone Mystery. 1989. 15.95 o.p. (0-89296-270-4) Mysterious Pr.

—There's Something in a Sunday: A Sharon McCone Mystery. 1990. 224p. reprint ed. mass mkt. 6.99 (0-445-40865-0) Warner Bks., Inc.

—Till the Butchers Cut Him Down: A Sharon McCone Mystery. 1994. 352p. 18.95 o.s.i (0-89296-455-3) Mysterious Pr.

—Till the Butchers Cut Him Down: A Sharon McCone Mystery. 1995. pap. (0-446-40034-3, Mysterious Pr. Paperback Bks.); 336p. reprint ed. mass mkt. 5.99 (0-446-60302-3) Warner Bks., Inc.

—Trophies & Dead Things: A Sharon McCowe Mystery. unabr. ed. 1999. audio 48.00 Books on Tape, Inc.

—Trophies & Dead Things: A Sharon McCowe Mystery. l.t. ed. 1991. (General Ser.). 379p. lib. bdg. 19.95 o.p. (0-8161-5134-2, Macmillan Reference USA) Gale Group.

—Trophies & Dead Things: A Sharon McCowe Mystery. 1990. 272p. 16.95 o.p. (0-89296-417-0) Mysterious Pr.

—Trophies & Dead Things: A Sharon McCowe Mystery. 1991. 272p. reprint ed. mass mkt. 5.99 o.s.i (0-446-40039-4) Warner Bks., Inc.

—A Walk Through the Fire. 1999. 362p. 23.00 o.s.i (0-89296-688-2) Mysterious Pr.

—Where Echoes Live. 1991. 17.95 o.p. (0-89296-418-9) Mysterious Pr.

—Where Echoes Live. 1992. 368p. reprint ed. mass mkt. 6.99 (0-446-40161-7) Warner Bks., Inc.

—While Other People Sleep. unabr. ed. 1999. (Sharon McCone Ser.). audio 48.00 (0-7366-4318-4, 4790) Books on Tape, Inc.

—While Other People Sleep. unabr. ed. 1998. (Sharon McCone Ser.). audio 25.95 (1-56740-061-2, 1, Bookcassette); audio 57.25 (1-56740-590-8, 1095, Unabridged Library Editions);Set. audio 17.95 o.p. (1-56740-786-2, 448, Nova Audio Bks.) Brilliance Audio.

—While Other People Sleep. 1998. (Sharon McCone Mysteries Ser.). 344p. 23.00 o.p. (0-89296-650-5) Mysterious Pr.

—While Other People Sleep. l.t. ed. 1998. (Mystery Ser.). 432p. 28.95 o.p. (0-7862-1615-8) Thorndike Pr.

—While Other People Sleep. 1999. 304p. reprint ed. mass mkt. 6.99 (0-446-60721-5) Warner Bks., Inc.

—A Wild & Lonely Place: A Sharon McCone Mystery. unabr. ed. 2000. (Sharon McCone Ser.: 16). audio 48.00 Books on Tape, Inc.

—A Wild & Lonely Place: A Sharon McCone Mystery. 1995. 300p. 19.95 o.s.i (0-89296-526-6) Mysterious Pr.

—A Wild & Lonely Place: A Sharon McCone Mystery. 1996. 336p. reprint ed. mass mkt. 6.99 (0-446-60328-7) Warner Bks., Inc.

—Wolf in the Shadows. 1993. 368p. 18.95 (0-89296-525-8) Mysterious Pr.

—Wolf in the Shadows. 1994. 384p. reprint ed. mass mkt. 5.50 (0-446-40383-0) Warner Bks., Inc.

Muller, Marcia & Pronzini, Bill. Double. unabr. ed. 1997. audio 64.00 (0-7366-3710-9, 4394) Books on Tape, Inc.

—Double. 1984. 288p. 13.95 o.p. (0-312-21807-9) St. Martin's Pr.

—Double. 1995. 288p. reprint ed. mass mkt. 5.50 o.s.i (0-446-40413-6) Warner Bks., Inc.

Mulligan, John. Shopping Cart Soldiers. 1997. 239p. 22.95 (1-880684-48-9) Curbstone Pr.

—Shopping Cart Soldiers. 1999. 256p. pap. 12.00 (0-684-85605-0, Touchstone) Simon & Schuster.

Nava, Michael. Goldenboy. 2003. (Henry Rios Mystery Ser.). 216p. pap. 12.95 (1-55583-829-4, Alyson Bks.) Alyson Pubns.

—The Little Death. 1986. 165p. pap. 7.95 o.p. (0-932870-96-1) Alyson Pubns.

—The Little Death: A Henry Rios Mystery. 2003. (Illus.). 168p. pap. 12.95 (1-55583-830-8, Alyson Bks.) Alyson Pubns.

Nelson, Curt. Darkstar. 2001. 390p. pap. 22.99 (0-7388-1825-9); text 32.99 (0-7388-1824-0) Xlibris Corp.

Nemec, David. Stonesifer. 2001. 276p. pap. 25.00 (1-885003-19-6) Reed, Robert D. Pubs.

Ng, Fae M. Bone: A Novel. 1993. 208p. (J). 19.95 o.p. (1-56282-944-0) Hyperion Pr.

—Bone: Novel, A. 1994. 208p. reprint ed. pap. 12.95 (0-06-097592-X, Perennial) HarperTrade.

Nichols, Linda. Handyman. 2000. 272p. mass mkt. 6.99 (0-440-23542-1) Dell Publishing.

—Handyman. abr. ed. 2000. audio 25.00 (0-694-52266-X, HarperAudio) HarperTrade.

—Handyman. l.t. ed. 2000. (Americana Ser.). 431p. 28.95 (0-7862-2503-3) Thorndike Pr.

Nisbet, Jim. Prelude to a Scream. 1997. 400p. 4.50 (0-7867-0408-X, Carroll & Graf Pubs.) Avalon Publishing Group.

—The Price of the Ticket. 2003. 230p. 30.00 (0-939767-43-0) McMillan, Dennis Pubns.

Norris, Frank. McTeague. 1976. lib. bdg. 18.95 o.s.i (0-89968-071-2, Lightyear Pr.) Buccaneer Bks., Inc.

—McTeague. E-Book 2.49 (1-58627-817-7) Electric Umbrella Publishing.

—McTeague. Collins, Carvel, ed. 1950. 343p. (C). pap. text 25.00 (0-03-009250-7) Harcourt College Pubs.

—McTeague. 2002. 312p. 96.99 (1-4043-1838-0); per. 91.99 (1-4043-1839-9) IndyPublish.com.

—McTeague. 1999. 201p. 14.95 (1-57002-135-X) University Publishing Hse., Inc.

—McTeague. 2004. 272p. pap. 5.95 (0-486-43408-7) Dover Pubns., Inc.

—McTeague. 2003. 368p. mass mkt. 7.95 (0-451-52891-3); 1969. mass mkt. 0.60 o.p. (0-451-50201-9); 1969. mass mkt. 0.75 o.p. (0-451-50381-3); 1969. mass mkt. 0.95 o.p. (0-451-50479-8); 1964. mass mkt. 1.25 o.p. (0-451-50752-5); 1964. mass mkt. 1.50 o.p. (0-451-50957-9); 1964. mass mkt. 1.75 o.p. (0-451-51119-0); 1964. mass mkt. 1.95 o.p. (0-451-51303-7); 1964. mass mkt. 2.25 o.p. (0-451-51574-9); 1964. mass mkt. 2.50 o.p. (0-451-51790-3); 1964. mass mkt. 2.75 o.p. (0-451-51860-8); 1964. mass mkt. 2.95 o.p. (0-451-52049-1); 1964. mass mkt. 3.50 o.p. (0-451-52178-1) NAL. (Signet Classics).

—McTeague. unabr. ed. 1998. (Classic Books on Cassettes Collection). audio 53.95 (1-55685-273-8) Audio Bk. Contractors, Inc.

—McTeague. unabr. ed. 1993. audio 69.95 (0-7861-0462-7, 1414) Blackstone Audio Bks., Inc.

—McTeague. unabr. ed. 1990. audio 79.95 (1-58081-104-3, RDP9) L. A. Theatre Works.

—McTeague. unabr. ed. 1997. 201p. reprint ed. pap. 14.95 o.p. (1-57002-056-6) University Publishing Hse., Inc.

—McTeague: A Story of California. 1971. 340p. lib. bdg. 20.00 (0-8376-0406-0) Bentley Pubs.

—McTeague: A Story of San Francisco. 1980. mass mkt. 2.25 o.s.i (0-449-30810-3, Fawcett) Ballantine Bks.

—McTeague: A Story of San Francisco. 1990. (Vintage-Library of America ). 324p. pap. 10.50 o.p. (0-679-73273-X, Vintage) Knopf Publishing Group.

—McTeague: A Story of San Francisco. 1964. mass mkt. 3.95 o.p. (0-451-52281-8); 352p. mass mkt. 6.95 o.s.i (0-451-52421-7, Signet Classics) NAL.

—McTeague: A Story of San Francisco. Pizer, Donald, ed. 1978. (C). pap. text o.p. (0-393-09136-8); 1977. 12.95 o.p. (0-393-04460-2) Norton, W. W. & Co., Inc.

—McTeague: A Story of San Francisco. Loving, Jerome, ed. 2001. (Oxford World's Classics Ser.). 384p. pap. 10.95 (0-19-284059-2) Oxford Univ. Pr., Inc.

—McTeague: A Story of San Francisco. Loving, Jerome, ed. & intro. by. 1996. 372p. pap. 9.95 o.p. (0-19-282356-6) Oxford Univ. Pr., Inc.

—McTeague: A Story of San Francisco. 2002. (Modern Library Classics). 544p. pap. 10.95 (0-375-76129-2) Random Hse., Inc.

—McTeague: A Story of San Francisco. 1992. (BCL1-PS American Literature Ser.). 442p. reprint ed. lib. bdg. 99.00 (0-7812-6809-5) Reprint Services Corp.

—McTeague: A Story of San Francisco. 1988. 18.75 o.p. (0-8446-2663-5) Smith, Peter Pub., Inc.

—McTeague: A Story of San Francisco. E-Book 5.00 (0-7410-0477-1) SoftBook Pr.

—McTeague: A Story of San Francisco. 1981. 12.05 o.p. (0-606-03855-8) Turtleback Bks.

—McTeague: A Story of San Francisco. Starr, Kevin, ed. & intro. by. 1994. (Penguin Twentieth-Century Classics Ser.). 496p. 10.95 (0-14-018769-3, Penguin Classics) Viking Penguin.

—McTeague: A Story of San Francisco. Starr, Kevin, ed. 1982. (American Library). 496p. pap. 9.95 o.p. (0-14-039017-0, Penguin Classics) Viking Penguin.

—McTeague: A Story of San Francisco: an Authoritative Text, Contexts, Criticism. Pizer, Donald, ed. 2nd ed. 1996. (Critical Editions Ser.). (C). pap. text 9.00 (0-393-97013-2) Norton, W. W. & Co., Inc.

Obenzinger, Hilton. Cannibal Eliot & the Lost Histories of San Francisco. 1993. 256p. (Orig.). pap. 12.95 (1-56279-047-1) Mercury Hse.

Offit, Avodah K. Virtual Love. 1994. 317p. 22.00 (0-671-87436-5, Simon & Schuster) Simon & Schuster.

O'Marie, Carol Anne. Advent of Dying: A Sister Mary Helen Mystery. 1987. 256p. mass mkt. 4.99 o.s.i (0-440-10052-6); 1986. 288p. 14.95 o.p. (0-385-29506-5, Delacorte Pr.) Dell Publishing.

—The Corporal Works of Murder. 2002. (Sister Mary Helen Mystery Ser.). 208p. 22.95 (0-312-20917-7, Saint Martin's Minotaur) St. Martin's Pr.

—Death Goes on Retreat. unabr. ed. 2001. (Sister Mary Helen Mystery Ser.). audio 29.95 (1-57270-187-0, N61187u, Audio Editions Mystery Masters) Audio Partners Publishing Corp.

—Death Goes on Retreat. unabr. ed. 2000. (Sister Mary Helen Mystery Ser.). audio 49.95 (0-7927-2213-2, CSL 102) Chivers Audio Bks. GBR. *Dist:* BBC Audiobooks America.

—Death Goes on Retreat: A Sister Mary Helen Mystery. 1996. 272p. mass mkt. 5.50 o.s.i (0-440-21610-9) Dell Publishing.

—Death of an Angel: A Sister Mary Helen Mystery. unabr. ed. 1998. audio 39.95 (0-7861-1452-5, 2314) Blackstone Audio Bks., Inc.

—Death of an Angel: A Sister Mary Helen Mystery. l.t. ed. 1997. pap. 23.95 (1-56895-442-5, Wheeler Publishing, Inc.) Gale Group.

—Death of an Angel: A Sister Mary Helen Mystery. 1996. 256p. 21.95 (0-312-15107-1, Saint Martin's Minotaur); 3rd ed. 1997. 304p. mass mkt. 6.50 (0-312-96396-3, St. Martin's Paperbacks) St. Martin's Pr.

—Death Takes up a Collection: A Sister Mary Helen Mystery. (Sister Mary Helen Mystery Ser.: Vol. 8). 1998. 224p. 21.95 o.p. (0-312-19256-8, Saint Martin's Minotaur); 1999. 256p. reprint ed. mass mkt. 6.50 (0-312-97193-1, St. Martin's Paperbacks) St. Martin's Pr.

SAN FRANCISCO (CALIF.)—FICTION

BOWKER'S GUIDE TO CHARACTERS IN FICTION 2004

Settings

—Death Takes up a Collection: A Sister Mary Helen Mystery. l.t. ed. 1999. (Mystery Ser.). 347p. 27.95 (0-7862-1663-8) Thorndike Pr.

—The Missing Madonna: A Sister Mary Helen Mystery. 1989. 272p. reprint ed. mass mkt. 4.99 o.s.i (0-440-20473-9) Dell Publishing.

—The Missing Madonna: A Sister Mary Helen Mystery. l.t. ed. 1990. (General Ser.). 371p. lib. bdg. 20.95 o.p. (0-8161-4814-7, Macmillan Reference USA) Gale Group.

—Murder in Ordinary Time: A Sister Mary Helen Mystery. 256p. 1992. mass mkt. 4.99 o.s.i (0-440-21353-3); 1991. 18.00 o.s.i (0-385-30226-6, Delacorte Pr.) Dell Publishing.

—Murder in Ordinary Time: A Sister Mary Helen Mystery. l.t. ed. 1992. (General Ser.). 352p. lib. bdg. 20.95 o.p. (0-8161-5425-2); lib. bdg. 16.95 o.p. (0-8161-5426-0) Gale Group. (Macmillan Reference USA).

—Murder Makes a Pilgrimage: A Sister Mary Helen Mystery, unabr. ed. 2000. audio 69.95 (0-7927-2325-2, CSL 214, Chivers Sound Library) BBC Audiobooks America.

—A Novena for Murder: A Sister Mary Helen Mystery. 1986. 192p. mass mkt. 4.99 o.s.i (0-440-16469-9) Dell Publishing.

—A Novena for Murder: A Sister Mary Helen Mystery. 1984. 224p. 12.95 o.s.i (0-684-18087-1, Macmillan Reference USA) Gale Group.

—Requiem at the Refuge: A Sister Mary Helen Mystery. 2000. (Sister Mary Helen Mystery Ser.). 276p. 23.95 (0-312-20906-1, Saint Martin's Minotaur) St. Martin's Pr.

—Requiem at the Refuge: A Sister Mary Helen Mystery. l.t. ed. 2000. (Mystery Ser.). 421p. 29.95 (0-7862-2844-X) Thorndike Pr.

Otto, Whitney. A Collection of Beauties at the Height of Their Popularity. 2002. E-Book 19.00 (1-58836-154-3) Random Hse., Inc.

—A Collection of Beauties at the Height of Their Popularity: A Novel. 2003. (Illus.). 320p. pap. 12.95 (0-8129-6681-3) Random House Adult Trade Publishing Group.

Outland, Orland. Death Wore a Fabulous New Fragrance. 1998. (Doan & Binky Mysteries Ser.). 208p. mass mkt. 5.99 o.s.i (0-425-16197-8, Prime Crime) Berkley Publishing Group.

—Death Wore a Smart Little Outfit. 1997. 224p. mass mkt. 5.50 o.s.i (0-425-15855-1, Prime Crime) Berkley Publishing Group.

—Every Man for Himself. 2000. 272p. pap. 13.00 (1-57566-553-0, Kensington Bks.) Kensington Publishing Corp.

Parkinson, T. L. The Man Upstairs. 240p. 1992. pap. 9.00 o.p. (0-452-26847-8, Plume); 1991. 18.95 o.p. (0-525-93349-2, Dutton) Dutton/Plume.

Patterson, James. Violets Are Blue. 2001. 400p. 27.95 o.p. (0-316-69323-5); 432p. 27.95 o.p. (0-316-68656-5) Little Brown & Co.

—Violets Are Blue. abr. ed. 2001. audio 25.98 (1-58621-195-1); audio 29.98 (1-58621-196-X); audio 32.98 (1-58621-197-8); audio 39.98 (1-58621-198-6) Time Warner AudioBooks.

—Violets Are Blue. 2001. pap. 16.00 o.s.i (0-446-67860-0) Warner Bks., Inc.

—1st to Die. 2001. 432p. 26.95 o.p. (0-316-66600-9) Little Brown & Co.

—1st to Die. l.t. ed. 2001. 464p. 32.95 (0-7862-3291-9); pap. 29.95 (0-7862-3292-7); (0-7540-1631-5); (0-7540-2486-5) Thorndike Pr.

—1st to Die. 2001. E-Book 4.95 (0-7595-8434-6) Time Warner Bk. Group.

—1st to Die. 2001. 432p. pap. 16.00 (0-446-67842-2); 2002. 488p. reprint ed. mass mkt. 7.99 (0-446-61003-8) Warner Bks., Inc.

—1st to Die. 2001. E-Book 4.95 (0-7595-6427-2) ereads.com.

—2nd Chance. 2002. 400p. pap. 16.00 (0-446-67876-7) Warner Bks., Inc.

Patterson, James & Gross, Andrew. 2nd Chance. 2002. 400p. 26.95 o.p. (0-316-69320-0); 512p. 26.95 o.p. (0-316-69597-1) Little Brown & Co.

—2nd Chance. abr. ed. 2002. audio 25.98 (1-58621-232-X); audio 29.98 (1-58621-233-8); audio 32.98 (1-58621-234-6); audio 39.98 (1-58621-235-4) Time Warner AudioBooks.

—2nd Chance. 2003. 432p. reprint ed. mass mkt. 7.99 (0-446-61279-0) Warner Bks., Inc.

—3rd Degree. 2004. 352p. 26.95 (0-316-60357-0); 400p. 27.95 (0-316-74386-0) Little Brown & Co.

—3rd Degree. unabr. ed. 2004. audio 26.98 (1-58621-598-1); audio compact disk 31.98 (1-58621-599-X) Time Warner AudioBooks.

—3rd Degree. 2004. pap. 16.00 (0-446-69258-1) Warner Bks., Inc.

Patterson, Richard North. Degree of Guilt. 1998. pap. 7.99 (0-345-91454-6); 1997. pap. 12.00 o.s.i (0-345-41811-5); 1992. mass mkt. o.s.i (0-345-38408-3); 1993. 544p. reprint ed. mass mkt. 7.99 (0-345-38184-X) Ballantine Bks.

—Degree of Guilt. unabr. collector's ed. 1994. audio 104.00 (0-7366-2612-3, 3354) Books on Tape, Inc.

—Degree of Guilt, Set. abr. ed. 1994. audio 8.99 o.s.i (0-679-43409-7, RH Audio) Random Hse. Audio Publishing Group.

—Degree of Guilt. l.t. ed. 1993. 25.00 o.s.i (0-679-42211-0) Random Hse., Inc.

—Eyes of a Child. 1998. pap. 7.99 (0-345-91463-5); 1997. pap. 12.00 o.s.i (0-345-41813-1); 1995. 576p. mass mkt. 7.99 (0-345-38613-2); 1995. mass mkt. 6.99 o.s.i (0-345-40007-0); 1994. mass mkt. o.p. (0-345-39526-3) Ballantine Bks.

—Eyes of a Child. abr. ed. 2003. audio compact disk 14.99 (0-7393-0377-5, RH Audio Price-Less); 1995. audio 17.00 o.s.i (0-679-43952-8, RH Audio); Set. 1997. audio 8.99 o.s.i (0-679-46021-7, RH Audio) Random Hse. Audio Publishing Group.

—Eyes of a Child. l.t. ed. 1995. pap. 23.00 o.s.i (0-679-76031-8) Random Hse., Inc.

Peak, John. Mortal Judgments. E-Book 23.95 (0-312-26461-5); 1999. 352p. 23.95 o.p. (0-312-19837-X) St. Martin's Pr.

Peak, John A. M & M: A Thriller. 2002. 320p. 24.95 (0-312-27674-5, Saint Martin's Minotaur) St. Martin's Pr.

—Spare Change. 1994. 512p. 24.95 o.p. (0-312-11071-5, Saint Martin's Minotaur) St. Martin's Pr.

Peart, Jane. Circle of Love. l.t. ed. 2002. (Christian Romance Ser.). 263p. 26.95 (0-7862-4110-1) Gale Group.

—Circle of Love. 1999. (Steeple Hill Love Inspired Ser.). 238p. per. (0-373-87093-0, 1-87093-0, Harlequin Bks.) Harlequin Enterprises, Ltd.

Pella, Judith. Blind Faith. 1996. (Portraits Ser.). 304p. pap. 8.99 o.p. (1-55661-880-8) Bethany Hse. Pubs.

—Blind Faith. l.t. ed. 2002. 581p. 26.95 o.p. (0-7862-4011-3) Gale Group.

Pence, Joanne. Cook in Time. 1999. (Angie Amalfi Mysteries Ser.). 352p. mass mkt. 6.99 (0-06-104454-7) HarperCollins Pubs.

—Cooking Most Deadly. 1996. (Angie Amalfi Mysteries Ser.). 256p. mass mkt. 6.50 (0-06-104395-8, HarperTorch) Morrow/Avon.

—Cooking up Trouble. 1995. (Angie Amalfi Mysteries Ser.). 320p. mass mkt. 6.99 (0-06-108200-7, HarperTorch) Morrow/Avon.

—Cook's Night Out. 1998. (Angie Amalfi Mysteries Ser.). 304p. mass mkt. 5.99 (0-06-104396-6) HarperCollins Pubs.

—Cooks Overboard. 1998. (Angie Amalfi Mysteries Ser.: Vol. 6). 304p. mass mkt. 5.99 (0-06-104453-9, HarperTorch) Morrow/Avon.

—Something's Cooking. 650th ed. 1993. (Angie Amalfi Mysteries Ser.). 336p. mass mkt. 6.50 (0-06-108096-9, HarperTorch) Morrow/Avon.

—Too Many Cooks. 1994. (Angie Amalfi Mysteries Ser.). 352p. mass mkt. 6.50 (0-06-108199-X, HarperTorch) Morrow/Avon.

Perison, Eben Paul. The Seventh Sin. 2000. 304p. mass mkt. 6.99 o.s.i (0-451-40912-4, Onyx) NAL.

Perkins, Michael C. Dark Matter. 2001. 256p. pap. 7.95 (1-56201-233-9, Blue Moon Bks.) Avalon Publishing Group.

Phillips, Claire. Black Market Babies. 1998. 182p. pap. 10.00 (0-9664488-0-4) Eleventh Hour Press.

Phillips, Clyde. Blindsided: A Mystery. 2000. 320p. 24.00 (0-688-17154-0, Morrow, William & Co.) Morrow/Avon.

—Fall from Grace: A Noir Thriller. 1998. 320p. 24.00 o.p. (0-688-15744-0, Morrow, William & Co.) Morrow/Avon.

—Fall from Grace: A Noir Thriller. 1999. 448p. reprint ed. pap. 6.50 (0-671-03428-6, Pocket) Simon & Schuster.

—Sacrifice. 2003. 320p. 24.95 (0-06-621237-5, Morrow, William & Co.) Morrow/Avon.

Pincus, Elizabeth. The Hangdog Hustle. 1995. (Neil Fury Ser.). 205p. (Orig.). pap. 9.95 (1-883523-05-2) Spinsters Ink Bks.

—The Solitary Twist. 1993. (Neil Fury Ser.). 225p. (Orig.). pap. 9.95 (0-933216-93-9) Spinsters Ink Bks.

—The Two Bit Tango. 1992. (Neil Fury Ser.). (Illus.). 193p. (Orig.). pap. 9.95 (0-933216-88-2) Spinsters Ink Bks.

Plate, Peter. The Angels of Catastrophe. 2001. 256p. 22.95 (1-58322-050-X); pap. 13.00 (1-58322-063-1) Seven Stories Pr.

—One Foot off the Gutter: Seven Stories. 1995. 200p. (Orig.). pap. 13.00 o.p. (1-884615-11-2) Incommunicado Pr.

—One Foot off the Gutter: Seven Stories. 2001. 184p. (Orig.). pap. 13.00 (1-58322-259-6) Seven Stories Pr.

—Police & Thieves: A Novel. 2002. 208p. pap. 13.00 (1-58322-482-3); 1999. 192p. text 20.00 (1-888363-95-9) Seven Stories Pr.

—Snitch Factory. 2001. 184p. pap. 13.00 (1-58322-258-8) Seven Stories Pr.

Poverman, C. E. On the Edge. 1997. 311p. 22.95 (0-86538-087-2) Ontario Review Pr.

—On the Edge. 1999. 368p. mass mkt. 6.99 (0-312-97089-7, St. Martin's Paperbacks) St. Martin's Pr.

Pronzini, Bill. Bindlestiff. 1983. 208p. 11.95 o.p. (0-312-07864-1) St. Martin's Pr.

—Bleeders. l.t. ed. 2002. 352p. 30.45 (0-7862-4119-5) Gale Group.

—Blowback. 1983. 149p. reprint ed. pap. 4.95 o.p. (0-88150-034-8) Countryman Pr.

—Blowback. 1977. 6.95 o.p. (0-394-40793-8) Random Hse., Inc.

—Blue Lonesome. l.t. ed. 2002. (Large Print Ser.). 28.95 (1-57490-453-1) Beeler, Thomas T. Publisher.

—Blue Lonesome. 240p. 1995. 21.95 o.p. (0-8027-3268-2); 1999. reprint ed. pap. 8.95 (0-8027-7561-6) Walker & Co.

—Bones. l.t. ed. 1991. 21.95 o.p. (0-7927-0937-3, CH0147); pap. 19.95 o.p. (0-7927-0938-1, CS0244) BBC Audiobooks America.

—Bones. 1985. (Nameless Detective Ser.). 224p. 12.95 o.p. (0-312-08769-1, 087691) St. Martin's Pr.

—Boobytrap: A "Nameless Detective" Mystery. 1998. (Nameless Detective Mystery Ser.). 256p. 23.00 (0-7867-0505-1, Carroll & Graf Pubs.) Avalon Publishing Group.

—Boobytrap: A "Nameless Detective" Mystery. unabr. ed. 1999. ("Nameless Detective" Mystery Ser.). audio 54.95 (0-7927-2269-8, CSL158, Chivers Sound Library) BBC Audiobooks America.

—Boobytrap: A "Nameless Detective" Mystery. l.t. ed. 1999. (Mystery Ser.). 317p. 28.95 (0-7862-1718-9) Thorndike Pr.

—Breakdown. l.t. ed. 1992. 19.95 o.p. (0-7927-1050-9); pap. 17.95 o.p. (0-7927-1051-7) BBC Audiobooks America.

—Breakdown. 1991. 256p. mass mkt. 4.50 o.s.i (0-440-21157-3) Dell Publishing.

—Carpenter & Quincannon, Professional Detective Services. 1998. 203p. 40.00 o.p. (1-885941-24-2) Crippen & Landru, Pubs.

—Crazybone: A "Nameless Detective" Mystery. l.t. ed. 2000. (Mystery Ser.). 317p. 29.95 (0-7862-2694-3) Thorndike Pr.

—Deadfall. 1986. 272p. 15.95 o.p. (0-312-18525-1) St. Martin's Pr.

—Demons: A "Nameless Detective" Mystery. 1994. 288p. mass mkt. 4.99 o.s.i (0-440-21118-2) Dell Publishing.

—Demons: A "Nameless Detective" Mystery. l.t. ed. 1994. 65.95 o.p. (0-7862-9982-7, Macmillan Reference USA) Gale Group.

—Dragonfire: A "Nameless Detective" Mystery. 1982. 208p. 10.95 o.p. (0-312-21893-1) St. Martin's Pr.

—Dragonfire & Casefile. 1990. (Nameless Detective Ser.). 576p. reprint ed. pap. 5.95 (1-877961-95-7) Knightsbridge Publishing.

—Epitaphs: A "Nameless Detective" Mystery. 1993. 304p. mass mkt. 4.99 o.s.i (0-440-21117-4); 1992. 240p. 19.00 o.s.i (0-385-30504-4, Delacorte Pr.) Dell Publishing.

—Hardcase. unabr. ed. 2000. (Nameless Detective Mystery Ser.). audio 49.95 (0-7927-2215-9, CSL 104) Chivers Audio Bks. GBR. *Dist:* BBC Audiobooks America.

—Hardcase. 1996. 288p. mass mkt. 5.50 o.s.i (0-440-22149-8) Dell Publishing.

—Hoodwink: A "Nameless Detective" Mystery. l.t. ed. 1990. pap. 17.95 o.p. (0-7927-0193-3, C0242) BBC Audiobooks America.

—Hoodwink: A "Nameless Detective" Mystery. 1981. 238p. 10.95 o.p. (0-312-38969-8) St. Martin's Pr.

—Illusions: A "Nameless Detective" Mystery. 1997. 256p. 23.00 o.p. (0-7867-0403-9, Carroll & Graf Pubs.) Avalon Publishing Group.

—Illusions: A "Nameless Detective" Mystery. unabr. ed. 2000. (Nameless Detective Mystery Ser.). audio 49.95 (0-7927-2234-5, CSL 123) Chivers Audio Bks. GBR. *Dist:* BBC Audiobooks America.

—Illusions: A "Nameless Detective" Mystery. 1999. 254p. lib. bdg. 26.95 (0-7351-0222-8) Replica Bks.

—Jackpot. 1990. 240p. reprint ed. mass mkt. 3.95 o.s.i (0-440-20821-1) Dell Publishing.

—Jackpot. l.t. ed. 1991. (General Ser.). 342p. lib. bdg. 20.95 (0-8161-5037-0, Macmillan Reference USA) Gale Group.

—Labyrinth. 2001. 186p. pap. 12.95 (1-931755-01-9) Mystery Vault, Inc.

—Labyrinth. 1980. 8.95 o.p. (0-312-46352-9) St. Martin's Pr.

—The Nameless Detective: Dragonfire-Bindlestiff. 1990. pap. 5.95 (1-877961-15-9) Knightsbridge Publishing.

—The Nameless Detective: Hoodwink & Scattershot. 1990. 560p. reprint ed. pap. 5.95 (1-877961-94-9) Knightsbridge Publishing.

—The Nameless Detective: Labyrinth & Bones. 1990. 560p. pap. 5.95 (1-877961-92-2) Knightsbridge Publishing.

—Nightshades: A "Nameless Detective" Mystery. 1984. 208p. 11.95 o.p. (0-312-57338-3) St. Martin's Pr.

—Quarry: A "Nameless Detective" Mystery. l.t. ed. 1992. 22.95 o.p. (0-7927-1392-3); pap. 20.95 o.p. (0-7927-1391-5) BBC Audiobooks America.

—Quarry: A "Nameless Detective" Mystery. 1992. 224p. mass mkt. 4.99 o.s.i (0-440-21116-6) Dell Publishing.

—Quicksilver: A "Nameless Detective" Mystery. 1984. 192p. 11.95 o.p. (0-312-66081-2) St. Martin's Pr.

—Scattershot: A "Nameless Detective" Mystery. l.t. ed. 1989. 18.95 o.p. (1-55504-833-1, 296) BBC Audiobooks America.

—Scattershot: A "Nameless Detective" Mystery. 1983. 176p. pap. 5.95 o.p. (0-312-70047-4, Saint Martin's Griffin); 1982. 182p. 10.95 o.p. (0-312-70046-6) St. Martin's Pr.

—Shackles: A "Nameless Detective" Mystery. 1988. 272p. 16.95 o.p. (0-312-01818-5, Saint Martin's Minotaur) St. Martin's Pr.

—The Snatch. 1984. (Nameless Detective Mystery Ser.). reprint ed. pap. 4.95 o.p. (0-88150-021-6) Countryman Pr.

—Spadework: A Collection of "Nameless Detective" Stories. 1996. 192p. pap. 16.00 (1-885941-07-2); 30.00 o.p. (1-885941-06-4) Crippen & Landru, Pubs.

—Undercurrent. 1984. 213p. pap. 4.95 o.p. (0-88150-033-X) Countryman Pr.

—The Vanished. 1984. (Nameless Detective Mystery Ser.). reprint ed. pap. 4.95 o.p. (0-88150-022-4) Countryman Pr.

—The Vanished. 1974. pap. 0.95 o.p. (0-671-77714-9, Pocket) Simon & Schuster.

—The Vanished. l.t. ed. 1999. (G. K. Hall Nightingale Ser.). 236p. pap. 20.95 (0-7838-8766-3) Thorndike Pr.

Pronzini, Bill & Wilcox, Collin. Two-Spot. 1993. 272p. mass mkt. 12.95 (0-7867-0042-4, Carroll & Graf Pubs.) Avalon Publishing Group.

—Two-Spot. 1978. 8.95 o.p. (0-399-12129-3) Putnam Publishing Group, The.

Racina, Thom. Snow Angel. 1996. 304p. 23.95 o.s.i (0-525-94030-8) Dutton/Plume.

—Snow Angel. 1997. 416p. mass mkt. 6.99 (0-451-18599-4, Signet Bks.) NAL.

Raphael, Neil & Raphael, Ray. Comic Cops. 1992. 182p. (Orig.). (J). (gr. 4-8). pap. 6.95 (1-881102-13-0) Real Bks.

Ray, Francis. The Turning Point. 2001. 432p. mass mkt. 6.99 (0-312-97862-6, St. Martin's Paperbacks) St. Martin's Pr.

Reed, Paul. Vertical Intercourse. 2001. 304p. pap. 16.00 (1-892723-06-9) Black Bks.

Reidinger, Paul. Good Boys. 272p. 1994. pap. 10.95 o.p. (0-452-27220-3, Plume); 1993. 20.00 o.p. (0-525-93616-5, Dutton) Dutton/Plume.

Rivers, Francine. Redeeming Love. 1991. 432p. mass mkt. 3.99 o.s.i (0-553-29368-0) Bantam Bks.

—Redeeming Love. l.t. ed. 1993. 670p. lib. bdg. 23.95 o.p. (0-8161-5823-1, Macmillan Reference USA) Gale Group.

—Redeeming Love. 2000. 464p. pap. 13.99 o.p. (1-57673-186-3, Multnomah Bks.) Multnomah Pubs., Inc.

Roberts, Lora. Murder Follows Money. 2000. (Liz Sullivan Mysteries Ser.). 240p. mass mkt. 6.50 o.s.i (0-449-00539-9, Fawcett) Ballantine Bks.

—Murder Follows Money. l.t. ed. 2001. 262p. pap. 24.95 (0-7838-9591-7, Macmillan Reference USA) Gale Group.

Robinson, Frank M., et al. Waiting. 1999. 303p. 23.95 (0-312-86652-6, Tor Bks.) Doherty, Tom Assocs., LLC.

Russo, Richard Paul. Carlucci 3 in 1. 2003. 624p. pap. 16.00 (0-441-01054-7) Ace Bks.

Saban, Cheryl. The Sins of the Mother. 1997. 256p. 19.95 o.p. (0-7871-1268-2) NewStar Media, Inc.

Sanders, Evelin. A Rainbow High. 1997. (YA). (gr. 9 up). pap. 9.99 (0-88092-345-8) Royal Fireworks Publishing Co.

Santora, The Good Daughter. 2002. 320p. per. 14.95 (0-9712357-0-8) Xipactli Publishing.

Sawyer, Meryl. A Kiss in the Dark. l.t. ed. 1995. 605p. 23.95 o.p. (0-7838-1371-6, Macmillan Reference USA) Gale Group.

Saxton, Alexander. Bright Web in the Darkness. 1997. (California Fiction Ser.). 312p. pap. text 15.95 (0-520-20931-1) Univ. of California Pr.

Schermerhorn, James. Night of the Cat. 1993. 224p. 18.95 o.p. (0-312-09887-1, Saint Martin's Minotaur) St. Martin's Pr.

Schneider, Bart. Blue Bossa. 240p. 1999. 12.95 (0-14-027570-3); 1998. 24.95 o.p. (0-670-87695-X) Viking Penguin.

—Secret Love. 2001. 288p. 25.95 o.s.i (0-670-89492-3, Viking) Viking Penguin.

Scholten, Jenny. Slay Me Tender. 2001. (Aubrey Lyle Mystery Ser.). 200p. pap. 11.95 (1-892281-15-5) New Victoria Pubs., Inc.

Seth, Vikram. The Golden Gate. 1987. 320p. pap. 5.95 o.p. (0-394-75063-2, Vintage) Knopf Publishing Group.

—The Golden Gate. 1991. 320p. pap. 14.00 (0-679-73457-0) Knopf, Alfred A. Inc.

Sheldon, Sidney. Nothing Lasts Forever. 1994. 398p. 23.00 o.p. (0-688-08491-5, Morrow, William & Co.) Morrow/Avon.

Shimoda, Todd A. & Shimoda, L. J. C. The Fourth Treasure. 2002. (Illus.). 349p. E-Book 22.50 (*0-385-50561-2*, Talese, Nan A.) Doubleday Publishing.

Shirley, John. City Come a Walkin' 2001. 216p. pap. 13.95 (*1-56858-191-2*) Four Walls Eight Windows.

Siegel, Sheldon. Criminal Intent. 2002. 416p. 25.95 (*0-399-14917-1*) Penguin Group (USA) Inc.

—Final Verdict. 2004. 432p. mass mkt. 7.99 (*0-451-21261-4*, Signet Bks.) NAL.

—Final Verdict. 2003. 400p. 25.95 (*0-399-15042-0*) Putnam Publishing Group, The.

—Incriminating Evidence. abr. ed. 2001. 400p. 24.95 o.s.i (*0-553-80144-9*) Bantam Bks.

—Incriminating Evidence. abr. ed. 2001. audio 25.95 (*0-553-52813-0*); audio compact disk 29.95 (*0-553-71437-6*) Random Hse. Audio Publishing Group. (RH Audio).

—Special Circumstances. 2001. 576p. reprint ed. mass mkt. 7.50 (*0-553-58192-9*) Bantam Bks.

Smith, Julie. Dead in the Water. (Orig.). 1993. pap. 4.99 o.p. (*0-8041-9804-7*); 1991. mass mkt. 4.99 o.s.i (*0-8041-0855-2*) Ballantine Bks. (Ivy Bks.).

—Death Turns a Trick. 1993. pap. 3.99 o.p. (*0-8041-9805-5*); 1992. reprint ed. mass mkt. 5.99 o.s.i (*0-8041-0856-0*) Ballantine Bks. (Ivy Bks.).

—Huckleberry Fiend. 1987. (Paul McDonald Mystery Ser.). 224p. 15.95 (*0-89296-237-2*) Mysterious Pr.

—Huckleberry Fiend. 1988. 224p. mass mkt. 5.50 (*0-445-40696-8*, Mysterious Pr. Paperback Bks.) Warner Bks., Inc.

—Other People's Skeletons. 1995. 240p. pap. 15.00 (*0-345-47164-4*); 1994. pap. 4.99 o.p. (*0-8041-9820-9*, Ivy Bks.); 1993. mass mkt. 5.99 o.s.i (*0-8041-1086-7*, Ivy Bks.) Ballantine Bks.

—Other People's Skeletons. 1999. (Mystery Ser.). 232p. 20.95 (*0-7862-1953-X*, Five Star) Gale Group.

—The Sourdough Wars. 1993. pap. 4.99 o.p. (*0-8041-9807-1*); 1992. mass mkt. 5.99 o.s.i (*0-8041-0929-X*) Ballantine Bks. (Ivy Bks.).

—Tourist Trap. 1993. pap. 4.99 o.p. (*0-8041-9806-3*); 1992. mass mkt. 5.99 o.s.i (*0-8041-0930-3*) Ballantine Bks. (Ivy Bks.).

—Tourist Trap. 1986. 240p. 15.45 o.p. (*0-89296-162-7*) Mysterious Pr.

—Tourist Trap. 1987. 240p. mass mkt. 3.95 o.s.i (*0-445-40640-2*, Mysterious Pr. Paperback Bks.) Warner Bks., Inc.

—True-Life Adventure. 1986. 15.45 o.p. (*0-89296-120-1*) Mysterious Pr.

—True-Life Adventure. 1986. 256p. reprint ed. mass mkt. 4.99 o.s.i (*0-445-40505-8*, Mysterious Pr. Paperback Bks.) Warner Bks., Inc.

Sparkle: The Queerest Book You'll Ever Love. 2002. 256p. pap. 19.95 (*0-7596-4531-0*) 1stBooks Library.

Spicer, Jack. The Tower of Babel. 1994. vi, 170p. (Orig.). lib. bdg. 33.95 (*1-883689-05-8*); pap. 12.95 (*1-883689-04-X*) Talisman Hse., Pubs.

Stadler, Matthew. Landscape: Memory. 1991. (Contemporary Fiction Ser.). (Illus.). 320p. pap. 9.95 o.p. (*0-452-26647-5*, Plume) Dutton/Plume.

—Landscape: Memory. 1990. (Illus.). 416p. 19.95 o.s.i (*0-684-19185-7*, Macmillan Reference USA) Gale Group.

Stansberry, Domenic. The Last Days of Il Duce. 1998. 168p. 22.00 (*1-57962-004-3*) Permanent Pr., The.

Stark, Elizabeth. Shy Girl. 1999. 212p. 22.00 o.p. (*0-374-26352-3*) Farrar, Straus & Giroux.

Steel, Danielle. Accident. 1995. 448p. mass mkt. 7.99 (*0-440-21754-7*); 1994. 312p. 23.95 (*0-385-30602-4*, Delacorte Pr.); 1994. 312p. 200.00 (*0-385-31215-6*, Delacorte Pr.) Dell Publishing.

—Accident. l.t. ed. 2004. 480p. 24.95 (*0-375-43320-1*) Random Hse. Large Print.

—Accident. 1995. 12.09 o.p. (*0-606-07173-3*) Turtleback Bks.

—Dating Game: A Novel. 2004. 464p. mass mkt. 7.99 (*0-440-24075-1*) Dell Publishing.

—Dating Game: A Novel. l.t. ed. 2004. 576p. pap. 14.95 (*0-375-43312-0*) Random Hse. Large Print.

—The House on Hope Street. 2000. 240p. 19.95 (*0-385-33306-4*, Delacorte Pr.) Dell Publishing.

—The House on Hope Street. l.t. ed. 2000. 336p. 19.95 (*0-375-43063-6*) Random Hse. Large Print.

—Irresistible Forces. 2000. 384p. mass mkt. 7.99 (*0-440-22486-1*); 2000. 18.87 (*0-385-33461-3*, Delacorte Pr.); 1999. 384p. 26.95 (*0-385-31960-6*, Delacorte Pr.); 1999. 384p. 200.00 (*0-385-33476-1*, Delacorte Pr.) Dell Publishing.

—Irresistible Forces, Set. abr. ed. 1999. audio 26.95 Highsmith Inc.

—Irresistible Forces. abr. ed. 1999. audio 26.95 (*0-553-47935-0*); audio compact disk 29.95 (*0-553-45574-5*); audio 39.95 (*0-553-50215-8*) Random Hse. Audio Publishing Group. (RH Audio).

—Irresistible Forces. l.t. ed. 528p. 2000. pap. 13.95 (*0-375-70787-5*); 1999. 26.95 (*0-375-40863-0*) Random Hse. Large Print.

—No Greater Love. l.t. ed. 1991. 608p. 27.50 o.s.i (*0-385-30509-5*, Delacorte Large Type) Bantam Doubleday Dell Large Print Group, Inc.

—No Greater Love. 1992. 400p. mass mkt. 7.99 (*0-440-21328-2*); 1992. mass mkt. o.s.i (*0-440-80329-2*); 1991. 408p. 23.00 (*0-385-29909-5*, Delacorte Pr.) Dell Publishing.

—No Greater Love. l.t. ed. 1994. (General Ser.). 483p. pap. 18.95 o.p. (*0-8161-5790-1*, Macmillan Reference USA) Gale Group.

—No Greater Love. 1991. 13.04 (*0-606-02811-0*) Turtleback Bks.

—Star. l.t. ed. 1989. 21.95 o.s.i (*0-440-50170-9*, Delacorte Large Type) Bantam Doubleday Dell Large Print Group, Inc.

—Star. 1989. 456p. 19.95 (*0-440-50072-9*, Delacorte Pr.); 1989. 100.00 (*0-440-50172-5*, Delacorte Pr.); 1990. 480p. reprint ed. mass mkt. 7.99 (*0-440-20557-3*, Dell Bks.) Dell Publishing.

—Star. l.t. ed. 1993. (Paperback Ser.). 683p. pap. 22.95 (*0-8161-5769-3*) Thorndike Pr.

—Star. 1989. 11.09 o.p. (*0-606-04546-5*) Turtleback Bks.

Steinke, Darcey. Suicide Blonde. 2000. 200p. pap. 12.00 (*0-8021-3664-8*, Grove Pr.); 1992. 191p. 19.00 o.p. (*0-87113-479-9*, Atlantic Monthly Pr.) Grove/Atlantic, Inc.

—Suicide Blonde. Rosenman, Jane, ed. 1994. 204p. reprint ed. pap. 10.00 (*0-671-87315-6*, Washington Square Pr.) Simon & Schuster.

Stone, Katherine. The Carlton Club. (Zebra Book Ser.). 544p. 1996. mass mkt. 6.99 o.s.i (*0-8217-5204-9*); 1988. mass mkt. 4.50 o.p. (*0-8217-2296-4*) Kensington Publishing Corp. (Zebra Bks.).

—Carlton Club. 1988. mass mkt. 4.95 o.s.i (*0-8217-3614-0*, Zebra Bks.) Kensington Publishing Corp.

—The Carlton Club. l.t. ed. 1997. pap. 24.95 (*1-56895-414-X*, Wheeler Publishing, Inc.) Gale Group.

—The Other Twin. 2003. 368p. mass mkt. (*1-55166-747-9*); 304p. (*1-55166-655-3*) Harlequin Enterprises, Ltd. (Mira Bks.).

—The Other Twin. 2003. (Basic Ser.). 433p. 29.95 (*0-7862-5393-2*) Thorndike Pr.

—Promises. l.t. ed. 1995. 23.95 o.p. (*0-7927-2018-0*); 1994. pap. 25.95 o.p. (*0-7927-2019-9*) BBC Audiobooks America.

Strupp, Joe. The City & County: A Novel of San Francisco's Newsmakers. 2001. 425p. per. 19.95 (*1-931333-01-7*) Dry Bones Pr.

Stubbs, Jean. The Golden Crucible. 1995. 280p. 18.50 o.p. (*0-7451-8664-5*, Black Dagger) BBC Audiobooks America.

—The Golden Crucible. 1977. (General Ser.). reprint ed. lib. bdg. 12.50 o.p. (*0-8161-6488-6*, Macmillan Reference USA) Gale Group.

—The Golden Crucible. 1976. 8.95 o.p. (*0-8128-1903-9*, Scarborough Hse.) Madison Bks., Inc.

Taylor, Elizabeth Atwood. The Cable Car Murder. 1988. 240p. reprint ed. mass mkt. 4.99 o.s.i (*0-8041-0281-3*, Ivy Bks.) Ballantine Bks.

—The Cable Car Murder. (Fingerprint Mysteries Ser.). 224p. 1983. pap. 5.95 o.p. (*0-312-11312-9*, Saint Martin's Griffin); 1981. 11.95 o.p. (*0-312-11311-0*) St. Martin's Pr.

—The Cable Car Murders. l.t. ed. 1982. 412p. reprint ed. 12.95 o.p. (*0-89621-360-9*) Thorndike Pr.

—Murder at Vassar. 1988. mass mkt. 4.95 o.s.i (*0-8041-0212-0*, Ivy Bks.) Ballantine Bks.

—Murder at Vassar. 1987. 256p. 15.95 o.p. (*0-312-00160-6*) St. Martin's Pr.

—The Northwest Murders. 1992. 288p. 18.95 o.p. (*0-312-07753-X*, Saint Martin's Minotaur) St. Martin's Pr.

Taylor, Jean. The Last of Her Lies: A Maggie Garrett Mystery. 1996. 238p. (Orig.). pap. 10.95 (*1-878067-75-3*, Seal Pr.) Avalon Publishing Group.

—We Know Where You Live. 1995. 240p. pap. 9.95 (*1-878067-62-1*, Seal Pr.) Avalon Publishing Group.

Taylor, Kathrine Kressmann. Address Unknown. 2001. (Illus.). 64p. reprint ed. pap. 8.95 (*0-7434-1271-0*, Washington Square Pr.) Simon & Schuster.

Taylor, Kathrine Kressmann. Address Unknown. 1995. 64p. 12.99 o.p. (*1-884910-17-3*, Story Pr.) F&W Pubns., Inc.

Tea, Michelle. Valencia. 2000. 202p. pap. 13.00 (*1-58005-035-2*, Seal Pr.) Avalon Publishing Group.

Thoreau, David. City at Bay. 1979. 9.95 o.p. (*0-87795-231-0*, Morrow, William & Co.) Morrow/Avon.

Tierney, Ronald. Eclipse of the Heart. 1995. pap. 8.95 o.p. (*0-312-11780-9*, Saint Martin's Griffin); 1993. 224p. 12.99 o.p. (*0-312-09792-1*, Saint Martin's Minotaur) St. Martin's Pr.

Toland, James. City Limits: Fictional Tales of Transition along San Francisco's Mission Street. 2000. 2000p. pap. 12.95 (*0-9702109-1-4*, Bridgeway Pr.) Toland Communications.

Tsukiyama, Gail. Night of Many Dreams. unabr. ed. 1999. audio 29.95 (*0-7861-1546-7*); pap. 44.95 incl. audio (*0-7861-1335-9*, 2229) Blackstone Audio Bks., Inc.

—Night of Many Dreams. 1999. E-Book 12.95 o.s.i (*0-312-20733-6*); 1998. 288p. 22.95 o.p. (*0-312-17194-3*); 1998. 288p. reprint ed. pap. 12.95 (*0-312-19940-6*, NPB 0230, Saint Martin's Griffin) St. Martin's Pr.

Tulchinsky, Karen X. Love & Other Ruins. 2003. 317p. pap. 15.95 (*1-55192-554-0*, Polestar Book Pubs.) Raincoast Bk. Distribution CAN. *Dist:* Publishers Group West.

Upton, Robert. Dead on the Stick. 256p. 1987. pap. 3.50 o.p. (*0-14-007601-8*, Penguin Bks.); 1986. 15.95 o.p. (*0-670-80331-6*) Viking Penguin.

—The Faberge Egg. 1988. 208p. 16.95 o.p. (*0-525-24692-4*, Dutton) Dutton/Plume.

—Fade Out. 1984. (Amos McGuffin Mystery Ser.). 13.95 o.p. (*0-670-30469-7*) Viking Penguin.

—Fade Out: An Amos McGuffin Mystery. 1986. 192p. pap. 3.95 o.p. (*0-14-008312-X*, Penguin Bks.) Viking Penguin.

—A Golden Fleecing. 1979. 10.95 o.p. (*0-312-33730-2*) St. Martin's Pr.

—A Killing in Real Estate: An Amos McGuffin Mystery. 1990. 192p. 17.95 o.p. (*0-525-24927-3*, Dutton) Dutton/Plume.

—Who'd Want to Kill Old George? 1982. 224p. pap. 2.50 o.p. (*0-523-41537-0*, Pinnacle Bks.) Kensington Publishing Corp.

—Who'd Want to Kill Old George? 1976. 7.95 o.p. (*0-399-11867-5*) Putnam Publishing Group, The.

Vardeman, Robert E. The Resonance of Blood. 1992. 224p. (Orig.). mass mkt. 4.50 (*0-380-75857-1*, Avon Bks.) Morrow/Avon.

Vasas-Brown, Cathy. Every Wickedness. 2002. 432p. mass mkt. (*0-7704-2864-9*) Seal Pr.

Vea, Alfredo, Jr. Reckoning of Angels. 1996. 352p. 24.95 o.s.i (*0-525-94077-4*, Dutton) Dutton/Plume.

Villatoro, Marcos McPeek. The Holy Spirit of My Uncle's Cojones. 1999. 298p. pap. 12.95 (*1-55885-283-2*) Arte Publico Pr.

Vollmann, William T. The Rainbow Stories. 1992. (Contemporay American Fiction Ser.). 560p. pap. 17.95 (*0-14-017154-1*) Penguin Group (USA) Inc.

—The Rainbow Stories. 1989. 541p. 19.95 o.s.i (*0-689-11961-5*, Scribner) Simon & Schuster.

—The Royal Family: A Novel. 2000. (Illus.). 566p. 40.00 o.s.i (*0-670-89167-3*) Viking Penguin.

Walker, Charlie. The Black Sicilian. 2003. 190p. 35.00 (*0-9673517-8-2*) Sur-Mount Pubs., Inc.

Walker, Walter. The Appearance of Impropriety. Rosenman, Jane, ed. 1993. 336p. 20.00 (*0-671-74042-3*, Atria) Simon & Schuster.

Washburn, Stan. Into Thin Air. 1996. 336p. mass mkt. 6.99 (*0-671-56246-0*, Pocket) Simon & Schuster.

Wells, Jess. AfterShocks: A Novel. 1992. 240p. (Orig.). pap. 9.95 o.p. (*1-879427-08-7*) 3rd Side Pr., Inc.

West, Mark. Union Gold. 1998. (Illus.). 288p. pap. 19.95 (*1-889901-02-4*) Glencannon Pr.

White, Gloria. Charged with Guilt. 1995. 336p. mass mkt. 5.50 o.s.i (*0-440-22049-1*) Dell Publishing.

—Money to Burn. 1993. 320p. mass mkt. 4.99 o.s.i (*0-440-21612-5*, Dell Bks.) Dell Publishing.

—Money to Burn. unabr. ed. 1993. (Ronnie Ventana Mystery Ser.). audio 36.00 (*0-9624010-6-4*, 752466) Reader's Chair, Inc., The.

—Murder on the Run. 1991. 288p. mass mkt. 5.50 o.s.i (*0-440-20983-8*) Dell Publishing.

—Murder on the Run. unabr. ed. 1993. (Ronnie Ventana Mystery Ser.). audio 30.00 (*0-9624010-4-8*) Reader's Chair, Inc., The.

—Murder on the Run. 1992. 304p. 20.00 o.p. (*0-7278-4317-6*) Severn Hse. Pubs., Ltd.

—Sunset & Santiago. 1997. 320p. mass mkt. 5.50 o.s.i (*0-440-22326-1*) Dell Publishing.

Wilcox, Collin. Aftershock. unabr. ed. 1997. (Frank Hastings Ser.). audio 48.00 (*0-7366-3554-8*, 4199) Books on Tape, Inc.

—Bernhardt's Edge. 1991. pap. 3.95 o.p. (*0-8125-1148-4*); 1988. 320p. 17.95 o.p. (*0-312-93076-3*) Doherty, Tom Assocs., LLC. (Tor Bks.).

—Calculated Risk. unabr. ed. 1996. (Frank Hastings Ser.). audio 48.00 (*0-7366-3203-4*, 3867) Books on Tape, Inc.

—Calculated Risk. 1995. 256p. 22.50 o.p. (*0-8050-3003-4*) Holt, Henry & Co.

—Dead Aim. unabr. ed. 1996. (Frank Hastings Ser.). audio 48.00 (*0-7366-3373-1*, 4023) Books on Tape, Inc.

—Dead Center. unabr. ed. 1993. (Frank Hastings Ser.). audio 48.00 (*0-7366-2519-4*, 3274) Books on Tape, Inc.

—Dead Center. 1995. pap. 5.95 o.p. (*0-8050-4232-6*, Owl Bks.); 1992. 256p. 18.95 o.p. (*0-8050-1615-5*) Holt, Henry & Co.

—A Death Before Dying. unabr. ed. 1992. (Frank Hastings Ser.). audio 56.00 (*0-7366-2212-8*, 3005) Books on Tape, Inc.

—A Death Before Dying. 1994. 231p. pap. 5.95 o.p. (*0-8050-3122-7*, Owl Bks.) Holt, Henry & Co.

—A Death Before Dying: A Lt. Hastings Mystery. 1990. 240p. 18.95 o.p. (*0-8050-0979-5*) Holt, Henry & Co.

—The Disappearance. 19.95 (*0-89190-580-4*) Amereon, Ltd.

—The Disappearance. unabr. ed. 1996. (Frank Hastings Ser.). audio 48.00 (*0-7366-3346-4*, 3996) Books on Tape, Inc.

—Doctor, Lawyer ... 1981. (Mystery Ser.). 192p. 1.95 o.s.i (*0-515-05194-2*, Jove) Berkley Publishing Group.

—Doctor, Lawyer ... 1977. 6.95 o.p. (*0-394-40061-5*) Random Hse., Inc.

—Doctor, Lawyer... unabr. ed. 1997. (Frank Hastings Ser.). audio 48.00 (*0-7366-3530-0*, 4168) Books on Tape, Inc.

—Except for the Bones. 1991. 288p. 18.95 o.p. (*0-312-93162-X*, Tor Bks.) Doherty, Tom Assocs., LLC.

—Find Her a Grave. 1993. 288p. 19.95 o.p. (*0-312-85244-4*, Forge Bks.) Doherty, Tom Assocs., LLC.

—Full Circle. 1994. 352p. 21.95 o.p. (*0-312-85521-4*, Forge Bks.) Doherty, Tom Assocs., LLC.

—Hiding Place. 20.95 (*0-89190-581-2*) Amereon, Ltd.

—Hiding Place. unabr. ed. 1996. (Frank Hastings Ser.). audio 48.00 (*0-7366-3404-5*, 4050) Books on Tape, Inc.

—Hire a Hangman. 1994. 248p. pap. 5.95 o.p. (*0-8050-3121-9*, Owl Bks.) Holt, Henry & Co.

—Hire a Hangman: A Lt. Hastings Mystery. Haun, Joann, ed. 1991. 256p. 18.95 o.p. (*0-8050-0980-9*) Holt, Henry & Co.

—The Lonely Hunter. unabr. ed. 1996. (Frank Hastings Ser.). audio 48.00 (*0-7366-3325-1*, 3977) Books on Tape, Inc.

—Long Way Down. unabr. ed. 1996. (Frank Hastings Ser.). audio 48.00 (*0-7366-3474-6*, 4117) Books on Tape, Inc.

—Mankiller. unabr. ed. 1997. (Frank Hastings Ser.). audio 48.00 (*0-7366-3788-5*, 4462) Books on Tape, Inc.

—Mankiller. 1980. 224p. 8.95 o.p. (*0-394-50550-6*) Random Hse., Inc.

—Night Games. 1986. 240p. 15.45 o.p. (*0-89296-160-0*) Mysterious Pr.

—Night Games. 1987. 240p. mass mkt. 3.95 o.s.i (*0-445-40590-2*, Mysterious Pr. Paperback Bks.) Warner Bks., Inc.

—The Pariah. 1988. 15.45 o.p. (*0-89296-280-1*) Mysterious Pr.

—The Pariah. 1989. mass mkt. 4.95 (*0-445-40790-5*, Mysterious Pr. Paperback Bks.) Warner Bks., Inc.

—Power Plays. 21.95 (*0-89190-582-0*) Amereon, Ltd.

—Power Plays. unabr. ed. 1997. (Frank Hastings Ser.). audio 48.00 (*0-7366-3737-0*, 4414) Books on Tape, Inc.

—Power Plays. 1979. 7.95 o.p. (*0-394-50172-1*) Random Hse., Inc.

—Silent Witness. 1992. mass mkt. 3.99 (*0-8125-1149-2*); 1990. 17.95 o.p. (*0-312-93161-1*) Doherty, Tom Assocs., LLC. (Tor Bks.).

—Stalking Horse: A Mystery. 1982. 10.50 o.p. (*0-394-51173-5*) Random Hse., Inc.

—Switchback. unabr. ed. 1994. (Frank Hastings Ser.). audio 56.00 (*0-7366-2701-4*, 3435) Books on Tape, Inc.

—Switchback. 1995. 89p. pap. 5.95 o.p. (*0-8050-4233-4*, Owl Bks.) Holt, Henry & Co.

—Switchback: A Lt. Hastings Mystery. 1993. 256p. 19.95 o.p. (*0-8050-2104-3*) Holt, Henry & Co.

—Victims. 1986. 14.95 o.p. (*0-89296-066-3*); pap. 3.95 o.p. (*0-445-40252-0*) Mysterious Pr.

Wings, Mary. She Came in a Flash. 1989. 208p. 17.95 o.p. (*0-453-00648-5*) NAL.

—She Came in Drag. 1999. (Emma Victor Mysteries Ser.). 352p. mass mkt. 6.50 o.s.i (*0-425-16935-9*) Berkley Publishing Group.

—She Came to the Castro. (Emma Victor Mysteries Ser.). 272p. 1998. mass mkt. 5.99 o.s.i (*0-425-16222-2*); 1997. 21.95 o.s.i (*0-425-15629-X*) Berkley Publishing Group. (Prime Crime).

Yan, Geling. The Lost Daughter of Happiness. 2002. 288p. pap. 13.95 (*0-7868-8757-5*) Hyperion Pr.

—The Lost Daughter of Happiness: A Novel. Silber, Cathy, tr. from CHI. 2001. 276p. 22.95 (*0-7868-6654-3*) Hyperion Pr.

Zackel, Fred. Cinderella After Midnight. 1980. 11.95 o.p. (*0-698-10990-2*) Putnam Publishing Group, The.

—Cocaine & Blue Eyes. 1983. 320p. mass mkt. 2.95 o.p. (*0-425-06241-4*) Berkley Publishing Group.

—Cocaine & Blue Eyes. 1978. 8.95 o.p. (*0-698-10934-1*) Putnam Publishing Group, The.

Zavala, Ann. The San Francisco Gold. 1995. 288p. 21.95 o.p. (*0-312-85441-2*, Forge Bks.) Doherty, Tom Assocs., LLC.

—San Francisco Gold. 1996. 286p. pap. text 5.99 (*0-8125-2360-1*, Forge Bks.) Doherty, Tom Assocs., LLC.

Zimler, Richard. The Angelic Darkness: A Novel. 1999. 256p. text 23.95 o.p. (*0-393-04817-9*) Norton, W. W. & Co., Inc.

Zimmerman, Bruce. Blood under the Bridge. 1989. 16.95 o.p. (*0-06-016087-X*) HarperTrade.

Settings

—Blood under the Bridge. 1990. mass mkt. 3.95 o.p. (*0-312-92244-2*, St. Martin's Paperbacks) St. Martin's Pr.
—Crimson Green: A Quinn Parker Novel of Suspense. 1994. 320p. 20.00 o.p. (*0-06-017069-7*) HarperCollins Pubs.
—Crimson Green: A Quinn Parker Suspense Novel. 1995. 368p. mass mkt. 4.50 o.p. (*0-06-109359-9*) HarperCollins Pubs.
—Thicker Than Water: A Novel of Suspense. 1991. 288p. 19.95 o.p. (*0-06-016387-9*) HarperTrade.
—Thicker Than Water: A Quinn Parker Mystery. 1993. 368p. mass mkt. 4.50 o.p. (*0-06-109026-3*, HarperTorch) Morrow/Avon.

## SANCTUARY (IMAGINARY PLACE)—FICTION

Abbey, Lynn. A Thieves World Epic Novel. 2003. (Thieve's World Ser.). 544p. mass mkt. 6.99 (*0-8125-6175-9*, Tor Bks.) Doherty, Tom Assocs., LLC.
Abbey, Lynn & Abbey, Elizabeth. Sanctuary: An Epic Novel of Thieves' World. 2002. 304p. 27.95 (*0-312-87491-X*, Tor Bks.) Doherty, Tom Assocs., LLC.
Abbey, Lynn, et al. Soul of City. 1986. (Thieves' World Ser.: No. 8). 256p. mass mkt. 4.50 o.s.i (*0-441-77581-0*) Ace Bks.
Asprin, Robert L. Thieves' World. mass mkt. 2.95 o.s.i (*0-441-80589-2*); 1985. 320p. mass mkt. 2.95 o.s.i (*0-441-80584-1*); 1984. mass mkt. 2.95 o.s.i (*0-441-80583-3*); 1984. mass mkt. 2.95 o.s.i (*0-441-80582-5*); 1983. mass mkt. 2.95 o.s.i (*0-441-80581-7*); 1982. mass mkt. 2.75 o.s.i (*0-441-80579-5*);No. 1. 1987. 320p. mass mkt. 4.99 o.s.i (*0-441-80591-4*);Nos. 1, 7, 8, 9, 10, 11. 1988. 21.00 o.s.i (*0-441-80572-8*) Ace Bks.
—Thieves' World No. 10: Aftermath. 1987. mass mkt. 3.95 o.s.i (*0-441-80597-3*) Ace Bks.
—Thieves' World No. 11: Uneasy Alliance. 1988. mass mkt. 3.95 o.s.i (*0-441-80610-4*) Ace Bks.
Asprin, Robert L. & Abbey, Lynn. Thieves' World. Reynolds, Kay & Sutton, Laurie, eds. 1985. (Thieves' World Graphics Ser.). (Illus.). 64p. No. 1. pap. 3.95 o.p. (*0-89865-415-7*); No. 2. pap. 3.95 o.p. (*0-89865-416-5*) Donning Co. Pubs. (Starblaze).
—Thieves' World No. 03: Shadows of Sanctuary. 1987. 352p. mass mkt. 3.95 o.s.i (*0-441-80601-5*) Ace Bks.
—Thieves' World No. 04: Storm Season. 1985. 320p. mass mkt. 4.50 o.s.i (*0-441-78713-4*) Ace Bks.
—Thieves' World No. 05: Face of Chaos. 1985. 256p. mass mkt. 4.50 o.s.i (*0-441-80587-6*) Ace Bks.
—Thieves' World Graphics. Sutton, Laurie, ed. 1987. (Thieves' World Graphics Ser.: No. 6). (Illus.). 64p. pap. 4.95 o.p. (*0-89865-522-6*, Starblaze) Donning Co. Pubs.
—Thieves' World Graphics. (Thieves' World Graphics Ser.). (Illus.). No. 1. 1986. 184p. pap. 12.95 o.p. (*0-89865-460-2*); No. 1. 1986. 184p. 40.00 o.p. (*0-89865-478-5*); No. 3. 1986. 64p. pap. 3.95 o.p. (*0-89865-457-2*); No. 4. 1986. 64p. pap. 3.95 o.p. (*0-89865-458-0*); No. 5. 1987. 64p. pap. 3.95 o.p. (*0-89865-521-8*) Donning Co. Pubs. (Starblaze).
Asprin, Robert L. & Abbey, Lynn, eds. Thieves' World No. 2: Tales from the Vulgar Unicorn. 1986. mass mkt. 4.99 o.s.i (*0-441-80590-6*) Ace Bks.
—Thieves' World No. 06: Wings of Omen. 1986. mass mkt. 4.99 o.s.i (*0-441-80596-5*) Ace Bks.
—Thieves' World No. 07: Dead of Winter. 1985. 272p. mass mkt. 4.99 o.s.i (*0-441-14089-0*) Ace Bks.
—Thieves' World No. 09: Blood Ties. 1987. mass mkt. 3.95 o.s.i (*0-441-80598-1*) Ace Bks.
—Thieves' World No. 12: Stealers' Sky. 1989. mass mkt. 3.95 o.s.i (*0-441-80612-0*) Ace Bks.
Drake, David. Dagger. 1988. (Thieves' World Ser.: No. 5). mass mkt. 3.50 o.s.i (*0-441-80609-0*) Ace Bks.
Morris, Janet. Beyond Sanctuary. Asprin, Robert L. & Abbey, Lynn, eds. 1987. (Thieves' World Ser.: No. 1). mass mkt. 3.95 o.s.i (*0-441-05636-9*) Ace Bks.
—Beyond Sanctuary. 1986. 272p. mass mkt. 2.95 o.s.i (*0-441-05635-0*) Ace Bks.
—Beyond the Veil. 1987. (Thieves' World Ser.: No. 2). 256p. mass mkt. 2.95 o.s.i (*0-441-05512-5*) Ace Bks.
—Beyond Wizardwall. 1987. (Thieves' World Ser.: No. 3). 256p. mass mkt. 2.95 o.s.i (*0-441-05722-5*) Ace Bks.
Offutt, Andrew J. Shadowspawn. 1987. (Thieves' World Ser.: No. 4). mass mkt. 4.50 o.s.i (*0-441-76039-2*) Ace Bks.

## SANTA BARBARA (CALIF.)—FICTION

Collins, Michael. The Cadillac Cowboy. 1995. 288p. 20.95 o.p. (*1-55611-461-3*) Fine, Donald I. Bks.
—Cassandra in Red. 1992. 256p. 19.95 o.p. (*1-55611-316-1*) Fine, Donald I. Bks.
Harper, Brian. Mortal Pursuit. 1997. 432p. mass mkt. 5.99 o.s.i (*0-451-18200-6*, Signet Bks.) NAL.
Martin, Kat. The Dream. l.t. ed. 2001. (G. K. Hall Romance Ser.). 429p. 27.95 o.p. (*0-7838-9535-6*, Macmillan Reference USA) Gale Group.
Muller, Marcia. The Legend of the Slain Soldiers: An Elena Oliverez Mystery. 1987. 224p. mass mkt. 3.50 o.p. (*0-451-15050-3*, Signet Bks.) NAL.
—The Legend of the Slain Soldiers: An Elena Oliverez Mystery. 1985. 181p. 13.95 o.p. (*0-8027-5617-4*) Walker & Co.
—The Legend of the Slain Soldiers: An Elena Oliverez Mystery. 1996. 192p. mass mkt. 5.99 (*0-446-40421-7*) Warner Bks., Inc.
—The Tree of Death. 1987. mass mkt. 3.50 o.p. (*0-451-14749-9*, Signet Bks.) NAL.
—The Tree of Death. 1983. (Mysteries Ser.). 192p. 12.95 o.s.i (*0-8027-5576-3*) Walker & Co.
—The Tree of Death. 1996. 208p. mass mkt. 5.99 o.s.i (*0-446-40420-9*) Warner Bks., Inc.
Muller, Marcia & Pronzini, Bill. Beyond the Grave. 240p. 1999. mass mkt. 5.95 (*0-7867-0650-3*); 1991. mass mkt. 3.95 o.p. (*0-88184-731-3*) Avalon Publishing Group. (Carroll & Graf Pubs.).
—Beyond the Grave. l.t. ed. 2001. 388p. pap. 24.95 (*0-7838-9537-2*, Macmillan Reference USA) Gale Group.
—Beyond the Grave. 1986. 224p. 15.95 o.p. (*0-8027-5651-4*) Walker & Co.
Perry, Thomas. Dead Aim. 2002. 384p. 24.95 (*1-4000-6003-6*) Random Hse., Inc.
—Dead Aim. l.t. ed. 2003. (Americana Ser.). 29.95 (*0-7862-5160-3*) Thorndike Pr.

## SANTA FE (N.M.)—FICTION

Ballantine, David. Chalk's Woman. 2000. 288p. 23.95 o.p. (*0-312-87348-4*, Forge Bks.) Doherty, Tom Assocs., LLC.
Gallegos, Eloy J. Jacona: An Epic Story of the Spanish Southwest. 1996. (Spanish Pioneers Ser.: Vol. I). (Illus.). 377p. pap. 13.50 (*1-882194-22-5*) Tennessee Valley Publishing.
Hamilton, Laurell K. Obsidian Butterfly: An Anita Blake Vampire Hunter Novel. 2000. (Anita Blake Ser.). 400p. 21.95 (*0-441-00684-1*); 608p. reprint ed. mass mkt. 7.50 o.s.i (*0-441-00781-3*) Ace Bks.
—Obsidian Butterfly: An Anita Blake Vampire Hunter Novel. 2002. 608p. mass mkt. 7.99 (*0-515-13450-3*) Berkley Publishing Group.
Harper, Karen. Empty Cradle. l.t. ed. 2000. 342p. 26.95 (*1-57490-282-2*, Beeler Large Print Bks.) Beeler, Thomas T. Publisher.
—Empty Cradle. 1998. 448p. mass mkt. 6.50 o.s.i (*0-451-19482-9*, Signet Bks.) NAL.
Jones, D. J. H. Murder in the New Age. 192p. 2000. pap. 13.95 (*0-8263-2236-0*); 1997. 19.95 (*0-8263-1813-4*) Univ. of New Mexico Pr.
Kowalski, William. Somewhere South of Here. 2001. 304p. 25.00 (*0-06-019356-5*) HarperCollins Pubs.
—Somewhere South of Here: A Novel. 2002. 304p. pap. 12.95 (*0-06-008437-5*, Perennial) HarperTrade.
Long, Goldberry M. Juniper Tree Burning. 464p. 2002. pap. 14.00 (*0-7432-2211-3*); 2001. 25.00 (*0-7432-0203-1*) Simon & Schuster. (Simon & Schuster).
Lovett, Sarah. Acquired Motives: A Novel. 1997. mass mkt. 5.99 o.s.i (*0-8041-1298-3*, Ivy Bks.) Ballantine Bks.
—Acquired Motives: A Novel. aut. ed. 1996. 22.95 o.s.i (*0-676-51776-5*, Villard Bks.) Random House Adult Trade Publishing Group.
—Acquired Motives: A Novel. 2003. (Illus.). 368p. pap. 6.99 (*0-7434-6335-8*, Pocket) Simon & Schuster.
—Dangerous Attachments. 1996. 344p. mass mkt. 5.99 o.s.i (*0-8041-1297-5*, Ivy Bks.) Ballantine Bks.
—Dangerous Attachments: A Dr. Sylvia Strange Novel. 2003. 400p. pap. 6.99 (*0-7434-6334-X*, Pocket) Simon & Schuster.
—A Desperate Silence: A Novel. 1998. mass mkt. 5.99 o.s.i (*0-8041-1299-1*, Ivy Bks.) Ballantine Bks.
—A Desperate Silence: A Novel. l.t. ed. 1998. 24.95 (*1-57490-152-4*) Beeler, Thomas T. Publisher.
—A Desperate Silence: A Novel. 2003. (Illus.). 400p. pap. 7.50 (*0-7434-6336-6*, Pocket) Simon & Schuster.
Major, Ann. Inseparable. 1999. 384p. mass mkt. (*1-55166-548-4*, 1-66548-8, Mira Bks.) Harlequin Enterprises, Ltd.
McGarrity, Michael. Hermit's Peak. l.t. ed. 2001. (Illus.). 310p. 27.95 (*1-57490-338-1*) Beeler, Thomas T. Publisher.
—Hermit's Peak. (Kevin Kerney Novels Ser.). 1999. (Illus.). 320p. 24.00 o.s.i (*0-684-85078-8*, Scribner); 2000. 368p. reprint ed. mass mkt. 6.99 (*0-671-02147-8*, Pocket) Simon & Schuster.
—The Judas Judge. abr. ed. 2000. (Kevin Kerney Novels Ser.). audio 25.00 o.s.i (*0-7435-0627-8*, Simon & Schuster Audioworks) Simon & Schuster Audio.
—The Judas Judge: A Kevin Kerney Novel. 2000. (Kevin Kerney Novels Ser.). 288p. 23.95 o.s.i (*0-525-94547-4*, Dutton) Dutton/Plume.
—Mexican Hat. l.t. ed. 2001. (Illus.). 302p. 26.95 (*1-57490-379-9*, Beeler Large Print Bks.) Beeler, Thomas T. Publisher.
—Mexican Hat. unabr. ed. 1998. (Kevin Kerney Mystery Ser.: Vol. 2). audio 51.00 (*0-7887-1892-4*, 95314E7) Recorded Bks., LLC.
—Mexican Hat. 1998. (Kevin Kerney Novels Ser.). (Illus.). 336p. mass mkt. 6.50 (*0-671-00253-8*, Pocket Star) Simon & Schuster.
—The Mexican Hat: A Novel. 1997. 304p. 22.95 (*0-393-04063-1*) Norton, W. W. & Co., Inc.
—Serpent Gate. l.t. ed. 2000. 307p. 27.95 (*1-57490-326-8*, Beeler Large Print Bks.) Beeler, Thomas T. Publisher.
—Serpent Gate. (Kevin Kerney Novels Ser.). 1999. (Illus.). 368p. mass mkt. 6.99 (*0-671-02146-X*, Pocket Star); 1998. 320p. 23.00 o.s.i (*0-684-85076-1*, Scribner); 1998. 22.50 o.p. (*0-684-85345-0*, Scribner) Simon & Schuster.
—Serpent Gate. 1999. 12.55 (*0-606-19062-7*) Turtleback Bks.
—Tularosa. l.t. ed. 1996. pap. 23.95 (*1-56895-372-0*, Wheeler Publishing, Inc.) Gale Group.
—Tularosa. 1996. 304p. 25.00 (*0-393-03922-6*) Norton, W. W. & Co., Inc.
—Tularosa. unabr. ed. 2000. (Kevin Kerney Mystery Ser.: Vol. 1). audio 51.00 (*0-7887-1767-7*, 95245E7) Recorded Bks., LLC.
—Tularosa. 1998. 3.99 (*0-671-02373-X*, Pocket); 1997. (Illus.). 336p. mass mkt. 6.99 (*0-671-00252-X*, Pocket Star) Simon & Schuster.
Miscione, Lisa. Angel Fire. E-Book 17.95 (*0-312-70416-X*); 2003. 288p. mass mkt. 6.50 (*0-312-98918-0*, St. Martin's Paperbacks); 2002. 288p. 23.95 (*0-312-28304-0*, Saint Martin's Minotaur) St. Martin's Pr.
Morrell, David. Extreme Denial. abr. ed. 1996. audio 24.95 o.p. (*0-7871-0582-1*) NewStar Media, Inc.
—Extreme Denial. 480p. 1996. 32.00 (*0-446-51962-6*); 1997. reprint ed. mass mkt. 7.50 (*0-446-60396-1*) Warner Bks., Inc.
Onley, Glen. Discovery Tree: A Novel of the Old West. 2001. (Illus.). 256p. pap. 18.95 (*0-86534-327-6*) Sunstone Pr.
Page, Jake. The Knotted Strings. 1995. mass mkt. 5.99 o.s.i (*0-345-38783-X*); 256p. 20.00 o.s.i (*0-345-38782-1*) Ballantine Bks.
—The Knotted Strings. abr. ed. 1995. audio 16.95 o.p. (*1-56100-406-5*, 1318, Nova Audio Bks.); audio 57.25 o.p. (*1-56100-238-0*, 921, Unabridged Library Editions); audio 23.95 o.p. (*1-56100-613-0*, 156, Bookcassette) Brilliance Audio.
—The Knotted Strings. abr. ed. 2000. audio 7.95 (*1-57815-016-7*, 1040, Media Bks. Audio Publishing) Media Bks., L. L. C.
—The Knotted Strings. 2003. 256p. pap. 13.95 (*0-8263-2862-8*) Univ. of New Mexico Pr.
—The Lethal Partner. 1996. 293p. mass mkt. 5.99 o.s.i (*0-345-38785-6*); 240p. 21.00 o.s.i (*0-345-38784-8*) Ballantine Bks.
—The Lethal Partner. unabr. ed. 1997. audio 48.00 (*0-913369-64-0*, 4305) Books on Tape, Inc.
—The Lethal Partner. 2003. 246p. pap. 13.95 (*0-8263-2863-6*) Univ. of New Mexico Pr.
—The Stolen Gods. (Southwest Mysteries Ser.). 1994. 272p. mass mkt. 4.99 o.s.i (*0-345-37929-2*); 1993. 256p. 19.00 o.s.i (*0-345-37928-4*) Ballantine Bks.
—The Stolen Gods. 2002. 260p. pap. 13.95 (*0-8263-2860-1*) Univ. of New Mexico Pr.
Rue, Nancy. The Mirage. 2001. (Christian Heritage Ser.). (Illus.). 192p. (J). (gr. 3-7). pap. 5.99 (*1-56179-863-0*) Bethany Hse. Pubs.
Satterthwait, Walter. Accustomed to the Dark. 1998. (WWL Mystery Ser.). per. (*0-373-26263-9*, 1-26263-3, Worldwide Library) Harlequin Enterprises, Ltd.
—Accustomed to the Dark. 1996. 256p. 21.95 o.p. (*0-312-14535-7*, Saint Martin's Minotaur) St. Martin's Pr.
—At Ease with the Dead. 1993. per. (*0-373-83266-4*, 1-83266-6); 1991. mass mkt. (*0-373-26072-5*) Harlequin Enterprises, Ltd. (Harlequin Bks.).
—At Ease with the Dead. 1990. 16.95 o.p. (*0-312-04260-4*, Saint Martin's Minotaur) St. Martin's Pr.
—At Ease with the Dead: A Joshua Croft Mystery. 2002. 256p. pap. 13.95 (*0-8263-2970-5*) Univ. of New Mexico Pr.
—A Flower in the Desert. 1993. (WWL Mystery Ser.). per. (*0-373-26134-9*, 1-26134-6, Harlequin Bks.) Harlequin Enterprises, Ltd.
—A Flower in the Desert. 1992. 240p. 17.95 o.p. (*0-312-07751-3*, Saint Martin's Minotaur) St. Martin's Pr.
—The Hanged Man: A Joshua Croft Mystery. 1995. (WWL Mystery Ser.). 250p. per. (*0-373-26173-X*, 1-26173-4, Harlequin Bks.) Harlequin Enterprises, Ltd.
—The Hanged Man: A Joshua Croft Mystery. 1993. 256p. 19.95 o.p. (*0-312-09827-8*, Saint Martin's Minotaur) St. Martin's Pr.
—The Hanged Man: A Joshua Croft Mystery. 2003. 258p. pap. 13.95 (*0-8263-3365-6*) Univ. of New Mexico Pr.
—Wall of Glass. 1993. per. (*0-373-83265-6*, 1-83265-8); 1989. mass mkt. (*0-373-26032-6*) Harlequin Enterprises, Ltd. (Harlequin Bks.).
—Wall of Glass. 1988. 256p. 16.95 o.p. (*0-312-01530-5*, Saint Martin's Minotaur) St. Martin's Pr.
—Wall of Glass: A Joshua Croft Mystery. 2002. 250p. pap. 13.95 (*0-8263-2887-3*) Univ. of New Mexico Pr.
Sharpe, Jon. Santa Fe Slaughter. 1988. (Trailsman Ser.: No. 73). 176p. mass mkt. 2.75 o.p. (*0-451-15139-9*, Signet Bks.) NAL.
Tallent, Elizabeth. Museum Pieces. 1986. 240p. pap. 7.95 o.p. (*0-03-008003-7*, Owl Bks.) Holt, Henry & Co.
—Museum Pieces. Goerner, Lee, ed. 1985. 206p. 14.95 o.s.i (*0-394-53928-1*) Knopf, Alfred A. Inc.
Woods, Stuart. Santa Fe Rules. 1992. 320p. 20.00 o.p. (*0-06-017963-5*) HarperTrade.
—Santa Fe Rules. 1993. 368p. mass mkt. 7.99 (*0-06-109089-1*, HarperTorch) Morrow/Avon.

## SANTA TERESA (CALIF.: IMAGINARY PLACE)—FICTION

Grafton, Sue. A Is for Alibi. 1987. (Kinsey Millhone Mystery Ser.). 224p. mass mkt. 7.99 (*0-553-27991-2*); mass mkt. 3.50 o.s.i (*0-553-26563-6*) Bantam Bks.
— A Is for Alibi. unabr. collector's ed. 1993. (Kinsey Millhone Mystery Ser.). audio 48.00 (*0-7366-2455-4*, 3219) Books on Tape, Inc.
— A Is for Alibi. 1994. (Kinsey Millhone Mystery Ser.). reprint ed. lib. bdg. 29.95 o.p. (*1-56849-284-7*) Buccaneer Bks., Inc.
— A Is for Alibi. l.t. ed. 1991. (Kinsey Millhone Mystery Ser.). 354p. 20.95 o.p. (*0-8161-5144-X*, Macmillan Reference USA) Gale Group.
— A Is for Alibi. 1982. (Kinsey Millhone Mystery Ser.). 256p. o.p. (*0-03-059048-5*); 288p. 27.00 (*0-8050-1334-2*) Holt, Henry & Co.
— A Is for Alibi. 1984. (Kinsey Millhone Mystery Ser.). 192p. mass mkt. 2.75 o.p. (*0-451-12862-1*) NAL.
— A Is for Alibi, Set. abr. ed. 1990. (Kinsey Millhone Mystery Ser.). audio 18.00 o.s.i (*0-394-57977-1*, 390310, RH Audio) Random Hse. Audio Publishing Group.
— A Is for Alibi. 2001. (Kinsey Millhone Mystery Ser.). 285p. (*0-7621-8860-X*) Reader's Digest Assn., Inc., The.
— A Is for Alibi. l.t. ed. 1988. (Kinsey Millhone Mystery Ser.). 432p. 15.95 o.p. (*0-7089-1744-5*, Ulverscroft) Thorpe, F. A. Pubs. GBR. *Dist:* Ulverscroft Large Print Bks., Ltd.
—B Is for Burglar. 1986. (Kinsey Millhone Mystery Ser.). 224p. mass mkt. 7.99 (*0-553-28034-1*); mass mkt. 3.50 o.s.i (*0-553-26061-8*) Bantam Bks.
—B Is for Burglar. 1994. (Kinsey Millhone Mystery Ser.). reprint ed. lib. bdg. 29.95 (*1-56849-283-9*) Buccaneer Bks., Inc.
—B Is for Burglar. l.t. ed. 1991. (Kinsey Millhone Mystery Ser.). 20.95 o.p. (*0-8161-5145-8*, Macmillan Reference USA) Gale Group.
—B Is for Burglar. 1985. (Kinsey Millhone Mystery Ser.). 240p. 27.00 (*0-8050-1632-5*) Holt, Henry & Co.
—B Is for Burglar. l.t. ed. 1988. (Kinsey Millhone Mystery Ser.). 448p. 17.95 o.p. (*0-7089-1786-0*, Ulverscroft) Thorpe, F. A. Pubs. GBR. *Dist:* Ulverscroft Large Print Bks., Ltd.
—C Is for Corpse. 1987. mass mkt. 3.50 o.s.i (*0-553-26468-0*); 224p. mass mkt. 7.99 (*0-553-28036-8*) Bantam Bks.
—C Is for Corpse. 1986. (Kinsey Millhone Mystery Ser.). 256p. 19.95 o.p. (*0-03-001888-9*); 258p. 27.00 (*0-8050-2818-8*) Holt, Henry & Co.
—C Is for Corpse. l.t. ed. 1991. (Kinsey Millhone Mystery Ser.). 371p. pap. 22.95 (*0-8161-5146-6*) Thorndike Pr.
—C Is for Corpse. l.t. ed. 1988. (Kinsey Millhone Mystery Ser.). 432p. 15.95 o.p. (*0-7089-1898-0*, Ulverscroft) Thorpe, F. A. Pubs. GBR. *Dist:* Ulverscroft Large Print Bks., Ltd.
—D Is for Deadbeat. 1988. (Kinsey Millhone Mystery Ser.). 256p. reprint ed. mass mkt. 7.99 (*0-553-27163-6*) Bantam Bks.
—D Is for Deadbeat. unabr. collector's ed. 1993. (Kinsey Millhone Mystery Ser.). audio 42.00 (*0-7366-2568-2*, 3317) Books on Tape, Inc.
—D Is for Deadbeat. l.t. ed. 1992. (Kinsey Millhone Mystery Ser.). 345p. 16.95 o.p. (*0-8161-5147-4*, Macmillan Reference USA) Gale Group.
—D Is for Deadbeat, Set. abr. ed. 1993. (Kinsey Millhone Mystery Ser.). audio 18.00 (*0-679-40354-X*, 390596, RH Audio) Random Hse. Audio Publishing Group.
—D Is for Deadbeat. l.t. ed. 1990. (Kinsey Millhone Mystery Ser.). 18.95 o.p. (*0-7089-2118-3*, Ulverscroft) Thorpe, F. A. Pubs. GBR. *Dist:* Ulverscroft Large Print Bks., Ltd.
—E Is for Evidence. 1989. (Kinsey Millhone Mystery Ser.). 208p. mass mkt. 7.99 (*0-553-27955-6*) Bantam Bks.
—E Is for Evidence. unabr. collector's ed. 1994. (Kinsey Millhone Mystery Ser.). audio 42.00 (*0-7366-2615-8*, 3357) Books on Tape, Inc.

—E Is for Evidence. l.t. ed. 1989. (Kinsey Millhone Mystery Ser.). 319p. 20.95 o.p. (*0-8161-4715-9*, Macmillan Reference USA) Gale Group.

—E Is for Evidence. 1988. (Kinsey Millhone Mystery Ser.). 240p. 27.00 (*0-8050-0459-9*) Holt, Henry & Co.

—E Is for Evidence. abr. ed. 1989. (Kinsey Millhone Mystery Ser.). audio 18.00 (*0-394-57982-8*, 390695, RH Audio) Random Hse. Audio Publishing Group.

—F Is for Fugitive. 1990. (Kinsey Millhone Mystery Ser.). 352p. mass mkt. 7.99 (*0-553-28478-9*) Bantam Bks.

—F Is for Fugitive. unabr. collector's ed. 1994. (Kinsey Millhone Mystery Ser.). audio 48.00 (*0-7366-2620-4*, 3360) Books on Tape, Inc.

—F Is for Fugitive. l.t. ed. 1990. (Kinsey Millhone Mystery Ser.). 368p. 21.95 (*0-8161-4901-1*, Macmillan Reference USA) Gale Group.

—F Is for Fugitive. 1989. (Kinsey Millhone Mystery Ser.). 272p. 25.00 (*0-8050-0460-2*) Holt, Henry & Co.

—F Is for Fugitive. abr. ed. 1989. (Kinsey Millhone Mystery Ser.). audio 18.00 (*0-394-57983-6*, 390742); audio 17.00 (*0-394-58173-3*) Random Hse. Audio Publishing Group. (RH Audio).

—G Is for Gumshoe. (Kinsey Millhone Mystery Ser.). 1997. pap. 12.95 o.s.i (*0-449-00062-1*); 1995. mass mkt. 6.99 o.p. (*0-449-45491-6*); 1993. mass mkt. 5.99 o.p. (*0-449-45161-5*); 1991. pap. 6.99 (*0-449-45764-8*); 1991. 352p. mass mkt. 7.99 (*0-449-21936-4*) Ballantine Bks. (Fawcett).

—G Is for Gumshoe. unabr. collector's ed. 1994. (Kinsey Millhone Mystery Ser.). audio 48.00 (*0-7366-2679-4*, 3415) Books on Tape, Inc.

—G Is for Gumshoe. l.t. ed. 1991. (Kinsey Millhone Mystery Ser.). 355p. 20.95 o.p. (*0-8161-5090-7*, Macmillan Reference USA) Gale Group.

—G Is for Gumshoe. 1990. (Kinsey Millhone Mystery Ser.). 272p. 27.00 (*0-8050-0461-0*) Holt, Henry & Co.

—G Is for Gumshoe. abr. ed. 1990. (Kinsey Millhone Mystery Ser.). audio 16.00 o.p. (*0-394-58632-8*);Set. audio 18.00 (*0-394-58563-1*, 390833) Random Hse. Audio Publishing Group. (RH Audio).

—G Is for Gumshoe. l.t. ed. 1991. (Kinsey Millhone Mystery Ser.). 355p. pap. 22.95 o.p. (*0-8161-5091-5*) Thorndike Pr.

—H Is for Homicide. (Kinsey Millhone Mystery Ser.). 1997. pap. 11.00 o.s.i (*0-449-00063-X*); 1995. mass mkt. 6.99 o.p. (*0-449-45492-4*); 1993. mass mkt. 5.99 o.p. (*0-449-45162-3*); 1992. pap. 6.99 (*0-449-45765-6*); 1992. 304p. mass mkt. 7.99 (*0-449-21946-1*) Ballantine Bks. (Fawcett).

—H Is for Homicide. unabr. collector's ed. 1994. (Kinsey Millhone Mystery Ser.). audio 48.00 (*0-7366-2728-6*, 3458) Books on Tape, Inc.

—H Is for Homicide. l.t. ed. 1992. (Kinsey Millhone Mystery Ser.). 390p. 16.95 o.p. (*0-8161-5281-0*, Macmillan Reference USA) Gale Group.

—H Is for Homicide. (Kinsey Millhone Mystery Ser.). 1991. 272p. 25.00 (*0-8050-1084-X*); 1992. 390p. lib. bdg. 20.95 (*0-8161-5280-2*) Holt, Henry & Co.

—H Is for Homicide, Set. abr. ed. 1991. (Kinsey Millhone Mystery Ser.). 18.00 incl. audio (*0-394-58698-0*, 390890, RH Audio) Random Hse. Audio Publishing Group.

—I Is for Innocent. (Kinsey Millhone Mystery Ser.). 1997. 304p. pap. 12.95 (*0-449-00064-8*); 1995. mass mkt. 6.99 o.p. (*0-449-45493-2*); 1994. mass mkt. 5.99 o.p. (*0-449-45335-9*); 1993. pap. 6.99 (*0-449-45766-4*); 1993. 352p. mass mkt. 7.99 (*0-449-22151-2*) Ballantine Bks. (Fawcett).

—I Is for Innocent. unabr. ed. 1993. (Kinsey Millhone Mystery Ser.). audio 56.00 (*0-7366-2433-3*, 3198) Books on Tape, Inc.

—I Is for Innocent. l.t. ed. 1994. (Kinsey Millhone Mystery Ser.). 373p. 16.95 o.p. (*0-8161-5538-0*, Macmillan Reference USA) Gale Group.

—I Is for Innocent. 1992. (Kinsey Millhone Mystery Ser.). 272p. 27.00 (*0-8050-1085-8*) Holt, Henry & Co.

—I Is for Innocent. abr. ed. 1992. (Kinsey Millhone Mystery Ser.). audio 18.00 (*0-679-41115-1*, 390946, RH Audio) Random Hse. Audio Publishing Group.

—I Is for Innocent. l.t. ed. 1993. (Kinsey Millhone Mystery Ser.). 373p. 24.95 (*0-8161-5537-2*) Thorndike Pr.

—J Is for Judgment. (Kinsey Millhone Mystery Ser.). 1997. pap. 11.00 o.s.i (*0-449-00065-6*); 1995. mass mkt. 6.99 o.p. (*0-449-45495-9*); 1994. pap. 6.99 (*0-449-45767-2*); 1994. 384p. mass mkt. 7.99 (*0-449-22148-2*) Ballantine Bks. (Fawcett).

—J Is for Judgment. unabr. ed. 1994. (Kinsey Millhone Mystery Ser.). audio 56.00 (*0-7366-2736-7*, 3463) Books on Tape, Inc.

—J Is for Judgment. l.t. ed. 1993. (Kinsey Millhone Mystery Ser.). lib. bdg. 23.95 o.p. (*0-8161-5750-2*, Macmillan Reference USA) Gale Group.

—J Is for Judgment. 1993. (Kinsey Millhone Mystery Ser.). 304p. 27.00 (*0-8050-1935-9*) Holt, Henry & Co.

—J Is for Judgment, Set. abr. ed. 1993. (Kinsey Millhone Mystery Ser.). audio 18.00 (*0-679-41368-5*, 390993, RH Audio) Random Hse. Audio Publishing Group.

—J Is for Judgment. l.t. ed. 1994. (Kinsey Millhone Mystery Ser.). 410p. pap. 20.95 (*0-8161-5751-0*) Thorndike Pr.

—K Is for Killer. (Kinsey Millhone Mystery Ser.). 1997. pap. 11.00 (*0-449-00066-4*); 1995. pap. 6.99 (*0-449-45768-0*); 1995. 320p. mass mkt. 7.99 (*0-449-22150-4*) Ballantine Bks. (Fawcett).

—K Is for Killer. unabr. ed. 1995. (Kinsey Millhone Mystery Ser.). audio 56.00 (*0-7366-3043-0*, 3725) Books on Tape, Inc.

—K Is for Killer. l.t. ed. 1994. (Kinsey Millhone Mystery Ser.). 26.95 o.p. (*1-56895-101-9*, Wheeler Publishing, Inc.) Gale Group.

—K Is for Killer. 1994. (Kinsey Millhone Mystery Ser.). 304p. 27.00 (*0-8050-1936-7*) Holt, Henry & Co.

—Kinsey Millhone Mystery Series Boxed Set: G Is for Gumshoe; H Is for Homicide; I Is for Innocent, 3 vols. 1993. (Kinsey Millhone Mystery Ser.). 23.97 o.s.i (*0-449-22262-4*, Fawcett) Ballantine Bks.

—L Is for Lawless. (Kinsey Millhone Mystery Ser.). 1997. pap. 11.00 o.s.i (*0-449-00067-2*); 1996. pap. 6.99 (*0-449-45769-9*); 1996. 336p. mass mkt. 7.99 (*0-449-22149-0*) Ballantine Bks. (Fawcett).

—L Is for Lawless. unabr. ed. 1996. (Kinsey Millhone Mystery Ser.). audio 56.00 (*0-7366-3305-7*, 3959) Books on Tape, Inc.

—L Is for Lawless. 1995. (Kinsey Millhone Mystery Ser.). 304p. 24.00 (*0-8050-1937-5*) Holt, Henry & Co.

—L Is for Lawless, Set. abr. ed. 1995. (Kinsey Millhone Mystery Ser.). audio 18.00 (*0-679-42462-8*, 393143, RH Audio) Random Hse. Audio Publishing Group.

—L Is for Lawless. 1997. (Kinsey Millhone Mystery Ser.). 5.98 o.p. (*0-7651-0722-8*) Smithmark Pubs., Inc.

—L Is for Lawless. l.t. ed. (Kinsey Millhone Mystery Ser.). 384p. 1996. pap. 26.95 (*0-7838-1383-X*); 1995. 29.95 (*0-7838-1382-1*) Thorndike Pr.

—M Is for Malice. 1997. (Kinsey Millhone Mystery Ser.). 352p. mass mkt. 7.99 (*0-449-22360-4*, Fawcett) Ballantine Bks.

—M Is for Malice. unabr. collector's ed. 1997. (Kinsey Millhone Mystery Ser.). audio 56.00 (*0-913369-70-5*, 4322) Books on Tape, Inc.

—M Is for Malice. 1996. (Kinsey Millhone Mystery Ser.). (Illus.). 304p. 27.00 (*0-8050-3637-7*) Holt, Henry & Co.

—M Is for Malice. l.t. ed. 1997. (Kinsey Millhone Mystery Ser.). 458p. pap. 27.95 (*0-7838-1834-3*); lib. bdg. 29.95 (*0-7838-1833-5*) Thorndike Pr.

—N Is for Noose. 1999. (Kinsey Millhone Mystery Ser.). mass mkt. (*0-449-00457-0*); 336p. mass mkt. 7.99 (*0-449-22361-2*) Ballantine Bks. (Fawcett).

—N Is for Noose. unabr. ed. 1998. (Kinsey Millhone Mystery Ser.). audio 56.00 (*0-7366-4141-6*, 4645) Books on Tape, Inc.

—N Is for Noose, unabr. ed. 1999. (Kinsey Millhone Mystery Ser.). audio 39.95 Highsmith Inc.

—N Is for Noose. 1998. (Kinsey Millhone Mystery Ser.). 320p. 25.00 (*0-8050-3650-4*) Holt, Henry & Co.

—N Is for Noose. abr. ed. 2002. audio compact disk 25.95 (*0-553-71339-6*); 1998. audio 24.00 (*0-375-40289-6*, 495734); 1998. audio 34.95 (*0-375-40326-4*, AD37D) Random Hse. Audio Publishing Group. (RH Audio).

—N Is for Noose. l.t. ed. (Kinsey Millhone Mystery Ser.). 455p. 1999. pap. 27.95 (*0-7862-1297-7*); 1998. 30.95 (*0-7862-1296-9*) Thorndike Pr.

—O Is for Outlaw. 2001. (Kinsey Millhone Mystery Ser.). 368p. mass mkt. 7.99 (*0-449-00378-7*, Ballantine Bks.) Ballantine Bks.

—O Is for Outlaw. 2000. (Kinsey Millhone Mystery Ser.). audio 39.95 Blackstone Audio Bks., Inc.

—O Is for Outlaw. 1999. (Kinsey Millhone Mystery Ser.). audio 44.95 Books on Tape, Inc.

—O Is for Outlaw. abr. ed. 1999. (Kinsey Millhone Mystery Ser.). audio 25.95. audio 39.95 Highsmith Inc.

—O Is for Outlaw. 1999. (Kinsey Millhone Mystery Ser.). 336p. 26.00 (*0-8050-5955-5*) Holt, Henry & Co.

—O Is for Outlaw. abr. ed. 2004. audio 17.99 (*0-7393-1219-7*, RH Audio Price-Less); 1999. audio compact disk 29.95 (*0-375-40661-1*, RH Audio); 1999. audio 25.95 (*0-375-40415-5*, RH Audio); 1999. audio 39.95 (*0-375-40662-X*, N160, RH Audio) Random Hse. Audio Publishing Group.

—O Is for Outlaw. l.t. ed. (Kinsey Millhone Mystery Ser.). 534p. 2000. 28.95 (*0-7862-2045-7*); 1999. 31.95 (*0-7862-2044-9*) Thorndike Pr.

—P Is for Peril. l.t. ed. 2001. (Kinsey Millhone Mystery Ser.). 352p. 33.95 (*0-7862-2931-4*) Thorndike Pr.

**SARANTIUM (IMAGINARY PLACE)—FICTION**

Kay, Guy Gavriel. Sailing to Sarantium. 1999. (Sarantine Mosaic Ser.: Bk. 1). 448p. 24.00 o.s.i (*0-06-105117-9*); 24.00 (*0-06-105127-6*) HarperCollins Pubs.

—Sailing to Sarantium. 2000. (Sarantine Mosaic Ser.: Bk. 1). 560p. mass mkt. 7.99 (*0-06-105990-0*, Eos) Morrow/Avon.

**SARATOGA SPRINGS (N.Y.)—FICTION**

Dobyns, Stephen. Saratoga Backtalk. unabr. collector's ed. 1995. audio 36.00 (*0-7366-2969-6*, 3660) Books on Tape, Inc.

—Saratoga Backtalk. l.t. ed. 1995. (Large Print Bks.). pap. 21.95 o.p. (*1-56895-089-6*, Wheeler Publishing, Inc.) Gale Group.

—Saratoga Backtalk. 1994. 221p. 19.95 o.p. (*0-393-03659-6*) Norton, W. W. & Co., Inc.

—Saratoga Backtalk. 1995. (Charlie Bradshaw Mystery Ser.). 224p. pap. 5.99 o.s.i (*0-14-024708-4*, Penguin Bks.) Penguin Group (USA) Inc.

—Saratoga Bestiary. unabr. collector's ed. 1994. audio 42.00 (*0-7366-2792-8*, 3507) Books on Tape, Inc.

—Saratoga Bestiary. (Charlie Bradshaw Mystery Ser.). 1990. 304p. pap. 4.50 o.p. (*0-14-010613-8*, Penguin Bks.); 1988. 272p. 16.95 o.p. (*0-670-82024-5*) Viking Penguin.

—Saratoga Fleshpot. unabr. collector's ed. 1996. audio 36.00 (*0-7366-3356-1*, 4007) Books on Tape, Inc.

—Saratoga Fleshpot. 1995. 220p. 21.00 (*0-393-03805-X*) Norton, W. W. & Co., Inc.

—Saratoga Fleshpot. 1996. (Charlie Bradshaw Mystery Ser.). 224p. pap. 5.95 o.p. (*0-14-025535-4*, Penguin Bks.) Penguin Group (USA) Inc.

—Saratoga Haunting. unabr. collector's ed. 1994. audio 36.00 (*0-7366-2836-3*, 3544) Books on Tape, Inc.

—Saratoga Haunting. 1994. (Charlie Bradshaw Mystery Ser.). 224p. pap. 6.95 o.p. (*0-14-017162-2*, Penguin Bks.) Penguin Group (USA) Inc.

—Saratoga Haunting. 1993. (Charlie Bradshaw Mystery Ser.). 224p. 19.00 o.p. (*0-670-84581-7*, Viking) Viking Penguin.

—Saratoga Headhunter. unabr. collector's ed. 1994. audio 36.00 (*0-7366-2754-5*, 3477) Books on Tape, Inc.

—Saratoga Headhunter. 1991. (Charlie Bradshaw Mystery Ser.). 224p. pap. 4.95 o.p. (*0-14-015606-2*, Penguin Bks.) Penguin Group (USA) Inc.

—Saratoga Headhunter. (Crime Monthly Ser.). 1986. pap. 3.50 o.p. (*0-14-007772-3*, Penguin Bks.); 1985. 13.95 o.p. (*0-670-80488-6*) Viking Penguin.

—Saratoga Hexameter. unabr. collector's ed. 1994. audio 48.00 (*0-7366-2890-8*, 3590) Books on Tape, Inc.

—Saratoga Hexameter. l.t. ed. 1991. (General Ser.). 391p. lib. bdg. 20.95 (*0-8161-5133-4*, Macmillan Reference USA) Gale Group.

—Saratoga Hexameter. 1991. (Crime Monthly Ser.). 256p. pap. 4.95 o.p. (*0-14-011691-5*, Penguin Bks.) Penguin Group (USA) Inc.

—Saratoga Hexameter. 1990. (Charlie Bradshaw Mystery Ser.). 256p. 16.95 o.p. (*0-670-82568-9*, Viking) Viking Penguin.

—Saratoga Longshot. unabr. collector's ed. 1994. audio 36.00 (*0-7366-2698-0*, 3432) Books on Tape, Inc.

—Saratoga Longshot. 1987. (Charlie Bradshaw Mystery Ser.). 256p. pap. 3.95 o.p. (*0-14-009627-2*, Penguin Bks.) Viking Penguin.

—Saratoga Snapper. unabr. collector's ed. 1994. audio 42.00 (*0-7366-2793-6*, 3508) Books on Tape, Inc.

—Saratoga Snapper. l.t. ed. 1988. 329p. 17.95 o.p. (*0-8161-4348-X*, Macmillan Reference USA) Gale Group.

—Saratoga Snapper. (Charlie Bradshaw Mystery Ser.). 1987. 272p. pap. 3.95 o.p. (*0-14-008812-1*, Penguin Bks.); 1986. 288p. 15.95 o.p. (*0-670-81059-2*) Viking Penguin.

—Saratoga Strongbox. l.t. ed. 2000. pap. 23.95 (*1-56895-848-X*, Wheeler Publishing, Inc.) Gale Group.

—Saratoga Strongbox. 1999. (Charlie Bradshaw Mysteries Ser.). 224p. pap. 5.99 o.s.i (*0-14-028012-X*) Penguin Group (USA) Inc.

—Saratoga Strongbox. 1998. (Charlie Bradshaw Mysteries Ser.). 208p. 21.95 o.p. (*0-670-87692-5*) Viking Penguin.

—Saratoga Swimmer. unabr. collector's ed. 1994. audio 36.00 (*0-7366-2753-7*, 3476) Books on Tape, Inc.

—Saratoga Swimmer. 1981. 12.95 o.p. (*0-689-11193-2*, Scribner) Simon & Schuster.

—Saratoga Swimmer. 1983. (Charlie Bradshaw Mystery Ser.). 224p. pap. 5.95 o.p. (*0-14-006357-9*, Penguin Bks.) Viking Penguin.

—Saratoga Trifecta. 1995. (Charlie Bradshaw Mystery Ser.). 544p. pap. 24.00 o.s.i (*0-14-025196-0*, Penguin Bks.) Penguin Group (USA) Inc.

Healy, R. Austin. The Ninth Race. 224p. 1995. pap. 12.95 o.p. (*0-8338-0217-8*); 1994. 21.95 o.p. (*0-8338-0211-9*) Marshall Jones Co.

—Sweetfeed: A Mike Flint Murder Mystery. 1996. 256p. 24.95 o.p. (*0-8338-0230-5*) Marshall Jones Co.

Wiggs, Susan. Enchanted Afternoon. l.t. ed. 2003. (Thorndike Romance Ser.). 562p. 29.95 (*0-7862-4985-4*) Gale Group.

—Enchanted Afternoon. 2002. 416p. mass mkt. (*1-55166-938-2*, Mira Bks.) Harlequin Enterprises, Ltd.

Witten, Matt. Breakfast at Madeline's. 1999. (Signet Book Ser.). 256p. mass mkt. 5.99 o.s.i (*0-451-19681-3*) NAL.

—Grand Illusion. 2000. (Jacob Burns Mysteries Ser.). 256p. mass mkt. 5.99 o.s.i (*0-451-19897-2*, Signet Bks.) NAL.

**SASKATCHEWAN—FICTION**

Bowen, Gail. A Colder Kind of Death. 2001. (Joanne Kilbourn Mystery Ser.). 224p. mass mkt. 7.95 (*0-7710-1495-3*) McClelland & Stewart/Tundra Bks.

—A Colder Kind of Death: A Joanne Kilbourn Mystery. 1999. 240p. 19.95 o.p. (*0-7710-1482-1*); 1995. 232p. mass mkt. 7.99 (*0-7710-1483-X*) McClelland & Stewart/Tundra Bks.

—Deadly Appearances. 2000. (Joanne Kilbourn Mystery Ser.). 280p. mass mkt. 7.99 (*0-7710-1491-0*) McClelland & Stewart/Tundra Bks.

—Deadly Appearances: A Joanne Kilbourn Mystery. 1992. mass mkt. 5.99 o.s.i (*0-7704-2433-3*) Bantam Bks.

—Deadly Appearances: A Joanne Kilbourn Mystery. (*0-88894-703-8*) Douglas & McIntyre, Ltd.

—Deadly Appearances: A Joanne Kilbourn Mystery. 1997. 280p. mass mkt. 7.99 (*0-7710-1485-6*) McClelland & Stewart/Tundra Bks.

—A Killing Spring. 1997. (Joanne Kilbourn Mystery Ser.). 272p. mass mkt. 5.95 (*0-7710-1486-4*) McClelland & Stewart/Tundra Bks.

—A Killing Spring: A Joanne Kilburn Mystery. 1997. 264p. 22.95 o.p. (*0-7710-1484-8*) McClelland & Stewart/Tundra Bks.

—Love & Murder. 1993. 224p. 17.95 o.p. (*0-312-09344-6*, Saint Martin's Minotaur) St. Martin's Pr.

—Murder at the Mendel. 2000. (Joanne Kilbourn Mystery Ser.). 216p. mass mkt. 7.99 (*0-7710-1492-9*) McClelland & Stewart/Tundra Bks.

—Murder at the Mendel: A Joanne Kilbourn Mystery. 1992. mass mkt. 7.99 o.s.i (*0-7710-1480-5*) McClelland & Stewart/Tundra Bks.

—Verdict in Blood. (Joanne Kilbourn Mystery Ser.). 264p. 1999. mass mkt. 7.95 (*0-7710-1489-9*); 1998. 20.95 o.s.i (*0-7710-1487-2*) McClelland & Stewart/Tundra Bks.

—The Wandering Soul Murders: A Joanne Kilbourn Mystery. 1993. 216p. mass mkt. 7.99 (*0-7710-1481-3*) McClelland & Stewart/Tundra Bks.

—The Wandering Soul Murders: A Joanne Kilbourn Mystery. 1994. 207p. 19.95 o.p. (*0-312-10574-6*, Saint Martin's Minotaur) St. Martin's Pr.

Dickinson, Donald Percy. Robbiestime. 2000. 324p. (*0-00-225509-X*) HarperCollins Pubs.

Glover, Ruth. Backroads to Bliss: A Novel. 2003. 272p. pap. 11.99 (*0-8007-5829-3*) Revell, Fleming H. Co.

—The Journey to Bliss. 2001. (Saskatchewan Saga Ser.: Vol. 3). 256p. (gr. 13 up). pap. 10.99 (*0-8007-5758-0*, Spire) Revell, Fleming H. Co.

—A Place Called Bliss. 2001. (Saskatchewan Saga Ser.: Vol. 1). 240p. (gr. 13 up). pap. 10.99 (*0-8007-5743-2*) Revell, Fleming H. Co.

—A Place to Call Home: Book 6. 1999. (Wildrose Ser.: 6). 212p. pap. 12.99 (*0-8341-1753-3*) Beacon Hill Pr. of Kansas City.

—Seasons of Bliss. 2002. (Saskatchewan Saga Ser.). 224p. (gr. 13 up). pap. 10.99 (*0-8007-5792-0*) Revell, Fleming H. Co.

—Second-best Bride: Book 5. 1997. (Wildrose Ser.: Bk. 5). 208p. pap. 12.99 (*0-8341-1628-6*) Beacon Hill Pr. of Kansas City.

—With Love from Bliss. 2001. (Saskatchewan Saga Ser.: Vol. 2). 240p. (gr. 13 up). pap. 10.99 (*0-8007-5744-0*) Revell, Fleming H. Co.

Glover, Ruth E. Bitter Thistle, Sweet Rose: Book 2. 1995. (Wildrose Ser.: 2). 208p. pap. 12.99 (*0-8341-1528-X*) Beacon Hill Pr. of Kansas City.

—The Shining Light: Book 1. 1993. (Wildrose Ser.: Vol. 1). 216p. pap. 12.99 (*0-8341-1514-X*) Beacon Hill Pr. of Kansas City.

—A Time To Dream: Book 3. 1995. (Wildrose Ser.: 3). 192p. pap. 12.99 (*0-8341-1572-7*) Beacon Hill Pr. of Kansas City.

—Turn Northward, Love: Book 4. 1997. (Wildrose Ser.: 4). 216p. (Orig.). pap. 12.99 (*0-8341-1590-5*) Beacon Hill Pr. of Kansas City.

Hay, Elizabeth. A Student of Weather. 2003. 384p. text 24.00 (*1-58243-123-X*, Counterpoint Pr.) Basic Bks.

—A Student of Weather. 2000. 376p. (*0-7710-3789-9*) McClelland & Stewart.

Malcolm, Murray J. Nine Dead Dogs. 2001. (Illus.). 240p. pap. 6.95 (*1-896300-41-3*) NeWest Pubs., Ltd. CAN. *Dist:* Strauss Consultants.



For book reviews, descriptive annotations, tables of contents, cover images, author biographies & additional information, updated daily, subscribe to **www.booksinprint.com** 1083

Slade, Arthur G. Dust. 2003. 192p. (J). (gr. 5). 15.95 (0-385-73004-7); lib. bdg. 17.99 (0-385-90093-7) Dell Publishing. (Delacorte Pr.).

**SAUDI ARABIA—FICTION**

Bond, Larry. Day of Wrath. unabr. ed. 1998. audio 96.00 (0-7366-4187-4, 4685) Books on Tape, Inc.

—Day of Wrath. abr. ed. 1998. 5p. audio 25.00 (0-671-58224-0, 495728, Simon & Schuster Audioworks) Simon & Schuster Audio.

—Day of Wrath. l.t. ed. 1999. (Mystery Ser.). 725p. 30.95 o.p. (0-7862-1616-6) Thorndike Pr.

—Day of Wrath. 1999. 528p. mass mkt. 7.99 (0-446-60705-3); 1998. 496p. 25.00 (0-446-51677-5) Warner Bks., Inc.

Briley, John. The First Stone: A Novel. 1997. 288p. 24.00 o.p. (0-688-15235-X, Morrow, William & Co.) Morrow/Avon.

Khashoggi, Soheir. Mirage. 1997. 438p. mass mkt. 6.99 (0-8125-5094-3, Forge Bks.) Doherty, Tom Assocs., LLC.

—Mirage. 1997. 13.04 (0-606-13081-0) Turtleback Bks.

Khashoggi, Soheir & Africano, Lillian. Mirage. 1996. 352p. 23.95 o.p. (0-312-85835-3, Forge Bks.) Doherty, Tom Assocs., LLC.

Nasrallah, Ibrahim. Prairies of Fever. Jayyusi, May & Reed, Jeremy, trs. from ARA. 1993. (Emerging Voices Ser.). 160p. 22.95 (1-56656-103-5); pap. 9.95 (1-56656-106-X) Interlink Publishing Group, Inc.

Palmer, Shirley. A Veiled Journey. 2002. 416p. mass mkt. (1-55166-924-2, 1-66924-1, Mira Bks.) Harlequin Enterprises, Ltd.

Singer, Randy D. Directed Verdict. 2002. 496p. pap. 13.99 (1-57856-633-9) WaterBrook Pr.

Wilkinson, David Marion. The Empty Quarter. Nawrocki, Sarah, ed. 2003. (Celestial Arts Ser.). 260p. 21.95 (0-9651879-2-6) Boaz Publishing Co.

**SAVANNAH (GA.)—FICTION**

Allen, Nancy Campbell. Echoes. 2001. 262p. 14.95 (1-57734-813-3) Covenant Communications.

Andrews, Mary Kay. Savannah Blues. 2002. 416p. 24.95 (0-06-019958-X) HarperCollins Pubs.

DePoy, Phillip. Too Easy. 1998. (Flap Tucker Mysteries Ser.). 288p. mass mkt. 5.99 o.s.i (0-440-22495-0) Dell Publishing.

Ellis, Julie. Savage Oaks. 1981. mass mkt. 2.25 o.s.i (0-449-23996-9, Fawcett) Ballantine Bks.

—Savage Oaks. l.t. ed. 2000. (G. K. Hall Romance Ser.). 453p. 26.95 (0-7838-9158-X, Macmillan Reference USA) Gale Group.

Fuhrman, Chris. The Dangerous Lives of Altar Boys: A Novel. Ng, Donna, ed. 1996. 192p. pap. 12.00 (0-671-52903-X, Washington Square Pr.) Simon & Schuster.

—The Dangerous Lives of Altar Boys: A Novel. 1994. 176p. 19.95 (0-8203-1632-6); 2001. 200p. reprint ed. 14.95 (0-8203-2338-1) Univ. of Georgia Pr.

Harris, William C., Jr. No Enemy but Time: A Novel of the South. 2003. 288p. pap. 14.95 (0-312-32012-4, Saint Martin's Griffin); 2002. (Illus.). 320p. 24.95 (0-312-26980-3) St. Martin's Pr.

Harris, William Charles, Jr. Delirium of the Brave. 2nd ed. 1999. xi, 366p. 24.95 (0-312-25495-4) St. Martin's Pr.

Hervey, Harry. The Damned Don't Cry. 2003. 35.00 (0-87797-305-9); pap. (0-87797-306-7) Cherokee Publishing Co.

Jones, Jill. Remember Your Lies. 2001. 320p. mass mkt. 6.50 (0-312-97715-8, St. Martin's Paperbacks) St. Martin's Pr.

London, Jeanie. About That Night... 2002. (Harlequin Blaze Ser.). mass mkt. (0-373-79057-0, Harlequin Bks.) Harlequin Enterprises, Ltd.

Rogers, Evelyn. Raven. 1995. 384p. mass mkt. 4.99 o.s.i (0-8217-4800-9, Zebra Bks.) Kensington Publishing Corp.

Rosen, Charles. The Cockroach Basketball League. 1992. 288p. 21.00 o.p. (1-55611-329-3) Fine, Donald I. Bks.

—The Cockroach Basketball League: A Novel. 1998. 240p. pap. 13.95 (1-888363-78-9) Seven Stories Pr.

Tan, Maureen. AKA. Jane. 1999. 336p. mass mkt. 6.50 (0-446-60667-7) Warner Bks., Inc.

—AKA Jane. 1997. 304p. 22.00 o.p. (0-89296-658-0) Mysterious Pr.

—AKA Jane. abr. ed. 1998. audio 23.00 (1-56876-070-1) Soundlines Entertainment, Inc.

—Run Jane Run. 1999. 274p. 22.00 o.s.i (0-89296-659-9) Mysterious Pr.

—Run Jane Run. 2000. 304p. mass mkt. 6.50 (0-446-60904-8); 1999. E-Book 4.95 (0-446-91276-X) Warner Bks., Inc.

Taylor, Janelle. Promise Me Forever. l.t. ed. 1997. (Romance Ser.). 554p. 24.95 (0-7862-0905-4, Five Star) Gale Group.

—Promise Me Forever. 1992. mass mkt. 5.99 o.s.i (0-8217-3764-3); 1991. mass mkt. 20.00 o.p. (0-8217-3553-5) Kensington Publishing Corp. (Zebra Bks.).

—Promise Me Forever. abr. ed. 1994. audio 5.99 (1-57096-007-0, RAZ 908) Romance Alive Audio.

**SCOTLAND—FICTION**

Abbott, Lee K., et al. The Putt at the End of the World. 2001. audio 24.98 (1-58621-019-X); 2000. audio 24.98 (1-57042-918-9) Time Warner AudioBooks.

—The Putt at the End of the World. Standiford, Les, ed. 2000. (Illus.). 256p. 23.95 o.p. (0-446-52600-2) Warner Bks., Inc.

—The Putt at the End of the World. 2000. E-Book 14.95 (0-446-91470-3) Warner Bks., Inc.

Abe, Shana. The Truelove Bride. 1999. 368p. mass mkt. 5.99 (0-553-58054-X) Bantam Bks.

Aboulela, Leila. The Translator. 2001. 184p. pap. text 12.95 (0-7486-6257-X) Polygon GBR. *Dist:* Interlink Publishing Group, Inc.

Anderson, Margaret J. The Druid's Gift. 1989. 192p. (J). 13.99 o.s.i (0-394-91936-X); 12.95 o.s.i (0-394-81936-5) Random Hse. Children's Bks. (Knopf Bks. for Young Readers).

Archer, Catherine. Dragon's Daughter. 2003. (Harlequin Historicals Ser.: No. 641). 304p. mass mkt. (0-373-29241-4, Harlequin Bks.) Harlequin Enterprises, Ltd.

Armstrong, Campbell. Last Darkness. 2002. 480p. pap. (0-00-226202-9) HarperCollins Pubs.

—The Last Darkness. 2002. 480p. (0-00-714265-X) HarperCollins Pubs.

Arnold, Margot, pseud. Lament for a Lady Laird. 1982. 224p. 2.50 (0-86721-132-6, Jove) Berkley Publishing Group.

—Lament for a Lady Laird. 1990. (Penny Spring & Sir Toby Glendower Mystery Ser.). 224p. reprint ed. pap. 7.95 (0-88150-159-X, Foul Play) Norton, W. W. & Co., Inc.

Atkinson, Kate. Emotionally Weird. 2000. 343p. 25.00 o.p. (0-312-20324-1) Picador.

Banks, Iain M. The Wasp Factory, 001. 1984. 184p. 13.95 o.p. (0-395-36296-2) Houghton Mifflin Co.

—The Wasp Factory. 1998. 192p. pap. 13.00 (0-684-85315-9, Simon & Schuster) Simon & Schuster.

—The Wasp Factory. 1986. 192p. mass mkt. 3.95 o.s.i (0-446-34087-1) Warner Bks., Inc.

Barker, Elspeth. O Caledonia. 1992. 18.95 o.s.i (0-15-167774-3) Harcourt Trade Pubs.

Barrie, J. M. The Little Minister. 1968. (Airmont Classics Ser.). (J). (gr. 10 up). mass mkt. 0.75 o.p. (0-8049-0187-2, CL-187) Airmont Publishing Co., Inc.

Bateman, Tracey Victoria. Highland Legacy: Four Generations of Love & Rooted in Scotland. 2004. 352p. pap. 6.97 (1-59310-082-5) Barbour Publishing, Inc.

Beaton, M. C., pseud. Death of a Cad. 1988. mass mkt. 4.99 o.s.i (0-8041-0225-2, Ivy Bks.) Ballantine Bks.

—Death of a Cad. l.t. ed. 1995. 265p. pap. 17.95 (0-7838-1457-7, Macmillan Reference USA) Gale Group.

—Death of a Cad. unabr. ed. 1999. audio 46.00 (0-7887-4080-6, H1074E7, Clipper Audio) Recorded Bks., LLC.

—Death of a Cad. 1986. 208p. 13.95 o.p. (0-312-00118-5) St. Martin's Pr.

—Death of a Cad. 2000. 222p. pap. 6.95 o.p. (0-553-40792-9) Transworld Publishers Ltd. GBR. *Dist:* Trafalgar Square.

—Death of a Cad. 2004. mass mkt. (0-446-60714-2) Warner Bks., Inc.

—Death of a Celebrity. l.t. ed. 2002. 264p. 26.95 (1-58724-152-8, Wheeler Publishing, Inc.) Gale Group.

—Death of a Celebrity. 2002. 272p. 23.95 (0-89296-676-9) Mysterious Pr.

—Death of a Celebrity. 2003. 304p. mass mkt. 6.99 (0-446-61204-9) Warner Bks., Inc.

—Death of a Charming Man. 2001. 208p. 18.95 (0-89296-529-0) Mysterious Pr.

—Death of a Charming Man. unabr. ed. 1997. (Hamish Macbeth Mystery Ser.). audio 44.00 (0-7887-1084-2, 95088E7) Recorded Bks., LLC.

—Death of a Charming Man. 1995. (Hamish Macbeth Mystery Ser.). 176p. reprint ed. mass mkt. 6.99 (0-446-40338-5) Warner Bks., Inc.

—Death of a Dentist. 2001. 256p. 22.00 (0-89296-643-2); E-Book 4.95 (0-446-92301-X); E-Book 4.95 (0-446-91295-6) Mysterious Pr.

—Death of a Dentist. unabr. ed. 1998. (Hamish Macbeth Mystery Ser.). audio 44.00 (0-7887-2044-9, 95408E7) Recorded Bks., LLC.

—Death of a Dentist. 1998. (Hamish Macbeth Mystery Ser.). 256p. mass mkt. 6.99 (0-446-60601-4); mass mkt. (0-446-40494-2, Mysterious Pr. Paperback Bks.) Warner Bks., Inc.

—Death of a Dustman. 2001. (Hamish Macbeth Mystery Ser.). 215p. 22.95 o.p. (0-89296-631-9) Mysterious Pr.

—Death of a Dustman. 2002. (Hamish Macbeth Mystery Ser.). 256p. reprint ed. mass mkt. 6.99 (0-446-60931-5) Warner Bks., Inc.

—Death of a Glutton. 1995. 176p. mass mkt. 6.50 (0-8041-1212-6, Ivy Bks.) Ballantine Bks.

—Death of a Glutton. l.t. ed. 1996. 17.95 o.p. (0-7838-1484-4, Macmillan Reference USA) Gale Group.

—Death of a Glutton. 1993. 152p. 16.95 o.p. (0-312-08761-6, Saint Martin's Minotaur) St. Martin's Pr.

—Death of a Glutton. 187p. pap. 6.95 o.p. (0-553-40972-7) Transworld Publishers Ltd. GBR. *Dist:* Trafalgar Square.

—Death of a Gossip. l.t. ed. 1986. 13.95 o.p. (0-89340-955-3, 254) BBC Audiobooks America.

—Death of a Gossip. 1988. 160p. reprint ed. mass mkt. 4.99 o.s.i (0-8041-0226-0, Ivy Bks.) Ballantine Bks.

—Death of a Gossip. l.t. ed. 1996. (Nightingale Ser.). 194p. pap. 17.95 o.p. (0-7838-1472-0, Macmillan Reference USA) Gale Group.

—Death of a Gossip. 1985. 192p. 12.95 o.p. (0-312-18637-1) St. Martin's Pr.

—Death of a Gossip. 1999. (Hamish Macbeth Mystery Ser.). 192p. reprint ed. mass mkt. 6.99 (0-446-60713-4) Warner Bks., Inc.

—Death of a Hussy. 1991. 160p. mass mkt. 6.99 (0-8041-0768-8, Ivy Bks.) Ballantine Bks.

—Death of a Hussy. 1990. 160p. 14.95 o.p. (0-312-05071-2, Saint Martin's Minotaur) St. Martin's Pr.

—Death of a Hussy. l.t. ed. 1999. (Nightingale Ser.). 208p. pap. 21.95 (0-7838-8664-0) Thorndike Pr.

—Death of a Hussy. 2000. pap. 6.95 (0-553-40967-0) Transworld Publishers Ltd. GBR. *Dist:* Trafalgar Square.

—Death of a Macho Man. 1996. (Hamish Macbeth Mystery Ser.). 224p. 4.95 o.p. (0-89296-531-2) Mysterious Pr.

—Death of a Macho Man. unabr. ed. 1997. (Hamish Macbeth Mystery Ser.: Vol. 12). audio 44.00 (0-7887-1749-9, 95227E7) Recorded Bks., LLC.

—Death of a Macho Man. 1997. (Hamish Macbeth Mystery Ser.). 240p. mass mkt. 6.99 (0-446-40340-7) Warner Bks., Inc.

—Death of a Nag. 2001. 192p. E-Book 4.95 (0-446-91296-4); 18.95 (0-89296-530-4); E-Book 4.95 (0-446-92302-8) Mysterious Pr.

—Death of a Nag. unabr. ed. 1997. (Hamish Macbeth Mystery Ser.). audio 44.00 (0-7887-1285-3, 95147E7) Recorded Bks., LLC.

—Death of a Nag. 1996. (Hamish Macbeth Mystery Ser.). 192p. mass mkt. 5.99 (0-446-40339-3) Warner Bks., Inc.

—Death of a Perfect Wife. 1990. mass mkt. 4.99 o.s.i (0-8041-0593-6, Ivy Bks.) Ballantine Bks.

—Death of a Perfect Wife. 1989. 224p. 15.95 o.p. (0-312-03322-2, Saint Martin's Minotaur) St. Martin's Pr.

—Death of a Perfect Wife. 2000. 202p. pap. 6.95 o.p. (0-553-40794-5) Transworld Publishers Ltd. GBR. *Dist:* Trafalgar Square.

—Death of a Poison Pen. 2004. 23.95 (0-89296-788-9) Mysterious Pr.

—Death of a Prankster. 1993. (Hamish Macbeth Mystery Ser.: Vol. 7). 176p. mass mkt. 6.50 (0-8041-1102-2, Ivy Bks.) Ballantine Bks.

—Death of a Prankster. l.t. ed. 1998. (Hamish Macbeth Mystery Ser.). pap. 19.95 o.p. (0-7838-8417-6, Macmillan Reference USA) Gale Group.

—Death of a Prankster. 1992. 160p. 16.95 o.p. (0-312-07701-7, Saint Martin's Minotaur) St. Martin's Pr.

—Death of a Prankster. 187p. pap. 6.95 o.p. (0-553-40969-7) Transworld Publishers Ltd. GBR. *Dist:* Trafalgar Square.

—Death of a Scriptwriter. 224p. 2001. 22.00 (0-89296-644-0); 2001. E-Book 4.95 (0-446-92314-1); 1999. E-Book 4.95 (0-446-91297-2) Mysterious Pr.

—Death of a Scriptwriter. unabr. ed. 1998. (Hamish Macbeth Mystery Ser.). audio 44.00 (0-7887-2175-5, 95471E7) Recorded Bks., LLC.

—Death of a Scriptwriter. 1999. (Hamish Macbeth Mystery Ser.). 224p. reprint ed. mass mkt. 6.99 (0-446-60698-7) Warner Bks., Inc.

—Death of a Snob. 1992. (Hamish Macbeth Mystery Ser.). 160p. mass mkt. 6.99 (0-8041-0912-5, Ivy Bks.) Ballantine Bks.

—Death of a Snob. l.t. ed. 2000. (G. K. Hall Nightingale Ser.). 210p. 30.00 (0-7838-8755-8, Macmillan Reference USA) Gale Group.

—Death of a Snob. 1991. 15.95 o.p. (0-312-05851-9, Saint Martin's Minotaur) St. Martin's Pr.

—Death of a Snob. 186p. pap. 6.95 o.p. (0-553-40968-9) Transworld Publishers Ltd. GBR. *Dist:* Trafalgar Square.

—Death of a Travelling Man. 1996. 176p. mass mkt. 6.99 (0-8041-1211-8, Ivy Bks.) Ballantine Bks.

—Death of a Travelling Man. 1993. (Hamish Macbeth Mystery Ser.). 208p. 17.95 o.p. (0-312-09783-2, Saint Martin's Minotaur) St. Martin's Pr.

—Death of a Village. 2003. 274p. 30.95 (1-58724-441-1) Gale Group.

—Death of a Village. 2003. (Hamish Macbeth Mystery Ser.). 256p. 23.95 (0-89296-677-7) Mysterious Pr.

—Death of a Village. 2004. 272p. mass mkt. 6.99 (0-446-61371-1) Warner Bks., Inc.

—Death of an Addict. 2001. (Hamish Macbeth Mystery Ser.). 224p. 22.00 o.p. (0-89296-675-0) Mysterious Pr.

—Death of an Addict. unabr. ed. 1999. (Hamish Macbeth Mystery Ser.). audio 46.00 (0-7887-3486-5, 95690E7) Recorded Bks., LLC.

—Death of an Addict. 2001. (Hamish Macbeth Mystery Ser.). 240p. reprint ed. mass mkt. 6.99 (0-446-60828-9) Warner Bks., Inc.

—Death of an Outsider. 1990. (Hamish Macbeth Mystery Ser.). 160p. mass mkt. 4.99 o.s.i (0-8041-0487-5, Ivy Bks.) Ballantine Bks.

—Death of an Outsider. l.t. ed. 1998. (Hamish Macbeth Mystery Ser.). pap. 19.95 o.p. (0-7838-8299-8); (0-7540-3136-5) Gale Group. (Macmillan Reference USA).

—Death of an Outsider. unabr. ed. 1999. (Hamish Macbeth Mystery Ser.). audio 38.00 (1-84197-009-3, H1009E7);Set. audio 38.00 Recorded Bks., LLC.

—Death of an Outsider. 1988. (Hamish Macbeth Mystery Ser.). 192p. 14.95 o.p. (0-312-02188-7, Saint Martin's Minotaur) St. Martin's Pr.

—Death of an Outsider. 2000. (Hamish Macbeth Mystery Ser.). 218p. pap. 6.95 o.p. (0-553-40793-7) Transworld Publishers Ltd. GBR. *Dist:* Trafalgar Square.

—Death of an Outsider: A Hamish Macbeth Mystery. 1991. (Hamish Macbeth Mystery Ser.). 3.99 o.p. (0-517-06864-8) Random Hse. Value Publishing.

—A Highland Christmas. (Hamish Macbeth Mystery Ser.). 2001. (Illus.). 128p. 16.95 o.p. (0-89296-699-8); 2000. E-Book 16.95 (0-446-96000-4); 1999. 128p. E-Book 9.95 (0-446-91480-0) Mysterious Pr.

—A Highland Christmas. 2002. 160p. mass mkt. 4.99 (0-446-60919-6) Warner Bks., Inc.

Beckwith, Lillian. An Island Apart. 2001. 192p. pap. 9.95 (0-7551-0284-3) House of Stratus, Inc. GBR. *Dist:* Midpoint Trade Bks., Inc.

—An Island Apart. 1993. 176p. 18.95 o.p. (0-312-10483-9) St. Martin's Pr.

Black, Laura. Albany. 1984. 256p. 11.95 o.p. (0-312-01708-1) St. Martin's Pr.

—The Falls of Gard. l.t. ed. 1987. 372p. 18.95 o.p. (0-8161-4236-X, Macmillan Reference USA) Gale Group.

—The Falls of Gard. 1986. 256p. 15.95 o.p. (0-312-28009-2) St. Martin's Pr.

—Ravenburn. 1980. (General Ser.). lib. bdg. 16.95 o.p. (0-8161-3129-5, Macmillan Reference USA) Gale Group.

—Ravenburn. 1978. 10.00 o.p. (0-312-66408-7) St. Martin's Pr.

—Strathgallant. 1981. 316p. 11.95 o.p. (0-312-76481-2) St. Martin's Pr.

—Wild Cat. 1979. 10.00 o.p. (0-312-88001-4) St. Martin's Pr.

Black, Veronica. A Vow of Sanctity: A Sister Joan Mystery. 1994. mass mkt. 4.99 o.s.i (0-8041-1244-4, Ivy Bks.) Ballantine Bks.

—A Vow of Sanctity: A Sister Joan Mystery. 1993. 192p. 16.95 (0-312-09408-6, Saint Martin's Minotaur) St. Martin's Pr.

—A Vow of Sanctity: A Sister Joan Mystery. l.t. ed. 1994. (Ulverscroft Large Print Ser.). 400p. 29.99 o.p. (0-7089-3197-9, Ulverscroft) Thorpe, F. A. Pubs. GBR. *Dist:* Ulverscroft Large Print Bks., Ltd., Ulverscroft Large Print Canada, Ltd.

Blair, Emma. An Apple from Eden. 1998. 362p. o.s.i (0-316-88239-9) Little Brown & Co.

—The Blackbird's Tale. l.t. ed. 1995. 876p. 22.95 o.p. (0-7838-1156-X, Macmillan Reference USA) Gale Group.

Bluehorse, Elizabeth. The View from the Hill. 2nd ed. 2002. 122p. pap. 13.98 (0-7596-0129-1) 1stBooks Library.

—The View from the Hill. 1998. 81p. 14.95 o.p. (0-533-12454-9) Vantage Pr., Inc.

Boucher, Rita. The Devil's Due. 1996. 224p. mass mkt. 4.99 o.s.i (0-451-18751-2, Signet Bks.) NAL.

Brandewyne, Rebecca. Destiny's Daughter. 2001. 402p. mass mkt. (1-55166-782-7, 1-66782-3, Mira Bks.) Harlequin Enterprises, Ltd.

Brandon, Paul. Swim the Moon. 384p. 2002. pap. 14.95 (0-312-87793-5); 2001. 25.95 (0-312-87794-3) Doherty, Tom Assocs., LLC. (Tor Bks.).

Braun, Lilian Jackson. The Cat Who Wasn't There. l.t. ed. 1993. (General Ser.). 367p. 17.95 o.p. (0-8161-5694-8, Macmillan Reference USA) Gale Group.

—The Cat Who Wasn't There. 1993. 13.04 (0-606-12649-X) Turtleback Bks.

Brockway, Connie. McClairen's Isle: The Passionate One. 1999. 400p. mass mkt. 6.99 (0-440-22629-5) Dell Publishing.

—McClairen's Isle: The Ravishing One. 2000. 384p. mass mkt. 6.99 (0-440-22630-9) Dell Publishing.

—McClairen's Isle: The Reckless One. 2000. 384p. mass mkt. 6.99 (0-440-22627-9) Dell Publishing.

Brockway, Connie & Berg, Patti. My Scottish Summer. 2001. 496p. E-Book 4.95 (0-7595-4484-0); E-Book 4.95 (0-7595-6481-7) Warner Bks., Inc.

Brookmyre, Christopher. Country of the Blind. 2002. 416p. pap. 12.00 (0-8021-3919-1, Grove Pr.) Grove/Atlantic, Inc.

—Quite Ugly One Morning. 2002. 224p. pap. 12.00 (*0-8021-3861-6*, Grove Pr.) Grove/Atlantic, Inc.

—Quite Ugly One Morning. 1996. 224p. o.s.i (*0-316-87883-9*) Little Brown & Co.

Brown, Debra Lee. A Rogue's Heart. 2002. (Harlequin Historicals Ser.). 304p. mass mkt. (*0-373-29225-2*, Harlequin Bks.) Harlequin Enterprises, Ltd.

Brown, George M. Beside the Ocean of Time. 1995. 224p. (*1-896209-12-2*) Bayeux Arts, Inc.

—Beside the Ocean of Time. l.t. unabr. ed. 1998. 240p. 21.95 (*1-85695-249-5*, 952495) ISIS Large Print Bks. GBR. *Dist:* Transaction Pubs.

—Beside the Ocean of Time. 1994. 224p. 19.95 o.p. (*0-7195-5368-7*) Murray, John Pubs., Ltd. GBR. *Dist:* Trafalgar Square.

—Magnus. 1999. 196p. pap. 11.95 (*0-86241-814-3*) Canongate Bks. GBR. *Dist:* Grove/Atlantic, Inc.

—Winter Tales. 1996. 247p. 25.95 o.p. (*0-7195-5435-7*) Murray, John Pubs., Ltd. GBR. *Dist:* Trafalgar Square.

Brown, John. Rab & His Friends. 1977. (Short Story Index Reprint Ser.). reprint ed. 23.95 (*0-8369-4193-4*) Ayer Co. Pubs., Inc.

Buchan, John. Castle Gay. 1993. pap. 7.00 (*0-7509-0483-6*) Sutton Publishing, Ltd. GBR. *Dist:* International Publishers Marketing.

—Huntingtower. Stonehouse, Ann F., ed. 1997. (Oxford World's Classics Ser.). (Illus.). 260p. pap. 8.95 o.p. (*0-19-283229-8*) Oxford Univ. Pr., Inc.

—Huntingtower. 1993. pap. 7.00 (*0-7509-0484-4*) Sutton Publishing, Ltd. GBR. *Dist:* International Publishers Marketing.

—The Island of Sheep. 22.95 (*0-8488-0926-2*) Amereon, Ltd.

—The Island of Sheep. unabr. ed. 2001. audio 61.95 (*1-85695-769-1*, 940503) ISIS Audio Bks. GBR. *Dist:* Ulverscroft Large Print Bks., Ltd.

—The Island of Sheep. Duncan, Ian, ed. 1997. (Oxford World's Classics Ser.). (Illus.). 268p. pap. (*0-19-282433-3*) Oxford Univ. Pr., Inc.

—The Island of Sheep. l.t. ed. 1970. (Ulverscroft Large Print Ser.). 432p. 29.99 o.p. (*0-85456-003-3*, Ulverscroft) Thorpe, F. A. Pubs. GBR. *Dist:* Ulverscroft Large Print Bks., Ltd., Ulverscroft Large Print Canada, Ltd.

—The Power-House & the 39 Steps. 2002. xxviii, 233p. pap. 11.95 (*1-873631-95-2*) B & W Publishing GBR. *Dist:* Interlink Publishing Group, Inc.

—Witch Wood. 1993. (Oxford World's Classics Ser.). 366p. pap. 4.99 (*0-19-282941-6*) Oxford Univ. Pr., Inc.

Burke, John. Death by Marzipan. l.t. ed. 2001. (Ulverscroft Large Print Ser.). 400p. 31.99 (*0-7089-4344-6*, Ulverscroft) Thorpe, F. A. Pubs. GBR. *Dist:* Ulverscroft Large Print Bks., Ltd., Ulverscroft Large Print Canada, Ltd.

Cabot, Patricia. Lady of Skye. 2001. (Sonnet Bks.). 464p. pap. 6.50 (*0-7434-1027-0*); reprint ed. E-Book 6.50 (*0-7434-2147-7*) Simon & Schuster. (Pocket).

Cadell, Elizabeth. The Marrying Kind. l.t. ed. 1980. (General Ser.). lib. bdg. 12.95 o.p. (*0-8161-3083-3*, Macmillan Reference USA) Gale Group.

Caird, Janet. The Umbrella-Maker's Daughter. 1980. 10.95 o.p. (*0-312-82855-1*) St. Martin's Pr.

—The Umbrella-Maker's Daughter. l.t. ed. 1983. (Ulverscroft Large Print Ser.). 464p. 29.99 o.p. (*0-7089-0943-4*, Ulverscroft) Thorpe, F. A. Pubs. GBR. *Dist:* Ulverscroft Large Print Bks., Ltd., Ulverscroft Large Print Canada, Ltd.

Campbell, Archibald Olrig. Tales from the Pit. 2002. 400p. pap. 16.95 (*1-899874-17-8*) Goblinshead GBR. *Dist:* Dufour Editions, Inc.

Campbell, Drew. Dead Letter House. 2002. 192p. pap. 15.00 (*1-903238-29-3*, 11:9) Wilson, Neil Publishing GBR. *Dist:* Interlink Publishing Group, Inc.

Canham, Marsha. Midnight Honor. 2001. 400p. mass mkt. 6.50 (*0-440-23522-7*) Dell Publishing.

Carter, Marie, ed. Word Jig: New Fiction from Scotland. 2003. 242p. 26.00 (*1-931236-26-7*); pap. 16.00 (*1-931236-25-9*) Hanging Loose Pr.

Cartland, Barbara. The Captive Heart. 1980. 1.75 o.s.i (*0-515-05566-2*, Jove) Berkley Publishing Group.

—The Chieftain Without a Heart. 1978. 6.95 o.p. (*0-525-07985-8*, Dutton) Dutton/Plume.

—The Chieftain Without a Heart. l.t. ed. 2000. (Paperback Ser.). 227p. pap. 23.95 (*0-7838-9141-5*) Thorndike Pr.

—The Eyes of Love. 1994. (Camfield Romance Ser.: No. 135). 176p. mass mkt. 3.99 o.s.i (*0-515-11496-0*, Jove) Berkley Publishing Group.

—The Heart of the Clan. 1981. (Barbara Cartland Ser.: No. 13). 192p. 1.75 o.s.i (*0-515-05929-3*, Jove) Berkley Publishing Group.

—The Heart of the Clan. l.t. ed. 2000. (Romance Ser.). 216p. 26.95 (*0-7862-2484-3*) Thorndike Pr.

—The Loveless Marriage. 1995. (Camfield Romance Ser.: No. 139). 176p. mass mkt. 3.99 o.s.i (*0-515-11572-X*, Jove) Berkley Publishing Group.

—The Loveless Marriage. l.t. ed. 1998. (Nightingale Ser.). 220p. pap. 21.95 (*0-7838-1893-9*) Thorndike Pr.

Castle, Linda Lea. Embrace the Sun. 2002. 352p. mass mkt. 5.99 o.s.i (*0-8217-7268-6*) Kensington Publishing Corp.

Charles, Caroline. Laird of Drumm. l.t. ed. 1996. 235p. pap. 20.95 o.p. (*0-7838-1896-3*, Macmillan Reference USA) Gale Group.

Chesterton, G. K. The Ball & the Cross. 1985. 384p. pap. 6.95 o.p. (*0-85115-236-8*) Academy Chicago Pubs., Ltd.

—The Ball & the Cross. reprint ed. lib. bdg. 98.00 (*0-7426-3015-3*); 2001. 403p. pap. text 28.00 (*0-7426-8015-0*) Classic Bks.

—The Ball & the Cross. unabr. ed. 1995. 192p. reprint ed. pap. 8.95 (*0-486-28805-6*) Dover Pubns., Inc.

Clarbe, Mary S. Piper to the Clan. 1970. 4.75 o.p. (*0-670-55660-2*) Viking Penguin.

Coffman, Elaine. The Bride of Black Douglas. l.t. ed. 2002. (Wheeler Large Print Book Ser.). pap. 23.95 (*1-58724-175-7*, Wheeler Publishing, Inc.) Gale Group.

—The Bride of Black Douglas. 2000. 448p. mass mkt. (*1-55166-596-4*, 1-66596-7, Mira Bks.) Harlequin Enterprises, Ltd.

Constant, Jan. MacKenzie's Woman. l.t. ed. 1993. 269p. lib. bdg. 15.95 (*0-8161-5842-8*, Macmillan Reference USA) Gale Group.

—Master of Craigraven. l.t. ed. 1994. 230p. lib. bdg. 16.95 (*0-8161-5844-4*, Macmillan Reference USA) Gale Group.

Cooper, James Fenimore. The Two Admirals. 1842. 504p. (YA). reprint ed. pap. text 34.00 (*1-4047-2388-9*) Classic Textbooks.

—The Two Admirals. 1990. (Works of James Fenimore Cooper). reprint ed. lib. bdg. 79.00 (*0-7812-2388-1*) Reprint Services Corp.

—The Two Admirals: A Tale. 1990. 511p. (C). (gr. 9-12). text 59.50 (*0-88706-905-3*); pap. text 20.95 (*0-88706-907-X*) State Univ. of New York Pr.

Copeland, Bonnie C. Lady of Moray. 1979. 13.95 o.p. (*0-689-10996-2*, Scribner) Simon & Schuster.

Coulter, Catherine. The Duke. 1997. (Star-Romance Ser.). 328p. 25.95 (*0-7862-0914-3*, Five Star); 26.95 (*1-56895-416-6*, Wheeler Publishing, Inc.) Gale Group.

—The Duke. 384p. 2002. mass mkt. 7.99 (*0-451-20663-0*); 1995. mass mkt. 7.99 o.s.i (*0-451-40617-6*, Topaz) NAL.

—The Heiress Bride. l.t. ed. 1993. 22.95 o.p. (*1-56895-019-5*, Wheeler Publishing, Inc.) Gale Group.

—The Heiress Bride. l.t. ed. 1996. (Magna Large Print Ser.). 500p. (*0-7505-0766-7*) Magna Large Print Bks. GBR. *Dist:* Ulverscroft Large Print Canada, Ltd.

—The Heiress Bride. 1993. 304p. 19.95 o.p. (*0-399-13778-5*, G. P. Putnam's Sons) Penguin Group (USA) Inc.

—The Heiress Bride. 19.95 o.s.i (*0-399-13999-0*) Putnam Publishing Group, The.

—The Scottish Bride. 2001. (Bride Trilogy Ser.: Vol. 4). 368p. mass mkt. 7.99 (*0-515-12993-3*, Jove) Berkley Publishing Group.

—The Scottish Bride. l.t. ed. 2001. (Thorndike American Ser.). 519p. 31.95 (*0-7862-3216-1*); pap. 28.95 (*0-7862-3217-X*) Thorndike Pr.

Courtney, Dayle. The Knife with Eyes. 1981. (Thorne Twins Adventure Bks.). (Illus.). 192p. (Orig.). (J). (gr. 5 up). pap. 2.98 o.p. (*0-87239-471-9*, 2716) Standard Publishing.

Crockett, S. R. The Grey Man. 1988. (C). 65.00 (*0-907526-15-2*); 1980. (Illus.). 328p. pap. 59.95 (*0-907526-14-4*) Alloway Publishing, Ltd. GBR. *Dist:* State Mutual Bk. & Periodical Service, Ltd.

Croft, Rachael. Mistress of Trennish. l.t. ed. 2001. (Linford Romance Large Print Ser.). 272p. pap. 19.99 (*0-7089-4549-X*, Ulverscroft) Thorpe, F. A. Pubs. GBR. *Dist:* Ulverscroft Large Print Bks., Ltd., Ulverscroft Large Print Canada, Ltd.

Crombie, Deborah. Now May You Weep. l.t. ed. 2004. lib. bdg. 29.95 (*1-58547-409-6*, Platinum) Ctr. Point Large Print.

—Now May You Weep. 2003. 384p. 23.95 (*0-06-052523-1*, Morrow, William & Co.) Morrow/Avon.

Crow, Donna Fletcher. The Fields of Bannockburn: A Novel of Christian Scotland from Its Origins to Independence. pap. 19.99 o.p. (*0-8024-7736-4*, 141) Moody Pr.

Davidson, Toni. Scar Culture. 2000. 247p. pap. 14.00 (*0-393-32089-8*, Norton Paperbacks) Norton, W. W. & Co., Inc.

Davis, Kathryn Lynn. Somewhere Lies the Moon. 1999. 544p. 24.95 o.s.i (*0-671-73605-1*, Atria); 2000. 720p. reprint ed. pap. 6.99 (*0-671-73606-X*, Pocket Star) Simon & Schuster.

Davis, Margaret Thomson. The Gourlay Girls. 2001. 256p. pap. 11.95 (*1-903265-09-6*) B & W Publishing GBR. *Dist:* Interlink Publishing Group, Inc.

Davis, Margaret Thomson. The Clydesiders. 2001. 278p. pap. 11.95 (*1-903265-06-1*) B & W Publishing GBR. *Dist:* Interlink Publishing Group, Inc.

Dawson, Geralyn. Sizzle All Day. 2000. (Illus.). 368p. pap. 6.50 (*0-671-03448-0*, Pocket) Simon & Schuster.

Delacroix, Claire. The Bride Quest: The Countess. 2000. (Bride Quest Ser.: Vol. 4). 384p. mass mkt. 6.50 (*0-440-23634-7*) Dell Publishing.

—The Damsel. 1999. (Bride Quest Ser.: No. 2). 384p. mass mkt. 6.50 (*0-440-22588-4*) Dell Publishing.

Dengler, Sandy. King of the Stars: St. Columba's Sojourn to Scotland. 1995. (Heroes of Misty Isle Ser.). pap. 9.99 o.p. (*0-8024-2296-9*) Moody Pr.

Derwent, Lavinia. The Boy from Sula. 2002. (Kelpies Ser.). (Illus.). 160p. (J). pap. (*0-86315-400-X*) Floris Bks. GBR. *Dist:* SteinerBooks, Inc.

—Sula. 1989. (Kelpie Ser.). 160p. pap. 6.95 o.p. (*0-86241-068-1*) Trafalgar Square.

Deveraux, Jude. The Duchess. l.t. ed. 1992. (General Ser.). 494p. 21.95 o.p. (*0-8161-5413-9*); 17.95 o.p. (*0-8161-5414-7*) Gale Group. (Macmillan Reference USA).

—The Duchess. Marrow, Linda, ed. 1992. 368p. mass mkt. 7.99 (*0-671-68972-X*, Pocket); 1991. 320p. 21.00 o.p. (*0-671-68971-1*, Atria) Simon & Schuster.

—The Duchess. abr. ed. 1999. audio 9.98 (*0-671-04415-X*); Set. 1991. audio 16.00 (*0-671-74751-7*, 390693) Simon & Schuster Audio. (Simon & Schuster Audioworks).

—Temptation. l.t. ed. 2001. (Large Print Book Ser.). 383p. 29.95 (*1-58724-021-1*, Wheeler Publishing, Inc.) Gale Group.

Dier, Debra. MacLaren's Bride. 2000. 368p. (Orig.). mass mkt. 5.50 (*0-8439-4768-3*, Leisure Bks.) Dorchester Publishing Co., Inc.

Dodd, Christina, et al. Scottish Brides. 1999. 384p. mass mkt. 6.99 (*0-380-80451-4*, Avon Bks.) Morrow/Avon.

Drake, Shannon. Come the Morning. abr. ed. 2000. audio 7.99 o.s.i (*1-56740-331-X*, 1956, Paperback Nova Audio Bks.); 1999. audio 17.95 o.p. (*1-56740-822-2*, 1601, Nova Audio Bks.); 1999. audio 89.25 (*1-56740-630-0*, 1599, Unabridged Library Editions); 1999. audio 28.95 (*1-56740-401-4*, 1598, Bookcassette) Brilliance Audio.

—Come the Morning. abr. ed. 1999. audio 17.95 Highsmith Inc.

—Come the Morning. 2000. 448p. mass mkt. 6.99 (*0-8217-6471-3*); 2000. mass mkt. 6.99 (*0-8217-6971-5*, Zebra Bks.); 1999. 384p. 17.95 o.s.i (*1-57566-383-X*) Kensington Publishing Corp.

—When Darkness Falls. 2000. 432p. mass mkt. 6.99 (*0-8217-6692-9*, Zebra Bks.) Kensington Publishing Corp.

Duffy, Margaret. Prospect of Death. 1996. 224p. 20.95 o.p. (*0-312-14396-6*, Saint Martin's Minotaur) St. Martin's Pr.

Dukthas, Ann. A Time for the Death of a King. 1995. 226p. mass mkt. 4.99 (*0-312-95613-4*, St. Martin's Paperbacks); 1994. viii, 226p. 19.95 o.p. (*0-312-11439-7*, Saint Martin's Minotaur) St. Martin's Pr.

Duncan, Bill. The Smiling School for Calvinists. 2001. xii, 199p. pap. (*0-7475-5757-8*) Bloomsbury Pr.

Dunlop, Eileen. The Valley of Deer. 1989. 152p. (J). (gr. 4-7). 13.95 o.p. (*0-8234-0766-7*) Holiday Hse., Inc.

Dunn, Douglas, ed. The Oxford Book of Scottish Short Stories. (Orig.). 1995. 506p. 35.00 o.p. (*0-19-214235-6*); 1996. 512p. reprint ed. pap. 15.95 o.p. (*0-19-282521-6*) Oxford Univ. Pr., Inc.

Dunnett, Dorothy. The Game of Kings. 1976. 22.95 o.p. (*0-8488-1298-0*) Amereon, Ltd.

—The Game of Kings. 1983. 425p. lib. bdg. 39.95 (*0-89966-318-4*) Buccaneer Bks., Inc.

—The Game of Kings. 1997. (Legendary Lymond Chronicles: Vol. 1). 560p. pap. 15.00 (*0-679-77743-1*, Vintage) Knopf Publishing Group.

—The Game of Kings. 1987. mass mkt. 5.95 o.s.i (*0-446-31459-5*) Warner Bks., Inc.

—Gemini: The Eighth Book of the House of Niccolo. 2001. (House of Niccolo Ser.: Vol. 8). (Illus.). 720p. reprint ed. pap. 15.00 (*0-375-70856-1*, Vintage) Knopf Publishing Group.

—Gemini: The Eighth Book of the House of Niccolo. 2000. (Illus.). 720p. 27.50 (*0-375-41083-X*) Knopf, Alfred A. Inc.

Dupont, Desiree. Love Me Forever. 1996. 142p. pap. 12.95 (*81-7328-065-7*) International Specialized Bk. Services.

Ellison, B. Eugene. Rings of the Templars. 2002. pap. 18.95 (*0-595-24050-X*, Writers Club Pr.) iUniverse, Inc.

Engel, Howard. Mr. Doyle & Dr. Bell: A Victorian Mystery. 2003. 214p. 24.95 (*1-58567-417-6*) Overlook Pr., The.

Ewing, Jean R. Flowers under Ice. 1999. 384p. mass mkt. 6.99 o.s.i (*0-425-17036-5*) Berkley Publishing Group.

Faber, Michel. Under the Skin: A Novel. 320p. 2000. 23.00 o.s.i (*0-15-100626-1*); 2001. reprint ed. pap. 13.00 (*0-15-601160-3*, Harvest Bks.) Harcourt Trade Pubs.

Faulkner, Colleen. Highland Lady. 2001. 352p. mass mkt. 5.99 o.s.i (*0-8217-6787-9*, Zebra Bks.) Kensington Publishing Corp.

Ferguson, Jo Ann. A Highland Folly. 2001. 228p. 26.95 (*0-7862-3710-4*, Five Star) Gale Group.

—A Highland Folly. 2001. (Zebra Regency Romance Ser.). 256p. mass mkt. 4.99 o.s.i (*0-8217-6862-X*) Kensington Publishing Corp.

Findlater, Jane H. Seven Scots Stories. 1977. (Short Story Index Reprint Ser.). 23.95 (*0-8369-3498-9*) Ayer Co. Pubs., Inc.

Fisher, Anne K. The Legend of Tommy Morris: A Mystical Tale of Timeless Love. 1996. 144p. 15.00 (*1-878424-29-7*) Amber-Allen Publishing.

Fletcher, Inglis. The Scotswoman. (Carolina Ser.). 414p. reprint ed. lib. bdg. 32.95 (*0-89244-008-2*, Queens Hse., Inc.) Amereon, Ltd.

Fletcher, Jessica & Bain, Donald. The Highland Fling Murders. 1997. (Murder She Wrote Ser.: 7). 304p. mass mkt. 6.50 (*0-451-18851-9*, Signet Bks.) NAL.

Fobes, Tracy. To Tame a Wild Heart. 2001. 384p. pap. 6.50 (*0-7434-1278-8*, Pocket) Simon & Schuster.

Follett, Ken. A Place Called Freedom. 1998. pap. 6.99 (*0-449-45861-X*, Fawcett); 1996. 464p. mass mkt. 7.99 (*0-449-22515-1*, Fawcett); 1996. mass mkt. (*0-449-22517-8*, Ballantine Bks.) Ballantine Bks.

—A Place Called Freedom. l.t. ed. 1995. 672p. 25.00 o.p. (*0-7838-1590-5*, Macmillan Reference USA) Gale Group.

—A Place Called Freedom. l.t. ed. 1995. 672p. 25.00 o.s.i (*0-679-76509-3*) Random Hse. Large Print.

Frame, Ronald. The Lantern Bearers. 2001. 224p. text 24.00 (*1-58243-155-8*, Counterpoint Pr.) Basic Bks.

Francis, Dick. To the Hilt. 1997. 352p. mass mkt. 6.99 (*0-515-12148-7*, Jove) Berkley Publishing Group.

—To the Hilt. unabr. ed. 1997. audio 56.00 (*0-913369-59-4*, 4287) Books on Tape, Inc.

—To the Hilt. 2015. 24.95 o.s.i (*0-399-14486-2*); 1996. 320p. 24.95 o.p. (*0-399-14185-5*, G. P. Putnam's Sons) Penguin Group (USA) Inc.

—To the Hilt. unabr. ed. 1997. audio 60.00 (*0-7887-0805-8*, 94954E7) Recorded Bks., LLC.

—To the Hilt. abr. ed. 1998. audio 14.40 (*0-671-57734-4*, 908766); 1996. audio 18.00 (*0-671-53630-3*, 394243) Simon & Schuster Audio. (Simon & Schuster Audioworks).

—To the Hilt. l.t. ed. (Paperback Bestsellers Ser.). 492p. 1998. pap. 26.95 (*0-7862-0893-7*); 1996. 28.95 (*0-7862-0892-9*) Thorndike Pr.

Fraser, Christine M. Rhanna. l.t. ed. 1987. 16.95 o.p. (*0-86009-819-2*, Macmillan Reference USA) Gale Group.

—Rhanna. 1990. 79p. mass mkt. 4.50 o.p. (*0-06-100053-1*, HarperTorch) Morrow/Avon.

—Rhanna at War. 1990. 79p. pap. 4.50 o.p. (*0-06-100091-4*, HarperTorch) Morrow/Avon.

Fraser, George MacDonald. The Candlemass Road. 1994. 180p. 20.00 o.p. (*0-00-271362-4*) HarperCollins Pubs. Ltd. GBR. *Dist:* HarperCollins Pubs.

Gabaldon, Diana. Diana Gabaldon, 3 vols., Set. 1995. pap. 17.97 (*0-440-36066-8*) Dell Publishing.

—Dragonfly in Amber. 1993. 960p. mass mkt. 7.99 (*0-440-21562-5*); 1992. 752p. 27.95 (*0-385-30231-2*, Delacorte Pr.) Dell Publishing.

—Dragonfly in Amber. abr. ed. 1995. audio 25.95 o.s.i (*0-553-47330-1*, 692850, RH Audio) Random Hse. Audio Publishing Group.

—Dragonfly in Amber. unabr. ed. 1998. audio 186.00 (*0-7887-2170-4*, 95466E7);Set. audio 87.00 (*0-7887-2472-X*, 95587) Recorded Bks., LLC.

—Drums of Autumn. 1997. 1088p. mass mkt. 9.99 (*0-7704-2775-8*) Bantam Bks.

—Drums of Autumn. 1997. 1088p. mass mkt. 7.99 (*0-440-22425-X*); 1996. 896p. 27.95 (*0-385-31140-0*, Delacorte Pr.) Dell Publishing.

—Drums of Autumn. abr. ed. 1996. audio 25.95 (*0-553-47332-8*, 694515, RH Audio) Random Hse. Audio Publishing Group.

—Drums of Autumn. unabr. ed. 1999. audio 198.00 (*0-7887-3473-3*, 95755E7) Recorded Bks., LLC.

—Outlander. 1998. 640p. pap. 14.95 (*0-385-31995-9*, Delacorte Pr.); 1996. 864p. mass mkt. 3.99 o.s.i (*0-440-22291-5*); 1992. 864p. mass mkt. 7.99 (*0-440-21256-1*); 1991. 640p. 27.95 (*0-385-30230-4*, Delacorte Pr.) Dell Publishing.

—Outlander. 2001. 640p. pap. (*0-385-65868-0*) Doubleday Canada, Ltd. CAN. *Dist:* Random Hse., Inc.

—Outlander. abr. ed. 1994. audio 21.98 o.s.i (*0-553-74580-8*); audio 25.95 (*0-553-47329-8*, 692279) Random Hse. Audio Publishing Group. (RH Audio).

—Outlander. unabr. ed. 1997. audio 175.00 (*0-7887-1298-5*, 95132E7) Recorded Bks., LLC.

—The Outlandish Companion: In Which Much Is Revealed Regarding Claire & Jamie Fraser, Their Lives & Times, Antecedents, Adventures, Companions & Progeny, with Learned Commentary (and Many Footnotes) by Their Humble Creator. 1999. (Illus.). 608p. 27.95 (*0-385-32413-8*, Delacorte Pr.) Dell Publishing.

—Voyager. 1994. 1072p. mass mkt. 7.99 (*0-440-21756-3*); 1993. 880p. 27.95 (*0-385-30232-0*, Delacorte Pr.) Dell Publishing.



For book reviews, descriptive annotations, tables of contents, cover images, author biographies & additional information, updated daily, subscribe to **www.booksinprint.com**

—Voyager. abr. ed. 1994. audio 25.95 o.s.i (*0-553-47331-X*, 693353, RH Audio) Random Hse. Audio Publishing Group.

—Voyager, unabr. ed. 2000. (Claire Randall Ser.: Vol. 3). audio 186.00 (*0-7887-2926-8*, 95657E7) Recorded Bks., LLC.

Galbraith, Douglas. The Rising Sun. 2002. 544p. pap. 13.00 (*0-8021-3864-0*, Grove Pr.) Grove/Atlantic, Inc.

—The Rising Sun. 2000. 520p. (*0-330-37297-1*) Picador.

—The Rising Sun: A Novel. 2001. 544p. 25.00 o.p. (*0-87113-781-X*, Atlantic Monthly Pr.) Grove/Atlantic, Inc.

Galford, Ellen. The Fires of Bride. 1988. 232p. (Orig.). lib. bdg. 18.95 (*0-932379-42-7*); pap. 8.95 (*0-932379-41-9*) Firebrand Bks.

Galloway, Janice. The Trick Is to Keep Breathing. 236p. 1995. pap. 12.95 (*1-56478-081-3*); 1994. 19.95 (*1-56478-046-5*) Dalkey Archive Pr.

—Where You Find It. 2002. (Illus.). 240p. 24.00 (*0-684-84450-8*, Simon & Schuster) Simon & Schuster.

Galt, John. Annals of the Parish. 2000. 252p. pap. 9.95 (*0-594-01423-9*) 1873 Pr.

—Annals of the Parish. 2001. 168p. 23.99 (*1-58827-576-0*); per. 18.99 (*1-58827-577-9*) IndyPublish.com.

—Annals of the Parish. 1986. 224p. (C). pap. 45.00 (*0-901824-48-8*) Mercat Pr. Bks. GBR. *Dist:* State Mutual Bk. & Periodical Service, Ltd.

—Annals of the Parish. 1986. (Oxford World's Classics Ser.). 272p. pap. 4.95 o.p. (*0-19-281735-3*) Oxford Univ. Pr., Inc.

—Annals of the Parish. (Ebook Classic Ser.). E-Book 5.00 (*0-7410-1187-5*) SoftBook Pr.

—The Annals of the Parish & the Ayrshire Legatees. 2000. 252p. E-Book 3.95 (*0-594-02243-6*) 1873 Pr.

—The Annals of the Parish & the Ayrshire Legatees. 1996. 352p. pap. 32.00 (*1-873644-31-0*) Mercat Pr. Bks. GBR. *Dist:* State Mutual Bk. & Periodical Service, Ltd.

—The Entail. Gordon, Ian A., ed. 1985. (Oxford World's Classics Ser.). pap. 7.95 o.p. (*0-19-281694-2*) Oxford Univ. Pr., Inc.

—The Provost. 2003. 148p. 22.95 (*1-59408-467-X*); 186p. pap. 14.00 (*1-59408-237-5*) Cork Hill Pr.

—The Provost. E-Book 2.49 (*0-7574-0385-9*) Electric Umbrella Publishing.

—The Provost. Gordon, Ian A., ed. 1983. (Oxford World's Classics Ser.). (C). pap. 5.95 o.p. (*0-19-281629-2*) Oxford Univ. Pr., Inc.

—The Provost. E-Book 5.00 (*0-7410-1318-5*) SoftBook Pr.

Garcia y Robertson, R. The Spiral Dance. 1991. 256p. 20.00 o.p. (*0-688-10902-0*, Morrow, William & Co.) Morrow/Avon.

Garnett, Juliana. The Laird. 2002. 320p. mass mkt. 6.99 (*0-515-13388-4*, Jove) Berkley Publishing Group.

Garwood, Julie. Ransom. l.t. ed. 1999. (Large Print Book Ser.). 29.95 (*1-56895-722-X*, Wheeler Publishing, Inc.) Gale Group.

—Ransom. abr. ed. 1999. audio 18.00 Highsmith Inc.

—Ransom. 1999. 496p. 24.00 o.s.i (*0-671-00335-6*, Atria); (Illus.). 576p. reprint ed. mass mkt. 7.99 (*0-671-00336-4*, Pocket) Simon & Schuster.

—Ransom. 2001. audio 9.98 (*0-7435-0861-0*); 1999. (*0-671-57685-2*, 399785) Simon & Schuster Audio. (Simon & Schuster Audioworks).

Gelder, Kenneth. R. L. Stevenson: The Scottish Stories & Essays. 1989. 300p. 40.00 o.p. (*0-85224-591-2*) Edinburgh Univ. Pr. GBR. *Dist:* Columbia Univ. Pr.

George, Margaret. Mary Queen of Scotland & the Isles: A Novel. 1993. pap. 13.95 (*0-312-95067-5*, Saint Martin's Griffin); 1992. 752p. 24.95 (*0-312-08262-2*); 4th ed. 1997. 870p. pap. 16.95 (*0-312-15585-9*, Saint Martin's Griffin) St. Martin's Pr.

Gibbon, Lewis G. Grey Granite. 1991. (Canongate Classic Ser.). 240p. pap. 9.95 o.p. (*0-86241-312-5*) Trafalgar Square.

—A Scots Quair: A Trilogy of Sunset Song, Cloud Howe & Grey Granite. 1987. 496p. (C). reprint ed. 16.95 o.p. (*0-8052-3661-9*, Schocken) Knopf Publishing Group.

Gibbon, Lewis Grassic. The Thirteenth Disciple. 2001. 274p. pap. 12.95 (*1-873631-55-3*) B & W Publishing GBR. *Dist:* Interlink Publishing Group, Inc.

Gillenwater, Sharon. Song of the Highlands. 1997. 428p. pap. 11.99 o.s.i (*0-88070-946-4*, Palisades) Multnomah Pubs., Inc.

Glass, Julia. Three Junes: A Novel. l.t. ed. 2003. (Romance Ser.). 28.95 (*1-58724-379-2*, Wheeler Publishing, Inc.) Gale Group.

—Three Junes: A Novel. 368p. 2002. 25.00 (*0-375-42144-0*, Pantheon); 2003. reprint ed. pap. 14.00 (*0-385-72142-0*, Anchor) Knopf Publishing Group.

—Three Junes: A Novel. 2002. 368p. 25.00 (*0-375-42241-2*) Knopf, Alfred A. Inc.

Graham, Heather. Devil's Mistress. 1986. 352p. mass mkt. 6.99 (*0-440-11740-2*) Dell Publishing.

—Devil's Mistress. l.t. ed. 2001. (Wheeler Large Print Book Ser.). 445p. 26.95 (*1-58724-011-4*, Wheeler Publishing, Inc.) Gale Group.

Graham, Vanessa. The Stand-In. l.t. ed. 1995. (Large Print Romance Ser.). 178p. pap. 16.95 (*0-8161-7451-2*, Macmillan Reference USA) Gale Group.

Grant-Adamson, Lesley. Wish You Were Here. 1996. 176p. 19.95 o.p. (*0-312-14075-4*, Saint Martin's Minotaur) St. Martin's Pr.

Gray, Alasdair. Janine, 1982. (Fiction Ser.). 352p. 1985. pap. 6.95 o.p. (*0-14-007110-5*, Penguin Bks.); 1984. 16.95 o.p. (*0-670-51387-3*) Viking Penguin.

—Lanark: A Life in Four Books. 560p. 1986. pap. 9.95 (*0-8076-1162-X*); 1985. reprint ed. 20.00 (*0-8076-1108-5*) Braziller, George Inc.

—Lanark: A Life in Four Books. 2002. (Illus.). 560p. pap. 16.00 (*1-84195-183-8*) Canongate Bks. GBR. *Dist:* Grove/Atlantic, Inc., Publishers Group West.

—Lanark: A Life in Four Books, 4 bks., Set. 1996. (Harvest Book Ser.). 576p. pap. 16.00 o.s.i (*0-15-600361-9*, Harvest Bks.) Harcourt Trade Pubs.

—Lanark: A Life in Four Books. 1981. 488p. pap. o.p. (*0-06-090862-9*, CN 862) HarperCollins Pubs.

—Poor Things. 2002. (British Literature Ser.). (Illus.). 319p. reprint ed. pap. 13.50 (*1-56478-307-3*) Dalkey Archive Pr.

—Poor Things: Episodes from the Early Life of Archibald McCandless M.D., Scottish Public Health Officer. 320p. 3.98 o.p. (*0-8317-3686-0*) Smithmark Pubs., Inc.

Gray, Alasdair, ed. Poor Things: Episodes from the Early Life of Archibald McCandless M.D., Scottish Public Health Officer. 1994. 336p. pap. 10.95 o.s.i (*0-15-600068-7*, Harvest Bks.); 1993. xiv, 317p. 21.95 o.s.i (*0-15-173076-8*) Harcourt Trade Pubs.

Greig, Andrew. Electric Brae. 1993. 304p. 24.95 o.p. (*0-86241-404-0*) Trafalgar Square.

—The Return of John MacNab. 1998. 279p. pap. 13.95 (*0-7472-5353-6*) Headline Bk. Publishing, Ltd. GBR. *Dist:* Trafalgar Square.

Greiman, Lois. Highland Enchantment. 1999. (Highland Brides Ser.). 384p. mass mkt. 5.99 (*0-380-80366-6*, Avon Bks.) Morrow/Avon.

—Highland Flame. 1996. (Scottish Ser.: No. 2). 384p. (Orig.). mass mkt. 5.50 (*0-380-78190-5*, Avon Bks.) Morrow/Avon.

—Highland Jewel. 1994. 384p. (Orig.). mass mkt. 4.50 (*0-380-77443-7*, Avon Bks.) Morrow/Avon.

—The Highland Rogues. 2001. 384p. mass mkt. 5.99 (*0-380-81540-0*, Avon Bks.) Morrow/Avon.

—Highland Scoundrel. 1998. (Highland Brides Ser.). mass mkt. 5.99 o.p. (*0-380-79435-7*, Avon Bks.) Morrow/Avon.

—Highland Wolf. 1997. 384p. mass mkt. 5.99 (*0-380-78191-3*, Avon Bks.) Morrow/Avon.

—The Lady & the Knight. 1997. (Highland Brides Ser.). 384p. mass mkt. 5.99 (*0-380-79433-0*, Avon Bks.) Morrow/Avon.

Grindal, Richard. The Tartan Conspiracy. l.t. ed. 1994. 311p. lib. bdg. 17.95 (*0-8161-5984-X*, Macmillan Reference USA) Gale Group.

—The Tartan Conspiracy. 1993. 224p. 19.95 o.p. (*0-312-10555-X*, Saint Martin's Minotaur) St. Martin's Pr.

Grindle, Lucretia. So Little to Die For. Issacson, Dana, ed. 1994. 256p. (Orig.). mass mkt. 4.99 (*0-671-74846-7*, Pocket) Simon & Schuster.

Gunn, Kirsty. Featherstone. 2003. 192p. pap. 14.00 (*0-571-21247-6*) Faber & Faber, Inc.

—Featherstone: A Novel. 2003. 272p. tchr. ed. 24.00 (*0-618-24692-4*) Houghton Mifflin Co.

—Featherstone: A Novel. 2004. 272p. pap. 12.00 (*0-618-44660-5*, Mariner Bks.) Houghton Mifflin Co. Trade & Reference Div.

Gunn, Neil M. Butcher's Broom. 1994. 432p. 25.95 o.p. (*0-8027-1291-6*) Walker & Co.

—Morning Tide. 1993. 256p. 19.95 o.s.i (*0-8027-1228-2*) Walker & Co.

—The Other Landscape. 1990. 318p. 19.95 (*0-8027-1108-1*) Walker & Co.

—Young Art & Old Hector. l.t. ed. 2002. (Dales Large Print Ser.). 368p. pap. 21.99 (*1-84262-177-7*) Dales Large Print Bks. GBR. *Dist:* Ulverscroft Large Print Bks., Ltd., Ulverscroft Large Print Canada, Ltd.

—Young Art & Old Hector. 1991. 255p. 21.95 o.s.i (*0-8027-1177-4*) Walker & Co.

Haining, Peter, ed. Clans of Darkness: Scottish Stories of Fantasy & Horror. 1971. 7.50 o.s.i (*0-8008-1621-8*) Taplinger Publishing Co., Inc.

Hamilton, Julia. Other People's Rules. 2000. 384p. 24.95 (*0-312-26627-8*) St. Martin's Pr.

Hammond, Gerald. Adverse Report. 1990. 2.99 o.p. (*0-517-05806-5*) Random Hse. Value Publishing.

—Adverse Report. 1989. 14.95 o.p. (*0-312-02858-X*, Saint Martin's Minotaur) St. Martin's Pr.

—Adverse Report. l.t. ed. 1990. (Ulverscroft Large Print Ser.). 29.99 o.p. (*0-7089-2119-1*, Ulverscroft) Thorpe, F. A. Pubs. GBR. *Dist:* Ulverscroft Large Print Bks., Ltd., Ulverscroft Large Print Canada, Ltd.

—Bloodlines. 1997. 224p. 20.95 o.p. (*0-312-18052-7*, Saint Martin's Minotaur) St. Martin's Pr.

—Bloodlines. l.t. ed. 1998. (General Ser.). 256p. pap. 23.95 (*0-7862-1497-X*) Thorndike Pr.

—A Brace of Skeet. 1990. 192p. 15.95 o.p. (*0-312-04688-X*, Saint Martin's Minotaur) St. Martin's Pr.

—A Brace of Skeet. l.t. ed. 1991. (Ulverscroft Large Print Ser.). 29.99 o.p. (*0-7089-2480-8*, Ulverscroft) Thorpe, F. A. Pubs. GBR. *Dist:* Ulverscroft Large Print Bks., Ltd., Ulverscroft Large Print Canada, Ltd.

—Carriage of Justice. l.t. ed. 1996. 221p. pap. 20.95 (*0-7838-1633-2*, Macmillan Reference USA) Gale Group.

—Carriage of Justice. 1995. 192p. 19.95 o.p. (*0-312-13941-1*, Saint Martin's Minotaur) St. Martin's Pr.

—Cousin Once Removed. 1984. 192p. 10.95 o.p. (*0-312-17055-6*) St. Martin's Pr.

—Cousin Once Removed. l.t. ed. 1988. (Linford Mystery Library). 256p. pap. 17.99 o.p. (*0-7089-6616-0*, Linford) Thorpe, F. A. Pubs. GBR. *Dist:* Ulverscroft Large Print Bks., Ltd., Ulverscroft Large Print Canada, Ltd.

—The Curse of the Cockers. unabr. ed. 1999. audio 44.95 (*0-7531-0479-2*, 981009) ISIS Audio Bks. GBR. *Dist:* Ulverscroft Large Print Bks., Ltd.

—The Curse of the Cockers. 1994. 192p. 18.95 o.p. (*0-312-10446-4*, Saint Martin's Minotaur) St. Martin's Pr.

—Dog in the Dark. 1992. 1.99 o.p. (*0-517-08390-6*) Random Hse. Value Publishing.

—Dog in the Dark. 1990. 192p. 14.95 o.p. (*0-312-03819-4*, Saint Martin's Minotaur) St. Martin's Pr.

—Dog in the Dark. l.t. ed. 1990. (Ulverscroft Large Print Ser.). 29.99 o.p. (*0-7089-2285-6*, Ulverscroft) Thorpe, F. A. Pubs. GBR. *Dist:* Ulverscroft Large Print Bks., Ltd., Ulverscroft Large Print Canada, Ltd.

—Doghouse. 1992. 192p. 16.95 o.p. (*0-312-07733-5*, Saint Martin's Minotaur) St. Martin's Pr.

—The Executor. 1987. 176p. 12.95 o.p. (*0-312-00593-8*) St. Martin's Pr.

—The Executor. l.t. ed. 1997. (Linford Mystery Library). 320p. pap. 17.99 o.p. (*0-7089-5155-4*, Ulverscroft) Thorpe, F. A. Pubs. GBR. *Dist:* Ulverscroft Large Print Bks., Ltd., Ulverscroft Large Print Canada, Ltd.

—Fair Game. 1982. 224p. 9.95 o.p. (*0-312-27961-2*) St. Martin's Pr.

—Fair Game. l.t. ed. 1983. (Ulverscroft Large Print Ser.). 336p. 29.99 o.p. (*0-7089-1014-9*, Ulverscroft) Thorpe, F. A. Pubs. GBR. *Dist:* Ulverscroft Large Print Bks., Ltd., Ulverscroft Large Print Canada, Ltd.

—Follow That Gun. l.t. ed. 1998. (General Ser.). 256p. pap. 23.95 (*0-7862-1374-4*) Thorndike Pr.

—The Game. 1982. 176p. 10.95 o.p. (*0-312-31590-2*) St. Martin's Pr.

—Grail for Sale. 2002. 224p. 25.99 (*0-7278-5807-6*); 28.99 (*0-7278-7163-3*) Severn Hse. Pubs., Ltd.

—Home to Roost. 1991. 160p. 16.95 o.p. (*0-312-06369-5*, Saint Martin's Minotaur) St. Martin's Pr.

—Hook or Crook. l.t. ed. 1995. 209p. pap. 19.95 o.p. (*0-7838-1174-8*, Macmillan Reference USA) Gale Group.

—Hook or Crook. 1995. 154p. 17.95 o.p. (*0-312-11825-2*, Saint Martin's Minotaur) St. Martin's Pr.

—Illegal Tender. 2001. 224p. 22.95 (*0-312-27292-8*, Saint Martin's Minotaur) St. Martin's Pr.

—Illegal Tender. l.t. ed. 2003. (Ulverscroft Large Print Ser.). 304p. 32.50 (*0-7089-4677-1*) Thorpe, F. A. Pubs. GBR. *Dist:* Ulverscroft Large Print Bks., Ltd., Ulverscroft Large Print Canada, Ltd.

—In Camera. l.t. ed. 1993. (Dales Large Print Ser.). 247p. pap. 19.99 o.p. (*1-85389-390-0*) Dales Large Print Bks. GBR. *Dist:* Ulverscroft Large Print Bks., Ltd., Ulverscroft Large Print Canada, Ltd.

—In Camera. 1992. 192p. 16.95 o.p. (*0-312-06997-9*, Saint Martin's Minotaur) St. Martin's Pr.

—Let Us Prey. 1991. 15.95 o.p. (*0-312-05891-8*, Saint Martin's Minotaur) St. Martin's Pr.

—Let Us Prey. l.t. ed. 1993. (Mystery Ser.). 256p. 29.99 o.p. (*0-7089-2893-5*, Ulverscroft) Thorpe, F. A. Pubs. GBR. *Dist:* Ulverscroft Large Print Bks., Ltd., Ulverscroft Large Print Canada, Ltd.

—Mad Dogs & Scotsmen. l.t. ed. 1996. 20.95 (*0-7838-1890-4*, Macmillan Reference USA) Gale Group.

—Mad Dogs & Scotsmen. 1996. 192p. 20.95 (*0-312-14818-6*, Saint Martin's Minotaur) St. Martin's Pr.

—Pursuit of Arms. 1985. 192p. 12.95 o.p. (*0-312-65697-1*) St. Martin's Pr.

—Pursuit of Arms. l.t. ed. 1998. (Linford Mystery Library). 320p. pap. 17.99 (*0-7089-5215-1*, Linford) Thorpe, F. A. Pubs. GBR. *Dist:* Ulverscroft Large Print Bks., Ltd., Ulverscroft Large Print Canada, Ltd.

—The Revenge Game. 1981. 192p. 9.95 o.p. (*0-312-67930-0*) St. Martin's Pr.

—The Reward Game. 1980. 224p. 9.95 o.p. (*0-312-68078-3*) St. Martin's Pr.

—The Reward Game. l.t. ed. 1981. (Ulverscroft Large Print Ser.). 326p. 29.99 o.p. (*0-7089-0717-2*, Ulverscroft) Thorpe, F. A. Pubs. GBR. *Dist:* Ulverscroft Large Print Bks., Ltd., Ulverscroft Large Print Canada, Ltd.

—Sauce for the Pigeon. 1985. 192p. 12.95 o.p. (*0-312-69977-8*) St. Martin's Pr.

—Sauce for the Pigeon. l.t. ed. 1989. (Linford Mystery Library). 305p. pap. 17.99 o.p. (*0-7089-6631-4*, Linford) Thorpe, F. A. Pubs. GBR. *Dist:* Ulverscroft Large Print Bks., Ltd., Ulverscroft Large Print Canada, Ltd.

—Silver City Scandal. 1986. 12.95 o.p. (*0-312-72588-4*) St. Martin's Pr.

—Silver City Scandal. l.t. ed. 1987. (Ulverscroft Large Print Ser.). 272p. 29.99 o.p. (*0-7089-1639-2*, Ulverscroft) Thorpe, F. A. Pubs. GBR. *Dist:* Ulverscroft Large Print Bks., Ltd., Ulverscroft Large Print Canada, Ltd.

—Sink or Swim. 1997. 176p. 19.95 o.p. (*0-312-15657-X*, Saint Martin's Minotaur) St. Martin's Pr.

—Sink or Swim. l.t. ed. 1997. (General Ser.). 224p. pap. 24.95 (*0-7862-1071-0*) Thorndike Pr.

—Snatch Crop. l.t. ed. 1993. (Mystery Ser.). 224p. pap. 19.99 o.p. (*1-85389-389-7*) Dales Large Print Bks. GBR. *Dist:* Ulverscroft Large Print Bks., Ltd., Ulverscroft Large Print Canada, Ltd.

—Snatch Crop. 1993. 154p. 16.95 o.p. (*0-312-08891-4*, Saint Martin's Minotaur) St. Martin's Pr.

—Sting in the Tail. 1995. 160p. 19.95 o.p. (*0-312-13189-5*, Saint Martin's Minotaur) St. Martin's Pr.

—Sting in the Tail. l.t. ed. 1996. (Ulverscroft Large Print Ser.). 368p. 29.99 o.p. (*0-7089-3517-6*, Ulverscroft) Thorpe, F. A. Pubs. GBR. *Dist:* Ulverscroft Large Print Bks., Ltd., Ulverscroft Large Print Canada, Ltd.

—Stray Shot. 1989. 192p. 14.95 o.p. (*0-312-03435-0*, Saint Martin's Minotaur) St. Martin's Pr.

—Stray Shot. l.t. ed. 1990. (Ulverscroft Large Print Ser.). 29.99 o.p. (*0-7089-2211-2*, Ulverscroft) Thorpe, F. A. Pubs. GBR. *Dist:* Ulverscroft Large Print Bks., Ltd., Ulverscroft Large Print Canada, Ltd.

—Thin Air. 1994. 144p. 17.95 o.p. (*0-312-11339-0*, Saint Martin's Minotaur) St. Martin's Pr.

—Twice Bitten. 1999. 230p. 22.95 (*0-312-24256-5*, Saint Martin's Minotaur) St. Martin's Pr.

—Whose Dog Are You? 1991. 15.95 o.p. (*0-312-05536-6*, Saint Martin's Minotaur) St. Martin's Pr.

—Whose Dog Are You? l.t. ed. 1992. (Ulverscroft Large Print Ser.). 288p. 29.99 o.p. (*0-7089-2575-8*, Ulverscroft) Thorpe, F. A. Pubs. GBR. *Dist:* Ulverscroft Large Print Bks., Ltd., Ulverscroft Large Print Canada, Ltd.

—The Worried Widow. 1988. 192p. 13.95 o.p. (*0-312-01541-0*, Saint Martin's Minotaur) St. Martin's Pr.

Hanley, Clifford. Another Street, Another Dance. 1984. 320p. 13.95 o.p. (*0-312-04198-5*) St. Martin's Pr.

Hardwick, Mollie. Charlie Is My Darling. 1977. 8.95 o.p. (*0-698-10867-1*) Putnam Publishing Group, The.

Harper, Karen. The Wings of Morning. 1993. 384p. 20.00 o.p. (*0-525-93614-9*, Dutton) Dutton/Plume.

—The Wings of Morning. l.t. ed. 1993. 100.95 (*0-7862-9995-9*, Macmillan Reference USA) Gale Group.

—The Wings of Morning. 1994. 432p. mass mkt. 5.99 o.s.i (*0-451-18065-8*, Signet Bks.) NAL.

Hendry, J. F. Fernie Brae: A Scottish Childhood. 1988. 190p. reprint ed. pap. 14.95 (*0-948275-13-8*) Dufour Editions, Inc.

Henley, Virginia. Tempted. 1993. 528p. mass mkt. 6.99 (*0-440-20625-1*) Dell Publishing.

—Wild Hearts. 1985. (Avon Romance Ser.). 400p. reprint ed. mass mkt. 6.99 (*0-380-89536-6*, Avon Bks.) Morrow/Avon.

—Wild Hearts. abr. ed. 1994. audio 5.99 (*1-57096-015-1*, RAZ 916) Romance Alive Audio.

—A Year & a Day. 1998. 496p. mass mkt. 6.99 (*0-440-22207-9*) Dell Publishing.

Higgs, Liz Curtis. Thorn in My Heart. abr. ed. 2003. audio 17.95 (*1-59086-783-1*, 4376); audio 44.25 (*1-59086-784-X*, 4377, CD Library Edition); audio compact disk 24.95 (*1-59086-785-8*, 4378, CD); audio compact disk 62.25 (*1-59086-786-6*, 4379, CD Library Edition) Brilliance Audio.

—Thorn in My Heart. 2003. (Illus.). 496p. pap. 13.99 (*1-57856-512-X*) WaterBrook Pr.

Hill, Pamela. Bailie's Wake. l.t. ed. 2000. (Nightingale Ser.). 158p. pap. 21.95 (*0-7838-9100-8*) Thorndike Pr.

—My Lady Glamis. l.t. ed. 1986. lib. bdg. 17.50 o.p. (*0-7451-0403-7*, Macmillan Reference USA) Gale Group.

—My Lady Glamis. 1986. 192p. 12.95 o.p. (*0-312-00162-2*) St. Martin's Pr.

—Sisters. l.t. ed. 1988. (Nightingale Ser.). 252p. 12.95 o.p. (*0-8161-4416-8*, Macmillan Reference USA) Gale Group.

Hind, Archie. The Dear Green Place. 2002. 248p. pap. 13.95 (*1-84158-071-6*) Birlinn, Ltd. GBR. *Dist:* Interlink Publishing Group, Inc.

Hird, Laura J. Nail & Other Stories. 2000. pap. 13.95 (*0-86241-677-9*); 195p. pap. 13.95 (*0-86241-850-X*) Canongate Bks. GBR. *Dist:* Interlink Publishing Group, Inc., Grove/Atlantic, Inc.

Hogg, James. Confessions of a Justified Sinner. 1992. (Everyman's Library). 272p. 15.00 (*0-679-41732-X*) Knopf, Alfred A. Inc.

—Confessions of a Justified Sinner. Cuddon, J. A., ed. 1995. 336p. pap. 6.50 (*0-460-87471-3*, Everyman's Classic Library in Paperback) Tuttle Publishing.

—The Private Memoirs & Confessions of a Justified Sinner. 1995. (Classics Ser.). (Illus.). 224p. pap. 11.00 (*0-86241-340-0*) Canongate Bks. GBR. *Dist:* Grove/Atlantic, Inc.

—The Private Memoirs & Confessions of a Justified Sinner. Garside, Peter & Campbell, Ian, eds. 2003. (Collected Works of James Hogg Ser.). 300p. 52.50 (*0-7486-1414-1*) Edinburgh Univ. Pr. GBR. *Dist:* Columbia Univ. Pr.

—The Private Memoirs & Confessions of a Justified Sinner. 2003. (Twelve-Point Ser.). lib. bdg. 25.00 (*1-58287-230-9*) North Bks.

—The Private Memoirs & Confessions of a Justified Sinner. Carey, John, ed. (Oxford World's Classics Ser.). 1999. (Illus.). 320p. pap. 10.95 (*0-19-283590-4*); 1982. 296p. pap. 7.95 o.p. (*0-19-281556-3*) Oxford Univ. Pr., Inc.

—The Private Memoirs & Confessions of a Justified Sinner. Wain, John, ed. & intro. by. 1983. (Penguin Classics Ser.). 256p. pap. 10.95 o.p. (*0-14-043198-5*, Penguin Classics) Viking Penguin.

—Private Memoirs & Confessions of a Justified Sinner. 2002. (New York Review Books Classics Ser.). 296p. pap. 12.95 (*1-59017-025-3*) New York Review of Bks., Inc., The.

—Private Memoirs & Confessions of a Justified Sinner. 2001. 192p. pap. 3.95 (*1-85326-188-2*) Wordsworth Editions, Ltd. GBR. *Dist:* Combined Publishing.

—The Private Memoirs & Confessions of a Justified Sinner. l.t. ed. 2003. (Large Print Ser.). lib. bdg. 26.00 (*1-58287-714-9*) North Bks.

—Tales of Love & Mystery. 1986. 216p. 29.95 (*0-86241-085-1*); pap. 14.95 (*0-86241-103-3*) Dufour Editions, Inc.

Holcombe, Elizabeth. Heaven & the Heather. 2002. 288p. mass mkt. 5.99 o.s.i (*0-515-13402-3*) Berkley Publishing Group.

Holling, Jen. Forever, My Lady. 2001. 384p. mass mkt. 5.99 (*0-06-101437-0*) HarperCollins Pubs.

—Tempted by Your Touch: Brides of the Bloodstone. 2002. (Brides of the Bloodstone Ser.). 400p. pap. 6.99 (*0-7434-3802-7*, Pocket) Simon & Schuster.

Home, Stewart. 69 Things to Do with a Dead Princess. 2001. (Illus.). 144p. pap. 13.00 (*1-84195-182-X*) Canongate Bks. GBR. *Dist:* Grove/Atlantic, Inc.

Hood, Evelyn. A Matter of Mischief. 1998. 252p. mass mkt. o.s.i (*0-7515-1892-1*) Little Brown & Co.

—A Matter of Mischief. l.t. ed. 1990. (Ulverscroft Large Print Ser.). 29.99 o.p. (*0-7089-2334-8*, Ulverscroft) Thorpe, F. A. Pubs. GBR. *Dist:* Ulverscroft Large Print Bks., Ltd., Ulverscroft Large Print Canada, Ltd.

—A Procession of One. l.t. ed. 2000. (Magna Large Print Ser.). 464p. (*0-7505-1516-3*) Magna Large Print Bks. GBR. *Dist:* Ulverscroft Large Print Canada, Ltd.

—Rowan Cottage. l.t. ed. 2000. (Magna Large Print Ser.). 288p. 31.99 (*0-7505-1505-8*) Magna Large Print Bks. GBR. *Dist:* Ulverscroft Large Print Bks., Ltd., Ulverscroft Large Print Canada, Ltd.

Hood-Stewart, Fiona. The Journey Home. 2000. 448p. mass mkt. (*1-55166-606-5*, 1-66606-4, Mira Bks.) Harlequin Enterprises, Ltd.

—The Lost Dreams. 2003. 448p. mass mkt. (*1-55166-670-7*, Mira Bks.) Harlequin Enterprises, Ltd.

—The Stolen Years. 2001. 448p. mass mkt. (*1-55166-833-5*, Mira Bks.) Harlequin Enterprises, Ltd.

Howard, Linda. Son of the Morning. 1997. 384p. pap. 7.99 (*0-671-79938-X*, Pocket) Simon & Schuster.

Howell, Hannah. Conqueror's Kiss. 1991. 384p. (Orig.). mass mkt. 4.50 (*0-380-76503-9*, Avon Bks.) Morrow/Avon.

—Highland Angel. 2003. 319p. mass mkt. 6.50 (*0-8217-7426-3*) Kensington Publishing Corp.

—Highland Honor. 1999. 304p. mass mkt. 5.99 (*0-8217-6095-5*) Kensington Publishing Corp.

—Highland Promise. 1999. 352p. mass mkt. 5.99 (*0-8217-6254-0*) Kensington Publishing Corp.

—Highland Vow. 2000. (Zebra Historical Romance Ser.). 352p. mass mkt. 5.99 (*0-8217-6614-7*) Kensington Publishing Corp.

Howell, Hannah, et al. Scottish Magic. 1999. 288p. pap. 12.00 o.s.i (*1-57566-387-2*) Kensington Publishing Corp.

Hughes, Gillian, ed. Tales of the Wars of Montrose. 2002. 312p. pap. 11.00 (*0-7486-6318-5*) Polygon GBR. *Dist:* Interlink Publishing Group, Inc.

Hunter, Mollie. The Kelpie's Pearls. l.t. ed. 1988. 176p. (J). (gr. 3 up). 16.95 o.p. (*0-7451-0758-3*, Galaxy Children's Large Print) BBC Audiobooks America.

Huth, Angela. Wives of the Fisherman. l.t. ed. 1998. (G. K. Hall Core Ser.). 468p. 26.95 o.p. (*0-7838-0309-5*, Macmillan Reference USA) Gale Group.

—Wives of the Fisherman. 1998. 320p. 23.95 o.p. (*0-312-19370-X*) St. Martin's Pr.

—Wives of the Fishermen. unabr. ed. 1999. audio 84.95 (*0-7540-0256-X*, CAB1679) BBC Audiobooks America.

—Wives of the Fishermen. 2000. 320p. pap. 12.50 (*0-380-73265-3*, Avon Bks.) Morrow/Avon.

Jacob, Violet. Flemington & Tales from Angus. 1999. (ENG.). 544p. pap. 14.95 (*0-86241-784-8*) Canongate Bks. GBR. *Dist:* Interlink Publishing Group, Inc.

Jamesson, Peter. Unplayable Lie: A Chief Inspector St. George Mystery. 2002. 224p. 22.95 (*1-58536-088-0*) Clock Tower Pr. LLC.

Jardine, Quintin. Murmuring the Judges. 2001. 407p. mass mkt. 8.95 (*0-7472-5962-3*) Headline Bk. Publishing, Ltd. GBR. *Dist:* Trafalgar Square.

—Skinner's Festival. 2001. (J). mass mkt. 8.95 (*0-7472-4140-6*) Headline Bk. Publishing, Ltd. GBR. *Dist:* Trafalgar Square.

—Skinner's Festival. 1995. 310p. 21.95 o.p. (*0-312-11892-9*, Saint Martin's Minotaur) St. Martin's Pr.

—Skinner's Ghosts. l.t. ed. 1999. (Ulverscroft Large Print Ser.). 416p. 31.99 o.p. (*0-7089-4159-1*, Ulverscroft) Thorpe, F. A. Pubs. GBR. *Dist:* Ulverscroft Large Print Bks., Ltd., Ulverscroft Large Print Canada, Ltd.

—Skinner's Mission. 2001. 406p. mass mkt. 9.95 (*0-7472-5043-X*) Headline Bk. Publishing, Ltd. GBR. *Dist:* Trafalgar Square.

—Skinner's Mission. unabr. ed. 1999. audio 83.95 (*1-85903-291-5*) Magna Story Sound GBR. *Dist:* Ulverscroft Large Print Bks., Ltd.

—Skinner's Mission. l.t. ed. 1998. (Ulverscroft Large Print Ser.). 512p. 29.99 o.p. (*0-7089-3914-7*, Ulverscroft) Thorpe, F. A. Pubs. GBR. *Dist:* Ulverscroft Large Print Bks., Ltd., Ulverscroft Large Print Canada, Ltd.

—Skinner's Ordeal. 2001. 438p. mass mkt. 8.95 (*0-7472-5042-1*) Headline Bk. Publishing, Ltd. GBR. *Dist:* Trafalgar Square.

—Skinner's Ordeal. l.t. ed. 1997. (Ulverscroft Large Print Ser.). 720p. 29.99 (*0-7089-3826-4*, Ulverscroft) Thorpe, F. A. Pubs. GBR. *Dist:* Ulverscroft Large Print Bks., Ltd., Ulverscroft Large Print Canada, Ltd.

—Skinner's Round. 2001. 436p. mass mkt. 9.95 (*0-7472-5041-3*) Headline Bk. Publishing, Ltd. GBR. *Dist:* Trafalgar Square.

—Skinner's Round. 1996. 304p. 23.95 (*0-312-14737-6*, Saint Martin's Minotaur) St. Martin's Pr.

—Skinner's Rules. 2001. mass mkt. 8.95 (*0-7472-4139-2*) Headline Bk. Publishing, Ltd. GBR. *Dist:* Trafalgar Square.

—Skinner's Rules. 1994. 320p. 21.95 o.p. (*0-312-11066-9*, Saint Martin's Minotaur) St. Martin's Pr.

—Skinner's Trail. 1996. 320p. 22.95 o.p. (*0-312-14417-2*, Saint Martin's Minotaur) St. Martin's Pr.

Jenkins, Robin. Guests of War. 1988. (Scottish Classic Ser.: No. 10). 286p. pap. text 19.95 o.p. (*0-7073-0544-6*) Ashgate Publishing Co.

—Guests of War. 2001. 298p. pap. 12.95 (*1-873631-70-7*) B & W Publishing GBR. *Dist:* Interlink Publishing Group, Inc.

—Matthew & Sheila. 1998. 160p. pap. 15.95 o.p. (*0-7486-6239-1*) Polygon GBR. *Dist:* Subterranean Co.

—The Thistle & the Grail. 1994. 296p. pap. 18.00 (*0-7486-6193-X*) Polygon GBR. *Dist:* Subterranean Co.

—A Would-Be Saint. 1980. 207p. 9.95 o.p. (*0-8008-8710-7*) Taplinger Publishing Co., Inc.

Johansen, Iris. The Magnificent Rogue. 1993. 416p. mass mkt. 7.50 (*0-553-29944-1*) Bantam Bks.

—The Magnificent Rogue. l.t. ed. 1993. 23.95 o.p. (*1-56895-051-9*, Wheeler Publishing, Inc.) Gale Group.

Johnson, Alison. The Wicked Generation. 1993. 262p. pap. 14.95 (*0-85640-398-9*) Blackstaff Pr., The IRL. *Dist:* Dufour Editions, Inc.

Johnson, Grace. Tempest at Stonehaven. l.t. ed. 1999. (Christian Mystery Ser.). 345p. 23.95 o.p. (*0-7862-1960-2*) Thorndike Pr.

—Tempest at Stonehaven. 1997. (Scottish Shores Ser.). 251p. pap. 9.99 o.p. (*0-8423-6250-9*) Tyndale Hse. Pubs.

Johnson, Susan. To Please a Lady. 1999. 352p. mass mkt. 5.99 (*0-553-57866-9*) Bantam Bks.

—To Please a Lady. l.t. ed. 2000. (Wheeler Large Print Book Ser.). 337p. pap. 25.95 (*1-56895-887-0*, Wheeler Publishing, Inc.) Gale Group.

Johnston, Paul. Boneyard. 2000. 304p. 23.95 (*0-312-20280-6*, Saint Martin's Minotaur) St. Martin's Pr.

Johnston, Velda. I Came to the Highlands. 1978. mass mkt. 1.95 o.p. (*0-451-08218-4*, J8218, Signet Bks.) NAL.

—I Came to the Highlands. l.t. ed. 2001. (Romance Ser.). 308p. 27.95 (*0-7862-3504-7*) Thorndike Pr.

Kay, Jackie. Why Don't You Stop Talking. 2002. 239p. (*0-330-37333-1*) Picador.

Kearsley, Susanna. Shadowy Horses. 1997. 384p. mass mkt. 8.99 (*0-7704-2747-2*) Bantam Bks.

—Shadowy Horses. 1999. 368p. mass mkt. 6.99 o.s.i (*0-515-12464-8*, Jove) Berkley Publishing Group.

Kelman, James. How Late It Was, How Late. 1994. 21.00 o.p. (*0-393-03817-3*) Norton, W. W. & Co., Inc.

Kennedy, A. L. Original Bliss: A Novel. 2000. 224p. pap. 12.00 (*0-375-70278-4*, Vintage) Knopf Publishing Group.

—Original Bliss: A Novel. 1999. 224p. 21.00 o.s.i (*0-375-40272-1*) Knopf, Alfred A. Inc.

Kesson, Jessie. Another Time, Another Place. 2001. 160p. pap. 9.95 (*1-873631-71-5*) B & W Publishing GBR. *Dist:* Interlink Publishing Group, Inc.

—Another Time, Another Place. l.t. ed. 1987. 16.95 o.p. (*0-86009-810-9*, Macmillan Reference USA) Gale Group.

—Another Time, Another Place. 1989. pap. o.p. (*0-7012-0835-X*) Random Hse. of Canada, Ltd. CAN. *Dist:* Random Hse., Inc.

—Jessie Kesson: An Omnibus. 1992. 500p. 29.95 o.p. (*0-7011-3783-5*) Chatto & Windus GBR. *Dist:* Trafalgar Square.

King, Susan. The Heather Moon. 1999. 352p. mass mkt. 6.99 o.s.i (*0-451-40774-1*, Topaz) NAL.

—Lady Miracle. 1998. (Romance Ser.). 26.95 (*0-7862-1398-1*, Five Star); 23.95 (*1-56895-552-9*, Wheeler Publishing, Inc.) Gale Group.

—Lady Miracle. 1997. 384p. mass mkt. 5.99 o.s.i (*0-451-40766-0*, Signet Bks.) NAL.

—The Stone Maiden. l.t. ed. 2000. (Large Print Book Ser.). 467p. pap. 25.95 (*1-56895-927-3*, Wheeler Publishing, Inc.) Gale Group.

—The Stone Maiden. 2000. 352p. mass mkt. 6.99 o.s.i (*0-451-19970-7*, Signet Bks.) NAL.

—Taming the Heiress. 2003. 352p. mass mkt. 6.99 (*0-451-20955-9*, Signet Bks.) NAL.

Kirkwood, Gwen. The Laird of Lochandee. 2002. 320p. 26.99 (*0-7278-5877-7*) Severn Hse. Pubs., Ltd.

Knight, Alanna. Blood Line: An Inspector Faro Mystery. 1989. 224p. 15.95 o.p. (*0-312-03295-1*, Saint Martin's Minotaur) St. Martin's Pr.

—The Bull Slayers: An Inspector Faro Mystery. l.t. ed. 1997. 290p. 21.95 (*0-7838-8045-6*, Macmillan Reference USA) Gale Group.

—Deadly Beloved. l.t. ed. 1992. (Mystery Ser.). 336p. 29.99 o.p. (*0-7089-2646-0*, Ulverscroft) Thorpe, F. A. Pubs. GBR. *Dist:* Ulverscroft Large Print Bks., Ltd., Ulverscroft Large Print Canada, Ltd.

—Enter Second Murderer. 1989. 14.95 o.p. (*0-312-03021-5*) St. Martin's Pr.

—Enter Second Murderer. l.t. ed. 1998. (General Ser.). 269p. pap. 23.95 (*0-7862-1308-6*) Thorndike Pr.

—Enter Second Murderer. l.t. ed. 1990. (Ulverscroft Large Print Ser.). 29.99 o.p. (*0-7089-2236-8*, Ulverscroft) Thorpe, F. A. Pubs. GBR. *Dist:* Ulverscroft Large Print Bks., Ltd., Ulverscroft Large Print Canada, Ltd.

—Enter Second Murderer: An Inspector Faro Mystery, Set. unabr. ed. 1999. audio 54.95 (*0-7540-0352-3*, CAB1775) BBC Audiobooks America.

—Estella. 1986. 240p. 14.95 o.p. (*0-312-26469-0*) St. Martin's Pr.

—Estella. l.t. ed. 1998. (General Ser.). 344p. pap. 23.95 (*0-7862-1313-2*) Thorndike Pr.

—The Evil That Men Do. l.t. ed. 1996. 281p. pap. 20.95 o.p. (*0-7838-1649-9*, Macmillan Reference USA) Gale Group.

—Killing Cousins: An Inspector Faro Mystery. l.t. ed. 1992. (Lythway Ser.). 248p. lib. bdg. 20.50 o.p. (*0-7451-1419-9*, Macmillan Reference USA) Gale Group.

—Killing Cousins: An Inspector Faro Mystery. 1991. 256p. 17.95 o.p. (*0-312-07008-X*, Saint Martin's Minotaur) St. Martin's Pr.

—The Missing Duchess. l.t. ed. 1996. pap. 20.95 (*0-7838-1650-2*, Macmillan Reference USA) Gale Group.

—Murder by Appointment: An Inspector Faro Mystery. l.t. ed. 1997. pap. 20.95 o.p. (*0-7838-8044-8*, Macmillan Reference USA) Gale Group.

Knight, Alanna & Lawhead, Stephen R. Deadly Beloved. 1990. 192p. 15.95 o.p. (*0-312-05069-0*, Saint Martin's Minotaur) St. Martin's Pr.

Knox, Bill. Blood Proof. l.t. ed. 1999. (Ulverscroft Large Print Ser.). 400p. 31.99 o.p. (*0-7089-4025-0*, Ulverscroft) Thorpe, F. A. Pubs. GBR. *Dist:* Ulverscroft Large Print Bks., Ltd., Ulverscroft Large Print Canada, Ltd.

—Crossfire Killings. 1986. (Crime Club Ser.). 192p. 12.95 o.p. (*0-385-23544-5*) Doubleday Publishing.

—Dead Man's Mooring. l.t. ed. 1990. (Ulverscroft Large Print Ser.). 29.99 o.p. (*0-7089-2123-X*, Ulverscroft) Thorpe, F. A. Pubs. GBR. *Dist:* Ulverscroft Large Print Bks., Ltd., Ulverscroft Large Print Canada, Ltd.

—The Interface Man. 1990. 14.95 o.s.i (*0-385-41091-3*) Doubleday Publishing.

—Sanctuary Isle. l.t. ed. 2003. 265p. pap. 24.45 (*0-7862-5425-4*) Thorndike Pr.

—Sanctuary Isle. l.t. ed. 1988. (Linford Mystery Library). 326p. pap. 17.99 o.p. (*0-7089-6502-4*, Ulverscroft) Thorpe, F. A. Pubs. GBR. *Dist:* Ulverscroft Large Print Bks., Ltd., Ulverscroft Large Print Canada, Ltd.

Knox, Elizabeth. Billie's Kiss. 2003. 400p. pap. 13.95 (*0-345-45051-5*); 2002. 352p. 24.00 (*0-345-45052-3*) Ballantine Bks. (Ballantine Bks.).

Knox, Ronald A. Double Cross Purposes. 1986. 320p. reprint ed. pap. 6.95 o.p. (*0-486-25032-6*) Dover Pubns., Inc.

Koplinka, Charlotte. The Silkies. 1978. (Illus.). 7.95 o.p. (*0-8397-7810-4*) Eriksson, Paul S. Pub.

Kurtz, Katherine. The Adept. 1991. (Adept Ser.: No. 1). 336p. mass mkt. 6.99 (*0-441-00343-5*) Ace Bks.

—Death of an Adept. 1996. (Adept Ser.: No. 5). 464p. 21.95 o.s.i (*0-441-00367-2*) Ace Bks.

—The Lodge of the Lynx. 1993. (Adept Ser.: No. 2). 20.00 o.p. (*0-7278-4420-2*) Severn Hse. Pubs., Ltd.

—The Templar Treasure. 1993. (Adept Ser.: No. 3). 320p. mass mkt. 6.99 (*0-441-00345-1*) Ace Bks.

—The Templar Treasure. 1994. (Adept Ser.: No. 3). reprint ed. lib. bdg. 20.00 o.p. (*0-7278-4632-9*) Severn Hse. Pubs., Ltd.

Kurtz, Katherine & Harris, Deborah T. The Adept, Bk. I. 1992. (Adept Ser.: No. 1). 336p. reprint ed. 20.00 o.p. (*0-7278-4378-8*) Severn Hse. Pubs., Ltd.

—Death of an Adept. 1997. (Adept Ser.: No. 5). 448p. mass mkt. 7.50 (*0-441-00484-9*) Ace Bks.

—The Lodge of the Lynx, Vol. 2. 1992. (Adept Ser.: No. 2). 432p. mass mkt. 6.99 (*0-441-00344-3*) Ace Bks.

—The Temple & the Stone. 1999. 560p. mass mkt. 6.99 (*0-446-60723-1*); 1998. 450p. 22.00 o.p. (*0-446-52260-0*) Warner Bks., Inc.

Lamb, Arnette. Beguiled. 1996. (Clan MacKenzie Trilogy Ser.). 320p. pap. 6.50 (*0-671-88219-8*, Pocket) Simon & Schuster.

—Betrayed. 1995. (Clan MacKenzie Trilogy Ser.). 320p. mass mkt. 6.50 (*0-671-88218-X*, Pocket) Simon & Schuster.

—Maiden of Inverness. Tolley, Carolyn, ed. 1995. 368p. (Orig.). mass mkt. 6.50 (*0-671-88220-1*, Pocket) Simon & Schuster.

Langan, Ruth. Highland Sword. 2003. (Harlequin Historicals Ser.: No. 654). 304p. mass mkt. (*0-373-29254-6*, Harlequin Bks.) Harlequin Enterprises, Ltd.

Larsson, Bjorn. The Celtic Ring. Simpson, George, tr. from SWE. (Mariner's Library Fiction Classics). 400p. 1992. 22.95 (*1-57409-024-0*); 2000. (Illus.). reprint ed. pap. 14.95 (*1-57409-114-X*) Sheridan Hse., Inc.

Laurens, Stephanie. Scandal's Bride. 2001. E-Book 6.99 (*0-06-009504-0*); E-Book 6.99 (*0-06-009503-2*); E-Book 6.99 (*0-06-009501-6*) HarperCollins General Bks. Group. (PerfectBound).

—Scandal's Bride. 1999. (Avon Historical Romance Ser.). 416p. mass mkt. 7.50 (*0-380-80568-5*, Avon Bks.) Morrow/Avon.

Lawhead, Stephen R. The Black Rood. 2000. (Celtic Crusades Ser.: Bk. II). (Illus.). 448p. 25.00 (*0-06-105034-2*) HarperCollins Pubs.

—The Black Rood. 2001. (Celtic Crusades Ser.: Vol. 2). 624p. mass mkt. 7.50 (*0-06-105110-1*, Eos) Morrow/Avon.

—The Black Rood. 2001. (Illus.). 448p. pap. 16.99 (*0-310-21783-0*) Zondervan.

—The Iron Lance. (Celtic Crusades Ser.: Bk. 1). 2000. 656p. mass mkt. 7.99 (*0-06-105109-8*); 1998. 512p. 24.00 (*0-06-105032-6*) Morrow/Avon. (Eos).

—The Iron Lance. 1999. (Celtic Crusades Ser.: Bk. 1). 512p. pap. 16.99 (*0-310-21782-2*) Zondervan.

Lawrence, Irene. World Without Love. l.t. ed. 1993. 18.95 o.p. (*0-7927-1773-2*); pap. 17.95 o.p. (*0-7927-1772-4*) BBC Audiobooks America.

Lee, Diana. A Taste for Blood. 2003. 370p. pap. 19.95 (*1-56023-461-X*, Alice Street Editions) Haworth Pr., Inc., The.

Lee, J. Ardian. Son of the Sword. 2003. 352p. mass mkt. 6.99 (*0-441-01050-4*); 2001. 336p. pap. 14.00 (*0-441-00838-0*) Ace Bks.

Lee, J. Ardian. Sword of King James. 2003. 336p. pap. 14.00 (*0-441-01059-8*) Ace Bks.

Lindsey, Johanna. A Gentle Feuding. 1984. 400p. mass mkt. 7.99 (*0-380-87155-6*, Avon Bks.) Morrow/Avon.

—A Gentle Feuding. 1999. 329p. 26.00 (*0-7278-5487-9*) Severn Hse. Pubs., Ltd.

—Love Me Forever. unabr. ed. 1996. audio 56.00 (*0-7366-3308-1*, 3962) Books on Tape, Inc.

—Love Me Forever. abr. ed. (Sherring Cross Ser.). 1996. audio 7.99 o.s.i (*1-56740-136-8*, 673, Paperback Nova Audio Bks.); 1995. audio 16.95 o.p. (*1-56100-864-8*, 1281, Nova Audio Bks.); 1995. audio 57.25 (*1-56100-293-3*, 931, Unabridged Library Editions); 1995. audio 23.95 (*1-56100-668-8*, 165, Bookcassette) Brilliance Audio.

—Love Me Forever. l.t. ed. 1995. 480p. 25.95 o.p. (*0-7838-1501-8*, Macmillan Reference USA) Gale Group.

—Love Me Forever. 1996. 400p. mass mkt. 7.99 (*0-380-72570-3*, Avon Bks.); 1995. 356p. 22.00 o.p. (*0-688-14286-9*, Morrow, William & Co.) Morrow/Avon.

—Love Me Forever. 1997. 5.98 o.p. (*0-7651-0785-6*) Smithmark Pubs., Inc.

Lister, Jenna. Dark Secret. l.t. ed. 2001. 163p. (*0-7540-4391-6*, Macmillan Reference USA) Gale Group.

—Dark Secret. l.t. ed. 2001. (Nightingale Ser.). 163p. pap. 22.95 (*0-7838-9332-9*) Thorndike Pr.

Livesey, Margot. Criminals. 1997. 288p. pap. 11.95 (*0-14-026277-6*) Penguin Group (USA) Inc.

—Eva Moves the Furniture: A Novel. 2001. 272p. 23.00 o.s.i (*0-8050-6801-5*) Holt, Henry & Co.

—Eva Moves the Furniture: A Novel. 2002. 240p. pap. 13.00 (*0-312-42103-6*) Picador.

Llewellyn, Sam. Dead Eye. 1991. 288p. 18.95 o.p. (*0-671-70660-8*) Summit Bks.

Lockhart, John G. The History of Matthew Wald. Bour, Isabelle, ed. 2001. (Scottish Studies International: Vol. 30). 182p. pap. 34.95 (*0-8204-4778-1*); (*3-631-36667-1*) Lang, Peter Publishing, Inc.

Logue, John. The Feathery Touch of Death. 1996. 272p. mass mkt. 5.50 o.s.i (*0-440-22063-7*) Dell Publishing.

Lynnford, Janet. The Bride of Fair Isle. 2002. 368p. (Orig.). mass mkt. 5.99 o.s.i (*0-451-41032-7*, Onyx) NAL.

—Spellbound Summer. 2002. 368p. mass mkt. 5.99 o.s.i (*0-451-41052-1*) NAL.

Macalister, Katie. Men in Kilts. 2003. 368p. mass mkt. 6.99 (*0-451-41113-7*, Onyx) NAL.

MacDonald, George. Alec Forbes of Howglen. 1995. (George MacDonald Original Works Ser.: Series V). 440p. reprint ed. 22.00 (*1-881084-33-7*) Johannesen Printing & Publishing.

—Alec Forbes of Howglen. 1988. (Sunrise Centenary Editions of the Works of George MacDonald.: Vol. 1). 489p. 29.50 (*0-940652-50-1*) Sunrise Bks.

—Alec Forbes of Howglen, 1865. Wolff, Robert L., ed. 1976. (Victorian Fiction Ser.). lib. bdg. 66.00 o.p. (*0-8240-1583-5*) Garland Publishing, Inc.

—Annals of a Quiet Neighbourhood. 1995. (George MacDonald Original Works Ser.: Series V). 600p. reprint ed. 24.00 (*1-881084-29-9*) Johannesen Printing & Publishing.

—Annals of a Quiet Neighbourhood. deluxe ed. 1992. (Sunrise Centenary Editions of the Works of George MacDonald.: Vol. 11). 39.50 (*0-940652-60-9*) Sunrise Bks.

—The Baronet's Song. 1995. (Hampshire Bks.). 256p. mass mkt. 5.99 o.p. (*1-55661-580-9*) Bethany Hse. Pubs.

—The Baronet's Song. Phillips, Michael, ed. abr. rev. ed. 1983. 208p. pap. 7.99 o.p. (*0-87123-291-X*) Bethany Hse. Pubs.

—The Boyhood of Ranald Bannerman. Hamilton, Dan, ed. 1987. 168p. pap. 4.95 o.p. (*0-89693-748-8*) Cook Communications Ministries.

—David Elginbrod. E-Book 2.49 (*0-7574-2946-7*) Electric Umbrella Publishing.

—David Elginbrod. 1995. (George MacDonald Original Works Ser.: Series VI). 459p. reprint ed. 22.00 (*1-881084-40-X*) Johannesen Printing & Publishing.

—David Elginbrod. 1999. (Sunrise Centenary Editions of the Works of George MacDonald: Vol. 2). (Illus.). 459p. reprint ed. 29.50 (*0-940652-51-X*) Sunrise Bks.

—The Elect Lady. Hamilton, Dan, ed. 1988. 204p. pap. text 5.95 o.p. (*0-89693-451-9*) Cook Communications Ministries.

—The Elect Lady. 1989. (Sunrise Centenary Ser.: Vol. 30). 28.50 (*0-940652-79-X*) Sunrise Bks.

—The Elect Lady. 2003. (Series II). 373p. reprint ed. lib. bdg. 24.00 (*1-881084-61-2*) Johannesen Printing & Publishing.

—The Genius of Willie MacMichael. Hamilton, Dan, ed. 1987. 168p. pap. 4.95 o.p. (*0-89693-750-X*) Cook Communications Ministries.

—George MacDonald: The Parish Papers: Edited for Today's Readers. Hamilton, Dan, ed. 1997. 500p. 14.99 (*1-56476-618-7*) Cook Communications Ministries.

—Heather & Snow. Hamilton, Dan, ed. 1987. 288p. pap. 5.95 o.p. (*0-89693-760-7*) Cook Communications Ministries.

—Heather & Snow. (George MacDonald Original Works Ser.: Series VII). 450p. reprint ed. 24.00 (*1-881084-42-6*) Johannesen Printing & Publishing.

—The Highlander's Last Song. Phillips, Michael, ed. 1986. 272p. pap. 8.99 o.p. (*0-87123-658-3*) Bethany Hse. Pubs.

—Lady of the Mansion. 1983. 160p. pap. 7.95 o.p. (*0-06-250564-5*, CN4056) HarperSanFrancisco.

—The Laird's Inheritance. Phillips, Michael R., ed. rev. ed. 1987. 352p. pap. 9.99 o.p. (*0-87123-903-5*) Bethany Hse. Pubs.

—The Last Castle. 1986. 288p. pap. 5.95 o.p. (*0-89693-267-2*) Cook Communications Ministries.

—The Maiden's Bequest. Phillips, Michael, ed. 1985. 288p. (Orig.). pap. 8.99 o.p. (*0-87123-823-3*) Bethany Hse. Pubs.

—Malcolm. 2001. 416p. pap. 12.99 (*0-7642-2559-6*) Bethany Hse. Pubs.

—Malcolm. 1995. (George MacDonald Original Works Ser.: Series V). 450p. reprint ed. 22.00 (*1-881084-31-0*) Johannesen Printing & Publishing.

—Malcolm. deluxe ed. 1988. (Sunrise Centenary Editions of the Works of George MacDonald.: Vol. 4). 29.50 (*0-940652-53-6*) Sunrise Bks.

—The Marquis of Lossie. 1995. (George MacDonald Original Works Ser.: Series V). 390p. reprint ed. 22.00 (*1-881084-32-9*) Johannesen Printing & Publishing.

—The Marquis of Lossie. 1994. (Sunrise Centenary Editions of the Works of George MacDonald.: Vol. 5). 27.50 (*0-940652-54-4*) Sunrise Bks.

—The Marquis' Secret. Phillips, Michael, ed. 1986. 240p. text 13.99 o.p. (*0-87123-914-0*) Bethany Hse. Pubs.

—The Musician's Quest. Phillips, Michael, ed. 1984. Orig. Title: Robert Falconer. 272p. reprint ed. pap. 8.99 o.p. (*0-87123-444-0*) Bethany Hse. Pubs.

—A Quiet Neighborhood. 1985. 240p. pap. 5.95 o.p. (*0-89693-328-8*) Cook Communications Ministries.

—Robert Falconer. Wolff, Robert L., ed. 1975. (Victorian Fiction Ser.). reprint ed. lib. bdg. 66.00 o.p. (*0-8240-1584-3*) Garland Publishing, Inc.

—Robert Falconer. 1995. (George MacDonald Original Works Ser.: Series VI). 417p. reprint ed. 22.00 (*1-881084-39-6*) Johannesen Printing & Publishing.

—Robert Falconer. 1990. (Sunrise Centenary Editions of the Works of George MacDonald.: Vol. 3). 27.50 (*0-940652-52-8*) Sunrise Bks.

—The Seaboard Parish. 1985. 240p. pap. 5.95 o.p. (*0-89693-329-6*) Cook Communications Ministries.

—The Seaboard Parish. 1995. (George MacDonald Original Works Ser.: Series V). 650p. reprint ed. 24.00 (*1-881084-30-2*) Johannesen Printing & Publishing.

—The Seaboard Parish. 2001. (Centenary Editions Ser.: Vol. 12). viii, 624p. 45.00 (*0-940652-61-7*) Sunrise Bks.

—The Shopkeeper's Daughter. 1986. 288p. pap. 5.95 o.p. (*0-89693-270-2*) Cook Communications Ministries.

—Sir Gibbie. 1996. (George MacDonald Original Works Ser.: Series I). 450p. reprint ed. 22.00 (*1-881084-01-9*) Johannesen Printing & Publishing.

—Sir Gibbie. 1989. (Sunrise Centenary Editions of the Works of George MacDonald.: Vol. 6). 35.00 (*0-940652-55-2*) Sunrise Bks.

—The Tutor's First Love. Phillips, Mike, ed. 1984. 240p. reprint ed. pap. 7.99 o.p. (*0-87123-596-X*) Bethany Hse. Pubs.

—The Vicar's Daughter. 1985. 216p. 5.95 o.p. (*0-89693-330-X*) Cook Communications Ministries.

—Wee Sir Gibbie of the Highlands. Phillips, Michael R., ed. 1990. (George MacDonald Classics Ser.). 240p. (J). (gr. 2-7). text 10.99 o.p. (*1-55661-139-0*) Bethany Hse. Pubs.

MacDonald, George & Phillips, Michael. The Marquis' Secret. (Hampshire Bks.). 1994. 256p. mass mkt. 5.99 o.p. (*1-55661-451-9*); 1982. 240p. reprint ed. pap. 7.99 o.p. (*0-87123-324-X*) Bethany Hse. Pubs.

—The Shepherd's Castle. 1995. 304p. mass mkt. 5.99 o.p. (*1-55661-633-3*) Bethany Hse. Pubs.

MacDonald, George & Phillips, Michael. The Shepherd's Castle. 1983. 288p. pap. 8.99 o.p. (*0-87123-579-X*) Bethany Hse. Pubs.

MacDougall, Carl. The Giant Book of Scottish Short Stories. 1989. 574p. 29.95 o.p. (*0-87226-327-4*, Bedrick, Peter Bks.) McGraw-Hill Children's Publishing.

MacGill, Patrick. Children of the Dead End. 2001. 323p. pap. 15.95 (*1-84158-000-7*) Birlinn, Ltd. GBR. *Dist:* Dufour Editions, Inc., Interlink Publishing Group, Inc.

—The Rat-Pit. 2001. xv, 319p. pap. 15.95 (*1-84158-004-X*) Birlinn, Ltd. GBR. *Dist:* Dufour Editions, Inc., Interlink Publishing Group, Inc.

Macintyre, Lorn. The Blind Bend. 1981. 272p. 11.95 o.p. (*0-312-08388-2*) St. Martin's Pr.

Mackie, Mary. Castle Kintyle. l.t. ed. 1994. 263p. lib. bdg. 16.95 (*0-8161-7452-0*, Macmillan Reference USA) Gale Group.

MacLean, Alistair. When Eight Bells Toll. l.t. ed. 1993. 20.95 o.p. (*0-7927-1666-3*); pap. 18.95 o.p. (*0-7927-1665-5*) BBC Audiobooks America.

MacPherson, Margaret M. Rough Road. 1966. (Illus.). (J). (gr. 7 up). 4.75 o.p. (*0-15-269147-2*) Harcourt Children's Bks.

Madden, Mickie. Hope Everlastin' 1999. 352p. mass mkt. 5.99 o.s.i (*0-7860-0653-6*) Kensington Publishing Corp.

Magruder, Owen. The Strange Case of Mr. Nobody. 2000. 212p. pap. 7.95 (*1-892059-01-0*) Edmonston Publishing, Inc.

Marsh, Ellen T. The Enchanted Prince. 2000. 448p. (Orig.). mass mkt. 5.99 (*0-505-52390-6*, Love Spell) Dorchester Publishing Co., Inc.

Marshall, Robert. The Haunted Major. 1998. (Illus.). 160p. pap. 12.95 (*0-86241-786-4*) Canongate Bks. GBR. *Dist:* Interlink Publishing Group, Inc.

—The Haunted Major. 1999. (Illus.). 208p. 23.00 (*0-88001-669-8*, Ecco) HarperTrade.

Massie, Allan. These Enchanted Woods. 1993. 206p. o.p. (*0-09-177411-X*) Random Hse. of Canada, Ltd. CAN. *Dist:* Random Hse., Inc.

May, Gideon S. The Croft & the Ceilidh. 1980. pap. 30.00 (*0-907526-60-8*) Alloway Publishing, Ltd. GBR. *Dist:* State Mutual Bk. & Periodical Service, Ltd.

McCrone, Guy. Aunt Bel. 2001. 256p. pap. 11.95 (*1-873631-39-1*) B & W Publishing GBR. *Dist:* Interlink Publishing Group, Inc.

McCrumb, Sharyn. Highland Laddie Gone. 1999. mass mkt. 5.99 o.s.i (*0-345-91575-5*); 1998. mass mkt. o.s.i (*0-345-42948-6*); 1991. 224p. mass mkt. 5.99 (*0-345-36036-2*, Ivy Bks.) Ballantine Bks.

—Highland Laddie Gone. l.t. ed. 2002. 28.95 (*1-58547-213-1*, Premier) Ctr. Point Large Print.

—Highland Laddie Gone. 1986. 192p. pap. 2.95 o.p. (*0-380-89910-8*, Avon Bks.) Morrow/Avon.

—Highland Laddie Gone. unabr. ed. 1992. audio 44.00 (*1-55690-678-1*, 92220E7) Recorded Bks., LLC.

—Highland Laddie Gone. 1993. 19.00 o.p. (*0-7278-4418-0*) Severn Hse. Pubs., Ltd.

McDermid, Val. The Distant Echo. Date not set. mass mkt. (*0-312-99483-4*, St. Martin's Paperbacks); 2003. 384p. 24.95 o.s.i (*0-312-30199-5*, Saint Martin's Minotaur) St. Martin's Pr.

McEwen, Todd. McX: A Romance of the Dour. 1990. 192p. 17.95 o.p. (*0-8021-1166-1*) Grove/Atlantic, Inc.

McGoldrick, May. The Dreamer, Vol. 1. 2000. (Highland Treasure Trilogy ). 336p. mass mkt. 5.99 (*0-451-19718-6*, Onyx) NAL.

—The Enchantress. 2000. (Highland Treasure Trilogy : Vol. 2). 336p. mass mkt. 6.99 (*0-451-19719-4*, Onyx) NAL.

—Highland Treasure: The Firebrand. 2000. (Highland Treasure Trilogy : Vol. 3). 336p. mass mkt. 6.99 (*0-451-40942-6*, Onyx) NAL.

McIlvanney, William. The Big Man. 1986. 320p. 16.95 o.p. (*0-688-06405-1*, Morrow, William & Co.) Morrow/Avon.

—Laidlaw. 1993. 224p. pap. 15.00 (*0-15-648109-X*) Harcourt Trade Pubs.

—Laidlaw. (International Crime Ser.). 1982. pap. 2.95 o.s.i (*0-394-73338-X*); 1977. 7.95 o.p. (*0-394-41253-2*) Knopf Publishing Group. (Pantheon).

—The Papers of Tony Veitch. 1993. 256p. pap. 9.95 (*0-15-670828-0*, Harvest Bks.) Harcourt Trade Pubs.

—The Papers of Tony Veitch. 1983. 256p. 12.95 o.p. (*0-394-42437-9*, Pantheon) Knopf Publishing Group.

—Strange Loyalties. 1993. (Harvest Book Ser.). 288p. pap. 9.95 (*0-15-685644-1*, Harvest Bks.) Harcourt Trade Pubs.

—Strange Loyalties. 1992. 20.00 o.p. (*0-688-11413-X*, Morrow, William & Co.) Morrow/Avon.

McKay, Reg & Ferris, Paul. Deadly Divisions. 2002. 224p. pap. 13.95 (*1-84018-601-1*) Mainstream Publishing Co., Ltd. GBR. *Dist:* Trafalgar Square.

McKenzie, Helen B. The Sassenach. 1989. (Kelpie Ser.). 166p. (J). (gr. 5-7). pap. 5.95 o.p. (*0-86241-115-7*) Trafalgar Square.

McLean, Duncan. Bucket of Tongues. 1999. 244p. pap. 13.00 (*0-393-31897-4*) Norton, W. W. & Co., Inc.

—Bunker Man. 1997. 297p. 13.00 (*0-393-31616-5*); 25.00 (*0-393-04121-2*) Norton, W. W. & Co., Inc.

McLellan, Robert. Linmill Stories. 1994. (Classics Ser.). 280p. pap. 11.95 (*0-86241-282-X*) Canongate Bks. GBR. *Dist:* Interlink Publishing Group, Inc.

McNeill, Elisabeth. Hot News. 2003. 288p. 25.99 (*0-7278-5939-0*) Severn Hse. Pubs., Ltd.

McNiven, Daniel A. The Kilted Ladies from Hell. l.t. ed. 1996. 176p. (Orig.). pap. 12.95 (*0-9654680-2-X*) Pilgrimage Pr.

Medeiros, Teresa. The Bride & the Beast. 2001. 352p. reprint ed. mass mkt. 6.99 (*0-553-58183-X*) Bantam Bks.

—The Bride & the Beast. l.t. ed. 2001. 398p. 28.95 (*0-7862-3519-5*) Thorndike Pr.

—A Whisper of Roses. 1993. 416p. mass mkt. 6.99 (*0-553-29408-3*) Bantam Bks.

Millington, Mil. A Certain Chemistry: A Novel. 2004. 384p. pap. 13.95 (*0-8129-6667-8*, Villard Bks.) Random House Adult Trade Publishing Group.

Mina, Denise. Exile. 2001. 364p. 25.00 (*0-7867-0838-7*); 2002. 368p. reprint ed. pap. 14.00 (*0-7867-0962-6*) Avalon Publishing Group. (Carroll & Graf Pubs.).

—Garnethill. 1999. 348p. 24.00 (*0-7867-0612-0*); 2001. 352p. reprint ed. pap. 14.00 (*0-7867-0839-5*) Avalon Publishing Group. (Carroll & Graf Pubs.).

—Garnethill. 1999. 448p. (gr. 9). mass mkt. (*0-553-50694-3*, Corgi) Bantam Bks.

—Sanctum. 2004. 24.95 (*0-316-73592-2*) Little Brown & Co.

Moffat, Gwen. Miss Pink at the Edge of the World. 1995. 208p. 19.50 (*0-7451-8667-X*, Black Dagger) BBC Audiobooks America.

—Miss Pink at the Edge of the World. 1993. (J). 6.95 o.p. (*0-684-14336-4*, Macmillan Reference USA) Gale Group.

—Miss Pink at the Edge of the World. l.t. ed. 1995. (Ulverscroft Large Print Ser.). 368p. 29.99 o.p. (*0-7089-3379-3*, Ulverscroft) Thorpe, F. A. Pubs. GBR. *Dist:* Ulverscroft Large Print Bks., Ltd., Ulverscroft Large Print Canada, Ltd.

—Over the Sea to Death. unabr. ed. 1996. audio 49.95 o.p. (*1-85903-099-8*, 30998) Magna Story Sound GBR. *Dist:* Ulverscroft Large Print Bks., Ltd.

—Over the Sea to Death. l.t. ed. 1994. (Ulverscroft Large Print Ser.). 368p. 29.99 o.p. (*0-7089-3137-5*, Ulverscroft) Thorpe, F. A. Pubs. GBR. *Dist:* Ulverscroft Large Print Bks., Ltd., Ulverscroft Large Print Canada, Ltd.

—Snare: A Miss Pink Mystery. l.t. ed. 2002. 292p. pap. 24.45 (*0-7862-3939-5*) Gale Group.

—Snare: A Miss Pink Mystery. 1988. 192p. 14.95 o.p. (*0-312-02284-0*, Saint Martin's Minotaur) St. Martin's Pr.

—Snare: A Miss Pink Mystery. l.t. ed. 1990. (Ulverscroft Large Print Ser.). 29.99 o.p. (*0-7089-2128-0*, Ulverscroft) Thorpe, F. A. Pubs. GBR. *Dist:* Ulverscroft Large Print Bks., Ltd., Ulverscroft Large Print Canada, Ltd.

Moning, Karen. Beyond the Highland Mist. 1999. 384p. mass mkt. 6.99 (*0-440-23480-8*) Dell Publishing.

Moning, Karen M. To Tame a Highland Warrior. 1999. 384p. mass mkt. 6.99 (*0-440-23481-6*) Dell Publishing.

Moning, Karen Marie. The Highlander's Touch. 2000. 384p. mass mkt. 6.99 (*0-440-23652-5*) Dell Publishing.

—Kiss of the Highlander. 2001. 416p. mass mkt. 6.99 (*0-440-23655-X*) Dell Publishing.

Monk, Karyn. Once a Warrior. 1997. 384p. mass mkt. 6.50 (*0-553-57422-1*, Fanfare) Bantam Bks.

—The Rose & the Warrior. 2000. 336p. mass mkt. 5.99 (*0-553-57761-1*) Bantam Bks.

—The Witch & the Warrior. 1998. 384p. mass mkt. 5.99 (*0-553-55760-2*); 352p. mass mkt. 6.50 (*0-553-57760-3*) Bantam Bks.

Morgan, Kathleen. Embrace the Dawn. 2002. 416p. pap. 12.99 (*0-8423-4097-1*) Tyndale Hse. Pubs.

Munro, Neil. Erchie: My Droll Friend. 2002. 558p. pap. (*1-84158-202-6*) Birlinn, Ltd.

Munro, Niel. Jimmy Swan. 2002. 208p. pap. 13.95 (*1-84158-203-4*) Birlinn, Ltd. GBR. *Dist:* Interlink Publishing Group, Inc.

Murray, Helen. Heart of a Nurse. l.t. ed. 1991. (Orig.). 18.95 o.p. (*0-7927-0696-X*, CH011); pap. 16.95 o.p. (*0-7927-0697-8*, CS0115) BBC Audiobooks America.

Murray, Ian, ed. The New Penguin Book of Scottish Short Stories. 2000. 336p. pap. 14.95 (*0-14-006411-7*) Penguin Bks., Ltd. GBR. *Dist:* Trafalgar Square.

Neri, Penelope. Highland Lovesong. 2000. 368p. mass mkt. 5.99 (*0-8439-4724-1*, Leisure Bks.) Dorchester Publishing Co., Inc.

Newman, Sharan. Cursed in the Blood. 2000. 370p. mass mkt. 6.99 (*0-8125-9020-1*, Forge Bks.); 1999. 23.95 (*0-312-87153-8*, Tor Bks.); 1998. 352p. 23.95 (*0-312-86567-8*, Forge Bks.) Doherty, Tom Assocs., LLC.

O'Farrell, Maggie. After You'd Gone. l.t. ed. 2001. (Magna Large Print Ser.). 432p. (*0-7505-1722-0*) Magna Large Print Bks. GBR. *Dist:* Ulverscroft Large Print Canada, Ltd.

—After You'd Gone. 2002. 384p. 13.00 (*0-14-200032-9*); 2001. 372p. 24.95 o.s.i (*0-670-89448-6*, Viking) Viking Penguin.

O'Hagan, Andrew. Our Fathers. 2001. 304p. pap. 13.00 (*0-15-601202-2*, Harvest Bks.) Harcourt Trade Pubs.

—Our Fathers: A Novel. 1999. 304p. 23.00 (*0-15-100494-3*, Harvest Bks.) Harcourt Trade Pubs.

—Personality. 320p. 2004. pap. (*0-15-602967-7*, Harvest Bks.); 2003. 25.00 (*0-15-101000-5*) Harcourt Trade Pubs.

The Original Miss Honeyford. 2002. 25.95 o.p. (*0-7862-3618-3*) Thorndike Pr.

Paige, Robin. Death at Glamis Castle. 352p. 2004. mass mkt. 6.50 (*0-425-19264-4*); 2003. 22.95 (*0-425-18847-7*, Prime Crime) Berkley Publishing Group.

Paul, William. Sleeping Dogs. 1995. 192p. 19.95 o.p. (*0-312-13603-X*, Saint Martin's Minotaur) St. Martin's Pr.

—Sleeping Partner. 1997. 192p. 19.95 o.p. (*0-312-15208-6*, Saint Martin's Minotaur) St. Martin's Pr.

—Sleeping Pretty. 1996. 192p. 19.95 o.p. (*0-312-14418-0*, Saint Martin's Minotaur) St. Martin's Pr.

Peters, Elizabeth, pseud. Legend in Green Velvet. l.t. ed. 1991. 21.95 o.p. (*0-7927-0688-9*, CH007); pap. 19.95 o.p. (*0-7927-0689-7*, CS0109) BBC Audiobooks America.

—Legend in Green Velvet. unabr. ed. 1998. audio 39.95 (*0-7861-1425-8*, 2301) Blackstone Audio Bks., Inc.

—Legend in Green Velvet. 1992. 242p. mass mkt. 5.99 (*0-8125-2441-1*, Forge Bks.); 1989. 256p. pap. 3.95 o.s.i (*0-8125-0750-9*, Tor Bks.) Doherty, Tom Assocs., LLC.

—Legend in Green Velvet. 2002. 352p. mass mkt. 6.99 (*0-380-73118-5*) Morrow/Avon.

—Legend in Green Velvet. 1995. 256p. reprint ed. 20.00 (*0-7278-4721-X*) Severn Hse. Pubs., Ltd.

Phillips, Michael & Phillips, Michael R. An Ancient Strife. 2000. (Caledonia Ser.). (Illus.). 544p. pap. 13.99 (*0-7642-2218-X*) Bethany Hse. Pubs.

Phillips, Michael R. Caledonia: An Epic Novel of Scotland. 1994. 512p. 19.99 (*0-345-39564-6*, Ballantine Bks.) Ballantine Bks.

—Flight from Stonewycke. 1994. (Stonewycke Trilogy Ser.). 288p. mass mkt. 5.99 o.p. (*1-55661-453-5*) Bethany Hse. Pubs.

—Legend of the Celtic Stone. 1999. (Caledonia Ser.: Vol. 1). 544p. text 19.99 o.p. (*0-7642-2250-3*); (Illus.). pap. 13.99 (*0-7642-2217-1*) Bethany Hse. Pubs.

—The Stonewycke Trilogy, 3 vols. in 1. 1996. 640p. 12.98 (*0-88486-133-3*, Arrowood Pr.) BBS Publishing Corp.

—The Stonewycke Trilogy, Vol. 1-3. 1986. (Stonewycke Trilogy Ser.). 26.99 o.p. (*0-87123-971-X*) Bethany Hse. Pubs.

—Stranger at Stonewycke. 1995. (Stonewycke Legacy Ser.). 384p. mass mkt. 6.99 o.p. (*1-55661-581-7*) Bethany Hse. Pubs.

Phillips, Michael R. & Pella, Judith. Flight from Stonewycke. 1985. (Stonewycke Trilogy Ser.). 256p. pap. 8.99 o.p. (*0-87123-837-3*) Bethany Hse. Pubs.

—Flight from Stonewycke. 2002. (Stonewycke Trilogy: Bk. 2). 26.95 (*0-7862-4721-5*) Thorndike Pr.

—Heather Hills of Stonewycke. (Stonewycke Trilogy Ser.). (Orig.). 1993. 272p. mass mkt. 5.99 o.p. (*1-55661-373-3*); 1985. 256p. pap. 8.99 o.p. (*0-87123-803-9*) Bethany Hse. Pubs.

—Heather Hills of Stonewycke. l.t. ed. 2002. (Orig.). 25.95 (*0-7862-4724-X*) Thorndike Pr.

—Jamie Macleod: Highland Lass. 1987. (Highland Collections). 352p. pap. 9.99 o.p. (*0-87123-918-3*) Bethany Hse. Pubs.

—The Lady of Stonewycke. 1986. (Stonewycke Trilogy Ser.: Vol. 3). 272p. pap. 8.99 o.p. (*0-87123-856-X*) Bethany Hse. Pubs.

—The Lady of Stonewycke. l.t. ed. 2003. (Stonewycke Trilogy: Bk. 3). 26.95 (*0-7862-4725-8*) Thorndike Pr.

—Robbie Taggart, Highland Sailor. 1987. (Highland Collections: Vol. 2). 384p. pap. 9.99 o.p. (*0-87123-919-1*) Bethany Hse. Pubs.

—Shadows over Stonewycke. (Stonewycke Legacy Ser.: Bk. 2). (Orig.). 1995. 464p. mass mkt. 6.99 o.p. (*1-55661-632-5*); 1988. 400p. pap. 9.99 o.p. (*0-87123-901-9*) Bethany Hse. Pubs.

—The Stonewycke Legacy, 3 vols. in 1. 1997. 720p. 12.99 (*0-88486-169-4*) BBS Publishing Corp.

—The Stonewycke Legacy, 3 vols. (Stonewycke Legacy Ser.). 2000. (Illus.). 784p. pap. 12.99 (*0-7642-2377-1*); Vols. 1-3. 1988. pap. 29.99 o.p. (*1-55661-755-0*, 252755) Bethany Hse. Pubs.

—The Stonewycke Trilogy. 2000. (Stonewycke Trilogy Ser.). (Illus.). 640p. pap. 12.99 (*0-7642-2324-0*) Bethany Hse. Pubs.

—Stranger at Stonewycke. 1987. (Stonewycke Legacy Ser.). 352p. pap. 9.99 o.p. (*0-87123-900-0*) Bethany Hse. Pubs.

—Treasure of Stonewycke. (Stonewycke Legacy Ser.: Bk. 3). (Orig.). 1995. 464p. mass mkt. 6.99 o.p. (*1-55661-634-1*); 1988. 400p. pap. 9.99 o.p. (*0-87123-902-7*) Bethany Hse. Pubs.

Piel, Stobie, et al. Scottish Magic. 1997. 288p. 21.95 o.s.i (*1-57566-182-9*) Kensington Publishing Corp.

—Scottish Magic: Lily/Isbel/Faerie Princess/Beneath the Midnight Sky. 1998. 320p. mass mkt. 5.99 o.s.i (*1-57566-278-7*) Kensington Publishing Corp.

Pilcher, Robin. An Ocean Apart. unabr. ed. 1999. audio 44.00 (*0-7871-1868-0*, Dove Audio) NewStar Media, Inc.

Pilcher, Robin. An Ocean Apart. abr. ed. 1999. audio 25.00 (*0-7871-1867-2*, 698452, Dove Audio) NewStar Media, Inc.

—An Ocean Apart. 1999. 512p. mass mkt. 6.99 (*0-312-97184-2*, St. Martin's Paperbacks); 1998. 470p. 24.95 o.p. (*0-312-19995-3*) St. Martin's Pr.

—An Ocean Apart. l.t. ed. 1999. (Basic Ser.). 699p. 30.95 (*0-7862-1911-4*) Thorndike Pr.

—Starting Over. E-Book 18.95 (*0-312-70405-4*); 2003. 416p. mass mkt. 6.99 (*0-312-98341-7*, St. Martin's Paperbacks); 2002. 400p. 24.95 (*0-312-26995-1*) St. Martin's Pr.

Pilcher, Rosamunde. September. unabr. ed. 1992. audio 124.95 (*0-7451-6197-9*, CAB 625) BBC Audiobooks America.

—September. unabr. ed. 1990. audio 120.00 (*0-7366-1777-9*, 2616) Books on Tape, Inc.

—September. 1990. audio 12.79 o.s.i (*0-553-19974-9*); 2000. audio 9.99 o.s.i (*0-553-52701-0*); 1990. audio 16.99 (*0-553-45241-X*, 391540) Random Hse. Audio Publishing Group. (RH Audio).

—September. 1991. mass mkt. 7.99 (*0-312-92480-1*, St. Martin's Paperbacks); 1990. 22.95 o.p. (*0-312-04419-4*) St. Martin's Pr.

—September. l.t. ed. 1991. (Paperback Bestsellers Ser.). 874p. pap. 19.95 (*1-56054-089-3*) Thorndike Pr.

—Winter Solstice. E-Book 27.95 (*0-312-70036-9*); E-Book 27.95 (*0-312-27839-X*); 2000. 454p. 27.95 (*0-312-24426-6*); 2001. 512p. reprint ed. mass mkt. 7.99 (*0-312-97838-3*, St. Martin's Paperbacks) St. Martin's Pr.

—Winter Solstice. l.t. ed. (Basic Ser.). 799p. 2001. 30.95 (*0-7862-2646-3*); 2000. 32.95 (*0-7862-2506-8*) Thorndike Pr.

Plaidy, Jean. The Thistle & the Rose. 2004. (Illus.). 320p. pap. 12.95 (*0-609-81022-7*, Three Rivers Pr.) Crown Publishing Group.

—The Thistle & the Rose. 1973. 4.00 (*0-399-11196-4*) Putnam Publishing Group, The.

Porter, Jane. The Scottish Chiefs. Smith, Nora A. & Wiggin, Kate Douglas, eds. & trs. by. from SCO. 1991. (Scribner Illustrated Classics Ser.). (Illus.). 520p. (YA). (gr. 7 up). 29.00 (*0-684-19340-X*, Atheneum) Simon & Schuster Children's Publishing.

Potter, Paticia. The Heart Queen. 2001. 432p. mass mkt. 6.99 (*0-515-13098-2*, Jove) Berkley Publishing Group.

Potter, Patricia. The Black Knave. 2000. 416p. mass mkt. 6.99 (*0-515-12864-3*, Jove) Berkley Publishing Group.

Pozzessere, Heather G. Never Sleep with Strangers. 1998. 384p. mass mkt. (*1-55166-445-3*, Mira Bks.) Harlequin Enterprises, Ltd.

The Provost. E-Book 2.49 (*0-7574-0477-4*) Electric Umbrella Publishing.

Pye, M. Rewire. 2002. 310p. mass mkt. 13.95 (*0-340-76611-5*) Hodder & Stoughton, Ltd. GBR. *Dist:* Trafalgar Square.

Radcliffe, Ann. Castles of Athlin & Dunbayne: A Highland Story. 1974. (Gothic Novels Ser.). reprint ed. 51.95 (*0-405-00808-2*) Ayer Co. Pubs., Inc.

—Castles of Athlin & Dunbayne: A Highland Story. Milbank, Alison, ed. 1995. (Oxford World's Classics Ser.). 146p. pap. 9.95 o.p. (*0-19-282357-4*) Oxford Univ. Pr., Inc.

Raife, Alexandra. Until the Spring. l.t. ed. 2000. 27.95 (*1-57490-300-4*, Beeler Large Print Bks.) Beeler, Thomas T. Publisher.

—Until the Spring. 2000. 368p. mass mkt. 5.99 o.s.i (*0-451-40914-0*, Onyx) NAL.

—The Way Home. 2003. 380p. pap. 13.00 (*0-340-82237-6*) Hodder & Stoughton, Ltd. GBR. *Dist:* Trafalgar Square.

—The Way Home. l.t. ed. 2003. (Charnwood Large Print Ser.). 432p. 32.50 (*0-7089-4964-9*) Thorpe, F. A. Pubs. GBR. *Dist:* Ulverscroft Large Print Bks., Ltd.

Ramsay, Eileen. Butterflies in December. 1996. 346p. mass mkt. o.s.i (*0-7515-1649-X*); 1995. 352p. o.s.i (*0-316-91422-3*) Little Brown & Co.

—Butterflies in December. l.t. ed. 1998. (Magna Large Print Ser.). 438p. (*0-7505-1223-7*) Magna Large Print Bks. GBR. *Dist:* Ulverscroft Large Print Canada, Ltd.

Rankin, Ian. Black & Blue. unabr. ed. 1998. audio 80.00 (*0-7366-4176-9*, 4675) Books on Tape, Inc.

—Black & Blue. Date not set. E-Book (*0-312-70694-4*); 1999. (Black & Blue Ser.: Vol. 1). 352p. mass mkt. 6.99 (*0-312-96677-6*, St. Martin's Paperbacks); 1997. (Inspector Rebus Novel Ser.). 394p. 24.95 (*0-312-16783-0*, Saint Martin's Minotaur) St. Martin's Pr.

—Black & Blue: An Inspector Rebus Novel. l.t. ed. 1998. (Mystery Ser.). 623p. 28.95 (*0-7838-8443-5*) Thorndike Pr.

—The Black Book. E-Book 6.50 (*0-312-70693-6*); 2000. 352p. mass mkt. 7.50 (*0-312-97675-5*, St. Martin's Paperbacks) St. Martin's Pr.

—The Black Book: An Inspector Rebus Novel. unabr. ed. 1995. audio 59.95 (*0-7451-6514-1*, CAB 1130) Chivers Audio Bks. GBR. *Dist:* BBC Audiobooks America.

—The Black Book: An Inspector Rebus Novel. 1994. 288p. reprint ed. 21.00 (*1-883402-77-8*, Scribner) Simon & Schuster.

—Dead Souls. 2000. 448p. mass mkt. 6.99 (*0-312-97420-5*, St. Martin's Paperbacks); 1999. 320p. 24.95 o.p. (*0-312-20293-8*, Saint Martin's Minotaur) St. Martin's Pr.

—Death Is Not Enough. mass mkt. (*0-312-97628-3*, St. Martin's Paperbacks) St. Martin's Pr.

—Death Is Not the End: An Instpector Rebus Novella. 2000. 73p. 11.95 (*0-312-26142-X*, Saint Martin's Minotaur) St. Martin's Pr.

—The Hanging Garden. unabr. ed. 1999. audio 64.00 Books on Tape, Inc.

—The Hanging Garden. E-Book 5.99 (*0-312-70698-7*); 1998. 352p. 24.95 o.p. (*0-312-19278-9*, Saint Martin's Minotaur); 1999. 384p. reprint ed. mass mkt. 6.99 (*0-312-96913-9*, St. Martin's Paperbacks) St. Martin's Pr.

—The Hanging Garden. l.t. ed. 1999. (Charnwood Large Print Ser.). 432p. 31.99 o.p. (*0-7089-9124-6*, Ulverscroft) Thorpe, F. A. Pubs. GBR. *Dist:* Ulverscroft Large Print Bks., Ltd., Ulverscroft Large Print Canada, Ltd.

—Hide & Seek. E-Book 6.50 (*0-312-70699-5*); 1997. 224p. mass mkt. 6.50 (*0-312-96397-1*, St. Martin's Paperbacks) St. Martin's Pr.

—Hide & Seek. l.t. ed. 1992. (General Ser.). 464p. 29.99 o.p. (*0-7089-2734-3*, Ulverscroft) Thorpe, F. A. Pubs. GBR. *Dist:* Ulverscroft Large Print Bks., Ltd., Ulverscroft Large Print Canada, Ltd.

—Hide & Seek: A John Rebus Mystery. 1994. 288p. reprint ed. 21.00 (*1-883402-74-3*, Scribner) Simon & Schuster.

—Knots & Crosses. 1987. (Crime Club Ser.). 192p. 12.95 o.s.i (*0-385-24307-3*) Doubleday Publishing.

—Knots & Crosses. 2002. E-Book 6.99 (*0-312-70721-5*); 1995. mass mkt. 7.50 o.s.i (*0-312-95673-8*, St. Martin's Paperbacks); 1995. pap. o.s.i (*0-312-95566-9*, St. Martin's Paperbacks) St. Martin's Pr.

—Let It Bleed. 1996. (Detective John Rebus Novels Ser.). 288p. 20.50 (*0-684-83055-8*, Simon & Schuster); 20.00 (*1-883402-76-X*, Scribner) Simon & Schuster.

—Let It Bleed. E-Book 6.50 (*0-312-70701-0*); 1998. 320p. mass mkt. 7.50 (*0-312-96665-2*, St. Martin's Paperbacks) St. Martin's Pr.

—Let It Bleed: An Inspector Rebus Novel. l.t. ed. 2000. (Mystery Ser.). 502p. 26.95 (*0-7862-2677-3*) Thorndike Pr.

—Mortal Causes. 1995. 21.50 (*1-883402-75-1*, Scribner) Simon & Schuster.

—Mortal Causes. E-Book 6.50 (*0-312-70702-9*); 3rd ed. 1997. 277p. mass mkt. 6.99 (*0-312-96094-8*, St. Martin's Paperbacks) St. Martin's Pr.

—Mortal Causes: A John Rebus Mystery. 1995. 288p. 22.00 o.p. (*0-684-81497-8*, Simon & Schuster) Simon & Schuster.

—Mortal Causes: An Inspector Rebus Novel. unabr. ed. 1996. audio 69.95 BBC Audiobooks America.

—Set in Darkness. E-Book 6.99 (*0-312-70703-7*, Tor Bks.) Doherty, Tom Assocs., LLC.

—Set in Darkness. l.t. ed. 2001. 583p. 29.95 (*0-7838-9406-6*, Macmillan Reference USA) Gale Group.

—Set in Darkness. 2000. 432p. 24.95 (*0-312-20609-7*, Saint Martin's Minotaur); 2001. reprint ed. mass mkt. 7.50 (*0-312-97789-1*, St. Martin's Paperbacks) St. Martin's Pr.

—Strip Jack. E-Book 6.50 (*0-312-70704-5*);Vol. 1. 1998. 272p. mass mkt. 6.99 (*0-312-96514-1*, St. Martin's Paperbacks) St. Martin's Pr.

—Strip Jack: An Inspector Rebus Novel. 1994. 272p. 20.95 o.p. (*0-312-10553-3*, Saint Martin's Minotaur) St. Martin's Pr.

—Tooth & Nail. E-Book 6.99 (*0-312-70705-3*); 1996. 304p. reprint ed. mass mkt. 7.50 (*0-312-95878-1*, St. Martin's Paperbacks) St. Martin's Pr.

Ranney, Karen. One Man's Love. 2001. 384p. mass mkt. 5.99 (*0-380-81300-9*, Avon Bks.) Morrow/Avon.

Reding, Jaclyn. White Mist. 2000. 336p. mass mkt. 5.99 o.s.i (*0-451-20157-4*, Signet Bks.) NAL.

Reid, Joyce M., ed. Classic Scottish Short Stories. 1990. 342p. pap. 13.95 o.p. (*0-19-282686-7*) Oxford Univ. Pr., Inc.

Reisert, Rebecca. The Third Witch. 2001. 320p. 25.00 (*0-7434-1771-2*); E-Book 25.00 (*0-7434-2305-4*) Simon & Schuster. (Washington Square Pr.).

Richards, Cinda. Dillon's Promise. l.t. ed. 1993. 19.95 o.p. (*0-7927-1630-2*); pap. 17.95 o.p. (*0-7927-1629-9*) BBC Audiobooks America.

Robb, Candace. A Trust Betrayed. 2002. 272p. pap. 12.95 (*0-446-67850-3*, Mysterious Pr. Paperback Bks.) Warner Bks., Inc.

—A Trust Betrayed: First Chapter of Margaret Kerr of Perth. 2001. 272p. E-Book 14.95 (*0-7595-4245-7*); E-Book 14.95 (*0-7595-9274-8*); E-Book 14.95 (*0-7595-6242-3*); E-Book 14.95 (*0-7595-8248-3*); E-Book 14.95 (*0-7595-0242-0*); (Illus.). 22.95 o.p. (*0-89296-708-0*) Mysterious Pr.

—A Trust Betrayed: First Chapter of Margaret Kerr of Perth. l.t. ed. 2001. (Illus.). 354p. 29.95 (*0-7862-3323-0*); 368p. (*0-7540-1663-3*); 368p. (*0-7540-9077-9*) Thorndike Pr.

Roberson, Jennifer. Lady of the Glen. 1998. 576p. mass mkt. 6.99 o.s.i (*1-57566-289-2*); 1997. 432p. pap. 14.95 o.p. (*1-57566-129-2*); 1996. 432p. pap. 23.95 o.p. (*1-57566-022-9*) Kensington Publishing Corp.

Roberts, Nora. Rebellion. 1999. 298p. mass mkt. (*0-373-83428-4*, 1-83428-2); 1998. mass mkt. (*0-373-83403-9*, 1-83403-5); 1988. mass mkt. (*0-373-28604-X*) Harlequin Enterprises, Ltd. (Harlequin Bks.).

Robertson, James. The Fanatic. 2003. 310p. pap. 12.00 (*1-84115-189-0*) Fourth Estate, Ltd. GBR. *Dist:* Trafalgar Square.

—Joseph Knight: A Novel. 2003. 352p. pap. (*0-00-715024-5*, Fourth Estate) HarperTrade.

Roe, C. F. Bad Blood. l.t. ed. 1993. (Magna Large Print Ser.). 366p. (*0-7505-0486-2*) Magna Large Print Bks. GBR. *Dist:* Ulverscroft Large Print Canada, Ltd.

—A Bonny Case of Murder: Dr. Jean Montrose Mystery. 1994. (Dr. Jean Montrose Mystery Ser.). 256p. (Orig.). mass mkt. 3.99 o.s.i (*0-451-18067-4*) NAL.

—A Classy Touch of Murder. 1993. (Dr. Jean Montrose Mystery Ser.: No. 3). 256p. mass mkt. 5.99 o.s.i (*0-451-17713-4*, Signet Bks.) NAL.

—A Classy Touch of Murder. 256p. 24.00 (*0-7278-5183-7*) Severn Hse. Pubs., Ltd.

—Death by Fire. l.t. ed. 1992. (Magna Large Print Ser.). 345p. (*0-7505-0128-6*) Magna Large Print Bks. GBR. *Dist:* Ulverscroft Large Print Canada, Ltd.

—A Fiery Hint of Murder. 1993. (Dr. Jean Montrose Mystery Ser.: No. 2). 256p. reprint ed. mass mkt. 5.50 o.s.i (*0-451-17606-5*, Signet Bks.) NAL.

—The Hidden Cause of Murder. 1996. (Dr. Jean Montrose Mystery Ser.). 256p. mass mkt. 5.50 o.s.i (*0-451-18633-8*, Signet Bks.) NAL.

—A Nasty Bit of Murder. 1992. (Dr. Jean Montrose Mystery Ser.). 288p. mass mkt. 5.50 o.s.i (*0-451-17468-2*, Signet Bks.) NAL.

—A Relative Act of Murder. 1995. (Dr. Jean Montrose Mystery Ser.). 256p. (Orig.). mass mkt. 5.50 o.s.i (*0-451-18183-2*, Signet Bks.) NAL.

—Tangled Knot of Murder. 1996. (Dr. Jean Montrose Mystery Ser.). 256p. mass mkt. 5.50 o.s.i (*0-451-19079-3*, Signet Bks.) NAL.

—A Torrid Piece of Murder: A Dr. Jean Montrose Mystery. 1994. (Dr. Jean Montrose Mystery Ser.). 256p. (Orig.). mass mkt. 5.50 o.s.i (*0-451-18182-4*, Signet Bks.) NAL.

Rogers, Jane. Island. 2001. (Illus.). 238p. reprint ed. pap. 13.00 (*0-618-13931-1*, Mariner Bks.) Houghton Mifflin Co. Trade & Reference Div.

—Island. 2000. 261p. 25.95 (*1-58567-076-6*) Overlook Pr., The.

Ross, Bess. A Bit of Crack & Car Culture. 2002. 168p. pap. 12.95 (*1-84158-043-0*) Birlinn, Ltd. GBR. *Dist:* Interlink Publishing Group, Inc.

Sabbagh, Karl. A Rum Affair: A True Story of Botanical Fraud. 2000. (Illus.). viii, 276p. 24.00 o.p. (*0-374-25282-3*) Farrar, Straus & Giroux.

Samson, Lisa. The Highlander & His Lady. 1994. pap. 9.99 o.s.i (*1-56507-206-5*) Harvest Hse. Pubs.

—The Temptation of Aaron Campbell. 1996. (Highlanders Ser.). (Orig.). pap. 9.99 o.p. (*1-56507-390-8*) Harvest Hse. Pubs.

Scarborough, Elizabeth Ann. The Lady in the Loch. 272p. 1998. 19.95 o.s.i (*0-441-00582-9*); 1999. reprint ed. mass mkt. 5.99 o.s.i (*0-441-00666-3*) Ace Bks.

Scott, Amanda. Border Fire. 2000. 384p. mass mkt. 5.99 o.s.i (*0-8217-6586-8*) Kensington Publishing Corp.

—The Secret Clan: Abducted Heiress. 2001. 432p. reprint ed. mass mkt. 5.99 (*0-446-61026-7*, Warner Romance) Warner Bks., Inc.

—The Secret Clan: Highland Bride. 2003. 448p. reprint ed. mass mkt. 5.99 (*0-446-61266-9*, Warner Romance) Warner Bks., Inc.

—The Secret Clan: Reiver's Bride. 2003. (Illus.). 400p. mass mkt. 5.99 (*0-446-61267-7*, Warner Romance) Warner Bks., Inc.

Scott, Manda. Hen's Teeth. 1999. 352p. mass mkt. 5.50 (*0-553-57967-3*) Bantam Bks.

—No Good Deed. 2003. 432p. mass mkt. 5.99 (*0-553-58468-5*); 2002. 320p. 22.95 (*0-553-80267-4*) Bantam Bks.

Scott, Walter, Sr. The Antiquary. 1977. reprint ed. 13.95 o.p. (*0-460-00126-4*, DEL-04014); 2.95 o.p. (*0-460-01126-X*, DEL_04015) Biblio Distribution.

—The Antiquary. (Works of Sir Walter Scott: Vol. 5). reprint ed. Pt. 1. 2001. (Illus.). 360p. pap. text 28.00 (*0-7426-5237-8*); Pt. 1. 1999. 360p. lib. bdg. 90.00 (*1-58201-237-7*); Pt. 2. 2001. (Illus.). 358p. pap. text 28.00 (*0-7426-5238-6*) Classic Bks.

—The Antiquary. Hewitt, David, ed. 1995. 544p. 52.50 o.p. (*0-231-10396-4*) Columbia Univ. Pr.

—The Antiquary. Watson, Nicola J., ed. & intro. by. 2002. (Oxford World's Classics Ser.). (Illus.). 528p. pap. 14.95 (*0-19-283187-9*) Oxford Univ. Pr., Inc.

—The Antiquary. 1999. (Penguin Classics Ser.). 512p. 15.00 (*0-14-043652-9*, Penguin Classics) Viking Penguin.

—The Bride of Lammermoor. 1999. (Works of Sir Walter Scott: Vol. 14). 544p. reprint ed. lib. bdg. 90.00 (*1-58201-246-6*) Classic Bks.

—The Bride of Lammermoor. Alexander, J. H., ed. 1996. 390p. 44.50 (*0-231-10572-X*) Columbia Univ. Pr.

—The Bride of Lammermoor. 1972. 5.95 o.p. (*0-460-01129-4*, Dutton) Dutton/Plume.



For book reviews, descriptive annotations, tables of contents, cover images, author biographies & additional information, updated daily, subscribe to **www.booksinprint.com** 1089

—The Bride of Lammermoor. l.t. ed. 1998. (Large Print Ser.). 480p. lib. bdg. 26.00 (*0-939495-55-4*); 397p. reprint ed. lib. bdg. 25.00 (*1-58287-007-1*) North Bks.

—The Bride of Lammermoor. Robertson, Fiona, ed. & intro. by. 1998. (Oxford World's Classics Ser.). 512p. pap. 11.95 (*0-19-283544-0*) Oxford Univ. Pr., Inc.

—The Bride of Lammermoor. Robertson, Fiona, ed. 1991. (Oxford World's Classics Ser.). 510p. pap. 9.95 o.p. (*0-19-281791-4*) Oxford Univ. Pr., Inc.

—The Bride of Lammermoor. 1993. 288p. pap. 7.95 (*0-460-87233-8*); 1991. 352p. pap. 7.95 o.p. (*0-460-87100-5*) Tuttle Publishing. (Everyman's Classic Library in Paperback).

—The Heart of Midlothian. lib. bdg. 33.95 (*0-8488-2026-6*) Amereon, Ltd.

—The Heart of Midlothian. 1956. 10.50 o.p. (*0-460-00134-5*, Dutton) Dutton/Plume.

—The Heart of Midlothian, 001. Raleigh, John H., ed. rev. ed. 9999. (C). pap. 13.16 o.p. (*0-395-05178-9*) Houghton Mifflin Co.

—The Heart of Midlothian. Lamont, Claire, ed. & intro. by. 1999. (Oxford World's Classics Ser.). (Illus.). 624p. pap. 12.95 (*0-19-283567-X*) Oxford Univ. Pr., Inc.

—The Heart of Midlothian. Lamot, Clare, ed. 1983. (Oxford World's Classics Ser.). (Illus.). 614p. pap. 12.95 o.p. (*0-19-281583-0*) Oxford Univ. Pr., Inc.

—The Heart of Midlothian. Parker, W. M., ed. 1991. 575p. pap. 9.95 (*0-460-87090-4*, Everyman's Classic Library in Paperback) Tuttle Publishing.

—The Heart of Midlothian. Inglis, Tony, ed. & intro. by. 1994. (Classics Ser.). (Illus.). 848p. 12.95 (*0-14-043129-2*, Penguin Classics) Viking Penguin.

—The Monastery. 1969. reprint ed. 9.95 o.p. (*0-460-00136-1*) Biblio Distribution.

—The Monastery. Fielding, Penny, ed. 2001. (Waverley Novels Ser.). 354p. 52.00 (*0-7486-0574-6*) Edinburgh Univ. Pr. GBR. *Dist:* Columbia Univ. Pr.

—Old Mortality. 1958. 5.00 o.p. (*0-460-00137-X*) Biblio Distribution.

—Old Mortality. 1998. (Cloth Bound Pocket Ser.). 7.95 (*3-8290-0900-3*, 520663) Konemann.

—Old Mortality. 1999. (Oxford World's Classics Ser.). 612p. pap. 11.95 o.p. (*0-19-283763-X*) Oxford Univ. Pr., Inc.

—Old Mortality. Stevenson, Jane & Davidson, Peter, eds. 1993. (Oxford World's Classics Ser.). 612p. pap. 11.95 o.p. (*0-19-282630-1*) Oxford Univ. Pr., Inc.

—Old Mortality. Calder, Angus, ed. 1975. (Penguin Classics Ser.). 608p. pap. 9.95 o.s.i (*0-14-043098-9*, Penguin Classics) Viking Penguin.

—Redgauntlet. 1999. (Works of Sir Walter Scott: Vol. 35). reprint ed. Pt. 1. 374p. lib. bdg. 90.00 (*1-58201-267-9*); Pt. 2. 394p. lib. bdg. 90.00 (*1-58201-268-7*) Classic Bks.

—Redgauntlet. Wood, G. A. & Hewitt, David, eds. 1996. 528p. 50.00 (*0-231-10720-X*) Columbia Univ. Pr.

—Redgauntlet. 1957. 14.50 o.p. (*0-460-00141-8*, Dutton) Dutton/Plume.

—Redgauntlet. 1998. (Oxford World's Classics Ser.). 512p. pap. 10.95 (*0-19-283690-0*) Oxford Univ. Pr., Inc.

—Redgauntlet. Sutherland, Kathryn, ed. 2nd ed. 1985. (WC-P Ser.). 510p. pap. 8.95 o.p. (*0-19-281668-3*) Oxford Univ. Pr., Inc.

—The Tale of Old Mortality. Mack, Douglas S., ed. 1993. 522p. 52.50 (*0-231-08470-6*) Columbia Univ. Pr.

—The Tale of Old Mortality. 2000. (Classics Ser.). (Illus.). 496p. 13.95 o.s.i (*0-14-043653-7*, Penguin Classics) Viking Penguin.

—The Two Drovers & Other Stories. Tulloch, Graham, ed. 1987. (Oxford World's Classics Ser.). 384p. pap. 6.95 o.p. (*0-19-281718-3*) Oxford Univ. Pr., Inc.

—Waverley. 1999. (Works of Sir Walter Scott: Vol. 1). reprint ed. Pt. 1. 410p. lib. bdg. 90.00 (*1-58201-233-4*); Pt. 2. 434p. lib. bdg. 90.00 (*1-58201-234-2*) Classic Bks.

—Waverley. Lamont, Claire, ed. & intro. by. (Oxford World's Classics Ser.). 1998. 456p. pap. 10.95 (*0-19-283601-3*); 1986. 496p. pap. 6.95 o.p. (*0-19-281722-1*) Oxford Univ. Pr., Inc.

—Waverley. 1981. 89.00 o.p. (*0-19-812643-3*) Oxford Univ. Pr., Inc.

—Waverley. Hook, Andrew, ed. & intro. by. 1981. (English Library). 608p. 10.95 (*0-14-043071-7*, Penguin Classics) Viking Penguin.

—Waverley. 1976. 8.95 o.p. (*0-460-01075-1*) Viking Penguin.

Scott, Walter, Sr. & Lamont, Claire. Chronicles of the Canongate. 2003. 480p. pap. 14.00 (*0-14-043989-7*, Penguin Classics) Viking Penguin.

Scullion, Ailie. When the Whistle Blows. l.t. ed. 2001. (Dales Large Print Ser.). 240p. pap. 21.99 (*1-84262-069-X*) Dales Large Print Bks. GBR. *Dist:* Ulverscroft Large Print Bks., Ltd., Ulverscroft Large Print Canada, Ltd.

Seymour, Ana. Master of Castle Glen. 2003. 272p. mass mkt. 5.99 (*0-515-13490-2*, Jove) Berkley Publishing Group.

Sharp, William. The Sin-Eater, & Other Tales & Episodes. 1977. (Short Story Index Reprint Ser.). reprint ed. 23.95 (*0-8369-3996-4*) Ayer Co. Pubs., Inc.

Shea, Michael. A Cold Conspiracy. 2001. 190p. 25.00 (*0-7278-5620-0*) Severn Hse. Pubs., Ltd.

Sheepshanks, Mary. Off Balance. 2002. 352p. mass mkt. 6.50 o.s.i (*0-312-98042-6*, St. Martin's Paperbacks); 2001. 336p. 23.95 (*0-312-26813-0*) St. Martin's Pr.

Sizemore, Susan. The Price of Passion. 2001. (Avon Romance Ser.). 384p. mass mkt. 5.99 (*0-380-81651-2*, Avon Bks.) Morrow/Avon.

Skye, Christina. Christmas Knight. 1998. 432p. mass mkt. 6.50 (*0-380-80022-5*, Avon Bks.) Morrow/Avon.

—Season of Wishes. 2000. 348p. 27.95 (*0-7862-2749-4*, Five Star) Gale Group.

—Season of Wishes. 1997. pap. 5.99 (*0-380-78281-2*, Avon Bks.) Morrow/Avon.

Smith, Haywood. Highland Princess. 2000. 321p. mass mkt. 5.99 (*0-312-97496-5*, St. Martin's Paperbacks) St. Martin's Pr.

Smith, Iain Crichton. The Black Halo: The Complete English Stories 1977-98. MacNeil, Kevin, ed. & intro. by. 2002. 708p. pap. 16.00 (*1-84158-171-2*) Birlinn, Ltd. GBR. *Dist:* Interlink Publishing Group, Inc.

—The Red Door: The Complete English Stories 1949-76. MacNeil, Kevin, ed. & intro. by. 2002. xxxiv, 570p. pap. 16.00 (*1-84158-160-7*) Birlinn, Ltd. GBR. *Dist:* Interlink Publishing Group, Inc.

—Thoughts of Murdo. 2001. 208p. pap. 12.95 (*1-84158-058-9*) Birlinn, Ltd. GBR. *Dist:* Interlink Publishing Group, Inc.

Smith, Janet Elaine. Dunnottar. FirstPublish, Inc. Staff, ed. 2000. (Illus.). 191p. pap. 19.95 o.p. (*1-929925-04-2*) FirstPublish.

—Dunnottar. 2002. 232p. per. 17.95 (*1-930252-80-3*) PageFree Publishing, Inc.

Spark, Muriel. The Prime of Miss Jean Brodie. unabr. ed. 1991. audio 19.95 o.p. (*0-945353-61-8*, M30361, Audio Editions Bks. on Cassette) Audio Partners Publishing Corp.

—The Prime of Miss Jean Brodie. 1998. 31.95 (*1-56849-698-2*) Buccaneer Bks., Inc.

—The Prime of Miss Jean Brodie. 1984. 192p. pap. 6.95 o.p. (*0-452-26179-1*); pap. 9.00 o.p. (*0-452-26451-0*) Dutton/Plume. (Plume).

—The Prime of Miss Jean Brodie. l.t. ed. 2002. 219p. 28.95 (*0-7862-4349-X*) Gale Group.

—The Prime of Miss Jean Brodie. 2000. (*0-06-099587-4*) HarperCollins Pubs.

—The Prime of Miss Jean Brodie. (Perennial Classics Ser.). 1999. 160p. pap. 13.00 (*0-06-093173-6*); 1994. 192p. pap. 13.00 o.p. (*0-06-092398-9*) HarperTrade. (Perennial).

—The Prime of Miss Jean Brodie. 1994. 192p. lib. bdg. 29.00 o.p. (*0-8095-9144-8*) Millefleurs.

—The Prime of Miss Jean Brodie. 1984. pap. 6.95 o.p. (*0-452-25589-9*) NAL.

—The Prime of Miss Jean Brodie. l.t. ed. 1985. 164p. 14.95 o.p. (*1-85089-051-X*) Transaction Pubs.

Spencer, John B. Tooth & Nail. 1998. 184p. pap. 15.95 (*1-899344-31-4*) Do-Not Pr., The GBR. *Dist:* Dufour Editions, Inc.

Steele, Hunter. Chasing the Guild Shadow. 1986. 352p. 16.95 o.p. (*0-312-13144-5*) St. Martin's Pr.

Stephen, David. Alba, the Last Wolf. 1985. 256p. o.p. (*0-7126-0454-5*) Random Hse. of Canada, Ltd. CAN. *Dist:* Random Hse., Inc.

Sterling, Jessica. The Asking Price. 1990. 280p. 17.95 o.p. (*0-312-03792-9*) St. Martin's Pr.

Stevenson, Robert Louis. Kidnapped. reprint ed. lib. bdg. 21.95 (*0-88411-998-X*) Amereon, Ltd.

—Kidnapped. 9.95 (*0-233-99268-5*) Andre Deutsch GBR. *Dist:* Trafalgar Square, Trans-Atlantic Pubns., Inc.

—Kidnapped. 1999. (Illus.). 208p. 19.95 (*1-85149-708-0*) Antique Collectors' Club.

—Kidnapped. 1982. (Prindle, Weber & Schmidt Series in Mathematics Ser.). 240p. mass mkt. 3.95 (*0-553-21260-5*, Bantam Classics) Bantam Bks.

—Kidnapped. unabr. ed. 1997. audio 47.95 (*1-86015-437-9*) Beeler, Thomas T. Publisher.

—Kidnapped. 1991. (Illus.). 3.95 (*0-425-12857-1*) Berkley Publishing Group.

—Kidnapped. unabr. ed. 1989. audio 39.95 (*0-7861-0064-8*, 1061) Blackstone Audio Bks., Inc.

—Kidnapped. unabr. ed. 1999. (Bookcassette Classic Collection). audio 57.25 (*1-56740-679-3*, 1820, Unabridged Library Editions); audio 17.95 (*1-56740-453-7*, 1819, Bookcassette) Brilliance Audio.

—Kidnapped. 1990. reprint ed. lib. bdg. 17.95 (*0-89968-553-6*) Buccaneer Bks., Inc.

—Kidnapped. (Works of Robert Louis Stevenson Valima Edition Ser.: Vol. 9). 168p. reprint ed. 2001. (Illus.). pap. text 28.00 (*0-7426-5167-3*); 1999. lib. bdg. 88.00 (*1-58201-167-2*) Classic Bks.

—Kidnapped. 1988. mass mkt. 4.95 (*1-55902-003-2*, Aerie) Doherty, Tom Assocs., LLC.

—Kidnapped. unabr. ed. 1996. (Audio Favorites Ser.). audio 9.99 (*1-55204-006-2*, 9006) Durkin Hayes Publishing Ltd.

—Kidnapped. l.t. ed. 2002. 364p. 28.95 (*0-7862-4280-9*) Gale Group.

—Kidnapped. 2002. 224p. 94.99 (*1-4043-1206-4*); per. 89.99 (*1-4043-1207-2*) IndyPublish.com.

—Kidnapped. 1989. audio 42.00 Jimcin Recordings.

—Kidnapped. Stemach, Jerry, ed. l.t. ed. 2002. text 150.00 (*1-58702-055-6*) Johnston, Don Inc.

—Kidnapped. 1998. (Cloth Bound Pocket Ser.). 240p. 7.95 (*3-89508-257-0*, 520182) Konemann.

—Kidnapped. l.t. ed. 1998. (Large Print Heritage Ser.). 350p. lib. bdg. 33.95 (*1-58118-023-3*, 22015) LRS.

—Kidnapped. E-Book 1.95 (*1-57799-897-9*) Logos Research Systems, Inc.

—Kidnapped, Level 2. 2001. pap. 7.67 (*0-582-42178-0*) Longman Publishing Group.

—Kidnapped. (Classics Ser.). 2000. 240p. mass mkt. 3.95 (*0-451-52768-2*, Signet Bks.); 1959. mass mkt. 1.75 o.p. (*0-451-51602-8*, Signet Classics); 1959. mass mkt. 0.60 o.p. (*0-451-50553-0*, Signet Classics); 1959. mass mkt. 0.75 o.p. (*0-451-50744-4*, Signet Classics); 1959. mass mkt. 0.95 o.p. (*0-451-50881-5*, Signet Classics); 1959. mass mkt. 1.25 o.p. (*0-451-51035-6*, Signet Classics); 1959. mass mkt. 1.50 o.p. (*0-451-51194-8*, Signet Classics); 1959. mass mkt. 0.50 o.p. (*0-451-50006-7*, Signet Classics); 1959. mass mkt. 1.50 o.p. (*0-451-51754-7*, Signet Classics) NAL.

—Kidnapped. unabr. ed. 1997. audio 20.00 (*0-7871-0738-7*, Dove Audio) NewStar Media, Inc.

—Kidnapped. l.t. ed. 1998. (Large Print Ser.). reprint ed. 390p. lib. bdg. 26.00 (*0-939495-64-3*); 230p. lib. bdg. 25.00 (*1-58287-084-5*) North Bks.

—Kidnapped. 1975. 240p. pap. 2.25 o.p. (*0-14-030034-1*, Puffin Bks.) Penguin Putnam Bks. for Young Readers.

—Kidnapped. abr. ed. 1995. (Classics on Cassette). pap. 16.95 o.s.i incl. audio (*0-453-00939-5*) Penguin/HighBridge.

—Kidnapped. Sharma, V. A., ed. 1996. 256p. pap. 25.00 (*81-209-0169-X*) Pitambar Publishing IND. *Dist:* State Mutual Bk. & Periodical Service, Ltd.

—Kidnapped. 1999. (Illus.). 404p. E-Book 3.99 incl. cd-rom (*1-57646-164-5*) Quiet Vision Publishing.

—Kidnapped. 2001. (Modern Library Classics). (Illus.). 432p. pap. 7.95 (*0-375-75725-2*, Modern Library) Random House Adult Trade Publishing Group.

—Kidnapped. 1989. (Illus.). 290p. reprint ed. text 12.98 o.p. (*0-89471-780-4*, Courage Bks.) Running Pr. Bk. Pubs.

—Kidnapped. l.t. ed. 1982. (Charnwood Classics Ser.). 319p. 29.99 o.p. (*0-7089-8058-9*, Ulverscroft) Thorpe, F. A. Pubs. GBR. *Dist:* Ulverscroft Large Print Bks., Ltd., Ulverscroft Large Print Canada, Ltd.

—Kidnapped. 1990. (Canongate Classic Ser.). (Illus.). 224p. pap. 8.95 (*0-86241-232-3*) Trafalgar Square.

—Kidnapped. 2000. (Signature Classics Ser.). 324p. 24.95 (*1-58279-092-2*); lib. bdg. 29.95 (*1-58279-087-6*) Trident Pr. International.

—Kidnapped. 1983. (Madhuban Abridged Classics Ser.). 130p. text 6.95 o.s.i (*0-7069-1820-7*) Vikas Publishing Hse. Private, Ltd. IND. *Dist:* South Asia Bks.

—Kidnapped. 1998. (Children's Classics). 224p. (YA). (ps up). pap. 3.95 (*1-85326-117-3*, 1173WW) Wordsworth Editions, Ltd. GBR. *Dist:* Advanced Global Distribution Services.

—Kidnapped & Catriona. Letley, Emma, ed. & intro. by. 1986. (Oxford World's Classics Ser.). (Illus.). 496p. pap. 6.95 o.p. (*0-19-281726-4*) Oxford Univ. Pr., Inc.

—The Master of Ballantrae. unabr. collector's ed. 1983. audio 48.00 (*0-7366-3968-3*, 9512) Books on Tape, Inc.

—The Master of Ballantrae. 2002. 212p. 94.99 (*1-4043-1786-4*); per. 89.99 (*1-4043-1787-2*) IndyPublish.com.

—The Master of Ballantrae. E-Book 5.00 (*0-7410-1198-0*) SoftBook Pr.

—The Master of Ballantrae. Poole, Adrian, ed. & intro. by. 1997. (Classics Ser.). 288p. 10.95 (*0-14-043446-1*, Penguin Classics) Viking Penguin.

—The Master of Ballantrae: A Winter's Tale. 22.95 (*0-89190-738-6*) Amereon, Ltd.

—The Master of Ballantrae: A Winter's Tale. 1976. reprint ed. 12.95 o.p. (*0-460-00764-5*); 3.50 o.p. (*0-460-01764-0*) Biblio Distribution.

—The Master of Ballantrae: A Winter's Tale. unabr. ed. 1988. audio 49.95 (*1-55686-253-9*, 253) Books in Motion.

—The Master of Ballantrae: A Winter's Tale. 1993. (Canongate Classics Ser.). xviii, 219p. pap. 11.95 o.p. (*0-86241-405-9*) Interlink Publishing Group, Inc.

—The Master of Ballantrae: A Winter's Tale. l.t. ed. (Large Print Ser.). reprint ed. 1992. 393p. lib. bdg. 26.00 (*0-939495-35-X*); 1998. 247p. lib. bdg. 25.00 (*1-58287-047-0*) North Bks.

—The Master of Ballantrae: A Winter's Tale. Letley, Emma, ed. & intro. by. 1983. (Oxford World's Classics Ser.). 288p. pap. 7.95 o.p. (*0-19-281635-7*) Oxford Univ. Pr., Inc.

—The Master of Ballantrae & Weir of Hermiston. 1992. (Everyman's Library). xlix, 373p. 17.00 (*0-679-41744-3*) Knopf, Alfred A. Inc.

—The Master of Ballantrae & Weir of Hermiston. 318p. 1994. pap. 6.95 o.p. (*0-460-87226-5*); 1925. pap. 5.95 o.p. (*0-460-11764-5*) Tuttle Publishing. (Everyman's Classic Library in Paperback).

—Robert Louis Stevenson's Kidnapped: or the Lad with the Silver Button: The Original Text. Menikoff, Barry, ed. & intro. by. 1999. (Illus.). lxvi, 334p. 29.95 (*0-87328-177-2*) Huntington Library Pr.

—The Supernatural Short Stories of Robert Louis Stevenson. Hayes, Michael, ed. & intro. by. 1986. 188p. (Orig.). pap. 11.95 o.p. (*0-7145-3550-8*) Riverrun Pr., Inc.

—Weir of Hermiston. Kerrigan, Catherine, ed. 1996. xxxvi, 178p. 51.00 (*0-7486-0473-1*) Edinburgh Univ. Pr. GBR. *Dist:* Columbia Univ. Pr.

—Weir of Hermiston. Miller, Karl, ed. 1997. (Penguin Classics Ser.). 176p. pap. 9.95 o.p. (*0-14-043560-3*) Viking Penguin.

—Weir of Hermiston: An Unfinished Romance. 1977. (Short Story Index Reprint Ser.). reprint ed. 19.95 (*0-8369-3861-5*) Ayer Co. Pubs., Inc.

—Weir of Hermiston: And Other Stories. Binding, Paul, ed. & intro. by. 1980. (English Library). 320p. pap. 10.95 o.s.i (*0-14-043138-1*, Penguin Classics) Viking Penguin.

—The Works of Robert Louis Stevenson: Treasure Island, Kidnapped, The Strange Case of Dr. Jekyll & Mr. Hyde. 1995. (Classic Bonded Leather Ser.). 800p. (YA). 24.95 o.p. (*0-681-10373-6*) Borders Pr.

Stevenson, Robert Louis & Meis, Timothy. Kidnapped. 2004. (Scribner Storybook Classic Ser.). (J). (*0-689-86542-2*, Atheneum) Simon & Schuster Children's Publishing.

Stewart, A. C. Ossian House. 1976. (J). (gr. 6 up). lib. bdg. 26.95 (*0-87599-219-6*) Phillips, S.G. Inc.

Stirling, Jessica. Call Home the Heart. 1977. 416p. 8.95 o.p. (*0-312-11427-3*) St. Martin's Pr.

—Creature Comforts. 1986. 372p. 16.95 o.p. (*0-312-17163-3*) St. Martin's Pr.

—The Good Provider. 1988. 352p. 18.95 o.p. (*0-312-02580-7*) St. Martin's Pr.

—Hearts of Gold. 1988. 416p. 18.95 o.p. (*0-312-01036-2*) St. Martin's Pr.

—Lantern for the Dark. l.t. ed. 1993. pap. 22.95 o.p. (*0-7927-1596-9*); 24.95 o.p. (*0-7927-1597-7*) BBC Audiobooks America.

—Lantern for the Dark. 1992. 368p. 19.95 o.p. (*0-312-07857-9*) St. Martin's Pr.

—The Marrying Kind. unabr. ed. 1996. audio 96.95 (*0-7451-6683-0*, CAB 1299) BBC Audiobooks America.

—The Marrying Kind. 1996. 384p. 23.95 o.p. (*0-312-14366-4*) St. Martin's Pr.

—The Pipers Tune. 2002. vi, 486p. 26.95 (*0-312-28870-0*) St. Martin's Pr.

—Prized Possessions. 2001. 416p. 25.95 (*0-312-28057-2*) St. Martin's Pr.

—Shadows on the Shore. unabr. ed. 1994. audio 84.95 (*0-7451-4314-8*, CAB 997) BBC Audiobooks America.

—Shadows on the Shore. 1994. 320p. 21.95 o.p. (*0-312-10546-0*) St. Martin's Pr.

—Sisters Three. Date not set. pap. (*0-312-31432-9*); mass mkt. (*0-312-98959-8*) St. Martin's Pr. (St. Martin's Paperbacks).

—The Sisters Three. 2002. 448p. 26.95 (*0-312-30523-0*) St. Martin's Pr.

—Strawberry Season. 2000. 480p. 25.95 o.p. (*0-312-26654-5*) St. Martin's Pr.

—Treasures of the Earth. 1985. 384p. 15.95 o.p. (*0-312-81651-0*) St. Martin's Pr.

—Treasures on Earth. l.t. ed. 1993. pap. 18.95 o.p. (*0-7927-1468-7*); 23.95 o.p. (*0-7927-1469-5*) BBC Audiobooks America.

—The Welcome Light. l.t. ed. 1992. 20.95 o.p. (*0-7927-1108-4*, E0030) BBC Audiobooks America.

—The Welcome Light. 1991. 304p. 18.95 o.p. (*0-312-06490-X*) St. Martin's Pr.

—The Workhouse Girl. unabr. ed. 1997. audio 110.95 (*0-7451-8786-2*, CAB 1421) BBC Audiobooks America.

—The Workhouse Girl. 1997. 472p. text 25.95 o.p. (*0-312-15698-7*) St. Martin's Pr.

—The Workhouse Girl. l.t. ed. 1998. (Romance Ser.). 616p. 28.95 (*0-7838-0124-6*) Thorndike Pr.

Stranger, Joyce. The Call of the Sea. 2003. 192p. 25.99 (*0-7278-5938-2*) Severn Hse. Pubs., Ltd.

Strong, Tony. The Death Pit. 2000. 448p. mass mkt. 6.50 (*0-440-22623-6*) Dell Publishing.

—The Death Pit. 2000. 448p. mass mkt. o.s.i (*0-7704-2861-4*) Seal Bks. CAN. *Dist:* Random Hse. of Canada, Ltd.

Tannahill, Reay. Fatal Majesty: A Novel of Mary, Queen of Scots. unabr. ed. 1998. audio 124.95 (*0-7540-0242-X*, CAB1665) BBC Audiobooks America.
—Fatal Majesty: A Novel of Mary, Queen of Scots. 480p. 2000. pap. 14.95 (*0-312-25386-9*, Saint Martin's Griffin); 1998. 25.95 o.p. (*0-312-19881-7*) St. Martin's Pr.
—In Still & Stormy Waters. 1994. 528p. 25.95 o.p. (*0-312-11411-7*) St. Martin's Pr.
Thomas, Graham. Malice in the Highlands. 1998. (Erskine Powell Mysteries Ser.: Vol. 1). 240p. mass mkt. 6.50 (*0-8041-1657-1*, Ivy Bks.) Ballantine Bks.
Thomas, Sue. Water. 240p. 1995. pap. 11.95 (*0-87951-600-3*); 1994. 21.95 (*0-87951-532-5*) Overlook Pr., The.
Thompson, Alice. Pharos: A Ghost Story. 2003. 160p. 21.95 (*0-312-31810-3*) St. Martin's Pr.
Thomson, Daisy Hicks. The Island of Love. l.t. ed. 2002. 23.95 (*0-7862-4253-1*) Thorndike Pr.
Thomson, George M. The Ball at Glenkerran. 1983. 229p. o.p. (*0-436-52044-3*) David & Charles Pubs.
Torrington, Jeff. Swing Hammer Swing! 416p. 1995. pap. 13.00 o.s.i (*0-15-600197-7*, Harvest Bks.); 1994. 23.95 o.s.i (*0-15-187427-1*) Harcourt Trade Pubs.
Tranter, Nigel. Bridal Path. 2002. 225p. pap. 11.95 (*1-873631-02-2*) B & W Publishing GBR. *Dist:* Interlink Publishing Group, Inc.
—Children of the Mist. 346p. mass mkt. 11.95 (*0-340-57099-7*); 1993. 224p. 27.50 (*0-340-55898-9*) Hodder & Stoughton, Ltd. GBR. *Dist:* Lubrecht & Cramer, Ltd., Trafalgar Square.
—Fast & Loose. 2001. 256p. pap. 11.95 (*1-873631-29-4*) B & W Publishing GBR. *Dist:* Interlink Publishing Group, Inc.
—James, by the Grace of God. 1986. 352p. 17.95 o.p. (*0-8253-0316-8*) Beaufort Bks., Inc.
—The Lion's Whelp. 320p. 1998. mass mkt. 11.95 (*0-340-65999-8*); 1997. 27.00 (*0-340-65998-X*) Hodder & Stoughton, Ltd. GBR. *Dist:* Lubrecht & Cramer, Ltd., Trafalgar Square.
—Lord in Waiting. 1995. 464p. mass mkt. 11.95 o.p. (*0-340-62587-2*); 384p. 25.95 o.p. (*0-340-58786-5*); 384p. 27.50 (*0-340-58785-7*) Hodder & Stoughton, Ltd. GBR. *Dist:* Lubrecht & Cramer, Ltd., Trafalgar Square.
—The MacGregor Trilogy. 1996. 612p. pap. 19.95 (*0-340-40572-4*) Hodder & Stoughton, Ltd. GBR. *Dist:* Lubrecht & Cramer, Ltd., Trafalgar Square.
—The Riven Realm. 1985. 352p. 16.95 o.p. (*0-8253-0260-9*) Beaufort Bks., Inc.
—The Stewart Trilogy. 1998. 612p. pap. 22.95 (*0-340-39115-4*) Hodder & Stoughton, Ltd. GBR. *Dist:* Lubrecht & Cramer, Ltd., Trafalgar Square.
—Tapestry of the Boar. 1993. 320p. 27.00 o.p. (*0-340-60106-X*); mass mkt. 11.95 (*0-340-60105-1*) Hodder & Stoughton, Ltd. GBR. *Dist:* Lubrecht & Cramer, Ltd., Trafalgar Square.
—Tapestry of the Boar. l.t. ed. 1995. (Ulverscroft Large Print Ser.). 688p. 29.99 o.p. (*0-7089-3340-8*, Ulverscroft) Thorpe, F. A. Pubs. GBR. *Dist:* Ulverscroft Large Print Bks., Ltd., Ulverscroft Large Print Canada, Ltd.
—Unicorn Rampant. 1984. 14.95 o.p. (*0-340-33720-6*) Beaufort Bks., Inc.
Trocchi, Alexander. Young Adam. 2001. 168p. pap. 11.00 (*0-86241-905-0*) Canongate Bks. GBR. *Dist:* Grove/Atlantic, Inc.
—Young Adam. 2003. 146p. 12.00 (*0-8021-3977-9*, Grove Pr.) Grove/Atlantic, Inc.
—Young Adam. rev. ed. 1991. 208p. mass mkt. 4.95 o.s.i (*1-878320-63-7*) Masquerade Bks., Inc.
—Young Adam. 1996. 152p. reprint ed. pap. 14.95 (*0-86241-624-8*) Rebel, Inc. GBR. *Dist:* AK Pr. Distribution.
—Young Adam. 1982. 256p. pap. 7.95 o.s.i (*0-7145-3925-2*) Riverrun Pr., Inc.
Turnbull, Peter. And Did Murder Him. 1991. 15.95 o.p. (*0-312-05813-6*, Saint Martin's Minotaur) St. Martin's Pr.
—And Did Murder Him. l.t. ed. 1993. (Mystery Ser.). 320p. 29.99 o.p. (*0-7089-2922-2*, Ulverscroft) Thorpe, F. A. Pubs. GBR. *Dist:* Ulverscroft Large Print Bks., Ltd., Ulverscroft Large Print Canada, Ltd.
—Big Money. 1984. 173p. 10.95 o.p. (*0-312-07846-3*) St. Martin's Pr.
—Big Money. l.t. ed. 1985. (Ulverscroft Large Print Ser.). 304p. 29.99 o.p. (*0-7089-1397-0*, Ulverscroft) Thorpe, F. A. Pubs. GBR. *Dist:* Ulverscroft Large Print Bks., Ltd., Ulverscroft Large Print Canada, Ltd.
—Condition Purple. 1989. 14.95 o.p. (*0-312-02892-X*, Saint Martin's Minotaur) St. Martin's Pr.
—Condition Purple. l.t. ed. 1991. (Ulverscroft Large Print Ser.). 29.99 o.p. (*0-7089-2380-1*, Ulverscroft) Thorpe, F. A. Pubs. GBR. *Dist:* Ulverscroft Large Print Bks., Ltd., Ulverscroft Large Print Canada, Ltd.
—Dead Knock. 1982. 208p. 10.95 o.p. (*0-312-18499-9*) St. Martin's Pr.
—Dead Knock. l.t. ed. 1984. (Ulverscroft Large Print Ser.). 336p. 29.99 o.p. (*0-7089-1148-X*, Ulverscroft) Thorpe, F. A. Pubs. GBR. *Dist:* Ulverscroft Large Print Bks., Ltd., Ulverscroft Large Print Canada, Ltd.
—Deep & Crisp & Even. 1982. 216p. 10.95 o.p. (*0-312-19092-1*) St. Martin's Pr.
—Deep & Crisp & Even. l.t. ed. 1982. (Ulverscroft Large Print Ser.). 339p. 29.99 o.p. (*0-7089-0830-6*, Ulverscroft) Thorpe, F. A. Pubs. GBR. *Dist:* Ulverscroft Large Print Bks., Ltd., Ulverscroft Large Print Canada, Ltd.
—Fair Friday. 1983. 189p. 10.95 o.p. (*0-312-27958-2*) St. Martin's Pr.
—Fair Friday. l.t. ed. 1984. (Ulverscroft Large Print Ser.). 320p. 29.99 o.p. (*0-7089-1219-2*, Ulverscroft) Thorpe, F. A. Pubs. GBR. *Dist:* Ulverscroft Large Print Bks., Ltd., Ulverscroft Large Print Canada, Ltd.
—The Killing Floor. l.t. ed. 1995. 303p. pap. 20.95 o.p. (*0-7838-1459-3*, Macmillan Reference USA) Gale Group.
—The Killing Floor. 1996. 252p. per. (*0-373-26215-9*, Worldwide Library) Harlequin Enterprises, Ltd.
—The Killing Floor. 1995. 203p. 18.95 o.p. (*0-312-11844-9*, Saint Martin's Minotaur) St. Martin's Pr.
—Long Day Monday. 1994. per. (*0-373-26160-8*, 1-26160-1, Harlequin Bks.) Harlequin Enterprises, Ltd.
—Long Day Monday. 1993. 181p. 16.95 o.p. (*0-312-08837-X*, Saint Martin's Minotaur) St. Martin's Pr.
—Long Day Monday. l.t. ed. 1994. (Ulverscroft Large Print Ser.). 320p. 29.99 o.p. (*0-7089-3175-8*, Ulverscroft) Thorpe, F. A. Pubs. GBR. *Dist:* Ulverscroft Large Print Bks., Ltd., Ulverscroft Large Print Canada, Ltd.
—Two Way Cut. 1988. 192p. 14.95 o.p. (*0-312-02306-5*, Saint Martin's Minotaur) St. Martin's Pr.
—Two Way Cut. l.t. ed. 1990. (Ulverscroft Large Print Ser.). 29.99 o.p. (*0-7089-2262-7*, Ulverscroft) Thorpe, F. A. Pubs. GBR. *Dist:* Ulverscroft Large Print Bks., Ltd., Ulverscroft Large Print Canada, Ltd.
Umberger, Carol. Circle of Honor: A Novel. 2002. (Scottish Crown Ser.: Bk. 1). 288p. pap. 12.99 (*1-59145-005-5*) Integrity Pubs.
—The Mark of Salvation. 2003. 304p. 12.99 (*1-59145-007-1*) Integrity Pubs.
—The Price of Freedom. 2002. v, 280p. 12.99 (*1-59145-006-3*) Integrity Pubs.
Urquhart, Fred. Full Score. 1989. 236p. pap. 40.00 (*0-08-037719-X*) Mercat Pr. Bks. GBR. *Dist:* State Mutual Bk. & Periodical Service, Ltd.
Wadley, Margot. The Gripping Beast. 2002. 208p. mass mkt. 6.50 (*0-312-97960-6*, St. Martin's Paperbacks) St. Martin's Pr.
—Gripping Beast. E-Book 21.95 (*0-312-70139-X*) St. Martin's Pr.
—The Gripping Beast: An Orkney Mystery. 2001. 200p. 21.95 (*0-312-27254-5*, Saint Martin's Minotaur) St. Martin's Pr.
Wallace, Brian. Labyrinth of Chaos. 2000. 288p. pap. 16.95 (*1-56184-148-X*) New Falcon Pubns.
Warner, Alan. Morvern Callar. 1997. 256p. (Orig.). pap. 12.95 (*0-385-48741-X*) Doubleday Publishing.
—The Sopranos. 1999. 256p. 24.00 o.p. (*0-374-26670-0*) Farrar, Straus & Giroux.
—The Sopranos. 2000. (Harvest Book Ser.). 336p. pap. 14.00 (*0-15-601201-4*, Harvest Bks.) Harcourt Trade Pubs.
—These Demented Lands. 1998. 224p. pap. 12.95 (*0-385-49146-8*) Doubleday Publishing.
Welfonder, Sue-Ellen. Bride of the Beast. 2003. 352p. reprint ed. mass mkt. 5.99 (*0-446-61232-4*, Warner Romance) Warner Bks., Inc.
—Knight in My Bed. 2002. 400p. reprint ed. mass mkt. 5.99 (*0-446-61034-8*, Warner Romance) Warner Bks., Inc.
Welsh, Irvine. The Acid House: Stories. Drechsler, Clara & Hellmann, Harald, trs. (GER.). 533p. pap. (*3-462-02814-6*) Kiepenheuer & Witsch GmbH & Company KG DEU. *Dist:* International Bk. Import Service, Inc.
—The Acid House: Stories. 2000. (Illus.). 81p. pap. 10.95 o.s.i (*0-413-72420-4*) Methuen Publishing Ltd. GBR. *Dist:* Consortium Bk. Sales & Distribution.
—The Acid House: Stories. 1995. 304p. pap. 13.00 (*0-393-31280-1*, Norton Paperbacks) Norton, W. W. & Co., Inc.
—Filth. 1998. 393p. pap. 14.00 (*0-393-31868-0*) Norton, W. W. & Co., Inc.
—The Marabou Stork Nightmares. 1997. 284p. pap. 14.00 (*0-393-31563-0*); 1996. 264p. 21.00 (*0-393-03845-9*) Norton, W. W. & Co., Inc.
—Trainspotting. Date not set. pap. 5.99 (*0-7493-2173-3*) Heinemann.
—Trainspotting. 23.95 (*0-393-05724-0*); 1996. 340p. pap. 13.95 (*0-393-31480-4*, Norton Paperbacks) Norton, W. W. & Co., Inc.
Welsh, Louise. The Cutting Room. 304p. 2004. pap. (*1-84195-474-8*); 2003. (*1-84195-383-0*) Canongate Bks.
—The Cutting Room. 2002. 304p. 24.00 (*1-84195-280-X*) Canongate Bks. GBR. *Dist:* Grove/Atlantic, Inc.
Whyte, Christopher. The Warlock of Strathearn. 256p. 1997. pap. 17.95 (*0-575-06506-0*); 1999. reprint ed. mass mkt. 10.95 (*0-575-40122-2*) Gollancz, Victor GBR. *Dist:* Trafalgar Square.
Wilhelm, Terri L. Highland Jewel. 1999. (Topaz Historical Romance Ser.). 320p. mass mkt. 5.99 o.s.i (*0-451-40834-9*, Topaz) NAL.
Williams, Jeanne. The Island Harp. 1991. 352p. 19.95 o.p. (*0-312-06570-1*) St. Martin's Pr.
Work, James C. The Tobermory Manuscript. 2000. (Five Star Western Ser.). 299p. 21.95 (*0-7862-2103-8*, Five Star) Gale Group.
Wright, Sally S. Pride & Predator. 1999. (Ben Reese Mysteries Ser.). 336p. mass mkt. 6.50 (*0-345-42589-8*) Ballantine Bks.
—Pride & Predator, 3 vols. 2003. (Ben Reese Mysteries Ser.: Vol. 2). 350p. pap. 9.99 (*1-57673-084-0*, Multnomah Bks.) Multnomah Pubs., Inc.
—Pride & Predator. l.t. ed. 1999. (Christian Mystery Ser.). 507p. 24.95 (*0-7862-1801-0*) Thorndike Pr.
Young, Arthur. The Surgeon's Knot. 1982. 288p. 14.95 o.p. (*0-312-77693-4*) St. Martin's Pr.
—The Surgeon's Knot. l.t. ed. 1983. (Ulverscroft Large Print Ser.). 448p. 29.99 o.p. (*0-7089-1037-8*, Ulverscroft) Thorpe, F. A. Pubs. GBR. *Dist:* Ulverscroft Large Print Bks., Ltd., Ulverscroft Large Print Canada, Ltd.

**SCOTTSDALE (ARIZ.)—FICTION**

Horowitz, Renee B. Deadly Rx. 2001. 172p. per. 13.75 (*0-7433-0363-6*) Clocktower Bks.
—Deadly Rx. 1997. mass mkt. 5.50 (*0-380-78620-6*, Avon Bks.) Morrow/Avon.
—Rx for Murder. 2001. 160p. per. 13.50 (*0-7433-0116-1*) Clocktower Bks.
—Rx for Murder. 1997. mass mkt. 5.50 (*0-380-78619-2*, Avon Bks.) Morrow/Avon.

**SEATTLE (WASH.)—FICTION**

Alexander, Gary. Kiet Goes West. 1992. 272p. 18.95 o.p. (*0-312-07851-X*, Saint Martin's Minotaur) St. Martin's Pr.
Alexie, Sherman. Indian Killer. 1996. 432p. 22.00 o.p. (*0-87113-652-X*, Atlantic Monthly Pr.) Grove/Atlantic, Inc.
—Indian Killer. 1998. 432p. reprint ed. pap. 14.95 (*0-446-67370-6*) Warner Bks., Inc.
Allen, Irene. Quaker Indictment: An Elizabeth Elliot Mystery. 256p. 1999. (Quaker Sojourn Ser.: 4). (Illus.). mass mkt. 5.99 (*0-312-96684-9*, St. Martin's Paperbacks); 1997. (Elizabeth Elliot Mystery Ser.). 21.95 o.p. (*0-312-16970-1*, Saint Martin's Minotaur) St. Martin's Pr.
Anders, Donna. Dead Silence. 2000. 384p. mass mkt. 6.99 (*0-671-03881-8*, Pocket) Simon & Schuster.
Bacho, Peter. Dark Blue Suit: And Other Stories. E-Book 14.95 (*0-295-97974-7*); 1997. 192p. 30.00 (*0-295-97664-0*); 1997. 152p. pap. 16.95 (*0-295-97637-3*) Univ. of Washington Pr.
Ballantyne, Sheila. Imaginary Crimes. (Contemporary American Fiction Ser.). 1983. 272p. pap. 9.95 o.p. (*0-14-006540-7*, Penguin Bks.); 1982. 288p. 13.95 o.p. (*0-670-48022-3*) Viking Penguin.
Beck, K. K. Amateur Night: A Jane Da Silva Mystery. 1993. 288p. 18.95 (*0-89296-480-4*) Mysterious Pr.
—Amateur Night: A Jane Da Silva Mystery. 1994. 256p. mass mkt. 5.50 o.s.i (*0-446-40145-5*) Warner Bks., Inc.
—The Body in the Cornflakes. 1994. (Northwest Mysteries Ser.). mass mkt. 4.99 o.s.i (*0-8041-1175-8*, Ivy Bks.) Ballantine Bks.
—The Body in the Cornflakes. pap. 15.95 (*0-312-29184-1*, Saint Martin's Griffin); 1992. 224p. 17.95 (*0-312-08146-4*, Saint Martin's Minotaur) St. Martin's Pr.
—The Body in the Volvo. 1989. 208p. pap. 3.50 o.s.i (*0-8041-0371-2*, Ivy Bks.) Ballantine Bks.
—The Body in the Volvo. 1987. 16.95 o.p. (*0-8027-5685-9*) Walker & Co.
—Cold Smoked: A Jane Da Silva Mystery. 1995. 320p. 18.95 o.s.i (*0-89296-537-1*) Mysterious Pr.
—Cold Smoked: A Jane Da Silva Mystery. 1996. (Jane da Silva Mystery Ser.). 240p. mass mkt. 5.99 (*0-446-40351-2*) Warner Bks., Inc.
—Electric City: A Jane Da Silva Mystery. 1994. 304p. 18.95 o.s.i (*0-89296-536-3*) Mysterious Pr.
—Electric City: A Jane Da Silva Mystery. 1995. 224p. mass mkt. 5.50 (*0-446-40350-4*) Warner Bks., Inc.
—A Hopeless Case. 1992. 18.95 o.p. (*0-89296-479-0*) Mysterious Pr.
—A Hopeless Case. 1993. 272p. mass mkt. 4.99 o.s.i (*0-446-40144-7*) Warner Bks., Inc.
—We Interrupt This Broadcast. 1997. 240p. 20.00 o.p. (*0-89296-642-4*) Mysterious Pr.
Beck, Kathrine, ed. Bad Neighbors. l.t. ed. 1997. (G. K. Hall Mystery Ser.). 363p. lib. bdg. 24.95 o.p. (*0-7838-2008-9*, Macmillan Reference USA) Gale Group.
Billings, Andrew. Carnage. 1999. 368p. mass mkt. 6.50 o.s.i (*0-515-12564-4*, Jove) Berkley Publishing Group.
Brooks, Terry. A Knight of the Word. E-Book 6.99 (*1-58945-521-5*) Adobe Systems, Inc.
—A Knight of the Word. 1999. mass mkt. (*0-345-42942-7*, Ballantine Bks.); 1999. (Trolltown Ser.: Vol. 2). 408p. mass mkt. 6.99 (*0-345-42464-6*); 1998. 25.95 o.s.i (*0-345-43005-0*) Ballantine Bks.
—A Knight of the Word. 2001. E-Book 6.99 (*0-345-44459-0*) Random Hse., Inc.
—A Knight of the Word. unabr. ed. 2000. audio 75.00 (*0-7887-2516-5*, 95589E7) Recorded Bks., LLC.
Burgess, W. A. Cowards. 1997. 197p. 20.95 (*0-312-15503-4*) St. Martin's Pr.
Byers, Michael. Long for This World: A Novel. 2003. 448p. tchr. ed. 24.00 (*0-395-89171-X*) Houghton Mifflin Co.
—Long for This World: A Novel. 2004. 448p. pap. 13.00 (*0-618-44648-6*, Mariner Bks.) Houghton Mifflin Co. Trade & Reference Div.
Cameron, Stella. Tell Me Why. l.t. ed. 2001. (Wheeler Large Print Book Ser.). 453p. 29.95 o.p. (*1-58724-117-X*, Wheeler Publishing, Inc.) Gale Group.
—Tell Me Why. 2002. 352p. mass mkt. 6.99 (*0-8217-6930-8*); 2001. 384p. 24.00 (*1-57566-820-3*) Kensington Publishing Corp.
Clausen, Lowen. First Avenue. 2000. 384p. mass mkt. 6.99 (*0-451-40948-5*, Onyx) NAL.
—First Avenue: A Novel. 1999. 352p. 21.95 (*0-9669919-0-7*) Watershed Bks.
Coburn, Randy Sue. Remembering Jody. 1999. 322p. 22.95 (*0-7867-0566-3*, Carroll & Graf Pubs.) Avalon Publishing Group.
Colbert, Curt. Rat City: A Jake Rossiter & Miss Jenkins Mystery. 2001. (Jake Rossiter & Miss Jenkins Mystery Ser.). 368p. pap. 15.00 (*0-9663473-5-8*) UglyTown.
—Sayonaraville. 2003. 14.95 (*0-9724412-1-2*) UglyTown.
Collins, Max Allan. Dark Angel: Skin Game. movie tie-in ed. 2003. 272p. mass mkt. 6.99 (*0-345-45183-X*, Ballantine Bks.) Ballantine Bks.
Copeland, Lori. June. E-Book 9.99 (*0-8423-5678-9*); 1999. (Brides of the West Ser.: Bk. 2). 272p. pap. 9.99 (*0-8423-0268-9*, HeartQuest) Tyndale Hse. Pubs.
—June: Brides of the West 1872. l.t. ed. 2002. (Christian Romance Ser.). 295p. 25.95 (*0-7862-3824-0*) Gale Group.
Daheim, Mary R. Auntie Mayhem. 1996. (Bed-and-Breakfast Mysteries Ser.). 272p. mass mkt. 6.99 (*0-380-77878-5*, Avon Bks.) Morrow/Avon.
—Bantam of the Opera. 1993. 256p. (Orig.). mass mkt. 6.99 (*0-380-76934-4*, Avon Bks.) Morrow/Avon.
—Creeps Suzette. 2000. (Bed & Breakfast Mystery Ser.). 336p. mass mkt. 6.99 (*0-380-80079-9*, Avon Bks.) Morrow/Avon.
—Dune to Death. 1993. (Bed-and-Breakfast Mysteries Ser.). 240p. (Orig.). mass mkt. 6.99 (*0-380-76933-6*, Avon Bks.) Morrow/Avon.
—A Fit of Tempera. 1994. (Bed-and-Breakfast Mysteries Ser.). 256p. reprint ed. mass mkt. 6.99 (*0-380-77490-9*, Avon Bks.) Morrow/Avon.
—Fowl Prey. 1991. (Bed-and-Breakfast Mysteries Ser.). 272p. (Orig.). mass mkt. 6.99 (*0-380-76296-X*, Avon Bks.) Morrow/Avon.
—Holy Terrors. 1999. (Bed-and-Breakfast Mysteries Ser.). 256p. (Orig.). mass mkt. 6.99 (*0-380-76297-8*, Avon Bks.) Morrow/Avon.
—Just Desserts. l.t. ed. 2001. (Beeler Large Print Mystery Ser.). 240p. 25.95 (*1-57490-351-9*, Beeler Large Print Bks.) Beeler, Thomas T. Publisher.
—Just Desserts. 1999. (Bed & Breakfast Mystery Ser.). 256p. mass mkt. 6.99 (*0-380-76295-1*, Avon Bks.) Morrow/Avon.
—Legs Benedict: A Bed-and-Breakfast Mystery. 1999. (Bed-and-Breakfast Mysteries Ser.). 320p. mass mkt. 6.50 (*0-380-80078-0*, Avon Bks.) Morrow/Avon.
—Major Vices. 1995. (Bed-and-Breakfast Mysteries Ser.). 256p. (Orig.). mass mkt. 6.50 (*0-380-77491-7*, Avon Bks.) Morrow/Avon.
—Murder, My Suite. l.t. ed. 2002. 26.95 (*1-57490-414-0*) Beeler, Thomas T. Publisher.
—Murder, My Suite. 1995. (Bed-and-Breakfast Mysteries Ser.). 272p. mass mkt. 6.50 (*0-380-77877-7*, Avon Bks.) Morrow/Avon.
—Nutty as a Fruitcake. 1996. (Bed-and-Breakfast Mysteries Ser.). 272p. mass mkt. 6.99 (*0-380-77879-3*, Avon Bks.) Morrow/Avon.
—September Mourn. 1997. (Bed-and-Breakfast Mysteries Ser.). (Illus.). 320p. mass mkt. 6.50 (*0-380-78518-8*, Avon Bks.) Morrow/Avon.
—Snow Place to Die: Where There's Ice... There's Vice. 1998. (Bed & Breakfast Mystery Ser.: No. 13). 304p. mass mkt. 6.99 (*0-380-78521-8*, Avon Bks.) Morrow/Avon.
—A Streetcar Named Expire. 2001. (Bed-and-Breakfast Mysteries Ser.). 320p. mass mkt. 6.99 (*0-380-80080-2*, Avon Bks.) Morrow/Avon.
Davis, Michael E. The Homeboy. 2001. 281p. pap. 21.99 (*0-7388-5827-7*); E-Book 8.00 (*0-7388-5828-5*) Xlibris Corp.

Deverell, William. Slander. 2003. 400p. pap. 15.95 (*1-55022-593-6*) ECW Pr. CAN. *Dist:* Independent Pubs. Group.

Dibdin, Michael. Dark Specter: A Novel. 1996. 352p. 4.99 o.s.i (*0-679-44221-9*, Pantheon) Knopf Publishing Group.

—Dark Specter: A Novel. 1996. o.s.i (*0-676-51374-3*) Random Hse., Inc.

Doig, Ivan. Mountain Time, abr. ed. 1999. 25.00 incl. audio (*0-7871-2016-2*, Dove Audio) NewStar Media, Inc.

—Mountain Time. 320p. 2000. pap. 13.00 (*0-684-86569-6*); 1999. 25.00 o.s.i (*0-684-83295-X*) Simon & Schuster. (Scribner).

—Mountain Time. l.t. ed. 1999. (Americana Ser.). 487p. 29.95 (*0-7862-2216-6*) Thorndike Pr.

Donnelly, Deborah. May the Best Man Die. 2003. 336p. mass mkt. 5.99 (*0-440-24129-4*) Dell Publishing.

Dovell, Michael. The Dahlia Connection: A Deacon Davenport Mystery. Dunn, Brian, ed. 1995. (Illus.). 212p. 24.95 (*1-877882-19-4*); pap. 11.95 (*1-877882-18-6*) SCW Pubns.

Elkins, Aaron. A Deceptive Clarity. 1993. mass mkt. 5.99 o.s.i (*0-449-14900-5*, Fawcett) Ballantine Bks.

—A Deceptive Clarity. 1989. 2.99 o.p. (*0-517-00558-1*) Random Hse. Value Publishing.

—A Deceptive Clarity. 1987. 15.95 o.p. (*0-8027-5666-2*) Walker & Co.

—A Glancing Light. 1994. mass mkt. o.s.i (*0-449-45458-4*); 1992. mass mkt. 4.99 o.s.i (*0-449-14829-7*) Ballantine Bks. (Fawcett).

—A Glancing Light. 1991. 368p. 18.95 o.s.i (*0-684-19278-0*, Macmillan Reference USA) Gale Group.

—Old Scores. unabr. ed. 1995. (Chris Norgren Mystery Ser.: Vol. 3). audio 51.00 (*0-7887-0166-5*, 94391E7) Recorded Bks., LLC.

—Old Scores: A Chris Norgren Mystery. l.t. ed. 1994. 22.95 o.p. (*0-7927-1944-1*); pap. 20.95 o.p. (*0-7927-1943-3*) BBC Audiobooks America.

—Old Scores: A Chris Norgren Mystery. 1994. (Northwest Mysteries Ser.). mass mkt. 5.99 o.s.i (*0-449-14899-8*, Fawcett) Ballantine Bks.

—Old Scores: A Chris Norgren Mystery. 1993. 256p. 20.00 o.p. (*0-684-19551-8*, Macmillan Reference USA) Gale Group.

Emerson, Earl. Catfish Cafe. 1999. 304p. mass mkt. 6.99 (*0-345-42212-0*); 1998. 272p. 22.00 o.p. (*0-345-42202-3*) Ballantine Bks.

—Deception Pass. 1998. (Thomas Black Mysteries Ser.). 304p. mass mkt. 6.99 (*0-345-40069-0*) Ballantine Bks.

—Deviant Behavior. 1990. (Thomas Black Mysteries Ser.). 224p. mass mkt. 6.50 (*0-345-36028-1*) Ballantine Bks.

—Deviant Behavior. 1988. 256p. 17.95 o.p. (*0-688-08335-8*, Morrow, William & Co.) Morrow/Avon.

—Fat Tuesday. 1988. (Thomas Black Mysteries Ser.). 288p. mass mkt. 6.99 (*0-345-35223-8*) Ballantine Bks.

—Fat Tuesday. 1987. 288p. 16.95 o.p. (*0-688-06770-0*, Morrow, William & Co.) Morrow/Avon.

—Into the Inferno. 2004. 384p. mass mkt. 6.99 (*0-345-44592-9*, Fawcett) Ballantine Bks.

—Into the Inferno. l.t. ed. 2003. 29.95 (*0-7862-5450-5*) Thorndike Pr.

—Into the Inferno: A Novel of Suspense. 2003. 352p. 23.95 (*0-345-44591-0*, Ballantine Bks.) Ballantine Bks.

—The Million-Dollar Tattoo. 1997. (Thomas Black Mysteries Ser.). 304p. mass mkt. 5.99 (*0-345-40067-4*) Ballantine Bks.

—The Million-Dollar Tattoo. unabr. ed. 1997. (Thomas Black Mystery Ser.: Vol. 9). audio 51.00 (*0-7887-0813-9*, 94963E7) Recorded Bks., LLC.

—Nervous Laughter. 1998. mass mkt. 3.99 o.s.i (*0-345-42945-1*); 1997. 288p. mass mkt. 6.50 (*0-345-41407-1*) Ballantine Bks.

—Nervous Laughter. 1986. mass mkt. 4.99 (*0-380-89906-X*, Avon Bks.) Morrow/Avon.

—The Portland Laugher. 1995. (Thomas Black Mysteries Ser.). 352p. mass mkt. 6.50 (*0-345-39782-7*) Ballantine Bks.

—Poverty Bay. 1998. mass mkt. 3.99 o.s.i (*0-345-42944-3*); 1997. 320p. mass mkt. 6.99 (*0-345-41406-3*) Ballantine Bks.

—Poverty Bay. 1985. 256p. mass mkt. 4.99 (*0-380-89647-8*, Avon Bks.) Morrow/Avon.

—Poverty Bay. unabr. ed. 1994. (Thomas Black Mystery Ser.: Vol. 2). audio 51.00 (*1-55690-980-2*, 94119E7) Recorded Bks., LLC.

—The Rainy City. 1998. mass mkt. 3.99 o.s.i (*0-345-42943-5*); 1997. 288p. mass mkt. 6.99 (*0-345-41405-5*) Ballantine Bks.

—The Rainy City. 1985. (Thomas Black Ser.). 240p. mass mkt. 4.99 (*0-380-89517-X*, Avon Bks.) Morrow/Avon.

—The Rainy City. unabr. ed. 1992. (Thomas Black Mystery Ser.: Vol. 1). audio 51.00 (*1-55690-723-0*, 92218E7) Recorded Bks., LLC.

—The Vanishing Smile. (Thomas Black Mysteries Ser.). 1996. 320p. mass mkt. 6.99 (*0-345-40453-X*); 1995. 272p. 21.00 o.s.i (*0-345-38486-5*) Ballantine Bks.

—Vertical Burn. 2003. 416p. mass mkt. 7.50 (*0-345-44590-2*); 2002. 352p. 24.95 (*0-345-44589-9*) Ballantine Bks. (Ballantine Bks.).

—Yellow Dog Party: A Thomas Black Mystery. 1992. (Thomas Black Mysteries Ser.). 256p. mass mkt. 6.99 (*0-345-37716-8*) Ballantine Bks.

—Yellow Dog Party: A Thomas Black Mystery. 1991. 288p. 19.00 o.p. (*0-688-09635-2*, Morrow, William & Co.) Morrow/Avon.

Fergusson, Bruce C. The Piper's Sons. 1999. 352p. 24.95 o.p. (*0-525-94431-1*) Dutton/Plume.

—The Piper's Sons. 1999. 432p. reprint ed. mass mkt. 6.99 o.s.i (*0-451-40875-6*, Signet Bks.) NAL.

Forbes, Edith. Navigating the Darwin Straights: A Novel. 2001. 282p. pap. 13.95 (*1-58005-049-2*, Seal Pr.) Avalon Publishing Group.

Ford, G. M. A Blind Eye: A Novel. 2003. 304p. 23.95 (*0-380-97875-X*) HarperCollins Pubs.

—The Bum's Rush. 1998. (Leo Waterman Mysteries Ser.). 320p. mass mkt. 5.99 (*0-380-72763-3*, Avon Bks.) Morrow/Avon.

—The Bum's Rush. 1997. (Leo Waterman Mysteries Ser.). 246p. 22.95 (*0-8027-3299-2*) Walker & Co.

—Cast in Stone. 1997. (Leo Waterman Mysteries Ser.). 304p. mass mkt. 5.99 (*0-380-72762-5*, Avon Bks.) Morrow/Avon.

—Cast in Stone. 1996. (Leo Waterman Mysteries Ser.). 288p. 21.95 (*0-8027-3267-4*) Walker & Co.

—The Deader the Better. (Leo Waterman Mysteries Ser.). 352p. 2000. 22.00 (*0-380-97723-0*); 2001. reprint ed. mass mkt. 6.99 (*0-380-80420-4*, Avon Bks.) Morrow/Avon.

—Fury. 2002. 384p. mass mkt. 6.99 (*0-380-80421-2*) Morrow/Avon.

—Fury: A Novel. 2001. 336p. 24.00 (*0-380-97724-9*, Morrow, William & Co.) Morrow/Avon.

—The Last Ditch. (Leo Waterman Mysteries Ser.). 2000. 320p. mass mkt. 5.99 (*0-380-79369-5*); 1999. 288p. 22.00 (*0-380-97557-2*) Morrow/Avon. (Avon Bks.).

—Slow Burn. (Leo Waterman Mysteries Ser.). 1999. 304p. mass mkt. 5.99 (*0-380-79367-9*); 1998. 288p. 20.00 (*0-380-97556-4*) Morrow/Avon. (Avon Bks.).

—Who in Hell Is Wanda Fuca? 1996. (Leo Waterman Mysteries Ser.). 320p. mass mkt. 5.99 (*0-380-72761-7*, Avon Bks.) Morrow/Avon.

—Who in Hell Is Wanda Fuca? 1995. 244p. 21.95 (*0-8027-3255-0*) Walker & Co.

Gabriel, Kristin. Seduced in Seattle. 2002. (Harlequin Temptation Ser.: No. 868). 218p. mass mkt. (*0-373-25968-9*, 1-25968-8, Harlequin Bks.) Harlequin Enterprises, Ltd.

Garrison, Leslie Ann. Mental Graffiti: Tall Tales Trilogy. l.t. ed. 1999. (Tall Tales Ser.: No. 2). E-Book 24.95 incl. cd-rom (*1-929077-27-0*, Books OnScreen) PageFree Publishing, Inc.

—Sniper's Candy: Tall Tales Trilogy. l.t. ed. 2000. (Tall Tales Ser.: No. 3). E-Book 24.95 incl. cd-rom (*1-929077-28-9*, Books OnScreen) PageFree Publishing, Inc.

—Visions of Murder: Tall Tales Trilogy. l.t. ed. 1999. (Tall Tales Ser.). E-Book 14.99 incl. cd-rom (*1-929077-26-2*, Books OnScreen) PageFree Publishing, Inc.

Gilpatrick, Noreen. Shadow of Death. 1995. 400p. 19.95 o.s.i (*0-89296-515-0*); 1993. 384p. 17.95 (*0-89296-514-2*) Mysterious Pr.

Greer, Andrew S. How It Was for Me: Stories. 2000. 224p. 23.00 (*0-312-24105-4*) Picador.

Guterson, David. East of the Mountains. 2001. 279p. 25.00 (*0-7881-9642-1*) DIANE Publishing Co.

—East of the Mountains. 304p. 2000. pap. 14.00 o.s.i (*0-15-601104-2*, Harvest Bks.); 1999. 25.00 (*0-15-100229-0*) Harcourt Trade Pubs.

—East of the Mountains. abr. ed. 1999. audio 25.00 Highsmith Inc.

—East of the Mountains. 2003. (Illus.). 304p. pap. 13.00 (*1-4000-3265-2*, Vintage) Knopf Publishing Group.

—East of the Mountains. abr. ed. 1999. audio 25.00 o.s.i (*0-553-52573-5*, 696038); audio compact disk 29.95 (*0-553-45618-0*); audio 34.95 (*0-553-50224-7*, 895847) Random Hse. Audio Publishing Group. (RH Audio).

—East of the Mountains. l.t. ed. 1999. (Basic Ser.). 424p. 30.95 (*0-7862-2038-4*) Thorndike Pr.

—East of the Mountains. 2000. 20.05 (*0-606-17641-1*) Turtleback Bks.

—East of the Mountains. abr. ed. 1999. audio 16.85 (*0-00-105559-3*) Ulverscroft Audio (U.S.A.).

Harris, E. Lynn. Abide with Me. 1999. (Abide with Me Ser.: Vol. 3). 368p. 24.95 (*0-385-48657-X*) Doubleday Publishing.

—Abide with Me. 2000. 368p. pap. 13.00 (*0-385-48658-8*, Knopf Bks. for Young Readers) Random Hse. Children's Bks.

—Abide with Me. 2003. (African American Ser.). 535p. 29.95 (*0-7862-5062-3*) Thorndike Pr.

Hawley, Michael A. The Double Bluff. 2002. 400p. (Orig.). mass mkt. 6.99 (*0-451-41047-5*, Onyx) NAL.

—The Double Bluff. 2000. 300p. (Orig.). pap. 14.95 o.p. (*0-595-09726-X*, Writer's Showcase Pr.) iUniverse, Inc.

—Silent Proof. 2003. 384p. mass mkt. 6.99 (*0-451-41104-8*, Onyx) NAL.

Hendricks, Judith Ryan. Bread Alone: A Novel. l.t. ed. 2002. (Wheeler Large Print Book Ser.). 27.95 (*1-58724-171-4*, Wheeler Publishing, Inc.) Gale Group.

—Bread Alone: A Novel. 2002. 368p. pap. 13.95 (*0-06-008440-5*, Perennial) HarperTrade.

—Bread Alone: A Novel. 2001. 368p. 25.00 (*0-06-018895-2*, Morrow, William & Co.) Morrow/Avon.

Heubner, Fredrick. Methods of Execution: A Novel. 1994. 284p. 22.00 (*0-671-86724-5*, Simon & Schuster) Simon & Schuster.

Holm, Stef Ann. Girls Night. 2002. 384p. mass mkt. (*1-55166-949-8*, Mira Bks.) Harlequin Enterprises, Ltd.

Hooper, Kay. Touching Evil. 2001. 384p. mass mkt. 7.50 (*0-553-58344-1*, Spectra) Bantam Bks.

—Touching Evil. l.t. ed. 2002. 31.95 (*0-7862-3718-X*) Gale Group.

—Touching Evil. l.t. ed. 2002. pap. 28.95 (*0-7862-3719-8*) Thorndike Pr.

Hoyt, Richard. Bigfoot. 1995. 246p. pap. text 4.99 (*0-8125-1948-5*, Forge Bks.); 1992. 224p. 17.95 o.p. (*0-312-85278-9*, Tor Bks.) Doherty, Tom Assocs., LLC.

—Decoys: A John Denson Mystery. 1980. 204p. 8.95 o.p. (*0-87131-330-8*) Evans, M. & Co., Inc.

—Decoys: A John Denson Mystery. 1984. (Crime Ser.). 208p. pap. 3.95 o.p. (*0-14-007217-9*, Penguin Bks.) Viking Penguin.

—Fish Story. 1987. 288p. reprint ed. pap. 3.95 o.p. (*0-8125-0491-7*, Tor Bks.) Doherty, Tom Assocs., LLC.

—Fish Story. 1985. (Mystery Ser.). 224p. 13.95 o.p. (*0-670-31672-5*) Viking Penguin.

—Siskiyou. 1984. 304p. (Orig.). pap. 3.50 o.p. (*0-8125-0487-9*, Tor Bks.) Doherty, Tom Assocs., LLC.

—Snake Eyes. (John Denson Mystery Ser.). 1996. 250p. mass mkt. 5.99 (*0-8125-5072-2*); 1995. 256p. 27.95 o.p. (*0-312-85805-1*) Doherty, Tom Assocs., LLC. (Forge Bks.).

—Thirty for a Harry: A John Denson Mystery. l.t. ed. 1991. 8.95 o.p. (*0-7451-9624-1*, 5043); pap. 10.95 o.p. (*0-7927-0024-4*, 647) BBC Audiobooks America.

—Thirty for a Harry: A John Denson Mystery. 1981. 192p. 8.95 o.p. (*0-87131-357-X*) Evans, M. & Co., Inc.

—Thirty for a Harry: A John Denson Mystery. 1984. (Crime Monthly Ser.). 192p. pap. 3.95 o.p. (*0-14-007216-0*, Penguin Bks.) Viking Penguin.

—Whoo? 2000. 224p. mass mkt. 5.99 (*0-8125-1276-6*, Forge Bks.); 1991. 17.95 o.p. (*0-312-85149-9*, Tor Bks.) Doherty, Tom Assocs., LLC.

Huebner, Frederick D. Methods of Execution. 1995. mass mkt. 5.99 o.s.i (*0-449-14939-0*, Fawcett) Ballantine Bks.

—Methods of Execution. unabr. ed. 1994. audio 56.00 (*0-7366-2882-7*, 3584) Books on Tape, Inc.

Jance, J. A. Birds of Prey: A Novel of Suspense. l.t. ed. 2001. 464p. pap. 24.00 (*0-06-018562-7*, HarperLargePrint) HarperTrade.

—Birds of Prey: A Novel of Suspense. 2002. 416p. mass mkt. 7.99 (*0-380-71654-2*); 2001. 390p. 24.00 (*0-380-97407-X*, Morrow, William & Co.) Morrow/Avon.

—Breach of Duty. unabr. ed. 1999. (J. P. Beaumont Mystery Ser.: Bk. 14). audio 49.95 (*1-55686-897-9*) Books in Motion.

—Breach of Duty. 1999. (J. P. Beaumont Mystery Ser.). 384p. mass mkt. 7.50 (*0-380-71843-X*); 352p. 23.00 (*0-380-97406-1*) Morrow/Avon. (Avon Bks.).

—Breach of Duty. 2002. (Famous Authors Ser.). 29.95 (*0-7862-4758-4*) Thorndike Pr.

—Dismissed with Prejudice. unabr. ed. 1993. (J. P. Beaumont Mystery Ser.: Bk. 7). audio 39.95 (*1-55686-474-4*, 752465) Books in Motion.

—Dismissed with Prejudice. 1989. (J. P. Beaumont Mystery Ser.). 384p. mass mkt. 7.50 (*0-380-75547-5*, Avon Bks.) Morrow/Avon.

—Dismissed with Prejudice. 2003. (J. P. Beaumont Mystery Ser.). 384p. 26.99 (*0-7278-5981-1*) Severn Hse. Pubs., Ltd.

—Failure to Appear. unabr. ed. 1995. (J. P. Beaumont Mystery Ser.: Bk. 11). audio 49.95 (*1-55686-562-7*, 892559) Books in Motion.

—Failure to Appear. unabr. collector's ed. 1998. (J. P. Beaumont Ser.: Vol. 11). audio 56.00 (*0-7366-4042-8*, 4541) Books on Tape, Inc.

—Failure to Appear. (J. P. Beaumont Mystery Ser.). 1994. 384p. mass mkt. 7.50 (*0-380-75839-3*, Avon Bks.); 1993. 269p. 20.00 o.p. (*0-688-12674-X*, Morrow, William & Co.) Morrow/Avon.

—Failure to Appear. 2003. (Famous Authors Ser.). 29.95 (*0-7862-4760-6*) Thorndike Pr.

—Hour of the Hunter. unabr. ed. 1994. (Joanna Brady Mystery Ser.). audio 64.95 (*1-55686-470-1*, 112714) Books in Motion.

—Hour of the Hunter. (J. P. Beaumont Mystery Ser.). 1992. 416p. mass mkt. 7.99 (*0-380-71107-9*, Avon Bks.); 1991. 356p. 20.00 o.p. (*0-688-09630-1*, Morrow, William & Co.) Morrow/Avon.

—Hour of the Hunter. l.t. ed. 2003. 669p. 29.95 (*0-7862-5321-5*) Thorndike Pr.

—Improbable Cause. unabr. ed. 1993. (J. P. Beaumont Mystery Ser.: Bk. 5). audio 39.95 (*1-55686-462-0*, 752414) Books in Motion.

—Improbable Cause. unabr. collector's ed. 1997. (J. P. Beaumont Ser.). audio 48.00 (*0-7366-3609-9*, 4266) Books on Tape, Inc.

—Improbable Cause. 2003. (J. P. Beaumont Mystery Ser.). 352p. mass mkt. 7.50 (*0-380-75412-6*, Avon Bks.) Morrow/Avon.

—Improbable Cause. 1992. 224p. reprint ed. 19.00 o.p. (*0-7278-4314-1*) Severn Hse. Pubs., Ltd.

—Injustice for All. unabr. ed. 1992. (J. P. Beaumont Mystery Ser.: Bk. 2). audio 39.95 (*1-55686-415-9*, 415) Books in Motion.

—Injustice for All. unabr. collector's ed. 1997. (J. P. Beaumont Ser.: Vol. 2). audio 56.00 (*0-7366-3568-8*, 4217) Books on Tape, Inc.

—Injustice for All. 1986. (J. P. Beaumont Mystery Ser.). 384p. mass mkt. 7.50 (*0-380-89641-9*, Avon Bks.) Morrow/Avon.

—Injustice for All. 1993. 19.00 o.p. (*0-7278-4431-8*) Severn Hse. Pubs., Ltd.

—Lying in Wait. unabr. ed. 1994. (J. P. Beaumont Mystery Ser.: Bk. 12). audio 49.95 (*1-55686-563-5*, 102592) Books in Motion.

—Lying in Wait. (J. P. Beaumont Mystery Ser.). 1996. 400p. mass mkt. 7.99 (*0-380-71841-3*, Avon Bks.); 1994. 303p. 17.95 o.p. (*0-688-02013-5*, Morrow, William & Co.) Morrow/Avon.

—Lying in Wait. l.t. ed. 2003. (J. P. Beaumont Mystery Ser.). 447p. 29.95 (*0-7862-4762-2*) Thorndike Pr.

—Minor in Possession. unabr. ed. 1993. (J. P. Beaumont Mystery Ser.). audio 49.95 (*1-55686-475-2*, 892536) Books in Motion.

—Minor in Possession. unabr. collector's ed. 1997. (J. P. Beaumont Ser.). audio 56.00 (*0-7366-3824-5*, 4492) Books on Tape, Inc.

—Minor in Possession. 1990. (J. P. Beaumont Mystery Ser.). 384p. mass mkt. 7.50 (*0-380-75546-7*, Avon Bks.) Morrow/Avon.

—A More Perfect Union. unabr. ed. 1993. (J. P. Beaumont Mystery Ser.: Bk. 6). audio 39.95 (*1-55686-466-3*, 752467) Books in Motion.

—A More Perfect Union. unabr. collector's ed. 1997. (J. P. Beaumont Ser.). audio 48.00 (*0-7366-3822-9*, 4490) Books on Tape, Inc.

—A More Perfect Union. 2003. (J. P. Beaumont Mystery Ser.). 352p. mass mkt. 7.50 (*0-380-75413-4*, Avon Bks.) Morrow/Avon.

—A More Perfect Union. 1992. 224p. reprint ed. 19.00 o.p. (*0-7278-4361-3*) Severn Hse. Pubs., Ltd.

—Name Withheld. l.t. ed. 2001. 320p. 28.95 (*1-57490-357-8*, Beeler Large Print Bks.) Beeler, Thomas T. Publisher.

—Name Withheld. unabr. ed. 1996. (J. P. Beaumont Mystery Ser.: Bk. 13). audio 46.95 (*1-55686-651-8*, 893938) Books in Motion.

—Name Withheld. (J. P. Beaumont Mystery Ser.). 1997. 400p. mass mkt. 6.99 (*0-380-71842-1*, Avon Bks.); 1996. 293p. 22.00 o.p. (*0-688-11460-1*, Morrow, William & Co.) Morrow/Avon.

—Partner in Crime. 2002. E-Book 19.95 (*0-06-009827-9*); E-Book 19.95 (*0-06-009825-2*); E-Book 19.95 (*0-06-009826-0*) HarperCollins General Bks. Group. (PerfectBound).

—Partner in Crime. l.t. ed. 2002. 512p. pap. 24.95 (*0-06-009393-5*, HarperLargePrint) HarperTrade.

—Partner in Crime. 2003. 400p. mass mkt. 7.99 (*0-380-80470-0*); 2002. 384p. 24.95 (*0-380-97730-3*) Morrow/Avon. (Morrow, William & Co.).

—Payment in Kind. unabr. ed. 1992. (J. P. Beaumont Mystery Ser.: Bk. 9). audio 49.95 (*1-55686-410-8*, 892515) Books in Motion.

—Payment in Kind. unabr. collector's ed. 1997. audio 56.00 (*0-7366-3825-3*, 4493) Books on Tape, Inc.

—Payment in Kind, Bk. 9. 1991. (J. P. Beaumont Mystery Ser.). 384p. mass mkt. 7.50 (*0-380-75836-9*, Avon Bks.) Morrow/Avon.

—Taking the Fifth. unabr. ed. 1993. (J. P. Beaumont Mystery Ser.: Bk. 4). audio 39.95 (*1-55686-458-2*, 752411) Books in Motion.

—Taking the Fifth. unabr. collector's ed. 1997. (J. P. Beaumont Ser.: Vol. 4). audio 48.00 (*0-7366-3626-9*, 4286) Books on Tape, Inc.

—Taking the Fifth. 1987. (J. P. Beaumont Mystery Ser.). 320p. mass mkt. 7.99 (*0-380-75139-9*, Avon Bks.) Morrow/Avon.

—Taking the Fifth. 320p. 25.99 (*0-7278-5944-7*) Severn Hse. Pubs., Ltd.

—Three Complete Novels. 1996. 13.99 o.s.i (*0-517-14764-5*) Random Hse. Value Publishing.

—Trial by Fury. unabr. ed. 1993. (J. P. Beaumont Mystery Ser.: Bk. 3). audio 39.95 (1-55686-456-6, 752468) Books in Motion.

—Trial by Fury. unabr. collector's ed. 1997. (J. P. Beaumont Ser.: Vol. 3). audio 48.00 (0-7366-3582-3, 4236) Books on Tape, Inc.

—Trial by Fury. 1986. (J. P. Beaumont Mystery Ser.). 384p. mass mkt. 7.99 (0-380-75138-0, Avon Bks.) Morrow/Avon.

—Trial by Fury. 384p. 26.00 (0-7278-5609-X) Severn Hse. Pubs., Ltd.

—Until Proven Guilty. l.t. ed. 1991. 21.95 o.p. (0-7927-0825-3, CH080); pap. 19.95 o.p. (0-7927-0826-1, CS0176) BBC Audiobooks America.

—Until Proven Guilty. unabr. ed. 1992. (J. P. Beaumont Mystery Ser.: Bk. 1). audio 39.95 (1-55686-414-0, 752460) Books in Motion.

—Until Proven Guilty. unabr. collector's ed. 1997. (J. P. Beaumont Ser.: Vol. 1). audio 48.00 (0-7366-3584-X, 4238) Books on Tape, Inc.

—Until Proven Guilty. 1985. (J. P. Beaumont Mystery Ser.). 352p. mass mkt. 7.99 (0-380-89638-9, Avon Bks.) Morrow/Avon.

—Without Due Process. unabr. ed. 1993. (J. P. Beaumont Mystery Ser.: Bk. 10). audio 49.95 (1-55686-476-0, 892538) Books in Motion.

—Without Due Process. unabr. collector's ed. 1998. (J. P. Beaumont Ser.). audio 56.00 (0-7366-4041-X, 4540) Books on Tape, Inc.

—Without Due Process. (J. P. Beaumont Mystery Ser.). 1993. 384p. mass mkt. 7.50 (0-380-75837-7, Avon Bks.); 1992. 302p. 20.00 o.p. (0-688-11459-8, Morrow, William & Co.) Morrow/Avon.

—Without Due Process. 4.98 o.p. (0-8317-8577-2) Smithmark Pubs., Inc.

Keegan, John E. A Good Divorce. 2003. 26.00 (1-57962-092-2) Permanent Pr., The.

Keith, Don & Wallace, George. Final Bearing. 2003. (Illus.). 512p. 27.95 (0-7653-0415-5, Forge Bks.) Doherty, Tom Assocs., LLC.

Kersey, Colin. Soul Catcher. 1995. 272p. 22.95 o.p. (0-312-13606-4) St. Martin's Pr.

Kirchner, Bharti. Darjeeling: A Novel. 2003. 320p. pap. 12.95 (0-312-31606-2, Saint Martin's Griffin) St. Martin's Pr.

Krentz, Jayne Ann. Absolutely, Positively. unabr. ed. 1996. audio 64.00 (0-7366-3436-3, 104621) Books on Tape, Inc.

—Absolutely, Positively. l.t. ed. 1996. 25.95 (1-56895-286-4, Wheeler Publishing, Inc.) Gale Group.

—Absolutely, Positively. 384p. 2003. mass mkt. 5.99 (0-7434-6737-X); 1997. pap. 7.99 (0-671-77873-0) Simon & Schuster. (Pocket).

—Absolutely, Positively. Zion, Claire, ed. 1996. 352p. 23.00 o.p. (0-671-55170-1, Atria) Simon & Schuster.

—Absolutely, Positively. abr. ed. 1997. audio 17.00 (0-671-88653-3, 394827, Simon & Schuster Audioworks) Simon & Schuster Audio.

—Flash. l.t. ed. 1998. (Wheeler Large Print Book Ser.). 26.95 o.p. (1-56895-593-6, Wheeler Publishing, Inc.) Gale Group.

—Flash. 2002. 432p. mass mkt. 7.99 (0-7434-5647-5, Pocket); 1999. (Illus.). 432p. pap. 7.99 (0-671-52309-0, Pocket Star); 1998. 368p. 24.00 o.s.i (0-671-52308-2, Atria) Simon & Schuster.

—Sharp Edges. l.t. ed. 1998. 26.95 (1-56895-549-9, Wheeler Publishing, Inc.) Gale Group.

—Sharp Edges. 1998. (Illus.). 400p. mass mkt. 7.50 (0-671-52409-7, Pocket Star); 320p. 24.00 (0-671-52310-4, Atria) Simon & Schuster.

—Sharp Edges. abr. ed. 1998. audio 18.00 o.s.i (0-671-57613-5, 395615, Simon & Schuster Audioworks) Simon & Schuster Audio.

—Trust Me. unabr. ed. 1996. audio 64.00 (0-7366-3334-0, 3985) Books on Tape, Inc.

—Trust Me. l.t. ed. 1995. (Large Print Bks.). 25.95 o.p. (1-56895-204-X, Wheeler Publishing, Inc.) Gale Group.

—Trust Me. 1998. per. 6.99 (0-671-01969-4); 1995. 368p. mass mkt. 7.99 (0-671-51692-2) Simon & Schuster. (Pocket).

—Trust Me. Zion, Claire, ed. 1995. 320p. 22.00 o.p. (0-671-51691-4, Atria) Simon & Schuster.

—Trust Me. 2001. audio 9.98 o.s.i (0-671-04437-0); Set. 1995. audio 17.00 (0-671-88652-5, 391817) Simon & Schuster Audio. (Simon & Schuster Audioworks).

Layton, J. A. Vortex One. 2001. 416p. mass mkt. 6.99 o.s.i (0-515-13204-7, Jove) Berkley Publishing Group.

Long, Goldberry M. Juniper Tree Burning. 464p. 2002. pap. 14.00 (0-7432-2211-3); 2001. 25.00 (0-7432-0203-1) Simon & Schuster. (Simon & Schuster).

Macomber, Debbie. Fallen Angel. 1996. 256p. per. (1-55166-180-2, 1-66180-0, Mira Bks.); 1990. (Silhouette Special Edition Ser.: No. 577). pap. (0-373-09577-5, Silhouette) Harlequin Enterprises, Ltd.

—Fallen Angel. l.t. ed. 2000. (Americana Ser.). 334p. 26.95 (0-7862-2601-3) Thorndike Pr.

Masiel, David. 2182 kHz. l.t. ed. 2002. 28.95 (0-7862-4475-5) Thorndike Pr.

—2182 kHz: A Novel. 2002. 304p. 22.95 (0-375-50606-3) Random Hse., Inc.

McCourtney, Lorena. Dear Silver. 1997. 286p. pap. 9.99 o.p. (1-57673-110-3, Palisades) Multnomah Pubs., Inc.

McIntosh, Matthew. Well. 2003. 276p. 23.00 (0-8021-1751-1, Grove Pr.) Grove/Atlantic, Inc.

Meyerding, Jane. Everywhere House. 1994. 256p. (Orig.). pap. 9.95 (0-934678-42-1) New Victoria Pubs., Inc.

Miller, Linda Lael. Courting Susannah. 2000. 352p. mass mkt. 7.99 (0-671-00400-X, Pocket) Simon & Schuster.

—Courting Susannah. l.t. ed. 2001. (Thorndike Americana Ser.). 477p. 30.95 (0-7862-3226-9) Thorndike Pr.

—Only Forever. 2001. 256p. mass mkt. (1-55166-857-2, Mira Bks.) Harlequin Enterprises, Ltd.

Moody, Skye Kathleen. Blue Poppy. 1998. (WWL Mystery Ser.: No. 293). per. (0-373-26293-0, 0-26293-1, Worldwide Library) Harlequin Enterprises, Ltd.

—Blue Poppy. 1997. (Pacific Northwest Mysteries Ser.). 256p. 23.95 (0-312-15479-8, Saint Martin's Minotaur) St. Martin's Pr.

—Habitat. 1999. (Illus.). 274p. 24.95 (0-312-20390-X, Saint Martin's Minotaur) St. Martin's Pr.

—Rain Dance. 1998. (WWL Mystery Ser.). per. (0-373-26278-7, 1-26278-1, Worldwide Library) Harlequin Enterprises, Ltd.

—Rain Dance. 1996. 256p. 21.95 (0-312-14713-9, Saint Martin's Minotaur) St. Martin's Pr.

—Wildcrafters. 1999. (WWL Mystery Ser.: Vol. 332). 272p. per. (0-373-26332-5, Harlequin Bks.) Harlequin Enterprises, Ltd.

—Wildcrafters. 1998. (Pacific Northwest Mysteries Ser.). 320p. 23.95 o.p. (0-312-19364-5, Saint Martin's Minotaur) St. Martin's Pr.

Nunnally, Tiina. Fate of Ravens: A Margit Andersson Mystery. 1998. (Suspense Ser.: Vol. 2). 220p. pap. 12.00 (0-940242-80-X) Fjord Pr.

—Runemaker. 1996. (Suspense Ser.: No. 1). 213p. (Orig.). pap. 12.00 (0-940242-77-X) Fjord Pr.

Oran, Daniel. Ulterior Motive. 1999. 384p. mass mkt. 5.99 o.s.i (0-7860-0657-9); 1998. 320p. mass mkt. 22.95 o.s.i (1-57566-302-3, Kensington Bks.) Kensington Publishing Corp.

—Ulterior Motive. 2001. E-Book 6.99 (0-7592-1210-4); 1998. 284p. per. 19.96 (0-7592-1215-5) ereads.com.

Orton, Thomas. The Lost Glass Plates of Wilfred Eng: A Novel. 256p. 1999. text 24.00 o.p. (1-58243-023-3); 2000. reprint ed. pap. text 14.00 (1-58243-125-6) Basic Bks. (Counterpoint Pr.).

Parker, T. Jefferson. Red Light. l.t. ed. 2003. lib. bdg. 29.95 (1-58547-308-1, Premier) Ctr. Point Large Print.

—Red Light. 2000. 326p. 23.95 (0-7868-6600-4); 2003. 384p. reprint ed. mass mkt. 7.99 (0-7868-8975-6) Hyperion Pr.

Pearson, Ridley. The Angel Maker. 1994. 464p. mass mkt. 7.50 o.s.i (0-440-21632-X) Dell Publishing.

—The Angel Maker. 2003. (Illus.). 368p. reprint ed. mass mkt. 6.99 (0-7868-9008-8) Hyperion Pr.

—The Angel Maker. abr. ed. 1999. audio 9.99 o.s.i (0-553-70195-9, RH Audio) Random Hse. Audio Publishing Group.

—The Art of Deception. 2003. 464p. mass mkt. 7.99 (0-7868-9000-2); 2003. E-Book 5.99 (1-4013-9837-5); 2003. E-Book 5.99 (1-4013-9839-1); 2003. E-Book 5.99 (1-4013-9838-3); 2003. E-Book (1-4013-9841-3); 2003. E-Book 5.99 (1-4013-9840-5); 2002. 384p. 23.95 (0-7868-6724-8) Hyperion Pr.

—The Art of Deception. 2003. (Basic Ser.). 31.95 (0-7862-4967-6) Thorndike Pr.

—Beyond Recognition. unabr. ed. 1998. audio 96.00 (0-7366-4092-4, 4599) Books on Tape, Inc.

—Beyond Recognition. abr. ed. 1997. (Lou Boldt & Daphne Matthews Mystery Ser.). 3p. audio 7.99 (1-56740-228-3, 627, Paperback Nova Audio Bks.); audio 16.95 o.p. (1-56100-970-9, 1134, Nova Audio Bks.); audio 27.95 (1-56100-733-1, 45, Bookcassette); audio 105.25 (1-56100-807-9, 809) Brilliance Audio.

—Beyond Recognition. 1997. 496p. 22.95 o.p. (0-7868-6240-8); 2003. 656p. reprint ed. mass mkt. 7.99 (0-7868-8928-4) Hyperion Pr.

—Blood of the Albatross. 1993. 307p. mass mkt. 6.99 (0-312-95183-3, St. Martin's Paperbacks); 1986. mass mkt. 3.95 o.s.i (0-312-90607-2, St. Martin's Paperbacks); 1986. 16.95 o.p. (0-312-08448-X); Vol. 1. 1992. mass mkt. 4.99 o.s.i (0-312-92974-9, St. Martin's Paperbacks) St. Martin's Pr.

—The Body of David Hayes. 2003. 23.95 (0-7868-6725-6) Hyperion Pr.

—The First Victim. aut. ltd. ed. 1999. 400p. 23.95 (0-7868-6558-X) Disney Pr.

—The First Victim. l.t. ed. 2001. (Large Print Bks.). 475p. pap. 23.95 (1-58724-099-8, Wheeler Publishing, Inc.) Gale Group.

—The First Victim. 2001. 400p. E-Book 5.95 (0-7868-7142-3); 2001. 400p. E-Book 5.95 (0-7868-7145-8); 2001. 400p. E-Book 5.95 (0-7868-7143-1); 2001. 400p. E-Book 5.95 (0-7868-7144-X); 2001. 400p. E-Book 5.95 (0-7868-7146-6); 1999. 381p. 23.95 (0-7868-6440-0); 2003. 416p. reprint ed. mass mkt. 7.99 (0-7868-8966-7) Hyperion Pr.

—Middle of Nowhere. l.t. ed. 2001. (Large Print Book Ser.). 516p. 29.95 (1-58724-013-0, Wheeler Publishing, Inc.) Gale Group.

—Middle of Nowhere. 2001. 384p. E-Book 5.95 (0-7868-7149-0); 2001. 384p. E-Book 5.95 (0-7868-7197-0); 2001. 384p. E-Book 5.95 (0-7868-7198-9); 2000. 375p. 23.95 (0-7868-6563-6); 2003. 384p. reprint ed. mass mkt. 7.99 (0-7868-8960-8) Hyperion Pr.

—No Witnesses. unabr. ed. 1995. (Lou Boldt & Daphne Matthews Mystery Ser.). audio 72.00 (0-7366-2950-5, 3644) Books on Tape, Inc.

—No Witnesses. 1996. 480p. mass mkt. 7.50 o.s.i (0-440-22142-0) Dell Publishing.

—No Witnesses. 1994. 384p. 22.95 (0-7868-6066-9); 2003. 480p. reprint ed. mass mkt. 6.99 (0-7868-9006-1) Hyperion Pr.

—No Witnesses. abr. ed. 1999. audio 9.99 o.s.i (0-553-70215-7, RH Audio) Random Hse. Audio Publishing Group.

—The Pied Piper. l.t. ed. 2000. pap. 23.95 (1-56895-834-X, Wheeler Publishing, Inc.) Gale Group.

—The Pied Piper. 1998. 497p. 23.95 (0-7868-6300-5); 2003. 528p. reprint ed. mass mkt. 7.99 (0-7868-8955-1) Hyperion Pr.

—The Pied Piper & Beyond Recognition. 1998. (0-7868-6433-8) Disney Pr.

—Undercurrents. 2000. E-Book 4.99 (1-58910-004-2) PreviewPort.com.

—Undercurrents. 1992. mass mkt. 6.99 (0-312-92958-7, St. Martin's Paperbacks); 1989. mass mkt. 4.95 o.s.i (0-312-91485-7, St. Martin's Paperbacks); 1988. 416p. 18.95 o.p. (0-312-01841-X) St. Martin's Pr.

Powell, Randy. Tribute to Another Dead Rock Star. l.t. ed. 2000. (Young Adult Ser.). 224p. (J). 21.95 (0-7862-2191-7) Thorndike Pr.

Raban, Jonathan. Waxwings: A Novel. 2003. 288p. 24.00 (0-375-41008-2, Pantheon) Knopf Publishing Group.

Reardon, Joyce. The Diary of Ellen Rimbauer: My Life at Rose Red. 2002. E-Book 14.95 (1-4013-9674-7) Hyperion Pr.

Reardon, Joyce, ed. The Diary of Ellen Rimbauer: My Life at Rose Red. 2002. lib. bdg. 28.95 (1-58547-231-X, Platinum) Ctr. Point Large Print.

—The Diary of Ellen Rimbauer: My Life at Rose Red. 2002. 272p. mass mkt. 6.99 (0-7868-9043-6); 288p. 22.95 (0-7868-6801-5) Hyperion Pr.

Rolofson, Kristine, et al. Date with Destiny: Transforming Frankie/Protecting Maria/Distracting Diana, 3 bks. in 1. 2003. 384p. mass mkt. (0-373-83561-2, Harlequin Bks.) Harlequin Enterprises, Ltd.

Saul, John. Black Lightning. Grey, Linda, ed. 1996. 448p. mass mkt. 7.99 (0-449-22504-6, Fawcett) Ballantine Bks.

Sheahan, Bernie. Spring Break. 1996. (Palisades University Ser.: No. 3). 186p. (gr. 7-11). pap. 5.99 o.p. (0-88070-950-2, Palisades) Multnomah Pubs., Inc.

Shepherd, Pamela. Zach at Risk. 2003. 202p. pap. 14.95 (1-56023-466-0, Alice Street Editions) Haworth Pr., Inc., The.

Siler, Jenny. Shot: A Novel. 2004. 288p. mass mkt. 6.99 (0-312-99354-4, Saint Martin's Minotaur) St. Martin's Pr.

Sizemore, Susan. Partners. 2000. (Laws of the Blood Ser.: No. 2). 288p. mass mkt. 6.50 (0-441-00783-X) Ace Bks.

Sloan, Susan R. Act of God. 2003. 608p. mass mkt. 7.99 (0-446-61260-X); 2002. 544p. 24.95 o.p. (0-446-52451-4) Warner Bks., Inc.

Smith, Janet L. Practice to Deceive. 1993. (Northwest Mysteries Ser.). mass mkt. 4.99 o.s.i (0-8041-0978-8, Ivy Bks.) Ballantine Bks.

—Sea of Troubles. 1991. 224p. mass mkt. 4.99 o.s.i (0-8041-0759-9, Ivy Bks.) Ballantine Bks.

—Sea of Troubles. 1990. 197p. pap. 8.95 o.p. (0-9602676-9-7, Perseverance Pr.) Daniel, John & Co., Pubs.

—Sea of Troubles. 1990. 200p. (C). reprint ed. lib. bdg. 29.00 o.p. (0-8095-4208-0) Millefleurs.

—A Vintage Murder. 1995. mass mkt. 5.99 o.s.i (0-8041-1385-8, Ivy Bks.); 1994. 240p. 20.00 o.s.i (0-449-90871-2, Fawcett) Ballantine Bks.

Speight, Bernice. The Architect's Other Hat: A Mystery. 1995. 128p. (Orig.). pap. 9.95 (1-56474-135-4) Fithian Pr.

Stekel, Peter. The Flower Lover. pap. 17.11 (0-7596-1163-7) 1stBooks Library.

Stewart, Jean. Emerald City Blues. 1996. 228p. pap. 11.99 (1-883061-09-1) Rising Tide Pr.

Thayer, James Stewart. Terminal Event. l.t. ed. 2000. 25.95 (1-57490-304-7, Beeler Large Print Bks.) Beeler, Thomas T. Publisher.

—Terminal Event. 1999. (Illus.). 352p. 25.00 (0-684-84210-6, Simon & Schuster); 2003. 448p. reprint ed. mass mkt. 7.99 (0-671-01371-8, Pocket) Simon & Schuster.

Thompson, Joyce. Bones. 320p. 1992. mass mkt. 4.50 (0-380-71147-8, Avon Bks.); 1991. 19.95 o.p. (0-688-09653-0, Morrow, William & Co.) Morrow/Avon.

Thornburg, Newton. A Man's Game. 1997. 300p. mass mkt. 6.99 (0-8125-5374-8); 1996. 304p. 22.95 o.p. (0-312-85923-6) Doherty, Tom Assocs., LLC. (Forge Bks.).

Wilbee, Brenda. Sweetbriar Hope. 1999. (Sweetbriar Ser.: No. 6). 320p. (gr. 13 up). pap. 11.99 o.p. (0-8007-5695-9) Revell, Fleming H. Co.

—Sweetbriar Summer. 1997. (Sweetbriar Ser.). (Illus.). 272p. (gr. 12 up). pap. 11.99 o.p. (0-8007-5619-3) Revell, Fleming H. Co.

Wilcox, Valerie. Sins of Betrayal: A Sailing Mystery. 1999. 304p. mass mkt. 6.50 o.s.i (0-425-16963-4, Prime Crime) Berkley Publishing Group.

—Sins of Deception. 2000. (Sailing Mystery Ser.). 288p. mass mkt. 5.99 o.s.i (0-425-17507-3, Prime Crime) Berkley Publishing Group.

**SECTOR GENERAL (IMAGINARY PLACE)—FICTION**

White, James. Code Blue - Emergency. 1987. 288p. (Orig.). mass mkt. 2.95 o.s.i (0-345-34172-4, Del Rey) Ballantine Bks.

—Double Contact. 1999. (Sector General Novels Ser.). 300p. 24.95 (0-312-87041-8, Tor Bks.) Doherty, Tom Assocs., LLC.

—The Galactic Gourmet: A Sector General Novel. (Sector General Novels Ser.). 1997. 312p. mass mkt. 5.99 (0-8125-6267-4); 1996. 288p. 22.95 o.p. (0-312-86167-2) Doherty, Tom Assocs., LLC. (Tor Bks.).

—Mind Changer. 304p. 1999. mass mkt. 6.99 (0-8125-4196-0); 1998. 23.95 (0-312-86663-1) Doherty, Tom Assocs., LLC. (Tor Bks.).

—Mind Changer. 1999. 6.99 (0-312-87170-8) St. Martin's Pr.

—Sector General. 1987. 208p. mass mkt. 2.95 o.s.i (0-345-34627-0); 1986. mass mkt. 2.95 o.s.i (0-345-33672-0); 1983. mass mkt. 2.75 o.s.i (0-345-30851-4) Ballantine Bks. (Del Rey).

—Star Surgeon. (Orig.). 1980. 160p. mass mkt. 1.95 o.s.i (0-345-29169-7, Del Rey); 1970. mass mkt. 0.75 o.s.i (0-345-22028-5) Ballantine Bks.

**SEVEN KINGDOMS (IMAGINARY PLACE)—FICTION**

Martin, George R. R. A Clash of Kings. (Song of Ice & Fire Ser.: Bk 2). 2000. 1040p. mass mkt. 7.99 (0-553-57990-8); 1999. (Illus.). 768p. 26.95 (0-553-10803-4) Bantam Bks. (Spectra).

—A Game of Thrones. 2002. 704p. 26.95 (0-553-10354-7, Spectra); 1997. (Song of Ice & Fire Ser.: No. 1). 864p. mass mkt. 7.99 (0-553-57340-3) Bantam Bks.

—A Storm of Swords. 2000. (Song of Ice & Fire Ser.: Bk. 3). (Illus.). 992p. 26.95 (0-553-10663-5) Bantam Bks.

**SHADY HILLS (N.J.: IMAGINARY PLACE)—FICTION**

Marshall, Evan. Hanging Hannah. (Jane Stuart & Winky Mystery Ser.). 2001. 32p. mass mkt. 5.99 (1-57566-663-4); 2000. (Illus.). 307p. 20.00 o.s.i (1-57566-550-6) Kensington Publishing Corp. (Kensington Bks.).

—Missing Marlene. (Jane Stuart & Winky Mystery Ser.). 2000. 336p. mass mkt. 5.99 (1-57566-555-7, Kensington Bks.); 1999. 309p. 20.00 o.s.i (1-57566-420-8) Kensington Publishing Corp.

**SHAKESPEARE (ARK.: IMAGINARY PLACE)—FICTION**

Harris, Charlaine. Shakespeare's Champion. 1998. 274p. pap. 19.00 o.s.i (0-440-61352-3, Delta); 272p. mass mkt. 5.99 (0-440-22421-7) Dell Publishing.

—Shakespeare's Champion. 1997. (Lily Bard Mysteries Ser.). 224p. 20.95 o.p. (0-312-17005-X, Saint Martin's Minotaur) St. Martin's Pr.

—Shakespeare's Champion. l.t. ed. 1998. (Cloak & Dagger Ser.). 327p. 26.95 (0-7862-1454-6) Thorndike Pr.

—Shakespeare's Christmas: A Lily Bard Mystery. 1999. (Lily Bard Mysteries Ser.). 256p. mass mkt. 5.99 (0-440-23499-9) Dell Publishing.

—Shakespeare's Christmas: A Lily Bard Mystery. 1998. 224p. 20.95 (0-312-19330-0, Saint Martin's Minotaur) St. Martin's Pr.

—Shakespeare's Landlord. 1997. 256p. pap. 19.00 (0-440-61406-6, Dell Bks.); mass mkt. 5.99 (0-440-22418-7) Dell Publishing.

—Shakespeare's Landlord. 1996. 224p. 20.95 o.p. (0-312-14415-6, Saint Martin's Minotaur) St. Martin's Pr.

—Shakespeare's Trollop. 2004. 208p. mass mkt. 5.99 (0-425-19699-2) Berkley Publishing Group.

—Shakespeare's Trollop. 2000. 227p. 23.95 (0-312-26228-0, Saint Martin's Minotaur) St. Martin's Pr.

—Shakespeare's Trollop. l.t. ed. 2000. (Mystery Ser.). (Illus.). 296p. 28.95 (*0-7862-3030-4*) Thorndike Pr.

**SHANGHAI (CHINA)—FICTION**

Agel, Jerome & Boe, Eugene. Deliverance in Shanghai. 1983. 362p. 14.95 o.p. (*0-934878-32-3*, Dembner Bks.) Barricade Bks., Inc.

Ballard, J. G. Empire of the Sun. unabr. ed. 1996. audio 64.00 (*0-7366-3319-7*, 3971) Books on Tape, Inc.

—Empire of the Sun. 1997. reprint ed. lib. bdg. 39.95 (*1-56849-663-X*) Buccaneer Bks., Inc.

—Empire of the Sun. unabr. ed. 2001. audio 59.95 (*0-7451-5767-X*, CAB 152) Chivers Audio Bks. GBR. *Dist:* BBC Audiobooks America.

—Empire of the Sun. 1987. 384p. mass mkt. 5.99 (*0-671-64877-2*, Pocket); 1984. 320p. 16.45 o.p. (*0-671-53051-8*, Simon & Schuster); 1985. reprint ed. mass mkt. 4.50 (*0-671-53053-4*, Washington Square Pr.) Simon & Schuster.

—Empire of the Sun. l.t. ed. 1985. 480p. 13.95 o.p. (*0-7089-8270-0*, Charnwood) Thorpe, F. A. Pubs. GBR. *Dist:* Ulverscroft Large Print Bks., Ltd.

Bull, Bartle. Shanghai Station. 2004. 340p. 26.00 (*0-7867-1314-3*, Carroll & Graf Pubs.) Avalon Publishing Group.

Caldwell, Bo. The Distant Land of My Father: A Novel of Shanghai. 2001. (Illus.). 384p. 23.95 (*0-8118-3240-6*) Chronicle Bks. LLC.

—The Distant Land of My Father: A Novel of Shanghai. l.t. ed. 2003. (Charnwood Large Print Ser.). 496p. 32.50 (*0-7089-9446-6*) Thorpe, F. A. Pubs. GBR. *Dist:* Ulverscroft Large Print Bks., Ltd., Ulverscroft Large Print Canada, Ltd.

Egleton, Clive. In the Red. 1991. 3.99 o.p. (*0-517-07811-2*) Random Hse. Value Publishing.

—In the Red. 1990. 17.95 o.p. (*0-312-04677-4*) St. Martin's Pr.

—In the Red. l.t. ed. 1991. (Ulverscroft Large Print Ser.). 624p. 29.99 o.p. (*0-7089-2461-1*, Ulverscroft) Thorpe, F. A. Pubs. GBR. *Dist:* Ulverscroft Large Print Bks., Ltd., Ulverscroft Large Print Canada, Ltd.

Grayson, George. The Revolutionary's Confession. 2000. 331p. 24.95 (*1-890768-21-9*, Intrigue Pr.) Corvus Publishing.

Harrison, Kathryn. The Binding Chair: or A Visit from the Foot Emancipation Society. l.t. ed. 2000. (Compass Press Large Print Book Ser.). 419p. 26.95 (*1-56895-139-6*, Wheeler Publishing, Inc.) Gale Group.

—The Binding Chair: or A Visit from the Foot Emancipation Society. 2001. 336p. pap. 13.00 (*0-06-093442-5*, Perennial) HarperTrade.

Hui, Wei. Shanghai Baby. Humes, Bruce, tr. 272p. 2002. pap. 13.00 (*0-7434-2157-4*, Washington Square Pr.); 2001. 24.00 (*0-7434-2156-6*, Atria) Simon & Schuster.

—Shanghai Baby. 2001. 272p. pap. 10.00 (*0-7432-2516-3*, Pocket); reprint ed. E-Book 25.00 (*0-7434-2415-8*, Atria) Simon & Schuster.

Ishiguro, Kazuo. When We Were Orphans. E-Book 19.95 (*1-58945-537-1*) Adobe Systems, Inc.

—When We Were Orphans. unabr. ed. 2000. audio 39.95 (*0-694-52384-4*, PH844, HarperAudio) HarperTrade.

—When We Were Orphans. 2001. 352p. reprint ed. pap. 14.00 (*0-375-72440-0*, Vintage) Knopf Publishing Group.

—When We Were Orphans. 2000. 352p. 25.00 (*0-375-41054-6*) Knopf, Alfred A. Inc.

—When We Were Orphans. 2001. E-Book 12.50 (*0-375-41265-4*) Random Hse., Inc.

Jose, Nicholas. The Red Thread: A Love Story. (Illus.). 2002. 256p. pap. 14.95 (*0-8118-3690-8*); 2000. 254p. 24.95 (*0-8118-2951-0*) Chronicle Bks. LLC.

Oakes, Andy. Dragon's Eye. 2004. 460p. 24.95 (*1-58567-495-8*) Overlook Pr., The.

Rotenberg, David. The Shanghai Murders. 1998. 320p. o.p. (*0-312-18661-4*); 24.95 o.p. (*0-312-18175-2*, 853565) St. Martin's Pr. (Saint Martin's Minotaur).

Tarrant, John. China Gold. 1991. 252p. 19.95 (*0-8128-4020-8*, Scarborough Hse.) Madison Bks., Inc.

Xiaolong, Qiu. Death of a Red Heroine: An Inspector Chen Investigation. 2001. 464p. pap. 14.00 (*1-56947-242-4*); 2000. 463p. 25.00 (*1-56947-193-2*) Soho Pr., Inc.

**SHANGRI-LA (IMAGINARY PLACE)—FICTION**

Dalrymple, Alfred J. Murder in the Highest Places. 2nd unabr. ed. 1999. 206p. pap. 8.00 (*0-9673338-1-4*) Dalrymple Bks.

Hilton, James. Lost Horizon. 1976. 20.95 (*0-8488-0284-5*) Amereon, Ltd.

—Lost Horizon. unabr. collector's ed. 1978. (J). audio 42.00 (*0-7366-0144-9*, 1146) Books on Tape, Inc.

—Lost Horizon. 1983. 231p. (ps up). reprint ed. lib. bdg. 28.95 (*0-89966-450-4*) Buccaneer Bks., Inc.

—Lost Horizon. 2004. pap. (*0-06-059452-7*, Perennial) HarperTrade.

—Lost Horizon. 1996. 272p. 24.00 (*0-688-14656-2*); 1934. (Illus.). reprint ed. 13.45 o.p. (*0-688-02007-0*) Morrow/Avon. (Morrow, William & Co.).

—Lost Horizon. 1987. (Radiobook Ser.). audio 4.98 (*0-929541-02-2*) Radiola Co.

—Lost Horizon. 1990. (World's Best Reading Ser.). 191 p. (*0-89577-361-9*) Reader's Digest Assn., Inc., The.

—Lost Horizon. 1988. 240p. mass mkt. 6.99 (*0-671-66427-1*); 1984. (gr. 11 up). mass mkt. 3.50 (*0-671-54148-X*) Simon & Schuster. (Pocket).

—Lost Horizon. 1979. mass mkt. 1.95 (*0-671-83201-8*); 1978. mass mkt. 2.25 (*0-671-49125-3*); 1976. mass mkt. 1.95 (*0-671-48807-4*); 1976. mass mkt. 1.75 (*0-671-48660-8*); 1974. mass mkt. 1.50 (*0-671-48505-9*); 1973. mass mkt. 1.25 (*0-671-78307-6*); 1972. mass mkt. 0.95 (*0-671-47875-3*) Simon & Schuster Children's Publishing. (Simon Pulse).

—Lost Horizon. 2001. audio 49.95 (*1-85496-119-5*, 61195); 1999. audio 49.95 Soundings, Ltd. GBR. *Dist:* Ulverscroft Large Print Bks., Ltd., ISIS Publishing.

—Lost Horizon. unabr. ed. 1993. (Audio Books Ser.). 46.95 o.p. incl. audio Thorndike Pr.

—Lost Horizon. l.t. ed. 1984. (Charnwood Large Print Ser.). 272p. 29.99 o.p. (*0-7089-8170-4*, Charnwood) Thorpe, F. A. Pubs. GBR. *Dist:* Ulverscroft Large Print Bks., Ltd., Ulverscroft Large Print Canada, Ltd.

—Lost Horizon. 1933. 12.04 (*0-606-02843-9*) Turtleback Bks.

**SHANNARA (IMAGINARY PLACE)—FICTION**

Brooks, Terry. Antrax. 2001. E-Book 21.95 (*0-345-44944-4*); (Voyage of the Jerle Shannara Ser.: Bk. 2). (Illus.). 384p. 26.95 (*0-345-39766-5*, Del Rey) Ballantine Bks.

—Antrax. abr. ed. 2001. (Voyage of the Jerle Shannara Ser.: Bk. 2). audio 25.95 (*0-553-52867-X*); audio compact disk 29.95 (*0-553-71455-4*) Random Hse. Audio Publishing Group. (RH Audio).

—The Druid of Shannara. 2002. (Heritage of Shannara Ser.: No. 2). E-Book 7.99 (*1-59061-735-5*) Adobe Systems, Inc.

—The Druid of Shannara. (Heritage of Shannara Ser.: Bk. 2). 1997. pap. 6.99 (*0-345-91131-8*); 1993. mass mkt. 5.99 o.p. (*0-345-01967-9*); 1992. 384p. mass mkt. 7.99 (*0-345-37559-9*) Ballantine Bks. (Del Rey).

—The Druid of Shannara. 1992. (Heritage of Shannara Ser.: Bk. 2). 13.04 (*0-606-01237-0*) Turtleback Bks.

—The Elf Queen of Shannara. 2002. (Heritage of Shannara Ser.: No. 3). E-Book 7.99 (*1-59061-736-3*) Adobe Systems, Inc.

—The Elf Queen of Shannara. (Heritage of Shannara Ser.: Bk. 3). 1997. pap. 6.99 (*0-345-91132-6*); 1993. 368p. mass mkt. 7.99 (*0-345-37558-0*) Ballantine Bks. (Del Rey).

—The Elf Queen of Shannara. abr. ed. 1993. (Heritage of Shannara Ser.: Bk.3). 15.95 o.p. (*1-55800-608-7*, 390708) NewStar Media, Inc.

—The Elf Queen of Shannara. 1994. mass mkt. 5.99 o.p. (*0-517-12801-2*) Random Hse. Value Publishing.

—The Elf Queen of Shannara. 1993. (Heritage of Shannara Ser.: Bk. 3). 13.04 (*0-606-02627-4*) Turtleback Bks.

—The Elfstones of Shannara. 2002. (Shannara Trilogy: No. 2). E-Book 7.99 (*1-59061-732-0*) Adobe Systems, Inc.

—The Elfstones of Shannara. (Shannara Trilogy: Bk. 2). 1997. mass mkt. 6.99 (*0-345-91128-8*, Del Rey); 1996. mass mkt. 6.99 (*0-345-90956-9*, Del Rey); 1985. pap. 9.95 o.s.i (*0-345-33716-6*); 1983. 576p. mass mkt. 7.99 (*0-345-28554-9*, Del Rey); 1982. pap. 4.95 o.p. (*0-345-28555-7*); No. 2. 1982. 23.00 o.p. (*0-345-30253-2*, Del Rey) Ballantine Bks.

—The Elfstones of Shannara. abr. ed. 1999. (Shannara Trilogy: Bk. 2). audio 18.00 (*0-7871-1914-8*, Dove Audio) NewStar Media, Inc.

—The Elfstones of Shannara. abr. ed. 2004. audio 25.95 (*0-7393-0428-3*, Listening Library) Random Hse. Audio Publishing Group.

—The Elfstones of Shannara. 1982. (Shannara Ser.: Bk. 2). 12.09 o.p. (*0-606-03402-1*) Turtleback Bks.

—First King of Shannara. 1997. (Shannara Ser.). 448p. mass mkt. 7.99 (*0-345-39653-7*, Del Rey) Ballantine Bks.

—First King of Shannara. 1997. 14.04 (*0-606-17127-4*) Turtleback Bks.

—The Heritage of Shannara. 2003. 1248p. 35.00 (*0-345-46554-7*, Del Rey) Ballantine Bks.

—The Heritage of Shannara. abr. ed. 1997. audio 39.95 (*0-7871-0246-6*, Dove Audio); Set. 1993. (Heritage of Shannara Ser.: Bks. 1 - 4). 19.95 o.p. (*1-55800-743-1*) NewStar Media, Inc.

—The Heritage of Shannara: The Scions of Shannara, The Druid of Shannara, The Elf Queen of Shannara, & The Talismans of Shannara. 9999. (Heritage of Shannara Ser.: Bks. 1 - 4). 23.92 o.s.i (*0-345-39263-9*) Ballantine Bks.

—Ilse Witch. (Voyage of the Jerle Shannara Ser.: Bk. 1). E-Book 21.50 (*1-930161-99-9*) Adobe Systems, Inc.

—Ilse Witch. 2000. (Voyage of the Jerle Shannara Ser.: Bk. 1). E-Book 22.50 (*0-345-44481-7*, Ballantine Bks.) Ballantine Bks.

—Ilse Witch. abr. ed. 2000. (Voyage of the Jerle Shannara Ser.: Bk. 1). audio 29.95 (*0-553-52765-7*, RH Audio) Random Hse. Audio Publishing Group.

—The Scions of Shannara. 2002. (Heritage of Shannara Ser.: No. 1). E-Book 7.99 (*1-59061-734-7*) Adobe Systems, Inc.

—The Scions of Shannara. (Heritage of Shannara Ser.: Bk. 1). 1997. pap. 6.99 (*0-345-91130-X*, Del Rey); 1991. 432p. mass mkt. 7.99 (*0-345-37074-0*, Del Rey); 1990. mass mkt. 5.95 o.s.i (*0-345-37116-X*) Ballantine Bks.

—The Scions of Shannara. abr. ed. 1993. (Heritage of Shannara Ser.: Bk. 1). 15.95 o.p. (*1-55800-431-9*, 391517) NewStar Media, Inc.

—The Scions of Shannara. 1992. 4.99 o.p. (*0-517-08368-X*) Random Hse. Value Publishing.

—The Scions of Shannara. 1991. (Heritage of Shannara Ser.: Bk. 1). 13.04 (*0-606-01236-2*) Turtleback Bks.

—The Shannara Trilogy: The Sword of Shannara, The Elfstone of Shannara, & Wishsong of Shannara, 3 vols., Set. 1988. (Shannara Trilogy: Bks. 1 - 3 ). pap. 17.97 (*0-345-35833-3*, Del Rey) Ballantine Bks.

—The Sword of Shannara. 1997. (Shannara Trilogy: Bk. 1). mass mkt. 6.99 (*0-345-91127-X*, Del Rey); 1996. (Shannara Trilogy: Bk. 1). mass mkt. 6.99 (*0-345-90957-7*, Del Rey); 1986. (Shannara Trilogy: Bk. 1). pap. 9.95 o.p. (*0-345-33686-0*, Del Rey); 1983. (Shannara Trilogy: Bk. 1). (Illus.). 736p. mass mkt. 7.99 (*0-345-31425-5*, Ballantine Bks.); 1980. mass mkt. 3.50 o.p. (*0-345-29024-0*, Del Rey); 1977. (Shannara Trilogy: Bk. 1). 12.95 o.p. (*0-394-41333-4*) Ballantine Bks.

—The Sword of Shannara. abr. ed. 1984. audio 12.95 (*0-694-50308-8*, SWC 1567, Caedmon) HarperTrade.

—The Sword of Shannara. abr. ed. 1999. (Shannara Trilogy: Bk. 1). audio 18.00 (*0-7871-1913-X*, Dove Audio) NewStar Media, Inc.

—The Sword of Shannara. abr. ed. 2003. audio 25.95 (*0-7393-0426-7*) Random Hse. Audio Publishing Group.

—The Sword of Shannara. 1977. (Shannara Trilogy: Bk. 1). 14.04 (*0-606-01377-6*) Turtleback Bks.

—The Sword of Shannara & The Elfstones of Shannara. E-Book 6.99 (*1-59061-834-3*) Adobe Systems, Inc.

—The Sword of Shannara Trilogy: The Sword of Shannara - The Elfstones of Shannara - The Wishsong of Shannara. unabr. ed. 1993. (Shannara Trilogy: Bks. 1 - 3). audio 19.95 NewStar Media, Inc.

—The Talismans of Shannara. 2002. (Heritage of Shannara Ser.: No. 4). E-Book 7.99 (*1-59061-737-1*) Adobe Systems, Inc.

—The Talismans of Shannara. (Heritage of Shannara Ser.: Bk. 4). 1997. pap. 6.99 (*0-345-91133-4*); 1994. 464p. mass mkt. 7.99 (*0-345-38674-4*) Ballantine Bks. (Del Rey).

—The Talismans of Shannara. abr. ed. 1993. (Heritage of Shannara Ser.: Bk. 4). 16.95 o.p. (*1-55800-747-4*, 391731) NewStar Media, Inc.

—The Wishsong of Shannara. 2002. (Shannara Trilogy: No. 3). E-Book 7.99 (*1-59061-733-9*) Adobe Systems, Inc.

—The Wishsong of Shannara. (Shannara Trilogy: Bk. 3). 1997. mass mkt. 6.99 (*0-345-91129-6*); 1996. mass mkt. 5.99 (*0-345-90959-3*); 1988. 512p. mass mkt. 7.99 (*0-345-35636-5*); 1987. 544p. pap. 9.95 o.p. (*0-345-33687-9*); 1985. 544p. pap. 8.95 o.p. (*0-345-30833-6*); No. 3. 1985. 512p. 23.00 o.p. (*0-345-31823-4*) Ballantine Bks. (Del Rey).

—The Wishsong of Shannara. abr. ed. 1999. (Shannara Trilogy: Bk. 3). audio 18.00 (*0-7871-1915-6*, Dove Audio) NewStar Media, Inc.

—The Wishsong of Shannara. 2003. audio compact disk 14.99 (*0-7393-0430-5*, Listening Library) Random Hse. Audio Publishing Group.

—The Wishsong of Shannara. 1992. (Shannara Trilogy: Bk. 3). 14.04 (*0-606-01232-X*) Turtleback Bks.

**SHILOH (ARK.: IMAGINARY PLACE)—FICTION**

Thoene, Bodie. In My Father's House. 1992. (Shiloh Legacy Ser.: No. 1). 432p. pap. 12.99 (*1-55661-189-7*) Bethany Hse. Pubs.

—In My Father's House. l.t. ed. 1993. (Inspirational Ser.). 626p. pap. 21.95 o.p. (*0-8161-5669-7*, Macmillan Reference USA) Gale Group.

—Say to This Mountain. 1993. (Shiloh Legacy Ser.: Vol. 3). 448p. (J). pap. 12.99 (*1-55661-191-9*) Bethany Hse. Pubs.

—Shiloh Autumn. 1999. (Galway Chronicles Ser.). 324p. pap. text 9.97 (*0-7852-6922-3*) Nelson, Thomas Pubs.

—The Shiloh Legacy, Vols. 1-3. 1993. (Shiloh Legacy Ser.). pap. 38.99 (*1-55661-774-7*, 252774) Bethany Hse. Pubs.

—A Thousand Shall Fall. 1992. (Shiloh Legacy Ser.: Vol. 2). 432p. pap. 12.99 (*1-55661-190-0*) Bethany Hse. Pubs.

—A Thousand Shall Fall. l.t. ed. 1993. (General Ser.). 606p. lib. bdg. 22.95 (*0-8161-5718-9*, Macmillan Reference USA) Gale Group.

Thoene, Bodie & Thoene, Brock. Shiloh Autumn. 1996. 480p. 21.99 o.p. (*0-7852-8066-9*); 24.99 o.p. incl. audio (*0-7852-7273-9*) Nelson, Thomas Inc.

—Shiloh Autumn. 1997. 480p. pap. 14.99 (*0-7852-7134-1*) Nelson, Thomas Pubs.

**SICILY (ITALY)—FICTION**

Alexander, Alfred, ed. & intro. Stories of Sicily. 1975. 208p. 10.95 o.p. (*0-8052-3592-2*, Schocken) Knopf Publishing Group.

Armanno, Venero. The Volcano. 2001. (Illus.). 677p. (*1-74051-053-4*) Knopf, Alfred A. Inc.

Bufalino, Gesualdo. The Plague-Sower. Sartarelli, Stephen, tr. from ITA. 1988. 186p. 22.00 o.p. (*0-941419-12-6*); pap. 13.00 (*0-941419-13-4*) Marsilio Pubs. (Eridanos Library).

Cardella, Lara. Good Girls Don't Wear Trousers. Di Carcaci, Diana, tr. from ITA. 1994. 128p. 16.95 (*1-55970-263-X*) Arcade Publishing, Inc.

Cusumano, Camille. The Last Cannoli: A Novel: A Sicilian American Family Comes of Age Through the Ancient Power of Storytelling. 1999. (Illus.). 237p. per. (*1-881901-20-3*) LEGAS.

Fletcher, David. Confetti for Cortorelli. 1957. 2.75 o.s.i (*0-394-81045-7*) Random Hse., Inc.

Gilman, Dorothy. Mrs. Pollifax & the Second Thief. 1995. 208p. mass mkt. 6.99 (*0-449-14905-6*, Fawcett) Ballantine Bks.

—Mrs. Pollifax & the Second Thief. abr. ed. 1993. audio 16.95 o.p. (*1-56100-351-4*, 1328); audio 57.25 o.p. (*1-56100-161-9*, 954, Unabridged Library Editions); audio 21.95 o.p. (*1-56100-533-9*, 354, Bookcassette) Brilliance Audio.

—Mrs. Pollifax & the Second Thief. 1993. 208p. 20.00 o.s.i (*0-385-47109-2*) Doubleday Publishing.

—Mrs. Pollifax & the Second Thief. l.t. ed. 1994. 228p. lib. bdg. 16.95 o.p. (*0-8161-5918-1*); lib. bdg. 21.95 (*0-8161-5917-3*) Gale Group. (Macmillan Reference USA).

—Mrs. Pollifax & the Second Thief. abr. ed. 2000. audio 7.95 (*1-57815-020-5*, 1005, Media Bks. Audio Publishing) Media Bks., L. L. C.

—Mrs. Pollifax & the Second Thief. unabr. ed. 1993. (Mrs. Pollifax Mystery Ser.: Vol. 10). audio 44.00 (*1-55690-911-X*, 93407E7) Recorded Bks., LLC.

Graves, Robert. Homer's Daughter. 283p. 1987. reprint ed. 14.95 o.p. (*0-89733-058-7*); 1998. pap. 16.00 (*0-89733-059-5*) Academy Chicago Pubs., Ltd.

—Homer's Daughter. unabr. collector's ed. 1986. audio 48.00 (*0-7366-1051-0*, 1979) Books on Tape, Inc.

Hodge, Jane Aiken. Escapade. 1993. 240p. 18.95 o.p. (*0-312-09799-9*) St. Martin's Pr.

Holland, Cecelia. Great Maria. 1987. 528p. pap. 8.95 o.s.i (*0-345-34110-4*) Ballantine Bks.

—Great Maria. 1974. 8.95 o.p. (*0-394-48509-2*, Knopf Bks. for Young Readers) Random Hse. Children's Bks.

—Great Maria. 1993. (Hera Ser.). 519p. pap. 17.00 (*0-939149-84-2*) Soho Pr., Inc.

—Great Maria. 1979. pap. 2.75 o.p. (*0-446-95203-6*) Warner Bks., Inc.

Ker, Madeleine. Fire of the Gods. l.t. ed. 1995. (Nightingale Ser.). 232p. pap. 17.95 (*0-7838-1221-3*, Macmillan Reference USA) Gale Group.

—Fire of the Gods. 1985. mass mkt. (*0-373-10795-1*, Harlequin Bks.) Harlequin Enterprises, Ltd.

Messina, Calogero. St. Giordano: A Sicilian Martyr in Nagasaki. 2002. 160p. pap. (*1-881901-27-0*) LEGAS.

Moore, Christine P. The Virgin Knows. 1995. 320p. 22.95 o.p. (*0-312-13203-4*) St. Martin's Pr.

Pasqualino, Fortunato. The Little Jesus of Sicily. Rozier, Louise, tr. from ITA. 1999. (Illus.). xiv, 90p. 22.00 (*1-55728-572-1*); pap. 16.95 (*1-55728-573-X*) Univ. of Arkansas Pr.

Prior, Lily. La Cucina: A Novel of Rapture. 2000. 288p. 24.00 (*0-06-019538-X*) HarperCollins Pubs.

—La Cucina: A Novel of Rapture. 2001. 288p. pap. 13.00 (*0-06-095369-1*, Ecco) HarperTrade.

Puzo, Mario. The Sicilian. 1985. 416p. mass mkt. 6.99 o.s.i (*0-553-25282-8*) Bantam Bks.

—The Sicilian. unabr. ed. 1985. audio 19.95 (*0-930435-13-3*, 357, Bookcassette); audio 73.25 o.p. (*1-56100-008-6*, 1042, Unabridged Library Editions) Brilliance Audio.

—The Sicilian. l.t. ed. 1985. (Special Editions Ser.). 560p. 19.95 o.p. (*0-8161-3837-0*, Macmillan Reference USA) Gale Group.

—The Sicilian. unabr. ed. 1992. audio 91.00 (*1-55690-730-3*, 92230E7) Recorded Bks., LLC.

—The Sicilian. 1984. 448p. 17.45 o.p. (*0-671-43564-7*, Simon & Schuster) Simon & Schuster.

—The Sicilian. l.t. ed. 1986. (Charnwood Large Print Ser.). 574p. 29.99 o.p. (*0-7089-8317-0*, Charnwood) Thorpe, F. A. Pubs. GBR. *Dist:* Ulverscroft Large Print Bks., Ltd., Ulverscroft Large Print Canada, Ltd.

Radcliffe, Ann. A Sicilian Romance. 1972. (Gothic Novels Ser.). reprint ed. 46.95 (*0-405-00809-0*) Ayer Co. Pubs., Inc.

—A Sicilian Romance. Milbank, Alison, ed. (Oxford World's Classics Ser.). 1999. 256p. pap. 10.95 (*0-19-283666-8*); 1993. 244p. (C). pap. 8.95 o.p. (*0-19-282212-8*) Oxford Univ. Pr., Inc.

—A Sicilian Romance, 1792, 2 vols. in 1. 2003. (Revolution & Romanticism Ser.). 498p. (*1-85477-190-6*) Woodstock Books.

Rotundi, Cesar. The Garden of Persephone. 1982. 340p. 19.95 o.p. (*0-312-31682-8*) St. Martin's Pr.

Timpanelli, Gioia. Sometimes the Soul: Two Novellas of Sicily. 1999. 192p. pap. 11.95 (*0-375-70722-0*) Knopf, Alfred A. Inc.

—Sometimes the Soul: Two Novellas of Sicily. 1998. 192p. 23.00 (*0-393-02744-9*) Norton, W. W. & Co., Inc.

Tosches, Nick. In the Hand of Dante. 384p. 2002. 24.95 (*0-316-89524-5*); 2003. reprint ed. pap. 13.95 (*0-316-73564-7*, Back Bay) Little Brown & Co.

Valens, Amy. Danilo the Fruit Man. (Illus.). 16p. (J). 3.98 o.p. (*0-8317-9395-3*) Smithmark Pubs., Inc.

Vansittart, Peter. Choice of Murder. 1993. 216p. 30.00 (*0-7206-0832-5*) Dufour Editions, Inc.

—A Choice of Murder. 1992. 216p. pap. 29.95 (*0-7206-0851-1*) Owen, Peter Ltd. GBR. *Dist:* Dufour Editions, Inc.

Verga, Giovanni. Little Novels of Sicily. Lawrence, D. H., tr. 1975. 226p. reprint ed. lib. bdg. 22.50 o.p. (*0-8371-8199-2*, VENS, Greenwood Pr.) Greenwood Publishing Group, Inc.

—Little Novels of Sicily. Lawrence, D. H., tr. from ITA. 3rd ed. 2000. (Steerforth Italia Ser.). 200p. pap. 12.00 (*1-883642-54-X*) Steerforth Pr.

Vittorini, Elio. Conversations in Sicily. Mason, Alane Salierno, tr. from ITA. 2000. (Classics Ser.). xv, 182p. pap. 12.95 (*0-8112-1455-9*) New Directions Publishing Corp.

**SINGAPORE—FICTION**

Barber, Noel. Tanamera. l.t. ed. 1992. 16.95 o.p. (*0-7927-0564-5*); 1991. 22.95 o.p. (*0-7927-0563-7*, ED004) BBC Audiobooks America.

—Tanamera. 1982. 688p. 3.95 o.p. (*0-553-20921-3*) Bantam Bks.

Cheong, Fiona. The Scent of the Gods. 1993. 256p. pap. 8.95 o.p. (*0-393-31012-4*) Norton, W. W. & Co., Inc.

—The Scent of the Gods: A Novel. 1991. 224p. 19.95 o.p. (*0-393-03024-5*) Norton, W. W. & Co., Inc.

—Shadow Theatre: A Novel. 2003. 256p. pap. 12.00 (*1-56947-319-6*); 2002. 304p. 24.00 (*1-56947-287-4*) Soho Pr., Inc.

Cher, Ming. Spider Boys. 1995. 22.00 o.p. (*0-688-12858-0*, Morrow, William & Co.) Morrow/Avon.

Chua, Rebecca. The Newspaper Editor & Other Stories. 1982. (Writing in Asia Ser.). vi, 180p. (Orig.). pap. text 5.50 o.p. (*9971-64-031-7*, 00266) Heinemann.

Drummond, Emma. Some Far Elusive Dawn. 1990. 18.95 o.p. (*0-312-05518-8*) St. Martin's Pr.

Farrell, J. G. Singapore Grip. 1986. 455p. pap. 4.95 o.p. (*0-88184-124-2*, Carroll & Graf Pubs.) Avalon Publishing Group.

—The Singapore Grip. 1980. 2.75 o.p. (*0-425-04503-X*) Berkley Publishing Group.

—The Singapore Grip. 1979. 11.95 o.p. (*0-394-50483-6*, Knopf Bks. for Young Readers) Random Hse. Children's Bks.

Kok, Marilyn. On Assignment. 1998. (Palisades Pure Romance Ser.). 266p. pap. 9.99 o.s.i (*1-57673-279-7*, Palisades) Multnomah Pubs., Inc.

—On Assignment. l.t. ed. 1999. (Christian Fiction Ser.). 383p. 24.95 (*0-7862-1966-1*) Thorndike Pr.

Lim, Catherine. The Bondmaid. 1997. 384p. 24.95 (*0-87951-790-5*) Overlook Pr., The.

—The Bondmaid. 1998. pap. (*0-446-67475-3*); 368p. mass mkt. 6.99 (*0-446-60734-7*) Warner Bks., Inc.

Loh, Vyvyane. Breaking the Tongue. 2004. 448p. text 24.95 (*0-393-05792-5*) Norton, W. W. & Co., Inc.

Overgard, William. The Man from Raffles: A Novel. 1991. 352p. 19.95 o.p. (*0-671-70511-3*, Simon & Schuster) Simon & Schuster.

Simon, Frank. The Raptor Virus: A Novel. 2001. vii, 344p. pap. 12.99 (*0-8054-2339-7*) Broadman & Holman Pubs.

Straub, Peter. Koko. 1988. 19.95 o.p. (*0-525-24660-6*, Dutton) Dutton/Plume.

—Koko. 1989. 608p. mass mkt. 7.99 (*0-451-16214-5*, 001, Signet Bks.) NAL.

—Koko. 1990. 4.99 o.p. (*0-517-05233-4*) Random Hse. Value Publishing.

—Koko. 1999. pap. 9.98 (*0-671-04461-3*); 1988. audio 14.95 (*0-671-65239-7*) Simon & Schuster Audio. (Simon & Schuster Audioworks).

Tan, Hwee Hwee. Foreign Bodies. 1999. 278p. 24.00 (*0-89255-236-0*) Persea Bks., Inc.

—Foreign Bodies. 2000. 304p. pap. 12.95 (*0-671-04170-3*, Washington Square Pr.) Simon & Schuster.

Yeo, Robert, ed. Singular Stories, Vol. One: Tales from Singapore. 1993. 20.00 o.p. (*0-89410-757-7*, Three Continents) Rienner, Lynne Pubs., Inc.

**SKOLIAN EMPIRE (IMAGINARY PLACE)—FICTION**

Asaro, Catherine. Ascendant Sun. 2000. (Management & Leadership in Education Ser.). (Illus.). 380p. 24.95 (*0-312-86824-3*, Tor Bks.) Doherty, Tom Assocs., LLC.

—Catch the Lightning. 1997. 320p. pap. 6.99 (*0-8125-5102-8*); 1996. 496p. 24.95 o.p. (*0-312-86043-9*) Doherty, Tom Assocs., LLC. (Tor Bks.).

—The Last Hawk. (Tor Science Fiction Ser.). 1998. (Illus.). 463p. pap. 7.99 (*0-8125-5110-9*); 1997. 448p. 25.95 o.p. (*0-312-86044-7*) Doherty, Tom Assocs., LLC. (Tor Bks.).

—Primary Inversion. 1996. 369p. pap. 6.99 (*0-8125-5023-4*); 1995. 320p. 14.30 o.p. (*0-312-85764-0*) Doherty, Tom Assocs., LLC. (Tor Bks.).

—The Radiant Seas. (Saga of the Skolian Empire Ser.). (Illus.). 1999. 512p. mass mkt. 6.99 (*0-8125-8036-2*); 1998. 463p. 26.95 (*0-312-86714-X*) Doherty, Tom Assocs., LLC. (Tor Bks.).

**SOUTH AFRICA—FICTION**

Abrahams, Lionel. Celibacy of Felix Greenspan. 1993. 181p. reprint ed. 21.95 (*0-89733-396-9*) Academy Chicago Pubs., Ltd.

Adams, Arthur. Quimby. 1988. 304p. 17.95 o.p. (*0-312-01504-6*) St. Martin's Pr.

Allinson, Sidney. Kruger's Gold: A Novel of the Anglo-Boer War. 2001. 298p. E-Book 8.00 (*0-7388-6587-7*); (Illus.). pap. 21.99 (*0-7388-6586-9*); (Illus.). text 31.99 (*0-7388-6585-0*) Xlibris Corp.

Badsha, Omar. To Dream Again: Imperial Ghetto - South African Images. 2002. (Illus.). 296p. pap. 10.95 (*0-7957-0137-3*) Kwela Bks. ZAF. *Dist:* Independent Pubs. Group.

Behr, Mark. The Smell of Apples. 1995. 200p. pap. o.s.i (*0-349-10756-4*) Little Brown & Co.

—The Smell of Apples. 1997. 200p. pap. 12.00 (*0-312-15209-4*) Picador.

—The Smell of Apples. 1995. 224p. 21.95 o.p. (*0-312-13604-8*) St. Martin's Pr.

Belchers, Glynnis. A Telling Time. 2003. 211p. pap. 19.95 (*1-59129-591-2*) PublishAmerica, Inc.

Bloom, Harry. Transvaal Episode. 24.95 (*0-8488-0918-1*) Amereon, Ltd.

—Transvaal Episode. 1981. 363p. reprint ed. 28.00 (*0-933256-24-8*); pap. 20.00 (*0-933256-25-6*) Second Chance Pr.

Bond, Larry. Vortex: A Novel. unabr. ed. 1991. Pt. 1. audio 80.00 (*0-7366-2031-1*, 2845-A); Pt. 2. audio 80.00; Pts. 1 & 2. audio 100.00 o.p. Books on Tape, Inc.

—Vortex: A Novel, Set. abr. ed. 1999. audio 15.95 (*0-671-73486-5*, 391860, Simon & Schuster Audioworks) Simon & Schuster Audio.

—Vortex: A Novel. 1992. 928p. mass mkt. 7.99 (*0-446-36304-9*); 1991. 21.95 o.p. (*0-446-51566-3*) Warner Bks., Inc.

Bosman, Herman Charles & MacKenzie, Craig. Mafeking Road & Other Stories. 1998. (Illus.). (*0-7981-3902-1*) Human & Rousseau.

Brasfield, Lynette. Nature Lessons: A Novel. 2003. 288p. 23.95 (*0-312-31034-X*) St. Martin's Pr.

Brink. Rights of Desire. 2004. pap. (*0-15-600749-5*, Harvest Bks.) Harcourt Trade Pubs.

Brink, André. An Act of Terror. 1993. pap. 14.00 o.s.i (*0-679-74429-0*, Vintage) Knopf Publishing Group.

—An Act of Terror. 1992. 848p. 25.00 o.p. (*0-671-74858-0*) Summit Bks.

—Cape of Storms: The First Life of Adamastor. 1993. 141p. 16.00 o.p. (*0-671-79907-X*, Simon & Schuster) Simon & Schuster.

—A Chain of Voices. 1983. 528p. pap. 23.00 o.s.i (*0-14-006538-5*, Penguin Bks.) Penguin Group (USA) Inc.

—The Devil's Valley. 1999. 416p. 24.00 o.s.i (*0-15-100440-4*) Harcourt Trade Pubs.

—A Dry White Season. 1984. 432p. 13.95 (*0-14-006890-2*) Viking Penguin.

—Imaginings of Sand. 1999. 432p. pap. 14.00 (*0-15-600658-8*, Harvest Bks.); 1996. 368p. 24.00 o.s.i (*0-15-100224-X*) Harcourt Trade Pubs.

—An Instant in the Wind. 1985. (Fiction Ser.). 256p. pap. 6.95 o.p. (*0-14-008014-7*, Penguin Bks.) Viking Penguin.

—The Rights of Desire. 2001. 320p. 25.00 (*0-15-100654-7*) Harcourt Trade Pubs.

—Rumors of Rain. 1984. 448p. pap. 6.95 o.p. (*0-14-006891-0*, Penguin Bks.) Viking Penguin.

Brown, James A. The Ridge of Gold. 1986. 336p. 17.95 o.p. (*0-312-68231-X*) St. Martin's Pr.

Buchan, John. Prester John. unabr. ed. 1994. audio 44.95 (*0-7861-0744-8*, 892516) Blackstone Audio Bks., Inc.

—Prester John. 1994. (Oxford World's Classics Ser.). (Illus.). 256p. pap. 8.95 o.p. (*0-19-282936-X*) Oxford Univ. Pr., Inc.

—Prester John. 1988. reprint ed. lib. bdg. 49.00 (*0-7812-0160-8*) Reprint Services Corp.

—Prester John. 1970. (Illus.). 65.00 (*0-403-00537-X*) Scholarly Pr., Inc.

Burgess, Yvonne. Say a Little Mantra for Me. 2nd ed. 1995. (Ravan Writers Ser.). 166p. reprint ed. pap. text 12.95 (*0-86975-467-X*) Ravan Pr. ZMB. *Dist:* Ohio Univ. Pr.

Calhoun, Tom. Africa's Rose: A Novel. 1999. 244p. pap. 21.99 (*0-7388-0549-1*); text 31.99 (*0-7388-0548-3*) Xlibris Corp.

Carter, Rosemary. Sweet Impostor. l.t. ed. 1991. 17.95 o.p. (*0-7451-8087-6*, AH0147); pap. 15.95 o.p. (*0-7927-0567-X*, AS0183) BBC Audiobooks America.

Cavanaugh, Jack. The Pride & the Passion: A Determined People Forge a New Destiny in South Africa. 1996. (African Covenant Ser.: No. 1). pap. 10.99 o.p. (*0-8024-0862-1*, 257) Moody Pr.

—Quest for the Promised Land: Oppressed by British Rule, the Van der Kemps Cross a Hostile Wilderness to Find a Home. 1997. (African Covenant Ser.: No. 2). 288p. pap. 10.99 o.p. (*0-8024-0863-X*, 261) Moody Pr.

Chapman, Michael, ed. The Drum Decade. 1990. 256p. pap. 19.95 (*0-86980-694-7*) Univ. of Natal Pr. ZAF. *Dist:* International Specialized Bk. Services.

Chase-Riboud, Barbara. Hottentot Venus: A Novel. 2003. 336p. 24.00 (*0-385-50856-5*) Doubleday Publishing.

Cloete, Stuart. Rags of Glory. 1973. pap. 1.50 o.p. (*0-380-01516-1*, 15792, Avon Bks.) Morrow/Avon.

Coetzee, J. M. Age of Iron. 1992. pap. 12.00 o.s.i (*0-679-73292-6*) McKay, David Co., Inc.

—Age of Iron. 1998. 208p. 12.95 (*0-14-027565-7*) Viking Penguin.

—Disgrace. 2000. 224p. pap. 13.00 (*0-14-029640-9*) Penguin Group (USA) Inc.

—Disgrace. 1999. 224p. 23.95 o.s.i (*0-670-88731-5*, Viking) Viking Penguin.

—Disgrace. 2000. 608p. pap. (*0-09-928952-0*) Vintage UK GBR. *Dist:* Random Hse., Inc.

—Dusklands. 1985. (Fiction Ser.). 144p. pap. 9.95 o.p. (*0-14-007114-8*, Penguin Bks.) Viking Penguin.

—Life & Times of Michael K. 1985. 192p. 13.00 (*0-14-007448-1*); 1984. 175p. 13.95 o.p. (*0-670-42789-6*) Viking Penguin.

Conyngham, John. The Arrowing of the Cane. 1989. 154p. pap. 7.95 o.p. (*0-671-68755-7*, Fireside) Simon & Schuster.

Coovadia, Imraan. The Wedding. 2001. 320p. 23.00 (*0-312-27219-7*) Picador.

—The Wedding. E-Book 10.00 (*0-312-70343-0*) St. Martin's Pr.

Courtenay, Bryce. The Power of One. 1996. 528p. pap. 14.95 (*0-345-41005-X*); 1990. 544p. mass mkt. 6.99 o.s.i (*0-345-35992-5*); 1989. mass mkt. 5.95 o.p. (*0-345-01848-6*) Ballantine Bks.

—Tandia. 1992. mass mkt. 6.99 o.s.i (*0-316-15840-2*); (*0-316-15828-3*) Little Brown & Co.

Crail, Archie. The Bonus Deal. 1993. 136p. pap. 10.95 (*1-55050-031-7*) Coteau Bks. CAN. *Dist:* General Distribution Services, Inc.

Crane, John Kenny. The Legacy of Ladysmith. unabr. ed. 1989. audio 91.00 (*1-55690-307-3*, 89190E7) Recorded Bks., LLC.

—The Legacy of Ladysmith. 1986. 17.45 o.p. (*0-671-60586-0*, Simon & Schuster) Simon & Schuster.

—The Legacy of Ladysmith. 1987. 400p. pap. 4.50 o.p. (*0-14-010064-4*, Penguin Bks.) Viking Penguin.

Cry the Beloved Country: Readers Group Guide. 1996. pap. (*0-684-00198-5*, Scribner Paper Fiction) Simon & Schuster.

Dangor, Achmat. Kafka's Curse: A Novel. 240p. 2000. pap. 12.00 o.s.i (*0-375-70462-0*, Vintage); 1999. 22.00 o.s.i (*0-375-40510-0*, Pantheon) Knopf Publishing Group.

—Kafka's Curse: A Novella & Three Other Stories. 1997. (Illus.). (*0-7957-0054-7*) Kwela Bks.

Denton, Kit. The Breaker. 1998. audio; 2001. audio (*1-86340-775-8*, 571129) Bolinda Publishing Pty, Ltd.

—The Breaker. 1982. reprint ed. mass mkt. 3.50 o.s.i (*0-671-44762-9*, Pocket) Simon & Schuster.

—The Breaker. 1981. 288p. 11.95 o.p. (*0-312-09517-1*) St. Martin's Pr.

DeSoto, Lewis. A Blade of Grass: A Novel. 2003. 400p. 24.95 (*0-06-055426-6*, Ecco) HarperTrade.

Devine, Thea. Bliss River. 2002. 384p. pap. 14.00 (*1-57566-801-7*) Kensington Publishing Corp.

Drummond, Emma. The Burning Land. l.t. ed. 1987. 688p. 17.95 o.p. (*0-7089-8379-0*, Charnwood) Thorpe, F. A. Pubs. GBR. *Dist:* Ulverscroft Large Print Bks., Ltd.

—A Captive Freedom. 1987. 320p. 17.95 o.p. (*0-312-00575-X*) St. Martin's Pr.

—A Distant Hero. 1997. 432p. 24.95 o.p. (*0-312-17177-3*) St. Martin's Pr.

Ebersohn, Wessel. Closed Circle. 1992. 224p. 23.95 o.p. (*0-575-04848-4*) Gollancz, Victor GBR. *Dist:* Trafalgar Square.

—Divide the Night. 1982. 224p. pap. 2.95 o.p. (*0-394-70810-5*, Vintage); 1981. 10.95 o.p. (*0-394-52076-9*, Pantheon) Knopf Publishing Group.

Eprile, Tony. Temporary Sojourner & Other South African Stories. 1989. 19.95 o.s.i (*0-671-68205-9*, Simon & Schuster); pap. 8.95 o.p. (*0-671-64596-X*, Fireside) Simon & Schuster.

Essop, Ahmed. Hajji Musa & the Hindu Fire-Walker. 1988. (Readers International Ser.). 280p. (Orig.). 16.95 (*0-930523-51-2*); pap. 8.95 (*0-930523-52-0*) Readers International.

Florman, Samuel C. The Aftermath: A Novel of Survival. (Illus.). 336p. 2003. pap. 13.95 (*0-312-31112-5*, Saint Martin's Griffin); 2001. 24.95 (*0-312-26652-9*) St. Martin's Pr.

Foden, Giles. The Last King of Scotland. 1999. 352p. pap. 13.00 (*0-375-70331-4*); 1998. 336p. 25.00 o.s.i (*0-375-40360-4*) Knopf, Alfred A. Inc.

Francis, Dick. Smokescreen. l.t. ed. 1993. 19.95 o.p. (*0-7927-1664-7*); 1993. pap. 17.95 o.p. (*0-7927-1663-9*); 1995. audio 54.95 (*0-7451-6832-9*, CAB 486) BBC Audiobooks America.

—Smokescreen. 1993. 272p. mass mkt. 6.99 (*0-449-22111-3*, Fawcett) Ballantine Bks.

—Smokescreen. unabr. ed. 1999. audio 32.95 (*0-7861-1514-9*, 2364) Blackstone Audio Bks., Inc.

—Smokescreen. unabr. ed. 1994. audio 42.00 (*0-7366-2838-X*, 3546) Books on Tape, Inc.

—Smokescreen. unabr. ed. 2000. audio 49.95 Chivers Audio Bks. GBR. *Dist:* BBC Audiobooks America.

—Smokescreen. 1973. (Harper Novel of Suspense Ser.). 224p. 8.95 o.p. (*0-06-011334-0*) HarperCollins Pubs.

—Smokescreen. 1990. audio 15.95; audio 15.95 o.p. (*1-55994-130-8*, CPN 2130) HarperTrade. (Harper-Audio).

—Smokescreen. unabr. ed. 1999. audio 32.95 Highsmith Inc.

—Smokescreen. abr. ed. 2000. audio 7.95 (*1-57815-049-3*, 1046, Media Bks. Audio Publishing) Media Bks., L. L. C.

—Smokescreen. unabr. ed. 2000. audio 44.00 (*0-7887-0231-9*, 94456E7) Recorded Bks., LLC.

—Smokescreen. 1990. mass mkt. 4.95 (*0-671-70470-2*); 1984. 224p. mass mkt. 3.50 (*0-671-50737-0*); 1982. mass mkt. 2.95 o.s.i (*0-671-45911-2*) Simon & Schuster. (Pocket).

—Smokescreen. l.t. ed. 1978. 12.00 o.p. (*0-7089-0126-3*, Ulverscroft) Thorpe, F. A. Pubs. GBR. *Dist:* Ulverscroft Large Print Bks., Ltd.

Freed, Lynn. The Bungalow. 1999. 240p. reprint ed. pap. 14.00 (*1-885266-76-6*) Story Line Pr.

—The Bungalow: A Novel. 1993. 237p. 21.00 (*0-671-75587-0*, Simon & Schuster) Simon & Schuster.

—Home Ground. 1986. 273p. (*0-434-27170-5*, Butterworth-Heinemann) Elsevier Science & Technology Bks.

—Home Ground. 2nd ed. 1999. 288p. reprint ed. pap. 14.00 (*1-885266-71-5*) Story Line Pr.

—Home Ground. 1986. 16.45 o.p. (*0-671-61965-9*) Summit Bks.

—Home Ground. 1987. 288p. pap. 7.95 o.p. (*0-14-008948-9*, Penguin Bks.) Viking Penguin.

—The Mirror. 1999. (Illus.). 256p. pap. 13.95 (*0-345-42689-4*) Ballantine Bks.

Fugard, Athol. Tsotsi. 1980. 168p. 8.95 o.p. (*0-394-51384-3*) Random Hse., Inc.

Fugard, Sheila. A Revolutionary Woman. 1985. 160p. 14.95 o.p. (*0-8076-1127-1*) Braziller, George Inc.

Galgut, Damon. The Good Doctor. 2003. 224p. 23.00 (*0-8021-1764-3*, Grove Pr.) Grove/Atlantic, Inc.

Godfrey, Peter. The Newtonian Egg & Other Cases of Rolf le Roux. 2002. 25.00 net. (*1-885941-68-4*); pap. 15.00 net. (*1-885941-69-2*) Crippen & Landru, Pubs.

Gool, Reshard. Cape Town Coolie. 1990. (African Writers Ser.). 185p. (Orig.). (C). pap. 7.95 (*0-435-90568-6*, 90568) Heinemann.

—Cape Town Coolie: A Novel. 1989. pap. text (*0-920661-09-2*) TSAR Pubns.

Gordimer, Nadine. Burger's Daughter. 2015. 10.95 o.p. (*0-670-19475-1*); 1980. 368p. 13.95 (*0-14-005593-2*) Viking Penguin.

—The House Gun. 1998. 294p. 24.00 (*0-374-17307-9*) Farrar, Straus & Giroux.

—The House Gun. l.t. ed. 1998. 26.95 o.p. (*1-56895-615-0*, Wheeler Publishing, Inc.) Gale Group.

—The House Gun. 1999. 304p. 14.00 (*0-14-027820-6*) Viking Penguin.

—July's People. 1991. pap. text 22.25 (*0-582-06011-7*) Addison-Wesley Longman, Ltd. GBR. *Dist:* Trans-Atlantic Pubns., Inc.

—July's People. l.t. ed. 1992. 18.95 o.p. (*0-7927-1299-4*); pap. 16.95 o.p. (*0-7927-1298-6*) BBC Audiobooks America.

—July's People. unabr. ed. 1993. audio 32.95 (*0-7861-0412-0*, 1364) Blackstone Audio Bks., Inc.

—July's People. 2015. 192p. 10.95 o.p. (*0-670-41048-9*); 1982. 176p. 13.00 (*0-14-006140-1*) Viking Penguin.

—Jump & Other Stories. 1991. 257p. 20.00 o.s.i (*0-374-18055-5*) Farrar, Straus & Giroux.

—Jump & Other Stories. l.t. ed. 1992. (General Ser.). 306p. 20.95 o.p. (*0-8161-5424-4*, Macmillan Reference USA) Gale Group.

—Jump & Other Stories. 1992. 272p. reprint ed. pap. 14.00 (*0-14-016534-7*, Penguin Bks.) Penguin Group (USA) Inc.
—Lifetimes under Apartheid. 1986. (Illus.). 115p. 29.95 o.s.i (*0-394-55406-X*) Knopf, Alfred A. Inc.
—Loot. 2003. 256p. 23.00 (*0-374-19090-9*) Farrar, Straus & Giroux.
—My Son's Story. 1990. 277p. 19.95 o.s.i (*0-374-21751-3*) Farrar, Straus & Giroux.
—My Son's Story. 1991. 292p. reprint ed. 12.95 (*0-14-015975-4*) Viking Penguin.
—None to Accompany Me. unabr. ed. 1994. audio 23.95 o.p. (*1-56100-600-9*, 197, Bookcassette); audio 73.25 o.p. (*1-56100-225-9*, 965, Unabridged Library Editions) Brilliance Audio.
—None to Accompany Me. 1996. (*0-14-771180-0*); 1995. 336p. pap. 15.00 o.s.i (*0-14-025039-5*, Penguin Bks.) Penguin Group (USA) Inc.
—The Pickup: A Novel. 2001. 224p. 24.00 (*0-374-23210-5*) Farrar, Straus & Giroux.
—The Pickup: A Novel. l.t. ed. 2002. 390p. 29.95 (*0-7862-3848-8*) Gale Group.
—The Pickup: A Novel. 2002. 288p. pap. 14.00 (*0-14-200142-2*) Penguin Group (USA) Inc.
—Selected Stories. 1976. 381p. 11.95 o.p. (*0-670-63197-3*) Viking Penguin.
—Six Feet of the Country. 1986. 112p. pap. 13.00 (*0-14-006559-8*, Penguin Bks.) Penguin Group (USA) Inc.
—A Soldier's Embrace. 1982. 144p. pap. 8.00 o.p. (*0-14-005925-3*, Penguin Bks.) Viking Penguin.
—Something Out There. 1984. 15.95 o.p. (*0-670-65660-7*) Viking Penguin.
—Sport of Nature. l.t. ed. 1988. (Mainstream Ser.). 656p. reprint ed. 18.95 o.p. (*1-85089-228-8*) ISIS Large Print Bks. GBR. *Dist:* Transaction Pubs.
—Sport of Nature. 1987. (*0-224-02447-7*) Random Hse. UK, Ltd. GBR. *Dist:* Trafalgar Square.
—Sport of Nature. 1988. 368p. pap. 12.95 o.s.i (*0-14-008470-3*, Penguin Bks.) Viking Penguin.
—Why Haven't You Written? Selected Stories, 1950-1970. 1993. 240p. pap. 11.00 o.s.i (*0-14-017657-8*, Penguin Bks.) Penguin Group (USA) Inc.
Graham, Mark. The Missing Sixth. 1992. 22.95 (*0-15-160576-9*) Harcourt Trade Pubs.
Gray, Stephen. War Child. 2001. 256p. pap. 14.95 (*1-897959-01-X*) Serif GBR. *Dist:* Interlink Publishing Group, Inc.
Haggard, H. Rider. King Solomon's Mines. Date not set. reprint ed. lib. bdg. 20.95 (*0-89190-703-3*, American Reprint Co.) Amereon, Ltd.
—King Solomon's Mines. Kay, Marilyn, ed. abr. ed. 1987. pap. 12.95 incl. audio (*1-882071-12-3*, 014) B&B Audio, Inc.
—King Solomon's Mines. unabr. ed. 2000. audio compact disk 56.00 (*0-7861-9882-6*, z2575); audio 44.95 (*0-7861-0610-7*, 2575) Blackstone Audio Bks., Inc.
—King Solomon's Mines. unabr. collector's ed. 1984. (J). audio 48.00 (*0-7366-0928-8*, 1872) Books on Tape, Inc.
—King Solomon's Mines. 1976. reprint ed. lib. bdg. 19.95 (*0-89968-513-7*) Buccaneer Bks., Inc.
—King Solomon's Mines. l.t. ed. 1986. (Mainstream Ser.). (Illus.). xi, 317p. 15.95 o.p. (*1-85089-063-3*) ISIS Large Print Bks. GBR. *Dist:* Transaction Pubs.
—King Solomon's Mines. 1989. audio 35.00 Jimcin Recordings.
—King Solomon's Mines. l.t. ed. 1998. (Large Print Heritage Ser.). 365p. lib. bdg. 33.95 (*1-58118-033-0*, 22014) LRS.
—King Solomon's Mines. 1981. (English As a Second Language Bk.). pap. text 5.95 o.p. (*0-582-53502-6*, 74101) Longman Publishing Group.
—King Solomon's Mines. l.t. ed. (Large Print Ser.). 1992. 382p. lib. bdg. 26.00 (*0-939495-49-X*); 1998. 240p. reprint ed. lib. bdg. 25.00 (*1-58287-044-6*) North Bks.
—King Solomon's Mines. Butts, Dennis, ed. & intro. by. 1998. (Oxford World's Classics Ser.). (Illus.). 368p. pap. 9.95 (*0-19-283485-1*) Oxford Univ. Pr., Inc.
—King Solomon's Mines. Butts, Dennis, ed. 1990. (Oxford World's Classics Ser.). (Illus.). 366p. pap. 5.95 o.p. (*0-19-282204-7*) Oxford Univ. Pr., Inc.
—King Solomon's Mines. 1988. pap. 4.95 o.p. (*0-19-581013-9*) Oxford Univ. Pr., Inc.
—King Solomon's Mines. 1999. (Gateway Movie Classics Ser.). 382p. pap. 14.95 (*0-89526-329-7*, Gateway Editions) Regnery Publishing, Inc., An Eagle Publishing Co.
—King Solomon's Mines. 1998. (Children's Classics). 224p. pap. 3.95 (*1-85326-105-X*, 105XWW) Wordsworth Editions, Ltd. GBR. *Dist:* Advanced Global Distribution Services.
Hansen, Brooks. The Chess Garden: Or, the Twilight Letters of Gustav Uyterhoeven. 1996. (Illus.). 480p. reprint ed. 16.00 (*1-57322-563-0*, Riverhead Trade (Paperbacks)) Berkley Publishing Group.
—The Chess Garden: Or, the Twilight Letters of Gustav Uyterhoeven. 1995. (Illus.). 496p. 23.00 o.p. (*0-374-16015-5*) Farrar, Straus & Giroux.
—Chess Garden Readers. 1995. pap. (*0-374-99817-5*) Farrar, Straus & Giroux.
Harries, Ann. Manly Pursuits. 2000. 339p. pap. 13.95 (*1-58234-073-0*); 1999. 24.95 (*1-58234-019-6*) Bloomsbury Publishing.
Havermann, Ernst. Bloodsong & Other Stories of South Africa. 1987. 13.95 o.p. (*0-395-43296-0*) Houghton Mifflin Co.
Head, Bessie. The Cardinals. 1995. (African Writers Ser.). 141p. pap. 10.95 (*0-435-90967-3*, 90967) Heinemann.
Hirson, Denis, ed. South African Short Stories. 1994. (African Writers Ser.). 300p. pap. 10.95 (*0-435-90672-0*, 90672, African Writers Series) Heinemann.
Hodge, Norman, ed. To Kill a Man's Pride & Other Stories from Southern Africa. 1984. 226p. (C). pap. text 14.95 (*0-86975-146-8*) Ravan Pr. ZMB. *Dist:* Ohio Univ. Pr.
Jacobs, Rayda. Middle Children. 1994. 250p. pap. text 12.95 (*0-929005-59-7*) Second Story Pr. CAN. *Dist:* LPC/InBook.
Jardin, Martine. Yesterday's Tears, Tomorrow's Pearls. 2001. pap. (*1-59109-167-5*, PO 00006) Zumaya Pubns.
Jones, J. D. The Buchan Papers. 1997. 192p. 21.95 o.p. (*0-312-15071-7*, Saint Martin's Minotaur) St. Martin's Pr.
Jooste, Pamela. Frieda & Min. 2001. 348p. pap. 13.00 (*0-552-99758-7*) Transworld Publishers Ltd. GBR. *Dist:* Trafalgar Square.
—People Like Ourselves. 2003. 329p. pap. 19.95 (*0-385-60540-4*) Random Hse. UK, Ltd. GBR. *Dist:* Trafalgar Square.
—People Like Ourselves. 2003. 318p. 24.95 (*0-385-60148-4*) Transworld Publishers Ltd. GBR. *Dist:* Trafalgar Square.
Joubert, Elsa. Poppie Nongena. 1986. 15.95 o.p. (*0-393-02242-0*) Norton, W. W. & Co., Inc.
—Poppie Nongena. 1990. 3.99 o.p. (*0-517-05163-X*) Random Hse. Value Publishing.
—Poppie Nongena: A Novel of South Africa. 1987. 368p. pap. 8.95 o.p. (*0-8050-0230-8*, Owl Bks.) Holt, Henry & Co.
Kohler, Sheila. Cracks. 2000. 176p. pap. 12.00 o.p. (*1-58195-026-8*, Zoland Bks., Inc.) Steerforth Pr.
Kohler, Sheila. Cracks. 1999. 176p. 21.00 (*1-58195-008-X*, Zoland Bks., Inc.) Steerforth Pr.
Landsman, Anne. The Devil's Chimney. 1997. 320p. 24.00 (*1-56947-101-0*) Soho Pr., Inc.
—The Devil's Chimney: A Novel. 1999. 304p. pap. 12.95 o.s.i (*0-14-027746-3*) Penguin Group (USA) Inc.
Langa, Mandla. The Memory of Stones: A Novel. 2000. vii, 366p. pap. 16.00 (*0-89410-866-2*, Three Continents) Rienner, Lynne Pubs., Inc.
Leanne, Shelly. Joshua's Bible. 2003. 384p. 23.95 (*0-446-53032-8*, Walk Worthy Pr.) Warner Bks., Inc.
Leith, Prue. Sisters: A Novel. 2002. 304p. 23.95 (*0-312-28779-8*) St. Martin's Pr.
Lessing, Doris. The Sweetest Dream. 2002. E-Book 19.95 (*0-06-008494-4*); E-Book 19.95 (*0-06-008493-6*); E-Book 19.95 (*0-06-008492-8*); E-Book 19.95 (*0-06-050455-2*) HarperCollins General Bks. Group. (PerfectBound).
—The Sweetest Dream. 2002. 496p. 26.95 (*0-06-621334-7*) HarperCollins Pubs.
—The Sweetest Dream. 2003. 496p. pap. 13.95 (*0-06-093755-6*, Perennial) HarperTrade.
Magona, Sindiwe. Living, Loving & Lying Awake at Night. 1994. (Emerging Voices Ser.). 208p. 24.95 (*1-56656-147-7*); pap. 11.95 (*1-56656-141-8*) Interlink Publishing Group, Inc.
—Mother to Mother. (Bluestreak Ser.). 216p. 2000. pap. 13.00 (*0-8070-0949-0*); 1999. 20.00 o.p. (*0-8070-0948-2*) Beacon Pr.
—Push, Push. 2001. (Bluestreak Ser.). 168p. pap. 13.00 (*0-8070-0967-9*) Beacon Pr.
Magona, Sindiwe, et al, contrib. by. Mother to Mother. 1998. 210p. 22.00 (*0-86486-433-7*) Interlink Publishing Group, Inc.
Mankell, Henning. The White Lioness. Thompson, Laurie, tr. from SWE. 2003. (Kurt Wallander Mystery Ser.). Orig. Title: Den Vita Lejoninnan. (Illus.). 448p. reprint ed. pap. 13.00 (*1-4000-3155-9*, Vintage) Knopf Publishing Group.
—The White Lioness. Thompson, Laurie, tr. from SWE. 1998. (Kurt Wallander Mystery Ser.). Orig. Title: Den Vita Lejoninnan. 942p. 25.00 (*1-56584-424-6*) New Pr., The.
Mason, Alfred E. Ensign Knightley & Other Stories. 1977. (Short Story Index Reprint Ser.). 23.95 (*0-8369-3267-6*) Ayer Co. Pubs., Inc.
Maxwell, Marina. Land of the Long Grass. 2001. (Illus.). 500p. pap. 17.50 (*0-620-26087-4*) Covos-Day Bks. ZAF. *Dist:* BHB International, Inc.
McClure, James. The Artful Egg. l.t. ed. 1986. 19.95 o.p. (*1-55504-011-X*, 247) BBC Audiobooks America.
—The Artful Egg. 1985. 283p. 13.95 o.p. (*0-394-53472-7*, Pantheon) Knopf Publishing Group.
—The Artful Egg. 1986. 5.95 (*0-07-544541-7*) McGraw-Hill Cos., The.
—The Blood of an Englishman. 1981. 288p. 11.00 o.p. (*0-06-013046-6*) HarperCollins Pubs.
—The Blood of an Englishman. l.t. ed. 1982. (Ulverscroft Large Print Ser.). 498p. 29.99 o.p. (*0-7089-0744-X*, Ulverscroft) Thorpe, F. A. Pubs. GBR. *Dist:* Ulverscroft Large Print Bks., Ltd., Ulverscroft Large Print Canada, Ltd.
—The Caterpillar Cop. 1973. (Harper Novel of Suspense Ser.). 240p. 7.95 o.p. (*0-06-012897-6*) HarperCollins Pubs.
—The Caterpillar Cop. 1982. reprint ed. pap. 2.95 o.s.i (*0-394-71058-4*, Pantheon) Knopf Publishing Group.
—Four & Twenty Virgins. l.t. ed. 1990. (Magna Large Print Ser.). 258p. o.p. (*1-85057-723-4*) Magna Large Print Bks. GBR. *Dist:* Ulverscroft Large Print Canada, Ltd.
—The Gooseberry Fool. 1974. (Novel of Suspense Ser.). 224p. 7.95 o.p. (*0-06-012898-4*) HarperCollins Pubs.
—Imago. 1988. 16.95 o.p. (*0-89296-273-9*) Mysterious Pr.
—Imago. 1989. mass mkt. 4.50 o.s.i (*0-445-40729-8*, Mysterious Pr. Paperback Bks.) Warner Bks., Inc.
—Rogue Eagle. 1976. 256p. 8.95 o.p. (*0-06-012949-2*) HarperCollins Pubs.
—Snake. 1976. (Harper Novel of Suspense Ser.). 224p. o.p. (*0-06-012884-4*) HarperCollins Pubs.
—The Song Dog. l.t. ed. 1992. (General Ser.). 408p. 20.95 o.p. (*0-8161-5344-2*, Macmillan Reference USA) Gale Group.
—The Song Dog. 1991. 17.95 (*0-89296-274-7*) Mysterious Pr.
—The Song Dog. 1992. 304p. mass mkt. 4.99 o.s.i (*0-446-40186-2*, Mysterious Pr. Paperback Bks.) Warner Bks., Inc.
—The Steam Pig. 1972. (Harper Novel of Suspense Ser.). 256p. 7.95 o.p. (*0-06-012896-8*) HarperCollins Pubs.
—The Steam Pig. l.t. ed. 1990. (Magna Large Print Ser.). 373p. o.p. (*1-85057-635-1*) Magna Large Print Bks. GBR. *Dist:* Ulverscroft Large Print Canada, Ltd.
—The Sunday Hangman. 1977. (Harper Novel of Suspense Ser.). o.p. (*0-06-012859-3*) HarperCollins Pubs.
McCutchan, Philip. Ogilvie at War. 1999. 221p. 25.00 (*0-7278-5471-2*) Severn Hse. Pubs., Ltd.
—Ogilvie at War. l.t. ed. 2000. (General Ser.). 343p. pap. 23.95 (*0-7862-2567-X*); (*0-7540-4156-5*); (*0-7540-4157-3*) Thorndike Pr.
Mda, Zakes. The Heart of Redness: A Novel. 2002. (Illus.). 288p. spiral bd. 24.00 (*0-374-52834-9*) Farrar, Straus & Giroux.
—The Heart of Redness: A Novel. 2003. 288p. pap. 14.00 (*0-312-42174-5*) Picador.
—Ways of Dying. 1995. (Southern African Writing Ser.). 192p. (Orig.). pap. 10.95 o.p. (*0-19-571106-8*) Oxford Univ. Pr., Inc.
—Ways of Dying. 2002. 216p. (Orig.). pap. 13.00 (*0-312-42091-9*) Picador.
Mendels, Ora. Mandela's Children. 1987. 16.95 o.p. (*0-316-54506-6*) Little Brown & Co.
Michener, James A. The Covenant. 1987. 1248p. mass mkt. 7.99 (*0-449-21420-6*, Fawcett) Ballantine Bks.
—The Covenant, Pt. 2. unabr. ed. 1993. audio 104.00 Books on Tape, Inc.
—The Covenant. 1980. (Spanish Literary Reader Ser.). 35.00 o.p. (*0-394-51400-9*) Random Hse., Inc.
Mogotsi, Isaac. The Alexandra Tales. 1994. 172p. (Orig.). pap. text 14.95 (*0-86975-446-7*) Ravan Pr. ZMB. *Dist:* Ohio Univ. Pr.
Momple, Lilia. Neighbours: The Story of a Murder. 2001. (African Writers Ser.). 134p. pap. 13.95 (*0-435-91209-7*) Greenwood Publishing Group, Inc.
Moore, William. Bush War! 1986. 172p. 13.95 o.s.i (*0-8027-0870-6*) Walker & Co.
Mpe, Phaswane. Welcome to Our Hillbrow. 2001. 132p. pap. 12.95 (*0-86980-995-4*) Univ. of Natal Pr. ZAF. *Dist:* International Specialized Bk. Services.
Mphahlele, Es'kia. Modern African Stories. Komey, Ellis A., ed. 1966. 228p. pap. o.p. (*0-571-11217-X*) Faber & Faber Ltd.
—Renewal Time. 1988. (Readers International Ser.). (Orig.). (C). 225p. 16.95 (*0-930523-55-5*); 215p. pap. 8.95 (*0-930523-56-3*) Readers International.
Murray, Stuart. White Fire. 2000. 336p. 26.00 (*1-884592-25-2*) Images from the Past, Inc.
Mzamane, Mbulelo. The Children of Soweto. 1995. (C). pap. 14.20 o.p. (*0-582-01680-0*); pap. 22.00 (*0-582-26434-0*) Addison-Wesley Longman, Inc.
Mzamane, Mbulelo, ed. Hungry Flames: And Other Black South African Short Stories. 1995. (Longman African Classics Ser.). (C). pap. 16.80 (*0-582-78590-1*, TG7153) Longman Publishing Group.
Navarro, John. Vaga Lomez & the Judge. 2000. 120p. pap. 13.00 (*0-8059-4959-3*) Dorrance Publishing Co., Inc.
Ndebele, Njabulo S. Fools & Other Stories. 1986. (Readers International Ser.). 280p. (C). reprint ed. 14.95 o.p. (*0-930523-19-9*); pap. 12.95 (*0-930523-20-2*) Readers International.
Ngcobo, Lauretta. And They Didn't Die. 1991. 246p. 19.95 (*0-8076-1263-4*) Braziller, George Inc.
—And They Didn't Die. 1999. (Women Writing Africa Ser.). 272p. 42.00 (*1-55861-212-2*); (ACE.). pap. 15.95 (*1-55861-213-0*) Feminist Pr. at The City Univ. of New York.
—And They Didn't Die. 1994. o.s.i (*1-85381-153-X*) Random Hse., Inc.
Paton, Alan. Ah, But Your Land Is Beautiful. 1982. 208p. 12.95 o.p. (*0-684-17336-0*, Macmillan Reference USA) Gale Group.
—Cry, the Beloved Country. 23.95 (*0-89190-379-8*) Amereon, Ltd.
—Cry, the Beloved Country. l.t. ed. 1987. 370p. reprint ed. lib. bdg. 19.95 (*1-55736-004-9*) Bantam Doubleday Dell Large Print Group, Inc.
—Cry, the Beloved Country. 1991. 300p. reprint ed. lib. bdg. 28.95 (*0-89966-788-0*) Buccaneer Bks., Inc.
—Cry, the Beloved Country. 1985. pap. 12.00 (*0-684-51544-X*); 1982. 304p. pap. 4.95 o.s.i (*0-684-17473-1*); 1977. 304p. 35.00 (*0-684-15559-1*); 1940. 304p. pap. 9.95 o.s.i (*0-684-71863-4*) Gale Group. (Macmillan Reference USA).
—Cry, the Beloved Country, 2 vols., Set. l.t. ed. reprint ed. 10.00 (*0-89064-021-1*) National Assn. for Visually Handicapped.
—Cry, the Beloved Country. 1961. 442p. pap. text 12.00 o.p. (*0-02-391810-1*, Macmillan College) Prentice Hall PTR.
—Cry, the Beloved Country. 2003. 320p. 26.00 (*0-7432-6195-X*); 2003. 320p. pap. 14.00 (*0-7432-6217-4*); 1995. pap. 6.99 o.s.i (*0-684-82977-0*); 1995. 320p. pap. 13.00 o.s.i (*0-684-81894-9*) Simon & Schuster. (Scribner).
—Cry, the Beloved Country. 1996. 19.05 (*0-606-00509-9*) Turtleback Bks.
—Too Late the Phalarope. 23.95 (*0-89190-392-5*) Amereon, Ltd.
—Too Late the Phalarope. unabr. collector's ed. 1982. audio 42.00 (*0-7366-0346-8*, 1332) Books on Tape, Inc.
—Too Late the Phalarope. 1996. 288p. pap. 13.00 (*0-684-81895-7*, Scribner); 1983. pap. 7.95 (*0-684-10455-5*); 1950. pap. 7.95 o.s.i (*0-684-71866-9*, Scribner Paper Fiction); 1985. 272p. reprint ed. pap. 5.95 o.s.i (*0-684-18500-8*, Scribner Paper Fiction) Simon & Schuster.
Petuchowski, Jakob J., ed. When Jews & Christians Meet. 1988. 160p. (C). pap. text 19.95 (*0-88706-633-X*) State Univ. of New York Pr.
Pieterse, Pieter. The Price of a Chicken: A Youth Novel. 1997. (Illus.). (*0-7981-3765-7*) Human & Rousseau.
Poland, Marguerite. Iron Love. 1999. (*0-670-88986-5*) Viking Penguin.
Pubs, Struik. Evolution: A Novel. 1998. 188p. (*1-86872-248-1*) Struik Pubs.
Ramogale, Marcus, ed. To Kill a Man's Pride & Other Stories from Southern Africa. 2nd rev. ed. 1996. 272p. pap. text 14.95 (*0-86975-460-2*) Ravan Pr. ZMB. *Dist:* Ohio Univ. Pr.
Rive, Richard. Advance, Retreat: Selected Short Stories. 1989. 131p. 19.95 o.p. (*0-312-03689-2*) Palgrave Macmillan.
Rooke, Daphne. Mittee. 1991. (Penguin Twentieth-Century Classics Ser.). 224p. pap. 9.95 o.p. (*0-14-018431-7*, Penguin Classics) Viking Penguin.
Rosenberg, Valerie. The Von Veltheim File. (*0-7981-3671-5*) Human & Rousseau.
Schmahmann, David. Empire Settings. 2001. 327p. 21.95 (*1-893996-16-6*) White Pine Pr.
Serote, Mongane. To Every Birth Its Blood. 1984. (African Writers Ser.). 206p. (Orig.). (C). pap. 10.95 (*0-435-90263-6*, 90263) Heinemann.
—To Every Birth Its Blood: A Novel. 1997. (Ravan Writers Ser.). 368p. (Orig.). pap. text 14.95 (*0-86975-216-2*) Ravan Pr. ZMB. *Dist:* Ohio Univ. Pr.
—To Every Birth Its Blood: A Novel of South Africa. 1989. 208p. 19.95 o.p. (*0-938410-71-7*); pap. 10.95 (*0-938410-70-9*) Avalon Publishing Group. (Thunder's Mouth Pr.).
Sharpe, Tom. Indecent Exposure. unabr. ed. 1992. audio 56.00 (*0-7366-2178-4*, 2975) Books on Tape, Inc.
—Indecent Exposure. 1987. 256p. pap. 13.00 (*0-87113-142-0*, Atlantic Monthly Pr.) Grove/Atlantic, Inc.
—Indecent Exposure. l.t. unabr. ed. 2000. 19.95 (*0-7531-5894-9*, 158941); 25.95 (*0-7531-5160-X*, 15160X) ISIS Large Print Bks. GBR. *Dist:* ISIS Publishing.
—Riotous Assembly. 1987. 256p. pap. 12.00 (*0-87113-143-9*, Atlantic Monthly Pr.) Grove/Atlantic, Inc.
Sher, Anthony. The Indoor Boy. 1992. 272p. 20.00 o.p. (*0-670-84456-X*, Viking) Viking Penguin.

Settings

Slovo, Gillian. Red Dust. 2002. 352p. 25.95 (*0-393-04148-4*); reprint ed. pap. 14.95 (*0-393-32399-4*) Norton, W. W. & Co., Inc.

Smith, Pauline. The Little Karoo. 1990. 192p. 15.95 o.p. (*0-312-04729-0*) Palgrave Macmillan.

—The Little Karoo. l.t. ed. 1997. 144p. text 21.95 (*1-56000-540-8*) Transaction Pubs.

Smith, Wilbur. Birds of Prey, Pt. 1. unabr. ed. 1997. (Courtney Novels). audio 72.00 (*0-7366-3740-0*, 4417-A) Books on Tape, Inc.

—Birds of Prey, 2 cass. 2001. audio 16.95 (*0-333-69866-5*) Macmillan U.K. GBR. *Dist:* Trafalgar Square.

—Birds of Prey. abr. ed. 1997. 25.00 o.p. (*0-7871-1468-5*) NewStar Media, Inc.

—Birds of Prey. 1997. 554p. 25.95 (*0-312-15791-6*); Vol. 1. 1998. 664p. mass mkt. 7.50 (*0-312-96381-5*, St. Martin's Paperbacks) St. Martin's Pr.

—Birds of Prey. l.t. ed. 1997. (Basic Ser.). 968p. lib. bdg. 29.95 (*0-7862-1190-3*) Thorndike Pr.

—The Blue Horizon. 2003. (Illus.). audio compact disk 37.95 (*1-55927-871-4*); audio 29.95 (*1-55927-873-0*) Audio Renaissance.

—The Blue Horizon. E-Book 18.70 (*0-312-71020-8*); 2003. 624p. 27.95 (*0-312-27824-1*) St. Martin's Pr.

—The Burning Shore. 1987. 512p. mass mkt. 7.50 (*0-449-21189-4*, Fawcett); 1986. mass mkt. 3.50 o.s.i (*0-449-21198-3*) Ballantine Bks.

—The Burning Shore, Pt. 1. unabr. collector's ed. 1988. (Courtney Novels). audio 64.00 (*0-7366-1256-4*, 2170-A) Books on Tape, Inc.

—The Burning Shore. 1985. 432p. 17.95 o.p. (*0-385-18738-6*) Doubleday Publishing.

—The Courtneys. 1988. 944p. 29.95 (*0-316-80182-8*) Little Brown & Co.

—Gold Mine. l.t. ed. 1993. 20.95 o.p. (*0-7927-1528-4*); pap. o.p. (*0-7927-1527-6*) BBC Audiobooks America.

—Golden Fox. 1993. 480p. mass mkt. 6.99 (*0-449-14906-4*, Fawcett) Ballantine Bks.

—Golden Fox. unabr. ed. 1993. (Courtney Novels). audio 120.00 (*0-7366-2524-0*, 3277) Books on Tape, Inc.

—Golden Fox. unabr. ed. 2000. (Sean Courtney Adventure Ser.). audio 89.95 (*0-7451-4160-9*, CAB 843) Chivers Audio Bks. GBR. *Dist:* BBC Audiobooks America.

—Golden Fox. 1993. 4.99 o.p. (*0-517-09806-7*) Random Hse. Value Publishing.

—Golden Fox. l.t. ed. 1991. (Charnwood Library). 29.99 o.p. (*0-7089-8584-X*, Ulverscroft) Thorpe, F. A. Pubs. GBR. *Dist:* Ulverscroft Large Print Bks., Ltd., Ulverscroft Large Print Canada, Ltd.

—Power of the Sword. Date not set. 671p. 36.95 (*0-8488-2394-X*) Amereon, Ltd.

—Power of the Sword. 1987. 672p. mass mkt. 6.99 o.s.i (*0-449-21414-1*, Fawcett); mass mkt. 3.95 o.s.i (*0-449-21427-3*) Ballantine Bks.

—Power of the Sword, Pt. 1. unabr. collector's ed. 1988. (Courtney Novels). audio 88.00 (*0-7366-1378-1*, 2272-A) Books on Tape, Inc.

—Power of the Sword. 1986. 19.95 (*0-316-80171-2*) Little Brown & Co.

—Rage. 1989. 672p. mass mkt. 6.99 o.s.i (*0-449-21613-6*, Fawcett) Ballantine Bks.

—Rage, Pt. 1. unabr. collector's ed. 1988. (Courtney Novels). audio 88.00 (*0-7366-1294-7*, 2202-A) Books on Tape, Inc.

—Rage. 1987. 640p. 19.95 (*0-316-80179-8*) Little Brown & Co.

—The Roar of Thunder. 1977. mass mkt. 2.95 o.s.i (*0-440-18146-1*) Dell Publishing.

—The Sound of Thunder. 1991. 416p. mass mkt. 6.99 (*0-449-14819-X*, Fawcett) Ballantine Bks.

—The Sound of Thunder. unabr. ed. 1998. audio 110.95 o.p. Brilliance Audio.

—The Sound of Thunder. unabr. ed. 1998. (Sean Courtney Adventure Ser.). audio 89.95 (*0-7540-0189-X*, CAB 1612) Chivers Audio Bks. GBR. *Dist:* BBC Audiobooks America.

—The Sound of Thunder. abr. ed. 2001. audio 16.95 (*0-333-90276-9*) Macmillan U.K. GBR. *Dist:* Trafalgar Square.

—A Sparrow Falls, Pt. 2. unabr. collector's ed. 1989. (Courtney Novels). audio 64.00 (*0-7366-1476-1*, 2353-B) Books on Tape, Inc.

—A Sparrow Falls. 1991. 608p. reprint ed. lib. bdg. 49.95 (*0-89966-779-1*) Buccaneer Bks., Inc.

—A Sparrow Falls. 1978. 10.95 o.p. (*0-385-13603-X*) Doubleday Publishing.

—A Sparrow Falls. 1995. mass mkt. 6.99 o.p. (*0-7493-2192-X*) Heinemann.

—A Sparrow Falls. abr. ed. 2001. audio 16.95 (*0-333-90277-7*) Macmillan U.K. GBR. *Dist:* Trafalgar Square.

—A Time to Die. 1991. 496p. mass mkt. 6.99 (*0-449-14761-4*, Fawcett) Ballantine Bks.

—A Time to Die. 1992. 5.99 o.p. (*0-517-08097-4*) Random Hse. Value Publishing.

—A Time to Die. l.t. ed. 1990. (Charnwood Large Print Ser.). 29.99 o.p. (*0-7089-8537-8*, Ulverscroft) Thorpe, F. A. Pubs. GBR. *Dist:* Ulverscroft Large Print Bks., Ltd., Ulverscroft Large Print Canada, Ltd.

—When the Lion Feeds. 1989. mass mkt. 5.95 o.s.i (*0-449-21553-9*, Ballantine Bks.) Ballantine Bks.

—When the Lion Feeds. unabr. collector's ed. 1989. (Courtney Novels). audio 104.00 (*0-7366-1477-X*, 2354) Books on Tape, Inc.

—When the Lion Feeds. unabr. ed. 2000. (Sean Courtney Adventure Ser.). audio 89.95 (*0-7540-0073-7*, CAB 1496) Chivers Audio Bks. GBR. *Dist:* BBC Audiobooks America.

—When the Lion Feeds. 1989. mass mkt. 6.99 (*0-7493-2292-6*) Heinemann.

—When the Lion Feeds. abr. ed. 2001. audio 16.95 (*0-333-90275-0*) Macmillan U.K. GBR. *Dist:* Trafalgar Square.

—When the Lion Feeds. 1964. 5.95 o.p. (*0-670-75974-0*) Viking Penguin.

—When the Lion Feeds. 1999. lib. bdg. 27.95 (*1-56723-133-0*, 144) Yestermorrow, Inc.

Sometimes When It Rains. 1987. 9.95 o.p. (*0-86358-198-6*) HarperSanFrancisco.

Stirling, Emma. Marriage of Secrets. l.t. ed. 1997. (Romance-Hall Ser.). 158p. lib. bdg. 23.95 o.p. (*0-7838-8267-X*, Macmillan Reference USA) Gale Group.

—Marriage of Secrets. 160p. 22.00 (*0-7278-5128-4*) Severn Hse. Pubs., Ltd.

Strachan, Harold, et al, contrib. by. Way Up, Way Out: A Satirical Novel. 1998. 165p. (*0-86486-355-1*) Interlink Publishing Group, Inc.

Trapido, Barbara. Frankie & Stankie. 2003. 307p. (*0-7475-6034-X*) Bloomsbury Pr.

Trollope, Joanna. The Steps of the Sun. 1984. 266p. 13.95 o.p. (*0-312-76165-1*) St. Martin's Pr.

—The Steps of the Sun. abr. ed. 1995. pap. 16.95 incl. audio (*1-85998-166-6*) Trafalgar Square.

Van der Vyver, Marita. Entertaining Angels. Knox, Catherine, tr. 1995. 224p. 20.95 o.p. (*0-525-93918-0*) Dutton/Plume.

Van Heerden, Etienne. Ancestral Voices. 1992. 272p. 21.00 o.p. (*0-670-82831-9*, Viking) Viking Penguin.

—The Long Silence of Mario Salviati. 2004. 416p. pap. 14.95 (*0-06-052978-4*, ReganBooks) HarperTrade.

—The Long Silence of Mario Salviati: A Novel. Knox, Catherine, tr. from AFR. 2003. (Illus.). 448p. 24.95 (*0-06-052973-3*, ReganBooks) HarperTrade.

Vernon, Claire. The Doctor Who Forgot. l.t. ed. 2000. (G. K. Hall Nightingale Ser.). 220p. pap. 20.95 (*0-7838-9192-X*); (*0-7540-4293-6*) Gale Group. (Macmillan Reference USA).

Wicomb, Zoe. David's Story. 2002. pap. 14.95 (*1-55861-398-6*); 2001. (Illus.). 224p. 19.95 (*1-55861-251-3*) Feminist Pr. at The City Univ. of New York.

—You Can't Get Lost in Cape Town. 2000. (Women Writing Africa Ser.). 42.00 (*1-55861-244-0*); 240p. pap. 13.95 (*1-55861-225-4*) Feminist Pr. at The City Univ. of New York.

Williams, Michael. Hijack City. 1999. 272p. pap. (*0-19-571591-8*) Oxford Univ. Pr., Inc.

Williams, Michael, contrib. by. The Secret Song. (*0-624-03541-7*) Tafelberg Pubs., Ltd.

Winter, Jenny. Coolcat Alley. 1997. (*0-7981-3675-8*) Human & Rousseau.

Zwi, Rose. Another Year in Africa. 1988. 172p. reprint ed. pap. 14.95 o.p. (*0-86975-316-9*) Ravan Pr. ZMB. *Dist:* Ohio Univ. Pr.

—Safe Houses. 1994. 250p. pap. 12.95 (*1-875559-21-3*) Spinifex Pr. AUS. *Dist:* Stackpole Bks.

—The Umbrella Tree. 1991. 120p. (Orig.). pap. 6.95 o.p. (*0-14-013410-7*) Penguin Group (USA) Inc.

## SOUTH AMERICA—FICTION

Bear, Greg. Dinosaur Summer. (Illus.). 1999. 400p. mass mkt. 6.99 o.s.i (*0-446-60666-9*); 1998. 304p. 23.00 o.p. (*0-446-52098-5*) Warner Bks., Inc.

Benedetti, Mario. La Tregua. 1995. Tr. of Truce. (SPA.). 202p. pap. 12.50 o.s.i (*0-679-76095-4*) Random Hse., Inc.

Bergmann, Eugene B. Rio Amazonas. 2001. 208p. pap. 21.99 (*0-7388-4040-8*) Xlibris Corp.

Cameron, Peter. The City of Your Final Destination. 2003. 320p. reprint ed. pap. 14.00 (*0-452-28430-9*, Plume) Dutton/Plume.

—The City of Your Final Destination. 2002. 320p. 24.00 (*0-374-28197-1*) Farrar, Straus & Giroux.

Chacko, David. White Gamma. 1989. mass mkt. 3.95 (*0-312-91577-2*, St. Martin's Paperbacks); 1988. 208p. 15.95 o.p. (*0-312-02317-0*) St. Martin's Pr.

Chaikin, Linda L. Island Bride. 1988. pap. o.s.i (*0-373-04155-1*, Harlequin Bks.) Harlequin Enterprises, Ltd.

—Island Bride. 1999. (Trade Wind Ser.: Vol. 3). 228p. pap. 8.99 o.p. (*0-7369-0004-7*) Harvest Hse. Pubs.

—Island Bride. l.t. ed. 2001. (Trade Winds Ser.). (Illus.). 376p. (J). 24.95 (*0-7862-3120-3*) Thorndike Pr.

Clancy, Tom. Clear & Present Danger. 704p. 1994. mass mkt. 7.50 o.s.i (*0-425-14437-2*); 1990. mass mkt. 7.99 (*0-425-12212-3*) Berkley Publishing Group.

—Clear & Present Danger. l.t. ed. 1990. (Magna Large Print Ser.). 1140p. o.p. (*1-85057-853-2*) Magna Large Print Bks. GBR. *Dist:* Ulverscroft Large Print Canada, Ltd.

—Clear & Present Danger. 1989. 544p. 27.95 (*0-399-13440-9*, G. P. Putnam's Sons) Penguin Putnam Bks. for Young Readers.

—Clear & Present Danger. 1990. 13.09 o.p. (*0-606-00980-9*) Turtleback Bks.

—Peligro Imminente. 6th ed. 1998. (Jet de Plaza & Janes Ser.: Vol. 150). Orig. Title: Clear & Present Danger. (SPA., Illus.). 617p. pap. 8.50 (*84-01-49525-3*) Plaza & Janés Editores, S.A. ESP. *Dist:* Lectorum Pubns., Inc.

Cole, Michael. A King's Ransom. 2003. 198p. pap. 14.95 (*1-55517-691-7*, 76917, Bonneville Bks.) Cedar Fort, Inc./CFI Distribution.

Cosgrove, Thomas H. Last Climb: A Novel of Suspense. 1999. 304p. 23.00 o.s.i (*0-684-83414-6*, Simon & Schuster) Simon & Schuster.

Cussler, Clive. Blue Gold: A Novel from the NUMA Files. E-Book 16.00 (*1-58945-135-X*) Adobe Systems, Inc.

—Blue Gold: A Novel from the NUMA Files. 2002. E-Book 9.99 (*0-7434-2308-9*, Pocket) Simon & Schuster.

Cussler, Clive & Kemprecos, Paul. Blue Gold: A Novel from the NUMA Files. 2001. 416p. 7.99 (*0-7434-3790-X*); 2000. (NUMA Files Ser.: Vol. 2). (Illus.). 400p. pap. 16.00 (*0-671-78546-X*); 2001. (NUMA Files Ser.: Vol. 2). 416p. reprint ed. mass mkt. 7.99 (*0-7434-1822-0*) Simon & Schuster. (Pocket).

Daley, Robert. A Faint Cold Fear. abr. ed. 1991. audio 15.95 o.p. (*1-55927-142-6*) Audio Renaissance.

—A Faint Cold Fear. 1990. 19.95 o.p. (*0-316-17184-0*) Little Brown & Co.

—A Faint Cold Fear. abr. ed. 1991. audio 7.95 (*1-57815-038-8*, 1010) Media Bks., L. L. C.

—A Faint Cold Fear. 1992. 480p. mass mkt. 5.99 o.s.i (*0-446-36219-0*) Warner Bks., Inc.

Davies, Ed. House of the Moon. E-Book (*1-84045-030-4*) Online Originals.

Davis, Richard Harding. Soldiers of Fortune. reprint ed. lib. bdg. 48.00 (*0-7426-1083-7*) Classic Bks.

—Soldiers of Fortune. l.t. ed. 1999. (Perennial Bestsellers Ser.). 319p. 25.95 (*0-7838-8498-2*) Thorndike Pr.

De Bernieres, Louis. The Troublesome Offspring of Cardinal Guzman. 1994. 363p. 25.00 o.p. (*0-688-12583-2*, Morrow, William & Co.) Morrow/Avon.

—The War of Don Emmanuel's Nether Parts: A Novel. 1997. 368p. pap. 14.00 (*0-375-70013-7*, Vintage) Knopf Publishing Group.

—The War of Don Emmanuel's Nether Parts: A Novel. 1992. 363p. 25.00 o.p. (*0-688-11129-7*, Morrow, William & Co.) Morrow/Avon.

Delgado Aparain, Mario. The Ballad of Johnny Sosa. 2002. 21.95 (*1-58567-224-6*) Overlook Pr., The.

Doyle, Arthur Conan. The Lost World. 2003. (Illus.). 272p. pap. 8.95 (*0-8129-6725-9*, Modern Library) Random House Adult Trade Publishing Group.

Farhi, Moris. Journey Through the Wilderness. 2002. 486p. pap. 16.95 (*0-86356-372-4*) I.B.Tauris & Co., Ltd. GBR. *Dist:* Holtzbrinck Pubs.

Faye, Charlet. The Chilling Adventures of Marshall McCaw. 2004. (Illus.). (J). 18.95 (*0-9655222-1-0*) FayeHouse. Pr. International.

Feehan, Christine, et al. Hot Blooded. 2004. 400p. mass mkt. 7.99 (*0-515-13696-4*, Jove) Berkley Publishing Group.

Fuentes, Carlos. The Campaign. 1991. 22.95 o.s.i (*0-374-11828-0*) Farrar, Straus & Giroux.

—The Campaign. 1992. 256p. pap. 12.00 o.p. (*0-06-097502-4*, Perennial) HarperTrade.

Galeano, Eduardo. Book of Embraces. 1991. 19.95 o.p. (*0-393-02960-3*) Norton, W. W. & Co., Inc.

—The Book of Embraces. Belfrage, Cedric & Schafer, Mark, trs. 1992. (Illus.). 288p. pap. 13.95 (*0-393-30855-3*) Norton, W. W. & Co., Inc.

Garcia Márquez, Gabriel. The General in His Labyrinth. 2003. Tr. of General en Su Laberinto. (Illus.). 304p. pap. 13.00 (*1-4000-3470-1*, Vintage) Knopf Publishing Group.

—The General in His Labyrinth. 1990. Tr. of General en Su Laberinto. 200.00 o.p. (*0-394-58951-3*) Knopf, Alfred A. Inc.

—The General in His Labyrinth. Grossman, Edith, tr. from SPA. 1991. (Great Books of the 20th Century Ser.).Tr. of General en Su Laberinto. 288p. reprint ed. pap. 13.95 o.p. (*0-14-014859-0*, PE8590, Penguin Bks.) Penguin Group (USA) Inc.

—Of Love & Other Demons. 1996. (*0-14-771138-X*) Penguin Group (USA) Inc.

—Of Love & Other Demons. Grossman, Edith, tr. 1996. (Penguin Great Books of the 20th Century Ser.). 160p. 13.00 (*0-14-025636-9*) Viking Penguin.

Guebel, Daniel. Cuerpo Cristiano. 1994. Tr. of Christians. (SPA., Illus.). (YA). 6.99 (*968-16-4268-6*) Fondo de Cultura Economica MEX. *Dist:* Continental Bk. Co., Inc.

Hamilton, Lyn. The Moche Warrior: An Archaeological Mystery. (Archaeological Mystery Ser.). 336p. 1999. 21.95 o.s.i (*0-425-16809-3*); 2000. reprint ed. mass mkt. 6.50 (*0-425-17308-9*) Berkley Publishing Group. (Prime Crime).

Hudson, William Henry. Green Mansions: A Romance of the Tropical Forest. reprint ed. 35.00 (*0-404-03402-0*) AMS Pr., Inc.

—Green Mansions: A Romance of the Tropical Forest. Date not set. lib. bdg. 23.95 (*0-8488-2146-7*) Amereon, Ltd.

—Green Mansions: A Romance of the Tropical Forest. Baxter, Beth, ed. abr. ed. 1993. audio 12.95 (*1-882071-06-9*, 008) B&B Audio, Inc.

—Green Mansions: A Romance of the Tropical Forest. 1989. audio 49.95 (*1-55686-293-8*, 293) Books in Motion.

—Green Mansions: A Romance of the Tropical Forest. unabr. collector's ed. 1982. audio 48.00 (*0-7366-3862-8*, 9069) Books on Tape, Inc.

—Green Mansions: A Romance of the Tropical Forest. 1982. reprint ed. lib. bdg. 25.95 (*0-89966-374-5*) Buccaneer Bks., Inc.

—Green Mansions: A Romance of the Tropical Forest. 2001. (Collected Works of W. H. Hudson ). reprint ed. pap. text 28.00 (*0-7426-8540-3*) Classic Bks.

—Green Mansions: A Romance of the Tropical Forest. 1989. 320p. pap. 8.95 (*0-486-25993-5*) Dover Pubns., Inc.

—Green Mansions: A Romance of the Tropical Forest. abr. ed. 1977. audio 12.95 o.p. (*0-694-50302-9*, SWC 1561, Caedmon) HarperTrade.

—Green Mansions: A Romance of the Tropical Forest. unabr. ed. 1982. audio 29.00 Jimcin Recordings.

—Green Mansions: A Romance of the Tropical Forest. l.t. ed. (Large Print Ser.). reprint ed. 1992. 410p. lib. bdg. 26.00 (*0-939495-40-6*); 1998. 245p. lib. bdg. 25.00 (*1-58287-032-2*) North Bks.

—Green Mansions: A Romance of the Tropical Forest. Duncan, Ian, ed. 1998. (Oxford World's Classics Ser.). 240p. pap. 9.95 (*0-19-283288-3*) Oxford Univ. Pr., Inc.

—Green Mansions: A Romance of the Tropical Forest. 1999. E-Book 3.99 incl. cd-rom (*1-891595-90-3*) Quiet Vision Publishing.

—Green Mansions: A Romance of the Tropical Forest. E-Book 5.00 (*0-7410-0873-4*) SoftBook Pr.

—Green Mansions: A Romance of the Tropical Forest. 1999. E-Book 5.99 (*0-8220-7269-6*, Cliff Notes) Wiley, John & Sons, Inc.

—The Purple Land. (The Modern Library of the World's Best Bks.). 389p. reprint ed. 98.00 (*0-7222-9617-7*) Best Bks.

—The Purple Land. 2002. (Illus.). 304p. pap. 19.95 (*0-299-18224-X*) Univ. of Wisconsin Pr.

Hurwitz, Gregg. Minutes to Burn. 2002. 496p. mass mkt. 7.50 (*0-06-101551-2*) HarperCollins Pubs.

—Minutes to Burn. 2001. (Illus.). 432p. 25.00 (*0-06-018886-3*, Morrow, William & Co.) Morrow/Avon.

Iparraguirre, Sylvia. La Tierra del Fuego. 1999. (SPA., Illus.). 286p. 21.95 (*950-511-414-1*) Alfaguara S.A. de Ediciones ARG. *Dist:* Libros Sin Fronteras, Santillana USA Publishing Co., Inc.

Jackson, Brenda. Fire & Desire. 320p. 2000. mass mkt. 5.99 (*1-58314-232-0*); 1999. mass mkt. 4.99 o.s.i (*1-58314-024-7*) BET Bks.

Jacobs, Mark. Cast of Spaniards. 1994. 208p. pap. 12.95 (*1-883689-18-X*); lib. bdg. 33.95 (*1-883689-19-8*) Talisman Hse., Pubs.

Jaffe, Harold. Dos Indios. 1983. 168p. 14.95 o.p. (*0-938410-11-3*); pap. 8.95 o.p. (*0-938410-10-5*) Avalon Publishing Group. (Thunder's Mouth Pr.).

Johnson, Debra A. I Dreamed I Was a Toucan. 1994. (I Dreamed I Was Ser.). (J). lib. bdg. 21.95 (*1-56239-304-9*) ABDO Publishing Co.

Jones, Mark E. Wings of the Valiant. l.t. ed. 1999. E-Book 14.99 incl. cd-rom (*1-929077-69-6*, Books OnScreen) PageFree Publishing, Inc.

Judd, Alan. Tango. 1924. o.s.i (*0-688-09254-3*, Morrow, William & Co.) Morrow/Avon.

—Tango. 1990. 17.95 o.p. (*0-671-70710-8*) Summit Bks.

Just, Ward S. Soldier of the Revolution. 2002. 208p. pap. text 12.00 (*1-58648-097-9*) PublicAffairs.

Keene, Carolyn & Dixon, Franklin W. Jungle of Evil. Arico, Diane, ed. 1985. (Nancy Drew & Hardy Boys: No. 7). (Illus.). 128p. (Orig.). (J). (gr. 3-7). pap. 2.95 (*0-671-55734-3*, Simon & Schuster Children's Publishing) Simon & Schuster Children's Publishing.

Keith, Don & Wallace, George. Final Bearing. 2003. (Illus.). 512p. 27.95 (*0-7653-0415-5*, Forge Bks.) Doherty, Tom Assocs., LLC.

Kennett, Shirley. Burning Rose. 2003. 232p. pap. 13.95 (*1-4104-0106-5*, Five Star Trade); 2002. 228p. 24.95 (*0-7862-3661-2*, Five Star) Gale Group.

Koster, R.M. Glass Mountain. 2001. 320p. 24.95 (*0-393-02007-X*) Norton, W. W. & Co., Inc.

LaFarge, Paul. The Artist of the Missing. 1999. (Illus.). 256p. pap. 13.00 (*0-374-52580-3*) Farrar, Straus & Giroux.

Lanigan, Catherine. The Legend Makers. 1999. 384p. mass mkt. (*1-55166-517-4*, 1-66517-3, Mira Bks.) Harlequin Enterprises, Ltd.

Marcinko, Richard & Weisman, John. Detachment Bravo. 2001. 352p. 25.95 o.s.i (*0-671-00071-3*, Atria) Simon & Schuster.

Marisol. The Lady, the Chef & the Courtesan. 2003. 256p. 21.95 (*0-06-053042-1*, Rayo) HarperTrade.

Matthiessen, Peter. At Play in the Fields of the Lord. 1991. 384p. pap. 14.00 (*0-679-73741-3*); 1987. pap. 10.95 o.p. (*0-394-75083-7*) Knopf Publishing Group. (Vintage).

—At Play in the Fields of the Lord. 1967. mass mkt. 1.25 o.p. (*0-451-03057-5*, Signet Bks.) NAL.

—At Play in the Fields of the Lord. unabr. ed. 1999. audio 91.00 (*1-55690-701-X*, 92414E7) Recorded Bks., LLC.

—At Play in the Fields of the Lord. 1992. 26.75 (*0-8446-6636-X*) Smith, Peter Pub., Inc.

Melville, Pauline. The Ventriloquist's Tale. 1999. pap. 13.95 (*1-58234-026-9*); 1998. 23.95 (*1-58234-009-9*) Bloomsbury Publishing.

—The Ventriloquist's Tale. unabr. ed. 1999. audio 69.95 (*0-7531-0513-6*, 990511) ISIS Audio Bks. GBR. *Dist:* Ulverscroft Large Print Bks., Ltd.

Michaels, Shauna. Hold onto the Night. 2000. 192p. pap. 10.50 (*1-893896-11-0*) ImaJinn Bks.

Miller, Carlos Ledson. Belize: A Novel. 2000. 402p. pap. 24.99 (*0-7388-0717-6*); text 34.99 (*0-7388-0716-8*) Xlibris Corp.

—Panama: A Novel. 1999. 326p. pap. 22.99 (*0-7388-0715-X*); text 32.99 (*0-7388-0714-1*) Xlibris Corp.

Molnar, Alexander, Jr. The Land Beyond Time Adventure in the Amazon: An Al Ranlom Action Adventure Novel. 2000. 288p. pap. 21.99 (*0-7388-1787-2*); text 31.99 (*0-7388-1786-4*); E-Book 8.00 (*0-7388-8626-2*) Xlibris Corp.

Montalbano, William. The Sinners of San Ramon. 1989. 288p. bds. 3.95 o.s.i (*0-671-66411-5*, Pocket) Simon & Schuster.

Morris, Robert G. Diplomatic Relations. 2002. 256p. 15.95 (*0-87714-259-9*); 2000. E-Book 6.95 (*0-87714-572-5*) Denlingers Pubs., Ltd.

Mueller, Marnie. The Climate of the Country: A Novel. 1999. 308p. 24.95 (*1-880684-58-6*); 1994. 318p. 19.95 (*1-880684-16-0*) Curbstone Pr.

—Green Fires: Assault on Eden: A Novel of the Ecuadorian Rainforest. 1999. 318p. pap. 13.95 (*1-880684-59-4*) Curbstone Pr.

Munves, James. Andes Rising. 1999. 192p. text 21.95 (*0-8112-1407-9*) New Directions Publishing Corp.

Murphy, Warren & Sapir, Richard, creators. Air Raid. 2002. (Destroyer Ser.: No. 126). 346p. mass mkt. (*0-373-63241-X*, 1-63241-3, Worldwide Library) Harlequin Enterprises, Ltd.

O'Brian, Patrick. The Unknown Shore. unabr. ed. 1996. audio 64.00 (*0-7366-3301-4*, 3956) Books on Tape, Inc.

—The Unknown Shore. l.t. ed. 1996. 25.95 (*1-56895-360-7*, Wheeler Publishing, Inc.) Gale Group.

—The Unknown Shore. abr. ed. 2001. audio 24.95 (*1-56511-583-X*) HighBridge Co.

—The Unknown Shore. 1996. text 23.00 (*0-07-048221-7*) McGraw-Hill Cos., The.

—The Unknown Shore. 1996. 316p. pap. 13.95 (*0-393-31538-X*); 1995. 288p. 24.00 (*0-393-03859-9*) Norton, W. W. & Co., Inc.

—The Unknown Shore. unabr. ed. 1996. audio 78.00 (*0-7887-0500-8*, 94693E7) Recorded Bks., LLC.

—The Unknown Shore. abr. ed. 1998. (Aubrey-Maturin Ser.). 331p. audio 21.95 (*1-55935-205-1*) Soundelux Audio Publishing.

O'Donnell, Peter. Last Day in Limbo. 2003. (Modesty Blaise Series Ser.). 256p. pap. 14.95 (*0-285-63675-8*) Souvenir Pr. Ltd. GBR. *Dist:* Independent Pubs. Group.

Oglesby, Virgil. Watch for the Jaguar. 2000. 200p. 18.95 (*1-58141-014-X*) Rivercross Publishing, Inc.

Olivella, Manuel Z. Chambacu: Black Slum. Tittler, Jonathan, tr. from SPA. 1989. (Discoveries Ser.). 128p. pap. 12.95 (*0-935480-39-0*) Latin American Literary Review Pr.

Olsen, Theodore V. Treasures of the Sun: A South-Western Story. 1998. 284p. 19.95 (*0-7862-0995-X*, Five Star) Gale Group.

—Treasures of the Sun: A South-Western Story. l.t. ed. 1999. (Western Ser.). 445p. 20.95 (*0-7862-1034-6*) Thorndike Pr.

Pallamary, Matthew J. Land Without Evil. unabr. ed. 2000. (Illus.). 358p. 23.95 (*0-912880-09-0*) Charles Publishing Co.

Patchett, Ann. Bel Canto: A Novel. Date not set. E-Book 10.95 (*0-06-000613-7*); Date not set. 350p. E-Book 1.00 (*0-06-000611-0*); 2001. 336p. 25.00 (*0-06-018873-1*); 2001. E-Book 19.95 (*0-06-000612-9*) HarperCollins Pubs.

—Bel Canto: A Novel. 2002. 336p. pap. 13.95 (*0-06-093441-7*, Perennial) HarperTrade.

—Bel Canto: A Novel. 2002. 30.95 (*0-7862-4792-4*) Thorndike Pr.

Patino, Ernesto. In the Shadow of a Stranger. 2002. 224p. 27.50 (*0-7090-6871-9*) Hale, Robert Ltd. GBR. *Dist:* Trafalgar Square.

Paul, Jim. Elsewhere in the Land of Parrots. 2004. 288p. pap. 13.00 (*0-15-602972-3*, Harvest Bks.); 2003. 320p. 24.00 (*0-15-100495-1*) Harcourt Trade Pubs.

Peri Rossi, Cristina. Panic Signs. Rowinsky-Geurts, Mercedes & Borras, Angelo A., trs. from SPA. 2002. 126p. pap. 18.95 (*0-88920-393-8*) Wilfrid Laurier Univ. Pr. CAN. *Dist:* Wilfrid Laurier Univ. Pr.

Peri Rossi, Cristina, et al. Panic Signs. 2002. E-Book 18.95 (*0-585-46951-2*) netLibrary, Inc.

Piglia, Ricardo. Money to Burn. Hopkinson, Amanda, tr. from SPA. 2003. 256p. pap. 14.95 (*1-86207-592-1*) Granta Bks. GBR. *Dist:* Publishers Group West.

Pollock, J. C. Threat Case. 1992. 368p. mass mkt. 5.99 o.s.i (*0-440-21204-9*) Dell Publishing.

Price, Richard & Price, Sally. Enigma Variations. (Illus.). 176p. 1995. (C). 18.95 (*0-674-25726-X*); 1997. reprint ed. 12.95 (*0-674-25728-6*) Harvard Univ. Pr.

Rathbone, Julian. Greenfinger. (Crime Ser.). 1988. 256p. pap. 3.95 o.p. (*0-14-009913-1*, Penguin Bks.); 1988. 39.50 o.p. (*0-14-778358-5*); 1987. 16.95 o.p. (*0-670-81588-8*) Viking Penguin.

Redfield, James & Adrienne, Carol. The Tenth Insight: Holding the Vision: an Experiential Guide. 1996. 384p. pap. 11.99 (*0-446-67299-8*) Warner Bks., Inc.

Reilly, Matthew. Temple. unabr. ed. 2001. audio 96.00 (*0-7366-6037-2*) Books on Tape, Inc.

—Temple. 1999. 616p. pap. (*0-7329-0971-6*) Macmillan Education Australia.

—Temple. E-Book 24.95 (*0-312-70060-1*); 2002. (Illus.). 560p. mass mkt. 6.99 (*0-312-98126-0*, St. Martin's Paperbacks); 2001. 416p. 24.95 (*0-312-26659-6*) St. Martin's Pr.

Restrepo, Laura. The Leopard in the Sun. 2000. (Vintage International Ser.). 256p. pap. 12.00 (*0-375-70508-2*, Vintage) Knopf Publishing Group.

Russo, Ethan. The Last Sorcerer: Echoes of the Rainforest. 2003. 392p. 39.95 (*0-7890-1269-3*); (Illus.). pap. 24.95 (*0-7890-1270-7*) Haworth Pr., Inc., The. (Haworth Integrative Healing Pr., The).

Schine, Cathleen. The Evolution of Jane. unabr. ed. 1998. audio 24.95 (*1-56740-087-6*, 1484, Bookcassette); audio 57.25 (*1-56740-616-5*, 1485, Unabridged Library Editions) Brilliance Audio.

—The Evolution of Jane. 1999. 224p. pap. 12.95 (*0-452-28120-2*, Plume) Dutton/Plume.

—The Evolution of Jane. 1998. 256p. tchr. ed. 24.00 o.s.i (*0-395-82657-8*) Houghton Mifflin Co.

Scorza, Manuel. Garabombo, the Invisible. Aldaz, Ana-Marie, tr. 1994. (American University Studies: Ser. XXII, Vol. 22). Tr. of Historia de Garabombo el Invisible. (ENG & SPA.). XIX, 230p. (C). text 51.95 (*0-8204-2157-X*) Lang, Peter Publishing, Inc.

Shakespeare, Nicholas. The Dancer Upstairs: A Novel. 1996. 368p. 21.95 o.s.i (*0-385-48513-1*, Talese, Nan A.) Doubleday Publishing.

—The Dancer Upstairs: A Novel. l.t. ed. 1997. 433p. 25.95 o.p. (*0-7838-8107-X*, Macmillan Reference USA) Gale Group.

Varela, Felix & Castillo-Feliu, Guillermo I. Xicotencatl: An Anonymous Historical Novel about the Events Leading up to the Conquest of the Aztec Empire. 1999. (Texas Pan American Ser.). 166p. 27.50 o.p. (*0-292-71213-8*); pap. 13.95 (*0-292-71214-6*) Univ. of Texas Pr.

Wheeler, Kate. When Mountains Walked. 2000. 256p. tchr. ed. 24.00 (*0-395-85991-3*) Houghton Mifflin Co.

Wishnia, K. J. A. Blood Lake: A Filomena Buscarsela Mystery. 2002. (Illus.). 272p. 24.95 (*0-312-28186-2*, Saint Martin's Minotaur) St. Martin's Pr.

Woolf, Virginia. Melymbrosia: An Early Version of "The Voyage Out" DeSalvo, Louise A., ed. & intro. by. 2002. 280p. 24.95 (*1-57344-148-1*) Cleis Pr.

—Melymbrosia: An Early Version of "The Voyage Out" DeSalvo, Louise A., ed. 1982. xliv, 299p. 20.00 o.p. (*0-87104-277-0*) New York Public Library.

—The Voyage Out, Set. unabr. ed. 1991. (YA). (gr. 9 up). audio 59.95 (*1-55685-194-4*) Audio Bk. Contractors, Inc.

—The Voyage Out. 1991. 448p. mass mkt. 4.95 o.s.i (*0-553-21394-6*, Bantam Classics) Bantam Bks.

—The Voyage Out. unabr. ed. 1997. audio 69.95 (*0-7861-1163-1*, 1932);Set. audio 69.95 Blackstone Audio Bks., Inc.

—The Voyage Out. (Collected Works of Virginia Woolf). reprint ed. lib. bdg. 98.00 (*0-7426-3267-9*) Classic Bks.

—The Voyage Out. 1968. 384p. reprint ed. pap. 12.00 (*0-15-693625-9*, Harvest Bks.) Harcourt Trade Pubs.

—The Voyage Out. 1991. 432p. mass mkt. 4.95 o.s.i (*0-451-52555-8*, Signet Classics) NAL.

—The Voyage Out. 1998. (Twelve-Point Ser.). 405p. reprint ed. lib. bdg. 25.00 (*1-58287-077-2*) North Bks.

—The Voyage Out. Sage, Lorna, ed. (Oxford World's Classics Ser.). 2001. 496p. pap. 10.95 (*0-19-283711-7*); 1996. 482p. (C). pap. 8.95 o.p. (*0-19-281834-1*) Oxford Univ. Pr., Inc.

—The Voyage Out. 2000. (Modern Library Ser.). 528p. 17.95 o.s.i (*0-679-64028-2*) Random Hse., Inc.

—The Voyage Out. Wheare, Jane, ed. 1992. (Twentieth Century Classics Ser.). 400p. pap. 11.95 (*0-14-018563-1*, Penguin Classics) Viking Penguin.

### SOUTH CAROLINA—FICTION

Alexander, Kathryn. Heart of a Husband. 2000. (Steeple Hill Love Inspired Ser.: Bk. 116). 256p. mass mkt. (*0-373-87122-8*, 1-87122-7, Steeple Hill) Harlequin Enterprises, Ltd.

Allison, Dorothy. Bastard Out of Carolina. unabr. ed. 1996. 10p. audio 73.25 o.p. (*1-56100-303-4*, 802, Unabridged Library Editions); audio 23.95 o.p. (*1-56100-678-5*, 38, Bookcassette) Brilliance Audio.

—Bastard Out of Carolina. 320p. 1996. pap. 18.00 (*0-452-27864-3*, Plume); 1993. pap. 14.00 (*0-452-26957-1*, Plume); 1992. 20.00 o.s.i (*0-525-93425-1*, Dutton) Dutton/Plume.

—Bastard Out of Carolina. 1997. (C). pap. text (*0-8013-3146-3*) Longman Publishing Group.

—Bastard Out of Carolina. abr. ed. 1993. (Classics on Cassette). 16.00 o.p. incl. audio (*0-453-00860-7*, 390002) Penguin/HighBridge.

—Bastard Out of Carolina. 1996. 19.00 (*0-606-19193-3*) Turtleback Bks.

Baldwin, William P. The Fennel Family Papers. 1996. 304p. tchr. ed. 19.95 o.p. (*1-56512-069-8*, 72069) Algonquin Bks. of Chapel Hill.

—The Hard to Catch Mercy. 1993. 448p. 19.95 o.p. (*1-56512-025-6*) Algonquin Bks. of Chapel Hill.

—The Hard to Catch Mercy. 1995. 464p. pap. 11.00 o.s.i (*0-449-90944-1*, Fawcett) Ballantine Bks.

Battle, Lois. Bed & Breakfast. l.t. ed. 1997. 384p. pap. 14.00 (*0-14-025911-2*) Penguin Group (USA) Inc.

—Bed & Breakfast. 1996. 384p. 23.95 o.s.i (*0-670-86074-3*) Viking Penguin.

Baxter, Mary Lynn. Tempting Janey. 2001. 384p. mass mkt. (*1-55166-809-2*, 1-66809-4, Mira Bks.) Harlequin Enterprises, Ltd.

Bodie, Idella. Ghost in the Capitol. 1986. (Illus.). 116p. (J). (gr. 5 up). pap. 6.95 (*0-87844-072-0*) Sandlapper Publishing Co., Inc.

Boyd, Blanche M. The Revolution of Little Girls. 1992. (Vintage Contemporaries Ser.). 224p. pap. 12.00 (*0-679-73812-6*, Vintage) Knopf Publishing Group.

Brockmann, Suzanne. Forever Blue. 2003. 256p. mass mkt. (*1-55166-680-4*, Mira Bks.) Harlequin Enterprises, Ltd.

Brown, Joe E., et al. Alibi Ike. 1999. audio 6.98 (*1-57019-205-7*, 4166) Radio Spirits, Inc.

Brown, Sandra. The Alibi. l.t. ed. 1999. pap. 25.00 o.p. (*0-7838-8689-6*, Macmillan Reference USA) Gale Group.

—The Alibi. abr. ed. 1999. audio 25.95 (*0-553-47827-3*); 1999. audio compact disk 29.95 (*0-553-45649-0*); 1999. audio 39.95 (*0-553-50231-X*); Set. 2000. audio compact disk 29.95 Random Hse. Audio Publishing Group.

—The Alibi. l.t. ed. 624p. 2000. pap. 14.95 (*0-375-72792-2*); 1999. 25.95 (*0-375-40860-6*) Random Hse. Large Print.

—The Alibi. 2000. 640p. E-Book 6.95 (*0-446-92405-9*) Time Warner Bk. Group.

—The Alibi. 14.04 (*0-606-19680-3*) Turtleback Bks.

—The Alibi. 2000. 640p. E-Book 6.95 (*0-446-92268-4*); 2000. E-Book 6.95 (*0-446-93142-X*); 2000. 640p. E-Book 6.95 (*0-446-92875-5*); 2000. 640p. E-Book 6.95 (*0-446-96101-9*); 2000. 640p. E-Book 6.95 (*0-446-91355-3*); 1999. 496p. 25.95 (*0-446-51980-4*); 2000. 592p. reprint ed. mass mkt. 7.99 (*0-446-60865-3*) Warner Bks., Inc.

—The Witness. abr. ed. 1995. 17.95 o.p. (*0-7871-0296-2*, 392959); 39.95 o.p. (*0-7871-0298-9*, 102973) NewStar Media, Inc.

—The Witness. 1995. 432p. 21.95 o.s.i (*0-446-51631-7*); 1996. 448p. reprint ed. mass mkt. 7.99 (*0-446-60330-9*) Warner Bks., Inc.

Casada, Jim & Rutledge, Archibald H., eds. America's Greatest Game Bird: Archibald Rutledge's Turkey-Hunting Tales. 1994. 222p. (YA). (gr. 10). 24.95 (*0-87249-983-9*) Univ. of South Carolina Pr.

Channer, Colin. Satisfy My Soul. 256p. 2003. pap. 12.95 (*0-345-43790-X*, Ballantine Bks.); 2002. 19.95 (*0-345-43789-6*, One World/Ballantine) Ballantine Bks.

—Satisfy My Soul. l.t. ed. 2003. 367p. 29.95 (*0-7862-5906-X*) Thorndike Pr.

Chappell, Ruth P. & Shipe, Bess P. The Mysterious Tail of a Charleston Cat. 1996. (Illus.). 80p. (J). (gr. 4-7). 15.95 (*0-87844-130-1*) Sandlapper Publishing Co., Inc.

Childs, Laura. Death by Darjeeling. 2001. 256p. mass mkt. 5.99 (*0-425-17945-1*) Berkley Publishing Group.

—Death by Darjeeling. l.t. ed. 2002. 379p. pap. 25.95 (*0-7862-4535-2*) Thorndike Pr.

Clary, Margie Willis. Searching the Lights. 1998. (Illus.). (J). (gr. 4-7). 12.95 (*0-87844-138-7*) Sandlapper Publishing Co., Inc.

Coburn, Randy Sue. Remembering Jody. 1999. 322p. 22.95 (*0-7867-0566-3*, Carroll & Graf Pubs.) Avalon Publishing Group.

Collins, Kevin & Guilds, John C., eds. The Cassique of Kiawah: A Colonial Romance. 2003. (Simms Ser.). 600p. pap. 34.95 (*1-55728-762-7*) Univ. of Arkansas Pr.

Conroy, Pat. Beach Music. 1996. (Illus.). 816p. reprint ed. mass mkt. 7.99 (*0-553-57457-4*) Bantam Bks.

—Beach Music, 2 Pts. unabr. ed. 1995. audio 152.00 (*0-7366-3080-5*, 3761A/B); audio 72.00. audio 80.00 Books on Tape, Inc.

—Beach Music. 1995. 640p. 32.50 (*0-385-41304-1*, Talese, Nan A.); 628p. 200.00 o.s.i (*0-385-47590-X*) Doubleday Publishing.

—Beach Music. abr. ed. 1995. audio 29.95 (*0-553-47270-4*, 892989); audio 27.50 o.s.i (*0-553-74619-7*) Random Hse. Audio Publishing Group. (RH Audio).

—Beach Music. unabr. ed. audio 158.00 (*0-7887-0335-8*, 94527E7) Recorded Bks., LLC.

—Beach Music. 628p. pap. 8.98 o.p. (*0-7651-0633-7*) Smithmark Pubs., Inc.

—Beach Music. 1996. 14.04 (*0-606-11096-8*) Turtleback Bks.

—The Lords of Discipline, 001. 1980. 544p. 12.95 o.p. (*0-395-29462-2*) Houghton Mifflin Co.

—The Prince of Tides. audio 8.95 American Audio Prose Library, Inc.

—The Prince of Tides. l.t. ed. 1993. pap. 21.95 o.p. (*0-7927-1358-3*); 1992. 24.95 o.p. (*0-7927-1359-1*) BBC Audiobooks America.

—The Prince of Tides. 1987. 672p. mass mkt. 7.99 (*0-553-26888-0*) Bantam Bks.

—The Prince of Tides. unabr. ed. 1988. Pt. A. audio 88.00 (*0-7366-1458-3*, 2339-A); Pt. B. audio 88.00 (*0-7366-1459-1*, 2339-B) Books on Tape, Inc.

—The Prince of Tides, 001. 1986. 576p. tchr. ed. 30.00 (*0-395-35300-9*) Houghton Mifflin Co.

—The Prince of Tides. 1987. audio 12.79 o.s.i (*0-553-19969-2*); audio 15.95 o.s.i (*0-553-74510-7*); audio 16.99 (*0-553-45096-4*, 391403) Random Hse. Audio Publishing Group. (RH Audio).

—The Prince of Tides. unabr. ed. 1988. audio 144.00 (*1-55690-425-8*, 88020E7) Recorded Bks., LLC.

—The Prince of Tides. 2002. E-Book 8.99 (*0-7953-0100-6*) RosettaBooks.

—The Prince of Tides. 1991. 14.04 (*0-606-03895-7*) Turtleback Bks.

Craig, Amanda. In a Dark Wood. 2002. 320p. 24.95 (*0-385-50262-1*, Talese, Nan A.) Doubleday Publishing.

—In a Dark Wood: A Novel. 2003. 320p. pap. 13.00 (*0-385-72117-X*) Doubleday Publishing.

—In a Dark Wood: A Novel. 2000. 276p. (*1-85702-682-9*) Fourth Estate, Ltd. GBR. *Dist:* Trafalgar Square.

Dash, Julie. Daughters of the Dust: The Making of an African American Woman's Film. 320p. 1999. pap. 13.95 o.s.i (*0-452-27607-1*, Plume); 1997. 24.95 o.p. (*0-525-94109-6*) Dutton/Plume.

DeLoach, Nora L. Mama Stalks the Past. 1998. 272p. mass mkt. 5.99 o.s.i (*0-553-57721-2*); 1997. 208p. 21.95 o.s.i (*0-553-10662-7*) Bantam Bks.

Dunn, Mark. Ella Minnow Pea: A Novel in Letters. 2002. 224p. pap. 12.00 (*0-385-72243-5*, Anchor) Knopf Publishing Group.

—Ella Minnow Pea: A Novel in Letters. 2001. 205p. 22.00 (*0-9673701-6-7*) MacAdam/Cage Publishing, Inc.

Durban, Pam. The Laughing Place. 1995. 352p. pap. 13.00 (*0-312-13110-0*) Picador.

—The Laughing Place: A Novel. Grossman, Barbara, ed. 1993. 352p. 21.00 (*0-684-19258-6*, Macmillan Reference USA) Gale Group.

Earle, Wilton. Manse: One Man's War. 1996. (Illus.). 416p. 24.00 (*0-9632422-2-9*) Adept, Inc.

Evanovich, Janet. Full Speed. l.t. ed. 2003. 563p. pap. 14.95 (*0-375-43284-1*, Random House Large Print) Random Hse. Large Print.

Farley, Benjamin W. Mercy Road & Other Stories. 1986. (Illus.). 136p. 13.95 (*0-87797-122-6*) Cherokee Publishing Co.

Farrow, David A. The Root of All Evil. 2002. E-Book 20.00 o.p. (*0-941711-54-4*); 1997. 350p. 23.95 (*0-941711-36-6*) Wyrick & Co.

Fast, Howard. Freedom Road. 1988. 5.95 o.s.i (*0-517-50689-0*, Crown) Crown Publishing Group.

—Freedom Road. 1995. (American History Through Literature Ser.). 294p. (J). 80.95 (*1-56324-602-3*); (C). (gr. 13). pap. 21.95 (*1-56324-440-3*) Sharpe, M.E. Inc.

Floyd, Blanche W. Tales Along the King's Highway of South Carolina. 1999. 148p. pap. text 12.95 (*1-878177-10-9*) Bandit Bks., Inc.

Fortune, Gwendoline Y. Growing up Nigger Rich. 2002. 256p. 22.00 (*1-56554-963-5*) Pelican Publishing Co., Inc.

Frank, Dorothea Benton. Isle of Palms: A Lowcountry Tale. l.t. ed. 2003. 701p. 31.95 (*0-7862-5876-4*) Thorndike Pr.

—Plantation. 2004. 544p. pap. 13.95 (*0-425-19418-3*) Berkley Publishing Group.

—Plantation: A Lowcountry Tale. 2001. (Illus.). 608p. mass mkt. 6.99 (*0-515-13108-3*, Jove) Berkley Publishing Group.

—Sullivan's Island. 2004. 464p. pap. 13.95 (*0-425-19394-2*); 2000. 416p. mass mkt. 7.99 (*0-515-12722-1*, Jove) Berkley Publishing Group.

—Sullivan's Island. l.t. ed. 2000. (Core Ser.). 567p. 31.95 (*0-7838-9078-8*, Macmillan Reference USA) Gale Group.

—Sullivan's Island. l.t. ed. 2001. 567p. pap. 29.95 (*0-7838-9079-6*) Thorndike Pr.

—Sullivan's Island: A Lowcountry Tale. abr. ed. 2003. audio 12.99 (*1-59086-013-6*, 3534, Brilliance Audio Paperback Audiobooks); 2002. audio 24.95 o.p. (*1-59086-011-X*, 3533, Nova Audio Bks.); 2002. audio 62.25 (*1-59086-012-8*, 3535, Library Edition) Brilliance Audio.

Godwin, Rebecca T. Keeper of the House. 288p. 1994. 19.95 o.p. (*0-312-11405-2*); 1995. reprint ed. pap. 13.95 (*0-312-13529-7*, NPB 0331, Saint Martin's Griffin) St. Martin's Pr.

—Private Parts. 1992. 18.95 o.p. (*1-56352-021-4*) Longstreet Pr., Inc.

Goodman, James H. The Rusty Charm. Zuber, Fred, ed. 1986. 272p. pap. 9.95 o.s.i (*0-89896-270-6*) Larksdale.

Green, Hubert. Magnolia, Magnolia, Where Are You? 2001. pap. text (*0-9720272-0-3*) Green, Hubert.

—Magnolia, Magnolia, Where Are You? 2003. 104p. pap. (*1-4120-0092-0*) Trafford Publishing.

Greene, Harlan. What the Dead Remember. 192p. 1992. pap. 9.00 o.p. (*0-452-26865-6*, Plume); 1991. 18.95 o.p. (*0-525-93378-6*, Dutton) Dutton/Plume.

Greer, Ben. Slammer. 2002. (Voices of the South Ser.). 280p. pap. 16.95 (*0-8071-2789-2*) Louisiana State Univ. Pr.

Habersham, Isabella Rae. The Gilded Coach: A Novel. 2002. (First Fiction Ser.). 192p. pap. 14.95 (*0-86534-348-9*) Sunstone Pr.

Hamilton, Elizabeth V. Storm Center. 1983. (Illus.). 200p. 12.50 (*0-937684-16-3*) Tradd Street Pr.

Hart, Carolyn. Murder Walks the Plank. 2004. 304p. 23.95 (*0-06-000474-6*, Morrow, William & Co.) Morrow/Avon.

Hart, Carolyn G. April Fool Dead. 2002. 304p. 23.95 (*0-380-97774-5*) Morrow/Avon.

—The Christie Caper. 1992. (Annie Darling Ser.). 400p. mass mkt. 6.99 (*0-553-29569-1*) Bantam Bks.

—The Christie Caper. unabr. ed. 1996. (Annie Laurance Darling Ser.). audio 64.00 (*0-7366-3457-6*, 4101) Books on Tape, Inc.

—Crime on Her Mind: A Collection of Short Stories. 1999. (Mystery Ser.). 268p. 21.95 (*0-7862-1735-9*, Five Star) Gale Group.

—Dead Man's Island. 1994. 352p. mass mkt. 6.99 (*0-553-56607-5*) Bantam Bks.

—Dead Man's Island. unabr. ed. 1997. (Henrie O Mysteries Ser.). audio 48.00 (*0-7366-3837-7*, 4557) Books on Tape, Inc.

—Dead Man's Island. l.t. ed. 1994. (G. K. Hall Mystery Ser.). 355p. lib. bdg. 23.95 o.p. (*0-8161-5874-6*, Macmillan Reference USA) Gale Group.

—Deadly Valentine. 1991. (Death on Demand Ser.). 272p. mass mkt. 6.99 incl. audio (*0-553-28847-4*) Bantam Bks.

—Deadly Valentine. l.t. ed. 1998. (Beeler Large Print Mystery Ser.). 25.95 (*1-57490-139-3*, Beeler Large Print Bks.) Beeler, Thomas T. Publisher.

—Deadly Valentine. unabr. ed. 1996. (Annie Laurance Darling Ser.). audio 48.00 (*0-7366-3407-X*, 4053) Books on Tape, Inc.

—Deadly Valentine. 1990. 192p. 14.95 o.s.i (*0-385-26518-2*) Doubleday Publishing.

—Death on Demand. 1989. 208p. mass mkt. 1.95 o.s.i (*0-553-18502-0*); 1987. 224p. mass mkt. 6.99 (*0-553-26351-X*) Bantam Bks.

—Death on Demand. l.t. ed. 2000. (Mystery Ser.). (Illus.). 227p. 26.95 (*1-57490-276-8*, Beeler Large Print Bks.) Beeler, Thomas T. Publisher.

—Death on Demand. l.t. ed. 2000. (Wheeler Softcover Ser.). 280p. pap. 24.95 (*1-56895-914-1*, Wheeler Publishing, Inc.) Gale Group.

—Design for Murder. 1988. 320p. mass mkt. 6.99 (*0-553-26562-8*) Bantam Bks.

—Design for Murder. l.t. ed. 2000. (Beeler Large Print Mystery Ser.). 208p. (*1-57490-291-1*, Beeler Large Print Bks.) Beeler, Thomas T. Publisher.

—Design for Murder. l.t. ed. 2001. (Large Print Bks.). (Illus.). 345p. pap. 23.95 o.p. (*1-58724-112-9*, Wheeler Publishing, Inc.) Gale Group.

—Engaged to Die. 2003. 320p. 23.95 (*0-06-000469-X*, Morrow, William & Co.) Morrow/Avon.

—A Little Class on Murder. l.t. ed. 1992. pap. 21.95 o.p. (*0-7927-1140-8*, CS0306); 1991. 23.95 o.p. (*0-7927-1139-4*, CH0234) BBC Audiobooks America.

—A Little Class on Murder. 1989. 272p. mass mkt. 6.99 (*0-553-28208-5*) Bantam Bks.

—A Little Class on Murder. unabr. collector's ed. 1996. (Annie Laurance Darling Ser.). audio 48.00 (*0-7366-3419-3*, 894409) Books on Tape, Inc.

—A Little Class on Murder. 1989. 12.95 o.s.i (*0-385-26452-6*) Doubleday Publishing.

—Mint Julep Murder. 1996. 256p. mass mkt. 6.99 (*0-553-57202-4*); 1995. 288p. 19.95 o.s.i (*0-553-09463-7*) Bantam Bks.

—Mint Julep Murder. unabr. ed. 1996. (Annie Laurance Darling Ser.). audio 48.00 (*0-7366-3498-3*, 4138) Books on Tape, Inc.

—Mint Julep Murder. l.t. ed. 1996. 362p. 23.95 o.p. (*0-7838-1496-8*, Macmillan Reference USA) Gale Group.

—Southern Ghost. 1993. (Annie Darling Ser.). 320p. mass mkt. 6.99 (*0-553-56275-4*) Bantam Bks.

—Southern Ghost. unabr. ed. 1996. (Annie Laurance Darling Ser.). audio 56.00 (*0-7366-3501-7*, 4141) Books on Tape, Inc.

—Sugarplum Dead. l.t. ed. 2001. (G. K. Hall Core Ser.). 472p. 30.95 (*0-7838-9377-9*, Macmillan Reference USA) Gale Group.

—Sugarplum Dead. 2000. (Death on Demand Mysteries Ser.). 352p. 24.00 (*0-380-97772-9*, Morrow, William & Co.) Morrow/Avon.

—White Elephant Dead. (Death on Demand Mysteries Ser.). 2000. 304p. mass mkt. 6.99 (*0-380-79325-3*); 1999. 277p. 23.00 (*0-380-97530-0*) Morrow/Avon. (Avon Bks.).

—White Elephant Dead. l.t. ed. 2000. (Mystery Ser.). 431p. 29.95 o.p. (*0-7862-2341-3*) Thorndike Pr.

—Yankee Doodle Dead. l.t. ed. 1999. pap. 24.95 (*1-56895-718-1*, Wheeler Publishing, Inc.) Gale Group.

—Yankee Doodle Dead. 1999. 304p. mass mkt. 6.99 (*0-380-79326-1*); 1998. 288p. 21.00 (*0-380-97529-7*) Morrow/Avon. (Avon Bks.).

Hazzard, Kevin M. Sleeping Dogs: A Novel. 2002. 128p. 20.00 (*0-86554-812-9*) Mercer Univ. Pr.

Hearon, Shelby. Life Estates. 1995. pap. 11.00 (*0-679-75796-1*, Vintage) Knopf Publishing Group.

—Life Estates. 1994. 231p. 22.00 o.s.i (*0-679-41539-4*) Knopf, Alfred A. Inc.

Heins, Henry C., Jr. Dr. Thomas Chalmers' Secret Diary. 1998. 213p. 20.00 (*1-887301-03-8*) Palmetto Bookworks.

Heyward, DeBose. Mamba's Daughters. 24.95 (*0-89190-749-1*) Amereon, Ltd.

—Mamba's Daughters: A Novel of Charleston. 1995. (Southern Classics Ser.). 334p. pap. 16.95 (*1-57003-042-1*) Univ. of South Carolina Pr.

Heyward, DuBose & Heyward, Dorothy. Porgy. 1980. (American Drama Ser.). Dell Publishing.

Heyward, DuBose. Porgy. Date not set. reprint ed. lib. bdg. 20.95 (*0-89190-684-3*, American Reprint Co.) Amereon, Ltd.

—Porgy. 1991. 196p. reprint ed. lib. bdg. 18.95 (*0-89966-768-6*) Buccaneer Bks., Inc.

—Porgy. 2nd ed. (Illus.). 192p. reprint ed. pap. 20.00 o.p. (*0-937684-22-8*, P23.H1587PO) Tradd Street Pr.

—Porgy. 2001. (Banner Bks.). 208p. reprint ed. pap. 18.00 (*1-57806-356-6*) Univ. Pr. of Mississippi.

Heyward, Dubose & Heyward, Dorothy. Porgy: A Gullah Version. Geraty, Virginia M., tr. & intro. by. 1990. 129p. pap. 8.95 (*0-941711-11-0*) Wyrick & Co.

Hightower, Lynn S. High Water: A Novel. 2002. 336p. 25.00 (*0-8050-6756-6*) Holt, Henry & Co.

Holmes, Jean E. Bound Fo' Glory. 1996. (Weldon Oaks Ser.: Pt. 5). pap. 4.97 o.p. (*0-8163-1275-3*) Pacific Pr. Publishing Assn.

—Deep River, Lawd. 1993. pap. 9.99 o.p. (*0-8163-1119-6*) Pacific Pr. Publishing Assn.

—Mornin' Star Risin' 1992. (Weldon Oaks Ser.: No. 1). 160p. pap. 4.97 (*0-8163-1064-5*) Pacific Pr. Publishing Assn.

—Sea Island Sanctuary. Woolsey, Raymond H., ed. 1988. 128p. (Orig.). (J). (gr. 6-8). pap. 6.95 o.p. (*0-8280-0436-6*) Review & Herald Publishing Assn.

Houston, Gloria M. Young Will: A Sunny Land with a Sunny Brook. 1995. (Illus.). (J). o.p. (*0-399-22740-7*, Philomel) Penguin Putnam Bks. for Young Readers.

Hughes, Charlotte. Hot Shot. 2002. 384p. mass mkt. (*1-55166-941-2*, Mira Bks.) Harlequin Enterprises, Ltd.

Humphreys, Josephine. The Fireman's Fair. 1992. 272p. pap. 13.00 (*0-14-016838-9*, Penguin Bks.) Penguin Group (USA) Inc.

—The Fireman's Fair. 1991. 272p. 19.95 o.p. (*0-670-83907-8*) Viking Penguin.

Hunnings, Vicky. Death on a Cellular Level. 2003. 304p. text 24.95 (*0-8034-9608-7*, Avalon Bks.) Bouregy, Thomas & Co., Inc.

Hunter, Gwen. Deadly Remedy. 2003. 384p. mass mkt. (*1-55166-669-3*, Mira Bks.) Harlequin Enterprises, Ltd.

—Delayed Diagnosis. 2001. 384p. mass mkt. (*1-55166-803-3*, Mira Bks.) Harlequin Enterprises, Ltd.

Jakes, John. Charleston. 2003. (Illus.). 464p. 26.95 o.s.i (*0-525-94650-0*, Dutton) Dutton/Plume.

—Charleston. 2002. 29.95 (*1-58724-355-5*, Wheeler Publishing, Inc.) Gale Group.

—Charleston. 2003. 760p. reprint ed. mass mkt. 7.99 (*0-451-20733-5*, 53560613, Signet Bks.) NAL.

—Charleston. 528p. (*0-7278-5966-8*) Severn Hse. Pubs., Ltd.

Johnston, Colleen L. Guardians. 1994. (Gairden Legacy Ser.: No. 2). mass mkt. 4.99 o.p. (*0-312-95125-6*, St. Martin's Paperbacks) St. Martin's Pr.

Johnston, Colleen L. Founders. 1993. mass mkt. 4.99 o.p. (*0-312-95060-8*, St. Martin's Paperbacks) St. Martin's Pr.

Julian, Donna. Slow Dance. 1995. 384p. (Orig.). mass mkt. 5.50 o.s.i (*0-451-18671-0*, Signet Bks.) NAL.

Kidd, Sue Monk. The Secret Life of Bees: A Novel. l.t. ed. 2002. 474p. 29.95 (*0-7862-4306-6*) Gale Group.

—The Secret Life of Bees: A Novel. 2003. 336p. pap. 14.00 (*0-14-200174-0*) Penguin Group (USA) Inc.

—The Secret Life of Bees: A Novel. 2002. pap. 24.95 (*0-670-03237-9*); 320p. 24.95 (*0-670-89460-5*, Viking) Viking Penguin.

Kilgo, James. Daughter of My People. 2000. 303p. reprint ed. pap. 13.95 o.s.i (*0-425-17266-X*) Berkley Publishing Group.

—Daughter of My People. 1998. 288p. 24.00 (*0-8203-2002-1*) Univ. of Georgia Pr.

King, Susan P. Gerald Gray's Wife & Lily: A Novel. 1993. 400p. text 69.95 (*0-8223-1407-X*); pap. text 21.95 (*0-8223-1411-8*) Duke Univ. Pr.

Lacy, Al & Lacy, JoAnna. Ransom of Love. 2003. (Mail Order Bride Ser.: Vol. 5). 336p. pap. 10.99 (*1-57673-609-1*, Multnomah Bks.) Multnomah Pubs., Inc.

Leland Wilder, Effie. Effie Leland Wilder Omnibus: Out to Pasture; Over What Hill?; Older but Wilder, 3 vols., Set. 2002. (Illus.). 560p. 13.99 (*0-517-22002-4*) Random Hse., Inc.

—Oh My Goodness! More Surprises from FairAcres. 2001. (Illus.). 192p. (J). 14.95 (*1-56145-255-6*) Peachtree Pubs., Ltd.

—Out to Pasture: But Not over the Hill. 1995. (Illus.). 177p. 14.95 (*1-56145-101-0*); 1996. audio 15.95 (*1-56145-136-3*) Peachtree Pubs., Ltd.

Lott, Bret. The Hunt Club. 1999. 351p. mass mkt. 5.99 (*0-06-101390-0*) HarperCollins Pubs.

—The Hunt Club. abr. ed. 2001. audio 12.99 (*1-57815-208-9*, Media Bks. Audio Publishing) Media Bks., L. L. C.

—The Hunt Club: A Novel. 1998. 243p. 23.00 o.s.i (*0-375-50014-6*, Villard Bks.) Random House Adult Trade Publishing Group.

Lott, Bret, abr. The Hunt Club. 1999. 256p. pap. 13.00 (*0-06-097770-1*, Perennial) HarperTrade.

Maxim, John R. Haven. abr. ed. 1998. audio 7.99 o.s.i (*1-56740-256-9*, 889, Paperback Nova Audio Bks.); 1997. audio 16.95 o.p. (*1-56740-750-1*, 519, Nova Audio Bks.); 1997. audio 89.25 (*1-56740-550-9*, 888, Unabridged Library Editions); 1997. audio 25.95 (*1-56100-771-4*, 329, Bookcassette) Brilliance Audio.

—Haven. 1998. 416p. mass mkt. 6.99 (*0-380-78669-9*); 1997. 384p. 24.00 (*0-380-97301-4*) Morrow/Avon. (Avon Bks.).

Mercer, Judy. Double Take. l.t. ed. 1997. (G. K. Hall Mystery Ser.). 561p. 26.95 o.p. (*0-7838-8368-4*, Macmillan Reference USA) Gale Group.

—Double Take. 1997. 352p. 22.00 (*0-671-55707-6*, Atria) Simon & Schuster.

Meriwether, Louise. Fragments of the Ark. Rosenman, Jane, ed. 1995. 352p. pap. 21.95 (*0-671-79948-7*, Pocket) Simon & Schuster.

—Fragments of the Ark. 1994. 352p. 21.00 o.s.i (*0-671-79947-9*, Atria) Simon & Schuster.

Mezrich, Ben. Threshold. 1996. 320p. 24.00 o.p. (*0-06-017302-5*) HarperCollins Pubs.

—Threshold. 1997. 352p. mass mkt. 6.99 o.s.i (*0-446-60521-2*) Warner Bks., Inc.

Michaels, Fern. Finders Keepers. l.t. ed. 1998. 27.95 (*1-56895-693-2*, Wheeler Publishing, Inc.) Gale Group.

—Finders Keepers. 2002. 432p. mass mkt. 7.50 (*0-8217-7364-X*); 1999. 432p. mass mkt. 6.99 o.s.i (*0-8217-6307-5*, Zebra Bks.); 1998. 352p. 24.00 o.s.i (*1-57566-323-6*, Kensington Bks.) Kensington Publishing Corp.

—Yesterday. l.t. ed. 1999. 26.95 (*1-56895-797-1*, Wheeler Publishing, Inc.) Gale Group.

—Yesterday. 1999. 373p. 24.00 o.s.i (*1-57566-467-4*, Kensington Bks.); 2001. 464p. reprint ed. mass mkt. 7.50 (*0-8217-6785-2*, Zebra Bks.) Kensington Publishing Corp.

Monroe, Mary Alice. Skyward. 2003. 416p. mass mkt. (*1-55166-700-2*, Mira Bks.) Harlequin Enterprises, Ltd.

—Skyward. l.t. ed. 2003. 618p. 28.95 (*0-7862-5869-1*) Thorndike Pr.

Morgan, Robert. Brave Enemies: A Novel of the American Revolution. 2003. (Illus.). 320p. 24.95 (*1-56512-356-5*, Shannon Ravenel Bks.) Algonquin Bks. of Chapel Hill.

—Gap Creek: The Story of a Marriage. 2000. (Oprah's Book Club Ser.). 324p. tchr. ed. 22.95 (*1-56512-296-8*) Algonquin Bks. of Chapel Hill.

—Gap Creek: The Story of a Marriage. abr. ed. 2000. 24.95 (*1-56511-386-1*) HighBridge Co.

—Gap Creek: The Story of a Marriage. unabr. ed. 2000. audio 76.00 Recorded Bks., LLC.

—Gap Creek: The Story of a Marriage. 2000. 336p. pap. 14.00 (*0-7432-0363-1*); pap. 7.99 (*0-7432-0334-8*) Simon & Schuster. (Touchstone).

—Gap Creek: The Story of a Marriage. l.t. ed. 2000. (Basic Ser.). 488p. 30.95 (*0-7862-2545-9*) Thorndike Pr.

Morris, Dorothy K. Secret Sins of the Mothers: A Novel. Finton, Kenneth H. & Thompson, Chaya, eds. 1999. 248p. 24.95 (*1-892977-03-6*) HT Communications.

Morris, Lynn & Morris, Gilbert. Toward the Sunrising. 1996. (Cheney Duvall, M. D. Ser.: Vol. 4). 368p. pap. 11.99 (*1-55661-425-X*) Bethany Hse. Pubs.

—Toward the Sunrising. 1998. (Cheney Duvall, M. D. Ser.: Vol. 4). 362p. 23.95 (*0-7862-1436-8*, Five Star) Gale Group.

Myers, Walter Dean. The Glory Field. 1994. 288p. (J). (gr. 7-9). pap. 14.95 (*0-590-45897-3*) Scholastic, Inc.

Naylor, Gloria. Mama Day. unabr. ed. 1989. audio 22.95 o.p. (*0-930435-54-0*, 400, Bookcassette); audio 73.25 o.p. (*1-56100-048-5*, 582) Brilliance Audio.

—Mama Day. l.t. ed. 1989. 496p. 19.95 o.p. (*0-8161-4692-6*, Macmillan Reference USA) Gale Group.

—Mama Day. 1988. 320p. 17.95 (*0-89919-716-7*) Houghton Mifflin Co.

—Mama Day. 1989. (Vintage Contemporaries Ser.). 336p. pap. 13.95 (*0-679-72181-9*, Vintage) Knopf Publishing Group.

Newton, David, ed. The Forayers or the Raid of the Dog Days. 2003. (Simms Ser.). (Illus.). 560p. pap. 34.95 (*1-55728-741-4*) Univ. of Arkansas Pr.

O'Dell, Darlene. I Followed Close Behind Her. 2003. 14.00 (*1-883523-60-5*) Spinsters Ink Bks.

O'Neal, Reagan, pseud. The Fallon Blood. 1995. 384p. 23.95 o.p. (*0-312-85973-2*, Forge Bks.) Doherty, Tom Assocs., LLC.

Peterkin, Julia. Black April. 24.95 (*0-89190-527-8*) Amereon, Ltd.

—Black April. 1998. 328p. reprint ed. pap. 15.95 (*0-8203-1953-8*) Univ. of Georgia Pr.

—Green Thursday. 1998. 200p. reprint ed. pap. 15.95 (*0-8203-1955-4*) Univ. of Georgia Pr.

Pilgrim, Millie W. All Kneel down & Pray. 1998. 186p. pap. 10.95 (*0-9613184-3-0*) H&M Enterprises.

Pinckney, Roger. Little Glory. 2003. 225p. 22.95 (*0-941711-63-3*) Wyrick & Co.

Porcelli, Joe. The Photograph. Wyrick, Charles L., Jr., ed. 1995. 346p. 22.95 (*0-941711-30-7*) Wyrick & Co.

Powell, Mark. Prodigals: A Novel. 2002. 193p. 26.95 (*1-57233-189-5*) Univ. of Tennessee Pr.

Powell, Padgett. Edisto Revisited. 1996. 160p. 20.00 o.s.i (*0-8050-4237-7*) Holt, Henry & Co.

Quinn, Eric S. Say Uncle. 336p. 1995. pap. 11.95 o.p. (*0-452-27166-5*, Plume); 1994. 20.95 o.p. (*0-525-93780-3*) Dutton/Plume.

Reichs, Kathy. Death du Jour. unabr. ed. 2002. audio compact disk 110.95; 2000. audio 96.95 (*0-7927-2346-5*, CSL235, Chivers Sound Library) BBC Audiobooks America.

—Death du Jour. unabr. ed. 2000. 12p. audio compact disk 110.95 (*0-7540-5330-X*, CCD 021) Chivers Audio Bks. GBR. *Dist:* BBC Audiobooks America.

—Death du Jour. 1999. 384p. mass mkt. 7.99 (*0-671-03472-3*, Pocket); 1999. E-Book 25.00 (*0-7432-0080-2*, Scribner); 1999. 384p. 25.00 (*0-684-84118-5*, Scribner); 1999. 384p. 25.00 (*0-684-86906-3*, Scribner); 2000. (Illus.). 480p. reprint ed. mass mkt. 7.99 (*0-671-01137-5*, Pocket) Simon & Schuster.

—Death du Jour, Set. abr. ed. 1999. audio 24.00 (*0-671-04370-6*, 599126, Simon & Schuster Audioworks) Simon & Schuster Audio.

—Death du Jour. l.t. ed. (Thorndike/G. K. Hall Paperback Bestsellers Ser.). 632p. 2000. (FRE.). pap. 27.95 (*0-7862-1997-1*); 1999. 30.95 (*0-7862-1996-3*) Thorndike Pr.

—Death du Jour. abr. ed. 1999. audio 24.35 (*1-85686-522-3*) Ulverscroft Audio (U.S.A.).

Reynolds, Sheri. The Rapture of Canaan. 336p. 1997. pap. 12.00 (*0-425-16244-3*); 1996. reprint ed. mass mkt. 7.99 (*0-425-15543-9*) Berkley Publishing Group.

—The Rapture of Canaan. 1997. audio 48.00. audio 48.00 (*0-913369-87-X*) Books on Tape, Inc.

—The Rapture of Canaan. 1999. 320p. reprint ed. pap. text 12.00 (*0-7881-6169-5*) DIANE Publishing Co.

Settings

—The Rapture of Canaan. unabr. ed. 1999. audio NorthStar Audio Bks.

—The Rapture of Canaan. 1997. 22.95 o.s.i (0-399-14352-1); 1996. 336p. 22.95 o.p. (0-399-14112-X, G. P. Putnam's Sons) Penguin Group (USA) Inc.

—The Rapture of Canaan. 2001. audio compact disk 78.00 (0-7887-5205-7, C1362E7); 1997. audio 48.00 (0-7887-1315-9, 95173E7) Recorded Bks., LLC.

—The Rapture of Canaan. l.t. ed. 1997. (Core Ser.). 364p. lib. bdg. 30.95 (0-7838-8270-X) Thorndike Pr.

Rhyne, Nancy. Alice Flagg: The Ghost of the Hermitage. 1990. 256p. 19.95 (0-88289-760-8) Pelican Publishing Co., Inc.

Robards, Karen. Nobody's Angel. 1992. 416p. mass mkt. 7.99 (0-440-20828-9) Dell Publishing.

—To Trust a Stranger. 2003. (Illus.). 448p. mass mkt. 7.99 (0-671-78660-1, Pocket Star); 2001. 352p. 25.00 (0-671-78653-9, Atria); 2002. 512p. pap. 25.00 (0-7434-6628-4, Pocket) Simon & Schuster.

Roberts, Nora. Carolina Moon. 2001. 480p. reprint ed. mass mkt. 7.99 (0-515-13038-9, Jove) Berkley Publishing Group.

—Carolina Moon. 2000. 448p. 24.95 o.p. (0-399-14592-3) Penguin Group (USA) Inc.

—Carolina Moon. 2002. 24.95 o.s.i (0-399-15030-7) Putnam Publishing Group, The.

—Carolina Moon. l.t. ed. 2000. (Basic Ser.). 712p. 31.95 (0-7862-2287-5) Thorndike Pr.

Robinson, Patricia. A Trick of the Light. 214p. 3.98 o.p. (0-8317-5136-3) Smithmark Pubs., Inc.

—A Trick of the Light. 1994. 240p. 19.95 o.p. (0-312-10564-9, Saint Martin's Minotaur) St. Martin's Pr.

Rubin, Louis D. The Heat of the Sun. 1995. 448p. 21.95 (1-56352-233-0) Longstreet Pr., Inc.

Rue, Nancy. The Trap. 1998. (Christian Heritage Ser.). 208p. (J). (gr. 3-7). pap. 5.99 (1-56179-567-4) Focus on the Family Publishing.

Rutledge, Archibald. Tom & I on the Old Plantation. 1977. (Black Heritage Library Collection). (Illus.). reprint ed. 18.95 (0-8369-9124-9) Ayer Co. Pubs., Inc.

Sanders, Dori. Her Own Place. 1994. 256p. reprint ed. pap. 11.95 (0-449-90875-5, Fawcett) Ballantine Bks.

—Her Own Place. l.t. ed. 1993. (Large Print Bks.). 249p. lib. bdg. 20.95 o.p. (0-8161-5754-5, Macmillan Reference USA) Gale Group.

—Her Own Place. unabr. ed. 1998. audio 44.00 (0-7887-0404-4, 94837E7) Recorded Bks., LLC.

—Her Own Place: A Novel. 1999. 252p. tchr. ed. 16.95 (1-56512-027-2, 72027) Algonquin Bks. of Chapel Hill.

Sawyer, David J. My Great-Grandfather Was Stonewall Jackson: The Story of a Negro Boy Growing up in the Segregated South. 1994. (Illus.). 288p. pap. 14.00 (0-9635159-1-8) Publishing Concepts.

Sayers, Valerie. Due East. 1988. mass mkt. 3.95 o.p. (0-425-10895-3) Berkley Publishing Group.

Schede, Carol M. The Runaway Princess. 2001. (Five Star First Edition Romance Ser.). 200p. 25.95 (0-7862-3321-4, Five Star) Gale Group.

Shange, Ntozake. Sassafrass, Cypress & Indigo. 2nd ed. 1996. 240p. pap. 13.00 (0-312-14091-6) Picador.

Siddons, Anne Rivers. Islands. 2004. 384p. 24.95 (0-06-621111-5); 2003. E-Book 19.95 (0-06-057675-8); 2003. E-Book 19.95 (0-06-057676-6); 2003. E-Book 19.95 (0-06-057677-4); 2003. E-Book 19.95 (0-06-057674-X); 2004. audio compact disk 29.95 (0-06-055458-4) HarperCollins Pubs.

—Islands. l.t. ed. 2004. 512p. pap. 24.95 (0-06-054545-3, HarperLargePrint) HarperTrade.

—Low Country. l.t. ed. 1998. 509p. (0-7540-2156-4) BBC Audiobooks America.

—Low Country. unabr. ed. 1998. audio 64.00 (0-7366-4236-6, 4733) Books on Tape, Inc.

—Low Country. 1998. 304p. 25.00 o.s.i (0-06-017616-4) HarperCollins Pubs.

—Low Country. abr. ed. 1998. audio 25.00 (0-694-51996-0, 696012, HarperAudio) HarperTrade.

—Low Country. 1999. 480p. mass mkt. 7.99 (0-06-109332-7, HarperTorch) Morrow/Avon.

—Low Country. unabr. ed. 1999. audio compact disk 89.00 (0-7887-3444-X, C1050E7); 1998. audio 70.00 (0-7887-2163-1, 95459E7) Recorded Bks., LLC.

—Low Country. l.t. ed. (Paperback Bestsellers Ser.). 1999. 511p. pap. 27.95 o.p. (0-7862-1425-2); 1998. 511p. 30.95 (0-7862-1424-4); 1998. (0-7540-1214-X) Thorndike Pr.

Simmons, Dawn L. She-Crab Soup. 1993. 260p. 16.95 (0-9629880-2-2) ACME Pr.

Simms, William Gilmore. Woodcraft. E-Book 3.95 (0-594-01550-2) 1873 Pr.

—Woodcraft. Watson, Charles S., ed. 1986. 288p. pap. 29.95 (0-8084-0423-7) Rowman & Littlefield Pubs., Inc.

—Woodcraft: or, Hawks about the Dovecote: A Story of the South at the Close of the Revolution. rev. ed. (Americans in Fiction Ser.). 518p. reprint ed. lib. bdg. 20.00 (0-8398-1862-9); 1986. pap. text 9.95 (0-8290-2000-4) Irvington Pubs.

—The Yemassee. 454p. reprint ed. lib. bdg. 98.00 (0-7222-4989-6) Best Bks.

—The Yemassee. Ridgely, Joseph V., ed. 1964. 240p. pap. 24.95 (0-8084-0337-0) Rowman & Littlefield Pubs., Inc.

—The Yemassee: A Romance of Carolina. Guilds, John C., ed. 1993. (Simms Ser.: Vol. 7). 504p. text 49.95 (1-55728-302-8) Univ. of Arkansas Pr.

Sinclair, Bennie L. The Lynching. 1992. 208p. 19.95 (0-8027-3201-1) Walker & Co.

Singleton, George. These People Are Us: Short Stories. 2001. 250p. 23.95 (1-880216-94-9) River City Publishing.

—These People Are Us: Stories. 2002. 256p. pap. 13.00 (0-15-601274-X, Harvest Bks.) Harcourt Trade Pubs.

Smalls, Irene. Ebony Sea. 1996. (Illus.). 32p. (J). (gr. 3-6). 12.95 o.p. (0-681-00679-X) Borders Pr.

Smith, Carl T. Lowcountry Boil: A Novel. 2003. 378p. 27.95 (1-57966-043-6) River City Publishing.

Smith, Derek. The Sentinels. 2001. 234p. 24.95 (1-929490-13-5) Beil, Frederic C. Pub., Inc.

Spaugh, Jean C. Something Blue. 1997. (Salem Selections Ser.). 19.95 (0-89587-167-X) Blair, John F. Pub.

—Something Blue: A Novel. 2000. 352p. pap. 13.95 (0-393-32007-3) Norton, W. W. & Co., Inc.

Specht, Robert. Soul of Betty Fairchild. 1991. 18.95 o.p. (0-312-05965-5) St. Martin's Pr.

Stahl, Hilda. The Women of Catawba. 1993. 240p. pap. 9.99 o.p. (0-8407-5080-3) Nelson, Thomas Inc.

Stahl, Laurie. Winds of Catawba. 1995. 240p. pap. 9.99 o.p. (0-8407-5081-1) Nelson, Thomas Inc.

Straight, Susan. I Been in Sorrow's Kitchen & Licked Out All the Pots. 1993. 368p. pap. 13.00 (0-385-47012-6) Doubleday Publishing.

—I Been in Sorrow's Kitchen & Licked Out All the Pots. 1992. 384p. 19.95 o.p. (1-56282-963-7) Hyperion Pr.

Tallent, Mary. The Secret at Robert's Roost. 1988. 161p. (J). (gr. 4-7). pap. 3.95 o.p. (0-941711-05-6) Wyrick & Co.

Thacker, Cathy Gillen. Her Bachelor Challenge. 2002. (Harlequin American Romance Ser.). 250p. mass mkt. (0-373-16937-X, Harlequin Bks.) Harlequin Enterprises, Ltd.

—His Marriage Bonus. 2002. (Harlequin American Romance Ser.). 249p. mass mkt. (0-373-16941-8, Harlequin Bks.) Harlequin Enterprises, Ltd.

Thompson, Laura J. Joseph's Charleston Adventure. 1998. (Illus.). 32p. (J). (ps-4). 16.95 (0-9607854-1-8) Junior League of Charleston, South Carolina, Inc.

Truax, Carlton W. Banjo on My Knee. 1995. 325p. (Orig.). pap. 12.95 (0-9636845-5-8) Senior Pr.

Turner, Jamie Langston. A Garden to Keep. 2001. 416p. pap. 12.99 (0-7642-2154-X) Bethany Hse. Pubs.

—Suncatchers. rev. ed. 2000. 400p. pap. 12.99 (0-7642-2415-8) Bethany Hse. Pubs.

Wall, Kathryn R. Perdition House: A Bay Tanner Mystery. 2003. 368p. 24.95 (0-312-31385-3, Saint Martin's Minotaur) St. Martin's Pr.

Walters, Tony. Burden. E-Book 10.95 (0-312-70439-9); 2002. 320p. 23.95 (0-312-28705-4) St. Martin's Pr.

—Burden. Beier, Elizabeth, ed. 2003. 320p. reprint ed. pap. 13.95 (0-312-30994-5, Saint Martin's Griffin) St. Martin's Pr.

Warlick, Ashley. The Distance from the Heart of Things. (Orig.). 1997. 272p. pap. 12.00 (0-395-86031-8); 1996. 256p. tchr. ed. 21.95 o.p. (0-395-74177-7) Houghton Mifflin Co.

Watts, Timothy. Cons. 1995. 232p. pap. 10.00 (1-56947-034-0); 1993. 231p. 19.95 (0-939149-70-2) Soho Pr., Inc.

Whitlow, Robert. Life Support. 2003. 392p. pap. 14.99 (0-8499-4374-4) W Publishing Group.

Whitney, Phyllis A. Woman Without a Past. 1992. 352p. mass mkt. 6.99 (0-449-22071-0, Fawcett) Ballantine Bks.

—Woman Without a Past. l.t. ed. 1991. 384p. 23.00 o.s.i (0-385-41988-0, Doubleday Large Type) Bantam Doubleday Dell Large Print Group, Inc.

—Woman Without a Past. unabr. ed. 1997. audio 49.95 (0-7861-1227-1, 1970) Blackstone Audio Bks., Inc.

—Woman Without a Past. unabr. ed. 1992. audio 23.95 o.p. (1-56100-459-6, 322, Bookcassette);Set. audio 57.25 o.p. (1-56100-093-0, 1104) Brilliance Audio.

—Woman Without a Past. unabr. ed. 2000. audio 59.95 (0-7451-6570-2, CAB 1186) Chivers Audio Bks. GBR. Dist: BBC Audiobooks America.

—Woman Without a Past. l.t. ed. 1994. 400p. pap. 19.95 (0-8161-5801-0, Macmillan Reference USA) Gale Group.

Wilder, Effie Leland. Older but Wilder: More Notes from the Pasture. l.t. ed. 2000. (G. K. Hall Paperback Ser.). (Illus.). 200p. 23.95 (0-7838-8959-3, Macmillan Reference USA) Gale Group.

—Older but Wilder: More Notes from the Pasture. 1998. (Illus.). 179p. 14.95 (1-56145-182-7, Peachtree Junior) Peachtree Pubs., Ltd.

—One More Time... Just for the Fun of It! Notes from Fairacres. l.t. ed. 2000. (G. K. Hall Paperback Ser.). 160p. pap. 23.95 (0-7838-8960-7, Macmillan Reference USA) Gale Group.

—One More Time... Just for the Fun of It! Notes from Fairacres. 1999. (Illus.). 175p. 14.95 (1-56145-213-0) Peachtree Pubs., Ltd.

—Over What Hill? Notes from the Pasture. l.t. ed. 1996. (Illus.). 180p. 14.95 (1-56145-131-2) Peachtree Pubs., Ltd.

Williams, Naomi. Two Rivers. 2002. 24.95 (1-891799-08-8) Harbor Hse.

Williams, Philip Lee. The True & Authentic History of Jenny Dorset. 1997. 512p. 24.95 (1-56352-365-5) Longstreet Pr., Inc.

—The True & Authentic History of Jenny Dorset: Consisting of a Narrative by a Retainer, Mr. Henry Hawthorne, along with the History of Two Households, That of Dorset & Smythe...: A Novel. 2001. 512p. reprint ed. pap. 17.95 (0-8203-2334-9) Univ. of Georgia Pr.

Williamson, Denise. The Dark Sun Rises: A Novel. 1999. (Roots of Faith Ser.: Bk. 1). 448p. pap. 12.99 (1-55661-882-4) Bethany Hse. Pubs.

Woodiwiss, Kathleen E. The Elusive Flame. abr. ed. 1999. audio 7.99 o.s.i (1-56740-316-6, 1866, Paperback Nova Audio Bks.); 1998. audio 39.95 (1-56740-407-3, 1492, Brilliance Audio Unabridged); 1998. 16p. audio 89.25 (1-56740-605-X, 1632, Unabridged Library Editions) Brilliance Audio.

—The Elusive Flame. l.t. ed. 1998. (Large Print Book Ser.). 27.95 o.p. (1-56895-692-4, Wheeler Publishing, Inc.) Gale Group.

—The Elusive Flame. 1999. 496p. mass mkt. 7.50 (0-380-80786-6); 1998. 432p. pap. 14.00 o.p. (0-380-76655-8) Morrow/Avon. (Avon Bks.).

—A Season Beyond a Kiss. l.t. ed. 2000. 576p. pap. 22.00 (0-06-019730-7) HarperCollins Pubs.

—A Season Beyond a Kiss. 2001. 496p. mass mkt. 7.99 (0-380-80794-7); 2000. 512p. pap. 14.00 (0-380-80793-9) Morrow/Avon. (Avon Bks.).

Zimler, Richard. Hunting Midnight: A Novel. 2003. 512p. 24.95 (0-385-33644-6); E-Book 19.95 (0-440-33428-4) Dell Publishing. (Delacorte Pr.).

Zuber, Isabel. Salt: A Novel. 2003. 352p. pap. 14.00 (0-312-31137-0) Picador.

## SOUTH DAKOTA—FICTION

Adams, Harold. The Barbed Wire Noose. l.t. ed. 1991. pap. 10.95 o.p. (0-7927-0073-2, C0125) BBC Audiobooks America.

—The Barbed Wire Noose. 192p. 1988. pap. 3.95 o.p. (0-445-40727-1); 1987. 15.45 (0-89296-250-X) Mysterious Pr.

—The Ditched Blonde. (Carl Wilcox Mystery Ser.). 168p. 1998. pap. 7.95 (0-8027-7555-1); 1995. 19.95 (0-8027-3263-1) Walker & Co.

—The Fourth Widow. 208p. 1987. pap. 3.50 o.p. (0-445-40581-3); 1986. 15.95 (0-89296-231-3) Mysterious Pr.

—Hatchet Job: A Carl Wilcox Mystery. 1996. (Carl Wilcox Mystery Ser.). 176p. 19.95 (0-8027-3286-0) Walker & Co.

—The Ice Pick Artist: A Carl Wilcox Mystery. 1997. (Carl Wilcox Mystery Ser.). 240p. 21.95 (0-8027-3310-7) Walker & Co.

—Lead, So I Can Follow. (Carl Wilcox Mystery Ser.). 2000. 224p. pap. 8.95 (0-8027-7596-9); 1999. 219p. 22.95 (0-8027-3336-0) Walker & Co.

—The Man Who Met the Train. (Carl Wilcox Mystery Ser.: No. 7). 240p. 1989. pap. 3.95 o.p. (0-445-40810-3); 1988. 15.95 (0-89296-251-8) Mysterious Pr.

—The Man Who Missed the Party. l.t. ed. 1992. 18.95 o.p. (0-7451-8330-1); pap. 16.95 o.p. (0-7927-1017-7) BBC Audiobooks America.

—The Man Who Missed the Party. 1990. 192p. mass mkt. 4.95 o.s.i (0-445-40885-5, Mysterious Pr. Paperback Bks.) Warner Bks., Inc.

—The Man Who Missed the Party: A Carol Wilcox Mystery. 1989. 192p. 16.95 (0-89296-252-6) Mysterious Pr.

—The Man Who Was Taller Than God. 1998. (Carl Wilcox Mystery Ser.). 156p. (gr. 8). pap. 7.95 (0-8027-7554-3) Walker & Co.

—The Man Who Was Taller Than God: A Carl Wilcox Mystery. 1992. (Carl Wilcox Mystery Ser.). 156p. 18.95 (0-8027-1239-8) Walker & Co.

—The Missing Moon. 1983. 256p. mass mkt. 2.50 o.s.i (0-441-53401-5) Ace Bks.

—The Missing Moon. l.t. ed. 1991. 17.95 o.p. (0-7451-9761-2, C0076); 1990. pap. 15.95 o.p. (0-7927-0216-6, C0224) BBC Audiobooks America.

—The Missing Moon. 1988. 256p. mass mkt. 3.95 o.s.i (0-445-40629-1, Mysterious Pr. Paperback Bks.) Warner Bks., Inc.

—Murder. 1981. 256p. 2.50 o.s.i (0-441-54706-0) Ace Bks.

—Murder. l.t. ed. 1991. pap. 8.95 o.p. (1-55504-839-0, 102); 1989. 16.95 o.p. (0-7451-9459-1, 340) BBC Audiobooks America.

—Murder. 1988. 224p. mass mkt. 3.95 o.s.i (0-445-40627-5, Mysterious Pr. Paperback Bks.) Warner Bks., Inc.

—The Naked Liar. 1986. 15.95 o.p. (0-89296-126-0) Mysterious Pr.

—The Naked Liar. 1986. mass mkt. 3.95 o.s.i (0-445-40126-5, Mysterious Pr. Paperback Bks.) Warner Bks., Inc.

—No Badge, No Gun. (Carl Wilcox Mystery Ser.). 1999. 212p. pap. 7.95 (0-8027-7575-6); 1998. (Illus.). 208p. 22.95 (0-8027-3321-2) Walker & Co.

—Paint the Town Red. 1988. 208p. 3.95 o.p. (0-445-40631-3) Mysterious Pr.

—A Perfectly Proper Murder: A Carl Wilcox Mystery. 1993. 18.95 (0-8027-3237-2) Walker & Co.

—When Rich Men Die. 1987. 240p. 16.95 o.s.i (0-385-24005-8) Doubleday Publishing.

—When Rich Men Die. l.t. ed. 1988. (Mainstream Ser.). 377p. reprint ed. lib. bdg. 19.95 o.p. (1-55736-085-5) ISIS Large Print Bks. GBR. Dist: Transaction Pubs.

—When Rich Men Die. 1988. 256p. pap. 3.50 (0-380-70539-7, Avon Bks.) Morrow/Avon.

Bly, Stephen A. Beneath a Dakota Cross. 1999. (Fortune of the Black Hills Ser.: Vol. 1). viii, 212p. pap. 9.99 (0-8054-1659-5) Broadman & Holman Pubs.

—Beneath a Dakota Cross. l.t. ed. 2001. lib. bdg. 26.95 (1-58547-083-X) Ctr. Point Large Print.

—Shadow of Legends. 2000. (Fortunes of the Black Hills Ser.: No. 2). viii, 212p. pap. 12.99 (0-8054-2174-2) Broadman & Holman Pubs.

—Shadow of Legends. l.t. ed. 2001. 304p. lib. bdg. 26.95 (1-58547-084-8) Ctr. Point Large Print.

Callen, Paulette. Charity. 1998. 320p. reprint ed. mass mkt. 6.99 o.s.i (0-425-16516-7) Berkley Publishing Group.

—Charity. 1997. 308p. 21.50 (0-684-82942-8, Simon & Schuster) Simon & Schuster.

Champlin, Tim. A Trail to Wounded Knee: A Western Story. 2002. 320p. 24.95 (0-7862-2402-9) Thorndike Pr.

Cook-Lynn, Elizabeth. Aurelia: A Crow Creek Trilogy. 1999. 416p. 27.50 (0-87081-539-3) Univ. Pr. of Colorado.

—Aurelia: A Crow Creek Trilogy. 2002. 462p. pap. 16.95 (0-87081-685-3) Univ. of Oklahoma Pr.

—Aurelia: A Crow Creek Trilogy. 1999. E-Book 27.50 (0-585-34185-0) netLibrary, Inc.

Cummings, Jean. Stardancer. unabr. ed. 2000. 313p. pap. 12.50 (0-9679959-1-4, 004) Rx Ranch Enterprises.

Dexter, Pete. Deadwood. 1989. 384p. pap. 13.95 o.s.i (0-14-012729-1, Penguin Bks.) Penguin Group (USA) Inc.

—Deadwood. l.t. ed. 1997. (Niagara Large Print Ser.). 584p. 29.50 o.p. (0-7089-5862-1, Linford) Thorpe, F. A. Pubs. GBR. Dist: Ulverscroft Large Print Bks., Ltd.

—Deadwood. 1987. 512p. pap. 4.95 o.p. (0-14-009910-7, Penguin Bks.) Viking Penguin.

Doane, Michael. Bullet Heart. 1995. 448p. mass mkt. 6.99 o.s.i (0-425-15099-2) Berkley Publishing Group.

Dreamwalker, Richard. Four Winds Returning: A Novel. 1996. 190p. (Orig.). pap. (1-887786-10-4) Sky & Sage Bks.

Eickhoff, Randy Lee. Then Came Christmas. 2003. 160p. 12.95 (0-7653-0142-3, Forge Bks.) Doherty, Tom Assocs., LLC.

Gillman, Jonathan. Grasslands. 1993. 186p. (C). 25.00 (0-8135-1926-8); pap. 9.95 (0-8135-1927-6) Rutgers Univ. Pr.

Johnson, Adam. Parasites Like Us. 2003. 368p. 24.95 (0-670-03235-2) Viking Penguin.

Jones, Douglas C. A Creek Called Wounded Knee. 1984. pap. 7.95 (0-684-18257-2, Macmillan Reference USA) Gale Group.

—A Creek Called Wounded Knee. 1996. 288p. mass mkt. 5.99 o.p. (0-06-101029-4, HarperTorch) Morrow/Avon.

—A Creek Called Wounded Knee. 1979. pap. 2.50 o.s.i (0-446-91121-6) Warner Bks., Inc.

Kastner, Deb. Black Hills Bride. 2000. (Steeple Hill Love Inspired Ser.: No. 90). mass mkt. (0-373-87096-5, 1-87096-3, Harlequin Bks.) Harlequin Enterprises, Ltd.

London, David. Sun Dancer. 1996. 320p. 23.00 o.p. (0-684-81458-7, Simon & Schuster) Simon & Schuster.

Louis, Adrian C. Skins. 2002. 320p. reprint ed. pap. 18.00 (0-944024-44-0) Ellis Pr., The.

—Wild Indians & Other Creatures. 1997. (Western Literature Ser.). 200p. reprint ed. pap. 18.00 (0-87417-303-5); 21.00 (0-87417-279-9) Univ. of Nevada Pr.

McCollum, Thomas C. Palmer Lake. 2002. 352p. 25.00 (0-9713797-1-8) Shoji Bks., Inc.

McDonald, Bill. Dakota Incarnate: A Collection of Short Stories. 1999. (Minnesota Voices Project Ser.: Vol. 92). 204p. pap. 12.95 (0-89823-196-5) New Rivers Pr.

Micheaux, Oscar. The Conquest: The Story of a Negro Pioneer. 1977. (Black Heritage Library Collection). 30.95 (0-8369-8632-6) Ayer Co. Pubs., Inc.

—The Conquest: The Story of a Negro Pioneer. 1994. (Illus.). 332p. pap. text 15.00 (0-8032-8209-5, Bison Bks.) Univ. of Nebraska Pr.

—The Conquest: The Story of a Negro Pioneer. 1994. E-Book 9.95 (0-585-26635-2) netLibrary, Inc.

—The Homesteader: A Novel. 1994. (Illus.). 533p. pap. 12.95 (0-8032-8208-7, Bison Bks.) Univ. of Nebraska Pr.

Nelson, Kent. Land That Moves, Land That Stands Still: A Novel. 2003. 352p. text 24.95 (0-670-03226-3, Viking) Viking Penguin.

Nickels, Tracy. Dancing Wheat. 1998. 200p. (YA). pap. 12.95 (1-928727-00-X) Get'n Even.

Oaks, Barbara. Queen City of the Plains. 1991. (Illus.). 175p. (Orig.). (C). pap. 7.95 o.p. (0-9618582-2-2) Oaks, Barbara.

O'Brien, Dan. Brendan Prairie. 1996. 256p. 22.00 o.p. (0-684-80368-2, Scribner) Simon & Schuster.

—In the Center of the Nation. 1991. 21.95 o.p. (0-87113-441-1) Grove/Atlantic, Inc.

Porter, Melinda C. Badlands. 1996. 256p. 22.00 (0-86316-149-9) Writers & Readers Publishing, Inc.

Richardson, Arleta. Prairie Homestead. 1994. (Orphans' Journey Ser.: Vol. 3). 144p. (J). (gr. 4-7). pap. 4.99 (0-7814-0091-0) Cook Communications Ministries.

Rolvaag, Ole Edvart. Giants in the Earth: A Saga of the Prairie. 1937. (J). 16.45 o.p. (0-06-013595-6) HarperCollins Pubs.

—Giants in the Earth: A Saga of the Prairie. 1999. (Perennial Classics Ser.). 560p. pap. 13.00 (0-06-093193-0, Perennial) HarperTrade.

—Giants in the Earth: A Saga of the Prairie. Rolvaag, Ole Edvart, tr. 1991. 192p. pap. 8.00 (0-06-083047-6, Perennial) HarperTrade.

—Giants in the Earth: A Saga of the Prairie. 1955. 19.05 (0-606-00702-4) Turtleback Bks.

—Peder Victorious: A Tale of the Pioneers 20 Years Later. Solum, Nora O., tr. 1973. 350p. reprint ed. 65.00 o.p. (0-8371-7067-2, ROPV, Greenwood Pr.) Greenwood Publishing Group, Inc.

—Peder Victorious: A Tale of the Pioneers 20 Years Later. Solum, Nora O., tr. from NOR. 1982. 325p. reprint ed. pap. 15.95 (0-8032-8906-5, Bison Bks.) Univ. of Nebraska Pr.

—Pure Gold. Erdahl, Sivert, tr. 1973. 346p. reprint ed. lib. bdg. o.p. (0-8371-7070-2, ROPG, Greenwood Pr.) Greenwood Publishing Group, Inc.

—Their Fathers' God. Ager, Trygve M., tr. 1973. 338p. reprint ed. o.p. (0-8371-7068-0, ROFG, Greenwood Pr.) Greenwood Publishing Group, Inc.

—Their Fathers' God. Ager, Trygve M., tr. 1983. 338p. reprint ed. pap. 15.95 (0-8032-8911-1, Bison Bks.) Univ. of Nebraska Pr.

—The Third Life of Per Smevik. Tweet, Ella V. & Zempel, Solweig, trs. from NOR. 1987. 144p. pap. 6.95 o.p. (0-06-097076-6, PL 7076, Perennial) HarperTrade.

Schaller, Bob. South Dakota. 1998. (Arlingtons Ser.). (Illus.). 128p. (J). (gr. 8-12). pap. text 7.95 o.p. (1-887002-76-6) Cross Training Publishing.

Smith, Michael A. New America. 1999. 352p. 25.95 (0-312-86821-9, Forge Bks.) Doherty, Tom Assocs., LLC.

Taylor, Kathleen. Cold Front. 2000. (Tory Bauer Mystery Ser.). 352p. mass mkt. 5.99 (0-380-81204-5, Avon Bks.) Morrow/Avon.

—Foreign Body: A Tory Bauer Mystery. 2001. 384p. mass mkt. 6.99 (0-380-81205-3, Avon Bks.) Morrow/Avon.

—Funeral Food. 1998. (Tory Bauer Mystery Ser.). 256p. mass mkt. 5.99 (0-380-79380-6, Avon Bks.) Morrow/Avon.

—Hotel South Dakota. 1997. (Tory Bauer Mystery Ser.). 304p. mass mkt. 6.50 (0-380-78356-8, Avon Bks.) Morrow/Avon.

—Mourning Shift. 1998. (Tory Bauer Mystery Ser.: No. 4). 288p. mass mkt. 5.99 (0-380-79943-X, Avon Bks.) Morrow/Avon.

—Sex & Salmonella. 1996. 288p. (Orig.). mass mkt. 5.50 (0-380-78355-X, Avon Bks.) Morrow/Avon.

Trainor, J. F. Corona Blue. 1995. mass mkt. 4.99 o.s.i (0-8217-5134-4); 1994. 357p. mass mkt. 16.95 o.s.i (0-8217-4739-8, Zebra Bks.) Kensington Publishing Corp.

Troy, Judy. From the Black Hills. 1999. 300p. pap. 19.00 (0-8129-9173-7) Random Hse., Inc.

—From the Black Hills. l.t. ed. 1999. (Americana Ser.). 341p. 27.95 (0-7862-2213-1) Thorndike Pr.

—From the Black Hills: A Novel. 1999. 284p. 23.95 o.s.i (0-375-50230-0) Random Hse., Inc.

## SOUTHERN STATES—FICTION

Abbott, Jeff. A Kiss Gone Bad. 2001. 416p. mass mkt. 6.99 (0-451-41010-6, Onyx); 1999. pap. 6.99 (0-451-20217-1, Signet Bks.) NAL.

Adams, D. J. Scenting Evil: From the Case Files of the Mind Tracker. 2001. 288p. pap. 14.95 (1-892123-71-1) Capital Bks., Inc.

Allen, Vicki L. For Molly. 370p. 2000. pap. 12.95 (0-9674880-4-4); 1999. 24.95 (0-9674880-3-6) Magnolia Publishing Co., Inc.

Allison, Dorothy. Trash: Stories & Poems. 2002. 224p. pap. 13.00 (0-452-28351-5, Plume) Dutton/Plume.

—Trash: Stories & Poems. 1988. 176p. pap. 12.95 (0-932379-51-6); lib. bdg. 24.95 (0-932379-52-4) Firebrand Bks.

Ames, Gwen Parker. Panhandle Dreams. 2002. 354p. pap. 18.95 (0-595-23473-9, Writer's Showcase Pr.) iUniverse, Inc.

Andrews, Mary Kay. Little Bitty Lies. 2003. 448p. 24.95 (0-06-019959-8, HarperCollins) HarperTrade.

Ansa, Tina McElroy. Baby of the Family. (Harvest Book Ser.). 1991. 276p. pap. 13.00 (0-15-610150-5, Harvest Bks.); 1989. 18.95 (0-15-110431-X) Harcourt Trade Pubs.

Arnold, Darrell. The Cowboy Kind. 2001. (Illus.). 130p. pap. 18.00 (0-87842-440-7) Mountain Pr. Publishing Co., Inc.

Auerbach, Paul S. Bad Medicine. 1998. 355p. pap. 16.95 (0-9639960-7-X) Specialized Pubns. Co.

Bahr, Howard. The Black Flower: A Novel of the Civil War. unabr. ed. 1999. audio 56.95 Blackstone Audio Bks., Inc.

—The Black Flower: A Novel of the Civil War. 1998. 272p. pap. 13.00 o.s.i (0-8050-5445-6, Owl Bks.) Holt, Henry & Co.

—The Black Flower: A Novel of the Civil War. 3rd ed. 1997. (Illus.). 230p. (YA). (gr. 10-12). 24.95 (1-877853-50-X) Nautical & Aviation Publishing Co. of America, Inc., The.

—The Black Flower: A Novel of the Civil War. 2000. 272p. pap. 13.00 (0-312-26507-7) Picador.

—The Black Flower: A Novel of the Civil War. l.t. ed. 1997. (Niagara Large Print Ser.). 464p. 29.50 o.p. (0-7089-5882-6, Ulverscroft) Thorpe, F. A. Pubs. GBR. *Dist:* Ulverscroft Large Print Bks., Ltd.

—The Black Flower: A Novel of the Civil War. 2000. 19.05 (0-606-21819-X) Turtleback Bks.

Baldacci, David. Wish You Well. 2000. 400p. 24.95 o.p. (0-446-52716-5) Warner Bks., Inc.

Ball, John. In the Heat of the Night. 1992. (Mystery Scene Bk.). 208p. mass mkt. 4.50 (0-88184-887-5, Carroll & Graf Pubs.) Avalon Publishing Group.

—In the Heat of the Night. 1992. 158p. reprint ed. lib. bdg. 14.95 (0-89966-916-6) Buccaneer Bks., Inc.

—In the Heat of the Night. 1985. 256p. pap. 4.50 o.p. (0-06-080735-0, P735, Perennial) HarperTrade.

Barton, Beverly. What She Doesn't Know. 2002. 384p. mass mkt. 6.50 (0-8217-7214-7, Zebra Bks.) Kensington Publishing Corp.

Barton, Marlin. A Broken Thing. 2003. 258p. 24.95 (1-929490-20-8) Beil, Frederic C. Pub., Inc.

Basso, Hamilton. The View from Pompey's Head. 1994. reprint ed. lib. bdg. 24.95 (1-56849-557-9) Buccaneer Bks., Inc.

—The View from Pompey's Head. 1985. 409p. reprint ed. lib. bdg. 22.50 o.p. (0-8371-3207-X, BAPH) Greenwood Publishing Group, Inc.

—The View from Pompey's Head. 1998. (Voices of the South Ser.). 416p. pap. 16.95 (0-8071-2334-X) Louisiana State Univ. Pr.

—The View from Pompey's Head. 1985. pap. 6.95 o.p. (0-87795-708-8, Morrow, William & Co.) Morrow/Avon.

—The View from Pompey's Head. l.t. ed. 1999. 568p. 32.95 (1-56000-472-X) Transaction Pubs.

Battle, Lois. The Florabama Ladies' Auxiliary & Sewing Circle. 2002. (Illus.). 384p. pap. 14.00 (0-14-200036-1) Penguin Group (USA) Inc.

—The Florabama Ladies' Auxiliary & Sewing Circle. l.t. ed. 2001. 358p. 30.95 (0-7862-3305-2) Thorndike Pr.

—The Florabama Ladies' Auxiliary & Sewing Circle. 2001. 352p. 24.95 o.s.i (0-670-89469-9, Viking) Viking Penguin.

Bausch, Richard. The Cry of an Occasion: Fiction from the Fellowship of Southern Writers. 2001. 222p. 29.95 (0-8071-2635-7) Louisiana State Univ. Pr.

Bell, Madison Smartt. Anything Goes: A Novel. 2002. 320p. 24.00 (0-375-42125-4, Pantheon) Knopf Publishing Group.

Bell, Vereen. Brag Dog & Other Stories: The Best of Vereen Bell. 2000. (Illus.). xi, 244p. (1-885106-84-X) PleaWilderness Adventures Pr., Inc.

Bennett, Oscar H. The Colored Garden. 2000. 264p. pap. 12.50 (0-9659701-9-1); (Illus.). pap. text (0-9659701-7-5) Laughing Owl Publishing, Inc.

Berry, Bertice. Jim & Louella's Homemade Heartfix Remedy. 2002. 224p. 22.95 (0-385-50377-6) Doubleday Publishing.

Berry, Minta Sue. Who Is My Neighbor? 2001. 200p. 22.50 (1-57233-115-1) Univ. of Tennessee Pr.

Bikis, Gwendolyn. Your Loving Arms. 2002. 247p. (C). 27.95 (1-56023-220-X); pap. 17.95 (1-56023-221-8) Haworth Pr., Inc., The. (Alice Street Editions).

Bloom, Harold. Toni Morrison's Beloved. 1999. (Bloom's Notes Ser.). pap. 4.95 (0-7910-5223-0) Chelsea Hse. Pubs.

Bloom, Harold, ed. & intro. Toni Morrison's Beloved. 1999. (Bloom's Notes Ser.). 90p. (YA). (gr. 8 up). lib. bdg. 21.95 (0-7910-4516-1) Chelsea Hse. Pubs.

Boswell, Marshall. Trouble with Girls. 2003. 320p. tchr. ed. 23.95 (1-56512-344-1, 72344) Algonquin Bks. of Chapel Hill.

—Trouble with Girls. 2004. 320p. pap. 12.00 (0-385-33783-3, Delta) Dell Publishing.

Bottoms, Greg. Sentimental, Heartbroken Rednecks: Stories. 2001. 235p. 21.95 (1-893956-15-6) Context Bks.

Bracy, Ihsan. Ibo Landing: A Offering of Short Stories by Ihsan Bracy. 1998. (Illus.). 170p. pap. 12.95 (1-887276-10-6) Cool Grove Publishing, Inc.

—Ibo Landing: An Offering of Short Stories by Ihsan Bracy. 1998. (Illus.). 154p. 22.95 (1-887276-11-4) Cool Grove Publishing, Inc.

Brewer, Sonny, ed. Stories from the Blue Moon Cafe: Anthology of Southern Writers. 2002. 385p. 25.00 (1-931561-09-5) MacAdam/Cage Publishing, Inc.

—Stories from the Blue Moon Cafe: Anthology of Southern Writers. 2003. 368p. pap. 14.00 (0-451-21042-5) NAL.

—Stories from the Blue Moon Cafe II: Anthology of Southern Writers. 2003. 25.00 (1-931561-43-5) MacAdam/Cage Publishing, Inc.

Brown, Billie Jeane. Southern Exposure: Wealthy Cattleman's Daughter - Striptease Artist. 2001. 358p. pap. 22.99 (0-7388-5449-2); text 32.99 (0-7388-5448-4) Xlibris Corp.

Brown, Charlotte H. Mammy: An Appeal to the Heart of the South; &, The Correct Thing to Do—to Say—to Wear. 1995. (African American Women Writers, 1910-1940 Ser.). 149p. 25.00 (0-8161-1632-6, Macmillan Reference USA) Gale Group.

Brown, Joe David. Paper Moon. 30th anniv. ed. 2002. (Illus.). 308p. reprint ed. pap. 13.95 (1-56858-230-7) Four Walls Eight Windows.

—Paper Moon. 1973. mass mkt. 1.25 o.p. (0-451-05822-4); mass mkt. 1.50 o.p. (0-451-06409-7); mass mkt. 1.50 o.p. (0-451-07448-3); mass mkt. 1.75 o.p. (0-451-08505-1); mass mkt. 1.25 o.p. (0-451-05418-0) NAL. (Signet Bks.).

—Paper Moon. l.t. ed. 2002. (Perennial Bestsellers Ser.). 480p. 28.95 (0-7862-4649-9) Thorndike Pr.

Brown, Mary Ward. It Wasn't All Dancing & Other Short Stories. 2002. (Deep South Books). 144p. 26.95 (0-8173-1124-6) Univ. of Alabama Pr.

Brown, William Wells. Clotelle: The Coloured Heroine. 1999. E-Book 2.49 (1-58627-252-7) Electric Umbrella Publishing.

Cable, A. W. John March, Southerner. 2000. 252p. E-Book 3.95 (0-594-02019-0) 1873 Pr.

Cable, George W. John March, Southerner. 2000. 252p. pap. 9.95 (0-594-00885-9) 1873 Pr.

—John March, Southerner. 1977. (Black Heritage Library Collection). 40.95 (0-8369-8529-X) Ayer Co. Pubs., Inc.

—John March, Southerner. 524p. pap. 19.95 (1-56554-973-2, Firebird Pr.) Pelican Publishing Co., Inc.

—John March, Southerner. 1994. reprint ed. 69.00 (0-403-04554-1) Somerset Pubs., Inc.

Caldwell, Erskine. Estherville. 1998. 147p. reprint ed. pap. 16.00 (1-892323-75-3) Vivisphere Publishing.

—Un Patelin Nomme Estherville. 1985. (FRE.). 213p. pap. 11.95 (0-7859-2019-6, 2070376850) French & European Pubns., Inc.

—Un Pauvre Type. 1980. (FRE.). 192p. pap. 10.95 (0-7859-1906-6, 2070371646) French & European Pubns., Inc.

—Terre Tragique. 1986. (FRE.). 224p. pap. 10.95 (0-7859-2049-8, 2070377733) French & European Pubns., Inc.

—Trouble in July. 1977. (Illus.). 160p. 25.00 (0-88322-025-3) Beehive Pr., The.

—Trouble in July. 1975. mass mkt. 1.25 o.p. (0-451-06527-1, Y6527); 1970. mass mkt. 0.25 o.p. (0-451-00567-8); 1970. mass mkt. 0.35 o.p. (0-451-01608-4); 1970. mass mkt. 0.50 o.p. (0-451-02616-0); 1970. mass mkt. 0.75 o.p. (0-451-04331-6) NAL. (Signet Bks.).

—Trouble in July. 1999. (Brown Thrasher Bks.). xxiii, 241p. pap. 14.95 (0-8203-2105-2) Univ. of Georgia Pr.

—Les Voies du Seigneur. 1981. (FRE.). 224p. pap. 10.95 (0-7859-1942-2, 2070373304) French & European Pubns., Inc.

Capote, Truman. Other Voices, Other Rooms. 1999. 245 p. (0-7540-3681-2) BBC Audiobooks America.

—Other Voices, Other Rooms. 1994. lib. bdg. 24.95 (1-56849-388-6) Buccaneer Bks., Inc.

—Other Voices, Other Rooms. 1994. 240p. pap. 12.00 (0-679-74564-5, Vintage) Knopf Publishing Group.

—Other Voices, Other Rooms. 1949. mass mkt. 2.95 o.p. (0-451-13451-6, ROC); mass mkt. 3.95 o.p. (0-451-14463-5, Signet Bks.); 240p. mass mkt. 4.99 o.p. (0-451-16189-0, J9961, Signet Bks.); mass mkt. 4.50 o.p. (0-451-15640-4, Signet Bks.) NAL.

—Other Voices, Other Rooms. 1968. 19.95 o.s.i (0-394-43949-X) Random Hse., Inc.

—Other Voices, Other Rooms. l.t. ed. 1999. (Perennial Bestsellers Ser.). 245p. 25.95 (0-7838-8491-5) Thorndike Pr.

Card, Orson Scott. Homebody. 1999. 13.04 (0-606-15862-6) Turtleback Bks.

—Homebody: A Novel. 1999. 448p. mass mkt. 6.99 (0-06-109399-8, HarperTorch) Morrow/Avon.

Carter, Jimmy. The Hornet's Nest: A Novel of the Revolutionary War. 2003. (Illus.). 480p. 27.00 (0-7432-5542-9, Simon & Schuster) Simon & Schuster.

—The Hornet's Nest: A Novel of the Revolutionary War. l.t. ed. 2004. 832p. 31.95 (0-7862-6154-4) Thorndike Pr.

Chastain, Sandra, et al. Sweet Tea & Jesus Shoes. 2000. 190p. pap. 14.95 (0-9673035-0-8, M-2000) BelleBks.

Chesnutt, Charles Waddell. The Conjure Woman. 1988. reprint ed. lib. bdg. 59.00 (0-7812-0047-4) Reprint Services Corp.

—The Conjure Woman. reprint ed. 45.00 (0-403-07386-3) Scholarly Pr., Inc.

—The Conjure Woman. 1969. (Ann Arbor Paperbacks Ser.). (Illus.). 256p. (C). pap. text 14.95 (0-472-06156-9, 06156) Univ. of Michigan Pr.

—The Conjure Woman. 2000. (Classics Ser.). 304p. 10.95 (0-14-118502-3, Penguin Classics) Viking Penguin.

—The Conjure Woman & Other Conjure Tales. 1993. 216p. pap. 15.95 (0-8223-1387-1); text 54.95 (0-8223-1378-2) Duke Univ. Pr.

—The House Behind the Cedars. 2002. 196p. 94.99 (1-4043-0866-0); per. 89.99 (1-4043-0867-9) IndyPublish.com.

—The House Behind the Cedars. Jackson Fossett, Judith, ed. 2003. 256p. pap. 12.95 (0-8129-6616-3, Modern Library) Random House Adult Trade Publishing Group.

—The House Behind the Cedars. l.t. ed. 1999. 440p. text 29.95 (1-56000-494-0) Transaction Pubs.

—The House Behind the Cedars. 2000. xxi, 294p. pap. 11.95 (0-8203-2194-X) Univ. of Georgia Pr.

—The House Behind the Cedars. Gibson, Donald, ed. & intro. by. 1993. (Twentieth Century Classics Ser.). 336p. 12.95 (0-14-018685-9, Penguin Classics) Viking Penguin.

—Tales of Conjure & the Color Line: 10 Stories. 1998. 128p. pap. 2.00 (0-486-40426-9) Dover Pubns., Inc.

Chesnutt, Charles Waddell & Andrews, William L. The House Behind the Cedars. 1988. (Brown Thrasher Bks.). 312p. reprint ed. pap. 14.95 o.s.i (0-8203-1021-2) Univ. of Georgia Pr.

Clayton, Clay Worthington. Prisoners of Hope. 1998. 277p. pap. 5.95 (1-888422-00-9) Frost Publishing.

Coe, Marian. Eve's Mountain: A Novel of Passion & Mystery in the Blue Ridge. 4th ed. 2002. (Illus.). 363p. 18.95 (0-9633341-7-4) SouthLore Pr.

—Marvelous Secrets. 2000. (Illus.). viii, 232p. 16.95 (0-9633341-8-2) SouthLore Pr.

Collins, Sheila Hebert. Cendrillon: A Cajun Cinderella. 1998. (Illus.). 32p. (J). (ps-3). 14.95 (1-56554-326-2) Pelican Publishing Co., Inc.

Colson, John. A Bend in the Willows. 2000. 144p. pap. 13.00 (0-8059-5000-1) Dorrance Publishing Co., Inc.

Connor, Beverly. Airtight Case. 2002. (Lindsay Chamberlain Novel Ser.). (Illus.). 480p. mass mkt. 7.99 (1-58182-295-2) Cumberland Hse. Publishing.

Cousins, Caroline. Fiddle Dee Death. 2003. 208p. 21.95 (0-89587-286-2); pap. 14.95 (0-89587-275-7) Blair, John F. Pub.

Dann, Jack. The Silent. 1999. 304p. reprint ed. pap. 19.00 (0-553-38038-9) Bantam Bks.

Davidson, Jane Mann. Wings of the Morning. 2000. 173p. pap. 15.00 (0-9668884-6-4) Wings Pubs., LLC.

Diether, John W. With Friends Like These. 2000. 179p. pap. 15.54 (1-58820-128-7) 1stBooks Library.

Dixon, Thomas, Jr. Clansman. 1976. 27.95 (0-8488-0263-2) Amereon, Ltd.

—The Clansman. 1990. 400p. reprint ed. lib. bdg. 27.95 o.p. (0-89966-677-9) Buccaneer Bks., Inc.

—The Clansman. (Best Sellers of 1905 Ser.). reprint ed. lib. bdg. 48.00 (0-7426-1140-X) Classic Bks.

—The Clansman. 1986. reprint ed. o.p. (0-403-08269-2) Scholarly Pr., Inc.

Dixon, Thomas. The Clansman: An Historical Romance of the Ku Klux Klan. 2000. (Illus.). 224p. 54.95 (0-7656-0614-3, Sharpe Professional) Sharpe, M.E. Inc.

Dixon, Thomas. The Clansman: An Historical Romance of the Ku Klux Klan. Wintz, Cary D., ed. & abr. by. 2000. (Illus.). xxxvii, 186p. 56.95 (0-7656-0616-X) Sharpe, M.E. Inc.

Dixon, Thomas. The Clansman: An Historical Romance of the Ku Klux Klan. Wintz, Cary D., ed. & abr. by. abr. ed. 2000. (Illus.). xxxvii, 186p. pap. 22.95 (0-7656-0617-8) Sharpe, M.E. Inc.

Dixon, Thomas, Jr. The Clansman: An Historical Romance of the Ku Klux Klan. 1970. (Novel as American Social History Ser.). 392p. reprint ed. pap. 22.00 (*0-8131-0126-3*) Univ. Pr. of Kentucky.

Dorrell, Linda. True Believers. 2001. 208p. (gr. 13 up). pap. 10.99 (*0-8010-6362-0*) Baker Bks.

Douglas, Ellen. Where the Dreams Cross. 2000. (Voices of the South Ser.). 303p. pap. 15.95 (*0-8071-2639-X*) Louisiana State Univ. Pr.

—Where the Dreams Cross. 1968. 12.50 o.p. (*0-89366-091-4*) Ultramarine Publishing Co., Inc.

Dufaux, Jean. Dixie Road, Vol. 2. Johnson, Joe, tr. from FRE. 2001. (Illus.). 48p. pap. 10.95 (*1-56163-301-1*) NBM Publishing Co.

Dunn, Mark. Welcome to Higby. 2002. 339p. 25.00 (*1-931561-17-6*) MacAdam/Cage Publishing, Inc.

—Welcome to Higby: A Novel. 2003. 352p. pap. 14.00 (*0-7432-4988-7*, Touchstone) Simon & Schuster, Ltd. GBR. *Dist:* Simon & Schuster, Inc.

Edelson, Julie. Courting Disaster. 1999. (Illus.). 320p. 24.00 o.p. (*1-58195-003-9*, Zoland Bks., Inc.) Steerforth Pr.

Edgerton, Clyde. The Floatplane Notebooks. 1988. 280p. 16.95 o.p. (*0-945575-00-9*) Algonquin Bks. of Chapel Hill.

—The Floatplane Notebooks. 288p. 1997. pap. 19.00 (*0-345-41906-5*); 1989. mass mkt. 6.99 (*0-345-35984-4*) Ballantine Bks.

Ellis, Virginia. The Wedding Dress. l.t. ed. 2002. (Women's Fiction Ser.). 321p. 29.95 (*0-7862-4705-3*) Thorndike Pr.

Ellison, Ralph. Juneteenth: A Novel. 2000. (International Ser.). 400p. pap. 14.00 (*0-375-70754-9*, Vintage) Knopf Publishing Group.

—Juneteenth: A Novel. Callahan, John F., ed. 1999. xxiii, 368p. 25.00 o.s.i (*0-394-46457-5*) Random Hse., Inc.

Elwood, Roger. Across Fields of Dixie. 2001. pap. 12.99 (*0-8054-1698-6*) Broadman & Holman Pubs.

Faulkner, William. The Reivers. unabr. ed. 1994. (Bookcassette Classic Collection). audio 59.25 o.p. (*1-56100-192-9*, 1005, Unabridged Library Editions); audio 19.95 o.p. (*1-56100-566-5*, 228, Bookcassette) Brilliance Audio.

—The Reivers. Polk & Millgate, Michael, eds. 1986. (William Faulkner Manuscripts). 416p. text 50.00 (*0-8240-6835-1*) Garland Publishing, Inc.

—The Reivers. Millgate, Michael et al, eds. 1986. (William Faulkner Manuscripts). 416p. text 50.00 (*0-8240-6834-3*) Garland Publishing, Inc.

—The Reivers. 1992. 320p. pap. 12.00 (*0-679-74192-5*); 1966. pap. 9.00 o.p. (*0-394-70339-1*, V339) Knopf Publishing Group. (Vintage).

—The Reivers. 1969. mass mkt. 0.95 o.p. (*0-451-04033-3*, Signet Bks.) NAL.

—The Reivers. 1962. 17.95 o.s.i (*0-394-44229-6*) Random Hse., Inc.

—The Reivers, unabr. ed. 1996. audio 78.00 (*0-7887-0611-X*, 94791E7) Recorded Bks., LLC.

—The Reivers. l.t. ed. 1995. 390p. lib. bdg. 21.95 (*0-7838-1302-3*) Thorndike Pr.

—The Reivers. 1992. 18.05 (*0-606-21899-8*) Turtleback Bks.

Feibleman, Peter S. The Daughters of Necessity. 1999. (Voices of the South Ser.). 318p. pap. 15.95 (*0-8071-2388-9*) Louisiana State Univ. Pr.

Fox, James. Five Sisters: The Langhornes of Virginia. 2001. (Illus.). 496p. pap. 16.00 (*0-7432-0042-X*, Simon & Schuster) Simon & Schuster.

Fox, William Price. Dixiana Moon. 2001. (Voices of the South Ser.). 288p. pap. 16.95 (*0-8071-2746-9*) Louisiana State Univ. Pr.

—Dixiana Moon. 1981. 256p. 11.95 o.p. (*0-670-27453-4*) Viking Penguin.

Frank, Waldo. Holiday. 2003. 240p. pap. text 16.95 (*0-252-07133-6*) Univ. of Illinois Pr.

Franklin, Tom. Poachers: Stories. 2000. (Illus.). 208p. pap. 12.95 (*0-688-17771-9*, Perennial) HarperTrade.

—Poachers: Stories. 1999. 192p. 22.00 (*0-688-16740-3*, Morrow, William & Co.) Morrow/Avon.

Freeman, Steve. Sacrafice: A Novel of the War for Southern Independence. 1999. 416p. pap. 14.95 (*1-56002-852-1*, University Editions) Aegina Pr., Inc.

A Fulfilling & Meaningful Sexual Endeavor: The Total Pillage of Eddie Smock. 2000. (Illus.). 160p. mass mkt. 9.95 (*0-9678222-0-3*) Mooney, Dave.

Gavin, William F. One Hell of a Candidate: A Novel of Politics. 2003. 336p. 24.95 (*0-312-31283-0*) St. Martin's Pr.

George, Anne. This One & Magic Life: A Novel of a Southern Family. 1999. 288p. 22.00 (*0-380-97599-8*, Morrow, William & Co.) Morrow/Avon.

George, Anne Carroll. This One & Magic Life: A Novel of a Southern Family. 2001. 288p. pap. 13.00 (*0-380-79540-X*, Perennial) HarperTrade.

Gibbons, Kaye. Ellen Foster. 1987. 168p. 14.95 o.p. (*0-912697-52-0*); tchr. ed. 16.95 (*1-56512-205-4*) Algonquin Bks. of Chapel Hill.

—Ellen Foster. l.t. ed. 1998. (G. K. Hall Core Ser.). 171p. 26.95 o.p. (*0-7838-0115-7*); (*0-7838-0116-5*) Gale Group. (Macmillan Reference USA).

—Ellen Foster. 1997. pap. o.p. (*0-375-70050-1*, Vintage) Knopf Publishing Group.

—Ellen Foster. 1988. pap. 7.95 o.p. (*0-394-75757-2*); 1990. 144p. pap. 9.00 o.p. (*0-679-72866-X*) Random Hse., Inc.

—Ellen Foster. unabr. ed. 2000. audio compact disk 36.00 (*0-7887-3965-4*, C1120E7); 1998. audio 32.00 (*0-7887-2019-8*, 95396E7) Recorded Bks., LLC.

—Ellen Foster. abr. ed. 1996. audio 18.00 (*0-671-88567-7*, 394197, Simon & Schuster Audioworks) Simon & Schuster Audio.

—Ellen Foster: A Novel. 1997. 144p. pap. 11.00 (*0-375-70305-5*, Vintage) Knopf Publishing Group.

—On the Occasion of My Last Afternoon. l.t. ed. 1998. (Large Print Book Ser.). 26.95 (*1-56895-624-X*, Wheeler Publishing, Inc.) Gale Group.

—On the Occasion of My Last Afternoon. 1999. 288p. reprint ed. pap. 13.00 (*0-380-73214-9*, Perennial) HarperTrade.

—On the Occasion of My Last Afternoon. 1998. 208p. 22.95 (*0-399-19408-8*); 288p. (YA). 22.95 o.s.i (*0-399-14299-1*) Penguin Group (USA) Inc. (G. P. Putnam's Sons).

Gilbert, Sarah. Summer Gloves. (Fresh Voices Ser.). 1994. 224p. mass mkt. 5.99 o.s.i (*0-446-36575-0*); 1993. 208p. 18.95 o.s.i (*0-446-51689-9*) Warner Bks., Inc.

Gilchrist, Ellen. The Cabal & Other Stories. 288p. 2000. (gr. 8). 24.95 o.p. (*0-316-31491-9*); 2002. reprint ed. pap. 13.95 (*0-316-16922-6*, Back Bay) Little Brown & Co.

—Collected Stories. 2000. 576p. 27.95 o.p. (*0-316-29948-0*) Little Brown & Co.

—Ellen Gilchrist: Collected Stories. 2001. 576p. reprint ed. pap. 16.95 (*0-316-19365-8*, Back Bay) Little Brown & Co.

—I, Rhoda Manning, Go Hunting with My Daddy: And Other Stories. 304p. 2002. 25.95 (*0-316-17358-4*); 2003. reprint ed. pap. 14.95 (*0-316-73868-9*, Back Bay) Little Brown & Co.

Gilmore, James Roberts. Among the Pines: Or, South in Secession-Time. 1977. (Black Heritage Library Collection). 18.95 (*0-8369-8579-6*) Ayer Co. Pubs., Inc.

Gilmore, James Roberts & Kirke, Edmund. Among the Pines: Or, South in Secession-Time. 1972. (American Literature Ser.: No. 49). reprint ed. lib. bdg. 75.00 (*0-8383-1219-5*) M.S.G. Haskell Hse.

Gilroy, Jack. The Wisdom Box. 2002. 277p. pap. 14.00 (*1-58684-234-X*) Global Academic Publishing.

Glasgow, Ellen. The Battle-ground. 2000. (Classics of Civil War Fiction Ser.). (Illus.). 540p. pap. text 22.50 (*0-8173-1041-X*) Univ. of Alabama Pr.

—The Battle-Ground. (Collected Works of Ellen Glasgow ). 457p. reprint ed. 2001. (Illus.). pap. text 28.00 (*0-7426-5631-4*); 1998. lib. bdg. 108.00 (*1-58201-631-3*) Classic Bks.

—Virgina. 1989. (Penguin Twentieth-Century Classics Ser.). 432p. pap. 12.95 o.p. (*0-14-039072-3*, Penguin Classics) Viking Penguin.

Godwin, Gail. Evensong. 2000. (Ballantine Reader's Circle Ser.). 432p. pap. 14.00 (*0-345-43477-3*) Ballantine Bks.

—Evensong. l.t. ed. 1999. (Basic Ser.). 29.95 o.p. (*0-7862-2008-2*, Macmillan Reference USA) Gale Group.

Goolsby, Bert. Harpers' Joy. 2003. 200p. 24.95 (*1-932162-17-8*) Benoy Publishing.

Grau, Shirley Ann. The Keepers of the House. 2003. 320p. pap. 13.00 (*1-4000-3074-9*, Vintage) Knopf Publishing Group.

—Roadwalkers. 2003. (Voices of the South Ser.). 292p. 17.95 (*0-8071-2913-5*) Louisiana State Univ. Pr.

Griffith, Michael. Spikes. 2002. 288p. pap. 12.95 (*1-55970-633-3*); 2001. 258p. 24.95 (*1-55970-536-1*) Arcade Publishing, Inc.

Gurganus, Allan. Oldest Living Confederate Widow Tells All. 1996. 736p. pap. 15.00 o.s.i (*0-449-91169-1*, Fawcett); 1994. pap. 6.99 o.p. (*0-8041-9826-8*, Ivy Bks.); 1990. 912p. mass mkt. 6.99 o.s.i (*0-8041-0643-6*, Ivy Bks.) Ballantine Bks.

—Oldest Living Confederate Widow Tells All. 2001. 736p. reprint ed. pap. 16.00 (*0-375-72663-2*, Vintage) Knopf Publishing Group.

—Oldest Living Confederate Widow Tells All. 1992. 5.99 o.p. (*0-517-08827-4*); 1991. 5.99 o.p. (*0-517-06769-2*) Random Hse. Value Publishing.

Haardt, Sara & Henley, Ann, contrib. by. Southern Souvenirs: Selected Stories & Essays. 1999. (Illus.). 317p. text 44.00 (*0-8173-0977-2*) Univ. of Alabama Pr.

Harper, M. A. For the Love of Robert E. Lee. 1994. 325p. pap. 13.00 (*1-56947-002-2*); 1992. 330p. 20.00 o.s.i (*0-939149-63-X*) Soho Pr., Inc.

—The Worst Day of My Life, So Far: My Mother, Alzheimer's & Me. 2002. (Harvest Book Ser.). 288p. reprint ed. pap. 14.00 (*0-15-600718-5*, Harvest Bks.) Harcourt Trade Pubs.

—The Worst Day of My Life, So Far: My Mother, Alzheimer's & Me. 2001. (Illus.). 228p. (YA). 24.00 (*1-892514-97-4*) Hill Street Pr., LLC.

Harris, Alex. A New Life: Stories & Photographs from the Suburban South. 1996. (Illus.). 240p. 29.95 (*0-393-04030-5*) Norton, W. W. & Co., Inc.

Harris, Joel Chandler. Tales of the Home Folks in Peace & War. 1977. (Short Story Index Reprint Ser.). 28.95 (*0-8369-3147-5*) Ayer Co. Pubs., Inc.

—Tales of the Home Folks in Peace & War. 1992. (Notable American Authors Ser.). reprint ed. lib. bdg. 75.00 (*0-7812-3020-9*) Reprint Services Corp.

Hatcher, Robin Lee. Stormy Surrender. 432p. 1994. pap. 4.99 (*0-8439-3573-1*); 1988. pap. 3.95 (*0-8439-2585-X*); 1984. (Spring Haven Saga Ser.: Vol. I). pap. 3.75 o.p. (*0-8439-2073-4*) Dorchester Publishing Co., Inc.

—Stormy Surrender. 1999. (Romances Ser.). pap. 25.95 (*0-7862-2087-2*, Five Star) Gale Group.

Hemphill, Paul. Long Gone: A Novel. 2002. 288p. reprint ed. pap. 14.95 (*1-56663-417-2*) Dee, Ivan R. Pub.

—Lost in the Lights. 2003. 208p. pap. 18.95 (*0-8173-1316-8*) Univ. of Alabama Pr.

Hermes, Myrlin A. Careful What You Wish For. 2000. 240p. pap. 12.95 o.s.i (*0-425-17647-9*) Berkley Publishing Group.

—Careful What You Wish For. 1999. 208p. 23.00 (*0-684-84932-1*, Simon & Schuster) Simon & Schuster.

Hinton, Lynne. The Things I Know Best: A Novel. 16th l.t. ed. 2002. 184p. lib. bdg. 27.95 (*1-58547-154-2*) Ctr. Point Large Print.

—The Things I Know Best: A Novel. 2002. 304p. mass mkt. 7.50 (*0-06-104101-7*) HarperCollins Pubs.

—The Things I Know Best: A Novel. 176p. 2003. pap. 12.95 (*0-06-251728-7*); 2001. 20.00 (*0-06-251727-9*) HarperSanFrancisco.

Hoag, Tami. Heart of Dixie. 1991. (Loveswept Ser.: No. 492). 192p. mass mkt. 2.75 o.s.i (*0-553-44163-9*) Bantam Bks.

—Heart of Dixie. l.t. ed. 2002. 266p. 29.95 (*0-7862-3487-3*) Gale Group.

Hoffman, Roy. Almost Family. 1983. 256p. 14.95 o.p. (*0-385-27664-8*) Doubleday Publishing.

—Almost Family. 2000. (Deep South Book Ser.). 248p. pap. 16.95 (*0-8173-1031-2*) Univ. of Alabama Pr.

Hood, Mary. And Venus Is Blue. 2001. 293p. reprint ed. pap. 14.95 (*0-8203-2308-X*) Univ. of Georgia Pr.

Hudson, Charles M. Conversations with the High Priest of Coosa. 2003. (Illus.). 0248p. 34.95 (*0-8078-2753-3*); pap. 17.95 (*0-8078-5421-2*) Univ. of North Carolina Pr.

Hudson, Suzanne. In a Temple of Trees. 2003. 23.00 (*1-931561-41-9*) MacAdam/Cage Publishing, Inc.

Hughes, Charlotte. Night Kills. 1998. mass mkt. 5.99 (*0-380-79220-6*, Avon Bks.) Morrow/Avon.

Innes, Hammond. The White South. Date not set. pap. text (*0-17-556587-2*) Addison-Wesley Longman, Inc.

—The White South. l.t. ed. 1971. (Ulverscroft Large Print Ser.). 29.99 o.p. (*0-85456-063-7*, Ulverscroft) Thorpe, F. A. Pubs. GBR. *Dist:* Ulverscroft Large Print Bks., Ltd., Ulverscroft Large Print Canada, Ltd.

Jackson, Joe. How I Left the Great State of Tennessee & Went on to Better Things. 2004. 336p. pap. 26.00 (*0-7867-1284-8*, Carroll & Graf Pubs.) Avalon Publishing Group.

Jernigan, Brenda. Every Good & Perfect Gift: A Novel. 2001. (Illus.). 288p. 23.00 (*0-609-60790-1*, Harmony) Crown Publishing Group.

Johnson-Coleman, Lorraine. Larissa's Breadbook: Baking Bread & Telling Tales with Women of the American South. 2001. (Illus.). 245p. 19.99 (*1-55853-845-3*) Rutledge Hill Pr.

Jones, Suzanne Whitmore, ed. & tr. Growing up in the South. 2003. 544p. mass mkt. 7.95 (*0-451-52873-5*) NAL.

Kantor, MacKinlay. If the South Had Won the Civil War. 1994. reprint ed. lib. bdg. 25.95 (*1-56849-528-5*) Buccaneer Bks., Inc.

—If the South Had Won the Civil War. 128p. 2002. (Illus.). pap. 9.95 (*0-312-86949-5*); 2001. 19.95 (*0-312-86553-8*) Doherty, Tom Assocs., LLC. (Forge Bks.).

Kay, Terry. The Runaway. abr. ed. 1998. audio 7.99 o.s.i (*1-56740-265-8*, 1564); 1997. audio 17.95 o.p. (*1-56740-754-4*, 504, Nova Audio Bks.); 1997. audio 25.95 o.p. (*1-56100-775-7*, 243, Bookcassette); 1997. audio 89.25 o.p. (*1-56740-554-1*, 1021, Unabridged Library Editions) Brilliance Audio.

—The Runaway. 1997. 448p. 24.00 o.p. (*0-688-15033-0*, Morrow, William & Co.); 1998. 496p. reprint ed. pap. 6.99 (*0-380-72904-0*, Avon Bks.) Morrow/Avon.

Keegan, Claire. Antarctica. 2001. 207p. 23.00 o.p. (*0-87113-779-8*, Atlantic Monthly Pr.); 2002. 224p. reprint ed. pap. 12.00 (*0-8021-3901-9*, Grove Pr.) Grove/Atlantic, Inc.

Keith, Don. The Forever Season. 2002. (A Deep South Book Ser.). 276p. (Orig.). reprint ed. pap. 18.95 (*0-8173-1242-0*) Univ. of Alabama Pr.

Kincaid, Nanci. Balls. 1998. 408p. tchr. ed. 21.95 (*1-56512-178-3*) Algonquin Bks. of Chapel Hill.

—Balls. 1999. 412p. pap. 23.00 (*0-385-33453-2*, Delacorte Pr.) Dell Publishing.

—Verbena. 2003. 368p. pap. 14.00 (*0-425-19171-0*, Berkley/Pacer) Berkley Publishing Group.

—Verbena: A Novel. 2002. 338p. tchr. ed. 24.95 (*1-56512-348-4*, Shannon Ravenel Bks.) Algonquin Bks. of Chapel Hill.

King, Cassandra. The Sunday Wife. 2004. mass mkt. 7.99 (*0-7868-9070-3*); 2002. 400p. 23.95 (*0-7868-6905-4*) Hyperion Pr.

—The Sunday Wife. 2003. (Core Ser.). 30.95 (*0-7862-5040-2*) Thorndike Pr.

King, Larry L. The One-Eyed Man: A Novel. 2001. (Texas Tradition Ser.: 30). 328p. reprint ed. pap. 17.95 (*0-87565-236-0*) Texas Christian Univ. Pr.

Knight, Michael. Goodnight, Nobody. 2004. 176p. pap. 12.00 (*0-8021-4055-6*, Grove Pr.); 2003. 192p. 23.00 (*0-87113-867-0*, Atlantic Monthly Pr.) Grove/Atlantic, Inc.

Knox, Dahk. The Danville Diaries Vol. 1: A Time of Turmoil. 2003. pap. 15.95 (*1-58275-125-0*) Black Forest Pr.

Koger, Lisa. Farlanburg Stories. 1990. 234p. 17.95 o.p. (*0-393-02856-9*) Norton, W. W. & Co., Inc.

Kolbaker, Genieva. Kisatchie: The Big Thicket. Eyster, Warren, ed. (Illus.). 238p. pap. 12.95 (*0-9725072-1-3*); 1992. 25.00 (*0-9725072-0-5*) Kildara Pr.

Lacy, Al. Beloved Enemy, 8 vols. (Battles of Destiny Ser.: Vol. 3). 356p. 2003. pap. 9.99 (*0-88070-809-3*); 1994. pap. 4.99 o.s.i (*0-88070-626-0*) Multnomah Pubs., Inc. (Multnomah Bks.).

—A Heart Divided: Mobile Bay, 8 vols. 2003. (Battles of Destiny Ser.: Vol. 2). 353p. pap. 9.99 (*0-88070-591-4*, Multnomah Bks.) Multnomah Pubs., Inc.

—Joy from Ashes: Fredericksburg, 8 vols. 2003. (Battles of Destiny Ser.: Vol. 5). 308p. pap. 9.99 (*0-88070-720-8*) Multnomah Pubs., Inc.

—A Promise Unbroken: A Battle of Destiny, 8 vols. 2003. (Battles of Destiny Ser.: Vol. 1). 307p. pap. 9.99 (*0-88070-581-7*, Multnomah Bks.) Multnomah Pubs., Inc.

—Season of Valor: Gettysburg, 8 vols., Vol. 6. 2003. (Battles of Destiny Ser.: No. 6). 294p. pap. 9.99 (*0-88070-865-4*, Multnomah Bks.) Multnomah Pubs., Inc.

—Shadowed Memories: Shiloh, 8 vols. 2003. (Battles of Destiny Ser.: Vol. 4). 307p. pap. 9.99 (*0-88070-657-0*, Multnomah Bks.) Multnomah Pubs., Inc.

—Turn of Glory, 8 vols. 2003. (Battles of Destiny Ser.: Vol. 8). 322p. pap. 9.99 (*1-57673-217-7*) Multnomah Pubs., Inc.

Lacy, Al & Lacy, Lew A. Wings of the Wind, 8 vols. 2003. (Battles of Destiny Ser.: Vol. 7). 366p. pap. 9.99 (*1-57673-032-8*, Multnomah Bks.) Multnomah Pubs., Inc.

L'Amour, Louis. The Haunted Mesa. 1988. 384p. reprint ed. mass mkt. 5.50 (*0-553-27022-2*) Bantam Bks.

Lancelotta, Victoria. Here in the World. 2003. 168p. pap. text 13.95 (*1-58243-293-7*, Counterpoint Pr.) Basic Bks.

—Here in the World: Thirteen Stories. 2000. 168p. text 23.00 (*1-58243-099-3*, Counterpoint Pr.) Basic Bks.

Lee, Harper. To Kill a Mockingbird. 1991. 300p. reprint ed. lib. bdg. 22.95 (*0-89966-858-5*) Buccaneer Bks., Inc.

—To Kill a Mockingbird. 1970. 80p. pap. 5.95 (*0-87129-920-8*, T91) Dramatic Publishing Co.

—To Kill a Mockingbird. 2002. (Perennial Classics Ser.). 336p. pap. 11.95 (*0-06-093546-4*, Perennial) HarperTrade.

—To Kill a Mockingbird. 1969. 312p. (*0-7710-5234-0*) McClelland & Stewart.

—To Kill a Mockingbird. l.t. ed. 1976. 12.00 o.p. (*0-85456-572-8*, Ulverscroft) Thorpe, F. A. Pubs. GBR. *Dist:* Ulverscroft Large Print Bks., Ltd.

Leonard, Elmore. Tishomingo Blues. 2002. E-Book 7.99 (*0-06-051229-6*); 368p. pap. 25.95 (*0-06-008331-X*) HarperCollins Pubs.

—Tishomingo Blues. abr. ed. 2002. 32p. audio 25.95 (*0-06-001115-7*); 208p. audio 29.95 (*0-06-001116-5*); (Illus.). audio 34.95 (*0-06-001117-3*) HarperTrade. (HarperAudio).

—Tishomingo Blues. 2003. 400p. mass mkt. 7.99 (*0-06-008394-8*); 2002. 320p. 25.95 (*0-06-000872-5*) Morrow/Avon. (Morrow, William & Co.).

Linsley, Clyde. Saving Louisa. 2003. 272p. mass mkt. 5.99 (*0-425-19309-8*) Berkley Publishing Group.

Little, Lloyd. Smokehouse Jam. 1989. pap. 5.95 o.s.i (*0-345-35980-1*) Ballantine Bks.

Lodge, Marc. Within the Bounds. 1994. 336p. mass mkt. 5.99 o.s.i (*0-425-14457-7*) Berkley Publishing Group.

—Within the Bounds. 1993. 352p. 22.95 o.p. (*0-399-13881-1*, G. P. Putnam's Sons) Penguin Group (USA) Inc.

Lorenzen, Rod & Parkhurst, Liz, eds. Homecoming: The Southern Family in Short Fiction. 1990. 17.95 o.p. (*0-87483-112-1*) August Hse. Pubs., Inc.

Lyon, George Ella. With a Hammer for My Heart. 1997. (Illus.). 224p. (J). pap. 21.95 o.p. (*0-7894-2460-6*) Dorling Kindersley Publishing, Inc.

—With a Hammer for My Heart. 1999. 224p. reprint ed. pap. 12.00 (*0-380-73217-3*, Avon Bks.) Morrow/Avon.

Malone, Michael. Red Clay, Blue Cadillac: Stories of Twelve Southern Women. 2002. 352p. pap. 15.00 (*1-57071-824-5*, Sourcebooks Landmark) Sourcebooks, Inc.

Manley, Frank. The Cockfighter. 1998. 224p. 19.95 (*1-56689-073-X*) Coffee Hse. Pr.

—The Cockfighter. 1999. 208p. pap. 11.95 o.s.i (*0-385-49420-3*) Doubleday Publishing.

Martin, Joe. Fire in the Rock. 2003. 272p. pap. 13.95 (*0-345-45691-2*, Ballantine Bks.) Ballantine Bks.

—Fire in the Rock. 2001. 300p. 21.95 (*0-9708972-1-9*) Novello Festival Pr.

Mayer, Patricia. Terminal Bend: A Novel. 2000. 256p. 26.00 (*0-942979-74-5*); pap. 14.00 (*0-942979-73-7*) Livingston Pr.

McCord, Charline & McCord, Judy, eds. A Very Southern Christmas: Stories for the Holidays. 2003. (Illus.). 15.95 (*1-56512-383-2*) Algonquin Bks. of Chapel Hill.

McCown, Clint. War Memorials. 2000. 220p. 23.95 (*1-55597-312-4*) Graywolf Pr.

—War Memorials. 2001. 240p. reprint ed. pap. 13.00 (*0-618-12847-6*, Mariner Bks.) Houghton Mifflin Co. Trade & Reference Div.

McCullers, Carson. The Member of the Wedding. 1984. 160p. (gr. 7-12). mass mkt. 6.50 (*0-553-25051-5*) Bantam Bks.

—The Member of the Wedding, 001. 9999. 9.95 o.p. (*0-395-07979-9*) Houghton Mifflin Co.

—The Member of the Wedding. unabr. ed. 2001. audio 22.95 (*1-58081-206-6*, TPT151); audio compact disk 24.95 (*1-58081-221-X*, CDTPT151) L. A. Theatre Works.

—The Member of the Wedding. 1963. pap. 8.95 (*0-8112-0093-0*, NDP153) New Directions Publishing Corp.

—The Member of the Wedding. 1950. 12.04 (*0-606-01060-2*) Turtleback Bks.

—Reflections in a Golden Eye. 1990. 160p. mass mkt. 4.99 o.s.i (*0-553-56968-6*) Bantam Bks.

—Reflections in a Golden Eye. 2000. 182p. pap. 10.00 (*0-618-08475-4*, Mariner Bks.) Houghton Mifflin Co. Trade & Reference Div.

McDonald, Jeanne. Water Dreams. 2003. 25.00 (*1-57806-548-8*) Univ. Pr. of Mississippi.

McGovern, Cammie. Among the Headhunters of Formosa. 288p. 2005. pap. 13.00 (*0-7432-4792-2*); 2004. (*0-7432-4791-4*) Simon & Schuster. (Scribner).

Means, Howard. C. S. A. Confederate States of America, Set. abr. ed. 1999. audio 25.00 Highsmith Inc.

—C. S. A. Confederate States of America. 1998. audio 25.00 (*0-7871-1825-7*, Dove Audio) NewStar Media, Inc.

—C. S. A. - Confederate States of America. 1998. 352p. 24.00 o.p. (*0-688-16187-1*, Morrow, William & Co.) Morrow/Avon.

Moorcock, Michael. Blood: A Southern Fantasy. 352p. 1996. pap. 12.00 o.p. (*0-380-78078-X*, Avon Bks.); 1995. 22.00 o.p. (*0-688-14362-8*, Morrow, William & Co.) Morrow/Avon.

Morris, Gilbert. Edge of Honor. 2000. 373p. 16.99 (*0-310-22589-2*) Zondervan.

—Jacob's Way. 2001. 416p. pap. 12.99 (*0-310-22696-1*) Zondervan.

Morrison, Toni. Sula. 2002. 192p. pap. 13.00 (*0-452-28386-8*) NAL.

Myers, Tamar. A Penny Urned. 2000. (Den of Antiquity Ser.). 288p. mass mkt. 6.50 (*0-380-81189-8*, Avon Bks.) Morrow/Avon.

—A Penny Urned: A Den of Antiquity Mystery. 2003. (Mystery Ser.). 28.95 (*0-7862-4753-3*) Thorndike Pr.

Neilson, Melany. The Persia Cafe: A Novel. 2002. 288p. pap. 13.95 (*0-312-28916-2*, Saint Martin's Griffin) St. Martin's Pr.

Norris, Helen. One Day in the Life of a Born Again Loser & Other Stories. 2000. 208p. text 27.50 (*0-8173-1029-0*) Univ. of Alabama Pr.

O'Connor, Flannery. A Good Man Is Hard to Find. (HBJ Book Ser.). 1992. 264p. 17.00 (*0-15-136504-0*); 1977. 264p. pap. 12.00 (*0-15-636465-4*, Harvest Bks.); 1955. 7.95 o.p. (*0-15-136503-2*) Harcourt Trade Pubs.

—A Good Man Is Hard to Find. mass mkt. 0.50 o.p. (*0-451-01965-2*); mass mkt. 0.35 o.p. (*0-451-01345-X*) NAL. (Signet Bks.).

—A Good Man Is Hard to Find. 1993. (Women Writers: Text & Contexts Ser.). 180p. pap. 14.00 (*0-8135-1977-2*); text 30.00 (*0-8135-1976-4*) Rutgers Univ. Pr.

—A Good Man Is Hard to Find. 1999. 18.05 (*0-606-20680-9*) Turtleback Bks.

Olds, Bruce. Raising Holy Hell. 1995. 335p. 22.50 o.p. (*0-8050-3856-6*) Holt, Henry & Co.

—Raising Holy Hell. 1997. 352p. pap. 17.00 o.s.i (*0-14-025908-2*) Penguin Group (USA) Inc.

—Raising Holy Hell. 2002. 352p. pap. 14.00 (*0-312-42093-5*) Picador.

Page, Thomas Nelson. In Ole Virginia: Or, Marse Chan & Other Stories. 2000. 252p. E-Book 3.95 (*0-594-06399-X*) 1873 Pr.

—In Ole Virginia: Or, Marse Chan & Other Stories. 1991. (Southern Classics Ser.). 254p. (C). reprint ed. pap. 10.95 (*1-879941-04-X*, Sanders, J. S. & Co., Inc.) Dee, Ivan R. Pub.

—In Ole Virginia: Or, Marse Chan & Other Stories. (Americans in Fiction Ser.). 230p. reprint ed. lib. bdg. 19.00 (*0-8398-1550-6*); 1986. (C). pap. text 7.95 (*0-8290-1864-6*) Irvington Pubs.

—In Ole Virginia: Or, Marse Chan & Other Stories. 1992. (BCL1-PS American Literature Ser.). 230p. reprint ed. lib. bdg. 79.00 (*0-7812-6822-2*) Reprint Services Corp.

Page, Thomas Nelson, et al. Stories of the South. 1977. (Short Story Index Reprint Ser.). 26.95 (*0-8369-3369-9*) Ayer Co. Pubs., Inc.

Pancake, Ann. Given Ground. 2001. 152p. 24.95 (*1-58465-118-0*) Univ. Pr. of New England.

Parker, Michael. The Geographical Cure: Novellas & Stories. 1994. 288p. 20.00 (*0-684-19682-4*, Macmillan Reference USA) Gale Group.

—The Geographical Cure: Novellas & Stories. 1995. 304p. pap. 16.00 o.s.i (*0-14-024390-9*, Penguin Bks.) Penguin Group (USA) Inc.

Patterson, Richard North. The Outside Man. 1997. pap. 12.00 o.s.i (*0-345-41815-8*); 1995. mass mkt. 6.99 o.p. (*0-345-90514-8*); 1985. mass mkt. 2.95 o.s.i (*0-345-32533-8*, Ballantine Bks.); 1982. 320p. mass mkt. 7.99 (*0-345-30020-3*) Ballantine Bks.

—The Outside Man. l.t. ed. 2000. (Wheeler Large Print Book Ser.). 324p. 29.95 o.p. (*1-56895-907-9*, Wheeler Publishing, Inc.) Gale Group.

—The Outside Man. 1981. 252p. 11.95 o.p. (*0-316-69362-6*) Little Brown & Co.

Peacock, Nancy. Home Across the Road. 1999. 249p. 18.95 (*1-56352-509-7*) Longstreet Pr., Inc.

Pearson, T. R. True Cross. 2003. 272p. 24.95 (*0-670-03238-7*, Viking) Viking Penguin.

Peltier-Draine, Elsaida. The Spirit & Butterfly Brooch. 2001. 274p. pap. 13.00 (*0-9643320-5-1*) Zenon Pubn. Co.

Pendarvis, Edwina D. & Gifford, James M., eds. Appalachian Love Stories. 2001. (Illus.). 207p. (*0-945084-89-7*) Stuart, Jesse Foundation, The.

Penley, Gary. Jubal. 2003. 272p. 23.00 (*1-58980-129-6*) Pelican Publishing Co., Inc.

Phillips, Dale R. My People's Waltz: Stories. 2000. 192p. pap. 13.00 (*0-380-73336-6*, Perennial) HarperTrade.

—My People's Waltz: Stories. 1999. 192p. 22.95 (*0-393-04715-6*) Norton, W. W. & Co., Inc.

Phillips, Susan Elizabeth. Just Imagine. 2001. 384p. mass mkt. 6.99 (*0-380-80830-7*, Avon Bks.) Morrow/Avon.

Phillips, Thomas H. The Loved & the Unloved. 1998. 260p. pap. 17.00 (*1-57806-056-7*, A Banner Bk.) Univ. Pr. of Mississippi.

Pickens, Cathy. Southern Fried. Date not set. mass mkt. (*0-312-99553-9*, St. Martin's Paperbacks); pap. (*0-312-32493-6*, St. Martin's Paperbacks); 2004. 304p. 23.95 (*0-312-32492-8*) St. Martin's Pr.

Plain, Belva. Fortune's Hand. unabr. ed. 2000. audio 69.95 (*0-7540-0415-5*, CAB 1838);Set. 8p. audio compact disk 99.95 (*0-7540-5324-5*, CCD 015) Chivers Audio Bks. GBR. *Dist:* BBC Audiobooks America.

—Fortune's Hand. 2000. 432p. mass mkt. 7.99 (*0-440-22641-4*); 1999. mass mkt. 7.99 (*0-440-29575-0*) Dell Publishing.

—Fortune's Hand, Set. abr. ed. 1999. audio 25.00 Highsmith Inc.

—Fortune's Hand. abr. ed. 1999. audio Random Hse. Audio Publishing Group.

—Fortune's Hand. l.t. ed. 2000. (Thorndike/G. K. Hall Paperback Bestsellers Ser.). 519p. pap. 30.95 (*0-7862-2013-9*) Thorndike Pr.

—Fortune's Hand. 2000. (Illus.). 14.04 (*0-606-18103-2*) Turtleback Bks.

Porter, William T., ed. Big Bear of Arkansas, & Other Sketches. reprint ed. 29.50 (*0-404-05079-4*) AMS Pr., Inc.

Powell, Padgett. Mrs. Hollingsworth's Men: A Novel. 2000. 148p. tchr. ed. 20.00 (*0-618-07168-7*, Mariner Bks.) Houghton Mifflin Co. Trade & Reference Div.

Predestine Seasons. 2002. 259p. pap. 12.00 (*0-9721745-0-8*) Finnie, Bettie Adams.

Preston, Fayrene. In the Heat of the Night. 1992. (Loveswept Ser.: No. 573). 192p. mass mkt. 2.79 o.s.i (*0-553-44172-8*) Bantam Bks.

Price, Reynolds. A Great Circle: The Mayfield Trilogy. 2001. 1200p. 50.00 (*0-7432-1186-3*, Scribner) Simon & Schuster.

Quinn, Jay. Rebel Yell 2: More Stories of Contemporary Southern Gay Men. 2002. 288p. (C). pap. 17.95 (*1-56023-159-9*, Southern Tier Editions) Haworth Pr., Inc., The.

Quinn, Jay, ed. Rebel Yell 2: More Stories of Contemporary Southern Gay Men. 2002. 278p. (C). lib. bdg. 29.95 (*1-56023-158-0*, Southern Tier Editions) Haworth Pr., Inc., The.

Reece, Byron H. The Hawk & the Sun: A Novel. 1985. 192p. reprint ed. 16.95 o.s.i (*0-87797-103-X*) Cherokee Publishing Co.

—The Hawk & the Sun: A Novel. 1994. (Brown Thrasher Bks.). 200p. reprint ed. pap. 16.00 (*0-8203-1656-3*) Univ. of Georgia Pr.

Reece, Colleen L. Legacy of Silver. l.t. ed. 2002. (Christian Romance Ser.). 254p. 24.95 (*0-7862-3823-2*) Gale Group.

Reed, Ishmael. Flight to Canada. 1989. 180p. pap. 11.00 (*0-689-70733-9*) Central Bureau voor Schimmelcultures NLD. *Dist:* Lubrecht & Cramer, Ltd.

—Flight to Canada. 1977. pap. 2.75 o.p. (*0-380-01798-9*, 52019, Avon Bks.) Morrow/Avon.

—Flight to Canada. 1998. 192p. pap. 11.00 (*0-684-84750-7*, Scribner) Simon & Schuster.

Reynolds, Sheri. A Gracious Plenty. unabr. ed. 1998. audio 32.00 (*0-7366-4143-2*, 4647) Books on Tape, Inc.

—A Gracious Plenty. 1999. 208p. pap. 12.00 (*0-609-80387-5*) Crown Publishing Group.

—A Gracious Plenty. l.t. ed. 1999. (General Ser.). 248p. pap. 23.95 (*0-7862-1683-2*) Thorndike Pr.

Richards, Ann Vaughan. Miss Woman. 2001. (Illus.). 240p. 26.00 (*0-942979-78-8*); pap. 12.95 (*0-942979-77-X*) Livingston Pr.

Richardson, Brenda L. Chesapeake Song. 371p. 1999. pap. 19.95 (*1-56743-040-6*); 1994. pap. 10.95 (*1-56743-063-5*) HarperTrade. (Amistad Pr.).

—Chesapeake Song. 1996. 480p. mass mkt. 5.99 o.s.i (*0-7860-0304-9*, Pinnacle Bks.) Kensington Publishing Corp.

Roberts, Clifford. Run Lee Run. 2001. 192p. pap. 20.99 (*1-4010-2560-9*); text 30.99 (*1-4010-2559-5*); E-Book 8.00 (*1-4010-2561-7*) Xlibris Corp.

Russell, Charlie L. The Worthy Ones: A Novel. 2002. (Illus.). 221p. 15.95 (*0-932693-11-3*) Jukebox Pr.

Rutledge, Archibald. Bird Dog Days, Wingshooting Ways. Casada, Jim, ed. 1998. (Illus.). 192p. 35.00 (*1-885106-68-8*) PleaWilderness Adventures Pr., Inc.

Sanders, Deon. Miss Mary Weather: A Southern Nightmare. 2001. 166p. pap. 19.95 (*1-58851-837-X*) PublishAmerica, Inc.

Schimel, Lawrence & Greenberg, Martin H., eds. Southern Blood: Vampire Stories from the American South. 1997. (American Vampire Ser.). (Illus.). 240p. (Orig.). pap. 12.95 (*1-888952-49-0*) Cumberland Hse. Publishing.

Sherrill, Steven. The Minotaur Takes a Cigarette Break. 2000. 313p. 19.95 (*0-89587-197-1*) Blair, John F. Pub.

—The Minotaur Takes a Cigarette Break: A Novel. 2002. 320p. pap. 14.00 (*0-312-30892-2*) Picador.

Sibley, William Jack. Any Kind of Luck. 2001. 288p. 23.00 (*1-57566-766-5*) Kensington Publishing Corp.

Siddons, Anne Rivers. Homeplace. 1988. mass mkt. 5.99 o.s.i (*0-345-35457-5*) Ballantine Bks.

—Homeplace. l.t. ed. 1988. (General Ser.). 512p. 19.95 o.p. (*0-8161-4473-7*, Macmillan Reference USA) Gale Group.

—Homeplace. 1987. 320p. 17.95 o.p. (*0-06-015758-5*) HarperTrade.

—Homeplace. 1996. 432p. mass mkt. 7.99 (*0-06-101141-X*, HarperTorch) Morrow/Avon.

—King's Oak. 1990. 21.95 o.p. (*0-06-016248-1*); 1991. audio 15.95 o.s.i (*1-55994-370-X*, CPN 2221, HarperAudio) HarperTrade.

—King's Oak. 1991. 608p. mass mkt. 7.99 (*0-06-109927-9*, HarperTorch) Morrow/Avon.

Simms, William Gilmore & Guilds, John Caldwell. The Simms Reader: Selections from the Writings of William Gilmore Simms. 2001. (Publications of the Southern Texts Society). (Illus.). x, 412p. 42.50 (*0-8139-2019-1*) Univ. Pr. of Virginia.

Singleton, George. The Half-Mammals of Dixie: Stories. 2002. 304p. tchr. ed. 22.95 (*1-56512-354-9*) Algonquin Bks. of Chapel Hill.

—The Half-Mammals of Dixie: Stories. 2003. 312p. pap. 13.00 (*0-15-602858-1*) Harcourt Trade Pubs.

Smith, Annette. Homemade Humble Pie: And Other Slices of Life. 2001. 208p. (gr. 13 up). pap. 11.99 (*0-8007-5771-8*, Spire) Revell, Fleming H. Co.

Smith, Deborah, et al. Mossy Creek. 2001. 368p. pap. 14.95 (*0-9673035-1-6*) BelleBks.

—Mossy Creek, Vol. 1. 2003. 240p. reprint ed. mass mkt. 6.99 (*0-425-18916-3*) Berkley Publishing Group.

Smith, Debra White. A Shelter in the Storm. 2001. (Seven Sisters Ser.: Vol. 3). 314p. pap. 9.99 (*0-7369-0278-3*) Harvest Hse. Pubs.

Smith, Lee. The Last Girls: A Novel. (Illus.). 2003. 384p. 24.95 (*1-56512-405-7*); 2002. 400p. tchr. ed. 24.95 (*1-56512-363-8*, 72363) Algonquin Bks. of Chapel Hill.

—The Last Girls: A Novel. 2003. 432p. pap. 14.95 (*0-345-46495-8*) Ballantine Bks.

—The Last Girls: A Novel. l.t. ed. 2002. 30.95 (*0-7862-4734-7*) Thorndike Pr.

Sorrells, Russell B. The Yelling Boys: A Story of the American Revolution in the South. 1998. 317p. 18.95 (*0-9640019-1-8*) Sorrells, Russell B. Happy Valley Publishing.

Spencer, Elizabeth. The Southern Woman: New & Selected Fiction. 2001. 480p. 23.95 (*0-679-64218-8*, Modern Library) Random House Adult Trade Publishing Group.

Sprinkle, Patricia. Who Invited the Dead Man? l.t. ed. 2002. pap. 23.95 (*1-58724-349-0*, Wheeler Publishing, Inc.) Gale Group.

—Who Invited the Dead Man? 2002. 272p. mass mkt. 5.99 (*0-451-20659-2*) NAL.

Stacy, Judith Minthorn. Betty Sweet Tells All. 2002. 256p. 22.95 (*0-06-018485-X*) HarperCollins Pubs.

—Betty Sweet Tells All. 2003. 256p. pap. 12.95 (*0-06-053615-2*, Perennial) HarperTrade.

Stewart, Frank. River Rising: A Cherokee Odyssey. 1998. (Illus.). 798p. 34.95 (*0-9663853-0-6*) Wohali Pr.

Stewart, Mike. Dog Island. 2002. 304p. reprint ed. mass mkt. 5.99 o.s.i (*0-425-18204-5*, Prime Crime) Berkley Publishing Group.

—Dog Island. 2001. 448p. 23.95 o.p. (*0-399-14645-8*) Penguin Group (USA) Inc.

—Sins of the Brother. 2001. 304p. mass mkt. 5.99 o.s.i (*0-425-17887-0*) Berkley Publishing Group.

Still, Mark. Son of the South. 1999. 88p. pap. 9.95 (*0-9669789-0-0*) Eusebius Publishing.

Stowe, Harriet Beecher. Uncle Tom's Cabin. 1997. (Classics Illustrated Notes). (Illus.). pap. text 4.99 (*1-57840-060-0*) Acclaim Bks.

—Uncle Tom's Cabin. 1997. (C). pap. text (*0-321-02606-3*) Addison-Wesley Educational Pubs., Inc.

—Uncle Tom's Cabin. 29.95 (*0-8488-0637-9*) Amereon, Ltd.

—Uncle Tom's Cabin. 1982. (Bantam Classics Ser.). 544p. reprint ed. mass mkt. 5.95 (*0-553-21218-4*) Bantam Dell Publishing Group.

—Uncle Tom's Cabin. E-Book 5.00 (*0-7607-1294-8*) Barnes & Noble, Inc.

—Uncle Tom's Cabin. 2002. pap. 4.50 (*1-59109-074-1*) Booksurge, LLC.

—Uncle Tom's Cabin. 1982. reprint ed. lib. bdg. 27.95 (*0-89966-378-8*) Buccaneer Bks., Inc.

—Uncle Tom's Cabin. 2003. (Barnes & Noble Classics Ser.). 560p. mass mkt. 5.95 (*1-59308-038-7*) Fine Communications.

—Uncle Tom's Cabin. 1970. 480p. mass mkt. 6.50 (*0-06-080618-4*, Perennial) HarperTrade.

—Uncle Tom's Cabin, 001. 1972. (Riverside Library). 512p. tchr. ed. 29.95 o.p. (*0-395-08129-7*) Houghton Mifflin Co.

—Uncle Tom's Cabin. 1995. (Everyman's Library). 538p. 20.00 (*0-679-44365-7*) Knopf, Alfred A. Inc.

—Uncle Tom's Cabin. 1991. E-Book 1.95 (*1-58515-015-0*) MesaView, Inc.

—Uncle Tom's Cabin. 1968. mass mkt. 0.75 o.p. (*0-451-50322-8*); 1968. mass mkt. 0.85 o.p. (*0-451-50369-4*); 1968. mass mkt. 0.75 o.p. (*0-451-50393-7*); 1966. mass mkt. 1.50 o.p. (*0-451-51009-7*); 1966. mass mkt. 2.25 o.p. (*0-451-51473-4*); 1966. mass mkt. 0.95 o.p. (*0-451-50714-2*); 1966. mass mkt. 2.25 o.p. (*0-451-51755-5*); 1966. mass mkt. 2.75 o.p. (*0-451-51973-6*); 1966. mass mkt. 2.75 o.p. (*0-451-51611-7*); 1966. mass mkt. 1.95 o.p. (*0-451-51182-4*) NAL. (Signet Classics).

—Uncle Tom's Cabin. Yellin, Jean F., ed. 1998. (Oxford World's Classics Ser.). 576p. pap. 7.95 (*0-19-282787-1*) Oxford Univ. Pr., Inc.

—Uncle Tom's Cabin. (Classics Ser.). 2001. 688p. pap. 8.95 (*0-375-75693-0*); 2000. E-Book 4.95 (*0-679-64198-X*) Random House Adult Trade Publishing Group. (Modern Library).

—Uncle Tom's Cabin. (Modern Library Ser.). 1996. 656p. 19.95 (*0-679-60200-3*); 1985. 552p. 20.00 o.s.i (*0-394-60527-6*) Random Hse., Inc.

—Uncle Tom's Cabin. 512p. 2004. mass mkt. 5.95 (*0-7434-8766-4*); 2005. (Illus.). reprint ed. pap. 5.99 (*0-7434-2190-6*) Simon & Schuster. (Pocket).

—Uncle Tom's Cabin. 1981. 12.00 (*0-606-02474-3*) Turtleback Bks.

—Uncle Tom's Cabin. 1997. (Classics Library). 432p. pap. 3.95 o.s.i (*1-85326-575-6*, 5756WW) Wordsworth Editions, Ltd. GBR. *Dist:* Combined Publishing.

Strange, George. Generations: Stories. 2002. 192p. 24.95 (*0-86554-791-2*, H598) Mercer Univ. Pr.

Stuart, Dabney. Sweet Lucy Wine: Stories. 1992. 128p. 18.95 (*0-8071-1707-2*) Louisiana State Univ. Pr.

Taylor, Laurie. The Lillie Pad: A Southern Tale. 2001. 262p. pap. 21.95 (*1-58851-858-2*) PublishAmerica, Inc.

Toole, John Kennedy. The Neon Bible. 1990. (Illus.). 176p. pap. 12.00 (*0-8021-3207-3*, Grove Pr.); 1989. 160p. 15.95 o.p. (*0-8021-1108-4*) Grove/Atlantic, Inc.

Toomer, Jean. Cane. 2000. 252p. E-Book 9.95 (*0-594-06102-4*) 1873 Pr.

—Cane. 2000. (Illus.). (*0-910457-41-7*) Arion Pr.

—Cane. 1993. 144p. (C). pap. 9.95 (*0-87140-151-7*); 1975. 116p. 7.95 o.p. (*0-87140-611-X*); 1975. 116p. pap. 5.95 o.p. (*0-87140-104-5*) Liveright Publishing Corp.

—Cane. Turner, Darwin T., ed. 1987. (Critical Editions Ser.). 320p. (C). pap. text (*0-393-95600-8*) Norton, W. W. & Co., Inc.

—Cane. 1994. 182p. 12.50 o.s.i (*0-679-60109-0*) Random Hse., Inc.

—Cane. 1990. 28.00 (*0-8446-6367-0*) Smith, Peter Pub., Inc.

Toomer, Jean & Hutchinson, George B. Cane. 1999. (Penguin Twentieth-Century Classics Ser.). 160p. pap. 7.95 (*0-14-118132-X*) Viking Penguin.

Trobaugh, Augusta. River Jordan. 2004. 272p. 23.95 (*0-525-94755-8*, Dutton) Dutton/Plume.

—Swan Place: A Novel. 2002. 272p. 23.95 (*0-525-94688-8*) Dutton/Plume.

Troubaugh, Augusta. Swan Place. 2004. 304p. pap. 13.00 (*0-452-28414-7*, Plume) Dutton/Plume.

Twain, Mark. The Adventures of Huckleberry Finn. 1985. (Modern Library Ser.). E-Book 4.95 (*0-679-64205-6*, Modern Library) Random House Adult Trade Publishing Group.

Varnes, Paul. Confederate Money. 2003. 269p. 18.95 (*1-56164-271-1*) Pineapple Pr., Inc.

Vasseur, Thomas Jeffrey. Discovering the World: Thirteen Stories. 2001. 352p. 25.00 (*0-86554-718-1*, MUP/H538) Mercer Univ. Pr.

Walker, Alice. The Color Purple. Bernard, Andre, ed. 2003. 300p. pap. 14.00 (*0-15-602835-2*, Harvest Bks.) Harcourt Trade Pubs.

—Everyday Use. 1994. (Women Writers: Text & Contexts Ser.). vi, 229p. (C). 30.00 o.p. (*0-8135-2075-4*); pap. text 14.00 (*0-8135-2076-2*) Rutgers Univ. Pr.

—Meridian. l.t. ed. 1987. 299p. reprint ed. lib. bdg. 19.95 o.p. (*1-55736-019-7*) Bantam Doubleday Dell Large Print Group, Inc.

—Meridian. Bernard, Andre, ed. 2003. 264p. pap. 13.00 (*0-15-602834-4*, Harvest Bks.) Harcourt Trade Pubs.

—Meridian. 1976. 256p. 18.95 o.p. (*0-15-159265-9*) Harcourt Trade Pubs.

—Meridian. Rubenstein, Julie, ed. 1990. 224p. mass mkt. 6.99 (*0-671-72701-X*, Pocket) Simon & Schuster.

—Meridian. 1989. 224p. mass mkt. 4.50 (*0-671-68765-4*, Pocket); 1983. 228p. mass mkt. 3.95 (*0-671-47256-9*, Pocket); 1981. mass mkt. 2.75 o.p. (*0-671-43750-X*, Washington Square Pr.) Simon & Schuster.

Walker, Jo N. Rare Birds. 2001. pap. 8.00 (*0-8059-5187-3*) Dorrance Publishing Co., Inc.

Warren, Robert Penn. All the King's Men. 15.95 (*0-8488-1504-1*) Amereon, Ltd.

—All the King's Men. 1981. 350p. reprint ed. lib. bdg. 35.95 (*0-89966-290-0*) Buccaneer Bks., Inc.

—All the King's Men. 1961. per. 6.50 (*0-8222-0018-X*) Dramatists Play Service, Inc.

—All the King's Men. Polk, Noel, ed. 656p. 2002. pap. 15.00 (*0-15-601295-2*, Harvest Bks.); 2001. 30.00 (*0-15-100610-5*) Harcourt Trade Pubs.

—All the King's Men. (HBJ Book Ser.). 1990. 540p. 19.00 (*0-15-104772-3*); 1983. 438p. pap. 11.00 o.s.i (*0-15-604762-4*, Harvest Bks.); 2nd anniv. ed. 1996. 456p. pap. 14.00 (*0-15-600480-1*, Harvest Bks.) Harcourt Trade Pubs.

—All the King's Men. 2nd ed. 1996. 20.05 (*0-606-00317-7*) Turtleback Bks.

—All the King's Men Play. 1960. 15.95 o.s.i (*0-394-40502-1*) Random Hse., Inc.

Watson, Sterling. Sweet Dream Baby. 2002. 320p. 22.00 (*1-4022-0017-X*, Sourcebooks Landmark) Sourcebooks, Inc.

Watts, Julia. Finding H. F. 2004. 165p. (YA). (gr. 7 up). pap. 12.95 (*1-55583-622-4*) Alyson Pubns.

Wells Brown, William. Clotelle: Or, the Colored Heroine. 2000. per. 12.50 (*1-58396-520-3*) Blue Unicorn Editions.

West, Michael Lee. Crazy Ladies: A Novel. 1991. mass mkt. 6.99 o.s.i (*0-8041-0829-3*, Ivy Bks.) Ballantine Bks.

—Crazy Ladies: A Novel. l.t. ed. 28.95 (*1-57490-395-0*) Beeler, Thomas T. Publisher.

—Crazy Ladies: A Novel. 2000. (Illus.). 416p. pap. 14.00 (*0-06-097774-4*, Perennial); audio 24.00 (*0-694-52252-X*, HarperAudio) HarperTrade.

—Crazy Ladies: A Novel. 1990. 325p. 18.95 o.p. (*0-929264-38-X*) Longstreet Pr., Inc.

Wilkes, John. The Star Chamber. 1998. pap. text 17.98 (*0-9668643-0-1*) Pepperdine Pr., Inc.

Wilkinson, Sylvia. Cale. 1986. 455p. 21.95 o.p. (*0-912697-25-3*); pap. 11.95 o.p. (*0-912697-29-6*) Algonquin Bks. of Chapel Hill.

Williams, Sherley A. Dessa Rose. 1987. mass mkt. 6.50 o.s.i (*0-425-10337-4*) Berkley Publishing Group.

—Dessa Rose. abr. ed. 2000. audio 7.95 (*1-57815-148-1*, 1107, Media Bks. Audio Publishing) Media Bks., L. L. C.

—Dessa Rose: A Novel. 1999. 240p. pap. 13.00 (*0-688-16643-1*, Quill) HarperTrade.

—Dessa Rose: A Riveting Story of the South During Slavery. 1986. 256p. 15.95 o.p. (*0-688-05113-8*, Morrow, William & Co.) Morrow/Avon.

Williams, Shirley A. Dessa Rose. abr. ed. 1993. audio 15.95 o.p. (*1-55800-001-1*, 40000, Dove Audio) NewStar Media, Inc.

Willocks, Tim. Bloodstained Kings. 1995. 311p. (*0-224-04160-6*) Cape, Jonathan Ltd. GBR. *Dist:* Trafalgar Square.

Young, L. M. Michael's Journal Bk. 1: Being the Journals of Michael Cooke Holt, 1917-1925. 2001. 148p. pap. 17.95 (*0-7596-4694-5*) 1stBooks Library.

## SOUTHWEST, NEW—FICTION

Abbey, Edward. Good News. 1991. 256p. pap. 14.00 (*0-452-26565-7*, Plume); 1980. 256p. 11.95 o.p. (*0-525-11583-8*, Dutton); 1980. 256p. 6.95 o.p. (*0-525-03467-6*, 0674-210, Dutton); 1980. pap. 10.95 o.p. (*0-525-48521-X*, Plume) Dutton/Plume.

—Good News. 1980. pap. 9.95 o.p. (*0-525-48234-2*) NAL.

Buffington, G. N. Virgin Spring. 2001. 351p. 23.95 (*0-9700717-0-1*) Pony-Up Pr.

Conquest, Ned. The Way of the Eagle. 1994. 319p. 19.95 (*0-9627485-2-8*) Apollonian Pr.

—The Way of the Eagle. 2003. (Illus.). 332p. pap. 18.95 (*0-86534-398-5*) Sunstone Pr.

Donaldson, Stephen R. The Man Who Fought Alone. 2002. E-Book 27.95 (*1-59061-751-7*) Adobe Systems, Inc.

—The Man Who Fought Alone. 2001. 464p. 27.95 (*0-7653-0202-0*); 2002. reprint ed. mass mkt. 7.99 (*0-7653-4124-7*) Doherty, Tom Assocs., LLC. (Forge Bks.).

Evans, Max. Spinning Sun, Grinning Moon. 1995. (Illus.). 360p. 19.95 o.p. (*1-878610-52-X*) Red Crane Bks., Inc.

Gallegos, Eloy J. Jacona: An Epic Story of the Spanish Southwest. 1996. (Spanish Pioneers Ser.: Vol. I). (Illus.). 377p. pap. 13.50 (*1-882194-22-5*) Tennessee Valley Publishing.

Glatt, John. Cries in the Desert. 2002. (St. Martin's True Crime Library). (Illus.). 256p. mass mkt. 6.99 (*0-312-97756-5*, St. Martin's Paperbacks) St. Martin's Pr.

Gonzales, Felipe C. Recess Is Not Forever. 2000. 372p. pap. 22.99 (*0-7388-1763-5*); (Illus.). text 32.99 (*0-7388-1762-7*) Xlibris Corp.

Haley, Michael C. The Gold of el Negro. Hansen, Marge D., ed. 2001. 332p. mass mkt. 6.99 (*0-9701862-1-5*) Poncha Pr.

Havill, Steven F. Before She Dies. 2001. 218p. pap. 14.95 (*1-890208-59-0*) Poisoned Pen Pr.

—Privileged to Kill. 2001. 200p. pap. 14.95 o.s.i (*1-890208-65-5*) Poisoned Pen Pr.

Johnstone, William W. Code Name: Survival. 2000. 336p. mass mkt. 5.99 (*0-7860-1151-3*, Pinnacle Bks.) Kensington Publishing Corp.

Lummis, Charles F. New Mexico David, & Other Stories, & Sketches of the South-West. 1977. (Short Story Index Reprint Ser.). 19.95 (*0-8369-3069-X*) Ayer Co. Pubs., Inc.

Mount, Guy. Coyote's Big Penis & Other Stories. 1989. 80p. per. 5.95 (*0-9604462-5-7*) Sweetlight Bks.

Porter, William T., ed. Big Bear of Arkansas, & Other Sketches. reprint ed. 29.50 (*0-404-05079-4*) AMS Pr., Inc.

Salaz, Ruben D. Heartland Stories of the Southwest. 1978. pap. 4.95 (*0-932492-01-5*) Blue Feather Pr.

Sojourner, Mary. Delicate: Stories of Light & Desire. 2001. 201p. pap. 14.95 (*0-9709084-7-4*) Nevermore Pr.

## SOUTHWEST, OLD—FICTION

Cohen, Hennig & Dillingham, William B. Humor of the Old Southwest. rev. ed. 1994. 528p. 50.00 (*0-8203-1604-0*); pap. 25.00 (*0-8203-1605-9*) Univ. of Georgia Pr.

Cohen, Hennig & Dillingham, William B., eds. Humor of the Old Southwest. 2nd ed. 1975. 456p. (C). reprint ed. pap. 10.00 o.p. (*0-8203-0358-5*) Univ. of Georgia Pr.

Hartmann, William K. Cities of Gold: A Novel of the Ancient & Modern Southwest. 2003. 512p. mass mkt. 7.99 (*0-7653-4068-2*, Forge Bks.) Doherty, Tom Assocs., LLC.

Simms, William Gilmore. The Wigwam & the Cabin. rev. ed. reprint ed. 37.50 (*0-404-06038-2*) AMS Pr., Inc.

—The Wigwam & the Cabin. (Americans in Fiction Ser.). 311p. reprint ed. pap. text 12.95 (*0-89197-976-X*); lib. bdg. 17.50 (*0-8398-1861-0*) Irvington Pubs.

Simms, William Gilmore & Guilds, John Caldwell. The Wigwam & the Cabin: Selected Fiction of William Gilmore Simms: Arkansas Edition. 2000. (Simms Ser.: Vol. 10). (Illus.). xxxiv, 413p. text 34.95 (*1-55728-624-8*) Univ. of Arkansas Pr.

## SOUTHWESTERN STATES—FICTION

Abbey, Edward. Hayduke Lives!, unabr. collector's ed. 1990. audio 80.00 (*0-7366-1824-4*, 2660) Books on Tape, Inc.

—Hayduke Lives! 1998. pap. 12.95 (*0-316-19138-8*, Back Bay); 1991. 308p. pap. 13.95 (*0-316-00413-8*); 1990. 18.95 o.p. (*0-316-00411-1*) Little Brown & Co.

—The Monkey Wrench Gang. 22.95 (*0-8488-0902-5*) Amereon, Ltd.

—The Monkey Wrench Gang. unabr. collector's ed. 1988. audio 88.00 (*0-7366-1329-3*, 2233) Books on Tape, Inc.

—The Monkey Wrench Gang. 1991. reprint ed. lib. bdg. 37.95 (*1-56849-083-6*) Buccaneer Bks., Inc.

—The Monkey Wrench Gang. rev. ed. (Illus.). 368p. reprint ed. 1999. 24.95 (*0-942688-18-X*); 1984. 75.00 o.p. (*0-942688-19-8*) Dream Garden Pr.

—The Monkey Wrench Gang. 1992. 368p. pap. 12.50 (*0-380-71339-X*); 1976. 387p. pap. 6.99 (*0-380-00741-X*) Morrow/Avon. (Avon Bks.).

Abbey, Edward & Brinkley, Douglas. The Monkey Wrench Gang. 2000. (Perennial Classics Ser.). 448p. pap. 14.00 (*0-06-095644-5*, Perennial) HarperTrade.

Candelaria, Nash. Memories of the Alhambra. 192p. 1977. 25.00 (*0-9601086-1-0*); 1982. reprint ed. pap. 15.00 (*0-916950-32-8*) Bilingual Pr./Editorial Bilingue.

Chavez Ballejos, Gilberto & Witt, Shirley H. El Indio Jesus: A Novel. 2000. (Politics & International Relations of Southeast Asia Ser.: Vol. 35). x, 257p. 29.95 (*0-8061-3230-2*) Univ. of Oklahoma Pr.

Chavez Ballejos, Gilberto & Witt, Shirley Hill. El Indio Jesus: A Novel. 2002. pap. 17.95 (*0-8061-3376-7*) Univ. of Oklahoma Pr.

Chavez, Denise. Face of an Angel. 1994. 356p. 23.00 o.p. (*0-374-15204-7*) Farrar, Straus & Giroux.

—The Face of an Angel. 1995. 480p. reprint ed. pap. 14.95 (*0-446-67185-1*) Warner Bks., Inc.

Courlander, Harold. Journey of the Grey Fox People. 2002. 256p. pap. 17.95 (*0-8263-2814-8*) Univ. of New Mexico Pr.

Cummins, Ann. Red Ant House: Stories. 2003. 192p. pap. 12.00 (*0-618-26925-8*, Mariner Bks.) Houghton Mifflin Co. Trade & Reference Div.

Forte-Escamilla, Kleya. The Storyteller with Nike Airs & Other Barrio Stories. 1994. 208p. (Orig.). pap. 8.95 (*1-879960-34-6*) Aunt Lute Bks.

Freedman, Leora. The Ivory Pomegranate. 2002. 288p. pap. 16.95 (*965-229-269-9*) Gefen Publishing Hse., Ltd ISR. *Dist:* Gefen Bks.

Gilb, Dagoberto. Woodcuts of Women: Stories. 2001. (Illus.). 167p. 23.00 o.p. (*0-8021-1679-5*) Grove/Atlantic, Inc.

Hart, Virginia. A Rocky Romance. 1998. 192p. 18.95 (*0-8034-9325-8*, Avalon Bks.) Bouregy, Thomas & Co., Inc.

Harty, Ryan. Bring Me Your Saddest Arizona. 2003. (John Simmons Short Fiction Award Ser.). 172p. pap. 15.95 (*0-87745-869-3*) Univ. of Iowa Pr.

Jackson, Donald. Valley Men: A Speculative Account of the Arkansas Expedition of 1807. 1983. (Illus.). 340p. 16.95 o.p. (*0-89919-198-3*) Houghton Mifflin Co.

La Farge, Oliver. Yellow Sun, Bright Sky: The Indian Country Stories of Oliver La Farge. Caffey, David L., ed. 1988. 212p. 22.50 o.p. (*0-8263-1101-6*); pap. 12.95 o.p. (*0-8263-1033-8*) Univ. of New Mexico Pr.

Mayo, Wendell. Centaur of the North. 1996. 140p. pap. 11.95 (*1-55885-165-8*) Arte Publico Pr.

McBrearty, Robert Garner. A Night at the Y. 1999. 160p. pap. 12.00 (*1-880284-36-7*) Daniel, John & Co., Pubs.

Rechy, John. The Fourth Angel. 1983. 160p. pap. 9.95 (*0-8021-5197-3*, Grove Pr.) Grove/Atlantic, Inc.

—The Fourth Angel. 1983. 160p. pap. 6.95 o.p. (*0-394-62469-6*) Holt, Henry & Co.

—The Fourth Angel. 1973. 5.95 o.p. (*0-670-32630-5*) Library of America, The.

Robson, Lucia St Clair. Ghost Warrior: Lozen of the Apaches. 2nd ed. 2002. 496p. 27.95 (*0-312-87186-4*, CPHC0689, Forge Bks.) Doherty, Tom Assocs., LLC.

Simpson, Dan. American Angels: A Novel. 2001. (*0-9644849-2-7*) Pendleton Clay Pubs.

Smith, C. W. Letters from the Horse Latitudes. 1994. 206p. (C). 19.95 (*0-87565-131-3*) Texas Christian Univ. Pr.

Webb, Betty. Desert Wives: A Lena Jones Mystery. 2003. (Illus.). 300p. 24.95 o.s.i (*1-59058-030-3*) Poisoned Pen Pr.

## SOVIET UNION—FICTION

Aleshkovsky, Yuz Iosif. The Hand. Brownsberger, Susan, tr. from RUS. 1990. 320p. 22.95 o.s.i (*0-374-16770-2*) Farrar, Straus & Giroux.

Alexander, Robert. The Kitchen Boy. 2004. 240p. pap. 14.00 (*0-14-200381-6*) Penguin Group (USA) Inc.

Allington, Maynard. The Grey Wolf. 1995. 256p. (Orig.). reprint ed. pap. 17.95 (*1-57488-042-X*) Brassey's, Inc.

—The Grey Wolf. 1986. 336p. (Orig.). mass mkt. 3.95 o.s.i (*0-446-34148-7*) Warner Bks., Inc.

Anatoli, A. Babi Yar: A Document in the Form of a Novel. Floyd, David, tr. from RUS. 1979. reprint ed. lib. bdg. 30.00 (*0-8376-0432-X*) Bentley Pubs.

—Babi Yar: A Document in the Form of a Novel. Floyd, David, tr. 1970. 478p. pap. 32.00 (*0-374-52817-9*) Farrar, Straus & Giroux.

Archer, Geoffrey. Skydancer. unabr. ed. 2000. 8p. audio 69.95 (*0-7540-0475-9*, CAB1898) BBC Audiobooks America.

—Skydancer. 1989. mass mkt. 4.95 o.p. (*0-8125-0025-3*, Tor Bks.) Doherty, Tom Assocs., LLC.

—Skydancer. l.t. ed. 1999. (Mystery Ser.). 424p. 26.95 (*0-7862-2226-3*); (*0-7540-1377-4*); (*0-7540-2282-X*) Thorndike Pr.

Bankoff, Peter N. A Soviet Assignment. 1988. 192p. 14.75 (*0-930950-19-4*); pap. 8.75 (*0-930950-20-8*) Nopoly Pr., Inc.

Bar-Zohar, Michael. Brothers. 1993. 400p. 21.00 o.s.i (*0-449-90511-X*, Fawcett) Ballantine Bks.

Bar-Zohar, Michael & Hastings, Michael. Brothers. 1995. mass mkt. 5.99 o.s.i (*0-449-14678-2*, Fawcett) Ballantine Bks.

Baranskaya, Natalya. Week Like Any Other: Novellas & Stories. Monks, Pieta, tr. 1989. 231p. 18.95 o.p. (*0-931188-81-4*); pap. 13.95 (*0-931188-80-6*) Avalon Publishing Group. (Seal Pr.).

Barwick, James. The Kremlin Contract. 1987. 256p. 17.95 o.p. (*0-399-13238-4*, G. P. Putnam's Sons) Penguin Putnam Bks. for Young Readers.

Batchelor, John Calvin. Peter Nevsky & the True Story of the Russian Moon Landing: A Novel. 1993. 480p. 25.00 o.p. (*0-8050-2141-8*) Holt, Henry & Co.

Belai, Margrita A., et al. Song of Nightingale: An Anthology of Modern Soviet Short Stories. Bhatnagar, Y. C., tr. 1987. 214p. (C). 17.50 (*81-202-0189-2*) Ajanta Pubns/Ajanta Bks. International IND. *Dist:* South Asia Bks.

Bely, Andrey. The Silver Dove. Reavey, George, tr. from RUS. 1974. pap. 7.95 o.p. (*0-394-17859-9*, E637) Grove/Atlantic, Inc.

Bercovici, Konrad. Volga Boatman. 1970. reprint ed. 15.00 (*0-403-00515-9*) Scholarly Pr., Inc.

Bernard, Rein. Iskry (The Sparks) I Pelena Upala S Nashikh Glaz (As If a Veil Have Fallen from Our Eye) 1996. (RUS.). 248p. 24.95 (*1-55779-087-6*); pap. 15.00 (*1-55779-090-6*) Hermitage Pubs.

Bitov, Andrei. Life in Windy Weather: Short Stories. Meyer, Priscilla, ed. & tr. by. from RUS. 1986. 371p. (C). 19.50 o.p. (*0-88233-691-6*) Ardis Pubs.

Borovsky, Natasha. A Daughter of the Nobility. 1985. 512p. o.p. (*0-03-003294-6*) Holt, Henry & Co.

Bradbury, Malcolm. To the Hermitage. 2001. xi, 498p. 27.95 (*1-58567-131-2*) Overlook Pr., The.

Breton, Thierry & Beneich, Denis. Softwar. Howson, Mark, tr. 1986. (FRE.). 256p. o.p. (*0-03-004998-9*) Holt, Henry & Co.

Brien, Alan. Lenin. 1988. 712p. 22.95 o.p. (*0-688-07944-X*, Morrow, William & Co.) Morrow/Avon.

Broder, Gloria K. & Broder, Bill. Remember This Time. 1991. 336p. 14.95 (*0-937858-23-4*) Newmarket Pr.

Brown, Dale. Chains of Command. 1994. 528p. reprint ed. mass mkt. 7.99 (*0-425-14207-8*) Berkley Publishing Group.

—Chains of Command. abr. ed. 1993. audio 24.95 o.p. (*1-55800-814-4*) NewStar Media, Inc.

—Chains of Command. 1993. 480p. 22.95 (*0-399-13822-6*, G. P. Putnam's Sons) Penguin Group (USA) Inc.

Burstein, Chaya M. Rifka Bangs the Teakettle. 1970. (Illus.). (J). (gr. 4-6). 4.95 o.p. (*0-15-266944-2*) Harcourt Children's Bks.

Cahan, Abraham. The Rise of David Levinsky. 2002. 464p. pap. 8.95 (*0-486-42517-7*) Dover Pubns., Inc.

—The Rise of David Levinsky. 2001. (Paperback Classics Ser.). 560p. pap. 13.95 (*0-375-75798-8*, Modern Library) Random House Adult Trade Publishing Group.

—The White Terror & Red. 2000. 252p. E-Book 3.95 (*0-594-05960-7*) 1873 Pr.

Carlisle, Henry, et al. The Idealists. 1999. 288p. 23.95 o.p. (*0-312-20054-4*) St. Martin's Pr.

Carlisle, Henry Olga. Idealists: A Novel of Revolutionary Russia. 2000. 256p. pap. 14.95 (*0-312-25394-X*, Saint Martin's Griffin) St. Martin's Pr.

Cassutt, Michael. Red Moon. E-Book 25.95 (*1-58945-617-3*) Adobe Systems, Inc.

—The Red Moon. 2001. 352p. 25.95 (*0-312-87440-5*, Forge Bks.) Doherty, Tom Assocs., LLC.

Chukovskaya, Lydia. Sofia Petrovna. Werth, Aline, tr. from RUS. 1994. (European Classics Ser.). 126p. pap. 16.00 (*0-8101-1150-0*) Northwestern Univ. Pr.

—Sofia Petrovna. Werth, Aline & Klose, Eliza K., trs. from RUS. 1987. 120p. reprint ed. pap. 16.00 o.p. (*0-8101-0794-5*) Northwestern Univ. Pr.

Cook, James. Fellow Travelers. 1999. 240p. pap. 18.00 (*1-57962-052-3*) Permanent Pr., The.

Coppel, Alfred. The Eighth Day of the Week. 1996. 448p. reprint ed. mass mkt. 5.99 (*0-8439-3952-4*) Dorchester Publishing Co., Inc.

—The Eighth Day of the Week. 1994. 384p. 22.50 o.p. (*1-55611-411-7*) Fine, Donald I. Bks.

—The Eighth Day of the Week. 1996. E-Book 9.95 (*0-585-29169-1*) netLibrary, Inc.

Creighton, Christopher & Hynd, Noel. The Khruschev Objective. 1987. 336p. o.s.i (*0-385-18013-6*) Doubleday Publishing.

Deaux, John. The Swine Flu Conspiracy. 1997. 18.95 o.s.i (*0-89896-262-5*) Larksdale.

Delahunt, Meaghan. In the Blue House. 2001. 308p. (*0-7475-5236-3*); pap. (*0-7475-5359-9*) Bloomsbury Pr.

DeMille, Nelson. The Charm School. l.t. ed. 1994. 881p. lib. bdg. 25.95 o.p. (*0-8161-7480-6*, Macmillan Reference USA) Gale Group.

—The Charm School, Set. abr. ed. 1990. audio 16.00 o.s.i (*0-394-58376-0*, 390509, RH Audio) Random Hse. Audio Publishing Group.

—The Charm School. 1989. 640p. 17.45 o.s.i (*0-446-51305-9*); 1999. 816p. reprint ed. pap. 14.99 (*0-446-67509-1*); 1989. 640p. reprint ed. mass mkt. 7.99 (*0-446-35320-5*) Warner Bks., Inc.

Denny, Robert. Night Run: A Novel in Honor of the Famed Night Witches of World War II. 1992. 400p. 21.00 o.p. (*1-55611-336-6*) Fine, Donald I. Bks.

Dostoyevsky, Fyodor. The Brothers Karamazov. Pevear, Richard & Volokhonsky, Larissa, trs. abr. ed. 1995. audio 26.95 (*0-944993-56-7*) Audio Literature.

—The Brothers Karamazov. unabr. ed. 1987. Pt. 1. audio 69.95 (*0-7861-0530-5*, 2029-A); Pt. 3. audio 62.95 (*0-7861-0532-1*, 2029-C) Blackstone Audio Bks., Inc.

—The Brothers Karamazov. McDuff, David, tr. abr. ed. 1997. (Classic, Audio Ser.). audio 23.95 (*0-14-086461-X*, Penguin AudioBooks) Viking Penguin.

—The Brothers Karamazov: A Dramatization. 1995. per. 6.50 (*0-8222-1425-3*) Dramatists Play Service, Inc.

—The Brothers Karamazov: A Novel in Four Parts with Epilogue. Pevear, Richard & Volokhonsky, Larissa, trs. from RUS. 1990. 832p. 40.00 o.s.i (*0-86547-422-2*, North Point Pr.) Farrar, Straus & Giroux.

—Crime & Punishment. Coulson, Jessie, tr. 1998. (Oxford World's Classics Ser.). (Illus.). 576p. pap. 10.95 (*0-19-283383-9*) Oxford Univ. Pr., Inc.

Dovlatov, Sergei. The Zone: A Prison Camp Guard's Story. Frydman, Anne, tr. from RUS. 1985. 192p. 14.95 o.s.i (*0-394-53522-7*) Knopf, Alfred A. Inc.

Dukas, Vytas, ed. & tr. from RUS. Twelve Contemporary Russian Stories. 1977. 130p. 25.00 (*0-8386-1491-4*) Fairleigh Dickinson Univ. Pr.

Edelson, Marjorie. Malkeh & Her Children: A Novel. 1992. 704p. (Orig.). pap. 29.00 (*0-345-37971-3*) Ballantine Bks.

Egan, Judith. Elena: A Love Story of the Russian Revolution. 1981. 320p. 11.95 o.p. (*0-89919-028-6*) Houghton Mifflin Co.

Ehrenburg, Iiya G. Ninth Wave. 1974. 895p. reprint ed. 69.50 o.s.i (*0-8371-7672-7*, EHNW, Greenwood Pr.) Greenwood Publishing Group, Inc.

Freeborn, Richard & Turgenev, Ivan. Fathers & Sons. 1998. E-Book 9.40 (*0-585-35312-3*) netLibrary, Inc.

Freemantle, Brian. Little Grey Mice. 1992. 368p. 21.95 o.p. (*0-312-07625-8*) St. Martin's Pr.

—The Watchmen. 432p. (*0-7278-5915-3*) Severn Hse. Pubs., Ltd.

—The Watchmen. 2002. 448p. 25.95 (*0-312-24274-3*) St. Martin's Pr.

Friel, Brian. Fathers & Sons. 1988. 104p. pap. 7.95 o.p. (*0-571-15079-9*) Faber & Faber, Inc.

Gaillard, Frye. The Secret Diary of Mikhail Gorbachev. Bledsoe, Jerry, ed. 1990. 175p. (Orig.). pap. 9.95 o.p. (*0-9624255-6-7*, Imprimatur Bks.) Down Home Pr.

Gerhardie, William. Futility. 1991. (Revived Modern Classic Ser.: Vol. 718). 208p. reprint ed. pap. 14.50 (*0-8112-1176-2*, NDP722) New Directions Publishing Corp.

—Futility. rev. ed. 1974. 205p. reprint ed. 7.95 o.p. (*0-312-31395-0*) St. Martin's Pr.

Ginsburg, Mirra, tr. Last Door to Aiya: A Selection of the Best New Science Fiction from the Soviet Union. 1968. (YA). (gr. 10 up). 26.95 (*0-87599-135-1*) Phillips, S.G. Inc.

Golding, Leila P. Shelly. 1986. (Heartsong Ser.). 176p. (Orig.). (YA). (gr. 9-12). mass mkt. 3.99 o.p. (*0-87123-867-5*) Bethany Hse. Pubs.

Gorey, Edward. The Iron Tonic: Or, a Winter Afternoon in Lonely Valley. 2000. (Illus.). 36p. 10.00 (*0-15-100437-4*) Harcourt Trade Pubs.

Gorky, Maxim. Foma Gordeyev. 1974. 264p. reprint ed. 76.95 (*0-8371-7670-0*, GOFG, Greenwood Pr.) Greenwood Publishing Group, Inc.

—Foma Gordeyev. 2002. (YID.). (C). reprint ed. pap. 29.00 (*0-657-06620-6*) National Yiddish Bk. Ctr.

—Orloff & His Wife: Tales of the Barefoot Brigade. Hapgood, Isabel F., tr. from RUS. 15th ed. 1977. (Short Story Index Reprint Ser.). reprint ed. 33.95 (*0-8369-4232-9*) Ayer Co. Pubs., Inc.

—Twenty-Six Men & a Girl & Other Stories. 1977. (Short Story Index Reprint Ser.). 25.95 (*0-8369-3252-8*) Ayer Co. Pubs., Inc.

Goscilo, Helena, ed. Balancing Acts: Contemporary Stories by Russian Women. 1989. 368p. pap. 17.95 o.p. (*0-253-20500-X*, MB-500) Indiana Univ. Pr.

Grant, Myrna. Ivan & the Daring Escape. 1976. (Ivan Ser.). (J). (gr. 3-8). pap. 3.50 o.p. (*0-8423-1847-X*) Tyndale Hse. Pubs.

Green, William M. The Romanov Connection. 1986. 320p. reprint ed. pap. 3.50 o.p. (*0-8125-0378-3*, Tor Bks.) Doherty, Tom Assocs., LLC.

—The Romanov Connection: A Novel. 1984. 320p. 16.95 o.p. (*0-8253-0221-8*) Beaufort Bks., Inc.

Grekova. Ship of Widows. 1987. o.s.i (*0-86068-492-X*) Random Hse., Inc.

Grekova, I. Ship of Widows. 1987. o.s.i (*0-86068-487-3*) Random Hse., Inc.

—The Ship of Widows. Porter, Cathy, tr. from RUS. 1994. (European Classics Ser.). 192p. reprint ed. pap. 18.00 (*0-8101-1144-6*) Northwestern Univ. Pr.

—Svezho Predanie: Roman. 1995. (RUS.). 216p. (Orig.). pap. 12.00 o.s.i (*1-55779-084-1*) Hermitage Pubs.

Gross, Martin. The Red Defector. 1991. mass mkt. 4.99 o.p. (*0-425-12893-8*) Berkley Publishing Group.

Henty, G. A. Through Russian Snows. 2000. 252p. (J). E-Book 9.95 (*0-594-02407-2*) 1873 Pr.

Hetzer, Michael. The Forbidden Zone: A Novel. 2000. 528p. mass mkt. 6.99 (*0-06-103045-7*) HarperCollins Pubs.

—The Forbidden Zone: A Novel. 2000. E-Book 25.00 (*0-684-86789-3*); 1999. (Illus.). 400p. 25.00 o.s.i (*0-684-85408-2*) Simon & Schuster. (Simon & Schuster).

High, John A. The Desire Notebooks: A Trilogy of Novellas. 1999. (Illus.). 287p. 29.95 (*1-881471-34-9*); pap. 14.95 (*1-881471-33-0*) Spuyten Duyvil.

Hill, Reginald. There Are No Ghosts in the Soviet Union. 1988. 230p. 16.95 o.p. (*0-88150-119-0*) Countryman Pr.

—There Are No Ghosts in the Soviet Union. 1989. 224p. pap. 3.95 (*0-380-70844-2*, Avon Bks.) Morrow/Avon.

Hlasko, Marek. The Eighth Day of the Week. 1975. 128p. 57.95 (*0-8371-7896-7*, HLED, Greenwood Pr.) Greenwood Publishing Group, Inc.

Hoffman, Allen. Two for the Devil. 256p. (J). 2000. pap. 12.95 (*0-7892-0641-2*); 1998. (Illus.). 24.95 (*0-7892-0397-9*) Abbeville Pr., Inc. (Abbeville Kids).

Hyman, Trina Schart, illus. The Water of Life. 1986. 40p. (J). (ps-3). pap. 5.95 (*0-8234-0907-4*) Holiday Hse., Inc.

Jackson, James O. Dzerzhinsky Square. 1986. 288p. 15.95 o.p. (*0-312-22439-7*) St. Martin's Pr.

Johnston, Barbara S. Babushka! Grandmother's Bench. 2000. 176p. pap. 12.95 (*1-58736-006-3*, Hats Off Bks.) Wheatmark, Inc.

Jones, Dennis. Winter Palace. 1988. 352p. 17.95 (*0-316-47295-6*) Little Brown & Co.

Jones, Kaylie. Quite the Other Way. 1990. 384p. mass mkt. 3.95 o.s.i (*0-449-21823-6*, Fawcett) Ballantine Bks.

Jordan, Aaron. A Dream of Freedom. 2003. 288p. pap. 17.95 (*1-55517-699-2*, 76992, Bonneville Bks.) Cedar Fort, Inc./CFI Distribution.

Joseph, Mark. Typhoon. 1991. 332p. pap. 22.00 (*0-671-70865-1*, Simon & Schuster) Simon & Schuster.

—Typhoon. McCarthy, Paul, ed. 1992. 320p. reprint ed. mass mkt. 5.99 (*0-671-70866-X*, Pocket) Simon & Schuster.

Kane, Carol J. Blood & Sable. 1988. 480p. text 17.95 o.p. (*0-07-037866-5*) McGraw-Hill Cos., The.

—Blood & Sable. 1989. mass mkt. 4.95 (*0-312-91715-5*, St. Martin's Paperbacks) St. Martin's Pr.

Koestler, Arthur. Darkness at Noon. Hardy, Daphne, tr. 1984. 224p. mass mkt. 6.99 (*0-553-26595-4*) Bantam Bks.

—Darkness at Noon. 1987. 288p. bds. 35.00 (*0-02-565210-9*, Macmillan Reference USA) Gale Group.

—Darkness at Noon. mass mkt. 0.35 o.p. (*0-451-01220-8*, Signet Bks.); mass mkt. 0.50 o.p. (*0-451-01638-6*, Signet Bks.); mass mkt. 0.50 o.p. (*0-451-50064-4*, Signet Classics); mass mkt. 0.60 o.p. (*0-451-50279-5*, Signet Classics); mass mkt. 0.25 o.p. (*0-451-00671-2*, Signet Bks.) NAL.

—Darkness at Noon. unabr. ed. 2000. audio 51.00 (*0-7887-3103-3*, 95814E7); 1999. audio compact disk 66.00 (*0-7887-3722-8*, C1079E7) Recorded Bks., LLC.

Krauthoff, Berndt. Strife & Glory: A Translation of Berndt Krauthoff's "Ich Befehle" 1985. 205p. pap. 4.95 o.p. (*0-533-06048-6*) Vantage Pr., Inc.

Kross, Jaan. Professor Martens' Departure. Hollo, Anselm, tr. 304p. 1995. pap. 13.95 (*1-56584-111-5*); 1994. text 25.00 o.p. (*1-56584-110-7*) New Pr., The.

Krotkov, Yuri. The Red Monarch: Scenes from the Life of Stalin. Mairs, Tanya E., tr. 1979. 10.95 o.p. (*0-393-08836-7*) Norton, W. W. & Co., Inc.

Kuraev, Mikhail. Night Patrol & Other Stories. Thompson, Margareta O., tr. from RUS. 1994. 296p. pap. 21.95 (*0-8223-1415-0*); text 64.95 (*0-8223-1402-9*) Duke Univ. Pr.

Kuznetsov, Anatolii. The Journey. Butler, William Elliott, tr. from RUS. 1984. 180p. 15.95 o.p. (*0-941320-20-0*) Transnational Pubs., Inc.

Kuznetsov, Anatolii. The Journey. Butler, William Elliott, tr. 1984. 15.95 o.p. (*0-88282-300-0*) New Horizon Pr. Pubs., Inc.

Kyle, Duncan. The King's Commissar. 1985. 352p. pap. 3.95 o.p. (*0-312-90212-3*, St. Martin's Paperbacks) St. Martin's Pr.

Lehr, Helene. Star of the North. 1990. 336p. 18.95 o.p. (*0-312-03939-5*) St. Martin's Pr.

Leon, Bonnie. Harvest of Truth. 2000. (Sowers Trilogy Ser.: Vol. 3). 320p. pap. 12.99 (*0-8054-1274-3*) Broadman & Holman Pubs.

—Where Freedom Grows. 1998. (Sowers Triology Ser.: Vol. 1). 300p. pap. 12.99 (*0-8054-1272-7*) Broadman & Holman Pubs.

Littell, Robert. The Revolutionist. 1989. mass mkt. 4.95 o.s.i (*0-553-27792-8*) Bantam Bks.

Lorme, Anna. A Traitor's Daughter. Bononno, Robert, tr. from FRE. 1993. (French Expressions Ser.). 208p. 18.95 (*0-8419-1294-7*) Holmes & Meier Pubs., Inc.

Lourie, Richard. The Autobiography of Joseph Stalin: A Novel. 1999. 272p. text 25.00 o.p. (*1-58243-004-7*, Counterpoint Pr.) Basic Bks.

—The Autobiography of Joseph Stalin: A Novel. 2000. 272p. pap. text 15.00 (*0-306-80997-4*) Da Capo Pr., Inc.

Lowndes, Natalya. Snow Red. 1992. 272p. 24.95 o.p. (*0-340-55977-2*) Hodder & Stoughton, Ltd. GBR. *Dist:* Lubrecht & Cramer, Ltd., Trafalgar Square.

Ludlum, Robert. The Tristan Betrayal: A Novel. Date not set. mass mkt. (*0-312-99774-4*, St. Martin's Paperbacks); 2003. 528p. 27.95 (*0-312-31669-0*); 2003. E-Book 27.95 (*0-312-71133-6*) St. Martin's Pr.

Luker, Nicholas, ed. An Anthology of Russian Neo-Realism: The "Znanie" School of Maxim Gorky. 1982. (Illus.). 283p. pap. 15.95 o.s.i (*0-88233-422-0*) Ardis Pubs.

Makine, Andrei. Confessions of a Fallen Standard-Bearer. Strachan, Geoffrey, tr. from FRE. 2000. viii, 130p. 21.95 (*1-55970-529-9*) Arcade Publishing, Inc.

—Confessions of a Fallen Standard-Bearer. 2001. 144p. reprint ed. pap. 12.00 (*0-14-200001-9*) Penguin Group (USA) Inc.

—The Hero's Daughter: A Novel. 2003. 224p. 23.95 (*1-55970-687-2*) Arcade Publishing, Inc.

—Once upon the River Love. Strachan, Geoffrey, tr. from FRE. 1998. 224p. 24.95 (*1-55970-438-1*) Arcade Publishing, Inc.

—Once upon the River Love. unabr. collector's ed. 1998. audio 40.00 (*0-7366-4255-2*, 4754) Books on Tape, Inc.

—Once upon the River Love. 1999. 224p. 12.95 (*0-14-028362-5*) Viking Penguin.

Malashenko, Alexei. The Last Red August: A Russian Mystery. Olcott, Anthony, tr. 1993. (RUS.). 250p. 21.00 o.p. (*0-684-19571-2*, Macmillan Reference USA) Gale Group.

Margolin, Miriam. Little Stories for Little Children. 1986. (Illus.). 32p. (J). (gr. k-3). reprint ed. 11.95 o.p. (*0-918825-53-9*) Moyer Bell.

McCann, Colum. Dancer: A Novel. 2003. 356p. 26.00 (*0-8050-6792-2*, Metropolitan Bks.) Holt, Henry & Co.

—Dancer: A Novel. 2004. 352p. pap. 14.00 (*0-312-42318-7*) Picador.

—Dancer: A Novel. 2003. 352p. (*1-897580-29-0*) Weidenfeld & Nicolson, Ltd.

Meade, Glenn. Snow Wolf, abr. ed. 1996. audio 19.95 (*1-55927-392-5*) Audio Renaissance.

—Snow Wolf. unabr. ed. 1997. audio 104.00 (*0-913369-65-9*, 4308) Books on Tape, Inc.

—Snow Wolf. l.t. ed. 1996. 855p. 26.95 o.p. (*0-7838-1791-6*, Macmillan Reference USA) Gale Group.

—Snow Wolf. 1997. 526p. mass mkt. 6.99 (*0-312-96211-8*, St. Martin's Paperbacks); 1996. 432p. 24.95 o.p. (*0-312-14421-0*) St. Martin's Pr.

Merullo, Roland. A Russian Requiem. 1993. xii, 356p. 22.95 o.p. (*0-316-56789-2*) Little Brown & Co.

Mills, James. The Power. 1992. mass mkt. 5.99 o.s.i (*0-446-36127-5*); 1990. 21.95 o.p. (*0-446-51393-8*) Warner Bks., Inc.

Moorcock, Michael. Byzantium Endures. 1981. (Illus.). 384p. 14.50 o.p. (*0-394-51972-8*) Random Hse., Inc.

Morris, M. E. Alpha Bug. 1986. 236p. 14.95 o.p. (*0-89141-270-0*, Presidio Pr.) Ballantine Bks.

Moscovit, Andrei. The Judgment Day Archives. Bowie, Robert, tr. from RUS. 1988. 402p. 18.95 o.p. (*0-916515-45-1*) Mercury Hse.

Muggeridge, Malcolm. Winter in Moscow. 2nd ed. 1987. 268p. reprint ed. pap. 9.95 o.p. (*0-8028-0263-X*) Eerdmans, William B. Publishing Co.

Muravyova, Irina. The Nomadic Soul. Dewey, John, tr. 2000. (Glas Ser.: Vol. 22). 253p. 14.95 (*1-56663-276-5*) Dee, Ivan R. Pub.

—The Nomadic Soul, 22. 240p. pap. 17.95 (*5-7172-0048-X*) GLAS Pubs. RUS. *Dist:* Northwestern Univ. Pr.

Nabokov, Vladimir. Glory: A Novel. 1971. pap. text 6.95 o.p. (*0-07-045733-6*) McGraw-Hill Cos., The.

—King, Queen, Knave. 1989. (Vintage International Ser.). 288p. pap. 13.00 (*0-679-72340-4*, Vintage) Knopf Publishing Group.

—King, Queen, Knave. 1969. (RUS.). text 6.95 o.p. (*0-07-045716-6*) McGraw-Hill Cos., The.

—Tyrants Destroyed & Other Stories. Nabokov, Dmitri, tr. from RUS. 1975. 252p. text 8.95 o.p. (*0-07-045739-5*) McGraw-Hill Cos., The.

O'Brien, Gregory. Lenin Lives! 1984. 156p. 10.95 o.p. (*0-8128-2949-2*); pap. 3.95 o.p. (*0-8128-8138-9*) Madison Bks., Inc. (Scarborough Hse.).

Olcott, Anthony. Rough Beast. 1992. 320p. text 20.00 (*0-684-19406-6*, Scribner) Simon & Schuster.

Pelevin, Victor. Omon Ra. 1996. 154p. 21.00 o.p. (*0-374-22592-3*) Farrar, Straus & Giroux.

—Omon Ra. Bromfield, Andrew, tr. from RUS. 1998. 160p. pap. 10.95 (*0-8112-1364-1*, NDP851) New Directions Publishing Corp.

Pelevin, Viktor, contrib. by. The Clay Machine-Gun. 1998. ix, 335p. (*0-571-19406-0*) Faber & Faber, Inc.

Pella, Judith. Passage into Light. 2001. (Russians Ser.). 352p. pap. 7.99 (*0-7642-2527-8*) Bethany Hse. Pubs.

—White Nights, Red Morning. 2001. (Russians Ser.). 448p. pap. 7.99 (*0-7642-2526-X*) Bethany Hse. Pubs.

Peters, Ralph. Flames of Heaven: Export Edition. 1993. mass mkt. 5.99 (*0-671-88063-2*, Pocket) Simon & Schuster.

Peters, Ralph. Flames of Heaven. 1994. mass mkt. 5.99 (*0-671-89270-3*, Pocket) Simon & Schuster.

—Flames of Heaven. McCarthy, Paul, ed. 1994. 464p. reprint ed. mass mkt. 5.99 (*0-671-73739-2*, Pocket) Simon & Schuster.

—Flames of Heaven. 406p. 4.98 o.p. (*0-8317-7759-1*) Smithmark Pubs., Inc.

—Flames of Heaven. 2003. 384p. pap. 14.95 (*0-8117-2684-3*) Stackpole Bks.

—Flames of Heaven: A Novel of the End of the Soviet Union. McCartay, Paul, ed. 1993. 416p. 22.00 (*0-671-73738-4*, Atria) Simon & Schuster.

—Red Army. 1989. 18.95 o.p. (*0-671-67668-7*, Atria) Simon & Schuster.

Pilnyak, Boris. Volga Falls to the Caspian Sea. reprint ed. 37.50 (*0-404-05047-6*) AMS Pr., Inc.

Plante, David. The Age of Terror. 1998. (Illus.). 224p. 24.95 o.p. (*0-312-19824-8*) St. Martin's Pr.

—The Age of Terror: Novel. 1999. 240p. pap. 13.95 (*0-312-25366-4*, Saint Martin's Griffin) St. Martin's Pr.

Platonov, Andrei. Soul. 2003. (Illus.). 208p. pap. 15.95 (*1-84343-038-X*) Harvill Pr., The GBR. *Dist:* Trafalgar Square.

Platonov, Andrei. The Fierce & Beautiful World. Barnes, Joseph, tr. from RUS. 2000. (New York Review Books Classics Ser.). xvii, 264p. pap. 12.95 (*0-940322-33-1*) New York Review of Bks., Inc., The.

Polevoi, Boris N. A Story about a Real Man. 1970. 558p. reprint ed. 82.95 o.s.i (*0-8371-3993-7*, PORM, Greenwood Pr.) Greenwood Publishing Group, Inc.

Quinnell, A. J. In the Name of the Father. 1988. mass mkt. 4.50 o.p. (*0-451-15595-5*, Signet Bks.); 1987. 17.95 o.p. (*0-453-00571-3*) NAL.

—In the Name of the Father. l.t. ed. 1989. (Large Print Contemporary Ser.). 414p. 21.50 o.p. (*0-7089-8517-3*, Charnwood) Thorpe, F. A. Pubs. GBR. *Dist:* Ulverscroft Large Print Bks., Ltd., Ulverscroft Large Print Canada, Ltd.

Rand, Ayn. We the Living. 1959. 19.95 o.p. (*0-394-45124-4*) Random Hse., Inc.

Rasputin, Valentin. Farewell to Matyora. Bouis, Antonina W., tr. from RUS. 1991. 227p. reprint ed. pap. 18.00 o.p. (*0-8101-0997-2*) Northwestern Univ. Pr.

—Farewell to Matyora: A Novel. Bouis, Antonina W., tr. 2nd ed. 1995. (European Classics Ser.). 227p. pap. 14.95 (*0-8101-1329-5*) Northwestern Univ. Pr.

—Live & Remember. Bouis, Antonina W., tr. from RUS. 1992. 225p. reprint ed. pap. 15.95 (*0-8101-1053-9*) Northwestern Univ. Pr.

Ratushinskaya, Irina. A Tale of Three Heads. Ignashev, Diane N., tr. & intro. by. 1986. Tr. of Skazka o Trekh Golovakh. (ENG & RUS.). 128p. pap. 7.50 (*0-938920-83-9*) Hermitage Pubs.

Ready, Oliver & Buida, Yuri. The Zero Train. 2001. 140p. pap. 11.99 (*1-903517-01-X*) Dedalus, Ltd.

Reiss, Bob. The Last Spy. 1993. 300p. 20.00 o.p. (*0-671-77622-3*, Simon & Schuster) Simon & Schuster.

—The Last Spy. 1994. mass mkt. 5.99 o.p. (*0-312-95231-7*, St. Martin's Paperbacks) St. Martin's Pr.



For book reviews, descriptive annotations, tables of contents, cover images, author biographies & additional information, updated daily, subscribe to **www.booksinprint.com** 1105

Rennie, K. H. Maclay. 2001. (Illus.). pap. 17.50 o.s.i (*0-9585805-8-8*) Indra Publishing AUS. *Dist:* International Specialized Bk. Services.

Rettino, Ernie & Kerner, Debby. Psalty in the Soviet Circus. 1991. (Psalty's Worldwide Adventure Ser.: Vol. 1). (Illus.). 40p. (J). (gr. 1-5). 6.99 o.p. (*0-8499-0892-2*) Nelson, Tommy.

Robbins, David L. War of the Rats. 2000. (Illus.). 512p. mass mkt. 6.99 (*0-553-58135-X*) Bantam Bks.

—The War of the Rats. 1999. 416p. 23.95 o.s.i (*0-553-10817-4*) Bantam Bks.

—War of the Rats. unabr. ed. 2000. audio compact disk 119.00 (*0-7887-4203-5*, C1132E7); 1999. audio 96.00 (*0-7887-3743-0*, 95925E7) Recorded Bks., LLC.

Roth, Joseph. The Silent Prophet. 2003. 220p. pap. 14.95 (*1-58567-421-4*) Overlook Pr., The.

—The Silent Prophet. Le Vay, David, tr. 1990. 224p. pap. 15.95 (*0-87951-384-5*); 1980. 216p. 27.95 o.p. (*0-87951-110-9*) Overlook Pr., The.

—The Silent Prophet. Le Vay, David, tr. from GER. 2002. (Peter Owen Modern Classics Ser.). 220p. reprint ed. pap. 18.95 (*0-7206-1135-0*) Owen, Peter Ltd. GBR. *Dist:* Dufour Editions, Inc.

Rovin, Jeff. Starik. 1989. mass mkt. 3.95 o.s.i (*1-55817-270-X*, Pinnacle Bks.) Kensington Publishing Corp.

Rovin, Jeff & Diamond, Sander. Starik. 1988. 288p. 17.95 o.p. (*0-525-24626-6*, Dutton) Dutton/Plume.

Rutherford, Edward. Russka, an Excerpt. 1992. o.s.i (*0-517-58615-0*) Crown Publishing Group.

Rutherfurd, Edward. Russka. unabr. ed. 1994. Pt. 1. audio 95.95 (*0-7861-0684-0*, 1469-A); Pt. 2. audio 89.95 (*0-7861-0685-9*, 1469-B) Blackstone Audio Bks., Inc.

—Russka. unabr. collector's ed. 1998. Pt. A. audio 120.00 (*0-7366-4165-3*, 4668-A); Pt. B. audio 104.00 (*0-7366-4166-1*, 4668-B) Books on Tape, Inc.

—Russka: The Novel of Russia. 1992. 960p. mass mkt. 7.99 (*0-8041-0972-9*, Ivy Bks.) Ballantine Bks.

Ryan, Charles. The Capricorn Quadrant. 1990. 356p. 18.95 o.p. (*0-453-00737-6*) NAL.

Rybakov, Anatoly. The Arbat Trilogy, Vol. 2: Fear. 1992. vi, 686p. 24.95 o.p. (*0-316-76377-2*) Little Brown & Co.

—Children of the Arbat. 1989. 656p. mass mkt. 4.95 o.s.i (*0-440-20353-8*) Dell Publishing.

—Children of the Arbat. 1988. 19.95 o.p. (*0-316-76372-1*) Little Brown & Co.

—Dust & Ashes. Bouis, Antonina W., tr. from RUS. 1996. (Arbat Trilogy Ser.: Vol. 3). 473p. 24.95 o.p. (*0-316-76379-9*) Little Brown & Co.

—Heavy Sand. 1982. 384p. pap. 7.95 o.p. (*0-14-005535-5*, Penguin Bks.) Viking Penguin.

—Heavy Sand. Shukman, Harold, tr. from RUS. 1981. 384p. 13.95 o.p. (*0-670-36499-1*) Viking Penguin.

Scholefield, Alan. Fire in the Ice. 1987. pap. 3.95 o.p. (*0-312-90459-2*, St. Martin's Paperbacks); 1985. 14.95 o.p. (*0-312-29101-9*) St. Martin's Pr.

—Fire in the Ice. l.t. ed. 1986. (Ulverscroft Large Print Ser.). 560p. 29.99 o.p. (*0-7089-1424-1*, Ulverscroft) Thorpe, F. A. Pubs. GBR. *Dist:* Ulverscroft Large Print Bks., Ltd., Ulverscroft Large Print Canada, Ltd.

Serge, Victor. Midnight in the Century. Greeman, Richard, tr. from FRE. 284p. 12.95 (*0-904613-95-X*) Writers & Readers Publishing, Inc.

Sholokhov, Mikhail. And Quiet Flows the Don. 1965. pap. 9.95 o.p. (*0-394-70330-8*) Random Hse., Inc.

—Quiet Flows the Don. Murphy, Brian, ed. Daglish, Robert, tr. rev. ed. 1996. 1376p. 35.00 o.p. (*0-7867-0360-1*, Carroll & Graf Pubs.) Avalon Publishing Group.

—Quiet Flows the Don, 2 vols., Set, Vols. 1 & 2. Daglish, Robert, tr. 1988. 1612p. (C). 130.00 (*0-569-09106-3*) State Mutual Bk. & Periodical Service, Ltd.

Shuksin, Vasily. Roubles in Words, Kopeks in Figures & Other Stories. Ward, Natasha & Iliffe, David, trs. from RUS. 1985. 224p. 14.95 o.p. (*0-7145-2813-7*) Boyars, Marion Pubs., Inc.

Smith, Martin Cruz. Gorky Park. 1993. mass mkt. 5.99 o.s.i (*0-345-90112-6*); 1982. 448p. mass mkt. 7.99 (*0-345-29834-9*) Ballantine Bks.

—Havana Bay. l.t. ed. pap. 25.95 o.p. (*0-7838-8547-4*, Macmillan Reference USA) Gale Group.

Solzhenitsyn, Aleksandr. Cancer Ward. 1969. mass mkt. 4.95 o.p. (*0-553-20655-9*) Bantam Bks.

—Cancer Ward. 9999. 640p. pap. 3.75 o.s.i (*0-440-31009-1*, Laurel) Dell Publishing.

—Cancer Ward. Frank, Rebecca, tr. from RUS. 1974. pap. 1.95 o.s.i (*0-440-01009-8*) Dell Publishing.

—Cancer Ward. 1968. 12.95 o.p. (*0-385-27252-9*) Doubleday Publishing.

—Cancer Ward. o.s.i (*0-374-11849-3*) Farrar, Straus & Giroux.

—Cancer Ward. Bethell, Nicholas & Burg, David, trs. from RUS. 560p. 1991. pap. 18.00 (*0-374-51199-3*); 1969. 10.00 o.p. (*0-374-11848-5*) Farrar, Straus & Giroux.

—Cancer Ward. Bethell, Nicholas & Burg, David, trs. 1984. 560p. 20.00 o.s.i (*0-394-60499-7*) Random Hse., Inc.

—Cancer Ward. Bethell, Nicholas & Burg, David, trs. l.t. ed. 1995. 560p. 18.00 o.s.i (*0-679-60163-5*) Random Hse., Inc.

—The First Circle. 1976. mass mkt. 4.95 o.p. (*0-553-24623-2*) Bantam Bks.

—The First Circle. Whitney, Thomas P., tr. 1968. (ENG & RUS.). 20.00 o.p. (*0-06-013949-8*) HarperCollins Pubs.

—The First Circle. 1990. 596p. reprint ed. pap. 17.00 o.p. (*0-06-091683-4*, Perennial) HarperTrade.

—The First Circle. Whitney, Thomas F., tr. 1990. 596p. (C). reprint ed. lib. bdg. 41.00 o.p. (*0-8095-9000-X*) Millefleurs.

—The First Circle. Whitney, Thomas P., tr. from RUS. 1997. (European Classics Ser.). 600p. pap. 22.00 (*0-8101-1590-5*) Northwestern Univ. Pr.

—Lenin in Zurich. Willetts, H. T., tr. from RUS. 1976. 309p. 8.95 o.p. (*0-374-18501-8*) Farrar, Straus & Giroux.

—One Day in the Life of Ivan Denisovich. 1997. (C). pap. text o.p. (*0-321-02589-X*) Addison-Wesley Educational Pubs., Inc.

—One Day in the Life of Ivan Denisovich. 1984. 224p. mass mkt. 5.99 (*0-553-24777-8*) Bantam Bks.

—One Day in the Life of Ivan Denisovich. 1963. 160p. mass mkt. 4.95 o.s.i (*0-451-52310-5*) Berkley Publishing Group.

—One Day in the Life of Ivan Denisovich. unabr. ed. 1992. audio 32.95 (*0-7861-0329-9*, 692275) Blackstone Audio Bks., Inc.

—One Day in the Life of Ivan Denisovich. Parker, Ralph, tr. 1971. reprint ed. 4.95 o.p. (*0-525-17088-X*, Dutton) Dutton/Plume.

—One Day in the Life of Ivan Denisovich. Willetts, H. T., tr. 1992. 25.00 o.s.i (*0-374-22643-1*); 188p. pap. 13.00 (*0-374-52195-6*) Farrar, Straus & Giroux.

—One Day in the Life of Ivan Denisovich. Aitken, Gillon, tr. from FRE. 1972. pap. 6.95 o.p. (*0-374-51842-4*); 1971. 174p. 15.00 o.p. (*0-374-22642-3*) Farrar, Straus & Giroux.

—One Day in the Life of Ivan Denisovich. Hingley, Ronald, tr. 1963. 234p. (gr. 10 up). pap. 2.95 o.p. (*0-275-62300-9*, P169, Praeger Pubs.) Greenwood Publishing Group, Inc.

—One Day in the Life of Ivan Denisovich. unabr. ed. 1984. audio 12.95 (*0-694-50262-6*, SWC 1447, Caedmon) HarperTrade.

—One Day in the Life of Ivan Denisovich. Willetts, H. T., tr. 1995. 192p. 16.00 (*0-679-44464-5*) Knopf, Alfred A. Inc.

—One Day in the Life of Ivan Denisovich. Parker, Ralph, tr. from RUS. 1998. (Classics Ser.). 160p. mass mkt. 5.95 (*0-451-52709-7*, Signet Classics) NAL.

—One Day in the Life of Ivan Denisovich. unabr. ed. 1999. audio 26.00 (*1-55690-393-6*, 82034E7) Recorded Bks., LLC.

—One Day in the Life of Ivan Denisovich. 9999. pap. 1.75 o.p. (*0-590-05190-3*) Scholastic, Inc.

—One Day in the Life of Ivan Denisovich. 8th ed. 1999. (RUS.). pap. 9.95 (*5-7684-0706-5*) Terra, Izdatel'skij centr - Izdatel'stvo Azbuka RUS. *Dist:* Distribooks, Inc.

—One Day in the Life of Ivan Denisovich. 1963. (Signet Bks.). (J). 11.00 (*0-606-04237-7*) Turtleback Bks.

Steel, Danielle. Granny Dan. 2000. 272p. mass mkt. 7.50 (*0-440-22482-9*); 1999. 240p. 19.95 (*0-385-31709-3*, Delacorte Pr.); 1999. 304p. 24.95 o.s.i (*0-385-33427-3*) Dell Publishing.

—Granny Dan, Set. unabr. ed. 1999. audio 25.00 Highsmith Inc.

—Granny Dan. unabr. ed. 1999. audio. audio 25.00 (*0-553-47931-8*); audio compact disk 29.95 (*0-553-45651-2*) Random Hse. Audio Publishing Group. (RH Audio).

Thomas, Craig. Winter Hawk. 1988. mass mkt. 4.95 (*0-380-70389-0*, Avon Bks.); 1987. 372p. 18.95 o.p. (*0-688-07091-4*, Morrow, William & Co.) Morrow/Avon.

Tolstaya, Tatyana. On the Golden Porch. 1990. (Vintage International Ser.). 208p. pap. 13.00 o.s.i (*0-679-72843-0*, Vintage) Knopf Publishing Group.

—On the Golden Porch. 1990. 2.99 o.p. (*0-517-05635-6*) Random Hse. Value Publishing.

Tolstoy, Leo. Anna Karenina. Pevear, Richard & Volokhonsky, Larissa, trs. from RUS. 2001. 864p. text 40.00 (*0-670-89478-8*, Viking) Viking Penguin.

—War & Peace. 1976. Vol. I. 9.95 o.p. (*0-460-00525-1*); Vol. II. 11.95 o.p. (*0-460-00526-X*); Vol. III. 13.95 o.p. (*0-460-00527-8*) Biblio Distribution.

—War & Peace. unabr. ed. 1998. Pt. 1. audio 99.95 (*0-7861-1251-4*, 2163A); Pt. 2. audio 89.95 (*0-7861-1252-2*, 2163B); Pt. 3. audio 85.95 (*0-7861-1253-0*, 2163C) Blackstone Audio Bks., Inc.

—War & Peace. unabr. ed. audio 360.00Pt. 2. 1982. audio 96.00 (*0-7366-0371-9*, 1352-B);Pt. 3. 1982. audio 96.00 (*0-7366-0372-7*, 1352-C);Pt. 4. 1982. audio 80.00 (*0-7366-0373-5*, 1352-D) Books on Tape, Inc.

—War & Peace. 1989. reprint ed. Vol. I. lib. bdg. 49.95 o.p. (*0-89966-646-9*); Vol. II. lib. bdg. 49.95 o.p. (*0-89966-647-7*) Buccaneer Bks., Inc.

—War & Peace. 2001. (Early Best Sellers Ser.). (Illus.). reprint ed. pap. text 28.00 (*0-7426-5355-2*) Classic Bks.

—War & Peace, 3 vols., Set. Maude, Louise & Maude, Aylmer, trs. from RUS. 1992. (Everyman's Library Children's Classics Ser.). 560p. 40.00 (*0-679-40573-9*) Knopf, Alfred A. Inc.

—War & Peace, 4 vols. 1999. (Cloth Bound Pocket Ser.). 240p. 29.95 (*3-89508-690-8*, 520052) Konemann.

—War & Peace. 1973. pap. 3.95 o.p. (*0-380-01608-7*, 18143, Avon Bks.) Morrow/Avon.

—War & Peace. 1968. mass mkt. 5.95 o.p. (*0-451-52116-1*) NAL.

—War & Peace. Dunnigan, Ann, tr. 1968. (Signet Classics). 1456p. mass mkt. 9.95 (*0-451-52326-1*, Signet Classics) NAL.

—War & Peace. abr. ed. 1995. (Classic Fiction Ser.). audio 22.98 (*962-634-542-X*, NA404214); audio compact disk 26.98 (*962-634-042-8*, NA404212) Naxos of America, Inc. (Naxos AudioBooks).

—War & Peace. 1966. (Critical Editions Ser.). (C). pap. text o.p. (*0-393-09672-6*, 9672) Norton, W. W. & Co., Inc.

—War & Peace. Gifford, Henry, ed. Maude, Louise & Maude, Aylmer, trs. (Oxford World's Classics Ser.). 1998. (Illus.). 1392p. pap. 12.95 (*0-19-283398-7*); 1991. (Illus.). 1,386p. pap. 10.95 o.p. (*0-19-282780-4*, 312); 1983. pap. 5.95 o.p. (*0-19-281614-4*) Oxford Univ. Pr., Inc.

—War & Peace. Maude, Louise & Maude, Aylmer, trs. 1968. (Illus.). 14.95 o.p. (*0-19-250898-9*) Oxford Univ. Pr., Inc.

—War & Peace, 2 vols., Vol. 1. Gifford, Henry, ed. Maude, Louise & Maude, Aylmer, trs. from RUS. 1983. (Oxford World's Classics Ser.). pap. 5.95 o.p. (*0-19-281582-2*) Oxford Univ. Pr., Inc.

—War & Peace. abr. ed. 1997. (BBC Radio Presents Ser.). audio 39.95 o.s.i (*0-553-47943-1*, 105698, RH Audio) Random Hse. Audio Publishing Group.

—War & Peace. Garnett, Constance, tr. 1994. (Modern Library Ser.). 1408p. 25.95 (*0-679-60084-1*) Random Hse., Inc.

—War & Peace. 1999. 1456p. pap. 8.99 (*0-671-03298-4*, Washington Square Pr.) Simon & Schuster.

—War & Peace. Simmons, Ernest J., ed. abr. ed. 1986. 656p. (gr. 10 up). mass mkt. 3.95 o.s.i (*0-671-41893-9*, Pocket) Simon & Schuster.

—War & Peace. 1982. (Signet Classics Ser.). 16.00 (*0-606-12566-3*) Turtleback Bks.

—War & Peace. Edmonds, Rosemary, tr. from RUS. (Penguin Classics Ser.). 1982. 1472p. pap. 13.95 (*0-14-044417-3*, Penguin Classics); Vol. 1. 1957. 736p. pap. 4.95 o.p. (*0-14-044062-3*, Penguin Bks.); Vol. 2. 1957. 736p. pap. 4.95 o.p. (*0-14-044063-1*, Penguin Bks.) Viking Penguin.

—War & Peace. 1997. (Classics Library). 986p. pap. 3.95 (*1-85326-062-2*, 0622WW) Wordsworth Editions, Ltd. GBR. *Dist:* Casemate Pubs. & Bk. Distributors, LLC.

Topol, Edward. The Jewish Lover. E-Book 25.95 (*0-312-24613-7*); 1998. 496p. 25.95 (*0-312-19291-6*); 1998. 25.95 o.p. (*0-312-15557-3*) St. Martin's Pr.

Trifonov, Yury V. Disappearance. Lowe, David A., tr. from RUS. 1991. 23.95 (*0-87501-089-X*) Ardis Pubs.

—Disappearance. Lowe, David A., tr. from RUS. 1997. 182p. pap. 18.00 (*0-8101-1469-0*) Northwestern Univ. Pr.

Tsypkin, Leonid. Summer in Baden-Baden: A Novel. 2003. 176p. pap. 13.95 (*0-8112-1548-2*) New Directions Publishing Corp.

—Summer in Baden-Baden: A Novel. Keys, Roger & Keys, Angela, trs. from RUS. 2001. 160p. 23.95 (*0-8112-1484-2*) New Directions Publishing Corp.

Turgenev, Ivan. Fathers & Sons. 2002. (World Digital Library). E-Book 3.95 (*0-594-08428-8*) 1873 Pr.

—Fathers & Sons. Garnett, Constance, tr. 1967. (Airmont Classics Ser.). mass mkt. 1.95 o.p. (*0-8049-0129-5*, CL-129) Airmont Publishing Co., Inc.

—Fathers & Sons. 20.95 (*0-88411-444-9*) Amereon, Ltd.

—Fathers & Sons. 1982. 224p. mass mkt. 1.95 o.s.i (*0-553-21089-0*, Bantam Classics) Bantam Bks.

—Fathers & Sons. Makanowitzky, Barbara, tr. from RUS. 1982. (Classics Ser.). 224p. mass mkt. 3.95 o.s.i (*0-553-21259-1*, Bantam Classics) Bantam Bks.

—Fathers & Sons. unabr. ed. 1999. (World Classic Literature Ser.). (RUS.). pap. 8.95 (*2-87714-262-0*) Bookking International FRA. *Dist:* Distribooks, Inc.

—Fathers & Sons. 1987. 206p. reprint ed. lib. bdg. 19.95 (*0-89966-578-0*) Buccaneer Bks., Inc.

—Fathers & Sons. 1965. (*0-521-06656-5*) Cambridge Univ. Pr.

—Fathers & Sons. 1999. (Cloth Bound Pocket Ser.). 240p. 7.95 (*3-89508-456-5*, 520003) Konemann.

—Fathers & Sons. Guerney, Bernard G., tr. 1950. (Modern Library College Editions Ser.). (C). pap. text 8.25 o.p. (*0-07-553634-X*, T38) McGraw-Hill Cos., The.

—Fathers & Sons. mass mkt. 0.50 o.p. (*0-451-01066-3*, Signet Bks.); 1968. mass mkt. 0.60 o.p. (*0-451-50399-6*, Signet Classics); 1968. mass mkt. 0.50 o.p. (*0-451-50050-4*, Signet Classics); 1961. 320p. mass mkt. 5.95 o.s.i (*0-451-52383-0*); 1961. mass mkt. 0.75 o.p. (*0-451-50816-5*, Signet Classics); 1961. mass mkt. 0.95 o.p. (*0-451-50972-2*, Signet Classics); 1961. mass mkt. 1.25 o.p. (*0-451-51058-5*, Signet Classics); 1961. mass mkt. 1.95 o.p. (*0-451-51500-5*, Signet Classics); 1961. mass mkt. 2.25 o.p. (*0-451-51915-9*, Signet Classics) NAL.

—Fathers & Sons. Reavey, George, tr. 1961. 208p. mass mkt. 6.95 (*0-451-52382-2*, Signet Classics) NAL.

—Fathers & Sons. l.t. ed. 1996. 450p. lib. bdg. 26.00 (*0-939495-92-9*); 1998. 235p. reprint ed. lib. bdg. 25.00 (*1-58287-029-2*) North Bks.

—Fathers & Sons. Katz, Michael R., ed. & tr. by. 1995. (Critical Editions Ser.). 343p. (C). pap. text 8.00 (*0-393-96752-2*) Norton, W. W. & Co., Inc.

—Fathers & Sons. Katz, Michael R., tr. 1993. 288p. 25.00 (*0-393-03559-X*) Norton, W. W. & Co., Inc.

—Fathers & Sons. 1966. (C). pap. o.p. (*0-393-09652-1*) Norton, W. W. & Co., Inc.

—Fathers & Sons. Matlaw, Ralph E., ed. & tr. by. 2nd ed. 1989. (Critical Editions Ser.). 345p. (C). pap. o.p. (*0-393-95795-0*) Norton, W. W. & Co., Inc.

—Fathers & Sons. Freeborn, Richard, tr. from RUS. 2000. (Oxford World's Classics Ser.: Vol. 17). 256p. 13.00 o.p. (*0-19-210040-8*) Oxford Univ. Pr., Inc.

—Fathers & Sons. Freeborn, Richard, tr. & intro. by. 1998. (Oxford World's Classics Ser.). 296p. pap. 8.95 (*0-19-283392-8*) Oxford Univ. Pr., Inc.

—Fathers & Sons. Freeborn, Richard, ed. & tr. by. 1991. (Oxford World's Classics Ser.). 294p. pap. 5.95 o.p. (*0-19-282256-X*) Oxford Univ. Pr., Inc.

—Fathers & Sons. 2001. (Modern Library Classics). 256p. pap. 10.95 (*0-375-75839-9*, Modern Library) Random House Adult Trade Publishing Group.

—Fathers & Sons. Edmonds, Rosemary, tr. from RUS. 1965. (Classics Ser.). 304p. pap. 11.00 (*0-14-044147-6*, Penguin Classics) Viking Penguin.

—Fathers & Sons. 1997. (Classics Library). 208p. pap. 3.95 (*1-85326-286-2*, 2862WW) Wordsworth Editions, Ltd. GBR. *Dist:* Combined Publishing.

Turgenev, Ivan & Garnett, Constance B. Fathers & Sons. 1998. (Thrift Editions Ser.). 176p. pap. 2.50 (*0-486-40073-5*) Dover Pubns., Inc.

Ulam, Adam B. The Kirov Affair. 1988. 416p. 19.95 (*0-15-147277-7*) Harcourt Trade Pubs.

Vinokur, Boris. Inside the Kremlin Walls. 1986. 256p. pap. 7.95 o.p. (*0-916829-06-5*) Chicago Review Pr., Inc.

Voinovich, Vladimir. The Fur Hat. 1991. 132p. pap. 17.00 (*0-15-634030-5*, Harvest Bks.); 1989. 192p. 17.95 (*0-15-139100-9*) Harcourt Trade Pubs.

—In Plain Russian. Lourie, Richard, tr. from RUS. 1979. 320p. 11.95 o.p. (*0-374-17580-2*) Farrar, Straus & Giroux.

—The Life & Extraordinary Adventures of Private Ivan Chonkin. Lourie, Richard, tr. from RUS. 316p. 1982. pap. 10.95 o.s.i (*0-374-51752-5*); 1977. 10.00 o.p. (*0-374-18621-9*) Farrar, Straus & Giroux.

—The Life & Extraordinary Adventures of Private Ivan Chonkin. Lourie, Richard, tr. 1995. (European Classics Ser.). 215p. reprint ed. pap. 19.00 (*0-8101-1243-4*) Northwestern Univ. Pr.

Voznesenskaya, Julia. The Women's Decameron. 1986. 304p. 18.95 o.p. (*0-87113-101-3*) Grove/Atlantic, Inc.

—The Women's Decameron. Linton, W. B., tr. 1987. 320p. pap. 14.95 o.p. (*0-8050-0601-X*, Owl Bks.) Holt, Henry & Co.

Watkins, Paul. The Story of My Disappearance. 224p. 1999. pap. 11.00 (*0-312-20026-9*); 1998. 21.00 o.p. (*0-312-17995-2*) Picador.

—Story of My Disappearance. unabr. ed. 1998. audio 51.00 (*0-7887-2179-8*, 95475E7 ) Recorded Bks., LLC.

Wiesel, Elie. The Testament. 1982. 272p. mass mkt. 3.95 o.s.i (*0-553-20810-1*) Bantam Bks.

—The Testament. Wiesel, Marion, tr. from FRE. 1999. 352p. pap. 13.00 (*0-8052-1115-2*, Schocken) Knopf Publishing Group.

—The Testament. Wiesel, Marion, tr. 1990. pap. 9.95 o.s.i (*0-671-65746-1*, Touchstone) Simon & Schuster.

—The Testament. Wiesel, Marion, tr. 1981. 13.95 o.s.i (*0-671-44833-1*) Summit Bks.

—Le Testament d'un Poete Juif Assassine. 1981. (FRE.). pap. 16.95 (*0-7859-2684-4*) French & European Pubns., Inc.

—Zavet. Sonin, N., tr. 1997. (RUS.). 272p. 12.50 (*0-938920-89-8*) Hermitage Pubs.

Yarmolinsky, Avrahm, ed. Soviet Short Stories. 1975. 301p. reprint ed. lib. bdg. 35.00 o.p. (*0-8371-8310-3*, YASS, Greenwood Pr.) Greenwood Publishing Group, Inc.

Zalygin, Sergei P. The Commission. Wilson, David G., tr. from RUS. 1993. 386p. (C). 35.00 (*0-87580-177-3*); pap. 18.50 (*0-87580-558-2*) Northern Illinois Univ. Pr.

Zernova, Ruth. Mute Phone Calls & Other Stories. Reeve, Helen et al, trs. 1991. (Rutgers Press Fiction Ser.). 280p. (C). pap. 13.95 (*0-8135-1736-2*); text 35.00 (*0-8135-1735-4*) Rutgers Univ. Pr.

**SPAIN—FICTION**

Alas Leopoldo Clarin, Leopoldo (Clarin), ed. The Moral Tales. Stackhouse, Kenneth A., tr. from SPA. 1988. 450p. (Orig.). 55.00 (*0-913969-12-5*) University Publishing Assocs., Inc.

Ali, Tariq. The Shadows of the Pomegranate Tree. 1993. 242p. (gr. 13). pap. 15.00 (*0-86091-676-6*) Verso.

Anderson, Scott. Triage. 1999. 240p. pap. 12.00 (*0-684-85653-0*, Scribner Paper Fiction) Simon & Schuster.

—Triage: A Novel. 1998. 240p. 23.00 (*0-684-84695-0*, Scribner) Simon & Schuster.

—Triage: A Novel. l.t. ed. 1999. (Ulverscroft Large Print Ser.). 408p. 31.99 o.p. (*0-7089-4117-6*, Ulverscroft) Thorpe, F. A. Pubs. GBR. *Dist:* Ulverscroft Large Print Bks., Ltd., Ulverscroft Large Print Canada, Ltd.

Andrzejewski, Jerzy. The Inquisitors. Syrop, Konrad, tr. from POL. 1976. reprint ed. lib. bdg. 22.50 o.p. (*0-8371-8868-7*, ANIN, Greenwood Pr.) Greenwood Publishing Group, Inc.

Arrabal, Fernando. The Red Virgin. Hurley, Andrew, tr. from FRE. 1993. Tr. of Vierge Rouge. 256p. pap. 15.00 o.p. (*0-14-017921-6*, Penguin Bks.) Penguin Group (USA) Inc.

Avellaneda, Alonso F. Don Quixote de la Mancha (Avellaneda's Continuation) Being the Spurious Continuation of Miguel de Cervantes's Part I. Server, Alberta Wilson & Keller, John Esten, trs. 1980. (Documentacion Cervantina Ser.: Vol. 2). (Illus.). xiv, 350p. (C). 18.95 (*0-936388-01-3*) Juan de la Cuesta-Hispanic Monographs.

Ballard, J. G. Cocaine Nights. 336p. 1999. pap. text 16.00 (*1-58243-017-9*); 1998. (Illus.). 23.00 (*1-887178-66-X*) Basic Bks. (Counterpoint Pr.).

Bantock, Nick. The Forgetting Room. (Illus.). 1999. 29.95 (*0-00-225491-3*); 1997. 112p. 22.00 o.p. (*0-00-225176-0*) HarperCollins Pubs.

—The Forgetting Room. 1998. (Illus.). 112p. pap. 14.00 (*0-06-093126-4*, Perennial); 1997. audio 12.00 (*0-694-51899-9*, CPN 10124, HarperAudio) HarperTrade.

Baroja y Nessi, Pio. Zalacain the Adventurer: The History of the Good Fortune & Wanderings of Martin Zalacain of Urbia. Diendl, James P., tr. from SPA. 1997. Tr. of Zalacain el Aventurero, la Historia de la Buena Fortuna y Viajes de Martin Zalcain de Urbia. 234p. pap. 16.95 (*1-882897-13-7*, BT7137) Lost Coast Pr.

Bazan, Emilia P. The House of Ulloa. O'Prey, Paul & Graves, Lucia, trs. from SPA. 1991. 288p. pap. 8.95 o.p. (*0-14-044502-1*, Penguin Classics) Viking Penguin.

Benet, Juan. Una Meditacion. 2001. (SPA.). 448p. 9.95 (*84-204-2182-0*) Alfaguara, Ediciones, S.A.- Grupo Santillana ESP. *Dist:* Santillana USA Publishing Co., Inc.

Bowen, Marjorie. A Knight of Spain. 2000. 252p. pap. 9.95 (*0-594-00042-4*) 1873 Pr.

Boyar, Jane & Boyar, Burt. Hitler Stopped by Franco. 2001. (Illus.). viii, 323p. (Orig.). pap. 19.95 (*0-9710392-0-8*) Marbella Hse.

Boyle, Elizabeth. Once Tempted. 2001. 384p. mass mkt. 5.99 (*0-380-81535-4*, Avon Bks.) Morrow/Avon.

Brack, O. M., ed. The History & Adventures of the Renowned Don Quixote. Cervantes Saavedra, Miguel de & Smollett, Tobias George, trs. from SPA. 2003. (Illus.). 1056p. 100.00 (*0-8203-2430-2*) Univ. of Georgia Pr.

Branham, Mary. Three Deadly Days in Spain: A Mystery. 2000. 127p. 26.95 (*0-86534-315-2*) Sunstone Pr.

Bremyer, Jay. The Dance of Created Lights: A Sufi Tale. 1996. (Illus.). 256p. (Orig.). pap. 14.95 (*1-56184-084-X*) New Falcon Pubns.

Brown, Alan. Princess. l.t. ed. 1991. 21.95 o.p. (*0-7927-0694-3*, CH010); pap. 19.95 o.p. (*0-7927-0695-1*, CS0112) BBC Audiobooks America.

Buitrago, Fanny. Senora Honeycomb. Peden, Margaret Sayers, tr. 1996. 232p. 18.00 o.p. (*0-06-017365-3*) HarperCollins Pubs.

Caminals-Heath, Roser. Once Remembered, Twice Lived. 1993. (Catalan Studies: Vol. 4). 258p. (Orig.). (C). pap. text 32.95 (*0-8204-1969-9*) Lang, Peter Publishing, Inc.

Cela, Camilo José. Boxwood. Haugaard, Patricia, tr. from SPA. 2002. 284p. 25.95 (*0-8112-1497-4*) New Directions Publishing Corp.

—San Camilo, 1936: The Eve, Feast, & Octave of St. Camillus of the Year 1936 in Madrid. Polt, John H., tr. 1991. 327p. pap. 21.95 (*0-8223-1196-8*); lib. bdg. 69.95 (*0-8223-1179-8*) Duke Univ. Pr.

Cervantes Saavedra, Miguel de. The Adventures of Don Quixote de la Mancha. Smollett, Tobias George, tr. from SPA. 1986. 845p. 24.50 o.p. (*0-374-14232-7*); pap. 18.00 o.s.i (*0-374-51943-9*) Farrar, Straus & Giroux.

—The Adventures of Don Quixote de la Mancha. Jones, Olive, ed. Cohen, J. M., tr. from SPA. 1980. (Illus.). 10.95 o.p. (*0-416-87910-1*, NO.0189) Routledge.

—The Adventures of Don Quixote de la Mancha. 1950. (J). 15.00 (*0-606-03005-0*) Turtleback Bks.

—The Adventures of Don Quixote de la Mancha. Cohen, John M., tr. from SPA. 1951. (Penguin Classics Ser.). 944p. pap. 8.95 o.s.i (*0-14-044010-0*, PE0100, Penguin Classics) Viking Penguin.

—Don Quijote de la Mancha. (SPA., Illus.). 160p. 11.95 (*84-7281-097-6*, AF1097) Auriga, Ediciones S.A. ESP. *Dist:* Continental Bk. Co., Inc.

—Don Quijote de la Mancha. 2000. (SPA.). per. 14.00 (*1-891355-12-0*) Blue Unicorn Editions.

—Don Quijote de la Mancha. unabr. ed. (SPA.). Vol. I. pap. 7.95 (*84-410-0004-2*); Vol. II. pap. 7.95 (*84-410-0005-0*) Bookking International FRA. *Dist:* Distribooks, Inc.

—Don Quijote de la Mancha. 2000. (SPA.). 720p. 10.95 (*84-8403-030-X*) Edimat Libros, S. A. ESP. *Dist:* Independent Pubs. Group.

—Don Quijote de la Mancha. 1990. (SPA.). pap. (*968-15-0812-2*) Editores Mexicanos Unidos.

—Don Quijote de la Mancha. (SPA.). stu. ed. 11.98 (*968-15-0087-3*) Editores Mexicanos Unidos MEX. *Dist:* Lectorum Pubns., Inc.

—Don Quijote de la Mancha. annot. ed. (Coleccion Centro Literario). (SPA.). Vol. I. pap., stu. ed. 7.95 (*958-02-0485-3*, CAR012); Vol. II. pap., stu. ed. 7.95 (*958-02-0539-6*, CAR013) Editorial Voluntad S.A. COL. *Dist:* Continental Bk. Co., Inc.

—Don Quijote de la Mancha. Blecua, Alberto, ed. (SPA.). 272p. (*84-239-1950-1*) Elliot's Bks.

—Don Quijote de la Mancha, 2 vols., Set. deluxe ed. 1989. (SPA., Illus.). 952p. 850.00 (*84-239-4133-7*) Elliot's Bks.

—Don Quijote de la Mancha. 1998. (Coleccion Austral Ser.: Vol. 150). (SPA., Illus.). 1152p. (*84-239-9599-2*) Espasa Calpe, S.A.

—Don Quijote de la Mancha. (SPA.). 19.95 (*84-239-0150-5*, ECS150) Espasa Calpe, S.A. ESP. *Dist:* Continental Bk. Co., Inc.

—Don Quijote de la Mancha. (SPA.). 848p. 31.95 (*84-241-2608-4*, EV9173); 2003. (Illus.). 336p. (*84-241-5930-6*, EV6500) Everest de Ediciones y Distribucion, S.L. ESP. *Dist:* Lectorum Pubns., Inc.

—Don Quijote de la Mancha. 1989. 1184p. pap. (*0-7859-5151-2*); Set. 1989. (SPA.). 22.95 o.p. (*0-8288-2562-9*, S50624); Set. 1984. (SPA.). 1096p. 29.95 o.p. (*0-8288-7040-3*, S37320); Vol. 2. 1990. 592p. pap. 15.95 (*0-7859-5999-8*, 8437601185) French & European Pubns., Inc.

—Don Quijote de la Mancha. Tardy, William T., ed. 2001. audio 15.00 (*0-8442-7071-7*) Glencoe/McGraw-Hill.

—Don Quijote de la Mancha. (SPA.). 19.50 o.p. incl. audio Interlingua Foreign Language AudioBooks.

—Don Quijote de la Mancha, Part I. Lathrop, Tom, ed. 1997. (Illus.). 423p. 12.00 o.p. (*0-936388-80-3*) Juan de la Cuesta-Hispanic Monographs.

—Don Quijote de la Mancha, 2 vols., Set. (SPA.). 1100p. 21.95 (*84-261-0513-0*, JV0513) Juventud, Editorial ESP. *Dist:* AIMS International Bks., Inc., Continental Bk. Co., Inc., Distribooks, Inc.

—Don Quijote de la Mancha. 2001. (SPA.). audio 16.95 Norton Pubs., Inc., Jeffrey /Audio-Forum.

—Don Quijote de la Mancha. Raffel, Burton, tr. from SPA. 1996. 752p. pap. 19.95 (*0-393-31509-6*) Norton, W. W. & Co., Inc.

—Don Quijote de la Mancha. deluxe gif. ed. (SPA.). 248p. 19.95 (*84-7189-285-5*, ORT002) Ortells, Alfredo Editorial S.L. ESP. *Dist:* Continental Bk. Co., Inc.

—Don Quijote de la Mancha. Parr, James A. & Fajardo, Salvador, eds. 1998. (Spanish Classical Texts Ser.: Vol. 3). (SPA.). 900p. (C). text 29.95 (*1-889818-11-9*) Pegasus Pr.

—Don Quijote de la Mancha. 1997. (Clasicos Ser.). (SPA.). 860p. pap. (*0-929441-91-5*) Publicaciones Puertorriquenas, Inc.

—Don Quijote de la Mancha. (SPA.). 160p. 14.95 (*84-321-2482-6*, ORT839) Rialp, Ediciones, S.A. ESP. *Dist:* Continental Bk. Co., Inc.

—Don Quijote de la Mancha. 1998. (Clasicos Esenciales Ser.). (SPA., Illus.). 232p. (YA). (gr. 9-12). 11.95 (*84-294-4559-5*) Santillana USA Publishing Co., Inc.

—Don Quijote de la Mancha. (Coleccion Estrella). (SPA., Illus.). 64p. 14.95 (*950-11-0004-9*, SGM004) Sigmar ARG. *Dist:* Continental Bk. Co., Inc.

—Don Quijote de la Mancha. (SPA.). 270p. 36.98 (*84-305-8682-2*) Susaeta Ediciones, S.A. ESP. *Dist:* AIMS International Bks., Inc.

—Don Quijote de la Mancha: A New Translation, Backgrounds & Contexts, Criticism. Raffel, Burton, tr. from SPA. 1999. (Critical Editions Ser.). pap. 12.50 (*0-393-97281-X*, WW81X) Norton, W. W. & Co., Inc.

—Don Quijote de la Mancha: Primera Parte, Level D. (Spanish Easy Reader Library: Level D). (SPA., Illus.). pap. 9.50 (*0-88436-056-3*, 70275) EMC/Paradigm Publishing.

—Don Quijote de la Mancha: Segunda Parte. 2000. (SPA.). per. 14.00 (*1-891355-15-5*) Blue Unicorn Editions.

—Don Quijote de la Mancha: Segunda Parte, Level D. 1989. (Spanish Easy Reader Library: Level D). (SPA., Illus.). pap. 9.50 (*0-88436-887-4*, 70276) EMC/Paradigm Publishing.

—Don Quijote de la Mancha I. (Clasicos Castalia). (SPA., Illus.). 640p. 18.50 (*84-7039-285-9*, CC512) Castalia, Editorial S.A. ESP. *Dist:* Continental Bk. Co., Inc.

—Don Quijote de la Mancha I. 19th ed. (SPA., Illus.). 592p. 16.95 (*84-376-0117-7*, CT1100) Ediciones Cátedra ESP. *Dist:* AIMS International Bks., Inc., Continental Bk. Co., Inc.

—Don Quijote de la Mancha I. annot. ed. (SPA., Illus.). 21.95 (*84-207-2888-8*, ANY024) Grupo Anaya, S.A. ESP. *Dist:* Continental Bk. Co., Inc.

—Don Quijote de la Mancha II. (Clasicos Castalia). (SPA., Illus.). 624p. 18.50 (*84-7039-286-7*, CC513) Castalia, Editorial S.A. ESP. *Dist:* Continental Bk. Co., Inc.

—Don Quijote de la Mancha II. 20th ed. (SPA., Illus.). 592p. 16.95 (*84-376-0118-5*, CT1101) Ediciones Cátedra ESP. *Dist:* AIMS International Bks., Inc., Continental Bk. Co., Inc.

—Don Quijote de la Mancha II. (SPA.). (*84-89163-45-6*) Grafalco, S.A.

—Don Quijote de la Mancha II, 2 vols. annot. ed. (SPA., Illus.). 21.95 (*84-207-2796-2*, ANY025) Grupo Anaya, S.A. ESP. *Dist:* Continental Bk. Co., Inc.

—Don Quixote. 1967. (Airmont Classics Ser.). mass mkt. 4.95 o.p. (*0-8049-0153-8*, CL-153) Airmont Publishing Co., Inc.

—Don Quixote. 1994. (Illustrated Classics Collection). 64p. pap. 4.95 (*0-7854-0776-6*, 40547) American Guidance Service, Inc.

—Don Quixote. unabr. collector's ed. 1990. Pt. 1. audio 104.00 (*0-7366-1658-6*, 2509A); Pt. 2. audio 112.00 (*0-7366-1659-4*, 2509B) Books on Tape, Inc.

—Don Quixote. 1981. reprint ed. lib. bdg. 37.95 o.s.i (*0-89966-383-4*) Buccaneer Bks., Inc.

—Don Quixote. E-Book 2.49 (*1-58744-084-9*) Electric Umbrella Publishing.

—Don Quixote, Pt. I, set. unabr. ed. audio 84.95 Halvorson Assocs.

—Don Quixote. Grossman, Edith & Bloom, Harold, trs. from SPA. 2003. 976p. 29.95 (*0-06-018870-7*, Ecco) HarperTrade.

—Don Quixote. abr. ed. 1997. (Classics Ser.). audio 16.95 (*1-56511-180-X*) HighBridge Co.

—Don Quixote. l.t. ed. 3017p. pap. 195.31 (*0-7583-0764-0*); 2357p. pap. 156.76 (*0-7583-0763-2*); 1841p. pap. 123.30 (*0-7583-0762-4*); 1344p. pap. 94.08 (*0-7583-0761-6*); 1075p. pap. 78.86 (*0-7583-0760-8*); 3711p. pap. 227.38 (*0-7583-0765-9*); 4564p. pap. 275.69 (*0-7583-0766-7*); 5294p. pap. 314.65 (*0-7583-0767-5*); 3711p. lib. bdg. 259.37 (*0-7583-0757-8*); 3017p. lib. bdg. 225.31 (*0-7583-0756-X*); 2357p. lib. bdg. 180.76 (*0-7583-0755-1*); 1841p. lib. bdg. 141.30 (*0-7583-0754-3*); 1344p. lib. bdg. 106.08 (*0-7583-0753-5*); 1075p. lib. bdg. 90.86 (*0-7583-0752-7*); 5294p. lib. bdg. 381.89 (*0-7583-0759-4*); 4564p. lib. bdg. 330.63 (*0-7583-0758-6*) Huge Print Pr.

—Don Quixote. abr. ed. 2000. audio 7.95 (*1-57815-116-3*, 1078, Media Bks. Audio Publishing) Media Bks., L. L. C.

—Don Quixote. 1999. E-Book 1.95 (*1-58515-213-7*) MesaView, Inc.

—Don Quixote. 2001. 1056p. mass mkt. 7.95 (*0-451-52786-0*); 1970. mass mkt. 1.65 o.p. (*0-451-50510-7*, Signet Classics); 1970. mass mkt. 1.25 o.p. (*0-451-50273-6*, Signet Classics) NAL.

—Don Quixote. Starkie, Walter, tr. 1968. mass mkt. 0.95 o.p. (*0-451-60814-3*); mass mkt. 0.50 o.p. (*0-451-60207-2*); mass mkt. 0.60 o.p. (*0-451-60407-5*) NAL. (Signet Bks.).

—Don Quixote. 1965. 1056p. mass mkt. 7.95 o.s.i (*0-451-52507-8*, Signet Bks.); 1965. mass mkt. 1.95 o.p. (*0-451-50622-7*, Signet Classics); 1965. mass mkt. 2.25 o.p. (*0-451-50777-0*, Signet Classics); 1965. mass mkt. 2.50 o.p. (*0-451-50945-5*, Signet Classics); 1965. mass mkt. 2.95 o.p. (*0-451-51210-3*, Signet Classics); 1965. mass mkt. 4.50 o.p. (*0-451-51682-6*, Signet Classics); 1965. mass mkt. 3.95 o.p. (*0-451-51521-8*, Signet Classics); 1965. mass mkt. 3.50 o.p. (*0-451-51364-9*, Signet Classics); 1957. mass mkt. 1.75 o.p. (*0-451-61528-X*, Signet Bks.) NAL.

—Don Quixote. Starkie, Walter, tr. 1957. mass mkt. 1.50 o.p. (*0-451-61378-3*); mass mkt. 3.50 o.p. (*0-451-62512-9*); mass mkt. 1.25 o.p. (*0-451-61163-2*); mass mkt. 1.95 o.p. (*0-451-61775-4*); mass mkt. 2.95 o.p. (*0-451-61987-0*) NAL. (Signet Bks.).

—Don Quixote. abr. ed. 1957. mass mkt. 3.95 o.p. (*0-451-62611-7*) NAL.

—Don Quixote. Starkie, Walter, tr. abr. ed. 1957. 432p. mass mkt. 6.99 (*0-451-62684-2*, Mentor) NAL.

—Don Quixote. unabr. ed. 1965. mass mkt. 4.95 o.p. (*0-451-51821-7*) NAL.

—Don Quixote. Starkie, Walter, tr. unabr. ed. 1965. mass mkt. 5.95 o.p. (*0-451-52371-7*, CE1821, Signet Classics) NAL.

—Don Quixote. abr. ed. (Classic Fiction Ser.). 1996. audio 17.98 (*962-634-522-5*, NA302214); 1995. audio compact disk 19.98 (*962-634-022-3*, NA302212) Naxos of America, Inc. (Naxos AudioBooks).

—Don Quixote, Set. abr. ed. 1997. audio 20.00 o.p. (*0-7871-1206-2*, 695117) NewStar Media, Inc.

—Don Quixote. 1975. (Oxford Progressive English Readers Ser.). (Illus.). pap. text 3.50 o.p. (*0-19-638224-6*) Oxford Univ. Pr., Inc.

—Don Quixote. 2000. E-Book 4.95 (*0-679-64122-X*, Modern Library) Random House Adult Trade Publishing Group.

—Don Quixote. annuals 1998. (Modern Library Ser.). 1280p. 25.95 (*0-679-60286-0*) Random Hse., Inc.

—Don Quixote. Motteux, Peter A., tr. from SPA. 1991. (Everyman's Library Pocket Poets Ser.). 1104p. 23.00 (*0-679-40758-8*, RH7588) Random Hse., Inc.

—Don Quixote. Putnam, Samuel, tr. & intro. by. 1978. 1043p. 17.95 o.s.i (*0-394-60438-5*) Random Hse., Inc.

—Don Quixote. Rutherford, John, tr. from SPA. 2001. (Classics Ser.). 1072p. pap. 13.00 o.s.i (*0-14-044804-7*, Penguin Classics) Viking Penguin.

—Don Quixote. 992p. pap. 5.95 (*1-85326-795-3*); 1997. 784p. pap. 3.95 (*1-85326-036-3*, 0363WW) Wordsworth Editions, Ltd. GBR. *Dist:* Combined Publishing, Casemate Pubs. & Bk. Distributors, LLC.

—Don Quixote: A Landmark New Translation. Rutherford, J., tr. from SPA. 2001. 1056p. pap. 10.00 o.s.i (*0-14-044561-7*, Penguin Classics) Viking Penguin.

—Don Quixote: The Ormsby Translation, Revised, Backgrounds & Sources, Criticism. Jones, Joseph R. & Douglas, Kenneth, eds. 1981. (Critical Editions Ser.). (C). pap. text o.p. (*0-393-09018-3*); 29.95 o.p. (*0-393-04514-5*) Norton, W. W. & Co., Inc.

—Don Quixote de la Mancha. 1976. 21.95 (*0-8488-0438-4*) Amereon, Ltd.

—Don Quixote de la Mancha. 1954. 9.95 o.p. (*0-460-00386-0*); Vol. 1. 1975. reprint ed. 9.95 o.p. (*0-460-00385-2*) Biblio Distribution.

—Don Quixote de la Mancha. unabr. ed. 1997. Pt. 1. audio 85.95 (*0-7861-1242-5*, 2150A); Pt. 2. audio 89.95 (*0-7861-1250-6*, 2150B) Blackstone Audio Bks., Inc.

—Don Quixote de la Mancha. Jarvis, Charles, tr. from SPA. 1999. (Oxford World's Classics Ser.: Vol. 8). 1126p. 20.00 o.p. (*0-19-210032-7*) Oxford Univ. Pr., Inc.

—Don Quixote de la Mancha. Riley, E. C., ed. & tr. by. 1998. (Oxford World's Classics Ser.). 1120p. pap. 7.95 (*0-19-283483-5*) Oxford Univ. Pr., Inc.

—Don Quixote de la Mancha. Riley, E. C., ed. Jarvis, Charles, tr. 1992. (Oxford World's Classics Ser.). 1,110p. pap. 7.95 o.p. (*0-19-282726-X*) Oxford Univ. Pr., Inc.

—Don Quixote de la Mancha. 2001. (Modern Library Classics). (Illus.). 1168p. pap. 11.95 (*0-375-75699-X*, Modern Library) Random House Adult Trade Publishing Group.

—Don Quixote de la Mancha. Pt. 1. 1985. 29.95 o.p. incl. audio (*0-295-75537-7*); Pt. 2. 1986. audio 29.95 o.p. (*0-295-75538-5*) Univ. of Washington Pr.

—Don Quixote de la Mancha: An Old Spelling Control Edition Based on the First Editions of Parts 1 & 2, 2 vols. Flores, R. M., ed. 1988. Set. 700p. (*0-7748-0301-0*); Vol. 2. 635p. (*0-7748-0314-2*) Univ. of British Columbia Pr.

—Don Quixote Readalong. 1994. (Illustrated Classics Collection). 64p. pap. 14.95 incl. audio (*0-7854-0792-8*, 40549) American Guidance Service, Inc.

—The First Part of the Life & Achievements of the Renowned Don Quixote De la Mancha. Motteux, Peter, tr. 1985. (Illus.). 587p. reprint ed. 17.95 o.p. (*0-89659-023-2*) Abbeville Pr., Inc.

—El Ingenioso Hidalgo Don Quijote de la Mancha. 1989. (SPA.). 7.95 (*0-8288-2561-0*) French & European Pubns., Inc.

—El Ingenioso Hidalgo Don Quijote de la Mancha, Pts. I & II. Lathrop, Tom, ed. unabr. ed. 2000. (Documentacion Cervantina Ser.: Vol. 16). xlviii, 871p. pap. 16.00 o.p. (*0-936388-87-0*) Juan de la Cuesta-Hispanic Monographs.

Cervantes Saavedra, Miguel de & De Riquer, Martin. Don Quijote de la Mancha. 17th ed. 1997. (Clasicos Universales Ser.). (SPA., Illus.). 1224p. (*84-08-01882-5*) GeoPlaneta, Editorial, S. A.

Cervantes Saavedra, Miguel de, et al. Don Quixote. 1949. 12.50 o.p. (*0-670-27880-7*) Viking Penguin.

Chacel, Rosa. The Maravillas District. Demers, D. A., tr. from SPA. 1992. (European Women Writers Ser.). 286p. pap. 14.95 (*0-8032-6353-8*, Bison Bks.); xxiii, 286p. text 40.00 o.p. (*0-8032-1449-9*) Univ. of Nebraska Pr.

Coelho, Paulo. The Alchemist: A Fable about Following Your Dream. Clarke, Alan R., tr. l.t. ed. 1995. 165p. lib. bdg. 20.95 o.p. (*0-7838-1195-0*, Macmillan Reference USA) Gale Group.

—The Alchemist: A Fable about Following Your Dream. 2002. 192p. 18.00 (*0-06-053377-3*); 1993. o.p. (*0-06-250253-0*); 10th abr. ed. 2001. audio compact disk 27.50 (*0-694-52444-1*) HarperCollins Pubs.

—The Alchemist: A Fable about Following Your Dream. Clarke, Alan R., tr. 10th anniv. ed. 2003. 192p. pap. 13.00 (*0-06-250218-2*) HarperSanFrancisco.

—The Alchemist: A Fable about Following Your Dream. 10th anniv. ed. 1993. 192p. 18.00 (*0-06-250217-4*) HarperSanFrancisco.

—The Alchemist: A Fable about Following Your Dream. 1995. 19.05 (*0-606-20474-1*) Turtleback Bks.

—By the River Piedra I Sat down & Wept. Clarke, Alan R., tr. from POR. 1996. 224p. 20.00 o.s.i (*0-06-251398-2*) HarperSanFrancisco.

—By the River Piedra I Sat down & Wept. 1997. 192p. pap. 13.00 (*0-06-097726-4*, Perennial) HarperTrade.

—By the River Piedra I Sat down & Wept, Set. unabr. ed. 1996. 24.95 o.p. (*0-7871-1176-7*, 494322) NewStar Media, Inc.

Cohen, Matt. The Spanish Doctor. 1985. 352p. 16.95 o.p. (*0-8253-0227-7*) Beaufort Bks., Inc.

Comins, Ethel M. Caroline: Oxbow's American Bonaparte. 1985. 208p. 13.95 o.p. (*0-912526-38-6*) Library Research Assocs., Inc.

Conrad, Barnaby. Last Boat to Cadiz. 2003. 250p. 25.95 (*1-59266-032-0*) Capra Pr.

Cordell, Alexander. To Slay the Dreamer. 1980. 294p. 10.95 o.p. (*0-312-80741-4*) St. Martin's Pr.

—To Slay the Dreamer. l.t. ed. 1982. (Ulverscroft Large Print Ser.). 511p. 29.99 o.p. (*0-7089-0766-0*, Ulverscroft) Thorpe, F. A. Pubs. GBR. *Dist:* Ulverscroft Large Print Bks., Ltd., Ulverscroft Large Print Canada, Ltd.

Crockett, Samuel R. Adventurer in Spain. 1977. (Short Story Index Reprint Ser.). 23.95 (*0-8369-3319-2*) Ayer Co. Pubs., Inc.

Dakron, Ron. Infra. 1987. 239p. (Orig.). pap. 10.95 (*0-930773-04-7*) Black Heron Pr.

Davidsen, Leif. The Sardine Deception. Nunnally, Tiina & Murray, Steven T., trs. from DAN. 1986. Tr. of Uhellige Allliancer. 199p. pap. 6.95 (*0-940242-15-X*) Fjord Pr.

De Wohl, Louis. The Golden Thread: A Novel about St. Ignatius Loyola. 2002. 315p. pap. 14.95 (*0-89870-813-3*) Ignatius Pr.

Del Castillo, Michel. The Disinherited. 1991. 292p. pap. o.p. (*1-85242-102-9*) Serpent's Tail Ltd.

Delibes, Miguel. Five Hours with Mario. Lopez-Morillas, Frances M., tr. from SPA. 1988. (Twentieth-Century Continental Fiction Ser.). 224p. text 41.00 (*0-231-06828-X*) Columbia Univ. Pr.

—The Wars of Our Ancestors: A Novel by Miguel Delibes. Moncy, Agnes, tr. from SPA. 1992. 312p. 40.00 o.p. (*0-8203-1418-8*) Univ. of Georgia Pr.

Di Perna, Paula. The Discoveries of Mrs. Christopher Columbus. 1994. 224p. 24.00 (*1-877946-48-6*) Permanent Pr., The.

Don Quixote: LIFETIME SERIES CLASSICS. 2002. text (*0-924967-71-4*) JMW Group, Inc.

Donoso, José. The Garden Next Door: A Novel. 1992. 243p. 18.95 o.p. (*0-8021-1238-2*) Grove/Atlantic, Inc.

Doyle, Peter R. Chased by the Jewel Thieves. 1997. (Daring Adventure Ser.: Bk. 11). (J). (gr. 4). pap. 5.99 o.p. (*1-56179-547-X*) Focus on the Family Publishing.

Eastlake, William. Jack Armstrong in Tangier & Other Escapes. 1984. 13.00 (*0-917453-01-8*); pap. 6.50 (*0-917453-02-6*); 20.00 o.p. (*0-917453-00-X*) Bamberger Bks.

Eisner, Michael Alexander. The Crusader: A Novel. (Illus.). 336p. 2003. pap. 13.00 (*0-385-72141-2*); 2001. 24.95 (*0-385-50281-8*, Currency) Doubleday Publishing.

—The Crusader: A Novel. l.t. ed. 2002. 567p. 29.95 (*0-7862-3991-3*) Gale Group.

Elizondo, Salvador. Farabeuf: The Chronicle of an Instant. Incledon, John, tr. 1992. (Library of World Literature in Translation: Vol. 27). (SPA.). 125p. text 15.00 (*0-8240-0459-0*) Garland Publishing, Inc.

—Farabeuf, o la Cronica de un Instante. 1981. (SPA.). 183p. 8.00 o.s.i (*84-85859-18-9*, 2005) Ediciones del Norte.

Eskinazi, Salamon. Sepharad: The Embezzled Land. 1997. (Illus.). 488p. pap. 29.95 o.p. (*1-882897-17-X*) Lost Coast Pr.

Espinosa, Maria. Incognito: Journey of a Secret Jew. 2002. 190p. (C). pap. 17.95 (*0-930324-79-X*) Wings Pr.

Feldman, Ian. Rendezvous in Majorca. 2004. (Illus.). 495p. pap. 7.99 (*0-9743673-7-0*, 0-9743673-7-0); cd-rom 19.95 (*0-9743673-8-9*, 0-9743673-8-9); cd-rom 19.95 (*0-9743673-9-7*, 1); 29.95 (*0-9743673-6-2*, 0-9743673-6-2) SSI, Inc. Publishing.

Fitzgerald, Kenny. The Brave Dogs: Los Perros Bravos. 2002. (Illus.). 616p. pap. (*1-55369-625-5*) Trafford Publishing.

Flores, Angel, ed. Spanish Stories (Cuentos Espanoles) A Dual-Language Book. 1987. (ENG & SPA.). 336p. reprint ed. pap. 10.50 (*0-486-25399-6*, 25399-6) Dover Pubns., Inc.

Forester, C. S. The Gun. 1940. 22.95 (*0-88411-634-4*) Amereon, Ltd.

—The Gun. unabr. collector's ed. 1992. audio 42.00 (*0-7366-2176-8*, 2973) Books on Tape, Inc.

—The Gun. 2001. 290p. reprint ed. pap. 29.95 (*1-931313-25-3*) Simon Pubns., Inc.

—The Gun. l.t. ed. 1973. (Ulverscroft Large Print Ser.). 29.99 o.p. (*0-85456-206-0*, Ulverscroft) Thorpe, F. A. Pubs. GBR. *Dist:* Ulverscroft Large Print Bks., Ltd., Ulverscroft Large Print Canada, Ltd.

—Rifleman Dodd. 1976. 18.95 (*0-8488-1008-2*) Amereon, Ltd.

—Rifleman Dodd. 1989. (Great War Stories Ser.). 160p. reprint ed. 19.95 (*0-933852-76-2*) Nautical & Aviation Publishing Co. of America, Inc., The.

Galdós, Benito Pérez. The Campaign of the Maestrazgo. Guzman, Lila W., tr. from SPA. 1990. 282p. text 39.95 o.p. (*0-89341-595-2*); pap. text 19.95 o.p. (*0-89341-596-0*) Hollowbrook Publishing. (Longwood Academic).

—The Cape of Don Francisco Torquemada. Trimble, Robert G., tr. from SPA. 1997. vi, 626p. pap. 49.00 o.p. (*0-913960-47-0*) Millefleurs.

—Fortunata & Jacinta: Two Stories of Married Women. Gullon, Agnes M., tr. from SPA. 1986. Tr. of Fortunata y Jacinta. 840p. 35.00 o.p. (*0-8203-0783-1*) Univ. of Georgia Pr.

—Gerona. Racz, G. J., tr. from SPA. 1993. (Hispanic Literature Ser.: Vol. 17). 208p. text 89.95 (*0-7734-9251-8*) Mellen, Edwin Pr., The.

—A Royalist Volunteer: Un Voluntario Realista. Guzman, Lila W., tr. from SPA. 1993. 488p. 109.95 (*0-7734-9360-3*) Mellen, Edwin Pr., The.

Gambaro, Griselda. The Impenetrable Madam X. Garfield, Evelyn P., tr. 1991. (Latin American Literature & Culture Ser.). 149p. 19.95 (*0-8143-2126-7*) Wayne State Univ. Pr.

Gonzalez, Bea. The Bitter Taste of Time. 2000. 256p. pap. 18.00 (*0-00-648150-7*) HarperCollins Pubs.

Goytisolo, Juan. The Garden of Secrets. 2003. 160p. pap. 14.00 (*1-85242-809-0*) Serpent's Tail Ltd. GBR. *Dist:* Consortium Bk. Sales & Distribution.

Grandes, Almudena. The Ages of Lulu. Soto, Sonia, tr. from SPA. 1994. 224p. 18.00 o.p. (*0-8021-1553-5*, Grove Pr.) Grove/Atlantic, Inc.

Greene, A. C. They Are Ruining Ibiza: A Novella. 1998. 123p. 21.95 (*1-57441-042-3*) Univ. of North Texas Pr.

Greene, Graham. Monsignor Quixote. unabr. ed. 1993. 54.95 incl. audio (*0-7451-5991-5*, CSL 027) BBC Audiobooks America.

—Monsignor Quixote. unabr. ed. 1988. audio 48.00 (*0-7366-1273-4*, 2182) Books on Tape, Inc.

—Monsignor Quixote. unabr. ed. 2000. audio 49.95 Chivers Audio Bks. GBR. *Dist:* BBC Audiobooks America.

—Monsignor Quixote. l.t. ed. 1983. (General Ser.). lib. bdg. 14.95 o.p. (*0-8161-3535-5*, Macmillan Reference USA) Gale Group.

—Monsignor Quixote. 1990. 221p. mass mkt. 5.50 (*0-671-72223-9*, Pocket); 1983. pap. 3.95 (*0-671-47470-7*, Pocket); 1982. 75.00 o.p. (*0-671-45984-8*, Simon & Schuster); 1982. 12.50 o.s.i (*0-671-45818-3*, Simon & Schuster) Simon & Schuster.

Gutierrez, Jorge A. & Omiya, James K. The Falconer: A Novel. Smith, James C., Jr., ed. 1991. (Illus.). 200p. pap. 14.95 (*0-86534-149-4*) Sunstone Pr.

Halevi, Z'ev ben Shimon. The Annointed: A Kabbalistic Novel. 2001. (Illus.). 256p. pap. 16.95 (*1-57863-228-5*, Red Wheel) Red Wheel/Weiser.

—Anointed. 1988. 256p. pap. 7.95 o.p. (*0-14-019001-5*, Penguin Bks.) Viking Penguin.

Hall, David A. Return Trip Ticket. 1992. 176p. 16.95 o.p. (*0-312-08283-5*, Saint Martin's Minotaur) St. Martin's Pr.

Heaven, Constance. Castle of Doves. 1985. 336p. 16.95 o.p. (*0-399-13072-1*) Putnam Publishing Group, The.

Hemingway, Ernest. The Fifth Column & Four Stories of the Spanish Civil War. 160p. 1978. 40.00 (*0-684-15815-9*); 1972. pap. 9.95 (*0-684-12723-7*) Gale Group. (Macmillan Reference USA).

—The Sun Also Rises. 256p. 22.95 o.s.i (*0-8488-2455-5*) Amereon, Ltd.

—The Sun Also Rises. 2003. E-Book 9.99 (*0-7432-3733-1*, Scribner); 2003. (Illus.). 256p. pap. 13.00 (*0-684-80071-3*, Scribner); 1996. 224p. 25.00 (*0-684-83051-5*, Scribner); 1984. pap. 3.95 o.s.i (*0-684-18260-2*, Scribner Paper Fiction); 1984. pap. 47.40 o.s.i (*0-684-18261-0*, Scribner Paper Fiction); 1982. 256p. pap. 4.95 o.s.i (*0-684-17472-3*, Scribner Paper Fiction); 1977. 248p. 35.00 (*0-684-15327-0*, Scribner); 1920. 256p. 20.00 o.s.i (*0-684-10250-1*, Scribner); 1920. 256p. pap. 10.95 o.s.i (*0-684-71808-1*, Scribner Paper Fiction) Simon & Schuster.

—The Sun Also Rises. l.t. ed. 1994. 310p. lib. bdg. 23.95 (*0-8161-5969-6*) Thorndike Pr.

—The Sun Also Rises. 1995. 18.05 (*0-606-05064-7*) Turtleback Bks.

Hemingway, Ernest & DeFazio, Albert J. Literary Masterpieces: The Sun Also Rises. 2000. (Literary Masterpieces Ser.: Vol. 2). (Illus.). xi, 166p. (YA). (gr. 9 up). 55.00 (*0-7876-3962-1*, GML00502-113768) Gale Group.

Hernández, Ramón. Invitation to Die. Freeman, Marion, tr. 1990. (World Literature in Translation Ser.). 216p. text 20.00 (*0-8240-2995-X*) Garland Publishing, Inc.

Herrick, William. Hermanos! 1985. 316p. pap. 20.00 (*0-933256-42-6*); 1983. 310p. reprint ed. 21.95 o.p. (*0-933256-38-8*) Second Chance Pr.

Hewson, David. Semana Santa. (GER.). pap. (*3-548-24562-5*) Ullstein-Taschenbuch-Verlag DEU. *Dist:* International Bk. Import Service, Inc.

Higgins, Jack. The Khufra Run. Rubenstein, Julie, ed. 1990. 224p. reprint ed. mass mkt. 5.99 (*0-671-72453-3*, Pocket) Simon & Schuster.

Howson, G. Arms for Spain. 1999. (Illus.). xi, 354p. 25.95 o.p. (*0-312-24177-1*) St. Martin's Pr.

Hunter, Stephen. The Spanish Gambit. 1986. 352p. 3.95 o.s.i (*0-441-77776-7*, Diamond Bks.) Berkley Publishing Group.

—The Spanish Gambit. 1986. 2.99 o.p. (*0-517-55731-2*) Random Hse. Value Publishing.

—Tapestry of Spies. 1997. Orig. Title: The Spanish Gambit. 464p. mass mkt. 7.99 (*0-440-22185-4*) Dell Publishing.

Irving, Washington. Bracebridge Hall. Smith, Herbert F., ed. 1977. (Critical Editions Program Ser.). lib. bdg. 26.00 o.p. (*0-8057-8506-X*, Macmillan Reference USA) Gale Group.

—Bracebridge Hall. reprint ed. 24.00 o.p. (*0-404-03508-6*) AMS Pr., Inc.

—Bracebridge Hall. (Illus.). 320p. reprint ed. 12.00 o.p. (*0-912882-35-2*) Sleepy Hollow Pr.

—Bracebridge Hall, Or the Humorists. 1992. (BCL1-PS American Literature Ser.). 561p. reprint ed. lib. bdg. 99.00 (*0-7812-6753-6*) Reprint Services Corp.

—Bracebridge Hall, Or the Humorists. 1902. reprint ed. 10.00 (*0-403-00239-7*) Scholarly Pr., Inc.

—Bracebridge Hall, Tales of a Traveller & the Alhambra. Myers, Andrew B., ed. 1991. (Library of America: Vol. 52). 1104p. 35.00 (*0-940450-59-3*) Library of America, The.

Jardine, Quintin. On Honeymoon with Death. 2002. 352p. mass mkt. 8.95 (*0-7472-6471-6*); 245p. 29.95 (*0-7472-7176-3*) Headline Bk. Publishing, Ltd. GBR. *Dist:* Trafalgar Square.

Jeffries, Roderic. Almost Murder. l.t. ed. 1990. (Lythway Ser.). 280p. 20.95 o.p. (*0-7451-1198-X*, Macmillan Reference USA) Gale Group.

—Almost Murder. 1986. 192p. 12.95 o.p. (*0-312-02137-2*) St. Martin's Pr.

—The Ambiguity of Murder: An Inspector Alvarez Novel. 2001. 208p. 22.95 (*0-312-26968-4*, Saint Martin's Minotaur) St. Martin's Pr.

—The Ambiguity of Murder: An Inspector Alvarez Novel. l.t. ed. 2001. 297p. pap. 24.95 (*0-7862-3328-1*); 278p. (*0-7540-4505-6*); 278p. (*0-7540-4506-4*) Thorndike Pr.

—Arcadian Death. 1995. 192p. 19.95 o.p. (*0-312-13922-5*, Saint Martin's Minotaur) St. Martin's Pr.

—An Arcadian Death: An Inspector Alvarez Novel. l.t. ed. 1996. (Nightingale Ser.). 248p. pap. 17.95 o.p. (*0-7838-1698-7*, Macmillan Reference USA) Gale Group.

—An Artful Death: An Inspector Alvarez Mystery. 2000. 211p. (*0-00-232703-1*) HarperCollins Pubs.

—An Artful Death: An Inspector Alvarez Mystery. 2002. 224p. 22.95 (*0-312-30745-4*, Saint Martin's Minotaur) St. Martin's Pr.

—An Artistic Way to Go: An Inspector Alvarez Novel, Vol. 1. 1997. (Artistic Way to Go Ser.: Vol. 1). 192p. 20.95 (*0-312-15472-0*, Saint Martin's Minotaur) St. Martin's Pr.

—An Artistic Way to Go: An Inspector Alvarez Novel. l.t. ed. 1998. (Mystery Ser.). 288p. 26.95 (*0-7862-1545-3*) Thorndike Pr.

—Dead Clever. 1990. 2.99 o.p. (*0-517-05814-6*) Random Hse. Value Publishing.

—Dead Clever. 1989. 14.95 o.p. (*0-312-02899-7*) St. Martin's Pr.

—Deadly Petard. unabr. ed. 2000. audio 44.95 (*1-86042-650-6*, 26506) Soundings, Ltd. GBR. *Dist:* Ulverscroft Large Print Bks., Ltd.

—Deadly Petard. 1983. 160p. 10.95 o.p. (*0-312-18531-6*) St. Martin's Pr.

—Death Takes Time. l.t. ed. 1995. 256p. pap. 18.95 o.p. (*0-7838-1197-7*, Macmillan Reference USA) Gale Group.

—Death Takes Time. 1994. (Inspector Alvarez Mystery Ser.). 208p. 18.95 o.p. (*0-312-11260-2*, Saint Martin's Minotaur) St. Martin's Pr.

—Death Trick. l.t. ed. 1990. 256p. lib. bdg. 20.95 o.p. (*0-7451-1091-6*, Macmillan Reference USA) Gale Group.

—Death Trick. 1988. 192p. 14.95 o.p. (*0-312-02189-5*, Saint Martin's Minotaur) St. Martin's Pr.

—Definitely Deceased: An Inspector Alvarez Novel. 2002. 28.99 (*0-7278-7123-4*); 2001. 250p. 25.99 (*0-7278-5730-4*) Severn Hse. Pubs., Ltd.

—An Enigmatic Disappearance. 2000. 176p. 21.95 (*0-312-26583-2*, Saint Martin's Minotaur) St. Martin's Pr.

—A Fatal Fleece. l.t. ed. 1994. (Dales Large Print Ser.). 340p. pap. 19.99 o.p. (*1-85389-489-3*) Dales Large Print Bks. GBR. *Dist:* Ulverscroft Large Print Bks., Ltd., Ulverscroft Large Print Canada, Ltd.

—A Fatal Fleece. 1992. 208p. 17.95 o.p. (*0-312-08192-8*, Saint Martin's Minotaur) St. Martin's Pr.

—An Intriguing Murder. 2002. 256p. 26.99 (*0-7278-5907-2*) Severn Hse. Pubs., Ltd.

—Layers of Deceit. l.t. ed. 1986. lib. bdg. 17.50 o.p. (*0-7451-0405-3*, Macmillan Reference USA) Gale Group.

—Layers of Deceit: An Inspector Alvarez Novel. 1985. 192p. 12.95 o.p. (*0-312-47571-3*) St. Martin's Pr.

—A Maze of Murders. 1997. (Inspector Alvarez Mystery Ser.). 176p. 19.95 (*0-312-18135-3*, Saint Martin's Minotaur) St. Martin's Pr.

—A Maze of Murders. l.t. ed. 1998. (General Ser.). 240p. pap. 23.95 (*0-7862-1381-7*) Thorndike Pr.

—Murder Begets Murder. 1979. 8.95 o.p. (*0-312-55288-2*) St. Martin's Pr.

—Murder Confounded. l.t. ed. 1994. 279p. lib. bdg. 16.95 (*0-8161-5902-5*, Macmillan Reference USA) Gale Group.

—Murder Confounded. 1993. 176p. 17.95 o.p. (*0-312-09877-4*, Saint Martin's Minotaur) St. Martin's Pr.

—Murder's Long Memory. 1992. 192p. 16.95 o.p. (*0-312-07039-X*, Saint Martin's Minotaur) St. Martin's Pr.

—Relatively Dangerous. l.t. ed. 1988. (Nightingale Ser.). 302p. 12.95 o.p. (*0-8161-4393-5*, Macmillan Reference USA) Gale Group.

—Relatively Dangerous. 1987. 192p. 13.95 o.p. (*0-312-01080-X*, Saint Martin's Minotaur) St. Martin's Pr.

—Seeing is Deceiving. 2002. (Inspector Alvarez Novel Ser.). 256p. 26.99 (*0-7278-5811-4*) Severn Hse. Pubs., Ltd.

—Three & One Make Five: An Inspector Alvarez Novel. 1984. 188p. 11.95 o.p. (*0-312-80240-4*) St. Martin's Pr.

—Too Clever by Half. l.t. ed. 1992. (Lythway Ser.). 272p. 20.50 (*0-7451-1418-0*, Macmillan Reference USA) Gale Group.

—Too Clever by Half. 1992. 1.99 o.p. (*0-517-08492-9*) Random Hse. Value Publishing.

—Too Clever by Half. 1990. 192p. 15.95 o.p. (*0-312-04987-0*, Saint Martin's Minotaur) St. Martin's Pr.

—Troubled Deaths. 1983. 208p. pap. 5.95 o.p. (*0-312-81995-1*, Saint Martin's Griffin); 1978. 7.95 o.p. (*0-312-81994-3*) St. Martin's Pr.

—Two-Faced Death. l.t. ed. 1995. (Dales Large Print Ser.). 332p. pap. o.p. (*1-85389-586-5*) Dales Large Print Bks. GBR. *Dist:* Ulverscroft Large Print Canada, Ltd.

—Unseemly End. 1982. 210p. 9.95 o.p. (*0-312-83372-5*) St. Martin's Pr.

Joyce, Brenda. House of Dreams. l.t. ed. 2001. (Large Print Book Ser.). 624p. 26.95 (*1-58724-036-X*, Wheeler Publishing, Inc.) Gale Group.

—House of Dreams. mass mkt. 3.99 (*0-312-99885-6*, St. Martin's Paperbacks); E-Book 23.95 (*0-312-27166-2*); 2001. 416p. mass mkt. 6.99 (*0-312-97740-9*, St. Martin's Paperbacks); 2000. 416p. 23.95 o.p. (*0-312-26247-7*) St. Martin's Pr.

Kistler, Mary. A Stranger at My Door. l.t. ed. 2001. (Candlelight Ser.). 184p. 22.95 (*0-7862-3441-5*) Thorndike Pr.

Laforet, Carmen. Nada. 25th ed. (Classicos Contemporaneos Comentados Ser.). (SPA., Illus.). 276p. pap. 19.95 (*84-233-0989-4*, DE2057) Ediciones Destino ESP. *Dist:* Continental Bk. Co., Inc.

—Nada. Ennis, Glafyra, tr. from SPA. 1993. (Catalan Studies: Vol. 8). 250p. (C). pap. text 29.95 (*0-8204-2064-6*) Lang, Peter Publishing, Inc.

—Nada. 1958. 286p. (gr. 11-12). pap. text 22.95 (*0-19-500942-8*) Oxford Univ. Pr., Inc.

Levi, Jonathan. A Guide for the Perplexed. 1993. pap. 12.00 o.p. (*0-679-73969-6*, Vintage) Knopf Publishing Group.

Lewis, Matthew G., ed. The Monk. 1999. (Classics Ser.). 416p. 9.95 (*0-14-043603-0*, Penguin Classics) Viking Penguin.

Llewellyn, Sam. Death Roll. unabr. ed. 1990. audio 69.95 (*0-7451-6108-1*) BBC Audiobooks America.

—Death Roll. Chelius, Jane, ed. 1991. 256p. reprint ed. bds. 3.95 (*0-671-67043-3*, Pocket) Simon & Schuster.

—Death Roll. 1990. 247p. 18.95 o.p. (*0-671-67045-X*) Summit Bks.

Lopez-Medina, Sylvia. Siguiriya: A Novel. 1997. 320p. 24.00 o.p. (*0-06-017271-1*) HarperCollins Pubs.

Mahoney, Dan. The Protectors. E-Book 18.95 (*0-312-70763-0*); 2002. 352p. 24.95 (*0-312-28450-0*) St. Martin's Pr.

Malraux, André. Man's Hope. Gilbert, Stuart & MacDonald, Alastair, trs. from FRE. 1979. reprint ed. pap. 12.50 o.s.i (*0-394-17093-8*, E740) Grove/Atlantic, Inc.

—Man's Hope. Gilbert, Stuart & Macdonald, Alastair, trs. 1984. 511p. 10.95 o.s.i (*0-394-60478-4*) Random Hse., Inc.

Manuel, David. A Matter of Principle: A Faith Abbey Mystery. 2003. 19.95 (*1-55725-346-3*) Paraclete Pr., Inc.

Marks, William. The Marbella Conspiracy. 2003. 244p. pap. 14.00 (*0-9706969-1-4*) Golden Era Bks.

Martin Gaite, Carmen. The Back Room. Lane, Helen, tr. from SPA. 2000. Tr. of Cuarto de Atras. 216p. pap. 11.95 (*0-87286-371-9*) City Lights Bks.

—The Back Room. Lane, Helen R., tr. from SPA. 1987. (Twentieth-Century Continental Fiction Ser.).Tr. of Cuarto de Atras. 200p. text 41.00 o.p. (*0-231-05458-0*); pap. text 16.50 o.p. (*0-231-05459-9*) Columbia Univ. Pr.

Marias, Javier. A Heart So White. Costa, Margaret Jull, tr. from SPA. 2000. 278p. 24.95 (*0-8112-1452-4*) New Directions Publishing Corp.

—A Heart So White. Costa, Jull, tr. 2002. 280p. reprint ed. pap. 14.95 (*0-8112-1505-9*) New Directions Publishing Corp.

—Tomorrow in the Battle Think of Me. Costa, Margaret Jull, tr. from SPA. 1997. 320p. 24.00 o.s.i (*0-15-100276-2*) Harcourt Trade Pubs.

Masters, Anthony. The Confessional. 1994. 240p. 19.95 o.p. (*0-312-10956-3*, Saint Martin's Minotaur) St. Martin's Pr.

Matute, Ana M. Celebration in the Northwest. Porter, Phoebe A., tr. & intro. by. (European Women Writers Ser.).Tr. of Fiesta Al Noroeste. 1998. 139p. pap. 12.00 (*0-8032-8229-X*, Bison Bks.); 1997. 86p. text 40.00 (*0-8032-3180-6*); 1997. 86p. pap. text 14.95 (*0-8032-8196-X*, BT196X) Univ. of Nebraska Pr.

—The Heliotrope Wall & Other Stories. Doyle, Michael S., tr. 1989. 160p. text 44.50 o.p. (*0-231-06556-6*) Columbia Univ. Pr.

Mendoza, Eduardo. The City of Marvels. Molloy, Bernard, tr. 1988. 432p. 19.95 (*0-15-118040-7*) Harcourt Trade Pubs.

Michaels, Fern. Tender Warrior. 2001. 384p. mass mkt. 6.99 (*0-345-30358-X*, Ivy Bks.) Ballantine Bks.

—Tender Warrior. 384p. 25.00 (*0-7278-5220-5*) Severn Hse. Pubs., Ltd.

Michener, James A. Miracle in Seville. l.t. ed. 1995. 208p. 22.00 o.p. (*0-7838-1584-0*, Macmillan Reference USA) Gale Group.

—Miracle in Seville. l.t. ed. 1995. 208p. pap. 22.00 o.s.i (*0-679-76510-7*) Random Hse. Large Print.

Montalban, Manuel Vazquez. The Angst-Ridden Executive. Emery, Ed, tr. from SPA. 1990. (Masks Noir Ser.). 240p. pap. o.p. (*1-85242-159-2*) Serpent's Tail Ltd.

—Murder in the Central Committee. 1985. 203p. 13.95 o.p. (*0-89733-125-7*) Academy Chicago Pubs., Ltd.

—Murder in the Central Committee. Camiller, Patrick, tr. from SPA. 1999. 203p. (*1-85242-731-0*) Gallery Pr.

—Murder in the Central Committee. 1997. (Mask Noir Ser.). 224p. pap. text (*1-85242-131-2*) Serpent's Tail Ltd.

—Off Side. 2001. 278p. (Orig.). pap. 13.00 (*1-85242-742-6*) Serpent's Tail Ltd. GBR. *Dist:* Consortium Bk. Sales & Distribution.

—Olympic Death. 2000. (Mask Noir Ser.). 207p. pap. o.p. (*1-85242-257-2*) Serpent's Tail Ltd.

—Southern Seas. 2000. 214p. pap. (*1-85242-700-0*) Serpent's Tail Ltd.

—Southern Seas. Camiller, Patrick, tr. from SPA. 1990. 224p. pap. o.p. (*1-85242-132-0*) Serpent's Tail Ltd.

—Southern Seas. 1990. pap. 9.95 o.p. (*0-7453-0204-1*) Westview Pr.

Montero, Rosa. Absent Love: A Chronicle. De la Torre, Cristina & Glad, Diana, trs. 1991. (European Women Writers Ser.). 214p. pap. 66.40 (*0-608-05115-2*, 20656740005) Bks. on Demand.

—Absent Love: A Chronicle. De la Torre, Cristina & Glad, Diana, trs. from SPA. 1991. (European Women Writers Ser.). xxiv, 188p. pap. 9.95 o.p. (*0-8032-8176-5*, Bison Bks.); text 30.00 o.p. (*0-8032-3141-5*) Univ. of Nebraska Pr.

—The Delta Function. Easton, Kari A. & Gavilan, Yolanda M., trs. from SPA. 1992. (European Women Writers Ser.). 267p. pap. 14.95 (*0-8032-8183-8*, Bison Bks.); text 50.00 (*0-8032-3152-0*) Univ. of Nebraska Pr.

Monteros, Maria. Flamenco. 1999. 80p. pap. 8.00 o.p. (*0-8059-4740-X*) Dorrance Publishing Co., Inc.

Murray, Yxta Maya. The Conquest. 2003. 320p. pap. 12.95 (*0-06-009360-9*); 2002. 304p. 24.95 (*0-06-009359-5*) HarperTrade. (Rayo).

Naipaul, V. S. A House for Mr. Biswas. 1984. pap. 10.95 o.s.i (*0-394-72050-4*, Vintage) Knopf Publishing Group.

—A House for Mr. Biswas. 1995. (Everyman's Library: Vol. 213). 508p. 20.00 (*0-679-44458-0*) Knopf, Alfred A. Inc.

—A House for Mr. Biswas. (Penguin Twentieth-Century Classics Ser.). 1993. 608p. pap. 13.95 o.s.i (*0-14-018604-2*, Penguin Classics); 1976. 592p. pap. 10.95 o.p. (*0-14-003025-5*, Penguin Bks.) Viking Penguin.

—A House for Mr. Biswas: A Novel. 2001. 576p. pap. 15.00 (*0-375-70716-6*, Vintage) Knopf Publishing Group.

Newman, Sharan. Strong As Death. unabr. collector's ed. 1999. (Catherine LeVendeur Ser.: 4). audio 72.00 (*0-7366-4862-3*, 5189) Books on Tape, Inc.

—Strong As Death. (Catherine Levendeur Mystery Ser.). 384p. 1997. mass mkt. 5.99 (*0-8125-3935-4*); 1996. 23.95 o.p. (*0-312-86179-6*) Doherty, Tom Assocs., LLC. (Forge Bks.).

O'Brien, Kate. Talk of Angels: A Novel. 1997. 368p. (J). pap. 12.95 o.p. (*0-7868-6191-6*) Hyperion Pr.

Oliver, Maria-Antonia. Antipodes. McNerney, Kathleen, tr. from SPA. 1989. (International Women's Crime Ser.). 224p. (Orig.). reprint ed. pap. 8.95 o.p. (*0-931188-82-2*, Seal Pr.) Avalon Publishing Group.

—Study in Lilac. McNerney, Kathleen, tr. from CAT. 1987. (International Women's Crime Ser.). 161p. pap. 16.95 o.p. (*0-931188-53-9*); pap. 8.95 o.p. (*0-931188-52-0*) Avalon Publishing Group. (Seal Pr.).

O'Marie, Carol Anne. Murder Makes a Pilgrimage: A Sister Mary Helen Mystery. 1994. 320p. mass mkt. 5.50 o.s.i (*0-440-21613-3*) Dell Publishing.

—Murder Makes a Pilgrimage: A Sister Mary Helen Mystery. l.t. ed. 1994. 336p. lib. bdg. 21.95 o.p. (*0-8161-5951-3*, Macmillan Reference USA) Gale Group.

Pardo Bazán, Emilia. The House of Ulloa: A Novel by Emilia Pardo Bazan. 1992. 352p. 35.00 o.p. (*0-8203-1372-6*) Univ. of Georgia Pr.

Pawel, Rebecca. Law of Return. 2004. 288p. 24.00 (*1-56947-343-9*) Soho Pr., Inc.

Perutz, Leo. The Marquis of Bolibar. Brownjohn, John, tr. from GER. 1989. 192p. lib. bdg. 17.95 o.s.i (*1-55970-015-7*) Arcade Publishing, Inc.

Pilcher, Rosamunde. Sleeping Tiger. unabr. ed. 2000. audio 24.95 (*1-57270-134-X*, M41134u, Audio Editions Bks. on Cassette) Audio Partners Publishing Corp.

—Sleeping Tiger. l.t. ed. 1994. pap. 18.95 o.p. (*0-7927-1891-7*); 1994. 19.95 o.p. (*0-7927-1892-5*); 1996. audio 54.95 (*0-7451-6710-1*, CAB1326) BBC Audiobooks America.

—Sleeping Tiger. 1975. mass mkt. 1.25 o.s.i (*0-345-24749-3*) Ballantine Bks.

—Sleeping Tiger. unabr. ed. 1991. audio 30.00 (*0-7366-2082-6*, 2887) Books on Tape, Inc.

—Sleeping Tiger. 1989. 288p. mass mkt. 5.50 o.s.i (*0-440-20247-7*) Dell Publishing.

—Sleeping Tiger. 1992. audio 12.79 o.s.i (*0-553-70064-2*); 2000. audio 9.99 (*0-553-52726-6*); 1999. audio 9.99 o.s.i (*0-553-70200-9*) Random Hse. Audio Publishing Group. (RH Audio).

—Sleeping Tiger. 1974. 6.50 o.p. (*0-312-72905-7*); 3rd ed. 1996. 288p. mass mkt. 6.99 (*0-312-96125-1*, St. Martin's Paperbacks) St. Martin's Pr.

—Sleeping Tiger. l.t. ed. 1977. (Ulverscroft Large Print Ser.). 12.00 o.p. (*0-7089-0022-4*, Ulverscroft) Thorpe, F. A. Pubs. GBR. *Dist:* Ulverscroft Large Print Bks., Ltd., Ulverscroft Large Print Canada, Ltd.

Plante, David. The Foreigner. 1986. pap. 8.95 o.p. (*0-525-48209-1*, Obelisk) NAL.

—The Foreigner. 1984. 256p. 12.95 o.p. (*0-689-11491-5*, Scribner) Simon & Schuster.

Porcel, Baltasar. Springs & Autumns. Getman, John L., tr. from CAT. 2000. xiii, 202p. pap. 24.95 (*1-55728-609-4*) Univ. of Arkansas Pr.

Posadas, Carmen. Little Indiscretions: A Novel. Andrews, Christopher, tr. from SPA. 2003. 320p. 23.95 (*0-375-50885-6*) Random House Adult Trade Publishing Group.

Posse, Abel. Daimon. 1992. 288p. 20.00 o.p. (*0-689-12123-7*, Scribner) Simon & Schuster.

Potocki, Jan. The Manuscript Found in Saragossa. Maclean, Ian, tr. 1995. 656p. 27.95 o.p. (*0-670-83428-9*, Viking) Viking Penguin.

Prado, Benjamin. Never Shake Hands with a Left-Handed Gunman. Cordero, Kristina, tr. from SPA. 1998. 176p. 19.95 (*0-312-20084-6*) St. Martin's Pr.

Pérez Galdós, Benito. The Golden Fountain Cafe. Miller, Yvette E., ed. Rubin, Walter S., tr. from SPA. 1989. (Discoveries Ser.). 125p. 17.95 o.s.i (*0-935480-36-6*) Latin American Literary Review Pr.

Pérez-Reverte, Arturo. Flanders Panel. 1994. 294p. 21.95 o.s.i (*0-15-148926-2*) Harcourt Trade Pubs.

—The Flanders Panel. Costa, Margaret Jull, tr. from SPA. 1996. Tr. of Tabla de Flandes. (Illus.). 304p. pap. 13.95 (*0-553-37786-8*) Bantam Bks.

—The Seville Communion. Soto, Sonia, tr. from SPA. (Illus.). 1999. 416p. (C). pap. 14.00 (*0-15-600639-1*, Harvest Bks.); 1998. 400p. 24.00 (*0-15-100283-5*) Harcourt Trade Pubs.

—The Seville Communion. abr. ed. 1999. audio 25.00 (*0-7871-1910-5*, Dove Audio) NewStar Media, Inc.

Rann, Sheila. Anything for Love. 1995. 288p. 21.95 o.p. (*0-446-51830-1*) Warner Bks., Inc.

Raphael, David. The Alhambra Decree: A Historical Novel about the Expulsion of the Jews from Spain. 1988. 358p. (C). 25.00 (*0-9620772-0-8*) Carmi Hse. Pr.

—Cavalier of Malaga. 1989. 190p. 15.00 (*0-9620772-1-6*) Carmi Hse. Pr.

—El Decreto de la Alhambra: Novela Historica Sobre la Expulsion de los Judios de Espana en 1492. Santacruz, Daniel M., tr. from ENG. 1992. (SPA.). 357p. 25.00 (*0-9620772-4-0*); pap. 15.00 (*0-9620772-5-9*) Carmi Hse. Pr.

Rathbone, Julian. Carnival. 1976. 7.95 o.p. (*0-312-12250-0*) St. Martin's Pr.

—Lying in State. 1986. 16.95 o.p. (*0-399-13156-6*) Putnam Publishing Group, The.

Rayner, Claire. Nurse in the Sun. l.t. ed. 2000. 256p. 32.50 (*0-7531-6119-2*) ISIS Large Print Bks. GBR. *Dist:* Ulverscroft Large Print Bks., Ltd., Ulverscroft Large Print Canada, Ltd.

—Nurse in the Sun. l.t. ed. 2001. 256p. pap. 21.99 o.p. (*0-7531-6336-5*) Thorpe, F. A. Pubs. GBR. *Dist:* Ulverscroft Large Print Bks., Ltd., Ulverscroft Large Print Canada, Ltd.

Reilly, Bernard. Secret of Santiago: A Novel of Medieval Spain. 1997. (Medieval Military Library). 256p. text 24.95 o.p. (*0-938289-60-8*, 289608, Combined Publishing) Da Capo Pr., Inc.

—Treasure of the Vanquished: A Novel of Visigothic Spain. 1993. 256p. text o.p. (*0-938289-27-6*, 289276, Combined Publishing) Da Capo Pr., Inc.

Rodoreda, Mercé. Camellia Street: A Novel. Rosenthal, David H., tr. from SPA. & intro. by. 1993. 256p. 20.00 o.p. (*1-55597-192-X*) Graywolf Pr.

—The Time of the Doves. Rosenthal, David H., tr. from CAT. 1986. 208p. reprint ed. pap. 14.00 (*0-915308-75-4*) Graywolf Pr.

—The Time of the Doves. Rosenthall, David, tr. 1980. 8.95 o.s.i (*0-8008-7731-4*) Taplinger Publishing Co., Inc.

Roe, Caroline. An Antidote for Avarice. 1999. (Prime Crime Mysteries Ser.: 3). 288p. mass mkt. 6.50 o.s.i (*0-425-17260-0*, Prime Crime) Berkley Publishing Group.

—Cure for a Charlatan. 1999. (Chronicles of Issac of Girona Ser.: 2). 272p. mass mkt. 6.50 (*0-425-16734-8*, Prime Crime) Berkley Publishing Group.

—Remedy for Treason. 1998. (Chronicles of Issac of Girona Ser.: Vol. 1). 272p. mass mkt. 5.99 o.s.i (*0-425-16295-8*, Prime Crime) Berkley Publishing Group.

Ross, Dorien. Returning to A. 1995. (Illus.). 180p. 18.95 (*0-87286-306-9*); pap. 9.95 (*0-87286-307-7*) City Lights Bks.

Rossi, Christina P. Dostoevsky's Last Night: A Novel. 1995. Tr. of Ultima Noche de Dostoievski. 192p. 20.00 o.p. (*0-312-13054-6*) Picador.

Sender, Ramón J. Requiem Por un Campesino Espanol, Level C. 1997. (Spanish Easy Reader Library: Level C). (SPA., Illus.). pap. 9.50 (*0-88436-055-5*, 70273) EMC/Paradigm Publishing.

—Seven Red Sundays. 1990. 288p. 9.95 (*0-929587-29-4*, Elephant Paperbacks) Dee, Ivan R. Pub.

Serafin, David. The Angel of Torremolinos. 1988. 192p. 13.95 o.p. (*0-312-01730-8*, Saint Martin's Minotaur) St. Martin's Pr.

—The Body in Cadiz Bay: A Superintendent Bernal Novel. 1985. 224p. 13.95 o.p. (*0-312-08742-X*) St. Martin's Pr.

—Madrid Underground. 1984. 224p. 11.95 o.p. (*0-312-50401-2*) St. Martin's Pr.

—Port of Light. 1987. 208p. 14.95 o.p. (*0-312-01077-X*, Saint Martin's Minotaur) St. Martin's Pr.

—Saturday of Glory. 1981. 224p. 9.95 o.p. (*0-312-69975-1*) St. Martin's Pr.

—Saturday of Glory. l.t. ed. 1981. (Ulverscroft Large Print Ser.). 29.99 o.p. (*0-7089-0577-3*, Ulverscroft) Thorpe, F. A. Pubs. GBR. *Dist:* Ulverscroft Large Print Bks., Ltd., Ulverscroft Large Print Canada, Ltd.

Serasin, David. Christmas Rising. 1983. 224p. 10.95 o.p. (*0-312-13414-2*) St. Martin's Pr.

Sheckley, Robert. The Alternative Detective. 256p. 1997. pap. 13.95 o.p. (*0-312-85381-5*); 1993. 19.95 o.p. (*0-312-85023-9*) Doherty, Tom Assocs., LLC. (Forge Bks.).

Sheldon, Sidney. The Sands of Time. 1988. 320p. 22.95 (*0-688-06571-6*, Morrow, William & Co.) Morrow/Avon.

—The Sands of Time. abr. ed. 1993. 16.95 o.p. (*1-55800-731-8*); audio 15.95 o.p. (*1-55800-104-2*, 40400, Dove Audio) NewStar Media, Inc.

—The Sands of Time. 1989. 448p. reprint ed. mass mkt. 7.99 (*0-446-35683-2*) Warner Bks., Inc.

Shellabarger, Samuel. Captain from Castile: The Best-Selling Historical Epic. 2002. reprint ed. 640p. 18.95 (*1-882593-62-6*); 433p. pap. 32.50 (*1-882593-63-4*) Bridge Works Publishing Co., Inc.

Sherwood, John. The Hanging Garden: A Celia Grant Mystery. 1993. 192p. 20.00 o.p. (*0-684-19429-5*); 1994. 375p. lib. bdg. 16.95 (*0-8161-5903-3*) Gale Group. (Macmillan Reference USA).

Sostres, Salvador. Lucia. 2001. (SPA., Illus.). 120p. pap. (*84-350-0886-X*) Edhasa.

Stewart, Sally. Castles in Spain. 2001. 224p. 25.99 (*0-7278-5740-1*); 29.99 (*0-7278-7126-9*) Severn Hse. Pubs., Ltd.

Tate, Ellalice. The Scarlet Cloak. l.t. ed. 1994. (Core Collection). 560p. lib. bdg. 22.95 o.p. (*0-7838-1161-6*, Macmillan Reference USA) Gale Group.

—The Scarlet Cloak. 1992. 336p. 21.95 o.p. (*0-399-13783-1*, G. P. Putnam's Sons) Penguin Group (USA) Inc.

Thomas, Rosie. The White Dove. 1986. 640p. 18.95 o.p. (*0-670-80013-9*) Viking Penguin.

Toibin, Colm. The South. 240p. 1991. 18.95 o.p. (*0-670-83870-5*, Viking); 1992. reprint ed. 13.00 (*0-14-014986-4*) Viking Penguin.

Trollope, Joanna. A Spanish Lover. 1994. 384p. pap. 12.95 (*0-552-99549-5*) Bantam Bks.

—A Spanish Lover. 1998. 368p. mass mkt. 6.99 (*0-425-16234-6*); 2001. 384p. reprint ed. pap. 14.00 (*0-425-18170-7*) Berkley Publishing Group.

Tusquets, Esther. The Same Sea As Every Summer. Jones, Margaret E., tr. from SPA. 1990. (European Women Writers Ser.). 196p. pap. 9.95 o.p. (*0-8032-9416-6*, Bison Bks.); 194p. text 25.00 o.p. (*0-8032-4422-3*) Univ. of Nebraska Pr.

Unamuno, Miguel de. Ficciones: Four Stories & a Play. Kerrigan, Anthony, tr. 1987. (Bollingen Ser.: Vol. LXXXV, No. 7). 344p. pap. 12.95 o.p. (*0-691-01874-X*) Princeton Univ. Pr.

Valtos, William M. La Magdalena. 2002. (Theo Nikonos Mystery Ser.). 408p. pap. 15.95 (*1-57174-278-6*) Hampton Roads Publishing Co., Inc.

VandenBroeck, Andre. Breaking Through: A Narrative of the Great Work. 1996. 400p. pap. 15.95 (*0-87286-319-0*) City Lights Bks.

Whalley, Peter. Crooks. 1990. 192p. pap. 3.50 (*0-380-70617-2*, Avon Bks.) Morrow/Avon.

—Crooks. 1988. 15.95 (*0-8027-1038-7*) Walker & Co.

Wilson, Barbara. Gaudi Afternoon: A Cassandra Reilly Mystery. 1990. (Cassandra Reilly Mysteries Ser.). 172p. pap. 11.95 (*0-931188-89-X*, Seal Pr.) Avalon Publishing Group.

Wilson, Robert. The Blind Man of Seville. 2003. 448p. 25.00 (*0-15-100835-3*) Harcourt Trade Pubs.

Wolff, Milton. Another Hill: An Autobiographical Novel. 424p. 2002. (Illus.). pap. text 18.95 (*0-252-06983-8*); 1994. text 29.95 (*0-252-02091-X*) Univ. of Illinois Pr.

Yarbro, Chelsea Quinn. Come Twilight: A Novel of Count Saint-Germain. (Illus.). 2000. 479p. 27.95 (*0-312-87330-1*); 2001. 480p. reprint ed. pap. 17.95 (*0-312-87371-9*) Doherty, Tom Assocs., LLC. (Tor Bks.).

**SPOKANE (WASH.)—FICTION**

Oliver, Steve. Moody Gets the Blues. 1996. (Illus.). 256p. 21.95 (*0-9644138-7-6*) OffByOne Pr.

—Moody Gets the Blues, Vol. 1. 1998. 256p. pap. 5.99 (*0-312-96502-8*, St. Martin's Paperbacks) St. Martin's Pr.

Walter, Jess. Over Tumbled Graves. 2002. 416p. mass mkt. 7.50 (*0-06-103200-X*) HarperCollins Pubs.

—Over Tumbled Graves. 2001. (*0-06-039417-X*); 384p. 25.00 (*0-06-039386-6*) HarperTrade. (Regan-Books).

**SPRINGWATER STATION (IMAGINARY PLACE)—FICTION**

Miller, Linda Lael. Jessica. 1999. (Springwater Seasons Ser.: Bk. 4). 151p. pap. 3.99 o.s.i (*0-671-02687-9*, Pocket) Simon & Schuster.

—Jessica. l.t. ed. 1999. (Americana Ser.). 175p. 28.95 (*0-7862-2160-7*) Thorndike Pr.

—Miranda. 1999. (Springwater Seasons Ser.: Bk. 3). 142p. pap. 3.99 o.s.i (*0-671-02686-0*, Pocket) Simon & Schuster.

—Miranda Bk. 3: Springwater Seasons. l.t. ed. 1999. (Americana Ser.). 173p. 27.95 (*0-7862-2159-3*) Thorndike Pr.

—Rachel. 1999. (Springwater Seasons Ser.: Bk. 1). 145p. pap. 3.99 o.s.i (*0-671-02684-4*, Pocket) Simon & Schuster.

—Rachel. l.t. ed. 1999. (Americana Ser.). 189p. 27.95 (*0-7862-2157-7*) Thorndike Pr.

—Savannah. 1999. (Springwater Seasons Ser.: Bk. 2). 144p. mass mkt. 3.99 o.s.i (*0-671-02685-2*, Pocket) Simon & Schuster.

—Savannah. l.t. ed. 1999. (Americana Ser.). 184p. 27.95 (*0-7862-2158-5*) Thorndike Pr.

—Springwater. l.t. ed. 1999. (Wheeler Large Print Book Ser.). 280p. 26.95 (*1-56895-786-6*, Wheeler Publishing, Inc.) Gale Group.

—Springwater. 1998. 304p. mass mkt. 6.99 (*0-671-02751-4*, Pocket) Simon & Schuster.

—A Springwater Christmas. 1999. (Springwater Seasons Ser.). 320p. mass mkt. 6.99 (*0-671-02752-2*, Pocket) Simon & Schuster.

—Springwater Seasons Omnibus. 2000. 592p. mass mkt. 7.99 (*0-7434-0362-2*, Pocket) Simon & Schuster.

**SRI LANKA—FICTION**

Gunesekera, Romesh. The Sandglass. 1998. 288p. 21.95 (*1-56584-484-X*) New Pr., The.

—The Sandglass. 1999. 288p. 12.95 o.s.i (*1-57322-758-7*, Riverhead Bks. (Hardcovers)) Putnam Publishing Group, The.

—The Sandglass. 1998. 278p. 22.00 (*0-670-88173-2*, Viking) Viking Penguin.

Hower, Edward. A Garden of Demons. 2003. 220p. 22.95 (*0-86538-106-2*) Ontario Review Pr.

—Shadows & Elephants. 2002. 317p. pap. 14.95 (*0-9679520-3-4*) Leapfrog Pr.

Meidav, Edie. The Far Field: A Novel of Ceylon. 2001. 608p. tchr. ed. 25.00 (*0-618-01366-0*) Houghton Mifflin Co.

Merrick, Gordon. Now Let's Talk about Music. 1997. 256p. reprint ed. pap. 12.95 o.p. (*1-55583-293-8*) Alyson Pubns.

—Now Let's Talk about Music. 1981. 432p. mass mkt. 4.95 o.p. (*0-380-77867-X*, 60055-2, Avon Bks.) Morrow/Avon.

Ondaatje, Michael. Anil's Ghost. E-Book 11.50 (*1-58945-539-8*) Adobe Systems, Inc.

—Anil's Ghost. 2000. 320p. 25.00 (*0-375-41053-8*, Everyman's Library) Knopf Publishing Group.

—Anil's Ghost. 2001. E-Book 11.50 (*0-375-41267-0*) Random Hse., Inc.

—Anil's Ghost. 443p. 2000. (*0-7540-1494-0*); 2001. 27.95 o.p. (*0-7862-2791-5*); 2000. 29.95 (*0-7862-2790-7*); 2000. (*0-7540-2377-X*) Thorndike Pr.

—Anil's Ghost: A Novel. 2001. 320p. reprint ed. pap. 13.00 (*0-375-72437-0*, Vintage) Knopf Publishing Group.

Selvadurai, Shyam. Cinnamon Gardens. 2000. (Harvest Book Ser.). 368p. pap. 14.00 (*0-15-601328-2*, Harvest Bks.) Harcourt Trade Pubs.

—Cinnamon Gardens. 1999. 400p. 23.95 (*0-7868-6473-7*) Hyperion Pr.

—Funny Boy: A Novel in Six Stories. 1997. (Harvest Book Ser.). 320p. pap. 13.00 (*0-15-600500-X*, Harvest Bks.) Harcourt Trade Pubs.

—Funny Boy: A Novel in Six Stories. 1996. 320p. 23.00 o.p. (*0-688-14595-7*, Morrow, William & Co.) Morrow/Avon.

Swan, Rose. Message of Love. l.t. ed. 2001. 141p. (*0-7540-4393-2*); (*0-7540-4394-0*) Gale Group. (Macmillan Reference USA).

—Message of Love. l.t. ed. 2001. (Nightingale Ser.). 141p. pap. 22.95 (*0-7838-9336-1*) Thorndike Pr.

**STAGGERFORD (MINN.: IMAGINARY PLACE)—FICTION**

Hassler, Jon. Dear James. 1996. pap. 12.95 o.s.i (*0-345-41013-0*); 1994. 432p. mass mkt. 6.99 o.s.i (*0-345-37708-7*) Ballantine Bks.

—A Green Journey. 1996. 304p. pap. 12.95 (*0-345-41041-6*); 1993. mass mkt. 5.99 o.p. (*0-345-90023-5*); 1986. 304p. mass mkt. 5.99 o.s.i (*0-345-33372-1*) Ballantine Bks.

—A Green Journey. 1985. 320p. 15.95 o.p. (*0-688-03982-0*, Morrow, William & Co.) Morrow/Avon.

—Staggerford. 1997. pap. 12.00 o.s.i (*0-345-41824-7*); 1986. 304p. mass mkt. 6.99 (*0-345-33375-6*) Ballantine Bks.

—Staggerford. 1977. 8.95 o.p. (*0-689-10793-5*, Atheneum) Simon & Schuster Children's Publishing.

—The Staggerford Flood. 2003. 208p. pap. 13.00 (*0-452-28462-7*, Plume) Dutton/Plume.

—The Staggerford Flood. 2002. 208p. 24.95 (*0-670-03125-9*, Viking) Viking Penguin.

—Staggerford's Indian. ltd. ed. 1988. (Winter Bks.: No. 1). (Illus.). 36p. 60.00 o.s.i (*1-879832-18-6*); pap. 25.00 o.s.i (*1-879832-19-4*) Minnesota Ctr. for Bk. Arts.

**STOCKHOLM (SWEDEN)—FICTION**

Marklund, Liza. The Bomber. von Hofsten, Kajsa, tr. 2001. 336p. 24.95 (*0-7434-1783-6*, Atria) Simon & Schuster.

—The Bomber. reprint ed. 2002. 448p. mass mkt. 6.99 (*0-7434-1784-4*, Pocket); 2001. E-Book 24.95 (*0-7434-1785-2*, Atria) Simon & Schuster.

Peters, Elizabeth, pseud. Silhouette in Scarlet. 1990. mass mkt. 4.50 (*0-8125-0940-4*, Tor Bks.) Doherty, Tom Assocs., LLC.

—Silhouette in Scarlet. l.t. ed. 1986. 10.00 o.p. (*0-8161-3592-4*, Macmillan Reference USA) Gale Group.

—Silhouette in Scarlet. unabr. ed. (Vicky Bliss Mystery Ser.: Vol. 3). audio 44.00 (*0-7887-0160-6*, 94385E7) Recorded Bks., LLC.

—Silhouette in Scarlet. l.t. ed. 1985. (Ulverscroft Large Print Ser.). 29.99 o.p. (*0-7089-1315-6*, Ulverscroft) Thorpe, F. A. Pubs. GBR. *Dist:* Ulverscroft Large Print Bks., Ltd., Ulverscroft Large Print Canada, Ltd.

—Silhouette in Scarlet. 1994. 224p. mass mkt. 5.50 o.p. (*0-446-36482-7*) Warner Bks., Inc.

Sjowall, Maj & Wahloo, Per. The Abominable Man. 21.95 (*0-89190-378-X*) Amereon, Ltd.

—The Abominable Man. 1993. reprint ed. lib. bdg. 17.95 o.p. (*1-56849-222-7*) Buccaneer Bks., Inc.

—The Abominable Man. 1980. (Martin Beck Detective Ser.). pap. 3.95 o.s.i (*0-394-74273-7*, Vintage) Knopf Publishing Group.

—Cop Killer. 1978. pap. 3.95 o.s.i (*0-394-72444-5*, Vintage) Knopf Publishing Group.

—Cop Killer: The Story of a Crime. 23.95 (*0-89190-377-1*) Amereon, Ltd.

—The Fire Engine That Disappeared. 1977. pap. 4.95 o.s.i (*0-394-72340-6*, Vintage) Knopf Publishing Group.

—The Laughing Policeman. Blair, Alan, tr. from SWE. l.t. ed. 1993. (Nightingale Ser.). 378p. lib. bdg. 16.95 o.p. (*0-8161-5767-7*, Macmillan Reference USA) Gale Group.

—The Laughing Policeman. 1992. 224p. pap. 12.00 (*0-679-74223-9*); 1977. pap. 4.95 o.p. (*0-394-72341-4*) Knopf Publishing Group. (Vintage).

—The Locked Room. 1980. pap. 4.95 o.p. (*0-394-74274-5*, Vintage) Knopf Publishing Group.

—The Locked Room: The Story of a Crime. Austin, Paul B., tr. from SWE. 1992. (Crime - Black Lizard Ser.). 320p. pap. 12.95 (*0-679-74222-0*, Vintage) Knopf Publishing Group.

—The Man on the Balcony. Date not set. lib. bdg. 18.95 (*0-8488-2163-7*) Amereon, Ltd.

—The Man on the Balcony. 1976. pap. 4.50 o.p. (*0-394-71777-5*, Vintage) Knopf Publishing Group.

—The Man on the Balcony: The Story of a Crime. Blair, Alan, tr. 1993. (Vintage Crime/Black Lizard Ser.). 192p. pap. 11.95 (*0-679-74596-3*, Vintage) Knopf Publishing Group.

—The Man Who Went up in Smoke. Date not set. lib. bdg. 18.95 (*0-8488-2164-5*) Amereon, Ltd.

—The Man Who Went up in Smoke. Tate, Joan, tr. from SWE. 1993. (Vintage Crime/Black Lizard Ser.). 192p. pap. 11.00 (*0-679-74597-1*, Vintage) Knopf Publishing Group.

—The Man Who Went up in Smoke. 1976. pap. 3.95 o.p. (*0-394-71778-3*, Vintage) Knopf Publishing Group.

—Murder at the Savoy. 1977. pap. 5.95 o.s.i (*0-394-72342-2*, Vintage) Knopf Publishing Group.

—Roseanna. Roth, Lois, tr. from SWE. 1993. (Vintage Crime/Black Lizard Ser.). 224p. pap. 12.95 (*0-679-74598-X*, Vintage) Knopf Publishing Group.

—Roseanna. 1976. pap. 4.95 o.p. (*0-394-71779-1*, Vintage) Knopf Publishing Group.

—The Terrorists. 1977. pap. 4.95 o.s.i (*0-394-72452-6*, Vintage); 1976. 320p. 7.95 o.p. (*0-394-48532-7*, Pantheon) Knopf Publishing Group.

**STONY MAN FARM (VA.: IMAGINARY PLACE)—FICTION**

Donnelly, Jane. Flash Point. 1982. (SuperBolan Ser.: No. 12). 352p. pap. o.p. (*0-373-02456-8*, Harlequin Bks.) Harlequin Enterprises, Ltd.

Pendleton, Don. Betrayal: Stony Man. 1999. (StonyMan Ser.: Bk. 40). per. (*0-373-61924-3*, 1-61924-6, Harlequin Bks.) Harlequin Enterprises, Ltd.

Pendleton, Don. Asian Storm. 1997. (StonyMan Ser.: Vol. 27). 352p. per. (*0-373-61911-1*, 1-61911-3, Worldwide Library) Harlequin Enterprises, Ltd.

—Bird of Prey. 1996. (StonyMan Ser.: No. 24). per. (*0-373-61908-1*, Worldwide Library) Harlequin Enterprises, Ltd.

—Blind Eagle. 1994. (StonyMan Ser.). mass mkt. (*0-373-61896-4*, 1-61896-6, Harlequin Bks.) Harlequin Enterprises, Ltd.

—Blood Debt. 1995. (StonyMan Ser.). mass mkt. (*0-373-61899-9*, 1-61899-0, Harlequin Bks.) Harlequin Enterprises, Ltd.

—Conflagration. 2000. (SuperBolan Ser.: No. 72). 352p. per. (*0-373-61472-1*, Gold Eagle) Harlequin Enterprises, Ltd.

—Conflict Imperative. 2000. (StonyMan Ser.: Vol. 48). 352p. mass mkt. (*0-373-61932-4*, 1-61932-9, Worldwide Library) Harlequin Enterprises, Ltd.

—Deadly Agent. 1994. (StonyMan Ser.). per. (*0-373-61898-0*, 1-61898-2, Harlequin Bks.) Harlequin Enterprises, Ltd.

—Deep Alert. 1995. (StonyMan Ser.). mass mkt. (*0-373-61900-6*, 1-61900-6, Harlequin Bks.) Harlequin Enterprises, Ltd.

—Don Pendleton's Mack Bolan: Anvil of Hell. 1988. (Gold Eagle Ser.). 352p. pap. o.s.i (*0-373-61411-X*, Harlequin Bks.) Harlequin Enterprises, Ltd.

—Enemy Within No. 38: Stony Man. 1998. (StonyMan Ser.: Vol. 38). per. (*0-373-61922-7*, 1-61922-0, Harlequin Bks.) Harlequin Enterprises, Ltd.

—The Executioner. 2000. audio 21.00 (*1-55204-936-1*) Durkin Hayes Publishing Ltd.

—The Executioner, 12 vols. (Executioner Ser.). 1998. per. (*0-373-91954-9*); 1997. per. (*0-373-91376-1*); 1997. per. (*0-373-90285-9*) Harlequin Enterprises, Ltd. (Gold Eagle).

—Eye of the Ruby. 1997. (StonyMan Ser.: No. 29). per. (*0-373-61913-8*, 1-61913-9, Worldwide Library) Harlequin Enterprises, Ltd.

—Flashback. 1996. (StonyMan Ser.: No. 26). mass mkt. (*0-373-61910-3*, 1-61910-5, Worldwide Library) Harlequin Enterprises, Ltd.

—Flight Seven Four One. 1986. (SuperBolan Ser.). 384p. pap. o.s.i (*0-373-61405-5*, Harlequin Bks.) Harlequin Enterprises, Ltd.

—Law of Last Resort. 1997. (StonyMan Ser.: No. 32). per. (*0-373-61916-2*, 1-61916-2, Worldwide Library) Harlequin Enterprises, Ltd.

—Mack Bolan: Stony Man Doctrine. abr. ed. audio 16.99 (*0-88646-173-1*, 7174) Durkin Hayes Publishing Ltd.

—Mack Bolan: Terminal Velocity. 1984. (Gold Eagle Ser.: No. 2). 384p. mass mkt. o.s.i (*0-373-61402-0*, Harlequin Bks.) Harlequin Enterprises, Ltd.

—Mack Bolan: The Executioner. 1998. (*0-373-96225-8*, Harlequin Bks.) Harlequin Enterprises, Ltd.

—Message to America. 1998. (StonyMan Ser.). per. (*0-373-61919-7*, 1-61919-6, Worldwide Library) Harlequin Enterprises, Ltd.

—Message to Medellin. 1991. (Executioner Ser.: No. 151). mass mkt. (*0-373-61151-X*, Harlequin Bks.) Harlequin Enterprises, Ltd.

—Nuclear Nightmare. 1995. (StonyMan Ser.). 349p. per. (*0-373-61903-0*, 1-61903-0, Worldwide Library) Harlequin Enterprises, Ltd.

—Punitive Measures. 1998. (StonyMan Ser.: No. 33). per. (*0-373-61917-0*, 1-61917-0, Worldwide Library) Harlequin Enterprises, Ltd.

—Reprisal. 1998. (StonyMan Ser.: Vol. 34). per. (*0-373-61918-9*, 0-61918-9, Worldwide Library) Harlequin Enterprises, Ltd.

—Resurrection Day. 1985. (SuperBolan Ser.: No. 3). 384p. mass mkt. o.s.i (*0-373-61403-9*, Harlequin Bks.) Harlequin Enterprises, Ltd.

—Satan's Thrust. 1996. (StonyMan Ser.: Vol. 21). 346p. per. (*0-373-61905-7*, 1-61905-5, Worldwide Library) Harlequin Enterprises, Ltd.

—Silent Invader: (Stony Man #41) 1999. (StonyMan Ser.: Bk. 41). 352p. per. (*0-373-61925-1*, 1-61925-3, Worldwide Library) Harlequin Enterprises, Ltd.

—Skylance. 1996. (StonyMan Ser.: No. 52). per. (*0-373-61909-X*, 1-61909-7, Worldwide Library) Harlequin Enterprises, Ltd.

—Stony Man, No. III. 1991. mass mkt. (*0-373-61887-5*, Harlequin Bks.) Harlequin Enterprises, Ltd.

—Stony Man II. 1991. (StonyMan Ser.: Vol. 2). per. (*0-373-61886-7*, Harlequin Bks.) Harlequin Enterprises, Ltd.

—Stony Man IV. 1992. (StonyMan Ser.: No. 888). per. (*0-373-61888-3*, 1-61888-3, Harlequin Bks.) Harlequin Enterprises, Ltd.

—Stony Man V. 1992. (StonyMan Ser.). mass mkt. o.s.i (*0-373-61889-1*, 1-61889-1, Harlequin Bks.) Harlequin Enterprises, Ltd.

—Stony Man VI. 1993. mass mkt. (*0-373-61890-5*, 1-61890-9, Harlequin Bks.) Harlequin Enterprises, Ltd.

—Stony Man VII. 1993. mass mkt. (*0-373-61891-3*, 1-61891-7, Harlequin Bks.) Harlequin Enterprises, Ltd.

—Stony Man VIII. 1993. mass mkt. (*0-373-61892-1*, 1-61892-5, Harlequin Bks.) Harlequin Enterprises, Ltd.

—Storm Front. 2000. (SuperBolan Ser.: Bk. 73). 352p. per. (*0-373-61473-X*, 1-61473-4, Worldwide Library) Harlequin Enterprises, Ltd.

—Stranglehold. 1998. (StonyMan Ser.: Vol. 36). per. (*0-373-61920-0*, 1-61920-4, Worldwide Library) Harlequin Enterprises, Ltd.

—Stringer. 1995. (StonyMan Ser.: Vol. 18). mass mkt. (*0-373-61902-2*, Harlequin Bks.) Harlequin Enterprises, Ltd.

—Sudden Death. 1987. (SuperBolan Ser.: No. 7). 384p. mass mkt. o.s.i (*0-373-61407-1*, Harlequin Bks.) Harlequin Enterprises, Ltd.

—Sunflash. 1996. (StonyMan Ser.: No. 22). per. (*0-373-61906-5*, 1-61906-3, Worldwide Library) Harlequin Enterprises, Ltd.

—Terms of Survival. 1995. (StonyMan Ser.). 349p. per. (*0-373-61904-9*, 1-61904-8, Worldwide Library) Harlequin Enterprises, Ltd.

—Tropic Heat. 1987. (SuperBolan Ser.: No. 9). 384p. mass mkt. o.s.i (*0-373-61409-8*, Harlequin Bks.) Harlequin Enterprises, Ltd.

—Zero Hour. 1999. (StonyMan Ser.: No. 43). per. (*0-373-61927-8*, 1-61927-9, Worldwide Library) Harlequin Enterprises, Ltd.

Pendleton, Laura & Pendleton, Don. Night of the Jaguar. 1997. (StonyMan Ser.: No. 31). per. (*0-373-61915-4*, 1-61915-4, Worldwide Library) Harlequin Enterprises, Ltd.

**SWEDEN—FICTION**

Almqvist, C. J. L. The Queen's Tiara. 2001. 464p. pap. 15.99 (*1-900850-42-7*) Arcadia Bks. GBR. *Dist:* Consortium Bk. Sales & Distribution.

Bergman, Ingmar. The Best Intentions. Tate, Joan, tr. from SWE. 1994. 304p. pap. 11.95 (*1-55970-249-4*) Arcade Publishing, Inc.

—The Best Intentions. 1993. 304p. 22.95 (*1-55970-207-9*) Arcade Publishing, Inc.

Beskow, Elsa. Pelle's New Suit. Woodburn, Marion L., tr. from SWE. 1989. (Illus.). 32p. (J). reprint ed. 17.95 (*0-86315-092-6*) Floris Bks. GBR. *Dist:* Gryphon Hse., Inc.

Bremer, Frederika. The Neighbours: A Story of Every Day Life. Howitt, Mary, tr. from SWE. 4th ed. 1977. (Short Story Index Reprint Ser.). reprint ed. 28.95 (*0-8369-3835-6*) Ayer Co. Pubs., Inc.

Dahlin, Doris. The Sit-In Game. Tate, Joan, tr. from SWE. 1974. 96p. (J). (gr. 7 up). 4.95 o.p. (*0-670-64730-6*) Viking Penguin.

Ekman, Kerstin. Blackwater. 1999. pap. (*0-312-24519-X*) Picador.

—Blackwater. Tate, Joan, tr. 1996. 448p. pap. 15.00 (*0-312-15247-7*) Picador.

—Under the Snow, Set. 1999. pap. (*0-312-20244-X*, Saint Martin's Griffin) St. Martin's Pr.

Ekman, Kerstin & Tate, Joan. Under the Snow. 1999. 224p. pap. 12.00 o.s.i (*0-312-20038-2*) Picador.

Fredriksson, Marianne. Hannah's Daughters: A Novel of Three Generations. Tate, Joan, tr. 1998. 352p. (YA). (gr. 9 up). 24.00 o.s.i (*0-345-42664-9*) Ballantine Bks.

—Simon's Family: A Novel of Mothers & Sons. 2000. 368p. pap. 14.00 (*0-345-43630-X*) Ballantine Bks.

Fridegard, Jan. Land of Wooden Gods. Bjork, Robert E., tr. from SWE. 1989. (Modern Scandinavian Literature in Translation Ser.: Vol. 1). viii, 210p. text 23.50 o.p. (*0-8032-1970-9*); pap. 8.95 o.p. (*0-8032-6870-X*, Bison Bks.) Univ. of Nebraska Pr.

—People of the Dawn. Bjork, Robert E., tr. from SWE. 1990. (Modern Scandinavian Literature in Translation Ser.). x, 203p. text 25.00 o.p. (*0-8032-1980-6*); pap. 8.95 o.p. (*0-8032-6871-8*) Univ. of Nebraska Pr.

—Sacrificial Smoke. Bjork, Robert E., tr. from SWE. 1990. (Modern Scandinavian Literature in Translation Ser.). x, 191p. text 27.50 o.p. (*0-8032-1981-4*); pap. 9.95 o.p. (*0-8032-6872-6*, Bison Bks.) Univ. of Nebraska Pr.

Fulton, Robin, ed. Preparations for Flight & Other Swedish Stories. 1990. 176p. (Orig.). pap. 19.95 (*0-948259-66-3*) Dufour Editions, Inc.

Gustafsson, Lars. Stories of Happy People. Sandstroem, Yvonne L. & Weinstock, John, trs. from SWE. 1986. 160p. reprint ed. 9.95 (*0-8112-0977-6*); pap. 7.95 o.s.i (*0-8112-0978-4*, NDP616) New Directions Publishing Corp.

—A Tiler's Afternoon. Geddes, Tom, tr. from SWE. 1993. 128p. (Orig.). pap. 8.95 (*0-8112-1240-8*, NDP761) New Directions Publishing Corp.

Heidenstam, Verner. Charles Men. 2000. 252p. E-Book 9.95 (*0-594-02349-1*) 1873 Pr.

Jersild, P. C. The Animal Doctor. Paul, David M. & Paul, Margareta, trs. 1988. iv, 267p. 25.00 o.p. (*0-8032-2573-3*); 267p. pap. 8.95 (*0-8032-7569-2*, Bison Bks.) Univ. of Nebraska Pr.

Johnson, Barry L. The Visit of the Tomten. 1990. 46p. (J). reprint ed. pap. 7.95 o.p. (*0-8358-0439-9*) Upper Room Bks.

Kjell-Olof, Bornemark. The Dividing Line. 1988. 16.95 o.p. (*0-942637-05-4*, Dembner Bks.) Barricade Bks., Inc.

Lagerkvist, Par. The Holy Land. Walford, Naomi, tr. from SWE. 1982. (Illus.). 96p. pap. 2.95 o.p. (*0-394-70819-9*, Vintage) Knopf Publishing Group.

Lagerlof, Selma. From a Swedish Homestead. Brochner, Jessie, tr. 1977. (Short Story Index Reprint Ser.). 26.95 (*0-8369-3463-6*) Ayer Co. Pubs., Inc.

—Jerusalem. 1970. viii, 396p. reprint ed. 128.00 (*0-7426-4477-4*) Classic Bks.

—Jerusalem. Brochner, Jessie, tr. 1970. 396p. reprint ed. 65.00 o.s.i (*0-8371-3120-0*, LAJE, Greenwood Pr.) Greenwood Publishing Group, Inc.

—The Wonderful Adventures of Nils. Howard, Velma S., tr. from SWE. 1995. (Illus.). xii, 219p. (J). (gr. 4-12). pap. text 6.95 (*0-486-28611-8*) Dover Pubns., Inc.

Larsen, Hanna A., ed. Sweden's Best Stories: An Introduction to Swedish Fiction. Stork, Charles W., tr. from SWE. 1977. (Short Story Index Reprint Ser.). reprint ed. 25.95 (*0-8369-4087-3*) Ayer Co. Pubs., Inc.

Lidman, Sara. Naboth's Stone. Tate, Joan, tr. from SWE. 1990. (Norvik Press Series B: No. 7). 262p. (Orig.). pap. 19.95 (*1-870041-12-7*) Norvik Pr. GBR. *Dist:* Dufour Editions, Inc.

Lindgren, Astrid. Emil in the Soup Tureen. Seaton, Lilian, tr. 1989. (Illus.). 96p. (J). (gr. 3-7). 10.95 o.p. (*0-670-82658-8*, Viking Children's Bks.) Penguin Putnam Bks. for Young Readers.

—Lotta's Bike. 1989. (Illus.). 32p. (J). 12.95 o.p. (*91-29-59600-9*) R & S Bks. SWE. *Dist:* Farrar, Straus & Giroux, Holtzbrinck Pubs.

—Seacrow Island. 1969. 5.63 o.p. (*0-670-62592-2*, Viking); 5.95 o.p. (*0-670-62591-4*) Viking Penguin.

Lindgren, Torgny. Light: A Novel. Geddes, Tom, tr. 1993. 288p. 24.00 o.p. (*0-00-271171-0*) HarperCollins Pubs. Ltd. GBR. *Dist:* HarperCollins Pubs.

Lo-Johansson, Ivar. Only a Mother. Bjork, Robert E., tr. from SWE. 1991. (Modern Scandinavian Literature in Translation Ser.). viii, 505p. text 45.00 o.p. (*0-8032-2882-1*) Univ. of Nebraska Pr.

Mankell, Henning. Faceless Killers. 2003. (Illus.). 279p. pap. 17.95 (*1-86046-756-3*) Harvill Pr., The GBR. *Dist:* Trafalgar Square.

—Faceless Killers: A Kurt Wallander Mystery. 2003. 288p. pap. 13.00 (*1-4000-3157-5*, Vintage) Knopf Publishing Group.

—Faceless Killers: A Kurt Wallander Mystery. Murray, Steven T., tr. (Kurt Wallander Mystery Ser.). 288p. 2000. pap. 14.95 (*1-56584-605-2*); 1997. text 23.00 (*1-56584-341-X*) New Pr., The.

—The Fifth Woman: A Kurt Wallander Mystery. Murray, Steven T., tr. from SWE. 2000. (Kurt Wallander Mystery Ser.). 392p. 24.95 (*1-56584-547-1*) New Pr., The.

—Firewall. 2003. 416p. pap. 13.00 (*1-4000-3153-2*, Vintage) Knopf Publishing Group.

—One Step Behind: A Kurt Wallander Mystery. 2003. 448p. pap. 13.00 (*1-4000-3151-6*, Vintage) Knopf Publishing Group.

—One Step Behind: A Kurt Wallander Mystery. Segerberg, Ebba, tr. from SWE. 2001. 416p. text 24.95 (*1-56584-652-4*) New Pr., The.

—Sidetracked: A Kurt Wallander Mystery. Murray, Steven T., tr. from SWE. 2003. (Vintage Crime/Black Lizard Ser.). (Illus.). 432p. reprint ed. pap. 13.00 (*1-4000-3156-7*, Vintage) Knopf Publishing Group.

—Sidetracked: A Kurt Wallander Mystery. Murray, Steven T., tr. (Kurt Wallander Mystery Ser.). 352p. 2000. pap. 14.95 (*1-56584-611-7*); 1999. text 25.00 (*1-56584-507-2*) New Pr., The.

—The White Lioness. Thompson, Laurie, tr. from SWE. 2003. (Kurt Wallander Mystery Ser.). Orig. Title: Den Vita Lejoninnan. (Illus.). 448p. reprint ed. pap. 13.00 (*1-4000-3155-9*, Vintage) Knopf Publishing Group.

—The White Lioness. Thompson, Laurie, tr. from SWE. 1998. (Kurt Wallander Mystery Ser.). Orig. Title: Den Vita Lejoninnan. 942p. 25.00 (*1-56584-424-6*) New Pr., The.

Moberg, Vilhelm. The Emigrants. 1988. 384p. mass mkt. 5.95 o.s.i (*0-446-31492-7*) Warner Bks., Inc.

—Emigrants. 1984. mass mkt. 3.62 (*0-446-38115-2*) Warner Bks., Inc.

—The Emigrants. 1995. (Emigrant Novels Ser.: Bk. 1). xxxiii, 366p. reprint ed. pap. 15.95 (*0-87351-319-3*, Borealis Bk.) Minnesota Historical Society Pr.

—Emigrants. 1999. reprint ed. lib. bdg. 37.95 (*1-56849-312-6*) Buccaneer Bks., Inc.

—Unto a Good Land. 1994. reprint ed. lib. bdg. 29.95 (*1-56849-313-4*) Buccaneer Bks., Inc.

—Unto a Good Land. 1995. (Emigrant Novels Ser.: Bk. 2). xxvii, 372p. reprint ed. pap. 15.95 (*0-87351-320-7*, Borealis Bk.) Minnesota Historical Society Pr.

—Unto a Good Land. 1986. 416p. mass mkt. 4.95 o.s.i (*0-446-31446-3*); 1984. mass mkt. 3.62 (*0-446-38116-0*) Warner Bks., Inc.

Niemi, Mikael. Popular Music from Vittula. 2003. 240p. 21.95 (*1-58322-523-4*) Seven Stories Pr.

Sjowall, Maj & Wahloo, Per. The Abominable Man. 21.95 (*0-89190-378-X*) Amereon, Ltd.

—The Abominable Man. 1993. reprint ed. lib. bdg. 17.95 o.p. (*1-56849-222-7*) Buccaneer Bks., Inc.

—The Abominable Man. 1980. (Martin Beck Detective Ser.). pap. 3.95 o.s.i (*0-394-74273-7*, Vintage) Knopf Publishing Group.

—Cop Killer. 1978. pap. 3.95 o.s.i (*0-394-72444-5*, Vintage) Knopf Publishing Group.

—Cop Killer: The Story of a Crime. 23.95 (*0-89190-377-1*) Amereon, Ltd.

—The Fire Engine That Disappeared. 1977. pap. 4.95 o.s.i (*0-394-72340-6*, Vintage) Knopf Publishing Group.

—The Laughing Policeman. Blair, Alan, tr. from SWE. l.t. ed. 1993. (Nightingale Ser.). 378p. lib. bdg. 16.95 o.p. (*0-8161-5767-7*, Macmillan Reference USA) Gale Group.

—The Laughing Policeman. 1992. 224p. pap. 12.00 (*0-679-74223-9*); 1977. pap. 4.95 o.p. (*0-394-72341-4*) Knopf Publishing Group. (Vintage).

—The Locked Room. 1980. pap. 4.95 o.p. (*0-394-74274-5*, Vintage) Knopf Publishing Group.

—The Locked Room: The Story of a Crime. Austin, Paul B., tr. from SWE. 1992. (Crime - Black Lizard Ser.). 320p. pap. 12.95 (*0-679-74222-0*, Vintage) Knopf Publishing Group.

—The Man on the Balcony. Date not set. lib. bdg. 18.95 (*0-8488-2163-7*) Amereon, Ltd.

—The Man on the Balcony. 1976. pap. 4.50 o.p. (*0-394-71777-5*, Vintage) Knopf Publishing Group.

—The Man on the Balcony: The Story of a Crime. Blair, Alan, tr. 1993. (Vintage Crime/Black Lizard Ser.). 192p. pap. 11.95 (*0-679-74596-3*, Vintage) Knopf Publishing Group.

—The Man Who Went up in Smoke. Date not set. lib. bdg. 18.95 (*0-8488-2164-5*) Amereon, Ltd.

—The Man Who Went up in Smoke. Tate, Joan, tr. from SWE. 1993. (Vintage Crime/Black Lizard Ser.). 192p. pap. 11.00 (*0-679-74597-1*, Vintage) Knopf Publishing Group.

—The Man Who Went up in Smoke. 1976. pap. 3.95 o.p. (*0-394-71778-3*, Vintage) Knopf Publishing Group.

—Murder at the Savoy. 1977. pap. 5.95 o.s.i (*0-394-72342-2*, Vintage) Knopf Publishing Group.

—Roseanna. Roth, Lois, tr. from SWE. 1993. (Vintage Crime/Black Lizard Ser.). 224p. pap. 12.95 (*0-679-74598-X*, Vintage) Knopf Publishing Group.

—Roseanna. 1976. pap. 4.95 o.p. (*0-394-71779-1*, Vintage) Knopf Publishing Group.

—The Terrorists. 1977. pap. 4.95 o.s.i (*0-394-72452-6*, Vintage); 1976. 320p. 7.95 o.p. (*0-394-48532-7*, Pantheon) Knopf Publishing Group.

Soderberg, Hjalmar. Doctor Glas: A Novel. 2002. 160p. pap. 12.00 (*0-385-72267-2*, Anchor) Knopf Publishing Group.

Strindberg, August. The People of Hemso. Schubert, Elspeth H., tr. 1974. 220p. reprint ed. lib. bdg. 35.00 o.p. (*0-8371-7252-7*, STPH, Greenwood Pr.) Greenwood Publishing Group, Inc.

Tunstrom, Goran. The Christmas Oratorio. Hoover, Paul, tr. from SWE. 1994. (Verba Mundi Ser.). 320p. 23.95 (*1-56792-008-X*) Godine, David R. Pub.

Tursten, Helen. Detective Inspector Huss. Murray, Steven T., tr. from SWE. 2003. 320p. 25.00 (*1-56947-303-X*) Soho Pr., Inc.

Uria, Fernando. Carnaval en Canarias, Level 4. 1998. (Leer en Espanol Ser.: Level 4). (SPA., Illus.). 48p. (YA). (gr. 9-12). 8.95 (*84-294-3438-0*, 70321) Santillana USA Publishing Co., Inc.

Von Heidenstam, Verner. Charles Men. 2000. 252p. pap. 9.95 (*0-594-00471-3*) 1873 Pr.

—Charles Men, 2 Vols, Set. Stork, Charles W., tr. from SWE. 1977. (Short Story Index Reprint Ser.). 41.95 (*0-8369-3551-9*) Ayer Co. Pubs., Inc.

—King & His Campaigners. Tegnier, Axel, tr. 1977. (Short Story Index Reprint Ser.). 19.95 (*0-8369-3405-9*) Ayer Co. Pubs., Inc.

**SWITZERLAND—FICTION**

Augsburger, Myron S. I'll See You Again. 1989. 248p. pap. 7.95 o.p. (*0-8361-3489-3*) Herald Pr.

Brookner, Anita. Hotel du Lac. 1995. pap. text 50.95 (*0-582-25406-X*) Addison-Wesley Longman, Ltd. GBR. *Dist:* Trans-Atlantic Pubns., Inc.

—Hotel du Lac. unabr. ed. 2000. audio 34.95 (*0-7451-5810-2*, CAB 217) Chivers Audio Bks. GBR. *Dist:* BBC Audiobooks America.

—Hotel du Lac. 1986. pap. 7.95 o.p. (*0-525-48497-3*, Dutton) Dutton/Plume.

—Hotel du Lac. l.t. ed. 1996. (French Ser.). (FRE.). 320p. pap. 30.99 o.p. (*2-84011-163-2*) Feryane, SA, Editions FRA. *Dist:* Ulverscroft Large Print Bks., Ltd., Ulverscroft Large Print Canada, Ltd.

—Hotel du Lac. 1995. 192p. pap. 12.00 (*0-679-75932-8*, Vintage) Knopf Publishing Group.

—Hotel du Lac. 1986. pap. 6.95 o.p. (*0-525-48204-0*, Obelisk) NAL.

—Hotel du Lac. unabr. ed. 1988. audio 44.00 (*1-55690-236-0*, 88330E7) Recorded Bks., LLC.

Brown, Sandra. Not Even for Love. 1982. mass mkt. (*0-373-44515-6*, Harlequin Bks.) Harlequin Enterprises, Ltd.

—Not Even for Love. 2004. mass mkt. (*0-446-61291-X*, Warner Vision); 2003. 192p. 19.95 (*0-446-53162-6*) Warner Bks., Inc.

Cohen, Albert. Belle du Seigneur. 1986. (FRE.). 110.00 (*0-8288-3464-4*, F73582) French & European Pubns., Inc.

—Belle du Seigneur. 2000. (FRE.). pap. 23.95 (*2-07-040402-1*) Gallimard, Editions FRA. *Dist:* Distribooks, Inc.

—Belle du Seigneur. 1968. (Gallimard Ser.). (FRE.). pap. 44.95 (*2-07-026917-5*) Schoenhof's Foreign Bks., Inc.

—Belle du Seigneur. Coward, David, tr. from FRE. & intro. by. 1998. (Penguin Twentieth-Century Classics Ser.). (SPA.). 992p. pap. 15.95 o.s.i (*0-14-018871-1*, Penguin Classics) Viking Penguin.

—Belle du Seigneur. 1996. 992p. 34.95 o.s.i (*0-670-82187-X*) Viking Penguin.

Dessaix, Robert. Night Letters: A Journey Through Switzerland & Italy. 1999. 276p. pap. 13.00 o.s.i (*0-312-19939-2*) Picador.

—Night Letters: A Journey Through Switzerland & Italy. 1997. 276p. 22.95 (*0-312-16950-7*) St. Martin's Pr.

Durrenmatt, Friedrich. The Pledge. 2000. 176p. pap. 12.00 o.s.i (*0-425-17898-6*) Berkley Publishing Group.

Erdman, Paul. The Swiss Account. abr. ed. 1992. audio 16.95 o.p. (*1-55927-215-5*) Audio Renaissance.

—The Swiss Account. abr. ed. 1996. audio 7.95 (*1-57815-041-8*, 1021) Media Bks., L. L. C.

Erdman, Paul E. The Set up. 1998. 420p. mass mkt. 6.99 (*0-312-96805-1*, St. Martin's Paperbacks); 1997. 352p. 24.95 o.p. (*0-312-15110-1*) St. Martin's Pr.

—The Set Up. l.t. ed. 1997. pap. 24.95 (*1-56895-502-2*, Wheeler Publishing, Inc.) Gale Group.

—The Set Up. abr. ed. 1997. 25.00 o.p. (*0-7871-1332-8*, 695115) NewStar Media, Inc.

—The Swiss Account. 1993. 376p. mass mkt. 5.99 (*0-8125-2016-5*); 1992. 320p. 21.95 o.p. (*0-312-85321-1*) Doherty, Tom Assocs., LLC. (Tor Bks.).

Fell, Doris Elaine. Before Winter Comes. 1994. (Seasons of Intrigue Ser.: Vol. 2). 320p. pap. 9.99 o.p. (*0-89107-815-0*) Crossway Bks.

Findley, Timothy. Pilgrim. 1999. 496p. 25.00 (*0-06-019197-X*) HarperCollins Pubs.

—Pilgrim. 2001. 496p. pap. 14.00 (*0-06-092937-5*, Perennial) HarperTrade.

Fisher, Nancy. Side Effects. 1994. 384p. mass mkt. 4.99 o.s.i (*0-451-18130-1*, Signet Bks.) NAL.

—Side Effects. 2000. 384p. pap. 22.95 (*0-595-09230-6*, Backinprint.com) iUniverse, Inc.

Gerstner, Edna. Idelette: The Life of Mrs. John Calvin. 2nd ed. 1992. 160p. reprint ed. pap. 10.95 o.p. (*1-877611-54-9*) Soli Deo Gloria Pubns.

Gilman, Dorothy. A Palm for Mrs. Pollifax. 1985. 192p. mass mkt. 6.50 (*0-449-20864-8*, Fawcett) Ballantine Bks.

—A Palm for Mrs. Pollifax. (Black Dagger Crime Ser.). 232p. 12.95 o.p. (*0-86220-742-8*) Chivers Pr. GBR. *Dist:* BBC Audiobooks America.

—A Palm for Mrs. Pollifax. 1973. 240p. 5.95 o.p. (*0-385-09134-6*) Doubleday Publishing.

—A Palm for Mrs. Pollifax. l.t. ed. 1994. 281p. lib. bdg. 14.95 o.p. (*0-8161-5353-1*, Macmillan Reference USA) Gale Group.

Gunn, Robin Jones. Until Tomorrow. 2000. (Christy & Todd:College Yr Ser.: Vol. 1). (Illus.). 288p. pap. 11.99 (*0-7642-2272-4*) Bethany Hse. Pubs.

—Until Tomorrow. l.t. ed. 2002. 277p. 24.95 (*0-7862-4455-0*) Thorndike Pr.

Jaeggy, Fleur. Last Vanities. Parks, Tim, tr. from ITA. 1998. 96p. pap. 11.95 (*0-8112-1374-9*, NDP856) New Directions Publishing Corp.

—Sweet Days of Discipline. Parks, Tim, tr. from ITA. 1993. (Ndp Ser.: Vol. 758). 112p. pap. 10.95 (*0-8112-1235-1*, NDP758) New Directions Publishing Corp.

Jouve, Pierre J. & Davis, Lydia. The Desert World. 1996. 130p. 28.00 (*0-8101-6018-8*, Marlboro Pr., The) Northwestern Univ. Pr.

King, Peter. A Healthy Place to Die: A Gourmet Detective Mystery. 2000. (Culinary Mysteries Ser.). 230p. 22.95 (*0-312-24269-7*, Saint Martin's Minotaur) St. Martin's Pr.

Knox, Bill. A Pay-Off in Switzerland. l.t. ed. 1997. (Linford Mystery Library). 320p. pap. 17.99 (*0-7089-5061-2*, Ulverscroft) Thorpe, F. A. Pubs. GBR. *Dist:* Ulverscroft Large Print Bks., Ltd., Ulverscroft Large Print Canada, Ltd.

Koning, Hans. The Affair. 2002. 227p. pap. 14.00 (*1-58838-051-3*) NewSouth, Inc.

Laurie, Hugh. The Gun Seller. 1998. 368p. pap. 14.00 (*0-671-02082-X*, Washington Square Pr.) Simon & Schuster.

—The Gun Seller. 1997. 340p. 24.00 (*1-56947-087-1*) Soho Pr., Inc.

Ludlum, Robert. The Sigma Protocol. 2001. E-Book 27.95 (*1-59061-355-4*) Adobe Systems, Inc.

—The Sigma Protocol. abr. ed. 2001. audio 24.95 (*1-55927-686-X*); audio compact disk 39.95 (*1-55927-687-8*); audio 59.95 (*1-55927-688-6*) Audio Renaissance.

—The Sigma Protocol. l.t. ed. 2002. (Basic Ser.). 897p. 32.95 (*0-7862-3888-7*) Gale Group.

—The Sigma Protocol. E-Book 27.95 (*0-312-70314-7*); 2002. mass mkt. 7.99 (*0-312-98251-8*, St. Martin's Paperbacks); 2002. mass mkt. 7.99 (*0-312-98452-9*, St. Martin's Paperbacks); 2001. 528p. 27.95 o.s.i (*0-312-27688-5*) St. Martin's Pr.

—The Sigma Protocol. l.t. ed. 2002. 29.95 (*0-7862-3893-3*) Thorndike Pr.

MacNeill, Alistair. Damage Control. l.t. ed. 1999. (Magna Large Print Ser.). 432p. (*0-7505-1447-7*) Magna Large Print Bks. GBR. *Dist:* Ulverscroft Large Print Canada, Ltd.

Nabokov, Vladimir. Look at the Harlequins! 1990. (Vintage International Ser.). 272p. pap. 14.00 (*0-679-72728-0*, Vintage) Knopf Publishing Group.

—Look at the Harlequins! (McGraw-Hill Paperbacks). 1981. pap. text 5.95 o.p. (*0-07-045717-4*); 1974. 262p. text 7.95 o.p. (*0-07-045738-7*) McGraw-Hill Cos., The.

O'Reilly, Victor. Games of the Hangman. 1992. 512p. mass mkt. 7.50 o.s.i (*0-425-13456-3*) Berkley Publishing Group.

—Games of the Hangman. 1991. 512p. 19.95 o.p. (*0-8021-1431-8*) Grove/Atlantic, Inc.

Pacinelli, Donna. Heidi. 1988. (J). (ps-3). 5.95 o.p. (*0-88101-079-0*) Unicorn Publishing Hse., Inc., The.

Phillips, Michael. Heathersleigh Homecoming. 1999. (Secrets of Heathersleigh Hall Ser.: Vol. 3). (Illus.). 432p. text 17.99 o.p. (*0-7642-2237-6*);3. pap. 13.99 (*0-7642-2045-4*) Bethany Hse. Pubs.

Plain, Belva. Legacy of Silence. unabr. ed. 2000. audio 84.95 (*0-7540-0329-9*, CAB 1752) Chivers Audio Bks. GBR. *Dist:* BBC Audiobooks America.

—Legacy of Silence. 1999. mass mkt. 7.99 o.s.i (*0-440-29557-2*); 432p. mass mkt. 7.99 (*0-440-22640-6*) Dell Publishing.

—Legacy of Silence. l.t. ed. (Paperback Bestsellers Ser.). 471p. 1999. pap. 27.95 (*0-7862-1512-7*); 1998. 30.95 (*0-7862-1511-9*) Thorndike Pr.

Pye, Michael. The Pieces from Berlin. 2004. 352p. pap. 14.00 (*0-375-71416-2*, Vintage) Knopf Publishing Group.

—The Pieces from Berlin. 2003. 352p. 24.00 (*0-375-41436-3*) Knopf, Alfred A. Inc.

Reich, Christopher. Numbered Account. 2001. E-Book 7.99 (*1-58945-901-6*) Adobe Systems, Inc.

—Numbered Account. 1998. 768p. reprint ed. mass mkt. 7.99 (*0-440-22529-9*) Dell Publishing.

—Numbered Account. abr. ed. 1998. audio 24.95 (*0-553-47956-3*, RH Audio) Random Hse. Audio Publishing Group.

—Numbered Account. 1999. E-Book 7.99 (*0-440-33405-5*) Random Hse., Inc.

—Numbered Account, unabr. ed. 1998. audio 125.00 (*0-7887-1972-6*, 95359E7) Recorded Bks., LLC.

—Numbered Account. l.t. ed. 1998. (Basic Ser.). 896p. 30.95 (*0-7862-1505-4*) Thorndike Pr.

Schaeffer, Frank. Saving Grandma. 1997. 368p. pap. 14.00 o.s.i (*0-425-15776-8*) Berkley Publishing Group.

Schreiner, Samuel A., Jr. Angelica. 1978. 9.95 o.p. (*0-87795-194-2*, Morrow, William & Co.) Morrow/Avon.

Shaw, Patricia. Never Paint a Stranger. 1989. 15.95 o.p. (*0-312-93182-4*, Tor Bks.) Doherty, Tom Assocs., LLC.

Shelley, Mary Wollstonecraft. Frankenstein. l.t. unabr. ed. 2001. (Large Print Classics Ser.). xv, 283p. pap. 9.95 (*0-486-41562-7*) Dover Pubns., Inc.

Silva, Daniel. The English Assassin. l.t. ed. 2002. (Wheeler Large Print Book Ser.). 29.95 (*1-58724-185-4*, Wheeler Publishing, Inc.) Gale Group.

—The English Assassin. 2003. 416p. reprint ed. mass mkt. 7.99 (*0-451-20818-8*, Signet Bks.) NAL.

—The English Assassin. 2002. 400p. 25.95 o.s.i (*0-399-14851-5*) Putnam Publishing Group, The.

Spyri, Johanna. Heidi. 1989. (Grosset & Dunlap Junior Classics Ser.). 128p. (J). (gr. 2-6). 2.95 o.p. (*0-448-11076-8*, Grosset & Dunlap) Penguin Putnam Bks. for Young Readers.

Spyri, Johanna & Blaisdell, Robert. Heidi. 1998. (Illus.). (J). 1.00 (*0-486-40166-9*) Dover Pubns., Inc.

Spyri, Jonanna. Heidi. E-Book 2.49 (*1-58627-596-8*) Electric Umbrella Publishing.

Szczypiorski, Andrzej. Self-Portrait with Woman. Johnson, Bill, tr. 1996. 224p. 21.00 o.p. (*0-8021-1567-5*, Grove Pr.) Grove/Atlantic, Inc.

—Self-Portrait with Woman. Johnston, Bill, tr. from POL. 1997. 256p. reprint ed. pap. 12.00 (*0-8021-3488-2*, Grove Pr.) Grove/Atlantic, Inc.

Thor, Brad. The Lions of Lucerne. 2002. 432p. 25.00 (*0-7434-3673-3*, Atria); (Illus.). 544p. reprint ed. pap. 6.99 (*0-7434-3674-1*, Pocket Star) Simon & Schuster.

—The Lions of Lucerne. abr. ed. 2002. audio 26.00 (*0-7435-2103-X*); audio compact disk 30.00 (*0-7435-2104-8*) Simon & Schuster Audio. (Simon & Schuster Audioworks).

Weber, Katherine. Objects in Mirror Are Closer Than They Appear. 1996. 272p. pap. 12.00 (*0-312-14383-4*) Picador.

Webster, Noah. A Pay-Off in Switzerland. 1977. 6.95 o.p. (*0-385-13246-8*) Doubleday Publishing.

Williams, Amanda K. A Singular Spy. 1992. 192p. pap. 8.95 o.p. (*1-56280-008-6*) Naiad Pr., Inc.

**SYDNEY (N.S.W.)—FICTION**

Anderson, Jessica. The Only Daughter. (Fiction Ser.). 256p. 1986. pap. 6.95 o.p. (*0-14-006333-1*, Penguin Bks.); 1985. 15.95 o.p. (*0-670-80431-2*) Viking Penguin.

—Tirra Lirra by the River. 1984. 16p. pap. 8.95 o.p. (*0-14-006945-3*, Penguin Bks.) Viking Penguin.

Clancy, Tom. Rainbow Six. 1999. 7.99 (*0-425-17005-5*); 912p. reprint ed. mass mkt. 8.50 (*0-425-17034-9*) Berkley Publishing Group.

—Rainbow Six. l.t. ed. 1999. pap. 27.95 o.p. (*0-7838-0160-2*, Macmillan Reference USA) Gale Group.

—Rainbow Six. 1998. 752p. 27.95 (*0-399-14390-4*); 800p. 150.00 (*0-399-14413-7*) Penguin Group (USA) Inc. (G. P. Putnam's Sons).

—Rainbow Six. l.t. ed. 1998. 800p. pap. 27.95 (*0-375-70324-1*) Random Hse. Large Print.

—Rainbow Six. 1998. 14.55 (*0-606-17207-6*) Turtleback Bks.

Cleary, Jon. Autumn Maze: A Scobie Malone Mystery. 1995. 320p. 22.00 o.p. (*0-688-13697-4*, Morrow, William & Co.) Morrow/Avon.

—Babylon South. 1990. 352p. 19.95 o.p. (*0-688-08976-3*, Morrow, William & Co.) Morrow/Avon.

—Bleak Spring. l.t. ed. 1994. 416p. lib. bdg. 22.95 (*0-8161-7437-7*, Macmillan Reference USA) Gale Group.

—Bleak Spring. 1994. 22.00 o.p. (*0-688-12332-5*, Morrow, William & Co.) Morrow/Avon.

—Dark Summer. 1993. 269p. 20.00 o.p. (*0-688-11414-8*, Morrow, William & Co.) Morrow/Avon.

—A Different Turf. unabr. ed. 2001. audio (*1-86340-796-0*, 580336) Bolinda Publishing Pty, Ltd.

—Dilemma. l.t. ed. 2000. (G. K. Hall Core Ser.). 393p. 28.95 (*0-7838-9069-9*, Macmillan Reference USA) Gale Group.

—Dilemma. 2000. 272p. 23.00 (*0-688-17192-3*, Morrow, William & Co.) Morrow/Avon.

—Dragons at the Party. 1988. 320p. 17.95 o.p. (*0-688-07487-1*, Morrow, William & Co.) Morrow/Avon.

—Dragons at the Party. unabr. ed. 1999. audio 79.95 Soundings, Ltd. GBR. *Dist:* Ulverscroft Large Print Bks., Ltd.

—Dragons at the Party. l.t. ed. 1988. (Charnwood Large Print Ser.). 464p. 29.99 o.p. (*0-7089-8474-6*, Ulverscroft) Thorpe, F. A. Pubs. GBR. *Dist:* Ulverscroft Large Print Bks., Ltd., Ulverscroft Large Print Canada, Ltd.

—Endpeace: A Scobie Malone Mystery. 1997. 272p. 23.00 (*0-688-14710-0*, Morrow, William & Co.) Morrow/Avon.

—Endpeace: A Scobie Malone Mystery. l.t. ed. 1998. (Core Ser.). 421p. 28.95 (*0-7838-8369-2*) Thorndike Pr.

—Five Ring Circus, unabr. ed. 2001. audio (*1-86442-364-1*, 590270) Bolinda Publishing Pty, Ltd.

—Five-Ring Circus: Suspense Down Under. 1999. 256p. 23.00 (*0-688-16468-4*, Morrow, William & Co.) Morrow/Avon.

—Five-Ring Circus: Suspense down Under. l.t. ed. 1999. (Core Ser.). 399p. 28.95 (*0-7838-8617-9*) Thorndike Pr.

—The High Commissioner. audio 33.95 o.p. Ulverscroft Audio (U.S.A.).

—Murder Song. l.t. ed. 1992. pap. 21.95 o.p. (*0-7927-1183-1*); 23.95 o.p. (*0-7927-1182-3*, CH0243) BBC Audiobooks America.

—Murder Song. 1990. 288p. 18.95 o.p. (*0-688-09458-9*, Morrow, William & Co.) Morrow/Avon.

—Now & Then, Amen. 1989. 320p. 18.95 o.p. (*0-688-08390-0*, Morrow, William & Co.) Morrow/Avon.

—Now & Then, Amen. l.t. ed. 1989. (Charnwood Large Print Ser.). 29.99 o.p. (*0-7089-8528-9*, Charnwood) Thorpe, F. A. Pubs. GBR. *Dist:* Ulverscroft Large Print Bks., Ltd., Ulverscroft Large Print Canada, Ltd.

—Pride's Harvest. 1991. (Scobie Malone Mystery Ser.). 336p. 20.00 o.p. (*0-688-10408-8*, Morrow, William & Co.) Morrow/Avon.

—Pride's Harvest. unabr. ed. 2001. audio 69.95 (*1-85496-811-4*, 68114) Soundings, Ltd. GBR. *Dist:* Ulverscroft Large Print Bks., Ltd.

—Pride's Harvest. l.t. ed. 1993. (Charnwood Large Print Ser.). 432p. 29.99 o.p. (*0-7089-8690-0*, Charnwood) Thorpe, F. A. Pubs. GBR. *Dist:* Ulverscroft Large Print Bks., Ltd., Ulverscroft Large Print Canada, Ltd.

—Winter Chill. l.t. ed. 1996. 24.95 o.p. (*1-56895-331-3*, Wheeler Publishing, Inc.) Gale Group.

—Winter Chill: A Scobie Malone Mystery. 1996. 269p. 23.00 o.p. (*0-688-14311-3*, Morrow, William & Co.) Morrow/Avon.

English, Robert. More Deaths Than One. 1995. 408p. pap. 5.95 o.p. (*1-86373-651-4*) Independent Pubs. Group.

Geason, Susan. Dogfish. 1993. 208p. (Orig.). pap. 9.95 o.p. (*1-86373-088-5*) Allen & Unwin Pty., Ltd. AUS. *Dist:* Independent Pubs. Group.

—Sharkbait. 1994. 176p. pap. 9.95 o.p. (*1-86373-632-8*) Independent Pubs. Group.

—Shaved Fish. 1993. 168p. (Orig.). pap. 9.95 o.p. (*0-04-442274-1*) Allen & Unwin Pty., Ltd. AUS. *Dist:* Independent Pubs. Group.

Halligan, Marion. The Golden Dress. 1999. 380p. (*0-14-027302-6*) Penguin Group (USA) Inc.

Jaivin, Linda. Miles Walker, You're Dead. 2001. 272p. pap. 13.95 (*0-312-28274-5*, Saint Martin's Griffin) St. Martin's Pr.

Keneally, Thomas. An Angel in Australia. 2002. 336p. o.s.i (*1-86471-001-2*) Doubleday Publishing.

Lower, Lennie. Here's Luck. 2001. 286p. 14.95 (*1-85375-428-5*) Prion GBR. *Dist:* Trafalgar Square.

McKinley, Tamara. Windflowers: A Novel of Australia. 2002. 480p. 26.95 (*0-312-30750-0*) St. Martin's Pr.

McLaren, Philip. Scream Black Murder: A WorldKrime Mystery. 2002. 288p. 21.95 (*1-890768-42-1*, Intrigue Pr.) Corvus Publishing.

McNab, Claire. Cop Out. 1991. (Detective Inspector Carol Ashton Mysteries Ser.: Vol. 4). 224p. (Orig.). pap. 10.95 (*0-941483-84-3*) Naiad Pr., Inc.

—Death down Under. 1990. (Detective Inspector Carol Ashton Mysteries Ser.: Vol. 3). 240p. pap. 11.95 (*0-941483-39-8*) Naiad Pr., Inc.

—Fatal Reunion. 1989. (Detective Inspector Carol Ashton Mysteries Ser.: Vol. 2). 224p. pap. 11.95 (*0-941483-40-1*) Naiad Pr., Inc.

—Lessons in Murder. 1988. (Detective Inspector Carol Ashton Mysteries Ser.: Vol. 1). 216p. pap. 11.95 (*0-941483-14-2*) Naiad Pr., Inc.

Naylor, Clare. Dog Handling. 2004. 336p. mass mkt. 6.99 (*0-345-46539-3*); 2002. 352p. pap. 12.95 (*0-345-45338-7*) Ballantine Bks.

Ng, Lillian. Swallowing Clouds. 1999. 306p. o.p. (*0-88001-644-2*, Ecco) HarperTrade.

Niles, Chris. Run Time. 1999. 272p. reprint ed. mass mkt. 5.99 o.s.i (*0-425-17119-1*, Prime Crime) Berkley Publishing Group.

Pike, Arthur L. A River to Cross. 2001. 192p. pap. 17.50 o.s.i (*0-9578735-1-4*) International Specialized Bk. Services.

Ryan, Richard. Funnelweb. 1997. 339p. (*0-7329-0888-4*) Macmillan Education Australia.

**SYRACUSE (N.Y.)—FICTION**

Abu-Jaber, Diana. Arabian Jazz: A Novel. 2003. 384p. pap. 14.95 (*0-393-32422-2*) Norton, W. W. & Co., Inc.

Block, Barbara. Chutes & Adders. 1995. mass mkt. 4.99 o.s.i (*0-8217-4997-8*) Kensington Publishing Corp.

—Chutes & Adders: A Robin Light Mystery. 1994. 320p. mass mkt. 16.95 o.s.i (*0-8217-4533-6*) Kensington Publishing Corp.

—Endangered Species: A Robin Light Mystery. 1999. (Robin Light Mystery Ser.). 320p. 20.00 o.s.i (*1-57566-449-6*, Kensington Bks.) Kensington Publishing Corp.

—In Plain Sight: A Robin Light Mystery. (Robin Light Mystery Ser.). 1997. 336p. mass mkt. 5.50 o.s.i (*1-57566-199-3*); 1996. 321p. 18.95 o.p. (*1-57566-059-8*, Kensington Bks.) Kensington Publishing Corp.

—The Scent of Murder. 336p. 1999. mass mkt. 5.99 o.s.i (*1-57566-331-7*); 1997. 18.95 o.s.i (*1-57566-195-0*) Kensington Publishing Corp.

—Twister. 1996. (Robin Light Mystery Ser.). 304p. mass mkt. 4.99 (*1-57566-062-8*, Kensington Bks.) Kensington Publishing Corp.

—Twister: A Robin Light Mystery. 1995. mass mkt. 16.95 o.p. (*0-8217-4989-7*, Zebra Bks.) Kensington Publishing Corp.

—Vanishing Act. 1998. (Robin Light Mystery Ser.). 352p. 20.00 o.s.i (*1-57566-326-0*, Kensington Bks.) Kensington Publishing Corp.

—Vanishing Act: A Robin Light Mystery. 1999. (Robin Light Mystery Ser.). 320p. mass mkt. 5.99 (*1-57566-442-9*) Kensington Publishing Corp.

Litman, Robert B. Allergy Shots. 1993. 254p. (Orig.). pap. text 9.95 (*0-918921-04-X*) Ivy League Pr., Inc.

Oates, Joyce Carol. I'll Take You There. 304p. 2003. pap. 13.95 (*0-06-050118-9*); 2002. 25.95 (*0-06-050117-0*) HarperTrade. (Ecco).

# T

**TAHITI—FICTION**

Elkins, Aaron. Twenty Blue Devils. unabr. ed. 2000. audio 59.95 (*0-7927-2218-3*, CSL 107) Chivers Audio Bks. GBR. *Dist:* BBC Audiobooks America.

—Twenty Blue Devils. l.t. ed. 1997. (Cloak & Dagger Ser.). 421p. 25.95 o.p. (*0-7862-1091-5*) Thorndike Pr.

—Twenty Blue Devils. 1997. 288p. mass mkt. 5.99 o.s.i (*0-446-40526-4*); 22.00 o.p. (*0-89296-467-7*) Warner Bks., Inc.

Loti, Pierre. Tahiti. 2002. (Kegan Paul Asia Library). (Illus.). 200p. 76.50 (*0-7103-0821-3*) Kegan Paul International Ltd. GBR. *Dist:* Columbia Univ. Pr.

Maugham, W. Somerset. The Moon & Sixpence. 22.95 (*0-8488-2653-1*) Amereon, Ltd.

—The Moon & Sixpence. 1977. (Works of W. Somerset Maugham). reprint ed. 23.95 (*0-405-07816-1*) Ayer Co. Pubs., Inc.

—The Moon & Sixpence. 1995. 256p. mass mkt. 4.95 o.s.i (*0-553-21441-1*, Bantam Classics) Bantam Bks.

—The Moon & Sixpence. unabr. ed. 1995. (Thrift Editions Ser.). 176p. reprint ed. pap. text 2.00 (*0-486-28731-9*) Dover Pubns., Inc.

—The Moon & Sixpence. 2002. 244p. 18.99 (*1-4043-1902-6*); per. 13.99 (*1-4043-1903-4*) IndyPublish.com.

—The Moon & Sixpence. 2000. (Dover Thrift Editions Ser.). 288p. pap. 12.00 (*0-375-72456-7*, Vintage) Knopf Publishing Group.

—The Moon & Sixpence. 1993. 288p. mass mkt. 4.95 o.s.i (*0-451-52567-1*, Signet Classics) NAL.

—The Moon & Sixpence. 1998. 242p. reprint ed. lib. bdg. 25.00 (*1-58287-050-0*) North Bks.

—The Moon & Sixpence. 1997. (Ghosts of Fear Street Ser.: Vol. 22). 128p. (J). (gr. 3-6). pap. 3.99 (*0-671-00851-X*, Aladdin) Simon & Schuster Children's Publishing.

—The Moon & Sixpence. unabr. ed. 1997. 156p. reprint ed. pap. 14.95 o.p. (*1-57002-016-7*) University Publishing Hse., Inc.

—The Moon & Sixpence. (Twentieth Century Classics Ser.). 224p. 1993. 9.95 (*0-14-018597-6*, Penguin Classics); 1977. pap. 5.95 o.p. (*0-14-000468-8*, Penguin Bks.) Viking Penguin.

Patterson, Rosemary I. Mission Mururoa: An Adventure Novel Set in Tahiti. 2001. 180p. E-Book 8.00 (*0-7388-6400-5*) Xlibris Corp.

**TAHOE, LAKE (CALIF. AND NEV.)—FICTION**

O'Shaughnessy, Perri. Acts of Malice. abr. ed. 1999. audio 17.95 o.p. (*1-56740-852-4*, 1759, Nova Audio Bks.); audio 73.25 (*1-56740-668-8*, 1758, Unabridged Library Editions); audio 26.95 (*1-56740-442-1*, 1757, Bookcassette) Brilliance Audio.

—Acts of Malice. 2000. 480p. mass mkt. 7.99 (*0-440-22581-7*) Dell Publishing.

—Acts of Malice. l.t. ed. 1999. 503p. 27.95 (*1-56895-766-1*, Wheeler Publishing, Inc.) Gale Group.

—Acts of Malice, Set. abr. ed. 1999. audio 17.95. audio 73.25 Highsmith Inc.

—Breach of Promise. 1999. 560p. mass mkt. 7.99 (*0-440-22473-X*) Broadway Bks.

—Breach of Promise. l.t. ed. 1999. pap. 23.95 (*1-56895-808-0*, Wheeler Publishing, Inc.) Gale Group.

—Invasion of Privacy. 1997. 544p. mass mkt. 7.99 (*0-440-22069-6*) Dell Publishing.

—Motion to Suppress. 1996. 480p. mass mkt. 7.99 (*0-440-22068-8*) Dell Publishing.

—Motion to Suppress. l.t. ed. 1999. pap. 24.95 (*1-56895-755-6*, Wheeler Publishing, Inc.) Gale Group.

—Move to Strike. 2001. 512p. reprint ed. mass mkt. 7.99 (*0-440-22582-5*) Dell Publishing.

—Move to Strike. l.t. ed. 2000. (Wheeler Large Print Book Ser.). 540p. 27.95 (*1-56895-988-5*, Wheeler Publishing, Inc.) Gale Group.

—Obstruction of Justice. abr. ed. 1998. audio 7.99 o.s.i (*1-56740-240-2*, 1333, Paperback Nova Audio Bks.); 1997. audio 16.95 o.p. (*1-56740-753-6*, 498, Nova Audio Bks.); 1997. audio 89.25 (*1-56740-553-3*, 969, Unabridged Library Editions); 1997. audio 25.95 (*1-56100-774-9*, 201, Bookcassette) Brilliance Audio.

—Obstruction of Justice. 1998. 512p. reprint ed. mass mkt. 7.99 (*0-440-22472-1*) Dell Publishing.

—Obstruction of Justice. 1997. 400p. 23.95 o.s.i (*0-385-31870-7*) Doubleday Publishing.

—Obstruction of Justice. l.t. ed. 2000. 27.95 (*1-56895-845-5*, Wheeler Publishing, Inc.) Gale Group.

—Obstruction of Justice. unabr. ed. 1999. audio 89.25 Highsmith Inc.

**TAIPEI (TAIWAN)—FICTION**

Lu, Alvin. The Hell Screens: A Novel. 2000. 196p. 24.00 (*1-56858-167-X*, No Exit Pr.) Four Walls Eight Windows.

**TAIWAN—FICTION**

Chang, Ta-chun. Wild Kids: Two Novels about Growing Up. Berry, Michael, tr. from CHI. 2000. (Modern Chinese Literature from Taiwan Ser.). (CHI & ENG., Illus.). xii, 255p. 22.95 (*0-231-12096-6*) Columbia Univ. Pr.

Chang, Ta-chun, contrib. by. Wild Kids: Two Novels About Growing Up. 2002. (Modern Chinese Literature from Taiwan Ser.). (CHI & ENG., Illus.). 280p. pap. 15.95 (*0-231-12097-4*) Columbia Univ. Pr.

Ch'ing-wen, Cheng. Three-Legged Horse. (Modern Literature from Taiwan Ser.). 240p. 1999. (Illus.). 25.50 (*0-231-11386-2*); 2000. reprint ed. pap. 15.95 (*0-231-11387-0*) Columbia Univ. Pr.

Dalton, John. Heaven Lake. 2005. 416p. pap. 14.00 (*0-7432-4635-7*, Scribner) Simon & Schuster.

—Heaven Lake: A Novel. 2004. 464p. 26.00 (*0-7432-4634-9*, Scribner) Simon & Schuster.

Hsiao, Li-hung. A Thousand Moons on a Thousand Rivers. Wu, Michelle, tr. from CHI. 2000. (Modern Chinese Literature from Taiwan Ser.). xi, 304p. 24.95 (*0-231-11792-2*) Columbia Univ. Pr.

Hunt, E. Howard. Dragon Teeth. 1997. 480p. 26.95 o.s.i (*1-55611-523-7*) Fine, Donald I. Bks.

Hyde, Anthony. Formosa Straits. 1996. 341p. mass mkt. 5.99 o.s.i (*0-449-22576-3*, Fawcett) Ballantine Bks.

Lu, Alvin. The Hell Screens: A Novel. 2000. 196p. 24.00 (*1-56858-167-X*, No Exit Pr.) Four Walls Eight Windows.

Robinson, Patrick. The Shark Mutiny. 2002. 512p. mass mkt. 7.99 (*0-06-103066-X*); 2001. (Illus.). 480p. 26.00 (*0-06-019631-9*) HarperCollins Pubs.

—The Shark Mutiny. l.t. ed. 2001. 672p. 25.00 (*0-06-621021-6*, HarperLargePrint) HarperTrade.

—The Shark Mutiny. 2001. 385p. o.s.i (*0-7126-8038-1*) Random Hse. of Canada, Ltd.

**TAVISCOMBE (ENGLAND: IMAGINARY PLACE)—FICTION**

Holt, Hazel. The Cruellest Month. l.t. ed. 1992. 240p. 14.95 o.p. (*0-7451-1491-1*, Macmillan Reference USA) Gale Group.

—The Cruellest Month. 1992. (Mrs. Malory Mystery Ser.). 224p. mass mkt. 4.50 o.s.i (*0-451-40313-4*, Onyx) NAL.

—The Cruellest Month. 1991. 15.95 o.p. (*0-312-05840-3*, Saint Martin's Minotaur) St. Martin's Pr.

—Death among Friends, 1 vol. 1999. (Sheila Malory Mysteries Ser.). 256p. mass mkt. 5.99 o.s.i (*0-451-19691-0*) NAL.

—Death among Friends. l.t. ed. 1999. (General Ser.). 232p. pap. 24.95 (*0-7862-1979-3*); (*0-7540-3816-5*); (*0-7540-3815-7*) Thorndike Pr.

—Mrs. Malory: Death of a Dean. l.t. ed. 1996. (Mrs. Malory Mystery Ser.). 194p. 22.95 o.s.i (*0-525-94150-9*, Dutton) Dutton/Plume.

—Mrs. Malory: Death of a Dean. l.t. ed. 1996. pap. 23.95 (*1-56895-392-5*, Wheeler Publishing, Inc.) Gale Group.

—Mrs. Malory: Death of a Dean. 1997. (Sheila Malory Mysteries Ser.). 176p. mass mkt. 5.99 o.s.i (*0-451-19109-9*) NAL.

—Mrs. Malory: Detective in Residence. 1994. (Mrs. Malory Mystery Ser.). 192p. 18.95 o.p. (*0-525-93903-2*) Dutton/Plume.

—Mrs. Malory: Detective in Residence. 1995. (Sheila Malory Mysteries Ser.). 256p. mass mkt. 4.99 o.s.i (*0-451-18017-8*, Signet Bks.) NAL.

—Mrs. Malory & the Fatal Legacy: A Sheila Malory Mystery. 2000. (Sheila Malory Mysteries Ser.). 256p. mass mkt. 5.99 (*0-451-20002-0*, Signet Bks.) NAL.

—Mrs. Malory & the Festival Murders. 1994. (Mrs. Malory Mystery Ser.). 224p. mass mkt. 3.99 o.s.i (*0-451-18015-1*, Signet Bks.) NAL.

—Mrs. Malory & the Festival Murders. 1993. 171p. 17.95 o.p. (*0-312-08852-3*, Saint Martin's Minotaur) St. Martin's Pr.

—Mrs. Malory & the Only Good Lawyer. 1997. (Mrs. Malory Mystery Ser.). 192p. 22.95 o.p. (*0-525-94151-7*) Dutton/Plume.

—Mrs. Malory & the Only Good Lawyer. 1998. (Sheila Malory Mysteries Ser.). 256p. mass mkt. 5.99 o.s.i (*0-451-19264-8*, Signet Bks.) NAL.

—Mrs. Malory Investigates. 1991. (Mrs. Malory Mystery Ser.). 224p. mass mkt. 5.50 o.s.i (*0-451-40269-3*, Onyx) NAL.

—Mrs. Malory Investigates. 1990. 192p. 14.95 o.p. (*0-312-03894-1*, Saint Martin's Minotaur) St. Martin's Pr.

—Mrs. Malory Wonders Why. 1995. (Mrs. Malory Mystery Ser.). 192p. 20.95 o.s.i (*0-525-93932-6*, Dutton) Dutton/Plume.

—Mrs. Malory Wonders Why. 1996. (Sheila Malory Mysteries Ser.). 256p. mass mkt. 5.50 o.s.i (*0-451-18286-3*) NAL.

—Mrs. Malory's Shortest Journey. 1995. (Mrs. Malory Mystery Ser.). 256p. mass mkt. 4.99 o.s.i (*0-451-18395-9*, Signet Bks.) NAL.

—The Shortest Journey: A Mrs. Malory Mystery. l.t. ed. 1995. 232p. pap. 17.95 o.p. *(0-7838-1138-1*, Macmillan Reference USA) Gale Group.

—The Shortest Journey: A Mrs. Malory Mystery. 1994. 224p. 19.95 o.p. *(0-312-11140-1*, Saint Martin's Minotaur) St. Martin's Pr.

**TEKUMEL (IMAGINARY PLACE)—FICTION**

Barker, M. A. Flamesong. 1985. (Empire of the Petal Throne Ser.). mass mkt. 3.50 o.p. *(0-88677-076-9)* DAW Bks., Inc.

—The Man of Gold. 1984. (Empire of the Petal Throne Ser.). mass mkt. 3.95 o.p. *(0-88677-082-3)* DAW Bks., Inc.

**TENNESSEE—FICTION**

Adams, Deborah. All the Blood Relations. 1996. mass mkt. 5.50 o.s.i *(0-345-40378-9)* Ballantine Bks.

—All the Crazy Winters. 1992. (Holiday Mysteries Ser.). mass mkt. 5.50 o.s.i *(0-345-37076-7*, Ballantine Bks.) Ballantine Bks.

—All the Dark Disguises. 1993. mass mkt. 4.99 o.s.i *(0-345-37765-6)* Ballantine Bks.

—All the Deadly Beloved. 1995. mass mkt. 5.99 *(0-345-39222-1)*; 240p. pap. 15.00 *(0-345-47170-9)* Ballantine Bks.

—All the Great Pretenders. 1991. (Orig.). mass mkt. 5.99 o.s.i *(0-345-37075-9*, Ballantine Bks.) Ballantine Bks.

—All the Hungry Mothers. 1994. (Southern Mysteries Ser.). mass mkt. 4.99 o.s.i *(0-345-38552-7)* Ballantine Bks.

—All the Hungry Mothers. 1999. 192p. pap. 14.95 *(1-57072-122-X)*; reprint ed. 24.95 *(1-57072-106-8)* Overmountain Pr. (Silver Dagger Mysteries).

Alther, Lisa. Kinflicks. 1996. 528p. pap. 13.95 o.p. *(0-452-27677-2*, Plume) Dutton/Plume.

—Kinflicks. 1977. mass mkt. 2.25 o.p. *(0-451-07390-8)*; mass mkt. 2.50 o.p. *(0-451-08445-4)*; mass mkt. 2.75 o.p. *(0-451-08984-7)*; mass mkt. 2.95 o.p. *(0-451-09474-3)*; mass mkt. 3.50 o.p. *(0-451-11241-5)*; mass mkt. 3.95 o.p. *(0-451-11985-1)*; 528p. reprint ed. mass mkt. 5.99 o.p. *(0-451-15685-4)* NAL. (Signet Bks.).

—Kinflicks. 1976. 8.95 o.p. *(0-394-49836-4*, Knopf Bks. for Young Readers) Random Hse. Children's Bks.

—Original Sins. 1996. 608p. pap. 13.95 o.p. *(0-452-27676-4*, Plume) Dutton/Plume.

—Original Sins. 1981. 608p. 13.95 o.s.i *(0-394-51685-0)* Knopf, Alfred A. Inc.

—Original Sins. 1982. mass mkt. 4.50 o.p. *(0-451-13966-6*, AE1448); mass mkt. 3.95 o.p. *(0-451-11448-5)*; mass mkt. 1.95 o.p. *(0-451-13372-2)*; 576p. reprint ed. mass mkt. 5.99 o.p. *(0-451-15517-3)* NAL. (Signet Bks.).

Armistead, Bob. Warrior Forrest. 1998. (Illus.). 268p. text 24.00 *(0-9660098-0-0)* Armistead, Bob.

Arvin, Reed. The Wind in the Wheat. 1994. (YA). 12.99 o.p. *(0-7852-8146-0)* Nelson, Thomas Inc.

Atkins, Ace. Dark End of the Street. 2004. 416p. mass mkt. 7.50 *(0-06-000461-4*, HarperTorch); 2002. 336p. 23.95 *(0-06-000460-6*, Morrow, William & Co.) Morrow/Avon.

Belanus, Betty J. Seasonal: A Novel. 2002. 192p. *(0-9716852-0-7)* Round Barn Pr.

Bell, Madison Smartt. A Soldier's Joy. 1989. 480p. 19.95 o.p. *(0-89919-836-8)* Houghton Mifflin Co.

—A Soldier's Joy. 1990. 480p. pap. 11.95 o.s.i *(0-14-013359-3*, Penguin Bks.) Viking Penguin.

Blaylock, Ronald K. Charity's Reward. 2002. 290p. 24.95 *(0-9716965-5-1)* Knob Hill Pr.

Bonner, Sherwood. Dialect Tales. 1977. (Black Heritage Library Collection). reprint ed. 23.95 *(0-8369-8998-8)* Ayer Co. Pubs., Inc.

—Dialect Tales & Other Stories. Frank, William L., ed. 1991. 164p. pap. 26.95 *(0-8084-0427-X)* Rowman & Littlefield Pubs., Inc.

Brooks, Skip. Monteith's Mountains: Death Stalks the Southern Appalachians. 2002. (Illus.). 288p. 21.95 *(0-9713045-4-8)* High Country Pubs., Ltd.

Brown, Larry. The Rabbit Factory: A Novel. 2003. 352p. 25.00 o.s.i *(0-7432-5004-4*, Free Pr.) Simon & Schuster.

Burton, Linda, ed. Stories from Tennessee. 1983. 432p. text 32.50 o.p. *(0-87049-376-0)*; pap. 16.95 o.p. *(0-87049-377-9)* Univ. of Tennessee Pr.

Carter, Alden R. Bright Starry Banner: A Novel of the Civil War. 2004. 488p. 27.00 *(1-56947-355-2)* Soho Pr., Inc.

Clifford, Emmett. Night Whispers: A Novel of Evil. 1998. 448p. 22.95 *(1-888952-81-4)* Cumberland Hse. Publishing.

Connor, Beverly. Airtight Case. 2000. (Lindsay Chamberlain Mysteries Ser.). (Illus.). 423p. 22.95 *(1-58182-123-9)* Cumberland Hse. Publishing.

—Questionable Remains. 2001. (WWL Mystery Ser.: No. 385). 248p. mass mkt. *(0-373-26385-6*, 1-26385-4, Worldwide Library) Harlequin Enterprises, Ltd.

Cook, Gary W. Oakseeds: Stories from the Land. 1993. (Outdoor Tennessee Ser.). (Illus.). 208p. (C). pap. 17.95 *(0-87049-802-9)*; text 30.00 *(0-87049-801-0)* Univ. of Tennessee Pr.

Crawford, Dianna. An Echo of Hope. 2003. (HeartQuest Ser.). 336p. pap. 9.99 *(0-8423-6012-3)* Tyndale Hse. Pubs.

—Freedom's Promise. 2001. (HeartQuest Ser.). 336p. pap. 9.99 *(0-8423-1918-2)* Tyndale Hse. Pubs.

—A Home in the Valley. 2002. (HeartQuest Ser.). 352p. pap. 9.99 *(0-8423-6010-7)* Tyndale Hse. Pubs.

—Lady of the River. 2003. (HeartQuest Ser.). 352p. pap. 9.99 *(0-8423-6011-5)* Tyndale Hse. Pubs.

Darty, Peggy. Angel Valley. 1995. (Palisades Pure Romance Ser.). 262p. pap. 9.99 o.s.i *(0-88070-778-X*, Palisades) Multnomah Pubs., Inc.

Delffs, Dudley J. Forgiving August. 1993. 254p. (Orig.). pap. 10.00 o.p. *(0-89109-747-3)* Pinon Pr.

—The Judas Tree. 1999. (Father Grif Mystery Ser.: Vol. 2). 320p. pap. 10.99 o.p. *(0-7642-2087-X)* Bethany Hse. Pubs.

—The Judas Tree. l.t. ed. 2002. 557p. 25.95 *(0-7862-4245-0)* Gale Group.

Donald, Elsie Burch. Nashborough. 2002. 560p. mass mkt. 7.99 *(0-06-103162-3)*; 2001. 416p. 26.00 *(0-06-018633-X)* HarperCollins Pubs.

Dow, Rosey. Reaping the Whirlwind: A Trent Tyson Historical Mystery. 2000. (Illus.). 399p. pap. 15.99 *(1-57921-296-4)* WinePress Publishing.

Drake, Robert. Amazing Grace: Twenty-Fifth Anniversary Edition. 1989. xxiv, 116p. text 25.00 o.s.i *(0-86554-364-X*, MUP/H302) Mercer Univ. Pr.

Duff, Gerald. Memphis Ribs. 2000. E-Book 7.00 *(1-930486-02-2)*; 1999. 205p. pap. 12.95 *(0-9664520-1-1)* Salvo Pr.

Dunn, Robert. Pink Cadillac. 2001. 375p. pap. 14.95 *(0-9708293-0-2)* Coral Pr.

Elliott, Scott. Coiled in the Heart. 2003. 304p. 23.95 *(0-399-15038-2*, Putnam & Grosset) Putnam Publishing Group, The.

Eulo, Elena Y. A Southern Woman. 1993. 21.95 o.p. *(0-312-08751-9)* St. Martin's Pr.

Files, Lolita. Child of God: A Novel. 2001. 320p. 23.00 *(0-684-84143-6*, Simon & Schuster) Simon & Schuster.

Flowers, Arthur R. Another Good Loving Blues. 1994. 224p. pap. 15.00 o.s.i *(0-345-38103-3)* Ballantine Bks.

—Another Good Loving Blues. 1993. 224p. 20.00 o.p. *(0-670-84821-2*, Viking) Viking Penguin.

Foote, Shelby. Shiloh: A Novel. 1985. 23.95 *(0-8488-0158-X*, Carroll, J. M. Company) Amereon, Ltd.

—Shiloh: A Novel. 1991. 240p. pap. 12.00 *(0-679-73542-9*, Vintage) Knopf Publishing Group.

—Shiloh: A Novel. 1994. 6.99 o.p. *(0-517-13170-6)* Random Hse. Value Publishing.

—Shiloh: A Novel. unabr. ed. 2000. audio compact disk 42.00 *(0-7887-3963-8*, C1118E7); 1992. audio 35.00 *(1-55690-653-6*, 92341E7) Recorded Bks., LLC.

Foreman, Walter C., Jr. Fairy Tale. 2003. 350p. 22.95 *(1-880909-63-4)* Baskerville Pubs., Inc.

Fox, Les & Fox, Sue. Return to Sender: The Secret Son of Elvis Presley. 1996. 350p. 21.95 *(0-9646986-0-9)* West Highland Publishing Co., Inc.

Garlock, Dorothy. Tenderness, Set. unabr. ed. 1997. audio 69.95 *(0-7927-2221-3*, CSL 110, Chivers Sound Library) BBC Audiobooks America.

—Tenderness. unabr. ed. 2000. audio 59.95 Chivers Audio Bks. GBR. *Dist:* BBC Audiobooks America.

—Tenderness. l.t. ed. 1993. 434p. lib. bdg. 20.95 o.p. *(0-8161-5851-7*, Macmillan Reference USA) Gale Group.

—Tenderness. 384p. 1998. mass mkt. 3.99 *(0-446-60685-5)*; 1993. mass mkt. 6.99 *(0-446-36370-7)* Warner Bks., Inc.

Gay, William. I Hate to See That Evening Sun Go Down: Collected Stories. 320p. 2003. pap. 13.00 *(0-7432-4292-0)*; 2002. 24.00 *(0-7432-4088-X)* Simon & Schuster. (Free Pr.).

—The Long Home. 2000. 257p. pap. 13.50 *(1-878448-05-6)*; 1999. 250p. 24.95 *(1-878448-91-9)* MacMurray & Beck, Inc.

Gordon, Caroline. Green Centuries. 1972. reprint ed. 23.50 o.p. *(0-8154-0398-4)* Cooper Square Pubs., Inc.

—Green Centuries. 1992. (Cumberland & Westmorland Antiquarian & Ar Ser.). 489p. reprint ed. pap. 14.95 *(1-879941-05-8*, Sanders, J. S. & Co., Inc.) Dee, Ivan R. Pub.

Grisham, John. The Rainmaker. abr. ed. audio 22.95 Books on Tape, Inc.

—The Rainmaker. 1996. 608p. mass mkt. 7.99 *(0-440-22165-X)*; 1995. (YA). mass mkt. 9.99 o.s.i *(0-440-91092-7)* Dell Publishing.

—The Rainmaker. 1995. (YA). mass mkt. 7.50 *(0-440-29542-4)*; 448p. 27.95 *(0-385-42473-6)*; 784p. 29.95 o.s.i *(0-385-47512-8)*; (YA). 250.00 o.s.i *(0-385-47513-6)* Doubleday Publishing.

—The Rainmaker. unabr. ed. 1999. audio 49.95 Highsmith Inc.

—The Rainmaker, Level 5. 2000. (Penguin Reader Ser.). pap. 7.93 *(0-582-36412-4)* Longman Publishing Group.

—The Rainmaker. abr. ed. 1995. audio 27.95 *(0-553-47305-0*, 692837, RH Audio) Random Hse. Audio Publishing Group.

Haley, Alex & Stevens, David. Mama Flora's Family. 1999. 464p. mass mkt. 6.99 *(0-440-23543-X)*; (Illus.). 462p. pap. 23.00 *(0-440-61409-0*, Delta) Dell Publishing.

—Mama Flora's Family. 1998. 400p. 25.00 o.s.i *(0-684-83471-5*, Scribner) Simon & Schuster.

Hall, James Baker. Yates Paul, His Grand Flights, His Tootings. 2002. 288p. reprint ed. pap. 19.95 *(0-8131-9035-5)* Univ. Pr. of Kentucky.

Hamilton, Laurell K. Blue Moon. 1998. (Anita Blake Vampire Hunter Ser.: Bk. 8). 432p. mass mkt. 6.99 o.s.i *(0-441-00574-8)* Ace Bks.

Handeland, Lori. A Sheriff in Tennessee. 2002. (Harlequin Superromance Ser.: No. 1063). 298p. mass mkt. *(0-373-71063-1*, 1-71063-1, Harlequin Bks.) Harlequin Enterprises, Ltd.

Hart, Carolyn G. Scandal in Fair Haven. 1995. 352p. mass mkt. 6.99 *(0-553-56537-0)* Bantam Bks.

—Scandal in Fair Haven. unabr. ed. 1998. (Henrie O Mysteries Ser.). audio 56.00 *(0-7366-4144-0*, 4648) Books on Tape, Inc.

—Scandal in Fair Haven. l.t. ed. 1994. 414p. lib. bdg. 20.95 o.p. *(0-8161-7406-7*, Macmillan Reference USA) Gale Group.

Hawkes, Judith. My Soul to Keep. 1996. 336p. 23.95 o.p. *(0-525-93957-1*, Dutton) Dutton/Plume.

Herring, Robert. McCampbell's War. 1986. 256p. 16.95 o.p. *(0-670-80501-7)* Viking Penguin.

Hess, Joan. Misery Loves Maggody. 1999. 288p. 22.00 *(0-684-84562-8*, Simon & Schuster); 2000. (Illus.). 304p. reprint ed. pap. 6.99 *(0-671-01684-9*, Pocket) Simon & Schuster.

Hightower, Lynn S. Satan's Lambs. 1995. 256p. mass mkt. 4.99 o.p. *(0-425-14557-3*, Prime Crime) Berkley Publishing Group.

—Satan's Lambs, Set. l.t. ed. 1994. (Studio Ser.). 64.95 o.p. incl. audio *(0-7862-9993-2*, Macmillan Reference USA) Gale Group.

—Satan's Lambs. 1993. 256p. 19.95 o.p. *(0-8027-1229-0)* Walker & Co.

Holland, John D. Child of the Depression. 1997. 150p. 15.95 o.p. *(0-944957-65-X)* Rivercross Publishing, Inc.

Hooper, Kay. Out of the Shadows. 2000. (Shadows Trilogy Ser.). 368p. mass mkt. 7.50 *(0-553-57695-X)* Bantam Bks.

—Out of the Shadows. l.t. ed. 504p. 2002. pap. 28.95 *(0-7862-3060-6)*; 2001. 31.95 *(0-7862-3059-2)* Thorndike Pr.

Hunter, David. A Sonnet for Shasta. 2001. iii, 186p. pap. 13.95 *(1-57072-181-5)* Overmountain Pr.

Jones, Madison. A Cry of Absence: Novel. 1989. (Voices of the South Ser.). 288p. (C). reprint ed. pap. 11.95 *(0-8071-1579-7)* Louisiana State Univ. Pr.

—Nashville 1864: The Dying of the Light. 1997. 143p. 17.95 *(1-879941-35-X*, Sanders, J. S. & Co., Inc.) Dee, Ivan R. Pub.

—Nashville 1864: The Dying of the Light. 1999. 144p. pap. 9.95 o.s.i *(0-14-027880-X)* Penguin Group (USA) Inc.

Judd, Cameron. The Border Men. 1992. 480p. mass mkt. 5.99 o.s.i *(0-553-29533-0)* Bantam Bks.

—The Overmountain Men. 1991. 416p. mass mkt. 5.99 o.s.i *(0-553-29081-9)* Bantam Bks.

—The Overmountain Men. 2000. (Tennessee Frontier Trilogy Ser.). (Illus.). 410p. pap. 16.95 *(1-58182-097-6*, Cumberland Hearthside) Cumberland Hse. Publishing.

—The Phantom Legion. 1997. (Mountain War Ser.: No. 2). 432p. mass mkt. 5.99 o.s.i *(0-553-57389-6*, Fanfare) Bantam Bks.

—Season of Reckoning No. 3: Mountain War, Vol. 3. 1997. (Mountain War Ser.: Vol. 3). 496p. mass mkt. 5.99 o.s.i *(0-553-57390-X)* Bantam Bks.

—The Shadow Warriors, Vol. 1. 1997. (Mountain War Ser.: Vol. 1). 480p. mass mkt. 5.99 o.s.i *(0-553-57698-4)* Bantam Bks.

Kijewski, Karen. Honky Tonk Kat. 1997. (Kat Colorado Mysteries Ser.). 368p. mass mkt. 6.99 o.s.i *(0-425-15860-8)* Berkley Publishing Group.

—Honky Tonk Kat. 1996. viii, 323p. 22.95 o.s.i *(0-399-14133-2*, G. P. Putnam's Sons) Penguin Group (USA) Inc.

—Honky Tonk Kat. 22.95 o.s.i *(0-399-14424-2)* Putnam Publishing Group, The.

—Honky Tonk Kat. abr. ed. 1996. (Kat Colorado Mysteries Ser.). 5p. audio 23.00 *(1-56876-059-0)* Soundlines Entertainment, Inc.

Kline, Christina B. Sweet Water. l.t. ed. 1993. 22.95 o.p. *(0-7927-1738-4)*; pap. 20.95 o.p. *(0-7927-1737-6)* BBC Audiobooks America.

—Sweet Water: A Novel. 1993. 288p. 20.00 o.p. *(0-06-019033-7)* HarperTrade.

Landrum, Graham Gordon. The Famous DAR Murder Mystery. 1995. 198p. mass mkt. 4.50 *(0-312-95568-5*, St. Martin's Paperbacks); 1992. 208p. 18.95 o.p. *(0-312-06968-5*, Saint Martin's Minotaur) St. Martin's Pr.

—The Garden Club Mystery. l.t. ed. 1999. 23.95 o.p. *(1-56895-642-8*, Wheeler Publishing, Inc.) Gale Group.

—The Sensational Music Club Mystery. l.t. ed. 1995. 250p. lib. bdg. 21.95 *(0-7838-1278-7*, Macmillan Reference USA) Gale Group.

—The Sensational Music Club Mystery. 208p. 1994. 18.95 o.p. *(0-312-11331-5*, Saint Martin's Minotaur); Vol. 1. 1997. (Sensational Music Club Murder Ser.: Vol. 1). mass mkt. 5.99 *(0-312-96261-4*, St. Martin's Paperbacks) St. Martin's Pr.

Landrum, Graham Gordon & Landrum, Robert. The Garden Club Mystery. 1998. 224p. 20.95 *(0-312-18570-7*, Saint Martin's Minotaur) St. Martin's Pr.

Levitsky, Ronald. The Wisdom of Serpents: A Nate Rosen Mystery. 1992. 256p. text 19.00 *(0-684-19411-2*, Scribner) Simon & Schuster.

Lynn, Bunkie. A Comedy of Heirs. 2002. 500p. pap. 15.95 *(0-9721301-0-1)* LadyBug Publishing LLC.

Majors, Inman. Swimming in Sky. 2000. 192p. 19.95 *(0-87074-455-0)* Southern Methodist Univ. Pr.

Marion, Stephen. Hollow Ground: A Novel. 2002. 320p. tchr. ed. 23.95 *(1-56512-323-9)* Algonquin Bks. of Chapel Hill.

—Hollow Ground: A Novel. 2003. 320p. pap. 14.00 *(0-312-42235-0)* Picador.

Marius, Richard. An Affair of Honor. 2001. 608p. 26.95 *(0-375-41239-5)* Knopf, Alfred A. Inc.

—After the War. 1994. 640p. (J). reprint ed. pap. 16.95 o.s.i *(1-55853-273-0)* Rutledge Hill Pr.

—Coming of Rain. 1977. mass mkt. 1.95 o.p. *(0-451-07474-2*, J7474); 1971. mass mkt. 1.25 o.p. *(0-451-04716-8)* NAL. (Signet Bks.).

—The Coming of Rain. 1991. 448p. reprint ed. pap. 12.95 o.p. *(1-55853-142-4)* Rutledge Hill Pr.

Marshall, Catherine. Christy. abr. ed. 1995. pap. 19.95 o.p. incl. audio *(1-55927-324-0)* Audio Renaissance.

—Christy. 1994. reprint ed. lib. bdg. 35.95 *(1-56849-309-6)* Buccaneer Bks., Inc.

—Christy. 1967. text 14.95 o.p. *(0-07-040605-7)* McGraw-Hill Cos., The.

—Christy. 1976. 512p. mass mkt. 6.99 *(0-380-00141-1*, Avon Bks.) Morrow/Avon.

—Christy. 1968. 348p. mass mkt. 4.50 o.p. *(0-8007-8008-6)*; 1995. (Illus.). 160p. (J). (gr. 6-9). 10.99 o.p. *(0-8007-1708-2)* Revell, Fleming H. Co.

—Christy. 1968. 13.04 *(0-606-00470-X)* Turtleback Bks.

—Christy. 2001. 512p. pap. 12.99 *(0-310-24163-4)* Zondervan.

—Christy: The Collectors Edition. 2001. (Illus.). 480p. (gr. 13 up). 24.99 *(0-8007-9290-4)* Chosen Bks.

—Christy: The Collectors Edition. l.t. ed. 1987. 721p. 20.95 o.p. *(0-8161-4186-X*, Macmillan Reference USA) Gale Group.

—Christy: The Young Readers Edition. 2001. (Illus.). 160p. (J). (gr. 6-9). 9.99 *(0-8007-9293-9)* Chosen Bks.

—Christy Books. 1995. pap. 19.99 *(0-8499-3947-X)* W Publishing Group.

—Christy's Choice. 1996. (Christy Fiction Ser.: No. 6). 128p. (Orig.). (J). (gr. 4-8). mass mkt. 4.99 *(0-8499-3919-4)* Nelson, Tommy.

—The Macmillan International Film Encyclopedia. 4th ed. 2001. 1520p. reprint ed. pap. 12.99 *(0-333-90690-X*, HarperResource) HarperInformation.

Mauro, Jack L. Spite Hall. 2001. 196p. pap. 13.95 *(0-595-19322-6)* iUniverse, Inc.

McCarthy, Cormac. Child of God. 1984. (Neglected Books of the 20th Century Ser.). 197p. reprint ed. pap. 7.50 o.p. *(0-88001-065-7)* HarperCollins Pubs.

—Child of God. 1993. 208p. pap. 12.00 *(0-679-72874-0*, Vintage) Knopf Publishing Group.

—Child of God. 1994. 26.25 *(0-8446-6750-1)* Smith, Peter Pub., Inc.

—The Orchard Keeper. reprint ed. lib. bdg. 29.95 o.s.i *(1-56849-686-9)* Buccaneer Bks., Inc.

—The Orchard Keeper. 1982. (Neglected Books of the 20th Century Ser.). 225p. reprint ed. pap. 8.50 o.p. *(0-88001-009-6)* HarperCollins Pubs.

—The Orchard Keeper. 1993. 256p. pap. 13.00 *(0-679-72872-4*, Vintage) Knopf Publishing Group.

—The Orchard Keeper. 1965. 8.95 o.p. *(0-394-43936-8)* Random Hse., Inc.

—The Orchard Keeper. 1994. 25.50 *(0-8446-6751-X)* Smith, Peter Pub., Inc.

McCrumb, Sharyn. The Ballad of Frankie Silver, unabr. ed. 1998. audio 62.95 *(0-7861-1443-6*, 2305) Blackstone Audio Bks., Inc.

—The Ballad of Frankie Silver. 1998. 304p. 23.95 o.p. *(0-525-93969-5)* Dutton/Plume.

—The Ballad of Frankie Silver. l.t. ed. 1998. (Large Print Book Ser.). 27.95 *(1-56895-656-8*, Wheeler Publishing, Inc.) Gale Group.

—The Ballad of Frankie Silver. 1999. 416p. reprint ed. mass mkt. 7.99 (*0-451-19739-9*, Signet Bks.) NAL.

—The Ballad of Frankie Silver. abr. ed. 1998. audio 25.00 (*0-7871-1713-7*, Dove Audio) NewStar Media, Inc.

—The Ballad of Frankie Silver. unabr. ed. 1999. audio compact disk 109.00 (*0-7887-3437-7*, C1043E7); 1998. audio 94.00 (*0-7887-2475-4*, 95550E7) Recorded Bks., LLC.

—Bimbos of the Death Sun. 1996. 224p. mass mkt. 6.50 (*0-345-41215-X*) Ballantine Bks.

—Bimbos of the Death Sun. unabr. ed. 1988. audio 35.00 (*0-7887-3758-9*, 95942E7) Recorded Bks., LLC.

—Bimbos of the Death Sun. 1988. pap. 3.95 o.p. (*0-88038-455-7*) Wizards of the Coast.

—The Hangman's Beautiful Daughter: A Novel of Suspense. l.t. ed. 1996. lib. bdg. 23.95 (*1-57490-069-2*, Beeler Large Print Bks.) Beeler, Thomas T. Publisher.

—The Hangman's Beautiful Daughter: A Novel of Suspense. 1992. 288p. 19.00 (*0-684-19407-4*, Macmillan Reference USA) Gale Group.

—The Hangman's Beautiful Daughter: A Novel of Suspense. 1993. 384p. mass mkt. 7.99 (*0-451-40370-3*, Onyx) NAL.

—The Hangman's Beautiful Daughter: A Novel of Suspense. unabr. ed. 1993. audio 60.00 (*1-55690-786-9*, 93104E7) Recorded Bks., LLC.

—The Hangman's Beautiful Daughter: A Novel of Suspense. 1992. 13.55 (*0-606-06147-9*) Turtleback Bks.

—If Ever I Return, Pretty Peggy-O. 1998. mass mkt. 6.99 (*0-345-91352-3*); 1995. mass mkt. 5.99 o.p. (*0-345-90215-7*); 1991. 336p. mass mkt. 6.99 (*0-345-36906-8*) Ballantine Bks.

—If Ever I Return, Pretty Peggy-O. 1990. 324p. 17.95 o.s.i (*0-684-19104-0*, Macmillan Reference USA) Gale Group.

—If Ever I Return, Pretty Peggy-O. unabr. ed. 1993. audio 70.00 (*1-55690-921-7*, 93417E7) Recorded Bks., LLC.

—The Rosewood Casket. 2003. audio compact disk 19.95 (*0-7861-9651-3*); 1999. audio 49.95 (*0-7861-0994-7*, 1771); 1996. audio compact disk 72.00 (*0-7861-9844-3*, 1771) Blackstone Audio Bks., Inc.

—The Rosewood Casket. 1998. 303p. text 24.00 (*0-7881-5352-8*) DIANE Publishing Co.

—The Rosewood Casket. 1996. (Illus.). 320p. 23.95 o.p. (*0-525-94011-1*) Dutton/Plume.

—The Rosewood Casket. l.t. ed. 1996. 435p. lib. bdg. 25.95 o.p. (*0-7838-1826-2*, Macmillan Reference USA) Gale Group.

—The Rosewood Casket. 1997. 432p. mass mkt. 7.99 (*0-451-18471-8*, Signet Bks.) NAL.

—The Rosewood Casket. unabr. ed. 1996. (Ballad Ser.: Vol. 4). audio 78.00 (*0-7887-0522-9*, 94717E7) Recorded Bks., LLC.

—The Rosewood Casket. abr. ed. 1996. audio 16.95 o.p. (*0-14-086386-9*, Penguin AudioBooks) Viking Penguin.

—She Walks These Hills. unabr. ed. 1998. audio 56.95 (*0-7861-1351-0*, 2254) Blackstone Audio Bks., Inc.

—She Walks These Hills. abr. ed. 1994. audio 16.95 o.p. (*1-56100-394-8*, 1368, Nova Audio Bks.); audio 73.25 o.p. (*1-56100-228-3*, 1040, Unabridged Library Editions); audio 23.95 o.p. (*1-56100-603-3*, 262, Bookcassette) Brilliance Audio.

—She Walks These Hills. l.t. ed. 1996. (Large Print Bks.). 24.95 o.p. (*1-56895-357-7*, Wheeler Publishing, Inc.) Gale Group.

—She Walks These Hills. abr. ed. 2000. audio 7.95 (*1-57815-025-6*, 1027, Media Bks. Audio Publishing) Media Bks., L. L. C.

—She Walks These Hills. 1995. 448p. mass mkt. 7.99 (*0-451-18472-6*, Signet Bks.) NAL.

—She Walks These Hills. unabr. ed. 1999. audio 78.00 (*0-7887-0229-7*, 94454E7) Recorded Bks., LLC.

—She Walks These Hills. 1994. 320p. 21.00 (*0-684-19556-9*, Scribner) Simon & Schuster.

—Zombies of the Gene Pool. 1993. 288p. mass mkt. 6.99 (*0-345-37914-4*) Ballantine Bks.

Mcdonald, Gregory. Skylar. unabr. ed. 1997. audio 48.00 (*0-7366-3790-7*, 4464) Books on Tape, Inc.

—Skylar. abr. ed. 1996. audio 7.99 o.p. (*1-56740-124-4*, 1374, Paperback Nova Audio Bks.); 1995. audio 16.95 o.p. (*1-56100-446-4*, 1373, Nova Audio Bks.); 1995. audio 23.95 o.p. (*1-56100-652-1*, 335, Bookcassette); 1995. audio 57.25 o.p. (*1-56100-277-1*, 1048, Unabridged Library Editions) Brilliance Audio.

—Skylar. 1997. mass mkt. 5.99 (*0-380-72524-X*, Avon Bks.); 1995. 22.00 o.p. (*0-688-14163-3*, Morrow, William & Co.) Morrow/Avon.

McIntire, Dennis P. Lee at Chattanooga: A Novel of What Might Have Been. 2002. (Illus.). 320p. pap. 16.95 (*1-58182-257-X*) Cumberland Hse. Publishing.

McMillan, Rosalyn. This Side of Eternity. 2002. 464p. reprint ed. pap. 6.99 (*0-671-03436-7*, Pocket) Simon & Schuster.

—This Side of Eternity: A Novel. 2001. 320p. 24.00 o.s.i (*0-684-86288-3*, Free Pr.) Simon & Schuster.

Meador, Dale. Along Dusty Roads: Stories of Brothers & Friends. 2001. 184p. pap. 18.50 (*0-7596-3666-4*) 1stBooks Library.

Michaels, Fern. Finders Keepers. l.t. ed. 1998. 27.95 (*1-56895-693-2*, Wheeler Publishing, Inc.) Gale Group.

—Finders Keepers. 2002. 432p. mass mkt. 7.50 (*0-8217-7364-X*); 1999. 432p. mass mkt. 6.99 o.s.i (*0-8217-6307-5*, Zebra Bks.); 1998. 352p. 24.00 o.s.i (*1-57566-323-6*, Kensington Bks.) Kensington Publishing Corp.

Mirvis, Tova. The Ladies Auxiliary. 2000. (Ballantine Reader's Circle Ser.). 336p. pap. 14.00 (*0-345-44126-5*, Ballantine Bks.) Ballantine Bks.

—The Ladies Auxiliary. 1999. 352p. 23.95 (*0-393-04814-4*) Norton, W. W. & Co., Inc.

—The Ladies Auxiliary. 2000. 20.05 (*0-606-19737-0*) Turtleback Bks.

Monahan, Brent. The Bell Witch: An American Haunting. 2000. 208p. pap. 11.95 (*0-312-26292-2*, Saint Martin's Griffin) St. Martin's Pr.

Monahan, Brent, ed. The Bell Witch: An American Haunting. 1997. (Illus.). 208p. 20.95 (*0-312-15061-X*) St. Martin's Pr.

Morsi, Pamela. Sweetwood Bride. l.t. ed. 2000. (Wheeler Large Print Book Ser.). 443p. 26.95 (*1-56895-855-2*, Wheeler Publishing, Inc.) Gale Group.

—Sweetwood Bride. 1999. 416p. mass mkt. 6.99 (*0-06-101365-X*) HarperCollins Pubs.

Murfree, Mary N. Frontiersmen. 1977. (Short Story Index Reprint Ser.). 26.95 (*0-8369-3467-9*) Ayer Co. Pubs., Inc.

—In the Tennessee Mountains. 360p. reprint ed. 111.60 (*0-608-16850-5*, 202756000055) Bks. on Demand.

—In the Tennessee Mountains. (Americans in Fiction Ser.). (Illus.). 322p. reprint ed. pap. text 9.95 o.p. (*0-89197-793-7*); lib. bdg. 14.95 o.p. (*0-8398-1270-1*) Irvington Pubs.

—In the Tennessee Mountains. (Notable American Authors Ser.). reprint ed. 1999. lib. bdg. 125.00 (*0-7812-4591-5*); 1992. 322p. lib. bdg. 89.00 (*0-7812-6803-6*) Reprint Services Corp.

—In the Tennessee Mountains. 1970. (Tennesseana Editions Ser.). (Illus.). 18.50 o.p. (*0-87049-105-9*) Univ. of Tennessee Pr.

Nelscott, Kris. A Dangerous Road. 2001. 336p. mass mkt. 6.50 (*0-312-97643-7*, St. Martin's Paperbacks); 2000. 325p. 24.95 (*0-312-26264-7*, Saint Martin's Minotaur) St. Martin's Pr.

Nelson, Betty P. Changing Seasons, 1954-1980. 1996. 368p. 23.95 o.p. (*0-312-13942-X*) St. Martin's Pr.

—Private Knowledge. 256p. 1993. pap. 11.95 o.p. (*0-312-09897-9*, Saint Martin's Griffin); 1990. 16.95 o.p. (*0-312-03913-1*) St. Martin's Pr.

—Pursuit of Bliss. 1994. 360p. pap. 10.95 o.p. (*0-312-11049-9*, Saint Martin's Griffin); 1992. 288p. 18.95 o.p. (*0-312-08169-3*) St. Martin's Pr.

—Uncertain April. 1994. 336p. 20.95 (*0-312-11084-7*); 20.95 o.p. (*0-312-11086-3*) St. Martin's Pr.

—The Weight of Light. 1993. 320p. pap. 12.95 o.p. (*0-312-09936-3*, Saint Martin's Griffin); 1992. 336p. 21.95 o.p. (*0-312-07121-3*) St. Martin's Pr.

Nichols, Frank Reed. The Knell. 2000. 151p. 22.95 (*0-923687-54-8*) Celo Valley Bks.

Nighbert, David F. Shutout. 1995. 307p. 21.95 o.p. (*0-312-11890-2*, Saint Martin's Minotaur) St. Martin's Pr.

Patchett, Ann. Taft. 1999. 272p. pap. 13.00 o.s.i (*0-345-43353-X*, Ballantine Bks.); 1995. mass mkt. 5.99 o.s.i (*0-8041-1388-2*, Ivy Bks.) Ballantine Bks.

—Taft. 2003. 256p. pap. 12.95 (*0-06-054076-1*, Perennial) HarperTrade.

—Taft. 1994. 288p. 21.95 o.p. (*0-395-69461-2*) Houghton Mifflin Co.

Ross, Dana Fuller, pseud. Tennessee! 1986. (Wagons West Ser.: No. 17). 320p. mass mkt. 4.99 o.s.i (*0-553-25622-X*) Bantam Bks.

—Tennessee! l.t. ed. 1987. 384p. 16.95 o.p. (*0-8161-4193-2*, Macmillan Reference USA) Gale Group.

Rowan, William. Incident at Roan High Bluff. 2003. 273p. (YA). pap. 15.95 (*0-7414-1695-6*) Buy Bks. on the Web.Com.

—Incident at Roan High Bluff. 2000. 272p. pap. 14.50 (*0-9662860-2-2*) Cenografix.

Shankman, Sarah. I Still Miss My Man, but My Aim Is Getting Better. 1997. 288p. pap. 5.99 (*0-671-89750-0*, Pocket); 1996. 272p. 21.00 o.p. (*0-671-89751-9*, Atria) Simon & Schuster.

Simpson, Bland. Heart of the Country: A Novel of Southern Music. 1996. 320p. pap. 19.95 o.p. (*0-8203-1825-6*) Univ. of Georgia Pr.

Skinner, Margaret. Molly Flanagan & the Holy Ghost. 1995. 252p. tchr. ed. 17.95 o.p. (*1-56512-026-4*) Algonquin Bks. of Chapel Hill.

—Old Jim Canaan. 1990. 288p. 18.95 o.p. (*0-945575-37-8*) Algonquin Bks. of Chapel Hill.

Smith, Beecher, ed. Monsters from Memphis. ltd. ed. 1997. 345p. 12.95 (*1-880964-21-X*, ZP/HBP022) Hot Biscuit Productions, Inc.

Smith, Deborah. When Venus Fell. 1999. 464p. mass mkt. 6.99 (*0-553-56279-7*) Bantam Bks.

Speart, Jessica. Black Delta Night. l.t. ed. 2002. 332p. pap. 24.95 (*0-7862-4181-0*) Gale Group.

Steele, William O. Far Frontier. 1959. (Illus.). (J). (gr. 3-7). 5.50 o.p. (*0-15-227171-6*) Harcourt Children's Bks.

—The Lone Hunt. 1976. (Illus.). 176p. (J). (gr. 4-6). reprint ed. pap. 1.75 o.p. (*0-15-652983-1*, Voyager Bks./Libros Viajeros) Harcourt Children's Bks.

Stern, Steve. Plague of Dreamers: 3 Novellas. 1997. (Library of Modern Jewish Literature). 267p. pap. 17.95 (*0-8156-0453-X*) Syracuse Univ. Pr.

Stern, Steve & Grossman, B. A Plague of Dreamers: 3 Novellas. 1994. 256p. 20.00 o.p. (*0-684-19532-1*, Scribner) Simon & Schuster.

Stewart, Leah. Body of a Girl. 2000. 320p. 23.95 (*0-670-89164-9*, Viking) Viking Penguin.

Stone, Beatrice. The Sensual Thread: A Novel. 1994. 224p. (Orig.). pap. 10.95 o.p. (*1-879427-18-4*) 3rd Side Pr., Inc.

Strunk, Frank C. Throwback. 1996. 320p. mass mkt. 20.00 o.s.i (*0-06-101057-X*, HarperTorch) Morrow/Avon.

Sullivan, Walter. Sojourn of a Stranger. 2003. (Voices of the South Ser.). 316p. pap. 17.95 (*0-8071-2917-8*) Louisiana State Univ. Pr.

—Time to Dance: A Novel. 1995. 195p. 22.95 (*0-8071-1985-7*) Louisiana State Univ. Pr.

Taylor, Peter. In the Tennessee Country. 1994. 208p. 21.00 o.s.i (*0-394-56264-X*) Knopf, Alfred A. Inc.

—In the Tennessee Country. 1995. 208p. pap. 10.00 (*0-312-13521-1*) Picador.

—A Summons to Memphis. 1987. 234p. mass mkt. 6.99 o.s.i (*0-345-34660-2*); 224p. mass mkt. 4.95 (*0-345-90171-1*) Ballantine Bks.

—A Summons to Memphis. l.t. ed. 1987. (General Ser.). 319p. 18.95 o.p. (*0-8161-4305-6*, Macmillan Reference USA) Gale Group.

—A Summons to Memphis. 1999. (Vintage International Ser.). 224p. pap. 12.00 (*0-375-70117-6*) Knopf, Alfred A. Inc.

—A Summons to Memphis. 1999. 18.05 (*0-606-21893-9*) Turtleback Bks.

Tishy, Cecelia. Cryin' Time. 1998. (Kate Banning Mystery Ser.: No. 2). 336p. 23.95 (*1-891847-01-5*) Dowling Pr., Inc.

—Cryin' Time. 1999. (Kate Banning Mysteries Ser.). 304p. mass mkt. 5.99 o.s.i (*0-451-19832-8*, Signet Bks.) NAL.

—Fall to Pieces. 1999. (Kate Banning Mystery Ser.). 319p. 24.00 (*1-891847-07-4*) Dowling Pr., Inc.

—Fall to Pieces. 2000. (Kate Banning Mysteries Ser.). 304p. mass mkt. 5.99 o.s.i (*0-451-20094-2*, Signet Bks.) NAL.

—Jealous Heart. Sachs, Susan, ed. 1997. 304p. 24.00 o.p. (*0-9646452-5-4*) Dowling Pr., Inc.

—Jealous Heart. 1999. 272p. mass mkt. 5.99 o.s.i (*0-451-19678-3*, Signet Bks.) NAL.

Warren, Robert Penn. Flood. 2003. (Voices of the South Ser.). 440p. pap. 19.95 (*0-8071-2918-6*) Louisiana State Univ. Pr.

—Flood. mass mkt. 0.95 o.p. (*0-451-02611-X*, Signet Bks.) NAL.

—Flood. 1964. 10.00 o.s.i (*0-394-42519-7*) Random Hse., Inc.

West, Michael L. American Pie: A Novel. 1996. 79p. 24.00 o.p. (*0-06-018357-8*) HarperCollins Pubs.

Whorton, James C. Approximately Heaven: A Novel. 2003. 240p. 23.00 (*0-7432-4446-X*, Free Pr.) Simon & Schuster.

Williford, Carolyn. Jordan's Bend. 1995. pap. 12.99 o.p. (*0-7852-7707-2*) Nelson, Thomas Inc.

Wimberly, Clara. The Jeweled Heart of Rosemont Castle. l.t. ed. 1994. 391p. pap. 18.95 (*0-8161-7493-8*, Macmillan Reference USA) Gale Group.

—The Jeweled Heart of Rosemont Castle. 1992. 288p. mass mkt. 3.99 o.s.i (*0-8217-4000-8*, Zebra Bks.) Kensington Publishing Corp.

Womack, Steven. Chain of Fools. (Harry James Denton Mysteries Ser.). 320p. 1996. mass mkt. 6.50 (*0-345-39687-1*); 1995. pap. 19.00 (*0-345-46187-8*, Ballantine Bks.) Ballantine Bks.

—Chain of Fools. l.t. ed. 1997. (Ulverscroft Large Print Ser.). 544p. 29.99 (*0-7089-3730-6*, Ulverscroft) Thorpe, F. A. Pubs. GBR. *Dist:* Ulverscroft Large Print Bks., Ltd., Ulverscroft Large Print Canada, Ltd.

—Dead Folks' Blues. 272p. 1995. pap. 19.00 (*0-345-46186-X*, Ballantine Bks.); 1992. mass mkt. 5.99 o.s.i (*0-345-37674-9*) Ballantine Bks.

—Dead Folks' Blues. Haywood, Richard, ed. abr. ed. 1995. (Harry Denton Trilogy Ser.). audio 17.00 (*1-883268-25-7*) Spellbinders, Inc.

—Dirty Money. 2000. 320p. pap. 19.00 (*0-345-46190-8*, Ballantine Bks.); mass mkt. 6.50 (*0-345-41448-9*, Fawcett) Ballantine Bks.

—Murder Manual. 1998. (Harry James Denton Mysteries Ser.). 336p. mass mkt. 5.99 (*0-345-41447-0*); pap. 19.00 (*0-345-46189-4*, Ballantine Bks.) Ballantine Bks.

—Torch Town Boogie. 288p. 1995. pap. 19.00 (*0-345-46317-X*); 1993. mass mkt. 6.50 o.s.i (*0-345-38010-X*) Ballantine Bks.

—Torch Town Boogie. abr. ed. 1997. audio 17.00 (*1-883268-32-X*) Spellbinders, Inc.

—Torch Town Boogie. l.t. ed. 1996. (Ulverscroft Large Print Ser.). 480p. 29.99 o.p. (*0-7089-3600-8*, Ulverscroft) Thorpe, F. A. Pubs. GBR. *Dist:* Ulverscroft Large Print Bks., Ltd., Ulverscroft Large Print Canada, Ltd.

—Way Past Dead. 1995. 352p. pap. 19.00 (*0-345-46188-6*, Ballantine Bks.); 272p. mass mkt. 6.50 (*0-345-39043-1*) Ballantine Bks.

—Way Past Dead. abr. ed. 1997. audio 17.00 (*1-883268-30-3*) Spellbinders, Inc.

Yount, John. Toots in Solitude. 1985. 192p. pap. 5.95 o.p. (*0-312-80905-0*, Saint Martin's Griffin); 1983. 224p. 13.95 o.p. (*0-312-80904-2*) St. Martin's Pr.

—Toots in Solitude: A Novel. 1995. 200p. pap. 10.95 (*0-87074-384-8*) Southern Methodist Univ. Pr.

## TERREILLE (IMAGINARY PLACE)—FICTION

Bishop, Anne. Daughter of the Blood. 1998. (Black Jewels Trilogy Ser.: 1). 416p. mass mkt. 6.99 (*0-451-45671-8*, ROC) NAL.

—Heir to the Shadows. 1999. (Black Jewels Trilogy Ser.: 2). 496p. mass mkt. 6.99 (*0-451-45672-6*) NAL.

—Queen of the Darkness, Vol. 3. 2000. (Black Jewels Trilogy Ser.: Vol. 3). 448p. (J). mass mkt. 6.99 (*0-451-45673-4*, ROC) NAL.

## TEXAS—FICTION

Abbott, Jeff. Distant Blood. 1996. 352p. mass mkt. 6.99 (*0-345-39470-4*) Ballantine Bks.

—Do unto Others. 1994. (Southwest Mysteries Ser.). 256p. mass mkt. 6.99 (*0-345-38948-4*) Ballantine Bks.

—The Only Good Yankee. 1995. 256p. mass mkt. 6.50 (*0-345-39438-0*, Del Rey) Ballantine Bks.

—Promises of Home. 1996. 288p. mass mkt. 6.99 (*0-345-39469-0*) Ballantine Bks.

Abreu, Ciao Fernando. Whatever Happened to Dulce Veiga? A B-Novel. Frizzi, Adia, tr. from POR. & afterword by by. 2001. (Texas Pan American Ser.). 206p. 35.00 o.p. (*0-292-70500-X*) Univ. of Texas Pr.

Abreu, Ciao Fernando & Frizzi, Adria. Whatever Happened to Dulce Veiga? A B-Novel. 2001. (Texas Pan American Ser.). 206p. pap. 15.95 (*0-292-70501-8*) Univ. of Texas Pr.

Adams, Marcia. Shadow Patterns: A Novel of Dallas & Padre Island. 1997. pap. 18.95 (*1-57860-022-7*) Emmis Bks.

Albert, Susan Wittig. Chile Death. 1999. (West Coast Crime Ser.: No. 7). 320p. reprint ed. mass mkt. 6.99 (*0-425-17147-7*, Prime Crime) Berkley Publishing Group.

—Chile Death: A China Bayles Mystery. 1998. (China Bayles Mystery Ser.). 320p. 21.95 o.s.i (*0-425-16539-6*, Prime Crime) Berkley Publishing Group.

—Chile Death: A China Bayles Mystery. l.t. ed. 2001. 435p. 29.95 (*0-7862-3161-0*) Thorndike Pr.

—Hangman's Root: A China Bayles Mystery. 1995. 272p. mass mkt. 6.99 (*0-425-14898-X*) Berkley Publishing Group.

—Hangman's Root: A China Bayles Mystery. 1994. 256p. 20.00 (*0-684-19677-8*); 1995. 319p. pap. 19.95 (*0-7838-1246-9*) Gale Group. (Macmillan Reference USA).

—Indigo Dying. 2004. 288p. mass mkt. 6.99 (*0-425-19377-2*); 2003. 320p. 22.95 (*0-425-18828-0*) Berkley Publishing Group.

—Lavender Lies. 2000. (Prime Crime Mysteries Ser.). 320p. reprint ed. mass mkt. 6.99 (*0-425-17700-9*) Berkley Publishing Group.

—Lavender Lies: A China Bayles Mystery. 1999. (China Bayles Mystery Ser.: No. 8). 320p. 21.95 o.s.i (*0-425-17032-2*, Prime Crime) Berkley Publishing Group.

—Lavender Lies: A China Bayles Mystery. l.t. ed. 2001. 437p. o.p. (*0-7862-3162-9*) Thorndike Pr.

—Love Lies Bleeding: A China Bayles Mystery. (China Bayles Mystery Ser.). 1997. 320p. 21.95 o.s.i (*0-425-15969-8*); 1998. 336p. reprint ed. mass mkt. 6.99 (*0-425-16611-2*) Berkley Publishing Group. (Prime Crime).

—Mistletoe Man: A China Bayles Mystery. 2000. (China Bayles Ser.). 304p. 21.95 o.s.i (*0-425-17673-8*) Berkley Publishing Group.

—Mistletoe Man: A China Bayles Mystery. l.t. ed. 2001. (Thorndike Mystery Ser.). 408p. 29.95 (*0-7862-3163-7*) Thorndike Pr.

—Rosemary Remembered: A China Bayles Mystery. 304p. 1996. mass mkt. 6.99 (*0-425-15405-X*); 1995. 19.95 o.p. (*0-425-14937-4*, Prime Crime) Berkley Publishing Group.

—Rueful Death: A China Bayles Mystery. 1996. 320p. 21.95 o.p. (*0-425-15469-6*); 1997. 304p. reprint ed. mass mkt. 6.99 (*0-425-15941-8*, Prime Crime) Berkley Publishing Group.

—Thyme of Death: A Mystery Introducing China Bayles. 1994. (West Coast Crime Ser.). 320p. mass mkt. 6.99 (*0-425-14098-9*) Berkley Publishing Group.

—Thyme of Death: A Mystery Introducing China Bayles. 1992. 256p. bds. 20.00 o.s.i (*0-684-19522-4*, Scribner) Simon & Schuster.

—Unthymely Death: And Other Garden Mysteries. 2003. 272p. pap. 14.00 (*0-425-19002-1*) Berkley Publishing Group.

—Witches' Bane: A China Bayles Mystery. 1994. 272p. reprint ed. mass mkt. 6.99 (*0-425-14406-2*, Prime Crime) Berkley Publishing Group.

—Witches' Bane: A China Bayles Mystery. 1993. 256p. bds. 20.00 o.p. (*0-684-19636-0*, Scribner) Simon & Schuster.

Alcala, Kathleen. Spirits of the Ordinary. 1998. (Harvest Book Ser.). 256p. pap. 13.00 (*0-15-600568-9*) Harcourt Trade Pubs.

—Spirits of the Ordinary: A Tale of Casas Grandes. 1997. 204p. 22.95 o.p. (*0-8118-1447-5*) Chronicle Bks. LLC.

Algren, Nelson. The Texas Stories of Nelson Algren. Drew, Bettina, ed. & intro. by. 1995. 179p. 27.50 (*0-292-71577-3*); pap. 12.95 o.p. (*0-292-70468-2*) Univ. of Texas Pr.

All the Pretty Horses. 2000. 11.95 (*1-56137-914-X*) Novel Units, Inc.

Allen, Tricia. Texas Weather. 2000. 318p. 14.95 (*1-929976-00-3*) Top Pubns., Ltd.

Alter, Judith M. Luke & the Van Zandt County War. 1984. (Chaparral Bks.). (Illus.). 132p. (J). (gr. 4 up). 14.95 (*0-912646-88-8*) Texas Christian Univ. Pr.

Altsheler, Joseph A. The Texan Scouts. 2000. 252p. E-Book 9.95 (*0-594-02939-2*) 1873 Pr.

—The Texan Scouts. 26.95 (*0-8488-0730-8*); 1985. 21.95 (*0-8488-0202-0*) Amereon, Ltd.

—The Texan Scouts. 1993. reprint ed. lib. bdg. 21.95 (*0-89968-569-2*) Buccaneer Bks., Inc.

Amey, Linda. At Dead of Night. 1995. 448p. mass mkt. 5.99 o.s.i (*0-553-56474-9*) Bantam Bks.

—At Dead of Night. 1993. 240p. pap. 9.99 o.p. (*0-7459-2622-3*) Lion Publishing.

—At Dead of Night. 2002. 296p. pap. 19.95 (*0-595-24037-2*, Mystery Writers of America Presents) iUniverse, Inc.

Anderson, Dillon. I & Claudie. 2000. (Double Mountain Bks.). (Illus.). vii, 247p. 15.95 (*0-89672-429-8*) Texas Tech Univ. Pr.

Anderson, Patrick. Rich As Sin. 1991. 21.95 o.p. (*0-671-69531-2*, Simon & Schuster) Simon & Schuster.

—Rich As Sin. 1994. mass mkt. 4.99 o.p. (*0-312-95236-8*, St. Martin's Paperbacks) St. Martin's Pr.

Anthony, Patricia. Happy Policeman. 1996. 288p. mass mkt. 5.99 o.s.i (*0-441-00321-4*) Ace Bks.

—Happy Policeman. 1994. 288p. 21.95 o.s.i (*0-15-138478-9*) Harcourt Trade Pubs.

Antoni, Robert. My Grandmother's Erotic Folktales. 224p. 2001. 24.00 o.p. (*0-8021-1687-6*); 2002. reprint ed. pap. 13.00 (*0-8021-3900-0*) Grove/Atlantic, Inc. (Grove Pr.).

Arnold, Janis. Daughters of Memory. (Front Porch Paperback Ser.). 378p. 1999. pap. 9.95 (*1-56512-031-0*); 1991. 16.95 (*0-945575-68-8*) Algonquin Bks. of Chapel Hill.

—Excuse Me for Asking. 1997. (Front Porch Paperback Ser.). 364p. pap. 10.95 (*1-56512-172-4*, 72172) Algonquin Bks. of Chapel Hill.

—Excuse Me for Asking: A Novel. 1994. 378p. 18.95 o.p. (*1-56512-057-4*) Algonquin Bks. of Chapel Hill.

Arnold, Ron. The Grand Prairie Years. 2nd ed. 1987. (Illus.). 722p. 19.95 (*0-936783-01-X*) Merril Pr.

Axler, James. Salvation Road. 2002. (Deathlands Ser.: No. 58). mass mkt. (*0-373-62568-5*, 1-62568-0, Worldwide Library) Harlequin Enterprises, Ltd.

Bagdon, Paul. Long Road to LaRosa. 2003. (West Texas Sunrise Ser.). 192p. pap. 11.99 (*0-8007-5815-3*) Revell, Fleming H. Co.

—Stallions at Burnt Rock: A Novel. 2003. (West Texas Sunrise Ser.). 192p. pap. 11.99 (*0-8007-5798-X*) Revell, Fleming H. Co.

—The Stranger from Medina: A Novel. 2003. 192p. pap. 11.99 (*0-8007-5835-8*) Revell, Fleming H. Co.

—Thunder on the DOS Gatos: A Novel. 2003. 192p. pap. 11.99 (*0-8007-5834-X*) Revell, Fleming H. Co.

Bagwell, Stella. The Heiress & the Sheriff. 2000. (Fortunes of Texas Ser.: No. 8). 256p. per. (*0-373-65037-X*, Silhouette) Harlequin Enterprises, Ltd.

—Just for Christmas. 2000. (Harlequin American Romance Ser.: Bk. 4). 256p. mass mkt. (*0-373-65065-5*, 1-65065-4, Harlequin Bks.) Harlequin Enterprises, Ltd.

Bain, Darrell. Life on Santa Claus Lane. 2001. 159p. per. 13.95 (*0-9711915-8-1*, Lighthouse Editions) Lighthouse Pr., Inc.

—Life on Santa Claus Lane. E-Book 7.95 (*1-930756-16-X*); 1999. E-Book 4.95 (*1-930364-23-7*) McGraw Publishing, Inc. (Bookmice).

—Tales from a Texas Christmas Tree Farm. 1999. (Illus.). 120p. pap. 10.85 (*1-58500-439-1*) 1stBooks Library.

—Tales from a Texas Christmas Tree Farm. E-Book 7.95 (*1-930756-17-8*); 1999. E-Book 4.95 (*1-930364-24-5*) McGraw Publishing, Inc. (Bookmice).

Baisden, Michael. God's Gift to Women: A Novel. 2002. pap. 22.95 (*0-9643675-9-9*) Legacy Publishing.

—God's Gift to Women: A Novel. 2002. 312p. 22.95 (*0-7432-4692-6*, Touchstone) Simon & Schuster.

Balough, et al. The Gifts of Christmas. 1998. per. (*0-373-83372-5*, 1-83372-2, Harlequin Bks.) Harlequin Enterprises, Ltd.

Banks, Carolyn. Death by Dressage. 1993. mass mkt. 5.50 o.s.i (*0-449-14843-2*, Fawcett) Ballantine Bks.

—Death on the Diagonal. 1996. mass mkt. 4.99 o.s.i (*0-449-14968-4*, Fawcett) Ballantine Bks.

—Groomed for Death. 1994. 192p. mass mkt. 6.50 o.s.i (*0-449-14913-7*, Fawcett) Ballantine Bks.

—A Horse to Die For. 1996. 182p. mass mkt. 5.50 o.s.i (*0-449-14969-2*, Fawcett) Ballantine Bks.

—Murder Well-Bred. 1995. mass mkt. 5.50 o.s.i (*0-449-14914-5*, Fawcett) Ballantine Bks.

Barbieri, Elaine. The Wild One. 2001. (Secret Fires Ser.: Bk. 1). 400p. mass mkt. 5.99 (*0-8439-4826-4*, Leisure Bks.) Dorchester Publishing Co., Inc.

—The Wild One. l.t. ed. 2001. (Romance Ser.: Vol. 1). 393p. 28.95 o.p. (*0-7862-3592-6*) Thorndike Pr.

Barr, Nevada. Track of the Cat. abr. ed. 2002. audio 25.00 (*1-59040-249-9*) Audio Literature.

—Track of the Cat. 2003. 272p. mass mkt. 6.99 (*0-425-19083-8*) Berkley Publishing Group.

—Track of the Cat. l.t. ed. 1998. pap. 23.95 o.p. (*1-56895-572-3*, Wheeler Publishing, Inc.) Gale Group.

—Track of the Cat. 2002. (Anna Pigeon Mysteries Ser.: No. 1). 320p. reprint ed. mass mkt. 6.99 o.s.i (*0-380-72164-3*, Avon Bks.) Morrow/Avon.

—Track of the Cat. 1993. 240p. 19.95 o.s.i (*0-399-13824-2*, G. P. Putnam's Sons) Penguin Group (USA) Inc.

—Track of the Cat. unabr. ed. 2000. (Anna Pigeon Mystery Ser. : No. 1). audio 51.00 (*0-7887-1778-2*, 95252E7) Recorded Bks., LLC.

Barrett, Anna Pearl. The Middlebatchers: Throw a Party for the Marriage of Hetty Wish & Lester Leg, Vol. 1. Darst, Shelia S., ed. 1984. (Illus.). 118p. (Orig.). (J). (gr. 3-7). pap. 7.95 (*0-89896-105-X*) Larksdale.

Barrett, Neal, Jr. Dead Dog Blues. 1994. 368p. 22.95 o.p. (*0-312-10963-6*, Saint Martin's Minotaur) St. Martin's Pr.

Barthelme, Frederick. Natural Selection. 2001. 224p. pap. text 14.00 (*1-58243-131-0*, Counterpoint Pr.) Basic Bks.

—Natural Selection. 1990. 256p. 18.95 o.p. (*0-670-83113-1*, Viking) Viking Penguin.

Barton, Beverly. In the Arms of a Hero. 2000. (Fortunes of Texas Ser.: No. 10). 256p. per. (*0-373-65039-6*, Harlequin Bks.) Harlequin Enterprises, Ltd.

Barton, Wayne. Manhunt. 2000. 240p. (Orig.). mass mkt. 5.99 o.s.i (*0-425-17339-9*) Berkley Publishing Group.

Barton, Wayne & Williams, Stan. Live by the Gun. l.t. ed. 1992. 331p. pap. 14.95 o.p. (*0-8161-5465-1*, Macmillan Reference USA) Gale Group.

—Live by the Gun. 1989. bds. 2.95 o.s.i (*0-671-65216-8*, Pocket) Simon & Schuster.

—Manhunt. Grad, Doug, ed. 1992. 224p. (Orig.). mass mkt. 3.50 (*0-671-74576-X*, Pocket) Simon & Schuster.

Bass, Milton. Gunfighter Jory. 1987. 192p. mass mkt. 2.75 o.p. (*0-451-15053-8*, Signet Bks.) NAL.

—Jory. 1987. mass mkt. 2.75 o.p. (*0-451-14932-7*); 224p. mass mkt. 2.95 o.p. (*0-451-16130-0*) NAL. (Signet Bks.).

—Sheriff Jory. 1987. mass mkt. 2.75 o.p. (*0-451-14817-7*, Signet Bks.) NAL.

Bass, Milton R. Mister Jory. 1987. 192p. mass mkt. 2.75 o.p. (*0-451-14965-3*, Signet Bks.) NAL.

—Mister Jory. 1976. 7.95 o.p. (*0-399-11702-4*) Putnam Publishing Group, The.

Bauer, Douglas. The Very Air. 1997. 384p. per. 16.00 (*0-8050-7113-X*); pap. 14.00 o.s.i (*0-8050-4301-2*, Owl Bks.) Holt, Henry & Co.

—The Very Air. 380p. 4.98 o.p. (*0-8317-8604-3*) Smithmark Pubs., Inc.

—The Very Air: A Novel. 1993. 378p. 20.00 o.p. (*0-688-09460-0*, Morrow, William & Co.) Morrow/Avon.

Bauld, Jane S. Hector's Escapades: The First Night Out. 1997. (Illus.). 39p. (J). 14.95 (*1-57168-185-X*) Eakin Pr.

Baxter, Mary L., et al. Texas Heat: Slow Burn; Baby Makes Perfect; Everything but Time, 3 bks. in 1. 1999. per. (*0-373-20168-0*, 1-20168-0, Harlequin Bks.) Harlequin Enterprises, Ltd.

Bean, Fred. Black Gold. 384p. 1998. mass mkt. 5.99 (*0-8125-4597-4*); 1997. 23.95 o.p. (*0-312-86062-5*) Doherty, Tom Assocs., LLC. (Forge Bks.).

Bean, Frederic. The Hangman's Tree. 2000. 288p. mass mkt. 5.99 o.s.i (*0-553-58020-5*) Bantam Bks.

—Hard Luck. 1992. 164p. 19.95 o.s.i (*0-8027-1232-0*) Walker & Co.

Bell, Nancy. Biggie & the Devil Diet. E-Book 16.95 (*0-312-70885-8*) St. Martin's Pr.

—Biggie & the Devil Diet. 2003. (Mystery Ser.). 30.95 (*0-7862-4831-9*) Thorndike Pr.

—Biggie & the Devil Diet: A Mystery. 2002. (Biggie Ser.). 224p. 22.95 (*0-312-30184-7*, Saint Martin's Minotaur) St. Martin's Pr.

—Biggie & the Fricasseed Fat. 1998. 224p. 20.95 o.p. (*0-312-19238-X*, Saint Martin's Minotaur) St. Martin's Pr.

—Biggie & the Fricasseed Fatman. 1999. (St. Martin's Minotaur Mysteries Ser.). 240p. (J). mass mkt. 5.99 (*0-312-96937-6*, St. Martin's Paperbacks) St. Martin's Pr.

—Biggie & the Fricasseed Fatman. l.t. ed. 2000. (Thorndike Senior Lifestyle Ser.). 272p. 27.95 (*0-7862-2561-0*) Thorndike Pr.

—Biggie & the Mangled Mortician. (Dead Letter Mysteries Ser.). 1998. 208p. mass mkt. 5.99 (*0-312-96491-9*, St. Martin's Paperbacks); 1997. 201p. text 20.95 o.p. (*0-312-15477-1*, Saint Martin's Minotaur) St. Martin's Pr.

—Biggie & the Mangled Mortician. l.t. ed. 2000. (Thorndike Senior Lifestyle Ser.). (Illus.). 288p. 27.95 (*0-7862-2562-9*) Thorndike Pr.

—Biggie & the Meddlesome Mailman. 1999. 214p. 22.95 (*0-312-20880-4*, Saint Martin's Minotaur) St. Martin's Pr.

—Biggie & the Meddlesome Mailman. l.t. ed. 2000. (Mystery Ser.). 274p. 28.95 (*0-7862-2552-1*) Thorndike Pr.

—Biggie & the Poisoned Politician. (Dead Letter Mysteries Ser.). 1997. 192p. mass mkt. 5.50 (*0-312-96219-3*, St. Martin's Paperbacks); 1996. 208p. text 21.95 o.p. (*0-312-14285-4*, Saint Martin's Minotaur) St. Martin's Pr.

—Biggie & the Poisoned Politician. l.t. ed. 2000. (Thorndike Senior Lifestyle Ser.). 253p. 28.95 o.p. (*0-7862-2550-5*) Thorndike Pr.

—Biggie & the Quincy Ghost. 2001. 224p. 22.95 (*0-312-26560-3*, Saint Martin's Minotaur) St. Martin's Pr.

—Biggie & the Quincy Ghost. l.t. ed. 2002. (Mystery Ser.). 254p. 30.45 (*0-7862-3842-9*) Thorndike Pr.

Beraru, Elise Dee. The Hero's Best Friend. 2001. E-Book 4.75 incl. disk (*1-58749-027-7*); E-Book 4.75 (*1-58749-028-5*) Awe-Struck E-Bks.

Berg, Elizabeth. Durable Goods. l.t. ed. 2000. 248p. lib. bdg. 25.95 (*1-58547-049-X*) Ctr. Point Large Print.

—Durable Goods. 1997. pap. 6.99 (*0-380-72884-2*); 1999. 208p. reprint ed. pap. 13.00 o.s.i (*0-380-72308-5*) Morrow/Avon. (Avon Bks.).

—Durable Goods. 2003. 224p. pap. 12.95 (*0-8129-6814-X*) Random House Adult Trade Publishing Group.

Bickmore, Barbara. Deep in the Heart. l.t. ed. 1996. lib. bdg. 24.95 (*1-57490-067-6*, Beeler Large Print Bks.) Beeler, Thomas T. Publisher.

—Deep in the Heart. 1997. 448p. mass mkt. 5.99 o.s.i (*1-57566-225-6*); 1996. 358p. 22.95 o.s.i (*1-57566-039-3*) Kensington Publishing Corp.

Bingham, Linda S. Born on the Island. 2002. cd-rom 14.95 (*1-930430-24-8*) Waltsan Publishing, LLC.

Bittner, Rosanne. Texas Passions. 1999. 320p. mass mkt. 5.99 o.s.i (*0-8217-6166-8*) Kensington Publishing Corp.

Black, Jim. River Season: A Novel. 2003. 208p. 23.95 (*0-670-03227-1*, Viking) Viking Penguin.

—There's a River Down in Texas. 2000. (Illus.). 178p. pap. 12.00 (*0-9703052-0-6*) Black, Jim.

Blake, Glenn. Drowned Moon. 2002. (Poetry & Fiction Ser.). 112p. text 44.00 (*0-8018-6549-2*); pap. 13.00 (*0-8018-7093-3*) Johns Hopkins Univ. Pr.

Blake, James C. In the Rogue Blood. 1998. pap. 12.50 (*0-380-79241-9*); 1997. 352p. 23.00 (*0-380-97492-4*) Morrow/Avon. (Avon Bks.).

—The Pistoleer. 1996. 397p. mass mkt. 6.99 o.s.i (*0-425-15412-2*); 1995. 368p. pap. 12.00 o.p. (*0-425-14782-7*) Berkley Publishing Group.

—The Pistoleer. l.t. ed. 1996. (Niagara Large Print Ser.). 560p. 29.50 o.p. (*0-7089-5823-0*, Ulverscroft) Thorpe, F. A. Pubs. GBR. *Dist:* Ulverscroft Large Print Bks., Ltd.

Blakely, Mike. Shortgrass Song. 1994. 448p. 23.95 o.p. (*0-312-85541-9*, Forge Bks.) Doherty, Tom Assocs., LLC.

—The Summer of Pearls. 2000. 224p. 22.95 (*0-312-87516-9*, Forge Bks.) Doherty, Tom Assocs., LLC.

—Too Long at the Dance. 1998. 532p. mass mkt. 6.50 (*0-8125-4832-9*); 1996. 352p. 23.95 o.p. (*0-312-86093-5*) Doherty, Tom Assocs., LLC. (Forge Bks.).

Blakely, Mike & Goldman, Mary Elizabeth, eds. Forever Texas: Texas, the Way Those Who Lived It Wrote It. 2001. 336p. reprint ed. pap. 13.95 (*0-312-87685-8*, Forge Bks.) Doherty, Tom Assocs., LLC.

Boltd, Frazee. Alamo. 2004. 320p. mass mkt. 5.99 (*0-7868-9082-7*) Hyperion Pr.

Bonds, Parris A. For All Time. l.t. ed. 1996. 22.95 o.p. (*1-56895-124-8*, Wheeler Publishing, Inc.) Gale Group.

Bonner, Cindy. Lily. 1992. 350p. 17.95 (*0-945575-95-5*) Algonquin Bks. of Chapel Hill.

—Looking after Lily. 1999. 336p. tchr. ed. 18.95 (*1-56512-045-0*) Algonquin Bks. of Chapel Hill.

—Looking after Lily. l.t. ed. 1994. 22.95 o.p. (*0-7927-2076-8*); pap. 21.95 o.p. (*0-7927-2075-X*) BBC Audiobooks America.

—Looking after Lily. 1995. 320p. mass mkt. 4.99 o.s.i (*0-451-40587-0*, Signet Bks.) NAL.

—The Passion of Dellie O'Barr. 1996. 362p. tchr. ed. 18.95 (*1-56512-103-1*, 72103) Algonquin Bks. of Chapel Hill.

—Right from Wrong: A Novel. 1999. 336p. tchr. ed. 19.95 (*1-56512-104-X*, 72104) Algonquin Bks. of Chapel Hill.

—Right from Wrong: A Novel. l.t. ed. 1999. (Basic Ser.). 472p. 28.95 (*0-7862-1990-4*) Thorndike Pr.

Boothe, Ben B. Confessions of a Banker. Boothe, Paulette, ed. 2nd ed. 1991. 270p. reprint ed. 16.95 (*0-89015-767-7*) Unicorn Pr. U.S.A.

Borders, Lisa. Cloud Cuckoo Land: A Novel. 2002. 453p. 27.95 (*1-57966-030-4*) River City Publishing.

Borthwick, J. S. The Case of the Hook-Billed Kites. 1982. 256p. 12.95 o.p. (*0-312-12335-3*) St. Martin's Pr.

—The Case of the Hook-Billed Kites. 1983. 256p. pap. 3.95 o.p. (*0-14-006785-X*, Penguin Bks.) Viking Penguin.

Bowman, David. Let the Dog Drive. 1993. 295p. (C). 25.00 (*0-8147-1205-3*) New York Univ. Pr.

—Let the Dog Drive. 1994. 320p. reprint ed. pap. 10.95 o.p. (*0-14-023724-0*, Penguin Bks.) Penguin Group (USA) Inc.

Bowman, Doug. The Guns of Billy Free. 2000. 288p. mass mkt. 5.99 (*0-8125-9028-7*); 1998. 320p. 23.95 o.p. (*0-312-86573-2*) Doherty, Tom Assocs., LLC. (Forge Bks.).

—Pilgrim. 2001. 288p. 23.95 (*0-312-87864-8*, Forge Bks.) Doherty, Tom Assocs., LLC.

—The Quest of Jubal Kane. 315p. 2000. mass mkt. 5.99 (*0-8125-4047-6*); 1999. 22.95 (*0-312-86546-5*) Doherty, Tom Assocs., LLC. (Forge Bks.).

Boyd, Jim. Companions of the Blest. 2002. 281p. 28.95 (*1-57168-734-3*); pap. 22.95 (*1-57168-733-5*) Eakin Pr. (Eakin Pr.).

Bradley, Lynn. Stand-In for Murder. 1996. (WWL Mystery Ser.). per. (*0-373-26199-3*, 1-26199-9, Worldwide Library) Harlequin Enterprises, Ltd.

—Stand-In for Murder: A Cole January Mystery. 1994. 214p. 19.95 o.p. (*0-8027-3189-9*) Walker & Co.

Bragg, William F. & House, R. C. Drumm's War. 1992. (Novel of the West Ser.). 16.95 o.p. (*0-87131-695-1*) Evans, M. & Co., Inc.

Brammer, Billy L. The Gay Place. 1983. 544p. pap. 7.95 o.s.i (*0-394-72223-X*, Vintage) Knopf Publishing Group.

—The Gay Place: Being Three Related Novels. 1994. 560p. (Orig.). pap. 24.95 (*0-292-70831-9*) Univ. of Texas Pr.

Brandon, Jay. Angel of Death. 1999. 383p. mass mkt. 6.99 (*0-8125-4043-3*); 1998. 384p. 24.95 (*0-312-86541-4*) Doherty, Tom Assocs., LLC. (Forge Bks.).

—Defiance County. 1997. 288p. pap. 6.99 (*0-671-53655-9*, Pocket); 1996. 384p. 23.00 o.p. (*0-671-53654-0*, Atria) Simon & Schuster.

—Fade the Heat. 1991. 368p. mass mkt. 6.99 (*0-671-70261-0*, Pocket) Simon & Schuster.

—Fade the Heat. Gross, Bill, ed. 1990. 352p. 18.95 o.p. (*0-671-70260-2*, Atria) Simon & Schuster.

—Fade the Heat. abr. ed. 1990. audio 14.95 (*0-671-70893-7*, Simon & Schuster Audioworks) Simon & Schuster Audio.

—Local Rules. 1996. 320p. mass mkt. 5.99 (*0-671-88409-3*, Pocket); 1995. 304p. 22.00 o.p. (*0-671-88408-5*, Atria) Simon & Schuster.

—Loose among the Lambs. Grose, Bill, ed. 1993. 384p. 22.00 (*0-671-76032-7*, Atria); 1994. 400p. reprint ed. mass mkt. 5.99 (*0-671-76033-5*, Pocket); 1994. reprint ed. pap. 6.50 (*0-671-88315-1*, Pocket) Simon & Schuster.

—Predator's Waltz. Isaacson, Dana, ed. 1992. 304p. reprint ed. mass mkt. 4.99 (*0-671-70889-9*, Pocket) Simon & Schuster.

—Predator's Waltz. 1989. 288p. 17.95 o.p. (*0-312-03413-X*, Saint Martin's Minotaur) St. Martin's Pr.

—Sliver Moon. 2nd ed. 2003. (Chris Sinclair Ser.). 400p. 25.95 (*0-312-87436-7*, Forge Bks.) Doherty, Tom Assocs., LLC.

Brashear, Jean. The Healer. 2003. (Harlequin Superromance Ser.: No. 1105). 304p. mass mkt. o.s.i (*0-373-71105-0*, Harlequin Bks.) Harlequin Enterprises, Ltd.

Braun, Matt. El Paso. l.t. ed. 1991. (General Ser.). 366p. lib. bdg. 19.95 o.p. (*0-8161-5170-9*, Macmillan Reference USA) Gale Group.

Breihan, Carl W. & Garwood, W. R. West Wandering Wind. 1986. (Double D Western Ser.). 192p. 12.95 o.p. (*0-385-23504-6*) Doubleday Publishing.

Brett, Bill. This Here's a Good'un. (Illus.). 2000. 120p. pap. 15.95 (*1-58544-074-4*, Reveille Bks.); 1983. 112p. 12.95 o.p. (*0-89096-162-X*) Texas A&M Univ. Pr.

Brito, Aristeo. The Devil in Texas: El Diablo en Texas. 1992. 112p. pap. 8.00 o.s.i (*0-385-42015-3*) Doubleday Publishing.

Broadrick, Annette. Daughters of Texas: Megan's Marriage, Instant Mommy, The Groom, I Presume? 2000. 608p. mass mkt. o.s.i (*0-373-20170-2*, 1-20170-6, Harlequin Bks.) Harlequin Enterprises, Ltd.

—Sons of Texas: Callaway Country. 2000. per. (*0-373-48407-0*, Silhouette) Harlequin Enterprises, Ltd.

—Sons of Texas: Cowboys & Wedding Bells, 2 bks. in 1. 1999. per. (*0-373-20157-5*, 1-20157-3, Harlequin Bks.) Harlequin Enterprises, Ltd.

—Sons of Texas: Love & Courtship, 2 bks. in 1. 1998. per. (*0-373-20148-6*, 1-20148-2, Harlequin Bks.) Harlequin Enterprises, Ltd.

—Sons of Texas: Rogues & Ranchers. 1996. per. (*0-373-48336-8*, Harlequin Bks.) Harlequin Enterprises, Ltd.

Broday, Linda. Knight on the Texas Plains. 2002. 320p. mass mkt. 5.99 (*0-8439-5120-6*, Leisure Bks.) Dorchester Publishing Co., Inc.

Brown, Dee. Wave High the Banner: A Novel of Davy Crockett. 1999. (Illus.). 367p. 35.00 (*0-8263-2012-0*); pap. 15.95 (*0-8263-2013-9*) Univ. of New Mexico Pr.

Brown, Parry A. The Shirt off His Back: A Novel. 2001. 256p. pap. 13.95 (*0-375-75659-0*, Villard Bks.) Random House Adult Trade Publishing Group.

Brown, Rosellen. Half a Heart. 2000. (*0-374-93384-7*); 2000. 368p. 24.00 o.p. (*0-374-29987-0*); 2000. 402p. (*0-374-44013-1*); 1999. o.p. (*0-374-16772-9*) Farrar, Straus & Giroux.

—Half a Heart. abr. ed. 2000. audio 25.00 (*0-7435-0579-4*, Simon & Schuster Audioworks) Simon & Schuster Audio.

Brown, Sam. The Big Lonely. 1994. mass mkt. 3.99 (*0-671-89467-6*, Pocket) Simon & Schuster.

—The Big Lonely. Grad, Doug, ed. 1994. 256p. reprint ed. mass mkt. 5.99 (*0-671-86547-1*, Pocket) Simon & Schuster.

—The Big Lonely. Haywood, Richard, ed. unabr. ed. 1996. audio 17.00 (*1-883268-35-4*, 394644) Spellbinders, Inc.

—The Big Lonely. 1993. 203p. 19.95 (*0-8027-1234-7*) Walker & Co.

—Crime of Coy Bell. 1992. 192p. 19.95 (*0-8027-4115-0*) Walker & Co.

—The Crime of Coy Bell. 192p. 2002. pap. 4.99 (*0-7434-5732-3*); 1993. reprint ed. mass mkt. 3.99 (*0-671-78543-5*) Simon & Schuster. (Pocket).

—The Long Drift. 1996. 256p. mass mkt. 4.50 o.p. (*0-06-101003-0*, HarperTorch) Morrow/Avon.

—The Long Drift. abr. ed. 1997. audio 17.00 (*1-883268-45-1*) Spellbinders, Inc.

—The Long Drift. l.t. ed. 1995. (G. K. Hall Western Ser.). 339p. 23.95 (*0-7838-1448-8*) Thorndike Pr.

—The Long Drift. 1995. 192p. 20.95 (*0-8027-4146-0*) Walker & Co.

Brown, Sandra. Charade. abr. ed. 1993. audio 16.95 o.p. (*0-7871-0015-3*, 390507, Dove Audio); 1994. 39.95 o.p. (*0-7871-0101-X*, 112717) NewStar Media, Inc.

—Charade. 1994. 416p. 21.95 o.s.i (*0-446-51656-2*); 1995. 496p. reprint ed. mass mkt. 7.99 (*0-446-60185-3*) Warner Bks., Inc.

—In a Class by Itself. 2000. 224p. mass mkt. 6.99 (*0-553-57602-X*) Bantam Bks.

—In a Class by Itself, Set. abr. ed. 1999. audio 18.00 Highsmith Inc.

—In a Class by Itself. abr. ed. 2003. audio compact disk 14.99 (*0-7393-0378-3*, RH Audio Price-Less); 1999. audio 18.00 (*0-553-52659-6*, RH Audio) Random Hse. Audio Publishing Group.

—In a Class by Itself. l.t. ed. 240p. 2000. pap. 11.95 (*0-375-70790-5*); 1999. 18.95 (*0-375-40867-3*) Random Hse. Large Print.

—Mirror Image. 1991. reprint ed. 21.95 o.p. (*0-7278-4192-0*) Severn Hse. Pubs., Ltd.

—Mirror Image. 1990. 448p. reprint ed. mass mkt. 6.99 (*0-446-35395-7*) Warner Bks., Inc.

—The Rana Look. 2003. 256p. mass mkt. 7.50 (*0-553-57605-4*); 2002. 224p. 19.95 (*0-553-10424-1*, Spectra) Bantam Bks.

—The Rana Look. 2002. audio 28.00 (*0-7366-8854-4*) Books on Tape, Inc.

—The Rana Look. pap. o.p. (*0-7862-4701-0*); 2003. 32.95 (*0-7862-4700-2*) Thorndike Pr.

—Shadows of Yesterday. reprint ed. 1997. 272p. mass mkt. 3.99 (*0-446-60566-2*); 1992. 256p. mass mkt. 6.99 (*0-446-36071-6*) Warner Bks., Inc.

—Texas Chase. 1991. 352p. mass mkt. 6.99 (*0-553-28990-X*) Bantam Bks.

—Texas Chase. 1995. (Select Sound, Dove Ser.). 4.99 o.p. (*0-7871-0319-5*) Penguin Group (USA) Inc.

—Texas Lucky. 1991. 288p. mass mkt. 7.50 (*0-553-28951-9*) Bantam Bks.

—Texas Lucky. 1990. 192p. 14.95 o.s.i (*0-385-41406-4*) Doubleday Publishing.

—Texas Lucky. 1995. (Select Sound, Dove Ser.). 4.99 o.p. (*0-7871-0308-X*) Penguin Group (USA) Inc.

—Texas Sage. 1992. 352p. mass mkt. 7.50 (*0-553-29500-4*) Bantam Bks.

—Texas Sage. 1995. (Select Sound, Dove Ser.). 4.99 o.p. (*0-7871-0309-8*) Penguin Group (USA) Inc.

—Where There's Smoke. abr. ed. 1993. 16.95 o.p. (*1-55800-645-1*) NewStar Media, Inc.

—Where There's Smoke. 418p. 5.98 o.p. (*0-7651-0140-8*) Smithmark Pubs., Inc.

—Where There's Smoke. l.t. ed. 1994. (Paperback Bestsellers Ser.). 660p. lib. bdg. 17.95 (*1-56054-782-0*) Thorndike Pr.

—Where There's Smoke. 1993. 432p. 19.95 o.s.i (*0-446-51655-4*); 1994. 512p. reprint ed. mass mkt. 7.99 (*0-446-60034-2*) Warner Bks., Inc.

Brown, Will C. Think Fast Ranger. 1999. 191p. pap. 19.00 (*0-7540-8061-7*) BBC Audiobooks America.

—Think Fast, Ranger! l.t. ed. 1998. (Nightingale Ser.). 274p. pap. 20.95 (*0-7838-8378-1*) Thorndike Pr.

—Trouble on the Brazos. l.t. ed. 2000. (G. K. Hall Nightingale Ser.). 232p. pap. 20.95 (*0-7838-8850-3*, Macmillan Reference USA) Gale Group.

Bruni, Mary-Ann S. Rosita's Christmas Wish. 1985. (Texas Ser.). (Illus.). 48p. (J). (gr. k-8). 13.95 (*0-935857-00-1*) TexArt Services, Inc.

Bryan, J. Y. Come to the Bower: A Novel of the Texas Revolution. 1986. 474p. 14.95 o.p. (*0-89015-550-X*) Eakin Pr.

Bryant, Joy L. & Day, A. Steven. Whiskey Row. Diaz, Arthur S., ed. 2001. IX,520p. 27.95 (*0-9705259-5-8*) St. Aztec Publishing.

Buechner, Frederick. Open Heart. 1984. (Books of Bebb). mass mkt. 3.95 o.p. (*0-06-061166-9*, P-5008) HarperSanFrancisco.

—Open Heart. 1972. 5.95 o.p. (*0-689-10498-7*, Atheneum) Simon & Schuster Children's Publishing.

Bunkley, Anita Richmond. Balancing Act. 1997. 352p. 23.95 o.p. (*0-525-94010-3*) Dutton/Plume.

—Balancing Act. 1998. 400p. mass mkt. 6.99 o.s.i (*0-451-18483-1*, Signet Bks.) NAL.

—Black Gold. 1994. 416p. 21.95 o.p. (*0-525-93752-8*) Dutton/Plume.

—Black Gold. l.t. ed. 1994. 592p. reprint ed. lib. bdg. 23.95 (*0-8161-7434-2*, Macmillan Reference USA) Gale Group.

—Black Gold. 1995. 448p. mass mkt. 6.99 o.s.i (*0-451-17973-0*); 1951. mass mkt. 0.25 o.p. (*0-451-00853-7*) NAL. (Signet Bks.).

—Emily: The Yellow Rose. 1999. 243p. 19.99 (*0-9624012-1-8*); 1989. 224p. pap. 12.95 o.p. (*0-9624012-0-X*) Rinard Publishing.

Burandt, Harriet, et al. Tales from the Homeplace: Adventures of Texas Farm Girl. 1999. 160p. (gr. 4-6). pap. text 3.99 (*0-440-41494-6*, Dell Books for Young Readers) Random Hse. Children's Bks.

Burke, James Lee. Cimarron Rose. l.t. ed. 1998. (Large Print Book Ser.). 27.95 (*1-56895-527-8*, Wheeler Publishing, Inc.) Gale Group.

—Cimarron Rose. (Dave Robicheaux Mysteries Ser.). 1998. 406p. mass mkt. 7.99 (*0-7868-8930-6*); 1997. 304p. 24.95 (*0-7868-6258-0*) Hyperion Pr.

—Cimarron Rose. 1997. 278p. 15.95 (*0-7528-0486-3*) Orion Media.

—Cimarron Rose. unabr. ed. 1998. audio 75.00 (*0-7887-1746-4*, 95224E7) Recorded Bks., LLC.

—Cimarron Rose. abr. ed. 1997. (Dave Robicheaux Mystery Ser.). 5p. audio 25.00 (*0-671-57630-5*, 495292, Simon & Schuster Audioworks) Simon & Schuster Audio.

—Cimarron Rose. ltd. ed. 1997. 288p. 150.00 (*0-9631925-9-0*) Trice, B.E. Publishing.

—Heartwood. unabr. ed. 2000. 8p. audio 69.95 (*0-7927-2363-5*, CSL 252, Chivers Sound Library) BBC Audiobooks America.

—Heartwood. 2000. (Dave Robicheaux Mysteries Ser.). 400p. mass mkt. 7.50 (*0-440-22401-2*) Dell Publishing.

—Heartwood. l.t. ed. 1999. pap. 24.95 o.p. (*0-7838-8690-X*, Macmillan Reference USA) Gale Group.

—Heartwood, Set. abr. ed. 1999. audio 25.00 Highsmith Inc.

—Heartwood. l.t. ed. 1999. 560p. 24.95 (*0-375-40849-5*) Random Hse. Large Print.

—Heartwood. abr. ed. 1999. (Dave Robicheaux Mystery Ser.). audio 25.00 (*0-671-58107-4*, Simon & Schuster Audioworks) Simon & Schuster Audio.

—Heartwood. ltd. ed. 1999. 341p. 150.00 (*1-890885-08-8*) Trice, B.E. Publishing.

—Lay down My Sword & Shield. Date not set. lib. bdg. 24.95 (*0-8488-1779-6*) Amereon, Ltd.

—Lay down My Sword & Shield. 1989. 272p. reprint ed. pap. 8.95 o.p. (*0-88150-150-6*) Countryman Pr.

—Lay down My Sword & Shield. 1999. 389p. mass mkt. 6.50 (*0-7868-8950-0*); 1995. 240p. (J). pap. 10.95 o.p. (*0-7868-8039-2*) Hyperion Pr.

—Two for Texas. l.t. ed. 2002. 293p. 29.95 (*0-7862-3402-4*) Gale Group.

—Two for Texas. 1995. 148p. pap. 10.95 (*0-7868-8011-2*) Hyperion Pr.

Calhoun, Tom. The Waco Gang, Bk. 2. 2002. (Texas Tracker Ser.). 192p. mass mkt. 4.99 (*0-515-13349-3*, Jove) Berkley Publishing Group.

Camp, Candace. Smooth-Talking Texan. 2002. (Silhouette Intimate Moments Ser.: No. 1153). mass mkt. (*0-373-27223-5*, 1-27223-6, Silhouette) Harlequin Enterprises, Ltd.

Camp, Will. Blood of Texas. 1996. 288p. mass mkt. 4.50 o.p. (*0-06-100992-X*, HarperTorch) Morrow/Avon.

—Lone Survivor. l.t. ed. 2001. (G. K. Hall Western Ser.). 232p. 25.95 (*0-7838-9411-2*, Macmillan Reference USA) Gale Group.

—Lone Survivor. 1995. 208p. mass mkt. 4.50 o.p. (*0-06-100888-5*, HarperTorch) Morrow/Avon.

Campbell, Helen. The Blue Yonder Inn. 2002. 256p. text 26.95 (*0-87013-641-0*) Michigan State Univ. Pr.

Campbell, John N. Gator the Cowpony Goes to School. 1990. (Illus.). 72p. (J). (gr. 4-7). 9.95 (*0-89015-699-9*) Eakin Pr.

Cannell, Stephen J. The Devil's Workshop, Set. abr. ed. 1999. audio 25.00 Highsmith Inc.

—The Devil's Workshop. 1999. viii, 421p. 25.00 (*0-688-16618-0*, Morrow, William & Co.); 2000. 448p. reprint ed. mass mkt. 6.99 (*0-380-73221-1*) Morrow/Avon.

Cantu, Norma Elia. Canicula: Snapshots of a Girlhood en la Frontera. 1995. (Illus.). (C). 144p. 22.50 o.p. (*0-8263-1592-5*); 132p. pap. 14.95 (*0-8263-1828-2*) Univ. of New Mexico Pr.

Capps, Benjamin. The Brothers of Uterica. 1988. (Southwest Life & Letters Ser.). 320p. reprint ed. pap. 10.95 (*0-87074-258-2*) Southern Methodist Univ. Pr.

—The Brothers of Uterica: A Novel. 1988. (Southwest Life & Letters Ser.). 320p. reprint ed. 22.50 (*0-87074-257-4*) Southern Methodist Univ. Pr.

—Sam Chance. 1980. mass mkt. 1.95 o.s.i (*0-441-74940-2*) Ace Bks.

—Sam Chance. 1986. 272p. mass mkt. 2.50 o.s.i (*0-441-74920-8*, Diamond Bks.) Berkley Publishing Group.

—Sam Chance. l.t. ed. 2002. lib. bdg. 27.95 (*1-58547-108-9*, Western) Ctr. Point Large Print.

—Sam Chance. 1987. (Southwest Life & Letters Ser.). 282p. reprint ed. 22.50 (*0-87074-250-7*); pap. 10.95 (*0-87074-251-5*) Southern Methodist Univ. Pr.

—The Trail to Ogallala. 1986. 2.50 o.s.i (*0-441-82139-1*, Diamond Bks.) Berkley Publishing Group.

—The Trail to Ogallala. l.t. ed. 2002. 302p. lib. bdg. 26.95 (*1-58547-109-7*) Ctr. Point Large Print.

—The Trail to Ogallala. 1985. (Texas Tradition Ser.: No. 3). 286p. reprint ed. 16.95 (*0-87565-012-0*); pap. 9.95 (*0-87565-013-9*) Texas Christian Univ. Pr.

Carleen, Sally. Porcupine Ranch. 1997. per. (*0-373-19221-5*, 1-19221-0, Silhouette) Harlequin Enterprises, Ltd.

Carmichael, Kathy. Chasing Charlie. 2001. 184p. text 19.95 (*0-8034-9464-5*, Avalon Bks.) Bouregy, Thomas & Co., Inc.

—Chasing Charlie. l.t. ed. 2002. 24.95 (*0-7862-4089-X*) Gale Group.

Casad, Mary Brooke. Bluebonnet at the Alamo. 1984. (Illus.). 40p. (J). (gr. 4-7). 11.95 o.p. (*0-89015-445-7*) Eakin Pr.

Casper, K. N. The First Family of Texas (Home on the Ranch) 2000. (Harlequin Superromance Ser.: Vol. 951). mass mkt. (*0-373-70951-X*, Harlequin Bks.) Harlequin Enterprises, Ltd.

Cates, Kimberly. Only Forever. 1992. 320p. mass mkt. 5.99 (*0-671-74083-0*, Pocket) Simon & Schuster.

Cattarulla, Kay, ed. Texas Bound: Nineteen Texas Stories. 1994. (Southwest Life & Letters Ser.). 262p. 22.50 (*0-87074-367-8*); pap. 10.95 (*0-87074-368-6*) Southern Methodist Univ. Pr.

—Texas Bound: 22 Texas Stories. 2001. (Southwest Life & Letters Ser.). 280p. pap. 12.95 (*0-87074-459-3*) Southern Methodist Univ. Pr.

—Texas Bound Bk. II: 22 Texas Stories. 1998. 280p. 22.50 (*0-87074-426-7*); pap. 12.95 (*0-87074-427-5*) Southern Methodist Univ. Pr.

Cattarulla, Kay, et al, readers. Texas Bound, Eight by Eight Stories by Texas Writers, Read by Texas Actors. 1994. (Southwest Life & Letters Ser.). audio 15.95 (*0-87074-369-4*) Southern Methodist Univ. Pr.

—Texas Bound II, Eight by Eight: More Stories by Texas Writers, Read by Texas Actors. 1996. (Southwest Life & Letters Ser.). audio 16.95 (*0-87074-394-5*) Southern Methodist Univ. Pr.

Caves, Roger W. Exploring Urban America: An Introductory Reader. 1994. 538p. 120.00 (*0-8039-5637-1*, 4975); pap. 61.95 (*0-8039-5638-X*, 4976) Sage Pubns., Inc.

Chancellor, Victoria. The Prince's Texas Bride. 2003. (Harlequin American Romance Ser.: No. 959). 256p. mass mkt. (*0-373-16959-0*, Harlequin Bks.) Harlequin Enterprises, Ltd.

Chappell, Henry C. The Callings. 2002. (Illus.). 224p. 24.95 (*0-89672-494-8*) Texas Tech Univ. Pr.

Chariton, Wallace O. Forget the Alamo. 1990. (Regional Bks.). 312p. 18.95 o.p. (*1-55622-134-7*) Wordware Publishing, Inc.

Child, Lee. Echo Burning. l.t. ed. 2001. 510p. lib. bdg. 29.95 (*1-58547-135-6*) Ctr. Point Large Print.

—Echo Burning. 2001. (Illus.). 384p. 24.95 o.p. (*0-399-14726-8*) Penguin Group (USA) Inc.

Child, Maureen. Did You Say Twins? 2001. (Fortunes of Texas Ser.). (Illus.). 183p. mass mkt. (*0-373-76408-1*, Harlequin Bks.) Harlequin Enterprises, Ltd.

Christenberry, Judy. The Last Bachelor. 2003. (Silhouette Special Releases Ser.: No. 9). (Illus.). 256p. mass mkt. (*0-373-61360-1*, Silhouette) Harlequin Enterprises, Ltd.

—Saved by a Texas-Sized Wedding. 2003. (Harlequin American Romance Ser.: No. 969). (Illus.). 256p. mass mkt. (*0-373-16969-8*, Harlequin Bks.) Harlequin Enterprises, Ltd.

Chupp, Charles. For Land's Sake. 2001. 138p. (*1-57168-955-9*) Eakin Pr.

Clark, L. D. A Bright Tragic Thing: A Tale of Civil War Texas. 1992. 304p. (Orig.). pap. 14.95 (*0-938317-17-2*); pap. text 24.95 (*0-938317-18-0*) Cinco Puntos Pr.

Clemmons, Caroline. The Most Unsuitable Wife. 2003. 32p. mass mkt. 5.99 o.s.i (*0-8217-7443-3*) Kensington Publishing Corp.

Close, Bob. Don't Look Back. 2000. 148p. pap. 20.99 (*0-7388-2897-1*) Xlibris Corp.

Coffman, Elaine. Someone Like You. 1998. 345p. mass mkt. 5.99 o.s.i (*0-449-15006-2*, Fawcett) Ballantine Bks.

—Someone Like You. l.t. ed. 1998. pap. 24.95 (*1-56895-543-X*, Wheeler Publishing, Inc.) Gale Group.

Cole, Jackson. The Death Riders. 1999. 167 p. (*0-7540-3651-0*); pap. (*0-7540-3652-9*) BBC Audiobooks America.

—The Death Riders. l.t. ed. 1999. (Nightingale Ser.). 176p. pap. 20.95 (*0-7838-0445-8*) Thorndike Pr.

—The Devil's Legion. l.t. ed. 1996. (Nightingale Ser.). pap. 17.95 (*0-7838-1617-0*, Macmillan Reference USA) Gale Group.

—Fast Draw. l.t. ed. 2002. 180p. pap. 22.95 (*0-7862-3941-7*) Gale Group.

—Hell in Paradise. l.t. ed. 2001. 195p. pap. 22.95 (*0-7838-9566-6*) Thorndike Pr.

—Thunder Range: A Jim Hatfield Texas Ranger Western. l.t. ed. 1998. (Nightingale Ser.). 168p. pap. 20.95 (*0-7838-0244-7*) Thorndike Pr.

—Two-Gun Devil. l.t. ed. 2000. (G. K. Hall Nightingale Ser.). 208p. pap. 20.95 (*0-7838-8847-3*); (*0-7540-4015-1*) Gale Group. (Macmillan Reference USA).

Conner, Robert P., Sr. Cut to the Bone: A Novel. 2002. 200p. pap. 13.95 (*1-55583-695-X*) Alyson Pubns.

Conrad, Linda. Desperado Dad. 2002. (Silhouette Desire Ser.: No. 1458). 192p. mass mkt. (*0-373-76458-8*, Silhouette) Harlequin Enterprises, Ltd.

—Secrets, Lies... & Passion. 2002. (Silhouette Desire Ser.). mass mkt. (*0-373-76470-7*, Silhouette) Harlequin Enterprises, Ltd.

Conrad, Roxanne, tr. Exile, Texas. 2003. 302p. 25.95 (*1-59414-071-5*, Five Star) Gale Group.

Conwell, Kent. The Alamo Trail. 2000. 184p. 18.95 (*0-8034-9401-7*, Avalon Bks.) Bouregy, Thomas & Co., Inc.

Cook, Christopher. Robbers. 2000. 372p. 24.95 (*0-7867-0776-3*, Carroll & Graf Pubs.) Avalon Publishing Group.

—Robbers. 2002. 368p. pap. 14.00 (*0-425-18346-7*) Berkley Publishing Group.

Cook, Will. The Texas Pistol. l.t. ed. 2000. 194p. 20.95 (*1-57490-269-5*, Sagebrush Large Print Westerns) Beeler, Thomas T. Publisher.

—Until Darkness Disappears. (Saga of Texas Ser.). 2001. 316p. 23.95 (*0-7862-2403-7*, Five Star); 2002. 450p. 24.95 (*0-7838-8952-6*) Gale Group.

—Until Day Breaks: A Saga of Texas. 1999. (Western Ser.). 240p. 19.95 (*0-7862-1794-4*, Five Star) Gale Group.

—Until Day Breaks: A Saga of Texas. l.t. ed. 2000. (Western Ser.). 338p. 21.95 (*0-7862-1795-2*); (*0-7540-4105-0*); (*0-7540-4106-9*) Thorndike Pr.

—Until Shadows Fall Book 2: A Saga of Texas. 2000. (Five Star Western Ser.: Vol. 2). 296p. 21.95 (*0-7862-1847-9*, Five Star) Gale Group.

Coomer, Joe. Apologizing to Dogs. 1999. (Illus.). 288p. 22.00 o.s.i (*0-684-85946-7*, Scribner) Simon & Schuster.

—Apologizing to Dogs. l.t. ed. 2000. (Americana Ser.). 416p. 26.95 (*0-7862-2367-7*) Thorndike Pr.

—Apologizing to Dogs: A Novel. 2000. E-Book 22.00 (*0-684-87123-8*, Scribner) Simon & Schuster.

—The Loop. 228p. 1993. pap. 10.95 o.p. (*0-571-19823-6*); 1992. 21.95 o.p. (*0-571-12949-8*) Faber & Faber, Inc.

Cooner, Donna D. Twelve Days in Texas. 1994. (Illus.). 32p. (J). (ps up). pap. 12.95 (*0-937460-85-0*) Hendrick-Long Publishing Co.

Cooper, J. California. The Wake of the Wind: A Novel. 384p. 1999. pap. 13.95 (*0-385-48705-3*); 1998. 22.95 o.s.i (*0-385-48704-5*) Doubleday Publishing.

Cooper, Susan Rogers. A Crooked Little House. 1999. (E. J. Pugh Mysteries Ser.: No. 6). 352p. mass mkt. 5.99 o.s.i (*0-380-79469-1*, Avon Bks.) Morrow/Avon.

—Funny as a Dead Relative. 1994. 224p. 19.95 o.p. (*0-312-11438-9*, Saint Martin's Minotaur) St. Martin's Pr.

—Hickory Dickory Stalk. 1996. (E. J. Pugh Mysteries Ser.). (Orig.). mass mkt. 5.50 o.s.i (*0-380-78155-7*, Avon Bks.) Morrow/Avon.

—Home Again, Home Again. 1997. (E. J. Pugh Mysteries Ser.). mass mkt. 5.99 o.s.i (*0-380-78156-5*, Avon Bks.) Morrow/Avon.

—Not in My Backyard. 1999. (E. J. Pugh Mysteries Ser.). 256p. mass mkt. 5.99 o.s.i (*0-380-80532-4*, Avon Bks.) Morrow/Avon.

—One, Two, What Did Daddy Do? 1996. (E. J. Pugh Mysteries Ser.). mass mkt. 5.50 o.s.i (*0-380-78417-3*, Avon Bks.) Morrow/Avon.

—One, Two, What Did Daddy Do? 1992. 224p. 17.95 o.p. (*0-312-08209-6*, Saint Martin's Minotaur) St. Martin's Pr.

—There Was a Little Girl. 1998. (E. J. Pugh Mysteries Ser.). 224p. mass mkt. 5.50 o.s.i (*0-380-79468-3*, Avon Bks.) Morrow/Avon.

Cooper, Virgil R. Virg-4 Pettiquah Crossing. per. 4.99 (*0-9668804-5-5*) A-bar-V Publishing.

Copeland, Lori. Faith. l.t. ed. 2002. (Christian Romance Ser.). 372p. 25.95 (*0-7862-3826-7*) Gale Group.

—Faith. E-Book 7.99 (*0-8423-5653-3*) Tyndale Hse. Pubs.

—Promise Me Tomorrow. (Orig.). 1998. mass mkt. o.s.i (*0-449-00505-4*); 1993. mass mkt. 5.99 o.s.i (*0-449-14752-5*, Fawcett) Ballantine Bks.

—Promise Me Tomorrow. l.t. ed. 1994. (Orig.). 22.95 o.p. (*1-56895-064-0*, Wheeler Publishing, Inc.) Gale Group.

Cord, Barry. Six Bullets Left. l.t. ed. 2001. 121p. pap. 23.95 (*0-7838-9507-0*, Macmillan Reference USA) Gale Group.

—Two Graves for a Gunman. l.t. ed. 2002. (Nightingale Ser.). 22.95 (*0-7862-4192-6*) Thorndike Pr.

Cotrell, Georgia. Shoulders. 1987. 258p. (Orig.). lib. bdg. 20.95 (*0-932379-26-5*); pap. 9.95 (*0-932379-25-7*) Firebrand Bks.

Craven, Jerry. Snake Mountain: A Novel. 2000. 236p. 24.50 (*0-87565-221-2*) Texas Christian Univ. Pr.

Crawford, Max. Lords of the Plain. 1985. 352p. 14.95 o.s.i (*0-689-11475-3*, Scribner) Simon & Schuster.

—Lords of the Plains: A Novel. 1997. 320p. 14.95 (*0-8061-2908-5*) Univ. of Oklahoma Pr.

—Waltz Across Texas: A Novel. 2002. (Literature of the American West Ser.: Vol. 10). 393p. 19.95 (*0-8061-3417-8*) Univ. of Oklahoma Pr.

—Wamba: A Novel. 2002. (Literature of the American West Ser.: Vol. 8). 313p. 29.95 (*0-8061-3391-0*) Univ. of Oklahoma Pr.

Crider, Bill. Booked for a Hanging. 1992. 224p. 17.95 o.p. (*0-312-08149-9*, Saint Martin's Minotaur) St. Martin's Pr.

—Cursed to Death. 1990. 176p. mass mkt. 3.95 o.s.i (*0-8041-0424-7*, Ivy Bks.) Ballantine Bks.

—Cursed to Death. 1988. 16.95 o.s.i (*0-8027-5698-0*) Walker & Co.

—A Dangerous Thing. 1996. per. (*0-373-26216-7*, 1-26216-1, Worldwide Library) Harlequin Enterprises, Ltd.

—A Dangerous Thing. 1994. 200p. 19.95 (*0-8027-3187-2*) Walker & Co.

—Dead on the Island. unabr. ed. 1995. audio 17.00 (*1-883268-19-2*) Spellbinders, Inc.

—Dead on the Island. 1991. 193p. 18.95 (*0-8027-5787-1*) Walker & Co.

—Death by Accident. l.t. ed. 1998. (Large Print Book Ser.). pap. 23.95 (*1-56895-663-0*, Wheeler Publishing, Inc.) Gale Group.

—Death by Accident. 2000. (WWL Mystery Ser.: Vol. 343). 256p. per. (*0-373-26343-0*, Harlequin Bks.) Harlequin Enterprises, Ltd.

—Death by Accident. 1998. (Sheriff Dan Rhodes Mysteries Ser.). 288p. 22.95 o.p. (*0-312-18080-2*, Saint Martin's Minotaur) St. Martin's Pr.

—Death on the Move. 1990. mass mkt. 3.95 o.s.i (*0-8041-0425-5*, Ivy Bks.) Ballantine Bks.

—Death on the Move. 1989. 204p. 17.95 o.p. (*0-8027-5730-8*) Walker & Co.

—Dying Voices. 1989. 192p. 14.95 o.p. (*0-312-03328-1*, Saint Martin's Minotaur) St. Martin's Pr.

—Evil at Root. 1992. 2.99 o.p. (*0-517-09041-4*) Random Hse. Value Publishing.

—Evil at Root. 1990. 15.95 o.p. (*0-312-04314-7*, Saint Martin's Minotaur) St. Martin's Pr.

—Evil at the Root. 1991. 192p. mass mkt. 3.95 o.s.i (*0-8041-0764-5*, Ivy Bks.) Ballantine Bks.

—Gator Kill. Haywood, Richard, ed. unabr. ed. 1995. (Truman Smith Trilogy Ser.). audio 17.00 (*1-883268-27-3*) Spellbinders, Inc.

—Gator Kill: A Truman Smith. 1992. 202p. 18.95 (*0-8027-3213-5*) Walker & Co.

—A Ghost of a Chance: A Sheriff Dan Rhodes Mystery. 2000. (Sheriff Dan Rhodes Mysteries Ser.). 263p. 23.95 (*0-312-20889-8*, Saint Martin's Minotaur) St. Martin's Pr.

—Murder Is an Art. 1999. 256p. 21.95 o.p. (*0-312-19927-9*, Saint Martin's Minotaur) St. Martin's Pr.

—Murder Most Fowl. 1994. 208p. 18.95 o.p. (*0-312-11387-0*, Saint Martin's Minotaur) St. Martin's Pr.

—Murder Takes a Break: A Truman Smith Mystery. 1997. (Truman Smith Mystery Ser.). 246p. 21.95 (*0-8027-3308-5*) Walker & Co.

—One Dead Dean. 1988. 208p. 17.95 (*0-8027-5711-1*) Walker & Co.

—The Prairie Chicken Kill: A Truman Smith Mystery. 1996. (Truman Smith Mystery Ser.). 216p. 20.95 (*0-8027-3282-8*) Walker & Co.

—A Romantic Way to Die. 2002. (WWL Mystery Ser.: No. 440). 256p. mass mkt. (*0-373-26440-2*, Worldwide Library) Harlequin Enterprises, Ltd.

—A Romantic Way to Die: A Sheriff Dan Rhodes Mystery. 2001. 240p. 22.95 (*0-312-20907-X*) St. Martin's Pr.

—Shotgun Saturday Night. 1989. 176p. mass mkt. 3.95 o.s.i (*0-8041-0423-9*, Ivy Bks.) Ballantine Bks.

—Shotgun Saturday Night. 1987. 16.95 (*0-8027-5684-0*) Walker & Co.

—The Texas Capitol Murders. 1992. 336p. 21.95 o.p. (*0-312-07093-4*, Saint Martin's Minotaur) St. Martin's Pr.

—Too Late to Die. 1989. 192p. mass mkt. 3.95 o.s.i (*0-8041-0422-0*, Ivy Bks.) Ballantine Bks.

—Too Late to Die. 1986. 192p. 14.95 (*0-8027-5650-6*) Walker & Co.

—When Old Men Die. abr. ed. 1997. audio 17.00 (*1-883268-33-8*) Spellbinders, Inc.

—When Old Men Die. 1994. 192p. 19.95 (*0-8027-3195-3*) Walker & Co.

—Winning Can Be Murder. 2000. (Sheriff Dan Rhodes Mysteries Ser.: Bk. 354). 256p. per. (*0-373-26354-6*, 1-26354-0, Worldwide Library) Harlequin Enterprises, Ltd.

—Winning Can Be Murder. 1996. 240p. 21.95 o.p. (*0-312-14072-X*, Saint Martin's Minotaur) St. Martin's Pr.

Crook, Elizabeth. Promised Lands: A Novel of the Texas Rebellion. 1995. (Southwest Life & Letters Ser.). 528p. pap. 12.95 (*0-87074-385-6*) Southern Methodist Univ. Pr.

Crumley, James. Bordersnakes. 1996. 336p. 22.00 o.p. (*0-89296-573-8*) Warner Bks., Inc.

—The Final Country. l.t. ed. 2003. 25.95 (*1-58724-412-8*, Wheeler Publishing, Inc.) Gale Group.

—The Final Country. 2001. 320p. 24.95 (*0-89296-666-1*) Mysterious Pr.

—The Final Country. 2002. 320p. pap. 12.95 (*0-446-67964-X*, Mysterious Pr. Paperback Bks.) Warner Bks., Inc.

Culbert, Steven T. Lovesong for the Giant Contessa. 1997. 280 p. 20.00 (*1-56858-082-7*) Four Walls Eight Windows.

Cullin, Mitch. Tideland: A Novel. 2000. 192p. 22.00 (*0-8023-1335-3*) Dufour Editions, Inc.

Cunningham, Eugene. Pistol Passport. l.t. ed. 1994. 321p. pap. 17.95 o.p. (*0-8161-7418-0*, Macmillan Reference USA) Gale Group.

—Ranger Way. l.t. ed. 1998. (Large Print Western Ser.). 227 p. (*0-7540-3433-X*) BBC Audiobooks America.

—Ranger Way. l.t. ed. 1998. (Nightingale Ser.). 232p. pap. 20.95 (*0-7838-0243-9*) Thorndike Pr.

—Texas Sheriff. 1994. 17.50 o.p. (*0-7451-4614-7*, Gunsmoke) BBC Audiobooks America.

Curtis, Jack. Paradise Valley. l.t. ed. 2001. (Sagebrush Large Print Westerns Ser.). 180p. 20.95 (*1-57490-346-2*, Sagebrush Large Print Westerns) Beeler, Thomas T. Publisher.

—Pepper Tree Rider. 1997. 176p. reprint ed. pap. 3.99 (*0-8439-4270-3*, Leisure Bks.) Dorchester Publishing Co., Inc.

—Pepper Tree Rider. l.t. ed. 1994. 224p. lib. bdg. 19.95 (*0-7838-1130-6*, Macmillan Reference USA) Gale Group.

—Pepper Tree Rider. 1994. 144p. 19.95 (*0-8027-4137-1*) Walker & Co.

Dalrymple, Terence. Fishing for Trouble. 1992. 160p. 13.95 o.p. (*0-8329-0474-0*) New Win Publishing, Inc.

Dalton, Richard Merrill, Jr. Cattle War: A Novel about the Border War with Mexico in the 1870's. 2000. 256p. E-Book 8.00 (*0-7388-9506-7*) Xlibris Corp.

—Jornada del Muerto: Texas - 1841. 2001. 297p. pap. 21.99 (*0-7388-6473-0*); text 31.99 (*0-7388-6472-2*); E-Book 8.00 (*0-7388-6474-9*) Xlibris Corp.

Darby, Maribeth. The Land of the Magic Sand: Salt, Yesterday & Today. 1994. 120p. (J). (gr. 5-6). 12.95 o.p. (*0-89015-973-4*) Eakin Pr.

—Land of Whistlepunks & Wild Things: Forests Yesterday & Today. 1997. (Illus.). 128p. (J). 14.95 (*1-57168-112-4*) Eakin Pr.

Dark Winter. 1991. 208p. 15.00 o.s.i (*0-385-26568-9*) Doubleday Publishing.

Davenport, Bill. Love Song Blue. 2001. 320p. lib. bdg. 22.95 (*0-9707390-2-8*) Daugherty, Royce Publishing.

Davis, Austin. Shoveling Smoke: A Clay Parker Crime Novel. 2003. 320p. 23.95 (*0-8118-4152-9*) Chronicle Bks. LLC.

Davis, Dee. Midnight Rain. 2002. 384p. mass mkt. 6.99 (*0-8041-1977-5*, Ivy Bks.) Ballantine Bks.

Davis, Kaye. Devil's Leg Crossing. 1997. (Maris Middleton Mysteries Ser.). 240p. pap. 11.95 o.p. (*1-56280-158-9*) Naiad Pr., Inc.

—Possessions: A Maris Middleton Mystery. 1998. (Maris Middleton Mysteries Ser.). 240p. (Orig.). pap. 11.95 (*1-56280-192-9*) Naiad Pr., Inc.

—Shattered Illusions: A Maris Middleton Mystery. 1999. (Maris Middleton Mysteries Ser.: No. 4). 240p. pap. 11.95 (*1-56280-252-6*) Naiad Pr., Inc.

—Until the End: A Maris Middleton Mystery. 1999. (Maris Middleton Mysteries Ser.: No. 3). 224p. pap. 11.95 (*1-56280-222-4*) Naiad Pr., Inc.

Davis, Mollie Evelyn Moore. Under the Man Fig. Grider, Sylvia A., ed. 2000. (Texas Tradition Ser.: Vol. 28). 324p. reprint ed. pap. 15.95 (*0-87565-222-0*) Texas Christian Univ. Pr.

Davis, T. L. Home to Texas. 1997. 304p. (Orig.). (C). pap. 13.00 (*0-9656536-6-8*) F&S Pr.

—Shadow Soldier. 1997. 312p. 19.95 (*0-9656536-4-1*) F&S Pr.

Dawson, Carol. Body of Knowledge. 1994. 480p. tchr. ed. 22.95 (*1-56512-054-X*) Algonquin Bks. of Chapel Hill.

—Body of Knowledge. 1996. 480p. pap. (*0-671-53572-2*, Washington Square Pr.) Simon & Schuster.

—The Waking Spell. 1992. 312p. 19.95 o.p. (*0-945575-65-3*) Algonquin Bks. of Chapel Hill.

Dawson, Geralyn. The Bad Luck Wedding Dress. 1996. 352p. mass mkt. 4.99 o.s.i (*0-553-56792-6*) Bantam Bks.

—The Kissing Stars. 1999. (Sonnet Bks.). (Illus.). 416p. pap. 6.50 (*0-671-01518-4*, Pocket) Simon & Schuster.

—The Wedding Ransom. 1998. (Illus.). 368p. pap. 6.50 (*0-671-00127-2*, Pocket) Simon & Schuster.

de Paola, Tomie. The Legend of the Bluebonnet: An Old Tale of Texas. 1983. (J). 13.14 (*0-606-01690-2*) Turtleback Bks.

Dearen, Patrick. When Cowboys Die. l.t. ed. 1995. 253p. 19.95 (*0-7838-1514-X*, Macmillan Reference USA) Gale Group.

—When Cowboys Die. Haywood, Richard, ed. unabr. ed. 1996. audio 17.00 (*1-883268-36-2*) Spellbinders, Inc.

—When Cowboys Die: An Evans Novel of the West. 1994. 196p. 18.95 o.p. (*0-87131-756-7*) Evans, M. & Co., Inc.

Deleva, John. Hours Like Diamonds. 2000. 169p. (Orig.). pap. 11.77 (*0-9701668-0-X*) Johnsbook.com.

Dellin, Genell. The Renegades: Rafe. 2001. 384p. mass mkt. 5.99 (*0-380-81849-3*, Avon Bks.) Morrow/Avon.

DeNosky, Kathie. Cowboy Boss. 2002. (Silhouette Desire Ser.: No. 1457). 192p. mass mkt. (*0-373-76457-X*, Silhouette) Harlequin Enterprises, Ltd.

Denton, Bradley. Blackburn: A Novel. 1995. 304p. pap. 12.00 (*0-312-13029-5*) Picador.

—Blackburn: A Novel. 1993. 19.95 o.p. (*0-312-08705-5*) St. Martin's Pr.

—Lunatics. unabr. ed. 1998. audio 64.00 (*0-7366-4036-3*, 4535) Books on Tape, Inc.

—Lunatics. 1996. 336p. 23.95 (*0-312-14363-X*) St. Martin's Pr.

—Lunatics: A Novel. 1997. 352p. pap. 19.00 (*0-553-37891-0*) Bantam Bks.

Devlin, Linda. Jed. 2001. (Rock Creek Six Ser.). (Illus.). 32p. mass mkt. 5.99 o.s.i (*0-8217-6744-5*) Kensington Publishing Corp.

Dewlen, Al. The Bone Pickers. 2002. (Double Mountain Bks.). 424p. pap. 19.95 (*0-89672-479-4*, Double Mountain Bks.) Texas Tech Univ. Pr.

Dickerson, Zell G. Rise of Dark Shadows. 1985. 208p. (Orig.). pap. 9.95 o.p. (*0-934955-03-4*) Watercress Pr.

Dickson, Athol. Whom Shall I Fear? A Garr Reed Mystery. 1996. (Garr Reed Mystery Ser.). 352p. pap. 10.99 (*0-310-20760-6*) Zondervan.

Dilmore, John. Parts Unknown. 1999. 165p. pap. 13.95 (*0-88739-182-6*) Creative Arts Bk. Co.

DuCharme, Dede Fox. The Treasure in the Tiny Blue Tin. 1998. (Chaparral Books for Young Readers). 144p. (J). (gr. 5-8). pap. 11.95 (*0-87565-180-1*) Texas Christian Univ. Pr.

Duff, Gerald. Graveyard Working. 1994. 185p. 18.00 (*1-880909-15-4*) Baskerville Pubs., Inc.

Durr, Ben M., et al. Miss Emily, the Yellow Rose of Texas: A Novel. 2001. 319p. 28.95 (*0-86534-322-5*) Sunstone Pr.

Duval, John C. Early Times in Texas; or, the Adventures of Jack Dobell. Major, Mabel & Smith, Rebecca W., eds. 1986. (Illus.). reprint ed. 286p. pap. 14.95 (*0-8032-6567-0*, Bison Bks.); xxviii, 284p. text 30.00 o.p. (*0-8032-1673-4*) Univ. of Nebraska Pr.

Edson, J. T. The Code of Dusty Fog. 1989. 2.95 (*1-55773-288-4*, Diamond Bks.) Berkley Publishing Group.

—Cure the Texas Fever. 1996. 208p. mass mkt. 4.50 o.s.i (*0-440-22215-X*) Dell Publishing.

—Cure the Texas Fever. 1997. 192p. 22.00 (*0-7278-5130-6*) Severn Hse. Pubs., Ltd.

—Go Back to Hell. (Orig.). 1986. 192p. mass mkt. 2.50 o.s.i (*0-425-09101-5*); 1982. mass mkt. 1.95 o.s.i (*0-425-05618-X*); 1979. mass mkt. 1.75 o.s.i (*0-425-04110-7*) Berkley Publishing Group.

—Go Back to Hell. 1992. 192p. (Orig.). mass mkt. 3.50 o.s.i (*0-440-21033-X*) Dell Publishing.

—The Small Texan. 1985. 192p. mass mkt. 2.50 o.p. (*0-425-07594-X*) Berkley Publishing Group.

—The Small Texan. l.t. ed. 1983. (Ulverscroft Large Print Ser.). 304p. 29.99 o.p. (*0-7089-0956-6*, Ulverscroft) Thorpe, F. A. Pubs. GBR. *Dist:* Ulverscroft Large Print Bks., Ltd., Ulverscroft Large Print Canada, Ltd.

—Texas Warrior. 1997. mass mkt. 5.50 (*0-440-22396-2*); 240p. mass mkt. 5.50 o.s.i (*0-440-22399-7*) Dell Publishing.

—The Trouble Busters. 1990. 2.95 (*1-55773-297-3*, Diamond Bks.); 1984. 192p. mass mkt. 2.25 o.s.i (*0-425-06849-8*); 1982. mass mkt. 1.95 o.s.i (*0-425-05227-3*) Berkley Publishing Group.

Egbert, Kathlyn W. The Twenty-Third Dream: A Novel. 1993. (Southwest Life & Letters Ser.). 216p. (Orig.). pap. 10.95 (*0-87074-360-0*); pap. text 22.50 (*0-87074-352-X*) Southern Methodist Univ. Pr.

Eickhoff, Randy Lee & Lewis, Leonard C. Bowie. 2000. 352p. mass mkt. 6.99 (*0-8125-7784-1*); 1998. 304p. 23.95 (*0-312-86619-4*) Doherty, Tom Assocs., LLC. (Forge Bks.).

—Bowie. 1999. 6.99 (*0-312-87097-3*) St. Martin's Pr.

Englade, Ken. To Hatred Turned. 1994. mass mkt. 4.99 o.p. (*0-312-95132-9*, St. Martin's Paperbacks) St. Martin's Pr.

—To Hatred Turned: A True Story of Love & Death in Texas. 1993. (Illus.). 368p. 21.95 o.p. (*0-312-09924-X*) St. Martin's Pr.

Eppes, Cindy. South of Reason. 2002. 288p. 24.00 (*0-7434-3799-3*, Atria); 2002. E-Book 24.00 (*0-7434-4612-7*, Atria); 2003. 304p. reprint ed. pap. 13.00 (*0-7434-3973-2*, Washington Square Pr.) Simon & Schuster.

Erdman, Loula G. The Edge of Time. 1981. (Westerns Ser.). lib. bdg. o.s.i (*0-8398-2675-3*, Macmillan Reference USA) Gale Group.

—The Edge of Time. 1989. (Texas Tradition Ser.: No. 11). 282p. pap. 13.95 (*0-87565-031-7*) Texas Christian Univ. Pr.

Erickson, John R. The Devil in Texas & Other Cowboy Tales. 1983. (Illus.). 96p. pap. 5.95 (*0-9608612-0-3*); (J). 13.95 incl. audio (*0-916941-24-8*) Maverick Bks., Inc.

Estes, Winston M. Another Part of the House. 1978. (J). pap. 1.75 o.p. (*0-380-01959-0*, 38406, Avon Bks.) Morrow/Avon.

—Another Part of the House. 1988. (Texas Tradition Ser.: No. 10). 272p. reprint ed. pap. 10.95 (*0-87565-027-9*) Texas Christian Univ. Pr.

Evans, Max. My Pardner. 1972. (Illus.). 104p. (J). (gr. 5-9). 3.95 (*0-395-13725-X*) Houghton Mifflin Co.

—My Pardner. 1984. (Zia Bks.). (Illus.). 111p. (J). reprint ed. pap. 5.95 o.p. (*0-8263-0699-3*) Univ. of New Mexico Pr.

Evey, Ethel L. Stowaway to Texas. Darst, Shelia S., ed. 1986. 201p. (J). (gr. 4-7). 11.95 (*0-89896-102-5*, Post Oak Pr.) Larksdale.

—Thistles & Bluebonnets. 1996. (Illus.). 128p. (J). (gr. 5-6). 14.95 (*1-57168-037-3*) Eakin Pr.

Fenady, Andrew J. There Came a Stranger. 2001. 288p. 23.95 (*0-312-87752-8*, Forge Bks.) Doherty, Tom Assocs., LLC.

—There Came a Stranger. l.t. ed. 2001. (Thorndike Press Large Print Western Ser.). 459p. 25.95 (*0-7862-3482-2*) Gale Group.

Ferguson, Nancy. Alana: A Novel. 2001. 239p. pap. 14.95 (*1-56474-361-6*) Fithian Pr.

Ferrarella, Marie. Dad by Choice. 2000. (Harlequin American Romance Ser.: Vol. 1). 256p. mass mkt. (*0-373-65062-0*, 1-65062-1, Harlequin Bks.) Harlequin Enterprises, Ltd.

—Expecting... in Texas. 1999. (Fortunes of Texas Ser.: No. 3). per. (*0-373-65032-9*, 1-65032-4, Harlequin Bks.) Harlequin Enterprises, Ltd.

Flynn, Robert. In the House of the Lord. 1991. (Texas Tradition Ser.: No. 16). 212p. (*0-87565-249-2*); reprint ed. pap. 16.95 (*0-87565-087-2*) Texas Christian Univ. Pr.

—Living with the Hyenas. 1995. 232p. 22.50 (*0-87565-144-5*) Texas Christian Univ. Pr.

—North to Yesterday. Haywood, Richard, ed. unabr. ed. 1993. audio 59.95 (*1-883268-00-1*) Spellbinders, Inc.

—North to Yesterday. 1985. (Texas Tradition Ser.: No. 4). 340p. reprint ed. 19.95 (*0-87565-014-7*); pap. 14.95 (*0-87565-015-5*) Texas Christian Univ. Pr.

—The Sounds of Rescue, the Signs of Hope. 1989. (Texas Tradition Ser.: No. 12). 278p. reprint ed. pap. 11.95 (*0-87565-039-2*) Texas Christian Univ. Pr.

—Tie-Fast Country: A Novel. 2001. 360p. 24.50 (*0-87565-244-1*) Texas Christian Univ. Pr.

Flynn, Robert & Klepper, Dan. The Devils Tiger. 2000. 332p. 24.50 (*0-87565-224-7*) Texas Christian Univ. Pr.

Fold, Gaylord. Bay of Sorrows. 1995. 272p. 21.00 o.p. (*0-312-11751-5*, Saint Martin's Minotaur) St. Martin's Pr.

Fossen, Delores. Saddled. 2001. (Illus.). 320p. mass mkt. 4.99 (*0-505-52430-9*, Love Spell) Dorchester Publishing Co., Inc.

Foster, Barbara Spencer. Pecos Queen: A Novel. 2003. 192p. pap. 18.95 (*0-86534-391-8*) Sunstone Pr.

Foster, Bennett. The Mexican Saddle: A Western Story. 1999. (Western Ser.). 200p. 19.95 (*0-7862-1328-0*, Five Star); 245p. 20.00 (*0-7838-8397-8*, Macmillan Reference USA) Gale Group.

Foster, Lori. Married to the Boss. 2000. (Harlequin American Romance Ser.: Bk. 3). 256p. mass mkt. (*0-373-65064-7*, 1-65064-7, Harlequin Bks.) Harlequin Enterprises, Ltd.

Fowler, Zinita. The Last Innocent Summer. 1990. (Chaparral Book for Young Readers Ser.). 144p. (J). (gr. 4-7). pap. 11.95 (*0-87565-045-7*) Texas Christian Univ. Pr.

Foxx, Nina. Dippin' My Spoon. 2000. 256p. pap. 14.00 (*0-9678959-4-4*) Manisy Willows Bks.

Freedom's Fire: An Historical Novel Based upon the True Story of the Palm Sunday Massacre on March 27, 1836, at Fort La Bahia, Goliad, Texas. 1999. (Illus.). lxxv, 180p. (gr. 7-12). 30.00 (*0-9675023-0-6*) Kalcolby, Pat.

Freeman, Peggy P. The Coldest Day in Texas. 1997. (Chaparral Books for Young Readers). 126p. (J). (gr. 4-7). pap. 12.95 (*0-87565-169-0*) Texas Christian Univ. Pr.

Friedman, Kinky. Armadillos & Old Lace. 1995. 256p. mass mkt. 7.50 (*0-553-57447-7*) Bantam Bks.

—Armadillos & Old Lace. 1994. 240p. 21.00 (*0-671-86923-X*, Simon & Schuster) Simon & Schuster.

Fromm, Pete. How All This Started. 2001. 320p. pap. 14.00 (*0-312-27697-4*); 2000. 305p. 23.00 o.s.i (*0-312-20933-9*) Picador.

Gaddy, Eve. A Marriage Made in Texas. 2002. (Harlequin Superromance Ser.). mass mkt. (*0-373-71090-9*, Harlequin Bks.) Harlequin Enterprises, Ltd.

—Trouble in Texas. 2001. mass mkt. (*0-373-71031-3*, Harlequin Bks.) Harlequin Enterprises, Ltd.

Garcia, Lionel G. The Day They Took My Uncle & Other Short Stories. 2001. x, 234p. 22.50 (*0-87565-235-2*) Texas Christian Univ. Pr.

—Hardscrub. 1990. 300p. pap. 10.00 (*1-55885-005-8*) Arte Publico Pr.

—A Shroud in the Family. 1987. 319p. pap. text 10.00 o.p. (*0-934770-71-9*); 2nd ed. 1994. 320p. pap. 10.00 (*1-55885-113-5*) Arte Publico Pr.

—To a Widow with Children. 1994. 238p. 19.95 (*1-55885-069-4*) Arte Publico Pr.

Gardner, Mary. Boat People: A Novel. 1995. 288p. 21.00 (*0-393-03738-X*) Norton, W. W. & Co., Inc.

—Boat People: A Novel. 1997. 280p. pap. 15.95 (*0-8203-1881-7*) Univ. of Georgia Pr.

Garland, Sherry. A Line in the Sand: The Alamo Diary of Lucinda Lawrence, Gonzales, Texas, 1836. 1998. (Dear America Ser.). (Illus.). 201p. (YA). (gr. 4-9). pap. 10.95 (*0-590-39466-5*, Scholastic Pr.) Scholastic, Inc.

Garlock, Dorothy. This Loving Land. l.t. ed. 2000. 360p. lib. bdg. 27.95 (*1-58547-012-0*) Ctr. Point Large Print.

—This Loving Land. 1981. pap. 2.75 o.p. (*0-671-43563-9*, Pocket) Simon & Schuster.

—This Loving Land. 1996. (Illus.). 288p. reprint ed. mass mkt. 6.99 (*0-446-36525-4*) Warner Bks., Inc.

Gaylord, Louise. Anacacho: An Allie Armington Mystery. 2002. 288p. 21.95 (*0-9720227-0-8*) Little Moose Pr.

Gentry, Georgina. To Tame a Texan. l.t. ed. 2003. 421p. 29.95 (*1-58724-494-2*, Wheeler Publishing, Inc.) Gale Group.

—To Tame a Texan. 2003. (Illus.). 348p. mass mkt. 5.99 (*0-8217-7402-6*) Kensington Publishing Corp.

Geyer, Andrew. Whispers in Dust & Bone. 2003. 192p. 24.95 (*0-89672-496-4*) Texas Tech Univ. Pr.

Gibbons, Reginald. Sweetbitter. 2003. (Voices of the South Ser.). 440p. pap. 18.95 (*0-8071-2871-6*) Louisiana State Univ. Pr.

—Sweetbitter. 1996. 432p. pap. 21.00 o.s.i (*0-14-025242-8*, Viking) Penguin Group (USA) Inc.

Gibson, Rachel. Daisy's Back in Town. 2004. 384p. mass mkt. 6.99 (*0-06-000925-X*, Avon Bks.) Morrow/Avon.

Gipson, Fred. Hound-Dog Man. 1980. viii, 247p. reprint ed. pap. 4.95 o.p. (*0-8032-7005-4*, BB 748, Bison Bks.) Univ. of Nebraska Pr.

—Old Yeller. abr. ed. 1995. (J). audio 16.95 (*1-55927-347-X*, 393873) Audio Renaissance.

—Old Yeller. unabr. ed. 1989. (J). (gr. 4-7). audio 30.00 (*0-7366-1648-9*, 2500) Books on Tape, Inc.

—Old Yeller. 1990. (Trophy Bk.). (Illus.). 192p. (J). (gr. 5 up). pap. 5.99 (*0-06-440382-3*, Harper Trophy) HarperCollins Children's Bk. Group.

—Old Yeller, unabr. ed. 1991. (J). (gr. 5). audio 27.00 (*1-55690-389-8*, 91104E7) Recorded Bks., LLC.

—Old Yeller Reissue. 1989. 192p. (J). (gr. 4-7). reprint ed. pap. 5.50 (*0-06-080971-X*, P 971, Perennial) HarperTrade.

Gire, Ken. McKinney High, 1946: A Novel. 1993. 256p. 17.99 o.p. (*0-310-59040-X*); pap. 11.99 o.p. (*0-310-59041-8*) Zondervan.

Glancy, Diane H. The Only Piece of Furniture in the House. 2001. 160p. pap. 10.95 (*1-55921-294-2*); 1996. 124p. 18.95 o.p. (*1-55921-183-0*) Moyer Bell.

Glasscock, Sarah. Anna L. M. N. O. 1988. 352p. 17.95 o.s.i (*0-394-55930-4*) Random Hse., Inc.

—Anna L.M.N.O. Rosenman, Jane, ed. 1990. 352p. reprint ed. pap. (*0-671-68868-5*, Washington Square Pr.) Simon & Schuster.

Goldring, Kat. Work of the Angels. 2003. 288p. mass mkt. 5.99 (*0-425-19214-8*) Berkley Publishing Group.

Gonzalez, Genaro. The Quixote Cult. 1998. 224p. pap. 12.95 (*1-55885-254-9*) Arte Publico Pr.

—Rainbow's End. 1988. 182p. pap. 9.50 (*0-934770-81-6*) Arte Publico Pr.

Gonzalez, Jovita. Dew on the Thorn. Limon, Jose E., ed. & intro. by. 1997. (Recovering the U.S. Hispanic Literary Heritage Project Publi Ser.). 181p. pap. 12.95 (*1-55885-175-5*) Arte Publico Pr.

Gonzalez, Jovita & Raleigh, Eve. Caballero: A Historical Novel. Limon, Jose E. & Cotera, Maria, eds. 1996. (Illus.). (C). 400p. 19.95 o.p. (*0-89096-701-6*); 392p. pap. 19.95 (*0-89096-700-8*) Texas A&M Univ. Pr.

Goyen, William. Come, the Restorer. 1996. 180p. pap. 18.00 (*0-8101-5064-6*, TriQuarterly Bks.) Northwestern Univ. Pr.

—The House of Breath. anniv. ed. 1999. 208p. pap. 15.95 (*0-8101-5067-0*, TriQuarterly Bks.) Northwestern Univ. Pr.

—The House of Breath. 1975. (Illus.). 194 p. (J). o.p. (*0-394-49699-X*) Random Hse., Inc.

Goyne, Minetta A. Tales from the Sunday House. 1997. 148p. (Orig.). pap. 15.95 (*0-87565-173-9*) Texas Christian Univ. Pr.

Graham, Don, ed. South by Southwest: 24 Stories from Modern Texas. 1986. 300p. (C). 22.50 o.p. (*0-292-77600-4*); pap. 11.95 o.p. (*0-292-77601-2*) Univ. of Texas Pr.

Graham, Heather. Summer Fires: Dark Stranger; Rides a Hero; Apache Summer, 3 bks. in 1. 2001. 776p. mass mkt. (*0-373-83478-0*, 1-83478-7, Harlequin Bks.) Harlequin Enterprises, Ltd.

Graham, Jerry M. For the Love of the Children. 1993. 120p. 12.95 o.p. (*0-944957-41-2*) Rivercross Publishing, Inc.

Grape, Jan. Austin City Blues. l.t. ed. 2001. (Five Star First Edition Mystery Ser.). 224p. 23.95 (*0-7862-3014-2*) Thorndike Pr.

Grattan-Dominguez, Alejandro. Breaking Even. 1997. 250p. (YA). (gr. 9 up). pap. 11.95 (*1-55885-213-1*) Arte Publico Pr.

—The Dark Side of the Dream. 1995. 434p. 11.50 (*1-55885-140-2*); o.p. (*0-15-588514-6*) Arte Publico Pr.

Graves, Lonnie. Aunt Millipus & Her Will. 2002. 17.95 (*1-57168-720-3*, Eakin Pr.) Eakin Pr.

Gray, A. W. Bino. 1988. 208p. 16.95 o.p. (*0-525-24590-1*, Dutton) Dutton/Plume.

—Bino. 1989. mass mkt. 3.95 o.p. (*0-451-40129-8*, Onyx) NAL.

—Bino's Blues. 1995. 256p. 20.00 (*0-671-88186-8*, Simon & Schuster) Simon & Schuster.

—In Defense of Judges. 1990. 18.95 o.p. (*0-525-24875-7*, Dutton) Dutton/Plume.

—In Defense of Judges. 1991. 368p. mass mkt. 5.99 o.s.i (*0-451-40271-5*, Onyx) NAL.

—Killings. 1993. 304p. 20.00 o.p. (*0-525-93625-4*, Dutton) Dutton/Plume.

—Killings. 1994. 384p. mass mkt. 4.99 o.p. (*0-451-40525-0*, Onyx) NAL.

—The Man Offside. 1991. 240p. 18.95 o.p. (*0-525-93310-7*) Dutton/Plume.

—The Man Offside. 1992. 336p. mass mkt. 4.99 o.s.i (*0-451-40318-5*, Onyx) NAL.

—Prime Suspect. 1992. 256p. 20.00 o.p. (*0-525-93531-2*, Dutton) Dutton/Plume.

—Size. 1989. 208p. 16.95 o.p. (*0-525-24728-9*, Dutton) Dutton/Plume.

Gray, Ginna. The Prodigal Daughter. 2000. 384p. mass mkt. (*1-55166-603-0*, 1-66603-1, Mira Bks.) Harlequin Enterprises, Ltd.

Gray, William. Shares. 1996. 320p. 22.00 o.p. (*0-684-81096-4*, Simon & Schuster) Simon & Schuster.

Green, Chloe. Going Out in Style. 2000. (Dallas O'Connor Mysteries Ser.). 316p. 20.00 o.s.i (*1-57566-574-3*) Kensington Publishing Corp.

Green, Tim. The Letter of the Law. l.t. ed. 2000. (Wheeler Large Print Book Ser.). 341p. 28.95 (*1-56895-956-7*, Wheeler Publishing, Inc.) Gale Group.

—The Letter of the Law. 352p. 2000. E-Book 14.95 (*0-7595-0027-4*); 2000. E-Book 14.95 (*0-7595-9027-3*); 2000. E-Book 14.95 (*0-7595-8027-8*); 2000. 24.95 o.p. (*0-446-52299-6*); 2001. reprint ed. mass mkt. 7.99 (*0-446-60995-1*) Warner Bks., Inc.

—Outlaws. 1997. 512p. mass mkt. 5.99 o.p. (*0-06-101213-0*, HarperTorch) Morrow/Avon.

—Outlaws. 1999. 496p. mass mkt. 6.99 o.s.i (*0-446-60635-9*) Warner Bks., Inc.

—The Red Zone. abr. ed. 1998. audio 17.98 (*1-57042-594-9*) Time Warner AudioBooks.

—The Red Zone. 1999. 384p. mass mkt. 7.50 (*0-446-60756-8*); 1998. 325p. 24.00 o.p. (*0-446-52298-8*) Warner Bks., Inc.

Greenwood, Leigh. Cowboys. 2001. (Cowboys Ser.). 400p. mass mkt. 5.99 (*0-8439-4877-9*) Dorchester Publishing Co., Inc.

Gregory, Sarah. Capitol Scandal. 1999. 384p. mass mkt. 6.99 o.s.i (*0-451-19009-2*, Signet Bks.) NAL.

—Public Trust. 1997. 400p. mass mkt. 5.99 o.s.i (*0-451-19076-9*) NAL.

Grey, Zane. Last of the Duanes. unabr. ed. 1999. 9p. audio 29.99 (*0-88646-549-4*, DHA-6549) Durkin Hayes Publishing Ltd.

—Last of the Duanes. 1996. (Western Ser.). 230p. 17.95 (*0-7862-0627-6*, Five Star) Gale Group.

—Last of the Duanes. l.t. ed. 1997. (Western Ser.). 401p. 22.95 o.p. (*0-7862-0629-2*) Thorndike Pr.

—Rangers of the Lone Star. 1999. 320p. mass mkt. 4.99 (*0-8439-4556-7*, Leisure Bks.) Dorchester Publishing Co., Inc.

—Rangers of the Lone Star. 1999. E-Book 9.95 (*0-585-30678-8*) netLibrary, Inc.

—Shadow on the Trail. l.t. ed. 1987. 395p. 17.95 o.p. (*0-8161-4124-X*, Macmillan Reference USA) Gale Group.

—Shadow on the Trail. 1992. 352p. mass mkt. 3.99 o.p. (*0-06-100443-X*, HarperTorch) Morrow/Avon.

—Shadow on the Trail. 1982. mass mkt. 2.50 (*0-671-45644-X*, Pocket) Simon & Schuster.

—Shadow on the Trail. l.t. ed. 1994. (Western Ser.). 465p. lib. bdg. 22.95 (*0-7862-0074-X*) Thorndike Pr.

—Shadow on the Trail. l.t. ed. 1975. (Ulverscroft Large Print Ser.). 12.00 o.p. (*0-85456-332-6*, Ulverscroft) Thorpe, F. A. Pubs. GBR. *Dist:* Ulverscroft Large Print Bks., Ltd., Ulverscroft Large Print Canada, Ltd.

Griffith, Patricia B. The World Around Midnight. 1991. 256p. 22.95 o.p. (*0-399-13590-1*, G. P. Putnam's Sons) Penguin Group (USA) Inc.

Griggs, Winnie. Something More. 2001. 320p. mass mkt. 4.99 (*0-8439-4934-1*, Leisure Bks.) Dorchester Publishing Co., Inc.

—What Matters Most. 2001. 320p. mass mkt. 4.99 (*0-8439-4829-9*, Leisure Bks.) Dorchester Publishing Co., Inc.

Grisham, John. Bleachers. unabr. ed. 2003. audio 25.20 (*0-7366-9658-X*) Books on Tape, Inc.

—Bleachers. 2003. 176p. 175.00 (*0-385-51197-3*) Doubleday Canada, Ltd. CAN. *Dist:* Random Hse., Inc.

—Bleachers. 2003. 176p. 19.95 (*0-385-51161-2*) Doubleday Publishing.

—Bleachers. unabr. ed. 2003. audio compact disk 24.95 (*0-7393-1016-X*, RH Audio) Random Hse. Audio Publishing Group.

—Bleachers. l.t. ed. 2003. 288p. 21.95 (*0-375-43330-9*, 53859850) Random Hse. Large Print.

Grissom, Ken. Drowned Man's Key: A John Rodrigue Novel. 1992. 288p. 17.95 o.p. (*0-312-06955-3*, Saint Martin's Minotaur) St. Martin's Pr.

Grove, Fred. The Great Horse Race. 1982. 2.25 o.p. (*0-441-30267-X*); 1978. mass mkt. 1.75 o.s.i (*0-441-30259-9*) Ace Bks.

—The Great Horse Race. 1977. (Double D Western Ser.). 5.95 o.p. (*0-385-12101-6*) Doubleday Publishing.

—The Great Horse Race. l.t. ed. 2000. (G. K. Hall Western Ser.). 292p. 25.95 (*0-7838-9132-6*) Thorndike Pr.

Gurasich, Marjorie A. Letters to Oma: A Young German Girl's Account of Her First Year in Texas, 1847. 1989. (Chaparral Book Ser.). (Illus.). 162p. (J). (gr. 7-12). pap. 12.95 (*0-87565-037-6*) Texas Christian Univ. Pr.

Haddaway, Rich. Where the River Bends: A Novel. 2002. 22.50 (*0-87074-470-4*) Southern Methodist Univ. Pr.

Hailey, Elizabeth Forsythe. A Woman of Independent Means. l.t. ed. 1979. (YA). (gr. 7-12). 18.95 o.p. (*0-8161-6716-8*, Macmillan Reference USA) Gale Group.

—A Woman of Independent Means. 1978. 17.95 o.p. (*0-670-77795-1*) Viking Penguin.

Hailey, Elizabeth Forsythe. A Woman of Independent Means. 1995. 272p. 19.95 o.p. (*0-670-86604-0*) Viking Penguin.

Haley, James L. Final Refuge: A Novel of Eco-Terrorism. 1994. 304p. 20.95 o.p. (*0-312-11275-0*) St. Martin's Pr.

Haley, Wendy. Shadow Vengeance. 1993. 384p. mass mkt. 4.50 o.s.i (*0-8217-4097-0*, Zebra Bks.) Kensington Publishing Corp.

Hall, Linda. Chat Room. 2003. (Teri Blake-Addision Mystery Series, Book 2 Ser.). 290p. pap. 11.99 (*1-59052-200-1*) Multnomah Pubs., Inc.

Hannah, James. Sign Languages: Stories. 1993. 168p. (C). 22.50 o.p. (*0-8262-0900-9*) Univ. of Missouri Pr.

Hardy, Robin. Padre: A Novel. 1994. 288p. (Orig.). pap. 10.00 o.p. (*0-89109-799-6*) NavPress Publishing Group.

Harper, Jo & Harper, Josephine. Prairie Dog Pioneers. 2000. (SPA., Illus.). 48p. (J). (ps-3). 16.95 (*1-890515-10-8*) Turtle Bks.

Harrigan, Stephen. The Gates of the Alamo. E-Book 20.95 (*1-58945-819-2*) Adobe Systems, Inc.

—The Gates of the Alamo. 2000. 580p. pap. 14.00 (*0-7567-5898-X*) DIANE Publishing Co.

—The Gates of the Alamo. 2000. (Illus.). 592p. 25.00 (*0-679-44717-2*) Knopf, Alfred A. Inc.

—The Gates of the Alamo. 2001. 592p. reprint ed. pap. 14.00 (*0-14-100002-3*, Penguin Classics) Penguin Group (USA) Inc.

—The Gates of the Alamo, Set. abr. ed. 2000. audio compact disk 29.95 (*0-375-41560-2*, RH Audio) Random Hse. Audio Publishing Group.

—The Gates of the Alamo: A Novel. abr. ed. 2000. audio 25.95 o.s.i (*0-375-41559-9*, RH Audio) Random Hse. Audio Publishing Group.

Harrington, William. Partners. 1980. 352p. 12.45 o.p. (*0-87223-586-6*) Putnam Publishing Group, The.

Hart, Carolyn G. Death on the River Walk. l.t. ed. 2000. (Large Print Book Ser.). pap. 23.95 (*1-56895-822-6*, Wheeler Publishing, Inc.) Gale Group.

—Death on the River Walk. 2000. 336p. mass mkt. 6.99 (*0-380-79005-X*); 1999. 256p. 22.00 (*0-380-97415-0*) Morrow/Avon. (Avon Bks.).

Hart, Matthew S. Gunmetal Justice. l.t. ed. 1993. (Cody's Law Ser.). 318p. lib. bdg. 15.95 (*0-8161-5835-5*, Macmillan Reference USA) Gale Group.

—Gunmetal Justice: Cody's Law. 1991. (Cody's Law Ser.: Vol. 1). 224p. mass mkt. 3.50 o.s.i (*0-553-29030-4*) Bantam Bks.

Harte, Amanda. Strings Attached. 2000. 186p. 18.95 (*0-8034-9394-0*, Avalon Bks.) Bouregy, Thomas & Co., Inc.

—Strings Attached. l.t. ed. 2002. (Candlelights Ser.). 244p. 24.95 (*0-7862-4095-4*) Thorndike Pr.

Haseloff, Cynthia. The Kiowa Verdict. 2000. 272p. mass mkt. 4.50 (*0-8439-4767-5*, Leisure Bks.) Dorchester Publishing Co., Inc.

—The Kiowa Verdict. unabr. ed. 1999. audio 29.99 (*0-88646-547-8*, DHA-6547) Durkin Hayes Publishing Ltd.

—The Kiowa Verdict. 1997. (Western Ser.). 263p. lib. bdg. 18.95 (*0-7862-0752-3*, Five Star) Gale Group.

—The Kiowa Verdict. l.t. ed. 1998. (Western Ser.). 367p. 24.95 (*0-7862-0775-2*) Thorndike Pr.

Hauptman, William. Storm Season. 2001. (Southwestern Writers Collection). (Illus.). 318p. (C). pap. 21.95 (*0-292-73453-0*) Univ. of Texas Pr.

—The Storm Season. 1993. 336p. mass mkt. 5.99 o.s.i (*0-553-56386-6*) Bantam Bks.

Hayes, Penny. The Long Trail. 1986. 248p. pap. 8.95 (*0-930044-76-2*) Naiad Pr., Inc.

Haynes, Melinda. Willem's Field. 2003. 416p. (Orig.). 24.00 (*0-7432-3849-4*, Free Pr.) Simon & Schuster.

Hearon, Shelby. Hug Dancing. 1993. 256p. pap. 9.99 o.s.i (*0-446-39457-2*) Warner Bks., Inc.

—Life Estates. 1995. pap. 11.00 (*0-679-75796-1*, Vintage) Knopf Publishing Group.

—Life Estates. 1994. 231p. 22.00 o.s.i (*0-679-41539-4*) Knopf, Alfred A. Inc.

—A Prince of a Fellow. 1978. 7.95 o.p. (*0-385-12538-0*) Doubleday Publishing.

—A Prince of a Fellow. 1980. pap. o.p. (*0-671-82773-1*, Pocket) Simon & Schuster.

—A Prince of a Fellow. 1992. (Texas Tradition Ser.: No. 18). 206p. reprint ed. pap. 14.95 (*0-87565-099-6*) Texas Christian Univ. Pr.

—The Second Dune. 2003. (Texas Tradition Ser.: No. 33). 200p. pap. 17.95 (*0-87565-273-5*) Texas Christian Univ. Pr.

Heath, Lorraine. A Rogue in Texas. 1999. 384p. mass mkt. 6.99 (*0-380-80329-1*, Avon Bks.) Morrow/Avon.

Heinemann, Larry. Paco's Story. 1986. 224p. 15.95 o.s.i (*0-374-22847-7*) Farrar, Straus & Giroux.

Hemlin, Tim. A Catered Christmas. 1998. (Culinary Mysteries Ser.). 272p. mass mkt. 5.99 o.s.i (*0-345-42001-2*) Ballantine Bks.

—Dead Man's Broth. 1999. (Culinary Mysteries Ser.). 304p. mass mkt. 5.99 o.s.i (*0-345-42002-0*) Ballantine Bks.

—If Wishes Were Horses. 1996. mass mkt. 5.50 o.s.i (*0-345-40318-5*) Ballantine Bks.

—People in Glass Houses. 1997. (Culinary Mysteries Ser.). 230p. mass mkt. 5.50 o.s.i (*0-345-40902-7*) Ballantine Bks.

—A Whisper of Rage. 1997. (Culinary Mysteries Ser.). mass mkt. 5.50 o.s.i (*0-345-40319-3*) Ballantine Bks.

Hennech, Michael C., ed. Texas Short Fiction: A World in Itself: Texas Short Story Anthology by 21 Authors. 1993. 256p. (Orig.). pap. 12.95 (*1-881301-04-4*) Ale Publishing Co.

Henry, Will. The Blue Mustang. 1988. mass mkt. 2.95 o.s.i (*0-553-27732-4*) Bantam Bks.

—The Blue Mustang. l.t. ed. 1997. (G. K. Hall Nightingale Ser.). 305p. pap. 19.95 (*0-7838-8205-X*) Thorndike Pr.

Hepinstall, Kathy. The Absence of Nectar. l.t. ed. 2002. 28.95 (*1-58724-157-9*, Wheeler Publishing, Inc.) Gale Group.

—The Absence of Nectar. 2001. 304p. 23.95 o.p. (*0-399-14801-9*, G. P. Putnam's Sons) Penguin Group (USA) Inc.

Herndon, Nancy. C. O. P. Out. 1998. (Elena Jarvis Ser.). 304p. mass mkt. 5.99 o.s.i (*0-425-16293-1*, Prime Crime) Berkley Publishing Group.

—Casanova Crimes. 1999. 288p. mass mkt. 5.99 o.s.i (*0-425-16812-3*, Prime Crime) Berkley Publishing Group.

—Hunting Game. 1996. 288p. (Orig.). mass mkt. 5.99 o.s.i (*0-425-15579-X*, Prime Crime) Berkley Publishing Group.

—Lethal Statues. 1996. 304p. mass mkt. 5.99 o.s.i (*0-425-15384-3*) Berkley Publishing Group.

—Time Bombs. 1997. 320p. mass mkt. 5.99 o.s.i (*0-425-15965-5*, Prime Crime) Berkley Publishing Group.

—Widow's Watch. 1995. 304p. mass mkt. 5.50 o.s.i (*0-425-14900-5*) Berkley Publishing Group.

—Widow's Watch. 260p. 2002. pap. 6.99 (*0-7592-3636-4*); 2002. E-Book 6.99 (*0-7592-3633-X*); 2002. E-Book 6.99 (*0-7592-3632-1*); 2001. E-Book 6.99 (*0-7592-3631-3*) ereads.com.

Hickey, Dave. Prior Convictions: Stories from the Sixties. 1989. (Southwest Life & Letters Ser.). 200p. 17.95 (*0-87074-286-8*) Southern Methodist Univ. Pr.

Hicks, David L. & Parkinson, Dan. The Texians. 1981. 272p. 25.00 (*0-89896-000-2*) Larksdale.

Hill, Billy Bob & Champion, Laurie, eds. Texas Short Stories. 1997. (American Regional Book Ser.: Vol. 2). 571p. pap. 16.95 (*0-9651359-1-8*) Browder Springs Bks.

—Texas Short Stories 2. 1999. (American Regional Book Ser.: Vol. 6). 578p. 32.95 (*0-9651359-5-0*, 1306); pap. 18.95 (*0-9651359-6-9*, 1307) Browder Springs Bks.

Hill, Sandra. Truly, Madly Viking. 2000. (Time of Your Life Ser.). 400p. mass mkt. 5.99 (*0-505-52387-6*, Love Spell) Dorchester Publishing Co., Inc.

Hime, James. The Night of the Dance: A Novel. 2003. 320p. 24.95 (*0-312-31322-5*, Saint Martin's Minotaur) St. Martin's Pr.

Hingle, Metsy. The Marriage Profile. 2003. (Silhouette Special Releases Ser.: No. 11). 256p. mass mkt. (*0-373-61362-8*, Silhouette) Harlequin Enterprises, Ltd.

Hinojosa, Rolando. Los Amigos de Becky. 1991. (Klail City Death Trip Ser.). (SPA.). 128p. pap. 9.50 o.p. (*1-55885-021-X*) Arte Publico Pr.

—Ask a Policeman: A Rafe Buenrostro Mystery. 1998. (Rafe Buenrostro Mysteries Ser.). 256p. pap. text 12.95 (*1-55885-226-3*) Arte Publico Pr.

—Becky & Her Friends. 1990. (Klail City Death Trip Ser.). 160p. pap. 9.50 (*1-55885-006-6*) Arte Publico Pr.

—Claros Varones de Belken: Fair Gentlemen of Belken County, Bilingual Edition. Cruz, Julia, tr. 1986. (United States Hispanic Creative Literature Ser.).Tr. of Fair Gentlemen of Belken County. (ENG & SPA.). 224p. pap. text 16.00 (*0-916950-65-4*); 223p. lib. bdg. 26.00 (*0-916950-64-6*) Bilingual Pr./Editorial Bilingue.

—El Condado de Belken-Klail City. 1994. (Clasicos Chicanos - Chicano Classics Ser.: No. 8). 168p. 25.00 (*0-927534-33-9*); pap. 15.00 (*0-927534-34-7*) Bilingual Pr./Editorial Bilingue.

—Dear Rafe. 1985. 136p. pap. 8.50 (*0-934770-38-7*) Arte Publico Pr.

—Estampas del Valle. 1994. (Clasicos Chicanos - Chicano Classics Ser.: No. 7). (SPA.). 144p. 24.00 (*0-927534-24-X*); pap. 13.00 (*0-927534-25-8*) Bilingual Pr./Editorial Bilingue.

—Klail City. 1987. (Klail City Death Trip Ser.). 144p. pap. 9.00 (*0-934770-54-9*) Arte Publico Pr.

—Mi Querido Rafa. 1981. (Klail City Death Trip Ser.). (SPA.). 112p. (C). pap. 8.50 o.p. (*0-934770-10-7*) Arte Publico Pr.

—Partners in Crime. 1985. 248p. (C). pap. 10.00 (*0-934770-37-9*) Arte Publico Pr.

—Rites & Witnesses. 1982. (Klail City Death Trip Ser.). 112p. pap. 8.50 o.p. (*0-934770-19-0*) Arte Publico Pr.

—The Useless Servants. 1993. 192p. (C). 8.95 (*1-55885-068-6*) Arte Publico Pr.

—The Valley. 1983. (Klail City Death Trip Ser.). 112p. 18.00 (*0-916950-37-9*); pap. 10.00 (*0-916950-38-7*) Bilingual Pr./Editorial Bilingue.

Hoffman, Lee. Wiley's Move. l.t. ed. 2001. (Western Ser.). 250p. 24.95 (*0-7838-9355-8*) Thorndike Pr.

Hoffmann, Kate. Daddy Wanted. 2001. (Harlequin Special Releases Ser.: No. 4). mass mkt. (*0-373-65081-7*, 1-65081-1, Harlequin Bks.) Harlequin Enterprises, Ltd.

Hogan, Helen M. Warning Shot: A Novel of South Texas. 2001. 460p. pap. 24.99 (*0-7388-4097-1*) Xlibris Corp.

Hogan, Ray. The Doomsday Marshal & the Comancheros. l.t. ed. 1992. 227p. pap. 14.95 o.p. (*0-8161-5356-6*, Macmillan Reference USA) Gale Group.

—Texas Guns. 1980. mass mkt. 1.75 o.p. (*0-451-09257-0*, Signet Bks.) NAL.

Hoggard, James. Riding the Wind & Other Tales. 1997. (Tarleton State University Southwestern Studies in the Humanities: No. 9). 176p. 19.95 (*0-89096-781-4*) Texas A&M Univ. Pr.

Hohl, Joan. Handsome Devil. 1999. (Men at Work Ser.: Vol. 16). per. (*0-373-81028-8*, Harlequin Bks.); 1990. (Silhouette Desire Ser.: No. 612). mass mkt. (*0-373-05612-5*, Silhouette) Harlequin Enterprises, Ltd.

Horgan, Paul. Whitewater. 1970. 337p. (YA). (gr. 8 up). 6.95 o.p. (*0-374-28970-0*) Farrar, Straus & Giroux.

Horsley, David. Conquistador: A Novel. unabr. ed. 2003. 196p. pap. 15.95 (*1-931823-06-5*) Halcyon Pr.

Howard, Linda. Almost Forever. 2002. 256p. mass mkt. (*1-55166-934-X*, Mira Bks.) Harlequin Enterprises, Ltd.

Hudson, Wayne. The Beams of Our House. 2003. per. 13.95 (*1-888237-46-5*) Baxter Pr.

—The Beams of Our House. 2002. 165p. pap. 12.99 (*0-9705259-8-2*) St. Aztec Publishing.

Huffines, Alan C. A Pilgrim Shadow. 2001. (Illus.). 144p. (C). pap. 16.95 (*1-57168-529-4*, Eakin Pr.) Eakin Pr.

Humphrey, William. Home from the Hill. 1989. mass mkt. 9.95 o.s.i (*0-440-55044-0*); 1989. 312p. pap. 9.95 o.s.i (*0-385-29733-5*); 1984. mass mkt. 4.50 o.s.i (*0-440-33672-4*, Laurel) Dell Publishing.

—Home from the Hill. 1958. 10.00 o.p. (*0-394-42906-0*, Knopf Bks. for Young Readers) Random Hse. Children's Bks.

—Home from the Hill: Novel. 1996. (Voices of the South Ser.). 320p. (C). pap. 12.95 (*0-8071-2067-7*) Louisiana State Univ. Pr.

—Ordways. 1989. mass mkt. 9.95 o.s.i (*0-440-55046-7*); 1989. 384p. pap. 9.95 o.s.i (*0-385-29734-3*, Delta); 1984. mass mkt. 4.50 o.s.i (*0-440-36713-1*, Laurel) Dell Publishing.

—The Ordways. 1977. pap. 1.95 o.p. (*0-671-81245-9*, Pocket) Simon & Schuster.

—The Ordways: Novel. 1997. (Voices of the South Ser.). 376p. pap. 14.95 (*0-8071-2161-4*) Louisiana State Univ. Pr.

Hunter, Stephen. Dirty White Boys. 1995. 496p. mass mkt. 7.99 (*0-440-22179-X*) Dell Publishing.

—Dirty White Boys. abr. ed. 1994. audio 17.00 (*1-57042-192-7*, 4-521927) Time Warner AudioBooks.

Ingold, Jeanette. Pictures, 1918. D'Andrade, Diane, ed. 1998. 160p. (YA). (gr. 5-9). 16.00 (*0-15-201809-3*) Harcourt Children's Bks.

—Pictures, 1918. 2000. 160p. (J). (gr. 7-12). pap. 5.99 (*0-14-130695-5*) Penguin Putnam Bks. for Young Readers.

—Pictures, 1918. 2000. 12.04 (*0-606-17866-X*) Turtleback Bks.

Irving, Clifford. Trial. 1990. 19.95 o.p. (*0-671-66422-0*) Summit Bks.

Izzard, Kathryn, ed. Adobe Walls Wars. 4th ed. 1993. (Illus.). 116p. mass mkt. 10.00 (*1-891584-00-6*) Tangleaire Pr.

—Heroes Here Have Been. 2nd ed. 1993. (Illus.). ix, 112p. pap. 10.00 (*1-891584-01-4*) Tangleaire Pr.

James, Arlene. Corporate Daddy. 1999. (Fortunes of Texas Ser.: No. 5). (Illus.). 256p. per. (*0-373-65034-5*, 1-65034-5, Harlequin Bks.) Harlequin Enterprises, Ltd.

Jarrett, Norma L. Sunday Brunch. 1999. 238p. pap. 15.95 (*0-9671923-5-8*) Jarrett, Norma L.

Jenkins, Dan. Fast Copy. 1988. 400p. 19.95 o.p. (*0-671-60206-3*, Simon & Schuster) Simon & Schuster.

—Rude Behavior: A Novel. 1999. 544p. mass mkt. 7.50 o.s.i (*0-440-23560-X*) Dell Publishing.

Jensen, Muriel. Billion Dollar Bride. 2001. (Harlequin American Romance Ser.: Vol. 8). mass mkt. (*0-373-65069-8*, Harlequin Bks.) Harlequin Enterprises, Ltd.

Johnson, Charles. Another River to Cross. 2002. pap. 12.99 (*0-7684-3002-X*) Destiny Image Pubs.

Johnston, Joan. Comanche Woman. 2002. 416p. mass mkt. 7.50 (*0-440-23680-0*, Delta) Dell Publishing.

—Comanche Woman. 2003. (Americana Ser.). 605p. 28.95 (*0-7862-5260-X*) Thorndike Pr.

—Hawk's Way Rogues: Honey & the Hired Hand; The Cowboy Take a Wife; The Temporary Groom, 3 bks. in 1. 2001. 364p. pap. (*0-373-48445-3*, 1-48445-0, Silhouette) Harlequin Enterprises, Ltd.

—A Little Time in Texas. 2000. 256p. mass mkt. (*1-55166-629-4*, 1-66629-6, Mira Bks.); 1992. (Silhouette Desire Ser.: No. 710). pap. (*0-373-05710-5*, 5-05710-4, Harlequin Bks.) Harlequin Enterprises, Ltd.

—Sisters Found. l.t. ed. 2003. 30.95 (*1-58724-429-2*, Wheeler Publishing, Inc.) Gale Group.

—Sisters Found. 2002. 384p. mass mkt. (*1-55166-937-4*, Mira Bks.) Harlequin Enterprises, Ltd.

—The Texan. 2001. 368p. reprint ed. mass mkt. 6.99 (*0-440-23471-9*, Delta) Dell Publishing.

—The Texan. l.t. ed. 2001. 423p. 31.95 (*0-7838-9560-7*) Thorndike Pr.

Jones, Annie. The Double Heart Diner. 2000. 218p. 23.95 (*0-7862-2883-0*, Five Star) Gale Group.

Jones, Gayl. Mosquito. Atwan, Helene, ed. (Bluestreak Ser.). 2000. 624p. pap. 18.00 (*0-8070-8347-X*); 1999. 616p. 28.50 o.p. (*0-8070-8346-1*) Beacon Pr.

—Mosquito. unabr. collector's ed. 1999. Pt. 1. audio 64.00 (*0-7366-4830-5*, 5176-A); Pt. 2. audio 72.00 (*0-7366-4899-2*, 5176-B) Books on Tape, Inc.

Jones, Linda. One Day, My Prince. 2000. (Faerie Tale Romance Ser.). 400p. mass mkt. 5.99 (*0-505-52388-4*, Love Spell) Dorchester Publishing Co., Inc.

Jones, Martha Tannery. The Mystery of Y'Barbo's Tunnel. 1991. (Illus.). 110p. (J). (gr. 3-7). 9.95 (*0-937460-68-0*) Hendrick-Long Publishing Co.

Kahn, Sharon. Don't Cry for Me, Hot Pastrami. 2002. (Ruby, the Rabbi's Wife Mystery Ser.). 240p. reprint ed. mass mkt. 5.99 (*0-425-18715-2*, Prime Crime) Berkley Publishing Group.

—Don't Cry for Me, Hot Pastrami: A Ruby, the Rabbi's Wife Mystery. 2001. 304p. 24.00 o.s.i (*0-684-87155-6*); E-Book 24.00 (*0-7432-1825-6*) Simon & Schuster. (Scribner).

—Don't Cry for Me, Hot Pastrami: A Ruby, the Rabbi's Wife Mystery. l.t. ed. 2001. (G.K. Hall Large Print Core Ser.). 339p. 27.95 o.p. (*0-7838-9679-4*) Thorndike Pr.

—Fax Me a Bagel: A Ruby the Rabbi's Wife Mystery. 2001. 272p. mass mkt. 5.99 (*0-425-18046-8*) Berkley Publishing Group.

—Fax Me a Bagel: A Ruby the Rabbi's Wife Mystery. 1998. (Ruby, the Rabbi's Wife Mysteries Ser.). 256p. 22.00 (*0-684-84737-X*); 22.00 (*0-684-85498-8*) Simon & Schuster. (Scribner).

—Never Nosh a Matzo Ball: A Ruby the Rabbi's Wife Mystery. 2000. 304p. 22.00 o.s.i (*0-684-84738-8*, Scribner) Simon & Schuster.

Kelton, Elmer. Badger Boy. E-Book 23.95 (*1-58945-577-0*) Adobe Systems, Inc.

—Badger Boy. pap. text 23.95 (*0-312-70067-9*, Tor Bks.); 2002. mass mkt. 5.99 (*0-8125-7750-7*, Forge Bks.); 2001. 272p. 23.95 (*0-312-87319-0*, Forge Bks.) Doherty, Tom Assocs., LLC.

—Bitter Trail. 1986. 2.50 o.s.i (*0-441-06364-0*); 1984. 2.50 o.s.i (*0-441-06363-2*) Ace Bks.

—Bitter Trail. l.t. ed. 2002. lib. bdg. 28.95 (*1-58547-190-9*, Western) Ctr. Point Large Print.

—Bitter Trail. 1997. 217p. pap. 5.99 (*0-8125-5118-4*, Forge Bks.) Doherty, Tom Assocs., LLC.

—Bitter Trail. 1999. 12.04 (*0-606-19645-5*) Turtleback Bks.

—The Buckskin Line. l.t. ed. 2001. lib. bdg. 26.95 (*1-58547-112-7*) Ctr. Point Large Print.

—The Buckskin Line. 2000. 393p. mass mkt. 5.99 (*0-8125-4020-4*); 2nd ed. 1999. 287p. 22.95 (*0-312-86522-8*) Doherty, Tom Assocs., LLC. (Forge Bks.).

—The Buckskin Line. abr. ed. 1999. 25.00 incl. audio (*0-7871-2005-7*, Dove Audio) NewStar Media, Inc.

—The Buckskin Line. 2000. 12.04 (*0-606-19646-3*) Turtleback Bks.

—Captain's Rangers. l.t. ed. 2001. (G. K. Hall Western Ser.). 269p. 25.95 (*0-7838-9425-2*, Macmillan Reference USA) Gale Group.

—Captain's Rangers. 1999. 12.04 (*0-606-19648-X*) Turtleback Bks.

—Cloudy in the West. 1999. 244p. mass mkt. 5.99 (*0-8125-7594-6*); 1997. 255p. 21.95 (*0-312-86239-3*) Doherty, Tom Assocs., LLC. (Forge Bks.).

—Cloudy in the West. l.t. ed. 1997. (Wheeler Large Print Book Ser.). pap. 24.95 (*1-56895-462-X*, Wheeler Publishing, Inc.) Gale Group.

—Cloudy in the West. abr. ed. 2002. audio 16.95 (*1-56511-594-5*) HighBridge Co.

—Cloudy in the West. 1999. 12.04 (*0-606-19650-1*) Turtleback Bks.

—The Day the Cowboys Quit. 1985. 320p. 2.50 o.s.i (*0-441-13909-4*) Ace Bks.

—The Day the Cowboys Quit. 1992. 336p. mass mkt. 5.50 o.s.i (*0-553-29669-8*) Bantam Bks.

—The Day the Cowboys Quit. 1987. 320p. mass mkt. 2.75 o.s.i (*0-515-09221-5*, Jove) Berkley Publishing Group.

—The Day the Cowboys Quit. 1999. 288p. mass mkt. 5.99 (*0-8125-7450-8*, Forge Bks.) Doherty, Tom Assocs., LLC.

—The Day the Cowboys Quit. l.t. ed. 1993. (General Ser.). 378p. 20.95 o.p. (*0-8161-5670-0*, Macmillan Reference USA) Gale Group.

—The Day the Cowboys Quit. Holland, Stephen, ed. abr. ed. 1993. audio 24.95 (*1-883268-03-6*) Spellbinders, Inc.

—The Day the Cowboys Quit. 1986. (Texas Tradition Ser.: No. 7). 248p. reprint ed. 19.50 (*0-87565-053-8*); pap. 14.95 (*0-87565-054-6*) Texas Christian Univ. Pr.

—The Far Canyon nan. 1995. 368p. mass mkt. 5.50 o.s.i (*0-553-57259-8*) Bantam Bks.

—The Far Canyon nan. 1994. 336p. 22.95 o.s.i (*0-385-24895-4*) Doubleday Publishing.

—The Good Old Boys. 1995. 304p. mass mkt. 5.50 o.s.i (*0-553-57189-3*) Bantam Bks.

—The Good Old Boys. 1987. 256p. 2.50 o.s.i (*0-441-29857-5*, Diamond Bks.) Berkley Publishing Group.

—The Good Old Boys. 1999. 320p. mass mkt. 5.99 (*0-8125-7599-7*, Forge Bks.) Doherty, Tom Assocs., LLC.

—The Good Old Boys. 1978. 8.95 o.p. (*0-385-13315-4*) Doubleday Publishing.

—The Good Old Boys. 1985. (Texas Tradition Ser.: No. 1). 258p. (C). reprint ed. 19.95 (*0-912646-96-9*); pap. 12.95 (*0-912646-97-7*) Texas Christian Univ. Pr.

—The Good Old Boys. l.t. ed. 1999. (Western Ser.). 455p. 24.95 (*0-7862-2027-9*) Thorndike Pr.

—The Good Old Boys. 1999. 12.04 (*0-606-19655-2*) Turtleback Bks.

—Honor at Daybreak. 1992. 432p. mass mkt. 5.50 o.s.i (*0-553-29547-0*) Bantam Bks.

—Honor at Daybreak. 2002. (Texas Tradition Ser.: No. 32). 400p. 25.00 (*0-87565-254-9*); pap. 17.95 (*0-87565-263-8*) Texas Christian Univ. Pr.

—Llano River. 1982. (Western Ser.). 160p. mass mkt. 2.95 o.s.i (*0-553-27119-9*) Bantam Bks.

—Llano River. l.t. ed. 2000. (Western Ser.). 256p. 25.95 (*0-7862-2585-8*) Thorndike Pr.

—The Man Who Rode Midnight. 1996. 272p. mass mkt. 5.50 o.s.i (*0-553-27713-8*) Bantam Bks.

—The Man Who Rode Midnight. 1987. 264p. 16.95 o.s.i (*0-385-24020-1*) Doubleday Publishing.

—The Man Who Rode Midnight. l.t. ed. 1990. (Large Print Books General Ser.). 387p. lib. bdg. 19.95 o.p. (*0-8161-5023-0*, Macmillan Reference USA) Gale Group.

—The Man Who Rode Midnight. 1990. (Texas Tradition Ser.: No. 14). 196p. reprint ed. 19.95 (*0-87565-047-3*); pap. 11.95 (*0-87565-048-1*) Texas Christian Univ. Pr.

—Manhunters. 1996. 176p. mass mkt. 4.99 o.s.i (*0-553-27218-7*) Bantam Bks.

—Manhunters. 1994. (Texas Tradition Ser.: Vol. 22). 196p. (C). 19.95 (*0-87565-132-1*); pap. 12.95 (*0-87565-134-8*) Texas Christian Univ. Pr.

—Massacre at Goliad. 1972. mass mkt. 0.75 o.p. (*0-345-22742-5*) Ballantine Bks.

—Massacre at Goliad. 1989. 176p. mass mkt. 2.95 o.s.i (*0-553-26999-2*) Bantam Bks.

—Massacre at Goliad. l.t. ed. 2001. (G. K. Hall Western Ser.). 267p. 25.95 (*0-7838-9363-9*) Thorndike Pr.

—The Pumpkin Rollers. 301p. 1997. mass mkt. 5.99 (*0-8125-4399-8*); 1996. 22.95 (*0-312-86076-5*) Doherty, Tom Assocs., LLC. (Forge Bks.).

—The Pumpkin Rollers. 1997. 12.04 (*0-606-19667-6*) Turtleback Bks.

—Slaughter. l.t. ed. 1995. 652 p. (*0-7451-2927-7*) BBC Audiobooks America.

—Slaughter. 1994. 464p. mass mkt. 5.50 o.s.i (*0-553-56547-8*) Bantam Bks.

—Slaughter. 1993. audio 79.95 o.p. (*1-56054-869-X*) Thorndike Pr.

—The Smiling Country. l.t. ed. 2001. 279p. lib. bdg. 27.95 (*1-58547-111-9*) Ctr. Point Large Print.

—Stand Proud. 1991. 304p. mass mkt. 3.99 o.s.i (*0-553-25460-X*) Bantam Bks.

—Stand Proud. (Gunsmoke Western Ser.). 12.95 o.p. (*0-85997-839-7*, C1009) Chivers Pr. GBR. *Dist:* BBC Audiobooks America.

—Stand Proud. Holland, Stephen, ed. abr. ed. 1994. audio 24.95 (*1-883268-02-8*) Spellbinders, Inc.

—Stand Proud. 1990. (Texas Tradition Ser.: No. 13). 286p. reprint ed. 17.95 o.s.i (*0-87565-043-0*); pap. 19.95 o.p. (*0-87565-044-9*) Texas Christian Univ. Pr.

—The Time It Never Rained. 1993. 432p. mass mkt. 5.50 o.s.i (*0-553-56320-3*) Bantam Bks.

—The Time It Never Rained. 1990. mass mkt. 3.95 o.s.i (*0-515-10002-1*, Jove) Berkley Publishing Group.

—The Time It Never Rained. 1999. 416p. mass mkt. 5.99 (*0-8125-7451-6*, Forge Bks.) Doherty, Tom Assocs., LLC.

—The Time It Never Rained. l.t. ed. 1988. (General Ser.). 536p. 19.95 o.p. (*0-8161-4451-6*, Macmillan Reference USA) Gale Group.

—The Time It Never Rained, Set. abr. ed. 1997. audio 17.00 (*1-883268-04-4*, 394607) Spellbinders, Inc.

—The Time It Never Rained. 1984. (Chisholm Trail Ser.: No. 2). 378p. (C). reprint ed. 24.50 (*0-912646-91-8*); pap. 15.95 (*0-912646-89-6*) Texas Christian Univ. Pr.

—The Time It Never Rained. 1999. 12.04 (*0-606-19670-6*) Turtleback Bks.

—Wagon Tongue. 1996. 160p. mass mkt. 5.50 o.s.i (*0-553-27467-8*) Bantam Bks.

—Wagontongue. 1982. pap. 1.95 o.p. (*0-553-22525-1*) Bantam Bks.

—Wagontongue. 1996. (Texas Tradition Ser.: No. 23). 239p. reprint ed. 21.95 (*0-87565-165-8*); pap. 14.95 (*0-87565-166-6*) Texas Christian Univ. Pr.

—Wagontongue. l.t. ed. 1998. (Western Ser.). 293p. 24.95 (*0-7862-1358-2*) Thorndike Pr.

—The Way of the Coyote. 2001. 288p. 23.95 (*0-312-87318-2*, Forge Bks.) Doherty, Tom Assocs., LLC.

Kelton, Elmer & Spearman, Frank H. Massacre at Goliad. 1999. 224p. pap. text 5.99 (*0-8125-7489-3*, Forge Bks.) Doherty, Tom Assocs., LLC.

Kenner, Julie. Reckless. 2000. (Harlequin Temptation Ser.: Bk. 801). mass mkt. (*0-373-25901-8*, 1-25901-9, Harlequin Bks.) Harlequin Enterprises, Ltd.

Kerr, Rita. Buttercup & Bully Goat. 1995. (Illus.). 64p. (J). (gr. 3-4). 13.95 (*1-57168-056-X*) Eakin Pr.

—Texas Forever. 1993. 96p. (J). (gr. 4-5). 13.95 (*0-89015-921-1*) Eakin Pr.

—Texas Marvel. Roberts, Melissa, ed. 1987. 64p. (J). (gr. 5-6). 13.95 (*0-89015-597-6*) Eakin Pr.

Ketteman, Helen. Bubba the Cowboy Prince: A Fractured Texas Tale. 1997. (Illus.). 32p. (J). (gr. k-3). pap. 15.95 (*0-590-25506-1*) Scholastic, Inc.

Kiecolt-Glaser, Janice K. Detecting Lies. 1997. 256p. (Orig.). mass mkt. 5.50 (*0-380-78991-4*, Avon Bks.) Morrow/Avon.

—Unconscious Truths. 1998. mass mkt. 5.99 (*0-380-78992-2*, Avon Bks.) Morrow/Avon.

Kimmel, Fred N. Red River Ranger. l.t. ed. 2000. iv, 258p. pap. 19.95 (*0-9661115-4-0*) Zantanon Pr.

Knaggs, John R. Kingmakers: A Novel of Political Ambition & Corruption. 1992. 300p. (Orig.). pap. 12.95 o.p. (*1-55622-245-9*) Wordware Publishing, Inc.

Kok, Marilyn. Heaven's Song. 1997. (Portraits Ser.). 240p. pap. 8.99 o.p. (*1-55661-990-1*) Bethany Hse. Pubs.

—Heaven's Song. l.t. ed. 2000. (Christian Mystery Ser.). 352p. 23.95 (*0-7862-2517-3*) Thorndike Pr.

Krentz, Jayne Ann, et al. Witchcraft: Witchcraft/Last Chance Cafe/Bayou Moon, 3 bks. in 1. 2003. 352p. mass mkt. (*0-373-83542-6*, Harlequin Bks.) Harlequin Enterprises, Ltd.

Lackey, Mercedes. Burning Water. 1992. 314p. pap. text 6.99 (*0-8125-2485-3*, Tor Bks.) Doherty, Tom Assocs., LLC.

—Children of the Night. 1992. 313p. pap. text 6.99 (*0-8125-2272-9*); 1990. mass mkt. 3.95 o.s.i (*0-8125-2112-9*) Doherty, Tom Assocs., LLC. (Tor Bks.).

—Jinx High. 1991. 314p. (Orig.). pap. text 4.99 o.s.i (*0-8125-2114-5*, Tor Bks.) Doherty, Tom Assocs., LLC.

Lacy, Al & Lacy, JoAnna. Ransom of Love. l.t. ed. 2001. (Thorndike Christian Fiction Ser.). 495p. 24.95 (*0-7862-3251-X*) Thorndike Pr.

LaFoy, Leslie. Maddie's Justice. 2000. 416p. mass mkt. 5.50 (*0-553-58045-0*, Fanfare) Bantam Bks.

L'Amour, Louis. Bowdrie. 1990. 192p. mass mkt. 4.50 (*0-553-28106-2*); 1983. mass mkt. 2.95 o.s.i (*0-553-23368-8*) Bantam Bks.

—Bowdrie. l.t. ed. 1984. (General Ser.). lib. bdg. 12.95 o.p. (*0-8161-3660-2*, Macmillan Reference USA) Gale Group.

—Bowdrie Follows a Cold Trail. 1992. audio 7.99 o.s.i (*0-553-70001-4*); 2003. audio 9.99 (*0-553-47053-1*) Random Hse. Audio Publishing Group. (RH Audio).

—Bowdrie Passes Through. 1988. audio 7.99 o.s.i (*0-553-70002-2*); audio 9.99 o.s.i (*0-553-45124-3*) Random Hse. Audio Publishing Group. (RH Audio).

—Bowdrie's Law. 1984. 224p. mass mkt. 4.50 (*0-553-24550-3*) Bantam Bks.

—Bowdrie's Law. l.t. ed. 1985. 13.95 o.p. (*0-8161-3878-8*, Macmillan Reference USA) Gale Group.

—Case Closed - No Prisoners. abr. ed. 1987. audio 9.99 o.s.i (*0-553-45060-3*, RH Audio) Random Hse. Audio Publishing Group.

—Chick Bowdrie. abr. ed. 1990. 21.99 o.s.i incl. audio (*0-553-45193-6*, RH Audio) Random Hse. Audio Publishing Group.

—Down Sonora Way. abr. ed. 1994. audio 9.99 o.s.i (*0-553-47286-0*); audio 9.98 o.s.i (*0-553-74621-9*) Random Hse. Audio Publishing Group. (RH Audio).

—More Brains Than Bullets. abr. ed. 1996. audio 9.99 o.s.i (*0-553-47186-4*, RH Audio) Random Hse. Audio Publishing Group.

—The Outlaws of Poplar Creek. 1993. audio 7.99 o.s.i (*0-553-70052-9*); audio 9.99 o.s.i (*0-553-47184-8*) Random Hse. Audio Publishing Group. (RH Audio).

—Rain on the Mountain Fork. 1993. audio 7.99 o.s.i (*0-553-70051-0*); 2001. audio 9.99 (*0-553-47149-X*) Random Hse. Audio Publishing Group. (RH Audio).

—A Ranger Rides for Justice. abr. ed. 1993. 23.99 o.s.i incl. audio (*0-553-47168-6*, RH Audio) Random Hse. Audio Publishing Group.

—A Ranger Rides to Town. abr. ed. 2004. audio 7.99 (*0-553-45219-3*, RH Audio) Random Hse. Audio Publishing Group.

—The Road to Casa Piedras. abr. ed. 1990. (Bowdrie's Law Collection). audio 9.99 (*0-553-45239-8*, RH Audio) Random Hse. Audio Publishing Group.

—South of Deadwood. abr. ed. 1986. audio 9.99 (*0-553-45021-2*, 395502, RH Audio) Random Hse. Audio Publishing Group.

—Strawhouse Trail. abr. ed. 1997. audio 9.99 o.s.i (*0-553-47869-9*, 394643, RH Audio) Random Hse. Audio Publishing Group.

—Too Tough to Brand. 1989. audio 7.99 o.s.i (*0-553-70015-4*); 1999. audio 9.99 (*0-553-45161-8*) Random Hse. Audio Publishing Group. (RH Audio).

—A Trail to the West. abr. ed. 1986. audio 9.99 o.s.i (*0-553-45009-3*, RH Audio) Random Hse. Audio Publishing Group.

—Where Buzzards Fly: A Chick Bowdrie Story. abr. ed. 1986. audio 9.99 o.s.i (*0-553-45015-8*, RH Audio) Random Hse. Audio Publishing Group.

Landrey, Wanda A. Lost in the Big Thicket: A Mystery & Adventure in the Big Thicket of Texas. 1997. (Illus.). 104p. (Orig.). (J). (gr. 5-6). pap. 10.95 (*1-57168-116-7*) Eakin Pr.

Langan, Ruth R. Snowbound Cinderella. 2000. (Fortunes of Texas Ser.: No. 6). 250p. per. (*0-373-65035-3*, 1-65035-7, Harlequin Bks.) Harlequin Enterprises, Ltd.

Lansdale, Joe R. Bad Chili. 1997. 288p. 22.00 o.p. (*0-89296-619-X*) Mysterious Pr.

—Bad Chili. 1998. 272p. mass mkt. 6.99 (*0-446-60602-2*); 1997. mass mkt. (*0-446-60421-6*) Warner Bks., Inc.

—The Bottoms. l.t. ed. 2001. (Wheeler Large Print Book Ser.). 401p. 28.95 o.p. (*1-58724-093-9*, Wheeler Publishing, Inc.) Gale Group.

—The Bottoms. 2000. 336p. 24.95 (*0-89296-704-8*); 304p. E-Book 14.95 (*0-446-92859-3*); E-Book 14.95 (*0-446-96088-8*); 304p. E-Book 14.95 (*0-446-91367-7*); E-Book 14.95 (*0-446-93137-3*); 304p. E-Book 14.95 (*0-446-92368-0*) Mysterious Pr.

—The Bottoms. ltd. unabr. ed. 2000. (Illus.). 350p. 150.00 (*1-892284-60-X*) Subterranean Pr.

—The Bottoms. 2001. 336p. reprint ed. pap. 13.95 (*0-446-67792-2*) Warner Bks., Inc.

—The Bottoms: Lettered Edition. deluxe unabr. ed. 2000. (Illus.). 350p. 400.00 (*1-892284-61-8*) Subterranean Pr.

—Captains Outrageous. 2001. 336p. 24.45 o.p. (*0-89296-728-5*) Mysterious Pr.

—Captains Outrageous. 2003. 336p. pap. 12.95 (*0-446-67963-1*, Mysterious Pr. Paperback Bks.) Warner Bks., Inc.

—A Fine Dark Line. l.t. ed. 2003. 31.95 (*1-58724-419-5*, Wheeler Publishing, Inc.) Gale Group.

—A Fine Dark Line. 2003. 320p. 24.95 (*0-89296-729-3*) Mysterious Pr.

—A Fine Dark Line. 2003. 320p. pap. 12.95 (*0-446-69167-4*, Mysterious Pr. Paperback Bks.) Warner Bks., Inc.

—Mucho Mojo. 1994. 320p. 19.95 o.s.i (*0-89296-490-1*) Mysterious Pr.

—Mucho Mojo. 1995. 304p. mass mkt. 5.99 (*0-446-40187-0*) Warner Bks., Inc.

—Rumble Tumble. 1998. 244p. 22.00 o.p. (*0-89296-620-3*) Mysterious Pr.

—Rumble Tumble. 1999. 272p. mass mkt. 6.50 o.s.i (*0-446-60757-6*) Warner Bks., Inc.

—Savage Season. 1990. mass mkt. 4.50 o.s.i (*0-553-28563-7*) Bantam Bks.

—Savage Season. 1995. 192p. mass mkt. 5.50 o.p. (*0-446-40431-4*) Warner Bks., Inc.

—Savage Season. 1990. 200p. 25.00 o.p. (*0-929480-23-6*) Ziesing, Mark V.

—Sunset & Sawdust. 2004. 320p. 22.00 (*0-375-41453-3*) Knopf Publishing Group.

—The Two-Bear Mambo. 1995. 273p. 19.95 o.s.i (*0-89296-491-X*) Mysterious Pr.

—The Two-Bear Mambo. 1996. 288p. mass mkt. 5.99 (*0-446-40188-9*) Warner Bks., Inc.

Lantigua, John. Twister: A Novel. 1992. 288p. 18.00 o.p. (*0-671-73722-8*, Simon & Schuster) Simon & Schuster.

Lash, John D. Cowboy Stories from East Texas. 1991. (Illus.). 80p. (J). (gr. 1-4). pap. 10.95 (*1-885777-27-2*); reprint ed. lib. bdg. 14.95 o.p. (*0-937460-66-4*) Hendrick-Long Publishing Co.

Latham, Aaron. Code of the West. 2002. 496p. pap. 13.95 (*0-425-18513-3*) Berkley Publishing Group.

Lattany, Kristin Hunter. Do unto Others. E-Book 19.95 (*1-58945-572-X*) Adobe Systems, Inc.

—Do unto Others. E-Book 19.50 (*0-345-44329-2*, Ballantine Bks.) Ballantine Bks.

Law, Susan K. Heaven in West Texas. 1997. 304p. mass mkt. 5.50 o.p. (*0-06-108474-3*, HarperTorch) Morrow/Avon.

Le May, Alan. The Searchers. 1985. 352p. mass mkt. 3.50 o.s.i (*0-425-07968-6*) Berkley Publishing Group.

—The Searchers. l.t. ed. 2001. lib. bdg. 25.95 (*1-58547-080-5*) Ctr. Point Large Print.

—The Searchers. 1978. lib. bdg. 9.95 o.p. (*0-8398-2464-5*, Macmillan Reference USA) Gale Group.

Lea, Tom. The Wonderful Country. 1979. lib. bdg. 9.95 o.p. (*0-8398-2587-0*, Macmillan Reference USA) Gale Group.

—The Wonderful Country. 1984. (Illus.). 400p. reprint ed. 15.95 o.p. (*0-89096-185-9*) Texas A&M Univ. Pr.

—The Wonderful Country. 2002. (Texas Tradition Ser.: No. 33). (Illus.). 400p. 24.95 (*0-87565-261-1*); pap. 17.95 (*0-87565-255-7*) Texas Christian Univ. Pr.

Leclaire, Day. The Nine-Dollar Daddy: Texas Grooms Wanted! 1999. (Harlequin Romance Ser.: No. 3543). mass mkt. (*0-373-03543-8*, 1-03543-5); (Harlequin Large Print Ser.: No. 389). mass mkt. (*0-373-15789-4*, 1-15789-0) Harlequin Enterprises, Ltd. (Harlequin Bks.).

—The Nine-Dollar Daddy: Texas Grooms Wanted! l.t. ed. 1999. (Mills & Boon Large Print Ser.). 288p. 25.99 o.p. (*0-263-16139-0*) Harlequin Mills & Boon, Ltd. GBR. *Dist:* Ulverscroft Large Print Bks., Ltd., Ulverscroft Large Print Canada, Ltd.

Lee, Linda Francis. Looking for Lacey. 2003. 352p. mass mkt. 6.99 (*0-8041-1996-1*, Ivy Bks.) Ballantine Bks.

Leedom, John H. Whose Water. 2002. 401p. 29.95 (*0-9717028-0-2*) Nesbett Heights, Inc.

Lehman, M M. Texans on the Powder. unabr. ed. 1989. audio 39.95 (*1-55686-327-6*, 327) Books in Motion.

—Texans on the Powder. l.t. ed. 1999. E-Book 24.95 incl. cd-rom (*1-929077-62-9*, Books OnScreen) PageFree Publishing, Inc.

Lehrer, Jim. White Widow. 2000. 224p. pap. text 12.00 (*1-891620-41-X*) PublicAffairs.

Lehrer, Kate. Confessions of a Bigamist: A Novel. 2004. 288p. 24.00 (*1-4000-5025-1*) Crown Publishing Group.

Leigh, Ana. The Mackenzies: Zach. 2001. (Mackenzies Ser.). 384p. mass mkt. 5.99 (*0-380-81103-0*, Avon Bks.) Morrow/Avon.

Liles, Maurine W. The Littlest Vaquero: A Story of the First Texas Cowboys, Longhorns, & the American Revolution. 1996. (Illus.). 120p. (J). (gr. 4-6). 15.95 (*1-57168-103-5*) Eakin Pr.

—Rebecca of Blossom Prairie: Grandmother of a Vice President. Roberts, M., ed. 1990. (Illus.). 105p. (J). (gr. 5-6). 15.95 (*0-89015-754-5*) Eakin Pr.

Lindsey, David L. An Absence of Light. 1995. 576p. mass mkt. 6.99 (*0-553-56941-4*) Bantam Bks.

—An Absence of Light. unabr. ed. 1994. audio 105.25 (*1-56100-195-3*, 785, Unabridged Library Editions) Brilliance Audio.

—Animosity. l.t. ed. 2001. (Americana Ser.). 447p. 28.95 o.p. (*0-7862-3324-9*) Thorndike Pr.

—Animosity. 2001. 352p. 24.95 o.p. (*0-446-52791-2*) Warner Bks., Inc.

—Black Gold, Red Death. 1986. 256p. mass mkt. 5.99 o.s.i (*0-449-13121-1*, Fawcett) Ballantine Bks.

—Body of Truth. 1993. 480p. mass mkt. 6.99 (*0-553-28964-0*) Bantam Bks.

—A Cold Mind. 1994. 368p. mass mkt. 6.99 (*0-553-56081-6*) Bantam Bks.

—A Cold Mind. 1996. pap. o.s.i (*0-385-48406-2*) Doubleday Publishing.

—A Cold Mind. 1990. 352p. mass mkt. 5.99 (*0-671-73338-9*); 1984. mass mkt. 3.95 (*0-671-49933-5*) Simon & Schuster. (Pocket).

—Heat from Another Sun. 1996. 384p. mass mkt. 6.99 (*0-553-56790-X*) Bantam Bks.

—Heat from Another Sun. 1984. 256p. 14.95 o.p. (*0-06-015346-6*) HarperTrade.

—Heat from Another Sun. 1985. mass mkt. 5.95 (*0-671-54632-5*, Pocket) Simon & Schuster.

—In the Lake of the Moon. 1990. 400p. mass mkt. 6.50 o.s.i (*0-553-28344-8*) Bantam Bks.

—In the Lake of the Moon. 1988. 320p. 17.95 o.s.i (*0-689-11626-8*, Scribner) Simon & Schuster.

—Requiem for a Glass Heart. 1997. 448p. mass mkt. 6.99 (*0-553-57594-5*) Bantam Bks.

—Requiem for a Glass Heart. l.t. ed. 1996. (Core Collection). 681p. lib. bdg. 28.95 (*0-7838-1885-8*) Thorndike Pr.

—The Rules of Silence. 2003. 10p. pap. 84.95 (*0-7927-2880-7*); 12p. pap. 10.95 (*0-7927-2881-5*) BBC Audiobooks America.

—The Rules of Silence. 2004. mass mkt. (*0-446-61292-8*); 2003. 416p. 24.95 (*0-446-53163-4*) Warner Bks., Inc.

—Spiral. (Orig.). 1990. mass mkt. 5.99 (*0-671-73337-0*, Pocket); 1988. 416p. mass mkt. 4.50 (*0-671-64666-4*, Pocket); 1986. 320p. pap. 16.95 o.p. (*0-689-11625-X*, Scribner) Simon & Schuster.

Lindsey, Johanna. All I Need Is You, abr. ed. 1998. (Straton Ser.). audio 7.99 o.s.i (*1-56740-260-7*, 1550, Paperback Nova Audio Bks.) Brilliance Audio.

—All I Need Is You. 1997. 384p. 22.00 (*0-380-97534-3*, Avon Bks.) Morrow/Avon.

—All I Need Is You. abr. ed. 1997. (Straton Ser.). audio 17.95 o.p. (*1-56100-994-6*, 455, Nova Audio Bks.) Brilliance Audio.

—All I Need Is You. unabr. ed. 1997. (Straton Ser.). audio 23.95 (*1-56100-768-4*, 30, Bookcassette); 9p. audio 57.25 (*1-56100-843-5*, 793, Unabridged Library Editions) Brilliance Audio.

—All I Need Is You, Set. unabr. ed. 1999. audio 57.25 Highsmith Inc.

—All I Need Is You. 1998. 416p. reprint ed. mass mkt. 6.99 (*0-380-76260-9*, Avon Bks.) Morrow/Avon.

—All I Need Is You. l.t. ed. 1998. (Basic Ser.). 459p. 29.95 o.p. (*0-7862-1284-5*) Thorndike Pr.

—Angel. l.t. ed. 1993. (Romance Ser.). 362p. lib. bdg. 24.95 (*0-8161-5760-X*, Macmillan Reference USA) Gale Group.

—Angel. 1992. 416p. mass mkt. 7.99 (*0-380-75628-5*, Avon Bks.) Morrow/Avon.

Logan, Jake. Showdown in Texas, Vol. 263. 2001. (Jake Logan Ser.: Vol. 263). 192p. mass mkt. 4.99 o.s.i (*0-515-13000-1*, Jove) Berkley Publishing Group.

Long, Jeff. Empire of Bones: A Novel of Sam Houston & the Texas Revolution. 1993. 256p. 22.00 o.p. (*0-688-12252-3*, Morrow, William & Co.) Morrow/Avon.

Lovelace, Merline. Texas Hero. 2002. (Silhouette Intimate Moments Ser.: No. 1165). mass mkt. (*0-373-27235-9*, Silhouette) Harlequin Enterprises, Ltd.

—Texas... Now & Forever. 2003. (Silhouette Special Releases Ser.: No. 12). 256p. mass mkt. (*0-373-61363-6*, Silhouette) Harlequin Enterprises, Ltd.

—Texas Now & Forever. l.t. ed. 2003. 259p. 28.95 (*0-7862-5850-0*) Thorndike Pr.

Lundy, Mike. Baby Farm. 1988. mass mkt. 3.95 o.p. (*0-425-10896-1*) Berkley Publishing Group.

Lyons, Michael. Cultivating the Texas Twister Hybrid. 1998. 175p. pap. 20.00 (*0-9655842-0-8*) HiT MoteL Pr.

MacAllister, Heather. Hand-Picked Husband: Texas Grooms Wanted! 1998. mass mkt. (*0-373-03535-7*, 1-03535-1, Mira Bks.); 1999. (Harlequin Large Print Ser.: Vol. 429). 253p. mass mkt. (*0-373-15829-7*, 1-15829-4, Mira Bks.); 1998. (Harlequin Large Print Ser.). mass mkt. (*0-373-15781-9*, 1-15781-7, Harlequin Bks.) Harlequin Enterprises, Ltd.

Macomber, Debbie. Caroline's Child. abr. ed. 1999. (Harlequin Romance Ser.). audio 7.99 o.p. (*1-56740-530-4*, 1824, Harlequin Romance Audio) Brilliance Audio.

—Caroline's Child. 1998. (Promo Ser.). 217p. per. (*0-373-83344-X*, 1-83344-1, Harlequin Bks.) Harlequin Enterprises, Ltd.

—Caroline's Child. l.t. ed. 1999. (Mills & Boon Large Print Ser.). 288p. 25.99 o.p. (*0-263-16104-8*) Harlequin Mills & Boon, Ltd. GBR. *Dist:* Ulverscroft Large Print Bks., Ltd., Ulverscroft Large Print Canada, Ltd.

—Dr. Texas. abr. ed. 1999. (Heart of Texas Ser.). audio 7.99 o.p. (*1-56740-534-7*, 1831, Harlequin Romance Audio) Brilliance Audio.

—Dr. Texas. 1998. (Promo Ser.). 216p. per. (*0-373-83345-8*, 1-83345-8, Harlequin Bks.) Harlequin Enterprises, Ltd.

—Dr. Texas. l.t. ed. (Mills & Boon Large Print Ser.). 1999. 288p. 25.99 o.p. (*0-263-16141-2*); 1998. 187p. 6.25 (*0-263-16130-7*) Harlequin Mills & Boon, Ltd. GBR. *Dist:* Ulverscroft Large Print Bks., Ltd., Ulverscroft Large Print Canada, Ltd., Ulverscroft Large Print Bks., Ltd.

—Lone Star Baby. abr. ed. 2000. (Harlequin Romance Ser.). audio 7.99 o.p. (*1-56740-545-2*, 1846, Harlequin Romance Audio) Brilliance Audio.

—Lone Star Baby. 1998. (Harlequin Ser.). per. (*0-373-83347-4*, Harlequin Bks.) Harlequin Enterprises, Ltd.

—Lone Star Baby. l.t. ed. 1999. (Mills & Boon Large Print Ser.). 288p. 25.99 o.p. (*0-263-16208-7*) Harlequin Mills & Boon, Ltd. GBR. *Dist:* Ulverscroft Large Print Bks., Ltd., Ulverscroft Large Print Canada, Ltd.

—Lonesome Cowboy. abr. ed. 1998. (Harlequin Romance Ser.: Vol. 2). audio 7.99 o.p. (*1-56740-032-9*, 779, Harlequin Romance Audio) Brilliance Audio.

—Lonesome Cowboy. 1998. (Promo Ser.). per. (*0-373-83342-3*, 1-83342-5, Harlequin Bks.) Harlequin Enterprises, Ltd.

—Lonesome Cowboy. l.t. ed. 1999. (Mills & Boon Large Print Ser.). 25.99 o.p. (*0-263-16058-0*) Harlequin Mills & Boon, Ltd. GBR. *Dist:* Ulverscroft Large Print Bks., Ltd., Ulverscroft Large Print Canada, Ltd.

—Nell's Cowboy. abr. ed. 2000. (Harlequin Romance Ser.). audio 7.99 o.p. (*1-56740-539-8*, 1839, Harlequin Romance Audio) Brilliance Audio.

—Nell's Cowboy. 1998. (Harlequin Ser.: No. 5). per. (*0-373-83346-6*, 1-83346-6, Harlequin Bks.) Harlequin Enterprises, Ltd.

—Nell's Cowboy. l.t. ed. 1999. (Mills & Boon Large Print Ser.). 288p. 25.99 o.p. (*0-263-16173-0*) Harlequin Mills & Boon, Ltd. GBR. *Dist:* Ulverscroft Large Print Bks., Ltd., Ulverscroft Large Print Canada, Ltd.

—Promise, Texas. unabr. ed. 1999. audio 7.99 (*1-55204-187-5*, MIR-1187) Durkin Hayes Publishing Ltd.

—Promise, Texas. 384p. 2003. mass mkt. (*1-55166-976-5*); 1999. mass mkt. (*1-55166-502-6*) Harlequin Enterprises, Ltd. (Mira Bks.).

—Return to Promise. 2000. 256p. (*1-55166-613-8*, 1-66613-0, Mira Bks.) Harlequin Enterprises, Ltd.

—Sooner or Later. l.t. ed. 2000. (Wheeler Softcover Ser.). 346p. pap. 25.95 (*1-56895-141-8*, Wheeler Publishing, Inc.) Gale Group.

—Sooner or Later. 1998. 368p. mass mkt. 3.99 o.p. (*0-06-104475-X*) HarperCollins Pubs.

—Sooner or Later. 1996. 368p. mass mkt. 6.99 (*0-06-108345-3*, HarperTorch) Morrow/Avon.

—Texas Two-Step. abr. ed. 1998. (Harlequin Romance Ser.: Vol. 2). audio 7.99 o.p. (*1-56740-039-6*, 1543, Harlequin Romance Audio) Brilliance Audio.

—Texas Two-Step. 1998. (Promo Ser.: Vol. 2). 219p. per. (*0-373-83343-1*, 1-83343-3, Harlequin Bks.) Harlequin Enterprises, Ltd.

—Texas Two-Step. l.t. ed. 1999. (Mills & Boon Large Print Ser.). 288p. 25.99 o.p. (*0-263-16081-5*) Harlequin Mills & Boon, Ltd. GBR. *Dist:* Ulverscroft Large Print Bks., Ltd., Ulverscroft Large Print Canada, Ltd.

Madame Justice. 2000. (Andy Ser.: No. 3). 336p. (C). mass mkt. 7.99 (*0-9673506-4-6*) Trent Martin Pubns.

Major, Ann. Marry a Man Who Will Dance. 2002. 256p. mass mkt. (*1-55166-956-0*, Mira Bks.) Harlequin Enterprises, Ltd.

Makris, Kathryn. A Different Way. 1989. 192p. (J). pap. 2.95 (*0-380-75728-1*, Avon Bks.) Morrow/Avon.

Mallery, Susan. Lone Star Millionaire. 1999. (World's Most Eligible Ser.: No. 10). per. (*0-373-65027-2*, 1-65027-4, Harlequin Bks.) Harlequin Enterprises, Ltd.

Malone, Paul S. In an Arid Land: Thirteen Stories of Texas. 1995. 232p. 21.50 (*0-87565-140-2*) Texas Christian Univ. Pr.

Malone, Paul Scott. This House of Women. 2001. 392p. 27.95 (*0-89672-458-1*) Texas Tech Univ. Pr.

Manning, Jason. Texas Bound. 1997. (Falconer Ser.). mass mkt. 5.99 o.s.i (*0-451-19142-0*) NAL.

Marlow, Herb. Dillon's Revenge. 1997. (Illus.). (J). (*1-56763-275-0*); pap. (*1-56763-276-9*) Ozark Publishing.

Marshall, Marion. Cimarron Surrender. 2000. E-Book 3.99 (*1-58608-228-0*); 213p. E-Book 5.80 incl. disk (*1-58608-008-3*) New Concepts Publishing.

Martin, Allana. Death of a Healing Woman: A Texana Jones Mystery. l.t. ed. 1997. (G. K. Hall Mystery Ser.). 290p. lib. bdg. 25.95 o.p. (*0-7838-8216-5*, Macmillan Reference USA) Gale Group.

—Death of a Healing Woman: A Texana Jones Mystery. 1998. (WWL Mystery Ser.). per. (*0-373-26281-7*, 1-26281-5, Worldwide Library) Harlequin Enterprises, Ltd.

—Death of a Healing Woman: A Texana Jones Mystery. l.t. ed. 1996. 224p. 20.95 (*0-312-14581-0*, Saint Martin's Minotaur) St. Martin's Pr.

—Death of a Myth Maker: A Texana Jones Mystery. 2001. (WWL Mystery Ser.: No. 380). 252p. mass mkt. (*0-373-26380-5*, 1-26380-5, Worldwide Library) Harlequin Enterprises, Ltd.

—Death of a Myth Maker: A Texana Jones Mystery. 2000. (Texana Jones Mystery Ser.). (Illus.). 272p. 23.95 (*0-312-25241-2*, Saint Martin's Minotaur) St. Martin's Pr.

—Death of a Saint Maker. 1999. (gr. 3). per. (*0-373-26299-X*, Harlequin Bks.) Harlequin Enterprises, Ltd.

—Death of a Saint Maker: A Texana Jones Mystery. 1997. (Texana Jones Mystery Ser.). 288p. 22.95 o.p. (*0-312-18083-7*, Saint Martin's Minotaur) St. Martin's Pr.

—Death of an Evangelista. 2000. (WWL Mystery Ser.: No. 335). mass mkt. (*0-373-26335-X*, 1-26335-9, Worldwide Library) Harlequin Enterprises, Ltd.

—Death of an Evangelista. 1999. 272p. 22.95 o.p. (*0-312-19853-1*, Saint Martin's Minotaur) St. Martin's Pr.

—Death of the Last Villista. 2002. (WWL Mystery Ser.: No. 434). 256p. mass mkt. (*0-373-26434-8*, Worldwide Library) Harlequin Enterprises, Ltd.

—Death of the Last Villista. 2001. (Texana Jones Mystery Ser.). 224p. 22.95 (*0-312-26573-5*, Saint Martin's Minotaur) St. Martin's Pr.

Martin, LaJoyce. Two Scars Against One. 1995. 192p. (Orig.). pap. 9.99 (*1-56722-025-8*) Word Aflame Pr.

Martin, Lee. Bird in a Cage. 1996. per. (*0-373-26225-6*, 1-26225-2, Worldwide Library) Harlequin Enterprises, Ltd.

—Bird in a Cage. 1995. 240p. 20.95 o.p. (*0-312-13028-7*, Saint Martin's Minotaur) St. Martin's Pr.

—A Conspiracy of Strangers. 1986. 208p. 13.95 o.p. (*0-312-16433-5*) St. Martin's Pr.

—The Day that Dusty Died. 1994. 304p. 20.95 o.p. (*0-312-09779-4*, Saint Martin's Minotaur) St. Martin's Pr.

—Death Warmed Over. 1991. mass mkt. (*0-373-26065-2*, Harlequin Bks.) Harlequin Enterprises, Ltd.

—Death Warmed Over. 1988. 224p. 15.95 o.p. (*0-312-02221-2*, Saint Martin's Minotaur) St. Martin's Pr.

—Deficit Ending. 1992. (Mystery Ser.: No. 101). mass mkt. (*0-373-26101-2*, Harlequin Bks.) Harlequin Enterprises, Ltd.

—Deficit Ending. 1990. 208p. 15.95 o.p. (*0-312-03813-5*, Saint Martin's Minotaur) St. Martin's Pr.

—Genealogy of Murder. 1997. (WWL Mystery Ser.: No. 239). per. (*0-373-26239-6*, 1-26239-3, Worldwide Library) Harlequin Enterprises, Ltd.

—Genealogy of Murder. 1996. 240p. 22.95 o.p. (*0-312-13975-6*, Saint Martin's Minotaur) St. Martin's Pr.

—Hacker. 1993. (WWL Mystery Ser.). per. (*0-373-26135-7*, 1-26135-3, Harlequin Bks.) Harlequin Enterprises, Ltd.

—Hacker: A Deb Ralston Mystery. 1992. 192p. 16.95 o.p. (*0-312-06990-1*, Saint Martin's Minotaur) St. Martin's Pr.

—Hal's Own Murder Case. 1991. mass mkt. (*0-373-26087-3*, Harlequin Bks.) Harlequin Enterprises, Ltd.

—Hal's Own Murder Case. 1989. 14.95 o.p. (*0-312-02925-X*, Saint Martin's Minotaur) St. Martin's Pr.

—Inherited Murder. 1994. (Deb Ralston Mystery Ser.). 304p. 19.95 o.p. (*0-312-11415-X*, Saint Martin's Minotaur) St. Martin's Pr.

—The Mensa Murders. 1993. mass mkt. (*0-373-26115-2*, 1-26115-5, Harlequin Bks.) Harlequin Enterprises, Ltd.

—The Mensa Murders. 1990. 192p. 15.95 o.p. (*0-312-05126-3*, Saint Martin's Minotaur) St. Martin's Pr.

—Murder at the Blue Owl. 1990. mass mkt. (*0-373-26054-7*, Harlequin Bks.) Harlequin Enterprises, Ltd.

—Murder at the Blue Owl. 1988. 208p. 14.95 o.p. (*0-312-01795-2*) St. Martin's Pr.

—Quakertown: A Novel. 2002. 304p. pap. 14.00 (*0-452-28336-1*, Plume); 2001. (Illus.). 320p. 23.95 o.p. (*0-525-94583-0*) Dutton/Plume.

—Too Sane a Murder. 1984. 192p. 12.95 o.p. (*0-312-80901-8*) St. Martin's Pr.

Martinello, Marian L. Ready's Gifts. 2003. (Illus.). 158p. (YA). (gr. 8 up). per. 12.95 (*0-9724113-0-5*) MindCatcher Pr.

Martinez, Max. Layover. 1997. 140p. 22.95 (*1-55885-199-2*); 284p. pap. 11.95 o.p. (*1-55885-200-X*) Arte Publico Pr.

—White Leg. 1996. 257p. 19.95 (*1-55885-098-8*) Arte Publico Pr.

Matheson, Richard. The Gun Fight. 1993. (Evans Novel of the West Ser.). 196p. 16.95 o.p. (*0-87131-726-5*) Evans, M. & Co., Inc.

—The Gunfight. 1993. 256p. mass mkt. 4.99 o.p. (*0-425-13901-8*) Berkley Publishing Group.

Mathis, Edward G. The Fifth Level: A Dan Roman Mystery. 1992. 256p. text 20.00 (*0-684-19386-8*, Macmillan Reference USA) Gale Group.

Matlock, Curtiss Ann. Lost Highways. 1999. mass mkt. (*1-55166-499-2*, 1-66499-4, Mira Bks.) Harlequin Enterprises, Ltd.

Mayhar, Ardath. Slewfoot Sally & the Flying Mule: And Other Tales from Cotton County. Richards, J., ed. 1995. (Illus.). 226p. (Orig.). (YA). (gr. 7-12). pap. 12.00 (*1-887303-00-6*) Blue Lantern Publishing.

Maynard, Roy. The Old Man. 1994. (Emerson Dunn Mystery Ser.). 192p. pap. 7.99 o.p. (*0-89107-772-3*) Crossway Bks.

—A Quick Thirty Seconds. 1993. (Emerson Dunn Mystery Ser.). 192p. (YA). pap. 7.99 o.p. (*0-89107-745-6*) Crossway Bks.

—Thirty-Eight Caliber. 1992. (Emerson Dunn Mystery Ser.). 192p. (Orig.). pap. 7.99 o.p. (*0-89107-674-3*) Crossway Bks.

—Twenty-Two Automatic. 1993. (Emerson Dunn Mystery Ser.). 192p. pap. 7.99 o.p. (*0-89107-696-4*) Crossway Bks.

McAdoo, Ron & McAdoo, Caryl. The Apple Orchard Bed & Breakfast. 2002. (Five Star First Edition Romance Ser.). 300p. 26.95 (*0-7862-4234-5*, Five Star) Gale Group.

McAfee, John P. On Rims of Empty Moons. 1997. 267p. 25.95 (*0-89672-386-0*) Texas Tech Univ. Pr.

McBride, Jule. Prescription Baby. 2000. (Harlequin American Romance Ser.: Vol. 5). 256p. mass mkt. (*0-373-65066-3*, 1650662, Harlequin Bks.) Harlequin Enterprises, Ltd.

McCandless, Bruce. So Many Things to Say: A Novel. 2000. 240p. pap. 21.99 (*0-7388-2826-2*); text 31.99 (*0-7388-2825-4*) Xlibris Corp.

McCarthy, Cormac. All the Pretty Horses. l.t. ed. 1993. 24.95 o.p. (*0-7927-1576-4*); pap. 22.95 o.p. (*0-7927-1575-6*) BBC Audiobooks America.

—All the Pretty Horses. unabr. collector's ed. 1993. audio 48.00 (*0-7366-2416-3*, 3183) Books on Tape, Inc.

—All the Pretty Horses. unabr. ed. 2000. audio 34.95 (*0-694-52280-5*); (Border Trilogy: Vol. 1). audio compact disk 50.00 (*0-694-52344-5*) HarperTrade. (HarperAudio).

—All the Pretty Horses. movie tie-in ed. 1993. (Border Trilogy: Vol. 1). 320p. pap. 14.00 (*0-679-74439-8*, Vintage) Knopf Publishing Group.

—All the Pretty Horses. abr. ed. 2000. (Border Trilogy: Vol. 1). audio 18.00 (*0-679-42568-3*, 390333);Set. audio compact disk 21.95 (*0-375-41587-4*) Random Hse. Audio Publishing Group. (RH Audio).

—All the Pretty Horses. 1992. (Border Trilogy: Vol. 1). 320p. 27.50 (*0-394-57474-5*) Random Hse., Inc.

—All the Pretty Horses. unabr. ed. 1999. (Border Trilogy: Vol. 1). audio 60.00 (*1-55690-660-9*, 92403E7) Recorded Bks., LLC.

—All the Pretty Horses. 1993. 19.05 (*0-606-20069-X*) Turtleback Bks.

—All the Pretty Horses. 2000. (CliffsNotes Ser.). (Illus.). 80p. pap. 5.99 (*0-7645-8551-7*, Cliff Notes) Wiley, John & Sons, Inc.

—Cities of the Plain. 1999. (Border Trilogy: Vol. 3). 304p. pap. 13.00 (*0-679-74719-2*, Vintage) Knopf Publishing Group.

—Cities of the Plain. 1998. (Border Trilogy : Vol.3). 304p. 27.50 (*0-679-42390-7*) Knopf, Alfred A. Inc.

—Cities of the Plain. ltd. ed. 1998. 292p. 195.00 (*1-890885-04-5*) Trice, B.E. Publishing.

McCauley, Barbara. In Blackhawk's Bed. 2002. (Silhouette Desire Ser.). 192p. mass mkt. (*0-373-76447-2*, Silhouette) Harlequin Enterprises, Ltd.

McCord, John S. Texas Comebacker. 1991. 192p. 15.00 o.s.i (*0-385-41497-8*) Doubleday Publishing.

McCorquodale, Robin. Stella Landry. 1992. 20.00 o.p. (*0-688-11528-4*, Morrow, William & Co.) Morrow/Avon.

McDaniel, Sylvia. The Outlaw Takes a Wife. 2001. (Burnett Brides Ser.). 32p. mass mkt. 5.50 o.s.i (*0-8217-6766-6*) Kensington Publishing Corp.

McEachin, James. Farewell to the Mockingbirds. 1997. 512p. 27.00 (*0-9656661-9-0*) Rharl Publishing Group.

McGhee, George C. Dance of the Billions: Texas Oil Creed. Seidl, Tony, ed. 1989. 288p. 17.95 o.p. (*0-89015-692-1*) Eakin Pr.

McGinnis, Bruce. Reflections in Dark Glass: The Life & Times of John Wesley Hardin. 1996. 180p. 24.95 (*1-57441-008-3*) Univ. of North Texas Pr.

McGuire, Tim. Gold of Cortes. 2000. 288p. mass mkt. 5.99 (*0-8439-4729-2*, Leisure Bks.) Dorchester Publishing Co., Inc.

McMurtry, Larry. Comanche Moon. unabr. ed. 1999. Pt. 1. audio 72.00; Pt. 2. (Lonesome Dove Ser.: No. 2). audio 64.00 Books on Tape, Inc.

—Comanche Moon, Set. unabr. ed. 1999. (Lonesome Dove Ser.: No. 2). audio 45.00 Highsmith Inc.

—Comanche Moon. 2000. (Lonesome Dove Ser.: No. 2). 720p. pap. 16.00 (*0-684-85755-3*, Simon & Schuster); 1998. (Lonesome Dove Ser.: No. 2). 816p. pap. 7.99 (*0-671-02064-1*, Pocket); 1998. mass mkt. 6.99 (*0-671-02049-8*, Pocket); 1997. (Lonesome Dove Ser.: No. 2). 752p. 28.50 (*0-684-80754-8*, Simon & Schuster) Simon & Schuster.

—Comanche Moon. unabr. ed. 1997. (Lonesome Dove Ser.: No. 2). 24p. audio 60.00 (*0-671-57730-1*, 135489, Simon & Schuster Audioworks) Simon & Schuster Audio.

—Comanche Moon. l.t. ed. 1999. (Paperback Bestsellers Ser.: No. 2). 921p. pap. 28.95 (*0-7862-1392-2*) Thorndike Pr.

—Comanche Moon. 1998. 14.04 (*0-606-16182-1*) Turtleback Bks.

—Dead Man's Walk. unabr. ed. 1996. audio 80.00 (*0-7366-3211-5*, 3874) Books on Tape, Inc.

—Dead Man's Walk. l.t. ed. (Lonesome Dove Ser.: No. 1). 1999. 800p. 27.95 o.p. (*0-7838-1510-7*); 1996. pap. 25.95 o.p. (*0-7838-1511-5*) Gale Group. (Macmillan Reference USA).

—Dead Man's Walk. (Lonesome Dove Ser.: No. 1). 2000. 464p. pap. 15.00 (*0-684-85754-5*, Simon & Schuster); 1995. 480p. 26.00 (*0-684-80753-X*, Simon & Schuster); 1996. 528p. pap. 7.99 (*0-671-00116-7*, Pocket) Simon & Schuster.

—Dead Man's Walk. unabr. ed. 1995. (Lonesome Dove Ser.: No. 1). audio 45.00 (*0-671-55169-8*, 113285, Simon & Schuster Audioworks) Simon & Schuster Audio.

—Dead Man's Walk. l.t. ed. 1998. (Lonesome Dove Ser.: No. 1). 5.98 o.p. (*0-7651-0771-6*) Smithmark Pubs., Inc.

—Dead Man's Walk. 2000. 21.05 (*0-606-20274-9*) Turtleback Bks.

—Duane's Depressed. 2002. 431p. reprint ed. 26.00 (*0-7567-5630-8*) DIANE Publishing Co.

—Duane's Depressed. l.t. ed. 1999. (Core Ser.: No. 3). 574p. 30.95 (*0-7838-8631-4*, Macmillan Reference USA) Gale Group.

—Duane's Depressed. 2003. 432p. pap. 14.00 (*0-7432-3015-9*, Simon & Schuster); 1999. (Last Picture Show Trilogy: No. 3). 528p. pap. 7.99 (*0-671-02557-0*, Pocket); 1999. mass mkt. 7.99 (*0-671-03461-8*, Pocket); 1999. (Last Picture Show Trilogy: No. 3). 432p. 26.00 (*0-684-85497-X*, Simon & Schuster) Simon & Schuster.

—Duane's Depressed. 1999. (Last Picture Show Trilogy: No. 3). 14.04 (*0-606-19049-X*) Turtleback Bks.

—The Evening Star: A Novel. unabr. ed. audio 94.95 o.p. BBC Audiobooks America.

—The Evening Star: A Novel. unabr. ed. 1993. audio 120.00 (*0-7366-2472-4*, 3235) Books on Tape, Inc.

—The Evening Star: A Novel. l.t. ed. 1993. (General Ser.). 765p. pap. 18.95 (*0-8161-5649-2*); lib. bdg. 25.95 (*0-8161-5648-4*) Gale Group. (Macmillan Reference USA).

—The Evening Star: A Novel. 1999. 640p. pap. 15.00 (*0-684-85751-0*, Simon & Schuster); 1996. 624p. pap. 6.99 (*0-671-00427-1*, Pocket); 1992. 448p. pap. 23.00 (*0-671-68519-8*, Simon & Schuster) Simon & Schuster.

—The Evening Star: A Novel. Rubenstein, ed. 1993. 624p. reprint ed. mass mkt. 7.99 o.s.i (*0-671-79904-5*, Pocket) Simon & Schuster.

—The Evening Star: A Novel. unabr. ed. 1999. audio 19.98 (*0-671-04544-X*); 1997. audio 45.00 (*0-671-57651-8*) Simon & Schuster Audio. (Simon & Schuster Audioworks).

—The Last Picture Show. 1976. (Last Picture Show Trilogy: No. 1). 22.95 (*0-89190-889-7*) Amereon, Ltd.

—The Last Picture Show. 1999. (Last Picture Show Trilogy: Bk. 1). (*0-7540-1321-9*); pap. (*0-7540-2238-2*) BBC Audiobooks America.

—The Last Picture Show. unabr. collector's ed. 1984. (Last Picture Show Trilogy: No. 1). audio 48.00 (*0-7366-0764-1*, 1721) Books on Tape, Inc.

—The Last Picture Show. 1997. (Last Picture Show Trilogy: No. 1). 35.95 o.p. (*1-56849-688-5*) Buccaneer Bks., Inc.

—The Last Picture Show. unabr. ed. 1989. (Last Picture Show Trilogy). audio 51.00 (*1-55690-304-9*, 89810E7) Recorded Bks., LLC.

—The Last Picture Show. (Thalia Trilogy Ser.: No. 1). 2003. 288p. pap. 13.00 (*0-684-85386-8*, Simon & Schuster); 1999. pap. 11.00 (*0-684-00817-3*, Simon & Schuster); 1992. 224p. pap. 10.00 (*0-671-75487-4*, Simon & Schuster); 1992. 320p. mass mkt. 7.99 o.s.i (*0-671-75381-9*, Pocket); 1989. 280p. 18.95 o.p. (*0-671-67604-0*, Simon & Schuster) Simon & Schuster.

—The Last Picture Show. 1979. (Last Picture Show Trilogy: No. 1). 224p. pap. 8.95 o.p. (*0-14-005183-X*, Penguin Bks.) Viking Penguin.

—Leaving Cheyenne. 1976. 22.95 (*0-8488-0373-6*) Amereon, Ltd.

—Leaving Cheyenne. unabr. collector's ed. 1983. audio 48.00 (*0-7366-0763-3*, 1720) Books on Tape, Inc.

—Leaving Cheyenne. unabr. ed. 1993. audio 70.00 (*1-55690-847-4*, 93214E7) Recorded Bks., LLC.

—Leaving Cheyenne. 304p. 2002. pap. 14.00 (*0-684-85387-6*); 1992. pap. 12.00 (*0-671-75490-4*) Simon & Schuster. (Simon & Schuster).

—Leaving Cheyenne. Grose, Bill, ed. 1992. 320p. reprint ed. mass mkt. 7.99 (*0-671-75380-0*, Pocket) Simon & Schuster.

—Leaving Cheyenne. 1986. (Southwest Landmark Ser.: No. 3). 312p. reprint ed. 15.95 o.p. (*0-89096-242-1*) Texas A&M Univ. Pr.

—Leaving Cheyenne. 1979. (Contemporary American Fiction Ser.). 256p. pap. 8.95 o.p. (*0-14-005221-6*, Penguin Bks.) Viking Penguin.

—Moving On, Pt. 1. unabr. collector's ed. 1992. audio 80.00 (*0-7366-2185-7*, 2981-A) Books on Tape, Inc.

—Moving On. Grose, Bill, ed. 1991. mass mkt. 7.99 (*0-671-74408-9*, Pocket) Simon & Schuster.

For book reviews, descriptive annotations, tables of contents, cover images, author biographies & additional information, updated daily, subscribe to **www.booksinprint.com** 1121

—Moving On. 800p. 1987. pap. 11.00 (*0-671-63320-1*, Touchstone); 1999. reprint ed. pap. 15.00 (*0-684-85388-4*, Simon & Schuster) Simon & Schuster.
—Some Can Whistle. l.t. ed. 1990. (General Ser.). 399p. 13.95 o.p. (*0-8161-5010-9*); lib. bdg. 20.95 o.p. (*0-8161-4987-9*) Gale Group. (Macmillan Reference USA).
—Some Can Whistle. 1989. 19.95 o.p. (*0-671-64267-7*, Simon & Schuster) Simon & Schuster.
—Some Can Whistle. Grose, William, ed. 1990. 384p. reprint ed. mass mkt. 6.99 (*0-671-72213-1*, Pocket) Simon & Schuster.
—Texasville. unabr. collector's ed. 1989. (Last Picture Show Trilogy: No. 2). audio 112.00 (*0-7366-1653-5*, 2504) Books on Tape, Inc.
—Texasville. l.t. ed. 1999. (Core Ser.: No. 2). 663p. 30.95 (*0-7838-8633-0*, Macmillan Reference USA) Gale Group.
—Texasville. (Thalia Trilogy Ser.: No. 2). 2003. 544p. pap. 14.00 (*0-684-85750-2*, Simon & Schuster); 1990. mass mkt. 5.95 o.s.i (*0-671-72474-6*, Pocket) Simon & Schuster.
—Texasville. Grose, Bill, ed. 1990. (Last Picture Show Trilogy: No. 2). 576p. mass mkt. 7.99 o.s.i (*0-671-73517-9*, Pocket) Simon & Schuster.
—Texasville. 1987. (Last Picture Show Trilogy: No. 2). mass mkt. 3.95 o.s.i (*0-671-64878-0*, Pocket); 512p. 18.45 o.p. (*0-671-62533-0*, Simon & Schuster) Simon & Schuster.
McMurtry, Larry & Prichard, Michael. Some Can Whistle. unabr. collector's ed. 1990. audio 56.00 (*0-7366-1803-1*, 2640) Books on Tape, Inc.
McNaught, Judith. Remember When. 2003. 432p. mass mkt. 5.99 (*0-7434-6728-0*, Pocket); 1996. 400p. 24.00 (*0-671-52570-0*, Atria); 1997. 432p. reprint ed. mass mkt. 7.99 (*0-671-79555-4*, Pocket) Simon & Schuster.
—Remember When. abr. ed. 1997. audio 14.40 (*0-671-57739-5*, 908769); 1995. audio 18.00 (*0-671-53699-0*, 393282) Simon & Schuster Audio. (Simon & Schuster Audioworks).
—Remember When. l.t. ed. 1997. 704p. pap. 28.95 (*0-7862-0569-5*) Thorndike Pr.
McWilliams, A. L. Eye of the Cat. 2000. (First Edition Romance Ser.). 347p. 25.95 (*0-7862-2495-9*, Five Star) Gale Group.
Meredith, Doris R. The Homefront Murders. 1994. (Southwest Mysteries Ser.). mass mkt. 4.99 o.s.i (*0-345-38050-9*) Ballantine Bks.
—Murder by Deception. 1989. mass mkt. 4.99 o.s.i (*0-345-35243-2*) Ballantine Bks.
—Murder by Deception. 2004. 288p. mass mkt. 6.99 (*0-7434-7999-8*) ibooks, Inc.
—Murder by Impulse. 1987. 288p. mass mkt. 4.99 o.s.i (*0-345-34671-8*) Ballantine Bks.
—Murder by Impulse. Holland, Steve, ed. abr. ed. 1993. audio 24.95 (*1-883268-05-2*) Spellbinders, Inc.
—Murder by Impulse. 2003. 288p. mass mkt. 6.99 (*0-7434-7968-8*) ibooks, Inc.
—Murder by Masquerade. 1990. (John Lloyd Branson Ser.). 256p. mass mkt. 4.99 o.s.i (*0-345-35986-0*) Ballantine Bks.
—Murder by Masquerade. Holland, Stephen, ed. abr. ed. 1994. audio 24.95 (*1-883268-11-7*) Spellbinders, Inc.
—Murder by Reference. 1991. 272p. mass mkt. 4.99 o.s.i (*0-345-36861-4*) Ballantine Bks.
—Murder by Reference. abr. ed. 1997. audio 25.00 (*1-883268-28-1*) Spellbinders, Inc.
—Murder by Sacrilege. 1993. mass mkt. 4.99 o.s.i (*0-345-37693-5*) Ballantine Bks.
—Murder in Volume. 2000. (Prime Crime Mysteries Ser.). 256p. mass mkt. 6.50 (*0-425-17309-7*, Prime Crime) Berkley Publishing Group.
—Murder Past Due. 2001. 240p. mass mkt. 5.99 (*0-425-17800-5*, Prime Crime) Berkley Publishing Group.
—The Sheriff & the Branding Iron Murders. 1992. mass mkt. 3.99 o.s.i (*0-345-36950-5*) Ballantine Bks.
—The Sheriff & the Branding Iron Murders. l.t. ed. 1997. (Nightingale Ser.). pap. 18.95 o.p. (*0-7838-2044-5*, Macmillan Reference USA) Gale Group.
—The Sheriff & the Branding Iron Murders. 1986. 160p. pap. 2.95 (*0-380-70050-6*, Avon Bks.) Morrow/Avon.
—The Sheriff & the Branding Iron Murders. Holland, Stephen, ed. abr. ed. 1994. audio 24.95 (*1-883268-12-5*) Spellbinders, Inc.
—The Sheriff & the Branding Iron Murders. 1985. 159p. 14.95 (*0-8027-4050-2*) Walker & Co.
—The Sheriff & the Folsom Man Murders. 1992. mass mkt. 3.99 o.s.i (*0-345-36949-1*) Ballantine Bks.
—The Sheriff & the Folsom Man Murders. 1987. 208p. pap. 2.95 (*0-380-70364-5*, Avon Bks.) Morrow/Avon.
—The Sheriff & the Folsom Man Murders. 1989. 2.99 o.p. (*0-517-00603-0*) Random Hse. Value Publishing.
—The Sheriff & the Folsom Man Murders. l.t. ed. 1999. 261p. pap. 24.95 (*0-7838-8582-2*) Thorndike Pr.
—The Sheriff & the Folsom Man Murders. 1987. 192p. 16.95 (*0-8027-5663-8*) Walker & Co.
—The Sheriff & the Panhandle Murders. l.t. ed. 1986. 13.95 o.p. (*1-55504-028-4*, 317) BBC Audiobooks America.
—The Sheriff & the Panhandle Murders. 1991. mass mkt. 4.99 o.s.i (*0-345-36951-3*) Ballantine Bks.
—The Sheriff & the Panhandle Murders. 1985. 224p. pap. 2.95 o.p. (*0-380-69929-X*, Avon Bks.) Morrow/Avon.
—The Sheriff & the Panhandle Murders. Holland, Stephen, ed. abr. ed. 1994. audio 24.95 (*1-883268-08-7*) Spellbinders, Inc.
—The Sheriff & the Panhandle Murders. 1984. 192p. 12.95 o.s.i (*0-8027-4036-7*) Walker & Co.
—The Sheriff & the Pheasant Hunt Murders. 1993. mass mkt. 4.50 o.s.i (*0-345-36948-3*) Ballantine Bks.
—The Sheriff & the Pheasant Hunt Murders. Holland, Stephen, ed. abr. ed. 1994. audio 24.95 (*1-883268-07-9*) Spellbinders, Inc.
Merritt, Jackie. A Willing Wife. 1999. (Fortunes of Texas Ser.: No. 4). (Illus.). 250p. per. (*0-373-65033-7*, Silhouette) Harlequin Enterprises, Ltd.
Meyer, Charles. Beside the Still Waters. 1997. (Reverend Lucas Holt Mystery Ser.). 232p. pap. 6.50 (*0-9631149-4-8*) Stone Angel Bks.
—Blessed Are the Merciless. 1996. 272p. mass mkt. 5.50 o.s.i (*0-425-15140-9*) Berkley Publishing Group.
—Blessed Are the Merciless. 2nd ed. 1997. (Reverend Lucas Holt Mystery Ser.). 266p. reprint ed. pap. 6.50 (*0-9631149-5-6*) Stone Angel Bks.
—The Saints of God Murders. 1995. 256p. (Orig.). mass mkt. 5.99 o.s.i (*0-425-14869-6*, Prime Crime) Berkley Publishing Group.
Michaels, Fern. Texas Fury. 1996. pap. 8.95 o.s.i (*0-345-40569-2*); 1989. 512p. mass mkt. 6.99 (*0-345-31375-5*, Ballantine Bks.) Ballantine Bks.
—Texas Fury. 1991. reprint ed. 21.95 o.p. (*0-7278-4269-2*) Severn Hse. Pubs., Ltd.
—Texas Heat. 1989. mass mkt. 4.95 o.p. (*0-345-01028-0*); 1986. 512p. mass mkt. 6.99 (*0-345-33100-1*) Ballantine Bks.
—Texas Heat. 1989. reprint ed. 20.00 o.p. (*0-7278-4007-X*) Severn Hse. Pubs., Ltd.
—Texas Rich. 1995. pap. 8.95 o.p. (*0-345-40114-X*); 1987. 576p. mass mkt. 6.99 (*0-345-33540-6*, Ivy Bks.) Ballantine Bks.
—Texas Rich. 1989. reprint ed. 19.95 o.p. (*0-7278-1758-2*) Severn Hse. Pubs., Ltd.
—Texas Sunrise. 1994. 384p. mass mkt. 7.50 (*0-345-36593-3*) Ballantine Bks.
—Texas Trilogy. 1989. pap. 17.93 o.p. (*0-345-36424-4*) Ballantine Bks.
Michaels, Kasey. His Innocent Temptress. 2001. (Harlequin American Romance Ser.: No. 869). 251p. mass mkt. (*0-373-16869-1*, Harlequin Bks.) Harlequin Enterprises, Ltd.
Michener, James A. Texas. 1987. 1344p. mass mkt. 7.99 (*0-449-21092-8*, Fawcett) Ballantine Bks.
—Texas. unabr. ed. 1992. Pt. 1. audio 120.00; Pt. 2. audio 120.00; Pt. 3. audio 120.00 Books on Tape, Inc.
—Texas. 2002. 1120p. pap. 14.95 (*0-375-76141-1*) Random House Adult Trade Publishing Group.
—Texas. abr. ed. 1999. audio 8.99 o.s.i (*0-375-40572-0*, 391752); 1987. audio 18.00 o.s.i (*0-394-56056-6*) Random Hse. Audio Publishing Group. (RH Audio).
—Texas, 2 vols. 1986. (Illus.). 943p. 125.00 o.p. (*0-292-78071-0*) Univ. of Texas Pr.
Miller, J. P. Surviving Joy. 1995. 256p. 21.50 o.s.i (*1-55611-448-6*) Fine, Donald I. Bks.
Miller, Rex. Stone Shadow. 1989. mass mkt. 3.95 o.p. (*0-451-40164-6*, 036, Onyx) NAL.
—Stone Shadow. E-Book 6.99 (*0-7592-0797-6*); 2000. pap. 19.95 (*1-58586-164-2*); 2000. E-Book 6.99 (*1-58586-162-6*); 2000. E-Book 6.99 (*1-58586-163-4*); 2000. E-Book 6.99 (*1-58586-280-0*) eread-s.com.
Milne, Peter. Of Gold & Men. 9.95 (*0-9726927-0-3*) Clairvoyant Publishing.
Miralejos, Carlos. Texas, 2077: A Futuristic Novel. 1998. 220p. 20.95 (*0-9625266-4-9*, 97F002) Outer Space Pr.
Mitchard, Jacquelyn. The Most Wanted. l.t. ed. 1998. (Large Print Bks.). 407p. 27.95 (*1-56895-605-3*, Wheeler Publishing, Inc.) Gale Group.
—The Most Wanted. 1999. 416p. reprint ed. mass mkt. 7.99 o.s.i (*0-451-19685-6*, Signet Bks.) NAL.
—The Most Wanted. 1998. 448p. (gr. 9). 24.95 o.s.i (*0-670-87884-7*, Viking) Viking Penguin.
Mitchell, Kathryn. Proud & Angry Dust. 2001. 233p. 24.95 o.p. (*0-87081-608-X*) Univ. Pr. of Colorado.
Mogan, Jewel. Beyond Telling: Stories. 1995. 173p. 19.95 (*0-86538-082-1*) Ontario Review Pr.
Mojtabai, A. G. Called Out. 1994. 224p. 22.00 o.s.i (*0-385-47430-X*, Talese, Nan A.) Doubleday Publishing.
Moore Davis, Mollie E. The Wire Cutters. 1997. 384p. pap. 16.95 (*0-89096-796-2*) Texas A&M Univ. Pr.
Moore, Laurie. Constable's Apprehension. 2003. 452p. 26.95 (*0-7862-5334-7*, Five Star) Gale Group.
—Constable's Run. 2003. 335p. pap. 13.95 (*1-4104-0120-0*, Five Star Trade); 2002. 304p. 25.95 (*0-7862-4641-3*, Five Star) Gale Group.
—The Lady Godiva Murder. 2002. (Five Star First Edition Mystery Ser.). 327p. 25.95 (*0-7862-4827-0*, Five Star) Gale Group.
Moreland, Peggy. Rugrats & Rawhide. 1997. 243p. per. (*0-373-24084-8*, 1-24084-5, Silhouette) Harlequin Enterprises, Ltd.
—The Texan's Tiny Secret. 2001. (Silhouette Desire Ser.: No. 1394). mass mkt. (*0-373-76394-8*, Silhouette) Harlequin Enterprises, Ltd.
Morgan, Neal. Karankawa County: Short Stories from a Corner of Texas. 152p. 2002. pap. 16.95 (*1-58544-204-6*); 1990. 19.95 (*0-89096-423-8*) Texas A&M Univ. Pr.
—Karankawa County: Short Stories from a Corner of Texas. 1990. E-Book 19.95 (*0-585-17453-9*) netLibrary, Inc.
Morris, David. Last Flight of the Liberators: The Seventh Flag Over Texas. 2000. 228p. E-Book 8.00 (*0-7388-8711-0*) Xlibris Corp.
Morris, Gilbert. Deep in the Heart. 2003. 400p. 13.99 (*1-59145-112-4*) Integrity Pubs.
Morsi, Pamela. No Ordinary Princess. l.t. ed. 1998. (Large Print Book Ser.). 26.95 (*1-56895-519-7*, Wheeler Publishing, Inc.) Gale Group.
—No Ordinary Princess. 1997. 384p. mass mkt. 5.99 (*0-380-78643-5*, Avon Bks.) Morrow/Avon.
—Sealed with a Kiss. 1998. 400p. mass mkt. 5.99 (*0-380-79638-4*, Avon Bks.) Morrow/Avon.
Morsi, Pamela, et al. Matters of the Heart: With Marriage in Mind; You're My Baby; I'm Going to Be a... What?! 2001. 384p. mass mkt. (*0-373-48427-5*, Harlequin Bks.) Harlequin Enterprises, Ltd.
Munroe, Kirk. With Crockett & Bowie. 2000. 252p. pap. 9.95 (*0-594-01299-6*); E-Book 3.95 (*0-594-02687-3*) 1873 Pr.
Munson, Sammye. Hej Texas, Goodbye Sweden. 1994. 128p. (J). (gr. 5-6). 13.95 (*0-89015-948-3*) Eakin Pr.
Myers, Helen R. Lost. 2000. 408p. mass mkt. (*1-55166-572-7*, Mira Bks.) Harlequin Enterprises, Ltd.
—More Than You Know. 1999. (Mira Bks.). 400p. mass mkt. (*1-55166-504-2*, Mira Bks.) Harlequin Enterprises, Ltd.
—No Sanctuary. 2003. 384p. mass mkt. (*1-55166-659-6*, Mira Bks.) Harlequin Enterprises, Ltd.
Nagle, P. G. Galveston. 2003. (Civil War in the Far West Ser.). (Illus.). 384p. mass mkt. 6.99 o.s.i (*0-8125-6573-8*, Forge Bks.) Doherty, Tom Assocs., LLC.
—Red River. E-Book (*0-312-71090-9*, Tor Bks.); 2003. 384p. 25.95 (*0-7653-0344-2*, Forge Bks.) Doherty, Tom Assocs., LLC.
Neggers, Carla. Stonebrook Cottage. l.t. ed. 2003. (Wheeler Romance Ser.). 381p. 29.95 (*1-58724-365-2*, Wheeler Publishing, Inc.) Gale Group.
—Stonebrook Cottage. 2002. 384p. mass mkt. (*1-55166-923-4*, Mira Bks.) Harlequin Enterprises, Ltd.
Nelson, Barney, ed. God's Country or Devil's Playground: The Best Nature Writing from the Big Bend of Texas. 2002. (Corrie Herring Hooks Ser.: No. 54). (Illus.). 400p. 60.00 (*0-292-75577-5*); pap. 22.95 (*0-292-75580-5*) Univ. of Texas Pr.
Newcomb, Kerry. The Red Ripper. 1999. 288p. 23.95 o.p. (*0-312-20575-9*) St. Martin's Pr.
—Red Ripper. E-Book 23.95 (*0-312-26465-8*) Picador.
—Texas Anthem. 2000. 288p. mass mkt. 5.99 (*0-312-97682-8*, St. Martin's Paperbacks) St. Martin's Pr.
Nighbert, David F. Squeezeplay: A Mystery. 1992. 272p. 18.95 o.p. (*0-312-07847-1*, Saint Martin's Minotaur) St. Martin's Pr.
Nofziger, Lyn. Tackett & the Teacher. 1998. (Ground Source Chronicles Ser.). pap. 19.95 (*0-915463-81-4*) Jameson Bks., Inc.
—Tackett & the Teacher. 1994. 192p. 16.95 (*0-89526-488-9*) Regnery Publishing, Inc., An Eagle Publishing Co.
Nye, Nelson C. The Texas Gun. l.t. ed. 2001. 228p. pap. 23.95 (*0-7838-9586-0*, Macmillan Reference USA) Gale Group.
—The Texas Gun - Gringo. 1995. 320p. pap. 4.99 (*0-8439-3822-6*) Dorchester Publishing Co., Inc.
O'Banyon, Constance. The Agreement. 2001. (Secret Fires Ser.). 400p. mass mkt. 5.99 (*0-8439-4878-7*) Dorchester Publishing Co., Inc.
—Ride the Wind. 2000. 400p. mass mkt. 5.99 (*0-8439-4777-2*, Leisure Bks.) Dorchester Publishing Co., Inc.
O'Donnell, Jodi. The Come-Back Cowboy. 2002. (Silhouette Special Edition Ser.). 256p. mass mkt. (*0-373-24494-0*, Silhouette) Harlequin Enterprises, Ltd.
—His Best Friend's Bride. 2002. 192p. mass mkt. 3.99 o.s.i (*0-373-19625-3*, Silhouette) Harlequin Enterprises, Ltd. CAN. *Dist:* Simon & Schuster.
—The Rancher's Promise. 2002. (Silhouette Romance Ser.). 192p. mass mkt. (*0-373-19619-9*, Silhouette) Harlequin Enterprises, Ltd.
O'Donnell, Mary King. Quincie Bolliver. 2001. (Double Mountain Bks.). xvi, 425p. pap. text 19.95 (*0-89672-449-2*, Double Mountain Bks.) Texas Tech Univ. Pr.
Olsen, Theodore V. McGivern. 1987. mass mkt. 2.50 o.s.i (*0-449-13077-0*); 1982. 160p. mass mkt. 2.25 o.s.i (*0-449-14465-8*, Fawcett) Ballantine Bks.
—McGivern. l.t. ed. 2001. (G. K. Hall Western Ser.). 216p. 24.95 (*0-7838-9412-0*, Macmillan Reference USA) Gale Group.
—McGivern. 1994. E-Book 9.95 (*0-585-28968-9*) netLibrary, Inc.
—McGivern - The Hard Men, 2 bks. in 1. 1994. 320p. pap. 4.99 (*0-8439-3612-6*) Dorchester Publishing Co., Inc.
—Starbuck's Brand. 1997. 192p. reprint ed. mass mkt. 3.99 (*0-8439-4326-2*, Leisure Bks.) Dorchester Publishing Co., Inc.
—Starbuck's Brand. 1973. (Western Ser.). 185p. (J). o.p. (*0-385-07012-8*) Doubleday Publishing.
—Starbuck's Brand. l.t. ed. 1992. (Nightingale Ser.). 311p. pap. 14.95 o.p. (*0-8161-5594-1*, Macmillan Reference USA) Gale Group.
Orcutt, Jane. The Living Stone. 2000. 352p. pap. 10.95 (*1-57856-292-9*) WaterBrook Pr.
Owens, Virginia Stem. At Point Blank: A Suspense Novel. 1992. 240p. 14.99 o.p. (*0-8010-6724-3*); (gr. 10). pap. 9.99 o.p. (*0-8010-6752-9*) Baker Bks.
Owens, William A. Look to the River. Trautman, R., ed. 1970. (Reading Shelf Ser.: No. 1). o.p. (*0-07-065133-7*) McGraw-Hill Cos., The.
—Look to the River. 1988. (Texas Tradition Ser.: No. 8). 134p. reprint ed. pap. 11.95 (*0-87565-026-0*) Texas Christian Univ. Pr.
—Walking on Borrowed Land. 1988. (Texas Tradition Ser.: No. 9). 320p. reprint ed. pap. 11.95 (*0-87565-028-7*) Texas Christian Univ. Pr.
Page, Patricia. Hope's Cadillac: A Novel. 1996. 264p. 25.00 o.p. (*0-393-03974-9*) Norton, W. W. & Co., Inc.
Paige, Laurie. The Baby Pursuit. 1999. (Fortunes of Texas Ser.: No. 2). 256p. per. (*0-373-65031-0*, Silhouette) Harlequin Enterprises, Ltd.
—Heartbreaker. 2002. (Silhouette Special Releases Ser.). 256p. mass mkt. (*0-373-61355-5*, Silhouette) Harlequin Enterprises, Ltd.
Palfrey, Evelyn. The Price of Passion. 1997. 350p. pap. 14.95 o.p. (*0-9654190-1-0*) Moon Child Bks.
—The Price of Passion. 2002. 384p. E-Book 9.99 (*0-7434-2716-5*, Atria); 2000. (Illus.). 384p. pap. 12.95 (*0-671-04220-3*, Atria); 1999. mass mkt. (*0-671-04221-1*, Pocket) Simon & Schuster.
Palmer, Diana. The Cowboy & the Lady. 2001. 256p. mass mkt. (*1-55166-804-1*, 1-66804-5, Mira Bks.) Harlequin Enterprises, Ltd.
—Desperado. 2002. 29.95 (*1-58724-345-8*, Wheeler Publishing, Inc.) Gale Group.
—Desperado. 2003. 384p. mass mkt. (*1-55166-692-8*, Mira Bks.) Harlequin Enterprises, Ltd.
—Diamond Spur. l.t. ed. 2003. 30.95 (*1-58724-408-X*, Wheeler Publishing, Inc.) Gale Group.
—Diamond Spur. 2002. 416p. mass mkt. (*1-55166-950-1*, Mira Bks.) Harlequin Enterprises, Ltd.
—Lawless. 2003. 304p. (*1-55166-708-8*, Mira Bks.) Harlequin Enterprises, Ltd.
—A Long Tall Texan Summer. 1997. (Illus.). 367p. per. (*0-373-48342-2*, 1-48342-9, Harlequin Bks.) Harlequin Enterprises, Ltd.
—A Long Tall Texan Summer: Tom Walker/Drew Morris/Jobe Dodd, 3 bks. in 1. 2002. 378p. mass mkt. (*0-373-21838-9*, Harlequin Bks.) Harlequin Enterprises, Ltd.
—Long Tall Texans. 1994. per. (*0-373-48320-1*, 1-48320-5, Silhouette) Harlequin Enterprises, Ltd.
—Long Tall Texans: Calhoun; Justin; Tyler, 3 bks. in 1. 2001. (Silhouette Special Releases Ser.). 462p. pap. (*0-373-48446-1*, 1-48446-8, Silhouette) Harlequin Enterprises, Ltd.
—Long, Tall Texans: Emmett; Regan; Burke, 3 bks. in 1. rev. ed. 1999. mass mkt. (*0-373-20158-3*, 1-20158-1, Harlequin Bks.) Harlequin Enterprises, Ltd.
—Long, Tall Texans: Harden, Evan, Donavan. 1999. mass mkt. (*0-373-48393-7*, 1-48393-2); 1997. per. (*0-373-20137-0*, 1-20137-5) Harlequin Enterprises, Ltd. (Harlequin Bks.).
—Most Wanted. 2000. 434p. pap. (*1-55166-612-X*, Mira Bks.) Harlequin Enterprises, Ltd.
—Rage of Passion. unabr. ed. 1999. audio 7.99 (*1-55204-186-7*, MIR-1186) Durkin Hayes Publishing Ltd.
—Rage of Passion. 1999. 251p. mass mkt. (*1-55166-556-5*, 1-66556-1, Mira Bks.); 1986. per. (*0-373-05325-8*, Harlequin Bks.) Harlequin Enterprises, Ltd.
—The Winter Soldier. 2001. (Silhouette Desire Ser.: No. 1351). mass mkt. (*0-373-76351-4*, Silhouette) Harlequin Enterprises, Ltd.
Paredes, Americo. George Washington Gomez. 1990. 302p. pap. 12.95 (*1-55885-012-0*) Arte Publico Pr.

Parker, F. M. Blood & Dust. l.t. ed. 2001. 19.95 o.p. (*1-58724-089-0*, Wheeler Publishing, Inc.) Gale Group.
—Blood & Dust. 2000. 384p. mass mkt. 5.99 o.s.i (*0-7860-1152-1*, Pinnacle Bks.) Kensington Publishing Corp.
—The Far Battleground. 1988. mass mkt. 3.50 o.p. (*0-451-15675-7*, Signet Bks.); 15.95 o.p. (*0-453-00585-3*) NAL.
Parks, Suzan-Lori. Getting Mother's Body: A Novel. 2004. 288p. pap. 12.95 (*0-8129-6800-X*, Random Hse. Trade Paperbacks) Random House Adult Trade Publishing Group.
—Getting Mother's Body: A Novel. 2003. 272p. 23.95 (*1-4000-6022-2*) Random Hse., Inc.
Pavie, Theodore. Tales of the Sabine Borderlands: Early Louisiana & Texas Fiction. Klier, Betje B., ed. & tr. by. Marsh, Anne C. et al, trs. 1998. (Centennial Series of the Association of Former Students: No. 79). (Illus.). 144p. 29.95 (*0-89096-837-3*); pap. 15.95 (*0-89096-854-3*) Texas A&M Univ. Pr.
Pella, Judith. Frontier Lady. 1993. (Lone Star Legacy Ser.: Bk. 1). 400p. (Orig.). (gr. 7-12). pap. 10.99 o.p. (*1-55661-293-1*) Bethany Hse. Pubs.
—Stoner's Crossing. 1994. (Lone Star Legacy Ser.: Bk. 2). 384p. pap. 10.99 o.p. (*1-55661-294-X*) Bethany Hse. Pubs.
—Texas Angel. 1999. 352p. pap. 12.99 (*0-7642-2278-3*) Bethany Hse. Pubs.
Perry, George S. Walls Rise Up: A Novel. 1994. (Texas Tradition Ser.: No. 21). 154p. 19.95 (*0-87565-126-7*) Texas Christian Univ. Pr.
Peterson, Tracie. Controlling Interests. 1998. 256p. (YA). (gr. 10 up). pap. 8.99 o.p. (*0-7642-2064-0*) Bethany Hse. Pubs.
—Controlling Interests. l.t. ed. 1999. (Christian Mystery Ser.). 456p. 24.95 o.p. (*0-7862-1999-8*) Thorndike Pr.
Petrick, Neila Skinner. Jane Long of Texas. 2nd ed. (Illus.). 299p. 23.95 (*0-9642905-0-2*) Prime Time Pr.
—Jane Long of Texas, 1798-1880. 2000. 312p. pap. 19.95 (*1-56554-758-6*) Pelican Publishing Co., Inc.
Philips, Ingram. Beyond Sundown. 2000. 280p. pap. 16.00 o.p. (*0-7388-1159-9*); text 25.00 o.p. (*0-7388-1158-0*) Xlibris Corp.
Phillips, Susan Elizabeth. Heaven, Texas: Where Even a Angel Can Raise a Little Hell... l.t. ed. 1998. pap. 26.95 (*1-56895-699-1*, Wheeler Publishing, Inc.) Gale Group.
—Lady Be Good. l.t. ed. 1999. (Large Print Book Ser.). 27.95 (*1-56895-733-5*, Wheeler Publishing, Inc.) Gale Group.
—Lady Be Good. 2002. E-Book 6.99 (*0-06-621215-4*); E-Book 6.99 (*0-06-621213-8*); E-Book 6.99 (*0-06-009835-X*); E-Book 6.99 (*0-06-621210-3*) HarperCollins General Bks. Group. (PerfectBound).
—Lady Be Good. 1999. (Avon Romance Ser.). 384p. mass mkt. 6.99 (*0-380-79448-9*, Avon Bks.) Morrow/Avon.
Pierre, D. B. C. Vernon God Little. 2003. 23.00 (*1-84195-460-8*) Canongate Bks. GBR. *Dist:* Publishers Group West.
—Vernon God Little. 2003. 279p. pap. (*0-571-21642-0*) Faber & Faber, Inc.
Pilkington, Tom, ed. & intro. Careless Weeds: Six Texas Novellas. 1993. (Southwest Life & Letters Ser.). 352p. text 35.00 (*0-87074-338-4*); pap. 14.95 (*0-87074-339-2*) Southern Methodist Univ. Pr.
Pipkin, Turk. Fast Greens. 1994. 192p. pap. 8.95 o.p. (*1-881484-06-8*) Softshoe Publishing.
Porter, Cheryl A. Captive Angel. 1999. 320p. mass mkt. 5.99 (*0-312-96906-6*, St. Martin's Paperbacks) St. Martin's Pr.
Poston, Jeffrey A. The Peacekeeper. unabr. ed. 1998. audio 26.95 (*1-55686-819-7*) Books in Motion.
—The Peacekeeper. 1997. 192p. 20.95 o.p. (*0-8027-4160-6*) Walker & Co.
Potter, Patricia. Diablo. 1996. 368p. mass mkt. 5.99 o.s.i (*0-553-56602-4*) Bantam Bks.
—Diablo. l.t. ed. 1997. (Romance Ser.). 618p. lib. bdg. 26.95 (*0-7862-0924-0*) Thorndike Pr.
Powell, Mary C. Auslander: A Novel. 2000. 295p. 24.50 (*0-87565-215-8*) Texas Christian Univ. Pr.
Preston, Fayrene. The Barons of Texas: Kit. 2001. (Silhouette Desire Ser.: No. 1342). 187p. mass mkt. (*0-373-76342-5*, 1-76342-4, Silhouette) Harlequin Enterprises, Ltd.
Priddy, Laurance L. Son of Durango: A Novel. 1996. 176p. 22.95 (*0-86534-242-3*) Sunstone Pr.
—Winning Passion: A Novel. 1994. 288p. pap. 14.95 (*0-86534-200-8*) Sunstone Pr.
Pronzini, Bill & Greenberg, Martin H., eds. The Texans: The Best of the West. 1988. mass mkt. 3.50 o.s.i (*0-449-13470-9*, Fawcett) Ballantine Bks.
Proulx, E. Annie. That Old Ace in the Hole: A Novel. 2003. 352p. pap. 12.00 (*0-7432-4147-9*); 2003. mass mkt. 7.99 (*0-7432-4148-7*); 2002. 384p. 26.00 (*0-684-81307-6*); 2002. 560p. 26.00 (*0-7432-4092-8*) Simon & Schuster. (Scribner).
Quinn, Tara Taylor. Cassidy's Kids. 2000. (Harlequin American Romance Ser.: No. 2). 256p. mass mkt. (*0-373-65063-9*, 1-65063-9, Harlequin Bks.) Harlequin Enterprises, Ltd.
—The Rancher's Bride. 2002. (Harlequin Special Releases Ser.: No. 11). mass mkt. (*0-373-65088-4*, 1-65088-6, Harlequin Bks.) Harlequin Enterprises, Ltd.
Rae Rao, Linda. The Eagle Stirs Her Nest. 1997. (Eagle Wings Ser.). 256p. (gr. 10). pap. 10.99 o.p. (*0-8007-5607-X*) Revell, Fleming H. Co.
Randle, Kevin & Cornett, Robert. Remember the Alamo! 1986. 240p. 3.50 o.s.i (*0-441-71325-4*, Diamond Bks.) Berkley Publishing Group.
Randle, Kevin D. & Cornett, Robert. Remember the Alamo! l.t. ed. 1997. 21.95 (*0-7838-8351-X*, Macmillan Reference USA) Gale Group.
Rawlins, Debbi. Hands On: Trueblood Texas. 2002. (Harlequin Blaze Ser.). mass mkt. (*0-373-79064-3*, Harlequin Bks.) Harlequin Enterprises, Ltd.
Ray, Francis. I Know Who Holds Tomorrow. 2nd ed. 2002. 352p. pap. 13.95 (*0-312-30050-6*, CPB1181, Saint Martin's Griffin) St. Martin's Pr.
—Only Hers. 1996. (Arabesque Ser.). mass mkt. 5.99 (*1-58314-181-2*) Kensington Publishing Corp.
Reasoner, James. Hell's Half Acre. 1999. (Walker, Texas Ranger Ser.: Vol. 2). 224p. mass mkt. 5.99 o.s.i (*0-425-16972-3*) Berkley Publishing Group.
—Walker, Texas Ranger: The Novel. 1999. (Walker, Texas Ranger Ser.). 256p. (Orig.). mass mkt. 5.99 o.s.i (*0-425-16815-8*) Berkley Publishing Group.
Rechy, John. The Life & Adventures of Lyle Clemens. 2003. (Illus.). 352p. 24.00 (*0-8021-1746-5*, Grove Pr.) Grove/Atlantic, Inc.
Redd, Louise. Playing the Bones. 1997. 256p. pap. 11.95 o.s.i (*0-452-27824-4*, Plume) Dutton/Plume.
—Playing the Bones: A Novel. 1996. 256p. 21.95 o.p. (*0-316-73511-6*) Little Brown & Co.
Reeves, Joan. Summer's Fortune. 2002. (Five Star Romance Ser.). 239p. 25.95 (*0-7862-4450-X*, Five Star) Gale Group.
Rehder, Ben. Bone Dry: A Blanco County Texas Novel. 2003. 320p. 23.95 (*0-312-29132-9*, Saint Martin's Minotaur) St. Martin's Pr.
—Buck Fever. E-Book 17.95 (*0-312-70797-5*); 2003. 288p. mass mkt. 6.99 (*0-312-99220-3*, St. Martin's Paperbacks) St. Martin's Pr.
Reinbolt, William, III. Moses Rose. Danbury, Richard S., ed. 1996. 220p. (Orig.). pap. text 10.95 (*0-89754-125-1*, 12077354-0998) Dan River Pr.
Reynolds, Clay. Ars Poetica: A Postmodern Parable. 2003. 296p. (Orig.). pap. 16.95 (*1-881515-48-6*) Texas Review Pr.
—Monuments. 2000. 382p. 29.95 (*0-89672-433-6*) Texas Tech Univ. Pr.
—The Players. 1997. 432p. 24.00 o.p. (*0-7867-0407-1*, Carroll & Graf Pubs.) Avalon Publishing Group.
—Players. 1998. 448p. mass mkt. 5.99 o.s.i (*0-7860-0598-X*, Pinnacle Bks.) Kensington Publishing Corp.
—The Tentmaker. 2002. 400p. pap. 14.00 (*0-425-18270-3*) Berkley Publishing Group.
—Threading the Needle. 2003. (Sandhill Chronicle Ser.). 288p. 27.95 (*0-89672-498-0*) Texas Tech Univ. Pr.
—The Vigil. 1988. (Southwest Life & Letters Ser.). 232p. reprint ed. pap. 8.95 o.p. (*0-87074-269-8*) Southern Methodist Univ. Pr.
—The Vigil. 2001. (Illus.). 240p. pap. 17.95 (*0-89672-457-3*) Texas Tech Univ. Pr.
Reynolds, R. C. The Vigil. 1985. 224p. 13.95 o.p. (*0-312-84639-8*) St. Martin's Pr.
Rice, James. Cowboy Night Before Christmas. 2nd ed. 1986. (Night Before Christmas Ser.). Orig. Title: Praire Night Before Christmas. (Illus.). 32p. (J). (ps-3). reprint ed. 14.95 (*0-88289-811-6*) Pelican Publishing Co., Inc.
Rice, James, tr. & illus. Trail Boss: J. M. Daugherty. 2003. (J). (*1-57168-769-6*, Eakin Pr.) Eakin Pr.
Richardson, Doug. Dark Horse. abr. ed. 1997. audio 16.95 o.p. (*1-56100-907-5*, 1169, Nova Audio Bks.); audio 89.25 o.p. (*1-56100-323-9*, 854, Unabridged Library Editions); audio 25.95 o.p. (*1-56100-698-X*, 82, Bookcassette) Brilliance Audio.
Richardson, Douglas. Dark Horse. 1997. 384p. 24.00 o.p. (*0-380-97314-6*, Avon Bks.) Morrow/Avon.
Rimmer, Christine. Stroke of Fortune. 2002. (Silhouette Special Releases Ser.: No. 1). 256p. mass mkt. (*0-373-61352-0*, 1-61352-0, Silhouette) Harlequin Enterprises, Ltd.
Riordan, Rick. The Last King of Texas. 2001. 400p. mass mkt. 6.99 (*0-553-57991-6*) Bantam Bks.
—The Widower's Two-Step. 1998. 416p. mass mkt. 6.50 (*0-553-57645-3*) Bantam Bks.
Rios, Reyna. Destination: Love. 2000. (Encanto Ser.). 28p. mass mkt. 3.99 o.s.i (*0-7860-1155-6*); mass mkt. 3.99 o.s.i (*0-7860-1159-9*) Kensington Publishing Corp. (Pinnacle Bks.).
Ripley, J. R. Lost in Austin: Tony Kozol Mystery. 2001. (Tony Kozol Mystery Ser.: Vol. 3). 246p. 19.95 (*1-892695-06-5*) Long Wind Publishing.
Ritchie, James A. The Last Free Range. l.t. ed. 1996. 295p. 20.95 o.p. (*0-7838-1843-2*, Macmillan Reference USA) Gale Group.
—The Last Free Range. 1995. 224p. 19.95 (*0-8027-4150-9*) Walker & Co.
Robenalt, Jeff. Ranger: The Saga of a Texas Ranger. 2000. 428p. E-Book 8.00 (*0-7388-7775-1*) Xlibris Corp.
Roberts, Kelsey. The Best Man in Texas. 2002. (Harlequin Special Releases Ser.: No. 6). 251p. mass mkt. (*0-373-65083-3*, 1-65083-7, Harlequin Bks.) Harlequin Enterprises, Ltd.
Roderus, Frank. Duster. 1987. (Chaparral Bks.). (Illus.). 266p. (J). (gr. 6 up). reprint ed. pap. 10.95 (*0-87565-095-3*) Texas Christian Univ. Pr.
Rodgers, Joni. Sugar Land. 1999. 352p. pap. 12.00 (*1-883523-32-X*) Spinsters Ink Bks.
Rogers, Chris. Bitch Factor. 1998. 336p. mass mkt. 5.99 (*0-553-58001-9*) Bantam Bks.
—The Chill Factor. 2001. 416p. reprint ed. mass mkt. 6.50 o.s.i (*0-553-58073-6*) Bantam Bks.
—The Rage Factor. 2000. 400p. mass mkt. 5.99 (*0-553-58070-1*) Bantam Bks.
Rogers, Evelyn. Flame. 1994. 448p. mass mkt. 4.50 o.s.i (*0-8217-4491-7*, Zebra Bks.) Kensington Publishing Corp.
Rogers, Kenny & Davenport, Donald. Christmas in Canaan. 2002. 336p. (J). (gr. 6-9). 15.99 (*0-06-000746-X*) HarperCollins Children's Bk. Group.
Rolofson, Kristine. Blame It on Texas. 2001. 304p. mass mkt. (*0-373-83462-4*, Harlequin Bks.) Harlequin Enterprises, Ltd.
—The Texan Takes a Wife. 1999. 256p. per. (*0-373-83420-9*, 1-83420-9); 1996. per. (*0-373-25704-X*, 1-25704-7) Harlequin Enterprises, Ltd. (Harlequin Bks.).
Rosenberg, Nancy Taylor. Trial by Fire. unabr. ed. 1996. audio 64.00 (*0-7366-3433-9*, 4077) Books on Tape, Inc.
—Trial by Fire. 1996. 352p. 22.95 o.p. (*0-525-93767-6*) Dutton/Plume.
—Trial by Fire. l.t. ed. 1996. (Large Print Bks.). 27.95 (*1-56895-305-4*, Wheeler Publishing, Inc.) Gale Group.
—Trial by Fire. 1996. 448p. mass mkt. 7.99 (*0-451-18005-4*, Signet Bks.) NAL.
—Trial by Fire, unabr. ed. audio 78.00 (*0-7887-0521-0*, 94716E7) Recorded Bks., LLC.
—Trial by Fire. abr. ed. 1996. audio 16.95 o.s.i (*0-14-086200-5*, Penguin AudioBooks) Viking Penguin.
Ross, Carol. Wild Woman. 2001. (Five Star Romance Ser.). 212p. 26.95 (*0-7862-3474-1*, Five Star) Gale Group.
Ross, Dana Fuller, pseud. Texas! 1984. mass mkt. 3.99 o.s.i (*0-553-80005-1*); 368p. mass mkt. 4.99 o.s.i (*0-553-26070-7*) Bantam Bks.
—Texas! 1982. (Reader's Request Ser.). lib. bdg. 16.95 o.p. (*0-8161-3318-2*, Macmillan Reference USA) Gale Group.
Ross, David W. Eye of the Hawk. 1994. 512p. mass mkt. 5.99 (*0-380-72232-1*, Avon Bks.) Morrow/Avon.
—Eye of the Hawk. 1992. 512p. 22.00 o.p. (*0-671-75513-7*, Simon & Schuster) Simon & Schuster.
Roszel, Renee. Bridegroom on Her Doorstep. 2002. (Harlequin Romance Ser.). 192p. mass mkt. (*0-373-03725-2*, Harlequin Bks.) Harlequin Enterprises, Ltd.
—Bridegroom on Her Doorstep. l.t. ed. 2003. (Harlequin II Romance Ser.). 25.95 (*0-263-17898-6*) Harlequin Mills & Boon, Ltd. GBR. *Dist:* Thorndike Pr.
Ruby, Lois. Swindletop. 2000. E-Book 15.95 (*0-585-27649-8*) netLibrary, Inc.
Ruffin, Paul. Islands, Women & God. 2001. 254p. (*0-9651359-8-5*, 005); 247p. pap. (*0-9651359-9-3*) Browder Springs Bks.
Rumbley, Rose-Mary. What? No Chili? rev. ed. 2000. (Illus.). 144p. (J). (gr. 6-8). pap. 16.95 (*0-89015-992-0*) Eakin Pr.
Rushing, Jane G. Against the Moon. 1979. pap. 1.95 o.p. (*0-380-42812-1*, 42812, Avon Bks.) Morrow/Avon.
—Against the Moon. 1991. (Texas Tradition Ser.: No. 17). 222p. reprint ed. pap. 14.95 (*0-87565-094-5*) Texas Christian Univ. Pr.
—Walnut Grove. 1979. pap. 1.95 o.p. (*0-380-44164-0*, 44164, Avon Bks.) Morrow/Avon.
—Walnut Grove. 1992. xiv, 255p. reprint ed. pap. 12.00 (*0-89672-278-3*) Texas Tech Univ. Pr.
Rye, Edgar. The Quirt & the Spur: Vanishing Shadows of the Texas Frontier. 2000. (Double Mountain Bks.). (Illus.). x, 372p. pap. 17.95 (*0-89672-441-7*) Texas Tech Univ. Pr.
Sabin, Edwin L. With Sam Houston in Texas. E-Book 3.95 (*0-594-04589-4*) 1873 Pr.
Sanderson, Jim. La Mordida. 2002. 254p. 22.95 (*0-8263-2815-6*) Univ. of New Mexico Pr.
—Nevin's History: A Novel of Texas. 2004. (*0-89672-518-9*) Texas Tech Univ. Pr.
Sanford, Winifred M. & Miles, Emerett S. Windfall & Other Stories. 1988. (Southwest Life & Letters Ser.). 204p. reprint ed. pap. 10.95 (*0-87074-268-X*) Southern Methodist Univ. Pr.
Sanford, Winifred W. Windfall & Other Stories. 1988. (Southwest Life & Letters Ser.). 204p. reprint ed. 17.95 (*0-87074-267-1*) Southern Methodist Univ. Pr.
Saylor, Steven. Have You Seen Dawn? 2003. 256p. 24.00 (*0-7432-1366-1*, Simon & Schuster) Simon & Schuster.
—Have You Seen Dawn? l.t. ed. 2003. 28.95 (*0-7862-5467-X*) Thorndike Pr.
—A Twist at the End: A Novel of O. Henry. 2000. 464p. 25.00 o.s.i (*0-684-85681-6*, Simon & Schuster) Simon & Schuster.
Scarborough, Dorothy. Can't Get a Red Bird. (Labor Movement in Fiction & Non-Fiction Ser.). reprint ed. 45.00 (*0-404-58468-3*) AMS Pr., Inc.
Schumacher, Aileen. Affirmative Reaction. 2000. (Tory Travers/David Alvarez Mysteries Ser.: Bk. 355). 256p. mass mkt. (*0-373-26355-4*, 1-26355-7, Worldwide Library) Harlequin Enterprises, Ltd.
—Affirmative Reaction. 1999. (Travers/Alvarez Mystery Ser.: No. 4). 310p. 24.95 o.p. (*1-885173-69-5*) Write Way Publishing.
—Engineered for Murder. 1996. 293p. 21.95 o.p. (*1-885173-17-2*); mass mkt. 5.95 o.p. (*1-885173-43-1*) Write Way Publishing.
—Framework for Death. 1998. (Tory Travers/David Alvarez Mysteries Ser.). 360p. 23.95 o.p. (*1-885173-55-5*) Write Way Publishing.
Scofield, Sandra J. Opal on Dry Ground. 1995. mass mkt. 5.99 o.s.i (*0-8041-1360-2*, Ivy Bks.) Ballantine Bks.
—Walking Dunes. 1993. (Contemporary Fiction Ser.). 256p. pap. 10.00 o.p. (*0-452-27027-8*, Plume) Dutton/Plume.
—Walking Dunes. 1992. 247p. 22.00 o.p. (*1-877946-12-5*); 2000. 248p. reprint ed. pap. 18.00 (*1-57962-027-2*) Permanent Pr., The.
Scott, Bradford. Dead Man's Trail: A Walt Slade Texas Ranger Western. l.t. ed. 2000. (G. K. Hall Nightingale Ser.). 151p. pap. 20.95 (*0-7838-8848-1*, Macmillan Reference USA) Gale Group.
—The Pecos Trail. l.t. ed. 2000. 153p. 20.95 (*1-57490-310-1*, Sagebrush Large Print Westerns) Beeler, Thomas T. Publisher.
Scott, D. Travers. Execution, Texas, 1987. (Stonewall Inn Editions Ser.). 1999. 224p. pap. 11.95 (*0-312-19878-7*, Saint Martin's Griffin); 1997. 208p. 20.95 o.p. (*0-312-16830-6*) St. Martin's Pr.
Sealsfield, Charles & Postel, Karl. The Cabin Book: Das Kajutenbuch. Lich, Glen, ed. 1985. (GER., Illus.). 300p. 14.95 o.p. (*0-89015-525-9*) Eakin Pr.
Searcy, David. Last Things. 2003. 336p. pap. 14.00 (*0-452-28463-5*, Plume) Dutton/Plume.
Searle, Don L. Light in the Harbor. 1991. viii, 245p. (Orig.). (J). pap. 8.95 o.p. (*0-87579-528-5*) Deseret Bk. Co.
Sharpe, Jon. Texas Hell Country. 1989. (Trailsman Ser.: No. 86). 176p. mass mkt. 2.95 o.p. (*0-451-15812-1*, Signet Bks.) NAL.
—Texas Hellion. 1999. (Trailsman Ser.: Vol. 214). 176p. mass mkt. 4.99 o.s.i (*0-451-19758-5*) NAL.
—Texas Tinhorns. 2000. (Trailsman Ser.: Vol. 224). 176p. mass mkt. 4.99 o.s.i (*0-451-20041-1*, Signet Bks.) NAL.
—The Texas Train. 1989. (Trailsman Ser.: No. 93). mass mkt. 3.50 o.p. (*0-451-16154-8*, Signet Bks.) NAL.
—Texas Triggers. 1993. (Trailsman Ser.: No. 136). 176p. (Orig.). mass mkt. 3.50 o.s.i (*0-451-17565-4*, Signet Bks.) NAL.
—The Trailsman No. 158: Texas Terror. 1995. (Trailsman Ser.). 176p. (Orig.). mass mkt. 3.99 o.s.i (*0-451-18215-4*, Signet Bks.) NAL.
Shaw, Allie. The Impossible Bride. 2002. 352p. mass mkt. 6.99 (*0-8041-1965-1*, Ivy Bks.) Ballantine Bks.
—The Impossible Texan. 2001. 304p. mass mkt. 6.99 (*0-8041-1964-3*, Ivy Bks.) Ballantine Bks.
Shayne, Maggie. Million Dollar Marriage. 1999. (Fortunes of Texas Ser.: No. 1). (Illus.). 244p. per. (*0-373-65030-2*, 1-65030-8, Harlequin Bks.) Harlequin Enterprises, Ltd.
—That Mysterious Texas Brand Man: World's Most Eligible Bachelors. 1998. (World's Most Eligible Ser.: No. 4). per. (*0-373-65021-3*, 1-65021-7, Harlequin Bks.) Harlequin Enterprises, Ltd.
Shelron, Gene. Last Gun. 1991. 192p. 14.95 o.s.i (*0-385-41410-2*) Doubleday Publishing.
Shelton, Gene. Tascosa Gun. 1999. 288p. mass mkt. 5.99 o.s.i (*0-425-17257-0*) Berkley Publishing Group.
—Texas Legends: Captain Jack, Vol. 2. 1993. 208p. mass mkt. 4.50 o.s.i (*0-515-11192-9*, Jove) Berkley Publishing Group.
—Texas Legends: Last Gun, Vol. 1. 1993. 224p. mass mkt. 4.50 o.s.i (*0-515-11100-7*, Jove) Berkley Publishing Group.

Sheriff, Jack. Brazos Guns. l.t. ed. 1998. (Dales Large Print Ser.). 257p. pap. 19.99 (*1-85389-848-1*) Dales Large Print Bks. GBR. *Dist:* Ulverscroft Large Print Bks., Ltd., Ulverscroft Large Print Canada, Ltd.

Sherman, Jory. The Baron Brand. 2001. 374p. mass mkt. 6.99 o.s.i (*0-8125-3924-9*); 2000. 317p. 24.95 (*0-312-86356-X*); 2000. 24.95 (*0-312-86736-0*) Doherty, Tom Assocs., LLC. (Forge Bks.).

—The Baron War. 2003. mass mkt. (*0-7653-4349-5*); 2002. 320p. 25.95 (*0-7653-0255-1*) Doherty, Tom Assocs., LLC. (Forge Bks.).

—The Barons of Texas. 1999. 384p. pap. 5.99 (*0-8125-2075-0*); 1997. 320p. 23.95 (*0-312-85361-0*) Doherty, Tom Assocs., LLC. (Forge Bks.).

—Grass Kingdom. 1993. 416p. 23.95 o.p. (*0-312-85360-2*, Forge Bks.) Doherty, Tom Assocs., LLC.

Shrake, Bud. Billy Boy. 2001. (Illus.). 240p. 21.00 (*0-7432-2480-9*, Simon & Schuster) Simon & Schuster.

Shrake, Edwin. The Borderland: A Novel of Texas. 2001. 432p. pap. 14.95 (*0-7868-8493-2*); 2000. 416p. 24.95 (*0-7868-6579-2*) Hyperion Pr.

—But Not for Love. 2000. (Texas Tradition Ser.: Vol. 29). x, 377p. reprint ed. pap. 16.95 (*0-87565-233-6*) Texas Christian Univ. Pr.

Simmons, Trana Mae. Southern Charms. 1999. (Magical Love Ser.). 304p. mass mkt. 5.99 o.s.i (*0-515-12516-4*, Jove) Berkley Publishing Group.

Smith, Barbara B. Celebration in Purple Sage. 1996. 272p. 21.95 o.p. (*0-312-14562-4*, Saint Martin's Minotaur) St. Martin's Pr.

—Celebration in Purple Sage: A Jolie Wyatt Mystery. 1997. per. (*0-373-26261-2*, 1-26261-7, Worldwide Library) Harlequin Enterprises, Ltd.

—Dust Devils of the Purple Sage. 1997. per. (*0-373-26234-5*, 1-26234-4, Worldwide Library) Harlequin Enterprises, Ltd.

—Dust Devils of the Purple Sage. 1995. 256p. 21.95 o.p. (*0-312-13476-2*, Saint Martin's Minotaur) St. Martin's Pr.

—Mauve & Murder. 2000. (Five Star Mystery Ser.). 271p. 21.95 (*0-7862-2690-0*, Five Star) Gale Group.

—Mistletoe from Purple Sage. 1997. 304p. 22.95 o.p. (*0-312-16930-2*, Saint Martin's Minotaur) St. Martin's Pr.

—Writers of the Purple Sage. 1996. (Mystery Ser.). per. (*0-373-26214-0*, Worldwide Library) Harlequin Enterprises, Ltd.

—Writers of the Purple Sage. 1994. 304p. 20.95 o.p. (*0-312-11352-8*, Saint Martin's Minotaur) St. Martin's Pr.

Smith, Bobbi. The Half Breed. 2001. (Secret Fires Ser.: Bk. 2). 400p. mass mkt. 5.99 (*0-8439-4853-1*, Leisure Bks.) Dorchester Publishing Co., Inc.

—The Half-Breed. l.t. ed. 2001. (Thorndike Press Large Print Romance Ser.). 373p. 28.95 o.p. (*0-7862-3584-5*) Thorndike Pr.

Smith, C. W. The Thin Men of Haddam. 1980. pap. 1.50 o.p. (*0-380-00422-4*, 24943, Avon Bks.) Morrow/Avon.

—The Thin Men of Haddam. 1990. (Texas Tradition Ser.: No. 15). 336p. reprint ed. pap. 15.95 (*0-87565-078-3*) Texas Christian Univ. Pr.

Smith, Cotton. Pray for Texas. 2000. 272p. mass mkt. 4.50 (*0-8439-4710-1*, Leisure Bks.) Dorchester Publishing Co., Inc.

—Pray for Texas. 2000. E-Book 9.95 (*0-585-28575-6*) netLibrary, Inc.

Smith, Mark. Riddle. 1992. (Illus.). vi, 78p. (Orig.). pap. 6.95 (*0-9634181-0-6*) Argo Pr.

Smith, Mary-Ann Tirone. Love Her Madly. 2002. 320p. 25.00 (*0-8050-6648-9*) Holt, Henry & Co.

—Love Her Madly. 2004. 320p. mass mkt. 6.99 (*0-7860-1657-4*, Pinnacle Bks.) Kensington Publishing Corp.

Snyder, Midori. The Flight of Michael McBride. 1994. 320p. (YA). 21.95 o.p. (*0-312-85410-2*, Tor Bks.) Doherty, Tom Assocs., LLC.

Sodowsky, Roland. Interim in the Desert. 1990. 288p. 19.95 (*0-87565-079-1*) Texas Christian Univ. Pr.

Southern, Terry. Texas Summer. 1992. 192p. 17.95 o.p. (*1-55970-150-1*) Arcade Publishing, Inc.

Southwick, Teresa. Sky Full of Promise. 2002. (Silhouette Romance Ser.). 192p. mass mkt. 3.99 o.s.i (*0-373-19624-5*, Silhouette) Harlequin Enterprises, Ltd. CAN. *Dist:* Simon & Schuster.

Speart, Jessica. Border Prey. l.t. ed. 2003. (Mystery Ser.). 27.95 (*1-57490-523-6*) Beeler, Thomas T. Publisher.

—Border Prey. Nuding, M. N., ed. 2000. (Rachel Porter Mysteries Ser.). 288p. mass mkt. 5.99 (*0-380-81040-9*, Avon Bks.) Morrow/Avon.

Spencer, LaVyrle & Freed, Jan. Harlequin 50th Anniversary Collection, 2 bks. in 1, No. 2. 1999. per. (*0-373-83410-1*, Harlequin Bks.) Harlequin Enterprises, Ltd.

Stacy, Judith. The Last Bride in Texas. 2000. (Harlequin Historicals Ser.: Vol. 541). 296p. mass mkt. (*0-373-29141-8*, 1291418, Harlequin Bks.) Harlequin Enterprises, Ltd.

Stan, Wayne, et al. Manhunt. l.t. ed. 1997. (G. K. Hall Western Ser.). 293p. 22.95 (*0-7838-8305-6*) Thorndike Pr.

Steele, Tex. Texas Rebellion. 1992. 13.95 o.p. (*0-7451-4535-3*, Gunsmoke); 18.95 o.p. (*0-7451-8382-4*); pap. 16.95 o.p. (*0-7927-1122-X*) BBC Audiobooks America.

Stem, Jacqueline. The Haunted Tunnel. 1994. 96p. (J). (gr. 5-6). 12.95 o.p. (*0-89015-959-9*) Eakin Pr.

Sterling, Cynthia. Titled Texans: Last Chance Ranch. 2000. (Titled Texans Ser.). 32p. mass mkt. 5.50 o.s.i (*0-8217-6698-8*, Zebra Bks.) Kensington Publishing Corp.

—Titled Texans: Nobility Ranch. 2000. (Titled Texans Ser.). 320p. mass mkt. 5.50 o.s.i (*0-8217-6646-5*, Zebra Bks.) Kensington Publishing Corp.

—Titled Texans: Runaway Ranch. 2001. (Titled Texans Ser.). 32p. mass mkt. 5.50 o.s.i (*0-8217-6764-X*) Kensington Publishing Corp.

Stolz, Karen. World of Pies: A Novel. 2000. (Illus.). 161p. 18.95 (*0-7868-6550-4*) Hyperion Pr.

—World of Pies: A Novel. l.t. ed. 2000. (Core Ser.). 227p. 28.95 (*0-7838-9171-7*) Thorndike Pr.

Stone, Katherine. Pearl Moon. 1996. mass mkt. 5.99 o.s.i (*0-449-22415-5*, Fawcett) Ballantine Bks.

—Pearl Moon. l.t. ed. (Large Print Bks.). 24.95 o.p. (*1-56895-165-5*, Wheeler Publishing, Inc.) Gale Group.

Storey, Gail D. God's Country Club. 1999. 238p. reprint ed. pap. 12.95 (*0-89255-242-5*) Persea Bks., Inc.

—God's Country Club: A Novel. 1996. 224p. 22.95 (*0-89255-219-0*) Persea Bks., Inc.

—The Lord's Motel. 1993. reprint ed. pap. 12.95 (*0-89255-194-1*) Persea Bks., Inc.

—The Lord's Motel: A Novel. 1992. 224p. 19.95 o.p. (*0-89255-178-X*) Persea Bks., Inc.

Stout, Janis. Home Truth. 1993. 3.49 o.p. (*0-517-10834-8*) Random Hse. Value Publishing.

—Home Truth. 1992. 256p. 19.95 o.p. (*0-939149-66-4*) Soho Pr., Inc.

Stowers, Carlton. Careless Whispers. 2001. (St. Martin's True Crime Library). (Illus.). 480p. mass mkt. 6.99 (*0-312-97704-2*, St. Martin's Paperbacks) St. Martin's Pr.

Sublett, Jesse. Rock Critic Murders. 1990. 240p. mass mkt. 3.50 o.s.i (*0-440-20703-7*) Dell Publishing.

—Rock Critic Murders. 1989. pap. 3.95 o.p. (*0-14-011208-1*) Penguin Group (USA) Inc.

—Rock Critic Murders. 1989. 240p. 16.95 o.p. (*0-670-82302-3*) Viking Penguin.

—Tough Baby. 1999. pap. 4.95 (*0-14-012397-0*); 1990. 256p. 16.95 o.p. (*0-670-83325-8*) Viking Penguin. (Viking).

Swanson, Doug J. Big Town. 1995. 288p. mass mkt. 4.50 o.p. (*0-06-109213-4*, HarperTorch) Morrow/Avon.

—Big Town: A Novel of Suspense. 1994. 224p. 18.00 o.p. (*0-06-017749-7*) HarperTrade.

—Dreamboat. 1996. 256p. mass mkt. 4.99 o.p. (*0-06-109214-2*); 1995. 288p. 20.00 o.p. (*0-06-017748-9*) HarperCollins Pubs.

—House of Corrections. 2001. (Jack Flippo Mysteries Ser.). 240p. mass mkt. 6.50 o.s.i (*0-425-17947-8*) Berkley Publishing Group.

—The House of Corrections. 2000. (Jack Flippo Mysteries Ser.). 304p. 24.95 o.s.i (*0-399-14615-6*) Penguin Group (USA) Inc.

—Umbrella Man. 1999. (Jack Flippo Mysteries Ser.: Vol. 4). 273p. 23.95 o.p. (*0-399-14503-6*, G. P. Putnam's Sons) Penguin Group (USA) Inc.

—96 Tears. 1996. 208p. 22.50 o.p. (*0-06-017511-7*) HarperCollins Pubs.

Swindle, Howard. Doin' Dirty. 2000. 292p. 22.95 (*0-312-20389-6*, Saint Martin's Minotaur) St. Martin's Pr.

—Jitter Joint. unabr. ed. 2000. audio compact disk 69.00; 1999. audio 56.00 (*0-7887-3481-4*, 95875E7) Recorded Bks., LLC.

—Jitter Joint. E-Book 5.99 (*0-312-26457-7*); 2000. 272p. mass mkt. 5.99 (*0-312-97611-9*, St. Martin's Paperbacks); 1999. 256p. 21.95 (*0-312-20066-8*, Saint Martin's Minotaur) St. Martin's Pr.

Taylor, Chuck. The Lights of the City. 1984. 125p. (Orig.). lib. bdg. 12.95 (*0-941720-15-2*) Slough Pr.

Taylor, Janelle. Follow the Wind. 1990. mass mkt. 16.95 o.s.i (*0-8217-3204-8*, Zebra Bks.) Kensington Publishing Corp.

Taylor, Robert. All We Have Is Now. Date not set. pap. (*0-312-31968-1*, St. Martin's Paperbacks); 2002. 288p. 24.95 (*0-312-28481-0*) St. Martin's Pr.

Terry, Marshall. Dallas Stories. 1987. (Southwest Life & Letters Ser.). 168p. 17.95 o.p. (*0-87074-254-X*); pap. 8.95 o.p. (*0-87074-255-8*) Southern Methodist Univ. Pr.

Thacker, Cathy Gillen. Texas Vows: A McCabe Family Saga. 2001. 304p. mass mkt. (*0-373-83463-2*, Harlequin Bks.) Harlequin Enterprises, Ltd.

Thomas, Jodi. Beneath the Texas Sky. 2001. 384p. mass mkt. 6.50 (*0-8217-7149-3*) Kensington Publishing Corp.

—The Texan's Dream. 2001. 352p. (J). mass mkt. 6.99 (*0-515-13176-8*, Jove) Berkley Publishing Group.

—To Kiss a Texan. 1999. (Texas Brothers Trilogy Ser.). 320p. mass mkt. 6.50 (*0-515-12503-2*, Jove) Berkley Publishing Group.

—To Wed in Texas. 2000. mass mkt. 6.50 (*0-515-12762-0*, Jove); 320p. mass mkt. 6.50 (*0-425-17516-2*) Berkley Publishing Group.

—When a Texan Gambles. 2003. 336p. mass mkt. 6.99 (*0-515-13629-8*, Jove) Berkley Publishing Group.

—The Widows of Wichita County. 2003. 384p. mass mkt. (*1-55166-715-0*, Mira Bks.) Harlequin Enterprises, Ltd.

Thompson, Cole. Chocolate Lizards. E-Book 22.95 (*0-312-26825-4*); 1999. 256p. 22.95 o.p. (*0-312-20052-8*) St. Martin's Pr.

Thompson, E. V. Republic! A Novel of Texas. 1985. 448p. 16.95 o.p. (*0-531-09795-1*, Watts, Franklin) Scholastic Library Publishing.

Thompson, Jim. South of Heaven. 1994. 240p. pap. 11.00 (*0-679-74017-1*, Vintage) Knopf Publishing Group.

—South of Heaven. E-Book 6.99 (*0-7592-0792-5*); 2000. E-Book 9.99 (*1-58586-151-0*); 2000. E-Book 6.99 (*1-58586-152-9*); 2000. E-Book 6.99 (*1-58586-275-4*) ereads.com.

—Texas by the Tail. 1994. 224p. pap. 11.00 (*0-679-74011-2*, Vintage) Knopf Publishing Group.

Thompson, Thomas. Bitter Water. l.t. ed. 1992. (Nightingale Ser.). 235p. pap. 14.95 o.p. (*0-8161-5405-8*, Macmillan Reference USA) Gale Group.

Thompson, Vicki Lewis, et al. Return to Crystal Creek: She Used to Be Mine/Made for Lovin' You/ I'll Take Texas, 3 bks. in 1. 2002. 384p. mass mkt. (*0-373-83510-8*, Harlequin Bks.) Harlequin Enterprises, Ltd.

Tilman, G. Wayne. Zack Bodeway, Texas Ranger. 2001. 216p. pap. 14.95 (*1-928704-86-7*, Fusion Pr.) Authorlink.

Tippette, Giles. Heavens Gold. 1996. 384p. 24.95 o.p. (*0-312-86047-1*, Forge Bks.) Doherty, Tom Assocs., LLC.

—Heaven's Gold. 1998. 380p. mass mkt. 5.99 o.p. (*0-8125-4917-1*, Forge Bks.) Doherty, Tom Assocs., LLC.

—Southwest of Heaven. 400p. 2001. mass mkt. 6.99 (*0-8125-4920-1*); 2000. 25.95 (*0-312-86048-X*) Doherty, Tom Assocs., LLC. (Forge Bks.).

Tompkins, Walker A. . Texas Renegade. 1999. 219p. 19.00 (*0-7540-8069-2*, Gunsmoke) BBC Audiobooks America.

—West of Texas Law. l.t. ed. 2001. 214p. 21.95 (*1-57490-407-8*, Sagebrush Large Print Westerns) Beeler, Thomas T. Publisher.

Toth, Pamela. Wedlocked?! 2000. (Fortunes of Texas Ser.: No. 11). (Illus.). 256p. per. (*0-373-65040-X*, 1-65040-7, Harlequin Bks.) Harlequin Enterprises, Ltd.

Townsend, Tom. The Dark Ships. 1988. 112p. (J). (gr. 4-5). pap. 6.95 (*0-89015-579-8*) Eakin Pr.

—Fair Wind to Glory. 1994. (Illus.). 136p. (J). (gr. 4-7). lib. bdg. 6.95 (*0-89015-975-0*) Eakin Pr.

Turner, Nancy E. The Water & the Blood: A Novel. 2002. 416p. pap. 13.95 (*0-06-098902-5*) HarperCollins Pubs.

—The Water & the Blood: A Novel. 2001. 416p. 26.00 (*0-06-039430-7*, ReganBooks) HarperTrade.

Vanzant, Lorele. Net Stalkings. E-Book 6.95 (*1-4033-0467-X*); 2002. 708p. pap. 30.95 (*1-4033-0468-8*) 1stBooks Library.

Vazquez, Diego. Growing Through the Ugly. 1997. 224p. 21.00 (*0-393-03963-3*) Norton, W. W. & Co., Inc.

Vazquez, Diego. Growing Through the Ugly. 1998. 208p. pap. 12.00 o.s.i (*0-8050-5744-7*, Owl Bks.) Holt, Henry & Co.

Verne, Jules. From the Earth to the Moon. 1967. (Airmont Classics Ser.). (YA). (gr. 8 up). mass mkt. 1.75 (*0-8049-0142-2*, CL-142) Airmont Publishing Co., Inc.

—From the Earth to the Moon. (Illus.). reprint ed. lib. bdg. 21.95 (*0-88411-901-7*) Amereon, Ltd.

—From the Earth to the Moon. 1993. 208p. mass mkt. 5.95 (*0-553-21420-9*, Bantam Classics) Bantam Bks.

—From the Earth to the Moon. 1975. (Dent's Illustrated Children's Classics Ser.). (Illus.). 192p. (YA). reprint ed. 9.00 o.p. (*0-460-05088-5*) Biblio Distribution.

—From the Earth to the Moon. l.t. ed. 2000. (LRS Large Print Heritage Ser.). 223p. (YA). (gr. 7-12). lib. bdg. 27.95 (*1-58118-070-5*) LRS.

—From the Earth to the Moon. E-Book 2.95 (*1-57799-848-0*) Logos Research Systems, Inc.

—From the Earth to the Moon. E-Book 1.95 (*1-58515-183-1*) MesaView, Inc.

—From the Earth to the Moon. 1999. (Twelve-Point Ser.). 245p. lib. bdg. 25.00 (*1-58287-103-5*); 400p. lib. bdg. 26.00 (*0-939495-96-1*) North Bks.

—From the Earth to the Moon. l.t. ed. 2000. (Science Fiction Ser.). 245p. 25.95 (*0-7838-9075-3*) Thorndike Pr.

—From the Earth to the Moon & a Trip Round It! E-Book 2.49 (*1-58627-446-5*) Electric Umbrella Publishing.

—From the Earth to the Moon & a Trip Round It! 1998. (Pocket Classics). xi, 208p. pap. 10.95 (*0-7509-0824-6*) Sutton Publishing, Ltd. GBR. *Dist:* International Publishers Marketing.

Vliet, R. G. Soledad, or Solitudes. rev. ed. 1986. (Texas Tradition Ser.: No. 6). 270p. 19.50 (*0-87565-063-5*) Texas Christian Univ. Pr.

Von Herzen, Lane. Copper Crown. 1992. (Contemporary Fiction Ser.). 240p. pap. 10.95 o.p. (*0-452-26916-4*, Plume) Dutton/Plume.

—Copper Crown. 1991. 288p. 19.00 o.p. (*0-688-10688-9*, Morrow, William & Co.) Morrow/Avon.

Wade, Mary Dodson. I'm Going to Texas: Yo Voy a Tejas. Quintanilla, Quadalupe C., tr. 1995. (ENG & SPA., Illus.). 24p. (J). (ps-4). 16.95 (*1-882539-17-6*) Colophon Hse.

Waggoner, Bill. Sweet Death. 1992. 192p. 19.95 o.s.i (*0-8027-3208-9*) Walker & Co.

Wainscott, Tina. In a Heartbeat. 1999. 320p. mass mkt. 5.99 (*0-312-97008-0*, St. Martin's Paperbacks) St. Martin's Pr.

Walker, Mary Willis. All the Dead Lie Down. unabr. ed. 1998. audio 64.00 (*0-7366-4220-X*, 4718) Books on Tape, Inc.

—All the Dead Lie Down. l.t. ed. 1998. (Large Print Bks.). 26.95 (*1-56895-669-X*, Wheeler Publishing, Inc.) Gale Group.

—All the Dead Lie Down, unabr. ed. 1998. audio 78.00 (*0-7887-2166-6*, 95462E7) Recorded Bks., LLC.

—The Red Scream. 1995. 416p. mass mkt. 6.99 (*0-553-57172-9*, Crimeline) Bantam Bks.

—The Red Scream. unabr. ed. 1996. audio 64.00 (*0-7366-3381-2*, 4031) Books on Tape, Inc.

—The Red Scream. 1994. 19.95 o.s.i (*0-385-46858-X*) Doubleday Publishing.

—The Red Scream, unabr. ed. 1996. audio 85.00 (*0-7887-0468-0*, 94661E7) Recorded Bks., LLC.

—The Red Scream. l.t. ed. 1997. (Niagara Large Print Ser.). 524p. 29.50 o.p. (*0-7089-5814-1*, Ulverscroft) Thorpe, F. A. Pubs. GBR. *Dist:* Ulverscroft Large Print Bks., Ltd., Ulverscroft Large Print Canada, Ltd.

—Under the Beetle's Cellar. 1996. 368p. reprint ed. mass mkt. 6.50 (*0-553-57173-7*, Crimeline) Bantam Bks.

—Under the Beetle's Cellar. unabr. ed. 1996. audio 64.00 (*0-7366-3382-0*, 4032) Books on Tape, Inc.

—Under the Beetle's Cellar. l.t. ed. 1996. pap. 22.95 o.p. (*1-56895-313-5*, Wheeler Publishing, Inc.) Gale Group.

—Under the Beetle's Cellar. unabr. ed. audio 75.00 (*0-7887-0515-6*, 94709E7); 1999. audio compact disk 99.00 (*0-7887-3410-5*, C1016E7) Recorded Bks., LLC.

—Zero at the Bone. 1997. 336p. mass mkt. 6.50 (*0-553-57505-8*) Bantam Bks.

—Zero at the Bone. unabr. ed. 1998. audio 56.00 (*0-7366-4131-9*, 4634) Books on Tape, Inc.

—Zero at the Bone. 1993. (Mystery Ser.). mass mkt. (*0-373-26122-5*, 1-26122-1, Harlequin Bks.) Harlequin Enterprises, Ltd.

—Zero at the Bone. 1991. 336p. 18.95 (*0-312-06495-0*, Saint Martin's Minotaur) St. Martin's Pr.

—Zero at the Bone. l.t. ed. 1998. (Niagara Large Print Ser.). 392p. 29.50 o.p. (*0-7089-5830-3*, Ulverscroft) Thorpe, F. A. Pubs. GBR. *Dist:* Ulverscroft Large Print Bks., Ltd., Ulverscroft Large Print Canada, Ltd.

Walker, Rivers. Bubba. 2001. 264p. pap. 15.95 (*0-87714-202-5*) Denlingers Pubs., Ltd.

Wall, Judith Henry. My Mother's Daughter. 2000. 432p. 25.00 (*0-684-83766-8*, Simon & Schuster) Simon & Schuster.

—My Mother's Daughter: A Novel. l.t. ed. 2001. 504p. 28.95 (*1-57490-372-1*, Beeler Large Print Bks.) Beeler, Thomas T. Publisher.

Walraven, Bill. Real Texans Don't Drink Scotch in Their Dr. Pepper: Don't Drink Scotch in Their Dr. Pepper. 1994. 96p. 4.95 o.p. (*0-89015-701-4*) Eakin Pr.

Ward, Amanda Eyre. Sleep Toward Heaven. 2004. 304p. pap. 12.95 (*0-06-058229-4*, Perennial) HarperTrade.

—Sleep Toward Heaven. 2003. 295p. 24.00 (*1-931561-23-0*) MacAdam/Cage Publishing, Inc.

Ward, Dorys. Mike's Oil Patch. 1993. 96p. (J). 13.95 (*0-89015-920-3*) Eakin Pr.

Ward, Jonas. Buchanan Calls the Shots. (Buchanan Ser.). 1981. 144p. mass mkt. 1.95 o.s.i (*0-449-14210-8*, Fawcett); 1978. mass mkt. 1.25 o.s.i (*0-449-13760-0*) Ballantine Bks.

—Buchanan Calls the Shots. l.t. ed. 1990. (Linford Western Large Print Ser.). pap. 17.99 (*0-7089-6943-7*, Linford) Thorpe, F. A. Pubs. GBR. *Dist:* Ulverscroft Large Print Bks., Ltd., Ulverscroft Large Print Canada, Ltd.

—Buchanan Gets Mad. 1981. (Buchanan Ser.). mass mkt. 1.95 o.s.i (*0-449-14209-4*, Fawcett) Ballantine Bks.

—Buchanan Gets Mad. l.t. ed. 1996. (Western Ser.). 199p. 23.95 (*0-7838-1661-8*) Thorndike Pr.

—Buchanan on the Prod. (Buchanan Ser.). 1981. 144p. mass mkt. 1.95 o.s.i (*0-449-14107-1*, Fawcett); 1975. mass mkt. 1.25 o.s.i (*0-449-13472-5*) Ballantine Bks.

—Buchanan on the Prod. l.t. ed. 1985. (Linford Western Library). 304p. pap. 17.99 (*0-7089-6144-4*, Linford) Thorpe, F. A. Pubs. GBR. *Dist:* Ulverscroft Large Print Bks., Ltd., Ulverscroft Large Print Canada, Ltd.

—Buchanan on the Run. (Buchanan Ser.). 1981. mass mkt. 1.75 o.s.i (*0-449-14208-6*, Fawcett); 1975. mass mkt. 1.25 o.s.i (*0-449-13474-1*) Ballantine Bks.

—Buchanan Says No. (Buchanan Ser.). 1981. mass mkt. 1.95 o.s.i (*0-449-14164-0*, Fawcett); 1978. mass mkt. 1.25 o.s.i (*0-449-13862-3*); 1974. mass mkt. 0.95 o.s.i (*0-449-13022-3*) Ballantine Bks.

—Buchanan Says No. l.t. ed. 1985. (Linford Western Library). 256p. pap. 17.99 (*0-7089-6140-1*, Linford) Thorpe, F. A. Pubs. GBR. *Dist:* Ulverscroft Large Print Bks., Ltd., Ulverscroft Large Print Canada, Ltd.

—Buchanan Takes Over. 1981. mass mkt. 1.95 o.s.i (*0-449-14063-6*, Fawcett) Ballantine Bks.

—Buchanan Takes Over. l.t. ed. 1989. (Linford Western Large Print Ser.). pap. 17.99 (*0-7089-6772-8*, Linford) Thorpe, F. A. Pubs. GBR. *Dist:* Ulverscroft Large Print Bks., Ltd., Ulverscroft Large Print Canada, Ltd.

—Buchanan's Big Fight. 1981. mass mkt. 1.95 o.s.i (*0-449-14406-2*, Fawcett) Ballantine Bks.

—Buchanan's Big Fight. l.t. ed. 1990. (Linford Western Large Print Ser.). pap. 17.99 (*0-7089-6868-6*, Linford) Thorpe, F. A. Pubs. GBR. *Dist:* Ulverscroft Large Print Bks., Ltd., Ulverscroft Large Print Canada, Ltd.

—Buchanan's Big Showdown. 1981. (Buchanan Ser.). 176p. mass mkt. 1.95 o.s.i (*0-449-14109-8*, Fawcett) Ballantine Bks.

—Buchanan's Black Sheep. 1984. (Buchanan Ser.). 176p. mass mkt. 2.50 o.s.i (*0-449-12412-6*, Fawcett) Ballantine Bks.

—Buchanan's Black Sheep. l.t. ed. 1990. (Linford Western Large Print Ser.). pap. 17.99 (*0-7089-6938-0*, Linford) Thorpe, F. A. Pubs. GBR. *Dist:* Ulverscroft Large Print Bks., Ltd., Ulverscroft Large Print Canada, Ltd.

—Buchanan's Gamble. (Buchanan Ser.). 1981. mass mkt. 1.95 o.s.i (*0-449-14177-2*, Fawcett); 1975. mass mkt. 1.25 o.s.i (*0-449-13473-3*) Ballantine Bks.

—Buchanan's Gamble. l.t. ed. 1989. (Linford Western Library). 305p. pap. 17.99 (*0-7089-6683-7*, Linford) Thorpe, F. A. Pubs. GBR. *Dist:* Ulverscroft Large Print Bks., Ltd., Ulverscroft Large Print Canada, Ltd.

—Buchanan's Gun. 1982. (Buchanan Ser.). 160p. mass mkt. 1.95 o.s.i (*0-449-14211-6*, Fawcett) Ballantine Bks.

—Buchanan's Gun. l.t. ed. 1976. (Ulverscroft Large Print Ser.). 29.99 o.p. (*0-85456-437-3*, Ulverscroft) Thorpe, F. A. Pubs. GBR. *Dist:* Ulverscroft Large Print Bks., Ltd., Ulverscroft Large Print Canada, Ltd.

—Buchanan's Manhunt. 1981. mass mkt. 1.75 o.s.i (*0-449-14119-5*, Fawcett) Ballantine Bks.

—Buchanan's Manhunt. l.t. ed. 1989. (Linford Western Library). pap. 17.99 (*0-7089-6760-4*, Linford) Thorpe, F. A. Pubs. GBR. *Dist:* Ulverscroft Large Print Bks., Ltd., Ulverscroft Large Print Canada, Ltd.

—Buchanan's Range War. 1980. (Buchanan Ser.). 224p. mass mkt. 1.75 o.s.i (*0-449-14357-0*, Fawcett) Ballantine Bks.

—Buchanan's Range War. l.t. ed. 1987. (Linford Western Library). 240p. pap. 17.99 o.p. (*0-7089-6351-X*, Linford) Thorpe, F. A. Pubs. GBR. *Dist:* Ulverscroft Large Print Bks., Ltd., Ulverscroft Large Print Canada, Ltd.

—Buchanan's Revenge. 1982. (Buchanan Ser.). 144p. mass mkt. 2.25 o.s.i (*0-449-12361-8*, Fawcett) Ballantine Bks.

—Buchanan's Revenge. l.t. ed. 1996. (G. K. Hall Western Ser.). 227p. 21.95 (*0-7838-1877-7*) Thorndike Pr.

—Buchanan's Revenge. l.t. ed. 1985. (Ulverscroft Large Print Ser.). 496p. 29.99 o.p. (*0-7089-1291-5*, Ulverscroft) Thorpe, F. A. Pubs. GBR. *Dist:* Ulverscroft Large Print Bks., Ltd., Ulverscroft Large Print Canada, Ltd.

—Buchanan's Showdown. 1976. mass mkt. 1.25 o.s.i (*0-449-13553-5*) Ballantine Bks.

—Buchanan's Siege. 1982. 160p. mass mkt. 2.25 o.s.i (*0-449-14086-5*, Fawcett) Ballantine Bks.

—Buchanan's Siege. l.t. ed. 1990. (Linford Western Library). pap. 17.99 (*0-7089-6804-X*, Linford) Thorpe, F. A. Pubs. GBR. *Dist:* Ulverscroft Large Print Bks., Ltd., Ulverscroft Large Print Canada, Ltd.

—Buchanan's Stage Line. 1986. (Buchanan Ser.). 176p. mass mkt. 2.50 o.s.i (*0-449-12847-4*, Fawcett) Ballantine Bks.

—Buchanan's Stage Line. l.t. ed. 1987. (Linford Western Library). 272p. pap. 17.99 o.p. (*0-7089-6427-3*, Linford) Thorpe, F. A. Pubs. GBR. *Dist:* Ulverscroft Large Print Bks., Ltd., Ulverscroft Large Print Canada, Ltd.

—Buchanan's Stolen Railway. 1979. (Buchanan Ser.). mass mkt. 1.75 o.s.i (*0-449-13977-8*, Fawcett) Ballantine Bks.

—Buchanan's Texas Treasure. 1982. (Buchanan Ser.). 160p. mass mkt. 2.25 o.s.i (*0-449-14175-6*, Fawcett) Ballantine Bks.

—Buchanan's Texas Treasure. l.t. ed. 1991. (Linford Western Large Print Ser.). pap. 17.99 (*0-7089-6960-7*, Ulverscroft) Thorpe, F. A. Pubs. GBR. *Dist:* Ulverscroft Large Print Bks., Ltd., Ulverscroft Large Print Canada, Ltd.

—Buchanan's War. (Buchanan Ser.). 1981. mass mkt. 1.95 o.s.i (*0-449-14137-3*, Fawcett); 1974. mass mkt. 0.95 o.s.i (*0-449-13025-8*) Ballantine Bks.

—Buchanan's War. l.t. ed. 1997. (G. K. Hall Western Ser.). 233p. lib. bdg. 20.95 (*0-7838-1878-5*) Thorndike Pr.

—Get Buchanan! 1979. (Buchanan Ser.). mass mkt. 1.50 o.s.i (*0-449-14062-8*, Fawcett) Ballantine Bks.

—Get Buchanan! l.t. ed. 1990. (Linford Western Library). pap. 17.99 o.p. (*0-7089-6811-2*, Ulverscroft) Thorpe, F. A. Pubs. GBR. *Dist:* Ulverscroft Large Print Bks., Ltd., Ulverscroft Large Print Canada, Ltd.

—The Name's Buchanan. (Buchanan Ser.). 1980. 128p. mass mkt. 1.75 o.s.i (*0-449-14135-7*, Fawcett); 1977. mass mkt. 1.25 o.s.i (*0-449-13858-5*) Ballantine Bks.

—The Name's Buchanan. l.t. ed. 1995. 204p. 18.95 (*0-7838-1471-2*, Macmillan Reference USA) Gale Group.

—Trap for Buchanan. 1979. (Buchanan Ser.). 144p. mass mkt. 1.50 o.s.i (*0-449-14082-2*, Fawcett) Ballantine Bks.

—Trap for Buchanan. l.t. ed. 1989. (Linford Western Library). 256p. pap. 17.99 (*0-7089-6715-9*, Linford) Thorpe, F. A. Pubs. GBR. *Dist:* Ulverscroft Large Print Bks., Ltd., Ulverscroft Large Print Canada, Ltd.

Watt, Donley. Can You Get There from Here? Stories. 1994. (Southwest Life & Letters Ser.). 176p. (Orig.). pap. 9.95 (*0-87074-377-5*); pap. text 19.95 (*0-87074-376-7*) Southern Methodist Univ. Pr.

—Journey of Hector Rabinal. 1994. 194p. (Orig.). (C). pap. 12.95 (*0-87565-125-9*) Texas Christian Univ. Pr.

—Reynolds: A Novel. 2002. (Illus.). 200p. 24.50 (*0-87565-256-5*) Texas Christian Univ. Pr.

Webb, Don. Endless Honeymoon. 2001. 243p. 23.95 (*0-312-26582-4*, Saint Martin's Minotaur) St. Martin's Pr.

Webb, Paula. Domestic Life. 1992. 224p. 20.00 o.s.i (*0-671-74433-X*, Simon & Schuster) Simon & Schuster.

Westland, Lynn. The Heart of Texas. l.t. ed. 1992. 18.95 o.p. (*0-7451-8353-0*); pap. 16.95 o.p. (*0-7927-1100-9*) BBC Audiobooks America.

WhiteFeather, Sheri. Lone Wolf. 2003. (Silhouette Special Releases Ser.: No. 10). (Illus.). 256p. mass mkt. (*0-373-61361-X*, Silhouette) Harlequin Enterprises, Ltd.

Whittington, Brad. Welcome to Fred: A Novel. 2003. 256p. pap. 12.99 (*0-8054-2555-1*) Broadman & Holman Pubs.

Wick, Lori. City Girl. l.t. ed. 2002. 385p. (Yellow Rose Trilogy: No. 3). pap. 17.95 (*1-4104-0017-4*, Walker Large Print); 27.95 (*0-7862-2943-8*) Gale Group.

—City Girl, No. 3. 2001. (Yellow Rose Trilogy Ser.: Vol. 3). 288p. (YA). pap. 10.99 (*0-7369-0255-4*) Harvest Hse. Pubs.

—Every Little Thing about You. l.t. ed. 2002. (Yellow Rose Trilogy). 484p. pap. 17.95 (*1-4104-0019-0*, Walker Large Print) Gale Group.

—Every Little Thing about You. 1999. (Yellow Rose Trilogy Ser.: Vol. 1). 299p. pap. 10.99 (*0-7369-0104-3*) Harvest Hse. Pubs.

—Every Little Thing about You. l.t. ed. 2001. (Yellow Rose Trilogy Ser.: Vol. 1). 299p. 26.95 (*0-7862-2876-8*) Thorndike Pr.

—A Texas Sky. l.t. ed. 404p. 2002. (Yellow Rose Trilogy: No. 2). pap. 17.95 (*1-4104-0013-1*, Walker Large Print); 2001. 25.95 (*0-7862-2934-9*) Gale Group.

—A Texas Sky. 2000. (Yellow Rose Trilogy Ser.: Vol. 2). 288p. pap. 10.99 (*0-7369-0187-6*) Harvest Hse. Pubs.

Wiggs, Susan. Home Before Dark. 2004. 416p. mass mkt. (*0-7783-2019-7*, Mira Bks.); 2003. 384p. (*1-55166-673-1*) Harlequin Enterprises, Ltd.

Wilkinson, D. Marion. Not Between Brothers: An Epic Novel of Texas. (Celestial Arts Ser.). 680p. 2003. pap. 15.95 (*0-9651879-3-4*); 1996. (Illus.). 27.95 (*0-9651879-0-X*) Boaz Publishing Co.

Wilkinson, D. Marion. Not Between Brothers: An Epic Novel of Texas. 1999. 656p. reprint ed. mass mkt. 6.99 o.s.i (*0-451-19686-4*, Signet Bks.) NAL.

Williams, Lori Aurelia. When Kambia Elaine Flew in from Neptune. l.t. ed. 2001. 369p. 22.95 (*0-7862-3657-4*) Thorndike Pr.

Williamson, Ermal Walden. The Man from the Brazos. 2001. 394p. pap. 7.95 (*1-931643-02-4*) Seven Locks Pr.

Willocks, Tim. Green River Rising. abr. ed. 1994. audio 16.95 o.p. (*1-56100-380-8*, 1314, Nova Audio Bks.); audio 23.95 o.p. (*1-56100-581-9*, 128, Bookcassette); audio 57.25 o.p. (*1-56100-206-2*, 884, Unabridged Library Editions) Brilliance Audio.

—Green River Rising. abr. ed. 2000. audio 7.95 (*1-57815-034-5*, 1051, Media Bks. Audio Publishing) Media Bks., L. L. C.

—Green River Rising. 1995. 400p. mass mkt. 5.99 (*0-380-72357-3*, Avon Bks.); 1994. 23.00 o.p. (*0-688-13571-4*, Morrow, William & Co.) Morrow/Avon.

Wind, Ruth. In the Midnight Rain. l.t. ed. 2001. 350p. 26.95 (*1-57490-359-4*, Beeler Large Print Bks.) Beeler, Thomas T. Publisher.

—In the Midnight Rain. 2000. 416p. mass mkt. 6.99 (*0-06-103012-0*) HarperCollins Pubs.

Windle, Janice Woods. Hill Country: A Novel. 1998. (Illus.). 416p. 25.00 (*1-56352-522-4*) Longstreet Pr., Inc.

—Hill Country: A Novel. 2000. (Illus.). 480p. pap. 14.00 (*0-684-86605-6*, Touchstone) Simon & Schuster.

—True Women. 1994. 432p. mass mkt. 6.99 (*0-8041-1308-4*, Ivy Bks.) Ballantine Bks.

—True Women. l.t. ed. 1994. 657p. lib. bdg. 24.95 o.p. (*0-8161-7425-3*, Macmillan Reference USA) Gale Group.

—True Women. 1994. 464p. 22.95 o.p. (*0-399-13813-7*) Penguin Group (USA) Inc.

—True Women Cookbook: Original Antique Recipes, Photographs & Family Folklore. 1997. (Illus.). pap. text 22.95 (*1-880092-41-7*) Bright Bks., Inc.

Wingate, Anne. The Buzzards Must Also be Fed. 1992. 256p. mass mkt. 3.99 o.p. (*0-06-104099-1*, HarperTorch) Morrow/Avon.

—The Buzzards Must Also be Fed. 1991. 192p. 18.95 o.s.i (*0-8027-5773-1*) Walker & Co.

—Death by Deception. 1991. 208p. mass mkt. 3.95 o.p. (*0-06-100146-5*, Perennial) HarperTrade.

—Death by Deception. 1988. 192p. 17.95 o.p. (*0-8027-5714-6*) Walker & Co.

—Exception to Murder. pap. 2.98 o.p. (*0-8317-8133-5*) Smithmark Pubs., Inc.

—Exception to Murder. 1992. 192p. 19.95 (*0-8027-3203-8*) Walker & Co.

—The Eye of Anna. 1991. 208p. mass mkt. 3.95 o.p. (*0-06-100165-1*, HarperTorch) Morrow/Avon.

—The Eye of Anna. 1990. 192p. 17.95 o.p. (*0-8027-5749-9*) Walker & Co.

—Yakuza, Go Home! A Mark Shigata Mystery. 1993. 218p. 19.95 o.p. (*0-8027-3226-7*) Walker & Co.

Winn, Bonnie K. Family Ties. 2002. (Steeple Hill Love Inspired Ser.: No. 186). mass mkt. (*0-373-87193-7*, Steeple Hill) Harlequin Enterprises, Ltd.

—Promise of Grace. 2003. (Steeple Hill Love Inspired Ser.: No. 222). 256p. mass mkt. (*0-373-87229-1*, Steeple Hill) Harlequin Enterprises, Ltd.

Winship, Robert. Flannery's Crossing. 2003. 144p. (Orig.). pap. 16.95 (*1-881515-41-9*) Texas Review Pr.

Wisler, G. Clifton. Antelope Springs. 1986. 192p. 14.95 (*0-8027-4062-6*) Walker & Co.

—The Wetherbys. 1992. mass mkt. 4.99 o.s.i (*0-449-14830-0*, Fawcett) Ballantine Bks.

—The Wetherbys. l.t. ed. 2000. 22.95 o.p. (*1-56895-835-8*, Wheeler Publishing, Inc.) Gale Group.

Witt, Wilbur W. Cigar Box. 2001. 301p. pap. 15.95 (*0-595-16844-2*) iUniverse, Inc.

Wolverton, Cheryl. For Love of Mitch. 2000. (Steeple Hill Love Inspired Ser.: Bk. 105). per. (*0-373-87111-2*, 1-87111-0, Steeple Hill) Harlequin Enterprises, Ltd.

Wood, Jane Roberts. Dance a Little Longer, Vol. 3. unabr. ed. 1995. audio 51.00 (*0-7887-0396-X*, 94588E7) Recorded Bks., LLC.

—Dance a Little Longer. 3rd ed. 2000. (Lucinda Richards Trilogy Ser.: Vol. 3). iv, 211p. reprint ed. pap. 15.95 (*1-57441-080-6*) Univ. of North Texas Pr.

—Grace. 2001. 240p. 22.95 o.s.i (*0-525-94602-0*) Dutton/Plume.

—Grace. l.t. ed. 2001. (Americana Ser.). 397p. 28.95 (*0-7862-3457-1*) Thorndike Pr.

—A Place Called Sweet Shrub. 1991. 320p. pap. 10.00 o.s.i (*0-440-50305-1*, Dell Bks.) Dell Publishing.

—A Place Called Sweet Shrub, Set. unabr. ed. 1996. audio 67.00 Recorded Bks., LLC.

—A Place Called Sweet Shrub. 3rd ed. 2000. (Lucinda Richards Trilogy Ser.: Vol. 2). 286p. reprint ed. pap. 15.95 (*1-57441-079-2*) Univ. of North Texas Pr.

—The Train to Estelline. 1988. 240p. pap. 11.95 o.s.i (*0-385-31289-X*, Delta); reprint ed. pap. 10.00 o.s.i (*0-440-50033-8*, Laurel) Dell Publishing.

—The Train to Estelline. unabr. ed. 1995. audio 44.00 (*0-7887-0164-9*, 94389E7) Recorded Bks., LLC.

—The Train to Estelline. 1987. 240p. 19.95 (*0-936650-05-2*) Temple, Ellen C. Publishing, Inc.

—The Train to Estelline. 3rd ed. 2000. (Lucinda Richards Trilogy Ser.: Vol. 1). 209p. reprint ed. pap. 15.95 (*1-57441-078-4*) Univ. of North Texas Pr.

—The Train to Estelline. 1987. E-Book 19.95 (*0-585-16344-8*) netLibrary, Inc.

Woolley, Bryan. Time & Place. 1985. (Texas Tradition Ser.: No. 2). 246p. (C). reprint ed. 16.95 (*0-912646-98-5*); pap. 9.95 (*0-912646-99-3*) Texas Christian Univ. Pr.

Worcester, Don. Gone to Texas. 1992. 224p. 16.95 o.p. (*0-87131-697-8*) Evans, M. & Co., Inc.

Worth, Lenora. His Brother's Wife. 1999. (Steeple Hill Love Inspired Ser.: Vol. 82). mass mkt. (*0-373-87082-5*, Steeple Hill) Harlequin Enterprises, Ltd.

Wouk, Herman. A Hole in Texas: A Novel. 2004. 25.00 (*0-316-00072-8*) Little Brown & Co.

Wyse, Sharon. The Box Children. 2002. 160p. 18.95 o.s.i (*1-57322-219-4*, Riverhead Bks. (Hardcovers)) Putnam Publishing Group, The.

—The Box Children: A Novel. 2003. 192p. reprint ed. pap. 13.00 (*1-57322-996-2*, Riverhead Trade (Paperbacks)) Berkley Publishing Group.

Young, Karen. Kiss & Kill: A Kiss Before Dying. 2000. 384p. mass mkt. 5.99 o.s.i (*0-8217-6658-9*) Kensington Publishing Corp.

—Private Lives. 2003. 448p. mass mkt. (*1-55166-679-0*, Mira Bks.) Harlequin Enterprises, Ltd.

Yount, J. Steven. Wandering Star. 1994. 400p. 22.00 o.s.i (*0-345-38301-X*) Ballantine Bks.

Yount, Steven. Wandering Star. 1995. mass mkt. 5.99 o.s.i (*0-345-39437-2*, Del Rey) Ballantine Bks.

—Wandering Star. audio o.p. National Humanities Ctr.

Zesch, Scott. Alamo Heights. 1999. 322p. 24.50 (*0-87565-194-1*) Texas Christian Univ. Pr.

## THAILAND—FICTION

Banomyong, Pridi. The King of the White Elephant. 2000. 128p. pap. 12.00 (*974-7449-22-6*) Committees on the Project for the National Celebration on the Occasion of the Centennial Anniversary of Pridi Banomyong THA. *Dist:* Lantern Bks.

Barrett, Dean. Kingdom of Make-Believe. 1999. 344p. pap. 11.95 (*0-9661899-0-6*) Village East Bks.

Block, Lawrence. The Scoreless Thai: An Evan Tanner Novel. 2000. 160p. reprint ed. 30.00 (*1-892284-99-5*) Subterranean Pr.

Burdett, John. Bangkok 8: A Novel. 336p. 2004. pap. 12.95 (*1-4000-3290-3*, Vintage); 2003. 24.95 (*1-4000-4044-2*) Knopf Publishing Group.

Carr, Richard J. Wyndedanse: A Royal Chronicle of 17th Century Siam. 2000. 616p. pap. 28.99 (*0-7388-1241-2*); text 38.99 (*0-7388-1240-4*) Xlibris Corp.

Chua, Lawrence. Gold by the Inch. 224p. 1999. pap. 12.00 (*0-8021-3649-4*); 1998. 20.00 o.p. (*0-8021-1626-4*) Grove/Atlantic, Inc. (Grove Pr.).

Culler, Al. Speedin' A Strange & Savage Trip Thru the Thai & Cambodian Badlands. 2000. 168p. pap. 20.99 (*0-7388-2633-2*) Xlibris Corp.

Dokmaisot. A Secret Past. Strehlow, Ted, tr. from THA. 1992. (Southeast Asia Program Ser.: No. 9). 72p. pap. text 12.00 (*0-87727-126-7*) Cornell Univ., Southeast Asia Program Pubns.

Forman, Craig. War Stories. 1999. 327p. pap. 22.99 (*0-7388-0659-5*); text 32.99 (*0-7388-0658-7*) Xlibris Corp.

Fowler, William. Speedin' A Strange & Savage Trip Thru the Thai & Cambodian Badlands. 2000. 168p. E-Book 8.00 (*0-7388-8972-5*) Xlibris Corp.

Gilman, Dorothy. Mrs. Pollifax & the Golden Triangle. 1989. 208p. mass mkt. 6.99 (*0-449-21515-6*, Fawcett) Ballantine Bks.

Hamilton, Lyn. The Thai Amulet. 2004. 288p. mass mkt. 6.99 (*0-425-19487-6*); 2003. 256p. 22.95 (*0-425-19006-4*, Prime Crime) Berkley Publishing Group.

Joyce, Graham. Smoking Poppy. 288p. 2003. pap. 14.00 (*0-671-03940-7*, Washington Square Pr.); 2002. 23.00 (*0-671-03939-3*, Atria) Simon & Schuster.

Keeley, Edmund. A Wilderness Called Peace. 1985. 16.45 o.p. (*0-671-47416-2*, Simon & Schuster) Simon & Schuster.

Keeley, Edmund. A Wilderness Called Peace. 1987. 368p. reprint ed. mass mkt. 4.95 o.s.i (*0-440-39376-0*, Laurel) Dell Publishing.

Mathews, Francine. The Secret Agent. 2003. 528p. mass mkt. 6.99 (*0-553-58153-8*); 2002. (Illus.). 416p. 23.95 (*0-553-10913-8*) Bantam Bks.

Perry, Fred E. Prisoner of the Poppy. 2001. 512p. pap. 26.99 (*0-7388-6117-0*) Xlibris Corp.

Topley, Donald. Horse Passing. 2001. 320p. 19.95 (*1-58345-633-3*); pap. 15.95 (*1-58345-570-1*) Domhan Bks.

Tuck, Lily. Siam: Or the Woman Who Shot a Man. 1999. (Sewanee Writers' Ser.). 192p. (C). 23.95 (*0-87951-723-9*) Overlook Pr., The.

Wilson, Robert Charles. The Chronoliths. Date not set. E-Book (*0-312-70191-8*); 2001. 301p. 23.95 (*0-312-87384-0*); 1999. mass mkt. 6.99 (*0-8125-4524-9*) Doherty, Tom Assocs., LLC. (Tor Bks.).

**THALIA (TEX.: IMAGINARY PLACE)—FICTION**

McMurtry, Larry. Duane's Depressed. 2002. 431p. reprint ed. 26.00 (*0-7567-5630-8*) DIANE Publishing Co.

—Duane's Depressed. l.t. ed. 1999. (Core Ser.: No. 3). 574p. 30.95 (*0-7838-8631-4*, Macmillan Reference USA) Gale Group.

—Duane's Depressed. 2003. 432p. pap. 14.00 (*0-7432-3015-9*, Simon & Schuster); 1999. (Last Picture Show Trilogy: No. 3). 528p. pap. 7.99 (*0-671-02557-0*, Pocket); 1999. mass mkt. 7.99 (*0-671-03461-8*, Pocket); 1999. (Last Picture Show Trilogy: No. 3). 432p. 26.00 (*0-684-85497-X*, Simon & Schuster) Simon & Schuster.

—Duane's Depressed. 1999. (Last Picture Show Trilogy: No. 3). 14.04 (*0-606-19049-X*) Turtleback Bks.

—The Last Picture Show. 1976. (Last Picture Show Trilogy: No. 1). 22.95 (*0-89190-889-7*) Amereon, Ltd.

—The Last Picture Show. 1999. (Last Picture Show Trilogy: Bk. 1). (*0-7540-1321-9*); pap. (*0-7540-2238-2*) BBC Audiobooks America.

—The Last Picture Show. unabr. collector's ed. 1984. (Last Picture Show Trilogy: No. 1). audio 48.00 (*0-7366-0764-1*, 1721) Books on Tape, Inc.

—The Last Picture Show. 1997. (Last Picture Show Trilogy: No. 1). 35.95 o.p. (*1-56849-688-5*) Buccaneer Bks., Inc.

—The Last Picture Show. l.t. ed. 1999. (Core Ser.: No. 1). 381p. 29.95 o.p. (*0-7838-8632-2*, Macmillan Reference USA) Gale Group.

—The Last Picture Show. unabr. ed. 1989. (Last Picture Show Trilogy). audio 51.00 (*1-55690-304-9*, 89810E7) Recorded Bks., LLC.

—The Last Picture Show. (Thalia Trilogy Ser.: No. 1). 2003. 288p. pap. 13.00 (*0-684-85386-8*, Simon & Schuster); 1999. pap. 11.00 (*0-684-00817-3*, Simon & Schuster); 1992. 224p. pap. 10.00 (*0-671-75487-4*, Simon & Schuster); 1992. 320p. mass mkt. 7.99 o.s.i (*0-671-75381-9*, Pocket); 1989. 280p. 18.95 o.p. (*0-671-67604-0*, Simon & Schuster) Simon & Schuster.

—The Last Picture Show. 1979. (Last Picture Show Trilogy: No. 1). 224p. pap. 8.95 o.p. (*0-14-005183-X*, Penguin Bks.) Viking Penguin.

—Some Can Whistle. l.t. ed. 1990. (General Ser.). 399p. 13.95 o.p. (*0-8161-5010-9*); lib. bdg. 20.95 o.p. (*0-8161-4987-9*) Gale Group. (Macmillan Reference USA).

—Some Can Whistle. 1989. 19.95 o.p. (*0-671-64267-7*, Simon & Schuster) Simon & Schuster.

—Some Can Whistle. Grose, William, ed. 1990. 384p. reprint ed. mass mkt. 6.99 (*0-671-72213-1*, Pocket) Simon & Schuster.

—Texasville. l.t. ed. 1999. (Core Ser.: No. 2). 663p. 30.95 (*0-7838-8633-0*, Macmillan Reference USA) Gale Group.

—Texasville. (Thalia Trilogy Ser.: No. 2). 2003. 544p. pap. 14.00 (*0-684-85750-2*, Simon & Schuster); 1990. mass mkt. 5.95 o.s.i (*0-671-72474-6*, Pocket) Simon & Schuster.

—Texasville. Grose, Bill, ed. 1990. (Last Picture Show Trilogy: No. 2). 576p. mass mkt. 7.99 o.s.i (*0-671-73517-9*, Pocket) Simon & Schuster.

—Texasville. 1987. (Last Picture Show Trilogy: No. 2). mass mkt. 3.95 o.s.i (*0-671-64878-0*, Pocket); 512p. 18.45 o.p. (*0-671-62533-0*, Simon & Schuster) Simon & Schuster.

**THRUSH GREEN (IMAGINARY PLACE)—FICTION**

Read, Miss. Affairs at Thrush Green. unabr. ed. 1993. (Thrush Green Chronicles Ser.). 54.95 incl. audio (*0-7451-6213-4*, CAB 083) BBC Audiobooks America.

—Affairs at Thrush Green. 1984. 13.95 o.p. (*0-395-36554-6*) Houghton Mifflin Co.

—Affairs at Thrush Green. l.t. ed. 1993. (General Fiction Ser.). 258p. 19.95 o.p. (*0-7505-0205-3*) Magna Large Print Bks. GBR. *Dist:* Ulverscroft Large Print Bks., Ltd.

—At Home in Thrush Green. unabr. ed. 1993. (Thrush Green Chronicles Ser.). 54.95 incl. audio (*0-7451-6214-2*, CAB 160) BBC Audiobooks America.

—At Home in Thrush Green, 001. 1986. 16.95 o.p. (*0-395-41224-2*) Houghton Mifflin Co.

—Battles at Thrush Green. unabr. ed. 2000. audio 24.95 (*1-57270-126-9*, M41126u, Audio Editions Bks. on Cassette) Audio Partners Publishing Corp.

—Battles at Thrush Green. unabr. ed. 1993. audio 54.95 (*0-7451-6215-0*, CAB 227) BBC Audiobooks America.

—Celebrations at Thrush Green. l.t. ed. 1994. 18.95 o.p. (*0-7927-1921-2*); pap. o.p. (*0-7927-1920-4*) BBC Audiobooks America.

—Celebrations at Thrush Green. unabr. ed. 2000. (Thrush Green Chronicles). audio 34.95 (*0-7451-4191-9*, CAB 874) Chivers Audio Bks. GBR. *Dist:* BBC Audiobooks America.

—Celebrations at Thrush Green. 1993. (Illus.). 151p. 19.95 o.p. (*0-395-65030-5*) Houghton Mifflin Co.

—Celebrations at Thrush Green. 1993. pap. 11.00 (*0-14-015798-0*) Penguin Bks., Ltd. GBR. *Dist:* Trafalgar Square.

—Encounters at Thrush Green. (Illus.). 448p. 29.95 o.p. (*0-7181-4334-5*) Joseph, Michael Ltd. GBR. *Dist:* Trafalgar Square.

—Friends at Thrush Green. 1991. (Illus.). 256p. 21.95 o.p. (*0-395-57381-5*) Houghton Mifflin Co.

—Gossip from Thrush Green. l.t. ed. 1993. pap. 16.95 o.p. (*0-7927-1375-3*); 1992. 18.95 o.p. (*0-7927-1376-1*) BBC Audiobooks America.

—Gossip from Thrush Green. unabr. ed. 1983. audio 53.95 o.p. (*0-8161-9766-0*, Macmillan Reference USA) Gale Group.

—Gossip from Thrush Green, 001. 1982. 13.50 o.p. (*0-395-32215-4*) Houghton Mifflin Co.

—News from Thrush Green. 1990. (Illus.). 240p. reprint ed. pap. 12.00 (*0-89733-334-9*) Academy Chicago Pubs., Ltd.

—News from Thrush Green. lib. bdg. 21.95 (*0-8488-1455-X*) Amereon, Ltd.

—News from Thrush Green. 1983. 291p. reprint ed. lib. bdg. 16.95 o.p. (*0-89966-465-2*) Buccaneer Bks., Inc.

—News from Thrush Green. l.t. ed. (General Ser.). 1993. (Illus.). 325p. lib. bdg. 21.95 (*0-8161-5503-8*); 1993. 22.00 (*0-8161-5504-6*); 1976. reprint ed. lib. bdg. 10.95 o.p. (*0-8161-6432-0*) Gale Group. (Macmillan Reference USA).

—A Peaceful Retirement, Set. abr. ed. 1998. (Fairacre Chronicles). audio 24.95 (*0-7540-7522-2*) BBC Audiobooks America.

—A Peaceful Retirement. unabr. ed. 2000. (Fairacre Chronicles). audio 39.95 (*0-7451-8784-6*, CAB 1419) Chivers Audio Bks. GBR. *Dist:* BBC Audiobooks America.

—A Peaceful Retirement. l.t. ed. 1997. 189p. 26.95 o.p. (*0-7838-8276-9*, Macmillan Reference USA) Gale Group.

—A Peaceful Retirement. 1997. 160p. 22.00 o.p. (*0-395-85062-2*) Houghton Mifflin Co.

—Return to Thrush Green. l.t. ed. 1993. pap. 15.95 o.p. (*0-7927-1266-8*); 1992. 18.95 o.p. (*0-7927-1267-6*) BBC Audiobooks America.

—Return to Thrush Green, 001. 1979. 8.95 o.p. (*0-395-27627-6*) Houghton Mifflin Co.

—Return to Thrush Green. unabr. ed. 1998. audio 69.95 o.p. (*1-872672-08-6*) Magna Story Sound GBR. *Dist:* Ulverscroft Large Print Bks., Ltd.

—The School at Thrush Green. 1988. (Illus.). 272p. 17.95 o.p. (*0-395-46108-1*) Houghton Mifflin Co.

—Tales from a Village School. 1996. audio 24.95 (*0-7451-2844-0*) BBC Audiobooks America.

—Tales from a Village School. unabr. ed. 2000. (Fairacre Chronicles). audio 34.95 (*0-7451-6540-0*, CAB 1156) Chivers Audio Bks. GBR. *Dist:* BBC Audiobooks America.

—Tales from a Village School. l.t. ed. 1995. 226p. 24.95 o.p. (*0-7838-1441-0*, Macmillan Reference USA) Gale Group.

—Tales from a Village School. 1995. (Illus.). 176p. 19.95 o.p. (*0-395-71762-0*) Houghton Mifflin Co.

—Tales from a Village School. l.t. ed. 1996. (Paperback Bestsellers Ser.). 190p. pap. 23.95 (*0-7838-1442-9*) Thorndike Pr.

—Thrush Green. 1987. (Illus.). 226p. pap. 9.00 o.s.i (*0-89733-263-6*) Academy Chicago Pubs., Ltd.

—Thrush Green. Date not set. lib. bdg. 21.95 (*0-8488-1692-7*) Amereon, Ltd.

—Thrush Green. l.t. ed. 1992. pap. 14.95 o.p. (*0-7927-0867-9*); 18.95 o.p. (*0-7927-0866-0*, E0019) BBC Audiobooks America.

—Thrush Green. 1982. reprint ed. lib. bdg. 25.95 (*0-89966-435-0*) Buccaneer Bks., Inc.

—Thrush Green, Set. unabr. ed. 1998. audio 69.95 o.p. (*1-872672-02-7*) Magna Story Sound GBR. *Dist:* Ulverscroft Large Print Bks., Ltd.

—Thrush Green. 1988. 10.95 o.p. (*0-7181-0370-X*) Viking Penguin.

—Winter in Thrush Green. 1987. (Illus.). 226p. pap. 9.00 o.p. (*0-89733-264-4*) Academy Chicago Pubs., Ltd.

—Winter in Thrush Green. 1982. reprint ed. lib. bdg. 25.95 (*0-89966-436-9*) Buccaneer Bks., Inc.

—Winter in Thrush Green, Set. unabr. ed. 1998. audio 69.95 o.p. (*1-872672-12-4*) Magna Story Sound GBR. *Dist:* Ulverscroft Large Print Bks., Ltd.

—The World of Thrush Green. l.t. ed. 1993. (Illus.). 326p. lib. bdg. 17.95 o.p. (*0-8161-5508-9*); 22.95 (*0-8161-5507-0*) Gale Group. (Macmillan Reference USA).

—The World of Thrush Green. 1989. (Illus.). 208p. 24.95 o.p. (*0-395-50228-4*) Houghton Mifflin Co.

—The World of Thrush Green. l.t. ed. 1992. (Magna Large Print Ser.). 350p. o.p. (*0-7505-0179-0*) Magna Large Print Bks. GBR. *Dist:* Ulverscroft Large Print Canada, Ltd.

—The Year at Thrush Green. 1996. 272p. 21.95 o.p. (*0-395-79570-2*) Houghton Mifflin Co.

—The Year at Thrush Green: A Thrush Green Chronicle. 1998. 31p. audio 29.95 (*0-7540-7516-8*) BBC Audiobooks America.

Read, Miss & Goodall, J. S. Winter in Thrush Green. 1999. (J). 21.95 (*0-8488-1456-8*) Amereon, Ltd.

Read, Miss & Watford, Gwen. The School at Thrush Green. unabr. ed. 1989. (Thrush Green Chronicles Ser.). audio 54.95 (*0-7451-6222-3*, CAB 363) BBC Audiobooks America.

**TIMBERDALE RETIREMENT CENTER (OKLA.: IMAGINARY PLACE)—FICTION**

Miles, John. A Most Deadly Retirement. 1997. per. (*0-373-26252-3*, 1-26252-6, Worldwide Library) Harlequin Enterprises, Ltd.

—A Most Deadly Retirement: A Laura Michaels Mystery. 1995. 246p. 22.95 (*0-8027-3258-5*) Walker & Co.

—Murder in Retirement. 1997. (WWL Mystery Ser.: No. 243). per. (*0-373-26243-4*, 1-26243-5, Worldwide Library) Harlequin Enterprises, Ltd.

—Murder in Retirement: A Laura Michaels Mystery. 1994. 246p. 19.95 (*0-8027-3246-1*) Walker & Co.

—A Permanent Retirement. 1997. (Laura Michaels Mystery Ser.). 256p. per. (*0-373-26228-0*, 1-26228-6, Worldwide Library) Harlequin Enterprises, Ltd.

—A Permanent Retirement. 1992. 230p. 19.95 (*0-8027-1243-6*) Walker & Co.

**TINKER'S COVE (ME.: IMAGINARY PLACE)—FICTION**

Meier, Leslie. Back to School Murder: A Lucy Stone Mystery. (Lucy Stone Mysteries Ser.). 1998. 272p. mass mkt. 5.99 (*1-57566-330-9*); 1997. 256p. 18.95 o.s.i (*1-57566-216-7*) Kensington Publishing Corp.

—Christmas Cookie Murder, Vol. 1. 1999. (Lucy Stone Mysteries Ser.). 256p. (J). pap. 20.00 o.s.i (*1-57566-476-3*) Kensington Publishing Corp.

—Mail-Order Murder. 1999. pap. 5.95 (*0-14-015832-4*, Viking) Viking Penguin.

—Mail-Order Murder: A Christmas Mystery. 1991. 192p. 18.95 o.p. (*0-670-84111-0*, Viking) Viking Penguin.

—Mail Order Murders. 1993. 256p. mass mkt. 4.99 o.s.i (*0-440-21452-1*) Dell Publishing.

—Mistletoe Murder. 1998. Orig. Title: Mail-Order Murder. 224p. mass mkt. 6.50 (*0-7582-0337-3*); mass mkt. 5.99 o.s.i (*1-57566-370-8*, Kensington Bks.) Kensington Publishing Corp.

—Tippy Toe Murder. (Lucy Stone Mysteries Ser.). 1999. 352p. mass mkt. 5.99 (*1-57566-392-9*); 1996. 256p. mass mkt. 4.99 o.s.i (*1-57566-099-7*) Kensington Publishing Corp.

—Tippy Toe Murder. 1994. 240p. 18.95 o.p. (*0-670-84791-7*, Viking) Viking Penguin.

—Trick or Treat Murder. (Lucy Stone Mysteries Ser.). 256p. 1997. mass mkt. 5.99 (*1-57566-219-1*); 1996. 18.95 o.s.i (*1-57566-093-8*, Kensington Bks.) Kensington Publishing Corp.

—Valentine Murder. (Lucy Stone Mysteries Ser.). 2000. 272p. mass mkt. 5.99 (*1-57566-499-2*); 1999. 248p. 20.00 o.s.i (*1-57566-390-2*) Kensington Publishing Corp.

**TIR-NAN-OG (IMAGINARY PLACE)—FICTION**

Deitz, Tom. Darkthunder's Way. 1989. pap. 3.95 (*0-380-75508-4*, Avon Bks.) Morrow/Avon.

—Dreamseeker's Road. 2000. 20.00 (*0-380-97254-9*); 1996. 368p. mass mkt. 5.99 (*0-380-77484-4*, Avon Bks.); 1995. 356p. 20.00 o.p. (*0-688-14155-2*, Morrow, William & Co.) Morrow/Avon.

—Fireshaper's Doom. 1987. 320p. pap. 3.95 (*0-380-75329-4*, Avon Bks.) Morrow/Avon.

—Ghostcountry's Wrath. 1995. 400p. (Orig.). mass mkt. 5.50 o.p. (*0-380-76838-0*, Avon Bks.) Morrow/Avon.

—Landslayer's Law. 1997. 304p. mass mkt. 5.99 (*0-380-78649-4*, Avon Bks.) Morrow/Avon.

—Stoneskin's Revenge. 1991. 320p. pap. 3.95 (*0-380-76063-0*, Avon Bks.) Morrow/Avon.

—Sunshaker's War. 1990. 368p. mass mkt. 3.95 (*0-380-76062-2*, Avon Bks.) Morrow/Avon.

—Warstalker's Track. 1999. 384p. mass mkt. 6.50 o.s.i (*0-380-78650-8*, Eos) Morrow/Avon.

—Windmaster's Bane. 1986. (Orig.). pap. 4.99 (*0-380-75029-5*, Avon Bks.) Morrow/Avon.

**TOKYO (JAPAN)—FICTION**

Adamson, Isaac. Dreaming Pachinko. 2003. 368p. pap. 12.95 (*0-06-051623-2*, Perennial) HarperTrade.

—Tokyo Suckerpunch. 2000. 336p. pap. 13.00 (*0-380-81291-6*, Perennial) HarperTrade.

Blensdorf, Jan. My Name Is Sei Shonagon. 2003. 248p. 19.95 (*1-58567-443-5*) Overlook Pr., The.

Castro, Brian. Stepper. 1997. (*0-09-183502-X*) Trafalgar Square.

Furutani, Dale. Kill the Shogun. 2000. (Samurai Mysteries Ser.). 240p. 23.00 o.s.i (*0-688-15819-6*, Morrow, William & Co.) Morrow/Avon.

—Kill the Shogun: A Samurai Mystery. l.t. ed. 2001. (Thorndike Mystery Ser.). 327p. 27.95 (*0-7862-3190-4*) Thorndike Pr.

Gallagher, Fred. Megatokyo, Vol. 2. 2003. 140p. 9.95 (*1-929090-48-X*) International Comics & Entertainment L.L.C.

Gallagher, Fred & Caston, Rodney. Megatokyo, Vol. 1. 2003. (Illus.). 144p. pap. 9.95 (*1-929090-30-7*) International Comics & Entertainment L.L.C.

Gibson, William. Idoru. 2003. 320p. pap. 13.95 (*0-425-19045-5*) Berkley Publishing Group.

Hamill, Pete. Tokyo Sketches. Shaw, S., ed. 1995. 168p. pap. 10.00 (*4-7700-1950-5*) Kodansha America, Inc.

—Tokyo Sketches. 1993. 224p. 20.00 o.s.i (*4-7700-1697-2*) Kodansha America, Inc.

Haylock, John. Uneasy Relations. 1993. 223p. 30.00 (*0-7206-0880-5*) Owen, Peter Ltd. GBR. *Dist:* Dufour Editions, Inc.

Highbridge, Dianne. In the Empire of Dreams. 2000. 248p. pap. 12.00 (*1-56947-190-8*); 1999. 288p. 24.00 (*1-56947-146-0*) Soho Pr., Inc.

Hill, Tobias. The Love of Stones. 2001. 400p. pap. (*0-571-19454-0*) Faber & Faber, Inc.

—The Love of Stones. 2002. 416p. 25.00 (*0-312-28773-9*) Picador.

—The Love of Stones: A Novel. 2003. 400p. pap. 14.00 (*0-312-31131-1*) Picador.

Jones, Susanna. The Earthquake Bird. 2001. 224p. 22.45 o.p. (*0-89296-742-0*) Mysterious Pr.

—The Earthquake Bird. l.t. ed. 2002. 236p. 28.95 (*0-7862-4136-5*) Thorndike Pr.

—The Earthquake Bird. 2003. 224p. pap. 12.95 (*0-446-67975-5*, Mysterious Pr. Paperback Bks.) Warner Bks., Inc.

Kramer, Gavin. Shopping. 215p. 1999. pap. text (*1-85702-958-5*); 1998. (*1-85702-807-4*) Fourth Estate, Ltd. GBR. *Dist:* Trafalgar Square.

—Shopping. 2000. 215p. 22.00 (*1-56947-189-4*); 2001. 224p. reprint ed. pap. 13.00 (*1-56947-229-7*) Soho Pr., Inc.

Massey, Sujata. The Floating Girl. 2000. 304p. 24.00 (*0-06-019229-1*) HarperCollins Pubs.

—The Floating Girl. 2001. 384p. mass mkt. 6.99 (*0-06-109735-7*, Avon Bks.) Morrow/Avon.

—The Flower Master. 1999. 304p. 24.00 (*0-06-019228-3*) HarperCollins Pubs.

—The Flower Master. 2000. 400p. mass mkt. 6.99 (*0-06-109734-9*, HarperTorch) Morrow/Avon.

—The Flower Master. 2000. 13.04 (*0-606-21840-8*) Turtleback Bks.

—The Salaryman's Wife. 1997. 432p. mass mkt. 7.50 (*0-06-104443-1*, HarperTorch) Morrow/Avon.

—Salarymans Wife Arc. 2000. 368p. pap. 5.99 (*0-06-104384-2*) HarperCollins Pubs.

—Zen Attitude. 1998. 320p. mass mkt. 6.99 (*0-06-104444-X*, HarperTorch) Morrow/Avon.

Meigs, Henry. Gate of the Tigers. 1992. 416p. 21.00 o.p. (*0-670-83620-6*, Viking) Viking Penguin.

Mitchell, David. Number 9 Dream. 2001. E-Book 19.95 (*1-58836-215-9*) Random Hse., Inc.

—Number 9 Dream: A Novel. 2003. 416p. pap. 13.95 (*0-8129-6692-9*) Random House Adult Trade Publishing Group.

Mori Ogai. The Wild Goose (Gan) 1995. (Michigan Monograph Series in Japanese Studies: No. 14). 166p. 28.95 (*0-939512-70-X*) Univ. of Michigan, Ctr. for Japanese Studies.

—The Wild Goose (Gan) Watson, Burton, tr. 1995. (Michigan Monograph Series in Japanese Studies: No. 14). 166p. pap. 14.95 (*0-939512-71-8*) Univ. of Michigan, Ctr. for Japanese Studies.

Murakami, Haruki. The Hard-Boiled Wonderland & the End of the World. Birnbaum, Alfred T., tr. from JPN. 1993. 416p. pap. 14.00 (*0-679-74346-4*, Vintage) Knopf Publishing Group.

—The Hard-Boiled Wonderland & the End of the World. Birnbaum, Alfred T., tr. from JPN. 1991. 416p. 21.95 o.s.i (*4-7700-1544-5*) Kodansha America, Inc.

Murakami, Ryu. Coin Locker Babies. Snyder, Stephen, tr. from JPN. 1995. 400p. 23.00 (*4-7700-1590-9*) Kodansha America, Inc.

—Coin Locker Babies. Snyder, Stephen, tr. 1998. 400p. pap. 13.00 (*4-7700-2308-1*) Kodansha International JPN. *Dist:* Kodansha America, Inc.

—Coin Locker Babies. 2002. 400p. reprint ed. pap. 18.00 (*4-7700-2896-2*) Kodansha International JPN. *Dist:* Kodansha America, Inc.

Namban, Akahige. Tokyo Story. 2001. 224p. mass mkt. 7.95 (*1-56201-266-5*, Blue Moon Bks.) Avalon Publishing Group.

Oe, Kenzaburo. Rouse up O Young Men of the New Age! 2003. pap. 13.00 (*0-8021-3968-X*) Grove/Atlantic, Inc.

Shannon, William. One Summer in Tokyo. 2000. 332p. E-Book 8.00 (*0-7388-8756-0*) Xlibris Corp.

Shimada, Masahiko. Dream Messenger. Luke, Elmer, ed. Gabriel, Philip, tr. from JPN. 1992. 304p. 22.00 (*4-7700-1535-6*) Kodansha America, Inc.

—Dream Messenger. 1994. pap. (*0-446-60062-8*); 293p. pap. 10.99 o.s.i (*0-446-67010-3*) Warner Bks., Inc.

Smith, Martin Cruz. December 6: A Novel. 2003. 558p. pap. 13.95 (*1-4104-0170-7*, Wheeler Publishing, Inc.) Gale Group.

—December 6: A Novel. 2003. E-Book 26.00 (*0-7432-5006-0*); 2002. (Illus.). 352p. 26.00 (*0-684-87253-6*); 2002. (Illus.). 352p. 26.00 (*0-7432-4352-8*); 2002. 352p. 26.00 (*0-7432-4284-X*) Simon & Schuster. (Simon & Schuster).

—December 6: A Novel. l.t. ed. 2003. (Basic Ser.). 632p. 32.95 (*0-7862-4683-9*) Thorndike Pr.

Takagi, Akimitsu. The Informer. 2001. 256p. pap. 13.00 (*1-56947-243-2*) Soho Pr., Inc.

—The Informer. Mizuguchi, Sadako, tr. from JPN. 1999. 272p. 22.00 (*1-56947-155-X*) Soho Pr., Inc.

Tasker, Peter. Dragon Dance. 2003. 272p. 22.95 (*4-7700-2948-9*) Kodansha International JPN. *Dist:* Kodansha America, Inc.

—Samurai Boogie. 2002. 394p. mass mkt. 13.00 (*0-7528-3676-5*) Orion Publishing Group, Ltd. GBR. *Dist:* Trafalgar Square.

Van Lustbader, Eric. The Kaisho. abr. ed. 1993. audio 16.95 o.p. (*1-55800-889-6*) NewStar Media, Inc.

—The Kaisho. 1998. 3.99 (*0-671-02329-2*, Pocket) Simon & Schuster.

—The Kaisho. Zion, Claire, ed. 1993. 496p. 22.00 (*0-671-86806-3*, Atria); 1994. 592p. reprint ed. mass mkt. 6.99 (*0-671-86807-1*, Pocket Star) Simon & Schuster.

Wolbers, Marian. Rider. 1996. 192p. 21.95 o.p. (*0-312-14718-X*) St. Martin's Pr.

**TOMBSTONE (ARIZ.)—FICTION**

Berrington, Patricia. The Famous Rose Callahan. 1997. 485p. lthr. 27.95 (*0-9658379-0-4*) Silver Rose Productions.

Boxleitner, Bruce. Frontier Earth. 2001. (Babylon 5 Ser.). 336p. reprint ed. mass mkt. 6.99 o.s.i (*0-441-00794-5*) Ace Bks.

—Frontier Earth: A Novel. 1999. 336p. 21.95 o.s.i (*0-441-00589-6*) Ace Bks.

—Frontier Earth: Searcher. 2001. 336p. 23.95 o.s.i (*0-441-00799-6*) Ace Bks.

Estleman, Loren D. Bloody Season. Set. unabr. ed. 1999. audio 54.95 (*0-7927-2304-X*, CSL193, Chivers Sound Library) BBC Audiobooks America.

—Bloody Season. 1989. mass mkt. 3.95 o.s.i (*0-553-27494-5*) Bantam Bks.

—Bloody Season. 1999. 256p. mass mkt. 5.99 o.s.i (*0-515-12531-8*, Jove) Berkley Publishing Group.

Nye, Nelson C. Gunfight at the O. K. Corral. 1982. 244p. pap. 1.95 o.p. (*0-8439-1093-3*) Dorchester Publishing Co., Inc.

—The Seven Six-Gunners. 1987. 144p. 2.50 o.s.i (*0-441-75972-6*, Diamond Bks.) Berkley Publishing Group.

—The Seven Six-Gunners. l.t. ed. 2000. (Paperback Ser.). 199p. 23.95 (*0-7838-9179-2*) Thorndike Pr.

West, Paul. O. K. The Corral, the Earps & Doc Holliday. 2000. 304p. 24.00 (*0-684-84865-1*, Scribner) Simon & Schuster.

**TORONTO (ONT.)—FICTION**

Ali, Ansara. The Sacred Adventures of a Taxi Driver. rev. ed. 1993. (Illus.). 544p. reprint ed. 27.95 o.s.i (*0-9636170-1-X*); pap. 16.95 (*0-9636170-0-1*) Royal Rags Publishing.

Alibrandi, Tom. Killshot. 1979. pap. 2.25 o.p. (*0-523-40375-5*, Pinnacle Bks.) Kensington Publishing Corp.

Armstrong, Kelley. Bitten. unabr. ed. 2001. audio 34.95 (*1-56740-383-2*, 2182, Brilliance Audio Unabridged) Brilliance Audio.

—Bitten. 2002. 384p. pap. 13.00 (*0-452-28348-5*, Plume) Dutton/Plume.

—Bitten. 2001. 400p. 24.95 o.s.i (*0-670-89471-0*, Viking) Viking Penguin.

Atwood, Margaret. Cat's Eye. 1995. 480p. pap. 10.95 o.s.i (*0-553-37790-6*); 1989. 464p. mass mkt. 6.50 o.s.i (*0-553-28247-6*); 1989. 464p. mass mkt. 8.99 o.s.i (*0-7704-2334-5*) Bantam Bks.

—Cat's Eye. 1998. 480p. pap. 13.95 (*0-385-49102-6*); 1989. 312p. 18.95 o.s.i (*0-385-26007-5*) Doubleday Publishing.

—Cat's Eye. l.t. ed. 1990. (Large Print Bks.). 573p. lib. bdg. 20.95 o.p. (*0-8161-4890-2*, Macmillan Reference USA) Gale Group.

—Cat's Eye. 1996. 19.00 (*0-606-00533-1*) Turtleback Bks.

Aubert, Rosemary. The Feast of Stephen. 2001. 272p. mass mkt. 6.99 o.s.i (*0-425-17799-8*, Prime Crime) Berkley Publishing Group.

—The Feast of Stephen: An Ellis Portal Mystery. 1999. (Ellis Portal Mystery Ser.). 224p. 22.95 (*1-882593-27-8*) Bridge Works Publishing Co., Inc.

—The Ferryman Will Be There. 2002. 272p. reprint ed. mass mkt. 6.99 o.s.i (*0-425-18402-1*) Berkley Publishing Group.

—The Ferryman Will Be There: An Ellis Portal Mystery. 2001. (Ellis Portal Mystery Ser.: Vol. 3). 264p. 22.95 (*1-882593-44-8*) Bridge Works Publishing Co., Inc.

—Free Reign. 1998. 304p. mass mkt. 6.99 o.s.i (*0-425-16427-6*) Berkley Publishing Group.

—Free Reign: A Suspense Novel. 1997. (Ellis Portal Mystery Ser.). 240p. 21.95 o.s.i (*1-882593-18-9*) Bridge Works Publishing Co., Inc.

Baker, Nancy. The Night Inside. 1994. 320p. 20.00 o.p. (*0-449-90904-2*, Fawcett) Ballantine Bks.

Barnao, Jack. Hammerlocke. 1987. 256p. 3.50 o.s.i (*0-441-31609-3*, Diamond Bks.) Berkley Publishing Group.

—Hammerlocke. 1986. 240p. 13.95 o.s.i (*0-684-18683-7*, Macmillan Reference USA) Gale Group.

—Lockestep. 1989. 3.50 (*1-55773-159-4*, Diamond Bks.) Berkley Publishing Group.

—Lockestep. 1988. (John Locke Mystery Ser.). 240p. 15.95 o.s.i (*0-684-18782-5*, Macmillan Reference USA) Gale Group.

—Lockestep. 186p. 2002. pap. 6.99 (*0-7592-1432-8*); 2002. E-Book 6.99 (*0-7592-1430-1*); 2002. E-Book 6.99 (*0-7592-1429-8*); 2001. E-Book 6.99 (*0-7592-1428-X*) ereads.com.

—Timelocke: A John Locke Mystery. 1991. 256p. 18.95 o.s.i (*0-684-19298-5*, Scribner) Simon & Schuster.

Bell, Mary S. Sonata for Mind & Heart. 1992. 224p. (YA). (gr. 7 up). lib. bdg. 14.95 o.s.i (*0-689-31734-4*, Atheneum) Simon & Schuster Children's Publishing.

Bowen, Gail. Striking Out. 1996. 256p. mass mkt. 5.99 (*0-7710-3415-6*) McClelland & Stewart/Tundra Bks.

Bush, Catherine. The Rules of Engagement. 2002. pap. 24.00 (*0-374-52870-5*); 2000. 302p. 24.00 o.s.i (*0-374-25280-7*) Farrar, Straus & Giroux.

Carpenter, J. D. The Devil in Me: A Campbell Young Mystery. 2002. 320p. mass mkt. (*0-7710-1923-8*) McClelland & Stewart/Tundra Bks.

Clarke, Austin. Nine Men Who Laughed. 1987. 240p. pap. 6.95 o.p. (*0-14-008560-2*, Penguin Bks.) Viking Penguin.

Denoon, Anne. Back Flip: A Novel. 2002. (Illus.). 336p. pap. 24.95 (*0-88984-238-8*) Porcupine's Quill, Inc. CAN. *Dist:* Univ. of Toronto Pr.

Deverell, William. Street Legal: The Betrayal. 1996. 344p. 22.95 o.p. (*0-7710-2669-2*) McClelland & Stewart/Tundra Bks.

Eddie, David. Chump Change: A Novel. 1999. 230p. 13.00 (*1-57322-736-6*, Riverhead Trade (Paperbacks)) Berkley Publishing Group.

Findley, Timothy. Headhunter. 1994. 23.00 o.s.i (*0-517-59827-2*) Crown Publishing Group.

Foster, Marion. Legal Tender. 1992. 240p. (Orig.). pap. 9.95 (*1-56341-010-9*); pap. text 20.95 (*1-56341-011-7*) Firebrand Bks.

Gibson, Graeme. Gentleman Death. 1995. 256p. pap. 12.95 (*0-7710-3312-5*) McClelland & Stewart/Tundra Bks.

Gordon, Alison. The Dead Pull Hitter. 1991. 256p. mass mkt. 3.99 o.p. (*0-451-40240-5*, Onyx) NAL.

—The Dead Pull Hitter. 1989. 224p. 15.95 o.p. (*0-312-03319-2*, Saint Martin's Minotaur) St. Martin's Pr.

—The Dead Pull Hitter: A Kate Henry Mystery. 1996. 224p. mass mkt. 6.99 (*0-7710-3420-2*) McClelland & Stewart/Tundra Bks.

—Prairie Hardball. 1998. (Kate Henry Mysteries Ser.: Bk. 5). 288p. mass mkt. 6.95 (*0-7710-3413-X*) McClelland & Stewart/Tundra Bks.

—Prairie Hardball: A Kate Henry Mystery. 1998. (Kate Henry Mystery Ser.). 288p. 20.95 o.p. (*0-7710-3412-1*) McClelland & Stewart/Tundra Bks.

—Safe at Home. 1991. 17.95 o.p. (*0-312-05959-0*, Saint Martin's Minotaur) St. Martin's Pr.

—Safe at Home: A Kate Henry Mystery. 1996. 248p. mass mkt. 5.95 (*0-7710-3417-2*) McClelland & Stewart/Tundra Bks.

—Striking Out: A Kate Henry Mystery. 1995. 240p. 19.95 o.p. (*0-7710-3423-7*) McClelland & Stewart/Tundra Bks.

Green, Terence M. Blue Limbo. 1998. (Blue Limbo Ser.: Vol. 1). 288p. mass mkt. 5.99 (*0-8125-7134-7*); 1996. 253p. 22.95 o.p. (*0-312-86282-2*) Doherty, Tom Assocs., LLC. (Tor Bks.).

—Blue Limbo. 1999. 5.99 (*0-312-87119-8*) St. Martin's Pr.

—A Witness to Life. (Illus.). 240p. 2000. pap. 12.95 (*0-312-87300-X*); 1999. 20.95 (*0-312-86672-0*) Doherty, Tom Assocs., LLC. (Forge Bks.).

Harvor, Elisabeth. Excessive Joy Injures the Heart. 2002. 336p. 25.00 (*0-15-100894-9*) Harcourt Trade Pubs.

—Excessive Joy Injures the Heart. 2000. 352p. (*0-7710-3963-8*) McClelland & Stewart.

Humphreys, Helen. Leaving Earth. 1998. 224p. 22.00 o.s.i (*0-8050-5957-1*, Metropolitan Bks.) Holt, Henry & Co.

—Leaving Earth. 2000. 256p. pap. 13.00 (*0-312-25500-4*) Picador.

Jennings, Maureen. Except the Dying. 1997. 288p. 23.95 (*0-312-16829-2*, 737113, Saint Martin's Minotaur) St. Martin's Pr.

—Except the Dying: A Mystery. 1999. 336p. mass mkt. 5.99 (*0-06-109739-X*, HarperTorch) Morrow/Avon.

—Poor Tom Is Cold. E-Book 23.95 (*1-58945-671-8*) Adobe Systems, Inc.

—Poor Tom Is Cold. E-Book 23.95 (*0-312-70097-0*); 2001. vii, 278p. 23.95 (*0-312-26892-0*, Saint Martin's Minotaur) St. Martin's Pr.

—Under the Dragon's Tail. 1999. 304p. mass mkt. 5.99 (*0-06-109740-3*, HarperTorch) Morrow/Avon.

—Under the Dragon's Tail. 1998. 256p. 21.95 o.p. (*0-312-19348-3*, Saint Martin's Minotaur) St. Martin's Pr.

Kosar, Richelle. The Drum King. 1998. 416p. pap. 15.95 (*0-88801-220-9*) Turnstone Pr. CAN. *Dist:* General Distribution Services, Inc.

Leonard, Elmore. Killshot. l.t. ed. 1990. (General Ser.). 432p. reprint ed. lib. bdg. 20.95 o.p. (*0-8161-4865-1*, Macmillan Reference USA) Gale Group.

—Killshot. 1999. 288p. pap. 12.00 (*0-688-16638-5*, Quill) HarperTrade.

—Killshot. 2003. 416p. mass mkt. 7.50 (*0-06-051224-5*, HarperTorch); 1989. 288p. 18.95 o.p. (*1-55710-041-1*, Morrow, William & Co.) Morrow/Avon.

—Killshot. abr. ed. 1999. audio 7.99 (*0-7871-2047-2*); 1993. audio 14.95 o.p. (*1-55800-156-5*, 40640, Dove Audio); Set. 1998. audio 18.00 (*0-7871-1740-4*, Dove Audio) NewStar Media, Inc.

—Killshot. 1994. (Super Sound Buy, Dove Ser.). 8.99 o.p. (*0-7871-0112-5*) Penguin Group (USA) Inc.

—Killshot. 1991. 4.99 o.p. (*0-517-07549-0*) Random Hse. Value Publishing.

—Killshot. 1990. 352p. reprint ed. mass mkt. 5.95 (*0-446-35041-9*) Warner Bks., Inc.

MacKay, Scott. Fall Guy: A Barry Gilbert Mystery. 2001. 384p. 24.95 (*0-312-28155-2*, Saint Martin's Minotaur) St. Martin's Pr.

—Old Scores. 2003. 320p. 24.95 (*0-312-30841-8*, Saint Martin's Minotaur) St. Martin's Pr.

Mahoney, Dan. The Two Chinatowns. 2001. E-Book 24.95 (*1-59061-043-1*) Adobe Systems, Inc.

—The Two Chinatowns. 2002. 432p. mass mkt. 6.99 (*0-312-98361-1*, St. Martin's Paperbacks); 2001. 342p. 24.95 (*0-312-26134-9*) St. Martin's Pr.

Millar, Margaret. The Iron Gates. l.t. ed. 1999. (Mystery Ser.). 320p. 27.95 (*0-7862-1779-0*) Thorndike Pr.

Moritsugu, Kim. Old Flames. 1999. 212p. 17.95 (*0-88984-203-5*) Porcupine's Quill, Inc. CAN. *Dist:* Univ. of Toronto Pr.

Ondaatje, Michael. In the Skin of a Lion: A Novel. 1987. 16.95 o.s.i (*0-394-56363-8*) Knopf, Alfred A. Inc.

—In the Skin of a Lion: A Novel. 1997. 256p. pap. 12.00 (*0-679-77266-9*) McKay, David Co., Inc.

—In the Skin of a Lion: A Novel. abr. ed. 1998. audio 15.00 (*0-333-72603-0*) Ulverscroft Audio (U.S.A.).

—In the Skin of a Lion: A Novel. 1988. 256p. pap. 10.95 o.p. (*0-14-011309-6*, Penguin Bks.) Viking Penguin.

—In the Skin of a Lion & Running in the Family. unabr. ed. 1993. audio 13.95 (*1-55644-385-4*, 13021) American Audio Prose Library, Inc.

Persaud, S. Canada Geese & Apple Chutney. 1998. 159p. pap. (*0-920661-72-6*) TSAR Pubns.

Redhill, Michael. Martin Sloane. 2001. 288p. pap. (*0-385-25987-5*, Anchor Canada) Doubleday Canada, Ltd. CAN. *Dist:* Random Hse., Inc.

—Martin Sloane. 2002. 288p. pap. 13.95 (*0-316-73936-7*, Back Bay) Little Brown & Co.

Ricci, Nino. Where She Has Gone. 336p. 1999. pap. 13.00 o.s.i (*0-312-20681-X*); 1998. 25.00 o.p. (*0-312-18700-9*) Picador.

Sakamoto, Kerri. The Electrical Field. 2000. 320p. pap. text 13.00 (*0-393-32048-0*, Norton Paperbacks); 1999. 305p. 23.95 o.p. (*0-393-04692-3*) Norton, W. W. & Co., Inc.

Sale, Medora. Murder in a Good Cause. 1990. 224p. 18.95 o.s.i (*0-684-19216-0*) Macmillan Information.

—Murder in Focus. 1989. 288p. 17.95 o.s.i (*0-684-19082-6*, Macmillan Reference USA) Gale Group.

—Murder on the Run. unabr. ed. 1998. (Inspector John Sanders Mystery Ser.). audio 39.95 (*1-55686-825-1*) Books in Motion.

—Pursued by Shadows. 1992. (Inspector John Sanders Mystery Ser.). 256p. text 20.00 (*0-684-19505-4*, Scribner) Simon & Schuster.

—Shortcut to Santa Fe. 1994. 256p. 20.00 (*0-684-19680-8*, Scribner) Simon & Schuster.

—Sleep of the Innocent. unabr. ed. 1999. (Inspector John Sanders Mystery Ser.). audio 49.95 (*1-55686-906-1*) Books in Motion.

—Sleep of the Innocent. 1991. 256p. 18.95 o.s.i (*0-684-19305-1*, Scribner) Simon & Schuster.

Sawyer, Robert J. Calculating God. 2001. 352p. mass mkt. 6.99 (*0-8125-8035-4*); 2000. 320p. reprint ed. 23.95 (*0-312-86713-1*, NHC 0160) Doherty, Tom Assocs., LLC. (Tor Bks.).

—Factoring Humanity. 352p. 1999. pap. 6.99 (*0-8125-7129-0*); 1998. 23.95 o.p. (*0-312-86458-2*) Doherty, Tom Assocs., LLC. (Tor Bks.).

—Factoring Humanity. 1999. (Illus.). (J). 12.04 (*0-606-18640-9*) Turtleback Bks.

Smith, Brad. One-Eyed Jacks. 2001. 272p. (gr. 9). pap. 13.95 (*0-385-25921-2*) Doubleday Publishing.

Warsh, Sylvia Maultash. To Die in Spring. 2001. 255p. pap. 14.95 (*0-9705049-3-4*) Avocet Pr., Inc.

—To Die in Spring. 2000. 170p. pap. text 9.99 (*0-88882-216-2*) Hounslow Pr. CAN. *Dist:* Lone Pine Publishing.

Wilson, Doug. Labour of Love. 1994. 208p. pap. 8.95 o.p. (*0-312-11408-7*, Saint Martin's Griffin); 1993. 224p. 18.95 o.p. (*0-312-09839-1*) St. Martin's Pr.

Wright, Eric. A Body Surrounded by Water. (Inspector Charlie Salter Mystery Ser.). 1987. 208p. 14.95 o.s.i (*0-684-18873-2*); 1992. 264p. pap. 14.95 o.p. (*0-8161-5319-1*) Gale Group. (Macmillan Reference USA).

—A Body Surrounded by Water. 1989. mass mkt. 3.95 o.p. (*0-451-16385-0*, Signet Bks.) NAL.

—Death by Degrees. 1995. 192p. reprint ed. mass mkt. 6.99 o.s.i (*0-7704-2601-8*) Bantam Bks.

—Death by Degrees. 1993. 192p. o.s.i (*0-385-25436-9*) Doubleday Canada, Ltd. CAN. *Dist:* Random Hse., Inc.

—Death by Degrees. 1993. 256p. 24.95 o.p. (*0-385-25433-4*) Doubleday Publishing.

—Death by Degrees. 1993. (Inspector Charlie Salter Mystery Ser.). 224p. 20.00 (*0-684-19648-4*, Macmillan Reference USA) Gale Group.

—Death by Degrees. 1995. (WWL Mystery Ser.). 251p. mass mkt. (*0-373-26169-1*, 1-26169-2, Harlequin Bks.) Harlequin Enterprises, Ltd.

—Death of a Sunday Writer. 1996. 224p. text 21.00 (*0-88150-377-0*) Norton, W. W. & Co., Inc.

—Death on the Rocks: A Lucy Trimble Mystery. 1999. 240p. 15.95 (*0-312-20525-2*, Saint Martin's Minotaur) St. Martin's Pr.

—Death on the Rocks: A Lucy Trimble Mystery. l.t. ed. 1999. (Mystery Ser.). 343p. 27.95 (*0-7862-2205-0*) Thorndike Pr.

—Final Cut: An Inspector Charlie Salter Novel. 1991. 256p. 22.50 o.s.i (*0-385-25289-7*) Doubleday Publishing.

—Final Cut: An Inspector Charlie Salter Novel. 1991. 256p. 18.95 o.s.i (*0-684-19300-0*, Macmillan Reference USA) Gale Group.

—Final Cut: An Inspector Charlie Salter Novel. 1992. (Inspector Charlie Salter Mystery Ser.). reprint ed. per. (*0-373-26107-1*, Harlequin Bks.) Harlequin Enterprises, Ltd.

—A Fine Italian Hand. l.t. ed. 1993. 21.95 o.p. (*0-7927-1564-0*); pap. 19.95 o.p. (*0-7927-1563-2*) BBC Audiobooks America.

—A Fine Italian Hand. 1993. 240p. mass mkt. 6.99 o.s.i (*0-7704-2569-0*) Bantam Bks.

—A Fine Italian Hand. 1992. 192p. 23.50 o.s.i (*0-385-25371-0*) Doubleday Publishing.

—A Fine Italian Hand. 1992. (Inspector Charlie Salter Mystery Ser.). 192p. text 20.00 (*0-684-19504-6*, Macmillan Reference USA) Gale Group.

—A Fine Italian Hand. 1994. mass mkt. (*0-373-26143-8*, Harlequin Bks.) Harlequin Enterprises, Ltd.

—The Kidnapping of Rosie Dawn: A Joe Barley Mystery. 2000. 213p. pap. 12.95 (*1-880284-40-5*, Perseverance Pr.) Daniel, John & Co., Pubs.

—The Kidnapping of Rosie Dawn: A Joe Barley Mystery. l.t. ed. 2001. 306p. 27.95 (*0-7862-3478-4*); 296p. (*0-7540-4673-7*); 296p. (*0-7540-4674-5*) Thorndike Pr.

—The Last Hand: Charlie Salter Turns in His Badge. 2002. 256p. 23.95 (*0-312-28330-X*, Saint Martin's Minotaur) St. Martin's Pr.

—The Man Who Changed His Name. l.t. ed. 1987. (Nightingale Ser.). 288p. 11.95 o.p. (*0-8161-4285-8*, Macmillan Reference USA) Gale Group.

—The Man Who Changed His Name. 1987. 224p. mass mkt. 3.50 o.p. (*0-451-14930-0*, Signet Bks.) NAL.

—The Night the Gods Smiled. 1983. 192p. 12.95 o.s.i (*0-684-18009-X*, Macmillan Reference USA) Gale Group.

—The Night the Gods Smiled. 1985. mass mkt. 2.95 o.p. (*0-451-13409-5*, Signet Bks.) NAL.

—A Question of Murder. l.t. ed. 1992. 330p. pap. 14.95 o.p. (*0-8161-5372-8*, Macmillan Reference USA) Gale Group.

—A Question of Murder. 1989. mass mkt. (*0-373-26039-3*, Harlequin Bks.) Harlequin Enterprises, Ltd.

—A Question of Murder. 1988. 208p. 15.95 o.s.i (*0-684-19000-1*, Scribner) Simon & Schuster.

—A Sensitive Case. 1990. 224p. 22.95 o.s.i (*0-385-25250-1*) Doubleday Publishing.

—A Sensitive Case. 1991. (Inspector Charlie Salter Mystery Ser.). 224p. mass mkt. (*0-373-26083-0*, Harlequin Bks.) Harlequin Enterprises, Ltd.

—A Sensitive Case: A Charlie Salter Novel. l.t. ed. 1991. (Magna Large Print Ser.). 284p. *(0-7505-0119-7)* Magna Large Print Bks. GBR. *Dist:* Ulverscroft Large Print Canada, Ltd.

—A Sensitive Case: A Charlie Salter Novel. 1990. 224p. 17.95 o.s.i *(0-684-19132-6,* Scribner) Simon & Schuster.

—Smoke Detector. l.t. ed. 1985. (Nightingale Ser.). 286p. 10.95 o.p. *(0-8161-3900-8,* Macmillan Reference USA) Gale Group.

—Smoke Detector. 1986. mass mkt. 2.95 o.p. *(0-451-14123-7,* Signet Bks.) NAL.

Wynveen, Tim. Balloon. 1999. 344p. pap. *(1-55263-096-X)* Key Porter Bks. CAN. *Dist:* BookWorld Services, Inc.

### TRANTORIAN EMPIRE (IMAGINARY PLACE)—FICTION

Asimov, Isaac. The Currents of Space. 1985. mass mkt. 4.95 o.s.i *(0-345-33544-9,* Del Rey); 1983. mass mkt. 2.95 o.s.i *(0-345-31195-7,* Del Rey); 1983. mass mkt. 2.50 o.s.i *(0-449-20351-4)*; 1981. mass mkt. 2.25 o.s.i *(0-449-23829-6,* Fawcett); 1975. mass mkt. 1.25 o.s.i *(0-449-22495-3)* Ballantine Bks.

—The Currents of Space. 1991. 304p. mass mkt. 5.99 o.s.i *(0-553-29341-9)* Bantam Bks.

—Fundacion. 5th ed. 1998. (Jet de Plaza & Janes Ser.). (SPA.). pap. 9.50 *(84-01-49678-0,* JP9128) Plaza & Janés Editories, S.A. ESP. *Dist:* Lectorum Pubns., Inc.

—Fundacion. 2002. (SPA.). 264p. mass mkt. 6.95 *(1-4000-0082-3)* Random Hse., Inc.

—Fundacion. 1998. (SPA.). 15.55 *(0-606-21870-X)* Turtleback Bks.

—Fundacion e Imperio. 3rd ed. 1998. (Jet de Plaza & Janes Ser.). Orig. Title: Foundation & Empire. (SPA.). 336p. *(84-01-46332-7)* Plaza & Janés Editories, S.A.

—Fundacion e Imperio. 1994. Orig. Title: Foundation & Empire. (SPA.). 256p. 10.50 *(84-01-49652-7)* Plaza & Janés Editories, S.A. ESP. *Dist:* Astran, Inc.

—Pebble in the Sky. 1986. mass mkt. 3.95 o.s.i *(0-345-33563-5)*; 1983. mass mkt. 2.95 o.s.i *(0-345-31196-5,* Del Rey); 1982. mass mkt. 2.95 o.s.i *(0-449-23423-1,* Fawcett); 1975. mass mkt. 1.50 o.s.i *(0-449-22828-2)* Ballantine Bks.

—Pebble in the Sky. 1991. 336p. mass mkt. 5.99 o.s.i *(0-553-29342-7)* Bantam Bks.

—Pebble in the Sky. 1982. 224p. reprint ed. 16.00 *(0-8376-0462-1)* Bentley Pubs.

—The Stars, Like Dust. 1986. mass mkt. 3.95 o.s.i *(0-345-33929-0,* Del Rey); 1983. mass mkt. 2.95 o.s.i *(0-345-31194-9,* Del Rey); 1981. mass mkt. 2.25 o.s.i *(0-449-23595-5,* Fawcett) Ballantine Bks.

—The Stars, Like Dust. 1991. 304p. mass mkt. 4.99 o.s.i *(0-553-29343-5)* Bantam Bks.

### TREASURE ISLAND (IMAGINARY PLACE)—FICTION

Bryan, Francis. The Curse of Treasure Island. l.t. ed. 2002. (Adventure Ser.). 494p. 28.95 *(0-7862-4477-1)* Thorndike Pr.

—The Curse of Treasure Island. 2002. 304p. 24.95 *(0-670-03089-9)* Viking Penguin.

Stevenson, Robert Louis. Treasure Island. 1985. pap. 1.25 o.p. *(0-553-15400-1)* Bantam Bks.

—Treasure Island. 1970. (Illus.). reprint ed. 1.95 o.p. *(0-460-01763-2)* Biblio Distribution.

—Treasure Island. reprint ed. lib. bdg. 48.00 *(0-7426-1049-7)*; 2001. (Illus.). pap. text 28.00 *(0-7426-6049-4)* Classic Bks.

—Treasure Island. 1988. mass mkt. 4.95 *(0-938819-81-X,* Aerie) Doherty, Tom Assocs., LLC.

—Treasure Island. (English As a Second Language Bk.). 1981. pap. text 4.46 net. o.p. *(0-582-52676-0)*; 1991. per. 6.50 *(0-8222-1170-X)* Dramatists Play Service, Inc.

—Treasure Island. 1998. 288p. 50.00 *(0-7486-0837-0)* Edinburgh Univ. Pr. GBR. *Dist:* Columbia Univ. Pr.

—Treasure Island. l.t. ed. 2002. 28.95 *(0-7862-4103-9)* Gale Group.

—Treasure Island. 1997. pap. 12.00 *(0-00-273016-2)* HarperCollins Pubs.

—Treasure Island. Stemach, Jerry, ed. 2000. pap., tchr.'s training gde. ed. 8.00 *(1-58702-550-7)*; 2000. text 65.00 incl. audio, cd-rom *(1-893376-22-2)*; 2000. audio compact disk 200.00 *(1-58702-428-4)*; 2002. (Illus.). text 150.00 *(1-58702-012-2)*; 2000. (Illus.). text 50.00 *(1-58702-430-6)*; 2000. (Illus.). 128p. text 10.00 *(1-893376-03-6)* Johnston, Don Inc.

—Treasure Island. E-Book 2.95 *(1-57799-805-7)* Logos Research Systems, Inc.

—Treasure Island. 2nd rev. ed. 1996. (Longman Fiction Ser.). pap. text 5.90 o.s.i *(0-582-27529-6)* Longman Publishing Group.

—Treasure Island. 1991. 22.50 o.p. *(0-07-158548-6)* McGraw-Hill Cos., The.

—Treasure Island. 1965. mass mkt. 1.50 o.p. *(0-451-51729-6)*; mass mkt. 1.50 o.p. *(0-451-51450-5)*; mass mkt. 1.25 o.p. *(0-451-51139-5)*; mass mkt. 0.95 o.p. *(0-451-50926-9)*; mass mkt. 0.60 o.p. *(0-451-50713-4)*; mass mkt. 0.50 o.p. *(0-451-50272-8)*; mass mkt. 0.75 o.p. *(0-451-50841-6)*; mass mkt. 1.75 o.p. *(0-451-51610-9)* NAL. (Signet Classics).

—Treasure Island. Letley, Emma, ed. & intro. by. 1998. (Oxford World's Classics Ser.). 256p. pap. 7.95 *(0-19-283380-4)* Oxford Univ. Pr., Inc.

—Treasure Island. 2000. (Illustrated Junior Library Ser.). 9.99 o.s.i *(0-448-42447-9,* Grosset & Dunlap) Penguin Putnam Bks. for Young Readers.

—Treasure Island. 2001. (Modern Library Classics). (Illus.). 240p. pap. 5.95 *(0-375-75682-5,* Modern Library) Random House Adult Trade Publishing Group.

—Treasure Island. 1995. (Literary Classics Ser.). 208p. 5.98 o.p. *(1-56138-510-7,* Courage Bks.) Running Pr. Bk. Pubs.

—Treasure Island. Shefter, ed. 1984. 304p. mass mkt. 2.95 o.s.i *(0-671-48932-1,* Pocket) Simon & Schuster.

—Treasure Island. 1974. reprint ed. pap. 0.75 o.s.i *(0-671-46621-6,* Washington Square Pr.) Simon & Schuster.

—Treasure Island. (Ebook Classic Ser.). E-Book 5.00 *(0-7410-0485-2)* SoftBook Pr.

—Treasure Island: Masters of Literature. 1996. (Masters of Literature Ser.). pap. 5.00 *(81-207-1884-4)* Sterling Pubs. Pvt., Ltd. IND. *Dist:* South Asia Bks.

—Treasure Island: With Story of the Treasure of Normon Island. 1986. 5.99 o.s.i *(0-517-41376-0)* Random Hse. Value Publishing.

—Treasure Island: With Story of the Treasure of Normon Island. 1985. 2.98 o.p. *(0-671-07203-X)* Simon & Schuster.

Stevenson, Robert Louis & Katz, Wendy R. Treasure Island. 1998. E-Book 60.00 *(0-585-10287-2)* netLibrary, Inc.

Stevenson, Robert Louis, et al. Treasure Island: With Story of the Treasure of Normon Island. 1998. (Illus.). 190p. pap. 19.95 *(0-926330-01-2)* Mapes Monde Editore.

### TRENTON (N.J.)—FICTION

Evanovich, Janet. Four to Score. abr. ed. audio *(1-55927-963-X)*; 1999. (Stephanie Plum Novel Ser.: No. 4). audio 17.95 *(1-55927-544-8)* Audio Renaissance.

—Four to Score. abr. ed. 2001. audio compact disk 11.99 *(1-57815-544-4,* 1111); audio 7.95 *(1-57815-263-1)* Media Bks., L. L. C.

—Four to Score. (Stephanie Plum Novel Ser.: No. 4). 2000. audio compact disk 89.00 *(0-7887-4749-5,* C1235E7); 1999. audio 66.00 *(0-7887-2593-9,* 95613E7) Recorded Bks., LLC.

—Four to Score. 1999. E-Book 23.95 o.s.i *(0-312-20762-X)*; 1998. (Stephanie Plum Novel Ser.: No. 4). 304p. 24.95 *(0-312-18586-3)*; 1999. (Stephanie Plum Novel Ser.: No. 4). 352p. reprint ed. mass mkt. 7.99 *(0-312-96697-0,* St. Martin's Paperbacks) St. Martin's Pr.

—Four to Score. abr. ed. 1998. (Stephanie Plum Novel Ser.: No. 4). audio 15.00 *(0-333-74772-0)* Ulverscroft Audio (U.S.A.).

—Hard Eight. abr. ed. 2002. (Illus.). audio 17.95 o.s.i *(1-55927-723-8)*; audio 36.95 *(1-55927-725-4)*; audio compact disk 40.00 *(1-55927-724-6)* Audio Renaissance.

—Hard Eight. abr. ed. 2001. (Stephanie Plum Ser.: Vol. 7). audio 19.95 o.p. *(1-58788-531-X,* 2802, Nova Audio Bks.); audio compact disk 27.95 o.p. *(1-58788-532-8,* 2803, CD); audio 69.25 *(1-58788-530-1,* 2801, Unabridged Library Editions); audio 29.95 *(1-58788-529-8,* 2800, Brilliance Audio Unabridged) Brilliance Audio.

—Hard Eight. l.t. ed. 2002. 432p. 25.95 *(0-375-43170-5)* Random Hse., Inc.

—Hard Eight. unabr. ed. 2002. (Stephanie Plum Ser.: Vol. #8). audio 37.95 *(1-4025-2386-6,* RG083); audio compact disk 89.00 *(1-4025-2965-1,* C1854) Recorded Bks., LLC.

—Hard Eight. 2003. 352p. mass mkt. 7.99 *(0-312-98386-7,* St. Martin's Paperbacks); 2003. mass mkt. 7.99 *(0-312-98894-X,* St. Martin's Paperbacks); 2002. 320p. 25.95 *(0-312-26585-9)*; 2002. mass mkt. 7.99 *(0-312-98451-0,* St. Martin's Paperbacks) St. Martin's Pr.

—High Five. abr. ed. audio *(1-55927-964-8)*; 1999. (Stephanie Plum Novel Ser.: No. 5). audio 17.95 *(1-55927-545-6)* Audio Renaissance.

—High Five. abr. ed. 2001. audio *(0-333-76587-7)* Macmillan U.K. GBR. *Dist:* Macmillan Publishing Co., Inc.

—High Five. abr. ed. 2002. audio compact disk 11.99 *(1-57815-545-2)*; 2001. audio 7.95 *(1-57815-264-X)* Media Bks., L. L. C.

—High Five. unabr. ed. (Stephanie Plum Novel Ser.: No. 5). 2000. audio compact disk 75.00 *(0-7887-4200-0,* C1129E7); 1999. audio 60.00 *(0-7887-3464-4,* 95857E7); 1999. audio 58.00 *(0-7887-3664-7)* Recorded Bks., LLC.

—High Five. (Stephanie Plum Novel Ser.: No. 5). 2000. 340p. mass mkt. 7.99 *(0-312-97134-6,* St. Martin's Paperbacks); 3rd ed. 1999. 292p. 24.95 *(0-312-20303-9)* St. Martin's Pr.

—High Five. l.t. ed. 1999. (Stephanie Plum Novel Ser.: No. 5). 419p. 30.95 *(0-7862-2107-0)* Thorndike Pr.

—Hot Six. abr. ed. audio *(1-55927-965-6)*; 2000. (Stephanie Plum Novel Ser.: No. 6). audio 17.95 *(1-55927-605-3)* Audio Renaissance.

—Hot Six. l.t. ed. 2000. (Stephanie Plum Novel Ser.: No. 6). 350p. 31.95 *(0-7838-9083-4,* Macmillan Reference USA) Gale Group.

—Hot Six. abr. ed. 2001. audio *(0-333-78251-8)* Macmillan U.K. GBR. *Dist:* Macmillan Publishing Co., Inc.

—Hot Six. abr. ed. 2002. audio 7.95 *(1-57815-265-8)* Media Bks., L. L. C.

—Hot Six. unabr. ed. 2001. audio compact disk 78.00 *(0-7887-6173-0)*; 2000. (Stephanie Plum Novel Ser.: No. 6). audio 67.00 *(0-7887-4848-3,* 96103E7) Recorded Bks., LLC.

—Hot Six. 2001. (Stephanie Plum Novel Ser.: No. 6). 352p. mass mkt. 7.99 *(0-312-97627-5,* St. Martin's Paperbacks); 2000. (Stephanie Plum Novel Ser.: No. 6). x, 294p. 24.95 *(0-312-20540-6)*; 2000. 0.01 *(0-312-26526-3)* St. Martin's Pr.

—Hot Six. l.t. ed. 2001. (Stephanie Plum Novel Ser.: No. 6). 350p. pap. 29.95 *(0-7838-9082-6)* Thorndike Pr.

—One for the Money. abr. ed. 2001. audio *(0-333-78015-9)* Macmillan U.K. GBR. *Dist:* Macmillan Publishing Co., Inc.

—One for the Money. 2002. (Stephanie Plum Novel Ser.: No. 1). 304p. mass mkt. 7.99 o.s.i *(0-06-100905-9,* HarperTorch) Morrow/Avon.

—One for the Money. unabr. ed. (Stephanie Plum Novel Ser.: No. 1). 1999. audio compact disk 66.00 *(0-7887-3406-7,* C1012E7); 1995. audio 51.00 *(0-7887-0449-4,* 94639E7) Recorded Bks., LLC.

—One for the Money. (Stephanie Plum Novel Ser.: No. 1). 2000. E-Book 20.00 *(0-684-86731-1)*; 1994. 288p. 25.00 *(0-684-19639-5)* Simon & Schuster. (Scribner).

—One for the Money. abr. ed. (Stephanie Plum Novel Ser.: No. 1). 2000. audio compact disk 9.98 *(0-7435-1838-1)*; 1996. audio 17.00 o.s.i *(0-671-56255-X,* 393338) Simon & Schuster Audio. (Simon & Schuster Audioworks).

—One for the Money. Date not set. pap. *(0-312-31635-6)*; 2003. (Illus.). 352p. reprint ed. mass mkt. 7.99 *(0-312-99045-6)* St. Martin's Pr. (St. Martin's Paperbacks).

—One for the Money. l.t. ed. 1995. (Stephanie Plum Novel Ser.: No. 1). 333p. 23.95 *(0-7838-1186-1)* Thorndike Pr.

—Seven Up. l.t. ed. 2001. (Stephanie Plum Novel Ser.: Bk. 7). 400p. 24.95 *(0-375-43111-X)* Random Hse. Large Print.

—Seven Up. 2001. (Stephanie Plum Novel Ser.: Bk. 7). 309p. 24.95 *(0-312-26584-0)* St. Martin's Pr.

—Three Plums in One: One for the Money, Two for the Dough, Three to Get Deadly. 2001. 800p. 23.00 *(0-7432-1639-3)*; E-Book 9.99 *(0-7432-1666-0)* Simon & Schuster. (Scribner).

—Three Plums in One: One for the Money, Two for the Dough, Three to Get Deadly, Set. abr. ed. 2001. audio compact disk 39.95 *(0-7435-0947-1,* Simon & Schuster Audioworks) Simon & Schuster Audio.

—Three to Get Deadly. l.t. ed. 1997. (Stephanie Plum Novel Ser.: No. 3). 25.95 o.p. *(1-56895-429-8,* Wheeler Publishing, Inc.) Gale Group.

—Three to Get Deadly. 2001. audio *(0-333-78011-6)* Macmillan U.K. GBR. *Dist:* Macmillan Publishing Co., Inc.

—Three to Get Deadly. unabr. ed. (Stephanie Plum Novel Ser.: No. 3). 2000. audio compact disk 89.00 *(0-7887-3964-6,* C1119E7); 1997. audio 60.00 *(0-7887-0927-5,* 95067E7) Recorded Bks., LLC.

—Three to Get Deadly. (Stephanie Plum Novel Ser.: No. 3). 1998. E-Book 24.00 *(0-684-86860-1)*; 1997. 304p. 25.00 *(0-684-82265-2)*; 1997. 24.00 o.s.i *(0-684-84466-4)* Simon & Schuster. (Scribner).

—Three to Get Deadly. abr. ed. (Stephanie Plum Novel Ser.: No. 3). 2000. audio 9.98 *(0-7435-1839-X)*; 1994. audio 18.00 *(0-671-57520-1,* 394533) Simon & Schuster Audio. (Simon & Schuster Audioworks).

—Three to Get Deadly. 1998. (Stephanie Plum Novel Ser.: No. 3). 352p. reprint ed. mass mkt. 7.99 *(0-312-96609-1,* St. Martin's Paperbacks) St. Martin's Pr.

—Two for the Dough. l.t. ed. 1998. (Stephanie Plum Novel Ser.: No. 2). 25.95 *(1-57490-151-6,* Beeler Large Print Bks.) Beeler, Thomas T. Publisher.

—Two for the Dough. unabr. ed. (Stephanie Plum Novel Ser.: No. 2). 2000. audio 51.00 *(0-7887-0617-9,* 94788E7); 1999. audio compact disk 69.00 *(0-7887-3723-6,* C1080E7) Recorded Bks., LLC.

—Two for the Dough. (Stephanie Plum Novel Ser.: No. 2). 2000. E-Book 22.00 *(0-684-86853-9,* Scribner); 1996. 304p. 22.00 *(0-684-82592-9,* Scribner); 1996. 304p. 25.00 *(0-684-19638-7,* Scribner); 1996. 336p. reprint ed. mass mkt. 7.99 *(0-671-00179-5,* Pocket) Simon & Schuster.

—Two for the Dough. (Stephanie Plum Novel Ser.: No. 2). 1999. audio 9.98 *(0-671-04420-6)*; Set. 1996. audio 17.00 *(0-671-56258-4,* 393428) Simon & Schuster Audio. (Simon & Schuster Audioworks).

### TSCHAI (IMAGINARY PLACE)—FICTION

Vance, Jack. City of the Chasch. 1979. (Science Fiction Ser.). mass mkt. 1.75 o.p. *(0-87997-461-3,* UE1461) DAW Bks., Inc.

—The Dirdir: Tschai, Planet of Adventure: 3. 1979. (Science Fiction Ser.). mass mkt. 1.75 o.p. *(0-87997-478-8,* UE1478) DAW Bks., Inc.

—The Dirdir: Tschai, Planet of Adventure: 3. 1983. 240p. lib. bdg. 15.95 o.p. *(0-934438-24-2)* Underwood Bks., Inc.

—Planet of Adventure. 1993. 541p. pap. 15.95 *(0-312-85488-9,* Orb Bks.) Doherty, Tom Assocs., LLC.

—Planet of Adventure: City of the Chasch; Servants of the Wankh the Dirdir; The Pnume. 1993. 24.95 o.p. *(0-312-85487-0,* Tor Bks.) Doherty, Tom Assocs., LLC.

—The Pnume. 1983. 224p. lib. bdg. 15.95 o.p. *(0-934438-57-9)* Underwood Bks., Inc.

—Servants of the Wankh: Tschai, Planet of Adventure, No. 2. 1979. (Science Fiction Ser.). mass mkt. 1.75 o.p. *(0-87997-467-2,* UE1467) DAW Bks., Inc.

### TUCSON (ARIZ.)—FICTION

Farrier, Nancy J. Tucson: Four Romances in the Old Southwest. 2003. (Historical Collections). 464p. pap. 6.97 *(1-58660-964-5)* Barbour Publishing, Inc.

Jance, J. A. Kiss of the Bees. l.t. ed. 2001. (Large Print Book Ser.). 585p. pap. 23.95 o.p. *(1-58724-033-5,* Wheeler Publishing, Inc.) Gale Group.

—Kiss of the Bees. 2000. 389p. 24.00 *(0-380-97747-8,* Morrow, William & Co.) Morrow/Avon.

—Kiss of the Bees: A Novel of Suspense. 2001. 464p. mass mkt. 7.50 *(0-380-80599-5,* Avon Bks.) Morrow/Avon.

Krentz, Jayne Ann. Call It Destiny. 2000. 256p. mass mkt. *(1-55166-563-8)*; 1993. mass mkt. *(0-373-45153-9,* 1-45153-3); 1984. mass mkt. *(0-373-25121-1)* Harlequin Enterprises, Ltd. (Harlequin Bks.).

—Call It Destiny. l.t. ed. 2002. 334p. 29.95 *(0-7862-3971-9)* Thorndike Pr.

Monroe, Debra. Newfangled: A Novel. 304p. 2000. pap. 12.00 *(0-684-85197-0,* Touchstone); 1998. 22.00 *(0-684-81905-8,* Simon & Schuster) Simon & Schuster.

Parrish, Richard. The Dividing Line. 1993. 368p. 20.00 o.p. *(0-525-93561-4)* Dutton/Plume.

—The Dividing Line. 1994. 432p. mass mkt. 5.99 o.s.i *(0-451-40430-0,* Onyx) NAL.

—Nothing but the Truth. 1995. (Joshua Rabb Ser.). 304p. 20.95 o.p. *(0-525-93852-4,* Dutton) Dutton/Plume.

—Nothing but the Truth. 1996. (Joshua Rabb Ser.). 352p. mass mkt. 5.99 o.s.i *(0-451-40538-2,* Onyx) NAL.

Pickard, Nancy. The Twenty-Seven Ingredient Chili con Carne Murders. 1994. (Eugenia Potter Mysteries Ser.). 288p. mass mkt. 5.99 *(0-440-21641-9)* Dell Publishing.

Turner, Elizabeth. Rebel's Treasure. 2002. 384p. mass mkt. 5.99 o.s.i *(0-8217-6839-5,* Zebra Bks.) Kensington Publishing Corp.

### TULSA (OKLA.)—FICTION

Askew, Rilla. Fire in Beulah. 2001. 352p. 25.95 o.p. *(0-670-88843-5,* Viking) Viking Penguin.

Bernhardt, William. Blind Justice. 1997. mass mkt. 3.50 o.s.i *(0-345-41806-9)*; 1992. 320p. mass mkt. 6.99 *(0-345-37483-5)* Ballantine Bks.

—Blind Justice. unabr. ed. 1998. (Justice Ser.: Vol. 2). audio 48.00 *(0-7366-4106-8,* 4611) Books on Tape, Inc.

—Blind Justice. unabr. ed. 2001. (Attorney Ben Kincaid Mystery Ser.). audio Chivers Audio Bks. GBR. *Dist:* BBC Audiobooks America.

—Blind Justice. l.t. ed. 1993. 80.95 o.p. *(0-7862-9989-4,* Macmillan Reference USA) Gale Group.

—Cruel Justice. 1997. mass mkt. 3.50 o.s.i *(0-345-41807-7)*; 1996. 480p. mass mkt. 7.50 *(0-345-40803-9)* Ballantine Bks.

—Cruel Justice. unabr. ed. 1998. (Justice Ser.). audio 72.00 *(0-7366-4180-7,* 4678) Books on Tape, Inc.

—Cruel Justice. l.t. ed. 1996. pap. 23.95 *(1-56895-323-2,* Wheeler Publishing, Inc.) Gale Group.

—Dark Justice. 1999. 448p. mass mkt. 6.99 *(0-345-43476-5)* Ballantine Bks.

—Deadly Justice. 1997. mass mkt. 3.50 o.s.i *(0-345-41808-5)*; 1993. 320p. mass mkt. 7.50 *(0-345-38027-4)* Ballantine Bks.

—Deadly Justice. unabr. ed. 1998. (Justice Ser.: Vol. 3). audio 48.00 *(0-7366-4107-6,* 4612) Books on Tape, Inc.

—Deadly Justice. l.t. ed. 1994. 65.95 o.p. (*0-7862-9988-6*, Macmillan Reference USA) Gale Group.
—Double Jeopardy. 1996. 416p. mass mkt. 7.99 (*0-345-39784-3*) Ballantine Bks.
—Double Jeopardy. l.t. ed. 1996. (Niagara Large Print Ser.). 431p. 29.50 o.p. (*0-7089-5828-1*, Ulverscroft) Thorpe, F. A. Pubs. GBR. *Dist:* Ulverscroft Large Print Bks., Ltd.
—Extreme Justice. 1998. (Ben Kincaid Ser.). 384p. mass mkt. 6.99 (*0-345-42481-6*) Ballantine Bks.
—Hate Crime. 2004. 368p. 25.95 (*0-345-45147-3*, Ballantine Bks.) Ballantine Bks.
—Hate Crime. l.t. ed. 2004. 592p. 27.95 (*0-375-43341-4*) Random Hse. Large Print.
—Murder One. 2001. 416p. reprint ed. mass mkt. 7.50 (*0-345-42815-3*, Ballantine Bks.) Ballantine Bks.
—Naked Justice. 1997. 448p. mass mkt. 6.99 (*0-449-00087-7*, Fawcett) Ballantine Bks.
—Naked Justice. unabr. ed. 1997. (Justice Ser.). audio 88.00 (*0-7366-3789-3*, 4463) Books on Tape, Inc.
—Naked Justice. l.t. ed. 1997. (Niagara Large Print Ser.). 688p. 29.50 o.p. (*0-7089-5879-6*, Ulverscroft) Thorpe, F. A. Pubs. GBR. *Dist:* Ulverscroft Large Print Bks., Ltd.
—Perfect Justice. 1997. mass mkt. 3.50 o.s.i (*0-345-41809-3*) Ballantine Bks.
—Perfect Justice. unabr. ed. 1998. (Justice Ser.: Vol. 4). audio 56.00 (*0-7366-4108-4*, 4613) Books on Tape, Inc.
—Perfect Justice, Set. l.t. ed. 1994. (Studio Ser.). 64.95 o.p. incl. audio (*0-7862-9987-8*, Macmillan Reference USA) Gale Group.
—Perfect Justice. 1995. 416p. mass mkt. 6.99 (*0-345-39133-0*, House of Collectibles) Random Hse. Information Group.
—Primary Justice. 1997. mass mkt. 3.50 o.s.i (*0-345-41810-7*); 1991. 320p. mass mkt. 6.99 (*0-345-37479-7*) Ballantine Bks.
—Primary Justice. unabr. ed. 1998. (Justice Ser.: Vol. 1). audio 48.00 (*0-7366-4105-X*, 4610) Books on Tape, Inc.
—Primary Justice. (Mystery Ser.). 1998. 309p. 22.95 (*0-7862-1659-X*, Five Star); Set. 1993. 79.95 o.p. incl. audio (*0-7862-9991-6*, Macmillan Reference USA) Gale Group.
Carr, Pat M. If We Must Die: A Novel. 2002. (Chaparral Book for Young Readers Ser.). 168p. (J). 15.95 (*0-87565-262-X*) Texas Christian Univ. Pr.
Sanders, William. Blood Autumn. 1995. 272p. 21.00 o.p. (*0-312-11755-8*, Saint Martin's Minotaur) St. Martin's Pr.
—A Death on 66: A Taggart Roper Mystery. 1993. 256p. 20.95 o.p. (*0-312-10452-9*, Saint Martin's Minotaur) St. Martin's Pr.
—The Next Victim. 1993. 240p. 17.95 o.p. (*0-312-08861-2*, Saint Martin's Minotaur) St. Martin's Pr.

### TUNISIA—FICTION

Benton, Kenneth. Craig & the Tunisian Tangle. l.t. ed. 2002. 275p. pap. 24.45 (*0-7862-3944-1*) Gale Group.
Cartland, Barbara. Love in the Ruins. l.t. ed. 1999. (Candlelight Romance Ser.). 192p. 21.95 o.p. (*0-7862-2266-2*) Thorndike Pr.
Hamilton, Lyn. The African Quest: An Archaeological Mystery. 2001. (Archaeological Mystery Ser.). (Illus.). 304p. 21.95 o.s.i (*0-425-17806-4*) Berkley Publishing Group.
Kurata, Phillip. The Reluctant Agent. 2001. 248p. (*0-931846-61-7*) Washington Writers' Publishing Hse.
Memmi, Albert. The Pillar of Salt: A Novel. 1992. 352p. reprint ed. pap. 21.00 (*0-8070-8327-5*) Beacon Pr.
—The Scorpion, or the Imaginary Confession. Levieux, Eleanor, tr. 1986. (Folio Ser.: No. 1715). (FRE.). 270p. pap. 10.95 (*2-07-037715-6*) Schoenhof's Foreign Bks., Inc.
Miller, Alex. Conditions of Faith. 2002. 400p. reprint ed. pap. 13.95 (*0-425-18177-4*) Berkley Publishing Group.
—Conditions of Faith. 2000. (Illus.). 352p. 25.00 o.s.i (*0-684-86935-7*, Scribner) Simon & Schuster.
Taleb, Mirza. Hannibal, Man of Destiny. 1974. 300p. 25.95 o.p. (*0-8283-1501-9*) Branden Bks.
Webster, Elizabeth A. Escape into Light. 1991. 304p. 19.95 o.p. (*0-312-06964-2*) St. Martin's Pr.

### TURKEY—FICTION

Ali, Tariq. The Stone Woman. 2001. 288p. pap. 12.00 (*1-85984-364-6*) Verso.
—The Stone Woman: A Novel. 2000. (Islamic Quartet Ser.). 274p. 23.00 (*1-85984-764-1*) Verso.
Bell, Albert A., Jr. All Roads Lead to Murder: A Case from the Notebooks of Pliny the Younger. 2002. (Illus.). 246p. 21.95 (*0-9713045-3-X*) High Country Pubs., Ltd.
Cohen, Rose Mary H. The Survivor. Mitchell, Sara, ed. 2002. (Illus.). 200p. 24.95 (*0-9667361-2-5*) LICO Publishing.
De Osa, Veronica. Sinan: The Turkish Michelangelo. 1981. 10.95 o.p. (*0-533-04655-6*) Vantage Pr., Inc.
Eskinazi, Salamon. The Reluctant Messiah. 2002. ix, 354p. pap. 30.00 (*0-7657-6168-8*) Aronson, Jason Pubs.
Farrar, Frederick W. Gathering Clouds. E-Book 3.95 (*0-594-02203-7*) 1873 Pr.
Gilman, Dorothy. The Amazing Mrs. Pollifax. 1986. pap. 2.95 o.p. (*0-449-44215-2*); 1985. 176p. mass mkt. 6.50 (*0-449-20912-1*) Ballantine Bks. (Fawcett).
—The Amazing Mrs. Pollifax. 1970. 5.95 o.p. (*0-385-02907-1*) Doubleday Publishing.
—The Amazing Mrs. Pollifax. (Nightingale Ser.). 1983. 284p. pap. 9.95 o.p. (*0-8161-3371-9*); 1992. 286p. 17.95 o.p. (*0-8161-5355-8*) Gale Group. (Macmillan Reference USA).
—The Amazing Mrs. Pollifax. unabr. ed. 1989. (Mrs. Pollifax Mystery Ser.: Vol. 2). audio 44.00 (*1-55690-011-2*, 89740E7) Recorded Bks., LLC.
Goshgarian, Diane. The Arbitrary Sword. 2000. 496p. (Orig.). pap. 15.95 (*0-9665742-0-6*) Vision Pr.
Hunt, E. Howard. Izmir: A Jack Novak Adventure. 1996. (Jack Novak Adventure Ser.). 240p. 21.95 o.p. (*1-55611-474-5*) Fine, Donald I. Bks.
Illinik, C. J. The Tablets of Ararat. 2002. 352p. 12.99 (*0-8254-2908-0*) Kregel Pubns.
Karasu, Bilge. Death in Troy. Aji, Aron, tr. from TUR. 2002. 116p. pap. 11.95 (*0-87286-401-4*) City Lights Bks.
—Night: A Novel. Gun, Guneli, tr. 1994. 152p. (C). 19.95 (*0-8071-1849-4*) Louisiana State Univ. Pr.
Karnezis, Panos. The Maze. 2004. 224p. 24.00 (*0-374-20480-2*) Farrar, Straus & Giroux.
Kazan, Frances. Halide's Gift: A Novel. 2002. 376p. pap. 12.95 (*0-375-75997-2*) Random House Adult Trade Publishing Group.
—Halide's Gift: A Novel. 2001. E-Book 19.95 (*1-58836-018-0*) Random Hse., Inc.
Kelly, Clint. Power & the Glory. 1999. (In Shadow of the Mountain Ser.: Vol. 2). 272p. pap. 11.99 o.p. (*1-55661-956-1*) Bethany Hse. Pubs.
Kemal, Yashar. The Sea-Crossed Fisherman. 1985. 286p. 16.95 o.s.i (*0-8076-1122-0*) Braziller, George Inc.
—They Burn the Thistles: Memed My Hawk, Part II. pap. 6.95 (*0-906495-47-4*) Writers & Readers Publishing, Inc.
Marcom, Micheline Aharonian. Three Apples Fell from Heaven. 2001. (Illus.). 208p. 23.95 o.p. (*1-57322-186-4*, Riverhead Bks. (Hardcovers)) Putnam Publishing Group, The.
O'Donnelly, Kristina. The Scorpion Child. 2000. pap. 15.95 (*1-930574-01-0*); (Illus.). 320p. 27.95 (*1-930574-11-8*) Rose International Publishing Hse., Inc.
Pamuk, Orhan. The New Life. Gun, Guneli, tr. 1997. 296p. 24.00 o.p. (*0-374-22129-4*) Farrar, Straus & Giroux.
—The New Life. Gun, Guneli, tr. 1998. 304p. pap. 13.95 (*0-375-70171-0*, Vintage) Knopf Publishing Group.
—The White Castle. Holbrook, Victoria, tr. from TUR. 1991. 162p. 17.50 (*0-8076-1264-2*) Braziller, George Inc.
—The White Castle: A Novel. Holbrook, Victoria, tr. from TUR. 1998. 176p. pap. 12.00 (*0-375-70161-3*, Vintage) Knopf Publishing Group.
Parker, Gary E. Ephesus Fragment. 1999. 368p. pap. 11.99 (*0-7642-2256-2*) Bethany Hse. Pubs.
—The Ephesus Fragment. l.t. ed. 2000. (Christian Mystery Ser.). 663p. 23.95 o.p. (*0-7862-2889-X*) Thorndike Pr.
Payne, Holly. The Virgin's Knot. 2002. 336p. 23.95 o.s.i (*0-525-94657-8*, Dutton) Dutton/Plume.
—Virgins Knot: A Novel. 2003. 320p. reprint ed. pap. 14.00 (*0-452-28445-7*, Plume) Dutton/Plume.
Schreyer, Lothar. Der Untergang Von Byzanz. 2001. (Lothar Schreyer Edition Ser.: Vol. 5). (Illus.). 324p. 99.95 (*0-7734-1358-8*) Mellen, Edwin Pr., The.
Settle, Mary Lee. Blood Tie. 1983. mass mkt. 3.95 o.s.i (*0-345-30143-9*); 1979. mass mkt. 2.50 o.s.i (*0-345-28154-3*) Ballantine Bks.
—Blood Tie. 1986. (Signature Editions Ser.). 400p. pap. 7.95 o.p. (*0-684-18662-4*, Macmillan Reference USA) Gale Group.
—Blood Tie. 1977. 10.95 o.p. (*0-395-25401-9*) Houghton Mifflin Co.
—Blood Tie. 1995. (Mary Lee Settle Collection). 386p. reprint ed. pap. 12.95 (*1-57003-097-9*) Univ. of South Carolina Pr.
Sobin, Gustaf. In Pursuit of Vanishing a Star: A Novel. 2002. 192p. 23.95 (*0-393-04204-9*) Norton, W. W. & Co., Inc.
Tekin, Latife. Berji Kristin: Tales from the Garbage Hills. Christie, Ruth & Paker, Saliha, trs. from TUR. 1993. 176p. 21.95 (*0-7145-2944-3*) Boyars, Marion Pubs., Inc.
Tekin, Latife & Christie, Ruth. Berji Kristin: Tales from the Garbage Hills. Parker, Salina, tr. from TUR. 1996. 162p. reprint ed. pap. 12.95 (*0-7145-3011-5*) Boyars, Marion Pubs., Inc.
Wallach, Janet. Seraglio. l.t. ed. 2003. 28.95 (*0-7862-5424-6*) Thorndike Pr.
—Seraglio: A Novel. 2003. 336p. 24.95 (*0-385-49046-1*, Talese, Nan A.) Doubleday Publishing.
Whitney, Phyllis A. Black Amber. 1982. 224p. mass mkt. 3.95 o.s.i (*0-449-20219-4*); 1981. mass mkt. 2.75 o.s.i (*0-449-23943-8*); 1977. mass mkt. 1.75 o.s.i (*0-449-23430-4*); 1975. mass mkt. 1.50 o.s.i (*0-449-22604-2*) Ballantine Bks. (Fawcett).
—Black Amber. 1994. 336p. mass mkt. 4.99 o.p. (*0-06-100264-X*, HarperTorch) Morrow/Avon.
—Black Amber. l.t. ed. 1976. (Ulverscroft Large Print Ser.). 12.00 o.p. (*0-85456-493-4*, Ulverscroft) Thorpe, F. A. Pubs. GBR. *Dist:* Ulverscroft Large Print Bks., Ltd., Ulverscroft Large Print Canada, Ltd.

## U

### UKRAINE—FICTION

Berman, Leonard H. Consider My Servant. 2001. 437p. pap. 24.99 (*0-7388-1680-9*); text 34.99 (*0-7388-1679-5*); E-Book 8.00 (*0-7388-8569-X*) Xlibris Corp.
Brown, Dale. Chains of Command. 1994. 528p. reprint ed. mass mkt. 7.99 (*0-425-14207-8*) Berkley Publishing Group.
—Chains of Command. abr. ed. 1993. audio 24.95 o.p. (*1-55800-814-4*) NewStar Media, Inc.
—Chains of Command. 1993. 480p. 22.95 (*0-399-13822-6*, G. P. Putnam's Sons) Penguin Group (USA) Inc.
Bulgakov, Mikhail Afanasevich. The White Guard. Gleeny, Michael, tr. from RUS. 2000. 319p. reprint ed. pap. 16.95 (*0-89733-246-6*) Academy Chicago Pubs., Ltd.
—The White Guard. Glenny, Michael, tr. 1975. (ENG & RUS.). 320p. reprint ed. pap. o.p. (*0-07-008853-5*) McGraw-Hill Cos., The.
Foer, Jonathan Safran. Everything Is Illuminated: A Novel. 2003. 288p. pap. 13.95 (*0-06-052970-9*, Perennial) HarperTrade.
—Everything Is Illuminated: A Novel. 2002. (Illus.). 288p. tchr. ed. 24.00 (*0-618-17387-0*) Houghton Mifflin Co.
Gorenstein, Friedrich. Traveling Companions. 1991. 21.95 (*0-15-191074-X*) Harcourt Trade Pubs.
Klein, Olaf G. Aftertime. Dembo, Margot B., tr. from GER. 1999. 124p. 28.00 (*0-8101-1504-2*, Hydra Bks.) Northwestern Univ. Pr.
Kotsiubynsky, Mykhailo. Shadows of Forgotten Ancestors. Carynnk, Marco, tr. 1981. (Ukrainian Classics in Translation Ser.: No. 4). 127p. pap. 9.50 o.p. (*0-87287-258-0*); lib. bdg. 14.50 o.p. (*0-87287-205-X*) Libraries Unlimited, Inc.
Kurkov, Andreaei. Death & the Penguin. 2001. 192p. pap. 13.00 (*1-86046-945-0*) Harvill Pr., The GBR. *Dist:* Trafalgar Square.
Leviant, Curt. The Man Who Thought He Was Messiah. 1990. 226p. 9.95 (*0-8276-0371-1*) Jewish Pubn. Society.
Zabytko, Irene. The Sky Unwashed. 2000. 263p. tchr. ed. 22.95 (*1-56512-246-1*, 72246) Algonquin Bks. of Chapel Hill.

### UNITED STATES—FICTION

Abraham, Pearl. Giving America. 1998. 309p. 22.95 o.p. (*1-57322-121-X*, Riverhead Bks. (Hardcovers)) Putnam Publishing Group, The.
Alcott, Louisa May. Alternative Alcott. Showalter, Elaine, ed. & intro. by. 1988. (American Women Writers Ser.). 400p. 45.00 o.p. (*0-8135-1271-9*); pap. text 16.00 (*0-8135-1272-7*) Rutgers Univ. Pr.
—Behind a Mask: The Unknown Thrillers of Louisa May Alcott. Stern, Madeleine B., ed. & afterword by. 1997. 320p. reprint ed. pap. 13.95 (*0-688-15132-9*, Quill) HarperTrade.
Allan, Clarke. The First Man to Be First Lady. 1999. 309p. pap. 17.95 (*0-7414-0157-6*) Buy Bks. on the Web.Com.
Anderson, Donald. Fire Road. 2001. (John Simmons Short Fiction Award Ser.). 216p. pap. 15.95 (*0-87745-778-6*) Univ. of Iowa Pr.
Andrews, Robert. Last Spy Out. 1991. 384p. mass mkt. 4.99 o.s.i (*0-553-29126-2*) Bantam Bks.
Archer, Jeffrey. The Eleventh Commandment. 1999. 448p. mass mkt. 7.99 (*0-06-101331-5*); 1998. 368p. 26.00 o.s.i (*0-06-019150-3*) HarperCollins Pubs.
—The Eleventh Commandment, Set. abr. ed. 1998. audio 25.00 (*0-694-51973-1*, 696013, HarperAudio) HarperTrade.
—The Eleventh Commandment. unabr. ed. 1999. audio compact disk 83.00 (*0-7887-3440-7*, C1046E7); 1998. audio 75.00 (*0-7887-1968-8*, 95355E7) Recorded Bks., LLC.
—The Eleventh Commandment. l.t. ed. (Paperback Bestsellers Ser.). 567p. 1999. pap. 28.95 (*0-7862-1593-3*); 1998. 30.95 (*0-7862-1592-5*) Thorndike Pr.
—Honor among Thieves. l.t. ed. 1993. 26.95 o.p. (*1-56895-045-4*, Wheeler Publishing, Inc.) Gale Group.
—Honor among Thieves. 1993. 416p. 276.00 o.p. (*0-06-017771-3*); 414.00 o.p. (*0-06-017756-X*) HarperCollins Pubs.
—Honor among Thieves. 1993. 416p. 23.00 o.p. (*0-06-017945-7*) HarperTrade.
—Honor among Thieves. 1994. 480p. mass mkt. 7.99 (*0-06-109204-5*, HarperTorch) Morrow/Avon.
—Honor among Thieves. unabr. ed. 1994. audio 75.00 (*1-55690-968-3*, 94111E7) Recorded Bks., LLC.
Atherton, Gertrude Franklin Horn. The Conqueror. 2000. 252p. E-Book 3.95 (*0-594-01840-4*) 1873 Pr.
Axler, James. Damnation Road Show. 2003. (Deathlands Ser.: No. 62). 352p. mass mkt. (*0-373-62572-3*, 1-62572-2, Gold Eagle) Harlequin Enterprises, Ltd.
Baker, Calvin. Naming the New World. 1999. E-Book 9.95 (*0-312-20732-8*); 1997. 128p. 18.95 o.p. (*0-312-15178-0*) St. Martin's Pr.
Barnes, Steven. Lion's Blood: A Novel of Slavery & Freedom in an Alternate America. 2003. 624p. mass mkt. 6.99 (*0-446-61221-9*, Aspect) Warner Bks., Inc.
—Zulu Heart. 2004. 656p. mass mkt. 6.99 (*0-446-61195-6*); 2003. (Illus.). 480p. 24.95 (*0-446-53122-7*) Warner Bks., Inc. (Aspect).
Barolini, Helen. Umbertina. 1983. audio 13.95 (*1-55644-064-2*, 3021) American Audio Prose Library, Inc.
—Umbertina. 1989. 432p. (C). reprint ed. pap. 12.95 (*0-88143-107-9*) Ayer Co. Pubs., Inc.
—Umbertina. 1985. 448p. pap. 2.75 o.p. (*0-553-13817-0*) Bantam Bks.
Barolini, Helena. Umbertina. 1998. 464p. 35.00 (*1-55861-204-1*); pap. 18.95 (*1-55861-205-X*) Feminist Pr. at The City Univ. of New York.
Baxter, Charles. Through the Safety Net. 1998. 224p. pap. 13.00 (*0-679-77649-4*, Vintage) Knopf Publishing Group.
—Through the Safety Net. 1985. 208p. 14.95 o.p. (*0-670-80477-0*) Viking Penguin.
Beggs, Beth. Just Passing Through. 1994. 248p. (gr. 4-7). pap. 10.95 (*1-55622-376-5*, Seaside Pr.) Wordware Publishing, Inc.
Benson, Ann. The Burning Road. 2000. 720p. mass mkt. 6.50 (*0-440-22591-4*) Dell Publishing.
Bowyer, Mathew J. General George Washington's Great Secret. 1999. E-Book 6.95 (*0-87714-376-5*) Denlingers Pubs., Ltd.
—General George Washington's Great Secret: The Man Who Twizzled America. 2000. 260p. pap. 15.95 (*0-87714-528-8*); 1999. E-Book 6.95 (*0-87714-351-X*) Denlingers Pubs., Ltd.
Brodsky, Michael. * * * A Novel. 1994. 368p. 26.95 (*1-56858-000-2*); pap. 13.95 (*1-56858-001-0*) Four Walls Eight Windows.
Brown, Jason. Driving the Heart: And Other Stories. 1999. 192p. 23.00 (*0-393-04721-0*) Norton, W. W. & Co., Inc.
Brown, Rita Mae. Dolley: A Novel of Dolley Madison in Love & War. 1995. 432p. mass mkt. 6.50 (*0-553-56949-X*) Bantam Bks.
Brown, Sandra. French Silk. abr. ed. 1993. audio 15.95 o.p. (*1-55800-601-X*) NewStar Media, Inc.
—French Silk. 2000. 512p. pap. 12.95 (*0-446-67744-2*) Warner Bks., Inc.
Broyard, Bliss. My Father, Dancing. 2000. (Harvest Book Ser.). 208p. pap. 13.00 (*0-15-601396-7*, Harvest Bks.) Harcourt Trade Pubs.
Bruckheimer, Linda. Dreaming Southern. 1999. 240p. 23.95 o.p. (*0-525-94453-2*, Dutton) Dutton/Plume.
—Dreaming Southern: A Novel. 2000. 272p. pap. 12.95 (*0-452-28036-2*, Plume) Dutton/Plume.
Card, Orson Scott. Alvin Journeyman. (Tales of Alvin Maker Ser.: No. 4). 1996. 416p. mass mkt. 6.99 (*0-8125-0923-4*); 1995. 384p. 23.95 o.p. (*0-312-85053-0*); 1995. 200.00 (*0-312-86005-6*) Doherty, Tom Assocs., LLC. (Tor Bks.).
—Alvin Journeyman. 1996. (Tales of Alvin Maker Ser.: No. 4). 13.04 (*0-606-11033-X*) Turtleback Bks.
—Enchantment. 2000. 432p. mass mkt. 6.99 (*0-345-41688-0*); 1999. 400p. 25.00 o.s.i (*0-345-41687-2*) Ballantine Bks. (Del Rey).
—Enchantment, Set. abr. ed. 1999. audio 25.00 Highsmith Inc.
—Enchantment. abr. ed. 1999. audio 25.00 (*0-7871-1942-3*, 694163, Dove Audio) NewStar Media, Inc.
—Enchantment. 2000. (Illus.). (J). 13.04 (*0-606-18096-6*) Turtleback Bks.
—Heartfire. (Tales of Alvin Maker Ser.: No. 5). 1999. 352p. mass mkt. 6.99 (*0-8125-0924-2*); 1998. 304p. 24.95 o.p. (*0-312-85054-9*); 1999. 200.00 (*0-312-86728-X*) Doherty, Tom Assocs., LLC. (Tor Bks.).
—Prentice Alvin. 1989. (Tales of Alvin Maker Ser.: No. 3). 352p. mass mkt. 6.99 (*0-8125-0212-4*); 17.95 o.p. (*0-312-93141-7*) Doherty, Tom Assocs., LLC. (Tor Bks.).
—Prentice Alvin. 1989. (Tales of Alvin Maker Ser.: No. 3). 13.04 (*0-606-11761-X*) Turtleback Bks.

—Red Prophet. (Tales of Alvin Maker Ser.: No. 2). 320p. 1992. mass mkt. 6.99 (*0-8125-2426-8*); 1987. 17.95 o.p. (*0-312-93043-7*) Doherty, Tom Assocs., LLC. (Tor Bks.).

—Red Prophet. 1988. (Tales of Alvin Maker Ser.: No. 2). 13.04 (*0-606-11784-9*) Turtleback Bks.

—Seventh Son. 2003. (Alvin Maker Ser.). 256p. (YA). mass mkt. 3.99 o.s.i (*0-7653-4775-X*, Tor Bks.); 2003. mass mkt. 6.99 (*0-7653-4565-X*, Tor Teen); 1993. (Tales of Alvin Maker Ser.: No. 1). 256p. mass mkt. 6.99 (*0-8125-3305-4*, Tor Bks.); 1988. (Tales of Alvin Maker Ser.: No. 1). (Illus.). 256p. pap. 3.95 o.s.i (*0-8125-3353-4*, Tor Bks.); 1987. (Tales of Alvin Maker Ser.: No. 1). 17.95 o.p. (*0-312-93019-4*, Tor Bks.) Doherty, Tom Assocs., LLC.

—Seventh Son. 1987. (Tales of Alvin Maker Ser.: No. 1). 13.04 (*0-606-04134-6*) Turtleback Bks.

Carton, Paul. Death of the Woodstock Generation. 1994. 80p. (Orig.). pap. 6.95 (*0-9641889-0-2*) Van Cortlandt Bks.

Cheever, John. The Wapshot Chronicle. 1986. mass mkt. 2.95 o.s.i (*0-345-29408-4*) Ballantine Bks.

—The Wapshot Chronicle. 1979. o.p. (*0-06-010741-3*); 1973. reprint ed. pap. 2.25 o.p. (*0-06-080295-2*, P295) HarperCollins Pubs.

—The Wapshot Chronicle. 2003. (Perennial Classics Ser.). 368p. pap. 12.95 (*0-06-052887-7*, Perennial) HarperTrade.

—The Wapshot Chronicle. l.t. ed. 1999. (Perennial Bestsellers Ser.). 448p. 26.95 (*0-7838-8488-5*) Thorndike Pr.

Churchill, Winston. Mr. Crewe's Career. 2001. (Best Sellers of 1908 Ser.). reprint ed. pap. text 28.00 (*0-7426-6171-7*) Classic Bks.

—Mr. Crewe's Career. 2002. 464p. 28.99 (*1-4043-2004-0*); per. 23.99 (*1-4043-2005-9*) IndyPublish-.com.

Cobb, William. Wings of Morning. 2001. 255p. 26.95 (*1-57587-177-7*) Crane Hill Pubs.

Coonts, Stephen. Fortunes of War. 1998. audio compact disk 112.00 (*0-7366-8040-3*); audio 96.00 (*0-7366-4207-2*, 4704) Books on Tape, Inc.

—Fortunes of War, Set. abr. ed. 1999. audio 25.00 Highsmith Inc.

—Fortunes of War, Set. abr. ed. 1998. audio 25.00 (*0-7871-1731-5*, 695766, Dove Audio) NewStar Media, Inc.

—Fortunes of War. 1999. 436p. mass mkt. 7.99 (*0-312-96941-4*, St. Martin's Paperbacks); 1998. 368p. 24.95 (*0-312-18583-9*) St. Martin's Pr.

Coppel, Alfred. The Eighth Day of the Week. 1996. 448p. reprint ed. mass mkt. 5.99 (*0-8439-3952-4*) Dorchester Publishing Co., Inc.

—The Eighth Day of the Week. 1994. 384p. 22.50 o.p. (*1-55611-411-7*) Fine, Donald I. Bks.

—The Eighth Day of the Week. 1996. E-Book 9.95 (*0-585-29169-1*) netLibrary, Inc.

De Grazia, Sebastian. Country with No Name. 1999. 432p. pap. 17.00 (*0-679-74422-3*) Knopf, Alfred A. Inc.

—A Country with No Name: Tales from the Constitution. 1997. 27.50 o.s.i (*0-679-41977-2*, Pantheon) Knopf Publishing Group.

Domini, John. Highway Trade. 1998. 192p. pap. 14.95 (*1-888996-07-2*) Red Hen Pr.

Dos Passos, John. 1919. 2000. (U. S. A. Trilogy Ser.: Vol. 2). 464p. pap. 13.00 (*0-618-05682-3*) Houghton Mifflin Co.

—1919. 1969. (USA Ser.). mass mkt. 1.25 o.p. (*0-451-50630-8*); mass mkt. 1.95 o.p. (*0-451-51059-3*); mass mkt. 3.50 o.p. (*0-451-51508-0*); mass mkt. 3.95 o.p. (*0-451-51803-9*); mass mkt. 0.95 o.p. (*0-451-50445-3*) NAL. (Signet Classics).

—The 42nd Parallel. 2000. (U. S. A. Trilogy Ser.: Vol. 1). 448p. pap. 13.00 (*0-618-05681-5*) Houghton Mifflin Co.

—The 42nd Parallel. 1969. (USA Ser.). mass mkt. 1.25 o.p. (*0-451-50561-1*); mass mkt. 1.50 o.p. (*0-451-50648-0*); mass mkt. 1.75 o.p. (*0-451-50998-6*); mass mkt. 2.25 o.p. (*0-451-51344-4*); mass mkt. 2.95 o.p. (*0-451-51580-3*); mass mkt. 3.95 o.p. (*0-451-51810-1*); mass mkt. 0.95 o.p. (*0-451-50444-5*) NAL. (Signet Classics).

Dreher, Sarah. Bad Company: A Stoner McTavish Mystery. 1995. 235p. pap. 10.95 (*0-934678-66-9*); trans. 19.95 (*0-934678-67-7*) New Victoria Pubs., Inc.

—A Captive in Time. 1990. (Stoner McTavish Mystery Ser.). 256p. (Orig.). pap. 10.95 (*0-934678-22-7*) New Victoria Pubs., Inc.

—Gray Magic. 1987. (Stoner McTavish Mystery Ser.). 282p. (Orig.). pap. 9.95 (*0-934678-11-1*) New Victoria Pubs., Inc.

—Otherworld. 1993. (Stoner McTavish Mystery Ser.). 256p. (Orig.). pap. 10.95 (*0-934678-44-8*) New Victoria Pubs., Inc.

—Shaman's Moon. 1998. (Stoner McTavish Mystery Ser.). 197p. pap. 12.95 (*0-934678-91-X*) New Victoria Pubs., Inc.

—Something Shady. 1986. (Stoner McTavish Mystery Ser.). 272p. pap. 8.95 (*0-934678-07-3*) New Victoria Pubs., Inc.

—Stoner McTavish. 1985. (Stoner McTavish Mystery Ser.). 200p. pap. 9.95 (*0-934678-06-5*) New Victoria Pubs., Inc.

DuBois, Brendan. Resurrection Day. unabr. ed. 2000. audio 96.95 (*0-7927-2328-7*, CSL 217, Chivers Sound Library) BBC Audiobooks America.

—Resurrection Day. 2000. 480p. mass mkt. 7.50 o.s.i (*0-515-12949-6*, Jove) Berkley Publishing Group.

—Resurrection Day. 1999. 400p. (YA). 23.95 o.p. (*0-399-14498-6*) Penguin Group (USA) Inc.

Estleman, Loren D. Billy Gashade. 1998. 320p. mass mkt. 5.99 (*0-8125-4915-5*); 1997. 384p. 23.95 (*0-312-85997-X*) Doherty, Tom Assocs., LLC. (Forge Bks.).

Fender, J. E. Audacity, Privateer out of Portsmouth Vol. II: The Chronicles of Geoffrey Frost. 2003. (Hardscrabble Books). 3634p. text 26.95 (*1-58465-316-7*) Univ. Pr. of New England.

Fitzgerald, F. Scott. Jazz Age Stories. O'Donnell, Patrick, ed. & intro. by. 1998. (Twentieth Century Classics Ser.). 400p. 9.95 (*0-14-118048-X*, Penguin Classics) Viking Penguin.

—Tales of the Jazz Age. 1996. (Bibelots Ser.). 96p. pap. 8.00 (*0-8112-1333-1*, NDP830) New Directions Publishing Corp.

Fleming, Thomas J. Promises to Keep. 1978. 10.00 o.p. (*0-385-13555-6*) Doubleday Publishing.

—Promises to Keep. 1980. 400p. pap. 2.50 o.s.i (*0-446-91192-5*) Warner Bks., Inc.

—Remember the Morning. 1998. 544p. mass mkt. 6.99 (*0-8125-0849-1*); 1997. 384p. 24.95 o.p. (*0-312-86308-X*) Doherty, Tom Assocs., LLC. (Forge Bks.).

—Remember the Morning. 1999. 24.95 (*0-312-87100-7*) St. Martin's Pr.

—The Spoils of War. 1986. 640p. mass mkt. 4.50 (*0-380-70065-4*, Avon Bks.) Morrow/Avon.

—The Spoils of War. 1985. 528p. 18.95 o.p. (*0-399-12968-5*, G. P. Putnam's Sons) Penguin Putnam Bks. for Young Readers.

—The Wages of Fame. 1999. 688p. mass mkt. 6.99 (*0-8125-7182-7*); 1998. 461p. 26.95 (*0-312-86309-8*) Doherty, Tom Assocs., LLC. (Forge Bks.).

Follett, Ken. A Place Called Freedom. 1998. pap. 6.99 (*0-449-45861-X*, Fawcett); 1996. 464p. mass mkt. 7.99 (*0-449-22515-1*, Fawcett); 1996. mass mkt. (*0-449-22517-8*, Ballantine Bks.) Ballantine Bks.

—A Place Called Freedom. l.t. ed. 1995. 672p. 25.00 o.p. (*0-7838-1590-5*, Macmillan Reference USA) Gale Group.

—A Place Called Freedom. l.t. ed. 1995. 672p. 25.00 o.s.i (*0-679-76509-3*) Random Hse. Large Print.

Forester, C. S. The Good Shepherd. 1999. 222p. 21.95 (*0-8488-2267-6*) Amereon, Ltd.

—The Good Shepherd. Sweetman, Jack, ed. 1989. (Classics of Naval Literature Ser.). 288p. 32.95 o.p. (*0-87021-230-3*) Naval Institute Pr.

—The Good Shepherd. 2001. 310p. reprint ed. pap. 29.95 (*1-931313-27-X*) Simon Pubns., Inc.

—The Good Shepherd. l.t. ed. 1998. (Perennial Bestsellers Ser.). 349p. 26.95 (*0-7838-0363-X*) Thorndike Pr.

Frost, Mark. The Six Messiahs. 1996. pap. 6.99 (*0-380-72229-1*, Avon Bks.); 1995. 448p. 23.00 o.p. (*0-688-13092-5*, Morrow, William & Co.) Morrow/Avon.

—The Six Messiahs. abr. ed. 1995. 24.95 o.p. (*0-7871-0399-3*) NewStar Media, Inc.

Gavin, Thomas. Breathing Water. 1994. 320p. 21.95 (*1-55970-232-X*) Arcade Publishing, Inc.

Goldberg, Ed. Better Dead. 2001. (West Coast Crime Ser.). 304p. 23.95 (*0-936085-60-6*, West Coast Crime) Blue Heron Publishing.

Grey, Zane. George Washington, Frontiersman: An Epic of the Colonial Frontier Is Completed after Nearly a Century. 2001. 304p. pap. 13.95 (*0-7653-0023-0*, Forge Bks.) Doherty, Tom Assocs., LLC.

Hale, Robert D. Elm at the Edge of the Earth. 1990. 351p. 18.95 (*0-393-02861-5*) Norton, W. W. & Co., Inc.

Hanley, Tom. Flyboys. 1999. 225p. pap. 21.99 (*0-7388-0865-2*); text 31.99 (*0-7388-0864-4*) Xlibris Corp.

Hergé. Tintin im Amerika.Tr. of Tintin in America. (GER., Illus.). 62p. (J). pap. 24.95 (*0-8288-4999-4*) French & European Pubns., Inc.

Hershman, Marcie. Safe in America: A Novel. 1996. 304p. pap. 13.00 (*0-06-092734-8*, Perennial); 1995. 320p. 24.00 o.p. (*0-06-017144-8*) HarperTrade.

Hinman, Wilbur F., contrib. by. Corporal Si Klegg & His "Pard" How They Lived & Talked & What They Did & Suffered While Fighting for the Flag. 1997. (Illus.). (*0-9656727-0-0*) Henry, J. W. Publishing, Inc.

Hlasko, Marek. The Eighth Day of the Week. 1975. 128p. 57.95 (*0-8371-7896-7*, HLED, Greenwood Pr.) Greenwood Publishing Group, Inc.

Houston, Patty, contrib. by. Every Good Blessing: A Collection of Short Stories. (*0-9633551-4-7*) Cincinnati Writers' Project.

Hughes, Richard Arthur Warren. The Wooden Shepherdess. 1973. 389 p. (*0-7011-1946-2*) Chatto & Windus GBR. *Dist:* Trafalgar Square.

—The Wooden Shepherdess. 1973. 400p. 10.00 o.p. (*0-06-011986-1*) HarperCollins Pubs.

—The Wooden Shepherdess. 2000. (New York Review Books Classics Ser.). 419p. pap. 14.95 (*0-940322-30-7*) New York Review of Bks., Inc., The.

Ignatius, David. The Bank of Fear. l.t. ed. 1995. (G. K. Hall Core Ser.). 576p. 23.95 (*0-7838-1185-3*, Macmillan Reference USA) Gale Group.

—The Bank of Fear. 1994. 20.00 o.p. (*0-688-13136-0*, Morrow, William & Co.); 1995. 400p. reprint ed. mass mkt. 5.99 (*0-380-72280-1*, Avon Bks.) Morrow/Avon.

—The Bank of Fear. unabr. ed. audio 78.00 (*0-7887-0300-5*, 94493E7) Recorded Bks., LLC.

Jackson, Bruce. Growing up Free in America. 1998. 144p. pap. 11.95 (*0-916397-48-3*) Manic D Pr.

Jarrard, Kyle. Rolling the Bones. 2001. 336p. 26.00 (*1-58642-026-7*) Steerforth Pr.

Kaye, Judith & Gelshenen, Rosemary, eds. Discovering Fiction 1: A Reader of American Short Stories. 2001. (Discovering Fiction Ser.). (Illus.). 240p. pap., stu. ed. 22.00 (*0-521-00559-0*) Cambridge Univ. Pr.

Kohler, Sheila. Stories from Another World. 2003. 150p. 22.95 (*0-86538-110-0*) Ontario Review Pr.

Kotzwinkle, William. The Bear Went over the Mountain. 1996. 288p. 22.50 o.s.i (*0-385-48428-3*) Doubleday Publishing.

—The Bear Went over the Mountain. 1997. 320p. pap. 15.00 (*0-8050-5438-3*, Owl Bks.) Holt, Henry & Co.

Lachnit, Carroll. Akin to Death. 1998. 384p. mass mkt. 6.50 o.s.i (*0-425-16409-8*) Berkley Publishing Group.

—A Blessed Death. 1996. 336p. mass mkt. 5.99 o.s.i (*0-425-15347-9*, Prime Crime) Berkley Publishing Group.

—Janie's Law. 1999. (Prime Crime Mysteries Ser.: No. 4). 336p. mass mkt. 6.50 o.s.i (*0-425-17150-7*, Prime Crime) Berkley Publishing Group.

—Murder in Brief. 1995. 272p. (Orig.). mass mkt. 4.99 o.s.i (*0-425-14790-8*) Berkley Publishing Group.

Lane, Jim R. Blindside: A Novel. 2002. 240p. pap. 25.95 (*1-882593-59-6*) Bridge Works Publishing Co., Inc.

Lanigan, Catherine. Wings of Destiny. 1999. viii, 506p. tchr. ed. 24.00 (*1-55874-690-0*) Health Communications, Inc.

Leavitt, David. Arkansas: Three Novellas. 1997. 224p. tchr. ed. 23.00 o.p. (*0-395-83704-9*) Houghton Mifflin Co.

—Arkansas: Three Novellas. 1998. 208p. pap. 12.00 (*0-395-90128-6*, Mariner Bks.) Houghton Mifflin Co. Trade & Reference Div.

Leon, Bonnie. Where Freedom Grows. 1998. (Sowers Triology Ser.: Vol. 1). 300p. pap. 12.99 (*0-8054-1272-7*) Broadman & Holman Pubs.

Lester, Julius. And All Our Wounds Forgiven. 1994. 256p. 19.95 (*1-55970-258-3*) Arcade Publishing, Inc.

—And All Our Wounds Forgiven. 1996. (Harvest Book Ser.). 240p. pap. 12.00 o.s.i (*0-15-600330-9*, Harvest Bks.) Harcourt Trade Pubs.

Levitt, Paul M. Chin Music: A Novel of the Jazz Age. 2002. 64p. pap. 24.95 (*1-57098-404-2*) Rinehart, Roberts Inc.

Lilliefors, Jim. Bananaville. 1996. 288p. text 22.95 o.p. (*0-312-14548-9*, Saint Martin's Minotaur) St. Martin's Pr.

Locklin, Gerald. A Simpler Time, a Simpler Place: Three Mid-century Stories. 2000. (*1-880391-25-2*) Event Horizon Pr.

Locust Alley: A Novel of the Civil War. 2000. 268p. pap. 15.00 (*0-9677103-0-8*) Wordsmith & Penn.

Lopez, Barry. Winter Count. 1999. (Illus.). 128p. pap. 11.00 (*0-679-78141-2*, Vintage) Knopf Publishing Group.

—Winter Count. 128p. 1993. pap. 8.00 o.p. (*0-380-71937-1*); 1982. mass mkt. 4.95 (*0-380-58107-8*) Morrow/Avon. (Avon Bks.).

—Winter Count. 1981. (Illus.). 112 p. 9.95 o.p. (*0-684-16817-0*) Simon & Schuster.

Macomber, Debbie. Between Friends: A Novel. l.t. ed. 2002. (Wheeler Hardcover Ser.). 489p. 28.95 (*1-58724-363-6*, Wheeler Publishing, Inc.) Gale Group.

McCarthy, Mary. Birds of America. 1981. 352p. pap. 3.95 o.p. (*0-380-55459-3*, 55459, Avon Bks.) Morrow/Avon.

—The Groves of Academe. 1974. pap. 3.95 o.p. (*0-452-25084-6*, 25084, Plume) Dutton/Plume.

—The Groves of Academe. 1992. 312p. pap. 14.00 o.s.i (*0-15-637211-8*, Harvest Bks.); 1952. 320p. 9.50 o.s.i (*0-15-137331-0*) Harcourt Trade Pubs.

—The Groves of Academe. 1981. 240p. pap. 2.95 o.p. (*0-380-52522-4*, 52522-0, Avon Bks.) Morrow/Avon.

—The Groves of Academe. 2000. 330p. text 27.95 (*1-56000-455-X*) Transaction Pubs.

McGrory, Brian. The Incumbent. 2003. E-Book 6.99 (*0-7434-8363-4*, Atria); 2001. 448p. reprint ed. mass mkt. 7.99 (*0-7434-0351-7*, Pocket Star) Simon & Schuster.

Metalious, Grace. Peyton Place. 1991. 300p. reprint ed. lib. bdg. 38.95 (*0-89966-861-5*) Buccaneer Bks., Inc.

—Peyton Place. 1999. 384p. pap. 15.95 (*1-55553-400-7*) Northeastern Univ. Pr.

—Peyton Place. 1988. 7.95 o.p. (*0-671-56683-0*, Simon & Schuster) Simon & Schuster.

—Peyton Place: And Return to Peyton Place. 1999. (Modern Classics Ser.). (Illus.). 640p. 10.99 (*0-517-20477-0*) Random Hse. Value Publishing.

Moore, Lorrie. Birds of America: Stories. 1998. 304p. 23.00 o.s.i (*0-679-44597-8*) Knopf, Alfred A. Inc.

—Birds of America: Stories. 2nd ed. 1999. (Illus.). 304p. pap. 14.00 (*0-312-24122-4*) Picador.

Morgan, Richard. Sailing Away. 2000. 124p. pap. 14.95 (*0-9668612-4-8*) Lost Horse Pr.

Morris, Gilbert. The Captive Bride. 1987. (House of Winslow Ser.: Bk. 2). 240p. (Orig.). pap. 11.99 (*0-87123-978-7*) Bethany Hse. Pubs.

—The Dixie Widow. 1991. (House of Winslow Ser.: Bk. 9). 320p. pap. 11.99 (*1-55661-115-3*) Bethany Hse. Pubs.

—The Gentle Rebel. 1988. (House of Winslow Ser.: Vol. 4). 288p. pap. 11.99 (*1-55661-006-8*) Bethany Hse. Pubs.

—The Honorable Imposter. 1987. (House of Winslow Ser.: No. 1). 336p. pap. 11.99 (*0-87123-933-7*) Bethany Hse. Pubs.

—The Honorable Imposter. l.t. ed. 1993. (General Ser.). 464p. lib. bdg. 20.95 o.p. (*0-8161-5672-7*, Macmillan Reference USA) Gale Group.

—The Indentured Heart. 1988. (House of Winslow Ser.: Vol. 3). 288p. pap. 11.99 (*1-55661-003-3*) Bethany Hse. Pubs.

—The Last Confederate. 1990. (House of Winslow Ser.: Vol. 8). 336p. pap. 11.99 (*1-55661-109-9*) Bethany Hse. Pubs.

—The Rough Rider, Vol. 18. 1995. (House of Winslow Ser.: Vol. 18). 304p. pap. 11.99 (*1-55661-394-6*) Bethany Hse. Pubs.

—The Rough Rider. l.t. ed. 1996. 458p. lib. bdg. 22.95 (*0-7838-1853-X*, Macmillan Reference USA) Gale Group.

—The Saintly Buccaneer. 1989. (House of Winslow Ser.: Vol. 5). 304p. pap. 11.99 (*1-55661-048-3*) Bethany Hse. Pubs.

—The Union Belle. 1992. (House of Winslow Ser.: No. 11). 336p. pap. 11.99 (*1-55661-186-2*) Bethany Hse. Pubs.

—White Hunter. 1999. (House of Winslow Ser.: Vol. 22). (Illus.). 320p. pap. 11.99 (*1-55661-909-X*) Bethany Hse. Pubs.

—The Yukon Queen. 1995. (House of Winslow Ser.: Bk. 17). 288p. (J). pap. 11.99 (*1-55661-393-8*) Bethany Hse. Pubs.

Morris, Lynn & Morris, Gilbert. The Stars for a Light. 1994. (Cheney Duvall, M. D. Ser.: Bk. 1). 320p. pap. 11.99 (*1-55661-422-5*) Bethany Hse. Pubs.

—The Stars for a Light. 1999. (Christian Fiction Ser.: Vol. 1). (Illus.). 344p. 23.95 (*0-7862-1828-2*, Five Star); 1995. 355p. 21.95 o.p. (*0-7838-1376-7*, Macmillan Reference USA) Gale Group.

Mueller, Daniel. How Animals Mate. (Sewanee Writers' Ser.). 2000. 191p. 13.95 (*1-58567-055-3*); 1999. 224p. 23.95 (*0-87951-925-8*) Overlook Pr., The.

Mugg, Berthinia. A Visit to Spitesville: A Murder Mystery. 2000. 148p. pap. 20.99 (*0-7388-0829-6*); text 30.99 (*0-7388-0828-8*) Xlibris Corp.

Nevin, David. The Eagle's Cry: A Novel of the Louisianna Purchase. 2000. 448p. 25.95 (*0-312-85511-7*, Forge Bks.) Doherty, Tom Assocs., LLC.

Norris, Lisa. Toy Guns: Winner of the Willa Cather Fiction Prize. 2000. (Winner of the 1999 Willa Cather Fiction Prize Ser.). 145p. pap. 12.95 (*1-884235-31-X*) Helicon 9 Editions.

Oates, Joyce Carol. My Heart Laid Bare. 1999. 544p. pap. 15.00 (*0-452-28006-0*, Plume); 1998. 420p. 26.95 o.p. (*0-525-94442-7*, Abrahams, William Bks.) Dutton/Plume.

Park, Yongsoo. Boy Genius. 2002. 228p. pap. 14.95 (*1-888451-24-6*) Akashic Bks.

Pate, Alexs D. Losing Absalom. 1995. 320p. mass mkt. 7.50 o.s.i (*0-425-15013-5*) Berkley Publishing Group.

—Losing Absalom. 1994. 220p. 5.00 (*1-56689-017-9*) Coffee Hse. Pr.

Portis, Charles. The Dog of the South. 1999. 246p. 15.95 (*0-87951-931-2*) Overlook Pr., The.

Reese, Jim. This Ain't No Shoe Store! 2000. pap. 8.95 o.p. (*0-533-13341-6*) Vantage Pr., Inc.

Richard, Mark. Charity. 1999. 160p. pap. 11.00 (*0-385-42570-8*) Doubleday Publishing.

Riis, Jacob A. Children of the Tenements. 1977. (Short Story Index Reprint Ser.). (Illus.). 25.95 (*0-8369-3565-9*) Ayer Co. Pubs., Inc.

—Children of the Tenements. (Illus.). reprint ed. lib. bdg. 22.00 (*0-8398-1757-6*) Irvington Pubs.

Romo, Ito. El Puente - The Bridge. 2002. 128p. pap. 12.95 (*0-8263-2253-0*); 2000. (SPA.). 149p. 18.95 (*0-8263-2252-2*) Univ. of New Mexico Pr.

Rosen, Charley. Barney Polan's Game: A Novel of the 1951 College Basketball Scandals. 1999. (Harvest Book Ser.). 264p. pap. 13.00 (*0-15-600688-X*, Harvest Bks.) Harcourt Trade Pubs.

Ross-Russell, Noel, contrib. by. A Voice Within. 1998. (*1-871871-39-5*) Open Gate Pr. GBR. *Dist:* Paul & Co. Pubs. Consortium, Inc.

Rowson, Susanna Hoswell. Charlotte Temple. E-Book 2.49 (*1-58627-767-7*) Electric Umbrella Publishing.

Rusch, Kristine K. Stories for an Enchanted Afternoon. 2001. 295p. 24.95 (*1-930846-02-9*) Golden Gryphon Pr.

Safire, William. Freedom: A Novel of Abraham Lincoln & the Civil War. unabr. ed. 1994. Pt. 1. audio 95.95 (*0-7861-0463-5*, 1415-A); Pt. 2. audio 95.95 (*0-7861-0735-9*, 1415-B) Blackstone Audio Bks., Inc.

—Freedom: A Novel of Abraham Lincoln & the Civil War. 1988. mass mkt. 7.99 (*0-380-70584-2*); 2000. (Illus.). 1152p. reprint ed. pap. 15.00 (*0-380-71938-X*) Morrow/Avon. (Avon Bks.).

Sanford, Annette. Crossing Shattuck Bridge: Stories. 1999. 176p. 17.95 (*0-87074-442-9*) Southern Methodist Univ. Pr.

Scholastic, Inc. Staff. My Dear America Diary. 1998. 144p. pap. 7.95 (*0-590-25989-X*) Scholastic, Inc.

Sherwood, Ben. The Man Who Ate the 747. 2004. 288p. pap. 10.00 (*0-553-38262-4*); 2002. 272p. reprint ed. mass mkt. 6.50 (*0-553-58280-1*) Bantam Bks.

Sidhwa, Bapsi. American Brat. 1993. 334p. 21.95 o.p. (*0-915943-73-5*) Milkweed Editions.

—An American Brat. 1995. 336p. pap. 15.95 o.s.i (*1-57131-005-3*) Milkweed Editions.

Stafford, Tim. The Stamp of Glory: A Novel of the Abolitionist Movement. 2000. (River of Freedom Ser.). 380p. 14.99 (*0-7852-6905-3*) Nelson, Thomas Pubs.

Stein, Gertrude. The Making of Americans: An Opera & a Play from the Novel by Gertrude Stein. 1995. (American Literature Ser.). 925p. pap. 16.95 (*1-56478-088-0*) Dalkey Archive Pr.

—The Making of Americans: An Opera & a Play from the Novel by Gertrude Stein. 1966. reprint ed. pap. 6.45 o.p. (*0-87110-099-1*) Ultramarine Publishing Co., Inc.

Stephenson, John S. Intentional Change. 2000. 232p. text 31.99 (*0-7388-0796-6*) Xlibris Corp.

Stern, Daniel. One Day's Perfect Weather: More Twice-Told Tales. 1999. 224p. 19.95 (*0-87074-445-3*) Southern Methodist Univ. Pr.

Thane, Elswyth. Dawn's Early Light. reprint ed. lib. bdg. 26.95 (*0-88411-974-2*) Amereon, Ltd.

—Dawn's Early Light. 1982. 352p. pap. 2.95 o.p. (*0-553-22581-2*) Bantam Bks.

—Dawn's Early Light. 1996. lib. bdg. 28.95 (*1-56849-475-0*) Buccaneer Bks., Inc.

—Dawn's Early Light. 1943. 10.00 o.p. (*0-8015-1957-8*, Dutton) Dutton/Plume.

—Dawn's Early Light. 1981. (Reader's Request Ser.). lib. bdg. 16.95 o.p. (*0-8161-3167-8*, Macmillan Reference USA) Gale Group.

—Ever After. 1976. reprint ed. lib. bdg. 26.95 (*0-88411-958-0*) Amereon, Ltd.

—Ever After. 1983. mass mkt. 3.50 o.s.i (*0-553-22933-8*) Bantam Bks.

—Ever After. 1993. reprint ed. lib. bdg. 31.95 (*1-56849-230-8*) Buccaneer Bks., Inc.

—Ever After. 1981. (Reader's Request Ser.). lib. bdg. 17.95 o.p. (*0-8161-3165-1*, Macmillan Reference USA) Gale Group.

—Homing. 272p. reprint ed. lib. bdg. 23.95 (*0-88411-969-6*) Amereon, Ltd.

—Homing. 1994. lib. bdg. 29.95 (*1-56849-479-3*) Buccaneer Bks., Inc.

—Homing. l.t. ed. 1981. lib. bdg. 15.95 o.p. (*0-8161-3164-3*, Macmillan Reference USA) Gale Group.

—Kissing Kin. 374p. reprint ed. lib. bdg. 27.95 (*0-88411-970-X*) Amereon, Ltd.

—Kissing Kin. 1994. lib. bdg. 29.95 (*1-56849-477-7*) Buccaneer Bks., Inc.

—Kissing Kin. 1981. (Reader's Request Ser.: No. 5). lib. bdg. 16.95 o.p. (*0-8161-3162-7*, Macmillan Reference USA) Gale Group.

—The Light Heart. 1974. reprint ed. lib. bdg. 26.95 (*0-88411-951-3*) Amereon, Ltd.

—The Light Heart. 1996. lib. bdg. 29.95 (*1-56849-476-9*) Buccaneer Bks., Inc.

—The Light Heart. 1977. 10.00 o.p. (*0-8015-4543-9*, Dutton) Dutton/Plume.

—The Light Heart. 1981. (Williamsburg Ser.: No. 4). lib. bdg. 17.95 o.p. (*0-8161-3163-5*, Macmillan Reference USA) Gale Group.

—This Was Tomorrow. 1976. reprint ed. lib. bdg. 24.95 (*0-88411-962-9*) Amereon, Ltd.

—This Was Tomorrow. 1994. lib. bdg. 29.95 (*1-56849-478-5*) Buccaneer Bks., Inc.

—This Was Tomorrow. 1981. (Williamsburg Ser.: No. 6). lib. bdg. 14.95 o.p. (*0-8161-3161-9*, Macmillan Reference USA) Gale Group.

—Yankee Stranger. 1976. reprint ed. lib. bdg. 25.95 (*0-88411-963-7*) Amereon, Ltd.

—Yankee Stranger. 1993. reprint ed. lib. bdg. 31.95 (*1-56849-229-4*) Buccaneer Bks., Inc.

—Yankee Stranger. 1981. (Williamsburg Ser.: No. 2). lib. bdg. 16.95 o.p. (*0-8161-3166-X*, Macmillan Reference USA) Gale Group.

—Yankee Stranger. unabr. ed. 2001. audio 84.95 (*1-85089-622-4*, 91014) ISIS Audio Bks. GBR. *Dist:* Ulverscroft Large Print Bks., Ltd.

Tibbetts, Peggy. Rumors of War. 2000. 310p. pap. 19.95 (*0-9677868-0-0*) Lunatic Fringe Publishing.

Tougias, Michael J. Until I Have No Country: A Novel of King Philip's War in New England. 1996. 256p. (Orig.). pap. 12.95 (*0-924771-80-1*, Covered Bridge Pr.) Douglas Charles, Ltd.

Trainor, J. F. Dynamite Pass. 1993. 384p. mass mkt. 3.99 o.s.i (*0-8217-4227-2*, Zebra Bks.) Kensington Publishing Corp.

—Target for Murder. 1993. 288p. mass mkt. 3.99 o.s.i (*0-8217-4069-5*, Zebra Bks.) Kensington Publishing Corp.

—Whiskey Jack. 1994. 384p. mass mkt. 3.99 o.s.i (*0-8217-4439-9*, Zebra Bks.) Kensington Publishing Corp.

Tufts, Kingsley. Ephraim's Magic. 2nd ed. 2000. 288p. reprint ed. pap. 12.00 (*1-880284-28-6*) Daniel, John & Co., Pubs.

Tyler, Anne. Ladder of Years. 1997. 416p. mass mkt. 7.99 (*0-8041-1347-5*, Ivy Bks.); 1996. 352p. pap. 14.95 (*0-449-91057-1*); 1996. mass mkt. 6.99 o.s.i (*0-8041-1492-7*, Ivy Bks.); Bk. 5. Date not set. pap. (*0-449-91056-3*, Fawcett) Ballantine Bks.

—Ladder of Years. deluxe l.t. ed. 1995. 23.00 o.s.i (*0-676-50229-6*) Random Hse., Inc.

Uris, Leon. A God in Ruins. 1999. 483p. 26.00 (*0-06-018377-2*); 656p. pap. 27.50 (*0-06-093304-6*) HarperCollins Pubs.

—A God in Ruins. Set. abr. ed. 1999. audio 25.00 (*0-694-52040-3*, HarperAudio) HarperTrade.

—A God in Ruins. 2000. 528p. mass mkt. 7.99 (*0-06-109793-4*, Avon Bks.) Morrow/Avon.

Werry, Howard W. Sharp Cheese & Soda Crackers. 1998. (Illus.). 256p. lib. bdg. 13.00 (*1-57087-399-2*) Wilmot Publishing Co.

Williams, Jeanne. Wind Water. 1997. 352p. 23.95 (*0-312-14765-1*) St. Martin's Pr.

—Wind Water. l.t. ed. 1998. (Romance Ser.). 523p. 27.95 (*0-7862-1379-5*) Thorndike Pr.

—Wind Water. 2000. 324p. pap. 19.95 (*0-595-09585-2*, Backinprint.com) iUniverse, Inc.

Wilson, Edmund. The Memoirs of Hecate County. 1995. 411p. pap. 30.00 (*0-374-52432-7*) Farrar, Straus & Giroux.

—The Memoirs of Hecate County. l.t. ed. 1990. 196p. 22.95 (*1-85290-020-2*) ISIS Large Print Bks. GBR. *Dist:* Transaction Pubs.

—Memoirs of Hecate County. 1980. 472p. reprint ed. pap. 7.95 o.p. (*0-87923-315-X*) Godine, David R. Pub.

—The Memoirs of Hecate County. rev. ed. 1979. reprint ed. lib. bdg. 29.00 o.p. (*0-374-98656-8*) Hippocrene Bks., Inc.

—Memoirs of Hecate County. unabr. ed. 1986. audio 80.00 (*0-7366-0545-2*, 1519) Books on Tape, Inc.

Wings, Mary. She Came by the Book. (Mistery Ser.). 272p. 1996. 21.95 o.p. (*0-425-15147-6*, Prime Crime); 1996. pap. 10.00 o.p. (*0-425-15144-1*); 1997. reprint ed. mass mkt. 5.99 o.s.i (*0-425-15697-4*, Prime Crime) Berkley Publishing Group.

—She Came Too Late. 1987. (WomanSleuth Mystery Ser.). 208p. reprint ed. 20.95 o.p. (*0-89594-244-5*); pap. 7.95 o.p. (*0-89594-243-7*) Crossing Pr., Inc., The.

—She Came Too Late: An Emma Victor Mystery. 2000. (Emma Victor Mysteries Ser.: No. 1). 263p. reprint ed. pap. 10.95 o.p. (*1-55583-547-3*, Alyson Bks.) Alyson Pubns.

Winter Count. Incl. Searching for Ancestors. audio Short Manifesto. audio Trying the Land. audio 1985. 1985. Set audio 13.95 (*1-55644-124-X*, 5021) American Audio Prose Library, Inc.

Wise, Robert L. Tail of the Dragon. 2000. (Illus.). 288p. (J). pap. 9.97 (*0-7852-6833-2*) Nelson, Thomas Inc.

Wise, Robert L. & Wilson, William Louis. The Tail of the Dragon: A Novel. 2000. x, 271p. pap. 12.99 (*0-7852-6983-5*) Nelson, Thomas Pubs.

Worden, Mike. The Heroes of Henley's Woods. 1998. 208p. pap. text 14.95 (*1-886769-20-6*) Gold Leaf Pr.

**UNITED STATES—SOCIAL LIFE AND CUSTOMS—FICTION**

Adams, Alice. The Stories of Alice Adams. 2002. 640p. 30.00 (*0-375-41285-9*) Knopf, Alfred A. Inc.

Addonizio, Kim. In the Box Called Pleasure. 1999. 150p. pap. 12.95 (*1-57366-081-7*) Fiction Collective Two, Inc.

Alcott, Louisa May. Louisa May Alcott on Race, Sex, & Slavery. Elbert, Sarah, ed. & intro. by. 1997. (Illus.). 160p. text 42.50 (*1-55553-308-6*); pap. text 17.95 (*1-55553-307-8*) Northeastern Univ. Pr.

Aldrich, Thomas Bailey. Marjorie Daw & Other People. E-Book 3.95 (*0-594-04263-1*) 1873 Pr.

—Marjorie Daw & Other People. 1977. (Short Story Index Reprint Ser.). 22.95 (*0-8369-3230-7*) Ayer Co. Pubs., Inc.

—Marjorie Daw & Other People. (Works of Thomas Bailey Aldrich). reprint ed. 243p. 44.00 (*0-7812-0819-X*); 1989. lib. bdg. 79.00 (*0-7812-1665-6*) Reprint Services Corp.

Alexie, Sherman. The Toughest Indian in the World. 2000. 238p. 24.00 o.p. (*0-87113-801-8*, Atlantic Monthly Pr.); 2001. 256p. reprint ed. pap. 12.00 (*0-8021-3800-4*, Grove Pr.) Grove/Atlantic, Inc.

Allen, Dwight. The Green Suit. 2000. 274p. tchr. ed. 22.95 (*1-56512-274-7*) Algonquin Bks. of Chapel Hill.

Allen, Preston L. Churchboys & Other Sinners. 2003. (Illus.). 152p. 15.95 (*0-932112-44-7*) Carolina Wren Pr.

Auchincloss, Louis. The Anniversary & Other Stories. 1999. 208p. tchr. ed. 25.00 o.p. (*0-395-97074-1*) Houghton Mifflin Co.

—Her Infinite Variety. 2002. 240p. pap. 13.00 (*0-618-22488-2*, Mariner Bks.) Houghton Mifflin Co. Trade & Reference Div.

Bachelder, Chris. Bear V. Shark. 256p. 2002. E-Book (*0-7432-2370-5*); 2001. 23.00 (*0-7432-1946-5*) Simon & Schuster. (Scribner).

Baida, Peter. A Nurse's Story & Others. 2001. viii, 238p. 26.00 (*1-57806-318-3*) Univ. Pr. of Mississippi.

Bank, Melissa. The Girls' Guide to Hunting & Fishing. unabr. ed. 1999. (Chivers Sound Library American Collections). audio 54.95 (*0-7927-2331-7*, CSL 220, Chivers Sound Library) BBC Audiobooks America.

—The Girls' Guide to Hunting & Fishing. unabr. ed. 2000. audio compact disk 64.95 (*0-7540-5328-8*, CCD 019) Chivers Audio Bks. GBR. *Dist:* BBC Audiobooks America.

—The Girls' Guide to Hunting & Fishing. l.t. ed. (Bestsellers Ser.). 2000. 325p. 27.95 (*0-7862-2169-0*); 1999. (Illus.). 325p. 30.95 (*0-7862-2168-2*); 1999. (*0-7540-1360-X*); 1999. (*0-7540-2269-2*) Thorndike Pr.

—The Girls' Guide to Hunting & Fishing. 2000. 19.00 (*0-606-19483-5*) Turtleback Bks.

—The Girls' Guide to Hunting & Fishing. 2000. (Illus.). 288p. (YA). 12.95 (*0-14-029324-8*); 1999. 288p. 23.95 (*0-670-88300-X*); 1999. 2p. audio 24.95 o.s.i (*0-14-180028-3*, Penguin AudioBooks) Viking Penguin.

Barthelme, Frederick. Law of Averages: New & Selected Stories. 2000. 352p. text 25.00 o.p. (*1-58243-115-9*, Counterpoint Pr.) Basic Bks.

Bass, Rick. The Hermit's Story. 2002. 192p. tchr. ed. 22.00 (*0-618-13932-X*) Houghton Mifflin Co.

—The Hermit's Story. 2003. 192p. pap. 12.00 (*0-618-38044-2*, Mariner Bks.) Houghton Mifflin Co. Trade & Reference Div.

Bausch, Richard. Someone to Watch over Me: Stories. 2000. 224p. pap. 13.00 (*0-06-093070-5*, Perennial) HarperTrade.

—The Stories of Richard Bausch: New & Selected Stories. 2003. 672p. 29.95 (*0-06-019649-1*, HarperCollins) HarperTrade.

Bean, Barbara. Dream House. 2001. (Contemporary Fiction Ser.). 178p. 22.00 (*0-87081-617-9*) Univ. Pr. of Colorado.

Bellow, Saul. Collected Stories. Bellow, Janis Freedman, ed. 2002. 464p. 15.00 (*0-14-200164-3*) Viking Penguin.

—Collected Stories. 2001. 464p. text 30.00 o.s.i (*0-670-89486-9*, Viking) Viking Penguin.

Benedict, Elizabeth. Almost: A Novel. 2002. 260p. pap. 13.00 (*0-618-23161-7*, Mariner Bks.) Houghton Mifflin Co. Trade & Reference Div.

Berg, Elizabeth. Ordinary Life: Stories. 2002. 208p. 22.95 (*0-679-43746-0*); E-Book 19.95 (*1-58836-142-X*) Random Hse., Inc.

Bloom, Amy. A Blind Man Can See How Much I Love You. 2001. 176p. reprint ed. pap. 12.00 (*0-375-70557-0*, Vintage) Knopf Publishing Group.

—A Blind Man Can See How Much I Love You: Stories. l.t. ed. 2001. (Thorndike Press Large Print Women's Fiction Ser.). 199p. 29.95 (*0-7862-3290-0*) Thorndike Pr.

Boyle, T. Coraghessan. After the Plague. 2002. 320p. 14.00 (*0-14-200141-4*); 2001. 256p. 25.95 o.s.i (*0-670-03005-8*, Viking) Viking Penguin.

—Descent of Man. 1979. 9.95 o.p. (*0-316-10469-8*) Little Brown & Co.

—Descent of Man. 1979. 228p. pap. text 4.95 o.p. (*0-07-006956-5*) McGraw-Hill Cos., The.

—Descent of Man. 2015. (Illus.). 864p. pap. 10.95 (*0-14-043631-6*, Penguin Classics); 1990. 480p. 12.95 (*0-14-029994-7*); 1987. 256p. pap. 6.95 o.p. (*0-14-009286-2*, Penguin Bks.) Viking Penguin.

—Drop City. 2004. 512p. pap. 14.00 (*0-14-200380-8*) Penguin Group (USA) Inc.

Brennan, Maeve. The Rose Garden: Short Stories. 1999. 320p. text 23.00 o.p. (*1-58243-050-0*, Counterpoint Pr.) Basic Bks.

—Rose Garden: Short Stories. 2001. 320p. pap. text 14.50 (*1-58243-119-1*, Counterpoint Pr.) Basic Bks.

Brodkey, Harold. First Love & Other Sorrows. 1998. 288p. pap. 14.00 o.s.i (*0-8050-6010-3*, Owl Bks.) Holt, Henry & Co.

—First Love & Other Sorrows. (Contemporaries Ser.). 1988. reprint ed. pap. 13.00 o.s.i (*0-679-72075-8*); Vol. 970. 1986. pap. 5.95 o.s.i (*0-394-72970-6*) Knopf Publishing Group. (Vintage).

Broughton, T. Alan. Suicidal Tendencies: Stories. 2003. (Series in Contemporary Fiction). 311p. 23.95 (*1-885635-05-2*) Ctr. for Literary Publishing, Colorado State Univ.

Brown, Rebecca. The End of Youth. 2003. 144p. pap. 11.95 (*0-87286-418-9*) City Lights Bks.

Bruce, Annette J. & Brooks, J. Stephen, eds. Sandspun: Florida Tales by Florida Tellers. 2001. xix, 149p. 16.95 (*1-56164-242-8*); pap. 9.95 (*1-56164-243-6*) Pineapple Pr., Inc.

Burford, Miles. Dark Mountain & Other Stories. 2003. 168p. 19.95 (*1-56474-432-9*) Fithian Pr.

—Flying Lessons: Stories. 2001. 131p. 19.95 (*1-56474-370-5*) Fithian Pr.

Carlson, Ron. A Kind of Flying: Selected Stories. 2003. 352p. pap. 15.95 (*0-393-32479-6*) Norton, W. W. & Co., Inc.

Carson, Tom. Gilligan's Wake: A Novel. 352p. 2004. pap. 14.00 (*0-312-31114-1*); 2003. 25.00 (*0-312-29123-X*) Picador.

Chabon, Michael. Werewolves in Their Youth: Stories. 2000. 224p. pap. 12.00 (*0-312-25438-5*) Picador.

Chopin, Kate. Complete Novels & Stories. 2002. 1071p. 35.00 (*1-931082-21-9*) Library of America, The.

Clark, Howard. Crowded Lives & Other Stories of Desperation & Danger. 2000. (Five Star Mystery Ser.). 219p. 20.95 (*0-7862-2366-9*, Five Star) Gale Group.

Cobb, Thomas. Acts of Contrition. 2003. (*1-881515-59-1*) Texas Review Pr.

Cohen, Robert. The Varieties of Romantic Experience: Stories. 2003. 224p. pap. 12.00 (*1-4000-3184-2*) Knopf Publishing Group.

Cohen, Shari. Rhythm of the Sea. 2001. 250p. per. 19.95 (*1-888725-63-X*, MacroPrintBooks); 147p. (*1-888725-55-9*, BeachHouse Bks.) Science & Humanities Pr.

Coshnear, Daniel. Jobs & Other Preoccupations: Stories. 2001. 213p. pap. 12.95 (*1-884235-34-4*) Helicon 9 Editions.

Cox, Elizabeth. Bargains in the Real World: Thirteen Stories. 2001. E-Book 15.95 (*1-58945-765-X*) Adobe Systems, Inc.

—Bargains in the Real World: Thirteen Stories. 2001. E-Book 15.95 (*0-375-50696-9*) Random Hse., Inc.

Crane, Elizabeth. When the Messenger Is Hot: Stories. 2003. 224p. 21.95 (*0-316-09652-0*); 2004. 240p. reprint ed. pap. 12.95 (*0-316-60846-7*, Back Bay) Little Brown & Co.

Davis, Jennifer S. Her Kind of Want. 2002. (Iowa Short Fiction Award Ser.). 160p. pap. 15.95 (*0-87745-818-9*) Univ. of Iowa Pr.

Dobyns, Stephen. Eating Naked: Stories. 2000. 276p. 23.00 o.s.i (*0-8050-6022-7*, Metropolitan Bks.) Holt, Henry & Co.

—Eating Naked: Stories. 2001. 288p. pap. 13.00 (*0-312-27829-2*) Picador.

Doctorow, E. L. Five Stories. 2004. 160p. 24.95 (*1-4000-6204-7*) Random Hse., Inc.

Dodd, Susan. O Careless Love: Stories & a Novella. 1999. 274p. 22.00 o.p. (*0-688-16999-6*, Morrow, William & Co.) Morrow/Avon.

Earle, Steve. Doghouse Roses: Stories. 2001. 206p. tchr. ed. 22.00 (*0-618-04026-9*) Houghton Mifflin Co.

—Doghouse Roses: Stories. 2002. 224p. pap. 12.00 (*0-618-21924-2*, Mariner Bks.) Houghton Mifflin Co. Trade & Reference Div.

Epstein, Joseph. Fabulous Small Jews: Stories. 2003. 352p. tchr. ed. 24.00 (*0-395-94402-3*) Houghton Mifflin Co.

—Fabulous Small Jews: Stories. 2004. 352p. pap. 13.00 (*0-618-44658-3*, Mariner Bks.) Houghton Mifflin Co. Trade & Reference Div.

Erian, Alicia. Untitled Alicia Erian. 2004. 288p. 25.00 (*0-7432-4494-X*, Simon & Schuster) Simon & Schuster.

Estleman, Loren D., ed. & intro. American West: Twenty New Stories from the Western Writers of America. 2000. 384p. 25.95 (*0-312-87317-4*, Forge Bks.) Doherty, Tom Assocs., LLC.

French, Marilyn. Her Mother's Daughter. 1996. mass mkt. 6.99 (*0-345-91019-2*); 1988. 770p. mass mkt. 6.99 o.s.i (*0-345-35362-5*); 1988. mass mkt. 4.95 o.s.i (*0-345-35662-4*) Ballantine Bks.

—Her Mother's Daughter. 1990. 4.99 o.p. (*0-517-05544-9*) Random Hse. Value Publishing.

—Her Mother's Daughter. 1987. 21.45 o.p. (*0-671-63051-2*) Summit Bks.

Friedman, Paul. And If Defeated Allege Fraud: Stories. fac. ed. 1994. 154p. pap. 47.80 (*0-7837-7623-3*, 204737500007) Bks. on Demand.

Settings

—And If Defeated Allege Fraud: Stories. 1971. 146p. 17.95 (*0-252-00159-1*) Univ. of Illinois Pr.

Fulton, John. Retribution. 2002. 208p. pap. 13.00 (*0-312-30068-9*); 2001. 240p. 23.00 (*0-312-27680-X*) Picador.

Furman, Laura. Drinking with the Cook. 2001. 262p. 24.00 (*0-9701525-2-3*); pap. 16.00 (*0-9701525-3-1*) Winedale Publishing.

Gates, David. The Wonders of the Invisible World: Stories. 2000. (Contemporaries Ser.). 272p. pap. 12.00 (*0-679-75644-2*, Vintage) Knopf Publishing Group.

—The Wonders of the Invisible World: Stories. 1999. 272p. 23.00 o.s.i (*0-679-43668-5*) Knopf, Alfred A. Inc.

Gavell, Mary Ladd. I Cannot Tell a Lie, Exactly: And Other Stories. 2002. 240p. pap. 12.95 (*0-375-75822-4*) Random House Adult Trade Publishing Group.

Gay, William. I Hate to See That Evening Sun Go Down: Collected Stories. 320p. 2003. pap. 13.00 (*0-7432-4292-0*); 2002. 24.00 (*0-7432-4088-X*) Simon & Schuster. (Free Pr.).

Gibney, Art. Skin of the Earth: Stories from Nevada's Back Country. 2002. (Western Literature Ser.). 132p. pap. 16.00 (*0-87417-513-5*) Univ. of Nevada Pr.

Gifford, Barry. American Falls: Collected Stories. 2002. 288p. 24.95 (*1-58322-470-X*) Seven Stories Pr.

Gills, Michael. Why I Lie: Stories. 2002. (Western Literature Ser.). 144p. pap. 16.00 (*0-87417-514-3*) Univ. of Nevada Pr.

Glancy, Diane. The Voice That Was in Travel: Stories. 1999. (American Indian Literature & Critical Studies Ser.: Vol. 33). x, 116p. 19.95 (*0-8061-3157-8*) Univ. of Oklahoma Pr.

—The Voice That Was in Travel: Stories. 1999. E-Book 19.95 (*0-585-11326-2*) netLibrary, Inc.

Glover, Douglas. Bad News of the Heart. 2003. 212p. pap. 13.95 (*1-56478-286-7*) Dalkey Archive Pr.

Greer, Robert. Isolation & Other Stories. 2002. (Illus.). 208p. pap. 18.00 (*1-888570-48-2*) Davies Group Pubs., The.

—Isolation & Other Stories. Davies Group Staff, ed. & des. by. ltd. ed. 2001. (Illus.). 208p. 29.95 (*1-888570-47-4*) Davies Group Pubs., The.

Grodstein, Lauren. The Best of Animals. 2002. 224p. 23.95 (*0-89255-281-6*) Persea Bks., Inc.

Gurganus, Allan. The Practical Heart: Four Novellas. 1993. (Illus.). 96p. 29.95 o.p. (*0-933598-49-1*) North Carolina Wesleyan College Pr.

—The Practical Heart: Four Novellas. 2002. 336p. pap. 14.00 (*0-375-72763-9*) Random Hse., Inc.

Hackenberger, Claus. A Long Walk. 2001. pap. 19.95 (*1-883697-69-7*) Hara Publishing Group.

Hall, Donald. Willow Temple: New & Selected Stories. 2003. 224p. tchr. ed. 24.00 (*0-618-32981-1*) Houghton Mifflin Co.

—Willow Temple: New & Selected Stories. 2004. 224p. pap. 12.00 (*0-618-44661-3*, Mariner Bks.) Houghton Mifflin Co. Trade & Reference Div.

Harrison, Jim. The Beast God Forgot to Invent. 2000. 274p. 24.00 o.p. (*0-87113-821-2*, Atlantic Monthly Pr.) Grove/Atlantic, Inc.

—The Beast God Forgot to Invent: Novellas. 2001. 288p. pap. 13.00 (*0-8021-3836-5*, Grove Pr.) Grove/Atlantic, Inc.

Hawkins, Odie. Ghetto Sketches. 2001. 300p. reprint ed. mass mkt. 8.50 (*1-892343-19-3*, Oak Tree Pr.) Oak Tree Publishing.

Hemphill, Paul. Lost in the Lights. 2003. 208p. pap. 18.95 (*0-8173-1316-8*) Univ. of Alabama Pr.

Hoffman, Alice. Seventh Heaven. 2003. 272p. pap. 13.00 (*0-425-18848-5*) Berkley Publishing Group.

Homes, A. M. Things You Should Know: A Collection of Stories. 2002. 224p. 23.95 (*0-688-16712-8*) HarperCollins Pubs.

—Things You Should Know: A Collection of Stories. 2003. 224p. pap. 12.95 (*0-06-052013-2*, Perennial) HarperTrade.

Honey, Maureen, ed. Breaking the Ties That Bind: Popular Stories of the New Woman, 1915-1930. 1998. (Illus.). xi, 352p. pap. 12.95 (*0-8061-3034-2*); 1992. (Illus.). xi, 339p. 26.95 o.p. (*0-8061-2467-9*); 1992. E-Book 27.95 (*0-8061-7105-7*) Univ. of Oklahoma Pr.

Howard, Clark. Challenge the Widow-Maker & Other Stories of People in Peril. 2000. (Illus.). 237p. pap. 16.00 (*1-885941-40-4*); 40.00 o.p. (*1-885941-39-0*) Crippen & Landru, Pubs.

Jaime-Becerra, M. Every Night Is Ladies' Night: Stories. 2004. 304p. 23.95 (*0-06-055962-4*, Rayo) HarperTrade.

Jewett, Sarah Orne. A White Heron & Other Stories. 1999. (Thrift Editions Ser.). 128p. pap. 1.50 (*0-486-40884-1*) Dover Pubns., Inc.

—A White Heron & Other Stories. 1988. (Collected Works of Sarah Orne Jewett). reprint ed. lib. bdg. 59.00 (*0-7812-1308-8*) Reprint Services Corp.

Johnson, Dana. Break Any Woman Down: Stories. 2001. 168p. 24.95 (*0-8203-2315-2*) Univ. of Georgia Pr.

Kamani, Ginu. Junglee Girl. 1995. 208p. 19.95 (*1-879960-41-9*); pap. 11.95 (*1-879960-40-0*) Aunt Lute Bks.

Kane, Jessica Francis. Bending Heaven: Stories. 2002. 208p. text 23.00 (*1-58243-206-6*, Counterpoint Pr.) Basic Bks.

Kees, Weldon. Selected Short Stories of Weldon Kees. Gioia, Dana, ed. & intro. by. 2002. 172p. reprint ed. pap. 12.00 (*0-8032-7806-3*, Bison Bks.) Univ. of Nebraska Pr.

Kelly, Leisha. Julia's Hope: A Novel. 2002. 320p. (gr. 13 up). pap. 12.99 (*0-8007-5820-X*) Revell, Fleming H. Co.

King, Martha. Little Tales of Family & War, 1990-1999. 2000. 89p. pap. 12.00 (*1-881471-47-0*) Spuyten Duyvil.

King, Stephen. Hearts in Atlantis. 2001. E-Book 9.99 (*1-59061-258-2*) Adobe Systems, Inc.

—Hearts in Atlantis. l.t. ed. (Thorndike/G. K. Hall Paperback Bestsellers Ser.). 2000. 760p. pap. 28.95 (*0-7838-8738-8*); 1999. 732p. 31.95 (*0-7838-8737-X*) Gale Group. (Macmillan Reference USA).

—Hearts in Atlantis. 1999. 528p. 28.00 (*0-684-85351-5*, Scribner); 1999. E-Book 28.00 (*0-684-84490-7*, Scribner); 2000. 688p. reprint ed. pap. 7.99 (*0-671-02424-8*, Pocket); 2000. 528p. reprint ed. 7.99 (*0-671-04214-9*, Pocket); 2001. 688p. reprint ed. mass mkt. 7.99 o.s.i (*0-7434-3621-0*, Pocket) Simon & Schuster.

—Hearts in Atlantis. 2001. pap. 49.95 incl. audio compact disk (*0-7435-0987-0*, Simon & Schuster Audioworks) Simon & Schuster Audio.

—Hearts in Atlantis. 2000. 14.04 (*0-606-19496-7*) Turtleback Bks.

Kirshenbaum, Binnie. Married Life & Other True Adventures. 1990. 128p. pap. 7.95 o.p. (*0-89594-397-2*); lib. bdg. 22.95 o.p. (*0-89594-398-0*) Crossing Pr., Inc., The.

Krouse, Erika. Come up & See Me Sometime: Stories. 208p. 2002. pap. 13.00 (*0-7434-2298-8*); 2001. 22.00 (*0-7432-0244-9*) Simon & Schuster. (Scribner).

Lee, Don. Yellow: Stories. 2002. 256p. pap. 13.95 (*0-393-32308-0*); 2001. 192p. 22.95 (*0-393-02562-4*) Norton, W. W. & Co., Inc.

Lewis, Trudy. The Bones of Garbo, & Other Stories. 2003. xi, 175p. 42.95 (*0-8142-0930-0*); 9.95 (*0-8142-9007-8*); pap. 22.95 (*0-8142-5109-9*) Ohio State Univ. Pr.

Lincoln, Christine. Sap Rising: Stories. 2002. 176p. pap. 11.00 (*0-375-72777-9*) Random Hse., Inc.

Makuck, Peter. Breaking & Entering: Stories. 1981. (Illinois Short Fiction Ser.). 172p. text 14.95 o.p. (*0-252-00898-7*); pap. text 14.95 o.p. (*0-252-00925-8*) Univ. of Illinois Pr.

—Costly Habits: Stories. 2002. 224p. (Orig.). pap. 19.95 (*0-8262-1446-0*) Univ. of Missouri Pr.

Marino, Assunta F. In the Heart of a Friend: A Collection of Short Stories. 2003. 16.95 (*0-936389-89-3*) Tudor Pubs., Inc.

Mason, Bobbie Ann. Zigzagging down a Wild Trail: Stories. 2001. E-Book 18.00 (*1-59061-174-8*) Adobe Systems, Inc.

McCullers, Carson. The Member of the Wedding. 1984. 160p. (gr. 7-12). mass mkt. 6.50 (*0-553-25051-5*) Bantam Bks.

—The Member of the Wedding, 001. 9999. 9.95 o.p. (*0-395-07979-9*) Houghton Mifflin Co.

—The Member of the Wedding. 1963. pap. 8.95 (*0-8112-0093-0*, NDP153) New Directions Publishing Corp.

—The Member of the Wedding. 1950. 12.04 (*0-606-01060-2*) Turtleback Bks.

McPherson, James Alan. Hue & Cry. 2001. 304p. pap. 14.00 (*0-06-093647-9*, Ecco) HarperTrade.

Miller, Adrienne, ed. Esquire's Big Book of Fiction. 2002. 544p. pap. 21.95 (*1-893956-26-1*) Context Bks.

Montemarano, Nicholas. The Worst Degree of Unforgivable. 2003. 224p. pap. 12.95 (*1-893956-41-5*) Context Bks.

Moody, Rick. The Ring of Brightest Angels Around Heaven: A Novella & Stories. 2002. 256p. reprint ed. pap. 13.95 (*0-316-70628-0*, Back Bay) Little Brown & Co.

Moore, Lorrie. Self-Help: Stories. 1986. 176p. pap. 9.00 o.p. (*0-452-25821-9*, Plume) Dutton/Plume.

Neider, Charles. Life as I Find It: A Treasury of Mark Twain Rarities. 2000. (Illus.). 411p. pap. 17.95 (*0-8154-1027-1*) Cooper Square Pubs., Inc.

Nesbitt, Marc. Gigantic. 2002. 192p. 24.00 (*0-8021-1709-0*, Grove Pr.) Grove/Atlantic, Inc.

Nevin, David. American Story, Vol. 5. Date not set. (*0-312-87657-2*, Forge Bks.) Doherty, Tom Assocs., LLC.

Nunez, Sigrid. A Feather on the Breath of God. 2004. pap. (*0-312-42273-3*) Picador.

Oates, Joyce Carol. Crossing the Border. 1978. mass mkt. 2.50 o.p. (*0-449-23751-6*, Fawcett) Ballantine Bks.

—Faithless: Tales of Transgression. 2001. E-Book 19.95 (*0-06-621320-7*); E-Book 19.95 (*0-06-621317-7*); E-Book 19.95 (*0-06-621318-5*) HarperCollins General Bks. Group. (PerfectBound).

—Faithless: Tales of Transgression. 2001. 400p. 27.00 (*0-06-018525-2*, Ecco) HarperTrade.

—The Hungry Ghosts. 1978. 200p. 14.00 o.p. (*0-87685-204-5*); pap. 5.00 o.p. (*0-87685-203-7*) Godine, David R. Pub. (Black Sparrow Pr.).

—I Am No One You Know: Stories. 2004. 304p. 24.95 (*0-06-059288-5*, Ecco) HarperTrade.

—Marriages & Infidelities. 1978. 416p. mass mkt. 2.50 o.s.i (*0-449-23724-9*, Fawcett) Ballantine Bks.

—The Seduction & Other Stories. 1981. 320p. mass mkt. 2.75 o.s.i (*0-449-24284-6*, Fawcett) Ballantine Bks.

—The Seduction & Other Stories. 1976. 275p. 14.00 o.p. (*0-87685-229-0*, Black Sparrow Pr.) Godine, David R. Pub.

—Upon the Sweeping Flood. 1977. pap. 1.75 o.s.i (*0-449-23274-3*, Fawcett); 1975. mass mkt. 1.25 o.s.i (*0-449-22463-5*) Ballantine Bks.

—Where Are You Going, Where Have You Been? Selected Early Stories. 1979. 352p. mass mkt. 1.75 o.s.i (*0-449-30795-6*, Fawcett) Ballantine Bks.

—Where Are You Going, Where Have You Been? Selected Early Stories. 522p. 2002. pap. 14.95 (*0-86538-078-3*); 1993. 24.95 (*0-86538-077-5*) Ontario Review Pr.

—Where Are You Going, Where Have You Been? Selected Early Stories. 1995. (Women Writers: Text & Contexts Ser.). 160p. (C). pap. text 14.00 (*0-8135-2135-1*) Rutgers Univ. Pr.

—Where Are You Going, Where Have You Been? Selected Early Stories. Showalter, Elaine, ed. & intro. by. 1995. (Women Writers: Text & Contexts Ser.). 160p. (C). text 30.00 (*0-8135-2134-3*) Rutgers Univ. Pr.

O'Brien, Tim. July, July: A Novel. 2002. 336p. tchr. ed. 26.00 (*0-618-03969-4*) Houghton Mifflin Co.

Ochsner, Gina. The Necessary Grace to Fall: Stories. 2002. (Winner of the Flannery O'Connor Award for Short Fiction Ser.). 192p. 24.95 (*0-8203-2314-4*) Univ. of Georgia Pr.

O'Connell, Mary. Living with Saints. 2001. 240p. 23.00 (*0-87113-826-3*, Atlantic Monthly Pr.) Grove/Atlantic, Inc.

O'Hara, John. Selected Short Stories of John O'Hara. 2003. 256p. pap. 12.95 (*0-8129-6697-X*, Modern Library) Random House Adult Trade Publishing Group.

Page, Thomas Nelson. The Burial of the Guns. E-Book 2.49 (*1-58627-733-2*) Electric Umbrella Publishing.

—The Burial of the Guns. 2002. 128p. per. 88.99 (*1-58827-207-9*); 93.99 (*1-58827-206-0*) IndyPublish.com.

—The Burial of the Guns. reprint ed. 1986. (C). pap. text 7.95 (*0-8290-1905-7*); 1972. 27.25 (*0-8422-8103-7*) Irvington Pubs.

Parks, John G. American Short Stories since 1945. 2001. 896p. pap. text 45.00 (*0-19-513132-0*) Oxford Univ. Pr., Inc.

Pearlman, Edith. Love among the Greats. 2002. 176p. pap. 15.95 (*0-910055-80-7*) Eastern Washington Univ. Pr.

Purdy, James. The Candles of Your Eyes. 1991. 160p. pap. 7.95 o.p. (*0-87286-256-9*) City Lights Bks.

—Candles of Your Eyes. 1986. 15.95 o.p. (*0-670-80804-0*, Viking) Viking Penguin.

—The Candles of Your Eyes: Stories. 1987. 160p. 14.95 o.s.i (*1-55584-066-3*) Grove/Atlantic, Inc.

—Color of Darkness. 1975. 175p. reprint ed. 60.95 (*0-8371-7874-6*, PUCD, Greenwood Pr.) Greenwood Publishing Group, Inc.

—Dream Palaces: Malcolm the Nephew & 63: Dream Palace. 1980. 19.95 o.p. (*0-670-28463-7*) Viking Penguin.

—Sixty-Three: Dream Palace & Other Stories. 1981. 192p. pap. 4.95 o.p. (*0-14-005732-3*, Penguin Bks.) Viking Penguin.

—Sixty-Three: Dream Palace, Selected Stories, 1956-1987. 1991. 356p. pap. 15.00 o.p. (*0-87685-844-2*); 35.00 o.p. (*0-87685-846-9*); 25.00 o.p. (*0-87685-845-0*) Godine, David R. Pub. (Black Sparrow Pr.).

Richter, Stacey. My Date with Satan. 1999. 224p. 22.00 (*0-684-85701-4*, Scribner) Simon & Schuster.

—My Date with Satan: Stories. 2000. 224p. pap. 11.00 (*0-684-85702-2*, Scribner) Simon & Schuster.

Rinehart, Steven. Kick in the Head: Stories. 2000. 240p. 22.00 o.s.i (*0-385-49853-5*) Doubleday Publishing.

—Kick in the Head: Stories. 2001. 240p. pap. 12.00 (*0-385-49854-3*, Knopf Bks. for Young Readers) Random Hse. Children's Bks.

Robinson, Ann. Ordinary Perils: Stories. 2002. 188p. pap. 16.95 (*1-931807-09-4*) Randall, Peter E. Pub.

Roorbach, Bill. Big Bend: Stories. 2002. 192p. reprint ed. pap. text 14.00 (*1-58243-257-0*, Counterpoint Pr.) Basic Bks.

Russo, Richard. The Whore's Child & Other Stories. 2003. 240p. reprint ed. pap. 12.95 (*0-375-72601-2*, Vintage) Knopf Publishing Group.

—The Whore's Child & Other Stories. 2002. 240p. 24.00 (*0-375-41168-2*) Knopf, Alfred A. Inc.

—The Whore's Child & Other Stories. 2002. (Americana Ser.). 29.95 (*0-7862-4890-4*) Thorndike Pr.

Sandlin, Tim. Honey Don't. 2004. 400p. pap. 14.00 (*1-59448-022-2*, Riverhead Trade (Paperbacks)) Berkley Publishing Group.

Schroeder, John. Cumberland County. pap. (*1-889924-05-9*) Paradigm Pr.

Scott, Daniel. Some of Us Have to Get up in the Morning: Short Stories. unabr. ed. 2001. 232p. (Orig.). pap. 15.95 (*1-885586-21-3*) Turtle Point Pr.

Smiley, Jane. A Thousand Acres. 2003. 384p. pap. 14.00 (*1-4000-3383-7*) Knopf Publishing Group.

Solomon, Barbara H., ed. American Families: Twenty-Eight Short Stories. 1989. 432p. mass mkt. 6.99 o.s.i (*0-451-62736-9*, 029) NAL.

Sontag, Susan. I, Etcetera. 2002. 256p. pap. 14.00 (*0-312-42010-2*) Picador.

Spencer, Elizabeth. The Southern Woman: New & Selected Fiction. 2001. 480p. 23.95 (*0-679-64218-8*, Modern Library) Random House Adult Trade Publishing Group.

Spofford, Harriet Elizabeth Prescott. The Amber Gods & Other Stories. Bendixen, Alfred, ed. 1989. (American Women Writers Ser.). 300p. (C). text 40.00 o.p. (*0-8135-1400-2*); pap. text 15.00 (*0-8135-1401-0*) Rutgers Univ. Pr.

—Amber Gods & Other Stories. 1977. (Short Story Index Reprint Ser.). 28.95 (*0-8369-3209-9*) Ayer Co. Pubs., Inc.

Stephens, Amanda. Justice for All. 2003. (Liberty's Kids Ser.: Vol. 1). (Illus.). 112p. (J). 6.99 (*0-448-43248-X*, Grosset & Dunlap) Penguin Putnam Bks. for Young Readers.

Stoddard, Elizabeth. Elizabeth Stoddard: Stories. Opfermann, Susanne & Roth, Yvonne, eds. 2003. 272p. text 45.00 (*1-55553-563-1*); pap. text 18.95 (*1-55553-562-3*) Northeastern Univ. Pr.

Stowe, Harriet Beecher. Oldtown Folks. 2000. 252p. pap. 9.95 (*0-594-01023-3*); E-Book 3.95 (*0-594-05614-4*) 1873 Pr.

—Oldtown Folks. reprint ed. 35.00 (*0-404-06293-8*) AMS Pr., Inc.

—Oldtown Folks. 1992. (BCL1-PS American Literature Ser.). 608p. reprint ed. lib. bdg. 109.00 (*0-7812-6873-7*) Reprint Services Corp.

—Oldtown Folks. Berkson, Dorothy, ed. 1987. (American Women Writers Ser.). 519p. (C). text 45.00 (*0-8135-1219-0*); pap. text 17.00 (*0-8135-1220-4*) Rutgers Univ. Pr.

—Oldtown Folks. 1969. reprint ed. 13.00 (*0-403-00053-X*) Scholarly Pr., Inc.

—Uncle Sam's Emancipation. 1977. (Black Heritage Library Collection). 24.95 (*0-8369-8719-5*) Ayer Co. Pubs., Inc.

—Uncle Sam's Emancipation. 9.00 o.p. (*0-403-00147-1*) Scholarly Pr., Inc.

Strauss, Darin. The Real McCoy: A Novel. 2003. 336p. reprint ed. pap. 14.00 (*0-452-28441-4*, Plume) Dutton/Plume.

Sutton, Joseph. The Immortal Mouth: And Other Stories. 2003. 200p. pap. 14.95 (*0-88739-310-1*) Creative Arts Bk. Co.

Tanner, Ron. A Bed of Nails: Stories. 2003. (*1-886157-42-1*) BkMk Pr. of the Univ. of Missouri-Kansas City.

Thomas, Dorothy. The Getaway & Other Stories. 2002. 120p. pap. 29.95 (*0-8032-9448-4*, Bison Bks.) Univ. of Nebraska Pr.

Tinsley, Molly Best. Throwing Knives. 2000. 184p. 36.95 (*0-8142-0847-9*); (Illus.). pap. 17.95 (*0-8142-5051-3*) Ohio State Univ. Pr.

Twa, Garth. Durable Beauty: Stories. 2001. 232p. 26.00 (*0-9648974-4-X*, Epiphany Pr.) Parissound Publishing.

Twain, Mark. The Mysterious Stranger & Other Stories. 2004. 272p. mass mkt. 4.95 (*0-451-52924-3*, Signet Classics) NAL.

Updike, John. The Early Stories, 1953-1975. 2003. (Illus.). 864p. 35.00 (*1-4000-4072-8*) Knopf, Alfred A. Inc.

—Licks of Love: Short Stories & a Sequel, "Rabbit Remembered" 2001. 368p. reprint ed. pap. 14.00 (*0-345-44201-6*, Ballantine Bks.) Ballantine Bks.

—Licks of Love: Short Stories & a Sequel, "Rabbit Remembered" 2000. 368p. 25.00 (*0-375-41113-5*) Knopf, Alfred A. Inc.

Valeri, Laura. The Kind of Things Saints Do. 2002. (John Simmons Short Fiction Award Ser.). (Illus.). 200p. pap. 16.95 (*0-87745-819-7*) Univ. of Iowa Pr.

Vapnyar, Lara. There Are Jews in My House: Stories. 2003. 160p. 17.95 (*0-375-42250-1*, Pantheon) Knopf Publishing Group.

Vonnegut, Kurt, Jr. Bagombo Snuff Box: Uncollected Short Fiction. 2000. 384p. pap. 13.95 (*0-425-17446-8*) Berkley Publishing Group.

—Bagombo Snuff Box: Uncollected Short Fiction. 13th abr. unabr. ed. 1999. 6p. audio 26.95 (*1-56511-329-2*) HighBridge Co.
—Bagombo Snuff Box: Uncollected Short Fiction. 1999. 150.00 (*0-399-14526-5*, Putnam & Grosset) Penguin Group (USA) Inc.
Warren, Elizabeth & Davenport, Sheri. On the Way to Woodstock. 2002. 445p. pap. 14.00 (*0-9712648-0-5*) Sisyphus Pr.
Washington, Ida H. Early Stories of Dorothy Caufield. 2000. 44p. pap. 8.00 (*0-9666832-3-4*) Cherry Tree Bks.
Wildman, Eugene. The World of Glass. 2003. 35.00 (*0-268-01970-3*); pap. 16.50 (*0-268-01971-1*) Univ. of Notre Dame Pr.
Williams, Miller. The Lives of Kelvin Fletcher: Stories Mostly Short. 2002. 224p. 24.95 (*0-8203-2439-6*) Univ. of Georgia Pr.
Winegardner, Mark. That's True of Everybody: Stories. 2002. 256p. 24.00 (*0-15-100864-7*) Harcourt Trade Pubs.
Wolfe, Tom. Hooking up Mobile. 2000. pap. (*0-374-93941-1*) Farrar, Straus & Giroux.
Yamamoto, Hisaye. Seventeen Syllables & Other Stories. (C). 1998. 150p. pap. 14.00 (*0-8135-2607-8*); 2001. xxiii, 178p. pap. text 16.00 (*0-8135-2953-0*) Rutgers Univ. Pr.
Yates, Richard. The Collected Stories of Richard Yates. 2001. 496p. 28.00 (*0-8050-6693-4*) Holt, Henry & Co.
—The Collected Stories of Richard Yates. 2002. 496p. pap. 16.00 (*0-312-42081-1*) Picador.
Yuknavitch, Lidia. Real to Reel. 2003. 175p. pap. 13.95 (*1-57366-107-4*) Fiction Collective Two, Inc.

**UTAH—FICTION**

Anderson, Launi K. Ellie's Gold. 1995. (Latter-Day Daughters Ser.). (J). pap. 4.95 (*1-56236-505-3*) Aspen Bks.
—Sadie's Trade. 1998. (Latter-Day Daughters Ser.). (J). o.p. (*1-57345-415-X*) Deseret Bk. Co.
—Violet's Garden. 1996. (Latter-Day Daughters Ser.). (Illus.). 80p. (J). (gr. 3-9). pap. 4.95 (*1-56236-506-1*) Aspen Bks.
Andrews, Sarah. Bone Hunter. 2nd ed. 1999. 320p. 24.95 (*0-312-20381-0*, Saint Martin's Minotaur) St. Martin's Pr.
—Bone Hunter: An Em Hansen Mystery. 2000. (Em Hansen Mysteries Ser.). 353p. mass mkt. 6.50 (*0-312-97317-9*, St. Martin's Paperbacks) St. Martin's Pr.
—An Eye for Gold. E-Book 24.95 (*0-312-27607-9*) St. Martin's Pr.
—Fault Line. 2003. 336p. mass mkt. 6.50 (*0-312-98445-6*, St. Martin's Paperbacks); 2002. 304p. 23.95 (*0-312-25350-8*, Saint Martin's Minotaur) St. Martin's Pr.
Arnold, Marilyn. Desert Song. 1998. 14.95 (*1-57734-254-2*, 01113348) Covenant Communications, Inc.
Arthur, Burt. Gunsmoke over Utah. l.t. ed. 1992. 18.95 o.p. (*0-7927-0763-X*); pap. 16.95 o.p. (*0-7927-0764-8*) BBC Audiobooks America.
Barrus, Emery. The Other Wife: A Novel. 1991. 288p. text 22.95 (*0-931832-87-X*) Fithian Pr.
Black, Angela K. Bitterbrush. 1994. 274p. (Orig.). pap. 9.95 (*0-9642571-0-6*) ABCDE Publishing.
Blevins, Win. The Rock Child. 1999. 464p. pap. 6.99 (*0-8125-4472-2*); 1997. 416p. 24.95 (*0-312-86400-0*) Doherty, Tom Assocs., LLC. (Forge Bks.).
Borg, Todd. Tahoe Deathfall. 2001. (Owen McKenna Mystery Thriller Ser.). (Illus.). 256p. per. 16.95 (*1-931296-11-1*) Thriller Pr.
Briggs, Betty. Quality Concealed. 1999. (Illus.). 203p. (J). (gr. 7-12). pap. 9.95 (*0-9656307-1-4*) Sunrise Selections.
Brown, Marilyn. Statehood. 1995. 304p. pap. 9.95 (*1-56236-308-5*) Aspen Bks.
—The Wine-Dark Sea of Grass: A People Struggling to Survive Suffer the Horror of the Mountain Meadows Massacre. 2000. 385p. 24.95 (*1-55517-529-5*, Salt Pr.) Cedar Fort, Inc./CFI Distribution.
Brown, Marilyn McMeen Miller. Ghosts of the Oquirrhs: A Novel. 2002. (Utah Witness Ser.). 211p. pap. 14.95 (*1-55517-658-5*, Salt Pr.) Cedar Fort, Inc./CFI Distribution.
Call, Jeff. Mormonville: A Big-City Reporter Spends a Year in Utah to Uncover the Truth about the LDS Church, but Uncovers Truths about Himself. 2002. 310p. pap. 16.95 (*1-55517-618-6*, 76186) Cedar Fort, Inc./CFI Distribution.
Civish, Fred. The Sunnyside War. 2003. 340p. pap. 19.95 (*1-55517-645-3*, 76453, Bonneville Bks.) Cedar Fort, Inc./CFI Distribution.
Crane, Cheri J. Kate's Turn: A Novel. 1994. (J). pap. 11.95 (*1-55503-715-1*, 019404) Covenant Communications, Inc.
Decker, Rod. An Environment for Murder. 1994. 236p. (Orig.). pap. 14.95 o.p. (*1-56085-063-9*) Signature Bks., Inc.
Edwards, Jaroldeen. Hannah: Mormon Midwife. 1997. 328p. 16.95 (*1-57345-280-7*, Shadow Mountain) Deseret Bk. Co.
Edwards, William H. Perry & the Professor: A Prairie Dog Story. 2000. (Illus.). 51p. (J). pap. 10.95 o.p. (*1-888106-55-7*) Agreka Bks., LLC.
Evans, Eric C. Endangered. 1997. 184p. lib. bdg. 18.95 (*0-8034-9358-4*, Avalon Bks.) Bouregy, Thomas & Co., Inc.
Evans, Richard Paul. The Carousel. 2000. 336p. 18.95 (*0-684-86891-1*, Simon & Schuster); 2001. 368p. reprint ed. pap. 6.99 (*0-7434-2870-6*, Pocket) Simon & Schuster.
—The Carousel. abr. ed. 2000. audio 18.00 (*0-7435-0050-4*, Simon & Schuster Audioworks) Simon & Schuster Audio.
—The Carousel. l.t. ed. 2001. (Illus.). 416p. 32.50 o.p. (*0-7432-0090-X*) Thorpe, F. A. Pubs. GBR. *Dist:* Ulverscroft Large Print Bks., Ltd.
—The Locket. l.t. ed. (Wheeler Large Print Bks.). 2000. 10.95 (*1-56895-970-2*); 1999. 26.95 o.p. (*1-56895-702-5*) Gale Group. (Wheeler Publishing, Inc.).
—The Locket. 1998. 240p. 15.95 (*0-684-00786-X*, Simon & Schuster); 1998. (Illus.). 368p. 17.95 o.s.i (*0-684-83473-1*, Simon & Schuster); 2003. (Illus.). 448p. reprint ed. pap. 7.99 (*0-671-00423-9*, Pocket) Simon & Schuster.
—The Locket. abr. ed. 1998. 240p. audio 16.00 (*0-671-04326-9*, Simon & Schuster Audioworks) Simon & Schuster Audio.
Fagg, Ellen, ed. The Way We Live: Stories by Utah Women. 1994. 224p. (Orig.). pap. 14.95 (*1-56085-062-0*) Signature Bks., Inc.
Farris, John. Solar Eclipse. 1999. 399p. 25.95 o.p. (*0-312-85072-7*, Forge Bks.) Doherty, Tom Assocs., LLC.
Freeman, Judith. Red Water: A Novel. 336p. 2002. (Illus.). 24.00 (*0-375-42092-4*, Pantheon); 2003. reprint ed. pap. 14.00 (*0-385-72069-6*, Anchor) Knopf Publishing Group.
Gardner, Lynn. Diamonds & Danger, Set. 1997. audio 11.98 (*1-57734-109-0*, 07001509) Covenant Communications, Inc.
—Diamonds & Danger: A Novel. 1997. 300p. pap. 11.95 (*1-57734-108-2*, 01112805) Covenant Communications, Inc.
Gardner, Willard Boyd. Pursuit of Justice: A Novel. 2003. 231p. 14.95 (*1-59156-154-X*) Covenant Communications.
Gates, John. Brigham's Day. 2000. 187p. 23.95 (*0-8027-3344-1*) Walker & Co.
—Sister Wife: A Brigham Bybee Novel. 2001. 228p. 23.95 (*0-8027-3363-8*) Walker & Co.
Gordon, Leo V. Powderkeg: Novel of Old West. 1991. 368p. 19.95 o.p. (*0-89141-435-5*, Presidio Pr.) Ballantine Bks.
Grey, Zane. Wild Horse Mesa. 1992. (Gunsmoke Western Ser.). 13.95 o.p. (*0-7451-4518-3*) BBC Audiobooks America.
—Wild Horse Mesa. l.t. ed. 1981. lib. bdg. 12.95 o.p. (*0-8161-3239-9*, Macmillan Reference USA) Gale Group.
—Wild Horse Mesa. l.t. ed. 1993. (Western Ser.). 452p. lib. bdg. 22.95 (*0-7862-0075-8*) Thorndike Pr.
Hannon, Steven M. Glen Canyon. 1997. (Illus.). x, 635p. 28.95 (*0-9655125-0-9*) Kokopelli Bks.
Hansen, Jennie. When Tomorrow Comes: A Novel. 1994. pap. 11.95 (*1-55503-725-9*, 019403) Covenant Communications, Inc.
Harris, Jeane. Delia Ironfoot. 1992. 224p. pap. 9.95 o.p. (*1-56280-014-0*) Naiad Pr., Inc.
Havens, Virginia. Roxey's Choice: A Novel. 1994. pap. 9.95 o.p. (*1-55503-712-7*) Covenant Communications, Inc.
Hill, Theresa S. Life & Times of Erastus Snow. l.t. ed. 1997. (Life & Times Ser.: Vol. I). (Illus.). 285p. 29.95 o.p. (*1-888106-18-2*) Agreka Bks., LLC.
Holmes, Perry. Mountains Against the Sun. 1997. 243p. lib. bdg. 17.95 o.p. (*0-7862-0754-X*, Five Star) Gale Group.
—Mountains Against the Sun. l.t. ed. 1998. (Western Ser.). 369p. 21.95 (*0-7862-0778-7*) Thorndike Pr.
Irvine, Robert. The Angels' Share. Isaacson, Dana, ed. 1990. 224p. reprint ed. bds. 3.95 (*0-671-69494-4*, Pocket) Simon & Schuster.
—The Angels' Share. 1989. 15.95 o.p. (*0-312-02862-8*, Saint Martin's Minotaur) St. Martin's Pr.
—Baptism for the Dead. 1990. 256p. mass mkt. 3.95 (*0-671-69495-2*, Pocket) Simon & Schuster.
—Called Home. 1991. 17.95 o.p. (*0-312-05829-2*, Saint Martin's Minotaur) St. Martin's Pr.
—Gone to Glory. Isaacson, Dana, ed. 1991. 224p. reprint ed. mass mkt. 3.95 (*0-671-72799-0*, Pocket) Simon & Schuster.
—Gone to Glory. 1990. 16.95 o.p. (*0-312-04321-X*, Saint Martin's Minotaur) St. Martin's Pr.
—The Great Reminder. 1993. 224p. 17.95 o.p. (*0-312-09302-0*, Saint Martin's Minotaur) St. Martin's Pr.
—The Hosanna Shout. 1994. 240p. 19.95 o.p. (*0-312-11418-4*, Saint Martin's Minotaur) St. Martin's Pr.
—Pillar of Fire: A Moroni Traveler Mystery. 1995. 272p. 21.95 o.p. (*0-312-13588-2*, Saint Martin's Minotaur) St. Martin's Pr.
—The Spoken Word. 1992. 224p. 17.95 o.p. (*0-312-07841-2*, Saint Martin's Minotaur) St. Martin's Pr.
Johnson, Sherrie. A House with Wings. 1995. (J). pap. 7.95 (*1-56236-309-3*) Aspen Bks.
L'Amour, Louis. The Empty Land. 1995. 192p. mass mkt. 4.50 (*0-553-25306-9*) Bantam Bks.
—The Empty Land. l.t. ed. 1999. (Western Ser.). 253p. 26.95 (*0-7838-1956-0*) Thorndike Pr.
Levitt, J. R. Carnivores. 1990. 256p. mass mkt. 3.95 o.p. (*0-451-16845-3*, Signet Bks.) NAL.
—Carnivores. 1989. 208p. 15.95 o.p. (*0-312-02553-X*, Saint Martin's Minotaur) St. Martin's Pr.
—Ten of Swords. 1991. 15.95 o.p. (*0-312-05386-X*, Saint Martin's Minotaur) St. Martin's Pr.
Linton, John. Vermillion Cliffs: A Tale of Triumph over Fear. 2003. (Illus.). 350p. pap. 19.95 (*1-55517-702-6*, 77026, Bonneville Bks.) Cedar Fort, Inc./CFI Distribution.
Lowell, Elizabeth. Reckless Love. l.t. ed. 2002. (Wheeler Large Print Book Ser.). 28.95 (*1-58724-207-9*, Wheeler Publishing, Inc.) Gale Group.
—Reckless Love. 2000. 384p. mass mkt. (*1-55166-525-5*, 1-66525-6, Mira Bks.); 1996. mass mkt. (*0-373-83328-8*, 1-83328-4, Harlequin Bks.); 1995. 376p. mass mkt. (*0-373-15308-2*, 1-15308-9, Harlequin Bks.); 1993. (Harlequin Historicals Ser.). mass mkt. (*0-373-28799-2*, 1-28799-4, Harlequin Bks.); 1989. (Harlequin Historicals Ser.: No. 38). mass mkt. (*0-373-28638-4*, Harlequin Bks.); 1989. 400p. mass mkt. o.p. (*0-373-97106-0*, Harlequin Bks.) Harlequin Enterprises, Ltd.
Lund, Gerald N. Praise to the Man. 2002. (Work & the Glory Ser.: Vol. 6). 732p. pap. 15.95 (*1-57345-875-9*, Bookcraft, Inc.) Deseret Bk. Co.
Lyon, Annette. Lost Without You: A Novel. 2002. 201p. 14.95 (*1-59156-019-5*) Covenant Communications.
Mailer, Norman. The Executioner's Song. 1998. 1072p. pap. 17.00 (*0-375-70081-1*, Vintage) Knopf Publishing Group.
—The Executioner's Song. 1979. 25.00 o.s.i (*0-316-54417-5*) Little Brown & Co.
—The Executioner's Song. 1993. (Modern Library Ser.). 1024p. 22.95 o.s.i (*0-679-42471-7*, Modern Library) Random House Adult Trade Publishing Group.
—The Executioner's Song. 1998. 22.05 (*0-606-19217-4*) Turtleback Bks.
—The Executioner's Song. 1986. mass mkt. 7.99 o.s.i (*0-446-34521-0*) Warner Bks., Inc.
Martin, Lee. Inherited Murder. 1994. (Deb Ralston Mystery Ser.). 304p. 19.95 o.p. (*0-312-11415-X*, Saint Martin's Minotaur) St. Martin's Pr.
McKendrick, Lisa. A Life of My Own: A Novel. 2003. 263p. 13.95 (*1-59156-159-0*) Covenant Communications.
McRae, John. Fire in the Snow. 1993. 239p. pap. 10.95 (*0-87579-752-0*) Deseret Bk. Co.
Millhiser, Marlys. Murder in a Hot Flash: A Charlie Greene Mystery. 1996. (Charlie Greene Ser.). 256p. pap. 5.95 o.s.i (*0-14-025138-3*) Penguin Group (USA) Inc.
—Murder in a Hot Flash: A Charlie Greene Mystery. 1995. 252p. 20.50 (*1-883402-29-8*, Scribner) Simon & Schuster.
Moffat, Gwen. The Stone Hawk. 1989. 224p. 15.95 o.p. (*0-312-03434-2*, Saint Martin's Minotaur) St. Martin's Pr.
Nelson, Lee. The Wasatch Savage. 2001. 161p. 17.95 (*1-55517-554-6*, Council Pr.) Cedar Fort, Inc./CFI Distribution.
Oberhansly, Curtis & Oberhansly, Dianne Nelson. Downwinders: An Atomic Tale. 2001. (Illus.). 425p. pap. 14.95 (*0-9707965-9-5*) Black Ledge Pr.
Palmer, Susan. The Tabernacle Bar: A Novel. 1997. 184p. pap. 17.95 (*1-56085-096-5*) Signature Bks., Inc.
Papanikolas, Helen. The Apple Falls from the Apple Tree: Stories. 1996. 250p. pap. 16.95 (*0-8040-0994-5*); text 27.95 (*0-8040-0993-7*) Swallow Pr.
Parkinson, Benson Y. The MTC: Set Apart. 1995. 302p. pap. 9.95 (*1-56236-310-7*) Aspen Bks.
Pearson, Carol L. A Lasting Peace. 1990. 158p. (YA). (gr. 9-12). reprint ed. pap. 5.95 o.p. (*0-87579-302-9*) Deseret Bk. Co.
Peterson, Levi S. Aspen Marooney. 1995. 222p. pap. 15.95 (*1-56085-078-7*) Signature Bks., Inc.
Poulson, Clair. Conflict of Interest: A Novel. 2003. 296p. 14.95 (*1-59156-209-0*) Covenant Communications.
—Samuel: Moroni's Young Warrior. 1993. pap. 10.95 (*1-55503-553-1*, 29004799) Covenant Communications, Inc.
Preston, Douglas J. Thunderhead, Set. abr. ed. 1999. audio 24.98 Highsmith Inc.
Preston, Douglas J. & Child, Lincoln. Thunderhead. 2001. audio 24.98 (*1-57042-899-9*); 1999. audio 24.98 (*1-57042-667-8*) Time Warner AudioBooks.
—Thunderhead. 1999. 496p. 32.00 (*0-446-52337-2*); 2000. 560p. reprint ed. mass mkt. 7.50 (*0-446-60837-8*) Warner Bks., Inc.
Pruitt, Robert G., Jr. Rivers of Stone: A Story of Adventure & Mineral Exploration in the American Southwest. 2002. (First Fiction Ser.). (Illus.). 160p. pap. 14.95 (*0-86534-347-0*) Sunstone Pr.
Ramstetter, Mary. Down the Valley of the Shadow: An American Novel. 2002. (Illus.). 488p. (C). per. 14.00 (*0-9643283-1-3*) C Lazy Three Pr.
Reece, Colleen L. Nurse Autumn's Secret Love. l.t. ed. 2001. 237p. 23.95 (*0-7862-3137-8*); (*0-7540-4457-2*) Thorndike Pr.
Richardson, Boyd C. Danger Trail: Knife Thrower's Journey West. 1995. (J). pap. 9.95 o.p. (*1-55503-777-1*, 01111795) Covenant Communications, Inc.
Robards, Karen. Heartbreaker. l.t. ed. 1997. 20.00 (*0-7838-8092-8*, Macmillan Reference USA) Gale Group.
Rowley, Brent. Light Traveler: The Adventure Begins: A Novel. 1998. 185 P. ;p. o.p. (*1-57734-310-7*) Covenant Communications, Inc.
—My Body Fell Off! A Novel. 1997. (J). 9.95 o.p. (*1-57734-130-9*) Covenant Communications, Inc.
Ruckman, Ivy. No Way Out. 1989. (Trophy Keypoint Bks.). 224p. (YA). (gr. 7 up). reprint ed. pap. 4.95 (*0-06-447003-2*, Harper Trophy) HarperCollins Children's Bk. Group.
Ryan, Nan. The Seduction of Ellen. 2001. 384p. mass mkt. (*1-55166-814-9*, 1-66814-4, Mira Bks.) Harlequin Enterprises, Ltd.
Savage, Douglas. Cedar City Rendezvous. 1998. 160p. reprint ed. mass mkt. 3.99 (*0-8439-4345-9*, Leisure Bks.) Dorchester Publishing Co., Inc.
—Cedar City Rendezvous. 1995. (Evans Novel of the West Ser.). 158p. 18.95 (*0-87131-762-1*) Evans, M. & Co., Inc.
Sharpe, Jon. Utah Slaughter. 1988. (Trailsman Ser.: No. 84). mass mkt. 2.95 o.p. (*0-451-15719-2*, Signet Bks.) NAL.
—Utah Uprising. 1998. (Trailsman Ser.: Vol. 19). 176p. mass mkt. 4.99 o.s.i (*0-451-19501-9*, Signet Bks.) NAL.
Smith, Marion. Riptide: A Novel. 2000. 204p. pap. 14.95 (*1-56085-131-7*) Signature Bks., Inc.
Stansfield, Anita. Where the Heart Leads. 2001. 246p. 14.95 (*1-57734-848-6*) Covenant Communications.
Stegner, Wallace. Recapitulation. 1980. mass mkt. 2.50 o.s.i (*0-449-24263-3*, Fawcett) Ballantine Bks.
—Recapitulation. 1979. 11.95 o.p. (*0-385-11580-6*) Doubleday Publishing.
—Recapitulation. 1997. 288p. pap. 14.00 (*0-14-026673-9*) Penguin Group (USA) Inc.
—Recapitulation. 1986. 280p. reprint ed. pap. 9.95 (*0-8032-9165-5*, Bison Bks.) Univ. of Nebraska Pr.
Stewart, Gary. The Tenth Virgin. 1983. 288p. 14.95 o.p. (*0-312-79122-4*) St. Martin's Pr.
—The Zarahemla Vision. 1986. 256p. 15.95 o.p. (*0-312-89851-7*) St. Martin's Pr.
Stucki, Warren J. Boy's Pond: A Novel. 2001. (Illus.). 256p. 26.95 (*0-86534-328-4*) Sunstone Pr.
Sullivan, Mark T. The Fall Line. 1995. mass mkt. 5.99 o.s.i (*0-7860-0176-3*, Pinnacle Bks.); 1994. mass mkt. 20.00 o.p. (*0-8217-4710-X*, Zebra Bks.) Kensington Publishing Corp.
Thayne, Carole. A Question of Trust: A Novel. 2003. 293p. 14.95 (*1-59156-210-4*) Covenant Communications.
Thoene, Brock. Hope Valley War: A Novel. 1996. 228p. pap. 12.99 o.p. (*0-7852-8071-5*) Nelson, Thomas Inc.
Thompson, Vicki Lewis, et al. Escapade: Shattered Vows; Loverboy; The Keeper; The Veranchetti Marriage, 4 bks. in 1. 1998. (Promo Ser.). 971p. per. (*0-373-83408-X*, 1-83408-4, Harlequin Bks.) Harlequin Enterprises, Ltd.
Williams, Carol Lynch. Caroline's Secret. 1997. (Latter-Day Daughters Ser.). 86 p. (J). pap. 4.95 (*1-57345-318-8*, Cinnamon Tree) Deseret Bk. Co.
—Esther's Celebration. 1996. (Latter-Day Daughters Ser.). (Illus.). 80p. (J). (gr. 3-9). pap. 4.95 (*1-56236-507-X*) Aspen Bks.
Yorgason, Blaine M. & Yorgason, Brenton G. In Search of Steenie Bergman. 1988. (Soderberg Ser.: No. 5). 258p. 3.99 o.p. (*0-87579-174-3*) Deseret Bk. Co.

## V

**VALDEMAR (IMAGINARY PLACE)—FICTION**

Lackey, Mercedes. Arrow's Fall. 1988. (Heralds of Valdemar Ser.). mass mkt. 3.50 o.p. (*0-88677-255-9*); mass mkt. 2.50 o.p. (*0-88677-342-3*);Vol. 3. 320p. reprint ed. mass mkt. 6.99 (*0-88677-400-4*) DAW Bks., Inc.
—Arrow's Flight. 1987. (Heralds of Valdemar Ser.). mass mkt. 3.50 o.p. (*0-88677-222-2*); mass mkt. 2.50 o.p. (*0-88677-338-5*); (Illus.). 320p. reprint ed. mass mkt. 6.99 (*0-88677-377-6*) DAW Bks., Inc.
—Arrows of the Queen, Vol. 1. 1987. (Heralds of Valdemar Ser.: Bk. 1). 320p. reprint ed. mass mkt. 6.99 (*0-88677-378-4*) DAW Bks., Inc.
—Brightly Burning. (Valdemar Novels Ser.). 2000. (Illus.). 416p. 24.95 (*0-88677-889-1*); 2001. 448p. reprint ed. mass mkt. 6.99 (*0-88677-989-8*) DAW Bks., Inc.

Settings

—By the Sword. 1991. (Kerowyn's Tale Ser.). 496p. mass mkt. 6.99 (0-88677-463-2) DAW Bks., Inc.

—Exile's Honor. 2003. 432p. mass mkt. 6.99 (0-7564-0113-5); 2002. 448p. 24.95 (0-7564-0085-6) DAW Bks., Inc.

—Exile's Valor: A Novel of Valdemar. 2003. (Valdemar Ser.). 416p. 24.95 (0-7564-0206-9) DAW Bks., Inc.

—Friends of Valdemar. 1997. (Daw Book Collectors Ser.: Vol. 1047). 352p. mass mkt. 6.99 (0-88677-720-8) DAW Bks., Inc.

—Heralds of Valdemar Trilogy, 3 vols. 1989. 11.85 o.p. (0-451-92307-3, Signet Bks.) NAL.

—The Mage Wars Trilogy: The Black Gryphon, The White Gryphon & The Silver Gryphon, 3 Vols. 1997. (Mage Wars Ser.). 161.73 o.s.i (0-451-93484-9) NAL.

—Magic's Pawn, Vol. 1. 1989. (Last Herald-Mage Trilogy Ser.: Bk. 1). 352p. mass mkt. 6.99 (0-88677-352-0) DAW Bks., Inc.

—Magic's Price, Vol. 3. 1990. (Last Herald-Mage Trilogy Ser.: Bk. 3). 352p. mass mkt. 6.99 (0-88677-426-8) DAW Bks., Inc.

—Magic's Promise. 1990. (Last Herald-Mage Trilogy Ser.: Bk. 2). 320p. mass mkt. 6.99 (0-88677-401-2) DAW Bks., Inc.

—The Oathbound. 1988. (Vows & Honor Ser.: Bk. 1). 304p. mass mkt. 6.99 (0-88677-414-4); 320p. mass mkt. 3.50 o.p. (0-88677-285-0) DAW Bks., Inc.

—Oathbreakers. 1989. (Vows & Honor Ser.). mass mkt. 3.95 o.p. (0-88677-319-9); 320p. mass mkt. 6.99 (0-88677-454-3) DAW Bks., Inc.

—Owlflight. 1998. 13.04 (0-606-18981-5) Turtleback Bks.

—Storm Breaking. (Mage Storms Ser.). 1996. (Illus.). 448p. 21.95 o.p. (0-88677-713-5); Vol. 3. 1997. 416p. mass mkt. 7.99 (0-88677-755-0) DAW Bks., Inc.

—Storm Rising. (Mage Storms Ser.). 1995. (Illus.). 416p. 21.95 o.p. (0-88677-660-0); Vol. 2. 1996. 432p. mass mkt. 6.99 (0-88677-712-7) DAW Bks., Inc.

—Storm Warning. (Mage Storms Trilogy Ser.: Bk. 1). 432p. 1995. mass mkt. 6.99 (0-88677-661-9); 1994. 21.95 o.p. (0-88677-611-2) DAW Bks., Inc.

—Vows & Honor. 1998. (Vows & Honor Ser.: Vol. 3). 400p. mass mkt. 6.99 (0-88677-773-9) DAW Bks., Inc.

—Winds of Change. 1992. (Mage Winds Ser.: Bk. 2). 576p. 20.00 o.p. (0-88677-534-5) DAW Bks., Inc.

—Winds of Fate. (Mage Winds Ser.: Bk. 1). 1991. (Illus.). 400p. 18.95 o.s.i (0-88677-489-6); Vol. 1. 1992. 464p. mass mkt. 7.99 (0-88677-516-7) DAW Bks., Inc.

—Winds of Fury. 1993. (Mage Winds Ser.). 400p. 20.00 o.p. (0-88677-562-0); 1994. (Mage Winds Ser.: Bk. 3). 432p. reprint ed. mass mkt. 6.99 (0-88677-612-0) DAW Bks., Inc.

Lackey, Mercedes & Dixon, Larry. The Black Gryphon. (Mage Wars Ser.). 464p. 1994. 22.00 o.p. (0-88677-577-9); Vol. 1. 1995. mass mkt. 6.99 (0-88677-643-0) DAW Bks., Inc.

—Owlflight. (Darian's Tale Ser.: Vol. 1). 1998. (Illus.). 352p. mass mkt. 6.99 (0-88677-804-2); 1997. 304p. 21.95 o.s.i (0-88677-754-2) DAW Bks., Inc.

—Owlknight. 1999. (Darian's Tale Ser.: Vol. 3). (Illus.). 336p. 24.95 o.s.i (0-88677-851-4, D A W Fiction); Vol. 3. 2000. 464p. reprint ed. mass mkt. 6.99 (0-88677-916-2) DAW Bks., Inc.

—Owlsight. (Darian's Tale Ser.: Vol. 2). 1999. 464p. mass mkt. 6.99 (0-88677-803-4, D A W Fiction); 1998. (Illus.). 304p. 24.95 o.s.i (0-88677-802-6) DAW Bks., Inc.

—The Silver Gryphon. (Mage Wars Ser.: Vol. 3). 1997. 400p. mass mkt. 6.99 (0-88677-685-6); 1996. 336p. 21.95 o.s.i (0-88677-684-8) DAW Bks., Inc.

—The White Gryphon. (Mage Wars Ser.). 400p. 1996. mass mkt. 6.99 (0-88677-682-1); 1995. 21.95 o.p. (0-88677-631-7) DAW Bks., Inc.

## VANCOUVER (B.C.)—FICTION

Blackbridge, Persimmon. Prozac Highway. 2000. 373p. pap. 14.95 (0-7145-3059-X) Boyars, Marion Pubs., Inc.

—Prozac Highway: A Novel. 1997. 256p. pap. (0-88974-078-X, Press Gang Pubs.) Raincoast Bk. Distribution.

Blair, Michael. If Looks Could Kill. 2001. 288p. 23.95 (0-7710-1127-X) McClelland & Stewart/Tundra Bks.

Bowers, Elisabeth. Ladies' Night. 1988. (International Women's Crime Ser.). 238p. pap. 8.95 o.p. (0-931188-65-2, Seal Pr.) Avalon Publishing Group.

—No Forwarding Address. 288p. 1991. 18.95 o.p. (1-878067-13-3); 1994. reprint ed. pap. 10.95 o.p. (1-878067-46-X) Avalon Publishing Group. (Seal Pr.).

Braithwaite, Lawrence Ytzhak. Ratz Are Nice (PSP) A Novel. 2000. 192p. pap. 11.95 (1-55583-554-6, Alyson Bks.) Alyson Pubns.

Cherrington, John. Vancouver at the Dawn. 1997. (Illus.). 208p. pap. (1-55017-157-7) Harbour Publishing Co., Ltd.

Choy, Wayson. The Jade Peony. 240p. 1998. pap. 12.00 o.s.i (0-312-18692-4); 1997. 22.00 o.p. (0-312-15556-5) Picador.

Coupland, Douglas. Hey Nostradamus! 2003. (Illus.). 240p. 21.95 (1-58234-358-6) Bloomsbury Publishing.

Cruise, David & Griffiths, Alison. Vancouver. 2003. 768p. 29.95 (0-06-019787-0, HarperCollins) HarperTrade.

D'anna, Lynnette. Belly Fruit. 2000. 247p. pap. 16.00 (0-921586-79-5) New Star Bks., Ltd. CAN. Dist: SPD-Small Pr. Distribution, Stackpole Bks.

Ferone, Joseph. Boomboom. 1998. 317p. pap. (0-9684336-0-X) Bitterroot Pr.

—Boomboom. 2000. 204p. pap. 13.95 (0-936085-64-9, West Coast Crime) Blue Heron Publishing.

Giroux, E. X. A Death for a Dancing Doll. 1992. mass mkt. 3.99 o.s.i (0-345-37609-9) Ballantine Bks.

—A Death for a Dancing Doll. 1991. 17.95 o.p. (0-312-05848-9, Saint Martin's Minotaur) St. Martin's Pr.

Gough, Laurence. Death on a No. 8 Hook. 2001. (Willows & Parker Mystery Ser.). 232p. mass mkt. 7.95 (0-7710-3533-0) McClelland & Stewart/Tundra Bks.

—The Goldfish Bowl. 2001. (Willows & Parker Mystery Ser.). 216p. mass mkt. 7.95 (0-7710-3532-2) McClelland & Stewart/Tundra Bks.

—The Goldfish Bowl. 1988. 192p. 13.95 o.p. (0-312-01434-1, Saint Martin's Minotaur) St. Martin's Pr.

—The Goldfish Bowl. 1990. 192p. pap. 3.95 o.p. (0-14-011596-X, Penguin Bks.) Viking Penguin.

—Heartbreaker. 1996. (Willows & Parker Mystery Ser.). 272p. mass mkt. 5.99 (0-7710-3447-4) McClelland & Stewart/Tundra Bks.

—Heartbreaker: A Willows & Parker Mystery. 1996. 272p. 22.95 o.p. (0-7710-3438-5) McClelland & Stewart/Tundra Bks.

—Hot Shots. 2002. 224p. mass mkt. 6.95 (0-7710-3545-4) McClelland & Stewart/Tundra Bks.

—Hot Shots. 1991. (Crime Monthly Ser.). 192p. pap. 4.95 o.p. (0-14-015488-4, Penguin Bks.) Penguin Group (USA) Inc.

—Hot Shots. 1990. 192p. 16.95 o.p. (0-670-83014-3) Viking Penguin.

—Karaoke Rap. 1998. (Willows & Parker Mystery Ser.). 368p. 20.95 o.p. (0-7710-3403-2) McClelland & Stewart/Tundra Bks.

—Killers. 1995. 256p. pap. 8.95 o.p. (0-575-05782-3) Gollancz, Victor GBR. Dist: Trafalgar Square.

—Killers. 1993. o.p. (0-7710-3439-3) McClelland & Stewart/Tundra Bks.

—Memory Lane. 1997. (Willows & Parker Mystery Ser.). 304p. mass mkt. 5.95 (0-7710-3404-0) McClelland & Stewart/Tundra Bks.

—Memory Lane: A Willows & Parker Mystery. 1997. 296p. 24.95 o.p. (0-7710-3437-7) McClelland & Stewart/Tundra Bks.

—Serious Crimes. 2002. 256p. mass mkt. 6.95 (0-7710-3546-2) McClelland & Stewart/Tundra Bks.

—Serious Crimes. 1999. pap. (0-670-83675-3) Viking Penguin.

—Shutterbug. 1999. (Willows & Parker Mystery Ser.). 288p. mass mkt. 7.95 (0-7710-3429-6) McClelland & Stewart/Tundra Bks.

—Shutterbug: A Willows & Parker Mystery. 1998. (Willows & Parker Mystery Ser.: Bk. 11). 288p. 20.95 o.p. (0-7710-3531-4) McClelland & Stewart/Tundra Bks.

—Silent Knives. 1988. 192p. 13.95 o.p. (0-312-01747-2, Saint Martin's Minotaur) St. Martin's Pr.

—Silent Knives. 1990. 192p. pap. 3.95 o.p. (0-14-012189-7, Penguin Bks.) Viking Penguin.

Haig-Brown, Roderick L. On the Highest Hill. 1994. (Northwest Reprints Ser.). 336p. reprint ed. 27.95 (0-87071-518-6); pap. 15.95 (0-87071-519-4) Oregon State Univ. Pr.

Heide, C. L. Terrorist Cove. 2002. 178p. pap. (1-55369-241-1) Trafford Publishing.

Ireland, Ann. Exile: A Novel. 2002. 300p. 34.99 (1-55002-400-0) Dundurn Pr. CAN. Dist: Univ. of Toronto Pr.

Keller, Better. Better the Devil You Know... 2001. (Illus.). 160p. pap. (0-920576-88-5) Caitlin Pr., Inc.

Kelly, Nora. Bad Chemistry, Vol. 21. 2000. (Missing Mysteries Ser.: Vol. 21). 240p. pap. 14.95 (1-890208-34-5) Poisoned Pen Pr.

—Bad Chemistry. 1994. 256p. 20.95 o.p. (0-312-10934-2, Saint Martin's Minotaur) St. Martin's Pr.

—In the Shadow of Kings. 2000. (Missing Mysteries Ser.: Vol. 12). 189p. pap. 14.95 (1-890208-22-1) Poisoned Pen Pr.

—In the Shadow of Kings. 1984. 12.95 o.p. (0-312-41171-5) St. Martin's Pr.

—In the Shadow of Kings. l.t. ed. 1995. (Linford Mystery Library). 400p. pap. 17.99 o.p. (0-7089-7733-2, Linford) Thorpe, F. A. Pubs. GBR. Dist: Ulverscroft Large Print Bks., Ltd., Ulverscroft Large Print Canada, Ltd.

—My Sister's Keeper. 2000. (Missing Mysteries Ser.: Vol. 15). 221p. pap. 14.95 (1-890208-28-0) Poisoned Pen Pr.

—My Sister's Keeper. 1992. 224p. 17.95 o.p. (0-312-08268-1, Saint Martin's Minotaur) St. Martin's Pr.

—Old Wounds. l.t. ed. 1999. (Magna Large Print Ser.). 464p. (0-7505-1410-8) Magna Large Print Bks. GBR. Dist: Ulverscroft Large Print Canada, Ltd.

—Old Wounds. 2000. 300p. pap. 12.95 (1-890208-25-6) Poisoned Pen Pr.

Lee, Nancy. Dead Girls. 2003. 296p. pap. (0-7710-5251-0) McClelland & Stewart.

MacDonald, Mark. Flat. 2001. (Illus.). 154p. pap. 11.95 (1-55152-090-7) Arsenal Pulp Pr., Ltd. CAN. Dist: Consortium Bk. Sales & Distribution.

McMahon, Donna. Dance of Knives. 2001. 416p. 25.95 (0-312-87431-6, Tor Bks.) Doherty, Tom Assocs., LLC.

—Dances of Knives. 2002. 416p. reprint ed. pap. 15.95 (0-312-87536-3, Tor Bks.) Doherty, Tom Assocs., LLC.

Munroe, Jim. Everyone in Silico. 2002. 256p. pap. 13.95 (1-56858-240-4) Four Walls Eight Windows.

Odhiambo, David N. Diss/Ed Banded Nation. 1999. 160p. pap. (1-896095-26-7, Polestar Book Pubs.) Raincoast Bk. Distribution.

Perrin, Kayla. Again, My Love. 1999. 286p. mass mkt. 5.99 (0-345-43255-X) Ballantine Bks.

—Again, My Love. 1998. (Indigo Love Stories Ser.). 212p. pap. 10.95 (1-885478-23-2) Genesis Pr., Inc.

Robinson, Margaret A. A Woman of Her Tribe. 1991. 160p. (YA). (gr. 7-12). mass mkt. 4.50 o.s.i (0-449-70405-X, Fawcett) Ballantine Bks.

—A Woman of Her Tribe. 1990. 144p. (YA). (gr. 7 up). mass mkt. 13.95 (0-684-19223-3, Atheneum) Simon & Schuster Children's Publishing.

Sattler, Gail. Vancouver: The Gem of Canada Is Aglow with Four Romances. 2003. (Contemporary Collection). 464p. pap. 6.97 (1-58660-963-7) Barbour Publishing, Inc.

Sinclair, Bertrand W., tr. Hidden Places. 2003. 251p. 24.95 (1-57490-496-5, Sagebrush Large Print Westerns) Beeler, Thomas T. Publisher.

Slade, Michael. Cutthroat. 1992. 400p. (Orig.). mass mkt. 5.99 o.s.i (0-451-17452-6, Signet Bks.) NAL.

—Evil Eye. 1997. 432p. mass mkt. 6.99 o.s.i (0-451-40695-8, Onyx) NAL.

—Ghoul. 1988. 416p. 18.95 o.p. (0-688-07550-9, Morrow, William & Co.) Morrow/Avon.

—Ghoul. 1989. 400p. mass mkt. 6.99 o.s.i (0-451-15959-4, Signet Bks.) NAL.

—Headhunter. 1985. (Illus.). 480p. 17.95 o.p. (0-688-04710-6, Morrow, William & Co.) Morrow/Avon.

—Headhunter. 1986. mass mkt. 3.95 o.p. (0-451-40005-4); mass mkt. 4.50 o.p. (0-451-40137-9); 424p. mass mkt. 6.99 o.s.i (0-451-40172-7, Onyx) NAL.

—Primal Scream: Scream If You Want, Live If You Can. 1998. 432p. mass mkt. 6.99 o.s.i (0-451-19566-3, Signet Bks.) NAL.

—Ripper. 1994. 416p. (Orig.). mass mkt. 4.99 o.s.i (0-451-17702-9, Signet Bks.) NAL.

Smith, Lyndsay. Proximate Causes. 1999. 302p. pap. (1-55017-214-X) Harbour Publishing Co., Ltd.

Svendsen, Linda. Marine Life. 1992. 180p. 17.00 o.p. (0-374-10088-8) Farrar, Straus & Giroux.

—Marine Life. 1993. (Contemporay American Fiction Ser.). 176p. pap. 9.00 o.p. (0-14-023048-3, Penguin Bks.) Penguin Group (USA) Inc.

Taylor, Timothy. Stanley Park. 432p. 2003. pap. text 15.00 (1-58243-290-2, Basic Civitas Bks.); 2002. text 25.00 (1-58243-207-4, Counterpoint Pr.) Basic Bks.

Zaremba, Eve. Beyond Hope. 1990. 184p. pap. 11.95 (0-921299-02-8) Second Story Pr. CAN. Dist: SCB Distributors.

—The Butterfly Effect: A Helen Keremos Detective Novel. 1994. 332p. pap. 9.95 (0-929005-56-2) Second Story Pr. CAN. Dist: SCB Distributors.

—Uneasy Lies: A Helen Keremos Mystery. 1994. 255p. pap. 11.95 (0-929005-17-1) Second Story Pr. CAN. Dist: LPC/InBook.

—White Noise: A Helen Keremos Mystery Novel. 1997. 248p. pap. 9.95 (0-929005-97-X) Second Story Pr. CAN. Dist: SCB Distributors.

—Work for a Million. (NFS Canada Ser.). 200p. pap. 11.95 o.p. (0-921299-00-1) Second Story Pr. CAN. Dist: SCB Distributors.

## VANDAREI (IMAGINARY PLACE)—FICTION

Chant, Joy. The Grey Mane of Morning. 1982. 352p. pap. 3.50 o.p. (0-553-22666-5) Bantam Bks.

—The Grey Mane of Morning. 1977. 12.50 o.p. (0-04-823137-1) Routledge.

—Red Moon & Black Mountain. 1978. mass mkt. 1.95 o.s.i (0-345-25785-5) Ballantine Bks.

—Red Moon & Black Mountain. 1976. 272p. 8.95 o.p. (0-525-38193-7, Dutton) Dutton/Plume.

—When Voiha Wakes. 1985. mass mkt. o.s.i (0-553-19847-5); 1983. pap. 2.95 o.p. (0-553-23647-4) Bantam Bks.

## VATICAN CITY—FICTION

Brown, Dan. Angels & Demons: A Novel. 2000. E-Book 24.95 (1-930161-13-1) Adobe Systems, Inc.

—Angels & Demons: A Novel. l.t. ed. 2003. 768p. 26.95 (0-375-43318-X) Random Hse. Large Print.

—Angels & Demons: A Novel. 2003. 592p. 17.95 (0-7434-8622-6, Atria); 2000. 448p. 24.95 o.s.i (0-671-02735-2, Atria); 2000. E-Book 6.29 (0-7434-1239-7, Atria); 2001. (Illus.). 608p. reprint ed. mass mkt. 7.99 (0-671-02736-0, Pocket Star) Simon & Schuster.

—Angels & Demons: A Novel. abr. ed. 2003. audio 26.00 (0-7435-3576-6); audio compact disk 30.00 (0-7435-3577-4) Simon & Schuster Audio. (Simon & Schuster Audioworks).

Cooney, John. Acts of Contrition. 1994. 416p. mass mkt. 5.99 (0-671-78316-5, Pocket) Simon & Schuster.

Flynn, Raymond & Moore, Robin. The Accidental Pope. 2000. 394p. 24.95 (0-312-26801-7) St. Martin's Pr.

Folsom, Allan. Day of Confession. l.t. ed. 1999. 27.95 (1-56895-648-7, Wheeler Publishing, Inc.) Gale Group.

—Day of Confession. 1998. 576p. (gr. 8). 25.00 (0-316-28755-5) Little Brown & Co.

—Day of Confession. 1999. 688p. mass mkt. 7.99 (0-446-60453-4) Warner Bks., Inc.

Greeley, Andrew M. White Smoke: A Novel about the Next Papal Conclave. 1997. 466p. mass mkt. 6.99 (0-8125-9055-4); 1996. 384p. 24.95 o.p. (0-312-85814-0) Doherty, Tom Assocs., LLC. (Forge Bks.).

—White Smoke: A Novel about the Next Papal Conclave, Set. abr. ed. 1996. audio 24.99 (0-88646-413-7, 693997) Durkin Hayes Publishing Ltd.

—White Smoke: A Novel about the Next Papal Conclave. 1997. 6.99 (0-312-87118-X) St. Martin's Pr.

Martin, Malachi. Vatican. 1988. mass mkt. 5.95 o.s.i (0-515-09654-7, Jove) Berkley Publishing Group.

—Vatican. 1986. 672p. 18.95 o.p. (0-06-015478-0) HarperTrade.

—Windswept House: A Vatican Novel. 656p. 1998. pap. 18.95 (0-385-49231-6); 1996. 24.95 o.s.i (0-385-48408-9) Doubleday Publishing.

Montalbano, William D. Basilica. 2000. 368p. reprint ed. mass mkt. 6.99 o.s.i (0-515-12723-X, Jove) Berkley Publishing Group.

—Basilica. 1998. 304p. 23.95 o.p. (0-399-14418-8) Penguin Group (USA) Inc.

Monteleone, Thomas F. Blood of the Lamb. 1993. 448p. mass mkt. 5.99 (0-8125-2222-2); 1992. 416p. 21.95 o.p. (0-312-85031-X) Doherty, Tom Assocs., LLC. (Tor Bks.).

Moore, Christine P. The Virgin Knows. 1995. 320p. 22.95 o.p. (0-312-13203-4) St. Martin's Pr.

Nassr, Donald. In the Shadows of the Cross. 1994. 410p. 24.95 (0-9642463-0-9) ICAM Publishing Co.

Tobin, Greg. Conclave. 2002. 453p. mass mkt. 7.99 (0-8125-7921-6, Tor Bks.); 2001. 432p. 25.95 (0-312-87352-2, Forge Bks.) Doherty, Tom Assocs., LLC.

West, Morris. Morris West: Three Complete Novels: The Shoes of the Fisherman, The Clowns of the Gods, Lazarus. 1993. 13.99 o.s.i (0-517-09390-1) Random Hse. Value Publishing.

## VENEZUELA—FICTION

Bickham, Jack M. The Davis Cup Conspiracy. 384p. 1996. pap. 6.99 o.p. (0-8125-5055-2); 1994. 22.95 o.p. (0-312-85727-6) Doherty, Tom Assocs., LLC. (Forge Bks.).

Cowcher, Helen. Jaguar. (BEN, CHI, ENG, GRE & GUJ., Illus.). 40p. (J). 16.95 (1-84059-009-2) Milet Publishing, Ltd. GBR. Dist: Pan Asia Pubns. (USA), Inc.

De la Parra, Teresa. Iphigenia: The Diary of a Young Lady Who Wrote Because She Was Bored. Acker, Bertie, tr. from POR. 1993. (Texas Pan American Ser.).Tr. of Ifigenia. (Illus.). 372p. (C). 37.50 o.p. (0-292-71570-6); pap. 19.95 (0-292-71571-4) Univ. of Texas Pr.

Freilich, Alicia. Claper. 1998. xiv, 182p. 39.95 (0-8263-1854-1); pap. 17.95 (0-8263-1855-X) Univ. of New Mexico Pr.

Gallegos, Rómulo. Canaima. Tello, Jaime, tr. 1986. (Illus.). 360p. reprint ed. 22.95 o.p. (0-8061-9928-8); pap. 11.95 (0-8061-2119-X) Univ. of Oklahoma Pr.

—Canaima. Minguet, Charles, ed. 1991. (Coleccion Archivos). (SPA.). 513p. 34.95 o.p. (84-00-07120-4) Univ. of Pittsburgh Pr.

Hill, Reginald. Traitor's Blood. 1986. 256p. 16.95 o.p. (0-88150-076-3) Countryman Pr.

—Traitor's Blood. l.t. ed. 1985. (Ulverscroft Large Print Ser.). 504p. 29.99 o.p. (0-7089-1297-4, Ulverscroft) Thorpe, F. A. Pubs. GBR. Dist: Ulverscroft Large Print Bks., Ltd., Ulverscroft Large Print Canada, Ltd.

—Traitor's Blood. 1987. 256p. mass mkt. 3.95 (*0-446-34719-1*) Warner Bks., Inc.

Nieto, Benigno S. Reina de la Vida. 2001. (Coleccion Caniqui Ser.). 334p. pap. 19.95 (*0-89729-940-X*, 940-X) Ediciones Universal.

Pollock, Daniel. Pursuit into Darkness. 1995. 368p. mass mkt. 5.99 (*0-671-70576-8*, Pocket) Simon & Schuster.

—Pursuit into Darkness. Grose, Bill, ed. 1994. 384p. 22.00 o.p. (*0-671-70575-X*, Atria) Simon & Schuster.

St. Aubin De Teran, Lisa. Keepers of the House. 1985. (Fiction Ser.). 192p. pap. 5.95 o.p. (*0-14-006372-2*, Penguin Bks.) Viking Penguin.

—The Long Way Home. 1983. (Fiction Ser.). 192p. 12.95 o.p. (*0-06-015124-2*) HarperTrade.

Torres, Ana Teresa. Dona Ines vs. Oblivion. Rabassa, Gregory, tr. from SPA. 2000. 256p. reprint ed. pap. 13.00 (*0-8021-3726-1*, Grove Pr.) Grove/Atlantic, Inc.

—Dona Ines vs. Oblivion. Rabassa, Gregory, tr. from SPA. 1999. (Pegasus Prize for Literature Ser.). 256p. 27.50 (*0-8071-2476-1*) Louisiana State Univ. Pr.

**VENICE (ITALY)—FICTION**

Alison, Jane. The Marriage of the Sea: A Novel. 2003. 272p. 24.00 (*0-374-19941-8*) Farrar, Straus & Giroux.

—The Marriage of the Sea: A Novel. 2004. 272p. pap. 13.00 (*0-312-42255-5*) Picador.

Begley, Louis. Mistler's Exit. 1999. 224p. pap. 12.95 (*0-449-00422-8*) Ballantine Bks.

Bhabra, H. S. Gestures: A Novel. 2003. 318p. 17.95 (*1-56792-235-X*) Godine, David R. Pub.

Brodkey, Harold. Profane Friendship. 1994. 387p. 23.00 o.p. (*0-374-23544-9*) Farrar, Straus & Giroux.

—Profane Friendship. 1995. 400p. reprint ed. pap. 14.00 o.p. (*1-56279-071-4*) Mercury Hse.

Cleveland, David Adams. With a Gem-Like Flame: A Novel of Venice & a Lost Masterpiece. 2001. 320p. 25.00 (*0-7867-0877-8*, Carroll & Graf Pubs.) Avalon Publishing Group.

Coleman, Jane Candia. The Italian Quartet. 2001. (Five Star First Edition Women's Fiction Ser.). 197p. 25.95 (*0-7862-3379-6*, Five Star) Gale Group.

Coover, Robert. Pinocchio in Venice. 1997. 336p. reprint ed. pap. 13.50 (*0-8021-3485-8*, Grove Pr.) Grove/Atlantic, Inc.

—Pinocchio in Venice. 1991. 336p. 19.95 o.p. (*0-671-64471-8*, Simon & Schuster) Simon & Schuster.

Crawford, F. Marion. Marietta: A Maid of Venice. rev. ed. 2000. 376p. E-Book 3.95 (*0-594-02055-7*) 1873 Pr.

—Marietta: A Maid of Venice. collector's ed. 2002. (Illus.). im. lthr. 38.85 (*1-4115-1226-X*); pap. 19.95 (*1-4115-0483-6*); 25.95 (*1-4115-0848-3*); pap. 17.95 (*1-4115-0261-2*) Polyglot Pr., Inc.

—Marietta: A Maid of Venice. 1990. (Works of Francis Marion Crawford). reprint ed. lib. bdg. 79.00 (*0-7812-2552-3*) Reprint Services Corp.

Drake, Shannon. Deep Midnight. l.t. ed. 2002. (Thorndike Romance Ser.). 616p. 29.95 (*0-7862-3908-5*) Gale Group.

—Deep Midnight. 2001. 480p. mass mkt. 3.99 (*0-8217-7739-4*, Zebra Bks.); mass mkt. 6.99 (*0-8217-6837-9*) Kensington Publishing Corp.

Dunham, Mikel. Casting for Murder. 1992. 320p. 18.95 o.p. (*0-312-06924-3*, Saint Martin's Minotaur) St. Martin's Pr.

Elegant, Robert S. Bianca: A Novel of Venice. 2000. 352p. 24.95 (*0-312-26127-6*) St. Martin's Pr.

—Bianca: A Novel of Venice. 1993. 348p. 24.95 o.p. (*1-85619-113-3*) Trafalgar Square.

Gallizier, Nathan. The Leopard Prince. 2000. 252p. pap. 9.95 (*0-594-00327-X*); E-Book 3.95 (*0-594-02235-5*) 1873 Pr.

Godden, Rumer. Pippa Passes. unabr. ed. 2001. audio 44.95 (*1-85695-933-3*, 950412) ISIS Audio Bks. GBR. *Dist:* Ulverscroft Large Print Bks., Ltd.

—Pippa Passes. 1994. 22.00 o.p. (*0-688-13397-5*, Morrow, William & Co.) Morrow/Avon.

Goldman, William. The Silent Gondoliers. 2001. 128p. pap. 10.00 (*0-345-44263-6*); 1985. mass mkt. 3.50 o.s.i (*0-345-32583-4*) Ballantine Bks. (Del Rey).

Hewson, David. Lucifer's Shadow. 2004. 288p. 21.95 (*0-385-33794-9*, Delacorte Pr.) Dell Publishing.

—Lucifer's Shadow. 2001. (Illus.). 408p. (*0-00-225622-3*); pap. (*0-00-711917-8*) HarperCollins Pubs.

Jaffe, Michele. The Stargazer. 1999. 400p. 18.00 o.s.i (*0-671-02739-5*, Atria); 2000. (Illus.). 480p. reprint ed. pap. 6.99 (*0-671-02740-9*, Pocket) Simon & Schuster.

James, Henry. The Wings of the Dove. 2003. 768p. pap. 9.95 (*0-8129-6719-4*, Modern Library) Random House Adult Trade Publishing Group.

Johnston, Velda. Masquerade in Venice. l.t. ed. 1987. (Nightingale Ser.). 299p. 12.95 o.p. (*0-8161-4339-0*, Macmillan Reference USA) Gale Group.

Jong, Erica. Serenissima. unabr. ed. 1987. audio 17.95 o.p. (*0-930435-33-8*, 389); audio 57.25 o.p. (*1-56100-028-0*, 571) Brilliance Audio.

—Serenissima. 1988. 384p. mass mkt. 4.95 o.s.i (*0-440-20104-7*) Dell Publishing.

—Serenissima. 1987. 225p. 16.95 o.p. (*0-395-42922-6*) Houghton Mifflin Co.

—Serenissima. 1989. 3.99 o.p. (*0-517-68552-3*) Random Hse. Value Publishing.

Langton, Jane. The Thief of Venice: A Homer Kelly Mystery. 2000. (Homer Kelly Mystery Ser.). (Illus.). 256p. pap. 5.99 (*0-14-029189-X*) Penguin Group (USA) Inc.

—The Thief of Venice: A Homer Kelly Mystery. 1999. (Homer Kelly Mystery Ser.). 256p. 22.95 o.p. (*0-670-88210-0*, Viking) Viking Penguin.

Lee, Tanith. A Bed of Earth. 2003. 345p. pap. 14.95 (*1-58567-455-9*) Overlook Pr., The.

—A Bed of Earth: The Gravedigger's Tale. 2002. (Secret Books of Venus Ser.: Bk. 3). 345p. 25.95 (*1-58567-261-0*) Overlook Pr., The.

—Venus Preserved. 2003. 352p. 25.95 (*1-58567-474-5*) Overlook Pr., The.

Leon, Donna. Acqua Alta. unabr. collector's ed. 1998. audio 48.00 (*0-7366-4294-3*, 4787) Books on Tape, Inc.

—Acqua Alta. 1996. 288p. 22.50 o.p. (*0-06-018651-8*) HarperCollins Pubs.

—Death & Judgement. unabr. ed. 1998. audio 44.95 Blackstone Audio Bks., Inc.

—Death & Judgement. 1995. 304p. 20.00 o.p. (*0-06-017796-9*) HarperCollins Pubs.

—Death & Judgement: A Question of Motive. unabr. ed. 2000. audio 29.95 (*0-7861-1549-1*) Blackstone Audio Bks., Inc.

—Death & Judgment. 1996. 304p. mass mkt. 4.99 o.p. (*0-06-109523-0*, HarperTorch) Morrow/Avon.

—Death at la Fenice. 1995. 288p. mass mkt. 6.99 (*0-06-104337-0*, HarperTorch) Morrow/Avon.

—Death at la Fenice. l.t. ed. 2003. (General Ser.). (FRE.). lib. bdg. 24.95 (*0-7862-5107-7*) Thorndike Pr.

—Death at La Fenice. unabr. ed. 1999. audio 27.95 (*0-7861-1538-6*); 1997. audio 44.95 (*0-7861-1193-3*, 1951) Blackstone Audio Bks., Inc.

—Death at La Fenice. unabr. collector's ed. 1998. (Guido Brunetti Mystery Ser.). audio 48.00 (*0-7366-4217-X*, 4715) Books on Tape, Inc.

—Death at La Fenice: A Novel of Suspense. 1992. 224p. 19.00 o.p. (*0-06-016871-4*) HarperTrade.

—Death in a Strange Country: A Guido Brunetti Mystery. unabr. ed. 1997. audio 44.95 (*0-7861-1228-X*, 1971) Blackstone Audio Bks., Inc.

—Death in a Strange Country: A Guido Brunetti Mystery. unabr. collector's ed. 1998. (Guido Brunetti Mystery Ser.). audio 48.00 (*0-7366-4218-8*, 4716) Books on Tape, Inc.

—Death in a Strange Country: A Guido Brunetti Mystery. 1993. 304p. 20.00 o.p. (*0-06-017008-5*) HarperTrade.

—Death in a Strange Country: A Guido Brunetti Mystery. 1995. 288p. mass mkt. 4.50 o.p. (*0-06-109406-4*, HarperTorch) Morrow/Avon.

—Dressed for Death. unabr. ed. 1997. audio 44.95 (*0-7861-1194-1*, 1953) Blackstone Audio Bks., Inc.

—Dressed for Death, , unabr. collector's ed. 1999. (Guido Brunetti Mystery Ser.). audio 48.00 (*0-7366-4317-6*, 4785) Books on Tape, Inc.

—Dressed for Death. 1994. 288p. 20.00 o.p. (*0-06-017795-0*) HarperTrade.

—Dressed for Death. 1995. 304p. mass mkt. 4.99 o.p. (*0-06-109418-8*, HarperTorch) Morrow/Avon.

—Uniform Justice. 2003. 280p. 19.95 (*0-87113-903-0*, Atlantic Monthly Pr.) Grove/Atlantic, Inc.

—Uniform Justice. 2004. 320p. mass mkt. 7.99 (*0-14-200422-7*) Penguin Group (USA) Inc.

Leviant, Curt. Partita in Venice: A Novel. unabr. ed. 198p. 2000. pap. 11.00 (*0-942979-63-X*); 1999. 24.00 (*0-942979-64-8*) Livingston Pr.

Lewitt, Shariann. Interface Masque. 2002. mass mkt. 6.99 (*0-7653-4459-9*); 1997. 350p. text 23.95 o.p. (*0-312-85627-X*) Doherty, Tom Assocs., LLC. (Tor Bks.).

—Interface Masque. 1999. 23.95 (*0-312-87139-2*) St. Martin's Pr.

Lovric, M. R. The Floating Book: A Novel of Venice. 2004. 496p. 25.95 (*0-06-057856-4*, ReganBooks) HarperTrade.

MacInnes, Helen. The Venetian Affair. 1985. 352p. mass mkt. 3.95 o.s.i (*0-449-20942-3*, Fawcett) Ballantine Bks.

—The Venetian Affair. 1987. 19.95 o.p. (*0-8161-4150-9*, Macmillan Reference USA) Gale Group.

—The Venetian Affair. 1963. 8.95 o.s.i (*0-15-193501-7*) Harcourt Trade Pubs.

Mann, Thomas. Death in Venice. Heller, Erich, tr. 1970. (Modern Library College Editions Ser.). 436p. (C). 11.25 (*0-07-553669-2*, T99, McGraw-Hill Humanities, Social Sciences & World Languages) McGraw-Hill Higher Education.

—Death in Venice & Other Stories. Luke, David, tr. & intro. by. 1988. 320p. mass mkt. 5.95 (*0-553-21333-4*) Bantam Bks.

—Death in Venice & Other Stories. 1991. 400p. 17.00 o.s.i (*0-679-40666-2*) Random Hse., Inc.

—Death in Venice & Other Tales. 1976. 13.95 (*0-8488-0574-7*) Amereon, Ltd.

—Death in Venice & Other Tales. 1983. 451p. reprint ed. lib. bdg. 16.95 (*0-89966-455-5*) Buccaneer Bks., Inc.

—Death in Venice & Other Tales. Chase, Jefferson S., tr. from GER. 1999. (Signet Classics). 256p. mass mkt. 5.95 (*0-451-52609-0*, Signet Classics) NAL.

—Death in Venice & Other Tales. Kolb, Clayton, ed. & tr. by. 1994. (Critical Editions Ser.). (C). pap. 13.50 (*0-393-96013-7*) Norton, W. W. & Co., Inc.

—Death in Venice & Other Tales. 1998. (Case Studies in Contemporary Criticism). 314p. 35.00 o.p. (*0-312-21064-7*) Palgrave Macmillan.

—Death in Venice & Other Tales. Neugroschel, Joachim, tr. unabr. ed. 2000. audio 85.00 (*0-7887-2482-7*, 95557E7) Recorded Bks., LLC.

—Death in Venice & Other Tales. 1999. 384p. pap. 11.00 (*0-14-118173-7*, Penguin Classics) Viking Penguin.

—Death in Venice & Other Tales. Neugroschel, Joachim, tr. from GER. 1998. 400p. 25.95 o.p. (*0-670-87424-8*) Viking Penguin.

Manning, Liza. The Glass Madonna. l.t. ed. 2000. (G. K. Hall Nightingale Ser.). 242p. pap. 20.95 (*0-7838-9193-8*); (*0-7540-4291-X*); (*0-7540-4292-8*) Gale Group. (Macmillan Reference USA).

—The Glass Madonna. 1987. per. (*0-373-02818-0*, Harlequin Bks.) Harlequin Enterprises, Ltd.

Mordden, Ethan. Venice Adriana. (Stonewall Inn Editions Ser.). 1999. 324p. pap. 13.95 (*0-312-20680-1*, Saint Martin's Griffin); 1998. 304p. 23.95 o.p. (*0-312-18202-3*) St. Martin's Pr.

Murphy, Haughton. A Very Venetian Murder. 1993. mass mkt. 4.50 o.s.i (*0-449-22066-4*, Fawcett) Ballantine Bks.

—A Very Venetian Murder. 1992. 256p. 19.00 o.p. (*0-671-70664-0*, Simon & Schuster) Simon & Schuster.

Nelson, Karen. Tea & Tiramisu. l.t. ed. 2002. 288p. pap. 24.95 (*0-7862-3688-4*) Gale Group.

Pippa Passes. audio HarperTrade.

Powell, Anthony. Temporary Kings. l.t. unabr. ed. 1999. 352p. 32.50 (*0-7531-5824-8*, 158248) ISIS Large Print Bks. GBR. *Dist:* Ulverscroft Large Print Bks., Ltd., Ulverscroft Large Print Canada, Ltd.

—Temporary Kings. 1973. 7.95 o.p. (*0-316-71547-6*) Little Brown & Co.

Pozzessere, Heather G. The Di Medici Bride. 1999. mass mkt. (*1-55166-469-0*, Mira Bks.) Harlequin Enterprises, Ltd.

—The Di Medici Bride. l.t. ed. 2000. (Americana Ser.). 427p. 28.95 (*0-7862-2610-2*) Thorndike Pr.

Rolfe, Frederick W. Desire & Pursuit of the Whole: A Romance of Modern Venice. Eburne, Andrew, ed. 1994. 300p. 20.00 (*0-8076-1331-2*) Braziller, George Inc.

—The Desire & Pursuit of the Whole: A Romance of Modern Venice. (Gay Experience Ser.). reprint ed. 25.50 (*0-404-61536-8*) AMS Pr., Inc.

—The Desire & Pursuit of the Whole: A Romance of Modern Venice. 1977. 299p. reprint ed. 35.00 o.s.i (*0-8371-9808-9*, RODP, Greenwood Pr.) Greenwood Publishing Group, Inc.

Rylands, Jane Turner. Venetian Stories. 304p. 2004. pap. 13.00 (*1-4000-3262-8*, Anchor); 2003. 22.00 (*0-375-42232-3*, Pantheon) Knopf Publishing Group.

Sand, George. Consuelo: A Romance of Venice. 1979. (Quality Paperbacks Ser.). 225p. pap. text 9.00 o.p. (*0-306-80102-7*) Da Capo Pr., Inc.

Schiller, Friedrich. The Man Who Sees Ghosts. 2003. 128p. pap. 14.00 (*1-901285-12-X*) Pushkin Pr., Ltd. GBR. *Dist:* Consortium Bk. Sales & Distribution.

Sklepowich, Edward. Deadly to the Sight: A Mystery of Venice. (*0-312-27774-1*) St. Martin's Pr.

Sklepowich, Edward. Black Bridge: A Mystery of Venice. 1995. 224p. 20.50 (*0-684-81520-6*); o.s.i (*1-883402-84-0*) Simon & Schuster. (Scribner).

—Deadly to the Sight: A Mystery of Venice. 2002. 320p. 23.95 (*0-312-26955-2*, Saint Martin's Minotaur) St. Martin's Pr.

—Death in a Serene City. 1992. 304p. pap. 4.50 (*0-380-71636-4*, Avon Bks.); 1990. 18.95 o.p. (*0-688-09180-6*, Morrow, William & Co.) Morrow/Avon.

—Death in the Palazzo: A Venetian Mystery. 1997. 250p. 21.50 o.p. (*0-684-83031-0*, Scribner) Simon & Schuster.

—Farewell to the Flesh: An Urbino Macintyre Mystery. 1993. 288p. pap. 4.99 (*0-380-71814-6*, Avon Bks.); 1991. 352p. 19.00 o.p. (*0-688-11006-1*, Morrow, William & Co.) Morrow/Avon.

—The Last Gondola: A Mystery of Venice. 2003. 384p. 24.95 (*0-312-29049-7*, Saint Martin's Minotaur) St. Martin's Pr.

—Liquid Desires: An Urbino Macintyre Mystery. 1993. 315p. 22.00 o.p. (*0-688-11165-3*, Morrow, William & Co.); 1994. 320p. reprint ed. mass mkt. 4.99 (*0-380-72150-3*, Avon Bks.) Morrow/Avon.

—Liquid Desires: An Urbino Macintyre Mystery. 316p. 4.98 o.p. (*0-7651-0268-4*) Smithmark Pubs., Inc.

Sollers, Philippe. Watteau in Venice. 1994. Orig. Title: Fete a Venise. 288p. text 22.00 (*0-684-19451-1*, Scribner) Simon & Schuster.

Spark, Muriel. Territorial Rights. 1984. 248p. pap. 6.95 o.p. (*0-399-50930-5*) Putnam Publishing Group, The.

St. Aubin De Teran, Lisa. The Palace. 272p. 2000. pap. 13.00 (*0-06-095653-4*); 1999. 23.95 o.p. (*0-88001-662-0*) HarperTrade. (Ecco).

Stern, Richard. Stitch. 1986. 205p. pap. 5.95 o.p. (*0-87795-837-8*, Morrow, William & Co.) Morrow/Avon.

Vickers, Salley. Miss Garnet's Angel. l.t. ed. 2001. (Illus.). 352p. 25.00 (*0-7867-0823-9*, Carroll & Graf Pubs.) Avalon Publishing Group.

—Miss Garnet's Angel. 2002. 352p. pap. 13.00 (*0-452-28297-7*) Dutton/Plume.

—Miss Garnet's Angel. l.t. ed. 2002. 320p. pap. 24.95 (*0-7862-3690-6*) Gale Group.

Von Hofmannsthal, Hugo. Andreas. Hottinger, Marie D., tr. 2001. 192p. pap. 14.00 (*1-901285-01-4*) Pushkin Pr., Ltd. GBR. *Dist:* Consortium Bk. Sales & Distribution.

—Andreas. Hottinger, Marie D., tr. from GER. 2000. 192p. pap. 12.95 (*1-885586-03-5*) Turtle Point Pr.

Williams, Niall. As It Is in Heaven. abr. ed. 2001. audio (*0-333-78257-7*) Macmillan U.K. GBR. *Dist:* Macmillan Publishing Co., Inc.

—As It Is in Heaven. 2000. 310p. E-Book 9.95 (*0-446-92334-6*); 1999. E-Book 9.95 (*0-446-96005-5*) Time Warner Bk. Group.

Wilson, Barbara. Case of the Orphaned Bassoonists. 2000. (Cassandra Reilly Mysteries Ser.). (Illus.). 224p. pap. 12.95 (*1-58005-046-8*, Seal Pr.) Avalon Publishing Group.

**VERMONT—FICTION**

Abrahams, Peter. Hard Rain. 1988. 384p. 18.95 o.p. (*0-525-24581-2*, Dutton) Dutton/Plume.

—Hard Rain. 1989. 352p. mass mkt. 4.50 o.p. (*0-451-40113-1*, Onyx) NAL.

Alberts, Laurie. The Price of Land in Shelby. (Illus.). 330p. 1997. pap. 15.95 (*0-87451-844-X*); 1996. text 35.00 o.p. (*0-87451-782-6*) Univ. Pr. of New England. (Hardscrabble Bks.).

Alpert, Stanley L. Mohop Mogande. 1998. 460p. 27.00 (*1-892666-03-0*) Alpert's Bookery, Inc.

Alther, Lisa. Other Women. 1996. 352p. pap. 13.95 o.s.i (*0-452-27678-0*, Plume) Dutton/Plume.

—Other Women. 1985. mass mkt. 4.50 o.p. (*0-451-13894-5*); mass mkt. 2.95 o.p. (*0-451-15451-7*) NAL. (Signet Bks.).

Baruth, Philip E. The Dream of the White Village: A Novel in Stories. 333p. 1999. pap. 14.00 (*0-9657144-2-X*); 1998. 24.00 (*0-9657144-1-1*) Onion River Pr.

Beattie, Ann. Love Always: A Novel. 1986. (Vintage Contemporaries Ser.). 256p. pap. 12.00 (*0-394-74418-7*, Vintage) Knopf Publishing Group.

Berger, Jason. Forested Moments. 2002. 137p. (*1-888725-79-6*); 124p. per. 14.95 (*1-888725-73-7*) Science & Humanities Pr. (BeachHouse Bks.).

Bohjalian, Chris. The Buffalo Soldier: A Novel. unabr. ed. 2002. audio 39.95 (*0-553-71500-3*) Random Hse. Audio Publishing Group.

—The Law of Similars. 1999. E-Book 11.50 (*0-609-60629-8*) Crown Publishing Group.

—The Law of Similars. l.t. ed. 1999. (Large Print Book Ser.). 27.95 (*1-56895-723-8*, Wheeler Publishing, Inc.) Gale Group.

—The Law of Similars. 2000. 336p. pap. 13.00 (*0-679-77147-6*, Vintage) Knopf Publishing Group.

—Midwives: A Novel. 1998. E-Book 11.50 (*0-609-60630-1*); 1997. 312p. 24.00 o.s.i (*0-517-70396-3*, Harmony) Crown Publishing Group.

—Midwives: A Novel. 1998. 384p. pap. 14.00 (*0-375-70677-1*); 400p. pap. 13.00 o.p. (*0-679-77146-8*) Knopf Publishing Group. (Vintage).

—Midwives: A Novel. l.t. ed. 1998. (Niagara Large Print Ser.). 496p. 29.50 o.p. (*0-7089-5880-X*, Ulverscroft) Thorpe, F. A. Pubs. GBR. *Dist:* Ulverscroft Large Print Bks., Ltd., Ulverscroft Large Print Canada, Ltd.

—Trans-Sister Radio. E-Book 12.50 (*1-58945-533-9*) Adobe Systems, Inc.

—Trans-Sister Radio. 2001. 368p. reprint ed. pap. 14.00 (*0-375-70517-1*, Vintage) Knopf Publishing Group.

—Trans-Sister Radio. 2001. E-Book 12.50 (*0-609-50408-8*) Random Hse., Inc.

Brandt, Nat & Brandt, Yanna. Land Kills. 1991. (Mitch Stevens Ser.). 260p. 18.95 o.p. (*0-88150-209-X*) Countryman Pr.

Bruchac, Joseph. The Waters Between: A Novel of the Dawn Land. 1998. 310p. pap. 14.95 (*1-58465-015-X*); text 26.00 o.p. (*0-87451-881-4*) Univ. Pr. of New England. (Hardscrabble Bks.).

Burnham, Janet Hayward. Love in the Mountains. l.t. ed. 2000. (G. K. Hall Paperback Ser.). 189p. 23.95 (*0-7838-9227-6*); (*0-7540-4348-7*); (*0-7540-4349-5*) Gale Group. (Macmillan Reference USA).

Burns, Michael. Gemini. Hansen, Marge D., ed. 2001. (Illus.). 387p. 24.95 (*0-9701862-4-X*) Poncha Pr.

Canfield, Dorothy. Understood Betsy. 1981. 219p. (J). (ps up). reprint ed. lib. bdg. 25.95 (*0-89966-342-7*) Buccaneer Bks., Inc.

Citro, Joseph A. Green Mountains, Dark Tales. 249p. 2001. pap. 14.95 (*1-58465-134-2*); 1999. (Illus.). text 26.00 (*0-87451-863-6*) Univ. Pr. of New England.

—Lake Monsters: A Novel. 2001. (Hardscrabble Bks.). (Illus.). 272p. reprint ed. pap. 14.95 (*1-58465-110-5*, Hardscrabble Bks.) Univ. Pr. of New England.

Comfort, Barbara. The Cashmere Kid. (Tish McWhinny Mystery Ser.). 224p. 1994. pap. 6.95 (*0-88150-321-5*); 1993. text 18.00 o.p. (*0-88150-254-5*) Norton, W. W. & Co., Inc. (Foul Play).

—Elusive Quarry. (Tish McWhinny Mystery Ser.). 224p. 1996. pap. 7.50 (*0-88150-370-3*); 1995. 19.00 o.p. (*0-88150-332-0*) Norton, W. W. & Co., Inc. (Foul Play).

—Grave Consequences. (Vermont Village Murders Ser.). (Orig.). 1989. 233p. pap. 5.95 (*0-9608726-4-7*); 1994. 240p. reprint ed. pap. 6.00 o.p. (*0-88150-296-0*, Foul Play) Norton, W. W. & Co., Inc.

—A Pair for the Queen. 1999. 221p. pap. 7.95 (*0-393-31913-X*); 1998. (Tish McWhinny Mystery Ser.: Vol. 5). 192p. 22.00 (*0-393-04627-3*) Norton, W. W. & Co., Inc.

—Phoebe's Knee. (Tish McWhinny Mystery Ser.). (Orig.). 1994. 224p. pap. 7.95 (*0-88150-295-2*, Foul Play); 1986. 220p. pap. 3.95 (*0-9608726-3-9*) Norton, W. W. & Co., Inc.

Comfort, Barbara, contrib. by. A Pair for the Queen. l.t. ed. 1999. (Senior Lifestyles Ser.). 320p. o.p. (*0-7862-2297-2*) Thorndike Pr.

Conde, Richard S. Shelburne, Vermont: A Novel. 1998. (*1-886166-06-4*) Pine Tree Pr.

Cook, Robin. Fatal Cure. abr. ed. 1994. audio 24.95 (*1-55927-263-5*, 692199) Audio Renaissance.

—Fatal Cure. 1995. 464p. mass mkt. 7.99 (*0-425-14563-8*) Berkley Publishing Group.

—Fatal Cure. unabr. ed. 1994. audio 96.00 (*0-7366-2774-X*, 3493) Books on Tape, Inc.

—Fatal Cure. l.t. ed. 618p. 1995. lib. bdg. 17.95 o.p. (*0-8161-5943-2*); 1994. lib. bdg. 22.95 o.p. (*0-8161-5942-4*) Gale Group. (Macmillan Reference USA).

—Fatal Cure. 1994. 432p. 22.95 o.p. (*0-399-13879-X*, G. P. Putnam's Sons) Penguin Group (USA) Inc.

—Fatal Cure: Library Edition. unabr. ed. 1994. audio 119.95 (*1-55927-279-1*) Audio Renaissance.

Corriveau, Art. Housewrights. 2002. 208p. 13.00 (*0-14-200209-7*) Viking Penguin.

Dank, Gloria. As the Sparks - Upward. 1992. 208p. 16.50 o.s.i (*0-385-42236-9*) Doubleday Publishing.

Danziger, Jeff. Teed Stories. 1988. (Illus.). 116p. (Orig.). pap. 7.95 (*0-933050-60-7*) New England Pr., Inc., The.

Davis, Thomas C. The Governor's Man. 2002. 290p. pap. 15.95 (*0-9709026-0-3*) Wildersburg Publishing Co.

Delinsky, Barbara. An Irresistible Impulse. l.t. ed. 1996. 260p. lib. bdg. 25.95 o.p. (*0-7838-1549-2*, Macmillan Reference USA) Gale Group.

—An Irresistible Impulse. 1983. mass mkt. (*0-373-53623-2*, Harlequin Bks.) Harlequin Enterprises, Ltd.

—An Irresistible Impulse. 1995. 336p. mass mkt. 7.99 (*0-06-100876-1*, HarperTorch) Morrow/Avon.

—An Irresistible Impulse. 240p. 26.00 (*0-7278-5673-1*) Severn Hse. Pubs., Ltd.

—Suddenly. l.t. ed. 1994. 567p. lib. bdg. 23.95 o.p. (*0-8161-7467-9*, Macmillan Reference USA) Gale Group.

—Suddenly. 1994. 480p. mass mkt. 7.99 (*0-06-104200-5*, HarperTorch) Morrow/Avon.

—Three Wishes. l.t. ed. 1997. (Core Ser.). 454p. 28.95 o.p. (*0-7838-8315-3*, Macmillan Reference USA) Gale Group.

—Three Wishes. 304p. 1997. 23.00 (*0-684-84507-5*, Simon & Schuster); 1998. (Illus.). mass mkt. 7.99 (*0-671-01665-2*, Pocket) Simon & Schuster.

—Three Wishes. l.t. ed. 1999. (Paperback Bestsellers Ser.). 422p. pap. 27.95 (*0-7838-8316-1*) Thorndike Pr.

Dequasie, Andrew. Vermont Mosaic: Whizzers & Other Short Fictional Tales of Vermont. 2000. 239p. pap. 21.99 (*0-7388-1471-7*); text 31.99 (*0-7388-1470-9*); E-Book 8.00 (*0-7388-8458-8*) Xlibris Corp.

Dimmick, Barbara. Heart-Side Up. 2002. 380p. 24.95 (*1-55597-362-0*) Graywolf Pr.

Faine, Edward Allan. Green Mountain Men: The Odyssey of Ethan Allen. 1997. 384p. 26.95 (*0-312-86078-1*, Forge Bks.) Doherty, Tom Assocs., LLC.

Farrow, Rachi. Charlie's Dream. 1978. (Illus.). (J). (gr. 1-5). lib. bdg. 5.99 o.p. (*0-394-93595-0*, Pantheon) Knopf Publishing Group.

Forbes, Edith. Nowle's Passing. 1997. 272p. pap. 12.00 (*1-878067-99-0*); 1996. 266p. 21.95 o.p. (*1-878067-72-9*) Avalon Publishing Group. (Seal Pr.).

Freeman, Castle, Jr. Judgment Hill: A Novel. 1997. 239p. text 26.00 (*0-87451-832-6*, Hardscrabble Bks.) Univ. Pr. of New England.

—My Life & Adventures: A Novel. 2002. 416p. 25.95 (*0-312-28261-3*) St. Martin's Pr.

Gardner, John. October Light. 1983. mass mkt. 3.95 o.s.i (*0-345-31550-2*); 1977. mass mkt. 2.50 o.p. (*0-345-27193-9*) Ballantine Bks.

—October Light. 1986. pap. 6.95 o.s.i (*0-394-74058-0*); 1989. reprint ed. pap. 15.00 o.s.i (*0-679-72133-9*) Knopf Publishing Group. (Vintage).

Greene, Thomas C. Mirror Lake. 2004. mass mkt. 6.99 (*0-7434-6461-3*, Pocket) Simon & Schuster.

Greene, Thomas Christopher. Mirror Lake. 2003. 224p. 22.00 (*0-7432-4427-3*, Simon & Schuster) Simon & Schuster.

Greenwood, T. Breathing Water. 1999. 276p. 23.95 o.p. (*0-312-20283-0*); 2000. 288p. reprint ed. pap. 13.95 (*0-312-26289-2*, NPB 0264, Saint Martin's Griffin) St. Martin's Pr.

Hayford, James. Gridley Firing. 1987. (Illus.). 160p. (Orig.). (J). (gr. 4 up). pap. 9.95 (*0-933050-49-6*) New England Pr., Inc., The.

Hays, Mary. Learning to Drive. 2003. 320p. 23.00 (*1-4000-4780-3*) Crown Publishing Group.

Heffernan, William. Beulah Hill. 2003. 301p. pap. 13.95 (*1-888451-40-8*) Akashic Bks.

—Beulah Hill. 2001. 304p. 24.00 o.s.i (*0-684-86226-3*, Simon & Schuster) Simon & Schuster.

—Blood Rose. 1991. 320p. 18.95 o.p. (*0-525-24962-1*, Dutton) Dutton/Plume.

—Blood Rose. 1992. 448p. mass mkt. 6.99 o.s.i (*0-451-17163-2*, Signet Bks.) NAL.

—Scarred. 1993. 384p. (Orig.). mass mkt. 5.99 o.s.i (*0-451-17863-7*, Signet Bks.) NAL.

Higgins, George V. Victories. 1990. 19.95 o.p. (*0-8050-1219-2*) Holt, Henry & Co.

Hoag, Tami. Mismatch. l.t. ed. 2002. 267p. 29.95 (*0-7862-3488-1*) Gale Group.

—Mismatch. l.t. ed. 2002. 275p. (*0-7540-4792-X*); 29.95 (*0-7540-4793-8*) Thorndike Pr.

Hummel, Maria. Wilderness Run: A Novel. 352p. 2003. pap. 13.95 (*0-312-32047-7*, Saint Martin's Griffin); 2002. 24.95 (*0-312-28757-7*) St. Martin's Pr.

Hurwitz, Johanna. Faraway Summer. 1998. (Illus.). 160p. (J). (gr. 3-7). 14.95 (*0-688-15334-8*) HarperCollins Children's Bk. Group.

Hustvedt, Siri. What I Loved: A Novel. 2003. 384p. 25.00 (*0-8050-7170-9*) Holt, Henry & Co.

—What I Loved: A Novel. 2004. 384p. pap. 14.00 (*0-312-42119-2*); 2003. mass mkt. 7.99 (*0-312-99387-0*) Picador.

Johnson, Allen, Jr. The Christmas Tree Express. (Illus.). (J). (gr. 4-8). 12.95 o.s.i (*1-878561-21-9*) Seacoast Publishing, Inc.

Kendall, Jay. The Secret Keepers. 1998. 250p. pap. 14.95 (*1-884540-39-2*) Haley's.

Kessler, Brad. The Woodcutter's Christmas. 2001. (Illus.). 54p. 14.95 (*1-57178-105-6*) Council Oak Bks.

Kinsey-Warnock, Natalie. If Wishes Were Horses. (J). 2002. 144p. pap. 5.99 (*0-14-230143-4*, Puffin Bks.); 2000. (Illus.). (gr. 6-12). 15.99 o.s.i (*0-525-46448-4*, Dutton Children's Bks.) Penguin Putnam Bks. for Young Readers.

—When I Remember. 2015. 32p. 15.99 (*0-525-65200-0*) Penguin Putnam Bks. for Young Readers.

Kramer, Kathryn. Sweet Water: A Novel. 1998. 311p. 24.00 (*0-375-40083-4*) Knopf, Alfred A. Inc.

Lasky, Kathryn. Sugaring Time. (Illus.). 64p. (J). (gr. 3-7). 1983. lib. bdg. 15.00 o.s.i (*0-02-751680-6*, Simon & Schuster Children's Publishing); 1986. reprint ed. pap. 6.99 (*0-689-71081-X*, Aladdin) Simon & Schuster Children's Publishing.

—Sugaring Time. 1986. (J). 12.14 (*0-606-03308-4*) Turtleback Bks.

Lee, Wendi. Habeas Campus. 2003. (WWL Mystery Ser.: No. 447). 256p. mass mkt. (*0-373-26447-X*, Worldwide Library) Harlequin Enterprises, Ltd.

Leitz, David E. Casting in Dead Water. 1996. mass mkt. 5.50 (*0-312-95779-3*, St. Martin's Paperbacks) St. Martin's Pr.

—Dying to Fly Fish: A Max Addams Fly-Fishing Mystery. 1996. (Dead Letter Mysteries Ser.). 292p. mass mkt. 5.99 (*0-312-95983-4*, St. Martin's Paperbacks) St. Martin's Pr.

—Fly-Fishing Can Be Fatal: A Max Addams Mystery. 1997. 260p. (Orig.). mass mkt. 5.99 (*0-312-96162-6*, St. Martin's Paperbacks) St. Martin's Pr.

—The Fly Fishing Corpse. 1994. 160p. 19.95 o.p. (*1-882418-15-8*); pap. 12.95 (*1-882418-13-1*) Centennial Pubns.

—Hooked on Death: A Max Addams Fly Fishing Mystery. 2000. 288p. pap. 21.99 (*0-7388-1797-X*); text 31.99 (*0-7388-1796-1*) Xlibris Corp.

Lent, Jeffrey. In the Fall. 2000. 560p. 25.00 o.p. (*0-87113-765-8*, Atlantic Monthly Pr.) Grove/Atlantic, Inc.

—In the Fall. 2000. pap. (*0-375-72589-X*, Vintage) Knopf Publishing Group.

—In the Fall. l.t. ed. 2000. (Americana Ser.). 967p. 28.95 (*0-7862-2783-4*) Thorndike Pr.

—In the Fall: A Novel. 2001. 528p. reprint ed. pap. 14.95 (*0-375-70745-X*, Vintage) Knopf Publishing Group.

Lipman, Elinor. The Inn at Lake Devine. 1999. 272p. pap. 13.00 (*0-375-70485-X*, Vintage) Knopf Publishing Group.

—The Inn at Lake Devine. 1998. 23.00 (*0-676-54572-6*) Random Hse., Inc.

—The Inn at Lake Devine: A Novel. 1998. 272p. 23.95 o.s.i (*0-679-45693-7*) Random Hse., Inc.

Lowenthal, Michael. Avoidance: A Novel. 2002. 272p. pap. 16.00 (*1-55597-367-1*) Graywolf Pr.

Malamud, Bernard. Dubin's Lives. 2003. 376p. pap. 15.00 (*0-374-52882-9*); 1979. 362p. 10.00 o.p. (*0-374-14414-1*) Farrar, Straus & Giroux.

—Dubin's Lives. 1980. 432p. pap. 2.50 o.p. (*0-380-48413-7*, 48413-7, Avon Bks.) Morrow/Avon.

—Dubin's Lives. 1994. (Penguin Twentieth-Century Classics Ser.). 400p. pap. 10.95 o.s.i (*0-14-018760-X*, Penguin Classics) Viking Penguin.

Mathes, Charles. The Girl at the End of the Line. 2000. (WWL Mystery Ser.: Vol. 341). 256p. per. (*0-373-26341-4*, Harlequin Bks.) Harlequin Enterprises, Ltd.

—The Girl at the End of the Line. 17.95 (*0-312-33171-1*); 1999. 288p. 22.95 o.p. (*0-312-19887-6*, Saint Martin's Minotaur) St. Martin's Pr.

Mayor, Archer. Bellows Falls. 1997. 224p. 22.00 o.p. (*0-89296-637-8*) Mysterious Pr.

—Bellows Falls. l.t. ed. 1998. (Mystery Ser.). 392p. 27.95 (*0-7838-8405-2*) Thorndike Pr.

—Bellows Falls. 1998. 352p. reprint ed. mass mkt. 6.99 (*0-446-60630-8*) Warner Bks., Inc.

—Borderlines. 1991. 320p. mass mkt. 4.50 (*0-380-71600-3*, Avon Bks.) Morrow/Avon.

—Borderlines. 1990. 256p. 19.95 o.s.i (*0-399-13553-7*, G. P. Putnam's Sons) Penguin Putnam Bks. for Young Readers.

—Borderlines. 1994. 336p. reprint ed. mass mkt. 6.99 (*0-446-40443-8*) Warner Bks., Inc.

—The Dark Root. 1995. 82p. 19.95 o.p. (*0-89296-558-4*) Mysterious Pr.

—The Dark Root. 1996. 400p. reprint ed. mass mkt. 6.99 (*0-446-40376-8*) Warner Bks., Inc.

—The Disposable Man. 1998. (Joe Gunther Mysteries Ser.). 294p. 22.00 o.p. (*0-89296-685-8*) Mysterious Pr.

—The Disposable Man. 1999. 336p. reprint ed. mass mkt. 6.99 (*0-446-60768-1*) Warner Bks., Inc.

—Fruits of the Poisonous Tree. 1994. 224p. 19.95 o.s.i (*0-89296-557-6*) Mysterious Pr.

—Fruits of the Poisonous Tree. 1995. (Joe Gunther Mysteries Ser.). 304p. reprint ed. mass mkt. 6.99 (*0-446-40374-1*) Warner Bks., Inc.

—Gatekeeper. 2003. (Joe Gunther Mysteries Ser.). 23.95 (*0-89296-766-8*) Mysterious Pr.

—The Marble Mask. l.t. ed. 2001. (Large Print Bks.). 347p. pap. 23.95 (*1-58724-129-3*, Wheeler Publishing, Inc.) Gale Group.

—The Marble Mask. 2000. 309p. 23.95 o.p. (*0-89296-723-4*); 336p. E-Book 14.95 (*0-7595-9011-7*); E-Book 14.95 (*0-7595-6011-0*) Mysterious Pr.

—The Marble Mask. 336p. 2000. E-Book 14.95 (*0-7595-8011-1*); 2001. reprint ed. mass mkt. 6.99 (*0-446-61029-1*) Warner Bks., Inc.

—Open Season. 1989. 320p. pap. 3.95 (*0-380-70756-X*, Avon Bks.) Morrow/Avon.

—Open Season. 1988. 304p. 18.95 o.p. (*0-399-13398-4*, G. P. Putnam's Sons) Penguin Putnam Bks. for Young Readers.

—Open Season. 1994. (Joe Gunther Mysteries Ser.). 320p. reprint ed. mass mkt. 6.99 (*0-446-40414-4*) Warner Bks., Inc.

—The Ragman's Memory. l.t. ed. 1997. (G. K. Hall Mystery Ser.). 483p. lib. bdg. 25.95 o.p. (*0-7838-8208-4*, Macmillan Reference USA) Gale Group.

—The Ragman's Memory. 1997. 368p. 6.50 (*0-446-40524-8*) Mysterious Pr.

—The Ragman's Memory. 1996. 336p. 22.00 o.p. (*0-89296-636-X*); 1997. 368p. reprint ed. mass mkt. 6.99 (*0-446-60590-5*) Warner Bks., Inc.

—Scent of Evil. 1992. 368p. 18.95 o.p. (*0-89296-471-5*) Mysterious Pr.

—Scent of Evil. 1993. (Joe Gunther Mysteries Ser.). 416p. reprint ed. mass mkt. 6.99 (*0-446-40335-0*) Warner Bks., Inc.

—The Skeleton's Knee. 1993. 320p. 18.95 (*0-89296-470-7*) Mysterious Pr.

—The Skeleton's Knee. 1994. (Joe Gunther Mysteries Ser.). 320p. reprint ed. mass mkt. 6.99 (*0-446-40099-8*) Warner Bks., Inc.

—Tucker Peak. 2001. 304p. 23.45 o.p. (*0-89296-724-2*) Mysterious Pr.

—Tucker Peak. 2002. 352p. reprint ed. mass mkt. 6.99 (*0-446-61208-1*) Warner Bks., Inc.

McNaughton, Brian. Buster Callan. 2002. 204p. 37.95 (*1-58715-556-7*) Wildside Pr.

Miller, John M. & Mosher, Howard Frank. Granite & Cedar: The Land & People of the Northeast Kingdom. 2001. (Illus.). 96p. 35.00 (*0-9705511-1-8*) Thistle Hill Pubns.

Miller, Sue. The World Below. 2001. E-Book 20.00 (*1-59061-312-0*) Adobe Systems, Inc.

—The World Below. 2001. 288p. 25.00 (*0-375-41094-5*) Knopf, Alfred A. Inc.

—The World Below. unabr. ed. 2001. audio 34.95 (*0-375-41993-4*); audio compact disk 39.95 (*0-375-41994-2*) Random Hse. Audio Publishing Group. (RH Audio).

—The World Below. l.t. ed. 2001. 448p. 25.00 (*0-375-43131-4*) Random Hse. Large Print.

—The World Below. 2002. 304p. pap. 13.95 (*0-345-44076-5*) Random Hse., Inc.

Morris, Mary McGarry. Songs in Ordinary Time. unabr. ed. 1997. Pt. 1. audio 80.00; Pt. 2. audio 80.00 Books on Tape, Inc.

—Songs in Ordinary Time. unabr. ed. 1997. audio 169.25 (*1-56740-560-6*, 1053, Unabridged Library Editions); audio 29.95 (*1-56100-781-1*, 272, Bookcassette) Brilliance Audio.

—Songs in Ordinary Time. 1996. 752p. pap. 13.95 (*0-14-024482-4*, Penguin Bks.) Penguin Group (USA) Inc.

—Songs in Ordinary Time. 1997. 26.95 (*0-670-87907-X*); 1995. 752p. 24.95 o.s.i (*0-670-86014-X*, Viking); 1997. audio 24.95 Viking Penguin.

Mosher, Howard Frank. The Fall of the Year: A Novel. 1999. 288p. tchr. ed. 24.00 (*0-395-98416-5*); E-Book 24.00 (*0-618-15331-4*) Houghton Mifflin Co.

—The Fall of the Year: A Novel. 2000. 288p. pap. 13.00 (*0-618-08236-0*, Mariner Bks.) Houghton Mifflin Co. Trade & Reference Div.

—Northern Borders. 1994. 304p. 22.95 o.s.i (*0-385-47337-0*) Doubleday Publishing.

—The True Account: A Novel of the Lewis & Clark & Kinneson Expeditions. 2003. 352p. tchr. ed. 24.00 (*0-618-19721-4*) Houghton Mifflin Co.

—The True Account: A Novel of the Lewis & Clark & Kinneson Expeditions. 2004. 352p. pap. 13.00 (*0-618-43123-3*, Mariner Bks.) Houghton Mifflin Co. Trade & Reference Div.

Neggers, Carla. The Carriage House. 384p. 2003. mass mkt. (*1-55166-972-2*); 2001. mass mkt. (*1-55166-790-8*, 1-66790-6) Harlequin Enterprises, Ltd. (Mira Bks.).

—The Waterfall. 384p. 2003. mass mkt. (*1-55166-971-4*); 2000. mass mkt. (*1-55166-582-4*) Harlequin Enterprises, Ltd. (Mira Bks.).

—The Waterfall. l.t. ed. 2004. 419p. 28.95 (*0-7862-6233-8*) Thorndike Pr.

Nicholson, Peggy. Don't Mess with Texans: By the Year 2000: Revenge, No. 834. 1999. (Harlequin Superromance Ser.: Vol. 834). per. (*0-373-70834-3*, Harlequin Bks.) Harlequin Enterprises, Ltd.

Noon, Jack. The Big Fish of Barston Falls. 1995. (Illus.). 289p. (C). 24.00 (*0-9642213-2-2*) Moose Country Pr.

—Old Sam's Thunder. unabr. ed. 1998. (Illus.). 328p. (YA). pap. 16.00 (*0-9642213-6-5*) Moose Country Pr.

Offill, Jenny. Last Things. 1999. 272p. 23.00 o.p. (*0-374-18405-4*) Farrar, Straus & Giroux.

Olshan, Joseph. In Clara's Hands. 2003. 305p. 26.00 (*0-7475-5497-8*); 2002. 320p. pap. 12.00 (*0-7475-5704-7*) Bloomsbury Publishing, Ltd. GBR. *Dist:* Trafalgar Square.

Peck, Robert Newton. A Day No Pigs Would Die. 1972. 160p. (gr. 7 up). 25.00 (*0-394-48235-2*) Knopf, Alfred A. Inc.

—A Day No Pigs Would Die. 1994. (Illus.). 160p. (gr. 4-7). mass mkt. 5.50 (*0-679-85306-5*, Random Hse. Bks. for Young Readers) Random Hse. Children's Bks.

—A Part of the Sky. 1997. 176p. (J). (gr. 5-9). mass mkt. 4.99 (*0-679-88696-6*, Random Hse. Bks. for Young Readers) Random Hse. Children's Bks.

Pizzuti, Suzy. Raising Cain... And His Sisters. l.t. ed. 2000. (Christian Fiction Ser.). 371p. 24.95 o.p. (*0-7862-2533-5*) Thorndike Pr.

Prendergast, John. Jump. 1995. (First Novel Ser.). 256p. (Orig.). pap. 14.00 (*0-922811-23-7*) Mid-List Pr.

Ramsay, Diana. Killing Words. 1994. 192p. 18.95 o.p. (*0-312-11015-4*, Saint Martin's Minotaur) St. Martin's Pr.

Rawlings, Ellen. Deadly Harvest. 1997. mass mkt. 5.99 o.s.i (*0-449-14987-0*, Fawcett) Ballantine Bks.

Roberts, Sherry. Maud's House. 216p. 1995. pap. 11.00 (*0-918949-28-9*); 1994. 18.00 (*0-918949-32-7*) Roberts, Sherry.

Robinson, Rowland E. Danvis Tales: Selected Stories. Budbill, David, ed. 1995. (Illus.). 320p. lib. bdg. 24.95 o.p. (*0-87451-718-4*, Hardscrabble Bks.) Univ. Pr. of New England.

Salter, Anna. Fault Lines. 1998. E-Book 22.00 (0-671-03696-3, Atria); 1998. 272p. 22.00 (0-671-00312-7, Atria); 1999. 368p. reprint ed. mass mkt. 6.99 o.s.i (0-671-00313-5, Pocket Star); Vol. 2. Date not set. (0-671-02352-7, Atria) Simon & Schuster.
—Shiny Water. 1998. 320p. per. 6.50 (0-671-00311-9, Pocket Star); 1997. 272p. 23.00 (0-671-00310-0, Atria) Simon & Schuster.
Schupack, Deborah. The Boy on the Bus. l.t. ed. 2003. (Basic Ser.). 28.95 (0-7862-5573-0) Thorndike Pr.
—The Boy on the Bus: A Novel. 2004. 256p. pap. 12.00 (0-7432-4221-1); 2003. 224p. 23.00 (0-7432-4220-3) Simon & Schuster. (Free Pr.).
Schwenke, Karl. In a Pig's Eye. l.t. ed. 1991. pap. 8.95 o.p. (1-55504-516-2, 855) BBC Audiobooks America.
—In a Pig's Eye. 1985. 160p. pap. 9.95 (0-930031-00-8) Chelsea Green Publishing.
Shaw, Terrence. Deadly Waters. 1998. (Illus.). v, 271p. 19.95 (0-9666018-0-7) Black Ponds Publishing.
Singerman, Philip. Proof Positive. 2001. 352p. 24.95 (0-312-87686-6, Forge Bks.) Doherty, Tom Assocs., LLC.
Spielberg, Elinor. Uninvited Daughter. 1993. 224p. 18.95 o.p. (0-312-09914-2) St. Martin's Pr.
Stone, Abigail. Recipes from the Dump. 1996. pap. 10.00 (0-380-72882-6, Avon Bks.) Morrow/Avon.
—Recipes from the Dump. pap. o.p. (0-393-31433-2); 1995. 224p. 18.00 o.p. (0-393-03854-8) Norton, W. W. & Co., Inc.
Stuart, Anne. Still Lake. l.t. ed. 2003. (Thorndike Romance Ser.). 402p. 28.95 (0-7862-4988-9) Gale Group.
—Still Lake. 2002. 384p. mass mkt. (1-55166-908-0, Mira Bks.) Harlequin Enterprises, Ltd.
Sullivan, Mark T. Ghost Dance. 2000. 352p. reprint ed. mass mkt. 6.99 o.s.i (0-380-79043-2) HarperCollins Pubs.
—Ghost Dance. 1999. 352p. 24.00 o.s.i (0-380-97429-0, Avon Bks.) Morrow/Avon.
Sumner, Mark. News from the Edge. 1999. (News from the Edge Ser.). 208p. mass mkt. 6.50 o.s.i (0-441-00628-0) Ace Bks.
Tartt, Donna. The Secret History: A Novel. 1996. 592p. pap. 14.95 (0-449-91151-9, Fawcett); 1993. 512p. mass mkt. 7.99 (0-8041-1135-9, Ivy Bks.) Ballantine Bks.
—The Secret History: A Novel. 1992. 544p. 27.95 (0-679-41032-5) Knopf, Alfred A. Inc.
—The Secret History: A Novel. 1994. 6.99 o.p. (0-517-11658-8) Random Hse. Value Publishing.
Tesler, Nancy. Slippery Slopes & Other Deadly Things: A Carrie Carlin Biofeedback Mystery. 2003. 264p. pap. 13.95 (1-880284-58-8, Perseverance Pr.) Daniel, John & Co., Pubs.
Thompson, Daniel P. The Green Mountain Boys. E-Book 3.95 (0-594-01065-9) 1873 Pr.
—The Green Mountain Boys. 1987. 496p. reprint ed. pap. 14.95 o.s.i (0-87797-145-5) Cherokee Publishing Co.
—The Green Mountain Boys. Washington, Carol E. & Washington, Ida H., eds. 2000. (Illus.). 242p. pap. 15.00 (0-9666832-4-2) Cherry Tree Bks.
Updike, John. Seek My Face. 2003. 288p. pap. 13.95 (0-345-46086-3, Ballantine Bks.) Ballantine Bks.
—Seek My Face. l.t. ed. 2003. lib. bdg. 29.95 (1-58547-318-9, Platinum) Ctr. Point Large Print.
—Seek My Face. 2002. 288p. 23.00 (0-375-41490-8) Knopf, Alfred A. Inc.
Walker, Mildred. The Body of a Young Man. 1997. 186p. pap. 9.00 (0-8032-9787-4, Bison Bks.) Univ. of Nebraska Pr.
—The Quarry. 1995. 341p. pap. 14.00 (0-8032-9779-3, Bison Bks.) Univ. of Nebraska Pr.
Webb, Charles. New Cardiff. 2002. (Illus.). 368p. pap. 14.00 (0-7434-4416-7, Washington Square Pr.) Simon & Schuster.
Wizowaty, Suzi. The Round Barn. 2002. (Hardscrabble Books). (Illus.). 256p. text 24.95 (1-58465-282-9) Univ. Pr. of New England.
Wood, Ted. Snowjob. 1995. (Mystery Ser.). 251p. per. (0-373-26182-9, 1-26182-5, Worldwide Library) Harlequin Enterprises, Ltd.
—Snowjob. 1993. 256p. 20.00 o.p. (0-684-19563-1, Scribner) Simon & Schuster.
Wright, Nancy M. Harvest of Bones: A Vermont Mystery. 1999. 256p. per. (0-373-26325-2, Worldwide Library) Harlequin Enterprises, Ltd.
—Harvest of Bones: A Vermont Mystery. 1998. 304p. 23.95 (0-312-19280-0, Saint Martin's Minotaur) St. Martin's Pr.
—Mad Season: A Mystery. 1998. (WWL Mystery Ser.). per. (0-373-26270-1, 1-26270-8, Worldwide Library) Harlequin Enterprises, Ltd.
—Mad Season: A Mystery. 1996. (Mad Season Ser.: Vol. 1). 208p. 20.95 o.p. (0-312-14819-4, Saint Martin's Minotaur) St. Martin's Pr.
—Poison Apples. 2000. 322p. 24.95 (0-312-26220-5, Saint Martin's Minotaur) St. Martin's Pr.
—Stolen Honey. 2003. (WWL Mystery Ser.: No. 453). 272p. mass mkt. (0-373-26453-4, Worldwide Library) Harlequin Enterprises, Ltd.
—Stolen Honey. 2002. 256p. 23.95 (0-312-26245-0, Saint Martin's Minotaur) St. Martin's Pr.
—Stolen Honey. l.t. ed. 2003. 465p. pap. 24.95 (0-7862-5681-8) Thorndike Pr.
Yorke, Christy. Magic Spells. 1999. 368p. mass mkt. 5.99 o.s.i (0-553-57842-1) Bantam Bks.
—Magic Spells. l.t. ed. 2000. (G. K. Hall Core Ser.). 477p. 27.95 (0-7838-9028-1) Thorndike Pr.

### VICTORIA SPRINGS (MO.: IMAGINARY PLACE)—FICTION

Hager, Jean. Blooming Murder. 1994. (Iris House Mystery Ser.). pap. 5.50 (0-380-77209-4, Avon Bks.) Morrow/Avon.
—Blooming Murder. l.t. ed. 2001. (Illus.). 339p. (0-7862-3215-3) Thorndike Pr.
—Bride & Doom. 2000. (Iris House Mystery Ser.: No. 2). 224p. mass mkt. 5.99 (0-380-80376-3, Avon Bks.) Morrow/Avon.
—Dead & Buried. 1995. (Iris House Mystery Ser.). mass mkt. 5.50 (0-380-77210-8, Avon Bks.) Morrow/Avon.
—Dead & Buried. l.t. ed. 2000. (Mystery Ser.). (Illus.). 339p. 27.95 (0-7862-2928-4) Thorndike Pr.
—Death on the Drunkard's Path. 1996. (Iris House Mystery Ser.: No. 3). pap. 5.50 (0-380-77211-6, Avon Bks.) Morrow/Avon.
—Death on the Drunkard's Path. l.t. ed. 2000. (Mystery Ser.). 328p. 26.95 (0-7862-2353-7) Thorndike Pr.
—The Last Noel. 1997. (Iris House Mystery Ser.). 224p. mass mkt. 5.99 (0-380-78637-0, Avon Bks.) Morrow/Avon.
—Sew Deadly. 1998. (Iris House Mystery Ser.). 224p. mass mkt. 5.99 (0-380-78638-9, Avon Bks.) Morrow/Avon.
—Weigh Dead. 2003. (Mystery Ser.). 27.95 (1-57490-468-X) Beeler, Thomas T. Publisher.
—Weigh Dead. 1999. (Iris House Mystery Ser.: Vol. 6). 224p. mass mkt. 5.99 (0-380-80375-5, Avon Bks.) Morrow/Avon.

### VICTORY (WYO.: IMAGINARY PLACE)—FICTION

Bean, Gregory. A Death in Victory: A Harry Starbranch Mystery. 1997. 323p. 24.95 o.p. (0-312-15512-3, Saint Martin's Minotaur) St. Martin's Pr.
—Grave Victory. 1998. (Harry Starbranch Mysteries Ser.). 336p. 23.95 (0-312-18590-1, Saint Martin's Minotaur) St. Martin's Pr.
—Long Shadows in Victory: A Harry Starbranch Mystery. (Dead Letter Mysteries Ser.). 1997. 336p. mass mkt. 5.99 (0-312-96217-7, St. Martin's Paperbacks); 1996. 352p. 23.95 o.p. (0-312-14348-6, Saint Martin's Minotaur) St. Martin's Pr.
—No Comfort in Victory: A Sheriff Harry Starbranch Mystery. 353p. 1996. mass mkt. 5.99 o.p. (0-312-95877-3, St. Martin's Paperbacks); 1995. 23.95 o.p. (0-312-13133-X, Saint Martin's Minotaur) St. Martin's Pr.

### VIDESSOS (IMAGINARY PLACE)—FICTION

Turtledove, Harry. An Emperor for the Legion. 1987. (Videssos Cycle Ser.: Bk. 2). 336p. (Orig.). mass mkt. 6.99 (0-345-33068-4, Del Rey) Ballantine Bks.
—Hammer & Anvil. 1996. (Time of Troubles Ser.: Bk. 2). 384p. (Orig.). mass mkt. 5.99 o.s.i (0-345-38048-7, Del Rey) Ballantine Bks.
—Krispos of Videssos. 1991. (Illus.). 368p. mass mkt. 5.95 o.s.i (0-345-36119-9, Del Rey) Ballantine Bks.
—Krispos Rising Bk. 1: The Tale of Krispos. 1991. (Videssos Science Fiction Ser.). 368p. (Orig.). mass mkt. 6.99 (0-345-36118-0, Del Rey) Ballantine Bks.
—Krispos the Emperor Bk. 3: The Tale of Krispos. 1994. 368p. mass mkt. 5.99 o.s.i (0-345-38046-0, Del Rey) Ballantine Bks.
—The Legion of Videssos. 1987. (Videssos Cycle Ser.: Bk. III). 432p. mass mkt. 5.99 (0-345-33069-2, Del Rey) Ballantine Bks.
—The Misplaced Legion: Book One of the Videssos Cycle. 1987. (Videssos Cycle Ser.: Vol. 1). 336p. (Orig.). mass mkt. 6.99 (0-345-33067-6, Del Rey) Ballantine Bks.
—The Stolen Throne. 1995. (Time of Troubles Ser.: Bk. 1). 368p. mass mkt. 5.99 o.s.i (0-345-38047-9, Del Rey) Ballantine Bks.
—Swords of the Legion. 1987. (Videssos Cycle Ser.: Bk. 4). 408p. mass mkt. 6.99 (0-345-33070-6, Del Rey) Ballantine Bks.
—The Thousand Cities. 1997. (Time of Troubles Ser.: Bk. 3). 416p. (Orig.). mass mkt. 6.99 o.s.i (0-345-38049-5, Del Rey) Ballantine Bks.
—Videssos Besieged. 1998. (Time of Troubles Ser.: Vol. 4). 384p. mass mkt. l.t. ed. 6.99 o.s.i (0-345-40299-5, Del Rey) Ballantine Bks.

### VIENNA (AUSTRIA)—FICTION

Bernhard, Thomas. Old Masters: A Comedy. Osers, Ewald, tr. 1992. (Phoenix Fiction Ser.). iv, 160p. pap. 15.00 (0-226-04391-6) Univ. of Chicago Pr.
Canetti, Veza. Yellow Street. Mitchell, Ian, tr. from GER. 1991. 144p. 18.95 (0-8112-1159-2); pap. 10.95 (0-8112-1160-6, NDP709) New Directions Publishing Corp.
Carroll, Jonathan. Sleeping in Flame. 1990. 288p. pap. 13.00 (0-679-72777-9, Vintage) Knopf Publishing Group.
—Sleeping in Flames. 1989. 288p. 17.95 o.s.i (0-385-24957-8) Doubleday Publishing.
Carter, Peter. Children of the Book. 1987. 272p. (J). (gr. 3-6). 13.95 o.p. (0-19-271456-2) Oxford Univ. Pr., Inc.
Davis, Dee. Just Breathe. 2001. 384p. mass mkt. 6.50 (0-8041-1967-8, Ivy Bks.) Ballantine Bks.
Davison, Geoffrey. The Last Waltz: Vienna, May 1945. 2001. 288p. E-Book 8.00 (0-7388-7396-9) Xlibris Corp.
Ebner, Jeannie. The Bengal Tiger. Bangerter, Lowell A., tr. & afterword by by. 1992. (Studies in Austrian Literature, Culture & Thought). (GER.). 101p. pap. 12.50 (0-929497-54-6) Ariadne Pr.
Fagan, Cary. Animals Waltz. 1996. 288p. 21.95 (0-312-13921-7) St. Martin's Pr.
Fell, Doris Elaine. Blue Mist on the Danube. 1999. (Sagas of a Kindred Heart Ser.). 448p. (gr. 13 up). pap. 11.99 o.p. (0-8007-5677-0) Revell, Fleming H. Co.
Heaven, Constance. Castle of Eagles. l.t. ed. 1993. 21.95 o.p. (0-7927-1480-6); pap. 19.95 o.p. (0-7927-1479-2) BBC Audiobooks America.
Ibbotson, Eva. Madensky Square. 1988. 256p. 16.95 o.p. (0-312-02246-8) St. Martin's Pr.
—The Morning Gift. 1993. 336p. 19.95 o.p. (0-312-09338-1) St. Martin's Pr.
—A Song for Summer. unabr. ed. 1998. audio 69.95 (0-7540-0229-2, CAB 1652) BBC Audiobooks America.
—A Song for Summer. 1999. mass mkt. (0-312-96987-2, St. Martin's Paperbacks); 1998. 288p. 22.95 (0-312-18181-7) St. Martin's Pr.
—A Song for Summer. l.t. ed. 1998. (Charnwood Large Print Ser.). 432p. 29.99 o.p. (0-7089-9041-X, Charnwood) Thorpe, F. A. Pubs. GBR. *Dist:* Ulverscroft Large Print Bks., Ltd., Ulverscroft Large Print Canada, Ltd.
Jelinek, Elfriede. The Piano Teacher. 1988. 18.95 o.p. (1-55584-052-3) Grove/Atlantic, Inc.
—The Piano Teacher. Neugroschez, Joachim, tr. from GER. 1992. 288p. reprint ed. pap. o.p. (1-85242-157-6) Serpent's Tail Ltd.
—The Piano Teacher. 280p. 2002. pap. 14.00 (1-85242-750-7); 5th ed. 1999. pap. 12.00 (1-85242-725-6) Serpent's Tail Ltd. GBR. *Dist:* Consortium Bk. Sales & Distribution.
Korber, Lili. Night over Vienna. Hertling, Viktoria & Stone, Kay M., trs. from GER. 1989. (Studies in Austrian Literature, Culture & Thought). 147p. pap. 14.95 (0-929497-12-0) Ariadne Pr.
Lauterstein, Ingeborg. Vienna Girl. 1986. 16.95 o.p. (0-393-02264-1) Norton, W. W. & Co., Inc.
McMullan, Margaret. In My Mother's House. Date not set. mass mkt. (0-312-99153-3, St. Martin's Paperbacks); 2003. 272p. 23.95 (0-312-31824-3) St. Martin's Pr.
Menkes, John H. After the Tempest: A Novel. 2003. 304p. 24.95 (1-56474-420-5) Fithian Pr.
Musil, Robert. The Man Without Qualities. 1965. pap. 12.00 o.p. (0-399-50152-5, Perigee Bks.) Berkley Publishing Group.
—The Man Without Qualities. Wilkins, Sophie & Pike, Burton, trs. 1996. (Man Without Qualities Ser.: Vol. 1). Vol. 1. 752p. pap. 20.00 (0-679-76787-8); Vol. 2. 1072p. pap. 24.00 (0-679-76802-5) Knopf Publishing Group. (Vintage).
Nagorski, Andrew. Last Stop Vienna. 2003. 288p. 25.00 (0-7432-3750-1, Simon & Schuster) Simon & Schuster.
—Last Stop Vienna. l.t. ed. 2003. 29.95 (0-7862-5489-0) Thorndike Pr.
Powers, Tim. The Drawing of the Dark. (Del Rey Impact Ser.). 1999. 336p. pap. 11.95 (0-345-43081-6); 1987. mass mkt. 3.99 o.s.i (0-345-35008-1, Del Rey) Ballantine Bks.
Ross, Philip. Talley's Truth. 1988. 256p. mass mkt. 3.50 (0-8125-8784-7); 1987. 288p. 15.95 o.p. (0-312-93015-1) Doherty, Tom Assocs., LLC. (Tor Bks.).
Roth, Joseph. The Tale of the 1002nd Night. 1999. 272p. pap. 14.00 (0-312-24494-0) Picador.
—The Tale of the 1002nd Night: A Novel. Hofmann, Michael, tr. 1998. 272p. 23.95 o.p. (0-312-19341-6) Picador.
—The Tale of the 1002nd Night: A Novel. Hofmann, Michael, tr. 1999. E-Book 23.95 (0-312-24618-8) St. Martin's Pr.
Schnitzler, Arthur. The Road into the Open. Byers, Roger, tr. 1992. 314p. (C). pap. 18.95 (0-520-07774-1); text 55.00 (0-520-07575-7) Univ. of California Pr.
—The Road to the Open. Samuel, Horace, tr. from GER. 1991. 416p. reprint ed. 35.00 o.p. (0-8101-0921-2) Northwestern Univ. Pr.
—Vienna, 1900: Games with Love & Death. 1974. 365p. pap. 3.95 o.p. (0-14-003759-4, Penguin Bks.) Viking Penguin.
—Viennese Idylls. Eisemann, Frederick, tr. 1977. (Short Story Index Reprint Ser.). reprint ed. 19.95 (0-8369-4226-4) Ayer Co. Pubs., Inc.
Seth, Vikram. An Equal Music. abr. ed. 1999. audio 25.00 o.s.i (0-553-52636-7, RH Audio) Random Hse. Audio Publishing Group.
—An Equal Music. unabr. ed. 2000. audio 102.00 (0-7887-4493-3, H1080E7, Clipper Audio) Recorded Bks., LLC.
—An Equal Music: A Novel. 2000. (International Ser.). 400p. pap. 14.00 (0-375-70924-X, Vintage) Knopf Publishing Group.
Shields, Jody. The Fig Eater: A Novel. l.t. ed. 2000. (Wheeler Hardcover Ser.). (Illus.). 432p. 25.95 (1-56895-961-3, Wheeler Publishing, Inc.) Gale Group.
—The Fig Eater: A Novel. 2001. 320p. E-Book 9.95 (0-7595-9238-1); 2001. 320p. E-Book 9.95 (0-7595-4212-0); 2001. 320p. E-Book 9.95 (0-7595-0209-9); 2001. 320p. E-Book 9.95 (0-7595-6209-1); 2001. (Illus.). 368p. pap. 13.95 (0-316-78526-1, Back Bay); 2000. 240p. 23.95 o.p. (0-316-78564-4) Little Brown & Co.
—The Fig Eater: A Novel. 2001. 320p. E-Book 9.95 (0-7595-8215-7) Mysterious Pr.
Silva, Daniel. A Death in Vienna. 2004. 416p. 25.95 (0-399-15143-5) Putnam Publishing Group, The.
Simon, Leonard. Thanatos. 2003. 304p. 22.00 (1-56858-255-2) Four Walls Eight Windows.
Thoene, Bodie. Vienna Prelude. (Zion Covenant Ser.: No. 1). 2000. 464p. pap. 7.99 (0-7642-2427-1); 1989. 416p. pap. 12.99 (1-55661-066-1) Bethany Hse. Pubs.

### VIETNAM—FICTION

Abrahams, Peter. Hard Rain. 1988. 384p. 18.95 o.p. (0-525-24581-2, Dutton) Dutton/Plume.
—Hard Rain. 1989. 352p. mass mkt. 4.50 o.p. (0-451-40113-1, Onyx) NAL.
Accardi, James. Saigon Landing. 2001. 307p. pap. 22.99 (0-7388-5053-5); text 32.99 (0-7388-5052-7); E-Book 8.00 (1-4010-0166-1) Xlibris Corp.
Barnes, Thomas. Tay Son: Rebellion in 18th Century Vietnam. 2000. 216p. E-Book 8.00 (0-7388-8462-6) Xlibris Corp.
Barrett, Dean. Kingdom of Make-Believe. 1999. 344p. pap. 11.95 (0-9661899-0-6) Village East Bks.
Bataille, Christophe. Annam. Howard, Richard, tr. from FRE. 1996. 112p. 15.95 (0-8112-1330-7) New Directions Publishing Corp.
Breuer, Charles. The Horse Soldiers of Vietnam. 2000. 188p. E-Book 8.00 (0-7388-7653-4) Xlibris Corp.
Butler, David E. The Fall of Saigon. 1986. 512p. mass mkt. 5.95 o.s.i (0-440-12431-X) Dell Publishing.
Butler, Robert Olen. The Alleys of Eden. 1983. 256p. mass mkt. 2.95 o.s.i (0-345-30774-7) Ballantine Bks.
—The Alleys of Eden. 1994. 256p. 25.00 o.p. (0-8050-3199-5); pap. 11.00 o.s.i (0-8050-3141-3, Owl Bks.) Holt, Henry & Co.
—The Deep Green Sea. l.t. ed. 240p. 1999. pap. 13.00 o.s.i (0-8050-6001-4, Owl Bks.); 1998. (Deep Green Sea Ser.: Vol. 1). 23.00 o.s.i (0-8050-3130-8) Holt, Henry & Co.
—The Deep Green Sea. l.t. ed. 1998. (Core Ser.). 216p. 27.95 (0-7838-8431-1) Thorndike Pr.
Butler, Robert Olen & Nemeroy, Howard. The Alleys of Eden. 1981. 12.95 o.p. (0-8180-0631-5) Horizon Pr.
Christman, Rick. Falling in Love at the End of the World: A Collection of Stories. 1994. (Minnesota Voices Project Ser.: Vol. 62). 160p. (Orig.). pap. 9.95 (0-89823-154-X) New Rivers Pr.
Christopher, Nicholas. A Trip to the Stars. 2001. 512p. pap. 14.00 (0-7432-0330-5, Touchstone) Simon & Schuster.
Clancy, Tom. Without Remorse. 1993. 640p. 25.95 (0-399-13825-0); 150.00 o.s.i (0-399-13840-4) Penguin Group (USA) Inc. (G. P. Putnam's Sons).
Coonts, Stephen. Flight of the Intruder. abr. ed. 1990. audio 9.95 (0-88690-314-9, A20203, Audio Editions Bks. on Cassette) Audio Partners Publishing Corp.
—Flight of the Intruder. unabr. collector's ed. 1987. audio 72.00 (0-7366-1175-4, 2097) Books on Tape, Inc.
—Flight of the Intruder. unabr. ed. 1987. audio 19.95 o.p. (0-930435-32-X, 110, Bookcassette);Set. audio 73.25 o.p. (1-56100-027-2, 840) Brilliance Audio.
—Flight of the Intruder. l.t. ed. 1987. 523p. 19.95 o.p. (0-8161-4295-5); 11.95 o.p. (0-8161-4296-3) Gale Group. (Macmillan Reference USA).
—Flight of the Intruder. 1986. 329p. 26.95 (0-87021-200-1) Naval Institute Pr.
—Flight of the Intruder, unabr. ed. 1986. audio 70.00 (1-55690-180-1, 86980E7) Recorded Bks., LLC.
—Flight of the Intruder. 1991. mass mkt. 5.95 (0-671-72470-3, Pocket) Simon & Schuster.

—Flight of the Intruder. McCarthy, Paul, ed. 1990. 448p. mass mkt. 6.99 o.s.i (0-671-70960-7, Pocket) Simon & Schuster.

—Flight of the Intruder. 1987. mass mkt. 4.95 (0-671-64012-7, Pocket) Simon & Schuster.

Couch, Dick. Seal Team 1. 1991. 288p. (Orig.). mass mkt. 5.99 o.p. (0-380-76115-7, Avon Bks.) Morrow/Avon.

Crew, Randolph E. A Killing Shadow. Parker, Nancy, ed. 1996. 369p. 23.95 (0-9651430-8-2) Artec Publishing.

DeMille, Nelson. Up Country. 2002. (Illus.). 720p. 26.95 o.p. (0-446-51657-0); 1184p. 26.95 o.p. (0-446-52993-1) Warner Bks., Inc.

Dinh, Linh. Fake House: Stories. 2000. 224p. 23.95 (1-58322-039-9) Seven Stories Pr.

Duong, Thu Huong. Paradise of the Blind: A Novel. 2002. 272p. pap. 12.95 (0-06-050559-1, Perennial) HarperTrade.

Eickhoff, Randy Lee. Return to Ithaca. 2001. 512p. 25.95 (0-312-87446-4); 2002. 496p. reprint ed. pap. 16.95 (0-312-87538-X) Doherty, Tom Assocs., LLC. (Forge Bks.).

Freadhoff, Chuck. Blue Rain. 2000. 368p. mass mkt. 6.99 (0-06-109727-6); 1999. 336p. 24.00 o.p. (0-06-019217-8) HarperCollins Pubs.

—Blue Rain. l.t. ed. 1999. (Americana Ser.). 493p. 26.95 (0-7862-2068-6) Thorndike Pr.

Gabriel, Richard. Sebastian's Cross. 2001. pap. 18.95 (0-595-19156-8) iUniverse, Inc.

Grey, Anthony. Saigon. 1982. 825p. 19.95 o.p. (0-316-32822-7) Little Brown & Co.

Hanh, Thich Nhat. Hermitage among the Clouds: An Historical Novel of 14th Century Vietnam. 1993. 145p. pap. 12.50 (0-938077-56-2) Parallax Pr.

Heath, Layne. The Blue Deep. 1994. 416p. mass mkt. 5.99 (0-380-71398-5, Avon Bks.); 1993. 384p. 20.00 o.p. (0-688-10313-8, Morrow, William & Co.) Morrow/Avon.

—The Blue Deep. abr. ed. 1993. audio 17.00 (0-671-86591-9, Simon & Schuster Audioworks) Simon & Schuster Audio.

—The Blue Deep. 382p. 4.98 o.p. (0-8317-8747-3) Smithmark Pubs., Inc.

Hillerman, Tony. Finding Moon. 1995. ix, 319p. 24.00 o.p. (0-06-017772-1); 288p. 432.00 o.p. (0-06-017669-5); 336p. 150.00 o.p. (0-06-017287-8) HarperCollins Pubs.

—Finding Moon. 1996. 368p. mass mkt. 6.99 (0-06-109261-4, HarperTorch) Morrow/Avon.

—Finding Moon. l.t. ed. 1996. (Basic Ser.). 448p. 28.95 (0-7862-0574-1) Thorndike Pr.

—Finding Moon. 1996. lib. bdg. 13.04 (0-606-16176-7) Turtleback Bks.

Ho Anh Thai. The Woman on the Island: A Novel. Karlin, Wayne et al, trs. from VIE. 2001. (Illus.). 176p. 30.00 (0-295-98086-9); pap. 16.95 (0-295-98108-3) Univ. of Washington Pr.

Hunter, Stephen. Time to Hunt. 1999. 608p. mass mkt. 7.99 (0-440-22645-7) Dell Publishing.

Huong, Duong Thu. Beyond Illusions. McPherson, Nina & Duong, Phan Huy, trs. from VIE. 2002. 356p. 24.95 (0-7868-6417-6) Hyperion Pr.

—Memories of a Pure Spring. McPherson, Nina & Duong, Phan Huy, trs. from VIE. 2000. 356p. text 23.95 (0-7868-6581-4) Hyperion Pr.

—Memories of a Pure Spring. McPherson, Nina & Duong, Phan Huy, trs. 2001. 368p. pap. 14.00 (0-14-029843-6) Penguin Group (USA) Inc.

Ihimaera, Witi. The Uncle's Story. 2000. 373p. (0-14-029892-4) Penguin Group (USA) Inc.

—The Uncle's Story. 2002. (Talanoa: Contemporary Pacific Literature Ser.). 384p. (C). pap. 15.95 (0-8248-2576-4) Univ. of Hawaii Pr.

Just, Ward. A Dangerous Friend. 1999. 256p. tchr. ed. 23.00 (0-395-85698-1) Houghton Mifflin Co. Trade & Reference Div.

Karlin, Wayne, et al, eds. The Other Side of Heaven: Postwar Fiction by Vietnamese & American Writers. 1995. 412p. pap. 17.95 (1-880684-31-4) Curbstone Pr.

Kirts, Donald K. Okay, Fine. 1999. pap. text 19.95 (1-58445-036-3) Pulpless.com, Inc.

Lane, Daniel. Black Silk Pajamas: The Autobiography of the Former First Lady of South Vietnam. 2001. 260p. E-Book 8.00 (0-7388-9316-1) Xlibris Corp.

Lang, Tam, et al. The Light of the Capital: Three Modern Vietnamese Classics from Old Hanoi. Lockhart, Greg & Lockhart, Monique, trs. 1996. (Oxford in Asia Paperbacks Ser.). 232p. pap. 12.95 o.p. (967-65-3093-X) Oxford Univ. Pr., Inc.

Lawton. A Lovely Country. 2001. pap. (0-15-600466-6) Harcourt Trade Pubs.

Lawton, David. A Lovely Country: A Novel. 1995. 272p. 22.00 o.s.i (0-15-100171-5) Harcourt Trade Pubs.

—A Lovely Country: A Novel of Vietnam. 1995. 262p. o.p. (0-15-100118-9) Harcourt Trade Pubs.

Logan, Chuck. The Price of Blood. 1997. 400p. 24.00 o.p. (0-06-017492-7) HarperCollins Pubs.

—The Price of Blood. 1998. 496p. mass mkt. 7.50 (0-06-109622-9, HarperTorch) Morrow/Avon.

Luu, Le. A Time Far Past. Hai, Ngo Vinh et al, eds. Chung, Nguyen Ba et al, trs. from VIE. 1997. Tr. of Thoi Xa Vang. 296p. 27.50 (1-55849-085-X) Univ. of Massachusetts Pr.

Mort, John. Soldier in Paradise. 1999. 192p. 19.95 (0-87074-440-2) Southern Methodist Univ. Pr.

Nagata, Linda. Limit of Vision. 2001. 384p. 24.95 (0-312-87688-2, Tor Bks.) Doherty, Tom Assocs., LLC.

Nelms, Stan. Shack Rat: A Novel of Vietnam. 2000. 364p. pap. 17.95 (1-893652-81-5, Writers Club Pr.) iUniverse, Inc.

Rast, Franklin D. Don's Nam. 1999. (Illus.). 399p. pap. 29.95 (1-58112-849-5) Upublish.com.

Riker, H. Jay. Bronze Star. 1995. (SEALs, the Warrior Breed Ser.: No. 3). 496p. mass mkt. 6.99 (0-380-76970-0, Avon Bks.) Morrow/Avon.

—Navy Cross. 1996. (SEALs, the Warrior Breed Ser.: No. 4). 448p. mass mkt. 5.99 (0-380-78555-2, Avon Bks.) Morrow/Avon.

Simpson, Howard R. Someone Else's War. 1995. 200p. 21.95 (1-57488-000-4) Brassey's, Inc.

Smith, Debra White. The Awakening. 2000. (Seven Sisters Ser.: Vol. 2). 332p. pap. 9.99 (0-7369-0277-5) Harvest Hse. Pubs.

Steel, Danielle. Message from Nam. l.t. ed. 1990. 672p. 24.95 o.s.i (0-385-30136-7); 408p. 21.95 (0-385-29907-9) Bantam Doubleday Dell Large Print Group, Inc. (Delacorte Large Type).

—Message from Nam. 1991. 432p. mass mkt. 7.99 (0-440-20941-2); 1990. 408p. 125.00 (0-385-30137-5, Delacorte Pr.) Dell Publishing.

—Message from Nam. l.t. ed. 1993. pap. 19.95 o.p. (0-8161-5794-4, Macmillan Reference USA) Gale Group.

—Message from Nam. abr. ed. 1994. audio 16.99 (0-553-45281-9, RH Audio) Random Hse. Audio Publishing Group.

Stone, Scott C. Song of the Wolf. 1985. 16.95 o.p. (0-87795-678-2, Morrow, William & Co.) Morrow/Avon.

—Song of the Wolf. 1987. mass mkt. 3.95 o.p. (0-451-14775-8, Signet Bks.) NAL.

—Song of the Wolf. 1999. 388p. reprint ed. pap. 13.95 (1-58348-001-3) iUniverse, Inc.

Thiep, Nguyen H. Crossing the River: Short Fiction. Cam, Nguyen Nguyet & Sachs, Dana, eds. 2003. (Voices from Vietnam Ser.: Vol. 5). 360p. pap. 16.95 (1-880684-92-6) Curbstone Pr.

—The General Retires & Other Stories: With an Introduction. 1993. 202p. pap. 11.95 o.p. (0-19-588580-5) Oxford Univ. Pr., Inc.

Tillery, Gary. Darkling Plain. 2001. 221p. pap. 21.99 (0-7388-1815-1); text 31.99 (0-7388-1814-3) Xlibris Corp.

Tourison, Sedgwick. Project Alpha, Vol. 1. 1997. (Project Alpha Ser.: Vol. 1). 432p. mass mkt. 6.99 (0-312-96262-2, St. Martin's Paperbacks) St. Martin's Pr.

Trigg, Louisa Hagner. The Real Dragon: A Novel of Viet Nam. 2001. (Illus.). 511p. 25.95 (1-56474-352-7) Fithian Pr.

Vu, Tran. The Dragon Hunt: Five Stories. 1999. 160p. text (0-7868-6501-6) Disney Pr.

—The Dragon Hunt: Five Stories. McPherson, Nina & Duong, Phan Huy, trs. from VIE. 1999. 160p. 21.00 (0-7868-6418-4) Hyperion Pr.

Washington, Geno. Blood Brothers, 1. 1999. 311p. pap. text 12.95 (1-899344-44-6) Dufour Editions, Inc.

Wright, Don. Blood on the Blue Grass. 2001. 251p. 21.95 (0-9702567-1-X) New Way Publishing.

## VIRGIN ISLANDS—FICTION

Brandt, Kathy. Swimming with the Dead. 2003. 272p. mass mkt. 5.99 (0-451-21020-4, Signet Bks.) NAL.

Fletcher, Jessica & Bain, Donald. Rum & Razors. l.t. ed. 1995. (Murder She Wrote Ser.). (Orig.). 22.95 o.p. (1-56895-219-8, Wheeler Publishing, Inc.) Gale Group.

—Rum & Razors. 1995. (Murder She Wrote Ser.: Vol. 2). 304p. (Orig.). mass mkt. 6.50 (0-451-18383-5) NAL.

Heyn, Jean. The Governor-General's Lady. 1988. (Orig.). pap. 9.95 o.p. (0-936784-68-7) Daniel, John & Co., Pubs.

Jevons, Marshall. Murder at the Margin: A Henry Spearman Mystery. 1993. 192p. text 47.50 o.p. (0-691-03391-9); pap. text 15.95 (0-691-00098-0) Princeton Univ. Pr.

Medlicott, Joan Avna. Virgin Islands Tales of Olden Days. 1997. 96 p. (0-9657695-1-8) Picara Point.

Phillips, T. J. Dance of the Mongoose. 1995. 288p. pap. 9.00 o.s.i (0-425-14921-8, Prime Crime) Berkley Publishing Group.

Phillips, T. J. Dance of the Mongoose. 288p. 1996. mass mkt. 5.99 o.s.i (0-425-15623-0); 1995. 19.95 o.p. (0-425-14786-X) Berkley Publishing Group. (Prime Crime).

Savage, Tom. Precipice. 1994. 290p. 19.95 o.p. (0-316-77160-0) Little Brown & Co.

—Precipice. 1995. 416p. mass mkt. 6.99 o.s.i (0-451-18333-9, Onyx) NAL.

## VIRGINIA—FICTION

Altsheler, Joseph A. The Guns of Bull Run. E-Book 3.95 (0-594-04990-3) 1873 Pr.

—The Guns of Bull Run. 1976. reprint ed. lib. bdg. 25.95 (0-88411-942-4) Amereon, Ltd.

—The Guns of Bull Run. 1990. reprint ed. lib. bdg. 21.95 (0-89968-458-0) Buccaneer Bks., Inc.

—The Guns of Bull Run. 2002. 244p. 24.99 (1-4043-0530-0); per. 20.99 (1-4043-0531-9) IndyPublish-.com.

Andrews, Donna. Murder with Peacocks. l.t. ed. 2002. (Mystery Ser.). 26.95 (1-57490-388-8, Beeler Large Print Bks.) Beeler, Thomas T. Publisher.

—Murder with Peacocks. (Meg Langslow Mysteries Ser.). 2000. 320p. mass mkt. 6.50 (0-312-97063-3, St. Martin's Paperbacks); 1998. 332p. 23.95 (0-312-19929-5, Saint Martin's Minotaur) St. Martin's Pr.

—Revenge of the Wrought-Iron Flamingos. l.t. ed. 2002. (Mystery Ser.). 419p. 29.95 (0-7862-3925-5) Gale Group.

—Revenge of the Wrought-Iron Flamingos. mass mkt. (0-312-98022-1, St. Martin's Paperbacks); 2002. 288p. mass mkt. 6.50 (0-312-98319-0, St. Martin's Paperbacks); 2001. 304p. 23.95 (0-312-27729-6, Saint Martin's Minotaur) St. Martin's Pr.

—We'll Always Have Parrots: A Meg Langslow Mystery. 2004. 304p. 23.95 (0-312-27732-6, Saint Martin's Minotaur) St. Martin's Pr.

Andrews, V. C. Dawn. unabr. ed. 1991. (Cutler Ser.). audio 64.00 (0-7366-1944-5, 2765) Books on Tape, Inc.

—Dawn. l.t. ed. 1991. (General Ser.). 472p. pap. 17.95 (0-8161-5186-5); lib. bdg. 20.95 (0-8161-5184-9) Gale Group. (Macmillan Reference USA).

—Dawn. 2003. audio 76.95 (0-7531-1772-X); audio compact disk 89.95 (0-7531-2231-6) ISIS Audio Bks. GBR. *Dist:* Ulverscroft Large Print Bks., Ltd.

—Dawn. 1990. 19.95 (0-671-67067-0, Atria) Simon & Schuster.

—Dawn. Marrow, Linda, ed. 1990. (Cutler Ser.). 416p. mass mkt. 7.99 (0-671-67068-9, Pocket) Simon & Schuster.

—Dawn. 1990. 14.04 (0-606-04649-6) Turtleback Bks.

—The End of the Rainbow. 2002. (Hudson Ser.: No. 4). E-Book 7.99 (1-59061-643-X) Adobe Systems, Inc.

—The End of the Rainbow. 2001. (Hudson Ser.: Vol. 4). 384p. 24.95 (0-671-03984-9, Atria); E-Book 24.95 (0-7434-2167-1, Pocket); (Illus.). 384p. reprint ed. pap. 7.99 (0-671-03985-7, Pocket) Simon & Schuster.

—The End of the Rainbow. l.t. ed. 2001. 430p. 31.95 (0-7838-9512-7) Thorndike Pr.

—The End of the Rainbow. 2001. (Hudson Family Ser.). 14.04 (0-606-20651-5) Turtleback Bks.

—Eye of the Storm. 2001. (Hudson Ser.: No. 3). E-Book 7.99 (1-59061-063-6) Adobe Systems, Inc.

—Eye of the Storm. l.t. ed. 2001. 435p. (0-7540-1580-7); (0-7540-2442-3) Gale Group. (Macmillan Reference USA).

—Eye of the Storm. 2000. (Hudson Family Ser.: Vol. 3). 400p. 24.95 (0-671-03982-2, Atria); pap. 7.99 (0-671-03983-0, Pocket) Simon & Schuster.

—Eye of the Storm. l.t. ed. 2001. (Hudson Ser.). 435p. 31.95 (0-7838-9328-0) Thorndike Pr.

—Eye of the Storm. 2000. (Hudson Family Ser.). 14.04 (0-606-20221-8) Turtleback Bks.

—Rain. 2000. (Hudson Family Ser.: Vol. 1). 448p. 24.00 (0-671-00764-5, Atria); pap. 7.99 (0-671-00767-X, Pocket) Simon & Schuster.

—Rain. l.t. ed. 2001. (Core Ser.). 510p. 30.95 (0-7838-9329-9) Thorndike Pr.

Ashcom, Robert L. Winter Run. 2002. 240p. tchr. ed. 19.95 (1-56512-328-X, 72328) Algonquin Bks. of Chapel Hill.

Austin, Lynn. Candle in the Darkness: A Novel. 2002. (Refiners Fire Ser.: No. 1). 432p. pap. 12.99 (1-55661-436-5) Bethany Hse. Pubs.

Baldacci, David. Wish You Well. l.t. ed. 2000. 624p. 24.95 (0-375-43091-1) Random Hse. Large Print.

—Wish You Well. 2001. 368p. E-Book 14.95 (0-7595-8012-X) Time Warner Bk. Group.

—Wish You Well. 2000. 368p. E-Book 14.95 (0-7595-9012-5) Warner Bks., Inc.

Baldwin, Lydia W. A Yankee School-Teacher in Virginia. 1977. (Black Heritage Library Collection). reprint ed. 22.95 (0-8369-8959-7) Ayer Co. Pubs., Inc.

Barr, Marleen S. Oy Pioneer! 2003. (Library of American Fiction). 19.95 (0-299-18910-4) Univ. of Wisconsin Pr.

Barth, John. Sabbatical. 1984. audio 8.95 American Audio Prose Library, Inc.

—Sabbatical: A Romance. 1983. 366p. pap. 5.95 o.p. (0-14-006619-5); 1982. 352p. 14.95 o.p. (0-399-12717-8); 1982. 50.00 o.p. (0-399-12723-2) Putnam Publishing Group, The.

—Sabbatical: A Romance. 1996. 366p. reprint ed. pap. 12.95 (1-56478-096-1) Dalkey Archive Pr.

—The Tidewater Tales: A Novel. 1988. 656p. pap. 15.00 o.s.i (0-449-90293-5, Fawcett) Ballantine Bks.

—The Tidewater Tales: A Novel. 1987. 624p. 21.95 o.p. (0-399-13247-3, G. P. Putnam's Sons) Penguin Putnam Bks. for Young Readers.

Barth, John & Johnston, Mary. The Tidewater Tales: A Novel. 1997. (Maryland Paperback Bookshelf Ser.). (Illus.). 655p. reprint ed. pap. 19.95 (0-8018-5556-X) Johns Hopkins Univ. Pr.

Bausch. The Gypsy Man. 2003. 512p. pap. 14.00 (0-15-602873-5) Harcourt Trade Pubs.

Bausch, Robert. The Gypsy Man. 2002. 512p. 25.00 (0-15-100172-3) Harcourt Trade Pubs.

—A Hole in the Earth. 2001. 368p. reprint ed. pap. 14.00 (0-15-601184-0, Harvest Bks.) Harcourt Trade Pubs.

Bear, Greg. Darwin's Children. 2004. 512p. mass mkt. 7.50 (0-345-44836-7); 2003. 400p. 24.95 (0-345-44835-9); 2003. E-Book 17.95 (0-345-46491-5) Ballantine Bks. (Del Rey).

Bernhard, Virginia. A Durable Fire. 1991. 528p. mass mkt. 4.95 (0-380-70873-6, Avon Bks.); 1990. 448p. 22.95 o.p. (0-688-08900-3, Morrow, William & Co.) Morrow/Avon.

Blain, W. Edward. Love Cools. 1992. 288p. 19.95 o.p. (0-399-13779-3, G. P. Putnam's Sons) Penguin Group (USA) Inc.

Blair, Sydney. Buffalo. 1991. 256p. 18.95 o.p. (0-670-83554-4) Viking Penguin.

Blanshard, Audrey. A Virginian at Venncombe. 1978. mass mkt. 1.50 o.s.i (0-449-23420-7, Fawcett) Ballantine Bks.

—A Virginian at Venncombe. l.t. ed. 1993. (Historical Romance Ser.). 336p. 29.99 o.p. (0-7089-2946-X, Ulverscroft) Thorpe, F. A. Pubs. GBR. *Dist:* Ulverscroft Large Print Bks., Ltd., Ulverscroft Large Print Canada, Ltd.

Bontemps, Arna. Black Thunder: Gabriel's Revolt: Virginia, 1800. 1992. 254p. pap. 19.00 (0-8070-6337-1) Beacon Pr.

Bontemps, Arna, ed. Black Thunder. 1968. pap. 14.95 o.p. (0-8070-6429-7) Beacon Pr.

Bowen, Marjorie. The Soldier of Virginia: A Novel on George Washington. 1997. pap. 12.90 (0-921100-99-X) Inheritance Pubns.

Brand, Irene. Come Gentle Spring. 1987. 224p. pap. 5.70 (0-310-47661-5, 15618P) Zondervan.

Briscoe, Connie. A Long Way from Home. 1999. 368p. 25.00 (0-06-017278-9) HarperCollins Pubs.

—A Long Way from Home. abr. ed. 1999. audio 18.00 (0-694-52149-3, HarperAudio) HarperTrade.

—A Long Way from Home. abr. ed. 1999. audio 18.00 Highsmith Inc.

—A Long Way from Home. 2000. 416p. mass mkt. 7.50 (0-06-103021-X, Avon Bks.) Morrow/Avon.

—A Long Way from Home. 2000. 13.04 (0-606-22863-2) Turtleback Bks.

Brown, Rita Mae. Cat on the Scent. 336p. 1999. (Illus.). 23.95 o.s.i (0-553-09971-X); 2000. reprint ed. mass mkt. 7.50 (0-553-57541-4) Bantam Bks.

—Cat on the Scent. l.t. ed. 1999. 26.95 o.p. (1-56895-749-1, Wheeler Publishing, Inc.) Gale Group.

—Catch as Cat Can. l.t. ed. 2002. 504p. 31.95 (0-7862-4045-8) Gale Group.

—Catch as Cat Can. l.t. ed. 2003. (Paperback Bestsellers Ser.). pap. 13.95 (0-7862-4044-X) Thorndike Pr.

—Claws & Effect. 2002. (Mrs. Murphy Mystery Ser.). (Illus.). 320p. reprint ed. mass mkt. 7.50 (0-553-58090-6) Bantam Bks.

—Claws & Effect. l.t. ed. 2001. (Illus.). 433p. 30.95 (0-7862-3484-9) Thorndike Pr.

—Hotspur. 352p. 2003. mass mkt. 6.99 (0-345-42823-4); 2002. (Illus.). 24.95 (0-345-42822-6) Ballantine Bks.

—Hotspur. 2003. (Basic Ser.). 31.95 (0-7862-5135-2) Thorndike Pr.

—Murder at Monticello, or, Old Sins. 1995. (Mrs. Murphy Mystery Ser.). 320p. mass mkt. 7.50 (0-553-57235-0, Crimeline) Bantam Bks.

—Murder on the Prowl. 1999. 400p. reprint ed. mass mkt. 7.50 (0-553-57540-6) Bantam Bks.

—Murder on the Prowl. l.t. ed. 1998. (Basic Ser.). 467p. 30.95 (0-7862-1458-9) Thorndike Pr.

—Murder, She Meowed. 1997. (Mrs. Murphy Mystery Ser.). (Illus.). 336p. mass mkt. 7.50 (0-553-57237-7) Bantam Bks.

—Outfoxed. l.t. ed. 2000. 27.95 (1-56895-844-7, Wheeler Publishing, Inc.) Gale Group.

—Pawing Through the Past. 2001. (Mrs. Murphy Mystery Ser.). 352p. mass mkt. 7.50 (0-553-58025-6) Bantam Bks.

—Pawing Through the Past. l.t. ed. 2000. (Wheeler Large Print Book Ser.). (Illus.). 360p. 28.95 o.p. (1-56895-134-5, Wheeler Publishing, Inc.) Gale Group.

—Pay Dirt. 1996. (Mrs. Murphy Mystery Ser.). 288p. mass mkt. 7.50 (0-553-57236-9, Crimeline) Bantam Bks.

—Rest in Pieces. 1993. (Mrs. Murphy Mystery Ser.). 368p. mass mkt. 7.50 (0-553-56239-8) Bantam Bks.

—Riding Shotgun. 1997. 368p. mass mkt. 6.99 (*0-553-57224-5*) Bantam Bks.
—Riding Shotgun. l.t. ed. 1996. (Large Print Bks.). pap. 23.95 o.p. (*1-56895-332-1*, Wheeler Publishing, Inc.) Gale Group.
—The Tail of the Tip-Off. 2004. (Illus.). 400p. mass mkt. 7.50 (*0-553-58285-2*) Bantam Bks.
—Venus Envy. 1994. 400p. mass mkt. 7.50 (*0-553-56497-8*) Bantam Bks.
—Whisker of Evil. 2004. (Illus.). 320p. 24.95 (*0-553-80161-9*) Bantam Bks.
—Wish You Were Here. l.t. ed. 1992. pap. 20.95 o.p. (*0-7927-1189-0*); 22.95 o.p. (*0-7927-1188-2*, CH0250) BBC Audiobooks America.
—Wish You Were Here. 1991. (Mrs. Murphy Mystery Ser.). 304p. mass mkt. 7.50 (*0-553-28753-2*) Bantam Bks.
Brown, Rita Mae & Brown, Sneaky Pie. Catch As Cat Can. 2003. (Illus.). 368p. mass mkt. 7.50 (*0-553-58028-0*, Bantam) Bantam Bks.
—Catch As Cat Can. 2002. (Illus.). 304p. 24.95 (*0-553-10744-5*) Bantam Dell Publishing Group.
—Catch as Cat Can. l.t. ed. 13.95 (*1-4104-0084-0*, Large Print Pr.) Thorndike Pr.
—The Tail of the Tip-Off. 2003. (Mrs. Murphy Mystery Ser.). E-Book 19.95 (*0-553-89725-X*); (Illus.). 320p. 24.95 (*0-553-80158-9*) Bantam Bks.
—The Tail of the Tip-Off. audio 29.99 (*1-4025-3628-3*) Recorded Bks., LLC.
—The Tail of the Tip-Off. l.t. ed. 2003. 32.95 (*0-7862-4991-9*) Thorndike Pr.
Burnham, Sophy. Revelations. 1992. 496p. 20.00 o.s.i (*0-345-37233-6*) Ballantine Bks.
Byron, Gilbert. Done Crabbin' Noah Leaves the River. 208p. 2000. pap. 16.95 (*0-8018-6528-X*); 1957. (gr. 9-12). text 40.00 o.p. (*0-8018-3988-2*) Johns Hopkins Univ. Pr.
Campbell, Phyllis. Come Home, My Heart. l.t. ed. 2001. (Candlelight Ser.). 207p. 22.95 (*0-7862-3627-2*) Thorndike Pr.
Cannon, Taffy. Guns & Roses: A Modern Mystery Set in Colonial Williamsburg. 2000. 240p. pap. 12.95 (*1-880284-34-0*) Daniel, John & Co., Pubs.
—Guns & Roses: An Irish Eyes Travel Mystery Set in Colonial Williamsburg. l.t. ed. 2001. 323p. 24.95 (*0-7838-9678-6*) Thorndike Pr.
Case, John. The Genesis Code. 1998. 480p. mass mkt. 7.99 (*0-345-42231-7*) Ballantine Bks.
—The Genesis Code. abr. ed. 1998. 3p. audio 7.99 o.p. (*1-56740-241-0*, 655, Paperback Nova Audio Bks.); 1997. audio 27.95 o.p. (*1-56100-753-6*, 121, Bookcassette); 1997. audio 105.25 o.p. (*1-56100-828-1*, 880, Unabridged Library Editions) Brilliance Audio.
—The Genesis Code. l.t. ed. 1997. (Basic Ser.). 761p. 26.95 o.p. (*0-7862-1205-5*) Thorndike Pr.
Chamberlain, Diane. Brass Ring. 1994. 416p. 21.00 o.p. (*0-06-017612-1*) HarperCollins Pubs.
—Brass Ring. 1995. 432p. mass mkt. 5.99 o.p. (*0-06-104281-1*, HarperTorch) Morrow/Avon.
Chappell, Helen. Oysterback Spoken Here. 1998. (Illus.). 208p. pap. 14.95 (*1-891521-01-2*) Woodholme Hse. Pubs.
—The Oysterback Tales. 1980. 128p. 22.95 (*0-8018-4815-6*) Johns Hopkins Univ. Pr.
Charbeneau, James A. Shouts & Whispers: Stories from the Southern Chesapeake Bay. 1997. (Illus.). 175p. (Orig.). pap. 12.95 (*1-883911-11-7*) Brandylane Pubs., Inc.
Charbonneau, Eileen. The Randolph Legacy. 1998. (Illus.). 499p. mass mkt. 6.50 o.p. (*0-8125-4467-6*); 1997. 416p. 24.95 (*0-312-86332-2*) Doherty, Tom Assocs., LLC. (Forge Bks.).
Chase-Riboud, Barbara. Sally Hemings: A Novel. 1994. 416p. reprint ed. pap. 12.00 o.s.i (*0-345-38971-9*) Ballantine Bks.
—Sally Hemings: A Novel. 1992. 300p. reprint ed. lib. bdg. 37.95 (*0-89966-915-8*) Buccaneer Bks., Inc.
—Sally Hemings: A Novel. 1980. 416p. mass mkt. 4.95 (*0-380-48686-5*, Avon Bks.) Morrow/Avon.
—Sally Hemings: A Novel. 2000. 368p. pap. 14.95 (*0-312-24704-4*, Saint Martin's Griffin) St. Martin's Pr.
—Sally Hemings: A Novel. 1979. 12.95 o.p. (*0-670-61605-2*) Viking Penguin.
Churchman, Deborah. Cross a Dark Bridge: A Novel. 1996. 130p. 14.95 (*0-918056-08-X*) Ariadne Pr.
Clark, Mary Higgins. Mount Vernon Love Story. 2003. 272p. mass mkt. 6.99 (*0-7434-4894-4*, Pocket); 2002. E-Book 9.99 (*0-7432-0630-4*, Simon & Schuster); 2002. (Illus.). 224p. 22.00 (*0-7432-2987-8*, Simon & Schuster); 2002. 352p. 22.00 (*0-7432-3380-8*, Simon & Schuster); 2002. 224p. 22.00 (*0-7432-4304-8*, Simon & Schuster) Simon & Schuster.
—Mount Vernon Love Story. abr. ed. 2002. audio 26.00 (*0-7435-2288-5*); audio compact disk 30.00 (*0-7435-2287-7*) Simon & Schuster Audio. (Simon & Schuster Audioworks).
Conley, Robert J. War Woman: A Novel of the Real People. 1998. 368p. pap. 15.95 (*0-312-19361-0*, Saint Martin's Griffin); 1997. 384p. 25.95 o.p. (*0-312-17058-0*) St. Martin's Pr.
—War Woman: A Novel of the Real People. 2001. 357p. pap. 17.95 (*0-8061-3369-4*) Univ. of Oklahoma Pr.
Conquest, Ned. Virginia, the Gray & the Green. 1990. 160p. 19.95 (*0-9627485-1-X*) Apollonian Pr.
Cooke, John Esten. My Lady Pokahontas. (Americans in Fiction Ser.). reprint ed. lib. bdg. 22.00 (*0-8398-0272-2*) Irvington Pubs.
—My Lady Pokohontos. 2000. 252p. E-Book 3.95 (*0-594-02031-X*) 1873 Pr.
—Surry of Eagle's Nest. 2000. 252p. pap. 9.95 (*0-594-00129-3*); E-Book 9.95 (*0-594-02033-6*) 1873 Pr.
—Surry of Eagle's Nest: Or, the Memoirs of a Staff Officer Serving in Virginia. (Americans in Fiction Ser.). 484p. reprint ed. lib. bdg. 37.00 (*0-8398-0273-0*); 1986. (C). pap. text 8.95 (*0-8290-2037-3*) Irvington Pubs.
—The Virginia Comedians. 2000. 252p. E-Book 9.95 (*0-594-03643-7*) 1873 Pr.
Coon, Alma S. Amy, Ben, & Catalpa the Cat: A Fanciful Story of This & That. 1990. (Illus.). 40p. (J). (ps-1). 8.95 (*0-87935-079-2*) Colonial Williamsburg Foundation.
Cornwell, Patricia. All That Remains. unabr. ed. 1996. 10p. audio 84.95 (*0-7451-6665-2*, CAB1281) BBC Audiobooks America.
—All That Remains. unabr. collector's ed. 1992. (Kay Scarpetta Mystery Ser.). audio 56.00 (*0-7366-2239-X*, 3029) Books on Tape, Inc.
—All That Remains. unabr. ed. 1992. audio 22.95 o.p. (*1-56100-468-5*, 421, Bookcassette); audio 57.25 o.p. (*1-56100-102-3*, 604, Unabridged Library Editions) Brilliance Audio.
—All That Remains. l.t. ed. 1992. (G. K. Hall Hardcover Ser.). 447p. 23.95 (*0-8161-5526-7*, Macmillan Reference USA) Gale Group.
—All That Remains. abr. ed. 1994. (Kay Scarpetta Mystery Ser.). audio 18.00 (*0-694-51471-3*, 390332, HarperAudio) HarperTrade.
—All That Remains. 1993. (Kay Scarpetta Mystery Ser.). 416p. mass mkt. 7.99 (*0-380-71833-2*, Avon Bks.) Morrow/Avon.
—All That Remains. unabr. ed. 1995. (Kay Scarpetta Mystery Ser. : Vol. 3). audio 78.00 (*0-7887-0168-1*, 94393E7) Recorded Bks., LLC.
—All That Remains. 1992. 416p. 26.00 (*0-684-19395-7*); 21.95 (*0-684-19515-1*) Simon & Schuster. (Scribner).
—Black Notice. 2000. 464p. mass mkt. 7.99 (*0-425-17540-5*) Berkley Publishing Group.
—Black Notice. unabr. ed. 1999. audio 72.00 (*0-7366-4581-0*, 4988) Books on Tape, Inc.
—Black Notice. l.t. ed. 1999. 25.95 o.p. (*0-7838-8688-8*, Macmillan Reference USA) Gale Group.
—Black Notice, Set. abr. ed. 1999. audio 24.95. audio 39.95 Highsmith Inc.
—Black Notice. abr. ed. 1999. 24.95 o.s.i (*0-399-14515-X*); 368p. 150.00 (*0-399-14522-2*, G. P. Putnam's Sons);Set. 5p. 39.95 o.s.i (*0-399-14516-8*, Putnam Berkley Audio) Penguin Group (USA) Inc.
—Black Notice. 2002. 25.95 o.s.i (*0-399-15031-5*); 1999. 415p. 25.95 o.p. (*0-399-14508-7*) Putnam Publishing Group, The.
—Black Notice. l.t. ed. 2000. 544p. pap. 13.95 (*0-375-70771-9*); 1999. 576p. 25.95 (*0-375-40845-2*) Random Hse. Large Print.
—Black Notice. unabr. ed. 2000. (Kay Scarpetta Mystery Ser. : Vol. 5). audio compact disk 112.00 (*0-7887-3975-1*, C1094E7); 1999. audio compact disk 112.00; 1999. (Kay Scarpetta Mystery Ser. : Vol. 5). audio 85.00 (*0-7887-3458-X*, 95881E7) Recorded Bks., LLC.
—Black Notice. 2000. 14.04 (*0-606-19510-6*) Turtleback Bks.
—The Body Farm. 1995. 368p. mass mkt. 7.99 (*0-425-14762-2*); 6.99 (*0-425-14863-7*, Prime Crime) Berkley Publishing Group.
—The Body Farm. unabr. ed. 1995. (Kay Scarpetta Mystery Ser.). audio 64.00 (*0-7366-3040-6*, 3722) Books on Tape, Inc.
—The Body Farm. 1994. 400p. 23.00 (*0-684-19597-6*); 403p. lib. bdg. 26.95 o.p. (*0-7838-1122-5*) Gale Group. (Macmillan Reference USA).
—The Body Farm. unabr. ed. 2002. audio 39.95 (*1-4025-2411-0*, RG096) Recorded Bks., LLC.
—The Body Farm. 1999. audio 9.98 (*0-671-04687-X*, Simon & Schuster Audioworks); 2002. audio 9.95 (*0-7435-2749-6*, Encore); Set. 1994. audio 17.00 o.p. (*0-671-86880-2*, 390161, Simon & Schuster Audioworks) Simon & Schuster Audio.
—The Body Farm. l.t. ed. 1996. (Paperback Bestsellers Ser.). pap. 20.95 (*0-7838-1123-3*) Thorndike Pr.
—Body of Evidence. unabr. ed. 1996. audio 69.95 (*0-7451-6580-X*, CAB1196) BBC Audiobooks America.
—Body of Evidence. unabr. collector's ed. 1991. (Kay Scarpetta Mystery Ser.). audio 56.00 (*0-7366-2001-X*, 2818) Books on Tape, Inc.
—Body of Evidence. unabr. ed. 1992. audio 22.95 o.p. (*1-56100-457-X*, 427); audio 57.25 o.p. (*1-56100-091-4*, 609) Brilliance Audio. (Bookcassette).
—Body of Evidence. 1991. 400p. 18.95 (*0-684-19240-3*); 1994. lib. bdg. 16.95 o.p. (*0-8161-5867-3*) Gale Group. (Macmillan Reference USA).
—Body of Evidence. abr. ed. 1995. audio 18.00 (*0-694-51592-2*, CPN 2267, HarperAudio) HarperTrade.
—Body of Evidence. 1992. (Kay Scarpetta Mystery Ser.). 416p. mass mkt. 6.99 (*0-380-71701-8*, Avon Bks.) Morrow/Avon.
—Body of Evidence. unabr. ed. 1994. audio 78.00 (*0-7887-0048-0*, 94247E7) Recorded Bks., LLC.
—Body of Evidence. Pocket Books Staff, ed. 1999. 416p. pap. 7.99 (*0-671-03856-7*, Pocket) Simon & Schuster.
—Body of Evidence. 1900. mass mkt. (*0-671-03880-X*, Pocket) Simon & Schuster.
—Body of Evidence. l.t. ed. 1994. (Mystery Ser.). lib. bdg. 26.95 (*0-8161-5866-5*) Thorndike Pr.
—Cause of Death. 1997. 368p. mass mkt. 7.99 (*0-425-15861-6*); 7.50 (*0-425-16198-6*) Berkley Publishing Group.
—Cause of Death. unabr. ed. 1996. audio 56.00 (*0-7366-3372-3*, 4022) Books on Tape, Inc.
—Cause of Death. l.t. ed. 1998. (Thorndike/G. K. Hall Paperback Bestsellers Ser.). 430p. pap. 25.95 o.p. (*0-7838-1793-2*, Macmillan Reference USA) Gale Group.
—Cause of Death, unabr. ed. 1999. audio 39.95 Highsmith Inc.
—Cause of Death. abr. unabr. ed. 2003. audio compact disk 49.95 (*1-59007-467-X*) New Millennium Entertainment.
—Cause of Death. 1996. 352p. 25.95 o.p. (*0-399-14146-4*); 340p. 150.00 (*0-399-14170-7*) Penguin Group (USA) Inc. (G. P. Putnam's Sons).
—Cause of Death. 25.95 o.s.i (*0-399-14482-X*) Putnam Publishing Group, The.
—Cause of Death. abr. ed. 1996. 23.50 o.s.i incl. audio (*0-679-44508-0*); audio compact disk 27.50 o.s.i (*0-679-45184-6*) Random Hse. Audio Publishing Group. (RH Audio).
—Cause of Death. unabr. ed. 2002. audio 24.99 (*1-4025-2893-0*, 02294); audio compact disk 34.99 (*1-4025-2894-9*, 00562) Recorded Bks., LLC.
—Cause of Death. 1998. 7.98 o.p. (*0-7651-1040-7*) Smithmark Pubs., Inc.
—Cause of Death. l.t. ed. 1996. (Core Collection). 407p. lib. bdg. 29.95 (*0-7838-1792-4*) Thorndike Pr.
—Cruel & Unusual. unabr. ed. 1996. audio 84.95 (*0-7451-4358-X*, CAB1041) BBC Audiobooks America.
—Cruel & Unusual. unabr. collector's ed. 1993. (Kay Scarpetta Mystery Ser.). audio 64.00 (*0-7366-2518-6*, 3273) Books on Tape, Inc.
—Cruel & Unusual. unabr. ed. 1993. audio 23.95 o.p. (*1-56100-506-1*, 76, Bookcassette); audio 73.25 o.p. (*1-56100-135-X*, 1164, Unabridged Library Editions) Brilliance Audio.
—Cruel & Unusual. 1993. 21.00 (*0-684-19599-2*); 448p. 23.00 (*0-684-19612-3*); 439p. 25.00 o.p. (*0-8161-5727-8*) Gale Group. (Macmillan Reference USA).
—Cruel & Unusual. abr. ed. 1993. (Kate Scarpetta Mystery Ser.). 3p. audio 18.00 (*1-55994-712-8*, 390583, HarperAudio) HarperTrade.
—Cruel & Unusual. 1994. 416p. mass mkt. 7.99 (*0-380-71834-0*, Avon Bks.) Morrow/Avon.
—Cruel & Unusual. unabr. ed. 2000. (Kay Scarpetta Mystery Ser. : No. 4). audio 70.00 (*1-55690-849-0*, 93217E7) Recorded Bks., LLC.
—Cruel & Unusual. 1993. 384p. 25.00 (*0-684-19530-5*, Scribner) Simon & Schuster.
—From Potter's Field. l.t. ed. 1996. 384p. mass mkt. 7.99 (*0-425-15409-2*) Berkley Publishing Group.
—From Potter's Field. unabr. ed. 1996. (Kay Scarpetta Mystery Ser.). audio 56.00 (*0-7366-3241-7*, 3900) Books on Tape, Inc.
—From Potter's Field. 1995. 29.50 (*0-684-81318-1*); 416p. 24.00 (*0-684-19598-4*, Scribner) Simon & Schuster.
—From Potter's Field. abr. ed. 1995. (Kay Scarpetta Mystery Ser.). audio 24.00 (*0-671-86881-0*, 493119, Simon & Schuster Audioworks) Simon & Schuster Audio.
—From Potter's Field. 1997. 7.98 o.p. (*0-7651-0544-6*) Smithmark Pubs., Inc.
—From Potter's Field. l.t. ed. (Thorndike/G. K. Hall Paperback Bestsellers Ser.). 434p. 1997. pap. 25.95 (*0-7838-1292-2*); 1995. 28.95 (*0-7838-1291-4*) Thorndike Pr.
—Isle of Dogs. l.t. ed. 2001. 663p. (*0-7540-1701-X*); (*0-7540-9101-5*) BBC Audiobooks America.
—Isle of Dogs. 2002. mass mkt. 7.99 (*0-425-18676-8*); 432p. reprint ed. mass mkt. 7.99 (*0-425-18290-8*) Berkley Publishing Group.
—Isle of Dogs. 2001. 368p. 26.95 (*0-399-14739-X*, Riverhead Bks. (Hardcovers)) Penguin Group (USA) Inc.
—Isle of Dogs. l.t. ed. 2002. 13.95 (*1-4104-0004-2*, Large Print Pr.); 2001. 663p. 32.95 (*0-7862-3358-3*); 2001. 663p. 29.95 (*0-7862-3359-1*) Thorndike Pr.
—The Last Precinct. 2001. 480p. mass mkt. 7.99 (*0-425-18063-8*) Berkley Publishing Group.
—The Last Precinct. ltd. ed. 2000. (Kay Scarpetta Ser.). 432p. 150.00 (*0-399-14639-3*) Penguin Group (USA) Inc.
—The Last Precinct. 2000. (Kay Scarpetta Ser.). 449p. 26.95 o.s.i (*0-399-14625-3*); E-Book 26.95 (*0-399-14756-X*) Putnam Publishing Group, The.
—The Last Precinct. l.t. ed. 2000. 736p. 26.95 (*0-375-43068-7*) Random Hse. Large Print.
—Patricia Cornwell: 3 Complete Novels: Postmortem; Body of Evidence; All That Remains. 1997. 832p. 14.98 (*0-7651-9112-1*) Smithmark Pubs., Inc.
—Point of Origin. l.t. ed. 1998. 542p. (*0-7540-2149-1*) BBC Audiobooks America.
—Point of Origin. 1999. 416p. reprint ed. mass mkt. 7.99 (*0-425-16986-3*) Berkley Publishing Group.
—Point of Origin, Set. abr. ed. 1999. audio 24.95. audio 39.95 Highsmith Inc.
—Point of Origin. 1998. 25.95 o.s.i (*0-399-14769-1*); 368p. 25.95 o.p. (*0-399-14394-7*, G. P. Putnam's Sons); 350p. 150.00 (*0-399-14412-9*, G. P. Putnam's Sons);Set. 24.95 o.p. (*0-399-14401-3*, 692891) Penguin Group (USA) Inc.
—Point of Origin. unabr. ed. 1998. (Kay Scarpetta Mystery Ser.). 39.95 incl. audio (*0-375-40353-1*, PC05M, RH Audio) Random Hse. Audio Publishing Group.
—Point of Origin. l.t. ed. (Paperback Bestsellers Ser.). 543p. 1999. pap. 28.95 (*0-7862-1478-3*); 1998. 31.95 (*0-7862-1477-5*) Thorndike Pr.
—Postmortem. unabr. ed. 1996. audio 69.95 (*0-7451-6482-X*, CAB 1098) BBC Audiobooks America.
—Postmortem. unabr. collector's ed. 1991. (Kay Scarpetta Mystery Ser.). audio 56.00 (*0-7366-2071-0*, 2879) Books on Tape, Inc.
—Postmortem. unabr. ed. 1993. 73.25 o.p. incl. audio (*1-56100-172-4*, 990, Unabridged Library Editions-);Set. audio 23.95 o.p. (*1-56100-545-2*, 217, Bookcassette) Brilliance Audio.
—Postmortem. 1999. (SPA.). pap. 14.95 (*970-05-0943-5*) Distribooks, Inc.
—Postmortem. l.t. ed. 1994. 441p. lib. bdg. 16.95 o.p. (*0-8161-5865-7*); lib. bdg. 23.95 o.p. (*0-8161-5864-9*) Gale Group. (Macmillan Reference USA).
—Postmortem. abr. ed. 1999. audio 18.00 (*0-694-52281-3*) HarperCollins Pubs.
—Postmortem, Set. abr. ed. 1992. audio 16.00 (*1-55994-528-1*, DCN 2268, HarperAudio) HarperTrade.
—Postmortem, Set. unabr. ed. 1999. audio 73.25 Highsmith Inc.
—Postmortem. 1991. 352p. pap. 6.49 (*0-380-71021-8*, Avon Bks.) Morrow/Avon.
—Postmortem. 2000. (Best Mysteries of All Time Ser.). 333p. (*0-7621-8859-6*) Reader's Digest Assn., Inc., The.
—Postmortem. unabr. ed. 1993. (Kay Scarpetta Mystery Ser. : Vol. 1). audio 70.00 (*1-55690-892-X*, 93334E7) Recorded Bks., LLC.
—Postmortem. 2004. 352p. mass mkt. 7.99 (*0-7434-7715-4*, Pocket); 1990. 293p. 21.00 o.s.i (*0-684-19141-5*, Scribner); 1998. 352p. mass mkt. 7.99 (*0-671-02361-6*, Pocket) Simon & Schuster.
—The Scarpetta Collection Vol. I: Postmortem & Body of Evidence. 2003. 640p. 26.95 (*0-7432-5580-1*, Scribner) Simon & Schuster.
—Scarpetta's Winter Table. 1998. (Illus.). 96p. 19.95 (*0-941711-42-0*) Penguin Group (USA) Inc.
—Southern Cross. 1999. audio compact disk (*0-7540-5316-4*, CCD007) BBC Audiobooks America.
—Southern Cross. 1999. 400p. mass mkt. 7.99 (*0-425-17254-6*) Berkley Publishing Group.
—Southern Cross. l.t. ed. (Wheeler Press Paperback Ser.). 2000. pap. 11.95 (*1-56895-973-7*); 1999. 458p. 29.95 (*1-56895-709-2*) Gale Group. (Wheeler Publishing, Inc.).
—Southern Cross, abr. ed. 1999. audio 24.95. audio 39.95 Highsmith Inc.
—Southern Cross. 1999. 368p. 25.95 o.p. (*0-399-14465-X*); 25.95 o.s.i (*0-399-14771-3*); 24.95 o.p. (*0-399-14478-1*, 696063); 39.95 o.p. (*0-399-14472-2*, 106043, Putnam Berkley Audio) Penguin Group (USA) Inc.
—Southern Cross. 1999. 24.95 o.s.i (*0-399-14773-X*); 39.95 o.s.i (*0-399-14772-1*, Putnam Berkley Audio) Putnam Publishing Group, The.
—Southern Cross. unabr. ed. 1999. audio 83.00 (*0-7887-2591-2*, 95612E7) Recorded Bks., LLC.
—Southern Cross. abr. ed. 1999. audio 16.85 (*1-85686-611-4*) Ulverscroft Audio (U.S.A.).
—Unnatural Exposure. 1998. 384p. mass mkt. 7.99 (*0-425-16340-7*) Berkley Publishing Group.
—Unnatural Exposure. unabr. ed. 1997. (Kay Scarpetta Mystery Ser.). audio 56.00 (*0-913369-71-3*, 4323) Books on Tape, Inc.
—Unnatural Exposure, Set. unabr. ed. 1999. audio 34.95 Highsmith Inc.
—Unnatural Exposure. abr. unabr. ed. 2003. audio compact disk 49.95 (*1-59007-468-8*) New Millennium Entertainment.

—Unnatural Exposure. 25.95 (*0-399-14544-3*); 1997. 352p. 25.95 o.p. (*0-399-14285-1*, G. P. Putnam's Sons); 1997. 352p. 150.00 (*0-399-14295-9*, G. P. Putnam's Sons) Penguin Group (USA) Inc.

—Unnatural Exposure. l.t. ed. (Paperback Bestsellers Ser.). 415p. 1998. pap. 28.95 (*0-7838-8088-X*); 1997. lib. bdg. 30.95 (*0-7838-8087-1*) Thorndike Pr.

—Unnatural Exposure: A Novel, Set. abr. ed. 1997. (Kay Scarpetta Mystery Ser.). audio 24.00 o.s.i (*0-679-44509-9*, 495252, RH Audio) Random Hse. Audio Publishing Group.

Crafts, Hannah. The Bondwoman's Narrative. l.t. ed. 2002. (African American Ser.). 29.95 (*0-7862-4471-2*) Thorndike Pr.

—The Bondwoman's Narrative. Gates, Henry Louis, Jr., ed. 2002. (Illus.). 416p. 24.95 (*0-446-53008-5*) Warner Bks., Inc.

—The Bondwoman's Narrative. Gates, Henry Louis, Jr., ed. & intro. by. fac. ed. 2003. (Illus.). 384p. 50.00 (*0-446-53173-1*) Warner Bks., Inc.

—The Bondwoman's Narrative. Gates, Henry Louis, Jr., ed. 2003. 464p. reprint ed. pap. 14.95 (*0-446-69029-5*) Warner Bks., Inc.

Crane, Stephen. The Red Badge of Courage. E-Book 3.95 (*0-594-03693-3*) 1873 Pr.

—The Red Badge of Courage. 1997. (Classics Illustrated Study Guides). (Illus.). mass mkt. 4.99 (*1-57840-040-6*) Acclaim Bks.

—The Red Badge of Courage. 17.95 (*0-89190-118-3*) Amereon, Ltd.

—The Red Badge of Courage. 1994. (Illustrated Classics Collection). 64p. pap. 4.95 (*0-7854-0669-7*, 40352) American Guidance Service, Inc.

—The Red Badge of Courage. unabr. ed. audio 23.80 Audio Bk. Co.

—The Red Badge of Courage. 1995. audio 29.95 (*1-55685-357-2*) Audio Bk. Contractors, Inc.

—The Red Badge of Courage. unabr. ed. audio 26.95 o.p. (*1-55656-094-X*, DAB007) BBC Audiobooks America.

—The Red Badge of Courage. 1997. 216p. pap. 14.95 incl. disk, cd-rom (*1-55701-230-X*) BNI Pubns., Inc.

—The Red Badge of Courage. 1986. (Bantam Classics Ser.). 208p. pap. 11.95 o.p. (*0-553-06415-0*) Bantam Bks.

—The Red Badge of Courage. Green, Frank & Seely, John, eds. 1999. (Classic Novels ). 200p. pap. 8.95 (*0-7641-1145-0*) Barron's Educational Series, Inc.

—The Red Badge of Courage. unabr. ed. 1994. audio 32.95 (*0-7861-0697-2*, 1479) Blackstone Audio Bks., Inc.

—The Red Badge of Courage. unabr. ed. audio 21.95 (*1-55686-111-7*, 111) Books in Motion.

—The Red Badge of Courage. 2002. pap. 3.93 (*1-59109-097-0*) Booksurge, LLC.

—The Red Badge of Courage. unabr. ed. 1993. (Bookcassette Classic Collection). 5p. audio 57.25 (*1-56100-119-8*, 1002, Unabridged Library Editions); audio 17.95 o.p. (*1-56100-485-5*, 225, Bookcassette) Brilliance Audio.

—The Red Badge of Courage. reprint ed. lib. bdg. 48.00 (*0-7426-1071-3*); 2001. pap. text 28.00 (*0-7426-6071-0*) Classic Bks.

—The Red Badge of Courage. unabr. ed. audio 21.95 o.s.i (*1-55656-054-0*); 1998. pap. 21.95 o.p. incl. audio (*1-55656-271-3*) Dercum Audio.

—The Red Badge of Courage. 1988. mass mkt. 4.95 (*0-938819-99-2*, Aerie) Doherty, Tom Assocs., LLC.

—The Red Badge of Courage. abr. ed. 1986. (J). (gr. 6-8). audio 29.99 (*0-88646-816-7*, R 7146); 2p. (gr. 4-7). audio 16.99 (*0-88646-145-6*, 7146) Durkin Hayes Publishing Ltd.

—The Red Badge of Courage. E-Book 2.49 (*1-58744-104-7*) Electric Umbrella Publishing.

—The Red Badge of Courage. audio 19.95 Filmic Archives.

—The Red Badge of Courage. (Reader's Request Ser.). 1980. lib. bdg. 8.95 o.p. (*0-8161-3078-7*); 2001. 155p. 27.95 (*0-7838-9527-5*) Gale Group. (Macmillan Reference USA).

—The Red Badge of Courage. unabr. ed. (J). audio 28.95 Halvorson Assocs.

—The Red Badge of Courage. abr. ed. audio 12.95 o.p. (*0-89845-247-3*, SWC 1040, Caedmon) HarperTrade.

—The Red Badge of Courage, Set. unabr. ed. 1999. audio 32.95 Highsmith Inc.

—The Red Badge of Courage. 1999. 150p. pap. 9.95 o.p. (*1-930128-09-6*, JNMedia Bks.) JNMedia, Inc.

—The Red Badge of Courage. unabr. ed. 1980. audio 24.00 Jimcin Recordings.

—The Red Badge of Courage. 1990. (Vintage-Library of America ). 168p. pap. 10.00 (*0-679-73223-3*, Vintage) Knopf Publishing Group.

—The Red Badge of Courage. 1998. (Cloth Bound Pocket Ser.). 7.95 (*3-89508-686-X*, 520038) Konemann.

—The Red Badge of Courage. l.t. ed. 1997. (Large Print Heritage Ser.). 233p. lib. bdg. 28.95 (*1-58118-019-5*, 21491) LRS.

—The Red Badge of Courage. E-Book 1.95 (*1-57799-934-7*) Logos Research Systems, Inc.

—The Red Badge of Courage, Level 3. 2000. pap. 11.67 (*0-582-34265-1*) Longman Publishing Group.

—The Red Badge of Courage. 1951. 187p. (C). pap. 7.50 (*0-07-555608-1*, McGraw-Hill Humanities, Social Sciences & World Languages) McGraw-Hill Higher Education.

—The Red Badge of Courage. 1994. 20.00 o.s.i (*0-679-43209-4*) McKay, David Co., Inc.

—The Red Badge of Courage. 1999. E-Book 1.95 (*1-58515-248-X*) MesaView, Inc.

—The Red Badge of Courage. Binder, Henry, ed. 1987. pap. 3.50 (*0-380-70432-3*); 1983. 192p. mass mkt. 6.95 o.p. (*0-380-64113-5*, 64113) Morrow/Avon. (Avon Bks.).

—The Red Badge of Courage. Willard, Throp, ed. & intro. by. 1969. pap. NAL.

—The Red Badge of Courage. 1960. mass mkt. 1.50 o.p. (*0-451-51304-5*); mass mkt. 1.75 o.p. (*0-451-51433-5*); mass mkt. 1.25 o.p. (*0-451-51127-1*); mass mkt. 0.95 o.p. (*0-451-50971-4*); mass mkt. 0.75 o.p. (*0-451-50812-2*); mass mkt. 0.60 o.p. (*0-451-50671-5*); mass mkt. 0.50 o.p. (*0-451-50016-4*) NAL. (Signet Classics).

—The Red Badge of Courage. l.t. ed. reprint ed. 10.00 (*0-89064-053-X*) National Assn. for Visually Handicapped.

—The Red Badge of Courage. Green, Frank, ed. 1996. (Thornes Classic Novels Ser.). (Illus.). 194p. pap. 16.75 (*0-7487-2423-0*) Nelson Thornes GBR. *Dist:* Trans-Atlantic Pubns., Inc.

—The Red Badge of Courage. (Super Sound Buy, Dove Ser.). 1993. 8.99 o.p. (*1-55800-685-0*); 1995. audio 16.95 o.p. (*0-7871-0421-3*) NewStar Media, Inc.

—The Red Badge of Courage. l.t. ed. 2000. reprint ed. 250p. lib. bdg. 25.00 (*0-939495-99-6*); 155p. lib. bdg. 24.00 (*1-58287-123-X*) North Bks.

—The Red Badge of Courage. 1999. 192p. pap. 10.95 (*0-393-31954-7*) Norton, W. W. & Co., Inc.

—The Red Badge of Courage. Binder, Henry, ed. 1982. (Critical Editions Ser.). 14.95 o.p. (*0-393-01345-6*) Norton, W. W. & Co., Inc.

—The Red Badge of Courage. Pizer, Donald, ed. 3rd ed. 1993. (Critical Editions Ser.). (C). pap. text 9.00 (*0-393-96430-2*) Norton, W. W. & Co., Inc.

—The Red Badge of Courage. l.t. ed. 2003. 177p. E-Book 3.99 (*1-932681-36-1*) NuVision Pubns.

—The Red Badge of Courage. 1987. (Classics for Young Readers Ser.). 186p. pap. 2.99 o.p. (*0-14-035055-1*, Puffin Bks.) Penguin Putnam Bks. for Young Readers.

—The Red Badge of Courage. 1982. (Classics Ser.). 3.95 o.p. (*0-442-82531-5*) Peter Pauper Pr. Inc.

—The Red Badge of Courage. text (*0-13-981606-2*) Prentice Hall (Schl. Div.).

—The Red Badge of Courage. Dixson, Robert James, ed. rev. ed. 1987. (American Classics: Bk. 10). (J). (gr. 9 up). audio 65.00 o.p. (*0-13-024795-2*, 58235) Prentice Hall, ESL Dept.

—The Red Badge of Courage. 1999. E-Book 3.99 incl. cd-rom (*1-57646-018-5*) Quiet Vision Publishing.

—The Red Badge of Courage. 1987. (Radiobook Ser.). audio 4.98 (*0-929541-23-5*) Radiola Co.

—The Red Badge of Courage. 1998. E-Book 4.95 (*0-679-64129-7*, Modern Library) Random House Adult Trade Publishing Group.

—The Red Badge of Courage. 1993. 252p. 13.50 o.s.i (*0-679-60044-2*); 1980. 251p. 10.95 o.s.i (*0-394-60493-8*) Random Hse., Inc.

—The Red Badge of Courage. 1982. (Illus.). 176p. 12.95 o.p. (*0-89577-155-1*) Reader's Digest Assn., Inc., The.

—The Red Badge of Courage. unabr. ed. 1981. audio 26.00 (*1-55690-437-1*, 81240E7) Recorded Bks., LLC.

—The Red Badge of Courage. 1990. (Works of Stephen Crane). reprint ed. lib. bdg. 79.00 (*0-7812-2426-8*) Reprint Services Corp.

—The Red Badge of Courage. (Literary Classics Ser.). 1992. 128p. text 5.98 o.p. (*1-56138-115-2*, Courage Bks.); 1986. 160p. pap. 4.95 o.p. (*0-89471-482-1*); 1986. 160p. lib. bdg. 12.90 o.p. (*0-89471-483-X*) Running Pr. Bk. Pubs.

—The Red Badge of Courage. 1967. reprint ed. 40.00 (*0-8201-1010-8*) Scholars' Facsimiles & Reprints.

—The Red Badge of Courage. Shefter, Harry, ed. 1990. (Enriched Classics Ser.). 224p. mass mkt. (*0-671-74081-4*, 44003, Washington Square Pr.) Simon & Schuster.

—The Red Badge of Courage. 1996. (Enriched Classics Ser.). 224p. reprint ed. mass mkt. 5.99 (*0-671-00275-9*, Pocket) Simon & Schuster.

—The Red Badge of Courage. (Ebook Classic Ser.). E-Book 5.00 (*0-7410-0452-6*) SoftBook Pr.

—The Red Badge of Courage. abr. ed. 1979. (Mind's Eye Ser.). audio 14.95 o.p. (*0-88142-379-3*) Soundelux Audio Publishing.

—The Red Badge of Courage. l.t. ed. 1997. 190p. text 24.95 (*1-56000-528-9*) Transaction Pubs.

—The Red Badge of Courage. 1987. 8.60 o.p. (*0-606-03448-X*) Turtleback Bks.

—The Red Badge of Courage. Bradbury, Malcolm & Bigsby, Christopher, eds. 1993. 152p. pap. 7.95 (*0-460-87381-4*, Everyman's Classic Library in Paperback) Tuttle Publishing.

—The Red Badge of Courage. 1983. 133p. pap. 1.95 o.p. (*0-460-87138-2*, Everyman's Classic Library in Paperback) Tuttle Publishing.

—The Red Badge of Courage. unabr. ed. 1997. 135p. reprint ed. pap. 9.95 (*1-57002-051-5*) University Publishing Hse., Inc.

—The Red Badge of Courage. 1983. (American Library). 224p. pap. 2.95 o.p. (*0-14-039021-9*, Penguin Classics) Viking Penguin.

—The Red Badge of Courage. 2002. 184p. 29.95 (*1-59224-793-8*) Wildside Pr.

—The Red Badge of Courage. (Classics Ser.). 1999. pap. 3.95 (*1-85326-084-3*); 1997. 128p. pap. 3.95 o.s.i (*1-85326-567-5*, 5675WW) Wordsworth Editions, Ltd. GBR. *Dist:* Combined Publishing.

—The Red Badge of Courage: An Annotated Text with Critical Essays. Bradley, Sculley et al, eds. rev. ed. (Critical Editions Ser.). 1977. 12.50 o.p. (*0-393-04435-1*); 1976. (C). pap. o.p. (*0-393-09182-1*) Norton, W. W. & Co., Inc.

—The Red Badge of Courage: An Episode of the American Civil War. 1998. (Modern Library Ser.). 304p. 16.95 (*0-679-60296-8*) Random Hse., Inc.

—The Red Badge of Courage: An Historically Annotated Edition. LaRocca, Charles J., ed. 1995. (Illus.). 212p. pap. 18.00 o.p. (*0-935796-68-1*) Purple Mountain Pr., Ltd.

—The Red Badge of Courage: And Four Stories. Stallman, R. W., ed. & notes by. rev. ed. 1997. (Signet Classics). 240p. mass mkt. 3.95 (*0-451-52647-3*, Signet Classics) NAL.

—The Red Badge of Courage: And Selected Prose & Poetry. Gibson, William M., ed. 3rd ed. 1968. 652p. (C). pap. text 26.50 (*0-03-073360-X*) Harcourt College Pubs.

—The Red Badge of Courage: And Selected Stories. 1960. (Signet Classics Ser.). 10.00 (*0-606-00225-1*) Turtleback Bks.

—The Red Badge of Courage: The Comprehensive Edition: The December 1894 Newspaper Serial & the Novel. 1999. (Ironweed American Classics Ser.). 189p. (Orig.). pap. 10.95 (*0-9655309-2-2*) Ironweed Pr., Inc.

—The Red Badge of Courage & Maggie, a Girl of the Streets. l.t. ed. 2001. per. 15.50 (*1-58396-129-1*); 2000. 250p. per. 9.90 (*1-58396-033-3*) Blue Unicorn Editions.

—The Red Badge of Courage & Other Stories. 1960. 224p. mass mkt. 3.95 o.p. (*0-451-52368-7*, CW1592, Signet Classics) NAL.

—The Red Badge of Courage & Other Stories. Robertson, Fiona & Mellors, Anthony, eds. 1998. (Oxford World's Classics Ser.). 320p. pap. 8.95 (*0-19-283315-4*) Oxford Univ. Pr., Inc.

—The Red Badge of Courage & Other Stories, Set. unabr. ed. 1999. audio 44.98 BBC Audiobooks America.

—The Red Badge of Courage & Selected Stories. 1987. 224p. reprint ed. lib. bdg. 21.95 (*0-89966-620-5*) Buccaneer Bks., Inc.

—The Red Badge of Courage & Selected Stories. 1960. mass mkt. 1.50 o.p. (*0-451-51592-7*) NAL.

—The Red Badge of Courage & the Veteran. 2000. (Modern Library Classics). 336p. pap. 8.95 (*0-679-78320-2*, Modern Library) Random House Adult Trade Publishing Group.

—The Red Badge of Courage Readalong. 1994. (Illustrated Classics Collection). 64p. pap. 14.95 incl. audio (*0-7854-0710-3*, 40354) American Guidance Service, Inc.

Crane, Stephen & Covici, Pascal, Jr. The Red Badge of Courage & Other Stories. Covici, Pascal, Jr., ed. 1991. (Classics Ser.). 336p. pap. 8.95 (*0-14-039081-2*, Penguin Classics) Viking Penguin.

Crane, Stephen, et al. The Red Badge of Courage & Other Stories. 1998. E-Book 8.35 (*0-585-36127-4*) netLibrary, Inc.

Crosswell, Jack. Murder of a Brother. 2001. 256p. 18.95 (*1-57197-265-X*) Pentland Pr., Inc.

D'Aguiar, Fred. The Longest Memory. 1995. 20.00 o.s.i (*0-679-43962-5*, Pantheon) Knopf Publishing Group.

—The Longest Memory. 1996. (J). pap. 10.00 o.p. (*0-380-72700-5*, Avon Bks.) Morrow/Avon.

Dailey, Janet. Tidewater Lover. l.t. ed. 2000. (G. K. Hall Core Ser.). 213p. 29.95 (*0-7838-9124-5*, Macmillan Reference USA) Gale Group.

—Tidewater Lover. 1992. per. (*0-373-89896-7*, 1-89896-4, Harlequin Bks.) Harlequin Enterprises, Ltd.

Davis, Patrick A. The Colonel. 2001. (Illus.). 384p. 24.95 o.p. (*0-399-14734-9*) Penguin Group (USA) Inc.

—The General. 1999. 416p. reprint ed. mass mkt. 6.99 (*0-425-16804-2*) Berkley Publishing Group.

—The General. abr. ed. 1999. audio 7.99 (*1-56740-284-4*, 1749, Paperback Nova Audio Bks.); 1998. audio 26.95 (*1-56740-063-9*, 1213, Bookcassette); 1998. 10p. audio 73.25 (*1-56740-592-4*, 1214, Unabridged Library Editions); Set. 1998. audio 17.95 o.p. (*1-56740-788-9*, 524, Nova Audio Bks.) Brilliance Audio.

—The General. 1998. 352p. 23.95 o.p. (*0-399-14411-0*, G. P. Putnam's Sons) Penguin Group (USA) Inc.

Davis, Thulani. 1959. 1992. 295p. 18.95 o.p. (*0-8021-1230-7*) Grove/Atlantic, Inc.

—1959: A Novel. 1993. 304p. pap. 11.00 o.p. (*0-06-097529-6*, Perennial) HarperTrade.

Dee, Jonathan. Palladio. 2002. 400p. 24.95 (*0-385-50179-X*) Doubleday Publishing.

—Palladio. 2003. 400p. pap. 14.00 (*0-375-72641-1*) Knopf, Alfred A. Inc.

Deutermann, P. T. Sweepers. abr. ed. 1998. audio 7.99 o.s.i (*1-56740-207-0*, 1385, Paperback Nova Audio Bks.); 1997. audio 16.95 o.p. (*1-56100-942-3*, 509, Nova Audio Bks.); 1997. audio 89.25 (*1-56100-825-7*, 1067, Unabridged Library Editions); 1997. audio 25.95 (*1-56100-750-1*, 285, Bookcassette) Brilliance Audio.

—Sweepers. 1999. E-Book 5.99 (*0-312-20745-X*); 1998. (Sweepers Ser.: Vol. 1). 464p. mass mkt. 6.99 (*0-312-96447-1*, St. Martin's Paperbacks); 1997. 322p. 23.95 (*0-312-15669-3*) St. Martin's Pr.

Deveraux, Jude. Counterfeit Lady. l.t. ed. 1985. (General Ser.). 496p. 17.95 o.p. (*0-8161-3826-5*, Macmillan Reference USA) Gale Group.

—Counterfeit Lady. 1998. (Illus.). 400p. mass mkt. 3.99 (*0-671-02011-0*, Pocket) Simon & Schuster.

—Counterfeit Lady. Marrow, Linda, ed. 1991. 384p. mass mkt. 7.99 (*0-671-73976-X*, Pocket) Simon & Schuster.

—Counterfeit Lady. 1990. mass mkt. 4.95 (*0-671-70674-8*, Pocket) Simon & Schuster.

—Counterfeit Lady. Marrow, Linda, ed. 1988. mass mkt. 4.50 (*0-671-67519-2*, Pocket) Simon & Schuster.

—Lost Lady. l.t. ed. 1985. (General Ser.). 371p. 14.95 o.p. (*0-8161-3950-4*, Macmillan Reference USA) Gale Group.

—Lost Lady. Marrow, Linda, ed. 1991. 352p. mass mkt. 7.99 (*0-671-73977-8*, Pocket) Simon & Schuster.

—Lost Lady. 1990. mass mkt. 4.95 (*0-671-70675-6*, Pocket) Simon & Schuster.

—Lost Lady. Marrow, Linda, ed. 1988. mass mkt. 4.50 (*0-671-67430-7*, Pocket) Simon & Schuster.

—River Lady. l.t. ed. 1986. (General Ser.). 431p. 17.95 o.p. (*0-8161-4138-X*, Macmillan Reference USA) Gale Group.

—River Lady. Marrow, Linda, ed. 1991. 320p. mass mkt. 7.99 (*0-671-73978-6*); 1988. mass mkt. 4.50 (*0-671-67297-5*) Simon & Schuster. (Pocket).

—Sweetbriar. 1990. mass mkt. 4.95 (*0-671-72402-9*); 1991. 352p. reprint ed. mass mkt. 7.99 (*0-671-74382-1*) Simon & Schuster. (Pocket).

Dickinson, Barbara M. A Rebellious House. 1999. (Illus.). 242p. pap. 19.95 o.s.i (*1-55618-185-X*) Brunswick Publishing Corp.

—A Rebellious House: A Novel. 1997. (Illus.). 242p. 24.95 o.s.i (*1-55618-165-5*) Brunswick Publishing Corp.

Donnell, Susan. Pocahontas. 1993. 416p. mass mkt. 6.50 o.s.i (*0-425-13620-5*); 1991. pap. 8.95 o.p. (*0-425-12617-X*) Berkley Publishing Group.

Doolittle, Jerome. Head Lock. Grose, Bill, ed. 1993. 272p. 20.00 (*0-671-79978-9*, Atria) Simon & Schuster.

—Head Lock. 1900. per. 4.99 (*0-671-50288-3*, Pocket) Simon & Schuster.

—Head Lock. 262p. 3.98 o.p. (*0-8317-2353-X*) Smithmark Pubs., Inc.

Dowdey, Clifford. Bugles Blow No More. 1990. 512p. reprint ed. 42.00 (*0-87797-176-5*) Cherokee Publishing Co.

Dyja, Tom. Meet John Trow. 2002. (Illus.). 336p. 24.95 (*0-670-03099-6*, Viking) Viking Penguin.

Edwards, Cassie. Midnight Falcon. 2001. 352p. mass mkt. 6.99 (*0-451-20382-8*, Signet Bks.) NAL.

Eggleston, George Cary. Dorothy South. 2000. 252p. pap. 9.95 (*0-594-04945-8*); E-Book 3.95 (*0-594-04948-2*) 1873 Pr.

—Dorothy South. 1992. (Notable American Authors Ser.). reprint ed. lib. bdg. 75.00 (*0-7812-2778-X*) Reprint Services Corp.

—The Master of Warlock. E-Book 3.95 (*0-594-02179-0*) 1873 Pr.

Elliott, James. Cold, Cold Heart. 1995. mass mkt. 5.99 o.s.i (*0-440-29537-8*) Dell Publishing.

—Cold Cold Heart. 1995. 416p. mass mkt. 5.99 o.s.i (*0-440-21863-2*) Dell Publishing.

—Cold, Cold Heart. abr. ed. 1994. audio 21.98 o.s.i (*0-553-74615-4*, RH Audio) Random Hse. Audio Publishing Group.

Ellis, Julie. Lasting Treasures. 1993. 464p. 22.95 o.p. (*0-399-13808-0*, G. P. Putnam's Sons) Penguin Group (USA) Inc.

Epps, Garrett. The Shad Treatment. 1977. 9.95 o.p. (*0-399-11829-2*) Putnam Publishing Group, The.

—The Shad Treatment: A Novel. 1997. (Virginia Bookshelf Ser.). 444p. reprint ed. pap. 17.95 (*0-8139-1776-X*) Univ. Pr. of Virginia.

Erickson, Steve. Arc d'X. 1993. 288p. 20.00 o.p. (*0-671-74296-5*, Simon & Schuster) Simon & Schuster.

—Arc'D X: A Novel. 1996. 304p. pap. 14.00 o.p. (*0-8050-4882-0*, Owl Bks.) Holt, Henry & Co.

Even, Aaron Roy. Bloodroot. 2000. 261p. 22.95 (*0-312-26561-1*) St. Martin's Pr.

Everett, Percival. Cutting Lisa. 1986. 228p. 14.95 o.p. (*0-89919-412-5*) Houghton Mifflin Co.

—Cutting Lisa. 2000. (Voices of the South Ser.). 147p. pap. 12.95 (*0-8071-2640-3*) Louisiana State Univ. Pr.

Farley, Benjamin W. Mercy Road & Other Stories. 1986. (Illus.). 136p. 13.95 (*0-87797-122-6*) Cherokee Publishing Co.

Fischer, Maribeth. The Language of Good-Bye. 352p. 2002. pap. 14.00 (*0-452-28309-4*, Plume); 2001. 23.95 o.p. (*0-525-94570-9*, Dutton) Dutton/Plume.

—The Language of Good-bye: A Novel. 2001. (Thorndike Press Large Print Women's Fiction Ser.). 573p. 28.95 (*0-7862-3759-7*) Thorndike Pr.

Freeburn, Chris. Parental Source. 2002. 272p. 24.95 o.p. (*0-9714296-1-8*); per. 24.95 (*0-9728819-2-1*) Quiet Storm Publishing Group.

Frey, Stephen. Silent Partner. 2004. 384p. mass mkt. 7.50 (*0-345-44327-6*, Fawcett); 2003. 320p. 24.95 (*0-345-44326-8*, Ballantine Bks.); 2002. E-Book 6.99 (*0-345-46322-6*, Ballantine Bks.) Ballantine Bks.

—Silent Partner. 2003. 31.95 (*0-7862-5239-1*) Thorndike Pr.

Fugate, Clara T. From Massacre to Matriarch: Six Weeks in the Life of Fanny Scott. Calvera, Elizabeth C., ed. Socarras-Roufagalas, Gilda, tr. 1989. (Tales of the Virginia Wilderness Ser.: No. 2). (ENG & SPA., Illus.). 98p. (Orig.). pap. 8.95 (*0-936015-08-X*) Pocahontas Pr., Inc.

Gaffney, Patricia. Circle of Three. l.t. ed. 2000. 608p. pap. 24.00 (*0-06-019706-4*) HarperCollins Pubs.

—Circle of Three. 2000. 432p. 24.00 (*0-06-019375-1*, HarperCollins) HarperTrade.

—Circle of Three: A Novel. 2001. 448p. mass mkt. 7.50 (*0-06-109836-1*, HarperTorch) Morrow/Avon.

Gaffney, Virginia. Carry Me Home. 1997. 300p. pap. 9.99 o.p. (*1-56507-562-5*) Harvest Hse. Pubs.

—Magnolia Dreams. 1998. (Richmond Chronicles Ser.: No. 4). 403p. pap. 9.99 o.p. (*1-56507-670-2*) Harvest Hse. Pubs.

—The Tender Rebel. 1997. (Richmond Chronicles: Bk. 3). 400p. pap. 9.99 o.p. (*1-56507-669-9*) Harvest Hse. Pubs.

—Under the Southern Moon. 1996. (Richmond Chronicles Ser.: Vol. 1). 375p. pap. 9.99 o.p. (*1-56507-507-2*) Harvest Hse. Pubs.

Gilstrap, John. Nathan's Run. 1996. 304p. 23.00 o.p. (*0-06-017385-8*) HarperCollins Pubs.

Gindlesperger, James. Escape from Libby Prison. 1996. 245p. 24.95 (*0-942597-91-5*, Burd Street Pr.) White Mane Publishing Co., Inc.

Glasgow, Ellen. Barren Ground. 1976. 28.95 (*0-88411-645-X*) Amereon, Ltd.

—Barren Ground. 1995. reprint ed. lib. bdg. 24.95 (*1-56849-623-0*) Buccaneer Bks., Inc.

—Barren Ground. (Collected Works of Ellen Glasgow ). 511p. reprint ed. 2001. (Illus.). pap. text 28.00 (*0-7426-5630-6*); 1998. lib. bdg. 118.00 (*1-58201-630-5*) Classic Bks.

—Barren Ground. 1957. (American Century Ser.). 409p. pap. 8.95 o.p. (*0-8090-0014-8*, Hill & Wang) Farrar, Straus & Giroux.

—Barren Ground. 1985. 540p. reprint ed. pap. 16.00 (*0-15-610685-X*, Harvest Bks.) Harcourt Trade Pubs.

—Barren Ground. 1990. 20.50 (*0-8446-4019-0*) Smith, Peter Pub., Inc.

—The Romantic Comedians. Hardwick, Elizabeth, ed. 1977. (Rediscovered Fiction by American Women Ser.). reprint ed. lib. bdg. 33.95 (*0-405-10047-7*) Ayer Co. Pubs., Inc.

—The Romantic Comedians. 1995. 288p. (C). pap. 14.95 (*0-8139-1615-1*) Univ. Pr. of Virginia.

—The Sheltered Life. 24.95 (*0-88411-646-8*) Amereon, Ltd.

—The Sheltered Life. 1985. 408p. reprint ed. pap. 23.00 (*0-15-681690-3*, Harvest Bks.) Harcourt Trade Pubs.

—The Sheltered Life. 1994. 352p. (C). pap. 14.95 (*0-8139-1514-7*) Univ. Pr. of Virginia.

—Vein of Iron. 1995. reprint ed. lib. bdg. 49.95 (*1-56849-624-9*) Buccaneer Bks., Inc.

—Vein of Iron. 1967. (Harvest Book Ser.). 416p. pap. 23.00 (*0-15-693476-0*, Harvest Bks.) Harcourt Trade Pubs.

—Vein of Iron. 1995. 408p. (C). pap. 14.95 (*0-8139-1636-4*) Univ. Pr. of Virginia.

—The Voice of the People. 2000. 252p. E-Book 9.95 (*0-594-06250-0*) 1873 Pr.

—The Voice of the People. reprint ed. lib. bdg. 29.95 (*0-89190-151-5*, Rivercity Pr.) Amereon, Ltd.

—The Voice of the People. (Collected Works of Ellen Glasgow ). 444p. reprint ed. 2001. (Illus.). pap. text 28.00 (*0-7426-5643-8*); 1998. lib. bdg. 108.00 (*1-58201-643-7*) Classic Bks.

—The Voice of the People. 444p. reprint ed. pap. text 7.50 o.p. (*0-8290-2049-7*); lib. bdg. 19.50 (*0-8398-0662-0*) Irvington Pubs.

—The Voice of the People. Godshalk, William, ed. 1972. pap. 26.95 (*0-8084-0031-2*) Rowman & Littlefield Pubs., Inc.

Goddard, Kenneth M. Cheater. 1997. 542p. mass mkt. 6.99 (*0-8125-5388-8*, Tor Bks.); 1996. 416p. 24.95 o.p. (*0-312-85945-7*, Forge Bks.) Doherty, Tom Assocs., LLC.

—Digger. 1991. 448p. mass mkt. 4.95 o.s.i (*0-553-28982-9*) Bantam Bks.

Godwin, Gail. Father Melancholy's Daughter. 1997. 416p. reprint ed. pap. 13.95 (*0-380-72986-5*, Perennial) HarperTrade.

—Father Melancholy's Daughter. 1992. pap. 5.99 (*0-380-70314-9*, Avon Bks.); 1991. 512p. 21.95 o.p. (*0-688-06531-7*, Morrow, William & Co.) Morrow/Avon.

Goodwin, Stephen. The Blood of Paradise. 1979. 8.95 o.p. (*0-525-06846-5*, Dutton) Dutton/Plume.

—The Blood of Paradise. 2000. (Virginia Bookshelf Ser.). xi, 242p. pap. 14.95 (*0-8139-1877-4*) Univ. Pr. of Virginia.

—Blood of Paradise. 1985. pap. 3.95 o.p. (*0-380-69890-0*, Avon Bks.) Morrow/Avon.

Graham, Heather. Haunted. 2003. 384p. mass mkt. (*1-55166-750-9*, Mira Bks.) Harlequin Enterprises, Ltd.

Gray, Muriel. Furnace. 2000. 400p. mass mkt. 6.99 (*0-312-96903-1*, St. Martin's Paperbacks) St. Martin's Pr.

—The Furnace. 1999. 496p. mass mkt. o.s.i (*0-7704-2785-5*) Bantam Bks.

Hall, Barbara. Better Place. 1994. 287p. 21.00 (*0-671-78422-6*, Simon & Schuster) Simon & Schuster.

—Close to Home. 1997. 320p. 23.00 (*0-684-80981-8*, Simon & Schuster) Simon & Schuster.

Halliday, Sylvia. The Ring. 1996. 320p. 21.95 o.p. (*1-57566-014-8*) Kensington Publishing Corp.

Hambly, Barbara. Wet Grave. 2003. 384p. mass mkt. 6.50 (*0-553-58159-7*); 2002. (Illus.). 304p. 23.95 (*0-553-10935-9*) Bantam Bks.

—Wet Grave. l.t. ed. 2003. 486p. 25.95 (*0-375-43274-4*, Random House Large Print) Random Hse. Large Print.

Handler, David. The Woman Who Fell from Grace. 1992. 240p. mass mkt. 4.99 o.s.i (*0-553-28914-4*) Bantam Bks.

—The Woman Who Fell from Grace. 1991. 240p. 15.00 o.s.i (*0-385-42115-X*) Doubleday Publishing.

—The Woman Who Fell from Grace. l.t. ed. 1992. (General Ser.). 19.95 o.p. (*0-8161-5511-9*); pap. 17.95 (*0-8161-5512-7*) Gale Group. (Macmillan Reference USA).

—The Woman Who Fell from Grace. unabr. ed. 1998. (Stewart Hoag Mystery Ser.: Vol. 4). audio 51.00 (*0-7887-2024-4*, 95399E7) Recorded Bks., LLC.

Hart, Alison. Pursuit. 2002. (Illus.). 96p. (gr. 3-5). lib. bdg. 11.99 (*0-679-99367-3*, Random Hse. Bks. for Young Readers) Random Hse. Children's Bks.

Hart, Lenore. Waterwoman. 2003. 256p. reprint ed. pap. 14.00 (*0-425-19007-2*) Berkley Publishing Group.

Hazelgrove, William E. Tobacco Sticks. 1997. 352p. reprint ed. mass mkt. 5.99 o.s.i (*0-553-57559-7*) Bantam Bks.

—Tobacco Sticks. 1995. 308p. 18.95 (*0-9630052-8-6*) Pantonne Pr., Inc.

Hermary-Vieille, Catherine. Nat Turner's Tragic Search for Freedom: From Deprivation to Vengeance. Bodkin, Robin Orr, tr. from FRE. 2002. 356p. pap. (*1-55212-977-2*) Trafford Publishing.

Higgs, Liz Curtis. Mixed Signals. 2003. (Alabaster Bks.). 376p. pap. 12.99 (*1-57673-401-3*, Alabaster) Multnomah Pubs., Inc.

Hite, Sid. Cecil in Space, ERS. 1999. (Cecil in Space Ser.). (Illus.). 160p. (YA). (gr. 6-9). 16.95 (*0-8050-5055-8*, Holt, Henry & Co. Bks. For Young Readers) Holt, Henry & Co.

Hoffman, William. Doors: Stories. 1999. 200p. pap. 19.95 (*0-8262-1238-7*) Univ. of Missouri Pr.

—Tidewater Blood. 1998. 300p. tchr. ed. 19.95 (*1-56512-187-2*, 72187) Algonquin Bks. of Chapel Hill.

—Tidewater Blood. 1999. 400p. mass mkt. 6.99 (*0-06-101371-4*) HarperCollins Pubs.

—Tidewater Blood, unabr. ed. 1998. audio 60.00 (*0-7887-2188-7*, 95484E7) Recorded Bks., LLC.

Holman, Sheri. The Mammoth Cheese. l.t. ed. 2003. 726p. 28.95 (*0-7862-6066-1*) Gale Group.

—The Mammoth Cheese. 2003. 592p. 24.00 (*0-87113-900-6*, Atlantic Monthly Pr.) Grove/Atlantic, Inc.

Hooper, Kay. Haunting Rachel. 1999. 368p. mass mkt. 7.50 (*0-553-57183-4*); 1998. 352p. 22.95 o.s.i (*0-553-09950-7*) Bantam Bks.

—Haunting Rachel. l.t. ed. 2000. (Wheeler Romance Ser.). 26.95 (*1-56895-987-7*, Wheeler Publishing, Inc.) Gale Group.

Hornig, Doug. Deep Dive. l.t. ed. 1989. (General Ser.). 373p. lib. bdg. 18.95 o.p. (*0-8161-4690-X*, Macmillan Reference USA) Gale Group.

—Deep Dive. 1988. 15.45 o.p. (*0-89296-257-7*) Mysterious Pr.

—Waterman. 1987. 352p. 16.95 (*0-89296-256-9*) Mysterious Pr.

—Waterman. 1988. mass mkt. 3.95 o.s.i (*0-445-40707-7*) Warner Bks., Inc.

Hunt, Angela Elwell. Jamestown. 1996. (Keepers of the Ring Ser.: Vol. 2). 432p. pap. 11.99 o.p. (*0-8423-2013-X*) Tyndale Hse. Pubs.

Johansen, Iris. Final Target. 2002. 416p. reprint ed. mass mkt. 7.50 (*0-553-58213-5*) Bantam Bks.

—Final Target. l.t. ed. 2001. 448p. 24.95 (*0-375-43114-4*) Random Hse. Large Print.

Johnston, Mary. Audrey. E-Book 3.95 (*0-594-02501-X*) 1873 Pr.

—Audrey. 1976. lib. bdg. 11.95 o.s.i (*0-89968-150-6*, Lightyear Pr.); 1977. 418p. reprint ed. lib. bdg. 16.95 o.p. (*0-89966-251-X*) Buccaneer Bks., Inc.

—Audrey. reprint ed. lib. bdg. 48.00 (*0-7426-1126-4*); 2001. pap. text 28.00 (*0-7426-6126-1*) Classic Bks.

—Prisoners of Hope: A Tale of Colonial Virginia. E-Book 3.95 (*0-594-02511-7*) 1873 Pr.

Joinson, Carla. March of Glory. 1994. 125p. (YA). (gr. 9-12). lib. bdg. 9.99 (*0-88092-082-3*) Royal Fireworks Publishing Co.

Jones, Edward P. The Known World. unabr. ed. 2003. audio 39.95 (*0-06-056943-3*) HarperCollins Pubs.

—The Known World. 2003. 400p. 24.95 (*0-06-055754-0*, Amistad Pr.) HarperTrade.

Joyce, Brenda. Double Take. l.t. ed. 2003. 566p. 30.95 (*1-58724-497-7*, Wheeler Publishing, Inc.) Gale Group.

—Double Take. Date not set. mass mkt. (*0-312-99145-2*, St. Martin's Paperbacks); 2003. 384p. 24.95 (*0-312-28474-8*) St. Martin's Pr.

Junkin, Tim. The Waterman. 1999. 300p. tchr. ed. 22.95 (*1-56512-230-5*) Algonquin Bks. of Chapel Hill.

Kafka, F. L. The Tunnel to Glory. 1992. 249p. 19.95 o.p. (*0-89141-442-8*, Presidio Pr.) Ballantine Bks.

Kegley, Mary B. Free in Chains. 2002. 266p. pap. 9.50 (*0-9641315-1-X*) Kegley Bks.

Keneally, Thomas. Confederates. 1983. mass mkt. 3.95 o.s.i (*0-425-06542-1*); 1981. mass mkt. 3.50 o.s.i (*0-425-05057-2*) Berkley Publishing Group.

—Confederates. 1980. 427p. 13.50 o.p. (*0-06-012299-4*); 1987. 448p. reprint ed. pap. 13.00 o.p. (*0-06-091446-7*, PL/1446, Perennial) HarperTrade.

—Confederates. 2000. (Illus.). 427p. pap. 18.95 (*0-8203-2263-6*) Univ. of Georgia Pr.

Kilian, Michael. The Ironclad Alibi: A Harrison Raines Civil War Mystery. 2002. 320p. 22.95 o.s.i (*0-425-18325-4*, Prime Crime) Berkley Publishing Group.

—Murder at Manassas: A Harrison Raines Civil War Mystery. 2000. (Harrison Raines Civil War Mysteries Ser.). 320p. mass mkt. 5.99 (*0-425-17743-2*); 306p. 21.95 o.s.i (*0-425-17233-3*) Berkley Publishing Group. (Prime Crime).

King, Benjamin. A Bullet for Stonewall. 2nd ed. 1990. 272p. reprint ed. 19.95 (*0-88289-768-3*) Pelican Publishing Co., Inc.

Klein, Marjorie. Test Pattern. 2001. 288p. pap. 13.00 (*0-06-095953-3*, Perennial) HarperTrade.

—Test Pattern: A Novel. 2000. 271p. 25.00 (*0-688-17284-9*, Morrow, William & Co.) Morrow/Avon.

Koen, Karleen. Now Face to Face. unabr. ed. 1997. audio 136.00 (*0-7366-3543-2*, 4190A/B) Books on Tape, Inc.

—Now Face to Face. unabr. ed. 1996. audio 137.25 o.p. (*1-56100-273-9*, 967, Unabridged Library Editions); audio 31.95 o.p. (*1-56100-648-3*, 199, Bookcassette) Brilliance Audio.

—Now Face to Face. 1997. 608p. mass mkt. 6.99 o.s.i (*1-57566-177-2*) Kensington Publishing Corp.

Kraus, Harry Lee. Could I Have This Dance? 2002. 416p. pap. 12.99 (*0-310-24089-1*) Zondervan.

—For the Rest of My Life. 2004. pap. 12.99 (*0-310-24978-3*) Zondervan.

Lacy, Al. Turn of Glory, 8 vols. 2003. (Battles of Destiny Ser.: Vol. 8). 322p. pap. 9.99 (*1-57673-217-7*) Multnomah Pubs., Inc.

Landrum, Graham Gordon. The Famous DAR Murder Mystery. 1995. 198p. mass mkt. 4.50 (*0-312-95568-5*, St. Martin's Paperbacks); 1992. 208p. 18.95 o.p. (*0-312-06968-5*, Saint Martin's Minotaur) St. Martin's Pr.

—The Historical Society Murder Mystery. 1996. 224p. text 21.95 o.p. (*0-312-14355-9*, Saint Martin's Minotaur) St. Martin's Pr.

—The Rotary Club Murder Mystery. 1996. 217p. pap. text 4.99 (*0-312-95796-3*, St. Martin's Paperbacks); 1993. 224p. 17.95 o.p. (*0-312-09375-6*, Saint Martin's Minotaur) St. Martin's Pr.

LeClaire, Anne D. Glamour Day at the Klip-n-Kurl. E-Book (*0-345-45861-3*) Ballantine Bks.

—Leaving Eden. 2003. 320p. pap. 13.95 (*0-345-44575-9*); 2002. 304p. 23.95 (*0-345-44574-0*) Ballantine Bks. (Ballantine Bks.).

—Leaving Eden. l.t. ed. 2003. (Women's Fiction Ser.). 341p. 29.95 (*0-7862-4871-8*) Gale Group.

Lee, Barbara. Death in Still Waters: A Chesapeake Bay Mystery. 1996. 226p. pap. text 5.50 (*0-312-95780-7*, St. Martin's Paperbacks); 1995. 240p. 20.95 o.p. (*0-312-13048-1*, Saint Martin's Minotaur) St. Martin's Pr.

—Final Closing. 1999. (WWL Mystery Ser.: No. 304). per. (*0-373-26304-X*, 1-26304-5, Worldwide Library) Harlequin Enterprises, Ltd.

—Final Closing: An Eve Elliot Mystery. 1997. (Eve Elliot Mystery Ser.). 304p. 22.95 o.p. (*0-312-16762-8*, Saint Martin's Minotaur) St. Martin's Pr.

Lee, Karen. Meredith's Wish. 2000. (Heartspell Ser.). 320p. mass mkt. 4.99 (*0-505-52405-8*, Love Spell) Dorchester Publishing Co., Inc.

Lehmann-Haupt, Christopher. Crooked Man. 1995. 351p. 23.00 (*0-671-73444-X*, Simon & Schuster) Simon & Schuster.

—A Crooked Man. 1996. 416p. mass mkt. 5.99 o.s.i (*1-57566-006-7*) Kensington Publishing Corp.

Lehrer, Jim. Last Debate. 2000. 368p. pap. text 13.00 (*1-58648-004-9*) PublicAffairs.

—Last Debate. l.t. ed. 1996. (Niagara Large Print Ser.). 485p. 29.50 o.p. (*0-7089-5838-9*, Ulverscroft) Thorpe, F. A. Pubs. GBR. *Dist:* Ulverscroft Large Print Bks., Ltd.

Light, Elliott. Chain Thinking: A Shep Harrington SmallTown Mystery. 2003. (Smalltown Mystery Ser.: 2). 211p. 19.95 (*1-890862-21-5*) Bancroft Pr.

—Lonesome Song: A Shep Harrington SmallTown Mystery. 2002. (Smalltown Mystery Ser.: 1). 204p. pap. 14.95 (*1-890862-17-7*) Bancroft Pr.

Massie, Elizabeth. SinEater. 1994. 352p. 21.00 o.p. (*0-7867-0061-0*, Carroll & Graf Pubs.) Avalon Publishing Group.

McCaig, Donald. Jacob's Ladder. abr. ed. 1998. pap. 24.95 o.p. incl. audio (*1-55927-508-1*, JM77D) Audio Renaissance.

—Jacob's Ladder. unabr. ed. 1999. audio 130.00 (*0-7887-2184-4*, 95480E7) Recorded Bks., LLC.

—Jacob's Ladder: A Story of Virginia During the War. 1998. 525p. 25.95 o.p. (*0-393-04629-X*) Norton, W. W. & Co., Inc.

McCann, Kenyon. Ride into Darkness. 1995. 232p. (Orig.). pap. 10.95 (*1-56002-470-4*, University Editions) Aegina Pr., Inc.

McCrumb, Sharyn. If I'd Killed Him When I Met Him... Date not set. pap. (*0-449-22537-2*, Fawcett); 1996. mass mkt. o.p. (*0-345-40451-3*); 1996. 288p. mass mkt. 6.99 (*0-449-14998-6*, Fawcett); 1995. 277p. 20.00 o.s.i (*0-345-38229-3*) Ballantine Bks.

—If I'd Killed Him When I Met Him... l.t. ed. 1997. (Large Print Book Ser.). pap. 24.95 (*1-56895-472-7*, Wheeler Publishing, Inc.) Gale Group.

—If I'd Killed Him When I Met Him... unabr. ed. 1996. audio 51.00 (*0-7887-0506-7*, 94699E7) Recorded Bks., LLC.

—Lovely in Her Bones. 1999. 5.99 (*0-345-91574-7*); 1998. mass mkt. o.s.i (*0-345-42947-8*); 1990. 224p. reprint ed. mass mkt. 5.99 (*0-345-36035-4*) Ballantine Bks.

—Lovely in Her Bones. l.t. ed. 2000. (Wheeler Large Print Book Ser.). 249p. pap. 23.95 (*1-56895-859-5*, Wheeler Publishing, Inc.) Gale Group.

—Lovely in Her Bones. 1985. 224p. pap. 2.95 o.p. (*0-380-89592-7*, Avon Bks.) Morrow/Avon.

—Lovely in Her Bones. 1993. 224p. lib. bdg. 20.00 o.p. (*0-7278-4495-4*) Severn Hse. Pubs., Ltd.

—MacPherson's Lament. (Elizabeth MacPherson Ser.). 304p. 1993. mass mkt. 6.99 (*0-345-38474-1*); 1992. 17.00 o.p. (*0-345-36576-3*) Ballantine Bks.

—MacPherson's Lament. l.t. ed. 2002. 30.95 (*1-58724-230-3*, Wheeler Publishing, Inc.) Gale Group.

—MacPherson's Lament. unabr. ed. 2000. audio 46.00 (*0-7887-3109-2*, 95820E7) Recorded Bks., LLC.

—Missing Susan. 2000. mass mkt. 6.99 (*0-345-91578-X*); 1992. 256p. reprint ed. mass mkt. 5.99 (*0-345-37945-4*) Ballantine Bks.

—Missing Susan. l.t. ed. 1993. (General Ser.). 408p. pap. 18.95 (*0-8161-5566-6*, Macmillan Reference USA) Gale Group.

—Missing Susan. unabr. ed. 1998. audio 51.00 (*0-7887-1993-9*, 95380E7) Recorded Bks., LLC.

—Paying the Piper. 1999. 5.99 (*0-345-91576-3*); 1988. 192p. mass mkt. 5.99 (*0-345-34518-5*) Ballantine Bks.

—Paying the Piper. unabr. ed. 1993. audio 35.00 (*1-55690-709-5*, 93109E7) Recorded Bks., LLC.

—Paying the Piper. 1991. reprint ed. 18.95 o.p. (*0-7278-4247-1*) Severn Hse. Pubs., Ltd.

—Sick of Shadows. 1999. 5.99 (*0-345-91573-9*); 1998. mass mkt. o.s.i (*0-345-42946-X*); 1989. 240p. mass mkt. 6.99 (*0-345-35653-5*) Ballantine Bks.

—Sick of Shadows. 240p. 1984. pap. 2.95 o.p. (*0-380-87189-0*, 87189); 1992. reprint ed. 19.00 o.p. (*0-7278-4334-6*) Severn Hse. Pubs., Ltd.

—Sick of Shadows. l.t. ed. 2000. (Basic Ser.). 352p. 29.95 (*0-7862-2370-7*) Thorndike Pr.

McMillan, Ann. Civil Blood: A Civil War Mystery. l.t. ed. 2001. (Thorndike Press Large Print Americana Ser.). (Illus.). 447p. 28.95 o.p. (*0-7862-3614-0*) Gale Group.

—Civil Blood: A Civil War Mystery. 2003. 320p. mass mkt. 6.99 (*0-14-200124-4*) Penguin Group (USA) Inc.

—Civil Blood: A Civil War Mystery. 2001. (Illus.). 224p. 22.95 o.p. (*0-670-89997-6*, Viking) Viking Penguin.

Michaels, Barbara, pseud. Houses of Stone. unabr. ed. 1995. audio 84.95 (*0-7451-6512-5*, CAB 1128) BBC Audiobooks America.

—Houses of Stone. 1994. 400p. reprint ed. mass mkt. 7.50 o.s.i (*0-425-14306-6*) Berkley Publishing Group.

—Houses of Stone, unabr. ed. 1995. audio 85.00 (*0-7887-0261-0*, 94470E7) Recorded Bks., LLC.

—Houses of Stone. 1993. 336p. 21.00 o.p. (*0-671-68949-5*, Simon & Schuster) Simon & Schuster.

—Houses of Stone. l.t. ed. (Paperback Bestsellers Ser.). 556p. 1995. 20.95 (*0-8161-5937-8*); 1994. lib. bdg. 25.95 (*0-8161-5936-X*) Thorndike Pr.

—Patriot's Dream. l.t. ed. 1995. pap. 21.95 o.p. (*0-7927-2020-2*); 1994. 22.95 o.p. (*0-7927-2021-0*) BBC Audiobooks America.

Michaels, Fern. Celebration. 1999. 368p. 24.00 o.s.i (*1-57566-402-X*) Kensington Publishing Corp.

Michener, James A. Chesapeake. 1986. 1024p. mass mkt. 7.99 (*0-449-21158-4*); 1984. mass mkt. 4.95 o.p. (*0-449-20668-8*); 1983. mass mkt. 3.95 o.p. (*0-449-20315-8*) Ballantine Bks. (Fawcett).

—Chesapeake. 1993. audio 96.00 (*0-7366-2421-X*); audio 96.00 (*0-7366-2422-8*);Pt. 1. audio 96.00 (*0-7366-2420-1*, 3187A);Pt. 2. audio 96.00Pt. 3. audio 96.00 Books on Tape, Inc.

—Chesapeake. 2003. (Illus.). 888p. pap. 14.95 (*0-8129-7043-8*, Random Hse. Trade Paperbacks) Random House Adult Trade Publishing Group.

—Chesapeake. 1987. audio 14.95 o.p. (*0-394-56383-2*); Set. 1986. audio 16.00 o.s.i (*0-394-55695-X*) Random Hse. Audio Publishing Group. (RH Audio).

—Chesapeake. 1978. 45.00 o.s.i (*0-394-50079-2*) Random Hse., Inc.

Mitchell, Kirk. Shadow on the Valley: A Civil War Thriller. 1993. 352p. 21.95 o.p. (*0-312-10542-8*) St. Martin's Pr.

Mitchell, Sara. Virginia Autumn. 2002. 416p. pap. 12.99 (*1-57856-485-9*) WaterBrook Pr.

—Virginia Autumn: The Sinclair Legacy, Bk. 2. l.t. ed. 2003. (Christian Fiction Ser.). 26.95 (*0-7862-4956-0*) Thorndike Pr.

Moore, Eva. Good Children Get Rewards: A Story of Colonial Times. 2001. (Hello Reader! Ser.). (Illus.). 40p. (J). (gr. 1-3). mass mkt. 3.99 (*0-590-92921-6*) Scholastic, Inc.

Moore, Laura. Ride a Dark Horse. 2001. 448p. pap. 6.99 (*0-671-04292-0*); reprint ed. E-Book 6.99 (*0-7434-2162-0*) Simon & Schuster. (Pocket).

Morgenroth, Kate. Kill Me First. 1999. 288p. pap. 15.00 (*0-06-103010-4*); 272p. 24.00 (*0-06-019275-5*) HarperCollins Pubs.

—Kill Me First. abr. ed. 1999. audio 18.00 o.s.i (*0-694-52213-9*, HarperAudio) HarperTrade.

—Kill Me First. 2000. 384p. mass mkt. 6.99 (*0-06-109774-8*, Avon Bks.) Morrow/Avon.

Morton, Virginia B. Marching Through Culpeper: A Novel of Culpeper, Virginia - Crossroads of the Civil War. 2nd ed. 2000. (Illus.). 542p. (C). 27.99 (*0-615-11642-6*) Edgehill Bks.

Mrazek, Robert J. Stonewall's Gold. l.t. ed. 2000. (G. K. Hall Paperback Ser.). (Illus.). 302p. pap. 23.95 (*0-7838-9288-8*, Macmillan Reference USA) Gale Group.

—Stonewall's Gold. unabr. ed. 2000. audio 53.00 (*0-7887-3119-X*, 95685E7) Recorded Bks., LLC.

—Stonewall's Gold. 2000. (Illus.). 240p. pap. 12.95 (*0-312-25422-9*, Saint Martin's Griffin); 1999. mass mkt. 4.99 (*0-312-97429-9*, St. Martin's Paperbacks); 1998. (Illus.). 240p. 22.95 (*0-312-20024-2*) St. Martin's Pr.

Nelson, James. The Pirate Round. 2003. 384p. pap. 13.95 (*0-06-053926-7*, Perennial) HarperTrade.

Nelson, James L. The Blackbirder. 2002. (Brethern of the Coast Ser.: BK. 3). 352p. pap. 13.95 (*0-06-000779-6*, Perennial) HarperTrade.

—The Blackbirder. 2001. (Brethren of the Coast Ser.: Bk. 2). (Illus.). 352p. 24.00 (*0-380-80453-0*, Morrow, William & Co.) Morrow/Avon.

—The Guardship. 2000. (Brethren of the Coast Ser.: Bk. 1). (Illus.). 384p. pap. 14.00 (*0-380-80452-2*, Avon Bks.) Morrow/Avon.

—The Pirate Round. 2002. (Brethren of the Coast Ser.: Bk. 3). 384p. 24.95 (*0-380-80454-9*, Morrow, William & Co.) Morrow/Avon.

Nichols, Linda. Not a Sparrow Falls. 2002. 352p. pap. 12.99 (*0-7642-2727-0*); 352p. text 16.99 o.p. (*0-7642-2755-6*); 544p. pap. 16.99 (*0-7642-2756-4*) Bethany Hse. Pubs.

—Not a Sparrow Falls. abr. ed. 2003. audio 7.99 (*1-59086-728-9*, 4319, Brilliance Audio Paperback Audiobooks); 2002. audio 17.95 (*1-59086-727-0*, 4318); 2002. audio 44.25 (*1-59086-729-7*, 4320, CD Library Edition); 2002. audio compact disk 62.25 (*1-59086-731-9*, 4322, CD Library Edition); 2002. audio compact disk 24.95 (*1-59086-730-0*, 4321) Brilliance Audio.

O'Brien, Judith. To Marry a British Lord. 1997. 320p. mass mkt. 5.99 o.s.i (*0-671-00039-X*, Pocket) Simon & Schuster.

Ore, Rebecca. Slow Funeral. 1994. 320p. 21.95 o.p. (*0-312-85201-0*, Tor Bks.) Doherty, Tom Assocs., LLC.

Owen, Howard. Fat Lightning. 1996. 192p. pap. 11.00 o.p. (*0-06-097676-4*) HarperCollins Pubs.

—Fat Lightning. 1994. 181p. 24.00 (*1-877946-41-9*) Permanent Pr., The.

Page, Thomas Nelson. In Ole Virginia: Or, Marse Chan & Other Stories. 2000. 252p. E-Book 3.95 (*0-594-06399-X*) 1873 Pr.

—In Ole Virginia: Or, Marse Chan & Other Stories. 1991. (Southern Classics Ser.). 254p. (C). reprint ed. pap. 10.95 (*1-879941-04-X*, Sanders, J. S. & Co., Inc.) Dee, Ivan R. Pub.

—In Ole Virginia: Or, Marse Chan & Other Stories. (Americans in Fiction Ser.). 230p. reprint ed. lib. bdg. 19.00 (*0-8398-1550-6*); 1986. (C). pap. text 7.95 (*0-8290-1864-6*) Irvington Pubs.

—In Ole Virginia: Or, Marse Chan & Other Stories. 1992. (BCL1-PS American Literature Ser.). 230p. reprint ed. lib. bdg. 79.00 (*0-7812-6822-2*) Reprint Services Corp.

—The Land of the Spirit. E-Book 3.95 (*0-594-05630-6*) 1873 Pr.

—The Land of the Spirit. 1999. (Notable American Authors Ser.). reprint ed. lib. bdg. 125.00 (*0-7812-4713-6*) Reprint Services Corp.

Park, Frances. When My Sister Was Cleopatra Moon. 2000. 243p. 22.95 (*0-7868-6647-0*) Talk Miramax Bks.

Parkhurst, Carolyn. The Dogs of Babel. 2004. 288p. pap. 15.00 (*0-316-77850-8*, Back Bay); 2003. 272p. (gr. 8 up). 21.95 (*0-316-16868-8*) Little Brown & Co.

—The Dogs of Babel. l.t. ed. 2003. 384p. 32.95 (*0-7862-5913-2*) Thorndike Pr.

Passarella, Lee. Swallowed up in Victory: A Civil War Narrative, Petersburg, 1864-1865. 2002. (Illus.). 273p. pap. 19.95 (*1-57249-301-1*, Burd Street Pr.) White Mane Publishing Co., Inc.

Pearce, Jean L. Swept under the Rug. 1998. 222p. text 21.00 (*1-887301-05-4*) Palmetto Bookworks.

Pearson, Emily C. Cousin Franck's Household: Or Scenes in the Old Dominion, by Pochanontas. 1977. (Black Heritage Library Collection). reprint ed. 28.95 (*0-8369-9041-2*) Ayer Co. Pubs., Inc.

Pearson, T. R. Blue Ridge. 2000. 240p. 24.95 o.s.i (*0-670-89269-6*, Viking) Viking Penguin.

Peart, Jane. Destiny's Bride. 1991. (Brides of Montclair Ser.: Vol. 8). 224p. pap. 15.99 (*0-310-67021-7*) Zondervan.

—Folly's Bride. 1994. 224p. mass mkt. 3.99 o.p. (*0-06-104314-1*, HarperTorch) Morrow/Avon.

—Folly's Bride. (Brides of Montclair Ser.: Vol. 4). 1990. 192p. pap. 15.99 (*0-310-66981-2*); No. 4. 2000. 3.99 (*0-310-21466-1*) Zondervan.

—Fortune's Bride. 1994. 320p. mass mkt. 3.99 o.p. (*0-06-104315-X*, HarperTorch) Morrow/Avon.

—Fortune's Bride. 1990. (Brides of Montclair Ser.: Vol. 3). 272p. pap. 15.99 (*0-310-66971-5*); 1987. 224p. mass mkt. 5.95 (*0-310-47431-0*, 15589P) Zondervan.

—Fortunes Bride, No. 3. 2000. (Brides of Montclair Ser.: Vol. 3). 3.99 (*0-310-21468-8*) Zondervan.

—Gallant Bride. 224p. (Orig.). 1990. (Brides of Montclair Ser.: Vol. 6). pap. 15.99 (*0-310-67001-2*); 1988. mass mkt. 5.95 (*0-310-46741-1*, 15673P) Zondervan.

—Hero's Bride. 1993. (Brides of Montclair Ser.: Vol. 11). 224p. pap. 15.99 (*0-310-67141-8*) Zondervan.

—Jubilee Bride. 1992. (Brides of Montclair Ser.: Vol. 9). 208p. pap. 15.99 (*0-310-67121-3*) Zondervan.

—Mirror Bride. 1993. (Brides of Montclair Ser.: Vol. 10). 208p. pap. 15.99 (*0-310-67131-0*) Zondervan.

—Ransomed Bride. 1994. (Brides of Montclair Ser.). 208p. mass mkt. 3.99 o.p. (*0-06-104316-8*, HarperTorch) Morrow/Avon.

—Ransomed Bride. l.t. ed. 2004. (Brides of Montclair Ser.: No. 2). 227p. 26.95 (*0-7862-6090-4*) Thorndike Pr.

—Ransomed Bride. (Brides of Montclair Ser.: Vol. 2). 1989. 176p. pap. 15.99 (*0-310-66961-8*); No. 2. 2000. 3.99 (*0-310-21498-X*) Zondervan.

—Shadow Bride. 1991. (Brides of Montclair Ser.: Vol. 7). 224p. pap. 15.99 (*0-310-67011-X*) Zondervan.

—Valiant Bride. l.t. ed. 2003. 299p. 25.95 (*0-7862-5765-2*); 1993. (Brides of Montclair - EasyRead Type Ser.: Bk. 1). 224p. reprint ed. pap. 8.95 o.p. (*0-8027-2673-9*, Walker Large Print) Gale Group.

—Valiant Bride. 1994. (Brides of Montclair Ser.). 240p. mass mkt. 3.99 o.p. (*0-06-104317-6*, HarperTorch) Morrow/Avon.

—Valiant Bride. 1989. (Brides of Montclair Ser.: Vol. 1). 192p. pap. 15.99 (*0-310-66951-0*); No. 1. 2000. (Brides of Montclair Ser.: Vol. 1). 3.99 (*0-310-21506-4*); No. 18. 1985. (Serenade Saga Ser.). pap. 2.50 (*0-310-46782-9*, 15537P) Zondervan.

—Yankee Bride. 1984. (Serenade Saga Ser.: No. 8). 192p. 1.49 o.p. (*0-310-46542-7*, 15514P) Zondervan.

—Yankee Bride & Rebel Bride: Montclair Divided. 1990. (Brides of Montclair Ser.: Vol. 5). 276p. pap. 15.99 (*0-310-66991-X*) Zondervan.

Peters, Elizabeth, pseud. Devil-May-Care. 1978. mass mkt. 1.75 o.s.i (*0-449-23581-5*, Fawcett) Ballantine Bks.

—Devil-May-Care. unabr. ed. 1998. audio 44.95 (*0-7861-1441-X*, 2303) Blackstone Audio Bks., Inc.

—Devil-May-Care. 1989. 250p. mass mkt. 4.50 (*0-8125-0789-4*, Tor Bks.) Doherty, Tom Assocs., LLC.

—Devil-May-Care. l.t. ed. 1990. (General Ser.). 381p. 19.95 (*0-8161-4907-0*, Macmillan Reference USA) Gale Group.

—Devil-May-Care. 1997. 256p. reprint ed. 24.00 o.p. (*0-7278-5108-X*) Severn Hse. Pubs., Ltd.

Pharr, Robert Deane. The Book of Numbers. 2001. (Virginia Bookshelf). 382p. reprint ed. pap. 18.95 (*0-8139-2046-9*) Univ. Pr. of Virginia.

Pinkney, Andrea Davis. Silent Thunder: A Civil War Story. 2001. (J). 12.04 (*0-606-21434-8*) Turtleback Bks.

Poe, Robert. The Black Cat. 1998. 278p. mass mkt. 6.99 (*0-8125-4932-5*, Tor Bks.); 1997. 384p. 23.95 (*0-312-86013-7*, Forge Bks.) Doherty, Tom Assocs., LLC.

—Return to the House of Usher. 1997. 284p. pap. text 6.99 (*0-8125-4931-7*, Tor Bks.); 1996. 288p. 22.95 o.p. (*0-312-86012-9*, Forge Bks.) Doherty, Tom Assocs., LLC.

Power, Nani. The Good Remains. 2002. 272p. 24.00 (*0-8021-1720-1*, Grove Pr.) Grove/Atlantic, Inc.

Preston, Margaret J. Aunt Dorothy: An Old Virginia Plantation Story. 1977. (Black Heritage Library Collection). (Illus.). reprint ed. 15.95 (*0-8369-9050-1*) Ayer Co. Pubs., Inc.

Reasoner, James. Manassas. 1999. (Civil War Battle Ser.: Vol. 1). 352p. 22.95 (*1-58182-008-9*) Cumberland Hse. Publishing.

The Red Badge of Courage & Other Stories. unabr. collector's ed. Incl. Blue Hotel. audio Bride Comes to Yellow Sky. audio Open Boat. audio 1984. 1978. Set audio 48.00 (*0-7366-0100-7*, 1108) Books on Tape, Inc.

The Red Badge of Courage & Other Stories. unabr. ed. Incl. Bride Comes to Yellow Sky. audio Mystery of Heroism. audio Open Boat. audio 1976. 1976. Set audio 44.98 (*0-8072-2998-9*, CXL 523CX, Listening Library) Random Hse. Audio Publishing Group.

Renich, T. Elizabeth. Word of Honor. 1994. (Shadowcreek Chronicles Ser.: Bk. 1). 300p. pap. 9.99 (*1-883002-10-9*) Emerald Bks.

Richards, Emilie. Fox River. 2001. 512p. mass mkt. (*1-55166-806-8*, Mira Bks.) Harlequin Enterprises, Ltd.

Roberts, Byrd. Commonwealth Chronicles: Short Stories of Virginia. 2002. per. 14.95 (*1-879194-74-0*) GLB Pubs.

Roberts, Carey & Seely, Rebecca. Tidewater Dynasty: A Biographical Novel of the Lees of Stratford Hall. (Harvest Book Ser.). 1983. 456p. pap. 23.00 (*0-15-690336-9*, Harvest Bks.); 1981. 19.95 o.s.i (*0-15-190294-1*) Harcourt Trade Pubs.

Roberts, Nora. Three Complete Novels. 2001. 852p. 14.98 (*0-399-14731-4*, Putnam & Grosset) Penguin Group (USA) Inc.

—True Betrayals. 1996. 432p. mass mkt. 7.99 (*0-515-11855-9*, Jove) Berkley Publishing Group.

—True Betrayals. abr. ed. 1996. audio 7.99 o.s.i (*1-56740-121-X*, 712, Paperback Nova Audio Bks.); 1995. audio 16.95 o.p. (*1-56100-421-9*, 1396, Nova Audio Bks.); 1995. audio 25.95 o.s.i (*1-56100-628-9*, 300, Bookcassette); 1995. audio 89.25 (*1-56100-253-4*, 1109, Unabridged Library Editions) Brilliance Audio.

—True Betrayals. 1995. 400p. 22.95 o.p. (*0-399-14059-X*, G. P. Putnam's Sons) Penguin Group (USA) Inc.

—True Betrayals. 22.95 o.s.i (*0-399-14293-2*) Putnam Publishing Group, The.

Robinson, Timothy M. He Took My Lickin' for Me. Sowards, Ben, tr. & illus. by. 2003. (J). (*1-57008-953-1*, Shadow Mountain) Deseret Bk. Co.

Roles, Joe B. Mary Jane's War. (*0-615-12327-9*) Roles, Joe B.

Santangello, Elena. Hang My Head & Cry. 2001. 322p. 24.95 (*0-312-26939-0*, Saint Martin's Minotaur) St. Martin's Pr.

Schott, Carolyn J. & Smith, Phillipa A. The Cracker Crumb Rescue. 1992. 40p. (J). (gr. 3-6). lib. bdg. 16.95 (*0-9632461-0-0*) Harbour Duck Specialties, Inc.

Schroeder, Joan V. Solitary Places. 1996. 368p. mass mkt. 6.99 o.s.i (*0-425-15157-3*) Berkley Publishing Group.

—Solitary Places. 1994. 288p. 22.95 o.s.i (*0-399-13987-7*, G. P. Putnam's Sons) Penguin Group (USA) Inc.

Scott, Willard. Murder in the Mist: A Stanley Waters Mystery. l.t. ed. 1999. (Thorndike Senior Lifestyle Ser.). 367p. 27.95 (*0-7862-1915-7*) Thorndike Pr.

Settle, Mary Lee. O Beulah Land. 1984. 304p. mass mkt. 4.95 o.s.i (*0-345-32490-0*); 1981. mass mkt. 3.50 o.s.i (*0-345-29311-8*) Ballantine Bks.

—O Beulah Land. 1987. 368p. pap. 8.95 o.s.i (*0-684-18846-5*, Macmillan Reference USA) Gale Group.

—O Beulah Land. 1996. (Beulah Quintet Ser.: Bk. II). 368p. pap. 14.95 (*1-57003-115-0*) Univ. of South Carolina Pr.

—O Beulah Land. 1956. 3.95 o.p. (*0-670-51886-7*) Viking Penguin.

Shea, Lisa. Hula. 1994. 15.00 o.p. (*0-393-03589-1*) Norton, W. W. & Co., Inc.

—Hula: A Novel. 2001. 160p. pap. 11.00 (*0-393-32130-4*) Norton, W. W. & Co., Inc.

Shepard, Karen. An Empire of Women. 2002. 272p. pap. 12.95 (*0-425-18456-0*) Berkley Publishing Group.

—An Empire of Women. l.t. ed. 2001. (Hardcover Ser.). 281p. 29.95 (*1-58724-077-7*, Wheeler Publishing, Inc.) Gale Group.

—An Empire of Women. 2000. 320p. 24.95 o.s.i (*0-399-14667-9*) Penguin Group (USA) Inc.

Shermer, Michael. The Science of Good & Evil: Why People Cheat, Share, Gossip, & Follow the Golden Rule. 2004. 384p. 26.00 (*0-8050-7520-8*, Times Bks.) Holt, Henry & Co.

Shores, Christopher & Ehrengardt, Chris. Fledgling Eagles: The Complete Account of the Air War over Western Europe & Scandinavia, Sept. 1939-August 1940. 1992. (Illus.). 400p. 45.00 (*0-948817-42-9*) Grub Street GBR. *Dist:* Casemate Pubs. & Bk. Distributors, LLC.

Shreve, Susan Richards. A Country of Strangers. 1990. 240p. (YA). pap. 9.95 o.s.i (*0-385-26775-4*) Doubleday Publishing.

—A Country of Strangers. 1989. 17.95 o.p. (*0-671-64409-2*, Simon & Schuster) Simon & Schuster.

Smith-Brown, Fern. Plantation. 1999. 219p. 21.95 (*0-9666721-3-5*); 2000. 224p. reprint ed. pap. 21.95 (*0-9666721-7-8*) GoldenIsle Pubs., Inc.

Smith, Lee. Oral History: A Novel. 1996. 320p. pap. 12.95 (*0-345-41028-9*); 1993. 304p. pap. 10.00 o.s.i (*0-345-38398-2*); 1984. 368p. mass mkt. 5.99 o.s.i (*0-345-31607-X*, Ballantine Bks.) Ballantine Bks.

—Oral History: A Novel. 1983. 288p. 14.95 o.p. (*0-399-12794-1*) Putnam Publishing Group, The.

—Oral History: A Novel. unabr. ed. 1998. audio 70.00 (*0-7887-2609-9*, 95619E7) Recorded Bks., LLC.

Smith, Mary B. Miss Ophelia. l.t. ed. 1998. (Core Ser.). 400p. 28.95 (*0-7838-8402-8*) Thorndike Pr.

Smith, Taylor. Guilt by Silence. 2000. 408p. mass mkt. (*1-55166-537-9*, 1-66537-1); 1995. 400p. per. (*1-55166-048-2*, 1-66048-9) Harlequin Enterprises, Ltd. (Mira Bks.).

Stark, Stephen. The Second Son. Rosenman, Jane, ed. 1994. 432p. reprint ed. pap. o.p. (*0-671-87119-6*, Washington Square Pr.) Simon & Schuster.

—Second Son: A Novel. 1992. 288p. 22.50 o.p. (*0-8050-1943-X*) Holt, Henry & Co.

Stewart, Michael. Belladonna: A Novel. 1992. 352p. 20.00 o.p. (*0-06-017982-1*) HarperTrade.

Stone, Katherine. Star Light, Star Bright. l.t. ed. 2002. 393p. 30.95 (*0-7862-4207-8*) Gale Group.

—Star Light, Star Bright. 2002. 384p. mass mkt. (*1-55166-954-4*); (*1-55166-875-0*) Harlequin Enterprises, Ltd. (Mira Bks.).

Styron, William. The Confessions of Nat Turner. 1981. 368p. mass mkt. 4.95 o.s.i (*0-553-26916-X*) Bantam Bks.

—The Confessions of Nat Turner. unabr. collector's ed. 1985. audio 96.00 (*0-7366-0933-4*, 1877) Books on Tape, Inc.

—The Confessions of Nat Turner. 1994. reprint ed. lib. bdg. 32.95 (*1-56849-344-4*) Buccaneer Bks., Inc.

—The Confessions of Nat Turner. 1992. 480p. pap. 14.00 (*0-679-73663-8*, Vintage) Knopf Publishing Group.

—The Confessions of Nat Turner. 1976. mass mkt. 1.95 o.p. (*0-451-07004-6*, Signet Bks.); 1968. mass mkt. 2.75 o.p. (*0-451-09554-5*, Signet Bks.); 1968. mass mkt. 2.25 o.p. (*0-451-07767-9*, E7767); 1968. mass mkt. 1.25 o.p. (*0-451-03596-8*, Signet Bks.) NAL.

—The Confessions of Nat Turner. 1994. (Modern Library Ser.). 480p. 18.95 (*0-679-60101-5*, Random Hse. Bks. for Young Readers) Random Hse. Children's Bks.

—The Confessions of Nat Turner. 2002. 448p. 23.00 (*0-375-50803-1*); 1967. 24.95 o.s.i (*0-394-42099-3*) Random Hse., Inc.

—The Confessions of Nat Turner. 2002. E-Book 8.99 (*0-7953-0310-6*) RosettaBooks.

—A Tidewater Morning: Three Tales from Youth. l.t. ed. 1993. 22.95 (*1-56895-048-9*, Wheeler Publishing, Inc.) Gale Group.
—A Tidewater Morning: Three Tales from Youth. 1994. 160p. pap. 11.00 (*0-679-75449-0*, Vintage) Knopf Publishing Group.
—A Tidewater Morning: Three Tales from Youth. ltd. ed. 1993. 100.00 o.s.i (*0-679-42963-8*) Random Hse., Inc.
Talley, Marcia. Sing It to Her Bones. l.t. ed. 2000. 27.95 (*1-57490-301-2*, Beeler Large Print Bks.) Beeler, Thomas T. Publisher.
—Sing It to Her Bones: A Hannah Ives Mystery. 1999. (Hannah Ives Mysteries Ser.). 304p. mass mkt. 5.99 (*0-440-23517-0*) Dell Publishing.
Theroux, Alexander. Darconville's Cat. 1996. 720p. pap. 16.00 o.s.i (*0-8050-4365-9*, Owl Bks.) Holt, Henry & Co.
Thom, James A. Follow the River. 1986. 416p. mass mkt. 7.99 (*0-345-33854-5*) Ballantine Bks.
Thom, James Alexander & Thom, Dark Rain. Warrior Woman: The Exceptional Life Story of Nonhelma, Shawnee Indian Woman Chief. 2003. 464p. 25.95 (*0-345-44554-6*, Ballantine Bks.) Ballantine Bks.
Tilghman, Christopher. Mason's Retreat. Date not set. (*0-679-45240-0*) McKay, David Co., Inc.
—Mason's Retreat. 1997. 304p. pap. 13.00 o.p. (*0-312-15586-7*) Picador.
—Mason's Retreat. 1995. 290p. 22.00 o.s.i (*0-679-45143-9*) Random Hse., Inc.
Trigiani, Adriana. Big Cherry Holler: A Big Stone Gap Novel. 2002. 320p. pap. 13.95 (*0-345-44584-8*, Ballantine Bks.) Ballantine Bks.
—Big Cherry Holler: A Big Stone Gap Novel. l.t. ed. 2001. 29.95 (*1-58724-141-2*, Wheeler Publishing, Inc.) Gale Group.
—Big Cherry Holler: A Big Stone Gap Novel. 2001. E-Book 19.95 (*1-58836-010-5*); 288p. 24.95 (*0-375-50617-9*) Random Hse., Inc.
—Big Stone Gap. unabr. ed. 2001. 8p. audio compact disk 94.95 (*0-7927-9957-7*, SLD 008); 2000. audio 69.95 (*0-7927-2406-2*, CSL 295) BBC Audiobooks America. (Chivers Sound Library).
—Big Stone Gap. l.t. ed. 2000. (Large Print Book Ser.). 395p. 27.95 (*1-56895-919-2*, Wheeler Publishing, Inc.) Gale Group.
—Big Stone Gap. abr. ed. 2000. audio compact disk 29.95 (*0-375-41006-6*); audio 25.00 (*0-375-40947-5*) Random Hse. Audio Publishing Group. (RH Audio).
—Big Stone Gap: A Novel. 2001. mass mkt. (*0-345-44301-2*); 320p. reprint ed. pap. 13.95 (*0-345-43832-9*) Ballantine Bks. (Ballantine Bks.).
—Big Stone Gap: A Novel. 2000. 288p. 23.95 (*0-375-50403-6*) Random Hse., Inc.
—Milk Glass Moon: A Big Stone Gap Novel. 2002. 272p. 24.95 (*0-375-50618-7*) Random Hse., Inc.
Tucker, Norma. Fledgling Eagle: Captain William Tucker & the New World Colony. 1995. 251p. 18.95 (*0-912526-71-8*) Library Research Assocs., Inc.
Underwood, J. Cabaniss. Gilbert: or Then & Now: A Thrilling Story of the Life & Achievements of a Virginia Negro. 1977. (Black Heritage Library Collection). reprint ed. 30.95 (*0-8369-9086-2*) Ayer Co. Pubs., Inc.
Vollmann, William T. Argall. 2002. (Illus.). 768p. 18.00 (*0-14-200150-3*) Viking Penguin.
Walther, Anne Newton. A Time for Treason: A Novel of the American Revolution. 2000. 451p. 24.95 (*0-9676703-0-6*) Tapestries.
Wells, Leslie. The Curing Season. 2002. 272p. pap. 13.95 (*0-446-67866-X*); 2001. 256p. 22.95 o.p. (*0-446-52693-2*) Warner Bks., Inc.
Wensyel, James W. Petersburg: Out of the Trenches. 1998. 169p. 24.95 (*1-57249-139-6*, Burd Street Pr.) White Mane Publishing Co., Inc.
Whitney, Phyllis A. The Ebony Swan. unabr. ed. 1995. audio 69.95 (*0-7451-6504-4*, CAB 1120) BBC Audiobooks America.
—The Ebony Swan. 1998. mass mkt. 3.99 o.s.i (*0-449-00507-0*); 1993. mass mkt. 5.99 o.s.i (*0-449-22197-0*) Ballantine Bks. (Fawcett).
—The Ebony Swan. l.t. ed. 1992. 352p. 24.00 o.p. (*0-385-42444-2*, Doubleday Large Type) Bantam Doubleday Dell Large Print Group, Inc.
—The Ebony Swan. unabr. ed. 1997. audio 49.95 (*0-7861-1237-9*, 1984) Blackstone Audio Bks., Inc.
—The Ebony Swan. l.t. ed. 1993. 354p. pap. 19.95 o.p. (*0-8161-5805-3*, Macmillan Reference USA) Gale Group.
Wicker, Tom. Unto This Hour. 1985. 752p. mass mkt. 4.95 o.s.i (*0-425-07583-4*) Berkley Publishing Group.
—Unto This Hour. 1984. (Illus.). 630p. 19.95 o.p. (*0-670-52193-0*) Viking Penguin.
—Unto This Hour: A Novel by Tom Wicker. 1997. 656p. reprint ed. pap. 24.95 (*0-8203-1964-3*) Univ. of Georgia Pr.
Wiggins, Marianne. Almost Heaven. 1999. 224p. pap. 14.00 (*0-671-03860-5*, Simon & Schuster) Simon & Schuster.
Wiggs, Susan. The Horsemaster's Daughter. unabr. ed. 1999. audio 7.99 (*1-55204-193-X*, MIR-1193) Durkin Hayes Publishing Ltd.
—The Horsemaster's Daughter. 1999. 401p. mass mkt. (*1-55166-534-4*, 1-66534-8, Mira Bks.) Harlequin Enterprises, Ltd.
Wolf, Joan. That Summer. 2003. (Illus.). 368p. mass mkt. 5.99 (*0-446-61044-5*, Warner Romance) Warner Bks., Inc.
Woodbridge, Annie & Woodbridge, Hensley C., eds. The Collected Short Stories of Mary Johnston. 1982. xxii, 340p. (C). 48.00 (*0-87875-204-8*) Whitston Publishing Co., Inc.
Woodiwiss, Kathleen E. Petals on the River. abr. ed. 1998. audio 7.99 o.s.i (*1-56740-268-2*, 1607, Paperback Nova Audio Bks.); 1997. audio 17.95 o.p. (*1-56740-752-8*, 501, Nova Audio Bks.); 1997. 18p. audio 105.25 (*1-56740-552-5*, 980, Unabridged Library Editions); 1997. audio 27.95 (*1-56100-773-0*, 208, Bookcassette) Brilliance Audio.
—Petals on the River. (Avon Historical Romance Ser.). 1998. 560p. mass mkt. 6.99 (*0-380-79828-X*); 1997. pap. 12.50 o.p. (*0-380-76654-X*) Morrow/ Avon. (Avon Bks.).
Woods, Sherryl. About that Man. 2001. 408p. mass mkt. (*1-55166-815-7*, Mira Bks.) Harlequin Enterprises, Ltd.
—Along Came Trouble. 2002. 400p. mass mkt. (*1-55166-955-2*, Mira Bks.) Harlequin Enterprises, Ltd.
Youmans, Marly. The Wolf Pit. 2001. 352p. 24.00 o.p. (*0-374-29195-0*) Farrar, Straus & Giroux.
—The Wolf Pit. 2003. 352p. pap. 14.00 (*0-15-602714-3*, Harvest Bks.) Harcourt Trade Pubs.

# W

## WALES—FICTION

Adams, Sam & Mathias, Roland. The Shining Pyramid. 1970. 163p. (C). pap. 22.00 (*0-85044-484-5*); pap. 30.00 (*0-85088-484-5*) Gomer Pr. GBR. *Dist:* State Mutual Bk. & Periodical Service, Ltd.
Amis, Kingsley. The Old Devils. 1994. 5.50 o.p. (*0-87129-407-9*, O51) Dramatic Publishing Co.
—The Old Devils. 1988. 304p. reprint ed. pap. 7.95 o.p. (*0-06-097146-0*, PL-7146, Perennial) HarperTrade.
—The Old Devils. 1987. 256p. 18.45 o.p. (*0-671-63704-5*) Summit Bks.
Ashworth, Elizabeth. So I Kissed Her Little Sister. 2000. 121p. pap. 11.95 (*1-902638-02-6*) Parthian Bks. GBR. *Dist:* Dufour Editions, Inc.
Attanasio, A. A. Kingdom of the Grail: A Novel. 1992. 608p. 23.00 o.p. (*0-06-017965-1*) HarperTrade.
Azzopardi, Trezza. The Hiding Place. l.t. ed. 2001. 360p. (*0-7838-9483-X*, Hall, G. K. & Co.) Gale Group.
—The Hiding Place. 288p. 2002. pap. 13.00 (*0-8021-3859-4*, Grove Pr.); 2001. 24.00 o.p. (*0-87113-815-8*) Grove/Atlantic, Inc.
—The Hiding Place. 2000. 282p. pap. 21.95 (*1-55263-161-3*) Key Porter Bks. CAN. *Dist:* Firefly Bks., Ltd.
—The Hiding Place. 2000. 282p. (*0-330-39075-9*) Picador.
Balogh, Mary. Slightly Married. 2003. (Bedwyn Family Bks.). 368p. mass mkt. 5.99 (*0-440-24104-9*) Bantam Dell Publishing Group.
—Slightly Married. l.t. ed. 2003. lib. bdg. 28.95 (*1-58547-338-3*, Platinum) Ctr. Point Large Print.
Becnel, Rexanne. The Bride of Rosecliffe. 1998. 378p. mass mkt. 6.50 (*0-312-96649-0*, St. Martin's Paperbacks) St. Martin's Pr.
Berridge, Elizabeth. Touch & Go. 2000. 220p. pap. 9.95 (*0-552-99648-3*) Transworld Publishers Ltd. GBR. *Dist:* Trafalgar Square.
Berridge, Elizabeth. Touch & Go. unabr. ed. 1996. audio 54.95 (*0-7451-6703-9*, CAB1319) BBC Audiobooks America.
Bessey, Sian Ann. Cover of Darkness. 2002. (Illus.). 230p. 14.95 (*1-57734-985-7*) Covenant Communications.
Bowen, Rhys. Evan & Elle. l.t. ed. 2000. (Beeler Large Print Mystery Ser.). 236p. 26.95 (*1-57490-319-5*, Beeler Large Print Bks.) Beeler, Thomas T. Publisher.
—Evan & Elle: A Constable Evans Mystery. 2001. 224p. reprint ed. mass mkt. 5.99 (*0-425-17888-9*, Prime Crime) Berkley Publishing Group.
—Evan & Elle: A Constable Evans Mystery. 2000. 274p. 22.95 (*0-312-25244-7*, Saint Martin's Minotaur) St. Martin's Pr.
—Evan Can Wait: A Constable Evans Mystery. l.t. ed. 2001. (G. K. Hall Core Ser.). 365p. 29.95 (*0-7838-9451-1*, Macmillan Reference USA) Gale Group.
—Evan Can Wait: A Constable Evans Mystery. 2001. 259p. 22.95 (*0-312-26587-5*, Saint Martin's Minotaur) St. Martin's Pr.
—Evan Help Us. l.t. ed. 1999. (Beeler Large Print Mystery Ser.). 25.95 (*1-57490-213-X*, Beeler Large Print Bks.) Beeler, Thomas T. Publisher.
—Evan Help Us. 1999. (Constable Evan Evans Mysteries Ser.). 224p. reprint ed. mass mkt. 5.99 (*0-425-17261-9*, Prime Crime) Berkley Publishing Group.
—Evan Help Us. 1998. (Constable Evans Mysteries Ser.). 224p. 21.95 (*0-312-19411-0*, Saint Martin's Minotaur) St. Martin's Pr.
—Evan Only Knows: A Constable Evans Mystery. 2004. 272p. mass mkt. 6.50 (*0-425-19607-0*) Berkley Publishing Group.
—Evan Only Knows: A Constable Evans Mystery. 2003. 256p. 23.95 (*0-312-30113-8*, Saint Martin's Minotaur) St. Martin's Pr.
—Evanly Choirs. l.t. ed. 1999. (Beeler Large Print Mystery Ser.). 249p. 25.95 (*1-57490-241-5*, Beeler Large Print Bks.) Beeler, Thomas T. Publisher.
—Evanly Choirs. 2000. (Constable Evan Evans Mysteries Ser.). 256p. mass mkt. 5.99 (*0-425-17613-4*) Berkley Publishing Group.
—Evanly Choirs. 1999. (Constable Evans Mysteries Ser.). x, 256p. 22.95 (*0-312-20539-2*, Saint Martin's Minotaur) St. Martin's Pr.
—Evans Above. l.t. ed. 1999. (Beeler Large Print Mystery Ser.). 218p. 25.95 (*1-57490-208-3*, Beeler Large Print Bks.) Beeler, Thomas T. Publisher.
—Evans Above. 1998. (Constable Evan Evans Mysteries Ser.). 224p. reprint ed. mass mkt. 5.99 (*0-425-16642-2*, Prime Crime) Berkley Publishing Group.
Bowen, Rhys & Bowen, J. Evans Above. 1997. (Evan Evans Ser.). 236p. 21.95 (*0-312-16828-4*, Saint Martin's Minotaur) St. Martin's Pr.
Brandewyne, Rebecca. Swan Road. 1995. (Illus.). 384p. reprint ed. 22.00 (*0-7278-4758-9*) Severn Hse. Pubs., Ltd.
—Swan Road. 1994. 384p. mass mkt. 5.99 (*0-446-32701-8*) Warner Bks., Inc.
Brook, Rhidian. The Testimony of Taliesin Jones. 2001. 208p. pap. 13.00 (*0-14-200157-0*) Penguin Group (USA) Inc.
Burke, Sean. Deadwater. 2002. 256p. pap. 14.00 (*1-85242-693-4*) Serpent's Tail Ltd. GBR. *Dist:* Consortium Bk. Sales & Distribution.
Cameron, Stella. Once & for Always. 2000. per. (*1-55166-580-8*); 1988. (Harlequin Superromance Ser.: No. 402). pap. (*0-373-70340-6*) Harlequin Enterprises, Ltd. (Harlequin Bks.).
Chadwick, Elizabeth. The Running Vixen. 1992. 336p. 19.95 o.p. (*0-312-07793-9*) St. Martin's Pr.
Collier, Catrin. Swansea Girls. l.t. ed. 2002. (Magna Large Print Ser.). 576p. 32.50 (*0-7505-1881-2*) Magna Large Print Bks. GBR. *Dist:* Ulverscroft Large Print Bks., Ltd., Ulverscroft Large Print Canada, Ltd.
—Swansea Girls. 392p. 29.95 (*0-7528-3232-8*); 2002. 486p. pap. (*0-7528-4484-9*); 2002. 392p. pap. 16.95 (*0-7528-4701-5*) Orion Publishing Group, Ltd. GBR. *Dist:* Trafalgar Square.
Cook, Linda. Silver Wind. 2001. (Zebra Historical Romance Ser.). 352p. mass mkt. 5.99 o.s.i (*0-8217-6870-0*) Kensington Publishing Corp.
Cory, Desmond. The Catalyst. 1991. 15.95 o.p. (*0-312-05832-2*, Saint Martin's Minotaur) St. Martin's Pr.
—The Dobie Paradox. 1994. 240p. 19.95 o.p. (*0-312-10969-5*, Saint Martin's Minotaur) St. Martin's Pr.
Coulter, Catherine. Secret Song. 384p. 2003. mass mkt. 7.99 (*0-451-20929-X*, Signet Bks.); 1991. mass mkt. 7.99 o.s.i (*0-451-40234-0*, Onyx) NAL.
—Secret Song. 1991. 21.95 o.p. (*0-7278-4185-8*) Severn Hse. Pubs., Ltd.
—Secret Song. l.t. ed. 2000. (Basic Ser.). 567p. 29.95 (*0-7862-2357-X*) Thorndike Pr.
Curzon, Clare. All Unwary. (*0-7540-3467-4*); 1999. 340p. pap. (*0-7540-3468-2*) BBC Audiobooks America.
—All Unwary. 1998. (Thames Valley Mystery Ser.). 256p. 21.95 o.p. (*0-312-18037-3*, Saint Martin's Minotaur) St. Martin's Pr.
—All Unwary. l.t. ed. 1999. (General Ser.). 352p. pap. 23.95 (*0-7862-1544-5*) Thorndike Pr.
Davies, Lewis. My Piece of Happiness. 2002. (Illus.). 226p. pap. 14.95 (*1-902638-20-4*); 2000. 220p. 19.95 (*1-902638-04-2*) Parthian Bks. GBR. *Dist:* Dufour Editions, Inc.
—Tree of Crows. 1997. 102p. pap. 9.95 (*0-9521558-3-4*) Dufour Editions, Inc.
Davies, Rhys. Ram with Red Horns. 1997. 180p. pap. 16.95 (*1-85411-165-5*) Seren Bks. GBR. *Dist:* Dufour Editions, Inc.
Davis, Kathryn. The Walking Tour: A Novel. 1999. 288p. tchr. ed. 23.00 (*0-395-94541-0*) Houghton Mifflin Co.
—The Walking Tour: A Novel. 2000. 288p. pap. 13.00 (*0-618-08238-7*, Mariner Bks.) Houghton Mifflin Co. Trade & Reference Div.
Ellis, Alice Thomas. Fairy Tale. 2001. (Common Reader Edition Ser.). 213p. reprint ed. pap. 14.95 (*1-888173-40-8*) Akadine Pr., The.
—Fairy Tale. 1998. 200p. 22.95 o.p. (*1-55921-254-3*) Moyer Bell.
—Fairy Tale. 2003. (General Ser.). lib. bdg. 24.95 (*0-7862-4826-2*) Thorndike Pr.
—The Sin Eater. 2001. 196p. pap. 14.95 (*1-888173-36-X*, Common Reader Editions) Akadine Pr., The.
—The Sin Eater. 1998. 192p. 22.95 (*1-55921-257-8*) Moyer Bell.
—Unexplained Laughter. 2002. pap. 15.95 (*1-888173-53-X*) Akadine Pr., The.
—Unexplained Laughter. 1987. 160p. 14.95 o.p. (*0-06-015722-4*) HarperTrade.
Evans, Caradoc. Capel Sion. 2002. 112p. pap. 13.95 (*1-85411-308-9*) Seren Bks. GBR. *Dist:* Dufour Editions, Inc.
—My Neighbors: Stories of the Welsh People. 1977. (Short Story Index Reprint Ser.). 19.95 (*0-8369-3495-4*) Ayer Co. Pubs., Inc.
—Nothing to Pay. 1995. (Revived Modern Classic Ser.: Vol. 800). 240p. pap. 11.95 (*0-8112-1290-4*, NDP800) New Directions Publishing Corp.
Evans, Dilys. Looking for Merlyn. 1997. (Illus.). (J). 14.95 (*0-590-60191-1*) Scholastic, Inc.
Evans, George Brinley. Boys of Gold. 2001. 78p. pap. 12.95 (*1-902638-12-3*) Parthian Bks. GBR. *Dist:* Dufour Editions, Inc.
Figgis, Paddy. On The Bright Road. 2000. (Illus.). 256p. 14.95 o.p. (*0-7145-3057-3*) Mari, Inc.
Fobes, Tracy. Daughter of Destiny. 2000. 416p. pap. 6.50 (*0-671-04174-6*, Pocket) Simon & Schuster.
Ford, John M. The Dragon Waiting. 1985. 400p. pap. 3.95 (*0-380-69887-0*, Avon Bks.) Morrow/Avon.
—The Dragon Waiting: A Masque of History. 1983. 368p. 15.50 (*0-671-47552-5*, Atria) Simon & Schuster.
Fraser, Anthea. Dangerous Deception. 1998. 224p. 24.00 (*0-7278-5318-X*) Severn Hse. Pubs., Ltd.
Gallie, Menna. In These Promiscuous Parts. 1986. 320p. 15.95 o.p. (*0-312-42537-6*) St. Martin's Pr.
Goddard, Robert. Hand in Glove. 1994. mass mkt. o.s.i (*0-552-14165-8*, Corgi); 528p. mass mkt. 7.99 (*0-552-13839-8*) Bantam Bks.
—Hand in Glove. unabr. ed. 2000. audio 89.95 (*0-7451-4362-8*, CAB 1045) Chivers Audio Bks. GBR. *Dist:* BBC Audiobooks America.
—Hand in Glove. 1993. 432p. 22.00 o.p. (*0-671-75070-4*, Simon & Schuster) Simon & Schuster.
—Hand in Glove. Rosenman, Jane, ed. 1994. 432p. reprint ed. pap. (*0-671-89037-9*, Washington Square Pr.) Simon & Schuster.
—Hand in Glove. l.t. ed. 1994. (Charnwood Large Print Ser.). 720p. 29.99 o.p. (*0-7089-8773-7*, Ulverscroft) Thorpe, F. A. Pubs. GBR. *Dist:* Ulverscroft Large Print Bks., Ltd., Ulverscroft Large Print Canada, Ltd.
Goodman, Lisl Marburg. Light at the End of the Tunnel. 2002. 220p. 25.00 (*0-939713-10-1*) Carriage Hse. Pr.
Gordon, Mary & Swinburne, Algernon Charles. The Children of the Chapel: A Tale. 1982. 1185p. (C). lib. bdg. 18.95 o.p. (*0-8214-0631-0*) Ohio Univ. Pr.
Gower, Iris. Black Gold. 1989. 384p. 18.95 o.p. (*0-312-02546-7*) St. Martin's Pr.
—Black Gold. 2000. pap. 8.95 (*0-552-13316-7*) Transworld Publishers Ltd. GBR. *Dist:* Trafalgar Square.
—The Copper Kingdom, Set. unabr. ed. 1998. audio 83.95 (*1-872672-10-8*) Magna Story Sound GBR. *Dist:* Ulverscroft Large Print Bks., Ltd.
—The Copper Kingdom. 1984. 320p. 13.95 o.p. (*0-312-16971-X*) St. Martin's Pr.
—The Copper Kingdom. 2000. pap. 10.95 (*0-552-12387-0*) Transworld Publishers Ltd. GBR. *Dist:* Trafalgar Square.
—Fiddler's Ferry. 1988. 384p. 17.95 o.p. (*0-312-01429-5*) St. Martin's Pr.
—Morgan's Woman. 1986. 384p. 17.95 o.p. (*0-312-00018-9*) St. Martin's Pr.
—Proud Mary. 1985. 14.95 o.p. (*0-312-65225-9*) St. Martin's Pr.
—A Royal Ambition. 1999. 222p. 25.00 (*0-7278-5503-4*) Severn Hse. Pubs., Ltd.
—A Royal Ambition. l.t. ed. 2000. (Romance Ser.). 293p. 25.95 (*0-7862-2647-1*) Thorndike Pr.
—Spinner's Wharf. 432p. 26.99 (*0-7278-5789-4*) Severn Hse. Pubs., Ltd.
—Spinner's Wharf. 1986. 384p. 16.95 o.p. (*0-312-75237-7*) St. Martin's Pr.
—Spinner's Wharf. 2000. (J). pap. 8.95 (*0-552-12638-1*) Transworld Publishers Ltd. GBR. *Dist:* Trafalgar Square.
Gower, Iris, contrib. by. A Royal Ambition. l.t. ed. 2000. 293p. (*0-7540-4233-2*); (*0-7540-4234-0*) Thorndike Pr.
Griffiths, Niall. Sheepshagger. 2001. 256p. pap. (*0-224-06105-4*) Random Hse. UK, Ltd.
—Sheepshagger. 2002. 288p. 23.95 (*0-312-30073-5*) St. Martin's Pr.
Howatch, Susan. The Wheel of Fortune. 1984. 1184p. 19.45 o.p. (*0-671-49989-0*, Simon & Schuster) Simon & Schuster.
Humphreys, Emyr. The Gift of a Daughter. 2000. 240p. 22.00 (*1-85411-222-8*) Seren Bks. GBR. *Dist:* Dufour Editions, Inc.

Jackson, Lisa. Dark Emerald. 352p. 2004. mass mkt. 6.99 (*0-451-20991-5*, Signet Bks.); 1999. mass mkt. 6.99 o.s.i (*0-451-40778-4*) NAL.

Jones, Anna. A World Away. 2001. (Illus.). 218p. 14.95 (*1-57734-817-6*) Covenant Communications.

Jones, Gwyn. Selected Short Stories. 1974. pap. 5.95 o.p. (*0-19-281162-2*) Oxford Univ. Pr., Inc.

Jones, John Sam. Welsh Boys Too. 2001. 91p. pap. 12.95 (*1-902638-11-5*) Parthian Bks. GBR. *Dist:* Dufour Editions, Inc.

Kearsley, Susanna. Named of the Dragon. 1999. 304p. mass mkt. 6.99 o.s.i (*0-425-17345-3*) Berkley Publishing Group.

—Named of the Dragon. 1998. 240p. o.p. (*0-385-25726-0*) Doubleday Canada, Ltd. CAN. *Dist:* Random Hse., Inc.

—Named of the Dragon. l.t. ed. 1999. (Magna Large Print Ser.). 432p. (*0-7505-1393-4*) Magna Large Print Bks. GBR. *Dist:* Ulverscroft Large Print Canada, Ltd.

Kelly, Carla Sue. The Lady's Companion. 1996. 224p. mass mkt. 4.99 o.s.i (*0-451-18684-2*, Signet Bks.) NAL.

Leiner, Catherine. Digging Out. 2004. 304p. pap. 12.95 (*0-451-21160-X*) NAL.

Lewis, Saunders. Monica. 1997. 107p. pap. 17.95 (*1-85411-195-7*) Seren Bks. GBR. *Dist:* Dufour Editions, Inc.

Linscott, Gillian. Hanging on the Wire. 1992. 215p. 17.95 o.p. (*0-312-08806-X*, Saint Martin's Minotaur) St. Martin's Pr.

Llewellyn, Richard. How Green Was My Valley. 1983. reprint ed. lib. bdg. 30.95 (*0-88411-936-X*) Amereon, Ltd.

—How Green Was My Valley. 1987. (Hudson River Editions Ser.). 512p. 40.00 (*0-02-573420-2*, Macmillan Reference USA) Gale Group.

—How Green Was My Valley. mass mkt. 1.25 o.p. (*0-451-03427-9*, Signet Bks.) NAL.

—How Green Was My Valley. 1997. 512p. pap. 14.00 (*0-684-82555-4*, Scribner) Simon & Schuster.

Mawer, Simon. The Fall. 2004. 400p. pap. 13.95 (*0-316-73559-0*, Back Bay); 2003. 384p. 24.95 (*0-316-09780-2*) Little Brown & Co.

Mayse, Susan. Awen: A Novel of Early Medieval Wales. 1997. (Illus.). 416p. 35.00 (*0-910055-37-8*) Eastern Washington Univ. Pr.

McReynolds, Glenna. The Chalice & the Blade. 1998. 512p. reprint ed. mass mkt. 6.50 (*0-553-57430-2*, Fanfare) Bantam Bks.

—Dream Stone. 2000. 496p. reprint ed. mass mkt. 6.50 (*0-553-57431-0*) Bantam Bks.

Medeiros, Teresa. The Fairest of Them All. 1995. 400p. mass mkt. 6.99 (*0-553-56333-5*) Bantam Bks.

—Fairest of Them All. l.t. ed. 1996. (Romance Ser.). lib. bdg. 24.95 (*0-7862-0864-3*, Five Star) Gale Group.

Meredith, Christopher. Griffri. 1995. 256p. 30.00 (*1-85411-059-4*) Dufour Editions, Inc.

—Shifts. 1997. 180p. pap. 17.95 (*1-85411-199-X*) Seren Bks. GBR. *Dist:* Dufour Editions, Inc.

Monger, Christopher. The Englishman Who Went up a Hill but Came down a Mountain. l.t. ed. 1996. 23.95 o.p. (*1-56895-321-6*, Wheeler Publishing, Inc.) Gale Group.

—The Englishman Who Went up a Hill but Came down a Mountain. 1995. 256p. pap. 9.95 o.p. (*0-7868-8140-2*) Hyperion Pr.

Neale, Linda. Briallen. 1958. 384p. 16.95 o.p. (*0-312-00110-X*) St. Martin's Pr.

Newby, P. H. Coming in with the Tide. 1991. 364p. o.p. (*0-09-174664-7*) Random Hse. of Canada, Ltd. CAN. *Dist:* Random Hse., Inc.

Norris, Leslie. Collected Stories. 1996. 260p. pap. 19.95 (*1-85411-133-7*) Seren Bks. GBR. *Dist:* Dufour Editions, Inc.

—The Girl from Cardigan: Sixteen Stories. 1988. 176p. 15.95 o.p. (*0-87905-296-1*) Smith, Gibbs Pub.

—The Girl from Cardigan: Sixteen Stories by Leslie Norris. 1989. 176p. reprint ed. pap. 8.95 o.p. (*0-87905-337-2*) Smith, Gibbs Pub.

O'Brian, Patrick. Testimonies. unabr. ed. 1993. audio 48.00 (*0-7366-2597-6*, 3342) Books on Tape, Inc.

—Testimonies. 224p. 1995. pap. 13.95 (*0-393-31316-6*, Norton Paperbacks); 1993. 20.95 (*0-393-03483-6*) Norton, W. W. & Co., Inc.

Pargeter, Edith. The Brothers of Gwynedd Quartet. 1990. 822p. pap. 16.95 (*0-7472-3267-9*) Headline Bk. Publishing, Ltd. GBR. *Dist:* Trafalgar Square.

Pawar, Ravi. Tilting at Windmills: New Welsh Short Fiction. 1995. 144p. pap. 9.95 (*0-9521558-1-8*) Dufour Editions, Inc.

Penman, Sharon Kay. Here Be Dragons. 1993. 720p. pap. 15.95 (*0-345-38284-6*) Ballantine Bks.

—Here Be Dragons. 1985. (Illus.). 704p. o.p. (*0-03-062773-7*) Holt, Henry & Co.

—Here Be Dragons. 1987. 784p. mass mkt. 4.95 (*0-380-70181-2*, Avon Bks.) Morrow/Avon.

Phillips, Pat. Love Waits at Penrhyn. l.t. ed. 1997. (Candlelight Romance Ser.). 217p. lib. bdg. 20.95 (*0-7862-1240-3*) Thorndike Pr.

Powell, Sophie. The Mushroom Man. 2004. 208p. pap. 14.00 (*0-425-19413-2*) Berkley Publishing Group.

—The Mushroom Man. 2003. 208p. 23.95 (*0-399-14963-5*, Putnam & Grosset) Putnam Publishing Group, The.

Powys, John Cowper. Owen Glendower. 777p. 2004. pap. 24.95 (*1-58567-521-0*); 2003. 35.00 (*1-58567-314-5*) Overlook Pr., The.

—Porius: A Romance of the Dark Ages. Albrecht, Wilbur, ed. 1994. 900p. text 48.95 (*0-912568-16-X*) Colgate Univ. Pr.

—Porius: A Romance of the Dark Ages. 1952. (*0-8022-2009-6*) Philosophical Library, Inc.

Preston, Fayrene. In Guilty Night. 1998. 352p. mass mkt. 5.99 o.s.i (*0-553-57582-1*) Bantam Bks.

Prichard, Caradog. One Moonlit Night. 1995. xv, 76 p. (*0-86241-530-6*) Canongate Bks.

—One Moonlit Night. Mitchell, Philip, tr. from WEL. 1997. (Classics Ser.). 304p. pap. 12.95 (*0-8112-1342-0*, NDP835) New Directions Publishing Corp.

Richards, Alun. Alun Richards: Selected Stories. 1996. 340p. pap. 17.95 (*1-85411-117-5*) Seren Bks. GBR. *Dist:* Dufour Editions, Inc.

Rickman, Phil. Candlenight. 1995. 480p. mass mkt. 5.99 o.s.i (*0-515-11715-3*, Jove) Berkley Publishing Group.

—Curfew. 1993. Orig. Title: Crybbe. 496p. 23.95 o.p. (*0-399-13861-7*, G. P. Putnam's Sons) Penguin Group (USA) Inc.

Robb, Candace. A Gift of Sanctuary: An Owen Archer Mystery. 2000. (Owen Archer Mystery Ser.: Vol. 6). 320p. mass mkt. 6.99 (*0-312-97477-9*, St. Martin's Paperbacks); 1998. 304p. 22.95 o.p. (*0-312-19266-5*, Saint Martin's Minotaur) St. Martin's Pr.

—A Gift of Sanctuary: An Owen Archer Mystery. l.t. ed. 1999. (Mystery Ser.). 475p. 28.95 (*0-7862-1910-6*); (*0-7540-1302-2*); (*0-7540-2226-9*) Thorndike Pr.

Roberts, Cynthia S. The Fox-Red Hills. 1993. 23.95 o.p. (*0-312-08784-5*) St. Martin's Pr.

Roberts, Kate. Tea in the Heather. Griffith, Wyn, tr. from WEL. 1998. 280p. pap. 14.95 (*0-8496-4486-0*) Beekman Pubs., Inc.

—Tea in the Heather. Griffiths, Wyn, tr. from WEL. 1997. 134p. pap. 6.95 (*1-871083-85-0*) Jones, John Publishing GBR. *Dist:* International Specialized Bk. Services.

—Tea in the Heather. 2002. 85p. pap. 13.95 (*1-85411-320-8*) Seren Bks. GBR. *Dist:* Dufour Editions, Inc.

Roberts, William. Pestilence. 2003. 192p. 19.95 (*1-56858-257-9*) Four Walls Eight Windows.

Roberts, William Owen. Pestilence. Roberts, Elisabeth, tr. from WEL. 2000. 214p. pap. 17.95 (*1-85411-198-1*) Seren Bks. GBR. *Dist:* Dufour Editions, Inc.

Ross, Caroline. Miss Nobody. 1982. mass mkt. 2.75 o.s.i (*0-345-30260-5*) Ballantine Bks.

Saxton, Judith A. First Love, Last Love. 1993. 22.95 o.p. (*0-312-08779-9*) St. Martin's Pr.

Small, Bertrice. A Memory of Love. 2002. 432p. mass mkt. 6.99 (*0-345-43518-4*); 2000. (Illus.). 368p. pap. 14.00 (*0-345-43434-X*) Ballantine Bks.

—A Moment in Time. 1994. 480p. mass mkt. 6.99 (*0-345-39079-2*); 1991. 516p. pap. 25.00 (*0-345-36863-0*, Ballantine Bks.) Ballantine Bks.

Taylor, Alison G. In Guilty Night. 1998. 352p. pap. 19.00 (*0-553-76266-4*) Bantam Bks.

—Simeon's Bride. 1996. 368p. mass mkt. 5.99 (*0-553-57579-1*) Bantam Bks.

Thomas, Dylan. Adventures in the Skin Trade & Other Stories. 1964. (C). pap. 9.95 (*0-8112-0202-X*, NDP183) New Directions Publishing Corp.

—The Collected Stories. 384p. 1986. pap. 16.95 (*0-8112-0998-9*, NDP626); 1984. 16.95 o.p. (*0-8112-0918-0*) New Directions Publishing Corp.

—Eight Stories. 1993. (Bibelots Ser.). 96p. reprint ed. pap. 7.00 (*0-8112-1245-9*, NDP766) New Directions Publishing Corp.

Trezise, Rachel. In & Out of the Goldish Bowl. 2002. 122p. pap. 12.95 (*1-902638-07-7*) Parthian Bks. GBR. *Dist:* Dufour Editions, Inc.

Trollope, Anthony. Cousin Henry, Set. unabr. ed. 1991. (YA). (gr. 8 up). audio 35.95 (*1-55685-215-0*) Audio Bk. Contractors, Inc.

—Cousin Henry, 2 vols. Hall, N. John, ed. 1981. (Selected Works of Anthony Trollope). reprint ed. lib. bdg. 55.95 (*0-405-14172-6*) Ayer Co. Pubs., Inc.

—Cousin Henry, 2. reprint ed. lib. bdg. 196.00 (*0-7426-2483-8*) Classic Bks.

—Cousin Henry. Thompson, Julian F., ed. (Oxford World's Classics Ser.). 336p. 2000. pap. 9.95 (*0-19-283846-6*); 1987. pap. 7.95 o.p. (*0-19-281784-1*) Oxford Univ. Pr., Inc.

—Cousin Henry. 1994. (Trollope Ser.). 288p. pap. 6.95 o.p. (*0-14-043842-4*, Penguin Classics) Viking Penguin.

Verge, Lisa A. The Faery Bride. 1996. 352p. mass mkt. 4.99 o.s.i (*0-8217-5261-8*) Kensington Publishing Corp.

Waldo, Anna Lee. Circle of Stones. 2000. (Illus.). 512p. mass mkt. 6.99 (*0-312-97061-7*, St. Martin's Paperbacks); 1999. (Druid Circle Ser.: Vol. 1). 448p. 25.95 o.p. (*0-312-19843-4*) St. Martin's Pr.

Walton, Evangeline. The Mabinogian Tetralogy. 2002. 980p. 35.00 (*1-58567-241-6*) Overlook Pr., The.

Watson, Rob. Slipping Away from Milford. 2000. 222p. pap. 17.95 (*1-85411-181-7*) Seren Bks. GBR. *Dist:* Dufour Editions, Inc.

White, Jon M. Whistling Past the Churchyard: Strange Tales from a Superstitious Welshman. 1992. xii, 227p. 21.00 o.p. (*0-87113-487-X*) Grove/Atlantic, Inc.

Williams, David. A Terminal Case. unabr. ed. 1999. audio 54.95 (*0-7540-0246-2*, CAB1669) BBC Audiobooks America.

—A Terminal Case. l.t. ed. 1998. (Nightingale Ser.). 304p. pap. 20.95 (*0-7838-0282-X*) Thorndike Pr.

Williams, John. Cardiff Dead. 2001. 246p. pap. 14.95 (*1-58234-145-1*) Bloomsbury Publishing.

—Cardiff Dead. 2001. 230p. pap. 14.95 (*0-7475-4997-4*) Bloomsbury Publishing, Ltd. GBR. *Dist:* Trafalgar Square.

—Five Pubs, Two Bars & a Nightclub. 1999. pap. 13.95 (*1-58234-027-7*) Bloomsbury Publishing.

## WALL STREET—FICTION

Ashbaugh, Regan C. In the Red. 1999. 480p. 24.00 o.s.i (*0-671-01890-6*, Atria); 2000. 608p. reprint ed. pap. 6.99 (*0-671-02774-3*, Pocket) Simon & Schuster.

Culp, Michael. Conflicted: A Novel. 2003. (Illus.). 419p. 30.00 (*0-9727961-8-5*) Mecox Bay Pr. LLC.

Doherty, Amy. Rory's Random Walk down Wall Street. 2000. (Illus.). 32p. (J). 16.95 (*0-9674572-0-3*) Playgroup Pr.

Finder, Joseph. The Zero Hour. abr. ed. 1996. audio 16.95 o.p. (*1-56100-888-5*, 1119, Nova Audio Bks.); 1996. audio 25.95 o.p. (*1-56100-687-4*, 326, Bookcassette); 1996. audio 89.25 o.p. (*1-56100-312-3*, 1118, Unabridged Library Editions); Set. 1997. audio 7.99 o.p. (*1-56740-165-1*, 721, Nova Audio Bks.) Brilliance Audio.

—The Zero Hour. l.t. ed. 1996. (G. K. Hall Core Ser.). 630p. lib. bdg. 25.95 (*0-7838-1825-4*, Macmillan Reference USA) Gale Group.

—The Zero Hour. 1997. pap. 6.99 (*0-380-72665-3*, Avon Bks.); 1996. 432p. 25.00 o.p. (*0-688-14450-0*, Morrow, William & Co.) Morrow/Avon.

Frey, Stephen. The Takeover. 1995. 400p. 19.95 o.p. (*0-525-93985-7*) Dutton/Plume.

—The Takeover. 1996. pap. 6.99 (*0-451-18928-0*, Signet Bks.); 448p. mass mkt. 7.99 (*0-451-18478-5*, Onyx) NAL.

—Trust Fund. E-Book 19.95 (*1-58945-513-4*) Adobe Systems, Inc.

—Trust Fund. 2001. E-Book 6.99 (*0-345-44714-X*) Random Hse., Inc.

—Trust Fund. l.t. ed. 2001. 496p. 30.95 (*0-7862-3168-8*) Thorndike Pr.

Goldsmith, Olivia. Pen Pals. 2002. (Illus.). 368p. 24.95 o.s.i (*0-525-94644-6*, Dutton) Dutton/Plume.

—Pen Pals. 2002. 432p. reprint ed. mass mkt. 7.99 (*0-451-20667-3*, Signet Bks.) NAL.

—Pen Pals. l.t. ed. 2002. (Basic Ser.). 716p. 29.95 (*0-7862-4206-X*) Thorndike Pr.

Jennings, Kate. Moral Hazard. 2002. 192p. 21.95 (*0-00-714108-4*) HarperCollins Pubs.

—Moral Hazard. 2003. 192p. pap. 11.95 (*0-00-715462-3*, Fourth Estate) HarperTrade.

—Moral Hazard. 2004. 160p. pap. 22.00 (*0-7434-4218-0*, Washington Square Pr.) Simon & Schuster.

Lasser, Scott. All I Could Get: A Novel. 2003. 256p. pap. 12.00 (*0-375-72787-6*, Vintage) Knopf Publishing Group.

Lathen, Emma. Double, Double Oil & Trouble. 1983. mass mkt. 2.95 o.s.i (*0-671-49990-4*, Pocket); 1978. 8.95 o.s.i (*0-671-24215-6*, Simon & Schuster) Simon & Schuster.

—Going for the Gold. 1981. (General Ser.). lib. bdg. 12.95 o.p. (*0-8161-3200-3*, Macmillan Reference USA) Gale Group.

—Going for the Gold. 1981. 12.95 o.p. (*0-671-41407-0*, Simon & Schuster) Simon & Schuster.

—Green Grow the Dollars. 1982. (General Ser.). lib. bdg. 14.95 o.p. (*0-8161-3397-2*, Macmillan Reference USA) Gale Group.

—Green Grow the Dollars. 1984. mass mkt. 3.95 o.s.i (*0-671-52767-3*, Pocket); 1983. mass mkt. 2.95 o.s.i (*0-671-45049-2*, Pocket); 1982. 12.95 o.p. (*0-671-44130-2*, Simon & Schuster) Simon & Schuster.

—The Longer the Thread. l.t. ed. 1984. (Nightingale Ser.). 328p. pap. 9.95 o.p. (*0-8161-3668-8*, Macmillan Reference USA) Gale Group.

—The Longer the Thread. 1988. 192p. mass mkt. 3.50 (*0-671-65053-X*, Pocket) Simon & Schuster.

—Murder to Go. 1983. mass mkt. 2.95 o.s.i (*0-671-45529-X*, Pocket) Simon & Schuster.

—Sweet & Low. 1983. mass mkt. 2.95 o.s.i (*0-671-45527-3*, Pocket); 1974. 6.95 o.s.i (*0-671-21785-2*, Simon & Schuster) Simon & Schuster.

Maxim, John R. The Shadow Box. 1997. mass mkt. 6.99 (*0-380-78668-0*); 1996. 384p. mass mkt. 23.00 o.p. (*0-380-97300-6*) Morrow/Avon. (Avon Bks.).

Payne, David. Confessions of a Taoist on Wall Street. 1996. pap. 15.00 o.s.i (*0-345-41038-6*); 1985. 864p. mass mkt. 5.99 o.s.i (*0-345-32696-2*) Ballantine Bks.

—Confessions of a Taoist on Wall Street: A Chinese American Romance, 001. 1984. 17.95 o.p. (*0-395-35562-1*) Houghton Mifflin Co.

Reich, Christopher. Numbered Account. 1998. 768p. reprint ed. mass mkt. 7.99 (*0-440-22529-9*) Dell Publishing.

Rhodes, Stephen. The Velocity of Money: A Novel of Wall Street. 1997. 352p. 24.00 (*0-688-15538-3*, Morrow, William & Co.) Morrow/Avon.

Robbins, Harold. Never Enough. 2001. 336p. 25.95 (*0-7653-0000-1*); 2002. reprint ed. mass mkt. 7.99 (*0-7653-4050-X*) Doherty, Tom Assocs., LLC. (Forge Bks.).

Rosenberg, Philip. House of Lords. 2002. 480p. 24.95 (*0-06-019415-4*) HarperCollins Pubs.

—The House of Lords. 2003. 496p. mass mkt. 7.50 (*0-06-109861-2*) HarperCollins Pubs.

Sanders, Lawrence. Three Complete Novels: The Timothy Files, Timothy's Game, Sullivan's Sting. 1999. 784p. 12.98 o.s.i (*0-399-14531-1*) Penguin Group (USA) Inc.

—The Timothy Files. 1988. mass mkt. 7.50 (*0-425-10924-0*) Berkley Publishing Group.

—The Timothy Files. l.t. ed. 1988. (General Ser.). 508p. 19.95 o.p. (*0-8161-4479-6*, Macmillan Reference USA) Gale Group.

—The Timothy Files. 1987. 384p. 18.95 o.p. (*0-399-13261-9*, G. P. Putnam's Sons) Penguin Putnam Bks. for Young Readers.

—Timothy's Game. 1989. 352p. mass mkt. 7.50 (*0-425-11641-7*) Berkley Publishing Group.

—Timothy's Game. l.t. ed. 1989. (General Ser.). 468p. lib. bdg. 19.95 o.p. (*0-8161-4757-4*, Macmillan Reference USA) Gale Group.

—Timothy's Game. 1988. 384p. 18.95 o.p. (*0-399-13368-2*, G. P. Putnam's Sons) Penguin Putnam Bks. for Young Readers.

—Timothy's Game. abr. ed. 1988. audio 14.95 (*0-671-67015-8*, Simon & Schuster Audioworks) Simon & Schuster Audio.

## WALNUT HILLS (CALIF.: IMAGINARY PLACE)—FICTION

Jacobs, Jonnie. Murder among Friends. 2001. 352p. mass mkt. 5.99 (*0-7582-0098-6*); 1996. 352p. mass mkt. 5.99 o.s.i (*1-57566-089-X*, Kensington Bks.); 1995. 304p. mass mkt. 16.95 o.s.i (*0-8217-5030-5*) Kensington Publishing Corp.

—Murder among Neighbors. 304p. 1995. mass mkt. 5.99 (*1-57566-275-2*); 1995. mass mkt. 4.99 o.s.i (*0-8217-5039-9*); 1994. mass mkt. 16.95 o.p. (*0-8217-4680-4*, Zebra Bks.) Kensington Publishing Corp.

—Murder among Strangers. 2000. (Kate Austen Mystery Ser.). 378p. 20.00 o.s.i (*1-57566-540-9*) Kensington Publishing Corp.

—Murder among Us: A Kate Austen Mystery. 1999. 304p. mass mkt. 5.99 (*1-57566-398-8*); 1998. 336p. 20.00 (*1-57566-276-0*) Kensington Publishing Corp.

## WARSAW (POLAND)—FICTION

Egleton, Clive. A Double Deception. 1992. 288p. 18.95 o.p. (*0-312-07736-X*, Saint Martin's Minotaur) St. Martin's Pr.

—A Double Deception. l.t. ed. 1994. (Charnwood Large Print Ser.). 496p. 29.99 o.p. (*0-7089-8769-9*, Ulverscroft) Thorpe, F. A. Pubs. GBR. *Dist:* Ulverscroft Large Print Bks., Ltd., Ulverscroft Large Print Canada, Ltd.

Elberg, Yehuda, tr. from YID. Ship of the Hunted. 1997. (Library of Modern Jewish Literature). 400p. reprint ed. 28.95 (*0-8156-0449-1*) Syracuse Univ. Pr.

Masterson, Graham. The Chosen Child. 2000. 320p. 23.95 o.p. (*0-312-87382-4*, Tor Bks.) Doherty, Tom Assocs., LLC.

Szczypiorski, Andrzej. The Beautiful Mrs. Seidenman. Glowczewska, Klara, tr. from POL. 208p. 1997. pap. 12.00 (*0-8021-3502-1*, Grove Pr.); 1990. 16.95 o.p. (*0-8021-1140-8*) Grove/Atlantic, Inc.

—The Beautiful Mrs. Seidenman. 1991. (Vintage International Ser.). 208p. pap. 9.95 o.s.i (*0-679-73214-4*, Vintage) Knopf Publishing Group.

—The Beautiful Mrs. Seidenman. 1993. 3.49 o.p. (*0-517-11006-7*) Random Hse. Value Publishing.

Uris, Leon. Mila 18. 1983. 576p. mass mkt. 7.99 (*0-553-24160-5*) Bantam Bks.

Wojdowski, Bogdan. Bread for the Departed. Levine, Madeline G., tr. from ENG. 1997. (Jewish Lives Ser.). 304p. 59.95 (*0-8101-1455-0*); pap. 24.00 (*0-8101-1456-9*) Northwestern Univ. Pr.

**WASHINGTON (D.C.)—FICTION**

Abercrombie, Neil & Hoyt, Richard. Blood of Patriots. 1997. 317p. pap. 6.99 (*0-8125-6795-1*); 1996. 352p. 24.95 o.p. (*0-312-86166-4*) Doherty, Tom Assocs., LLC. (Forge Bks.).

Abrahams, Peter. Hard Rain. 1988. 384p. 18.95 o.p. (*0-525-24581-2*, Dutton) Dutton/Plume.

—Hard Rain. 1989. 352p. mass mkt. 4.50 o.p. (*0-451-40113-1*, Onyx) NAL.

Ackerman, Karl. The Patron Saint of Unmarried Women. 1995. pap. 9.95 o.p. (*0-312-13142-9*, Saint Martin's Griffin); 1994. 304p. 20.95 o.p. (*0-312-11037-5*) St. Martin's Pr.

Adams, Henry. Democracy: An American Novel. 2000. 252p. pap. 9.95 (*0-594-04280-1*); E-Book 3.95 (*0-594-04283-6*) 1873 Pr.

—Democracy: An American Novel. 1968. (Airmont Classics Ser.). mass mkt. 2.50 o.p. (*0-8049-0164-3*, CL-164) Airmont Publishing Co., Inc.

—Democracy: An American Novel. Date not set. reprint ed. lib. bdg. 19.95 (*0-89190-525-1*, Queens Hse., Inc.) Amereon, Ltd.

—Democracy: An American Novel, Set. unabr. ed. 1992. audio 35.95 (*1-55685-255-X*) Audio Bk. Contractors, Inc.

—Democracy: An American Novel. 1983. pap. 3.50 o.p. (*0-452-00651-1*, Meridian Bks.); 192p. pap. 12.95 (*0-452-00942-1*, Plume) NAL.

—Democracy: An American Novel. reprint ed. 1988. lib. bdg. 59.00 (*0-7812-1437-8*); 1985. 374p. lib. bdg. 49.00 o.p. (*0-932051-17-0*) Reprint Services Corp.

—Democracy: An American Novel. Katopes, Peter, ed. 1991. 248p. pap. 19.95 (*0-8084-0430-X*) Rowman & Littlefield Pubs., Inc.

—Democracy: An American Novel. 1976. reprint ed. 59.00 (*0-403-05724-8*, Regency Pr.) Scholarly Pr., Inc.

Adkins, Jan E. Deadline for Final Art. 1990. 192p. 18.95 (*0-8027-5759-6*) Walker & Co.

Adler, Warren. American Quartet: A Fiona FitzGerald Mystery. 1982. 13.95 o.p. (*0-87795-365-1*, Morrow, William & Co.) Morrow/Avon.

—American Sextet: A Fiona FitzGerald Mystery. 1983. 256p. 13.95 o.p. (*0-87795-414-3*, Morrow, William & Co.) Morrow/Avon.

—Immaculate Deception: A Fiona FitzGerald Mystery. 1991. 18.95 o.p. (*1-55611-229-7*) Fine, Donald I. Bks.

—Immaculate Deception: A Fiona FitzGerald Mystery. 1992. 288p. mass mkt. 3.99 o.s.i (*0-8217-3935-2*, Zebra Bks.) Kensington Publishing Corp.

—Senator Love: A Fiona FitzGerald Mystery. 1991. 18.95 o.p. (*1-55611-244-0*) Fine, Donald I. Bks.

—Senator Love: A Fiona FitzGerald Mystery. 1992. 256p. reprint ed. mass mkt. 3.99 o.s.i (*0-8217-3998-0*, Zebra Bks.) Kensington Publishing Corp.

—The Ties That Bind: A Fiona FitzGerald Mystery. 1994. 224p. 19.95 o.p. (*1-55611-395-1*) Fine, Donald I. Bks.

—The Ties That Bind: A Fiona FitzGerald Mystery. 2001. E-Book 6.95 (*1-931304-20-3*); E-Book 6.95 (*1-931304-44-0*) Stonehouse Pr.

—The Ties That Bind: A Fiona FitzGerald Mystery. 2001. 0272p. 26.95 (*1-59006-020-2*) Stonehouse Pubns.

—The Witch of Watergate: A Fiona FitzGerald Mystery. 1992. 256p. 19.95 o.p. (*1-55611-296-3*) Fine, Donald I. Bks.

Aellen, Richard. The Cain Conversion. 1993. 21.95 o.p. (*1-55611-348-X*) Fine, Donald I. Bks.

—The Cain Conversion. 1994. 400p. mass mkt. 5.50 o.p. (*0-06-100711-0*, HarperTorch) Morrow/Avon.

—The Cain Conversion. 358p. pap. 4.98 o.p. (*0-7651-0602-7*) Smithmark Pubs., Inc.

Alderson, T. A. Subversion: A Romantic Suspense Story. 2001. 277p. 19.95 (*0-7679-0657-8*) Broadway Bks.

Aldridge, Sarah. Nina in the Wilderness. 1997. 288p. 18.00 (*0-9646648-4-4*); pap. 11.95 (*0-9646648-3-6*) A&M Bks.

Allbeury, Ted. Aid & Comfort. l.t. ed. 1998. (Mystery Ser.). 344p. 27.95 (*0-7838-0175-0*) Thorndike Pr.

Andrews, Donna. Click Here for Murder. 304p. 2004. mass mkt. 6.50 (*0-425-19529-5*); 2003. 22.95 (*0-425-18856-6*, Prime Crime) Berkley Publishing Group.

—You've Got Murder. 304p. 2003. mass mkt. 6.50 (*0-425-18945-7*, Prime Crime); 2002. 21.95 (*0-425-18191-X*) Berkley Publishing Group.

Andrews, Robert. A Murder of Honor. 2001. 304p. 23.95 o.s.i (*0-399-14684-9*, Wood, Marian Bks.) Penguin Group (USA) Inc.

—A Murder of Promise. 2003. 368p. mass mkt. 6.99 (*0-425-18942-2*) Berkley Publishing Group.

—A Murder of Promise. 2002. 384p. 24.95 o.s.i (*0-399-14832-9*, Wood, Marian Bks.) Putnam Publishing Group, The.

Andrews, V. C. Rain. 2000. (Hudson Family Ser.: Vol. 1). 448p. 24.00 (*0-671-00764-5*, Atria); pap. 7.99 (*0-671-00767-X*, Pocket) Simon & Schuster.

—Rain. l.t. ed. 2001. (Core Ser.). 510p. 30.95 (*0-7838-9329-9*) Thorndike Pr.

Archer, Jeffrey. Shall We Tell the President? 1985. 228p. mass mkt. 3.95 o.s.i (*0-449-20806-0*); 1983. mass mkt. 3.50 o.s.i (*0-449-20320-4*); 1982. mass mkt. 2.95 o.s.i (*0-449-20065-5*); 1982. mass mkt. 2.95 o.s.i (*0-449-23686-2*) Ballantine Bks. (Fawcett).

—Shall We Tell the President? l.t. ed. 1987. 415p. 17.95 o.p. (*0-8161-4311-0*, Macmillan Reference USA) Gale Group.

—Shall We Tell the President? 1999. 336p. mass mkt. 6.99 (*0-06-101370-6*) HarperCollins Pubs.

—Shall We Tell the President? 1987. 288p. mass mkt. 5.50 (*0-671-63305-8*, Pocket) Simon & Schuster.

—Shall We Tell the President? 1977. 8.95 o.p. (*0-670-63934-6*) Viking Penguin.

Atherton, Gertrude Franklin Horn. Senator North. 2000. 252p. E-Book 3.95 (*0-594-01842-0*) 1873 Pr.

Baldacci, David. Absolute Power. 1996. 480p. 22.95 o.p. (*0-446-51996-0*); 528p. reprint ed. mass mkt. 7.99 (*0-446-60358-9*) Warner Bks., Inc.

—Saving Faith. l.t. ed. 1999. pap. 25.00 o.p. (*0-7838-8700-0*, Macmillan Reference USA) Gale Group.

—Saving Faith. l.t. ed. 576p. 2000. pap. 13.95 (*0-375-72798-1*); 1999. 26.95 (*0-375-40866-5*) Random Hse. Large Print.

—Saving Faith. 2000. 528p. E-Book 7.95 (*0-446-92868-2*); 2000. 528p. E-Book 7.95 (*0-446-96096-9*); 2000. 528p. E-Book 7.95 (*0-446-92262-5*); 2000. E-Book 7.95 (*0-446-93135-7*, Warner Vision); 2000. 528p. E-Book 7.95 (*0-446-92401-6*); 1999. 464p. 26.95 (*0-446-52577-4*); 1999. 464p. mass mkt. 16.00 (*0-446-67647-0*); 2000. 528p. reprint ed. mass mkt. 7.99 (*0-446-60889-0*) Warner Bks., Inc.

—The Simple Truth. 1999. 680p. (*0-7540-2178-5*) BBC Audiobooks America.

—The Simple Truth. l.t. ed. 2000. (Bestsellers Ser.). 680p. pap. 26.95 (*0-7862-1696-4*) Thorndike Pr.

—The Simple Truth. 1998. 470p. 25.00 o.p. (*0-446-52332-1*); 1999. 544p. reprint ed. mass mkt. 7.99 (*0-446-60771-1*) Warner Bks., Inc.

Baldacci, David, contrib. by. The Simple Truth. (*0-7540-1244-1*) BBC Audiobooks America.

Banks, Carolyn. Mr. Right. 1999. 352p. 25.00 (*0-933256-91-4*) Second Chance Pr.

—Mr. Right. 1979. 9.95 o.p. (*0-670-49318-X*) Viking Penguin.

—Mr. Right. 1980. pap. 2.50 o.s.i (*0-446-91191-7*) Warner Bks., Inc.

Bardi, Abby. The Book of Fred: A Novel. 2001. 304p. 24.00 (*0-7434-1193-5*, Washington Square Pr.) Simon & Schuster.

Barrett, Neal, Jr. Bad Eye Blues, Vol. 1. (Wiley Moss Mystery Ser.). 1999. 352p. mass mkt. 5.99 o.s.i (*1-57566-484-4*); 1997. 288p. 21.95 o.p. (*1-57566-173-X*) Kensington Publishing Corp.

—Skinny Annie Blues. (Wiley Moss Mystery Ser.). 1997. 304p. mass mkt. 5.50 (*1-57566-134-9*); 1996. 256p. 21.95 o.p. (*1-57566-058-X*) Kensington Publishing Corp. (Kensington Bks.).

Bartolomeo, Christina. Cupid & Diana. 1998. (Illus.). 224p. 22.00 (*0-684-83977-6*, Scribner) Simon & Schuster.

—Cupid & Diana. l.t. ed. 1999. (Americana Ser.). 319p. 27.95 (*0-7862-1750-2*) Thorndike Pr.

—Cupid & Diana: A Novel. 1999. 224p. pap. 11.00 (*0-684-85622-0*, Scribner) Simon & Schuster.

—The Side of the Angels: A Novel. 304p. 2003. pap. 13.00 (*0-7432-0462-X*); 2002. 23.00 (*0-7432-0461-1*) Simon & Schuster. (Scribner).

Bayard, Louis. Fool's Errand: A Novel. 1999. 486p. pap. 12.95 o.p. (*1-55583-494-9*) Alyson Pubns.

Beattie, Ann. Chilly Scenes of Winter. 1991. (Vintage Contemporaries Ser.). 288p. pap. 13.00 (*0-679-73234-9*, Vintage) Knopf Publishing Group.

—Chilly Scenes of Winter. 1985. mass mkt. 3.95 o.s.i (*0-446-31343-2*) Warner Bks., Inc.

Beechcroft, William. Pursuit of Fear. 1990. 17.95 o.p. (*0-88184-510-8*, Carroll & Graf Pubs.) Avalon Publishing Group.

—Pursuit of Fear. l.t. ed. 1991. 17.95 o.p. (*0-7451-8094-9*, AH0155); pap. 15.95 o.p. (*0-7927-0600-5*, AS0191) BBC Audiobooks America.

Bell, James Scott. Deadlock. 2004. E-Book 10.99 (*0-310-25612-7*); 2004. E-Book 10.99 (*0-310-25613-5*); 2004. E-Book 10.99 (*0-310-25615-1*); 2003. E-Book 10.99 (*0-310-25614-3*); 2002. 320p. pap. 12.99 (*0-310-24388-2*) Zondervan.

Bennet, Rick. Lost Brother. 1996. 240p. 21.95 (*1-55970-367-9*) Arcade Publishing, Inc.

Benson, Chris. Special Interest. 2003. 288p. pap. 12.95 (*0-345-45727-7*) Ballantine Bks.

—Special Interest. 2001. 300p. pap. 15.95 (*0-88378-230-8*) Third World Press.

Berne, Suzanne. A Crime in the Neighborhood. 1997. 294p. tchr. ed. 17.95 (*1-56512-165-1*, 72165) Algonquin Bks. of Chapel Hill.

—A Crime in the Neighborhood. 1998. pap. (*0-8050-5852-4*); 304p. pap. 13.00 (*0-8050-5580-0*) Holt, Henry & Co. (Owl Bks.).

—A Crime in the Neighborhood. unabr. ed. 2000. audio 58.00 (*0-7887-4456-9*, 96277E7) Recorded Bks., LLC.

Bowen, Kevin. The Third Funeral. 2003. 288p. pap. 12.95 (*1-930892-14-4*) Engage Publishing.

—Wil's Bones. 2000. 256p. pap. 12.95 (*1-930892-12-8*) Engage Publishing.

Bowen, Michael. Collateral Damage. pap. 15.95 (*0-312-29181-7*, Saint Martin's Griffin); 1999. 224p. 22.95 (*0-312-20289-X*, Saint Martin's Minotaur) St. Martin's Pr.

—Corruptly Procured: A Richard Michaelson Mystery. 1994. 256p. 20.95 o.p. (*0-312-10524-X*, Saint Martin's Minotaur) St. Martin's Pr.

—Faithfully Executed. 1991. 240p. 17.95 o.p. (*0-312-07018-7*, Saint Martin's Minotaur) St. Martin's Pr.

—Washington Deceased. 1990. 10.95 o.p. (*0-312-05179-4*, Saint Martin's Minotaur) St. Martin's Pr.

—Worst Case Scenario. 1996. 224p. 24.00 o.s.i (*0-517-70149-9*) Random Hse., Inc.

—Worst Case Scenario: A Washington, D. C. Mystery. l.t. ed. 1997. 257p. 23.95 o.p. (*0-7838-8072-3*, Macmillan Reference USA) Gale Group.

Bradley, John E. Love & Obits. 1992. 276p. 21.95 o.p. (*0-8050-1680-5*) Holt, Henry & Co.

Brandon, Jay. Executive Privilege. (Chris Sinclair Ser.). 2003. mass mkt. 6.99 (*0-8125-7545-8*, Tor Bks.); 2001. 464p. 25.95 (*0-312-87425-1*, Forge Bks.) Doherty, Tom Assocs., LLC.

Branon, Bill. Let Us Prey. 1992. 327p. pap. 12.95 o.s.i (*1-880772-69-8*) Black Seal Pr.

—Let Us Prey. l.t. ed. 1994. 466p. reprint ed. lib. bdg. 24.95 (*0-8161-7432-6*, Macmillan Reference USA) Gale Group.

—Let Us Prey. 1994. 304p. 198.00 o.p. (*0-06-017779-9*) HarperCollins Pubs.

—Let Us Prey. 1994. 304p. 22.00 o.p. (*0-06-017759-4*) HarperTrade.

—Let Us Prey. 1995. 352p. mass mkt. 5.99 o.p. (*0-06-109250-9*, HarperTorch) Morrow/Avon.

—Let Us Prey. 4.98 o.p. (*0-8317-8573-X*) Smithmark Pubs., Inc.

Briscoe, Connie. Big Girls Don't Cry. 1999. 416p. mass mkt. 6.99 (*0-449-00564-X*, Fawcett); 1998. mass mkt. 6.99 (*0-449-00258-6*, Fawcett); 1998. mass mkt. o.s.i (*0-8041-1520-6*, Ivy Bks.); 1997. 384p. pap. 14.00 (*0-345-41362-8*) Ballantine Bks.

—Big Girls Don't Cry. l.t. ed. 1996. 25.95 o.p. (*1-56895-346-1*, Wheeler Publishing, Inc.) Gale Group.

—Big Girls Don't Cry. 1996. 384p. 23.00 o.s.i (*0-06-017277-0*); 207.00 o.p. (*0-06-017473-0*) HarperCollins Pubs.

—Sisters & Lovers. 416p. 1996. pap. 13.95 (*0-345-40969-8*); 1995. mass mkt. 6.99 (*0-8041-1334-3*, Ivy Bks.) Ballantine Bks.

—Sisters & Lovers. 1994. 352p. 22.00 o.p. (*0-06-017116-2*) HarperTrade.

—Sisters & Lovers. l.t. ed. 1997. (Niagara Large Print Ser.). 437p. 29.50 o.p. (*0-7089-5805-2*, Ulverscroft) Thorpe, F. A. Pubs. GBR. *Dist:* Ulverscroft Large Print Bks., Ltd., Ulverscroft Large Print Canada, Ltd.

Brophy, Beth. My Ex-Best Friend. 2003. 256p. 23.00 (*0-7432-4422-2*, Simon & Schuster) Simon & Schuster.

Brossard, Chandler. The Bold Saboteurs. 4th ed. 2001. 362p. reprint ed. pap. 15.00 (*1-928746-18-7*) Herodias.

Brown, Richard E. & Brown, Beverly A. The Rose Engagement. exp. ed. 1996. (Orig.). 205p. (C). pap. text 12.00 (*0-9654000-2-6*); 203p. pap. 12.00 (*0-9654000-1-8*) Kent Information Services, Inc.

Brown, Sandra. Exclusive, Set. unabr. ed. 1999. audio 49.95 Highsmith Inc.

—Exclusive, Set. abr. ed. 1996. 17.95 o.p. (*0-7871-0880-4*, 394140); 49.95 o.p. (*0-7871-0881-2*, 104018) NewStar Media, Inc.

—Exclusive. l.t. ed. 1996. (Basic Ser.). 688p. 28.95 (*0-7862-0698-5*) Thorndike Pr.

—Exclusive. 1996. 464p. 22.95 o.s.i (*0-446-51978-2*); 1997. 496p. reprint ed. mass mkt. 7.99 (*0-446-60423-2*) Warner Bks., Inc.

—Tiger Prince. l.t. ed. 29.95 (*1-58724-251-6*, Wheeler Publishing, Inc.) Gale Group.

—Tiger Prince. 1999. 298p. mass mkt. (*1-55166-531-X*, 1-66531-4, Mira Bks.); 1994. 251p. per. (*1-55166-023-7*, 1-66023-2, Mira Bks.); 1994. mass mkt. (*0-373-48295-7*, 5-48295-5, Silhouette) Harlequin Enterprises, Ltd.

Buckley, Christopher. Little Green Men. 2000. 320p. pap. 13.00 (*0-06-095557-0*, Perennial) HarperTrade.

—The White House Mess. l.t. ed. 1987. 373p. 18.95 o.p. (*0-8161-4194-0*, Macmillan Reference USA) Gale Group.

Buckley, William F., Jr. Mongoose R. I. P. A Blackford Oakes Novel. 1998. (Blackford Oakes Novel Ser.). 376p. reprint ed. pap. 12.95 (*1-888952-72-5*) Cumberland Hse. Publishing.

—Mongoose R. I. P. A Blackford Oakes Novel. 1993. 4.99 o.p. (*0-517-10701-5*) Random Hse. Value Publishing.

Callahan, David. State of the Union. 1997. 384p. 23.95 o.p. (*0-316-12490-7*) Little Brown & Co.

—State of the Union. 1998. 416p. mass mkt. 6.99 o.s.i (*0-451-19725-9*, Signet Bks.) NAL.

Cannell, Stephen J. The Plan. 1996. 464p. mass mkt. 7.99 (*0-380-72754-4*, Avon Bks.); 1995. 420p. 23.00 (*0-688-14046-7*, Morrow, William & Co.) Morrow/Avon.

—The Plan. abr. ed. 1995. 24.95 o.p. (*0-7871-0444-2*, 692957) NewStar Media, Inc.

Card, C. J. One Wish. 1998. (Magical Love Ser.: Vol. 4). 320p. mass mkt. 5.99 o.s.i (*0-515-12354-4*, Jove) Berkley Publishing Group.

Carroll, James. Firebird. 1989. 18.95 o.p. (*0-525-24726-2*, Dutton) Dutton/Plume.

—Firebird. l.t. ed. 1989. (General Ser.). 592p. lib. bdg. 20.95 o.p. (*0-8161-4845-7*, Macmillan Reference USA) Gale Group.

—Firebird. 1990. mass mkt. 5.95 o.p. (*0-451-16289-7*, Signet Bks.) NAL.

Case, John. The Eighth Day. E-Book (*0-345-45872-9*); 2002. 384p. 25.95 (*0-345-43309-2*) Ballantine Bks.

—The Eighth Day. 2003. (Basic Ser.). 29.95 (*0-7862-5130-1*) Thorndike Pr.

Cashdan, Linda. Special Interests. 1990. 18.95 o.p. (*0-312-04426-7*) St. Martin's Pr.

Chambers, Christopher. A Prayer for Deliverance: An Angela Bivens Thriller. 2003. 352p. 23.00 (*0-609-60850-9*, Crown) Crown Publishing Group.

Chase, Jack. Fatal Analysis. 1996. 368p. mass mkt. 5.99 o.s.i (*0-451-18764-4*, Signet Bks.) NAL.

Clancy, Tom. Clear & Present Danger. 704p. 1994. mass mkt. 7.50 o.s.i (*0-425-14437-2*); 1990. mass mkt. 7.99 (*0-425-12212-3*) Berkley Publishing Group.

—Clear & Present Danger. l.t. ed. 1990. (Magna Large Print Ser.). 1140p. o.p. (*1-85057-853-2*) Magna Large Print Bks. GBR. *Dist:* Ulverscroft Large Print Canada, Ltd.

—Clear & Present Danger. 1989. 544p. 27.95 (*0-399-13440-9*, G. P. Putnam's Sons) Penguin Putnam Bks. for Young Readers.

—Clear & Present Danger. 1990. 13.09 o.p. (*0-606-00980-9*) Turtleback Bks.

—Peligro Imminente. 6th ed. 1998. (Jet de Plaza & Janes Ser.: Vol. 150). Orig. Title: Clear & Present Danger. (SPA., Illus.). 617p. pap. 8.50 (*84-01-49525-3*) Plaza & Janés Editories, S.A. ESP. *Dist:* Lectorum Pubns., Inc.

Clark, Mary Higgins. Stillwatch. E-Book 9.95 (*1-930161-32-8*) Adobe Systems, Inc.

—Stillwatch. 1991. reprint ed. lib. bdg. 31.95 (*1-56849-070-4*) Buccaneer Bks., Inc.

—Stillwatch. 1992. mass mkt. o.s.i (*0-440-80340-3*); 1986. 368p. mass mkt. 6.99 o.s.i (*0-440-18305-7*) Dell Publishing.

—Stillwatch. l.t. ed. 1985. (General Ser.). 15.95 o.p. (*0-8161-3694-7*, Macmillan Reference USA) Gale Group.

—Stillwatch. 2000. E-Book 9.95 (*0-7432-0615-0*, Simon & Schuster); 1997. 368p. pap. 7.99 (*0-671-52820-3*, Pocket); 1984. 14.70 o.p. (*0-671-46952-5*, Simon & Schuster) Simon & Schuster.

—Stillwatch. 1997. 14.04 (*0-606-11914-0*) Turtleback Bks.

Clarke, Breena. River, Cross My Heart. 2000. 272p. mass mkt. 7.50 (*0-316-89816-3*) Hyperion Pr.

—River, Cross My Heart. 2000. 288p. E-Book 6.95 (*0-7595-0007-X*); 2000. 288p. E-Book 6.95 (*0-7595-8007-3*); 1999. 288p. 23.00 o.p. (*0-316-89999-2*); 1999. 256p. pap. 14.95 (*0-316-89998-4*) Little Brown & Co.

—River, Cross My Heart. 1999. 224p. 23.00 (*0-316-14423-1*) Little Brown Children's Bks.

—River, Cross My Heart. l.t. ed. 2000. (Thorndike General Ser.). 341p. pap. 28.95 (*0-7862-2432-0*); 30.95 (*0-7862-2431-2*) Thorndike Pr.

—River, Cross My Heart. 1999. 20.50 (*0-606-19030-9*) Turtleback Bks.

—River, Cross My Heart. 2000. 288p. E-Book 6.95 (*0-7595-9007-9*) Warner Bks., Inc.

Clements, Mark A. Lorelei. 1995. 304p. pap. 4.99 (*0-8439-3867-6*) Dorchester Publishing Co., Inc.

—Lorelei. 1994. 304p. 20.95 o.p. (*1-55611-410-9*) Fine, Donald I. Bks.

—Lorelei. 1995. E-Book 9.95 (*0-585-28857-7*) netLibrary, Inc.

Cohen, William S. Murder in the Senate, Vol. 1. 1994. mass mkt. 5.50 o.p. (*0-312-95319-4*, St. Martin's Paperbacks) St. Martin's Pr.

Collins, Max Allan. Majic Man. 1999. 304p. 23.95 o.p. (*0-525-94515-6*) Dutton/Plume.

—Majic Man. 2000. (Nathan Heller Ser.). 384p. mass mkt. 5.99 o.s.i (*0-451-19945-6*, Signet Bks.) NAL.

—Majic Man. l.t. ed. 2000. (Basic Ser.). 527p. 28.95 (*0-7862-2529-7*) Thorndike Pr.

Colson, Charles & Vaughn, Ellen S. Gideon's Torch: A Novel. 544p. 1996. pap. 12.99 (*0-8499-3977-1*); 1995. 21.99 o.p. (*0-8499-1146-X*) W Publishing Group.

Compton, David. Impaired Judgment. 2000. 352p. 24.95 o.s.i (*0-525-94457-5*) Dutton/Plume.

Conroy, Richard Timothy. Mr. Smithson's Bones. 1993. 208p. 17.95 o.p. (0-312-09341-1, Saint Martin's Minotaur) St. Martin's Pr.
—Old Ways in the New World. 1994. 320p. 21.95 o.p. (0-312-11038-3, Saint Martin's Minotaur) St. Martin's Pr.
—Smithsonian Snafu: A Mystery. 1992. 272p. 18.95 o.p. (0-312-07807-2, Saint Martin's Minotaur) St. Martin's Pr.
Coonts, Stephen. America: A Jake Grafton Novel. 2001. 390p. 25.95 (0-312-25341-9) St. Martin's Pr.
—America: A Jake Grafton Novel. l.t. ed. 2001. 657p. 31.95 (0-7862-3641-8); 28.95 (0-7862-3645-0) Thorndike Pr.
—Liberty. l.t. ed. 2003. 688p. 32.95 (1-58724-442-X, Wheeler Publishing, Inc.) Gale Group.
—Liberty. 2004. 544p. mass mkt. 7.99 (0-312-98970-9); 2003. mass mkt. 7.99 (0-312-99062-6) St. Martin's Pr. (St. Martin's Paperbacks).
—Liberty: A Jake Grafton Novel. 2003. (Jake Grafton Novels Ser.). 352p. 25.95 (0-312-28361-X) St. Martin's Pr.
—The Minotaur. unabr. ed. 1990. audio 88.00 (0-7366-1830-9, 2666) Books on Tape, Inc.
—The Minotaur. 448p. 1993. mass mkt. 3.99 o.s.i (0-440-21517-X); 1990. mass mkt. 7.99 (0-440-20742-8) Dell Publishing.
—The Minotaur. 1989. 18.95 o.s.i (0-385-26736-3) Doubleday Publishing.
—The Minotaur. l.t. ed. 1991. (Magna Large Print Ser.). 719p. o.p. (0-7505-0042-5) Magna Large Print Bks. GBR. Dist: Ulverscroft Large Print Canada, Ltd.
—The Minotaur. 1993. 4.99 o.p. (0-517-09881-4) Random Hse. Value Publishing.
—Under Siege. unabr. ed. 1991. audio 96.00 (0-7366-1906-2, 2732) Books on Tape, Inc.
—Under Siege. 1990. audio 12.79 o.s.i (0-553-19958-7); audio 15.99 o.s.i (0-553-45264-9) Random Hse. Audio Publishing Group. (RH Audio).
—Under Siege. 2002. 544p. mass mkt. 7.99 (0-7434-5720-X, Pocket) Simon & Schuster.
—Under Siege. McCarthy, Paul, ed. 1991. 544p. mass mkt. 7.99 (0-671-74294-9, Pocket); 1990. 416p. 19.95 o.p. (0-671-72229-8, Atria) Simon & Schuster.
Corn, David. Deep Background. 2000. E-Book 25.95 (0-312-26829-7) St. Martin's Pr.
Coulter, Catherine. Hemlock Bay. 2001. 300p. 23.95 o.s.i (0-399-14800-0) Penguin Group (USA) Inc.
—Hemlock Bay. 2001. 432p. 24.95 o.p. (0-399-14738-1) Putnam Publishing Group, The.
—Hemlock Bay. l.t. ed. 2001. 496p. 24.95 (0-375-43115-2) Random Hse. Large Print.
Cresswell, Jasmine. Dead Ringer. 2003. 400p. mass mkt. (1-55166-712-6, Mira Bks.) Harlequin Enterprises, Ltd.
Crider, Bill, et al. White House Horrors. Greenberg, Martin H., ed. 1996. 320p. mass mkt. 5.99 o.s.i (0-88677-659-7) DAW Bks., Inc.
Crittenden, Danielle. Amanda Bright @ Home: A Novel. 2003. 336p. 23.95 (0-446-53074-3) Warner Bks., Inc.
—Amanda Bright@Home. l.t. ed. 2003. 456p. 28.95 (0-7862-5685-0) Thorndike Pr.
—Amanda Bright@Home. 2004. (0-446-69246-8) Warner Bks., Inc.
Crosland, Susan. Dangerous Games. 1993. 3.99 o.p. (0-517-09793-1) Random Hse. Value Publishing.
Cullen, Robert. Heirs of the Fire. 1998. 357p. mass mkt. 6.99 o.s.i (0-8041-1445-5, Ivy Bks.); 1997. 368p. 23.00 o.p. (0-449-00025-7, Fawcett) Ballantine Bks.
Daheim, Mary R. Suture Self. 2002. 352p. mass mkt. 6.99 (0-380-81561-3, Avon Bks.) Morrow/Avon.
Dalton, James. City of Shadows. 2002. 480p. pap. 6.99 (0-8125-8957-2, Tor Bks.); 2000. 384p. 25.95 (0-312-87643-2, Forge Bks.) Doherty, Tom Assocs., LLC.
Darnton, John. The Experiment. 1999. 416p. 24.95 o.p. (0-525-94517-2) Dutton/Plume.
—The Experiment. l.t. ed. 2000. 26.95 (1-56895-819-6, Wheeler Publishing, Inc.) Gale Group.
—The Experiment. 2000. 496p. mass mkt. 6.99 (0-451-20010-1, Signet Bks.) NAL.
David, Peter. One Knight Only. 2003. 384p. 23.95 (0-441-01057-1) Ace Bks.
Davis, Patrick A. The General. 1999. 416p. reprint ed. mass mkt. 6.99 (0-425-16804-2) Berkley Publishing Group.
—The General. abr. ed. 1999. audio 7.99 (1-56740-284-4, 1749, Paperback Nova Audio Bks.); 1998. audio 26.95 (1-56740-063-9, 1213, Bookcassette); 1998. 10p. audio 73.25 (1-56740-592-4, 1214, Unabridged Library Editions); Set. 1998. audio 17.95 o.p. (1-56740-788-9, 524, Nova Audio Bks.) Brilliance Audio.
—The General. 1998. 352p. 23.95 o.p. (0-399-14411-0, G. P. Putnam's Sons) Penguin Group (USA) Inc.
Dean, Maureen. Capitol Secrets. 1992. 288p. 21.95 o.p. (0-399-13660-6, G. P. Putnam's Sons) Penguin Group (USA) Inc.
—Washington Wives. 1987. 416p. 17.95 o.p. (0-87795-721-5, Morrow, William & Co.) Morrow/Avon.
Deaver, Jeffery. Die Tranen des Teufels. 2003. (GER.). 448p. pap. 23.00 (1-4000-5510-5) Random Hse. Information Group.
Deutermann, P. T. Firefly. abr. ed. 2004. audio 12.99 (1-59086-117-5, 3691, Brilliance Audio Paperback Audiobooks); 2003. audio 24.95 (1-59086-116-7, 3690); 2003. audio compact disk 74.25 (1-59086-868-4, 4500, Brilliance Audio on CD Lib Ed); 2003. audio compact disk 26.95 (1-59086-867-6, 4499, Brilliance Audio on CD); 2003. audio 102.25 (1-59086-115-9, 3689, Brilliance Audio Unabridged Lib Ed); 2003. audio 34.95 (1-59086-114-0, 3688, Brilliance Audio Unabridged) Brilliance Audio.
—Firefly. Date not set. mass mkt. (0-312-99481-8, St. Martin's Paperbacks) St. Martin's Pr.
—The Firefly: A Novel. 2003. 352p. 24.95 (0-312-20377-2) St. Martin's Pr.
—Hunting Season. 2001. 402p. 24.95 (0-312-26979-X) St. Martin's Pr.
Dezenhall, Eric. Money Wanders. E-Book 13.95 (0-312-70428-3); 2002. 338p. 24.95 (0-312-28275-3) St. Martin's Pr.
Dinallo, Greg. Final Answers. 1993. 336p. mass mkt. 5.50 (0-671-73312-5, Pocket) Simon & Schuster.
—Final Answers. Grose, Ed & Grad, Doug, eds. 1992. 320p. 20.00 (0-671-73311-7, Atria) Simon & Schuster.
Dixon, Collen. Simon Says: A Novel of Intrigue, Betrayal... And Murder. 2003. 336p. pap. 12.95 (0-8129-6881-6, Villard Bks.) Random House Adult Trade Publishing Group.
Douglas, John E. Man Down: A Broken Wings Thriller. 2002. 336p. 24.00 (0-671-02392-6, Atria) Simon & Schuster.
Douglas, John E. & Olshaker, Mark. Broken Wings. l.t. ed. 2000. (G. K. Hall Core Ser.). 570p. 29.95 (0-7838-9027-3, Macmillan Reference USA) Gale Group.
—Broken Wings. 1999. 336p. 24.00 o.s.i (0-671-02391-8, Atria); 2001. 384p. reprint ed. pap. 7.99 (0-671-00395-X, Pocket) Simon & Schuster.
Drury, Allen. Advise & Consent. 1991. lib. bdg. 54.95 (1-56849-060-7) Buccaneer Bks., Inc.
—Advise & Consent. 1959. 16.95 o.s.i (0-385-05419-X) Doubleday Publishing.
—Preserve & Protect. 1968. 14.95 o.p. (0-385-01030-3) Doubleday Publishing.
—Preserve & Protect. l.t. ed. 1999. 690p. 34.95 (1-56000-471-1) Transaction Pubs.
Duarte, Stella Pope. Let Their Spirits Dance. 2003. 336p. pap. 12.95 (0-06-008948-2, Rayo) HarperTrade.
—Let Their Spirits Dance: A Novel. 2002. 336p. 24.95 (0-06-018637-2, Rayo) HarperTrade.
Elam, Patricia. Breathing Room. 2001. (Illus.). 352p. 24.95 (0-671-02842-1, Atria) Simon & Schuster.
Ellison, Ralph. Juneteenth: A Novel. 2000. (International Ser.). 400p. pap. 14.00 (0-375-70754-9, Vintage) Knopf Publishing Group.
—Juneteenth: A Novel. Callahan, John F., ed. 1999. xxiii, 368p. 25.00 o.s.i (0-394-46457-5) Random Hse., Inc.
English, Brenda H. Corruption of Faith. 1997. 272p. mass mkt. 5.99 o.s.i (0-425-16091-2, Prime Crime) Berkley Publishing Group.
—Corruption of Justice. 1999. 272p. mass mkt. 5.99 o.s.i (0-425-16811-5, Prime Crime) Berkley Publishing Group.
—Corruption of Power. 1998. (Sutton McPhee Mystery Ser.). 288p. mass mkt. 5.99 o.s.i (0-425-16398-9, Prime Crime) Berkley Publishing Group.
Estaver, Paul. His Third, Her Second. 1993. 2.99 o.p. (0-517-10833-X) Random Hse. Value Publishing.
—His Third, Her Second. 245p. 1990. pap. 9.95 o.p. (0-939149-45-1); 1989. 17.95 o.p. (0-939149-25-7) Soho Pr., Inc.
Everett, Percival. Erasure: A Novel. 2002. 304p. pap. 14.95 (0-7868-8815-6) Hyperion Pr.
—Erasure: A Novel. 2001. 277p. text 26.00 (1-58465-090-7) Univ. Pr. of New England.
Faulks, Sebastian. On Green Dolphin Street: A Novel. 2003. 368p. pap. 14.00 (0-375-70456-6, Vintage) Knopf Publishing Group.
—On Green Dolphin Street: A Novel. 2002. 368p. 24.95 (0-375-50225-4) Random Hse., Inc.
Fishkin, Shelley Fisher, ed. The Gilded Age (1873) 1996. (Oxford Mark Twain Ser.). (Illus.). 720p. 19.95 o.p. (0-19-510134-0) Oxford Univ. Pr., Inc.
Flynn, Vince. Separation of Power. l.t. ed. 2002. (Wheeler Large Print Book Ser.). 29.95 (1-58724-196-X, Wheeler Publishing, Inc.) Gale Group.
—Separation of Power. 2002. 368p. E-Book 25.00 (0-7434-4922-3, Atria); 2001. 368p. 25.00 (0-671-04733-7, Atria); 2001. 368p. 25.00 (0-7434-4837-5, Atria); 2002. (Illus.). 448p. reprint ed. mass mkt. 7.99 (0-671-04734-5, Pocket) Simon & Schuster.
—Term Limits. 1997. ix, 363p. 24.00 (0-9658510-0-1) Cloak & Dagger Pr., Inc.
—Term Limits. l.t. ed. 2003. 651p. 29.95 (0-7862-5873-X) Gale Group.
—Term Limits. (0-671-02539-2, Atria); 2001. 656p. E-Book 9.99 (0-7434-4923-1, Atria); 1999. (Illus.). 656p. mass mkt. 7.99 (0-671-02318-7, Pocket Star); 1998. 416p. 23.00 (0-671-02317-9, Atria) Simon & Schuster.
—Term Limits. 2002. pap. 14.95 incl. audio (0-7435-2750-X, Encore); 1998. 24.00 incl. audio (0-671-58225-9, Simon & Schuster Audioworks) Simon & Schuster Audio.
—Term Limits. 1999. 13.04 (0-606-19064-3) Turtleback Bks.
—The Third Option. 2001. 368p. E-Book 9.99 (0-7434-5158-9, Atria); 2000. 368p. 24.95 (0-671-04731-0, Atria); 2001. (Illus.). 432p. reprint ed. mass mkt. 7.99 (0-671-04732-9, Pocket Star) Simon & Schuster.
—Transfer of Power. 2001. 416p. E-Book 9.99 (0-7434-4924-X, Atria); 1999. (Illus.). 395p. pap. 24.00 (0-671-02319-5, Atria); 2000. (Illus.). 592p. reprint ed. mass mkt. 7.99 (0-671-02320-9, Pocket Star) Simon & Schuster.
—Transfer of Power. 2003. audio 14.95 (0-7435-3253-8, Encore); 2003. audio compact disk 14.95 (0-7435-3271-6, Encore); 1999. (Illus.). 416p. audio 24.00 o.s.i (0-671-04562-8, Simon & Schuster Audioworks) Simon & Schuster Audio.
—Transfer of Power. l.t. ed. 2004. 751p. 29.95 (0-7862-5872-1) Thorndike Pr.
Ford, Susan. Double Exposure. 2003. 320p. mass mkt. 6.99 (0-312-98827-3, St. Martin's Paperbacks) St. Martin's Pr.
—Sharp Focus: A First Daughter Mystery. 2003. 320p. 24.95 (0-312-28499-3, Saint Martin's Minotaur) St. Martin's Pr.
Ford, Susan & Hayden, Laura. Double Exposure. 2002. 240p. 23.95 (0-312-28471-3, Saint Martin's Minotaur) St. Martin's Pr.
Forrest, Katherine V. Liberty Square: A Kate Delafield Mystery. (Kate Delafield Mystery Ser.). 256p. 2000. pap. 13.00 o.s.i (0-425-17675-4); 1997. mass mkt. 5.99 o.s.i (0-425-15899-3); 1996. 21.95 o.s.i (0-425-15467-X) Berkley Publishing Group. (Prime Crime).
Frank, Jeffrey. The Columnist. 2002. (Harvest Book Ser.). 240p. reprint ed. pap. 13.00 (0-15-601198-0, Harvest Bks.) Harcourt Trade Pubs.
—The Columnist. 2001. (Illus.). 240p. 22.00 (0-7432-1253-3, Simon & Schuster) Simon & Schuster.
Freemantle, Brian. No Time for Heroes. l.t. ed. 1995. 648p. lib. bdg. 24.95 o.p. (0-7838-1276-0, Macmillan Reference USA) Gale Group.
—No Time for Heroes. 1996. 472p. mass mkt. 6.99 (0-312-95927-3, St. Martin's Paperbacks); 1995. 23.95 o.p. (0-312-11866-X) St. Martin's Pr.
Frey, Stephen. The Takeover. 1995. 400p. 19.95 o.p. (0-525-93985-7) Dutton/Plume.
—The Takeover. 1996. pap. 6.99 (0-451-18928-0, Signet Bks.); 448p. mass mkt. 7.99 (0-451-18478-5, Onyx) NAL.
—Trust Fund. E-Book 19.95 (1-58945-513-4) Adobe Systems, Inc.
—Trust Fund. 2001. E-Book 6.99 (0-345-44714-X) Random Hse., Inc.
—Trust Fund. l.t. ed. 2001. 496p. 30.95 (0-7862-3168-8) Thorndike Pr.
Friedlander, Mark P., Jr. & Kenny, Robert W. The Shakespeare Transcripts. 1993. 275p. 24.95 (0-918024-94-3) Ox Bow Pr.
Fullilove, Eric James. Blowback. 2001. 304p. 24.00 (0-06-621250-2, Amistad Pr.) HarperTrade.
Gaffney, Patricia. The Saving Graces. unabr. ed. 2000. audio 84.95 (0-7927-2344-9, CSL 233, Chivers Sound Library) BBC Audiobooks America.
—The Saving Graces. l.t. ed. 1999. 27.95 (1-56895-785-8, Wheeler Publishing, Inc.) Gale Group.
—The Saving Graces. 2000. pap. (0-06-099592-0); 2000. 528p. mass mkt. 7.99 (0-06-109710-1); 1999. 400p. 24.00 (0-06-019192-9) HarperCollins Pubs.
—The Saving Graces. abr. ed. 1999. audio 25.95 (0-375-40714-6, RH Audio) Random Hse. Audio Publishing Group.
Garnett, Griffin T. The Sandscrapers: A Forgotten Navy. Pruett, Robert H., ed. 1995. (Illus.). 432p. pap. 14.95 o.p. (1-883911-03-6) Brandylane Pubs., Inc.
—The Sandscrapers: A Forgotten Navy. 2nd ed. 1996. 432p. pap. 15.95 o.p. (1-883911-10-9) Brandylane Pubs., Inc.
—The Sandscrapers: A Forgotten Navy. 1999. 394p. pap. 17.95 (0-7414-0177-0) Buy Bks. on the Web.Com.
—The Sandscrapers: A Forgotten Navy. 2003. (Illus.). 420p. pap. 17.95 (1-929381-20-4, Third Millennium Publishing) Sci Fi-Arizona, Inc.
—Taboo Avenged. 1997. 320p. pap. 14.95 (1-883911-16-8) Brandylane Pubs., Inc.
Gifford, Thomas. Saints Rest. 1997. 448p. mass mkt. 6.99 o.s.i (0-553-57226-1) Bantam Bks.
—Saint's Rest. 1997. 448p. pap. 23.00 (0-553-76269-9, Crimeline) Bantam Bks.
Golden, Marita. Long Distance Life. 1999. mass mkt. 6.99 (0-345-36711-1); 1992. 336p. pap. 19.00 o.s.i (0-345-37616-1) Ballantine Bks.
—Long Distance Life. 1989. 336p. 18.95 o.s.i (0-385-19455-2) Doubleday Publishing.
—Long Distance Life. l.t. ed. 1990. (Large Print Bks.). 373p. lib. bdg. 19.95 o.p. (0-8161-5005-2, Macmillan Reference USA) Gale Group.
Goldstein, Frank R. Mournful Numbers. 1995. 129p. 15.95 o.p. (1-880664-08-9) E. M. Productions.
Goodrum, Charles. The Best Cellar: A Werner-Bok Library Mystery. 1988. 288p. reprint ed. mass mkt. 3.95 o.p. (0-06-080931-0, P 931, Perennial) HarperTrade.
—Carnage of the Realm: A Werner-Bok Library Mystery. 1988. 240p. reprint ed. mass mkt. 3.95 o.p. (0-06-080932-9, Perennial) HarperTrade.
—Dewey Decimated: A Werner-Bok Library Mystery. 1988. 304p. reprint ed. mass mkt. 3.95 o.p. (0-06-080933-7, P 933, Perennial) HarperTrade.
—A Slip of the Tong. 1992. 192p. 16.95 o.p. (0-312-07806-4); Vol. 1. 1958. 17.95 o.p. (0-312-08296-7) St. Martin's Pr. (Saint Martin's Minotaur).
Goodrum, Charles A. The Best Cellar: Murder & Mystery at the Werner-Bok Library. 1987. 160p. 13.95 o.p. (0-312-00008-1) St. Martin's Pr.
—Carnage of the Realm. 1988. 1.99 o.p. (0-517-53504-1) Random Hse. Value Publishing.
Goodwin, Stephen. Breaking Her Fall. 416p. 2004. pap. (0-15-602969-3, Harvest Bks.); 2003. 24.00 (0-15-100806-X) Harcourt Trade Pubs.
Gorman, Ed. The First Lady. 1995. 320p. 23.95 o.s.i (0-312-85777-2, Forge Bks.) Doherty, Tom Assocs., LLC.
—First Lady, Vol. 1. 1996. 370p. pap. text 6.99 o.p. (0-8125-5041-2, Forge Bks.) Doherty, Tom Assocs., LLC.
—Senatorial Privilege. 1999. 382p. mass mkt. 6.99 (0-8125-5042-0); 1997. 384p. 23.95 (0-312-85778-0) Doherty, Tom Assocs., LLC. (Forge Bks.).
Grady, James. Thunder. 1994. 400p. 21.95 o.s.i (0-446-51765-8) Warner Bks., Inc.
—White Flame. 1999. 320p. pap. 5.99 o.p. (0-7871-1420-0); 1996. 304p. 22.95 o.p. (0-7871-0903-7); Set. 1996. 24.95 o.p. (0-7871-0876-6, 628198) NewStar Media, Inc.
Greeley, Andrew M. The Bishop in the West Wing: A Blackie Ryan Story. l.t. ed. 2003. lib. bdg. 28.95 (1-58547-280-8, Platinum) Ctr. Point Large Print.
—The Bishop in the West Wing: A Blackie Ryan Story. E-Book 24.95 (0-312-70724-X, Tor Bks.); 2002. (Illus.). 288p. 24.95 (0-312-86873-1, Forge Bks.); 2003. (Illus.). 320p. reprint ed. mass mkt. 6.99 (0-8125-7598-9, Forge Bks.) Doherty, Tom Assocs., LLC.
Green, Tim. The First 48. 2004. 336p. 24.95 (0-446-53144-8) Warner Bks., Inc.
Greenberg, Martin H. Danger in D. C. Cat Crimes in the Nation's Capital. Gorman, Ed, ed. 1995. mass mkt. 5.99 o.s.i (0-8041-1277-0, Ivy Bks.) Ballantine Bks.
Greenberg, Martin H. & Gorman, Ed, eds. Danger in D. C. Cat Crimes in the Nation's Capital. 1993. 272p. 20.00 o.p. (1-55611-374-9) Fine, Donald I. Bks.
Griffith, Patricia B. Supporting the Sky. 1999. 288p. reprint ed. text 24.00 (0-7881-6631-X) DIANE Publishing Co.
—Supporting the Sky. 1996. 289p. 23.95 o.s.i (0-399-14128-6, G. P. Putnam's Sons) Penguin Group (USA) Inc.
Griffiths, John. The Presidential Archives. 1996. 384p. 23.00 (0-7867-0316-4, Carroll & Graf Pubs.) Avalon Publishing Group.
Grisham, John. The Street Lawyer. 1999. 464p. mass mkt. 7.99 (0-440-22570-1) Dell Publishing.
—The Street Lawyer. 1998. 352p. 27.95 (0-385-49099-2); 464p. 32.95 o.s.i (0-385-49100-X); 250.00 o.s.i (0-385-49101-8) Doubleday Publishing.
—The Street Lawyer, Level 4. 2001. pap. 7.66 (0-582-43404-1) Longman Publishing Group.
—The Street Lawyer. abr. ed. 1998. audio compact disk 29.95 (0-553-45571-0, RH Audio) Random Hse. Audio Publishing Group.
—The Street Lawyer. 1999. 14.04 (0-606-16227-5) Turtleback Bks.
Gross, Martin. Man of Destiny. 1997. 384p. mass mkt. 24.00 o.p. (0-380-97417-7, Avon Bks.) Morrow/Avon.
Grossman, Richard. The Alphabet Man: A Novel. 1993. 443p. 22.95 o.p. (0-932511-76-7); pap. 11.95 (0-932511-77-5) Fiction Collective Two, Inc.
Haddock, Richard. Arkalalah. 2002. 293p. pap. 16.95 (0-595-21522-X, Writers Club Pr.) iUniverse, Inc.
Haig, Brian. The Kingmaker. l.t. ed. 2003. lib. bdg. 29.95 (1-58547-312-X, Platinum) Ctr. Point Large Print.
—The Kingmaker. 2003. 496p. mass mkt. 6.99 (0-446-61290-1); 400p. 22.95 (0-446-53055-7) Warner Bks., Inc.
—Private Sector. 2003. 448p. 24.95 (0-446-53178-2) Warner Bks., Inc.

Hand, Elizabeth. Waking the Moon. Date not set. (0-06-105323-6) HarperCollins Pubs.

—Waking the Moon. 1996. 512p. mass mkt. 6.99 (0-06-105443-7); 1995. 80p. mass mkt. 19.00 o.p. (0-06-105214-0) Morrow/Avon. (Eos).

Hare, Neil. An Animal Cries. 1998. 250p. 27.50 (0-9653869-2-9) Castle Pacific Publishing.

Harrison, Richard C. Grass Roots. 1999. (Illus.). 318p. pap. 12.95 (1-891929-12-7) Four Seasons Pubs.

Haywood, Gar Anthony. Bad News Travels Fast. 1996. mass mkt. 5.99 o.s.i (0-425-15464-5) Berkley Publishing Group.

—Bad News Travels Fast. abr. ed. 1996. audio 7.99 o.p. (1-56740-122-8, 623, Paperback Nova Audio Bks.); 1995. audio 16.95 o.p. (1-56100-424-3, 1147, Nova Audio Bks.); 1995. audio 23.95 o.p. (1-56100-636-X, 36, Bookcassette); 1995. audio 57.25 o.p. (1-56100-261-5, 800, Unabridged Library Editions) Brilliance Audio.

—Bad News Travels Fast. 1995. 240p. 21.95 o.p. (0-399-14017-4, G. P. Putnam's Sons) Penguin Group (USA) Inc.

—Bad News Travels Fast. l.t. ed. 1996. (Niagara Large Print Ser.). 139p. 29.50 o.p. (0-7089-5837-0, Ulverscroft) Thorpe, F. A. Pubs. GBR. *Dist:* Ulverscroft Large Print Bks., Ltd.

Heggan, Christine. Suspicion. 1997. 378p. per. (1-55166-305-8, 0-66305-4, Mira Bks.) Harlequin Enterprises, Ltd.

Heller, Jean. Maximum Impact. 1995. 627p. pap. 5.99 (0-8125-1619-2); 1993. 432p. 22.95 o.p. (0-312-85203-7) Doherty, Tom Assocs., LLC. (Forge Bks.).

Hendricks, Judith Ryan. Bread Alone: A Novel. 2002. 368p. pap. 13.95 (0-06-008440-5, Perennial) HarperTrade.

Herron, Carolivia. Thereafter Johnnie. 2002. pap. 15.54 (0-7596-1485-7) 1stBooks Library.

—Thereafter Johnnie. 1992. (Vintage Contemporaries Ser.). pap. 10.00 o.s.i (0-679-74188-7, Vintage) Knopf Publishing Group.

Hill, Grace Livingston. Marigold. 299p. reprint ed. lib. bdg. 23.95 (0-89190-056-X, Rivercity Pr.) Amereon, Ltd.

—Marigold, No. 15. 1984. pap. 2.50 o.p. (0-553-23805-1) Bantam Bks.

—Marigold. l.t. ed. 2000. (Romance Ser.). 381p. 26.95 o.p. (0-7862-3022-3) Thorndike Pr.

—Marigold, No. 15. 1990. (Grace Livingston Hill Ser.: Vol. 15). 249p. mass mkt. 3.95 o.p. (0-8423-4037-8) Tyndale Hse. Pubs.

Hoopes, Roy. Our Man in Washington. 2001. 512p. mass mkt. 7.99 (0-8125-7562-8); 2000. 380p. 24.95 (0-312-86849-9) Doherty, Tom Assocs., LLC. (Forge Bks.).

—A Watergate Tape. E-Book 24.95 (0-312-70650-2, Tor Bks.); 2002. 384p. 24.95 (0-312-87899-0, Forge Bks.) Doherty, Tom Assocs., LLC.

Horn, Stephen. In Her Defense. 2001. 416p. mass mkt. 6.99 (0-06-109875-2, HarperTorch) Morrow/Avon.

—In Her Defense: A Novel. Marino, C., ed. 2000. 25.00 o.s.i (0-06-019754-4) HarperCollins Pubs.

—In Her Defense: A Novel. 2000. 376p. 25.00 (0-06-019440-5) HarperCollins Pubs.

Horrock, Henry. Potomac Fever. 2000. 352p. mass mkt. 6.99 o.s.i (0-7860-1105-X, Pinnacle Bks.) Kensington Publishing Corp.

—Potomac Fever. 1999. 304p. (gr. 8). 24.00 (0-316-35472-4) Little Brown & Co.

—Potomac Fever. l.t. ed. 1999. (Basic Ser.). 552p. 28.95 (0-7862-2175-5) Thorndike Pr.

Huddle, David. Tenorman: A Novella. 1995. 96p. 12.95 o.p. (0-8118-1027-5) Chronicle Bks. LLC.

Hunt, E. Howard. Guilty Knowledge: A Novel. 1999. 320p. 23.95 (0-312-86760-3, Forge Bks.) Doherty, Tom Assocs., LLC.

Hyde, Christopher. Hard Target. 1992. 464p. mass mkt. 4.99 (0-380-70900-7, Avon Bks.); 1991. 19.95 o.p. (0-688-09053-2, Morrow, William & Co.) Morrow/Avon.

Ignatius, David. A Firing Offense. 1998. mass mkt. 6.99 o.s.i (0-8041-1802-7, Ivy Bks.) Ballantine Bks.

—A Firing Offense. unabr. ed. 1998. audio 85.00 (0-7887-2167-4, 95463E7) Recorded Bks., LLC.

—The Sun King. E-Book 17.50 (1-58945-558-4) Adobe Systems, Inc.

—The Sun King. 2000. E-Book 17.50 (0-375-50455-9) Random Hse., Inc.

Insel, Deborah. Clouded Dreams. 1995. 273p. 20.00 (1-883285-04-6) Delphinium Bks., Inc.

Jasper, Kenji. Dark: A Novel. 2001. 256p. pap. 12.95 (0-7679-0707-8) Broadway Bks.

Jones, Edward P. Lost in the City: Stories. 2003. 256p. pap. 12.95 (0-06-056628-0, Amistad Pr.) HarperTrade.

Junkin, Tim. Good Counsel: A Novel. 2001. 304p. tchr. ed. 23.95 (1-56512-284-4, Shannon Ravenel Bks.) Algonquin Bks. of Chapel Hill.

Just, Ward. In the City of Fear. 1990. pap. 10.95 o.p. (0-393-30722-0) Norton, W. W. & Co., Inc.

—In the City of Fear. 1982. 264p. 14.95 o.p. (0-670-39679-6) Viking Penguin.

Just, Ward S. Echo House. 1997. 336p. pap. 13.00 (0-395-90138-3); 368p. tchr. ed. 25.00 o.p. (0-395-85697-3) Houghton Mifflin Co. Trade & Reference Div.

Kafka-Gibbons, Paul. Dupont Circle: A Novel. 2001. 256p. tchr. ed. 24.00 (0-395-86932-3) Houghton Mifflin Co.

—Dupont Circle: A Novel. 2002. 256p. pap. 13.00 (0-618-21918-8, Mariner Bks.) Houghton Mifflin Co. Trade & Reference Div.

Kaplan, Mindy. The Girl Next Door. 1996. 224p. pap. 10.95 o.p. (1-56280-140-6) Naiad Pr., Inc.

Karaim, Reed. If Men Were Angels. abr. ed. 2000. audio 7.99 o.s.i (1-56740-983-0, 2106, Paperback Nova Audio Bks.); 1999. audio 26.95 (1-56740-433-2, 1725, Bookcassette); 1999. audio 73.25 (1-56740-658-0, 1726, Unabridged Library Editions) Brilliance Audio.

—If Men Were Angels. 1999. 320p. 24.95 o.p. (0-393-04780-6) Norton, W. W. & Co., Inc.

Kauffman, Donna. The Cinderella Rules. 2003. 432p. pap. 11.00 (0-553-38234-9) Bantam Bks.

Kava, Alex. The Soul Catcher: A Maggie O'Dell Novel. 2003. 416p. mass mkt. (1-55166-701-0, Mira Bks.) Harlequin Enterprises, Ltd.

—The Soul Catcher: A Maggie O'Dell Novel. l.t. ed. 2003. (Basic Ser.). 628p. 28.95 (0-7862-4925-0) Thorndike Pr.

Killham, Nina. How to Cook a Tart: A Novel. 2002. 256p. 21.95 (1-58234-269-5) Bloomsbury Publishing.

Kimball, Stephen. Death Duty. 1996. 320p. 24.95 o.s.i (0-525-94230-0) Dutton/Plume.

—Death Duty. 1998. 400p. mass mkt. 5.99 o.s.i (0-451-19107-2, Signet Bks.) NAL.

King, Benjamin. Bullet for Lincoln. 1993. 304p. 19.95 (0-88289-927-9) Pelican Publishing Co., Inc.

King, Peter T. Deliver Us from Evil. 2002. 32p. 24.95 (1-57098-419-0) Rinehart, Roberts Pubs.

Krist, Gary. Bad Chemistry. 2000. 368p. reprint ed. mass mkt. 7.50 o.s.i (0-425-17300-3) Berkley Publishing Group.

—Chaos Theory. 2001. 352p. reprint ed. mass mkt. 7.50 o.s.i (0-515-13085-0, Jove) Berkley Publishing Group.

Law, Janice. Backfire. 1996. (WWL Mystery Ser.). per. (0-373-26201-9, 1-26201-3, Worldwide Library) Harlequin Enterprises, Ltd.

—Backfire. 1994. (Anna Peters Mystery Ser.). 208p. 18.95 o.p. (0-312-11474-5, Saint Martin's Minotaur) St. Martin's Pr.

Lee, Rachel. With Malice. 2003. 384p. mass mkt. (1-55166-658-8, Mira Bks.) Harlequin Enterprises, Ltd.

Lefcourt, Peter. The Woody: A Novel. 1999. 368p. pap. 14.00 (0-671-03855-9); 1998. 320p. 23.00 (0-684-85744-8); 1998. 320p. (gr. 6). 23.00 (0-684-85393-0) Simon & Schuster. (Simon & Schuster).

Lehrer, James. Blue Hearts: Novel. 2001. 240p. pap. text 13.00 (1-58648-031-6) PublicAffairs.

Lehrer, Jim. Purple Dots: A Novel. 2002. (Illus.). 240p. pap. text 13.00 (1-58648-032-4) PublicAffairs.

—Purple Dots: A Novel. l.t. ed. 1999. (Americana Ser.). 344p. 28.95 (0-7862-1809-6) Thorndike Pr.

Leuci, Bob. Double Edge. 1991. 272p. 19.95 o.p. (0-525-93383-2, Dutton) Dutton/Plume.

Leuci, Robert. Sweet Baby James. 2004. Orig. Title: Double Edge. 272p. reprint ed. pap. 10.95 (1-55921-299-3) Moyer Bell.

Lewis, Philip. Life of Death: A Novel. 1993. 253p. 18.95 (0-932511-74-0); pap. 10.95 (0-932511-75-9) Fiction Collective Two, Inc.

Lind, Michael. Powertown: A Novel. 1996. 79p. 23.00 o.p. (0-06-017510-9) HarperCollins Pubs.

Lorrance, Arleen. The Two. 2002. 492p. pap. 24.95 (0-916192-47-4, Teleos Imprint) LP Pubns.

Lucas, Daryl J. The Smithsonian Connection. 1991. (Choice Adventures Ser.: Vol. 2). 152p. (J). (gr. 3-7). pap. 4.99 o.p. (0-8423-5026-8) Tyndale Hse. Pubs.

Ludlum, Robert. Trevayne. 480p. 1992. mass mkt. 3.99 o.s.i (0-553-19955-2); 1989. mass mkt. 7.99 (0-553-28179-8) Bantam Bks.

MacKinnon, Douglas. First Victim. 1997. 320p. 19.95 (0-87131-824-5) Evans, M. & Co., Inc.

Maddison, Lauren. Deceptions: A Connor Hawthorne Mystery. 1999. (Connor Hawthorne Mysteries Ser.). 424p. pap. 14.95 (1-55583-490-6) Alyson Pubns.

Maddox, Muriel. Myra's Daughters: A Contemporary Novel. 2001. 280p. 22.95 (0-86534-323-3) Sunstone Pr.

Mallon, Thomas. Two Moons: A Novel. 2001. (Harvest Book Ser.). (Illus.). 368p. reprint ed. pap. 14.00 (0-15-601082-8, Harvest Bks.) Harcourt Trade Pubs.

Marshall, Leslie. A Girl Could Stand Up: A Novel. 2003. 384p. 24.00 (0-8021-1748-1, Grove Pr.) Grove/Atlantic, Inc.

McLaughlin, Ann L. The House on Q Street: A Novel. 2002. 292p. pap. 14.95 (1-880284-59-6) Daniel, John & Co., Pubs.

McMurtry, Larry. Cadillac Jack. 1995. reprint ed. lib. bdg. 27.95 o.p. (1-56849-648-6) Buccaneer Bks., Inc.

—Cadillac Jack. 2002. 400p. pap. 14.00 (0-684-85383-3, Simon & Schuster) Simon & Schuster.

—Cadillac Jack. Grose, Bill, ed. 1990. mass mkt. 7.99 (0-671-73902-6, Pocket) Simon & Schuster.

—Cadillac Jack. 1990. mass mkt. 4.95 (0-671-70825-2, Pocket); 1987. 400p. pap. 14.00 (0-671-63720-7, Simon & Schuster); 1985. pap. 8.95 o.s.i (0-671-55541-3, Touchstone); 1982. 416p. 75.00 o.p. (0-671-45983-X, Simon & Schuster) Simon & Schuster.

Meltzer, Brad. The First Counsel. l.t. ed. 2001. (Large Print Bks.). pap. 12.95 o.p. (1-56895-187-6); 593p. 31.95 (1-58724-000-9) Gale Group. (Wheeler Publishing, Inc.).

—The First Counsel. 2001. 496p. E-Book 14.95 (0-7595-6071-4); 496p. E-Book 14.95 (0-7595-9081-8); 496p. E-Book 14.95 (0-7595-4074-8); 496p. E-Book 14.95 (0-7595-8075-8); 496p. 25.95 o.p. (0-446-52728-9); 496p. pap. 16.00 (0-446-67763-9); 544p. reprint ed. mass mkt. 7.99 (0-446-61064-X) Warner Bks., Inc.

—The Tenth Justice. unabr. ed. 1997. audio 80.00 (0-7366-4054-1, 4565) Books on Tape, Inc.

—The Tenth Justice. l.t. ed. 1998. (Large Print Book Ser.). 27.95 (1-56895-518-9, Wheeler Publishing, Inc.) Gale Group.

—The Tenth Justice. abr. ed. 1997. audio 18.00 o.s.i (0-694-51807-7, CPN 2645, HarperAudio) HarperTrade.

—The Tenth Justice. 1997. 400p. 23.00 (0-688-15089-6, Morrow, William & Co.) Morrow/Avon.

—The Tenth Justice. 1998. 496p. reprint ed. mass mkt. 7.99 (0-446-60624-3) Warner Bks., Inc.

—The Zero Game. 311.40 (0-446-17410-6); 2004. 480p. 25.95 (0-446-53098-0); 2004. (0-446-70194-7); 2004. 688p. 25.95 (0-446-53316-5) Warner Bks., Inc.

Menos, Dennis. A Test of Allegiance. 1997. vii, 252p. pap. 15.00 (0-9660404-0-6) Vergina Pr.

Merlis, Mark. Man about Town. 2003. 368p. 24.95 (0-00-715611-1, Fourth Estate) HarperTrade.

Michaels, Barbara, pseud. Ammie, Come Home. l.t. ed. 1993. 18.95 o.p. (0-7927-1672-8); pap. 17.95 o.p. (0-7927-1671-X) BBC Audiobooks America.

—Ammie, Come Home. 1979. mass mkt. 1.95 o.s.i (0-449-23926-8, Fawcett) Ballantine Bks.

—Ammie, Come Home. 1987. 256p. mass mkt. 7.50 o.s.i (0-425-09949-0) Berkley Publishing Group.

—Shattered Silk. unabr. ed. 1993. 69.95 incl. audio (0-7451-6164-2, CAB 375); 1989. audio 64.95 o.s.i (0-8161-9465-3) BBC Audiobooks America.

—Shattered Silk. Warriner, Mercer, ed. 1988. 320p. mass mkt. 6.50 o.s.i (0-425-10476-1) Berkley Publishing Group.

—Shattered Silk. l.t. ed. 1987. 462p. 18.95 o.p. (0-8161-4286-6, Macmillan Reference USA) Gale Group.

—Shattered Silk. 1999. 320p. mass mkt. 6.99 (0-06-104473-3) HarperCollins Pubs.

—Shattered Silk. 1996. 320p. mass mkt. 6.50 (0-06-101008-1, HarperTorch) Morrow/Avon.

—Shattered Silk. 1986. 369p. bds. 15.95 o.p. (0-689-11620-9, Scribner) Simon & Schuster.

—Stitches in Time. unabr. ed. 1995. audio 72.00 (0-7366-3084-8, 3764) Books on Tape, Inc.

—Stitches in Time. l.t. ed. 1995. 527p. 25.95 o.p. (0-7838-1356-2, Macmillan Reference USA) Gale Group.

—Stitches in Time. 1999. 400p. mass mkt. 6.99 (0-06-104474-1); 1995. 307p. (YA). 22.00 o.p. (0-06-017763-2) HarperCollins Pubs.

—Stitches in Time. abr. ed. 1995. audio 17.00 (0-694-51553-1, HarperAudio) HarperTrade.

—Stitches in Time. 1996. 400p. mass mkt. 6.99 (0-06-109253-3, HarperTorch) Morrow/Avon.

—Stitches in Time, unabr. ed. audio 85.00 (0-7887-0339-0, 94531E7) Recorded Bks., LLC.

Mickelbury, Penny. One Must Wait. 1998. 256p. 22.00 (0-684-83741-2, Simon & Schuster) Simon & Schuster.

—One Must Wait. 1999. 304p. mass mkt. 6.50 (0-312-97186-9, St. Martin's Paperbacks) St. Martin's Pr.

—Paradise Interrupted. 2001. 288p. 23.00 (0-684-85991-2, Simon & Schuster) Simon & Schuster.

—The Step Between. 240p. 2002. pap. 17.95 (0-7432-4636-5); 2000. 22.00 (0-684-85990-4) Simon & Schuster. (Simon & Schuster).

—Where to Choose. 1999. 256p. 22.00 (0-684-83742-0, Simon & Schuster) Simon & Schuster.

Micklebury, Penny. Keeping Secrets. 1994. 240p. pap. 9.95 o.p. (1-56280-052-3) Naiad Pr., Inc.

—Night Songs. 1995. 224p. pap. 10.95 o.p. (1-56280-097-3) Naiad Pr., Inc.

Mikulski, Barbara & Oates, Marylouise. Capitol Offense. abr. ed. 1997. audio 7.99 o.p. (1-56740-184-8, 632, Paperback Nova Audio Bks.); 1996. audio 16.95 o.p. (1-56100-903-2, 820, Nova Audio Bks.); 1996. audio 23.95 o.p. (1-56100-693-9, 58, Bookcassette); 1996. audio 73.25 o.p. (1-56100-318-2, 1149, Unabridged Library Editions) Brilliance Audio.

—Capitol Offense. 1996. 320p. 23.95 o.s.i (0-525-94214-9) Dutton/Plume.

—Capitol Offense. 1997. 416p. mass mkt. 6.99 o.s.i (0-451-19032-7, Signet Bks.) NAL.

—Capitol Venture. 1997. 320p. 24.95 o.p. (0-525-94277-7) Dutton/Plume.

—Capitol Venture. 1999. 384p. mass mkt. 6.99 o.s.i (0-451-19183-8) NAL.

Mills, Charles. Stranger in the Shadows. 1998. (Shadow Creek Ranch Ser.: Vol. 11). 151p. (Orig.). (J). (gr. 4-7). pap. 5.99 (0-8280-1316-0) Review & Herald Publishing Assn.

Mitchell, Lauren Porosoff. Look at Me: A Novel. 2000. 198p. pap. 14.95 (0-9654578-1-8) Leapfrog Pr.

Mitchell, Michele. The Latest Bombshell: A Novel. 2003. 288p. 23.00 (0-8050-7321-3) Holt, Henry & Co.

Moffat, Gwen. Running Dogs. 1999. 192p. 25.00 (0-7278-5456-9) Severn Hse. Pubs., Ltd.

Moore, Marshall. The Concrete Sky. 2003. 274p. pap. 17.95 (1-56023-436-9); 273p. 44.95 (1-56023-435-0) Haworth Pr., Inc., The. (Southern Tier Editions).

Mrazek, Robert J. Unholy Fire: A Novel of the Civil War. 2003. 336p. 24.95 (0-312-30673-3) St. Martin's Pr.

—Unholy Fire: A Novel of the Civil War. l.t. ed. 2003. 543p. 28.95 (0-7862-5674-5) Thorndike Pr.

Myers, John L. Holy Family. 1992. 232p. (Orig.). pap. 8.95 o.p. (1-55583-200-8) Alyson Pubns.

Nesbit, Jeff. The Insider. 1996. 352p. pap. 12.99 o.p. (0-310-20098-9) Zondervan.

Nessen, Ron. Knight & Day. audio 24.95 (0-7861-1399-5) Blackstone Audio Bks., Inc.

—Knight & Day. 1996. 256p. mass mkt. 5.99 (0-8125-5053-6, Forge Bks.) Doherty, Tom Assocs., LLC.

—Press Corpse. 1997. (Knight & Day Mysteries Ser.). 215p. pap. 5.99 (0-8125-6793-5, Forge Bks.) Doherty, Tom Assocs., LLC.

Nessen, Ron & Neuman, Johanna. Death with Honors. unabr. ed. 1999. (Knight & Day Mystery Ser.: Vol. 3). audio 29.95 (0-7861-1534-3);Pt. 3. audio 44.95 (0-7861-1484-3, 2336) Blackstone Audio Bks., Inc.

—Death with Honors, No. 3. 1998. (Knight & Day Mysteries Ser.). 288p. 22.95 o.p. (0-312-85594-X, Forge Bks.) Doherty, Tom Assocs., LLC.

—Knight & Day, unabr. ed. 1996. audio 32.95 (0-7861-1009-0, 1788) Blackstone Audio Bks., Inc.

—Knight & Day. 1995. 256p. 21.95 o.p. (0-312-85588-5, Forge Bks.) Doherty, Tom Assocs., LLC.

—Press Corpse. unabr. ed. 2000. audio 27.95 (0-7861-1545-9); 1999. audio 39.95 Blackstone Audio Bks., Inc.

—Press Corpse. 1996. 256p. 21.95 o.p. (0-312-85592-3, Forge Bks.) Doherty, Tom Assocs., LLC.

Nienkemper, Robert C. Fatal Games. 2nd ed. 1998. 341p. reprint ed. mass mkt. 7.50 (1-892614-00-6, BWP-FG-2) Briarwood Pubns.

—Fatal Genes. 1999. 351p. pap. 7.50 (1-892614-15-4, BWP-FG) Briarwood Pubns.

O'Brien, Meg. Crimson Rain. 2002. 400p. mass mkt. (1-55166-932-3, Mira Bks.) Harlequin Enterprises, Ltd.

O'Brien, Patricia. Ladies Lunch. 1994. 22.00 (0-671-78906-6, Simon & Schuster) Simon & Schuster.

—Ladies Lunch. 1996. 310p. pap. text 5.99 (0-312-95789-0, St. Martin's Paperbacks) St. Martin's Pr.

Olshaker, Mark. The Edge. 1995. 448p. mass mkt. 5.99 o.s.i (0-553-57403-5) Bantam Bks.

O'Reilly, Victor. The Devil's Footprint. 1998. 448p. mass mkt. 7.50 o.s.i (0-425-16186-2) Berkley Publishing Group.

—The Devil's Footprint. 1997. 400p. 24.95 o.p. (0-399-14137-5, G. P. Putnam's Sons) Penguin Group (USA) Inc.

Parsons, Alexander. Leaving Disneyland. 2001. 256p. 23.95 (0-312-27855-1) St. Martin's Pr.

Patterson, James. Along Came a Spider. l.t. ed. (General Ser.). 486p. 1994. pap. 18.95 o.s.i (0-8161-5753-7); 1993. 22.95 o.p. (0-8161-5752-9) Gale Group. (Macmillan Reference USA).

—Along Came a Spider. abr. ed. 1993. audio 18.00 o.p. (1-55994-751-9, 390336, HarperAudio) HarperTrade.

—Along Came a Spider. 1993. 435p. 19.95 (0-316-69364-2) Little Brown & Co.

—Along Came a Spider. movie tie-in ed. 1993. 528p. reprint ed. mass mkt. 7.99 (0-446-36419-3) Warner Bks., Inc.

—The Big Bad Wolf. 2003. 400p. 27.95 (0-316-60290-6) Little Brown & Co.

—Cat & Mouse. unabr. ed. 1998. audio 56.00 (0-7366-4138-6, 4643) Books on Tape, Inc.

—Cat & Mouse. 1997. 400p. 24.95 o.p. (*0-316-69329-4*) Little Brown & Co.

—Cat & Mouse. unabr. ed. 1999. audio compact disk 69.00 (*0-7887-3411-3*, C1017E7); 1998. audio 70.00 (*0-7887-2022-8*, 95395E7) Recorded Bks., LLC.

—Cat & Mouse. l.t. ed. (Paperback Bestsellers Ser.). 472p. 1999. pap. 27.95 (*0-7838-8345-5*); 1998. 30.95 (*0-7838-8344-7*) Thorndike Pr.

—Cat & Mouse. abr. ed. 1999. audio (*1-57042-737-2*); 1997. audio 24.00 (*1-57042-577-9*, 695410) Time Warner AudioBooks.

—Cat & Mouse. 1998. 480p. reprint ed. mass mkt. 7.99 (*0-446-60618-9*) Warner Bks., Inc.

—Four Blind Mice. 2002. 400p. 27.95 (*0-316-69300-6*); 432p. 27.95 (*0-316-14786-9*) Little Brown & Co.

—Four Blind Mice. 2003. 416p. mass mkt. 7.99 (*0-446-61326-6*, Warner Vision); 2002. 400p. pap. 16.00 (*0-446-69052-X*) Warner Bks., Inc.

—Jack & Jill. 1997. audio compact disk 80.00 (*0-7366-8519-7*); audio 64.00 (*0-913369-41-1*, 4218) Books on Tape, Inc.

—Jack & Jill. 1996. 448p. 24.95 (*0-316-69371-5*) Little Brown & Co.

—Jack & Jill. unabr. ed. 1999. audio compact disk 99.00 (*0-7887-3415-6*, C1021E7); 1997. audio 85.00 (*0-7887-0804-X*, 94953E7) Recorded Bks., LLC.

—Jack & Jill. l.t. ed. 1998. (Paperback Bestsellers Ser.). 537p. pap. 27.95 (*0-7862-0939-9*) Thorndike Pr.

—Jack & Jill. abr. ed. 1996. (Alex Cross Mystery Ser.). (gr. 8 up). audio 17.00 (*1-57042-437-3*, 394457) Time Warner AudioBooks.

—Jack & Jill. 2003. E-Book 5.95 (*0-7595-4743-2*) Time Warner Bk. Group.

—Jack & Jill. 480p. 2003. pap. 13.95 (*0-446-69265-4*); 1997. reprint ed. mass mkt. 7.99 (*0-446-60480-1*) Warner Bks., Inc.

—Kiss the Girls. unabr. ed. 1995. audio 64.00 (*0-7366-3082-1*, 3762) Books on Tape, Inc.

—Kiss the Girls. l.t. ed. 2001. 432p. 31.95 o.p. (*0-7838-9437-6*, Macmillan Reference USA) Gale Group.

—Kiss the Girls. 1995. 451p. 22.95 (*0-316-69370-7*) Little Brown & Co.

—Kiss the Girls. unabr. ed. audio audio 78.00 (*0-7887-0340-4*, 94532E7) Recorded Bks., LLC.

—Kiss the Girls. abr. ed. 1995. (Alex Cross Mystery Ser.). (gr. 8 up). audio 17.00 (*1-57042-029-7*, 391029) Time Warner AudioBooks.

—Kiss the Girls. 2002. E-Book 4.95 (*0-7595-4718-1*) Time Warner Bk. Group.

—Kiss the Girls. 496p. reprint ed. 2000. pap. 13.95 (*0-446-67738-8*); 1995. mass mkt. 7.99 (*0-446-60124-1*) Warner Bks., Inc.

—The Lake House. 2003. 384p. (gr. 8). 27.95 (*0-316-60328-7*); 448p. 27.95 (*0-316-71113-6*) Little Brown & Co.

—The Lake House. 2003. E-Book 12.75 (*0-7595-4745-9*) Time Warner Bk. Group.

—The Lake House. 2004. 416p. mass mkt. 7.99 (*0-446-61390-8*) Warner Bks., Inc.

—Pop! Goes the Weasel. 1999. 432p. (YA). (gr. 8). 26.95 o.p. (*0-316-69328-6*) Little Brown & Co.

—Pop! Goes the Weasel. l.t. ed. 496p. 2000. pap. 13.95 (*0-375-72793-0*); 1999. 26.95 (*0-375-40854-1*) Random Hse. Large Print.

—Pop! Goes the Weasel. 2003. E-Book 5.95 (*0-7595-4739-4*) Time Warner Bk. Group.

—Pop! Goes the Weasel. 2000. 480p. reprint ed. mass mkt. 7.99 (*0-446-60881-5*) Warner Bks., Inc.

—Roses Are Red. 2000. 400p. 26.95 o.p. (*0-316-69325-1*); pap. 16.00 (*0-316-66620-3*) Little Brown & Co.

—Roses Are Red. l.t. ed. 2000. 448p. 26.95 (*0-375-43090-3*) Random Hse. Large Print.

—Roses Are Red. abr. ed. 2000. audio 29.98 (*1-57042-922-7*); audio 24.98 (*1-57042-920-0*); audio 32.98 (*1-57042-921-9*) Time Warner AudioBooks.

—Roses Are Red. 2001. 400p. reprint ed. mass mkt. 7.99 (*0-446-60548-4*) Warner Bks., Inc.

—Violets Are Blue. 2001. 400p. 27.95 o.p. (*0-316-69323-5*); 432p. 27.95 o.p. (*0-316-68656-5*) Little Brown & Co.

—Violets Are Blue. abr. ed. 2001. audio 25.98 (*1-58621-195-1*); audio 29.98 (*1-58621-196-X*); audio 32.98 (*1-58621-197-8*); audio 39.98 (*1-58621-198-6*) Time Warner AudioBooks.

—Violets Are Blue. 2001. pap. 16.00 o.s.i (*0-446-67860-0*) Warner Bks., Inc.

Patterson, Richard North. Balance of Power. 2004. 640p. mass mkt. 7.99 (*0-345-45018-3*); 2003. 624p. 27.95 (*0-345-45017-5*, Ballantine Bks.); 2003. E-Book 9.99 (*0-345-46988-7*, Ballantine Bks.) Ballantine Bks.

—Balance of Power. unabr. ed. 2003. audio 44.95 (*0-7393-0130-6*, Listening Library) Random Hse. Audio Publishing Group.

—Balance of Power. l.t. ed. 2003. 992p. 29.95 (*0-375-43208-6*) Random Hse. Large Print.

Pearson, Ridley. Hard Fall. unabr. ed. 1993. audio 80.00 (*0-7366-2528-3*, 3280) Books on Tape, Inc.

—Hard Fall. 1992. 416p. mass mkt. 6.99 o.s.i (*0-440-21262-6*) Dell Publishing.

Pease, William D. The Monkey's Fist. 1997. 448p. mass mkt. 6.99 o.s.i (*0-451-18872-1*, Signet Bks.) NAL.

—The Monkey's Fist. 1996. 368p. 23.95 o.s.i (*0-670-85129-9*, Viking) Viking Penguin.

Pelecanos, George P. The Big Blowdown. 1999. 320p. pap. 14.95 (*0-312-24291-3*, Saint Martin's Griffin); 1996. 304p. 24.95 o.p. (*0-312-14284-6*) St. Martin's Pr.

—Down by the River Where the Dead Men Go. 1998. 240p. pap. text o.p. (*1-85242-529-6*) Serpent's Tail Ltd.

—Down by the River Where the Dead Men Go. 1999. 216p. pap. 13.00 (*1-85242-716-7*) Serpent's Tail Ltd. GBR. *Dist:* Consortium Bk. Sales & Distribution.

—Down by the River Where the Dead Men Go. 1995. 240p. 20.95 o.p. (*0-312-13056-2*, Saint Martin's Minotaur) St. Martin's Pr.

—A Firing Offense. 1999. 224p. pap. 13.00 (*1-85242-715-9*); 1998. 216p. pap. text 12.99 o.p. (*1-85242-563-6*) Serpent's Tail Ltd. GBR. *Dist:* Consortium Bk. Sales & Distribution.

—A Firing Offense. 1992. 224p. 17.95 o.p. (*0-312-06970-7*, Saint Martin's Minotaur) St. Martin's Pr.

—Hard Revolution. 2004. 384p. 24.95 (*0-316-60897-1*) Little Brown & Co.

—Hard Revolution. abr. ed. 2004. audio 25.98 (*1-58621-600-7*); audio compact disk 31.98 (*1-58621-601-5*) Time Warner AudioBooks.

—Hell to Pay. 2002. E-Book 14.95 (*0-7595-8686-1*); 352p. 24.95 o.p. (*0-316-69506-8*) Little Brown & Co.

—Hell to Pay. l.t. ed. 2003. 536p. 30.45 (*0-7862-5615-X*) Thorndike Pr.

—Hell to Pay. 2003. 416p. mass mkt. 6.99 (*0-446-61132-8*) Warner Bks., Inc.

—King Suckerman. 1998. 336p. mass mkt. 6.99 (*0-440-22595-7*) Dell Publishing.

—King Suckerman. 1997. 288p. (gr. 8). 28.00 o.p. (*0-316-69590-4*) Little Brown & Co.

—Nick's Trip. 1998. 276p. pap. o.p. (*1-85242-562-8*) Serpent's Tail Ltd.

—Nick's Trip. 1999. 288p. pap. 13.00 (*1-85242-714-0*) Serpent's Tail Ltd. GBR. *Dist:* Consortium Bk. Sales & Distribution.

—Nick's Trip. 1993. 276p. 18.95 o.p. (*0-312-08862-0*, Saint Martin's Minotaur) St. Martin's Pr.

—Right As Rain. 2001. 336p. 24.95 (*0-316-69526-2*) Little Brown & Co.

—Right As Rain. l.t. ed. 2003. 525p. 30.45 (*0-7862-5609-5*) Thorndike Pr.

—Right As Rain. 2002. 384p. reprint ed. mass mkt. 6.99 (*0-446-61079-8*) Warner Bks., Inc.

—Shame the Devil. 2001. 384p. reprint ed. mass mkt. 6.99 (*0-440-23635-5*, Delta) Dell Publishing.

—Shame the Devil. 2000. 304p. 24.95 (*0-316-69523-8*) Little Brown & Co.

—Soul Circus. abr. ed. 2004. (Derek Strange/Terry Quinn Ser.). audio compact disk 14.99 (*1-59355-668-3*, 5287) Brilliance Audio.

—Soul Circus. 2003. 352p. 24.95 (*0-316-60843-2*) Little Brown & Co.

—Soul Circus. l.t. ed. 2003. (New York Times Bestseller Ser.). 533p. 30.95 (*0-7862-5614-1*) Thorndike Pr.

—Soul Circus. 2004. 416p. mass mkt. 7.50 (*0-446-61142-5*) Warner Bks., Inc.

—The Sweet Forever. 1999. 384p. mass mkt. 6.99 (*0-440-23493-X*) Dell Publishing.

—The Sweet Forever. 1998. 304p. (gr. 8). 23.95 (*0-316-69109-7*) Little Brown & Co.

Peters, Ralph. Traitor. 2000. 384p. mass mkt. 6.99 (*0-380-79738-0*); 1999. 320p. 23.00 (*0-380-97641-2*) Morrow/Avon. (Avon Bks.).

—Traitor. 2004. pap. (*0-8117-3107-3*) Stackpole Bks.

Petschull, Jurgen. The Martyr. Cappellari, Stephen G., tr. from GER. 1988. 296p. 18.95 o.p. (*0-916515-28-1*) Mercury Hse.

Poyer, David. Tomahawk. (Dan Lenson Novels Ser.). 2000. 480p. mass mkt. 6.99 (*0-312-96561-3*, St. Martin's Paperbacks); 1998. 384p. 24.95 (*0-312-17975-8*) St. Martin's Pr.

—Tomahawk. l.t. ed. 1998. (Americana Ser.). 672p. 28.95 (*0-7862-1457-0*) Thorndike Pr.

Quinn, Sally. Happy Endings. l.t. ed. 1992. 24.95 o.p. (*0-7927-1378-8*); pap. 21.95 o.p. (*0-7927-1377-X*) BBC Audiobooks America.

Racina, Thom. Hidden Agenda. 1998. 368p. 24.95 o.p. (*0-525-94031-6*) Dutton/Plume.

—Hidden Agenda. 1999. 368p. reprint ed. mass mkt. 6.99 o.s.i (*0-451-18600-1*) NAL.

Randle, Kevin D. Invasion Washington: UFOS over the Capitol. 2001. 320p. mass mkt. 7.50 (*0-380-81470-6*) Morrow/Avon.

Rawlings, Ellen. The Murder Lover. 1996. mass mkt. 5.99 o.s.i (*0-449-14988-9*, Fawcett) Ballantine Bks.

Redd, Mary Allen. The World of Holly Prickle: For Women Who Have Worked for Men. 1993. 290p. (Orig.). pap. 10.00 (*0-9636548-0-2*) Cascade Bks.

Reiss, Bob. The Last Spy. 1993. 300p. 20.00 o.p. (*0-671-77622-3*, Simon & Schuster) Simon & Schuster.

—The Last Spy. 1994. mass mkt. 5.99 o.p. (*0-312-95231-7*, St. Martin's Paperbacks) St. Martin's Pr.

Richards, Emilie. Prospect Street. 2003. 512p. mass mkt. (*1-55166-693-6*, Mira Bks.) Harlequin Enterprises, Ltd.

Richman, Phyllis C. The Butter Did It. unabr. ed. 1998. audio 49.95 (*0-7861-1293-X*, 2197) Blackstone Audio Bks., Inc.

—The Butter Did It: A Gastronomic Tale of Love & Murder. 1997. 320p. 23.00 o.s.i (*0-06-018370-5*) HarperCollins Pubs.

—The Butter Did It: A Gastronomic Tale of Love & Murder. 1998. (Chas Wheatley Mysteries Ser.). 384p. mass mkt. 6.99 (*0-06-109625-3*, HarperTorch) Morrow/Avon.

—The Butter Did It: A Gastronomic Tale of Love & Murder. l.t. ed. 1997. (Cloak & Dagger Ser.). 459p. 25.95 o.p. (*0-7862-1183-0*) Thorndike Pr.

—Murder on the Gravy Train. 1999. viii, 243p. 23.00 (*0-06-018390-X*) HarperCollins Pubs.

—Murder on the Gravy Train. 2000. 336p. mass mkt. 6.50 (*0-06-109783-7*, Avon Bks.) Morrow/Avon.

—Murder on the Gravy Train. l.t. ed. 1999. (Mystery Ser.). 416p. 29.95 (*0-7862-2208-5*) Thorndike Pr.

—Who's Afraid of Virginia Ham? 2001. (Illus.). 256p. 23.00 (*0-06-018389-6*) HarperCollins Pubs.

Ricks, Thomas E. A Soldier's Duty: A Novel. 2001. E-Book 19.95 (*1-58836-015-6*) Random Hse., Inc.

Ripley, Ann. Death of a Garden Pest. 1996. (Louise Eldridge Mystery Ser.). 288p. 22.95 (*0-312-14311-7*, Saint Martin's Minotaur) St. Martin's Pr.

—Death of a Garden Pest: A Gardening Mystery. 1997. (Gardening Mysteries Ser.). 304p. mass mkt. 5.99 o.s.i (*0-553-57730-1*, Crimeline) Bantam Bks.

—Death of a Political Plant: A Gardening Mystery. 1998. (Gardening Mysteries Ser.). 336p. mass mkt. 5.99 o.s.i (*0-553-57735-2*) Bantam Bks.

—The Garden Tour Affair: A Gardening Mystery. 1999. (Gardening Mysteries Ser.). 320p. mass mkt. 5.99 o.s.i (*0-553-57736-0*); 22.95 o.s.i (*0-553-10693-7*) Bantam Bks.

—Mulch. 1998. (Gardening Mysteries Ser.). (Illus.). 304p. reprint ed. mass mkt. 5.99 (*0-553-57734-4*) Bantam Bks.

—Mulch. 1994. 224p. 19.95 o.p. (*0-312-11029-4*, Saint Martin's Minotaur) St. Martin's Pr.

—The Perennial Killer: A Gardening Mystery. 2000. (Gardening Mysteries Ser.). 352p. mass mkt. 5.99 o.s.i (*0-553-57737-9*); 20.01 (*0-553-10694-5*) Bantam Bks.

Rivers, Caryl. Girls Forever Brave & True. 1986. 384p. 15.95 o.p. (*0-312-32728-5*) St. Martin's Pr.

Roberts, Carey. Pray God to Die: A Detective Anne Fitzhugh Mystery. 1993. 384p. 21.00 o.p. (*0-684-19562-3*, Scribner) Simon & Schuster.

Roberts, Nora. Brazen Virtue. 2002. 304p. mass mkt. 7.99 (*0-553-27283-7*, Spectra) Bantam Bks.

—Brazen Virtue. l.t. ed. 2001. 464p. 18.95 (*0-375-43112-8*) Random Hse. Large Print.

—Honest Illusions. 2002. 432p. pap. 13.95 (*0-425-18619-9*); 1993. 512p. mass mkt. 7.99 (*0-515-11097-3*, Jove) Berkley Publishing Group.

—Honest Illusions. abr. ed. 2001. audio 24.95 o.p. (*1-58788-404-6*, 2648, Nova Audio Bks.) Brilliance Audio.

—Honest Illusions. 1992. 384p. 19.95 o.p. (*0-399-13761-0*, G. P. Putnam's Sons) Penguin Group (USA) Inc.

—Honest Illusions. 19.95 o.s.i (*0-399-13958-3*) Putnam Publishing Group, The.

Robinson, C. Kelly. Between Brothers: A Novel. 2001. 384p. pap. 13.95 (*0-375-75772-4*); 256p. pap. 13.95 (*0-676-90055-0*) Random House Adult Trade Publishing Group. (Villard Bks.).

Roosevelt, Elliott. A First Class Murder. l.t. ed. 1992. (General Ser.). 339p. 20.95 o.p. (*0-8161-5317-5*); pap. 16.95 o.p. (*0-8161-5318-3*) Gale Group. (Macmillan Reference USA).

—A First Class Murder. 1993. 224p. reprint ed. pap. 4.99 (*0-380-71238-5*, Avon Bks.) Morrow/Avon.

—A First Class Murder. 1991. 17.95 o.p. (*0-312-05527-7*) St. Martin's Pr.

—The Hyde Park Murder. l.t. ed. 1986. (General Ser.). 390p. 16.95 o.p. (*0-8161-3991-1*, Macmillan Reference USA) Gale Group.

—The Hyde Park Murder. 1986. pap. 4.50 (*0-380-70058-1*, Avon Bks.) Morrow/Avon.

—The Hyde Park Murder. unabr. ed. 1986. (Eleanor Roosevelt Mystery Ser.: Vol. 2). audio 44.00 (*1-55690-243-3*, 86580E7) Recorded Bks., LLC.

—The Hyde Park Murder. 1985. 240p. 14.95 o.p. (*0-312-40160-4*) St. Martin's Pr.

—Murder & the First Lady. l.t. ed. 1985. (General Ser.). 14.95 o.p. (*0-8161-3785-4*, Macmillan Reference USA) Gale Group.

—Murder & the First Lady. 1985. (Eleanor Roosevelt Mystery Ser.). 240p. mass mkt. 4.99 (*0-380-69937-0*, Avon Bks.) Morrow/Avon.

—Murder & the First Lady. unabr. ed. 1986. (Eleanor Roosevelt Mystery Ser.: Vol. 1). audio 35.00 (*1-55690-357-X*, 86130E7) Recorded Bks., LLC.

—Murder & the First Lady. 1984. 208p. 12.95 o.p. (*0-312-55280-7*) St. Martin's Pr.

—Murder at Hobcaw Barony. l.t. ed. 1987. 379p. 17.95 o.p. (*0-8161-4195-9*, Macmillan Reference USA) Gale Group.

—Murder at Hobcaw Barony. 1987. (Eleanor Roosevelt Mystery Ser.). 224p. pap. 4.50 (*0-380-70021-2*, Avon Bks.) Morrow/Avon.

—Murder at Hobcaw Barony. unabr. ed. 1986. (Eleanor Roosevelt Mystery Ser.: Vol. 3). audio 51.00 (*1-55690-360-X*, 86680E7) Recorded Bks., LLC.

—Murder at Hobcaw Barony. 1986. (Eleanor Roosevelt Mystery Ser.). 240p. 15.95 o.p. (*0-312-55291-2*) St. Martin's Pr.

—Murder at Midnight: An Eleanor Roosevelt Mystery. (Eleanor Roosevelt Mystery Ser.). 1998. 240p. mass mkt. 5.99 (*0-312-96554-0*, St. Martin's Paperbacks); 1997. 224p. 20.95 o.p. (*0-312-15596-4*, Saint Martin's Minotaur) St. Martin's Pr.

—Murder at the Palace. l.t. unabr. ed. 1989. (General Ser.). 315p. 20.95 o.p. (*0-8161-4663-2*, Macmillan Reference USA) Gale Group.

—Murder at the Palace. 1989. pap. 4.99 (*0-380-70405-6*, Avon Bks.) Morrow/Avon.

—Murder at the Palace. unabr. ed. 1988. (Eleanor Roosevelt Mystery Ser.: Vol. 5). audio 44.00 (*1-55690-358-8*, 88882E7) Recorded Bks., LLC.

—Murder at the Palace. 1988. 240p. 15.95 o.p. (*0-312-01373-6*, Saint Martin's Minotaur) St. Martin's Pr.

—Murder at the President's Door. mass mkt. (*0-312-98275-5*, St. Martin's Paperbacks); E-Book 23.95 (*0-312-70355-4*); 2003. 240p. mass mkt. 6.50 (*0-312-98670-X*, St. Martin's Paperbacks) St. Martin's Pr.

—Murder in Georgetown. l.t. ed. 1999. (Illus.). pap. 23.95 (*1-56895-807-2*, Wheeler Publishing, Inc.) Gale Group.

—Murder in Georgetown. 2000. 240p. mass mkt. 5.99 (*0-312-97321-7*, St. Martin's Paperbacks); 1999. 230p. 23.95 o.p. (*0-312-24221-2*, Saint Martin's Minotaur) St. Martin's Pr.

—Murder in the Blue Room. l.t. ed. 1991. (General Ser.). 377p. 13.95 o.p. (*0-8161-5112-1*); lib. bdg. 21.95 (*0-8161-5100-8*) Gale Group. (Macmillan Reference USA).

—Murder in the Blue Room. 1992. 240p. pap. 4.99 (*0-380-71237-7*, Avon Bks.) Morrow/Avon.

—Murder in the Blue Room. 1990. 16.95 o.p. (*0-312-04354-6*, Saint Martin's Minotaur) St. Martin's Pr.

—Murder in the East Room. l.t. ed. 2001. (Large Print Book Ser.). 246p. pap. 22.95 (*1-58724-020-3*, Wheeler Publishing, Inc.) Gale Group.

—Murder in the East Room. (Eleanor Roosevelt Mystery Ser.). 1995. 244p. mass mkt. 4.99 (*0-312-95410-7*, St. Martin's Paperbacks); 1993. 208p. 18.95 o.p. (*0-312-09878-2*, Saint Martin's Minotaur) St. Martin's Pr.

—Murder in the Executive Mansion. 1998. 256 p. (*0-7540-3423-2*) BBC Audiobooks America.

—Murder in the Executive Mansion. 1996. 242p. mass mkt. 5.99 (*0-312-95578-2*, St. Martin's Paperbacks); 1995. 208p. 19.95 o.p. (*0-312-13128-3*, Saint Martin's Minotaur) St. Martin's Pr.

—Murder in the Executive Mansion. l.t. ed. 1998. (Nightingale Ser.). 264p. pap. 21.95 (*0-7838-0284-6*) Thorndike Pr.

—Murder in the Lincoln Bedroom: An Eleanor Roosevelt Mystery. 2002. 240p. mass mkt. 6.50 (*0-312-97919-3*, St. Martin's Paperbacks); 2000. (Illus.). 228p. 22.95 (*0-312-26130-0*, Saint Martin's Minotaur) St. Martin's Pr.

—Murder in the Lincoln Bedroom: An Eleanor Roosevelt Mystery. l.t. ed. 2001. (Thorndike Americana Ser.). 279p. 30.95 (*0-7862-3049-5*); (*0-7540-4446-7*); (*0-7540-4447-5*) Thorndike Pr.

—Murder in the Map Room: An Eleanor Roosevelt Mystery. l.t. ed. (Large Print Bks.). 2001. pap. 24.95 o.p. (*1-58724-097-1*); 1998. pap. 22.95 o.p. (*1-56895-619-3*) Gale Group. (Wheeler Publishing, Inc.).

—Murder in the Map Room: An Eleanor Roosevelt Mystery. (Eleanor Roosevelt Mystery Ser.). 256p. 1999. mass mkt. 5.99 (*0-312-96764-0*, St. Martin's Paperbacks); 1998. 21.95 (*0-312-18168-X*) St. Martin's Pr.

—Murder in the Oval Office. l.t. ed. 1989. (General Ser.). 392p. 20.95 o.p. (*0-8161-4853-8*, Macmillan Reference USA) Gale Group.

—Murder in the Oval Office. 1990. pap. 4.99 (*0-380-70528-1*, Avon Bks.) Morrow/Avon.

—Murder in the Oval Office. 1991. 3.99 o.p. (*0-517-07815-5*) Random Hse. Value Publishing.

—Murder in the Oval Office, unabr. ed. 1989. (Eleanor Roosevelt Mystery Ser.: Vol. 7). audio 44.00 (*1-55690-365-0*, 89940E7) Recorded Bks., LLC.

—Murder in the Oval Office. 1989. 256p. 17.95 o.p. (0-312-02259-X) St. Martin's Pr.
—Murder in the Red Room. l.t. ed. 2000. (Wheeler Large Print Book Ser.). 263p. pap. 25.95 (1-56895-901-X, Wheeler Publishing, Inc.) Gale Group.
—Murder in the Red Room. 1994. (Eleanor Roosevelt Mystery Ser.). 256p. mass mkt. 4.99 (0-380-72143-0, Avon Bks.) Morrow/Avon.
—Murder in the Red Room. 1992. (Eleanor Roosevelt Mystery Ser.). 256p. 18.95 o.p. (0-312-07637-1, Saint Martin's Minotaur) St. Martin's Pr.
—Murder in the Rose Garden. l.t. ed. 1990. (Eleanor Roosevelt Mystery Ser.). 384p. reprint ed. pap. 11.95 o.s.i (0-8161-5000-1); lib. bdg. 20.95 o.p. (0-8161-4998-4) Gale Group. (Macmillan Reference USA).
—Murder in the Rose Garden. 1991. (Eleanor Roosevelt Mystery Ser.). reprint ed. pap. 4.95 (0-380-70529-X, Avon Bks.) Morrow/Avon.
—Murder in the Rose Garden. 1989. (Eleanor Roosevelt Mystery Ser.). 240p. 16.95 o.p. (0-312-03406-7) St. Martin's Pr.
—Murder in the West Wing. l.t. ed. 2000. (Wheeler Large Print Book Ser.). 264p. pap. 24.95 (1-56895-994-X, Wheeler Publishing, Inc.) Gale Group.
—Murder in the West Wing. (Eleanor Roosevelt Mystery Ser.). 1993. mass mkt. 5.99 (0-312-95144-2, St. Martin's Paperbacks); 1992. 256p. 18.95 o.p. (0-312-08144-8, Saint Martin's Minotaur) St. Martin's Pr.
—New Deal for Death. l.t. ed. 2001. 264p. lib. bdg. 25.95 o.p. (1-58547-062-7) Ctr. Point Large Print.
—New Deal for Death. 1994. (Blackjack Endicott Ser.: No. 2). 288p. mass mkt. 4.99 (0-312-95238-4, St. Martin's Paperbacks); 1993. (Blackjack Endicott Novel Ser.). 256p. 18.95 o.p. (0-312-09267-9, Saint Martin's Minotaur) St. Martin's Pr.
—The President's Man: A "Blackjack" Endicott Novel. l.t. ed. 1992. (General Ser.). 354p. 20.95 o.p. (0-8161-5396-5); lib. bdg. 16.95 o.p. (0-8161-5397-3) Gale Group. (Macmillan Reference USA).
—The President's Man: A "Blackjack" Endicott Novel. 1992. 290p. mass mkt. 4.99 (0-312-92828-9, St. Martin's Paperbacks); 1991. 256p. 18.95 o.p. (0-312-06443-8) St. Martin's Pr.
—A Royal Murder. l.t. ed. 1995. 284p. 22.95 o.p. (1-56895-171-X, Wheeler Publishing, Inc.) Gale Group.
—A Royal Murder. 1994. 240p. 19.95 o.p. (0-312-10970-9, Saint Martin's Minotaur) St. Martin's Pr.
—The White House Pantry Murder. l.t. ed. 1988. (General Ser.). 327p. 17.95 o.p. (0-8161-4342-0, Macmillan Reference USA) Gale Group.
—The White House Pantry Murder. 1988. (Eleanor Roosevelt Mystery Ser.). pap. 4.50 (0-380-70404-8, Avon Bks.) Morrow/Avon.
—The White House Pantry Murder, unabr. ed. 1988. (Eleanor Roosevelt Mystery Ser.: Vol. 4). audio 44.00 (1-55690-561-0, 88120E7) Recorded Bks., LLC.
—The White House Pantry Murder. 1987. (Eleanor Roosevelt Mystery Ser.). 224p. 15.95 o.p. (0-312-00202-5) St. Martin's Pr.
Roosevelt, Elliott & Harrington, William. Murder at the President's Door. l.t. ed. 2002. 30.95 (0-7862-4093-8) Gale Group.
—Murder at the President's Door. 2001. 240p. 23.95 (0-312-27499-8, Saint Martin's Minotaur) St. Martin's Pr.
Ross, Dana Fuller, pseud. Honor! 1998. (Wagons West: The Empire Trilogy : Bk. 1). (Illus.). 400p. mass mkt. 5.99 o.s.i (0-553-57764-6) Bantam Bks.
—Honor! l.t. ed. 2001. (Thorndike Western Ser.). (Illus.). 576p. (J). 26.95 (0-7862-3116-5) Thorndike Pr.
Roussel, Peter. Ruffled Flourishes: A Novel. 2002. 280p. pap. 24.95 (1-57168-537-5, Eakin Pr.) Eakin Pr.
Ryan, Mary. Hope. mass mkt. (0-312-98744-7, St. Martin's Paperbacks) St. Martin's Pr.
—Hope: A Novel. 2003. 480p. 27.95 (0-312-30970-8) St. Martin's Pr.
Sanders, Lawrence. Capital Crimes. 1990. 352p. mass mkt. 7.50 o.s.i (0-425-12164-X) Berkley Publishing Group.
—Capital Crimes. l.t. ed. 1990. (General Ser.). 432p. 16.95 o.p. (0-8161-4929-1); lib. bdg. 21.95 o.p. (0-8161-4924-0) Gale Group. (Macmillan Reference USA).
—Capital Crimes. 1989. 19.95 o.p. (0-399-13426-3, G. P. Putnam's Sons) Penguin Putnam Bks. for Young Readers.
Sandford, John, pseud. The Hanged Man's Song. 2003. 336p. 25.95 (0-399-15139-7, Putnam & Grosset) Putnam Publishing Group, The.
Sandlin, Tim. Honey, Don't. 2003. 368p. 24.95 (0-399-14998-8, Putnam & Grosset) Putnam Publishing Group, The.
Saxton, Lisa. Caught in a Rundown. 1997. 287p. 20.50 (0-684-82967-3, Scribner) Simon & Schuster.
Schamess, Lisa. Borrowed Light: A Novel. 2002. 208p. 22.50 (0-87074-474-7) Southern Methodist Univ. Pr.
Schutz, Benjamin M. All the Old Bargains. 1987. 208p. mass mkt. 2.95 o.s.i (0-553-26335-8) Bantam Bks.
—All the Old Bargains. 1985. (Leo Haggerty Thriller Ser.). 208p. 13.95 o.p. (0-312-94014-9) Bluejay Bks.
—Embrace the Wolf. (Mystery Ser.). 208p. 1990. mass mkt. 2.25 o.s.i (0-553-18508-X); 1986. mass mkt. 2.95 o.s.i (0-553-26106-1) Bantam Bks.
—Embrace the Wolf. 1985. (Leo Haggerty Thriller Ser.). 208p. 13.95 o.p. (0-312-94137-4) Bluejay Bks.
—A Fistful of Empty. 1999. pap. 4.95 (0-14-012890-5); 1991. 208p. 17.95 o.p. (0-670-83111-5) Viking Penguin.
—Mexico Is Forever. 1994. 256p. 18.95 o.p. (0-312-10502-9, Saint Martin's Minotaur) St. Martin's Pr.
—Mexico Is Forever. 1999. pap. 3.95 (0-14-012891-3, Viking) Viking Penguin.
—A Tax in Blood. 1989. mass mkt. 3.95 o.s.i (0-553-28291-3) Bantam Bks.
—A Tax in Blood. 1987. (Leo Haggerty Thriller Ser.). 288p. 14.95 o.p. (0-312-94421-7, Tor Bks.) Doherty, Tom Assocs., LLC.
—The Things We Do for Love. 1990. mass mkt. 3.95 o.s.i (0-553-28489-4) Bantam Bks.
—The Things We Do for Love. 1989. 224p. 16.95 o.s.i (0-684-18990-9, Scribner) Simon & Schuster.
Shelby, Philip. Last Rights. 1998. 368p. pap. 6.99 (0-671-00131-0, Pocket); 1997. 336p. 23.00 (0-684-82939-8, Simon & Schuster) Simon & Schuster.
Sheldon, Sidney. The Sky Is Falling. 2000. 336p. pap. 16.00 (0-06-018523-6) HarperCollins Pubs.
—The Sky Is Falling. 2000. 336p. 26.00 (0-06-019834-6, Morrow, William & Co.); 400p. pap. 26.00 (0-06-019912-1) Morrow/Avon.
—The Sky Is Falling. 2001. 416p. mass mkt. 7.99 (0-446-61017-8) Warner Bks., Inc.
Shepard, Nathan. Step 339. 2002. 192p. pap. 18.50 (0-7596-2406-2) 1stBooks Library.
Shreve, Susan Richards. The Train Home. 1994. mass mkt. 4.99 o.s.i (0-8041-1294-0, Ivy Bks.) Ballantine Bks.
Smith, Mary-Ann Tirone. An American Killing. 1999. 352p. mass mkt. 6.99 (0-449-00579-8, Fawcett) Ballantine Bks.
—An American Killing. abr. ed. 1998. audio 17.95 o.p. (1-56740-801-X, 1447, Nova Audio Bks.); audio 26.95 o.s.i (1-56740-077-9, 1446, Bookcassette); audio 73.25 (1-56740-606-8, 1448, Unabridged Library Editions) Brilliance Audio.
—An American Killing. 1999. E-Book 6.99 (0-8050-6250-5); 1998. 368p. 23.00 o.s.i (0-8050-5702-1) Holt, Henry & Co.
—Love Her Madly. 2002. 320p. 25.00 (0-8050-6648-9) Holt, Henry & Co.
—Love Her Madly. 2004. 320p. mass mkt. 6.99 (0-7860-1657-4, Pinnacle Bks.) Kensington Publishing Corp.
Smith, Mitchell. Daydreams. 1987. 464p. 17.95 o.p. (0-07-059082-6) McGraw-Hill Cos., The.
—Daydreams. 1988. 448p. mass mkt. 5.99 o.s.i (0-451-40089-5, Onyx) NAL.
Spencer, Scott. Secret Anniversaries. 1990. 19.95 o.p. (0-394-57817-1) Knopf, Alfred A. Inc.
Spruill, Steven. My Soul to Take. l.t. ed. 1994. o.p. (0-7927-2093-8); pap. o.p. (0-7927-2092-X) BBC Audiobooks America.
—My Soul to Take. 1994. 304p. 22.00 o.p. (0-312-09879-0); Vol. 1. 1995. (My Soul to Take Ser.: Vol. 1). 295p. mass mkt. 5.50 (0-312-95253-8, St. Martin's Paperbacks) St. Martin's Pr.
—Rulers of Darkness. 1995. 357p. 22.95 o.p. (0-312-13163-1); Vol. 1. 1998. (Rulers of Darkness Ser.: Vol. 1). 352p. mass mkt. 6.50 (0-312-95668-1, St. Martin's Paperbacks) St. Martin's Pr.
Steel, Danielle. Journey. 2001. 368p. mass mkt. 7.99 (0-440-23702-5); 2000. 336p. 200.00 (0-385-33304-8, Delacorte Pr.); 2000. 336p. 26.95 (0-385-31687-9, Delacorte Pr.) Dell Publishing.
—Journey. abr. unabr. ed. 2000. audio compact disk 29.95 (0-553-71219-5); audio 39.95 (0-553-50260-3) Random Hse. Audio Publishing Group. (RH Audio).
—Journey. l.t. ed. 464p. 2001. pap. 13.95 (0-375-72807-4); 2000. 26.95 (0-375-43080-6) Random Hse. Large Print.
Stein, Harry. The Magic Bullet. 1996. 400p. mass mkt. 6.50 o.s.i (0-440-21808-X) Dell Publishing.
—The Magic Bullet. l.t. ed. 1995. 544p. lib. bdg. 24.95 (0-7838-1226-4, Macmillan Reference USA) Gale Group.
Stern, Mark. Inadmissible. 1994. 192p. 19.95 o.p. (0-7867-0057-2, Carroll & Graf Pubs.) Avalon Publishing Group.
Steven, Daniel. Final Remedy. 1996. 384p. pap. 5.50 o.p. (0-06-100878-8) HarperCollins Pubs.
—Final Remedy. Date not set. 384p. mass mkt. (0-06-101041-3, HarperTorch) Morrow/Avon.
Steven, Daniel, told to. Final Remedy. 2002. 383p. pap. 21.95 (0-595-22685-X, Mystery Writers of America Presents) iUniverse, Inc.
Stone, Eric. In a Heartbeat: A Thriller. 1996. 320p. 23.95 o.p. (0-89141-590-4, Presidio Pr.) Ballantine Bks.
Tarloff, Erik. Face-Time. 2000. 256p. reprint ed. pap. 12.95 (0-671-03978-4, Pocket) Simon & Schuster.
Taylor, Janelle. Night Moves. l.t. ed. 2002. (Wheeler Compass Ser.). 439p. 29.95 (1-58724-321-0, Wheeler Publishing, Inc.) Gale Group.
—Night Moves. 2002. 352p. mass mkt. 6.99 o.s.i (0-8217-7145-0) Kensington Publishing Corp.
Terry, Michael D. So Shine Before Men: A Novel. 2002. (First Fiction Ser.). 448p. 24.95 (0-86534-346-2) Sunstone Pr.
Thomas, Ross. Ah, Treachery! 1994. 288p. 21.95 o.s.i (0-89296-452-9) Mysterious Pr.
—Ah, Treachery!, unabr. ed. audio 51.00 (0-7887-0260-2, 94469E7) Recorded Bks., LLC.
—Ah, Treachery! 2004. 288p. pap. 13.95 (0-312-32704-8, Saint Martin's Griffin) St. Martin's Pr.
—Ah, Treachery! 1995. 272p. mass mkt. 5.99 o.s.i (0-446-40031-9) Warner Bks., Inc.
—Briarpatch. E-Book 13.95 (0-312-70960-9) Holtzbrinck Pubs.
—Briarpatch. 1984. 288p. 15.45 o.p. (0-671-53008-9, Simon & Schuster) Simon & Schuster.
—Briarpatch. 2003. 336p. pap. 13.95 (0-312-29031-4, Saint Martin's Griffin) St. Martin's Pr.
—Briarpatch. (Fiction Ser.). 1988. 38p. mass mkt. 5.95 o.p. (0-14-010581-6); 1985. 384p. pap. 6.95 o.p. (0-14-007990-4) Viking Penguin. (Penguin Bks.).
—Cast a Yellow Shadow. 1986. 192p. pap. 2.25 o.p. (0-380-02391-1, 57711-9, Avon Bks.) Morrow/Avon.
—Cast a Yellow Shadow. 1987. 272p. reprint ed. mass mkt. 5.99 o.s.i (0-445-40556-2) Warner Bks., Inc.
—No Questions Asked. 1993. 192p. mass mkt. 4.99 o.p. (0-446-40180-3, Mysterious Pr. Paperback Bks.) Warner Bks., Inc.
—Twilight at Mac's Place. 1990. 352p. 19.95 o.p. (0-89296-214-3); 75.00 (0-89296-434-0) Mysterious Pr.
—Twilight at Mac's Place. mass mkt. (0-312-99038-3, St. Martin's Paperbacks); 2003. 320p. pap. 13.95 (0-312-31584-8, Saint Martin's Griffin) St. Martin's Pr.
—Twilight at Mac's Place. 1991. 352p. mass mkt. 5.99 o.s.i (0-446-40059-9) Warner Bks., Inc.
Trackler, Richard. The Roll-Call Vote. 2001. 300p. pap. 17.95 (1-57197-277-3) Pentland Pr., Inc.
Truman, Margaret. Margaret Truman: Three Complete Mysteries. 1994. 640p. 13.99 o.s.i (0-517-11823-8) Random Hse. Value Publishing.
—Margaret Truman: Three Complete Novels. 1993. 11.99 (0-517-08480-5) Random Hse. Value Publishing.
—Murder at Ford's Theatre. E-Book (0-345-45870-2); 2003. 384p. mass mkt. 7.50 (0-449-00738-3); 2002. 336p. 24.95 (0-345-44489-2, Ballantine Bks.) Ballantine Bks.
—Murder at Ford's Theatre. 2003. 540p. pap. 13.95 (1-4104-0175-8, Wheeler Publishing, Inc.) Gale Group.
—Murder at Ford's Theatre. 2003. (Basic Ser.). 30.95 (0-7862-5038-0) Thorndike Pr.
—Murder at the FBI. 1986. (Capital Crime Myteries Ser.). 336p. mass mkt. 6.99 (0-449-20618-1, Fawcett) Ballantine Bks.
—Murder at the FBI. l.t. ed. 1985. 395p. 17.95 o.p. (0-8161-3925-3); 10.95 o.p. (0-8161-3933-4) Gale Group. (Macmillan Reference USA).
—Murder at the FBI. 1985. 15.95 o.p. (0-87795-680-4, Morrow, William & Co.) Morrow/Avon.
—Murder at the Kennedy Center. 1999. 6.99 (0-449-45926-8); 1990. 352p. mass mkt. 6.99 (0-449-21208-4) Ballantine Bks. (Fawcett).
—Murder at the Kennedy Center. 1993. audio 48.00 (1-56544-014-5, 250029); audio Literate Ear, Inc.
—Murder at the Kennedy Center. 1991. 4.99 o.p. (0-517-07459-1) Random Hse. Value Publishing.
—Murder at the Library of Congress. l.t. ed. 1999. pap. 25.00 o.p. (0-7838-8706-X, Macmillan Reference USA) Gale Group.
—Murder at the Library of Congress, abr. ed. 1999. audio 18.00 Highsmith Inc.
—Murder at the Library of Congress. abr. ed. 1999. audio 18.00 o.s.i (0-375-40564-X, RH Audio) Random Hse. Audio Publishing Group.
—Murder at the Library of Congress. l.t. ed. 1999. 384p. 25.00 o.s.i (0-375-40865-7) Random Hse. Large Print.
—Murder at the National Cathedral. 1999. 6.99 (0-449-45928-4); 1991. 336p. mass mkt. 6.99 (0-449-21939-9) Ballantine Bks. (Fawcett).
—Murder at the National Cathedral. abr. ed. 1990. (Capital Crime Ser.). audio 16.00 o.s.i (0-394-58561-5, RH Audio) Random Hse. Audio Publishing Group.
—Murder at the National Cathedral. 1993. 4.99 o.p. (0-517-08679-4); 5.99 o.p. (0-517-10676-0) Random Hse. Value Publishing.
—Murder at the National Gallery. 1997. mass mkt. 6.99 o.s.i (0-449-22328-0); 368p. mass mkt. 6.99 (0-449-21938-0) Ballantine Bks. (Fawcett).
—Murder at the National Gallery. l.t. ed. 1996. 486p. 23.00 o.p. (0-7838-1687-1, Macmillan Reference USA) Gale Group.
—Murder at the National Gallery. abr. ed. 1997. (Mac & Annabel Smith Mystery Ser.). audio 8.99 o.s.i (0-679-46023-3, 394047, RH Audio) Random Hse. Audio Publishing Group.
—Murder at the Pentagon. 1999. 6.99 (0-449-45927-6); 1994. mass mkt. 5.99 o.p. (0-449-45334-0); 1993. 336p. mass mkt. 6.99 (0-449-21940-2) Ballantine Bks. (Fawcett).
—Murder at the Pentagon. 1993. audio o.p. (0-679-42642-6); 1992. audio 16.00 o.p. (0-394-58672-7); Set. 1993. audio 8.99 o.s.i (0-679-42348-6) Random Hse. Audio Publishing Group. (RH Audio).
—Murder at the Pentagon. l.t. ed. 1992. 23.00 o.s.i (0-679-41357-X) Random Hse. Large Print.
—Murder at the Pentagon. 1994. 5.99 o.p. (0-517-11744-4) Random Hse. Value Publishing.
—Murder at the Watergate. 1999. (Capital Crime Myteries Ser.). 368p. mass mkt. 6.99 (0-449-00194-6, Fawcett) Ballantine Bks.
—Murder at the Watergate. l.t. ed. 1998. o.p. (0-7838-0157-2, Macmillan Reference USA) Gale Group.
—Murder in Foggy Bottom. l.t. ed. 2000. (Large Print Bks.). 396p. 28.95 o.p. (1-56895-947-8, Wheeler Publishing, Inc.) Gale Group.
—Murder in Georgetown. 1987. (Capital Crime Myteries Ser.). 336p. mass mkt. 7.50 (0-449-21332-3, Fawcett) Ballantine Bks.
—Murder in Georgetown. unabr. ed. 2000. audio 49.95 (0-7451-6334-3, CAB 404) Chivers Audio Bks. GBR. *Dist:* BBC Audiobooks America.
—Murder in Georgetown. l.t. ed. 1987. 359p. 10.95 o.p. (0-8161-4146-0, Macmillan Reference USA) Gale Group.
—Murder in Georgetown. 1986. 16.95 o.p. (0-87795-797-5, Morrow, William & Co.) Morrow/Avon.
—Murder in the CIA. 1999. 6.99 (0-449-45925-X); 1988. 320p. reprint ed. mass mkt. 6.99 (0-449-21275-0) Ballantine Bks. (Fawcett).
—Murder in the CIA. l.t. ed. 1988. (General Ser.). 412p. 19.95 o.p. (0-8161-4406-0); 11.95 o.p. (0-8161-4407-9) Gale Group. (Macmillan Reference USA).
—Murder in the CIA. 1993. audio. audio 49.00 (1-56544-013-7, 250030) Literate Ear, Inc.
—Murder in the CIA. abr. ed. 1988. audio 16.00 o.s.i (0-394-57184-3); Set. 1996. audio 8.99 o.s.i (0-679-45597-3, 391229) Random Hse. Audio Publishing Group. (RH Audio).
—Murder in the CIA, unabr. ed. 1991. audio 70.00 (1-55690-364-2, 91219E7) Recorded Bks., LLC.
—Murder in the House. 1998. (Capital Crime Myteries Ser.). 352p. mass mkt. 6.99 (0-449-00172-5, Fawcett) Ballantine Bks.
—Murder in the House, Set. abr. ed. 1997. (Mac & Annabel Smith Mystery Ser.). audio 18.00 o.s.i (0-679-46009-8, 395257, RH Audio) Random Hse. Audio Publishing Group.
—Murder in the House. l.t. ed. 1997. (Large Print Ser.). pap. 24.00 (0-679-77435-1) Random Hse. Large Print.
—Murder in the Smithsonian. (Capital Crime Myteries Ser.). 1985. 304p. mass mkt. 6.99 (0-449-20959-8, Fawcett); 1984. mass mkt. 3.50 o.s.i (0-449-20502-9) Ballantine Bks.
—Murder in the Smithsonian. l.t. ed. 1983. (General Ser.). 9.95 o.p. (0-8161-3631-9); 383p. lib. bdg. 14.95 o.p. (0-8161-3601-7) Gale Group. (Macmillan Reference USA).
—Murder in the Smithsonian. 1993. audio 44.20 (1-56544-035-8, 250024); audio Literate Ear, Inc.
—Murder in the Smithsonian. 1983. 304p. 14.95 o.p. (0-87795-475-5, Morrow, William & Co.) Morrow/Avon.
—Murder in the Supreme Court. (Capital Crime Myteries Ser.). 1985. 288p. mass mkt. 6.99 (0-449-20969-5); 1984. mass mkt. 3.50 o.p. (0-449-20476-6) Ballantine Bks. (Fawcett).
—Murder in the Supreme Court. l.t. ed. 1983. 8.95 o.p. (0-8161-3570-3); lib. bdg. 15.50 o.p. (0-8161-3516-9) Gale Group. (Macmillan Reference USA).
—Murder in the Supreme Court. 1993. audio 44.20 (1-56544-038-2, 250028); audio Literate Ear, Inc.
—Murder in the Supreme Court. 1982. 12.95 o.p. (0-87795-384-8, Morrow, William & Co.) Morrow/Avon.
—Murder in the White House. 2001. (Capital Crimes Ser.). 272p. mass mkt. 6.99 (0-345-44379-9, Fawcett) Ballantine Bks.
—Murder in the White House. l.t. ed. 1981. pap. 9.95 o.p. (0-8161-3281-X); 1980. lib. bdg. 13.95 o.p. (0-8161-3171-6) Gale Group. (Macmillan Reference USA).
—Murder in the White House. 1980. 9.95 o.p. (0-87795-245-0, Morrow, William & Co.) Morrow/Avon.

—Murder in the White House. 1988. mass mkt. 5.99 o.p. (*0-446-31488-9*) Warner Bks., Inc.
—Murder on Capitol Hill. 2001. (Capital Crimes Ser.). 336p. mass mkt. 6.99 (*0-345-44380-2*, Fawcett) Ballantine Bks.
—Murder on Capitol Hill. 1981. (General Ser.). lib. bdg. 14.95 o.p. (*0-8161-3323-9*, Macmillan Reference USA) Gale Group.
—Murder on Capitol Hill. 1981. 256p. 11.95 o.p. (*0-87795-312-0*, Morrow, William & Co.) Morrow/Avon.
—Murder on Capitol Hill. 1989. 288p. pap. 3.50 o.s.i (*0-446-31072-7*); mass mkt. 5.99 o.p. (*0-446-31518-4*) Warner Bks., Inc.
—Murder on Embassy Row. 1985. (Capital Crime Myteries Ser.). 352p. mass mkt. 6.99 (*0-449-20621-1*, Fawcett) Ballantine Bks.
—Murder on Embassy Row. l.t. ed. 1984. (General Ser.). 16.95 o.p. (*0-8161-3727-7*); 9.95 o.p. (*0-8161-3765-X*) Gale Group. (Macmillan Reference USA).
—Murder on Embassy Row. 1993. audio 49.00 (*1-56544-042-0*, 250027); audio Literate Ear, Inc.
—Murder on Embassy Row. 1984. 297p. 15.95 o.p. (*0-87795-594-8*, Morrow, William & Co.) Morrow/Avon.
—Murder on the Potomac. 1995. (Capital Crime Myteries Ser.). 352p. reprint ed. mass mkt. 6.99 (*0-449-21937-2*, Fawcett) Ballantine Bks.
—Murder on the Potomac. 1994. audio 17.00 o.p. (*0-679-41235-2*) McKay, David Co., Inc.
—Murder on the Potomac. abr. ed. 1995. (Mac & Annabel Smith Mystery Ser.). audio 8.99 o.s.i (*0-679-44347-9*, 391231, RH Audio) Random Hse. Audio Publishing Group.
—Murder on the Potomac. l.t. ed. 1994. 404p. pap. 22.00 o.s.i (*0-679-75387-7*) Random Hse. Large Print.
—Murder on the Potomac. unabr. ed. 1994. audio 53.00 (*0-7887-3759-7*, 95957E7) Recorded Bks., LLC.
Twain, Mark. The Gilded Age: A Tale of To-Day. 2002. (World Digital Library). E-Book 3.95 (*0-594-08668-X*) 1873 Pr.
—The Gilded Age: A Tale of To-Day, 2 vols. 1988. (Works of Mark Twain). reprint ed. 1. (*0-7812-1107-7*); 2. lib. bdg. 79.00 (*0-7812-1115-8*) Reprint Services Corp.
Twain, Mark & Fishkin, Shelley Fisher. The Gilded Age: A Tale of To-Day. 1997. (Oxford Mark Twain Ser.). (Illus.). 720p. text 25.00 o.p. (*0-19-511403-5*) Oxford Univ. Pr., Inc.
Twain, Mark & Warner, Charles Dudley. The Gilded Age: A Tale of To-Day. 2002. 436p. 21.99 (*1-4043-0434-7*); per. 16.99 (*1-4043-0435-5*) IndyPublish.com.
—The Gilded Age: A Tale of To-Day. 1985. pap. 4.95 o.p. (*0-452-00779-8*, Meridian Bks.); 1969. (Illus.). 456p. mass mkt. 3.50 o.p. (*0-451-51542-0*, CE1542, Signet Classics) NAL.
—The Gilded Age: A Tale of To-Day. Budd, Louis J., ed. & intro. by. 2001. (Classics Ser.). (Illus.). 512p. pap. 15.00 (*0-14-043920-X*, Penguin Classics) Viking Penguin.
Twain, Mark, et al. The Gilded Age: A Tale of To-Day. 1985. 456p. pap. 13.95 o.s.i (*0-452-00999-5*, Plume) NAL.
Tyree, Omar R. Capital City. 1993. 400p. (Orig.). pap. 12.95 (*1-56411-075-3*) Conquering Bks.
Urban Griot Staff, et al. The Underground: A Hardcore Novel. Chanel, Lisa & Penrice, Ronda Rasha, eds. 3rd ed. 2001. (Urban Groit Ser.). 400p. pap. 12.95 (*0-9710397-0-4*) Mars Productions.
Van Lustbader, Eric. The Kaisho. 1998. 3.99 (*0-671-02329-2*, Pocket) Simon & Schuster.
—The Kaisho. Zion, Claire, ed. 1993. 496p. 22.00 (*0-671-86806-3*, Atria); 1994. 592p. reprint ed. mass mkt. 6.99 (*0-671-86807-1*, Pocket Star) Simon & Schuster.
Vasile, Nick & Bain, Don. A Member of the Family. 1993. 320p. 21.95 o.p. (*0-312-85349-1*, Tor Bks.) Doherty, Tom Assocs., LLC.
Vaughn, Ellen S. The Strand. 1999. 336p. pap. 10.99 (*0-8499-3728-0*); 1997. 320p. 16.99 o.s.i (*0-8499-1328-4*) W Publishing Group.
Vidal, Gore. Empire. 1988. 480p. mass mkt. 6.99 o.s.i (*0-345-35472-9*) Ballantine Bks.
—Empire. unabr. ed. 1993. (American Chronicles Ser.: Vol. 3). audio 112.00 (*0-7366-2471-6*, 3234) Books on Tape, Inc.
—Empire. 2000. (International Ser.). 496p. pap. 16.00 (*0-375-70874-X*, Vintage) Knopf Publishing Group.
—Empire. 1988. audio 16.00 o.s.i (*0-394-57079-0*); audio 14.95 o.p. Random Hse. Audio Publishing Group.
—Empire. 1989. 3.99 o.p. (*0-517-68969-3*) Random Hse. Value Publishing.
—Empire. ltd. ed. 1987. 512p. 100.00 o.p. (*0-394-56127-9*) Random Hse., Inc.
—The Golden Age: A Novel. 2001. 480p. reprint ed. pap. 15.00 (*0-375-72481-8*, Vintage) Knopf Publishing Group.
—The Golden Age: A Novel. abr. ed. 2000. audio compact disk 29.95 (*0-553-71214-4*); audio 39.95 (*0-553-50265-4*) Random Hse. Audio Publishing Group. (RH Audio).
—The Golden Age: A Novel. l.t. ed. 2000. 720p. 27.50 (*0-375-43082-2*) Random Hse. Large Print.
—Washington, D. C. 1988. mass mkt. 4.95 o.p. (*0-345-00887-1*); 1986. 384p. mass mkt. 5.99 o.s.i (*0-345-34236-4*); 1983. mass mkt. 4.50 o.s.i (*0-345-31213-9*); 1981. mass mkt. 3.50 o.s.i (*0-345-30109-9*); 1978. mass mkt. 2.25 o.s.i (*0-345-27463-6*); 1976. mass mkt. 1.95 o.s.i (*0-345-25651-4*) Ballantine Bks.
—Washington, D. C. 2000. (International Ser.). 432p. pap. 15.00 (*0-375-70877-4*, Vintage) Knopf Publishing Group.
—Washington, D. C. (Modern Library Ser.). 1999. 464p. 24.95 o.s.i (*0-679-60291-7*); 1976. 14.95 o.s.i (*0-394-40689-3*) Random Hse., Inc.
—1876: A Novel. 1988. mass mkt. 4.95 o.p. (*0-345-00886-3*); 1987. 448p. mass mkt. 5.99 o.s.i (*0-345-34626-2*); 1982. mass mkt. 3.95 o.s.i (*0-345-30674-0*, Ballantine Bks.); 1977. mass mkt. 2.25 o.s.i (*0-345-25400-7*) Ballantine Bks.
—1876: A Novel. 2000. (Ace's Exambusters Ser.). 384p. pap. 15.00 (*0-375-70872-3*, Vintage) Knopf Publishing Group.
Viorst, Judith. Murdering Mr. Monti: A Merry Little Tale of Sex & Violence. 1994. 254p. 21.00 (*0-671-76074-2*, Simon & Schuster) Simon & Schuster.
Wakling, Christopher. The Immortal Part: A Novel of Suspense. 2003. 320p. 24.95 (*1-57322-239-9*, Riverhead Bks. (Hardcovers)) Putnam Publishing Group, The.
Walker, Robert W. Darkest Instinct. 1996. 464p. mass mkt. 6.99 o.s.i (*0-515-11856-7*, Jove) Berkley Publishing Group.
—Extreme Instinct. 1998. 400p. mass mkt. 6.99 o.s.i (*0-515-12195-9*, Jove) Berkley Publishing Group.
—Fatal Instinct. 1993. 5.99 o.s.i (*1-55773-950-1*, Diamond Bks.) Ace Bks.
—Fatal Instinct. 1995. 320p. mass mkt. 6.99 o.s.i (*0-515-11913-X*, Jove) Berkley Publishing Group.
—Killer Instinct. 1992. 336p. 5.99 o.s.i (*1-55773-743-6*, Diamond Bks.) Ace Bks.
—Killer Instinct. 1995. 336p. mass mkt. 6.99 o.s.i (*0-515-11790-0*, Jove) Berkley Publishing Group.
—Primal Instinct. 1994. 368p. (Orig.). pap. 5.99 o.s.i (*0-7865-0055-7*, Diamond Bks.) Ace Bks.
—Primal Instinct. 1995. 368p. (Orig.). mass mkt. 6.99 o.s.i (*0-515-11949-0*, Jove) Berkley Publishing Group.
—Pure Instinct. 1995. 432p. (Orig.). mass mkt. 6.99 (*0-515-11755-2*, Jove) Berkley Publishing Group.
Walter, Jess. Land of the Blind: A Novel. 2003. 304p. 24.95 (*0-06-039439-0*, ReganBooks) HarperTrade.
Weber, Janice. Hot Ticket. 2000. 384p. mass mkt. 6.50 (*0-446-60788-6*); 1998. 337p. 24.00 o.p. (*0-446-51773-9*) Warner Bks., Inc.
Weld, William. Big Ugly. 2002. 304p. reprint ed. pap. 7.99 (*0-7434-1037-8*, Pocket) Simon & Schuster.
West, Chassie. Killer Riches: A Leigh Ann Warren Mystery. 2001. 304p. mass mkt. 6.50 (*0-06-104391-5*, Avon Bks.) Morrow/Avon.
—Killing Kin. 2000. 336p. mass mkt. 5.99 (*0-06-104389-3*, Avon Bks.) Morrow/Avon.
Whitfield, Van. Guys in Suits. 2002. 272p. pap. 12.95 (*0-385-49847-0*, Anchor) Knopf Publishing Group.
Wickert, Gary L. Dark Redemption. 1999. 475p. pap. 19.95 (*0-936389-70-2*) Tudor Pubs., Inc.
Wiggs, Susan. Halfway to Heaven. l.t. ed. 2002. 505p. 30.95 (*0-7862-3995-6*) Gale Group.
—Halfway to Heaven. 2001. 408p. mass mkt. (*1-55166-837-8*, Mira Bks.) Harlequin Enterprises, Ltd.
Wilcox, Valerie. Sins of Betrayal: A Sailing Mystery. 1999. 304p. mass mkt. 6.50 o.s.i (*0-425-16963-4*, Prime Crime) Berkley Publishing Group.
Wilson, F. Paul. Implant. 1996. 437p. mass mkt. 6.99 (*0-8125-4470-6*); 1995. 352p. 23.95 o.p. (*0-312-89034-6*) Doherty, Tom Assocs., LLC. (Forge Bks.).
Wise, J. Call Me Coffy. 2002. 160p. (C). per. 12.00 (*0-9720298-0-X*) Wise, Jeanne M.
Witham, Larry. Dark Blossom. 1997. 260p. pap. 10.95 (*0-9640428-2-7*) Meridian Bks. of Maryland.
—Dark Blossom: A Novel of East & West. 1997. 260p. (Orig.). pap. text 17.95 (*0-9640428-1-9*) Meridian Bks. of Maryland.
Wood, Philip. Xultun. 2000. 349p. pap. 23.95 (*0-9677983-0-2*) Sun & Shore Pubns.
Woods, Sherryl. Wages of Sin. 1999. 254p. pap. 16.95 (*0-7351-0322-4*); reprint ed. 26.95 o.p. (*0-7351-0071-3*) Replica Bks.
—Wages of Sin. 1994. 272p. mass mkt. 5.50 (*0-446-60088-1*) Warner Bks., Inc.
Woods, Stuart. Capital Crimes. unabr. ed. 2003. (Will Lee Ser.). audio 29.95 (*1-59086-736-X*, 4328, Brilliance Audio Unabridged); audio 69.25 (*1-59086-737-8*, 4329, Library Edition); audio compact disk 29.95 (*1-59086-738-6*, 4330, Brilliance Audio on CD Unabridged); audio compact disk 82.25 (*1-59086-739-4*, 4331, Brilliance Audio on CD Lib Ed) Brilliance Audio.
—Capital Crimes. l.t. ed. 2003. 408p. 32.95 (*1-58724-561-2*, Wheeler Publishing, Inc.) Gale Group.
—Capital Crimes. 2004. 368p. mass mkt. 7.99 (*0-451-21156-1*, Signet Bks.) NAL.
—Capital Crimes. 2003. 304p. 25.95 (*0-399-15090-0*, Putnam & Grosset) Putnam Publishing Group, The.
Wouk, Herman. Inside, Outside. 1985. 656p. 27.95 o.p. (*0-316-95504-3*) Little Brown & Co.
Zigman, Laura. Her: A Novel. 2002. 226p. pap. o.s.i (*0-09-179398-X*) Hutchinson GBR. *Dist:* Random Hse. of Canada, Ltd.
—Her: A Novel. 2003. 224p. reprint ed. pap. 12.00 (*0-375-71322-0*, Anchor) Knopf Publishing Group.
—Her: A Novel. abr. unabr. ed. 2002. audio compact disk 29.95 (*0-553-71341-8*, RH Audio) Random Hse. Audio Publishing Group.

## WASHINGTON (STATE)—FICTION

Alexander, Gary. Kiet Goes West. 1992. 272p. 18.95 o.p. (*0-312-07851-X*, Saint Martin's Minotaur) St. Martin's Pr.
Alexie, Sherman. Indian Killer. 1996. 432p. 22.00 o.p. (*0-87113-652-X*, Atlantic Monthly Pr.) Grove/Atlantic, Inc.
—Indian Killer. 1998. 432p. reprint ed. pap. 14.95 (*0-446-67370-6*) Warner Bks., Inc.
—The Lone Ranger & Tonto Fistfight in Heaven. 2001. E-Book 7.95 (*1-4014-0042-6*); E-Book 7.95 (*1-4014-0043-4*); E-Book 7.95 (*1-4014-0044-2*) Barnes & Noble Digital.
—The Lone Ranger & Tonto Fistfight in Heaven. 1993. 223p. 21.00 o.p. (*0-87113-548-5*, Atlantic Monthly Pr.) Grove/Atlantic, Inc.
—The Lone Ranger & Tonto Fistfight in Heaven. 1994. 240p. pap. 13.00 (*0-06-097624-1*, Perennial) HarperTrade.
—Reservation Blues. 1996. 320p. reprint ed. pap. 13.99 (*0-446-67235-1*) Warner Bks., Inc.
—Reservation Blues: A Novel. 1995. 306p. 21.00 o.p. (*0-87113-594-9*, Atlantic Monthly Pr.) Grove/Atlantic, Inc.
Allen, Irene. Quaker Indictment: An Elizabeth Elliot Mystery. 256p. 1999. (Quaker Sojourn Ser.: 4). (Illus.). mass mkt. 5.99 (*0-312-96684-9*, St. Martin's Paperbacks); 1997. (Elizabeth Elliot Mystery Ser.). 21.95 o.p. (*0-312-16970-1*, Saint Martin's Minotaur) St. Martin's Pr.
Bacher, June M. When Morning Comes Again. l.t. ed. 1993. (Orig.). 22.95 o.p. (*0-7927-1613-2*); pap. 20.95 o.p. (*0-7927-1612-4*) BBC Audiobooks America.
—When Morning Comes Again. 1989. (Orig.). pap. 6.99 o.p. (*0-89081-694-8*) Harvest Hse. Pubs.
Bacho, Peter. Dark Blue Suit: And Other Stories. E-Book 14.95 (*0-295-97974-7*); 1997. 192p. 30.00 (*0-295-97664-0*); 1997. 152p. pap. 16.95 (*0-295-97637-3*) Univ. of Washington Pr.
Ballantyne, Sheila. Imaginary Crimes. (Contemporary American Fiction Ser.). 1983. 272p. pap. 9.95 o.p. (*0-14-006540-7*, Penguin Bks.); 1982. 288p. 13.95 o.p. (*0-670-48022-3*) Viking Penguin.
Baum, Thomas. Out of Body. unabr. ed. 1997. audio 42.00 (*0-7366-3768-0*, 4441) Books on Tape, Inc.
—Out of Body. unabr. ed. 1997. audio 24.95 (*1-57511-029-6*) Publishing Mills, Inc., The.
—Out of Body. 1999. E-Book 21.95 o.s.i (*0-312-20736-0*) St. Martin's Pr.
Baum, Tom. Out of Body. 1999. (Out of Body Ser.: Vol. 1). 256p. mass mkt. 5.99 (*0-312-96735-7*, St. Martin's Paperbacks); 1997. 224p. 22.95 o.p. (*0-312-15620-0*) St. Martin's Pr.
Beck, K. K. Amateur Night: A Jane Da Silva Mystery. 1993. 288p. 18.95 (*0-89296-480-4*) Mysterious Pr.
—Amateur Night: A Jane Da Silva Mystery. 1994. 256p. mass mkt. 5.50 o.s.i (*0-446-40145-5*) Warner Bks., Inc.
—The Body in the Cornflakes. 1994. (Northwest Mysteries Ser.). mass mkt. 4.99 o.s.i (*0-8041-1175-8*, Ivy Bks.) Ballantine Bks.
—The Body in the Cornflakes. pap. 15.95 (*0-312-29184-1*, Saint Martin's Griffin); 1992. 224p. 17.95 (*0-312-08146-4*, Saint Martin's Minotaur) St. Martin's Pr.
—The Body in the Volvo. 1989. 208p. pap. 3.50 o.s.i (*0-8041-0371-2*, Ivy Bks.) Ballantine Bks.
—The Body in the Volvo. 1987. 16.95 o.p. (*0-8027-5685-9*) Walker & Co.
—Cold Smoked: A Jane Da Silva Mystery. 1995. 320p. 18.95 o.s.i (*0-89296-537-1*) Mysterious Pr.
—Cold Smoked: A Jane Da Silva Mystery. 1996. (Jane da Silva Mystery Ser.). 240p. mass mkt. 5.99 (*0-446-40351-2*) Warner Bks., Inc.
—Electric City: A Jane Da Silva Mystery. 1994. 304p. 18.95 o.s.i (*0-89296-536-3*) Mysterious Pr.
—Electric City: A Jane Da Silva Mystery. 1995. 224p. mass mkt. 5.50 (*0-446-40350-4*) Warner Bks., Inc.
—A Hopeless Case. 1992. 18.95 o.p. (*0-89296-479-0*) Mysterious Pr.
—A Hopeless Case. 1993. 272p. mass mkt. 4.99 o.s.i (*0-446-40144-7*) Warner Bks., Inc.
—We Interrupt This Broadcast. 1997. 240p. 20.00 o.p. (*0-89296-642-4*) Mysterious Pr.
Beck, Kathrine, ed. Bad Neighbors. l.t. ed. 1997. (G. K. Hall Mystery Ser.). 363p. lib. bdg. 24.95 o.p. (*0-7838-2008-9*, Macmillan Reference USA) Gale Group.
Billings, Andrew. Carnage. 1999. 368p. mass mkt. 6.50 o.s.i (*0-515-12564-4*, Jove) Berkley Publishing Group.
Bly, Stephen A. & Bly, Janet. Fox Island. 1996. (Hidden West Ser.: Vol. 1). 240p. pap. 10.99 o.p. (*0-89283-941-4*, Vine Bks.) Servant Pubns.
Boone, M. Broughton. Tahoma. 2000. 165p. pap. 12.95 (*0-9671203-0-6*) Cape Winds Pr., Inc.
Brooks, Patricia. But for the Grace. 2000. (Molly Piper Mysteries Ser.). 240p. mass mkt. 5.99 o.s.i (*0-440-22608-2*) Dell Publishing.
—Falling from Grace. 1998. (Molly Piper Mysteries Ser.). 256p. mass mkt. 5.99 o.s.i (*0-440-22607-4*) Dell Publishing.
Brooks, Terry. A Knight of the Word. E-Book 6.99 (*1-58945-521-5*) Adobe Systems, Inc.
—A Knight of the Word. 1999. mass mkt. (*0-345-42942-7*, Ballantine Bks.); 1999. (Trolltown Ser.: Vol. 2). 408p. mass mkt. 6.99 (*0-345-42464-6*); 1998. 25.95 o.s.i (*0-345-43005-0*) Ballantine Bks.
—A Knight of the Word. 2001. E-Book 6.99 (*0-345-44459-0*) Random Hse., Inc.
—A Knight of the Word. unabr. ed. 2000. audio 75.00 (*0-7887-2516-5*, 95589E7) Recorded Bks., LLC.
Brown, Carrie. The Dark. 1995. 279p. 21.00 o.p. (*0-312-11769-8*, Saint Martin's Minotaur) St. Martin's Pr.
Brown, Marilyn McMeen Miller. House on the Sound: A Novel. 2002. 235p. 22.50 (*1-55517-584-8*, Salt Pr.) Cedar Fort, Inc./CFI Distribution.
Burgess, W. A. Cowards. 1997. 197p. 20.95 (*0-312-15503-4*) St. Martin's Pr.
Burton, Hal. Cave of Secrets. 2002. 224p. pap. 13.85 (*0-9725707-0-5*) Burton, Hal Publishing.
Cady, Jack. The Haunting of Hood Canal. 2001. 304p. 23.95 (*0-312-28079-3*) St. Martin's Pr.
Carson, Rob. The Living Mountain. 1992. (Illus.). 72p. (J). (gr. k-8). pap. 10.95 (*0-9623072-9-7*) Storytellers Ink, Inc.
Chance, Megan. A Season in Eden. 1999. 352p. mass mkt. 5.99 (*0-06-108705-X*) HarperCollins Pubs.
—A Season in Eden. l.t. ed. 2000. (Americana Ser.). 443p. 29.95 (*0-7862-2477-0*) Thorndike Pr.
Clausen, Lowen. First Avenue. 2000. 384p. mass mkt. 6.99 (*0-451-40948-5*, Onyx) NAL.
—First Avenue: A Novel. 1999. 352p. 21.95 (*0-9669919-0-7*) Watershed Bks.
Coburn, Randy Sue. Remembering Jody. 1999. 322p. 22.95 (*0-7867-0566-3*, Carroll & Graf Pubs.) Avalon Publishing Group.
Colbert, Curt. Rat City: A Jake Rossiter & Miss Jenkins Mystery. 2001. (Jake Rossiter & Miss Jenkins Mystery Ser.). 368p. pap. 15.00 (*0-9663473-5-8*) UglyTown.
Collette, Rondi. The Meadow Dancers. 2001. 250p. pap. 14.95 (*0-9705031-0-5*) Hawthorne Pubs.
Copeland, Lori. June. E-Book 9.99 (*0-8423-5678-9*); 1999. (Brides of the West Ser.: Bk. 2). 272p. pap. 9.99 (*0-8423-0268-9*, HeartQuest) Tyndale Hse. Pubs.
Coyle, Daniel. Waking Samuel. 2003. 304p. 23.95 (*1-58234-281-4*) Bloomsbury Publishing.
Daheim, Mary R. The Alpine Advocate. 1992. (Emma Lord Mysteries Ser.). 240p. mass mkt. 6.99 (*0-345-37672-2*) Ballantine Bks.
—The Alpine Betrayal. 1993. (Emma Lord Mysteries Ser.). 240p. mass mkt. 6.99 (*0-345-37937-3*) Ballantine Bks.
—The Alpine Christmas. 1993. (Emma Lord Mysteries Ser.). 272p. mass mkt. 6.99 (*0-345-38270-6*) Ballantine Bks.
—The Alpine Decoy. 1994. (Emma Lord Mysteries Ser.). 256p. mass mkt. 6.99 (*0-345-38841-0*) Ballantine Bks.
—The Alpine Escape. 1995. (Emma Lord Mysteries Ser.). 288p. (Orig.). mass mkt. 6.99 (*0-345-38842-9*) Ballantine Bks.
—The Alpine Fury. 1995. 320p. (Orig.). mass mkt. 6.99 (*0-345-38843-7*) Ballantine Bks.
—The Alpine Gamble. 1996. (Emma Lord Mysteries Ser.). 304p. mass mkt. 6.99 (*0-345-39641-3*) Ballantine Bks.
—The Alpine Gamble. l.t. ed. 1999. (Beeler Large Print Mystery Ser.). (*1-57490-210-5*, Beeler Large Print Bks.) Beeler, Thomas T. Publisher.
—The Alpine Hero. 1996. (Emma Lord Mysteries Ser.). 320p. mass mkt. 6.99 (*0-345-39642-1*) Ballantine Bks.
—The Alpine Hero. l.t. ed. 1999. (Beeler Large Print Mystery Ser.). 25.95 (*1-57490-203-2*, Beeler Large Print Bks.) Beeler, Thomas T. Publisher.
—The Alpine Icon. 1997. (Emma Lord Mysteries Ser.). 336p. mass mkt. 6.99 (*0-345-39643-X*) Ballantine Bks.

—The Alpine Icon. l.t. ed. 1998. 353p. 24.95 (*1-57490-138-9*, Beeler Large Print Bks.) Beeler, Thomas T. Publisher.
—The Alpine Journey. 1998. (Emma Lord Mysteries Ser.). 320p. mass mkt. 6.99 (*0-345-39644-8*) Ballantine Bks.
—Alpine Journey. l.t. ed. 2003. 512p. 25.95 (*0-375-43268-X*, Random House Large Print) Random Hse. Large Print.
—The Alpine Kindred. l.t. ed. 2004. 448p. 25.95 (*0-375-43253-1*) Random Hse. Large Print.
—The Alpine Kindred: An Emma Lord Mystery. 1998. (Emma Lord Mysteries Ser.). 320p. mass mkt. 6.99 (*0-345-42122-1*) Ballantine Bks.
—The Alpine Legacy. 1999. (Emma Lord Mysteries Ser.). 320p. mass mkt. 6.99 (*0-345-42123-X*, Ballantine Bks.) Ballantine Bks.
—The Alpine Nemesis. 2001. (Emma Lord Mystery Ser.). 320p. mass mkt. 6.99 (*0-345-42125-6*) Ballantine Bks.
—Auntie Mayhem. 1996. (Bed-and-Breakfast Mysteries Ser.). 272p. mass mkt. 6.99 (*0-380-77878-5*, Avon Bks.) Morrow/Avon.
—Bantam of the Opera. 1993. 256p. (Orig.). mass mkt. 6.99 (*0-380-76934-4*, Avon Bks.) Morrow/Avon.
—Creeps Suzette. 2000. (Bed & Breakfast Mystery Ser.). 336p. mass mkt. 6.99 (*0-380-80079-9*, Avon Bks.) Morrow/Avon.
—Dune to Death. 1993. (Bed-and-Breakfast Mysteries Ser.). 240p. (Orig.). mass mkt. 6.99 (*0-380-76933-6*, Avon Bks.) Morrow/Avon.
—A Fit of Tempera. 1994. (Bed-and-Breakfast Mysteries Ser.). 256p. reprint ed. mass mkt. 6.99 (*0-380-77490-9*, Avon Bks.) Morrow/Avon.
—Fowl Prey. 1991. (Bed-and-Breakfast Mysteries Ser.). 272p. (Orig.). mass mkt. 6.99 (*0-380-76296-X*, Avon Bks.) Morrow/Avon.
—Holy Terrors. 1999. (Bed-and-Breakfast Mysteries Ser.). 256p. (Orig.). mass mkt. 6.99 (*0-380-76297-8*, Avon Bks.) Morrow/Avon.
—Just Desserts. l.t. ed. 2001. (Beeler Large Print Mystery Ser.). 240p. 25.95 (*1-57490-351-9*, Beeler Large Print Bks.) Beeler, Thomas T. Publisher.
—Just Desserts. 1999. (Bed & Breakfast Mystery Ser.). 256p. mass mkt. 6.99 (*0-380-76295-1*, Avon Bks.) Morrow/Avon.
—Legs Benedict: A Bed-and-Breakfast Mystery. 1999. (Bed-and-Breakfast Mysteries Ser.). 320p. mass mkt. 6.50 (*0-380-80078-0*, Avon Bks.) Morrow/Avon.
—Major Vices. 1995. (Bed-and-Breakfast Mysteries Ser.). 256p. (Orig.). mass mkt. 6.50 (*0-380-77491-7*, Avon Bks.) Morrow/Avon.
—Murder, My Suite. l.t. ed. 2002. 26.95 (*1-57490-414-0*) Beeler, Thomas T. Publisher.
—Murder, My Suite. 1995. (Bed-and-Breakfast Mysteries Ser.). 272p. mass mkt. 6.50 (*0-380-77877-7*, Avon Bks.) Morrow/Avon.
—Nutty as a Fruitcake. 1996. (Bed-and-Breakfast Mysteries Ser.). 272p. mass mkt. 6.99 (*0-380-77879-3*, Avon Bks.) Morrow/Avon.
—September Mourn. 1997. (Bed-and-Breakfast Mysteries Ser.). (Illus.). 320p. mass mkt. 6.50 (*0-380-78518-8*, Avon Bks.) Morrow/Avon.
—Snow Place to Die: Where There's Ice... There's Vice. 1998. (Bed & Breakfast Mystery Ser.: No. 13). 304p. mass mkt. 6.99 (*0-380-78521-8*, Avon Bks.) Morrow/Avon.
—A Streetcar Named Expire. 2001. (Bed-and-Breakfast Mysteries Ser.). 320p. mass mkt. 6.99 (*0-380-80080-2*, Avon Bks.) Morrow/Avon.
—Suture Self. 2001. (Bed-and-Breakfast Mysteries Ser.). 304p. 23.00 (*0-380-97866-0*, Morrow, William & Co.) Morrow/Avon.
Dalton, Margot. Third Choice. 1998. (Jackie Kaminsky Mysteries Ser.). 384p. mass mkt. (*1-55166-441-0*, 1-66441-6, Harlequin Bks.) Harlequin Enterprises, Ltd.
Dereske, Jo. Final Notice, Bk. 3. 1998. (Miss Zukas Mystery Ser.). 240p. mass mkt. 5.99 (*0-380-78245-6*, Avon Bks.) Morrow/Avon.
—Miss Zukas & Stroke of Death. 1995. (Miss Zukas Mystery Ser.: No. 3). 224p. mass mkt. 6.50 (*0-380-77033-4*, Avon Bks.) Morrow/Avon.
—Miss Zukas & the Island Murders. 1995. (Miss Zukas Mystery Ser.). 224p. (Orig.). mass mkt. 5.99 (*0-380-77031-8*, Avon Bks.) Morrow/Avon.
—Miss Zukas & the Library Murders. l.t. ed. 2003. (Mystery Ser.). (Orig.). 27.95 (*1-57490-511-2*) Beeler, Thomas T. Publisher.
—Miss Zukas & the Library Murders. 1994. (Miss Zukas Mystery Ser.). 224p. (Orig.). mass mkt. 5.99 (*0-380-77030-X*, Avon Bks.) Morrow/Avon.
—Miss Zukas & the Raven's Dance. 1996. (Miss Zukas Mystery Ser.). 256p. mass mkt. 5.99 (*0-380-78243-X*, Avon Bks.) Morrow/Avon.
—Miss Zukas in Death's Shadow. 1999. 224p. mass mkt. 5.99 (*0-380-80472-7*, Avon Bks.) Morrow/Avon.
—Miss Zukas Shelves the Evidence. l.t. ed. 2002. (Paperback Ser.). 310p. pap. 25.95 (*0-7838-9734-0*) Gale Group.
—Miss Zukas Shelves the Evidence. 2001. (Miss Zukas Mystery Ser.). 256p. mass mkt. 5.99 (*0-380-80474-3*, Avon Bks.) Morrow/Avon.
—Out of Circulation. 1997. (Miss Zukas Mystery Ser.). mass mkt. 5.99 (*0-380-78244-8*, Avon Bks.) Morrow/Avon.
Dibdin, Michael. Dark Specter: A Novel. 1996. o.s.i (*0-676-51374-3*) Random Hse., Inc.
Dillard, Annie. The Living. unabr. ed. 1993. audio 83.95 (*0-7861-0639-5*, 130298) Blackstone Audio Bks., Inc.
—The Living. abr. ed. audio 16.00 o.p. (*1-55994-608-3*, HarperAudio) HarperTrade.
—The Living: A Novel. 1993. 416p. pap. 72.00 o.p. (*0-06-092422-5*) HarperCollins Pubs.
—The Living: A Novel. 1993. 464p. pap. 14.95 (*0-06-092411-X*, Perennial); 1992. 416p. 22.50 o.p. (*0-06-016870-6*); 1992. 416p. 100.00 o.p. (*0-06-017993-7*) HarperTrade.
Doig, Ivan. Mountain Time. abr. ed. 1999. 25.00 incl. audio (*0-7871-2016-2*, Dove Audio) NewStar Media, Inc.
—Mountain Time. 320p. 2000. pap. 13.00 (*0-684-86569-6*); 1999. 25.00 o.s.i (*0-684-83295-X*) Simon & Schuster. (Scribner).
—Mountain Time. l.t. ed. 1999. (Americana Ser.). 487p. 29.95 (*0-7862-2216-6*) Thorndike Pr.
Dovell, Michael. The Dahlia Connection: A Deacon Davenport Mystery. Dunn, Brian, ed. 1995. (Illus.). 212p. 24.95 (*1-877882-19-4*); pap. 11.95 (*1-877882-18-6*) SCW Pubns.
Duckworth, Marion. Remembering the Roses. 1998. (Palisades Pure Romance Ser.). 294p. pap. 9.99 o.s.i (*1-57673-236-3*, Palisades) Multnomah Pubs., Inc.
—Remembering the Roses. l.t. ed. 1999. (Christian Fiction Ser.). 416p. 24.95 (*0-7862-2057-0*) Thorndike Pr.
Duncan, David J. The Brothers K. 1993. 736p. mass mkt. 6.99 o.s.i (*0-553-56314-9*); 1996. 656p. reprint ed. pap. 14.95 (*0-553-37849-X*) Bantam Bks.
Duncan, Sharon. A Deep Blue Farewell. 2002. 304p. mass mkt. 5.99 (*0-451-20677-0*) NAL.
Elkins, Aaron. The Dark Place. 1983. 192p. 13.95 o.s.i (*0-8027-5565-8*) Walker & Co.
—The Dark Place. 1994. 208p. mass mkt. 5.99 o.s.i (*0-446-40403-9*); 1989. mass mkt. 4.50 o.s.i (*0-445-20955-0*) Warner Bks., Inc.
—A Deceptive Clarity. 1993. mass mkt. 5.99 o.s.i (*0-449-14900-5*, Fawcett) Ballantine Bks.
—A Deceptive Clarity. 1989. 2.99 o.p. (*0-517-00558-1*) Random Hse. Value Publishing.
—A Deceptive Clarity. 1987. 15.95 o.p. (*0-8027-5666-2*) Walker & Co.
—A Glancing Light. 1994. mass mkt. o.s.i (*0-449-45458-4*); 1992. mass mkt. 4.99 o.s.i (*0-449-14829-7*) Ballantine Bks. (Fawcett).
—A Glancing Light. 1991. 368p. 18.95 o.s.i (*0-684-19278-0*, Macmillan Reference USA) Gale Group.
—Old Scores. unabr. ed. 1995. (Chris Norgren Mystery Ser.: Vol. 3). audio 51.00 (*0-7887-0166-5*, 94391E7) Recorded Bks., LLC.
—Old Scores: A Chris Norgren Mystery. l.t. ed. 1994. 22.95 o.p. (*0-7927-1944-1*); pap. 20.95 o.p. (*0-7927-1943-3*) BBC Audiobooks America.
—Old Scores: A Chris Norgren Mystery. 1994. (Northwest Mysteries Ser.). mass mkt. 5.99 o.s.i (*0-449-14899-8*, Fawcett) Ballantine Bks.
—Old Scores: A Chris Norgren Mystery. 1993. 256p. 20.00 o.p. (*0-684-19551-8*, Macmillan Reference USA) Gale Group.
Emerson, Earl. Black Hearts & Slow Dancing. 1997. 256p. mass mkt. 5.99 (*0-380-72937-7*, Avon Bks.); 1988. 320p. 17.95 o.p. (*0-688-07533-9*, Morrow, William & Co.) Morrow/Avon.
—Black Hearts & Slow Dancing. 1989. 272p. pap. 5.95 o.p. (*0-14-011732-6*, Penguin Bks.) Viking Penguin.
—Catfish Cafe. 1999. 304p. mass mkt. 6.99 (*0-345-42212-0*); 1998. 272p. 22.00 o.p. (*0-345-42202-3*) Ballantine Bks.
—The Dead Horse Paint Company. 1997. (Mac Fontana Mystery Ser.: No. 5). 272p. 24.00 (*0-688-13751-2*, Morrow, William & Co.); 1998. (Mac Fontana Mystery Ser.). 288p. reprint ed. mass mkt. 5.99 o.s.i (*0-380-72438-3*, Avon Bks.) Morrow/Avon.
—Deception Pass. 1998. (Thomas Black Mysteries Ser.). 304p. mass mkt. 6.99 (*0-345-40069-0*) Ballantine Bks.
—Deviant Behavior. 1990. (Thomas Black Mysteries Ser.). 224p. mass mkt. 6.50 (*0-345-36028-1*) Ballantine Bks.
—Deviant Behavior. 1988. 256p. 17.95 o.p. (*0-688-08335-8*, Morrow, William & Co.) Morrow/Avon.
—Fat Tuesday. 1988. (Thomas Black Mysteries Ser.). 288p. mass mkt. 6.99 (*0-345-35223-8*) Ballantine Bks.
—Fat Tuesday. 1987. 288p. 16.95 o.p. (*0-688-06770-0*, Morrow, William & Co.) Morrow/Avon.
—Going Crazy in Public. 1997. 288p. mass mkt. 5.99 (*0-380-72437-5*, Avon Bks.); 1996. 256p. 24.00 o.p. (*0-688-13750-4*, Morrow, William & Co.) Morrow/Avon.
—Help Wanted: Orphans Preferred. 1990. 320p. 17.95 o.p. (*0-688-09333-7*, Morrow, William & Co.); 1991. 288p. reprint ed. mass mkt. 4.99 o.p. (*0-380-71047-1*, Avon Bks.) Morrow/Avon.
—The Million-Dollar Tattoo. 1997. (Thomas Black Mysteries Ser.). 304p. mass mkt. 5.99 (*0-345-40067-4*) Ballantine Bks.
—The Million-Dollar Tattoo. unabr. ed. 1997. (Thomas Black Mystery Ser.: Vol. 9). audio 51.00 (*0-7887-0813-9*, 94963E7) Recorded Bks., LLC.
—Morons & Madmen: A Mac Fontana Mystery. 1993. 18.00 o.p. (*0-688-09334-5*, Morrow, William & Co.); 1994. 256p. reprint ed. mass mkt. 4.99 (*0-380-72075-2*, Avon Bks.) Morrow/Avon.
—Morons & Madmen: A Mac Fontana Mystery. 268p. pap. 3.98 o.p. (*0-7651-0494-6*) Smithmark Pubs., Inc.
—Nervous Laughter. 1998. mass mkt. 3.99 o.s.i (*0-345-42945-1*); 1997. 288p. mass mkt. 6.50 (*0-345-41407-1*) Ballantine Bks.
—Nervous Laughter. 1986. mass mkt. 4.99 (*0-380-89906-X*, Avon Bks.) Morrow/Avon.
—The Portland Laugher. 1995. (Thomas Black Mysteries Ser.). 352p. mass mkt. 6.50 (*0-345-39782-7*) Ballantine Bks.
—Poverty Bay. 1998. mass mkt. 3.99 o.s.i (*0-345-42944-3*); 1997. 320p. mass mkt. 6.99 (*0-345-41406-3*) Ballantine Bks.
—Poverty Bay. 1985. 256p. mass mkt. 4.99 (*0-380-89647-8*, Avon Bks.) Morrow/Avon.
—Poverty Bay. unabr. ed. 1994. (Thomas Black Mystery Ser.: Vol. 2). audio 51.00 (*1-55690-980-2*, 94119E7) Recorded Bks., LLC.
—The Rainy City. 1998. mass mkt. 3.99 o.s.i (*0-345-42943-5*); 1997. 288p. mass mkt. 6.99 (*0-345-41405-5*) Ballantine Bks.
—The Rainy City. 1985. (Thomas Black Ser.). 240p. mass mkt. 4.99 (*0-380-89517-X*, Avon Bks.) Morrow/Avon.
—The Rainy City. unabr. ed. 1992. (Thomas Black Mystery Ser.: Vol. 1). audio 51.00 (*1-55690-723-0*, 92218E7) Recorded Bks., LLC.
—The Vanishing Smile. (Thomas Black Mysteries Ser.). 1996. 320p. mass mkt. 6.99 (*0-345-40453-X*); 1995. 272p. 21.00 o.s.i (*0-345-38486-5*) Ballantine Bks.
—Yellow Dog Party: A Thomas Black Mystery. 1992. (Thomas Black Mysteries Ser.). 256p. mass mkt. 6.99 (*0-345-37716-8*) Ballantine Bks.
—Yellow Dog Party: A Thomas Black Mystery. 1991. 288p. 19.00 o.p. (*0-688-09635-2*, Morrow, William & Co.) Morrow/Avon.
Fergusson, Bruce C. The Piper's Sons. 1999. 352p. 24.95 o.p. (*0-525-94431-1*) Dutton/Plume.
—The Piper's Sons. 1999. 432p. reprint ed. mass mkt. 6.99 o.s.i (*0-451-40875-6*, Signet Bks.) NAL.
Ford, G. M. The Bum's Rush. 1998. (Leo Waterman Mysteries Ser.). 320p. mass mkt. 5.99 (*0-380-72763-3*, Avon Bks.) Morrow/Avon.
—The Bum's Rush. 1997. (Leo Waterman Mysteries Ser.). 246p. 22.95 (*0-8027-3299-2*) Walker & Co.
—Cast in Stone. 1997. (Leo Waterman Mysteries Ser.). 304p. mass mkt. 5.99 (*0-380-72762-5*, Avon Bks.) Morrow/Avon.
—Cast in Stone. 1996. (Leo Waterman Mysteries Ser.). 288p. 21.95 (*0-8027-3267-4*) Walker & Co.
—The Deader the Better. (Leo Waterman Mysteries Ser.). 352p. 2000. 22.00 (*0-380-97723-0*); 2001. reprint ed. mass mkt. 6.99 (*0-380-80420-4*, Avon Bks.) Morrow/Avon.
—Fury. 2002. 384p. mass mkt. 6.99 (*0-380-80421-2*) Morrow/Avon.
—Fury: A Novel. 2001. 336p. 24.00 (*0-380-97724-9*, Morrow, William & Co.) Morrow/Avon.
—The Last Ditch. (Leo Waterman Mysteries Ser.). 2000. 320p. mass mkt. 5.99 (*0-380-79369-5*); 1999. 288p. 22.00 (*0-380-97557-2*) Morrow/Avon. (Avon Bks.).
—Slow Burn. (Leo Waterman Mysteries Ser.). 1999. 304p. mass mkt. 5.99 (*0-380-79367-9*); 1998. 288p. 20.00 (*0-380-97556-4*) Morrow/Avon. (Avon Bks.).
—Who in Hell Is Wanda Fuca? 1996. (Leo Waterman Mysteries Ser.). 320p. mass mkt. 5.99 (*0-380-72761-7*, Avon Bks.) Morrow/Avon.
—Who in Hell Is Wanda Fuca? 1995. 244p. 21.95 (*0-8027-3255-0*) Walker & Co.
French, Linda. Coffee to Die For. 1998. (Professor Teodora Morelli Mystery Ser.: No. 2). 224p. mass mkt. 5.99 (*0-380-79575-2*, Avon Bks.) Morrow/Avon.
—Steeped in Murder. 1999. (Professor Teodora Morelli Mystery Ser.). 256p. mass mkt. 5.99 (*0-380-79576-0*, Avon Bks.) Morrow/Avon.
—Talking Rain: A Professor Teodora Morelli Mystery. 1998. (Professor Teodora Morelli Mystery Ser.). 224p. mass mkt. 5.99 (*0-380-79573-6*, Avon Bks.) Morrow/Avon.
Garrison, Leslie Ann. Mental Graffiti: Tall Tales Trilogy. l.t. ed. 1999. (Tall Tales Ser.: No. 2). E-Book 24.95 incl. cd-rom (*1-929077-27-0*, Books OnScreen) PageFree Publishing, Inc.
—Sniper's Candy: Tall Tales Trilogy. l.t. ed. 2000. (Tall Tales Ser.: No. 3). E-Book 24.95 incl. cd-rom (*1-929077-28-9*, Books OnScreen) PageFree Publishing, Inc.
—Visions of Murder: Tall Tales Trilogy. l.t. ed. 1999. (Tall Tales Ser.). E-Book 14.99 incl. cd-rom (*1-929077-26-2*, Books OnScreen) PageFree Publishing, Inc.
Gilpatrick, Noreen. Shadow of Death. 1995. 400p. 19.95 o.s.i (*0-89296-515-0*); 1993. 384p. 17.95 (*0-89296-514-2*) Mysterious Pr.
Gloss, Molly. Wild Life: A Novel. 2000. (Illus.). 256p. 24.00 (*0-684-86798-2*, Simon & Schuster) Simon & Schuster.
—Wild Life: A Novel. l.t. ed. 2000. (Basic Ser.). (Illus.). 463p. 28.95 (*0-7862-2872-5*) Thorndike Pr.
Grant, Vanessa. Seeing Stars. 2001. (Romance Ser.). 256p. mass mkt. 4.99 o.p. (*0-8217-6778-X*) Kensington Publishing Corp.
Greer, Andrew S. How It Was for Me: Stories. 2000. 224p. 23.00 (*0-312-24105-4*) Picador.
Grippando, James M. Under Cover of Darkness. 2001. 480p. mass mkt. 7.50 (*0-06-109747-0*) Morrow/Avon.
Guterson, David. East of the Mountains. 1999. 304p. 25.00 (*0-15-100229-0*) Harcourt Trade Pubs.
—East of the Mountains. abr. ed. 1999. audio 25.00 Highsmith Inc.
—East of the Mountains. abr. ed. 1999. audio 25.00 o.s.i (*0-553-52573-5*, 696038); audio compact disk 29.95 (*0-553-45618-0*); audio 34.95 (*0-553-50224-7*, 895847) Random Hse. Audio Publishing Group. (RH Audio).
—East of the Mountains. l.t. ed. 1999. (Basic Ser.). 424p. 30.95 (*0-7862-2038-4*) Thorndike Pr.
—East of the Mountains. 2000. 20.05 (*0-606-17641-1*) Turtleback Bks.
—East of the Mountains. abr. ed. 1999. audio 16.85 (*0-00-105559-3*) Ulverscroft Audio (U.S.A.).
—Our Lady of the Forest. 2003. 336p. 25.95 (*0-375-41211-5*) Knopf, Alfred A. Inc.
—Our Lady of the Forest. unabr. ed. 2003. audio 39.95 (*0-7393-0637-5*) Random Hse. Audio Publishing Group.
—Our Lady of the Forest. l.t. ed. 2003. 544p. 27.95 (*0-375-43293-0*) Random Hse. Large Print.
—Snow Falling on Cedars. unabr. ed. 1996. audio 84.95 (*0-7451-2752-5*, SAB 118, Sterling Audio Bks.) BBC Audiobooks America.
—Snow Falling on Cedars. unabr. ed. 1996. audio 80.00 (*0-913369-19-5*, 4165) Books on Tape, Inc.
—Snow Falling on Cedars. 1999. 352p. 20.00 o.s.i (*0-15-100443-9*, Harvest Bks.); 1994. 100.00 o.s.i (*0-15-100242-8*); 1994. 368p. 21.95 (*0-15-100100-6*) Harcourt Trade Pubs.
—Snow Falling on Cedars. 1998. 512p. pap. 14.00 (*0-676-57609-5*); 1995. 480p. pap. 14.00 (*0-679-76402-X*) Knopf Publishing Group. (Vintage).
—Snow Falling on Cedars, Level 6. 2000. pap. 7.93 (*0-582-41928-X*) Longman Publishing Group.
—Snow Falling on Cedars. abr. ed. 1995. audio 18.00 (*0-679-44775-X*, 393149); 1998. audio 39.95 (*0-375-40468-6*); Set. 1999. audio compact disk 21.95 (*0-375-40811-8*) Random Hse. Audio Publishing Group. (RH Audio).
—Snow Falling on Cedars. unabr. ed. audio 91.00 (*0-7887-0585-7*, 94738E7); 2000. audio compact disk 116.00 (*0-7887-3718-X*, C1075E7) Recorded Bks., LLC.
—Snow Falling on Cedars. 1995. (Vintage Contemporaries Ser.). 20.05 (*0-606-12140-4*) Turtleback Bks.
—Snow Falling on Cedars. abr. ed. 1998. audio 16.85 (*0-00-105207-1*) Ulverscroft Audio (U.S.A.).
Hannah, Kristin. If You Believe. 2004. 384p. mass mkt. 4.99 (*0-345-46710-8*); 1995. mass mkt. 2.99 o.s.i (*0-449-14971-4*, Fawcett); 1993. 384p. mass mkt. 6.99 (*0-449-14837-8*, Fawcett) Ballantine Bks.
—If You Believe. l.t. ed. 1994. 415p. lib. bdg. 21.95 o.p. (*0-8161-5965-3*, Macmillan Reference USA) Gale Group.
—On Mystic Lake. 2004. 432p. pap. 13.95 (*0-345-47117-2*); 2000. 416p. mass mkt. 6.99 (*0-449-14967-6*, Ballantine Bks.) Ballantine Bks.
—On Mystic Lake. abr. ed. 2000. audio 7.99 (*1-56740-328-X*, 1954, Paperback Nova Audio Bks.); 1999. audio 17.95 o.p. (*1-56740-826-5*, 1604, Nova Audio Bks.); 1999. audio 39.95 (*1-56740-406-5*, 1602, Brilliance Audio Unabridged); 1999. 10p. audio 73.25 (*1-56740-634-3*, 1603, Unabridged Library Editions) Brilliance Audio.
—On Mystic Lake. l.t. ed. 1999. (Large Print Book Ser.). 27.95 (*1-56895-631-2*, Wheeler Publishing, Inc.) Gale Group.
—On Mystic Lake, abr. ed. 1999. audio 17.95 Highsmith Inc.
—Summer Island. 2002. 416p. mass mkt. 6.99 (*0-345-44113-3*) Ballantine Bks.

Settings

—Summer Island. unabr. ed. 2001. audio 69.25 (1-58788-301-5, 2539, Unabridged Library Editions) Brilliance Audio.

—Summer Island. l.t. ed. 2001. 368p. lib. bdg. 29.95 (1-58547-107-0); 367p. 17.97 (1-74030-498-5) Ctr. Point Large Print.

—Summer Island: A Novel. 2001. 336p. 21.00 o.s.i (0-609-60737-5, Crown) Crown Publishing Group.

Harper, Karen. The Falls. l.t. ed. 2003. 472p. pap. 25.95 (1-58724-537-X, Wheeler Publishing, Inc.) Gale Group.

—The Falls. 2003. 400p. mass mkt. (1-55166-695-2, Mira Bks.) Harlequin Enterprises, Ltd.

Harris, E. Lynn. Abide with Me. 1999. (Abide with Me Ser.: Vol. 3). 368p. 24.95 (0-385-48657-X) Doubleday Publishing.

—Abide with Me. 2000. 368p. pap. 13.00 (0-385-48658-8, Knopf Bks. for Young Readers) Random Hse. Children's Bks.

—Abide with Me. 2003. (African American Ser.). 535p. 29.95 (0-7862-5062-3) Thorndike Pr.

Hawley, Michael A. The Double Bluff. 2002. 400p. (Orig.). mass mkt. 6.99 (0-451-41047-5, Onyx) NAL.

Hegi, Ursula. Salt Dancers. 1997. 240p. pap. 12.00 (0-684-84482-6, Touchstone); 1996. pap. (0-684-00289-2, Scribner Paper Fiction); 1996. 240p. per. 11.00 (0-684-82530-9, Scribner Paper Fiction); 1995. 240p. 22.00 (0-684-80209-0, Simon & Schuster) Simon & Schuster.

Hendricks, Judith Ryan. Bread Alone: A Novel. l.t. ed. 2002. (Wheeler Large Print Book Ser.). 27.95 (1-58724-171-4, Wheeler Publishing, Inc.) Gale Group.

—Bread Alone: A Novel. 2001. 368p. 25.00 (0-06-018895-2, Morrow, William & Co.) Morrow/Avon.

Heubner, Fredrick. Methods of Execution: A Novel. 1994. 284p. 22.00 (0-671-86724-5, Simon & Schuster) Simon & Schuster.

Higginson, Ella. From the Land of the Snow-Pearls: Tales from Puget Sound. 1977. (Short Story Index Reprint Ser.). 19.95 (0-8369-3553-5) Ayer Co. Pubs., Inc.

Hoyt, Richard. Bigfoot. 1995. 246p. pap. text 4.99 (0-8125-1948-5, Forge Bks.); 1992. 224p. 17.95 o.p. (0-312-85278-9, Tor Bks.) Doherty, Tom Assocs., LLC.

—Decoys: A John Denson Mystery. 1980. 204p. 8.95 o.p. (0-87131-330-8) Evans, M. & Co., Inc.

—Decoys: A John Denson Mystery. 1984. (Crime Ser.). 208p. pap. 3.95 o.p. (0-14-007217-9, Penguin Bks.) Viking Penguin.

—Fish Story. 1987. 288p. reprint ed. pap. 3.95 o.p. (0-8125-0491-7, Tor Bks.) Doherty, Tom Assocs., LLC.

—Fish Story. 1985. (Mystery Ser.). 224p. 13.95 o.p. (0-670-31672-5) Viking Penguin.

—Siskiyou. 1984. 304p. (Orig.). pap. 3.50 o.p. (0-8125-0487-9, Tor Bks.) Doherty, Tom Assocs., LLC.

—Snake Eyes. (John Denson Mystery Ser.). 1996. 250p. mass mkt. 5.99 (0-8125-5072-2); 1995. 256p. 27.95 o.p. (0-312-85805-1) Doherty, Tom Assocs., LLC. (Forge Bks.).

—Thirty for a Harry: A John Denson Mystery. l.t. ed. 1991. 8.95 o.p. (0-7451-9624-1, 5043); pap. 10.95 o.p. (0-7927-0024-4, 647) BBC Audiobooks America.

—Thirty for a Harry: A John Denson Mystery. 1981. 192p. 8.95 o.p. (0-87131-357-X) Evans, M. & Co., Inc.

—Thirty for a Harry: A John Denson Mystery. 1984. (Crime Monthly Ser.). 192p. pap. 3.95 o.p. (0-14-007216-0, Penguin Bks.) Viking Penguin.

—Whoo? 2000. 224p. mass mkt. 5.99 (0-8125-1276-6, Forge Bks.); 1991. 17.95 o.p. (0-312-85149-9, Tor Bks.) Doherty, Tom Assocs., LLC.

Huebner, Frederick D. Methods of Execution. 1995. mass mkt. 5.99 o.s.i (0-449-14939-0, Fawcett) Ballantine Bks.

—Methods of Execution. unabr. ed. 1994. audio 56.00 (0-7366-2882-7, 3584) Books on Tape, Inc.

—Shades of Justice. 2003. 384p. mass mkt. 6.99 (0-451-20768-8, Signet Bks.) NAL.

—Shades of Justice. 2001. 368p. 24.00 o.s.i (0-684-81847-7, Simon & Schuster) Simon & Schuster.

Hughes, Dean. Lucky's Mud Festival. 1991. (Lucky Ladd Ser.: Bk. 5). 141p. (Orig.). (J). (gr. 3-6). pap. text o.p. (0-87579-566-8, Cinnamon Tree) Deseret Bk. Co.

Jackson, Lisa. A Twist of Fate. 2003. (Illus.). 256p. mass mkt. (1-55166-705-3, Mira Bks.) Harlequin Enterprises, Ltd.

Jance, J. A. Birds of Prey: A Novel of Suspense. l.t. ed. 2001. 464p. pap. 24.00 (0-06-018562-7, HarperLargePrint) HarperTrade.

—Birds of Prey: A Novel of Suspense. 2002. 416p. mass mkt. 7.99 (0-380-71654-2); 2001. 390p. 24.00 (0-380-97407-X, Morrow, William & Co.) Morrow/Avon.

—Breach of Duty. unabr. ed. 1999. (J. P. Beaumont Mystery Ser.: Bk. 14). audio 49.95 (1-55686-897-9) Books in Motion.

—Breach of Duty. 1999. (J. P. Beaumont Mystery Ser.). 384p. mass mkt. 7.50 (0-380-71843-X); 352p. 23.00 (0-380-97406-1) Morrow/Avon. (Avon Bks.).

—Breach of Duty. 2002. (Famous Authors Ser.). 29.95 (0-7862-4758-4) Thorndike Pr.

—Failure to Appear. unabr. ed. 1995. (J. P. Beaumont Mystery Ser.: Bk. 11). audio 49.95 (1-55686-562-7, 892559) Books in Motion.

—Failure to Appear. unabr. collector's ed. 1998. (J. P. Beaumont Ser.: Vol. 11). audio 56.00 (0-7366-4042-8, 4541) Books on Tape, Inc.

—Failure to Appear. (J. P. Beaumont Mystery Ser.). 1994. 384p. mass mkt. 7.50 (0-380-75839-3, Avon Bks.); 1993. 269p. 20.00 o.p. (0-688-12674-X, Morrow, William & Co.) Morrow/Avon.

—Failure to Appear. 2003. (Famous Authors Ser.). 29.95 (0-7862-4760-6) Thorndike Pr.

—Hour of the Hunter. unabr. ed. 1994. (Joanna Brady Mystery Ser.). audio 64.95 (1-55686-470-1, 112714) Books in Motion.

—Hour of the Hunter. (J. P. Beaumont Mystery Ser.). 1992. 416p. mass mkt. 7.99 (0-380-71107-9, Avon Bks.); 1991. 356p. 20.00 o.p. (0-688-09630-1, Morrow, William & Co.) Morrow/Avon.

—Hour of the Hunter. l.t. ed. 2003. 669p. 29.95 (0-7862-5321-5) Thorndike Pr.

—Improbable Cause. unabr. ed. 1993. (J. P. Beaumont Mystery Ser.: Bk. 5). audio 39.95 (1-55686-462-0, 752414) Books in Motion.

—Improbable Cause. unabr. collector's ed. 1997. (J. P. Beaumont Ser.). audio 48.00 (0-7366-3609-9, 4266) Books on Tape, Inc.

—Improbable Cause. 2003. (J. P. Beaumont Mystery Ser.). 352p. mass mkt. 7.50 (0-380-75412-6, Avon Bks.) Morrow/Avon.

—Improbable Cause. 1992. 224p. reprint ed. 19.00 o.p. (0-7278-4314-1) Severn Hse. Pubs., Ltd.

—Injustice for All. unabr. ed. 1992. (J. P. Beaumont Mystery Ser.: Bk. 2). audio 39.95 (1-55686-415-9, 415) Books in Motion.

—Injustice for All. unabr. collector's ed. 1997. (J. P. Beaumont Ser.: Vol. 2). audio 56.00 (0-7366-3568-8, 4217) Books on Tape, Inc.

—Injustice for All. 1986. (J. P. Beaumont Mystery Ser.). 384p. mass mkt. 7.50 (0-380-89641-9, Avon Bks.) Morrow/Avon.

—Injustice for All. 1993. 19.00 o.p. (0-7278-4431-8) Severn Hse. Pubs., Ltd.

—Lying in Wait. unabr. ed. 1994. (J. P. Beaumont Mystery Ser.: Bk. 12). audio 49.95 (1-55686-563-5, 102592) Books in Motion.

—Lying in Wait. (J. P. Beaumont Mystery Ser.). 1996. 400p. mass mkt. 7.99 (0-380-71841-3, Avon Bks.); 1994. 303p. 17.95 o.p. (0-688-02013-5, Morrow, William & Co.) Morrow/Avon.

—Lying in Wait. l.t. ed. 2003. (J. P. Beaumont Mystery Ser.). 447p. 29.95 (0-7862-4762-2) Thorndike Pr.

—Minor in Possession. unabr. ed. 1993. (J. P. Beaumont Mystery Ser.). audio 49.95 (1-55686-475-2, 892536) Books in Motion.

—Minor in Possession. unabr. collector's ed. 1997. (J. P. Beaumont Ser.). audio 56.00 (0-7366-3824-5, 4492) Books on Tape, Inc.

—Minor in Possession. 1990. (J. P. Beaumont Mystery Ser.). 384p. mass mkt. 7.50 (0-380-75546-7, Avon Bks.) Morrow/Avon.

—A More Perfect Union. unabr. ed. 1993. (J. P. Beaumont Mystery Ser.: Bk. 6). audio 39.95 (1-55686-466-3, 752467) Books in Motion.

—A More Perfect Union. unabr. collector's ed. 1997. (J. P. Beaumont Ser.). audio 48.00 (0-7366-3822-9, 4490) Books on Tape, Inc.

—A More Perfect Union. 2003. (J. P. Beaumont Mystery Ser.). 352p. mass mkt. 7.50 (0-380-75413-4, Avon Bks.) Morrow/Avon.

—A More Perfect Union. 1992. 224p. reprint ed. 19.00 o.p. (0-7278-4361-3) Severn Hse. Pubs., Ltd.

—Name Withheld. l.t. ed. 2001. 320p. 28.95 (1-57490-357-8, Beeler Large Print Bks.) Beeler, Thomas T. Publisher.

—Name Withheld. unabr. ed. 1996. (J. P. Beaumont Mystery Ser.: Bk. 13). audio 46.95 (1-55686-651-8, 893938) Books in Motion.

—Name Withheld. (J. P. Beaumont Mystery Ser.). 1997. 400p. mass mkt. 6.99 (0-380-71842-1, Avon Bks.); 1996. 293p. 22.00 o.p. (0-688-11460-1, Morrow, William & Co.) Morrow/Avon.

—Payment in Kind. unabr. ed. 1992. (J. P. Beaumont Mystery Ser.: Bk. 9). audio 49.95 (1-55686-410-8, 892515) Books in Motion.

—Payment in Kind. unabr. collector's ed. 1997. audio 56.00 (0-7366-3825-3, 4493) Books on Tape, Inc.

—Payment in Kind, Bk. 9. 1991. (J. P. Beaumont Mystery Ser.). 384p. mass mkt. 7.50 (0-380-75836-9, Avon Bks.) Morrow/Avon.

—Taking the Fifth. unabr. ed. 1993. (J. P. Beaumont Mystery Ser.: Bk. 4). audio 39.95 (1-55686-458-2, 752411) Books in Motion.

—Taking the Fifth. unabr. collector's ed. 1997. (J. P. Beaumont Ser.: Vol. 4). audio 48.00 (0-7366-3626-9, 4286) Books on Tape, Inc.

—Taking the Fifth. 1987. (J. P. Beaumont Mystery Ser.). 320p. mass mkt. 7.99 (0-380-75139-9, Avon Bks.) Morrow/Avon.

—Taking the Fifth. 320p. 25.99 (0-7278-5944-7) Severn Hse. Pubs., Ltd.

—Three Complete Novels. 1996. 13.99 o.s.i (0-517-14764-5) Random Hse. Value Publishing.

—Trial by Fury. unabr. ed. 1993. (J. P. Beaumont Mystery Ser.: Bk. 3). audio 39.95 (1-55686-456-6, 752468) Books in Motion.

—Trial by Fury. unabr. collector's ed. 1997. (J. P. Beaumont Ser.: Vol. 3). audio 48.00 (0-7366-3582-3, 4236) Books on Tape, Inc.

—Trial by Fury. 1986. (J. P. Beaumont Mystery Ser.). 384p. mass mkt. 7.99 (0-380-75138-0, Avon Bks.) Morrow/Avon.

—Trial by Fury. 384p. 26.00 (0-7278-5609-X) Severn Hse. Pubs., Ltd.

—Until Proven Guilty. l.t. ed. 1991. 21.95 o.p. (0-7927-0825-3, CH080); pap. 19.95 o.p. (0-7927-0826-1, CS0176) BBC Audiobooks America.

—Until Proven Guilty. unabr. ed. 1992. (J. P. Beaumont Mystery Ser.: Bk. 1). audio 39.95 (1-55686-414-0, 752460) Books in Motion.

—Until Proven Guilty. unabr. collector's ed. 1997. (J. P. Beaumont Ser.: Vol. 1). audio 48.00 (0-7366-3584-X, 4238) Books on Tape, Inc.

—Until Proven Guilty. 1985. (J. P. Beaumont Mystery Ser.). 352p. mass mkt. 7.99 (0-380-89638-9, Avon Bks.) Morrow/Avon.

—Without Due Process. unabr. ed. 1993. (J. P. Beaumont Mystery Ser.: Bk. 10). audio 49.95 (1-55686-476-0, 892538) Books in Motion.

—Without Due Process. unabr. collector's ed. 1998. (J. P. Beaumont Ser.). audio 56.00 (0-7366-4041-X, 4540) Books on Tape, Inc.

—Without Due Process. (J. P. Beaumont Mystery Ser.). 1993. 384p. mass mkt. 7.50 (0-380-75837-7, Avon Bks.); 1992. 302p. 20.00 o.p. (0-688-11459-8, Morrow, William & Co.) Morrow/Avon.

—Without Due Process. 4.98 o.p. (0-8317-8577-2) Smithmark Pubs., Inc.

Kalpakian, Laura. Educating Waverly. 2002. 336p. 24.95 (0-380-97768-0, Morrow, William & Co.) Morrow/Avon.

—Steps & Exes: A Novel of Family. 2000. 336p. pap. 13.00 (0-380-80659-2, Perennial) HarperTrade.

—Steps & Exes: A Novel of Family. 1999. 336p. 23.00 (0-380-97767-2, Avon Bks.) Morrow/Avon.

Kersey, Colin. Soul Catcher. 1995. 272p. 22.95 o.p. (0-312-13606-4) St. Martin's Pr.

Kilby, Joan. Child of Her Dreams. 2002. (Harlequin Superromance Ser.: No. 1076). 304p. mass mkt. (0-373-71076-3, Harlequin Bks.) Harlequin Enterprises, Ltd.

Krentz, Jayne Ann. Absolutely, Positively. unabr. ed. 1996. audio 64.00 (0-7366-3436-3, 104621) Books on Tape, Inc.

—Absolutely, Positively. l.t. ed. 1996. 25.95 (1-56895-286-4, Wheeler Publishing, Inc.) Gale Group.

—Absolutely, Positively. 384p. 2003. mass mkt. 5.99 (0-7434-6737-X); 1997. pap. 7.99 (0-671-77873-0) Simon & Schuster. (Pocket).

—Absolutely, Positively. Zion, Claire, ed. 1996. 352p. 23.00 o.p. (0-671-55170-1, Atria) Simon & Schuster.

—Absolutely, Positively, abr. ed. 1997. audio 17.00 (0-671-88653-3, 394827, Simon & Schuster Audioworks) Simon & Schuster Audio.

—The Adventurer. 1998. 249p. mass mkt. (1-55166-462-3, 1-66562-2, Mira Bks.); 1990. (Harlequin Temptation Ser.: No. 293). pap. (0-373-25393-1, Harlequin Bks.) Harlequin Enterprises, Ltd.

—The Adventurer. l.t. ed. 2000. (Famous Authors Ser.). 293p. 27.95 (0-7862-2602-1) Thorndike Pr.

—Deep Waters. l.t. ed. 1997. (Large Print Book Ser.). 26.95 (1-56895-437-9, Wheeler Publishing, Inc.) Gale Group.

—Deep Waters. 2002. 400p. mass mkt. 7.99 (0-7434-5722-6, Pocket); 1997. (Illus.). 400p. mass mkt. 7.99 (0-671-52420-8, Pocket Star); 1997. 352p. 23.00 (0-671-52419-4, Atria) Simon & Schuster.

—Deep Waters. abr. ed. 1997. 3p. audio 18.00 (0-671-57523-6, 394871, Simon & Schuster Audioworks) Simon & Schuster Audio.

—Flash. l.t. ed. 1998. (Wheeler Large Print Book Ser.). 26.95 (1-56895-593-6, Wheeler Publishing, Inc.) Gale Group.

—Flash. 2002. 432p. mass mkt. 7.99 (0-7434-5647-5, Pocket); 1999. (Illus.). 432p. pap. 7.99 (0-671-52309-0, Pocket Star); 1998. 368p. 24.00 o.s.i (0-671-52308-2, Atria) Simon & Schuster.

—The Golden Chance; Silver Linings: Omnibus Edition. 2001. 528p. pap. 12.95 o.s.i (0-7434-2295-3, Pocket) Simon & Schuster.

—Hidden Talents. unabr. collector's ed. 1996. audio 64.00 (0-7366-3448-7, 4092) Books on Tape, Inc.

—Hidden Talents. l.t. ed. 1994. 23.95 o.p. (1-56895-056-X, Wheeler Publishing, Inc.) Gale Group.

—Hidden Talents. 416p. 1997. mass mkt. 7.99 (0-671-01965-1); 1993. mass mkt. 6.99 (0-671-77871-4) Simon & Schuster. (Pocket).

—Hidden Talents Promotion. 1997. (Illus.). 432p. mass mkt. 3.99 (0-671-01135-9, Pocket) Simon & Schuster.

—Sharp Edges. l.t. ed. 1998. 26.95 (1-56895-549-9, Wheeler Publishing, Inc.) Gale Group.

—Sharp Edges. 1998. (Illus.). 400p. mass mkt. 7.50 (0-671-52409-7, Pocket Star); 320p. 24.00 (0-671-52310-4, Atria) Simon & Schuster.

—Sharp Edges. abr. ed. 1998. audio 18.00 o.s.i (0-671-57613-5, 395615, Simon & Schuster Audioworks) Simon & Schuster Audio.

—Trust Me. unabr. ed. 1996. audio 64.00 (0-7366-3334-0, 3985) Books on Tape, Inc.

—Trust Me. l.t. ed. 1995. (Large Print Bks.). 25.95 o.p. (1-56895-204-X, Wheeler Publishing, Inc.) Gale Group.

—Trust Me. 1998. per. 6.99 (0-671-01969-4); 1995. 368p. mass mkt. 7.99 (0-671-51692-2) Simon & Schuster. (Pocket).

—Trust Me. Zion, Claire, ed. 1995. 320p. 22.00 o.p. (0-671-51691-4, Atria) Simon & Schuster.

—Trust Me. 2001. audio 9.98 o.s.i (0-671-04437-0); Set. 1995. audio 17.00 (0-671-88652-5, 391817) Simon & Schuster Audio. (Simon & Schuster Audioworks).

Leon, Bonnie. In Fields of Freedom. 1999. (Sowers Triology Ser.: No. 2). 320p. pap. 12.99 (0-8054-1273-5) Broadman & Holman Pubs.

Macomber, Debbie. Between Friends: A Novel. 2002. 384p. (1-55166-905-6, 1-66905-0, Mira Bks.) Harlequin Enterprises, Ltd.

—Fallen Angel. 1996. 256p. per. (1-55166-180-2, 1-66180-0, Mira Bks.); 1990. (Silhouette Special Edition Ser.: No. 577). pap. (0-373-09577-5, Silhouette) Harlequin Enterprises, Ltd.

—Fallen Angel. l.t. ed. 2000. (Americana Ser.). 334p. 26.95 (0-7862-2601-3) Thorndike Pr.

—16 Lighthouse Road. l.t. ed. 2002. (Americana Ser.). 486p. 31.95 (0-7862-3904-2) Gale Group.

—16 Lighthouse Road. 2001. 384p. mass mkt. (1-55166-830-0, Mira Bks.) Harlequin Enterprises, Ltd.

—204 Rosewood Lane. 2002. 384p. mass mkt. (1-55166-929-3, Mira Bks.) Harlequin Enterprises, Ltd.

—204 Rosewood Lane. 2003. (Americana Ser.). 31.95 (0-7862-4966-8) Thorndike Pr.

—311 Pelican Court. l.t. ed. 2003. 511p. 31.95 (0-7862-6068-8) Gale Group.

—311 Pelican Court. 2003. 384p. mass mkt. (1-55166-719-3, Mira Bks.) Harlequin Enterprises, Ltd.

Martin, Nora. Flight of the Fisherbird. 2003. (Illus.). 200p. (J). 16.95 (1-58234-814-6, Bloomsbury Children) Bloomsbury Publishing.

Martini, Steve. Critical Mass. 1999. reprint ed. 384p. mass mkt. 7.99 (0-515-12648-9); 7.99 (0-515-12583-0) Berkley Publishing Group. (Jove).

—Critical Mass. l.t. ed. 1998. 28.95 (1-56895-668-1, Wheeler Publishing, Inc.) Gale Group.

—Critical Mass. 1998. 448p. 25.95 o.p. (0-399-14362-9) Penguin Group (USA) Inc.

Masiel, David. 2182 kHz. l.t. ed. 2002. 28.95 (0-7862-4475-5) Thorndike Pr.

—2182 kHz: A Novel. 2002. 304p. 22.95 (0-375-50606-3) Random Hse., Inc.

Maxwell, Evan. Season of the Swan. l.t. ed. 1998. 23.95 (1-57490-132-X, Beeler Large Print Bks.) Beeler, Thomas T. Publisher.

—Season of the Swan. 256p. 1998. mass mkt. 6.50 o.s.i (0-06-109975-9); 1997. 19.00 o.p. (0-06-017529-X) HarperCollins Pubs.

—Season of the Swan, unabr. ed. 1998. audio 51.00 (0-7887-2005-8, 95392E7) Recorded Bks., LLC.

McCourtney, Lorena. Dear Silver. 1997. 286p. pap. 9.99 o.p. (1-57673-110-3, Palisades) Multnomah Pubs., Inc.

McGrory, Brian. The Incumbent. 2000. 352p. 24.95 o.s.i (0-7434-0350-9, Atria) Simon & Schuster.

Mead, Dave. Dead Even. E-Book 6.50 (0-9671113-4-X) Electric Umbrella Publishing.

—Dead Even. 1999. E-Book 6.00 (1-929374-04-6) Fire Mountain Pr.

Meyerding, Jane. Everywhere House. 1994. 256p. (Orig.). pap. 9.95 (0-934678-42-1) New Victoria Pubs., Inc.

Michael, Judith, pseud. Acts of Love. l.t. ed. 1997. 480p. mass mkt. 7.99 (0-8041-1787-X, Ivy Bks.) Ballantine Bks.

—Acts of Love. abr. ed. 1997. (Civil War Ser.). 3p. audio 7.99 o.p. (1-56740-225-9, 618, Paperback Nova Audio Bks.); audio 16.95 o.p. (1-56100-968-7, 1128, Nova Audio Bks.); audio 105.25 o.p. (1-56100-809-5, 787, Unabridged Library Editions); audio 27.95 o.p. (1-56100-731-5, 25, Bookcassette) Brilliance Audio.

—Acts of Love. l.t. ed. 1997. 6624p. pap. 24.00 o.s.i (0-679-77418-1) Random Hse., Inc.

Miller, Linda Lael. Courting Susannah. 2000. 352p. mass mkt. 7.99 (0-671-00400-X, Pocket) Simon & Schuster.

—Courting Susannah. l.t. ed. 2001. (Thorndike Americana Ser.). 477p. 30.95 (0-7862-3226-9) Thorndike Pr.

—Daniel's Bride. 1996. 400p. mass mkt. 3.99 (*0-671-00814-5*, Pocket) Simon & Schuster.
—Daniel's Bride. Marrow, Linda, ed. 1992. 400p. mass mkt. 6.99 o.s.i (*0-671-73166-1*, Pocket) Simon & Schuster.
—Fletcher's Woman. 1997. mass mkt. 3.99 (*0-671-01004-2*); 1991. 320p. mass mkt. 6.99 (*0-671-73768-6*); 1990. mass mkt. 4.50 (*0-671-70632-2*) Simon & Schuster. (Pocket).
—Yankee Wife. l.t. ed. 2002. lib. bdg. 28.95 (*1-58547-195-X*, Premier) Ctr. Point Large Print.
Moody, Skye Kathleen. Blue Poppy. 1998. (WWL Mystery Ser.: No. 293). per. (*0-373-26293-0*, 0-26293-1, Worldwide Library) Harlequin Enterprises, Ltd.
—Blue Poppy. 1997. (Pacific Northwest Mysteries Ser.). 256p. 23.95 (*0-312-15479-8*, Saint Martin's Minotaur) St. Martin's Pr.
—Habitat. 1999. (Illus.). 274p. 24.95 (*0-312-20390-X*, Saint Martin's Minotaur) St. Martin's Pr.
—Rain Dance. 1998. (WWL Mystery Ser.). per. (*0-373-26278-7*, 1-26278-1, Worldwide Library) Harlequin Enterprises, Ltd.
—Rain Dance. 1996. 256p. 21.95 (*0-312-14713-9*, Saint Martin's Minotaur) St. Martin's Pr.
—Wildcrafters. 1999. (WWL Mystery Ser.: Vol. 332). 272p. per. (*0-373-26332-5*, Harlequin Bks.) Harlequin Enterprises, Ltd.
—Wildcrafters. 1998. (Pacific Northwest Mysteries Ser.). 320p. 23.95 o.p. (*0-312-19364-5*, Saint Martin's Minotaur) St. Martin's Pr.
Morgan, Mary. Deeper Waters. E-Book 23.95 (*0-312-70683-9*); 2002. 304p. 23.95 (*0-312-29035-7*, Saint Martin's Minotaur) St. Martin's Pr.
Nordberg, Bette. Thin Air. 2002. 320p. pap. 11.99 (*0-7642-2398-4*) Bethany Hse. Pubs.
Nunnally, Tiina. Fate of Ravens: A Margit Andersson Mystery. 1998. (Suspense Ser.: Vol. 2). 220p. pap. 12.00 (*0-940242-80-X*) Fjord Pr.
—Runemaker. 1996. (Suspense Ser.: No. 1). 213p. (Orig.). pap. 12.00 (*0-940242-77-X*) Fjord Pr.
O'Brien, Meg. Gathering Lies. 2001. (Illus.). 408p. mass mkt. (*1-55166-807-6*, 1-66807-8, Mira Bks.) Harlequin Enterprises, Ltd.
Oliver, Steve. Moody Forever. 2003. 258p. pap. 13.95 (*0-9644138-1-7*, Dark City Bks.) OffByOne Pr.
—Moody Forever. (St. Martin's Minotaur Mysteries Ser.). 272p. 1999. mass mkt. 5.99 (*0-312-96923-6*, St. Martin's Paperbacks); 1998. 22.95 o.p. (*0-312-19301-7*, Saint Martin's Minotaur) St. Martin's Pr.
—Moody Gets the Blues. 1996. (Illus.). 256p. 21.95 (*0-9644138-7-6*) OffByOne Pr.
—Moody Gets the Blues, Vol. 1. 1998. 256p. pap. 5.99 (*0-312-96502-8*, St. Martin's Paperbacks) St. Martin's Pr.
Oran, Daniel. Ulterior Motive. 1999. 384p. mass mkt. 5.99 o.s.i (*0-7860-0657-9*); 1998. 320p. mass mkt. 22.95 o.s.i (*1-57566-302-3*, Kensington Bks.) Kensington Publishing Corp.
—Ulterior Motive. 2001. E-Book 6.99 (*0-7592-1210-4*); 1998. 284p. per. 19.96 (*0-7592-1215-5*) eread-s.com.
Orton, Thomas. The Lost Glass Plates of Wilfred Eng: A Novel. 256p. 1999. text 24.00 o.p. (*1-58243-023-3*); 2000. reprint ed. pap. text 14.00 (*1-58243-125-6*) Basic Bks. (Counterpoint Pr.).
Parker, T. Jefferson. Red Light. l.t. ed. 2003. lib. bdg. 29.95 (*1-58547-308-1*, Premier) Ctr. Point Large Print.
—Red Light. 2000. 326p. 23.95 (*0-7868-6600-4*); 2003. 384p. reprint ed. mass mkt. 7.99 (*0-7868-8975-6*) Hyperion Pr.
Parks, Mary A. The Circle Leads Home. 1998. (Women's West Ser.: Vol. 3). 224p. 22.50 o.p. (*0-87081-488-5*) Univ. Pr. of Colorado.
Paul, Jasmine. A Girl in Parts: A Novel. 2003. 248p. pap. text 14.95 (*1-58243-285-6*); 2002. 256p. text 24.00 (*1-58243-218-X*) Basic Bks. (Counterpoint Pr.).
Pearson, Ridley. The Angel Maker. 1994. 464p. mass mkt. 7.50 o.s.i (*0-440-21632-X*) Dell Publishing.
—The Angel Maker. 2003. (Illus.). 368p. reprint ed. mass mkt. 6.99 (*0-7868-9008-8*) Hyperion Pr.
—The Angel Maker. abr. ed. 1999. audio 9.99 o.s.i (*0-553-70195-9*, RH Audio) Random Hse. Audio Publishing Group.
—Beyond Recognition. unabr. ed. 1998. audio 96.00 (*0-7366-4092-4*, 4599) Books on Tape, Inc.
—Beyond Recognition. abr. ed. 1997. (Lou Boldt & Daphne Matthews Mystery Ser.). 3p. audio 7.99 (*1-56740-228-3*, 627, Paperback Nova Audio Bks.); audio 16.95 o.p. (*1-56100-970-9*, 1134, Nova Audio Bks.); audio 27.95 (*1-56100-733-1*, 45, Bookcassette); audio 105.25 (*1-56100-807-9*, 809) Brilliance Audio.
—Beyond Recognition. 1997. 496p. 22.95 o.p. (*0-7868-6240-8*); 2003. 656p. reprint ed. mass mkt. 7.99 (*0-7868-8928-4*) Hyperion Pr.
—Blood of the Albatross. 1993. 307p. mass mkt. 6.99 (*0-312-95183-3*, St. Martin's Paperbacks); 1986. mass mkt. 3.95 o.s.i (*0-312-90607-2*, St. Martin's Paperbacks); 1986. 16.95 o.p. (*0-312-08448-X*); Vol. 1. 1992. mass mkt. 4.99 o.s.i (*0-312-92974-9*, St. Martin's Paperbacks) St. Martin's Pr.
—The Body of David Hayes. 2003. 23.95 (*0-7868-6725-6*) Hyperion Pr.
—The First Victim. aut. ltd. ed. 1999. 400p. 23.95 (*0-7868-6558-X*) Disney Pr.
—The First Victim. l.t. ed. 2001. (Large Print Bks.). 475p. pap. 23.95 (*1-58724-099-8*, Wheeler Publishing, Inc.) Gale Group.
—The First Victim. 1999. 381p. 23.95 (*0-7868-6440-0*); 2003. 416p. reprint ed. mass mkt. 7.99 (*0-7868-8966-7*) Hyperion Pr.
—No Witnesses. unabr. ed. 1995. (Lou Boldt & Daphne Matthews Mystery Ser.). audio 72.00 (*0-7366-2950-5*, 3644) Books on Tape, Inc.
—No Witnesses. 1996. 480p. mass mkt. 7.50 o.s.i (*0-440-22142-0*) Dell Publishing.
—No Witnesses. 1994. 384p. 22.95 (*0-7868-6066-9*); 2003. 480p. reprint ed. mass mkt. 6.99 (*0-7868-9006-1*) Hyperion Pr.
—No Witnesses. abr. ed. 1999. audio 9.99 o.s.i (*0-553-70215-7*, RH Audio) Random Hse. Audio Publishing Group.
—The Pied Piper. l.t. ed. 2000. pap. 23.95 (*1-56895-834-X*, Wheeler Publishing, Inc.) Gale Group.
—The Pied Piper. 1998. 497p. 23.95 (*0-7868-6300-5*); 2003. 528p. reprint ed. mass mkt. 7.99 (*0-7868-8955-1*) Hyperion Pr.
—The Pied Piper & Beyond Recognition. 1998. (*0-7868-6433-8*) Disney Pr.
—Undercurrents. 2000. E-Book 4.99 (*1-58910-004-2*) PreviewPort.com.
—Undercurrents. 1992. mass mkt. 6.99 (*0-312-92958-7*, St. Martin's Paperbacks); 1989. mass mkt. 4.95 o.s.i (*0-312-91485-7*, St. Martin's Paperbacks); 1988. 416p. 18.95 o.p. (*0-312-01841-X*) St. Martin's Pr.
Pereira, Peter, et al, eds. Pontoon, Number Two: An Anthology of Washington State Poets. 1998. 96p. pap. 7.00 (*0-9647199-5-9*) Floating Bridge Pr.
Plowman, Mary S. White Powder. Goodfellow, Pamela R., ed. 1996. pap. 9.99 (*0-9639882-6-3*) Goodfellow Pr., Inc.
Radke, Nancy. Turnagain Love. 1998. 337p. E-Book 4.99 (*1-57343-010-2*) LionHearted Publishing, Inc.
Reardon, Joyce. The Diary of Ellen Rimbauer: My Life at Rose Red. 2002. E-Book 14.95 (*1-4013-9675-5*) Hyperion Pr.
Reece, Colleen L. The Hills of Hope. l.t. ed. 2001. (Christian Fiction Ser.). 259p. 25.95 (*0-7862-3071-1*) Thorndike Pr.
Reynolds, Marjorie. The Civil Wars of Jonah Moran. 2001. 336p. reprint ed. pap. 13.95 o.s.i (*0-425-17834-X*) Berkley Publishing Group.
Roberts, Nora. River's End. 2000. 480p. mass mkt. 7.99 (*0-515-12783-3*, Jove) Berkley Publishing Group.
—River's End. abr. ed. 2000. audio 7.99 (*1-56740-986-5*, 2156, Paperback Nova Audio Bks.); 1999. audio 17.95 o.p. (*1-56740-828-1*, 1622, Nova Audio Bks.); 1999. audio 39.95 (*1-56740-412-X*, 1621, Brilliance Audio Unabridged); 1999. 14p. audio 73.25 (*1-56740-640-8*, 1635, Unabridged Library Editions) Brilliance Audio.
—River's End. abr. ed. 1999. audio 17.95. audio 39.95 Highsmith Inc.
—River's End. 2001. (*0-399-15029-3*); 1999. 420p. 23.95 o.s.i (*0-399-14470-6*) Penguin Group (USA) Inc.
—River's End. l.t. ed. (Paperback Bestsellers Ser.). 2000. 664p. 28.95 (*0-7862-1862-2*); 1999. 714p. pap. 31.95 (*0-7862-1861-4*) Thorndike Pr.
Ross, Dana Fuller, pseud. Washington! 1983. (General Ser.). lib. bdg. 15.95 o.p. (*0-8161-3507-X*); pap. 8.95 o.p. (*0-8161-3577-0*) Gale Group. (Macmillan Reference USA).
Ross, JoAnn. Homeplace. 1999. (Illus.). 416p. pap. 6.99 (*0-671-02706-9*, Pocket) Simon & Schuster.
Rushford, Patricia H. Red Sky in Mourning. 1997. (Helen Bradley Mysteries Ser.: Vol. 2). 240p. pap. 9.99 o.p. (*1-55661-731-3*) Bethany Hse. Pubs.
—Red Sky in Mourning. l.t. ed. 1999. (Christian Mystery Ser.). 360p. 23.95 o.p. (*0-7862-1693-X*) Thorndike Pr.
Saul, John. Black Lightning. Grey, Linda, ed. 1996. 448p. mass mkt. 7.99 (*0-449-22504-6*, Fawcett) Ballantine Bks.
Sheahan, Bernie. Spring Break. 1996. (Palisades University Ser.: No. 3). 186p. (gr. 7-11). pap. 5.99 o.p. (*0-88070-950-2*, Palisades) Multnomah Pubs., Inc.
Sherman, Charlotte W. One Dark Body: A Novel. 1993. 224p. 20.00 o.p. (*0-06-016924-9*) HarperTrade.
Simonson, Sheila. Larkspur. 1991. 224p. reprint ed. mass mkt. (*0-373-26074-1*, Harlequin Bks.) Harlequin Enterprises, Ltd.
—Larkspur: A Mystery. 1990. 16.95 o.p. (*0-312-04338-4*, Saint Martin's Minotaur) St. Martin's Pr.
—Meadowlark. 1997. (WWL Mystery Ser.: No. 240). per. (*0-373-26240-X*, 1-26240-1, Worldwide Library) Harlequin Enterprises, Ltd.
—Meadowlark. 1996. 256p. 21.95 o.p. (*0-312-14013-4*, Saint Martin's Minotaur) St. Martin's Pr.
—Skylark. 1994. per. (*0-373-26145-4*, 1-26145-2, Harlequin Bks.) Harlequin Enterprises, Ltd.
—Skylark. 1992. 272p. 17.95 o.p. (*0-312-08294-0*, Saint Martin's Minotaur) St. Martin's Pr.
Sloan, Susan R. Act of God. 2002. 544p. 24.95 o.p. (*0-446-52451-4*) Warner Bks., Inc.
Smith, Janet L. Practice to Deceive. 1993. (Northwest Mysteries Ser.). mass mkt. 4.99 o.s.i (*0-8041-0978-8*, Ivy Bks.) Ballantine Bks.
—Sea of Troubles. 1991. 224p. mass mkt. 4.99 o.s.i (*0-8041-0759-9*, Ivy Bks.) Ballantine Bks.
—Sea of Troubles. 1990. 197p. pap. 8.95 o.p. (*0-9602676-9-7*, Perseverance Pr.) Daniel, John & Co., Pubs.
—Sea of Troubles. 1990. 200p. (C). reprint ed. lib. bdg. 29.00 o.p. (*0-8095-4208-0*) Millefleurs.
—A Vintage Murder. 1995. mass mkt. 5.99 o.s.i (*0-8041-1385-8*, Ivy Bks.); 1994. 240p. 20.00 o.s.i (*0-449-90871-2*, Fawcett) Ballantine Bks.
Speight, Bernice. The Architect's Other Hat: A Mystery. 1995. 128p. (Orig.). pap. 9.95 (*1-56474-135-4*) Fithian Pr.
Stewart, Jean. Emerald City Blues. 1996. 228p. pap. 11.99 (*1-883061-09-1*) Rising Tide Pr.
Stokes, Naomi M. Listening Ones. 1997. 416p. 25.95 (*0-312-86108-7*, Forge Bks.) Doherty, Tom Assocs., LLC.
—The Listening Ones. 1999. 493p. mass mkt. 6.99 (*0-8125-4295-9*, Tor Bks.) Doherty, Tom Assocs., LLC.
Stoks, Peggy. Romy's Walk. 2001. (Abounding Love Ser.: Vol. 2). (Illus.). 288p. pap. 9.99 (*0-8423-1943-3*) Tyndale Hse. Pubs.
Thayer, James Stewart. Terminal Event. l.t. ed. 2000. 25.95 (*1-57490-304-7*, Beeler Large Print Bks.) Beeler, Thomas T. Publisher.
—Terminal Event. 1999. (Illus.). 352p. 25.00 (*0-684-84210-6*, Simon & Schuster); 2003. 448p. reprint ed. mass mkt. 7.99 (*0-671-01371-8*, Pocket) Simon & Schuster.
Thompson, Joyce. Bones. 320p. 1992. mass mkt. 4.50 (*0-380-71147-8*, Avon Bks.); 1991. 19.95 o.p. (*0-688-09653-0*, Morrow, William & Co.) Morrow/Avon.
Thornburg, Newton. A Man's Game. 1997. 300p. mass mkt. 6.99 (*0-8125-5374-8*); 1996. 304p. 22.95 o.p. (*0-312-85923-6*) Doherty, Tom Assocs., LLC. (Forge Bks.).
Thorp, Roderick. River: A Novel of the Green River Killings. 1996. mass mkt. o.p. (*0-8041-0985-0*, Ivy Bks.); mass mkt. 5.99 o.p. (*0-449-22514-3*, Fawcett); mass mkt. 5.99 o.s.i (*0-8041-1535-4*, Ivy Bks.) Ballantine Bks.
Tobin, Brian. The Missing Person. 1994. 21.95 o.p. (*0-312-09872-3*); 1994. 320p. 21.95 o.p. (*0-312-11028-6*); 1993. 268p. 18.95 o.p. (*0-312-09874-X*) St. Martin's Pr. (Saint Martin's Minotaur).
Tompkins, Walker A. . West of Texas Law. l.t. ed. 2001. 214p. 21.95 (*1-57490-407-8*, Sagebrush Large Print Westerns) Beeler, Thomas T. Publisher.
Van Winkel, Nance. Curtain Creek Farm. 2000. 186p. 22.00 (*0-89255-250-6*) Persea Bks., Inc.
Walter, Jess. Over Tumbled Graves. 2000. pap. 13.00 (*0-06-098867-3*) HarperCollins Pubs.
Wiggs, Susan. The Lightkeeper. l.t. ed. 2002. (Americana Ser.). 554p. 29.95 (*0-7862-4235-3*) Thorndike Pr.
Wilbee, Brenda. Sweetbriar. 1983. (Pioneer Romance Ser.). 208p. (Orig.). pap. 6.99 (*0-89081-336-1*) Harvest Hse. Pubs.
—Sweetbriar Autumn. 1998. (Sweetbriar Ser.). 288p. (gr. 12 up). pap. 11.99 o.p. (*0-8007-5661-4*) Revell, Fleming H. Co.
—The Sweetbriar Bride. 1986. (Pioneer Romance Ser.). 240p. (Orig.). pap. 6.99 o.p. (*0-89081-482-1*) Harvest Hse. Pubs.
—Sweetbriar Hope. 1999. (Sweetbriar Ser.: No. 6). 320p. (gr. 13 up). pap. 11.99 o.p. (*0-8007-5695-9*) Revell, Fleming H. Co.
—Sweetbriar Summer. 1997. (Sweetbriar Ser.). (Illus.). 272p. (gr. 12 up). pap. 11.99 o.p. (*0-8007-5619-3*) Revell, Fleming H. Co.
Wilcox, Valerie. Sins of Deception. 2000. (Sailing Mystery Ser.). 288p. mass mkt. 5.99 o.s.i (*0-425-17507-3*, Prime Crime) Berkley Publishing Group.

### WATERDEEP (IMAGINARY PLACE)—FICTION

Awlinson, Richard. Shadowdale. 1989. (Forgotten Realms Avatar Trilogy Ser.: Bk. 1). 335p. pap. 6.99 (*0-88038-730-0*) Wizards of the Coast.
—Tantras. 1989. (Forgotten Realms Avatar Trilogy Ser.: Bk. 2). 338p. mass mkt. 6.99 (*0-88038-748-3*) Wizards of the Coast.
—Waterdeep. 1989. (Forgotten Realms Avatar Trilogy Ser.: Bk. 3). 341p. mass mkt. 7.99 (*0-88038-759-9*) Wizards of the Coast.

### WATERSHIP DOWN (IMAGINARY PLACE)—FICTION

Adams, Richard. Tales from Watership Down. l.t. ed. 1997. 24.95 (*1-56895-449-2*, Wheeler Publishing, Inc.) Gale Group.
—Tales from Watership Down. 1996. 23.00 o.s.i (*0-679-45125-0*) Knopf, Alfred A. Inc.
—Tales from Watership Down. 1998. 352p. mass mkt. 6.99 (*0-380-72934-2*, Avon Bks.) Morrow/Avon.
—Tales from Watership Down. 1998. 13.04 (*0-606-13835-8*) Turtleback Bks.
—Watership Down. unabr. collector's ed. 1990. audio 88.00 (*0-7366-1700-0*, 2545) Books on Tape, Inc.
—Watership Down. 1994. reprint ed. lib. bdg. 37.95 (*1-56849-250-2*) Buccaneer Bks., Inc.
—Watership Down. abr. ed. 2001. audio 19.95 o.p. (*1-56511-586-4*) HighBridge Co.
—Watership Down. 1976. 496p. mass mkt. 7.99 (*0-380-00293-0*); 20th anniv. ed. 480p. pap. 12.00 (*0-380-00428-3*) Morrow/Avon. (Avon Bks.).
—Watership Down. 1996. (Scribner Classics). 448p. 27.50 (*0-684-83605-X*, Scribner) Simon & Schuster.
—Watership Down. 1975. 13.55 (*0-606-05080-9*) Turtleback Bks.

### WELL-BUILT CITY (IMAGINARY PLACE)—FICTION

Ford, Jeffrey. The Beyond. 304p. 2002. pap. 12.95 (*0-380-81288-6*); 2001. 24.00 (*0-380-97897-0*) Morrow/Avon. (Eos).
—Memoranda. 1999. 240p. pap. 12.00 (*0-380-80262-7*); 2000. 256p. reprint ed. mass mkt. 5.99 (*0-380-81368-8*) Morrow/Avon. (Eos).
—Memoranda. l.t. ed. 2003. 392p. 27.95 (*0-7862-5777-6*) Thorndike Pr.
—The Physiognomy. 1998. 256p. mass mkt. 5.99 (*0-380-79332-6*, Eos); 1997. 218p. pap. 12.00 (*0-380-79331-8*, Avon Bks.) Morrow/Avon.
—The Physiognomy. 2002. (Science Fiction Ser.). 27.95 (*0-7862-4907-2*) Thorndike Pr.

### WELL WORLD (IMAGINARY PLACE)—FICTION

Chalker, Jack L. Echoes of the Well of Souls. 1993. (Watchers at the Well Ser.: Bk. 1). 320p. mass mkt. 5.99 o.s.i (*0-345-38686-8*); 352p. pap. 19.00 (*0-345-36201-2*) Ballantine Bks. (Del Rey).
—Exiles at the Well of Souls. 1984. (Saga of the Well World Ser.: Bk. 2). mass mkt. 5.99 o.s.i (*0-345-32437-4*); 1983. mass mkt. 2.50 o.p. (*0-345-31239-2*) Ballantine Bks. (Del Rey).
—Ghost of the Well of Souls. 2000. (Well World Ser.: Vol. 2). 352p. mass mkt. 6.99 (*0-345-39485-2*, Del Rey) Ballantine Bks.
—Gods of the Well of Souls. (Watchers at the Well Ser.: Bk. 3). 1995. mass mkt. 5.99 o.s.i (*0-345-38850-X*); 1994. 448p. pap. 10.00 o.p. (*0-345-36203-9*) Ballantine Bks. (Del Rey).
—Midnight at the Well of Souls. 1985. (Saga of the Well World Ser.: Bk. 1). mass mkt. 5.99 o.s.i (*0-345-32445-5*, Del Rey) Ballantine Bks.
—Quest for the Well of Souls. Baen, James P., ed. 2003. 352p. mass mkt. 7.99 (*0-7434-7153-9*) Baen Bks.
—Quest for the Well of Souls. 1985. (Saga of the Well World Ser.: Bk. 3). mass mkt. 5.99 o.s.i (*0-345-32450-1*); 1983. mass mkt. 2.50 o.p. (*0-345-31120-5*) Ballantine Bks. (Del Rey).
—The Return of Nathan Brazil. 1986. (Return of Nathan Brazil Ser.: Bk. 4). mass mkt. 5.99 o.s.i (*0-345-34105-8*, Del Rey) Ballantine Bks.
—The Sea Is Full of Stars. 1999. (Well World Ser.). 352p. mass mkt. 6.99 (*0-345-39486-0*) Ballantine Bks.
—Shadow of the Well of Souls. 1994. (Watchers at the Well Ser.: Bk. 2). (Orig.). 368p. mass mkt. 5.99 o.s.i (*0-345-38846-1*); 345p. pap. 10.00 o.s.i (*0-345-36202-0*, Del Rey) Ballantine Bks.
—Twilight at the Well of Souls: The Legacy of Nathan Brazil. 1986. (Saga of the Well World Ser.: Bk. 5). 320p. mass mkt. 5.99 o.s.i (*0-345-34408-1*, Del Rey) Ballantine Bks.

### WENDAR (IMAGINARY PLACE)—FICTION

Elliott, Kate, pseud. The Burning Stone. (Crown of Stars Ser.: Vol. 3). 2000. 816p. mass mkt. 7.99 (*0-88677-815-8*); 1999. 768p. 24.95 o.s.i (*0-88677-813-1*) DAW Bks., Inc.
—Child of Flame. 2000. (Crown of Stars Ser.: Vol. 4). (Illus.). 864p. 24.95 o.s.i (*0-88677-892-1*) DAW Bks., Inc.
—King's Dragon. (Crown of Stars Ser.: Vol. 1). 1998. 640p. mass mkt. 7.99 (*0-88677-771-2*); 1997. 544p. mass mkt. 22.95 o.s.i (*0-88677-727-5*) DAW Bks., Inc.
—Prince of Dogs. (Crown of Stars Ser.). 1998. 544p. 23.95 o.p. (*0-88677-770-4*); Vol. 2. 1999. 640p. mass mkt. 7.99 (*0-88677-816-6*) DAW Bks., Inc.

### WENTWORTH (OHIO: IMAGINARY PLACE)—FICTION

Bachman, Richard, pseud. The Regulators. 1996. 480p. 24.95 o.s.i (*0-525-94190-8*); 325.00 o.s.i (*0-525-94224-6*) Dutton/Plume.
—The Regulators. 1997. (Illus.). 512p. mass mkt. 7.99 (*0-451-19101-3*, Signet Bks.) NAL.
—The Regulators, unabr. ed. 1997. audio 80.00 (*0-7887-1163-6*, 95006E7) Recorded Bks., LLC.

—The Regulators. l.t. ed. 1997. (Thorndike/G. K. Hall Paperback Bestsellers Ser.). 598p. pap. 26.95 (0-7862-0845-7) Thorndike Pr.

—The Regulators. 1996. (Illus.). 466p. text 24.95 (0-670-87281-4); 6p. pap. 29.95 o.p. incl. audio (0-14-086322-2, Penguin AudioBooks) Viking Penguin.

**WERNER-BOK LIBRARY (WASHINGTON, D.C.: IMAGINARY PLACE)—FICTION**

Goodrum, Charles. The Best Cellar: A Werner-Bok Library Mystery. 1988. 288p. reprint ed. mass mkt. 3.95 o.p. (0-06-080931-0, P 931, Perennial) HarperTrade.

—Carnage of the Realm: A Werner-Bok Library Mystery. 1988. 240p. reprint ed. mass mkt. 3.95 o.p. (0-06-080932-9, Perennial) HarperTrade.

—Dewey Decimated: A Werner-Bok Library Mystery. 1988. 304p. reprint ed. mass mkt. 3.95 o.p. (0-06-080933-7, P 933, Perennial) HarperTrade.

—A Slip of the Tong. 1992. 192p. 16.95 o.p. (0-312-07806-4); Vol. 1. 1958. 17.95 o.p. (0-312-08296-7) St. Martin's Pr. (Saint Martin's Minotaur).

Goodrum, Charles A. The Best Cellar: Murder & Mystery at the Werner-Bok Library. 1987. 160p. 13.95 o.p. (0-312-00008-1) St. Martin's Pr.

—Carnage of the Realm. 1988. 1.99 o.p. (0-517-53504-1) Random Hse. Value Publishing.

**WESSEX (ENGLAND)—FICTION**

Boumelha, Penny & Hardy, Thomas. Jude the Obscure: Thomas Hardy. 2000. (New Casebooks Ser.). 224p. 59.95 (0-312-22701-9) Palgrave Macmillan.

Carnegie, Dale. Tess of the d'Urbervilles. Hardy, Thomas, ed. 1998. (Enriched Classics Ser.). (Illus.). 480p. reprint ed. mass mkt. 5.99 (0-671-01546-X, Pocket) Simon & Schuster.

Grindle, Juliet, et al. Tess of the d'Urbervilles. Hardy, Thomas, ed. 1998. E-Book 7.30 (0-585-35555-X) netLibrary, Inc.

Hardy, Thomas. The Bedside Thomas Hardy. Leeson, Edward, ed. 1979. 15.00 o.p. (0-312-07131-0) St. Martin's Pr.

—Desperate Remedies, 3. reprint ed. lib. bdg. 294.00 (0-7426-2783-7); 2001. pap. text 84.00 (0-7426-7783-4) Classic Bks.

—Desperate Remedies. 1975. 448 p. (J). 12.50 (0-333-17760-6) Macmillan U.K. GBR. *Dist:* Trans-Atlantic Pubns., Inc.

—Desperate Remedies. 1977. (Hardy New Wessex Editions Ser.). pap. 3.95 o.p. (0-312-19494-3, Saint Martin's Griffin) St. Martin's Pr.

—Desperate Remedies. Rimmer, Mary, ed. & intro. by. 1998. (Classics Ser.). (Illus.). 512p. 15.00 (0-14-043523-9, Penguin Classics) Viking Penguin.

—Far from the Madding Crowd. 1983. 384p. mass mkt. 5.95 (0-553-21331-8, Bantam Classics) Bantam Bks.

—Far from the Madding Crowd. 1895. 475p. (YA). reprint ed. pap. text 28.00 (1-4047-7546-3) Classic Textbooks.

—Far from the Madding Crowd. Adams, Richard, ed. 1989. (Study Texts Ser.). pap. 4.46 o.p. (0-582-00263-X, 73903) Longman Publishing Group.

—Far from the Madding Crowd. 1967. mass mkt. 0.60 o.p. (0-451-03273-X, Signet Bks.); 1961. mass mkt. 0.50 o.p. (0-451-50044-X, Signet Classics); 1961. mass mkt. 0.60 o.p. (0-451-50356-2, Signet Classics); 1961. mass mkt. 0.95 o.p. (0-451-50572-7, Signet Classics); 1961. mass mkt. 1.25 o.p. (0-451-50997-8, Signet Classics); 1961. mass mkt. 1.95 o.p. (0-451-51329-0, Signet Classics); 1961. mass mkt. 2.50 o.p. (0-451-51505-6, Signet Classics); 1961. mass mkt. 2.75 o.p. (0-451-51660-5, Signet Classics) NAL.

—Far from the Madding Crowd. 1991. (Everyman's Library: Vol. 21). 512p. 20.00 (0-679-40576-3); 1998. 410p. 16.00 o.s.i (0-679-60307-7) Random Hse., Inc.

—Far from the Madding Crowd. 2003. (Illus.). 480p. pap. 8.00 (0-14-143965-3, Penguin Classics) Viking Penguin.

—Far from the Madding Crowd: Penguin Readers Level 4. 1998. pap. 7.00 (0-14-081531-7) Longman Publishing Group.

—The Hand of Ethelberta. 2002. 392p. 27.99 (1-4043-0606-4); per. 22.99 (1-4043-0607-2) IndyPublish-.com.

—The Hand of Ethelberta. 1978. (Hardy New Wessex Editions Ser.). pap. 3.95 o.p. (0-312-35736-2, Saint Martin's Griffin) St. Martin's Pr.

—The Hand of Ethelberta. 1998. pap. 7.50 (0-460-87645-7) Tuttle Publishing.

—The Hand of Ethelberta. 1998. (Classics Ser.). (Illus.). 512p. 13.95 (0-14-043502-6, Penguin Classics) Viking Penguin.

—The Hand of Ethelberta: A Comedy in Chapters. reprint ed. lib. bdg. 196.00 (0-7426-2787-X) Classic Bks.

—The Hand of Ethelberta: A Comedy in Chapters. 1990. (New Wessex Edition Ser.). 362p. 42.50 (0-333-17767-3) Macmillan U.K. GBR. *Dist:* Trans-Atlantic Pubns., Inc.

—An Indiscretion in the Life of an Heiress & Other Stories. Dalziel, Pamela, ed. 1999. (Oxford World's Classics Ser.). (Illus.). 320p. pap. 9.95 (0-19-283685-4) Oxford Univ. Pr., Inc.

—An Indiscretion in the Life of an Heiress & Other Stories. Dalziel, Pamela, ed. & intro. by. 1995. (Oxford World's Classics Ser.). (Illus.). 312p. pap. 9.95 o.p. (0-19-282344-2) Oxford Univ. Pr., Inc.

—Jude the Obscure. 1966. (Airmont Classics Ser.). (YA). (gr. 11 up). mass mkt. 1.95 o.p. (0-8049-0108-2, CL-108) Airmont Publishing Co., Inc.

—Jude the Obscure. 1976. 27.95 (0-8488-0515-1) Amereon, Ltd.

—Jude the Obscure. 1985. 448p. (gr. 8-12). mass mkt. 5.95 (0-553-21191-9, Bantam Classics) Bantam Bks.

—Jude the Obscure. Watts, Cedric, ed. 1999. (Literary Texts Ser.). text (1-55111-313-9); (Illus.). 517p. pap. (1-55111-171-3) Broadview Pr.

—Jude the Obscure. 1990. 400p. reprint ed. lib. bdg. 25.95 (0-89966-665-5) Buccaneer Bks., Inc.

—Jude the Obscure. reprint ed. lib. bdg. 98.00 (0-7426-2798-5); 2001. pap. text 28.00 (0-7426-7798-2) Classic Bks.

—Jude the Obscure. 2003. (Barnes & Noble Classics Ser.). 464p. pap. 6.95 (1-59308-035-2) Fine Communications.

—Jude the Obscure. Howe, Irving, ed. 1972. (YA). (gr. 9 up). pap. 16.36 (0-395-05191-6, Riverside Editions) Houghton Mifflin Co.

—Jude the Obscure. 1996. 522p. 20.00 (0-676-51620-3); 1992. 560p. 20.00 (0-679-40993-9) Knopf, Alfred A. Inc.

—Jude the Obscure. 2000. (Cloth Bound Pocket Ser.). (Illus.). 7.95 (3-8290-3007-X, 521123) Konemann.

—Jude the Obscure. 1998. 144p. (C). pap. 7.66 (0-582-40264-6) Longman Publishing Group.

—Jude the Obscure. 1961. mass mkt. 0.75 o.p. (0-451-50095-4, Signet Classics); 1961. mass mkt. 0.95 o.p. (0-451-50570-0, Signet Classics); 1961. mass mkt. 2.25 o.p. (0-451-51394-0, Signet Classics); 1961. mass mkt. 2.75 o.p. (0-451-51589-7, Signet Classics); 1961. mass mkt. 2.95 o.p. (0-451-51783-0); 1961. 416p. mass mkt. 5.95 o.s.i (0-451-52370-9, Signet Classics); 1961. mass mkt. 1.75 o.p. (0-451-51208-1, Signet Classics); 1961. mass mkt. 1.25 o.p. (0-451-50934-X, Signet Classics); 1999. 448p. mass mkt. 5.95 (0-451-52725-9, Signet Classics) NAL.

—Jude the Obscure. l.t. ed. 1998. (Large Print Ser.). reprint ed. 575p. lib. bdg. 26.00 (0-939495-69-4); 457p. lib. bdg. 25.00 (1-58287-092-6) North Bks.

—Jude the Obscure. Page, Norman, ed. 1978. (Critical Editions Ser.). (Illus.). (C). o.p. (0-393-04473-4); 468p. pap. text o.p. (0-393-09089-2) Norton, W. W. & Co., Inc.

—Jude the Obscure. Ingham, Patricia, ed. 1985. (Oxford World's Classics Ser.). (Illus.). 492p. pap. 5.95 o.p. (0-19-281670-5) Oxford Univ. Pr., Inc.

—Jude the Obscure. 2003. o.p. (0-333-16897-6) Pan Macmillan.

—Jude the Obscure. 2001. (Paperback Classics Ser.). (Illus.). 528p. pap. 7.95 (0-375-75741-4, Modern Library) Random House Adult Trade Publishing Group.

—Jude the Obscure. Slack, Robert C., ed. 1978. 6.95 o.s.i (0-394-60462-8) Random Hse., Inc.

—Jude the Obscure. 1992. (BCL1-PR English Literature Ser.). 503p. reprint ed. lib. bdg. 99.00 (0-7812-7547-4) Reprint Services Corp.

—Jude the Obscure. 1977. (Hardy New Wessex Editions Ser.). pap. 2.95 o.p. (0-312-44661-6, Saint Martin's Griffin) St. Martin's Pr.

—Jude the Obscure. 1995. (Sun & Moon Classics Ser.: No. 77). 496p. pap. 12.95 o.p. (1-55713-203-8) Sun & Moon Pr.

—Jude the Obscure. l.t. ed. 1982. (Charnwood Large Print Ser.). 640p. 29.99 o.p. (0-7089-8067-8, Ulverscroft) Thorpe, F. A. Pubs. GBR. *Dist:* Ulverscroft Large Print Bks., Ltd., Ulverscroft Large Print Canada, Ltd.

—Jude the Obscure. 1961. (Signet Classics Ser.). 12.00 (0-606-03696-2) Turtleback Bks.

—Jude the Obscure. Hands, Timothy, ed. 1995. (Everyman Paperback Classics Ser.). 528p. (C). pap. 5.95 (0-460-87567-1, Everyman's Classic Library in Paperback) Tuttle Publishing.

—Jude the Obscure. Taylor, Dennis, ed. & intro. by. 1998. (Classics Ser.). 528p. pap. 7.95 (0-14-043538-7, Penguin Classics) Viking Penguin.

—Jude the Obscure. Sisson, C. H., ed. 1978. (Penguin Classics Ser.). 512p. (C). pap. 7.95 o.s.i (0-14-043131-4, Penguin Classics) Viking Penguin.

—Jude the Obscure. abr. ed. 1997. pap. 23.95 o.s.i incl. audio (0-14-086455-5, Penguin AudioBooks) Viking Penguin.

—Jude the Obscure. 1998. (Classics Library). pap. 3.95 (1-85326-261-7, 2617WW) Wordsworth Editions, Ltd. GBR. *Dist:* Casemate Pubs. & Bk. Distributors, LLC.

—Jude the Obscure. Hands, Timothy, ed. rev. ed. 1993. 528p. pap. 5.95 (0-460-87413-6, Everyman's Classic Library in Paperback) Tuttle Publishing.

—Jude the Obscure, Set. 1995. audio 65.95 (1-55685-364-5) Audio Bk. Contractors, Inc.

—Jude the Obscure, Set. unabr. ed. 1995. audio 96.95 (1-56054-914-9, SAB 028, Sterling Audio Bks.) BBC Audiobooks America.

—Jude the Obscure. unabr. ed. 1997. audio 76.95 (0-7861-1249-2, 2158) Blackstone Audio Bks., Inc.

—Jude the Obscure. unabr. collector's ed. 1983. (YA). audio 96.00 (0-7366-3978-0, 9526) Books on Tape, Inc.

—Jude the Obscure. Ingham, Patricia, ed. & intro. by. 2nd ed. 1998. (Oxford World's Classics Ser.). (Illus.). 496p. pap. 6.95 o.p. (0-19-283379-0) Oxford Univ. Pr., Inc.

—A Laodicean, 3. (Collected Works of Thomas Hardy). reprint ed. lib. bdg. 294.00 (0-7426-2790-X); 2001. pap. text 84.00 (0-7426-7790-7) Classic Bks.

—A Laodicean. 2002. 428p. 21.99 (1-4043-1290-0); per. 16.99 (1-4043-1291-9) IndyPublish.com.

—A Laodicean. 2003. o.p. (0-333-17765-7) Macmillan U.K. GBR. *Dist:* Trafalgar Square.

—A Laodicean. Gatewood, Jane, ed. 1992. (Oxford World's Classics Ser.). 506p. pap. 9.95 o.p. (0-19-282783-9) Oxford Univ. Pr., Inc.

—A Laodicean. 1978. (Hardy New Wessex Editions Ser.). pap. 3.95 o.p. (0-312-46936-5, Saint Martin's Griffin) St. Martin's Pr.

—A Laodicean. Stape, J. H., ed. 1997. (Everyman Paperback Classics Ser.). 432p. pap. 8.50 (0-460-87637-6, Everyman's Classic Library in Paperback) Tuttle Publishing.

—A Laodicean: A Story of Today. 1975. (New Wessex Ser.). 461p. (J). 12.50 (0-333-17759-2) Macmillan U.K. GBR. *Dist:* Trans-Atlantic Pubns., Inc.

—The Life & Death of the Mayor of Casterbridge: A Story of a Man of Character. 1962. 12.00 (0-606-01055-6) Turtleback Bks.

—The Mayor of Casterbridge. 8.97 (0-673-58355-4); 1991. pap. text (0-17-556573-2) Addison-Wesley Longman, Inc.

—The Mayor of Casterbridge. 1994. pap. text 34.60 (0-582-22586-8) Addison-Wesley Longman, Ltd. GBR. *Dist:* Trans-Atlantic Pubns., Inc.

—The Mayor of Casterbridge. 1965. (Airmont Classics Ser.). mass mkt. 1.95 o.p. (0-8049-0063-9, CL-63) Airmont Publishing Co., Inc.

—The Mayor of Casterbridge. reprint ed. lib. bdg. 25.95 (0-88411-560-7) Amereon, Ltd.

—The Mayor of Casterbridge. 1981. (Bantam Classics Ser.). 336p. mass mkt. 5.99 (0-553-21024-6, Bantam Classics) Bantam Bks.

—The Mayor of Casterbridge. Page, Norman, ed. 1997. (Literary Texts Ser.). 411p. (C). pap. (1-55111-122-5) Broadview Pr.

—The Mayor of Casterbridge. 1990. 326p. reprint ed. lib. bdg. 24.95 (0-89966-719-8) Buccaneer Bks., Inc.

—The Mayor of Casterbridge, 2. reprint ed. lib. bdg. 196.00 (0-7426-2792-6) Classic Bks.

—The Mayor of Casterbridge. E-Book 2.49 (1-58627-417-1) Electric Umbrella Publishing.

—The Mayor of Casterbridge, 001. Heilman, Robert B., ed. 1962. (gr. 9 up). pap. 16.36 (0-395-05158-4, Riverside Editions) Houghton Mifflin Co.

—The Mayor of Casterbridge. l.t. ed. 335p. pap. 27.96 (0-7583-1488-4); 423p. pap. 32.94 (0-7583-1489-2); 583p. pap. 40.73 (0-7583-1490-6); 969p. pap. 69.29 (0-7583-1492-2); 1469p. pap. 92.92 (0-7583-1494-9); 750p. pap. 50.07 (0-7583-1491-4); 1734p. pap. 112.29 (0-7583-1495-7); 1196p. pap. 81.06 (0-7583-1493-0); 1196p. lib. bdg. 93.06 (0-7583-1485-X); 969p. lib. bdg. 81.29 (0-7583-1484-1); 583p. lib. bdg. 46.73 (0-7583-1482-5); 423p. lib. bdg. 38.94 (0-7583-1481-7); 335p. lib. bdg. 33.96 (0-7583-1480-9); 1469p. lib. bdg. 104.92 (0-7583-1486-8); 1734p. lib. bdg. 130.29 (0-7583-1487-6); 750p. lib. bdg. 56.07 (0-7583-1483-3) Huge Print Pr.

—The Mayor of Casterbridge. 2002. 336p. 96.99 (1-4043-1836-4); per. 91.99 (1-4043-1837-2) IndyPublish.com.

—The Mayor of Casterbridge. 1993. (Everyman's Library). 17.00 (0-679-42035-5) Knopf, Alfred A. Inc.

—The Mayor of Casterbridge. l.t. ed. 2000. (LRS Large Print Heritage Ser.). 579p. (YA). (gr. 6-12). lib. bdg. 35.95 (1-58118-075-6, 23667) LRS.

—The Mayor of Casterbridge. Adams, Richard, ed. 1988. (Study Texts Ser.). pap. text 4.29 (0-582-33171-4, 72064) Longman Publishing Group.

—The Mayor of Casterbridge. (Classics Ser.). 1999. (Illus.). 384p. mass mkt. 5.95 (0-451-52735-6, Signet Classics); 1962. 336p. mass mkt. 5.95 o.s.i (0-451-52519-1, Signet Classics); 1962. mass mkt. 2.25 o.p. (0-451-52305-9, Signet Classics); 1962. mass mkt. 1.95 o.p. (0-451-51230-8) NAL.

—The Mayor of Casterbridge. l.t. ed. reprint ed. 1997. 468p. lib. bdg. 26.00 (0-939495-14-7); 1998. 265p. lib. bdg. 25.00 (1-58287-048-9) North Bks.

—The Mayor of Casterbridge. Robinson, James K., ed. 1977. (Critical Editions Ser.). (Illus.). 14.95 o.p. (0-393-04459-9); 436p. (C). pap. text 10.50 o.p. (0-393-09174-0) Norton, W. W. & Co., Inc.

—The Mayor of Casterbridge. 2nd ed. 2000. (Critical Editions Ser.). (Illus.). xvii, 461p. pap. 11.00 (0-393-97498-7, Norton Paperbacks) Norton, W. W. & Co., Inc.

—The Mayor of Casterbridge. 1999. (YA). 9.95 (1-56137-350-8) Novel Units, Inc.

—The Mayor of Casterbridge. Kramer, Dale, ed. & intro. by. 1998. (Oxford World's Classics Ser.). (Illus.). 464p. pap. 7.95 (0-19-283441-X) Oxford Univ. Pr., Inc.

—The Mayor of Casterbridge. (Oxford World's Classics Ser.). (Illus.). 1987. 456p. pap. 5.95 o.p. (0-19-281728-0); 2nd ed. 1993. 126p. pap. text 5.95 (0-19-585118-8) Oxford Univ. Pr., Inc.

—The Mayor of Casterbridge. 2003. o.p. (0-333-16892-5) Pan Macmillan.

—The Mayor of Casterbridge. 2001. E-Book 2.25 (1-58882-538-8) PublishingOnline.

—The Mayor of Casterbridge. 2002. (Paperback Classics Ser.). (Illus.). 416p. pap. 7.95 (0-375-76006-7, Modern Library) Random House Adult Trade Publishing Group.

—The Mayor of Casterbridge. 1984. (gr. 11-12). mass mkt. 1.75 o.s.i (0-671-41524-7, Pocket) Simon & Schuster.

—The Mayor of Casterbridge. (Ebook Classic Ser.). E-Book 5.00 (0-7410-0449-6) SoftBook Pr.

—The Mayor of Casterbridge. 1977. (Hardy New Wessex Editions Ser.). pap. 2.95 o.p. (0-312-52326-2, Saint Martin's Griffin) St. Martin's Pr.

—The Mayor of Casterbridge. l.t. ed. 1998. (Perennial Bestsellers Ser.). 512p. 27.95 (0-7838-0351-6) Thorndike Pr.

—The Mayor of Casterbridge. l.t. ed. 1982. 13.95 o.p. (0-7089-8021-X, Charnwood) Thorpe, F. A. Pubs. GBR. *Dist:* Ulverscroft Large Print Bks., Ltd.

—The Mayor of Casterbridge. l.t. ed. 1998. 492p. text 29.95 (1-56000-518-1) Transaction Pubs.

—The Mayor of Casterbridge. Norris, Pamela, ed. 1993. 448p. pap. 4.95 (0-460-87279-6, Everyman's Classic Library in Paperback) Tuttle Publishing.

—The Mayor of Casterbridge. 2000. 11.95 (81-85944-99-7) UBS Pubs. Distributions, Ltd. IND. *Dist:* South Asia Bks.

—The Mayor of Casterbridge. Wilson, Keith, ed. & intro. by. 1998. (Penguin Classics Ser.). (Illus.). 448p. 7.95 (0-14-043513-1, Penguin Classics) Viking Penguin.

—The Mayor of Casterbridge. Seymour-Smith, Martin, ed. 1978. (English Library). 448p. pap. 7.95 o.s.i (0-14-043125-X, Penguin Classics) Viking Penguin.

—The Mayor of Casterbridge. 1999. E-Book 5.99 (0-8220-7127-4, Cliff Notes) Wiley, John & Sons, Inc.

—The Mayor of Casterbridge. 1998. (Classics Library). 352p. pap. 3.95 (1-85326-098-3, 0983WW) Wordsworth Editions, Ltd. GBR. *Dist:* Casemate Pubs. & Bk. Distributors, LLC.

—The Mayor of Casterbridge: Digital Reprint of 1922 Harper & Brothers Edition. Exams Unlimited, Inc. Staff, ed. 2001. 391p. (C). reprint ed. cd-rom 6.95 (1-885343-92-2) Exams Unlimited, Inc.

—The Mayor of Casterbridge: The Life & Death of a Man of Character. 2001. (Collected Works of Thomas Hardy). reprint ed. pap. text 56.00 (0-7426-7792-3) Classic Bks.

—A Pair of Blue Eyes. 2001. per. 25.00 (1-891355-57-0) Blue Unicorn Editions.

—A Pair of Blue Eyes. E-Book 2.49 (1-58627-431-7) Electric Umbrella Publishing.

—A Pair of Blue Eyes. 2003. o.p. (0-333-17764-9) Macmillan U.K. GBR. *Dist:* Trafalgar Square.

—A Pair of Blue Eyes. Manford, Alan, ed. & intro. by. 1998. (Oxford World's Classics Ser.). (Illus.). 432p. pap. 7.95 (0-19-283482-7) Oxford Univ. Pr., Inc.

—A Pair of Blue Eyes. Manford, Alan, ed. 1985. (Oxford World's Classics Ser.). 426p. pap. 5.95 o.p. (0-19-281684-5) Oxford Univ. Pr., Inc.

—A Pair of Blue Eyes. 1979. (Hardy New Wessex Editions Ser.). pap. 3.95 o.p. (0-312-59466-6, Saint Martin's Griffin) St. Martin's Pr.

—A Pair of Blue Eyes. Dalziel, Pamela, ed. & intro. by. 1998. (Penguin Classics Ser.). 448p. pap. 10.00 (0-14-043529-8, Penguin Classics) Viking Penguin.

—A Pair of Blue Eyes. Ebbatson, Roger, ed. & intro. by. 1986. (Penguin Classics Ser.). 480p. pap. 7.95 o.s.i (0-14-043266-3, Penguin Classics) Viking Penguin.

—Pair of Blue Eyes. 1998. (Classics Library). pap. 3.95 (1-85326-277-3, 2773WW) Wordsworth Editions, Ltd. GBR. *Dist:* Casemate Pubs. & Bk. Distributors, LLC.

—A Pair of Blue Eyes. l.t. ed. 2000. per. 15.50 (1-58396-224-7) Blue Unicorn Editions.

—The Return of the Native. reprint ed. lib. bdg. 28.95 (0-88411-561-5) Amereon, Ltd.

—The Return of the Native. 1994. (Illustrated Classics Collection). 64p. pap. 4.95 (*0-7854-0753-7*, 40512); pap. 3.60 o.p. (*1-56103-600-5*) American Guidance Service, Inc.
—The Return of the Native. 1982. 384p. mass mkt. 1.95 o.s.i (*0-553-21080-7*) Bantam Bks.
—The Return of the Native. 1992. reprint ed. lib. bdg. 24.95 (*0-89968-264-2*, Lightyear Pr.) Buccaneer Bks., Inc.
—The Return of the Native. Milne, John, ed. 1980. (Heinemann Guided Readers Ser.). pap. text 3.00 o.p. (*0-435-27061-3*) Heinemann.
—The Return of the Native. 1997. text 8.25 (*0-03-051494-0*) Holt, Rinehart & Winston.
—The Return of the Native. 1992. (Everyman's Library). 20.00 (*0-679-41730-3*) Knopf, Alfred A. Inc.
—The Return of the Native. 2003. o.p. (*0-333-16894-1*) Macmillan U.K. GBR. *Dist:* Trafalgar Square.
—The Return of the Native. 1959. 416p. mass mkt. 4.95 o.s.i (*0-451-52471-3*, Signet Classics); 1959. 414p. mass mkt. 2.50 o.p. (*0-451-52307-5*, Signet Classics); 1999. 416p. mass mkt. 5.95 (*0-451-52738-0*) NAL.
—The Return of the Native. l.t. ed. (Large Print Ser.). reprint ed. 1992. 573p. lib. bdg. 26.00 (*0-939495-36-8*); 1998. 433p. lib. bdg. 25.00 (*1-58287-064-0*) North Bks.
—The Return of the Native. Gindin, James, ed. 1969. (Critical Editions Ser.). (Illus.). 7.00 o.p. (*0-393-04300-2*); 512p. (C). pap. text 10.50 (*0-393-09791-9*, 9791) Norton, W. W. & Co., Inc.
—The Return of the Native. Gatrell, Simon, ed. & intro. by. 1998. (Oxford World's Classics Ser.). (Illus.). 512p. pap. 8.95 (*0-19-283406-1*) Oxford Univ. Pr., Inc.
—The Return of the Native. 1990. (Oxford World's Classics Ser.). (Illus.). 510p. pap. 6.95 o.p. (*0-19-282717-0*) Oxford Univ. Pr., Inc.
—The Return of the Native. (Paperback Classics Ser.). 2001. (Illus.). 448p. pap. 8.95 (*0-375-75718-X*); 2000. E-Book 4.95 (*0-679-64152-1*) Random House Adult Trade Publishing Group. (Modern Library).
—The Return of the Native. 1992. (BCL1-PR English Literature Ser.). 485p. reprint ed. lib. bdg. 99.00 (*0-7812-7548-2*) Reprint Services Corp.
—The Return of the Native. 1979. (Hardy New Wessex Editions Ser.). pap. 2.95 o.p. (*0-312-67901-7*, Saint Martin's Griffin) St. Martin's Pr.
—The Return of the Native. 1959. 12.00 (*0-606-03347-5*) Turtleback Bks.
—The Return of the Native. Hodgson, Amanda, ed. 1995. pap. 4.95 o.p. (*0-460-87531-0*, Everyman's Classic Library in Paperback) Tuttle Publishing.
—The Return of the Native. 1999. (Classics Ser.). (Illus.). 496p. pap. 8.95 (*0-14-043518-2*, Penguin Classics) Viking Penguin.
—The Return of the Native. Woodcock, George, ed. 1978. (Penguin Classics Ser.). 496p. pap. 8.95 o.s.i (*0-14-043122-5*, Penguin Classics) Viking Penguin.
—The Return of the Native. 1998. (Classics Library). 510p. pap. 3.95 (*1-85326-238-2*, 2382WW) Wordsworth Editions, Ltd. GBR. *Dist:* Casemate Pubs. & Bk. Distributors, LLC.
—The Return of the Native Readalong. 1994. (Illustrated Classics Collection). 64p. pap. 13.50 o.p. incl. audio (*1-56103-602-1*); pap. 14.95 incl. audio (*0-7854-0769-3*, 40514) American Guidance Service, Inc.
—Selected Stories of Thomas Hardy. 1980. pap. 3.95 (*0-312-71119-0*, Saint Martin's Griffin) St. Martin's Pr.
—Tess of the d'Urbervilles. 1991. 560p. 20.00 (*0-679-40586-0*, Everyman's Library) Knopf Publishing Group.
—Tess of the d'Urbervilles. 1979. 8.95 o.s.i (*0-394-60484-9*) Random Hse., Inc.
—Tess of the d'Urbervilles: A Pure Woman. 1999. (Signet Classics). 432p. mass mkt. 4.95 (*0-451-52722-4*, Signet Classics) NAL.
—Tess of the d'Urbervilles: A Pure Woman. 2001. (Paperback Classics Ser.). (Illus.). 544p. pap. 7.95 (*0-375-75679-5*, Modern Library) Random House Adult Trade Publishing Group.
—Tess of the d'Urbervilles: A Pure Woman. 1998. (Modern Library Ser.). 544p. 16.95 o.s.i (*0-679-60318-2*) Random Hse., Inc.
—Tess of the d'Urbervilles: A Pure Woman. 1985. (Illus.). 368p. 12.95 o.p. (*0-89577-215-9*) Reader's Digest Assn., Inc., The.
—Tess of the d'Urbervilles: A Pure Woman. 1995. (Literary Classics Giant Ser.). 528p. text 8.98 o.p. (*1-56138-653-7*, Courage Bks.) Running Pr. Bk. Pubs.
—Tess of the d'Urbervilles: A Pure Woman. 1998. 9.00 (*81-85944-57-1*) UBS Pubs. Distributions, Ltd. IND. *Dist:* South Asia Bks.
—Thomas Hardy: Three Complete Novels. 1995. 704p. 12.99 o.s.i (*0-517-12419-X*) Random Hse., Inc.
—The Thomas Hardy Omnibus. 1979. 15.00 o.p. (*0-312-80157-2*) St. Martin's Pr.
—The Trumpet-Major. l.t. unabr. ed. 1992. (Isis Large Print Bks.). 384p. 29.99 (*1-85089-387-X*, 89387X) ISIS Large Print Bks. GBR. *Dist:* Ulverscroft Large Print Bks., Ltd., Ulverscroft Large Print Canada, Ltd.
—The Trumpet-Major. 2003. o.p. (*0-333-16890-9*) Macmillan U.K. GBR. *Dist:* Trafalgar Square.
—The Trumpet-Major. Nemesvari, Richard, ed. & intro. by. 1999. (Oxford World's Classics Ser.). (Illus.). 416p. pap. 5.95 o.p. (*0-19-283635-8*) Oxford Univ. Pr., Inc.
—The Trumpet-Major. (Oxford World's Classics Ser.). 1998. pap. 5.95 (*0-19-283135-6*); 1991. (Illus.). 410p. pap. 5.95 o.p. (*0-19-282718-9*) Oxford Univ. Pr., Inc.
—The Trumpet-Major. 1977. (Hardy New Wessex Editions Ser.). pap. 3.95 (*0-312-82146-8*, Saint Martin's Griffin) St. Martin's Pr.
—The Trumpet-Major. Rimmer, Mary, ed. 2000. 432p. pap. 6.95 (*0-460-87790-9*, Everyman's Classic Library in Paperback) Tuttle Publishing.
—The Trumpet-Major. Shires, Linda M., ed. 1998. (Penguin Classics Ser.). 416p. pap. 7.95 o.p. (*0-14-043540-9*, Penguin Classics) Viking Penguin.
—The Trumpet-Major. 1989. 400p. pap. 6.95 o.s.i (*0-14-043273-6*, Penguin Classics) Viking Penguin.
—The Trumpet-Major. 1998. (Classics Library). 410p. pap. 3.95 (*1-85326-246-3*, 2463WW) Wordsworth Editions, Ltd. GBR. *Dist:* Casemate Pubs. & Bk. Distributors, LLC.
—The Trumpet-Major & Robert His Brother. 1975. pap. text 10.95 o.p. (*0-312-82145-X*) St. Martin's Pr.
—The Trumpet-Major & Robert his Brother. 1985. (Nonfiction Ser.). 320p. pap. 4.95 o.p. (*0-14-043142-X*, Penguin Classics) Viking Penguin.
—Two on a Tower. 1999. (Everyman Paperback Classics Ser.). 288p. pap. (*0-460-87784-4*) Dent, J.M. & Sons.
—Two on a Tower. 1990. (New Wessex Edition Ser.). 264p. text 42.50 o.s.i (*0-333-17763-0*) Macmillan U.K. GBR. *Dist:* Trans-Atlantic Pubns., Inc.
—Two on a Tower. Ahmad, Suleiman M., ed. 1999. (Oxford World's Classics Ser.). 352p. pap. 10.95 (*0-19-283641-2*) Oxford Univ. Pr., Inc.
—Two on a Tower. 1993. (Oxford World's Classics Ser.). 350p. pap. 9.95 o.p. (*0-19-282919-X*) Oxford Univ. Pr., Inc.
—Two on a Tower. 1977. (Hardy New Wessex Editions Ser.). pap. 3.95 o.p. (*0-312-82742-3*, Saint Martin's Griffin) St. Martin's Pr.
—Two on a Tower. 2000. (Classics Ser.). (Illus.). 336p. 10.95 (*0-14-043536-0*, Penguin Classics) Viking Penguin.
—Under the Greenwood Tree. 1976. 22.95 (*0-8488-0517-8*) Amereon, Ltd.
—Under the Greenwood Tree. unabr. ed. 1998. audio 29.95 (*1-55685-600-8*) Audio Bk. Contractors, Inc.
—Under the Greenwood Tree. l.t. ed. 2003. 302p. 29.95 (*0-7862-6007-6*) Gale Group.
—Under the Greenwood Tree. 1998. (Penguin Readers Ser.: Level 2 ). 144p. (J). pap. 7.66 (*0-582-40161-5*) Longman Publishing Group.
—Under the Greenwood Tree. 2003. (Twelve-Point Ser.). lib. bdg. 25.00 (*1-58287-235-X*); lib. bdg. 26.00 (*1-58287-719-X*) North Bks.
—Under the Greenwood Tree. Gatrell, simon, ed. & intro. by. 1999. (Oxford World's Classics Ser.). (Illus.). 256p. pap. 4.95 (*0-19-283517-3*) Oxford Univ. Pr., Inc.
—Under the Greenwood Tree. Gatrell, Simon, ed. & intro. by. 1985. (Oxford World's Classics Ser.). (Illus.). 250p. pap. 4.95 o.p. (*0-19-281706-X*) Oxford Univ. Pr., Inc.
—Under the Greenwood Tree. 1977. (Hardy New Wessex Editions Ser.). pap. 3.95 o.p. (*0-312-82987-6*, Saint Martin's Griffin) St. Martin's Pr.
—Under the Greenwood Tree. 1999. (Penguin Classics Ser.). 288p. pap. 5.95 o.s.i (*0-14-043553-0*) Viking Penguin.
—Under the Greenwood Tree. Wright, David, ed. 1978. (Penguin Classics Ser.). 256p. pap. 5.95 o.s.i (*0-14-043123-3*, Penguin Classics) Viking Penguin.
—Under the Greenwood Tree. 1998. (Classics Library). 250p. pap. 3.95 (*1-85326-227-7*, 2277WW) Wordsworth Editions, Ltd. GBR. *Dist:* Casemate Pubs. & Bk. Distributors, LLC.
—Under the Greenwood Tree, Our Exploits at West Poley & Short Stories. Gibson, James, ed. 1997. (Everyman Paperback Classics Ser.). 296p. pap. 5.95 o.p. (*0-460-87575-2*, Everyman's Classic Library in Paperback) Tuttle Publishing.
—Wessex Tales. l.t. ed. 1987. (Mainstream Ser.). 242p. 15.95 o.p. (*1-85089-148-6*) ISIS Large Print Bks. GBR. *Dist:* Transaction Pubs.
—Wessex Tales. 1998. 288p. pap. 7.95 (*0-19-283558-0*) Oxford Univ. Pr., Inc.
—The Withered Arm & Other Stories. Brady, Kristin, ed. & intro. by. 1999. (Classics Ser.). (Illus.). 464p. 11.95 (*0-14-043532-8*, Penguin Classics) Viking Penguin.
—The Woodlanders, 3. reprint ed. lib. bdg. 294.00 (*0-7426-2793-4*) Classic Bks.
—The Woodlanders. 1998. (Everyman's Library: Vol. 233). 20.00 (*0-375-40082-6*) Knopf, Alfred A. Inc.
—The Woodlanders. Pinion, F. B., ed. 1975. (Students' Hardy Ser.). 494p. (J). 12.50 (*0-333-17265-5*) Macmillan U.K. GBR. *Dist:* Trans-Atlantic Pubns., Inc.
—The Woodlanders. 1974. 416p. (J). 12.50 (*0-333-16883-6*) Macmillan U.K. GBR. *Dist:* Trans-Atlantic Pubns., Inc.
—The Woodlanders. Kramer, Dale, ed. (Oxford World's Classics Ser.). 2001. (Illus.). 448p. pap. 7.95 (*0-19-283504-1*); 1985. 342p. pap. 6.95 o.p. (*0-19-281600-4*); 1981. 506p. text 98.00 o.p. (*0-19-812504-6*) Oxford Univ. Pr., Inc.
—The Woodlanders. abr. ed. pap. 23.95 incl. audio (*0-14-086576-4*, Penguin AudioBooks) Penguin Group (USA) Inc.
—The Woodlanders. 1998. 20.00 (*0-375-40319-1*) Random Hse., Inc.
—The Woodlanders. 1978. (Hardy New Wessex Editions Ser.). pap. 3.95 o.p. (*0-312-88901-1*, Saint Martin's Griffin) St. Martin's Pr.
—The Woodlanders. 1995. pap. 5.50 o.p. (*0-460-87459-4*) Tuttle Publishing.
—The Woodlanders. Ingham, Patricia, ed. & intro. by. 1998. (Classics Ser.). (Illus.). 464p. pap. 7.95 (*0-14-043547-6*, Penguin Classics) Viking Penguin.
—The Woodlanders. Gibson, James, ed. 1981. (English Library). 464p. pap. 7.95 o.s.i (*0-14-043145-4*, Penguin Classics) Viking Penguin.
—The Woodlanders. 1998. (Classics Library). 352p. pap. 3.95 (*1-85326-293-5*, 2935WW) Wordsworth Editions, Ltd. GBR. *Dist:* Combined Publishing.
Hardy, Thomas, ed. Far from the Madding Crowd. 1967. (Airmont Classics Ser.). (YA). (gr. 11 up). mass mkt. 2.50 o.p. (*0-8049-0136-8*, CL-136) Airmont Publishing Co., Inc.
—Far from the Madding Crowd. 1976. 26.95 (*0-8488-0514-3*) Amereon, Ltd.
—Far from the Madding Crowd. 1999. (Literature Made Easy Ser.). (Illus.). x, 85p. (YA). pap. 4.95 o.p. (*0-7641-0824-7*) Barron's Educational Series, Inc.
—Far from the Madding Crowd. 1988. 380p. reprint ed. lib. bdg. 26.95 (*0-89966-625-6*) Buccaneer Bks., Inc.
—Far from the Madding Crowd, 2. reprint ed. lib. bdg. 196.00 (*0-7426-2786-1*); 2001. pap. text 56.00 (*0-7426-7786-9*) Classic Bks.
—Far from the Madding Crowd. 2000. E-Book 2.49 (*1-58744-123-3*) Electric Umbrella Publishing.
—Far from the Madding Crowd. 1942. 12.95 o.p. (*0-06-011755-9*); 2000. 576p. pap. 24.00 (*0-06-095696-8*, HarperCollins) HarperTrade.
—Far from the Madding Crowd. l.t. ed. 2062p. pap. 125.06 (*0-7583-0879-5*); 1659p. pap. 112.27 (*0-7583-0878-7*); 1428p. pap. 90.93 (*0-7583-0877-9*); 900p. pap. 65.07 (*0-7583-0875-2*); 1161p. pap. 77.69 (*0-7583-0876-0*); 405p. pap. 31.92 (*0-7583-0872-8*); 700p. pap. 46.56 (*0-7583-0874-4*); 405p. lib. bdg. 37.92 (*0-7583-0864-7*); 509p. lib. bdg. 43.80 (*0-7583-0865-5*); 700p. lib. bdg. 52.56 (*0-7583-0866-3*); 900p. lib. bdg. 77.07 (*0-7583-0867-1*); 1428p. lib. bdg. 102.93 (*0-7583-0869-8*); 2062p. lib. bdg. 147.16 (*0-7583-0871-X*); 1161p. lib. bdg. 89.69 (*0-7583-0868-X*) Huge Print Pr.
—Far from the Madding Crowd. unabr. ed. 1998. (Wordsworth Classics Ser.). (YA). (gr. 6-12). 5.27 (*0-89061-067-3*, R0673WW) Jamestown.
—Far from the Madding Crowd, Level 4. 2003. (Illus.). v, 56p. pap. 7.67 (*0-582-41764-3*) Longman Publishing Group.
—Far from the Madding Crowd. 2002. 400p. mass mkt. 5.95 (*0-451-52856-5*, Signet Classics); 1961. 384p. mass mkt. 5.95 o.s.i (*0-451-52360-1*, Signet Classics); 1961. mass mkt. 2.95 o.p. (*0-451-52115-3*) NAL.
—Far from the Madding Crowd. l.t. ed. (Large Print Ser.). reprint ed. 1993. 523p. lib. bdg. 26.00 (*0-939495-46-5*); 1998. (Illus.). 440p. lib. bdg. 25.00 (*1-58287-028-4*) North Bks.
—Far from the Madding Crowd. 2001. E-Book 2.25 (*1-58882-536-1*) PublishingOnline.
—Far from the Madding Crowd. (Modern Library Classics). 2001. (Illus.). 512p. pap. 9.95 (*0-375-75797-X*); 2000. E-Book 4.95 (*0-679-64150-5*) Random House Adult Trade Publishing Group. (Modern Library).
—Far from the Madding Crowd. 1978. (Hardy New Wessex Editions Ser.). pap. 2.95 (*0-312-28246-X*, Saint Martin's Griffin) St. Martin's Pr.
—Far from the Madding Crowd. l.t. ed. 1983. 608p. o.p. (*0-7089-8092-9*, Charnwood) Thorpe, F. A. Pubs.
—Far from the Madding Crowd. 1968. (Signet Classics Ser.). 12.00 (*0-606-03206-1*) Turtleback Bks.
—Far from the Madding Crowd. 1997. (Classics Ser.). (Illus.). 360p. pap. 3.95 (*1-85326-067-3*, 0673WW) Wordsworth Editions, Ltd. GBR. *Dist:* Combined Publishing.
—Tess of the d'Urbervilles. 1993. (Longman Literature Ser.). pap. text 7.00 (*0-582-09715-0*) Addison-Wesley Longman, Ltd. GBR. *Dist:* Trans-Atlantic Pubns., Inc.
—Tess of the d'Urbervilles. 1963. (Airmont Classics Ser.). (gr. 11 up). mass mkt. 3.50 (*0-8049-0082-5*, CL-82) Airmont Publishing Co., Inc.
—Tess of the d'Urbervilles. 1976. 29.95 (*0-8488-0516-X*) Amereon, Ltd.
—Tess of the d'Urbervilles. 1984. (Bantam Classics Ser.). 448p. (gr. 9-12). mass mkt. 4.95 (*0-553-21168-4*, Bantam Classics) Bantam Bks.
—Tess of the d'Urbervilles. pap. 4.95 (*0-7910-4167-0*) Chelsea Hse. Pubs.
—Tess of the d'Urbervilles. 1980. pap. 1.50 o.p. (*0-440-38626-8*) Dell Publishing.
—Tess of the d'Urbervilles. 1998. audio 44.95 Filmic Archives.
—Tess of the d'Urbervilles. 1989. audio 65.00 Jimcin Recordings.
—Tess of the d'Urbervilles. 1999. (Cloth Bound Pocket Ser.). (Illus.). 7.95 (*3-8290-3008-8*, 521260) Konemann.
—Tess of the d'Urbervilles. 1993. audio 66.40 (*1-56544-032-3*, 350025) Literate Ear, Inc.
—Tess of the d'Urbervilles. E-Book 1.95 (*1-57799-944-4*) Logos Research Systems, Inc.
—Tess of the d'Urbervilles. 1988. (Study Texts Ser.). pap. text 5.95 (*0-582-01978-8*) Longman Publishing Group.
—Tess of the d'Urbervilles. 2003. (*0-333-16896-8*) Macmillan U.K. GBR. *Dist:* Trafalgar Square.
—Tess of the d'Urbervilles. 1964. 432p. mass mkt. 4.95 o.s.i (*0-451-52546-9*, Signet Classics); mass mkt. 3.50 o.p. (*0-451-52429-2*); mass mkt. 2.95 o.p. (*0-451-51924-8*, CE1686, Signet Classics) NAL.
—Tess of the d'Urbervilles. 2001. E-Book 2.25 (*1-58882-541-8*) PublishingOnline.
—Tess of the d'Urbervilles. 2000. E-Book 4.95 (*0-679-64151-3*, Modern Library) Random House Adult Trade Publishing Group.
—Tess of the d'Urbervilles. (Ebook Classic Ser.). E-Book 5.00 (*0-7410-0563-8*) SoftBook Pr.
—Tess of the d'Urbervilles. 1978. (Hardy New Wessex Editions Ser.). pap. 2.95 o.p. (*0-312-79346-4*, Saint Martin's Griffin) St. Martin's Pr.
—Tess of the d'Urbervilles. 1973. (Washington Square Press Enriched Classic Ser.). 11.00 (*0-606-01449-7*) Turtleback Bks.
—Tess of the d'Urbervilles. 1984. 447p. pap. 3.95 o.p. (*0-460-87122-6*, Everyman's Classic Library in Paperback) Tuttle Publishing.
—Tess of the d'Urbervilles. abr. ed. 1996. 4p. 23.95 incl. audio (*0-14-086040-1*, Penguin AudioBooks) Viking Penguin.
—Tess of the d'Urbervilles. 1997. (Classics Library). 384p. pap. 3.95 (*1-85326-005-3*, 0053WW) Wordsworth Editions, Ltd. GBR. *Dist:* Casemate Pubs. & Bk. Distributors, LLC.
—Tess of the D'Urbervilles. abr. ed. 1997. (Classic Fiction Ser.). audio 17.98 o.p. (*962-634-647-7*, NA314714); audio compact disk 19.98 o.p. (*962-634-147-5*, NA314712) Naxos of America, Inc. (Naxos AudioBooks).
—Tess of the d'Urbervilles, Set. unabr. ed. 1991. (YA). (gr. 8 up). audio 65.95 (*1-55685-094-8*) Audio Bk. Contractors, Inc.
—Tess of the d'Urbervilles. unabr. ed. 1998. audio 39.95 (*1-57270-067-X*, F91067u, Cover to Cover Classics) Audio Partners Publishing Corp.
—Tess of the d'Urbervilles. unabr. ed. audio 94.95 o.p. (*1-85549-969-X*, CTC 054) BBC Audiobooks America.
—Tess of the d'Urbervilles. unabr. ed. 1982. audio 83.95 (*0-7861-0516-X*, 2016) Blackstone Audio Bks., Inc.
—Tess of the d'Urbervilles. unabr. collector's ed. 1982. (YA). audio 96.00 (*0-7366-3868-7*, 9075) Books on Tape, Inc.
—Tess of the d'Urbervilles. 1987. 432p. reprint ed. lib. bdg. 35.95 (*0-89966-624-8*) Buccaneer Bks., Inc.
—Tess of the d'Urbervilles, Set. unabr. ed. 2000. audio 79.95 (*0-7451-2744-4*, SAB 110) Chivers Audio Bks. GBR. *Dist:* BBC Audiobooks America.
—Tess of the d'Urbervilles, Set. unabr. ed. 1999. audio 83.95 Highsmith Inc.
—Tess of the d'Urbervilles, Set. abr. ed. 1996. (Ultimate Classics Ser.). 19.95 o.p. (*0-7871-0899-5*, 694329) NewStar Media, Inc.
—Tess of the d'Urbervilles. unabr. ed. 1994. audio 97.00 (*0-7887-0034-0*, 94233E7) Recorded Bks., LLC.
—Tess of the d'Urbervilles. l.t. ed. 1982. (Classics Ser.). 649p. 13.95 o.p. (*0-7089-8038-4*, Charnwood) Thorpe, F. A. Pubs. GBR. *Dist:* Ulverscroft Large Print Bks., Ltd.
Hardy, Thomas, et al, eds. Tess of the d'Urbervilles. (Oxford World's Classics Ser.). (Illus.). 1988. 450p. pap. 5.95 o.p. (*0-19-281826-0*); 1983. 754p. text 194.50 o.p. (*0-19-812495-3*); 1998. 456p. reprint ed. pap. 6.95 (*0-19-283362-6*) Oxford Univ. Pr., Inc.

Settings

Settings

Hardy, Thomas & Blythe, Ronald, eds. Far from the Madding Crowd. 1978. (Penguin English Library). 496p. pap. 9.95 o.s.i (0-14-043126-8, Penguin Classics) Viking Penguin.

Hardy, Thomas & Buckler, William E., eds. Tess of the d'Urbervilles. 1960. (YA). (gr. 9 up). pap. 16.36 (0-395-05144-4, Riverside Editions) Houghton Mifflin Co.

Hardy, Thomas & Dolin, Tim, eds. Tess of the d'Urbervilles. 1999. (Classics Ser.). (Illus.). 592p. 7.95 (0-14-043514-X, Penguin Classics) Viking Penguin.

Hardy, Thomas & Elledge, Scott, eds. Tess of the d'Urbervilles. (Critical Editions Ser.). 1978. (Illus.). (C). pap. o.p. (0-393-09044-2); 2nd ed. 1979. (Illus.). 14.95 o.p. (0-393-04507-2); 3rd ed. 1990. 492p. (C). pap. text 11.50 (0-393-95903-1) Norton, W. W. & Co., Inc.

Hardy, Thomas & Falck-Yi, Suzanne B., eds. Far from the Madding Crowd. (Oxford World's Classics Ser.). (Illus.). 1998. 528p. pap. 6.95 o.p. (0-19-283391-X); 1993. 514p. (C). pap. 4.95 o.p. (0-19-282782-0) Oxford Univ. Pr., Inc.

Hardy, Thomas & George, Pat, eds. Far from the Madding Crowd. 1996. (Cambridge Literature Ser.). (Illus.). 432p. pap. text 11.95 o.p. (0-521-56767-X) Cambridge Univ. Pr.

Hardy, Thomas & Gibson, James, eds. Far from the Madding Crowd. 1993. 416p. pap. 3.95 o.p. (0-460-87255-9, Everyman's Classic Library in Paperback) Tuttle Publishing.

—Tess of the d'Urbervilles. 1993. 447p. pap. 4.95 o.p. (0-460-87344-X, Everyman's Classic Library in Paperback) Tuttle Publishing.

Hardy, Thomas & Gibson, Rex, eds. Tess of the d'Urbervilles. 1996. (Cambridge Literature Ser.). (Illus.). 448p. pap. text 11.95 o.p. (0-521-56714-9) Cambridge Univ. Pr.

Hardy, Thomas & Hedge, Tricia, eds. Far from the Madding Crowd. (Illus.). 1992. 96p. pap. text 5.95 (0-19-422687-5); Level 5. 2000. 112p. (YA). pap. text 5.95 (0-19-423064-3) Oxford Univ. Pr., Inc.

—Far from the Madding Crowd. 1992. (BCL1-PR English Literature Ser.). 475p. reprint ed. lib. bdg. 99.00 (0-7812-7546-6) Reprint Services Corp.

Hardy, Thomas & Maier, Sarah, eds. Tess of the d'Urbervilles. 1996. (Illus.). 280p. pap. (1-55111-066-0) Broadview Pr.

Hardy, Thomas & Moody, Rick. The Mayor of Casterbridge. 2001. (Oxford World's Classics Ser.). 464p. 18.00 (0-19-514810-X) Oxford Univ. Pr., Inc.

Hardy, Thomas & Morgan, Rosemarie, eds. Far from the Madding Crowd. 2000. (Penguin Classics Ser.). (Illus.). 480p. 7.95 (0-14-043521-2, Penguin Bks.) Viking Penguin.

Hardy, Thomas & Page, Norman. Jude the Obscure: An Authoritative Text: Backgrounds & Contexts Criticism. 2nd ed. 1999. (Critical Editions Ser.). (Illus.). xii, 468p. pap. 11.00 (0-393-97278-X) Norton, W. W. & Co., Inc.

Hardy, Thomas & Riquelme, John P., eds. Tess of the d'Urbervilles. 1998. 528p. (C). pap. text 9.50 (0-312-10688-2) Bedford/Saint Martin's.

—Tess of the d'Urbervilles. 1998. (Case Studies in Contemporary Criticism). 528p. (C). 35.00 (0-312-16375-4) Palgrave Macmillan.

Hardy, Thomas & Schweik, Robert C., eds. Far from the Madding Crowd. 1986. (Critical Editions Ser.). 472p. (C). pap. text 10.50 (0-393-95408-0) Norton, W. W. & Co., Inc.

Hardy, Thomas & Skilton, David, eds. Tess of the d'Urbervilles. 1978. (Penguin Classics Ser.). 544p. pap. 7.95 o.s.i (0-14-043135-7, Penguin Classics) Viking Penguin.

Hardy, Thomas & Widdowson, Peter, eds. Tess of the d'Urbervilles. 1993. (New Casebooks Ser.). 528p. 49.95 o.p. (0-312-09092-7) Palgrave Macmillan.

Shefter, Harry. Tess of the d'Urbervilles. Hardy, Thomas, ed. 1973. (Enriched Classics Ser.). pap. 0.95 o.s.i (0-671-47905-9, Washington Square Pr.) Simon & Schuster.

Shires, Linda M. Far from the Madding Crowd. Hardy, Thomas & Falck-Yi, Suzanne B., eds. 2nd ed. 2003. (Oxford World's Classics Ser.). (Illus.). 528p. pap. 7.95 (0-19-280149-X) Oxford Univ. Pr., Inc.

## WEST (U.S.)—FICTION

Abbey, Edward. The Brave Cowboy: An Old Tale in a New Time. deluxe ltd. ed. 1993. (Illus.). 304p. reprint ed. 95.00 o.p. (0-942688-88-0) Dream Garden Pr.

—The Brave Cowboy: An Old Tale in a New Time. 1977. (Zia Bks.). 292p. reprint ed. pap. 10.95 o.p. (0-8263-0448-6) Univ. of New Mexico Pr.

Adams, Andy. Andy Adams' Campfire Tales. Hudson, Wilson M., ed. 1976. (Illus.). reprint ed. xxxii, 296p. 30.00 o.p. (0-8032-0870-7); 296p. pap. 15.95 o.p. (0-8032-5835-6, Bison Bks.) Univ. of Nebraska Pr.

—Cattle Brands: A Collection of Western Campfire Stories. 2000. 252p. E-Book 3.95 (0-594-04428-6) 1873 Pr.

—Cattle Brands: A Collection of Western Campfire Stories. 1977. (Short Story Index Reprint Ser.). reprint ed. 19.95 (0-8369-3831-3) Ayer Co. Pubs., Inc.

—The Log of a Cowboy: A Narrative of the Old Trail Days. 1969. (Airmont Classics Ser.). (YA). (gr. 7 up). mass mkt. 1.95 o.p. (0-8049-0201-1, CL-201) Airmont Publishing Co., Inc.

—The Log of a Cowboy: A Narrative of the Old Trail Days. 1987. (Classics of the Old West Ser.). (J). lib. bdg. 17.27 o.p. (0-8094-3979-4) Silver, Burdett & Ginn, Inc.

—Wells Brothers: The Young Cattle Kings. 1997. (Illus.). 370p. pap. 12.95 (0-8032-5929-8, Bison Bks.) Univ. of Nebraska Pr.

Agee, Jonis. The Weight of Dreams. 2000. 448p. 13.95 (0-14-029188-1); 1999. 368p. 24.95 o.s.i (0-670-88233-X) Viking Penguin.

Alpert, Bill. Castle Garden. 1996. 346p. 28.00 (1-877946-67-2) Permanent Pr., The.

Alter, Judy. Cherokee Rose. 1997. 432p. mass mkt. 5.99 o.s.i (0-553-57319-5) Bantam Bks.

—Cherokee Rose: A Novel of America's First Cowgirl. 1996. 400p. pap. 9.95 o.s.i (0-553-37560-1) Bantam Bks.

Alter, Judy & Row, A. T., eds. Unbridled Spirits: Short Fiction about Women in the Old West. 1994. 366p. (C). pap. 17.95 (0-87565-124-0) Texas Christian Univ. Pr.

Altsheler, Joseph A. The Rifleman of the Ohio. 2000. 252p. pap. 9.95 (0-594-06414-7); E-Book 3.95 (0-594-06415-5) 1873 Pr.

—The Rifleman of the Ohio. 25.95 (0-8488-1239-5) Amereon, Ltd.

—The Rifleman of the Ohio. (Young Trailer Ser.). reprint ed. 1984. 319p. lib. bdg. 35.95 o.p. (0-89966-483-0); 1981. 432p. lib. bdg. 35.95 (0-89968-226-X, Lightyear Pr.) Buccaneer Bks., Inc.

Anderson, Leone C. Sean's War. 1998. (Illus.). 192p. (J). (gr. 3-9). 16.95 (0-9638819-4-9); pap. 10.95 (0-9638819-5-7) ShadowPlay Pr.

Athanas, Verne. Pursuit: Western Stories. Tuska, Jon, ed. 1999. (Five Star Western Ser.). 216p. 19.95 (0-7862-1842-8, Five Star) Gale Group.

Athanas, Verne & Tuska, Jon. Pursuit: Western Stories. l.t. ed. 2000. (G. K. Hall Western Ser.). 273p. 23.95 (0-7838-9134-2, Macmillan Reference USA) Gale Group.

Bacher, June M. Gently Love Beckons. l.t. ed. 1994. (Orig.). 22.95 o.p. (0-7927-2048-2); pap. 21.95 o.p. (0-7927-2047-4) BBC Audiobooks America.

Bailey, Larry. San Poil Chronicle. 1998. 640p. pap. 28.99 (0-7388-0050-3); text 38.99 (0-7388-0049-X) Xlibris Corp.

Baker, Madeline. Chase the Wind. 2000. 400p. mass mkt. 5.99 (0-505-52401-5, Love Spell) Dorchester Publishing Co., Inc.

Ballantyne, R. M. The Norsemen in the West. E-Book 3.95 (0-594-02074-3) 1873 Pr.

Barr, Nevada. Bittersweet. 1999. 368p. pap. 13.95 (0-380-79950-2) Morrow/Avon.

—Bittersweet. 1989. 344p. reprint ed. pap. 9.95 o.p. (0-933216-64-5) Spinsters Ink Bks.

Barton, Wayne. Fairchild's Passage. 1997. 384p. 24.95 o.p. (0-312-86141-9, Forge Bks.) Doherty, Tom Assocs., LLC.

Barton, Wayne & Williams, Stan. Fairchilds Passage. 2000. 384p. mass mkt. 6.99 (0-8125-4422-6, Forge Bks.) Doherty, Tom Assocs., LLC.

Beach, Rex Ellingwood. Pardners. 1977. (Short Story Index Reprint Ser.). 22.95 (0-8369-3180-7) Ayer Co. Pubs., Inc.

—Pardners. (Collected Works of Rex Ellingwood Beach ). 278p. reprint ed. 2001. (Illus.). pap. text 28.00 (0-7426-5538-5); 1998. lib. bdg. 88.00 (1-58201-538-4) Classic Bks.

Bean, Frederic. Hell's Half Acre. 1996. 256p. (Orig.). mass mkt. 5.99 o.s.i (0-425-15584-6) Berkley Publishing Group.

—Tom Spoon. 1990. 192p. 18.95 o.p. (0-8027-4103-7) Walker & Co.

Bechko, Peggy A. Blown to Hell. l.t. ed. 1994. 19.95 o.p. (0-7927-1812-7); pap. 17.95 o.p. (0-7927-1813-5) BBC Audiobooks America.

—The Eye of the Hawk. 1998. (Western Ser.). 218p. 19.95 (0-7862-0991-7, Five Star) Gale Group.

—The Eye of the Hawk: A Western Story. l.t. ed. 1999. (Western Ser.). 317p. pap. 19.95 o.p. (0-7862-1030-3) Thorndike Pr.

Bendall, Molly & Wronsky, Gail. Calamity & Belle. 1993. 48p. 17.95 o.p. (0-87905-558-8) Smith, Gibbs Pub.

Benedict, Rex. Good Luck Arizona Man. 1972. (J). (gr. 5 up). 4.50 o.p. (0-394-82441-5, Pantheon) Knopf Publishing Group.

Benshoof-Holler, Margaret. Burning of the Marriage Hat: A Novel of High Plains Women. 2002. (Illus.). 381p. pap. 14.95 (0-9714473-2-2) Wind Women Pr.

Berger, Thomas. Little Big Man. 30.95 (0-8488-0429-5) Amereon, Ltd.

—Little Big Man. 1982. mass mkt. 3.75 o.s.i (0-449-20026-4); 1981. 448p. mass mkt. 3.50 o.s.i (0-449-23854-7) Ballantine Bks. (Fawcett).

—Little Big Man. 1985. 448p. mass mkt. 5.95 o.s.i (0-440-34976-1, Laurel) Dell Publishing.

—Little Big Man, unabr. collector's ed. 1988. audio 96.00 (0-7366-2706-5, 3439) Books on Tape, Inc.

—Little Big Man. 1979. 10.95 o.s.i (0-385-28606-6, Delacorte Pr.) Dell Publishing.

—Little Big Man. 25th ed. 1989. 480p. pap. 15.95 (0-385-29829-3, Delta) Dell Publishing.

—The Return of Little Big Man: A Novel. 448p. 2000. pap. 13.95 (0-316-09117-0, Back Bay); 1999. (YA). (gr. 8 up). 25.00 o.p. (0-316-09844-2) Little Brown & Co.

—The Return of Little Big Man: A Novel. l.t. ed. 1999. (Core Ser.). 695p. 30.95 (0-7838-8600-4) Thorndike Pr.

Bergren, Lisa Tawn. Deep Harbor. 1999. (Northern Lights Ser.: Vol. 2). 384p. pap. 10.95 (1-57856-045-4) WaterBrook Pr.

Bittner, Rosanne. Mystic Dreamers. 2000. 384p. mass mkt. 6.99 (0-8125-6540-1, Tor Bks.); 1999. (Mystic Dreamers Ser.: Vol. 1). (Illus.). 288p. 23.95 (0-312-86511-2, Forge Bks.) Doherty, Tom Assocs., LLC.

—Mystic Visions, Bk. 2. 2000. (Mystic Dreamers Ser.: Vol. 2). (Illus.). 320p. 23.95 o.s.i (0-312-86512-0, Forge Bks.) Doherty, Tom Assocs., LLC.

—Mystic Warriors. 2001. 352p. 24.95 (0-312-86513-9, Forge Bks.); 2002. reprint ed. mass mkt. 6.99 (0-8125-6543-6, Tor Bks.) Doherty, Tom Assocs., LLC.

Black, Baxter. Hey, Cowboy, Wanna Get Lucky. 1995. 240p. pap. 13.00 (0-14-025093-X, Penguin Bks.) Penguin Group (USA) Inc.

—Hey Cowboy, Wanna Get Lucky? 1994. 240p. 21.00 o.s.i (0-517-59377-7, Crown) Crown Publishing Group.

—Hey Cowboy, Wanna Get Lucky? A Rodeo Novel, Set. abr. ed. 1996. 180p. audio 16.99 o.s.i (0-553-47693-9, 393414, RH Audio) Random Hse. Audio Publishing Group.

Blackburn, Thomas Wakefield. El Segundo. 1997. (Gunsmoke Western Ser.). 203p. 17.50 o.p. (0-7451-8714-5, Gunsmoke) BBC Audiobooks America.

—El Segundo. 1978. pap. 1.25 o.p. (0-440-13491-9) Dell Publishing.

—El Segundo. l.t. ed. 2000. (G. K. Hall Paperback Ser.). 256p. pap. 23.95 (0-7838-9041-9, Macmillan Reference USA) Gale Group.

Blake, Michael. Marching to Valhalla: A Novel of Custer's Last Days. l.t. ed. 1997. 304p. pap. 19.00 (0-449-00044-3, Fawcett) Ballantine Bks.

—Marching to Valhalla: A Novel of Custer's Last Days. 2002. 261p. 24.95 (0-9724753-3-8) Hrymfaxe.

—Marching to Valhalla: A Novel of Custer's Last Days. l.t. ed. 1997. (G. K. Hall Western Ser.). 403p. 25.95 (0-7838-8091-X) Thorndike Pr.

Blakely, Mike. Shortgrass Song. 1994. 448p. 23.95 o.p. (0-312-85541-9, Forge Bks.) Doherty, Tom Assocs., LLC.

—Too Long at the Dance. 1998. 532p. mass mkt. 6.50 (0-8125-4832-9); 1996. 352p. 23.95 o.p. (0-312-86093-5) Doherty, Tom Assocs., LLC. (Forge Bks.).

Blevins, Win. Ravenshadow. 2000. 423p. mass mkt. 6.99 (0-8125-9017-1); 1999. 448p. 25.95 (0-312-86565-1) Doherty, Tom Assocs., LLC. (Forge Bks.).

Blum, Ivon B. River of Souls: A Novel of the American Myth. Smith, James C., ed. 1999. 320p. 24.95 (0-86534-281-4) Sunstone Pr.

Bly, Stephen A. Columbia Falls. l.t. ed. 1999. (Christian Fiction Ser.). 373p. 24.95 (0-7862-2055-4) Thorndike Pr.

—Coyote True, No. 2. 1992. (Nathan T. Riggins Western Adventure Ser.: Bk. 2). 128p. (J). (gr. 4-7). pap. 4.99 o.p. (0-89107-680-8) Crossway Bks.

—False Claims at the Little Stephen Mine. 1992. (Stuart Brannon Western Adventure Ser.: No. 2). 192p. pap. 7.99 o.p. (0-89107-642-5) Crossway Bks.

—False Claims at the Little Stephen Mine. l.t. ed. 1994. 269p. lib. bdg. 18.95 (0-8161-7405-9, Macmillan Reference USA) Gale Group.

—Friends & Enemies: A Novel. 2002. (Fortune of the Black Hills Ser.: Vol. 4). 272p. pap. 12.99 (0-8054-2437-7) Broadman & Holman Pubs.

—Last Hanging at Paradise Meadow. 1992. (Stuart Brannon Western Adventure Ser.: Vol. 3). 192p. pap. 8.99 o.p. (0-89107-672-7) Crossway Bks.

—Last Hanging at Paradise Meadow. l.t. ed. 1995. 254p. lib. bdg. 19.95 o.p. (0-7838-1249-3, Macmillan Reference USA) Gale Group.

—The Long Trail Home: A Novel. l.t. ed. 2002. 280p. lib. bdg. 27.95 (1-58547-085-6) Ctr. Point Large Print.

—Standoff at Sunrise Creek. 1993. (Stuart Brannon Western Ser.: Vol. 4). 192p. pap. 8.99 (0-89107-695-6) Crossway Bks.

—Standoff at Sunrise Creek. l.t. ed. 1995. 270p. 20.95 o.p. (0-7838-1275-2, Macmillan Reference USA) Gale Group.

—Strangers & Pilgrims. 2002. 304p. pap. 11.99 (1-58134-426-0) Crossway Bks.

—Sweet Carolina. 1998. (Heroines of the Golden West Ser.: Vol. 1). 224p. (gr. 7-12). pap. 10.99 (0-89107-973-4) Crossway Bks.

—Sweet Carolina. l.t. ed. 1999. (Western Ser.). 327p. 25.95 (0-7838-0410-5) Thorndike Pr.

—Trouble in Quartz Mountain Tunnel. 1901. (Making Choices Ser.). (Illus.). 124p. (J). (gr. 4-8). pap. 3.50 o.p. (0-89191-979-1, 59790) Cook Communications Ministries.

Bly, Stephen A. & Bly, Janet. Columbia Falls. 1998. (Hidden West Ser.). 250p. pap. 10.99 o.p. (1-56955-069-7, Vine Bks.) Servant Pubns.

Boggs, Johnny D. The Lonesome Chisholm Trail: A Western Story. l.t. ed. 2002. 329p. 25.95 (0-7838-8950-X) Gale Group.

Bojer, Johan. The Emigrants. Jayne, A. G., tr. 1974. 351p. reprint ed. 35.00 o.s.i (0-8371-6194-0, BOTE, Greenwood Pr.) Greenwood Publishing Group, Inc.

—The Emigrants. 1991. (Borealis Bks.). xii, 351p. reprint ed. pap. 12.95 (0-87351-260-X, Borealis Bk.) Minnesota Historical Society Pr.

—The Emigrants. Jayne, A. G., tr. 1978. xviii, 355p. reprint ed. pap. 8.95 o.p. (0-8032-6051-2, BB 673) Univ. of Nebraska Pr.

Boling, Fredrick W. Incident at Crazy Woman Creek: A Historical Western Novel. 1999. 273p. pap. 16.95 o.p. (0-7414-0046-4) Buy Bks. on the Web.Com.

Bonham, Frank. The Best Western Stories of Frank Bonham. Pronzini, Bill & Greenberg, Martin H., eds. (Western Writers Ser.). 288p. 1990. pap. 15.95 (0-8040-0930-9); 1989. 24.95 (0-8040-0929-5) Swallow Pr.

—The Canon of Maverick Brands. 1997. (Western Ser.). 213p. lib. bdg. 18.95 (0-7862-0746-9, Five Star) Gale Group.

—The Canon of Maverick Brands. l.t. ed. 1998. (Western Ser.). 328p. 20.95 (0-7862-0769-8) Thorndike Pr.

—One Ride Too Many & Twelve Other Action Stories of the Wild West. Greenberg, Martin H. & Pronzini, Bill, eds. 1995. 270p. pap. 12.00 (1-56980-034-0) Barricade Bks., Inc.

Bowen, Peter. Yellowstone Kelly. 1990. 320p. mass mkt. 3.95 o.s.i (0-553-28597-1) Bantam Bks.

—Yellowstone Kelly. 1988. (Frontier Library). 260p. 17.95 o.s.i (0-915463-40-7, Frontier Library, The) Jameson Bks., Inc.

Bower, B. M. Chip, of the Flying U. 1999. 256p. 19.00 (0-7540-8066-8, Gunsmoke) BBC Audiobooks America.

—Chip, of the Flying U. 1975. lib. bdg. 16.95 o.p. (0-89966-012-6) Buccaneer Bks., Inc.

—Chip, of the Flying U. l.t. ed. 2003. lib. bdg. 26.95 (1-58547-343-X, Western) Ctr. Point Large Print.

—Chip, of the Flying U. 1995. (Illus.). 264p. pap. 8.95 (0-8032-6121-7, Bison Bks.) Univ. of Nebraska Pr.

—The Flying U Ranch. 1996. (Illus.). 253p. pap. 10.00 (0-8032-6129-2, Bison Bks.) Univ. of Nebraska Pr.

—Happy Family of the Flying U. 1996. (Illus.). 323p. pap. 12.00 (0-8032-6130-6, Bison Bks.) Univ. of Nebraska Pr.

Bowers, Terrell L. The Secret of Snake Canyon. l.t. ed. 1994. 201p. lib. bdg. 17.95 o.p. (0-8161-5921-1, Macmillan Reference USA) Gale Group.

—The Secret of Snake Canyon. 1993. 168p. 19.95 (0-8027-1264-9) Walker & Co.

Boyer, G. G. Morgette in the Yukon. 2001. 176p. mass mkt. 3.99 (0-8439-4886-8, Leisure Bks.) Dorchester Publishing Co., Inc.

Brand, Max. The Abandoned Outlaw. l.t. ed. 1997. (Sagebrush Large Print Westerns Ser.). lib. bdg. 20.95 (1-57490-095-1) Beeler, Thomas T. Publisher.

—The Abandoned Outlaw. 1998. 240p. mass mkt. 4.50 (0-8439-4465-X, Leisure Bks.) Dorchester Publishing Co., Inc.

—The Black Rider & Other Stories. l.t. ed. 1996. (G. K. Hall Western Ser.). 346p. 25.95 (0-7838-1844-0) Thorndike Pr.

—Dan Barry's Daughter. 1976. reprint ed. lib. bdg. 25.95 (0-88411-516-X) Amereon, Ltd.

—Farewell, Thunder Moon. l.t. ed. 1998. (Sagebrush Large Print Westerns Ser.). 18.95 (1-57490-123-0) Beeler, Thomas T. Publisher.

—Farewell, Thunder Moon. 1996. 84p. (C). text 40.00 (0-8032-1267-4) Univ. of Nebraska Pr.

—The Fugitive's Mission. 1997. (Western Ser.). 250p. lib. bdg. 18.95 (0-7862-0750-7, Five Star) Gale Group.

—The Fugitive's Mission. l.t. ed. 1998. (Western Ser.). 400p. 24.95 (0-7862-0773-6) Thorndike Pr.

—The Geraldi Trail. 2003. 272p. mass mkt. 4.99 (0-8439-5123-0) Dorchester Publishing Co., Inc.

—The Geraldi Trail. 1999. (Western Ser.). 272p. 19.95 (0-7862-1576-3, Five Star) Gale Group.
—The Geraldi Trail. l.t. ed. 2000. (G. K. Hall Western Ser.). 351p. 25.95 (0-7838-0314-1) Thorndike Pr.
—The Ghost Wagon & Other Great Western Adventures, Set. abr. ed. 1997. audio 16.99 (0-88646-439-0, 7439) Durkin Hayes Publishing Ltd.
—The Ghost Wagon & Other Great Western Adventures. Tuska, Jon, ed. l.t. ed. 1996. (G. K. Hall Western Ser.). 452p. 24.95 (0-7838-1862-9) Thorndike Pr.
—The Ghost Wagon & Other Great Western Adventures. Tuska, Jon, ed. & frwd. by. 1996. 246p. (C). text 40.00 (0-8032-1265-8) Univ. of Nebraska Pr.
—The Lost Valley. 1998. (Western Ser.). 264p. 19.95 (0-7862-0997-6, Five Star) Gale Group.
—Max Brand's Best Western Stories. Vol. I. 1981. 10.95 o.p. (0-396-07984-9); Vol. II. 1985. 182p. 13.95 o.p. (0-396-08500-8); Vol. III. 1987. 15.95 o.p. (0-396-08948-8) Penguin Putnam Bks. for Young Readers. (G. P. Putnam's Sons).
—Men Beyond the Law. 2001. 256p. mass mkt. 4.50 (0-8439-4873-6, Leisure Bks.) Dorchester Publishing Co., Inc.
—Men Beyond the Law. l.t. ed. 1997. (Western Ser.). 251p. 18.95 (0-7862-0742-6, Five Star) Gale Group.
—Men Beyond the Law. l.t. ed. 1998. (Western Ser.). 399p. 24.95 (0-7862-0765-5); (0-7540-3351-1); (0-7540-3352-X) Thorndike Pr.
—The One-Way Trail. l.t. ed. 1996. (Sagebrush Large Print Westerns Ser.). 256p. lib. bdg. 20.95 (1-57490-014-5) Beeler, Thomas T. Publisher.
—The One-Way Trail. 1998. 240p. reprint ed. mass mkt. 4.50 (0-8439-4379-3, Leisure Bks.) Dorchester Publishing Co., Inc.
—Outlaws All. unabr. ed. 1997. audio 64.00 Books on Tape, Inc.
—Outlaws All. unabr. ed. 1996. audio 57.25 o.p. (1-56100-317-4, 975, Unabridged Library Editions); audio 19.95 o.p. (1-56100-692-0, 205, Bookcassette) Brilliance Audio.
—Outlaws All. 1998. 272p. reprint ed. mass mkt. 5.50 (0-8439-4398-X, Leisure Bks.) Dorchester Publishing Co., Inc.
—Outlaws All. l.t. ed. 1996. (Western Ser.). 273p. 17.95 (0-7862-0592-X, Five Star) Gale Group.
—Outlaws All. l.t. ed. 1997. (Western Ser.). 362p. lib. bdg. 24.95 (0-7838-1575-1) Thorndike Pr.
—The Rock of Kiever. l.t. ed. 1998. (Sagebrush Large Print Westerns Ser.). 246 p. 20.95 (1-57490-122-2) Beeler, Thomas T. Publisher.
—The Rock of Kiever. 2000. 224p. mass mkt. 4.50 (0-8439-4719-5, Leisure Bks.) Dorchester Publishing Co., Inc.
—Safety McTee. l.t. ed. 1998. (Sagebrush Large Print Westerns Ser.). 20.95 (1-57490-116-8, Sagebrush Large Print Westerns) Beeler, Thomas T. Publisher.
—Safety McTee. 1999. 240p. mass mkt. 4.50 (0-8439-4528-1, Leisure Bks.) Dorchester Publishing Co., Inc.
—Slumber Mountain. 2000. 242p. 19.00 (0-7540-8078-1) BBC Audiobooks America.
—Slumber Mountain. l.t. ed. (Sagebrush Large Print Westerns Ser.). 1997. lib. bdg. 18.95 (1-57490-109-5, Beeler Large Print Bks.); 1998. audio 47.95 (1-57490-220-2) Beeler, Thomas T. Publisher.
—Slumber Mountain. 1998. 320p. reprint ed. mass mkt. 4.99 (0-8439-4442-0, Leisure Bks.) Dorchester Publishing Co., Inc.
—Stolen Gold. 1999. (Western Ser.). 255p. 19.95 (0-7862-1333-7, Five Star) Gale Group.
—Stolen Gold. l.t. ed. 2000. (Western Ser.). 384p. 24.95 (0-7862-1341-8); (0-7540-4103-4); (0-7540-4104-2) Thorndike Pr.
—Tales of the Wild West. l.t. ed. 1997. (Circle V Western Ser.). lib. bdg. 20.95 (1-57490-078-1, Beeler Large Print Bks.) Beeler, Thomas T. Publisher.
—Tales of the Wild West. 2000. 240p. mass mkt. 4.50 (0-8439-4769-1, Leisure Bks.) Dorchester Publishing Co., Inc.
—Two Sixes. l.t. ed. (Sagebrush Large Print Westerns Ser.). 1997. lib. bdg. 21.95 (1-57490-088-9); 1999. audio 47.95 (1-57490-225-3) Beeler, Thomas T. Publisher.
—Two Sixes. 1999. 320p. mass mkt. 4.99 (0-8439-4508-7, Leisure Bks.) Dorchester Publishing Co., Inc.
—Two Sixes. 1999. E-Book 9.95 (0-585-29666-9) netLibrary, Inc.
—The Wolf Strain. l.t. ed. 1996. 218p. 17.95 (0-7862-0662-4, Five Star) Gale Group.
Brand, Max & Tuska, Jon. The Black Rider & Other Stories. 1996. 193p. text 40.00 (0-8032-1263-1) Univ. of Nebraska Pr.
Brandewyne, Rebecca. Desperado. 2000. 384p. mass mkt. 5.99 (0-505-52376-0, Love Spell) Dorchester Publishing Co., Inc.
—Desperado. 1996. 384p. 24.00 (0-7278-4846-1) Severn Hse. Pubs., Ltd.
Brandwyne, Rebecca. Desperado. 2000. E-Book 9.95 (0-585-31293-1) netLibrary, Inc.
Braverman, Kate. Wonders of the West. 1993. 280p. 20.00 o.s.i (0-449-90656-6, Fawcett) Ballantine Bks.
British Library Staff, et al. Imagining the West: A Guide to Printed Materials in the British Library on the Literature of the American West. 1997. 60p. (0-7123-4413-6) British Library Research & Development Department.
Brown, Bill. Reading the West: An Anthology of Dime Westerns. 1997. (Bedford Cultural Editions Ser.). (Illus.). 516p. pap. text 14.50 (0-312-13761-3) Bedford/Saint Martin's.
—Reading the West: An Anthology of Dime Westerns. 1997. (Bedford Cultural Editions Ser.). (Illus.). 507p. 45.00 o.p. (0-312-16373-8) Palgrave Macmillan.
—Reading the West: An Anthology of Dime Westerns. 1997. (Bedford Cultural Editions Ser.). pap. 18.95 o.p. (0-312-15462-3) St. Martin's Pr.
Brown, Karen. A Hard Dry Road. 2003. 171p. 26.95 (0-7862-5337-1, Five Star) Gale Group.
Brown, Sam. The Trail to Honk Ballard's Bones. Grad, Doug, ed. 1991. 224p. reprint ed. mass mkt. 3.50 (0-671-69359-X, Pocket) Simon & Schuster.
—The Trail to Honk Ballard's Bones. 1990. 192p. 17.95 (0-8027-4101-0) Walker & Co.
Brusso, Clifton. Tales from the U. S. Mid West. 1992. 123p. (Orig.). pap. 4.95 (0-9633548-1-7) Iroquois Pr.
Buntline, Ned. Buffalo Bill: His Adventures in the West. 1975. (Popular Culture in America Ser.). (Illus.). 320p. (YA). (gr. 7 up). reprint ed. 25.95 (0-405-06366-0) Ayer Co. Pubs., Inc.
Byrd, Max. Shooting the Sun. 2003. 320p. 23.95 (0-553-80208-9) Bantam Bks.
Calder, Stephen. The High-Steel Hazard. 1993. (Bonanza Bk.: No. 3). 288p. mass mkt. 3.99 o.s.i (0-553-29043-6) Bantam Bks.
—The High-Steel Hazard. l.t. ed. 1995. (Bonanza Ser.: No. III). 380p. 19.95 o.p. (0-7838-1389-9, Macmillan Reference USA) Gale Group.
—Journey of the Horse. l.t. ed. 1996. (Bonanza Ser.: No. IV). 329p. 20.95 o.p. (0-7838-1513-1, Macmillan Reference USA) Gale Group.
—The Pioneer Spirit. l.t. ed. 1995. (Bonanza Ser.: No. I). 395p. lib. bdg. 18.95 o.p. (0-7838-1204-3, Macmillan Reference USA) Gale Group.
—The Ponderosa Empire. l.t. ed. 1995. (Bonanza Ser.: No. II). 329p. lib. bdg. 18.95 o.s.i (0-7838-1205-1, Macmillan Reference USA) Gale Group.
Calvert, Patricia. The Snowbird. 1982. (Illus.). 192p. (YA). (gr. 9-12). mass mkt. 2.95 o.p. (0-451-15531-9, Signet Bks.) NAL.
—The Snowbird. 1989. 160p. (YA). (gr. 7 up). lib. bdg. 16.00 o.p. (0-684-19120-2, Atheneum) Simon & Schuster Children's Publishing.
Cameron, Lou. The Spirit Horses. 1976. mass mkt. 1.25 o.p. (0-345-24915-1) Ballantine Bks.
—The Spirit Horses. 1986. 192p. 2.50 o.s.i (0-441-77809-7, Diamond Bks.) Berkley Publishing Group.
—The Spirit Horses. l.t. ed. 2000. (Western Ser.). 291p. 20.95 (0-7862-2424-X) Thorndike Pr.
Carlson, Nolan. Lewis & Clark & Davey Hutchins. 1994. (Illus.). 158p. (Orig.). (J). (gr. 4-8). pap. 6.95 (1-882420-08-X, 1-882420-08-X) Hearth Publishing.
Carroll, Lenore. Abduction From Fort Union. 24.95 (0-8027-4080-4) Walker & Co.
Carter, Forrest. Josey Wales: Two Westerns by Forrest Carter. 1989. 419p. reprint ed. pap. 15.95 (0-8263-1168-7) Univ. of New Mexico Pr.
Cather, Willa. A Lost Lady. 2001. (Modern Classics). 92p. pap. 13.95 (0-86068-126-2) Virago Pr., Ltd. GBR. Dist: Trafalgar Square.
Caves, Roger W. Exploring Urban America: An Introductory Reader. 1994. 538p. 120.00 (0-8039-5637-1, 4975); pap. 61.95 (0-8039-5638-X, 4976) Sage Pubns., Inc.
Charyn, Jerome. Darlin' Bill: A Love Story of the Wild West. 1985. 320p. pap. 8.95 o.p. (0-917657-40-3, Fine, Donald I.) Dutton/Plume.
—Darlin' Bill: A Love Story of the Wild West. 1980. 11.95 o.p. (0-87795-283-3, Morrow, William & Co.) Morrow/Avon.
Cheshire, Gifford Paul. Renegade River: Western Stories. Pronzini, Bill, ed. 1998. (Western Ser.). 261p. 19.95 (0-7862-0992-5, Five Star) Gale Group.
—Renegade River: Western Stories. l.t. ed. 1999. (Western Ser.). 388p. 19.95 (0-7862-1031-1) Thorndike Pr.
Chiaventone, Frederick J. Moon of the Bitter Cold. 2002. (Illus.). 400p. 26.95 (0-7653-0093-1, Forge Bks.) Doherty, Tom Assocs., LLC.
Clarke, Richard. The Oldest Treachery. l.t. ed. 1994. 18.95 o.p. (0-7927-1836-4); pap. 16.95 o.p. (0-7927-1835-6) BBC Audiobooks America.
Cleary, Rita. River Walk. 2000. (Five Star Western Ser.). 268p. 21.95 (0-7862-1845-2, Five Star) Gale Group.
Clyde, Mary. Survival Rate Stories. 2001. 288p. pap. 12.00 (0-393-32084-7) Norton, W. W. & Co., Inc.
—Survival Rates: Stories. 1999. 184p. 24.95 (0-8203-2049-8) Univ. of Georgia Pr.
Coburn, Walt. The Secret of Crutcher's Cabin: A Western Trio. 1999. (Western Ser.). 288p. 19.95 (0-7862-1326-4, Five Star) Gale Group.
—The Secret of Crutcher's Cabin: A Western Trio. l.t. ed. 1999. (G. K. Hall Western Ser.). 381p. 23.95 (0-7838-8396-X) Thorndike Pr.
Coldsmith, Dan. Fort de Chastaigne. l.t. ed. 1993. (Nightingale Ser.). 237p. lib. bdg. 15.95 o.p. (0-8161-5773-1, Macmillan Reference USA) Gale Group.
Coldsmith, Don. Raven Mocker. 2002. (Spanish Bit Saga: Bk. 2). 272p. reprint ed. mass mkt. 6.50 (0-553-29472-5) Bantam Bks.
—Raven Mocker. 2001. 253p. 22.95 (0-8061-3316-3) Univ. of Oklahoma Pr.
—Spanish Bit Saga: Fort de Chastaigne, Vol. 16. 1990. 192p. 14.95 o.s.i (0-385-24576-9) Doubleday Publishing.
Coleman, Jane Candia. Desperate Acts. 2001. (First Edition Romance Ser.). 305p. 25.95 (0-7862-3210-2, Five Star) Gale Group.
—I, Pearl Hart. 1998. (Western Ser.). 222p. 19.95 (0-7862-0987-9, Five Star) Gale Group.
—I, Pearl Hart: A Western Story. l.t. ed. 1999. (Western Ser.). 312p. 20.95 o.p. (0-7862-1026-5) Thorndike Pr.
—Moving On: Stories of the West. 1999. (Love Spell Ser.). 320p. mass mkt. 4.99 (0-8439-4545-1, Leisure Bks.) Dorchester Publishing Co., Inc.
—Moving On: Stories of the West. l.t. ed. 1997. (Western Ser.). 274p. 18.95 (0-7862-0732-9, Five Star) Gale Group.
—Moving On: Stories of the West. l.t. ed. 1998. (Western Ser.). 379p. 25.95 (0-7838-8383-8) Thorndike Pr.
—Stories from Mesa Country. 160p. 1991. 28.95 (0-8040-0949-X); 1992. reprint ed. pap. 14.95 (0-8040-0957-0) Swallow Pr.
Coleman, Rhea. Gutsy's Luck. Smith, James C., Jr., ed. 1993. 196p. (Orig.). pap. 12.95 o.p. (0-86534-187-7) Sunstone Pr.
Colson, Constance. Chase the Dream. 1996. 462p. pap. 11.99 o.s.i (0-88070-928-6, Multnomah Bks.) Multnomah Pubs., Inc.
Combs, Harry. The Scout. 1996. 736p. mass mkt. 6.99 (0-440-21729-6) Dell Publishing.
Comfort, Will L. Apache. 1976. reprint ed. lib. bdg. 23.95 (0-89190-851-X, Rivercity Pr.) Amereon, Ltd.
—Apache. 1980. lib. bdg. 11.95 o.p. (0-8398-2678-8, Macmillan Reference USA) Gale Group.
—Apache. 1986. 274p. reprint ed. pap. 11.95 o.p. (0-8032-6319-8, Bison Bks.) Univ. of Nebraska Pr.
Compton, Ralph. The Old Spanish Trail. abr. ed. 1999. (Trail Drive Ser.: Vol. 2). audio (1-890990-22-1) Otis Audio, Inc.
—The Old Spanish Trail, Vol. 1. 1998. (Trail Drive Ser.). (Illus.). 288p. mass mkt. 6.50 (0-312-96408-0, St. Martin's Paperbacks) St. Martin's Pr.
—The Old Spanish Trail. l.t. ed. 2000. (Charnwood Large Print Ser.). 368p. 31.99 (0-7089-9206-4, Ulverscroft) Thorpe, F. A. Pubs. GBR. Dist: Ulverscroft Large Print Bks., Ltd., Ulverscroft Large Print Canada, Ltd.
Comstock, Will. The Man from Wells Fargo. 1984. 224p. mass mkt. 2.25 o.s.i (0-8439-2170-6) Dorchester Publishing Co., Inc.
—The Man from Wells Fargo. l.t. ed. 1998. (Five Star Western Ser.). 245p. 19.95 (0-7862-0680-2, Five Star) Gale Group.
Conley, Robert J. Broke Loose. 2000. 256p. mass mkt. 4.50 (0-8439-4756-X, Leisure Bks.) Dorchester Publishing Co., Inc.
—Cherokee Dragon: A Novel of the Real People. 2000. ix, 289p. 23.95 (0-312-20884-7) St. Martin's Pr.
—Cherokee Dragon: A Novel of the Real People. 2001. ix, 289p. pap. 14.95 (0-8061-3370-8) Univ. of Oklahoma Pr.
Cooper, Virgil R. Virg-1 Promised Land. per. 4.99 (0-9668804-4-7) A-bar-V Publishing.
—Virg-2 A Helping Hand. per. 4.99 (0-9668804-3-9) A-bar-V Publishing.
Coover, Robert. Ghost Town: A Novel. 2000. 160p. pap. 12.00 (0-8021-3666-4, Grove Pr.) Grove/Atlantic, Inc.
—Ghost Town: A Novel. 1998. 160p. 24.00 o.p. (0-8050-5884-2) Holt, Henry & Co.
Corle, Edwin. Billy the Kid. 1979. (Zia Bks.). 306p. reprint ed. pap. 8.95 o.p. (0-8263-0509-1) Univ. of New Mexico Pr.
Cotton, Ralph W. While Angels Dance: The Life & Times of Jeston Nash. 1995. 344p. pap. text 5.50 o.p. (0-312-95461-1, St. Martin's Paperbacks); 1994. 352p. 21.95 o.p. (0-312-11098-7) St. Martin's Pr.
Critser, David. Border Town Law. 1994. 160p. 19.95 o.s.i (0-8027-1278-9) Walker & Co.
Cross, Virgil S. The McKennas. 1997. (Orig.). pap. 22.50 (1-880664-22-4) E. M. Productions.
Cullum, Ridgwell. The Watchers of the Plains. 2000. 252p. E-Book 3.95 (0-594-02077-8) 1873 Pr.
Cummings, Jack. The Deserter Troop. 1993. 256p. mass mkt. 3.50 o.s.i (1-55817-715-9) Kensington Publishing Corp.
—The Deserter Troop. 1991. 192p. 18.95 (0-8027-4121-5) Walker & Co.
—Escape from Yuma. 1993. 224p. mass mkt. 3.50 o.p. (1-55817-697-7, Pinnacle Bks.) Kensington Publishing Corp.
—Escape from Yuma. 1990. 187p. 18.95 o.p. (0-8027-4111-8) Walker & Co.
—The Rough Rider. 1991. mass mkt. 3.50 o.p. (1-55817-481-8, Pinnacle Bks.) Kensington Publishing Corp.
—The Rough Rider. l.t. ed. 1993. (Linford Western Large Print Ser.). 352p. pap. 17.99 (0-7089-7357-4, Linford) Thorpe, F. A. Pubs. GBR. Dist: Ulverscroft Large Print Bks., Ltd., Ulverscroft Large Print Canada, Ltd.
—The Rough Rider. 1988. 192p. 17.95 o.p. (0-8027-4089-8) Walker & Co.
Cunningham, Eugene. Trails West: A Western Trio. 2000. (Five Star Western Ser.). 232p. 21.95 (0-7862-1899-1, Five Star) Gale Group.
—Trails West: Western Stories. l.t. ed. 2001. (Thorndike Western Ser.). 304p. 23.95 (0-7862-3095-9) Thorndike Pr.
Cushman, Dan. Badlands Justice. 2000. (Gunsmoke Western Ser.). 190p. 19.00 (0-7540-8075-7, Gunsmoke) BBC Audiobooks America.
Dailey, Janet. Big Sky Country: Montana. 1992. (Janet Dailey Americana Ser.: No. 876). per. (0-373-89876-2, 1-89876-6, Harlequin Bks.) Harlequin Enterprises, Ltd.
Dale, Ruth Jean. Shane's Last Stand. 2000. (Harlequin Heart of the West Ser.: No. 8). per. (0-373-82592-7, 1-82592-6, Harlequin Bks.) Harlequin Enterprises, Ltd.
Davis, Tim. Tales from Dust River Gulch. 1997. (Illus.). 102p. (J). (gr. 4-7). pap. 6.49 (0-89084-896-3, 102517) Jones, Bob Univ. Pr.
Dawson, Les. Ghost Brand of the Wishbones. l.t. ed. 1999. (Western Ser.). 360p. 20.95 (0-7862-1171-7) Thorndike Pr.
Dawson, Peter. Angel Peak. 1999. (Western Ser.). 256p. 19.95 (0-7862-1572-0, Five Star) Gale Group.
—Angel Peak: Western Stories. l.t. ed. 2000. (G. K. Hall Western Ser.). 320p. 12.48 (0-7838-0312-5) Thorndike Pr.
DeCalves, Don A., et al. The Narrative of Don Alonso DeCalves, John Van Delure & Capt, James Vanleason. 1996. 17.95 (0-87770-582-8); pap. 12.95 (0-87770-583-6) Ye Galleon Pr.
Delton, Judy. Wild, Wild West. 1999. (Pee Wee Scouts Ser.: No. 37). (Illus.). 112p. (gr. 2-5). pap. text 3.99 o.s.i (0-440-41342-7, Dell Books for Young Readers) Random Hse. Children's Bks.
—Wild, Wild West. 1999. (Pee Wee Scouts Ser.: No. 37). (J). (gr. 2-5). 10.04 (0-606-16585-1) Turtleback Bks.
Dengler, Sandy. Socorro Island Treasure. 1983. (Daniel Tremain Adventures Ser.). 128p. (J). (gr. 5-8). pap. 3.95 o.p. (0-8024-7813-1) Moody Pr.
DeRosso, H. A. Riders of the Shadowlands: Western Stories. 1999. (Western Ser.). 229p. 19.95 (0-7862-1329-9, Five Star) Gale Group.
—Riders of the Shadowlands: Western Stories. l.t. ed. 2000. (Western Ser.). 325p. 22.95 (0-7862-1338-8) Thorndike Pr.
—Under the Burning Sun. 2000. 288p. mass mkt. 4.50 (0-8439-4712-8, Leisure Bks.) Dorchester Publishing Co., Inc.
—Under the Burning Sun. l.t. ed. 1998. (Western Ser.). 304p. 22.95 o.p. (0-7838-8381-1, Macmillan Reference USA) Gale Group.
—Under the Burning Sun. 2000. E-Book 9.95 (0-585-29812-2) netLibrary, Inc.
Detter, Thomas. Nellie Brown: Or the Jealous Wife, with Other Sketches. 1996. (Blacks in the American West Ser.). 122p. (C). text 35.00 (0-8032-1704-8) Univ. of Nebraska Pr.
Deveraux, Jude. Mountain Laurel. l.t. ed. 1991. (General Ser.). 405p. lib. bdg. 21.95 (0-8161-5124-5, Macmillan Reference USA) Gale Group.
—Mountain Laurel. Marrow, Linda, ed. 1990. 320p. 18.95 o.p. (0-671-68975-4, Atria); 1991. 384p. reprint ed. mass mkt. 7.99 (0-671-68976-2, Pocket) Simon & Schuster.
—Mountain Laurel. 2003. audio compact disk 9.95 (0-7435-3274-0, Encore); 2003. audio 9.95 (0-7435-3245-7, Encore); 1990. 14.95 incl. audio (0-671-70872-4, Simon & Schuster Audioworks) Simon & Schuster Audio.
Downing, Sybil. Ladies of the Goldfield Stock Exchange. 1997. 352p. 23.95 o.p. (0-312-86331-4, Forge Bks.) Doherty, Tom Assocs., LLC.
—The Ladies of the Goldfield Stock Exchange. 1998. 320p. (gr. 8). mass mkt. 5.99 (0-8125-3927-3, Forge Bks.) Doherty, Tom Assocs., LLC.
Durham, Leslie L. Heart of a Western Woman. 1987. 72p. pap. 9.00 o.p. (0-937179-01-9) Blue Scarab Pr.

Edwards, Lynn. Bacon, Beans, Tobacco 'n' Whiskey. 1998. pap. 16.95 (*0-9652942-2-6*) WordsWorth.
Edwards, Page, Jr. The Search for Kate Duval. 1996. 208p. pap. 14.95 o.p. (*0-7145-3000-X*) Boyars, Marion Pubs., Inc.
Eickhoff, Randy Lee. The Fourth Horseman. 1999. 624p. mass mkt. 6.99 (*0-8125-7183-5*); 1998. 416p. 24.95 o.p. (*0-312-85301-7*) Doherty, Tom Assocs., LLC. (Forge Bks.).
Eidson, Tom. The Last Ride. 1995. 352p. mass mkt. 6.99 o.s.i (*0-515-11741-2*, Jove) Berkley Publishing Group.
—The Last Ride. l.t. ed. 1995. (Large Print Bks.). 23.95 (*1-56895-241-4*, Wheeler Publishing, Inc.) Gale Group.
—The Last Ride. 1995. 21.95 o.p. (*0-399-14057-3*, G. P. Putnam's Sons) Penguin Group (USA) Inc.
Elder, Gary. Tending the Dream. 1998. 115p. pap. 9.95 (*0-931896-17-7*) Cove View Pr.
Ell, Flynn J. Dakota Scouts. 1992. 192p. 18.95 (*0-8027-4130-4*) Walker & Co.
Emshwiller, Carol. Ledoyt. 1995. (Illus.). 224p. pap. 14.95 (*1-56279-081-1*) Mercury Hse.
Estleman, Loren D. The Best Western Stories of Loren D. Estleman. Pronzini, Bill & Greenberg, Martin H., eds. l.t. ed. 1990. (Nightingale Ser.). 224p. 11.95 o.p. (*0-8161-4848-1*, Macmillan Reference USA) Gale Group.
—The Best Western Stories of Loren D. Estleman. Pronzini, Bill & Greenberg, Martin H., eds. 1990. (Best Western Stories Ser.). 135p. 22.95 o.p. (*0-8040-0911-2*) Swallow Pr.
—The Best Western Stories of Loren D. Estleman. Pronzini, Bill, ed. 1990. (Best Western Stories Ser.). 135p. pap. 11.95 o.p. (*0-8040-0912-0*) Swallow Pr.
—Journey of the Dead. 16th l.t. ed. 2001. 270p. lib. bdg. 27.95 (*1-58547-072-4*) Ctr. Point Large Print.
—Journey of the Dead. 256p. 1999. mass mkt. 5.99 (*0-8125-4916-3*); 1998. 21.95 o.p. (*0-312-85999-6*) Doherty, Tom Assocs., LLC. (Forge Bks.).
—This Old Bill. 1999. 272p. mass mkt. 5.99 o.s.i (*0-515-12508-3*, Jove) Berkley Publishing Group.
—This Old Bill. 1990. mass mkt. 3.95 o.s.i (*1-55817-422-2*); 1985. 288p. pap. 2.95 o.p. (*0-523-42575-9*) Kensington Publishing Corp. (Pinnacle Bks.).
—This Old Bill. 1984. 203p. 25.00 (*0-385-19165-0*) Ultramarine Publishing Co., Inc.
Estleman, Loren D., ed. & intro. American West: Twenty New Stories from the Western Writers of America. 2000. 384p. 25.95 (*0-312-87317-4*); 2002. 368p. reprint ed. pap. 15.95 (*0-312-87281-X*) Doherty, Tom Assocs., LLC. (Forge Bks.).
Evans, Max. The Rounders 3. 1990. 256p. 14.95 o.s.i (*0-385-26723-1*) Doubleday Publishing.
—Rounders 3: Cattle Drive. abr. ed. 1997. 24.95 o.p. (*0-7871-0750-6*, 685787) NewStar Media, Inc.
Everett, Percival. God's Country. 2nd ed. 2003. 240p. pap. 14.00 (*0-8070-8363-1*) Beacon Pr.
—God's Country. 1994. 204p. 21.95 o.s.i (*0-571-19832-5*) Faber & Faber, Inc.
Fackler, Elizabeth. Backtrail. 1993. (Novel of the West Ser.). 238p. 16.95 o.p. (*0-87131-716-8*) Evans, M. & Co., Inc.
—Badlands. 1996. 352p. 23.95 o.p. (*0-312-86230-X*, Forge Bks.) Doherty, Tom Assocs., LLC.
—Blood Kin. 1992. (Novel of the West Ser.). 208p. 16.95 o.p. (*0-87131-667-6*) Evans, M. & Co., Inc.
—Breaking Even. 448p. 1998. 25.95 o.p. (*0-312-85911-2*); 2001. reprint ed. pap. 17.95 (*0-312-87509-6*) Doherty, Tom Assocs., LLC. (Forge Bks.).
—Road from Betrayal: An Evans Novel of the West. 1994. 238p. 18.95 o.p. (*0-87131-734-6*) Evans, M. & Co., Inc.
Farraday, Tess. Blue Rain. 1999. (Magical Love Ser.). 286p. mass mkt. 5.99 o.s.i (*0-515-12652-7*, Jove) Berkley Publishing Group.
Fenady, Andrew J. Claws of the Eagle: A Novel of Tom Horn & the Apache Kid. l.t. ed. 2004. 274p. 25.95 (*0-7862-5933-7*) Thorndike Pr.
—Claws of the Eagle: A Novel of Tom Horn & the Apache Kid. 1984. (Western Ser.). 192p. 12.95 o.p. (*0-8027-4027-8*) Walker & Co.
Fergus, Jim. One Thousand White Women: The Journals of May Dodd. 1998. 304p. 24.95 (*0-312-18008-X*); 3rd ed. 1999. 320p. pap. 14.95 (*0-312-19943-0*, Saint Martin's Griffin) St. Martin's Pr.
Finley, Mary Peace. Meadow Lark. 2003. (YA). 15.95 (*0-86541-070-4*) Filter Pr., LLC.
Fisher, Clay Henry Will. Red Blizzard. l.t. ed. 1994. 20.95 o.p. (*0-7927-1811-9*); pap. 18.95 o.p. (*0-7927-1810-0*) BBC Audiobooks America.
Fisher, Vardis. Mountain Man. 1976. reprint ed. lib. bdg. 24.95 (*0-89190-832-3*, Rivercity Pr.) Amereon, Ltd.
—Mountain Man. 1993. reprint ed. lib. bdg. 27.95 (*1-56849-196-4*) Buccaneer Bks., Inc.
—Mountain Man. 1990. 320p. (YA). (gr. 10 up). mass mkt. 4.95 (*0-671-73907-7*, Pocket) Simon & Schuster.
—Mountain Man. 1977. 384p. 12.95 o.p. (*0-918522-52-8*) Univ. of Idaho Pr.
Flynn, Robert. North to Yesterday. Haywood, Richard, ed. unabr. ed. 1993. audio 59.95 (*1-883268-00-1*) Spellbinders, Inc.
—North to Yesterday. 1985. (Texas Tradition Ser.: No. 4). 340p. reprint ed. 19.95 (*0-87565-014-7*); pap. 14.95 (*0-87565-015-5*) Texas Christian Univ. Pr.
Flynn, T. T. Long Journey to Deep Canon: A Western Quartet. 1997. (Western Ser.). 246p. lib. bdg. 18.95 (*0-7862-0751-5*, Five Star) Gale Group.
—Long Journey to Deep Canon: A Western Quartet. l.t. ed. 1998. (Western Ser.). 365p. 20.95 (*0-7862-0774-4*) Thorndike Pr.
—Rawhide: A Western Quintet. 1996. (Western Ser.). 246p. 17.95 (*0-7862-0660-8*, Five Star) Gale Group.
—Rawhide: A Western Quintet. l.t. ed. 1997. (Western Ser.). 327p. lib. bdg. 21.95 (*0-7862-1193-8*) Thorndike Pr.
Fox, Kathryn. The Mounties: The First Time. 2000. (Romances Ser.). 32p. mass mkt. 5.50 o.s.i (*0-8217-6731-3*) Kensington Publishing Corp.
—The Seduction. 2002. 34p. mass mkt. 5.99 o.s.i (*0-8217-7243-0*) Kensington Publishing Corp.
Fraser, George MacDonald. Flashman & the Redskins. unabr. ed. 1995. (Flashman Ser.). audio 96.00 (*0-7366-3007-4*, 3693) Books on Tape, Inc.
—Flashman & the Redskins. 1983. (Flashman Ser.). 480p. pap. 8.95 o.p. (*0-452-26066-3*); 480p. pap. 14.00 (*0-452-26487-1*); pap. 7.95 o.p. (*0-452-25431-0*) Dutton/Plume. (Plume).
—Flashman & the Redskins. l.t. ed. 1983. (Charnwood Large Print Ser.). 708p. 29.99 o.p. (*0-7089-8127-5*, Ulverscroft) Thorpe, F. A. Pubs. GBR. *Dist:* Ulverscroft Large Print Bks., Ltd., Ulverscroft Large Print Canada, Ltd.
Frazee, Steve. The Best Western Stories of Steve Frazee. Pronzini, Bill & Greenberg, Martin H., eds. 1984. (Western Writers Ser.). 219p. 16.95 o.p. (*0-8093-1174-7*) Southern Illinois Univ. Pr.
—The Best Western Stories of Steve Frazee. Pronzini, Bill & Greenberg, Martin H., eds. 1989. (Best Western Stories Ser.). 294p. reprint ed. pap. 12.95 o.p. (*0-8040-0914-7*) Swallow Pr.
—Ghost Mine: A Western Story. 2000. (Five Star Western Ser.). 231p. 21.95 (*0-7862-2472-X*, Five Star) Gale Group.
—Smoke in the Valley. 1995. 191p. 17.50 o.p. (*0-7451-4651-1*, Gunsmoke) BBC Audiobooks America.
—Smoke in the Valley: An Original Gold Medal Novel. l.t. ed. 1997. (Nightingale Ser.). pap. 17.95 o.p. (*0-7838-2046-1*, Macmillan Reference USA) Gale Group.
Gale Group Staff, contrib. by. El Desconocido: Butch Cassidy. l.t. ed. 2002. (Five Star First Edition Western Ser.). (Illus.). 263p. 24.95 (*0-7862-2731-1*, Five Star) Gale Group.
Gardner, Erle Stanley. Pay Dirt: And Other Whispering Sands Stories of Gold Fever & the Western Desert. Waugh, Charles G. & Greenberg, Martin H., eds. 1983. 324p. 15.95 o.p. (*0-688-01981-1*, Morrow, William & Co.) Morrow/Avon.
Garland, Hamlin. Main-Travelled Roads. 1962. 272p. mass mkt. 4.95 o.p. (*0-451-52271-0*, Signet Classics) NAL.
—Prairie Song & Western Story. 1977. (Short Story Index Reprint Ser.). (Illus.). reprint ed. 25.95 (*0-8369-3940-9*) Ayer Co. Pubs., Inc.
—Wayside Courtships. 1977. (Short Story Index Reprint Ser.). 22.95 (*0-8369-3251-X*) Ayer Co. Pubs., Inc.
—Wayside Courtships. 1988. (Collected Works of Hamlin Garland). reprint ed. lib. bdg. 79.00 (*0-7812-1224-3*) Reprint Services Corp.
Garlock, Dorothy. Nightrose. l.t. ed. 1997. 26.95 (*0-7838-8098-7*, Macmillan Reference USA) Gale Group.
—Nightrose. abr. ed. 1994. audio 5.99 (*1-57096-020-8*, RAZ 917) Romance Alive Audio.
—Nightrose. 1990. 384p. reprint ed. mass mkt. 6.99 (*0-446-35607-7*) Warner Bks., Inc.
—River of Tomorrow. l.t. ed. 1999. (Romance Ser.). 483p. 29.95 o.p. (*0-7838-8839-2*, Macmillan Reference USA) Gale Group.
—River of Tomorrow. 1991. 19.95 o.p. (*0-7278-4189-0*) Severn Hse. Pubs., Ltd.
—River of Tomorrow. 1988. 376p. mass mkt. 6.99 (*0-445-20366-8*) Warner Bks., Inc.
—Yesteryear. 384p. 1995. mass mkt. 6.99 (*0-446-36371-5*); 1998. reprint ed. mass mkt. 3.99 (*0-446-60651-0*) Warner Bks., Inc.
Garwood, Julie. One Red Rose. 1997. per. 2.66 (*0-671-02024-2*); 160p. mass mkt. 2.99 o.s.i (*0-671-01010-7*) Simon & Schuster. (Pocket).
Garwood, William R. Kill Him, Again. 1980. 315p. 9.95 (*0-937618-00-4*) Bath Street Pr.
Gear, Kathleen O'Neal & Gear, W. Michael. People of the Silence. (First North Americans Ser.). 1997. 650p. mass mkt. 7.99 (*0-8125-1559-5*, Tor Bks.); 1996. 448p. 25.95 o.p. (*0-312-85853-1*, Forge Bks.) Doherty, Tom Assocs., LLC.
—People of the Silence, Set. 1996. audio 19.95 o.p. (*1-55935-235-3*) Soundelux Audio Publishing.
Gear, W. Michael. Coyote Summer. 1999. (Illus.). 660p. mass mkt. 6.99 (*0-8125-7115-0*); 1997. 432p. 25.95 o.p. (*0-312-86330-6*) Doherty, Tom Assocs., LLC. (Forge Bks.).
—The Morning River. 1997. (Illus.). 490p. mass mkt. 6.99 (*0-8125-5153-2*); 1996. 384p. 24.95 o.p. (*0-312-89039-7*) Doherty, Tom Assocs., LLC. (Forge Bks.).
—People of the Sea, Vol. 1. 1958. 425p. 22.95 o.p. (*0-312-93122-0*, Tor Bks.) Doherty, Tom Assocs., LLC.
Giambastiani, Kurt R. A. The Year the Cloud Fell. 2001. (Illus.). 352p. mass mkt. 6.99 o.s.i (*0-451-45821-4*, Onyx) NAL.
Gilchrist, Micaela. Good Journey. 2001. (Illus.). 400p. 24.00 (*0-684-87143-2*, Simon & Schuster) Simon & Schuster.
Gish, Robert F. Dreams of Quivira: Stories in Search of the Golden West. 1997. 216p. 24.95 (*0-940666-97-9*); (Illus.). pap. 14.95 (*0-940666-98-7*) Clear Light Pubs.
—First Horses: Stories of the New West. 1993. (Western Literature Ser.). 144p. 19.95 o.p. (*0-87417-210-1*); 152p. pap. 15.00 (*0-87417-211-X*) Univ. of Nevada Pr.
Glasrud, Bruce A. & Champion, Laurie, eds. The African American West: A Century of Short Stories. 2000. xi, 463p. 29.95 (*0-87081-559-8*) Univ. Pr. of Colorado.
Golden Spurs: Best Short Western Stories Selected by The Western Writers of America. 1990. 17.95 o.p. (*0-922066-36-1*) Wynwood.
Gonzalez, Ray. The Ghost of John Wayne & Other Stories. 2001. (Camino del Sol). (Illus.). 150p. 29.95 (*0-8165-2065-8*); pap. 17.95 (*0-8165-2066-6*) Univ. of Arizona Pr.
Goodloe, Abbie C. At the Foot of the Rockies. 1977. (Short Story Index Reprint Ser.). reprint ed. 25.95 (*0-8369-4177-2*) Ayer Co. Pubs., Inc.
Gorman, Ed. The Best Western Stories of Ed Gorman. Pronzini, Bill & Greenberg, Martin H., eds. 1992. (Western Writers Ser.). 160p. (C). 26.95 (*0-8040-0959-7*) Swallow Pr.
—Blood Game. 2000. 384p. mass mkt. 4.99 (*0-8125-4827-2*); 2001. 176p. reprint ed. pap. 12.95 (*0-312-87748-X*) Doherty, Tom Assocs., LLC. (Forge Bks.).
—Blood Game. 1989. (Novel of the West Ser.). 180p. 14.95 o.p. (*0-87131-596-3*) Evans, M. & Co., Inc.
—Blood Game. 1992. 2.99 o.p. (*0-517-09416-9*) Random Hse. Value Publishing.
—Dark Trail. 1990. (Novel of the West Ser.). 192p. 15.95 o.p. (*0-87131-635-8*) Evans, M. & Co., Inc.
—Dark Trail. 1992. 2.99 o.p. (*0-517-09423-1*) Random Hse. Value Publishing.
—The Dark Trail. 1997. (Evans Novel of the West Ser.). 215p. pap. 5.99 (*0-8125-4826-4*, Forge Bks.) Doherty, Tom Assocs., LLC.
—Gunslinger & Nine Other Action-Packed Stories of the Wild West. Greenberg, Martin H. & Pronzini, Bill, eds. 1995. 132p. pap. 12.00 (*1-56980-036-7*) Barricade Bks., Inc.
—Ride into Yesterday. 1999. 192p. pap. 3.99 (*0-8439-4488-9*, Leisure Bks.) Dorchester Publishing Co., Inc.
—Wolf Moon. 1999. mass mkt. 4.99 (*0-449-45909-8*); 1993. 163p. mass mkt. 4.99 o.s.i (*0-449-14836-X*) Ballantine Bks. (Fawcett).
—Wolf Moon. l.t. ed. 1999. pap. 22.95 o.p. (*1-56895-783-1*, Wheeler Publishing, Inc.) Gale Group.
Gorman, Ed, ed. Westeryear: Stories about the West, Past & Present. l.t. ed. 1990. (Large Print Bks.). 425p. lib. bdg. 19.95 o.p. (*0-8161-5024-9*, Macmillan Reference USA) Gale Group.
Grant, Ken. The Deer Mouse. 1997. 208p. pap. 16.00 (*1-57962-015-9*); 205p. 24.00 (*1-877946-84-2*) Permanent Pr., The.
—The Deer Mouse. 160p. 2002. pap. 6.99 (*0-7592-1334-8*); 2002. E-Book 6.99 (*0-7592-1330-5*); 2002. E-Book 6.99 (*0-7592-1331-3*); 2001. E-Book 6.99 (*0-7592-1329-1*) ereads.com.
Grattan-Dominguez, Alejandro. Breaking Even. 1997. 250p. (YA). (gr. 9 up). pap. 11.95 (*1-55885-213-1*) Arte Publico Pr.
Graulich, Melody, selected by. Western Trails: A Collection of Short Stories by Mary Austin. 1987. (Western Literature Ser.). 320p. 24.95 o.p. (*0-87417-127-X*) Univ. of Nevada Pr.
Great American Writers: Wild West Stories. 1989. 5.98 o.p. (*0-8317-9422-4*) Smithmark Pubs., Inc.
The Great Railroad Race: The Diary of Libby West. 2003. (J). lib. bdg. 12.95 (*0-439-55533-7*) Scholastic, Inc.
Greenberg, Martin H., ed. Great Stories of the American West: Stories by John Jakes, Elmore Leonard, Marcia Muller, John D. MacDonald & Many Others. 1996. 400p. mass mkt. 6.99 o.s.i (*0-515-11840-0*, Jove); Vol. 2. 1997. (Great Stories of the American West Ser.: Vol. 2). 496p. mass mkt. 6.99 o.s.i (*0-425-15936-1*) Berkley Publishing Group.
—Great Stories of the American West: Stories by John Jakes, Elmore Leonard, Marcia Muller, John D. MacDonald & Many Others. 1994. 304p. 22.50 o.s.i (*1-55611-417-6*) Fine, Donald I. Bks.
—Great Stories of the American West II. 1996. 304p. 22.95 o.p. (*1-55611-481-8*) Fine, Donald I. Bks.
Greenberg, Martin H. & Walker, Dale C., eds. The Western Hall of Fame: An Anthology of Classic Western Stories Selected by the Western Writers of America. 1997. 288p. mass mkt. 5.99 o.s.i (*0-425-15906-X*) Berkley Publishing Group.
Gregory, Jill. Cold Night, Warm Stranger. 1999. 400p. mass mkt. 6.50 (*0-440-22440-3*) Dell Publishing.
Grey, Zane. The Camp Robber & Other Stories. l.t. ed. 1991. 12.95 o.p. (*0-7927-0127-5*, 4532) BBC Audiobooks America.
—Code of the West. 1978. (Zane Grey Western Ser.). 561p. (J). (*0-89340-138-2*) BBC Audiobooks America.
—Code of the West. l.t. ed. 1995. (Sagebrush Large Print Westerns Ser.). 392p. lib. bdg. 18.95 o.s.i (*1-57490-002-1*) Beeler, Thomas T. Publisher.
—The Last of the Plainsmen. 1976. reprint ed. lib. bdg. 24.95 (*0-89190-753-X*) Amereon, Ltd.
—The Last of the Plainsmen. 1990. 208p. mass mkt. 2.95 o.s.i (*0-553-28546-7*) Bantam Bks.
—The Last of the Plainsmen. unabr. ed. 2000. audio 44.95 (*0-7861-1804-0*, 2603); audio compact disk 56.00 (*0-7861-9863-X*, z2603) Blackstone Audio Bks., Inc.
—The Last of the Plainsmen. 1990. reprint ed. lib. bdg. 20.95 (*0-89968-511-0*) Buccaneer Bks., Inc.
—The Last of the Plainsmen. 1994. 288p. mass mkt. 4.99 (*0-8125-3537-5*, Tor Bks.) Doherty, Tom Assocs., LLC.
—Silvermane & Other Stories. l.t. ed. 1991. (General Ser.). 218p. lib. bdg. 17.95 (*0-8161-5076-1*, Macmillan Reference USA) Gale Group.
—Tigre & Other Stories. l.t. ed. 1988. 18.95 o.p. (*1-55504-487-5*); pap. 16.95 o.p. (*1-55504-488-3*) BBC Audiobooks America.
Grimes, Martha. Biting the Moon. unabr. ed. 1999. audio 64.00 (*0-7366-4567-5*, 4974) Books on Tape, Inc.
—Biting the Moon. l.t. ed. 1999. (Wheeler Large Print Book Ser.). 442p. 27.95 (*1-56895-775-0*, Wheeler Publishing, Inc.) Gale Group.
—Biting the Moon. 1999. 305p. 25.00 o.s.i (*0-8050-5621-1*) Holt, Henry & Co.
Grimes, Martha, contrib. by. Biting the Moon. 2000. 320p. mass mkt. 13.00 (*0-451-40913-2*, Onyx) NAL.
Gunn, Gay G. Nowhere to Run. 1997. 261p. pap. 10.95 (*1-885478-13-5*) Genesis Pr., Inc.
Guthrie, A. B., Jr. The Way West. 1992. 350p. reprint ed. lib. bdg. 32.95 (*0-89968-305-3*, Lightyear Pr.) Buccaneer Bks., Inc.
—The Way West. 1993. 352p. pap. 13.00 o.p. (*0-395-65662-1*) Houghton Mifflin Co.
Guthrie, A. B. The Way West. 1979. reprint ed. 18.00 o.p. (*0-89783-005-9*) Larlin Corp.
Guthrie, Alfred B., Jr. The Big Sky. 2002. (Illus.). 400p. reprint ed. pap. 14.00 (*0-618-15463-9*, Mariner Bks.) Houghton Mifflin Co. Trade & Reference Div.
Haake, Katharine. The Height & Depth of Everything. 2001. (Western Literature Ser.). 216p. pap. 17.00 (*0-87417-488-0*) Univ. of Nevada Pr.
Hagan, Patricia. Orchids in Moonlight. l.t. ed. 1994. 22.95 o.p. (*1-56895-059-4*, Wheeler Publishing, Inc.) Gale Group.
—Orchids in Moonlight. 1993. 384p. mass mkt. 5.50 o.p. (*0-06-108038-1*, HarperTorch) Morrow/Avon.
Hailes, Steve. The Quicksilver Kid: A Gold Rush Adventure. 2000. 193p. pap. 20.99 (*0-7388-0811-3*); text 30.99 (*0-7388-0810-5*) Xlibris Corp.
Hall, Oakley M. Separations. 1997. (Western Literature Ser.). 288p. pap. 17.00 (*0-87417-292-6*) Univ. of Nevada Pr.
Handeland, Lori. Nate. 2002. 352p. mass mkt. 5.99 o.s.i (*0-8217-7275-9*) Kensington Publishing Corp.
Hanlon, Julia. Mine for All Time. 2000. 320p. mass mkt. 5.99 o.s.i (*0-8217-6523-X*, Zebra Bks.) Kensington Publishing Corp.
Hannah, Barry. Boomerang & Never Die. 1994. (Banner Bk.). 320p. pap. 20.00 (*0-87805-702-1*) Univ. Pr. of Mississippi.
—Never Die. 1991. 288p. 18.95 o.p. (*0-395-51560-2*) Houghton Mifflin Co.
Hansen, Ron. The Assassination of Jesse James by the Coward Robert Ford. 1984. 368p. mass mkt. 3.95 o.s.i (*0-345-29626-5*) Ballantine Bks.
—The Assassination of Jesse James by the Coward Robert Ford. 1997. 320p. pap. 13.00 (*0-06-097699-3*, Perennial) HarperTrade.
—The Assassination of Jesse James by the Coward Robert Ford. 1990. pap. 8.95 o.p. (*0-393-30679-8*) Norton, W. W. & Co., Inc.
—Desperadoes. 1984. 288p. mass mkt. 3.50 o.s.i (*0-345-32500-1*); 1980. mass mkt. 2.50 o.p. (*0-345-28675-8*) Ballantine Bks.
—Desperadoes. 1997. 288p. pap. 14.00 (*0-06-097698-5*, Perennial) HarperTrade.

—Desperadoes. 1990. pap. 8.95 o.p. (0-393-30680-1) Norton, W. W. & Co., Inc.

—Desperadoes. l.t. ed. 1981. (Ulverscroft Large Print Ser.). 470p. 29.99 o.p. (0-7089-0644-3, Ulverscroft) Thorpe, F. A. Pubs. GBR. *Dist:* Ulverscroft Large Print Bks., Ltd., Ulverscroft Large Print Canada, Ltd.

Hanson, Jacquelyn. Matilda's Story: A Biographical Novel. 1997. (Illus.). 672p. 24.95 (0-9637265-3-6, 9704); pap. 12.95 (0-9637265-4-4, 9704) Glenhaven Pr.

Harper, Karen. River of Sky. 1994. 416p. 21.95 o.p. (0-525-93822-2, Dutton) Dutton/Plume.

—River of Sky. 1995. 448p. mass mkt. 5.99 o.s.i (0-451-18490-4, Signet Bks.) NAL.

Harris, Jana. The Pearl of Ruby City. 1998. 368p. 23.95 (0-312-19315-7, Saint Martin's Minotaur) St. Martin's Pr.

Hart, Catherine. Night Flame. 2000. 480p. mass mkt. 5.99 (0-505-52386-8, Love Spell) Dorchester Publishing Co., Inc.

Harte, Bret. Ancestors of Peter Atherly & Other Tales. 1977. (Short Story Index Reprint Ser.). reprint ed. 31.95 (0-8369-4235-3) Ayer Co. Pubs., Inc.

—Colonel Starbottle's Client & Some Other People. 1977. (Short Story Index Reprint Ser.). 22.95 (0-8369-3347-8) Ayer Co. Pubs., Inc.

—Condensed Novels. 1977. (Short Story Index Reprint Ser.). (Illus.). 19.95 (0-8369-3548-9) Ayer Co. Pubs., Inc.

—Maruja & Other Tales. 1977. (Short Story Index Reprint Ser.: Vol. 1). 32.95 (0-8369-3400-8) Ayer Co. Pubs., Inc.

—Mr. Jack Hamlin's Mediation. 1977. (Short Story Index Reprint Ser.). reprint ed. 26.95 (0-8369-4218-3) Ayer Co. Pubs., Inc.

—Mr. Jack Hamlin's Mediation. 2002. 296p. per. 29.95 (1-58963-864-6) Fredonia Bks.

—Mr. Jack Hamlin's Mediation. 2002. 144p. 16.99 (1-4043-1918-2); per. 12.99 (1-4043-1919-0) IndyPublish.com.

—Mr. Jack Hamlin's Mediation. 1999. (Works of Bret Harte: Vol. 12). 508p. reprint ed. lib. bdg. 90.00 (0-7812-7844-9) Reprint Services Corp.

—On the Frontier. 1977. (Short Story Index Reprint Ser.). reprint ed. 19.95 (0-8369-4147-0) Ayer Co. Pubs., Inc.

—On the Frontier. 2002. 132p. 93.99 (1-4043-2268-X); per. 88.99 (1-4043-2269-8) IndyPublish.com.

—Tales of the West. Atkins, Mary, ed. 1991. 12.99 o.s.i (0-517-05289-X) Random Hse. Value Publishing.

—Tales of Trail & Town. 1977. (Short Story Index Reprint Ser.). 25.95 (0-8369-3519-5) Ayer Co. Pubs., Inc.

Haseloff, Cynthia. Man Without Medicine. 1999. 240p. mass mkt. 4.50 (0-8439-4581-8, Leisure Bks.) Dorchester Publishing Co., Inc.

—Man Without Medicine. l.t. ed. 1999. 20.00 o.p. (0-7838-1675-8, Macmillan Reference USA) Gale Group.

—Man Without Medicine. 1999. E-Book 9.95 (0-585-28583-7) netLibrary, Inc.

—Man Without Medicine: A Western Story. l.t. ed. 1997. (Western Ser.). 309p. lib. bdg. 21.95 (0-7862-1192-X) Thorndike Pr.

—Satanta's Woman. unabr. ed. 1999. audio 29.99 (0-88646-527-3, DHA-6527) Durkin Hayes Publishing Ltd.

—Satanta's Woman. 1998. (Western Ser.). 284p. 19.95 (0-7862-1335-3); 18.95 o.p. (0-7862-1319-1) Gale Group. (Five Star).

—Satanta's Woman Vol. 1: A Western Story. l.t. ed. 1999. (G. K. Hall Western Ser.). 360p. 22.95 (0-7838-8400-1) Thorndike Pr.

Haycox, Ernest. Burnt Creek. 2000. 256p. mass mkt. 4.50 (0-8439-4798-5, Leisure Bks.) Dorchester Publishing Co., Inc.

—Burnt Creek. l.t. ed. 1997. (Western Ser.). 344p. 20.95 (0-7862-1119-9) Thorndike Pr.

—New Hope. 1998. (Western Ser.). 255p. 20.95 (0-7862-0994-1, Five Star) Gale Group.

—New Hope. l.t. ed. 1999. (Western Ser.). 387p. 21.95 (0-7862-1033-8) Thorndike Pr.

—Pioneer Loves. l.t. ed. 1997. (Western Ser.). 239p. 20.95 (0-7862-1078-8) Thorndike Pr.

Hedges, Mackey. Last Buckaroo. 352p. 1995. 22.95 o.s.i (0-87905-661-4); 2nd ed. 1998. reprint ed. pap. 10.95 (0-87905-667-3) Smith, Gibbs Pub.

Henderson, Eva Pendleton. Wild Horses: Turn of the Century Prairie Girlhood. 1983. (Illus.). 96p. pap. 8.95 (0-86534-013-7) Sunstone Pr.

Henley, Patricia. Friday Night at Silver Star. 1986. (Short Fiction Ser.). 144p. (Orig.). pap. 8.50 o.p. (0-915308-84-3) Graywolf Pr.

—The Secret of Cartwheels: Short Stories. 1992. 224p. pap. 11.00 o.p. (1-55597-168-7) Graywolf Pr.

Henry, Will. The Gates of the Mountains. 1991. 352p. mass mkt. 4.50 o.s.i (0-553-29181-5); 1979. pap. 1.75 o.p. (0-553-12565-6) Bantam Bks.

—The Gates of the Mountains. l.t. ed. 2001. 352p. lib. bdg. 26.95 (1-58547-082-1) Ctr. Point Large Print.

—The Gates of the Mountains. 1999. 320p. mass mkt. 4.99 (0-8439-4653-9, Leisure Bks.) Dorchester Publishing Co., Inc.

—The Gates of the Mountains. 1980. lib. bdg. 13.95 o.p. (0-8398-2689-3, Macmillan Reference USA) Gale Group.

—I, Tom Horn. 1992. 400p. mass mkt. 4.99 o.s.i (0-553-29835-6); 1980. pap. 1.75 o.p. (0-553-12013-1) Bantam Bks.

—I, Tom Horn. unabr. ed. 1994. audio 78.00 (0-7887-0039-1, 94238E7) Recorded Bks., LLC.

—I, Tom Horn. 1996. 341p. pap. 12.00 (0-8032-7283-9, Bison Bks.) Univ. of Nebraska Pr.

—Tumbleweeds: Frontier Stories. 1999. (Western Ser.). 251p. 19.95 (0-7862-1327-2, Five Star) Gale Group.

Higdon, Lisa. Unforsaken. 2000. 320p. mass mkt. 5.99 o.s.i (0-8217-6660-0) Kensington Publishing Corp.

High Cotton. 2003. 267p. pap. 15.95 (1-930846-17-7) Golden Gryphon Pr.

Hill, Billy Bob & Champion, Laurie, eds. Texas Short Stories. 1997. (American Regional Book Ser.: Vol. 2). 571p. pap. 16.95 (0-9651359-1-8) Browder Springs Bks.

—Texas Short Stories 2. 1999. (American Regional Book Ser.: Vol. 6). 578p. 32.95 (0-9651359-5-0, 1306); pap. 18.95 (0-9651359-6-9, 1307) Browder Springs Bks.

Hillerman, Tony. Due West. 1994. 288p. 23.00 o.p. (0-06-017785-3) HarperTrade.

Hillerman, Tony, intro. The Best of the West: An Anthology of Classic Writing from the American West. 1992. 544p. pap. 18.00 (0-06-092352-0, Perennial); 1991. 448p. 27.50 o.p. (0-06-016664-9) HarperTrade.

Hirsh, M. E. Dreaming Back. 1996. (WWL Mystery Ser.). per. (0-373-26195-0, 1-26195-7, Worldwide Library) Harlequin Enterprises, Ltd.

—Dreaming Back. 1993. 320p. 19.95 o.p. (0-312-09789-1, Saint Martin's Minotaur) St. Martin's Pr.

Hoagland, Edward. Seven Rivers West. 1986. 320p. 18.45 o.p. (0-671-60753-7) Summit Bks.

—Seven Rivers West. 1987. 320p. pap. 6.95 o.p. (0-14-010276-0, Penguin Bks.) Viking Penguin.

Hoffman, Lee. Bred to Kill. 1981. mass mkt. 1.75 o.p. (0-345-29547-1) Ballantine Bks.

—Bred to Kill. l.t. ed. 2000. 156p. 19.95 (1-57490-272-5) Beeler, Thomas T. Publisher.

—Bred to Kill. l.t. ed. 1999. (Paperback Ser.). 197p. pap. 22.95 (0-7838-8603-9) Thorndike Pr.

Hogan, Ray. Betrayal in Tombstone. 1995. 190p. 15.95 o.p. (0-7451-4634-1) BBC Audiobooks America.

—Betrayal in Tombstone. l.t. ed. 1993. (Nightingale Ser.). 224p. 14.95 o.p. (0-8161-5625-5, Macmillan Reference USA) Gale Group.

—Legend of a Bad Man. 1997. (Western Ser.). 243p. lib. bdg. 18.95 (0-7862-0747-7, Five Star) Gale Group.

—Legend of a Bad Man. l.t. ed. 1998. (Western Ser.). 352p. 21.95 (0-7862-0770-1) Thorndike Pr.

—Soldier in Buckskin. unabr. ed. 1997. audio 64.00 (0-7366-3815-6, 105783) Books on Tape, Inc.

—Soldier in Buckskin. abr. ed. (Five Star Westerns Ser.). 1997. audio 7.99 o.p. (1-56740-172-4, 700, Paperback Nova Audio Bks.); 1996. audio 16.95 o.p. (1-56100-897-4, 1377, Nova Audio Bks.) Brilliance Audio.

—Soldier in Buckskin. 1998. 304p. reprint ed. mass mkt. 4.99 (0-8439-4387-4, Leisure Bks.) Dorchester Publishing Co., Inc.

—Soldier in Buckskin. 1996. (Western Ser.). 296p. 17.95 (0-7862-0619-5, Five Star) Gale Group.

Holl, Kristi. Danger at Hanging Rock. 1989. 96p. (YA). (gr. 7-9). pap. 3.99 o.p. (1-55513-067-4) Cook Communications Ministries.

Holland, Cecelia. An Ordinary Woman: The Remarkable Story of the First American Woman in California. 224p. 1999. 21.95 (0-312-86528-7); 2001. reprint ed. pap. 13.95 (0-312-87417-0) Doherty, Tom Assocs., LLC. (Forge Bks.).

Holmes, L. P. Brandon's Empire. l.t. ed. 1997. (Western Ser.). 311p. lib. bdg. 18.95 o.p. (0-7862-1196-2) Thorndike Pr.

—Brandon's Empire. 1986. pap. 2.95 o.s.i (0-446-31356-4) Warner Bks., Inc.

Hotchkiss, Bill. Ammahabas. 1983. 15.95 o.p. (0-393-01718-4) Norton, W. W. & Co., Inc.

—The Medicine Calf. 1981. 13.95 o.p. (0-393-01389-8) Norton, W. W. & Co., Inc.

Hough, Emerson. Heart's Desire: The Story of a Contented Town, Certain Peculiar Citizens, & Two Fortunate Lovers. 1981. (Illus.). xx, 381p. 30.00 o.p. (0-8032-2315-3); pap. 6.95 o.p. (0-8032-7209-X) Univ. of Nebraska Pr.

Houston, Pam. Cowboys Are My Weakness. abr. ed. 2000. audio 7.95 (1-57815-151-1, 1110, Media Bks. Audio Publishing) Media Bks., L. L. C.

—Cowboys Are My Weakness, Set. unabr. ed. 1993. audio 15.95 (1-879371-31-6, 390568) Publishing Mills, Inc., The.

—Cowboys Are My Weakness. Rosenman, Jane, ed. 1993. 176p. reprint ed. pap. 14.00 (0-671-79388-8, Washington Square Pr.) Simon & Schuster.

—Cowboys Are My Weakness: Stories. 1992. 192p. 19.95 o.p. (0-393-03077-6) Norton, W. W. & Co., Inc.

Hubalek, Linda K. Trail of Thread: A Woman's Westward Journey. 1995. (Trail of Thread Ser.: Bk. 1). (Illus.). 124p. (Orig.). pap. 9.95 (1-886652-06-6) Butterfield Bks., Inc.

Huebner, Andrew. American by Blood. E-Book 23.00 (1-58945-121-X) Adobe Systems, Inc.

—American by Blood. 256p. 2001. pap. 13.00 (0-684-85771-5); 2000. (Illus.). 23.00 (0-684-85770-7) Simon & Schuster. (Simon & Schuster).

Huebner, Kenneth H. & Andrew. American by Blood. 2000. 256p. 23.00 (0-684-87358-3, Simon & Schuster) Simon & Schuster.

Hunter, Dia. The Gentle Season. 2000. 320p. mass mkt. 4.99 (0-8439-4705-5, Leisure Bks.) Dorchester Publishing Co., Inc.

—The Gentle Season. 2000. E-Book 9.95 (0-585-28332-X) netLibrary, Inc.

Iversen, Cap. Arson! 1992. (Dakota Ser.: No. 1). 233p. pap. 7.95 o.p. (1-55583-197-4) Alyson Pubns.

—Silver Saddles. 1993. (Dakota Ser.: No. 2). 222p. pap. 7.95 o.p. (1-55583-213-X) Alyson Pubns.

Jackson, Dave. Lost River Conspiracy. 1995. 220p. (YA). pap. 8.95 (1-56148-183-1) Good Bks.

Jakes, John. The Best Western Stories of John Jakes. Pronzini, Bill & Greenberg, Martin H., eds. 1991. (Western Writers Ser.). 291p. 24.95 o.p. (0-8214-0982-4); pap. 14.95 (0-8214-0983-2) Ohio Univ. Pr.

—The Big Country. 1993. 416p. mass mkt. 5.99 o.s.i (0-553-29485-7) Bantam Bks.

—In the Big Country. unabr. collector's ed. 1994. audio 56.00 (0-7366-2822-3, 3532) Books on Tape, Inc.

—In the Big Country: The Best Western Stories of John Jakes. Pronzini, Bill & Greenberg, Martin H., eds. l.t. ed. 1993. Orig. Title: The Best Western Stories of John Jakes. 367p. lib. bdg. 20.95 o.p. (0-8161-5812-6, Macmillan Reference USA) Gale Group.

Jakes, John, et al. Great Stories of the American West: Stories by John Jakes, Elmore Leonard, Marcia Muller, John D. MacDonald & Many Others. Greenberg, Martin H., ed. l.t. ed. 1995. 507p. 22.95 o.p. (0-7838-1355-4, Macmillan Reference USA) Gale Group.

James, Frederic & Nixon, James F. Champion of Justice. 1997. pap. 13.95 (0-9656586-0-0) Nixon, James F.

James, Will. Big Enough. 1993. reprint ed. lib. bdg. 18.95 (1-56849-238-3) Buccaneer Bks., Inc.

—Big Enough. McKenna, Gwen, ed. 1997. (Tumbleweed Ser.). (Illus.). 290p. (YA). (gr. 4 up). pap. 16.00 (0-87842-369-9, 692); pap. 30.00 o.s.i (0-87842-368-0, 693) Mountain Pr. Publishing Co., Inc.

—Cow Country. 1976. 22.95 (0-8488-1060-0) Amereon, Ltd.

—Cow Country. unabr. collector's ed. 1999. (Tumbleweed Ser. ). audio 32.00 (0-7366-4401-6, 4862) Books on Tape, Inc.

—Cow Country. 1995. (Tumbleweed Ser.). (Illus.). 260p. (gr. 7-12). reprint ed. pap. 14.00 (0-87842-330-3, 684); 25.00 (0-87842-331-1, 685) Mountain Pr. Publishing Co., Inc.

—Cow Country. 1973. (Illus.). xii, 242p. reprint ed. pap. 7.95 o.p. (0-8032-5774-0, Bison Bks.) Univ. of Nebraska Pr.

—The Drifting Cowboy, , unabr. collector's ed. 1999. (Tumbleweed Ser. ). audio 32.00 (0-7366-4400-8, 4861) Books on Tape, Inc.

—The Drifting Cowboy. 1995. (Tumbleweed Ser.). (Illus.). 244p. (gr. 7-12). (YA). pap. 14.00 (0-87842-326-5, 682); pap. 25.00 (0-87842-325-7, 683) Mountain Pr. Publishing Co., Inc.

—Flint Spears: Cowboy Rodeo Contestant. 2002. (Illus.). 291p. 30.00 (0-87842-450-4); pap. 15.00 (0-87842-449-0) Mountain Pr. Publishing Co., Inc.

—Sun-Up: Tales of the Cow Camps. 1997. (Tumbleweed Ser.). (Illus.). 342p. (gr. 9-12). 30.00 (0-87842-364-8, 691) Mountain Pr. Publishing Co., Inc.

—Sun Up: Tales of the Cow Camps. 1997. (Illus.). 342p. (YA). (gr. 9-12). pap. 16.00 o.s.i (0-87842-365-6, 690) Mountain Pr. Publishing Co., Inc.

Janke, James A. McHenry's Last Shoot-Out. 1992. 192p. 13.95 o.p. (0-8034-8928-5) Bouregy, Thomas & Co., Inc.

Jensen, Muriel. His Bodyguard. 1999. (Harlequin Heart of the West Ser.: Bk. 4). 256p. pap. (0-373-82588-9, Harlequin Bks.) Harlequin Enterprises, Ltd.

Johnson, Denis. Jesus' Son. 1993. 176p. reprint ed. pap. 12.00 (0-06-097577-6, Perennial) HarperTrade.

—Jesus' Son: Stories. 1992. 160p. 19.00 o.p. (0-374-17892-5) Farrar, Straus & Giroux.

Johnson, Dorothy M. The Hanging Tree. 1979. mass mkt. 1.95 o.s.i (0-345-28621-9); 1977. mass mkt. 1.75 o.s.i (0-345-25737-5); 1973. mass mkt. 0.95 o.s.i (0-345-23663-7) Ballantine Bks.

—The Hanging Tree. 1980. lib. bdg. 9.95 o.p. (0-8398-2616-8, Macmillan Reference USA) Gale Group.

—The Hanging Tree. 1995. 273p. pap. 18.95 (0-8032-7584-6, Bison Bks.) Univ. of Nebraska Pr.

—The Hanging Tree & Other Stories. 1985. mass mkt. 2.50 o.s.i (0-345-32855-8) Ballantine Bks.

Johnson, Ryerson. The Best Western Stories of Ryerson Johnson. Pronzini, Bill & Greenberg, Martin H., eds. 1990. (Western Writers Ser.). 246p. 24.95 (0-8040-0937-6) Swallow Pr.

—The Best Western Stories of Ryerson Johnson. Pronzini, Bill & Greenberg, Martin H., eds. l.t. ed. 1995. (Paperback Ser.). 294p. pap. 22.95 (0-7838-1381-3) Thorndike Pr.

—Torture Trek: And Eleven Other Tales of the Wild West. Greenberg, Martin H. & Pronzini, Bill, eds. 1995. 226p. pap. 12.00 (1-56980-033-2) Barricade Bks., Inc.

Johnston, Terry C. Buffalo Palace. 1997. 576p. mass mkt. 7.50 (0-553-57283-0) Bantam Bks.

—Carry the Wind. 1997. (Illus.). 704p. mass mkt. 7.50 (0-553-25572-X) Bantam Bks.

—Carry the Wind. 1982. 571p. 18.95 o.s.i (0-89803-106-0, Frontier Library, The) Jameson Bks., Inc.

—Carry the Wind. abr. ed. 1994. audio 9.98 (1-57042-075-0, 4-520750) Time Warner AudioBooks.

—Dance on the Wind. 1996. 640p. mass mkt. 7.50 (0-553-57281-4); 1995. 528p. 21.95 o.s.i (0-553-09071-2) Bantam Bks.

—One-Eyed Dream. 1994. 592p. mass mkt. 7.50 (0-553-28139-9) Bantam Bks.

—One-Eyed Dream. 1988. (Frontier Library). 450p. 19.95 (0-915463-38-5, Frontier Library, The) Jameson Bks., Inc.

—Turn the Stars Upside Down: The Last Days & Tragic Death of Crazy Horse. 2001. (Plainsmen Ser.: Bk. 16). (Illus.). 384p. 24.95 (0-312-27757-1) St. Martin's Pr.

Johnstone, William W. Dreams of Eagles. 1998. 412p. mass mkt. 5.99 (0-8217-6086-6); 1994. 416p. mass mkt. 4.99 o.s.i (0-8217-4619-7) Kensington Publishing Corp.

—Eyes of Eagles. 2000. mass mkt. 5.99 (0-7860-1364-8, Pinnacle Bks.); 1993. 480p. mass mkt. 4.99 o.s.i (0-8217-4285-X, Zebra Bks.) Kensington Publishing Corp.

—Rage of Eagles. 1998. (Arabesque Ser.). 320p. mass mkt. 5.99 (0-7860-0507-6, Pinnacle Bks.) Kensington Publishing Corp.

—Scream of Eagles. 1997. 320p. mass mkt. 5.99 o.s.i (0-7860-0447-9, Pinnacle Bks.); 1996. 320p. pap. 19.95 o.p. (1-57566-016-4); 1996. mass mkt. 19.95 o.s.i (0-8217-5253-7) Kensington Publishing Corp.

—Song of Eagles. 1999. 320p. mass mkt. 5.99 (0-7860-1012-6); 304p. mass mkt. 5.99 o.s.i (0-7860-0639-0) Kensington Publishing Corp.

—Talons of Eagles. 1996. mass mkt. 5.99 (0-7860-0249-2, Pinnacle Bks.); 1995. 352p. mass mkt. 18.95 o.p. (0-8217-4890-4) Kensington Publishing Corp.

Jones, Douglas C. The Search for Temperance Moon. 1991. 320p. 22.00 o.s.i (0-8050-1387-3) Holt, Henry & Co.

—Season of Yellow Leaf. 1983. (Illus.). 323p. o.p. (0-03-060042-1) Holt, Henry & Co.

Jones, Robert F. Tie My Bones to Her Back. l.t. ed. 1996. 256p. 23.00 o.p. (0-374-27759-1) Farrar, Straus & Giroux.

—Tie My Bones to Her Back. l.t. ed. 1997. (Western Ser.). 380p. 24.95 (0-7838-1986-2) Thorndike Pr.

Karr, Kathleen. The Great Turkey Walk. 2000. (J). 11.00 (0-606-20132-7) Turtleback Bks.

Keegan, Christopher. Ride into Yesterday. 1992. 137p. 18.95 o.p. (0-8027-4132-0) Walker & Co.

Kelton, Elmer. The Time It Never Rained. 1993. 432p. mass mkt. 5.50 o.s.i (0-553-56320-3) Bantam Bks.

—The Time It Never Rained. 1990. mass mkt. 3.95 o.s.i (0-515-10002-1, Jove) Berkley Publishing Group.

—The Time It Never Rained. 1999. 416p. mass mkt. 5.99 (0-8125-7451-6, Forge Bks.) Doherty, Tom Assocs., LLC.

—The Time It Never Rained. l.t. ed. 1988. (General Ser.). 536p. 19.95 o.p. (0-8161-4451-6, Macmillan Reference USA) Gale Group.

—The Time It Never Rained, Set. abr. ed. 1997. audio 17.00 (1-883268-04-4, 394607) Spellbinders, Inc.

—The Time It Never Rained. 1984. (Chisholm Trail Ser.: No. 2). 378p. (C). reprint ed. 24.50 (0-912646-91-8); pap. 15.95 (0-912646-89-6) Texas Christian Univ. Pr.

—The Time It Never Rained. 1999. 12.04 (0-606-19670-6) Turtleback Bks.

Kerslake, Susan. Seasoning Fever. 2002. (Illus.). 320p. pap. 24.95 (0-88984-234-5) Porcupine's Quill, Inc. CAN. *Dist:* Univ. of Toronto Pr.

Kilgore, John. Nightrider's Moon. l.t. ed. 1993. 19.95 o.p. (0-7451-1714-7) Chivers Large Print GBR. *Dist:* BBC Audiobooks America.

Kilpatrick, Terrence. Swimming Man Burning: A Rip-Roaring Novel of the American West. 1993. (Western Literature Ser.). 248p. reprint ed. pap. 18.00 (0-87417-219-5) Univ. of Nevada Pr.

For book reviews, descriptive annotations, tables of contents, cover images, author biographies & additional information, updated daily, subscribe to **www.booksinprint.com** 1159

Kimball, Philip. Liar's Moon: A Long Story. 1999. (Marian Wood Book Ser.). 304p. 23.00 o.s.i (*0-8050-6148-7*) Holt, Henry & Co.
—Liar's Moon: A Novel. 2000. 304p. pap. 12.95 o.s.i (*0-452-28183-0*, Plume) Dutton/Plume.
Kinder, Chuck. The Honeymooners: A Cautionary Tale. 2001. 384p. 24.00 o.p. (*0-374-17258-7*) Farrar, Straus & Giroux.
Kingsolver, Barbara. The Bean Trees. l.t. ed. 1989. (Large Print Bks.). 397p. 17.95 o.p. (*0-8161-4672-1*, Macmillan Reference USA) Gale Group.
—The Bean Trees. 10th anniv. ed. 1998. 272p. 19.95 (*0-06-017579-6*) HarperCollins Pubs.
—The Bean Trees. 1988. 232p. 16.95 o.p. (*0-06-015863-8*); 1989. 256p. reprint ed. pap. 13.00 (*0-06-091554-4*, PL 1554, Perennial) HarperTrade.
—The Bean Trees. 1998. 336p. mass mkt. 7.99 (*0-06-109731-4*, HarperTorch) Morrow/Avon.
—The Bean Trees. 1998. 13.04 (*0-606-17362-5*); 1989. 19.05 (*0-606-00846-2*) Turtleback Bks.
Kingsolver, Barbara, reader. The Bean Trees, Set. unabr. ed. audio 58.00 (*1-78870-054-6*, 94253R4) Recorded Bks., LLC.
Kittredge, William. The Portable Western Reader. 1997. (Portable Library). 592p. 17.00 (*0-14-023026-2*, Penguin Classics) Viking Penguin.
Knox, Etta R. Homesteading on Grasshopper Flats. 1984. (Illus.). 182p. 12.95 (*0-940920-03-4*) Drollery Pr.
Kohler, George. The Texan. 2003. 638p. 27.95 (*0-9729518-0-6*, (734) 945-2189) El Paso City Bks., LLC.
Kurtz, Jane. I'm Sorry, Almira Ann, ERS. 1999. (Illus.). 120p. (J). (gr. 4-7). 15.95 (*0-8050-6094-4*, Holt, Henry & Co. Bks. For Young Readers) Holt, Henry & Co.
La Farge, Oliver. All the Young Men. reprint ed. 36.00 (*0-404-14566-3*) AMS Pr., Inc.
La Plante, Royal. The Myrtlewood Grove. 1994. pap. text 12.95 (*1-881116-94-8*) Black Forest Pr.
Lacy, Al. Captive Set Free, 10 vols. 2003. (Angel of Mercy Ser.: Vol. 3). 278p. pap. 10.99 (*0-88070-872-7*, Multnomah Bks.) Multnomah Pubs., Inc.
—Suffer the Little Children, 10 vols. 2003. (Angel of Mercy Ser.: Vol. 5). 294p. pap. 10.99 (*1-57673-039-5*, Multnomah Bks.) Multnomah Pubs., Inc.
Lacy, Al & Lacy, JoAnna. The Tender Flame, 10 vols. 2003. (Mail Order Bride Ser.: Vol. 3). 288p. pap. 10.99 (*1-57673-399-8*) Multnomah Pubs., Inc.
—The Tender Flame. l.t. ed. 1999. (Christian Fiction Ser.). 424p. 24.95 (*0-7862-2156-9*) Thorndike Pr.
Lamb, F. Bruce. Kid Curry: Life & Times of Harvey Logan & the Wild Bunch. 1991. (Illus.). 381p. 19.95 o.p. (*1-55566-073-8*); pap. 11.95 o.p. (*1-55566-084-3*) Johnson Bks.
L'Amour, Louis. End of the Drive. 1998. 272p. reprint ed. mass mkt. 4.99 (*0-553-57898-7*) Bantam Bks.
—End of the Drive. l.t. ed. 1997. 26.95 o.p. (*1-56895-490-5*, Wheeler Publishing, Inc.) Gale Group.
—Jubal Sackett. 1986. mass mkt. 3.95 o.s.i (*0-553-25673-4*); 368p. mass mkt. 5.50 (*0-553-27739-1*) Bantam Bks.
—Jubal Sackett. l.t. ed. 1986. (General Ser.). 448p. pap. 17.95 o.p. (*0-8161-3976-8*, Macmillan Reference USA) Gale Group.
—Jubal Sackett. unabr. ed. 2000. (Sacketts Ser.). audio 27.50 (*0-553-50248-4*, RH Audio) Random Hse. Audio Publishing Group.
—Jubal Sackett. 1986. 11.55 (*0-606-02260-0*) Turtleback Bks.
—The Outlaws of Mesquite: Frontier Stories. l.t. ed. 1993. 257p. pap. 17.95 o.p. (*0-8161-5795-2*, Macmillan Reference USA) Gale Group.
—Reilly's Luck. 1985. 224p. mass mkt. 4.50 (*0-553-25305-0*, Spectra) Bantam Bks.
—Valley of the Sun: Frontier Stories. 1996. 192p. mass mkt. 4.99 (*0-553-57444-2*) Bantam Bks.
—Valley of the Sun: Frontier Stories. abr. ed. 1995. (Illus.). audio 9.99 o.s.i (*0-553-47390-5*, RH Audio) Random Hse. Audio Publishing Group.
—Valley of the Sun: Frontier Stories. l.t. ed. 1996. (Western Ser.). 271p. 23.95 (*0-7862-0587-3*) Thorndike Pr.
—Valley of the Sun: Frontier Stories. 1996. 11.04 (*0-606-10010-5*) Turtleback Bks.
—West of Dodge. abr. ed. 1996. audio 9.99 o.s.i (*0-553-47720-X*, RH Audio) Random Hse. Audio Publishing Group.
—West of Dodge: Frontier Stories. 1997. 240p. mass mkt. 4.99 (*0-553-57697-6*) Bantam Bks.
—West of Dodge: Frontier Stories. l.t. ed. 1996. (Western Ser.). 347p. 23.95 (*0-7862-0803-1*) Thorndike Pr.
Langan, Ruth. Badlands Legend. 2002. (Harlequin Historicals Ser.). 304p. mass mkt. (*0-373-29228-7*, Harlequin Bks.) Harlequin Enterprises, Ltd.
Lansdale, Joe R., ed. The New Frontier: The Best of Today's Western Fiction, Vol. 2. 1989. 12.95 o.s.i (*0-385-24569-6*) Doubleday Publishing.
LaPlante, Royal. The Myrtlewood Grove. 3rd ed. 2001. 360p. pap. 12.95 (*1-58275-060-2*) Black Forest Pr.
—The Myrtlewood Grove: Final Episode. 2001. 248p. per. 12.95 (*1-58275-063-7*) Black Forest Pr.
—The Myrtlewood Grove-Revisited. Inbody, Mary, ed. 2000. 226p. pap. 12.95 (*1-58275-015-7*) Black Forest Pr.
—The Myrtlewood Grove Trilogy, 3 vols. 2001. 800p. per. 34.95 (*1-58275-062-9*) Black Forest Pr.
Lattimore, Steve. Circumnavigation. 224p. 1998. pap. 12.00 (*0-395-92621-1*); 1997. tchr. ed. 22.00 o.p. (*0-395-85407-5*) Houghton Mifflin Co.
Laymon, Richard. Savage. 1993. 352p. 21.95 o.p. (*0-312-10537-1*) St. Martin's Pr.
Le May, Alan. Spanish Crossing. 1998. (Western Ser.). 240p. 19.95 (*0-7862-1158-X*, Five Star) Gale Group.
—Spanish Crossing Vol. 1: Western Stories. l.t. ed. 1999. (Western Ser.). 315p. 23.95 (*0-7862-1170-9*) Thorndike Pr.
Leclaire, Day. The Perfect Solution: Heart of the West. 2000. (Harlequin Heart of the West Ser.: Vol. 10). 256p. per. (*0-373-82594-3*, Harlequin Bks.) Harlequin Enterprises, Ltd.
Lee, Grem, illus. The Rounders 3. 1997. 304p. 24.95 (*0-87081-455-9*) Univ. Pr. of Colorado.
Lee, Rachel. The Catch of Conard County. 1998. (Harlequin World's Most Eligible Ser.). per. (*0-373-65018-3*, Harlequin Bks.) Harlequin Enterprises, Ltd.
Lee, Wendi. Outlaw's Fortune. 1993. 154p. 19.95 (*0-8027-1270-3*) Walker & Co.
—Rancher's Blood. l.t. ed. 1994. (Linford Western Large Print Ser.). 288p. pap. 17.99 (*0-7089-7579-8*, Linford) Thorpe, F. A. Pubs. GBR. *Dist:* Ulverscroft Large Print Bks., Ltd., Ulverscroft Large Print Canada, Ltd.
—Rancher's Blood. 1991. 192p. 18.95 o.p. (*0-8027-4120-7*) Walker & Co.
—Robber's Trail. 1992. 150p. 18.95 o.p. (*0-8027-4133-9*) Walker & Co.
—Rogue's Gold. 1989. 192p. 17.95 (*0-8027-4096-0*) Walker & Co.
—Rustler's Venom. l.t. ed. 1994. (Linford Western Large Print Ser.). 336p. pap. 17.99 (*0-7089-7491-0*, Linford) Thorpe, F. A. Pubs. GBR. *Dist:* Ulverscroft Large Print Bks., Ltd., Ulverscroft Large Print Canada, Ltd.
—Rustler's Venom. 1990. 192p. 18.95 o.p. (*0-8027-4112-6*) Walker & Co.
Leonard, Elmore. Elmore Leonard's Western Roundup No. 1: The Bounty Hunters, Forty Lashes Less One. 1998. (Elmore Leonard's Roundup Ser.). 512p. pap. 13.95 o.s.i (*0-385-33322-6*) Dell Publishing.
—Elmore Leonard's Western Roundup No. 2: Escape from Five Shadows, Last Stand at Sabre River, the Law at Randado. 1998. (Elmore Leonard's Roundup Ser.). 496p. pap. 13.95 o.s.i (*0-385-33323-4*) Dell Publishing.
—Elmore Leonard's Western Roundup No. 3: Valdez is Coming, Hombre. 1998. (Elmore Leonard's Roundup Ser.). 304p. pap. 13.95 o.s.i (*0-385-33324-2*) Dell Publishing.
—The Tonto Woman & Other Western Stories. 1998. 352p. pap. 12.95 o.s.i (*0-385-32387-5*) Dell Publishing.
—The Tonto Woman & Other Western Stories. 2004. mass mkt. (*0-380-82235-0*, HarperTorch) Morrow/Avon.
Lewis, Jon E., ed. The Mammoth Book of the Western. 1991. 576p. pap. 9.95 o.p. (*0-88184-791-7*, Carroll & Graf Pubs.) Avalon Publishing Group.
Lewis, Preston. The Lady & Doc Holliday. 1989. 300p. 15.95 o.p. (*0-89015-727-8*) Eakin Pr.
Litherland, Donna. Walker Pass Lodge. 1996. 220p. (Orig.). pap. 11.95 (*0-9607888-4-0*) Barney Pr.
Logan, Jake. Slocum's Close Call, Vol. 254. 2000. (Jake Logan Ser.: Vol. 254). 192p. mass mkt. 4.99 o.s.i (*0-515-12789-2*, Jove) Berkley Publishing Group.
London, Jack. In a Far Country: Jack London's Tales of the West. Walker, Dale, ed. 2002. 304p. (Orig.). pap. 8.95 o.p. (*0-915463-36-9*, Frontier Library, The) Jameson Bks., Inc.
Loveday, John. Halo. 1994. 286p. pap. 9.95 (*0-15-600113-6*, Harvest Bks.); 19.95 (*0-15-100070-0*) Harcourt Trade Pubs.
Lynch, Willie. Sheriff Skinner & the Puzzle River Water War. Kleincheck, M., ed. 2003. (Sheriff Skinner Westerns Ser.). 300p. pap. 12.95 (*0-9715542-2-6*, 3) Primer Cap Pistol Publishing.
MacAllister, Heather. The Rancher & the Rich Girl. 1999. (Harlequin Heart of the West Ser.: Bk. 7). 256p. per. (*0-373-82591-9*, 1-82591-8, Harlequin Bks.) Harlequin Enterprises, Ltd.
MacDonald, William Colt, contrib. by. Ridin' Through. 1999. 228p. (*0-7540-3537-9*) BBC Audiobooks America.
Malecot, Andre. Eye on the Western Stars: A Novel. 1995. 176p. (Orig.). pap. 10.95 (*1-56474-113-3*) Fithian Pr.
Mallery, Susan. Wild West Wife. 2001. 304p. mass mkt. (*0-373-83486-1*, Harlequin Bks.) Harlequin Enterprises, Ltd.
Manfred, Frederick. Lord Grizzly. 1983. (Illus.). 285p. reprint ed. pap. 9.95 o.p. (*0-8032-8118-8*, Bison Bks.) Univ. of Nebraska Pr.
Marius, Richard. Bound for the Promised Land. 1977. mass mkt. 2.25 o.p. (*0-451-07459-9*, Signet Bks.) NAL.
—Bound for the Promised Land. 1976. 10.95 o.p. (*0-394-48344-8*, Knopf Bks. for Young Readers) Random Hse. Children's Bks.
—Bound for the Promised Land. 1993. 436p. reprint ed. pap. 14.95 o.p. (*1-55853-226-9*) Rutledge Hill Pr.
Marshall, Joseph, III. Winter of the Holy Iron. 1994. (Literature Ser.). (Illus.). 304p. 19.95 (*1-878610-44-9*) Red Crane Bks., Inc.
Martin, L. Joyce. Light in the Evening Time. 1995. 224p. pap. 9.99 (*1-56722-132-7*) Word Aflame Pr.
Martin, LaJoyce. The Broken Bow. 1996. 192p. (Orig.). pap. 9.99 (*1-56722-139-4*, 1567221394) Word Aflame Pr.
—Love's Golden Wings. 1987. (Pioneer Trilogy Ser.). (Illus.). 256p. (Orig.). (YA). (gr. 7 up). pap. 9.99 (*0-932581-19-6*) Word Aflame Pr.
—Love's Mended Wings. 1987. (Pioneer Trilogy Ser.: Vol. Bk. 2). (Illus.). 272p. (Orig.). pap. 9.99 (*0-932581-09-9*) Word Aflame Pr.
—Ordered Steps. 1996. (Path of Promise Ser.). 208p. pap. 9.99 (*1-56722-190-4*) Word Aflame Pr.
—To Love a Bent Winged Angel. 1986. (Pioneer Trilogy Ser.: Vol. Bk. 1). (Illus.). 288p. (Orig.). pap. 9.99 (*0-912315-99-7*) Word Aflame Pr.
—To Strike a Match. 1997. 192p. pap. 9.99 (*1-56722-206-4*) Word Aflame Pr.
Martin, Larry J. Rush to Destiny. 1992. 400p. mass mkt. 3.99 o.s.i (*0-553-29410-5*) Bantam Bks.
Martin, Larry Jay. Rush to Destiny. 1998. 312p. reprint ed. lib. bdg. 29.95 (*0-7351-0028-4*) Replica Bks.
—Rush to Destiny. 2002. 431p. pap. 17.95 (*1-885339-03-8*) Wolfpack Publishing.
Maybury, Anne. Someone Waiting. 1980. mass mkt. 2.25 o.s.i (*0-441-77474-1*) Ace Bks.
—Someone Waiting. l.t. ed. 1983. 299p. reprint ed. 12.95 o.p. (*0-89621-422-2*) Thorndike Pr.
McAllister, Anne. The Cowboy's Code: Cowboys Don't Quit; Cowboys Don't Stay; The Cowboy & the Kid, 3 bks. in 1. 2001. 576p. mass mkt. o.s.i (*0-373-20189-3*, Harlequin Bks.) Harlequin Enterprises, Ltd.
McBride, Jule. Hitched by Christmas, No. 6. 1999. (Harlequin Heart of the West Ser.: Vol. 6). mass mkt. (*0-373-82590-0*, Harlequin Bks.) Harlequin Enterprises, Ltd.
McCarthy, Cormac. Blood Meridian or the Evening Redness in the West. 1986. 337p. reprint ed. pap. 9.50 o.p. (*0-88001-092-4*) HarperCollins Pubs.
—Blood Meridian or the Evening Redness in the West. 1992. 352p. pap. 14.00 (*0-679-72875-9*, Vintage) Knopf Publishing Group.
—Blood Meridian or the Evening Redness in the West. 1985. 327p. 17.95 o.p. (*0-394-54482-X*) Random Hse., Inc.
—Blood Meridian or the Evening Redness in the West. 1994. 26.50 (*0-8446-6793-5*) Smith, Peter Pub., Inc.
McCarthy, Gary. Blue Bullet. unabr. ed. 1994. (Horsemen Ser.: No. 4). audio 39.95 (*1-55686-518-X*) Books in Motion.
—Cherokee Lighthorse. 1992. (Horsemen Ser.: Bk. 2). 192p. 3.99 o.p. (*1-55773-797-5*, Diamond Bks.) Ace Bks.
—Cherokee Lighthorse. unabr. ed. 1994. (Horsemen Ser.: Bk. 2). audio 26.95 (*1-55686-528-7*) Books in Motion.
—The Horsemen, Bk. 1. 1992. 3.99 o.p. (*1-55773-733-9*, Diamond Bks.) Ace Bks.
—The Horsemen. unabr. ed. 1994. (Horsemen Ser.: Bk. 1). audio 26.95 (*1-55686-530-9*) Books in Motion.
—Stallion Valley, Bk. 5. 1994. (Horsemen Ser.). 192p. (Orig.). mass mkt. 3.99 o.s.i (*0-515-11434-0*, Jove) Berkley Publishing Group.
—Texas Mustangers. unabr. ed. 1994. (Horsemen Ser.: Bk. 3). audio 26.95 (*1-55686-534-1*) Books in Motion.
McKee, Mac. Wolfer. 1995. (Evans Novel of the West Ser.). 192p. 19.95 (*0-87131-778-8*) Evans, M. & Co., Inc.
—Wolfer. l.t. ed. 1998. (Western Ser.). 240p. 22.95 (*0-7838-8435-4*) Thorndike Pr.
McMath, Meredith B. Marilla: Celebrating the American Woman. 1996. (Celebrating the American Woman Ser.: Bk. 3). 300p. pap. 11.99 o.p. (*0-89283-896-5*, Vine Bks.) Servant Pubns.
McMurtry, Larry. Buffalo Girls. unabr. ed. 1997. audio 69.95 o.p. BBC Audiobooks America.
—Buffalo Girls. unabr. collector's ed. 1990. audio 56.00 (*0-7366-1851-1*, 2684) Books on Tape, Inc.
—Buffalo Girls. l.t. ed. 1991. (General Ser.). 436p. 15.95 o.p. (*0-8161-5242-X*); 14.95 o.p. (*0-8161-5243-8*) Gale Group. (Macmillan Reference USA).
—Buffalo Girls. 1995. mass mkt. 7.50 o.s.i (*0-671-53615-X*, Pocket); 1990. 19.95 o.p. (*0-671-68518-X*, Simon & Schuster) Simon & Schuster.
—Buffalo Girls. Grose, Bill, ed. 1991. 352p. reprint ed. mass mkt. 6.99 o.s.i (*0-671-73527-6*, Pocket) Simon & Schuster.
—Buffalo Girls. unabr. ed. 1990. 12p. audio 29.95 (*0-671-72781-8*, 102603, Simon & Schuster Sound Ideas) Simon & Schuster Audio.
—Horseman, Pass By. 1976. 20.95 (*0-8488-0372-8*) Amereon, Ltd.
—Horseman, Pass By. unabr. collector's ed. 1984. audio 42.00 (*0-7366-0762-5*, 1719) Books on Tape, Inc.
—Horseman, Pass By. unabr. ed. 1993. audio 51.00 (*1-55690-811-3*, 93120E7) Recorded Bks., LLC.
—Horseman, Pass By. 192p. 2002. pap. 12.00 (*0-684-85385-X*); 1992. pap. 12.00 o.s.i (*0-671-75499-8*) Simon & Schuster. (Simon & Schuster).
—Horseman, Pass By. Grose, Bill, ed. 1992. 256p. reprint ed. mass mkt. 7.99 (*0-671-75384-3*, Pocket) Simon & Schuster.
—Horseman, Pass By. 1988. (Southwest Landmark Ser.: No. 1). 192p. reprint ed. 13.95 o.p. (*0-89096-241-3*) Texas A&M Univ. Pr.
—Horseman, Pass By. 1979. (Contemporary American Fiction Ser.). 144p. pap. 8.95 o.p. (*0-14-004691-7*, Penguin Bks.) Viking Penguin.
—Lonesome Dove, Pt. 1. unabr. collector's ed. 1986. audio 56.00 (*0-7366-0582-7*, 1552-A) Books on Tape, Inc.
—Lonesome Dove. unabr. ed. 1993. (Lonesome Dove Ser.: No. 3). Vol. 1. 49.95 o.p. (*1-55800-481-5*); Vol. 2. 49.95 o.p. (*1-55800-622-2*); Vols. 1 & 2. audio 69.95 o.p. (*1-55800-719-9*) NewStar Media, Inc.
—Lonesome Dove. Grose, Bill, ed. 2000. (Lonesome Dove Ser.: No. 3). 960p. mass mkt. 7.99 (*0-671-79589-9*, Pocket) Simon & Schuster.
—Lonesome Dove. 2000. (Simon & Schuster Classic Editions: No. 3). (Illus.). 864p. 30.00 (*0-684-87122-X*, Simon & Schuster); 2000. (Lonesome Dove Ser.: No. 3). 864p. pap. 16.00 (*0-684-85752-9*, Simon & Schuster); 1993. (Lonesome Dove Ser.: No. 3). mass mkt. 6.99 (*0-671-74471-2*, Pocket); 1985. (Lonesome Dove Ser.: No. 3). 848p. 28.00 (*0-671-50420-7*, Simon & Schuster); No. 3. 1988. 960p. mass mkt. 7.99 (*0-671-68390-X*, Pocket) Simon & Schuster.
—Sin Killer: A Novel. 2002. (Berrybender Narratives Ser.: Bk. 1). 30.95 (*1-58724-301-6*, Wheeler Publishing, Inc.) Gale Group.
—Sin Killer: A Novel. (Berrybender Narratives Ser.: Bk. 1). 2003. 368p. mass mkt. 7.99 (*0-7434-5141-4*, Pocket Star); 2002. (Illus.). 304p. 25.00 (*0-7432-3302-6*, Simon & Schuster) Simon & Schuster.
—Still Wild: Short Fiction of the American West - 1950 to Present. 2000. 416p. 26.00 o.s.i (*0-684-86882-2*, Simon & Schuster) Simon & Schuster.
—Streets of Laredo. l.t. ed. 1994. (Lonesome Dove Ser.: No. 4). 795p. lib. bdg. 19.95 (*0-8161-5956-4*); lib. bdg. 25.95 o.p. (*0-8161-5955-6*) Gale Group. (Macmillan Reference USA).
—Streets of Laredo. (Lonesome Dove Ser.: No. 4). 2000. 544p. pap. 15.00 (*0-684-85753-7*, Simon & Schuster); 1995. 560p. mass mkt. 7.99 (*0-671-53746-6*, Pocket); 1994. 560p. mass mkt. 6.99 o.s.i (*0-671-79282-2*, Pocket); 1993. 589p. pap. 25.00 o.p. (*0-671-79281-4*, Simon & Schuster) Simon & Schuster.
—Streets of Laredo. unabr. ed. (Lonesome Dove Ser.: No. 4). 1995. audio 50.00 (*0-671-86998-1*, Simon & Schuster Audioworks); 1995. audio 45.00 (*0-671-56871-X*, Simon & Schuster Audioworks); 1993. audio 45.00 Simon & Schuster Audio.
—Streets of Laredo. 1993. (Lonesome Dove Ser.: No. 4). 14.04 (*0-606-06771-X*) Turtleback Bks.
—Terms of Endearment. 1982. audio 13.95 (*1-55644-048-0*, 2081) American Audio Prose Library, Inc.
—Terms of Endearment. unabr. collector's ed. 1985. audio 80.00 (*0-7366-1014-6*, 1945) Books on Tape, Inc.
—Terms of Endearment. l.t. ed. 1984. (General Ser.). 18.95 o.p. (*0-8161-3708-0*, Macmillan Reference USA) Gale Group.
—Terms of Endearment. 1988. mass mkt. 4.50 o.p. (*0-451-15817-2*); 1983. mass mkt. 2.95 o.p. (*0-451-15778-8*); 1976. mass mkt. 1.95 o.p. (*0-451-07173-5*) NAL. (Signet Bks.).
—Terms of Endearment. unabr. ed. audio 85.00 (*1-55690-507-6*, 90067E7) Recorded Bks., LLC.
—Terms of Endearment. 1999. 416p. pap. 13.00 (*0-684-85390-6*, Simon & Schuster) Simon & Schuster.
—Terms of Endearment. Grose, Bill, ed. 1992. 432p. mass mkt. 7.99 (*0-671-75872-1*, Pocket) Simon & Schuster.
—Terms of Endearment. 1989. 416p. pap. 11.00 (*0-671-68208-3*); 1975. 448p. 9.95 o.s.i (*0-671-22102-7*) Simon & Schuster. (Simon & Schuster).
—The Wandering Hill. l.t. ed. 2003. (Berrybender Narratives Ser.: Bk. 2). 421p. 31.95 (*1-58724-437-3*, Wheeler Publishing, Inc.) Gale Group.

—The Wandering Hill. 2003. (Berrybender Narratives Ser.: Bk. 2). 432p. mass mkt. 7.99 (*0-7434-5142-2*, Pocket Star); (Illus.). 320p. 26.00 (*0-7432-3303-4*, Simon & Schuster) Simon & Schuster.

Meier, Mary Jane. Catch a Dream. 2001. 352p. mass mkt. 6.99 o.s.i (*0-451-40975-2*, Onyx) NAL.

Meloy, Maile. Half in Love: Stories. 176p. 2003. pap. 12.00 (*0-7432-4685-3*); 2002. 23.00 (*0-7432-1647-4*) Simon & Schuster. (Scribner).

Merritt, Judy. Mountain Rising: A Novel. 1996. 250p. (Orig.). pap. (*1-887786-09-0*) Sky & Sage Bks.

Meschery, Joanne. A Gentleman's Guide to the Frontier. 1990. 19.95 o.p. (*0-671-46369-1*, Simon & Schuster) Simon & Schuster.

Michaels, Fern. Paint Me Rainbows. abr. ed. 2000. (Silhouette Romance Ser.). audio 7.99 o.s.i (*1-56740-540-1*, 1840, Silhouette Romance Audio) Brilliance Audio.

—Paint Me Rainbows. l.t. ed. 1982. (Nightingale Ser.). pap. 8.95 o.p. (*0-8161-3391-3*, Macmillan Reference USA) Gale Group.

—Paint Me Rainbows. 1999. 256p. mass mkt. (*0-373-48398-8*, 1-48398-1, Harlequin Bks.); 1994. mass mkt. (*0-373-48316-3*, 5-48316-9, Silhouette); 1994. 256p. per. (*1-55166-003-2*, 1-66003-4, Mira Bks.) Harlequin Enterprises, Ltd.

Miller, Dawn. The Journal of Callie Wade. 1996. 336p. 20.00 o.s.i (*0-671-52100-4*, Atria) Simon & Schuster.

—The Journal of Callie Wade. 1998. 12.55 (*0-606-19497-5*) Turtleback Bks.

Miller, Linda Lael. Daniel's Bride. 1996. 400p. mass mkt. 3.99 (*0-671-00814-5*, Pocket) Simon & Schuster.

—Daniel's Bride. Marrow, Linda, ed. 1992. 400p. mass mkt. 6.99 o.s.i (*0-671-73166-1*, Pocket) Simon & Schuster.

—One Wish. l.t. ed. 2000. 27.95 (*1-56895-878-1*, Wheeler Publishing, Inc.) Gale Group.

—One Wish. 2000. (Illus.). 368p. mass mkt. 6.99 (*0-671-53786-5*, Pocket) Simon & Schuster.

—Two Brothers: The Gunslinger. l.t. ed. 1999. 26.95 (*1-56895-812-9*, Wheeler Publishing, Inc.) Gale Group.

—Two Brothers: The Lawman. l.t. ed. 1999. 27.95 (*1-56895-747-5*, Wheeler Publishing, Inc.) Gale Group.

—Two Brothers: The Lawman & the Gunslinger. 1998. 320p. pap. 12.00 (*0-671-00401-8*); 2001. (Illus.). 432p. reprint ed. mass mkt. 7.99 (*0-7434-1154-4*) Simon & Schuster. (Pocket).

Milne, A. A., pseud. The Pooh Story Book. 1965. (Illus.). 80p. (J). (ps-3). 15.99 (*0-525-37546-5*, Dutton Children's Bks.) Penguin Putnam Bks. for Young Readers.

Mitchell, Kirk. Cry Dance. 2000. (Illus.). 368p. mass mkt. 6.50 (*0-553-57914-2*) Bantam Bks.

—Cry Dance. l.t. ed. 2003. 560p. 25.95 (*0-375-43265-5*) Random Hse. Large Print.

—The Cry Dance: A Novel of Suspense. 1999. 368p. 23.95 o.s.i (*0-553-10810-7*) Bantam Bks.

Monroe, Mary Alice. The Book Club. l.t. ed. 2003. 496p. pap. 25.95 (*1-58724-510-8*, Wheeler Publishing, Inc.) Gale Group.

—The Book Club. 2003. 368p. pap. (*1-55166-721-5*); 1999. 408p. mass mkt. (*1-55166-530-1*, 1-66530-6) Harlequin Enterprises, Ltd. (Mira Bks.).

Moody, Ralph. The Fields of Home. 1991. 340p. reprint ed. lib. bdg. 29.95 (*0-89966-831-3*) Buccaneer Bks., Inc.

—The Fields of Home. 1993. (Illus.). 335p. (C). o.p. (*0-8032-3170-9*); pap. 13.95 (*0-8032-8194-3*) Univ. of Nebraska Pr. (Bison Bks.).

—The Home Ranch. 1994. (Illus.). 279p. pap. 12.95 (*0-8032-8210-9*, Bison Bks.) Univ. of Nebraska Pr.

Morris, Alan & Morris, Gilbert. Imperial Intrigue. 1996. (Katy Steele Adventures Ser.: Vol. 2). 275p. pap. 8.99 o.p. (*0-8423-2040-7*) Tyndale Hse. Pubs.

—Tracks of Deceit. l.t. ed. 1998. (Christian Fiction Ser.). 357p. 24.95 (*0-7862-1412-0*) Thorndike Pr.

—Tracks of Deceit. 1996. (Katy Steele Adventures Ser.: No. 1). 256p. pap. 8.99 o.p. (*0-8423-2039-3*) Tyndale Hse. Pubs.

Morris, Gilbert. The Crossed Sabres. 1993. (House of Winslow Ser.: No. 13). 320p. pap. 11.99 (*1-55661-309-1*) Bethany Hse. Pubs.

—The Holy Warrior. 1989. (House of Winslow Ser.: Vol. 6). 288p. pap. 11.99 (*1-55661-054-8*) Bethany Hse. Pubs.

—Jeweled Spur. 1994. (House of Winslow Ser.: Vol. 16). 304p. pap. 11.99 (*1-55661-392-X*) Bethany Hse. Pubs.

—Lone Wolf. 1995. (Reno Western Saga Ser.: Vol. 6). 236p. pap. 7.99 o.p. (*0-8423-1997-2*) Tyndale Hse. Pubs.

—The Reluctant Bridegroom. 1990. (House of Winslow Ser.: Vol. 7). 304p. pap. 11.99 (*1-55661-069-6*) Bethany Hse. Pubs.

Morris, Gilbert & Ferguson, J. Landon. Above the Clouds. 1999. (Chronicles of the Golden Frontier Ser.: Bk. 3). 319p. pap. 11.99 (*1-58134-108-3*) Crossway Bks.

—Riches Untold: Chronicles of the Golden Frontier. 1998. (Chronicles of the Golden Frontier Ser.: Vol. 1). 368p. pap. 11.99 o.p. (*1-58134-014-1*) Crossway Bks.

—The Silver Thread. 2000. (Chronicles of the Golden Frontier Ser.: Bk. 4). 316p. pap. 11.99 (*1-58134-212-8*) Crossway Bks.

Morris, Neil. Longhorn on the Move. 1989. (Tales of the Old West Ser.). (Illus.). 32p. (J). (gr. 3-8). lib. bdg. 9.95 o.p. (*1-85435-166-4*) Cavendish, Marshall Corp.

—On the Trapping Trail. 1989. (Tales of the Old West Ser.). (Illus.). 32p. (J). (gr. 3-8). lib. bdg. 9.95 o.p. (*1-85435-164-8*) Cavendish, Marshall Corp.

—Tales of the American West. 1989. (J). 5.99 o.s.i (*0-517-68024-6*) Random Hse. Value Publishing.

Morris, Wright. Three Easy Pieces. 1993. 328p. (C). 25.00 (*0-87685-924-4*);signed ed. 35.00 (*0-87685-925-2*) Godine, David R. Pub. (Black Sparrow Pr.).

—Three Easy Pieces. 1993. 328p. (C). pap. 15.00 (*0-87685-923-6*) HarperCollins Pubs.

Mosher, Howard Frank. The True Account: A Novel of the Lewis & Clark & Kinneson Expeditions. 2003. 352p. tchr. ed. 24.00 (*0-618-19721-4*) Houghton Mifflin Co.

—The True Account: A Novel of the Lewis & Clark & Kinneson Expeditions. 2004. 352p. pap. 13.00 (*0-618-43123-3*, Mariner Bks.) Houghton Mifflin Co. Trade & Reference Div.

Mosiman, Billie Sue & Greenberg, Martin H., eds. Blowout in Little Man Flats: And Other Spine-Tingling Stories of Murder in the West. 1998. 224p. pap. 9.95 o.p. (*1-55853-573-X*) Rutledge Hill Pr.

Moss, Marissa. True Heart. 1999. (Illus.). 32p. (J). (gr. k-4). 16.00 (*0-15-201344-X*, Silver Whistle) Harcourt Children's Bks.

Muller, Marcia & Pronzini, Bill, eds. She Won the West: An Anthology of Western & Frontier Stories by Women. 1985. 17.95 o.p. (*0-688-04701-7*, Morrow, William & Co.) Morrow/Avon.

Munn, Vella. Blackfeet Season. 2000. 376p. mass mkt. 5.99 (*0-8125-7065-0*, Tor Bks.); 1999. (Illus.). 400p. 25.95 (*0-312-86734-4*, Forge Bks.) Doherty, Tom Assocs., LLC.

Murphy, Pat. Nadya Wolf Chronicles. 1996. 384p. 23.95 o.p. (*0-312-86226-1*, Tor Bks.) Doherty, Tom Assocs., LLC.

Myers, J. Jay. Altered Brand. 1993. 142p. 19.95 o.s.i (*0-8027-1271-1*) Walker & Co.

Nance, John J. Fire Flight. 2003. 368p. 25.00 (*0-7432-5050-8*, Simon & Schuster) Simon & Schuster.

Nesbitt, John D. One Foot in the Stirrup: Western Stories. 1998. 126p. reprint ed. pap. 7.95 (*0-9651856-3-X*) R.R. Productions.

Nevin, David. Dream West. 1984. 576p. 17.95 o.p. (*0-399-12742-9*, G. P. Putnam's Sons) Penguin Putnam Bks. for Young Readers.

Nichols, Hugh, ed. Passages West: Nineteen Stories of Youth & Identity. 1990. pap. 12.95 o.s.i (*0-917652-76-2*) Confluence Pr., Inc.

Nolan, William F. Max Brand's Best Western Short Stories, Vol. II. l.t. ed. 1986. (General Ser.). 305p. 15.95 o.p. (*0-8161-4011-1*, Macmillan Reference USA) Gale Group.

Norris, Frank. Deal in Wheat. (Illus.). reprint ed. 21.50 (*0-404-04788-2*) AMS Pr., Inc.

—A Deal in Wheat & Other Stories of New & Old West. 1977. 272p. 16.95 (*0-8369-3410-5*) Ayer Co. Pubs., Inc.

—Deal in Wheat & Other Stories of the New & Old West. 1971. (Illus.). reprint ed. 16.00 (*0-403-00675-9*) Scholarly Pr., Inc.

Oke, Janette. The Bluebird & the Sparrow. 2003. (Classics for Girls Ser.). (Illus.). 176 p. (J). 9.99 (*0-7642-2712-2*); 1998. (Women of the West Ser.: Bk. 10). 288p. mass mkt. 5.99 o.p. (*0-7642-2099-3*, 202099); 1995. (Women of the West Ser.: Vol. 10). 256p. pap. 11.99 (*1-55661-612-0*); 1995. (Women of the West Ser.). 336p. (J). pap. 12.99 o.p. (*1-55661-613-9*) Bethany Hse. Pubs.

—The Bluebird & the Sparrow. l.t. ed. 1995. 305p. 22.95 (*0-7838-1479-8*, Macmillan Reference USA) Gale Group.

—A Gown of Spanish Lace. (Classics for Girls Ser.). 2002. 176p. (J). 9.99 (*0-7642-2711-4*); 1997. 288p. mass mkt. 5.99 o.p. (*0-7642-2017-9*); 1995. audio 15.99 o.p. (*1-55661-826-3*); 1995. 256p. text 14.99 o.p. (*1-55661-690-2*); 1995. 256p. pap. 11.99 (*1-55661-683-X*); 1995. 368p. pap. 12.99 o.p. (*1-55661-684-8*) Bethany Hse. Pubs.

—A Gown of Spanish Lace. l.t. ed. 1996. 367p. 22.95 (*0-7838-1595-6*, Macmillan Reference USA) Gale Group.

—A Gown of Spanish Lace. 2001. audio 42.95 NorthStar Audio Bks.

—Too Long a Stranger. (Women of the West Ser.). 2000. 288p. pap. 5.99 (*0-7642-2385-2*); 1994. 304p. pap. 10.99 (*1-55661-456-X*); 1994. 384p. pap. 14.99 o.p. (*1-55661-457-8*) Bethany Hse. Pubs.

—Too Long a Stranger. l.t. ed. 1995. 337p. 21.95 o.p. (*0-7838-1158-6*, Macmillan Reference USA) Gale Group.

—Too Long a Stranger. unabr. ed. 2001. audio 46.95 NorthStar Audio Bks.

—Too Long a Stranger. unabr. ed. 1997. audio 51.00 (*0-7887-0820-1*, 94970E7) Recorded Bks., LLC.

Olds, Bruce. Bucking the Tiger. 2001. (Illus.). 240p. 25.00 (*0-374-11727-6*) Farrar, Straus & Giroux.

—Bucking the Tiger. 2002. 384p. pap. 14.00 (*0-312-42024-2*) Picador.

Oliphant, B. J., pseud. A Ceremonial Death. 1995. mass mkt. 5.99 o.s.i (*0-449-14897-1*, Fawcett) Ballantine Bks.

Olsen, Theodore V. Lone Hand: Frontier Stories. l.t. ed. 1997. (Western Ser.). 274p. 18.95 (*0-7862-0738-8*, Five Star) Gale Group.

—Lone Hand: Frontier Stories. l.t. ed. 1998. (Western Ser.). 392p. 21.95 (*0-7862-0761-2*) Thorndike Pr.

O'Neill, Robert. The Sheriff: Longman Structural Readers. Stage 1. 1983. (American Structural Readers Ser.: Stage 1). (Illus.). 16p. pap. text 5.72 o.p. (*0-582-79819-1*, 75069) Longman Publishing Group.

Overholser, Stephen. Dark Embers at Dawn. 1999. 208p. mass mkt. 4.50 (*0-8439-4657-1*, Leisure Bks.) Dorchester Publishing Co., Inc.

—Dark Embers at Dawn. 1998. (Western Ser.). 199p. 19.95 (*0-7862-1163-6*, Five Star) Gale Group.

—Dark Embers at Dawn. l.t. ed. 1999. (Western Ser.). 287p. 20.95 (*0-7862-1175-X*) Thorndike Pr.

—Dark Embers at Dawn. 1999. E-Book 9.95 (*0-585-28435-0*) netLibrary, Inc.

—Dark Embers at Dawn: A Western Story. l.t. ed. 1999. (*0-7540-3872-6*); (*0-7540-3873-4*) Chivers Large Print GBR. *Dist:* BBC Audiobooks America.

Overholser, Wayne D. The Best Western Stories of Wayne D. Overholser. Pronzini, Bill & Greenberg, Martin H., eds. 1984. (Western Writers Ser.). 224p. 16.95 o.p. (*0-8093-1145-3*) Southern Illinois Univ. Pr.

Paine, Lauran. Nightrider's Moon. 1988. 160p. 16.95 o.p. (*0-8027-4083-9*) Walker & Co.

—The Prairieton Raid. 1994. 192p. 19.95 (*0-8027-4139-8*) Walker & Co.

—Trail of the Freighters. l.t. ed. 1999. (*0-7540-3769-X*) BBC Audiobooks America.

Palmer, Bernard. Kid Breckenridge. 1984. (Breck Western Ser.). 276p. pap. 3.50 o.p. (*0-8423-2059-8*) Tyndale Hse. Pubs.

Palmer, Diana. September Morning. l.t. ed. 2000. 192p. (*0-7540-4360-6*); (*0-7540-4361-4*) Gale Group. (Macmillan Reference USA).

—September Morning. 1996. (Here Come the Grooms Ser.: No. 12). per. (*0-373-30112-X*, 1-30112-6); 1992. (Silhouette Desire Ser.: No. 222). mass mkt. o.p. (*0-373-15222-1*) Harlequin Enterprises, Ltd. (Harlequin Bks.).

Patten, Lewis B. Trail to Vicksburg: A Western Duo. 2000. (Leisure Western Ser.). 256p. mass mkt. 4.50 (*0-8439-4700-4*, Leisure Bks.) Dorchester Publishing Co., Inc.

—Trail to Vicksburg: A Western Duo. l.t. ed. 1997. (Western Ser.). 224p. 18.95 (*0-7862-0741-8*, Five Star) Gale Group.

—Trail to Vicksburg: A Western Duo. l.t. ed. 1998. (Western Ser.). 365p. 20.95 (*0-7862-0764-7*); (*0-7540-3357-0*); (*0-7540-3358-9*) Thorndike Pr.

—Trail to Vicksburg: A Western Duo. 2000. E-Book 9.95 (*0-585-29772-X*) netLibrary, Inc.

Paulsen, Gary. Murphy. 1988. 160p. mass mkt. 2.75 o.s.i (*0-671-64432-7*, Pocket) Simon & Schuster.

—Murphy. 1987. 192p. 14.95 o.s.i (*0-8027-4068-5*) Walker & Co.

—Murphy's Stand. 1993. 128p. 17.95 o.s.i (*0-8027-1277-0*) Walker & Co.

Peart, Jane. A Distant Dawn. 1995. (Westward Dreams Ser.: Vol. 4). 240p. pap. 18.99 (*0-310-41301-X*) Zondervan.

—Homeward the Seeking Heart. 1990. (Orphan Train West Ser.). 192p. (gr. 10 up). pap. 7.99 o.p. (*0-8007-5374-7*) Revell, Fleming H. Co.

—Homeward the Seeking Heart. l.t. ed. 2000. (Christian Fiction Ser.). 291p. (YA). 24.95 (*0-7862-2531-9*) Thorndike Pr.

—Where Tomorrow Waits. 1995. (Westward Dreams Ser.: Vol. 3). 224p. reprint ed. pap. 18.99 (*0-310-41291-9*) Zondervan.

Pelegrimas, Marthayn. On the Strength of Wings. 2001. (Five Star First Edition Women's Fiction Ser.). 288p. 25.95 (*0-7862-3378-8*, Five Star) Gale Group.

Pelham, Howard. Judas Guns. 1990. 192p. 18.95 o.p. (*0-8027-4104-5*) Walker & Co.

Pella, Judith. Warrior's Song. 1996. (Lone Star Legacy Ser.: Vol. 3). 384p. (Orig.). pap. 10.99 o.p. (*1-55661-655-4*) Bethany Hse. Pubs.

Pendleton, Don. Zero Hour. 1999. (StonyMan Ser.: No. 43). per. (*0-373-61927-8*, 1-61927-9, Worldwide Library) Harlequin Enterprises, Ltd.

Peretti, Frank E. The Legend of Annie Murphy. 1997. (Cooper Kids Adventures Ser.: Vol. 7). (Illus.). 160p. (J). (gr. 5-7). 5.99 (*0-8499-3645-4*) Nelson, Tommy.

Phillips, Michael. Grayfox. (Journals of Corrie Belle Hollister). 304p. 1997. text 14.99 o.p. (*1-55661-950-2*); 1993. pap. 10.99 o.p. (*1-55661-368-7*) Bethany Hse. Pubs.

Piekarski, Vicki. Westward the Women: An Anthology of Western Stories by Women. 1988. E-Book 11.95 (*0-585-18793-2*) netLibrary, Inc.

Piekarski, Vicki, ed. Westward the Women. l.t. ed. 1985. lib. bdg. 13.95 o.p. (*0-89340-903-0*, 88) BBC Audiobooks America.

—Westward the Women: An Anthology of Western Stories by Women. 1984. (Double D Western Ser.). 192p. 11.95 o.p. (*0-385-19187-1*) Doubleday Publishing.

—Westward the Women: An Anthology of Western Stories by Women. 1988. 186p. reprint ed. pap. 13.95 (*0-8263-1063-X*) Univ. of New Mexico Pr.

Popham, Melinda W. Skywater. 1990. 224p. (C). 17.95 o.p. (*1-55597-127-X*) Graywolf Pr.

Potter, Patricia. Chase the Wind: Chase the Thunder; Against the Wind, 2 vols. in 1. 2000. 480p. mass mkt. o.s.i (*0-373-21705-6*, 1-21705-8, Harlequin Bks.) Harlequin Enterprises, Ltd.

Powell, Talmage. Six-Gun Ladies: Tales of the Range. 1996. pap. text 9.95 (*1-57090-029-9*) aBOOKS Distributing.

Powers, Tim. Earthquake Weather. (Tor Fantasy Ser.). 1998. 640p. mass mkt. 6.99 (*0-8125-5519-8*); 1997. 384p. 24.95 (*0-312-86163-X*) Doherty, Tom Assocs., LLC. (Tor Bks.).

Pronzini, Bill. The Best Western Stories of Bill Pronzini. Greenberg, Martin H., ed. l.t. ed. 1991. (Nightingale Ser.). 287p. pap. 14.95 o.p. (*0-8161-5115-6*, Macmillan Reference USA) Gale Group.

—The Best Western Stories of Bill Pronzini. 1991. (Best Western Stories Ser.). 200p. pap. 14.95 (*0-8040-0933-3*) Swallow Pr.

—The Best Western Stories of Bill Pronzini. Greenberg, Martin M., ed. 1990. (Best Western Stories Ser.). 200p. 24.95 (*0-8040-0932-5*) Swallow Pr.

—Christmas Out West. 1991. 240p. mass mkt. 3.99 o.s.i (*0-553-29372-9*) Bantam Bks.

—Christmas Out West. 1990. 192p. 14.95 o.s.i (*0-385-41561-3*) Doubleday Publishing.

—The Montanans. 1991. 224p. (Orig.). mass mkt. 3.50 o.s.i (*0-449-14643-X*, Fawcett) Ballantine Bks.

—The Northwesterners. Greenberg, Martin H., ed. 1990. 240p. (Orig.). mass mkt. 3.50 o.s.i (*0-449-14642-1*, Fawcett) Ballantine Bks.

Pronzini, Bill, ed. Great Tales of the West. 1994. 10.98 (*0-88365-702-3*, Galahad Bks.) BBS Publishing Corp.

Pronzini, Bill & Greenberg, Martin H., eds. The Arbor House Treasury of Great Western Stories. 1982. 17.95 o.p. (*0-87795-439-9*); pap. 8.95 o.p. (*0-87795-410-0*) Morrow/Avon. (Morrow, William & Co.).

—The Best of the West III: More Stories That Inspired Classic Western Films. 1990. 224p. mass mkt. 3.95 o.p. (*0-451-16858-5*, Signet Bks.) NAL.

—The Best Western Stories of Ed Gorman. l.t. ed. 1995. (G. K. Hall Nightingale Ser.). 200p. pap. 18.95 o.p. (*0-7838-1283-3*, Macmillan Reference USA) Gale Group.

—The Best Western Stories of Lewis B. Patten. l.t. ed. 1989. 336p. pap. 13.95 o.p. (*0-8161-4781-7*, Macmillan Reference USA) Gale Group.

—The Best Western Stories of Lewis B. Patten. 1987. (Western Writers Ser.). 184p. 18.95 o.p. (*0-8093-1358-8*) Southern Illinois Univ. Pr.

—The Gunfighters: The Best of the West. l.t. ed. 1991. 400p. lib. bdg. 20.95 o.p. (*0-8161-5273-X*, Macmillan Reference USA) Gale Group.

—The Western Hall of Fame: An Anthology of Classic Western Stories Selected by the Western Writers of America. 1984. 360p. 17.95 o.p. (*0-688-02220-0*, Morrow, William & Co.) Morrow/Avon.

Ptacek, Kathy. Women of the West. 1990. 192p. 14.95 o.s.i (*0-385-24647-1*) Doubleday Publishing.

Punke, Michael. The Revenant: A Novel of Revenge. 2002. (Illus.). 320p. 25.00 (*0-7867-1027-6*, Carroll & Graf Pubs.) Avalon Publishing Group.

Ramstetter, Mary. Down the Valley of the Shadow: An American Novel. 2002. (Illus.). 488p. (C). per. 14.00 (*0-9643283-1-3*) C Lazy Three Pr.

—Over the Mountains of the Moon: An American Novel. 1998. (Illus.). 496p. (C). reprint ed. per. 14.00 (*0-9643283-0-5*) C Lazy Three Pr.

Reasoner, J. L. Healer's Calling. 1996. 352p. mass mkt. 5.99 o.s.i (*0-425-15487-4*) Berkley Publishing Group.

Reavis, Cheryl. The Captive Heart. 2000. (Harlequin Historicals Ser.: Vol. 512). 296p. pap. (*0-373-29112-4*, Harlequin Bks.) Harlequin Enterprises, Ltd.

Recknor, Ellen. Prophet Annie. 2000. 352p. mass mkt. 6.99 (*0-380-81122-7*); 1999. 330p. pap. 12.00 (*0-380-79513-2*) Morrow/Avon. (Avon Bks.).

—Prophet Annie. l.t. ed. 1999. (Americana Ser.: Vol. 1). 551p. 27.95 (*0-7862-1992-0*) Thorndike Pr.

Remington, Frederic. Crooked Trails. 1998. (Short Story Index Reprint Ser.). 3.95 (*0-8369-3208-0*) Ayer Co. Pubs., Inc.

—Crooked Trails. 2001. 257p. E-Book 4.95 (*1-58218-297-3*); (Illus.). 260p. reprint ed. 27.95 (*1-58218-299-X*) Digital Scanning, Inc.

—Crooked Trails. 1992. (Illus.). 226p. reprint ed. pap. 18.00 (*1-55613-566-1*) Heritage Bks.

—Crooked Trails. 1979. (Illus.). reprint ed. lib. bdg. 20.00 (*0-8398-1753-3*) Irvington Pubs.

Richter, Conrad. The Rawhide Knot & Other Stories. 1985. 207p. reprint ed. pap. 6.50 o.p. (*0-8032-8916-2*, Bison Bks.) Univ. of Nebraska Pr.

Riefe, Barbara. Against All Odds: The Lucy Scott Mitchum Story. 2000. 288p. mass mkt. 5.99 (*0-8125-5522-8*); 1996. 304p. 22.95 (*0-312-86075-7*) Doherty, Tom Assocs., LLC. (Forge Bks.).

—Westward Hearts: The Amelia Dale Archer Story. 1999. 256p. mass mkt. 5.99 (*0-8125-5530-9*, Forge Bks.) Doherty, Tom Assocs., LLC.

Ritchie, James A. Over on the Lonesome Side. 1991. 192p. 19.95 (*0-8027-4118-5*) Walker & Co.

—The Wagon Wars: A Sequel to "The Last Free Range" 1997. 190p. 20.95 (*0-8027-4157-6*) Walker & Co.

Rizzuto, R. Why She Left Us: A Novel. 2000. 304p. pap. 13.00 (*0-06-093182-5*, Perennial) Harper-Trade.

Rizzuto, Rahna Reiko. Why She Left Us: A Novel. 1999. 304p. 24.00 o.s.i (*0-06-019370-0*) Harper-Collins Pubs.

Roberts, C. New Mexico. 1989. (Illus.). 220p. pap. 16.95 (*0-8263-1145-8*) Univ. of New Mexico Pr.

Robson, Lucia St Clair. Fearless: A Novel of Sarah Bowman. 1998. 400p. 24.95 o.p. (*0-345-39771-1*, Ballantine Bks.) Ballantine Bks.

—Ghost Warrior: Lozen of the Apaches. 2nd ed. 2002. 496p. 27.95 (*0-312-87186-4*, CPHC0689, Forge Bks.) Doherty, Tom Assocs., LLC.

Roche, George. A Reason for Living. 1990. 156p. 17.95 (*0-89526-545-1*) Regnery Publishing, Inc., An Eagle Publishing Co.

Rockwell, Barbara. Sarah's Gold: A Woman Pioneer of Vision. 2000. (Illus.). 300p. pap. 22.99 (*0-7388-1829-1*); text 32.99 (*0-7388-1828-3*) Xlibris Corp.

Roddy, Lee. Days of Deception. 1998. (Pinkerton Lady Chronicles Ser.: 1). 320p. (*1-56476-686-1*) Cook Communications Ministries.

—Days of Deception. l.t. ed. 2002. (Pinkerton Lady Chronicles: No. 1). 477p. pap. 16.95 (*1-4104-0018-2*, Walker Large Print) Gale Group.

—Days of Deception. l.t. ed. 2001. (Pinkerton Lady Chronicles Ser.). 477p. 23.95 (*0-7862-3186-6*) Thorndike Pr.

—Tomorrow's Promise. (Pinkerton Lady Chronicles Ser.: 3). 363p. pap. 10.99 (*1-56476-688-8*) Cook Communications Ministries.

—Yesterday's Shadows. (Pinkerton Lady Chronicles Ser.: 2). 320p. pap. 10.99 (*1-56476-635-7*); 335p. pap. 10.99 (*1-56476-687-X*) Cook Communications Ministries.

—Yesterday's Shadows. l.t. ed. 2002. (Pinkerton Lady Chronicles: No. 2). 470p. pap. 16.95 (*1-4104-0037-9*, Walker Large Print) Gale Group.

—Yesterday's Shadows. l.t. ed. 2001. (Pinkerton Lady Chronicles Ser.). 467p. 23.95 (*0-7862-3208-0*) Thorndike Pr.

Roegdke, Soren & Busse, Kay. Quien Es? The True Story of Billy the Kid. 1991. 403p. (Orig.). pap. 20.00 o.s.i (*0-9629242-0-2*) WKB Enterprises, Inc.

Rosenbloom, Joseph. Deputy Dan & the Bank Robbers. 1985. (Step into Reading Step 3 Bks.). (Illus.). 48p. (ps-3). pap. 3.99 o.s.i (*0-394-87045-X*, Random Hse. Bks. for Young Readers) Random Hse. Children's Bks.

Ross, David W. Beyond the Stars. 1991. 528p. mass mkt. 5.95 (*0-380-71471-X*, Avon Bks.) Morrow/Avon.

—Beyond the Stars. 1990. 19.95 o.p. (*0-671-70314-5*, Simon & Schuster) Simon & Schuster.

Rubinsky, Holley. At First I Hope for Rescue. 256p. 1999. pap. 12.00 (*0-312-19967-8*); 1998. 22.00 o.p. (*0-312-18043-8*) Picador.

Rushing, Jane G. Mary Dove. 1974. 216p. 9.95 o.p. (*0-385-08302-5*) Doubleday Publishing.

—Mary Dove. 2003. 224p. pap. 16.95 (*0-89672-503-0*) Texas Tech Univ. Pr.

Russell, Helen D. Come in This House. 1982. 230p. (J). (gr. 6-12). lib. bdg. 15.95 (*0-934188-07-6*) Evans Pubns.

Ryan, Nan. Desert Storm. 1987. 432p. mass mkt. (*0-373-97038-2*, Harlequin Bks.) Harlequin Enterprises, Ltd.

—Desert Storm. 1997. 400p. mass mkt. 5.50 o.p. (*0-06-108514-6*, HarperTorch) Morrow/Avon.

Saban, Vera. Test of the Tenderfoot. 1989. (Illus.). 147p. (YA). (gr. 5-8). 6.95 (*0-914565-35-4*, Timbertrails) Capstan Pubns.

Sandoz, Mari. Capital City. 1982. 343p. reprint ed. pap. 6.95 (*0-8032-9126-4*, Bison Bks.); text 40.00 (*0-8032-4130-5*) Univ. of Nebraska Pr.

—The Tom-Walker. 1984. 372p. reprint ed. pap. 8.95 o.p. (*0-8032-9147-7*, Bison Bks.); text 40.00 (*0-8032-4150-X*) Univ. of Nebraska Pr.

Sargent, Pamela. Climb the Wind. 1999. 512p. mass mkt. 6.99 o.s.i (*0-06-105808-4*) HarperCollins Pubs.

—Climb the Wind. 1999. 448p. 25.00 o.s.i (*0-06-105029-6*, Eos) Morrow/Avon.

Savage, Douglas. Highpockets. 1998. 176p. reprint ed. mass mkt. 3.99 (*0-8439-4400-5*, Leisure Bks.) Dorchester Publishing Co., Inc.

—Highpockets: An Evans Novel of the West. 1994. (Evans Novel of the West Ser.). 168p. 18.95 (*0-87131-757-5*) Evans, M. & Co., Inc.

Savage, Les, Jr. The Best Western Stories of Les Savage Jr. Pronzini, Bill & Greenberg, Martin H., eds. 1991. (Western Writers Ser.). 248p. 29.95 (*0-8040-0950-3*) Swallow Pr.

—The Return of Senorita Scorpion: A Western Trio. l.t. ed. 1997. (Sagebrush Large Print Westerns Ser.). lib. bdg. 19.95 (*1-57490-089-7*) Beeler, Thomas T. Publisher.

—Six-Gun Bride of the Teton Bunch, & Seven Other Action-Packed Stories of the Wild West. Greenberg, Martin H. & Pronzini, Bill, eds. 1995. 220p. pap. 12.00 (*1-56980-035-9*) Barricade Bks., Inc.

Schwartz, Warren E. In the Far Country: A Portrait of Three Generations. 1984. (Illus.). 228p. (Orig.). pap. 12.00 (*0-914222-14-7*) American Historical Society of Germans from Russia.

Seelye, John. Stories of the Old West. 1999. pap. 22.95 (*0-670-83647-8*) Viking Penguin.

Seelye, John, ed. Stories of the Old West: Tales of the Mining Camp & Cattle Ranch. 1994. 512p. pap. 13.95 o.p. (*0-14-014550-8*, Penguin Bks.) Penguin Group (USA) Inc.

Seelye, John D. Stories of the Old West: Tales of the Mining Camp, Cavalry Troop & Cattle Ranch. 2000. 512p. pap. 15.95 (*0-8061-3283-3*) Univ. of Oklahoma Pr.

Shaw, Patricia. Fires of Fortune. 1996. 416p. 24.95 o.p. (*0-312-14336-2*) St. Martin's Pr.

Shelby, Kermit. Covered Wagon Boy. 1984. pap. 3.95 o.p. (*0-89051-096-2*) Master Bks.

Shepard, Lucius. Two Trains Running. 2004. 125p. 22.95 (*1-930846-23-1*) Golden Gryphon Pr.

Shepard, Sam. Great Dream of Heaven: Stories. 2003. 160p. pap. 12.00 (*0-375-70452-3*, Vintage) Knopf Publishing Group.

—Great Dream of Heaven: Stories. 2002. 160p. 20.00 (*0-375-40505-4*) Knopf, Alfred A. Inc.

—Great Dream of Heaven: Stories. 2003. 28.95 (*0-7862-5194-8*) Thorndike Pr.

Sherman, Jory. Horne's Law. unabr. ed. 1996. (Horne Ser.: Bk. 2). audio 26.95 (*1-55686-670-4*) Books in Motion.

—Horne's Law. 1990. 186p. mass mkt. 3.50 (*0-8125-1169-7*, Tor Bks.) Doherty, Tom Assocs., LLC.

—Horne's Law. 1988. 192p. 17.95 (*0-8027-4087-1*) Walker & Co.

—Trapper's Moon. 1995. 286p. mass mkt. 5.99 (*0-8125-8877-0*); 1994. 288p. 20.95 o.p. (*0-312-85773-X*) Doherty, Tom Assocs., LLC. (Forge Bks.).

Sherman, Steve. Tempered Iron. 1989. 192p. 18.95 o.p. (*0-8027-4100-2*) Walker & Co.

Sickles, Noelle. Walking West. 1995. 320p. 22.95 o.p. (*0-312-13208-5*) St. Martin's Pr.

Silko, Leslie Marmon. Almanac of the Dead: A Novel. 1992. (Contemporary American Fiction Ser.). 784p. reprint ed. pap. 16.00 (*0-14-017319-6*, Penguin Bks.) Penguin Group (USA) Inc.

—Almanac of the Dead: A Novel. 1991. 25.00 o.p. (*0-671-66608-8*, Simon & Schuster) Simon & Schuster.

—Gardens in the Dunes. 1999. 480p. 25.00 (*0-684-81154-5*, Simon & Schuster) Simon & Schuster.

—Gardens in the Dunes: A Novel. 2000. 480p. pap. 14.00 (*0-684-86332-4*, Simon & Schuster) Simon & Schuster.

Skarie, Heidi. Red Willow's Quest. 2000. (Illus.). ix, 261p. pap. 14.95 (*1-888604-10-7*) SunShine Pr. Pubns., Inc.

Skimin, Robert. Apache Autumn. 1994. 399p. pap. text 4.99 o.p. (*0-312-95195-7*, St. Martin's Paperbacks) St. Martin's Pr.

—Apache Autumn: A Novel of the Apache Nation. 1992. 426p. 22.95 o.p. (*0-312-08697-0*) St. Martin's Pr.

Skinner, Jose. Flight & Other Stories. 2001. (Western Literature Ser.). (Illus.). ix, 186p. pap. 15.00 (*0-87417-359-0*) Univ. of Nevada Pr.

Slotkin, Richard. The Return of Henry Starr. 1988. 524p. 24.95 o.p. (*0-689-11811-2*, Scribner) Simon & Schuster.

Snyder, Midori. The Flight of Michael McBride. 1994. 320p. (YA). 21.95 o.p. (*0-312-85410-2*, Tor Bks.) Doherty, Tom Assocs., LLC.

Sparrow, Rose. Shoshoni Man: A Tale of Self-Discovery & Love. 1994. 13.95 (*1-885275-10-2*) Howie, C.J. Co.

Spatz, Gregory. No One but Us. 1995. 224p. (YA). tchr. ed. 17.95 (*1-56512-037-X*, 72037) Algonquin Bks. of Chapel Hill.

Speer, Bonnie S. The Killing of Ned Christie: Cherokee Outlaw. 2nd ed. 1999. (Illus.). 168p. (Orig.). pap. 12.95 (*1-889683-13-2*) Reliance Pr.

Stahl, Hilda. Kayla O'Brian & the Runaway Orphans. 1991. (Kayla O'Brian Adventure Ser.). 128p. (J). (gr. 4-7). pap. 4.99 o.p. (*0-89107-631-X*) Crossway Bks.

Steber, Rick. Tall Tales. 1997. (Tales of the Wild West Ser.: No. 13). (Illus.). 60p. pap. 4.95 (*0-945134-13-4*); lib. bdg. 14.95 (*0-945134-91-6*) Bonanza Publishing.

Stegner, Wallace. The Big Rock Candy Mountain. 1995. reprint ed. lib. bdg. 39.95 (*1-56849-671-0*) Buccaneer Bks., Inc.

—The Big Rock Candy Mountain. 1973. reprint ed. 8.95 o.p. (*0-385-07905-2*) Doubleday Publishing.

—The Big Rock Candy Mountain. 1991. (Contemporary American Fiction Ser.). 576p. pap. 15.00 (*0-14-013939-7*, Penguin Classics) Penguin Group (USA) Inc.

—The Big Rock Candy Mountain. 1977. pap. 2.75 o.s.i (*0-671-82804-5*, Pocket) Simon & Schuster.

—The Big Rock Candy Mountain. 1983. vi, 563p. reprint ed. pap. 12.95 o.p. (*0-8032-9144-2*, Bison Bks.) Univ. of Nebraska Pr.

—City of the Living & Other Stories. 1977. (Short Story Index Reprint Ser.). 3.95 (*0-8369-3028-2*) Ayer Co. Pubs., Inc.

—The Collected Stories of Wallace Stegner. 1991. (Contemporary American Fiction Ser.). 544p. pap. 16.00 (*0-14-014774-8*, Penguin Classics) Penguin Group (USA) Inc.

—The Collected Stories of Wallace Stegner. 1994. 542p. 13.99 o.s.i (*0-517-12188-3*); 1992. 9.99 o.p. (*0-517-08823-1*) Random Hse. Value Publishing.

—The Women on the Wall. 1981. 279p. reprint ed. pap. 12.95 (*0-8032-9110-8*, Bison Bks.) Univ. of Nebraska Pr.

Steinbeck, John. Of Mice & Men. (Steinbeck's Centennial Ser.). 2002. 112p. pap. 11.00 (*0-14-200067-1*); 1963. pap. 1.45 o.p. (*0-670-00125-2*) Penguin Group (USA) Inc.

—The Red Pony. l.t. ed. 1994. 107p. pap. 14.95 (*0-8161-5900-9*, Macmillan Reference USA) Gale Group.

—The Red Pony. l.t. ed. 1994. 107p. lib. bdg. 20.95 (*0-8161-5899-1*) Thorndike Pr.

—The Red Pony. 1994. (Great Books of the 20th Century Ser.). 128p. 10.00 (*0-14-018739-1*, Penguin Classics) Viking Penguin.

Stephens, Jackie. Apache Angel. 2001. (Zebra Historical Romance Ser.). 384p. mass mkt. 5.99 o.s.i (*0-8217-6763-1*, Zebra Bks.) Kensington Publishing Corp.

Stewart, William D. Edward Warren. Barbour, Bart & Blevins, Winfred, eds. 1986. (Classics of the Fur Trade Ser.). 455p. 26.95 o.p. (*0-87842-183-1*) Tamarack Bks., Inc.

Striker, Fran. The Lone Ranger & the Mystery Ranch. 1976. reprint ed. lib. bdg. 22.95 (*0-89190-501-4*, Rivercity Pr.) Amereon, Ltd.

Svee, Gary D. Incident at Pishkin Creek. 1989. 192p. 18.95 (*0-8027-4095-2*) Walker & Co.

Swayne, Zoa L. Do Them No Harm! Lewis & Clark among the Nez Perce. Bates, Carol Ann Goodrich, ed. 2003. (Illus.). 350p. pap. 16.95 (*0-87004-427-3*) Caxton Pr.

Taylor, Janelle. Savage Ecstasy. l.t. ed. 2000. (G. K. Hall Romance Ser.). 600p. 27.95 (*0-7838-9306-X*, Macmillan Reference USA) Gale Group.

—Savage Ecstasy. 1996. 528p. mass mkt. 5.99 o.s.i (*0-8217-5453-X*); 1991. mass mkt. 4.95 o.s.i (*0-8217-3496-2*, Zebra Bks.); 1982. mass mkt. 4.50 o.p. (*0-8217-3306-0*, Zebra Bks.); 1982. mass mkt. 3.50 o.p. (*0-89083-824-0*, Zebra Bks.); 1982. mass mkt. 3.95 o.p. (*0-8217-2671-4*, Zebra Bks.) Kensington Publishing Corp.

—Three Complete Western Love Stories. 1996. 13.99 o.s.i (*0-517-14924-9*) Random Hse. Value Publishing.

—Wild Winds. (Zebra Historical Romance Ser.). 1998. 384p. mass mkt. 6.99 o.s.i (*0-8217-6026-2*); 1998. 320p. mass mkt. 6.99 (*0-8217-5861-6*); 1997. 384p. 21.95 o.s.i (*1-57566-190-X*) Kensington Publishing Corp.

—Wild Winds. l.t. ed. 1998. (Romance Ser.). 461p. 29.95 (*0-7838-0303-6*) Thorndike Pr.

Taylor, Robert. Loving Belle Starr. 1984. 224p. 14.95 o.p. (*0-912697-07-5*) Algonquin Bks. of Chapel Hill.

Thacker, Cathy Gillen. A Baby by Chance. 2000. (Harlequin Heart of the West Ser.: Vol. 9). 256p. per. (*0-373-82593-5*, Harlequin Bks.) Harlequin Enterprises, Ltd.

Thanet, Octave, pseud. Stories of a Western Town. 2000. 252p. pap. 9.95 (*0-594-06386-8*); E-Book 3.95 (*0-594-06387-6*) 1873 Pr.

—Stories of a Western Town. 1972. reprint ed. pap. text 8.50 (*0-8290-0673-7*); lib. bdg. 30.50 (*0-8422-8055-3*) Irvington Pubs.

—Stories of a Western Town. 11.00 o.p. (*0-403-04295-X*) Somerset Pubs., Inc.

Thayer, Patricia. The Cowboy's Courtship. 1995. (Harlequin Romance Ser.). per. (*0-373-19064-6*, 1-19064-4, Silhouette) Harlequin Enterprises, Ltd.

Truett, John H. To Die in Dinetah: A Novel. 1994. 256p. pap. 14.95 (*0-86534-225-3*) Sunstone Pr.

Tuska, Jon. The Big Book of Western Action Stories. 1995. 560p. 24.00 (*1-56980-048-0*) Barricade Bks., Inc.

—The Big Book of Western Action Stories. 2001. (Illus.). 559p. 24.00 (*0-7858-1365-9*) Book Sales, Inc.

—The Big Book of Western Action Stories. 1999. 559p. reprint ed. text 24.00 (*0-7881-6767-7*) DIANE Publishing Co.

—The Morrow Anthology of Great Western Short Stories. 1997. 672p. 32.00 (*0-688-14783-6*, Morrow, William & Co.) Morrow/Avon.

—Shadow of the Lariat: A Treasury of Frontier Tales. 1995. 592p. reprint ed. 25.00 (*0-7867-0256-7*, Carroll & Graf Pubs.) Avalon Publishing Group.

—Star Western. 1995. 448p. 12.99 o.s.i (*0-517-14688-6*) Random Hse. Value Publishing.

Tuska, Jon, ed. The Western Story: A Chronological Treasury. l.t. ed. 1997. (Sagebrush Large Print Westerns Ser.). 19.95 (*1-57490-093-5*); (*0-15-749009-2*) Beeler, Thomas T. Publisher. (Sagebrush Large Print Westerns).

—The Western Story: A Chronological Treasury. 1995. 404p. pap. 15.00 (*0-8032-9439-5*) Univ. of Nebraska Pr.

—The Western Story Vol. 1: A Chronological Treasury, 1892-1939. l.t. ed. 1997. (Sagebrush Large Print Westerns Ser.). 19.95 (*1-57490-092-7*, Sagebrush Large Print Westerns) Beeler, Thomas T. Publisher.

Tuska, Jon, ed. & intro. The Western Story: A Chronological Treasury. 1995. 404p. text 40.00 o.p. (*0-8032-4428-2*) Univ. of Nebraska Pr.

Tuska, Jon & Piekarski, Vicki, eds. The First Five Star Western Corral: Western Stories. l.t. ed. 2001. (Western Ser.). 335p. 23.95 o.p. (*0-7862-3097-5*); (*0-7540-4433-5*); (*0-7540-4434-3*) Thorndike Pr.

Tuska, Jon, et al. The Frontier Experience: A Reader's Guide to the Life & Literature of the American West. 1984. 448p. lib. bdg. 29.95 o.p. (*0-89950-118-4*) McFarland & Co., Inc. Pubs.

Ullman, Elwood & Collins, Monty. Phony Express. 1992. (Three Stooges Ser.). lib. bdg. 19.94 o.p. (*1-56239-162-3*) ABDO Publishing Co.

Underwood, Phillip. Lee Tanner. 1989. 192p. 18.95 (*0-8027-4099-5*) Walker & Co.

Van Gieson, Judith. The Stolen Blue: A Claire Reynier Mystery. 2000. (Claire Reynier Mysteries Ser.). 256p. mass mkt. 5.99 (*0-451-20001-2*, Signet Bks.) NAL.

—The Stolen Blue: A Claire Reynier Mystery. l.t. ed. 2001. (Senior Lifestyles Ser.). 320p. 28.95 (*0-7862-3586-1*) Thorndike Pr.

—The Stolen Blue: A Claire Reynier Mystery. 2000. 197p. 22.95 o.p. (*0-8263-2233-6*) Univ. of New Mexico Pr.

Van Leeuwen, Jean. Going West. 1997. (Picture Puffin Ser.). 12.14 (*0-606-11398-3*) Turtleback Bks.

Veltfort, Ruhama. The Promised Land. 2001. 300p. pap. 13.95 (*1-57131-035-5*) Milkweed Editions.

Vernon, John. The Great Unknown. 2001. 352p. tchr. ed. 24.00 (*0-618-10940-4*) Houghton Mifflin Co.

—The Last Canyon: A Novel. 2002. 352p. pap. 13.00 (*0-618-25774-8*, Mariner Bks.) Houghton Mifflin Co. Trade & Reference Div.

Victor, Frances F. Women of the Gold Rush: "The New Penelope" & Other Stories. Egli, Ida R., ed. 1998. 192p. reprint ed. pap. 12.95 (*1-890771-03-1*) Heyday Bks.

Vories, Eugene C. Saddle a Whirlwind. 1990. 192p. 18.95 (*0-8027-4106-1*) Walker & Co.

Wade, Rebecca. A Wanted Woman. 2000. 384p. mass mkt. 5.99 (*0-380-81618-0*, Avon Bks.) Morrow/Avon.

Walker, Jim. The Dreamgivers. l.t. ed. 1994. (Wells Fargo Trail Ser.: No. 1). 224p. pap. 8.99 o.p. (*1-55661-428-4*) Bethany Hse. Pubs.

—The Dreamgivers. l.t. ed. 1997. 255p. 19.95 o.p. (*0-7838-1997-8*, Macmillan Reference USA) Gale Group.

—The Oyster Pirates. 1996. (Wells Fargo Trail Ser.: Bk. 6). 336p. pap. 8.99 (*1-55661-701-1*) Bethany Hse. Pubs.

—The Rail Kings. 1995. (Wells Fargo Trail Ser.: Bk. 3). 304p. pap. 8.99 o.p. (*1-55661-430-6*) Bethany Hse. Pubs.

—The Warriors, Vol. 7. 1997. (Wells Fargo Trail Ser.). 352p. pap. 8.99 o.p. (*1-55661-702-X*) Bethany Hse. Pubs.

Waller, Robert James. A Thousand Country Roads: An Epilogue to the Bridges of Madison County. unabr. ed. 2003. audio 9.99 (*1-59355-089-8*, 4667, Brilliance Audio Paperback Audiobooks); 2003. audio compact disk 14.99 (*1-59355-090-1*, 4668,

Brilliance Audio on CD Value Priced); 2002. audio 22.95 o.p. (*1-59086-264-3*, 3843, Brilliance Audio Unabridged); 2002. audio 49.25 (*1-59086-265-1*, 3849, Unabridged Library Editions); 2002. audio compact disk 27.95 o.p. (*1-59086-266-X*, 3850, CD Unabridged); 2002. audio compact disk 69.25 (*1-59086-267-8*, 3851, CD Unabridged Library Edition) Brilliance Audio.

—A Thousand Country Roads: An Epilogue to the Bridges of Madison County. l.t. ed. 2002. 30.95 (*0-7862-4410-0*) Gale Group.

—A Thousand Country Roads: An Epilogue to the Bridges of Madison County. 2002. 178p. 19.95 (*0-9717667-1-1*); 40.00 (*0-9717667-0-3*) Hardy, John M. Publishing Co.

—A Thousand Country Roads: An Epilogue to the Bridges of Madison County. l.t. ed. 2003. 240p. pap. 13.95 (*0-7862-4411-9*) Thorndike Pr.

—A Thousand Country Roads: An Epilogue to the Bridges of Madison County. 2003. 208p. mass mkt. 5.99 (*0-446-61306-1*) Warner Bks., Inc.

Watkins, T. W. & Watkins, Joan P. The West: A Treasury of Art & Literature. 1994. (Illus.). 384p. 75.00 o.p. (*0-88363-794-4*) Levin, Hugh Lauter Assocs.

Watson, Esther Pearl. The Adventures of Jules & Gertie. 1999. (Illus.). 36p. (J). (gr. k-3). 16.00 o.s.i (*0-15-201975-8*) Harcourt Children's Bks.

Weld, John. The Missionary. 1980. 180p. 15.00 (*0-89002-176-7*); pap. 7.95 (*0-89002-175-9*) American History Pr.

Wells, Lee E. Tonto Riley. l.t. ed. 1993. 20.95 o.p. (*0-7927-1511-X*) BBC Audiobooks America.

West, Joseph A. Johnny Blue & the Hanging Judge. l.t. ed. 2001. (Wheeler Large Print Book Ser.). 19.95 (*1-58724-073-4*, Wheeler Publishing, Inc.) Gale Group.

—Johnny Blue & the Hanging Judge. 2001. 352p. mass mkt. 5.99 o.s.i (*0-451-20328-3*, Signet Bks.) NAL.

Western Writers of America Staff. Branded West: An Anthology. Ward, Don, ed. 1977. (Short Story Index Reprint Ser.). 22.95 (*0-8369-3471-7*) Ayer Co. Pubs., Inc.

—Hoof Trails & Wagon Tracks: Stories of the Western Trails by Members of the Western Writers of America. Ward, Don, ed. 1977. (Short Story Index Reprint Ser.). reprint ed. 19.95 (*0-8369-3999-9*) Ayer Co. Pubs., Inc.

—Spurs West. 1977. (Short Story Index Reprint Ser.). 26.95 (*0-8369-3421-0*) Ayer Co. Pubs., Inc.

—Tales of the American West: The Best of Spur Award-Winning Authors. Wheeler, Richard S., ed. 2001. 320p. mass mkt. 5.99 o.s.i (*0-451-20327-5*) NAL.

Western Writers of America Staff, ed. The Golden Spurs: The Best of Western Short Fiction. 1991. 320p. 19.95 o.p. (*0-312-85251-7*, Tor Bks.) Doherty, Tom Assocs., LLC.

Western Writers of America Staff, et al. The Golden Spurs. 1992. 320p. mass mkt. 4.99 o.p. (*0-8125-2303-2*, Tor Bks.) Doherty, Tom Assocs., LLC.

Wheeler, Richard S. Eclipse: A Novel of Lewis & Clark. mass mkt. 6.99 (*0-8125-7771-X*); 2002. 384p. 27.95 (*0-312-87846-X*) Doherty, Tom Assocs., LLC. (Forge Bks.).

Whitson, Stephanie G. Red Bird: A Novel. 1997. (Prairie Winds Ser.: 3). 288p. pap. 10.99 (*0-7852-7484-7*) Nelson, Thomas Pubs.

—Soaring Eagle. 1996. (Prairie Winds Ser.: Bk. 2). 312p. pap. 10.99 (*0-7852-7617-3*) Nelson, Thomas Pubs.

—Walks the Fire: A Novel. 1994. (Prairie Winds Ser.: Bk. 1). 301p. pap. 9.99 (*0-7852-7981-4*) Nelson, Thomas Pubs.

Whitson, Stephanie Grace. Valley of the Shadow: A Novel. 2001. (Dakota Moons Ser.: Bk 1). viii, 295p. (C). pap. 12.99 (*0-7852-6822-7*) Nelson, Thomas Pubs.

Wick, Lori. Promise Me Tomorrow. 1997. (Rocky Mountain Memories Ser.: Vol. 4). 400p. pap. 10.99 (*1-56507-695-8*) Harvest Hse. Pubs.

Wieland, Liza. You Can Sleep While I Drive. 1999. 256p. pap. 19.95 (*0-87074-441-0*) Southern Methodist Univ. Pr.

Wilhelmsen, Romain. The Curse of Destiny: The Betrayal of General George Armstrong Custer - a Novel. 2000. 223p. pap. 18.95 (*0-86534-314-4*) Sunstone Pr.

Wilkins, Gina F. It Takes a Cowboy. 1999. (Harlequin Heart of the West Ser.: No. 5). per. (*0-373-82589-7*, 1-82589-2, Harlequin Bks.) Harlequin Enterprises, Ltd.

Williams, Philip L. All the Western Stars. 1989. 288p. mass mkt. 3.95 o.s.i (*0-345-35869-4*) Ballantine Bks.

—All the Western Stars. 1988. 338p. 15.95 (*0-934601-47-X*) Peachtree Pubs., Ltd.

Wister, Owen. The Jimmyjohn Boss & Other Stories. 2000. 252p. pap. 9.95 (*0-594-06360-4*); E-Book 3.95 (*0-594-06361-2*) 1873 Pr.

—The Jimmyjohn Boss & Other Stories. 1999. E-Book 2.49 (*1-58627-489-9*) Electric Umbrella Publishing.

—The Jimmyjohn Boss & Other Stories. 2002. 184p. 93.99 (*1-4043-1122-X*); per. 89.99 (*1-4043-1123-8*) IndyPublish.com.

—The Jimmyjohn Boss & Other Stories. 1972. reprint ed. lib. bdg. 19.00 o.p. (*0-8422-8127-4*) Irvington Pubs.

—The Jimmyjohn Boss & Other Stories. 20.00 o.p. (*0-403-04123-6*) Somerset Pubs., Inc.

—The Virginian. E-Book 2.49 (*1-58627-363-9*) Electric Umbrella Publishing.

—The West of Owen Wister: Selected Short Stories. 1972. xviii, 247p. (C). 23.00 o.p. (*0-8032-0808-1*) Univ. of Nebraska Pr.

Woods, Duanne. Charlie Three Hats. Crook-Gandette, Kathy, ed. & illus. by. 1998. 38p. pap., mass mkt. 8.95 (*0-913301-05-1*) Strawberry Productions.

Worcester, Donald E. War Pony. 1984. (Chaparral Bks.). (Illus.). 96p. (J). (gr. 4 up). reprint ed. 10.95 (*0-912646-85-3*) Texas Christian Univ. Pr.

Work, James C. Ride West to Dawn: A Western Story. 2001. (Five Star First Edition Western Ser.). 291p. 23.95 (*0-7862-3264-1*, Five Star) Gale Group.

Work, James C., ed. Gunfight! Thirteen Western Stories. 1996. 184p. text 25.00 o.p. (*0-8032-4780-X*) Univ. of Nebraska Pr.

Yates, Alma J. Horse Thieves. 1986. 172p. (J). (gr. 9 up). 8.95 o.p. (*0-87747-921-6*) Deseret Bk. Co.

Yorgason, Blaine M. Gabriel's Well. 2000. 160p. 15.95 (*1-57345-641-1*, Shadow Mountain) Deseret Bk. Co.

Zimmer, Michael. Cottonwood Station. l.t. ed. 1994. 19.95 o.p. (*0-8161-5920-3*, Macmillan Reference USA) Gale Group.

—Cottonwood Station. 1994. 224p. mass mkt. 3.99 o.p. (*0-06-100794-3*, HarperTorch) Morrow/Avon.

—Cottonwood Station. 1993. 182p. 19.95 o.p. (*0-8027-1273-8*) Walker & Co.

Zollinger, Norman. Meridian. 1997. 416p. 25.95 o.p. (*0-312-86131-1*, Forge Bks.) Doherty, Tom Assocs., LLC.

—Meridian: A Novel of Kit Carson's West. 1998. (Illus.). 622p. mass mkt. 6.99 (*0-8125-4287-8*, Forge Bks.) Doherty, Tom Assocs., LLC.

**WEST INDIES—FICTION**

Anthony, Michael. In the Heat of the Day. 1996. (Caribbean Writers Ser.). 250p. pap. 11.95 (*0-435-98944-8*) Heinemann.

Antoni, Robert. Blessed Is the Fruit. 1997. 399p. 25.00 o.p. (*0-8050-4925-8*) Holt, Henry & Co.

Baldeosingh, Kevin. The Autobiography of Paras P. 1996. (Caribbean Writers Ser.). 180p. pap. 10.95 (*0-435-98818-2*) Heinemann.

Bergren, Lisa Tawn. Treasure. l.t. ed. 1997. 22.95 (*0-7838-8066-9*, Macmillan Reference USA) Gale Group.

—Treasure. 1994. 273p. pap. 9.99 o.p. (*0-88070-725-9*, Palisades) Multnomah Pubs., Inc.

Cartland, Barbara. Secret Harbor. l.t. ed. 2001. 197p. 23.95 (*0-7838-9664-6*) Thorndike Pr.

Chamoiseau, Patrick. School Days. Coverdale, Linda, tr. 1997. 146p. pap. 13.95 (*0-8032-6376-7*); text 45.00 (*0-8032-1477-4*) Univ. of Nebraska Pr.

Christie, Agatha. A Caribbean Mystery. unabr. ed. 1997. (Miss Marple Mysteries Ser.). audio 54.95 o.p. (*0-7451-6813-2*, CAB 581) BBC Audiobooks America.

—A Caribbean Mystery. l.t. ed. (Agatha Christie Ser.). 1990. 312p. 12.95 o.p. (*0-8161-4538-5*); 1989. 273p. lib. bdg. 20.95 o.p. (*0-8161-4537-7*) Gale Group. (Macmillan Reference USA).

—A Caribbean Mystery. 2000. (Miss Marple Mysteries Ser.). 224p. mass mkt. 5.99 (*0-451-19992-8*, Signet Bks.) NAL.

—A Caribbean Mystery. 1987. (Agatha Christie Ser.). 224p. 14.95 o.s.i (*0-396-09156-3*, G. P. Putnam's Sons) Penguin Putnam Bks. for Young Readers.

—A Caribbean Mystery. 1990. 224p. mass mkt. 3.95 o.s.i (*0-671-70598-9*); 1982. mass mkt. 2.95 o.s.i (*0-671-46920-7*) Simon & Schuster. (Pocket).

—A Caribbean Mystery. l.t. ed. 1967. (Ulverscroft Large Print Ser.). 313p. 12.00 (*0-85456-587-6*, Ulverscroft) Thorpe, F. A. Pubs. GBR. *Dist:* Ulverscroft Large Print Bks., Ltd., Ulverscroft Large Print Canada, Ltd.

—A Caribbean Mystery. 1992. (Miss Marple Mysteries Ser.). 12.04 (*0-606-12212-5*) Turtleback Bks.

—A Caribbean Mystery: A Miss Marple Murder Mystery. unabr. ed. 2001. audio 24.95 (*1-57270-110-2*, N41110u, Audio Editions Bks. on Cassette) Audio Partners Publishing Corp.

Coulter, Catherine. Calypso Magic. 416p. 2004. mass mkt. 7.99 (*0-451-21094-8*, Signet Bks.); 1999. mass mkt. 7.99 (*0-451-40877-2*, Topaz); 1988. reprint ed. mass mkt. 6.99 o.s.i (*0-451-40087-9*, Onyx) NAL.

—Calypso Magic. 1999. 416p. 26.00 (*0-7278-2247-0*) Severn Hse. Pubs., Ltd.

—Calypso Magic. l.t. ed. 2000. (Romance Ser.). 552p. 28.95 (*0-7862-2347-2*) Thorndike Pr.

De Nijs, E. Breton, et al. Faded Portraits: A Novel of the East Indies. 1999. (Library of the Indies ). Orig. Title: Vergeelde Portretten Uit Een Indisch Familie-Album. 176p. pap. 14.95 (*962-593-511-8*) Tuttle Publishing.

Duncker, Patricia. The Doctor. 2000. 384p. 24.00 (*0-06-019601-7*, Ecco) HarperTrade.

Foy, George. Coaster. 1986. mass mkt. 3.95 o.s.i (*0-671-62326-5*, Pocket) Simon & Schuster.

—Coaster. 1986. 320p. 16.95 o.p. (*0-670-80491-6*) Viking Penguin.

Glissant, Edouard. The Fourth Century. Wing, Betsy, tr. from FRE. 2001. 295p. pap. 20.00 (*0-8032-7083-6*, Bison Bks.) Univ. of Nebraska Pr.

Hearn, Lafcadio. Youma: The Story of a West Indian Slave. E-Book 3.95 (*0-594-02347-5*) 1873 Pr.

—Youma: The Story of a West Indian Slave. reprint ed. 45.00 (*0-404-03208-7*) AMS Pr., Inc.

—Youma: The Story of a West Indian Slave. 1890. 193p. (YA). reprint ed. pap. text 28.00 (*1-4047-6737-1*) Classic Textbooks.

—Youma: The Story of a West Indian Slave. 1992. (BCL1-PS American Literature Ser.). 193p. reprint ed. lib. bdg. 69.00 (*0-7812-6737-4*) Reprint Services Corp.

Hopkinson, Nalo. Skin Folk. 2001. 320p. E-Book 9.95 (*0-7595-0631-0*); 320p. E-Book 9.95 (*0-7595-6632-1*); 320p. E-Book 9.95 (*0-7595-8641-1*); 320p. E-Book 9.95 (*0-7595-9702-2*); 320p. E-Book 9.95 (*0-7595-4634-7*); 272p. reprint ed. pap. 12.95 (*0-446-67803-1*, Aspect) Warner Bks., Inc.

Jenkins, Edward. Lutchmee & Dilloo: A Study of West Indian Life. Dabydeen, David, ed. 2003. pap. 15.00 (*0-333-91937-8*) Macmillan Caribbean GBR. *Dist:* Interlink Publishing Group, Inc.

Kempadoo, Oonya. Tide Running. 2004. 224p. pap. 14.00 (*0-8070-8373-9*) Beacon Pr.

—Tide Running. 2001. 201p. 24.95 (*0-330-48252-1*) Pan Macmillan GBR. *Dist:* Trans-Atlantic Pubns., Inc.

—Tide Running: A Novel. 2003. 224p. 22.00 (*0-374-27757-5*) Farrar, Straus & Giroux.

Markham, E. A. Taking the Drawing Room Through Customs: Selected Short Stories, 1970-2000. 2002. 300p. pap. 14.95 (*1-900715-69-4*) Peepal Tree Pr., Ltd. GBR. *Dist:* Independent Pubs. Group, Paul & Co. Pubs. Consortium, Inc.

Nijs, E. Breton de. Faded Portraits. Beekman, E. M., ed. Sturtevant, Donald & Sturtevant, Elsje, trs. from DUT. 1982. (Library of the Indies). Orig. Title: Vergeelde Portretten Uit Een Indisch Familie-Album. 192p. text 35.00 (*0-87023-363-7*) Univ. of Massachusetts Pr.

Nunez, Elizabeth. Bruised Hibiscus: A Novel. 2000. 300p. 24.95 (*1-58005-036-0*, Seal Pr.) Avalon Publishing Group.

Phillips, Caryl. Cambridge. 1993. 192p. pap. 13.00 (*0-679-73689-1*) Random Hse., Inc.

Scott, Michael. Tom Cringle's Log. 1998. (Classics of Nautical Fiction Ser.). 512p. pap. 14.95 (*0-935526-51-X*) McBooks Pr., Inc.

**WEST VIRGINIA—FICTION**

Anderson, Linda. The Secrets of Sadie Maynard. 1999. (Illus.). 480p. pap. 6.50 (*0-671-02768-9*, Pocket) Simon & Schuster.

Baggott, Julianna. The Madam. 2004. pap. 14.00 (*0-7434-5458-8*, Washington Square Pr.); 2003. 304p. 24.00 (*0-7434-5457-X*, Atria) Simon & Schuster.

Banks, Russell. Cloudsplitter: A Novel, abr. ed. 1998. audio 25.95 (*1-57453-270-7*) Audio Literature.

—Cloudsplitter: A Novel, Pt. 1. unabr. collector's ed. 1998. audio 72.00 (*0-7366-4252-8*, 4751-A) Books on Tape, Inc.

—Cloudsplitter: A Novel. 1998. 768p. o.s.i (*0-06-016860-9*, HarperFlamingo) HarperCollins Pubs. Canada, Ltd.

—Cloudsplitter: A Novel. 1999. 768p. pap. 16.00 (*0-06-093086-1*, Perennial) HarperTrade.

—Cloudsplitter: A Novel. 1999. 22.05 (*0-606-21709-6*) Turtleback Bks.

Barkley, Brad. Alison's Automotive Repair Manual: A Novel. 288p. 2004. pap. 13.95 (*0-312-32579-7*, Saint Martin's Griffin); 2003. (Illus.). 23.95 (*0-312-29138-8*) St. Martin's Pr.

Benedict, Pinckney. Dogs of God. unabr. ed. 1995. audio 96.95 (*0-7862-9973-8*, CSL 084) BBC Audiobooks America.

—Dogs of God. 1993. 368p. pap. 19.00 (*0-385-51113-2*, Talese, Nan A.) Doubleday Publishing.

—Dogs of God. 1995. 368p. pap. 13.00 o.s.i (*0-452-27370-6*, Plume) Dutton/Plume.

—The Wrecking Yard: And Other Short Stories. 1991. 224p. 19.00 o.s.i (*0-385-42021-8*) Doubleday Publishing.

—The Wrecking Yard: And Other Short Stories. 1995. 224p. pap. 10.95 o.p. (*0-452-27435-4*, Plume) Dutton/Plume.

Billheimer, John W. The Contrary Blues: An Owen Allison Mystery. 1999. 288p. mass mkt. 5.99 o.s.i (*0-440-23504-9*) Dell Publishing.

—The Contrary Blues: An Owen Allison Mystery. 1998. (Owen Allison Mysteries Ser.). 256p. 21.95 o.p. (*0-312-18565-0*, Saint Martin's Minotaur) St. Martin's Pr.

—Dismal Mountain. 2002. (WWL Mystery Ser.: No. 431). 304p. mass mkt. (*0-373-26431-3*, Worldwide Library) Harlequin Enterprises, Ltd.

—Drybone Hollow: An Owen Allison Mystery. 2003. 320p. 24.95 (*0-312-29121-3*, Saint Martin's Minotaur) St. Martin's Pr.

—Highway Robbery. E-Book 5.99 (*0-312-27349-5*) St. Martin's Pr.

—Highway Robbery: An Owen Allison Mystery. 2000. (Owen Allison Mysteries Ser.). 290p. 24.95 (*0-312-25247-1*, Saint Martin's Minotaur) St. Martin's Pr.

—Land Butchers: Dismal Mountain: An Owen Allison Mystery. 2001. (Owen Allison Mysteries Ser.). 304p. 23.95 (*0-312-26981-1*, Saint Martin's Minotaur) St. Martin's Pr.

Bookout, Alice M. The Little Sisters of Little Bethel. 1999. 70p. pap. 8.00 (*1-56002-850-5*, University Editions) Aegina Pr., Inc.

Burke, James Lee. To the Bright & Shining Sun. 1995. 224p. (J). pap. 10.95 (*0-7868-8012-0*) Hyperion Pr.

Chamberlain, Diane. The Courage Tree. 2002. 416p. mass mkt. (*1-55166-869-6*, 1-66869-8); 2001. 384p. (*1-55166-799-1*, 1-66799-7) Harlequin Enterprises, Ltd. (Mira Bks.).

Chambers, Rick. Casey's Grudge. 1995. (Open Door Bks.). pap. 4.75 (*1-56212-131-6*, 350705, Faith Alive Christian Resources) CRC Pubns.

Cliff, Michelle. Free Enterprise. 1993. 224p. 19.00 o.p. (*0-525-93704-8*, Dutton) Dutton/Plume.

Coberly, Lenore M. The Handywoman Stories. 2002. (Illus.). 192p. pap. 16.95 (*0-8040-1041-2*) Swallow Pr.

—The Handywoman Stories: An Astounding Collection of Appalachian Stories. 2002. (Illus.). 192p. pap. 16.95 (*0-8040-1044-7*) Swallow Pr.

Deutermann, P. T. Hunting Season. 2001. 402p. 24.95 (*0-312-26979-X*) St. Martin's Pr.

Eberhart, Mignon G. Family Fortune. reprint ed. lib. bdg. 22.95 (*0-88411-769-3*) Amereon, Ltd.

—Family Fortune. l.t. ed. 2000. (G. K. Hall Romance Ser.). 384p. 27.95 (*0-7838-9044-3*, Macmillan Reference USA) Gale Group.

—Family Fortune. 1976. 7.95 o.p. (*0-394-40723-7*) Random Hse., Inc.

Fraser, George MacDonald. Flashman & the Angel of the Lord: From the Flashman Papers, 1958-59. unabr. ed. 1995. (Flashman Ser.). audio 80.00 (*0-7366-3131-3*, 3806) Books on Tape, Inc.

—Flashman & the Angel of the Lord: From the Flashman Papers, 1958-59. 1996. 400p. pap. 13.95 (*0-452-27440-0*, Plume) Dutton/Plume.

—Flashman & the Angel of the Lord: From the Flashman Papers, 1958-59. 1995. 394p. 24.00 o.s.i (*0-679-44172-7*) Knopf, Alfred A. Inc.

Furner, Emmitt. The Widow's Son. 2003. 279 p. pap. 21.95 (*1-59129-676-5*) PublishAmerica, Inc.

Gaddis, Mike. Jenny Willow: A Novel. 288p. 2004. pap. 14.95 (*1-59228-492-2*, Lyons Pr.); 2002. 24.95 (*1-58574-451-4*) Globe Pequot Pr., The.

Giardina, Denise. Fallam's Secret: A Novel. 2003. 356p. 24.95 (*0-393-05206-0*) Norton, W. W. & Co., Inc.

—Storming Heaven: A Novel. 1987. (Illus.). 16.95 o.p. (*0-393-02440-7*) Norton, W. W. & Co., Inc.

—The Unquiet Earth. 1999. pap. (*0-449-00492-9*, Fawcett); 1994. 352p. mass mkt. 6.99 (*0-8041-1144-8*, Ivy Bks.) Ballantine Bks.

—The Unquiet Earth. 1992. 480p. 22.95 (*0-393-03096-2*) Norton, W. W. & Co., Inc.

Grubb, David. You Never Believe Me. 1989. 16.95 o.p. (*0-312-02997-7*) St. Martin's Pr.

Harrington, William. Town on Trial. 1994. 272p. 20.95 o.p. (*1-55611-393-5*) Fine, Donald I. Bks.

Henderson, C. J. The Cabin: Misery on the Mountain, vol. 1. 1999. (Cabin Ser.). 272p. (Orig.). (C). pap. 7.99 (*0-87012-633-4*) McClain Printing Co.

Hoff, B. J. Storm at Daybreak. unabr. ed. 1998. (Daybreak Mystery Ser.: Bk. 1). audio 39.95 (*1-55686-830-8*) Books in Motion.

—Storm at Daybreak. 1992. 208p. pap. 6.99 o.p. (*0-7814-0519-X*); 196p. pap. 6.95 o.p. (*0-89636-217-5*) Cook Communications Ministries.

—Storm at Daybreak. l.t. ed. 1998. (Christian Mystery Ser.). 280p. 23.95 (*0-7862-1317-5*) Thorndike Pr.

—Storm at Daybreak. 1996. (Daybreak Mysteries Ser.: Vol. 1). 195p. pap. 8.99 o.p. (*0-8423-7192-3*) Tyndale Hse. Pubs.

—The Tangled Web. unabr. ed. 1998. (Daybreak Mystery Ser.: Bk. 3). audio 39.95 (*1-55686-838-3*) Books in Motion.

—The Tangled Web. 1991. (Daybreak Mystery Ser.: No. 3). 207p. pap. 6.95 o.p. (*0-89636-242-6*) Cook Communications Ministries.

—The Tangled Web. l.t. ed. 1998. (Christian Mystery Ser.). 279p. 23.95 (*0-7862-1473-2*) Thorndike Pr.

—The Tangled Web. 1997. (Daybreak Mysteries Ser.). 189p. pap. 8.99 o.p. (*0-8423-7194-X*) Tyndale Hse. Pubs.

—Vow of Silence. 1992. 208p. pap. 6.99 o.p. (*0-7814-0528-9*); (Daybreak Mystery Ser.: No. 4). 194p. pap. 6.95 o.p. (*0-89636-234-5*) Cook Communications Ministries.

—Vow of Silence. l.t. ed. 1998. (Christian Mystery Ser.). 280p. 23.95 (*0-7862-1563-1*) Thorndike Pr.

—Vow of Silence. l.t. ed. 1990. (Linford Mystery Large Print Ser.). pap. 17.99 o.p. (*0-7089-6902-X*, Ulverscroft) Thorpe, F. A. Pubs. GBR. *Dist:* Ulverscroft Large Print Bks., Ltd., Ulverscroft Large Print Canada, Ltd.

—Vow of Silence. 1997. (Daybreak Mysteries Ser.: No. 4). 193p. pap. 8.99 o.p. (*0-8423-7195-8*) Tyndale Hse. Pubs.

Hoffman, William. Blood & Guile. 2000. 256p. 24.00 (*0-06-019794-3*) HarperCollins Pubs.

—Blood & Guile. l.t. ed. 2001. (Thorndike Mystery Ser.). 357p. 29.95 (*0-7862-3172-6*) Thorndike Pr.

Hollingsworth, Harold M. Glory Creek. 2000. 228p. (Orig.). pap. 12.50 (*0-87012-603-2*) McClain Printing Co.

Hunter, Dan. The Magic Blue Giant. 1991. (Illus.). 80p. (Orig.). (J). (gr. 3-6). pap. 7.00 (*1-56002-107-1*) Aegina Pr., Inc.

Iles, Robert L. Dead Wrong. E-Book 4.00 (*1-929613-17-2*, Mosaic); 1999. 195p. mass mkt. 5.50 (*1-929613-15-6*); 1999. E-Book (*1-929613-16-4*, Mosaic) Avid Pr., LLC.

Kessler, Brad. Lick Creek. (Illus.). 304p. 2002. pap. 14.00 (*0-7432-1775-6*); 2001. 24.00 (*0-7432-0160-4*) Simon & Schuster. (Scribner).

Kincaid, John. Mountain Yarns: Home-Spun Stories Woven from the Threads of Life. 1996. 169p. (Orig.). pap. 8.95 (*0-9651707-0-5*) Kincaid Kountry Bks.

Labovitz, Trudy. Deadly Embrace: A Zoe Kergulin Mystery. 2000. (Zoe Kergulin Mystery Ser.: Vol. 1). vi, 200p. pap. 12.00 (*1-883523-38-9*) Spinsters Ink Bks.

—Ordinary Justice: A Zoe Kergulin Mystery. 1999. 248p. pap. 12.00 (*1-883523-31-1*) Spinsters Ink Bks.

Lehrer, Jim. Purple Dots: A Novel. 2002. (Illus.). 240p. pap. text 13.00 (*1-58648-032-4*) PublicAffairs.

—Purple Dots: A Novel. l.t. ed. 1999. (Americana Ser.). 344p. 28.95 (*0-7862-1809-6*) Thorndike Pr.

Lepp, Bil. Inept, Impaired, Overwhelmed: Tall Tales from West Virginia & Beyond. 2001. 164p. per. 9.95 (*1-891852-17-5*) Quarrier Pr.

MacPherson, Rett. A Misty Mourning. l.t. ed. 2001. (Beeler Large Print Mystery Ser.). 251p. 25.95 (*1-57490-353-5*, Beeler Large Print Bks.) Beeler, Thomas T. Publisher.

—A Misty Mourning. (Torie O'Shea Mysteries Ser.). 2000. 244p. 22.95 (*0-312-26619-7*, Saint Martin's Minotaur); 2001. 272p. reprint ed. mass mkt. 6.50 (*0-312-97784-0*, St. Martin's Paperbacks) St. Martin's Pr.

Maillard, Keith. The Clarinet Polka. Date not set. pap. (*0-312-30890-6*, Saint Martin's Griffin); mass mkt. (*0-312-98689-0*, St. Martin's Paperbacks) St. Martin's Pr.

—The Clarinet Polka: A Novel. 2003. 384p. 24.95 (*0-312-30889-2*) St. Martin's Pr.

—Gloria. 1999. 665p. (J). pap. (*0-00-648175-2*) HarperCollins Pubs. Canada, Ltd.

—Gloria. 2001. 656p. pap. 15.00 (*0-06-093597-9*, Perennial) HarperTrade.

—Gloria. 2000. 643p. 27.00 (*1-56947-206-8*) Soho Pr., Inc.

—Hazard Zone: A Novel. 1996. 80p. (Orig.). pap. 14.00 o.p. (*0-00-224397-0*) HarperSanFrancisco.

Mollohan, Marie. Death of the Circuit Rider. 1997. 168p. pap. 12.00 (*0-87012-580-X*) McClain Printing Co.

Moore, Ruth N. Mystery at Indian Rocks. 1981. (Illus.). 192p. (J). (gr. 5-10). pap. 4.95 o.p. (*0-8361-1944-4*) Herald Pr.

Mosby, Katherine. Private Altars. 2000. 352p. pap. 13.95 o.s.i (*0-425-17126-4*); 1996. 384p. mass mkt. 6.99 o.s.i (*0-425-15236-7*) Berkley Publishing Group.

—Private Altars. 1995. 322p. 21.00 o.s.i (*0-679-42896-8*) Random Hse., Inc.

Mullenax, Foster. Capasheea's Leadmine. 1989. 200p. (Orig.). pap. 9.95 (*0-87012-484-6*) McClain Printing Co.

—Sugarlands. 1980. 422p. pap. 15.00 (*0-87012-387-4*) McClain Printing Co.

Naylor, Phyllis Reynolds. Shiloh. 1998. (Shiloh Ser.: No. 1). 160p. (gr. 4-7). mass mkt. 2.99 o.s.i (*0-440-22811-5*, Yearling) Random Hse. Children's Bks.

—Shiloh. 1991. (Shiloh Ser.: No. 1). (J). (gr. 4-7). 10.09 (*0-606-01016-5*) Turtleback Bks.

O'Rourke, Erin. Seeing Pink. 2003. (Five Star First Edition Women's Fiction Ser.). 434p. 27.95 (*0-7862-5632-X*, Five Star) Gale Group.

Paige, Laurie. Sally's Beau. 1993. pap. (*0-373-08923-6*, 5-08923-0, Silhouette) Harlequin Enterprises, Ltd.

Pancake, Breece D'J. The Stories of Breece D'J Pancake. 1984. 192p. pap. 9.95 o.p. (*0-8050-0720-2*); pap. o.p. (*0-03-070623-8*) Holt, Henry & Co. (Owl Bks.).

—The Stories of Breece D'J Pancake. 1983. 15.95 o.s.i (*0-316-69012-0*); 2002. 192p. reprint ed. pap. 13.95 (*0-316-71597-2*, Back Bay) Little Brown & Co.

Paul, Jasmine. A Girl in Parts: A Novel. 2003. 248p. pap. text 14.95 (*1-58243-285-6*); 2002. 256p. text 24.00 (*1-58243-218-X*) Basic Bks. (Counterpoint Pr.).

Phillips, Jayne Anne. Machine Dreams. l.t. ed. 1985. (General Ser.). 456p. 18.95 o.p. (*0-8161-3819-2*, Macmillan Reference USA) Gale Group.

—Machine Dreams. 1999. 352p. pap. 14.00 (*0-375-70525-2*) Knopf, Alfred A. Inc.

—Machine Dreams. 1984. 352p. 16.95 o.p. (*0-525-24252-X*, 01646-490, Seymour Lawrence) NAL.

—Machine Dreams. 1985. mass mkt. 3.95 (*0-671-53290-1*, Pocket) Simon & Schuster.

—Machine Dreams. Rosenman, Jane, ed. 1992. 400p. reprint ed. pap. (*0-671-74235-3*, Pocket) Simon & Schuster.

—Shelter. 1995. 336p. pap. 11.95 o.s.i (*0-385-31389-6*, Delta) Dell Publishing.

—Shelter. 1994. 288p. 21.95 o.p. (*0-395-48890-7*) Houghton Mifflin Co.

—Shelter. 1994. 288p. (*0-7710-6997-9*) McClelland & Stewart/Tundra Bks.

—Shelter. 2002. 336p. pap. 13.00 (*0-375-72739-6*) Random Hse., Inc.

Ramey, Jim. Junior. 1995. (Illus.). 56p. pap. 8.00 o.p. (*0-8059-3745-5*) Dorrance Publishing Co., Inc.

Riley, Margaret L. Charlie's Way. l.t. ed. 1999. (Illus.). E-Book incl. cd-rom (*1-929077-60-2*, Books OnScreen) PageFree Publishing, Inc.

Settle, Mary Lee. Charley Bland. 1991. 208p. pap. 8.95 o.p. (*0-88184-709-7*, Carroll & Graf Pubs.) Avalon Publishing Group.

—Charley Bland. 1989. 18.95 o.p. (*0-374-12078-1*) Farrar, Straus & Giroux.

—Charley Bland. 1996. (Mary Lee Settle Collection). 208p. pap. 12.95 (*1-57003-149-5*) Univ. of South Carolina Pr.

—The Scapegoat. 1982. 288p. mass mkt. 3.95 o.s.i (*0-345-29802-0*) Ballantine Bks.

—The Scapegoat. 1988. (Beulah Quintet - Signature Edition Ser.). 288p. pap. 9.95 o.s.i (*0-684-18848-1*, Scribner Paper Fiction) Simon & Schuster.

—The Scapegoat. 1996. (Beulah Quintet Ser.: Bk. IV). 278p. pap. 12.95 (*1-57003-117-7*) Univ. of South Carolina Pr.

Shuster, Bud. Chances. 2002. 240p. 24.95 (*1-57249-314-3*, Burd Street Pr.) White Mane Publishing Co., Inc.

Ware, Cheryl. Flea Circus Summer. 1997. 144p. (J). (gr. 4-6). pap. 15.95 (*0-531-30032-3*); lib. bdg. 16.99 (*0-531-33032-X*) Scholastic, Inc. (Orchard Bks.).

—Sea Monkey Summer. 1996. 144p. (J). (gr. 4-6). mass mkt. 15.99 o.p. (*0-531-08868-5*); mass mkt. 14.95 o.p. (*0-531-09518-5*) Scholastic, Inc. (Orchard Bks.).

Whitehead, Colson. John Henry Days: A Novel. 2002. 400p. pap. 14.00 (*0-385-49820-9*, Knopf Bks. for Young Readers) Random Hse. Children's Bks.

Whitney, Phyllis A. Daughter of the Stars. unabr. ed. 1995. audio 54.95 (*0-7451-6522-2*, CAB 1138) BBC Audiobooks America.

—Daughter of the Stars. 1995. 320p. mass mkt. 6.99 o.s.i (*0-449-22344-2*, Fawcett) Ballantine Bks.

—Daughter of the Stars. unabr. ed. 1997. audio 39.95 (*0-7861-1221-2*, 2162) Blackstone Audio Bks., Inc.

—Daughter of the Stars. unabr. ed. 1995. 29.95 o.p. (*0-7871-0939-8*) NewStar Media, Inc.

—Daughter of the Stars. l.t. ed. 1994. 480p. 19.00 o.s.i (*0-679-75648-5*) Random Hse. Large Print.

Wiggs, Susan. The Horsemaster's Daughter. 1999. 401p. mass mkt. (*1-55166-534-4*, 1-66534-8, Mira Bks.) Harlequin Enterprises, Ltd.

Williams, Thomas H. Greenbrier! Valley of Hope. 1997. 256p. pap. 12.95 (*1-880404-14-1*) Bookwrights Pr.

Yep, Laurence. Dream Soul. 2002. 256p. (J). (gr. 3-7). pap. 6.99 (*0-06-440788-8*) HarperCollins Children's Bk. Group.

**WESTLANDS (IMAGINARY PLACE)—FICTION**

Kerr, Katharine. The Black Raven. 2000. (Dragon Mage Ser.: Bk. 20). 432p. mass mkt. 6.99 (*0-553-57919-3*) Bantam Bks.

—The Black Raven. 2000. (Dragon Mage Ser.: Bk. 2). 13.04 (*0-606-19271-9*) Turtleback Bks.

—Daggerspell. 1987. (Deverry Ser.: No. 1). 384p. mass mkt. 4.99 o.s.i (*0-345-34430-8*, Del Rey) Ballantine Bks.

—Daggerspell. 1993. (Deverry Ser.: No. 1). 480p. mass mkt. 6.99 (*0-553-56521-4*, Spectra) Bantam Bks.

—Daggerspell. 1986. (Deverry Ser.: No. 1). (Illus.). xi, 414p. 16.95 o.s.i (*0-385-23108-3*) Doubleday Publishing.

—Darkspell. 1988. (Deverry Ser.: No. 2). mass mkt. 4.99 o.s.i (*0-345-34431-6*, Del Rey) Ballantine Bks.

—Darkspell. 1994. (Deverry Ser.: No. 2). 432p. mass mkt. 6.99 (*0-553-56888-4*, Spectra) Bantam Bks.

—Darkspell. 1987. (Deverry Ser.: No. 2). (Illus.). xi, 369p. 17.95 o.s.i (*0-385-23109-1*) Doubleday Publishing.

—Dawnspell: The Bristling Wood. 1990. (Deverry Ser.: No. 3). 384p. mass mkt. 6.99 (*0-553-28581-5*, Spectra) Bantam Bks.

—Days of Air & Darkness. (Deverry Ser.: No. 8). 1995. 432p. mass mkt. 6.99 (*0-553-57262-8*); 1994. (Illus.). xiii, 415p. pap. 12.95 o.s.i (*0-553-37289-0*) Bantam Bks.

—Days of Blood & Fire. (Deverry Ser.: No. 7). 1994. 528p. mass mkt. 6.99 (*0-553-29012-6*); 1993. 416p. pap. 11.95 o.s.i (*0-553-37204-1*) Bantam Bks.

—The Dragon Revenant. 1991. (Deverry Ser.: No. 4). 432p. mass mkt. 6.99 (*0-553-28909-8*, Spectra) Bantam Bks.

—The Dragon Revenant. 1990. (Deverry Ser.: No. 4). 416p. pap. 19.00 (*0-385-41098-0*) Broadway Bks.

—The Dragon Revenant. 1990. (Deverry Ser.: No. 4). xi, 403p. 18.95 o.s.i (*0-385-26140-3*) Doubleday Publishing.

—The Red Wyvern. 1998. (Dragon Mage Ser.: Bk. 1). 416p. mass mkt. 6.99 (*0-553-57264-4*) Bantam Bks.

—A Time of Exile. 1992. (Deverry Ser.: No. 5). 432p. mass mkt. 6.99 (*0-553-29813-5*, Spectra) Bantam Bks.

—A Time of Exile. 1991. (Deverry Ser.: No. 5). 444p. pap. 19.00 (*0-385-41464-1*) Broadway Bks.

—A Time of Exile. 1991. (Deverry Ser.: No. 5). 444p. 22.00 o.s.i (*0-385-41463-3*) Doubleday Publishing.

—A Time of Omens. (Deverry Ser.: No. 6). 1993. 432p. mass mkt. 6.99 (*0-553-29011-8*); 1992. xi, 406p. 22.50 o.s.i (*0-553-08913-7*, Spectra); 1992. xi, 406p. pap. 11.00 o.s.i (*0-553-35235-0*, Spectra) Bantam Bks.

**WESTRIA (IMAGINARY PLACE)—FICTION**

Paxson, Diana L. Silverhair the Wanderer. 1986. 320p. (Orig.). mass mkt. 2.95 (*0-8125-4860-4*, Tor Bks.) Doherty, Tom Assocs., LLC.

Paxson, Diana L. The Earthstone. 1987. 288p. (Orig.). pap. 3.50 o.p. (*0-8125-4862-0*, Tor Bks.) Doherty, Tom Assocs., LLC.

—The Jewel of Fire. 1992. (Westria Ser.: No. 7). mass mkt. 3.99 o.p. (*0-8125-1110-7*, Tor Bks.) Doherty, Tom Assocs., LLC.

—Lady of Light & Darkness. 1982. 256p. (Orig.). pap. 8.95 o.p. (*0-671-45883-3*, Pocket) Simon & Schuster.

—The Sea Star. 1988. 384p. mass mkt. 3.50 (*0-8125-4864-7*, Tor Bks.) Doherty, Tom Assocs., LLC.

—Wind Crystal. 1990. pap. 3.95 o.p. (*0-8125-0040-7*, Tor Bks.) Doherty, Tom Assocs., LLC.

**WILDROSE (SASKATCHEWAN: IMAGINARY PLACE)—FICTION**

Glover, Ruth. A Place to Call Home: Book 6. 1999. (Wildrose Ser.: 6). 212p. pap. 12.99 (*0-8341-1753-3*) Beacon Hill Pr. of Kansas City.

—Second-Best Bride. 2004. (Wildrose Ser.). 232p. 25.95 (*1-59414-055-3*, Five Star) Gale Group.

—Second-best Bride: Book 5. 1997. (Wildrose Ser.: Bk. 5). 208p. pap. 12.99 (*0-8341-1628-6*) Beacon Hill Pr. of Kansas City.

Glover, Ruth E. Bitter Thistle, Sweet Rose: Book 2. 1995. (Wildrose Ser.: 2). 208p. pap. 12.99 (*0-8341-1528-X*) Beacon Hill Pr. of Kansas City.

—The Shining Light: Book 1. 1993. (Wildrose Ser.: Vol. 1). 216p. pap. 12.99 (*0-8341-1514-X*) Beacon Hill Pr. of Kansas City.

—A Time To Dream: Book 3. 1995. (Wildrose Ser.: 3). 192p. pap. 12.99 (*0-8341-1572-7*) Beacon Hill Pr. of Kansas City.

—Turn Northward, Love: Book 4. 1997. (Wildrose Ser.: 4). 216p. (Orig.). pap. 12.99 (*0-8341-1590-5*) Beacon Hill Pr. of Kansas City.

**WISCONSIN—FICTION**

Addy, Sharon Hart. Right Here on This Spot. 1999. (Illus.). 32p. (J). (ps-3). lib. bdg., tchr. ed. 15.00 (*0-395-73091-0*) Houghton Mifflin Co.

Ansay, A. Manette. Midnight Champagne. 1999. 240p. 24.00 (*0-688-15244-9*, Morrow, William & Co.) Morrow/Avon.

—Midnight Champagne: A Novel. 2000. (Illus.). 240p. pap. 13.00 (*0-380-72975-X*, Perennial) HarperTrade.

—Read This & Tell Me What It Says. 1998. 160p. reprint ed. pap. 11.00 (*0-380-73077-4*, Perennial) HarperTrade.

—Read This & Tell Me What It Says: Stories. 1996. 176p. pap. 13.95 o.p. (*1-55849-039-6*); 1995. 160p. text 22.95 (*0-87023-988-0*) Univ. of Massachusetts Pr.

—River Angel: A Novel. 1998. 224p. 24.00 (*0-688-15243-0*, Morrow, William & Co.); 1999. 256p. reprint ed. pap. 12.50 (*0-380-72974-1*, Avon Bks.) Morrow/Avon.

—Sister. 1997. 240p. pap. 13.00 (*0-380-72976-8*, Perennial) HarperTrade.

—Sister. 1996. 224p. 24.00 o.p. (*0-688-14449-7*, Morrow, William & Co.) Morrow/Avon.

—Vinegar Hill. 1998. 256p. pap. 13.00 (*0-380-73013-8*, Perennial); 1999. audio 25.00 (*0-694-52343-7*, HarperAudio); 2000. 6p. audio 25.00 (*0-694-52338-0*, HarperAudio) HarperTrade.

—Vinegar Hill. 1999. (Oprah's Book Club Ser.). 256p. 24.00 (*0-688-18063-9*, Morrow, William & Co.) Morrow/Avon.

—Vinegar Hill. unabr. ed. 2000. audio 36.00 Recorded Bks., LLC.

—Vinegar Hill. l.t. ed. 2000. (Basic Ser.). 341p. 30.95 (*0-7862-2511-4*) Thorndike Pr.

—Vinegar Hill. 1999. 15.99 (*0-606-19124-0*) Turtleback Bks.

—Vinegar Hill. 1999. pap. 9.95 (*0-14-023239-7*); 1994. 256p. 22.95 o.p. (*0-670-85253-8*) Viking Penguin. (Viking).

—Vinegar Hill Oprah, Vol. 28. 2000. 240p. pap. 13.00 (*0-380-29976-3*, Avon Bks.) Morrow/Avon.

Armstrong, Margaret D. Tales from an Irish Wake. 1990. 256p. 19.95 (*0-912526-45-9*) Library Research Assocs., Inc.

Best, Steven M. When Philosophers Were Kings. 2002. (Illus.). 384p. 28.95 (*0-86534-362-4*) Sunstone Pr.

Bukoski, Anthony. Polonaise: Stories. 1998. 192p. 19.95 (*0-87074-434-8*) Southern Methodist Univ. Pr.

—Time Between Trains. 2003. 200p. 22.50 (*0-87074-479-8*) Southern Methodist Univ. Pr.

Calhoun, Jackie. By Reservation Only. 1998. 256p. pap. 11.95 o.p. (*1-56280-191-0*) Naiad Pr., Inc.

Cameron, Ann. The Secret Life of Amanda K. Woods. 1999. (Illus.). 208p. (YA). (gr. 5-9). pap. 5.99 (*0-14-130642-4*, Puffin Bks.) Penguin Putnam Bks. for Young Readers.

Canin, Ethan. Blue River. 1991. 224p. 19.95 o.s.i (*0-395-49854-6*) Houghton Mifflin Co.

—Blue River. 1992. 240p. reprint ed. pap. 12.99 o.p. (*0-446-39447-5*) Warner Bks., Inc.

Carrier, Warren. Death of a Poet. 2001. 160p. pap. 9.95 (*0-87714-209-2*) Denlingers Pubs., Ltd.

—Justice at Christmas. 2001. 140p. pap. 8.95 (*0-87714-240-8*); 2000. E-Book 6.95 (*0-87714-507-5*) Denlingers Pubs., Ltd.

—Murder at the Strawberry Festival. 2003. 295p. 19.95 (*1-878044-14-1*) Mayhaven Publishing.

Carter, Alden R. Crescent Moon. 1999. 153p. (J). (gr. 5-9). tchr. ed. 16.95 (*0-8234-1521-X*) Holiday Hse., Inc.

Cherry, Kelly. The Society of Friends: Stories. 1999. 208p. pap. 19.95 (*0-8262-1243-3*) Univ. of Missouri Pr.

Chester, Laura. The Story of the Lake. 1995. 380p. 24.95 o.s.i (*0-571-19861-9*) Faber & Faber, Inc.

Cooke, John Peyton. The Chimney Sweeper. 1995. 320p. 21.95 o.s.i (*0-89296-523-1*) Mysterious Pr.

—The Chimney Sweeper. 1996. 288p. mass mkt. 5.99 (*0-446-40388-1*) Warner Bks., Inc.

Cote, Lyn. Autumn's Shadow. 2003. (Northern Intrigue Ser.). 286p. pap. 9.99 (*0-8423-3557-9*) Tyndale Hse. Pubs.

—Winter's Secret. 2002. (Northern Intrigue HeartQuest Ser.: Bk. 1). (Illus.). 288p. pap. 9.99 (*0-8423-3556-0*) Tyndale Hse. Pubs.

Craft, Michael. Body Language. 1999. (Mark Manning Mystery Ser.). 273p. 22.00 o.s.i (*1-57566-419-4*) Kensington Publishing Corp.

—Boy Toy. 2002. 272p. pap. 13.95 o.s.i (*0-312-28709-7*, Saint Martin's Griffin) St. Martin's Pr.

—Boy Toy: A Mark Manning Mystery. 2001. (Mark Manning Mystery Ser.). 272p. 23.95 (*0-312-26917-X*) St. Martin's Pr.

—Hot Spot: A Mark Manning Mystery. 288p. 2003. pap. 13.95 (*0-312-31364-0*, Saint Martin's Griffin); 2002. 23.95 (*0-312-28900-6*, Saint Martin's Minotaur) St. Martin's Pr.

Derleth, August. The Hills Stand Watch. 2000. (August Derleth Library ). 25.00 (*1-55246-140-8*); pap. 17.00 (*1-55246-141-6*) Battered Silicon Dispatch Box, The.

—The Hills Stand Watch. 1993. reprint ed. lib. bdg. 21.95 (*1-56849-124-7*) Buccaneer Bks., Inc.

DeSmet, Christine. Spirit Lake. 2000. E-Book 6.00 (*1-58200-544-3*) Hard Shell Word Factory.

Faust, Ron. Split Image. 2000. 224p. pap. 12.95 (*0-312-87719-6*, Forge Bks.); 1999. mass mkt. (*0-8125-4924-4*, Tor Bks.); 1997. 224p. 20.95 o.p. (*0-312-86011-0*, Forge Bks.) Doherty, Tom Assocs., LLC.

Fine, Africa. Katrina. 2001. (Romance Ser.). 210p. 26.95 (*0-7862-3027-4*, Five Star) Gale Group.

Fortney, Steven. The Gazebo: The Passing of Shadows. 2001. 372p. 19.95 (*1-878569-74-0*, Waubesa Pr.) Badger Bks., Inc.

Gilligan, Sharon. Faces of Love. 1992. 192p. (Orig.). pap. 8.95 (*0-9628938-4-6*) Rising Tide Pr.
Gorman, Ed. Ghost Town. l.t. ed. 2002. (Thorndike Western Ser.). 353p. 25.95 (*0-7862-3838-0*) Gale Group.
Greenlief, K. C. Death at the Door: A Swenson & Smith Mystery. 2003. (Illus.). 304p. 23.95 (*0-312-31809-X*) St. Martin's Pr.
Gregg, Andy. Cannibal Lake: A Thriller. 2003. 214p. 25.95 (*1-59414-059-6*, Five Star) Gale Group.
Hall, Brenda. Cold Hunter's Moon. 2002. 320p. 23.95 (*0-312-27847-0*) St. Martin's Pr.
Halvorson, Jerry. Abandoned: Now Stutter My Orphan. 1999. (Illus.). 250p. 15.95 (*0-9664894-1-1*) Halvorson Farms of Wisconsin, Inc.
Hamilton, Jane. A Map of the World. (Oprah's Book Club Ser.). 1999. 400p. 24.95 o.s.i (*0-385-50076-9*); 1994. 432p. 22.00 o.s.i (*0-385-47310-9*); 1992. 400p. pap. 12.95 o.p. (*0-385-47311-7*) Doubleday Publishing.
—A Map of the World. l.t. ed. 1995. (G. K. Hall Core Ser.). 587p. 24.95 o.p. (*0-7838-1189-6*, Macmillan Reference USA) Gale Group.
—A Map of the World. abr. ed. 1999. audio 9.99 o.s.i (*0-553-70206-8*); 1995. audio 18.00 (*0-553-52737-1*) Random Hse. Audio Publishing Group. (RH Audio).
—A Map of the World. 1999. 400p. pap. 12.95 (*0-385-72010-6*, Knopf Bks. for Young Readers) Random Hse. Children's Bks.
—A Map of the World. unabr. ed. 1995. audio 97.00 (*0-7887-0195-9*, 94419K8) Recorded Bks., LLC.
—A Map of the World. 1995. 19.00 (*0-606-18125-3*) Turtleback Bks.
—The Short History of a Prince: A Novel. l.t. ed. 1998. 496p. 23.00 o.p. (*0-7838-8343-9*, Macmillan Reference USA) Gale Group.
—The Short History of a Prince: A Novel. 1999. 368p. pap. 12.95 (*0-385-47948-4*, Knopf Bks. for Young Readers) Random Hse. Children's Bks.
Harsch, Rick. Billy Verite. 1999. (Illus.). 263p. pap. 13.00 (*1-883642-57-4*) Steerforth Pr.
—Billy Verite: A Novel. 1998. 230p. 22.00 o.p. (*1-883642-92-2*) Steerforth Pr.
—The Driftless Zone. 1999. 201p. pap. 12.00 (*1-883642-58-2*); 1997. 200p. 21.00 o.p. (*1-883642-32-9*) Steerforth Pr.
Hart, Ellen. A Small Sacrifice. 1994. (Jane Lawless Mysteries Ser.). 300p. 20.95 (*1-878067-55-9*, Seal Pr.) Avalon Publishing Group.
Houston, Victoria. Dead Angler. 2000. (Loon Lake Fishing Mysteries Ser.). 272p. mass mkt. 6.50 (*0-425-17355-0*, Prime Crime) Berkley Publishing Group.
—Dead Creek. 2000. (Loon Lake Fishing Mysteries Ser.). 288p. mass mkt. 6.50 (*0-425-17703-3*, Prime Crime) Berkley Publishing Group.
Howard, Sara. Fantasy Man. 2001. (Romance Ser.). 256p. mass mkt. 4.99 o.p. (*0-8217-6793-3*) Kensington Publishing Corp.
Isaacs, Susan. Red, White & Blue. unabr. ed. 1999. audio 83.95 (*0-7861-1519-X*, 2369) Blackstone Audio Bks., Inc.
Kerr, Simon. The Rainbow Singer: A Novel. 2003. pap. (*0-7868-8682-X*); 2002. 304p. 23.95 (*0-7868-6798-1*) Hyperion Pr.
King, Stephen. Black House. 2003. 688p. pap. 15.95 (*0-345-47063-X*) Ballantine Bks.
King, Stephen & Straub, Peter. Black House. 2001. E-Book 19.95 (*1-59061-169-1*) Adobe Systems, Inc.
—Black House. 2002. 672p. mass mkt. (*0-345-45925-3*); mass mkt. 7.99 (*0-345-44103-6*, Ballantine Bks.) Ballantine Bks.
—Black House, 2 vols. deluxe ed. 2001. 225.00 (*1-880418-52-5*) Grant, Donald M. Pub., Inc.
—Black House. unabr. ed. 2001. audio 54.98. audio compact disk 80.00 (*0-7393-0011-3*); audio 54.95 (*0-7393-0010-5*) Random Hse. Audio Publishing Group. (RH Audio).
—Black House. l.t. ed. 2001. 1056p. 28.95 (*0-375-43151-9*) Random Hse. Large Print.
—Black House. 2002. 672p. mass mkt. 7.99 (*0-345-45121-X*); 2001. E-Book 19.95 (*1-58836-054-7*) Random Hse., Inc.
Kokoris, Jim. Sister North: A Novel. 2003. (Illus.). 256p. 23.95 (*0-312-27540-4*) St. Martin's Pr.
Kopetz, Mark. Trolls at the Door: A Door County Story. 1995. (Illus.). 62p. (Orig.). (YA). pap. 8.95 (*0-940473-29-1*) Caxton, Wm Ltd.
Kringle, Karen. Vital Ties. 1992. 280p. (Orig.). pap. 10.95 (*0-933216-90-4*) Spinsters Ink Bks.
Kunkel, Jeff. Bless Ewe: More Stories. 2000. 181p. 18.95 (*1-883953-31-6*, Face to Face Bks.) Midwest Traditions, Inc.
Lee, Rachel. Conard County: Boots & Badges. abr. ed. 1999. (Silhouette Romance Ser.). audio 7.99 o.p. (*1-56740-522-3*, 1827, Silhouette Romance Audio) Brilliance Audio.
Logue, Mary. Blood Country. 2001. (WWL Mystery Ser.: No. 381). 251p. mass mkt. (*0-373-26381-3*, 1-26381-3, Worldwide Library) Harlequin Enterprises, Ltd.
—Blood Country. 1999. (Clare Watkins Mysteries Ser.). 312p. 23.95 (*0-8027-3339-5*) Walker & Co.
—Dark Coulee. l.t. ed. 2001. (Thorndike Mystery Ser.). 351p. 28.95 (*0-7862-3176-9*) Thorndike Pr.
—Dark Coulee. 2000. (Claire Watkins Mystery Ser.). 231p. 23.95 (*0-8027-3351-4*) Walker & Co.
Milofsky, David. A Friend of Kissinger: A Novel. 2003. (Library of American Fiction). 222p. 24.95 (*0-299-18520-6*) Univ. of Wisconsin Pr.
Monroe, Debra. A Wild, Cold State: Stories. 272p. 1996. pap. 11.00 (*0-684-81511-7*, Scribner Paper Fiction); 1995. 21.00 (*0-671-89717-9*, Simon & Schuster) Simon & Schuster.
Nevins, Francis M. Beneficiaries' Requiem. 2000. (Five Star Mystery Ser.). 219p. 20.95 (*0-7862-2373-1*, Five Star) Gale Group.
Nunez, Elizabeth. Beyond the Limbo Silence. 1998. 320p. 24.00 o.p. (*1-58005-017-4*); pap. 12.00 (*1-58005-013-1*) Avalon Publishing Group. (Seal Pr.).
—Beyond the Limbo Silence. 2003. 336p. pap. 13.95 (*0-345-45108-2*, One World/Ballantine) Ballantine Bks.
O'Nan, Stewart. A Prayer for the Dying: A Novel. l.t. ed. 2000. (Wheeler Large Print Book Ser.). 196p. 26.95 (*1-56895-841-2*, Wheeler Publishing, Inc.) Gale Group.
—A Prayer for the Dying: A Novel. 1999. 195p. 22.00 o.s.i (*0-8050-6147-9*) Holt, Henry & Co.
—A Prayer for the Dying: A Novel. 2000. 208p. pap. 13.00 (*0-312-25501-2*) Picador.
Packer, Ann. The Dive from Clausen's Pier. 2002. 384p. 24.00 (*0-375-41282-4*) Knopf, Alfred A. Inc.
Ridley, Elizabeth. Rainey's Lament. 1999. 300p. 24.95 (*0-87951-949-5*) Overlook Pr., The.
—Rainey's Lament. 1998. 300p. pap. o.s.i (*1-86049-412-9*) Virago Pr., Ltd. GBR. *Dist:* Little Brown & Co.
—Throwing Roses. 1993. 131p. 24.00 (*1-877946-29-X*) Permanent Pr., The.
Riederer, Joe. Restoration in the Barrens: The Story of a Young Teen's Struggle to Rebuild His Life While Helping to Rebuild a Local Prairie. 1999. 144p. pap. 14.95 (*0-9671386-0-4*) Big Bluestem Pr.
Riggs, John R. Cold Hearts & Gentle People. 1994. 272p. 17.95 (*1-56980-021-9*) Barricade Bks., Inc.
—Dead Letter. 1992. 15.95 (*0-942637-40-2*) Barricade Bks., Inc.
—Dead Letter. 1994. 208p. mass mkt. 4.50 o.s.i (*0-515-11280-1*, Jove) Berkley Publishing Group.
—A Dragon Lives Forever. 1992. (Garth Ryland Mystery Ser.). 344p. 17.95 (*0-942637-78-X*) Barricade Bks., Inc.
—A Dragon Lives Forever. 1994. 224p. reprint ed. mass mkt. 4.50 o.p. (*0-425-14301-5*, Prime Crime) Berkley Publishing Group.
—Glory Hound. 1986. (Garth Ryland Mystery Ser.). 14.95 o.p. (*0-934878-78-1*, Dembner Bks.) Barricade Bks., Inc.
—Haunt of the Nightingale. (Garth Ryland Mystery Ser.). 224p. 15.95 o.p. (*0-934878-97-8*, Dembner Bks.) Barricade Bks., Inc.
—Haunt of the Nightingale. 1992. 192p. mass mkt. 3.99 o.s.i (*0-515-10953-3*, Jove) Berkley Publishing Group.
—He Who Waits: A Garth Ryland Mystery. 1997. (Garth Ryland Mystery Ser.). 288p. 17.95 (*1-56980-096-0*) Barricade Bks., Inc.
—Killing Frost: A Garth Ryland Mystery. 1995. 304p. 17.95 (*1-56980-053-7*) Barricade Bks., Inc.
—The Last Laugh. l.t. ed. 1992. 19.95 o.p. (*0-7927-1394-X*); pap. 17.95 o.p. (*0-7927-1393-1*) BBC Audiobooks America.
—The Last Laugh. 1984. (Garth Ryland Mystery Ser.). 191p. 13.95 o.p. (*0-934878-37-4*, Dembner Bks.) Barricade Bks., Inc.
—The Last Laugh. 1993. 192p. mass mkt. 3.99 o.s.i (*0-515-11134-1*, Jove) Berkley Publishing Group.
—The Last Laugh. 1988. mass mkt. 2.95 (*0-312-91131-9*, St. Martin's Paperbacks) St. Martin's Pr.
—Let Sleeping Dogs Lie. 1986. (Garth Ryland Mystery Ser.). 14.95 o.p. (*0-934878-67-6*, Dembner Bks.) Barricade Bks., Inc.
—Let Sleeping Dogs Lie. 1993. mass mkt. 4.50 o.s.i (*0-515-11211-9*, Jove) Berkley Publishing Group.
—Let Sleeping Dogs Lie. 1988. mass mkt. 3.50 (*0-312-91140-8*, St. Martin's Paperbacks) St. Martin's Pr.
—The Lost Scout: A Garth Ryland Mystery. 1998. 352p. 17.95 (*1-56980-121-5*) Barricade Bks., Inc.
—One Man's Poison. 1991. (Garth Ryland Mystery Ser.). 17.95 o.p. (*0-942637-31-3*, Dembner Bks.) Barricade Bks., Inc.
—One Man's Poison, No. 4. 1993. 208p. mass mkt. 3.99 o.s.i (*0-515-11078-7*, Jove) Berkley Publishing Group.
—Snow on the Roses: A Garth Ryland Mystery. 1996. 272p. 17.95 (*1-56980-072-3*) Barricade Bks., Inc.
—Wolf in Sheep's Clothing. 1993. 192p. (Orig.). mass mkt. 3.99 o.s.i (*0-515-11016-7*, Jove) Berkley Publishing Group.
—Wolf in Sheep's Clothing: A Garth Ryland Mystery. 1989. 16.95 o.p. (*0-942637-16-X*, Dembner Bks.) Barricade Bks., Inc.
Rizzo, Kay D. Seasons of the Heart. 1987. (Destiny Ser.). 96p. pap. 4.99 o.p. (*0-8163-0703-2*) Pacific Pr. Publishing Assn.
Rolofson, Kristine, et al. Tyler Brides: Meant for Each Other; Behind Closed Doors; The Bride's Surprise, 3 bks. in 1. 2001. 378p. mass mkt. (*0-373-83457-8*, 1-83457-1, Harlequin Bks.) Harlequin Enterprises, Ltd.
Ross, Dana Fuller, pseud. Wisconsin! 1987. (Wagons West Ser.: No. 19). 320p. mass mkt. 4.95 o.s.i (*0-553-26533-4*) Bantam Bks.
—Wisconsin! l.t. ed. 1988. 420p. 17.95 o.p. (*0-8161-4384-6*, Macmillan Reference USA) Gale Group.
Rubino, Jane, et al. Homicide for the Holidays: Fruitcake; Milwaukee Winters Can Be Murder; A Perfect Time for Murder. 2000. (WWL Mystery Ser.: Vol. 362). 512p. mass mkt. (*0-373-26362-7*, 1-26362-3, Worldwide Library) Harlequin Enterprises, Ltd.
Russell, D. Dreamdust. 2001. 201p. pap. (*1-55212-637-4*) Trafford Publishing.
Schulenburg, Marnie. Murder off the Record. 1998. 304p. 23.95 o.p. (*1-885173-50-4*) Write Way Publishing.
Schwarz, Christina. Drowning Ruth: A Novel. 2001. (Reader's Circle Ser.). 368p. pap. 14.95 (*0-345-43910-4*, Ballantine Bks.) Ballantine Bks.
—Drowning Ruth: A Novel. 2000. 352p. 23.95 o.s.i (*0-385-49971-X*) Doubleday Publishing.
—Drowning Ruth: A Novel. l.t. ed. (Wheeler Press Paperback Ser.). 2001. pap. 12.95 (*1-56895-179-5*); 2000. 422p. 28.95 (*1-56895-959-1*) Gale Group. (Wheeler Publishing, Inc.).
—Drowning Ruth: A Novel. 2001. 20.05 (*0-606-21165-9*) Turtleback Bks.
Simpson, Mona. Off Keck Road. E-Book 15.95 (*1-58945-518-5*) Adobe Systems, Inc.
—Off Keck Road. 2001. E-Book 10.00 (*0-375-41263-8*) Random Hse., Inc.
—Off Keck Road. l.t. ed. 2001. (Thorndike Press Large Print Women's Fiction Ser.). 229p. (*0-7862-3242-0*) Thorndike Pr.
—Off Keck Road: A Novella. 2001. 176p. reprint ed. pap. 11.00 (*0-375-70906-1*, Vintage) Knopf Publishing Group.
Snyder, Mary. Glare Ice: A Claire Watkins Mystery. 2001. 240p. 23.95 (*0-8027-3371-9*) Walker & Co.
Steuber, William. The Landlooker. 2nd ed. 1991. (Prairie Classics Ser.: Vol. 1). 372p. pap. 12.95 (*1-879483-04-1*) Prairie Oak Pr., Inc.
Thayer, Steve. The Wheat Field. 2002. 288p. 24.95 o.s.i (*0-399-14841-8*) Putnam Publishing Group, The.
—The Wheat Field, 5 cass. 2002. audio 24.99 (*1-4025-1179-5*, 01244) Recorded Bks., LLC.
—The Wheat Field. l.t. ed. 2002. (Mystery Ser.). 408p. 30.45 (*0-7862-4438-0*) Thorndike Pr.
—Wolf Pass. 2004. 368p. mass mkt. 7.99 (*0-451-41131-5*, Onyx) NAL.
—Wolf Pass. 2003. 304p. 24.95 (*0-399-14991-0*) Penguin Group (USA) Inc.
—Wolf Pass. 2003. (Mystery Ser.). 380p. 30.45 (*0-7862-5254-5*) Thorndike Pr.
Thompson, Craig. Blankets. 2003. (Illus.). 592p. pap. 29.95 (*1-891830-43-0*) Top Shelf Productions.
Tracy, P. J. Monkeewrench. 2004. 432p. mass mkt. 6.99 (*0-451-21157-X*, Signet Bks.) NAL.
—Monkeewrench. 2003. 384p. 23.95 (*0-399-14978-3*, Putnam & Grosset) Putnam Publishing Group, The.
—Monkeewrench. l.t. ed. 2003. 547p. 28.95 (*0-7862-5645-1*) Thorndike Pr.
Van Meter, Homer. Day of the Little Guy. 1996. 196p. 18.50 (*1-880664-16-X*) E. M. Productions.
Wanderer, Pauline. Dream Girl at Mystery Lake: A Door County Adventure. 1995. (J). pap. 8.95 (*0-940473-28-3*) Caxton, Wm Ltd.
Watson, Larry. Orchard: A Novel. 2004. 256p. pap. 13.95 (*0-375-75854-2*, Random Hse. Trade Paperbacks) Random House Adult Trade Publishing Group.
—Orchard: A Novel. 2003. 256p. 24.95 (*0-375-50723-X*) Random Hse., Inc.
Wescott, Glenway. The Grandmothers. 1986. pap. 6.95 o.p. (*0-87795-799-1*, Morrow, William & Co.) Morrow/Avon.
—The Grandmothers: A Family Portrait. 1962. pap. 1.45 o.p. (*0-689-70205-1*, 11, Atheneum) Simon & Schuster Children's Publishing.
—The Grandmothers: A Family Portrait. 1996. 412p. 49.95 (*0-299-15020-8*); pap. 19.95 (*0-299-15024-0*) Univ. of Wisconsin Pr.
Wick, Lori. The Long Road Home. 1991. (Fireside Ser.). 224p. pap. 6.99 o.s.i (*0-89081-885-1*); 1997. (Place Called Home Ser.: Vol. 3). 192p. reprint ed. pap. 8.99 (*1-56507-590-0*) Harvest Hse. Pubs.
—The Long Road Home. l.t. ed. 2001. (Christian Romance Ser.). (Illus.). 288p. 25.95 o.p. (*0-7862-2956-X*) Thorndike Pr.
—A Song for Silas. 204p. 1996. (Place Called Home Ser.: Vol. 2). pap. 8.99 (*1-56507-589-7*); 1990. pap. 6.99 o.s.i (*0-89081-839-8*) Harvest Hse. Pubs.
—A Song for Silas. l.t. ed. 2000. (Christian Romance Ser.). (Illus.). 270p. 25.95 (*0-7862-2728-1*) Thorndike Pr.
—Sophie's Heart. 1995. 425p. pap. 10.99 (*1-56507-311-8*); 2nd ed. 2003. reprint ed. mass mkt. 6.99 (*0-7369-1279-7*) Harvest Hse. Pubs.
—Sophie's Heart. l.t. ed. 1999. (Romance Ser.). 643p. 28.95 (*0-7838-0432-6*) Thorndike Pr.
Wilkes, Maria D. Frontier Family. 2000. (Little House Chapter Bks.: No. 3). (Illus.). 80p. (J). (gr. 3-6). lib. bdg. 14.89 (*0-06-028157-X*) HarperCollins Children's Bk. Group.
—Frontier Family. 1999. (Little House Chapter Bks.: No. 3). (Illus.). (J). (gr. 3-6). 10.40 (*0-606-18681-6*) Turtleback Bks.
Wright, Scott. The Lynching of John Hanson. 1986. 160p. (Orig.). pap. 9.95 o.p. (*1-55618-000-4*) Brunswick Publishing Corp.
Zettel, Sarah. The Usurper's Crown: A Novel of Isavalta. 2003. (Isavalta Ser.). 528p. 27.95 (*0-312-87442-1*, Tor Bks.) Doherty, Tom Assocs., LLC.
Zimmerman, R. D. Mindscream. 1989. 288p. 17.95 o.p. (*1-55611-137-1*) Fine, Donald I. Bks.
—Mindscream. 1990. mass mkt. 3.95 o.s.i (*0-8217-3099-1*, Zebra Bks.) Kensington Publishing Corp.
—Mindscream. 1991. 3.99 o.p. (*0-517-07483-4*) Random Hse. Value Publishing.

**WITCH WORLD (IMAGINARY PLACE)—FICTION**

Norton, Andre. The Crystal Gryphon. 1973. (Science Fiction Ser.). mass mkt. 2.25 o.p. (*0-87997-701-9*, UE1701); mass mkt. 0.95 o.p. (*0-87997-076-6*); mass mkt. 1.25 o.p. (*0-87997-187-8*); mass mkt. 1.75 o.p. (*0-87997-428-1*); mass mkt. 1.95 o.p. (*0-87997-586-5*) DAW Bks., Inc.
—The Crystal Gryphon. 1985. 256p. reprint ed. mass mkt. 2.95 (*0-8125-4738-1*, Tor Bks.) Doherty, Tom Assocs., LLC.
—Four from the Witch World. 1989. (Witch World). 288p. mass mkt. 5.99 o.s.i (*0-8125-1006-2*); 16.95 o.p. (*0-312-93153-0*) Doherty, Tom Assocs., LLC. (Tor Bks.).
—The Gate of the Cat. (Illus.). 256p. 1988. mass mkt. 3.50 o.s.i (*0-441-27380-7*); 1987. 16.95 o.p. (*0-441-27376-9*) Ace Bks.
—The Gates of Witch World. 2001. (Witch World). (Illus.). 464p. 27.95 (*0-7653-0050-8*, Tor Bks.) Doherty, Tom Assocs., LLC.
—Gryphon in Glory. 1986. 224p. mass mkt. 2.95 o.s.i (*0-345-34243-7*); 1983. mass mkt. 2.50 o.p. (*0-345-30950-2*) Ballantine Bks. (Del Rey).
—The Jargoon Pard. 1983. 224p. mass mkt. 2.95 o.s.i (*0-345-31192-2*); 1980. mass mkt. 1.95 o.p. (*0-449-23615-3*, Fawcett) Ballantine Bks.
—Lore of the Witch World. 1980. (Witchworld Ser.). mass mkt. 1.95 o.p. (*0-87997-560-1*); mass mkt. 2.25 o.p. (*0-87997-634-9*); mass mkt. 2.50 o.p. (*0-87997-750-7*); mass mkt. 2.95 o.p. (*0-88677-012-2*); mass mkt. 2.50 o.p. (*0-88677-335-0*); mass mkt. 3.50 o.p. (*0-88677-243-5*) DAW Bks., Inc.
—Sorceress of the Witch World. 1986. (Witch World Ser.: 6). 288p. mass mkt. 3.50 o.s.i (*0-441-77558-6*); 1981. mass mkt. 2.50 o.s.i (*0-441-77556-X*) Ace Bks.
—Spell of the Witch World. 1972. (Science Fiction Ser.). 224p. (Orig.). mass mkt. 3.50 o.p. (*0-88677-242-7*) DAW Bks., Inc.
—Tales of the Witch World. 1989. 343p. mass mkt. 5.99 o.s.i (*0-8125-4757-8*); No. 3. 1991. mass mkt. 3.95 (*0-8125-1336-3*); No.3. 1990. 18.95 o.p. (*0-312-85044-1*) Doherty, Tom Assocs., LLC. (Tor Bks.).
—Three Against the Witch World. 1977. lib. bdg. 10.50 o.p. (*0-8398-2358-4*, Macmillan Reference USA) Gale Group.
—The Warding of Witch World. (Secrets of the Witch World Ser.: Vol. 3). 2001. 590p. pap. 4.95 (*0-446-51991-X*); 1998. 608p. mass mkt. 6.99 (*0-446-60369-4*) Warner Bks., Inc.
—Warlock of the Witch World. 1986. (Witch World Ser.: No. 5). mass mkt. 3.50 o.s.i (*0-441-87316-2*) Ace Bks.
—Web of the Witch World. 1986. (Witch World Ser.: 2). mass mkt. 3.50 o.s.i (*0-441-87879-2*) Ace Bks.
—Witch World. 1986. 288p. mass mkt. 3.50 o.s.i (*0-441-89708-8*); 1984. mass mkt. 2.50 o.s.i (*0-441-89707-X*); 1982. mass mkt. 2.50 o.s.i (*0-441-89706-1*); No. 3. 1981. mass mkt. 3.50 o.s.i (*0-441-94255-5*) Ace Bks.
—Witch World No. 4: Three Against Witch World. 1986. mass mkt. 3.50 o.s.i (*0-441-80808-5*) Ace Bks.
—Witch World No. 8: Zarsthor's Bane. 1986. mass mkt. 3.50 o.s.i (*0-441-95493-6*) Ace Bks.
—The Witch World Novels. 1979. 65.00 o.p. (*0-8398-7000-0*, Macmillan Reference USA) Gale Group.
—Witch World Omnibus, No. 2. Date not set. (*0-7653-0052-4*, Tor Bks.) Doherty, Tom Assocs., LLC.

—Year of the Unicorn. 1989. (Witch World Ser.: No. 3). 288p. mass mkt. 2.75 o.s.i (0-441-94256-3) Ace Bks.

Norton, Andre, ed. Tales of the Witch World. 1988. 352p. 16.95 o.p. (0-312-93078-X, Tor Bks.) Doherty, Tom Assocs., LLC.

Norton, Andre & Crispin, A. C. Songsmith. 1993. 294p. mass mkt. 4.99 (0-8125-1107-7); 1992. 304p. 19.95 (0-312-85123-5) Doherty, Tom Assocs., LLC. (Tor Bks.).

Norton, Andre & Griffin, P. M. Storms of Victory. (Witch World: Vol. 1). 1992. mass mkt. 4.99 (0-8125-1109-3); 1991. 19.95 o.p. (0-312-93171-9) Doherty, Tom Assocs., LLC. (Tor Bks.).

Norton, Andre & McConchie, Lyn. Ciara's Song: A Chronicle of Witch World. 1998. (Witch World Ser.). 256p. mass mkt. 6.50 (0-446-60644-8) Warner Bks., Inc.

Norton, Andre, et al. Flight of Vengeance. 1994. 383p. pap. text 4.99 o.s.i (0-8125-0706-1); 1992. (Witch World: Vol. 2). 384p. 21.95 o.p. (0-312-85014-X) Doherty, Tom Assocs., LLC. (Tor Bks.).

—On Wings of Magic: Witch World, the Turning, Bk. 3. 1993. 448p. 23.95 o.p. (0-312-85026-3, Tor Bks.) Doherty, Tom Assocs., LLC.

**WORLD OF TIERS (IMAGINARY PLACE)—FICTION**

Farmer, Philip Jose. Behind the Walls of Terra. 1981. mass mkt. 2.50 o.s.i (0-441-05374-2) Ace Bks.

—Behind the Walls of Terra. 1984. 224p. 2.75 o.s.i (0-425-07558-3) Berkley Publishing Group.

—Behind the Walls of Terra. 1993. reprint ed. lib. bdg. 18.95 (0-89968-400-9, Lightyear Pr.) Buccaneer Bks., Inc.

—Behind the Walls of Terra, No. 4. 1982. (World of Tiers Ser.). 18.00 o.p. (0-932096-13-1) Phantasia Pr.

—The Gates of Creation. 1983. 224p. mass mkt. 2.75 o.s.i (0-441-27390-4) Ace Bks.

—The Gates of Creation. 1984. (World of Tiers Ser.: No. 2). 192p. 2.75 o.s.i (0-425-07193-6) Berkley Publishing Group.

—The Gates of Creation. 1993. reprint ed. lib. bdg. 18.95 (0-89968-398-3, Lightyear Pr.) Buccaneer Bks., Inc.

—The Gates of Creation, No. 2. 1981. (World of Tiers Ser.). 15.00 (0-932096-08-5) Phantasia Pr.

—The Lavalite World. 1983. (World of Tiers Ser.). 288p. mass mkt. 2.75 o.s.i (0-441-47422-5) Ace Bks.

—The Lavalite World. 1985. (World of Tiers Ser.: No. 5). 288p. 2.95 o.p. (0-425-08625-9); 2.75 o.s.i (0-425-07515-X) Berkley Publishing Group.

—The Lavalite World. 1993. reprint ed. lib. bdg. 18.95 (0-89968-401-7, Lightyear Pr.) Buccaneer Bks., Inc.

—The Lavalite World. 1983. (World of Tiers Ser.: No. 5). 18.00 (0-932096-21-2) Phantasia Pr.

—The Maker of Universes. 1984. (World of Tiers Ser.: No. 1). 256p. 2.75 o.p. (0-425-07378-5) Ace Bks.

—The Maker of Universes. 1993. reprint ed. lib. bdg. 18.95 (0-89968-397-5, Lightyear Pr.) Buccaneer Bks., Inc.

—The Maker of Universes. Del Rey, Lester, ed. 1975. (Library of Science Fiction). lib. bdg. 21.00 o.p. (0-8240-1408-1) Garland Publishing, Inc.

—The Maker of Universes. rev. ed. 1980. (World of Tiers Ser.: No. 1). 224p. reprint ed. 15.00 (0-932096-07-7) Phantasia Pr.

—More Than Fire: A World of Tiers Novel. 1995. 320p. pap. 5.99 (0-8125-1959-0); 1993. 304p. 20.95 o.p. (0-312-85280-0) Doherty, Tom Assocs., LLC. (Tor Bks.).

—A Private Cosmos. 1981. 288p. mass mkt. 2.50 o.s.i (0-441-67954-4) Ace Bks.

—A Private Cosmos. 1993. reprint ed. lib. bdg. 18.95 (0-89968-399-1, Lightyear Pr.) Buccaneer Bks., Inc.

—A Private Cosmos, No. 3. 1981. (World of Tiers Ser.). 18.00 (0-932096-10-7) Phantasia Pr.

—Red Orc's Rage. 1991. 18.95 o.p. (0-312-85036-0); 1992. 288p. reprint ed. mass mkt. 4.99 (0-8125-0890-4) Doherty, Tom Assocs., LLC. (Tor Bks.).

**WORLD OF TWO MOONS (IMAGINARY PLACE)—FICTION**

Auklandus, Joellyn, et al. Wild Hunt. Pini, Wendy, ed. 2000. (Elfquest Reader's Collection: Bk. 11b). (Illus.). 240p. pap. 13.95 (0-936861-70-3, Wolfrider Bks.) Warp Graphics, Inc.

Cerriteli, Elizabeth. Sea Elves: A Complete Culture for Elfquest. Kahn, Sherman, ed. 1985. (Illus.). 48p. pap. 7.95 o.p. (0-933635-24-9) Chaosium, Inc.

Cerritelli, Elizabeth & Petersen, Sandy. Elf War: Hubward Adventures of the World of Two Moons. Willis, Lynn, ed. 1987. (Illus.). 40p. (Orig.). (YA). (gr. 9 up). pap. 7.95 o.p. (0-933635-32-X, 2604) Chaosium, Inc.

Decker, Dwight, ed. Elfquest Gatherum, Vol. 1. 1987. 144p. reprint ed. pap. 8.95 o.p. (0-936861-02-9, Father Tree Pr.) Warp Graphics, Inc.

Elfquest V02 Digest Size. 1988. pap. 5.95 o.p. (0-89865-715-6) Donning Co. Pubs.

Harkins, Bern. Skyward Shadow. Pini, Richard, ed. 1999. (Elfquest Reader's Collection: Bk. 13a). (Illus.). 160p. pap. 11.95 (0-936861-49-5, Wolfrider Bks.) Warp Graphics, Inc.

Harkins, Bern, et al. The Rebels. 1998. (Elfquest Graphic Novels Ser.: Bk. 13). (Illus.). 160p. pap. text 11.95 (0-936861-47-9, Wolfrider Bks.) Warp Graphics, Inc.

Lee, Wendy. Elfquest Bedtime Stories. Pini, Richard, ed. 1994. (Illus.). 128p. (J). pap. 19.95 (0-936861-37-1, Father Tree Pr.) Warp Graphics, Inc.

Littlegreen, Inc. Think Tank Staff. Transfiguration Diet. 1986. (Illus.). 176p. (Orig.). pap. 7.95 (0-936863-04-8, Littlegreen) Christopher Publishing.

Perrin, Steve. Elfquest. Chodak, Yurek, ed. 1984. (Illus.). 136p. 19.95 o.p. (0-933635-09-5, 2601-X) Chaosium, Inc.

—Elfquest: The Official Roleplaying Game. Chodak, Yurek, ed. 2nd ed. 1989. (Elfquest Roleplaying Game System Ser.). (Illus.). 192p. (YA). (gr. 9 up). pap. 19.95 o.p. (0-933635-54-0, 2605) Chaosium, Inc.

Perrin, Steve & Petersen, Steve. The Elfquest Companion. D'Arn, Gigi, ed. 1985. (Illus.). 40p. pap. 6.00 o.p. (0-933635-19-2) Chaosium, Inc.

Pini, Richard. Dark Hours: Blood of Ten Chiefs. 1993. (Elfquest Ser.: Vol. 5). pap. 7.99 o.p. (0-8125-2341-5, Tor Bks.) Doherty, Tom Assocs., LLC.

—Elfquest: Against the Wind, Vol. 4. 1990. pap. 7.95 o.p. (0-8125-4906-6, Tor Bks.) Doherty, Tom Assocs., LLC.

—Elfquest: Winds of Change, Vol. 3. 1990. 384p. mass mkt. 4.50 (0-8125-0700-2); 1989. pap. 7.95 o.p. (0-8125-4905-8) Doherty, Tom Assocs., LLC. (Tor Bks.).

—Elfquest Gatherum, Vol. 2. 1988. 144p. (Orig.). pap. 8.95 o.p. (0-936861-03-7, Father Tree Pr.) Warp Graphics, Inc.

—Wolfsong, Vol. 2. 1989. (Elfquest Ser.: Vol. 2). 307p. mass mkt. 4.50 (0-8125-0377-5, Tor Bks.) Doherty, Tom Assocs., LLC.

Pini, Richard, ed. Big Elfquest Gatherum. 1995. (Illus.). 244p. 19.95 o.p. (0-936861-13-4, Father Tree Pr.) Warp Graphics, Inc.

Pini, Richard, et al, eds. Elfquest: Blood of Ten Chiefs, Vol. 1. (Orig.). 1987. pap. 3.50 o.p. (0-8125-3043-8); 1986. 320p. pap. 6.95 o.p. (0-8125-3041-1) Doherty, Tom Assocs., LLC. (Tor Bks.).

—Elfquest: Wolfsong, Vol. 2. 1988. 320p. pap. 7.95 o.p. (0-8125-3037-3, Tor Bks.) Doherty, Tom Assocs., LLC.

Pini, Richard & Auklandus, Joellyn. Huntress. 1999. (Elfquest Reader's Collection: Bk. 11a). (Illus.). 176p. pap. 11.95 (0-936861-46-0, Wolfrider Bks.) Warp Graphics, Inc.

Pini, Richard & Murphy, Vickie. Wave Dancers. 2000. (Elfquest Graphic Novels Ser.: Bk. 16). (Illus.). 176p. pap. 11.95 (0-936861-71-1, Wolfrider Bks.) Warp Graphics, Inc.

Pini, Richard & Pini, Wendy. Captives of Blue Mountain - Elfquest, Bk. 3. 1999. (Elfquest Graphic Novels Ser.: 3). (Illus.). 176p. (YA). pap. text 11.95 (0-936861-57-6, Wolfrider Bks.) Warp Graphics, Inc.

—Fire & Flight. 1999. (Elfquest Reader's Collection: Bk. 1). (Illus.). 176p. pap. text 11.95 (0-936861-55-X, Wolfrider Bks.) Warp Graphics, Inc.

—Quest's End. 1999. (Elfquest Reader's Collection: Bk. 4). (Illus.). 192p. pap. text 11.95 (0-936861-58-4, Wolfrider Bks.) Warp Graphics, Inc.

—The Secret of Two-Edge. 1999. (Elfquest Reader's Collection: Bk. 6). (Illus.). 128p. pap. text 11.95 (0-936861-60-6, Wolfrider Bks.) Warp Graphics, Inc.

—Shards: Elfquest Reader's Collection. 1998. (Elfquest Graphic Novels Ser.: Vol. 10). (Illus.). 256p. pap. text 13.95 (0-936861-42-8, Wolfrider Bks.) Warp Graphics, Inc.

—Siege at Blue Mountain. 1999. (Elfquest Reader's Collection: Bk. 5). (Illus.). 128p. pap. text 11.95 (0-936861-59-2, Wolfrider Bks.) Warp Graphics, Inc.

Pini, Richard, et al. Elfquest Readers Collection 15A: Dream's End. 2001. (Elfquest Reader's Collection: Bk. 15a). (Illus.). 208p. pap. 12.95 (0-936861-65-7, Wolfrider Bks.) Warp Graphics, Inc.

—Forevergreen. 1999. (Elfquest Reader's Collection: Bk. 15). 224p. pap. 12.95 (0-936861-64-9) Warp Graphics, Inc.

Pini, Wendy. Ascent - Elfquest. Pini, Richard, ed. 1999. (Elfquest Readers Collection: 12). 208p. (YA). pap. 12.95 (0-936861-43-6, Wolfrider Bks.) Warp Graphics, Inc.

—The Cry from Beyond. 1999. (Elfquest Reader's Collection: Bk. 7). 128p. pap. 11.95 (0-936861-61-4, Wolfrider Bks.); 1991. (Elfquest Ser.). 17.95 o.s.i (0-936861-23-1) Warp Graphics, Inc.

—Elfquest. 1986. 3.50 o.s.i (0-425-09039-6); 1985. 2.95 o.s.i (0-425-08458-2); 1984. 2.95 o.s.i (0-425-07009-3) Berkley Publishing Group.

—Elfquest Bk. 1. 1988. pap. 5.95 o.p. (0-89865-626-5) Donning Co. Pubs.

—Elfquest 1998 Calendar: To Hunt, to Howl, to Live Free. 1997. pap. text 11.99 o.p. (0-936861-41-X) Warp Graphics, Inc.

—A Gift of Her Own: An Elfquest Story. 1996. (Illus.). 48p. (J). (gr. 4-7). 16.95 (0-936861-38-X) Warp Graphics, Inc.

—Kings of the Broken Wheel. 1999. (Elfquest Reader's Collection: Bk. 8). 160p. pap. text 11.95 (0-936861-62-2, Wolfrider Bks.) Warp Graphics, Inc.

—Mindcoil. 1999. (Elfquest Reader's Collection: Bk. 14a). (Illus.). 160p. pap. 11.95 (0-936861-50-9, Wolfrider Bks.) Warp Graphics, Inc.

—Quest Begins. 1997. (Elfquest Ser.). 240p. mass mkt. 5.99 o.s.i (0-441-00418-0) Ace Bks.

—Reunion. 1999. (Elfquest Reader's Collection: Bk. 12a). 208p. pap. 12.95 (0-936861-44-4, Wolfrider Bks.) Warp Graphics, Inc.

Pini, Wendy & Ostrander, John. Jink. 1999. (Elfquest Reader's Collection: Bk. 14). (Illus.). 160p. pap. text 11.95 (0-936861-48-7) Warp Graphics, Inc.

Pini, Wendy & Pini, Richard. Captives of Blue Mountain. 1997. (Elfquest Ser.: No. 3). 240p. (Orig.). mass mkt. 5.99 o.s.i (0-441-00492-X) Ace Bks.

—Captives of Blue Mountain - Elfquest, Book 3. rev. ed. 1988. (Elfquest Graphic Novels Ser.: 3). (Illus.). 192p. (Orig.). pap. 17.95 o.s.i (0-936861-08-8, Father Tree Pr.) Warp Graphics, Inc.

—The Complete ElfQuest. Reynolds, Kay, ed. ltd. ed. 1985. (ElfQuest Ser.). (Illus.). 652p. 120.00 o.p. (0-89865-453-X, Starblaze) Donning Co. Pubs.

—The Cry from Beyond, Bk. 7. 1993. (Elfquest Ser.). (Illus.). 160p. (J). (gr. 4 up). 19.95 o.s.i (0-936861-17-7) Warp Graphics, Inc.

—Dreamtime - Elfquest Book. 1998. (Elfquest Reader's Collection: 8A). (Illus.). 176p. (YA). pap. 11.95 (0-936861-52-5, Wolfrider Bks.) Warp Graphics, Inc.

—Elfquest. Reynolds, Kay, ed. (Illus.). Book 1. 1981. 35.00 o.p. (0-89865-166-2); Book 1. 1981. pap. 14.95 o.p. (0-89865-140-9); Book 2. 1982. 172p. (J). (gr. 5 up). pap. 14.95 o.p. (0-89865-245-6, Starblaze); Book 4. 1984. 172p. (J). (gr. 5 up). 40.00 o.p. (0-89865-378-9, Starblaze); Book 4. 1984. 172p. (J). (gr. 5 up). pap. 14.95 o.p. (0-89865-377-0, Starblaze) Donning Co. Pubs.

—Elfquest: Captives of Blue Mountain, Vol. 3. rev. ed. 1994. (Elfquest Graphic Novel Ser.: 3). (Illus.). 192p. (J). (gr. 4 up). 19.95 o.s.i (0-936861-19-3, Father Tree Pr.) Warp Graphics, Inc.

—Elfquest No. 2: The Quest Begins. 1996. 272p. (Orig.). pap. 11.00 o.p. (0-441-00294-3) Ace Bks.

—Elfquest Novel - Journey to Sorrow's End. 1993. 320p. mass mkt. 5.99 o.s.i (0-441-18371-9) Ace Bks.

—Fire & Flight. rev. ed. (Illus.). 192p. 1988. pap. 17.95 o.p. (0-936861-06-1, Father Tree Pr.); Bk. 1. 1993. (J). 19.95 o.s.i (0-936861-16-9) Warp Graphics, Inc.

—The Forbidden Grove. 1999. (Elfquest Reader's Collection: Bk. 2). 192p. pap. text 11.95 (0-936861-56-8, Wolfrider Bks.); 1988. (Illus.). 208p. pap. 17.95 o.p. (0-936861-07-X, Father Tree Pr.); Bk. 2. 1994. (Elfquest Ser.). (Illus.). 208p. (J). 19.95 o.s.i (0-936861-18-5) Warp Graphics, Inc.

—Kings of the Broken Wheel. (Elfquest Ser.). (Illus.). 160p. (J). 1992. 17.95 o.s.i (0-936861-24-X); Bk. 8. 1994. pap. 19.95 o.s.i (0-936861-36-3) Warp Graphics, Inc.

—Quest's End. rev. ed. (Elfquest Ser.). (Illus.). 208p. 1994. (J). 19.95 o.p. (0-936861-15-0); 1988. pap. 17.95 o.p. (0-936861-09-6, Father Tree Pr.) Warp Graphics, Inc.

—Rogue's Challenge, Bk. 9. 1994. (Elfquest Ser.). (Illus.). 160p. 19.95 o.s.i (0-936861-26-6) Warp Graphics, Inc.

—The Secret of Two-Edge. (Illus.). 144p. 1988. pap. 16.95 o.p. (0-936861-11-8, Father Tree Pr.); Bk. 6. 1994. (J). 19.95 o.s.i (0-936861-35-5) Warp Graphics, Inc.

—Siege at Blue Mountain. (Illus.). 144p. 1988. pap. 16.95 o.p. (0-936861-10-X, Father Tree Pr.); Bk. 5. 1994. (J). 19.95 o.s.i (0-936861-34-7) Warp Graphics, Inc.

—Wolfrider. 1999. (Elfquest Reader's Collection: Bk. 9a). (Illus.). 176p. pap. 11.95 (0-936861-67-3, Wolfrider Bks.) Warp Graphics, Inc.

Pini, Wendy & Pini, Richard, eds. Elfquest: New Blood. 1993. (Illus.). 176p. (YA). 19.95 (0-936861-31-2, Father Tree Pr.) Warp Graphics, Inc.

Pini, Wendy, et al. Elfquest Bk. 3. Reynolds, Kay, ed. 1983. (Illus.). 172p. 40.00 o.p. (0-89865-328-2); pap. 14.95 o.p. (0-89865-329-0) Donning Co. Pubs. (Starblaze).

—Kahvi. 2000. (Elfquest Readers Collection: Bk. 9c). (Illus.). 272p. pap. 13.95 (0-936861-74-6, Wolfrider Bks.) Warp Graphics, Inc.

—Legacy. 1998. (Elfquest Reader's Collection: Bk. 11). (Illus.). 176p. pap. text 11.95 (0-936861-45-2, Wolfrider Bks.) Warp Graphics, Inc.

—Rogue's Curse. 2000. (Elfquest Readers Collection: Bk. 9). (Illus.). 272p. (YA). pap. 13.95 (0-936861-72-X, Wolfrider Bks.) Warp Graphics, Inc.

—Shadowstalker. 2000. (Elfquest Reader's Collection: Bk. 11c). (Illus.). 176p. pap. 12.95 (0-936861-75-4, Wolfrider Bks.) Warp Graphics, Inc.

—Worldpool: An Elfquest Reader's Collection Special. 2000. (Elfquest Reader's Collection). (Illus.). 192p. pap. 12.95 (0-936861-73-8, Wolfrider Bks.) Warp Graphics, Inc.

Robeson, Theresa. Wolfrider's Guide to the World of Elfquest. 1997. (J). 19.95 o.p. (0-936861-39-8) Warp Graphics, Inc.

**WYOMING—FICTION**

Andrews, Sarah. Tensleep: An Em Hansen Mystery. 1995. (Em Hansen Mystery Ser.). 304p. mass mkt. 4.99 o.s.i (0-451-18606-0, Signet Bks.) NAL.

—Tensleep: An Em Hansen Mystery. 1994. 288p. 20.00 (1-883402-33-6, Scribner) Simon & Schuster.

Bausch, Richard. Rebel Powers. 1993. 352p. 21.95 o.p. (0-395-59508-8) Houghton Mifflin Co.

—Rebel Powers. 1994. 400p. pap. 12.00 o.s.i (0-679-75253-6, Vintage) Knopf Publishing Group.

Bean, Gregory. A Death in Victory: A Harry Starbranch Mystery. 1997. 323p. 24.95 o.p. (0-312-15512-3, Saint Martin's Minotaur) St. Martin's Pr.

—Grave Victory. 1998. (Harry Starbranch Mysteries Ser.). 336p. 23.95 (0-312-18590-1, Saint Martin's Minotaur) St. Martin's Pr.

—Long Shadows in Victory: A Harry Starbranch Mystery. (Dead Letter Mysteries Ser.). 1997. 336p. mass mkt. 5.99 (0-312-96217-7, St. Martin's Paperbacks); 1996. 352p. 23.95 o.p. (0-312-14348-6, Saint Martin's Minotaur) St. Martin's Pr.

—No Comfort in Victory: A Sheriff Harry Starbranch Mystery. 353p. 1996. mass mkt. 5.99 o.p. (0-312-95877-3, St. Martin's Paperbacks); 1995. 23.95 o.p. (0-312-13133-X, Saint Martin's Minotaur) St. Martin's Pr.

Benshoof-Holler, Margaret. Burning of the Marriage Hat: A Novel of High Plains Women. 2002. (Illus.). 381p. pap. 14.95 (0-9714473-2-2) Wind Women Pr.

Blakely, Mike. Snowy Range Gang. 1992. (Evans Novel of the West Ser.). 192p. 16.95 o.p. (0-87131-670-6) Evans, M. & Co., Inc.

Bly, Stephen A. Beneath a Dakota Cross. 1999. (Fortune of the Black Hills Ser.: Vol. 1). viii, 212p. pap. 9.99 (0-8054-1659-5) Broadman & Holman Pubs.

—Beneath a Dakota Cross. l.t. ed. 2001. lib. bdg. 26.95 (1-58547-083-X) Ctr. Point Large Print.

—Shadow of Legends. 2000. (Fortunes of the Black Hills Ser.: No. 2). viii, 212p. pap. 12.99 (0-8054-2174-2) Broadman & Holman Pubs.

—Shadow of Legends. l.t. ed. 2001. 304p. lib. bdg. 26.95 (1-58547-084-8) Ctr. Point Large Print.

—Stay Away from That City. . . They Call It Cheyenne. 1996. (Code of the West Ser.: Vol. 4). 192p. pap. 9.99 o.p. (0-89107-890-8) Crossway Bks.

Bowen, Judith & Roszel, Renee. Cowboy Country: The Man from Blue River; To Lasso a Lady, 2 bks. in 1. 2002. 496p. mass mkt. o.s.i (0-373-21726-9, 1-21726-4, Harlequin Bks.) Harlequin Enterprises, Ltd.

Bowen, Peter. Kelly & the Three-Toed Horse. 2001. 326p. 23.95 (0-312-24106-2) St. Martin's Pr.

Box, C. J. Open Season. 2002. 304p. reprint ed. mass mkt. 6.50 (0-425-18546-X, Prime Crime) Berkley Publishing Group.

—Open Season. 2002. lib. bdg. 28.95 (1-58547-248-4, Premier) Ctr. Point Large Print.

—Open Season. 2001. 304p. 23.95 (0-399-14748-9) Penguin Group (USA) Inc.

—Savage Run: A Joe Pickett Novel. 2003. 304p. mass mkt. 6.50 (0-425-18924-4, Prime Crime) Berkley Publishing Group.

—Savage Run: A Joe Pickett Novel. 2002. 288p. 23.95 (0-399-14887-6) Penguin Group (USA) Inc.

—Winterkill. 2004. 352p. mass mkt. 6.99 (0-425-19595-3) Berkley Publishing Group.

—Winterkill. abr. ed. 2004. (Joe Pickett Ser.). audio 12.99 (1-59086-949-4, 4551, Brilliance Audio Paperback Audiobooks); 2003. (Joe Pickett Series: Vol. 3). audio 24.95 (1-59086-948-6, 4550, Brilliance Audio); 2003. (Joe Pickett Series: Vol. 3). audio 32.95 (1-59086-946-X, 4548, Brilliance Audio Unabridged); 2003. (Joe Pickett Series: Vol. 3). audio 87.25 (1-59086-947-8, 4549, Unabridged Library Editions) Brilliance Audio.

—Winterkill. 2003. 239.50 (0-399-19746-X) Putnam Publishing Group, The.

—Winterkill: A Joe Pickett Novel. 2003. 384p. 23.95 (0-399-15045-5) Putnam Publishing Group, The.

Bragg, William F. Wyoming: Wild & Wooly. 1983. (Illus.). 168p. 14.95 o.p. (0-87108-628-X); pap. 7.95 o.p. (0-87108-631-X) Pruett Publishing Co.

Brooks, Bill. Leaving Cheyenne. 1999. 304p. mass mkt. 5.99 o.s.i (0-440-22652-X) Dell Publishing.

Brouwer, Sigmund. Evening Star. 2000. (Sam Keaton Ser.: Vol. 1). (Illus.). 320p. pap. 10.99 (*0-7642-2366-6*) Bethany Hse. Pubs.

—Morning Star. 1994. (Ghost Rider Ser.). 312p. (Orig.). pap. 9.99 (*1-56476-340-4*, 6-3340) Cook Communications Ministries.

—Silver Moon. 2000. (Sam Keaton Ser.: Vol. 2). (Illus.). 320p. pap. 10.99 (*0-7642-2365-8*) Bethany Hse. Pubs.

—Sun Dance. 2000. (Sam Keaton Ser.: Vol. 3). 304p. pap. 10.99 (*0-7642-2367-4*) Bethany Hse. Pubs.

—Sun Dance. 1995. (Illus.). 312p. pap. 9.99 o.p. (*1-56476-427-3*, 6-3427) Cook Communications Ministries.

—Thunder Voice. 2000. (Sam Keaton Ser.: Vol. 4). 304p. pap. 10.99 (*0-7642-2368-2*) Bethany Hse. Pubs.

—Thunder Voice. 1995. (Ghost Rider Ser.). (Illus.). 312p. pap. 9.99 o.p. (*1-56476-426-5*, 6-3426) Cook Communications Ministries.

Brown, Corinne Joy. MacGregor's Lantern. 2001. (Five Star First Edition Western Ser.). 392p. 26.95 (*0-7862-3227-7*, Five Star) Gale Group.

Castle, Linda Lea. Bogus Brides: Addie & the Laird. 2000. (Ballad Romances Ser.). 320p. mass mkt. 5.50 o.s.i (*0-8217-6715-1*) Kensington Publishing Corp.

Chandler, Jon. Wyoming Wind: A Story of Tom Horn: A Western Story. 2003. 208p. mass mkt. 5.50 (*0-8439-5165-6*, Leisure Bks.) Dorchester Publishing Co., Inc.

—Wyoming Wind: A Story of Tom Horn: A Western Story. 2002. (Five Star First Edition Western Ser.). 201p. 24.95 (*0-7862-3769-4*, Five Star) Gale Group.

Coel, Margaret. The Dream Stalker. 1997. 256p. 21.95 o.s.i (*0-425-15967-1*); 1998. 272p. reprint ed. mass mkt. 6.50 (*0-425-16533-7*) Berkley Publishing Group. (Prime Crime).

—The Dream Stalker. unabr. ed. 1999. (O'Malley Mystery Ser.). audio 39.95 (*1-55686-873-1*) Books in Motion.

—The Eagle Catcher. 1996. (Arapaho Indian Mysteries Ser.). 256p. mass mkt. 6.50 (*0-425-15463-7*) Berkley Publishing Group.

—The Eagle Catcher. 16th l.t. ed. 2002. 248p. lib. bdg. 28.95 (*1-58547-159-3*) Ctr. Point Large Print.

—The Eagle Catcher. 1995. (Arapaho Indian Mysteries Ser.). 224p. 22.50 (*0-87081-367-6*) Univ. Pr. of Colorado.

—The Eagle Catcher. 1995. E-Book 22.50 (*0-585-02336-0*) netLibrary, Inc.

—The Ghost Walker. 256p. 1996. 21.95 o.p. (*0-425-15468-8*); 1997. reprint ed. mass mkt. 6.50 (*0-425-15961-2*) Berkley Publishing Group. (Prime Crime).

—The Ghost Walker. unabr. ed. 1999. (O'Malley Mystery Ser.). audio 39.95 (*1-55686-865-0*) Books in Motion.

—Killing Raven. 2004. 304p. mass mkt. 6.99 (*0-425-19750-6*); 2003. 288p. 22.95 (*0-425-19261-X*, Prime Crime) Berkley Publishing Group.

—The Lost Bird. 2000. 304p. mass mkt. 6.50 (*0-425-17030-6*) Berkley Publishing Group.

—The Lost Bird. l.t. ed. 2000. (G. K. Hall Core Ser.). 332p. 28.95 (*0-7838-8958-5*, Macmillan Reference USA) Gale Group.

—The Lost Bird: A Mystery. 1999. 304p. 21.95 o.s.i (*0-425-17059-4*, Prime Crime) Berkley Publishing Group.

—The Shadow Dancer. 2002. 304p. 22.95 (*0-425-18640-7*, Prime Crime) Berkley Publishing Group.

—The Shadow Dancer. l.t. ed. 2003. lib. bdg. 28.95 (*1-58547-284-0*, Platinum) Ctr. Point Large Print.

—The Spirit Woman. 2000. 272p. 21.95 o.s.i (*0-425-17597-9*); 2001. 304p. reprint ed. mass mkt. 6.50 (*0-425-18090-5*, Prime Crime) Berkley Publishing Group.

—The Spirit Woman. l.t. ed. 2001. 294p. lib. bdg. 28.95 (*1-58547-063-5*) Ctr. Point Large Print.

—The Story Teller. (Wind River Arapaho Ser.). 256p. 1998. 21.95 o.s.i (*0-425-16538-8*); 1999. reprint ed. mass mkt. 6.50 (*0-425-17025-X*) Berkley Publishing Group. (Prime Crime).

—The Story Teller. unabr. ed. 1999. (O'Malley Mystery Ser.). audio 49.95 (*1-55686-891-X*) Books in Motion.

—The Thunder Keeper. 2001. 256p. 22.95 o.s.i (*0-425-18188-X*, Prime Crime) Berkley Publishing Group.

Conley, Robert J. Wilder & Wilder. l.t. ed. 2002. (Paperback Ser.). 247p. pap. 24.95 (*0-7862-4424-0*) Thorndike Pr.

Connors, Cathleen. A Home of Her Own. 2002. (Steeple Hill Love Inspired Ser.: No. 167). mass mkt. (*0-373-87174-0*, Steeple Hill) Harlequin Enterprises, Ltd.

Coolidge, Dane. Man from Wyoming. 2001. 208p. reprint ed. mass mkt. 3.99 (*0-8439-4938-4*, Leisure Bks.) Dorchester Publishing Co., Inc.

—Man from Wyoming. 2000. (Five Star Western Ser.). (Illus.). 207p. 21.95 (*0-7862-2115-1*, Five Star) Gale Group.

Curry, Peggy S. LandMarked: Stories of Peggy Simson Curry. 1992. 320p. (Orig.). pap. 12.95 (*0-931271-17-7*) High Plains Pr.

Cushman, Dan. North Fork to Hell. l.t. ed. 2001. (Sagebrush Large Print Westerns Ser.). 221p. 20.95 (*1-57490-347-0*, Sagebrush Large Print Westerns) Beeler, Thomas T. Publisher.

Dalton, Margot. Best Man in Wyoming. 2000. (Harlequin Heart of the West Ser.: Vol. 12). 256p. per. (*0-373-82596-X*, Harlequin Bks.) Harlequin Enterprises, Ltd.

DeAndrea, William L. The Fatal Elixir: A Lobo Blacke-Quinn Booker Mystery. 1997. (Lobo Black/Quinn Booker Mystery Ser.). 208p. 22.95 (*0-8027-3289-5*) Walker & Co.

—Written in Fire: A Lobo Blacke-Quinn Booker Mystery. 1995. 168p. 19.95 (*0-8027-3270-4*) Walker & Co.

Eagle, Kathleen. The Last Good Man. 2001. (Illus.). 400p. mass mkt. 6.99 (*0-380-81014-X*); 2000. 374p. 23.00 (*0-380-97815-6*) Morrow/Avon.

—The Last True Cowboy. 1999. 400p. mass mkt. 6.50 (*0-380-78492-0*); 1998. 211p. 20.00 (*0-380-97522-X*) Morrow/Avon. (Avon Bks.).

Erickson, Lynn. Courting Callie. 1999. (Harlequin Heart of the West Ser.: Vol. 2). per. (*0-373-82586-2*, 1-82586-8, Harlequin Bks.) Harlequin Enterprises, Ltd.

Galvin, James. The Meadow. l.t. ed. 1993. 21.95 o.p. (*0-7927-1570-5*); pap. 19.95 o.p. (*0-7927-1569-1*) BBC Audiobooks America.

—The Meadow. 1992. (Illus.). 192p. 19.95 o.p. (*0-8050-1684-8*) Holt, Henry & Co.

Garland, Kit. Sweeter Than Sin. 1999. 368p. mass mkt. 5.99 o.s.i (*0-440-22365-2*) Dell Publishing.

Garlock, Dorothy. Forever, Victoria. 1983. mass mkt. 3.50 o.s.i (*0-515-07444-6*, Jove) Berkley Publishing Group.

—Forever, Victoria. l.t. ed. 1994. 362p. pap. 17.95 o.p. (*0-8161-7463-6*, Macmillan Reference USA) Gale Group.

—The Listening Sky. l.t. ed. 1996. 25.95 o.p. (*1-56895-317-8*, Wheeler Publishing, Inc.) Gale Group.

Gist, John. Crowheart. 1999. 301p. 29.95 (*0-916781-45-3*, 2001) Andmar Pr.

Grant, Ken. The Deer Mouse. 1997. 208p. pap. 16.00 (*1-57962-015-9*); 205p. 24.00 (*1-877946-84-2*) Permanent Pr., The.

—The Deer Mouse. 160p. 2002. pap. 6.99 (*0-7592-1334-8*); 2002. E-Book 6.99 (*0-7592-1330-5*); 2002. E-Book 6.99 (*0-7592-1331-3*); 2001. E-Book 6.99 (*0-7592-1329-1*) ereads.com.

Grayson, Elizabeth. Color of the Wind. 1999. 432p. mass mkt. 5.99 o.s.i (*0-553-58010-8*) Bantam Bks.

Greenwood, Leigh. Wyoming Wildfire. 2001. 464p. reprint ed. mass mkt. 5.99 (*0-505-52459-7*, Love Spell) Dorchester Publishing Co., Inc.

—Wyoming Wildfire. 1987. (Heartfire Romance Ser.). mass mkt. 3.75 o.p. (*0-8217-2107-0*, Zebra Bks.) Kensington Publishing Corp.

Grey, Zane. Wyoming. (Gunsmoke Western Ser.). 17.50 o.p. (*0-86220-929-3*, C0716, Gunsmoke); 1990. pap. 10.95 o.p. (*0-89340-280-X*, C0161) BBC Audiobooks America.

—Wyoming. l.t. ed. 2001. 304p. 21.95 (*1-57490-333-0*, Sagebrush Large Print Westerns) Beeler, Thomas T. Publisher.

—Wyoming. 1994. 320p. mass mkt. 3.99 o.p. (*0-06-100340-9*, HarperTorch) Morrow/Avon.

Hageman, Vee. A Child of Caurus. Keskinen, Mindy & Gentle, Audrey, eds. 2001. 198p. pap. 12.95 (*0-9703306-0-X*) Antelope Publishing.

Hardy, Edward. Geyser Life: A Novel. 1996. 288p. 21.95 (*1-882593-16-2*) Bridge Works Publishing Co., Inc.

Hart, Diana. Bad Medicine. 1999. (Wyoming Wilde Ser.: Vol. 2). E-Book 5.50 (*1-58200-240-1*) Hard Shell Word Factory.

Haycox, Ernest. The Wild Bunch. l.t. ed. 1983. 400p. lib. bdg. 14.95 o.p. (*0-8161-3443-X*, Macmillan Reference USA) Gale Group.

—The Wild Bunch. 1974. mass mkt. 1.25 o.p. (*0-451-06164-0*); 1970. mass mkt. 0.35 o.p. (*0-451-01557-6*); 1970. mass mkt. 0.75 o.p. (*0-451-04232-8*) NAL. (Signet Bks.).

Haynie, Barbara. The Terrain of Paradise. 2003. 263p. pap. 13.95 (*1-4104-0127-8*, Five Star Trade); 2002. 259p. 25.95 (*0-7862-4474-7*, Five Star) Gale Group.

Hays, Clark & McFall, Kathleen. The Cowboy & the Vampire: A Very Unusual Romance. Hill, Connie, ed. 336p. pap. 12.95 (*1-56718-451-0*, K451) Llewellyn Pubns.

Henderson, William H. Native. 256p. 1994. pap. 9.95 o.p. (*0-452-27139-8*, Plume); 1993. 20.00 o.p. (*0-525-93574-6*) Dutton/Plume.

Henry, Will. The Bear Paw Horses. l.t. ed. 1995. (G. K. Hall Nightingale Ser.). 329p. pap. 16.95 (*0-7838-1121-7*, Macmillan Reference USA) Gale Group.

Hess, Norah. Storm. 2000. 432p. mass mkt. 5.99 (*0-505-52396-5*, Love Spell) Dorchester Publishing Co., Inc.

Hobbet, Anastasia. Pleasure of Believing. 1997. 336p. 24.00 o.p. (*1-56947-085-5*) Soho Pr., Inc.

Hohl, Joan. Silver Thunder. l.t. ed. 2002. 418p. pap. 23.95 (*1-58724-330-X*, Wheeler Publishing, Inc.) Gale Group.

—Silver Thunder. 2001. mass mkt. 6.99 (*0-8217-7201-5*) Kensington Publishing Corp.

Horton, J. Royal. Murder in Jackson Hole. 1993. 224p. (Orig.). pap. 12.95 o.p. (*0-943972-23-X*) Homestead Publishing.

Hough, Donald. The Cocktail Hour in Jackson Hole. 1993. (Illus.). 253p. reprint ed. pap. 11.95 o.p. (*1-881019-02-0*) High Plains Publishing Co., Inc.

Howard, Linda. Mackenzie's Mountain. l.t. ed. 1993. (Senses Ser.). 17.95 o.p. (*0-373-58800-3*) BBC Audiobooks America.

—Mackenzie's Mountain. 2000. 256p. mass mkt. (*1-55166-574-3*); 1989. mass mkt. (*0-373-07281-3*) Harlequin Enterprises, Ltd. (Harlequin Bks.).

Howell, Hannah. Wild Roses. l.t. ed. 2001. (Five Star Romance Ser.). 336p. 26.95 (*0-7862-3702-3*, Five Star) Gale Group.

Isaacs, Susan. Red, White & Blue. 1998. 416p. 25.00 o.s.i (*0-06-017608-3*) HarperCollins Pubs.

—Red, White & Blue. abr. ed. 1998. audio 25.00 (*0-694-51982-0*, 696054, HarperAudio) HarperTrade.

—Red, White & Blue. abr. ed. 1999. audio 25.00 Highsmith Inc.

—Red, White & Blue. l.t. ed. (Thorndike/G. K. Hall Paperback Bestsellers Ser.). 749p. 2000. pap. 27.95 (*0-7862-1742-1*); 1999. 30.95 (*0-7862-1741-3*) Thorndike Pr.

—Red, White & Blue: A Novel. 1999. 592p. mass mkt. 6.99 (*0-06-109310-6*, HarperTorch) Morrow/Avon.

Johnstone, William W. Creed of the Mountain Man, 1. 1999. 256p. mass mkt. 4.99 o.s.i (*0-8217-6258-3*) Kensington Publishing Corp.

—Ordeal of the Mountain Man. 1996. 288p. mass mkt. 4.99 o.s.i (*0-8217-5373-8*, Zebra Bks.) Kensington Publishing Corp.

—Pursuit of the Mountain Man. l.t. ed. 2000. (G. K. Hall Western Ser.). 320p. 25.95 (*0-7838-9274-8*, Macmillan Reference USA) Gale Group.

—Pursuit of the Mountain Man. 2001. 256p. mass mkt. 5.99 (*0-7860-1305-2*); 1998. 256p. mass mkt. 4.99 o.s.i (*0-8217-6011-4*); 1996. 256p. mass mkt. 4.99 o.s.i (*0-8217-5246-4*); 1991. mass mkt. 3.50 o.s.i (*0-8217-3515-2*, Zebra Bks.) Kensington Publishing Corp.

Jones, Allen Morris. Last Year's River. 2001. 256p. 23.00 (*0-618-17449-4*); tchr. ed. 24.00 (*0-618-13161-2*) Houghton Mifflin Co.

Joseph, Stephen C. Summer of Fifty-seven: Coming of Age in Wyoming's Shining Mountains. 2002. (Illus.). 184p. 24.95 (*0-86534-367-5*) Sunstone Pr.

Kellogg, Marne Davis. Bad Manners. 1998. 270p. reprint ed. lib. bdg. 29.95 (*0-7351-0056-X*) Replica Bks.

—Bad Manners. 1996. (Illus.). 288p. mass mkt. 5.99 o.s.i (*0-446-60357-0*); 1995. 272p. 21.45 o.p. (*0-446-51836-0*) Warner Bks., Inc.

—Birthday Party: A Lilly Bennett Mystery. 2000. 272p. mass mkt. 5.99 o.s.i (*0-553-58049-3*) Bantam Bks.

—Birthday Party: A Lilly Bennett Mystery. 1999. (Lilly Bennett Mysteries Ser.). 272p. 21.95 o.s.i (*0-385-49333-9*) Doubleday Publishing.

—Curtsey. 1996. 272p. 21.95 o.p. (*0-446-51837-9*) Warner Bks., Inc.

—Tramp. 1998. (Lilly Bennett Mysteries Ser.). 352p. mass mkt. 5.99 o.s.i (*0-553-57992-4*) Bantam Bks.

Kerr, Baine. Wrongful Death. 2002. 384p. 25.00 (*0-7432-1117-0*, Scribner) Simon & Schuster.

Kuban, Karla. Marchlands: A Novel. 272p. 1999. pap. 12.00 o.s.i (*0-684-85444-9*); 1998. 23.00 (*0-684-83165-1*) Simon & Schuster. (Scribner).

Lacy, Al. Pillow of Stone, 8 vols. 2003. (Hannah of Fort Bridger Ser.: Vol. 4). 312p. pap. 10.99 (*1-57673-234-7*, Multnomah Fiction) Multnomah Pubs., Inc.

Lacy, Al & Lacy, JoAnna. Beyond the Valley. 2003. (Hannah of Fort Bridger Ser.: Vol. 7). 320p. pap. 10.99 (*1-57673-618-0*, Multnomah Bks.) Multnomah Pubs., Inc.

—Consider the Lilies, 8 vols. 2003. (Hannah of Fort Bridger Ser.: Vol. 2). 308p. pap. 10.99 (*1-57673-049-2*, Multnomah Bks.) Multnomah Pubs., Inc.

—Damascus Journey, 8 vols. 2003. (Hannah of Fort Bridger Ser.: Vol. 8). 294p. pap. 10.99 (*1-57673-630-X*) Multnomah Pubs., Inc.

—No Place for Fear, 8 vols. 2003. (Hannah of Fort Bridger Ser.: Vol. 3). 322p. pap. 10.99 (*1-57673-083-2*, Multnomah Fiction) Multnomah Pubs., Inc.

—The Perfect Gift, 8 vols. 2003. (Hannah of Fort Bridger Ser.: Vol. 5). 336p. pap. 10.99 (*1-57673-407-2*) Multnomah Pubs., Inc.

—Touch of Compassion. 2003. (Hannah of Fort Bridger Ser.: Vol. 6). 308p. pap. 10.99 (*1-57673-422-6*) Multnomah Pubs., Inc.

Lacy, Al, et al. Under the Distant Sky. 2003. (Hannah of Fort Bridger Ser.: Vol. 1). 280p. pap. 10.99 (*1-57673-033-6*, Multnomah Bks.) Multnomah Pubs., Inc.

Lambert, Page. Shifting Stars. 1997. 384p. 23.95 (*0-312-86324-1*, Forge Bks.) Doherty, Tom Assocs., LLC.

Landreth, Marsha. A Clinic for Murder. 1993. (Dr. Sam Turner Mystery Ser.). 212p. 19.95 o.s.i (*0-8027-3241-0*) Walker & Co.

—French Creek. 1992. 16.95 o.p. (*0-87131-696-X*) Evans, M. & Co., Inc.

—Vial Murders. 1994. (Doctor Samantha Turner Mystery Ser.). 224p. 19.95 (*0-8027-3199-6*) Walker & Co.

Langan, Ruth R. The Wildes of Wyoming—Hazard. 2000. (Silhouette Intimate Moments Ser.: No.997). 248p. mass mkt. (*0-373-27067-4*, Silhouette) Harlequin Enterprises, Ltd.

Lee, Rachel. Conard County. 1999. mass mkt. (*0-373-48383-X*, 1-48383-3, Harlequin Bks.) Harlequin Enterprises, Ltd.

—A Conard County Homecoming. 1999. mass mkt. (*0-373-48394-5*, 1-48394-0, Harlequin Bks.) Harlequin Enterprises, Ltd.

—A Conard County Reckoning. 1996. mass mkt. (*0-373-48317-1*, 1-48317-1, Worldwide Library) Harlequin Enterprises, Ltd.

Lethem, Jonathan. Amnesia Moon. 1996. 247p. pap. 12.95 (*0-312-86220-2*, Tor Bks.) Doherty, Tom Assocs., LLC.

—Amnesia Moon. 1995. 256p. 20.00 o.s.i (*0-15-100091-3*) Harcourt Trade Pubs.

London, Cait. It Happened at Midnight. 2000. 384p. mass mkt. 5.99 (*0-380-81550-8*, Avon Bks.) Morrow/Avon.

London, David. Sun Dancer. 1996. 320p. 23.00 o.p. (*0-684-81458-7*, Simon & Schuster) Simon & Schuster.

Lovelace, Merline. The Horse Soldier. 2001. 384p. mass mkt. o.s.i (*1-55166-784-3*, 1-66784-9, Mira Bks.) Harlequin Enterprises, Ltd.

Mazza, Cris. Girl Beside Him. 2001. 269p. pap. 13.95 (*1-57366-092-2*) Fiction Collective Two, Inc.

McAllister, Anne. The Stardust Cowboy. 1999. (Silhouette Desire Ser.: No. 1219). 186p. per. (*0-373-76219-4*, 1-76219-4, Silhouette) Harlequin Enterprises, Ltd.

McClendon, Lise. Nordic Nights. 1999. (Alix Thorssen Mysteries Ser.). 292p. 23.95 (*0-8027-3340-9*) Walker & Co.

—Painted Truth: An Alix Thorssen Mystery. 1996. per. (*0-373-26222-1*, 1-26222-9, Worldwide Library) Harlequin Enterprises, Ltd.

—Painted Truth: An Alix Thorssen Mystery. 1995. 252p. 22.95 (*0-8027-3271-2*) Walker & Co.

McElrath, Frances. The Rustler: A Tale of Love & War in Wyoming. 2002. (Illus.). 193p. pap. 19.95 (*0-8032-8284-2*, Bison Bks.) Univ. of Nebraska Pr.

McKinney, Meagan. Fair Is the Rose. l.t. ed. 1993. 12.95 o.p. (*1-56895-031-4*, Wheeler Publishing, Inc.) Gale Group.

McKinzie, Clinton. The Edge of Justice. 2003. 448p. mass mkt. 6.99 (*0-440-23723-8*); 2002. 336p. 21.95 (*0-385-33625-X*, Delacorte Pr.) Dell Publishing.

—The Edge of Justice. abr. ed. 2002. audio compact disk 29.95 (*0-553-71344-2*, RH Audio) Random Hse. Audio Publishing Group.

—Trial by Ice & Fire. 2004. 400p. mass mkt. 6.99 (*0-440-23727-0*, Dell Bks.); 2003. 320p. 21.95 (*0-385-33735-3*, Delacorte Pr.) Dell Publishing.

—Trial by Ice & Fire. l.t. ed. 2003. 559p. 29.95 (*0-7862-6064-5*) Gale Group.

McLinn. My Heart Remembers. 2001. (Wyoming Wildflowers Ser.). mass mkt. (*0-373-24439-8*, Harlequin Bks.) Harlequin Enterprises, Ltd.

Mondello, Lisa. Nothing but Trouble. E-Book 6.00 (*1-58345-324-5*); 2000. 148p. 18.95 (*1-58345-360-1*); 1999. 120p. pap. 10.00 (*1-58345-350-4*) Domhan Bks.

Mone, Gregory. The Wages of Genius. 2004. pap. 13.00 (*0-7867-1327-5*); 2003. 208p. 25.00 (*0-7867-1136-1*) Avalon Publishing Group. (Carroll & Graf Pubs.).

Moore, Stanford W. Blue Vistas, Wyoming Territory. 2001. 176p. pap. 20.99 (*0-7388-4273-7*); E-Book 8.00 (*0-7388-9639-X*) Xlibris Corp.

Morris, Gilbert. The Valiant Gunman. 1993. (House of Winslow Ser.: Bk. 14). 320p. pap. 11.99 (*1-55661-310-5*) Bethany Hse. Pubs.

Murray, Earl P. Spirit of the Moon. 1996. 304p. text 23.95 o.p. (*0-312-86189-3*, Forge Bks.) Doherty, Tom Assocs., LLC.

Nance, John J. Fire Flight. abr. ed. 2004. audio 12.99 (*1-59086-760-2*, 4361, Brilliance Audio Paperback Audiobooks); 2003. audio 24.95 (*1-59086-759-9*, 4360); 2003. audio 34.95 (*1-59086-757-2*, 4358, Brilliance Audio Unabridged); 2003. audio 87.25 (*1-59086-758-0*, 4359, Brilliance Audio Unabridged Lib Ed) Brilliance Audio.

Neff, Mindy. The Cowboy Is a Daddy. 1998. mass mkt. (*0-373-16759-8*, 1-16759-2, Mira Bks.) Harlequin Enterprises, Ltd.

Nesbitt, John D. Man from Wolf River. 2001. 256p. mass mkt. 4.50 (*0-8439-4871-X*, Leisure Bks.) Dorchester Publishing Co., Inc.

—North of Cheyenne. 2000. 256p. mass mkt. 4.50 (*0-8439-4783-7*, Leisure Bks.) Dorchester Publishing Co., Inc.

—One-Eyed Cowboy Wild. l.t. ed. 1994. 221p. pap. 18.95 (*0-8161-7477-6*, Macmillan Reference USA) Gale Group.

—One-Eyed Cowboy Wild. 1994. 180p. 19.95 (*0-8027-4135-5*) Walker & Co.

—Wild Rose of Ruby Canyon. 1997. 179p. 20.95 (*0-8027-4159-2*) Walker & Co.

Olson, Ted. Ranch on the Laramie. 1973. x, 240p. (*0-316-65052-8*) Little Brown & Co.

Palmer, Diana. Heart of Ice. 1995. (Western Lovers Ser.). mass mkt. (*0-373-88524-5*, 1-88524-3, Harlequin Bks.) Harlequin Enterprises, Ltd.

—Paper Rose. unabr. ed. 1999. audio 7.99 (*1-55204-195-6*, MIR-1195) Durkin Hayes Publishing Ltd.

—Paper Rose. 1999. 379p. mass mkt. o.s.i (*1-55166-539-5*, Mira Bks.) Harlequin Enterprises, Ltd.

Patten, Lewis B. Gun Proud. l.t. ed. 1994. (General Ser.). 243p. lib. bdg. 16.95 (*0-8161-5924-6*, Macmillan Reference USA) Gale Group.

Peterson, Tracie. A Shelter of Hope. 1998. (Westward Chronicles Ser.: Vol. 1). 304p. pap. 11.99 (*0-7642-2112-4*) Bethany Hse. Pubs.

—A Shelter of Hope. 2001. 364p. 24.95 (*0-7862-3680-9*, Five Star) Gale Group.

Potter, Patricia. Wanted. 1994. 448p. mass mkt. 5.50 o.s.i (*0-553-56600-8*) Bantam Bks.

—Wanted. l.t. ed. 1995. (Large Print Bks.). pap. 21.95 o.p. (*1-56895-125-6*, Wheeler Publishing, Inc.) Gale Group.

Proulx, E. Annie. Close Range: Wyoming Stories. l.t. ed. 1999. (Core Ser.). (Illus.). 379p. 29.95 o.p. (*0-7838-8677-2*, Macmillan Reference USA) Gale Group.

—Close Range: Wyoming Stories. 2000. 288p. pap. 14.00 (*0-684-85222-5*); 1999. 336p. pap. 7.99 (*0-684-86726-5*); 1999. (Illus.). 288p. 25.00 (*0-684-85221-7*) Simon & Schuster. (Scribner).

—Close Range: Wyoming Stories. unabr. ed. 1999. audio 25.00 o.s.i (*0-671-04449-4*, 696741, Simon & Schuster Audioworks) Simon & Schuster Audio.

Reece, Colleen L. A Girl Called Cricket. l.t. ed. 2001. (Thorndike Candlelight Romance Ser.). 245p. 22.95 (*0-7862-3277-3*); (*0-7540-4517-X*) Thorndike Pr.

—A Girl Called Cricket & the Hills of Hope, 2 bks. in 1. (Romance Reader Ser.: No. 8). 7.95 o.p. (*1-55748-228-4*) Barbour Publishing, Inc.

—Storm Clouds over Chantel. l.t. ed. 2002. 282p. pap. 14.95 (*1-4104-0031-X*, Walker Large Print) Gale Group.

—Storm Clouds over Chantel. l.t. ed. 2002. (Christian Fiction Ser.). 282p. 25.95 (*0-7862-4527-1*) Thorndike Pr.

Rice, Luanne. Dream Country. l.t. ed. 557p. 2002. pap. 29.95 (*0-7838-9385-X*); 2001. 32.95 (*0-7838-9384-1*) Gale Group. (Macmillan Reference USA).

Rigoni, Orlando. The Big Brand. l.t. ed. 1992. 18.95 o.p. (*0-7451-8329-8*); pap. 16.95 o.p. (*0-7927-1012-6*) BBC Audiobooks America.

Ritchie, James A. Kerrigan. 1993. 19.95 (*0-8027-1276-2*) Walker & Co.

Robbins, David. The Return of the Virginian. l.t. ed. 1994. 535p. lib. bdg. 20.95 o.p. (*0-8161-5997-1*, Macmillan Reference USA) Gale Group.

Roderus, Frank. Charlie & the Sir. 1988. (Double D Western Ser.). 12.95 o.s.i (*0-385-23960-2*) Doubleday Publishing.

—Charlie & the Sir. l.t. ed. 1993. (Nightingale Ser.). pap. 15.95 o.p. (*0-8161-5774-X*, Macmillan Reference USA) Gale Group.

Romtvedt, David. Crossing Wyoming. 1992. 263p. pap. 12.00 (*1-877727-23-7*) White Pine Pr.

Rooke, Leon. The Fall of Gravity: A Novel. 2000. 271p. tchr. ed. (*0-919028-36-5*) Allen, Thomas & Son, Ltd.

Rosenthal, C. P. Elena of the Stars. 1996. 192p. pap. 10.95 (*0-312-14592-6*, Saint Martin's Griffin) St. Martin's Pr.

—Elena of the Stars: A Novel. 1995. 192p. 18.95 o.p. (*0-312-13482-7*) St. Martin's Pr.

Ross, Dana Fuller, pseud. Wyoming! 1983. mass mkt. 3.99 o.s.i (*0-553-80003-5*); 384p. mass mkt. 4.95 o.s.i (*0-553-26242-4*) Bantam Bks.

—Wyoming! (Reader's Request Ser.). 1982. lib. bdg. 16.95 o.p. (*0-8161-3316-6*); 1993. 50.95 o.p. (*0-7838-1107-1*) Gale Group. (Macmillan Reference USA).

Roundy, Shaun B. Gone but Not Forgotten. 1998. (Not Forgotten Ser.: No. 1). 110p. pap. 5.95 (*1-893594-00-9*) University of Life, The.

Ryan, Courtney. Absolute Beginners, No. 462. 1989. 2.50 o.p. (*0-425-11591-7*) Berkley Publishing Group.

—Absolute Beginners. l.t. ed. 2000. (Romance Ser.). 220p. 25.95 (*0-7862-2489-4*) Thorndike Pr.

Saban, Vera. Johnny Egan of the Paintrock. 1986. (This Is America Ser.). (Illus.). 130p. (Orig.). (J). (gr. 4-8). pap. 6.95 (*0-914565-13-3*, Timbertrails) Capstan Pubns.

—The Westering: Jamie. Crane, Kitty, ed. 1996. (This Is America: The Westering Ser.: Vol. 3). (Illus.). 600p. (Orig.). pap. 15.95 (*0-914565-46-X*, Timbertrails) Capstan Pubns.

—The Westering: Rebecca. Crane, Kitty, ed. 1995. (This Is America, the Westering Ser.: Vol. 2). (Illus.). 650p. (Orig.). pap. 15.95 (*0-914565-45-1*, Timbertrails) Capstan Pubns.

Sandlin, Tim. Skipped Parts. 1991. 320p. 19.95 o.p. (*0-8050-1086-6*) Holt, Henry & Co.

—Sorrow Floats. 352p. 4.98 o.p. (*0-8317-7748-6*) Smithmark Pubs., Inc.

—Sorrow Floats: A Novel. 1994. 368p. pap. 10.00 o.s.i (*0-449-90890-9*, Fawcett) Ballantine Bks.

Savage, Les, Jr. Medicine Wheel. 1998. 224p. mass mkt. 4.50 (*0-8439-4444-7*, Leisure Bks.) Dorchester Publishing Co., Inc.

—Medicine Wheel. (Western Ser.). 1996. 218p. 17.95 (*0-7862-0657-8*, Five Star); 1999. 20.00 (*0-7838-1668-5*, Macmillan Reference USA) Gale Group.

Schaller, Bob. Wyoming. 1998. (Arlingtons Ser.). (Illus.). 128p. (J). (gr. 8-12). pap. text 7.95 o.p. (*1-887002-79-0*) Cross Training Publishing.

Sharpe, Jon. The Trailsman: Wyoming Wolfpack, Vol. 259. 2003. 176p. mass mkt. 4.99 (*0-451-20860-9*, Signet Bks.) NAL.

—Wyoming Conspiracy. 1992. (Canyon O'Grady Ser.: No. 21). 176p. (Orig.). mass mkt. 3.50 o.p. (*0-451-17370-8*, Signet Bks.) NAL.

—Wyoming War Cry. 2000. (Trailsman Ser.: Vol. 228). 176p. mass mkt. 4.99 o.s.i (*0-451-20148-5*, Signet Bks.) NAL.

—Wyoming Whirlwind, No. 242. 2001. (Trailsman Ser.). 176p. mass mkt. 4.99 o.s.i (*0-451-20522-7*) NAL.

—Wyoming Wildcats. 1998. (Trailsman Ser.: Vol. 199). 176p. mass mkt. 4.99 o.s.i (*0-451-19502-7*, Signet Bks.) NAL.

Smith, Diane. Letters from Yellowstone. 272p. 2000. (Illus.). 13.00 (*0-14-029181-4*); 1999. 24.95 o.s.i (*0-670-88631-9*) Viking Penguin.

Sorensen, Michele R. Broken Lance. 1997. xi, 285p. 15.95 (*1-57345-270-X*) Deseret Bk. Co.

Spence, Gerry. Half-Moon & Empty Stars. 2001. 416p. 27.00 (*0-7432-0276-7*, Scribner); 2002. 576p. reprint ed. mass mkt. 7.99 (*0-7434-1035-1*, Pocket) Simon & Schuster.

Standiford, Les. Black Mountain. 2001. 288p. mass mkt. 5.99 o.s.i (*0-425-17853-6*, Prime Crime) Berkley Publishing Group.

—Black Mountain. 2000. 336p. 23.95 o.s.i (*0-399-14584-2*) Penguin Group (USA) Inc.

Steele, Danielle. The Ranch. 1997. 432p. 25.95 (*0-385-31634-8*, Delacorte Pr.) Dell Publishing.

Swift, Virginia. Bad Company. 2002. 336p. 24.95 (*0-06-019554-1*) HarperCollins Pubs.

—Bad Company. 2003. 384p. mass mkt. 6.99 (*0-06-103029-5*, Avon Bks.) Morrow/Avon.

Talcott, Deanna. Her Last Chance. 2002. (Silhouette Romance Ser.). 192p. mass mkt. (*0-373-19628-8*, Silhouette) Harlequin Enterprises, Ltd.

Thacker, Cathy Gillen. A Baby by Chance. 2000. (Harlequin Heart of the West Ser.: Vol. 9). 256p. per. (*0-373-82593-5*, Harlequin Bks.) Harlequin Enterprises, Ltd.

Thompson, Vicki Lewis. Bachelor Father. 1999. (Harlequin Special Releases Ser.). per. (*0-373-82587-0*, 1-82587-6, Harlequin Bks.) Harlequin Enterprises, Ltd.

Trevanian. Incident at Twenty Mile. 1998. 309p. 24.95 o.p. (*0-312-19233-9*) St. Martin's Pr.

—Incident at Twenty-Nine. 1999. 352p. mass mkt. 6.99 (*0-312-97023-4*, St. Martin's Paperbacks) St. Martin's Pr.

Vetter, Craig. Striking It Rich: A Novel. 1991. 256p. 18.00 o.p. (*0-688-10609-9*, Morrow, William & Co.) Morrow/Avon.

Whipple, Dan. Click: A Novel. 2001. 258p. 35.00 (*0-87081-632-2*); pap. 16.95 (*0-87081-652-7*) Univ. Pr. of Colorado.

White, Richard W. Mister Grey. 1992. 300p. 18.95 o.p. (*0-941423-71-9*) Four Walls Eight Windows.

Wister, Owen. The Virginian: A Horseman on the Plains. 100th anniv. ed. 2002. (Illus.). 304p. 29.95 (*1-57098-415-8*); 112p. pap. 150.00 (*1-57098-416-6*) Rinehart, Roberts Pubs.

Woods, Sherryl. After Tex. unabr. ed. 1999. audio 7.99 (*1-55204-191-3*, MIR-1191) Durkin Hayes Publishing Ltd.

—After Tex. 1999. 408p. mass mkt. (*1-55166-542-5*, Worldwide Library) Harlequin Enterprises, Ltd.

Zane, Carolyn. Taking on Twins. 2002. (Harlequin Special Releases Ser.: No. 8). 256p. mass mkt. o.s.i (*0-373-38711-3*, 1-38711-7, Harlequin Bks.) Harlequin Enterprises, Ltd.

# X

## XANTH (IMAGINARY PLACE)—FICTION

Anthony, Piers. Castle Roogna. (Xanth Novels Ser.). 1997. pap. 11.00 o.s.i (*0-345-41851-4*, Del Rey); 1987. 336p. mass mkt. 6.99 (*0-345-35048-0*, Del Rey); 1986. mass mkt. 3.50 o.p. (*0-345-33748-4*, Del Rey); 1985. mass mkt. 2.95 o.s.i (*0-345-32435-8*); 1981. mass mkt. 2.75 o.p. (*0-345-30283-4*, Del Rey); 1979. mass mkt. 1.95 o.p. (*0-345-27925-5*, Del Rey) Ballantine Bks.

—Castle Roogna. 1987. audio 14.95 o.p. (*0-394-29962-0*); 1985. audio 14.95 o.p. Random Hse. Audio Publishing Group.

—Castle Roogna. 1979. (Magic of Xanth Ser.). 13.04 (*0-606-02463-8*) Turtleback Bks.

—Centaur Aisle. 1997. (Xanth Novels Ser.: Vol. 4). pap. 11.00 o.s.i (*0-345-41852-2*, Del Rey); 1987. (Xanth Novels Ser.: Vol. 4). 304p. mass mkt. 6.99 (*0-345-35246-7*, Del Rey); 1986. mass mkt. 3.50 (*0-345-33571-6*); 1984. mass mkt. 2.95 o.p. o.s.i (*0-345-31808-0*, Del Rey); 1981. mass mkt. 2.75 o.p. (*0-345-29770-9*, Del Rey) Ballantine Bks.

—Centaur Aisle. (Illus.). 304p. 24.00 (*0-7278-5127-6*) Severn Hse. Pubs., Ltd.

—Centaur Aisle. 1979. (Magic of Xanth Ser.). 13.04 (*0-606-02462-X*) Turtleback Bks.

—The Color of Her Panties. 1992. (Xanth Ser.: No. 15). 288p. 23.00 o.p. (*0-688-10916-0*, Morrow, William & Co.);Bk. 15. 352p. mass mkt. 6.99 (*0-380-75949-7*, Avon Bks.) Morrow/Avon.

—The Continuing Xanth Saga. 1997. (Xanth Novels Ser.). 736p. 13.99 o.s.i (*0-517-18337-4*) Random Hse. Value Publishing.

—Crewel Lye: A Caustic Yarn. 1987. (Xanth Novels Ser.). 320p. mass mkt. 6.99 (*0-345-34599-1*, Del Rey) Ballantine Bks.

—Crewel Lye: A Caustic Yarn. 1984. (Magic of Xanth Ser.). 13.04 (*0-606-02461-1*) Turtleback Bks.

—The Dastard. (Xanth Novels Ser.). 2000. (Illus.). 303p. 24.95 (*0-312-86900-2*); 2001. 384p. reprint ed. mass mkt. 6.99 (*0-8125-7473-7*) Doherty, Tom Assocs., LLC. (Tor Bks.).

—Demons Don't Dream. 1994. (Xanth Novels Ser.: Vol. 16). 340p. mass mkt. 6.99 (*0-8125-3483-2*); 1993. 304p. 19.95 o.p. (*0-312-85389-0*) Doherty, Tom Assocs., LLC. (Tor Bks.).

—Demons Don't Dream, 16. 1994. (Xanth Ser.). 12.04 (*0-606-11249-9*) Turtleback Bks.

—Dragon on a Pedestal. (Xanth Novels Ser.). 1987. 320p. mass mkt. 6.99 (*0-345-34936-9*); 1983. mass mkt. 2.95 o.p. (*0-345-31107-8*) Ballantine Bks. (Del Rey).

—Dragon on a Pedestal. 1983. (Magic of Xanth Ser.). 13.04 (*0-606-02477-8*) Turtleback Bks.

—A Dragon on a Pedestal. 1985. 320p. mass mkt. 3.50 o.p. (*0-345-33553-8*, Del Rey) Ballantine Bks.

—Faun & Games. 1998. 352p. mass mkt. 167.76 (*0-8125-7059-6*); 1998. 352p. mass mkt. 6.99 (*0-8125-5511-2*); 1997. 320p. 23.95 o.p. (*0-312-86162-1*) Doherty, Tom Assocs., LLC. (Tor Bks.).

—Faun & Games. 1998. (Magic of Xanth Ser.). 13.04 (*0-606-16886-9*) Turtleback Bks.

—Geis of the Gargoyle. 1995. (Xanth Novels Ser.). mass mkt. 6.99 (*0-8125-3485-9*); 320p. 22.95 o.p. (*0-312-85391-2*); mass mkt. 22.95 (*0-8125-5271-7*) Doherty, Tom Assocs., LLC. (Tor Bks.).

—Geis of the Gargoyle. 1995. (Xanth Ser.). 13.04 (*0-606-11360-6*) Turtleback Bks.

—Golem in the Gears. 1997. (Xanth Novels Ser.). pap. 11.00 o.s.i (*0-345-41857-3*, Del Rey) Ballantine Bks.

—Golem in the Gears. 1986. (Xanth Ser.). 13.04 (*0-606-01025-4*) Turtleback Bks.

—Harpy Thyme. 1995. (Xanth Novels Ser.: bk. 17). 352p. mass mkt. 5.99 (*0-8125-3484-0*); 1993. 320p. 21.95 o.p. (*0-312-85390-4*) Doherty, Tom Assocs., LLC. (Tor Bks.).

—Harpy Thyme. 1995. (Magic of Xanth Ser.). 12.04 (*0-606-11439-4*) Turtleback Bks.

—Heaven Cent. 2000. (Xanth Novels Ser.). 352p. mass mkt. 6.99 (*0-8125-7498-2*, Tor Bks.) Doherty, Tom Assocs., LLC.

—Heaven Cent. 2000. (Illus.). 13.04 (*0-606-18643-3*) Turtleback Bks.

—Isle of View. 1990. 19.95 o.p. (*0-688-10134-8*, Morrow, William & Co.);Bk. 13. (Xanth Ser.: No. 13). 352p. mass mkt. 6.99 (*0-380-75947-0*, Avon Bks.) Morrow/Avon.

—Man from Mundania. 2000. 344p. mass mkt. 6.99 (*0-8125-7497-4*, Tor Bks.) Doherty, Tom Assocs., LLC.

—Man from Mundania. 1989. pap. 5.99 (*0-380-75289-1*, Avon Bks.) Morrow/Avon.

—Night Mare. 1997. (Xanth Novels Ser.: Vol. 6). pap. 11.00 o.s.i (*0-345-41854-9*); 1987. (Xanth Novels Ser.: Vol. 6). 320p. mass mkt. 6.99 (*0-345-35493-1*); 1982. mass mkt. 2.95 o.p. (*0-345-30456-X*) Ballantine Bks. (Del Rey).

—Night Mare. 1982. (Magic of Xanth Ser.). (J). 13.04 (*0-606-02597-9*) Turtleback Bks.

—Ogre, Ogre. 1997. (Xanth Novels Ser.: Vol. 5). pap. 11.00 o.s.i (*0-345-41853-0*); 1987. (Xanth Novels Ser.: Vol. 5). 320p. mass mkt. 6.99 (*0-345-35492-3*, Del Rey); 1986. mass mkt. 3.50 o.p. (*0-345-33509-0*, Del Rey); 1982. (Magic of Xanth Ser.). 320p. mass mkt. 2.95 o.s.i (*0-345-30187-0*, Del Rey) Ballantine Bks.

—Ogre, Ogre. 1982. (Magic of Xanth Ser.). (J). 13.04 (*0-606-02599-5*) Turtleback Bks.

—Question Quest. 1991. (Xanth Ser.: Vol. 14). (Orig.). 420p. pap. 20.00 o.p. (*0-688-10898-9*, Morrow, William & Co.);Bk. 14. 368p. mass mkt. 6.99 (*0-380-75948-9*, Avon Bks.) Morrow/Avon.

—Roc & a Hard Place. 1995. 320p. 23.95 o.p. (*0-312-85392-0*); Vol. 1. 1996. 344p. mass mkt. 6.99 (*0-8125-3486-7*) Doherty, Tom Assocs., LLC. (Tor Bks.).

—Roc & a Hard Place. 1996. 13.04 (*0-606-11804-7*) Turtleback Bks.

—The Source of Magic. 1997. (Xanth Novels Ser.: Vol. 2). pap. 11.00 o.s.i (*0-345-41850-6*); 1987. (Xanth Novels Ser.: Vol. 2). 336p. mass mkt. 6.99 (*0-345-35058-8*); 1983. mass mkt. 2.95 o.p. (*0-345-31321-6*); 1981. mass mkt. 2.50 o.p. (*0-345-30074-2*); 1979. mass mkt. 2.25 o.p. (*0-345-28765-7*); 1979. mass mkt. 1.95 o.p. (*0-345-27284-6*) Ballantine Bks. (Del Rey).

—Source of Magic. 1979. (Magic of Xanth Ser.). (J). 13.04 (*0-606-02647-9*) Turtleback Bks.

—A Spell for Chameleon. 1997. (Xanth Novels Ser.: Vol. 1). pap. 11.00 o.s.i (*0-345-41849-2*); 1987. (Xanth Novels Ser.: Vol. 1). 352p. mass mkt. 7.50 (*0-345-34753-6*); 1984. mass mkt. 2.95 o.p. (*0-345-31771-8*); 1981. mass mkt. 2.75 o.p. (*0-345-30422-5*); 1981. mass mkt. 2.50 o.p. (*0-345-30075-0*); 1979. mass mkt. 2.25 o.p. (*0-345-28766-5*); 1979. mass mkt. 1.95 o.p. (*0-345-25855-X*) Ballantine Bks. (Del Rey).

—A Spell for Chameleon. 1987. audio 14.95 o.p. (*0-394-29985-X*, RH Audio) Random Hse. Audio Publishing Group.

—A Spell for Chameleon. 1977. (Magic of Xanth Ser.). (J). 13.04 (*0-606-02492-1*) Turtleback Bks.

—Swell Foop. 2001. 304p. 24.95 (*0-312-86906-1*, Tor Bks.) Doherty, Tom Assocs., LLC.

—Up in a Heaval. 2002. (Xanth Novels Ser.: No. 26). (Illus.). 352p. 24.95 (*0-312-86904-5*, Tor Bks.) Doherty, Tom Assocs., LLC.

—Vale of the Vole. 2000. (Xanth Novels Ser.). 352p. mass mkt. 6.99 (*0-8125-7496-6*, Tor Bks.) Doherty, Tom Assocs., LLC.

—Vale of the Vole. 1987. pap. 5.99 (*0-380-75287-5*, Avon Bks.) Morrow/Avon.

—Xone of Contention. 1999. (Xanth Novels Ser.). 304p. 24.95 o.p. (*0-312-86691-7*, Tor Bks.) Doherty, Tom Assocs., LLC.

—The Xone of Contention. 2000. (Xanth Novels Ser.). 376p. mass mkt. 6.99 (*0-8125-5523-6*, Tor Bks.) Doherty, Tom Assocs., LLC.

—Yon Ill Wind. (Xanth Novels Ser.). 1997. 352p. mass mkt. 6.99 (*0-8125-5510-4*); 1996. 320p. 23.95 o.p. (*0-312-86227-X*) Doherty, Tom Assocs., LLC. (Tor Bks.).

—Zombie Lover, 48 vols. 1999. 341p. mass mkt. 6.99 (*0-8125-5512-0*); No. 22. 1998. (Xanth Novels Ser.: Vol. 22). 304p. 23.95 (*0-312-86690-9*) Doherty, Tom Assocs., LLC. (Tor Bks.).

—Zombie Lover. 1999. (Magic of Xanth Ser.). 13.04 (*0-606-17458-3*) Turtleback Bks.

Pini, Richard. Return to Centaur. 1990. (Xanth Graphic Novel Ser.: Vol. 1). (Illus.). 80p. (J). pap. 9.95 o.p. (*0-936861-20-7*, Father Tree Pr.) Warp Graphics, Inc.

## XANTIC EMPIRE (IMAGINARY PLACE)—FICTION

Wylie, Jonathan. Dark Fire. 1994. mass mkt. o.s.i (*0-552-13978-5*, Corgi) Bantam Bks.

—Echoes of Flame. 1994. mass mkt. o.s.i (*0-552-13979-3*, Corgi) Bantam Bks.

—The Last Augury. 1994. mass mkt. o.s.i (*0-552-13980-7*, Corgi) Bantam Bks.

# Y

## YOKNAPATAWPHA COUNTY (IMAGINARY PLACE)—FICTION

Faulkner, William. Absalom, Absalom! Date not set. 320p. 24.95 (*0-8488-2606-X*) Amereon, Ltd.

—Absalom, Absalom! 2002. audio 72.00 (*0-7366-8955-9*); 2002. audio compact disk 80.00 (*0-7366-9123-5*); 1993. audio 88.00 (*0-7366-2456-2*, 3220) Books on Tape, Inc.

—Absalom, Absalom! (William Faulkner Annotations to Novels Ser.). 1991. 192p. text 15.00 o.p. (*0-8240-4235-2*); 1987. text 163.00 o.p. (*0-8240-6817-3*) Garland Publishing, Inc.

—Absalom, Absalom! 1991. (Vintage International Ser.). 320p. pap. 12.95 (*0-679-73218-7*, Vintage) Knopf Publishing Group.

—Absalom, Absalom! Polk, Noel, ed. 1987. (Illus.). 384p. pap. 8.95 o.p. (*0-394-74775-5*, Vintage) Knopf Publishing Group.
—Absalom, Absalom! 1972. pap. 3.95 o.p. (*0-394-71780-5*, Vintage) Knopf Publishing Group.
—Absalom, Absalom! 1966. 378p. (C). pap. 7.50 (*0-07-553657-9*, McGraw-Hill Humanities, Social Sciences & World Languages) McGraw-Hill Higher Education.
—Absalom, Absalom! 2002. (Illus.). 392p. 22.00 (*0-375-50872-4*); 1993. (Illus.). 432p. 16.95 (*0-679-60072-8*); 1966. 17.95 o.s.i (*0-394-41400-4*); 1951. 3.95 o.s.i (*0-394-60271-4*) Random Hse., Inc.
—Absalom, Absalom! Polk, Noel, ed. rev. ed. 1986. 320p. 25.00 o.s.i (*0-394-55634-8*) Random Hse., Inc.
—Absalom, Absalom! l.t. ed. 1997. (Perennial Ser.). 496p. 24.95 (*0-7838-8138-X*) Thorndike Pr.
—Absalom, Absalom! 1972. 18.05 (*0-606-00781-4*) Turtleback Bks.
—As I Lay Dying. unabr. ed. 1994. audio 48.00 (*0-7366-2664-6*, 3401) Books on Tape, Inc.
—As I Lay Dying. 1987. (William Faulkner Manuscripts). 504p. text 65.00 o.p. (*0-8240-6809-2*) Garland Publishing, Inc.
—As I Lay Dying. 1991. (Vintage International Ser.). 288p. pap. 11.95 (*0-679-73225-X*, Vintage) Knopf Publishing Group.
—As I Lay Dying. Polk, Noel, ed. 1987. (Illus.). 256p. pap. 7.95 o.p. (*0-394-74745-3*, Vintage) Knopf Publishing Group.
—As I Lay Dying. annuals 2000. 288p. 16.95 (*0-375-50452-4*) Knopf, Alfred A. Inc.
—As I Lay Dying. 1967. 3.95 o.s.i (*0-394-60378-8*) Random Hse., Inc.
—As I Lay Dying. 1964. 17.05 (*0-606-02171-X*) Turtleback Bks.
—Go down, Moses. 1991. (Vintage International Ser.). 384p. pap. 12.00 (*0-679-73217-9*, Vintage) Knopf Publishing Group.
—Go down, Moses. 1955. 4.95 o.s.i (*0-394-60175-0*, Modern Library) Random House Adult Trade Publishing Group.
—Go down, Moses. 1995. 364p. 16.95 o.s.i (*0-679-60174-0*); 1942. 17.95 o.s.i (*0-394-42646-0*) Random Hse., Inc.
—Go down, Moses. unabr. ed. 1995. audio 85.00 (*0-7887-0217-3*, 94442E7) Recorded Bks., LLC.
—The Hamlet. 1991. (Vintage International Ser.). 432p. pap. 13.00 (*0-679-73653-0*, Vintage) Knopf Publishing Group.
—The Hamlet. 1956. pap. 8.00 o.p. (*0-394-70139-9*, V139); 1940. 16.95 o.s.i (*0-394-42759-9*) Random Hse., Inc.
—The Hamlet, unabr. ed. 2001. audio 97.00 (*1-55690-916-0*, 93412E7) Recorded Bks., LLC.
—Light in August. unabr. ed. 1994. audio 59.25 o.p. (*1-56100-213-5*, 1269, Unabridged Library Editions); audio 19.95 o.p. (*1-56100-588-6*, 163, Bookcassette) Brilliance Audio.
—Light in August. 1987. (Faulkner Manuscripts). 45.00 o.p. (*0-8240-6813-0*) Garland Publishing, Inc.
—Light in August. Blotner, Joseph Leo, ed. 1987. (Faulkner Manuscripts). 480p. text 60.00 o.p. (*0-8240-6814-9*) Garland Publishing, Inc.
—Light in August. 1985. (Book Notes Ser.). (gr. 10-12). pap. 2.50 o.p. (*0-8120-3521-6*) Library of America, The.
—Light in August. 1965. 480p. (C). pap. 11.25 (*0-07-553648-X*, McGraw-Hill Humanities, Social Sciences & World Languages) McGraw-Hill Higher Education.
—Light in August. 2002. 528p. 19.95 (*0-679-64248-X*); 1931. 3.95 o.s.i (*0-394-60088-6*) Random House Adult Trade Publishing Group. (Modern Library).
—Light in August. 1987. pap. 8.95 o.p. (*0-394-74743-7*); 1967. 16.95 o.s.i (*0-394-43335-1*); Vol. 189. 1972. pap. 4.95 o.p. (*0-394-71189-0*) Random Hse., Inc.
—Light in August, unabr. ed. 1994. audio 97.00 (*0-7887-0037-5*, 94236E7) Recorded Bks., LLC.
—Light in August: The Corrected Text. 1991. (Vintage International Ser.). 528p. pap. 13.95 (*0-679-73226-8*, Vintage) Knopf Publishing Group.
—Light in August: The Corrected Text. 1959. 19.05 (*0-606-01720-8*) Turtleback Bks.
—The Mansion, 2 vols. 1986. 752p. 110.00 o.p. (*0-8240-1833-8*) Garland Publishing, Inc.
—The Mansion. Millgate, Michael, ed. 1986. (William Faulkner Manuscripts). 1088p. text 135.00 (*0-8240-6832-7*) Garland Publishing, Inc.
—The Mansion. 1965. 448p. mass mkt. 12.00 (*0-394-70282-4*); 1959. 10.00 o.s.i (*0-394-43514-1*) Random Hse., Inc.
—Novels, 1930-1935: As I Lay Dying, Sanctuary, Light in August, Pylon. Blotner, Joseph & Polk, Noel, eds. 1985. (Library of America). 1056p. 35.00 (*0-940450-26-7*) Library of America, The.
—Novels, 1936-1940: Absalom, Absalom!; If I Forget Thee, Jerusalem (The Wild Palms); The Unvanquished; The Hamlet. Blotner, Joseph & Polk, Noel, eds. 1990. (Library of America: Vol. 48). 1148p. 37.50 (*0-940450-55-0*) Library of America, The.
—Novels, 1957-1962: The Town; The Mansion; The Reivers. Polk, Noel, ed. 1999. (Library of America: Vol. 112). 1020p. 35.00 (*1-883011-69-8*) Library of America, The.
—The Portable Faulkner. 2003. 688p. pap. 17.00 (*0-14-243728-X*, Penguin Classics) Viking Penguin.
—The Portable Faulkner. Cowley, Malcolm, ed. rev. ed. 1967. 14.95 o.p. (*0-670-31002-6*) Viking Penguin.
—Pylon. 1984. (FRE.). pap. 12.95 (*0-7859-2486-8*, 2070375315) French & European Pubns., Inc.
—Pylon. Polk, Noel, ed. 1987. (William Faulkner Manuscripts). 360p. text 50.00 (*0-8240-6816-5*) Garland Publishing, Inc.
—Pylon. mass mkt. 0.35 o.p. (*0-451-01485-5*, Signet Bks.); mass mkt. 0.25 o.p. (*0-451-00863-4*, Signet Bks.); 1968. mass mkt. 0.95 o.p. (*0-451-50415-1*, Signet Classics) NAL.
—Pylon. 1965. 13.95 o.s.i (*0-394-44156-7*) Random Hse., Inc.
—Pylon: The Corrected Text. Polk, Noel, ed. 1987. (Illus.). 336p. mass mkt. 9.00 (*0-394-74741-0*, Vintage) Knopf Publishing Group.
—Sanctuary. unabr. ed. 1995. (Bookcassette Classic Collection). audio 17.95 o.p. (*1-56100-631-9*, 245, Bookcassette); audio 57.25 o.p. (*1-56100-256-9*, 1024, Unabridged Library Editions) Brilliance Audio.
—Sanctuary. 6.95 o.p. (*0-453-00321-4*, Dutton) Dutton/Plume.
—Sanctuary. 1993. 336p. pap. 12.00 (*0-679-74814-8*, Vintage) Knopf Publishing Group.
—Sanctuary. Polk, Noel, ed. 1987. (Illus.). 320p. pap. 7.00 o.p. (*0-394-74744-5*, Vintage) Knopf Publishing Group.
—Sanctuary. mass mkt. 0.25 o.p. (*0-451-00632-1*, Signet Bks.); 1971. mass mkt. 1.25 o.p. (*0-451-04511-4*, Signet Bks.); 1968. mass mkt. 1.25 o.p. (*0-451-50685-5*, Signet Classics); 1968. mass mkt. 0.95 o.p. (*0-451-50413-5*, Signet Classics) NAL.
—Sanctuary. 1966. 10.00 o.s.i (*0-394-44368-3*); Vol. 381. 1967. pap. 4.95 o.p. (*0-394-70381-2*) Random Hse., Inc.
—Sanctuary. 1993. 18.05 (*0-606-19219-0*) Turtleback Bks.
—Sanctuary & Requiem for a Nun. 1976. 25.95 (*0-8488-0999-8*) Amereon, Ltd.
—Sanctuary & Requiem for a Nun. mass mkt. 0.50 o.p. (*0-451-01486-3*); mass mkt. 0.75 o.p. (*0-451-01900-8*); mass mkt. 0.35 o.p. (*0-451-01079-5*) NAL. (Signet Bks.).
—The Town. 1961. (ACE.). 384p. mass mkt. 11.00 (*0-394-70184-4*, V184, Vintage) Knopf Publishing Group.
—The Town. 1957. 13.95 o.s.i (*0-394-42452-2*) Random Hse., Inc.
—Uncollected Stories of William Faulkner. Blotner, Joseph L., ed. 1981. 732p. pap. 20.00 o.s.i (*0-394-74656-2*) Knopf, Alfred A. Inc.
—The Unvanquished. (Vintage International Ser.). 1991. 272p. pap. 12.95 (*0-679-73652-2*); Vol. 351. 1966. (Illus.). pap. 8.00 o.p. (*0-394-70351-0*, V351) Knopf Publishing Group. (Vintage).
—The Wild Palms. McHaney, Thomas, ed. 1986. (William Faulkner Manuscripts). 356p. text 50.00 (*0-8240-6818-1*); 408p. text 60.00 (*0-8240-6819-X*) Garland Publishing, Inc.
—The Wild Palms. 1984. 339p. 20.00 o.s.i (*0-394-60513-6*, V262, Vintage) Knopf Publishing Group.
—The Wild Palms. 1964. 352p. pap. 8.00 o.s.i (*0-394-70262-X*) Random Hse., Inc.
Faulkner, William & Blotner, Joseph. Uncollected Stories of William Faulkner. anniv. ed. 1997. 736p. pap. 19.00 (*0-375-70109-5*, Vintage) Knopf Publishing Group.
Faulkner, William & Oatman, Eric F. As I Lay Dying. 1985. (Barron's Book Notes Ser.). (gr. 10-12). pap. 2.50 o.p. (*0-8120-3502-X*) Barron's Educational Series, Inc.

**YS (IMAGINARY PLACE)—FICTION**

Anderson, Poul & Anderson, Karen. Dahut. 1988. (King of YS Ser.: Bk. III). (Orig.). pap. 3.95 o.s.i (*0-671-65371-7*) Baen Bks.
—Gallicenae. 1987. (King of YS Ser.: Bk. II). 384p. (Orig.). pap. 3.95 o.s.i (*0-671-65342-3*) Baen Bks.
—The King of Ys. 1996. 1216p. pap. 15.00 (*0-671-87729-1*) Baen Bks.
—Roma Mater. 1986. (King of YS Ser.: Bk. I). 480p. pap. 3.95 o.s.i (*0-671-65602-3*) Baen Bks.
Guyot, Charles. The Legend of the City of Ys. Cavanagh, Deirdre, tr. from FRE. & illus. by. 1979. 128p. lib. bdg. 12.00 o.p. (*0-87023-264-9*) Univ. of Massachusetts Pr.

**YUGOSLAVIA—FICTION**

Bradford, Barbara Taylor. Where You Belong. 2000. 464p. mass mkt. 7.99 (*0-440-23515-4*) Dell Publishing.
—Where You Belong. abr. ed. 2000. audio 25.00 (*0-553-52603-0*); audio compact disk 29.95 (*0-553-45674-1*) Random Hse. Audio Publishing Group. (RH Audio).
—Where You Belong. l.t. ed. 2000. 528p. pap. 13.95 (*0-375-72797-3*); 24.95 (*0-375-40974-2*) Random Hse. Large Print.
Franklin, Yelena. A Bowl of Sour Cherries. 1998. (New American Voices Ser.: Vol. 2). 242p. pap. text 14.00 (*1-877727-81-4*) White Pine Pr.
Handke, Peter. Repetition. Manheim, Ralph, tr. from GER. 1988. 225p. 18.95 o.s.i (*0-374-24934-2*) Farrar, Straus & Giroux.
Ireland, Perrin. Ana Imagined. 2000. vii, 195p. 22.95 (*1-55597-300-0*) Graywolf Pr.
Kauffman, Christmas Carol. Hidden Rainbow. 1997. 411p. (YA). mass mkt. 5.95 (*0-87813-958-3*) Christian Light Pubns., Inc.
—Hidden Rainbow. 1963. pap., mass mkt. 6.99 o.p. (*0-8024-3807-5*) Moody Pr.
Tesich, Nadja. Native Land. 1997. 320p. (Orig.). pap. 15.95 (*1-57129-042-7*, Lumen Editions) Brookline Bks., Inc.
Tisma, Aleksandar. The Book of Blam. 2000. 240p. pap. 13.00 o.s.i (*0-15-600841-6*) Harcourt Trade Pubs.
—The Book of Blam. Heim, Michael H., tr. from CRO. 1998. 240p. (C). 23.00 (*0-15-100235-5*) Harcourt Trade Pubs.

**YURT (IMAGINARY PLACE)—FICTION**

Brittain, C. Dale. A Bad Spell in Yurt. 1991. 320p. pap. 5.99 (*0-671-72075-9*) Baen Bks.
—Daughter of Magic. 1996. 352p. pap. 5.99 (*0-671-87720-8*) Baen Bks.
—Mage Quest. 1993. 368p. (Orig.). mass mkt. 4.99 o.s.i (*0-671-72169-0*) Baen Bks.
—The Witch & the Cathedral. 1995. 352p. (Orig.). mass mkt. 5.99 o.s.i (*0-671-87661-9*) Baen Bks.
—The Wood Nymph & the Cranky Saint. 1993. 320p. pap. 4.99 (*0-671-72156-9*) Baen Bks.

# Z

**ZANZIBAR—FICTION**

Foden, Giles. Zanzibar. 2002. 384p. (*0-571-20512-7*) Faber & Faber, Inc.
Fouchet, Lorraine. Le Phare de Zanzibar. l.t. ed. 1999. (French Ser.). (FRE.). 458p. pap. 30.99 (*2-84011-280-9*) Feryane, SA, Editions FRA. *Dist:* Ulverscroft Large Print Bks., Ltd., Ulverscroft Large Print Canada, Ltd.
Kaye, M. M. Trade Wind. 1985. mass mkt. 4.95 o.s.i (*0-553-25311-5*) Bantam Bks.
—Trade Wind. 1984. lib. bdg. 19.95 o.p. (*0-8161-3636-X*, Macmillan Reference USA) Gale Group.
Palmer, Catherine. A Whisper of Danger. 2003. (Christian Mystery Ser.). 26.95 (*0-7862-4874-2*) Thorndike Pr.
—A Whisper of Danger. 2000. (Treasures of the Heart Ser.). (Illus.). 384p. pap. 9.99 (*0-8423-3886-1*) Tyndale Hse. Pubs.

**ZENDA (IMAGINARY PLACE)—FICTION**

Colman, Ronald. The Prisoner of Zenda. audio National Recording Co.
Hope-Hawkins, Anthony. The Heart of Princess Osra. 1976. 18.95 (*0-8488-1370-7*) Amereon, Ltd.
—The Heart of Princess Osra. unabr. ed. 1991. audio 39.95 (*1-55686-384-5*, 384) Books in Motion.
—The Heart of Princess Osra. 1983. 250p. reprint ed. lib. bdg. 17.95 o.p. (*0-89966-477-6*) Buccaneer Bks., Inc.
—The Heart of Princess Osra. 2001. (Works of Sir Anthony Hope Hawkins ). reprint ed. pap. text 28.00 (*0-7426-8461-X*) Classic Bks.
—The Heart of Princess Osra. 2000. pap. 19.95 (*1-889439-12-6*); (Illus.). 24.95 (*1-889439-13-4*) Paper Tiger, The.
—The Prisoner of Zenda. 1976. 21.95 (*0-8488-0819-3*) Amereon, Ltd.
—The Prisoner of Zenda. 1994. (Illustrated Classics Collection). 64p. pap. 4.95 (*0-7854-0752-9*, 40509); pap. 3.60 o.p. (*1-56103-597-1*) American Guidance Service, Inc.
—The Prisoner of Zenda. unabr. ed. 1996. audio 54.95 (*0-7451-2745-2*, SAB111, Sterling Audio Bks.) BBC Audiobooks America.
—The Prisoner of Zenda. unabr. ed. 1997. audio 39.95 (*0-7861-1049-X*, 1821) Blackstone Audio Bks., Inc.
—The Prisoner of Zenda. 2000. per. 12.50 (*1-58396-534-3*) Blue Unicorn Editions.
—The Prisoner of Zenda. unabr. ed. 1989. audio 26.95 (*1-55686-298-9*, 298) Books in Motion.
—The Prisoner of Zenda. unabr. collector's ed. 1982. (J). audio 36.00 (*0-7366-3847-4*, 9013) Books on Tape, Inc.
—The Prisoner of Zenda. 1988. lib. bdg. 21.95 (*0-89966-226-9*) Buccaneer Bks., Inc.
—The Prisoner of Zenda. (Best Sellers of 1895 Ser.). reprint ed. lib. bdg. 48.00 (*0-7426-1061-6*); 2001. (Illus.). pap. text 28.00 (*0-7426-6061-3*) Classic Bks.
—The Prisoner of Zenda. abr. ed. audio 15.95 o.p. (*0-88646-098-0*, TC-LFP 7027); 1986. (YA). (gr. 7-9). audio 29.95 o.p. (*0-88646-789-6*, R 7027) Durkin Hayes Publishing Ltd.
—The Prisoner of Zenda. E-Book 2.49 (*0-7574-0382-4*) Electric Umbrella Publishing.
—The Prisoner of Zenda. l.t. ed. 1988. (Mainstream Ser.). 230p. reprint ed. 18.95 (*1-85089-208-3*) ISIS Large Print Bks. GBR. *Dist:* Transaction Pubs.
—The Prisoner of Zenda. 1989. audio 35.00 Jimcin Recordings.
—The Prisoner of Zenda. E-Book 1.95 (*1-58515-025-8*) MesaView, Inc.
—The Prisoner of Zenda. Watkins, Tony, ed. (Oxford World's Classics Ser.). 2002. 208p. pap. 8.95 (*0-19-283904-7*); 1994. 196p. pap. 7.95 o.p. (*0-19-282933-5*) Oxford Univ. Pr., Inc.
—The Prisoner of Zenda. E-Book 5.00 (*0-7410-0499-2*) SoftBook Pr.
—The Prisoner of Zenda. abr. ed. 1995. mass mkt. 16.95 incl. audio (*1-85998-202-6*) Trafalgar Square.
—The Prisoner of Zenda. 1994. 256p. pap. 4.95 o.p. (*0-460-87534-5*, Everyman's Classic Library in Paperback) Tuttle Publishing.
—The Prisoner of Zenda. 2002. 212p. pap. 19.95 (*1-59224-898-5*); lib. bdg. 29.95 (*1-59224-899-3*) Wildside Pr.
—The Prisoner of Zenda & Rupert of Hentzau. 2000. (Classics Ser.). 400p. 7.95 (*0-14-043755-X*, Penguin Classics) Viking Penguin.
—The Prisoner of Zenda Readalong. 1994. (Illustrated Classics Collection). 64p. pap. 13.50 o.p. incl. audio (*1-56103-599-8*); pap. 14.95 incl. audio (*0-7854-0768-5*, 40511) American Guidance Service, Inc.
—Rupert of Hentzau, unabr. ed. 1989. audio 47.95 (*1-55685-137-5*) Audio Bk. Contractors, Inc.
—Rupert of Hentzau: (Sequel to Prisoner of Zenda) 1976. 22.95 (*0-8488-1040-6*) Amereon, Ltd.
—Rupert of Hentzau: (Sequel to Prisoner of Zenda) 1987. lib. bdg. 25.95 (*0-89966-227-7*) Buccaneer Bks., Inc.
Sabatini, Rafael & Hope-Hawkins, Anthony. The Prisoner of Zenda. 1999. (Gateway Movie Classics Ser.). 384p. pap. 14.95 (*0-89526-309-2*, Gateway Editions) Regnery Publishing, Inc., An Eagle Publishing Co.

# PUBLISHER NAME INDEX

**1stBooks Library,** *( 1-58500; 0-9675669; 1-58721; 1-58820; 0-7596; 1-4033; 1-4107; 1-4140 )* Div. of Advanced Marketing Technologies, 2595 Vernal Pike, Bloomington, IN 47403 (SAN 253-7605) Fax: 812-961-1023; Toll Free: 800-839-8640
E-mail: 1stbooks@1stbooks.com
Web site: http://www.1stbooks.com

**21st Century Pr.,** *( 0-9717009; 0-9725719; 0-9728899 )* 3308 S. Meadowlark Ave., Springfield, MO 65807 Tel 417-889-4803; Fax: 417-889-2210; Toll Free: 800-658-0284
E-mail: lee@21stcenturypress.com
Web site: http://www.21stcenturypress.com.

**7-Fold Publishing,** *( 0-9667938 )* 7732 S. Cottage Grove, Suite 121, Chicago, IL 60619 Tel 773-723-5202; Fax: 773-723-4738
E-mail: viifoldterrence@aol.com
Web site: http://www.7foldpublishing.com.

**A & B Books** *See* **A & B Distributors & Pubs. Group**

**A & B Distributors & Pubs. Group,** *( 1-881316; 1-886433 )* Div. of A&B Distributors, 1000 Atlantic Ave., Brooklyn, NY 11238 (SAN 630-9216) Tel 718-783-7808; Fax: 718-783-7267; Toll Free: 877-542-6657; 146 Lawrence St., Brooklyn, NY 11201 (SAN 631-385X)
E-mail: maxtay@webspan.net
*Dist(s):* **D&J Bk. Distributors**
   **Red Sea Pr..**

**A & C Black (GBR)** *( 0-245; 0-333; 0-510; 0-7136; 0-85177; 0-85314; 0-212; 0-85146; 0-85147; 0-85317; 0-86019; 0-946716; 0-9507160; 1-85691 )* Dist. by Lubrecht & Cramer.

**A&M Bks.,** *( 0-9646648 )* Orders Addr.: P.O. Box 283, Rehoboth Beach, DE 19971 Tel 302-227-2893; Toll Free: 800-489-7662; Edit Addr.: 212 Laurel St., Rehoboth Beach, DE 19971.

**ABCDE Publishing,** *( 0-9642571 )* 456 E. 100 S, Spanish Fork, UT 84660.

**A Banner Bk. Imprint of Univ. Pr. of Mississippi**

**A Bison Original Imprint of Univ. of Nebraska Pr.**

**A E I/TITAN,** *( 0-9703056 )* 9601 Wilshire Blvd., No. 1202, Beverly Hills, CA 90210 Tel 323-932-0407; Fax: 323-932-0321
E-mail: webaei@aol.com
Web site: http://www.aeionline.com.

**AIMS International Bks., Inc.,** *( 0-922852 )* 7709 Hamilton Ave., Cincinnati, OH 45231-3103 (SAN 630-270X) Tel 513-521-5590; Fax: 513-521-5592; Toll Free: 800-733-2067
E-mail: aimsbooks@fuse.net
Web site: http://www.aimsbooks.com
*Dist(s):* **Shen's Bks..**

**AK Peters, Ltd.,** *( 1-56881 )* 63 South Ave., Natick, MA 01760 (SAN 299-1810) Tel 508-655-9933 All inquiries; Fax: 508-655-5847
E-mail: service@akpeters.com
Web site: http://www.akpeters.com.

**AM & K Publishing,** *( 0-9717610 )* 1113 Murfreesboro Rd., Suite 106-325, Franklin, TN 37064 Fax: 615-599-6603
E-mail: sales@amkpublishing.com
Web site: http://www.amkpublishing.com.

**AMG Pubs.,** *( 0-89957 )* Subs. of CLW Communications Group, Inc., Orders Addr.: P.O. Box 22000, Chattanooga, TN 37422 Tel 423-894-6060; Fax: 423-894-9511; Toll Free Fax: 800-265-6690; Toll Free: 800-266-4977; Edit Addr.: 6815 Shallowford Rd., Chattanooga, TN 37421 (SAN 211-3074) Toll Free Fax: 800-395-2682
E-mail: sales@AMGpublishers.com; info@ampgpublishers.com
Web site: http://www.amgpublishers.com; http://www.followinggod.com
*Dist(s):* **Anchor Distributors**
   **Appalachian Bk. Distributors**
   **Christian Bk. Distributors**
   **FaithWorks**
   **Riverside**
   **Spring Arbor Distributors, Inc.**
   **Twentieth Century Christian Bks..**

**†AMS Pr., Inc.,** *( 0-404 )* Brooklyn Navy Yard Bldg. 292, Suite 417, 63 Flushing Ave., New York, NY 11205 (SAN 106-6706) Tel 718-875-8100; Fax: 212-995-5413 Do not confuse with companies with the same or similar name in Los Angeles, CA, Pittsburgh, PA
E-mail: amserve@earthlink.net ; *CIP.*

**A New Hope Publishing,** *( 1-929279 )* 133-41 Rockaway Ave., No 2A, Brooklyn, NY 11233 Tel 718-498-2408
E-mail: newhopepublish@aol.com
Web site: http://www.anewhopepublishing.com.

**APKA Pubs., Translators & Bk. Distributors,** *( 1-888244 )* 110 Overhill Rd., Providence, RI 02906 Tel 401-331-8783 (phone/fax)
E-mail: david_shrayer@brown.edu.

**†A.R.E. Pr.,** *( 0-87604 )* Orders Addr.: 215 67th St., Virginia Beach, VA 23451-2061 Tel 757-428-3588 (Ext. 7355); Fax: 757-491-0689; Toll Free: 888-273-3400
E-mail: kkelly@edgarcayce.org
Web site: http://www.edgarcayce.org
*Dist(s):* **Baker & Taylor Bks.**
   **Brodart Co.**
   **DeVorss & Co.**
   **Midwest Library Service**
   **New Concepts Bks. & Tapes Distributors**
   **New Leaf Distributing Co., Inc.**
   **Red Wheel/Weiser** ; *CIP.*

**AAcorn Bks.,** *( 0-9663666 )* P.O. Box 647, Micaville, NC 28755-0647 Fax: 828-675-0026
E-mail: aacorn2@excite.com
*Dist(s):* **Parnassus Bk. Distributors.**

**A&B Bahr & Co. Imprint of Factor Pr.**

**Aardwolfe Bks.,** *( 0-9707776 )* P.O. Box 471, Aiea, HI 96701 Do not confuse with Aardwolf Books in Roseville, MN
E-mail: publisher@aardwolfe.com
Web site: http://www.aardwolfe.com
*Dist(s):* **Independent Pubs. Group.**

**A.B. Espanola, Editorial S.L. (ESP)** *( 84-89691 ) Dist. by* **Lectorum Pubns.**

**A-bar-V Publishing,** *( 0-9668804 )* 614 W. Cherry St., Drumright, OK 74030-2416 (SAN 299-7665) Tel 918-352-3988
E-mail: vrcooper@swbell.net.

**Abbeville Kids Imprint of Abbeville Pr., Inc.**

**†Abbeville Pr., Inc.,** *( 0-7892; 0-89659; 1-55859 )* 116 W. 23rd St., Suite 500, New York, NY 10011 (SAN 211-4755) Tel 646-375-2039; Fax: 646-375-2040; Toll Free: 800-278-2665; *Imprints:* Artabras (Artabras); Abbeville Kids (Abbeville Kids)
E-mail: service@abbeville.com; abbeville@abbeville.com
Web site: http://www.abbeville.com
*Dist(s):* **Client Distribution Services** ; *CIP.*

**Abdo & Daughters Publishing** *See* **ABDO Publishing Co.**

**†ABDO Publishing Co.,** *( 0-939179; 1-56239; 1-57765; 1-59197 )* Div. of the Abdo Consulting Group, Inc., Orders Addr.: P.O. Box 398166, Minneapolis, MN 55439-8166 (SAN 662-9164) Tel 952-831-2120; Fax: 952-831-1632; Toll Free: 800-800-1312; P.O. Box 56510, Vaughan, ON L4 8V3 Tel 905-851-4660; Fax: 905-851-5507; Edit Addr.: 4940 Viking Dr., Suite 622, Edina, MN 55435 (SAN 662-9172) Tel 952-831-2120 ext. 1; Fax: 952-831-1632; 938 Woodbridge Ave., Vaughan, ON L4L 8V3
E-mail: info@abdopub.com
Web site: http://www.abdopub.com ; *CIP.*

**Abelard Pr., The,** *( 0-9648817 )* P.O. Box 242, Manchester, NH 03105-0242 Tel 603-645-0143 Do not confuse with Abelard Pr., Bellevue, WA
*Dist(s):* **Alamo Square Distributors.**

**†Abingdon Pr.,** *( 0-687 )* Div. of United Methodist Publishing Hse., Orders Addr.: P.O. Box 801, Nashville, TN 37202-3919 (SAN 201-0054) Tel 615-749-6409; Fax: 615-749-6056; Toll Free Fax: 800-836-7802; Toll Free: 800-251-3320; Edit Addr.: 201 Eighth Ave., S., Nashville, TN 37202 (SAN 699-9956)
E-mail: info@abingdon.org
Web site: http://www.abingdonpress.com/
*Dist(s):* **CRC Pubns.** ; *CIP.*

**aBOOKS Distributing,** *( 1-57090 )* Div. of Creativity, Inc., 65 Macedonia Rd., Alexander, NC 28701 Tel 828-252-9515; Fax: 828-255-8719; Toll Free: 800-472-0438; *Imprints:* Farthest Star (Farthest Star)
E-mail: sales@abooks.com
Web site: http://www.abooks.com
*Dist(s):* **Midpoint Trade Bks., Inc..**

**Abrahams, William Bks. Imprint of Dutton/Plume**

**Abrams, Harry N. , Inc.,** *( 0-8109 )* 100 Fifth Ave., New York, NY 10011 (SAN 200-2434) Tel 212-206-7715; Fax: 212-645-8437
E-mail: webmaster@abramsbooks.com
Web site: http://www.abramsbooks.com
*Dist(s):* **Time Warner Bk. Group.**

**Absey & Co.,** *( 1-888842 )* 23011 Northcrest, Spring, TX 77389 Tel 281-257-2340; Fax: 281-251-4676; Toll Free: 888-412-2739
E-mail: Abseyandco@aol.com
Web site: http://www.absey.com
*Dist(s):* **Baker & Taylor Bks.**
   **Brodart Co.**
   **Follett Library Resources.**

*Names*

**Acacia Publishing, Inc.,** ( 0-9666572; 0-9671187 ) 1366 E. Thomas Rd., Suite 305, Phoenix, AZ 85014 Tel 602-265-4553; Fax: 602-274-1598; Toll Free: 866-265-4553
E-mail: editor@acaciapublishing.com; nic@hiredpen.com; karen@hiredpen.com

**Academica Pr., LLC,** ( 1-930901 ) 7831 Woodmont Ave., Suite 381, Bethesda, MD 20814 Tel 202-337-6811; Fax: 202-296-7490
E-mail: academicapress@aol.com
Web site: http://www.academica.com
*Dist(s):* **Books International, Incorporated.**

†**Academy Chicago Pubs., Ltd.,** ( 0-89733; 0-915864 ) 363 W. Erie St., Chicago, IL 60610-3125 (SAN 213-2001) Tel 312-751-7300; Fax: 312-751-7306; Toll Free: 800-248-7323 (Orders, outside Illinois)
E-mail: info@academychicago.com
Web site: http://www.academychicago.com
*Dist(s):* **Baker & Taylor Bks.**
**Brodart Co. ; CIP.**

**Acadia Publishing Co.,** ( 0-934745 ) Div. of World Three, Inc., P.O. Box 170, Bar Harbor, ME 04609 (SAN 694-1648) Tel 207-288-9025; Fax: 207-288-1132
E-mail: sales@acadiapublishing.com
Web site: http://www.acadiapublishing.com.

**Acclaim Bks.,** ( 1-57840 ) Div. of Acclaim Comics, Inc., 1 Acclaim Plaza, Glen Cove, NY 11542-2777 Tel 516-656-5000; Fax: 516-656-2037
*Dist(s):* **Penguin Group (USA) Inc..**

**Acclaim Comics, Incorporated** *See* **Acclaim Bks.**

**Accolade Bks.,** ( 0-9712082 ) 17005 Westland Ave., Southfield, MI 48075-7626 Tel 248-569-1432; Toll Free: 888-318-4794 Do not confuse with Accolade Books in Niceville, FL
E-mail: accoladebooks@qix.net
Web site: http://www.qix.net/accoladebooks.

†**Ace Bks.,** ( 0-441 ) Div. of Berkley Publishing Group, Orders Addr.: 405 Murray Hill Pkwy, East Rutherford, NJ 07073 Toll Free: 800-526-0275 (orders); Edit Addr.: 375 Hudson St., New York, NY 10014 (SAN 665-6404) Tel 212-366-2000; *Imprints:* Diamond Books (DiamondBks)
Web site: http://www.penguinputnam.com/
*Dist(s):* **Penguin Group (USA) Inc. ; CIP.**

**Ace/Putnam Imprint of Penguin Group (USA) Inc.**

**Acirfa Pubs.,** ( 0-9658573 ) Orders Addr.: P.O. Box 152141, San Diego, CA 92195-2141 Tel 619-263-7621; Fax: 619-263-7699; Edit Addr.: 2481 Kathleen Pl., San Diego, CA 92105
E-mail: aaacirfa@msn.com.

**ACME Pr.,** ( 0-9629880 ) Orders Addr.: P.O. Box 1702, Westminster, MD 21158 Tel 410-848-7577; Edit Addr.: 1116 E. Deep Run Rd., Westminster, MD 21158.

**Acorn Alliance,** 549 Old North Rd., Kingston, RI 02881-1220 Tel 401-783-5480; Fax: 401-284-0959; Fulfillment Addr.: Client Distribution Services 193 Edwards Dr., Jackson, TN 38301 Toll Free Fax: 800-351-5073; Toll Free: 800-343-4499
E-mail: contact@moyerbellbooks.com
Web site: http://www.moyerbellbooks.com
*Dist(s):* **Client Distribution Services.**

**Acorn Media Publishing, Inc.,** ( 0-945716; 1-56938 ) 801 Roeder Rd., Suite 700, Silver Spring, MD 20910 (SAN 247-4476) Tel 301-608-2115; Fax: 301-608-9312; Toll Free: 800-474-2277
E-mail: info@acornmedia.com
Web site: http://www.acornmedia.com
*Dist(s):* **Baker & Taylor Bks.**
**Critics' Choice Video, Inc.**
**Follett Media Distribution**
**Karol Video**
**Library Video Co.**
**Tapeworm Video Distributor, Inc.**
**Valley Media, Inc..**

**Acorn Publishing,** ( 0-9678801; 0-9710988; 0-9728969 ) Div. of Development Initiatives, 186 N. 23rd St., Battle Creek, MI 49015-1711 Tel 269-962-8184 (phone fax); Toll Free: 877-700-2219 Do not confuse with companies with the same or similar name in Broomfield, CO, Midvale, UT, Montpelier, VT, Sisters, OR, Suffern, NY, Salt Lake City, UT, Portland, OR, Sping Lake, MI
E-mail: editor@acornpublishing.com
Web site: http://www.acornpublishing.com
*Dist(s):* **Baker & Taylor Bks..**

**Ad Center, The** *See* **Leathers Publishing**

**Adamant Media,** ( 1-4021 ) 50 Cutler Ln., Chestnut Hill, MA 02467; *Imprints:* Elibron Classics (Elibron Class)
Web site: http://www.elibron.com.

**Adams, Scott Charles,** ( 0-9673045 ) P.O. Box 611, Maple Shade, NJ 08052 Tel 856-979-3841
E-mail: scott@neverdream.com
Web site: http://www.neverdream.com.

**Adams-Finnie, Bettie** *See* **Finnie, Bettie Adams**

**Addison-Wesley Educational Pubs., Inc.,** ( 0-321; 0-328; 0-673 ) Div. of Addison Wesley Longman, Inc., One Jacob Way, Reading, MA 01867 Tel 781-944-3700; Fax: 781-942-1117; Toll Free: 800-447-2226
Web site: http://www.awl.com.

†**Addison-Wesley Longman, Inc.,** ( 0-201; 0-321; 0-582; 0-673; 0-8013; 0-8053; 0-9654123 ) Orders Addr.: 200 Old Tappan Rd., Old Tappan, NJ 07675 (SAN 299-4739) Toll Free: 800-922-0579; Edit Addr.: 75 Arlington St., Suite 300, Boston, MA 02116 (SAN 200-2000) Tel 617-848-7500; Toll Free: 800-447-2226
E-mail: pearsoned@eds.com; orderdeptnj@pearsoned.com
Web site: http://www.awl.com
*Dist(s):* **Continental Bk. Co., Inc.**
**Pearson Education**
**Trans-Atlantic Pubns., Inc. ; CIP.**

**Addison-Wesley Longman, Ltd. (GBR)** ( 0-582 ) Dist. by **Trans-Atl Phila.**

**Addison-Wesley Publishing Company, Incorporated** *See* **Addison-Wesley Longman, Inc.**

**Adept, Inc.,** ( 0-9632422 ) Orders Addr.: P.O. Box 176, Starr, SC 29684 Fax: 864-352-2643; Edit Addr.: 750 Whall Rd., Starr, SC 29684
E-mail: sales@adeptbooks.com; wearle@wctel.net
Web site: http://www.adeptbooks.com; http://www.wiltonearle.com
*Dist(s):* **Baker & Taylor Bks.**
**Parnassus Bk. Distributors**
**Sandlapper Publishing Co., Inc..**

**Adirondack Empire, Inc.,** ( 0-9663423 ) 20 Excelsior Spring Ave., Saratoga Springs, NY 12866 Tel 518-587-5819; *Imprints:* Creative Bloc Press (Creative Bloc Pr)
*Dist(s):* **North Country Bks., Inc..**

**Adler & Adler Pubs., Inc.,** ( 0-917561 ) 5530 Wisconsin Ave., Suite 1460, Chevy Chase, MD 20815-4301 (SAN 656-5298) Tel 301-654-4271
*Dist(s):* **Biblio Distribution.**

**Admiral Hse. Publishing,** ( 0-9659602 ) Orders Addr.: 4281 7th Avenue SW, Naples, FL 34119 (SAN 299-4496) Fax: 239-455-3585
E-mail: admhouse@swfla.rr.com
*Dist(s):* **Barnes & Noble Bks.-Imports**
**Baker & Taylor Bks.**
**Book Warehouse**
**Bookazine Co., Inc.**
**Brodart Co.**
**Ingram Bk. Co..**

**Adobe Systems, Inc.,** ( 1-58039; 1-930161; 1-931208; 1-58945; 1-59061 ) 1601 Trapelo Rd., Waltham, MA 02451 (SAN 663-1975) Fax: 508-544-7053.

**Advanced Global Distribution Services,** 5880 Oberlin Dr., San Diego, CA 32121 Toll Free Fax: 800-499-3822; Toll Free: 800-284-3580.

**Adventure Hse.,** ( 1-886937 ) 914 Laredo Rd., Silver Spring, MD 20901-1867 Tel 301-754-1589; Fax: 815-361-5199
E-mail: sales@adventurehouse.com
Web site: http://www.adventurehouse.com
*Dist(s):* **Diamond Comic Distributors, Inc..**

**Adventures In Creative Living,** ( 0-9714319 ) 157 Timber Trail, Blanchester, OH 45107 Tel 937-289-9035; Toll Free: 866-289-9035.

**Advocacy Pr.,** ( 0-911655 ) Div. of Girls Inc. of Greater Santa Barbara, P.O. Box 236, Santa Barbara, CA 93102 (SAN 263-9114) Tel 805-962-2728; Fax: 805-963-3580; Toll Free: 800-676-1480
E-mail: advpress@impulse.net
Web site: http://www.advocacypress.com
*Dist(s):* **Baker & Taylor Bks.**
**Bookpeople**
**Wieser Educational, Inc..**

**Advocate Bks. Imprint of Alyson Pubns.**

**Aegina Pr., Inc.,** ( 0-916383; 1-56002 ) 1905 Madison Ave., Huntington, WV 25704 (SAN 665-469X) Fax: 304-429-7234; *Imprints:* University Editions (Univ Edtns)
E-mail: tommcat28@aol.com.

**Aeonian Pr. Imprint of Amereon, Ltd.**

**Aerial Imprint of Farrar, Straus & Giroux**

**Aerie Imprint of Doherty, Tom Assocs., LLC**

**Af-Am Links Pr.,** ( 0-9669613 ) 3100 SW Bracken Ct., No. 10, Topeka, KS 66614-6011 (SAN 299-8041)
E-mail: freedomships@aol.com; rdcarey@aol.com
*Dist(s):* **Booksurge, LLC.**

**Affiliated Writers of America, Incorporated** *See* **Alexander & Fraser, Inc.**

**Africa World Pr.,** ( 0-86543; 1-59221 ) 541 W. Ingham Ave., Trenton, NJ 08638 (SAN 692-3925) Tel 609-695-3200; Fax: 609-695-6466
E-mail: awprsp@africanworld.com
Web site: http://www.africanworld.com.

**African Writers Series Imprint of Heinemann**

**Africana Pub. Imprint of Holmes & Meier Pubs., Inc.**

**Afton Historical Society Pr.,** ( 0-9639338; 1-890434 ) Orders Addr.: P.O. Box 100, Afton, MN 55001 Tel 651-436-8443; Fax: 651-436-7354; Toll Free: 800-436-8443; Edit Addr.: 3321 Saint Croix Trail, S., Afton, MN 55001
E-mail: aftonpress@aftonpress.com
Web site: http://www.aftonpress.com
*Dist(s):* **Bookmen, Inc.**
**Brodart Co.**
**Coutts Library Service, Inc.**
**Eastern Bk. Co.**
**Galda Library Services, Inc.**
**Partners Pubs. Group, Inc..**

**Agate Publishing, Incorporated,** ( 0-9724562 ) 1501 Madison St., Evanston, IL 60202 Tel 847-363-1830
E-mail: agatepub@ameritech.net
*Dist(s):* **Consortium Bk. Sales & Distribution.**

**Agawa Pr.,** ( 0-9642436 ) 1246 Wenniway, Box 39, Mackinaw City, MI 49701 Tel 616-436-7032
*Dist(s):* **Partners Pubs. Group, Inc..**

**Agents of Change,** ( 1-928992 ) Div. of Granite Publishing, LLC, P.O. Box 1429, Columbus, NC 28722-1429 Tel 828-894-3088; Fax: 828-894-8454; Toll Free: 800-366-0264
E-mail: brian@5thworld.com
Web site: http://www.5thworld.com
*Dist(s):* **Bookpeople**
**New Leaf Distributing Co., Inc..**

**Agreka Imprint of Agreka Bks., LLC**

**Agreka Bks., LLC,** ( 1-888106 ) P.O. Drawer 39, Sandy, UT 84091-0039 Tel 801-733-0708; Toll Free Fax: 888-771-7758; Toll Free: 800-360-5284; *Imprints:* Agreka (Agreka)
E-mail: info@agreka.com
Web site: http://www.utahbooks.com; http://www.agreka.com; http://www.historypreserved.com
*Dist(s):* **Baker & Taylor Bks.**
**Quality Bks., Inc..**

**Aguilar Editorial (MEX)** ( 968-19 ) Dist. by **Santillana.**

**Aihole Publishing,** ( 0-9722925 ) 219 Lewis Wharf, Boston, MA 02110.

**Airmont Publishing Co., Inc.,** ( 0-8049 ) 160 Madison Ave., New York, NY 10016 (SAN 206-8710) Tel 212-598-0222; Fax: 212-979-1862
E-mail: customerservice@avalonbooks.com; orderdept@avalonbooks.com
Web site: http://www.avalonbooks.com/.

**Airplay,** ( 1-885608 ) 110 W. 86th St., 12th Flr., New York, NY 10024-4049 Tel 212-879-1201; Fax: 212-879-1013; Toll Free: 800-459-4925
*Dist(s):* **Barnes & Noble Bks.-Imports**
**Baker & Taylor Bks.**
**Bookazine Co., Inc.**
**Borders, Inc.**
**Brodart Co.**
**Koen Bk. Distributors.**

**Ajanta Pubns/Ajanta Bks. International (IND)** ( 81-202 ) Dist. by **S Asia.**

**AK Pr. Distribution,** ( 1-873176; 1-902593 ) 674-A 23rd St., Oakland, CA 94612-1163 (SAN 298-2234) Tel 510-208-1700; Fax: 510-208-1701
E-mail: akpress@akpress.org
Web site: http://www.akpress.org
*Dist(s):* **Consortium Bk. Sales & Distribution**
**SPD-Small Pr. Distribution.**

**Akadine Pr., The,** ( 1-888173; 1-58579 ) 141 Tompkins Ave., Pleasantville, NY 10570-3154 Tel 914-747-0777 ; Fax: 914-747-0778; Toll Free: 800-832-7323; *Imprints:* Common Reader Editions (Common Reader Eds)
E-mail: acr@akadine.com
Web site: http://www.acommonreader.com
*Dist(s):* **Trafalgar Square.**

**Akal Pubns.,** ( 0-9660942 ) P.O. Box 130563, Ann Arbor, MI 48113-0563 Tel 313-761-9357; Fax: 313-763-9224
E-mail: singh@caen.umich.engin.edu.

**Akashic Bks.,** ( *1-888451* ) P.O. Box 1456, New York, NY 10009 Tel 718-622-6463 (phone/fax) E-mail: akashic7@aol.com Web site: http://www.akashicbooks.com
*Dist(s):* **Baker & Taylor Bks.**
**Bookazine Co., Inc.**
**Bookpeople**
**Consortium Bk. Sales & Distribution**
**Koen Bk. Distributors**
**Last Gasp Eco-Funnies, Inc.**
**SPD-Small Pr. Distribution.**

**Akili Publishing,** ( *0-9659118* ) 4613 Sutherland Cir., Upper Marlboro, MD 20772 Tel 301-627-7461; Toll Free: 800-429-9367 (ext. 627-1130) E-mail: akilip@bellatlantic.net.

**Akimac Publishing,** ( *0-9662578* ) P.O. Box 41062, Dallas, TX 75241 Tel 972-441-3464; Toll Free: 800-583-3519.

**Alabaster Imprint of Multnomah Pubs., Inc.**

**Alamo Square Pr.,** ( *0-9624751; 1-886360* ) 103 FR 321, Tajique, NM 87016 (SAN 298-1289) Tel 505-384-9766 E-mail: alamosquare@earthlink.net
*Dist(s):* **Bookazine Co., Inc.**
**Bookpeople**
**New Leaf Distributing Co., Inc..**

**Alaska Northwest Bks. Imprint of Graphic Arts Ctr. Publishing Co.**

**Alcazar Audioworks,** ( *0-9724995; 0-9746806* ) 3032 Alcazar Dr., Burlingame, CA 94010-5814 Tel 650-692-1166; Fax: 650-692-7911 E-mail: bfrohman@pacbell.net Web site: http://www.alcazaraudioworks.com.

**Ale Publishing Co.,** ( *1-881301* ) P.O. Box 1396, Alto, NM 88312-1396 Tel 505-336-1698; Fax: 505-336-1847.

**Alef Design Group,** ( *1-881283* ) 4423 Fruitland Ave., Los Angeles, CA 90058 Tel 323-582-1200; Fax: 323-585-0327; Toll Free: 800-845-0662 E-mail: jane@torahaura.com Web site: http://www.torahaura.com.

**Alexander & Fraser, Inc.,** ( *1-879915* ) 507 Barlow, Wichita, KS 67207 Tel 316-706-7875; Fax: 316-686-1974 E-mail: jayfraser16@hotmail.com
*Dist(s):* **Baker & Taylor Bks..**

**Alexander Bks.,** ( *1-57090* ) Div. of Creativity, Inc., 65 Macedonia Rd., Alexander, NC 28701 Tel 828-252-9515; Fax: 828-255-8719
*Dist(s):* **Midpoint Trade Bks., Inc..**

**Alexander Distributing** *See* **aBOOKS Distributing**

**Alfaguara, Ediciones, S.A.- Grupo Santillana (ESP)** ( *84-204; 958-704* ) *Dist. by* **Lectorum Pubns.**

**Alfaguara, Ediciones, S.A.- Grupo Santillana (ESP)** ( *84-204; 958-704* ) *Dist. by* **Santillana.**

**Alfaguara S.A. de Ediciones (ARG)** ( *950-511* ) *Dist. by* **Santillana.**

†**Algonquin Bks. of Chapel Hill,** ( *0-7611; 0-912697; 0-945575; 1-56512* ) Div. of Workman Publishing Co., Inc., Orders Addr.: 708 Broadway, New York, NY 10003 Tel 212-254-5900 (orders, customer service); Fax: 212-614-7783; Toll Free Fax: 800-521-1832 (fax orders, customer sevice); Toll Free: 800-722-7202 (orders, customer service); Edit Addr.: P.O. Box 2225, Chapel Hill, NC 27515-2225 (SAN 282-7506) Tel 919-967-0108 (editorial, publicity, marketing); Fax: 919-933-0272 (editorial, publicity, marketing); 127 Kingston Dr., Suite 105, Chapel Hill, NC 27514 (SAN 662-2011); *Imprints:* Shannon Ravenel Books (Shannon Ravenel Bks) E-mail: dialogue@algonquin.com Web site: http://www.booksellerscorner.com; http://www.algonquin.com ; *CIP.*

**Alianza Editorial, S. A. (ESP)** ( *84-206* ) *Dist. by* **Lectorum Pubns.**

**Alianza Editorial, S. A. (ESP)** ( *84-206* ) *Dist. by* **Distribks Inc.**

**Alice Street Editions Imprint of Haworth Pr., Inc., The**

**Allen & Unwin Pty., Ltd. (AUS)** ( *0-04; 0-86861; 1-85242; 1-86373; 1-86448; 1-875680; 1-875889; 0-7299; 1-86508; 1-74114* ) *Dist. by* **IPG Chicago.**

**Allen & Unwin Pty., Ltd. (AUS)** ( *0-04; 0-86861; 1-85242; 1-86373; 1-86448; 1-875680; 1-875889; 0-7299; 1-86508; 1-74114* ) *Dist. by* **Paul & Co Pubs.**

**Alliance Hse., Inc.,** ( *0-9665234* ) 220 Ferris Ave., Suite 201, White Plains, NY 10603 Tel 914-328-5456; Fax: 914-946-1929 E-mail: alliancehs@aol.com.

**Allison & Busby, Ltd. (GBR)** ( *0-7490; 0-85031* ) *Dist. by* **Intl Pubs Mktg.**

**Alloway Publishing, Ltd. (GBR)** ( *0-907526* ) *Dist. by* **St Mut.**

†**Allyn & Bacon, Inc.,** ( *0-205; 0-321* ) Div. of Pearson Education Corp. Commun, Orders Addr.: 200 Old Tappan Rd., Old Tappan, NJ 07675 Toll Free Fax: 800-445-6991; Toll Free: 800-666-9433 (ordering); 800-922-0579 (customer service); 111 Tenth St., Des Moines, IA 50309 Tel 515-284-6751; Toll Free: 515-284-2607; Toll Free: 800-278-3525; Edit Addr.: 75 Arlington St., Suite 300, Boston, MA 02116 (SAN 201-2510) Tel 781-848-6000 E-mail: ab_webmaster@abacon.com Web site: http://www.abacon.com
*Dist(s):* **Pearson Education** ; *CIP.*

**Alpert's Bookery, Inc.,** ( *1-892666* ) P.O. Box 215, Nanuet, NY 10954 Tel 845-371-4209 E-mail: AlpertBook@aol.com Web site: http://www.alpertsbookery.com.

**Alpha Bks.,** ( *0-02; 0-672; 0-7357; 0-7897; 1-56761; 1-57595; 0-7431; 1-59257* ) Div. of Pearson Technology Group, 201 W. 103rd St., Indianapolis, IN 46290 (SAN 219-6298) Tel 317-581-3500 Toll Free: 800-571-5840 (orders) Web site: http://www.idiotsguides.com
*Dist(s):* **Libros Sin Fronteras**
**Penguin Group (USA) Inc.**
**Sams Technical Publishing, LLC**
**netLibrary, Inc..**

**Alpha Imagery,** ( *0-9703805* ) P.O. Box 61, Edmonds, WA 98020 Tel 425-640-6606 E-mail: jimhauge@aol.com.

**AltaMira Pr.,** ( *0-7619; 0-910050; 0-942063; 0-7425; 0-7591* ) Div. of Rowman & Littlefield Publishing Group, Orders Addr.: 67 Mowat Ave., Suite 241, Toronto, ON M6K 3E3 Tel 416-534-1660; Fax: 416-534-3699; 15200 NBN Way, Blue Ridge Summit, PA 17214 Tel 717-794-3800 (phone/fax); Toll Free Fax: 800-338-4550; Toll Free: 800-462-6420; Edit Addr.: 1630 N. Main St., No. 367, Walnut Creek, CA 94596 (SAN 299-4054) Tel 925-938-7243; Fax: 925-933-9720 E-mail: explore@altamirapress.com Web site: http://www.altamirapress.com
*Dist(s):* **National Bk. Network**
**Rowman & Littlefield Pubs., Inc..**

**Althouse Pr.,** ( *1-59087* ) 2251 Dick George Rd., Cave Junction, OR 97523 Tel 541-592-4142; Fax: 541-592-2597 E-mail: noah@oism.org Web site: http://www.robinsonbooks.org.

**Alyson Bks. Imprint of Alyson Pubns.**

**Alyson Pubns.,** ( *0-932870; 1-55583; 1-59350* ) Div. of Liberation Pubns., Inc., Orders Addr.: P.O. Box 4371, Los Angeles, CA 90078 (SAN 213-6546) Tel 323-860-6070; Fax: 323-467-0152; Toll Free: 800-464-4574 (orders only); Edit Addr.: 6922 Hollywood Blvd., Suite 100, Los Angeles, CA 90028; *Imprints:* Alyson Wonderland (Alyson Wonderland); Alyson Books (Alyson Bks); Advocate Books (Advocate) E-mail: mail@alyson.com Web site: http://www.alyson.com
*Dist(s):* **Consortium Bk. Sales & Distribution.**

**Alyson Wonderland Imprint of Alyson Pubns.**

**Amaro Bks.,** ( *0-9620556; 1-883203* ) 9765-C SW 92nd Ct., Ocala, FL 34481-8623 (SAN 249-2032) Tel 352-237-9840; Fax: 352-237-1810 E-mail: amarobooks@aol.com
*Dist(s):* **Book Warehouse.**

**Amazing Dreams Publishing,** ( *0-9719628* ) P.O. Box 1811, Asheville, NC 28802 E-mail: contact@amazingdreamspublishing.com Web site: http://www.amazingdreamspublishing.com.

**Ambassador-Emerald, International Imprint of Emerald Hse. Group, Inc.**

**Amber Bks.,** ( *0-9655064; 0-9702224; 0-9727519* ) 1334 E. Chandler Blvd., Suite 5-D67, Phoenix, AZ 85048 Tel 480-460-1660; Fax: 480-283-0991 E-mail: amberbk@aol.com Web site: http://www.amberbooks.com
*Dist(s):* **A & B Distributors & Pubs. Group**
**Baker & Taylor Bks.**
**Brodart Co.**
**Culture Plus Bks.**
**D&J Bk. Distributors**
**Follett Library Resources**
**Koen Bk. Distributors**
**Midwest Library Service.**

**Amber-Allen Publishing,** ( *1-878424* ) P.O. Box 6657, San Rafael, CA 94903-0657 Tel 415-499-4657; Fax: 415-499-3174; Toll Free: 800-624-8855 E-mail: joyce@amberallen.com Web site: http://www.amberallen.com
*Dist(s):* **Bookpeople**
**Publishers Group West.**

**Amereon, Ltd.,** ( *0-8488; 0-88411; 0-89190* ) Orders Addr.: P.O. Box 1200, Mattituck, NY 11952 (SAN 201-2413) Tel 631-298-5100; Fax: 631-298-5631; Edit Addr.: 800 Wickham Ave., Mattituck, NY 11952; *Imprints:* Carroll, J. M. Company (J M C & Co); Queens House, Incorporated (Queens House); Rivercity Press (Rivercity Pr); Aeonian Press (Aeonian Pr); American Reprint Company (Am Repr) E-mail: amereon@aol.com.

**American Audio Prose Library, Inc.,** ( *1-55644* ) Orders Addr.: P.O. Box 842, Columbia, MO 65205 (SAN 693-8205) Tel 573-443-0361; Fax: 573-499-0579; Toll Free: 800-447-2275; Edit Addr.: 600 Crestland Ave., Columbia, MO 65201 E-mail: aaplinc@gte.net Web site: http://www.americanaudioprose.com.

**American Biography Service, Incorporated** *See* **Reprint Services Corp.**

**American Book Publishing** *See* **American Bk. Publishing Group**

**American Bk. Publishing Group,** ( *1-930586; 1-58982* ) P.O. Box 65624, Salt Lake City, UT 84165 (SAN 254-4725) Fax: 801-382-0881; Toll Free: 800-296-1248; *Imprints:* American University & College Press (Amer Univ & Coll Pr) E-mail: info@american-book.com; orders@american-book.com; operations@american-book.com Web site: http://www.american-book.com.

**American Girl Imprint of Pleasant Co. Pubns.**

**American Guidance Service, Inc.,** ( *0-7854; 0-88671; 0-913476; 0-942277; 1-56269* ) 4201 Woodland Rd., Circle Pines, MN 55014-1796 (SAN 201-694X) Tel 763-786-4343; Fax: 763-786-9077; Toll Free: 800-328-2560 E-mail: ags@mr.net Web site: http://www.agsnet.com.

**American Historical Society of Germans from Russia,** ( *0-914222* ) 631 D St., Lincoln, NE 68502-1199 (SAN 204-7543) Tel 402-474-3363; Fax: 402-474-7229 E-mail: ahsgr@aol.com Web site: http://www.ahsgr.org.

**American History Pr.,** ( *0-89002* ) Div. of Conservatory of American Letters, 24 Thachter, Thomaston, ME 04861-0088 (SAN 241-6077) Tel 207-354-0998; Fax: 207-354-8953.

**American International Publishing Group,** ( *1-59040* ) 370 W. San Bruno Ave., Suite F, San Bruno, CA 94066 Tel 650-583-9700; Fax: 650-583-0235; *Imprints:* Phoenix Audio (Phoenix Audio) *Dist(s):* **Publishers Group West.**

**American Literary Pr., Inc.,** ( *1-56167* ) 8019 Belair Rd., Suite 10, Baltimore, MD 21236-3711 Tel 410-882-7700; Fax: 410-882-7703; Toll Free: 800-873-2003; *Imprints:* Five Star Special Edition (Five Star Spec Ed) E-mail: amerlit@erols.com Web site: http://www.erols.com/amerlit
*Dist(s):* **Baker & Taylor Bks.**
**Children's Library of Poetry**
**Temme Haus Pr..**

**American Pictures Foundation,** P.O. Box 2123, New York, NY 10009 (SAN 659-1957) Tel 212-614-0438.

†**American Psychological Assn.,** ( *0-912704; 0-945354; 1-55798; 1-59147* ) Orders Addr.: P.O. Box 92984, Washington, DC 20090-2984 (SAN 685-3137) Tel 202-336-6123; 202-336-5510; Fax: 202-336-5502 (orders); Toll Free: 800-374-2721; Edit Addr.: 750 First St., NE, Washington, DC 20002-4241 (SAN 255-5921) Tel 202-336-5836 E-mail: ghughes@spa.org Web site: http://www.apa.org ; *CIP.*

**American Reprint Co. Imprint of Amereon, Ltd.**

**American Univ. & College Pr. Imprint of American Bk. Publishing Group**

**American Univ. in Cairo Pr. (EGY)** ( *977-424* ) *Dist. by* **Bks Intl VA.**

**American World Geographic Publishing** *See* **Farcountry Pr.**

**Americana Publishing, Inc.,** ( *1-58807; 1-58943* ) 303 San Mateo NE, Suite 104A, Albuquerque, NM 87108 Tel 505-265-6121 (ext. 171); Fax: 505-255-6189; Toll Free: 888-883-8203 (ext. 171) E-mail: editor@americanbooks.com Web site: http://www.americanabooks.com.

**Ameritonia Inspirations,** ( *0-9701345* ) Div. of Alex Muriuki Memorial Trust, 2 High Plain St., Box 415, Norwood, MA 02062 Tel 781-784-0663 (phone/fax) E-mail: inspire@ameritonia.com Web site: http://ameritonia.com.

**Amherst Pr.,** ( *0-910122; 0-942495; 1-930596* ) Div. of
The Guest Cottage, Inc., Orders Addr.: P.O. Box 848,
Woodruff, WI 54568 (SAN 213-9820) Tel
715-358-5195; Fax: 715-358-9456; Toll Free:
800-333-8122; Edit Addr.: 8821 Hwy. 47, Woodruff,
WI 54568 (SAN 666-6450) Do not confuse with
companies with the same name in Amherst, NY, North
Hampton, NH
E-mail: sales@theguestcottage.com
Web site: http://www.theguestcottage.com.

**Amistad Pr. Imprint of HarperTrade**

**Amok Pr., Inc.,** ( *0-941693* ) Orders Addr.: P.O. Box 51,
New York, NY 10276 (SAN 666-5063).

**Ampersand Pr.,** ( *0-9650224* ) P.O. Box 91445, City of
Industry, CA 91715-1445 Tel 626-913-4005; Fax:
818-913-4465 Do not confuse with companies with
the same name in Princeton, NJ, Parker, CO.

**Anabasis,** ( *1-930259* ) P.O. Box 216, Oysterville, WA
98641-0216 Tel 360-665-3248; Toll Free:
800-527-6274
E-mail: anabasis@pacifier.com.

**Anacade International,** ( *0-9666192* ) Orders Addr.: P.O.
Box 6724, Santa Barbara, CA 93105; Edit Addr.: 3775
Modoc Rd., Suite 135, Santa Barbara, CA 93105-4462
Tel 805-569-5689; Fax: 805-569-9908; Toll Free:
877-705-7298
E-mail: helenhgordon@reporters.net;
helenhgordon@earthlink.net
Web site: http://www.anacade.com.

**Anchor Imprint of Knopf Publishing Group**

**Anchor Bible Imprint of Doubleday Publishing**

**Anchor Watch Pr.,** ( *0-9631460* ) Orders Addr.: P.O. Box
1230, Orange, VA 22960 Tel 540-672-1099; Fax:
540-672-4403
E-mail: anchor@ns.gemlink.com.

**Anchorage Pr.,** ( *0-87602* ) Orders Addr.: P.O. Box 2901,
Louisville, KY 40201-2901 (SAN 203-4727) Tel
502-583-2288; Fax: 502-583-2281 Do not confuse
with Anchorage Pr., Houston, TX
E-mail: applays@bellsouth.net.

**Andmar Pr.,** ( *0-916781* ) Orders Addr.: P.O. Box 217,
Mills, WY 82644 (SAN 654-2123) Tel 307-472-0890;
Fax: 307-472-0891; Edit Addr.: 2941 Pilot Dr.,
Casper, WY 82604 Tel 307-472-3107
E-mail: fjozwik@cs.com; fjozwik@compuser.com
Web site: http://www.andmar.com
*Dist(s):* **Baker & Taylor Bks.**

**Andover Pr.,** ( *0-9703512* ) Div. of SAC, Inc., Orders
Addr.: P.O. Box 588, Wharton, NJ 07885 (SAN
253-3243) Tel 908-852-7645; 973-361-0068; Fax:
973-361-0181; Edit Addr.: 361 W. Dewey Ave., Bldg
5, Wharton, NJ 07885 Do not confuse with companies
with the same name in New York, NY, Portland, OR
E-mail: pschneider@nac.net
Web site: http://www.andoverpress.com
*Dist(s):* **Alliance Hse., Inc..**

**Andre Deutsch (GBR)** ( *0-233* ) *Dist. by* **Trafalgar.**

**Andre Deutsch (GBR)** ( *0-233* ) *Dist. by* **Trans-Atl
Phila.**

**†Andrews McMeel Publishing,** ( *0-8362; 0-7407* )
Orders Addr.: c/o Simon & Schuster, Inc., 100 Front
St., Riverside, NJ 08075 Toll Free Fax: 800-943-9831
; Toll Free: 800-943-9839 (Customer Service;
800-897-7650 (Credit Dept.); Edit Addr.: 4520 Main
St., Kansas City, MO 64111-7701 (SAN 202-540X)
Tel 816-932-6600; Fax: 816-932-6749; Toll Free:
800-851-8923
Web site: http://www.AndrewsMcMeel.com
*Dist(s):* **AMCAL, Inc.**
        **Simon & Schuster, Inc. ;** *CIP.*

**Angel Bks. (GBR)** ( *0-88064; 0-946162* ) *Dist. by*
**Dufour**

**Angle Publishing Company, Incorporated** *See*
**Welcome Rain Pubs.**

**Angus & Robertson, Ltd. (GBR)** ( *0-207* ) *Dist. by*
**Consort Bk Sales.**

**Angus Publishing,** ( *0-9703526* ) 450 E. Lionshead Cir.,
No. 2D, Vail, CO 81657 Tel 970-476-6258; Fax:
970-476-1562 Do not confuse with companies with
the same or similar name in Salt Lake City, UT,
Marionville, MO
E-mail: tedmcfadden@compuserve.com
*Dist(s):* **Fulfillment Services, Inc..**

**Animazing Entertainment, Inc.,** ( *1-58083* ) 2221
Niagara Falls Blvd., Niagara Falls, NY 14304 Tel
716-731-5137; Fax: 716-731-9180.

**Annick Pr., Ltd. (CAN)** ( *0-920236; 0-920303; 1-55037*
) *Dist. by* **Firefly Bks Limited.**

**Anoai Pr.,** ( *0-9653971; 0-9702618* ) 3349-A Anoai Pl.,
Honolulu, HI 96822 Tel 808-988-6109; Fax:
808-988-1119
E-mail: kukui@lava.net
Web site: http://www.anoaipress.com
*Dist(s):* **Booklines Hawaii, Ltd..**

**Antelope Publishing,** ( *0-9703306* ) P.O. Box 1447,
Douglas, WY 82633
E-mail: fhageman@netcommander.com.

**Anthroposophic Press, Incorporated** *See* **SteinerBooks,
Inc.**

**Antioch Publishing Co.,** ( *0-7824; 0-89954; 1-4017* )
Div. of The Antioch Co., Orders Addr.: P.O. Box 28,
Yellow Springs, OH 45387-0028 (SAN 654-7214) Tel
937-767-7379; Fax: 937-767-6137; Toll Free:
800-543-1515; 800-543-2397; Edit Addr.: 888 Dayton
St., Yellow Springs, OH 45387 Do not confuse with
Antioch Publishing Co., Torrance, CA
Web site: http://www.antioch.com.

**Antipodes Bks. & Beyond,** 9707 Fairway Ave., Silver
Spring, MD 20901-3001 Tel 301-602-9519; Fax:
301-565-0160
E-mail: Antipode@antipodesbooks.com
Web site: http://www.antipodesbooks.com.

**Antique Collectors' Club,** ( *0-902028; 0-907462;
1-85149* ) Orders Addr.: 91 Market St. Industrial Park,
Wappingers Falls, NY 12590 (SAN 630-7787) Tel
845-297-0003; Fax: 845-297-0068; Toll Free:
800-252-5231 (orders)
E-mail: info@antiquecc.com
Web site: http://www.antiquecc.com;
http://www.antiquecc.com.

**AOL Time Warner Book Group** *See* **Time Warner Bk.
Group**

**Apache Beach Pubns.,** ( *0-9674503; 1-930253* ) 105
Matthews Point, No. 12, New Baltimore, NY 12124
Tel 845-353-2693
E-mail: apachebeach@aol.com.

**A-Peak Publishing,** ( *0-9667407* ) Orders Addr.: P.O.
Box 511, Johnstown, NY 12095 Tel 518-762-5309;
Fax: 518-762-5317; Edit Addr.: 2533 State Hwy. 29,
Johnstown, NY 12095
E-mail: apeak@superior.net
*Dist(s):* **North Country Bks., Inc..**

**APG Sales and Fulfillment,** Div. of Warehousing and
Fulfillment Specialists, LLC (WFS, LLC), 1501
County Hospital Rd., Nashville, TN 37218 (SAN
630-818X) Tel 615-254-2450; Fax: 615-254-2405;
Toll Free: 800-327-5113
E-mail: sswift@agpbooks.com
Web site: http://www.apgbooks.com.

**Apollonian Pr.,** ( *0-9627485* ) Orders Addr.: P.O. Box
25010, Washington, DC 20007; Edit Addr.: 1547 33rd
St., NW, Washington, DC 20007 Tel 202-338-4911.

**Appalachian Consortium Pr.,** ( *0-913239* ) Div. of
Appalachian Consortium, Inc., Appalachian State
Univ., University Hall, Boone, NC 28608 (SAN
285-8150) Tel 828-262-2064; Fax: 828-262-6564
E-mail: Burlesonec@appstate.edu.

**Applause Theatre Bk. Pubs.,** ( *0-936839; 1-55783* )
Orders Addr.: 151 W. 46th St., 8th Flr., New York, NY
10036 (SAN 658-3245) Tel 212-575-9265; Fax:
646-562-5852
E-mail: info@applausepub.com
Web site: http://www.applausepub.com
*Dist(s):* **Continental Bk. Co., Inc.
        Leonard, Hal Corp..**

**Appledore Bks.,** ( *0-9627162; 0-9741488* ) Orders Addr.:
P.O. Box 174, Hancock, NH 03449-0174 Tel
603-525-3581 (phone/fax); Edit Addr.: 7 Hosley Rd.,
Hancock, NH 03449
E-mail: appledorebooks@aol.com
Web site: http://www.appledorebooks.com
*Dist(s):* **Baker & Taylor Bks.
        Koen Bk. Distributors.**

**Apples & Oranges, Inc.,** ( *0-929637* ) Orders Addr.: P.O.
Box 2296H, Valley Center, CA 92082 (SAN
249-7662) Tel 760-751-8868; Fax: 760-751-8866
E-mail: mary@bajadestinations.com
Web site: http://www.bajadestinations.com
*Dist(s):* **Alpen Bks
        Angler's Bk. Supply
        Baker & Taylor Bks.
        Ingram Bk. Co.
        Pacific Bks..**

**Appletree Pr., Ltd. (IRL)** ( *0-86281; 0-904651* ) *Dist. by*
**IPG Chicago.**

**†Applewood Bks.,** ( *0-918222; 1-55709* ) 128 The Great
Rd., Bedford, MA 01730 (SAN 210-3419) Tel
781-271-0055; Fax: 781-271-0056; Toll Free:
800-277-5312
E-mail: applewood@awb.com
Web site: http://www.awb.com
*Dist(s):* **Consortium Bk. Sales & Distribution ;** *CIP.*

**Arabesque Imprint of BET Bks.**

**Arania Bks.,** ( *1-893530* ) Orders Addr.: P.O. Box 15691,
Fort Wayne, IN 46885-5691 (SAN 299-8327) Tel
219-486-3554 (phone/fax); Toll Free: 888-637-8208;
Edit Addr.: 6306 Old Brook Dr., Fort Wayne, IN
46835
E-mail: arania@earthlink.net.

**Arc Pr.,** ( *0-938041* ) Orders Addr.: 13581 Tyree
Mountain Rd., Lincoln, AR 72744 Tel 501-824-3821
Do not confuse with companies with the same or
similar names in Kent, OH, Kenmore, WA
Web site: http://www.solectec.com

**†Arcade Publishing, Inc.,** ( *1-55970; 1-58996* ) Orders
Addr.: c/o Time Warner Trade Publishing, 3 Center
Plaza, Boston, MA 02108 Toll Free Fax:
800-890-0875; Toll Free: 800-759-0190; Edit Addr.:
141 Fifth Ave., New York, NY 10010 (SAN
252-2012) Tel 212-475-2633; Fax: 212-353-8148
E-mail: arcadeinfo@arcadepub.com
Web site: http://www.arcadepub.com
*Dist(s):* **Publishers Group West
        Time Warner Interactive
        Time Warner Bk. Group ;** *CIP.*

**Arcadia Bks. (GBR)** ( *1-900850* ) *Dist. by* **Consort Bk
Sales.**

**Archer Bks.,** ( *0-9662299; 1-931122* ) Orders Addr.: P.O.
Box 1254, Santa Maria, CA 93456-1254 Tel
805-934-9977 (phone/fax)
E-mail: info@archerbooks.ccm;
rosemary.tribulato@verizon.net;
ab@archer-books.com
Web site: http://www.archer-books.com
*Dist(s):* **Midpoint Trade Bks., Inc.
        SPD-Small Pr. Distribution.**

**Archipelago Bks.,** ( *0-9728692* ) 239 W. 12th St., 3C,
New York, NY 10014 (SAN 255-4852)
E-mail: info@archipelagobooks.org
Web site: http://www.archipelagobooks.org
*Dist(s):* **Consortium Bk. Sales & Distribution.**

**Arco Imprint of Peterson's**

**Ardis Pubs.,** ( *0-87501; 0-88233* ) Orders Addr.: One
Overlook Dr., Woodstock, NY 12498 Tel
845-679-6838; Fax: 845-679-8571; Toll Free:
800-877-7133; 800-473-1312; Edit Addr.: c/o
Overlook Press, 141 Wooster St., New York, NJ
10012 (SAN 201-1492) Tel 212-673-2210; Fax:
212-673-2252
E-mail: publisher@ardisbooks.com
Web site: http://www.ardisbooks.com.

**Ardmore Pr.,** ( *0-8025* ) Div. of Illustrated World
Encyclopedia, Inc., 311 Crossways Park Dr.,
Woodbury, NY 11797 (SAN 204-5494) Tel
516-364-1800.

**Ardor Books.com** *See* **Sadorian Pubns.**

**Argo Pr.,** ( *0-9634181* ) Orders Addr.: P.O. Box 4201,
Austin, TX 78765-4201; Edit Addr.: 2208 Saratoga
Dr., Austin, TX 78733 Tel 512-263-5027
E-mail: mikeargo@Flash.net.

**Argonaut Pr.,** ( *1-882206* ) 369 11th St., San Francisco,
CA 94103-4313
*Dist(s):* **Publishers Group West.**

**†Ariadne Pr.,** ( *0-918056* ) 4817 Tallahassee Ave.,
Rockville, MD 20853 (SAN 210-1661) Tel
301-949-2514 (phone/fax); 301 949 2514 Do not
confuse with Ariadne Pr., Riverside, CA ; *CIP.*

**Ariadne Pr.,** ( *0-929497; 1-57241* ) 270 Goins Ct.,
Riverside, CA 92507 (SAN 249-5791) Tel
909-684-9202; Fax: 909-779-0449 Do not confuse
with Ariadne Pr., Rockville, MD
E-mail: bookinfo@ariadnepress.com
Web site: http://www.ariadnepress.com.

**Ariel Pr.,** ( *0-89804* ) Subs. of Light, P.O. Box 297,
Marble Hill, GA 30148-0297 (SAN 219-8460) Toll
Free: 800-336-7769 Do not confuse with companies
with the same or similar names in Bedrod, NH,
Berkeley, CA, Muscatine, IA.

**Arion Pr.,** ( *0-910457* ) 1802 Hays St., San Francisco,
CA 94129 (SAN 203-1361) Tel 415-561-2542; Fax:
415-777-2545
E-mail: arionpress@aol.com
Web site: http://www.arionpress.com.

**Arizona Highways,** ( *0-916179; 1-893860; 1-932082* )
Div. of Arizona Dept. of Transportation, 2039 W.
Lewis Ave., Phoenix, AZ 85009 (SAN 294-8974) Tel
602-712-2038; 602-712-2050; Fax: 602-254-4505
E-mail: pkmcmahon@dot.state.az.us
Web site: http://www.arizonahighways.com.

**Arizona State Univ. Ctr. for Asian Studies,** ( *0-939252*
) Arizona State Univ. Ctr. for Asian Studies, Tempe,
AZ 85287-1702 (SAN 220-1623) Tel 480-965-7184;
Fax: 480-965-8317
E-mail: asian.studies@asu.edu
Web site: http://www.asu.edu/clas/asian/cas.html.

**Ark Works, Inc.,** ( *1-887146* ) Orders Addr.: P.O. Box 1215, Orleans, MA 02653; Edit Addr.: 46 Main St., Orleans, MA 02653 Tel 508-240-1987 E-mail: Sales@ArkWorks.com. Web site: http://www.Arkworks.com.

**Arkham Hse. Pubs.,** ( *0-87054* ) Orders Addr.: P.O. Box 546, Sauk City, WI 53583 (SAN 206-9741) Tel 608-643-4500; Fax: 608-643-5043; *Imprints:* Mycroft & Moran (Mycroft & Moran) E-mail: sales@arkhamhouse.com. Web site: http://www.arkhamhouse.com.

**Armistead, Bob,** ( *0-9660098* ) 1907 Division St., Nashville, TN 37203 Tel 615-321-0639; Fax: 615-321-4023; Toll Free: 800-854-7832 E-mail: SouthernHistorical@Nashville.com. Web site: http://www.Southernhistorical.com.

**Arnica Publishing, Inc.,** ( *0-9726535; 0-9745686* ) 620 SW Main, Suite 345, Portland, OR 97205 (SAN 255-0091) Tel 503-225-9900 (phone/fax); Toll Free: 800-323-6554 (orders) E-mail: matt@arnicapublishing.com Web site: http://arnicapublilshing.com *Dist(s):* **Kumarian Pr., Inc..**

**Arnold Pubs. (IND)** *Dist. by* **S Asia.**

**Aronson, Jason Pubs.,** ( *0-7657; 0-87668; 1-56821* ) Orders Addr.: P.O. Box 1539, Fort Lee, NJ 07024-2539 (SAN 665-6536) Fax: 201-840-7242; Toll Free: 800-782-0015; Edit Addr.: 230 Livingston St., Northvale, NJ 07647 (SAN 201-0127) Tel 201-767-4093; Fax: 201-767-4330 Do not confuse with companies with similar name in Highmount, NY, Arcade, NY, Santa Monica, CA E-mail: editor@aronson.com. Web site: http://www.aronson.com.

**Arrowmist Publishing, Inc.,** ( *1-880144* ) Orders Addr.: P.O. Box 818, Lake Stevens, WA 98258 (SAN 297-4657) Tel 206-334-3157; Edit Addr.: 11702 20th NE, Lake Stevens, WA 98258.

**Arrowood Pr. Imprint of BBS Publishing Corp.**

**Arroyo Pr.,** ( *0-9623682; 1-887045* ) Orders Addr.: P.O. Box 433, Las Cruces, NM 88003 Tel 505-522-2348; Toll Free: 800-795-2692; Edit Addr.: 4932 Tobosa Rd., Las Cruces, NM 88001 E-mail: lgharris@lascruces.com *Dist(s):* **Baker & Taylor Bks.** **Sunbelt Pubns., Inc.** **Univ. of New Mexico Pr..**

**Arsenal Pulp Pr., Ltd. (CAN)** ( *0-88978; 1-55152* ) *Dist. by* **Consort Bk Sales.**

**Art of Hearing, Inc.,** 4905 N. Classen Blvd., Oklahoma City, OK 73118 Tel 405-843-7568; Fax: 405-843-7367; Toll Free: 800-949-1122 E-mail: studiop@earthlink.net Web site: http://www.studiop.com/art.html.

**Artabras Imprint of Abbeville Pr., Inc.**

**Artana Productions,** ( *1-877954* ) P.O. Box 1054, Marshfield, MA 02050 (SAN 630-9275) Tel 781-837-0962; Fax: 781-837-1238; Toll Free: 800-626-5356 E-mail: jay@ocallahan.com Web site: http://www.ocallahan.com *Dist(s):* **High Windy Audio** **Rounder Kids Music Distribution** **Yellow Moon Pr..**

†**Arte Publico Pr.,** ( *0-934770; 1-55885* ) Univ. of Houston, 452 Cullen Performance Hall, Houston, TX 77204 (SAN 213-4594) Tel 713-743-2841; Fax: 713-743-3080; 713-743-2847; Toll Free: 800-633-2783; *Imprints:* Piñata Books (Pinata Bks) E-mail: cebaker@uh.edu Web site: http://www.arte.uh.edu *Dist(s):* **Baker & Taylor International** **Bookpeople** **Coutts Library Service, Inc.** **Empire Publishing Service** **Follett Library Resources** **Lectorum Pubns., Inc.** **Libros Sin Fronteras** **Midwest Library Service** **Blackwell North America** **Quality Bks., Inc.** **SPD-Small Pr. Distribution** ; **CIP.**

**Artec Publishing,** ( *0-9651430* ) Orders Addr.: P.O. Box 25103, Greenville, SC 29616 Tel 864-288-2111; Toll Free: 800-445-0234; Edit Addr.: 15 Vintage Ave., Greenville, SC 29607.

**Artesian Pr.,** ( *1-58659* ) Div. of R. F. Dawn, Inc., 7300 Artesia Blvd., Buena Park, CA 90621 (SAN 253-1259) Tel 714-562-0415; Fax: 714-562-0237; Toll Free Fax: 888-462-0226; Toll Free: 888-734-9355 E-mail: MillerEduc@aol.com Web site: http://www.millereducational.com.

**Artex Press** *See* **Artex Publishing, Inc.**

**Artex Publishing, Inc.,** ( *0-930401; 1-57745* ) 4410 17th Ave., N., Saint Petersburg, FL 33713-4621 (SAN 670-9397).

**Arthur Mann Kaye,** ( *0-9632962* ) North Carolina Wesleyan College, Dept. of English, Rocky Mount, NC 27804 Tel 919-985-5193; Fax: 919-977-3701 *Dist(s):* **North Carolina Wesleyan College Pr..**

**Artspace Bks.,** ( *0-9631095; 1-891273* ) 33 Filbert Ave., Sausalito, CA 94965 Tel 415-331-3031; Fax: 415-332-7119 *Dist(s):* **Distributed Art Pubs./D.A.P..**

**Arx Publishing,** ( *0-9644234; 1-889758* ) 10 Canal St., Bristol, PA 19007 Tel 215-781-8600; Fax: 215-781-8602 E-mail: info@arxpub.com; info@evolpub.com Web site: http://www.arxpub.com; http://www.evolpub.com.

†**Ashgate Publishing Co.,** ( *0-566; 0-85331; 0-906909* ) Subs. of Ashgate Publishing, Ltd., Orders Addr.: 2252 Ridge Rd., Brookfield, VT 05036-9704 Tel 802-276-3162; Fax: 802-276-3837; Toll Free: 800-535-9544 (Orders - US & Canada); Edit Addr.: 101 Cherry St., Suite 420, Burlington, VT 05401-4405 (SAN 213-4446) Tel 802-865-7641; Fax: 802-865-7847 E-mail: ash.cs@aidcvt.com; info@ashgate.com; ash.orders@aidcvt.com Web site: http://www.ashgatechem.com; http://www.ashgate.com *Dist(s):* **American International Distribution Corp.** ; **CIP.**

**Ashgate Publishing, Ltd. (GBR)** ( *0-291; 0-566; 0-7512; 0-85331; 0-85417; 0-85967; 0-86078; 1-84014; 1-85521; 1-85628; 1-85928; 1-85972; 0-7546* ) *Dist. by* **Ashgate Pub Co.**

**Ashleigh-Reid Pubs.,** ( *0-9636031* ) 7142 Harlan Ln., Sykesville, MD 21784 Tel 410-552-0203.

**Ashley Bks., Inc.,** ( *0-87949* ) Orders Addr.: 4600 W. Commercial Blvd., Fort Lauderdale, FL 33319 (SAN 201-1409); Edit Addr.: P.O. Box 223580, Hollywood, FL 33022-3580.

**Asia Literary Pr., U.S.A,** ( *0-9671947* ) 20533 Biscayne Blvd., No. 160, Aventura, FL 33180 Tel 305-936-1618 ; Fax: 305-932-3033 E-mail: Asialit@webtv.net.

**Asian Educational Services (IND)** ( *81-206* ) *Dist. by* **S Asia.**

**Asiapac (SGP)** ( *981-3029; 9971-9; 981-3068; 981-229* ) *Dist. by* **China Bks.**

**Askeladd Pr.,** ( *0-9619327* ) 437 W. First St., Saint Charles, MN 55972 (SAN 243-7589) Tel 507-932-4099.

**Aspect Imprint of Warner Bks., Inc.**

**Aspen Bks.,** ( *1-56236* ) Div. of Worldwide Pubs., Inc., P.O. Box 1271, Bountiful, UT 84011-1271 Toll Free: 800-748-4850 E-mail: jasay@qwest.net; prawlins@aspenbook.com *Dist(s):* **Origin Bk. Sales, Inc..**

†**Aspen Pubs., Inc.,** ( *0-444; 0-7896; 0-8342; 0-87189; 0-87622; 0-89443; 0-912862* ) Subs. of Wolters Kluwer Nv, Orders Addr.: 7210 McKinney Cir., Frederick, MD 21704 Fax: 301-417-7550; Toll Free Fax: 800-901-9075; Toll Free: 800-638-8437; 800-234-1660 (Customer Service); Edit Addr.: 1185 Avenue of the Americas, 37th Flr., New York, NY 10036 (SAN 203-4999) Tel 212-597-0200; Fax: 212-597-0338 E-mail: customer.service@aspenpubl.com Web site: http://www.aspenpublishers.com ; **CIP.**

**Associated Publishers Group** *See* **APG Sales and Fulfillment**

**Associated Univ. Presses,** ( *0-8453* ) 2010 Eastpark Blvd., Cranbury, NJ 08512 (SAN 281-2959) Tel 609-655-4770; Fax: 609-655-8366; *Imprints:* Cornwall Books (Cornwall Bks) E-mail: aup440@aol.com Web site: http://arts.fdu.edu/aup/; http://www.aupresses.com.

**AST, Izdatel'stvo, OOO, firma (RUS)** ( *5-237; 5-7841* ) *Dist. by* **Distribks Inc.**

**Astarte Shell Pr.,** ( *0-9624626; 1-885349* ) HC 63, Box 89, Bath, ME 04530-9503 Tel 207-828-1992; Fax: 207-442-7260; Toll Free: 800-349-0941 E-mail: INTP@Biddeford.com Web site: http://www.HighwayTech.comAstarteShell *Dist(s):* **Snow Pocket Distributors.**

**Astor-Honor, Inc.,** ( *0-8392* ) 16 E. 40th St., Third Flr., New York, NY 10016 (SAN 203-5022) Tel 212-840-8800; Fax: 212-840-7246.

**Astran, Inc.,** 591 SW Eighth St., Miami, FL 33130-3413 (SAN 169-1082) Tel 305-858-4300; Fax: 305-858-0405; Toll Free: 800-431-4957 Web site: http://www.astranbooks.com.

**Asylum Arts,** ( *1-878580* ) 5847 Sawmill Rd., Paradise, CA 95969-5333 (SAN 297-2816) Tel 530-876-1454 E-mail: asyarts@sunset.net Web site: http://www.asylumartsbooks.com *Dist(s):* **SPD-Small Pr. Distribution.**

**Ata Bks.,** ( *0-931688* ) 1928 Stuart St., Berkeley, CA 94703 (SAN 211-4801) Tel 510-841-9613; Fax: 510-548-9846 E-mail: dorbob@flash.net.

**Athenean Pr., Inc.,** ( *0-9701466; 1-932108* ) 4160 S. Pecos Rd., Suite 20, Las Vegas, NV 89121 Tel 866-700-3076; Fax: 615-754-8592 E-mail: atheneanpress@aol.com Web site: http://www.atheneanpress.com *Dist(s):* **Ingram Bk. Co..**

**Atlantean Pr.,** ( *0-9626854; 1-885862* ) Orders Addr.: P.O. Box 7336, Golden, CO 80403 Tel 303-604-0788; Toll Free: 800-621-5535; Edit Addr.: 44 Rudi Ln., Golden, CO 80403.

**Atlantic Monthly Pr. Imprint of Grove/Atlantic, Inc.**

**Atlantida (ARG)** ( *950-08* ) *Dist. by* **Lectorum Pubns.**

**Atlas Video, Incorporated** *See* **Acorn Media Publishing, Inc.**

**AtRandom Imprint of Random House Adult Trade Publishing Group**

**Atria Imprint of Simon & Schuster**

**AttaGirl Pr.,** ( *0-929435* ) Div. of Damron Co., P.O. Box 422458, San Francisco, CA 94142-2458 Tel 415-255-0404; Fax: 415-703-9049; Toll Free: 800-462-6654 (ext. 29) E-mail: attagirlpress@aol.com Web site: http://www.attagirlpress.com.

**Attakapas Pr.,** ( *0-9667806* ) 1323 W. Saint Mary Blvd., Lafayette, LA 70506 Tel 318-237-6749; Fax: 318-235-1276 *Dist(s):* **BookMasters, Inc.** **Forest Sales & Distributing Co..**

**Aubrey Hse.,** ( *0-9675448* ) 3 Hillcrest St., Ashland, OR 97520 Tel 541-488-3842; Fax: 541-488-1953 E-mail: AubreyPub@aol.com.

**Auckland Univ. Pr. (NZL)** ( *1-86940* ) *Dist. by* **Paul & Co Pubs.**

**Audenreed Pr.,** ( *1-879418* ) Div. of Biddle Publishing Co., PMB 103, Box 1305, Brunswick, ME 04011 Tel 207-833-5016; Toll Free: 888-315-0582 (orders only) Web site: http://www.biddle-audenreed.com *Dist(s):* **Baker & Taylor Bks..**

**Audio Book Club Publishing** *See* **MediaBay Audio Publishing**

**Audio Bk. Co.,** ( *0-89926* ) 125 N. Aspen Ave., Suite 2, Azusa, CA 91702 (SAN 158-1414) Fax: 626-969-6099; Toll Free: 800-423-8273 E-mail: sales@audiobookco.com Web site: http://www.audiobookco.com.

**Audio Bk. Contractors, Inc.,** ( *1-55685* ) P.O. Box 40115, Washington, DC 20016-0115 (SAN 687-0376) Tel 202-363-3429 (phone/fax) E-mail: flogibsonABC@aol.com.

**Audio Editions Bks. on Cassette Imprint of Audio Partners Publishing Corp.**

**Audio Editions Mystery Masters Imprint of Audio Partners Publishing Corp.**

**Audio File, The,** ( *1-57816* ) Orders Addr.: P.O. Box 93, Glenview, IL 60025-0093 Tel 847-759-9288; Fax: 847-759-9289; Toll Free Fax: 800-997-8273; Toll Free: 800-555-3179; Edit Addr.: 1310 Callen Ln., Des Plaines, IL 60016-8737 E-mail: Audfile@aol.com.

**Audio Language Studies, Incorporated** *See* **Durkin Hayes Publishing Ltd.**

**Audio Literature,** ( *0-944993; 1-57453* ) 370 W. San Bruno Ave., Suite F, San Bruno, CA 94066 (SAN 245-9825) Tel 650-583-9700; Fax: 650-583-0235; Toll Free: 800-383-0174 E-mail: audiolit@aol.com Web site: http://www.audiouniverse.com *Dist(s):* **Baker & Taylor Bks.** **Landmark Audiobooks** **New Leaf Distributing Co., Inc.** **Publishers Group West.**

**Audio Partners, Incorporated** *See* **Audio Partners Publishing Corp.**

Names

**Audio Partners Publishing Corp.,** ( *0-88690; 0-945353; 1-57270* ) P.O. Box 6930, Auburn, CA 95604-6930 (SAN 253-4622) Tel 530-888-7803; Fax: 530-888-1840; Toll Free: 800-882-1840; Toll Free: 800-231-4261 (orders only); *Imprints:* Audio Editions Books on Cassette (Audio Editions); Cover to Cover Classics (Cvr to Cvr Classics); Audio Editions Mystery Masters (Audio Edits Mystry) E-mail: info@audiopartners.com
Web site: http://www.audiopartners.com
*Dist(s):* **Baker & Taylor Bks.**
**Landmark Audiobooks**
**Publishers Group West.**

**Audio Pr., The,** ( *0-939643* ) P.O. Box 666, Niwot, CO 80544 (SAN 663-5717) Tel 303-652-3050; Fax: 303-652-3923.

**Audio Renaissance,** ( *0-940687; 1-55927; 1-59397* ) Div. of Holtzbrinck Publishers, Orders Addr.: 16365 James Madison Hwy., Gordonsville, VA 22942-8501 Toll Free Fax: 800-672-2054; Toll Free: 888-330-8477; Edit Addr.: 175 Fifth Ave., Suite 315, New York, NY 10010 (SAN 665-1275) Tel 212-674-5151; Fax: 917-534-0980
*Dist(s):* **Holtzbrinck Pubs.**
**Landmark Audiobooks.**

**Audio-Forum** *See* **Norton Pubs., Inc., Jeffrey /Audio-Forum**

**Audioscope,** ( *1-57375* ) Div. of K-tel International (USA), Inc., 2605 Fernbrook Ln., N., No. H-O, Plymouth, MN 55447 Tel 612-559-6888; Fax: 612-559-6848; Toll Free: 800-328-6640
Web site: http://www.ktel.com.

**Augsburg Bks. Imprint of Augsburg Fortress, Pubs.**

†**Augsburg Fortress, Pubs.,** ( *0-8006; 0-8066* ) Orders Addr.: P.O. Box 1209, Minneapolis, MN 55440-1209 (SAN 169-4081) Tel 612-330-3300; Fax: 612-330-3455; Toll Free Fax: 800-722-7766; Toll Free: 800-328-4648 (orders only); Edit Addr.: 100 S. Fifth St., Suite 700, Minneapolis, MN 55402; *Imprints:* Fortress Press (Fortress Pr); Augsburg Books (Augsburg Bks) E-mail: info@augsburgfortress.org; productinfo@augsburgfortress.org; subscriptions@augsburgfortress.org; customerservice@augsburgfortress.com
Web site: http://www.augsburgfortress.org
*Dist(s):* **CRC Pubns. ; CIP.**

**Augsburg Fortress Publishers, Publishing House of The Evangelical Lutheran Church in America** *See* **Augsburg Fortress, Pubs.**

†**August Hse. Pubs., Inc.,** ( *0-87483; 0-935304* ) Orders Addr.: P.O. Box 3223, Little Rock, AR 72203-3223 (SAN 223-7288) Tel 501-372-5450; Fax: 501-372-5579; Toll Free: 800-284-8784; Edit Addr.: 201 E. Markham St., Little Rock, AR 72201 E-mail: order@augusthouse.com; ahinfo@augusthouse.com
Web site: http://www.augusthouse.com
*Dist(s):* **Continental Bk. Co., Inc. ; CIP.**

†**Aunt Lute Bks.,** ( *0-918040; 0-933216; 1-879960* ) Div. of Aunt Lute Foundation, Orders Addr.: P.O. Box 410687, San Francisco, CA 94141 Tel 415-826-1300; Fax: 415-826-8300; Edit Addr.: 2180 Bryant St., San Francisco, CA 94110-2128
E-mail: books@auntlute.com
Web site: http://www.auntlute.com
*Dist(s):* **Bookpeople**
**Consortium Bk. Sales & Distribution**
**SPD-Small Pr. Distribution ; CIP.**

**Aunt Strawberry Bks.,** ( *0-9669988* ) Orders Addr.: P.O. Box 819, Boulder, CO 80306-0819 (SAN 299-9811) Tel 303-449-3574; Fax: 303-444-9221; Edit Addr.: 3255 20th St., Boulder, CO 80304 E-mail: samthe1@hotmail.com.

**Auriga, Ediciones S.A. (ESP)** ( *84-7281* ) Dist. by **Continental Bk.**

**Authorlink,** ( *1-928704* ) 3720 Millswood Dr., Irving, TX 75062-7537 Tel 972-650-1986; Fax: 972-650-1622; *Imprints:* Fusion Press (Fusion Pr); Authorlink Press (Authorlink Pr) E-mail: dbooth@authorlink.com
Web site: http://www.authorlink.net; http://www.authorlink.com.

**Authorlink Pr. Imprint of Authorlink**

**Authors & Artists Publishers of New York,** ( *0-9708053; 0-9724922* ) 3 Kimberly Dr., Suite B, Dryden, NY 13053 Tel 607-273-2870 E-mail: authorsartists@aol.com
Web site: http://www.aapny.com.

**Authors & Artists Publishing of New York** *See* **Authors & Artists Publishers of New York**

**Authors Choice Pr. Imprint of iUniverse, Inc.**

**Autumn Bks. Imprint of Pontalba Pr.**

**AV Concepts Corp.,** ( *0-931334; 1-55576* ) 30 Montauk Blvd., Oakdale, NY 11769 (SAN 655-5888) Tel 516-567-7227; Fax: 516-567-8745
*Dist(s):* **Continental Bk. Co., Inc..**

**Avalon Bks. Imprint of Bouregy, Thomas & Co., Inc.**

**Avalon Publishing Group,** ( *0-7867; 0-88184; 0-929654; 0-931188; 0-938410; 1-56025; 1-56201; 1-56924; 1-58005; 1-878067* ) Div. of Avalon Publishing Group Inc., 161 William St., 16th Flr., New York, NY 10038 Tel 646-375-2570; Fax: 646-375-2571; *Imprints:* Blue Moon Books (Blue Moo); Thunder's Mouth Press (Thunders Mouth); Seal Press (Seal); Carroll & Graf Publishers (Carr & Graf); Marlowe & Company (Marl & Co) Web site: http://www.sealpress.com; http://www.carrollandgraf.com; http://www.marlowepub.com; http://www.thundersmouth.com; http://www.avalonpub.com
*Dist(s):* **Bilingual Pubns. Co., The**
**Publishers Group West**
**netLibrary, Inc..**

**Ave Maria Pr.,** ( *0-87793; 0-939516; 1-59471* ) P.O. Box 428, Notre Dame, IN 46556-0428 (SAN 201-1255) Tel 547-287-2831; Fax: 574-239-2908; Toll Free Fax: 800-282-5681; Toll Free: 800-282-1865; *Imprints:* Forest of Peace Publishing (For Peace Pubng); More, Thomas (Thomas More) E-mail: avemariapress.1@nd.edu
Web site: http://www.avemariapress.com.

**Aventura Bks. Imprint of Great Marsh Pr.**

**Avery Color Studios, Inc.,** ( *0-932212; 1-892384* ) 511 D Ave., Gwinn, MI 49841 (SAN 211-1470) Tel 906-346-3908; Fax: 906-346-3015; Toll Free: 800-722-9925
E-mail: avery@portup.com
*Dist(s):* **Partners Pubs. Group, Inc.**
**Hale, Robert & Co., Inc..**

**Avid Pr., LLC,** ( *1-929613; 1-931419* ) 5470 Red Fox Dr., Brighton, MI 48114-9079 Tel 810-801-1177; Fax: 503-210-6765; Toll Free: 888-284-3257 (888-AVIDBKS (orders); *Imprints:* Mosaic (Mosaic MI) Do not confuse with Avid Pr., New Paltz, NY E-mail: cgs@avidpress.com
Web site: http://www.avidpress.com.

**Avisson Pr., Inc.,** ( *1-888105* ) Orders Addr.: P.O. Box 38816, Greensboro, NC 27438-8816 (SAN 298-8127) Tel 336-288-6989; Fax: 336-288-6989; Edit Addr.: 3007 Taliaferro Rd., Greensboro, NC 27408 (SAN 298-8097).

**Avocet Pr., Inc.,** ( *0-9661072; 0-9677346; 0-9705049; 0-9725078* ) 19 Paul Ct., Pearl River, NY 10965-1539 (SAN 299-4631) Fax: 845-735-6807; Toll Free: 877-428-6238
E-mail: books@avocetpress.com
Web site: http://www.avocetpress.com
*Dist(s):* **Words Distributing Co..**

**Avon Bks. Imprint of Morrow/Avon**

**Awe-Struck E-Bks.,** ( *1-928670; 1-58749* ) 2458 Cherry St., Dubuque, IA 52001-5749
E-mail: kdstruck@home.com
Web site: http://www.awe-struck.net.

**Ayer Co. Pubs., Inc.,** ( *0-88143* ) Orders Addr.: c/o IDS, 300 Bedford St., Suite B-213, Manchester, NH 03101 (SAN 211-1936) Fax: 603-669-7945; Toll Free: 888-267-7323
E-mail: cservice@ayerpub.com
Web site: http://www.ayerpub.com.

**B&B Audio, Inc.,** ( *1-882071* ) 3175 Commercial Ave., Suite 107B, Northbrook, IL 60062 (SAN 248-207X) Tel 847-562-9516; Fax: 847-562-9517; Toll Free: 800-354-7836 (orders) E-mail: info@bandbaudio.com
Web site: http://www.bandbaudio.com
*Dist(s):* **Landmark Audiobooks.**

**B & R Samizdat Express,** ( *0-915232; 0-931968* ) P.O. Box 161, West Roxbury, MA 02132 (SAN 207-1037) Tel 617-469-2269
E-mail: seltzer@samizdat.com
Web site: http://www.samizdat.com.

**B & W Publishing (GBR)** ( *1-873631; 0-9515151; 1-903265* ) Dist. by **Interlink Pub.**

**B Ediciones S.A. (ESP)** ( *84-406; 84-7735; 84-666* ) Dist. by **Lectorum Pubns.**

**B Ediciones S.A. (ESP)** ( *84-406; 84-7735; 84-666* ) Dist. by **Distribks Inc.**

**BNI Pubns., Inc.,** ( *1-55701; 1-878088* ) 1612 S. Clementine St., Anaheim, CA 92802 (SAN 664-2624) Tel 714-517-0970; Fax: 714-535-8078; Toll Free: 888-246-2665; 800-873-6397; 629 Highland Ave., Needham Heights, MA 02494 Tel 781-455-1466; Fax: 781-455-1493; Toll Free: 800-873-6397 E-mail: sales@bnibooks.com
Web site: http://www.bni-books.com
*Dist(s):* **BookWorld Services, Inc.**
**Craftsman Bk. Co..**

**BS Bk. Publishing,** ( *0-9667203* ) 975 Village Sq S., Palm Springs, CA 92262-7599
E-mail: stamplee@aol.com
*Dist(s):* **Baker & Taylor Bks..**

**Back Alley Bks. Imprint of Barbadoes Hall Communications**

**Back Bay Imprint of Little Brown & Co.**

**Backinprint.com Imprint of iUniverse, Inc.**

**Badboy Imprint of Masquerade Bks., Inc.**

**Badger Bks., Inc.,** ( *1-878569; 1-932542* ) Orders Addr.: P.O. Box 192, Oregon, WI 53575 (SAN 297-9055) Tel 608-835-3638 (phone/fax); Toll Free: 800-928-2372; Edit Addr.: 350 Richards Rd., Oregon, WI 53575; *Imprints:* Waubesa Press (Waubesa Pr) E-mail: books@badgerbooks.com
Web site: http://www.badgerbooks.com
*Dist(s):* **Midpoint Trade Bks., Inc..**

**Baen Bks.,** ( *0-671; 1-55594; 0-7434* ) Orders Addr.: c/o Simon & Schuster, 200 Old Tappan Rd., Old Tappan, NJ 07675 Fax: 800-445-6991; Toll Free: 800-223-2336; Edit Addr.: c/o Simon & Schuster, 1230 Ave. of the Americas, New York, NY 10020 (SAN 658-8417) Tel 212-698-7000; Toll Free: 800-223-2348 (customer service); *Imprints:* Starline (Starline NY) Web site: http://www.simonsays.com/
*Dist(s):* **Simon & Schuster, Inc..**

**Bagehot Council** *See* **Griffon Hse. Pubns.**

**Baggetts Investigative Enterprises, Ltd.,** ( *0-9666111* ) Orders Addr.: P.O. Box 448, Ringgold, LA 71068 Tel 318-894-9370; Edit Addr.: 233 Haynes Rd., Ringgold, LA 71068
E-mail: oleirv@juno.com.

**BainBridgeBooks,** ( *1-891696* ) 311 Bainbridge St., Philadelphia, PA 19147 Tel 215-925-5083; Fax: 215-925-7412; 215-925-1912 Do not confuse with Bainbridge Books, Jacksboro, TX E-mail: order@transpub.comatlabtic
Web site: http://www.transatlanticpub.com
*Dist(s):* **Trans-Atlantic Pubns., Inc..**

**Baker & Taylor Bks.,** ( *0-8480* ) Orders Addr.: Commerce Service Ctr., 251 Mt. Olive Church Rd., Commerce, GA 30599-9988 (SAN 169-1503) Tel 404-335-5000; Toll Free: 800-775-1800 (orders); 800-775-1200 (customer service); Reno Service Ctr., 1160 Trademark Dr., Reno, NV 89511 (SAN 169-4464) Tel 775-850-3800; Fax: 775-850-3826 (customer service); Toll Free Fax: 800-775-7480 (orders); Edit Addr.: National Sales Hdqtrs., 5 Lakepointe Plaza, Suite 500, 2709 Water Ridge Pkwy., Charlotte, NC 28217 (SAN 169-5606) Fax: 704-329-8989; Toll Free: 800-775-1800 (information) ; 1120 US Hwy. 22, E., Bridgewater, NJ 08807 (SAN 169-4901) Toll Free: 800-775-1500 (customer service) E-mail: btinfo@btol.com
Web site: http://www.btol.com.

**Baker Bks.,** ( *0-8010; 0-913686* ) Div. of Baker Bk. Hse., Orders Addr.: P.O. Box 6287, Grand Rapids, MI 49516-6287 (SAN 299-1500) Toll Free Fax: 800-398-3111 (orders only); Toll Free: 800-877-2665 (orders only); Edit Addr.: 6030 E. Fulton, Ada, MI 49301 (SAN 201-4041) Tel 616-676-9185; Fax: 616-676-9573
Web site: http://www.bakerbooks.com
*Dist(s):* **Baker Bk. Hse., Inc.**
**CRC Pubns.**
**Twentieth Century Christian Bks..**

**Baker, George** *See* **Kildara Pr.**

**Baker Street Irregulars, The,** ( *0-9648788* ) 7938 Mill Stream Cir., Indianapolis, IN 46278 Tel 317-293-2212.

**Balance Publishing Co.,** ( *1-878298* ) 1346 S. Quality Ave., Sanger, CA 93657 Tel 559-876-1577 phone/fax Do not confuse with companies with similar names in Naples, FL, Port Charlotte, FL E-mail: balance02@sprynet.com
Web site: http://www.balancepublishing.com.

**Bald Eagle Pr.,** ( *0-9666739* ) Orders Addr.: P.O. Box 422, Louisianna, MO 63353 Tel 217-367-4588; 605 W. Pennsylvania Ave., Urbana, IL 61801 E-mail: baldeagle@big-river.net
Web site: http://www.whiteroot.com.

**Ballantine Bks. Imprint of Ballantine Bks.**

**Names**

†**Ballantine Bks.**, ( *0-345; 0-449; 0-8041; 0-87637; 1-4000* ) Div. of Random Hse., Inc., Orders Addr.: 400 Hahn Rd., Westminster, MD 21157 Tel 410-848-1900; Toll Free Fax: 800-767-4465; Toll Free: 800-726-0600 (customer service); 800-733-3000 (orders); Edit Addr.: 1540 Broadway, 11th Flr., New York, NY 10036 (SAN 214-1175) Tel 212-782-9000; Fax: 212-940-7539; Toll Free: 800-733-3000; *Imprints:* Del Rey (Del Rey); Ballantine Books (Ballantine Bks); Fawcett (Fawcett); Ivy Books (Ivy); One World/Ballantine (OneWorl-Bal); Presidio Press (Presid Pr)
E-mail: bfi@randomnhouse.com;
thenry@randomhouse.com
Web site: http://www.randomhouse.com
*Dist(s):* **Random Hse., Inc. ; CIP.**

**Ballantine Publishing Group** *See* **Ballantine Bks.**

**Balsam Press, Incorporated** *See* **Master Communications Group, Inc.**

**Bamberger Bks.**, ( *0-917453* ) P.O. Box 1126, Flint, MI 48501-1126 Tel 810-232-5396
*Dist(s):* **SPD-Small Pr. Distribution.**

**Bamboo Ridge Pr.**, ( *0-910043* ) P.O. Box 61781, Honolulu, HI 96839-1781 (SAN 240-8740) Tel 808-626-1481 (phone/fax)
E-mail: brinfo@bambooridge.com
Web site: http://www.bambooridge.com
*Dist(s):* **Booklines Hawaii, Ltd.**
**SPD-Small Pr. Distribution**
**Univ. of Hawaii Pr..**

**Bancroft Pr.**, ( *0-9631246; 0-9635376; 1-890862* ) P.O. Box 65360, Baltimore, MD 21209-9945 Tel 410-358-0658; Fax: 410-764-1967; Toll Free: 800-637-7377 Do not confuse with Bancroft Pr., San Rafael, CA
E-mail: bruceb@bancroftpress.com
Web site: http://www.bancroftpress.com
*Dist(s):* **Baker & Taylor Bks.**
**Book Hse., Inc., The**
**Brodart Co.**
**Fell, Frederick Pubs., Inc.**
**Yankee Bk. Peddler, Inc..**

**Bandit Bks., Inc.**, ( *1-878177* ) Orders Addr.: P.O. Box 11721, Winston-Salem, NC 27116-1721 Tel 910-785-7417; Edit Addr.: 2324 Union Cross Rd., Winston-Salem, NC 27107 Do not confuse with Bandit Bk., Inc., Virginia Beach, VA
*Dist(s):* **Blair, John F. Pub..**

**Banis & Associates** *See* **Science & Humanities Pr.**

**Banks Channel Bks.**, ( *0-9635967; 1-889199* ) 2314 Waverly Dr., Wilmington, NC 28403 Tel 910-762-4677
E-mail: bankschan@ec.rr.com
*Dist(s):* **Blair, John F. Pub..**

**Banned Bks. Imprint of Edward-William Publishing Co.**

**Banner of Truth, The,** ( *0-85151* ) Orders Addr.: P.O. Box 621, Carlisle, PA 17013 Tel 717-249-5747; Fax: 717-249-0604; Toll Free: 800-263-8085; Edit Addr.: 63 E. Louther St., Carlisle, PA 17013 (SAN 112-1553)
E-mail: info@banneroftruth.org
Web site: http://www.banneroftruth.co.uk
*Dist(s):* **Spring Arbor Distributors, Inc..**

**Bantam Imprint of Bantam Bks.**

†**Bantam Bks.**, ( *0-553; 0-593; 0-7704; 1-4000* ) Div. of Bantam Dell Publishing Group, Orders Addr.: 400 Hahn Rd., Westminster, MD 21157 Tel 410-848-1900 ; Toll Free: 800-726-0600; Edit Addr.: 1540 Broadway, New York, NY 10036-4094 Tel 212-354-6500; Fax: 212-492-8941; Toll Free Fax: 800-233-3294; Toll Free: 800-223-6834 (Bulk orders); 800-726-0600 (Orders/Customer service); *Imprints:* Spectra (Spectra); Bantam Classics (Bantam Classics); Bantam (Bant); Fanfare (Fanfare); Crimeline (Crimeline); Corgi (Crgi); Domain (Domain)
E-mail: bantampublicity@randomhouse.com
Web site: http://www.bantam.com
*Dist(s):* **Random Hse., Inc. ; CIP.**

**Bantam Classics Imprint of Bantam Bks.**

†**Bantam Dell Publishing Group,** ( *0-440; 0-553; 0-593; 0-7704; 1-4000* ) Div. of Random House, Inc., Orders Addr.: 400 Hahn Rd., Westminster, MD 21157 (SAN 201-3983) Tel 410-848-1900; Toll Free: 800-726-0600 ; Edit Addr.: 1540 Broadway, New York, NY 10036-4094 (SAN 201-0097) Tel 212-354-6500; Fax: 212-492-8941
*Dist(s):* **Giron Bks.**
**Random Hse., Inc. ; CIP.**

**Bantam Doubleday Dell Large Print Group, Inc.**, ( *0-385* ) Orders Addr.: 2451 S. Wolf Rd., Des Plaines, IL 60018 Toll Free: 800-323-9872 (orders); 800-258-4233 (EDI ordering); Edit Addr.: 1540 Broadway, New York, NY 10036-4094 Tel 212-354-6500; Toll Free: 800-223-5780; *Imprints:* Bantam Large Type (Bantam LT); Doubleday Large Type (Doubleday LT); Delacorte Large Type (Delacorte LT)
*Dist(s):* **Beeler, Thomas T. Publisher.**

**Bantam Large Type Imprint of Bantam Doubleday Dell Large Print Group, Inc.**

**Bantam Pr., Ltd. (GBR)** ( *0-593* ) *Dist. by* **Trafalgar.**

**Barbadoes Hall Communications,** ( *0-9710159* ) 7026 High Oaks Dr., Weddington, NC 28104-7959 Tel 704-846-9616; *Imprints:* Back Alley Books (Back Alley)
E-mail: barhallcom@aol.com.

**Barbary Coast Bks.**, ( *0-936041* ) P.O. Box 3645, Oakland, CA 94609 (SAN 697-0060) Tel 510-653-8048; Fax: 510-653-6313 Do not confuse with Barbary Coast Pr. in San Francisco, CA
Web site: http://www.71034.456@compuserve.com.

**Barbour & Company, Incorporated** *See* **Barbour Publishing, Inc.**

**Barbour Publishing, Inc.**, ( *0-916441; 1-55748; 1-57748; 1-58660; 1-59310* ) P.O. Box 719, Uhrichsville, OH 44683 (SAN 295-7094) Tel 740-922-6045; Fax: 740-922-5948; Toll Free Fax: 800-220-5948; Toll Free: 800-847-8270; *Imprints:* Promise Press (Promise Pr)
E-mail: info@barbourbooks.com
Web site: http://www.barbourbooks.com
*Dist(s):* **Anchor Distributors**
**Appalachian Bk. Distributors**
**Baker & Taylor Bks.**
**Riverside**
**Spring Arbor Distributors, Inc..**

**Barclay Bks., LLC,** ( *1-931402* ) 6161 51st St., S., Saint Petersburg, FL 33715 Tel 727-867-0518; Fax: 727-866-9673 Do not confuse with Barclay Books, Ann Arbor, MI
E-mail: drrsmcneel@aol.com
Web site: http://www.BarclayBooks.com
*Dist(s):* **Baker & Taylor Bks..**

**Bard Pubns.**, ( *0-9727079* ) 687 E. 800 N., Orem, UT 84097 Tel 801-221-4798
E-mail: mhcook@mstar2.net; mhcook@mstarz.net
Web site: http://users.mstar2.net/mhcook/.

**Bardsong Pr.**, ( *0-9660371* ) P.O. Box 775396, Steamboat Springs, CO 80477 Tel 970-870-1401; Fax: 970-879-2657
E-mail: celts@bardsongpress.com
Web site: http://www.bardsongpress.com.

**Barefoot Bks., Inc.**, ( *1-84148; 1-898000; 1-901223; 1-902283* ) 3 Bow St., 3rd Flr., Cambridge, MA 02138 Tel 866-417-2369; Fax: 888-346-9138
E-mail: ussales@barefoot-books.com
Web site: http://www.barefoot-books.com
*Dist(s):* **American Bk. Ctr.**
**Distribution Solutions Group**
**Lectorum Pubns., Inc.**
**Ten Speed Pr..**

**Barker Creek Publishing, Inc.**, ( *0-9639307; 1-928961* ) Orders Addr.: P.O. Box 2610, Poulsbo, WA 98370 (SAN 298-4628) Tel 360-692-5833; Fax: 360-613-2542; Toll Free: 800-692-5833
E-mail: marketing@barkercreek.com
Web site: http://www.barkercreek.com
*Dist(s):* **Appalachian Bk. Distributors**
**Baker & Taylor Bks.**
**Koen Bk. Distributors.**

**Barn Peg Pr., The,** ( *0-9665943* ) PMB 231, 221 E. Market St., Iowa City, IA 52245-2166 Fax: 319-358-7332; Toll Free: 800-318-4668
E-mail: barnpeg@barnpegpress.com
Web site: http://www.barnpegpress.com.

**Barnaby & Co.**, ( *0-9642836* ) P.O. Box 3198, Nantucket, MA 02584 Tel 508-228-5114; Fax: 508-325-0011
E-mail: barnaby@nantucket.net
Web site: http://www.barnabybear.com.

**Barnaby Books** *See* **Barnaby & Co.**

**Barnes & Noble Bks.-Imports,** ( *0-389* ) Div. of Rowman & Littlefield Pubs., Inc., 4720 Boston Way, Lanham, MD 20706 (SAN 206-7803) Tel 301-459-3366; Toll Free: 800-462-6420.

**Barnes & Noble Digital,** ( *1-4014* ) 76 Ninth Ave., 9th Flr., New York, NY 10011 Tel 212-414-6668; Fax: 212-414-8230
Web site: http://www.ebooks.barnesandnoble.com/bn_digital.

**Barnes & Noble, Inc.**, ( *0-7607; 0-88029; 1-4028* ) 122 Fifth Ave., New York, NY 10011 (SAN 141-3651) Tel 212-633-3300
E-mail: staylor@bn.com
*Dist(s):* **Bookazine Co., Inc.**
**Sterling Publishing Co., Inc..**

**Barney Pr.**, ( *0-9607888* ) R.R. 4, Box 269b., Pel Rapids, MN 56572-8826 (SAN 238-1443) Do not confuse with Barney Pr., Dallas, TX.

**Barney Pr.**, ( *0-9611110* ) 5211 Vanderbilt, Dallas, TX 75206 (SAN 282-8677) Tel 214-824-2882 Do not confuse with Barney Pr., Bakersfield, CA.

**Barney Publishing** *See* **Lyric Publishing**

**Barnhardt & Ashe Publishing, Inc.**, ( *0-9715402* ) 444 Brickell Ave., Sutie 51, PMB 432, Miami, FL 33131-2492 Tel 410-707-6686
E-mail: barnhardtashe@aol.com
Web site: http://www.barnhardtashepublishing.com.

†**Barricade Bks., Inc.**, ( *0-934878; 0-942637; 0-9623032; 1-56980* ) 185 Bridge Plaza N., Suite 308A, Fort Lee, NJ 07024 (SAN 299-1780) Tel 201-944-7600; Fax: 201-944-6363; Toll Free: 800-592-6657; *Imprints:* Dembner Books (Dembner NY)
E-mail: customerservice@barricadebooks.com
Web site: http://www.barricadebooks.com
*Dist(s):* **Paladin Pr. ; CIP.**

**Barrier Reef Publishing,** ( *0-9707311* ) P.O. Box 142061, Austin, TX 78714-2041 Tel 512-458-0156
E-mail: brain_s_78714@yahoo.com;
brian-sc-78714@yahoo.com.

†**Barron's Educational Series, Inc.**, ( *0-7641; 0-8120* ) 250 Wireless Blvd., Hauppauge, NY 11788-3917 (SAN 201-453X) Tel 631-434-3311; Fax: 631-434-3723; 631-434-3217 (orders); Toll Free: 800-645-3476 Do not confuse with BARRONS, Monroe, WA
E-mail: info@barronseduc.com;
barrons@barronseduc.com
Web site: http://www.barronseduc.com
*Dist(s):* **Continental Bk. Co., Inc.**
**Giron Bks.**
**Lectorum Pubns., Inc.**
**Production Assocs., Inc.**
**netLibrary, Inc. ; CIP.**

**Barrytown, Ltd.**, ( *1-58177; 1-886449* ) 94 Station Hill Rd., Barrytown, NY 12507 Tel 845-758-5840; Fax: 845-758-8163
E-mail: publishers@stationhill.org
Web site: http://www.stationhill.org
*Dist(s):* **Midpoint Trade Bks., Inc.**
**SPD-Small Pr. Distribution.**

**Bartels, Carolyn M.** *See* **Two Trails Publishing**

**Bartleby Pr.**, ( *0-910155* ) 11141 Georgia Ave., Suite A-3, Silver Spring, MD 20902 (SAN 241-2098) Tel 301-949-2443; Fax: 301-949-2205; Toll Free: 800-953-9929
E-mail: Inquiries@bartlebythepublisher.com
Web site: http://www.BartlebythePublisher.com.

**Bartleby.com,** ( *1-58734* ) P.O. Box 13, New York, NY 10034-0013
E-mail: webmaster@bartleby.com
Web site: http://www.bartleby.com.

†**Basic Bks.**, ( *0-465* ) A Member of Perseus Books Group, Orders Addr.: 5500 Central Ave., Boulder, CO 80301-2877 Fax: 303-449-3356 (customer service); Toll Free: 800-386-5656 (customer service); Edit Addr.: 387 Park Ave., S., New York, NY 10016 (SAN 201-4521) Tel 212-340-8100; Fax: 212-340-8135; *Imprints:* Counterpoint Press (Count Pr); Basic Civitas Books (BasCiviBks)
E-mail: westview.orders@perseusbooks.com
Web site: http://www.counterpointpress.com;
http://www.perseusbooksgroup.com
*Dist(s):* **Cobblestone Publishing Co.**
**HarperCollins Pubs. ; CIP.**

**Basic Civitas Bks. Imprint of Basic Bks.**

**Baskerville Pubs., Inc.**, ( *0-9627509; 1-880909* ) 2711 Park Hill Dr., Fort Worth, TX 76109 Tel 817-923-1064; Fax: 817-921-9114; *Imprints:* Basset Books (Basset Bks)
E-mail: baskerville@baskervillepublishers.com
Web site: http://www.baskervillepublishers.com.

**Baskerville Publishing Company, Incorporated** *See* **Baskerville Pubs., Inc.**

**Basset Bks. Imprint of Baskerville Pubs., Inc.**

**Bath Street Pr.**, ( *0-937618* ) 1016 Bath St., Ann Arbor, MI 48103 (SAN 215-2967) Tel 313-663-2071.

**Battered Silicon Dispatch Box, The,** ( *1-55246; 1-896648* ) P.O. Box 122, Sauk City, WI 53583 Fax: 608-643-5080
E-mail: gav@bmts.com.

Bauhan, William L. Inc., ( 0-87233 ) P.O. Box 443, Dublin, NH 03444-0443 (SAN 204-384X) Tel 877-832-3738; 603-563-8020; Fax: 603-563-8026 E-mail: info@bauhanpublishing.com. Web site: http://www.bauhanpublishing.com.

Baxter Pr., ( 1-888237 ) 700 S. Friendswood Dr., Suite C, Friendswood, TX 77546 Tel 281-992-0628; Fax: 281-992-0615 E-mail: baxter2@flash.net *Dist(s):* FaithWorks.

Bay Books & Tapes, Incorporated *See* Bay Soma Publishing

Bay Island Bks., ( 0-9654694 ) P.O. Box 485, Corte Madera, CA 94976-0485 Tel 415-924-9026 E-mail: bayisland@earthlink.net *Dist(s):* Alamo Square Distributors
  Baker & Taylor Bks.
  Koen Bk. Distributors
  New Leaf Distributing Co., Inc..

Bay Soma Publishing, ( 0-912333; 1-57959 ) Div. of Windmere Durable Holdings, Inc., 444 DeHaro St., Suite 130, San Francisco, CA 94107 (SAN 265-1246) Tel 415-252-4350; Fax: 415-252-4352; Toll Free: 888-242-1295 E-mail: catalog@baybooks.com; info@baybooks.com Web site: http://www.baybooks.com. *Dist(s):* Publishers Group West.

Baylor Univ. Pr., ( 0-918954; 1-878804 ) Member of Texas A & M University Press Consortium, Orders Addr.: P.O. Box 97363, Waco, TX 76798-7363 Tel 254-710-3164; Fax: 254-710-3440; Edit Addr.: 1920 S. Fourth St., Waco, TX 76798 E-mail: Diane_Smith@baylor.edu Web site: http://www.baylorpress.com *Dist(s):* Texas A&M Univ. Pr..

†BBC Audiobooks America, ( 0-563; 0-7540; 0-7927; 0-89340; 1-55504 ) Orders Addr.: P.O. Box 1450, Hampton, NH 03843-1450 (SAN 208-4864) Tel 603-926-8744; Fax: 603-929-3890; Toll Free: 800-621-0182; Edit Addr.: 1 Lafayette Rd., Hampton, NH 03843; *Imprints:* Gunsmoke (Gunsmoke); Black Dagger (Black Dagger); Galaxy Children's Large Print (Galaxy Child Lrg Print); Sterling Audio Books (Sterling Audio); Chivers Children's Audio Books (Chivers Child Audio); Chivers Sound Library (Chivers Sound Lib) E-mail: customerservice@bbcaudiobooksamerica.com Web site: http://www.bbcaudiobooksamerica.com *Dist(s):* Landmark Audiobooks ; CIP.

BBC Bk. Publishing (GBR) ( 0-563 ) *Dist. by* Ulverscroft US.

BBC Worldwide Americas, ( 0-563; 1-882335 ) Subs. of BBC Enterprises, Inc., 747 Third Ave., 6th Flr., New York, NY 10017 Tel 212-705-9300; Fax: 212-888-0576; Toll Free Fax: 800-216-1222 *Dist(s):* Diamond Distributors, Inc.
  London Bridge
  Trafalgar Square.

BBS Publishing Corp., ( 0-88365; 0-88394; 0-88486; 1-57866 ) 450 Raritan Center Pkwy., Edison, NJ 08837 Tel 732-346-1912; Fax: 732-346-1913; *Imprints:* Galahad Books (Galah Bks); Arrowood Press (Arrow Pr) *Dist(s):* Publishers Group West.

Beach Holme Pubs., Ltd. (CAN) ( 0-88878 ) *Dist. by* StackpoleBks.

Beach Holme Pubs., Ltd. (CAN) ( 0-88878 ) *Dist. by* Strauss Cnslts.

Beachfront Publishing, ( 1-892339 ) Div. of Words, Words, Words, Inc., Orders Addr.: P.O. Box 811922, Boca Raton, FL 33481 E-mail: info@beachfrontentertainment.com Web site: http://www.beachfrontentertainment.com *Dist(s):* Biblio Distribution.

BeachHouse Bks. Imprint of Science & Humanities Pr.

Beacon Hill Pr. of Kansas City, ( 0-8341 ) Div. of Nazarene Publishing Hse., 2923 Troost, Kansas City, MO 64109 (SAN 241-6328) Tel 816-931-1900; Fax: 816-753-4071; Toll Free: 800-877-0700 (orders only) E-mail: inquiry@bhillkc.com; nphdirect@nph.com; orders@nph.com Web site: http://www.nph.com; http://www.bhillkc.com

Beacon Pr., ( 0-8070 ) 25 Beacon St., Boston, MA 02108-2892 (SAN 201-4483) Tel 617-742-2110; Fax: 617-723-3097 Web site: http://www.beacon.org *Dist(s):* Continental Bk. Co., Inc.
  Houghton Mifflin Co. Trade & Reference Div.
  netLibrary, Inc..

Beaconridge Pr., ( 0-9704135 ) P.O. Box 6937, Boston, MA 02106-6937 E-mail: beaconridgepress@aol.com Web site: http//www.beaconridgepress.com.

Bear & Co. Imprint of Bear & Co.

†Bear & Co., ( 0-939680; 1-879181; 1-59143 ) Orders Addr.: One Park St., Rochester, VT 05767 (SAN 216-7174) Tel 802-767-3174; Fax: 802-767-3726; Toll Free: 800-246-8648; *Imprints:* Bear & Company (Bear & Company) Do not confuse with Bear & Co. in Bedford, NH E-mail: info@innertraditions.com; jeanie@innertraditions.com Web site: http://www.innertraditions.com *Dist(s):* Ten Speed Pr. ; CIP.

Beaufort Bks., Inc., ( 0-8253 ) 27 W. 20th St., Suite 1102, New York, NY 10011 (SAN 215-2304) Tel 212-727-0190; Fax: 212-727-0195 E-mail: midpointny@aol.com *Dist(s):* Midpoint Trade Bks., Inc..

Beaver Pond Publishing & Printing, Inc., ( 1-881399 ) Orders Addr.: P.O. Box 224, Greenville, PA 16125 Tel 724-588-3492; Fax: 724-588-2486; Edit Addr.: 454 Hadley Rd., Greenville, PA 16125 (SAN 630-9305) E-mail: beaverpond@pathway.net Web site: http://www.bookblender.com.

Beavercreek Pub. Co., ( 0-9646470 ) 16045 S. Neibur Rd., Beavercreek, OR 97045 Tel 503-631-3209 Do not confuse with companies with the same name in Hatton, ND, Bradleyville, MO.

Bedford/Saint Martin's, ( 0-312 ) Div. of Holtzbrinck Publishers, Orders Addr.: 16365 James Madison Hwy., Gordonsville, VA 22942 Tel 540-672-7600; Toll Free Fax: 800-672-2054; Toll Free: 888-330-8477; Edit Addr.: 33 Irving Pl., New York, NY 10003 Tel 212-375-7000; Fax: 212-614-1885; Toll Free: 800-223-1115; 75 Arlington St., Boston, MA 02116 Tel 617-399-4000; Fax: 617-426-8582; Toll Free: 800-779-7440 E-mail: communication@bedfordstmartins.com Web site: http://www.bfwpub.com *Dist(s):* Holtzbrinck Pubs..

Bedrick, Peter Bks. Imprint of McGraw-Hill Children's Publishing

Bedrock Books, Incorporated *See* Dry, Paul Bks., Inc.

Bee Con Bks., ( 0-9715838 ) P.O. Box 27708, Philadelphia, PA 19118 (SAN 254-4954) Tel 215-381-0768; Fax: 215-247-0680 E-mail: beeconbooks@aol.com Web site: http://www.BeeConBooks.com.

Beech Seal Press, Incorporated *See* Images from the Past, Inc.

Beehive Pr., The, ( 0-88322 ) 321 Barnard St., Savannah, GA 31401 (SAN 201-7547) Tel 912-236-4870; Fax: 912-236-4747 Do not confuse with Beehive Pr., Las Vegas, NV Web site: http://www.beehivepress.org.

BeeJay Enterprises, ( 0-9659042 ) Orders Addr.: P.O. Box 1373, Alpharetta, GA 30239-1373 Tel 770-346-8626; Fax: 770-410-4995; Edit Addr.: 1306 Cobb Crossing, Smyrna, GA 30080 E-mail: beejaypub@aol.com.

Beekman Pubs., Inc., ( 0-8464 ) P.O. Box 888, Woodstock, NY 12498-0888 (SAN 170-1622) Tel 845-679-2300; Fax: 845-679-2301; Toll Free: 888-233-5626 E-mail: beekman@beekmanpublishers.com Web site: http://www.beekmanpublishers.comw; http://www.beekman.net.

Beeler Large Print Bks. Imprint of Beeler, Thomas T. Publisher

Beeler, Thomas T. Publisher, ( 1-57490 ) Orders Addr.: P.O. Box 659, Hampton Falls, NH 03844-0659; Edit Addr.: 22 King St., Hampton Falls, NH 03844-2414 Tel 603-772-1175; Fax: 603-778-9025; Toll Free: 800-818-7574; *Imprints:* Sagebrush Large Print Westerns (Sagebrush LP West); Beeler Large Print Books (Beeler LP Bks) E-mail: tombeeler@hotmail.com Web site: http://www.beelerpub.com.

Beginning II End Publishing Company *See* Beginning II End Publishing, Inc.

Beginning II End Publishing, Inc., ( 0-9706847; 0-9746704 ) 800 N. Rainbow, No. 208, Las Vegas, NV 89107 Tel 702-647-3694; Fax: 702-648-7164 E-mail: raineypublisher@aol.com Web site: http://www.beginning2endpub.com *Dist(s):* Partners/West.

Behrman Hse., Inc., ( 0-87441 ) 11 Edison Pl., Springfield, NJ 07081 (SAN 201-4459) Tel 973-379-7200; Fax: 973-379-7280; Toll Free: 800-221-2755 E-mail: webmaster@behrmanhouse.com Web site: http://www.behrmanhouse.com.

Beijing Foreign Languages Pr. (CHN) ( 7-119 ) *Dist. by* China Bks.

Beil, Frederic C. Pub., Inc., ( 0-913720; 1-929490 ) 609 Whitaker St., Savannah, GA 31401 (SAN 240-9909) Tel 912-233-2446 (phone/fax); *Imprints:* Sandstone Press (Sandstone Pr) E-mail: beilbook@beil.com Web site: http://www.beil.com.

Belecam & Assocs., ( 0-9720821 ) 3741 Jamestown Ct. Aspen Commons, Doraville, GA 30340-2816 Tel 770-451-6729; Fax: 770-457-7485 E-mail: lemba241@aol.com

Belgrave Hse., ( 0-9660643; 0-9741068 ) 190 Belgrave Ave., San Francisco, CA 94117-4228 Tel 415-661-5025; Fax: 415-661-5703 E-mail: neff@belgravehouse.com Web site: http://www.belgravehouse.com.

Believer's Ink, ( 0-9718023 ) P.O. Box 2393, Chesterfield, VA 23832 Tel 804-777-9150.

Belknap Pr. Imprint of Harvard Univ. Pr.

Bell Buckle Pr., ( 0-9624100; 1-882845 ) P.O. Box 486, Bell Buckle, TN 37020 Tel 931-389-6878.

Bella Bks., Inc., ( 0-9677753; 1-931513; 1-59493 ) Orders Addr.: P.O. Box 10543, Tallahassee, FL 32302 Tel 850-539-5965; Fax: 850-539-9731; Toll Free: 800-729-4992; Edit Addr.: 186 Sheline Dr., Havana, FL 32333 E-mail: Linda@BellaBooks.com Web site: http://www.bellabooks.com. *Dist(s):* Client Distribution Services.

BelleBks., ( 0-9673035 ) Orders Addr.: P.O. Box 67, Smyrna, GA 30081 Tel 770-384-1348; Fax: 901-344-9068; Edit Addr.: 4128 Manson Ave., Smyrna, GA 30082 E-mail: Marthashld@aol.com Web site: http://www.BelleBooks.com.

Bell-Forsythe Publishing Co., ( 0-9657619 ) Div. of Croskery & Assocs., Inc., 5300 Hamilton Ave., Suite 1000, Cincinnati, OH 45224 Tel 513-542-9819; Fax: 513-542-9890 E-mail: 102545.277@compuserve.com.

BenBella Bks., ( 1-932100 ) 6440 N. Central Expressway, Suite 508, Dallas, TX 75206 Tel 214-750-3600; Fax: 214-750-3645 E-mail: info@benbellabooks.com Web site: http://www.benbellabooks.com *Dist(s):* Independent Pubs. Group.

Bench Pr., The, ( 0-930769 ) 2507 Brighton Ln., Beaufort, SC 29902 (SAN 677-6663) Tel 843-322-0532 Do not confuse with companies with the same name in Eastpoint, FL, Valdez, AK, Iowa City, IA, Tarzana, CA E-mail: slesin@islc.net *Dist(s):* Parnassus Bk. Distributors
  SPD-Small Pr. Distribution.

Benmir Bks., ( 0-917883 ) P.O. Box 515, Walnut Creek, CA 94597 (SAN 656-9641) Tel 510-736-1914; Fax: 510-736-4405.

Bennerson, Denise, ( 0-9646279 ) Orders Addr.: P.O. Box 3164, Frederiksted, VI 00841 E-mail: justdoit@viaccess.net Web site: http://www.homelandcollections.com/children_books.htm *Dist(s):* Century Bk. Distribution.

Bennett-Edwards, ( 0-9617271 ) 3731 N. County Club Dr., Suite 2227, Aventura, FL 33180-1745 (SAN 663-4508) Tel 305-931-7038.

Benoy Publishing, ( 0-9720809; 1-932162 ) 735 Bragg Dr., Unit H, Wilmington, NC 28412 Tel 910-796-0424 (phone/fax) E-mail: bbppdodo@aol.com Web site: http://www.benoypublishing.com.

Ben-Simon Pubns., ( 0-914539 ) P.O. Box 2124, Port Angeles, WA 98362 (SAN 289-1492) Tel 250-652-6332; Fax: 360-452-2502 E-mail: bensimon@pinc.com Web site: http://www.swifty.com/bensimon/index.html.

Bentley Pubs., ( 0-8376 ) 1734 Massachusetts Ave., Cambridge, MA 02138-1804 (SAN 213-9839) Tel 617-547-4170; Fax: 617-876-9235; Toll Free: 800-423-4595 E-mail: Sales@bentleypublishing.com Web site: http://www.bentleypublishers.com.

Bentley, Robert Incorporated, Publishers *See* Bentley Pubs.

Berdine Publishing Co., ( 0-9631802 ) A5 Woodcrest Addition, Princeton, WV 24740-3968 Tel 304-425-5750.

Bergquist Publishing, ( 0-9615483 ) 414 W. Seventh, Willmar, MN 56201 (SAN 696-0952) Tel 612-235-4516.

Berkeley Hills Bks., ( 0-9653774; 1-893163 ) Orders Addr.: P.O. Box 9877, Berkeley, CA 94709 Tel 510-848-7303; Fax: 510-525-2948; Toll Free: 888-848-7303 (orders) E-mail: rfdobb@berkeleyhills.com Web site: http://www.berkeleyhills.com *Dist(s):* **Publishers Group West.**

†Berkley Publishing Group, ( 0-425; 0-515 ) Div. of Penguin Putnam, Inc., Orders Addr.: 405 Murray Hill Pkwy., East Rutherford, NJ 07073 Toll Free: 800-788-6262 (individual consumer sales); 800-847-5515 (orders); 800-631-8571 (customer service); Edit Addr.: 375 Hudson St., New York, NY 10014 (SAN 201-3991) Tel 212-366-2000; Fax: 212-366-2385; *Imprints:* Berkley/Pacer (Berkley/Pacer); Splash (Splash); Classics Illustrated (Classics Illus); Prime Crime (Prime Crime); Perigee Books (Perigee Bks); Riverhead Trade (Paperbacks) (Riverhd Trade); Jove (Jove); Diamond Books (DiamondBks) E-mail: online@penguinputnam.com Web site: http://www.penguinputnam.com *Dist(s):* **Penguin Group (USA) Inc.** **Perelandra, Ltd. ; CIP.**

Berkley/Pacer Imprint of Berkley Publishing Group

Berliner, Harold, ( 0-933861 ) P.O. Box 6, Nevada City, CA 95959-0006 (SAN 692-705X) Tel 530-273-2278; Fax: 530-273-0303 E-mail: berliner@jps.net Web site: http://www.berlinerpress.com.

Bess Pr., Inc., ( 0-935848; 1-57306; 1-880188 ) 3565 Harding Ave., Honolulu, HI 96816 (SAN 239-4111) Tel 808-734-7159; Fax: 808-732-3627; Toll Free: 800-910-2377 E-mail: info@besspress.com Web site: http://www.besspress.com *Dist(s):* **Aha Punana Leo** **Booklines Hawaii, Ltd.** **Fell, Frederick Pubs., Inc.** **Univ. of Hawaii Pr..**

Best Bks., ( 0-7222 ) Orders Addr.: P.O. Box 893520, Temecula, CA 92589-3520 (SAN 254-0258) Toll Free Fax: 888-265-3540; Toll Free: 888-265-3531; Edit Addr.: 26111 Ynez B14, Temecula, CA 92592 Do not confuse with companies with similar name in Henderson, NV, South Birmingham, AL, North Highlands, CA E-mail: sales@thebbooks.net.

BET Bks., ( 1-58314 ) 1900 W. Pl., NE., Washington, DC 20018 Tel 202-608-2000; Fax: 202-608-2533; *Imprints:* Arabesque (Arabesq); Sepia (Sepia); New Spirit (New Spirit) E-mail: kelli.richardson@internetmci.com Web site: http://msbet.com *Dist(s):* **Kensington Publishing Corp.** **Penguin Group (USA) Inc..**

†Bethany Hse. Pubs., ( 0-7642; 0-87123; 1-55661; 1-56179; 1-57778; 1-880089; 1-59066 ) Div. of Baker Book House, Inc., Orders Addr.: P.O. Box 6287, Grand Rapids, MI 49516-6287 Toll Free: 800-877-2665; Edit Addr.: 11400 Hampshire Ave., S., Bloomington, MN 55438-2455 (SAN 201-4416) Tel 952-829-2500; Fax: 952-996-1393; Toll Free: 800-877-2665 E-mail: orders@bakerbooks.com Web site: http://www.bethanyhouse.com *Dist(s):* **Anchor Distributors** **Appalachian Bible Co.** **Baker & Taylor Bks.** **Baker Bk. Hse., Inc.** **Brodart Co.** **CRC Pubns.** **Follett Library Resources** **Permabound Bks.** **Riverside Bk. & Bible Resource** **Spring Arbor Distributors, Inc.** **Beeler, Thomas T. Publisher ; CIP.**

Bethlehem Bks., ( 1-883937; 1-932350 ) Div. of Bethlehem Community, Orders Addr.: 10194 Garfield St. S., Bathgate, ND 58216-4031 Tel 701-265-3725; Fax: 701-265-3716; Toll Free: 800-757-6831 Do not confuse with bethlehem Books in Richmond, VA E-mail: inquiry@bethlehembooks.com Web site: http://www.bethlehembooks.com *Dist(s):* **Ignatius Pr.** **Spring Arbor Distributors, Inc..**

Better Bks. Bureau, ( 0-9707111 ) 8417 Xylon Cir., Bloomington, MN 55438 Tel 952-942-8613; Fax: 952-942-7218 E-mail: publisher@betterbooksbyreav.dizland.com; larrystoller@betterbooksbureau.bizland.com Web site: http://betterbooksbureau.bizland.com.

BHB International, Inc., Orders Addr.: 302 W. North 2nd St., Seneca, SC 29678 (SAN 631-0915) Tel 864-885-9444; Fax: 864-885-1090 E-mail: bhbbooks@aol.com Web site: http://www.bhbinternational.com.

Bibleline Pubns., ( 0-9717235 ) 1438 Baylor Dr., Colorado Springs, CO 80909 Tel 719-597-8211 (phone/fax) E-mail: bibleline@earthlink.net Web site: http://home.earthlink.net/~bibleline/ index.html.

Biblio Distribution, Div. of National Book Network, Orders Addr.: 15200 NBN Way, Blue Ridge Summit, PA 17214 Toll Free Fax: 800-338-4550; Toll Free: 800-462-6420; Edit Addr.: 4501 Forbes Blvd., Suite 200, Lanham, MD 20706 (SAN 211-724X) Tel 301-459-3366; Fax: 301-429-5746 E-mail: custserv@nbnbooks.com Web site: http://www.bibliodistribution.com

Biblio Distribution Center *See* Biblio Distribution

Biblio Pr., the Jewish Women's Pub., ( 0-930395; 0-9602036 ) Orders Addr.: P.O. Box 20195, New York, NY 10011 (SAN 217-0892) Tel 212-989-2755; Toll Free: 800-698-7781 (orders) E-mail: Bibook@aol.com *Dist(s):* **Bloch Publishing Co.** **Holmes & Meier Pubs., Inc.** **New Leaf Distributing Co., Inc..**

Bibliotheca Islamica, Inc., ( 0-88297 ) Orders Addr.: P.O. Box 14474, Minneapolis, MN 55414 (SAN 202-4063) Tel 651-221-9883; Fax: 651-665-9886.

Biblo & Tannen Booksellers & Pubs., ( 0-8196 ) P.O. Box 302, Cheshire, CT 06410 (SAN 202-4071) Tel 203-250-1647 (phone/fax); Toll Free: 800-272-8778 E-mail: biblo.moser@gte.net.

Bifulco Books *See* Bifulco, Michael

Bifulco, Michael, ( 0-9619596 ) 1708 Simmons Ave., NE, Grand Rapids, MI 49505-7618 (SAN 245-4858) E-mail: bif35film@aol.com.

Big Ben Audio, Inc., ( 1-885546 ) Orders Addr.: P.O. Box 969, Ashland, OR 97520 Tel 541-488-6022; Fax: 541-734-2537; Edit Addr.: 31 Mistletoe, Ashland, OR 97520.

Big Bluestem Pr., ( 0-9671386 ) 12321 87th St., South, Wisconsin Rapids, WI 54494-9415 Tel 715-325-5749 ; Fax: 715-325-3109 E-mail: info@bigbluestempress.com Web site: http://www.bigbluestempress.com.

Big Bridge Pr., ( 1-878471 ) 2000 Cabrillo Hwy., Pacifica, CA 94044 Tel 650-355-4857; Fax: 650-355-4931; 2000 Hwy. 1, Pacifica, CA 94044 E-mail: poezine@bigbridge.org Web site: http://www.bigbridge.org.

Big Entertainment, Inc., ( 0-9645175; 1-57780 ) 2255 Glades Rd., Suite 237W, Boca Raton, FL 33431-7395 Tel 407-998-8000; Fax: 407-998-2974 *Dist(s):* **Kable News Co., Inc..**

BIG RADIO Productions, Inc., ( 1-888928 ) 10 Mace Pl., No. 2, Lynn, MA 01902-3110.

Bigwater Publishing, ( 0-923048 ) Orders Addr.: P.O. Box 177, Caledonia, MI 49316 (SAN 251-608X) Tel 616-891-1113; Fax: 616-891-8015 E-mail: bigpub@att.net.

Bilingual Pr./Editorial Bilingue, ( 0-916950; 0-927534; 1-931010 ) Orders Addr.: Arizona State Univ., Hispanic Research Ctr., P.O. Box 872702, Tempe, AZ 85287-2702 (SAN 208-5526) Tel 480-965-3867; Fax: 480-965-8309; Edit Addr.: c/o University Commons, 215 E. Seventh St., Rm. 212, Tempe, AZ 85281 E-mail: brp@asu.edu Web site: http://www.asu.edu/brp *Dist(s):* **Libros Sin Fronteras** **SPD-Small Pr. Distribution.**

Bill Barry's Compass Bks., ( 0-944099 ) Subs. of Adventure Feature Syndicate, Orders Addr.: P.O. Box 2524, Waldport, OR 97394 (SAN 242-2999); Edit Addr.: 385 NW Grant St., No. 4, Waldport, OR 97394 Tel 541-563-7282 E-mail: barrytoons@hotmail.com Web site: http://www.BlackBeard-the-Pirate.com *Dist(s):* **Diamond Distributors, Inc..**

Bimini Twist Adventures, Inc., ( 0-9676853; 0-9728564 ) 2911 NW 27th Ave., Boca Raton, FL 33434 Tel 561-451-3452; Fax: 954-964-3900; Toll Free: 800-558-5885 E-mail: pjm@biminitwist.com Web site: http://www.biminitwist.com.

Binford & Mort Publishing, ( 0-8323 ) Orders Addr.: P.O. Box 91580, Portland, OR 97291; Edit Addr.: 5245 NE Elam Young Pkwy., Suite C, Hillsboro, OR 97124 (SAN 201-4386) Tel 503-844-4960; Fax: 503-844-4959; Toll Free: 888-221-4514 Web site: http://www.binfordandmort.com/ *Dist(s):* **Baker & Taylor Bks.** **Maverick Distributors** **Partners/West.**

Binford & Mort Publishing; Metropolitan Press *See* Binford & Mort Publishing

Birch Lane Pr. Imprint of Kensington Publishing Corp.

Birlinn, Ltd. (GBR) ( 1-874744; 1-84158; 1-84341 ) *Dist. by* Dufour.

Birlinn, Ltd. (GBR) ( 1-874744; 1-84158; 1-84341 ) *Dist. by* Interlink Pub.

Bison Bks. Imprint of Univ. of Nebraska Pr.

†BkMk Pr. of the Univ. of Missouri-Kansas City, ( 0-933532; 1-886157 ) Univ. Hse., 5100 Rockhill Rd., Kansas City, MO 64110-2499 (SAN 207-7914) Tel 816-235-2558; Fax: 816-235-2611; *Imprints:* Wallaroo Books (Wallaroo Bks) E-mail: bkmk@umkc.edu *Dist(s):* **Baker & Taylor Bks. ; CIP.**

Black Belt Communications Group *See* River City Publishing

Black Belt Pr. Imprint of River City Publishing

Black Bks., ( 0-9637401; 1-892723 ) P.O. Box 31155, San Francisco, CA 94131-0155 (SAN 299-5778) Tel 415-431-0171; Fax: 415-431-0172 E-mail: info@blackbooks.com; orders@blackbooks.com Web site: http://www.blackbooks.com *Dist(s):* **LPC Group.**

Black Butterfly Pr., ( 0-9647576 ) 2605 W. 102nd St., Inglewood, CA 90303 Tel 213-242-9917 (phone/fax) E-mail: maxtho@aol.com Web site: http://www.maxinethompson.com.

Black Classic Pr., ( 0-933121; 1-57478 ) Orders Addr.: P.O. Box 13414, Baltimore, MD 21203 (SAN 219-5836) Tel 410-358-0980; Fax: 410-358-0987; Toll Free: 800-476-8870 E-mail: bcp@charm.net Web site: http://www.blackclassic.com *Dist(s):* **Publishers Group West.**

Black Dagger Imprint of BBC Audiobooks America

Black Deer Bks., ( 0-9729455 ) P.O. Box 6156, North Babylon, NY 11703 Tel 252-432-1518 E-mail: blackdeerbooks@aol.com *Dist(s):* **Ingram Bk. Co..**

Black Dog & Leventhal Pubs., Inc., ( 0-9637056; 1-57912; 1-884822 ) 151 W. 19th St., New York, NY 10011-4106 Tel 212-647-9336; Fax: 212-647-9332 *Dist(s):* **Workman Publishing Co., Inc..**

Black Dome Pr. Corp., ( 0-9628523; 1-883789 ) 1011 Rte. 296, Hensonville, NY 12439 Tel 518-734-6357; Fax: 518-734-5802; Toll Free: 800-513-9013 E-mail: blackdomep@aol.com Web site: http://www.blackdomepress.com *Dist(s):* **Baker & Taylor Bks.** **Koen Bk. Distributors** **North Country Bks., Inc..**

Black Forest Pr., ( 1-58275; 1-881116 ) Div. of Black Forest Enterprises, Orders Addr.: P.O. Box 6342, Chula Vista, CA 91909-6342 Fax: 619-482-8704; Toll Free: 888-808-5440 (Book Sales, Marketing and Promotion); 800-451-9404 (General Information, Submission Inquiries and Acquisitions); Edit Addr.: 914 Nolan Way, Chula Vista, CA 91911-2408 (SAN 298-8445) Tel 619-656-8048 E-mail: bfp@blackforestpress.com; dknox@blackforestpress.com Web site: http://www.blackforestpress.com *Dist(s):* **Ingram Bk. Co..**

Black Heron Pr., ( 0-930773 ) Orders Addr.: P.O. Box 95676, Seattle, WA 98145 (SAN 677-623X) Tel 206-363-5210 (phone/fax); Edit Addr.: 3032 NE 140th St., No. 402, Seattle, WA 98125 (SAN 241-9866) Web site: http://mav.net/blackheron *Dist(s):* **Client Distribution Services.**

Black Ice Bks. Imprint of Fiction Collective Two, Inc.

Black, Jim, ( 0-9703052 ) 4809 Windsong Dr., Wichita Falls, TX 76310 Tel 940-692-7092 E-mail: jbodie1@aol.com

Black Lace (GBR) ( 0-352 ) *Dist. by* London Brdge.

Black Ledge Pr., ( 0-9707965 ) P.O. Box 58009, Salt Lake City, UT 84158 (SAN 253-7176) Tel 801-582-1169; Fax: 801-583-0928 E-mail: delrio@blackledgepress.com Web site: http://www.blackledgepress.com.

Black Mask Imprint of Creative Arts Bk. Co.

Names

**Black Moss Pr. (CAN)** ( *0-88753* ) *Dist. by* **Firefly Bks Limited.**

**Black Oaks Publishing,** ( *0-9652673* ) Orders Addr.: P.O. Box 803, Hillsboro, MO 63050 Tel 514-789-2052 ; Fax: 314-645-3280; Toll Free: 800-275-4055; Edit Addr.: 5564 Hillsboro-Hematite Rd., DeSoto, MO 63020
Web site: http://www.csss-inc.com/blackoakspublishing
*Dist(s):* **CSSS, Inc..**

**Black Ponds Publishing,** ( *0-9666018* ) P.O. Box 50190, Summerville, SC 29485-0190
E-mail: steinbeckmicky@webtv.net.

**Black Print Publishing,** ( *0-9722071; 0-9748051* ) 289 Livingston St., Brooklyn, NY 11217
Web site: http://www.blackprintpublishing.com.

**Black Seal Pr.,** ( *1-880772* ) 9308 Eagle Ridge Rd., Las Vegas, NV 89134 Fax: 402-255-8665.

**Black Skimmer Pr.,** ( *0-9709554* ) 3270 Cargo St., Fort Myers, FL 33916 Tel 941-334-4311; Fax: 941-334-4611
*Dist(s):* **BookWorld Services, Inc..**

**Black Sparrow Pr. Imprint of Godine, David R. Pub.**

**Black Swan (GBR)** ( *0-552* ) *Dist. by* **Trafalgar.**

**Black Swan Bks., Ltd.,** ( *0-933806* ) P.O. Box 327, Redding Ridge, CT 06876 (SAN 213-4675) Tel 203-938-9548.

**BlackAmber Bks. (GBR)** ( *1-901969* ) *Dist. by* **SPD-Small Pr Dist.**

**Blackstaff Pr., The (IRL)** ( *0-85640* ) *Dist. by* **Dufour.**

**Blackstone Audio Bks., Inc.,** ( *0-7861* ) Orders Addr.: c/o Dept. LJ, P.O. Box 969, Ashland, OR 97520 Tel 541-482-9239; Fax: 541-482-9294; Toll Free: 800-729-2665; Edit Addr.: 31 Mistletoe Rd., Ashland, OR 97520 (SAN 173-2811)
E-mail: sales@blackstoneaudio.com
Web site: http://www.blackstoneaudio.com
*Dist(s):* **Landmark Audiobooks.**

**Blackwell Publishers** *See* **Blackwell Publishing**

†**Blackwell Publishing,** ( *0-631; 0-7456; 0-85012; 1-55786; 1-57718; 1-878975; 1-4051* ) Orders Addr.: c/o AIDC, P.O. Box 20, Williston, VT 05495-0020 (SAN 680-5035) Tel 802-862-0095; Fax: 802-864-7626; Toll Free Fax: 800-864-7626; Toll Free: 800-216-2522; Edit Addr.: 350 Main St., 6th Flr., Malden, MA 02148-5018 (SAN 680-5035) Tel 781-388-8200; Fax: 781-388-8210
E-mail: books@blackwellpub.com
Web site: http://www.blackwellpub.com
*Dist(s):* **American International Distribution Corp.**
**Iowa State Pr.**
**Lightning Source, Inc.**
**netLibrary, Inc.** ; *CIP.*

**BlackWords, Incorporated** *See* **BlackWords Pr.**

**BlackWords Pr.,** ( *1-888018* ) P.O. Box 21, Alexandria, VA 22313-0021
E-mail: info@blackwordsonline.com; blackwords@juno.com
Web site: http://www.blackwordsonline.com
*Dist(s):* **Afrikan World Bk. Distributor**
**Biblio Distribution**
**Bookazine Co., Inc.**
**Culture Plus Bks.**
**Koen Bk. Distributors**
**National Bk. Network**
**SPD-Small Pr. Distribution.**

**Blair, John F. Pub.,** ( *0-89587; 0-910244* ) 1406 Plaza Dr., Winston-Salem, NC 27103 (SAN 201-4319) Tel 336-768-1374; Fax: 336-768-9194; Toll Free: 800-222-9796
E-mail: blairpub@blairpub.com
Web site: http://www.blairpub.com.

**Blake Printing & Publishing, Incorporated** *See* **Blake Publishing, Inc.**

**Blake Publishing, Inc.,** ( *0-918303* ) 2222 Beebee, Saint Louis Obispo, CA 93401 (SAN 657-2618) Tel 805-543-6843; Toll Free: 800-234-3320
*Dist(s):* **Bookpeople**
**Quality Bks., Inc..**

**Blandford Pr. (GBR)** ( *0-7137* ) *Dist. by* **Sterling.**

**Bloch Publishing Co.,** ( *0-8197* ) 118 E. 28th St., Suite 501-503, New York, NY 10016-8413 (SAN 214-204X) Tel 212-532-3977; Fax: 212-779-9169
E-mail: BlochPub@worldnet.att.net
Web site: http://www.blochpub.com/.

**Blom Pubns. (GBR)** ( *0-405* ) *Dist. by* **Ayer.**

**Blood & Guts Pr.,** ( *0-940941* ) 11706 San Vicente Blvd., Los Angeles, CA 90049-5006 (SAN 665-1453) Tel 310-475-2700; Fax: 310-442-4846
E-mail: vagabondbooks@aol.com
*Dist(s):* **Vagabond Bks..**

**Bloodaxe Bks. (GBR)** ( *0-906427; 1-85224* ) *Dist. by* **Dufour.**

**Bloody Mist Pr.,** ( *1-932306* ) 2961 Industrial Rd., No. 445, Las Vegas, NV 89109 Toll Free: 866-890-0659
Web site: http://www.bloodymistpress.com.

**Bloomsbury Children Imprint of Bloomsbury Publishing**

**Bloomsbury Pr.,** ( *0-9667039* ) 4340 Anza St., No. 6, San Francisco, CA 94121 Do not confuse with Bloomsberry Pr., Madison, WI.

**Bloomsbury Publishing,** ( *1-58234* ) Orders Addr.: 16365 James Madison Hwy., Gordonsville, VA 22942-8501 Toll Free: 888-330-8477; Edit Addr.: 175 Fifth Ave., Suite 300, New York, NY 10010 Tel 212-674-5151 (ext. 782); Fax: 212-780-0115; Toll Free: 800-221-7945; *Imprints:* Bloomsbury Children (Bloom Child)
E-mail: alona.fryman@bloomsburyusa.com
Web site: http://www.bloomsbury.com/usa
*Dist(s):* **St. Martin's Pr..**

**Bloomsbury Publishing, Ltd. (GBR)** ( *0-7475* ) *Dist. by* **Trafalgar.**

**Blue & Grey Bk. Shoppe,** ( *1-929264* ) 107 W. Lexington, Independence, MO 64050 Tel 816-252-9909
E-mail: vbeck@qni.com
Web site: http://www.blueandgrey.com.

**Blue Bear Pr.,** ( *0-9666294* ) 22 E. Levering Mill Rd., Bala Cynwyd, PA 19004 Tel 715-374-3059.

†**Blue Bird Publishing,** ( *0-933025; 0-9615578* ) 10820 Farragut Hills Blvd., Knoxville, TN 37922 (SAN 200-5603) Tel 865-777-5218; Fax: 865-777-5219
E-mail: bluebird@bluebird1.com
Web site: http://www.bluebird1.com ; *CIP.*

**Blue Dolphin Publishing, Inc.,** ( *0-931892; 1-57733* ) Orders Addr.: P.O. Box 8, Nevada City, CA 95959 (SAN 223-2480) Tel 530-265-6925; Fax: 530-265-0787; Toll Free: 800-643-0765; Edit Addr.: 12428 Nevada City Hwy., Grass Valley, CA 95945 (SAN 696-009X); *Imprints:* Pelican Pond (Pelican Pond)
E-mail: bdolphin@netshel.net; clemens@netshel.net
Web site: http://www.bluedolphinpublishing.com
*Dist(s):* **Baker & Taylor Bks.**
**Booklines Hawaii, Ltd.**
**Bookpeople**
**Koen Bk. Distributors**
**Koen Pacific**
**New Concepts Bks. & Tapes Distributors**
**New Leaf Distributing Co., Inc.**
**Quality Bks., Inc.**
**Red Wheel/Weiser**
**Vision Distributors.**

**Blue Feather Pr.,** ( *0-932482* ) 2884 Trades West Rd., Santa Fe, NM 87505-3124 (SAN 211-9293) Tel 505-471-7519; Fax: 505-984-8010
E-mail: gok@arrowweb.com
*Dist(s):* **Quest, The.**

**Blue Heron Pr.,** ( *0-9621724; 1-884725* ) Orders Addr.: 302 Thoroughbred Park Dr., Thibodaux, LA 70301 (SAN 252-1199) Tel 504-446-8201; Toll Free: 888-273-2352 Do not confuse with companies with the same name in Bellingham, WA, Phoenix, MD, Albuquerque, NM, Shokan, NY, Mercer Island, WA, Commerce Township, MI, Grand Rapids, MI
E-mail: cpgorman@charter.net.

**Blue Heron Publishing,** ( *0-936085* ) Orders Addr.: 1234 SW Stark St., Suite 1, Portland, OR 97205 Tel 503-223-2098; Fax: 503-223-9474; Edit Addr.: 4205 SW Washington St., Suite 303, Portland, OR 97204 (SAN 696-6446) Tel 503-221-6841; Fax: 503-221-6843; *Imprints:* West Coast Crime (West Coast Crime)
E-mail: pjt@blueheron.com
Web site: http://www.blueheron.com/.

**Blue Knight Enterprises,** ( *1-892775* ) 7 Carriage House Ct., Hyde Park, NY 12538-1505 Tel 914-229-0244
E-mail: blue_knight_ent@hotmail.com.

**Blue Lantern Publishing,** ( *1-887303* ) Orders Addr.: P.O. Box 5833, Kingwood, TX 77325-5833 Tel 281-358-2583; Fax: 281-361-5746; Edit Addr.: 4015 Pecan Pk., Kingwood, TX 77345
E-mail: lanternblu@aol.com
Web site: http://www.geocities.com/SoHo/den/5463.

**Blue Moon Bks. Imprint of Avalon Publishing Group**

**Blue Moon Pr., Inc.,** ( *0-933188* ) Div. of Confluence Pr., Inc., Orders Addr.: Lewis Clark State College, 500 Eighth Ave., Lewiston, ID 83501-2698 (SAN 213-0157) Tel 208-799-2336; Fax: 208-799-2850 Do not confuse with companies with the same or similiar names in Denver, CO, Buffalo, NY, Rye, NH, Scottsdale, AZ, Huntingdon, PA, Scottsdale, AZ, Hilton, NY
E-mail: conpress@lcsc.edu
Web site: http://www.confluencepress.com.

**Blue Murder Pr.,** ( *0-9678809* ) Div. of Loft Works, Inc., 2340 NW Thurman St., Portland, OR 97210 Tel 503-944-6682; 503-292-6987
E-mail: dave@dsi-ads.com; dfirks@saw.net
Web site: http://www.bluemurder.com
*Dist(s):* **Baker & Taylor Bks..**

**Blue Pacific Pr.,** ( *0-9633351* ) P.O. Box 462018, Los Angeles, CA 90046-8018 (SAN 297-7591) Tel 213-654-1988; Fax: 213-654-3174
*Dist(s):* **Baker & Taylor Bks..**

**Blue Planet Bks., Inc.,** ( *1-930501* ) 4619 W. McRae Way, Glendale, AZ 85308 Tel 623-780-0053; Fax: 623-780-0468
E-mail: vijayaschartz@az.rmci.net
Web site: http://www.blueplanetbooks.net.

**Blue Scarab Pr.,** ( *0-937179* ) P.O. Box 4966, Pocatello, ID 83205-4966 (SAN 658-4640) Tel 208-775-3216
E-mail: jswhpw@srv.net.

**Blue Sky Pr., The Imprint of Scholastic, Inc.**

**Blue Steel Pr.,** ( *0-9743199* ) 1648 W. Bloomingdale Ave., Chicago, IL 60622 Tel 773-252-6480; Fax: 773-252-7166
E-mail: bluesteelpress@aol.com.

**Blue Unicorn Editions,** ( *1-891355; 1-58396* ) 1403 NW Ninth Ave., Gainesville, FL 32605 Fax: 352-371-1154 (orders)
E-mail: blueunicorn@instabook.net
Web site: http://www.blue-unicorn-editions.com/.

**Blue Wind Pr.,** ( *0-912652* ) 820 Miramar Ave., Berkeley, CA 94707-1807 (SAN 206-7099) Tel 510-525-2098; Fax: 510-525-1150
E-mail: gmd@dnai.com
*Dist(s):* **Baker & Taylor Bks.**
**SPD-Small Pr. Distribution.**

**Bluegrass Bks.,** ( *0-9643683* ) P.O. Box 784, Pewee Valley, KY 40056 Fax: 502-255-7657.

**BlueHen Bks. Imprint of Putnam Publishing Group, The**

**Bluejay Bks.,** 26 Douglas Rd., Chappaqua, NY 10514-3105 (SAN 293-0188).

**BlueOak Publishing,** ( *1-929117* ) P.O. Box 2012, Paso Robles, CA 93447-2012 Tel 805-238-1162; Fax: 805-238-7634
E-mail: gemroot@tcsn.net.

**Bluewater Publishing,** ( *0-9677814* ) Orders Addr.: P.O. Box 638, Eastlake, CO 80614-0638
E-mail: jpjacob@dimensional.com.

**BOA Editions, Ltd.,** ( *0-918526; 1-880238; 1-929918* ) 260 East Ave., Rochester, NY 14604 (SAN 281-3351) Tel 585-546-3410; Fax: 585-546-3913
E-mail: info@boaeditions.org; boaedit@frontiernet.net
Web site: http://www.boaeditions.org
*Dist(s):* **Consortium Bk. Sales & Distribution**
**SPD-Small Pr. Distribution.**

**Boaz Publishing Co.,** ( *0-9651879; 1-893448* ) Orders Addr.: P.O. Box 7123, Berkeley, CA 94606 Tel 510-559-1600; Fax: 510-525-4588; Toll Free: 800-841-2665; Edit Addr.: 1111 Eighth St., Berkeley, CA 94710
E-mail: order@tenspeed.com
*Dist(s):* **Ten Speed Pr..**

**Bodhisattva Pr., The,** ( *0-9676590* ) 53 Blaine St., Cranston, RI 02920 Tel 401-943-9179 (phone/fax).

**Boffin Bks.,** ( *0-9653109* ) Div. of Claypool Comics, 647 Grand Ave., Leonia, NJ 07605 Tel 201-947-1321 (phone/fax); *Imprints:* Claypool Comics (Claypool Comics)
E-mail: claypool@sonic.net
Web site: http://www.luckymojo.com/comicswarehouse5.html
*Dist(s):* **Diamond Book Distributors, Inc.**
**Hobbies Hawaii Distributors.**

†**Bolchazy-Carducci Pubs.,** ( *0-86516* ) 1000 Brown St., Unit 101, Wauconda, IL 60084 (SAN 219-7685) Tel 847-526-4344; Fax: 847-526-2867; Toll Free: 800-392-6453
E-mail: info@bolchazy.com
Web site: http://www.bolchazy.com ; *CIP.*

**Bonanza Publishing,** ( *0-945134* ) Orders Addr.: P.O. Box 204, Prineville, OR 97754 (SAN 246-0858) Tel 541-447-3115; Fax: 541-416-0822; Edit Addr.: 4393 NE Wainwright Rd., Prineville, OR 97754 (SAN 246-0866)
E-mail: bonanza@transport.com
Web site: http://www.ricksteber.com
*Dist(s):* **Baker & Taylor Bks.**
**Maverick Distributors.**

**Bond, Ed Books** *See* **Pulp Adventures, Inc.**

**Bonneville Bks. Imprint of Cedar Fort, Inc./CFI Distribution**

Names

**Bonus Bks., Inc.,** ( *0-929387; 0-931028; 0-933893; 1-56625* ) 875 N. Michigan Ave., Suite 1416, Chicago, IL 60611 (SAN 630-0804) Tel 312-467-0580 ; Fax: 312-467-9271
E-mail: richard@bonus-books.com
Web site: http://www.bonus-books.com
*Dist(s):* **National Bk. Network.**

**Book Bin - Pacifica, The,** ( *0-9621818* ) 228 SW Third St., Corvallis, OR 97333-4630 Tel 541-752-0045; Fax: 541-754-4115
E-mail: seasia@bookbin.com.

**Book Guild, Ltd. (GBR)** ( *1-85776; 0-86332* ) *Dist. by* **Trans-Atl Phila.**

**Book Montana,** ( *0-9670759* ) 663 N. Warren, Helena, MT 59601 Tel 406-442-0949
E-mail: architec@initco.net
*Dist(s):* **Partners/West.**

†**Book Publishing Co., The,** ( *0-913990; 1-57067; 0-9669317; 0-9673108* ) P.O. Box 99, Summertown, TN 38483 (SAN 202-439X) Tel 931-964-3571; Fax: 931-964-3518; Toll Free: 888-260-8458 Do not confuse with Book Publishing Co., Seattle, WA
E-mail: bookpub@bookpubco.com
Web site: http://www.bookpubco.com
*Dist(s):* **Baker & Taylor Bks.**
        **Bookpeople**
        **Borders, Inc.**
        **New Leaf Distributing Co., Inc.**
        **Nutri-Bks. Corp.**
        **Treasure Chest Bks.** *; CIP.*

**Book Sales, Inc.,** ( *0-7858; 0-89009; 1-55521* ) Orders Addr.: 114 Northfield Ave., Edison, NJ 08837 (SAN 169-488X) Tel 732-225-0530; Fax: 212-779-6058; 732-225-2257; Toll Free: 800-526-7257; Edit Addr.: 276 Fifth Ave., Suite 206, New York, NY 10001 (SAN 299-4062) Tel 212-779-4972; Fax: 212-779-6058
E-mail: booksales@eclipse.net
Web site: http://www.booksales.com
*Dist(s):* **Continental Bk. Co., Inc..**

**Book Tree, The,** ( *1-885395; 1-58509* ) Orders Addr.: P.O. Box 16476, San Diego, CA 92176 Tel 619-280-1263; Fax: 619-280-1285; Toll Free: 800-700-8733
E-mail: booktree@cts.com
Web site: http://www.thebooktree.com
*Dist(s):* **New Leaf Distributing Co., Inc..**

**Book Wholesalers, Inc.,** ( *0-7587; 1-4046; 1-4131; 1-4155; 1-4156* ) 1847 Mercer Rd., Lexington, KY 40511-1001 (SAN 135-5449) Toll Free: 800-888-4478
E-mail: jcarrico@bwibooks.com; nb
Web site: http://www.bwibooks.com

**Book World, Inc.,** ( *1-881542* ) 9666 E. Riggs Rd., Box 194, Sun Lakes, AZ 85248 Tel 480-895-7995; Fax: 480-895-6991; Toll Free: 888-472-2665 Do not confuse with companies with the same or similar name in Layfayette, IN, Roanoke, VA
E-mail: bst@bluestarproductions.net
Web site: http://www.bluestarproductions.net
*Dist(s):* **Bookpeople**
        **New Leaf Distributing Co., Inc..**

**Bookbooters Pr.,** ( *1-931297; 1-59281* ) 14 E. Tomstead Rd., Simsbury, CT 06070 Fax: 860-658-2736
E-mail: sales@bookbooters.com;
temden@bookbooters.com;
postmaster@bookbooters.com
Web site: http://www.bookbooters.com.

**Bookbooters.com** *See* **Bookbooters Pr.**

**Bookcassette Imprint of Brilliance Audio**

**Bookcraft, Inc. Imprint of Deseret Bk. Co.**

**Bookking International (FRA)** *Dist. by* **Distribks Inc.**

**Booklines Hawaii, Ltd.,** ( *1-929844; 1-58849* ) 269 Pali'i St., Mililani, HI 96789 (SAN 630-6624) Tel 877-828-4852; Fax: 808-676-2031
E-mail: cynthiar@booklines.com
Web site: http://www.booklineshawaii.com.

**Booklocker.com, Inc.,** ( *1-929072; 1-931391; 1-59113* ) P.O. Box 2399, Bangor, ME 04402 (SAN 254-363X) Fax: 207-262-5544
E-mail: writersweekly@writersweekly.com;
booklocker@booklocker.com
Web site: http://www.booklocker.com;
http://www.writersweekly.com.

**Bookmice Imprint of McGraw Publishing, Inc.**

**Book-On-Disc.Com,** ( *1-58519* ) 3624 Simcoe Ct., Palm Harbor, FL 34684 Tel 727-785-2217
E-mail: Book@book-on-disc.com
Web site: http://www.book-on-disc.com.

**Bookpublisher.com** *See* **Wheatmark, Inc.**

**Books in Motion,** ( *1-55686; 1-58116* ) Div. of Classic Ventures, Ltd., 9922 E. Montgomery, Suite 31, Spokane, WA 99206 (SAN 677-8909) Tel 509-922-1646; Fax: 509-922-1445; Toll Free: 800-752-3199
E-mail: sales@booksinmotion.com
*Dist(s):* **Landmark Audiobooks.**

**Books International, Incorporated,** ( *1-891078* ) Orders Addr.: P.O. Box 605, Herndon, VA 20172-0605 (SAN 131-761X) Tel 703-661-1500; Fax: 703-661-1501
E-mail: mgreenwald@sorosny.org.

**Books of Wonder,** ( *0-929605* ) 216 W. 18th St., Rm. 806, New York, NY 10011 (SAN 249-9916) Tel 212-989-3270; 212-989-3475; Fax: 212-989-1203
E-mail: wholesale@booksofwonder.com
Web site: http://www.booksofwonder.com.

**Bks. on Demand,** ( *0-608; 0-7837; 0-8357; 0-598* ) Div. of UMI, 300 N. Zeeb Rd., Ann Arbor, MI 48106-1346 Tel 734-761-4700; Fax: 734-665-5022; Toll Free: 800-521-0600
E-mail: info@umi.com
Web site: http://wwwlib.umi.com/bod; http://www.umi.com.

**Books on Tape, Inc.,** ( *0-7366; 0-913369; 1-4159* ) Div. of Random House, Inc., Orders Addr.: P.O. Box 25122, Santa Ana, CA 92799-5122 Fax: 714-825-0764 ; Toll Free: 800-541-5525; Edit Addr.: 2910 W. Garry Ave., Santa Ana, CA 92704-6510 (SAN 107-0460) Tel 714-825-0021; Fax: 714-825-0756; Toll Free: 800-626-3333
E-mail: botcs@booksontape.com
Web site: http://www.booksontape.com; http://library.booksontape.com.

**Books OnScreen Imprint of PageFree Publishing, Inc.**

**Books West Southwest,** ( *0-9632966* ) P.O. Box 40250, Tucson, AZ 85717-0250
E-mail: bkswest@ix.netcom.com.

**Booksurge, LLC,** ( *1-59109; 1-59457* ) 5341 Dorchester Rd., Suite 16, North Charleston, SC 29418 (SAN 255-2132) Tel 843-579-0000; Fax: 843-577-7506; Toll Free: 866-308-6235
E-mail: editor@booksurge.com;
info@imprintbooks.com
Web site: http://www.booksurge.com;
http://www.imprintbooks.com
*Dist(s):* **BookWorld Services, Inc..**

**BookWorld Distribution Services, Incorporated** *See* **BookWorld Services, Inc.**

**BookWorld Services, Inc.,** ( *1-884962* ) 1933 Whitfield Pk. Loop, Sarasota, FL 34243 (SAN 173-0568) Tel 941-758-8094; Fax: 941-753-9396; Toll Free Fax: 800-777-2525; Toll Free: 800-444-2524 (orders only)
E-mail: central@bookworld.com;
sales@bookworld.com
Web site: http://www.bookworld.com.

**Bookwrights Pr.,** ( *1-880404* ) 2255 Westover Dr., Charlottesville, VA 22901-9504 Tel 804-823-8223; Toll Free: 888-823-2977
E-mail: editor@bookwrights.com
Web site: http://www.bookwrights.com
*Dist(s):* **Midpoint Trade Bks., Inc..**

**Boomer Pubns.,** ( *0-9656648* ) 7204 Cobalt Way, Citrus Heights, CA 95621 Tel 916-723-3720; Fax: 914-725-7014 Do not confuse with Boomer Pubns. Corp., Marietta, GA
E-mail: XZBM96D@Prodigy.com
Web site: http://www.BooksAmerica.com.

**Boone, M. Broughton Publishing** *See* **Cape Winds Pr., Inc.**

**Borderlands Pr.,** ( *1-880325* ) Orders Addr.: P.O. Box 1529, Grantham, NH 03753-1529 Tel 603-863-9879; Fax: 603-863-9886; Toll Free: 800-528-3310; Edit Addr.: 6 Winter Hill, Grantham, NH 03753 Do not confuse with companies with the same name in Gulf Breeze, FL, San Antonio, TX
E-mail: scribe@srnet.com; skyfamily.com/dddd
*Dist(s):* **Alliance Hse., Inc.**
        **Baker & Taylor Bks.**
        **Bookpeople**
        **Brodart Co.**
        **Capital City**
        **Diamond Book Distributors, Inc..**

**Borders Pr.,** ( *0-681* ) Div. of Borders Group, Inc., 100 Phoenix Dr., Ann Arbor, MI 48108
Web site: http://www.bordersgroupinc.com; http://www.bordersstores.com; http://www.borders.com.

**Bordighera, Inc.,** ( *1-884419* ) Orders Addr.: P.O. Box 1374, Lafayette, IN 47902-1374; Edit Addr.: Languages and Linguistics, Florida Atlantic Univ., 777 Glades Rd., Boca Raton, FL 33431; *Imprints:* VIA Folios (VIA Folios)
E-mail: dstarewich@aol.com
*Dist(s):* **SPD-Small Pr. Distribution.**

**Borealis Imprint of White Wolf Publishing, Inc.**

**Borealis Bk. Imprint of Minnesota Historical Society Pr.**

**Borgo Press** *See* **Millefleurs**

**Boson Bks. Imprint of C&M Online Media, Inc.**

**Bosworth Publishing Co.,** ( *0-9717693* ) 5863 Erlanger St., San Diego, CA 92122
E-mail: sales@newcenturypress.com;
gzabka@aol.com
*Dist(s):* **New Century Pr..**

**Boulevard Bks.,** ( *0-910278* ) P.O. Box 89, Topanga, CA 90290 (SAN 202-4179) Tel 310-455-1036; Fax: 310-455-0426 Do not confuse with companies with the same name in New York, NY, Panama City, FL
E-mail: blvdbooks@yahoo.com.

**Boulevard Bks.,** ( *0-399; 0-425; 1-57297* ) Div. of Berkley Publishing Group, Orders Addr.: 405 Murray Hill Pkwy., East Rutherford, NJ 07073; Edit Addr.: 200 Madison Ave., 14th Flr., New York, NY 10016 Fax: 212-545-8917; Toll Free: 800-788-6262 Do not confuse with Boulevard Bks. in Topanga, CA
Web site: http://www.penguinputnam.com/
*Dist(s):* **Penguin Group (USA) Inc..**

**Bouregy, Thomas & Co., Inc.,** ( *0-8034* ) 160 Madison Ave., New York, NY 10016 (SAN 201-4173) Tel 212-598-0222; Fax: 212-979-1862; Toll Free: 800-223-5251; *Imprints:* Avalon Books (Avalon Bks)
E-mail: custserv@avalonbooks.com
Web site: http://www.avalonbooks.com.

**Boyars, Marion Pubs., Inc.,** ( *0-7145; 0-905223* ) 237 E. 39th St., No. 1A, New York, NY 10016-2110 (SAN 284-981X) Tel 212-697-1599; Fax: 212-808-0664; Toll Free: 800-283-3572 (orders only)
*Dist(s):* **Consortium Bk. Sales & Distribution.**

**Boydell & Brewer, Inc.,** ( *0-85115; 0-85991; 0-86193; 0-907239; 1-870252* ) Div. of Boydell & Brewer, Inc., 668 Mount Hope Ave., Rochester, NY 14620-2731 Tel 585-275-0419; Fax: 585-271-8778
E-mail: boydell@boydellusa.com
Web site: http://www.boydell.co.uk.

**Boyds Mills Pr.,** ( *1-56397; 1-878093; 1-59078* ) Div. of Highlights For Children, Inc., 815 Church St., Honesdale, PA 18431 Tel 717-253-1164; 570-253-1164; Fax: 570-253-0179; Toll Free: 800-490-5111
E-mail: admin@boydsmillspress.com
Web site: http://www.boydsmillspress.com
*Dist(s):* **Cheng & Tsui Co.**
        **Lectorum Pubns., Inc..**

**Bradford Pr.,** ( *0-9705618* ) Orders Addr.: P.O. Box 6802, South Bend, IN 46660-6802 Do not confuse with companies with same name in Bradford, MA, Palm Beach, FL, Chicago, IL
E-mail: BradfordPress@myvine.com.

**Bradley, Robert L.,** ( *0-9702912* ) Orders Addr.: P.O. Box 25768, Saint Louis, MO 63136.

**Brady Computer Books** *See* **Brady Publishing**

**Brady Publishing,** ( *0-8359; 0-87618; 0-87619; 0-89303; 0-913486; 1-56686; 0-7440* ) Div. of Prentice Hall, 201 W. 103rd St., Indianapolis, IN 46290 Tel 317-581-3500; Fax: 317-705-6290; Toll Free Fax: 800-835-3202; Toll Free: 800-428-5331 (orders)
E-mail: janet.eshenour@bradygames.com
Web site: http://www.bradygames.com
*Dist(s):* **Alpha Bks..**

**Branden Bks.,** ( *0-8283* ) P.O. Box 812094, Wellesley, MA 02482 (SAN 201-4106) Tel 781-235-3634; Fax: 781-790-1056
E-mail: branden@branden.com
Web site: http://www.branden.com.

**Branden Publishing Company** *See* **Branden Bks.**

**Brandon Bk. Pubs., Ltd. (IRL)** ( *0-86322* ) *Dist. by* **Irish Bks Media.**

**Brandylane Pubs., Inc.,** ( *0-9627635; 1-883911* ) Orders Addr.: P.O. Box 261, White Stone, VA 23223; Edit Addr.: 1711 E. Main St., Suite 9, Richmond, VA 23223 Tel 804-644-3090; Fax: 804-644-3092; Toll Free: 800-553-6922 (orders only)
E-mail: thpruett@hotmail.com; brandy@crosslink.net
Web site: http://www.brandylanepublishers.com
*Dist(s):* **Baker & Taylor International**
        **Parnassus Bk. Distributors.**

**Brandywine Publishing,** ( *0-9679745* ) 420 Fletcher Ct., Salt Lake City, UT 84102 Do not confuse with Brandywine Publishing, Sarasota, FL
E-mail: Brandywinepub@aol.com.

Names

**Brassey's, Inc.,** ( *0-02; 1-57488* ) Orders Addr.: P.O. Box 960, Herndon, VA 20172-0605 Toll Free: 800-775-2518; Edit Addr.: 22841 Quicksilver Dr., Dulles, VA 20166 (SAN 200-741X) Tel 703-661-1500 ; Fax: 703-661-1501
E-mail: brasseys@presswarehouse.com
Web site: http://www.brasseysinc.com
*Dist(s):* **Libros Sin Fronteras**
    **MBI Distribution Services.**

**Brassey's, UK Ltd. (GBR)** ( *0-08; 1-85753; 0-904609* )
*Dist. by* **Brasseys Inc.**

**BraZen,** ( *0-9676268* ) Orders Addr.: 13234 US Hwy. 80, E., Pike Road, TX 36064
E-mail: reggiec4@juno.com;
webstercarter@juno.com.

**Braziller, George Inc.,** ( *0-8076* ) 171 Madison Ave., Suite 1103, New York, NY 10016 (SAN 201-9310) Tel 212-889-0909; Fax: 212-689-5405
*Dist(s):* **Norton, W. W. & Co., Inc..**

**Breakaway Bks.,** ( *1-55821; 1-891369* ) P.O. Box 24, Halcottsville, NY 12438 Tel 607-326-4805; Fax: 212-898-0408; Toll Free: 800-548-4348 (voicemail) Do not confuse with Breakaway Bks., Albany, TX
E-mail: information@breakawaybooks.com
Web site: http://www.breakawaybooks.com
*Dist(s):* **Consortium Bk. Sales & Distribution.**

**Breaux Bks., LLC,** ( *0-9701709* ) P.O. Box 67, Fairburn, GA 30213 Tel 770-842-4792; Fax: 770-964-1875
E-mail: magbreaux@mindspring.com
Web site: http://www.familycurse.com
*Dist(s):* **Hervey's Booklink & Cookbook**
    **Warehouse.**

**Breeding, Robert L.** *See* **Thriftecon Publications**

**Breese Bks., Ltd. (GBR)** ( *0-947533* ) *Dist. by* **Midpt Trade.**

**Brendan Bks.,** ( *0-9626136* ) P.O. Box 221143, Carmel, CA 93922-1143 (SAN 297-2298) Tel 408-624-5781
E-mail: regilligan@aol.com
*Dist(s):* **Otter B Bks..**

**Brentwood Communications Group,** ( *0-916573; 1-55630* ) 4000 Bealwood Ave., Columbus, GA 31904 (SAN 297-1895) Tel 706-576-7887; Fax: 706-317-5808; Toll Free: 800-334-2828
E-mail: brentwood@aol.com
Web site: http://www.brentwoodbooks.com.

**Breslov Research Institute,** ( *0-930213; 1-928822* ) P.O. Box 587, Monsey, NY 10952-0587 (SAN 670-7890) Tel 845-425-4258; Fax: 845-425-3018; Toll Free: 800-332-7375
E-mail: info@rebbenachman.com
Web site: http://www.rebbenachman.com
*Dist(s):* **Moznaim Publishing Corp..**

**Briarwood Pubns,** ( *1-892614* ) 150 W. College St., Rocky Mount, VA 24151 (SAN 299-8068) Tel 540-483-3606; Fax: 540-489-4692 ext. 51 Do not confuse with Briarwood Pubns., Terre Haute, IN
E-mail: bturner@swva.net
Web site: http://www.briarwoodva.com.

**Bridge Imprint of Bridge-Logos Pubs.**

**Bridge Publishing, Incorporated/LOGOS** *See* **Bridge-Logos Pubs.**

**Bridge Works Publishing Co., Inc.,** ( *1-882593* ) P.O. Box 1798, Bridgehampton, NY 11932 Tel 631-537-3418 Do not confuse with Bridge Works Publishing in Indianapolis, IN
E-mail: bap@hamptons.com
*Dist(s):* **National Bk. Network.**

**Bridge-Logos Pubs.,** ( *0-88270; 0-912106* ) Orders Addr.: 17310 NW 32nd Ave., Newberry, FL 32669 Toll Free Fax: 800-935-6467 (orders only); Toll Free: 800-631-5802 (orders only); Edit Addr.: P.O. Box 141630, Gainesville, FL 32614 (SAN 253-5254) Tel 352-472-7900; Fax: 352-472-7908; *Imprints:* Bridge (Bridge)
E-mail: editor@bridgelogos.com;
info@bridgelogos.com; mail@bridgelogos.com
Web site: http://www.bridgelogos.com
*Dist(s):* **Anchor Distributors**
    **Appalachian Bible Co.**
    **Baker & Taylor Bks.**
    **Riverside**
    **Spring Arbor Distributors, Inc..**

**Bridgeway Pr. Imprint of Toland Communications**

**Bright Bks., Inc.,** ( *1-880092* ) 2313 Lake Austin Blvd., Austin, TX 78703 Tel 512-499-4164; Fax: 512-477-9975 Do not confuse with companies with the same name in Akron, IN, Folsom, CA
*Dist(s):* **Partners Pubs. Group, Inc..**

**Bright Hill Pr.,** ( *0-9646844; 1-892471* ) Orders Addr.: P.O. Box 193, Treadwell, NY 13846-0193 Tel 607-746-7306; Fax: 607-746-7274; Edit Addr.: R.R. 1, Box 545, Delhi, NY 13753
E-mail: http://www.brighthillpress.org;
wordthur@catskill.net
*Dist(s):* **Baker & Taylor Bks.**
    **North Country Bks., Inc.**
    **SPD-Small Pr. Distribution**
    **Small Pr. Alliance.**

**Bright Mountain Bks., Inc.,** ( *0-914875* ) 206 Riva Ridge Dr., Fairview, NC 28730 (SAN 289-0674) Tel 828-628-1768; Fax: 828-628-1755; *Imprints:* Historical Images (Historical Images)
E-mail: BooksBMB@charter.net
*Dist(s):* **Appalachian Bk. Distributors**
    **Baker & Taylor Bks.**
    **Parnassus Bk. Distributors.**

**Brighton Publishing,** ( *0-9706544* ) Orders Addr.: P.O. Box 30959, Laughlin, NV 89028-0959 Do not confuse with Brighton Publishing Co. in Corvallis, OR
E-mail: annhovi@brightonpublishing.com;
annahovi@brightonpublishing.com
Web site: http://www.brightonpublishing.com.

**†Brill Academic Pubs., Inc.,** ( *0-391; 0-916846* ) Subs. of Brill Academic Publishing Co., The Netherlands, 112 Water St., Suite 400, Boston, MA 02109 (SAN 254-6922) Tel 617-263-2323; Fax: 617-263-2324; Toll Free: 800-962-4406
E-mail: cs@brillusa.com
Web site: http://www.brill.nl
*Dist(s):* **Books International, Incorporated** ; *CIP.*

**Brill, E. J. U. S. A., Incorporated** *See* **Brill Academic Pubs., Inc.**

**Brilliance Audio,** ( *0-930435; 1-56100; 1-56740; 1-58788; 1-59086; 1-59355* ) 1704 Eaton Dr., Grand Haven, MI 49417 (SAN 690-1395) Tel 616-846-5256 ; Fax: 616-846-0630; Toll Free: 800-648-2312 (phone/fax, retail & library orders); *Imprints:* Bookcassette (Bkcassette); Nova Audio Books (Nova Audio Bks); Unabridged Library Editions (Unabridge Lib Edns); Paperback Nova Audio Books (Abridged) (Pprback Nova); Silhouette Romance Audio (Silhouette Romance); Harlequin Romance Audio (Harlequin Romance); Brilliance Audio Unabridged (BAU); CD Unabridged (CD Unabridged); CD (CD); Library Edition (Lib Edit); CD Unabridged Library Edition (CD Unabrid Lib Ed); CD Library Edition (CD Lib Edit); Brilliance Audio (Brill Audio); Brilliance Audio Paperback Audiobooks (Bri Audio Pbk Audbks); Brilliance Audio on CD Unabridged (Bril Audio CD Unabri); Brilliance Audio on CD (BACD); Brilliance Audio on CD Value Priced (BCD Value Price); Brilliance Audio Unabridged Lib Ed (BrilAudUnabridg); Brilliance Audio on CD Unabridged Lib Ed (BriAudCD Unabrid); Brilliance Audio on CD Lib Ed (BACDLib Ed)
E-mail: catalogcustomerservice@brillianceaudio.com; sales@brillianceaudio.com
Web site: http://www.brillianceaudio.com
*Dist(s):* **American Wholesale Bk. Co.**
    **BPDI**
    **Baker & Taylor Bks.**
    **Bookazine Co., Inc.**
    **Ingram Bk. Co.**
    **Koen Bk. Distributors**
    **Landmark Audiobooks**
    **Partners/West**
    **Southern Bk. Service.**

**Brilliance Audio Imprint of Brilliance Audio**

**Brilliance Audio on CD Imprint of Brilliance Audio**

**Brilliance Audio on CD Lib Ed Imprint of Brilliance Audio**

**Brilliance Audio on CD Unabridged Imprint of Brilliance Audio**

**Brilliance Audio on CD Unabridged Lib Ed Imprint of Brilliance Audio**

**Brilliance Audio on CD Value Priced Imprint of Brilliance Audio**

**Brilliance Audio Paperback Audiobooks Imprint of Brilliance Audio**

**Brilliance Audio Unabridged Imprint of Brilliance Audio**

**Brilliance Audio Unabridged Lib Ed Imprint of Brilliance Audio**

**Brilliance Corporation** *See* **Brilliance Audio**

**Brimax Bks., Ltd.,** ( *0-86112; 0-900195; 0-904494; 1-85854* ) Member of Reed Elsevier Group, 2284 Black River Rd., Bethlehem, PA 18015
*Dist(s):* **Libros Sin Fronteras.**

**British American Publishing, Ltd.,** ( *0-945167* ) 4 British American Blvd., Latham, NY 12110 (SAN 246-3008) Tel 518-786-6000; Fax: 518-786-6001
E-mail: info@bapublish.com
Web site: http://www.bapublish.com
*Dist(s):* **Midpoint Trade Bks., Inc..**

**British Bk. Co., Inc.,** ( *1-930468* ) 149 Palos Verdes Blvd., Suite B, Redondo Beach, CA 90277 Tel 310-373-5917; Fax: 310-373-7342; Toll Free: 877-990-1299
E-mail: tony310@earthlink.com
Web site: http://www.firstnovels.com.

**†Broadman & Holman Pubs.,** ( *0-8054; 0-87981; 1-55819; 1-58640; 0-8400* ) Div. of LifeWay Christian Resources of the Southern Baptist Convention, 127 Ninth Ave., N., Nashville, TN 37234 (SAN 201-937X) Tel 615-251-2520; Fax: 615-251-5026 (Books Only); 615-251-2036 (Bibles Only); 615-251-2413 (Gifts/Supplies Only); Toll Free: 800-296-4036 (orders/returns); 800-251-3225; 800-725-5416
E-mail: broadmanholman@lifeway.com
Web site: http://www.broadmanholman.com
*Dist(s):* **CRC Pubns.**
    **Christian Bk. Distributors**
    **Twentieth Century Christian Bks.** ; *CIP.*

**Broadway Bks.,** ( *0-385; 0-553; 0-7679; 1-4000* ) Div. of Doubleday Broadway Publishing Group, Orders Addr.: 400 Hahn Rd., Westminster, MD 21157 Tel 410-848-1900; Toll Free: 800-726-0600; Edit Addr.: 1540 Broadway, New York, NY 10036 Tel 212-354-6500; Fax: 212-782-8338; Toll Free: 800-223-6834; *Imprints:* Harlem Moon (Harlem Moo); Main Street Books (MainStreet)
Web site: http://www.bdd.com
*Dist(s):* **Random Hse., Inc..**

**Brodart Co.,** ( *0-87272* ) Orders Addr.: 500 Arch St., Williamsport, PA 17705 (SAN 169-7684) Tel 717-326-2461; 570-326-2461 (International); Fax: 570-326-1479; 519-759-1144 (Canada); Toll Free Fax: 800-999-6799; Toll Free: 800-233-8467 (US & Canada)
E-mail: bookinfo@brodart.com
Web site: http://www.brodart.com.

**Brooke, Gabriella,** ( *0-9719988* ) 4704 S. Dyer Rd., Spokane, WA 99223 Tel 509-448-1028; *Imprints:* Malgari Press (Malgari Pr)
E-mail: malgaripress@icehouse.net
*Dist(s):* **Partners/West.**

**Brookfield Reader, Inc., The,** ( *0-9660172; 1-930093* ) 137 Peyton Rd., Sterling, VA 20165-5605 (SAN 299-4445) Tel 703-430-0202; Fax: 703-430-7315; Toll Free: 888-389-2741
E-mail: info@brookfieldreader.com;
hbaggett@erols.com
Web site: http://www.brookfieldreader.com
*Dist(s):* **Book Wholesalers, Inc.**
    **BookWorld Services, Inc.**
    **Brodart Co.**
    **International Publishers Marketing**
    **Quality Bks., Inc..**

**Brookhaven Pr.,** ( *1-58103; 1-4035* ) Div. of NMT Corp., Orders Addr.: 2004 Kramer St., LaCrosse, WI 54603 (SAN 287-6817) Tel 608-781-0850; Fax: 608-781-3883; Toll Free: 800-236-0850
E-mail: brookhaven@nmt.com
Web site: http://www.brookhavenpress.com.

**†Brookline Bks., Inc.,** ( *0-914797; 1-57129* ) Orders Addr.: P.O. Box 97, Newton Upper Falls, MA 02464 (SAN 289-0690) Tel 617-558-8010; Fax: 617-558-8011; Toll Free: 800-666-2665; Edit Addr.: 29 Ware St., Cambridge, MA 02138; *Imprints:* Lumen Editions (Lumen Eds)
E-mail: brbooks@yahoo.com
Web site: http://www.brooklinebooks.com ; *CIP.*

**Browder Springs Bks.,** ( *0-9651359; 0-9709645* ) 6238 Glennox Ln., Dallas, TX 75214-2144 Tel 214-368-4360; Fax: 214-739-9149
E-mail: browder@airmail.net
Web site: http://www.browdersprings.com
*Dist(s):* **Hervey's Booklink & Cookbook**
    **Warehouse.**

**Brown Bear Books,** ( *0-9670861* ) 325 High St., Santa Cruz, CA 95060 Tel 831-457-1135
E-mail: brwnbear@sasquatch.com

**Brown, David Bk. Co.,** Orders Addr.: P.O. Box 511, Oakville, CT 06779 (SAN 630-9461) Tel 860-945-9329; Fax: 860-945-9468; Toll Free: 800-791-9354
E-mail: david.brown.bk.co@snet.net
Web site: http://www.oxbowbooks.com.

**Browne Bks. in The Hollow,** ( *0-9636621* ) 12469 The Hollow Rd., Grass Valley, CA 95945-9334 Tel 916-273-2909.

Names

**Brownlow Publishing Co., Inc.,** ( *0-910444; 0-915720; 1-57051; 1-877719; 1-59177* ) 6309 Airport Freeway, Fort Worth, TX 76117 (SAN 207-5105) Tel 817-831-3831; Fax: 817-831-7025; Toll Free: 800-433-7610
E-mail: jcerneka@brownlowgift.com; jroser@brownlowgift.com
Web site: http://www.brownlowgift.com
*Dist(s):* **Appalachian Bible Co.**
    **Riverside**
    **Spring Arbor Distributors, Inc.**

**Bruccoli Clark Layman, Inc.,** ( *0-89723* ) 2006 Sumter St., Columbia, SC 29201 (SAN 209-3987) Tel 803-771-4642; Fax: 803-799-6953.

**Brunswick Publishing Corp.,** ( *0-931494; 1-55618* ) 1386 Lawrenceville Plank Rd., Lawrenceville, VA 23868 (SAN 211-6332) Tel 434-848-3865; Fax: 434-848-0607
E-mail: brunswickbooks@earthlink.net
Web site: http://www.brunswickbooks.com/
*Dist(s):* **Breakfast Poems.**

**Buccaneer Bks., Inc.,** ( *0-89966; 0-89967; 0-89968; 1-56849* ) P.O. Box 168, Cutchogue, NY 11935 (SAN 209-1542) Tel 631-734-5724; Fax: 631-734-7920;
*Imprints:* Lightyear Press (Lghtyr Pr); Harmony Raine & Company (Harmony Raine)
E-mail: BuccBooks@aol.com
Web site: http://www.BuccaneerBooks.com
*Dist(s):* **National Bk. Network.**

**Buckingham Classics, Limited** *See* **B&B Audio, Inc.**

**Bucknell Univ. Pr.,** ( *0-8387* ) 440 Forsgate Dr., Cranbury, NJ 08512 Tel 609-655-4770
Web site:
http://www.department.bucknell.edu/univ_press/
*Dist(s):* **Associated Univ. Presses**
    **Baker & Taylor International.**

**Bullion Bks.,** ( *0-9651376* ) 4833 Saratoga Blvd., No. 602, Corpus Christi, TX 78413 Tel 361-949-8309
E-mail: success@bullionbooks.com
*Dist(s):* **Midpoint Trade Bks., Inc..**

**Burd Street Pr. Imprint of White Mane Publishing Co., Inc.**

**Burford Bks.,** ( *1-58080* ) 32 Morris Ave., Springfield, NJ 07081 Tel 973 258 0960; 973-258-0960; Fax: 973-258-0113; Toll Free: 888-672-5247
E-mail: orders@burfordbooks.com; info@burfordbooks.com
Web site: http://www.burfordbooks.com
*Dist(s):* **National Bk. Network.**

**Burke, Arleen,** ( *0-9721881* ) 85 Ardsmoor Rd., Melrose, MA 02176.

**Burns-Cole Pubs.,** ( *0-9645876* ) P.O. Box 5275, Bozeman, MT 59717-5275 Tel 406-587-5997
*Dist(s):* **Baker & Taylor Bks.**
    **Bookmen, Inc.**
    **Brodart Co.**
    **Koen Bk. Distributors.**

**Burton, Hal Publishing,** ( *0-9725707* ) 61 N. Picnic Dr., Lilliwaup, WA 98555.

**Butterfield Bks., Inc.,** ( *1-886652* ) Box 407, Lindsborg, KS 67456 Tel 785-227-2707; Fax: 785-227-2017
E-mail: linda@bookkansas.com
Web site: http://www.bookkansas.com
*Dist(s):* **Baker & Taylor Bks.**
    **Booksource, The**
    **Skandisk, Inc..**

**Butterworth-Heinemann Imprint of Elsevier Science & Technology Bks.**

**Buttonwillow Books** *See* **Wolfpack Publishing**

**Buy Bks. on the Web.Com,** ( *0-9665678; 1-892896; 0-7414* ) 519 W. Lancaster Ave., Haverford, PA 19041 Tel 610-520-2500; Fax: 610-519-0261; Toll Free: 877-289-2665
E-mail: info@buybooksontheweb.com
Web site: http://buybooksontheweb.com.

**ByteLady Publishing,** ( *0-9704891* ) 3885-J Cochran St., No. 326, Simi Valley, CA 93063 Fax: 805-522-0814; Toll Free: 866-298-3523
E-mail: bytelady@earthlink.net
Web site: http://www.bytelady.com/.

**C&M Online Media, Inc.,** ( *0-917990; 1-886420; 1-932482* ) 3905 Meadow Field Ln., Raleigh, NC 27606 Tel 919-233-8164; Fax: 919-233-8578;
*Imprints:* Boson Books (Boson Bks)
E-mail: nancy@cmonline.com
Web site: http://www.cmonline.com;
http://www.bosonbooks.com;
http://www.bosonromances.com
*Dist(s):* **Amazon.Com**
    **netLibrary, Inc..**

**C C Comics/C C Publishing** *See* **C C Publishing**

**C C Publishing,** ( *0-9634183* ) Orders Addr.: P.O. Box 542, Loveland, OH 45140-0542; Edit Addr.: 6304 Councilridge Ct., Loveland, OH 45140 Tel 513-248-4170; *Imprints:* Journey Book Press (Jrny Bk Pr)
Web site: http://www.mysterypublishers.com/CC
*Dist(s):* **Spring Arbor Distributors, Inc..**

**CEDCO Publishing,** ( *0-7683; 0-915865; 1-55912* ) 100 Pelican Way, San Rafael, CA 94901 (SAN 293-9495) Tel 415-451-3176; Fax: 415-457-4839; Toll Free: 800-227-6162
E-mail: sales@cedco.com
Web site: http://www.cedco.com.

**C.E. Publishing Group,** ( *0-9652655* ) P.O. Box 57, Advance, NC 27006-0057 Tel 336-998-2679; Fax: 336-998-2055
E-mail: cepublishing@aol.com.

**CIS Communications, Inc.,** ( *0-935063; 1-56062* ) 180 Park Avenue, Lakewood, NJ 08701 (SAN 694-5953) Tel 732-905-3000; Fax: 732-367-6666.

**CJH Enterprises,** ( *0-9643250; 1-890683* ) 6064 Mayberry Ln., Milton, FL 32570-8875 Tel 850-626-2700; Fax: 850-626-7040; Toll Free: 888-258-2784
E-mail: altarvin@pcola.gulf.net
Web site: http://www.pcola.gulf.net/~altarvin
*Dist(s):* **Baker & Taylor Bks..**

**C Lazy Three Pr.,** ( *0-9643283* ) 5957 Crawford Gulch, Golden, CO 80403 (SAN 255-5271) Tel 303-277-0134 (phone/fax)
E-mail: clazy3@earthlink.net
*Dist(s):* **Baker & Taylor Bks.**
    **Books West.**

**C. M. Publishing,** ( *0-9663480* ) 132 Sandpiper Cir., Corte Madera, CA 94925 Tel 415-927-7667; Fax: 415-945-0667
*Dist(s):* **Baker & Taylor Bks.**
    **Bookpeople.**

†**CRC Pr. LLC,** ( *0-8493; 0-87819; 0-935184; 1-57491; 1-58488* ) Subs. of Taylor & Francis, Inc., 2000 Corporate Blvd., NW, Boca Raton, FL 33431 (SAN 202-1994) Tel 561-994-0555; Fax: 561-989-8732 (outside USA); Toll Free Fax: 800-374-3401 (inside USA); Toll Free: 800-272-7737
E-mail: orders@crcpress.com
Web site: http://www.crcpress.com ; *CIP.*

†**CRC Pubns.,** ( *0-930265; 0-933140; 1-56212* ) 2850 Kalamazoo Ave., SE, Grand Rapids, MI 49560 (SAN 212-727X) Tel 616-224-0724; Fax: 616-224-0834; Toll Free Fax: 888-642-8606; Toll Free: 800-333-8300; P.O. Box 5070, Burlington, ON L7R 3Y8; *Imprints:* Faith Alive Christian Resources (Faith Alive Christian)
E-mail: sales@crcpublications.org
Web site: http://www.crcpublications.org ; *CIP.*

†**CSS Publishing Co.,** ( *0-7880; 0-89536; 1-55673* ) Orders Addr.: P.O. Box 4503, Lima, OH 45802-4503 (SAN 207-0707) Tel 419-227-1818; Tel 419-228-9184; Toll Free: 800-241-4056; Edit Addr.: 517 S. Main St., Lima, OH 45804-4503 Do not confuse with CSS Publishing in Tularosa, NM
E-mail: editor@csspub.com; csspub@csspub.com; info@csspub.com
Web site: http://www.csspub.com
*Dist(s):* **BookWorld Services, Inc.**
    **Spring Arbor Distributors, Inc.** ; *CIP.*

**CVK Publishing,** ( *0-9654364* ) Orders Addr.: P.O. Box 74-8086, Rego Park, NY 11374 Tel 718-533-7442
Web site: http://www.outcrybookreview.com/CVKpublishing.htm.

**Caedmon Imprint of HarperTrade**

**Cahill, James Publishing,** ( *0-9640454; 1-893205* ) 31 Golden Rain, Aliso Viejo, CA 92656-2118 Tel 949-716-6686
E-mail: cahillfilms@home.com.

**Caledonia Pr.,** ( *0-932282* ) P.O. Box 245, Racine, WI 53401 (SAN 211-8432) Tel 414-637-6200.

**California Artists Radio Theater Productions,** 1224 N. Lincoln St., Burbank, CA 91506 Toll Free: 800-200-8868.

**California State Univ. Fullerton, Ctr. for Oral & Public History,** ( *0-930046* ) Orders Addr.: P.O. Box 6486, Fullerton, CA 92834-6846; Edit Addr.: Ctr. for Oral and Public History California State Univ., Fullerton, CA 92834-6846 (SAN 210-3982) Tel 714-278-3580; Fax: 714-278-5069
E-mail: ahansen@fullerton.edu
Web site: http://coph.fullerton.edu.

**California State University Fullerton, Oral History Program** *See* **California State Univ. Fullerton, Ctr. for Oral & Public History**

**Calli Callul** *See* **Hughes Henshaw Pubns.**

**Calyx Bks.,** ( *0-934971* ) Div. of Calyx, Inc., Orders Addr.: P.O. Box B, Corvallis, OR 97339 (SAN 695-1171) Tel 541-753-9384; Fax: 541-753-0515; Toll Free: 888-336-2665; Edit Addr.: 216 SW Madison, No. 7, Corvallis, OR 97333 (SAN 242-0643)
E-mail: calyx@proaxis.com
Web site: http://www.proaxis.com/~calyx
*Dist(s):* **Bookpeople**
    **Consortium Bk. Sales & Distribution**
    **Koen Bk. Distributors**
    **SPD-Small Pr. Distribution.**

**Cambeira, Alan B.** *See* **Belecam & Assocs.**

**Cambridge Cornerstone Pr.,** ( *0-9662870* ) P.O. Box 400351, Cambridge, MA 02140 Tel 617-497-8846
E-mail: cambridgepress@aol.com.

†**Cambridge Univ. Pr.,** ( *0-521; 0-511* ) Orders Addr.: 100 Brook Hill Dr., West Nyack, NY 10994-2133 (SAN 281-3769) Tel 845-353-7500; Fax: 845-353-4141; Toll Free: 800-872-7423 (orders, returns, credit & accounting); 800-937-9600; Edit Addr.: 40 W. 20th St., New York, NY 10011-4211 (SAN 200-206X) Tel 212-924-3900; Fax: 212-691-3239
E-mail: orders@cup.org; information@cup.org; customer_service@cup.org
Web site: http://www.cup.org
*Dist(s):* **netLibrary, Inc.** ; *CIP.*

**Camden Hse.,** ( *0-938100; 1-57113; 1-879751* ) Orders Addr.: 668 Mt. Hope Ave., Rochester, NY 14620 Tel 716-275-0419; Fax: 716-271-8778; Edit Addr.: P.O. Box 41026, Rochester, NY 14604-4126
E-mail: CamdenHouse2@Compuserve.com
Web site: http://www.boydell.co.uk/CAMDEN.HTM
*Dist(s):* **Boydell & Brewer, Inc..**

**Camelback Gallery,** ( *0-9639966* ) P.O. Box 13476, Scottsdale, AZ 85267 Tel 602-602-960-2400; Fax: 602-451-8070
E-mail: sgottlieb@aol.com.

**Camino Bks., Inc.,** ( *0-940159* ) Orders Addr.: P.O. Box 59026, Philadelphia, PA 19102-9026 (SAN 664-225X) Tel 215-413-1917; Fax: 215-413-3255
E-mail: camino@caminobooks.com
Web site: http://www.caminobooks.com

**Campaign Pr. Pubns.,** ( *0-9642115* ) 7513 Clayton Dr., Oklahoma City, OK 73132-5636 (SAN 298-315X) Tel 405-721-0044.

**Campbell Comics, Eddie (AUS)** ( *0-9585783; 0-9577896* ) *Dist. by* **Top Shelf Prodns.**

**Candlelight Pr.,** ( *0-9637101; 1-930843* ) Orders Addr.: P.O. Box 50187, Irvine, CA 92619-0187 Tel 949-552-4266 (phone/fax); Edit Addr.: 34 Cresthaven, Irvine, CA 92604-3315 Do not confuse with companies with the same or similar name in New York, NY, Campbell, CA
E-mail: shigezawa@worldnet.att.net; candlelightpress@yahoo.com.

†**Candlewick Pr.,** ( *0-7636; 1-56402* ) Div. of Walker Bks., London, England, 2067 Massachusetts Ave., Cambridge, MA 02140 Tel 617-661-3330; Fax: 617-661-0565 Do not confuse with Candlewick Pr., Crystal Lake, IL
E-mail: bigbear@candlewick.com; salesinfo@candlewick.com
Web site: http://www.candlewick.com/
*Dist(s):* **Lectorum Pubns., Inc.**
    **Penguin Group (USA) Inc.** ; *CIP.*

**Cane Hill Pr.,** ( *0-943433* ) 225 Varick St., 11th Flr., New York, NY 10014 (SAN 668-4599) Tel 212-316-5513.

**Canmore Pr.,** ( *1-887774* ) Orders Addr.: P.O. Box 510794, Melbourne Beach, FL 32951-0794 Tel 321-729-0078; Fax: 321-724-1162
E-mail: publish@canmorepress.com
Web site: http://www.canmorepress.com.

**Canongate Bks. (GBR)** ( *0-86241; 0-903937; 1-84195* ) *Dist. by* **Publishers Group.**

**Canongate Bks. (GBR)** ( *0-86241; 0-903937; 1-84195* ) *Dist. by* **Grove-Atltic.**

**Cantelon Hse. Pubs.,** ( *0-9642116* ) 2818 Vallette St., Bellingham, WA 98225 Tel 360-671-4735; Toll Free: 800-265-8371.

**Cantus Verus Bks.,** ( *0-9642577* ) P.O. Box 30853, Albuquerque, NM 87190-0853 Tel 505-291-0016
E-mail: Glitter@swcp.com
Web site: http://www.swc/.com/~mmontano
*Dist(s):* **Baker & Taylor Bks..**

**Canyon Publishing Co.,** ( *0-942568* ) 8561 Eatough Ave., Canoga Park, CA 91304 (SAN 240-0685) Tel 818-702-0171 (phone/fax) Do not confuse with Canyon Publishing Co., Canyonville, OR
E-mail: mmmcauley@msn.com.

**Cape, Jonathan Ltd. (GBR)** ( *0-224; 0-206* ) *Dist. by* **Trafalgar.**

Cape Winds Pr., Inc., ( *0-9671203; 1-58972* ) P.O. Box 1087, Flagler Beach, FL 32136
E-mail: cwpeditor@yahoo.com
*Dist(s):* **Baker & Taylor Bks..**

Capital Bks., Inc., ( *1-892123; 1-931868* ) Orders Addr.: P.O. Box 605, Herndon, VA 20172-0605 Tel 703-661-1586; Fax: 703-661-1547; Edit Addr.: 22841 Quicksilver Dr., Sterling, VA 20166 Do not confuse with Capital Bks., Jacksonville Beach, FL
E-mail: noemi@booksintl.com
Web site: http://www.capital-books.com
*Dist(s):* **International Publishers Marketing.**

Capper's Bks., ( *0-941678* ) 1503 SW 42nd St., Topeka, KS 66608 (SAN 239-1694) Tel 295-274-4300; Fax: 913-274-4305; Toll Free: 800-678-5779
Web site: http://www.cappers.com.

Cappetta, Gary Michael Incorporated *See* **Little Bro' Ltd.**

Capra Pr., ( *0-9722503; 1-59266* ) 815 De La Vina St., Santa Barbara, CA 93101 Tel 805-892-2722; Fax: 805-892-2721 Do not confuse with Capra Press, Santa Barbara, CA
E-mail: richardbarre@caprapress.com
Web site: http://www.caprapress.com
*Dist(s):* **SCB Distributors.**

Capstan Pubns., ( *0-914565* ) P.O. Box 306, Basin, WY 82410 (SAN 289-162X) Tel 307-568-2604; *Imprints:* Timbertrails (Timbertrails).

Capstone Publishing, Inc., ( *1-880450* ) 1376 S. Beach Dr., Camano Island, WA 98292-7601 Do not confuse with Capstone Publishing Co. in New York, NY
*Dist(s):* **Bookpeople.**

Carbapr., ( *0-9672603* ) 3680 SW 26th St., Miami, FL 33133 Tel 305-774-1464 (phone/fax)
E-mail: http://www.arlescarballo.net
Web site: http://www.arlescarballo.com.

Carcanet Pr., Ltd. (GBR) ( *0-85635; 0-902145; 1-85754; 1-903101* ) *Dist. by* **Paul & Co Pubs.**

Career Pr., Inc., ( *1-56414* ) Orders Addr.: 3 Tice Rd., Franklin Lakes, NJ 07417-1322 (SAN 694-3640) Tel 201-848-0310; Fax: 201-848-1727; Toll Free: 800-227-3371 (outside New Jersey); Edit Addr.: P.O. Box 687, Franklin Lakes, NJ 07417; *Imprints:* New Page Books (New Page Bks)
E-mail: Bbrienza@nisusa.net
Web site: http://www.careerpress.com; http://www.newpagebooks.com
*Dist(s):* **Ten Speed Pr..**

Carmi Hse. Pr., ( *0-9620772* ) Orders Addr.: P.O. Box 4796, Valley Village, CA 91617 (SAN 249-714X) Tel 818-752-8643; Fax: 818-509-8849
E-mail: kfarnetter@aol.com.

Carnegie-Mellon Univ. Pr., ( *0-88748; 0-915604* ) Orders Addr.: P.O. Box 21, Pittsburgh, PA 15213-3799 (SAN 211-2329) Tel 412-268-2861 (phone/fax); Toll Free: 800-666-2211 (orders only)
E-mail: cynthia@andrew.cmu.edu
Web site: http://www.cmu.edu/universitypress
*Dist(s):* **CUP Services**
          **Cornell Univ. Pr..**

†Carolina Wren Pr., ( *0-932112* ) 120 Morris St., Durham, NC 27701 (SAN 213-0327) Tel 919-560-2738; Fax: 919-560-2759
E-mail: carolinawrenpress@compuserve.com; carolinawrenpress@carolinawrenpress.org
Web site: http://www.carolinawrenpress.org
*Dist(s):* **Baker & Taylor Bks.**
          **SPD-Small Pr. Distribution** ; *CIP.*

Carolrhoda Bks. Imprint of Lerner Publishing Group

Carriage Hse. Pr., ( *0-939713* ) One Carriage Ln., East Hampton, NY 11937 (SAN 663-6152) Tel 516-267-8773 Do not confuse with companies with the same name in Brookline, MA, Mount Vernon, OH
E-mail: hwsatter@yahoo.com; tedkheel@aol.com.

Carroll & Graf Pubs. Imprint of Avalon Publishing Group

Carroll, J. M. Company Imprint of Amereon, Ltd.

Cartwheel Bks. Imprint of Scholastic, Inc.

Cascade Bks., ( *0-9636548* ) 4271 Vintage Dr., Provo, UT 84604-5669 Tel 801-222-9990
*Dist(s):* **Baker & Taylor Bks..**

Casemate Pubs. & Bk. Distributors, LLC, ( *0-9711709; 1-932033* ) Orders Addr.: 2114 Darby Rd., 2nd Flr., Havertown, PA 19083 Tel 610-853-9131; Fax: 610-853-9146
E-mail: casemate@casematepublishing.com
Web site: http://www.casematepublishing.com.

Cass, Frank Pubs. (GBR) ( *0-7146; 0-85303* ) *Dist. by* **Intl Spec Bk.**

Cassell P L C (GBR) ( *0-304; 1-86047; 1-84188* ) *Dist. by* **Trafalgar.**

Cassell P L C (GBR) ( *0-304; 1-86047; 1-84188* ) *Dist. by* **Sterling.**

---

Cassette Book Company *See* **Audio Bk. Co.**

Castalia, Editorial S.A. (ESP) ( *84-7039* ) *Dist. by* **Continental Bk.**

Castle Pacific Publishing, ( *0-9653869* ) 1301 Fifth Ave., Seattle, WA 98101 Tel 206-839-0984; Fax: 206-839-0743; Toll Free: 888-756-2665
E-mail: glenn@castlepacific.com
Web site: http://www.castlepacific.com
*Dist(s):* **Baker & Taylor Bks..**

Catbird Pr., ( *0-945774* ) 16 Windsor Rd., North Haven, CT 06473 (SAN 247-607X) Tel 203-230-2391; 201-572-0816; Fax: 203-230-8029; Toll Free: 800-360-2391
E-mail: catbird@pipeline.com
Web site: http://www.catbirdpress.com
*Dist(s):* **Independent Pubs. Group.**

Cathedral Audio Bks., Inc., ( *1-886175* ) 341 Beirut Ave., Pacific Palisades, CA 90272 Tel 310-281-3770; Fax: 310-281-3777; Toll Free: 800-479-0099.

Cauldron Pubns., ( *0-9621470* ) Orders Addr.: P.O. Box 282, San Geronimo, CA 94963 (SAN 251-6772); Edit Addr.: 330 Meadow Way, San Geronimo, CA 94963 (SAN 251-6780) Tel 415-488-9641; Fax: 415-456-9492
E-mail: topaz3@aol.com
Web site: http://www.cauldronpublications.com
*Dist(s):* **Baker & Taylor Bks.**
          **Bookpeople**
          **New Leaf Distributing Co., Inc..**

Cavendish Children's Bks. Imprint of Cavendish, Marshall Corp.

†Cavendish, Marshall Corp., ( *0-7614; 0-85685; 0-86307; 1-85435* ) Member of Times Publishing Group, 99 White Plains Rd., P.O. Box 2001, Tarrytown, NY 10591-9001 (SAN 238-437X) Tel 914-332-8888; Fax: 914-332-8882; Toll Free: 800-821-9881; *Imprints:* Cavendish Children's Books (Cav Child Bks)
E-mail: mcc@marshallcavendish.com
Web site: http://www.marshallcavendish.com ; *CIP.*

†Caxton Pr., ( *0-87004* ) Div. of Caxton Printers. Ltd., 312 Main St., Caldwell, ID 83605-3299 (SAN 201-9698) Tel 208-459-7421; Fax: 208-459-7450; Toll Free: 800-657-6465
E-mail: wcornell@caxtonpress.com; sgipson@caxtonpress.com; publish@caxtonpress.com
Web site: http://www.caxtonpress.com; http://www.caxtonprinters.com ; *CIP.*

Caxton Printers, Limited *See* **Caxton Pr.**

Caxton, Wm Ltd., ( *0-940473* ) P.O. Box 220, Ellison Bay, WI 54210-0220 (SAN 135-1303) Tel 920-854-2955.

Cay-Bel Publishing Co., ( *0-918768; 0-941216* ) 272 Center St., Bangor, ME 04401 (SAN 238-9215) Tel 207-947-0008; Fax: 207-223-9004.

CD Imprint of Brilliance Audio

CD Library Edition Imprint of Brilliance Audio

CD Unabridged Imprint of Brilliance Audio

CD Unabridged Library Edition Imprint of Brilliance Audio

Cedar Fort, Inc./CFI Distribution, ( *0-934126; 1-55517* ) 925 N. Main St., Springville, UT 84663-1051 (SAN 170-2858) Tel 801-489-4084; Fax: 801-489-1097; Toll Free Fax: 800-388-3727; Toll Free: 800-759-2665; *Imprints:* Council Press (Council Pr); Bonneville Books (Bonneville Bks); Salt Press (Salt Press)
E-mail: sales@cedarfort.com; cedarfort@cedarfort.com; editorial@cedarfort.com
Web site: http://www.cedarfort.com
*Dist(s):* **Todd Communications.**

†Celestial Arts Publishing Co., ( *0-89087; 0-912310; 1-58761* ) Div. of Ten Speed Pr., Orders Addr.: P.O. Box 7123, Berkeley, CA 94707 (SAN 159-8333) Tel 510-559-1600; Fax: 510-559-1637; Toll Free: 800-841-2665; Edit Addr.: 999 Harrison St., Berkeley, CA 94710 Fax: 510-524-1052
E-mail: order@tenspeed.com
Web site: http://www.tenspeed.com ; *CIP.*

Celo Valley Bks., ( *0-923687* ) 160 Ohle Rd., Burnsville, NC 28714 (SAN 251-7973) Tel 828-675-5918
E-mail: Marilynb@main.nc.us.

Cemetery Dance Pubns., ( *1-881475; 1-58767* ) Orders Addr.: 132-B Industry Ln., Unit 7, Forest Hills, MD 21050 Tel 410-588-5901; Fax: 410-588-5904
E-mail: info@cemeterydance.com; cdancepub@aol.com
Web site: http://www.cemeterydance.com.

Cenografix, ( *0-9662860* ) Orders Addr.: 5000 Bearberry Point, Greensboro, NC 27455
E-mail: cgfix@earthlink.net
Web site: http://www.cenografix.com

---

Centennial Pubns., ( *0-9629439; 1-882418* ) 256 Nashua Ct., Grand Junction, CO 81503-3809 Tel 970-243-6503; Fax: 970-243-8572 Do not confuse with Centennial Pubns., Fort Collins, CO
E-mail: spurr@classic-angler.com.

†Ctr. for Chinese Studies Pubns., ( *0-89264* ) Univ. Michigan, 202 S. Thayer St., Ann Arbor, MI 48104-1608 (SAN 208-2772) Tel 734-998-7181; Fax: 734-998-7263
E-mail: ccs.publications@umich.edu; telf@umich.edu
Web site: http://www.umich.edu/~iinet/ccs/ccspubs.htm
*Dist(s):* **Chicago Distribution Ctr.**
          **Univ. of Michigan Pr.** ; *CIP.*

Ctr. for Learning, The, ( *1-56077* ) Orders Addr.: P.O. Box 910, Villa Maria, PA 16155 Tel 724-964-8083; Toll Free Fax: 888-767-8080; Toll Free: 800-767-9090 (ordering); Edit Addr.: 24600 Detroit Rd., Suite 201, Westlake, OH 44145 (SAN 248-2029) Tel 440-259-9341; Fax: 440-250-9715
E-mail: cfl@stratos.net
Web site: http://www.centerforlearning.org.

Ctr. for Literary Publishing, Colorado State Univ., ( *1-885635* ) Center for Literary Publishing, Department of English, Colorado State University, Fort Collins, CO 80523 Tel 970-491-5449; Fax: 970-491-0283
E-mail: creview@colostate.edu
Web site: http://www.coloradoreview.com.

Ctr. for Middle Eastern Studies, ( *0-915943* ) 430 First Ave. N., Suite 668, Minneapolis, MN 5r5401-1743
*Dist(s):* **Univ. of Texas Pr..**

Ctr. for Western Studies, ( *0-931170* ) Box 727, Augustana College, Sioux Falls, SD 57197 (SAN 211-4844) Tel 605-274-4007; Fax: 605-274-4999; Toll Free: 800-727-2844 (Ext. 4007)
E-mail: cws@inst.augie.edu
Web site: http://inst.augie.edu/cws/
*Dist(s):* **Bookmen, Inc.**
          **Dakota West Bks..**

Ctr. Point Large Print, ( *1-58547* ) P.O. Box 1, Thorndike, ME 04986-0001 Tel 207-568-3717; Fax: 207-568-3727; Toll Free: 800-929-9108; *Imprints:* Premier (Premier); Platinum (Platinm); Western (Western)
E-mail: centerpoint@uninets.net.

Center Point Publishing *See* **Ctr. Point Large Print**

Central Bureau voor Schimmelcultures (NLD) ( *90-70351* ) *Dist. by* **Lubrecht & Cramer.**

Century (GBR) ( *0-7126; 1-84413* ) *Dist. by* **Trafalgar.**

CeShore Imprint of SterlingHouse Pubs., Inc.

Chain Sales Marketing, Inc., ( *1-55836* ) 149 Madison Ave., Suite 810, New York, NY 10016 (SAN 245-1328) Tel 212-696-4230; Fax: 212-696-4391.

Chalet Publishing, ( *0-9648327* ) P.O. Box 1154, Old Forge, NY 13420-1154 Tel 315-369-3903; Toll Free: 800-237-5802 Do not confuse with Chalet Publishing, Manitou Springs, CO
E-mail: jbrnt@earthlink.Net
*Dist(s):* **North Country Bks., Inc..**

Chanakya Publications (IND) ( *81-7001* ) *Dist. by* **S Asia.**

Chance22 Publishing, ( *0-9664587* ) Orders Addr.: P.O. Box 30717, Philadelphia, PA 19104 Tel 215-238-0759 (phone/fax)
E-mail: info@chance22.com
Web site: http://www.chance22.com
*Dist(s):* **Biblio Distribution.**

ChanceTwenty Two Publishing *See* **Chance22 Publishing**

Chaosium Fiction Series Imprint of Chaosium, Inc.

Chaosium, Inc., ( *0-933635; 1-56882* ) Orders Addr.: 895 B St., No. 423, Hayward, CA 94541 (SAN 692-6460) Tel 510-583-1000; Fax: 510-583-1101; *Imprints:* Chaosium Fiction Series (Chaosium Fiction)
E-mail: chaosium@chaosium.com
Web site: http://www.chaosium.com.

Chapel Hill Pr., ( *1-880849* ) 1829 E. Franklin St., Bldg. 300A, Chapel Hill, NC 27514-5863 Tel 919-942-8389 ; Fax: 919-942-2506
E-mail: publisher@chapelhillpress.com; dmcgill@chapelhillpress.com
Web site: http://www.chapelhillpress.com.

CharFaye Publishing, Incorporated *See* **FayeHouse Pr. International**

Chariton Review Pr., ( *0-933428* ) Truman State Univ., Kirksville, MO 63501 (SAN 212-4890) Tel 816-785-4499.

Charles Publishing Co., ( *0-912880* ) 1308 Stewart St., Oceanside, CA 92054 (SAN 201-9779) Tel 760-433-5757; Fax: 760-433-3636 E-mail: NTMcharlespub@aol.com; charlespublishing@hotmail.com *Dist(s):* **Baker & Taylor Bks. Univ. of New Mexico Pr..**

Charlesbridge Publishing, Inc., ( *0-88106; 0-935508; 1-57091; 1-58089; 1-879085* ) Orders Addr.: 85 Main St., Watertown, MA 02472 (SAN 240-5474) Tel 617-926-0329; Fax: 617-926-5720; Toll Free Fax: 800-926-5775; Toll Free: 800-225-3214; *Imprints:* Talewinds (Talewinds); Whispering Coyote (Whispering Coyote) E-mail: books@charlesbridge.com; orders@charlesbridge.com Web site: http://www.charlesbridge.com *Dist(s):* **Continental Bk. Co., Inc. Lectorum Pubns., Inc..**

Charnel Hse., ( *0-927389* ) Orders Addr.: P.O. Box 633, Lynbrook, NY 11563; Edit Addr.: 44 Carpenter Ave., Lynbrook, NY 11563 Tel 516-887-2565 Web site: http://www.charnelhouse.com/.

†Chatham Bookseller, ( *0-911860* ) 8 Green Village Rd., Madison, NJ 07940 (SAN 203-641X) Tel 973-822-1361 ; *CIP.*

Chatto & Windus (GBR) ( *0-7011; 0-7012; 1-85619* ) *Dist. by Trafalgar.*

Cheap Street, ( *0-941826* ) Rte. 2, Box 1293, New Castle, VA 24127 (SAN 239-1783) E-mail: jg@cheapst.com Web site: http://www.cheapst.com.

†Checkerboard Pr., Inc., ( *1-56288* ) 1560 Revere Rd., Yardley, PA 19067-4351 ; *CIP.*

Chelsea Green Publishing, ( *0-930031; 1-890132; 1-931498; 88-86283* ) Orders Addr.: P.O. Box 428, White River Junction, VT 05001 (SAN 669-7631) Tel 802-295-6300; Fax: 802-295-6444; Toll Free: 800-639-4099; Edit Addr.: 205 Gates-Briggs Bldg., Main St., White River Junction, VT 05001 Web site: http://www.chelseagreen.com *Dist(s):* **Baker & Taylor Bks. Koen Bk. Distributors.**

†Chelsea Hse. Pubs., ( *0-7910; 0-87754; 1-55546* ) Div. of Main Line Bk. Co., 1974 Sproul Rd., Suite 400, Broomall, PA 19008-0914 (SAN 206-7609) Tel 610-353-5166; Fax: 610-359-1439; Toll Free: 800-848-2665 E-mail: info@chelseahouse.com Web site: http://www.chelseahouse.com *Dist(s):* **Baker & Taylor Bks. Brodart Co. Follett Library Resources Wolverine Distributing, Inc.;** *CIP.*

Cheng & Tsui Co., ( *0-646; 0-88727; 0-917056* ) 25 West St., Boston, MA 02111-1213 (SAN 169-3387) Tel 617-988-2401; Fax: 617-426-3669 E-mail: service@cheng-tsui.com Web site: http://www.cheng-tsui.com.

Cherokee Bks., ( *0-9640458; 1-930052* ) Orders Addr.: P.O. Box 463, Little Creek, DE 19961 Tel 302-734-8782; Fax: 302-734-3198; Edit Addr.: 231 Meadow Ridge Pkwy., Dover, DE 19904 Do not confuse with Cherokee Bks., Ponca City, OK E-mail: milthanna@aol.com Web site: http://www.cherokeebooks.com.

†Cherokee Publishing Co., ( *0-87797* ) Orders Addr.: P.O. Box 1730, Marietta, GA 30061-1730 (SAN 650-0404) Tel 404-467-4189; Fax: 404-237-1062; Toll Free: 800-653-3952; Edit Addr.: 800 Miami Cir., NE, Suite 100, Atlanta, GA 30324-3055 Do not confuse with Cherokee Publishing Co., Antioch, CA E-mail: books@mgci.com; *CIP.*

Cherokee Publishing Company *See* Cherokee Bks.

Cherry Lane Books *See* Cherry Lane Music Co.

Cherry Lane Music Imprint of Cherry Lane Music Co.

†Cherry Lane Music Co., ( *0-89524; 1-57560* ) 6 E. 32nd St., 11 Flr., New York, NY 10016 (SAN 219-0788) Tel 212-561-3000; *Imprints:* Cherry Lane Music (Cher Ln) Web site: http://www.cherrylane.com *Dist(s):* **Leonard, Hal Corp.;** *CIP.*

Cherry Tree Bks., ( *0-9666832* ) 433 Perkins Rd., Weybridge, VT 05753 Tel 802-545-2474 E-mail: idahw@pshift.com; lmwash@together.net Web site: http://www.cherrytreebooks.net.

†Cherry Valley Editions, ( *0-916156* ) Orders Addr.: P.O. Box 303, Cherry Valley, NY 13320; *CIP.*

Chevy Chase Publishing Co., ( *0-9657743* ) 2307 Ashboro Dr., Chevy Chase, MD 20815 Tel 301-589-2921.

†Chicago Review Pr., Inc., ( *0-914090; 0-914091; 1-55652; 1-56976* ) 814 N. Franklin St., Chicago, IL 60610 (SAN 213-5744) Tel 312-337-0747; Fax: 312-337-5985; Toll Free: 800-888-4741 (orders only); *Imprints:* Hill, Lawrence Books (Lawrence Hill) E-mail: orders@ipgbook.com; frontdesk@ipgbook.com Web site: http://www.ipgbook.com *Dist(s):* **Cobblestone Publishing Co. Gryphon Hse., Inc. Independent Pubs. Group;** *CIP.*

Chicago Spectrum Pr., ( *1-58374; 1-886094* ) Div. of Evanston Publishing Inc., 4824 Brownsboro Ctr., Louisville, KY 40207 Tel 502-899-1919; Fax: 502-896-0246; Toll Free: 888-266-5780 (888-BOOKS-80); 800-594-5190 E-mail: info@evanstonpublishing.com; EvanstonPB@aol.com Web site: http://www.EvanstonPublishing.com *Dist(s):* **Baker & Taylor Bks. Independent Pubs. Group Paladin Pr. Partners/West.**

Chick Pubns., Inc., ( *0-937958; 0-7589* ) P.O. Box 3500, Ontario, CA 91761-1019 (SAN 211-7770) Tel 909-987-0771; Fax: 909-941-8128; Toll Free: 800-932-3050 E-mail: orderdesk@chick.com Web site: http://www.chick.com.

Chick Springs Publishing, ( *0-9670273; 0-9712521* ) Orders Addr.: P.O. Box 1130, Taylors, SC 29687 (SAN 299-9579); Edit Addr.: 103 Berrywood Ct., Greer, SC 29650 Web site: http://www.chicksprings.com; http://www.susanchase.com *Dist(s):* **Baker & Taylor Bks..**

Chicken Soup Pr., Inc., ( *0-9646904; 1-893337* ) Orders Addr.: P.O. Box 164, Circleville, NY 10919 (SAN 298-6787) Tel 914-692-6320; Fax: 914-692-7574; Edit Addr.: 17 Todd Dr., Middletown, NY 10941 E-mail: poet@warwick.net Web site: http://www.chickensouppress.com *Dist(s):* **Baker & Taylor Bks. Brodart Co. Hervey's Booklink & Cookbook Warehouse Quality Bks., Inc..**

Chicory Blue Pr., Inc., ( *0-9619111; 1-887344* ) 795 East St. N., Goshen, CT 06756 (SAN 243-0339) Tel 860-491-2271; Fax: 860-491-8619 E-mail: sondraz@optonline.net Web site: http://www.chicorybluepress.com *Dist(s):* **SPD-Small Pr. Distribution.**

Chimera Pubns. (GBR) ( *1-901388; 1-903931* ) *Dist. by Client Dist Srvs.*

†China Bks. & Periodicals, Inc., ( *0-8351* ) 2929 24th St., San Francisco, CA 94110-4126 (SAN 145-0557) Tel 415-282-2994; Fax: 415-282-0994 E-mail: info@chinabooks.com Web site: http://www.chinabooks.com; *CIP.*

Chivers Audio Bks. (GBR) ( *0-7451; 0-7540; 0-85119; 0-85594; 0-85997* ) *Dist. by BBC Audiobks.*

Chivers Children's Audio Bks. Imprint of BBC Audiobooks America

Chivers Large Print (GBR) ( *0-7451* ) *Dist. by BBC Audiobks.*

Chivers North America *See* BBC Audiobooks America

Chivers Pr. (GBR) ( *0-7451; 0-7540; 0-85046; 0-85119; 0-85594; 0-86220* ) *Dist. by BBC Audiobks.*

Chivers Sound Library Imprint of BBC Audiobooks America

Chosen Bks., ( *0-8007; 1-58743* ) Div. of Baker Bk. Hse., Orders Addr.: P.O. Box 6287, Grand Rapids, MI 49516-6287 Toll Free Fax: 800-398-3111 (orders only); Toll Free: 800-877-2665 (orders only); Edit Addr.: 6030 E. Fulton, Ada, MI 49301 Tel 616-676-9185; Fax: 616-676-9573 E-mail: orders@bakerbooks.com; retail@bakerbooks.com Web site: http://www.bakerbooks.com *Dist(s):* **Baker Bk. Hse., Inc..**

Christian Light Pubns., Inc., ( *0-87813* ) 1066 Chicago Ave., Harrisonburg, VA 22802 (SAN 206-7315) Tel 540-434-0768; Fax: 540-433-8896 E-mail: johnh@clp.org.

Christian Literature Crusade, Inc., ( *0-87508* ) Div. of CLC Publications, Orders Addr.: P.O. Box 1449, Fort Washington, PA 19034-8449 Tel 215-542-1242; Fax: 215-542-7580; Toll Free: 800-659-1240; Edit Addr.: 701 Pennsylvania Ave., Fort Washington, PA 19034 (SAN 169-7358) E-mail: joinclc@juno.com Web site: http://www.clcusa.org *Dist(s):* **Anchor Distributors Appalachian Bible Co. Calvary Distribution Riverside Spring Arbor Distributors, Inc..**

Christian Pubns., Inc., ( *0-87509; 0-88965* ) 3825 Hartzdale Dr., Camp Hill, PA 17011-7830 (SAN 202-1617) Tel 717-761-7044; Fax: 717-761-7273; Toll Free Fax: 800-865-8799 (orders only); Toll Free: 800-233-4443 (orders only); *Imprints:* Horizon Books (Horizon Bks) E-mail: orders@cpi-horizon.com; salemktg@cpi-horizon.com Web site: http://www.christianpublications.com *Dist(s):* **Christian Literature Crusade, Inc. Spring Arbor Distributors, Inc..**

Christopher Publishing, ( *0-936863* ) Orders Addr.: P.O. Box 412, Springville, UT 84663 (SAN 200-2787) Tel 801-489-4254; Toll Free: 800-453-1406; Edit Addr.: 188 S. Main, Springville, UT 84663 (SAN 242-0996) ; *Imprints:* Littlegreen (Littlegreen) Do not confuse with Christopher Publishing, Corona del Mar, CA *Dist(s):* **Distributors, The New Leaf Distributing Co., Inc. Nutri-Bks. Corp..**

Christopher Publishing Hse., ( *0-8158* ) 24 Rockland St., Hanover, MA 02339 (SAN 202-1625) Tel 781-826-7474; Fax: 781-826-5556 E-mail: cph@atigroupinc.com Web site: http://atigroupinc.com.

†Chronicle Bks. LLC, ( *0-8118; 0-87701; 0-938491* ) 85 Second St., San Francisco, CA 94105 (SAN 202-165X) Tel 415-537-4200; Fax: 415-537-4460; Toll Free Fax: 800-858-7787; Toll Free: 800-722-6657 (orders only) E-mail: orders@chroniclebooks.com Web site: http://www.chroniclebooks.com *Dist(s):* **Continental Bk. Co., Inc. Lectorum Pubns., Inc.;** *CIP.*

Chuckduck Storytellers, ( *0-9740176* ) 325 Kevin Rd., Silver City, NC 27344 Tel 919-663-1576 E-mail: chuckduk@centernet.net.

Chutzpah Publishing, ( *0-9703078* ) 19355 NE 36th St., No 21K, Aventura, FL 33180 Fax: 305-935-8986 E-mail: enosotro@aol.com *Dist(s):* **Biblio Distribution.**

Cimino Publishing Group, ( *1-878427* ) P.O. Box 174, Carle Place, NY 11514 (SAN 630-3722) Tel 516-997-3721; Fax: 516-997-3420 E-mail: cimpub@juno.com *Dist(s):* **CPG Publishing, Inc..**

Cincinnati Writers' Project, ( *0-9633551* ) Orders Addr.: P.O. Box 29920, Cincinnati, OH 45229 Tel 513-281-4767; Edit Addr.: 582 McAlyin Ave., Cincinnati, OH 45220.

Cinco Puntos Pr., ( *0-938317* ) 701 Texas Ave., El Paso, TX 79901 (SAN 661-0080) Tel 915-838-1625; Fax: 915-838-1635; Toll Free: 800-566-9072 E-mail: bbyrd@cincopuntos.com; leebyrd@cincopuntos.com Web site: http://www.cincopuntos.com *Dist(s):* **Consortium Bk. Sales & Distribution.**

Cinnamon Moon, ( *0-9650366* ) Orders Addr.: P.O. Box 878, Kodak, TN 37764 Tel 423-932-1636; Fax: 423-386-0381; Toll Free: 800-396-4626; Edit Addr.: 3326 Bentwood Dr., Kodak, TN 37764 *Dist(s):* **Midpoint National, Inc..**

Cinnamon Tree Imprint of Deseret Bk. Co.

Circlet Pr., Inc., ( *0-9633970; 1-885865* ) 1770 Massachusetts Ave., PMB 278, Cambridge, MA 02140 Tel 617-864-0492; Fax: 617-864-0485; Toll Free: 800-664-4330 (orders only) E-mail: info@circlet.com Web site: http://www.circlet.com *Dist(s):* **SCB Distributors.**

Citadel Pr. Imprint of Kensington Publishing Corp.

†City Lights Bks., ( *0-87286* ) 261 Columbus Ave., San Francisco, CA 94133 (SAN 202-1684) Tel 415-362-1901; Fax: 415-362-4921 E-mail: staff@citylights.com Web site: http://www.citylights.com *Dist(s):* **Consortium Bk. Sales & Distribution SPD-Small Pr. Distribution Subterranean Co.;** *CIP.*

**Names**

**Clagon, Angelena E.,** ( *0-9724301* ) Orders Addr.: P.O. Box 1063, Plymouth, NC 27962 Tel 252-793-5300 (phone/fax); Edit Addr.: 18 Autumn Dr., Plymouth, NC 27962
E-mail: angelenaec@yahoo.com.

**Clairvoyant Publishing,** ( *0-9726927* ) Orders Addr.: 5628 Andover Way, Chino Hills, CA 91709 Tel 909-597-6540; 213-216-7991; Edit Addr.: 10250 Central Ave., Montclair, CA 91763 (SAN 255-3236) Tel 909-482-1467 (phone/fax)
E-mail: peter_mil@msn.com; peter-mil@msn.com.

**Clarendon Press** Imprint of Oxford Univ. Pr., Inc.

**Clarion Bks.** Imprint of Houghton Mifflin Co. Trade & Reference Div.

**Clark City Pr.,** ( *0-944439* ) Orders Addr.: P.O. Box 1358, Livingston, MT 59047 (SAN 243-699X) Tel 406-222-7412; Fax: 406-222-4719; Toll Free: 800-835-0814; Edit Addr.: 109 W. Callender St., Livingston, MT 59047 (SAN 243-7007)
E-mail: sally@russellchatham.com; info@clarkcitypress.com
Web site: http://www.clarkcitypress.com.

**Clark, I. E. Pubns.,** ( *0-88680* ) P.O. Box 246, Schulenburg, TX 78956-0246 (SAN 282-7433) Tel 979-743-3232; Fax: 979-743-4765
E-mail: ieclark@cvtv.net
Web site: http://www.ieclark.com.

**Classic Bks.,** ( *1-58201; 0-7426* ) Orders Addr.: P.O. Box 130, Murrieta, CA 92564-0130 Tel 888-265-3547; Fax: 888-265-3550.

**Classic Specialties,** ( *1-888728* ) P.O. Box 19058, Cincinnati, OH 45219 Tel 513-281-4757; Fax: 513-281-5797; Toll Free: 877-233-3823
E-mail: sherlock@sherlock-holmes.com.
Web site: http://www.sherlock-holmes.com.

**Classic Textbooks,** ( *1-4047* ) Div of Classic Books, Orders Addr.: P.O. Box 130, Murrieta, CA 92564-0130 Tel 909-296-9628; Fax: 909-296-3528; Toll Free Fax: 888-265-3550; Edit Addr.: 26111 Ynez B14, Temecula, CA 92591
E-mail: 4classic@gte.net.

**Classics Illustrated** Imprint of Berkley Publishing Group

**Claypool Comics** Imprint of Boffin Bks.

**Cle International (FRA)** ( *2-09; 2-19* ) *Dist. by* Continental Bk.

**Clear Creek Pr.,** ( *0-9651240; 0-9713694* ) Orders Addr.: P.O. Box 1081, Mena, AR 71953 Tel 501-394-4992 (phone/fax); Edit Addr.: 142 Amber Ln., Mena, AR 71953
E-mail: reisig@ipa.net
Web site: http://www.michael-reisig.com.

**Clear Light Pubs.,** ( *0-940666; 1-57416* ) 823 Don Diego, Santa Fe, NM 87501 (SAN 219-7758) Tel 505-989-9590; Fax: 505-989-9519; Toll Free: 800-253-2747 Do not confuse with Clear Light Pub., Seattle, WA
E-mail: service@clearlightbooks.com
Web site: http://www.clearlightbooks.com.

**Cleis Pr.,** ( *0-939416; 1-57344* ) P.O. Box 14684, San Francisco, CA 94114-0684 (SAN 284-9976) Tel 415-575-4700; Fax: 415-575-4705; Toll Free: 800-780-2279
E-mail: cleis@cleispress.com
Web site: http://www.cleispress.com
*Dist(s):* **Baker & Taylor Bks.**
**Bookpeople**
**Publishers Group West.**

**Client Distribution Services,** 425 Madison Ave., New York, NY 10017 (SAN 631-760X) Tel 212-223-2969; Fax: 212-223-1504 Do not confuse with Client Distribution Services, Jackson, TN.
E-mail: skail@cds.aeneas.com;
tflowers@cdsbooks.com
Web site: http://www.cdsbooks.com/.

**Cliff Notes** Imprint of Wiley, John & Sons, Inc.

**Cliffrose Pubns.,** ( *0-9632052* ) 6321 Alonzo Ave., Reseda, CA 91335 Tel 818-705-7794.

**Clifton Brusso** *See* **Iroquois Pr.**

**Clifton, Robert T. Company, Incorporated** *See* **Pretani**

**Clinton Publishing,** ( *0-9645624* ) 8076 Priem Rd., Strongsville, OH 44136 Tel 216-238-4885.

**Clipper Audio** Imprint of Recorded Bks., LLC

**Clo Iar-Chonnachta Teo (IRL)** ( *1-874700; 1-900693; 1-902420* ) *Dist. by* **Dufour.**

**Cloak & Dagger Pr., Inc.,** ( *0-9658510* ) 3900 W. 28th St., Minneapolis, MN 55416-3903 Tel 612-690-0849
E-mail: vflynn@mn.uswest.net
*Dist(s):* **Bookmen, Inc..**

**Clock Tower Pr. LLC,** ( *1-932202* ) Orders Addr.: 3622 W. Liberty Rd., Ann Arbor, MI 48103 (SAN 254-8526) Fax: 734-769-5607
E-mail: lynne@clocktowerpress.com
Web site: http://www.clocktowerpress.com.

**Clocktower Bks.,** ( *0-7433* ) 6549 Mission Gorge Rd., PMB 260, San Diego, CA 92120
E-mail: johncullen@candcpublishers.com
Web site: http://www.clocktowerfiction.com.

**Clocktower Fiction** *See* **Clocktower Bks.**

**Closson Pr.,** ( *0-933227; 1-55856* ) 1935 Sampson Dr., Apollo, PA 15613-9208 (SAN 297-1712) Tel 724-337-4482; Fax: 724-337-9484
E-mail: rclosson@nb.net
Web site: http://www.clossonpress.com.

**Clove Pubns.,** ( *1-889191* ) 60 Falcon Hills Dr., Littleton, CO 80162
E-mail: clovepublication@aol.com
*Dist(s):* **Baker & Taylor Bks..**

**Coastal Carolina Pr.,** ( *1-928556* ) Orders Addr.: 2231 Wrightville Ave., Wilmington, NC 28403 Tel 910-362-9298; Fax: 910-362-9497
E-mail: books@coastalcarolinapress.org
Web site: http://www.coastalcarolinapress.org
*Dist(s):* **Baker & Taylor Bks.**
**Parnassus Bk. Distributors.**

**Coastal Plains Publishing Co.,** ( *0-9607300* ) 3116-27 Dockside Cir., Raleigh, NC 27613 (SAN 239-183X)
E-mail: mkale@bellsouth.net.

**Cobblestone Pr.,** ( *0-929613* ) 4516 Washington St., Midland, MI 48642 (SAN 250-0930) Tel 989-832-0166; Fax: 989-832-4944 Do not confuse with Cobblestone Pr., Indianapolis, IN
*Dist(s):* **Baker & Taylor Bks.**
**Partners Pubs. Group, Inc..**

**Codex (GBR)** ( *1-899598* ) *Dist. by* **SCB Distributors.**

**Coe Review Pr.,** ( *0-9636959; 1-889678* ) Coe College, Dept. of English, Cedar Rapids, IA 52402 Tel 319-399-8591; Fax: 319-399-8557
E-mail: theller@coe.edu
Web site: http://www.public.coc.edu/~theller/crp-home.htm.

**Coffee Hse. Pr.,** ( *0-918273; 1-56689* ) 27 N. Fourth St., Suite 400, Minneapolis, MN 55401 (SAN 206-3883) Tel 612-338-0125; Fax: 612-338-4004
Web site: http://www.coffeehousepress.org
*Dist(s):* **Consortium Bk. Sales & Distribution**
**SPD-Small Pr. Distribution.**

**Coffee Table Bks.,** ( *0-9666002* ) 6595 Plantation Dr., Boise, ID 83703 Tel 208-853-1732; Fax: 208-343-4376 Do not confuse with Coffee Table Bks., Gold Beach, OR.

**Coghlan Group, The** *See* **Phoenix International, Inc.**

**Colbert Hse., The,** ( *1-887399* ) Orders Addr.: P.O. Box 150, Norman, OK 73070-0150 Tel 405-329-7999; Fax: 405-329-6977; Toll Free: 800-698-2644; Edit Addr.: 1005 N. Flood, Suite 138, Norman, OK 73069
E-mail: customerservice@greatbargainbooks.com
Web site: http://www.greatbargainbooks.com
*Dist(s):* **Anchor Distributors**
**Appalachian Bk. Distributors**
**Baker & Taylor Bks.**
**FaithWorks.**

**Colgate Univ. Pr.,** ( *0-912568* ) 13 Oak Dr., 315A Lawrence Hall, Hamilton, NY 13346-1398 (SAN 204-3181) Tel 315-824-7268.

**College Publishing,** ( *0-9679121* ) Orders Addr.: c/o Port City Fulfillment Services, 35 Ash Dr., Kimball, MI 48074 Fax: 810-388-9502; Edit Addr.: 12309 Lynwood Dr., Glen Allen, VA 23059 (SAN 254-458X) Tel 804-364-8410; Fax: 804-364-8408
E-mail: collegepub@mindspring.com.

**Collins Pr., The (IRL)** ( *0-9516306; 1-898256; 1-903464* ) *Dist. by* **Dufour.**

**Collins Willow (GBR)** ( *0-00; 0-01* ) *Dist. by* **Trafalgar.**

†**Colonial Williamsburg Foundation,** ( *0-87935; 0-910412* ) P.O. Box 3532, Williamsburg, VA 23187-3532 (SAN 128-4630) Fax: 757-565-8999 (orders only); Toll Free: 800-446-9240 (orders only)
Web site: http://www.colonialwilliamsburg.com
*Dist(s):* **Antique Collectors' Club**
**Baker & Taylor Bks.**
**Koen Bk. Distributors***; CIP.*

**Colonnade Bks.,** ( *0-9663058* ) 812 Masselin Ave., Los Angeles, CA 90036 Tel 323-931-1962; Fax: 213-931-1962
E-mail: editors@colonnadebooks.com
Web site: http://www.colonnadebooks.com
*Dist(s):* **Baker & Taylor Bks.**
**Partners Pubs. Group, Inc.**
**Partners/West.**

**Colophon Hse.,** ( *1-882539* ) 17522 Brushy River Ct., Houston, TX 77095 Tel 281-304-9502; Fax: 281-256-3442
E-mail: marydwade@aol.com
Web site: http://www.wadeco.com/colophon.htm
*Dist(s):* **Baker & Taylor Bks.**
**Brodart Co.**
**Follett Library Resources**
**Lectorum Pubns., Inc..**

**Colorado Associated University Press** *See* **Univ. Pr. of Colorado**

**Colorado State University, Center for Literary Publishing** *See* **Ctr. for Literary Publishing, Colorado State Univ.**

**Columbia Pubns.,** ( *0-9659454; 1-892651* ) Orders Addr.: P.O. Box 3026, Urbana, IL 61803-3026 Tel 217-337-5245; Fax: 217-337-5101; Edit Addr.: 3728 Faulkner Dr., Nashville, TN 37211-4938
E-mail: lmlowhorn@aol.com.

†**Columbia Univ. Pr.,** ( *0-231* ) 61 W. 62nd St., New York, NY 10023 (SAN 212-2472) Tel 212-459-0600; Fax: 212-459-3678
Web site: http://www.columbia.edu/cu/cup
*Dist(s):* **Continental Bk. Co., Inc.**
**netLibrary, Inc.***; CIP.*

**Combined Publishing** Imprint of Da Capo Pr., Inc.

**Comic Art Publishing Company** *See* **Bill Barry's Compass Bks.**

**Comics Lit** Imprint of NBM Publishing Co.

**Committees on the Project for the National Celebration on the Occasion of the Centennial Anniversary of Pridi Banomyong (THA)** ( *974-7449* ) *Dist. by* Lantern Books.

**Common Reader Editions** Imprint of Akadine Pr., The

**Commonwealth Publishing,** ( *0-9664475* ) Orders Addr.: P.O. Box 1234, Hyannis, MA 02601 Fax: 207-933-4600; Toll Free: 800-890-1403; Edit Addr.: 450 Wilson Pond Rd., North Monmouth, ME 04265
E-mail: pmars@juno.com
*Dist(s):* **Tabby Hse. Bks..**

**Communication Service Corporation** *See* **Gryphon Hse., Inc.**

**Communications Plus USA,** 2103 N. Decatur Rd., Suite 335, Decatur, GA 30033 (SAN 631-6735) Tel 404-727-7289.

**Commuter's Library** *See* **Sound Room Pubs., Inc.**

**Commuters Library** Imprint of Sound Room Pubs., Inc.

**Compass American Guides, Inc.** Imprint of Fodor's Travel Pubns.

**Compass Point Mysteries** Imprint of Quincannon Publishing Group

**Comprehensive Health Education Foundation,** ( *0-935529; 1-57021* ) 22419 Pacific Hwy. S., Seattle, WA 98198-5106 (SAN 696-3668) Tel 206-824-2907; Fax: 206-824-3072; Toll Free: 800-323-2433
E-mail: chefstaff@chef.org
Web site: http://www.chef.org/.

**Concentric Pubns.,** ( *0-9661744* ) P.O. Box 13458, Silver Spring, MD 20911-3458 (SAN 299-5034) Tel 301-563-3091; Fax: 301-563-3022
*Dist(s):* **Baker & Taylor Bks..**

**Concepts 'N' Publishing,** ( *1-879940* ) Orders Addr.: P.O. Box 1552, Seaside, CA 93955 Tel 831-899-1118; Edit Addr.: 582 Lighthouse Ave., Suite 7, Pacific Grove, CA 93950.

**Concordia Publishing Hse.,** ( *0-570; 0-7586* ) Subs. of Lutheran Church Missouri Synod, 3558 S. Jefferson Ave., Saint Louis, MO 63118-3968 (SAN 202-1781) Tel 314-268-1000; Fax: 314-268-1360; Toll Free Fax: 800-490-9889 (orders only); Toll Free: 800-325-0191; 800-325-3040 (orders only)
E-mail: cphorder@cph.org
Web site: http://www.cph.org
*Dist(s):* **National Bk. Network.**

†**Confluence Pr., Inc.,** ( *0-917652; 1-881090* ) 500 Eighth Ave., Lewiston, ID 83501-2698 (SAN 209-5467) Tel 208-799-2336; Fax: 208-799-2850
E-mail: conpress@lcsc.edu
Web site: http://www.confluencepress.com
*Dist(s):* **Midpoint Trade Bks., Inc.***; CIP.*

**Conjunctions,** ( *0-941964* ) Bard College, Annandale-on-Hudson, New York, NY 12504 (SAN 239-5169) Tel 914-758-1539; Fax: 914-758-2660
E-mail: conjunctions@bard.edu
Web site: http://www.conjunctions.com
*Dist(s):* **Distributed Art Pubs./D.A.P.**
**SPD-Small Pr. Distribution.**

Conquering Bks., ( 1-56411 ) 26070 Barhams Hill Rd., Drewyville, VA 23844 (SAN 630-6748) Tel 757-329-7200 (cell phone); 434-658-4934 (phone/fax) ; 210 E. Arrowhead Dr., No. 01, Charlotte, NC 28213 Tel 704-509-2226
E-mail: khalifah@kbabooks.com
Web site: http://www.conqueringbooks.com.

Conroca Publishing, ( 1-892617 ) 132 Ridge Trail, Boerne, TX 78006 Tel 830-537-5917 (phone/fax); Toll Free: 877-762-2782 (phone/fax)
E-mail: info@conrocapub.com;
conrocapub@yahoo.com
Web site: http://www.conrocapub.com
Dist(s): Baker & Taylor Bks..

Consortium Bk. Sales & Distribution, Orders Addr.: 1045 Westgate Dr., Suite 90, Saint Paul, MN 55114-1065 (SAN 200-6049) Tel 651-221-9035; Fax: 651-221-0124; (Toll Free: 800-283-3572 (orders)
E-mail: consortium@cbsd.com
Web site: http://www.cbsd.com.

Consortium, Inc., ( 0-9632707 ) c/o The Distributors, 702 S. Michigan, South Bend, IN 46601.

Conspiracy, Incorporated, The See Rams Head Pr., International, The

Contemporary Bks. Imprint of McGraw-Hill Trade

Context Bks., ( 1-893956 ) 368 Broadway, Suite 314, New York, NY 10013 Tel 212-233-4880; Fax: 212-964-1810; Toll Free: 888-240-6032
E-mail: info@contextbooks.com;
simnyc@interport.net
Web site: http://www.contextbooks.com
Dist(s): Publishers Group West.

Continental Bk. Co., Inc., ( 0-9626800 ) Eastern Div., 80-00 Cooper Ave., Bldg. No. 29, Glendale, NY 11385 (SAN 169-5436) Tel 718-326-0560; Fax: 718-326-4276; Toll Free: 800-364-0350; Western Div., 625 E. 70th Ave., No. 5, Denver, CO 80229 (SAN 630-2882) Tel 303-289-1761; Fax: 303-289-1764 Do not confuse with Continental Book Company, Denver, CO
E-mail: esl@continentalbook.com;
bonjour@continentalbook.com;
tag@continentalbook.com; hola@continentalbook.com
Web site: http://www.continentalbook.com.

Continental Historical Society, ( 0-9609900 ) 3145 Geary Blvd., No. 126, San Francisco, CA 94118 (SAN 269-3607) Tel 415-389-9817.

†Continuum International Publishing Group, Inc., ( 0-304; 0-7201; 0-8044; 0-8264 ) Orders Addr.: 22883 Quicksilver Dr., Dulles, VA 20166 (SAN 253-3391) Fax: 703-661-1501; Toll Free: 800-561-7704; Edit Addr.: 370 Lexington Ave., New York, NY 10017-6503 (SAN 213-8220) Tel 212-953-5858; Fax: 212-953-5944
E-mail: info@continuum-books.com
Web site: http://www.continuum-books.com; CIP.

Continuum Publishing Company See Continuum International Publishing Group, Inc.

Converg Pubs., ( 0-9706546 ) 117 W. Outer Dr., Canyon Lake, TX 78133-4359 Tel 830-899-4706 (phone/fax)
E-mail: converg@converg.org.
Web site: http://www.converg.org.

Conversation Pr., Inc., ( 0-9634395 ) 1011 Oak St., Winnetka, IL 60093-2130 Tel 847-446-7561; Fax: 847-441-5617; Toll Free: 800-848-5224
E-mail: convpress@aol.com.

Cook Communications Ministries, ( 0-7459; 0-7814; 0-88207; 0-89191; 0-89693; 0-912692; 1-55513; 1-56476; 983-45027; 983-45018; 983-45031 ) 4050 Lee Vance View, Colorado Springs, CO 80918 Tel 719-536-0100; Fax: 719-536-3269; Toll Free: 800-708-5550; 55 Woodslee Ave., Paris, ON N3L 3E5 Toll Free Fax: 800-461-8575; Toll Free: 800-263-2664 Do not confuse with Cook Communications Ministries International, same address
E-mail: bergerj@cookministries.org
Web site: http://www.cookministries.com
Dist(s): CRC Pubns.
   Libros Sin Fronteras
   Twentieth Century Christian Bks..

†Cook, David C. Publishing Co., ( 0-7814; 0-88207; 0-89191; 0-89693; 0-912692; 1-55513; 1-56476; 983-45026; 5-503; 983-45027; 983-45023; 983-45019; 983-45018; 983-45013; 983-45012; 983-45016 ) Div. of Cook Communications Ministries, 4050 Lee Vance View, Colorado Springs, CO 80918-7102 (SAN 206-0981) Tel 719-536-0100; Fax: 719-536-3202; Toll Free: 800-708-5550
Web site: http://www.davidcook.com; CIP.

Cookbooks by Morris Press See Morris Publishing

Cool Grove Publishing, Inc., ( 1-887276 ) 512 Argyle Rd., Brooklyn, NY 11218 Tel 718-287-7221; Imprints: Coolgrove Press (Coolgrve Pr)
E-mail: thaza@rcn.com
Web site: http://www.coolgrove.com
Dist(s): Independent Pubs. Group
   SPD-Small Pr. Distribution.

Coolgrove Pr. Imprint of Cool Grove Publishing, Inc.

†Cooper Square Pubs., Inc., ( 0-8154; 0-87833 ) Member of Rowman & Littlefield Publishing Group, Orders Addr.: 15200 NBN Way, Blue Ridge Summit, PA 17214 Tel 717-794-3800; 717-794-3803; Toll Free Fax: 800-338-4550; 67 Mowat Ave., Suite 241, Toronto, ON M6K 3E3 Tel 416-534-1660; Fax: 416-534-3699; Edit Addr.: 200 Park Ave., S., Suite 1109, New York, NY 10003-1503 (SAN 281-5621) Tel 212-529-3888; Fax: 212-529-4223; Toll Free: 800-462-6420 (orders)
E-mail: custservrl@rowman.com
Web site: http://www.coopersquarepress.com
Dist(s): National Bk. Network; CIP.

Copley Editions Imprint of Copley Publishing Group, Inc.

Copley Publishing Group, Inc., ( 0-87411; 1-58152; 1-58390 ) 138 Great Rd, Acton, MA 01720 (SAN 687-4959) Tel 978-263-9090; Fax: 978-263-9190; Toll Free: 800-562-2147; Imprints: Copley Editions (Copley Editions)
E-mail: textbook@copleypublishing.com;
publish@copleycustom.com
Web site: http://www.copleyeditions.com;
http://www.copleycustom.com; http://
www.copleypublishing.com.

Coral Pr., ( 0-9708293 ) 530 W. End Ave., Suite 7A, New York, NY 10024 Tel 212-769-0489; Fax: 212-877-2080
E-mail: rgdunn@aol.com
Web site: http://www.coralpress.com
Dist(s): Biblio Distribution.

Corgi Imprint of Bantam Bks.

Corgi Bks. Ltd. (GBR) ( 0-552 ) Dist. by Trafalgar.

Corinthian Bks. Imprint of Cote Literary Group, The

Cork Hill Pr., ( 1-59408 ) 7520 E. 88th Pl., Suite 100, Indianapolis, IN 46256-1253 Tel 317-576-6910
Web site: http://www.corkhillpress.com
Dist(s): Ingram Bk. Co..

†Cornell Maritime Pr., Inc., ( 0-87033 ) P.O. Box 456, Centreville, MD 21617 (SAN 203-5901) Tel 410-758-1075; Fax: 410-758-6849; Toll Free: 800-638-7641; Imprints: Tidewater Publishers (Tidewtr Pubs)
E-mail: cornell@crosslink.net
Web site: http://www.cornellmaritimepress.com/
Dist(s): Hale, Robert & Co., Inc.; CIP.

†Cornell Univ. Pr., ( 0-8014; 0-87546 ) Orders Addr.: P.O. Box 6525, Ithaca, NY 14851 (SAN 281-5680) Tel 607-277-2211; Toll Free Fax: 800-688-2877; Edit Addr.: Sage House, 512 E. State St., Ithaca, NY 14851 (SAN 202-1862) Tel 607-277-2338; Imprints: ILR Press (ILR Press)
E-mail: orders@plymbridge.com;
cupress-sales@cornell.edu; cupressinfo@cornell.edu
Web site: http://www.cornellpress.cornell.edu
Dist(s): CUP Services; CIP.

Cornell Univ., Southeast Asia Program Pubns., ( 0-87727 ) Orders Addr.: 369 Pine Tree Rd., Ithaca, NY 14850; Edit Addr.: 640 Stewart Ave., Ithaca, NY 14850 (SAN 241-6700) Tel 607-255-8038; Fax: 607-255-7534; Toll Free: 877-865-2432
E-mail: med28@cornell.edu; SEAP-Pubs@cornell.edu
Web site: http://www.einaudi.cornell.edu/booktore/seap.

Cornerstone Bks. Imprint of Pages, Inc.

Cornerstone Pr. Chicago, ( 0-940895 ) 939 W. Willson, Chicago, IL 60640 (SAN 664-7200) Tel 773-989-4920; 773-561-2450; Fax: 773-989-2076; Toll Free: 888-407-7377
E-mail: cspress@jpusa.org
Web site: http://www.cornerstonepress.com
Dist(s): Baker & Taylor Bks.
   Midpoint Trade Bks., Inc.
   Riverside.

Cornerstone Publishing, ( 1-882185 ) Div. of Banner Enterprises, Orders Addr.: 2979 W. School House Ln., Suite K-605C, Philadelphia, PA 19144 (SAN 298-735X); P.O. Box 44353, Philadelphia, PA 19144 Do not confuse with companies with the same name in Decatur, GA, Altamonte Springs, FL, Wichita, KS
E-mail: cornerstone@bannerenterprises.com
Web site: http://www.cornerstonepublishing.com
Dist(s): Book Clearing Hse.
   Follett Library Resources.

Cornwall Bks. Imprint of Associated Univ. Presses

Coronet (GBR) ( 0-340 ) Dist. by Trafalgar.

Corvina Books (HUN) ( 963-13 ) Dist. by St Mut.

Corvus Publishing, ( 1-890768; 0-9725776 ) Orders Addr.: P.O. Box 102004, Denver, CO 80210 Tel 303-777-0539; Fax: 303-756-8011; Toll Free: 800-996-9783; Imprints: Intrigue Press (Intrigue)
E-mail: derek@corvuspublishing.com;
books@corvuspublishing.com
Web site: http://www.intriguepress.com;
http://www.corvuspublishing.com;
http://www.speckpress.com
Dist(s): Consortium Bk. Sales & Distribution.

Corvus Publishing Group See Corvus Publishing

Cosmic Concepts Pr., ( 0-9620507 ) 2531 Dover Ln., Saint Joseph, MI 49085 (SAN 248-6431) Tel 616-428-2792; Fax: 616-428-9671
E-mail: cosmicconcepts@atm.net
Dist(s): Baker & Taylor Bks.
   Bookpeople
   Distributors, The
   New Leaf Distributing Co., Inc..

Cosmos Books See Prime

Cote Literary Group, The, ( 1-929175 ) P.O. Box 1898, Mount Pleasant, SC 29465-1898 Tel 843-881-6080; Fax: 843-881-1899; Imprints: Corinthian Books (Corinthian Bks)
E-mail: editor@corinthianbooks.com;
dickcote@earthlink.net
Web site: http://www.corinthianbooks.com
Dist(s): Baker & Taylor Bks.
   Brodart Co.
   Follett Library Resources
   Parnassus Bk. Distributors
   Quality Bks., Inc.
   Sandlapper Publishing Co., Inc..

Cotler, Joanna Bks. Imprint of HarperCollins Children's Bk. Group

Council for Indian Education, ( 0-89992 ) Orders Addr.: 1240 Burlington Ave., Billings, MT 59102-4224 Tel 406-248-3465
E-mail: cie@cie-mt.org
Web site: http://www.cie-mt.org.

Council Oak Bks., ( 0-933031; 1-57178 ) Orders Addr.: 2105 E. 15th St., Suite B, Tulsa, OK 74104 (SAN 689-5522) Toll Free: 800-247-8850 (orders only); Edit Addr.: 5806 S. Perkins Rd., Stillwater, OK 74074
E-mail: sdennison@counciloakbooks.com
Web site: http://www.counciloakbooks.com
Dist(s): Baker & Taylor Bks.
   Koen Bk. Distributors
   New Leaf Distributing Co., Inc..

Council Pr. Imprint of Cedar Fort, Inc./CFI Distribution

Countertop Software See TOPICS Entertainment

†Countryman Pr., ( 0-88150; 0-914378; 0-936399; 0-942440; 1-58157 ) Div. of W. W. Norton & Co., Inc., P.O. Box 748, Woodstock, VT 05091-0748 (SAN 206-4901) Tel 802-457-4826 Toll Free: 800-245-4151 (Orders only)
E-mail: countrymanpress@wwnorton.com
Web site: http://www.countrypress.com
Dist(s): Norton, W. W. & Co., Inc.; CIP.

Courage Bks. Imprint of Running Pr. Bk. Pubs.

Court Street Pr. Imprint of NewSouth, Inc.

Cove Pr. Imprint of U.S. Games Systems, Inc.

†Cove View Pr., ( 0-931896 ) 883 Chamise Way, Redding, CA 96002-2146 (SAN 220-0422)
E-mail: geraldak@digital-star.com; CIP.

†Covenant Communications, ( 0-9649122 ) 1009 Jones St., Old Hickory, TN 37138 Tel 615-847-2066; Fax: 615-860-3601; Toll Free: 800-979-3882 Do nt oconfuse with Covenant Communications in Old Hickory, TN
Dist(s): Quality Bks., Inc.; CIP.

Covenant Communications, Inc., ( 1-55503; 1-57734; 1-59156 ) Orders Addr.: P.O. Box 416, American Fork, UT 84003-0416 (SAN 169-8540) Tel 801-756-9966; Fax: 801-756-1049; Toll Free: 800-662-9545; Edit Addr.: 920 E. State Rd., Suite F, American Fork, UT 84003 Do not confuse with Covenant Communications in American Fork, UT
E-mail: lindao@covenant-lds.com
Web site: http://www.covenant-lds.com.

Cover to Cover Cassettes, Ltd., ( 0-941935 ) 238 15th St., NE, No. 13, Atlanta, GA 30309 (SAN 666-7910) Tel 404-892-1637.

Cover to Cover Classics Imprint of Audio Partners Publishing Corp.

Covercraft Imprint of Perfection Learning Corp.

Covered Bridge Pr. Imprint of Douglas Charles, Ltd.

Covos-Day Bks. (ZAF) ( 0-620; 1-919874 ) Dist. by BHB Intl.

**Coward-McCann** Imprint of Putnam Publishing Group, The

**Cowles Creative Publishing, Incorporated** See **Creative Publishing international, Inc.**

†**Crane Hill Pubs.,** ( *0-9621455; 1-57587; 1-881548* ) 3608 Clairmont Ave., Birmingham, AL 35222-3508 Tel 205-714-3007; Fax: 205-714-3008; Toll Free Fax: 800-377-7981; Toll Free: 800-841-2682 E-mail: info@cranehill.com; cranies@cranehill.com Web site: http://www.cranehill.com *Dist(s):* **Blair, John F. Pub.**; *CIP.*

**Crazy Wolf Publishing,** ( *0-9674172* ) P.O. Box 3954, New Hyde Park, NY 11040 Fax: 718-418-9311 E-mail: TRStaab@aol.com Web site: http://www.crazywolfpublishing.com.

**Creation Bks.,** ( *1-84068; 1-871592* ) P.O. Box 1137, New York, NY 10156 Toll Free: 800-431-1579; 4th Flr., 72.80 Leather Ln., London, EC1N 7TR Tel (0) 20 7430 9878; Fax: (0) 20 7242 5527 E-mail: info@creationbooks.com Web site: http://www.creationbooks.com *Dist(s):* **Consortium Bk. Sales & Distribution Last Gasp Eco-Funnies, Inc. Subterranean Co..**

†**Creative Arts Bk. Co.,** ( *0-88739; 0-916870* ) 833 Bancroft Way, Berkeley, CA 94710 (SAN 208-4880) Tel 510-848-4777; Fax: 510-848-4844; Toll Free: 800-848-7789; *Imprints:* Black Mask (Black Mask) E-mail: staff@creativeartsbooks.com Web site: http://www.creativeartsbooks.com *Dist(s):* **Baker & Taylor Bks. Bookazine Co., Inc. Bookpeople Koen Bk. Distributors New Leaf Distributing Co., Inc. SPD-Small Pr. Distribution**; *CIP.*

**Creative Bk. Co. (IND)** ( *81-86318; 81-86798* ) *Dist. by* **S Asia.**

**Creative Bloc Pr.** Imprint of Adirondack Empire, Inc.

**Creative Co., The,** ( *0-87191; 0-88682; 1-56660; 1-56846* ) 123 S. Broad St., P.O. Box 227, Mankato, MN 56001 Tel 507-388-6273; Fax: 507-388-2746; Toll Free: 800-445-6209; *Imprints:* Creative Education (Creat Educ) Do not confuse with The Creative Co., Lawrenceburg, IN E-mail: CreativeCo@aol.com.

**Creative Education** Imprint of Creative Co., The

**Creative Outlet,** ( *0-9635106* ) 201 E. Burlington, Stillwater, MN 55082 Tel 651-430-9062; Fax: 651-430-2377; Toll Free: 888-553-2484 Web site: http://www.faithink.com .

**Creative Publishing** See **Lavelle Publishing**

**Creative Publishing international, Inc.,** ( *0-86573; 0-942802; 1-55971; 1-85434; 1-58728; 1-58923* ) 18755 Lake Dr., E., Chanhassen, MN 55317 (SAN 289-7148) Tel 952-936-4700; Fax: 952-933-1456; Toll Free: 800-328-0590; *Imprints:* NorthWord (NorthWord) E-mail: sales@creativepub.com Web site: http://www.two-canpublishing.com; http://www.creativepublishinginternational.com; http://www.northwordpress.com; http://www.howtobookstore.com; http://www.creativepub.com *Dist(s):* **Athena Productions, Inc. Book Travelers West DUX Sales & Marketing McLemore, Hollern & Assocs. New England Bk. Reps. Proe & Proe Southern Territory Assocs. Wybel Marketing Group.**

**Creatures at Large,** ( *0-940064* ) Orders Addr.: P.O. Box 687, Pacifica, CA 94044 (SAN 281-5788) Tel 415-355-7323; Fax: 415-355-4863; Edit Addr.: 1082 Grand Teton Dr., Pacifica, CA 94044 (SAN 281-577X) E-mail: creature@netwiz.net *Dist(s):* **SCB Distributors.**

**Cresent Hse. Publishing,** ( *0-9675884* ) 7941 Katy Freeway, No. 105, Houston, TX 77024 Tel 713-268-4763 E-mail: cresenthouse@usa.net Web site: http://www.bayoushadows.com *Dist(s):* **BookMasters, Inc..**

**Crime & Again Pr.,** ( *0-9665899* ) 245 Eighth Ave., Suite 283, New York, NY 10011 Tel 212-727-0151 E-mail: crimepress@aol.com *Dist(s):* **Midpoint Trade Bks., Inc..**

**Crimeline** Imprint of Bantam Bks.

**Crime-Zone Bks.,** ( *0-9634767* ) Subs. of Tug Pr., 4790 Irvine Blvd., Suite 105-339, Irvine, CA 92620 Tel 949-551-9591 E-mail: CrimeZone1@aol.com..

**Crippen & Landru, Pubs.,** ( *1-885941; 1-932009* ) Orders Addr.: P.O. Box 9315, Norfolk, VA 23505-9315 Tel 757-622-6656 (phone/fax); Toll Free: 877-622-6656 (phone/fax); Edit Addr.: 533 W. 24th, Norfolk, VA 23517 Tel 757-622-6656; Fax: 757-622-6656 E-mail: crippenl@pilot.infi.net Web site: http://www.crippenlandru.com.

**Crispin/Hammer Pr.,** ( *0-9706405* ) 5640 Imai Rd., Hood River, OR 97031-7468 Tel 541-354-6304 E-mail: crispinpub@gorge.net Web site: http://www.himalayandhaba.com.

**Criterion Hse.,** ( *1-884162* ) Orders Addr.: P.O. Box 586295, Oceanside, CA 92058 Tel 760-631-0555 (phone/fax); Edit Addr.: 4563 Dunhill Ct., Oceanside, CA 92056 E-mail: curt@criterionhouse.com Web site: http://www.criterionhouse.com.

**Crocodile Bks.** Imprint of Interlink Publishing Group, Inc.

**Cross Cultural Pubns., Inc.,** ( *0-940121* ) Orders Addr.: 53310 Peggy Ln., South Bend, IN 46635 Tel 219-273-6526; Edit Addr.: P.O. Box 506, Notre Dame, IN 46556 (SAN 664-2551) Tel 219-272-0889; Fax: 219-273-5973; Toll Free: 800-561-6526; *Imprints:* Cross Roads Books (Cross Roads Bks) E-mail: crosscult@crossculturalpub.com; crosscult@aol.com Web site: http://www.crossculturalpub.com *Dist(s):* **Barnes & Noble Bks.-Imports Baker & Taylor Bks. BookWorld Services, Inc. Coutts Library Service, Inc. Distributors, The Emery-Pratt Co. New Leaf Distributing Co., Inc..**

**Cross Dove Publishing Co., Inc.,** ( *0-9656513* ) Orders Addr.: P.O. Box 220, Manhattan Beach, CA 90267 Tel 310-546-5951; Fax: 310-316-0192.

**Cross Roads Books** Imprint of Cross Cultural Pubns., Inc.

**Cross Time** Imprint of Crossquarter Publishing Group

**Cross Training Publishing,** ( *1-887002; 1-929478* ) Orders Addr.: P.O. Box 1541, Grand Island, NE 68802 (SAN 298-7406) Tel 308-384-5762; Fax: 308-384-9974; Toll Free: 800-430-8588; Edit Addr.: 317 W. Second St., Grand Island, NE 68801 E-mail: crosstrainingpub@computer-concepts.com Web site: http://www.crosstrainingpub.com.

†**Crossing Pr., Inc., The,** ( *0-89594; 0-912278; 1-58091* ) Orders Addr.: 1201 Shaffer Rd., Suite B, Santa Cruz, CA 95060 (SAN 202-2060) Tel 831-420-1110; Fax: 831-420-1114; Toll Free: 800-777-1048 (orders only) E-mail: katie@crossingpress.com Web site: http://www.crossingpress.com *Dist(s):* **Baker & Taylor Bks. Bookpeople Koen Bk. Distributors New Leaf Distributing Co., Inc. Publishers Group West**; *CIP.*

**Crossquarter Breeze Publishing** See **Crossquarter Publishing Group**

**Crossquarter Publishing Group,** ( *1-890109* ) Orders Addr.: P.O. Box 8756, Santa Fe, NM 87504-8756 Tel 505-438-9846 (phone/fax); Edit Addr.: 1910 Sombra Ct., Santa Fe, NM 87505-5445; *Imprints:* Cross Time (Crosstime) E-mail: tfrancis@crossquarter.com Web site: http://www.crossquarter.com.

**Crossroad 8 Avenue** Imprint of Crossroad Publishing Co.

**Crossroad Carlisle** Imprint of Crossroad Publishing Co.

**Crossroad Classic** Imprint of Crossroad Publishing Co.

†**Crossroad Publishing Co.,** ( *0-8245* ) 481 Eighth Ave., Suite 1550, New York, NY 10001 (SAN 287-0118) Tel 212-868-1801; Fax: 212-868-2171; Toll Free: 800-395-0690 (Orders Only); *Imprints:* Crossroad Classic (Crossroad Classic); Crossroad 8 Avenue (Crossroad Gen); Crossroad Carlisle (CrossCarlisle) E-mail: ask@crossroadpublishing.com Web site: http://www.crossroadpublishing.com *Dist(s):* **ACTA Pubns. Abingdon Pr. FaithWorks National Bk. Network**; *CIP.*

**Crossroads Publishing Company** See **CrossroadsPub.com.**

**CrossroadsPub.com,** ( *1-58338* ) 505 W. Forest St., Roswell, NM 88203-3728.

†**Crossway Bks.,** ( *0-89107; 1-58134* ) Div. of Good News Pubs., 1300 Crescent St., Wheaton, IL 60187 (SAN 211-7991) Tel 630-682-4300; 708-682-4300; Fax: 630-682-4785; Toll Free: 800-323-3890 (sales only) Web site: http://www.crosswaybooks.org *Dist(s):* **LIM Productions, LLC Vision Video**; *CIP.*

**Crow Woods Publishing,** ( *0-9665871* ) P.O. Box 7049, Evanston, IL 60204 Tel 847-864-9147 (phone/fax) E-mail: crowwoods1@netscape.net Web site: http://mywebpage.netscape.com/crowwoods1/ *Dist(s):* **Baker & Taylor Bks..**

**Crown** Imprint of Crown Publishing Group

†**Crown Publishing Group,** ( *0-517; 0-609; 0-676; 1-4000* ) Div. of Random Hse., Inc., Orders Addr.: 400 Hahn Rd., Westminster, MD 21157 Tel 410-848-1900; Toll Free Fax: 800-659-2436; Toll Free: 800-733-3000; 800-726-0600; Edit Addr.: 299 Park Ave., New York, NY 10171 (SAN 200-2639) Tel 212-751-2600; Fax: 212-572-2165; *Imprints:* Crown (Crown); Three Rivers Press (Three River Pr); Shaye Areheart Books (Shaye Areheart Bks); Harmony (Harmon); Prima Lifestyles (PrimLife) E-mail: customerservice@randomnhouse.com Web site: http://www.randomhouse.com/ *Dist(s):* **Random Hse., Inc.**; *CIP.*

**Crown Publishing Group, Incorporated** See **Crown Publishing Group**

**Crum Creek Pr.,** ( *0-9625804; 1-932325* ) c/o The Mystery Company, 1323 S Rangeline Rd., Carmel, IN 46032 Toll Free: 800-643-6737 E-mail: info@droodreview.com Web site: http://www.droodreview.com.

**Crumb Elbow Publishing,** ( *0-89904* ) P.O. Box 294, Rhododendron, OR 97049 (SAN 679-128X) Tel 503-622-4798.

**CT Publishing (GBR)** ( *1-902002* ) *Dist. by* **Trafalgar.**

**Culter, Robert Bks.,** ( *0-9713235* ) 17505 Mines Rd., Livermore, CA 94550.

**Cumberland Hearthside** Imprint of Cumberland Hse. Publishing

†**Cumberland Hse. Publishing,** ( *1-58182; 1-888952* ) 431 Harding Industrial Park Dr., Nashville, TN 37211-3105 (SAN 254-4172) Tel 615-832-1171; Fax: 615-832-0633; Toll Free: 800-254-6716; Toll Free: 888-439-2665; *Imprints:* Cumberland Hearthside (Cumberland Hearthside) Do not confuse with Cumberland Hse. Publishing. Co., Inc. in Indianapolis, IN E-mail: twright@cumberlandhouse.com; CumbHouse@aol.com Web site: http://www.CumberlandHouse.com; *CIP.*

**Cune** See **Cune Pr., LLC**

**Cune Pr., LLC,** ( *1-885942* ) Div. of Scott Davis Co., P.O. Box 31024, Seattle, WA 98103 (SAN 298-3648) Tel 206-789-7055; Fax: 206-782-1330 E-mail: bowker@cunepress.com Web site: http://www.cunepress.com; http://www.cunepress.net.

**CUP Services,** 750 Cascadilla St., Ithaca, NY 14851 (SAN 630-6519) Tel 607-277-2211; Fax: 607-277-6292; Toll Free: 800-666-2211.

†**Curbstone Pr.,** ( *0-915306; 1-880684; 1-931896* ) 321 Jackson St., Willimantic, CT 06226 (SAN 209-4282) Tel 860-423-5110; Fax: 860-423-9242 E-mail: info@curbstone.org Web site: http://www.curbstone.org *Dist(s):* **Consortium Bk. Sales & Distribution SPD-Small Pr. Distribution**; *CIP.*

**Currency** Imprint of Doubleday Publishing

**Custom & Limited Editions,** ( *0-9623836; 1-881529* ) Div. of Jamaica Editions, Ltd., 41 Sutter St., Suite 1634, San Francisco, CA 94104 Tel 415-337-0177; Fax: 415-337-0805; Toll Free: 800-762-0177 E-mail: customltd@aol.com Web site: http://www.connieimboden.com *Dist(s):* **Baker & Taylor Bks. Publishers Group West.**

**Cyber Classics, Inc.,** ( *1-58855* ) 1612 S. Clementine St., Anaheim, CA 92802 Tel 714-517-0970; Fax: 714-535-8078; Toll Free: 800-873-6397 E-mail: tedw@bnibooks.com *Dist(s):* **Beeler, Thomas T. Publisher.**

†Cypress Hse., ( *1-879384* ) 155 Cypress St., Fort Bragg, CA 95437 (SAN 297-9004) Tel 707-964-9520; Fax: 707-964-7531; Toll Free: 800-773-7782 E-mail: cypresshouse@cypresshouse.com; forms@cypresshouse.com Web site: http://www.cypresshouse.com *Dist(s):* **Baker & Taylor Bks.**
**Partners Bk. Distributing, Inc.**
**Partners/West**
**Quality Bks., Inc.**
**Unique Bks., Inc.;** *CIP.*

DAW Bks., Inc., ( *0-8099; 0-87997; 0-88677; 0-7564* ) Affil. of Penguin Putnam, Inc., Orders Addr.: 405 Murray Hill Pkwy., East Rutherford, NJ 07073 Toll Free: 800-788-6262 (individual consumer sales); 800-526-0275 (reseller sales); 800-631-8571 (reseller customer service); Edit Addr.: 375 Hudson St., New York, NY 10014-3658 (SAN 665-6846) Fax: 212-366-2385; Toll Free: 800-253-6476; *Imprints:* D A W Fiction (DAW Fict); D A W Fantasy (DAW Fantasy) E-mail: daw@penguinputnam.com Web site: http://www.dawbooks.com *Dist(s):* **Penguin Group (USA) Inc..**

D A W Fantasy Imprint of DAW Bks., Inc.

D A W Fiction Imprint of DAW Bks., Inc.

D K Ink Imprint of Dorling Kindersley Publishing, Inc.

D K Publishing, Incorporated *See* Dorling Kindersley Publishing, Inc.

DPK Pubns., ( *1-882821* ) 118 47th St., NE, Washington, DC 20019 Tel 202-398-5487; Fax: 202-397-6621.

DRL Bks., ( *0-9631730* ) 5733 Sunbury Rd., Gahanna, OH 43230 Tel 614-478-0913 *Dist(s):* **Baker & Taylor Bks.**
**BookMasters, Inc..**

†Da Capo Pr., Inc., ( *0-306* ) A Member of Perseus Books Group, Orders Addr.: 5500 Central Ave., Boulder, CO 80301 Fax: 303-449-3356 (customer service); Toll Free: 800-386-5656 (customer service); Edit Addr.: 11 Cambridge Ctr., Cambridge, MA 02142 Tel 617-252-5200; Fax: 617-252-5285; *Imprints:* Combined Publishing (CombPubng) E-mail: westview.orders@perseusbooks.com Web site: http://www.perseusbooksgroup.com *Dist(s):* **HarperCollins Pubs.;** *CIP.*

Dada Foundation Imprints, LLC, ( *0-9658423* ) P.O. Box 621, Monterey, CA 93942 Tel 408-372-4778; Fax: 408-372-3138; 280 Grove Acre Ave., Pacific Grove, CA 93950 E-mail: dadaklub@aol.com Web site: http://www.Geocities.com/Athens/Agora/8103.

Daedalus Howell Co., ( *0-9671001* ) 40 Fourth St., No. 244, Petaluma, CA 94952 Tel 707-769-8053; Fax: 707-763-4950; Toll Free: 888-707-7226 E-mail: info@scam.com Web site: http://scam.com.

Dafina Imprint of Kensington Publishing Corp.

Dageforde Publishing, Inc., ( *0-9637515; 1-886225* ) 128 E. 13th St., Crete, NE 68333 Tel 402-826-2059; Fax: 402-826-4069; Toll Free: 800-216-8794 E-mail: info@dageforde.com Web site: http://www.dageforde.com *Dist(s):* **Baker & Taylor Bks.**
**Quality Bks., Inc.**
**Unique Bks., Inc..**

Dales Large Print Bks. (GBR) ( *1-85389; 1-84262* ) *Dist. by* Ulverscroft US.

†Dalkey Archive Pr., ( *0-916583; 1-56478* ) ISU Campus 8905, Normal, IL 61790 (SAN 296-4910) Tel 309-438-7555; Fax: 309-438-7422 E-mail: angela@dalleyarchive.com Web site: http://www.centerforbookculture.org; http://www.dalkeyarchive.com *Dist(s):* **SPD-Small Pr. Distribution**
**Univ. of Nebraska Pr.;** *CIP.*

Dalmatian Pr., ( *1-57759; 1-888567; 1-4037* ) 118 Seaboard Ln., Suite 118, Franklin, TN 37067-8218 Tel 615-370-9922; Fax: 615-370-8034 E-mail: derekadams@andersonpress.com.

Dalrymple Bks., ( *0-9673338* ) Orders Addr.: P.O. Box 2139, Ashland, OH 44905 Tel 907-581-3701; Fax: 907-581-5044; Edit Addr.: Eleanor Dr., Apt. 13, Unalaska, AK 99685 E-mail: Adalrymple@hotmail.com *Dist(s):* **BookMasters, Inc..**

Damien-Dutton Society for Leprosy Aid, Inc., ( *0-9606330* ) 616 Bedford Ave., Bellmore, NY 11710 (SAN 217-1694) Tel 516-221-5829; 516-221-9588; Fax: 516-221-5909.

Dan River Pr., ( *0-89754* ) Div. of Conservatory of American Letters, P.O. Box 298, Thomaston, ME 04861-0298 Tel 207-354-0998; Fax: 207-354-8953 E-mail: cal@americanletters.org Web site: http://www.americanletters.org.

Dancing Goat Pr., ( *0-9708160* ) 3013 SW Quail Creek Dr., Topeka, KS 66614 E-mail: cyoho@dancinggoatpress.com; cyoho@cjnetworks.com Web site: http://www.dancinggoatpress.com *Dist(s):* **Baker & Taylor Bks.**
**Bookmen, Inc..**

Dandelion Bks., LLC, ( *1-893302* ) Div. of Dandelion Enterprises, Inc., 5250 S. Hardy Dr., No. 3067, Tempe, AZ 85283-5217 Tel 480-897-4452; Fax: 480-897-4453; Toll Free: 800-861-7899 E-mail: cadler@mindspring.com Web site: http://www.dandelionbooks.net *Dist(s):* **Biblio Distribution**
**Booksurge, LLC.**

Danger Publishing, ( *0-9658727* ) 1014 S. Westlake Blvd., Suite 14 PMB 155, Westlake Village, CA 91361-3125 Tel 805-497-6483; Fax: 805-494-0745 E-mail: danger@dangerpub.com Web site: http://www.dangerpub.com.

Daniel, John & Co., Pubs., ( *0-936784; 1-880284* ) Div. of Daniel & Daniel Pubs., Inc., P.O. Box 21922, Santa Barbara, CA 93121 (SAN 215-1995) Tel 805-962-1780; Fax: 805-962-8835; Toll Free: 800-662-8351; *Imprints:* Perseverance Press (Perseverance Pr) E-mail: dandd@danielpublishing.com Web site: http://www.danielpublishing.com *Dist(s):* **SCB Distributors.**

Dante Univ. of America Pr., Inc., ( *0-937832* ) P.O. Box 812158, Wellesley, MA 02482 (SAN 220-150X) Tel 781-235-3634; Fax: 781-790-1256 E-mail: danteu@usa1.com; danteu@danteuniversity.org Web site: http://www1.USA1.COM/~DANTEU; http://www.danteuniversity.org *Dist(s):* **Baker & Taylor Bks..**

Danville Creek Publishing, ( *0-9656650* ) 20 Tea Tree Ct., Danville, CA 94526 Fax: 510-837-7619; Toll Free: 800-669-0773 E-mail: Mariek7734@aol.com Web site: http://www.Spannet.org/danvillecreek *Dist(s):* **Ad-Lib Pubns.**
**Baker & Taylor Bks..**

†Darby Creek Publishing, ( *0-87406; 1-58196* ) 7858 Industrial Pkwy., Plain City, OH 43064 (SAN 687-4592) Tel 614-873-7955 E-mail: editorial@darbycreekpublishing.com *Dist(s):* **Lerner Publishing Group;** *CIP.*

DARE Bks., ( *0-912444* ) Div. of Desmond A. Reid Enterprises, 33 Lafayette Ave., Brooklyn, NY 11217 Tel 718-625-4651; Fax: 718-625-0654.

Dark Alley Imprint of HarperTrade

Dark City Bks. Imprint of OffByOne Pr.

Dark Horse Comics, ( *1-56971; 1-878574; 1-59307* ) 10956 SE Main St., Milwaukie, OR 97222 Tel 503-652-8815; Fax: 503-654-9440 E-mail: daveye@dhorse.com Web site: http://www.darkhorse.com *Dist(s):* **Berkley Publishing Group**
**Diamond Book Distributors, Inc.**
**Diamond Comic Distributors, Inc.**
**LPC Group**
**Penguin Group (USA) Inc..**

Dark Oak Mysteries Imprint of Oak Tree Publishing

Dark River Publishing, ( *0-9663201* ) 6155 Pleasant View Dr., Clare, MI 48617 Tel 517-386-4540 E-mail: bigguy@voyager.net *Dist(s):* **Partners Pubs. Group, Inc.**
**Todd Communications.**

D'Asia Vu Reprint Library Imprint of EastBridge

Daugherty, Royce Publishing, ( *0-9707390* ) 126 E. Wing St., No. 162, Arlington Heights, IL 60004 (SAN 253-6439) Tel 847-358-9557; Fax: 847-358-0637 E-mail: rdnetbooks@aol.com.

Davenport Pr., ( *0-940827* ) Orders Addr.: P.O. Box 841, New York, NY 10156 (SAN 665-1011) Tel 212-725-5190; Fax: 212-725-5199.

Davies Associates Publishers *See* Davies Group Pubs., The

Davies Group Pubs., The, ( *0-9630076; 1-888570* ) Orders Addr.: P.O. Box 440140, Aurora, CO 80044-0140 Tel 303-750-8374; Fax: 303-337-0952 E-mail: daviesgroup@msn.com.

Davus Publishing, ( *0-915317* ) P.O. Box 1101, Buffalo, NY 14213-7101 (SAN 289-9787) Tel 519-426-2077; Fax: 519-426-0105; Toll Free: 800-565-9523 E-mail: davus@kwic.com Web site: http://www.kwic.com/~davus *Dist(s):* **Coutts Library Service, Inc..**

Dayal, Ravi Pub. (IND) ( *81-7530* ) *Dist. by* S Asia.

Daybreak Publishing, ( *0-9742233* ) P.O. Box 36634, Canton, OH 44735 Tel 330-479-8425 (phone/fax) Do not confuse with companies with the same name in Portland, OR, Georgetown, TX E-mail: daybreakpub@juno.com *Dist(s):* **Biblio Distribution.**

Days & Years Pr., The, ( *0-9645206* ) 7560 E. Canyon Meadow Cir., Pleasanton, CA 94588 Tel 925-463-0468; Fax: 925-463-0481 E-mail: gkaiper@comcast.net *Dist(s):* **Baker & Taylor Bks..**

Daystar House *See* Colbert Hse., The

DC Comics, ( *0-930289; 1-56389; 1-4012* ) Div. of Warner Bros.- A Time Warner Entertainment Co., 1700 Broadway, New York, NY 10019 Tel 212-636-5400; Fax: 212-636-5979; *Imprints:* Vertigo (Vertigo) Web site: http://www.dccomics.com *Dist(s):* **Diamond Book Distributors, Inc.**
**Eastern News Distributors**
**Time Warner Bk. Group**
**Warner Bks., Inc..**

Deaconess Press *See* Fairview Pr.

Dead End Street, LLC, ( *0-9665521; 1-929429* ) 813 Third St., Hoquiam, WA 98550 E-mail: jrutledge@deadendstreet.com Web site: http://www.deadendstreet.com.

Dead End Street Publications, LLC *See* Dead End Street, LLC

Deadly Alibi Pr., Ltd., ( *1-886199* ) Orders Addr.: P.O. Box 5947, Vancouver, WA 98668-5947 Tel 360-695-9004; Fax: 960-693-3354; Toll Free: 800-695-9003; Edit Addr.: 4000 NE 50th Ave., Vancouver, WA 98661-6450; *Imprints:* Madison Publishing Company (Madison Pub Co) E-mail: editor@deadlyalibipress.com; madison@teleport.com Web site: http://deadlyalibipress.com.

Debate, Editorial (ESP) ( *84-7444; 84-8306* ) *Dist. by* Lectorum Pubns.

Dedalus, Ltd., ( *0-946626; 1-873982; 1-903517* ) P.O. Box 160, Monroe, OR 97456 Tel 541-847-5274; Fax: 541-847-6018; 265 S. Fifth St., Monroe, OR 97456 E-mail: subco@clipper.net; dedaluslimited@compuserve.com *Dist(s):* **SCB Distributors.**

†Dee, Ivan R. Pub., ( *0-929587; 1-56663* ) Div. of Rowman & Littlefield Publishing Grp., Orders Addr.: 15200 NBN Way, Blue Ridge Summit, PA 17214 Tel 717-794-3800; Fax: 717-794-3803; Toll Free Fax: 800-338-4550; Toll Free: 800-462-6420; Edit Addr.: 1332 N. Halsted St., Chicago, IL 60622-2694 (SAN 249-535X) Tel 312-787-6262; Fax: 312-787-6269; *Imprints:* Elephant Paperbacks (Elephant Paperbacks); New Amsterdam Books (NAB); Sanders, J. S. & Company, Incorporated (J S Sanders & Co) E-mail: elephant@ivanrdee.com Web site: http://www.ivanrdee.com *Dist(s):* **National Bk. Network**
**Rowman & Littlefield Pubs., Inc.;** *CIP.*

Deerbridge Bks., ( *0-9668527* ) Orders Addr.: P.O. Box 2266, Pittsfield, MA 01201 Tel 413-449-2255; Fax: 413-442-5025; Toll Free: 877-499-2255 E-mail: info@deerbridgebooks.com.

Del Rey Imprint of Ballantine Bks.

Delacorte Large Type Imprint of Bantam Doubleday Dell Large Print Group, Inc.

Delacorte Pr. Imprint of Dell Publishing

Dell Bks. Imprint of Dell Publishing

Dell Books for Young Readers Imprint of Random Hse. Children's Bks.

†Dell Publishing, ( *0-440; 1-4000* ) Div. of Bantam Dell Publishing Group, Orders Addr.: 400 Hahn Rd., Westminster, MD 21157 Tel 410-848-1900; Toll Free: 800-726-0600; Edit Addr.: 1540 Broadway, New York, NY 10036-4094 Tel 212-782-9000; Fax: 212-492-9698; Toll Free: 800-223-6834 (Bulk orders); 800-223-5780 (Orders only); 800-323-9872 (Customer service); *Imprints:* Dell Books (Dell Bks.); Laurel (LE); Delta (Delta); Dial Books (Dial Bks.); Delacorte Press (Delacorte Pr) Web site: http://www.randomhouse.com *Dist(s):* **Random Hse., Inc.;** *CIP.*

**Delphi Bks.,** ( 0-9663397 ) Orders Addr.: P.O. Box 6435, Lee's Summit, MO 64064 Tel 816-478-2156 (phone/fax)
E-mail: delphibks@aol.com
Web site: http://www.TheAuthorsStudio.org/Delphi/
*Dist(s):* **Baker & Taylor Bks.**
**Brodart Co..**

**Delphi Productions, Ltd.,** ( 0-9639932; 1-57998 ) 3160 Fourth St., Boulder, CO 80304 Tel 303-443-2100; Fax: 303-443-4022; Toll Free: 888-443-2400
E-mail: info@delphivideo.com
Web site: http://www.delphivideo.com;
http://www.raisingthesparks.com
*Dist(s):* **Sunburst Communications, Inc..**

**Delphinium Bks., Inc.,** ( 1-883285 ) 127 W. 24th St., New York, NY 10011 Tel 212-255-6098 Do not confuse with Delphinium Pr. in Wellfleet, MA
E-mail: DelphBks@aol.com
*Dist(s):* **HarperCollins Pubs..**

**Delta Imprint of Dell Publishing**

**Dembner Bks. Imprint of Barricade Bks., Inc.**

**Demme Publishing Group,** ( 0-9677037 ) P.O. Box 1306, Antioch, TN 37011-1306 Tel 615-837-1840; Fax: 615-837-1841
E-mail: TheDemmeGroup@cs.com
Web site: http://www.demme.faithweb.com.

**Dempsey, William,** ( 0-9679895 ) 9760 Downing Pl., North Huntingdon, PA 15642 Tel 724-864-1942; Fax: 724-864-5201
E-mail: dempc@aol.com.

**Denlingers Pubs., Ltd.,** ( 0-87714 ) P.O. Box 1030, Edgewater, FL 32132-1030 (SAN 201-3150) Tel 386-424-1737; Fax: 386-428-3534; Toll Free Fax: 800-589-1911; Toll Free: 800-362-1810
E-mail: info@thebookden.com
Web site: http://www.thebookden.com
*Dist(s):* **Baker & Taylor Bks..**

**Dent, J.M. & Sons (GBR)** ( 0-460 ) *Dist. by* **Trafalgar.**

**Dercum Audio,** ( 1-55656 ) 1501 County Hospital Rd., Nashville, TN 37218 (SAN 658-7607) Tel 615-254-2408
E-mail: DawsonC@locc.com
Web site: http://www.bookcase.com/Dercum
*Dist(s):* **APG Sales and Fulfillment.**

**Dercum Press/Dercum Audio** *See* **Dercum Audio**

**Derrydale Pr., The,** ( 1-56416; 1-58667 ) Div. of Rowman & Littlefield Publishing Group, 4720 Boston Way, Lanham, MD 20706 Tel 301-459-3366; Fax: 301-306-5357
E-mail: sdriver@derrydalepress.com
Web site: http://www.derrydalepress.com
*Dist(s):* **National Bk. Network.**

**Derrynane Pr.,** ( 0-9651244 ) 348 Hartford Tpke., Hampton, CT 06247 Tel 860-455-0039; Fax: 860-455-9198; Toll Free: 800-418-9972; *Imprints:* Goldengrove Books (Gldengrove Bks).

†**Deseret Bk. Co.,** ( 0-87579; 0-87747; 1-57345; 1-59038 ) Div. of Deseret Management Corp., Orders Addr.: P.O. Box 30178, Salt Lake City, UT 84130 (SAN 150-763X) Tel 801-534-1515; 801-517-3165 (Wholesale Dept.); Fax: 801-517-3338; Toll Free: 800-453-3876; Edit Addr.: 40 E. South Temple, Salt Lake City, UT 84111; *Imprints:* Shadow Mountain (Shadow Mount); Cinnamon Tree (Cinnamon Tree); Bookcraft, Incorporated (Bkcraft Inc)
E-mail: dbwhsale@deseretbook.com;
wholesale@deseretbook.com
Web site: http://www.deseretbook.com
*Dist(s):* **BookWorld Services, Inc.;** *CIP.*

**Desert Bloom Pr.,** ( 0-9621452 ) P.O. Box 670, Cortaro, AZ 85652-0670 (SAN 251-3897) Tel 520-572-1597 (phone/fax)
E-mail: dbpress@dakotacom.net;
dbp@desertbloompress.com
Web site: http://www.dakotacom.net/~dbpress
*Dist(s):* **Baker & Taylor Bks..**

**Desert Island Bks. (GBR)** ( 1-874287 ) *Dist. by* **Griffin Skye Co.**

**Design Image Group, Inc., The,** ( 1-891946 ) 231 S. Frontage Rd., Suite 17, Burr Ridge, IL 60527 Tel 630-789-8991; Fax: 630-789-9013; Toll Free: 800-563-5455
E-mail: dig@designimagegroup.com
Web site: http://designimagegroup.com.

**Destiny Image Pubs.,** ( 0-7684; 0-914903; 1-56043; 0-9716036 ) Orders Addr.: P.O. Box 310, Shippensburg, PA 17257-0310 (SAN 289-1050); Edit Addr.: 167 Walnut Bottom Rd., Shippensburg, PA 17257 (SAN 253-4339) Tel 717-532-3040; Fax: 717-532-9291; Toll Free: 800-722-6774
E-mail: JLM@destinyimage.com
Web site: http://www.destinyimage.com
*Dist(s):* **Anchor Distributors**
**Appalachian Bible Co.**
**Riverside**
**Spring Arbor Distributors, Inc..**

**Determined Productions, Inc.,** ( 0-915696 ) P.O. Box 2150, San Francisco, CA 94126-2150 (SAN 212-7385) Tel 415-433-0660; Fax: 415-421-0929.

†**Devil Mountain Bks.,** ( 0-915685 ) P.O. Box 4115, Walnut Creek, CA 94596 (SAN 292-4803) Tel 925-939-3415; Fax: 925-937-4883
E-mail: cbsturges@aol.com
*Dist(s):* **SPD-Small Pr. Distribution**; *CIP.*

†**Devin-Adair Pubs., Inc.,** ( 0-8159 ) P.O. Box A, Old Greenwich, CT 06870 (SAN 112-062X) Tel 203-531-7755; Fax: 718-359-8568; *CIP.*

**Dial Bks. Imprint of Dell Publishing**

**Dial Bks. for Young Readers Imprint of Penguin Putnam Bks. for Young Readers**

**Diamond Bks. Imprint of Ace Bks.**

**Diamond Bks. Imprint of Berkley Publishing Group**

**Diamond Books** *See* **Penguin Putnam, Inc E-Books**

**DIANE Publishing Co.,** ( 0-7881; 0-941375; 1-56806; 0-7567 ) Orders Addr.: P.O. Box 1428, Collingdale, PA 19023-8428 (SAN 667-1217) Tel 610-461-6200; Fax: 610-461-6130; Toll Free: 800-782-3833; Edit Addr.: 330 Pusey Ave., Unit 3 Rear, Collingdale, PA 19023
E-mail: hbdjp220@hotmail.com.

**Dickens Publishing (GBR)** ( 0-9518525 ) *Dist. by* **A C Hood.**

**Digital Scanning, Inc.,** ( 1-58218 )
E-mail: info@digitalscanning.com
Web site: http://www.digitalscanning.com
*Dist(s):* **Amazon.Com**
**ebrary, Inc..**

**Dime Pubs.,** ( 0-615 ) Orders Addr.: P.O. Box 490, Cupertino, CA 95014 Tel 408-253-8237; Fax: 408-446-4455; Edit Addr.: 10353 Imperial Ave., Cupertino, CA 95014 Tel 408-253-8237
E-mail: rmblack@attbi.com.

**DIMI Pr.,** ( 0-931625 ) 3820 Oak Hollow Ln., SE, Salem, OR 97302-4774 (SAN 683-7271) Tel 503-364-7698; Fax: 503-364-9727; Toll Free: 800-644-3464 (orders only)
E-mail: dickbook@earthlink.net
Web site: http://home.earthlink.net/~dickbook.

**Diogenes Verlag AG (CHE)** ( 3-257 ) *Dist. by* **Intl Bk Import.**

**Dirty Creek Pubns. Co. Ltd.,** ( 0-9700935 ) 7010 Cornell Rd., Athens, OH 45701 Tel 740-593-7428
E-mail: jrichardson@eurekanet.com.

**Discipleship Journal Imprint of NavPress Publishing Group**

**Disc-Us Bks., Inc.,** ( 1-58444 ) 2570 Camino San Patricio, Santa Fe, NM 87505 Tel 505-474-9139
E-mail: books@disc-us.com
Web site: http://www.disc-us.com.

**DiskUs Publishing,** ( 0-9667995; 1-58495; 0-7572 ) Orders Addr.: P.O. Box 43, Albany, IN 47320 Tel 765-789-4064; Fax: 765-789-4993; Edit Addr.: 549 W. First St., Albany, IN 47320
E-mail: editor@diskuspublishing.com;
DiskUsMail@aol.com
Web site: http://www.diskuspublishing.com
*Dist(s):* **netLibrary, Inc..**

†**Disney Pr.,** ( 0-7868; 1-56282 ) Div. of Disney Bk. Publishing, Inc., A Walt Disney Co., 114 Fifth Ave., New York, NY 10011 Tel 212-633-4400; Fax: 212-633-4833; Toll Free: 800-759-0190
Web site:
http://www.disney.com/disneybooks/index.html
*Dist(s):* **Libros Sin Fronteras**
**Little Brown & Co.**
**Time Warner Bk. Group**; *CIP.*

**Dissertation.com,** ( 0-9658564; 1-58112 ) 7525 NW 61st Terr., Suite 2603, Parkland, FL 33067-2421 (SAN 299-3635) Tel 954-344-8203; Fax: 954-755-4059; Toll Free: 800-636-8329
E-mail: orders@dissertation.com;
publisher@dissertation.com
Web site: http://www.dissertation.com
*Dist(s):* **Baker & Taylor Bks..**

**Distinctive Publishing Corp.,** ( 0-942963 ) 1888 NW 21st St., 2nd Flr., Pompano Beach, FL 33069 Do not confuse with Distinctive Publishing, Sandy, UT.

**Distribooks, Inc.,** Div. of Midwest European Pubns., Inc., 8120 N. Ridgeway, Skokie, IL 60076 (SAN 630-9763) Tel 847-676-1596; Fax: 847-676-1195
E-mail: info@distribooks.com.

**Distribuidora Norma, Inc.,** ( 1-881700 ) Div. of Carvajal International, Orders Addr.: P.O. Box 195040, Hato Rey, PR 00919-5040 Tel 809-788-5050 ; Fax: 809-788-7161; Edit Addr.: Carr 869 Km 1.5 Bo. Palmas, Royal Industrial, Catano, PR 00962
E-mail: normapr@caribe.net.

**Distributed Art Pubs./D.A.P.,** ( 1-881616; 1-891024 ) Orders Addr.: a/o D.A.P. Book Distribution Ctr., 575 Prospect St., Lakewood, NJ 08701 Tel 732-363-5679; Toll Free: 800-338-2665; Edit Addr.: 155 Sixth Ave., 2nd Flr., New York, NY 10013-1507 (SAN 630-6446) Tel 212-627-1999; Fax: 212-627-9484
E-mail: dap@dapinc.com
Web site: http://www.artbook.com/.

**Distributors, The,** ( 0-942520 ) 702 S. Michigan, South Bend, IN 46601 (SAN 169-2488) Tel 219-232-8500; Fax: 312-803-0887; Toll Free: 800-348-5200.

**Diversity Pr.,** ( 0-936715 ) P.O. Box 25, Idabel, OK 74745 (SAN 699-9131) Tel 580-286-3148 Do not confuse with Diversity Pr., Cambridge, MA
E-mail: diversitypress@netscape.net
Web site: http://www.diversitypress.com.

**Divina,** ( 0-9659521 ) Div. of MacMurray & Beck, 4101 E. Louisiana Ave. Ste. 100, Denver, CO 80246-3400 Toll Free: 800-774-3777
*Dist(s):* **Words Distributing Co..**

**Doctor Who,** ( 0-8184 ) .

**Dog Hollow Pr.,** ( 0-9703993 ) Orders Addr.: P.O. Box 22287, Seattle, WA 98122-0287 (SAN 253-6986) Toll Free: 866-568-1195 (phone/fax); Edit Addr.: 2711 E. John St., Seattle, WA 98112 (SAN 253-7044) Tel 206-329-4883
E-mail: sales@doghollow.com; jcmaher@aol.com
Web site: http://doghollow.com
*Dist(s):* **Partners Bk. Distributing, Inc..**

**Dogwood Pr., LLC,** ( 0-9721611 ) 1022 Wakefield Pl., Brandon, MS 39047-7666 Do not confuse with companies with the same or similar names in Greensboro, NC, Hemphill, TX, Stone Mountain, GA.

**Doherty, Tom Assocs., LLC,** ( 0-312; 0-7653; 0-8125 ) Div. of Holtzbrinck Publishers, Orders Addr.: 16365 James Madison Hwy., Gordonsville, VA 22942-8501 Toll Free Fax: 800-672-2054; Toll Free: 888-330-8477; Edit Addr.: 175 Fifth Ave., New York, NY 10010 Tel 212-674-5151; Fax: 540-672-7540 (customer service); *Imprints:* Aerie (Aerie); Forge Books (Forge Bks); Orb Books (Orb Bks); Tor Books (Tor Books); Tor Classics (Tor Class); Starscape (Starscape); Tor Teen (Tor Teen)
*Dist(s):* **Holtzbrinck Pubs.**
**Libros Sin Fronteras.**

**Domain Imprint of Bantam Bks.**

**Domhan Bks.,** ( 1-58345 ) 9511 Shore Rd., Suite 514, Brooklyn, NY 11209 Tel 718-680-4362; Fax: 888-823-4770
E-mail: domhan@att.net
Web site: http://www.domhanbooks.com.

**Donning Co. Pubs.,** ( 0-89865; 0-915442; 1-57864 ) Subs. of Walsworth Publishing Co., Inc., 184 Business Park Dr., No. 106, Virginia Beach, VA 23462-6533 (SAN 211-6316) Tel 757-497-1789; Fax: 757-497-2542; Toll Free: 800-296-8572; *Imprints:* Starblaze (Starblaze)
E-mail: dcpr3@pilot.infi.net
Web site: http://www.donning.com
*Dist(s):* **Schiffer Publishing, Ltd..**

**Do-Not Pr., The (GBR)** ( 1-899344; 1-904316 ) *Dist. by* **Dufour.**

**Dorchester Publishing Co., Inc.,** ( 0-8439 ) 200 Madison Ave., Suite 2000, New York, NY 10016 (SAN 264-0090) Tel 212-725-8811; Fax: 212-532-1054; 610-995-9274 (Single copy orders); Toll Free: 800-481-9191; *Imprints:* Love Spell (Love Spell); Leisure Books (Leisure Bks)
E-mail: dorchesit@aol.com
Web site: http://www.dorchesterpub.com
*Dist(s):* **Comag Marketing Group**
**HarperCollins Pubs..**

†**Dorling Kindersley Publishing, Inc.,** ( 0-7894; 1-56458; 1-879431; 0-7566 ) Div. of The Penguin Group, 375 Hudson St., 2nd Flr., New York, NY 10014 (SAN 253-0791) Tel 212-213-4800; Fax: 212-213-5240; Toll Free: 877-342-5357 (orders only); *Imprints:* D K Ink (D K Ink)
E-mail: customer.service@dk.com;
Annemarie.Cancienne@dk.com
Web site: http://www.dk.com
*Dist(s):* **Continental Bk. Co., Inc.**
**Penguin Group (USA) Inc.**
**Hale, Robert & Co., Inc.**
**Sunburst Communications, Inc.;** *CIP.*

Names

**Dorn, William S.** *See* **Pencil Productions, Ltd.**

**Dorrance Publishing Co., Inc.,** *( 0-8059 )* 701
Smithfield St., Pittsburgh, PA 15222 (SAN 201-3363)
Tel 412-288-4543; Fax: 412-434-8430; Toll Free:
800-788-7654
E-mail: dorrorder@dorrancepublishing.com
Web site: http://www.dorrancepublishing.com.

**Double Mountain Bks. Imprint of Texas Tech Univ. Pr.**

**Double SS Pr.,** *( 0-945199 )* P.O. Box 1450, Wimberley,
TX 78676-1450 Tel 512-847-5173; Fax:
512-847-9099
E-mail: sspress1@aol.com
Web site: http://www.sspress.com
*Dist(s):* **Eakin Pr..**

**Doubleday** *See* **Doubleday Publishing**

**Doubleday Canada, Ltd. (CAN)** *( 0-385 ) Dist. by*
**Random.**

**Doubleday Large Type Imprint of Bantam Doubleday
Dell Large Print Group, Inc.**

†**Doubleday Publishing,** *( 0-385; 1-4000 ) Div. of*
Doubleday Broadway Publishing Group, Orders Addr.:
400 Hahn Rd., Westminster, MD 21157 (SAN
281-6083) Tel 410-848-1900; Toll Free:
800-726-0600; Edit Addr.: 1540 Broadway, New York,
NY 10036-4094 (SAN 201-0089) Tel 212-782-9000;
212-572-4961 Bulk orders; Toll Free Fax:
800-659-2436 Orders only; Toll Free: 800-726-0600
Customer service; 800-669-1536 Electronic orders;
*Imprints:* Image (ImageDD); Talese, Nan A. (N A
Talese); Anchor Bible (Anchor Bible); Currency (Curr
NY)
Web site: http://www.doubleday.com
*Dist(s):* **Random Hse., Inc.**; *CIP.*

**Douglas Charles, Ltd.,** *( 0-924771; 1-58066 )* 7
Adamsdale Rd., North Attleboro, MA 02760 Tel
508-761-5414; Fax: 508-761-6372; *Imprints:* Covered
Bridge Press (Covered Brdge Pr)
E-mail: cdurang@naisp.net.

**Dove Audio Imprint of NewStar Media, Inc.**

**Dove Audio, Incorporated** *See* **NewStar Media, Inc.**

†**Dover Pubns., Inc.,** *( 0-486 )* Orders Addr.: 31 E.
Second St., Mineola, NY 11501 (SAN 201-338X) Tel
516-294-7000; Fax: 516-742-5049 (orders only); Toll
Free: 800-223-3130 (Orders only)
Web site: http://www.doverpublications.com
*Dist(s):* **Continental Bk. Co., Inc.**
**Beeler, Thomas T. Publisher**; *CIP.*

**Dowling Pr., Inc.,** *( 0-9646452; 1-891847 )* 2817 West
End Ave., Suite 126-247, Nashville, TN 37203 Tel
615-297-9875; Fax: 615-297-2925
E-mail: dowlingprs@aol.com
Web site: http://www.dowlingpress.com
*Dist(s):* **Midpoint Trade Bks., Inc.**
**Music Sales Corp..**

**Down East Bks.,** *( 0-89272; 0-924357 ) Div. of Down*
East Enterprise, Inc., P.O. Box 679, Camden, ME
04843 (SAN 208-6301) Tel 207-594-9544; Fax:
207-594-0147; Toll Free: 800-766-1670 Wholesale
orders; Toll Free: 800-685-7962 Retail orders
E-mail: pblanchard@downeast.com;
tbregy@downeast.com
Web site: http://www.downeastbooks.com;
http://www.countrysportpress.com.

**Down Home Pr.,** *( 0-9624255; 1-878086 )* Orders Addr.:
P.O. Box 4126, Asheboro, NC 27204 Tel
336-672-6889; Fax: 336-672-2003; Edit Addr.: 1421
Randolph Tabernacle Rd., Asheboro, NC 27203;
*Imprints:* Imprimatur Books (Imprimatur Bks)
E-mail: downhompr@aol.com
*Dist(s):* **Blair, John F. Pub..**

**Down The Shore Publishing,** *( 0-945582; 0-9615208;
1-59322 )* Orders Addr.: P.O. Box 3100, Harvey
Cedars, NJ 08008 Tel 609-978-1233; Fax:
609-597-0422; Edit Addr.: 638 Teal St., Cedar Run,
NJ 08092 (SAN 661-082X)
E-mail: info@down-the-shore.com;
orders@down-the-shore.com; shore@att.net
Web site: http://www.down-the-shore.com
*Dist(s):* **Koen Bk. Distributors.**

**Downtown Pr. Imprint of Simon & Schuster**

**Dr. Leisure,** *( 0-9638802; 1-887471 )* P.O. Box 1137,
Kihei, HI 96753 Tel 808-879-4160
E-mail: drleisure@drleisure.com
Web site: http://www.drleisure.com.

**Dracula Pr.,** *( 0-9611944; 1-888893 ) Subs. of Dracula*
Unlimited, 29 Washington Sq. W., Penthouse N., New
York, NY 10011-9180 (SAN 219-4228) Tel
212-533-5018 (phone/fax)
E-mail: jeannekey@aol.com.

**Dragonfly Publishing, Inc.,** *( 0-9710473 )* P.O. Box 25,
Sparks, OK 74869 Do not confuse with companies
with the same or similar name in Mount Enterprise,
TX , Whethersfield, CT , San Antonio, TX ,
E-mail: publisher@dragonflypubs.com
Web site: http://www.dragonflyzone.com.

**Dragonhawk Publishing,** *( 1-888767 ) Div. of Life*
Magic Enterprises, Inc., P.O. Box 1316, Jackson, TN
38302 Tel 901-987-3334; Fax: 901-987-2484
*Dist(s):* **Baker & Taylor Bks.**
**Bookpeople**
**New Leaf Distributing Co., Inc.**
**Partners Pubs. Group, Inc..**

**Dramatic Publishing Co.,** *( 0-87129; 1-58342 )* Orders
Addr.: P.O. Box 129, Woodstock, IL 60098 Tel
815-338-7170; Fax: 815-338-8981; Toll Free Fax:
800-334-5302; Toll Free: 800-448-7469; Edit Addr.:
311 Washington St., Woodstock, IL 60098 (SAN
201-5676)
E-mail: dramaticpublishing.com
Web site: http://www.dramaticpublishing.com.

**Dramatists Play Service, Inc.,** *( 0-8222 )* 440 Park Ave.,
S., New York, NY 10016 (SAN 207-5717) Tel
212-683-8960; Fax: 212-213-1539
E-mail: postmaster@dramatists.com
Web site: http://www.dramatists.com.

**Drawn & Quarterly Pubns. (CAN)** *( 0-9696701;
1-896597; 1-894937 ) Dist. by* **Chronicle Bks.**

**Dream Garden Pr.,** *( 0-942688; 0-9604402 )* P.O. Box
27076, Salt Lake City, UT 84127 (SAN 217-1007) Tel
801-521-3819; Fax: 801-521-2606
E-mail: orders@dreamgarden.com
Web site: http://www.dreamgarden.com.

**Drollery Pr.,** *( 0-940920 )* 1524 Benton St., Alameda, CA
94501-2420 (SAN 223-1808) Tel 510-521-4087
*Dist(s):* **Publishers Group West.**

**Dry Bones Pr.,** *( 1-883938; 1-931333 )* P.O. Box 597,
Roseville, CA 95678 Tel 916-435-8355 (phone/fax)
E-mail: drybones@drybones.com;
DryBonesPress@egroups.com;
drynbones@drybones.com
Web site: http://www.drybones.com
*Dist(s):* **Spring Arbor Distributors, Inc..**

**Dry Creek Bks.,** *( 0-941885 )* 2532 Scenic Dr., Modesto,
CA 95352 (SAN 667-5921) Tel 209-522-2047.

**Dry, Paul Bks., Inc.,** *( 0-9664913; 0-9679675; 1-58988 )*
117 S. 17th St., Suite 1102, Philadelphia, PA 19103
Tel 215-231-9939; Fax: 215-231-9942
E-mail: pdb@pauldrybooks.com
Web site: http://www.pauldrybooks.com
*Dist(s):* **Independent Pubs. Group.**

**Dryad Pr.,** *( 0-931848; 1-928755 )* 15 Sherman Ave.,
Takoma Park, MD 20912 (SAN 206-197X) Tel
301-405-6374; Fax: 301-314-9581
E-mail: leffler@mdsg.umd.edu
*Dist(s):* **Univ. of Wisconsin Pr..**

**Dual Dolphin Publishing, Incorporated** *See* **Eye in the
Ear Inc.**

**Dubh Sith Ink,** *( 0-9656318 ) Div. of Wynd Feather Arts*
& Phantasm, P.O. Box 44046, Brooklyn, OH
44144-0046 Tel 216-556-5650
E-mail: dubhsith@wyndfeather.com
Web site: http://www.wyndfeather.com/dubhsith.

**Duckworth, Gerald & Co., Ltd. (GBR)** *( 0-7156;
1-86176 ) Dist. by* **Intl Pubs Mktg.**

†**Dufour Editions, Inc.,** *( 0-8023 )* P.O. Box 7, Chester
Springs, PA 19425-0007 (SAN 201-341X) Tel
610-458-5005; Fax: 610-458-7103; Toll Free:
800-869-5677
E-mail: dufour8023@aol.com;
info@dufoureditions.com
Web site: http://go.to/Dufour; http://members.aol.com/
Dufour8023/index.html; *CIP.*

**DuFour, Howard,** *( 0-9669965 )* 309 Madison St., New
Carlisle, OH 45344 Tel 937-845-1449.

†**Duke Univ. Pr.,** *( 0-8223 )* P.O. Box 90660, Durham,
NC 27708-0660 (SAN 201-3436) Tel 919-687-3600;
Fax: 919-688-4574
E-mail: orders@dukepress.edu;
subscriptions@dukepress.edu
Web site: http://www.dukeupress.edu; *CIP.*

**Dunne, Thomas Bks. Imprint of St. Martin's Pr.**

**Durand Pr., The,** *( 0-9633560; 0-9708324 )* 374 Dogford
Rd., Etna, NH 03750 Tel 603-643-6640; Fax:
603-643-1897
E-mail: DurandPress@aol.com
Web site: http://www.durandpress.com.

**Durban Hse. Publishing Co., Inc.,** *( 1-930754 )* 7502
Greenville Ave., Suite 500, Dallas, TX 75231 Tel
214-890-4050; Fax: 214-890-9295; *Imprints:* Durban
House (Durban)
E-mail: info@durbanhouse.com
Web site: http://www.durbanhouse.com
*Dist(s):* **Baker & Taylor Bks.**
**BookMasters.**

**Durban Hse. Imprint of Durban Hse. Publishing Co.,
Inc.**

**Durkin Hayes Publishing Ltd.,** *( 0-88625; 0-88646;
1-55204 )* 2221 Niagara Falls Blvd., Niagara Falls,
NY 14304-1696 (SAN 630-9518) Tel 716-731-9177;
Fax: 716-731-9180; Toll Free: 800-962-5200
E-mail: info@dhaudio.com
Web site: http://www.dhaudio.com
*Dist(s):* **Landmark Audiobooks.**

**Dutton Imprint of Fine, Donald I. Bks.**

**Dutton Imprint of Dutton/Plume**

**Dutton Studio Imprint of Dutton/Plume**

**Dutton/Plume,** *( 0-525 ) Div. of Penguin Putnam, Inc.,*
Orders Addr.: 405 Murray Hill Pkwy., East
Rutherford, NJ 07073-2136 Toll Free: 800-631-8571
(reseller customer service); 800-788-6262 (individual
consumer sales); 800-526-0275 (reseller sales); Edit
Addr.: 375 Hudson St., New York, NY 10014 Tel
212-366-2000; Fax: 212-366-2666; *Imprints:* Signet
Books (Sig); Meridian Books (Mer); Dutton Studio
(Dutton Studio); Dutton Children's Books (Dutton
Child); Dutton (Dutt); Fine, Donald I. (Don I Fine);
Plume (Plume); Abrahams, William Books (W
Abrahams Bks)
E-mail: online@penguinputnam.com
Web site: http://www.penguinputnam.com
*Dist(s):* **Lectorum Pubns., Inc.**
**Penguin Group (USA) Inc..**

**Dyne-American Pubns., Inc.,** *( 0-939891; 1-878970 )*
2070 Naamans Rd., Suite 103, Wilmington, DE 19810
Fax: 302-475-9066.

**E M C Publishing** *See* **EMC/Paradigm Publishing**

**E. M. Press, Incorporated** *See* **E. M. Productions**

**E. M. Productions,** *( 1-880664 )* 113 Derby Way,
Warrenton, VA 20186
E-mail: empress2@erols.com
Web site: http://www.empressinc.com.

**Eager Minds Pr. Imprint of Warehousing &
Fulfillment Specialists, LLC (WFS, LLC)**

**Eagle Bks.,** *( 0-910971 )* 6031 CR, 105, Carthage, MO
64836 (SAN 263-2160) Do not confuse with
companies with the same name in Hales Corners, WI,
Ridgewood, NJ.

**Eaglemont Pr.,** *( 0-9662257 )* 15600 NE 8th, No. B-1,
PMB 741, Bellevue, WA 98008-3900 (SAN 254-2102)
Tel 425-462-6618; Fax: 425-462-4950
E-mail: info@eaglemontpress.com
Web site: http://www.eaglemontpress.com
*Dist(s):* **National Bk. Network.**

**Eakin Pr. Imprint of Eakin Pr.**

†**Eakin Pr.,** *( 0-89015; 1-57168 )* P.O. Drawer 90159,
Austin, TX 78709-0159 (SAN 207-3633) Tel
512-288-1771; Fax: 512-288-1813; Toll Free:
800-880-8642; *Imprints:* Eakin Press (Eakin Pr)
E-mail: sales@eakinpress.com; tom@eakinpress.com
Web site: http://www.eakinpress.com
*Dist(s):* **Baker & Taylor Bks.**
**Follett Library Resources**
**Hervey's Booklink & Cookbook Warehouse**
**Twentieth Century Christian Bks.**
**Wolverine Distributing, Inc.**; *CIP.*

**Early English Text Society (EETS) (GBR)** *Dist. by*
**Boydell Brewer.**

**Earthen Vessel Production, Inc.,** *( 1-887400 )* 3620
Greenwood Dr., Kelseyville, CA 95451 Tel
707-277-7087; Fax: 707-277-7088; Toll Free:
800-233-6367
E-mail: request@earthsn.com; books@earthern.com
Web site: http://www.earthen.com.

**East Gate Bk. Imprint of Sharpe, M.E. Inc.**

**EastBridge,** *( 1-891936 );* *Imprints:* D'Asia Vu Reprint
Library (DAsia Vu)
E-mail: asia@eastbridgebooks.org
Web site: http://www.eastbridgebooks.org

†**Eastern National,** *( 0-915992; 1-888213; 1-59091 )* 470
Maryland Dr., Suite 1, Fort Washington, PA 19446
(SAN 630-4044)
Web site: http://www.easternnational.org; *CIP.*

**Eastern National Park & Monument Association** *See*
**Eastern National**

Names

**Eastern Washington Univ. Pr.,** ( *0-910055* ) Orders Addr.: MS 1, 705 W. First Ave., Spokane, WA 99201 (SAN 244-7967) Toll Free: 800-508-9095; Edit Addr.: Eastern Washington Univ. EWU, MS-1, 705 W. First Ave., Spokane, WA 99201 (SAN 241-2977) Tel 509-623-4286; Fax: 509-623-4283
E-mail: webadmin@mail.ewu.edu
Web site: http://www.ewu.edu/
*Dist(s):* **Univ. of Washington Pr..**

**Easy Break, First Time Publishing,** ( *0-9641606; 1-891571* ) Orders Addr.: P.O. Box 2005, Watsonville, CA 95077-200 Tel 831-722-2700; Fax: 831-768-0777 ; Toll Free: 888-777-9899; Edit Addr.: 271 Maher Rd., Royal Oaks, CA 95076 Fax: 831-768-0777; Toll Free: 888-777-9899
E-mail: ezbreak@pacbell.net
Web site: http://www.easybreak.com.

**EBOOKSITES.ORG,** ( *0-9713623* ) Orders Addr.: 503 E. 78th St., Suite 2A, New York, NY 10021-1175 Tel 212-396-4457
E-mail: bestbooks@ebooksites.com
Web site: http://www.ebooksites.com.

**EBW Assocs.,** ( *0-9657162* ) P.O. Box 2809, South Portland, ME 04106 Tel 207-799-8389.

**Ecco Imprint of HarperTrade**

**Econo-Clad Bks.,** ( *0-613; 0-7857; 0-8085; 0-8335; 0-88103* ) Div. of American Cos., Inc., Orders Addr.: P.O. Box 1777, Topeka, KS 66601 (SAN 169-2763) Tel 913-233-4252; Toll Free: 800-255-3502; Edit Addr.: 2101 N. Topeka Blvd., Topeka, KS 66608-1830 (SAN 249-2687)
E-mail: hkopperud@sagebrushcorp.com
Web site: http://www.sagebrushcorp.com.

**Econ-Verlag GmbH (DEU)** ( *3-430; 3-547; 3-612* ) *Dist. by* **Intl Bk Import.**

**Ecopress,** ( *0-9639705; 1-893272* ) P.O. Box 2004, Corvallis, OR 97339 (SAN 298-1238) Tel 541-791-4031; Fax: 541-791-2809; Toll Free: 800-326-9272
E-mail: ecopress@peak.org
Web site: http://www.ecopress.com
*Dist(s):* **Baker & Taylor Bks.**
**Midpoint Trade Bks., Inc..**

**Ecrivez!,** ( *1-889316* ) Orders Addr.: P.O. Box 247491, Columbus, OH 43224 Tel 614-253-0773; Fax: 614-253-0774; Edit Addr.: 2384 Gardendale Dr., Columbus, OH 43219
E-mail: ohialicia@ameritech.net.

**ECW Pr. (CAN)** ( *0-920763; 0-920802; 1-55022* ) *Dist. by* **IPG Chicago.**

**EDC Publishing,** ( *0-7460; 0-88110; 1-58086; 0-7945* ) Div. of Educational Development Corp., Orders Addr.: P.O. Box 470663, Tulsa, OK 74147-0663 (SAN 658-0505); Edit Addr.: 10302 E. 55th Pl., Tulsa, OK 74146-6515 (SAN 107-5322) Tel 918-622-4522; Fax: 918-665-7919; Toll Free: 800-475-4522
E-mail: edc@edcpub.com
Web site: http://www.edcpub.com
*Dist(s):* **Continental Bk. Co., Inc.**
**Lectorum Pubns., Inc.**
**Libros Sin Fronteras.**

**Edgehill Bks.,** ( *0-615* ) P.O. Box 1342, Orange, VA 22960-9998 Tel 540-825-9147 (phone/fax)
E-mail: morton@rappelec.com
Web site: http://www.edgehillbooks.com.

**Ediciones Cátedra (ESP)** ( *84-376* ) *Dist. by* **Continental Bk.**

**Ediciones Cátedra (ESP)** ( *84-376* ) *Dist. by* **Distribks Inc.**

**Ediciones del Norte,** ( *0-910061* ) P.O. Box 5130, Hanover, NH 03755 (SAN 241-2993).

**Ediciones Destino (ESP)** ( *84-233* ) *Dist. by* **Continental Bk.**

**Ediciones Era (MEX)** ( *968-411* ) *Dist. by* **Continental Bk.**

**Ediciones Joaquin Mortiz (MEX)** ( *968-27* ) *Dist. by* **Planeta.**

**Ediciones Universal,** ( *0-89729; 1-59388* ) Orders Addr.: P.O. Box 450353, Miami, FL 33245-0353 (SAN 658-0548); Edit Addr.: 3090 SW Eighth St., Miami, FL 33135 (SAN 207-2203) Tel 305-642-3355; Fax: 305-642-7978
E-mail: marta@ediciones.com
Web site: http://www.ediciones.com
*Dist(s):* **Lectorum Pubns., Inc..**

**Edimat Libros, S. A. (ESP)** ( *84-8403; 84-923200; 84-95002; 84-9764* ) *Dist. by* **IPG Chicago.**

**Edinborough Pr.,** ( *1-889020* ) P.O. Box 13790, Roseville, MN 55113-2293 (SAN 299-2825) Tel 651-415-1034; Toll Free Fax: 800-566-6145; Toll Free: 888-251-6336 (Orders Only)
E-mail: books@edinborough.com
Web site: http://www.edinborough.com.

**Edinburgh Univ. Pr. (GBR)** ( *0-7486; 0-85224* ) *Dist. by* **Col U Pr.**

**Editions de Fallois (FRA)** ( *2-87706* ) *Dist. by* **Distribks Inc.**

**Editions du Seuil (FRA)** ( *2-02* ) *Dist. by* **Distribks Inc.**

**Editions, Ltd.,** ( *0-915013; 0-9607938* ) P.O. Box 10150, Honolulu, HI 96816 (SAN 691-9510) Tel 808-735-7644; Fax: 808-732-2164 Do not confuse with Editions Limited in Pasadena, CA
*Dist(s):* **Booklines Hawaii, Ltd..**

**Editions Tom Thompson (AUS)** ( *1-875892* ) *Dist. by* **Intl Spec Bk.**

**Editores Mexicanos Unidos (MEX)** ( *968-15* ) *Dist. by* **Lectorum Pubns.**

**Editorial Gutenberg,** ( *9978-42* ) 300 South St., No. 306, Morris, MN 56267 Tel 320-589-6293; 320-589-3040; Fax: 425-675-6904.

**Editorial Mensaje,** ( *0-86515* ) 125 Queen St., Staten Island, NY 10314 (SAN 214-0063) Tel 718-761-0556.

**Editorial Planeta, S. A. (ESP)** ( *84-08; 84-320; 84-395* ) *Dist. by* **Giron Bks.**

**Editorial Seix Barral (ESP)** ( *84-322* ) *Dist. by* **Continental Bk.**

**Editorial Unilit,** ( *0-7899; 0-945792; 1-56063* ) Div. of Spanish Hse., Inc., 1360 NW 88th Ave., Miami, FL 33172-3093 (SAN 247-5979) Tel 305-592-6136; Fax: 305-592-0087; Toll Free: 800-767-7726
E-mail: sales1@unidial.com
Web site: http://www.editorialunilit.com/
*Dist(s):* **Bethany Hse. Pubs.**
**Harrison Hse., Inc.**
**Lectorum Pubns., Inc..**

**Editorial Voluntad S.A. (COL)** ( *958-02* ) *Dist. by* **Continental Bk.**

**Edmark, Limited** *See* **St. Barthelemey Pr., Ltd.**

**Edmonston Publishing, Inc.,** ( *0-9622393; 1-892059* ) Orders Addr.: P.O. Box 38, Hamilton, NY 13346 Tel 315-824-1965 (phone/fax); Edit Addr.: 1841 Preston Hill Rd., Hamilton, NY 13346
E-mail: shop@edmonstonpublishing.com
Web site: http://www.edmonstonpublishing.com
*Dist(s):* **Baker & Taylor Bks.**
**North Country Bks., Inc..**

**Educa Vision,** ( *1-881839; 1-58432* ) 7550 NW 47th Ave., Coconut Creek, FL 33073 Tel 954-725-0701; Fax: 954-427-6739; Toll Free: 800-983-3822
E-mail: educa@aol.com
Web site: http://www.educavision.com.

**Educational Developmental Laboratories, Inc.,** ( *1-55855; 1-56260; 1-928930* ) Orders Addr.: P.O. Box 210726, Columbia, SC 29221 (SAN 247-3763) Tel 803-781-4416; Fax: 803-781-3627; Edit Addr.: 411 Western Ln., Irmo, SC 29063
E-mail: east@conterra.com.

**Educational Materials Co.,** ( *0-937117* ) 784 River Rd., Windham, ME 04062-4747 (SAN 658-5175)
E-mail: eltottle@att.net
Web site: http://www.tottle.home.att.net.

**Edward-William Publishing Co.,** ( *0-934411* ) 8 Grays Farm Rd., Weston, CT 06883-3003 (SAN 693-8345); *Imprints:* Banned Books (Banned Bks).

**Eerdmans Bks For Young Readers Imprint of Eerdmans, William B. Publishing Co.**

†**Eerdmans, William B. Publishing Co.,** ( *0-8028* ) 255 Jefferson Ave., SE, Grand Rapids, MI 49503-4554 (SAN 220-0058) Tel 616-459-4591; Fax: 616-459-6540; Toll Free: 800-253-7521 (orders); *Imprints:* Eerdmans Books For Young Readers (Eerdmans Bks)
E-mail: info@eerdmans.com; customerservice@eerdmans.com; sales@eerdmans.com
Web site: http://www.eerdmans.com
*Dist(s):* **CRC Pubns.; CIP.**

**E-fect Publishing,** ( *0-9704995* ) P.O. Box 2425, Harvey, LA 70059-2425 (SAN 253-617X) Tel 504-433-1727
E-mail: efectpublishing@att.net; e.pete@att.net
Web site: http://www.e-fectpublishing.com
*Dist(s):* **Baker & Taylor Bks.**
**Brodart Co.**
**Forest Sales & Distributing Co..**

**1873 Pr.,** ( *0-594* ) Div. of Barnes & Noble.com, 76 Ninth Ave., 9th Flr., New York, NY 10011 (SAN 253-0635) Tel 212-414-6000; Fax: 212-414-6320.

**84, Editions (FRA)** ( *2-277; 2-290; 2-293* ) *Dist. by* **Distribks Inc.**

**El Paso City Bks., LLC,** ( *0-9729518* ) Orders Addr.: P.O. Box 156, Chelsea, MI 48118; Edit Addr.: 13271 Scio Church Rd., Chelsea, MI 48118 Tel 734-945-2189; Fax: 734-527-6063; *Imprints:* Olive Tree Books (Olive Tree Bks)
E-mail: editor@epcitybooks.com
Web site: http://www.epcitybooks.com
*Dist(s):* **Baker & Taylor Bks.**
**Partners Bk. Distributing, Inc..**

**Elderberry Pr., LLC,** ( *0-9658407; 1-930859; 1-932762* ) Orders Addr.: 1393 Old Homestead Dr., 2nd Flr., Oakland, OR 97462-9506 (SAN 254-6604) Tel 541-459-6043 (phone/fax) Do not confuse with Elderberry Pr., Encinitas, CA
E-mail: editor@elderberrypress.com
Web site: http://www.elderberrypress.com
*Dist(s):* **Baker & Taylor Bks.**
**Quality Bks., Inc..**

**Eldon Pubs.,** ( *0-9662541* ) 410 Tasker St., Philadelphia, PA 19148 Tel 215-389-4785; Fax: 215-574-9513
*Dist(s):* **Replica Bks..**

**Electric Umbrella, LLC, The** *See* **Electric Umbrella Publishing**

**Electric Umbrella Publishing,** ( *0-9671113; 1-929120; 1-58627; 1-58744; 0-7574* ) Div. of Mylero Corp., 520 Ericksen Ave., NE, Bainbridge, WA 98110 Tel 206-842-4322; Fax: 206-842-4279
E-mail: chris.vandyk@mylero.com; webmaster@electricumbrella.com; roxy@electricumbrella.com
Web site: http://www.mylero.com; http://www.electricumbrella.com.

**Elephant Paperbacks Imprint of Dee, Ivan R. Pub.**

**Elephant's Eye Imprint of Overlook Pr., The**

**Elevated Pr., The,** ( *0-9662408* ) Orders Addr.: P.O. Box 65218, Los Angeles, CA 90065 (SAN 299-6758) Tel 818-550-1963 (phone/fax); Toll Free: 800-547-1963; Edit Addr.: 1460 E. Glenoaks Blvd., Glendale, CA 91206 Do not confuse with Elevation Press, Phoenix, AZ
E-mail: mail@elevated.com; elevatedpr@aol.com
Web site: http://www.elevated.com
*Dist(s):* **Baker & Taylor Bks..**

**Eleventh Hour Press,** ( *0-9664488* ) P.O. Box 1503, Santa Monica, CA 90406-1503 Do not confuse with Eleventh Hour Pr., in El Segundo, CA
E-mail: pearldark@earthlink.net
*Dist(s):* **SPD-Small Pr. Distribution.**

**Elibron Classics Imprint of Adamant Media**

**Elliot's Bks.,** ( *0-911830* ) P.O. Box 6, Northford, CT 06472 (SAN 204-1529) Tel 203-484-2184; Fax: 203-484-7644
E-mail: outofprintbooks@mindspring.com.

**Ellis Pr., The,** ( *0-933180; 0-944024* ) Div. of Spoon River Poetry Pr., P.O. Box 6, Granite Falls, MN 56241 (SAN 214-008X) Tel 507-537-6463 Do not confuse with Ellis Pr., in Charlottesville, VA
E-mail: pichaske@southwest.msus.edu
Web site: http://www.southwest.msus.edu/faculty/ pichaske/plains.htm.

**Elm Tree Bks. Imprint of Viking Penguin**

**Elsevier Science & Technology Bks.,** 11830 Westline Industrial Dr., Saint Louis, MO 63146 Tel 314-872-8370; *Imprints:* Butterworth-Heinemann (Butter Sci Hein)
*Dist(s):* **Elsevier.**

**Elton-Wolf Publishing,** ( *1-58619* ) 2505 Second Ave., Suite 515, Seattle, WA 98121 Tel 206-748-0345; Fax: 206-748-0343
E-mail: hcox@elton-wolf.com
Web site: http://www.elton-wolf.com.

**Elysian Pr.,** ( *0-941692* ) Subs. of Professional Research Corp., P.O. Box 94, Cold Spring Harbor, NY 11724 (SAN 239-2844) Tel 212-831-0596 Do not confuse with Elysian Pr., Dallas, TX.

**Embiid Publishing,** ( *1-58787* ) P.O. Box 2149, Waianae, HI 96792-8149 Tel 808-696-6921
E-mail: us@embiid.com; richard@embiid.net
Web site: http://www.embiid.net.

†**EMC/Paradigm Publishing,** ( *0-7638; 0-8219; 0-88436; 0-912022; 1-56118* ) Div. of EMC Corp., 875 Montreal Way, Saint Paul, MN 55102-4245 (SAN 201-3800) Tel 651-290-2800; Fax: 651-290-2828
E-mail: publish@emcp.com; educate@emcp.com
Web site: http://www.emcp.com
*Dist(s):* **Continental Bk. Co., Inc.; CIP.**

For full information on wholesalers and distributors, refer to the Wholesaler and Distributor Name Index

**Names**

**Emerald Bks.,** ( *1-883002; 1-932096* ) Orders Addr.: P.O. Box 635, Lynnwood, WA 98046 (SAN 298-7538) Tel 425-771-1153; Fax: 425-775-2383; Toll Free: 800-922-2143; Edit Addr.: 7825 230th St. SW, Edmonds, WA 98026 Do not confuse with Emerald Bks. in Westfield, NJ
E-mail: emeraldbooks@seanet.com
Web site: http://www.ywampublishing.com
*Dist(s):* **YWAM Publishing.**

**Emerald Hse. Group, Inc.,** ( *1-889893; 1-932307* ) 427 Wade Hampton Blvd., Greenville, SC 29609 Tel 864-235-2434; Fax: 864-235-2491; Toll Free: 800-209-8570; *Imprints:* Ambassador-Emerald, International (Ambassador-Emerald)
E-mail: info@emeraldhouse.com
Web site: http://www.emeraldhouse.com
*Dist(s):* **FaithWorks.**

**Emerald Ink Publishing,** ( *1-885373* ) 9700 Almeda-Genoa Rd., No. 502, Houston, TX 77075-2400 Tel 713-946-8900; Fax: 713-946-6066; Toll Free: 800-324-5663
E-mail: emerald@emeraldink.com
Web site: http://www.emeraldink.com
*Dist(s):* **Baker & Taylor Bks.**
**Biblio Distribution**
**New Leaf Distributing Co., Inc..**

**Emerald Isle Pubs., Inc.,** ( *0-9674415* ) 1300 Woodmont Ave., Williamsport, PA 17701 Tel 570-326-7552 (phone/fax)
E-mail: cfconway@csrlink.net.

**Emmis Bks.,** ( *0-9617367; 1-57860; 1-878208* ) 10665 Andrade Dr., Zionsville, IN 46077-9230 (SAN 663-7965) Tel 317-733-4175; Fax: 317-733-4176; Toll Free: 800-913-9563
E-mail: info@guildpress.com; nbaxter@indymonthly.emmis.com
Web site: http://www.guildpress.com
*Dist(s):* **Client Distribution Services**
**Distributors, The**
**Hervey's Booklink & Cookbook Warehouse**
**Maus Tales**
**Partners Pubs. Group, Inc..**

**Empire Publishing Service,** ( *1-58690* ) P.O. Box 1344, Studio City, CA 91614-0344 (SAN 630-5687) Tel 818-784-8918
E-mail: empirepubsvc@att.net.

**Emprise Pubns.,** ( *0-938129* ) 820 Park Row, Suite 591, Salinas, CA 93901 (SAN 661-2423) Tel 831-422-0415
*Dist(s):* **Baker & Taylor Bks.**
**Sunbelt Pubns., Inc..**

**Empty Chair** *See* **Hrymfaxe**

**Encanto** Imprint of Kensington Publishing Corp.

**Encore** Imprint of Simon & Schuster Audio

**Encore Performance Publishing,** ( *1-57514* ) Orders Addr.: P.O. Box 692, Orem, UT 84059 Tel 801-785-9343; Fax: 801-785-9394
E-mail: encoreplay@aol.com
Web site: http://www.encoreplay.com

**Engage Publishing,** ( *1-930892* ) P.O. Box 1452, Port Townsend, WA 98368 (SAN 253-2875) Tel 360-379-1999; Fax: 360-379-5651; Toll Free: 877-536-4243
E-mail: info@engagepublishing.com
Web site: http://engagepublishing.com

**Enitharmon Pr. (GBR)** ( *0-905289; 1-870612; 1-900564; 0-901111* ) *Dist. by* **Dufour.**

**Enolam Group, Inc., The,** ( *0-9715536* ) P.O. Box 2008, Norwalk, CT 06852 (SAN 254-475X)
E-mail: rjg@enolam.com
Web site: http://www.enolam.com.

**†Enslow Pubs., Inc.,** ( *0-7660; 0-89490* ) Orders Addr.: P.O. Box 398, Berkeley Heights, NJ 07922-0398 (SAN 213-7518) Tel 908-771-9400; Fax: 908-771-0925; Toll Free: 800-398-2504; Edit Addr.: 40 Industrial Rd., Berkeley Heights, NJ 07922-0398
E-mail: mail@enslow.com
Web site: http://www.enslow.com
*Dist(s):* **Bollett Library Resources;** *CIP.*

**Enterprise Pr.,** ( *0-9604726* ) 8600 Fenner Rd., Laingsburg, MI 48848 (SAN 214-2406) Tel 517-651-2953; Fax: 517-651-5573.

**Entis Publishing,** ( *0-9652784* ) 448 W. Tenth St., Claremont, CA 91711 Tel 909-626-7264; Fax: 909-626-9804
E-mail: yalentis@cyberg8t.com
*Dist(s):* **Regina Bks..**

**Eos** Imprint of Morrow/Avon

**Epic OKC Pr. & Trust Co.,** ( *0-9704351* ) Orders Addr.: P.O. Box 4130, Nicoma Park, OK 73066 (SAN 253-4347) Tel 405-769-3365; Edit Addr.: 11927 SE 15th St., Choctaw, OK 73020.

**Epiphany Pr.** Imprint of Parissound Publishing

**Epiphany Publishing Hse. LLC,** ( *0-9710695* ) Orders Addr.: One Gateway Ctr., No. A-193, Newark, NJ 07102-5383 Fax: 973-824-4470; Toll Free: 888-501-7494; Edit Addr.: 111 Mulberry St., Suite 5-I, Newark, NJ 07102 (SAN 254-4563)
E-mail: toni@epiphanypublishing.net
Web site: http://www.epiphanypublishing.net.

**Epoch Pr.,** ( *0-9614068* ) 186 Almonte Blvd., Mill Valley, CA 94941-3559 (SAN 693-9996) Do not confuse with companies with the same or similar names in Orem, UT, St. Louis, MO.

**E-Pub2000,** ( *0-9679076; 0-9706622* ) 1228 Westloop, No. 274, Manhattan, KS 66502 Tel 785-776-1940
E-mail: e_pub_2000@yahoo.com
Web site: http://go.to/E-Pub2000.

**e-pulp** Imprint of Yellow Creek Publishing

**Equine Graphics Publishing,** ( *1-887932* ) Div. of Equine Graphics, Orders Addr.: P.O. Box 8016, Zanesville, OH 43702-8016 Tel 740-588-0181; Fax: 740-588-0183; Toll Free: 800-659-9442; *Imprints:* New Concord Press (New Concord Pr)
E-mail: editor@newconcordpress.com; toniweeone@smallhorse.com
Web site: http://www.smallhorse.com; http://www.newconcordpress.com.

**ereads.com,** ( *1-58586; 0-7592* ) 171 E. 74th St., New York, NY 10021 Tel 212-772-7363; Fax: 212-772-7393
E-mail: info@e-reads.com
Web site: http://www.e-reads.com.

**Eridanos Library** Imprint of Marsilio Pubs.

**Eridanos Press** *See* **Marsilio Pubs.**

**E-Rights/E-Reads, Limited** *See* **ereads.com**

**†Eriksson, Paul S. Pub.,** ( *0-8397* ) P.O. Box 125, Forest Dale, VT 05745 (SAN 201-6702) Tel 802-247-4210; Fax: 802-247-4256
E-mail: paulerikss@AOL.com
*Dist(s):* **Independent Pubs. Group;** *CIP.*

**Erskine Pr., The (GBR)** ( *1-85297; 0-948285; 0-9506104* ) *Dist. by* **St Mut.**

**Escape Media,** ( *0-9661861* ) P.O. Box 69, Morrison, CO 80465
E-mail: orders@escapemediapublishers.com; info@escapemediapublishers.com
Web site: http://www.escapemediapublishers.com
*Dist(s):* **Baker & Taylor Bks.**
**Partners/West.**

**Espasa Calpe, S.A. (ESP)** ( *84-239; 84-339; 84-8326; 84-670* ) *Dist. by* **Continental Bk.**

**Esrati Co.,** P.O. Box 20130, Shaker Heights, OH 44120 Tel 216-561-9393
E-mail: steve@esrati.com
Web site: members.tripod.com/—HIBAHILL/ esrati.html.

**Essential Series, The** Imprint of Marvel Enterprises

**Esstee Audios,** 3601 Clarks Ln., Suite 436, Baltimore, MD 21215 Tel 410-764-3343.

**Eusebius Publishing,** ( *0-9669789* ) 4744 Live Oak Canyon Rd., La Verne, CA 91750-2318.

**Evangel Press** *See* **Evangel Publishing Hse.**

**Evangel Publishing Hse.,** ( *0-916035; 1-928915* ) Div. of Board for Media Ministry of the Brethren in Christ Church, Orders Addr.: P.O. Box 189, Nappanee, IN 46550 (SAN 211-7940) Tel 574-773-3164; Fax: 574-773-5934; Toll Free: 800-253-9315 (order)
E-mail: sales@evangelpublishing.com; editorial@evangelpublishing.com
Web site: http://www.evangelpublishing.com
*Dist(s):* **Appalachian Bk. Distributors**
**Baker & Taylor Bks.**
**Riverside**
**Spring Arbor Distributors, Inc..**

**Evans Brothers, Ltd. (GBR)** ( *0-237* ) *Dist. by* **Trafalgar.**

**†Evans, M. & Co., Inc.,** ( *0-87131; 1-59077* ) 216 E. 49th St., New York, NY 10017 (SAN 203-4050) Tel 212-688-2810; Fax: 212-486-4544
E-mail: editorial@mevans.com
Web site: http://www.mevans.com/
*Dist(s):* **National Bk. Network;** *CIP.*

**Evans Pubns.,** ( *0-934188* ) P.O. Box 469, Barnsdall, OK 74002 (SAN 212-9019) Tel 918-847-2916; Fax: 918-847-2115 Do not confuse with Evans Pubns., Clearwater, FL.

**Event Horizon Pr.,** ( *0-9627501; 1-880391* ) P.O. Box 2006, Palm Springs, CA 92263-2006 (SAN 298-1351) Tel 760-329-3950; Fax: 760-329-1720 Do not confuse with Event Horizon Pubns., Council Bluffs, IA
E-mail: ziadina@earthlink.net
Web site: http://www.eventhorizonpress.com
*Dist(s):* **Baker & Taylor Bks.**
**Bookpeople**
**Quality Bks., Inc..**

**Everbind/Marco Bk. Co.,** ( *0-9710756; 0-9729765* ) 60 Industrail Rd., Lodi, NJ 07644 Tel 973-458-0485; Fax: 973-458-5289; Toll Free: 800-842-4234
E-mail: everbind5@aol.com.

**Everest de Ediciones y Distribucion, S.L. (ESP)** ( *84-241* ) *Dist. by* **Lectorum Pubns.**

**Everest Publishing,** ( *1-886295* ) 7041 E. Orange Blossom Ln., Scottsdale, AZ 85253-7042 Tel 602-994-5024; Fax: 602-941-5561; Toll Free: 800-240-2332 Do not confuse with Everest Publishing Co., Costa Mesa, CA
E-mail: info@sourcebook.com
Web site: http://www.sourcebook.com
*Dist(s):* **Lectorum Pubns., Inc..**

**Everyman's Classic Library in Paperback** Imprint of Tuttle Publishing

**Everyman's Library** Imprint of Knopf Publishing Group

**Evolution Publishing & Manufacturing** *See* **Arx Publishing**

**EvoraBooks, LLC,** ( *0-9725071* ) P.O. Box 397, Canton, CT 06019
E-mail: evorabooks@snet.net
Web site: http://www.evorabooks.com.

**Ex Machina,** ( *0-944287* ) Orders Addr.: P.O. Box 448, Sioux Falls, SD 57101 (SAN 243-3761) Tel 605-334-0869; Fax: 605-339-3219; Edit Addr.: 805 S. Sycamore, Sioux Falls, SD 57110-3180 (SAN 243-377X) Tel 605-334-0869
Web site: http://www.exmac.com
*Dist(s):* **Baker & Taylor Bks.**
**Barnes & Noble, Inc.**
**Bookmen, Inc.**
**Brodart Co..**

**Exams Unlimited, Inc.,** ( *1-885343; 1-59132* ) 1971 Western Ave., No. 191, Albany, NY 12203-5011 Tel 518-356-1486 (phone/fax)
E-mail: eui@eui.com
Web site: http://www.ebooks-etexts.com.

**Excelsior Music Publishing Company** *See* **Zinn Publishing Group**

**Eye in the Ear Inc.,** ( *1-884428* ) 215 State St., Portland, ME 04101 (SAN 630-8007) Tel 207-772-1826; Toll Free: 877-997-8679
E-mail: info@eyeintheear.com
Web site: http://www.eyeintheear.com
*Dist(s):* **Landmark Audiobooks.**

**Eynon Pubns.,** ( *0-9702918* ) 1 Eynon Ct., Hockessin, DE 19707 Tel 302-235-1943
E-mail: eynonpubs@hotmail.com; calebglass@hotmail.com.

**Eyrie Pr.,** ( *0-9619465* ) Orders Addr.: P.O. Box 805, Gainesville, VA 20156-0805 (SAN 245-016X)
E-mail: dgo@ix.netcom.com.

**FASA Corp.,** ( *0-931787; 1-55560* ) 1023 W. Vernon Park Pl. Apt. J, Chicago, IL 60607-3447 (SAN 684-8834)
E-mail: info@fasa.com
Web site: http://www.fasa.com
*Dist(s):* **McGraw-Hill/Contemporary.**

**F&S Pr.,** ( *0-9656536* ) Orders Addr.: P.O. Box 608, Brush, CO 80723-0608 Tel 970-867-9382; Toll Free: 800-404-1108; Edit Addr.: 14450 County Rd. 22, Fort Morgan, CO 80701
E-mail: Drill6@rmii.com
Web site: http://www.Americanwest.com/FSPress
*Dist(s):* **Baker & Taylor Bks..**

**F&W Pubns., Inc.,** ( *0-89134; 0-89879; 0-932620; 1-55870; 1-58180; 1-58297; 1-884910* ) Orders Addr.: 4700 E. Galbraith Rd., Cincinnati, OH 45236 Tel 513-531-2690; Fax: 513-531-4082; Toll Free Fax: 888-590-4082; Toll Free: 800-289-0963; c/o AERO Fulfillment Services, 2800 Henkle Dr., Lebanon, OH 45036; *Imprints:* Story Press (Story Press)
E-mail: marcia.jones@fwpubs.com
Web site: http://www.fwpublications.com; http://www.artistsmagazine.com; http://www.artistsnetwork.com; http://www.davidandcharles.co.uk; http://www.krause.com; http://www.familytreemagazine.com; http://www.howdesign.com; http://www.idonline.com; http://www.memorymakersmagazine.com; http://www.popularwoodworking.com; http://www.writersdigest.com; http://www.writersmarket.com; http://www.writersonlineworkshops.com.

Names

**FABER & FABER, INCORPORATED**

†Faber & Faber, Inc., ( 0-571 ) Affil. of Farrar, Straus & Giroux, LLC, Orders Addr.: c/o Van Holtzbrinck Publishing Services, 16365 James Madison Hwy., Gordonsville, VA 22942 Fax: 540-572-7540; Toll Free: 888-330-8477; Edit Addr.: 19 Union Sq., W, New York, NY 10003-3304 (SAN 218-7256) Tel 212-741-6900; Fax: 212-633-9385
Dist(s): **Continental Bk. Co., Inc.**
**Holtzbrinck Pubs.**; CIP.

**Face to Face Bks. Imprint of Midwest Traditions, Inc.**

Factor Pr., ( 0-9626531; 1-887650 ) Orders Addr.: P.O. Box 222, Salisbury, MD 21803 (SAN 631-466X) Toll Free: 800-304-0077; Edit Addr.: 5204 Dove Point Ln., Salisbury, MD 21801 Tel 410-334-6111; Imprints: A&B Bahr & Company (A&B Bahr)
E-mail: factorpress@earthlink.net.

Fairfax, C.H. Co., Inc., ( 0-935132 ) Orders Addr.: P.O. Box 7047, Baltimore, MD 21216-0047 (SAN 221-170X) Tel 410-728-6421 (phone/fax)
E-mail: chfairfaxco@hotmail.com
Web site: http://www.yougetpublished.com.

Fairfield Hse., ( 0-9602048 ) 3 Fairfield Dr., Baltimore, MD 21228-5026 (SAN 209-374X) Tel 410-747-6590.

FairHillBooks.com, ( 1-930351 ) 4907 Telegraph Rd., Elkton, MD 21921 Tel 410-620-1865
E-mail: bradytj@iximd.com.

†Fairleigh Dickinson Univ. Pr., ( 0-8386 ) 285 Madison Ave., Madison, NJ 07940 Tel 973-443-8564; Fax: 973-443-8364
E-mail: fdupress@fdu.edu
Web site: http://www.fdu.edu/newspubs/fdupress.html
Dist(s): **Associated Univ. Presses**
**Baker & Taylor International**; CIP.

Fairview Pr., ( 0-925190; 1-57749 ) 2450 Riverside Ave., Minneapolis, MN 55545 (SAN 298-170X) Tel 612-672-4180; Fax: 612-672-4980; Toll Free: 800-544-8207 Do not confuse with Fairview Pr., in Silver Spring, MD
E-mail: press@webx.fairview.org
Web site: http://www.fairviewpress.org
Dist(s): **National Bk. Network.**

**Faith Alive Christian Resources Imprint of CRC Pubns.**

Faith & Life Pr., ( 0-87303 ) Orders Addr.: P.O. Box 347, Newton, KS 67114-0347 (SAN 658-0637) Tel 316-283-5100; Fax: 316-283-0454; Toll Free: 800-743-2484 (orders only); Edit Addr.: 718 Main St., Newton, KS 67114-0347 (SAN 201-4726)
E-mail: flp@gcmc.org
Web site: http://www.2southwind.net/~gcmc/flp.html
Dist(s): **Spring Arbor Distributors, Inc..**

**Falcon Imprint of Globe Pequot Pr., The**

Falcon Creek Publishing Co., ( 0-9649756 ) 13504 Francisquito Ave., Suite E, Baldwin Park, CA 91706 Tel 626-337-8254
E-mail: namewhiz@namewhiz.com
Web site: http://www.falconcreek.com.

**Falcon Guides Imprint of Globe Pequot Pr., The**

**Fanfare Imprint of Bantam Bks.**

Fantagraphics Bks., ( 0-930193; 1-56097 ) 7563 Lake City Way, NE, Seattle, WA 98115 (SAN 251-5571) Tel 206-524-1967; Fax: 206-524-2104; Toll Free: 800-657-1100
E-mail: zura@fantagraphics.com; diva@eroscomix.com
Web site: http://www.fantagraphics.com; http://eroscomix.com
Dist(s): **Norton, W. W. & Co., Inc..**

Fantasma Bks., ( 0-9634982; 1-888214 ) 419 Amelia St., Key West, FL 33040 Tel 305-294-5269; Fax: 305-292-7665
E-mail: fantasmabooks@aol.com
Web site: http://www.fantasmabooks.com
Dist(s): **Baker & Taylor Bks.**
**Biblio Distribution.**

Farcountry Pr., ( 0-938314; 1-56037 ) Orders Addr.: P.O. Box 5630, Helena, MT 59604 (SAN 220-0732) Tel 406-443-2842; Fax: 406-443-5480; Toll Free: 800-654-1105; Edit Addr.: 3020 Bozeman Ave., Helena, MT 59601
Web site: http://www.montanamagazine.com; http://www.farcountrypress.com
Dist(s): **Mountain Pr. Publishing Co., Inc..**

Farmar, A. & A. (IRL) ( 1-899047 ) Dist. by **Irish Bks Media.**

†Farrar, Straus & Giroux, ( 0-374 ) Div. of Holtzbrinck Publishers, Orders Addr.: c/o Holtzbrinck Publishers, 16365 James Madison Hwy., Gordonsville, VA 22942 Toll Free Fax: 800-672-2054; Toll Free: 888-330-8477; Edit Addr.: 19 Union Sq., W., New York, NY 10003 (SAN 206-782X) Tel 212-741-6900; Fax: 212-463-0641; Imprints: Hill & Wang (Hil-Wang); North Point Press (N Point Pr); Aerial (AerFSG); Farrar, Straus & Giroux (BYR) (FSGBYR); Mirasol/Libros Juveniles (Mira Libros); Sunburst (SunbFSG)
E-mail: sales@fsgee.com; fsg.editorial@fsgee.com
Web site: http://www.fsbassociates.com/fsg/index.htm
Dist(s): **Continental Bk. Co., Inc.**
**Holtzbrinck Pubs.**
**Lectorum Pubns., Inc.**; CIP.

**Farrar, Straus & Giroux (BYR) Imprint of Farrar, Straus & Giroux**

**Farthest Star Imprint of aBOOKS Distributing**

Father & Son Publishing, ( 0-942407 ) 4909 N. Monroe St., Tallahassee, FL 32303 (SAN 667-0229) Tel 850-562-3927; Fax: 850-562-0916; Toll Free: 800-741-2712 (orders only)
E-mail: lance@fatherson.com
Web site: http://www.fatherson.com.

**Father Tree Pr. Imprint of Warp Graphics, Inc.**

**Fawcett Imprint of Ballantine Bks.**

FayeHouse. Pr. International, ( 0-9655222 ) 1568 St. Margaret's Rd., Annapolis, MD 21401 Tel 443-822-9144; Fax: 410-349-9413 (Call before faxing)
E-mail: Charletfaye@aol.com.

Feather Fables Publishing Company, ( 0-9634122; 1-885527 ) 954 Ryan Ct., Venice, FL 34293 Tel 941-493-7020 (phone/fax)
E-mail: FeatherFables@msn.com
Web site: http://community.webtv.net/FeatherFables.

Fedogan & Bremer, ( 1-878252 ) P.O. Box 6508, Minneapolis, MN 55406 Tel 612-822-2287; Fax: 612-822-2470
E-mail: fedbrem@usinternet.com.

Feedback Theatrebooks & Prospero Pr., ( 0-937657 ) Div. of Feedback Services, Orders Addr.: P.O. Box 220, Brooklin, ME 04616 Tel 207-359-2781; Fax: 207-359-5532
E-mail: feedback@hypernet.com
Web site: http://www.feedbacktheatrebooks.com
Dist(s): **Feedback Services.**

†Feldheim, Philipp Inc., ( 0-87306; 1-58330 ) 202 Airport Executive Pk., Nanuet, NY 10954 (SAN 106-6307) Tel 845-356-2282; Fax: 845-425-1908; Toll Free: 800-237-7149
E-mail: mike613@netvision.net.il
Web site: http://www.feldheim.com
Dist(s): **Libros Sin Fronteras**; CIP.

Feldheim Pubs., 200 Executive Park, Nanuet, NY 10954.

†Feminist Pr. at The City Univ. of New York, ( 0-912670; 0-935312; 1-55861 ) 365 Fifth Ave., New York, NY 10016 (SAN 213-6813) Tel 212-817-7915; Fax: 212-817-2988
E-mail: lglazer@gc.cuny.edu
Web site: http://www.feministpress.org
Dist(s): **Consortium Bk. Sales & Distribution**
**Continental Bk. Co., Inc.**
**Women Ink**; CIP.

Fernandez USA Publishing, ( 968-416; 970-03 ) 203 Argonne Ave., Suite B, PMB 151, Long Beach, CA 90803-1777 Tel 562-901-2370; Fax: 562-901-2372; Toll Free: 800-814-8080
Web site: http://www.fernandezusa.com
Dist(s): **Continental Bk. Co., Inc..**

†Fertig, Howard Inc., ( 0-86527 ) 80 E. 11th St., New York, NY 10003 (SAN 201-4777) Tel 212-982-7922; Fax: 212-982-1099; CIP.

Feryane, SA, Editions (FRA) ( 2-84011 ) Dist. by **Ulverscroft US.**

†Fiction Collective Two, Inc., ( 0-914590; 0-932511; 1-57366 ) Dept. of English, Florida State University, Tallahassee, FL 32306-1580 (SAN 201-4785) Tel 850-644-2260; Fax: 850-644-6808; Imprints: Black Ice Books (Black Ice Bks)
E-mail: fc2@english.fsu.edu
Web site: http://fc2.org
Dist(s): **Northwestern Univ. Pr.**
**SPD-Small Pr. Distribution**; CIP.

Fiction Works, The, ( 1-58124 ) Orders Addr.: 4665 SW Country Club Dr., Lake Tahoe, NV 97333
E-mail: fictionworks@comcast.net
Web site: http://www.fictionworks.com
Dist(s): **Brodart Co..**

Fictionwise, Inc., ( 1-930936; 1-59062 ) 407 Main St., Chatham, NJ 07928 Tel 973-701-6770; Fax: 973-701-6774
E-mail: scott@mindwise.com
Web site: http://www.fictionwise.com.

Fielder Group, ( 0-9639986 ) P.O. Box 510, Benton, KY 42025 Tel 888-255-9248; Fax: 270-362-7130; Toll Free: 888-255-9248
E-mail: barbara@thefieldergroupusa.com
Web site: http://www.thefieldergroupusa.com.

Fiesta Bk. Co., ( 0-88473 ) P.O. Box 490641, Key Biscayne, FL 33149 (SAN 201-8470) Tel 305-858-4843.

**Fiesta Publishing Corporation See Fiesta Bk. Co.**

52 Weeks Publishing Hse., ( 0-9665005 ) 7500 Calderon Ct., Alexandria, VA 22306
E-mail: kenyarc@tidalwave.net.

Filmic Archives, The Cinema Ctr., Botsford, CT 06404 Fax: 203-268-1796; Toll Free: 800-366-1920
Web site: http://www.filmicarchives.com.

Filter Pr., LLC, ( 0-86541; 0-910584 ) P.O. Box 95, Palmer Lake, CO 80133 (SAN 201-484X) Tel 719-481-2420 (phone/fax); Toll Free: 888-570-2663
E-mail: filter.press@prodigy.net.

Fine Communications, ( 1-56731; 1-59308 ) Div. of Fine Creative Media, Inc., 322 Eighth Ave., 15th Flr., New York, NY 10001 Tel 212-595-3500; Fax: 212-595-3779; Imprints: M J F Books (MJF Bks)
E-mail: mjf@mjfbooks; amy@mjfbooks.com
Dist(s): **Sterling Publishing Co., Inc..**

**Fine, Donald I. Imprint of Fine, Donald I. Bks.**

**Fine, Donald I. Imprint of Dutton/Plume**

†Fine, Donald I. Bks., ( 0-917657; 1-55611 ) Div. of Penguin Putnam, Inc., 375 Hudson St., New York, NY 10014-3658 (SAN 656-9749) Tel 212-366-2000; Fax: 212-366-2933; Imprints: Dutton (Dutt); Fine, Donald I. (Don I Fine)
Web site: http://www.booksnbytes.com/authors/fine_donaldi.htm
Dist(s): **Penguin Group (USA) Inc.**; CIP.

Finnie, Bettie Adams, ( 0-9721745 ) .

Fire Mountain Pr., ( 1-929374 ) Orders Addr.: P.O. Box 3851, Hillsboro, OR 97123 Tel 503-846-9057 (phone/fax); 503-219-5643 (phone/fax)
Web site: http://www.firemountainpress.com.

**Firebird Pr. Imprint of Pelican Publishing Co., Inc.**

†Firebrand Bks., ( 0-932379; 1-56341 ) 141 The Commons, Ithaca, NY 14850 (SAN 687-3855) Tel 607-272-0000; Toll Free: 800-663-1766
E-mail: firebrand@firebrandbooks.com
Web site: http://www.firebrandbooks.com
Dist(s): **Client Distribution Services**
**LPC Group**; CIP.

Firefall, ( 0-915090 ) Div. of California Street, 3213 Arundel Ave., Alexandria, VA 22306 Tel 510-549-2461; Fax: 415-673-8249
E-mail: firefallmedia@worldnet.att.net
Web site: http://www.firefallmedia.com
Dist(s): **Professional Media Service Corp..**

Firefly Bks., Ltd., ( 0-920668; 1-55209; 1-895565; 1-896284; 1-55297 ) 4 Daybreak Ln., Westport, CT 06880-2157
E-mail: service@fireflybooks.com
Web site: http://www.fireflybooks.com/
Dist(s): **Lectorum Pubns., Inc..**

**Firelight Publishing See Firelight Publishing, Inc.**

Firelight Publishing, Inc., ( 0-9707206 ) Orders Addr.: P.O. Box 444, Sublimity, OR 97385-0444 Toll Free: 866-347-3544; Edit Addr.: 226 Division St., SW, Sublimity, OR 97385-9637 Tel 503-767-0444; Fax: 503-769-8980; Toll Free: 866-347-3544
E-mail: firepub@teleport.com; orders@firelightpublishing.com; webmaster@firelightpublishing.com; editor@firelightpublishing.com; info@firelightpublishing.com
Web site: http://www.firelightpublishing.com
Dist(s): **Baker & Taylor Bks.**
**Partners/West.**

**Fireside Imprint of Simon & Schuster**

Fireweed Pr., ( 0-914221 ) P.O. Box 75418, Fairbanks, AK 99707 (SAN 287-4911) Tel 907-452-5070 Do not confuse with companies with the same name in Falls Church, VA, Madison, WI, Evergreen, CO
Dist(s): **Todd Communications.**

**First Page Press See Marblehead Publishing**

**FirstPublish,** ( *1-929925; 1-931743* ) 300 Sunport Ln., Orlando, FL 32809 Tel 407-240-1414; Fax: 407-240-1431 Do not confuse with First Publish, Inc in Evanston, IL
E-mail: submisson@firstpublish.com; orders@firstpublish.com; nick@firstpublish.com
Web site: http://www.firstpublish.com
*Dist(s):* **Baker & Taylor Bks..**

**Fisher Enterprises, Inc.,** ( *0-9651935* ) 1071 Fourth Ave., S., No. 303, Edmonds, WA 98020-4143 Tel 206-771-5382; *Imprints:* Prometheus Press (Prmetheus Pr)
E-mail: merlinstwr@aol.com.

**Fithian Pr.,** ( *0-931832; 1-56474* ) Div. of Daniel & Daniel Pubs., Inc., P.O. Box 1525, Santa Barbara, CA 93102 (SAN 211-6103) Tel 805-962-1780; Fax: 805-962-8835; Toll Free: 800-662-8351 (orders only)
E-mail: dandd@danielpublishing.com
Web site: http://www.danielpublishing.com
*Dist(s):* **SCB Distributors.**

**Fitzgerald & LaChapelle Publishing,** ( *0-9666202* ) 852 Elm St., No. 3, Manchester, NH 03101 Tel 603-669-6112; Fax: 603-641-4929.

**Five Star** Imprint of Gale Group

**Five Star Special Edition** Imprint of American Literary Pr., Inc.

**Five Star Trade** Imprint of Gale Group

†**Fjord Pr.,** ( *0-940242* ) P.O. Box 14630, Albuquerque, NM 87191 (SAN 220-3332) Tel 505-856-2550; Fax: 505-856-6855
E-mail: info@jfordpress.com; fjord@halcyon.com; sales@fjordpress.com
Web site: http://www.fjordpress.com; *CIP.*

**Flagg Mountain Pr.,** ( *0-9637154; 1-889455* ) 13 Louisburg Sq., Centerville, MA 02632 Tel 508-790-1351
E-mail: rpease@capecod.net.

**Flamingo (GBR)** ( *0-00; 0-01; 0-586* ) *Dist. by* **Trafalgar.**

**Flammarion et Cie (FRA)** ( *2-08* ) *Dist. by* **Continental Bk.**

**FLF Pr.** Imprint of Florida Literary Foundation

**Floating Bridge Pr.,** ( *0-9647199; 1-930446* ) Orders Addr.: P.O. Box 18814, Seattle, WA 98118-0814 Tel 206-860-0508 (phone/fax, call first to confirm)
E-mail: ppereira5@aol.com; floatingbridgepress@yahoo.com
Web site: http://www.scn.org/arts/floatingbridge
*Dist(s):* **Partners/West.**

**Florida Literary Foundation,** ( *1-877978; 1-891855* ) 1391 Blvd. of the Arts, Sarasota, FL 34236 Tel 941-957-1281; Fax: 941-955-3829; *Imprints:* STARbooks Press (STARbks Pr); FLF Press (FLF Pr)
E-mail: info@FLF.org; info@starbookspress.com
Web site: http://www.FLF.org; http://www.STARbooksPress.com
*Dist(s):* **Alamo Square Distributors**
    **Baker & Taylor Bks.**
    **Bookazine Co., Inc..**

**Floris Bks. (GBR)** ( *0-86315; 0-903540* ) *Dist. by* **SteinerBooks Inc.**

**Floris Bks. (GBR)** ( *0-86315; 0-903540* ) *Dist. by* **Gryphon Hse.**

**Flying Buttress Classics Library The** Imprint of NBM Publishing Co.

†**Focus on the Family Publishing,** ( *0-929608; 1-56179; 1-58997* ) 8605 Explorer Dr., Colorado Springs, CO 80920-1051 (SAN 250-0949) Fax: 719-531-3356; Toll Free: 800-232-6459
E-mail: edresources@fotf.org
Web site: http://www.family.org
*Dist(s):* **Bethany Hse. Pubs.**
    **Christian Bk. Distributors**
    **Honor Bks.**
    **Nelson, Tommy**
    **Tyndale Hse. Pubs.**
    **Vision Video**
    **Zondervan**; *CIP.*

**Fodor's Travel Guides** *See* **Fodor's Travel Pubns.**

**Fodor's Travel Pubns.,** ( *0-609; 0-676; 0-679; 0-7615; 1-878867; 1-4000* ) Div. of Random Hse., Information Group, Orders Addr.: 400 Hahn Rd., Westminster, MD 21157 Tel 410-848-1900; Toll Free: 800-726-0600; Edit Addr.: 280 Park Ave., Tenth Flr., New York, NY 10017 Tel 212-572-8784; Fax: 212-572-2248;
*Imprints:* Compass American Guides, Incorporated (Compass Amrcn)
Web site: http://www.fodors.com
*Dist(s):* **Libros Sin Fronteras**
    **Random Hse., Inc..**

**Folio, Editions (UKR)** ( *5-7150; 966-03* ) *Dist. by* **Distribks Inc.**

**Fondo de Cultura Economica (MEX)** ( *968-16* ) *Dist. by* **Continental Bk.**

**Fondo de Cultura Economica USA,** ( *968-16; 950-557; 956-7083; 9972-663* ) 2293 Verus St., San Diego, CA 92154 Tel 619-429-0827; Fax: 619-429-0455; Toll Free: 800-532-3872
E-mail: sales@fceusa.com; fceusa@fceusa.com
Web site: http://www.fceusa.com
*Dist(s):* **Giron Bks.**
    **Latin American Bk. Source, Inc.**
    **Lectorum Pubns., Inc.**
    **Libros Sin Fronteras**
    **Trucatriche.**

**Fordham Univ. Pr.,** ( *0-8232* ) University Box L, Bronx, NY 10458 (SAN 201-6516) Tel 718-817-4780; Fax: 718-817-4785
E-mail: mnoonan@fordham.edu
Web site: http://www.fordhampress.com
*Dist(s):* **BookMasters, Inc..**

**Forest Bks. (GBR)** ( *0-948259; 0-9509487; 1-85610* ) *Dist. by* **Dufour.**

**Forest of Peace Publishing** Imprint of Ave Maria Pr.

**Forge Bks.** Imprint of Doherty, Tom Assocs., LLC

**ForGen Productions,** ( *1-57479* ) 3654 Barham Blvd., Suite Q301, Los Angeles, CA 90068 Tel 323-851-1225 (phone/fax)
E-mail: forest@blackvillage.come; genevieve@forgen.com; forest@forgen.com
Web site: http://www.forgen.com; http://www.blackvillage.com.

**Fort Frederica Assn., Inc.,** ( *0-930803* ) Rte. 9, Box 286-C, Saint Simons Island, GA 31522 (SAN 677-6299) Tel 912-638-3639.

**Fortress Pr.** Imprint of Augsburg Fortress, Pubs.

**Foul Play** Imprint of Norton, W. W. & Co., Inc.

**Four Ravens** Imprint of Russell Dean & Co.

**Four Seasons Books, Incorporated** *See* **Four Seasons Bks., Inc.**

**Four Seasons Bks., Inc.,** ( *0-9666858; 1-893595* ) P.O. Box 395, Ben Wheeler, TX 75754 Tel 903-963-1442; Fax: 903-963-1525; Toll Free: 800-852-7484
E-mail: hcmarlow@yahoo.com
Web site: http://www.herbmarlow.com.

**Four Seasons Pubs.,** ( *0-9656811; 1-891929; 1-932497* ) Orders Addr.: P.O. Box 51, Titusville, FL 32781 Tel 321-267-9800; Fax: 321-267-8076; Edit Addr.: 4350 N. U.S. Hwy. 1, Cocoa, FL 32927
E-mail: fseasons@bellsouth.net
Web site: http://www.fourseasonspub.net
*Dist(s):* **Baker & Taylor Bks..**

†**Four Walls Eight Windows,** ( *0-941423; 1-56858* ) 39 W. 14th St., No. 503, New York, NY 10011 (SAN 667-6103) Tel 212-206-8965; Fax: 212-206-8799; Toll Free: 800-788-3123 (orders); *Imprints:* No Exit Press (No Exit Pr)
E-mail: edit@4w8w.com
Web site: http://www.4w8w.com
*Dist(s):* **Publishers Group West**; *CIP.*

**4D Publishing,** ( *0-9704141* ) 6245 Bristol Pkwy., No. 373, Culver City, CA 90230 (SAN 253-4010) Tel 310-236-9026; Fax: 818-487-9038
E-mail: divapublishing@aol.com
Web site: http://4divaspublishing.com.

**Fourth Estate** Imprint of HarperTrade

**Fourth Estate, Ltd. (GBR)** ( *0-947795; 1-85702; 1-872180; 1-84115* ) *Dist. by* **Trafalgar.**

**Fourth Lloyd Productions,** ( *0-9717806* ) 512 Old Glebe Point Rd., Burgess, VA 22432 Tel 804-453-6394 (phone/fax).

**FowlkesBooks,** ( *0-9723759* ) P.O. Box 862, Lithonia, GA 30058 Tel 770-982-8980
E-mail: rfowlkes@fowlkesbooks.com
Web site: http://www.Fowlkesbooks.com.

**Fredonia Bks.,** ( *1-58963; 1-4101* ) P.O. Box 025724, Miami, FL 33102-5724 Tel 407-650-2537 (phone/fax)
E-mail: fredoniabooks@cyberhaven.com.

**Free Pr.** Imprint of Simon & Schuster

**Free Reign Pr.,** ( *0-9701554* ) 800 Trenton Rd., No. 385, Langhorne, PA 19047
E-mail: steinslost@mindspring.com
Web site: http://www.freereignpress.com.

**Fremantle Arts Centre Pr. (AUS)** ( *1-86368; 0-909144; 0-949206; 1-920731* ) *Dist. by* **Intl Spec Bk.**

**French & European Pubns., Inc.,** ( *0-320; 0-7859; 0-8288* ) Rockefeller Ctr. Promenade, 610 Fifth Ave., New York, NY 10020-2497 (SAN 206-8109) Tel 212-581-8810; Fax: 212-265-1094
E-mail: frenchbookstore@aol.com
Web site: http://www.frencheuropean.com.

**French, Edward Inc.,** ( *0-9631737* ) 9209 Lakeview Terr., Chatsworth, CA 91311 Tel 818-340-3494.

**French, Samuel Inc.,** ( *0-573* ) 45 W. 25th St., New York, NY 10010-2751 Tel 212-206-8990; Fax: 212-206-1429
E-mail: samuelfrench@earthlink.net
Web site: http://www.samuelfrench.com.

†**Freundlich Bks.,** ( *0-88191* ) Div. of Lawrence Freundlich Pubns., Inc., 333 E. 30th St., Apt. 5-K, New York, NY 10016 (SAN 264-7419) Tel 212-686-4122; *CIP.*

**Friends of the Palace Pr.,** ( *0-941108* ) P.O. Box 9312, Santa Fe, NM 87504 (SAN 217-4332) Tel 505-827-6473.

†**Friends United Pr.,** ( *0-913408; 0-944350* ) 101 Quaker Hill Dr., Richmond, IN 47374 (SAN 201-5803) Tel 765-962-7573; Fax: 765-966-1293; Toll Free: 800-537-8839
E-mail: friendspress@fum.org; barbaram@fum.org
Web site: http://www.fum.org
*Dist(s):* **Independent Pubs. Group**; *CIP.*

†**Friendship Pr.,** ( *0-377* ) Subs. of National Council of the Churches of Christ USA, Orders Addr.: c/o Friendship Pr. Distribution Office, P.O. Box 37844, Cincinnati, OH 45222-0844 (SAN 201-5781) Tel 513-948-8733; Fax: 513-761-3722; Toll Free: 800-889-5733; Edit Addr.: 475 Riverside Dr., Rm. 860, New York, NY 10115 (SAN 201-5773) Tel 212-870-2496; Fax: 212-870-2550 Do not confuse with companies with the same name in Peoria, AZ, Santa Rosa, CA
Web site: http://www.ncccusa.org; *CIP.*

†**Frog in the Well,** ( *0-9603628* ) 420 King St., Santa Rosa, CA 95404-4331 (SAN 207-8295)
*Dist(s):* **Alamo Square Distributors**; *CIP.*

**Frog, Ltd.,** ( *1-883319; 1-58394* ) Div. of North Atlantic Bks., Orders Addr.: P.O. Box 12327, Berkeley, CA 94712 Tel 510-559-8277; Fax: 510-559-8279; Toll Free: 800-337-2665 (orders only)
E-mail: orders@northatlanticbooks.com
Web site: http://www.northatlanticbooks.com
*Dist(s):* **Paladin Pr.**
    **Publishers Group West.**

**From the Hse. of Ideas** Imprint of Marvel Enterprises

**Front Street, Inc.,** ( *1-886910; 1-932425* ) 862 Haywood Rd., Asheville, NC 28806 Tel 828-236-3097; Fax: 828-236-3098
E-mail: contactus@frontstreetbooks.com
Web site: http://www.frontstreetbooks.com
*Dist(s):* **Lectorum Pubns., Inc.**
    **Publishers Group West.**

**Frontier Library, The** Imprint of Jameson Bks., Inc.

**Frost, Anne Publisher** *See* **Frost Publishing**

**Frost Publishing,** ( *0-9614624; 1-888422* ) P.O. Box 909, Vero Beach, FL 32961-0902 (SAN 691-9073) Tel 407-644-9611; Fax: 407-628-3310 Do not confuse with Frost Publishing in Jordanville, NY
E-mail: frostwinn@aol.com.

**Fulcrum, Incorporated** *See* **Fulcrum Publishing**

†**Fulcrum Publishing,** ( *0-912347; 1-55591; 1-56373* ) 16100 Table Mountain Pkwy., Suite 300, Golden, CO 80403 (SAN 200-2825) Tel 303-277-1623; Fax: 303-279-7111; Toll Free Fax: 800-726-7112; Toll Free: 800-992-2908
E-mail: dianneh@fulcrum-books.com
Web site: http://www.fulcrum-books.com; http://www.fulcrum-gardening.com
*Dist(s):* **Lone Pine Publishing**; *CIP.*

**Full Moon Publishing,** ( *0-9666021* ) P.O. Box 408, Schererville, IN 46375 Fax: 219-922-6511; Toll Free: 888-922-1203; 800-247-6553 (orders) Do not confuse with Full Moon Publishing, Norton, MA
E-mail: order@bookmaster.com; fulmoonpub@aol.com
Web site: http://www.fullmoonpub.com/.

**Fusion Pr.** Imprint of Authorlink

**Futech Interactive Products, Inc.,** ( *1-58224; 1-879332* ) Div. of Futech Interactive Products, N16 W23390 Stoneridge Dr., Waukesha, WI 53188 Tel 414-544-2001; Fax: 414-544-2022; Toll Free: 800-541-2205.

**GAM Pubns.,** ( *0-87377* ) P.O. Box 25, Sterling, VA 20167 (SAN 204-6784) Toll Free: 888-689-2243.

**G. P. Putnam's Sons** Imprint of Penguin Group (USA) Inc.

**G. P. Putnam's Sons** Imprint of Penguin Putnam Bks. for Young Readers

**GRM Assocs.,** ( *0-933813; 0-929093* ) 290 W. End Ave., 16A, New York, NY 11111 Tel 212-874-5964; Fax: 212-874-6425; *Imprints:* Taylor Productions (Taylor Prods)
*Dist(s):* **Independent Pubs. Group.**

**Gabbard Enterprises** *See* **Gabbard Pubns.**

**Gabbard Pubns.,** ( *0-9622608* ) 1829 Grubb Rd., Lenoir City, TN 37771 Tel 423-988-0080; Fax: 423-988-5778.

**Galahad Bks. Imprint of BBS Publishing Corp.**

**Galaxy Children's Large Print Imprint of BBC Audiobooks America**

**Galaxy Publishing,** ( *0-9742655* ) 3128 Black Eagle Dr., Antelope, CA 95843
E-mail: rjd@surewest.net
*Dist(s):* **Biblio Distribution.**

**Galde Pr., Inc.,** ( *1-880090; 1-931942* ) Orders Addr.: P.O. Box 460, Lakeville, MN 55044-460 Tel 952-891-5991; Fax: 952-891-6091; Toll Free: 800-777-3454 (orders only)
E-mail: pgalde@galdepress.com
Web site: http://www.galdepress.com.

†**Gale Group,** ( *0-13; 0-7876; 0-8103; 0-936474; 1-57302; 1-878623; 1-59413; 1-59414; 1-59415; 1-4144* ) Subs. of The Thomson Corp., Orders Addr.: P.O. Box 9187, Farmington Hills, MI 48333-9187 Toll Free Fax: 800-414-5043; Toll Free: 800-877-4253; Edit Addr.: 27500 Drake Rd., Farmington Hills, MI 48331-3535 (SAN 213-4373) Tel 248-699-4253; a/o Wheeler Publishing, 295 Kennedy Memorial Dr., Waterville, ME 04901 Toll Free: 800-223-1244; *Imprints:* Macmillan Reference USA (Macmillan Ref); Hall, G. K. & Company (G K Hall & Company); Five Star (Five Star ME); Wheeler Publishing, Incorporated (Wheel); Walker Large Print (Walker Large Pt); Five Star Trade (Five Star Trade)
E-mail: galeord@galegroup.com
Web site: http://www.galegroup.com
*Dist(s):* **netLibrary, Inc.; CIP.**

**Galibren Written Treasures, LLC,** ( *0-9700849* ) P.O. Box 7644, Arlington, VA 22207 (SAN 253-3359) Tel 703-208-0503; Fax: 703-207-3306
E-mail: galibren@aol.com; info@galibren.com
Web site: http://www.galibren.com
*Dist(s):* **Baker & Taylor Bks..**

**Gallery Pr., The (IRL)** ( *0-902996; 0-904011; 1-85235* ) *Dist. by* **Dufour.**

**Gallery Pr.,** ( *0-913622* ) 1 River Rd., Essex, CT 06426 (SAN 207-0936) Tel 860-767-0313
E-mail: bergsma@bergsma.com

**Gallimard, Editions (FRA)** ( *2-07* ) *Dist. by* **Distribks Inc.**

**Games Workshop Imprint of Simon & Schuster**

**Ganley Pub.,** ( *0-932445* ) P.O. Box 149, Buffalo, NY 14226-0149 (SAN 686-7154) Tel 716-839-2415
E-mail: Wpaulg@aol.com.

**Garber Communications, Inc.,** ( *0-8334; 0-89345* ) Orders Addr.: 1 Union Sq., W., Suite 201, New York, NY 10003 (SAN 201-1824) Tel 212-414-2275; Fax: 212-414-2412; *Imprints:* Spiritual Literature Library (Spir Lit Lib)
E-mail: info@arthropress.org
*Dist(s):* **SteinerBooks, Inc..**

†**Garland Publishing, Inc.,** ( *0-8153; 0-8240* ) Member of Taylor & Francis, Inc., 29 W. 35th St., Flr. 10, New York, NY 10001-2299 Tel 212-216-7800; Fax: 212-564-7854; Toll Free: 800-627-6273 (orders)
E-mail: info@garland.com
Web site: http://www.garlandscience.com; http://www.garlandpub.com
*Dist(s):* **Taylor & Francis, Inc.**
**netLibrary, Inc.; CIP.**

**Garland S T P M Press** *See* **Garland Publishing, Inc.**

**Garrett County Pr.,** ( *1-891053* ) 828 Royal St., No. 248, New Orleans, LA 70116 Tel 504-598-4685; Fax: 504-522-0688
E-mail: books@gcpress.com
Web site: http://www.gcpress.com
*Dist(s):* **AK Pr. Distribution**
**Baker & Taylor Bks.**
**Koen Bk. Distributors**
**Last Gasp Eco-Funnies, Inc..**

†**Garrett Educational Corp.,** ( *0-944483; 1-56074* ) Orders Addr.: P.O. Box 1588, Ada, OK 74820 (SAN 169-6955) Tel 580-332-6884; Fax: 580-332-1560; Toll Free: 800-654-9366; Edit Addr.: 130 E. 13th St., Ada, OK 74820 (SAN 243-2722)
E-mail: mail@garrettbooks.com
Web site: http://www.garrettbooks.com; CIP.

**Gaslight Pubns.,** ( *0-934468* ) P.O. Box 1344, Studio City, CA 91614-0344 Tel 818-784-8918
*Dist(s):* **Empire Publishing Service**
**Players Pr., Inc..**

**Gasogene Press, Limited** *See* **Wessex Pr.**

**Gateway Editions Imprint of Regnery Publishing, Inc., An Eagle Publishing Co.**

†**Gaunt, Inc.,** ( *0-912004; 1-56169* ) 3011 Gulf Dr., Holmes Beach, FL 34217-2199 (SAN 202-9413) Tel 941-778-5211; Fax: 941-778-5252; Toll Free: 800-942-8683 (US & Canada)
E-mail: info@gaunt.com; sales@gaunt.com
Web site: http://www.gaunt.com; CIP.

**Gaunt, William W. & Sons, Incorporated** *See* **Gaunt, Inc.**

**Gauntlet, Inc.,** ( *0-9629659; 1-887368* ) 5307 Arroyo St., Colorado Springs, CO 80922 Tel 719-591-5566; Fax: 719-591-6676
E-mail: info@gauntletpress.com; gauntlet66@aol.com
Web site: http://www.gauntletpress.com
*Dist(s):* **Baker & Taylor Bks.**
**Independent Pubs. Group.**

**Gauntlett Pr.,** ( *0-9655893* ) Div. of WEB Enterprises, P.O. Box 209, Maryland Line, MD 21105-0209 Tel 717-993-3501; Fax: 717-993-5422
E-mail: webent@NFDC.NET
*Dist(s):* **New Leaf Distributing Co., Inc..**

†**Gay Sunshine Pr., Inc.,** ( *0-917342; 0-940567* ) P.O. Box 410690, San Francisco, CA 94141 (SAN 208-0915) Tel 415-626-1935; Fax: 415-626-1802
Web site: http://www.gaysunshine.com
*Dist(s):* **Bookazine Co., Inc.**
**Bookpeople**
**Koen Bk. Distributors; CIP.**

**Geckostufs, Incorporated** *See* **Words & Pictures Publishing, Inc.**

**Gefen Bks.,** ( *0-86343; 965-229* ) 12 New St., Hewlett, NY 11557-2012 Tel 516-295-2805; Fax: 516-295-2739; Toll Free: 800-477-5257
E-mail: gefenny@gefenpublishing.com
Web site: http://www.israelbooks.com

**Gefen Publishing Hse., Ltd (ISR)** ( *965-229* ) *Dist. by* **Gefen Bks.**

**Genesis Pr., Inc.,** ( *1-885478; 1-58571* ) 315 Third Ave., N., Columbus, MS 39701-3917 Tel 662-329-9927; Fax: 662-329-9399; *Imprints:* Love Spectrum (Love Spec); Indigo (Indigo MS) Do not confuse with Genesis Pr., Inc. in Honleah Gardens, FL
E-mail: books@genesis-press.com
Web site: http://www.genesis-press.com
*Dist(s):* **BookWorld Services, Inc..**

**GeoPlaneta, Editorial, S. A. (ESP)** ( *84-08; 84-320* ) *Dist. by* **Continental Bk.**

**GeoPlaneta, Editorial, S. A. (ESP)** ( *84-08; 84-320* ) *Dist. by* **Lectorum Pubns.**

**GeoPlaneta, Editorial, S. A. (ESP)** ( *84-08; 84-320* ) *Dist. by* **Planeta.**

**Georgia Literary Assn.,** ( *0-9668030* ) Div. of Porter & Prince Corp., Orders Addr.: P.O. Box 140544, Staten Island, NY 10314-0544; Edit Addr.: 75 Saint Mark's Pl., Staten Island, NY 10301 Tel 718-556-9410; Fax: 718-816-4092
E-mail: danforthpr@aol.com; georgialit@aol.com
Web site: http://www.GeorgiaLit.com
*Dist(s):* **Baker & Taylor Bks.**
**Bookazine Co., Inc..**

**Geringer, Laura Bk. Imprint of HarperCollins Children's Bk. Group**

**Get'n Even,** ( *1-928727* ) Orders Addr.: P.O. Box 55, Clark, SD 57225 Tel 801-544-9855 (orders); Fax: 801-531-3001; 605-532-5465; Edit Addr.: 410 SE Second Ave., Clark, SD 57225
E-mail: tnickels@worldnet.att.net.

**Ghost Town Pubns.,** ( *0-933818* ) P.O. Drawer 5998, Carmel, CA 93921 (SAN 209-4401)
E-mail: ghtownpub@aol.com
Web site: http://www.ghosttown.pub.com.

**Gill & MacMillan, Ltd. (IRL)** ( *0-7171* ) *Dist. by* **Irish Bks Media.**

**Giron Bks.,** ( *0-9741393* ) 2130 W. 21st. St., Chicago, IL 60608-2608 Tel 773-847-3000; Fax: 773-847-9197; Toll Free: 800-405-4276
E-mail: isbn_san@gironbooks.com
Web site: http://www.gironbooks.com.

**Glad Day Bks.,** ( *1-930180* ) Orders Addr.: P.O. Box 112, Thetford, VT 05074 Toll Free: 888-874-6904; Edit Addr.: Nichols Rd. Rte. 113, Thetford, VT 05074; P.O. Box 699, Enfield, VT 05748
E-mail: anarkiss@mindspring.com
*Dist(s):* **Enfield Publishing & Distribution Co., Inc..**

**GLAS Pubs. (RUS)** *Dist. by* **Northwestern U Pr.**

**GLB Pubs.,** ( *1-879194* ) Orders Addr.: P.O. Box 78212, San Francisco, CA 94107 Tel 415-621-8307; Fax: 415-621-8037; Edit Addr.: 1028 Howard St., No. 503, San Francisco, CA 94103 Toll Free: 888-621-9424
E-mail: warner@glbpubs.com; GLBpubs@mindspring.com
Web site: http://www.glbpubs.com
*Dist(s):* **Alamo Square Distributors**
**Bookazine Co., Inc..**

**Glenbridge Publishing, Ltd.,** ( *0-944435* ) 19923 E. Long Ave., Aurora, CO 80016 (SAN 243-5403) Tel 720-870-8381; Fax: 720-870-5598; Toll Free: 800-986-4135 (orders only)
E-mail: glenbr@eazy.net
Web site: http://www.glenbridgepublishing.com
*Dist(s):* **Baker & Taylor Bks..**

**Glencannon Pr.,** ( *0-9637586; 1-889901* ) Orders Addr.: P.O. Box 633, Benicia, CA 94510; *Imprints:* Palo Alto Books (Palo Alto)
E-mail: captjaff@pacbell.net
Web site: http://www.glencannon.com
*Dist(s):* **Baker & Taylor Bks.**
**Quality Bks., Inc..**

†**Glencoe/McGraw-Hill,** ( *0-02; 0-07* ) Div. of The McGraw-Hill Education Group, 8787 Orion Pl., Columbus, OH 43240-4027 Toll Free: 800-334-7344
E-mail: customer.service@mcgraw-hill.com
Web site: http://www.glencoe.com
*Dist(s):* **Libros Sin Fronteras; CIP.**

**Glenhaven Pr.,** ( *0-9637265; 0-9741279* ) 24871 Pylos Way, Mission Viejo, CA 92691 Tel 949-770-1486; Fax: 909-277-2849
E-mail: glenhavn@thevision.net; jacki@hydrasystems.com
*Dist(s):* **J&J Bk. Sales.**

**Global Academic Publishing,** ( *0-9633277; 1-883058; 1-58684* ) Institute of Global Cultural Studies, Binghamton Univ., Binghamton, NY 13902-6000 Tel 607-777-2745 (contact Barnes & Noble for orders); 607-777-4495; Fax: 607-777-2642; 607-777-6132
*Dist(s):* **Hesteria Records & Publishing Co..**

**Global City Pr.,** ( *0-9641292; 1-887369* ) Rifkind Ctr., City Coll. of NY, 138th St. & Convent Ave., New York, NY 10031 Tel 212-645-3865; Fax: 212-633-1236.

**Global Learning Systems, LLC,** ( *0-9679394* ) 1314 E. Las Olas Blvd., No. 15, Fort Lauderdale, FL 33301 Tel 954-522-2696; Fax: 954-522-7092
E-mail: keithob@bellsouth.net.

**Global Publications (S S I P S)** *See* **Global Academic Publishing**

**Globe Fearon Educational Publishing,** ( *0-13; 0-8224; 0-8359; 0-87065; 0-88102; 0-912925; 0-915510; 1-55555; 1-55675* ) Div. of Pearson Education Corporate Communications, Orders Addr.: 4350 Equity Dr., P.O. Box 2649, Columbus, OH 43216-2649 Toll Free Fax: 800-393-3156; Toll Free: 800-321-3106 (customer service); 800-848-9500; Edit Addr.: One Lake St., Upper Saddle River, NJ 07458
Web site: http://www.globefearon.com/
*Dist(s):* **Cambridge Bk. Co.**
**IFSTA**

†**Globe Pequot Pr., The,** ( *0-7627; 0-87106; 0-88742; 0-914788; 0-933469; 0-934802; 0-941130; 1-56440; 1-57034; 1-58574; 1-59228* ) Div. of Morris Communications Corp., Orders Addr.: P.O. Box 480, Guilford, CT 06437-0480 (SAN 201-9892) Toll Free Fax: 800-820-2329 (in Connecticut); Toll Free: 800-243-0495 (24 hours); Edit Addr.: 246 Goose Ln., Guilford, CT 06437 Tel 203-458-4500; Fax: 203-458-4604; *Imprints:* Lyons Press (Lyons); Falcon (Fal); Falcon Guides (Fal-Guides)
E-mail: info@globe-pequot.com; adessaint@globe-pequot.com
Web site: http://www.globe-pequot.com
*Dist(s):* **Paladin Pr.; CIP.**

**Gnomon Pr.,** ( *0-917788* ) P.O. Box 475, Frankfort, KY 40602-0475 (SAN 209-0104) Tel 502-223-1858 (phone/fax)
E-mail: jgnomon@aol.com
*Dist(s):* **SPD-Small Pr. Distribution.**

**Goblinshead (GBR)** ( *1-899874* ) *Dist. by* **Dufour.**

†**Godine, David R. Pub.,** ( *0-87923; 1-56792; 1-57423* ) Orders Addr.: P.O. Box 450, Jaffrey, NH 03452 Tel 603-532-4100; Fax: 603-532-5940; Toll Free Fax: 800-226-0934; Toll Free: 800-344-4771; Edit Addr.: 9 Hamilton Pl., Boston, MA 02108-4715 (SAN 213-4381) Tel 617-451-9600; Fax: 617-350-0250; *Imprints:* Hoc Volo (Hoc Volo); Non Pareil Books (Non Pareil Bk); Black Sparrow Press (Blk Spar Pr)
E-mail: info@godine.com; order@godine.com
Web site: http://www.godine.com
*Dist(s):* **Baker & Taylor International; CIP.**

**Gold Leaf Pr.,** ( *1-886769* ) Orders Addr.: 33 Crocker Blvd., Suite 33B-1, Mount Clemens, MI 48043 Tel 586-954-2921; Fax: 586-954-1085; Toll Free: 800-838-8854 Do not confuse with companies with the same name in Seattle, WA, Starke FL
E-mail: rebecca@goldleafpress.com
*Dist(s):* **QW, Inc..**

**Gold Star Pr.,** ( *0-915153* ) P.O. Box 433, New London, NC 28127 (SAN 289-9337) Tel 704-983-2287; Fax: 704-485-4799.

**Golden Bks. Imprint of Random Hse. Children's Bks.**

Names

**Golden Bks. Adult Publishing Group** Imprint of St. Martin's Pr.

**Golden Eagle Pr.,** ( *1-891940* ) P.O. Box 80187, Bakersfield, CA 93380 Tel 661-327-4290; Fax: 661-393-6157
E-mail: mapp@goldeneaglepress.com
Web site: http://www.goldeneaglepress.com.

**Golden Era Bks.,** ( *0-9706969* ) Orders Addr.: P.O. Box 5603, San Mateo, CA 94402-0603 (SAN 253-9616) Tel 650-578-8373; Fax: 650-578-8373; Edit Addr.: 1414 Bel Aire Rd., San Mateo, CA 94402 Tel 650-578-8373
E-mail: mrwill@goldenerabooks.com
Web site: http://www.goldenerabooks.com
*Dist(s):* **Baker & Taylor Bks.**
**New Leaf Distributing Co., Inc.**
**Quality Bks., Inc..**

**Golden Grove Publishing,** ( *0-9643010* ) P.O. Box 1637, Linden, NJ 07036
E-mail: info@goldengrove.com
Web site: http://www.goldengrove.com.

**Golden Gryphon Pr.,** ( *0-9655901; 1-930846* ) 3002 Perkins Rd., Urbana, IL 61802 (SAN 299-1829) Tel 217-384-4205 (phone/fax); Fax: 217-352-9748
E-mail: Gryphon@goldengryphon.com
Web site: http://www.goldengryphon.com
*Dist(s):* **Independent Pubs. Group.**

**Golden Guides from Saint Martin's Pr.** Imprint of St. Martin's Pr.

**Goldengrove Bks.** Imprint of Derrynane Pr.

**GoldenIsle Pubs., Inc.,** ( *0-9666721* ) R.R. 2, Box 560, Golden Isle Pkwy., N., Eastman, GA 31023 Tel 478-374-9455; Fax: 478-374-9720; Toll Free: 877-282-7586; 2395 Hawkinsville Hwy., Eastman, GA 31023
E-mail: jackjones@progressivetel.com
Web site: http://www.hom.net/~publish
*Dist(s):* **Baker & Taylor Bks..**

**Gollancz, Victor (GBR)** ( *0-575* ) Dist. by **Trafalgar.**

**Gollehon Pr.,** ( *0-914839* ) 6157 28th St., SE, Grand Rapids, MI 49546 (SAN 289-2170) Tel 616-949-3515 ; Fax: 616-949-8674
Web site: http://www.gollehonbooks.com.

**Gomer Pr. (GBR)** ( *0-85088; 0-86383; 1-85902* ) Dist. by **St Mut.**

†**Good Bks.,** ( *0-934672; 1-56148* ) Subs. of Good Enterprises, Ltd., Orders Addr.: P.O. Box 419, Intercourse, PA 17534 (SAN 693-9597) Tel 717-768-7171; Fax: 717-768-3433; Toll Free: 800-762-7171; Edit Addr.: 3510 Old Philadelphia Pike, Intercourse, PA 17534-0419
E-mail: custserv@goodbks.com;
mgood@goodbks.com
Web site: http://www.goodbks.com
*Dist(s):* **Baker & Taylor Bks.**
**Brodart Co.**
**Distributors, The**
**FaithWorks;** CIP.

**Goodfellow Catalog Pr., Inc.,** ( *0-936016* ) P.O. Box 4520, Berkeley, CA 94704 (SAN 206-4499) Tel 510-845-2062; Fax: 510-934-7650; *Imprints:* Liplop Press (Liplop)
E-mail: baysport@aol.com.

**Goodfellow Pr., Inc.,** ( *0-9639882; 1-891761* ) 9502 179th Pl., NE, No. 1, Redmond, WA 98052 Tel 425-881-7699; Fax: 425-881-8863
E-mail: info@goodfellowpress.com
*Dist(s):* **Partners Pubs. Group, Inc.**
**Partners/West.**

**Gothman Bks.,** ( *1-59240* ) Sub. of Penguin Putnam. Inc., 375 Hudson St., New York, NY 10014 Tel 212-366-2000; Fax: 212-366-2262; Toll Free: 800-631-8571
Web site: http://www.penguinputnam.com.

**Gramercy** Imprint of Random Hse. Value Publishing

**Gramercy Bks.,** ( *0-517* ) Div. of Random Hse. Value Publishing, 201 E. 50th St., New York, NY 10022 Tel 212-751-2600; Toll Free: 800-726-0600
*Dist(s):* **Empire Publishing Service.**

**Granite Publishing, LLC,** ( *0-926524; 0-9632310; 1-893183* ) P.O. Box 1429, Columbus, NC 28722 Tel 828-894-3088; Fax: 828-894-8454; Toll Free: 800-366-0264; *Imprints:* Wild Flower Press (Wild Flower Pr) Do not confuse with companies with same or similar names in Madison, WI, Orem, UT
E-mail: brian@5thworld.com
Web site: http://www.5thworld.com
*Dist(s):* **Baker & Taylor Bks.**
**Bookpeople**
**New Leaf Distributing Co., Inc..**

**Grant, Donald M. Pub., Inc.,** ( *0-937986; 1-880418* ) Orders Addr.: P.O. Box 187, Hampton Falls, NH 03844 (SAN 281-7535) Tel 603-778-7191 (phone/fax) ; Edit Addr.: 19 Surrey Ln.., Hampton Falls, NH 03844
E-mail: mail@grantbooks.com
Web site: http://www.grantbooks.com
*Dist(s):* **Baker & Taylor Bks.**
**Bookazine Co., Inc.**
**Dreamhaven Bks..**

**Granta,** ( *0-9645611; 1-86207; 1-929001* ) 1755 Broadway, 5th Flr., New York, NY 10019-3780 Tel 212-246-1313; Fax: 212-586-8003
E-mail: jhederman@nybooks.com;
granta@nybooks.com
Web site: http://www.nybooks.com
*Dist(s):* **Midpoint Trade Bks., Inc.**
**Publishers Group West.**

**Granta Bks. (GBR)** ( *0-14; 1-86207* ) Dist. by **Publishers Group.**

**Granta U. S. A., Limited** See **Granta**

**Graphic Arts Ctr. Publishing Co.,** ( *0-88240; 0-912856; 0-932575; 1-55868* ) Orders Addr.: P.O. Box 10306, Portland, OR 97296-0306 (SAN 201-6338) Tel 503-226-2402; Fax: 503-223-1410 (executive & editorial); Toll Free Fax: 800-355-9685 (sales office); Toll Free: 800-452-3032; *Imprints:* Alaska Northwest Books (Alaska NW Bks); West Winds Press (West Winds Pr)
E-mail: sales@gacpc.com
Web site: http://www.gacpc.com.

**Graphitti Designs,** ( *0-936211* ) 8045 E. Crystal Dr., Anaheim, CA 92807-2523 (SAN 697-1105) Tel 714-632-3356; Fax: 714-632-3403.

†**Graywolf Pr.,** ( *0-915308; 1-55597* ) 2402 University Ave., Suite 203, Saint Paul, MN 55114 (SAN 207-1665) Tel 651-641-0077; Fax: 651-641-0036
E-mail: wolves@graywolfpress.org
Web site: http://www.graywolfpress.org
*Dist(s):* **Farrar, Straus & Giroux**
**SPD-Small Pr. Distribution;** CIP.

**Great American Audio Corp.,** ( *1-55569; 0-7413* ) 33 Portman Rd., New Rochelle, NY 10801 (SAN 699-7198) Tel 914-576-7660; Fax: 914-576-7584; Toll Free: 800-675-2834
E-mail: inquiry@gaaudio.com
Web site: http://www.greatamericanaudio.com.

**Great Lakes Bks.,** ( *0-9606400* ) 5946 Alan Dr., No. 43, Brighton, MI 48116-8503 (SAN 222-9994) Tel 810-227-7471
*Dist(s):* **Wilderness Adventure Bks..**

**Great Lakes Publishing Co.,** ( *0-9620016* ) Orders Addr.: P.O. Box 128, Emmett, MI 48022 (SAN 247-428X); Edit Addr.: 3079 Washington St., Emmett, MI 48022 (SAN 247-4298) Tel 810-384-6416; Fax: 810-384-6005.

**Great Marsh Pr.,** ( *1-928863* ) Orders Addr.: P.O. Box 2144, New York, NY 10021 Tel 212-946-4522; *Imprints:* Aventura Books (Aventura Bks)
E-mail: mscrescent@aol.com
Web site: http://www.greatmarshpress.com.

**GreatUNpublished.com,** ( *1-58898; 1-59456* ) 5341 Dorchester Rd., Suite 16, North Charleston, SC 29418-5618 Tel 843-579-0000; Fax: 843-577-7506
E-mail: editorsdesk@greatunpublished.com
Web site: http://www.greatunpublished.com.

**Green Boat Pr.,** ( *0-9671411* ) P.O. Box 135, Manlius, NY 13104
E-mail: scrivneoir@aol.com
Web site: http://www.greenboatpress.com.

**Green Hill Publishers** See **Jameson Bks., Inc.**

**Green, Hubert,** ( *0-9720272* ) Orders Addr.: P.O. Box 271, Lynchburg, SC 29080 Tel 803-437-2213 (phone/fax); Edit Addr.: 40 Kingdom Ln.., Lynchburg, SC 29080.

**Green Integer,** ( *1-892295; 1-931243* ) Div. of Contemporary Arts Educational Project, Inc., 6026 Wilshire Blvd., Los Angeles, CA 90036 Tel 323-875-1115; 213 857 1115; Fax: 323-857-0143
E-mail: info@greeninteger.com
Web site: http://www.greeninteger.com
*Dist(s):* **Consortium Bk. Sales & Distribution**
**SPD-Small Pr. Distribution.**

**Green Mansion Pr. LLC,** ( *0-9714612; 0-9746457* ) 501 E. 79th St., Suite 16A, New York, NY 10021-0773 (SAN 254-2684) Tel 212-396-2667; Fax: 212-937-4685
E-mail: info@greenmansionpress.com
Web site: http://www.greenmansionpress.com
*Dist(s):* **Baker & Taylor Bks.**
**Ingram Bk. Co.**
**Midpoint Trade Bks., Inc..**

**Greene, J. R.,** ( *0-9609404; 1-884132* ) 26 Bearsden Rd., Athol, MA 01331 (SAN 262-6845) Tel 978-249-0156
E-mail: jrgo1331@webtv.net.

†**Greenfield Review Literary Ctr., Inc.,** ( *0-87886; 0-912678* ) 2 Middle Grove Rd., P.O. Box 308, Greenfield Center, NY 12833 (SAN 203-4506) Tel 518-583-1440; Fax: 518-583-9741; *Imprints:* Greenfield Review Press (Greenfld Rev Pr)
Web site: http://www.nativeauthors.com
*Dist(s):* **SPD-Small Pr. Distribution;** CIP.

**Greenfield Review Pr.** Imprint of Greenfield Review Literary Ctr., Inc.

**Greenleaf Pr.,** ( *1-882514* ) 3761 Hwy. 109 N., Lebanon, TN 37087 (SAN 297-8555) Tel 615-449-1617; Fax: 615-449-4018; Toll Free: 800-311-1508 Do not confuse with Greenleaf Pr., Breckenridge, CO
E-mail: info@greenleafpress.com
Web site: http://www.greenleafpress.com.

**Greenwood Pr.** Imprint of Greenwood Publishing Group, Inc.

**Greenwood Press, Incorporated** See **Greenwood Publishing Group, Inc.**

†**Greenwood Publishing Group, Inc.,** ( *0-275; 0-313; 0-8371; 0-86569; 0-89789; 0-89930; 1-56720* ) Orders Addr.: P.O. Box 5007, Westport, CT 06881-5007 (SAN 213-2028) Fax: 203-750-9790 (customer service and sales); Toll Free: 800-225-5800 (orders only); Edit Addr.: 88 Post Rd., W., Westport, CT 06881-5007 Tel 203-226-3571; Fax: 203-222-1502; 203-226-2540; *Imprints:* Greenwood Press (Greenwood Pr); Praeger Publishers (Praeger Pubs) Do not confuse with Greenwood Publishing in Glenview, IL
E-mail: customer-service@greenwood.com;
sales@greenwood.com
Web site: http://www.greenwood.com
*Dist(s):* **Libraries Unlimited, Inc.**
**National Bk. Network**
**netLibrary, Inc.;** CIP.

**Grenoble Books** See **Moonbeam Pubns., Inc.**

**Gresham Bks. (GBR)** Dist. by **St Mut.**

**Grey Castle Pr.,** ( *0-942545; 1-55905* ) Pocket Knife Sq., Lakeville, CT 06039 (SAN 667-383X) Tel 860-435-2518; Fax: 860-435-8093.

**Grey Matter Productions,** ( *0-9662157* ) 705 E. 72nd St., Kansas City, MO 64131 Tel 816-333-0814
E-mail: Menglish@juno.com.

**GreyCore Pr.,** ( *0-9671851; 0-9742074* ) 2646 New Prospect Rd., Pine Bush, NY 12566 Tel 845-744-5081 ; Fax: 845-744-8081
E-mail: joan123@frontiernet.net
*Dist(s):* **Client Distribution Services.**

**Greyfalcon Hse.,** ( *0-914870* ) 124 Waverly Pl., New York, NY 10011 (SAN 207-0723) Tel 212-777-9042; Fax: 212-691-8661
E-mail: anngrifalconi@aol.com.

**Griffin Skye Co.,** 1945 P St., Eureka, CA 95501 Tel 707-444-8768; Fax: 707-444-6600
E-mail: griffins@northcoast.com.

**Griffon Hse. Pubns.,** ( *0-918680; 1-932107* ) Orders Addr.: P.O. Box 468, Smyrna, DE 19977 (SAN 211-6685) Tel 302-659-1791 (phone/fax); Edit Addr.: 23 Village Dr., Smyrna, DE 19977
E-mail: griffonhse@aol.com.

**Grijalbo, Editorial (MEX)** ( *968-419; 970-05* ) Dist. by **AIMS Intl.**

**Grijalbo Mondadori, S.A.-Junior (ESP)** ( *84-253; 84-397; 84-7419; 84-478; 84-7423* ) Dist. by **Continental Bk.**

**Griot Audio** Imprint of Recorded Bks., LLC

**Grolier Publishing** See **Scholastic Library Publishing**

**Grosset & Dunlap** Imprint of Penguin Group (USA) Inc.

**Grosset & Dunlap** Imprint of Penguin Putnam Bks. for Young Readers

**Groundwood Bks. (CAN)** ( *0-88899* ) Dist. by **Publishers Group.**

**Grove Pr.** Imprint of Grove/Atlantic, Inc.

†**Grove/Atlantic, Inc.,** ( *0-8021; 0-87113; 1-55584* ) 841 Broadway, 4th Flr., New York, NY 10003-4793 (SAN 201-4890) Tel 212-614-7850; Fax: 212-614-7886; Toll Free: 800-521-0178; *Imprints:* Grove Press (Grove); Atlantic Monthly Press (Atlntc Mnthly)
*Dist(s):* **Continental Bk. Co., Inc.**
**Publishers Group West;** CIP.

**Grub Street (GBR)** ( *0-948817; 1-898697; 1-902304* ) Dist. by **Casemate Pubs.**

**Grupo Anaya, S.A. (ESP)** ( *84-207; 84-667* ) Dist. by **Continental Bk.**

**Gryphon Bks.,** ( *0-936071; 1-58250* ) Orders Addr.: P.O. Box 209, Brooklyn, NY 11228 (SAN 697-0834) Tel 718-646-6126
E-mail: GryphonBooks@worldnet.att.net
Web site: http://www.gryphonbooks.com.

*Names*

**Gryphon Hse., Inc.,** ( 0-87659; 1-58904 ) Orders Addr.: P.O. Box 207, Beltsville, MD 20704-0207 (SAN 169-3190) Tel 301-595-9500; Fax: 301-595-0051; Toll Free: 800-638-0928; Edit Addr.: 10726 Tucker St., Beltsville, MD 20705
E-mail: info@ghbooks.com
Web site: http://www.gryphonhouse.com
*Dist(s):* **Consortium Bk. Sales & Distribution.**

**Gryphon Publications** *See* **Gryphon Bks.**

**Guernica Editions, Inc.,** ( 0-919349; 0-920717; 1-55071; 2-89135 ) P.O. Box 117, Toronto, ON M5S 2S6 Tel 416-658-9888; Fax: 416-657-8885; Toll Free: 800-869-7553; 2250 Military Rd., Tonawanda, NY 14150-6000 Tel 716-693-2768 (orders only); Fax: 716-692-7479 (orders only); Toll Free Fax: 800-221-9985; Toll Free: 800-565-9523
E-mail: guernicaeditions@cs.com
Web site: http://www.guernicaeditions.com
*Dist(s):* **Independent Pubs. Group**
**Paul & Co. Pubs. Consortium, Inc..**

**Guild Press of Indiana, Incorporated** *See* **Emmis Bks.**

**Gulliver Bks. Imprint of Harcourt Children's Bks.**

**Gunsmoke Imprint of BBC Audiobooks America**

**Gutsoon! Entertainment, Inc.,** ( 0-9725037; 1-932454 ) 361 Van Ness Way, Suite 302, Torrance, CA 90501 Tel 310-328-3400; Fax: 310-618-2255; Toll Free: 877-488-7666; *Imprints:* Raijin Comics Collection (Raijin Comics)
E-mail: palmieri@gutsoon.com
Web site: http://www.gutsoon.com;
www.raijincomics.com
*Dist(s):* **Cold Cut Comics Distribution**
**Diamond Distributors, Inc.**
**Digital Manga Distribution**
**FM International.**

**H&M Enterprises,** ( 0-9613184 ) R.D. 6, Box 6009, East Stroudsburg, PA 18301-9108 (SAN 295-9569) Tel 717-223-0674 Do not confuse with companies with the same name in Stone Mountain, GA, Alton, IL.

**Hachai Publications, Incorporated** *See* **Hachai Publishing**

**Hachai Publishing,** ( 0-922613; 1-929628 ) 156 Chester Ave., Brooklyn, NY 11218 (SAN 251-3749) Tel 718-633-0100; Fax: 718-633-0103; Toll Free: 800-504-2242
E-mail: info@hachai.com
Web site: http://www.hachai.com
*Dist(s):* **Kerem Publishing.**

**Hachette Groupe Livre (FRA)** ( 2-01 ) Dist. by **Continental Bk.**

†**Hackett Publishing Co., Inc.,** ( 0-87220; 0-915144; 0-915145 ) Orders Addr.: P.O. Box 44937, Indianapolis, IN 46244-0937 (SAN 201-6044) Tel 317-635-9250; Fax: 317-635-9292; Toll Free Fax: 800-783-9213
E-mail: customer@hackettpublishing.com
Web site: http://www.hackettpublishing.com; CIP.

†**Hafner Pr.,** ( 0-02 ) Orders Addr.: c/o Macmillan Publishing Co., Inc., 100 Front St., Box 500, Riverside, NJ 08075-7500 (SAN 202-5582)
*Dist(s):* **Libros Sin Fronteras**; CIP.

**Hageman, Vee** *See* **Antelope Publishing**

**Hailey-Grey Bks.,** ( 0-9729480 ) 16781 Chagrin Blvd., No. 103, Shaker Heights, OH 44120 (SAN 255-2434)
Web site: http://www.hailey-grey-books.com
*Dist(s):* **Biblio Distribution.**

**Halcyon Pr.,** ( 0-941970 ) 18-05 215 St., Flushing, NY 11360 (SAN 238-244X) Tel 212-631-9640 Do not confuse with companies with same or similar name in Hendersonville, NC, Dallas, TX, Houston, TX.

**Hale, Robert Ltd. (GBR)** ( 0-7090; 0-7198 ) Dist. by **Trafalgar.**

**Haley's,** ( 0-9626308; 1-884540 ) Orders Addr.: P.O. Box 248, Athol, MA 01331 Tel 978-249-9400 (phone/fax); Toll Free: 800-215-8805 (phone/fax); Edit Addr.: 488 S. Main St., Athol, MA 01331
E-mail: haleyathol@aol.com
*Dist(s):* **Baker & Taylor Bks.**
**Follett Library Resources.**

**Hall Closet Bk. Co.,** ( 1-888348 ) Orders Addr.: P.O. Box 19335, Seattle, WA 98109 Tel 206-286-8915; Fax: 206-286-0656; Toll Free: 800-895-8915; Edit Addr.: 2005 13th Ave., W., No. 201, Seattle, WA 98119
E-mail: closetbk@aol.com

**Hall, G. K. & Co. Imprint of Gale Group**

**Halvorson Assocs.,** P.O. Box 518, Essex, CT 06426 (SAN 694-2369) Tel 860-767-7380 (phone/fax)
E-mail: w3dof@gateway.net

**Halvorson Farms of Wisconsin, Inc.,** ( 0-9664894 ) N3430 County Rd. O, Hager City, WI 54014 Tel 715-792-5177.

**Hamilton, Hamish Imprint of Viking Penguin**

**Hammarberg, Roger ,** ( 0-9671005 ) 1086 Udall Rd., Bay Shore, NY 11706-2714 Tel 516-586-8933.

**Hammond, Incorporated** *See* **Hammond World Atlas Corp.**

†**Hammond World Atlas Corp.,** ( 0-7230; 0-8437 ) Subs. of Langenscheidt Pubs., Inc., 95 Progress St., Union, NJ 07083 (SAN 202-2702) Tel 908-206-1300; Fax: 908-206-1104
E-mail: rstrung@americanmap.com
Web site: http://www.Hammondmap.com; CIP.

**Hampton Pr., Inc.,** ( 1-57273; 1-881303 ) 23 Broadway, Cresskill, NJ 07626 Tel 201-894-1686; Fax: 201-894-8732; Toll Free: 800-894-8955
E-mail: HamptonPr1@aol.com
Web site: http://www.hamptonpress.com
*Dist(s):* **Baker & Taylor Bks.**
**Blackwell North America.**

**Hampton Roads Publishing Co., Inc.,** ( 0-9624375; 1-57174; 1-878901 ) 1125 Stoney Ridge Rd., Charlottesville, VA 22902 (SAN 299-8874) Tel 434-296-2772; Fax: 434-296-1441; Toll Free Fax: 800-766-9042; Toll Free: 800-766-8009
E-mail: hrpc@hrpub.com; editorial@hrpub.com
Web site: http://www.hrpub.com
*Dist(s):* **Baker & Taylor Bks.**
**Book Warehouse**
**Bookazine Co., Inc.**
**Bookmen, Inc.**
**Bookpeople**
**Booksource, The**
**Brodart Co.**
**Christian Distribtuion Services, Inc.**
**DeVorss & Co.**
**Ingram Bk. Co.**
**Integral Yoga Pubns.**
**Koen Bk. Distributors**
**Levy Home Entertainment**
**Midwest Library Service**
**New Leaf Distributing Co., Inc.**
**Nutri-Bks. Corp.**
**Partners Pubs. Group, Inc.**
**Partners/West**
**Quality Bks., Inc.**
**Treasure Chest Bks.**
**Unique Bks., Inc.**
**Vision Distributors.**

**Handsel Bks. Imprint of Other Pr., LLC**

†**Hanging Loose Pr.,** ( 0-914610; 1-882413; 1-931236 ) 231 Wyckoff St., Brooklyn, NY 11217 (SAN 206-4960) Tel 212-206-8465; Fax: 212-243-7499
E-mail: print225@aol.com
Web site: http://www.omega.cc.umb.edu/~hangloos
*Dist(s):* **Bookpeople**
**Koen Bk. Distributors**
**Partners/West**
**SPD-Small Pr. Distribution**; CIP.

**Hannacroix Creek Bks., Inc.,** ( 1-889262 ) 1127 High Ridge Rd., PMB 110, Stamford, CT 06905-1203 (SAN 299-9560) Tel 203-321-8674; Fax: 203-968-0193
E-mail: Hannacroix@aol.com
Web site: http://www.hannacroix.com
*Dist(s):* **Baker & Taylor Bks.**
**Book Clearing Hse.**
**Book Hse., Inc., The**
**Brodart Co.**
**Follett Library Resources**
**Midwest Library Service**
**Quality Bks., Inc.**
**Replica Bks.**
**Unique Bks., Inc..**

**Hannibal Bks.,** ( 0-929292 ) Div. of KLMK Communications, Inc., P.O. Box 461592, Garland, TX 75046-1592 Tel 972-487-5710; Fax: 972-487-7960; Toll Free 800-747-0738
E-mail: hannibalbooks@earthlink.net; orders@hannibalbooks.com
Web site: http://www.hannibalbooks.com
*Dist(s):* **FaithWorks**
**Spring Arbor Distributors, Inc..**

**Hannover Hse. Imprint of Truman Pr., Inc.**

**Happy Bird Corp.,** ( 0-9741287 ) Orders Addr.: P.O. Box 86, Weston, MA 02493 Tel 781-899-7804; Fax: 781-899-8447; Edit Addr.: 55 Chest St., Weston, MA 02493
E-mail: sippers@theworld.com
Web site: http://world.std.com ~sippers
*Dist(s):* **Baker & Taylor Bks.**
**Ingram Bk. Co.**
**Powells.com.**

**Hara Publishing Group,** ( 1-883697; 1-887542; 0-9710724 ) Orders Addr.: P.O. Box 507, Lynnwood, WA 98046 (SAN 631-4953) Tel 425-398-3679; Fax: 425-672-8597; Edit Addr.: 18728 Bothell Way, NE, Bothell, WA 98011 Tel 425-775-7868; P.O. Box 19732, Seattle, WA 98109 Tel 425-775-7868; Fax: 425-398-1380
E-mail: harapub@foxinternet.net
Web site: http://www.harapublishing.com
*Dist(s):* **Todd Communications.**

†**Harbor Hill Bks.,** ( 0-916346 ) Div. of Purple Mountain Pr., P.O. Box 309, Fleischmanns, NY 12430-0378 (SAN 201-9159) Tel 914-254-4062; Fax: 914-254-4476; Toll Free: 800-325-2665
E-mail: Purple@catskill.net
Web site: http://www.catskill.net/purple; CIP.

**Harbor Hse.,** ( 1-891799 ) 629 Stevens Crossing, Martinez, GA 30907 Tel 706-738-0354 (phone/fax)
E-mail: harborBook@knology.net
Web site: http://www.harborhousebooks.com
*Dist(s):* **National Bk. Network.**

**Harbour Duck Specialties, Inc.,** ( 0-9632461 ) Orders Addr.: P.O. Box 511, Chester, VA 23831; Edit Addr.: 3224 Wooddale Rd., Chester, VA 23831.

**Harcourt Brace & Company** *See* **Harcourt Trade Pubs.**

**Harcourt Brace Jovanovich College Publishers** *See* **Harcourt College Pubs.**

**Harcourt College Pubs.,** ( 0-03; 0-15 ) Div. of Thomson Corp., The, Orders Addr.: 10650 Toebben Dr., Independence, KY 41051 (SAN 250-0086) Toll Free Fax: 800-487-8488 (customer service); Toll Free: 800-354-9706 (orders, inquiries); Edit Addr.: 301 Commerce St., Suite 3700 City Center Tower Two, Fort Worth, TX 76102 (SAN 297-4789) Tel 817-334-7500; Fax: 817-334-7844
E-mail: wlittle@harbrace.com
Web site: http://www.harcourtcollege.com/.

**Harcourt Paperbacks Imprint of Harcourt Children's Bks.**

†**Harcourt Trade Pubs.,** ( 0-15 ) Div. of Harcourt, Inc., Orders Addr.: 6277 Sea Harbor Dr., Orlando, FL 32887 (SAN 200-285X) Tel 619-699-6707; Toll Free Fax: 800-235-0256; Toll Free: 800-543-1918 (trade orders, inquiries, claims); Edit Addr.: 525 B St., Suite 1900, San Diego, CA 92101-4495 (SAN 200-2736) Tel 619-231-6616; 15 E. 26th St., 15th Flr., New York, NY 10010 Tel 212-592-1000; *Imprints:* Harvest Books (Harvest Bks)
E-mail: apbcs@harcourtbrace.com
Web site: http://www.harcourtbooks.com; CIP.

**Hard Candy Imprint of Masquerade Bks., Inc.**

**Hard Pr. Editions,** ( 0-9638433; 1-889097 ) Orders Addr.: P.O. Box 184, West Stockbridge, MA 01266 Tel 413-637-6927; Fax: 413-637-6973; Edit Addr.: 85 Church St., No. 1, West Stockbridge, MA 01240
E-mail: jongams@cultureport.com
Web site: http://www.cultureport.com
*Dist(s):* **National Bk. Network**
**SPD-Small Pr. Distribution.**

**Hard Press, Incorporated** *See* **Hard Pr. Editions**

**Hard Shell Word Factory,** ( 1-58200; 0-7599 ) Orders Addr.: P.O. Box 161, Amherst Junction, WI 54407 (SAN 631-4899) Tel 715-824-5552; Fax: 715-824-3875; Edit Addr.: 8941 Loberg Rd., Amherst Junction, WI 54407
E-mail: books@hardshell.com
Web site: http://www.hardshell.com.

**Hardscrabble Bks. Imprint of Univ. Pr. of New England**

**Hardy, John M. Publishing Co.,** ( 0-9657985; 0-9717667 ) 2 Riverway, Suite 500, Houston, TX 77056 Tel 713-625-7750; Fax: 713-871-1449
E-mail: jmh@hsoft.com
Web site: http://www.johnmhardypublishing.com
*Dist(s):* **Client Distribution Services.**

**Harkness Publishing Consultants, LLC,** ( 0-9651163 ) 2384 S. Redwood Rd., Salt Lake City, UT 84119 Tel 801-975-9261; Fax: 801-977-0611; Toll Free: 800-871-2522
*Dist(s):* **Origin Bk. Sales, Inc..**

**Harlan Publishing Co.,** ( 0-9676528; 0-9725609; 0-9747278 ) 5710-K No. 280 High Point Rd., Greensboro, NC 27407 Tel 336-643-5849; Fax: 336-643-1664
E-mail: harlan@northstate.net.

**Harlem Moon Imprint of Broadway Bks.**

**Harlequin Mills & Boon, Ltd. (GBR)** ( 0-263; 0-373; 0-204 ) Dist. by **BBC Audiobks.**

**Harlequin Mills & Boon, Ltd. (GBR)** ( 0-263; 0-373; 0-204 ) Dist. by **Thorndike Pr.**

**Harlequin Mills & Boon, Ltd. (GBR)** ( 0-263; 0-373; 0-204 ) Dist. by **Ulverscroft US.**

Harlequin Romance Audio Imprint of Brilliance Audio

Harmony Imprint of Crown Publishing Group

Harmony Raine & Co. Imprint of Buccaneer Bks., Inc.

Harper Religious Books *See* HarperSanFrancisco

HarperAudio Imprint of HarperTrade

HarperBusiness Imprint of HarperInformation

HarperCollins Imprint of HarperTrade

HarperCollins (NZL) *( 1-86950 ) Dist. by* **Antipodes Bks.**

HarperCollins General Bks. Group, *( 0-06 )* Subs. of HarperCollins US, 10 E. 53rd St., New York, NY 10022-5299 Fax: 212-207-7826; *Imprints:* PerfectBound (PerfectBound) *Dist(s):* **HarperCollins Pubs..**

†HarperCollins Pubs., *( 0-00; 0-06; 0-688; 0-690; 0-694; 0-7322 )* Div. of News Corp., Orders Addr.: 1000 Keystone Industrial Pk., Scranton, PA 18512-4621 (SAN 215-3742) Tel 570-941-1500; Toll Free Fax: 800-822-4090; Toll Free: 800-242-7737 (orders only); Edit Addr.: 10 E. 53rd St., New York, NY 10022-5299 (SAN 200-2086) Tel 212-207-7000 Web site: http://www.harpercollins.com *Dist(s):* **Comag Marketing Group;** *CIP.*

HarperCollins Pubs. Ltd. (GBR) *( 0-00; 0-06; 0-261 ) Dist. by* **Trafalgar.**

HarperCollins Pubs. Ltd. (GBR) *( 0-00; 0-06; 0-261 ) Dist. by* **HarperCollins Pubs.**

HarperEntertainment Imprint of Morrow/Avon

HarperInformation, *( 0-06 )* Div. of HarperCollins General Bks. Group, Orders Addr.: 1000 Keystone Industrial Pk., Scranton, PA 18512-4021 Toll Free Fax: 800-822-4090; Toll Free: 800-242-7737; Edit Addr.: 10 E. 53rd St., New York, NY 10022-5299 Tel 212-207-7000; *Imprints:* HarperBusiness (HarpBusn); HarperResource (HarpRes); Morrow Cookbooks, William (Morrow Cookbks) Web site: http://www.harpercollins.com/ *Dist(s):* **HarperCollins Pubs..**

HarperLargePrint Imprint of HarperTrade

HarperResource Imprint of HarperInformation

†HarperSanFrancisco, *( 0-06; 0-85924; 0-86683 )* Div. of HarperCollins General Bks. Group, Orders Addr.: 1000 Keystone Industrial Pk., Scranton, PA 18512 Toll Free Fax: 800-822-4090; Toll Free: 800-242-7737; Edit Addr.: 353 Sacramento St., Suite 500, San Francisco, CA 94111 Tel 415-477-4400; Fax: 415-477-4444 Web site: http://www.harpercollins.com *Dist(s):* **HarperCollins Pubs.;** *CIP.*

HarperTorch Imprint of Morrow/Avon

HarperTrade, *( 0-06; 0-688 )* Div. of HarperCollins General Bks. Group, Orders Addr.: 1000 Keystone Industrial Pk., Scranton, PA 18512-4021 Toll Free Fax: 800-822-4090; Toll Free: 800-242-7737; Edit Addr.: 10 E. 53rd St., New York, NY 10022 Tel 212-207-7000; Fax: 217-207-7633; Toll Free: 800-242-7737 (orders); *Imprints:* HarperCollins (HarpCollins); Perennial (Perennial); Quill (Quil); HarperLargePrint (Large Print Edns); Amistad Press (Amistad); HarperAudio (HarperAudio); Caedmon (Caed); Rayo (Rayo); Ecco (Ecco); ReganBooks (Regan); Fourth Estate (Four Est); Dark Alley (Dark Alley) Web site: http://www.harpercollins.com/ *Dist(s):* **Bilingual Pubns. Co., The**
  **Giron Bks.**
  **HarperCollins Pubs.**
  **Lectorum Pubns., Inc.**
  **Perelandra, Ltd.**
  **Thorndike Pr..**

Harrington Park Pr. Imprint of Haworth Pr., Inc., The

Harris, Antoinette S. *See* Epiphany Publishing Hse. LLC

Hartman, Claire, *( 0-9711586 )* 28576 Cano, Mission Viego, CA 92692 Tel 949-462-0709 E-mail: cahartman@juno.com.

†Harvard Univ. Pr., *( 0-674; 0-916724; 0-935617; 0-945454 )* Orders Addr.: c/o Triliteral LLC, 100 Maple Ridge Dr., Cumberland, RI 02864 Tel 401-531-2800; Fax: 401-531-2801; Toll Free Fax: 800-406-9145; Toll Free: 800-405-1619; 800-448-2242; Edit Addr.: 79 Garden St., Cambridge, MA 02138 (SAN 200-2043) Tel 617-495-2600; Fax: 617-495-5898; *Imprints:* Belknap Press (Belknap) E-mail: contact_hup@harvard.edu Web site: http://www.hup.harvard.edu *Dist(s):* **Univelt, Inc.;** *CIP.*

Harvest Bks. Imprint of Harcourt Trade Pubs.

Harvest Hse. Pubs., *( 0-7369; 0-89081; 1-56507 )* 990 Owen Loop, N., Eugene, OR 97402-9173 (SAN 207-4745) Tel 541-343-0123; Fax: 541-302-0731; Toll Free: 888-501-6991 E-mail: dietzm@harvesthousepubl.com Web site: http://www.harvesthousepubl.com *Dist(s):* **CRC Pubns.**
  **Twentieth Century Christian Bks..**

Harvest Moon Publishing, *( 0-9671345; 1-929750; 1-931436; 1-59300 )* P.O. Box 50998, Pasadena, CA 91115 Tel 310-319-9139; Fax: 310-868-2727 Do not confuse with Harvest Moon Publishing in Nashville, GA E-mail: online@harvestmoon.com Web site: http://www.harvestmoon.com.

Harvill Pr., The (GBR) *( 1-86046; 1-84343 ) Dist. by* **Trafalgar.**

Haskell Booksellers, Incorporated *See* M.S.G. Haskell Hse.

Hastings Hse. Daytrips Pubs., *( 0-8038 )* 2601 Wells Ave., Suite 161, Fern Park, FL 32730 Tel 407-339-3600; Fax: 407-339-5900; Toll Free: 800-206-7822 E-mail: hhousebks@aol.com Web site: http://www.daytripsbooks.com; http://www.hastingshousebooks.com *Dist(s):* **Midpoint Trade Bks., Inc.**
  **Publishers Group West.**

Hastings House Publishers *See* Hastings Hse. Daytrips Pubs.

Hatherleigh Co., Ltd., The, *( 1-57826; 1-886330 )* 5-22 46th Ave., Suite 200, Long Island City, NY 11101-5215 (SAN 298-878X) Tel 212-832-1584; Fax: 212-832-1502; Toll Free Fax: 800-621-8892; Toll Free: 800-367-2550; *Imprints:* Red Brick Press (Red Brick) E-mail: info@hatherleigh.com Web site: http://www.hatherleigh.com; http://www.getfitnow.com *Dist(s):* **Norton, W. W. & Co., Inc..**

Hatrack River Pubns., *( 0-9624049; 1-887473 )* Orders Addr.: P.O. Box 18184, Greensboro, NC 27419-8184 Tel 910-282-9848; Fax: 910-288-5470; Edit Addr.: 401 Willoughby Blvd., Greensboro, NC 27408.

Hats Off Bks. Imprint of Wheatmark, Inc.

Haven Bks., *( 0-9659480; 1-58436 )* 10153 1/2 Riverside Dr., Suite 629, North Hollywood, CA 91602 Tel 818-503-2518; Fax: 818-508-0299 E-mail: Havenbks@aol.com Web site: http://www.havenbooks.net.

Hawaiian Island Concepts, *( 1-878498 )* P.O. Box 1069, Wailuku, HI 96793-1069 (SAN 200-366X) Tel 808-572-2606; Fax: 808-573-1362 *Dist(s):* **Booklines Hawaii, Ltd..**

Haworth Integrative Healing Pr., The Imprint of Haworth Pr., Inc., The

†Haworth Pr., Inc., The, *( 0-7890; 0-86656; 0-917724; 1-56022; 1-56023; 1-56024 )* 10 Alice St., Binghamton, NY 13904-1580 (SAN 211-0156) Tel 607-722-5857; Fax: 607-722-6362; 607-722-1424; Toll Free Fax: 800-895-0582; Toll Free: 800-429-6784; *Imprints:* Harrington Park Press (Harrington Park); Southern Tier Editions (South Tier Edns); Alice Street Editions (Alice St Edns); Haworth Integrative Healing Press, The (Integrative Healing Pr) E-mail: getinfo@haworthpressinc.com Web site: http://www.haworthpressinc.com; http://www.haworthpressinc.com/journals/dds.asp *Dist(s):* **Barnes & Noble, Inc.**
  **BookWorld Services, Inc.**
  **Bookazine Co., Inc.**
  **Bookpeople**
  **Borders, Inc.**
  **Distributors, The**
  **Koen Bk. Distributors**
  **Matthews Medical Bk. Co.**
  **New Leaf Distributing Co., Inc.**
  **Quality Bks., Inc.**
  **Rittenhouse Bk. Distributors**
  **SPD-Small Pr. Distribution**
  **Unique Bks., Inc.**
  **Waldenbooks, Inc.;** *CIP.*

Hawthorne Bks. & Literary Arts, Inc., *( 0-9716915 )* 1312 SW Hessler Dr., Portland, OR 97201-2808 E-mail: hawthorn_kh@qwest.net Web site: http://www.hawthornebooks.com.

Hawthorne Pubs., *( 0-9705031 )* 16825 Tye St., SE, PMB 24, Monroe, WA 98272 Tel 360-863-1331; Fax: 425-258-3701.

HAYDEN Publishing, *( 1-930880 )* Div. of Hayden Companies, Inc., 117 Greenwich St., San Francisco, CA 94111 Tel 800-200-7441 E-mail: hillary@haydenpublishing.com Web site: http://www.haydenpublishing.com *Dist(s):* **Publishers Group West.**

Hazelden Information & Educational Services *See* Hazelden Publishing & Educational Services

†Hazelden Publishing & Educational Services, *( 0-89486; 0-89638; 0-935908; 0-942421; 1-56246; 1-56838; 1-59285 )* 15215 Pleasant Valley Rd., P.O. Box 176, Center City, MN 55012-0176 (SAN 209-4010) Fax: 651-213-4577; Toll Free: 800-328-9000 E-mail: kbuzick@hazeld.org Web site: http://www.hazelden.org *Dist(s):* **Health Communications, Inc.;** *CIP.*

Headline Bk. Publishing, Ltd. (GBR) *( 0-7472; 0-7553 ) Dist. by* **Trafalgar.**

†Health Communications, Inc., *( 0-922352; 0-932194; 0-941405; 1-55874; 0-7573 )* 3201 SW 15th St., Deerfield Beach, FL 33442-8157 (SAN 212-100X) Tel 954-360-0909; Fax: 954-360-0034; Toll Free: 800-851-9100; *Imprints:* Simcha Press (Simcha Press) Do not confuse with Health Communications, Inc., Edison, NJ E-mail: hci@hcibooks.com; terryy@hcibooks.com; lorig@hcibooks.com Web site: http://www.hcibooks.com *Dist(s):* **Continental Bk. Co., Inc.**
  **Lectorum Pubns., Inc.**
  **Landmark Audiobooks;** *CIP.*

Health Research, *( 0-7873 )* P.O. Box 850, Pomeroy, WA 99347 Tel 509-843-2385; Fax: 509-843-2387; Toll Free: 888-844-2386 E-mail: publish@pomeroy-wa.com Web site: http://www.healthresearchbooks.com.

Heart Wings Publishing, *( 0-9742005 )* P.O. Box 36634, Canton, OH 44735 Tel 330-479-8425 (phone/fax) E-mail: heartwings@cmh.net Web site: http://www.heartwingsbooks.com *Dist(s):* **Biblio Distribution.**

Hearth Publishing, *( 0-9627947; 1-882420 )* Orders Addr.: 212 N. Ash St., Hillsboro, KS 67063-1117 (SAN 631-4503).

Hearthstone Publishing, Ltd., *( 0-9624517; 1-57558; 1-879366 )* Div. of The Southwest Radio Church of the Air, P.O. Box 815, Oklahoma City, OK 73101 (SAN 298-7511) Tel 405-789-3885; Fax: 405-789-6502; Toll Free: 888-891-3300.

HeartQuest Imprint of Tyndale Hse. Pubs.

Heartwood Pr., *( 0-9661605 )* 3305 Stardust Dr., Austin, TX 78757 Tel 512-451-5985 Do not confuse with Heartwood Pr. in East Dummerston, VT E-mail: bredwolf@aol.com; forest@sover.net.

†Hebrew Publishing Co., *( 0-88482 )* P.O. Box 222, Spencertown, NY 12165-0222 (SAN 201-5404) Tel 518-392-3322; Fax: 518-392-4280; *CIP.*

Heian International Publishing, Inc., *( 0-89346 )* 1815 W. 205th St., Suite 301, Torrance, CA 90501-1518 (SAN 213-2036) Tel 310-782-6268; Fax: 310-782-6269 E-mail: heianemail@heian.com Web site: http://www.heian.com *Dist(s):* **Cheng & Tsui Co.**
  **SCB Distributors**
  **Weatherhill, Inc..**

†Heidelberg Graphics, *( 0-918606 )* 2 Stansbury Ct., Chico, CA 95928 (SAN 211-5654) Tel 530-342-6582 (phone/fax) E-mail: service@HeidelbergGraphics.com Web site: http://www.HeidelbergGraphics.com; *CIP.*

†Heinemann, *( 0-325; 0-435; 1-59469 )* Div. of Greenwood Publishing Group, Inc., Orders Addr.: P.O. Box 5007, Westport, CT 06881-5007 Toll Free: 800-793-2154; Edit Addr.: 361 Hanover St., Portsmouth, NH 03801 (SAN 210-5829) Tel 603-431-7894; Fax: 603-431-7840; *Imprints:* African Writers Series (African Write); Methuen Drama (Methuen Drama) E-mail: info@heinemann.com Web site: http://www.heinemann.com *Dist(s):* **National Bk. Network;** *CIP.*

Heinemann Educational Books, Incorporated *See* Heinemann

†Heinle, *( 0-8384; 0-88377; 0-912066; 1-4130 )* Div. of Thomson Learning, Orders Addr.: 10650 Toebben Dr., Independence, KY 41051 Toll Free Fax: 800-487-8488 E-mail: reply@heinle.com Web site: http://www.heinle.com *Dist(s):* **Thomson Learning;** *CIP.*

Heinle Publishing *See* Heinle

Heirloom Pr., *( 0-9615377 )* Orders Addr.: P.O. Box 28168, Minneapolis, MN 55428 (SAN 662-3492) Do not confuse with Heirloom Pr. in Glendale, CA.

Names

**Names**

**Helicon 9 Editions,** ( 0-9627460; 1-884235 ) Div. of Midwest Ctr. for the Literary Arts, Inc., Orders Addr.: P.O. Box 22412, Kansas City, MO 64113 Tel 816-753-1095; Fax: 816-753-1016; Edit Addr.: 3607 Pennsylvania, Kansas City, MO 64111 E-mail: helicon9@aol.com Web site: http://www.heliconnine.com *Dist(s):* **Baker & Taylor Bks.**
   **Booksource, The**
   **Brodart Co..**

**Hemed Books, Incorporated** *See* **Lambda Pubs., Inc.**

**Hemlock Hill Bk. Distributors,** Orders Addr.: P.O. Box 45, Millersville, PA 17551-0045.

†**Hendrick-Long Publishing Co.,** ( 0-937460; 1-885777 ) Orders Addr.: P.O. Box 1247, Friendswood, TX 77549 (SAN 281-7756) Tel 281-482-6187; Fax: 281-482-6169; Toll Free: 800-544-3770; Edit Addr.: 3905 Pear St., Suite 130, Pearland, TX 77581 (SAN 281-7748) E-mail: hendrick-long@worldnet.att.net Web site: http://www.hendricklongpublishing.com *Dist(s):* **Baker & Taylor Bks.**
   **Brodart Co.**
   **Follett Library Resources**
   **Hervey's Booklink & Cookbook Warehouse**
   **; CIP.**

**Hendricks Hse., Inc.,** ( 0-87532 ) Main St., Putney, VT 05346-0185 (SAN 206-9830) Tel 802-387-5232.

†**Hendrickson Pubs., Inc.,** ( 0-913573; 0-917006; 0-943575; 1-56563 ) Orders Addr.: P.O. Box 3473, Peabody, MA 01961-3473 (SAN 285-2772) Tel 978-532-6546; Fax: 978-531-8146; Toll Free: 800-358-3111; Edit Addr.: 140 Summit St., Peabody, MA 01960-3203 (SAN 663-6594) Fax: 978-573-8414 Do not confuse with Hendrickson Group, Sandy Hook, CT E-mail: orders@hendrickson.com Web site: http://www.hendrickson.com; *CIP.*

**Henry, Ian Pubns. (GBR)** ( 0-86025 ) *Dist. by* **Empire Pub Srvs.**

**Henry, J. W. Publishing, Inc.,** ( 0-9656727 ) Orders Addr.: P.O. Box 1501, Ashburn, VA 20146-1501 Tel 703-404-0542; Fax: 703-404-0543; Edit Addr.: 507 N. Brighton Ct., Sterling, VA 20164-3919 E-mail: 75361.755@compuserve.com.

†**Herald Pr.,** ( 0-8361 ) Div. of Mennonite Publishing Hse., 616 Walnut Ave., Scottdale, PA 15683-1999 (SAN 202-2915) Tel 412-887-8500; 724-887-8500; Fax: 724-887-3111; Toll Free: 800-245-7894 (orders only) Do not confuse with Herald Pr., Charlotte, NC E-mail: hp@mph.org Web site: http://www.mph.org *Dist(s):* **Baker & Taylor Bks.**
   **Spring Arbor Distributors, Inc.; CIP.**

†**Herald Publishing Hse.,** ( 0-8309 ) P.O. Box 390, Independence, MO 64051-0390 Tel 816-521-3015; Fax: 816-521-3066; Toll Free: 800-767-8181; 1001W. Walnut St., Independence, MO 64051-0390 (SAN 111-7556); *Imprints:* Independence Press (Indep Pr) E-mail: hhmark@heraldhouse.org Web site: http://www.heraldhouse.org; *CIP.*

**Heritage Bks.,** ( 0-7884; 0-917890; 0-940907; 1-55613; 1-888265; 1-58549 ) 1540 E Pointer Ridge Pl., Bowie, MD 20716-1800 (SAN 209-3367) Tel 301-390-7708; Toll Free Fax: 800-276-1760; Toll Free: 800-398-7709 E-mail: order@heritagebooks.com Web site: http://www.heritagebooks.com; http://www.WillowBendBooks.com

**Heritage Pubs., Inc.,** ( 0-929690 ) 5308 N. 12th St., Suite 400, Phoenix, AZ 85014 (SAN 249-9460) Tel 602-277-4780; Fax: 602-277-1659; Toll Free: 800-972-8507 E-mail: info@heritagepublishers.com; heritage@fastq.com Web site: http://www.heritagepublishers.com.

**Hermes Pr,** ( 1-929485 ) 840 Loma Alta Terr., Vista, CA 92083 Tel 760-726-3923 Do not confuse with companies with the same or similar name in Ferndale, MI, New Castle, PA, Brooks, ME E-mail: norman@hermes-press.com Web site: http://www.hermes-press.com.

**Hermitage** *See* **Hermitage Pubs.**

†**Hermitage Pubs.,** ( 0-938920; 1-55779 ) P.O. Box 310, Tenafly, NJ 07670 (SAN 239-4413) Tel 201-894-8247 ; Fax: 201-894-5591 E-mail: yefimovim@aol.com Web site: http://lexiconbridge.com/hermitage; *CIP.*

**Hern, Nick Bks. (GBR)** ( 1-85459 ) *Dist. by* **Theatre Comm.**

**Hern, Nick Bks. (GBR)** ( 1-85459 ) *Dist. by* **Consort Bk Sales.**

**Herodias,** ( 1-928746 ) Orders Addr.: 1603 79th St., Brooklyn, NY 11214; Edit Addr.: 346 First Ave., New York, NY 10009 Tel 212-995-5332 (phone/fax); Toll Free: 800-219-9116 (orders) E-mail: greatblue@acninc.net Web site: http://www.herodias.com *Dist(s):* **Mercedes Distribution Ctr., Inc..**

**Herzl Pr.,** ( 0-930832 ) Subs. of World Zionist Organization, 633 Third, 21st Flr., New York, NY 10022 (SAN 201-5374) Tel 212-339-6000; Fax: 212-318-6176.

**Hesperus Pr. (GBR)** ( 1-84391 ) *Dist. by* **Trafalgar.**

**Heyday Bks.,** ( 0-930588; 1-890771 ) Orders Addr.: P.O. Box 9145, Berkeley, CA 94709 (SAN 207-2351) Tel 510-549-3564; Fax: 510-549-1889; Edit Addr.: 2054 University Ave., Suite 400, Berkeley, CA 94704; *Imprints:* Roundhouse Press, The (Roundhse Pr) E-mail: heyday@heydaybooks.com Web site: http://www.heydaybooks.com *Dist(s):* **Bookpeople**
   **SPD-Small Pr. Distribution.**

**Hi.I.Que Publishing,** ( 0-9631333; 1-887492 ) Div. of The Guthrie Studio, P.O. Box 508, Claremont, CA 91711 Tel 909-622-7501; Fax: 909-622-4942 E-mail: hiiquepublish@aol.com Web site: http://www.hiiquepublishing.com.

**Hi Jinx Pr.,** ( 1-57650 ) P.O. Box 1814, Davis, CA 95617-1814 Tel 530-759-8514; Fax: 530-759-8639.

**Hidden Knowledge,** ( 0-9679159; 1-59500 ) 1181 Martin Ave., San Jose, CA 95126 Tel 408-298-3269 E-mail: mjward@hidden-knowledge.com Web site: http://www.hidden-knowledge.com *Dist(s):* **Lightning Source, Inc..**

**Higginson Bk. Co.,** ( 0-7404; 0-8328 ) 148 Washington St., Salem, MA 01970 (SAN 247-9400) Tel 978-745-7170; Fax: 978-745-8025 E-mail: higginsn@cove.com Web site: http://www.higginsonbooks.com.

**High Country Pubs., Ltd.,** ( 0-9713045; 1-932158 ) 197 New Market Ctr., No. 135, Boone, NC 28607 (SAN 254-3753) Tel 828-964-0590; Fax: 828-262-1973 Do not confuse with High Country Pubs., Lakewood, CO E-mail: editor@highcountrypublishers.com Web site: http://www.highcountrypublishers.com *Dist(s):* **Biblio Distribution.**

**High Plains Pr.,** ( 0-931271 ) P.O. Box 123, Glendo, WY 82213 (SAN 681-9907) Tel 307-735-4370; Fax: 307-735-4590; Toll Free: 800-552-7819 Do not confuse with companies with similar names in Norman, OK, Worland, WY, Fort Collins, CO, Long Beach, CA, Sugar Land, TX, Dodge City, KS E-mail: editor@highplainspress.com Web site: http://www.highplainspress.com *Dist(s):* **Baker & Taylor Bks..**

**High Plains Publishing Co., Inc.,** ( 0-9623333; 1-881019 ) Orders Addr.: P.O. Box 1860, Worland, WY 82401 Tel 307-347-3565 (phone/fax); Edit Addr.: 725 Bighorn Ave., Worland, WY 82401 Do not confuse companies with similar names in Glendo, WY, Norman, OK, Long Beach, CA, Sugar Land, TX, Dodge City, KS E-mail: larm@tritel.net.

**HighBridge Co.,** ( 0-942110; 1-56511 ) Subs. of Rivertown Trading Co., 33 S. Sixth St., CC-2205, Minneapolis, MN 55402 Tel 612-304-7163; Fax: 612-304-7175; Toll Free: 800-667-8433; *Imprints:* NAL Books (NAL Bks); Penguin Books (Penguin Bks); Penguin AudioBooks (Png AudioBks) E-mail: highbridge@highbridgeaudio.com Web site: http://www.highbridgeaudio.com *Dist(s):* **Penguin Group (USA) Inc..**

**High-Lonesome Bks.,** ( 0-944383 ) Orders Addr.: P.O. Box 878, Silver City, NM 88062 (SAN 243-3079) Tel 505-388-3763; Fax: 505-388-5705; Toll Free: 800-380-7323 (orders only) E-mail: Cherie@High-LonesomeBooks.com Web site: http://www.high-lonesomebooks.com *Dist(s):* **Johnson Bks..**

**Highsmith Inc.,** ( 0-913853; 0-917846; 1-57950; 1-932146 ) W5527 Hwy. 106 P.O. Box 800, Fort Atkinson, WI 53538 (SAN 159-8740) Tel 920-563-9571; Fax: 920-563-7395 Web site: http://www.highsmith.com *Dist(s):* **Women Ink.**

**Highsmith Press, LLC** *See* **Highsmith Inc.**

**Hightrees Bks. Imprint of Prism Corp.**

**Hill & Wang Imprint of Farrar, Straus & Giroux**

**Hill, Lawrence Bks. Imprint of Chicago Review Pr., Inc.**

**Hill Street Classics Imprint of Hill Street Pr., LLC**

**Hill Street Pr., LLC,** ( 1-892514; 1-58818 ) 191 E. Broad St., Suite 209, Athens, GA 30601 Tel 706-613-7200 (phone/fax); Fax: 706-613-7204; Toll Free: 800-295-0365; *Imprints:* Hill Street Classics (Hill St Class) E-mail: info@hillstreetpress.com Web site: http://www.hillstreetpress.com *Dist(s):* **Independent Pubs. Group**
   **Beeler, Thomas T. Publisher.**

**Hilliard & Harris,** ( 0-9704304; 1-59133 ) P.O. Box 3350, Frederick, MD 21705-3358 Tel 301-432-7080; Fax: 301-432-7505 E-mail: hilliardharris@aol.com; stephreill@hilliardandharris.com Web site: http://www.hilliardandharris.com.

**Hillsboro Pr. Imprint of Providence Hse. Pubs.**

**Hinterlands Pr.,** ( 0-9660829 ) 2525 Cnty. Rd. 775, Perrysville, OH 44864 Tel 419-938-7305 E-mail: Cwo51@aol.com.

†**Hippocrene Bks., Inc.,** ( 0-7818; 0-87052; 0-88254 ) 171 Madison Ave., New York, NY 10016-1002 (SAN 213-2060) Tel 718-454-2366 (sales); 212-685-4371 (editorial); Fax: 718-454-1391 (sales/order inquiry); 212-779-9338 (editorial) E-mail: hippocrenebooks.com; hippocre@ix.netcom.com; contact@hippocrenebooks.com Web site: http://www.hippocrenebooks.com *Dist(s):* **Continental Bk. Co., Inc.; CIP.**

**Hired Pen, Inc., The** *See* **Acacia Publishing, Inc.**

**Historical Images Imprint of Bright Mountain Bks., Inc.**

**History West Publishing Co.,** ( 0-9625069 ) P.O. Box 23133, Oklahoma City, OK 73123-2133 Tel 405-720-2954 E-mail: historywst@aol.com.

**HiT MoteL Pr.,** ( 0-9655842 ) 2267 28th Ave., San Francisco, CA 94116 Tel 415-664-6138 E-mail: mlyons@slip.net Web site: http://www.hitmotel.com.

**Hoc Volo Imprint of Godine, David R. Pub.**

**Hodder & Stoughton, Ltd. (GBR)** ( 0-340; 0-450; 0-7122; 0-7131 ) *Dist. by* **Trafalgar.**

**Hodder & Stoughton, Ltd. (GBR)** ( 0-340; 0-450; 0-7122; 0-7131 ) *Dist. by* **Lubrecht & Cramer.**

**Hodder Headline Audiobooks (GBR)** ( 1-85998; 1-84032 ) *Dist. by* **Trafalgar.**

**Hodder Headline Audiobooks (GBR)** ( 1-85998; 1-84032 ) *Dist. by* **Ulverscroft US.**

**Holdfast Bks.,** ( 1-929897 ) 2763 W. Ave., L, Suite 205, Lancaster, CA 93536 Tel 310-545-2446; Fax: 310-545-5256.

†**Holiday Hse., Inc.,** ( 0-8234 ) 425 Madison Ave., New York, NY 10017 (SAN 202-3008) Tel 212-688-0085; Fax: 212-688-0395 E-mail: bwalsh@holidayhouse.com Web site: http://www.holidayhouse.com *Dist(s):* **Lectorum Pubns., Inc.; CIP.**

**Holloway Hse. Publishing Co.,** ( 0-87067; 1-58520 ) 8060 Melrose Ave., Los Angeles, CA 90046 (SAN 206-8451) Tel 323-653-8060; Fax: 323-655-9452 E-mail: psi@loop.com Web site: http://www.hollowayhousebooks.com *Dist(s):* **All America Distributors Corp.**

†**Hollowbrook Publishing,** ( 0-88072; 0-89341 ) Div. of Hollowbrook Communications, Inc., 236 S. Third St., Unit 242, Montrose, CO 81401 Fax: 970-249-2041; *Imprints:* Longwood Academic (Longwood Academic) ; *CIP.*

**Hollym International Corp.,** ( 0-930878; 1-56591 ) 18 Donald Pl., Elizabeth, NJ 07208 (SAN 211-0172) Tel 908-353-1655; Fax: 908-353-0255 Do not confuse with Hollym Corporation Pubs., New York, NY E-mail: hollymint@aol.com Web site: http://www.hollym.com *Dist(s):* **Cheng & Tsui..**

†**Holmes & Meier Pubs., Inc.,** ( 0-8419 ) Orders Addr.: 41 Monroe Tpke., Trumbull, CT 06611 Tel 800-698-7781; Fax: 800-557-5601; Edit Addr.: 160 Broadway E. Bldg, 9th Flr.,, New York, NY 10038 (SAN 201-9280) Tel 212-374-0100; Fax: 212-374-1313; *Imprints:* Africana Pub. (Africana) E-mail: info@holmesandmeier.com Web site: http://www.holmesandmeier.com *Dist(s):* **H & M Distribution; CIP.**

**Holmes Publishing Group, LLC,** ( 0-916411; 1-55818 ) Orders Addr.: P.O. Box 623, Edmonds, WA 98020-0623 (SAN 655-8321) Tel 425-771-2701; Fax: 425-771-5651; Edit Addr.: 406 Main, Suite 116, Edmonds, WA 98020 (SAN 243-282X) Do not confuse with Holmes Publishing Co., Philadelphia, PA E-mail: jdh@jdholmes.com.

†**Holt, Henry & Co.,** *( 0-03; 0-8050 )* Div. of Holtzbrinck Publishers, Orders Addr.: 16365 James Madison Hwy., Gordonsville, VA 22942-8501 Toll Free Fax: 800-672-2054; Toll Free: 888-330-8477; Edit Addr.: 115 W. 18th St., 5th Flr., New York, NY 10011 (SAN 200-6472) Tel 212-886-9200; Fax: 540-672-7540 (customer service); *Imprints:* Owl Books (Owl); Metropolitan Books (Metropol Bks); Times Books (Times Bks); Holt, Henry & Company Books For Young Raders (HH Bks Yng Read) E-mail: info@hholt.com
Web site: http://www.henryholt.com
*Dist(s):* **Giron Bks.**
   **Holtzbrinck Pubs.**
   **Lectorum Pubns., Inc.**
   **Weston Woods Studios, Inc.***; CIP.*

**Holt, Rinehart & Winston,** *( 0-03 )* Div. of Harcourt, Inc., Orders Addr.: 6277 Sea Harbor Dr., Orlando, FL 32887-0001 Tel 407-345-3800; Fax: 407-352-3395; Toll Free Fax: 800-235-0256; Toll Free: 800-544-6678; Edit Addr.: a/o School Div., 10801 N. Mopac Expressway, Bldg. 3, Austin, TX 78759-5415 (SAN 297-4711) Tel 512-721-7000; Toll Free: 800-992-1627
E-mail: holtinfo@hrw.com
Web site: http://www.hrw.com
*Dist(s):* **Continental Bk. Co., Inc..**

**Holtzbrinck Pubs.,** *( 0-374 )* Orders Addr.: 16365 James Madison Hwy., Gordonsville, VA 22942 (SAN 631-5011) Tel 540-672-7600; Fax: 540-672-7540 (Customer Service); 540-672-7664; Toll Free Fax: 800-672-2054 (Order Dept.); Toll Free: 888-330-8477 ; Edit Addr.: 175 Fifth Ave., New York, NY 10010 Tel 212-674-5151; Fax: 212-677-6487; Toll Free: 800-488-5233
E-mail: dean.athans.@hbpubny.com
Web site: http://www.vhpsva.com/bookseller/.

†**Holy Cow! Pr.,** *( 0-930100 )* P.O. Box 3170, Duluth, MN 55803 (SAN 685-3315) Tel 218-724-1653 (phone/fax)
Web site: http://www.holycowpress.org
*Dist(s):* **Consortium Bk. Sales & Distribution**
   **SPD-Small Pr. Distribution***; CIP.*

**Homa & Sekey Bks.,** *( 0-9665421; 1-931907 )* P.O. Box 103, Dumont, NJ 07628 Tel 201-384-6692; Fax: 201-384-6055
E-mail: info@homabooks.com
Web site: http://www.homabooks.com
*Dist(s):* **Independent Pubs. Group.**

**Home Museum Pr.,** *( 0-943100 )* Div. of Advanced Research Corp., 1808 Makefield Rd., Yardley, PA 19067 (SAN 240-3889) Tel 215-295-7871.

**Homestead Publishing,** *( 0-943972 )* Box 193, Moose, WY 83012 (SAN 241-029X) Tel 307-733-6248 (phone/fax)
E-mail: homesteadpublishing@mac.com.

**Honey Bear Bks. Imprint of Modern Publishing**

**Honocan Pr.,** *( 0-9679879 )* 5856 College Ave., Oakland, CA 94618 Tel 510-655-5763; P.O. Box 240, Oakland, CA 94618
E-mail: falconbooks@hotmail.com.

**Hood, Alan C. & Co., Inc.,** *( 0-911469 )* P.O. Box 775, Chambersburg, PA 17201 (SAN 270-8221) Tel 717-267-0867; Fax: 717-267-0572.

**Hope & Nonthings,** *( 0-9707458 )* Div. of Panic Button Records, P.O. Box 148010, Chicago, IL 60614 Fax: 773-529-4248
E-mail: weaselcrue@mindspring.com
Web site: http://www.hopeandnonthings.com
*Dist(s):* **AK Pr. Distribution.**

**Horizon Bks. Imprint of Christian Pubns., Inc.**

**Horizon Pr.,** *( 0-9627628 )* 4561 N. Oraibi Pl., Tucson, AZ 85749 (SAN 297-3332) Tel 520-749-3033; Toll Free: 800-749-3036 Do not confuse with companies with the same name in Los Angeles, CA, Marietta, GA, New York, NY
E-mail: mast3033@aol.com; curtist@brooklynda.org.

**Horizon Pr.,** *( 1-890248 )* 10535 Wilshire Blvd., Apt. 1203, Los Angeles, CA 90024-4613 Do not confuse with companies with the same name in Tuscon, AZ, Marietta, GA, New York, NY
E-mail: seacourt@concentric.net.

**Horizon Pubs. & Distributors, Inc.,** *( 0-88290 )* Orders Addr.: P.O. Box 490, Bountiful, UT 84011-0490 Tel 801-295-9451; Fax: 801-295-0196; Toll Free: 800-453-0812
E-mail: horizonp@burgoyne.com
Web site: http://www.horizonpublishers.com
*Dist(s):* **Cornerstone Publishing & Distribution, Inc..**

**Hornkohl Communications,** *( 0-9701368 )* P.O. Box 2222, Traverse City, MI 49685 Tel 231-275-6186; *Imprints:* Written Word, The (Written Word MI) E-mail: cdbooks@triton.net; hornkohl@triton.net
Web site: http://www.hornkohl.com/index.html.

**Hot Biscuit Productions, Inc.,** *( 1-880964; 0-9671667 )* 5050 Poplar Ave., Suite 2400, Memphis, TN 38157-2401 Tel 901-537-7442; Fax: 901-537-7449 E-mail: beecherhbp@aol.com
Web site: http://members.aol.com/beecherhbp/mfm1.html.

†**Houghton Mifflin Co.,** *( 0-395; 0-87466; 0-9631591; 1-57630; 1-881527; 0-618 )* 222 Berkeley St., Boston, MA 02116 (SAN 215-3793) Tel 617-351-5000;
*Imprints:* Riverside Editions (RivEd)
Web site: http://www.hmco.com
*Dist(s):* **Chelsea Green Publishing**
   **Cheng & Tsui Co.**
   **Continental Bk. Co., Inc.**
   **Larousse Kingfisher Chambers, Inc.**
   **Lectorum Pubns., Inc.**
   **Perelandra, Ltd.**
   **netLibrary, Inc.***; CIP.*

**Houghton Mifflin Company (College Division)** *See* **Houghton Mifflin Co. Trade & Reference Div.**

**Houghton Mifflin Co. Trade & Reference Div.,** *( 0-395; 0-618 )* Orders Addr.: 181 Ballardvalle St., Wilmington, MA 01887 Tel 978-661-1300; Toll Free: 800-225-3362; Edit Addr.: 222 Berkeley St., Boston, MA 02116 (SAN 200-2388) Tel 617-351-5000; Fax: 617-227-5409; 215 Park Ave., S., New York, NY 10003 Tel 212-420-5800; Fax: 212-420-5855; *Imprints:* Clarion Books (Clarion Bks); Mariner Books (Mariner Bks); Lorraine, A. Walter (W Lorraine)
Web site: http://www.hmco.com/
*Dist(s):* **netLibrary, Inc..**

**Hounslow Pr. (CAN)** *( 0-88882 )* Dist. by **Lone Pine.**

**House of Collectibles Imprint of Random Hse. Information Group**

**House of REX/Cindered Monk** *See* **BraZen**

**House of Stratus, Inc. (GBR)** *( 1-84232; 0-7551 )* Dist. by **Midpt Trade.**

**House of Stratus, Inc.,** *( 1-84232; 0-7551 )* Orders Addr.: 1270 Avenue of the Americas, Suite 210, New York, NY 10020 Tel 212 218 7649; Fax: 212 218 7648
E-mail: EBottomley@houseofstratus.com; info@houseofstratus.com
Web site: http://www.houseofstratus.com.

**Howard Publishing Co.,** *( 1-58229; 1-878990 )* 3117 N. Seventh St., West Monroe, LA 71291-2227 (SAN 298-7597) Tel 318-396-4366; Fax: 318-396-1882; 318-396-0425; Toll Free Fax: 800-342-2067; Toll Free: 800-858-4109 Do not confuse with Howard Publishing, Ventura, CA
E-mail: info@howardpublishing.com
Web site: http://www.howardpublishing.com
*Dist(s):* **Anchor Distributors**
   **Appalachian Bible Co.**
   **Provident Music Distribution**
   **Riverside**
   **Spring Arbor Distributors, Inc.**
   **Twentieth Century Christian Bks..**

†**Howard Univ. Pr.,** *( 0-88258 )* Orders Addr.: c/o Hopkins Fullfillment Services, P.O. Box 50370, Baltimore, MD 21211-4370 Tel 410-516-6947; Fax: 410-516-6998; Toll Free: 800-537-5487; Edit Addr.: 2225 Georgia Ave., Suite 210, Washington, DC 20001 (SAN 202-3067) Tel 202-238-2570; Fax: 202-588-9849
E-mail: mnelson@howard.edu
Web site: http://www.founders.howard.edu/HUPRESS
*Dist(s):* **Baker & Taylor Bks.***; CIP.*

**Howie, C.J. Co.,** *( 1-885275 )* 1695 Quigley Rd., Columbus, OH 43227-3433 Tel 614-237-5474.

**Hrymfaxe,** *( 0-9724753 )* 340 S. Convent, Tucson, AZ 85701
Web site: http://www.emptychairllc.com.

**HT Communications,** *( 1-892977 )* Orders Addr.: P.O. Box 1401, Arvada, CO 80001 Tel 303-420-4888; Fax: 303-420-4845
E-mail: khf333@aol.com.

**Hubbard, Louis Publishing,** *( 0-9644751 )* 1350 S. Frontage Rd., Hastings, MN 55033-2426 Tel 612-521-4039; Fax: 612-522-6119
E-mail: rlbarnar@mn.rr.com.

**Huge Print Pr.,** *( 0-7583 )* 3052 Casmeg Way, Rancho San Diego, CA 92019 Tel 619-447-2300; Fax: 619-334-7764; Toll Free: 800-825-0057
E-mail: info@hugeprint.com
Web site: http://www.HugePrint.com.

**Hughes Henshaw Pubns.,** *( 0-9617223; 1-892693 )* 473 Birch Ave., SW, Palm Bay, FL 32908 Tel 321-956-8885; Fax: 321-956-2475
E-mail: hugheshenshaw@aol.com
Web site: http://www.hugheshenshaw.com
*Dist(s):* **Baker & Taylor Bks..**

**Humanity Bks. Imprint of Prometheus Bks., Pubs.**

**Humanoids, Inc.,** *( 0-9672401; 1-930652; 1-59465 )* Div. of Humanoids Group, Orders Addr.: P.O. Box 931658, Hollywood, CA 90093 Tel 323-850-5802; Fax: 323-850-5804; Edit Addr.: 12001 Ventura Pl., Suite 200, Studio City, CA 91604 Tel 818-655-9800; Fax: 818-655-9811
E-mail: cs@humanoids-publishing.com
Web site: http://www.humanoids-publishing.com
*Dist(s):* **Client Distribution Services.**

**Hungry Mind Press** *See* **Ruminator Bks.**

**Hungry Tiger Pr.,** *( 0-9644988; 1-929527 )* 5995 Dandridge Ln., Suite 121, San Diego, CA 92115-6575 E-mail: books@hungrytigerpress.com
Web site: http://www.hungrytigerpress.com.

**Hunt, Paul,** P.O. Box 10907, Burbank, CA 91510 (SAN 281-3777) Tel 818-845-6467; Fax: 818-845-0460.

**Hunter Publishing, Inc.,** *( 1-55650; 1-58843 )* Orders Addr.: 130 Campus Dr., Edison, NJ 08818 Tel 732-225-1900; Fax: 732-417-1744; Toll Free: 800-255-0343 Do not confuse with Hunter Publishing, Inc., Hobe Sound, FL
E-mail: hunterp@bellsouth.net
Web site: http://www.hunterpublishing.com
*Dist(s):* **netLibrary, Inc..**

**Huntington House** *See* **Huntington Hse. Pubs.**

**Huntington Hse. Pubs.,** *( 0-910311; 1-56384 )* Orders Addr.: P.O. Box 53788, Lafayette, LA 70505 (SAN 241-5208) Tel 337-237-7049; Fax: 337-237-7060; Toll Free: 800-749-4009; Edit Addr.: 104 Row 2, Suite A1 & A2, Lafayette, LA 70508
E-mail: joyced@xspedius.net;
admin@alphapublishingonline.com
Web site: http://www.alphapublishingonline.com
*Dist(s):* **Alpha Publishing, Inc.**
   **Riverside.**

**Huntington Library Pr.,** *( 0-87328 )* Div. of Huntington Library, Art Collections & Botanical Gardens, 1151 Oxford Rd., San Marino, CA 91108 (SAN 202-313X) Tel 626-405-2172; Fax: 626-585-0794
E-mail: booksales@huntington.org
Web site: http://www.Huntington.org/HEHPubs.html
*Dist(s):* **Sunbelt Pubns., Inc..**

**Huntington Library Publications** *See* **Huntington Library Pr.**

**Hutchinson (GBR)** *( 0-09 )* Dist. by **Trafalgar.**

**Hutchinson, Fred Cancer Research Ctr.,** *( 0-945278 )* Orders Addr.: P.O. Box 19023, Seattle, WA 98109 (SAN 246-0726) Tel 206-288-1148; Edit Addr.: 825 Eastlake Ave., E., G6-206, Seattle, WA 19023.

**Hydra Bks. Imprint of Northwestern Univ. Pr.**

†**Hyperion Pr.,** *( 0-7868; 1-56282; 1-4013 )* Div. of Disney Bk. Publishing, Inc., A Walt Disney Co., Orders Addr.: 3 Center Plaza, Boston, MA 02108 Toll Free: 800-759-0190; Edit Addr.: 77 W. 66th St., 11th Flr., New York, NY 10023-6298 Tel 212-456-0100; Fax: 212-456-0108
Web site: http://www.hyperionbooks.com
*Dist(s):* **Time Warner Bk. Group***; CIP.*

**I & L Publishing,** *( 0-9661244; 1-930002 )* 174 Oak Dr. Pkwy., Oroville, CA 95966 Tel 530-589-5048; Fax: 530-589-3551; Toll Free: 888-443-4722
E-mail: iolamoore@juno.com
*Dist(s):* **Morris Publishing.**

**ICAM Publishing Co.,** *( 0-9642463 )* P.O. Box 128, Rouse Point, NY 12979-1004 Tel 514-684-6235; Fax: 514-684-0014.

**IP Bks.,** *( 0-9653711 )* Orders Addr.: P.O. Box 32068, Cincinnati, OH 45232 Tel 513-681-3150; Fax: 513-542-5169; Toll Free: 888-222-7311; Edit Addr.: 4713 N. Edgewood Ave., Cincinnati, OH 45232-1738 E-mail: SRVGOD1@aol.com
*Dist(s):* **Barnes & Noble, Inc..**

**ISHK,** *( 0-86304; 0-900860; 1-883536 )* Div. of Institute for the Study of Human Knowledge, Orders Addr.: P.O. Box 381069, Cambridge, MA 02238-1069 (SAN 226-4536) Tel 617-497-4124; Fax: 617-876-2976; Toll Free Fax: 800-223-4200; Toll Free: 800-222-4745; Edit Addr.: P.O. Box 176, Los Altos, CA 94023 Tel 650-948-9428
E-mail: ishkbooks@aol.com; ishkorders@aol.com
Web site: http://www.ishkbooks.com
*Dist(s):* **Baker & Taylor Bks.**
   **Bookpeople**
   **Borders, Inc.**
   **New Leaf Distributing Co., Inc..**

**IAD Pr./Jukurrpa Bks. (AUS)** *( 0-949659; 1-86465; 0-9596206 )* Dist. by **Intl Spec Bk.**

**Iami Bks.,** *( 0-9633851 )* 114-35 198th St., Saint Albans, NY 11412 Tel 718-465-8167; Fax: 718-465-4050.

**ibooks, Inc.,** *( 0-671; 0-7434; 1-58824; 1-59176 )* 24 W. 25th St., 11th Flr., New York, NY 10010 Tel 212-645-9870; Fax: 212-645-9874
E-mail: aandrade@ipicturebooks.com
*Dist(s):* **Simon & Schuster, Inc..**

**Names**

**ibooks, Incorporated/ipictures.com** *See* **ibooks, Inc.**

**ICAN Press** *See* **Black Forest Pr.**

**Iceni Bks. Imprint of Wheatmark, Inc.**

**Ideals Pubns.,** ( *0-8249; 0-89542* ) Div. of Guideposts, 535 Metroplex Dr., Suite 250, Nashville, TN 37211 Tel 615-333-0478; Fax: 615-781-1447
E-mail: mflanagan@guideposts.org
Web site: http://www.idealspublications.com
*Dist(s):* **Appalachian Bk. Distributors**
**Baker & Taylor Bks.**
**Lectorum Pubns., Inc.**
**Riverside**
**Spring Arbor Distributors, Inc..**

**Ideals Publishing Corporation** *See* **Ideals Pubns.**

**IDKPr.,** ( *0-9710929* ) 10645 N. Tatum Blvd., Suite 200, Phoenix, AZ 85028 (SAN 253-8725) Tel 480-607-1830; Fax: 480-607-1906
E-mail: jbharding@earthlink.net; info@idkpress.com
Web site: http://www.idkpress.com;
http://www.escapefromparadise.com
*Dist(s):* **Baker & Taylor Bks..**

**Idyllwild Publishing Co.,** ( *1-931857* ) Div. of Wild Ink Productions, P.O. Box 355, Idyllwild, CA 92549 Tel 909-659-4950; Fax: 909-659-4920
E-mail: ipc@tazland.net
Web site: http://www.wildink.com
*Dist(s):* **Baker & Taylor Bks.**
**Books West**
**Partners/West**
**Sunbelt Pubns., Inc.**
**Wolverine Distributing, Inc..**

**Ignatius Pr.,** ( *0-89870; 1-58617* ) Div. of Guadalupe Assocs., Inc., Orders Addr.: P.O. Box 1339, Fort Collins, CO 80522-1339 Tel 970-221-3920; Fax: 970-221-3964; Toll Free Fax: 800-278-3566; Toll Free: 800-651-1531 (credit card orders, no minimum, individual orders); 877-320-9276 (bookstore orders); Edit Addr.: 2515 McAllister St., San Francisco, CA 94118 (SAN 214-3887) Tel 415-387-2324; Fax: 415-387-0896
E-mail: info@ignatius.com
Web site: http://www.ignatius.com
*Dist(s):* **Baker & Taylor Bks.**
**Midpoint Trade Bks., Inc.**
**Riverside**
**Spring Arbor Distributors, Inc..**

**III Publishing,** ( *0-9622937; 1-886625* ) P.O. Box 1581, Gualala, CA 95445 Tel 707-882-1818 (phone/fax)
E-mail: bill@publishing.com
Web site: http://www.iiipublishing.com
*Dist(s):* **Last Gasp Eco-Funnies, Inc.**
**Left Bank Distribution.**

**Illumination Arts Publishing Co., Inc.,** ( *0-935699; 0-9701907; 0-9740190* ) Orders Addr.: P.O. Box 1865, Bellevue, WA 98009 (SAN 696-2599) Tel 425-644-7185; Fax: 425-644-9274; Toll Free: 888-210-8216; Edit Addr.: 13256 Northup Way, No. 9, Bellevue, WA 98005
E-mail: liteinfo@illumin.com
Web site: http://www.illumin.com
*Dist(s):* **Baker & Taylor Bks.**
**DeVorss & Co.**
**Follett Library Resources**
**Koen Pacific**
**New Leaf Distributing Co., Inc.**
**Partners/West**
**Quality Bks., Inc..**

**ILR Pr. Imprint of Cornell Univ. Pr.**

**IM Pr. Imprint of Reader's Digest Assn., Inc., The**

**Image Imprint of Doubleday Publishing**

**Image Comics,** ( *1-58240; 1-887279* ) 1071 N. Batavia St., Suite A, Orange, CA 92867 Tel 714-288-0200; Fax: 714-288-2898
E-mail: brentimage@aol.com
*Dist(s):* **Diamond Book Distributors, Inc.**
**Diamond Comic Distributors, Inc.**
**LPC Group**
**Trucatriche.**

**Image Connection America, Inc.,** ( *0-9678238; 0-9702768; 1-931432* ) 456 Penn St., Yeadon, PA 19050 (SAN 253-8709) Tel 610-626-7770; Fax: 610-626-2778; Toll Free: 800-227-8178 Do not confuse with Image Connection, Lomita, CA
E-mail: imageco@earthlink.net.

**Image Imprints,** ( *0-9615233* ) 706 Eighth St., Fairmont, WV 26554-2505 (SAN 695-1767)
*Dist(s):* **Far West Bk. Service.**

**Images from the Past, Inc.,** ( *1-884592* ) 155 W. Main St., P.O. Box 137, Bennington, VT 05201-0137 Tel 802-442-3204 (phone/fax); Toll Free: 888-442-3204
E-mail: info@ImagesfromthePast.com
Web site: http://www.ImagesfromthePast.com
*Dist(s):* **Baker & Taylor Bks.**
**Koen Bk. Distributors.**

**Imaginary Pr., The,** ( *0-9656814* ) Orders Addr.: P.O. Box 509, East Setauket, NY 11733-0509 Tel 631-474-3621; Edit Addr.: 3 Quincy Ct., Setauket, NY 11733
E-mail: Wishnik@sunysuffolk.edu.

**ImaJinn Bks.,** ( *1-893896* ) P.O. Box 545, Canon City, CO 81215-0545 Toll Free: 877-625-3592
E-mail: orders@imajinnbooks.com
Web site: http://www.imajinnbooks.com.

**Impact Pubns.,** ( *0-942710; 1-57023* ) Div. of Development Concepts, Inc., 9104 Manassas Dr., Suite N, Manassas Park, VA 20111-5211 (SAN 240-1142) Tel 703-361-7300; Fax: 703-335-9486 Do not confuse with companies with the same name in Evanston, IL, Mandeville, LA
E-mail: impactp@impactpublications.com
Web site: http://www.impactpublications.com
*Dist(s):* **National Bk. Network.**

**Impress Imprint of Scriptorium Pr., The**

**Imprimatur Bks. Imprint of Down Home Pr.**

**In Audio Imprint of Sound Room Pubs., Inc.**

**In Between Bks.,** ( *0-935430* ) P.O. Box 790, Sausalito, CA 94966 (SAN 213-6236) Tel 415-383-8447; Fax: 415-381-3513; 415-381-1938
E-mail: inbetweenbooks@atthebutterflytree.com
Web site: http://www.atthebutterflytree.com.

**In His Steps Publishing,** ( *0-938645; 1-58535* ) Orders Addr.: P.O. Box 3563, Macon, GA 31205-3563 (SAN 661-633X) Tel 478-788-1848; Fax: 478-788-0925; Edit Addr.: 2249 Price Dr., Macon, GA 31206
E-mail: DrRev@msn.com.

**InChem Publishing Div.,** ( *0-9642058* ) Div. of Independent Chemical, Inc., Orders Addr.: P.O. Box 11565, Cleveland, OH 44111-0565 Fax: 216-941-6702 ; Edit Addr.: 4055 W. 166th St., Cleveland, OH 44135 Tel 216-941-6664.

**Incommunicado Pr.,** ( *1-888277* ) 326 Spring St., New York, NY 10013-1322 Fax: 212-925-5911
E-mail: info@incommunicado.com
Web site: http://www.onecity.com/incom
*Dist(s):* **SPD-Small Pr. Distribution.**

**Independence Pr. Imprint of Herald Publishing Hse.**

**Independent Pubs. Group,** Subs. of Chicago Review Pr., 814 N. Franklin, Chicago, IL 60610 (SAN 202-0769) Tel 312-337-0747; Fax: 312-337-5985; Toll Free: 800-888-4741
E-mail: lreardon@ipgbook.com; usold@ipgbook.com
Web site: http://www.ipgbook.com.

**Indian Historian Pr., Inc.,** ( *0-913436* ) 1493 Masonic Ave., San Francisco, CA 94117 (SAN 202-6929) Tel 415-626-5235.

†**Indiana Univ. Pr.,** ( *0-253* ) 601 N. Morton St., Bloomington, IN 47404-3797 (SAN 202-5647) Fax: 812-855-7931; Toll Free: 800-842-6796
E-mail: iuporder@indiana.edu
Web site: http://www.Indiana.edu/~iupress
*Dist(s):* **Baker & Taylor International**
**netLibrary, Inc.; CIP.**

**Indigo Imprint of Genesis Pr., Inc.**

**IndyPublish.com,** ( *1-58827; 1-4043; 1-4142* ) P.O. Box 410186, Cambridge, MA 02141
E-mail: info@indypublish.com
Web site: http://www.indypublish.com
*Dist(s):* **NuvoMedia**
**Replica Bks..**

**In-Fisherman, Inc.,** ( *0-929384; 0-9605254; 1-892947* ) 2 In-Fisherman Dr., Brainerd, MN 56401 (SAN 215-8965) Tel 218-825-2540; Fax: 218-829-2371; Toll Free: 800-814-8404.

**InfoNet Pubns.,** ( *0-9651190* ) 23852 Pacific Coast Hwy., PMB 330, Malibu, CA 90265 Tel 310-572-4125; Fax: 310-388-1026
E-mail: infonet@furthest.com
Web site: http://www.badbooks.com
*Dist(s):* **Partners/West.**

**Inheritance Pr., Inc.,** ( *0-9638086* ) 101 Henderson Ln., Trenton, NC 28585 Tel 919-448-3131; Fax: 919-448-1113.

**Inheritance Pubns.,** ( *0-921100* ) P.O. Box 366, Pella, IA 50219 Tel 780-674-3949 (phone/fax); Toll Free: 800-563-3594 (phone/fax)
E-mail: inhpubl@telusplanet.net
Web site: http://www.telusplanet.net/public/inhpubl/webip/ip..

**Innisfree Pr.,** ( *0-931055; 1-880913* ) 136 Roumfort Rd., Philadelphia, PA 19119 Tel 215-247-4085; Fax: 215-247-2343; Toll Free: 800-367-5872 (religious trade); 800-283-3572 (general)
E-mail: InnisfreeP@aol.com
Web site: http://www.innisfreepress.com
*Dist(s):* **Consortium Bk. Sales & Distribution.**

**Insomniac Pr. (CAN)** ( *1-895837; 1-894663* ) Dist. by **StackpoleBks.**

**Instantpublisher.com,** ( *1-59196* ) Orders Addr.: P.O. Box 985, Collierville, TN 38027 Tel 800-259-2592; Fax: 901-853-6196; Edit Addr.: 410 Hwy, 72 W., Collierville, TN 38017
E-mail: chris@instantpublisher.com
Web site: http://www.instantpublisher.com
*Dist(s):* **Dogwise Publishing.**

**Integra Pr.,** ( *0-9626148* ) 1702 W. Camelback, Suite 119, Phoenix, AZ 85015 Tel 602-841-7176; Fax: 602-841-2279
E-mail: info@integrapress.com
Web site: http://www.integrapress.com.

**Integrity Pubs.,** ( *1-59145* ) 5250 Virginia Way, Suite 110, Brentwood, TN 37027 (SAN 254-6264) Tel 615-370-3230; Fax: 615-370-3226
E-mail: jpaul@integinc.com
Web site: http://www.integrityincorporated.com.

**Interactive Knowledge** *See* **netLibrary, Inc.**

**Intercontinental Publishing, Inc.,** ( *1-881164* ) Orders Addr.: P.O. Box 7242, Fairfax Station, VA 22039 Tel 703-583-4800; Fax: 703-670-7825; Edit Addr.: 11681 Beacon Race Rd., Woodbridge, VA 22192
E-mail: icpub@worldnet.att.net
Web site: http://home.att.net/~icpub/index.html.

**Interlingua Foreign Language AudioBooks,** ( *1-58085* ) Orders Addr.: P.O. Box 4175, Arlington, VA 22204-0175 Tel 703-575-7849; Fax: 703-575-8919; Toll Free: 800-336-4400; Edit Addr.: 838 S. Monroe, Arlington, VA 22204
E-mail: altech@pressroom.com
Web site: http://www.foreign-audio-books.com; http://www.russianaudio.com.

**Interlink Publishing Group, Inc.,** ( *0-940793; 1-56656* ) 46 Crosby St., Northampton, MA 01060-1804 (SAN 664-8908) Tel 413-582-7054; Fax: 413-582-6731; Toll Free: 800-238-5465; *Imprints:* Crocodile Books (Crocodile Bks)
E-mail: info@interlinkbooks.com; editor@interlinkbooks.com
Web site: http://www.interlinkbooks.com.

†**International Bk. Ctr., Inc.,** ( *0-86685; 0-917062* ) 2007 Laurel Dr., P.O. Box 295, Troy, MI 48099 (SAN 169-4014) Tel 248-879-8436; Fax: 810-254-7230
E-mail: ibc@ibcbooks.com
Web site: http://www.ibcbooks.com; CIP.

**International Bk. Import Service, Inc.,** Orders Addr.: 161 Main St., P.O. Box 8188, Lynchburg, TN 37352-8188 (SAN 630-5679) Tel 931-759-7400; Fax: 931-759-7555; Toll Free: 800-277-4247
E-mail: IBIS@IBIService.com
Web site: http://www.IBIService.com.

**International Comics & Entertainment L.L.C.,** ( *1-929090; 1-932575* ) 1005 Mahone St., Fredericksburg, VA 22401 Tel 540-899-9186; Fax: 540-899-9196
E-mail: kblue@ic-ent.com
Web site: http://www.ic-ent.com
*Dist(s):* **Diamond Comic Distributors, Inc..**

**International Law & Taxation Pubs.,** ( *1-893713* ) P.O. Box 025207, Miami, FL 33102-5207 Tel 407-650-2537 (phone/fax); Dept. PTY 2624, Unit C-102 1601 NW 97th Ave., Miami, FL 33172
E-mail: internationallaw@cyberhaven.com
Web site: http://www.internationallawandtaxationpublishers.com.

†**International Polygonics, Ltd.,** ( *0-930330; 1-55882* ) P.O. Box 1563, New York, NY 10159 (SAN 211-0210) Tel 212-683-2914; Fax: 212-545-0429; *Imprints:* Library of Crime Classics (Lib Crime Classics)
*Dist(s):* **Independent Pubs. Group; CIP.**

**International Publishers Co., Inc.,** ( *0-7178* ) 239 W. 23rd St., 5th Flr., New York, NY 10011 (SAN 202-5655) Tel 212-366-9816; Fax: 212-366-9820
E-mail: service@intpubnyc.com
Web site: http://www.intpubnyc.com.

**International Publishers Marketing,** Orders Addr.: 22883 Quicksilver Dr., Dulles, VA 20166 (SAN 253-3375) Toll Free: 800-758-3756; Edit Addr.: P.O. Box 605, Herndon, VA 20172-0605 Fax: 703-661-1501.

**International Scholars Pubns.,** ( *1-57309; 1-85607; 1-883255* ) 4720 Boston, Lanham, MD 20706 Tel 301-459-3366; Fax: 301-459-5357; Toll Free Fax: 800-338-4550; Toll Free: 800-462-6420; *Imprints:* University Press for West Africa (U Pr W Africa)
E-mail: info@interscholars.com
Web site: http://www.interscholars.com
*Dist(s):* **National Bk. Network**
**Rowman & Littlefield Pubs., Inc.**
**Univ. Pr. of America.**

Names

**International Specialized Bk. Services,** 920 NE 58th Ave., Suite 300, Portland, OR 97213-3786 (SAN 169-7129) Tel 503-287-3093; Fax: 503-280-8832; Toll Free: 800-944-6190 E-mail: info@isbs.com. Web site: http://www.isbs.com.

**Internet Book Co., Inc.,** ( *1-930739; 1-931621* ) P.O. Box 327, Pacifica, CA 94044 Web site: http://www.internetbookco.

†**InterVarsity Pr.,** ( *0-8308; 0-87784* ) Div. of InterVarsity Christian Fellowship of the USA, Orders Addr.: P.O. Box 1400, Downers Grove, IL 60515 (SAN 202-7089) Tel 630-734-4000; Fax: 630-734-4200; Toll Free: 800-843-9487 (orders); 800-843-1019 (customer service); 800-873-0143 (electronic ordering); 800-843-7225 (other depts.) E-mail: mail@ivpress.com Web site: http://www.ivpress.com. *Dist(s):* **Baker & Taylor Bks. CRC Pubns. Riverside Bk. & Bible Resource***; CIP.*

**Intrigue Pr. Imprint of Corvus Publishing**

**Invisible Cities Pr.,** ( *0-9679683; 1-931229* ) 50 State St., Montpelier, VT 05602 Tel 802-223-2323 E-mail: editor@invisiblecitiespress.com Web site: http://www.invisiblecitiespress.com *Dist(s):* **Independent Pubs. Group.**

†**Iowa State Pr.,** ( *0-8138* ) 2121 S. State Ave., Ames, IA 50014-8300 (SAN 202-7194) Tel 515-292-0140; Fax: 515-292-3348 E-mail: orders@isupress.com Web site: http://www.iowastatepress.com*; CIP.*

**Iowa State University Press** *See* **Iowa State Pr.**

**ipicturebooks, LLC,** ( *1-58824; 1-59019; 1-59155; 1-59173* ) 24 W. 25th St., No. 12, New York, NY 10010 Tel 212-645-9870; Fax: 212-645-9874 E-mail: aandrade@ipicturebooks.com Web site: http://www.ipicturebooks.com *Dist(s):* **Time Warner Bk. Group.**

**Irish Academic Pr. (IRL)** ( *0-7165* ) Dist. by **Intl Spec Bk.**

**Irish American Bk. Co.,** Subs. of Roberts Rinehart Pubs., Inc., P.O. Box 666, Niwot, CO 80544-0666 Tel 303-652-2710; Fax: 303-652-2689; Toll Free: 800-452-7115 E-mail: irishbooks@aol.com Web site: http://www.irishvillage.com.

**Irish Bks. & Media, Inc.,** ( *0-937702* ) Orders Addr.: 1433 E. Franklin Ave., Suite 20, Minneapolis, MN 55404-2135 (SAN 111-8870) Tel 612-871-3505; Fax: 612-871-3358; Toll Free: 800-229-3505 Do not confuse with Irish Bks. in New York, NY E-mail: Irishbook@aol.com Web site: http://www.irishbook.com.

**Irite Publishing,** ( *0-9700957* ) P.O. Box 34195, Chicago, IL 60634 Tel 773-227-8040 E-mail: irite@mindspring.com Web site: http//www.makemeniceanovel.com *Dist(s):* **Alliance Hse.,**

**Ironweed Pr., Inc.,** ( *0-9655309; 1-931336* ) Orders Addr.: P.O. Box 754208, Forest Hills, NY 11375 Tel 718-544-1120; Fax: 718-268-2394; Toll Free: 800-650-5403; Edit Addr.: 77 Puritan Ave., Forest Hills, NY 11375 E-mail: iwpress@aol.com *Dist(s):* **Brodart Co..**

**Iroquois Pr.,** ( *0-9633548* ) 109 N. Iroquois St., Laurium, MI 49913 Tel 906-337-4536.

†**Irvington Pubs.,** ( *0-512; 0-8290; 0-8422; 0-89197* ) Orders Addr.: P.O. Box 286, New York, NY 10276-0286 Fax: 212-861-0998; Toll Free Fax: 800-455-5520; Toll Free: 800-472-6037*; CIP.*

**ISIS Audio Bks. (GBR)** ( *0-7531; 1-85089; 1-85695* ) Dist. by **Ulverscroft US.**

**ISIS Large Print Bks. (GBR)** ( *0-7531; 1-85089; 1-85695* ) Dist. by **Transaction Pubs.**

**ISIS Large Print Bks. (GBR)** ( *0-7531; 1-85089; 1-85695* ) Dist. by **Ulverscroft US.**

**Isis-Oasis (GBR)** ( *1-85089; 1-85695* ) Dist. by **Eye Ear.**

**Island Heritage Publishing,** ( *0-89610; 0-931548* ) Div. of The Madden Corp., 94-411 Koaki St., Waipahu, HI 96797 (SAN 211-1403) Tel 808-564-8888; Fax: 808-564-8999; Toll Free: 800-468-2800 E-mail: hawaii4u@islandheritage.com Web site: http://www.islandheritage.com/.

**Island Nation Pr., LLC,** ( *0-9657437; 1-892738* ) Orders Addr.: 144 Rowayton Woods Dr., Norwalk, CT 06854 Tel 203-852-0028; Fax: 203-852-0528; Toll Free: 800-356-1450 (Press 00 at the tone for orders.) E-mail: cvaleallen@earthlink.net Web site: http://www.charlottevaleallen.com.

**Israeli Trading Co.,** ( *1-880880* ) 4701 New Otrecht Ave., Brooklyn, NY 11219 Tel 718-437-9251; Fax: 718-437-4246; Toll Free: 800-892-4246.

**Italica Pr.,** ( *0-934977* ) 595 Main St., Suite 605, New York, NY 10044 (SAN 695-1805) Tel 212-935-4230; Fax: 212-838-7812 E-mail: inquiries@italicapress.com Web site: http://www.italicapress.com.

**iUniverse, Inc. Imprint of iUniverse, Inc.**

**iUniverse, Inc.,** ( *0-9665514; 1-58348; 0-9668591; 1-893652; 0-595* ) Orders Addr.: 2021 Pine Lake Rd., Suite 100, Lincoln, NE 68512 (SAN 254-9425) Tel 402-323-7800; Fax: 402-323-7824; Toll Free: 877-823-9235; *Imprints:* Writers Club Press (Writers Club Pr); Writer's Showcase Press (Writers Showcase); Backinprint.com (Backinprint); Authors Choice Press (Authors Choice Pr); Mystery Writers of America Presents (Myst Write Amer); Mystery & Suspense Press (Mystery & Suspense); iUniverse, Inc. (iUni Inc) E-mail: pubservices@iuniverse.com; custservice@iuniverse.com Web site: http://www.iUniverse.com.

**iUniverse.com, Incorporated** *See* **iUniverse, Inc.**

**Ivy Bks. Imprint of Ballantine Bks.**

**Ivy League Pr., Inc.,** ( *0-918921* ) P.O. Box 3326, San Ramon, CA 94583-8326 (SAN 670-0543) Tel 925-736-0601; Fax: 925-736-0602; Toll Free Fax: 888-489-7737; Toll Free: 800-489-7737 E-mail: IvyLeaguePress@worldnet.att.net *Dist(s):* **Baker & Taylor Bks..**

**J&J Bks.,** ( *1-878151* ) Div. of Burnt Rock Antiques, Orders Addr.: P.O. Box 76, Three Mile Bay, NY 13693; Edit Addr.: Burnt Rock Rd & Favret Rd., Cape Vincent, NY 13618 Tel 315-654-2305 Do not confuse with J & J Bks., Angola, IN, Grass Valley, CA *Dist(s):* **North Country Bks., Inc..**

**JMT Pubns.,** ( *0-9703045* ) 501 N. White St., Shirley, IN 47384 Do not confuse with JMT Pubns., Silver Spring, MD E-mail: jeantype@excite.com Web site: http://jmtpubs.hypermart.net.

**Jackson, Steve Games, Inc.,** ( *1-55634* ) P.O. Box 18957, Austin, TX 78760 (SAN 661-3292) Tel 512-447-7866; Fax: 512-447-1144 E-mail: sjgames@io.com Web site: http://www.sjgames.com.

**Jade Ram Publishing,** ( *1-877721* ) 3003 Wendy's Way, No. 9, Anchorage, AK 99517-1466 Tel 907-248-0979 ; Fax: 907-272-8432 E-mail: jaderam@alaska.net *Dist(s):* **Publication Consultants Todd Communications**

†**Jameson Bks., Inc.,** ( *0-89803; 0-915463; 0-916054* ) 722 Columbus St., P.O. Box 738, Ottawa, IL 61350 (SAN 281-7578) Tel 815-434-7905; Fax: 815-434-7907; Toll Free: 800-426-1357; *Imprints:* Frontier Library, The (Frontier Libr) E-mail: jamesonbooks@yahoo.com *Dist(s):* **Midpoint Trade Bks., Inc.;** *CIP.*

**Jamestown,** ( *0-02; 0-07; 0-8092; 0-8442; 0-89061; 0-913327; 0-941263; 1-56943* ) Div. of Glencoe/McGraw-Hill, Orders Addr.: P.O. Box 543, Blacklick, OH 43004-0543 Fax: 614-860-1877; Toll Free: 800-334-7344; Edit Addr.: P.O. Box 508, Columbus, OH 43216 Toll Free: 800-872-7323 Web site: jamestowneducation.com *Dist(s):* **Libros Sin Fronteras McGraw-Hill Cos., The.**

**Jane's Information Group, Inc.,** ( *0-354; 0-356; 0-7106* ) Subs. of Jane's Information Group, Ltd. (UK), 110 N. Royal St., Suite 200, Alexandria, VA 22314 (SAN 286-357X) Tel 703-683-3700; Fax: 703-836-0029; Toll Free: 800-824-0768 E-mail: order@janes.com Web site: http://www.janes.com *Dist(s):* **Univelt, Inc..**

**Jane's Publishing, Incorporated** *See* **Jane's Information Group, Inc.**

**Janus Publishing Co. (GBR)** ( *1-85756* ) Dist. by **Paul & Co Pubs.**

**Jarrett, Norma L.,** ( *0-9671923* ) P.O. Box 40147, Houston, TX 77240 Tel 713-957-5006; Fax: 713-681-6143 E-mail: nljarrett@hotmail.com Web site: http://www.pageturner.net/e-page/.

**J-D Publishing Co.,** ( *0-9669259* ) 1615 Poydras St., Suite 620, New Orleans, LA 70112 Tel 504-456-6125 ; Fax: 504-780-8739 E-mail: jdpublish@aol.com.

**Jersey Yarns Imprint of Quincannon Publishing Group**

**Jewel Publishing Co.,** ( *0-9614890* ) 165 Congress Run Rd., Cincinnati, OH 45215 (SAN 693-2460) Tel 513-521-1149 Do not confuse with companies with similar names in Denver, CO, New york, NY, Baltimore, MD *Dist(s):* **Baker & Taylor Bks. Distributors, The.**

†**Jewish Lights Publishing,** ( *1-58023; 1-879045* ) Div. of LongHill Partners, Inc., Sunset Farm Offices, Rte. 4, Woodstock, VT 05091 (SAN 242-6439) Tel 802-457-4000; Fax: 802-457-4004; Toll Free: 800-962-4544 (orders) E-mail: sales@jewishlights.com; everyone@longhillpartners.com Web site: http://www.jewishlights.com *Dist(s):* **Baker & Taylor Bks. Bookazine Co., Inc. New Leaf Distributing Co., Inc. Spring Arbor Distributors, Inc.;** *CIP.*

†**Jewish Pubn. Society,** ( *0-8276; 965-7157* ) Orders Addr.: 22883 Quicksilver Dr., Dulles, VA 20166 (SAN 253-9446) Tel 703-661-1529; 703-661-1165; Fax: 703-661-1501; Toll Free: 800-355-1165; Edit Addr.: 2100 Arch St., 2nd Flr., Philadelphia, PA 19103 Tel 215-832-0601; Fax: 215-568-2017; Toll Free: 800-234-3151 E-mail: shirleyb@ix.netcom.com; marketing@jewishpub.org; www.jewishpub.org Web site: http://www.jewishpub.org *Dist(s):* **Gefen Bks.;** *CIP.*

**Jews For The Preservation of Firearms Ownership, Inc.,** ( *0-9642304* ) P.O. Box 270143, Hartford, WI 53027 Tel 262-673-9745; Fax: 262-673-9746 E-mail: jpfo@execpc.com Web site: http://www.jpfo.org.

**Jimcin Recordings,** ( *1-55688* ) Orders Addr.: P.O. Box 536, Portsmouth, RI 02871 (SAN 694-2377) Toll Free: 800-538-3034; Edit Addr.: 240 Bramans Ln., Portsmouth, RI 02871 E-mail: jimcin@jimcin.com Web site: http://www.jimcin.com.

**Jimrose Publishing Co.,** ( *0-9675546* ) P.O. Box 388, Pine Lake, GA 30072 Tel 404-294-7528; Fax: 404-294-6819 E-mail: thunter142@aol.com Web site: http://www.travishunter.com.

**JMW Group, Inc.,** 3 New King St., White Plains, NY 10604 Tel 914-328-7200; Fax: 914-328-7686 E-mail: icct@net.att.net.

**JNMedia Bks. Imprint of JNMedia, Inc.**

**JNMedia, Inc.,** ( *1-930128* ) PMB 109 2124 Broadway, New York, NY 10023-1722 Fax: 916-404-6601; *Imprints:* JNMedia Books (JNMedia) E-mail: jnmediany@aol.com Web site: http://www.jnmedia.com.

**Joan of Arc Publishing,** ( *1-930185* ) 340 E. Sixth St., Apt. 5, New York, NY 10003 Toll Free: 866-888-9800 E-mail: WJoanDArc@cs.com *Dist(s):* **Baker & Taylor Bks..**

**Johannesen Printing & Publishing,** ( *1-881084* ) Orders Addr.: P.O. Box 24, Whitethorn, CA 95589 Tel 707-986-7465; Fax: 707-986-1656 E-mail: johannesen@humboldt.net Web site: http://www.johannesen.com.

**John James Co.,** ( *0-9675915* ) 79 Worth St., New York, NY 10013 Tel 212-966-5432; Fax: 212-625-9823 E-mail: JJPublishing@msn.com.

†**Johns Hopkins Univ. Pr.,** ( *0-8018* ) Div. of Johns Hopkins Univ., 2715 N. Charles St., Baltimore, MD 21218-4319 (SAN 202-7348) Tel 410-516-6900; Fax: 410-516-6998; Toll Free: 800-537-5487 E-mail: hfscustserv@mail.press.jhu.edu Web site: http://muse.jhu.edu/; http://www.jhupbooks.com *Dist(s):* **netLibrary, Inc.;** *CIP.*

**Johnsbook.com,** ( *0-9701668* ) 7429 SE 27th St., Mercer Island, WA 98040 Tel 206-232-8199; 206 232 8199; Fax: 206-232-8253 E-mail: mediawest@msn.com.

**Johnson Bks.,** ( *0-917895; 0-933472; 1-55566* ) Div. of Johnson Publishing Co., 1880 S. 57th Ct., Boulder, CO 80301 (SAN 201-0313) Tel 303-443-9766; Fax: 303-998-7594; Toll Free: 800-258-5830 E-mail: books@jpcolorado.com Web site: http://www.johnsonbooks.com.

**Johnston, Don Inc.,** ( *1-893376; 1-58702; 1-4105* ) Orders Addr.: 26799 W. Commerce Dr., Volo, IL 60073 Tel 847-740-0749; Fax: 847-740-7326; Toll Free: 800-999-4660 Web site: http://www.donjohnston.com.

**Jonathan Publishing Co.,** ( *0-9634206* ) 3524 Elmora Ave., Baltimore, MD 21213 Tel 410-563-4431 Do not confuse with Jonathan Pub. in Austin, TX.

Names

†**Jones, Bob Univ. Pr.,** ( *0-89084; 1-57924; 1-59166* ) 1700 Wade Hampton Blvd., Greenville, SC 29614 (SAN 223-7512) Tel 864-242-5731; Fax: 864-298-8398; Toll Free Fax: 800-525-8398; Toll Free: 800-845-5731 E-mail: bjup@bjup.com Web site: http://www.bjup.com; *CIP.*

**Jones, John Publishing (GBR)** ( *1-871083* ) *Dist. by* **Intl Spec Bk.**

**Jordan Pr.,** ( *0-9613427* ) 620 Sycamore Ave., Modesto, CA 95354-0151 (SAN 657-047X) Tel 209-571-2030 Do not confuse with companies with the same or similar names in Lake Worth, FL, San Mateo, CA, Baltimore, MD E-mail: danziger@toto.csustan.edu.

**Joseph, Beatrice Publishing,** ( *0-9729392* ) Orders Addr.: P.O. Box 191383, Boston, MA 02119 Tel 617-359-9331; Fax: 617-427-3165 E-mail: beatrice_joseph@earthlink.net.

**Joseph, Michael** Imprint of **Viking Penguin**

**Joseph, Michael Ltd. (GBR)** ( *0-7181* ) *Dist. by* **Trafalgar.**

**Journey Bk. Pr.** Imprint of **C C Publishing**

**Jove** Imprint of **Berkley Publishing Group**

**Joy Street Bks.** Imprint of **Little Brown & Co.**

**J-Pr. Publishing,** ( *0-9660111; 1-930922* ) 4796 N. 126th St., White Bear Lake, MN 55110 Toll Free: 888-407-1723 E-mail: Sjackson@Jpresspublishing.com Web site: http://www.jpresspublishing.com *Dist(s):* **Baker & Taylor Bks..**

**Juan de la Cuesta-Hispanic Monographs,** ( *0-936388; 1-58871* ) 270 Indian Rd., Newark, DE 19711 (SAN 221-4695) Tel 302-453-8695; Fax: 302-453-8601; Toll Free Fax: 800-784-4935; Toll Free: 800-784-4938 E-mail: libros@juandelacuesta.com Web site: http://www.juandelacuesta.com.

**Judaica Pr., Inc., The,** ( *0-910818; 1-880582; 1-932443* ) 123 Ditmas Ave., Brooklyn, NY 11218 (SAN 204-9856) Tel 718-972-6200; Fax: 718-972-6204; Toll Free: 800-972-6201 E-mail: info@judaicapress.com Web site: http://www.judaicapress.com.

†**Judson Pr.,** ( *0-8170* ) Div. of American Baptist Churches, U.S.A., P.O. Box 851, Valley Forge, PA 19482-0851 (SAN 201-0348) Tel 610-768-2118; Fax: 610-768-2107; Toll Free: 800-331-1053 Web site: http://www.judsonpress.com *Dist(s):* **Appalachian Bible Co.** **Riverside** **Spring Arbor Distributors, Inc.;** *CIP.*

**Jukebox Pr.,** ( *0-932693* ) P.O. Box 2069, Berkeley, CA 94702 (SAN 678-1969) Tel 510-528-7025; Fax: 510-528-3763 *Dist(s):* **SPD-Small Pr. Distribution.**

**July Blue Pr.,** ( *0-9656635* ) Orders Addr.: P.O. Box 2006, Arcadia, CA 91077 Tel 626-445-4420 E-mail: jlybl@earthlink.net *Dist(s):* **Baker & Taylor Bks.** **Small Pr. Alliance.**

**Junior League of Charleston, South Carolina, Inc.,** ( *0-9607854* ) 51 Folly Rd., Charleston, SC 29407 (SAN 218-8031) Tel 843-763-5284; Fax: 843-763-1626 E-mail: office@jlcharleston.org Web site: http://www.jlcharleston.org/.

**Junior League of Philadelphia, Inc.,** ( *0-9626959* ) 215 S 16th St., Philadelphia, PA 19102 Tel 215-731-1446; Fax: 215-731-1978 E-mail: jlphila@atxmail.com Web site: http://www.jphila.com.

**Justin, Charles & Co. Pubs.,** ( *1-932112* ) 20 Park Plaza, Suite 909, Boston, MA 02116 Tel 617-426-4406; *Imprints:* Kate's Mystery Books (Kate's Myst Bks) E-mail: info@justincharlesbooks.com Web site: http://www.justincharlesbooks.com *Dist(s):* **National Bk. Network.**

**Justpub,** ( *0-9702145* ) 137 Lynn-Justice Rd., Bainbridge, GA 31717-6731 (SAN 253-2999) Tel 912-246-5828 E-mail: justpub@surfsouth.com; justpub2surfsouth.com.

**Juventud, Editorial (ESP)** ( *84-261* ) *Dist. by* **Continental Bk.**

**KAC, Inc.,** ( *0-9622353* ) 3425 S. 94th Ave., Omaha, NE 68124 Tel 402-393-8537.

**KUNI/KHKE,** ( *0-9662041* ) Univ. of Northern Iowa, Cedar Falls, IA 50614-0359 Tel 319-273-6400; Fax: 319-273-2682; Toll Free: 800-772-2440 E-mail: jons.olsson@uni.edu; kuni@uni.edu Web site: http://www.uni.edu/kuni.

**Kachemak Country Pubns.,** ( *0-9651157* ) P.O. Box 3406, Homer, AK 99603-3406 Tel 907-235-8925.

**Kalcolby, Pat,** ( *0-9675023* ) Orders Addr.: P.O. Box 2206, Austin, TX 78768-2206; Edit Addr.: 7312 S. Hwy. 183, Suite 101, Austin, TX 78744.

**Kallman Publishing Co.,** ( *0-910824* ) 1614 W. University Ave., Box 14076, Gainesville, FL 32604 (SAN 203-9141) Tel 352-376-6066; Fax: 352-378-7446 E-mail: fbs@vector.net Web site: http://www.flbookstore.com.

**Kalos Pr.,** ( *0-9658820* ) 2331 W. Barry Ave., Chicago, IL 60618-8013.

**Kamalu'uluolele Pubs.,** ( *1-892174* ) 85-175 Farrington, No. A334, Makaha, HI 96792 Tel 808-696-8419 E-mail: Kumalu85@aol.com *Dist(s):* **Native Bks..**

†**Kane/Miller Bk. Pubs.,** ( *0-916291; 1-929132* ) Orders Addr.: P.O. Box 8515, La Jolla, CA 92038 (SAN 295-8945) Tel 858-456-0540; Fax: 858-456-9641; Toll Free: 800-968-1930 E-mail: kira@kanemiller.com Web site: http://www.kanemiller.com; http://www.everyonepoops.com *Dist(s):* **Cheng & Tsui Co.** **Distributors, The** **Lectorum Pubns., Inc.;** *CIP.*

**Kar-Ben Copies, Incorporated** *See* **Kar-Ben Publishing**

†**Kar-Ben Publishing,** ( *0-929371; 0-930494; 1-58013* ) Div. of Lerner Publishing Group, 1251 Washington Ave., N, Minneapolis, MN 55401 (SAN 210-7511) Tel 612-332-3344; Toll Free Fax: 800-332-1132; Toll Free: 800-452-7236 E-mail: karben@aol.com Web site: http://www.karben.com; *CIP.*

**Karger, S. AG,** ( *3-8055* ) 26 W. Avon Rd., Farmington, CT 06085 (SAN 281-8531) Tel 860-675-7834; Fax: 860-675-7302; Toll Free: 800-828-5479; Allschwilerstr 10, Basel, 4009 Tel 0761 452070; Fax: 0761 4520714 E-mail: karger@snet.net. Web site: http://www.karger.com.

**Karson Publishing,** ( *0-9642466* ) 14676 Superior Rd., Cleveland Heights, OH 44118 Tel 216-321-6881.

**Kasak, Richard Bks.** Imprint of **Masquerade Bks., Inc.**

**Kate, Incorporated** *See* **KAC, Inc.**

**Kate's Mystery Bks.** Imprint of **Justin, Charles & Co. Pubs.**

**Kav Books, Incorporated** *See* **Royal Fireworks Publishing Co.**

**Kaya Production,** ( *1-885030* ) 373 Broadway, No. F3, New York, NY 10013 Tel 212-343-9503; Fax: 212-343-8291 E-mail: sunyoung@kaya.com; kaya@kaya.com; julie@kaya.com Web site: http://www.kaya.com *Dist(s):* **Distributed Art Pubs./D.A.P.** **SPD-Small Pr. Distribution.**

**Kazi Pubns., Inc.,** ( *0-933511; 0-935782; 1-56744* ) 3023 W. Belmont Ave., Chicago, IL 60618 (SAN 162-3397) Tel 773-267-7001; Fax: 773-267-7002 E-mail: info@kazi.org Web site: http://www.kazi.org.

**Keats Publishing** Imprint of **McGraw-Hill Trade**

**Kegan Paul International Ltd. (GBR)** ( *0-7103* ) *Dist. by* **Col U Pr.**

**Kegley Bks.,** ( *0-9641315* ) Orders Addr.: P.O. Box 134, Wytheville, VA 24382; Edit Addr.: P.O. Box 134, Wytheville, VA 24382-0134.

**Kehot Pubn. Society,** ( *0-8266* ) Orders Addr.: 291 Kingston Ave., Brooklyn, NY 11213 Tel 718-778-0226; Fax: 718-778-4148; Toll Free: 877-463-7567 (877-4MERKOS); Edit Addr.: 770 Eastern Pkwy., Brooklyn, NY 11213 (SAN 220-7060) ; *Imprints:* Merkos L'Inyonei Chinuch (Merkos LInyonei Chinuch) E-mail: kehot@juno.com; orders@kehotonline.com Web site: http://www.kehotonline.com *Dist(s):* **Baker & Taylor Bks.** **Bookazine Co., Inc..**

†**Kelley, Augustus M. Pubs.,** ( *0-678* ) Orders Addr.: P.O. Box 1048, Fairfield, NJ 07004-1048 (SAN 206-9768) Tel 212-685-7202 (phone/fax); *CIP.*

†**Kelsey Street Pr.,** ( *0-932716* ) 50 Northgate, Berkeley, CA 94708 (SAN 212-6729) Tel 510-845-2260; Fax: 510-548-9185 E-mail: kelseyst@sirius.com Web site: http://www.kelseyst.com *Dist(s):* **SPD-Small Pr. Distribution;** *CIP.*

**Kennedy, Byron & Company** *See* **Southern Heritage Pr., Inc.**

**KenningHouse** Imprint of **Maasai, Inc.**

**Kensington Bks.** Imprint of **Kensington Publishing Corp.**

**Kensington Publishing,** ( *0-9635775* ) Townhouse No. 23, Union Wharf, Boston, MA 02109 Fax: 617-227-3899; Toll Free: 800-989-3513.

**Kensington Publishing Corp.,** ( *0-7860; 0-8184; 0-8217; 1-55817; 1-57566; 0-7582* ) 850 Third Ave., New York, NY 10022-6222 Tel 212-407-1500; Fax: 212-935-0699; Toll Free: 800-221-2647; *Imprints:* Citadel Press (Citadel Pr); Stuart, Lyle (L Stuart); Birch Lane Press (Birch Ln Pr); Zebra Books (Zebra Kensgtn); Pinnacle Books (Pinncle Kensgtn); Kensington Books (Knsington); Encanto (Encanto); Dafina (Dafina) E-mail: jmclean@kensingtonbooks.com Web site: http://www.kensingtonbooks.com *Dist(s):* **Penguin Group (USA) Inc.** **Worldwide Media Service, Inc..**

**Kent Information Services, Inc.,** ( *0-9654000; 1-892855* ) 237 E. Main St., Kent, OH 44240-2526 E-mail: email@kentis.com Web site: http://www.kentis.com.

†**Kent State Univ. Pr.,** ( *0-87338* ) Orders Addr.: c/o BookMasters, Inc., 30 Amberwood Pkwy., Ashland, OH 44805 Tel 419-281-1802; Fax: 419-281-6883; Toll Free: 800-247-6553; Edit Addr.: 307 Lowry Hall, Kent, OH 44242-0001 (SAN 201-0437) Tel 330-672-7913; Fax: 330-672-3104 Web site: http://bookmasters.com ksu-press *Dist(s):* **BookMasters, Inc.;** *CIP.*

**Kentucke Imprints,** ( *0-935680* ) 1115 McKee Rd., Berea, KY 40403 (SAN 209-8245) Tel 606-985-9059.

**Kerr, Charles H. Publishing Co.,** ( *0-88286* ) 1740 W. Greenleaf Ave., Chicago, IL 60626 (SAN 207-7043) Tel 773-465-7774; 312-988-7246 (orders) E-mail: chicagoare@attglobal.net *Dist(s):* **Chicago Review Pr., Inc..**

†**Kesend, Michael Publishing, Ltd.,** ( *0-935576* ) Orders Addr.: Raritan Industrial Pk., 100 Newfield Ave., Edison, NJ 08837 Tel 732-225-2727; Fax: 732-225-1562; Toll Free: 800-488-8040; Edit Addr.: 1025 Fifth Ave., New York, NY 10028 (SAN 213-6902) Tel 212-249-5150; Fax: 212-249-2129 E-mail: mkpublishing@yahoo.com; *CIP.*

**Kessinger Publishing Co.,** ( *0-7661; 0-922802; 1-56459* ) Orders Addr.: P.O. Box 609, Belle Fourche, SD 57717 (SAN 251-4621) Tel 605-892-0560; Fax: 208-439-2000 E-mail: sales@kessinger.net Web site: http://www.kessinger.net.

**Ketman Publishing** *See* **Wooster Bk. Co., The**

**Key Porter Bks. (CAN)** ( *0-88619; 0-919493; 0-919630; 1-55013; 1-55263; 1-85375; 1-55356* ) *Dist. by* **Firefly Bks Limited.**

**Key Porter Bks. (CAN)** ( *0-88619; 0-919493; 0-919630; 1-55013; 1-55263; 1-85375; 1-55356* ) *Dist. by* **BookWorld.**

**Khalifah's Booksellers & Associates** *See* **Conquering Bks.**

**Kids Can Pr., Ltd.,** ( *0-919964; 0-921103; 1-55074; 1-55337* ) 2250 Military Rd., Tonawanda, NY 14150 Toll Free Fax: 800-221-9985; Toll Free: 866-481-5827 E-mail: jcase@kidscan.com.

**Kiepenheuer & Witsch GmbH & Company KG (DEU)** ( *3-462* ) *Dist. by* **Intl Bk Import.**

**Kildara Pr.,** ( *0-9725072* ) 3763 Lanier Dr., Baton Rouge, LA 70814 Fax: 225-923-3053 E-mail: george.baker@mindspring.com.

**Kincaid Kountry Bks.,** ( *0-9651707* ) 105 Cherrywood Addition, Scott Depot, WV 25560 Tel 304-755-3976; Toll Free: 800-875-2704.

**Kindred Press** *See* **Kindred Productions**

**Kindred Productions,** ( *0-919797; 0-921788* ) Orders Addr.: 315 S. Lincoln St., Hillsboro, KS 67063 Tel 316-947-3151; Fax: 316-947-3266; Toll Free: 800-545-7322 E-mail: kindred@mbconf.ca Web site: http://www.mbconf.org/kindred.htm *Dist(s):* **Spring Arbor Distributors, Inc..**

**Kingsley, Jessica Pubs. (GBR)** ( *1-85302; 1-84310* ) *Dist. by* **Taylor and Fran.**

**Kisco Pubns.,** ( *1-893566* ) P.O. Box 405, Palermo, CA 95968 Tel 530-532-0953.

**Kissed Pubns.,** ( *0-9667609* ) Orders Addr.: P.O. Box 9819, Hampton, VA 23670 Tel 757-728-3770; Fax: 757-728-1189; Toll Free: 888-896-0072; Edit Addr.: 23 Braemar Dr., Hampton, VA 23669 E-mail: kissed@prodigy.net Web site: http://www.geocities.com/Athens/Oracle/8522.

**Names**

**Kitchen Sink Pr., Inc.,** ( *0-87816; 1-56862; 1-879450* ) Div. of Disappearing, Inc., 529 Belchertown Rd., Amherst, MA 01002-2705 (SAN 212-7784) Tel 413-586-9525; Fax: 413-586-7040
E-mail: service@deniskitchen.com
Web site: http://www.deniskitchen.com
*Dist(s):* **Baker & Taylor Bks.**
**Bayside Entertainment Distribution**
**Capital City**
**Last Gasp Eco-Funnies, Inc..**

**Kiva Publishing, Inc.,** ( *1-885772* ) 21731 E. Buckskin Dr., Walnut, CA 91789 Tel 909-595-6833; Fax: 909-860-5424; Toll Free: 800-634-5482
E-mail: kivapub@aol.com
Web site: http://www.kivapub.com
*Dist(s):* **Baker & Taylor Bks.**
**Bookpeople**
**Canyonlands Pubns.**
**New Leaf Distributing Co., Inc.**
**Quality Bks., Inc.**
**Treasure Chest Bks..**

**Kleworks Publishing Co.,** ( *0-9665157* ) 6127 N. Ozark Ave., Chicago, IL 60631 (SAN 299-8815) Tel 773-774-3372; Fax: 773-467-4496
E-mail: kleworks@aol.com
Web site: http://www.mysterykleworks.com.

†**Kluwer Academic Pubs.,** ( *0-412; 0-7923; 0-85200; 0-89838; 1-55608; 90-5576; 90-440; 1-4020* ) Orders Addr.: P.O. Box 358, Hingham, MA 02018-0358 (SAN 662-0647) Tel 781-871-6600; Fax: 781-681-9045 (Customer Service); 781-871 6528; Edit Addr.: 101 Philip Dr. Assinippi Park, Norwell, MA 02061 (SAN 211-481X); a/o Kluwer Academic/Plenum Pubs., 233 Spring St., 7th Flr., New York, NY 10013-1522 Tel 212-620-8000; *Imprints:* Kluwer Academic/Human Science Press (Kluwer Acad Hman Sci)
E-mail: kluwer@wkap.com
Web site: http://www.wkap.nl
*Dist(s):* **Aspen Pubs., Inc.**
**Lippincott Williams & Wilkins**
**netLibrary, Inc.***; CIP.*

**Kluwer Academic/Human Science Pr. Imprint of Kluwer Academic Pubs.**

**Knightsbridge Publishing,** ( *1-56129; 1-877961* ) 601 Ridge Rd., Tiburon, CA 94920 Tel 415-789-9040.

**Knob Hill Pr.,** ( *0-9716965* ) 380 Halstead Dr., Crossville, TN 38555 Tel 931-456-4768 (phone/fax)
E-mail: knobhillpress@crossville.com
*Dist(s):* **Baker & Taylor Bks..**

†**Knoll, Allen A. Pubs.,** ( *0-9627297; 1-888310* ) 200 W. Victoria St., Santa Barbara, CA 93101-3627 (SAN 299-0539) Tel 805-564-3377 (orders); Fax: 805-966-6657 (orders); Toll Free: 800-777-7623 (orders)
E-mail: bookinfo@knollpublishers.com
Web site: http://www.knollpublishers.com
*Dist(s):* **Baker & Taylor Bks.**
**Brodart Co.***; CIP.*

**Knopf Imprint of Knopf, Alfred A. Inc.**

**Knopf Imprint of Knopf Publishing Group**

†**Knopf, Alfred A. Inc.,** ( *0-375; 0-394; 0-676; 0-679* ) Div. of The Knopf Publishing Group, Orders Addr.: 400 Hahn Rd., Westminster, MD 21157 Tel 410-848-1900; Toll Free Fax: 800-659-2436; Toll Free: 800-733-3000 (orders); Edit Addr.: 299 Park Ave., New York, NY 10171 (SAN 202-5825) Tel 212-751-2600; Fax: 212-572-2593; Toll Free: 800-726-0600; *Imprints:* Knopf (KnoG)
E-mail: customerservice@randomhouse.com
Web site: http://www.randomhouse.com/knopf
*Dist(s):* **Libros Sin Fronteras***; CIP.*

**Knopf Publishing Group,** ( *0-375; 0-385; 1-4000* ) Orders Addr.: 400 Hahn Rd., Westminster, MD 21157 Tel 410-848-1900; Toll Free: 800-726-0600; Edit Addr.: 299 Park Ave., New York, NY 10171; *Imprints:* Knopf (KnoG); Everyman's Library (Everymns Lib); Pantheon (Pantheon); Schocken (Schocken); Vintage (Vin Bks); Anchor (AncKPG)
*Dist(s):* **Random Hse., Inc..**

**Knowledge Adventure, Inc.,** ( *1-56997* ) Div. of Vivendi Universal Interactive, 6060 Center Dr., Los Angeles, CA 90045 Tel 310-649-8000.

†**Kodansha America, Inc.,** ( *0-87011; 1-56836* ) 575 Lexington Ave., 23rd Flr., New York, NY 10022-6102 (SAN 201-0526) Tel 917-322-6200; Fax: 212-935-6929; Toll Free: 800-451-7556
E-mail: Kabooks@aol.com.

**Kodansha International (JPN)** ( *4-7700* ) Dist. by Kodansha.

**Kodansha, Ltd. (JPN)** ( *4-06* ) Dist. by Kodansha.

**Koenisha Pubns.,** ( *0-9700458; 0-9718758; 0-9741685* ) 3196-53rd St., Hamilton, MI 49419 Tel 269-951-4100 (phone/fax)
E-mail: koenisha@macatawa.org
Web site: http://www.koenisha.com
*Dist(s):* **Baker & Taylor Bks..**

**Kokopelli Bks.,** ( *0-9655125* ) Div. of Blackacre, Inc., A Colorado Corp., 1960 S. Balsam St., Lakewood, CO 80227 Tel 303-984-4650; Fax: 303-355-6422.

**Kokopelli Press** *See* **Kokopelli Bks.**

**KolorScope Publications** *See* **ShanKrys Publishing, Inc.**

**Kolowalu Bk. Imprint of Univ. of Hawaii Pr.**

**Konemann,** ( *3-89508; 3-8290* ) 137 W. 19th St., New York, NY 10011 Tel 212-367-8855; Fax: 212-367-8866; Toll Free: 888-317-8855
E-mail: mchin@konemann.com
*Dist(s):* **Bayside Entertainment Distribution**
**Daedalus Bks.**
**Koen Bk. Distributors**
**Lectorum Pubns., Inc.**
**Mel Bay Pubns., Inc.**
**Trucatriche.**

**Kramer, H.J. Inc.,** ( *0-915811; 1-932073* ) P.O. Box 1082, Tiburon, CA 94920 (SAN 294-0833) Fax: 415-435-5364; Toll Free: 800-972-6657; *Imprints:* Starseed Press (Starseed)
E-mail: hjkramer@jps.net
Web site: http://www.newworldlibrary.com
*Dist(s):* **Bookpeople**
**New Leaf Distributing Co., Inc.**
**New World Library**
**Publishers Group West.**

**Kraus Reprint** *See* **Periodicals Service Co.**

**Krause Pubns.,** ( *0-87341; 0-87349; 0-89689; 0-930625; 0-934466; 1-58221* ) 700 E. State St., Iola, WI 54990-0001 (SAN 202-6554) Tel 715-445-2214; Fax: 715-445-4087; Toll Free: 800-258-0929 (Phone Orders); 888-457-2873
E-mail: info@krause.com
Web site: http://www.krause.com.

†**Kregel Pubns.,** ( *0-8254* ) Div. of Kregel, Inc., Orders Addr.: P.O. Box 2607, Grand Rapids, MI 49501-2607 (SAN 206-9792) Tel 616-451-4775; Fax: 616-451-9330; Toll Free: 800-733-2607; Edit Addr.: 733 Wealthy St., SE., Grand Rapids, MI 49503-5553 (SAN 298-9115)
E-mail: kregelbooks@kregel.com
Web site: http://www.kregel.com
*Dist(s):* **Appalachian Bk. Distributors**
**CRC Pubns.**
**FaithWorks**
**National Bk. Network**
**Riverside**
**Spring Arbor Distributors, Inc.***; CIP.*

**Kresnak Pr., Ltd.,** ( *0-9670668* ) P.O. Box 187, Powell, OH 43015-0187 (SAN 299-8300) Tel 614-620-1576; Fax: 216-274-6398
E-mail: sales@kresnakpress.com
Web site: http://www.kresnakpress.com.

†**Krieger Publishing Co.,** ( *0-88275; 0-89464; 0-89874; 1-57524* ) P.O. Box 9542, Melbourne, FL 32902-9542 (SAN 202-6562) Tel 321-724-9542; Fax: 321-951-3671; Toll Free: 800-724-0025
E-mail: info@krieger-publishing.com
Web site: http://www.krieger-publishing.com
*Dist(s):* **Univelt, Inc.***; CIP.*

**Kruger, Wolfgang Verlag, GmbH (DEU)** ( *3-8105* ) Dist. by Intl Bk Import.

†**Ktav Publishing Hse., Inc.,** ( *0-87068; 0-88125* ) Orders Addr.: P.O. Box 6249, Hoboken, NJ 07030 (SAN 201-0038) Tel 201-963-9524; Fax: 201-963-0102; Toll Free Fax: 800-626-7517 (orders); Edit Addr.: 900 Jefferson St., Hoboken, NJ 07030 (SAN 200-8866)
E-mail: orders@ktav.com; editor@ktav.com; staff@ktav.com
Web site: http://www.ktav.com
*Dist(s):* **Baker & Taylor Bks.***; CIP.*

†**Ku Pa'a Publishing,** ( *0-914916* ) P.O. Box 37460, Honolulu, HI 96837 (SAN 209-4932) Tel 808-531-7985; Fax: 808-534-1463
*Dist(s):* **Booklines Hawaii, Ltd.***; CIP.*

**Kwela Bks. (ZAF)** ( *0-7957* ) Dist. by **IPG Chicago.**

**L. A. Theatre Works,** ( *1-58081* ) 681 Venice Blvd., Venice, CA 90291 Tel 310-827-0808; Fax: 310-827-4949; Toll Free: 800-708-8863
E-mail: audiosales@latw.org
Web site: http://www.latw.org
*Dist(s):* **Publishers Group West.**

**L. A. Weekly Bks. Imprint of St. Martin's Pr.**

**LICO Publishing,** ( *0-9667361* ) 1541 S. Robertson Blvd., Los Angeles, CA 90035 Tel 310-553-6636; Fax: 310-553-9621; Toll Free: 888-844-5426.

†**LP Pubns.,** ( *0-916192; 1-931619* ) Div. of Teleos Institute, 7119 E. Shea Blvd., Suite 109, PMB 418, Scottsdale, AZ 85254-6107 (SAN 207-2513) Tel 480-948-1800; Fax: 480-948-1870; *Imprints:* Teleos Imprint (Teleos Imprint)
E-mail: teleosinst@aol.com
Web site: http://www.consciousnesswork.com*; CIP.*

**L.T. Pubns.,** ( *1-881684* ) P.O. Box 302, Beverly Hills, CA 90213 Tel 310-652-7657; Fax: 310-360-0406; Toll Free: 877-463-2333 (orders) Do not confuse with L.T. Pubns., Los Angeles, CA
E-mail: LTownsend@Earthlink.net
Web site: http://www.larrytownsend.com
*Dist(s):* **Alamo Square Distributors**
**Bookazine Co., Inc.**
**Koen Bk. Distributors.**

**La Alameda Pr.,** ( *0-963909; 1-888809* ) 9636 Guadalupe Trail, NW, Albuquerque, NM 87114 Tel 505-897-0285; Fax: 505-897-0751
*Dist(s):* **SPD-Small Pr. Distribution**
**Univ. of New Mexico Pr..**

**La Caille Nous Publishing Co.,** ( *0-9647635; 0-9718191* ) 328 Flatbush Ave., Suite 240, Brooklyn, NY 11238 Tel 212-726-1293; Fax: 212-591-6465
E-mail: gcadet@lcnpub.com
*Dist(s):* **Biblio Distribution.**

**La Costa Pr., Inc.,** ( *1-56780* ) 21701 Pacific Coast Hwy., Malibu, CA 90265 Tel 310-456-5522; Fax: 310-456-5109.

**La Questa Pr.,** ( *0-9644348* ) 211 La Questa Way, Woodside, CA 94062 Tel 650-851-7705; Fax: 650-851-7757
E-mail: kabbe@batnet.com.

**La Villita Pubns.,** ( *0-9624727; 1-928792* ) 5520 Homerlee Ave., East Chicago, IN 46312 Tel 219-397-4649
E-mail: lavillita@webtv.net.

**Lady Chatterley's Library** *See* **Pigeonhole Pr.**

**Ladybird Bks. Imprint of Penguin Group (USA) Inc.**

**LadyBug Publishing LLC,** ( *0-9721301* ) 235 E. Main St., No. 162, Hendersonville, TN 37075 Tel 615-308-6750; Toll Free Fax: 866-826-2130
E-mail: ladybugpublisher@aol.com.

**Lake View Pr.,** ( *0-941702* ) P.O. Box 578279, Chicago, IL 60657-8279 (SAN 239-2488) Tel 773-935-2694; Fax: 773-935-8710 Do not confuse with Lake View Pr., Caroja, NY or Lakeview Pr. in New Orleans, LA
*Dist(s):* **Smyrna Pr..**

**Lambda Pubns., Inc.,** ( *0-915361; 1-55774* ) 3709 13th Ave., Brooklyn, NY 11218-3622 (SAN 291-0640) Tel 718-972-5449; Fax: 718-972-6307
E-mail: judaica@email.msn.com.

**Landfall Pr., Inc.,** ( *0-913428* ) 5171 Chapin St., Dayton, OH 45429 (SAN 202-6627) Tel 937-298-9123 Do not confuse with Landfall Pr. Inc., Chicago, IL.

**Landmark Editions, Inc.,** ( *0-933849* ) P.O. Box 270169, Kansas City, MO 64127-2135 (SAN 692-6916) Tel 816-241-4919; Fax: 816-483-3755; Toll Free: 800-653-2665 (orders only); 1402 Kansas Ave., Kansas City, MO 64127
Web site: http://www.landmarkeditions.com
*Dist(s):* **Baker & Taylor Bks.**
**Brodart Co.**
**Childswork/Childsplay.**

**Laney-Smith, Inc.,** ( *0-9624488; 1-891816* ) Orders Addr.: P.O. Box 18218, Charlotte, NC 28218 Tel 704-536-9832; Fax: 704-536-9834; Edit Addr.: 1370 Briar Creek Rd., Charlotte, NC 28205
E-mail: laneysmith@laneysmith.com
Web site: http://www.laneysmith.com
*Dist(s):* **Stowe, Daniel J. Foundation**
**Muses, The.**

†**Lang, Peter Publishing, Inc.,** ( *0-8204; 3-631* ) Subs. of Verlag Peter Lang AG (SZ), 275 Seventh Ave., 28th Flr., New York, NY 10001-6708 (SAN 241-5534) Tel 212-647-7700; Fax: 212-647-7707; Toll Free: 800-770-5264
E-mail: patty@plang.com
Web site: http://www.peterlang.com*; CIP.*

**LangMarc Publishing,** ( *1-880292* ) Orders Addr.: P.O. Box 90488, Austin, TX 78709 (SAN 297-519X) Tel 512-394-0989; Fax: 512-394-0829; Toll Free: 800-864-1648 (orders only); Edit Addr.: 7500 Shadowridge Run, No. 28, Austin, TX 78749 Tel 512-394-0898
E-mail: langmarc@booksails.com
Web site: http://www.langmarc.com
*Dist(s):* **Baker & Taylor Bks.**
**FaithWorks**
**Quality Bks., Inc.**
**Spring Arbor Distributors, Inc..**

Names

**Lantern Bks.**, ( *1-930051; 1-59056* ) Div. of Booklight, Inc., One Union Sq., W., Suite 201, New York, NY 10003-3303 Tel 212-414-2275; Fax: 212-414-2412 E-mail: martin@booklightinc.com. Web site: http://www.booklightinc.com.

**Larcom Pr.**, ( *0-9678199; 0-9714370* ) Orders Addr.: P.O. Box 161, Prides Crossing, MA 01915 Tel 978-927-8707; Fax: 978-927-8904; Toll Free: 800-935-0188; Edit Addr.: 3 Broadway St., Beverly, MA 01915 E-mail: amp@larcompress.com Web site: http://www.larcompress.com.

**Large Print Pr. Imprint of Thorndike Pr.**

†**Larksdale**, ( *0-89896* ) P.O. Box 801222, Houston, TX 77280 (SAN 220-0643) Tel 713-461-7200; Fax: 713-467-4770 (purchase orders); Toll Free: 877-461-7200; *Imprints*: Post Oak Press (Post Oak Pr) ; *CIP*.

†**Larlin Corp.**, ( *0-87419; 0-89783* ) P.O. Box 1730, Marietta, GA 30061 (SAN 201-4432); *CIP*.

**Latchpins Pr.**, ( *0-9625490* ) 708 Holly Hill Rd., Johnson City, TN 37604 Tel 423-283-4927.

†**Latin American Literary Review Pr.**, ( *0-935480; 1-891270* ) P.O. Box 17660, Pittsburgh, PA 15235 (SAN 215-2142) Tel 412-824-7903; Fax: 412-824-7909 E-mail: latin@angstrom.net Web site: http://www.lalrp.org *Dist(s)*: **Consortium Bk. Sales & Distribution** **Continental Bk. Co., Inc.** **SPD-Small Pr. Distribution**; *CIP*.

**Latitude 20 Bks. Imprint of Univ. of Hawaii Pr.**

**Laughing Fire Pr.**, ( *0-9674922* ) P.O. Box 319, Edmore, MI 48829-0319 Toll Free: 877-274-4806 (phone/fax) E-mail: jlewis@laughingfire.com. Web site: http://www.laughingfire.com.

**Laughing Owl Publishing, Inc.**, ( *0-9659701; 0-9679257* ) 12610 Hwy. 90, W., Grand Bay, AL 36541 Tel 334-865-1500; Fax: 334-865-6252; Toll Free: 888-865-4884 E-mail: info@laughingowl.com; owlbooks@juno.com Web site: http://www.laughingowl.com.

**Laurel Imprint of Dell Publishing**

**Laurel Leaf Imprint of Random Hse. Children's Bks.**

**Lavelle Publishing**, ( *0-9659254* ) 2350 Spring Rd., No. 30, Suite 250, Smyrna, GA 30080 Tel 404-230-9336; Fax: 404-659-1134 Do not confuse with Creative Publishing, Greenville, SC E-mail: LavellePbl@aol.com *Dist(s)*: **Culture Plus Bks.** **Lushena Bks.**.

**Leapfrog Pr.**, ( *0-9654578; 0-9679520; 0-9728984* ) Orders Addr.: P.O. Box 1495, Wellfleet, MA 02667-1495 Tel 508-349-1925; Fax: 508-349-1180; Edit Addr.: 95 Commercial St., Wellfleet, MA 02667-1495 Do not confuse with Leapfrog Pr., Wyandotte, MI E-mail: books@leapfrogpress.com Web site: http://www.leapfrogpress.com *Dist(s)*: **Consortium Bk. Sales & Distribution**.

**Leapfrog Press, Incorporated, The** *See* **Leapfrog Pr.**

**Learning, Inc.**, ( *0-913692* ) Learning Pl., 353 Seawall Rd., Manset, ME 04679 (SAN 201-5714) Tel 207-244-5015 *Dist(s)*: **Door Hse.**.

**Learning Links, Inc.**, ( *0-7675; 0-88122; 0-934048; 1-56982* ) 2300 Marcus Ave., New Hyde Park, NY 11042 (SAN 241-3302) Tel 516-437-9071; Fax: 516-437-5392; Toll Free: 800-724-2616 Web site: http://www.learninglinks.com.

**Learning Safari** *See* **Pages, Inc.**

**learningconnections** *See* **Bullion Bks.**

**Leathers Publishing**, ( *0-9646898; 1-890622; 1-58597* ) Div. of Ad Ctr., 4500 College Blvd., Overland Park, KS 66211-1760 Tel 913-498-2625; Fax: 913-498-1561; Toll Free: 888-888-7696 E-mail: leatherpub@aol.com Web site: http://www.leatherspublishing.com.

**LeClere Publishing Co.**, ( *0-9702501* ) Orders Addr.: P.O. Box 528222, Port Clinton, OH 43452 (SAN 253-3170) Tel 419-734-4588; Fax: 520-447-5257; Edit Addr.: 2855 Sand Rd., Port Clinton, OH 43452 E-mail: leclerepubco@thirdplanet.net Web site: http://www.leclerepublishing.com/ *Dist(s)*: **Biblio Distribution** **National Bk. Network.**

**Lectorum Pubns., Inc.**, ( *0-9625162; 1-880507; 1-930332* ) Subs. of Scholastic, Inc., 205 Chubb Ave., Lyndhurst, NJ 07071-3520 Tel 212-965-7322; Fax: 212-727-3035; Toll Free Fax: 877-532-8676; 877-532-8678; Toll Free: 800-345-5946 E-mail: info@lectorum.com Web site: http://www.lectorum.com *Dist(s)*: **Libros Sin Fronteras.**

**Lederer/Messianic Jewish Publishers & Distributors** *See* **Messianic Jewish Pubs.**

**Lee & Low Bks., Inc.**, ( *1-880000; 1-58430* ) 95 Madison Ave., New York, NY 10016 Tel 212-779-4400 (General info./Editorial); Fax: 212-683-1894 (orders); Toll Free: 888-320-3395 (orders) E-mail: info@leeandlow.com Web site: http://www.leeandlow.com *Dist(s)*: **Lectorum Pubns., Inc.**

**Leete's Island Bks.**, ( *0-918172* ) P.O. Box 3131, Branford, CT 06405-1731 (SAN 210-2285) E-mail: Pneill@compuserve.com Web site: http://www.leetesisland.com

**Legacy Publishing**, ( *0-9643675* ) Div. of Baisden Enterprises, P.O. Box 5544, Katy, TX 77491 Do not confuse with companies with the same or similar name in Birmingham, AL, West Chester, OH, Ojai, CA, Maitland, FL, Berkeley, CA, Fort Myers, FL, Baton Rouge, LA, Daty, TX, Athens, AL E-mail: mb@michaelbaisden.com; csmith@pclnet.net Web site: http://www.michaelbaisden.com *Dist(s)*: **Baker & Taylor Bks.** **Partners Pubs. Group, Inc.**.

**Leisure Bks. Imprint of Dorchester Publishing Co., Inc.**

**Lenox Pr.**, ( *0-9653470* ) Orders Addr.: P.O. Box 17016, Rockford, IL 61110-7016 Tel 815-965-7461; Fax: 815-965-7462; Edit Addr.: 2304 Benderwirt Ave., Rockford, IL 61103 E-mail: kroby1@aol.com Web site: http://www.tricomweb.com/kimroby.htm *Dist(s)*: **Baker & Taylor Bks.**.

†**Leonard, Hal Corp.**, ( *0-634; 0-7935; 0-88188; 0-9607350; 1-56516* ) Orders Addr.: P.O. Box 13819, Milwaukee, WI 53213-0819 Tel 414-774-3630; Fax: 414-774-3259; Toll Free: 800-524-4425; Edit Addr.: 7777 W. Bluemound Rd., Milwaukee, WI 53213 (SAN 239-250X) E-mail: halinfo@halleonard.com Web site: http://www.halleonard.com *Dist(s)*: **Giron Bks.**; *CIP*.

†**Lerner Publishing Group**, ( *0-8225; 0-87614; 0-929371; 0-930494; 1-57505; 1-58013* ) Orders Addr.: 1251 Washington Ave., N., Minneapolis, MN 55401 Toll Free Fax: 800-332-1132; Toll Free: 800-328-4929; *Imprints*: Lerner Publications (Lerner Publctns); Carolrhoda Books (Carolrhoda) E-mail: custserve@lernerbooks.com; http://www.karben.com; *CIP*.

**Lerner Publishing Group, The** *See* **Lerner Publishing Group**

**Lerner Pubns. Imprint of Lerner Publishing Group**

**Let's Go Pubns. Imprint of St. Martin's Pr.**

**Levin, Hugh Lauter Assocs.**, ( *0-88363* ) 9 Burr Rd., Westport, CT 06880-4220 (SAN 201-6109) E-mail: inquiries@hlla.com Web site: http://www.hlla.com *Dist(s)*: **F&W Pubns., Inc.** **Publishers Group West.**

**Levine, Arthur A. Bks. Imprint of Scholastic, Inc.**

**Lewis, Dewi Publishing (GBR)** ( *1-899235* ) *Dist. by* **Consort Bk Sales.**

**Lewis, Dewi Publishing (GBR)** ( *1-899235* ) *Dist. by* **Dist Art Pubs.**

**Lexington Pr., Inc.**, ( *0-9628089* ) P.O. Box 11365, Lexington, KY 40575 Do not confuse with Lexington Pr. in Columbus, OH.

**Lexington-Marshall Publishing**, ( *0-9656247* ) P.O. Box 339, Bozeman, MT 59771 Tel 406-586-1002 E-mail: sgwest@imt.net *Dist(s)*: **Bookmen, Inc.**.

**Leyland Pubns.**, ( *0-943595* ) P.O. Box 410690, San Francisco, CA 94141 (SAN 668-663X) Tel 415-626-1935; Fax: 415-626-1802 Web site: http://www.leylandpublications.com *Dist(s)*: **Bookazine Co., Inc.** **Bookpeople** **Koen Bk. Distributors.**

**Librairie Generale Francaise, LGF (FRA)** ( *2-253* ) *Dist. by* **Continental Bk.**

**Librairie Generale Francaise, LGF (FRA)** ( *2-253* ) *Dist. by* **Distribks Inc.**

†**Libraries Unlimited, Inc.**, ( *0-313; 0-87287; 1-56308; 1-59158* ) Div. of Greenwood Publishing Group, Orders Addr.: a/o Customer Service Group, Dept. 2229, P.O. Box 5007, Westport, CT 06881 Fax: 603-431-2214; Toll Free: 800-225-5800; Edit Addr.: 6931 S. Yosemite St., Englewood, CO 80112 Tel 303-770-1220; Fax: 303-220-8843 E-mail: lubooks@lu.com Web site: http://www.lu.com; *CIP*.

**Library Edition Imprint of Brilliance Audio**

**Library of America, The**, ( *0-940450; 1-883011; 1-931082* ) Div. of Literary Classics of the U. S., Inc., 14 E. 60th St., New York, NY 10022 (SAN 286-9918) Tel 212-308-3360; Fax: 212-750-8352 E-mail: info@loa.org Web site: http://www.loa.org *Dist(s)*: **Penguin Group (USA) Inc.**.

**Library of Crime Classics Imprint of International Polygonics, Ltd.**

**Library of New Atlantis, Inc.**, ( *1-57179; 1-883147* ) P.O. Box 1210, Pahrump, NV 89041 (SAN 159-4168) Tel 702-336-0514 E-mail: lonabooks@earthlink.net Web site: http://www.Lona-Inc.com *Dist(s)*: **Sonata Publishing.**

**Library Professional Pubns. Imprint of Shoe String Pr., Inc.**

†**Library Research Assocs., Inc.**, ( *0-89824; 0-912526* ) 474 Dunderberg Rd., Monroe, NY 10950-3703 (SAN 201-0887) Tel 845-783-1144; Fax: 845-782-3953; Toll Free: 800-914-3379 E-mail: lrainc@frontiernet.net; *CIP*.

**Libris, Ltd. (GBR)** ( *1-870352* ) *Dist. by* **Paul & Co Pubs.**

**Libros Sin Fronteras**, P.O. Box 2085, Olympia, WA 98507 Tel 360-357-4332; Fax: 360-357-4964 E-mail: info@librossinfronteras.com Web site: http://www.librossinfronteras.com.

**Life's Reflections, Incorporated** *See* **Heritage Pubs., Inc.**

**Light Pubns.**, ( *0-9702642* ) Orders Addr.: P.O. Box 2462, Providence, RI 02906 Tel 401-272-8707 E-mail: info@lightpublications.com Web site: http://www.lightpublications.com.

**Lighter Than Air, L.P.**, ( *0-9679535* ) P.O. Box 2362, Princeton, NJ 08543-2362 E-mail: litenair@aol.com Web site: http://lighterthanair.net.

**Lighthouse Editions Imprint of Lighthouse Pr., Inc.**

**Lighthouse Pr., Inc.**, ( *0-9676354; 0-9711915; 0-9714827; 1-932211* ) P.O. Box 910, Deerfield Beach, FL 33443 (SAN 254-0118) Fax: 954-782-2810 ; *Imprints*: Lighthouse Editions (Lghtse Ed) Do not confuse with companies with the same or similar names in Culver City, CA, Millersburg, OH, York, ME, Marblehead, MA, Nashville, TN, La Junta, CO, Rochester, NY, San Mateo, CA E-mail: lighthousepress@bellsouth.net Web site: http://www.TheLighthousePress.com *Dist(s)*: **Baker & Taylor Bks.**.

**Lightlines Publishing Co.**, ( *1-930126* ) S235a Stand Rock Rd., Wisc Dells, WI 53965-9203 Do not confuse with LightLines Publishing, Portsmouth, NH E-mail: voice@theinnervoice.com Web site: http://theinnervoice.com *Dist(s)*: **National Bk. Network.**

**Lightning Pubns.**, ( *0-9632702; 1-888574* ) 532 S. Raymond Ave., Fullerton, CA 92631 Tel 714-879-8300; Fax: 909-879-8305.

**Lightning Rod Limited Imprint of Windstorm Creative Ltd.**

**Lightning Source, Inc.**, 1246 Heil Quaker Blvd., LaVergne, TN 37086 (SAN 179-6976) Tel 615-213-4595; Fax: 615-213-4426.

**Lightyear Pr. Imprint of Buccaneer Bks., Inc.**

**Lilliput Pr., Ltd., The (IRL)** ( *0-946640; 1-874675; 1-901866; 1-84351* ) *Dist. by* **Dufour.**

**Lilliput Pr., Ltd., The (IRL)** ( *0-946640; 1-874675; 1-901866; 1-84351* ) *Dist. by* **Irish Bks Media.**

**Limbus Pr. (RUS)** ( *5-8370* ) *Dist. by* **Distribks Inc.**

**Limited Editions**, ( *0-9647515* ) 2003 16th St., Lubbock, TX 79401 Tel 806-763-3847 (phone/fax); Toll Free: 800-785-2254 (pin no. 9101) Do not confuse with companies with the same name in Milton, KY, Rocky Hill, CT E-mail: ltdeds@aol.com.

**Linden Pubns.**, ( *0-89642; 0-7949* ) 1750 N. Sycamore, Suite 305, Hollywood, CA 90028-8662 (SAN 206-7218) Tel 323-876-5190.

**Lindisfarne Bks. Imprint of SteinerBooks, Inc.**

Names

**Lintel,** ( 0-931642 ) 24 Blake Ln., Middletown, NY 10940 (SAN 213-6325) Tel 845-342-5224 (phone/fax).

†**Lion Publishing,** ( 0-7459; 0-85648 ) 4050 Lee Vance View, Colorado Springs, CO 80918-7102 (SAN 663-611X) Tel 719-536-0100; Toll Free: 800-437-4337
Web site: http://www.cookministries.com/
*Dist(s):* **Cook Communications Ministries**; CIP.

**Lion Publishing PLC (GBR)** ( 0-7459; 0-85648 ) Dist. by **Trafalgar.**

**Lionheart Television International, Incorporated** See **BBC Worldwide Americas**

**LionHearted Publishing, Inc.,** ( 1-57343 ) Orders Addr.: P.O. Box 618, Zephyr Cove, NV 89448-0618 Tel 775-588-1388; Fax: 775-588-1386; Toll Free: 888-546-6478 (phone/fax)
E-mail: admin@LionHearted.com.
Web site: http://www.LionHearted.com.

**Lion's Gate Publishing,** ( 0-9647183 ) 2981 Lake Tahuyeh Rd. NW, Bremerton, WA 98380 Tel 360-830-5612; Fax: 360-830-5611
E-mail: kope@sincom.com
Web site: http://www.everythingbooks.com.

**Liplop Pr.** Imprint of **Goodfellow Catalog Pr., Inc.**

**Lippincott** Imprint of **Lippincott Williams & Wilkins**

†**Lippincott Williams & Wilkins,** ( 0-316; 0-397; 0-683; 0-7817; 0-8067; 0-8121; 0-88167; 0-89004; 0-89313; 0-89640; 0-911216; 1-881063; 4-260 ) Orders Addr.: P.O. Box 1600, Hagerstown, MD 21741 Fax: 301-223-2400; Toll Free: 800-638-3030; Edit Addr.: 530 Walnut St., Philadelphia, PA 19106-3621 (SAN 201-0933) Tel 215-521-8300; Fax: 215-521-8902; Toll Free: 800-638-3030; 351 W. Camden St., Baltimore, MD 21201 Tel 410-528-4000; *Imprints:* Lippincott (Lippnctt)
E-mail: custserv@lww.com; orders@lww.com
Web site: http://www.lww.com
*Dist(s):* **Igaku-Shoin Medical Pubs.**; CIP.

**Lippincott-Raven Publishers** See **Lippincott Williams & Wilkins**

**Liquid Gravity Publishing,** ( 0-9716502 ) 6401 E. Lewis Ave., Scottsdale, AZ 85257 (SAN 254-6388) Tel 480-233-6734
E-mail: read@diereading.com; joey@diereading.com
Web site: http://www.diereading.com.

**Listen & Live Audio, Inc.,** ( 1-885408; 1-931953; 1-59316 ) Orders Addr.: P.O. Box 817, Roseland, NJ 07068 Tel 973-781-1444; Fax: 973-781-0333; Toll Free: 800-653-9400; Edit Addr.: 9B Great Meadow Ln., East Hanover, NJ 07936
E-mail: kellyr@listenandlive.com; Alfred@Listenandlive.com
Web site: http://www.listenandlive.com
*Dist(s):* **Baker & Taylor Bks.**
**Landmark Audiobooks**
**Quality Bks., Inc.**
**Unique Bks., Inc.**.

**Listening Library** Imprint of **Random Hse. Audio Publishing Group**

**Literate Ear, Inc.,** ( 1-56544 ) 8249 Fairview Rd., Elkins Park, PA 19117 Tel 215-635-4807; Fax: 215-635-4542; Toll Free: 800-777-8327.

**Little Bro' Ltd.,** ( 0-9703991 ) 683 Anderson Rd., Jackson, NJ 08527 Tel 732-928-6593; Toll Free: 800-746-4462
E-mail: bodyslams2000@aol.com
Web site: htttp://bodyslams.com
*Dist(s):* **Baker & Taylor Bks.**.

†**Little Brown & Co.,** ( 0-316; 0-8212 ) Div. of Time Warner Bk. Group, Orders Addr.: 3 Center Plaza, Boston, MA 02108-2084 (SAN 630-7248) Tel 617-227-0730; Toll Free Fax: 800-286-9471; Toll Free: 800-759-0190; Edit Addr.: Time & Life Bldg., 1271 Avenue of the Americas, New York, NY 10020 (SAN 200-2205) Tel 212-522-8700; Fax: 212-522-2067; Toll Free: 800-343-9204; *Imprints:* Joy Street Books (Joy St Bks); Back Bay (Back Bay)
E-mail: cust.service@littlebrown.com
Web site: http://www.littlebrown.com
*Dist(s):* **Continental Bk. Co., Inc.**
**Hastings Bks.**
**Lectorum Pubns., Inc.**
**Rounder Kids Music Distribution**
**Beeler, Thomas T. Publisher**
**Thorndike Pr.**
**Time Warner Bk. Group**
**Warner Bks., Inc.**; CIP.

**Little Brown U.K. (GBR)** ( 0-316; 0-349; 0-356; 0-7515 ) Dist. by **Trafalgar.**

**Little Moose Pr.,** ( 0-9720227 ) 269 S. Beverly Dr., No. 1065, Beverly Hills, CA 90212 (SAN 254-9778) Tel 310-278-6239; Toll Free: 866-234-0626
E-mail: info@littlemoosepress.com
Web site: http://www.littlemoosepress.com
*Dist(s):* **Biblio Distribution.**

**Little Simon** Imprint of **Simon & Schuster Children's Publishing**

**Little Tiger Pr.,** ( 1-888444; 1-58431 ) Div. of Futech Interactive Products, 39 S. La Salle St. Ste. 1410, Chicago, IL 60603-1706 Toll Free: 800-541-2205 Do not confuse Little Tiger Press in San Francisco, CA
E-mail: jody@futechsales.com
*Dist(s):* **Futech Educational Products, Inc.**
**Lectorum Pubns., Inc.**.

**Little White Hen & Company** See **White Hen & Co.**

**Littlegreen** Imprint of **Christopher Publishing**

**Live Oak Media,** ( 0-87499; 0-941078; 1-59112; 1-59519 ) Orders Addr.: P.O. Box 652, Pine Plains, NY 12567-0652 (SAN 217-3921) Tel 518-398-1010; Fax: 518-398-1070; Toll Free: 800-788-1121; Edit Addr.: P.O. Box 652, Pine Plains, NY 12567-0652 (SAN 669-1498)
E-mail: info@liveoakmedia.com
Web site: http://www.liveoakmedia.com
*Dist(s):* **BBC Audiobooks America**
**Greathall Productions, Inc.**
**Lectorum Pubns., Inc.**
**Weston Woods Studios, Inc.**.

†**Liveright Publishing Corp.,** ( 0-87140 ) Subs. of W. W. Norton Co., Inc., 500 Fifth Ave., New York, NY 10110 (SAN 201-0976) Tel 212-354-5500; Fax: 212-869-0856; Toll Free Fax: 800-458-6515; Toll Free: 800-233-4830
Web site: http://www.wwnorton.com
*Dist(s):* **Norton, W. W. & Co., Inc.**; CIP.

**Living Bks.** Imprint of **Tyndale Hse. Pubs.**

**Living Language** Imprint of **Random Hse. Information Group**

**Livingston Pr.,** ( 0-930501; 0-942979; 1-931982 ) Univ. of West Alabama, Sta. 22, Livingston, AL 35470 Tel 205-652-3470; Fax: 205-652-3717; Toll Free: 800-959-3245 Do not confuse with Livingston Pr., Anaheim, CA
E-mail: jwt@uwa.edu
Web site: http://www.livingstonpress.uwa.edu.

**Llano Pr.,** ( 0-9651770 ) Div. of Flying Zephyr Enterprises, Orders Addr.: P.O. Box 86, Penasco, NM 87553 Tel 505-587-1766; Edit Addr.: Sahd's Hwy. 75, Penasco, NM 87553.

†**Llewellyn Pubns.,** ( 0-7387; 0-87542; 1-56718; 1-892485 ) Div. of Llewellyn Worldwide, Ltd., Orders Addr.: P.O. Box 64383, Saint Paul, MN 55164-0383 (SAN 201-100X) Tel 651-291-1970; Fax: 651-291-1908; Toll Free: 800-843-6666; Edit Addr.: 84 S. Wabasha St., Saint Paul, MN 55107
E-mail: nweditor@llewellyn.com
Web site: http://www.llewellyn.com
*Dist(s):* **Agencia de Publicaciones de Puerto Rico**
**Baker & Taylor Bks.**
**Bilingual Pubns. Co., The**
**Bookazine Co., Inc.**
**Bookpeople**
**Ingram Bk. Co.**
**Koen Bk. Distributors**
**Lectorum Pubns., Inc.**
**Libros Sin Fronteras**
**National Bk. Network**
**New Leaf Distributing Co., Inc.**
**Partners/West**
**Perrone**
**Weiser Wholesale**; CIP.

**Lloyds of Louisiana,** ( 0-9660305 ) Orders Addr.: P.O. Box 7118, Monroe, LA 71211-7118 Tel 318-343-2476 ; Fax: 318-345-5204; Edit Addr.: 7207 Desiard, Monroe, LA 71203.

**Llumina Pr.** Imprint of **Media Creations, Inc.**

**Local History Co., The,** ( 0-9711835; 0-9744715 ) 112 N. Woodland Rd., Pittsburgh, PA 15232-2849 Tel 412-362-2294; Fax: 412-362-8192; Toll Free: 866-362-8192
Web site: www.TheLocalHistoryCompany.com.

**Locust Hill Pr.,** ( 0-933951; 0-9722289 ) P.O. Box 260, West Cornwall, CT 06796 (SAN 693-0646) Tel 860-672-0060; Fax: 860-672-4968; 419 Main St., Goshen Tpke., West Cornwall, CT 06796
E-mail: locusthill@optonline.net.

**Lodestone Catalog, The,** ( 0-9642427; 1-57677 ) Div. of Creative Audio Enterprises, Inc., 611 Empire Mill Rd., Bloomington, IN 47401 Tel 812-824-2400; Fax: 812-824-2401; Toll Free: 800-411-6463 (orders only)
E-mail: lodestone@lodestone-media.com
Web site: http://www.lodestone-media.com.

**Logan Hse.,** ( 0-9674123 ) Orders Addr.: Rte. 1, Box 154, Winside, NE 68790 Tel 402-580-5089; Edit Addr.: 1 Two Cow Rd., Winside, NE 68790
E-mail: loganhousepress@alltel.net
Web site: http://mockingbird.creighton.edu/new/reese.htm.

**Logos Research Systems, Inc.,** ( 1-57799 ) 715 SE Fidalgo Ave., Oak Harbor, WA 98277-4049 Tel 360-679-6575; Fax: 360-675-8169; Toll Free: 800-875-6467
E-mail: info@logos.com
Web site: http://www.logos.com.

**London Bridge,** Div. of General Distribution Services, Orders Addr.: 4500 Witmer Industrial EST, Niagara Falls, NY 14305-1386 Toll Free: 800-805-1083.

**London Circle Publishing,** ( 0-9667911; 1-930677 ) Div. of Benicia Hse., 17315 Henning Ct., Weed, CA 96094 Tel 530-938-2527; Fax: 530-938-1756
E-mail: publisher@londoncircle.com
Web site: http://www.londoncircle.com.

**Lone Pine Publishing,** ( 0-919433; 1-55105 ) 1808 B St., NW, Suite 140, Auburn, WA 98001 Tel 425-204-5965; Fax: 425-204-6036; Toll Free Fax: 800-548-1169; Toll Free: 800-518-3541
E-mail: rtruppner@lonepinepublishing.com
Web site: http://www.lonepinepublishing.com
*Dist(s):* **American West Bks.**
**Baker & Taylor Bks.**
**Bookmen, Inc.**
**Bookpeople**
**Koen Bk. Distributors**
**Partners Bk. Distributing, Inc.**
**Partners/West**
**Sunbelt Pubns., Inc.**.

**Long Wind Publishing,** ( 0-9658128; 1-892695 ) 108 N. Depot Dr., Box 13024, Fort Pierce, FL 34950 Tel 561-595-0268; Fax: 561-595-6246
E-mail: LongWndPub@aol.com
Web site: http://www.longwindpub.com.

†**Longman Publishing Group,** ( 0-13; 0-201; 0-321; 0-582; 0-8013; 1-74009 ) Div. of Addison Wesley Longman, Inc., The Longman Bldg., 10 Bank St., White Plains, NY 10606-1951 (SAN 202-6856) Tel 914-993-5000; Fax: 914-997-8115 800-922-0579 (college, bkstores, customer service only)
E-mail: orders@mcp.com
Web site: http://store.awl.com
*Dist(s):* **Coronet Bks.**
**Giron Bks.**
**Pearson Education**
**Trans-Atlantic Pubns., Inc.**; CIP.

**Longstreet Pr., Inc.,** ( 0-929264; 1-56352 ) Subs. of Cox Newspapers, Inc., 2140 Newmarket Pkwy., Suite 122, Marietta, GA 30067 (SAN 248-7640) Tel 770-980-1488; Fax: 770-859-9894; Toll Free: 800-927-1488
E-mail: rrichardson@longstreetpress.net
*Dist(s):* **National Bk. Network.**

**Longwood Academic** Imprint of **Hollowbrook Publishing**

**Lookout Pr.,** ( 1-882405 ) Orders Addr.: 900 53rd St., Sacramento, CA 95819 Tel 916-456-6991.

**Loose Change,** ( 0-944707 ) 936 Sixth St., Los Banos, CA 93635 (SAN 244-9692) Tel 209-826-3797; Fax: 209-826-1514.

**Lord & Allerton,** ( 0-9647139 ) P.O. Box 554, Harbor Springs, MI 49740 Tel 616-526-9922
*Dist(s):* **Baker & Taylor Bks.**
**Partners Pubs. Group, Inc.**.

**Lord John Pr.,** ( 0-935716 ) 19073 Los Alimos St., Northridge, CA 91326 (SAN 213-6333) Tel 818-360-5804
E-mail: herby11230@aol.

**Lorraine, A. Walter** Imprint of **Houghton Mifflin Co. Trade & Reference Div.**

**Los Hombres Pr.,** ( 0-9623497; 1-879603 ) P.O. Box 439016, San Diego, CA 92143-9016 Tel 619-688-1023.

**Lost Coast Pr.,** ( 1-882897 ) 155 Cypress St., Fort Bragg, CA 95437 Tel 707-964-9520; Fax: 707-964-7531; Toll Free: 800-773-7782
E-mail: forms@cypresshouse.com
Web site: http://www.cypresshouse.com
*Dist(s):* **Baker & Taylor Bks.**
**Continental Bk. Co., Inc.**
**New Leaf Distributing Co., Inc.**
**Partners/West.**

**Lost Horse Pr.,** ( 0-9668612; 0-9717265 ) 105 Lost Horse Ln., Sandpoint, ID 83864 Fax: 208-255-1560
*Dist(s):* **Lynx Hse. Pr.**
**SPD-Small Pr. Distribution.**

**Names**

†**Lost Roads Pubs.,** ( *0-918786* ) 351 Nayatt Rd., Barrington, RI 02806-4336 (SAN 680-0564) Tel 401-245-8069 (phone/fax)
E-mail: wrightcd@aol.com
Web site:
http://www.brown,edu/departments/english/road
*Dist(s):* **SPD-Small Pr. Distribution**; *CIP.*

**Lotus Lights Publications** *See* **Lotus Pr.**

**Lotus Pr.,** ( *0-910261; 0-914955; 0-940676; 0-940985; 0-941524* ) Div. of Lotus Brands, Inc., P.O. Box 325, Twin Lakes, WI 53181 (SAN 239-1120) Tel 262-889-2461; Fax: 262-889-8591; Toll Free: 800-824-6396 Do not confuse with companies with the same or similar name in Lotus, CA, Westerville, OH, Bokeelia, FL, Brattleboro, VT, Detroit, MI, Tobyhanna, PA
E-mail: lotuspress@lotuspress.com
Web site: http://www.lotuspress.com
*Dist(s):* **National Bk. Network**
　　　　　**Publishers Group West.**

**Lotus Pr., Inc.,** ( *0-916418* ) P.O. Box 21607, Detroit, MI 48221 Tel 313-861-1280; Fax: 313-861-4740 Do not confuse with companies with the same name or similar name in Westerville, OH, Lotus, CA, Bokeelia, FL, Brattleboro, VT, Detroit, MI, Tobyhanna, PA
E-mail: lotuspress@aol.com.

**Louisiana Literature Pr.,** ( *0-945083* ) Orders Addr.: c/o Southeastern Louisiana University, P.O. Box 10792, Hammond, LA 70403 (SAN 245-9116) Tel 985-549-5756; Fax: 985-549-5021.

†**Louisiana State Univ. Pr.,** ( *0-8071* ) P.O. Box 25053, Baton Rouge, LA 70894-5053 (SAN 202-6597) Tel 225-388-6295; Fax: 225-388-6461; Toll Free Fax: 800-305-4416 (orders); Toll Free: 800-861-3477 (orders)
E-mail: lsuprss@lsu.edu
Web site: http://lsupress.lsu.edu; *CIP.*

**Love Spectrum Imprint of Genesis Pr., Inc.**

**Love Spell Imprint of Dorchester Publishing Co., Inc.**

**Love Story Publishing,** ( *1-883111* ) Div. of Love Story Productions & Publishing, Orders Addr.: P.O. Box 300813, Denver, CO 80203 Tel 303-298-8612; Fax: 303-298-9768; Edit Addr.: 2770 California St., No. 211, Denver, CO 80205.

**Loveland Pr.,** ( *0-9662696; 0-9744851* ) P.O. Box 7001, Loveland, CO 80537-0001 Tel 970-593-9557 Toll Free: 800-593-9557
E-mail: info@lovelandpress.com
Web site: http://www.lovelandpress.com
*Dist(s):* **Baker & Taylor Bks..**

†**Loyola Pr.,** ( *0-8294* ) 3441 N. Ashland Ave., Chicago, IL 60657 (SAN 211-6537) Tel 773-281-1818; Fax: 773-281-0555; Toll Free: 800-621-1008
E-mail: customerservice@loyolapress.com
Web site: http://www.loyolapress.com
*Dist(s):* **Baker & Taylor Bks.**
　　　　　**Bookazine Co., Inc.**
　　　　　**Partners Pubs. Group, Inc.**
　　　　　**Riverside**
　　　　　**Spring Arbor Distributors, Inc.;** *CIP.*

**LRS,** ( *1-58118* ) 14214 S. Figueroa St., Los Angeles, CA 90061-1034 Tel 310-354-2610; Fax: 310-354-2601; Toll Free: 800-255-5002
E-mail: lrsprint@aol.com
Web site: http://www.lrs-largeprint.com

**LSA Publishing,** ( *1-890465* ) Div. of International Learning Trust, 200 Lime Quarry Rd., Madison, AL 35758 Tel 256-772-3373; Fax: 256-772-4436
E-mail: Ricky@lsapublishing.com
Web site: http://www.I-B-I.com.

**LTDBooks (CAN)** ( *1-55316* ) *Dist. by* **Baker & Taylor.**

**LTDBooks (CAN)** ( *1-55316* ) *Dist. by* **Lightn Source.**

**Lubbe, Gustav Verlag GmbH (DEU)** ( *3-7857; 3-404* ) *Dist. by* **Distribks Inc.**

**Lubrecht & Cramer, Ltd.,** ( *0-934454; 0-945345* ) 18 E. Main St., Port Jervis, NY 12771; Edit Addr.: P.O. Box 3110, Port Jervis, NY 12771 (SAN 214-1256) Toll Free: 800-920-9334; 350 Fifth Ave., Suite 3304, New York, NY 10118-0069
E-mail: lubrecht@frontiernet.net;
books@lubrechtcramer.com
Web site: http://www.lubrechtcramer.com.

**Lucky Pr., LLC,** ( *0-9676050; 0-9706377; 0-9713318* ) 126 S. Maple St., Lancaster, OH 43130 Fax: 740-689-2951
E-mail: books@luckypress.com
Web site: http://www.luckypress.com;
http://www.sleepy-dog.com
*Dist(s):* **National Bk. Network.**

**Lumen Editions Imprint of Brookline Bks., Inc.**

**Lunatic Fringe Publishing,** ( *0-9677868* ) 439 Orchard Ave., Silt, CO 81652 Tel 970-876-2196; Fax: 970-876-2208
E-mail: peggyt@sni.net
Web site: http://www.rumorsofwar.net.

**LuraMedia** *See* **Innisfree Pr.**

**Luthers,** ( *1-877633* ) 1009 N. Dixie Freeway, New Smyrna Beach, FL 32168-6221 (SAN 200-3961) Tel 386-423-1600 (phone/fax)
E-mail: luthers@n-jcenter.com.

**Lutherworth Pr., The (GBR)** ( *0-7188* ) *Dist. by* **Parkwest Pubns.**

†**Lynx Hse. Pr.,** ( *0-89924* ) 420 W. 24th Ave., Spokane, WA 99203-1922 (SAN 250-3344) Tel 309-624-4594; Fax: 309-623-4238
E-mail: cnhowell@mail.ewu.edu
*Dist(s):* **Michigan State Univ. Pr.**
　　　　　**SPD-Small Pr. Distribution**; *CIP.*

**Lyon, Jr., Lawrence B.,** ( *0-9656601* ) 114 Center St., Madison, WV 25130 Tel 304-369-2131.

**Lyons Pr. Imprint of Globe Pequot Pr., The**

**LyreBird Bks., Inc.,** ( *0-9664820* ) 155 Bank St., Suite 1007A, New York, NY 10014 Tel 212-741-8777; Fax: 212-367-7778
E-mail: LyreBirdBk@aol.com.

**Lyric Pr.,** P.O. Box 470493, Brookline Village, MA 02447 Tel 617-566-0233
E-mail: destiny@lyricpressbooks.com
Web site: http://www.lyricpressbooks.com.

**Lyrick Publishing,** ( *1-57064; 1-58668* ) Subs. of HIT Entertainment, 830 S. Greenville Ave., Allen, TX 75002 Tel 972-390-6794; Fax: 972-390-6030; Toll Free: 800-418-2371
E-mail: customerservice@HITEntertainment.com
Web site: http://www.HITEntertainment.com
*Dist(s):* **Lectorum Pubns., Inc..**

**MC Pr.,** ( *0-9670744* ) 34 W. 287 Sunset Dr., Batavia, IL 60510-3354 Tel 630-879-5323
E-mail: mailcoach@aol.com.

**ME Media LLC,** ( *1-58925* ) Orders Addr.: 1650 Bluegrass Lakes Pkwy., Alpharetta, GA 30004 Fax: 770-442-9742; Toll Free: 800-656-6479; Edit Addr.: 202 Old Ridgefield Rd., Wilton, CT 06897 (SAN 253-6382) Tel 203-834-0005; Fax: 203-834-0004; *Imprints:* Tiger Tales (Tiger Tales)
E-mail: etprial@tigertalesbooks.com
Web site: http://www.tigertalesbooks.com.

**M L E S** *See* **Pathway Bk. Service**

**M Q Pubns. (GBR)** ( *1-84072; 1-897954* ) *Dist. by* **IPG Chicago.**

**M.S.G. Haskell Hse.,** ( *0-8383* ) Orders Addr.: P.O. Box 190420, Brooklyn, NY 11219-0009 (SAN 202-2818) Tel 718-435-7878; Fax: 718-633-7050.

**Maasai, Inc.,** ( *0-9708008* ) 201 E. Bay Blvd., Provo, UT 84606 Tel 801-373-5655; Fax: 801-373-1387; *Imprints:* KenningHouse (KenningHouse)
E-mail: nwarner@profilemedia.com.

**MacAdam/Cage Publishing,** ( *0-9673701; 1-931561* ) 155 Sansome St., Suite 550, San Francisco, CA 94104 (SAN 299-9730) Tel 415-986-7502; Fax: 415-986-7414; Toll Free: 866-986-7470; 820 16th St., Suite 331, Denver, CO 80202 Tel 303-753-7565; Fax: 303-753-7566
E-mail: info@macadamcage.com
Web site: http://www.macadamcage.com
*Dist(s):* **American Wholesale Bk. Co.**
　　　　　**American West Bks.**
　　　　　**Baker & Taylor Bks.**
　　　　　**Book Warehouse**
　　　　　**Bookazine Co., Inc.**
　　　　　**Bookpeople**
　　　　　**Booksource, The**
　　　　　**Brodart Co.**
　　　　　**Koen Bk. Distributors**
　　　　　**Blackwell North America**
　　　　　**Partners Bk. Distributing, Inc.**
　　　　　**Sunbelt Pubns., Inc..**

**Macalester Park Publishing Co., Inc.,** ( *0-910924; 0-930286; 1-886158* ) 7317 Cahill Rd., Suite 201, Minneapolis, MN 55439 (SAN 110-8077) Tel 612-562-1234; Toll Free: 800-407-9078
*Dist(s):* **Baker & Taylor Bks.**
　　　　　**Bookmen, Inc.**
　　　　　**Riverside**
　　　　　**Spring Arbor Distributors, Inc..**

**Macaulay & Wittenstein Pubs., Inc.,** ( *1-885823* ) P.O. Box 57112, Oklahoma City, OK 73157 Tel 405-232-8550; Fax: 405-321-7771
*Dist(s):* **Baker & Taylor Bks..**

**MacDonald Sward Publishing Co.,** ( *0-945437* ) RD 3, Box 104A, Greensburg, PA 15601 (SAN 247-1973) Tel 724-832-7767
*Dist(s):* **Amazon.Com**
　　　　　**Baker & Taylor Bks..**

**Machibb Creations,** ( *1-930331* ) 27 Hancock Dr., Suite 553, West Milford, NJ 07480 Fax: 973-697-1477
E-mail: rickymac2@yahoo.com
Web site: http://www.caribbeanamericanbookclub.com
*Dist(s):* **GRM Group.**

**Maclay & Assocs.,** ( *0-940776* ) P.O. Box 16253, Baltimore, MD 21210 (SAN 219-6808) Tel 410-235-7985; Fax: 410-235-1390.

**Macmillan Caribbean (GBR)** ( *0-333* ) *Dist. by* **Interlink Pub.**

**Macmillan College Imprint of Prentice Hall PTR**

**Macmillan Information,** ( *0-02* ) 135 Mt. Zion Rd., Lebanon, IN 46052 (SAN 202-599X)
Web site: http://www.mcp.com/
*Dist(s):* **Libros Sin Fronteras.**

**Macmillan Reference USA Imprint of Gale Group**

**Macmillan U.K. (GBR)** ( *0-333; 1-4050* ) *Dist. by* **Trafalgar.**

**Macmillan U.K. (GBR)** ( *0-333; 1-4050* ) *Dist. by* **Trans-Atl Phila.**

**Macmillan USA** *See* **Alpha Bks.**

**MacMurray & Beck, Inc.,** ( *1-878448* ) 4101 E. Louisiana Ave., Suite 100, Denver, CO 80246 (SAN 200-3562) Tel 303-753-7565; Fax: 303-753-7566; Toll Free: 800-774-3777
E-mail: koffler@macmurraybeck.com
Web site: http://www.macmurraybeck.com.

**MacroPrintBooks Imprint of Science & Humanities Pr.**

**Madison Bks., Inc.,** ( *0-8128; 0-8191; 0-911572; 1-56833; 1-879511* ) Div. of Rowman & Littlefield Publishers, Inc., 200 Park Ave., S., Suite 1109, New York, NY 10003-1503 (SAN 246-7356) Tel 212-529-3888; Fax: 212-529-4223; Toll Free Fax: 800-338-4550; Toll Free: 800-462-6420; *Imprints:* Scarborough House (Scrbrough Hse)
Web site: http://www.univpress.com/
*Dist(s):* **National Bk. Network**
　　　　　**Rowman & Littlefield Pubs., Inc..**

**Madison Publishing Co. Imprint of Deadly Alibi Pr., Ltd.**

**Madison Publishing Company** *See* **Deadly Alibi Pr., Ltd.**

**Magabala Bks. (AUS)** ( *0-9588101; 1-875641* ) *Dist. by* **Intl Spec Bk.**

**Mage Pubs., Inc.,** ( *0-934211* ) 1032 29th St., NW, Washington, DC 20007 (SAN 693-0476) Tel 202-342-1642; Fax: 202-342-9269; Toll Free: 800-962-0922 (orders only)
E-mail: info@mage.com
Web site: http://www.mage.com
*Dist(s):* **Baker & Taylor Bks..**

**Magian Pr., The,** ( *0-917023* ) P.O. Box 117, Penn Laird, VA 22846 (SAN 655-2684) Tel 540-289-5596.

**Magic Attic Pr. Imprint of Millbrook Pr., Inc.**

**Magicimage Filmbooks,** ( *1-882127* ) 740 S. Sixth Ave., Absecon, NJ 08201 (SAN 249-8995) Tel 609-652-6500; Fax: 609-748-9776
E-mail: sales@magicimage.com
Web site: http://www.magicimage.com.

**Magna Large Print Bks. (GBR)** ( *0-7505; 0-86009; 1-84137; 1-85057* ) *Dist. by* **Ulverscroft US.**

**Magna Story Sound (GBR)** ( *1-85903; 1-872672* ) *Dist. by* **Ulverscroft US.**

**Magner Publishing** *See* **Magner Publishing & American Binding & Publishing**

**Magner Publishing & American Binding & Publishing,** ( *1-929416* ) P.O. Box 2259, Rockport, TX 78381-2259 Tel 361-729-3629; Toll Free: 800-863-3708
E-mail: rmagner@pyramid3.net
Web site: http://www.americanbindingpublishing.com.

**Magnolia Hill Pr.,** ( *0-9642231* ) Orders Addr.: P.O. Box 124, Kingston, TN 37763 Tel 423-376-3686; Fax: 423-376-2083; Toll Free: 800-946-1967
E-mail: booktalk@icx.net.

**Magnolia Productions,** ( *0-9611952* ) Orders Addr.: P.O. Box 651, New York, NY 10467 (SAN 253-5505) Tel 914-912-2120; 718-652-9827 Do not confuse with Magnolia Productions, Inc., Tallahassee, FL
E-mail: vivian@magnoliaholiday.com
Web site: http://www.magnoliaholiday.com.

**Magnolia Publishing Co., Inc.,** ( *0-9674880* ) P.O. Box 3758, Pineville, LA 71361 Tel 318-443-6333; Fax: 318-442-4212; Toll Free: 800-953-6246 Do not confuse with companies with the same or similar names in Magnolia, MA, Batesvilles, MS, Houston, TX, Macon, GA, Orlando, FL
E-mail: Magnoliapu@aol.com
Web site: http://www.Magnoliapublishing.com.

**Names**

**Magpie Pubns.,** ( *0-936480* ) P.O. Box 636, Alamo, CA 94507 (SAN 221-4091) Tel 925-838-9287 (phone/fax) ; Toll Free: 800-624-7435 (phone/fax) Web site: http://www.pp.ph.ic.ac.uk/~magpie.

**Main St. Bks. Imprint of Broadway Bks.**

**Maine Writers & Pubs. Alliance,** ( *0-9618592* ) 14 Maine St., No. 416, Brunswick, ME 04011-2054 (SAN 224-2303) Tel 207-729-6333; Fax: 207-725-1014.

**Mainesburg Pr.,** ( *0-9641632* ) 8370 Clouse Rd., New Albany, OH 43054 (SAN 298-3427) Tel 614-855-9809 ; Fax: 614-939-9329.

**Mainstream Publishing Co., Ltd. (GBR)** ( *0-906391; 1-85158; 1-84018* ) *Dist. by* **Trafalgar.**

**Malgari Pr. Imprint of Brooke, Gabriella**

**Malvern Publishing Co., Ltd. (GBR)** ( *0-947993* ) *Dist. by* **Brit Bk Co Inc.**

**Management Advisory Pubns.,** ( *0-940706* ) P.O. Box 81151, Wellesley Hills, MA 02481-001 (SAN 203-8692) Tel 781-235-2895; Fax: 781-235-5446 E-mail: jaykmasp@aol.com Web site: http://www.masp.com.

**Manic D Pr.,** ( *0-916397* ) Orders Addr.: P.O. Box 410804, San Francisco, CA 94141 (SAN 670-6932) Tel 415-648-8288 (phone/fax); Edit Addr.: 250 Banks St., San Francisco, CA 94110 E-mail: info@manicdpress.com Web site: http://www.manicdpress.com
*Dist(s):* **Baker & Taylor Bks.**
**Bookpeople**
**Last Gasp Eco-Funnies, Inc.**
**Publishers Group West**
**SPD-Small Pr. Distribution.**

**Manisy Willows Bks.,** ( *0-9678959* ) 701 Capital of Texas S., Box 1202, Bldg. C, Austin, TX 78746 (SAN 253-1739) Tel 512-347-9995; Fax: 512-347-9996 E-mail: manisywillowsbooks@austin.rr.com Web site: http://www.manisywillows.com; http://www.ninafoxx.com
*Dist(s):* **Biblio Distribution.**

**Manohar Pubns. (IND)** ( *81-7304; 81-85952; 81-85054; 81-85425* ) *Dist. by* **S Asia.**

**Mantis Pr.,** ( *0-9638900* ) P.O. Box 237132, New York, NY 10023-3031 Tel 212-874-6017.

**Manuel, Melissa,** ( *0-9702879* ) 6190 Radecke Ave., Baltimore, MD 21206-2932 E-mail: mma9899953@aol.com.

†**Manuscript Pr.,** ( *0-936414* ) P.O. Box 336, Mountain Home, TN 37684 (SAN 214-3224) Tel 423-926-7495 Do not confuse with Manuscript Pr., Nashville, TN E-mail: fnorwood@worldnet.att.net Web site: http://www.io.com/~norwoodr; *CIP.*

**Mapes Monde Editore,** ( *0-926330* ) Div. of Mapes Monde, Ltd., c/o MAPes MONDe, Ltd., P.O. Box 6545, 37 Dronningens gade, Saint Thomas, VI 00804 Tel 340-774-3280; Fax: 340-776-2959; Toll Free: 888-774-3280 (orders, outside Illinois).

**Mapletree Publishing Co.,** ( *0-9728071* ) 6233 Harvard Ln., Highlands Ranch, CO 80130 Tel 303-791-9024; Fax: 303-791-9028 E-mail: mail@mapletreepublishing.com Web site: http://www.mapletreepublishing.com.

**Marbella Hse.,** ( *0-9710392* ) 10450 Wilshire Blvd., PH-E, Los Angeles, CA 90024-4614 (SAN 254-086X) Tel 310-470-4353; Fax: 310-470-3089 E-mail: burtboyar@aol.com Web site: http://www.hitlerstoppedbyfranco.com.

**Marblehead Publishing,** ( *0-943335* ) 315 Blueridge Rd., Carrboro, NC 27510 (SAN 668-5471) Tel 919-929-1719; Fax: 919-933-2209 E-mail: smadon315@aol.com
*Dist(s):* **Parnassus Bk. Distributors.**

**Mari, Inc.,** ( *0-926706; 1-56096* ) 3215 Pico Blvd., Santa Monica, CA 90405 (SAN 134-6792) Tel 310-829-2212 E-mail: custserv@mariinc.com Web site: http://www.mariinc.com.

**Mariner Bks. Imprint of Houghton Mifflin Co. Trade & Reference Div.**

**Mariposa Printing & Publishing, Inc.,** ( *0-933553* ) 922 Baca St., Santa Fe, NM 87501 (SAN 691-8743) Tel 505-988-5582; Fax: 505-986-8774
*Dist(s):* **Continental Bk. Co., Inc..**

**Marketing Directions, Inc.,** ( *1-880218* ) 615 Queen St., Southington, CT 06489 Tel 860-276-2452; Fax: 860-276-2453; Toll Free: 800-562-4357 E-mail: info@strongbooks.com Web site: http://www.wstrongbooks.com.

**Marlboro Pr., The Imprint of Northwestern Univ. Pr.**

**Marlboro Pr., Inc., The,** ( *0-910395; 1-56897* ) 625 Colfax St., Evanston, IL 60208 (SAN 281-9813) Tel 847-491-2046; Fax: 847-491-8150
*Dist(s):* **Northwestern Univ. Pr..**

**Marlowe & Co. Imprint of Avalon Publishing Group**

**Mars Productions,** ( *0-9710397* ) Orders Addr.: P.O. Box 562823, Charlotte, NC 28256 Tel 704-549-0370; Fax: 704-548-8985; Edit Addr.: 2204 Cullendale Ct., Charlotte, NC 28262 (SAN 253-8393) Tel 704-549-0370 E-mail: omar8Tyree@aol.com; omar8tyree@aol.com Web site: http://www.omarTyree.com; http://www.TheUrbanGriot.com
*Dist(s):* **A & B Distributors & Pubs. Group.**

**Marsh Media,** ( *0-925159; 1-55942* ) Div. of Marsh Film Enterprises, Inc., P.O. Box 8082, Shawnee Mission, KS 66208 Tel 816-523-1059; Fax: 816-333-7421; Toll Free: 800-821-3303 (for orders/customer service only) E-mail: info@marshmedia.com Web site: http://www.marshmedia.com
*Dist(s):* **Baker & Taylor Bks..**

**Marshall Jones Co.,** ( *0-8338* ) Div. of Mountain Marketing, Inc., Orders Addr.: P.O. Box 12888, Prescott, AZ 86301; Edit Addr.: P.O. Box 17810, Tucson, AZ 85731 (SAN 206-8834) Tel 520-290-4569 ; Fax: 520-290-4592 E-mail: pegg@mountainnewsroom.com.

**Marshfilm Enterprises, Incorporated** *See* **Marsh Media**

**Marsilio Pubs.,** ( *0-941419; 1-56886* ) 853 Broadway, Suite 600, New York, NY 10003 Tel 718-522-3982; *Imprints:* Eridanos Library (Eridanos Library)
*Dist(s):* **SPD-Small Pr. Distribution.**

**MartinTate L.L.C.,** ( *0-9701496* ) 4555 Lake Forest Dr. Ste. 650, Cincinnati, OH 45242-3789 (SAN 253-5041) Toll Free: 877-626-7376 E-mail: pmartin@projectresults.com Web site: http://projectresult.com.

**MARUGE PUBLISHING,** ( *0-9721980* ) 2030 N. Heatherbrae Cir., Tucson, AZ 85715 Tel 520-298-8664 E-mail: marilynn@direcway.com.

**Marvel Enterprises,** ( *0-7851; 0-87135; 0-939766; 0-9604146* ) 10 E. 40th St. Flr. 9, New York, NY 10016-0201 (SAN 216-9088); *Imprints:* Marvel's Finest (Marvels Finest); Essential Series, The (Essential Series); From the House of Ideas (From the Hse) E-mail: mail@marvel.com Web site: http://www.marvel.com
*Dist(s):* **Client Distribution Services.**

**Marvel Entertainment Group, Incorporated** *See* **Marvel Enterprises**

**Marvel's Finest Imprint of Marvel Enterprises**

**Masquerade Bks., Inc.,** ( *1-56333; 1-878320* ) 801 Second Ave., New York, NY 10017 Tel 212-661-7878 ; Fax: 212-986-7355; *Imprints:* Hard Candy (Hard Candy); Badboy (Badboy); Rhinoceros (Rhinoceros); Kasak, Richard Books (R Kasak Bks); Masquerade SF (Masquerade SF) Do not confuse with Masquerade Bks. Gardena, CA E-mail: masqbks@aol.com Web site: http://www.masqueradebooks.com
*Dist(s):* **Bookazine Co., Inc.**
**Bookpeople.**

**Masquerade SF Imprint of Masquerade Bks., Inc.**

**Master Bks.,** ( *0-89051* ) P.O. Box 727, Green Forest, AR 72638-0727 (SAN 205-6119) Tel 870-438-5288; Fax: 870-438-5120; Toll Free: 800-999-3777 E-mail: nlp@newleafpress Web site: http://www.masterbooks.net.

**Master Communications Group, Inc.,** ( *0-9630340* ) 7322 Ohms Ln., Edina, MN 55439 Tel 612-835-6164; Fax: 612-835-9573; Toll Free: 800-862-6164 Web site: http://www.mastcom.com.

**Mastermind Publishing,** ( *0-9663214* ) Div. of Choose Integrity, Inc., Orders Addr.: P.O. Box 51722, Amarillo, TX 79159-1722 Tel 806-354-2305; Fax: 806-354-2536; Toll Free: 800-564-0498; Edit Addr.: 7913 Fenley Dr., Amarillo, TX 79121-1015 Do not confuse with Mastermind Publishing, Davenport, IA E-mail: cliff@nts-online.net Web site: http://www.DivineJustice.com.

**Mastery Education Corporation** *See* **Charlesbridge Publishing, Inc.**

**Masthof Pr.,** ( *1-883294; 1-930353* ) 219 Mill Rd., Morgantown, PA 19543-9701 Tel 610-286-0258; Fax: 610-286-6860 E-mail: mast@masthof.com Web site: http://www.ponyinvestigators.com; http://www.masthof.com.

**Matahari Pr.,** ( *0-9666160* ) Orders Addr.: P.O. Box 426, Diablo, CA 94528 Tel 925-837-4192; Fax: 925-837-0198.

**Maverick Bks.,** ( *0-9672355* ) P.O. Box 897, Woodstock, NY 12498 (SAN 253-9284) Toll Free: 866-478-9266 (phone/fax) Do not confuse with Maverick Books, Perryton, TX E-mail: maverickbooks@aol.com; hank1@ptsi.net.

**Maverick Bks., Inc.,** ( *0-916941; 0-9608612; 1-59188* ) Orders Addr.: Box 549, Perryton, TX 79070 (SAN 240-7183) Tel 806-435-7611; Fax: 806-435-2410; Edit Addr.: 402 S. Amherst, Suite 1, Perryton, TX 78070 Do not confuse with Maverick Books, Woodstock, NY E-mail: hank1@ptsi.net Web site: http://www.hankthecowdog.com
*Dist(s):* **Baker & Taylor Bks..**

**Maverick Press** *See* **Maverick Bks.**

**Maxit Publishing, Inc.,** ( *0-9700174; 0-9708904* ) P.O. Box 680, Solvang, CA 93463 (SAN 253-6811) Tel 310-275-1000; 805-686-5100; Fax: 805-686-5102 (for orders, bills & invoices); Toll Free: 866-686-5100 E-mail: info@maxitpublishing.com; wsimon@maxitpublishing.com Web site: http://www.maxitpublishing.com.

**Mayflower Pr.,** ( *0-9666055* ) 205 C Street, NE, Washington, DC 20002 Tel 202-546-0055 E-mail: mayflowerpress@erols.com Web site: http://www.mayflowerpress.com.

**Mayfly Productions,** ( *0-9624613* ) Orders Addr.: P.O. Box 380, Elmwood, IL 61529-0380 Tel 309-742-8126 ; Toll Free: 800-266-5564; Edit Addr.: 106 N. Althea, Elmwood, IL 61529
*Dist(s):* **Koen Bk. Distributors**
**Partners Pubs. Group, Inc.**
**Quality Bks., Inc..**

**Mayhaven Publishing,** ( *1-878044; 1-932278* ) Orders Addr.: P.O. Box 557, Mahomet, IL 61853 Tel 217-586-4493; Edit Addr.: 803 Buckthorn Cir., Mahomet, IL 61853 E-mail: mayhavenpublishing@mchsi.com Web site: http://www.mayhavenpublishing.com
*Dist(s):* **Baker & Taylor Bks.**
**Beyda & Assocs., Inc.**
**Booksource, The**
**Brodart Co.**
**Distributors, The**
**Forest Sales & Distributing Co.**
**Mumford Library Bks., Inc.**
**Quality Bks., Inc.**
**Unique Bks., Inc..**

**Mazda Pubs., Inc.,** ( *0-939214; 1-56859* ) Orders Addr.: P.O. Box 2603, Costa Mesa, CA 92628 (SAN 285-0524) Tel 714-751-5252; Fax: 714-751-4805 E-mail: hello@mazdapub.com Web site: http://www.mazdapub.com.

**McArthur & Co. (CAN)** ( *1-55278* ) *Dist. by* **Natl Bk Netwk.**

†**McBooks Pr., Inc.,** ( *0-935526; 1-59013* ) I.D. Booth Bldg. 520 N. Meadow St., Ithaca, NY 14850 (SAN 213-8573) Tel 607-272-2114; Fax: 607-273-6068; Toll Free: 888-266-5711 E-mail: mcbooks@mcbooks.com Web site: http://www.mcbooks.com
*Dist(s):* **National Bk. Network;** *CIP.*

**McClain Printing Co.,** ( *0-87012* ) P.O. Box 403, Parsons, WV 26287-0403 (SAN 203-9478) Tel 304-478-2881; Fax: 304-478-4658; Toll Free: 800-654-7179 E-mail: Mcclain@access.mountain.net Web site: http://www.McClainPrinting.com.

**McClelland & Stewart/Tundra Bks.,** ( *0-7710* ) P.O. Box 1030, Plattsburgh, NY 12901 Tel 416-598-1114; Fax: 416-598-4002 E-mail: salesdept@mcclelland.com Web site: http://www.mcclelland.com.

**McCormick-Armstrong Co., Inc.,** ( *0-911978* ) 1501 E. Douglas, Wichita, KS 67211 (SAN 220-8369) Tel 316-264-1363
*Dist(s):* **American Bonanza Society.**

**McDougal Littell Inc.,** ( *0-395; 0-8123; 0-86609; 0-88343; 0-618* ) Subs. of Houghton Mifflin Co., Orders Addr.: 1900 S. Batavia Ave., Geneva, IL 60134 Toll Free: 888-872-8380; Edit Addr.: P.O. Box 1667, Evanston, IL 60204 (SAN 202-2532) Toll Free: 800-462-6595 (customer service); 800-323-5435; 909 Davis St., Evanston, IL 60201 Tel 847-869-2300; Fax: 847-869-0841 Web site: http://www.mcdougallittell.com.

**McElderry, Margaret K. Imprint of Simon & Schuster Children's Publishing**

†**McFarland & Co., Inc. Pubs.,** ( *0-7864; 0-89950* ) P.O. Box 611, Jefferson, NC 28640 (SAN 215-093X) Tel 336-246-4460; Fax: 336-246-5018; Toll Free: 800-253-2187 (orders only) E-mail: vtomlinson@mcfarlandpub.com Web site: http://www.mcfarlandpub.com; *CIP.*

**McGee, Marcus Media,** ( *0-9673123* ) P.O. Box 231281, Sacramento, CA 95823 E-mail: Marcusmedia@prodigy.net.

**McGill-Queen's Univ. Pr. (CAN)** ( *0-7709; 0-7735; 0-88629; 0-88911; 1-55240* ) *Dist. by* **CUP Services.**

Names

**McGraw Publishing, Inc.,** ( *1-930364; 1-930756; 1-931071; 0-9707093* ) 51 Domingo Ave., Berkeley, CA 94702 Tel 510-644-9875; Fax: 281-340-2001; Toll Free: 866-815-2625; *Imprints:* Bookmice (Bookmic) E-mail: info@eldoradobooks.org Web site: http://www.eldoradobooks.org; http://www.mcgrawbooks.com.

†**McGraw-Hill Cos., The,** ( *0-02; 0-07* ) 6480 Jimmy Carter Blvd., Norcross, GA 30071-1701 (SAN 254-881X) Tel 614-755-5637; Fax: 614-755-5611; Orders Addr.: 860 Taylor Station Rd., Blacklick, OH 43004-0545 (SAN 200-254X) Tel 614-755-5645; Toll Free: 800-338-3987 (college); 800-525-5003 (subscriptions); 800-352-3566 (books - US/Canada orders); 800-722-4726 (orders & customer service); P.O. Box 545, Blacklick, OH 43004-0545 Fax: 614-759-3759; Toll Free: 877-833-5524 E-mail: customer.service@mcgraw-hill.com Web site: http://www.ebooks.mcgraw-hill.com/; http://www.mcgraw-hill.com *Dist(s):* **Libros Sin Fronteras McGraw-Hill Osborne McGraw-Hill Primis Custom Publishing Sams Technical Publishing, LLC;** *CIP.*

**McGraw-Hill Consumer Products** *See* **McGraw-Hill Children's Publishing**

**McGraw-Hill Higher Education,** ( *0-07* ) Div. of the McGraw-Hill Cos., Orders Addr.: P.O. Box 545, Blacklick, OH 43004-0545 Toll Free: 800-338-3987; Edit Addr.: 1333 Burr Ridge Pkwy., Burr Ridge, IL 60521; *Imprints:* McGraw-Hill/Dushkin (Dshkn McG-Hill); McGraw-Hill Humanities, Social Sciences & World Languages (Mc-H Human Soc) Web site: http://www.mhhe.com *Dist(s):* **McGraw-Hill Cos., The.**

**McGraw-Hill Humanities, Social Sciences & World Languages Imprint of McGraw-Hill Higher Education**

**McGraw-Hill Trade,** ( *0-07; 0-658; 0-8442* ) Div. of McGraw-Hill Professional, Orders Addr.: P.O. Box 545, Blacklick, OH 43004-0545 Tel 800-722-4726; Fax: 614-755-5645; Edit Addr.: 2 Penn Plaza, New York, NY 10121 Tel 212-904-2000; *Imprints:* Contemporary Books (Contemporary); Keats Publishing (Keats Pubng) Web site: http://www.books.mcgraw-hill.com *Dist(s):* **McGraw-Hill Cos., The.**

**McGraw-Hill/Contemporary,** ( *0-658; 0-8092; 0-8325; 0-8442; 0-88499; 0-89061; 0-913327; 0-940279; 0-941263; 0-9630646; 1-56606; 1-56943; 1-57028* ) Div. of McGraw-Hill Higher Education, 4255 W. Touhy Ave., Lincolnwood, IL 60712 (SAN 169-2208) Tel 847-679-5500; Fax: 847-679-2494; Toll Free Fax: 800-998-3103; Toll Free: 800-323-4900 E-mail: c_patton-vanbuskirk@mcgraw-hill.com; ntcpub@tribune.com Web site: http://www.ntc-cb.com *Dist(s):* **Continental Bk. Co., Inc. Giron Bks. Libros Sin Fronteras McGraw-Hill Cos., The netLibrary, Inc..**

**McGraw-Hill/Dushkin Imprint of McGraw-Hill Higher Education**

†**McKay, David Co., Inc.,** ( *0-679; 0-88326; 0-89440* ) Subs. of Random Hse., Inc., Orders Addr.: 400 Hahn Rd., Westminster, MD 21157 Tel 410-848-1900; Toll Free: 800-733-3000 (orders only); Edit Addr.: 201 E. 50th St., MD 4-6, New York, NY 10022 (SAN 200-240X) Tel 212-751-2600; Fax: 212-872-8026 *Dist(s):* **Libros Sin Fronteras;** *CIP.*

**McMillan, Dennis Pubns.,** ( *0-939767; 0-9609986* ) 4460 N. Hacienda del Sol (Guest House), Tucson, AZ 85718 (SAN 272-1686) Tel 520-529-6636 E-mail: dennismcmillan@aol.com Web site: http://dennismcmillan.com.

**McMillen Publishing,** ( *0-9635812; 1-888223* ) Orders Addr.: 304 Main St., Ames, IA 50010 (SAN 254-9085) Tel 515-232-0208; Fax: 515-232-0402 (orders); Toll Free: 800-750-6997 (In Iowa); 800-453-3960 (Outside Iowa) E-mail: denise.sunvold@sigler.com Web site: http://www.mcmillenbooks.com.

†**McPherson & Co.,** ( *0-914232; 0-929701* ) Orders Addr.: P.O. Box 1126, Kingston, NY 12402 (SAN 203-0624) Tel 845-331-5807; Toll Free: 800-613-8219 E-mail: bmcpher@ulster.net Web site: http://www.mcphersonco.com *Dist(s):* **SPD-Small Pr. Distribution;** *CIP.*

**McRoy & Blackburn, Pubs.,** ( *0-9632596; 0-9706712* ) Orders Addr.: P.O. Box 276, Ester City, AK 99725 Tel 907-479-2774; Fax: 907-479-2707; Edit Addr.: 404 Styx River Rd., Ester Dome, AK 99725 E-mail: mbe@mosquitonet.com Web site: http://www.alaskafiction.com *Dist(s):* **Partners/West Todd Communications Wizard Works.**

†**Meadowbrook Pr.,** ( *0-88166; 0-915658* ) 5451 Smetana Dr., Minnetonka, MN 55343 (SAN 207-3404) Tel 612-930-1100; Fax: 612-930-1940; Toll Free: 800-338-2232 E-mail: mballard@meadowbrookpress.com Web site: http://www.meadowbrookpress.com *Dist(s):* **Simon & Schuster Children's Publishing Simon & Schuster, Inc.;** *CIP.*

**Meadowcrest Books** *See* **Adams, Scott Charles**

**Mecox Bay Pr. LLC,** ( *0-9727961* ) P.O. Box 495, Southampton, NY 11969-0495 (SAN 255-092X) Tel 917-517-4422; Fax: 631-283-7425 E-mail: info@mecoxbaypress.com Web site: http://www.mecoxbaypress.com; http://www.conflictedthenovel.com; http://mecox-bay-press.com *Dist(s):* **Biblio Distribution.**

**Medea Publishing, Inc.,** ( *1-892358* ) Orders Addr.: P.O. Box 153, Princeton, MO 64673 Tel 660-382-4618; Edit Addr.: Rte. 1, Box 102, Cainsville, MO 64632 E-mail: jerry@jerryrobbins.com Web site: http://www.jerryrobbins.com.

**Media Bks. Audio Publishing Imprint of Media Bks., L. L. C.**

**Media Bks., L. L. C.,** ( *1-57815* ) 560 Sylvan Ave., Englewood, NJ 07632 Tel 201-894-8550; Fax: 201-894-1831; *Imprints:* Media Books Audio Publishing (Media Bks Audio) E-mail: clivefox@att.net.

**Media Creations, Inc.,** ( *0-9713099; 0-9718509; 1-932047; 1-932303; 1-932560; 1-59526* ) Orders Addr.: P.O. Box 772246, Coral Springs, FL 33077-2246 Tel 954-341-5636; Fax: 954-341-7987; Toll Free: 866-229-9244; Edit Addr.: 139 SW 98th Ln., Coral Springs, FL 33071; *Imprints:* Llumina Press (Llumina Pr) *Dist(s):* **Baker & Taylor Bks..**

**Media Publishing,** ( *0-939644* ) Div. of Trozzolo Resources, Inc., 802 Broadway St., Suite 300, Kansas City, MO 64105-1528 (SAN 216-6372) Tel 816-842-8111; Fax: 816-842-8188; Toll Free: 800-347-2665 Do not confuse with Media Publishing, Miami, FL *Dist(s):* **Baker & Taylor Bks..**

**Media Weavers LLC,** ( *0-9647212* ) P.O. Box 86190, Portland, OR 97286-0190 Tel 503-771-0428; Fax: 503-771-5156 E-mail: spudhow@alveus.com.

**MediaBay Audio Publishing,** ( *0-9668567; 1-930923* ) Div. of MediaBay, Inc., 2 Ridgedale Ave., Suite 300, Cedar Knolls, NJ 07927 Tel 973-539-9528; Fax: 973-539-1273 Do not confuse with Audio Book Club, Boca Raton, FL E-mail: mherrick@mediabay.com Web site: www.mediabay.com.

**Meisha Merlin Publishing, Inc.,** ( *0-9658345; 1-892065; 1-59222* ) Orders Addr.: P.O. Box 7, Decatur, GA 30031 Tel 404-634-1702 (phone/fax); Edit Addr.: 2332 Ava Pl., Decatur, GA 30033 E-mail: email@meishamerlin.com Web site: http://www.meishamerlin.com.

†**Mellen, Edwin Pr., The,** ( *0-7734; 0-88946; 0-935106* ) P.O. Box 450, Lewiston, NY 14092-0450 (SAN 207-110X) Tel 716-754-2788; 716-754-2266; Fax: 716-754-1860 E-mail: cs@wzrd.com; mellen@wzrd.com Web site: http://www.mellenpress.com *Dist(s):* **Continuum International Publishing Group, Inc.;** *CIP.*

**Mentor Imprint of NAL**

**Mercat Pr. Bks. (GBR)** ( *0-901824; 0-906664; 0-9505884; 1-84183; 1-873644* ) *Dist. by* **St Mut.**

**Merced de Mendez, Ana T.,** ( *0-9627442* ) 404 Darien St., Villa Borinquen, Rio Piedras, PR 00920 Tel 809-783-1513.

†**Mercer Univ. Pr.,** ( *0-86554* ) 6316 Peake Rd., Macon, GA 31210-3960 (SAN 220-0716) Tel 478-301-2880; Fax: 478-301-2264; Toll Free: 800-637-2378 (Ext. 2880 orders only); 800-342-0841 (Ext. 2880 in Georgia) E-mail: mupressorders@mercer.edu Web site: http://www.mupress.org; *CIP.*

†**Mercier Pr., Ltd., The (IRL)** ( *0-85342; 1-85635; 1-86023* ) *Dist. by* **Irish Bks Media.**

†**Mercury Hse.,** ( *0-916515; 1-56279* ) E-mail: mercury@hooked.net Web site: http://www.wenet.net/~mercury *Dist(s):* **Consortium Bk. Sales & Distribution Continental Bk. Co., Inc.;** *CIP.*

**Mercury Pr., The (CAN)** ( *0-920544; 1-55128* ) *Dist. by* **SPD-Small Pr Dist.**

**Meredith Pr.,** ( *0-9640884* ) 54 E. Elizabeth St., Skaneateles, NY 13152 Tel 315-685-3965 Do not confuse with Meredity Pr. in Des Moines, IA.

**Meridian Bks. Imprint of NAL**

**Meridian Bks. Imprint of Dutton/Plume**

**Meridian Books** *See* **Meridian Bks. of Maryland**

**Meridian Bks. of Maryland,** ( *0-9640428* ) 3816 Lansdale Ct., Burtonsville, MD 20866 *Dist(s):* **Baker & Taylor Bks..**

**Meriwether Publishing, Ltd.,** ( *0-916260; 1-56608* ) Orders Addr.: P.O. Box 7710, Colorado Springs, CO 80933 (SAN 208-4716) Tel 719-594-4422; Fax: 719-594-9916; Toll Free Fax: 888-594-4436; Toll Free: 800-937-5297; Edit Addr.: 885 Elkton Dr., Colorado Springs, CO 80907 E-mail: inzapel@aol.com; merpcds@aol.com Web site: http://www.contemporarydrama.com; http://www.meriwetherpublishing.com.

**Merkos L'Inyonei Chinuch Imprint of Kehot Pubn. Society**

**Merlin Pr. Ltd. (GBR)** ( *0-85036* ) *Dist. by* **Paul & Co Pubs.**

†**Merlin Pr.,** ( *0-930142* ) P.O. Box 5602, San Jose, CA 95150 (SAN 209-584X) Tel 408-289-9796; *CIP.*

**Merriam-Webster, Inc.,** ( *0-87779* ) Subs. of Encyclopaedia Britannica, Inc., 47 Federal St., P.O. Box 281, Springfield, MA 01102 (SAN 202-6244) Tel 413-734-3134; Fax: 413-734-2014; Toll Free: 800-201-5029 E-mail: tbishop@Merriam-Webster.com; sales@Merriam-Webster.com Web site: http://www.WordCentral.com; http://www.Merriam-Webster.com *Dist(s):* **Delmar Learning.**

**Merril Pr.,** ( *0-936783* ) 12500 NE Tenth Pl., Bellevue, WA 98005 (SAN 699-9387) Tel 425-454-7009; Fax: 425-451-3959 E-mail: editor@merrilpress.com Web site: http://www.merrilpress.com *Dist(s):* **Midpoint Trade Bks., Inc..**

**Merrill College,** Div. of Prentice Hall Higher Education, 75 Arlington St., Boston, MA 02116.

**Merriman Forest Development Corp.,** ( *0-9662661* ) Orders Addr.: P.O. Box 543, North Conway, NH 03860 Tel 603-356-5425; Fax: 603-356-8357; Toll Free: 800-322-6921; *Imprints:* MFDC Press (MFDC Pr).

**Mesa Vista Pr.,** ( *0-9668043* ) 874 Border Ave., Suite C-3, Joshua Tree, CA 92252-3405 Tel 760-362-5247; Fax: 775-542-7876 E-mail: kenrubin@published.com; thepress@published.com Web site: http://www.published.com *Dist(s):* **Partners/West.**

**MesaView, Inc.,** ( *1-58515* ) 12 Teak Dr., Nashua, NH 03062 Tel 603-674-8755 E-mail: 991199@msn.com Web site: http://www.mesaview.com.

**Mesorah Pubns., Ltd.,** ( *0-89906; 1-57819* ) 4401 Second Ave., Brooklyn, NY 11232 (SAN 213-1269) Tel 718-921-9000; Fax: 718-680-1875; Toll Free: 800-637-6724 E-mail: info@artscroll.com Web site: http://www.artscroll.com.

**Messianic Jewish Pubs.,** ( *1-880226* ) Div. of The Lewis & Harriet Lederer Foundation, Inc., 6204 Park Heights Ave., Baltimore, MD 21215 Tel 410-358-6471 ; Fax: 410-764-1376; Toll Free: 800-410-7367 (individual orders only) E-mail: booksinprint@messianicjewish.com Web site: http://www.MessianicJewish.net *Dist(s):* **Appalachian Bk. Distributors Christian Bk. Distributors Riverside Spring Arbor Distributors, Inc..**

**Methuen Drama Imprint of Heinemann**

**Methuen Publishing Ltd. (GBR)** ( *0-413* ) *Dist. by* **Consort Bk Sales.**

**Metropolitan Bks. Imprint of Holt, Henry & Co.**

**MFDC Pr. Imprint of Merriman Forest Development Corp.**

For full information on wholesalers and distributors, refer to the Wholesaler and Distributor Name Index

†**Micah Pubns.,** ( *0-916288* ) 255 Humphrey St., Marblehead, MA 01945 (SAN 209-1577) Tel 781-631-7601; Fax: 781-639-0772; Toll Free: 877-268-9963
E-mail: micah@micahbooks.com
Web site: http://www.micahbooks.com
*Dist(s):* **Book Publishing Co., The**
 **Jonathan David Pubs., Inc.;** *CIP.*

†**Michigan Slavic Pubns.,** ( *0-930042* ) Dept. of Slavic Languages & Literatures, 812 E. Washington, MLB 3040, Ann Arbor, MI 48109-1275 (SAN 210-4636) Tel 734-763-4496; Fax: 734-647-2127
E-mail: michsp@umich.edu
Web site: http://www.lsa.umich.edu/slavic/msp/ msp.html; *CIP.*

†**Michigan State Univ. Pr.,** ( *0-87013; 0-937191* ) 1405 S. Harrison Rd. Suite 25, East Lansing, MI 48823 (SAN 202-6295) Tel 517-355-9543; Fax: 517-432-2611
E-mail: msupress@msu.edu
Web site: http://www.msupress.msu.edu; *CIP.*

†**Middle Atlantic Pr.,** ( *0-912608; 0-9705804* ) Orders Addr.: c/o Koen Book Distributors, P.O. Box 600, Moorestown, NJ 08057 (SAN 667-4534) Tel 856-235-4444; Fax: 856-727-6914; Toll Free Fax: 800-257-8481; Edit Addr.: 213 Austin Ave., Barrington, NJ 08007 Tel 856-547-4122; Toll Free Fax: 800-225-3840
E-mail: tdoherty@koen.com; kbd@koen.com
Web site: http://www.koen.com/midat/index.html
*Dist(s):* **Koen Bk. Distributors**; *CIP.*

†**Middleburg Pr., The,** ( *0-931940* ) Box 166, Orange City, IA 51041 (SAN 212-9183); *CIP.*

**Midgard Pr.,** ( *0-9615948* ) 4218 Midway Ave., Grants Pass, OR 97527-9522 (SAN 696-8538) Tel 541-476-3603.

†**Mid-List Pr.,** ( *0-922811* ) 4324 12th Ave., S., Minneapolis, MN 55407-3218 (SAN 251-4605) Tel 612-822-3733; Fax: 612-823-8387; Toll Free: 888-543-1138
E-mail: guide@midlist.org
Web site: http://www.midlist.org
*Dist(s):* **SPD-Small Pr. Distribution**; *CIP.*

**Midpoint Trade Bks., Inc.,** Orders Addr.: 1263 Southwest Blvd., Kansas City, KS 66103 (SAN 631-3736) Tel 913-831-2233; Fax: 913-362-7401; Toll Free: 800-742-6139 (consumer orders); Edit Addr.: 27 W. 20th St., No. 1102, New York, NY 10011 (SAN 631-1075) Tel 212-727-0190; Fax: 212-727-0195; P.O. Box 411037, Kansas City, MO 64141-1037 (SAN 253-8539) Tel 913-362-7400; Fax: 913-362-7401
E-mail: midpointny1@aol.com
Web site: http://midpt.com.

**Midwest Traditions, Inc.,** ( *1-883953* ) 3147 S. Pennsylvania Ave., Milwaukee, WI 53207 Tel 414-294-4319 (phone/fax); Toll Free: 800-736-9189; *Imprints:* Face to Face Books (Face to Face)
*Dist(s):* **Partners Pubs. Group, Inc..**

**Mile Marker 12 Publishing,** ( *0-9659054* ) 6355 Long Island Dr., Atlanta, GA 30328 Tel 770-455-8606; Fax: 770-455-6893; Toll Free: 888-868-6612
E-mail: egypt47@mindspring.com
*Dist(s):* **Unique Bks., Inc..**

**Miles & Miles,** ( *0-936810* ) Orders Addr.: P.O. Box 6730, Eureka, CA 95502 (SAN 221-3834) Tel 707-442-5595; Edit Addr.: 3420 M St., Eureka, CA 95503 (SAN 691-9537).

**Miles, R & E** *See* **Miles & Miles**

**Milet Publishing, Ltd. (GBR)** ( *1-84059* ) *Dist. by* **Pan Asian Pubns.**

**Milkweed Editions,** ( *0-915943; 1-57131* ) 1011 Washington Ave. S., Suite 300, Minneapolis, MN 55415-1246 (SAN 294-0671) Tel 612-332-3192; Fax: 612-215-2550; Toll Free: 800-520-6455
E-mail: market@milkweed.org
Web site: http://www.worldashome.org; http://www.milkweed.org
*Dist(s):* **Publishers Group West.**

**Mill Creek Pr.,** ( *0-9705336* ) 3800 Centre Sq., W., 1500 Market St., Philadelphia, PA 19102 Tel 215-972-7713 ; Fax: 215-972-7725 Do not confuse with companies with the same or similar name in Springfield, Il, Salt Lake City, UT
E-mail: asolmssen@saul.com
*Dist(s):* **BookMobile.**

**Mill Street Forward, The,** ( *0-9654628* ) 15 1/2 Van Houten St., Apt. 117, Paterson, NJ 07505 Tel 973-345-9539.

†**Millbrook Pr., Inc.,** ( *0-7613; 1-56294; 1-878137; 1-878841* ) Orders Addr.: 2 Old New Milford Rd., Dept. LS, Brookfield, CT 06804 (SAN 299-9390) Tel 203-740-2220; Fax: 203-740-2223; Toll Free: 800-462-4703; 800-568-2665 (electronically transmitted orders); *Imprints:* Magic Attic Press (MagicAttPr); Twenty-First Century Books, Incorporated (TwentyFrstCent) Do not confuse with Mill Brook Pr., Highland Park, NJ
Web site: http://www.millbrookpress.com
*Dist(s):* **Simon & Schuster, Inc..**

†**Millefleurs,** ( *0-8095; 0-89370; 0-912134; 0-913330; 0-913960; 0-916732; 0-930261; 0-941028; 0-9616605; 1-55742; 1-877880* ) P.O. Box 2845, San Bernardino, CA 92406-2845 (SAN 208-9459) Fax: 909-888-4942
E-mail: borgopr@GTE.net
Web site: http://www.borgopress.com/; *CIP.*

**Millennium III Pubs., L.P.,** ( *0-9625220* ) Orders Addr.: P.O. Box 928, Simpsonville, SC 29681 Tel 864-967-7344; Toll Free: 800-967-7345; Edit Addr.: 174 N. Moore Rd., Simpsonville, SC 29680 Tel 803-967-7344
E-mail: willramsey@millennium.org
*Dist(s):* **BookWorld Services, Inc..**

**Miller, Charles F. Pub.,** ( *1-885611* ) 708 Westover Dr., Lancaster, PA 17601 Tel 717-285-2255.

**Milligan Bks.,** ( *1-881524; 0-9719749; 0-9725941; 0-9742811* ) 1425 W. Manchester Blvd., Suite C, Los Angeles, CA 90047 Tel 323-750-3592; Fax: 323-750-2886
E-mail: drrosie@aol.com
Web site: http://milliganbooks.com
*Dist(s):* **Baker & Taylor Bks..**

**Millivres Bks. (GBR)** ( *1-873741* ) *Dist. by* **Consort Bk Sales.**

**Millwood Publishing** *See* **Ruder Finn Pr.**

**MindCatcher Pr.,** ( *0-9724113* ) 284 Mattison Dr., Concord, MA 01742 Tel 978-369-7868
E-mail: marian@mindcatcherpress.com
Web site: http://www.mindcatcherpress.com; http://www.readylady.com.

**Minds Eye,** ( *1-883293* ) Div. of Collective Leisure, Inc., P.O. Box 2708, Menlo Park, CA 94026-2708 Fax: 415-365-7907; Toll Free: 800-542-7227.

**Mindwise Media, LLC** *See* **Fictionwise, Inc.**

**Miniver, Anne Pr.,** ( *0-9625794; 0-9720896* ) Orders Addr.: P.O. Box 381364, Cambridge, MA 02238-1364 Tel 617-497-8801; Edit Addr.: 16 Channin St., Cambridge, MA 02138
E-mail: billannt@mediaone.net
Web site: http://homepage.aol.com/cambridgepress.

**Minnesota Ctr. for Bk. Arts,** ( *1-879832* ) 1011 Washington Ave., S., Suite 100, Minneapolis, MN 55415 Tel 612-215-2520; Fax: 612-215-2545
E-mail: mcba@mnbookarts.org
Web site: http://www.mnbookarts.org
*Dist(s):* **Distributed Art Pubs./D.A.P.**

†**Minnesota Historical Society Pr.,** ( *0-87351* ) Orders Addr.: 11030 S. Langley Ave., Chicago, IL 60628 Toll Free Fax: 800-621-8476; Toll Free: 800-621-2736; Edit Addr.: 345 Kellogg Blvd., W., Saint Paul, MN 55102-1906 (SAN 202-6384) Tel 651-297-2221; Fax: 651-297-1345; Toll Free: 800-647-7827; *Imprints:* Borealis Book (Borealis Book)
E-mail: kevin.morrissey@mnhs.org
Web site: http://www.mnhs.org/mhspress
*Dist(s):* **Chicago Distribution Ctr.;** *CIP.*

**Mirasol/Libros Juveniles Imprint of Farrar, Straus & Giroux**

**Misty Hill Pr.,** ( *0-930079* ) 5024 Turner Rd., Sebastopol, CA 95472 (SAN 670-0942) Tel 707-823-7437
*Dist(s):* **Baker & Taylor Bks.**
 **Bookpeople.**

**Misty Mountain Publishing Co.,** ( *0-9635083* ) P.O. Box 111185, Anchorage, AK 99511 Fax: 907-278-2001; Toll Free: 800-750-8166
*Dist(s):* **Todd Communications.**

†**MIT Pr.,** ( *0-262* ) Orders Addr.: c/o Triliteral LLC, 100 Maple Ridge Dr., Cumberland, RI 02864 Tel 401-531-2800; Fax: 401-531-2801; Toll Free Fax: 800-406-9145; Toll Free: 800-405-1619; Edit Addr.: 5 Cambridge Ctr., Suite 4, Cambridge, MA 02142-1493 (SAN 202-6414) Tel 617-253-5646; Fax: 617-253-6779
E-mail: mitpress-orders@mit.edu
Web site: http://mitpress.mit.edu; *CIP.*

**Mitten, Peg Pr.,** ( *0-9665183* ) Orders Addr.: P.O. Box 436, Stonington, ME 04681 Tel 207-367-2838; Edit Addr.: 34 Indian Point Rd., Stonington, ME 04681
E-mail: critten@media2.hypernet.com.

**MJF Bks. Imprint of Fine Communications**

†**Modern Language Assn. of America,** ( *0-87352* ) 26 Broadway, 3rd Flr., New York, NY 10004-1789 (SAN 202-6422) Tel 646-576-5000; Fax: 646-458-0030
E-mail: info@mla.org
Web site: http://www.mla.org
*Dist(s):* **Baker & Taylor Bks.**
 **NACSCORP, Inc.;** *CIP.*

**Modern Library Imprint of Random House Adult Trade Publishing Group**

**Modern Publishing,** ( *0-7666; 0-87449; 1-56144* ) Div. of Unisystems, Inc., 155 E. 55th St., New York, NY 10022 (SAN 253-2921) Tel 212-826-0850; Fax: 212-759-9096; *Imprints:* Honey Bear Books (Honey Bear Bks)
E-mail: info@modernpublishing.com; rvreeland@modernpublishing.com
Web site: http://www.modernpublishing.com
*Dist(s):* **Worldwide Media Service, Inc..**

**Mohawk River Pr.,** ( *0-9662100* ) Orders Addr.: P.O. Box 4095, Clifton Park, NY 12065-0850 Tel 518-383-2254; Fax: 518-373-8018; Edit Addr.: 57 Carriage Rd., Clifton Park, NY 12065
E-mail: Jimlabate@hotmail.com
Web site: http://www.mohawkriverpress.com.

**Mokelumne Hill Press** *See* **Health Research**

**Molino, Editorial (ESP)** ( *84-272* ) *Dist. by* **AIMS Intl.**

**Momentum Books, Limited** *See* **Momentum Bks., LLC**

**Momentum Bks., LLC,** ( *0-9618726; 1-879094* ) 117 West Third St., Royal Oak, MI 48067 (SAN 668-7067) Tel 248-691-1800; Fax: 248-691-4531; Toll Free: 800-758-1870 (orders only); *Imprints:* Sabre Press (Sabre Pr)
E-mail: momentumbooks@glis.net
Web site: http://www.momentumbooks.com
*Dist(s):* **Baker & Taylor Bks.**
 **Partners Bk. Distributing, Inc..**

**Monbijou Pr.,** ( *0-9668251* ) PMB 256, 3579 E. Foothill Blvd., Pasadena, CA 91107 Tel 626-795-0459; Fax: 626-792-5989
E-mail: hornerwork@earthlink.net
Web site: http://home.earthlink.net/orhornerwork/.

**Mongolia Society, Inc., The,** ( *0-910980* ) Indiana Univ., 322 Goodbody Hall, Bloomington, IN 47405 (SAN 204-000X) Tel 812-855-4078; Fax: 812-855-7500.

**Mont Fort Press** *See* **Andmar Pr.**

**Monterey Home Video** *See* **Monterey Media, Inc.**

**Monterey Media, Inc.,** ( *1-56994* ) Div. of Monterey Media, Inc., 566 St. Charles Dr., Thousand Oaks, CA 91360-3901 Tel 805-494-7199; Fax: 805-496-6061; Toll Free: 800-424-2593; *Imprints:* Monterey SoundWorks (Monterey SoundWorks)
Web site: http://www.montereymedia.com
*Dist(s):* **Critics' Choice Video, Inc..**

**Monterey Publishing,** ( *0-9640537* ) Div. of Communicating Images, P.O. Box 3195, Monterey, CA 93942-3195
E-mail: DonEddy@Redshift.com.

**Monterey SoundWorks Imprint of Monterey Media, Inc.**

**Montevista Pr.,** ( *0-931551* ) 3467 Pinehurst Ct., Bellingham, WA 98226-4170 (SAN 682-191X)
*Dist(s):* **Todd Communications.**

†**Monthly Review Pr.,** ( *0-85345; 1-58367* ) Div. of Monthly Review Foundation, Inc., 122 W. 27th St., New York, NY 10001 (SAN 202-6481) Tel 212-691-2555; Fax: 212-727-3676; Toll Free: 800-670-9499
E-mail: promo@monthlyreview.org
Web site: http://www.monthlyreview.org
*Dist(s):* **Bookpeople**
 **New York Univ. Pr.;** *CIP.*

†**Moody Pr.,** ( *0-8024* ) Div. of Moody Bible Institute, 820 N. LaSalle Blvd., Chicago, IL 60610 (SAN 202-5604) Tel 312-329-2102; Fax: 312-329-2019; Toll Free: 800-678-8812
Web site: http://www.moodypress.org
*Dist(s):* **Jones, Bob Univ. Pr.;** *CIP.*

†**Moonbeam Pubns., Inc.,** ( *0-931013; 1-56271* ) 836 Hastings St., Traverse City, MI 49686-3441 (SAN 159-0308) Tel 231-922-0533; Fax: 231-922-0544; Toll Free: 800-334-9789; Toll Free: 800-445-2391
E-mail: moonbeam@chartermi.net
Web site: http://www.moonbeampublications.com
*Dist(s):* **Linx Educational Publishing, Inc.**
 **TMW Media Group, Inc.;** *CIP.*

**Mooney, Dave,** ( *0-9678222* ) 221 E. Elmwood Dr., Baltimore, OH 43105 Tel 740-862-4357
*Dist(s):* **Book Masters/El Rancho.**

**Moore, Lonnie W.** *See* **I & L Publishing**

**Moose Country Pr.,** ( *0-9642213; 1-893863* ) 73 Zerah
Fiske Rd., Shelburne, MA 01370 Tel 413-625-9569;
Fax: 413-774-3077; Toll Free: 800-346-6673
E-mail: moose@moosecountry.com.
Web site: http://moosecountry.com.

**More, Thomas Imprint of Ave Maria Pr.**

†**Morehouse Publishing,** ( *0-8192* ) Orders Addr.: P.O.
Box 1321, Harrisburg, PA 17105-1321 (SAN
202-6511) Tel 717-541-8130; Fax: 717-541-8128; Toll
Free: 800-877-0012; Edit Addr.: 4775 Linglestown
Rd., Harrisburg, PA 17112 Tel 717-541-8130;
717-236-0366; Fax: 717-541-8136
E-mail: morehouse@morehousegroup.com
Web site: http://www.morehousegroup.com; *CIP.*

**Morris Publishing,** ( *0-7392; 0-9631249; 1-57502;
1-885591* ) Subs. of Morris Pr. & Office Supplies,
3212 E. Hwy. 30, P.O. Box 2110, Kearney, NE 68847
Tel 308-236-7888; Fax: 308-237-0263; Toll Free:
800-650-7888 Do not confuse with companies with
the same or similar name in Sarveta, PA, Plymouth
Meeting, PA, Beecher City, IL, Urbana, IL, San
Francisco, CA
E-mail: publish@morrispublishing.com;
kimmyw414@yahoo.com; snowgers@mcn.org
Web site: http://morrispublishing.com.

**Morrow Cookbooks, William Imprint of
HarperInformation**

**Morrow, William & Co. Imprint of Morrow/Avon**

**Morrow/Avon,** ( *0-06; 0-380; 0-688* ) Div. of
HarperCollins General Bks. Grp., Orders Addr.: 1000
Keystone Industrial Pk., Scranton, PA 18512-4021
Toll Free Fax: 800-822-4090; Toll Free:
800-242-7737; Edit Addr.: 1350 Ave. of the Americas,
New York, NY 10019 Tel 212-261-6788; Fax:
570-941-1599 (customer service); Toll Free:
800-242-7737 (orders); *Imprints:* Morrow, William &
Company (Wm Morrow); Avon Books (Avon Bks);
HarperTorch (HarpTorch); Eos (Eos);
HarperEntertainment (HarpEntertain)
Web site: http://www.harpercollins.com/hc/
*Dist(s):* **HarperCollins Pubs.**
 **Lectorum Pubns., Inc..**

**Morton Bks.,** ( *1-929188* ) 47 Stewart Ave., Irvington,
NJ 07111 Tel 973-374-8327; Fax: 973-374-1125
E-mail: rmo1033555@aol.com
Web site: http://www.robmorton.com.

**Mosaic Imprint of Avid Pr., LLC**

**Mosaic Pr.,** ( *0-88962* ) Orders Addr.: PMB 145, 4500
Witmer Industrial Estates, Niagara Falls, NY 14305
Tel 905-825-2130 (phone/fax); Toll Free:
800-387-8992
E-mail: mosaicpress@on.aibn.com
Web site: http://w3.one.net~kirwin/mp.htm
*Dist(s):* **Midpoint Trade Bks., Inc.**
 **SCB Distributors.**

**Mother Lode Bks.,** ( *0-9663490* ) 7378 W. Atlantic
Blvd., Box 228, Margate, FL 33063 Tel
954-722-0624.

†**Mountain Pr. Publishing Co., Inc.,** ( *0-87842* ) Orders
Addr.: P.O. Box 2399, Missoula, MT 59806-2399
(SAN 202-8832) Tel 406-728-1900; Fax:
406-728-1635; Toll Free: 800-234-5308; Edit Addr.:
1301 S. Third West, Missoula, MT 59801 (SAN
662-0868)
E-mail: johnargyle@aol.com; mtnpress@montana.edu
Web site: http://www.mountainpresspublish.com
*Dist(s):* **Lone Pine Publishing;** *CIP.*

**Mountain Rose Publishing,** ( *0-9642147* ) P.O. Box
2738, Prescott, AZ 86302 Tel 520-445-5056.

**Mouse Works,** ( *0-7364; 1-57082* ) Div. of Disney Bk.
Publishing, Inc., A Walt Disney Co., 114 Fifth Ave.,
New York, NY 10011 (SAN 298-0797) Tel
212-633-4400; Fax: 212-633-4811
Web site: http://www.disneybooks.com.

†**Moyer Bell,** ( *0-918825; 1-55921* ) 549 Old North Rd.,
Kingston, RI 02881-1220 (SAN 630-1762) Tel
401-783-5480; Fax: 401-284-0959; Toll Free:
888-789-1945; *Imprints:* Papier-Mache Press
(Papier-Mache); Olmstead Press (Olmstead)
E-mail: contact@moyerbellbooks.com
Web site: http://www.moyerbellbooks.com/
*Dist(s):* **Acorn Alliance**
 **Alliance Hse., Inc.**
 **Client Distribution Services**
 **Wittenborn Art Bks.;** *CIP.*

**MTV Imprint of Simon & Schuster**

**Muehlberg Pr., The,** ( *0-9653342* ) Murray Hill Sta.,
P.O. Box 807, New York, NY 10156-0807 Fax:
212-689-4578
E-mail: richardm@nyc.rr.com.

**Multnomah Bks. Imprint of Multnomah Pubs., Inc.**

**Multnomah Fiction Imprint of Multnomah Pubs., Inc.**

**Multnomah Pubs., Inc.,** ( *0-88070; 0-930014; 0-945564;
1-57673; 1-885305; 1-58860; 1-59052* ) Orders Addr.:
P.O. Box 1720, Sisters, OR 97759 (SAN 247-123X)
Tel 541-549-1144; Fax: 541-549-8048; Toll Free:
800-929-0910; Edit Addr.: 204 W. Adams, Sisters, OR
97759; *Imprints:* Multnomah Books (Multnomah
Bks); Palisades (Palisades OR); Multnomah Fiction
(Multnomah Fiction); Alabaster (Alabaster)
E-mail: djacobson@multnomahbooks.com
Web site: http://multnomahbooks.com
*Dist(s):* **Christian Bk. Distributors**
 **GL Services**
 **Zondervan.**

**Munewata Pr.,** ( *0-9662707* ) Orders Addr.: P.O. Box
130, Cummington, MA 01026 Tel 413-634-5732; Fax:
413-634-5319; Edit Addr.: 11 Windsor Ave.,
Cummington, MA 01026
E-mail: RAPprr@aol.com.

**Murray, John Pubs., Ltd. (GBR)** ( *0-7195* ) *Dist. by*
**Trafalgar.**

**Muse Pubns.,** ( *0-9631750* ) Orders Addr.: P.O. Box 511,
Fort Yates, ND 58538 Tel 701-854-7435; Fax:
701-854-2004; Edit Addr.: 202 Main St., Fort Yates,
ND 58538 Do not confuse with Muse Pubns. in Alta
Loma, CA.
*Dist(s):* **New Leaf Distributing Co., Inc..**

**Music for Little People, Inc.,** ( *1-56628; 1-877737* ) 390
Lake Benbow Dr. No. C, Garberville, CA 95542 Tel
707-923-3991; Fax: 707-923-3241; Toll Free:
800-346-4445
Web site: http://www.mflp.com
*Dist(s):* **Bookpeople**
 **Educational Record Ctr., Inc.**
 **Goldenrod Music, Inc.**
 **Linden Tree Children's Records & Bks.**
 **Music Design, Inc.**
 **New Leaf Distributing Co., Inc.**
 **Rounder Kids Music Distribution**
 **Western Record Sales.**

**Mutual Publishing LLC,** ( *0-935180; 1-56647* ) 1215
Center St., Suite 210, Honolulu, HI 96816 (SAN
222-6359) Tel 808-732-1709; Fax: 808-734-4094
E-mail: mutual@lava.net
Web site: http://www.mutualpublishing.com
*Dist(s):* **Booklines Hawaii, Ltd..**

**mwynhad,** ( *0-9657993* ) 1615 43rd Ave., E., No. 101,
Seattle, WA 98112 Tel 206-328-6253 (phone/fax)
E-mail: mwynhad@juno.com
*Dist(s):* **Unique Bks., Inc..**

**Mycroft & Moran Imprint of Arkham Hse. Pubs.**

**Myers Hse. LLC,** ( *0-9721900* ) 2882 106th St., Suite
200, Des Moines, IA 50322 (SAN 255-0814) Tel
515-334-2687; Fax: 515-278-2245; Toll Free:
877-334-2687
E-mail: myershousemail@aol.com
Web site: http://www.disgracetotheprofession.com
*Dist(s):* **Brodart Co..**

**Mysterious Pr. Paperback Bks. Imprint of Warner
Bks., Inc.**

**Mysterious Pr.,** ( *0-446; 0-89296* ) Subs. of Warner Bks.,
Inc., Orders Addr.: 1271 Avenue of the Americas,
New York, NY 10020 (SAN 208-2152) Tel
212-522-7200; Fax: 212-522-7990; Toll Free Fax:
800-286-9471 (orders); Toll Free: 800-759-0190
(orders)
*Dist(s):* **Libros Sin Fronteras**
 **Little Brown & Co.**
 **Time Warner Bk. Group**
 **Warner Bks., Inc..**

**Mystery & Suspense Pr. Imprint of iUniverse, Inc.**

**Mystery Vault, Inc.,** ( *1-931755* ) 2621 Mall Dr.,
Sarasota, FL 34231 Tel 941-349-0838; Fax:
941-925-3145
Web site: http://www.mysteryvault.com.

**Mystery Writers of America Presents Imprint of
iUniverse, Inc.**

**Mystic Rose Press** *See* **Mountain Rose Publishing**

**NAL,** ( *0-451; 0-452; 0-453; 0-525; 0-8015* ) Div. of
Penguin Putnam, Inc., Orders Addr.: 405 Murray Hill
Pkwy., East Rutherford, NJ 07073 Toll Free:
800-788-6262 (individual consumer sales);
800-526-0275 (reseller sales); 800-631-8571 (reseller
customer service); Edit Addr.: 375 Hudson St., New
York, NY 10014-3657 Tel 212-366-2000; Fax:
212-366-2666; Toll Free: 800-331-4624 (Customer
service); *Imprints:* Seymour Lawrence (Seymour
Law); Obelisk (Obelisk); Signet Books (Sig); Signet
Classics (Sig Classics); ROC (ROC); Onyx (Onyx);
Mentor (Ment); Meridian Books (Mer); NAL Books
(NAL Bks); Signet Vista (Sig Vista); Topaz (Topaz);
Penguin Books (Penguin Bks); Penguin Classics
(Penguin Classics); Plume (Plume)
E-mail: online@penguinputnam.com
Web site: http://www.penguinputnam.com
*Dist(s):* **Penguin Group (USA) Inc..**

**N A L/Dutton** *See* **NAL**

**NBM Publishing Co.,** ( *0-918348; 1-56163* ) Orders
Addr.: 555 Eighth Ave., Suite 1202, New York, NY
10018-4312 (SAN 210-0835) Tel 212-643-5407; Fax:
212-643-1545; Toll Free: 800-886-1223; *Imprints:*
Comics Lit (Comics Lit); Flying Buttress Classics
Library The (Flying Buttress Class)
E-mail: catalog@nbmpublishing.com
Web site: http://www.nbmpub.com.

†**Naiad Pr., Inc.,** ( *0-930044; 0-941483; 1-56280* ) P.O.
Box 10543, Tallahassee, FL 32302 (SAN 206-801X)
Tel 850-539-5965; Fax: 850-539-9731; Toll Free:
800-533-1973
E-mail: naiadpress@aol.com
Web site: http://www.naiadpress.com
*Dist(s):* **Bookpeople**
 **Koen Bk. Distributors**
 **LPC Group;** *CIP.*

**NAL Bks. Imprint of NAL**

**NAL Bks. Imprint of HighBridge Co.**

**Napoleon Publishing/Rendezvous Pr. (CAN)** (
*0-929141; 1-894917* ) *Dist. by* **Words Distrib.**

**National Association for the Preservation of
Perpetuation of Storytelling** *See* **National
Storytelling Network**

**National Assn. for Visually Handicapped,** ( *0-89064* )
3201 Balboa St., San Francisco, CA 94121 (SAN
202-0971) Tel 415-221-3201; Fax: 415-221-8754; 22
W. 21st St., 6th Flr., New York, NY 10010 (SAN
669-1870) Tel 212-889-3141
E-mail: staff@navh.org
Web site: http://www.navh.org.

**National Bk. Network,** Div. of Rowman & Littlefield
Pubs., Inc., Orders Addr.: 15200 NBN Way, Blue
Ridge Summit, PA 17214 (SAN 630-0065) Tel
717-794-3800; Fax: 717-794-3803; Toll Free Fax:
800-338-4550; Toll Free: 800-462-6420; a/o Les
Petriw, 67 Mowat Ave., Suite 241, Toronto, ON M6P
3K3 Tel 416-534-1660; Fax: 416-534-3699; Edit
Addr.: 4501 Forbes Blvd., Suite 200, Lanham, MD
20706 Tel 301-459-3366; Fax: 301-429-5747
E-mail: lpetriw@nbnbooks.com
Web site: http://www.nbnbooks.com.

†**National Geographic Society,** ( *0-7922; 0-87044* ) 1145
17th St., NW, Washington, DC 20036 (SAN
202-8956) Tel 202-857-7000; Fax: 301-921-1575; Toll
Free: 800-647-5463; 800-548-9797 (TTD users only)
Web site: http://nationalgeographic.com
*Dist(s):* **Andrews McMeel Publishing**
 **Follett Media Distribution**
 **Lectorum Pubns., Inc.**
 **Simon & Schuster Children's Publishing**
 **Simon & Schuster, Inc.;** *CIP.*

**National Humanities Ctr.,** ( *0-912343* ) Orders Addr.:
P.O. Box 12256, Research Triangle Park, NC
27709-2256 (SAN 260-3489) Tel 919-549-0661; Edit
Addr.: 7 Alexander Dr., Research Triangle Park, NC
27709.

**National Recording Co.,** Orders Addr.: P.O. Box 395,
Glenview, IL 60025 (SAN 693-8175); Edit Addr.: 531
Pinar Dr., Orlando, FL 32825 Tel 407-282-3489.

**National Sahitya Akademi (IND)** *Dist. by* **S Asia.**

†**National Storytelling Network,** ( *1-879991* ) 101
Courthouse Sq., Jonesborough, TN 37659 (SAN
224-1978) Tel 423-913-8201; Fax: 423-753-9331; Toll
Free: 800-525-4514
E-mail: nsn@storynet.org
Web site: http://www.storynet.org; *CIP.*

**National Writers Pr., The,** ( *0-88100* ) Div. of National
Writers Assn., 3140 S. Peoria St., No. 294, Aurora,
CO 80014 (SAN 240-320X) Tel 720-851-1944; Fax:
303-841-2607
E-mail: AnitaEdits@aol.com
Web site: http://www.nationalwriters.com.

**National Yiddish Bk. Ctr.,** ( *0-657; 0-9655315* ) 1021
West St., Amherst, MA 01002-3375 Tel 413-256-4900
; Fax: 413-256-4700
E-mail: yiddish@bikher.org; orders@bikher.org
Web site: http://www.yiddishbookcenter.org.

**Native Planet Publishing,** ( *1-888298* ) Div. of Lotus
Foundation, Inc., 3917 Riverside Dr., Burbank, CA
91505 Tel 818-558-9543
*Dist(s):* **Bookpeople**
 **Quality Bks., Inc..**

**Naturegraph Pubs., Inc.,** ( *0-87961; 0-911010* ) Box
1047, 3543 Indian Creek Rd., Happy Camp, CA
96039 (SAN 202-8999) Tel 530-493-5353; Fax:
530-493-5240; Toll Free: 800-390-5353
E-mail: nature@sisqtel.net
Web site: http://www.naturegraph.com
*Dist(s):* **Gem Guides Bk. Co.**
 **New Leaf Distributing Co., Inc.**
 **Sunbelt Pubns., Inc..**

**Names**

†Nautical & Aviation Publishing Co. of America, Inc., The, ( 0-933852; 1-877853 ) 2055 Middleburg Ln., Mount Pleasant, SC 29464-4433 (SAN 213-3431) Tel 843-856-0561; Fax: 843-856-3164
E-mail: nauticalaviationpublishing@att.net
Web site: http://www.nauticalaviation.com; CIP.

†Naval Institute Pr., ( 0-87021; 1-55750; 1-59114 )
Orders Addr.: 2062 Generals Hwy., Annapolis, MD 21401 (SAN 662-0930) Tel 410-268-6110; Fax: 410-571-1703; Toll Free: 800-233-8764; Edit Addr.: 291 Wood Rd., Beach Hall, Annapolis, MD 21402-5034 (SAN 202-9006)
E-mail: psappington@usni.org
Web site: http://www.navalinstitute.org; CIP.

Navillus Pr., ( 0-9618152; 0-9677830 ) 1958 Onyx St., Eugene, OR 97403 (SAN 666-3788) Tel 541-683-6837
E-mail: sullivan@efn.org
Web site: http://oregonhiking.com.

NavPress Publishing Group, ( 0-89109; 1-57683 )
Orders Addr.: P.O. Box 35001, Colorado Springs, CO 80935 Tel 719-598-1212; Fax: 719-260-7223;
Imprints: Discipleship Journal (Diciple Jour)
Web site: http://www.navpress.com
Dist(s): CRC Pubns..

Naxos AudioBooks Imprint of Naxos of America, Inc.

Naxos of America, Inc., ( 962-634; 1-930838 ) Div. of HNH International, Cambridge House, Suite 7 1260 N. Forest Rd., Williamsville, NY 14221 (SAN 253-407X) Tel 716-634-3215; Fax: 716-634-3051;
Imprints: Naxos AudioBooks (Naxos AudioBooks)
E-mail: inquiries@naxosusa.com
Web site: http://www.naxosaudiobooks.com.

Necronomicon Pr., ( 0-940884 ) P.O. Box 1304, West Warwick, RI 02893 (SAN 210-315X) Tel 401-828-7161; Fax: 401-826-1151.

†Nel-Mar Publishing, ( 0-9615760; 1-877740 )
E-mail: Nelmar@gvtc.com
Dist(s): Baker & Taylor Bks.
Follett Library Resources; CIP.

Nelson Publishing Co., ( 0-9704237 ) 300 S. Washington Ave., Lot 224, Fort Meade, FL 33841-3174 Tel 863-285-5631 Do not confuse with companies with the same or similar names in Palouse, WA, Nokomis, FL, Northfield, VT
E-mail: nelpubco@juno.com; pegrog@juno.com
Web site: http://www.nelsonpublishingcompany.com.

†Nelson, Thomas Inc., ( 0-7852; 0-8407; 0-8499; 0-86605; 0-89840; 0-918956; 1-4003 ) Orders Addr.: P.O. Box 141000, Nashville, TN 37214-1000 (SAN 209-3820) Fax: 615-902-1866; Toll Free: 800-251-4000; Edit Addr.: 501 Nelson Pl., Nashville, TN 37214
E-mail: thomasnelson.com
Web site: http://www.thomasnelson.com
Dist(s): Christian Bk. Distributors
Twentieth Century Christian Bks.; CIP.

Nelson, Thomas Pubs., ( 0-7852; 0-8407 ) Div. of Thomas Nelson, Inc., Orders Addr.: P.O. Box 141000, Nashville, TN 37214-1000
Web site: http://ThomasNelsonPublishers.com
Dist(s): Nelson, Thomas Inc.
Vision Video.

Nelson Thornes (GBR) ( 0-17; 0-7487; 0-85950; 1-871402; 1-873732 ) Dist. by Trans-Atl Phila.

Nelson, Tommy, ( 0-7852; 0-8407; 0-8499; 1-4003 ) Div. of Thomas Nelson, Inc., Orders Addr.: P.O. Box 141000, Nashville, TN 37214 Fax: 615-902-3330; Edit Addr.: 501 Nelson Pl., Nashville, TN 37214 Tel 615-889-9000; Toll Free: 800-251-4000
E-mail: mduncan@tommynelson.com
Web site: http://www.tommynelson.com
Dist(s): CRC Pubns.
Nelson, Thomas Inc.
Twentieth Century Christian Bks..

Nepotist Bks., ( 0-9668772 ) P.O. Box 94759, Pasadena, CA 91009-9475 Tel 626-294-0990; Fax: 626-294-0626
E-mail: nepotist@aol.com.

Nesbett Heights, Inc., ( 0-9717028 ) 11012 Westmere Cir., Dallas, TX 75230 Tel 214-361-7755; Fax: 214-373-3141; Toll Free: 800-880-9400 (ext. 200)
E-mail: jleedom@worldweb.com

netLibrary, Inc., ( 0-585 ) 4888 Pearl East Cir., Boulder, CO 80301 (SAN 253-9497) Tel 303-415-2548; Fax: 303-381-7000; 303-381-8999; Toll Free: 800-413-4557
E-mail: mgilbert@netlibrary.com
Web site: http://www.netlibrary.com
Dist(s): ABC-CLIO, Inc..

Nevermore Pr., ( 0-9709084 ) HC 30, No. 14, Old Munds Hwy., Flagstaff, AZ 86001 Tel 520-779-5502 (phone/fax).

Nevraumont Publishing Co., ( 0-945223 ) 16 E. 23rd St., New York, NY 10010 (SAN 246-215X) Tel 212-529-0400.

New Amsterdam Bks Imprint of Dee, Ivan R. Pub.

New Amsterdam Publishing, Incorporated See Intercontinental Publishing, Inc.

New Ark Productions, ( 0-9659147 ) 148 Newman St., San Francisco, CA 94110 Tel 415-648-6834
E-mail: newarke@aol.com; elizane@aol.com.

New Century Pr., ( 1-890035 ) 1055 Bay Blvd., Suite C, Chula Vista, CA 91911-1628 Tel 619-476-7400; Fax: 619-476-7474; Toll Free: 800-519-2465 (orders) Do not confuse with companies with the same or similar name in Bermuda Dunes CA, New York NY
E-mail: sales@newcenturypress.com
Web site: http://www.newcenturypress.com.

New Concepts Publishing, ( 1-891020; 1-58608 ) 5202 Humphreys Rd., Lake Park, GA 31636 Tel 229-257-0367; Fax: 229-219-1097
E-mail: ncp@newconceptspublishing.com
Web site: http://www.newconceptspublishing.com
Dist(s): Baker & Taylor Bks..

New Concord Pr. Imprint of Equine Graphics Publishing

New Day Pubs., Philippines (PHL) ( 971-10 ) Dist. by Book Bin.

†New Directions Publishing Corp., ( 0-8112 ) 80 Eighth Ave., New York, NY 10011 (SAN 202-9081) Tel 212-255-0230; Fax: 212-255-0231; Toll Free: 800-233-4830
E-mail: nd@ndbooks.com
Web site: http://www.ndpublishing.com
Dist(s): Continental Bk. Co., Inc.
Norton, W. W. & Co., Inc.
SPD-Small Pr. Distribution; CIP.

†New England Pr., Inc., The, ( 0-933050; 1-881535 )
Orders Addr.: P.O. Box 575, Shelburne, VT 05482 (SAN 213-6376) Tel 802-863-2520; Fax: 802-863-1510
E-mail: nep@together.net
Web site: http://www.nepress.com; CIP.

New England Science Fiction Assn., Inc., ( 0-915368; 1-886778 ) P.O. Box 809, Framingham, MA 01701-0809 (SAN 223-8187) Tel 617-588-9350; Fax: 617-776-3243
E-mail: press@nesfa.org
Web site: http://www.nesfa.org/press/.

New English Library, Ltd. (GBR) ( 0-340; 0-450 ) Dist. by Trafalgar.

New Falcon Pubns., ( 0-941404; 0-9622452; 1-56184 ) 1739 E. Broadway Rd., No. 1-277, Tempe, AZ 85282 (SAN 262-0243) Tel 602-708-1409; Fax: 602-708-1410; Fulfillment Addr.: c/o JV Company, 1585 Linda Way, Sparks, NV 89431
E-mail: info@newfalcon.com
Web site: http://www.newfalcon.com
Dist(s): Baker & Taylor Bks.
Bookpeople
New Leaf Distributing Co., Inc.
Red Wheel/Weiser.

New Holland Pubs. (NZL) ( 0-908598; 1-877246; 0-908808; 1-84330; 1-877213; 1-86966 ) Dist. by BHB Intl.

New Hope See Woman's Missionary Union

New Hope Imprint of Woman's Missionary Union

New Horizon Pr. Pubs., Inc., ( 0-88282 ) Orders Addr.: P.O. Box 669, Far Hills, NJ 07931 (SAN 677-119X) Tel 908-604-6311; Fax: 908-604-6330; Toll Free: 800-533-7978 (orders only)
E-mail: nhp@newhorizonpressbooks.com
Web site: http://www.newhorizonpressbooks.com
Dist(s): Kensington Publishing Corp..

New Horizons Book Publishing Company See World Citizens

New Island Bks. (IRL) ( 1-85186; 1-874597; 1-902602; 1-904301 ) Dist. by Dufour.

New Island Bks. (IRL) ( 1-85186; 1-874597; 1-902602; 1-904301 ) Dist. by Irish Bks Media.

New Leaf Pr., ( 0-9660778 ) P.O. Box 361240, Los Angeles, CA 90036-9440 Tel 323-935-4067 (phone/fax) Do not confuse with companies with the same or similar name in Green Forest, AR, Stone Mountain, GA
E-mail: info@newleafpress.com
Web site: http://www.newleafpress.com.

New Letters on Air, 5101 Rockhill Rd., Kansas City, MO 64110 (SAN 695-4723) Tel 816-235-1159; Fax: 816-235-2611; Toll Free: 888-548-2477 (orders)
E-mail: ace@art.net; newletters@art.net
Web site: http://www.umkc.edu/newletters.

New Mill Publishing, ( 0-9711335 ) P.O. Box 101, Meadow Vista, CA 95722.

New Millennium Audio Imprint of New Millennium Entertainment

New Millennium Entertainment, ( 1-893224; 1-931056; 1-59007 ) 301 N. Canon Dr., Suite 214, Beverly Hills, CA 90210 Tel 310-273-7722; Fax: 310-273-7755;
Imprints: New Millennium Press (New Millenn Pr); New Millennium Audio (N Millennium Audio)
Dist(s): Client Distribution Services.

New Millennium Pr. Imprint of New Millennium Entertainment

New Millennium Publishing, ( 0-9639211 ) Orders Addr.: P.O. Box 3065, Portland, OR 97208 Fax: 503-297-0436; Edit Addr.: 8150 SW Barnes Rd., No. R105, Portland, OR 97225 Do not confuse with companies with the same name in North Miami Beach, FL, Venice, CA, Southfield, MI.

New Page Bks. Imprint of Career Pr., Inc.

New Pr., The, ( 1-56584 ) 38 Greene St., 4th Flr., New York, NY 10013 Tel 212-629-8802 Toll Free Fax: 800-458-6515; Toll Free: 800-233-4830
E-mail: newpress@thenewpress.com
Web site: http://www.thenewpress.com
Dist(s): Norton, W. W. & Co., Inc..

New Readers Pr., ( 0-88336; 1-56420 ) Div. of Laubach Literacy International, Orders Addr.: P.O. Box 888, Syracuse, NY 13210 (SAN 202-1064) Fax: 315-422-6369; Toll Free: 800-448-8878; Edit Addr.: 1320 Jamesville Ave., Syracuse, NY 13210 Tel 315-422-9121
E-mail: nrp@laubach.org
Web site: http://www.newreaderspress.com
Dist(s): CRC Pubns..

New Rivers Pr., ( 0-89823; 0-912284 ) Minnesota State University, Moorhead, 1104 Seventh Ave. South, Moorhead, MN 56563 (SAN 202-9138) Tel 218-236-4681; Fax: 218-236-2236; Toll Free: 800-339-2011
E-mail: davisa@mnstate.edu
Web site: http://www.newriverspress.org
Dist(s): Consortium Bk. Sales & Distribution
SPD-Small Pr. Distribution.

New Spirit Imprint of BET Bks.

New Star Bks., Ltd. (CAN) ( 0-919573; 0-919888; 0-921586; 1-55420 ) Dist. by SPD-Small Pr Dist.

†New Victoria Pubs., Inc., ( 0-934678; 1-892281 )
Orders Addr.: P.O. Box 27, Norwich, VT 05055 (SAN 212-1204) Tel 802-649-5297 (phone/fax); Toll Free: 800-326-5297 (phone/fax); Edit Addr.: 513 New Boston Rd., Norwich, VT 05055
E-mail: newvic@aol.com
Web site: http://www.newvictoria.com
Dist(s): LPC Group; CIP.

New Way Publishing, ( 0-9702567 ) 30 Amberwood Pkwy., Ashland, OH 44805 Tel 419-281-1802; Fax: 419-281-6883; Toll Free: 800-247-6553
E-mail: order@bookmaster.com;
dannetth@bookmaster.com
Dist(s): Amazon.Com.

†New Win Publishing, Inc., ( 0-8329; 0-87691 ) P.O. Box 5159, Clinton, NJ 08809 (SAN 217-1201) Tel 908-735-9701; Fax: 908-735-9703
Dist(s): Continental Bk. Co., Inc.; CIP.

†New York Botanical Garden, The, ( 0-89327 ) New York Botanical Garden, The, Bronx, NY 10458-5126 (SAN 205-7085) Tel 718-817-8700
Web site: http://www.nybg.org; CIP.

†New York Public Library, ( 0-87104 ) Pubns. Office, 6th Flr., 8 W. 40th St., New York, NY 10018 (SAN 202-926X) Tel 212-512-0202; Fax: 212-704-8620
E-mail: syoung@nypl.org; mciccone@nypl.org; sharrison@nypl.org
Web site: http://www.nypl.org; CIP.

New York Review of Bks., Inc., The, ( 0-940322; 1-59017 ) 1755 Broadway, 5th Flr., New York, NY 10019-3780 (SAN 220-3448) Tel 212-757-8070; Fax: 212-333-5374
E-mail: mail@nybooks.com
Web site: http://www.nybooks.com
Dist(s): Publishers Group West.

†New York Univ. Pr., ( 0-8147 ) Div. of New York Univ., 838 Broadway, 3rd Flr., New York, NY 10003-4812 (SAN 658-1293) Tel 212-998-2575; Fax: 212-995-3833; Toll Free: 800-996-6987
E-mail: orders@nyupress.nyu.edu
Web site: http://www.nyupress.nyu.edu
Dist(s): Slavica Pubs.; CIP.

Names

**NewCentury Pubs.,** ( *0-9679790* ) Orders Addr.: P.O. Box 751434, Petaluma, CA 94975 Tel 707-769-9808; Fax: 707-769-9779; Edit Addr.: 14 Boreal Pl., Petaluma, CA 94954
E-mail: editor@newcentutypublishers.com
Web site: http://www.newcenturypublishers.com
*Dist(s):* **Bookpeople**
    **DeVorss & Co.**
    **New Leaf Distributing Co., Inc.**
    **SCB Distributors.**

**Newconcept Pr., Inc.,** ( *0-931231* ) 10 Industrial Ave., Mahwah, NJ 07430-2262 (SAN 689-1705) Tel 212-265-6284; Fax: 212-265-6659; Toll Free: 800-926-6579
E-mail: orders@erlbaum.com
Web site: http://www.erlbaum.com
*Dist(s):* **Baker & Taylor Bks..**

**NeWest Pubs., Ltd. (CAN)** ( *0-920316; 0-920897; 1-896300* ) *Dist. by* **Strauss Cnslts.**

**†Newmarket Pr.,** ( *0-937858; 1-55704* ) Div. of Newmarket Publishing & Communications Corp., 18 E. 48th St., New York, NY 10017 (SAN 217-2585) Tel 212-832-3575; Fax: 212-832-3629; Toll Free Fax: 800-458-6515 (trade orders); Toll Free: 800-233-4830 (trade orders)
E-mail: mailbox@newmarketpress.com
Web site: http://www.newmarketpress.com
*Dist(s):* **Norton, W. W. & Co., Inc.;** *CIP.*

**Newport R&D, Inc.,** ( *0-9712696* ) 1 Maritime Dr., Portsmouth, RI 02871 Tel 401-683-9450; Fax: 401-683-5890.

**News Center Pubns.,** ( *0-9650053* ) Orders Addr.: Plaza G-190, Forest View, Bayamon, PR 00619 Tel 787-791-0204; Fax: 787-253-3872; Edit Addr.: General Delivery, Apt. 363004, San Juan, PR 00936-3004.

**NewSound, LLC,** 81 Demeritt Pl., Waterbury, VT 05676 Tel 802-244-7858; Fax: 802-244-1808; Toll Free: 800-342-0295 (wholesale orders)
E-mail: sales@newsoundmusic.com.

**NewSouth Bks. Imprint of NewSouth, Inc.**

**NewSouth, Inc.,** ( *1-58838* ) P.O. Box 1588, Montgomery, AL 36102-1588 Tel 334-834-3556; Fax: 334-834-3557; *Imprints:* NewSouth Books (NewSouth AL); Court Street Press (Court Street Pr)
E-mail: info@newsouthbooks.com
Web site: http://www.newsouthbooks.com.

**NewStar Media, Inc.,** ( *0-7871; 1-55800* ) 8955 Beverly Blvd., Los Angeles, CA 90048 (SAN 297-2913) Tel 310-786-1600; Fax: 310-247-2924; Toll Free: 800-368-3007; *Imprints:* NewStar Press (NewStar Pr); Dove Audio (Dove Audio)
E-mail: customerservice@audiouniverse.com
Web site: http://www.newstarmedia.com;
http://www.audiouniverse.com
*Dist(s):* **Lectorum Pubns., Inc.**
    **Landmark Audiobooks**
    **Penguin Group (USA) Inc..**

**NewStar Pr. Imprint of NewStar Media, Inc.**

**Nguoi Dan,** ( *1-889880* ) Orders Addr.: P.O. Box 2674, Costa Mesa, CA 92628 Tel 714-549-3443; Fax: 714-241-8505; Edit Addr.: 1825 W. Garry Ave., Santa Ana, CA 92704
E-mail: nguoidan@ix.netcom.com
Web site: http://www.nguoidan.net; http://www.nguoidan.com.

**Nickelodeon Press** *See* **Pony-Up Pr.**

**Night Tree Pr.,** ( *0-935939* ) P.O. Box 217, Boonville, NY 13309-0217 (SAN 661-4159) Tel 315-942-6001.

**Nine Muses Pr.,** ( *0-9644122* ) P.O. Box 1138, Occidental, CA 95465 Tel 707-829-8232 (phone/fax) Do not confuse with Nine Muses Pr., Long Beach, CA
E-mail: bronwen@9muses.com
Web site: http://www.9muses.com.

**Nite Owl Bks.,** ( *0-9661105* ) 4040 E. Camelback Rd., Suite 101, Phoenix, AZ 85018 (SAN 299-6413) Tel 602-840-0132; Fax: 602-957-1671; Toll Free: 888-927-9600
E-mail: theniteowl@juno.com
*Dist(s):* **KCS.**

**Nixon, James F.,** ( *0-9656586* ) 12625 Germane Ave. Apt. 7, Saint Paul, MN 55124-4377.

**No Dead Lines** *See* **Fithian Pr.**

**No Exit Pr. (GBR)** ( *0-948353; 1-874061; 1-901982; 1-84243* ) *Dist. by* **Trafalgar.**

**No Exit Pr. Imprint of Four Walls Eight Windows**

**Noble Hse.,** ( *1-56167* ) Div. of American Literary Pr., Inc., a/o Donna Wessel, 8019 Belair Rd. Suite 10, Baltimore, MD 21236-3711 Tel 410-882-7700; Fax: 410-882-7703; Toll Free: 800-873-2003 Do not confuse with Noble Hse., Jensen Beach, FL
E-mail: amerlit@erols.com
Web site: http://www.erols.com/amerlit
*Dist(s):* **Baker & Taylor Bks.**
    **Quality Bks., Inc.**
    **Unique Bks., Inc..**

**Noble Porter Pr.,** ( *0-9634147* ) 36-851 Palm View Rd., Rancho Mirage, CA 92270 Tel 760-770-6076; Fax: 760-770-4507
E-mail: drama@cyberg8t.com.

**Noble Pr., Inc., The,** ( *0-9622683; 1-879360* ) 636 N. Orleans St., No. 2SO, Chicago, IL 60610-3609 (SAN 200-3236) Tel 312-642-1168; Fax: 312-642-7682; Toll Free: 800-486-7737 Do not confuse with Noble Press, Inc., Coral Springs, FL.

**Noguer y Caralt Editores, S. A. (ESP)** ( *84-217; 84-279* ) *Dist. by* **Lectorum Pubns.**

**Non Pareil Bks. Imprint of Godine, David R. Pub.**

**Nonetheless Pr.,** ( *1-932053* ) 20332 W. 98th St., Lenexa, KS 66220-2650 Tel 913-254-7360; Fax: 913-393-3245
E-mail: mschutte@nonethelesspress.com
Web site: http://www.nonethelesspress.com.

**Nopoly Pr., Inc.,** ( *0-930950* ) 1 Wellington Rd., Wilmington, DE 19803-4129 (SAN 212-1220) Tel 302-764-2126; Fax: 302-764-2126
E-mail: nopoly@mindspring.com.

**Norma S.A. (COL)** ( *958-04* ) *Dist. by* **Lectorum Pubns.**

**Norma S.A. (COL)** ( *958-04* ) *Dist. by* **Distr Norma.**

**Normandy Hse. Pubs.,** ( *0-9708319* ) Div. of Grimbaldus Productions, P.O. Box 59-1066, Houston, TX 77259-1066 (SAN 253-6846) Tel 581-638-4622; Toll Free: 866-447-4622
E-mail: grimbaldus@aol.com
Web site: http://www.grimbaldus.com.

**†North Atlantic Bks.,** ( *0-913028; 0-938190; 0-942941; 1-55643; 1-883319* ) Div. of The Society of the Study of Native Art & Science, Orders Addr.: P.O. Box 12327, Berkeley, CA 94712 (SAN 203-1655) Tel 510-559-8277; Fax: 510-559-8279; Toll Free: 800-337-2665 (orders only); Edit Addr.: 1456 Fourth St., Berkeley, CA 94710
E-mail: orders@northatlanticbooks.com
Web site: http://www.northatlanticbooks.com
*Dist(s):* **Nutri-Bks. Corp.**
    **Publishers Group West**
    **SPD-Small Pr. Distribution;** *CIP.*

**North Bks.,** ( *0-939495; 1-58287* ) P.O. Box 1277, Wickford, RI 02852 (SAN 663-4052) Tel 401-294-3682; Fax: 401-294-9491.

**North Carolina Wesleyan College Pr.,** ( *0-933598* ) 3400 N. Wesleyan Blvd., Rocky Mount, NC 27804 (SAN 238-6364) Tel 919-985-5153; Fax: 919-977-3701.

**†North Country Bks., Inc.,** ( *0-925168; 0-932052; 0-9601158; 1-59531* ) 311 Turner St., Utica, NY 13501 (SAN 110-828X) Tel 315-735-4877
E-mail: ncbooks@adelphia.net; *CIP.*

**North Country Pr.,** ( *0-945980* ) Div. of Maine Fulfillment Corp., R.R. 1, Box 1395, Unity, ME 04988 (SAN 247-9680) Tel 207-948-2208; Fax: 207-948-2717; Toll Free: 800-722-2169 Do not confuse with North Country Pr., White Cloud, MI
E-mail: ncp@uninet.net
Web site: http://www.midcoast.com/~ncp/.

**North Point Pr. Imprint of Farrar, Straus & Giroux**

**North River Press, Incorporated** *See* **North River Pr. Publishing Corp., The**

**†North River Pr. Publishing Corp., The,** ( *0-88427* ) P.O. Box 567, Great Barrington, MA 01230 (SAN 202-1048) Tel 413-528-0034; Fax: 413-528-3163; Toll Free Fax: 800-266-5329; Toll Free: 800-486-2665
E-mail: agallagher@northriverpress.com
Web site: http://www.northriverpress.com; *CIP.*

**†North Star Pr. of St. Cloud,** ( *0-87839* ) P.O. Box 451, Saint Cloud, MN 56302-0451 (SAN 203-7491) Tel 320-558-9062; Fax: 320-558-9063; Toll Free: 888-820-1636
E-mail: nspress@cloudnet.com
*Dist(s):* **Adventure Pubns., Inc.**
    **Partners Bk. Distributing, Inc.**
    **Skandisk, Inc.;** *CIP.*

**†Northeastern Univ. Pr.,** ( *0-930350; 1-55553* ) Orders Addr.: 750 Cascadilla St., Ithaca, NY 14851 Tel 607-277-2211; Fax: 607-277-6292; Toll Free: 800-666-2211; Edit Addr.: 360 Huntington Ave., 416 Columbus Pl., Boston, MA 02115 (SAN 205-3764) Tel 617-373-5480; Fax: 617-373-5483
E-mail: univpress@nunet.neu.edu
Web site: http://www.neu.edu/nupress; *CIP.*

**†Northern Illinois Univ. Pr.,** ( *0-87580* ) 310 N. Fifth St., DeKalb, IL 60115-2854 (SAN 202-8875) Tel 815-753-1826; Fax: 815-753-1845
E-mail: bberg@niu.edu
Web site: http://www.niu.edu/univ_press/; *CIP.*

**Northern Liberties Pr. Imprint of Old City Publishing, Inc.**

**Northland Press** *See* **Northland Publishing**

**†Northland Publishing,** ( *0-87358* ) Orders Addr.: P.O. Box 1389, Flagstaff, AZ 86002-1389 Tel 928-774-5251; Fax: 928-774-0592; Toll Free Fax: 800-257-9082; Toll Free: 800-346-3257; *Imprints:* Rising Moon Books for Young Readers (Rising Moon Bks)
E-mail: info@northlandpub.com
Web site: http://www.northlandpub.com
*Dist(s):* **Lectorum Pubns., Inc.**
    **Libros Sin Fronteras;** *CIP.*

**†North-South Bks., Inc.,** ( *0-7358; 1-55858; 1-58717* ) 875 Sixth Ave., Suite 1901, New York, NY 10010 Tel 212-706-4545; Fax: 212-868-5951
E-mail: mnavarro@northsouth.com
Web site: http://www.northsouth.com
*Dist(s):* **Chronicle Bks. LLC**
    **Continental Bk. Co., Inc.**
    **Lectorum Pubns., Inc.**
    **Libros Sin Fronteras;** *CIP.*

**NorthStar Audio Bks.,** ( *1-58216* ) Orders Addr.: P.O. Box 129, Van Wyck, SC 29744 Tel 803-283-2858; Fax: 803-286-4151; Toll Free: 800-522-2979; Edit Addr.: 5055 Three Crow Rd., Van Wyck, SC 29744
E-mail: nsaudiobooks@comporium.net
*Dist(s):* **Bantam Doubleday Dell Publishing Group**
    **Landmark Audiobooks.**

**Northstar Bks.,** ( *0-9648145* ) 11940 N. Park Rd., NE, Alexandria, MN 56308 Tel 612-852-7139.

**Northwestern Univ. Pr.,** ( *0-8101* ) Orders Addr.: 11030 S. Langley Ave., Chicago, IL 60628 Tel 773-568-1550 ; Fax: 773-660-2235; Toll Free Fax: 800-621-8476; Toll Free: 800-621-2736; Edit Addr.: 625 Colfax St., Evanston, IL 60208-4210 (SAN 202-5787) Tel 847-491-5313; Fax: 847-491-8150; *Imprints:* Hydra Books (Hydra Bks); Marlboro Press, The (Marlboro); TriQuarterly Books (TriQuart)
E-mail: nupress@northwestern.edu
Web site: http://www.nupress.northwestern.edu
*Dist(s):* **Univ. of Chicago Pr..**

**Northwind Pr.,** ( *0-945887* ) Div. of OZ Enterprises, Inc., P.O. Box 637, Sandpoint, ID 83864 (SAN 247-8447) Tel 208-263-7756; Fax: 208-263-7751.

**NorthWord Imprint of Creative Publishing international, Inc.**

**Norton Paperbacks Imprint of Norton, W. W. & Co., Inc.**

**Norton Pubs., Inc., Jeffrey /Audio-Forum,** ( *0-88432; 1-57970* ) 96 Broad St., Guilford, CT 06437-2612 (SAN 213-957X) Tel 203-453-9794; Fax: 203-453-9774; Toll Free Fax: 888-453-4329; Toll Free: 800-243-1234
E-mail: info@audioforum.com
Web site: http://www.audioForum.com.

**†Norton, W. W. & Co., Inc.,** ( *0-393; 0-920256* ) Orders Addr.: 800 Keystone Industrial Pk., Scranton, PA 18512 (SAN 157-1869) Tel 570-346-2020; Fax: 570-346-1442; Toll Free Fax: 800-548-6515; Toll Free: 800-233-4830 (book orders only); Edit Addr.: 500 Fifth Ave., New York, NY 10110-0017 (SAN 202-5795) Tel 212-354-5500; Fax: 212-869-0856; Toll Free: 800-223-2584; *Imprints:* Norton Paperbacks (Norton Paperbks); Foul Play (Foul Play)
E-mail: webmaster@wwnorton.com
Tworrell@wwnorton.com
Web site: http://www.wwnorton.com/trade; http://www.wwnorton.com
*Dist(s):* **Continental Bk. Co., Inc.**
    **Peoples Publishing Group, Inc., The**
    **netLibrary, Inc.;** *CIP.*

**Norvik Pr. (GBR)** ( *1-870041* ) *Dist. by* **Dufour.**

**Nostos Bks.,** ( *0-932963* ) Box 19086, Minneapolis, MN 55419 (SAN 689-1500) Tel 612-824-2996.

**Nova Audio Bks. Imprint of Brilliance Audio**

**†Nova Science Pubs., Inc.,** ( *0-941743; 1-56072; 1-59033; 1-59454* ) 400 Oser Ave., Suite 1600, Hauppauge, NY 11788-3619 (SAN 666-0266) Fax: 631-231-8175
E-mail: novascience@earthlink.net
Web site: http://www.novapublishers.com
*Dist(s):* **Baker & Taylor Bks.;** *CIP.*

**Novel Units, Inc.,** ( *1-56137; 1-58310* ) Orders Addr.:
P.O. Box 791610, San Antonio, TX 78279-1610 (SAN
253-9276) Tel 830-438-4262; Fax: 830-438-4263; Toll
Free Fax: 877-688-3226; Toll Free: 800-688-3224
E-mail: novlunit@gvtc.com; editors@gvtc.com;
ecslearn@gvtc.com
Web site: http://www.educyberstor.com
*Dist(s):* **Lectorum Pubns., Inc.**
**Perma-Bound Bks..**

**NovelBooks, Inc.,** ( *1-931696; 1-59105* ) P.O. Box 661,
Douglas, MA 01516 Tel 508-476-1161; Fax:
508-476-3866
E-mail: publisher@novelbooksinc.com
Web site: http://www.novelbooksinc.com.

**Novello Festival Pr.,** ( *0-9708972* ) Div. of Public
Library of Charlotte & Mecklenburg County, 310 N.
Tryon St., Charlotte, NC 28202 (SAN 254-3206) Tel
704-336-4146; 704-432-0153; Fax: 704-336-2677
E-mail: rec@plcmc.org
Web site: http://www.novellofestival.net
*Dist(s):* **Blair, John F. Pub..**

**NTC/Contemporary Publishing Company** *See*
**McGraw-Hill/Contemporary**

**NUVENTURES Publishing,** ( *0-9625632* ) Div. of
NUVENTURES Consultants, Orders Addr.: P.O. Box
2489, La Jolla, CA 92038-2489 (SAN 200-3805) Fax:
619-459-0569; Toll Free: 800-338-9768; Edit Addr.:
6236 Cardeno Dr., La Jolla, CA 92037 (SAN
200-3813) Tel 619-454-9100.

**NuVision Pubns.,** ( *1-932681* ) 1304 Riverview Cir.,
Belle Fourche, SD 57717
E-mail: sales@nuvisionpublications.com
Web site: http://www.nuvisionpublications.com
*Dist(s):* **Lightning Source, Inc..**

**OMF Bks.,** ( *0-85363; 981-3009; 1-929122* ) Div. of
OMF International, 10 W. Dry Creek Cir., Littleton,
CO 80120-4413 (SAN 211-8351) Tel 303-730-4160;
Fax: 303-730-4165; Toll Free: 888-663-2665
E-mail: bookstore@omf.org
Web site: http://www.us.omf.org
*Dist(s):* **Christian Literature Crusade, Inc..**

**Oak Tree Pr. Imprint of Oak Tree Publishing**

**Oak Tree Publishing,** ( *1-892343* ) Orders Addr.: 2743
S. Veterans Pkwy., No. 135, Springfield, IL
62704-6402 Tel 217-824-8001; Fax: 217-824-3424;
*Imprints:* Oak Tree Press (Oaktreepress); Dark Oak
Mysteries (Dark Oak); Timeless Love (Timeless Love)
E-mail: oaktreepub@aol.com; info@oaktreebooks.com
Web site: http://www.oaktreebooks.com

**Oak Woods Media,** ( *0-88196* ) P.O. Box 19127,
Kalamazoo, MI 49019 (SAN 264-6285) Tel
616-375-5621; Fax: 616-375-7526
E-mail: oakwoods@net.link.net.

**Oaklea Pr., The,** ( *0-9646601; 1-892538* ) Orders Addr.:
P.O. Box 29334, Richmond, VA 23242-0334; Edit
Addr.: 6912-B Three Chopt Rd., Richmond, VA 23233
Tel 804-281-5872; Fax: 804-281-5686; Toll Free:
800-295-4066
E-mail: jgots@oakleapress.com
Web site: http://www.oakleapress.com
*Dist(s):* **Baker & Taylor Bks.**
**Bookpeople**
**New Leaf Distributing Co., Inc..**

**Oaks, Barbara,** ( *0-9618582* ) 3400 W. Ralph Rogers
Rd. Apt. 106, Sioux Falls, SD 57108-2639 (SAN
668-2898).

**Oasis Audio,** ( *1-55536; 1-886463; 1-58926* ) Div. of
Domain Communications, 289 S. Main Pl., Carol
Stream, IL 60188 Fax: 630-668-0158; Toll Free:
800-323-2500 (ext. 110)
E-mail: jelwell@oasisaudio.com;
info@oasisaudio.com
Web site: http://www.oasisaudio.com
*Dist(s):* **Baker & Taylor Bks..**

**Obelesk Bks.,** ( *1-887666* ) P.O. Box 1118, Elkton, MD
21922-1118 Tel 410-392-3640
E-mail: obelesk@tantalus.clark.net
*Dist(s):* **Alamo Square Distributors.**

**Obelisk Imprint of NAL**

**Obsidian Bks., Etc.,** ( *1-891480* ) 2053 Gilman Dr W.
Apt. B, Seattle, WA 98119-2740
E-mail: MJobsidian@aol.com
Web site: http://www.Horrornet.com/obsidian.htm.

**Octagon Pr., Ltd. (GBR)** ( *0-86304; 0-900860* ) *Dist. by*
**ISHK**

**Octagon Pr./ISHK Bk. Service** *See* **ISHK**

**Octavia Pr.,** ( *0-940601* ) 12127 Sperry Rd., Chesterland,
OH 44026-2230 (SAN 665-0236) Tel 440-729-3252;
Fax: 440-729-2003 Do not confuse with Octavia Pr.,
Miami Beach, FL.

**Oetinger, Annis,** ( *0-9634757* ) Orders Addr.: P.O. Box
3082, Sun River, OR 97707; Edit Addr.: 8 Yellow
Pine Ln., Sun River, OR 97707 Tel 541-593-3235
E-mail: annis@cmc.com.

**Offbeat Pr. Imprint of Santa Monica Pr.**

**OffByOne Pr.,** ( *0-9644138* ) 1325 W. First Ave., Suite A,
Spokane, WA 99201 Tel 509-747-7416; Fax:
509-747-7459; *Imprints:* Dark City Books (Drk City
Bks).

**Ohio Historical Society,** ( *0-87758* ) Ohio Historical Ctr.,
1982 Velma Ave., Columbus, OH 43211-2497 (SAN
202-1331) Tel 614-297-2300; Fax: 614-297-2569; Toll
Free: 800-OLDOHIO
E-mail: mdavis@ohiohistory.org
Web site: htttpw://www.ohiohistory.org.

†**Ohio State Univ. Pr.,** ( *0-8142* ) 1070 Carmack Rd.,
Columbus, OH 43210 (SAN 202-8158) Tel
614-292-6930; 773-568-1550 (orders); Fax:
614-292-2065; Toll Free Fax: 800-621-8476 (orders);
Toll Free: 800-621-2736 (orders); *Imprints:* Sandstone
Books (Sandstone Bks)
E-mail: ohiostatepress@osu.edu
Web site: http://www.ohiostatepress.org
*Dist(s):* **Univ. of Chicago Pr.**; *CIP.*

**Ohio Univ. Ctr. for International Studies Imprint of**
**Ohio Univ. Pr.**

†**Ohio Univ. Pr.,** ( *0-8214* ) Orders Addr.: 11030 S.
Langley Ave., Chicago, IL 60628 Tel 773-568-1559;
Fax: 773-660-2235; Toll Free Fax: 800-621-8476; Toll
Free: 800-621-2736; Edit Addr.: Scott Quadrangle,
Athens, OH 45701 (SAN 282-0773) Tel
740-593-1154; Fax: 740-593-4536; *Imprints:* Ohio
University Center for International Studies (Ohio U
Ctr Intl)
E-mail: gilbert@ohiou.edu
Web site: http://www.ohiou.edu/oupress/
*Dist(s):* **Univ. of Chicago Pr.**
**netLibrary, Inc.**; *CIP.*

**Okpaku Communications Corp.,** ( *0-89388* ) Div. of
Third Pr. Review of Bks. Co., 222 Forest Ave., New
Rochelle, NY 10804 (SAN 202-5701) Tel
914-632-2355; Fax: 914-632-2320
E-mail: okpaku@aol.com

**Old Berwick Historical Society,** ( *0-9636111* ) Orders
Addr.: P.O. Box 296, South Berwick, ME 03908; Edit
Addr.: 35 Wadleigh Ln., South Berwick, ME 03908
Tel 207-384-5162; Fax: 207-384-3220.

**Old City Publishing, Inc.,** ( *0-9704143* ) 628 N. Second
St., Philadelphia, PA 19123 Tel 215-925-4390; Fax:
215-925-4371; *Imprints:* Northern Liberties Press
(Northern Liberties Pr)
E-mail: ian@oldcitypublishing.com
Web site: http://www.oldcitypublishing.com.

**Old Earth Bks.,** ( *1-882968* ) Orders Addr.: P.O. Box
19951, Baltimore, MD 21211-0951; Edit Addr.: 2620
N. Calvert St., Baltimore, MD 21218-4616 Tel
410-889-4080 (phone/fax)
E-mail: publisher@oldearthbooks.com
Web site: http://www.oldearthbooks.com
*Dist(s):* **Koen Bk. Distributors.**

**Old New York Bk. Shop Pr.,** ( *0-937036* ) 660
Spindlewick Dr., Atlanta, GA 30350 Tel 770-393-2997
; Fax: 770-393-1288
E-mail: cgraubart@mindspring.com.

**Old Paths Pubns., Inc.,** ( *0-9632557; 1-889058* ) One
Bittersweet Path, Willow Street, PA 17584-9640 Tel
717-464-6963; Fax: 717-464-6964; Toll Free Fax:
800-999-2460; Toll Free: 800-999-4541
E-mail: oldpaths@flash.net
Web site: http://www.trinitybookservice.org/
oldpath.html.

**Oldcastle Bks., Ltd. (GBR)** ( *0-948353; 1-874061* )
*Dist. by* **Trafalgar.**

**Oldcastle Bks., Ltd. (GBR)** ( *0-948353; 1-874061* )
*Dist. by* **St Mut.**

**Olde Springfield Shoppe** *See* **Masthof Pr.**

**Olive Tree Bks. Imprint of El Paso City Bks., LLC**

**Olivia & Hill Pr., The,** ( *0-934034* ) Orders Addr.: P.O.
Box 7396, Ann Arbor, MI 48107; Edit Addr.: 905
Olivia Ave., Ann Arbor, MI 48104 (SAN 212-923X)
Tel 734-663-0235; Fax: 734-663-6590
E-mail: order@oliviahill.com
Web site: http://www.oliviahill.com.

**Olmstead Pr. Imprint of Moyer Bell**

**O'Mara, Michael Bks., Ltd. (GBR)** ( *1-85479;*
*0-946429; 0-948397; 1-84317; 1-903840* ) *Dist. by*
**Andrews McMeel.**

**Omnibus Enterprises, Ltd.,** ( *0-9702298* ) 12907 E.
36th St. Terr., Independence, MO 64055 Tel
816-252-6619 (phone/fax)
E-mail: WPaxton159@aol.com.

**Omnibus Printers Ltd.,** ( *0-9716771* ) 74 Deer Ridge
Ct., Getzville, NY 14068.

**Once Upon A Radio,** P.O. Box 1243, Cedar Falls, IA
50613-8571.

**One Eyed Pr.,** ( *0-9665430* ) 272 Rd. 6RT, Cody, WY
82414 Tel 307-587-6136; Toll Free: 800-247-6553
E-mail: one_eyed_press@yahoo.com
Web site: http://www.picaro.com;
http://www.one-eyed-press.com
*Dist(s):* **Booksurge, LLC**
**Todd Communications.**

**One Faithful Harp Publishing Co.,** ( *0-9666701* )
Orders Addr.: P.O. Box 20140, Scranton, PA
18502-0140 Tel 717-342-8156; Edit Addr.: 417
Moltke Ave., Scranton, PA 18505
E-mail: info@onefaithfulharp.com
Web site: http://www.onefaithfulharp.com.

**One Horse Rhino Pr.,** ( *0-9637981* ) 88 Howard St., No.
1510, San Francisco, CA 94105 Tel 415-243-4170;
Fax: 415-243-4183
E-mail: rhino@onehorse.com
Web site: http://www.onehorse.com
*Dist(s):* **Distributors, The.**

**One Peaceful World Pr.,** ( *0-9628528; 1-882984* )
Orders Addr.: P.O. Box 10, Becket, MA 01223 (SAN
631-2519) Tel 413-623-2322; Fax: 413-623-6042; Toll
Free: 888-322-4095; Edit Addr.: 308 Leland Rd.,
Becket, MA 01223
E-mail: opw@macrobiotics.org
Web site: http://www.macrobiotics.org.

**One World/Ballantine Imprint of Ballantine Bks.**

**Onion River Pr.,** ( *0-9657144* ) 21 Essex Way Ste. 106,
Essex Jct, VT 05452-3386 Toll Free: 877-266-5722
E-mail: bookrack@together.net
Web site: http://www.onionriverpress.com.

†**Ontario Review Pr.,** ( *0-86538* ) 9 Honey Brook Dr.,
Princeton, NJ 08540 (SAN 658-134X) Tel
609-737-7497; Fax: 609-737-2695
Web site: http://www.ontarioreviewpress.com
*Dist(s):* **Norton, W. W. & Co., Inc.**; *CIP.*

**Onyx Imprint of NAL**

**Open Gate Pr. (GBR)** ( *1-871871* ) *Dist. by* **Paul & Co**
**Pubs.**

**Optyon Bks.,** ( *0-9700207* ) 20 Surrey Rd., Great Neck,
NY 11020 Tel 516-298-3830; 516-487-1229; Fax:
516-482-2616
E-mail: info@optyonbooks.com;
msgabor@compuserve.com
Web site: http://www.optyonbooks.com
*Dist(s):* **Book Clearing Hse..**

**O'RaghaillIgh, Limited, Publishers** *See* **Magicimage**
**Filmbooks**

**Orb Bks. Imprint of Doherty, Tom Assocs., LLC**

**Orbit (GBR)** ( *0-09; 0-356; 0-7088; 0-7474; 1-85723;*
*1-84149* ) *Dist. by* **Trafalgar.**

**Orca Bk. Pubs.,** ( *0-920501; 1-55143* ) Orders Addr.:
P.O. Box 468, Custer, WA 98240-0468 (SAN
630-9674) Tel 250-380-1229; Fax: 250-380-1892; Toll
Free: 800-210-5277
E-mail: melanie@orcabook.com;
mcolgan@orcabook.com
Web site: http://www.orcabook.com.

**Orchard Bks. Imprint of Scholastic, Inc.**

**Orchid Isle Publishing Co.,** ( *1-887916* ) 131 Halai St.,
Hilo, HI 96720.

†**Orchises Pr.,** ( *0-914061; 1-932535* ) P.O. Box 20602,
Alexandria, VA 22320-1602 (SAN 287-4962) Fax:
703-993-1161
E-mail: lathbury@gmu.edu
Web site: http://mason.gmu.edu/rlathbur
*Dist(s):* **Washington Bk. Distributors**; *CIP.*

†**Oregon State Univ. Pr.,** ( *0-87071* ) Oregon State Univ.,
101 Waldo Hall, Corvallis, OR 97331 (SAN
202-8328) Tel 541-737-3166; Fax: 541-737-3170
E-mail: osu.press@oregonstate.edu
Web site: http://osu.orst.edu/dept/press
*Dist(s):* **American Society of Civil Engineers**
**Univ. of Arizona Pr.**; *CIP.*

**Organization for Economic Cooperation and**
**Development,** 2001 L St., NW, Suite 650,
Washington, DC 20036-4922 (SAN 202-1277) Tel
202-785-6323; 202-822-3865 SourceOECD; Fax:
202-785-0350; Toll Free: 800-456-6323
E-mail: washington.contact@oecd.org;
sales@oecd.org; ecmt.contact@oecd.org; info@iea.org
Web site: http://www.oecd.org/PUBS/PRINTPUBS/
period.html; http://www.oecd.org/dsti/itblurb.html;
http://www.oecd.org; http://www.oecd.org/com*;
http://www.oecd.org; http://www.oecdwash.org;
http://www.iea.org.

**Organization for Economic Cooperation &**
**Development (FRA)** ( *92-64; 92-821; 0-9501741* )
*Dist. by* **OECD.**

**Orion Media,** ( *0-7528; 1-887754* ) 4170 Jackdaw St.,
San Diego, CA 92103-1352 (SAN 299-0806) Tel
619-299-5585; Fax: 619-299-9473
E-mail: OrionMedia@aol.com
*Dist(s):* **Baker & Taylor Bks..**

**Orion Publishing Group, Ltd. (GBR)** *( 0-575; 0-7528; 1-85797; 1-85881 ) Dist. by* **Trafalgar.**

**Orloff Pr.,** *( 0-9642949 )* P.O. Box 2138, Corvallis, OR 97339-2138 Tel 541-753-4304
E-mail: orloffpress@comcast.net.

**Ortells, Alfredo Editorial S.L. (ESP)** *( 84-7189 ) Dist. by* **Continental Bk.**

**Ortiz, Oscar F.,** *( 1-928612 )* Orders Addr.: P.O. Box 126576, Hialeah, FL 33012-6576; Edit Addr.: 3382 W. 72nd Pl., Hialeah, FL 33018 Tel 305-231-0370 (phone/fax); *Imprints:* OSOR Productions (OSOR Productions)
E-mail: osor@msn.com
*Dist(s):* **Downtown Bk. Ctr., Inc..**

**Oshun Publishing Co., Inc.,** *( 0-9676028 )* Div. of Oshun Communications, P.O. Box 27606, Philadelphia, PA 19150
E-mail: oshuncom@aol.com.

**OSOR Productions Imprint of Ortiz, Oscar F.**

**Otero Pr.,** *( 0-9663156 )* 1212 San Juan Ave., La Junta, CO 81050-2849 Tel 719-384-2702.

**Other Pr., LLC,** *( 1-892746; 1-59051 )* Orders Addr.: 224 W. 20th St., New York, NY 10011 Tel 212-924-3344; Edit Addr.: 307 7th Ave., Suite 1807, New York, NY 10001 Tel 212-414-0054; Fax: 212-414-9654; *Imprints:* Handsel Books (Handsel Bks) Do not confuse with Other Press in Jersey City, NJ
E-mail: erica@otherpress.com; info@otherpress.com; Web site: http://www.otherbooks.com; http://www.otherpress.com.

**Other Voices,** *( 0-9708320 )* P.O. Box 2075, Decatur, GA 30031 Do not confuse with Other Voices, Highland, IL
E-mail: fordwilliams@hotmail.com
*Dist(s):* **Baker & Taylor Bks..**

**Otis Audio, Inc.,** *( 1-890990; 1-59183 )* 8712 S. Country Club Dr., Oklahoma City, OK 73159-6122 Tel 405-685-3888; Fax: 405-685-7676; Toll Free: 888-685-1789
E-mail: otisaudioinc@aol.com
*Dist(s):* **Baker & Taylor Bks.**
**Landmark Audiobooks.**

**Oughten Hse. Foundation, Inc.,** *( 1-880666 )* P.O. Box 1059, Coarsegold, CA 93614 Tel 559-641-7950; Fax: 559-641-7952
E-mail: info@oughtenhouse.com
Web site: http://www.oughtenhouse.com
*Dist(s):* **Bookpeople**
**Koen Pacific**
**New Leaf Distributing Co., Inc.**
**Partners Bk. Distributing, Inc..**

†**Our Child Pr.,** *( 0-9611872; 1-893516 )* P.O. Box 74, Wayne, PA 19087-0074 (SAN 682-272X) Tel 610-964-0606; Fax: 610-964-0938
E-mail: ocp98@aol.com
Web site: http://www.members.aol.com/ocp98/index.html; *CIP.*

**Our Power Pr.,** *( 0-9634075 )* Orders Addr.: P.O. Box 6680, Denver, CO 80206 Fax: 303-377-4150; Edit Addr.: 1337 Vine St., Denver, CO 80206 Tel 303-377-4107.

**Outer Space Pr.,** *( 0-9625266 )* Orders Addr.: P.O. Box 9593, Daytona Beach, FL 32120-9593 Tel 904-253-8179 (phone/fax); Edit Addr.: 15315 SW 106th Ter. Apt. 431, Miami, FL 33196-4580
E-mail: OSP9593@aol.com.

**Outlet Book Company, Incorporated** *See* **Random Hse. Value Publishing**

**Outrigger Publishing,** *( 1-59342 )* 15925 Garrett Dr., Apple Valley, MN 55124 Tel 612-747-3077; Fax: 413-702-7620
E-mail: outriggerpress@outriggerpress.com
Web site: http://www.outriggerpress.com.

†**Overlook Pr., The,** *( 0-87951; 1-58567; 1-59020 )* 141 Wooster St., 4th Flr., New York, NY 10012 (SAN 202-8360) Tel 212-673-2210; Fax: 212-673-2296; *Imprints:* Elephant's Eye (Elephants Eye)
Web site: http://www.overlookpress.com
*Dist(s):* **National Bk. Network**
**Penguin Group (USA) Inc.;** *CIP.*

**Overmountain Pr.,** *( 0-932807; 0-9644613; 1-57072 )* P.O. Box 1261, Johnson City, TN 37605 (SAN 687-6641) Tel 423-926-2691; Fax: 423-232-1252; Toll Free: 800-992-2691 (orders only); *Imprints:* Silver Dagger Mysteries (Silver Dagger)
E-mail: beth@overmtn.com
Web site: http://www.silverdaggermysteries.com; http://www.overmountainpress.com.

**Owen, Peter Ltd. (GBR)** *( 0-7206 ) Dist. by* **Dufour.**

**Owen, Richard C. Pubs., Inc.,** *( 0-913461; 1-57274; 1-878450 )* P.O. Box 585, Katonah, NY 10536 (SAN 285-1814) Tel 914-232-3903; Fax: 914-232-3977; Toll Free: 800-336-5588 (orders)
Web site: http://www.RCOwen.com
*Dist(s):* **Lectorum Pubns., Inc..**

**Owl Bks. Imprint of Holt, Henry & Co.**

**Owl Pr., The,** *( 1-884690 )* 1006 W. Main St., Madison, IN 47250 Do not confuse with Owl Press, Woodacre, CA
*Dist(s):* **Baker & Taylor Bks..**

**Ox Bow Pr.,** *( 0-918024; 1-881987 )* P.O. Box 4045, Woodbridge, CT 06525 (SAN 210-2501) Tel 203-387-5900; Fax: 203-387-0035
E-mail: oxbow@gte.net
Web site: http://www.oxbowpress-books.com.

**Oxford Univ. Pr., Inc.,** *( 0-19; 0-904147; 0-947946; 1-85221 )* Orders Addr.: 2001 Evans Rd., Cary, NC 27513 (SAN 202-5892) Tel 919-677-0977 (general voice); Fax: 919-677-1303 (customer service); Toll Free: 800-445-9714 (customer service - inquiry); 800-451-7556 (customer service - orders); Edit Addr.: 198 Madison Ave., New York, NY 10016-4314 (SAN 202-5884) Tel 212-726-6000 (general voice); Fax: 212-726-6440 (general fax); *Imprints:* Clarendon Press (Clarendon Pr)
E-mail: orders@oup-usa.org; custserv@oup-usa.org
Web site: http://www.oup-usa.org
*Dist(s):* **netLibrary, Inc..**

**Ozark Publishing,** *( 1-56763; 1-59381 )* P.O. Box 228, Prairie Grove, AR 72753 (SAN 298-4318) Tel 214-649-0188; Fax: 501-846-2853; Toll Free: 800-321-5671
E-mail: srg304@aol.com
Web site: http://www.ozarkpublishing.com
*Dist(s):* **Central Programs**
**Gumdrop Bks..**

**PAJ Pubns.,** *( 0-933826; 1-55554 )* Div. of Performing Arts Journal, Inc., c/o Johns Hopkins Univ. Pr., 2715 N. Charles St., Baltimore, MD 21218-4319 Tel 410-516-6900; Fax: 410-516-6998; Toll Free: 800-537-5487
Web site: http://www.press.jhu.edu
*Dist(s):* **Consortium Bk. Sales & Distribution.**

**P.I.A., Inc., Petticoat Pr.,** *( 0-9712148 )* 301 W. Branch Rd., Marquette, MI 49855 Tel 906-226-3965.

**PKA Pubns.,** *( 0-9651928 )* 301A Rolling Hills Pk., Prattsville, NY 12468 Tel 518-299-3103.

**Pace Group International,** *( 0-89209 )* P.O. Box 51, Arch Capp, OR 97201 (SAN 670-7041) Tel 503-436-1217; Fax: 503-436-2578
E-mail: pub@pacevideo.com
Web site: http://www.pacevideo.com.

**Pace International Research, Incorporated** *See* **Pace Group International**

**Pacific Century Press** *See* **EastBridge**

**Pacific Coast Pr.,** *( 0-9660851 )* P.O. Box 26857, San Jose, CA 95159-6857 Tel 408-244-3555; Fax: 408-244-3890
E-mail: blankenb@pacificcoastpress.com
Web site: http://www.pacificcoastpress.com
*Dist(s):* **Baker & Taylor Bks..**

†**Pacific Pr. Publishing Assn.,** *( 0-8163 )* P.O. Box 5353, Nampa, ID 83653-5353 (SAN 202-8409) Tel 208-465-2500; Fax: 208-465-2531; Toll Free: 800-447-7377
E-mail: sanhin@pacificpress.com
Web site: http://www.AdventistBookCenter.com
*Dist(s):* **Riverside**
**Spring Arbor Distributors, Inc.;** *CIP.*

**Padakami Pr.,** *( 0-9628914 )* 23 Dana St., Forty-Fort, Kingston, PA 18704 Tel 717-287-3668.

**Pageant Pr.,** *( 0-9703743 )* 27 Chestnut St., Binghamton, NY 13905-4445 (SAN 253-5947) Tel 607-772-8750 Do not confuse with Pageant Press, Brooklyn, NY.

**PageFree Publishing, Inc.,** *( 1-929077; 1-930252; 1-58961 )* 733 Howard St., Otsego, MI 49078 Tel 616-692-3926 (phone/fax); *Imprints:* Books OnScreen (Bks OnScreen)
E-mail: pagefreepublish@aol.com; publisher@pagefreepublishing.com
Web site: http://www.pagefreepublishing.com.

**Pages, Inc.,** *( 1-885885 )* P.O. Box 3572, Dublin, OH 43016-0284; *Imprints:* Cornerstone Books (Cornerstone FL).

**PAGES Publishing Group** *See* **Darby Creek Publishing**

**Paint Rock Publishing, Inc.,** *( 0-9649394 )* 3802 Calverton Bldg. No. 4, Bettsville, MD 20705 Tel 301-572-6116
*Dist(s):* **Baker & Taylor Bks.**
**Brodart Co.**
**Distributors, The.**

**Painted Leaf Pr.,** *( 0-9651558; 1-891305 )* Orders Addr.: P.O. Box 2480, New York, NY 10108-2480 Tel 212-594-4940 (phone/fax); Edit Addr.: 308 W. 40th St., New York, NY 10018
E-mail: cocadas@bway.net
*Dist(s):* **LPC Group.**

**Paladin Contemporaries,** *( 1-881048 )* Orders Addr.: P.O. Box 22780, Kansas City, MO 64113-2780; Edit Addr.: 7109 Pennsylvania Ave., Kansas City, MO 64114-1316 Tel 816-363-3110.

**Palancar,** *( 0-9643256 )* 1111 E. 80th St., New York, NY 10021 Tel 212-288-9730; Fax: 212-249-9501
*Dist(s):* **Norton, W. W. & Co., Inc..**

**Palgrave** *See* **Palgrave Macmillan**

**Palgrave Macmillan,** *( 0-312; 0-333; 1-4039 )* Div. of Saint Martin's Press, LLC, Orders Addr.: 16365 James Madison Hwy., Gordonsville, VA 22942-8501 Toll Free Fax: 800-672-2054; Toll Free: 888-330-8477; Edit Addr.: 175 Fifth Ave., New York, NY 10010 Tel 212-982-9300; Fax: 212-777-6359; Toll Free: 800-221-7945
Web site: http://www.palgrave.com
*Dist(s):* **Holtzbrinck Pubs.**
**Libros Sin Fronteras**
**Trans-Atlantic Pubns., Inc.**
**netLibrary, Inc..**

**Palisades Imprint of Multnomah Pubs., Inc.**

**Paljor Pubns. (IND)** *( 81-86230 ) Dist. by* **S Asia.**

**Palmaya Publishing,** *( 0-9707087 )* P.O. Box 773, Chapel Hill, NC 27514 Tel 919-933-1748
E-mail: snona@mindspring.com.

**Palmer Publications, Incorporated/Amherst Press** *See* **Amherst Pr.**

**Palmetto Bookworks,** *( 0-9623065; 1-887301 )* Orders Addr.: P.O. Box 2105, Lexington, SC 29071 Tel 803-951-3080; Fax: 810-815-6015
E-mail: palbook@aol.com
Web site: http://www.palmettobookworks.com.

**Palo Alto Bks. Imprint of Glencannon Pr.**

**Pan Asia Pubns. (USA), Inc.,** *( 1-57227 )* 29564 Union City Blvd., Union City, CA 94587 (SAN 173-685X) Tel 510-475-1185; Fax: 510-475-1489; Toll Free: 800-909-8088
E-mail: sales@panap.com
Web site: http://www.panap.com
*Dist(s):* **Lectorum Pubns., Inc..**

**Pan Bks. Ltd. (GBR)** *( 0-330 ) Dist. by* **Trafalgar.**

**Pan Bks. Ltd. (GBR)** *( 0-330 ) Dist. by* **Trans-Atl Phila.**

**Pan Macmillan (GBR)** *( 0-330; 0-333 ) Dist. by* **Trans-Atl Phila.**

**Pandora Pr. (GBR)** *( 0-04; 0-86358; 0-9698762 ) Dist. by* **Harper SF.**

**Panhelenic Pr.,** *( 0-9676723 )* PMB 101 171 Main St., Los Altos, CA 94022 Tel 408-268-4513; Fax: 408-323-9497
E-mail: Helenekrusich@aol.com.

**Pantheon Imprint of Knopf Publishing Group**

**Panther Creek Pr.,** *( 0-9678343; 0-9718361; 0-9747839 )* Orders Addr.: P.O. Box 130233, Spring, TX 77393-0233 (SAN 253-8520); Edit Addr.: 116 Tree Crest Cir., Spring, TX 77381
E-mail: panthercreek3@hotmail.com
Web site: http://www.panthercreekpress.com
*Dist(s):* **Baker & Taylor Bks..**

**Pantonne Pr., Inc.,** *( 0-9630052 )* 329 W. 18th St., Chicago, IL 60616 (SAN 297-5815) Tel 312-243-4430; Fax: 312-421-6823.

**Paper Tiger, Incorporated, The** *See* **Paper Tiger, The**

**Paper Tiger, The,** *( 1-889439 )* Orders Addr.: 335 Jefferson Ave., Cresskill, NJ 07626 Tel 201-567-5620
E-mail: fredweiss@papertig.com
Web site: http://www.papertig.com.

**Paperback Nova Audio Bks. Imprint of Brilliance Audio**

**Paperback Rack Bks.,** *( 0-9624878 )* 810 Annawood Dr., Tallahassee, FL 32311 Tel 904-224-3455
E-mail: pvl@nettally.com.

**Paperblank Bk. Co.,** *( 1-55156 )* P.O. Box 147, Point Roberts, WA 98281-0147 Tel 604-739-1771; Fax: 604-738-1913; Toll Free: 800-277-5887 (orders)
E-mail: info@hartleyandmarks.com
*Dist(s):* **Publishers Group West.**

**PaperStar Imprint of Penguin Putnam Bks. for Young Readers**

**Papier-Mache Pr. Imprint of Moyer Bell**

**Paraclete Pr., Inc.,** ( 0-941478; 1-55725 ) Orders Addr.: P.O. Box 1568, Orleans, MA 02653 (SAN 282-1508) Tel 508-255-4685; Fax: 508-255-5705; Toll Free: 800-451-5006; Edit Addr.: 36 Southern Eagle Cartway, Brewster, MA 02631 (SAN 664-6239) Do not confuse with companies with the same or similar names in Indianapolis, IN, Pentwater, MI E-mail: srmercy@paracletepress.com; miao@paracletepress.com Web site: http://www.paracletepress.com.

**Paradigm Bks.,** ( 0-9720151 ) 61 Columbine Ln., Ridgway, CO 81432 Tel 970-626-2349 E-mail: HM@montrose.net; markkimmel@ridgwayco.net; hm@montrose.net Web site: http://www.markkimmel.com; http://www.paradigmbooks.biz *Dist(s):* **Baker & Taylor Bks.**
**Books West**
**Ingram Bk. Co.**
**New Leaf Distributing Co., Inc.**
**Partners/West.**

**Paradigm Pr.,** ( 1-889924 ) Orders Addr.: P.O. Box 123, Ashland, WI 54806 Tel 715-682-6753; Edit Addr.: 916 Chapple Ave., Ashland, WI 54806 Do not confuse with companies with the same or similar names in Greenbrae, CA, Providence, RI, Carmichael, CA, Kent, WA, Doylestown, PA, E-mail: popglov@winbright.net.

**Paradise Pr., Inc.,** ( 1-57657; 1-884907 ) 1575 N. Park Dr., Suite 100, Weston, FL 33326-3230 Tel 954-476-5900; Fax: 954-476-0062 Do not confuse with companies with the same or similar names in Crested Butte, CO Corte Madera, CA, Santa Monica, CA, Ridgefield, CA, Chicago, IL, Herndon, VA.

**Parallax Pr.,** ( 0-938077; 1-888375 ) Orders Addr.: P.O. Box 7355, Berkeley, CA 94707 (SAN 663-4494) Tel 510-525-0101; Fax: 510-525-7129; Toll Free: 800-863-5290; Edit Addr.: 850 Talbot Ave., Albany, CA 94706 E-mail: parallax@parallax.org Web site: http://www.parallax.org *Dist(s):* **SCB Distributors**
**SPD-Small Pr. Distribution.**

**Parintel Bks.,** ( 0-9702160 ) 4195 Valley Fair St., Suite 104, Simi Valley, CA 93063 Tel 805-552-0030; Fax: 805-577-1954; Toll Free: 800-994-2477 E-mail: Dokeefe@236@aol.com; dokeefe@236.aol.com *Dist(s):* **Alliance Hse., Inc..**

**Parissound Publishing,** ( 0-9648974 ) Div. of K-Enterprises, Inc., 520 Tamalpais Dr., Corte Madera, CA 94925 (SAN 299-2663) Tel 415-945-9964; Fax: 415-945-9962; Toll Free: 888-544-5433; *Imprints:* Epiphany Press (Epiphany Press) E-mail: Parissound@aol.com Web site: http://www.parissound.com *Dist(s):* **Baker & Taylor Bks.**
**Bookpeople**
**New Leaf Distributing Co., Inc..**

**Park Avenue Pr.,** ( 0-9729076 ) 303 Park Avenue S., No. 1223, New York, NY 10010 Web site: http://www.ParkAvenuePress.net.

**Park Press** *See* **Solace Publishing, Inc.**

**Parker Distributing,** ( 1-878406 ) 11844 N. Delbert Rd., Parker, CO 80138 Tel 303-841-0246; Fax: 303-841-2607 E-mail: Sandywrter@aol.com.

**Parkstone Pr.,** ( 1-85995 ) Orders Addr.: P.O. Box 605, Herndon, VA 20172-6105; Edit Addr.: 16 W. 22nd St., 11th Flr., New York, NY 10010 Tel 212-807-7755; Fax: 212-620-0901; Toll Free: 800-844-2905 E-mail: parkstone@mindspring.com Web site: http://www.parkstone-online.com *Dist(s):* **Books International, Incorporated.**

**Parkway Pubs., Inc.,** ( 0-9635752; 1-887905 ) P.O. Box 3678, Boone, NC 28607 Tel 828-265-3993; Fax: 828-265-3993; Toll Free: 800-821-9155 E-mail: sales@parkwaypublishers.com; parkwaypub@hotmail.com Web site: http://www.parkwaypublishers.com *Dist(s):* **Baker & Taylor Bks..**

**Parkwest Pubns., Inc.,** ( 0-88186 ) 451 Communipaw Ave., Jersey City, NJ 07304 (SAN 264-6846) Tel 201-432-3257; Fax: 201-432-3708 E-mail: parkwest@parkwestpubs.com; info@parkwestpubs.com Web site: http://www.parkwestpubs.com.

**Parma Hse., Ltd,** ( 0-9701723 ) 1012 N. Summit, Suite C, Iowa City, IA 52245 (SAN 253-6951) Tel 319-337-7817; Fax: 319-327-9606 E-mail: parmahouse@paramahouse.com; jlluzkow@hotmail.com Web site: http://parmahouse.com.

**Parnassus Imprints,** ( 0-940160 ) 105 Cammett Rd., Marstons Mills, MA 02648-1519 (SAN 217-0809) Fax: 508-790-1176.

**Parthian Bks. (GBR)** ( 0-9521558; 1-902638 ) *Dist. by* Dufour.

**Passeggiata Pr.,** ( 1-57889 ) 222 W B St., Pueblo, CO 81003-3404 Tel 719-544-1038; Fax: 719-544-7911 E-mail: Passeggiata@compuserve.com.

**Paterson Museum for Italian Girls Press** *See* **Mill Street Forward, The**

**Pathway Bk. Service,** Div. of MLES, Inc., Orders Addr.: P.O. Box 89, Gilsum, NH 03448 Toll Free: 800-345-6665; Edit Addr.: 4 White Brook Rd., Gilsum, NH 03448 (SAN 170-0545) Tel 603-357-0236; Fax: 603-357-2073 E-mail: pbs@pathwaybook.com Web site: http://www.pathwaybook.com.

**Patterson, Andrew M. & Assocs.,** ( 0-9641679 ) P.O. Box 1193, Bellaire, TX 77402-1193 Tel 713-879-6237.

**Paul & Co. Pubs. Consortium, Inc.,** Div. of Independent Publishers Group, Orders Addr.: 814 N. Franklin St., Chicago, IL 60610 Tel 312-337-0747; Fax: 312-337-5985; Toll Free: 800-888-4741; Edit Addr.: P.O. Box 442, Concord, MA 01742 (SAN 630-5318) E-mail: frontdesk@ipgbook.com Web site: http://www.ipgbook.com *Dist(s):* **Independent Pubs. Group.**

†**Pauline Bks. & Media,** ( 0-8198 ) 50 St. Paul's Ave., Boston, MA 02130-3491 (SAN 203-8900) Tel 617-522-8911; Fax: 617-524-8035; Toll Free: 800-876-4463 (orders only) E-mail: jsmith@pauline.org; lilire@aol.com Web site: http://www.PAULINE.org *Dist(s):* **Alba Hse.;** *CIP.*

**Pavilion Bks., Ltd. (GBR)** ( 0-907516; 1-85145; 1-85793; 1-86205 ) *Dist. by* Trafalgar.

**Paws IV Publishing,** ( 0-934007 ) P.O. Box 2364, Homer, AK 99603 (SAN 692-7890) Tel 907-235-7697 ; Fax: 907-235-7698; Toll Free: 800-807-7297 E-mail: pawsiv@ptialaska.net *Dist(s):* **Publishers Group West.**

**Payback Pr. (GBR)** ( 0-86241; 0-903937; 1-84195 ) *Dist. by* AK Pr Dist.

**Peace Vision Bks. Imprint of Peace Vision Publishing**

**Peace Vision Publishing,** ( 1-931144 ) Div. of One Earth One People Peace Vision, Inc., P.O. Box 813, San Juan Bautista, CA 95045-0813 Tel 831-623-2379; Fax: 831-623-1807; *Imprints:* Peace Vision Books (Peace Vision Bks) E-mail: bluebirdwoman@iname.com Web site: http://peacevision.net.

**Peachtree Junior Imprint of Peachtree Pubs., Ltd.**

†**Peachtree Pubs., Ltd.,** ( 0-931948; 0-934601; 1-56145 ) 1700 Chattahoochee Ave., Atlanta, GA 30318-2112 (SAN 212-1999) Tel 404-876-8761; Fax: 404-875-2578; Toll Free Fax: 800-875-8909; Toll Free: 800-241-0113; *Imprints:* Peachtree Junior (Peachtree) E-mail: peachtree@mindspring.com Web site: http://www.peachtree-online.com *Dist(s):* **Lectorum Pubns., Inc.;** *CIP.*

**Peanut Butter Publishing,** ( 0-89716 ) Div. of Classic Day Publishing LLC, 2100 Westlake Ave. N., Suite 106, Seattle, WA 98109 (SAN 212-7881) Tel 206-860-4900; Fax: 206-285-2800; Toll Free: 800-328-4348 E-mail: elliottwolf@classicdaypublishing.com Web site: http://www.classicdaypublishing.com *Dist(s):* **Todd Communications.**

**Pearson Education,** ( 0-582 ) Orders Addr.: 200 Old Tappan Rd., Old Tappan, NJ 07675 (SAN 200-2175) Tel 201-767-5152; Toll Free Fax: 800-922-0579; 800-445-6991; Toll Free: 800-428-5331; Edit Addr.: One Lake St., Upper Saddle River, NJ 07458 Tel 201-236-7000; Fax: 201-236-6549 E-mail: eugene.wang@pearsonptr.com; carole.wilkins@phschool.com; emily.mcgee@pearson.ed.com; joann.kebrdle@pearsoned.com Web site: http://www.pearsoned.com *Dist(s):* **Gaunt, Inc.**
**Trans-Atlantic Pubns., Inc..**

**Pebble Beach Pr., Ltd.,** ( 1-883740 ) P.O. Box 1171, Pebble Beach, CA 93953-1171 Tel 408-372-5559; Fax: 408-375-4525.

**Peepal Tree Pr., Ltd. (GBR)** ( 0-948833; 1-900715 ) *Dist. by* IPG Chicago.

**Peepal Tree Pr., Ltd. (GBR)** ( 0-948833; 1-900715 ) *Dist. by* Paul & Co Pubs.

**Pegasus Pr.,** ( 1-889818 ) 101 Booter Rd., Fairview, NC 28730 Tel 828-628-3883; Fax: 828-628-3886 Do not confuse with companies with the same name in Vashon Island, WA, San Diego, CA, Kerrville, TX, Lake Forest, IL E-mail: dicesare1@mindspring.com Web site: http://www.pegpress.org.

**Peguis Pubs., Ltd.,** ( 0-919566; 0-920541; 1-895411 ) Box 6008, 120 N. Fourth St., Grand Forks, ND 58206-6008 Toll Free: 800-667-9673.

**Pelican Pond Imprint of Blue Dolphin Publishing, Inc.**

†**Pelican Publishing Co., Inc.,** ( 0-88289; 0-911116; 1-56554; 1-58980 ) Orders Addr.: P.O. Box 3110, Gretna, LA 70054 (SAN 212-0623) Tel 504-368-1175 ; Fax: 504-368-1195; Toll Free: 800-843-1724; 1000 Burmaster St., Gretna, LA 70053; *Imprints:* Firebird Press (Firebird Press) Do not confuse with companies with the same or similar names in Lowell, MA, Dallas, TX E-mail: promo@pelicanpub.com; Sales@pelicanpub.com Web site: http://www.bedandbreakfastguide.com; http://www.epelican.com; http://www.eirishbooks.com *Dist(s):* **Continental Bk. Co., Inc.;** *CIP.*

**Pella Publishing Co., Inc.,** ( 0-918618; 0-933824 ) 337 W. 36th St., New York, NY 10018-6401 (SAN 210-6183) Tel 212-279-9586; Fax: 212-594-3602.

**Pemberley Pr,** ( 0-9702727 ) P.O. Box 1027, Corona del Mar, CA 92625 Fax: 949-675-6431 Do not confuse with Pemberly Press, New York, NY E-mail: orders@pemberleypress.com; editor@pemberleypress.com Web site: http://www.pemberleypress.com.

**PenArtProductions, Incorporated** *See* **Dandelion Bks., LLC**

**Pencil Productions, Ltd.,** ( 0-9619318 ) 2045 S. Monroe St., Denver, CO 80210-3734 (SAN 243-7678) Tel 303-756-1097; Fax: 303-756-2662 E-mail: pencilprod@aol.com Web site: http://www.thesherlockstore.com; http://www.thesherlockstore.com bowkerpage.htm.

**Pendleton Bks.,** ( 1-893221 ) 666 Fifth Ave., Suite 365, New York, NY 10103 Toll Free: 800-690-7090 E-mail: editor@pendletonbooks.com Web site: http://www.pendletonbooks.com.

**Pendleton Clay Pubs.,** ( 0-9644849 ) Div. of The Publishing Cooperative, 1836 Blake St., Suite 200, Denver, CO 80202 Tel 303-297-1233; Fax: 303-297-3997.

**Pendulum Pr.,** ( 0-9712538; 0-9740105 ) 2700 W. 44th St., No. 412, Minneapolis, MN 55410-1946 Tel 612-926-3289 Do not confuse with companies with the same or similar name in Palm Coast, FL ,West Haven, CT, Jacksonville, FL E-mail: marilyn@pendulumpress.com Web site: http://www.pendulumpress.com *Dist(s):* **Biblio Distribution.**

**Pendulum Pr., Inc.,** ( 0-87232; 0-88301 ) Academic Bldg., Saw Mill Rd., West Haven, CT 06516 (SAN 202-8808) Tel 203-933-2551 Do not confuse with companies with same or similar names in Jacksonville, FL, Palm Coast, FL, Minneapolis, MN.

**Penfield Pr.,** ( 0-941016; 0-9603858; 1-57216 ) 215 Brown St., Iowa City, IA 52245 (SAN 221-6671) Tel 319-337-9998; Fax: 319-351-6846; Toll Free: 800-728-9998 E-mail: penfield@penfieldpress.com Web site: http://www.penfieldpress.com *Dist(s):* **Bookmen, Inc..**

**Penguin AudioBooks Imprint of Viking Penguin**

**Penguin AudioBooks Imprint of HighBridge Co.**

**Penguin AudioBooks Imprint of Penguin Group (USA) Inc.**

**Penguin Bks. Imprint of NAL**

**Penguin Bks. Imprint of Viking Penguin**

**Penguin Bks. Imprint of HighBridge Co.**

**Penguin Bks. Imprint of Penguin Group (USA) Inc.**

**Penguin Bks., Ltd. (GBR)** ( 0-14 ) *Dist. by* Trafalgar.

**Penguin Classics Imprint of NAL**

**Penguin Classics Imprint of Viking Penguin**

**Penguin Classics Imprint of Penguin Group (USA) Inc.**

Names

**Penguin Group (USA) Inc.,** ( *0-14* ) Orders Addr.: 405 Murray Hill Pkwy., East Rutherford, NJ 07073-2136 (SAN 282-5074) Fax: 201-933-2903 (customer service); Toll Free Fax: 800-227-9604; Toll Free: 800-788-6262 (individual consumer sales); 800-526-0275 (reseller sales); 800-631-8571 (reseller customer service); Edit Addr.: 375 Hudson St., New York, NY 10014 Tel 212-366-2000; Fax: 212-366-2666; *Imprints:* Perigee Books (Perigee Bks); Signet Books (Sig); Ace/Putnam (Ace-Putnam); Viking (Viking); Penguin Books (Penguin Bks); Penguin Classics (Penguin Classics); Ladybird Books (Ladybrd); Riverhead Books (Hardcovers) (Riverhead Books); Putnam Berkley Audio (Putnam Berkley Audio); Putnam & Grosset (Putnam & Grosset); Philomel (Philomel); Puffin Books (PuffinBks); G. P. Putnam's Sons (G P Putnam); Penguin AudioBooks (Png AudioBks); Wood, Marian Books (Marian Wood); Grosset & Dunlap (G & D)
E-mail: pmccarthy@penguinputman.com
Web site: http://www.penguinputnam.com
*Dist(s):* **Viking Penguin.**

**Penguin Putnam, Incorporated** *See* **Penguin Group (USA) Inc.**

**Penguin Putnam, Inc E-Books,** ( *0-7865* ) Div. of Berkley Publishing Group, 200 Madison Ave., New York, NY 10016 Do not confuse with companies with the same name in Salt Lake City, UT, Berkeley, CA.

**Penguin/HighBridge,** ( *0-453* ) 1000 Westgate Dr., Saint Paul, MN 55114 Tel 651-637-4722; Fax: 651-659-4495; Toll Free: 800-782-5756 (orders only)
E-mail: highbridgeaudio@rivertrade.com
Web site: http://www.penguinclassics.com/
*Dist(s):* **Landmark Audiobooks**
     **Penguin Group (USA) Inc..**

**Penman Publishing, Inc.,** ( *0-9700486; 0-9707646; 0-9712808; 0-9720775; 1-932496* ) 8-A Francis St., Chattanooga, TN 37419 Tel 423-400-3292; Fax: 423-825-2004
E-mail: maryleehm@comcast.net
Web site: http://www.penmanpub.com.

**Penmarin Bks.,** ( *1-883955* ) 1044 Magnolia Way, Roseville, CA 95661 Tel 916-771-5869; Fax: 916-771-5879
E-mail: penmarin@jps.net
Web site: http://www.penmarin.com
*Dist(s):* **Midpoint Trade Bks., Inc..**

†**Pennsylvania State Univ. Pr.,** ( *0-271* ) 820 N. University Dr., USB-1 Suite C, University Park, PA 16802 (SAN 213-5760) Tel 814-865-1327; Fax: 814-863-1408; Toll Free: 800-326-9180 (orders only)
E-mail: ajs23@psu.edu
Web site: http://www.psupress.org; *CIP.*

**Pentland Pr., Inc.,** ( *1-57197* ) 5122 Bur Oak Cir., Raleigh, NC 27612 (SAN 298-5063) Tel 919-782-0281; Fax: 919-781-9042; Toll Free: 800-948-2786
E-mail: janetevans@mindspring.com
Web site: http://www.pentlandpressusa.com
*Dist(s):* **Baker & Taylor Bks.**
     **Midpoint Trade Bks., Inc..**

**Penton Overseas, Inc.,** ( *0-939001; 1-56015; 1-59125* ) 2470 Impala Dr., Carlsbad, CA 92008 (SAN 631-0826) Tel 760-431-0060; Fax: 760-431-8110; Toll Free: 800-748-5804
Web site: http://www.pentonoverseas.com.

**Penury Pr.,** ( *0-9676344* ) P.O. Box 23058, Richfield, MN 55423 Tel 612-869-7979.

**Pepperdine Pr., Inc.,** ( *0-9668643* ) P.O. Box 3143, Fayetteville, AR 72702-3143 Tel 501-443-9706; Fax: 501-443-7522
Web site: http://www.pepperdinepress.com.

**Peralta Publishing Co.,** ( *0-9667631* ) P.O. Box 694, Bellingham, MA 02019-0689 Tel 508-928-1022
E-mail: peralta@peraltapub.com
Web site: http://www.peraltapub.com.

**Perception Pr.,** ( *1-893518* ) 11839 Hillbrook Dr., Houston, TX 77070-1255 (SAN 253-3804) Do not confuse with companies with the same name in Chicago, IL, Port Bolivar, TX
E-mail: wheeler@infosel.net.mx.

**Perennial Imprint of HarperTrade**

**PerfectBound Imprint of HarperCollins General Bks. Group**

**Perfection Form Company, The** *See* **Perfection Learning Corp.**

**Perfection Learning Corp.,** ( *0-7807; 0-7891; 0-89598; 1-56312; 0-7569* ) 1000 N. Second Ave., Logan, IA 51546 (SAN 221-0010) Tel 712-644-3553; Fax: 712-644-2122; Toll Free: 800-831-4190; *Imprints:* Covercraft (Covercraft)
E-mail: rfetter@logan.phonline.com
Web site: http://www.perfectionlearning.com.

**Pergamon Brassey's International Defense Publishers** *See* **Brassey's, Inc.**

**Perigee Bks. Imprint of Berkley Publishing Group**

**Perigee Bks. Imprint of Penguin Group (USA) Inc.**

†**Periodicals Service Co.,** ( *0-527; 0-8115; 3-262; 3-601* ) 11 Main St., Germantown, NY 12526 (SAN 164-8608) Tel 518-537-4700; Fax: 518-537-5899
E-mail: psc@backsets.com
Web site: http://www.backsets.com; *CIP.*

**Periplus Editions (HK), Ltd. (HKG)** ( *0-945971; 962-593; 0-7946* ) *Dist. by* **Tuttle Pubng.**

**Perky Pr.,** ( *0-9668854* ) 328 Elizabeth St., Key West, FL 33040 Tel 305-292-6591; Fax: 305-294-0190
E-mail: jteggers@earthlink.net.

**Permanent Pr., The,** ( *0-932966; 1-57962; 1-877946* ) Affil. of Second Chance Pr., 4170 Noyac Rd., Sag Harbor, NY 11963 (SAN 212-2995) Tel 631-725-1101 ; Fax: 631-725-8215 Do not confuse with companies with the same name in Santurce, PR, San Francisco, CA, Brooklyn, NY, Santa Fe, NM
E-mail: info@thepermanentpress.com
Web site: http://www.thepermanentpress.com.

†**Persea Bks., Inc.,** ( *0-89255* ) 853 Broadway, Suite 604, New York, NY 10003 (SAN 212-8233) Tel 212-260-9256; Fax: 212-260-1902
E-mail: info@perseabooks.com
Web site: http://www.perseabooks.com
*Dist(s):* **Norton, W. W. & Co., Inc.;** *CIP.*

**Perseus Books** *See* **Perseus Publishing**

**Perseus Bks. Group,** Orders Addr.: 5500 Central Ave., Boulder, CO 80301 Fax: 720-406-7336 (customer service); Toll Free: 800-386-5656 (customer service); Edit Addr.: 387 Park Ave., S., 12th Flr., New York, NY 10016-8810 Tel 212-340-8100; Fax: 212-340-8105
Web site: http://www.perseusbooksgroup.com
*Dist(s):* **HarperCollins Pubs..**

**Perseus Publishing,** ( *0-7382* ) A Member of Perseus Bks. Grp., Orders Addr.: 5500 Central Ave., Boulder, CO 80301 Fax: 303-449-3356; Toll Free: 800-386-5656; Edit Addr.: c/o Perseus Books Publishing, 11 Cambridge Ctr., Cambridge, MA 02142 Tel 617-252-5200; Fax: 617-252-5285
E-mail: westview.orders@perseusbooks.com
Web site: http://www.perseusbooks.com
*Dist(s):* **HarperCollins Pubs.**
     **netLibrary, Inc..**

**Perseverance Pr. Imprint of Daniel, John & Co., Pubs.**

**Petals of Life Publishing,** ( *1-892745* ) 42 Clearfield Dr., Jackson, TN 38305 Tel 901-664-3240; Fax: 901-664-2743
E-mail: petals@petalsoflife.com
Web site: http://www.petalsoflife.com.

**Peter Pauper Pr. Inc.,** ( *0-88088; 1-59359* ) 202 Mamaroneck Ave., Suite 400, White Plains, NY 10601 (SAN 204-9449) Tel 914-681-0144; Fax: 914-681-0389; Toll Free: 800-833-2311
E-mail: LBeilenson@peterpauper.com
Web site: http://www.peterpauper.com.

†**Peterson's,** ( *0-02; 0-7689; 0-87866; 1-56079* ) Div. of Thomson Learning, P.O. Box 67005, Lawrenceville, NJ 08648-6105 (SAN 200-2167); 2000 Lenox Dr., Lawrenceville, NJ 08648 (SAN 297-5661) Tel 609-896-1800; Fax: 609-896-1811; Toll Free: 877-433-8277; *Imprints:* Arco (Arco)
E-mail: support@petersons.com;
accounts.payable@petersons.com
Web site: http://www.petersons.com
*Dist(s):* **Giron Bks.;** *CIP.*

**Phantasia Pr.,** ( *0-932096* ) 5536 Crispin Way, West Bloomfield, MI 48323 (SAN 211-755X) Tel 248-855-3737.

**Pharos Bks.,** ( *0-9675200* ) 8657 SE Merritt Way, Jupiter, FL 33458-1007 (SAN 253-0317) Tel 561-575-3430; Fax: 561-575-3458 Do not confuse with Pharos Books in New Haven, CT
E-mail: jsnyder@adelphia.net
*Dist(s):* **FaithWorks.**

**Pharos Books/Pharoscan Incorporated** *See* **Pharos Bks.**

**Phillips, S.G. Inc.,** ( *0-87599* ) P.O. Box 416, Ghent, NY 12075 (SAN 293-3152) Tel 518-392-3068; Fax: 518-392-6493
E-mail: sgp@taconic.net.

**Philomel Imprint of Penguin Group (USA) Inc.**

**Philomel Imprint of Penguin Putnam Bks. for Young Readers**

†**Philosophical Library, Inc.,** ( *0-8022* ) P.O. Box 1789, New York, NY 10010 (SAN 201-999X) Tel 212-886-1873; Fax: 212-873-6070
*Dist(s):* **Kensington Publishing Corp.;** *CIP.*

**Phoenix,** ( *0-9632237* ) 4557 Deborah Ct., Union City, CA 94587 Tel 510-475-0959.

**Phoenix Audio Imprint of American International Publishing Group**

**Phoenix Hse. (GBR)** ( *0-460; 0-7538; 1-85799; 1-86159; 1-897580* ) *Dist. by* **Trafalgar.**

**Phoenix International, Inc.,** ( *0-9650485; 0-9713470* ) 1501 Stubblefield Rd., Fayetteville, AR 72703 Tel 501-521-2204 (phone/fax) Do not confuse with companies with the same or similar names in Oxon Hill, MD, Nampa, ID
E-mail: john@phoenixbase.com
Web site: http://www.phoenixbase.com
*Dist(s):* **Hudson Hills Pr. LLC.**

**Photosensitive,** ( *1-889252* ) Div. of Birth Of America Audiobooks, Orders Addr.: P.O. Box 7008, Hemet, CA 92545 Tel 909-765-0950 (phone/fax); Toll Free: 877-742-6241
E-mail: photosensitive@worldnet.att.net
Web site: http://www.home.att.net/~photosensitive.

**Phunn Pubs.,** ( *0-931762* ) P.O. Box 6, Viroqua, WI 54665-0006 (SAN 212-128X) Tel 608-637-8742; Fax: 608-637-8867
E-mail: Jeribill@frontiernet.net.

**Piñata Books Imprint of Arte Publico Pr.**

**Picador (GBR)** ( *0-330* ) *Dist. by* **Trans-Atl Phila.**

**Picador,** ( *0-312* ) Div. of Holtzbrinck Publishers, Orders Addr.: 16365 James Madison Hwy., Gordonsville, VA 22942-8501 Fax: 800-672-2054; Toll Free: 888-330-8477; Edit Addr.: 175 Fifth Ave., New York, NY 10010 Tel 212-674-5151; Fax: 540-672-7540 (customer service)
Web site: http://www.picadorusa.com
*Dist(s):* **Holtzbrinck Pubs.**
     **Libros Sin Fronteras.**

**Picador USA** *See* **Picador**

**Picara Point,** ( *0-9657695* ) Orders Addr.: P.O. Box 355, Barnardsville, NC 28709 Tel 704-626-2877; Fax: 704-645-6759; Edit Addr.: 180 Poverty Branch Rd., Barnardsville, NC 28709
E-mail: cookschoice@msn.com.

**Picardy Pr.,** ( *0-9633494* ) 235 Angell St., Providence, RI 02906-2112 Tel 401-273-7808
E-mail: picardyprs@aol.com
Web site: http://www.members.aol.com/picardyprs/home.html.

**Picaro Press** *See* **One Eyed Pr.**

**Pickering & Chatto Pubs., Ltd. (GBR)** ( *1-85196* ) *Dist. by* **Ashgate Pub Co.**

**Picton Pr.,** ( *0-89725; 0-912274; 0-929539; 0-9614281* ) Div. of Picton Corp., P.O. Box 250, Rockport, ME 04856-0250 (SAN 249-6321) Tel 207-236-6565; Fax: 207-236-6713
E-mail: sales@pictonpress.com
Web site: http://www.pictonpress.com.

**Pictorial Legends,** ( *0-939031* ) Subs. of Event Co., 435 Holland Ave., Los Angeles, CA 90042 (SAN 662-8486) Tel 213-254-4416
*Dist(s):* **Igram Pr.**

**Pierce, Ken Bks.,** ( *0-912277* ) P.O. Box 320125, Franklin, WI 53132 (SAN 265-0835) Tel 414-529-3056; Fax: 414-529-8506
E-mail: books@kenpiercebooks.com
Web site: http://www.kenpiercebooks.com.

**Pierian Quality Reprints,** ( *0-9668579* ) 115 North Ave., Fairhope, AL 36532 Tel 251-928-0087
E-mail: judyrchrds@aol.com.

†**Pierpont Morgan Library,** ( *0-87598* ) 29 E. 36th St., New York, NY 10016 (SAN 204-8957) Tel 212-685-0008; 212-685-0610; Fax: 212-685-4740; Toll Free: 800-861-0001
E-mail: nyc@mediabridge.com
Web site: http://www.morganlibrary.org; *CIP.*

**Pigeonhole Pr.,** ( *0-9664332* ) c/o Doug Clegg, P.O. Box 263, Jersey City, NJ 07303-0263 Fax: 203-861-2191
E-mail: ParisPoet@aol.com
Web site: http://www.readcipservice.com.

**Pilgrim Enterprises** *See* **H&M Enterprises**

**Pilgrimage Pr.,** ( *0-9654680* ) 4380 Latimer Ave., San Jose, CA 95130 Tel 408-379-1642; Fax: 408-379-7748
E-mail: dmcniven@aol.com;
pilgrimagepress@juno.com.

**Pilot Bks.,** ( *0-9678838* ) Orders Addr.: P.O. Box 817, Vienna, VA 22183-0817 (SAN 253-1445) Tel 202-232-7650; Fax: 202-232-7651 Do not confuse with Pilot Books, Greenport, NY
E-mail: jridout@ix.netcom.com
*Dist(s):* **Biblio Distribution**
     **Bookazine Co., Inc..**

**Pimsleur Imprint of Simon & Schuster Audio**

Pine Curtain Audiobooks, ( 0-9650850 ) Subs. of New Age Productions, Inc., Orders Addr.: 1015 W. Saint Germain St., Suite 410, Saint Cloud, MN 56301; Edit Addr.: P.O. Box 1974, Saint Cloud, MN 56302 Tel 612-255-9703; Fax: 612-255-1021; Toll Free: 800-495-7463.

Pine Hill Pr., Inc., ( 1-57579 ) 4000 W. 57th St., Sioux Falls, SD 57106 Tel 605-362-9200; Fax: 605-362-9222 Do not confuse with Pine Hill Pr., Lafayette, CA
E-mail: print@pinehillpress.com
Web site: http://www.pinehillpress.com
Dist(s): BookWorld Services, Inc.

Pine Island Pr., ( 0-9620092; 1-880836 ) 4294 N. High St., Suite 101, Columbus, OH 43214 (SAN 247-5510) Tel 614-262-0199; Fax: 614-262-0186.

Pine Tree Pr., ( 0-9629159; 1-886166 ) Div. of North Country Bks., Orders Addr.: c/o North Country Books, P.O. Box 217, Utica, NY 13501-1729 Tel 315-735-4877; Edit Addr.: 311 Turner St., Utica, NY 13501-1729 Do not confuse with companies with the same name in Minnetonka, MN, Los Angeles, CA, Alexander, NC, Annapolis, MD.

Pineapple Pr., Inc., ( 0-910923; 1-56164 ) P.O. Box 3889, Sarasota, FL 34230-3889 (SAN 285-0850) Tel 941-359-0886; Fax: 941-351-9988; Toll Free: 800-746-3275 Do not confuse with companies with same or similar names in Saint Johns, MI, Middletown, RI, Northampton, MA
E-mail: info@pineapplepress.com
Web site: http://www.pineapplepress.com
Dist(s): American Wholesale Bk. Co.
    Baker & Taylor Bks..

Pingry Pr., ( 0-942861 ) Orders Addr.: P.O. Box 803, Andover, NY 14806 (SAN 667-8327) Tel 607-478-8516; Edit Addr.: Pingry Hill Corners, Andover, NY 14806 (SAN 667-8335)
E-mail: warrenrl@eznet.net.

Pinhook Publishing Co., ( 0-9655917 ) P.O. Box 1545, Huntsville, AL 35807 Tel 256-534-1365.

Pink Flamingo Pr., ( 0-9665724 ) 6917 Hosmer Ave., Cleveland, OH 44105 Tel 216-441-1916 Do not confuse with Pink Flamingo Pr., Stillwater, MN
E-mail: cielec@hotmail.com.

Pinnacle Bks. Imprint of Kensington Publishing Corp.

Pinon Pr., ( 0-89109; 1-57683 ) Div. of NavPress Publishing Group, Orders Addr.: P.O. Box 35007, Colorado Springs, CO 80935 Tel 719-548-9222; Fax: 719-260-7223; Toll Free: 800-366-7788 (orders only) Do not confuse with Pinon Press Los Alamos, NM
Web site: http://www.navpress.org
Dist(s): Spring Arbor Distributors, Inc..

Pinto Pr., ( 0-9632476 ) 35 Stewart Pl., Suite 503, Mount Kisco, NY 10549 Tel 914-241-8549 (phone/fax)
E-mail: pintopotter@icnt.net
Dist(s): Koen Bk. Distributors
    North Country Bks., Inc..

Pippin Pr., ( 0-945912 ) Orders Addr.: P.O. Box 1347, New York, NY 10028 (SAN 247-8366) Tel 212-288-4920; Fax: 732-225-1562; Edit Addr.: 229 E. 85th St., New York, NY 10028.

Pitambar Publishing (IND) ( 81-209 ) Dist. by St Mut.

Pitspopany Pr., ( 0-943706; 965-465; 1-930143; 1-932687 ) Orders Addr.: 40 E. 78th St., Suite 16D, New York, NY 10021-1830 (SAN 238-373X) Tel 212-472-4959; Fax: 212-472-6253; Toll Free: 800-232-2931
E-mail: pitspop@netvision.net.il;
popany@netvision.net.il; pitspopany@aol.com
Web site: http://www.pitspopany.com;
http://www.devorapublishing.com
Dist(s): Baker & Taylor Bks.
    Bookazine Co., Inc..

Plain View Pr., ( 0-911051; 1-891386 ) Orders Addr.: P.O. Box 33311, Austin, TX 78764 (SAN 264-3073) Tel 512-441-2452; Toll Free: 800-878-3605; Edit Addr.: 2009 Arthur Ln., Austin, TX 78704 (SAN 665-7591)
E-mail: sbpvp@eden.com
Web site: http://www.eden.com/~sbpvp
Dist(s): Baker & Taylor Bks.
    In Between Bks.
    Yankee Peddler Bookshop.

Planeta Publishing Corp., ( 0-9715256; 0-9719950 ) 2057 NW 87th Ave., Miami, FL 33172 Tel 305-470-0016; 305-571-8400; Fax: 305-470-6267; Toll Free: 800-407-4770
E-mail: mnormanppc@aol.com
Web site: http://www.planetapublishing.com.

Platinum Imprint of Ctr. Point Large Print

Platinum Pr., Inc., ( 1-879582 ) Div. of Bobley-Harmann Publishing & Marketing Co., 311 Crossways Park Dr., Woodbury, NY 11797 Tel 516-364-1800; Fax: 516-364-1899.

†Playboy Enterprises, Inc., ( 0-87223 ) 680 N. Lake Shore Dr., Chicago, IL 60611 (SAN 213-2656) Tel 312-751-8000; Fax: 312-751-2818; Toll Free: 800-621-4105
E-mail: feedback@marketguide.com
Web site: http://www.marketguide.com/
Dist(s): Warner Publishing Services; CIP.

Pl;ayboy Press See Playboy Enterprises, Inc.

Players Pr., Inc., ( 0-88734 ) P.O. Box 1132, Studio City, CA 91614-0132 (SAN 239-0213) Tel 818-789-4980
E-mail: Playerspress@att.net.

Playgroup Pr., ( 0-9674572 ) 3220 Seven Eagles, Charlotte, NC 28210 Tel 704-643-1008; Fax: 704-643-0059
E-mail: playgrouppress@carolina.rr.com
Web site: http://www.playgrouppress.com
Dist(s): Biblio Distribution
    National Bk. Network.

Playmore, Inc., Pubs., ( 0-86611; 1-59060 ) 230 Fifth Ave., Suite 711, New York, NY 10001-7704 (SAN 219-340X) Tel 212-251-0600; Fax: 212-251-0966
E-mail: customerservice@playmorebooks.com.

Plaza & Janés Editories, S.A. (ESP) ( 84-01 ) Dist. by Astran.

Plaza & Janés Editories, S.A. (ESP) ( 84-01 ) Dist. by Continental Bk.

Plaza & Janés Editories, S.A. (ESP) ( 84-01 ) Dist. by Lectorum Pubns.

Plaza & Janés Editories, S.A. (ESP) ( 84-01 ) Dist. by AIMS Intl.

Plaza & Janés Editories, S.A. (ESP) ( 84-01 ) Dist. by Distribks Inc.

Plaza & Janés Editories, S.A. (ESP) ( 84-01 ) Dist. by Libros Fronteras.

†Pleasant Co. Pubns., ( 0-937295; 1-56247; 1-58485; 1-59369 ) Subs. of Mattel, Inc., Orders Addr.: P.O. Box 620991, Middleton, WI 53562-0991 Tel 608-836-4848; Toll Free Fax: 800-257-3865; Toll Free: 800-233-0264; Edit Addr.: 8400 Fairway Pl., Middleton, WI 53562-0998 (SAN 298-6337) Tel 608-836-4848; Fax: 608-831-7089; Imprints: American Girl (Amer Girl)
Web site: http://www.pleasantcopublications.com/
Dist(s): American Wholesale Bk. Co.
    Anderson News Co.
    Baker & Taylor Bks.
    Brodart Co.
    Follett Library Resources
    Koen Bk. Distributors
    Lectorum Pubns., Inc.
    Levy Home Entertainment
    Riverside
    Spring Arbor Distributors, Inc.; CIP.

Pleasure Boat Studio See Pleasure Boat Studio: A Literary Pr.

Pleasure Boat Studio: A Literary Pr., ( 0-912887; 0-9651413; 1-929355 ) 201 W. 89th St., No. 6F, New York, NY 10024 Toll Free: 888-810-5308 (phone/fax) ; 721 Mt. Pleasant Rd., Port Angeles, WA 98362 (SAN 299-0075)
E-mail: pleasboat@nyc.rr.com
Web site: http://www.pbstudio.com
Dist(s): Baker & Taylor Bks.
    Partners/West
    SPD-Small Pr. Distribution
    Todd Communications.

PleaWilderness Adventures Pr., Inc., ( 1-885106; 1-932098 ) 45 Buckskin Rd., Belgrade, MT 59714 Tel 406-388-0112; Fax: 406-388-0120; Toll Free Fax: 800-390-7558; Toll Free: 800-925-3339
E-mail: books@wildadv.com
Web site: http://www.wildadv.com
Dist(s): Baker & Taylor Bks.
    Partners Pubs. Group, Inc.
    Partners/West
    Sunbelt Pubns., Inc..

Plexus Publishing, Inc., ( 0-937548; 0-9666748 ) 143 Old Marlton Pike, Medford, NJ 08055 (SAN 212-436X) Tel 609-654-6500; Fax: 609-654-4309 Do not confuse with Plexus Publishing, Limited in London, United Kingdom
E-mail: patp@plexuspub.com
Web site: http://www.plexuspublishing.com
Dist(s): Independent Pubs. Group
    Koen Bk. Distributors.

Plimsoll Pr., ( 0-9647147 ) Orders Addr.: P.O. Box 742, White Sulphur Springs, WV 24986 Tel 304-536-2069 ; Fax: 304-536-3801; Toll Free: 800-327-6345; Edit Addr.: 220 Pleasant Valley Rd., White Sulphur Springs, WV 24986.

Plover Pr., ( 0-917635 ) 592 Kaimalino St., Kailua, HI 96734 (SAN 656-9005) Tel 808-254-5725; Fax: 808-254-5725.

Plume Imprint of NAL

Plume Imprint of Dutton/Plume

Pluto Pr. (GBR) ( 0-7453; 0-86104; 0-902818; 0-904383; 1-85305 ) Dist. by Stylus Pub VA.

Plymouth Rock Publishing, ( 1-890791 ) Orders Addr.: P.O. Box 1298, Plymouth, MA 02362 Tel 781-329-2272; Fax: 508-224-5200; Toll Free: 877-879-1620 (877-TRY-1620)
E-mail: alevenson@alumni.tufts.edu;
alevinson@alumni.tufts.edu
Web site: http://www.plymouthrockpublishing.com.

PMC Bks. & Music, ( 0-615; 0-9741543 ) 801 Cheever Ave., Geneva, IL 60134
E-mail: cookpmc@ameritech.net.

Pocahontas Pr., Inc., ( 0-936015 ) Orders Addr.: P.O. Box Drawer F, Blacksburg, VA 24063-1020 (SAN 630-124X) Tel 540-951-0467; Fax: 540-961-2847; Toll Free: 800-446-0467; Edit Addr.: 832 Hutcheson Dr., Blacksburg, VA 24063-1020
E-mail: mchollim@vt.edu
Dist(s): Baker & Taylor Bks.
    Coutts Library Service, Inc.
    Koen Bk. Distributors
    Quality Bks., Inc..

Pocket Imprint of Simon & Schuster

†Pocket Bks., ( 0-671; 0-7432; 0-7434; 1-4165 ) Div. of Simon & Schuster, Inc., Orders Addr.: 100 Front St., Riverside, NJ 08075 Toll Free Fax: 800-943-9831; Toll Free: 800-223-2336; Edit Addr.: 1230 Ave. of the Americas, New York, NY 10020 (SAN 202-5922) Tel 212-698-7000
E-mail: ssonline_feedback@simonsays.com
Web site: http://www.simonsays.com
Dist(s): Simon & Schuster
    Thorndike Pr.; CIP.

Pocket Essentials (GBR) ( 1-903047; 1-904048 ) Dist. by Trafalgar.

Pocket Star Imprint of Simon & Schuster

PocketPCpr., ( 1-58929 ) Div. of D P C, Inc., 4312 Branson St., Edina, MN 55424
E-mail: doug@pocketpcpress.com
Web site: http://www.pocketpcpress.com.

Poisoned Pen Pr., ( 1-890208; 1-929345; 1-59058 ) 6962 E. First Ave., Suite 103, Scottsdale, AZ 85251 (SAN 299-6898) Tel 480-945-3375 (ext. 210); Fax: 480-949-1707; Toll Free: 800-421-3976
E-mail: info@poisonedpenpress.com
Web site: http://www.poisonedpenpress.com
Dist(s): Baker & Taylor Bks..

Polaris Bks., ( 0-9741443 ) 11111 W. 8th Ave., Unit A, Lakewood, CO 80215-5516 Tel 303-980-0890; Fax: 303-980-0753
E-mail: zubrin@aol.com
Web site: http://www.polarisbooks.net.

Politico's Publishing Ltd. (GBR) ( 1-902301; 1-84275 ) Dist. by Intl Spec Bk.

†Poltroon Pr., ( 0-918395 ) P.O. Box 5476, Berkeley, CA 94705 (SAN 218-2475) Tel 510-845-8097
E-mail: poltroon@earthlink.net
Web site: http://www.poltroonpress.com
Dist(s): Independent Pubs. Group
    SPD-Small Pr. Distribution; CIP.

Polyglot Pr., Inc., ( 1-931927; 1-4115 ) 427 Queen St., Philadelphia, PA 19147 Tel 215-755-7559; Fax: 215-755-5569 Do not confuse with Polyglot Press in Fairfax, VA
E-mail: david@polyglotpress.com
Web site: http://www.polyglotpress.com.

Polygon (GBR) ( 0-7486; 0-85224; 0-904919; 0-948275; 0-9501890; 1-902930 ) Dist. by Interlink Pub.

Polygon (GBR) ( 0-7486; 0-85224; 0-904919; 0-948275; 0-9501890; 1-902930 ) Dist. by AK Pr Dist.

Pomegranate Communications, Inc, ( 0-7649; 0-87654; 0-917556; 1-56640 ) Orders Addr.: P.O. Box 6099, Rohnert Park, CA 94927-6099 (SAN 211-0857) Tel 707-586-5500; Fax: 707-586-5522; 707-586-5518; Toll Free: 800-227-1428; Edit Addr.: 210 Classic Ct., Rohnert Park, CA 94928
E-mail: info@pomegranate.com
Web site: http://www.pomegranate.com.

Poncha Pr., ( 0-9701862 ) P.O. Box 280, Morrison, CO 80465-0280 (SAN 253-3588) Tel 303-697-2384; Fax: 303-697-2385
E-mail: info@ponchapress.com
Web site: http://www.ponchapress.com
Dist(s): Baker & Taylor Bks.
    Brodart Co..

Names

**Pontalba Pr.,** ( *0-9653145; 1-891643* ) 4417 Dryades St., New Orleans, LA 70115 Tel 504-899-7970; Fax: 212-957-4671 (New York Office); 504-899-6573; Toll Free Fax: 888-240-5935; Toll Free: 888-436-3724; 888-249-6281 (New York Office); *Imprints:* Autumn Books (Autumn Bks) E-mail: wayne@pontalbapress.com Web site: http://www.pontalbapress.com *Dist(s):* **Forest Sales & Distributing Co.**.

**Pony-Up Pr.,** ( *0-9700717* ) 369 Montezuma Ave., No. 306, Sante Fe, NM 87501-2626 Tel 505-986-8717 (phone/fax) *Dist(s):* **Alliance Hse., Inc.**.

**Poolbeg Pr. (IRL)** ( *0-905169; 0-907085; 1-85371; 1-84223* ) *Dist. by* Dufour.

**Poole & Smith Publishing,** ( *0-9669658; 1-930392* ) 1152 Wilkinson Rd., Richmond, VA 23227 Fax: 804-262-3494.

**Popular E Commerce, Inc.,** ( *0-87380* ) P.O. Box 1901, Boerne, TX 78006 Tel 830-537-3411.

**Popular Pr. Imprint of Univ. of Wisconsin Pr.**

**Porphyrion Pr.,** ( *0-913884* ) 339 Middle Grove Rd., Middle Grove, NY 12850 (SAN 206-6823) Tel 518-587-9809 E-mail: propress@aol.com Web site: propress.com

**Portable Press** *See* **Akashic Bks.**

**Portmanteau Editions,** ( *0-945942* ) P.O. Box 665, Somers, NY 10589 (SAN 248-0395) Do not confuse with Portmanteau Pr. in New York, NY.

**Post Oak Pr. Imprint of Larksdale**

**Post-Apollo Pr., The,** ( *0-942996* ) 35 Marie St., Sausalito, CA 94965 (SAN 240-429X) Tel 415-332-1458; Fax: 415-332-8540 E-mail: tpapress@dnai.com Web site: http://www.dnai.com/~tpapress/ *Dist(s):* **SPD-Small Pr. Distribution.**

**Posterity Pr., Inc.,** ( *1-889274* ) P.O. Box 71081, Chevy Chase, MD 20813 Tel 301-652-2384; Fax: 301-652-2543 Do not confuse with companies with the same name in Emerald Isle, NC, Buffalo, NY E-mail: Publisher@PosterityPress.com Web site: http://www.PosterityPress.com *Dist(s):* **Koen Bk. Distributors.**

**Pozzi Pr. Corp.,** ( *0-9659465* ) 1508 Park Ave., Baltimore, MD 21217 Tel 410-837-1140; Fax: 410-669-6068 E-mail: chalumot@aol.com.

**Praeger Pubs. Imprint of Greenwood Publishing Group, Inc.**

**Prairie Imprints,** ( *0-9615098* ) P.O. Box 481, Stillwater, OK 74076 (SAN 692-9672) Tel 405-377-3750.

†**Prairie Oak Pr., Inc.,** ( *1-879483* ) 821 Prospect Pl., Madison, WI 53703 Tel 608-255-2288; Fax: 608-255-4204; Toll Free: 888-833-9118 E-mail: popjama@aol.com; *CIP.*

**Precocious Publishing Co.,** ( *0-9634969* ) 8817 Dartford Pl., Inglewood, CA 90305 Tel 310-672-1726; Fax: 310-672-0642.

**Premier Imprint of Ctr. Point Large Print**

**Premier Publishing** *See* **Futech Interactive Products, Inc.**

**Prentice Hall Imprint of Prentice Hall PTR**

**Prentice Hall, ESL Dept.,** ( *0-13; 0-88345* ) 240 Frisch Ct., Paramus, NJ 07652-5240 Tel 201-236-7000; Fax: 201-592-0904; Toll Free: 800-922-0579 Web site: http://vig.prenhall.com *Dist(s):* **Continental Bk. Co., Inc. Pearson Education.**

†**Prentice Hall PTR,** ( *0-13; 0-201; 0-672* ) Div. of Pearson Technology Group, Orders Addr.: 200 Old Tappan Rd., Old Tappan, NJ 07675 Fax: 416-447-2819 (orders - Canada); Toll Free Fax: 800-445-6991 (government orders); 800-835-5327 (individual single copy orders - US); Toll Free: 800-567-3800 (orders - Canada); 800-282-0693 (individual single copy orders - US); 800-922-0579 (government orders); Edit Addr.: 240 Frisch Ct., Paramus, NJ 07652-5240; *Imprints:* Macmillan College (Macmillan Coll); Prentice Hall (Prentice Hall) Web site: http://www.prenhall.com *Dist(s):* **Cambridge Bk. Co. Continental Bk. Co., Inc. IFSTA Pearson Education Penguin Group (USA) Inc.**; *CIP.*

**Prentice Hall (Schl. Div.),** ( *0-13* ) Orders Addr.: 4350 Equity Dr., Columbus, OH 43216-2649 Fax: 614-771-7361; Toll Free: 800-848-9500; P.O. Box 2649, Columbus, OH 43216-2649; Edit Addr.: 160 Gould St. (Northeast Region), Needham Heights, MA 02194-2310 Tel 617-455-1300; 8445 Freeport Pkwy., Suite 400 (South Central Region), Irving, TX 75063 Tel 214-915-4255 Web site: http://www.phschool.com/.

**Prentice-Hall** *See* **Prentice Hall PTR**

**PREP Publishing,** ( *1-885288* ) Div. of PREP, Inc., 1110 1/2 Hay St., PMB 66, Fayetteville, NC 28305 Tel 910-483-6611; Fax: 910-483-2439; Toll Free: 800-533-2814 E-mail: preppub@aol.com Web site: http://www.prep-pub.com *Dist(s):* **Baker & Taylor Bks.**.

**Presidio Pr. Imprint of Ballantine Bks.**

†**Press Pacifica, Ltd.,** ( *0-916630* ) Orders Addr.: P.O. Box 47, Kailua, HI 96734 (SAN 249-292X) Tel 808-261-6594 *Dist(s):* **Booklines Hawaii, Ltd.;** *CIP.*

**Presses Pocket (FRA)** ( *2-266* ) *Dist. by* Distribks Inc.

**Prestige Bks. (IND)** ( *81-85218; 81-7551* ) *Dist. by* S Asia.

**Preston-Speed Pubns.,** ( *1-887159; 1-931587* ) 51 Ridge Rd., Mill Hall, PA 17751 Tel 570-726-7844; Fax: 570-726-3547 E-mail: Preston@cub.kcnet.org Web site: http://www.prestonspeed.com *Dist(s):* **Greathall Productions, Inc.**

**Prestwick Hse., Inc.,** ( *1-58049* ) Orders Addr.: P.O. Box 246, Cheswold, DE 19936 Tel 302-736-2665; Fax: 302-734-0549; Toll Free: 800-932-4593; Edit Addr.: 604 Forrest Ave., Dover, DE 19404 E-mail: books@prestwickhouse.com Web site: http://www.prestwickhouse.com.

**Pretani,** ( *0-9634992; 1-892276* ) P.O. Box 7, Lakeport, CA 95453-0007 Tel 707-263-0514 E-mail: pretani@jps.net Web site: http://www.jps.net/pretani.

**PreviewPort.com,** ( *1-58910* ) 35 E. Wacker Dr., 16th Flr., Chicago, IL 60601 Tel 312-726-5336; Fax: 312-726-5446; Toll Free Fax: 888-408-7678 E-mail: contact@previewport.com Web site: http://www.previewport.com.

**Price Stern Sloan Imprint of Penguin Putnam Bks. for Young Readers**

**Prickly Pr.,** ( *1-893463* ) 7911 W. 92nd Terr., Overland Park, KS 66212 Tel 913-648-2034 (phone/fax) E-mail: ikesmith@kc.rr.com Web site: http://www.readwest.com/flouncesmith.thm.

**Pride & Imprints** *See* **Windstorm Creative Ltd.**

**Prima Games Imprint of Random Hse. Information Group**

**Prima Lifestyles Imprint of Crown Publishing Group**

**Prime,** ( *0-9668968; 1-930997; 1-894815* ) Orders Addr.: P.O. Box 36503, Canton, OH 44735 Fax: 801-340-1771; Edit Addr.: 2917 Parklane St., NW, Apt. F, Canton, OH 44709; 113 Brelus Dr., Dunnville, ON N1A 2S1 Tel 905-774-2663 E-mail: saw@neo.rr.com Web site: http://www.primebooks.net.

**Prime Crime Imprint of Berkley Publishing Group**

**Prime Time Pr.,** ( *0-9642905* ) 2102 Toulouse Dr., Austin, TX 78748-6005 Tel 512-451-0741.

**Primer Cap Pistol Publishing,** ( *0-9715542* ) 925 Freedom Blvd., B-309, Watsonville, CA 95076 Tel 831-724-3291.

**Princeton Architectural Pr.,** ( *0-907259; 0-910413; 0-9636372; 1-56898; 1-878271; 1-885232* ) 37 E. Seventh St., New York, NY 10003 (SAN 260-1176) Tel 212-995-9620; Fax: 212-995-9454; Toll Free: 800-722-6657 E-mail: sales@papress.com Web site: http://www.papress.com *Dist(s):* **Chronicle Bks. LLC.**

†**Princeton Univ. Pr.,** ( *0-691* ) Orders Addr.: California-Princeton Fulfillment Services, 1445 Lower Ferry Rd., Ewing, NJ 08618 Tel 800-777-4726; Fax: 800-999-1958; Edit Addr.: 41 William St., Princeton, NJ 08540 (SAN 202-0254) Tel 609-258-4900; Fax: 609-258-6305 E-mail: webmaster@pupress.princeton.edu Web site: http://www.pup.princeton.edu *Dist(s):* **California Princeton Fulfillment Services Tuttle Publishing netLibrary, Inc.;** *CIP.*

**PrinnyWorld Pr.,** ( *0-9668005* ) Orders Addr.: P.O. Box 248, Saraland, AL 36571 Tel 334-675-5967; Fax: 334-675-6909; Edit Addr.: 10385K Army Rd., Ext. S, Chunchula, AL 36521 E-mail: prinnywrld@aol.com Web site: http://members.aol.com/prinnywrld/intro.html *Dist(s):* **Baker & Taylor Bks.**.

**Prion (GBR)** ( *1-85375* ) *Dist. by* Trafalgar.

**Prism Corp.,** ( *0-9652778* ) Orders Addr.: P.O. Box 10775, New York, NY 10021-0775 (SAN 299-1535) Tel 212-517-5828; Fax: 212-628-0819; Toll Free: 888-638-4377; *Imprints:* Hightrees Books (Hightrees Bks) Do not confuse with companies with the same or similar name in Gladwin, MI, Baltimore, MD, Edison, NJ, Houston, TX, Dayton, NJ, Minneapolis, MN, Detroit, MI, Boulder, CO *Dist(s):* **Unique Bks., Inc.**.

**Proctor Pubns.,** ( *1-882792; 1-928623* ) Div. of Proctor Publications, LLC, Orders Addr.: P.O. Box 2498, Ann Arbor, MI 48106-2498 Tel 734-480-9900; Fax: 734-480-9811; Toll Free: 800-343-3034; Edit Addr.: 1832 Midvale, Ypsilanti, MI 48197 E-mail: dproctor9552@comcast.net Web site: http://www.proctorpublications.com *Dist(s):* **Baker & Taylor Bks. Follett Library Resources Quality Bks., Inc. Wayne State Univ. Pr.**.

**Professional Business Consultant** *See* **Milligan Bks.**

**Professional Pr.,** ( *1-57087; 1-880365* ) Orders Addr.: P.O. Box 4371, Chapel Hill, NC 27515-4371 Fax: 919-942-8020; Toll Free: 800-277-8960; Edit Addr.: 314 Warren Way, Chapel Hill, NC 27516 Do not confuse with Professional Pr., New York, NY E-mail: tag@geldermann.com *Dist(s):* **Sunbelt Pubns., Inc.**.

**Profile Entertainment, Inc.,** ( *0-88013; 0-931064; 0-934551* ) 475 Park Ave., S., 8th Flr., New York, NY 10016 (SAN 212-1247) Tel 212-689-2830; Fax: 212-889-7933 E-mail: dee.erwine@starloggroup.com *Dist(s):* **Kable News Co., Inc.**.

†**Prometheus Bks., Pubs.,** ( *0-87975; 1-57392; 1-59102* ) 59 John Glenn Dr., Amherst, NY 14228-2197 (SAN 202-0289) Tel 716-691-0133; Fax: 716-691-0137; Toll Free: 800-421-0351; *Imprints:* Humanity Books (Humanity Bks) E-mail: mhall@prometheusmail.com Web site: http://www.prometheusbooks.com *Dist(s):* **Paladin Pr.; CIP.**

**Prometheus Pr. Imprint of Fisher Enterprises, Inc.**

**Promise Pr. Imprint of Barbour Publishing, Inc.**

**Pro-Q Publishing,** ( *0-9711675* ) P.O. Box 510588, Saint Louis, MO 63151-0588 Tel 314-416-8875; Fax: 314-416-0182 E-mail: proqfineart@aol.com Web site: http://www.geocities.com/proqfineart/.

**Protea Publishing Co.,** ( *1-883707; 1-931768; 1-59344* ) 6920-B Peachtree Industrial Blvd., No. 648, Atlanta, GA 30341-2235 (SAN 253-7141) E-mail: kaolink@msn.com Web site: http://www.proteapublishing.com *Dist(s):* **Baker & Taylor Bks. Lightning Source, Inc. Replica Bks.**.

**Providence Hse. Pubs.,** ( *1-57736; 1-881576* ) 238 Seaboard Ln., Franklin, TN 37067 Tel 615-771-2020; Fax: 615-771-2002; Toll Free: 800-321-5692; *Imprints:* Hillsboro Press (Hillsboro Pr) E-mail: books@providencehouse.com Web site: http://www.providencehouse.com.

†**Pruett Publishing Co.,** ( *0-87108* ) 7464 Arapahoe Rd., Suite A9, Boulder, CO 80303-1500 (SAN 205-4035) Tel 303-449-4919; Fax: 303-443-9019; Toll Free: 800-592-9727 (orders) E-mail: pruettbks@aol.com Web site: http://www.pruettpublishing.com; *CIP.*

**Psychological Counseling Services, Inc.,** ( *0-9652879* ) 7530 E. Angus Dr., Scottsdale, AZ 85251 Tel 602-947-5739; Fax: 602-946-7795.

**Publicaciones Puertorriquenas, Inc.,** ( *0-929441; 1-881713; 1-881720; 1-932243* ) Calle Mayaguez, No. 44, San Juan, PR 00918 (SAN 249-4272) Tel 787-759-9673; Fax: 787-250-6498 E-mail: pubpr@tld.net Web site: http://www.tld.net/users/pubpr/2/.

**Names**

**PublicAffairs,** ( *1-891620; 1-58648* ) A Member of Perseus Books Group, 250 W. 57th St., Suite 1321, New York, NY 10107 Tel 212-397-6666; Fax: 212-397-4277; Toll Free: 877-782-1234 E-mail: westview.orders@perseusbooks.com; pubaff@interport.net Web site: http://www.publicaffairsbooks.com *Dist(s):* **HarperCollins Pubs..**

**PublishAmerica, Inc.,** ( *1-893162; 1-58851; 1-59129; 1-59286; 1-4137* ) Div. of America Hse. Bk. Pubs., 230 E. Patrick St., Frederick, MD 21701 Tel 240-529-1030; Fax: 301-631-9073 Web site: http://www.publishamerica.com.

**Publishers Group West,** Subs. of Publishers Group Inc., 1700 Fourth St., Berkeley, CA 94710 (SAN 202-8522) Tel 510-528-1444; Fax: 510-528-3444; Toll Free: 800-788-3123; 800-788-3122 (electronic orders) Web site: http://www.pgw.com.

**Publishing Concepts,** ( *0-9635159* ) 112 Elmhurst Rd., Baltimore, MD 21210 Tel 410-467-2269; Fax: 410-366-8622; Toll Free: 800-960-3003 E-mail: cdroke9819@aol.com *Dist(s):* **Hood, Alan C. & Co., Inc.** **Baker & Taylor Bks..**

**Publishing Directions, LLC,** ( *1-928782* ) 615 Queen St., Southington, CT 06489 Tel 860-276-2452; Fax: 203-267-1387; Toll Free: 800-562-4357 E-mail: info@strongbooks.com Web site: http://www.strongbooks.com *Dist(s):* **Midpoint Trade Bks., Inc..**

**Publishing Mills, Inc., The,** ( *0-9627187; 1-57511; 1-879371* ) Div. of New Millennium Entertainment, 301 N. Canon Dr., Suite 214, Beverly Hills, CA 90210 Tel 310-273-7722; Fax: 310-273-7755 E-mail: editor@pubmills.com Web site: http://www.publishingmills.com *Dist(s):* **Client Distribution Services** **Landmark Audiobooks.**

**PublishingOnline,** ( *1-929939; 1-58882; 1-4011* ) 1200 S. 192nd St., Suite 300, Seattle, WA 98148 Tel 206-439-9257; Fax: 206-246-8154; Toll Free: 888-730-7266 E-mail: tamaraf@publishingonline.com Web site: http://www.publishingonline.com.

**Puffin Bks.** Imprint of Penguin Group (USA) Inc.

**Puffin Bks.** Imprint of Penguin Putnam Bks. for Young Readers

**Pulp Adventures, Inc.,** ( *1-891729* ) P.O. Box 45495, Madison, WI 53744-5495 (SAN 254-5500) E-mail: pulpadventures@charter.net Web site: http://www.pulpadventures.com *Dist(s):* **Baker & Taylor Bks.** **Diamond Book Distributors, Inc..**

**Pulp Collector Press** *See* **Adventure Hse.**

**Pulp Faction (GBR)** ( *1-899571* ) *Dist. by* **AK Pr Dist.**

**Pulpless.com, Inc.,** ( *1-58445* ) 775 E. Blithedale, Suite 508, Mill Valley, CA 94941 Tel 310-839-7653 (phone/fax) E-mail: jneil@pulpless.com Web site: http://www.pulpless.com.

**Purple Mountain Pr., Ltd.,** ( *0-916346; 0-935796; 1-930098* ) Orders Addr.: P.O. Box 309, Fleischmanns, NY 12430-0309 (SAN 222-3716) Tel 845-254-4062; Fax: 845-254-4476; Toll Free: 800-325-2665 Do not confuse with Purple Mountain Pr., Carson City, NV E-mail: purple@catskill.net Web site: http://www.catskill.net/purple *Dist(s):* **Baker & Taylor Bks.** **Koen Bk. Distributors.**

**Pushcart Pr., The,** ( *0-916366; 1-888889* ) P.O. Box 380, Wainscott, NY 11975 (SAN 202-9871) Tel 631-324-9300 *Dist(s):* **Norton, W. W. & Co., Inc..**

**Pushkin Pr., Ltd. (GBR)** ( *1-901285* ) *Dist. by* **Consort Bk Sales.**

**Pussywillow Publishing Hse.,** ( *0-934739* ) 621 Leisure World, Mesa, AZ 85206-3153 (SAN 694-1702) Tel 480-641-9049; Fax: 480-854-1222 *Dist(s):* **Baker & Taylor Bks..**

**Putnam & Grosset** Imprint of Putnam Publishing Group, The

**Putnam & Grosset** Imprint of Penguin Group (USA) Inc.

**Putnam Berkley Audio** Imprint of Putnam Publishing Group, The

**Putnam Berkley Audio** Imprint of Penguin Group (USA) Inc.

†**Putnam Publishing Group, The,** ( *0-399; 0-698; 0-89828* ) Div. of Penguin Putnam, Inc., Orders Addr.: 405 Murray Hill Pkwy., East Rutherford, NJ 07073-2136 Toll Free Fax: 800-227-9604; Toll Free: 800-788-6262 (individual consumer sales); 800-631-8571 (reseller customer service); 800-526-0275 (reseller sales); Edit Addr.: 375 Hudson St., New York, NY 10014 (SAN 202-5531) Tel 212-366-2000; Fax: 212-366-2643; *Imprints:* Coward-McCann (Coward); Tuffy Books (Tuffy); Riverhead Books (Hardcovers) (Riverhead Books); Putnam Berkley Audio (Putnam Berkley Audio); Putnam & Grosset (Putnam & Grosset); Wood, Marian Books (Marian Wood); BlueHen Books (BlueHen) E-mail: online@penguinputnam.com Web site: http://www.penguinputnam.com *Dist(s):* **Continental Bk. Co., Inc.** **Hastings Bks.** **Lectorum Pubns., Inc.** **Landmark Audiobooks** **Penguin Group (USA) Inc.** **Rounder Kids Music Distribution** **Beeler, Thomas T. Publisher;** *CIP.*

**Puuiki Pr.,** ( *0-9662021* ) Orders Addr.: P.O. Box 718, Hana, HI 96713 Tel 808-248-7893; Edit Addr.: 718 Hana Hwy., Hana, HI 96713 E-mail: ldean@mauigateway.com.

†**Pyncheon Hse.,** ( *1-881119* ) 6 University Dr., Suite 105, Amherst, MA 01002 (SAN 297-6269) E-mail: davidrrhodes@hotmail.com *Dist(s):* **Baker & Taylor Bks.;** *CIP.*

**Quail Ridge Pr., Inc.,** ( *0-937552; 1-893062* ) Orders Addr.: P.O. Box 123, Brandon, MS 39043 Tel 601-825-2063; Fax: 601-825-3091; Toll Free Fax: 800-864-1082; Toll Free: 800-343-1583 E-mail: info@quailridge.com Web site: http://www.quailridge.com *Dist(s):* **Gibson, Dot Pubns.** **Forest Sales & Distributing Co.** **Partners Pubs. Group, Inc.** **Southwest Cookbook Distributors.**

**Quality Words In Print,** ( *0-9713160* ) P.O. Box 2707, Costa Mesa, CA 92628-2704 Tel 714-436-5700; Fax: 714-668-9448 E-mail: qwip@earthlink.net *Dist(s):* **Biblio Distribution.**

**Quarrier Pr.,** ( *0-938985; 0-9646197; 1-891852* ) 1416 Quarrier St., Charleston, WV 25301 Tel 304-342-1848 ; Fax: 304-343-0594; Toll Free: 888-982-7472 E-mail: wvbooks@ntelos.net *Dist(s):* **Pictorial Histories Distribution.**

**Quartet Bks., Ltd. (GBR)** ( *0-7043* ) *Dist. by* **Interlink Pub.**

†**Queens Hse./Focus Service,** ( *0-89244* ) P.O. Box 145, Dana Point, CA 92629 (SAN 208-2802) Tel 949-240-3242; *CIP.*

**Queens Hse., Inc.** Imprint of Amereon, Ltd.

**Quellen Co., The,** ( *0-9618473* ) 817 E. Eighth St., Holtville, CA 92250 (SAN 667-979X) Tel 760-356-1138; Fax: 760-356-2778.

**Quellen Enterprises** *See* **Quellen Co., The**

**Quest Bks.** Imprint of Theosophical Publishing Hse.

**Questar Publishers, Incorporated** *See* **Multnomah Pubs., Inc.**

**Quiet Storm Publishing Group,** ( *0-9714296; 0-9728819; 0-9744084* ) 1045 Needmore Rd., Martinsburg, WV 25401; P.O. Box 1666, Martinsburg, WV 25402 Tel 304-283-3838; Fax: 208-498-9259 E-mail: marketing@quietstormpublishing.com; quietstormbooks@aol.com Web site: http://www.quietstormpublishing.com *Dist(s):* **Baker & Taylor Bks..**

**Quiet Vision Publishing,** ( *1-57646; 1-891595* ) 12155 Mountain Shadow Rd., Sandy, UT 84092-5812 Tel 801-572-4018; Fax: 801-571-8625; Toll Free: 800-442-4018 E-mail: john@quietvision.com; info@quietvision.com Web site: http://www.quietvision.com *Dist(s):* **Baker & Taylor Bks.** **Sprout, Inc..**

**Quill** Imprint of HarperTrade

**Quincannon Publishing Group,** ( *1-878452* ) P.O. Box 8100, Glen Ridge, NJ 07028 Tel 973-669-8367 (phone/fax); *Imprints:* Jersey Yarns (Jersey Yarns); Rune-Tales (Rune-Tales); Compass Point Mysteries (Compass Point Mysteries) E-mail: editors@quincannongroup.com Web site: http://www.quincannongroup.com *Dist(s):* **Baker & Taylor Bks.** **Brodart Co.** **Hammond Castle Museum.**

†**Quintessence Pubns.,** ( *0-918466* ) Box 356, Amador City, CA 95601 (SAN 209-5947) Tel 209-267-5470; *CIP.*

**R & E Pubs., Inc.,** ( *0-88247; 1-56875* ) Div. of R & E Research Assocs., Inc., 2132 O'Toole Ave., San Jose, CA 95131-1302 (SAN 293-3195).

**R. N. M., Incorporated** *See* **Onion River Pr.**

**R.R. Productions,** ( *0-9651856* ) P.O. Box 973, Torrington, WY 82240 Tel 307-532-2667 E-mail: jnesbitt@ewc.cc.wy.us *Dist(s):* **Bookmen, Inc.** **Books West.**

**RVS Bks., Inc.,** ( *0-9634257* ) P.O. Box 683, Lebanon, TN 37088-0683 (SAN 298-7325) Tel 615-449-6725; Fax: 615-449-6910.

**Radical Romantic Pr., The,** ( *1-891021* ) Orders Addr.: P.O. Box 66693, Los Angeles, CA 90066 Tel 310-390-4245; Edit Addr.: 12226 Pacific Ave., No. 1, Los Angeles, CA 90066 E-mail: drgulbraa@aol.com.

**Radio Spirits, Inc.,** ( *1-57019* ) P.O. Box 87993, Carol Stream, IL 60188-7993 Tel 847-524-0200; Fax: 847-524-8245; Toll Free: 800-723-4648; Fulfillment Addr.: 974 Estes Ct., Schaumburg, IL 60193 (SAN 253-9144) Web site: http://www.radiospirits.com *Dist(s):* **Landmark Audiobooks.**

**Radio Theatre Productions - John L. Williams,** ( *0-9634652* ) 1706 Ski Slope, Austin, TX 78733 Tel 512-263-2911.

**Radiola Co.,** ( *0-929541* ) Div. of MediaBay, Inc., P.O. Box C, Sandy Hook, CT 06482 Tel Toll Free: 800-243-0987.

**raflki Bks.,** ( *0-9657999* ) 29 Henry St., Sag Harbor, NY 11963 Tel 516-725-2620; Fax: 516-725-2688 *Dist(s):* **Bookazine Co., Inc..**

**Raijin Comics Collection** Imprint of Gutsoon! Entertainment, Inc.

**Rainbow Bks., Inc.,** ( *0-935834; 1-56825* ) P.O. Box 430, Highland City, FL 33846-0430 (SAN 213-3515) Tel 863-648-4420; Fax: 863-647-5951; Toll Free: 888-613-2665 (888-613-BOOK) Do not confuse with Rainbow Bks., Inc. in Amsterdam, NY E-mail: RBIbooks@aol.com Web site: http://www.rainbowbooksinc.com *Dist(s):* **Baker & Taylor Bks.** **Book Clearing Hse..**

**Rainbow Pr.,** ( *0-943156* ) 222 Edwards Dr., Fayetteville, NY 13066 (SAN 240-4354) Do not confuse with companies with the same name in Southampton, NY, Snover, MI, Sparta, NJ, Saco, ME, Boise, ID *Dist(s):* **Baker & Taylor Bks..**

**Raincoast Bk. Distribution (CAN)** ( *0-920417; 1-55192; 1-895714* ) *Dist. by* **Publishers Group.**

†**Raintree Pubs.,** ( *0-8114; 0-8172; 0-8393; 0-7398* ) Div. of Harcourt, Inc., Orders Addr.: P.O. Box 26015, Austin, TX 78755 Toll Free Fax: 877-578-2638; Toll Free: 888-363-4266; Edit Addr.: 10801 N. Mopac Expressway, Bldg. 3, Austin, TX 78759 (SAN 658-1757) Tel 512-343-8227; Fax: 646-935-3713 Web site: http://www.raintreelibrary.com; *CIP.*

**Raintree Steck-Vaughn Publishers** *See* **Raintree Pubs.**

**Rams Head Pr., International, The,** ( *0-9648623; 1-57915* ) Orders Addr.: P.O. Box 12227, Atlanta, GA 30355 Tel 404-233-8023; Fax: 404-816-9994; Toll Free: 800-726-7432 (orders only); Edit Addr.: 2995 Slaton Dr., NW, Atlanta, GA 30305 *Dist(s):* **BookWorld Services, Inc..**

†**Randall, Peter E. Pub.,** ( *0-914339; 1-931807* ) Orders Addr.: P.O. Box 4726, Portsmouth, NH 03802; Edit Addr.: 5 Greenlead Woods Dr., No. 102, Portsmouth, NH 03802 (SAN 223-0496) Tel 603-431-5667; Fax: 603-431-3566 E-mail: deidre@perpublisher.com Web site: http://www.perpublisher.com *Dist(s):* **Univ. Pr. of New England;** *CIP.*

**Random House** Imprint of Random House Adult Trade Publishing Group

**Random House Adult Trade Publishing Group,** ( *0-375; 0-679; 0-8129; 1-4000* ) Orders Addr.: 400 Hahn Rd., Westminster, MD 21157 Tel 410-848-1900 ; Toll Free 800-726-0600; Edit Addr.: 299 Park Ave., New York, NY 10171 Tel 212-751-2600; Fax: 212-572-4949; Toll Free: 800-726-0600; *Imprints:* AtRandom (AtRandom); Random House Trade Paperbacks (RH Trade Bks); Modern Library (Mod Lib); Villard Books (Villard Books); Random House (Random House) *Dist(s):* **Libros Sin Fronteras** **Random Hse., Inc..**

Names

**Random Hse. Audio Publishing Group,** ( *0-375; 0-553; 1-4000* ) Div. of Random Hse., Diversified Pub. Group, Orders Addr.: 400 Hahn Rd., Westminster, MD 21157 (SAN 201-3975) Tel 410-848-1900; Toll Free: 800-726-0600; Edit Addr.: 1540 Broadway, New York, NY 10036; *Imprints:* RH Audio Price-Less (RH Aud Price); RH Audio (Random AudioBks); Listening Library (Listening Lib)
Web site: http://www.randomhouse.com/audio
*Dist(s):* **Random Hse., Inc.**.

†**Random Hse., Inc.,** ( *0-307; 0-345; 0-375; 0-394; 0-553; 0-676; 0-679; 0-87665; 1-58836; 1-4000* ) Div. of Bertelsmann AG, Orders Addr.: 400 Hahn Rd., Westminster, MD 21157 (SAN 202-5515) Tel 410-848-1900; Toll Free Fax: 800-659-2436; Toll Free: 800-726-0600 (customer service/orders); Edit Addr.: 1540 Broadway, New York, NY 10036 (SAN 202-5507) Tel 212-782-9000; Fax: 212-302-7985
E-mail: customerservice@randomhouse.com
Web site: http://www.randomhouse.com
*Dist(s):* **Giron Bks.**
**Knopf, Alfred A. Inc.**
**Libros Sin Fronteras**; *CIP.*

**Random Hse. Information Group,** ( *0-375; 0-679; 1-4000* ) Div. of Random Hse., Inc., Orders Addr.: 400 Hahn Rd., Westminster, MD 21157 Tel 410-848-1900; Toll Free: 800-726-0600; Edit Addr.: 280 Park Ave., New York, NY 10022 Tel 212-751-2600; Toll Free: 800-726-0600; *Imprints:* Prima Games (PrimGames); House of Collectibles (Hse Collectbls); Living Language (LivingLang)
E-mail: customerservice@randomhouse.com
Web site: http://www.randomhouse.com/
*Dist(s):* **Bilingual Pubns. Co., The**
**Libros Sin Fronteras**
**Random Hse., Inc.**.

**Random Hse. Large Print,** ( *0-375; 0-679; 1-4000* ) Div. of Random Hse., Diversified Pub. Group, Orders Addr.: 400 Hahn Rd., Westminster, MD 21157 Tel 410-848-1900; Toll Free Fax: 800-659-2436; Toll Free: 800-733-3000 (customer service/orders); Edit Addr.: 1540 Broadway, New York, NY 10036-4094 Fax: 212-572-8797; *Imprints:* Random House Large Print (RHLP)
E-mail: editor@randomhouse.com; customerservice@randomhouse.com
Web site: http://www.randomhouse.com
*Dist(s):* **Libros Sin Fronteras**
**Random Hse., Inc.**
**Thorndike Pr.**.

**Random House Large Print Imprint of Random Hse. Large Print**

**Random House Reference & Information Publishing** *See* **Random Hse. Information Group**

†**Random Hse. Value Publishing,** ( *0-517; 0-609; 0-87000; 1-4000* ) Div. of Random Hse., Diversified Pub. Group, Orders Addr.: 400 Hahn Rd., Westminster, MD 21157 Toll Free: 800-733-3000 (orders); 800-726-0600 (customer service, credit, electronic ordering dept.); Edit Addr.: 280 Park Ave., 11th Flr., New York, NY 10017 Tel 212-572-2400; *Imprints:* Gramercy (Gram)
Web site: http://www.randomhouse.com
*Dist(s):* **Random Hse., Inc.**; *CIP.*

**Random Hse. of Canada, Ltd. (CAN)** ( *0-09; 0-375; 0-394; 0-676; 0-679* ) *Dist. by* **Random.**

**Random Hse. Trade Paperbacks Imprint of Random House Adult Trade Publishing Group**

**Random Hse. UK, Ltd. (GBR)** ( *0-09; 0-224; 0-7126* ) *Dist. by* **Trafalgar.**

**Ravan Pr. (ZMB)** ( *0-86975* ) *Dist. by* **Ohio U Pr.**

**Raven Tree Pr., LLC,** ( *0-9701107; 0-9720192; 0-9724973; 0-9741992* ) 200 S. Washington St., Suite 306, Green Bay, WI 54301 (SAN 253-6005) Tel 920-438-1605; Fax: 920-438-1607; Toll Free: 877-256-0579
E-mail: amy@raventreepress.com; dawn@raventreepress.com
Web site: http://www.raventreepress.com
*Dist(s):* **Baker & Taylor Bks.**
**FaithWorks**
**Follett Media Distribution.**

**Rayo Imprint of HarperTrade**

**Reader's Chair, Inc., The,** ( *0-9624010; 1-885585* ) 1808 W. Quartet Dr., North Las Vegas, NV 89032 Toll Free: 800-616-1350
E-mail: CustomerService@ReadersChair.com
Web site: http://www.ReadersChair.com
*Dist(s):* **Landmark Audiobooks.**

---

†**Reader's Digest Assn., Inc., The,** ( *0-7621; 0-89577; 0-86438* ) Orders Addr.: Reader's Digest Rd., Pleasantville, NY 10570 (SAN 282-2091) Toll Free: 800-334-9599 (Magazines); 800-463-8820; *Imprints:* IM Press (IM PrMystery)
Web site: http://www.readersdigest.com
*Dist(s):* **Leonard, Hal Corp.**
**Penguin Group (USA) Inc.**
**Simon & Schuster, Inc.**; *CIP.*

**Readers International,** ( *0-930523; 1-887378* ) Orders Addr.: P.O. Box 959, Columbia, LA 71418-0959 Tel 318-649-7288 (phone/fax); Edit Addr.: c/o Carroll Clinic, 415 Main St., Columbia, LA 71418; 8 Srathray Gardens, London, NW3 4NY
E-mail: readers@globalnet.co.uk
Web site: http://www.users.globalnet.co.uk/~readers
*Dist(s):* **BHB International, Inc.**
**Consortium Bk. Sales & Distribution.**

**Real Bks.,** ( *1-881102* ) Orders Addr.: P.O. Box 979, Redway, CA 95560 (SAN 297-5920); Edit Addr.: 80 Barnes Ln., Redway, CA 95560 Tel 707-923-3995
E-mail: raphael@asis.com.

**Real Life Storybooks,** ( *1-882388* ) 8370 Kentland Ave., West Hills, CA 91304 Tel 818-887-6431; Fax: 818-887-4541.

**Really Great Bks.,** ( *1-893329* ) Orders Addr.: P.O. Box 861302, Los Angeles, CA 90086 Tel 323-660-0620; Fax: 323-660-2571; Toll Free: 800-422-0505; Edit Addr.: 792 1/2 E. Kensington Rd., Los Angeles, CA 90026
E-mail: MariBooks@aol.com
Web site: http://www.reallygreatbooks.com
*Dist(s):* **SCB Distributors.**

**Rebel, Inc. (GBR)** *Dist. by* **AK Pr Dist.**

**Rebel Publishing Company, Incorporated** *See* **Scurlock Publishing Co., Inc.**

**Recorded Bks., LLC,** ( *0-7887; 1-55690; 1-84197; 1-4025* ) 270 Skipjack Rd., Prince Frederick, MD 20678 (SAN 677-8887) Toll Free: 800-638-1304; *Imprints:* Clipper Audio (Clipper Audio); Griot Audio (Griot Aud)
E-mail: recordedbooks@recordedbooks.com
Web site: http://www.recordedbooks.com.

**Red Apple Publishing,** ( *1-880222* ) 15010 113th St., KPN, Gig Harbor, WA 98329 Tel 253-884-1450; Fax: 253-884-1451
E-mail: peggy@redapplepublishing.com; redapple@wa.net
Web site: http://www.redapplepublishing.com.

**Red Bone Press** *See* **RedBone Pr.**

**Red Brick Pr. Imprint of Hatherleigh Co., Ltd., The**

†**Red Crane Bks., Inc.,** ( *1-878610* ) Orders Addr.: P.O. Box 33590, Santa Fe, NM 87954; Edit Addr.: 2008 Rosina St., Suite C, Santa Fe, NM 87505 Tel 505-988-7070; Fax: 505-989-7476; Toll Free: 800-922-3392
E-mail: publish@redcrane.com
Web site: http://www.redcrane.com
*Dist(s):* **Consortium Bk. Sales & Distribution**
**Continental Bk. Co., Inc.**
**Libros Sin Fronteras**; *CIP.*

†**Red Hen Pr.,** ( *0-931093* ) P.O. Box 454, Big Sur, CA 93920 (SAN 678-9420) Tel 831-667-2726 (phone/fax) Do not confuse with Red Hen Pr., Casa Grande, AZ
E-mail: HopeHen@aol.com
*Dist(s):* **Baker & Taylor Bks.**
**Book Wholesalers, Inc.**
**Brodart Co.**
**Follett Library Resources**; *CIP.*

**Red Hen Pr.,** ( *1-888996* ) P.O. Box 3537, Granada Hills, CA 91394 Tel 818-831-0649; Fax: 818-831-6659
E-mail: editors@redhen.org
Web site: http://www.redhen.org
*Dist(s):* **SPD-Small Pr. Distribution**
**Valentine Publishing Group.**

**Red Lake Pr.,** ( *0-9671068* ) Orders Addr.: P.O. Box 951, Navajo, NM 87328 Tel 520-724-3638; Fax: 520-724-3605; Edit Addr.: 953 F Old Red Lake Rd., Apache County, AZ 85220
E-mail: avrum@navcha.navajo.ihs.gov.

**Red Moon Pr.,** ( *0-9657818; 1-893959* ) Orders Addr.: P.O. Box 2461, Winchester, VA 22604-1661 Tel 540-722-2156; Fax: 708-810-8992; Edit Addr.: 131 Rostel Rd., Winchester, VA 22601
E-mail: redmoon@shentel.net
*Dist(s):* **Weatherhill, Inc.**.

**Red Quill Publishing,** ( *0-9668159* ) Orders Addr.: P.O. Box 4191, Enterprise, FL 32725 Tel 407-324-2837; Fax: 407-331-4176; Edit Addr.: 201 Sheryl Dr., Deltona, FL 32738
E-mail: redquill@aol.com
*Dist(s):* **Southern Bk. Service.**

---

**Red River Pr.,** ( *0-9671506* ) Orders Addr.: P.O. Box 1694, Fort Worth, TX 76182 Tel 917-498-5052; Edit Addr.: 2901 Hurstview Dr., Hurst, TX 76054 Do not confuse with Red River Pr., Wichita Falls, TX
*Dist(s):* **Hervey's Booklink & Cookbook Warehouse.**

**Red Sea,** ( *1-887478* ) 114 Oak St., Patchogue, NY 11772 Tel 516-475-1142; Fax: 516-475-9673; *Imprints:* WiseAcre Books (WiseAcre)
E-mail: wiseacre@redsea.com
Web site: http://users.aol.com/wiseacrebk/.

**Red Sea Pr.,** ( *0-932415; 1-56902* ) 11 Princess Rd., Suites D, E & F, Lawrenceville, NJ 08648 (SAN 630-1983) Tel 609-844-9583; Fax: 609-844-0198
E-mail: africawpress@nyo.com
Web site: http://www.africanworld.com/.

**Red Wheel Imprint of Red Wheel/Weiser**

†**Red Wheel/Weiser,** ( *0-87728; 0-943233; 1-57324; 1-57863; 1-59003* ) Div. of Weiser Bks., Orders Addr.: P.O. Box 612, York Beach, ME 03910-0612 Tel 207-363-4393; Fax: 207-363-5799; Toll Free Fax: 877-337-3309; Toll Free: 800-423-7087 (orders only); *Imprints:* Red Wheel (Red)
E-mail: customerservice@redwheelweiser.com
Web site: http://www.redwheelweiser.com; http://www.weiserbooks.com
*Dist(s):* **Abyss Distribution**
**Baker & Taylor Bks.**
**Bookpeople**
**Koen Bk. Distributors**
**New Leaf Distributing Co., Inc.**
**Publishers Group West**
**Ten Speed Pr.**
**netLibrary, Inc.**; *CIP.*

**RedBone Pr.,** ( *0-9656659* ) P.O. Box 15571, Washington, DC 20003 Tel 202-667-0392; Fax: 301-559-5239
E-mail: redbonepress@yahoo.com
*Dist(s):* **Alamo Square Distributors**
**Bookpeople.**

**Redux Pubns.,** ( *0-9645502* ) 2025 Griggs, SE, Grand Rapids, MI 49506 Tel 616-774-4560.

**Reed, Robert D. Pubs.,** ( *1-885003; 1-931741* ) 750 La Playa St., Suite 647, San Francisco, CA 94121-3262 Tel 650-994-6570; Fax: 650-994-6579; Toll Free: 800-774-7336
E-mail: 4bobreed@msn.com
Web site: http://www.rdrpublishers.com
*Dist(s):* **Midpoint Trade Bks., Inc.**
**Todd Communications.**

**Regal Publications** *See* **University Publishing Hse., Inc.**

**ReganBooks Imprint of HarperTrade**

**Regency Pr. Imprint of Scholarly Pr., Inc.**

**Regency Pr.,** ( *1-929085* ) P.O. Box 18908, Cleveland Heights, OH 44118-0908 Tel 216-932-5319 (phone/fax); Toll Free: 877-343-6299 Do not confuse with companies with the same name in Mobile, AL, Bandera, TX
E-mail: editor@regency-press.com
Web site: http://www.regency-press.com.

**Regenesis Pr.,** ( *0-9704662* ) P.O. Box 9742, Laguna Beach, CA 92652-7729
E-mail: mickemn@cox.net
Web site: http://www.regenesispress.com
*Dist(s):* **Baker & Taylor Bks.**
**Emery-Pratt Co.**.

**Regent Pr.,** ( *0-916147; 1-889059; 1-58790* ) 6020-A Adeline St., Oakland, CA 94608 (SAN 294-9717) Tel 510-547-7602; Fax: 510-547-6357 Do not confuse with Regent Pr., Oxnard, CA
E-mail: regentpress@mindspring.com
Web site: http://www.regentpress.net
*Dist(s):* **AK Pr. Distribution**
**Baker & Taylor Bks.**
**Bookpeople**
**Quality Bks., Inc.**.

**Regnery Gateway, Incorporated** *See* **Regnery Publishing, Inc., An Eagle Publishing Co.**

†**Regnery Publishing, Inc., An Eagle Publishing Co.,** ( *0-89526* ) Subs. of Phillips Publishing International, One Massachusetts Ave., NW, Suite 600, Washington, DC 20001 (SAN 210-5578) Tel 202-216-0600; Fax: 202-216-0612; *Imprints:* Gateway Editions (Gateway Editions)
E-mail: info@regnery.com
Web site: http://www.regnery.com/
*Dist(s):* **Continental Bk. Co., Inc.**
**FaithWorks**
**National Bk. Network**; *CIP.*

**Reid, Carol A.** *See* **Believer's Ink**

---

For full information on wholesalers and distributors, refer to the Wholesaler and Distributor Name Index

**Reliance Pr.,** ( *0-9619639; 1-889683* ) 2201 Forest Cir., Norman, OK 73069-6420 (SAN 245-7172)
E-mail: bonny@oklahoma.net
*Dist(s):* **Baker & Taylor Bks.**
**Hervey's Booklink & Cookbook Warehouse**
**Quality Bks., Inc..**

**Remploy Pr. (CAN)** *Dist. by* **St Mut.**

**Renaissance Alliance Publishing, Inc.,** ( *0-9674196; 1-930928* ) PMB 238, 8691 Ninth Ave., Port Arthur, TX 77642-8025
E-mail: director@regalcrest.biz
Web site: http://www.rapbooks.biz
*Dist(s):* **Baker & Taylor Bks..**

**Renaissance Bks. Imprint of St. Martin's Pr.**

**Renaissance E Bks.,** ( *1-929670; 1-58873* ) Div. of Renaissance Enterprises, P.O. Box 494, Clemmons, NC 27012-0494
E-mail: ddyer1@triad.rr.com
Web site: http://www.renebooks.com.

**Renegade Bks.,** ( *0-9708929* ) 40 Middlefield St., Middletown, CT 06457-2394 Tel 860-347-1490
E-mail: thewindowpain01@hotmail.com
Web site: http://steveperry.tv.

**Replica Bks.,** ( *0-7351* ) Div. of Baker & Taylor, Orders Addr.: 1200 US Hwy., 22 E., Bridgewater, NJ 08807 Tel 908-541-7392; Fax: 908-541-7875; Toll Free: 800-775-1800; Edit Addr.: P.O. Box 6885, Bridgewater, NJ 08807-0885
E-mail: btinfo@baker-taylor.com.

†**Reprint Co.,** ( *0-87152* ) 611 Perrin Dr., P.O. Box 5401, Spartanburg, SC 29304 (SAN 203-3828) Tel 864-579-4433; *CIP.*

†**Reprint Services Corp.,** ( *0-7812; 0-932051* ) P.O. Box 890820, Temecula, CA 92589-0820 (SAN 686-2640) Tel 909-296-3388; Fax: 909-767-0133; Toll Free: 800-273-6635
Web site: http://www.reprintservices.com; *CIP.*

**Research Triangle Publishing,** ( *1-884570* ) Orders Addr.: P.O. Box 1130, Fuquay Varina, NC 27526 Fax: 919-557-2161; Toll Free: 800-941-0020; Edit Addr.: 503 N. Ennis St., Fuquay Varina, NC 27526
E-mail: info@tripub.com
Web site: http://www.RTPWeb.com/BooksExpress.

**Reveille Bks. Imprint of Texas A&M Univ. Pr.**

**Revelation I Publishing,** ( *1-890795* ) P.O. Box 3, Antlers, OK 74523 Tel 405-298-6222.

†**Revell, Fleming H. Co.,** ( *0-8007; 0-922066; 1-58743* ) Div. of Baker Bk. Hse., Orders Addr.: P.O. Box 6287, Grand Rapids, MI 49516-6287 Toll Free Fax: 800-398-3111; Toll Free: 800-877-2665; Edit Addr.: 6030 E. Fulton, Ada, MI 49301 Tel 616-676-9185; Fax: 616-676-9573; *Imprints:* Spire (Spire)
E-mail: sharlow@bakerbooks.com
Web site: http://www.bakerbooks.com
*Dist(s):* **Baker Bk. Hse., Inc.;** *CIP.*

†**Review & Herald Publishing Assn.,** ( *0-8127; 0-8280* ) 55 W. Oak Ridge Dr., Hagerstown, MD 21740 (SAN 203-3798) Tel 301-393-3000
E-mail: Information@rhpa.org
Web site: http://www.reviewandherald.com/
*Dist(s):* **Spring Arbor Distributors, Inc.;** *CIP.*

**Revive Publishing,** ( *0-9654299* ) 4012 Neptune Dr., Oklahoma City, OK 73116-1658 Toll Free: 800-541-0558 Do not confuse with Revive Publishing, Capitol Heights, MD
E-mail: revivepublishing.com
Web site:
http://www.geocities.com/Athens/Acropolis/5685/main.htm
*Dist(s):* **Baker & Taylor Bks..**

**Reynolds & Hearn (GBR)** ( *1-903111* ) *Dist. by* **Trafalgar.**

**RH Audio Imprint of Random Hse. Audio Publishing Group**

**RH Audio Price-Less Imprint of Random Hse. Audio Publishing Group**

**Rharl Publishing Group,** ( *0-9656661* ) 16161 Ventura Blvd., No. 550, Encino, CA 91436 Tel 818-990-5254; Fax: 818-990-5078
E-mail: RharlPub@aol
*Dist(s):* **Biblio Distribution.**

**Rhiannon Pubns.,** ( *1-890538* ) P.O. Box 1191, Newport, KY 41071 Tel 606-491-0158
Web site: http://www.rhiannonbook.com.

**Rhino Entertainment,** ( *0-7379; 0-930589; 1-56826* ) 10635 Santa Monica Blvd., Los Angeles, CA 90025-4900 (SAN 677-5454) Tel 310-474-4778; 888-622-9647; Fax: 310-441-6575
Web site: http://www.rhino.com.

**Rhinoceros Imprint of Masquerade Bks., Inc.**

**Rhwymbooks,** ( *1-889298* ) P.O. Box 1706, Cambridge, MA 02238-1706 Tel 617-623-5894 (phone/fax)
E-mail: post@rhwymbooks.com
Web site: http://www.rhwymbooks.com.

**Rialp, Ediciones, S.A. (ESP)** ( *84-320; 84-321* ) *Dist. by* **Continental Bk.**

**Ribbon Ridge Pr.,** ( *0-9630986* ) Div. of Dewey Kelly & Assocs., 4021 SW Comus St., Portland, OR 97219 Tel 503-244-6203.

†**Rice Univ. Pr.,** ( *0-89263; 0-911216* ) Rice Univ., P.O. Box 1892, Houston, TX 77251 (SAN 204-689X) Tel 713-285-5147
*Dist(s):* **Texas A&M Univ. Pr.;** *CIP.*

**Richelieu Court Pubns., Inc.,** ( *0-911519* ) P.O. Box 13264, Albany, NY 12212-3264 (SAN 264-3480) Tel 518-449-2073; Fax: 518-449-3284
*Dist(s):* **Baker & Taylor Bks..**

†**Ridgeway Pr.,** ( *1-56439* ) P.O. Box 120, Roseville, MI 48066 Tel 313-577-7713; Fax: 810-294-0474 Do not confuse with companies with the same name in Los Alamitos, CA, Dayton, OH
E-mail: mlliebler@aol.com
*Dist(s):* **Baker & Taylor Bks.**
**Partners Pubns. Group, Inc.;** *CIP.*

†**Rienner, Lynne Pubs., Inc.,** ( *0-89410; 0-931477; 1-55587; 1-58826* ) 1800 30th St., Suite 314, Boulder, CO 80301-1026 (SAN 683-1869) Tel 303-444-6684; Fax: 303-444-0824; *Imprints:* Three Continents (Three Contnts)
E-mail: sglover@rienner.com; questions@rienner.com; cservice@rienner.com
Web site: http://www.rienner.com
*Dist(s):* **Women Ink;** *CIP.*

**Rinard Publishing,** ( *0-9624012* ) Orders Addr.: P.O. Box 821248, Houston, TX 77282-1248; Edit Addr.: 3554 Ashfield Dr., Houston, TX 77082 Tel 281-531-0566; Fax: 281-531-9049
Web site: http://www.rinard.com
*Dist(s):* **Replica Bks..**

**Rinehart, Roberts Int.,** ( *0-911797; 1-57098; 1-879373; 1-58979* ) 4501 Forbes Blvd., Suite 200, Lanham, MD 20706 Tel 301-459-3366; Fax: 301-429-5747; Toll Free Fax: 800-338-4550; Toll Free: 800-462-6420
*Dist(s):* **National Bk. Network**
**netLibrary, Inc..**

**Rinehart, Roberts International Imprint of Rinehart, Roberts Pubs.**

**Rinehart, Roberts Pubs.,** ( *0-911797; 0-943173; 1-57098; 1-57140; 1-879373; 1-58979* ) Orders Addr.: 4720 Boston Way, Lanhan, MD 20706 Tel 301-459-3366; Toll Free Fax: 800-238-4650; Toll Free: 800-462-6420; Edit Addr.: c/o Rowman & Littlefield Publishing Group, 5360 Manhattan Cir., No. 101, Boulder, CO 80303 (SAN 264-3510) Tel 303-543-7835; *Imprints:* Rinehart, Roberts International (R Rinehart Intl)
E-mail: books@robertsrinehart.com
Web site: http://www.robertsrinehart.com
*Dist(s):* **National Bk. Network**
**Rowman & Littlefield Pubns., Inc.**
**netLibrary, Inc..**

**Rising Tide Pr.,** ( *0-9628938; 1-883061* ) P.O. Box 30457, Tucson, AZ 85751 (SAN 298-3885) Tel 520-888-1140; Fax: 520-888-1123 Do not confuse with Rising Tide Pr. in Santa Fe, NM
E-mail: milestonepress@earthlink.net
Web site: http://www.risingtidepress.com
*Dist(s):* **Alamo Square Distributors**
**Baker & Taylor Bks.**
**BookWorld Services, Inc.**
**Bookpeople**
**Koen Bk. Distributors.**

**River Bend Pr., Inc.,** ( *0-9679875* ) Orders Addr.: P.O. Box 296, Calvin, OK 74531-0296 Tel 405-645-2311 (phone/fax); Edit Addr.: 304 S. Elder, Calvin, OK 74531-0296 Do not confuse with River Bend Press in Naperville, IL
E-mail: CelestaFurgerson@aol.com.

**River Boat Bks.,** ( *0-9654756* ) P.O. Box 65314, Saint Paul, MN 55165-0314 Tel 651-690-5013; Fax: 651-224-3567
*Dist(s):* **Bookmen, Inc..**

**River City Publishing,** ( *0-913515; 0-9622815; 1-57966; 1-880216; 1-881320* ) 1719 Mulberry St., Montgomery, AL 36106 (SAN 631-4910) Tel 334-265-6753; Fax: 334-265-8880; Toll Free: 877-408-7078; *Imprints:* Black Belt Press (Black Belt) Do not confuse with companies with the same or similar names in Richland, WA, South Bend, IN
E-mail: sales@rivercitypublishing.com
Web site: http://www.rivercitypublishing.com.

**River Road Pubns., Inc.,** ( *0-938682* ) 830 E. Savidge St., Spring Lake, MI 49456 (SAN 253-8172) Tel 616-842-6920; Fax: 616-842-0084; Toll Free: 800-373-8762
E-mail: socialstudies@riverroadpublications.com
Web site: http://www.riverroadpublications.com
*Dist(s):* **Partners Pubns. Group, Inc.**

**Rivercity Pr. Imprint of Amereon, Ltd.**

†**Rivercross Publishing, Inc.,** ( *0-944957; 1-58141* ) 6214 Wynfield Ct., Orlando, FL 32819 (SAN 245-6826) Tel 407-876-7720; Fax: 407-876-7758; Toll Free: 800-451-4522
E-mail: editor@rivercross.com
Web site: http://www.rivercross.com; *CIP.*

**Riverdale Electronic Bks.,** ( *0-9712207; 1-932606* ) P.O. Box 962085, Riverdale, GA 30296
E-mail: kzrider@mindspring.com; jtm@riverdalebooks.com
Web site: http://www.riverdaleebooks.com.

**Riverhead Bks. (Hardcovers) Imprint of Putnam Publishing Group, The**

**Riverhead Bks. (Hardcovers) Imprint of Penguin Group (USA) Inc.**

**Riverhead Trade (Paperbacks) Imprint of Berkley Publishing Group**

**RiverOak Publishing,** ( *1-58919* ) Div. of Honor Bks., 2448 E. 81st St., Suite 4400, Tulsa, OK 74137-4322 Toll Free Fax: 877-663-1241; Toll Free: 800-493-2813
*Dist(s):* **Cook Communications Ministries.**

**Riverrun Pr., Inc.,** ( *0-7145; 0-86676* ) Affil. of Calder Pubns., 1200 Cty. Rd., Rte. 523, Flemington, NJ 08822 (SAN 240-9917) Tel 908-788-5753 Do not confuse with companies with same name in San Francisco, CA, Piermont, CA, Pepper Pike, OH
E-mail: wcbooks@aol.com;
info@calderpublications.com
Web site: http://www.calderpublications.com
*Dist(s):* **SPD-Small Pr. Distribution**
**Whitehurst & Clark.**

**Riverside Editions Imprint of Houghton Mifflin Co.**

**Riverview Publishing,** ( *0-9635160* ) Orders Addr.: P.O. Box 750308, Forest Hills, NY 11375-0308; Edit Addr.: 110-45 Queens Blvd., Suite 205, Forest Hills, NY 11375-5519 Tel 718-268-1821 Do not confuse with Riverview Pub. in Chattanooga, TN
*Dist(s):* **Baker & Taylor Bks.**
**Cokesbury.**

†**Rivilo Bks.,** ( *0-9630731* ) 7307 Pinewood St., Falls Church, VA 22046 Tel 843-757-7022; Fax: 843-757-7033
*Dist(s):* **Baker & Taylor Bks.**
**Raintree Pubs.**
**Solafide Bk.;** *CIP.*

†**Rizzoli International Pubns., Inc.,** ( *0-8478* ) Subs. of RCS Rizzoli Editore Corp., 300 Park Ave., S., 3rd Flr., New York, NY 10010 (SAN 111-9192) Tel 212-387-3400; Fax: 212-387-3535
*Dist(s):* **Distributed Art Pubs./D.A.P.**
**St. Martin's Pr.;** *CIP.*

**Roberts, Sherry,** 1305 Valleymede Rd., Greensboro, NC 27410-4745 Tel 910-292-1150; Fax: 910-632-9488.

**ROC Imprint of NAL**

**Rock Spring Collection Imprint of Stone Bridge Pr.**

†**Rodale Pr., Inc.,** ( *0-87596; 0-87857; 1-57954; 1-59486* ) Orders Addr.: 16365 James Madison Hwy., Gordonsville, VA 22942-8501 Toll Free Fax: 800-672-2054; Toll Free: 888-330-8471; Edit Addr.: 33 E. Minor St., Emmaus, PA 18098-0099 (SAN 200-2477) Tel 610-967-5171; Fax: 215-967-8963; Toll Free: 800-222-4997
E-mail: info@rodale.com
Web site: http://www.rodalepress.com
*Dist(s):* **Bilingual Pubns. Co., The**
**FaithWorks**
**Penguin Group (USA) Inc.**
**St. Martin's Pr.;** *CIP.*

**Rodgers & Nelsen Publishing Company** *See* **Loveland Pr.**

**Roles, Joe B.,** ( *0-615* ) 7450 Adams Park Ct., Annandale, VA 22003 Tel 703-304-6100; Fax: 703-914-2087
E-mail: joeroles@aol.com.

**Rolf, Gerald,** ( *0-9661836* ) 8610 N. New Braunfels, Suite 207, San Antonio, TX 78217 Tel 210-824-6032; Fax: 210-822-3441
E-mail: arolf91437@aol.com
Web site:
http://members.aol.com/arolf91437/event.htm
*Dist(s):* **Hervey's Booklink & Cookbook Warehouse.**

**Romance Alive Audio,** ( *1-57096* ) 1126 Pittsfield Ln., Ventura, CA 93001-3868.

**Names**

**Roscoe Village Foundation, Inc.,** ( *1-880443* ) 381 Hill St., Coshocton, OH 43812 Tel 614-622-7644; Fax: 614-622-2222.

**Rose International Publishing Hse., Inc.,** ( *1-930574* ) 3580 W. Hwy 44, Inverness, FL 34453 Tel 352-637-7237
E-mail: publisher@ladyliterature.com
Web site: http://www.roseinternational-graphicartsdesignpublishing.com; http://www.ladyliterature-films.com.

†**Rosen Publishing Group, Inc., The,** ( *0-8239; 1-4042* ) a/o Dept. C234561, 29 E. 21st St., New York, NY 10010 (SAN 203-3720) Tel 212-777-3017; Fax: 212-777-0277; Toll Free: 800-237-9932
E-mail: ginas@rosenpub.com
Web site: http://www.rosenpublishing.com
*Dist(s):* **Lectorum Pubns., Inc.; CIP.**

**RosettaBooks,** ( *0-7953* ) 845 Third Ave., 15th Flr., New York, NY 10022 Tel 212-751-4545; Fax: 212-755-2972
E-mail: ldwyer@rosettabooks.com
Web site: http://rosettabooks.com
*Dist(s):* **netLibrary, Inc..**

**Ross & Perry, Inc.,** ( *1-931641; 1-931839; 1-932080; 1-932109* ) 216 G St., NE, Washington, DC 20002 (SAN 253-8555) Tel 202-675-8300; Fax: 202-675-8400
E-mail: jstevenson@rossperry.com
Web site: http://www.rossperry.com; http://www.gporeprints.com
*Dist(s):* **Baker & Taylor Bks..**

†**Rossel Bks.,** ( *0-940646* ) Div. of R. C. C., Inc., 1228 Hardscrabble Rd., Chappaqua, NY 10514 Tel 914-238-3852; Toll Free: 800-221-2755 (orders only)
E-mail: srossel@rossel.net
Web site: http://www.rossel.net
*Dist(s):* **Behrman Hse., Inc.; CIP.**

**Roth Publishing, Inc.,** ( *0-8486; 0-89609* ) Orders Addr.: P.O. Box 406, Great Neck, NY 11022 (SAN 241-7073) Toll Free: 800-899-7684; Edit Addr.: 175 Great Neck Rd., Great Neck, NY 11021 (SAN 210-9735) Tel 516-466-3676; Fax: 516-829-7746
E-mail: rothpub@aol.com
Web site: http://www.rothpoem.com.

**Rough Guides Imprint of Viking Penguin**

**Round Barn Pr.,** ( *0-9716852* ) 18122 Cashell Rd., Rockville, MD 20853 Tel 301-924-5471
E-mail: behyb@folklife.si.edu.

**Roundhouse Pr., The Imprint of Heyday Bks.**

**Rourke Publishing, LLC,** ( *0-86592; 0-86593; 0-86625; 1-55916; 1-57103; 1-58952; 1-59515* ) Orders Addr.: P.O. Box 3328, Vero Beach, FL 32963 Tel 561-234-6001; Fax: 561-234-6622; Toll Free: 800-394-7055
E-mail: rourke@rourkepublishing.com
Web site: http://www.rourkepublishing.com.

**Route 66 Publishing, Ltd.,** ( *0-9644293* ) Orders Addr.: P.O. Box 25222, Albuquerque, NM 87125-5222 Tel 505-266-6128; Fax: 505-341-2608; Toll Free: 800-687-2665
E-mail: bren&ric@aol.com.

†**Routledge,** ( *0-04; 0-413; 0-415; 0-7100; 0-86861; 0-87830* ) Mem. of Taylor & Frances Group, Orders Addr.: 7625 Empire Dr., Florence, KY 41042 Toll Free Fax: 800-248-4724 (orders, customer serv.); Toll Free: 800-634-7064 (orders, customer serv.); Edit Addr.: 29 W. 35th St., New York, NY 10001-2299 (SAN 213-196X) Tel 212-216-7800; Fax: 212-564-7854
E-mail: info@routledge-ny.com; cserve@routledge-ny.com
Web site: http://www.routledge-ny.com
*Dist(s):* **Taylor & Francis, Inc.**
 **Women Ink**
 **netLibrary, Inc.; CIP.**

**Rowdy Hse. Publishing,** ( *0-9675215* ) P.O. Box 251293, Los Angeles, CA 90025
E-mail: kanesusan@aol.com.

†**Rowman & Littlefield Pubns., Inc.,** ( *0-8476; 0-87471; 0-7425* ) Div. of University Press of America, P.O. Box 191, Blue Ridge Summit, PA 17214-0191 Tel 717-794-3800; Fax: 717-794-3801; Orders Addr.: 15200 NBN Way, Blue Ridge Summit, PA 17214 Tel 717-794-3800; Fax: 717-794-3803; Toll Free Fax: 800-338-4550; Toll Free: 800-462-6420; 67 Mowat Ave., Suite 241, Toronto, ON M6K 3E3 Tel 416-534-1660; Fax: 416-534-3699; Edit Addr.: 4501 Forbes Blvd., Suite 200, Lanham, MD 20706 (SAN 203-3704) Tel 301-459-3366; Fax: 301-429-5747
E-mail: Rogers@univpress.com
Web site: http://www.rowmanlittlefield.com
*Dist(s):* **National Bk. Network**
 **University Publishing Assocs., Inc.; CIP.**

**Royal Fireworks Publishing Co.,** ( *0-88092; 0-89824* ) Orders Addr.: P.O. Box 399, Unionville, NY 10988 (SAN 240-2394) Tel 845-726-4444; Fax: 845-726-3824; Edit Addr.: 1 First Ave., Unionville, NY 10988
E-mail: rfpress@frontiernet.net
*Dist(s):* **Baker & Taylor Bks..**

**Royal Rags Publishing,** ( *0-9636170; 1-886704* ) Orders Addr.: P.O. Box 594, Emigrant, MT 59027 (SAN 297-8784) Tel 406-333-4296; Toll Free: 888-518-6100; Edit Addr.: 65 Capricorn Dr., Emigrant, MT 59027.

**RST Indiaink Publishing (IND)** ( *81-86939* ) *Dist. by* **S Asia.**

**Rubicon Media,** ( *0-9663454* ) Orders Addr.: P.O. Box 1823, New York, NY 10101 Tel 212-977-3175; Fax: 212-956-1360
*Dist(s):* **Bookazine Co., Inc..**

**Rubicon Pr., The (GBR)** ( *0-948695* ) *Dist. by* **David Brown.**

**Rubin, Ken Company, The** *See* **Mesa Vista Pr.**

**Ruder Finn Pr.,** ( *0-9640952; 0-9720119; 1-932646* ) Div. of Ruder Finn Group, Inc., The, c/o Ruder Finn, Inc., 301 E. 57th St., New York, NY 10022 Tel 212-583-2709; Fax: 212-715-1681
E-mail: finnd@ruderfinn.com; slacks@ruderfinn.com
*Dist(s):* **National Bk. Network.**

**Rue Morgue Pr.,** ( *0-915230* ) Orders Addr.: P.O. Box 4119, Boulder, CO 80304; Edit Addr.: 305 Hawthorn Ave., Boulder, CO 80304 (SAN 207-737X) Tel 303-443-5757; Fax: 303-443-4010; Toll Free: 800-699-6214
E-mail: Tomenid@attbi.com.

**Rugged Land,** ( *1-59071* ) Orders Addr.: 16365 James Madison Hwy., Gordonsville, VA 22942-8501 Toll Free Fax: 800-672-2054; Toll Free: 888-330-8477; Edit Addr.: 276 Canal St., 5th Flr., New York, NY 10013 Tel 212-334-8228; Fax: 212-334-5749
Web site: http://www.ruggedland.com
*Dist(s):* **St. Martin's Pr..**

**Ruminator Bks.,** ( *1-886913* ) Orders Addr.: Consortium Book Sales & Distribution, 1045 Westgate Dr. Suite 90, Saint Paul, MN 55114-1065 Tel 651-221-9035; Fax: 651-221-0124; Toll Free: 800-283-3572; Edit Addr.: 1648 Grand Ave., Saint Paul, MN 55105 Tel 651-699-7038; 651-699-0587; Fax: 651-699-7190
E-mail: books@ruminator.com; info.ruminator.com
Web site: http://www.ruminator.com
*Dist(s):* **Consortium Bk. Sales & Distribution**
 **Irish Bks. & Media, Inc..**

**Rune-Tales Imprint of Quincannon Publishing Group**

†**Running Pr. Bk. Pubs.,** ( *0-7624; 0-89471; 0-914294; 1-56138* ) Div. of Perseus Books Group, 125 S. 22nd St., Philadelphia, PA 19103-4399 (SAN 204-5702) Tel 215-567-5080; Fax: 215-568-2919; Toll Free Fax: 800-453-2884; Toll Free: 800-345-5359 customer service; *Imprints:* Courage Books (Courage)
E-mail: support@runningpress.com
Web site: http://www.runningpress.com
*Dist(s):* **HarperCollins Pubns.; CIP.**

**Ruroanik Pubs.,** ( *1-889361* ) Orders Addr.: P.O. Box 122605, San Diego, CA 92112 Tel 858-646-7637 (phone/fax); Toll Free: 800-484-3670 (Code 3057); Edit Addr.: 4360 Campus Ave., Suite 17, San Diego, CA 92101; 5075 Shoreham Pl., Suite 200, San Diego, CA 92122
E-mail: ruroanik@aol.com
Web site: http://www.ruroanikpublisher.com.

**Russell Dean & Co.,** ( *1-891954* ) Orders Addr.: P.O. Box 318, Santa Margarita, CA 93453 Tel 805-438-4115; Fax: 805-438-3745; Toll Free: 888-438-4115; Edit Addr.: 22595 K St., Santa Margarita, CA 93453; *Imprints:* Four Ravens (Four Ravens)
E-mail: russelldean@sgmp
Web site: http://www.sgmp.com/ntr/russelldean.

**Russian Hill Pr.,** ( *0-9653524; 1-891488* ) 1510 Guerrero St., San Francisco, CA 94110-4327 Tel 415-487-0480 ; Fax: 415-487-0290
E-mail: editors@russianhill.com
Web site: http://www.russianhill.com.

†**Rutgers Univ. Pr.,** ( *0-8135* ) 100 Joyce Kilmer Ave., Piscataway, NJ 08854-8099 (SAN 253-2115) Tel 732-445-7762; Fax: 732-445-7039; Toll Free Fax: 888-471-9014; Toll Free: 800-446-9323 (orders)
Web site: http://rutgerspress.rutgers.edu; *CIP.*

**Rutherford Pr.,** ( *0-9660582* ) 12423 Country Club Dr., Charlevoix, MI 49720 Tel 231-547-3851
E-mail: TWalker@Freeway.net
*Dist(s):* **Partners Bk. Distributing, Inc..**

**Rutledge Hill Pr.,** ( *0-934395; 1-55853; 1-4016* ) 501 Nelson Pl., Nashville, TN 37214 Tel 615-889-9000; 615-244-2700; Toll Free: 800-251-4000
E-mail: NelsonDirect@ThomasNelson.com
Web site: http://www.rutledgehillpress.com.

**Ruwanga Trading,** ( *0-9615102; 0-9701528* ) P.O. Box 1027, Puunene, HI 96784 (SAN 694-2776)
*Dist(s):* **Booklines Hawaii, Ltd..**

**Rx Ranch Enterprises,** ( *0-9679959* ) 2609 E. Fruitport Rd., Spring Lake, MI 49456 Tel 231-865-6798
E-mail: jcumming32@aol.com.

**Ryter, A. E.** *See* **Hunt, Paul**

**SAL Productions,** ( *0-9665404* ) 5902 Monterey Rd., No. 209, Los Angeles, CA 90042-4943 Tel 213-258-4656
E-mail: sproduction@aol.com.

**SCW Pubns.,** ( *1-877882* ) 1011 Boren Ave., Suite 155, Seattle, WA 98104 Tel 206-682-1268
E-mail: info@poetswest.com
Web site: http://www.poetswest.com
*Dist(s):* **Partners/West.**

**SMS Cos., Inc.,** ( *0-9669595* ) P.O. Box 1184, Smyrna, GA 30081 Tel 770-384-0668; Fax: 770-384-1537; *Imprints:* S M S Marketing & Publishing (SMS Mrktg)
E-mail: JMBryant@bellsouth.net
Web site: http://www.smsbooks.com; http://www.singlemanscreaming.com
*Dist(s):* **Follett Library Resources.**

**S M S Marketing & Publishing Imprint of SMS Cos., Inc.**

**SPD-Small Pr. Distribution,** ( *0-914068* ) 1341 Seventh St., Berkeley, CA 94710-1409 (SAN 204-5826) Tel 510-524-1668; Fax: 510-524-0852; Toll Free: 800-869-7553 (orders)
E-mail: orders@spdbooks.org
Web site: http://www.spdbooks.org.

**SPI Bks.,** ( *0-944007; 1-56171* ) 99 Spring St., 3rd Flr., New York, NY 10012 Tel 212-431-5011; Fax: 212-431-8646
E-mail: ian@spibooks.com
Web site: http://www.spibooks.com
*Dist(s):* **APG Sales and Fulfillment Weatherhill, Inc..**

**sa martin assocs.,** ( *0-9726510* ) 411 Pulpit Rock Rd., Cape Elizabeth, ME 04107 Tel 207-767-1995 (phone/fax); Toll Free: 888-406-3526
E-mail: www.samartin@mainerr.com
Web site: http://www.sallyfmartin.com.

**Sabre Pr. Imprint of Momentum Bks., LLC**

**Saddleback Publishing, Inc.,** ( *1-56254* ) Three Watson, Irvine, CA 92618-2716 Tel 949-860-2500; Fax: 949-860-2508; Toll Free: 800-637-8715
E-mail: info@sdlback.com
Web site: http://www.sdlback.com.

**Sadorian Pubns.,** ( *0-9700102; 0-9718148; 0-9741714* ) P.O. Box 2443, Durham, NC 27715 (SAN 253-7834) Fax: 208-988-8455; Toll Free: 866-723-6742
E-mail: sadroianllc@aol.com; sadorianllc@aol.com
Web site: http://www.sadorian.com
*Dist(s):* **Baker & Taylor Bks..**

**Safe Harbor Bks.,** ( *0-9665798* ) Orders Addr.: P.O. Box 2568, New London, NH 03257 Tel 603-526-4874; Fax: 603-525-3452; Edit Addr.: 101 Main St., New London, NH 03257
E-mail: safeharbor@cedarville.net
*Dist(s):* **Enfield Publishing & Distribution Co., Inc..**

†**Sage Pubns., Inc.,** ( *0-7619; 0-8039; 1-4129* ) 2455 Teller Rd., Thousand Oaks, CA 91320-2218 (SAN 204-7217) Tel 805-499-9774; 800-818-7243; Fax: 800-583-2665; 805-499-0871
E-mail: info@sagepub.com
Web site: http://www.sagepub.com
*Dist(s):* **Baker & Taylor Bks.**
 **Red Toad Road Co.**
 **Yankee Bk. Peddler, Inc.; CIP.**

**Sagebrush Large Print Westerns Imprint of Beeler, Thomas T. Publisher**

**Sagebrush Large Print Westerns,** ( *1-57490* ) .

**Sahara Publishing,** ( *0-9639497* ) 4151 Beltline Rd., Suite 124-188, Dallas, TX 75244 Tel 972-380-5716; Fax: 972-458-2644 Do not confuse with Sahara Publishing in Wilmington, DE.

**Saifer, Albert Pub.,** ( *0-87556* ) P.O. Box 7125, Watchung, NJ 07060 (SAN 204-7225).

**St. Aztec Publishing,** ( *0-9705259* ) P.O. Box 711528, Santee, CA 92072-1528 (SAN 253-5297) Tel 619-562-5932 (phone/fax); Toll Free Fax: 888-574-8426
E-mail: staztec@home.com
*Dist(s):* **BookWorld Services, Inc..**

Names

**St. Barthelemey Pr., Ltd.,** ( *1-887617* ) 2971 Flowers Rd., S., Suite 100, Atlanta, GA 30341 Tel 770-451-1922; Fax: 770-457-9808; Toll Free: 800-451-1923
E-mail: fullerws@aol.com
Web site: http://www.stbarthelemypress.com
*Dist(s):* **Biblio Distribution.**

†**St. Bede's Pubns.,** ( *0-932506; 1-879007* ) Orders Addr.: P.O. Box 9345, Framingham, MA 01701-9345 Fax: 419-281-6883; Toll Free: 800-247-6553; Edit Addr.: 271 N. Main St., Petersham, MA 01366-0606
*Dist(s):* **Fordham Univ. Pr.**
**Spring Arbor Distributors, Inc.;** *CIP.*

**St. Clair Pr.,** ( *0-9632357* ) Div. of Little Stirrup Cay, Ltd., Saint Clair Ave., Beverly Shores, IN 46301-0527 Tel 219-874-5139; Fax: 219-872-8437.

**St. Expedite Pr.,** ( *0-9652052* ) 4017 Swanee St., Lake Charles, LA 70607 (SAN 299-0326) Tel 318-477-6313
E-mail: fgf01@gnofn.org
*Dist(s):* **Forest Sales & Distributing Co..**

**St. Jude Media,** ( *0-9646316* ) Div. of the Mary Foundation, P.O. Box 26120, Fairview Park, OH 44126 Tel 440-333-4723; Fax: 440-333-8550.

**Saint Martin's Griffin Imprint of St. Martin's Pr.**

**Saint Martin's Minotaur Imprint of St. Martin's Pr.**

**St. Mary's Pr.,** ( *0-88489* ) 702 Terrace Heights, Winona, MN 55987-1320 (SAN 203-073X) Tel 507-457-7900; Toll Free Fax: 800-344-9225; Toll Free: 800-533-8095
E-mail: smpress@smp.org
Web site: http://www.smp.org.

**Saint Paul Books & Media** *See* **Pauline Bks. & Media**

**SakonnetPr., Inc.,** ( *0-9709333* ) 541 W. Main Rd., Little Compton, RI 02837 Tel 401-635-4908
E-mail: mallace1@aol.com
Web site: http://www.sakonnetpress.com.

**Salmon Publishing (IRL)** ( *0-948339; 1-897648; 1-903392* ) *Dist. by* Dufour.

**Salt Marsh Pubns.,** ( *1-929202* ) 163 Grand Oak Cir., Venice, FL 34292 Tel 941-484-9953; Toll Free: 888-441-2436
E-mail: smp@coastalnet.com
*Dist(s):* **Baker & Taylor Bks.**
**Parnassus Bk. Distributors**
**Southern Bk. Service.**

**Salt Pr. Imprint of Cedar Fort, Inc./CFI Distribution**

**Salvo Pr.,** ( *0-9664520; 1-930486* ) Orders Addr.: 61428 Elder Ridge St., Bend, OR 97702
E-mail: schmidt@salvopress.com
Web site: http://www.salvopress.com
*Dist(s):* **Baker & Taylor Bks..**

**Samaritan Pr.,** ( *1-881379* ) 8516 Baron Dr., Knoxville, TN 37923-1747.

**Sams,** ( *0-672; 0-8104* ) Div. of Pearson Technology Group, 201 W. 103rd St., Indianapolis, IN 46290-1097 Tel 317-581-3500; Toll Free Fax: 800-882-8583; Toll Free: 800-428-5331 (orders)
Web site: http://www.samspublishing.com
*Dist(s):* **Alpha Bks.**
**Pearson Education**
**Sams Technical Publishing, LLC.**

†**San Diego State Univ. Pr.,** ( *0-916304; 1-879691* ) 5500 Campanile Dr., San Diego, CA 92182-8141 (SAN 202-0637) Tel 619-594-6220
E-mail: sheila.d@sdsu.edu; *CIP.*

**Sanctuary Bks.,** ( *1-57988* ) P.O. Box 270575, Nashville, TN 37227-0575 Tel 615-871-0097; Fax: 615-843-1179; Toll Free: 888-758-7646
*Dist(s):* **BookWorld Services, Inc..**

**Sanders, J. S. & Co., Inc. Imprint of Dee, Ivan R. Pub.**

†**Sandlapper Publishing Co., Inc.,** ( *0-87844* ) Orders Addr.: P.O. Box 730, Orangeburg, SC 29115 (SAN 203-2678) Toll Free Fax: 800-337-9420 (orders); Toll Free: 800-849-7263 (orders); Edit Addr.: 1281 Amelia St., NE., Orangeburg, SC 29116 Tel 803-533-1658; Fax: 803-534-5223
*Dist(s):* **Baker & Taylor Bks.**
**Parnassus Bk. Distributors;** *CIP.*

**SANDS Publishing, LLC,** ( *1-59025* ) Orders Addr.: P.O. Box 92, Alpine, CA 90913 Tel 619-445-4105; 760-591-9277 (Invoice & PO information); Fax: 619-445-6017; Edit Addr.: 2121 Star Ln., Alpine, CA 91901
E-mail: ssnetbookbiz@aol.com
Web site: http://www.sandspublishing.com
*Dist(s):* **Baker & Taylor Bks.**
**Brodart Co.**
**Todd Communications.**

**Sandstone Bks. Imprint of Ohio State Univ. Pr.**

**Santa Monica Pr.,** ( *0-9639946; 1-891661* ) P.O. Box 1076, Santa Monica, CA 90406-1076 (SAN 298-1459) Tel 310-230-7759; Fax: 310-230-7761; Toll Free: 800-784-9553; *Imprints:* Offbeat Press (Offbeat)
E-mail: books@santamonicapress.com
Web site: http://www.santamonicapress.com
*Dist(s):* **Baker & Taylor Bks.**
**Independent Pubs. Group**
**Quality Bks., Inc..**

**Santillana USA Publishing Co., Inc.,** ( *0-88272; 1-56014; 1-58105; 84-294; 1-58986; 1-59437* ) Div. of Grup Santillana De Ediciones, S.A., 2105 NW 86th Ave., Miami, FL 33122 (SAN 205-1133) Tel 305-591-9522; Fax: 305-591-9145; Toll Free Fax: 800-530-8099 (orders); Toll Free: 800-245-8584
E-mail: customerservice@santillanausa.com
Web site: http://www.santillanausa.com/
*Dist(s):* **Baker & Taylor Bks.**
**Barnes & Noble, Inc.**
**Bilingual Pubns. Co., The**
**Continental Bk. Co., Inc.**
**Follett Library Resources**
**Lectorum Pubns., Inc.**
**Libros Sin Fronteras.**

**Sarabande Bks., Inc.,** ( *0-9641151; 1-889330; 1-932511* ) 2234 Dundee Rd., Suite 200, Louisville, KY 40205 Tel 502-458-4028; Fax: 502-458-4065
E-mail: sarabandek@aol.com
Web site: http://www.sarabandebooks.org
*Dist(s):* **Consortium Bk. Sales & Distribution.**

**Sarff, Extry R.,** ( *0-9662515* ) Orders Addr.: P.O. Box WWP, Ketchikan, AK 99950-0280 Tel 907-846-5311.

**Saroff, Raymond Pub.,** ( *1-878352* ) Acorn Hill Rd., Box 461, Olive Bridge, NY 12461 Tel 914-657-7023; Toll Free: 800-613-8219
*Dist(s):* **McPherson & Co..**

**Sattre Pr.,** ( *0-9718305* ) 2962 Middle Sattre Rd., Decorah, IA 52101-7644
E-mail: info@sattre-press.com; wmcclain@salamander.com
Web site: http://www.sattre-press.com/.

**Savvy Pr.,** ( *0-9669877* ) Orders Addr.: 473 17th St., No. 6, Brooklyn, NY 11215-6226 Tel 718-965-3756; Fax: 443-238-0770; 413-294-7541
E-mail: info@gowanusbooks.com; info@savvypress.com
Web site: http://www.gowanusbooks.com; http://www.savvypress.com.

**Saybrook Publishing Co., Inc.,** ( *0-933071* ) 5307 McCommas Blvd., Dallas, TX 75206 (SAN 689-7924) Tel 214-823-4388; Fax: 214-528-6532
E-mail: saybrookpub@aol.com
*Dist(s):* **Norton, W. W. & Co., Inc..**

**Scala Hse. Pubs., LLC,** ( *0-9720287* ) P.O. Box 17964, Seattle, WA 98107 Tel 206-706-7597
E-mail: tamara@scalahousepress.com
Web site: http://www.scalahousepress.com
*Dist(s):* **Biblio Distribution.**

**Scam.com:SoCo Arts & Media** *See* **Daedalus Howell Co.**

**Scarborough Hse. Imprint of Madison Bks., Inc.**

†**Scarecrow Pr., Inc.,** ( *0-8108; 1-57886* ) Div. of Rowman & Littlefield Publishing Group, Orders Addr.: 15200 NBN Way, Box 191, Blue Ridge Summit, PA 17214 Tel 717-794-3800; Fax: 717-794-3803; Toll Free Fax: 800-338-4550; Toll Free: 800-462-6420; Edit Addr.: 4501 Forbes Blvd., Suite 200, Lanham, MD 20706-4310 (SAN 203-2651) Tel 301-459-3366; Fax: 301-429-5747
E-mail: custserv@rowman.com
Web site: http://www.scarecrowpress.com
*Dist(s):* **Rowman & Littlefield Pubs., Inc.;** *CIP.*

**SCB Distributors,** 15608 S. New Century Dr., Gardena, CA 90248-2129 (SAN 630-4818) Tel 310-532-9400; Fax: 310-532-7001; Toll Free: 800-729-6423 (orders only)
E-mail: aaron@scbdistributors.com; info@scbdistributors.com
Web site: http://www.scbdistributors.com.

**Scheherazade AudioVisions, Inc.,** ( *0-9658148* ) 988 E. 18th St., Brooklyn, NY 11230 Tel 718-253-8116 (phone/fax)
E-mail: audiovisions@yahoo.com
*Dist(s):* **Landmark Audiobooks**
**Penton Overseas, Inc..**

**Schiffer Publishing, Ltd.,** ( *0-7643; 0-88740; 0-916838* ) 4880 Lower Valley Rd., Atglen, PA 19310 (SAN 208-8428) Tel 610-593-1777; Fax: 610-593-2002
E-mail: schifferii@aol.com
Web site: http://www.schifferbooks.com.

**Schmul Publishing Co., Inc.,** ( *0-88019* ) Orders Addr.: P.O. Box 716, Salem, OH 44460-0716 (SAN 180-2771) Tel 330-222-2249; Fax: 330-222-0001; Toll Free: 800-772-6657; Edit Addr.: 3583 Newgarden Rd., Salem, OH 44460
E-mail: spchale@valunet.com
Web site: http://www.wesleyanbooks.com.

**Schocken Imprint of Knopf Publishing Group**

**Schoenhof's Foreign Bks., Inc.,** ( *0-87774* ) Subs. of Editions Gallimard, 486 Green St., Cambridge, MA 02139 (SAN 212-0062) Tel 617-547-8855; Fax: 617-547-8551
E-mail: info@schoenhofs.com
Web site: http://www.schoenhofs.com
*Dist(s):* **Distribooks, Inc..**

†**Scholarly Pr., Inc.,** ( *0-403* ) P.O. Box 160, Saint Clair Shores, MI 48080 (SAN 209-0473) Tel 810-231-3728 (phone/fax); *Imprints:* Regency Press (Regency)
*Dist(s):* **North American Bk. Distributors;** *CIP.*

†**Scholars' Facsimiles & Reprints,** ( *0-8201* ) Subs. of Academic Resources Corp., 410 Lenawee Dr., Ann Arbor, MI 48104 (SAN 203-2627) Tel 734-741-0344
E-mail: nm320@columbia.edu; *CIP.*

**Scholastic en Espanola Imprint of Scholastic, Inc.**

†**Scholastic, Inc.,** ( *0-439; 0-590* ) Orders Addr.: c/o HarperCollins, 1000 Keystone Industrial Pk., Scranton, PA 18512 Toll Free: 800-242-7737; Edit Addr.: 557 Broadway, New York, NY 10012-3999 (SAN 202-5442) Tel 212-343-6100; Fax: 212-343-6802; Toll Free: 800-325-6149 (customer service); *Imprints:* Cartwheel Books (Cartwheel); Blue Sky Press, The (Blue Sky Press); Levine, Arthur A. Books (A A Levine); Orchard Books (Orchard Bks); Scholastic Press (Scholastic Pr); Scholastic en Espanola (Scholastic en Espanola); Scholastic Paperbacks (Schol Pbk)
Web site: http://www.scholastic.com; *CIP.*

**Scholastic Library Publishing,** ( *0-516; 0-531* ) 90 Old Sherman Tpke., Danbury, CT 06816 (SAN 253-8865) Tel 203-797-3500; Fax: 203-797-3657; Toll Free: 800-621-1115; *Imprints:* Children's Press (Childrens Pr); Watts, Franklin (Frank Watts)
E-mail: agraham@grolier.com
Web site: http://www.scholasticlibrary.com
*Dist(s):* **Lectorum Pubns., Inc..**

**Scholastic Paperbacks Imprint of Scholastic, Inc.**

**Scholastic Pr. Imprint of Scholastic, Inc.**

**Schreiber Publishing, Inc.,** ( *0-88400; 1-887563* ) 51 Monroe St., Suite 101, Rockville, MD 20850 (SAN 298-6876) Tel 301-424-7737; Fax: 301-424-2336; Toll Free: 800-822-3213; *Imprints:* Shengold Books (Shengold Bks)
E-mail: spbooks@aol.com
Web site: http://www.schreibernet.com
*Dist(s):* **Baker & Taylor Bks.**
**Fell, Frederick Pubs., Inc.**
**Libros Sin Fronteras**
**National Bk. Network**
**Quality Bks., Inc..**

**Sci Fi-Arizona, Inc.,** ( *1-929381* ) 1931 E. Libra Dr., Tempe, AZ 85283 Tel 480-838-6558; *Imprints:* Third Millennium Publishing (Third Millen Pubng)
E-mail: mccollum@scifi-az.com
Web site: http://www.3mpub.com; http://www.scifi-az.com.

**Science & Humanities Pr.,** ( *1-888725* ) Subs. of Banis & Assocs., Orders Addr.: P.O. Box 7151, Chesterfield, MO 63006-7151 (SAN 299-8459) Tel 636-394-4950; Fax: 636-394-1381; Edit Addr.: 1023 Stuyvesant Ln., Manchester, MO 63011-3601 Tel 636-394-4950; Fax: 636-394-1381; *Imprints:* MacroPrintBooks (MacroPrintBks); BeachHouse Books (BeachHouse Bks)
E-mail: sales@sciencehumanitiespress.com; pub@macroprintbooks.com; banis@banis-associates.com
Web site: http://www.stressmyth.com; http://www.normajeanebook.com; http://www.route66book.com; http://www.accessible-travel.com; http://www.banis-associates.com; http://www.sciencehumanitiespress.com; http://www.macroprintbooks.com
*Dist(s):* **Beeler, Thomas T. Publisher.**

**Scientists of New Atlantis** *See* **Library of New Atlantis, Inc.**

**Scopcraeft Pr.,** ( *1-881604* ) Orders Addr.: P.O. Box 1091, Portales, NM 88130 Tel 505-359-0901; Edit Addr.: 1400 S. Main Ave., Portales, NM 88130-6666 Tel 505-562-2532.

**Scott, D.&F. Publishing, Inc.,** ( *0-941037; 1-930566* )
Orders Addr.: P.O. Box 821653, North Richland Hills,
TX 76182-1653 (SAN 665-2875) Tel 817-788-2280;
Fax: 817-788-9232; Toll Free: 888-788-2280; Edit
Addr.: 6513-C Smithfield Rd., North Richland Hills,
TX 76180; *Imprints:* Smithfield Press (Smithfield Pr)
E-mail: info@dfscott.com
Web site: http://www.dfscott.com
*Dist(s):* **Spring Arbor Distributors, Inc..**

**Scribner** Imprint of Simon & Schuster

**Scribner Paper Fiction** Imprint of Simon & Schuster

**Scriptorium Pr., The,** ( *0-9651877* ) 3425 University
Blvd., Dallas, TX 75205 Tel 214-521-6996; Fax:
214-521-3543; *Imprints:* Impress (Impres) Do not
confuse with Scriptorium Pr., Alfred, NY.

**Scurlock Publishing Co., Inc.,** ( *0-9605666; 1-880655* )
R.R. 5, Box 347M, Texarkana, TX 75503-9403 (SAN
239-4804) Tel 903-832-4726; Fax: 903-831-3177; Toll
Free: 800-228-6389
E-mail: scurlockpubl@txk.net
Web site: http://www.muzzleloadermag.com.

**Seacoast Publishing, Inc.,** ( *1-878561; 1-59421* ) Orders
Addr.: P.O. Box 26492, Birmingham, AL 35260 Tel
205-979-2909; Fax: 205-979-3706; Edit Addr.: 1149
Mountain Oaks Dr., Birmingham, AL 35226 Do not
confuse with companies with the same name in
Monterey, CA, East Hampton, NY
E-mail: seacoast@charter.net
*Dist(s):* **Booksource, The**
**Hervey's Booklink & Cookbook**
**Warehouse.**

**Seagull Publishing Co.,** ( *0-9612698* ) 2915 Stanford
Ave., Suite 7, Marina del Rey, CA 90291 (SAN
295-0235) Do not confuse with Seagull Publishing in
Santa Cruz, CA.

**Seal Pr.** Imprint of Avalon Publishing Group

†**Seal Pr.,** ( *0-930364* ) 6505 Jaliut St., Cypress, CA
90630 (SAN 210-9522) Tel 714-894-4856; Fax:
714-894-2165 Do not confuse with Seal Pr. in Seattle,
WA
E-mail: kates40below@aol.com
Web site: http://www.kates40below.com; *CIP.*

**Seanachaoi Pr.,** ( *0-9656040* ) P.O. Box 404, Dexter, MI
48130 Tel 313-426-3620; Fax: 313-426-6765
E-mail: SeanaPress@aol.com
*Dist(s):* **Partners Pubs. Group, Inc..**

**Seaside Pr.** Imprint of Wordware Publishing, Inc.

**Second Chance Pr.,** ( *0-933256* ) 4170 Noyac Rd., Sag
Harbor, NY 11963 (SAN 213-1633) Tel 631-725-1101
; Fax: 631-725-8215
E-mail: shepard@thepermanentpress.com
Web site: http://www.thepermanentpress.com.

**Second Renaissance Bks.,** ( *1-56114* ) 17 George
Washington Plaza, Gaylordsville, CT 06755-1500 Tel
860-354-5448; Fax: 860-355-7161; Toll Free:
800-729-6149
E-mail: mail@rationalmind.com
Web site: http://www.rationalmind.com.

**Second Story Pr. (CAN)** ( *0-921299; 0-929005;*
*1-896764* ) *Dist. by* **SCB Distributors.**

**Second Story Pr. (CAN)** ( *0-921299; 0-929005;*
*1-896764* ) *Dist. by* **Orca Bk Pubs.**

**Seconda Donna, Inc.,** ( *0-9666591* ) 233 E. 70th St., No.
5R, New York, NY 10021 Tel 212-570-5765
E-mail: teresar@erols.com

**2ndsightbooks.com,** ( *0-9706854* ) P.O. Box 5277,
Berkely, CA 94705
E-mail: jwayshatch@yahoo.com
Web site: http://2ndsightbooks.com
*Dist(s):* **Baker & Taylor Bks..**

**See Sharp Pr.,** ( *0-9613289; 1-884365* ) P.O. Box 1731,
Tucson, AZ 85702-1731 (SAN 653-8134) Tel
520-628-8720 (phone/fax)
E-mail: cb@seesharppress.com
Web site: http://www.seesharppress.com
*Dist(s):* **Independent Pubs. Group.**

**Semiotexte/Smart Art,** ( *1-58435* ) 2571 W. Fifth St.,
Los Angeles, CA 90057 Tel 216-487-5203; Fax:
216-487-5204
E-mail: nativeagent@earthlink.net
*Dist(s):* **Autonomedia**
**MIT Pr.**
**SPD-Small Pr. Distribution.**

**Senior Pr.,** ( *0-9636845* ) Orders Addr.: P.O. Box 21362,
Hilton Head Island, SC 29925 Tel 803-681-5970; Edit
Addr.: 8 Fiddlers Way, Hilton Head Island, SC 29926
Fax: 803-681-3971
*Dist(s):* **Baker & Taylor Bks..**

**Sensory Publishing, Inc.,** ( *1-58853* ) 2000 Jefferson
Davis Hwy., Suite D, Alexandria, VA 22301-1004
Fax: 208-361-6381; Toll Free: 800-832-2823
E-mail: Publisher@SensoryPublishing.com
Web site: http://www.SensoryPublishing.com/.

**Separating Sickness Foundation** See **Anoai Pr.**

**Sepia** Imprint of BET Bks.

**Seren Bks. (GBR)** ( *0-907476; 1-85411* ) *Dist. by*
**Dufour.**

**Serendipity Systems,** ( *0-942871* ) Orders Addr.: P.O.
Box 140, San Simeon, CA 93452 (SAN 667-8610) Tel
805-927-5259; Edit Addr.: Highway 1, Big Sur, CA
93920 (SAN 667-8629)
E-mail: bookware@thegrid.net
Web site: http://www.thegrid.net/bookware/
bookware.htm.

**Sergeant Kirkland's Museum & Historical Society,**
**Incorporated** See **Sergeant Kirkland's Pr.**

**Sergeant Kirkland's Pr.,** ( *0-9632137; 1-887901* ) Div.
of Sergeant Kirkland's Museum & Historical Society,
Inc., 8 Yakama Trail, Spotsylvania, VA 22553-2422
(SAN 152-6324) Tel 540-582-6296; Fax:
540-582-8312
Web site: http://www.kirklands.org.

**Serif (GBR)** ( *1-897959* ) *Dist. by* **Interlink Pub.**

**Serpent's Tail Ltd. (GBR)** ( *1-85242* ) *Dist. by* **Consort**
**Bk Sales.**

†**Servant Pubns.,** ( *0-89283; 1-56955* ) Div. of Servant
Ministries, Inc., Orders Addr.: P.O. Box 8617, Ann
Arbor, MI 48107-8617 (SAN 208-9246) Tel
734-677-6490; Toll Free Fax: 800-315-8505; Edit
Addr.: 1143 Highland Dr., Suite E, Ann Arbor, MI
48108 (SAN 208-9238) Fax: 734-677-6685; Toll Free:
800-458-8505; *Imprints:* Vine Books (Vine Bks)
E-mail: dgriffin@servantpub.com
Web site: http://www.servantpub.com/
*Dist(s):* **Anchor Distributors**
**Appalachian Bible Co.**
**Baker & Taylor Bks.**
**Brodart Co.**
**CRC Pubns.**
**Riverside**
**Spring Arbor Distributors, Inc.;** *CIP.*

†**Seven Locks Pr.,** ( *0-929765; 0-932020; 0-9615964;*
*1-931643* ) 3100 W. Warner Ave., Suite 8, Santa Ana,
CA 92704 (SAN 211-9781) Tel 714-545-2526; Fax:
714-545-1572; Toll Free: 800-354-5348
E-mail: sevenlocks@aol.com
Web site: http://sevenlockspress.com
*Dist(s):* **Baker & Taylor Bks.**
**Koen Bk. Distributors;** *CIP.*

**Seven Stories Pr.,** ( *1-58322; 1-888363* ) 140 Watts St.,
New York, NY 10013 Tel 212-226-8760; Fax:
212-226-1411; Toll Free: 800-596-7437
E-mail: info@sevenstories.com
Web site: http://www.sevenstories.com
*Dist(s):* **Consortium Bk. Sales & Distribution**
**Continental Bk. Co., Inc.**
**Libros Sin Fronteras.**

**Severn Hse. Pubs., Ltd.,** ( *0-7278* ) Orders Addr.: c/o
Chivers North America, P.O. Box 1450, Hampton, NH
03843-1450 Tel 603-926-8744; Fax: 603-929-3890;
Toll Free: 800-830-3044; Edit Addr.: 595 Madison
Ave., 15th Flr., New York, NY 10022 Tel
212-888-4042; Fax: 212-759-5422; Toll Free:
800-830-3044 (customer service)
E-mail: chivers@rcn.com
*Dist(s):* **BBC Audiobooks America.**

**Seymour Lawrence** Imprint of NAL

**Shadow Mountain** Imprint of Deseret Bk. Co.

**ShadowPlay Pr.,** ( *0-9638819* ) P.O. Box 647, Forreston,
IL 61030 Tel 815-938-3151; Fax: 815-371-1440
E-mail: sheilawelch@juno.com;
ericwelch2@juno.com
Web site: http://www.shadowplay.userworld.com.

†**Shambhala Pubns., Inc.,** ( *0-87773; 1-56957; 1-57062;*
*1-59030* ) Horticultural Hall, 300 Massachusetts Ave.,
Boston, MA 02115 (SAN 203-2481) Tel
617-424-0030; Fax: 617-236-1563
E-mail: editors@shambhala.com
Web site: http://www.shambhala.com
*Dist(s):* **Random Hse., Inc.**
**Sounds True, Inc.;** *CIP.*

**Shangri-La Pubns.,** ( *0-9677201; 0-9714683; 0-9719496*
) Orders Addr.: P.O. Box 65, Warren Center, PA
18851-0065 Toll Free: 866-966-6288; Edit Addr.: 3
Coburn Hill Rd., PMB 65, Warren Center, PA 18851
Tel 570-395-3423; Fax: 570-395-0146
E-mail: gosline@egypt.net; shangrila@egypt.net;
shangri_la_book@hotmail.com
Web site: http://www.shangri-la.0catch.com/
*Dist(s):* **Independent Pubs. Group.**

**ShanKrys Publishing, Inc.,** ( *0-9666503* ) 1525 Aviation
Blvd., No. A106, Redondo Beach, CA 90278-2800 Tel
310-213-2515; Fax: 310-514-1399
E-mail: shankryspublishing@aol.com

**Shannon Ravenel Bks.** Imprint of Algonquin Bks. of
**Chapel Hill**

†**Sharpe, M.E. Inc.,** ( *0-7656; 0-87332; 1-56324* ) 80
Business Park Dr., Armonk, NY 10504 (SAN
202-7100) Tel 914-273-1800; Fax: 914-273-2106; Toll
Free: 800-541-6563; *Imprints:* East Gate Book (East
Gate Bk); Sharpe Professional (Sharpe Prof)
E-mail: mesinfo@usa.com
Web site: http://www.mesharpe.com
*Dist(s):* **Women Ink;** *CIP.*

**Sharpe Professional** Imprint of Sharpe, M.E. Inc.

**Shasta Abbey Pr.,** ( *0-930066* ) Orders Addr.: P.O. Box
1163, Mount Shasta, CA 96067; Edit Addr.: 3724
Summit Dr., Mount Shasta, CA 96067-9102 (SAN
210-6655) Tel 530-926-4208; Fax: 530-926-0428;
530-926-2663; Toll Free: 800-653-3315
E-mail: supplies@buddhistsupplies.com
Web site: http://www.buddhistsupplies.com
*Dist(s):* **Shasta Abbey Buddhist Supplies**
**Tuttle Publishing.**

**Shaw** Imprint of WaterBrook Pr.

**Shaye Areheart Bks.** Imprint of Crown Publishing
**Group**

**She Bear Publishing,** ( *0-9658876* ) 4493 E. Cedar Lake
Dr., Greenbush, MI 48738 Tel 517-739-8636
E-mail: SheBear@mail.theenchantedforest.com
Web site: http://www.theenchantedforest.com/
SheBearPublishing.

†**Shearer Publishing,** ( *0-940672* ) 406 Post Oak Rd.,
Fredericksburg, TX 78624 Tel 830-997-6529; Fax:
830-997-9752; Toll Free: 800-458-3808
E-mail: shearer@shearerpub.com
*Dist(s):* **Texas A&M Univ. Pr.;** *CIP.*

**Sheba Pr., Ltd.,** ( *1-880613* ) P.O. Box 59637, Potomac,
MD 20859-9637 Tel 703-734-1956; Fax:
301-469-9227.

**Shelby Hse.,** ( *0-942179* ) Affil. of St. Lukes Pr., 3522
Lucy Rd., Millington, TN 38053-7817 (SAN
666-8895).

**Shengold Bks.** Imprint of Schreiber Publishing, Inc.

†**Sheridan Hse., Inc.,** ( *0-911378; 0-924486; 1-57409* )
145 Palisade St., Dobbs Ferry, NY 10522 (SAN
204-5915) Tel 914-693-2410; Fax: 914-693-0776; Toll
Free: 888-743-7425 (orders only) Do not confuse with
Sheridan House, Inc., in Ft. Lauderdale, FL
E-mail: Sheribks@aol.com
Web site: http://www.sheridanhouse.com; *CIP.*

**Sherman Asher Publishing,** ( *0-9644196; 1-890932* )
P.O. Box 31725, Santa Fe, NM 87594-1725
E-mail: westernedge@santa-fe.net
Web site: http://www.shermanasher.com
*Dist(s):* **Baker & Taylor Bks.**
**Koen Bk. Distributors**
**Partners/West.**

**Shippen Pr.,** ( *0-9660861* ) 2395 S. Milwaukee St.,
Denver, CO 80210 Tel 303-757-1225
E-mail: peterhdkpr@aol.com.

†**Shoe String Pr., Inc.,** ( *0-208* ) 2 Linsley St., North
Haven, CT 06473-2517 (SAN 213-2079) Tel
203-239-2702; Fax: 203-239-2568; *Imprints:* Library
Professional Publications (Lib Prof Pubns)
E-mail: books@shoestringpress.com
Web site: http://www.shoestringpress.com; *CIP.*

**Shoemaker & Hoard,** ( *1-59376* ) Div. of Avalon
Publishing Group Inc., 3704 Macomb St., NW, Suite
4, Washington, DC 20016 Tel 202-364-4464; Fax:
202-364-4484
E-mail: thoard@shoemakerhoard.com
*Dist(s):* **Publishers Group West.**

**Shoji Bks., Inc.,** ( *0-9713797* ) Chase Publishing, L L C,
2123 Ivy Rd., Suite B-108, Charlottesville, VA 22903
*Dist(s):* **Biblio Distribution.**

**Shoreline Pr.,** ( *1-887671* ) Orders Addr.: P.O. Box
27735, Providence, RI 02907; Edit Addr.: P.O. Box
23220, Providence, RI 02903-0395 Tel 401-783-5994
; Fax: 401-782-4577 Do not confuse with Shoreline
Press in Soquel, CA
E-mail: kennethproudfoot@hotmail.com.

**Shyflower Pr., The,** ( *0-9707413* ) Div. of Shyflower's
Enterprises, Ltd., 411 Liberty, Winona, MN 55987 Tel
507-454-3151
E-mail: shy@shyflowersgarden.com; shy@luminet.net
Web site: http://shyflowersgarden.com.

**Sick Puppy Pr.,** ( *0-9708750* ) 209 West Dixie Ave.,
Marietta, GA 30060 Tel 404-456-6954
E-mail: jonathanpenton@yahoo.com;
jonathonpenton@yahoo.com
Web site: http://www.sickpuppypress.com.

**Sidgwick & Jackson, Ltd. (GBR)** ( *0-283* ) *Dist. by*
**Trans-Atl Phila.**

†**Sierra Club Bks.,** ( *0-375; 0-87156; 1-57805* ) 85
Second St., San Francisco, CA 94105 (SAN
203-2406) Tel 415-977-5500; Fax: 415-977-5792
E-mail: information@sierraclub.org
Web site: http://www.sierraclub.org/books
*Dist(s):* **Univ. of California Pr.;** *CIP.*

**Sierra Club Bks. for Children,** ( *0-87156; 1-57805* ) Div. of Sierra Club Bks., 85 Second Street, San Francisco, CA 94105 Tel 415-977-5500; Fax: 415-977-5793
Web site: http://www.sierraclub.org/books
*Dist(s):* **Smith, Gibbs Pub..**

**Sierra Oaks Publishing Co.,** ( *0-940113* ) P.O. Box 736, Newcastle, CA 95658-0736 (SAN 664-063X) Tel 916-663-1474; Fax: 916-663-1476
E-mail: sierraoak@aol.com
Web site: http://www.sierraoaks.com.

**Sierra Raconteur Publishing,** ( *1-58365; 1-58582* ) Orders Addr.: P.O. Box 452, Greenfield, IN 46140 Tel 317-462-0037; *Imprints:* Timeless Romance (Timeless Romance)
E-mail: LASoard@aol.com; LoriSoard@aol.com.

**Sigler Printing & Publishing, Incorporated** *See* **McMillen Publishing**

**Sigmar (ARG)** ( *950-11* ) *Dist.* by **Continental Bk.**

†**Signature Bks., Inc.,** ( *0-941214; 1-56085* ) 564 West 400 N., Salt Lake City, UT 84116-3411 (SAN 217-4391) Tel 801-531-1483; Fax: 801-531-1488; Toll Free: 800-356-5687 (orders only)
E-mail: people@signaturebooks.com
Web site: http://www.signaturebooksinc.com
*Dist(s):* **Baker & Taylor Bks.; CIP.**

**Signet Bks. Imprint of NAL**

**Signet Bks. Imprint of Penguin Group (USA) Inc.**

**Signet Bks. Imprint of Dutton/Plume**

**Signet Classics Imprint of NAL**

**Signet Vista Imprint of NAL**

**Siles Pr.,** ( *1-890085* ) Div. of Sillman-James Pr., 3624 Shannon Rd., Los Angeles, CA 90027 Tel 323-661-9922; Fax: 323-661-9933
E-mail: silmanjamespress@earthlink.net
*Dist(s):* **SCB Distributors.**

**Silhouette Bks. (GBR)** ( *0-340; 0-373* ) *Dist.* by **Thorndike Pr.**

**Silhouette Romance Audio Imprint of Brilliance Audio**

**Silicon Pr.,** ( *0-929306; 0-9615336* ) 25 Beverly Rd., Summit, NJ 07901 (SAN 695-1538) Tel 908-273-8919 ; Fax: 908-273-6149.

**Silo Pr.,** ( *0-9725811* ) Div. of Market Street Associates, Inc., c/o Market St., Associates, Inc., 2208 NW Market St., Suite 505, Seattle, WA 98107
Web site: http://www.LowenClausen.com.

†**Silver, Burdett & Ginn, Inc.,** ( *0-382; 0-663* ) Orders Addr.: P.O. Box 2500, Lebanon, IN 46052 Toll Free Fax: 800-841-8939; Toll Free: 800-552-2259; Edit Addr.: P.O. Box 480, Parsippany, NJ 07054 (SAN 204-5982); 108 Wilmot Rd., Suite 380, Midwest Div., Deerfield, IL 60015 (SAN 111-6517) Tel 708-945-1240
E-mail: customerservice@scottforesman.com
Web site: http://www.scottforesman.com/; *CIP.*

**Silver Dagger Mysteries Imprint of Overmountain Pr.**

**Silver Dawn Media,** ( *0-9623139* ) 6752 Teasdale St., Quartz Hill, CA 93536-1246.

**Silver Mountain Pr.,** ( *1-883721* ) Orders Addr.: P.O. Box 12994, Tucson, AZ 85745 (SAN 297-9470) Tel 520-798-1513; Fax: 520-798-1514 Do not confuse with Silver Mountain Pr. in New York, NY
*Dist(s):* **Baker & Taylor Bks.**
        **Bookpeople.**

**Silver Peach Publishing** *See* **Writing Minds**

**Silver River Bks.,** ( *0-9662817; 1-931753* ) Div. of Silver River, Inc., 1619 Meadowview Dr., Medford, OR 97504 Tel 541-857-6668.

**Silver Rose Productions,** ( *0-9658379* ) P.O. Box 3326, Las Cruces, NM 88003 Tel 505-522-8592
E-mail: silver-rose@ntdata.com

**Silver Spring Bks. Imprint of Truck Pr.**

**Silver Whistle Imprint of Harcourt Children's Bks.**

**SilverRoads Publishing,** ( *0-9729145* ) 3029 Prospect Ave. E., Cleveland, OH 44115 Tel 216-588-0099; Fax: 216-391-1636; Toll Free: 866-409-3434
E-mail: james@silverroads.com
Web site: http://www.silverroads.com
*Dist(s):* **Baker & Taylor Bks.**
        **New Leaf Distributing Co., Inc..**

**Simcha Pr. Imprint of Health Communications, Inc.**

**Simmons Publishing Co.,** ( *0-9667463* ) 915 Cole St., No. 199, San Francisco, CA 94117 (SAN 299-7274) Tel 415-731-6015; Fax: 415-566-9776.

**Simon & Pierre Publishing Co., Ltd. (CAN)** ( *0-88924; 0-9690454* ) *Dist.* by **Empire Pub Srvs.**

**Simon & Schuster,** ( *0-671; 0-684; 0-689; 0-914676; 0-7432* ) Div. of Simon & Schuster, Inc., Orders Addr.: 100 Front St., Riverside, NJ 08075 (SAN 200-2442) Toll Free Fax: 800-943-9831; Toll Free: 800-223-2348 (customer service); 800-223-2336 (ordering); Edit Addr.: 1230 Avenue of the Americas, New York, NY 10020 (SAN 200-2450) Tel 212-698-7000; Fax: 212-698-7007; Toll Free: 800-897-7650 (customer financial services); *Imprints:* Games Workshop (GameWork); WWE (WWE); Atria (Atria Bks); Downtown Press (Downtown); MTV (MTV Bks); Pocket (PB); Pocket Star (Pocket Star Bks); Star Trek (Star Trek); Washington Square Press (Wash Sq Pr); Fireside (Fireside); Free Press (Free Pr); Scribner (Scribner); Scribner Paper Fiction (ScriPapFic); Simon & Schuster (SimSchu); Touchstone (Touchstone)
E-mail: ssonline_feedback@simonsays.com; consumer.customerservice@simonandschuster.com
Web site: http://www.simonandschuster.com/ebooks; http://www.oasis.simonandschuster.com; http://www.simonsays.com
*Dist(s):* **Giron Bks.**
        **Libros Sin Fronteras**
        **Simon & Schuster, Inc.**
        **Thorndike Pr..**

**Simon & Schuster Imprint of Simon & Schuster**

**Simon & Schuster Audio,** ( *0-671; 0-7435* ) Div. of Simon & Schuster New Media, Orders Addr.: 100 Front St., Riverside, NJ 08075 Toll Free Fax: 800-943-9831 (orders); Toll Free: 800-223-2336 (customer service); Edit Addr.: 1230 Avenue of the Americas, New York, NY 10020 Tel 212-698-7000; Fax: 212-698-2370; *Imprints:* Simon & Schuster Sound Ideas (Sound Ideas); Simon & Schuster Audioworks (Audioworks); Pimsleur (Pimsleur); Encore (S&S Encore)
Web site: http://www.simonsays.com/subs/index.cfm?areaid=45
*Dist(s):* **Simon & Schuster, Inc..**

**Simon & Schuster Audioworks Imprint of Simon & Schuster Audio**

†**Simon & Schuster, Inc.,** ( *0-671* ) Div. of Viacom Co., Orders Addr.: 100 Front St., Riverside, NJ 08075 Toll Free Fax: 800-943-9831; Toll Free: 800-223-2336 (orders); 800-223-2348 (customer service); Edit Addr.: 1230 Ave. of the Americas, New York, NY 10020; *CIP.*

**Simon & Schuster, Ltd. (GBR)** ( *0-671; 0-684; 0-689; 0-7432; 0-7434* ) *Dist.* by **SandS Inc.**

**Simon & Schuster Sound Ideas Imprint of Simon & Schuster Audio**

**Simon & Schuster Trade** *See* **Simon & Schuster**

**Simon, Andrew Publications** *See* **Simon Pubns., Inc.**

**Simon Pubns., Inc.,** ( *0-9665734; 1-931313; 1-931541; 0-9725189; 1-932512* ) 1719 Anglers Ct., Safety Harbor, FL 34695 Tel 727-712-9543; Fax: 727-724-1618 Do not confuse with Simon Pubns., Glen Echo, MD
E-mail: simonar@simonpublications.com
Web site: http://www.simonpublications.com
*Dist(s):* **Baker & Taylor Bks..**

**Sinclair-Stevenson, Ltd. (GBR)** ( *1-85619* ) *Dist.* by **Trafalgar.**

**Siruela, Ediciones S.A. (ESP)** ( *84-7844; 84-85876* ) *Dist.* by **Lectorum Pubns.**

**SistahGirl Publishing Co.,** ( *0-9655545* ) Orders Addr.: P.O. Box 250593, Atlanta, GA 30325 Tel 770-815-9216
E-mail: sistahgirl@sistahgirl.com
Web site: http://www.sistahgirl.com.

**Sisyphus Pr.,** ( *0-9712648* ) 1309 W. Albion Ave., Suite 200, Chicago, IL 60626-4701 Tel 773-743-5550; Fax: 773-743-1466 Do not ocnfuse with companies with the same name in San Francisco, CA, State College, PA
E-mail: warrenee@aol.com
Web site: http://www.onthewaytowoodstock.com
*Dist(s):* **Bookpeople.**

**SK Publications** *See* **St Kitts Pr.**

**Skald Bks.,** ( *0-9719155* ) 1973 S. Kenton Ct., Aurora, CO 80014-4709 Tel 303-306-7294
E-mail: jsnoopy626@pol.net; jsoopy626@pol.net.

**Skandisk, Inc.,** ( *0-9615394; 1-57534* ) 6667 W. Old Shakopee Rd., Suite 109, Bloomington, MN 55438-2622 (SAN 695-4405) Tel 952-829-8998; Fax: 952-829-8992; Toll Free: 800-468-2424 (orders)
E-mail: lhamnes@skandisk.com; tomten@skandisk.com
Web site: http://www.skandisk.com
*Dist(s):* **Adventure Pubns., Inc..**

**Sky & Sage Bks.,** ( *1-887786* ) 918 Fourth St., Rapid City, SD 57701 Tel 605-343-5176
E-mail: libyad817@aol.com
*Dist(s):* **Baker & Taylor Bks.**
        **Bookpeople.**

**Sky Blue Pr.,** ( *0-9652364* ) 3438 Kilmer, Troy, MI 48083 Tel 248-619-9918
E-mail: paul@skybluepress.com; sara@skybluepress.com; skybluepress@skybluepress.com
Web site: http://www.skybluepress.com.

**Skylark Imprint of Random Hse. Children's Bks.**

†**Slawson Communications, Inc.,** ( *0-915391; 0-932238* ) P.O. Box 28459, San Diego, CA 92198-0459 (SAN 200-6901); *CIP.*

†**Sleepy Hollow Pr.,** ( *0-912882* ) Div. of Historic Hudson Valley, 150 White Plains Rd., Tarrytown, NY 10591 (SAN 250-3379) Tel 914-631-8200
*Dist(s):* **Fordham Univ. Pr.; CIP.**

**Slough Pr.,** ( *0-941720* ) Subs. of Slough Productions, 3009 Normand Dr., College Station, TX 77845 (SAN 239-3131) Tel 979-693-6321
E-mail: budbruce@usa.net.

**Slow Dancer Pr. (GBR)** ( *0-9507479; 1-871033* ) *Dist.* by **Dufour.**

**Small Press Distribution** *See* **SPD-Small Pr. Distribution**

**Smarr Pubs.,** ( *0-9663784; 1-929579* ) 211 Collins Ridge Dr., Forsyth, GA 31029 Tel 912-994-8981; Fax: 912-994-3762; Toll Free: 888-366-7627
E-mail: order@smarrpublishers.com
Web site: http://www.smarrpublishers.com/.

**Smile Awhile Enterprises,** ( *0-9719091* ) 1620 Countryside Ln., Heber City, UT 84032 Tel 435-657-9768
E-mail: kddavis@shadowlink.net
Web site: http://smileawhile.net.

**Smith, Florence B.** *See* **Prickly Pr.**

†**Smith, Gibbs Pub.,** ( *0-87905; 1-58685* ) Orders Addr.: P.O. Box 667, Layton, UT 84041 (SAN 201-9906) Toll Free Fax: 800-213-3023 (orders); Toll Free: 800-748-5439 (orders); Edit Addr.: 1877 E. Gentile St., Layton, UT 84040 Tel 801-544-9800; Fax: 801-546-8853
E-mail: info@gibbs-smith.com; text@gibbs-smith.com
Web site: http://www.gibbs-smith.com
*Dist(s):* **Athena Productions, Inc.; CIP.**

**Smith, Kenneth,** ( *0-9740335* ) 760 Campbell Rd., China Grove, NC 28023.

**Smith, Peter Pub., Inc.,** ( *0-8446* ) Five Lexington Ave., Magnolia, MA 01930 (SAN 206-8885) Tel 978-525-3562; Fax: 978-525-3674.

**Smith, The,** ( *0-912292; 1-882986* ) Subs. of Generalist Assn., Inc., Orders Addr.: P.O. Box 162, Newton, MA 02468 Tel 508-885-9904; Edit Addr.: 69 Joralemon St., Brooklyn, NY 11201-4003 (SAN 202-7747) Tel 718-834-1212
E-mail: thesmith@aol.com
*Dist(s):* **Arts End Bks..**

**Smith, W. H. Publishers, Incorporated** *See* **Smithmark Pubs., Inc.**

**Smithfield Pr. Imprint of Scott, D.&F. Publishing, Inc.**

**Smithmark Pubs., Inc.,** ( *0-7651; 0-8317* ) Div. of US Media Holdings, 115 W. 18th St., 5th Flr., New York, NY 10011-4113 (SAN 176-0912) Tel 212-519-1300; Fax: 212-519-1310; Toll Free: 800-932-0070 (customer service); Raritan Plaza 111, Fieldcrest Ave., Edison, NJ 08837 (SAN 658-1625) Tel 732-225-6499 (phone/fax); Toll Free Fax: 800-732-8688
*Dist(s):* **Continental Bk. Co., Inc..**

†**Smoky Valley Historical Pubns.,** ( *0-918331* ) Subs. of Smoky Valley Historical Assn., Inc., P.O. Box 255, Lindsborg, KS 67456-0255 (SAN 657-3037) Tel 785-227-2302; *CIP.*

**Smooth Stone Pr.,** ( *0-9619401* ) P.O. Box 19875, Saint Louis, MO 63144 (SAN 244-4259) Tel 314-968-2596
*Dist(s):* **Baker & Taylor Bks.**
        **Bookpeople**
        **Koen Bk. Distributors**
        **Midwest Library Service**
        **New Leaf Distributing Co., Inc.**
        **Nutri-Bks. Corp..**

†**Smyth & Helwys Publishing, Inc.,** ( *0-9628455; 1-57312; 1-880837* ) 6316 Peake Rd., Macon, GA 31210-3960 (SAN 298-7732) Tel 478-301-2117; Fax: 478-301-2264; Toll Free: 800-747-3016
E-mail: griff@helwys.com
Web site: http://www.helwys.com; *CIP.*

**Smythe, Colin Ltd. (GBR)** ( *0-85105; 0-86140; 0-900675; 0-901072* ) *Dist.* by **Dufour.**

Names

**Snow Lion Graphics/SLG Bks.,** ( *0-943389; 0-9617066* ) Orders Addr.: P.O. Box 9465, Berkeley, CA 94709 (SAN 662-8729) Tel 510-525-1134; Fax: 510-525-2632; Toll Free: 800-603-9903 E-mail: roger@slgbooks.com Web site: http://www.snowliongraphics.com; http://www.slgbooks.com *Dist(s):* **Bookpeople** **Publishers Group West.**

**Snowy Creek Pr.,** ( *0-9703497* ) P.O. Box 87555, Canton, MI 48187-0555 Tel 734-455-6467 (phone/fax).

**So There Bks.,** ( *0-9679073* ) 4545 Connecticut Ave. NW, No. 722, Washington, DC 20008 Tel 202-248-6730; Fax: 202-248-6731 E-mail: info@sotherebooks.com Web site: http://www.sotherebooks.com.

**Soft Skull Pr., Inc.,** ( *1-887128; 1-932360* ) 71 Bond St., Brooklyn, NY 11217 Tel 718-643-1599; Fax: 718-643-0879 E-mail: richard@softskull.com Web site: http://www.softskull.com *Dist(s):* **Publishers Group West** **SPD-Small Pr. Distribution.**

**SoftBook Pr.,** ( *0-7410* ) 900 Island Dr., Redwood City, CA 94065-5150 Web site: http://www.softbook.com.

**Softshoe Publishing,** ( *1-881484* ) 2600 Cuernavaca Dr., Austin, TX 78733 Tel 512-263-3691; Fax: 512-263-5763.

**Soho Crime Imprint of Soho Pr., Inc.**

**Soho Pr., Inc.,** ( *0-939149; 1-56947* ) Orders Addr.: 16365 James Madison Hwy., Gordonsville, VA 22942 Tel 888-330-8477; Fax: 540-672-7600; Edit Addr.: 853 Broadway, New York, NY 10003 (SAN 662-5088) Tel 212-260-1900; Fax: 212-260-1902; *Imprints:* Soho Crime (Soho Crime) E-mail: bdevendorf@sohopress.com Web site: http://www.sohopress.com/ *Dist(s):* **Consortium Bk. Sales & Distribution.**

**Solace Publishing, Inc.,** ( *0-9630287* ) Orders Addr.: P.O. Box 567, Folsom, CA 95763-0567 (SAN 297-4940) Toll Free: 800-984-9015; Edit Addr.: 12024 Old Eureka Wy, Gold River, CA 95670.

**Soli Deo Gloria Pubns.,** ( *1-57358; 1-877611* ) Div. of Soli Deo Gloria Ministries, Inc., Orders Addr.: P.O. Box 451, Morgan, PA 15064 (SAN 298-7589) Tel 412-221-1901; Fax: 412-221-1902; Toll Free: 888-266-5734; Edit Addr.: 451 Millers Run Rd., Morgan, PA 15064-9722 E-mail: joel@sdgbooks.com Web site: http://www.SDGbooks.com.

**Solmssen, A. R. G.** *See* **Mill Creek Pr.**

**Solo Zone Publishing,** ( *1-886163* ) P.O. Box 410792, San Francisco, CA 94141-0792 Tel 415-864-0797 E-mail: sales@solozone.com; charlie@solozone.com Web site: http://www.solozone.com.

**Solomon, James,** ( *0-615* ) 1072 Egret's Walk Cir., No. 203, Naples, FL 34108-2498 E-mail: jsol123@aol.com.

†**Somerset Pubs., Inc.,** ( *0-403* ) 1532 State St., Santa Barbara, CA 93101 (SAN 204-6105) Toll Free: 800-937-7947 Web site: http://www.somersetpubl.com *Dist(s):* **North American Bk. Distributors**; *CIP.*

**Songs of Sottongs,** ( *0-9624136* ) 709 Parsons Ln., Signal Mountain, TN 37377 Tel 423-886-2208.

†**Sophia Institute Pr.,** ( *0-918477; 1-928832* ) Orders Addr.: P.O. Box 5284, Manchester, NH 03108 (SAN 657-7172) Tel 603-641-9344; Fax: 603-641-8108; Toll Free: 800-888-9344; Edit Addr.: 300 Bedford St., Suite 540, Manchester, NH 03101 Do not confuse with Sophia Pr., Durham, NH E-mail: production@sophiainstitute.com; sipress@grolen.com Web site: http://www.sophiainstitute.com; *CIP.*

**Sorrells, Russell B. Happy Valley Publishing,** ( *0-9640019* ) 238 Happy Valley Rd., Bell Buckle, TN 37020-4319 Tel 931-389-9163 E-mail: lsorrell@edge.net.

**Soulmate Audio Bks., Inc.,** ( *1-59335* ) 18623 Cambridge Dr., Spring Lake, MI 49456 E-mail: kgosh@soulmateaudio.com Web site: http://www.soulmateaudio.com.

**Sound Room Pubs., Inc.,** ( *1-883049; 1-58472* ) Orders Addr.: P.O. Box 3168, Falls Church, VA 22043 Tel 540-722-2535; Fax: 540-722-0903; Toll Free: 800-643-0295; Edit Addr.: 100 Weems Ln., Winchester, VA 22601; *Imprints:* Commuters Library (Commuters Library); In Audio (In Aud) E-mail: commuterslib@worldnet.att.net Web site: http://commuterslibrary *Dist(s):* **Baker & Taylor Bks.** **Distributors, The** **Follett Media Distribution.**

**Soundelux Audio Publishing,** ( *0-88142; 1-55935; 1-880690* ) Div. of Soundelux Entertainment Group, 55 Mitchell Blvd., Suite 18, San Rafael, CA 94903-2010 Toll Free: 800-227-2020 E-mail: ibriggin@soundelux.com Web site: http://www.soundelux.com/ *Dist(s):* **Landmark Audiobooks.**

**Soundings, Ltd. (GBR)** ( *1-85496; 1-86042; 1-84283* ) *Dist. by* **Ulverscroft US.**

**Soundlines Entertainment, Inc.,** ( *1-56876* ) 10573 W. Pico Blvd., No. 821, Los Angeles, CA 90064 Tel 310-452-3305; Fax: 310-452-3505; Toll Free: 800-428-3467 *Dist(s):* **Landmark Audiobooks.**

†**Sourcebooks, Inc.,** ( *0-942061; 0-9629162; 0-9629803; 1-57071; 1-57248; 1-883518; 1-887166; 1-4022* ) 1935 Brookdale Rd., Suite 139, Naperville, IL 60563 (SAN 666-7864) Tel 630-961-3900; Fax: 630-961-2168; Toll Free: 800-432-7444; *Imprints:* Sourcebooks Landmark (Sourcebks Land); Sourcebooks MediaFusion (MediaFusion) E-mail: info@sourcebooks.com Web site: http://www.sourcebooks.com/ *Dist(s):* **Continental Bk. Co., Inc.** **Libros Sin Fronteras;** *CIP.*

**Sourcebooks Landmark Imprint of Sourcebooks, Inc.**

**Sourcebooks MediaFusion Imprint of Sourcebooks, Inc.**

**South Asia Bks.,** ( *0-8364; 0-88386* ) P.O. Box 502, Columbia, MO 65205 (SAN 207-4044) Tel 573-474-0116; Fax: 573-474-8124 E-mail: sabooks@juno.com Web site: http://www.southasiabooks.com.

†**South End Pr.,** ( *0-89608* ) Orders Addr.: c/o Consortium Book Sales & Distribution, 1045 Westgate Dr., Saint Paul, MN 55114-3572 Fax: 651-221-0124; Edit Addr.: 7 Brookline St., No. 1, Cambridge, MA 02139-4146 (SAN 211-979X) Tel 617-547-4002; Fax: 617-547-1333; Toll Free Fax: 800-334-3892; Toll Free: 800-283-3572 E-mail: southend@igc.org Web site: http://www.southendpress.org *Dist(s):* **Consortium Bk. Sales & Distribution**; *CIP.*

**Southeastern Louisiana University Press** *See* **Louisiana Literature Pr.**

**Southern Heritage Pr.,** ( *0-9631963; 1-889332* ) 4035 Emerald Dr., Murfreesboro, TN 37130 Tel 615-895-5642 (phone/fax) Do not confuse with Southern Heritage Pr. in St. Augustine, FL E-mail: rebeljohn@home.com *Dist(s):* **aBOOKS Distributing.**

**Southern Heritage Pr., Inc.,** ( *0-941072* ) P.O. Box 10937, Saint Petersburg, FL 33733 (SAN 217-3875) Tel 813-823-1938; Fax: 813-821-2379; Toll Free: 800-282-2823 E-mail: byronkennedy@hotmail.com Web site: http://www.southernheritagepress.com *Dist(s):* **Southern Bk. Service.**

†**Southern Illinois Univ. Pr.,** ( *0-8093* ) Div. of Southern Illinois Univ., Orders Addr.: P.O. Box 3697, Carbondale, IL 62902-3697 (SAN 203-3623) Tel 618-453-6624; Fax: 618-453-1221; Toll Free: 800-346-2680; Edit Addr.: 200 McLafferty Rd., Carbondale, IL 62902-3623 Toll Free Fax: 800-346-2681 Web site: http://www.siu.edu/~siupress; *CIP.*

†**Southern Methodist Univ. Pr.,** ( *0-87074* ) Orders Addr.: c/o Texas A&M Univ. Pr., 4354 TAMU, College Sta., TX 77843-4354 Toll Free Fax: 888-617-2421; Toll Free: 800-826-8911; Edit Addr.: P.O. Box 750415, Dallas, TX 75275-0415 (SAN 203-3615) Tel 214-768-1432; Fax: 214-768-1428 Web site: http://www.tamu.edu/upress *Dist(s):* **Texas A&M Univ. Pr.;** *CIP.*

**Southern Tier Editions Imprint of Haworth Pr., Inc., The**

**SouthLore Pr.,** ( *0-9633341* ) 730 Grouse Moor Dr., Banner Elk, NC 28604 (SAN 299-3945) Tel 828-898-3490; Fax: 828-898-3490 E-mail: southlore@skybest.com Web site: http://www.marioncoe.com *Dist(s):* **Biblio Distribution.**

**Southmont Publishing,** ( *0-9662145* ) Orders Addr.: P.O. Box 33024, Tulsa, OK 74153-1024 Tel 918-492-8614 ; Fax: 918-492-2104; Edit Addr.: 5711 E. 62nd Pl., Tulsa, OK 74136 E-mail: jehager@aol.com.

**Southwest Publishing,** ( *0-9659789* ) 11215 Research Blvd., Suite 1096, Austin, TX 78759 Tel 512-795-8527 Do not confuse with Southwest Publishing, Brownsville, TX.

**Souvenir Pr. Ltd. (GBR)** ( *0-285* ) *Dist. by* **IPG Chicago.**

**Sovereign Grace Pubs., Inc.,** ( *1-878442; 1-58960* ) 4427 E. 200 N., Lafayette, IN 47905 (SAN 299-6847) Tel 765-429-4122; Fax: 765-429-4142; Toll Free: 800-447-9142 Do not confuse with Sovereign Grace Pubns., Lexington, KY E-mail: jaygreenxx@iquest.net Web site: http://www.sovgracepub.com.

**Sovereign Pubs.,** ( *0-9709840* ) P.O. Box 8342, Erie, PA 16505-0342 E-mail: info@sovereignpublishers.com Web site: http://www.sovereignpublishers.com.

**Spanish Hse. Distributors,** 1360 NW 88th Ave., Miami, FL 33172-3093 (SAN 169-1171) Tel 305-592-6136; Fax: 305-592-0087; Toll Free: 800-767-7726.

**Spark Publishing Group,** ( *1-58663* ) Div. of Spark Notes, LLC, 120 5th Ave., 8th Flr., New York, NY 10011 Tel 212-414-6535; Fax: 212-414-6018 Web site: http://www.soarknotes.com *Dist(s):* **Sterling Publishing Co., Inc..**

**Special Pubns., Inc.,** ( *0-9636339; 1-892937* ) Orders Addr.: P.O. Box 4649, Ocala, FL 34478 Tel 352-622-2995; Fax: 352-622-9200; Edit Addr.: 743 SE Fort King St., Ocala, FL 34471 Tel 904-622-2995 E-mail: todaymag@earthlink.net Web site: http://www.ocalamagazine.net.

**Specialized Pubns. Co.,** ( *0-9639960* ) 5215 NW Crooked Rd., Parkville, MO 64152-3447 Tel 816-741-5151; Fax: 816-741-6458; Toll Free: 800-444-9932 E-mail: gary@spc-mag.com.

**Spectra Imprint of Bantam Bks.**

**Spellbinders, Inc.,** ( *1-883268* ) P.O. Box 8552, Wichita Falls, TX 76307-8552 Tel 940-723-1567; Fax: 940-766-3870; Toll Free: 800-887-7692 *Dist(s):* **Landmark Audiobooks** **Penton Overseas, Inc..**

†**Speller, Robert & Sons, Pubs., Inc.,** ( *0-8315* ) Orders Addr.: P.O. Box 411, New York, NY 10159 (SAN 203-2295) Tel 212-473-0333; P.O. Box 461, New York, NY 10108 (SAN 203-2309); *CIP.*

**Spellmount Pubs. (GBR)** *Dist. by* **Casemate Pubs.**

**Spinifex Pr. (AUS)** ( *1-875559; 1-876756* ) *Dist. by* **StackpoleBks.**

**Spinifex Pr. (AUS)** ( *1-875559; 1-876756* ) *Dist. by* **Strauss Cnslts.**

**Spinsters Ink** *See* **Spinsters Ink Bks.**

†**Spinsters Ink Bks.,** ( *0-918040; 0-933216; 1-883523* ) P.O. Box 22005, Denver, CO 80222 (SAN 212-6923) Tel 303-762-7284; Fax: 303-761-5284; Toll Free: 800-301-6860 E-mail: spinster@spinsters-ink.com Web site: http://www.spinsters-ink.com *Dist(s):* **SPD-Small Pr. Distribution** **Words Distributing Co.;** *CIP.*

**Spire Imprint of Revell, Fleming H. Co.**

**Spirit Song Publishing,** ( *0-9664412* ) Orders Addr.: P.O. Box 9622, Fort Collins, CO 80525-9622 Tel 970-226-1389 (phone/fax-on-demand); Edit Addr.: 1531 Centennial Rd., Fort Collins, CO 80525-2417 E-mail: SpiritPubl@aol.com.

**Spiritseeker Publishing, Inc.,** ( *0-9630419; 1-883064* ) Orders Addr.: P.O. Box 2441, Fargo, ND 58108-2441 Tel 701-232-5966; Fax: 701-232-0633; Toll Free: 800-538-6415; Edit Addr.: 412 Eighth Ave., S., Fargo, ND 58103.

**Spiritual Literature Library Imprint of Garber Communications, Inc.**

**Splash Imprint of Berkley Publishing Group**

**Spoken Arts, Inc.,** ( *0-8045* ) 8 Lawn Ave., New Rochelle, NY 10801-0100 (SAN 205-079X) Tel 914-633-4516; Toll Free: 800-326-4090 Web site: http://www.spokenartsmedia.com/Home.htm *Dist(s):* **Follett Media Distribution** **Lectorum Pubns., Inc.** **Weston Woods Studios, Inc..**

**Spotlight Books** *See* **Hannacroix Creek Bks., Inc.**

**Spring Creek Pubns.,** ( *0-945184* ) Orders Addr.: P.O. Box 243, Rose Hill, KS 67133 (SAN 246-6309) Edit Addr.: 5810 S. Webb, Derby, KS 67037 (SAN 246-6317) Tel 316-788-2812 Do not confuse with companies with the same or similar name in Bozeman, MT, Payson, UT.

Names

**Spring Harbor Pr.,** *( 0-935891 )* Div. of Spring Harbor, Ltd., Orders Addr.: P.O. Box 346, Delmar, NY 12054 (SAN 695-9768) Tel 518-478-7817 (phone/fax) E-mail: info@springharborpress.com; springharbor@global2000.net Web site: http://www.springharborpress.com *Dist(s):* **Baker & Taylor Bks.**

**Spring Publishing,** *( 0-9666946 )* P.O. Box 458, Independence, OR 97351 (SAN 299-7150) Tel 503-838-4231; Fax: 503-838-0659 E-mail: spring@transport.com.

†**Springer-Verlag New York, Inc.,** *( 0-387; 0-8176; 3-211; 3-540; 3-7908; 4-431; 1-85233 )* Subs. of Springer-Verlag GmbH & Co. KG, Orders Addr.: P.O. Box 2485, Secaucus, NJ 07096-2485 (SAN 665-7842) Tel 201-348-4033; Fax: 201-348-4505; Toll Free: 800-777-4643; Edit Addr.: 175 Fifth Ave., New York, NY 10010 (SAN 203-2228) Tel 212-460-1500; Fax: 212-473-6272 E-mail: service@springer-ny.com; orders@springer.de Web site: http://www.springer.de/; http://www.springer-ny.com; *CIP.*

**Spuyten Duyvil,** *( 1-881471; 0-9720662 )* Orders Addr.: P.O. Box 1852, New York, NY 10025 (SAN 237-9481) Toll Free: 800-886-5304; Edit Addr.: 42 St. John's Pl., Garden, Brooklyn, NY 11217 E-mail: spuytenduyvil@lycos.com Web site: http://www.spuytenduyvil.net *Dist(s):* **Biblio Distribution**
**SPD-Small Pr. Distribution.**

**SRA/McGraw-Hill,** *( 0-02; 0-383 )* Div. of The McGraw-Hill Education Group, Orders Addr.: 220 E. Daniel Dale Rd., DeSoto, TX 75115-2490 Fax: 972-228-1982; Toll Free: 800-843-8855; Edit Addr.: 8787 Orion Pl., Columbus, OH 43240-4027 Tel 614-430-6600; Fax: 614-430-6621; Toll Free: 800-468-5850 E-mail: sra@mcgraw-hill.com Web site: http://www.mcgraw-hill.com/education/sra.html *Dist(s):* **Libros Sin Fronteras**
**Weston Woods Studios, Inc..**

**SSI, Incorporated** *See* **SSI, Inc. Publishing**

**SSI, Inc. Publishing,** *( 0-9743673; 1-932623 )* 880 Holcomb Bridge Rd., Suite 135-B, Roswell, GA 30076 (SAN 255-7363) Web site: http://www.theskyclub.cc.

**St Kitts Pr.,** *( 0-9661879; 1-931206 )* Div. of SK Pubns., Orders Addr.: P.O. Box 8173, Wichita, KS 67208 Tel 316-685-3201; Fax: 316-685-6650; Toll Free: 888-705-4887; Edit Addr.: 4200 E. 24th, Wichita, KS 67220 Do not confuse with SK Pubns., Northfield, OH E-mail: stkitts@skpub.com Web site: http://www.stkittspress.com *Dist(s):* **Baker & Taylor Bks.**
**Book Wholesalers, Inc.**
**Brodart Co.**
**Coutts Library Service, Inc.**
**Emery-Pratt Co.**
**Follett Library Resources.**

**St. Martin's Paperbacks Imprint of St. Martin's Pr.**

†**St. Martin's Pr.,** *( 0-312; 0-8050; 0-940687; 0-9603648; 1-55927; 1-58063; 1-58238 )* Div. of Holtzbrinck Publishers, Orders Addr.: 16365 James Madison Hwy., Gordonville, VA 22942 Tel 540-672-7600; Fax: 540-672-7540 (customer service) ; Toll Free Fax: 800-672-2054; Toll Free: 888-330-8477; Edit Addr.: 175 Fifth Ave., New York, NY 10010 (SAN 200-2132) Tel 212-726-0200 (College Div.); 212-674-5151 (Trade Div.); Fax: 212-686-9491 (College Div.); 212-674-3179 (Trade Div.); Toll Free: 800-470-4767 (College Div.); 800-221-7945 (Trade Div.); *Imprints:* Saint Martin's Griffin (St Martin Griffin); Saint Martin's Paperbacks (St Martins Paperbacks); Let's Go Publications (Lets Go Pubns); Dunne, Thomas Books (Thomas Dunne); Saint Martin's Minotaur (Minotaur); Golden Books Adult Publishing Group (Golden Adult); L. A. Weekly Books (L A Weekly); Golden Guides from Saint Martin's Press (Gldn Guides); Renaissance Books (Rena Bks) E-mail: webmaster@stmartins.com; enquiries@stmartins.com Web site: http://www.smpcollege.com; http://www.stmartins.com *Dist(s):* **Comag Marketing Group**
**Holtzbrinck Pubs.**
**Libros Sin Fronteras;** *CIP.*

**St. Padraic Pr.,** *( 0-9704155 )* P.O. Box 43351, Cincinnati, OH 45204-0351 Tel 513-985-9316 E-mail: mgray64632@aol.com.

**ST Productions** *See* **LSA Publishing**

†**Stackpole Bks.,** *( 0-8117 )* 5067 Ritter Rd., Mechanicsburg, PA 17055 (SAN 202-5396) Tel 717-796-0411; Fax: 717-796-0412 E-mail: sales@stackpolebooks.com Web site: http://www.stackpolebooks.com *Dist(s):* **Pennsylvania Capitol Preservation Committee;** *CIP.*

†**Standard Publishing,** *( 0-7847; 0-87239; 0-87403 )* Div. of Standex International Corp., 8121 Hamilton Ave., Cincinnati, OH 45231-2323 (SAN 110-5515) Tel 513-931-4050; Fax: 513-931-0950; Toll Free Fax: 877-867-5751 (customer service); Toll Free: 800-543-1301; 800-543-1353 (customer service) Do not confuse with Standard Publishing Corp., Boston, MA E-mail: customerservice@standardpub.com; trolfes@standardpub.com Web site: http://www.standardpub.com *Dist(s):* **Twentieth Century Christian Bks.;** *CIP.*

**Standard Publishing Company** *See* **Standard Publishing**

**Standstone Pr. Imprint of Beil, Frederic C. Pub., Inc.**

†**Stanford Univ. Pr.,** *( 0-8047 )* Stanford Univ. Pr. 1450 Page Mill Rd., Palo Alto, CA 94304 (SAN 203-3526) Tel 650-723-9434; Fax: 650-725-3457 Web site: http://www.sup.org *Dist(s):* **Univ. of Chicago Pr.;** *CIP.*

**Star Quest Entertainment,** *( 0-9661287 )* 7805 Mason Ave., Winnetka, CA 91306-2221 E-mail: pjacob@iopener.net.

**Star Trek Imprint of Simon & Schuster**

**Starblaze Imprint of Donning Co. Pubs.**

**STARbooks Pr. Imprint of Florida Literary Foundation**

**Starcherone Bks.,** *( 0-9703165 )* P.O. Box 3032, Buffalo, NY 14201 (SAN 255-5514) Tel 716-885-2726 E-mail: publisher@starcherone.com Web site: http://www.starcherone.com.

**Starline Imprint of Baen Bks.**

**Starlog Group, Incorporated** *See* **Profile Entertainment, Inc.**

**Starmount Pr.,** *( 0-9669050 )* Orders Addr.: P.O. Box 3451, Littleton, CO 80161-3451; Edit Addr.: 7288 S. Sundown Cir., Littleton, CO 80120 Tel 303-738-9366 (phone/fax) E-mail: starmountpress@worldnet.att.net; isternberg@worldnet.att.net *Dist(s):* **Baker & Taylor Bks.**
**Books West.**

**Starnes Publishing Co.,** *( 0-9657613 )* 3550 Berkeley Park Ct., Duluth, GA 30096 E-mail: hgs1953ars@aol.com.

**Starscape Imprint of Doherty, Tom Assocs., LLC**

**Starseed Pr. Imprint of Kramer, H.J. Inc.**

**StarsEnd Creations,** *( 1-889120 )* 8547 E. Arapahoe Rd., No. J224, Greenwood Village, CO 80112 (SAN 298-962X) Tel 303-694-1664; Fax: 303-694-4098 E-mail: info@starsend.com Web site: http://www.starsend.com, http://www.pantrypress.com *Dist(s):* **Anderson News Co.**
**Baker & Taylor Bks..**

**State Mutual Bk. & Periodical Service, Ltd.,** *( 0-7855; 0-89771 )* Orders Addr.: P.O. Box 1199, Bridgehampton, NY 11932-1199.

†**State Univ. of New York Pr.,** *( 0-7914; 0-87395; 0-88706 )* Orders Addr.: c/o CUP Services, P.O. Box 6525, Ithaca, NY 14851 (SAN 203-3496) Tel 607-277-2211; Fax: 607-277-6292; Edit Addr.: 90 State St., Suite 700, Albany, NY 12207 (SAN 658-1730) Tel 518-472-5000; Fax: 518-472-5038 E-mail: info@sunypress.edu; orderbook@cupscrve.org Web site: http://www.sunypress.edu *Dist(s):* **Baker & Taylor Bks.**
**Pegasus Pr.**
**netLibrary, Inc.;** *CIP.*

**Staten, LaWanda M.,** *( 0-9664722 )* 19425 Hillford Ave., Carson, CA 90746 Tel 310-608-0904.

†**Station Hill Pr.,** *( 0-88268; 0-930794 )* Station Hill Rd., Barrytown, NY 12507 (SAN 214-1485) Tel 845-758-5840; Fax: 845-758-8163 E-mail: buun@stationhill.org Web site: http://www.stationhill.org/ *Dist(s):* **BookWorld Services, Inc.**
**Bookpeople**
**SPD-Small Pr. Distribution**
**Writers & Bks.;** *CIP.*

**Steerforth Italia Imprint of Steerforth Pr.**

**Steerforth Pr.,** *( 1-883642; 1-58642 )* 105-106 Chelsea St., P.O. Box 70, South Royalton, VT 05068 Tel 802-763-2808; Fax: 802-763-2818; *Imprints:* Steerforth Italia (Steerforth Italia); Zoland Books, Incorporated (Zoland) E-mail: helga@steerforth.com; info@steerforth.com Web site: http://www.steerforth.com *Dist(s):* **Publishers Group West.**

†**SteinerBooks, Inc.,** *( 0-8334; 0-88010; 0-89345; 0-910142; 1-58420; 1-85584; 0-9701097 )* Orders Addr.: P.O. Box 960, Herndon VA, 20172-0960 Tel 703-661-1594 (orders); Fax: 702-661-1501; Toll Free Fax: 800-277-7947 (orders); Toll Free: 800-856-8664 (orders); Edit Addr.: P.O. Box 799, Great Barrington, MA 01230 Tel 413-528-8233; Fax: 413-528-8826; Fulfillment Addr.: 22883 Quicksilver Dr., Dulles, VA 20166 (SAN 253-9519) Tel 703-661-1529; Fax: 703-996-1010; *Imprints:* Lindisfarne Books (Lindisfarne) E-mail: service@steinerbooks.org Web site: http://www.lindisfarne.org; http://www.bellpondbooks.com; http://www.steinerbooks.org *Dist(s):* **Bookpeople**
**New Leaf Distributing Co., Inc.**
**Red Wheel/Weiser;** *CIP.*

†**Stemmer Hse. Pubs., Inc.,** *( 0-88045; 0-916144 )* 4 White Brook Rd., Gilsum, NH 03448 (SAN 207-9623) Tel 603-357-0236; Fax: 603-357-2073 E-mail: stemmerhouse@home.com Web site: http://stemmer.com *Dist(s):* **Pathway Bk. Service;** *CIP.*

**Stephens Publishing Co.,** *( 0-9700572 )* Orders Addr.: P.O. Box 2126, Litchfield Park, AZ 85340 Tel 623-935-6842; Edit Addr.: 12555 Roanoke Dr., Litchfield Park, AZ 85340 E-mail: Nathan.stephens@luke.af.mil.

**Sterling Audio Bks. Imprint of BBC Audiobooks America**

**Sterling House Publishing** *See* **SterlingHouse Pubs., Inc.**

**Sterling Pubs.,** *( 0-9720310 )* 10 N. Main, Penthouse Rm. 6, West Hartford, CT 06107 Tel 860-712-6088; Fax: 707-982-1507 E-mail: tbmarquis@hotmail.com *Dist(s):* **Biblio Distribution.**

†**Sterling Publishing Co., Inc.,** *( 0-8069; 1-4027 )* 387 Park Ave., S., New York, NY 10016-8810 (SAN 211-6324) Tel 212-532-7160; Fax: 212-213-2495; Toll Free Fax: 800-775-8736 (warehouse); *Imprints:* Sterling/Main Street (Sterling-Main St) Do not confuse with companies with similar names in Falls Church, VA, Fallbrook, CA, Lewisville, TX E-mail: custservice@sterlingpub.com Web site: http://www.sterlingpub.com; *CIP.*

**Sterling Publishing Company, Incorporated** *See* **Sterling Publishing Co., Inc.**

**Sterling Pubs. Pvt., Ltd. (IND)** *( 81-207 )* Dist. by **S Asia.**

**SterlingHouse Pubs., Inc.,** *( 1-56315 )* Div. of Lee Shore Agency, 7436 Washington Ave., Suite 200, Pittsburgh, PA 15218 Tel 412-271-8800; Fax: 412-271-8600; Toll Free: 888-542-2665; *Imprints:* CeShore (CeShore) E-mail: info@sterlinghousepublisher.com Web site: http://www.sterlinghousepublisher.com *Dist(s):* **Fell, Frederick Pubs., Inc.**
**Partners Pubs. Group, Inc..**

**Sterling/Main St. Imprint of Sterling Publishing Co., Inc.**

**Sterling-Miller Publishing Company** *See* **Sterling-Miller Publishing Company, Inc.**

†**Sterling-Miller Publishing Company, Inc.,** *( 0-931791 )* 12573 Woodmill Dr., Palm Beach Gardens, FL 33418 (SAN 254-6493) Tel 561-622-1949; Fax: 561-775-0839 E-mail: stuart.sandow@sterling-miller.com Web site: http://www.campdaviddiaries.com; *CIP.*

†**Stevens, Gareth Inc.,** *( 0-8368; 0-918831; 1-55532 )* 330 W. Olive St., Suite 100, Milwaukee, WI 53212 (SAN 696-1592) Tel 414-332-3520; Fax: 414-332-3567; Toll Free: 800-542-2595 E-mail: info@gsinc.com *Dist(s):* **Lectorum Pubns., Inc.;** *CIP.*

**Stewart Masters Publishing, Ltd.,** *( 0-9718185 )* 27 Hampton Ct., Alameda, CA 94502 Web site: http://www.stewartmasters.com.

†**Stewart, Tabori & Chang,** *( 0-941434; 0-941807; 1-55670; 1-899791; 1-58479 )* Div. of Harry N. Abrams, Inc., 115 W. 18th St., 5th Flr., New York, NY 10011 (SAN 293-4000) Tel 212-519-1200; Fax: 212-519-1210 *Dist(s):* **Time Warner Bk. Group;** *CIP.*

Names

**Stickman Graphics,** ( *0-9675423* ) 141 16th St., Brooklyn, NY 11215-5302 (SAN 253-0228) Tel 718-788-8858 (phone/fax) E-mail: stickman@stickmangraphics.com Web site: http://www.stickmangraphics.com *Dist(s):* **Baker & Taylor Bks., Inc.**
**Book Wholesalers, Inc.**
**Cold Cut Comics Distribution**
**Diamond Book Distributors, Inc.**
**FM International.**

**Stone Angel Bks.,** ( *0-9631149* ) P.O. Box 27392, Austin, TX 78755-2392 Tel 512-345-4208; Fax: 512-345-7808; 7507 Stonecliff Cir., Austin, TX 78731 E-mail: stonangbks@aol.com *Dist(s):* **Bookmen, Inc.**
**Independent Pubs. Marketing.**

†**Stone Bridge Pr.,** ( *0-9628137; 1-880656* ) P.O. Box 8208, Berkeley, CA 94707 Tel 510-524-8732; Fax: 510-524-8711; Toll Free: 800-947-7271 (orders); *Imprints:* Rock Spring (Rock Spring Collect) do not confuse with Stone Bridge Press in Naples, FL E-mail: sbpsales@stonebridge.com Web site: http://www.stonebridge.com *Dist(s):* **Art Media Resources, Ltd.**
**Consortium Bk. Sales & Distribution**
**SPD-Small Pr. Distribution**; *CIP.*

**Stone Edge Pr.,** ( *0-9666435* ) Orders Addr.: P.O. Box 1632A, New York, NY 10027 Fax: 212-987-8904.

**Stone House Pr., Inc,** ( *0-9675060* ) RR 1, Box 247, Richville, MN 56576 Tel 218-495-2855; Fax: 218-495-3035 E-mail: joliejim@djam.com.

**Stonehall Publishing,** ( *0-9669930* ) 5156 Allyne Rd., Virginia Bch, VA 23462-3602 *Dist(s):* **Baker & Taylor Bks.**
**BookMasters, Inc..**

**Stonehill Publishing Co.,** ( *0-9643394* ) P.O. Box 3111, Traverse City, MI 49685 Do not confuse with Stonehill Publishing in Ephraim, WI.

**Stonehouse Pr.,** ( *1-931304; 1-59006* ) 300 E. 56th St., Suite 22F, New York, NY 10022 Tel 908-294-1818; 212-350-9357; 140 W. 69th St., No. 68B, New York, NY 10023 Tel 212-769-3997; Fax: 212-769-1313 E-mail: GoldmanEthan@aol.com; adlernovel@aol.com Web site: http://www.warrenadler.com.

**Stonehouse Pr., Inc.,** ( *0-89057* ) 336 W. Passaic St., Rochelle Park, NJ 07662 (SAN 222-9064) Tel 212-704-9640.

**Stonehouse Pubns.,** ( *0-9603236* ) Timber Butte Rd., Sweet, ID 83670 (SAN 206-1058) Tel 208-584-3344 E-mail: Skwatson@idfishnhunt.com.

**Stones Point Pr.,** ( *1-882521* ) Orders Addr.: P.O. Box 384, Belfast, ME 04915-0384 (SAN 297-8024) Tel 207-338-1921; Fax: 207-338-8379; Edit Addr.: 71 Congress St., Belfast, ME 04915 E-mail: stonespt@mint.net; haaron@mint.net *Dist(s):* **Baker & Taylor Bks..**

**Story Line Pr.,** ( *0-934257; 1-885266; 1-58654* ) Orders Addr.: P.O. Box 1240, Ashland, OR 97520-0055 (SAN 242-0465) Tel 541-512-8792; Fax: 541-512-8793; Edit Addr.: Three Oaks Farm, Ashland, OR 97520 E-mail: mail@storylinepress.com Web site: http://www.storylinepress.com *Dist(s):* **Consortium Bk. Sales & Distribution.**

**Story Pr. Imprint of F&W Pubns., Inc.**

**Storytellers Ink, Inc.,** ( *0-9623072; 1-880812; 1-930767* ) Orders Addr.: a/o Quinn Currie, P.O. Box 33398, Seattle, WA 98133-0398 Tel 206-365-8265; Fax: 206-363-0830 Do not confuse with Storytellers Ink, Inc. in Kansas City, MO E-mail: publisher@storytellers-ink.com Web site: http://www.storytellers-ink.com.

†**Stowe-Day Foundation,** ( *0-917482* ) 77 Forest St., Hartford, CT 06105 (SAN 209-052X) Tel 860-522-9258; *CIP.*

**Strategic Enterprise Consulting,** ( *0-9663167* ) 21141 Saratoga Hills Rd., Saratoga, CA 95070 Tel 408-741-5805; Fax: 408-741-1490 E-mail: gisnesheim@aol.com Web site: http://www.startupweb.com.

**Stratford Bks.,** ( *0-9627060* ) 175 Fairway Dr., Princeton, NJ 08540-2409 Tel 609-924-4290; Fax: 609-497-0805 Do not confuse with Stratford Bks. in Winston-Salem, NC.

**Strauss Consultants,** 48 W. 25th St., 11th Flr., New York, NY 10010-2708 Toll Free Fax: 888-528-8273; Toll Free: 800-236-7918 E-mail: strausscon@aol.com.

†**Strawberry Hill Pr.,** ( *0-89407* ) 21 Isis St. Apt. 102, San Francisco, CA 94103-4365 (SAN 238-8103); *CIP.*

**Strawberry Productions,** ( *0-913301* ) P.O. Box 380, Black Canyon City, AZ 85324 (SAN 285-8665) Tel 623-374-9494.

**Stuart, Jesse Foundation, The,** ( *0-945084; 1-931672* ) Orders Addr.: P.O. Box 669, Ashland, KY 41105 (SAN 245-8837) Tel 606-326-1667; Fax: 606-325-2519; Edit Addr.: 1645 Winchester Ave., Ashland, KY 41101 (SAN 245-8845) E-mail: jsf@inet99.net Web site: http://www.jsfbooks.com.

**Stuart, Lyle Imprint of Kensington Publishing Corp.**

**Studio Ironcat L.L.C.** *See* **International Comics & Entertainment L.L.C.**

**Stylus Publishing, LLC,** ( *1-57922* ) Orders Addr.: P.O. Box 605, Herndon, VA 20172-0605; Edit Addr.: 22883 Quicksilver Dr., Sterling, VA 20166-2012 (SAN 299-1853) Tel 703-661-1581; Fax: 703-661-1501 Do not confuse with companies with the same name in Sunnyvale, CA, Quakertown, PA E-mail: stylusmail@presswarehouse.com Web site: http://styluspub.com.

**Subterranean Pr.,** ( *1-880060* ) 501 Francisco St., San Francisco, CA 94133 Tel 415-474-9682 Do not confuse with Subterranean Pr., Burton, MI.

**Subterranean Pr.,** ( *0-9649890; 1-892284; 1-931081* ) P.O. Box 190106, Burton, MI 48519 Tel 810-232-1489; Fax: 810-232-1447 Do not confuse with Subterranean Pr., San Francisco, CA E-mail: publisher@subterraneanpress.com Web site: http://www.subterraneanpress.com.

**Sudamericana (Sudamericana - Planeta) (ARG)** ( *950-07; 950-37* ) Dist. by AIMS Intl.

**Suma de Letras, S.L. (ESP)** ( *84-663; 84-95501* ) *Dist. by Lectorum Pubns.*

**Summa Pubns.,** ( *0-917786; 1-883479* ) Orders Addr.: P.O. Box 660725, Birmingham, AL 35266-0725 (SAN 662-0124) Tel 205-822-0463 (phone/fax) E-mail: tmhines@samford.edu; tom62836@aol.com.

†**Summit Bks.,** ( *0-671* ) Div. of Simon & Schuster, Inc., 1230 Ave. of the Americas, New York, NY 10020 (SAN 206-1244) Tel 212-698-7000; Fax: 212-698-7501; Toll Free: 800-223-2336 Do not confuse with companies with the same name in Toledo, OH, Tempe, AZ Web site: http://www.simonsays.com/; *CIP.*

†**Summit Publishing Group - Legacy Bks.,** ( *0-9626219; 1-56530* ) 3649 Conflans Rd., No. 103, Irving, TX 75061 (SAN 631-1253) Tel 972-399-8856 ; Fax: 972-313-9060 Do not confuse with Summit Publishing, Los Angeles, CA E-mail: info@summitbooks.com Web site: http://www.summitbooks.com *Dist(s):* **BookWorld Services, Inc.**
**Tapestry Pr.;** *CIP.*

†**Sun & Moon Pr.,** ( *0-940650; 1-55713* ) 6026 Wilshire Blvd., Los Angeles, CA 90036 (SAN 630-3234) Tel 323-857-1115; Fax: 323-857-0143 E-mail: djmess@sunmoon.com Web site: http://www.sunmoon.com *Dist(s):* **Consortium Bk. Sales & Distribution**
**SPD-Small Pr. Distribution;** *CIP.*

**Sun & Shore Pubns.,** ( *0-9677983* ) 160 W. McKay Rd., Suite 4, Shelbyville, IN 46176 Tel 317-421-0966; 317-955-5100; Fax: 317-955-5101 E-mail: CRSPhil@prodigy.com *Dist(s):* **Hearthland Bks..**

**Sunbelt Media, Incorporated** *See* **Eakin Pr.**

†**Sunbelt Pubns., Inc.,** ( *0-916251; 0-932653; 0-9606704; 0-9620402* ) 1250 Fayette St., El Cajon, CA 92020-1511 (SAN 630-0790) Tel 619-258-4911; Fax: 619-258-4916; Toll Free: 800-626-6579 E-mail: sunbeltpub@prodigy.net Web site: http://www.sunbeltpub.com *Dist(s):* **Baker & Taylor Bks.**
**Pacific Bks.**
**Quality Bks., Inc.;** *CIP.*

**Sunburst Imprint of Farrar, Straus & Giroux**

**Sundance Publishing,** ( *0-7608; 0-88741; 0-940146; 1-56801* ) Orders Addr.: P.O. Box 1326, Littleton, MA 01460 (SAN 169-3484) Tel 978-486-9201; Fax: 978-486-1053; Toll Free Fax: 800-456-2419; Toll Free: 800-343-8204 Do not confuse with Sundance Publishing, Inc., Patchogue, NY E-mail: info@sundancepub.com Web site: http://www.sundancepub.com/ *Dist(s):* **Lectorum Pubns., Inc..**

**Sundown Canyon Productions, Inc.,** ( *0-9716030* ) Orders Addr.: P.O. Box 572, Grand Island, NY 14072 Tel 716-282-7476; Edit Addr.: 1715 Pine Ave., No.2, Niagara Falls, NY 14301-2279.

**Sunflower Pr.,** ( *0-9647783* ) Div. of Sunflower Foods, 13000 Tilghman, Austin, TX 78729-4635 Tel 512-918-2483 Do not confuse with companies with the same or similar names in Boise, ID, Meridian, ID, Newton, MA, Lafayette, LA E-mail: info@sfpressaustin.com.

**Sunflower Univ. Pr.,** ( *0-89745* ) Subs. of Journal of the West, Inc., 1531 Yuma, Box 1009, Manhattan, KS 66505-1009 (SAN 218-5075) Tel 785-539-1888; Fax: 785-539-2233; Toll Free: 800-258-1232 (orders) Web site: http://www.sunflower-univ-press.org.

**Sunlight Publishing, Inc.,** ( *0-9643978* ) 102 S. Tejon St., Suite 1100, Colorado Springs, CO 80903 Tel 307-734-6411 Do not confuse with companies with the same or similar names in Northglenn, CO, Philadelphia, PA, Schaumburg, IL E-mail: sburns@iex.net Web site: http://www.sunlightpublishing.com *Dist(s):* **Books West.**

**Sunny Bks.,** ( *0-9665513* ) 590 Madison Ave., 21st Flr., New York, NY 10022 Fax: 847-566-8990; Toll Free: 888-407-2665 E-mail: sunnybooks@ameritech.net.

**Sunrise Bks.,** ( *0-940652* ) 1707 "E" St., Eureka, CA 95501 (SAN 665-7893) Tel 707-442-4004 (phone/fax) Do not confuse with companies with the same name in Lebanon, VA, Lake Bluff, IL.

**Sunrise Selections,** ( *0-9656307* ) Orders Addr.: P.O. Box 51602, Provo, UT 84605-1602 Tel 801-852-6141; Fax: 801-489-9517; Edit Addr.: 1102 N. Main, Mapleton, UT 84664 E-mail: sunrise-selections@mindspring.com Web site: http://www.sunrise-selections.com *Dist(s):* **Evans Bk. Distribution & Pubs., Inc..**

**Sunset Products,** ( *0-939755* ) 157 Santa Ana Ave., Long Beach, CA 90803 Tel 310-433-0697 *Dist(s):* **Landmark Audiobooks.**

**SunShine Pr. Pubns., Inc.,** ( *0-9615743; 1-888604* ) P.O. Box 333, Hygiene, CO 80533-0333 (SAN 696-0510) Fax: 303-772-3556 (phone/fax) Do not confuse with Sunshine Pr., Malibu, CA E-mail: sunshinepress@sunshinepress.com Web site: http://www.sunshinepress.com *Dist(s):* **Baker & Taylor Bks.**
**Bookpeople**
**Books West**
**New Leaf Distributing Co., Inc..**

**Sunstar Publishing, Ltd.,** ( *0-9638502; 1-887472* ) Div. of 1st World Library, Orders Addr.: 8015 Shoal Creek Blvd., No.100, Austin, TX 78757; Edit Addr.: 809 S. 2nd St., Box 2211, Fairfield, IA 52556 Tel 641-472-8868; 641-469-3131; 512-339-4000; Toll Free: 800-532-4734 Do not confuse with SunStar Publishing in Oakland, CA E-mail: worldlibrary@lisco.com; rodney@1stworldlibrary.org Web site: http://www.sustarpub.com; http://www.1stworldlibrary.com; http://www.newage.com *Dist(s):* **Baker & Taylor Bks.**
**Bookpeople**
**Brodart Co.**
**Lightning Source, Inc.**
**Midpoint National, Inc.**
**New Leaf Distributing Co., Inc.**
**Quality Bks., Inc.**
**Spring Arbor Distributors, Inc..**

†**Sunstone Pr.,** ( *0-86534; 0-913270* ) Orders Addr.: 239 Johnson St., Santa Fe, NM 87504-2321; Edit Addr.: P.O. Box 2321, Santa Fe, NM 87504-2321 (SAN 214-2090) Tel 505-988-4418; Fax: 505-988-1025; Toll Free: 800-243-5644 (orders only) E-mail: jsmith@sunstonepress.com Web site: http://www.sunstonepress.com *Dist(s):* **Baker & Taylor Bks.**
**Bookpeople**
**Brodart Co.**
**New Leaf Distributing Co., Inc.**
**Quality Bks., Inc.**
**Treasure Chest Bks.;** *CIP.*

**Superior Bk. Publishing Co.,** ( *0-9661504* ) Orders Addr.: 16417 Superior St., North Hills, CA 91343-1836 E-mail: billndi@pacbell.net Web site: http://www.home.pacbell.net/billndi.

**SuperiorBooks.com, Inc.,** ( *1-931055* ) Route 30, P.O. Box 299, Indian Lake, NY 12842-0299 (SAN 193-4252) Tel 518-648-5648; Fax: 518-648-5256 E-mail: rbpurdue@juno.com Web site: http://www.superiorbooks.com *Dist(s):* **Lightning Source, Inc.**
**Replica Bks..**

Names

**Sur-Mount Pubs., Inc.,** ( *0-9673517; 0-9740107* ) P.O. Box 99396, Emeryville, CA 94662-9396 Tel 510-472-7125; Fax: 410-428-9092 E-mail: info@surmountpublishersincorporated.com Web site: http://www.surmountpublishersincorporated.com *Dist(s):* **Baker & Taylor Bks..**

**Susaeta Ediciones, S.A. (ESP)** ( *84-305* ) *Dist. by* **AIMS Intl.**

**Suspect Thoughts Pr.,** ( *0-9710846; 0-9746388* ) 2215-R Market St., No. 544, San Francisco, CA 94114-1612 Tel 415-713-7159; Fax: 415-703-9049 E-mail: gregw@suspectthoughts.com Web site: http://www.suspectthoughtspress.com *Dist(s):* **Publishers Distributing Co..**

**Susquehanna Univ. Pr.,** ( *0-941664; 0-945636; 1-57591* ) Affil. of Associated Univ. Presses, Orders Addr.: 440 Forsgate Dr., Cranbury, NJ 08512 Tel 609-655-4770; Fax: 609-655-8366 Web site: http://www.susqu.edu/su_press *Dist(s):* **Baker & Taylor International.**

**Sutton Publishing,** ( *0-7509; 0-86299; 0-904387* ) Subs. of Sutton Publishing, Ltd., 260 Fifth Ave., 6th Flr., New York, NY 10001 Do not confuse with companies with same names in Old Greenwich, CT, Eugene, OR E-mail: Suttonus@mindspring.com Web site: http://www.suttonpublishing.co.uk/ *Dist(s):* **National Bk. Network.**

†**Swallow Pr.,** ( *0-8040* ) Ohio Univ. Pr., Scott Quadrangle, Athens, OH 45701 (SAN 202-5663) Tel 740-593-1158; Fax: 740-593-4536; Toll Free: 800-621-2736 E-mail: arnold@ohio.edu Web site: http://www.ohio~.edu/oupress/ *Dist(s):* **Ohio Univ. Pr.**
        **Univ. of Chicago Pr.;** *CIP.*

**Sweet Valley** Imprint of Random Hse. Children's Bks.

**Sweetlight Bks.,** ( *0-9604462; 1-877714* ) 16625 Heitman Rd., Cottonwood, CA 96022 (SAN 215-1154) Tel 916-529-5392 E-mail: swtlight@snowcrest.net Web site: http://www.snowcrest.net/swtlight *Dist(s):* **Baker & Taylor Bks.**
        **Bookpeople**
        **New Leaf Distributing Co., Inc..**

**Syndicate Media Group, The,** ( *1-930306* ) 6605 Hollywood Blvd., Suite 220, Los Angeles, CA 90028 Tel 323-993-8390; Fax: 323-993-8399 E-mail: MGerald102@aol.com

**SynergEbks.,** ( *0-7443; 0-9702385; 1-931540* ) Orders Addr.: 1235 Flat Shoals Rd., King, NC 27021 (SAN 254-4962) Fax: 336-994-8403; Toll Free: 888-812-2533 E-mail: SynergEbooks@aol.com Web site: http://www.SynergEbooks.com *Dist(s):* **Book Clearing Hse..**

†**Synergistic Pr., Inc.,** ( *0-912184* ) 3965 Sacramento St., San Francisco, CA 94118 (SAN 205-4116) Tel 415-387-8180; Fax: 415-751-8505 E-mail: goodreading@synergisticbooks.com Web site: http://www.synergisticbooks.com *Dist(s):* **Baker & Taylor Bks.;** *CIP.*

†**Syracuse Univ. Pr.,** ( *0-8156* ) 621 Skytop Rd., Suite 110, Syracuse, NY 13244-5290 (SAN 206-9776) Tel 315-443-2597; Fax: 315-443-5545 E-mail: supress@syr.edu Web site: http://www.sumweb.syr.edu/su_press/ *Dist(s):* **Gryphon Hse., Inc.**
        **Music Sales Corp.**
        **Penguin Group (USA) Inc.;** *CIP.*

**T. Bo Publishing,** ( *0-9702882* ) Orders Addr.: P.O. Box 25, Gainesville, FL 32602-0025 Tel 352-335-5084; Fax: 352-371-3221; Edit Addr.: 2910 SE 21st Ave., Gainesville, FL 32641 E-mail: bothewriter@aol.com.

†**TQS Pubns., Eclectic Chicano Literature,** ( *0-88412; 0-89229* ) Div. of Tonatiuh/Quinto Sol International, Inc., P.O. Box 9275, Berkeley, CA 94709 (SAN 203-3984) Tel 510-655-8036; Fax: 510-601-6938 Web site: http://www.tqsbooks.com *Dist(s):* **Baker & Taylor Bks.**
        **Continental Bk. Co., Inc.;** *CIP.*

**TSR, Inc.,** ( *0-7869; 0-88038; 0-935696; 1-56076* ) Subs. of Wizards of the Coast, Orders Addr.: P.O. Box 707, Renton, WA 98057-0707 Tel 425-226-6500; Edit Addr.: 1801 Lind Ave., SW, Renton, WA 98055 Tel 425-226-2650 Do not confuse with T S R, Inc. in Agoyra Hills, CA E-mail: custserv@wizards.com Web site: http://www.wizards.com/.

**Tabby Hse. Bks.,** ( *0-9627974; 1-881539* ) Orders Addr.: 4429 Shady Ln., Charlotte Harbor, FL 33980 Tel 941-629-7646; Fax: 941-629-4270 E-mail: publisher@tabbyhouse.com Web site: http://www.tabbyhouse.com *Dist(s):* **Baker & Taylor Bks. Distributors, The.**

**Tales Pr.,** ( *0-9641423* ) 2609 N. High Cross Rd., Urbana, IL 61802-9643 Tel 217-384-5820; Fax: 217-384-7996 E-mail: tales@soltec.net Web site: http://www.talespress.com *Dist(s):* **Biblio Distribution.**

**Talese, Nan A.** Imprint of Doubleday Publishing

**Talewinds** Imprint of Charlesbridge Publishing, Inc.

**Talisman Hse., Pubs.,** ( *1-883689; 1-58498* ) Orders Addr.: P.O. Box 3157, Jersey City, NJ 07303-3157 Tel 201-938-0698; Fax: 201-938-1693; Edit Addr.: 129 Wayne St., Jersey City, NJ 07302 E-mail: talismaned@aol.com *Dist(s):* **Acorn Alliance**
        **Client Distribution Services**
        **LPC Group**
        **SPD-Small Pr. Distribution.**

**Talk Miramax Bks.,** ( *0-7868* ) Div. of Disney Bk. Publishing, Inc., A Walt Disney Co., 77 W. 66th St., 11th Flr., New York, NY 10023 Tel 212-456-0133 *Dist(s):* **Time Warner Bk. Group.**

**Tamarack Bks., Inc.,** ( *0-9634839; 1-886609* ) Orders Addr.: P.O. Box 190313, Boise, ID 83719-0313 (SAN 297-8792) Tel 208-922-2229; Fax: 208-922-5880; Toll Free: 800-962-6657; Edit Addr.: 2715 E. Deer Flat Rd., Kuna, ID 83634 E-mail: sales@tamarackbooks.com Web site: http://www.tamarackbooks.com.

**Tamarind,** ( *0-9667484* ) P.O. Box 75442, Honolulu, HI 96836 Tel 808-942-1794 E-mail: dcasey7@concentric.net *Dist(s):* **Native Bks..**

**Tana Lake Publishing,** ( *0-9651007* ) P.O. Box 782, Oxen Hill, MD 20750-0782.

**Tangleaire Pr.,** ( *1-891584* ) 2605 S. Hughes, Amarillo, TX 79109 Tel 806-376-7139.

**Tantor Media, Inc.,** ( *1-4001* ) 1315 Avenida De Verdes, San Clemente, CA 92672 (SAN 254-0509) Tel 949-481-2770; Fax: 949-481-2790 E-mail: kevin@tantor.com Web site: http://www.tantor.com.

**Tapestries,** ( *0-9676703* ) 3636 Buchanan St., San Francisco, CA 94123 (SAN 253-1992) Tel 415-921-8689; Fax: 415-921-1990 Web site: http://www.tapestriespublishing.com.

†**Taplinger Publishing Co., Inc.,** ( *0-8008* ) P.O. Box 175, Marlboro, NJ 07746 Tel 201-432-3257; Fax: 201-432-3708 E-mail: info@parkwestpubs.com Web site: http://www.parkwestpubs.com/ *Dist(s):* **Parkwest Pubns., Inc.;** *CIP.*

**Targum Pr., Inc.,** ( *0-944070; 1-56871* ) 22700 W. Eleven Mile Rd., Southfield, MI 48034 (SAN 242-8997) Tel 248-355-2266; Toll Free Fax: 888-298-9992 E-mail: targum@elronet.co.il Web site: http://www.targum.com *Dist(s):* **Feldheim, Philipp Inc..**

**Tatsch Assocs.,** ( *0-912890* ) 210 Edgewood Dr., Fredericksburg, TX 78624 (SAN 202-7623) Tel 210-997-8785.

**Tattersall Publishing,** ( *0-9640513; 0-9679775* ) P.O. Box 308194, Denton, TX 76203-8194 Tel 940-565-0804; Fax: 940-320-8604 E-mail: cwolfe@tattersallpub.com; cwood@tattersallpub.com Web site: http://www.tattersallpub.com.

†**Taylor & Francis, Inc.,** ( *0-335; 0-415; 0-8448; 0-85066; 0-89116; 0-903796; 0-905273; 1-56032; 1-85000* ) Orders Addr.: 10650 Toebben Dr., Independence, KY 41051 Toll Free Fax: 800-248-4724; Toll Free: 800-634-7064; Edit Addr.: 325 Chestnut St., Philadelphia, PA 19106 (SAN 241-9246) Tel 215-625-8900; Fax: 215-625-2940; 29 W. 35th St., New York, NY 10001 Tel 212-216-7800; Fax: 212-564-7854 E-mail: info@taylorandfrancis.com Web site: http://www.taylorandfrancis.com *Dist(s):* **netLibrary, Inc.;** *CIP.*

**Taylor Productions** Imprint of GRM Assocs.

**Taylor, W. Thomas Inc.,** ( *0-935072* ) P.O. Box 249, Barksdale, TX 78828-0249 (SAN 211-1454) Tel 210-234-3250 *Dist(s):* **Oak Knoll Pr..**

**Teacher Created Materials, Inc.,** ( *0-87673; 1-55734; 1-57690; 0-7439* ) 6421 Industry Way, Westminster, CA 92683-3608 (SAN 665-5270) Tel 714-891-7895; Fax: 714-892-0283; Toll Free: 800-662-4321 E-mail: ppulido@teachercreated.com Web site: http://www.teachercreated.com.

**Teleos Imprint** Imprint of LP Pubns.

**Temeron Bks., Inc.,** ( *1-895510* ) P.O. Box 896, Bellingham, WA 98227 Tel 360-738-4016.

**Temple, Ellen C. Publishing, Inc.,** ( *0-936650* ) 736 Crown Colony Dr., Suite 100, Lufkin, TX 75901 (SAN 215-1162) Tel 409-639-4707; Fax: 409-639-4716 E-mail: ectemple@icc.com *Dist(s):* **Eakin Pr..**

**Temple Productions** *See* **Temple Publishing**

**Temple Publishing,** ( *0-9709394* ) Orders Addr.: 25852 Mcbean Pkwy., No. 149, Santa Clarita, CA 91355-3705 E-mail: templepublishing@aol.com Web site: http://www.templebookpublishing.com.

†**Temple Univ. Pr.,** ( *0-87722; 1-56639; 1-59213* ) 1601 N. Broad St., Univ. Services Bldg., Rm. 305, Philadelphia, PA 19122-6099 (SAN 202-7666) Tel 215-204-3389; Fax: 215-204-4719; Toll Free: 800-447-1656 E-mail: charles.ault@temple.edu Web site: http://www.temple.edu/tempress *Dist(s):* **Baker & Taylor Bks.**
        **Koen Bk. Distributors;** *CIP.*

**Templegate Pubs.,** ( *0-87243* ) 302 E. Adams St., Springfield, IL 62705 (SAN 213-1994) Tel 217-522-3353; Fax: 217-522-3362; Toll Free: 800-367-4844 (orders only) E-mail: wisdom@templegate.com Web site: http://www.templegate.com *Dist(s):* **Partners Pubs. Group, Inc..**

†**Ten Speed Pr.,** ( *0-89815; 0-913668; 1-58008* ) Orders Addr.: P.O. Box 7123, Berkeley, CA 94707 (SAN 202-7674) Fax: 510-559-1629 (orders); Toll Free: 800-841-2665; 555 Richmond St., W. Suite 405, Box 702, Toronto, ON M5V 3B1 Tel 416-703-7775; Fax: 416-703-9992 E-mail: order@tenspeed.com; alan@tenspeed.ca; greg@tenspeed.com Web site: http://www.tenspeed.com; *CIP.*

**Tennessee Valley Publishing,** ( *1-882194; 1-932604* ) Orders Addr.: P.O. Box 52527, Knoxville, TN 37950-2527 Tel 865-584-5235; Fax: 865-584-0113; Toll Free: 800-762-7079; Edit Addr.: 5710 Kingston Pike, Suite F, Knoxville, TN 37950 E-mail: info@typ1.com; info@tvp1.com Web site: http://www.tvp1.com.

**Terra, Izdatel'skij centr - Izdatel'stvo Azbuka (RUS)** ( *5-7684* ) *Dist. by* **Distribks Inc.**

**Terrace Bks.** Imprint of Univ. of Wisconsin Pr.

**Tetu, Randeane,** 41 Old Turnpike Rd., Haddam, CT 06438-1244 Tel 203-343-5808.

**TexArt Services, Inc.,** ( *0-935857* ) P.O. Box 17423, San Antonio, TX 78217-0423 (SAN 696-0022) Tel 210-826-2889.

†**Texas A&M Univ. Pr.,** ( *0-89096; 1-58544* ) 4354 TAMU John H. Lindsey Bldg., Lewis St., College Station, TX 77843-4354 (SAN 658-1919) Tel 979-845-1436; Fax: 979-847-8752; Toll Free Fax: 888-617-2421 (orders); Toll Free: 800-826-8911 (orders); *Imprints:* Reveille Books (Reveille Books) E-mail: wjl@tampress.tamu.edu Web site: http://www.tamu.edu/upress/ *Dist(s):* **netLibrary, Inc.;** *CIP.*

†**Texas Christian Univ. Pr.,** ( *0-87565; 0-912646* ) P.O. Box 298300, Fort Worth, TX 76129 (SAN 202-7690) Tel 817-257-7822; Fax: 817-257-5075 E-mail: j.alter@tcu.edu; s.petty@tcu.edu Web site: http://www.prs.tcu.edu/prs *Dist(s):* **Texas A&M Univ. Pr.;** *CIP.*

**Texas Review Pr.,** ( *1-881515* ) Div. of Sam Houston State Univ., English Dept., Sam Houston State Univ. English Dept., Box 2146, Huntsville, TX 77341-2146 Tel 936-294-1992; Fax: 936-294-1414 E-mail: eng_pdr@shsu.edu Web site: http://www.tamu.edu/upress/TR/trgen.htm/ *Dist(s):* **Texas A&M Univ. Pr..**

†**Texas Tech Univ. Pr.,** ( *0-89672* ) Affil. of Texas Tech Univ., Orders Addr.: P.O. Box 41037, Lubbock, TX 79409-1037 (SAN 218-5899) Tel 806-742-2982; Fax: 806-742-2979; Toll Free: 800-832-4042; Edit Addr.: 2903 Fourth St., Lubbock, TX 79409-1037; *Imprints:* Double Mountain Books (Double Mtn Bks) E-mail: ttup@ttu.edu Web site: http://www.ttup.ttu.edu; *CIP.*

**Texture Pr.,** ( 0-9641837; 0-9712061 ) P.O. Box 720157, Norman, OK 73072 Tel 405-366-7730; Fax: 405-364-3627
E-mail: susan@beyondutopia.com
Web site: http://www.beyondutopia.com.

†**Theatre Communications Group, Inc.,** ( 0-88754; 0-913745; 0-930452; 0-948230; 1-55936; 1-84002; 1-85459; 1-870259; 1-899791 ) 355 Lexington Ave., New York, NY 10017-6603 (SAN 210-9387) Tel 212-697-5230; Fax: 212-983-4847
Web site: http://www.tcg.org
*Dist(s):* **Consortium Bk. Sales & Distribution**; *CIP.*

†**Theosophical Publishing Hse.,** ( 0-8356; 81-7059; 0-7229 ) Div. of Theosophical Society in America, 306 W. Geneva Rd., P.O. Box 270, Wheaton, IL 60189-0270 (SAN 202-5698) Tel 630-665-0130; Fax: 630-665-8791; Toll Free: 800-669-9425; *Imprints:* Quest Books (Quest)
E-mail: questoperations@theosmail.net; questbooks@aol.com; questbooks@theosophia.org
Web site: http://www.theosophical.org
*Dist(s):* **National Bk. Network**; *CIP.*

**Theytus Bks., Ltd. (CAN)** ( 0-919441; 1-894778 ) *Dist. by Orca Bk Pubs.*

**Third Millennium Publishing Imprint of Sci Fi-Arizona, Inc.**

**3rd Side Pr., Inc.,** ( 1-879427 ) 2250 W. Farragut, Chicago, IL 60625-1863 Tel 773-271-3029; Fax: 773-271-0459
E-mail: ThirdSide@aol.com.

**3rd Woman Pr.,** ( 0-943219 ) 1329 Ninth St., Berkeley, CA 94710 (SAN 668-3045) Tel 510-524-2677; Fax: 510-524-2817
E-mail: karina@thirdwomanpress.com.

**Third World Press,** ( 0-88378 ) P.O. Box 19730, Chicago, IL 60619 (SAN 202-778X) Tel 773-651-0700; Fax: 773-651-7286
Web site: http://www.thirdworldpress.com.

**Thirsty Horse LLC,** ( 0-9723127 ) 1220 N. Market St., Suite 606, Wilmington,, DE 19801-2598 (SAN 254-7767) Tel 302-428-1222
E-mail: orders@thirsty-horse.com
Web site: http://www.thirsty-horse-media.com.

**Thirteenth Bomb Squadron Assn. (Korea),** ( 0-9653649 ) c/o West Pr., 1663 W. Grant Rd., Tucson, AZ 85745 Tel 520-624-4939; Fax: 520-624-2715
E-mail: info@13thbombsquadron.org
Web site: http://www.13thbombsquadron.org/
*Dist(s):* **West Pr..**

**3300 Pr.,** ( 0-9646017 ) 3300 Mission St., San Francisco, CA 94110 Tel 415-826-6886; 300 Vicksburg St., No. 5, San Francisco, CA 94114.

**Thistle Hill Pubns.,** ( 0-9705511 ) 477 Thistle Hill Rd., North Pomfret, VT 05053-0307 Tel 802 457 4892; 802-457-2050; Fax: 802-457-3653; Fulfillment Addr.: P.O. Box 428, White River Junction, VT 05001
E-mail: crowl@together.net
Web site: http://www.thistlehillpub.com
*Dist(s):* **Chelsea Green Publishing**
**Univ. Pr. of New England.**

**Thorby Enterprises, Inc.,** ( 0-9666443 ) 16 Technology Dr., Suite 134, Irvine, CA 92618 Tel 949-753-0725; Fax: 949-753-0782
E-mail: webmaster@thorby.com
Web site: http://www.thorby.com.

†**Thorndike Pr.,** ( 0-7838; 0-7862; 0-8161; 0-89621; 1-56054 ) Div. of Gale Group, 295 Kennedy Memorial Dr., Waterville, ME 04901 Tel 207-859-1053; 207-859-1020; 207-859-1000; Toll Free Fax: 800-558-4676; Toll Free: 800-223-1244 (ext. 15); 800-877-4253 (customer resource ctr.); *Imprints:* Large Print Press (Lrg Print Pr)
E-mail: knobloch@galegroup.com; barb.littfield@galegroup.com
Web site: http://www.galegroup.com/thorndike; *CIP.*

**Thornfield Pr.,** ( 0-9613075 ) 21 Steele Ave., Staten Island, NY 10306-2326 (SAN 294-6815) Tel 718-351-2477; Toll Free: 800-356-9315 (orders only)
*Dist(s):* **Baker & Taylor Bks..**

†**Thorp Springs Pr.,** ( 0-914476 ) 1400 Cullen Ave., Austin, TX 78757 (SAN 202-781X) Tel 512-459-6243 ; Fax: 512-832-0936
E-mail: skankypossum@hotmail.com; *CIP.*

**Thorpe, F. A. Pubs. (GBR)** ( 0-7089; 0-85456 ) *Dist. by Ulverscroft US.*

**Three Arts Pr.,** ( 0-9669576 ) 1100 Maple Ave., Downers Grove, IL 60515 Fax: 630-968-1623; Toll Free: 800-777-2997.

**Three Continents Imprint of Rienner, Lynne Pubs., Inc.**

**Three Forks Pr.,** ( 0-9637629; 1-893451 ) Orders Addr.: P.O. Box 823461, Dallas, TX 75382 Tel 214-503-0738 ; Fax: 214-503-8534; Toll Free: 800-687-0903; Edit Addr.: 9021 Gunnison Dr., Dallas, TX 75231
E-mail: dpayne@mail.smu.edu
*Dist(s):* **Baker & Taylor Bks.**
**Hervey's Booklink & Cookbook Warehouse.**

**Three Rivers Pr. Imprint of Crown Publishing Group**

**Three Swans Publishing Co.,** ( 0-9661380 ) Div. of First Fleet Enterprises (FFE), 3412 Snowy Egret Ct., Palm Harbor, FL 34683 Tel 727-773-9744
E-mail: RMAtwater@aol.com
Web site: http://www.3swanspublishing.com
*Dist(s):* **Koen Bk. Distributors.**

**Thrifteon Publications,** ( 1-880258 ) 405 Ascot Ct., Knoxville, TN 37923-5807 Tel 423-539-9932
E-mail: RBreed4217@AOL.com.

**Thriller Pr.,** ( 1-931296 ) Orders Addr.: P.O. Box 612711, South Lake Tahoe, CA 96152 (SAN 253-9667) Tel 530-541-1454; Fax: 530-541-8709; Edit Addr.: 3440 Lake Tahoe Blvd., South Lake Tahoe, CA 96150 Tel 530-541-1454
E-mail: tyler@thrillerpress.com; thrillerpress@hotmail.com
Web site: http://www.thrillerpress.com.

**Thumbprint Pr.,** ( 0-9654951 ) 7 Brookside Dr., San Anselmo, CA 94960-1414 Tel 415-458-8724; Fax: 317-581-9853 Do not confuse with Thumbprint Pr., Sherman Oaks, CA.

**Thunder's Mouth Pr. Imprint of Avalon Publishing Group**

**Tickerwick Pubns.,** ( 1-885084 ) P.O. Box 100695, Denver, CO 80250 Tel 303-761-9940
E-mail: druid@henge.com
*Dist(s):* **Bookpeople**
**New Leaf Distributing Co., Inc..**

**Tidal Pr.,** ( 0-930954 ) Orders Addr.: P.O. Box 160, Cranberry Isles, ME 04625 (SAN 211-3783) Tel 207-244-3090 (May through October); Edit Addr.: 129 Mount Vernon St., Boston, MA 02108 Tel 617-523-7995 (November through April) Do not confuse with companies with the same name in San Diego, CA, Wilmington, NC
E-mail: jfnance@aol.com.

**Tidewater Pubs. Imprint of Cornell Maritime Pr., Inc.**

**Tiger Tales Imprint of ME Media LLC**

**Tilbury Hse. Pubs.,** ( 0-88448; 0-937966 ) 2 Mechanic St., No. 3, Gardiner, ME 04345 Tel 207-582-1899; Fax: 207-582-8227; Toll Free: 800-582-1899 (orders)
E-mail: tilbury@tilburyhouse.com; sbeach@tilburyhouse.com
Web site: http://www.tilburyhouse.com
*Dist(s):* **Lectorum Pubns., Inc..**

**Timbertrails Imprint of Capstan Pubns.**

**Timberwolf Pr., Inc.,** ( 0-9653210; 1-58752 ) 202 N. Allen Dr., Suite A, Allen, TX 75013 (SAN 254-0789) Tel 972-359-0911 (ext. 101); Toll Free: 888-808-0912
E-mail: sales@timberwolfpress.com; patrick@timberwolfpress.com
Web site: http://www.Timberwolfpress.com
*Dist(s):* **Ingram Entertainment, Inc..**

**Time Travelers,** ( 0-9674552 ) Orders Addr.: P.O. Box 361, Columbiana, OH 44408 Tel 330-482-3708 (phone/fax); Edit Addr.: 125 Hawkins Ln., Columbiana, OH 44408 Tel 330-482-3708
E-mail: Gertrud418@aol.com
Web site: http://www.timetravelersinc.com
*Dist(s):* **Baker & Taylor Bks.**
**Brodart Co..**

**Time Warner AudioBooks,** ( 1-57042; 1-58621; 1-59483 ) Div. of Time Warner, Inc., 135 W. 50th St., 4th Flr., New York, NY 10020 Fax: 212-522-7994
Web site: http://www.mytimewarneraudio.com
*Dist(s):* **Libros Sin Fronteras**
**Landmark Audiobooks**
**Warner Bks., Inc..**

**Time Warner Bks. UK (GBR)** ( 0-316 ) *Dist. by Trafalgar.*

**Time Warner Bks. UK (GBR)** ( 0-316 ) *Dist. by Little.*

**Time Warner Bk. Group,** ( 0-446 ) Orders Addr.: 3 Center Plaza, Boston, MA 02108 Toll Free Fax: 800-286-9471; Toll Free: 800-759-0190; Edit Addr.: 135 W. 50th St. Sports Illustrated Building, New York, NY 10020-1393 Tel 212-522-7381; Toll Free Fax: 800-477-5925
Web site: http://www.timewarner.com.

**TimeBridges Pubs. LLC,** ( 0-9707662 ) 1001 Cooper Point Rd., SW, Suite 140- No.176, Olympia, WA 98502 Tel 360-867-1883; Fax: 360-867-1221
E-mail: info@timebridgespublishers.com
Web site: http://www.timebridgespublishers.com
*Dist(s):* **Pathway Bk. Service.**

**TimeFare Audio Bk. Productions,** ( 0-932079 ) 215 W. 19th Ave., Kennewick, WA 99337 (SAN 686-2632) Tel 509-375-0808
E-mail: timefarebooks@aol.com
Web site: http://www.timefareinc.com; http://www.timefareproductions.com.

**TimeFare Books** *See* **TimeFare Audio Bk. Productions**

**Timeless Love Imprint of Oak Tree Publishing**

**Timeless Romance Imprint of Sierra Raconteur Publishing**

**Times Bks. Imprint of Holt, Henry & Co.**

**Titan Bks. Ltd. (GBR)** ( 0-907610; 1-84023; 1-85286; 1-900097 ) *Dist. by Client Dist Srvs.*

**Toby Pr.,** ( 1-902881; 1-59264 ) Orders Addr.: P.O. Box 8531, New Milford, CT 06776-8531 (SAN 253-9985) Fax: 203-830-8512 (questions & orders); Toll Free: 800-810-7191 (consumer orders)
E-mail: toby@tobypress.com
Web site: http://www.tobypress.com.

**TOKYOPOP, Inc.,** ( 1-892213; 1-931514; 1-59182; 1-59532 ) Div. of Mixx Entertainment, Inc., 5900 Wilshire Blvd., Suite 2000, Los Angeles, CA 90036 Tel 323-692-6700; Fax: 323-692-6701
*Dist(s):* **Client Distribution Services.**

**Tokyopop Press** *See* **TOKYOPOP, Inc.**

**Toland Communications,** ( 0-9702109 ) 1001 Bridgeway, PMB 214, Sausalito, CA 94965-0000; *Imprints:* Bridgeway Press (Bridgewy Pr)
E-mail: tolandweb@aol.com
Web site: http://www.tolan.com.

**Tombouctou Bks.,** ( 0-939180 ) 1472 Creekview Ln., Santa Cruz, CA 95062 (SAN 282-4647) Tel 408-476-4144
*Dist(s):* **Bookpeople**
**SPD-Small Pr. Distribution.**

†**Top of the Mountain Publishing,** ( 0-914295; 1-56087 ) P.O. Box 2244, Pinellas Park, FL 33780-2244 (SAN 287-590X) Tel 727-391-3958; Fax: 727-391-4598
E-mail: orders@abcinfo.com
Web site: http://www.abcinfo.com; http://www.10-10-net.com
*Dist(s):* **Baker & Taylor Bks.**
**Brodart Co.**
**Emery-Pratt Co.**
**New Leaf Distributing Co., Inc.**; *CIP.*

**Top Pubns., Ltd.,** ( 0-9666366; 1-929976 ) Div. of Top Ventures, Ltd., 3100 Independence Pkwy., No. 311-349, Plano, TX 75075-9152 Tel 972-960-2240; Fax: 972-233-0713; Toll Free: 877-490-9686
E-mail: victoria@toppub.com; bill@toppub.com
Web site: http://toppub.com
*Dist(s):* **Baker & Taylor Bks..**

**Top Shelf Productions,** ( 1-891830; 961-90436 ) Orders Addr.: P.O. Box 1282, Marietta, GA 30061-1282 Tel 770-425-0551; Fax: 770-427-6395; Edit Addr.: 1109 Grand Oaks Glen, Marietta, GA 30064 Tel 770-425-0551; Fax: 770-427-6395
E-mail: staros@bellsouth.net
Web site: http://www.topshelfcomix.com
*Dist(s):* **Diamond Book Distributors, Inc.**
**Diamond Comic Distributors, Inc..**

**Topaz Imprint of NAL**

**Topgallant Publishing Company, Limited** *See* **Ku Pa'a Publishing**

**TOPICS Entertainment,** ( 1-886089; 1-931102; 1-59150 ) 1600 SW. 43rd St., Renton, WA 98055 Tel 425-656-3621; Fax: 425-656-8013
E-mail: info@topics-ent.com; beth@topics-ent.com
Web site: http://www.topics-ent.com.

**Topsail Pr.,** ( 0-9662818 ) 739 Castle Blvd., Akron, OH 44313 Tel 330-836-6735
*Dist(s):* **Partners Pubs. Group, Inc..**

**Tor Bks. Imprint of Doherty, Tom Assocs., LLC**

**Tor Classics Imprint of Doherty, Tom Assocs., LLC**

**Tor Teen Imprint of Doherty, Tom Assocs., LLC**

**Tory Corner Editions** *See* **Quincannon Publishing Group**

**Total Sports Publishing,** ( 0-9656949; 1-892129; 1-930844 ) 45 Birch St. Apt. 5H, Kingston, NY 12401-1053
E-mail: us@ts-pub.com
Web site: http://www.totalsportspublishing.com.

**Touchstone Imprint of Simon & Schuster**

**Tout Paris/Palancar** *See* **Palancar**

**Tower Publishing,** ( 0-89442; 1-881758; 1-932056 ) 588 Saco Rd., Standish, ME 04084-6239 Tel 207-642-5400; 207-969-8693; Fax: 207-642-5463; Toll Free: 800-969-8693 Do not confuse with Tower Publishing Co. in Chula, GA
E-mail: info@towerpub.com; info@towrpub.com
Web site: http://www.towerpub.com.

**Tower Publishing of New Hampshire** *See* **Tower Publishing**

**TowleHouse Publishing Co.,** *( 0-9668774; 1-931249 )* 1312 Bell Grimes Ln., Nashville, TN 37207 (SAN 299-7797) Tel 615-612-3005; Fax: 615-612-0067 E-mail: vermonte@aol.com Web site: http://towlehouse.com *Dist(s):* **Fell, Frederick Pubs., Inc.** **FaithWorks** **National Bk. Network.**

**Townsend, J.N. Publishing,** *( 0-9617426; 1-880158 )* 4 Franklin St., Exeter, NH 03833 (SAN 630-303X) Tel 603-778-9883; Fax: 603-772-1980; Toll Free: 800-333-9883 (orders only) E-mail: townsendpub@aol.com Web site: http://www.jntownsendpublishing.com *Dist(s):* **Hood, Alan C. & Co., Inc..**

**Townsend Pr.,** *( 0-944210; 1-59194 )* 1038 Industrial Dr., West Berlin, NJ 08091-9164 (SAN 243-0444) Toll Free Fax: 800-225-8894; Toll Free: 800-772-6410 E-mail: townsendcs@aol.com Web site: http://www.townsendpress.com.

**Tradd Street Pr.,** *( 0-937684 )* 8376 Meadows Rd., Warrenton, VA 20186-7425 (SAN 205-4469) E-mail: info@vernergallery.com Web site: http://www.vernergallery.com.

**Tradition Publishing Co.,** *( 1-59187 )* Orders Addr.: P.O. Box 370, Maple Plain, MN 55359 *Dist(s):* **Child's World, Inc..**

**Trafalgar Square,** *( 0-943955; 1-57076 )* Orders Addr.: P.O. Box 257, North Pomfret, VT 05053 (SAN 213-8859) Tel 802-457-1911; Fax: 802-457-1913; Toll Free: 800-423-4525; Edit Addr.: Howe Hill Rd., North Pomfret, VT 05053; *Imprints:* Trafalgar Square Publishing (Trafalgar Sq Pub) E-mail: tsquare@sover.net Web site: http://www.trafalgarsquarebooks.com.

**Trafalgar Square Publishing Imprint of Trafalgar Square**

†**Transaction Pubs.,** *( 0-7658; 0-87855; 0-88738; 1-56000; 1-4128 )* 390 Campus Dr., Somerset, NJ 08873 (SAN 202-7941) Tel 732-445-2280; Fax: 732-445-3138; Toll Free: 888-999-6778 E-mail: orders@transactionpub.com; agarbie@transactionpub.com Web site: http://www.transactionpub.com; *CIP.*

**Transatlantic Arts, Inc.,** *( 0-693 )* P.O. Box 6086, Albuquerque, NM 87197 (SAN 202-7968) Tel 505-898-2289 Do not confuse with Trans-Atlantic Pubns., Inc., Philadelphia, PA. E-mail: books@transatlantic.com Web site: http://www.transatlantic.com/direct.

**Trans-Atlantic Pubns., Inc.,** 311 Bainbridge St., Philadelphia, PA 19147 (SAN 694-0234) Tel 215-925-5083; Fax: 215-925-1912 Do not confuse with Transatlantic Arts, Inc., Albuquerque, NM E-mail: order@transatlanticpub.com Web site: http://www.transatlanticpub.com *Dist(s):* **Baker & Taylor Bks..**

†**Transnational Pubs., Inc.,** *( 0-941320; 1-57105 )* 410 Saw Mill River Rd., Ardsley, NY 10502 (SAN 226-2967) Tel 914-693-5100; Fax: 914-693-4430; Toll Free: 800-914-8186 E-mail: info@transnationalpubs.com Web site: http://www.transnationalpubs.com *Dist(s):* **Baker & Taylor Bks.;** *CIP.*

**Transworld Publishers Ltd. (GBR)** *( 0-552 )* *Dist. by* **Trafalgar.**

**Treasure Chest Bks.,** *( 0-918080; 1-887896; 0-9700750 )* Orders Addr.: P.O. Box 5250, Tucson, AZ 85703-0250 (SAN 209-3251) Tel 520-623-9558; Fax: 520-624-5888; Toll Free Fax: 800-715-5888; Toll Free: 800-969-9558; Edit Addr.: 451 N. Bonita Ave., Tucson, AZ 85745 Tel 602-623-9558 E-mail: info@treasurechestbooks.com; info@rionuevo.com Web site: http://www.rionuevo.com/; http://www.treasurechestbooks.com *Dist(s):* **Norton, W. W. & Co., Inc..**

**Treasure Chest Publications** *See* **Treasure Chest Bks.**

**Treasure Coast Mysteries, Inc.,** *( 0-9715136 )* 43 Kindred St., Stuart, FL 34994 Tel 772-288-1066; Fax: 772-288-5015; Toll Free: 800-526-7979 E-mail: mtallpaul@aol.com Web site: http://www.treasurecoastmysteries.com *Dist(s):* **Baker & Taylor Bks..**

**Tree Garden Workshop,** *( 0-9642169 )* P.O. Box 4351, Philadelphia, PA 19118-8351 *Dist(s):* **Native Bks..**

**Treeless Pr.,** *( 1-58505 )* 2887 College Ave., No. 1, Suite 295, Berkeley, CA 94705 Tel 510-848 6692 E-mail: admin@treelesspress.com; sgarthp@inkyfingers.com Web site: http://www.treelesspress.com.

---

**Trent Martin Pubns.,** *( 0-9673506 )* P.O. Box 201281, San Antonio, TX 78220-8281 Tel 210-648-5994; Fax: 210-648-2088 E-mail: jomccall@idworld.net Web site: http://www.geocities.com/WestHollywood/ Stonewall/7523/.

**Tribeca Hse.,** *( 0-9701706 )* P.O. Box 364, Neptune, NJ 07754 Fax: 973-763-7478 E-mail: sibyllad@earthlink.net Web site: http://www.tribecahouse.com *Dist(s):* **Afrikan World Bk. Distributor** **Baker & Taylor Bks..**

**Trice, B.E. Publishing,** *( 0-9631925; 1-890885 )* 2727 Prytania St., New Orleans, LA 70130 Tel 504-895-0111 E-mail: betbooks@aol.com.

**Tricycle Pr.,** *( 1-58246; 1-883672 )* Div. of Ten Speed Pr., Orders Addr.: P.O. Box 7123, Berkeley, CA 94707 Tel 510-559-1600; Fax: 510-559-1629 Web site: http://www.tenspeed.com *Dist(s):* **Gryphon Hse., Inc.** **Ten Speed Pr.** **Wolverine Distributing, Inc..**

**Trident Pr. International,** *( 1-58279; 1-888777; 1-86091 )* Orders Addr.: 801 12th Ave., S., Suite 400, Naples, FL 34102 Tel 239-649-7077; Fax: 239-649-5832; Toll Free Fax: 800-494-4226; Toll Free: 800-593-3662; Edit Addr.: 395 W. Mayes St., Jackson, MO 39213 E-mail: tridentpress@worldnet.att.net Web site: http://www.schoolbookzone.com; http://www.secondworldwar.net; http:// www.trident-international.com.

**Trill Pr.,** *( 0-914485 )* 653 Robertson Way, Sacramento, CA 95818 (SAN 240-1673) Tel 916-448-2018 *Dist(s):* **Suttertown Publishing.**

**Trillium Pr.,** *( 1-881692 )* 620 Edgehill Dr., Saint Albans, WV 25177 Tel 304-722-6346 Do not confuse with companies with the same or similar names in Unionville, KY, Brisbane, CA.

†**Trinity Univ. Pr.,** *( 0-911536; 0-939980; 1-59534 )* One Trinity Pl., San Antonio, TX 78212 (SAN 205-4590) Tel 210-999-8881; Fax: 210-999-8182 Do not confuse with Trinity University Press in Bannockburn, IL E-mail: sarah.nawrocki@trinity.edu; *CIP.*

**TripleCrown Pubns.,** *( 0-9702472; 0-9747895 )* 422 S. 18th St., Columbus, OH 43205 Tel 614-258-8611 E-mail: carmenaparee@aol.com Web site: http://www.triplecrownpublications.com *Dist(s):* **A & B Distributors & Pubs. Group.**

**TriQuarterly Bks. Imprint of Northwestern Univ. Pr.**

**Tropical Pr., Inc.,** *( 0-9666173 )* P.O. Box 161174, Miami, FL 33116-1174 Tel 305-253-2325; Fax: 305-378-1595 E-mail: tropicbooks@aol.com Web site: http://www.tropicalpress.com.

**Truck Pr.,** *( 0-916562 )* c/o LPC Group, 8 Gray's Farm Rd., Weston, CT 06883 Tel 203-878-6417; Fax: 203-874-2308; Toll Free: 800-243-0138; *Imprints:* Silver Spring Books (Silver Spring) E-mail: dw@lpcgroup.com; wilk@optonline.net Web site: http://www.coolbooks.com *Dist(s):* **Acorn Alliance** **LPC Group.**

**True Arts Graphics & Printing,** *( 1-889858 )* 2545 W. 237th St., Suite H, Torrance, CA 90505 Tel 310-534-1680; Fax: 310-534-4081 E-mail: CDrombooks@aol.com.

**Truebekon Bks.,** *( 0-9675174 )* P.O. Box 353, American Fork, UT 84003 E-mail: TruebekonBooks@ranunes.com Web site: http://www.ranunes.com/ truebekonbooks.html.

**Truman Press** *See* **Truman Pr., Inc.**

**Truman Pr., Inc.,** *( 0-9637846 )* 15445 Ventura Blvd., Suite 905, Sherman Oaks, CA 91403 Tel 818-907-1889; Fax: 818-907-8046; Toll Free: 888-454-3345; *Imprints:* Hannover House (Hann Hse) E-mail: hannoverhouse@aol.com Web site: http://www.HannoverHouse.com.

**Tubman, Harriet Pr.,** *( 1-893562 )* Univ. of Richmond RC Box 56, 28 Westhampton Way, Richmond, VA 23173 Tel 804-287-6885; Fax: 804-287-6020.

**Tudor Pubs., Inc.,** *( 0-936389 )* 3109 Shady Lawn Dr., Greensboro, NC 27408 (SAN 697-3035) Tel 336-282-5907; Fax: 336-333-1099 E-mail: Eepfaff@aol.com *Dist(s):* **Baker & Taylor Bks.** **Brodart Co..**

**Tuffy Bks. Imprint of Putnam Publishing Group, The**

---

**Tundra Bks. of Northern New York,** *( 0-88776; 0-89541; 0-912766 )* Affil. of Tundra Bks., Inc., P.O. Box 1030, Plattsburgh, NY 12901 Tel 416-598-4786; Fax: 416-598-0247 E-mail: mail@mcclelland.com Web site: http://www.tundrabooks.com *Dist(s):* **Baker & Taylor Bks.** **Bookmen, Inc.** **Borders, Inc.** **Brodart Co.** **Random Hse., Inc..**

**Turtle Bks.,** *( 1-890515 )* 866 United Nations Plaza, Suite 525, New York, NY 10017 Tel 212-644-2020; Fax: 212-223-4387 E-mail: turtlebook@aol.com Web site: http://www.turtlebooks.com *Dist(s):* **Lectorum Pubns., Inc.** **Publishers Group West.**

**Turtle Point Pr.,** *( 0-9627987; 1-885586; 1-885983 )* 233 Broadway, Rm. 946, New York, NY 10279 E-mail: countomega@aol.com Web site: http://www.turtlepoint.com *Dist(s):* **Distributed Art Pubs./D.A.P.** **Lightning Source, Inc.** **SPD-Small Pr. Distribution** **Sprout, Inc..**

**Turtle Pr.,** *( 1-880336 )* Div. of S. K. Productions, Inc., Orders Addr.: P.O. Box 290206, Wethersfield, CT 06129-0206 Tel 860-721-1198; Fax: 860-529-3756; Toll Free Fax: 877-778-8785; Toll Free: 800-778-8785 (orders only) Do not confuse with companies with the same name in in New York, NY, Nordland, WA, Warren, MI, Seattle, WA E-mail: customerservice@turtlepress.com; sales@turtlepress.com Web site: http://www.turtlepress.com *Dist(s):* **Paladin Pr.** **Weatherhill, Inc..**

**Turtleback Bks.,** *( 0-606 )* Orders Addr.: P.O. Box 14260, Madison, WI 53714-0260 Toll Free Fax: 800-828-0401; Toll Free: 800-448-8939; Edit Addr.: 2810 Crossroads Dr., Suite 2700, Madison, WI 5378-7942 Fax: 608-241-0666 Do not confuse with Turtleback Bks., Friday Harbor, WA. Turtleback Books are available only to schools and libraries. Not available to the retail market. E-mail: turtleback@demco.com Web site: http://www.turtlebackbooks.com/.

**Tuttle Publishing,** *( 0-8048; 4-900737 )* Orders Addr.: 364 Innovation Dr., North Clarendon, VT 05759-9436 Tel 802-773-8930; Fax: 802-773-6993; Toll Free Fax: 800-329-8885; Toll Free: 800-526-2778; Edit Addr.: 153 Milk St., 4th Flr., Boston, MA 02109 (SAN 213-2621) Tel 617-951-4080; Fax: 617-951-4045; Toll Free: 800) 247 1060; *Imprints:* Everyman's Classic Library in Paperback (Everyman's Classic Lib) E-mail: info@tuttlepublishing.com Web site: http://www.tuttlemartialarts.com; http://www.tuttlepublishing.com *Dist(s):* **Cheng & Tsui Co.** **Continental Bk. Co., Inc..**

**TV Bks., L.L.C.,** *( 1-57500 )* 1619 Broadway, 9th Flr., New York, NY 10019 Tel 212-603-1824; Fax: 212-245-7281 E-mail: mail@tvbooks.com Web site: http://www.tvbooks.com *Dist(s):* **HarperCollins Pubs.** **Simon & Schuster, Inc..**

**Twenty Penny Pr., Inc.,** *( 0-9712910; 0-9726666 )* 159 Leslie Ln., Sequim, WA 98382 (SAN 254-752X) Tel 360-683-2287 E-mail: editor@twentypennypress.com Web site: http://www.twentypennypress.com.

**21st Century Bks., Inc. Imprint of Millbrook Pr., Inc.**

**21 UK (GBR)** *( 1-901785 )* *Dist. by* **Dist Art Pubs.**

**23 Hse.,** *( 0-9669705; 0-9706729 )* 7602 N. Jupiter Rd., Suite 114-303, Garland, TX 75044 (SAN 299-8084) Tel 972-680-6817 E-mail: mitchel@23house.com Web site: http://www.23house.com.

**Two Trails Publishing,** *( 0-9636780; 1-929311 )* c/o C.M. Bartels, 1108 Appleton Ave., Independence, MO 64053 Tel 816-836-8258; 816-252-0591; Fax: 816-252-5314 E-mail: cwbklady@aol Web site: http://erospros.com/2trails *Dist(s):* **Amazon.Com** **Baker & Taylor Bks.** **Booksource, The.**

**Tyndale Audio Imprint of Tyndale Hse. Pubs.**

**Names**

†**Tyndale Hse. Pubs.,** ( *0-8423; 1-4143* ) Orders Addr.: P.O. Box 80, Wheaton, IL 60189-0080 (SAN 206-7749) Tel 630-668-8310; Fax: 630-668-3245; Toll Free: 800-323-9400; Edit Addr.: 351 Executive Dr., Wheaton, IL 60188; *Imprints:* HeartQuest (HeartQuest); Tyndale Kids (Tyndale Kids); Tyndale Audio (Tyndale Audio); Living Books (Living Bks IL) Web site: http://www.tyndale.com
*Dist(s):* **Appalachian Bk. Distributors**
 **CRC Pubns.**
 **Christian Bk. Distributors**
 **Riverside**
 **Spring Arbor Distributors, Inc.**
 **Beeler, Thomas T. Publisher**; *CIP.*

**Tyndale Kids Imprint of Tyndale Hse. Pubs.**

†**UAHC Pr.,** ( *0-8074* ) 633 Third Ave., New York, NY 10017 (SAN 203-3291) Tel 212-650-4121; Fax: 212-650-4119; Toll Free: 888-489-8242 E-mail: rabrams@uahc.org; press@uahc.org Web site: http://www.uahcpress.org; *CIP.*

**U.S. Games Systems, Inc.,** ( *0-88079; 0-913866; 1-57281* ) 179 Ludlow St., Stamford, CT 06902 (SAN 158-6483) Tel 203-353-8400; Fax: 203-353-8431; Toll Free: 800-544-2637; *Imprints:* Cove Press (Cove Pr CT) E-mail: usgames@aol.com Web site: http://www.usgamesinc.com
*Dist(s):* **Bookpeople**
 **New Leaf Distributing Co., Inc..**

**UBS Pubs. Distributions, Ltd. (IND)** ( *81-7476; 81-85273; 81-85674; 81-85944; 81-86112; 81-87374; 83-640* ) *Dist. by* **S Asia.**

**UglyTown,** ( *0-9663473; 0-9724412* ) 2148 1/2 W. Sunset Blvd., Suite 204, Los Angeles, CA 90026 Tel 213-484-8334; Fax: 213-484-8333 E-mail: mayorsoffice@uglytown.com Web site: http://www.uglytown.com
*Dist(s):* **Words Distributing Co..**

**UglyTown Productions** *See* **UglyTown**

**Ullstein-Taschenbuch-Verlag (DEU)** ( *3-548* ) *Dist. by* **Intl Bk Import.**

**Ultramarine Publishing Co., Inc.,** ( *0-89366; 0-911499* ) P.O. Box 303, Hastings-on-Hudson, NY 10706 (SAN 208-8762) Tel 914-478-1339; Fax: 914-478-1365.

**Ulverscroft Audio (U.S.A.),** P.O. Box 1230, West Seneca, NY 14224-1230 Tel 716-674-4270; Fax: 716-674-4195; Toll Free: 800-955-9659 E-mail: sales@ulverscroftusa.com Web site: http://www.ulverscroft.com/.

**Ulverscroft Large Print Bks., Ltd.,** ( *0-7089* ) Div. of F. A Thorpe, Orders Addr.: P.O. Box 1230, West Seneca, NY 14224-1230; Edit Addr.: 1881 Ridge Rd., West Seneca, NY 14224-1230 (SAN 208-3035) Tel 716-674-4270; Fax: 716-674-4195; Toll Free: 800-955-9659 E-mail: enquiries@ulverscroft.co.uk Web site: http://www.ulverscroft.co.uk.

**Ulverscroft Soundings (U.S.A.)** *See* **Ulverscroft Audio (U.S.A.)**

**Unabridged Library Editions Imprint of Brilliance Audio**

**Underwood Bks., Inc.,** ( *0-88733; 0-934438; 1-887424* ) P.O. Box 1609, Grass Valley, CA 95945 Tel 530-274-7997; Fax: 530-274-7179
*Dist(s):* **Publishers Group West.**

**Ungar, Frederick A Bk.,** ( *0-8044* ) Orders Addr.: 22883 Quicksilver Dr., Dulles, VA 20166.

†**Unicorn Pr., Inc.,** ( *0-87775* ) 223 Milstead Rd., Newport News, VA 23606 (SAN 203-3313) Tel 757-930-9618 Do not confuse with companies with the same or similar name in Holland, PA, Santa Ana, CA, Northville, MI E-mail: UnicornPr0@aol.com; *CIP.*

**Unicorn Pr. U.S.A.,** ( *1-878162* ) 6715 Camp Bowie Blvd., Fort Worth, TX 76116-7112 Tel 817-738-9595; Fax: 817-738-7773 E-mail: 74323.2707@compuserve.com.

†**Unicorn Publishing Hse., Inc., The,** ( *0-88101* ) 120 American Way, Morris Plains, NJ 07950 (SAN 240-4567) Tel 973-292-6861; Fax: 973-984-6194; *CIP.*

**Unicycle Pr., Inc.,** ( *0-9664661* ) P.O. Box 2105, Media, PA 19063 Fax: 610-627-2521 E-mail: cyclepress@aol.com Web site: http://www.members.aol.com/cyclepress.

†**Union College Pr.,** ( *0-912756* ) 807 Union St., Schenectady, NY 12308 (SAN 665-8008) Tel 518-388-6131; Fax: 518-388-7092; *CIP.*

**Unique Pubns.,** ( *0-86568* ) Subs. of CFW Enterprises, Inc., 4201 Vanowen Pl., Burbank, CA 91505 (SAN 214-3313) Tel 818-845-2656; Fax: 818-845-7761; Toll Free Fax: 800-249-7761; Toll Free: 800-332-3330.

**United, Inc.,** ( *1-883103* ) Orders Addr.: P.O. Box 18646, Charlotte, NC 28218 Tel 704-536-3214; Fax: 704-535-1980; Toll Free: 800-244-6274; Edit Addr.: 2049 Birchcrest Dr., Charlotte, NC 28205 E-mail: jerry.stokes@www.worldnet.att.net Web site: http://www.bookzone.com/.

**U.S. Tennis Assn.,** ( *0-938822* ) 70 W. Red Oak Ln., White Plains, NY 10604 (SAN 207-6551) Fax: 914-696-7027.

**Univ. of Exeter Pr. (GBR)** ( *0-85989; 0-900771; 0-902414; 0-9501308* ) *Dist. by* **David Brown.**

**Univ. of Natal Pr. (ZAF)** ( *0-86980; 0-620; 1-86914* ) *Dist. by* **Intl Spec Bk.**

**Univ. of Otago Pr. (NZL)** ( *0-908569; 1-877133; 1-877276* ) *Dist. by* **Intl Spec Bk.**

**Univ. of Queensland Pr. (AUS)** ( *0-7022* ) *Dist. by* **Intl Spec Bk.**

**Univ. of Western Australia Pr. (AUS)** ( *0-85564; 0-86422; 0-909751; 1-875560; 1-876268; 1-920694* ) *Dist. by* **Intl Spec Bk.**

**Universe Publishing,** ( *0-7893; 0-87663; 1-55550* ) Div. of Rizzoli International Pubns., Inc., 300 Park Ave. S., 3rd Flr., New York, NY 10010 (SAN 202-537X) Tel 212-387-3400; Fax: 212-387-3444 Do not confuse with similar names in North Hollywood, CA, Englewood, NJ, Mendocino, CA
*Dist(s):* **Andrews McMeel Publishing**
 **Simon & Schuster, Inc.**
 **St. Martin's Pr..**

**University Editions Imprint of Aegina Pr., Inc.**

**Univ. Editions,** ( *0-615; 0-9711659* ) 1003 W. Centennial Dr., Peoria, IL 61614-2828 Tel 309-692-0621; Fax: 309-693-0628 Do not confuse with University Editions in Huntington, WV E-mail: mikruc@aol.com Web site: http://www.terrythetractor.com.

†**University Microfilms, Inc.,** ( *0-608; 0-7837; 0-8357* ) Div. of Bell & Howell, Orders Addr.: P.O. Box 1307, Ann Arbor, MI 48106 (SAN 241-8797); Edit Addr.: 300 N. Zeeb Rd., Ann Arbor, MI 48106 (SAN 212-2464) Tel 313-761-4700; Fax: 313-665-5022; Toll Free: 800-521-0600; 800-343-5299 (in Canada) Web site: http://www.umi.com; *CIP.*

†**Univ. of Alabama Pr.,** ( *0-8173* ) Orders Addr.: 11030 S. Langley, Chicago, IL 60628; Edit Addr.: P.O. Box 870380, Tuscaloosa, AL 35487-0380 (SAN 202-5272) Tel 205-348-5180; Fax: 205-348-9201 E-mail: jkramer@uapress.ua.edu; pjmcwill@uapress.ua.edu Web site: http://www.uapress.ua.edu
*Dist(s):* **Univ. of Chicago Pr.; CIP.**

**Univ. of Alaska Pr.,** ( *0-912006; 1-889963* ) P.O. Box 756240, Fairbanks, AK 99775-6240 (SAN 203-3011) Tel 907-474-5831; Fax: 907-474-5502; Toll Free: 888-252-6657 E-mail: fypress@uaf.edu Web site: http://www.uaf.edu/uapress.

**Univ. of Arizona, Ctr. for Mineral Resources & U.S. Geological Survey,** ( *0-9661233* ) Univ. of Arizona, Gould-Simpson Bldg., Tucson, AZ 85721 Tel 520-670-5506; Fax: 520-670-5571 E-mail: eforce@swfo.arizona.edu
*Dist(s):* **Univ. of Arizona Pr..**

†**Univ. of Arizona Pr.,** ( *0-8165* ) 355 S. Euclid Ave., Suite 103, Tucson, AZ 85719 (SAN 205-468X) Tel 520-621-1441; Fax: 520-621-8899 E-mail: orders@uapress.arizona.edu Web site: http://www.uapress.arizona.edu
*Dist(s):* **Continental Bk. Co., Inc.**
 **Many Feathers Bks. & Maps**
 **Univ of Arizona Critical Languages Program; CIP.**

†**Univ. of Arkansas Pr.,** ( *0-938626; 1-55728* ) 201 Ozark Ave., Fayetteville, AR 72701 (SAN 239-3972) Tel 479-575-3246; Fax: 479-575-6044; Toll Free: 800-626-0090 E-mail: uaprinfo@cavern.uark.edu Web site: http://www.uark.edu/~uaprinfo; http://www.uapress.com
*Dist(s):* **Baker & Taylor Bks.**
 **Yankee Peddler Bookshop; CIP.**

**Univ. of California, American Indian Studies Ctr.,** ( *0-935626* ) 3220 Campbell Hall, Box 951548, Los Angeles, CA 90095-1548 (SAN 220-1283) Tel 310-206-7508; Fax: 310-206-7060 E-mail: aiscpubs@ucla.edu Web site: http://www.sscnet.ucla.edu/esp/aisc/index.html
*Dist(s):* **Bookpeople**
 **SPD-Small Pr. Distribution.**

†**Univ. of California Pr.,** ( *0-520* ) Orders Addr.: 1445 Lower Ferry Rd., Ewing, NJ 08618 Tel 609-883-1759 (Customer Service); Fax: 609-883-7413; Toll Free Fax: 800-999-1958 ( U.S. & Canada); Toll Free: 800-777-4726 ( U.S. & Canada); Edit Addr.: 2120 Berkeley Way, Berkeley, CA 94720 Tel 510-642-4247; 510-643-7154 (Journals); Fax: 510-643-7127; 510-642-1144 (Marketing); 510-642-9917 (Journals) E-mail: orders@cpfs.pupress.princeton.edu; journals@ucop.edu; askucp@ucpress.edu Web site: http://www.ucpress.edu
*Dist(s):* **California Princeton Fulfillment Services; CIP.**

†**Univ. of Chicago Pr.,** ( *0-226; 0-89065; 0-943056; 1-892850* ) Orders Addr.: 11030 S. Langley Ave., Chicago, IL 60628 (SAN 202-5280) Tel 773-568-1550 ; Fax: 773-660-2235; Toll Free Fax: 800-621-8476 (US & Canada); Toll Free: 800-621-2736 (US & Canada); Edit Addr.: 1427 E. 60th St., Chicago, IL 60637 (SAN 202-5299) Tel 773-702-7700; Fax: 773-702-9756 E-mail: general@press.uchicago.edu; kh@press.uchicago.edu Web site: http://www.press.uchicago.edu
*Dist(s):* **Giron Bks.**
 **netLibrary, Inc.; CIP.**

†**Univ. of Delaware Pr.,** ( *0-87413* ) 326 Hullihen Hall, Newark, DE 19716 (SAN 203-4476) Tel 302-831-1149; Fax: 302-831-6549 E-mail: udpress@udel.edu Web site: http://www.udpress.udel.edu/udpress/index.html
*Dist(s):* **Associated Univ. Presses**
 **Baker & Taylor International; CIP.**

†**Univ. of Georgia Pr.,** ( *0-8203* ) 330 Research Dr., Suite B100, Athens, GA 30602-4901 (SAN 203-3054) Tel 706-369-6130; Fax: 706-369-6131 E-mail: books@ugapress.uga.edu Web site: http://www.ugapress.uga.edu; http://www.uga.edu; *CIP.*

†**Univ. of Hawaii Pr.,** ( *0-8248; 0-87022* ) Orders Addr.: 2840 Kolowalu St., Honolulu, HI 96822-1888 (SAN 202-5353) Tel 808-956-8255; Fax: 808-988-6052; *Imprints:* Kolowalu Book (Kolowalu Bk); Latitude Twenty Book (Latitude Twenty) E-mail: uhpmkt@hawaii.edu; uhpbooks@hawaii.edu Web site: http://www.uhpress.hawaii.edu; *CIP.*

**Univ. of Idaho Pr.,** ( *0-89301* ) P.O. Box PO Box 1107, Moscow, ID 83844-1107 (SAN 208-905X) Tel 208-885-5939; Fax: 208-885-9059; Toll Free: 800-847-7377 E-mail: uipress@uidaho.edu; marys@uidaho.edu Web site: http://www.uidaho.edu/~uipress; http://www.members.aol.com/sbeegel/hemrev.htm.

†**Univ. of Illinois Pr.,** ( *0-252* ) Orders Addr.: P.O. Box 50370, Baltimore, MD 21211 Fax: 410-516-6969; Toll Free: 800-537-5487; Edit Addr.: 1325 S. Oak St., Champaign, IL 61820 (SAN 202-5310) Tel 217-333-0950; Fax: 217-244-8082 E-mail: uipress@uiuc.edu Web site: http://www.uiuc.edu/providers/uipress; http://www.press.uillinois.edu; *CIP.*

†**Univ. of Iowa Pr.,** ( *0-87745; 1-58729* ) Div. of The University of Iowa, Orders Addr.: c/o Chicago Distribution Ctr. 11030 S. Langley Ave., Chicago, IL 60628 Toll Free Fax: 800-621-8476; Toll Free: 800-621-2736; Edit Addr.: 100 Kuhl Hse. 119 W. Parker Rd., Iowa City, IA 52242-1000 (SAN 203-3070) Tel 319-335-2000; Fax: 319-335-2055 Do not confuse with Univ. of Iowa, Pubns. Dept. at same address E-mail: holly-carver@uiowa.edu Web site: http://www.uiowa.edu/~uipress
*Dist(s):* **Univ. of Chicago Pr.**
 **netLibrary, Inc.; CIP.**

**University of Life, The,** ( *1-893594* ) 409 N. 1200 E., Orem, UT 84097 Tel 801-809-2557; Fax: 801-764-9985 E-mail: press@uoflife.com Web site: http://www.uoflife.com/press.

**Univ. of Maine Pr.,** ( *0-89101* ) 5717 Corbett Hall, Rm. 326, Orono, ME 04469 (SAN 207-2971) Tel 207-581-1408; Fax: 207-581-1490 E-mail: umpress@umit.maine.edu Web site: http://www.umaine.edu/umpress.

†**Univ. of Massachusetts Pr.,** ( *0-87023; 1-55849* ) Orders Addr.: P.O. Box 429, Amherst, MA 01004 (SAN 203-3089) Tel 413-545-2219 (orders); 413-545-2217 (editorial); Fax: 413-545-1226; Toll Free Fax: 800-488-1144 E-mail: orders@umpress.umass.edu Web site: http://www.umass.edu/umpress; *CIP.*

†Univ. of Michigan, Ctr. for Japanese Studies, ( 0-939512; 1-929280 ) 202 S. Thayer St., Ann Arbor, MI 48104-1608 (SAN 216-7018) Tel 734-998-7265; Fax: 734-998-7982
E-mail: cjspubs@umich.edu
Web site: http://www.umich.edu/~iinet/cjs/pubs/CJSpubs.html; CIP.

†Univ. of Michigan Pr., ( 0-472 ) Orders Addr.: P.O. Box 1104, Ann Arbor, MI 48106-1104 (SAN 282-4884) Tel 734-764-4388; Fax: 734-936-0456; Edit Addr.: 839 Greene St., Ann Arbor, MI 48106
E-mail: um.press@umich.edu
Web site: http://www.press.umich.edu/
Dist(s): Chicago Distribution Ctr.; CIP.

†Univ. of Minnesota Pr., ( 0-8166 ) Affil. of Univ. of Minnesota, 111 Third Ave. S., Suite 290, Minneapolis, MN 55401-2520 (SAN 213-2648) Tel 612-627-1970; Fax: 612-627-1980; Toll Free: 800-621-2736 (customer service only)
E-mail: ump@staff.tc.umn.edu
Web site: http://www.upress.umn.edu
Dist(s): Chicago Distribution Ctr.
Continental Bk. Co., Inc.
Univ. of Chicago Pr.; CIP.

†Univ. of Missouri Pr., ( 0-8262 ) 2910 LeMone Blvd., Columbia, MO 65201 (SAN 203-3143) Tel 573-882-7641; Fax: 573-884-4498; Toll Free: 800-828-1894 (orders only)
E-mail: order@ext.missouri.edu
Web site: http://www.system.missouri.edu/upress
Dist(s): East-West Export Bks.
netLibrary, Inc.; CIP.

†Univ. of Nebraska Pr., ( 0-8032 ) P.O. Box 880484, Lincoln, NE 68588-0484 (SAN 202-5337); 233 N. Eighth St., Lincoln, NE 68588-0255 Tel 402-472-3581; Imprints: Bison Books (Bison Books); A Bison Original (A Bison Orig)
E-mail: pressmail@unl.edu
Web site: http://www.nebraskapress.unl.edu
Dist(s): Continental Bk. Co., Inc.
netLibrary, Inc.; CIP.

†Univ. of Nevada Pr., ( 0-87417 ) Mail Stop 166, Reno, NV 89557 (SAN 203-316X) Tel 775-784-6573; Fax: 775-784-6200; Toll Free: 877-682-6657 (orders only)
E-mail: nvinfo@nvbooks.nevada.edu
Web site: www.nvbooks.nevada.edu
Dist(s): netLibrary, Inc.; CIP.

†Univ. of New Mexico Pr., ( 0-8263 ) 3721 Spirit Dr., SE, Albuquerque, NM 87106-5631 Tel 505-277-4810 (orders); Fax: 505-277-3350; Toll Free Fax: 800-622-8667; Toll Free: 800-249-7737 (orders only); Edit Addr.: 1720 Lomas Blvd., NE, Albuquerque, NM 87131-1591 (SAN 213-9588) Tel 505-277-2346; Fax: 505-277-9270
E-mail: unmpress@unm.edu
Web site: http://www.unmpress.com
Dist(s): Baker & Taylor Bks.
Continental Bk. Co., Inc.
Distributed Art Pubs./D.A.P.
Treasure Chest Bks.; CIP.

Univ. of New Mexico, Schl. of Medicine, Biomedical Communications, Orders Addr.: c/o Health Science Ctr., P.O. Box 719, Albuquerque, NM 87131 Tel 505-277-3633.

†Univ. of North Carolina Pr., ( 0-8078 ) P.O. Box 2288, Chapel Hill, NC 27515-2288 (SAN 203-3151) Tel 919-966-3561; Fax: 919-966-3829; Toll Free: 800-848-6224 (orders)
E-mail: uncpress@unc.edu
Web site: http://www.uncpress.unc.edu
Dist(s): Replica Bks.
netLibrary, Inc.; CIP.

Univ. of North Texas Pr., ( 0-929398; 1-57441 ) Orders Addr.: 4354 Tamus, College Station, TX 77843-4354 (SAN 249-4299) Fax: 888-617-2421; Toll Free: 800-826-8911 (orders only); Edit Addr.: P.O. Box 311336, Denton, TX 76203 (SAN 249-4280) Tel 940-565-2142; Fax: 940-565-4590
E-mail: kdevinney@unt.edu; poates@unt.edu; rchrisman@unt.edu
Web site: http://www.unt.edu/untpress
Dist(s): Texas A&M Univ. Pr..

†Univ. of Notre Dame Pr., ( 0-268 ) Orders Addr.: 11030 S. Langley Ave., Chicago, IL 60628 Tel 773-568-1550 ; Toll Free Fax: 800-621-8476; Toll Free: 800-621-2736; Edit Addr.: 310 Flanner Hall, Notre Dame, IN 46556 (SAN 203-3178) Tel 219-631-6346; Fax: 219-631-8148
E-mail: undpress.1@nd.edu
Web site: http://www.undpress.nd.edu
Dist(s): Chicago Distribution Ctr.
Univ. of Chicago Pr.
netLibrary, Inc.; CIP.

†Univ. of Oklahoma Pr., ( 0-8061 ) Orders Addr.: 4100 28th Ave., NW, Norman, OK 73069-8218 (SAN 203-3194) Tel 405-325-2000; Fax: 405-364-5798; Toll Free: 800-627-7377; Edit Addr.: 1005 Asp Ave., Norman, OK 73019-6051 Fax: 405-325-4000
Web site: http://www.oupress.com
Dist(s): Baker & Taylor Bks.
Continental Bk. Co., Inc.
netLibrary, Inc.; CIP.

†Univ. of Pennsylvania Pr., ( 0-8122; 0-940663 ) Orders Addr.: c/o Hopkins Fullfillment Srvc., P.O. Box 50370, Baltimore, MD 21211-4370 Tel 410-516-6948 ; Fax: 410-516-6998; Toll Free: 800-537-5487; Edit Addr.: 4200 Pine St., Philadelphia, PA 19104-4011 (SAN 202-5345) Tel 215-898-6261; Fax: 215-898-0404
E-mail: custserv@pobox.upenn.edu
Web site: http://www.upenn.edu/pennpress; CIP.

†Univ. of Pittsburgh Pr., ( 0-8229 ) 3400 Forbes Ave., Eureka Bldg., Fifth Flr., Pittsburgh, PA 15260 (SAN 203-3216) Tel 412-383-2456; Fax: 412-383-2466
E-mail: press+@pitt.edu
Web site: http://www.pitt.edu/~press/
Dist(s): Chicago Distribution Ctr.; CIP.

†Univ. of Puerto Rico Pr., ( 0-8477 ) Subs. of Univ. of Puerto Rico, Orders Addr.: P.O. Box 23322, Rio Piedras, PR 00931-3322 (SAN 208-1245) Tel 787-758-6932; Fax: 787-753-9116
Web site: http://www.press.uchicago.edu/journals/presses/puerto_rico/
Dist(s): Lectorum Pubns., Inc.
Libros Sin Fronteras; CIP.

†Univ. of South Carolina Pr., ( 0-87249; 1-57003 ) Orders Addr.: 718 Devine St., Columbia, SC 29208 Tel 803-777-1774; Fax: 803-777-0026; Toll Free Fax: 800-868-0740; Toll Free: 800-768-2500; Edit Addr.: 937 Assembly St., Carolina Plaza, 8th Flr., Columbia, SC 29208 (SAN 203-3224) Tel 803-777-5243; Fax: 803-777-0160; Toll Free Fax: 800-868-0740; Toll Free: 800-768-2500
E-mail: cdibble@sc.edu
Web site: http://www.sc.edu/uscpress/; CIP.

†Univ. of Tennessee Pr., ( 0-87049; 1-57233 ) Div. of Univ. of Tennessee & Member of Assn. of American Univ. Presses, Orders Addr.: 11030 S. Langley, Chicago, IL 60628 Tel 773-568-1550; Toll Free Fax: 800-621-8471; Toll Free: 800-621-2736 (orders only); Edit Addr.: 110 Conference Ctr. Bldg., Knoxville, TN 37996-0325 (SAN 212-9930) Tel 865-974-3321; Fax: 865-974-3724
E-mail: mcmillan@utpress.org; hannah@utpress.org
Web site: http//www.utpress.org
Dist(s): Univ. of Chicago Pr.; CIP.

†Univ. of Texas Pr., ( 0-292 ) Orders Addr.: P.O. Box 7819, Austin, TX 78713-7819 (SAN 212-9876) Tel 512-471-7233; Fax: 512-320-0668; Toll Free: 800-252-3206; Edit Addr.: University of Texas at Austin, Austin, TX 78713-7819
E-mail: utpress@utpress.ppb.utexas.edu
Web site: http://www.utexas.edu/utpress
Dist(s): Continental Bk. Co., Inc.
Urban Land Institute
netLibrary, Inc.; CIP.

†Univ. of Utah Pr., ( 0-87480 ) 1795 E. South Campus Dr., Rm. 101, Salt Lake City, UT 84112-9402 (SAN 220-0023) Tel 801-581-6771; Fax: 801-581-3365; Toll Free: 800-773-6672
E-mail: info@upress.utah.edu
Web site: http://www.upress.utah.edu
Dist(s): Baker & Taylor Bks.
Treasure Chest Bks.; CIP.

†Univ. of Washington Pr., ( 0-295; 1-902716 ) Orders Addr.: P.O. Box 50096, Seattle, WA 98145-5096 (SAN 212-2502); Edit Addr.: 1326 Fifth Ave., Suite 555, Seattle, WA 98101 Tel 206-543-8870; Fax: 206-685-3460; Toll Free Fax: 800-669-7993; Toll Free: 800-441-4115; 1126 N. 98th St., Seattle, WA 98103
E-mail: uwpord@u.washington.edu
Web site: http://www.washington.edu/uwpress
Dist(s): Urban Land Institute
netLibrary, Inc.; CIP.

†Univ. of Wisconsin Pr., ( 0-299 ) Orders Addr.: c/o Chicago Dist Ctr., 11030 S. Langley Ave., Chicago, IL 60628 Tel 773-568-1550; Fax: 773-660-2235; Toll Free Fax: 800-621-8476 (orders only); Toll Free: 800-621-2736 (orders only); Edit Addr.: 1930 Monroe St., 3rd Flr., Madison, WI 53711 Tel 608-263-1110; Fax: 608-263-1132; Imprints: Popular Press (Pop Pr); Terrace Books (Terrace Bks)
E-mail: uwiscpress@uwpress.wisc.edu
Web site: http://www.wisc.edu/wisconsinpress/
Dist(s): Chicago Distribution Ctr.
Distributed Art Pubs./D.A.P.
International Brecht Society
Sheridan Hse., Inc.
Univ. of Chicago Pr.; CIP.

University Pr. for West Africa Imprint of International Scholars Pubns.

†Univ. Pr. of America, ( 0-7618; 0-8191; 1-879691 ) Orders Addr.: 15200 NBN Way, P.O. Box 190, Blue Ridge Summit, PA 17214-0190 (SAN 253-2387) Tel 717-794-3800; Fax: 717-794-3803; Toll Free Fax: 800-338-4550; Toll Free: 800-462-6420; Edit Addr.: 4501 Forbes Blvd., Suite 200, Lanham, MD 20706 (SAN 200-2256) Tel 301-459-3366; Fax: 301-429-5747
E-mail: custserv@rowman.com
Web site: http://www.univpress.com
Dist(s): National Bk. Network
Rowman & Littlefield Pubs., Inc.; CIP.

Univ. Pr. of Colorado, ( 0-87081 ) Orders Addr.: c/o Univ. Press of Colorado, 4100 28th Ave., NW, Norman, OK 73069-8218 Toll Free Fax: 800-735-0476; Toll Free: 800-627-7377; Edit Addr.: 5589 Arapahoe Ave., Suite 206C, Boulder, CO 80303 (SAN 658-0343) Tel 720-406-8849
Web site: http://www.upcolorado.com
Dist(s): Univ. of Oklahoma Pr..

†Univ. Pr. of Florida, ( 0-8130 ) 15 NW 15th St., Gainesville, FL 32611-0279 (SAN 207-9275) Tel 352-392-1351; Fax: 352-392-7302; Toll Free: 800-226-3822
E-mail: info@upf.com
Web site: http://www.upf.com
Dist(s): netLibrary, Inc.; CIP.

†Univ. Pr. of Kansas, ( 0-7006 ) 2501 W. 15th St., Lawrence, KS 66049 (SAN 203-3267) Tel 785-864-4154; 785-864-4155 (orders); Fax: 785-864-4586
E-mail: jpigza@ukans.edu
Web site: http://www.kansaspress.ku.edu; CIP.

†Univ. Pr. of Kentucky, ( 0-8131; 0-912839; 0-916968 ) Orders Addr.: P.O. Box 11578, Lexington, KY 40576-1578 Tel 859-257-8400; Fax: 859-257-8481; Toll Free: 800-839-6855; Edit Addr.: 663 S. Limestone St., Lexington, KY 40508-4008 (SAN 203-3275) Tel 859-257-5200; Fax: 859-323-4981; Toll Free Fax: 800-870-4981
E-mail: leilas@pop.uky.edu
Web site: http://www.kentuckypress.com
Dist(s): CUP Services
netLibrary, Inc.; CIP.

†Univ. Pr. of Mississippi, ( 0-87805; 1-57806 ) 3825 Ridgewood Rd., Jackson, MS 39211-6492 (SAN 203-1914) Tel 601-432-6205; Fax: 601-432-6217; Toll Free: 800-737-7788 (orders only); Imprints: A Banner Book (Banner Bk)
E-mail: kerr@ihl.state.ms.us
Web site: http://www.upress.state.ms.us; CIP.

†Univ. Pr. of New England, ( 0-87451; 0-915032; 1-58465 ) Orders Addr.: 37 Lafayette St., Lebanon, NH 03766-1405 Tel 603-643-7100 (Sales Director); Toll Free: 800-421-1561; Edit Addr.: 23 S. Main St., Hanover, NH 03755-2048 (SAN 203-3283) Tel 603-448-1533; Fax: 603-643-1540; Imprints: Hardscrabble Books (Hardscrabble)
E-mail: University.Press@Dartmouth.edu
Web site: http://www.upne.com; CIP.

Univ. Pr. of the Pacific, ( 0-89875; 1-4102 ) Orders Addr.: P.O. Box 025724, Miami, FL 33102-5724 Fax: 407-650-2537 (phone/fax); Edit Addr.: 4440 NW 73rd Ave., PTY 362, Miami, FL 33166-6437
E-mail: universitypress@cyberhaven.com.

Univ. Pr. of the South, Inc., ( 1-889431; 1-931948 ) 2132 Broadway, New Orleans, LA 70118 Tel 504-866-2791; Fax: 504-866-2750; Toll Free: 877-803-6266
E-mail: unprsouth@aol.com
Web site: http://www.unprsouth.com.

†Univ. Pr. of Virginia, ( 0-8139; 0-912759; 1-57814 ) Orders Addr.: P.O. Box 400318, Charlottesville, VA 22904-4318 (SAN 202-5361) Tel 804-924-3468; Fax: 804-982-2655
E-mail: upress@virginia.edu
Web site: http://www.upress.virginia.edu
Dist(s): BookWorld Services, Inc.
Ediciones Universal; CIP.

University Publishing Assocs., Inc., ( 0-8026 ) 4720 Boston Way, Lanham, MD 20706 (SAN 630-1878) Tel 301-459-3366
Dist(s): Rowman & Littlefield Pubs., Inc..

University Publishing Hse., Inc., ( 1-57002; 1-877767 ) P.O. Box 1664, Mannford, OK 74044-1664 Tel 918-865-4726 (phone/fax)
E-mail: upub@juno.com.

Names

**Upper Access, Inc.,** ( *0-942679* ) Orders Addr.: P.O. Box 457, Hinesburg, VT 05461 (SAN 667-1195) Tel 802-482-2988; Fax: 802-482-7730; Toll Free Fax: 800-310-8320 (orders only); Edit Addr.: 87 Upper Access Rd., Hinesburg, VT 05461 Toll Free: 800-310-8320
E-mail: info@upperaccess.com
Web site: http://www.upperaccess.com.

**Upper Room Bks.,** ( *0-8358* ) Div. of The Upper Room, 1908 Grand Ave., Nashville, TN 37212 (SAN 203-3364) Tel 615-340-7256; 615-340-7204; Fax: 615-340-7266; Toll Free: 800-972-0433 (customer service, orders); 1650 Bluegrass Lakes Pkwy., Alphretta, GA 30201 Do not confuse with Upper Room Education for Parenting, Inc. in Derry, NH
E-mail: sarah_schaller-linn@gbod.org;
kwatts@upperroom.org.
Web site: http://www.upperroom.org.

**Upper Room Publishing Company** *See* **In His Steps Publishing**

**Upublish.com,** ( *1-58112* ) Div. of Dissertation.com, 7525 NW 61st Terr., Suite 2603, Parkland, FL 33067-2421 Tel 954-344-8203; Fax: 954-755-4059; Toll Free: 800-636-8329
E-mail: orders@upublish.com
Web site: http://www.upublish.com
*Dist(s):* **Baker & Taylor Bks.**
  **Slavica Pubs.**
  **Universal Publishing Group, The.**

**Urban Research Pr., Inc.,** ( *0-941484* ) 840 E. 87th St., Chicago, IL 60619 (SAN 239-0515) Tel 773-994-7200 ; Fax: 773-994-5191
Web site: http://www.urbanresearchpress.com.

**USA Bks.,** ( *1-59209* ) 244 Fifth Ave., Suite M 232, New York, NY 10001-7604 (SAN 254-6507) Tel 212-561-0849
E-mail: usabook@aol.com
Web site: http://www.usabook.net
*Dist(s):* **Baker & Taylor Bks..**

†**Utah State Univ. Pr.,** ( *0-87421* ) 7800 Old Main Hill, Logan, UT 84322-7800 (SAN 202-9294) Tel 435-797-1362; Fax: 435-797-0313; Toll Free: 800-239-9974
E-mail: brooke.bigelow@usu.edu
Web site: http://www.usu.edu/usupress; *CIP.*

**V H P S Holtzbrinck Publishers** *See* **Holtzbrinck Pubs.**

**Vacation Spot Publishing,** ( *0-9637688; 1-893622* ) Orders Addr.: P.O. Box 17011, Alexandria, VA 22302 Tel 703-684-8142; Fax: 703-684-7955; Toll Free: 800-441-1949; Edit Addr.: 2600 Russell Rd., Alexandria, VA 22301
E-mail: mail@VSPBooks.com
Web site: http://www.vspbooks.com
*Dist(s):* **Baker & Taylor Bks.**
  **Bookazine Co., Inc.**
  **Follett Library Resources**
  **Keith Distributors**
  **Koen Bk. Distributors.**

**Vallentine Mitchell Pubs. (GBR)** ( *0-85303* ) Dist. by Intl Spec Bk.

**Van Cortlandt Bks.,** ( *0-9641889* ) 20 Shagbark Ct., Rockville, MD 20852-4149 Tel 301-770-0799
E-mail: masterprintsg@yahoo.com
*Dist(s):* **Baker & Taylor Bks..**

**Van Neste Bks.,** ( *0-9657639; 1-929871* ) 612 W. Franklin St., Suite 6B, Richmond, VA 23220 Tel 804-343-2118 (phone/fax)
E-mail: kuno@aol.com.

**Vandamere Pr.,** ( *0-918339* ) Subs. of AB Assocs., P.O. Box 5243, Arlington, VA 22205 (SAN 657-3088) Tel 703-538-5750; Fax: 703-536-9644; Toll Free: 800-551-7776.

**VanderWyk & Burnham,** ( *0-9641089; 1-889242* ) Orders Addr.: P.O. Box 2789, Acton, MA 01720-6789 (SAN 298-2218) Tel 978-263-7595; Fax: 978-263-0696; Toll Free: 800-789-7916
E-mail: info@VandB.com
Web site: http://www.VandB.com
*Dist(s):* **BookWorld Services, Inc..**

**VanderWyk & Burnham Publishing Company** *See* **VanderWyk & Burnham**

**Vanessapress,** ( *0-940055* ) P.O. Box 82761, Fairbanks, AK 99708-2761 (SAN 696-5040) Tel 907-452-5070
Web site:
http://www.mospuitonet.com/~inkworks/vanessa.html
*Dist(s):* **Alaska News Agency, Inc.**
  **Todd Communications**
  **Wizard Works.**

**Vantage Pr., Inc.,** ( *0-533* ) 516 W. 34th St., New York, NY 10001 (SAN 206-8893) Tel 212-736-1767; Fax: 212-736-2273; Toll Free: 800-882-3273
Web site: http://www.vantagepress.com
*Dist(s):* **Dr. Leisure.**

**VanTine Publishing Co.,** ( *0-9629398* ) Orders Addr.: P.O. Box 40022, Bay Village, OH 44140 (SAN 297-4169) Tel 216-835-5711; Fax: 216-333-0099; Edit Addr.: 29005 Wayside Ln., Bay Village, OH 44140.

**Varangon Corp.,** ( *1-59096* ) 5050 Poplar Ave., Suite 1510, Memphis, TN 38157 (SAN 254-0010) Tel 901-374-9027; Fax: 901-374-0508
E-mail: jimweeks12@msn.com
*Dist(s):* **Independent Pubs. Group.**

**Vasso Studios,** ( *0-9660865* ) 319 Rector St., Philadelphia, PA 19128.

**Vedantic Shores Pr.,** ( *1-931816* ) P.O. Box 493100, Redding, CA 96049-3100 (SAN 254-0665) Tel 530-549-4757; Fax: 530-549-5743; Toll Free: 866-549-4757
E-mail: info@vedanticshorespress.com
Web site: http://www.vedanticshorespress.com.

**VeloPress,** ( *0-9622630; 1-884737; 1-931382* ) Div. of Inside Communications, Inc., 1830 55th St., Boulder, CO 80301-2700 Tel 303-440-0601; Fax: 303-444-6788; Toll Free: 800-811-4210
E-mail: velopress@7dogs.com
Web site: http://www.velogear.com
*Dist(s):* **Publishers Group West.**

**Vergina Pr.,** ( *0-9660404* ) P.O. Box 34101, West Bethesda, MD 20827 Tel 301-530-1704
E-mail: verginapr@aol.com
Web site: http://members.aol.com/denmenos.

**Veritie Pr.,** ( *0-915964* ) P.O. Box 222, Novelty, OH 44072 (SAN 207-6977) Tel 216-338-3374.

**Verso,** ( *0-86091; 0-902308; 1-85984* ) 180 Varick St., New York, NY 10014-4606 Tel 212-807-9680; Fax: 212-807-9152; Toll Free: 800-233-4830
E-mail: versoinc@aol.com
Web site: http://www.versobooks.com
*Dist(s):* **Norton, W. W. & Co., Inc..**

**Vertical, Inc.,** ( *1-932234* ) 257 Park Ave. S., 8th Flr., New York, NY 10010 Tel 212-529-2350; Fax: 212-529-3475
E-mail: info@vertical-inc.com
Web site: http://www.vertical-inc.com
*Dist(s):* **National Bk. Network.**

**Vertigo Imprint of DC Comics**

**Veterans Pr.,** ( *1-880483* ) 7111 W. 98th Terr., Suite 140, Overland Park, KS 66212-6158 Tel 913-385-7990; Fax: 913-327-7997; 135 N. Harvey Ave., Oak Park, IL 60302 Tel 708-386-1474
E-mail: Jon@tomesDvorak.com.

**VIA Folios Imprint of Bordighera, Inc.**

**Vikas Publishing Hse. Private, Ltd. (IND)** ( *81-259; 0-7069* ) Dist. by **S Asia.**

**Viking Imprint of Viking Penguin**

**Viking,** ( *0-670* ) .

**Viking Imprint of Penguin Group (USA) Inc.**

**Viking Compass Imprint of Viking Penguin**

†**Viking Penguin,** ( *0-14; 0-670* ) Div. of Penguin Group (USA) Inc., Orders Addr.: 405 Murray Hill Pkwy., East Rutherford, NJ 07073 Toll Free: 800-788-6262 (individual consumer sales); 800-631-8571 (reseller customer service); 800-526-0275 (reseller sales); Edit Addr.: 375 Hudson St., New York, NY 10014-3657 (SAN 298-0258) Tel 212-366-2000; Fax: 212-366-2952; Toll Free: 800-331-4624; *Imprints:* Viking (Viking); Penguin Books (Penguin Bks); Joseph, Michael (M Joseph); Hamilton, Hamish (H Hamilton); Elm Tree Books (Elm Tree Bks); Penguin Classics (Penguin Classics); Rough Guides (Rough Guides); Penguin AudioBooks (Png AudioBks); Viking Compass (Viking Compass)
E-mail: publicity@warnerbooks.com
Web site: http://www.penguinputnam.com/
*Dist(s):* **Cheng & Tsui Co.**
  **Continental Bk. Co., Inc.**
  **Lectorum Pubns., Inc.**
  **Penguin Group (USA) Inc.;** *CIP.*

**Village East Bks.,** ( *0-9661899* ) Countryside No.520, 8775 20th St., Vero Beach, FL 32966
E-mail: Villageeast@hotmail.com
Web site: http://www.deanbarrettmystery.com
*Dist(s):* **Midpoint Trade Bks., Inc..**

**Villard Bks. Imprint of Random House Adult Trade Publishing Group**

**Vine Bks. Imprint of Servant Pubns.**

**Vineyard Pr.,** ( *0-9673334; 1-930067* ) 106 Vineyard Pl., Port Jefferson, NY 11777 Tel 631-928-3460 (phone/fax) Do not confuse with companies with same name in Eureka Springs, AR, Vineyard, UT
E-mail: vineyard@portjeff.net
Web site: http://www.vineyardpress.com.

**Vintage Imprint of Knopf Publishing Group**

**Vintage UK (GBR)** ( *0-09* ) Dist. by **Random.**

**Virago Pr., Ltd. (GBR)** ( *0-86068; 1-85381; 1-86049* ) Dist. by **Trafalgar.**

**Virgin Bks. (GBR)** ( *0-426; 0-7535; 0-86369; 1-85227; 0-907080* ) Dist. by **London Brdge.**

**Virginia Publishing Corp.,** ( *0-9631448; 1-891442* ) P.O. Box 4538, Saint Louis, MO 63108 Tel 314-367-6612; Fax: 314-367-0727 Do not confuse with Virginia Publishing Co. in Lynchburg, VA
E-mail: jfister@westendword.com
Web site: http://www.wordnews.com
*Dist(s):* **Booksource, The.**

**Virtual Publishing Group, Inc.,** ( *1-930916* ) P.O. Box 88-0213, San Francisco, CA 94188-0231 Tel 415-244-3058
E-mail: virtualpublishing@n2books.com
Web site: http://ebooks2go.com

**Vision (IND)** ( *81-7094* ) Dist. by **S Asia.**

**Vision Bks. International,** ( *1-56550* ) 775 E. Blithedale Ave., No. 342, Mill Valley, CA 94941 (SAN 297-6447) Tel 415-383-0962; Fax: 415-383-4521
E-mail: publisher@vbipublishing.com
Web site: http://www.vbipublishing.com
*Dist(s):* **Baker & Taylor Bks.**
  **Brodart Co.**
  **Quality Bks., Inc..**

**Vision Pr.,** ( *0-9665742* ) 32 Vernon St., Brookline, MA 02446-4908 (SAN 253-7257) Tel 617-739-8424; Fax: 617-734-8070 Do not confuse with companies with the similar name in Tucson, AZ, Northport, AL, Redford, MI, Hillside, NJ, Los Angeles, CA, Kenosha, WI, Los Angeles, CA
E-mail: visionpress2000@aol.com
Web site: http://www.arbitrarysword.com.

**Vista Press Ventures, Incorporated** *See* **Eaglemont Pr.**

**Vista Publishing, Inc.,** ( *1-880254* ) 422 Morris Ave., Suite 1, Long Branch, NJ 07740 Tel 732-229-6500; Fax: 732-229-9647; Toll Free: 800-634-2498
E-mail: info@vistapubl.com
Web site: http://www.vistapubl.com.

**Vivisphere Publishing,** ( *1-892323; 1-58776* ) Div. of Net Pub Corp., Orders Addr.: 2 Neptune Rd., Poughkeepsie, NY 12601 (SAN 253-441X) Tel 845-463-1100; Fax: 845-463-0018; Toll Free: 800-724-1100
E-mail: cs@vivisphere.com
Web site: http://www.vivisphere.com.

**Viv-Poo, Incorporated** *See* **Magnolia Productions**

**Viz Comics Imprint of Viz Communications, Inc.**

**Viz Communications, Inc.,** ( *0-929279; 1-56931; 1-59116* ) Subs. of Shogakukan, Inc., 655 Bryant St., San Francisco, CA 94107-1612 (SAN 248-8604) Tel 415-546-7073; Fax: 415-546-7086; Toll Free: 800-788-3123 (Ext. 262 or 220); *Imprints:* Viz Comics (Viz Comics)
E-mail: dallas@viz.com
Web site: http://www.viz.com
*Dist(s):* **Publishers Group West.**

**Voice of Triumph, Inc., The,** ( *0-9608028* ) P.O. Box 78, Mayo, FL 32066 (SAN 239-9504) Tel 386-294-1236; Fax: 386-294-1112
E-mail: geneneill@earthlink.net
Web site: http//:www.go-to-jail.org.

†**Volcano Pr.,** ( *0-912078; 1-884244* ) Orders Addr.: P.O. Box 270, Volcano, CA 95689 (SAN 220-0015) Tel 209-296-4991; Fax: 209-296-4995; Toll Free: 800-879-9636; Edit Addr.: 21496 National St., Volcano, CA 95689
E-mail: sales@volcanopress.com;
info@volcanopress.com
Web site: http://www.volcanopress.com
*Dist(s):* **Baker & Taylor Bks.**
  **Bookpeople**
  **New Leaf Distributing Co., Inc.**
  **Quality Bks., Inc.;** *CIP.*

**Volo Imprint of Hyperion Bks. for Children**

**Voyager Bks./Libros Viajeros Imprint of Harcourt Children's Bks.**

**Voyageur Pr., Inc.,** ( *0-89658* ) Orders Addr.: P.O. Box 338, Stillwater, MN 55082 Toll Free: 800-888-9653; Edit Addr.: 123 N. Second St., Stillwater, MN 55082 (SAN 287-2668) Tel 651-430-2210; Fax: 651-430-2211
E-mail: books@voyageurpress.com
Web site: http://www.voyageurpress.com.

**Voyageur Publishing Co.,** ( *0-929146* ) 2227 Belmont Blvd., Nashville, TN 37212 (SAN 248-6709) Tel 615-463-3179
E-mail: vikar@bellsouth.net
*Dist(s):* **Biblio Distribution.**

**WKB Enterprises, Inc.,** ( *0-9629242* ) 790 SE Webber, No. 206, Portland, OR 97202 Tel 503-231-9095.

**W M Books** *See* **Sierra Raconteur Publishing**

Names

**W Publishing Group,** ( 0-8499; 0-87680 ) Div. of Thomas Nelson, Inc., P.O. Box 141000, Nashville, TN 37214-1000 (SAN 203-283X) Tel 615-902-3400; Fax: 615-902-3200 Do not confuse with Word Publishing Co. in Greenville, MS
Web site: http://www.wordpublishing.com; http://www.thomasnelson.com
*Dist(s):* **Christian Bk. Distributors.**

**Wabokat Publishing,** ( 0-9664753 ) Orders Addr.: P.O. Box 80573, San Diego, CA 92138 Tel 619-574-1405; Fax: 619-295-7667; Edit Addr.: 3902 Clark St., San Diego, CA 92103 (SAN 299-6863)
E-mail: Wabokat@aol.com
*Dist(s):* **Baker & Taylor Bks..**

**Wadjet Publishing,** ( 0-615 ) 253 Molimo Dr., San Francisco, CA 94127 Tel 415-586-4154
E-mail: mbfontaine@aol.com; mbfontawe@aol.com
*Dist(s):* **Wilson & Assocs..**

**Wainwright Pr.,** ( 0-9632830 ) 401 S. Second St., Emmaus, PA 18049 (SAN 297-7257) Tel 610-965-7792.

**Wakefield Pr. Pty, Ltd. (AUS)** ( 0-949268; 1-86254 ) *Dist. by* **BHB Intl.**

**Waldenbooks Company, Incorporated** *See* **Waldenbooks, Inc.**

**Waldenbooks, Inc.,** ( 0-681 ) Div. of Borders Group, Inc., a/o Calendar Orders, 455 Industrial Blvd., Ste. C, LaVergne, TN 37086 (SAN 179-3373); Orders Addr.: One Waldenbooks Dr., LaVergne, TN 37096; 11625 Venture, Mira Loma, CA 91752 Tel 909-361-4025; Edit Addr.: 100 Phoenix Dr., Ann Arbor, MI 48108-2202 (SAN 200-8858) Tel 734-477-1100
E-mail: customerservice@waldenbooks.com
Web site: http://www.waldenbooks.com; http://www.preferredreader.com

**Walk Worthy Pr. Imprint of Warner Bks., Inc.**

**Walkabout Pr.,** ( 0-9655833 ) 315 Clear Creek Dr., Meridian, ID 83642-5209.

†**Walker & Co.,** ( 0-8027 ) 435 Hudson St., New York, NY 10014-3941 (SAN 202-5213) Tel 212-727-8300; Fax: 212-727-0984; Toll Free Fax: 800-218-9367; Toll Free: 800-289-2553 (orders)
E-mail: orders@walkerbooks.com
Web site: http://www.walkerbooks.com
*Dist(s):* **Beeler, Thomas T. Publisher**; **CIP.**

**Walker Large Print Imprint of Gale Group**

**Walker Publishers** *See* **WP**

**Walker Publishing Company** *See* **Walker & Co.**

**Walker Publishing Co., Inc.,** ( 0-915379 ) P.O. Box 1192, Marble Falls, TX 78654 (SAN 291-4611) Tel 830-693-5113 Do not confuse with companies with the same or similar names in Reno, NV, Farmington Hills, MI, Indianapolis, IN.

**Wallace, Aldora,** ( 0-9706587 ) P.O. Box 699, Enfield, NH 03748 Tel 603-632-7377; Fax: 603-632-5611; Edit Addr.: R.R. 2, PMB Box 98-C, Canaan, NH 03741 Tel 603-523-9885; Fax: 603-523-8380
E-mail: enfield@ConnRiver.Net
Web site: http://www.dirtycops.net
*Dist(s):* **Enfield Publishing & Distribution Co., Inc..**

**Wallace, Connie,** ( 0-9668039 ) 3865 Franz Valley Rd., Santa Rosa, CA 95404 Tel 707-545-6294
E-mail: cjwallace@jpg.net.

**Wallaroo Bks. Imprint of BkMk Pr. of the Univ. of Missouri-Kansas City**

**Waltsan Publishing, LLC,** ( 1-930430 ) 5000 Barnett St., Fort Worth, TX 76103-2006 Tel 817-654-3099 (phone/fax)
E-mail: sandra@waltsan.com
Web site: http://www.waltsan.com

**Ward & Ward,** ( 0-9621126 ) 12949 W. Geauga Trail, Chesterland, OH 44026 (SAN 250-6629) Tel 440-729-1224; Fax: 440-729-6435.

**Ward Hill Pr.,** ( 0-9623380; 1-886747 ) 40 Willis Ave., Staten Island, NY 10301 (SAN 200-3139) Tel 718-816-9449; Fax: 718-816-4056; Toll Free: 800-535-4340
E-mail: wardhill@rcn.com
Web site: http://www.bookzone.com/wardhill.

**Warehousing & Fulfillment Specialists, LLC (WFS, LLC),** ( 1-57102; 1-58029; 1-59093 ) 1501 County Hospital Rd., Nashville, TN 37218 Tol Free Fax: 800-510-3650; Toll Free: 800-327-5113; *Imprints:* Eager Minds Press (Eager Minds)
E-mail: vhill@apgbooks.com
Web site: http://www.apgbooks.com
*Dist(s):* **APG Sales and Fulfillment.**

**Warne, Frederick Imprint of Penguin Putnam Bks. for Young Readers**

**Warner Bks. (GBR)** ( 0-7515 ) *Dist. by* **Trafalgar.**

†**Warner Bks., Inc.,** ( 0-445; 0-446 ) Div. of Time Warner Bk. Group, Orders Addr.: c/o Little Brown & Co., 3 Center Plaza, Boston, MA 02108-2084 Tel 800-286-9471; Toll Free: 800-759-0190; Edit Addr.: 1271 Avenue of the Americas, New York, NY 10020 (SAN 281-8892) Tel 212-522-7200; *Imprints:* Mysterious Press Paperback Books (Mysterious Paperbk); Aspect (Aspect); Warner Vision (Warner Vision); Walk Worthy Press (Walk Worthy); Warner Faith (Warner Faith); Warner Romance (Warner Forever)
Web site: http://www.warnerbooks.com
*Dist(s):* **Lectorum Pubns., Inc.**
  **Libros Sin Fronteras**
  **Little Brown & Co.**
  **Perelandra, Ltd.**
  **Beeler, Thomas T. Publisher**
  **Thorndike Pr.**
  **Time Warner Bk. Group;** *CIP.*

**Warner Bros. Pubns.,** ( 0-7604; 0-7692; 0-87487; 0-89724; 0-89898; 0-910957; 0-913277; 1-55122; 1-57623; 0-7579 ) Div. of AOL Time Warner, 15800 NW 48th Ave., Miami, FL 33014-6422 (SAN 203-0586) Tel 305-620-1500; Fax: 305-621-1094; Toll Free: 800-327-7643; 800-468-5010
Web site: http://warnerbrospub.com.

**Warner Faith Imprint of Warner Bks., Inc.**

**Warner Futura (GBR)** ( 0-7515 ) *Dist. by* **Trafalgar.**

**Warner Romance Imprint of Warner Bks., Inc.**

**Warner Vision Imprint of Warner Bks., Inc.**

**Warp Graphics, Inc.,** ( 0-936861 ) 515 Haight Ave., Poughkeepsie, NY 12603 (SAN 699-9204) Tel 914-473-9277; Fax: 914-473-9280; *Imprints:* Father Tree Press (Father Tree Pr); Wolfrider Books (Wolfrider Bks)
E-mail: elfquest@elfquest.com
Web site: http://www.elfquest.com.

**Warwick Hse. Publishing,** ( 0-9638455; 1-890306 ) 720 Court St., Lynchburg, VA 24504 Tel 434-846-1200; Fax: 434-846-0300
E-mail: whp720@aol.com.

**Washington Square Pr. Imprint of Simon & Schuster**

†**Washington State Univ. Pr.,** ( 0-87422 ) P.O. Box 645910, Pullman, WA 99164-5910 (SAN 206-6688) Tel 509-335-3518; Fax: 509-335-8568; Toll Free: 800-354-7360
E-mail: wsupress@wsu.edu; lawton@wsu.edu
Web site: http://wsupress.wsu.edu
*Dist(s):* **Baker & Taylor Bks.**
  **Benjamin News Group**
  **Partners/West;** *CIP.*

**Washington Writers' Publishing Hse.,** ( 0-931846 ) P.O. Box 15271, Washington, DC 20003 (SAN 211-9250) Tel 301-652-5636; 703-527-3208 (fiction only)
Web site: http://www.wwph.org
*Dist(s):* **Baker & Taylor Bks..**

**Water Row Pr.,** ( 0-934953 ) Subs. of Water Row Bks., P.O. Box 438, Sudbury, MA 01776 (SAN 694-6011) Tel 508-485-8515; Fax: 508-229-0885
E-mail: waterrow@aol.com
Web site: http://www.waterowbooks.com.

**Water Tower Press** *See* **Orloff Pr.**

**WaterBrook Pr.,** ( 0-87788; 1-57856; 1-4000 ) Div. of Random Hse., Inc., Orders Addr.: 400 Hahn Rd., Westminster, MD 21157 Tel 410-848-1900; Toll Free: 800-726-0600; Edit Addr.: 2375 Telstar Dr., Suite 160, Colorado Springs, CO 80920 (SAN 299-4682) Tel 719-590-4999; Fax: 719-590-8977; Toll Free Fax: 800-294-5686; Toll Free: 800-603-7051; *Imprints:* Shaw (ShawRH) Do not confuse with WaterBrook Pr., Great Falls, VA
Web site: randomhouse.com/waterbrook
*Dist(s):* **Random Hse., Inc..**

**Watercress Pr.,** ( 0-934955 ) 111 Grotto Blvd., San Antonio, TX 78216-7131 (SAN 694-4116) Tel 210-344-5338; Fax: 210-320-9536
E-mail: ace@watercresspress.com
Web site: http://watercresspress.com

**Watermark Pr.,** ( 1-57553; 1-58235; 0-7951 ) 6 Gwynns Mill Ct., Owings Mills, MD 21117 Tel 410-363-2330; Fax: 410-363-2342 Do not confuse with companies with same or similar names in Wichita KS, Seattle, WA
E-mail: emueck@circapress.com
Web site: http://www.poetry.com/.

**Watermark Pr., Inc.,** ( 0-922820 ) 149 N. Broadway, Wichita, KS 67202 (SAN 251-4265) Tel 316-263-3007 Do not confuse with companies with similar name in Owings Mill, MD, Seattle, WA.

**Watershed Bks.,** ( 0-9622344 ) 1770 W. State St., No. 330, Boise, ID 83702 Tel 208-863-1100 Do not confuse with companies with same name in San Jose, CA, Marietta, OH, Kansas City, MO, Coloma, CA, Seattle, WA , Marbleton, GA, Wheaton, IL.

**Watershed Bks.,** ( 0-9669919 ) 4642 First Ave., NE, Seattle, WA 98105 Tel 206-633-0503; Fax: 206-633-4803 Do not confuse with companies with the same name in Marietta, OH, Garden Valley, ID, San Jose, CA, Kansas City, MO, Coloma, CA, Boise, ID, Marbleton, GA, Wheaton, IL
E-mail: ajarrela@macconnect.com

**Waterton Pr.,** ( 0-9667235 ) P.O. Box 847, Danville, CA 94526-0847 (SAN 253-1070) Tel 925-838-4102; Fax: 925-838-8034
E-mail: sjwaterton@msn.com
Web site: http://www.danoconnor.com.

†**Watson-Guptill Pubns., Inc.,** ( 0-8174; 0-8230 ) Div. of VNU Business Media, Inc., 770 Broadway, New York, NY 10003 (SAN 282-5384)
E-mail: skerner@watsonguptill.com
Web site: http://www.watsonguptill.com; *CIP.*

**Watts, Franklin Imprint of Scholastic Library Publishing**

**Waubesa Pr. Imprint of Badger Bks., Inc.**

**Waubesa Press** *See* **Badger Bks., Inc.**

**Wave Publishing,** ( 0-9642359; 0-9722430 ) Div. of Caroy, Inc., 4 Yawl St., Venice, CA 90292 (SAN 298-3788) Tel 310-306-0699; Fax: 310-822-4921 Do not confusw with Wave Publishing Comopany in Waiahu, HI
*Dist(s):* **Baker & Taylor Bks..**

**Waverly Hse. Publishing Co.,** ( 0-9650970 ) P.O. Box 1053, Glenside, PA 19038 Tel 215-884-5873; Fax: 215-735-4796; Toll Free: 800-858-2253
E-mail: info@natsel.com
Web site: http://www.natsel.com
*Dist(s):* **Africa World Pr.**
  **Baker & Taylor Bks..**

†**Wayne State Univ. Pr.,** ( 0-8143 ) Leonard N. Simons Bldg., 4809 Woodward Ave., Detroit, MI 48201-1309 (SAN 202-5221) Tel 313-577-6120; Fax: 313-577-6131; Toll Free: 800-978-7323 (customer orders)
E-mail: j.stephenson@wayne.edu
Web site: http://wsupress.wayne.edu
*Dist(s):* **East-West Export Bks.;** *CIP.*

†**Weatherhill, Inc.,** ( 0-8348 ) 41 Monroe Tpke., Trumbull, CT 06611-1315 (SAN 202-9529) Tel 203-459-5090; Fax: 203-459-5095; Toll Free: 800-437-7840
E-mail: weatherhill@weatherhill.com
Web site: http://www.weatherhill.com; *CIP.*

**Weatherhill, John Incorporated** *See* **Weatherhill, Inc.**

†**Webb Research Group Pubs.,** ( 0-936738 ) P.O. Box 314, Medford, OR 97501 (SAN 222-1934) Tel 541-664-5205; Fax: 541-664-9131
E-mail: anybody@pnwbooks.com
Web site: http://www.pnwbooks.com; *CIP.*

**Weddle, Virginia B.,** ( 0-9640352 ) Orders Addr.: P.O. Box 607, Kamiah, ID 83536; Edit Addr.: 33 Spruce St., Kamiah, ID 83536 Tel 208-935-0629.

**Weidenfeld & Nicolson, Ltd. (GBR)** ( 0-297; 0-575; 0-303; 1-84188 ) *Dist. by* **Trafalgar.**

**Weiser, Samuel Incorporated** *See* **Red Wheel/Weiser**

**Welcome Rain Pubs.,** ( 1-56649 ) 532 LaGuardia Pl., No. 473, New York, NY 10012 (SAN 299-9528) Tel 212-989-0089; Fax: 212-889-0869
*Dist(s):* **National Bk. Network.**

**Well There It Is Pubs.,** ( 0-9674817 ) P.O. Box 1304, Del Valle, TX 78617 Fax: 512-247-5877
E-mail: LBERDOLL@aol.com; lberdoll@aol.com.

**Wellington Publishing, Inc.,** ( 0-922984 ) Orders Addr.: P.O. Box 14877, Chicago, IL 60614-0877 (SAN 251-7795) Tel 773-472-4820; Fax: 773-472-4924; Edit Addr.: 707 W. Junior Terr., Chicago, IL 60613 (SAN 251-7809)
E-mail: wellingt@interaccess.com.

**Wellspring Bks.,** ( 0-9715676 ) P.O. Box 51496, Albuquerque, NM 87181-1496 Tel 505-293-2653 Do not confuse with companies with the same or similar names in Pound Ridge, NJ, Albuquerque, NM, Adelphia, NJ, Woburn, MA, Groton, VT
Web site: http://www.wellspringbooks.com.

**Wesleyan Univ. Pr.,** ( 0-8195 ) 110 Mount Vernon St., Middletown, CT 06459-0433 Tel 860-685-2420; Fax: 860-685-2421
E-mail: Lstarr@wesleyan.edu
Web site: http://www.upne.com/order.html; http://www.wesleyan.edu
*Dist(s):* **SPD-Small Pr. Distribution**
  **Univ. Pr. of New England.**

**Wesoomi Publishing,** ( 0-9653732 ) P.O. Box 656, Ortonville, MI 48462 Tel 248-627-5804
E-mail: editor@wesoomi.com
Web site: http://www.wesoomi.com/
*Dist(s):* **Partners Pubs. Group, Inc..**

**Wessex Pr.,** ( *0-938501* ) P.O. Box 68308, Indianapolis, IN 46268 (SAN 661-2717)
E-mail: WessexPress@earthlink.net.

**West Beach Bks.,** ( *0-9665333; 1-931875* ) Orders Addr.: P.O. Box 68406, Indianapolis, IN 46268 (SAN 299-7355) Tel 619-665-3567; Fax: 772-594-7769
E-mail: svon@westbeachbooks.com
Web site: http://www.westbeachbooks.com
*Dist(s):* **Bookpeople.**

**West Coast Crime Imprint of Blue Heron Publishing**

**West Emerald Pr.,** ( *0-9704677* ) P.O. Box 4741, Englewood, CO 80155-4741 Tel 303-430-2897
E-mail: westemeraldpress@yahoo.com.

**West End Games, Inc.,** ( *0-87431* ) Subs. of Bucci Imports, R.D. 3, Box 2345, Honesdale, PA 18431 (SAN 687-8466) Tel 717-253-6990; Fax: 717-253-5104
E-mail: dspweg@hotmail.com
Web site: http://www.westendgames.net.

**West End Pr.,** ( *0-931122; 0-9705344* ) Orders Addr.: Box 27334, Albuquerque, NM 87125 (SAN 211-3406) Tel 505-345-5729 (phone/fax); Edit Addr.: 2309 Headingly NW, Albuquerque, NM 87107
E-mail: jcrawford@unm.edu
*Dist(s):* **SPD-Small Pr. Distribution**
**Univ. of New Mexico Pr..**

**West Highland Publishing Co., Inc.,** ( *0-9646986; 1-892141* ) P.O. Box 36, Midland Park, NJ 07432 Tel 201-891-7170; Fax: 201-891-6211.

**West Pr.,** ( *0-9740164* ) 1663 W. Grant Rd., Tucson, AZ 85745 (SAN 631-6794) Toll Free: 888-637-0337
E-mail: joel@westpress.com
Web site: http://www.westpress.com.

**West Winds Pr. Imprint of Graphic Arts Ctr. Publishing Co.**

**Western Imprint of Ctr. Point Large Print**

**Western Reflections Publishing Co.,** ( *1-890437; 1-932738* ) Orders Addr.: 219 Main St., Montrose, CO 81401 Tel 970-249-7180 Toll Free: 800-993-4490
Web site: http://www.westernreflectionspub.com
*Dist(s):* **Baker & Taylor Bks.**
**Books West**
**Partners/West**
**Quality Bks., Inc.**
**Treasure Chest Bks..**

†**Westminster John Knox Pr.,** ( *0-664; 0-8042* ) Div. of Presbyterian Publishing Corp., Orders Addr.: 100 Witherspoon St., Louisville, KY 40202-1396 (SAN 202-9669) Tel 502-569-5058; 502-569-5052 (outside U.S. for ordering); Fax: 502-569-5113 (outside U.S. for faxed orders); Toll Free: 800-541-5113 (toll-free U.S. faxed orders); Toll Free: 800-523-1631
E-mail: ppc@ctr.pcusa.org; BFalvey@ctr.pcus.org; SHardin@ctr.pcusa.org
Web site: http://www.wjk.org
*Dist(s):* **CRC Pubns.**
**Presbyterian Publishing Corp.; CIP.**

†**Westview Pr.,** ( *0-8133; 0-86531; 0-89158* ) A Member of Perseus Books Group, 5500 Central Ave., Boulder, CO 80301-2877 (SAN 219-970X) Tel 303-444-3541; Fax: 303-449-3356; Toll Free: 800-386-5656 orders only
E-mail: westview.orders@perseusbooks.com; meegan.finnegan@perseusbooks.com
Web site: http://www.perseusbooksgroup.com; http://www.westviewpress.com
*Dist(s):* **HarperCollins Pubs.**
**Women Ink; CIP.**

**Wexford College Pr.,** ( *0-9709917; 0-9721786; 0-9726596* ) 401 Merito Pl., Journalism Bldg., Palm Springs, CA 92262
E-mail: books@wexfordcollegepress.com
Web site: http://www.wexfordcollegepress.com.

**Wheatmark, Inc.,** ( *1-58736* ) 610 E. Delano St., Suite 104, Tucson, AZ 85705 (SAN 253-1054) Tel 520-798-0888; Fax: 520-798-3394; Toll Free: 888-934-0888; *Imprints:* Hats Off Books (Hats Off Bks), Iceni Books (Iceni Bks)
E-mail: editor@bookpublisher.com; orders@bookpublisher.com; shenrie@bookpublisher.com
Web site: http://www.bookpublisher.com
*Dist(s):* **Baker & Taylor Bks..**

**Wheeler Publishing, Inc. Imprint of Gale Group**

**Whereabouts,** ( *1-883513* ) 1111 Eight St., Suite D, Berkeley, CA 94710-1455
E-mail: info@whereaboutspress.com
Web site: http://www.whereaboutspress.com
*Dist(s):* **Consortium Bk. Sales & Distribution**
**SPD-Small Pr. Distribution.**

**Whispering Coyote Imprint of Charlesbridge Publishing, Inc.**

**Whispering Willows, Ltd., Co.,** ( *0-9653990* ) Orders Addr.: P.O. Box 890294, Oklahoma City, OK 73189-0294 Tel 405-239-2531; Fax: 405-236-0502; Toll Free: 800-368-1053; Edit Addr.: 2517 S. Central, Oklahoma City, OK 73129
E-mail: wwillows@telepath.com
*Dist(s):* **Hervey's Booklink & Cookbook Warehouse.**

**Whispers Pr.,** ( *0-918372* ) 70 Highland Ave., Binghamtom, NY 13905 (SAN 210-6272) Tel 607-729-6920; Fax: 607-754-3083.

**Whitaker Hse.,** ( *0-88368* ) 30 Hunt Valley Cir., New Kensington, PA 15068 (SAN 203-2104) Tel 724-334-7000; Fax: 724-334-1200
E-mail: marketing@anchordistributors.com; sharon@whitakerhouse.com
Web site: http://www.whitakerhouse.com; http://www.anchordistributors.com
*Dist(s):* **Anchor Distributors.**

**White Cloud Pr.,** ( *1-883991* ) Orders Addr.: P.O. Box 3400, Ashland, OR 97520; Edit Addr.: 240 E. Hersey St., Unit 17, Ashland, OR 97520-3041 Tel 541-488-6415; Toll Free: 800-380-8286 Do not confuse with White Cloud Pr. in Hobbs, NM
E-mail: sscholl@jeffnet.org
Web site: http://www.whitecloudpress.com
*Dist(s):* **SCB Distributors.**

**White Hen & Co.,** ( *0-9707941* ) 1171 W. Leisure Dr., Hayden, ID 83835 Tel 208-762-0919.

**White Mane Publishing Co., Inc.,** ( *0-942597; 1-57249* ) Orders Addr.: P.O. Box 708, Shippensburg, PA 17257 (SAN 667-1926) Tel 717-532-2237; Fax: 717-532-6110; Toll Free: 888-948-6263; *Imprints:* Burd Street Press (Burd St Pr); WM Kids (WM Kids)
E-mail: marketing@whitemane.com
Web site: http://www.whitemane.com/.

**White Oak Pr.,** ( *0-935069* ) P.O. Box 188, Reeds Springs, MO 65737 (SAN 694-695X) Tel 417-538-4220 Do not confuse with White Oak Pr., imprint of Candeur Manuscripts, Spring Valley, NY.

**White Pine Pr.,** ( *0-934834; 1-877027; 1-893996* ) P.O. Box 236, Buffalo, NY 14201-0236 (SAN 209-8067) Tel 716-627-4665 (phone/fax) Do not confuse with companies with the same name in West Linn, OR, Dellwood, MN
E-mail: wpine@whitepine.org; whitepinepress@qwest.net
Web site: http://www.whitepine.org
*Dist(s):* **Consortium Bk. Sales & Distribution**
**SPD-Small Pr. Distribution.**

**White Willow Enterprises,** ( *0-9640583* ) P.O. Box 1602, Rutherford, NJ 07070 Tel 201-935-7476; Toll Free: 800-824-2482 (outside New Jersey).

**White Wolf Publishing, Inc.,** ( *0-9627790; 1-56504; 1-58846* ) 1554 Litton Dr., Stone Mountain, GA 30083 (SAN 299-1349) Tel 404-292-1819; Fax: 678-382-3882; Toll Free: 800-454-9653; *Imprints:* World of Darkness (Wrld of Darkness); Borealis (Borealis) Do not confuse with White Wolf Publishing, Cresson, TX
E-mail: dianez@white-wolf.com
Web site: http://www.white-wolf.com.

**Whitehorse Pr.,** ( *0-9621834; 1-884313* ) 107 E. Conway Rd., P.O. Box 60, North Conway, NH 03860-0060 Tel 603-356-6556; Fax: 603-356-6590; Toll Free: 800-531-1133
E-mail: customerservice@whitehorsepress.com; orders@whitehorsepress.com
Web site: http://www.whitehorsepress.com
*Dist(s):* **MBI Distribution Services.**

†**Whitman, Albert & Co.,** ( *0-8075* ) 6340 Oakton St., Morton Grove, IL 60053-2723 (SAN 201-2049) Tel 847-581-0033; Fax: 847-581-0039; Toll Free: 800-255-7675
E-mail: mail@awhitmanco.com
Web site: http://www.albertwhitman.com
*Dist(s):* **Lectorum Pubns., Inc.; CIP.**

**Whitston Publishing Co., Inc.,** ( *0-87875* ) 1717 Central Ave., Suite 201, Albany, NY 12205-4759 (SAN 203-2120) Tel 518-452-1900; Fax: 518-452-1777
E-mail: whitston@capital.net; jwolcott@nycap.rr.com
Web site: http://www.whitston.com.

†**Wiener, Markus Pubs., Inc.,** ( *0-910129; 1-55876* ) 231 Nassau St., Princeton, NJ 08542 (SAN 282-5465) Tel 609-921-1141; Fax: 609-921-1140
E-mail: INFO@MARKUSWIENER.COM; PUBLISHER@MARKUSWIENER.COM
Web site: http://www.markuswiener.com; *CIP.*

**Wiese, Michael Productions,** ( *0-941188* ) 11288 Ventura Blvd., Suite 821, Studio City, CA 91604 (SAN 237-9716) Tel 818-379-8799; Fax: 818-986-3408; Toll Free: 800-379-8808; 800-833-5738 (24 hours)
E-mail: mwpsales@earthlink.net
Web site: http://www.mwp.com
*Dist(s):* **National Bk. Network.**

**WigWam Publishing Co.,** ( *1-930076* ) Orders Addr.: P.O. Box 6992, Villa Park, IL 60181 Tel 630-832-8337 Do not confuse with companies with the same or similar names in Weyauwega, WI, Cheyenne, WY
E-mail: tbasile@newleafbooks.net
Web site: http://www.newleafbooks.net.

**Wild Flower Pr. Imprint of Granite Publishing, LLC**

**Wildcat Pr.,** ( *0-9641099; 1-889135* ) Div. of Wildcat International, 8306 Wilshire Blvd., No. 8306, Beverly Hills, CA 90211 Tel 323-966-2466; Fax: 323-966-2467 Do not confuse with Wildcat Pr., Summit, NJ
E-mail: wildcatprs@aol.com
Web site: http://www.wildcatpress.com
*Dist(s):* **Alamo Square Distributors**
**Baker & Taylor Bks.**
**Bookazine Co., Inc.**
**Bookpeople**
**Brodart Co.**
**Emery-Pratt Co.**
**Koen Bk. Distributors.**

**Wildcat Publishing Co., Inc.,** ( *0-941968* ) P.O. Box 366, Greens Farms, CT 06436 (SAN 238-2776) Tel 203-255-0680
*Dist(s):* **National Bk. Network.**

†**Wilderness Adventure Bks.,** ( *0-923568; 0-9611596* ) P.O. Box 856, Manchester, MI 48158 (SAN 110-8883) Tel 734-433-1595; Fax: 734-433-0946; Toll Free: 800-852-8652
E-mail: sales@wildernessbooks.org; ddmpub@aol.com
Web site: http://www.wildernessbooks.org
*Dist(s):* **Partners Pubs. Group, Inc.; CIP.**

**Wilderness Adventures Press, Incorporated** *See* **PleaWilderness Adventures Pr., Inc.**

**Wildersburg Publishing Co.,** ( *0-9709026* ) 1588 Hazeltine Ct., Murrells Inlet, SC 29576 Tel 843-650-0207.

**Wildside Pr.,** ( *1-880448; 1-58715; 1-59224* ) Orders Addr.: P.O. Box 301, Holicong, PA 18928-0301 Tel 215-345-5645; Edit Addr.: 4355 Burnt House Hill Rd., Doylestown, PA 18901
E-mail: wildside@sff.net
Web site: http://www.wildsidepress.com
*Dist(s):* **Baker & Taylor Bks.**
**Ingram Bk. Co.**
**NACSCORP, Inc..**

**WildWest Publishing,** ( *0-9721800* ) P.O. Box 11658, Olympia, WA 98508
E-mail: clamityJan@aol.com
Web site: http://www.CalamityJan.com
*Dist(s):* **Biblio Distribution.**

†**Wiley, John & Sons, Inc.,** ( *0-02; 0-470; 0-471; 0-7645; 0-8260; 0-88422; 0-937721; 0-939246; 1-55828; 1-56561; 1-56884; 1-57313; 1-878058; 3-527* ) Orders Addr.: 1 Wiley Dr., Somerset, NJ 08875-1272 Tel 732-469-4400; Fax: 732-302-2300; Toll Free: 800-225-5945 (orders); Edit Addr.: 111 River St., Hoboken, NJ 07030 (SAN 200-2272) Tel 201-748-6276 (Retail and Wholesale); 201-748-6000; Fax: 201-748-8641 (Retail and Wholesale); 201-748-6088; *Imprints:* Cliff Notes (Cliff)
E-mail: bookinfo@wiley.com; compbks@wiley.com
Web site: http://www.wiley.com; http://www.wiley.com/compbooks/; http://www.interscience.wiley.com
*Dist(s):* **American Society of Civil Engineers**
**Aspen Pubs., Inc.**
**Peoples Publishing Group, Inc., The**
**Urban Land Institute**
**netLibrary, Inc.; CIP.**

**Williams, Carolyn D.,** ( *0-9705620* ) 3318 Parkgate Ct., Richmond, CA 94806-1989 Tel 510-758-0310; Fax: 510-758-3632
E-mail: cwilliams@locality.com
*Dist(s):* **iUniverse.**

†**Willow Creek Pr., Inc.,** ( *0-932558; 1-57223* ) Orders Addr.: P.O. Box 147, Minocqua, WI 54548-0147 (SAN 255-4038) Tel 715-358-7010; Fax: 715-358-2807; Toll Free: 800-850-9453; Edit Addr.: 9931 Hwy. 70, W., Minocqua, WI 54548-0147 Do not confuse with Willowcreek Pr. in Aloha, OR
E-mail: info@willowcrewpress.com
Web site: http://www.willowcreekpress.com; *CIP.*

**Willow Creek Press of Washington** *See* **Lion's Gate Publishing**

**Willowgate Pr.,** ( *1-930008* ) P.O. Box 6529, Holliston, MA 01746 (SAN 253-0376); 120 Brook Rd., Port Jefferson, NY 11777-1665
E-mail: willowgatepress@yahoo.com
Web site: http://www.willowgatepress.com
*Dist(s):* **Biblio Distribution.**

For full information on wholesalers and distributors, refer to the Wholesaler and Distributor Name Index

**Wilmot Publishing Co.,** ( *0-916405* ) 14321 Hazeltine Ct., Orlando, FL 32826 (SAN 295-5555) Tel 407-380-3411.

**Wilshire House of Arkansas** *See* **Ozark Publishing**

**Wilson, Neil Publishing (GBR)** ( *1-897784; 1-903238* ) *Dist.* by **Interlink Pub.**

**Win or Lose Ink,** ( *0-9655342* ) Orders Addr.: P.O. Box 638, Abbeville, LA 70511-0638 Tel 318-893-5066; Fax: 318-893-0030; Edit Addr.: 111 Concord St., Suite B, Abbeville, LA 70510.

**Wind Canyon Bks., Inc.,** ( *0-943691; 1-891118* ) P.O. Box 511, Brawley, CA 92227 Toll Free Fax: 888-289-7086; Toll Free: 800-952-7007
E-mail: books@windcanyon.com
Web site: http://www.windcanyon.com/.

**Wind River Pr.,** ( *0-9721513* ) 254 Dogwood Dr., Hershey, PA 17033-2617 Do not confuse with companies with the same name in Longboat Key, FL, Austin, TX
E-mail: editor@windriverpress.com
Web site: http://www.windriverpress.com
*Dist(s):* **Baker & Taylor Bks.**
**Booksurge, LLC.**

**Wind River Publications** *See* **Hawthorne Pubs.**

**Wind Women Pr.,** ( *0-9714473* ) P.O. Box 191812, San Francisco, CA 94119 (SAN 254-1238) Toll Free: 866-946-3966
E-mail: windwomenpress@earthlink.net;
windowmenpress@earthlink.net
Web site: http://www.windwomenpress@earthlink.net
*Dist(s):* **Baker & Taylor Bks.**
**Bookpeople.**

**Windows on History Pr., Inc.,** ( *0-9654499* ) 604 Brookwood Dr., Durham, NC 27707-3919 (SAN 299-7258) Tel 919-489-7759 (phone/fax); Toll Free: 888-398-7110 (phone/fax)
E-mail: jtetel@duke.edu
Web site: http://www.fatlikeus.com;
http://www.generationbooks.com.

**Windsor-Brooke Bks.,** ( *0-9676737* ) Five Piedmont Ctr. Suite 700, Atlantic, GA 30305 Tel 404-239-7520
E-mail: allbookedup@comcast.net;
office@windsor-brooke.com;
wbbpublishing@big-inc.com
Web site: http://www.windsor-brooke.com
*Dist(s):* **Baker & Taylor Bks.**
**Midpoint Trade Bks., Inc.**
**Publishers Group West.**

**Windsor's Golden Series,** ( *0-9620881* ) Orders Addr.: P.O. Box 310393, Atlanta, GA 30331 (SAN 249-3608) Tel 770-969-2293; Fax: 770-969-5677; Edit Addr.: 6555 Newborn Dr., College Park, GA 30349
E-mail: windsorgs@mindspring.com
*Dist(s):* **A & B Distributors & Pubs. Group**
**Baker & Taylor Bks.**
**Lushena Bks..**

**Windstorm Creative Ltd.,** ( *1-883573; 1-886383; 1-59092* ) 7419 Ebbert Dr., SE, Port Orchard, WA 98367 (SAN 299-1330) Tel 360-769-7174 (phone/fax) ; *Imprints:* Lightning Rod Limited (Lightning Rod)
E-mail: wsc@windstormcreative.com
Web site: http://www.windstormcreative.com
*Dist(s):* **Alamo Square Distributors**
**Baker & Taylor Bks.**
**Bookpeople.**

**Windswept Hse. Pubs.,** ( *0-932433; 1-883650* ) P.O. Box 159, Mount Desert, ME 04660 (SAN 687-4363) Tel 207-244-5027; Fax: 207-244-3369
E-mail: windswt@acadia.net
Web site: http://www.booknotes.com/windswept/.

**Winedale Publishing,** ( *0-9657468; 0-9701525* ) Orders Addr.: P.O. Box 130220, Houston, TX 77219 Tel 713-529-0024; Fax: 713-529-0728; Edit Addr.: Texas A&M Univ. Pr. Consortium Lindsay Bldg. Lewis St., college Station, TX 77843
E-mail: editors@winedalebooks.com
Web site: http://www.winedalebooks.com
*Dist(s):* **Texas A&M Univ. Pr..**

**WinePress Publishing,** ( *0-9622413; 1-57921; 1-883893* ) Orders Addr.: P.O. Box 428, Enumclaw, WA 98022 Tel 360-802-9758; Fax: 360-802-9992; Toll Free: 800-326-4674
E-mail: info@winepresspub.com;
jhughes@winepresspub.com;
adean@winepresspub.com
Web site: http://www.winepresspub.com
*Dist(s):* **Appalachian Bk. Distributors**
**Baker & Taylor Bks.**
**Riverside**
**Spring Arbor Distributors, Inc..**

**Wings Pr.,** ( *0-930324* ) 627 E. Guenther, San Antonio, TX 78210 (SAN 209-4975) Tel 210-271-7805 Do not confuse with companies with the same or similar name in Northhampton, MA, UNion, ME, Lusk, WY
E-mail: milligan@wingspress.com
Web site: http://www.wingspress.com
*Dist(s):* **SPD-Small Pr. Distribution.**

**Wings Pubs., LLC,** ( *0-9668884; 1-930897* ) 3555 Knollwood Dr., NW, Atlanta, GA 30305 Tel 404-231-1802; Fax: 404-231-1256
E-mail: wingsgtw@aol.com
Web site: http://www.wingspublishers.com
*Dist(s):* **Green Leaves Pr..**

**Winn Bks.,** ( *0-916947* ) Div. of Winn Corp., P.O. Box 80157, Seattle, WA 98108 (SAN 655-7864) Tel 206-763-9544; Toll Free: 800-426-4150
*Dist(s):* **Bookpeople.**

**Winslow Pr.,** ( *1-890817; 1-58837* ) Div. of Foundation for Concepts in Education, Inc., The, 115 E. 23rd St., 10th Flr., New York, NY 10010 Tel 212-254-2025; Fax: 212-254-1595; Toll Free: 800-617-3947
E-mail: winslow@winslowpress.com
Web site: http://www.winslowpress.com.

**Winter Street Pr.,** ( *0-9701057* ) Orders Addr.: P.O. Box 222103, Valencia, CA 91322-2103 Tel 818-831-6659 (phone/fax); Edit Addr.: 18535 Dvonshire St., Northridge, CA 91324.

**WinterSun Pr.,** ( *0-9658014; 1-929705* ) Orders Addr.: P.O. Box 2626, Overland Park, KS 66221 Fax: 413-691-2928; Edit Addr.: 14405 Stearns, Overland Park, KS 66221
E-mail: books@wintersunpress.com
Web site: http://www.wintersunpress.com.

**Wipf & Stock Pubs.,** ( *0-9653517; 1-57910; 1-59244* ) 199 W. 8th Ave., Suite 3, Eugene, OR 97401 Tel 541-344-1528; Fax: 541-344-1506
E-mail: jtedrick@wipfandstock.com;
jtedrick@theologybooks.com
Web site: http://www.wipfandstock.com
*Dist(s):* **Ingram Bk. Co.**
**Spring Arbor Distributors, Inc..**

**Wise, Jeanne M.,** ( *0-9720298* ) P.O. Box 575, Abingdon, MD 21009-0575 Tel 443-512-0126; Toll Free: 877-470-0126
E-mail: jwise@jwiseenterprise.com
Web site: http://www.Jwiseenterprise.com.

**WiseAcre Bks. Imprint of Red Sea**

**Wizards of the Coast,** ( *0-7869; 1-57530; 1-880992; 0-7430* ) Orders Addr.: P.O. Box 707, Renton, WA 98057-0709 Toll Free: 800-821-8028; Edit Addr.: 1801 Lind Ave., SW, Renton, WA 98055 (SAN 299-4410) Tel 425-226-6500
E-mail: angella@wizards.com
Web site: http://www.wizards.com
*Dist(s):* **Diamond Comic Distributors, Inc.**
**Holtzbrinck Pubs.**
**Doherty, Tom Assocs., LLC.**

**WM Kids Imprint of White Mane Publishing Co., Inc.**

**Wohali Pr.,** ( *0-9663853* ) Div. of Stewart, Scott & Henley, Inc., P.O. Box 3730, Burbank, CA 91508-3730 Tel 818-953-4242 (phone/fax); Toll Free: 877-964-2547
E-mail: wohalipress@mindspring.com
Web site: http://www.cherokee7.com
*Dist(s):* **Baker & Taylor Bks..**

**Woldt Corporation** *See* **Florida Literary Foundation**

**Wolf Moon Press** *See* **WinterSun Pr.**

**Wolfe Publishing Co.,** ( *0-935632; 1-879356* ) 2625 Stearman Rd. Ste. A, Prescott, AZ 86301-6155 (SAN 289-7083) Toll Free: 800-899-7810 Do not confuse with companies with the same name in Fernandina Beach, FL, Santa Monica, CA
E-mail: circ@riflemagazine.com;
info@riflemagazine.com
Web site: http://www.riflemag.com.

**Wolff, Renate,** ( *0-615* ) 199 Ormond St., Frostburg, MD 21532 Tel 301-689-5928
E-mail: renate@vtechworld.com.

**Wolfhound Pr. (IRL)** ( *0-86327; 0-905473; 0-9503454* ) *Dist.* by **Interlink Pub.**

**Wolfhound Pr. (IRL)** ( *0-86327; 0-905473; 0-9503454* ) *Dist.* by **Irish Amer Bk.**

**Wolfpack Publishing,** ( *1-885339* ) 48 Rock Creek Rd., Clinton, MT 59825-9629
E-mail: wolfpack@gunrack.net
Web site: http://www.ljmartin.com.

**Wolfrider Bks. Imprint of Warp Graphics, Inc.**

**WolfStar Pr.,** ( *0-9656422* ) 256 Bates Rd., Manhattan, MT 59741-8651 (SAN 299-2027) Toll Free: 888-965-3782
E-mail: wolfstarpr@aol.com
Web site: http://www.wolfsterpress.com
*Dist(s):* **Baker & Taylor Bks.**
**New Leaf Distributing Co., Inc.**
**Quality Bks., Inc.**
**Unique Bks., Inc..**

**Woman's Missionary Union,** ( *0-936625; 1-56309* ) Orders Addr.: c/o Carol Causey, P.O. Box 830010, Birmingham, AL 35283-0010 (SAN 699-7015) Tel 205-991-8100; Fax: 205-995-4841; Toll Free: 800-968-7301; Edit Addr.: Hwy. 280 E., 100 Missionary Ridge, Birmingham, AL 35242-5235 (SAN 699-7023); *Imprints:* New Hope (New Hope)
E-mail: cwhite@wmu.com
Web site: http://www.wmu.com
*Dist(s):* **Broadman & Holman Pubs..**

**Women In Translation,** ( *1-879679* ) 523 N. 84th St., Seattle, WA 98103 Tel 206-781-9612; Fax: 206-781-3112
E-mail: wit@scn.org
*Dist(s):* **Consortium Bk. Sales & Distribution.**

**Women's Pr., Ltd., The (GBR)** ( *0-7043* ) *Dist.* by **Trafalgar.**

**Wood, Marian Bks. Imprint of Putnam Publishing Group, The**

**Wood, Marian Bks. Imprint of Penguin Group (USA) Inc.**

**Woodbridge Pr. Publishing Co.,** ( *0-88007; 0-912800* ) c/o Woodbridge Press Shurgard Center, 7065 SW 105th Ave., No. 180, Beaverton, OR 97005 (SAN 212-9892); 12900 SW Ninth St., No. 321, Beaverton, OR 97005 Tel 503-641-5821; Fax: 503-644-5999; Toll Free Fax: 888-817-7724; Toll Free: 800-237-6053
E-mail: woodpress@aol.com
Web site: http://www.woodbridgepress.com.

**Woodholme Hse. Pubs.,** ( *0-9656342; 1-891521* ) 131 Village Square I Village of Cross Keys, Baltimore, MD 21210 Tel 410-532-5018; Fax: 410-532-9741; Toll Free: 800-488-0051
E-mail: info@woodholmehouse.com
*Dist(s):* **Koen Bk. Distributors**
**Washington Bk. Distributors.**

**Woodhouse,** ( *0-9667458* ) 69 Bank St., No. 103, New York, NY 10014 Tel 212-741-6637; Fax: 212-243-4963
E-mail: TyPak@aol.com.

**Woodley, Bob Memorial Pr., The,** ( *0-939391* ) Div. of Bob Woodley Memorial Foundation, Washburn Univ., Topeka, KS 66621 (SAN 663-1266) Tel 785-234-1032
E-mail: zzlaws@washburn.edu
Web site: http://www.wuacc.edu/reference/woodley-press/index.html.

**Woods Hole Historical Collection,** ( *0-9611374* ) P.O. Box 185, Woods Hole, MA 02543 (SAN 283-1791) Tel 508-548-7270 (phone/fax)
E-mail: woods_hole_historical@hotmail.com
Web site: www.woodsholemuseum.org.

**Wooster Bk. Co., The,** ( *1-888683; 1-59098* ) 205 W. Liberty St., Wooster, OH 44691-4831 Tel 330-262-1688; Fax: 330-264-9753; Toll Free: 800-982-6651 (800-WUBook-1)
E-mail: mail@woosterbook.com
Web site: http://www.woosterbook.com.

**Word Aflame Pr.,** ( *0-912315; 0-932581; 1-56722; 0-7577* ) Subs. of Pentecostal Publishing Hse., 8855 Dunn Rd., Hazelwood, MO 63042 (SAN 212-0046) Tel 314-837-7300; Fax: 314-837-6574
E-mail: pph@upci.org
Web site: http://www.upci.org/pph.

**Word Play Pubns.,** ( *0-9642922; 1-892847* ) One Sutter St., San Francisco, CA 94104 Tel 415-397-3716; Fax: 415-291-8377
Web site: http://www.word-play.com
*Dist(s):* **Bookpeople**
**Diamond Book Distributors, Inc.**
**Last Gasp Eco-Funnies, Inc.**
**Quality Bks., Inc.**
**Unique Bks., Inc..**

**Word Publishing** *See* **W Publishing Group**

**Word Wright International** *See* **WordWright.biz, Inc.**

**Words & Pictures Publishing, Inc.,** ( *0-9621280* ) P.O. Box 61444, Honolulu, HI 96839 (SAN 250-9326) Tel 808-955-4742; Fax: 808-951-6541
E-mail: gecko@aloha.net
Web site: http://www.brucehale.com
*Dist(s):* **Booklines Hawaii, Ltd.**
**Sunbelt Pubns., Inc..**

Names

**Words Distributing Co.,** ( *0-914728* ) Div. of Bookpeople, 7900 Edgewater Dr., Oakland, CA 94621 (SAN 154-7763) Tel 510-632-4700; Fax: 510-632-1281; Toll Free: 800-999-4650; 800-593-9673 (orders)
*Dist(s):* **Bookpeople.**

**Wordsmith & Penn,** ( *0-9677103* ) 501 Coolidge St., Chapel Hill, NC 27514
E-mail: nsnave@mindspring.com.

**WordsWorth,** ( *0-9652942* ) 1285 Sheridan Ave., No. 275, Cody, WY 82414 Tel 307-587-3932; Fax: 307-587-3801 Do not confuse with San Geronimo, CA, Newton, KS, Ridgewood, NJ.

**Wordsworth Editions, Ltd. (GBR)** ( *1-85326; 1-84022* ) *Dist. by* **Casemate Pubs.**

**Wordsworth Editions, Ltd. (GBR)** ( *1-85326; 1-84022* ) *Dist. by* **Advanced Global.**

†**Wordware Publishing, Inc.,** ( *0-915381; 1-55622; 0-556* ) 2320 Los Rios Blvd., Suite 200, Plano, TX 75074-3557 (SAN 291-4786) Tel 972-423-0090; Fax: 972-881-9147; Toll Free: 800-229-4949 (orders);
*Imprints:* Seaside Press (Seaside Pr)
E-mail: info@wordware.com
Web site: http://www.wordware.com
*Dist(s):* **Hervey's Booklink & Cookbook Warehouse**
**National Bk. Network**
**ibooks.com;** *CIP.*

**WordWright.biz, Inc.,** ( *0-9700615; 0-9713832; 0-9717868; 1-932196* ) P.O. Box 1785, Georgetown, TX 78627 Fax: 512-260-3080 (phone/fax)
E-mail: jnwriter@aol.com; snwriter@earthlink.net
Web site: http://www.wordwright.biz.

**World Almanac Bks.,** ( *0-88687; 0-911818* ) Div. of World Almanac Education Group, 512 Seventh Ave., New York, NY 10018 Tel 201-529-6900; Fax: 201-529-6901
E-mail: info@waegroup.com
Web site: http://www.worldalmanac.com; http://www.worldalmanacforkids.com
*Dist(s):* **St. Martin's Pr..**

**World Citizens,** ( *0-932279* ) 96 La Verne Ave., Mill Valley, CA 94941 (SAN 686-547X) Tel 415-380-8020 ; Toll Free: 800-247-6553 (orders only)
*Dist(s):* **Baker & Taylor Bks.**
**BookMasters, Inc.**
**Bookpeople**
**Social Studies Schl. Service.**

**World of Darkness Imprint of White Wolf Publishing, Inc.**

**World Pubns., Inc.,** ( *0-7669; 0-9640034; 1-57215; 0-7429; 1-4132* ) Orders Addr.: P.O. Box 622, North Dighton, MA 02764; Edit Addr.: 455 Somerset Ave., Bldg. 2A, North Dighton, MA 02764 (SAN 631-7014) Tel 508-880-5555; Fax: 508-880-0469 Do not confuse with World Publications, Inc., Winter Park, FL
E-mail: sales@wrldpub.com
Web site: http://www.wrldpub.com/.

**World Wide Distributors, Limited** *See* **Island Heritage Publishing**

**WorldComm,** ( *1-56664* ) Div. of Creativity, Inc., 65 Macedonia Rd., Alexander, NC 28701 Tel 828-252-9515; Fax: 828-255-8719; Toll Free: 800-472-0438 (phone/fax)
E-mail: sales@abooks.com
Web site: http://www.abooks.com.

**Worldscape Productions** *See* **Kensington Publishing**

**WP,** ( *0-9679527* ) 1281 Kensington Dr., Knoxville, TN 37922 Tel 865-694-4108; Toll Free: 800-743-1574 (phone/fax)
E-mail: michaelks@aol.com
Web site: http://www.wpbooks.com.

**Wright Group, The,** ( *0-322; 0-7802; 0-940156; 1-55624; 1-55911; 1-4045* ) Div. of The McGraw-Hill Education Group, 19201 120th Ave., NE, Suite 100, Bothell, WA 98011 Tel 425-486-8011; Fax: 425-486-6804; Toll Free Fax: 800-543-7323
Web site: http://www.wrightgroup.com/.

**Write Together Publishing,** ( *0-930142; 1-931718* ) 533 Inwood Dr., Nashville, TN 37211 Fax: 520-223-4850
E-mail: paul.clere@writetogether.com
Web site: http://www.writetogether.com.

**Write Way Publishing,** ( *1-885173* ) Orders Addr.: P.O. Box 441278, Aurora, CO 80044 Tel 303-617-0497; Fax: 303-617-1440; Toll Free: 800-680-1493 Do not confuse with Write Way Publishing, Charleston, WV
E-mail: staff@writewaypub.com; writewy@aol.com
Web site: http://www.writewaypub.com
*Dist(s):* **Midpoint Trade Bks., Inc..**

**Writers & Readers Publishing, Inc.,** ( *0-86316; 0-904613; 0-906386; 0-906495* ) 457 Washington St., New York, NY 10013-1344 (SAN 665-813X) Tel 212-982-3158; Fax: 212-777-4924
*Dist(s):* **Publishers Group West.**

**Writers Block, The,** ( *0-9659721* ) 1329 Stevenson Rd., Franklin, KY 42134 Tel 270-598-5861; Fax: 270-598-5862
E-mail: writersbl@aol.com.

**Writers Club Pr. Imprint of iUniverse, Inc.**

**Writers' Collective, The,** ( *0-9716734; 1-932133; 1-59411* ) 780 Reservoir Ave., Suite 243, Cranston, RI 02910 Tel 401-785-4440
E-mail: factotum@writerscollective.org
Web site: http://www.writerscollective.org
*Dist(s):* **Baker & Taylor Bks..**

**Writers Pr., Inc.,** ( *1-885101; 1-931041* ) 2309 Mountainview Dr., Suite 185, Boise, ID 83706 Tel 208-327-0566; Fax: 208-327-3477; Toll Free: 800-574-1715 Do not confuse with companies with the same or similar name in Washington, DC, Victorville, CA
E-mail: publisher@writerspress.com; info@writerspress.com
Web site: http://www.writerspress.com
*Dist(s):* **Baker & Taylor Bks..**

**Writer's Press Service** *See* **Writers Pr., Inc.**

**Writer's Publishing Hse.,** ( *0-9606510* ) 615 N.E. 15th Court, Ft. Lauderdale, FL 33304 (SAN 217-2186) Tel 954-764-4824
E-mail: Douglashyoung@att.net.

**Writer's Showcase Pr. Imprint of iUniverse, Inc.**

**Writer's Unlimited Publishing,** ( *0-9639917* ) 731 Bode Cir., Suite 216, Hoffman Estates, IL 60194 Tel 847-781-7446 Do not confuse with Writer's Unlimited, San Andreas, CA .

**Writing Minds,** ( *0-9664355* ) P.O. Box 38001, Charlotte, NC 28278 Tel 704-625-3077; Toll Free: 888-663-5509
E-mail: silverpeach@bellsouth.net
Web site: http://www.writingminds.com
*Dist(s):* **Culture Plus Bks.**
**Hervey's Booklink & Cookbook Warehouse.**

**Written Word, The Imprint of Hornkohl Communications**

**WWE Imprint of Simon & Schuster**

**Wynwood,** ( *0-922066* ) Orders Addr.: P.O. Box 6287, Grand Rapids, MI 49516-6287 (SAN 203-3801) Toll Free Fax: 800-398-3111 (orders only); Toll Free: 800-877-2665 (orders only); Edit Addr.: 6030 E. Fulton, Ada, MI 49301 Tel 616-676-9185; Fax: 616-676-9573
Web site: http://www.bakerbooks.com
*Dist(s):* **Baker Bk. Hse., Inc..**

**Wyrick & Co.,** ( *0-941711* ) Orders Addr.: P.O. Box 89, Charleston, SC 29402 (SAN 666-2412) Tel 843-722-0881; Fax: 843-722-6771; Toll Free: 800-227-5898; Edit Addr.: 284-A Meeting St., Charleston, SC 29401 (SAN 666-2420)
E-mail: wyrickco@bellsouth.net
*Dist(s):* **Independent Pubs. Group**
**Putnam Publishing Group, The.**

**X Pr., The (GBR)** ( *1-874509; 1-902934* ) *Dist. by* **Natl Bk Netwk.**

**Xenos Bks.,** ( *1-879378* ) Orders Addr.: 22632 Robin Way., Grand Terrace, CA 92324 Tel 909-370-2229; Edit Addr.: Box 52152, Riverside, CA 92517 Tel 909-370-2094; Fax: 909-370-2229
E-mail: info@xenosbooks.com
Web site: http://www.xenosbooks.com
*Dist(s):* **SPD-Small Pr. Distribution.**

**Xipactli Publishing,** ( *0-9712357* ) 255 Banks St., San Francisco, CA 94110 (SAN 253-9993) Fax: 954-212-8260
E-mail: xequina@earthmonsterbooks.com
Web site: http://earthmonsterbooks.com.

**Xlibris Corp.,** ( *0-7388; 0-9663501; 1-4010; 1-4134* ) 436 Walnut St., 11th Flr., Philadelphia, PA 19106 (SAN 299-5522) Tel 215-923-4686; Fax: 215-923-4685; Toll Free: 888-795-4274
E-mail: info@xlibris.com; orders@xlibris.com
Web site: http://www.xlibris.com
*Dist(s):* **Baker & Taylor Bks..**

**Xulon Pr., Inc.,** ( *1-931232; 1-59160; 1-59467* ) 10640 Main St., Suite 204, Fairfax, VA 22030 Tel 703-934-4411; Fax: 703-934-0174; Toll Free: 866-381-2665
E-mail: lelizalde@xulonpress.com; tfreiling@xulonpress.com
Web site: http://www.xulonpress.com
*Dist(s):* **FaithWorks.**

†**Yale Univ. Pr.,** ( *0-300* ) Orders Addr.: c/o Triliteral LLC, 100 Maple Ridge Dr., Cumberland, RI 02864 Tel 401-531-2800; Fax: 401-531-2801; Toll Free Fax: 800-406-9145; Toll Free: 800-405-1619; Edit Addr.: 302 Temple St., New Haven, CT 06511 (SAN 203-2740) Tel 203-432-0960; Fax: 203-432-0948
E-mail: yupmkt@yale.edu
Web site: http://www.yale.edu/yup/index.html; http://www.yale.edu/yup/
*Dist(s):* **Cheng & Tsui Co.**
**netLibrary, Inc.;** *CIP.*

**Yankee Bks.,** ( *0-89909; 0-911658* ) Affil. of Rodale Pr., 33 E. Minor St., Emmaus, PA 18098 (SAN 200-8343) Tel 610-967-5171; Fax: 610-967-8963; Toll Free: 800-527-8200
Web site: http://www.rodalestore.com/.

**Yardbird Bks.,** ( *0-9620251; 1-882611* ) 601 Kennedy Rd., Airville, PA 17302 (SAN 248-0182) Toll Free: 800-622-6044 (orders only)
E-mail: info@yardbird.com
Web site: http://www.yardbird.com/.

**Yarrow Pr.,** ( *1-878274* ) 101 Monterey Ave., Pelham, NY 10803 Tel 914-738-3884 Do not confuse with Yarrow Press in Richwood, WV.

†**Ye Galleon Pr.,** ( *0-87770* ) Orders Addr.: P.O. Box 287, Fairfield, WA 99012 (SAN 205-5597) Tel 509-283-2422 (phone/fax); Toll Free: 800-829-5586 (orders only)
E-mail: galleon@mt.arias.net
*Dist(s):* **Kendall Whaling Museum;** *CIP.*

**Yearling Imprint of Random Hse. Children's Bks.**

**Yellow Brick Road Press** *See* **Pitspopany Pr.**

**Yellow Creek Publishing,** ( *1-929782* ) P.O. Box 1261, Bath, OH 44210 Fax: 248-334-9002; *Imprints:* e-pulp (e-pulp)
E-mail: info@e-pulp.com
Web site: http://www.e-pulp.com
*Dist(s):* **NuvoMedia.**

**Yellow Moon Pr.,** ( *0-938756* ) P.O. Box 381316, Cambridge, MA 02238 (SAN 216-4809) Tel 617-776-2230; Fax: 617-776-8246; Toll Free: 800-497-4385 (orders)
E-mail: story@yellowmoon.com
Web site: http://www.yellowmoon.com
*Dist(s):* **Words Distributing Co..**

**Yerba Buena Pr.,** ( *0-9631242* ) 1560 Stannage Ave., Berkeley, CA 94702 Tel 510-525-3724.

**YES! Entertainment Corp.,** ( *1-57234; 1-883366* ) 1601 Elm St., Suite 4000, Dallas, TX 75201-7202.

**Yestermorrow, Inc.,** ( *1-56723* ) Orders Addr.: P.O. Box 700, Princess Anne, MD 21853.

**Zantanon Pr.,** ( *0-9661115* ) P.O. Box 97, Stony Creek, NY 12878 Tel 518-696-5007; Fax: 716-637-6555.

**Zebra Bks. Imprint of Kensington Publishing Corp.**

**Zenar Bks.,** ( *0-9637134* ) Orders Addr.: P.O. Box 686, Rancho Cordova, CA 95741 Tel 916-852-1816; Fax: 916-852-1871; Edit Addr.: P.O. Box 190, Jefferson, OR 97352-0190
E-mail: zenar@pacbell
*Dist(s):* **Baker & Taylor Bks..**

**Zenon Pubn. Co.,** ( *0-9643320* ) Orders Addr.: P.O. Box 8499, Kansas City, MO 64114 Tel 816-361-3253; Toll Free: 800-496-2662
E-mail: zenonn@juno.com.

**Zephyr Pr.,** ( *0-939010* ) 50 Kenwood St., Brookline, MA 02446 (SAN 239-7668) Tel 617-713-2813 (phone/fax) Do not confuse with companies with the same name in New York, NY, Tucson, AZ, Kansas City, MO, Canton, OH
E-mail: editors@zephyrpress.org
Web site: http://www.zephyrpress.org
*Dist(s):* **Consortium Bk. Sales & Distribution**
**SPD-Small Pr. Distribution.**

**Zero-g Pr.,** ( *1-892086* ) 6605 N. Rustic Oak Ct., Peoria, IL 61614-2344 Tel 309-692-2953
E-mail: scifi20@prodigy.net
Web site: http://www.bradley.bradley.edu/~dlb/steven.html
*Dist(s):* **Baker & Taylor Bks.**
**Partners Pubs. Group, Inc..**

**Ziesing, Mark V.,** ( *0-929480; 0-9612970* ) P.O. Box 76, Shingletown, CA 96088 (SAN 292-7446) Tel 530-474-1580
*Dist(s):* **Baker & Taylor Bks..**

**Ziggurat Productions,** ( *1-884214* ) P.O. Box 292, Topanga, CA 90290-0290 Tel 310-455-2689; Fax: 786-551-8177
E-mail: info@zigguratproductions.com
Web site: http://www.zigguratproductions.com
*Dist(s):* **Baker & Taylor Bks.**
**Brodart Co..**

Names

**Zilch Publishing, Inc.,** *( 1-930410 )* 1465 Rte. 23, Wayne, NJ 07470 Tel 973-696-4266; Fax: 973-696-4228
E-mail: zilchpublishing@aol.com
*Dist(s):* **Baker & Taylor Bks..**

**Zimmermann Publishing,** *( 0-9644793 )* 2701 Ave. J, Brooklyn, NY 11210 Tel 212-268-9900; Fax: 212-268-6106
Web site: http://ttx.com/bookzone/10000424.html.

**Zinn Publishing Group,** *( 0-87165; 0-935016 )* Div. of Zinn Communications, Inc., 35-19 215th Pl., Bayside, NY 11361 (SAN 241-693X) Tel 718-428-6121; Fax: 718-428-2857
*Dist(s):* **APG Sales and Fulfillment BookWorld Services, Inc. Empire Publishing Service.**

**Ziplow Productions,** *( 1-889974 )* Orders Addr.: P.O. Box 7765, Hilton Head Island, SC 29938 Tel 843-785-8190; Fax: 843-785-8197; Toll Free: 800-717-2434; Edit Addr.: 1032 William Hilton Pkwy., Hilton Head Island, SC 29928
E-mail: ziplow@ziplow.com
Web site: http://www.ziplow.com
*Dist(s):* **Penton Overseas, Inc..**

**Zoland Bks., Inc. Imprint of Steerforth Pr.**

**Zon Bks.,** *( 0-310 )* 5300 Patterson Ave., SE, Grand Rapids, MI 49530.

†**Zondervan,** *( 0-310; 0-937336 )* Subs. of HarperCollins US, c/o Zondervan, Order Processing-B36, 5300 Patterson Ave., SE, Grand Rapids, MI 49530 (SAN 203-2694) Tel 616-698-6900; Fax: 616-698-3439; Toll Free Fax: 800-934-6381 (fax orders); Toll Free: 800-727-1309 (orders & customer service)
E-mail: zprod@zph.com
Web site: http://www.zondervan.com
*Dist(s):* **Baker & Taylor Bks.
CRC Pubns.
Christian Bk. Distributors
HarperCollins Pubs.
Spring Arbor Distributors, Inc.
Twentieth Century Christian Bks.
Vida Pubs.
Vision Video;** *CIP.*
**Zondervan Publishing House** *See* **Zondervan**

Names

**21st Century Antiques,** Orders Addr.: P.O. Box 70, Hatfield, MA 01038 (SAN 110-8085); Edit Addr.: 11 1/2 Main St., Hatfield, MA 01038 (SAN 243-248X) Tel 413-247-9396.

**21st Century Pubns.,** ( *0-933278* ) Orders Addr.: P.O. Box 702, Fairfield, IA 52556-0702 Tel 515-472-5105; Fax: 515-472-8443; Toll Free: 800-593-2665; Edit Addr.: 401 N. Fourth St., Fairfield, IA 52556 Do not confuse with Twenty First Century Pubns., Tolland, CT
E-mail: books21st@lisco.com.
Web site: http://www.21stbooks.com.

**3M Sportsman's Video Collection,** 3M Ctr., Bldg. 223-4NE-05, Saint Paul, MN 55144-1000 (SAN 159-8929) Tel 612-733-7412; Fax: 612-736-7479; Toll Free: 800-940-8273 (orders only).

**A & B Books,** *See* **A & B Distributors & Pubs. Group**

**A & B Distributors & Pubs. Group,** ( *1-881316; 1-886433* ) Div. of A&B Distributors, 1000 Atlantic Ave., Brooklyn, NY 11238 (SAN 630-9216) Tel 718-783-7808; Fax: 718-783-7267; Toll Free: 877-542-6657; 146 Lawrence St., Brooklyn, NY 11201 (SAN 631-385X)
E-mail: maxtay@webspan.net.

**A & M Church Supplies,** 220 E. Genesee Ave., Saginaw, MI 48607-1228 (SAN 157-0145) Tel 517-753-4672; Fax: 517-753-4799; Toll Free: 800-345-4694.

**A B C-Clio Information Services,** *See* **ABC-CLIO, Inc.**

**A B S Corporation,** *See* **Budgetext**

**A K J Book Fare, Incorporated,** *See* **AKJ Educational Services, Inc.**

**ABC-CLIO, Inc.,** ( *0-87436; 0-903450; 1-57607; 1-85109* ) 130 Cremona Dr., Santa Barbara, CA 93117 (SAN 301-5467) Tel 805-968-1911; Fax: 805-685-9685; Toll Free: 800-368-6868
E-mail: customerservice@abc-clio.com.
Web site: http://www.abc-clio.com.

**Abel Love, Inc.,** Orders Addr.: P.O. Box 2250, Newport News, VA 23609 (SAN 158-4081) Tel 757-877-2939; Toll Free: 800-520-2939; Edit Addr.: 935 Lucas Creek Rd., Newport News, VA 23608 Fax: 804-877-2939.

**Abingdon Pr.,** ( *0-687* ) Div. of United Methodist Publishing Hse., Orders Addr.: P.O. Box 801, Nashville, TN 37202-3919 (SAN 201-0054) Tel 615-749-6409; Fax: 615-749-6056; Toll Free Fax: 800-836-7802; Toll Free: 800-251-3320; Edit Addr.: 201 Eighth Ave. S., Nashville, TN 37202 (SAN 699-9956)
E-mail: info@abingdon.org
Web site: http://www.abingdonpress.com/.

**aBOOKS Distributing,** ( *1-57090* ) Div. of Creativity, Inc., 65 Macedonia Rd., Alexander, NC 28701 Tel 828-252-9515; Fax: 828-255-8719; Toll Free: 800-472-0438
E-mail: sales@abooks.com.
Web site: http://www.abooks.com.

**Abyss Distribution,** ( *1-932548* ) P.O. Box 48, Middlefield, MA 01243-0048 (SAN 630-9925) Tel 413-623-2155; Fax: 413-623-2156; Toll Free: 800-326-0804
E-mail: abyssdist@aol.com.
Web site: http://www.azuregreen.com.

**Academic Bk. Ctr., Inc.,** 5600 NE Hassalo St., Portland, OR 97213-3640 (SAN 169-7145) Tel 503-287-6657; Fax: 503-284-8859; Toll Free: 800-547-7704
E-mail: orders@acbc.com.
Web site: http://www.abc.com.

**Academic Bk. Services, Inc.,** 5490 Fulton Industrial Blvd., Atlanta, GA 30336 (SAN 631-0591) Tel 404-344-8317; Fax: 404-349-2127.

**Academi-Text Medical Wholesalers,** 333 N. Superior, Toledo, OH 43604 (SAN 135-2415) Tel 419-255-9755 ; Fax: 419-255-9606; Toll Free: 800-552-8398 (out of state).

**Acorn Alliance,** 549 Old North Rd., Kingston, RI 02881-1220 Tel 401-783-5480; Fax: 401-284-0959; Fulfillment Addr.: Client Distribution Services 193 Edwards Dr., Jackson, TN 38301 Toll Free Fax: 800-351-5073; Toll Free: 800-343-4499
E-mail: contact@moyerbellbooks.com
Web site: http://www.moyerbellbooks.com.

**ACTA Pubns.,** ( *0-87946; 0-914070; 0-915388* ) 4848 N. Clark St., Chicago, IL 60640-4711 (SAN 204-7489) Tel 773-271-1030; Fax: 773-271-7399; Toll Free Fax: 800-397-0079; Toll Free: 800-397-2282
E-mail: actapublications@aol.com.
Web site: http://www.actapublications.com.

**Action Products International, Inc.,** 344 Cypress Rd., Ocala, FL 34472-3108 (SAN 630-8805) Tel 352-687-4961; Toll Free: 800-772-2846
E-mail: sales@apii.com.

**Adams Bk. Co., Inc.,** 537 Sackett St., Brooklyn, NY 11217 (SAN 107-7171) Tel 718-875-5464; Fax: 718-852-3212; Toll Free: 800-221-0909
E-mail: sales@adamsbook.com.
Web site: http://www.adamsbook.com.

**Adams News,** 1555 W. Galer St., Seattle, WA 98119 (SAN 169-8842) Tel 206-284-7617; Fax: 206-284-7599; Toll Free: 800-533-7617.

**Adams, Robert Henry Fine Art,** ( *0-9713010* ) 715 N. Franklin St., Chicago, IL 60610 (SAN 159-6918) Tel 312-642-8700; Fax: 312-642-8785
E-mail: info@adamsfineart.com
Web site: http://www.adamsfineart.com.

**Addison-Wesley Longman, Inc.,** ( *0-201; 0-321; 0-582; 0-673; 0-8013; 0-8053; 0-9654123* ) Orders Addr.: 200 Old Tappan Rd., Old Tappan, NJ 07675 (SAN 299-4739) Toll Free: 800-922-0579; Edit Addr.: 75 Arlington St., Suite 300, Boston, MA 02116 (SAN 200-2000) Tel 617-848-7500; Toll Free: 800-447-2226
E-mail: pearsoned@eds.com;
orderdeptnj@pearsoned.com.
Web site: http://www.awl.com.

**Addison-Wesley Publishing Company, Incorporated,** *See* **Addison-Wesley Longman, Inc.**

**Adelman, Joseph,** 217-17 82nd Ave., Jamaica, NY 11427 (SAN 285-8002) Tel 212-465-1711.

**Adler, Leo,** P.O. Box 10308, Eugene, OR 97440-2308 (SAN 169-7021).

**Adler's Foreign Bks., Inc.,** ( *0-8417* ) 915 Foster St., Evanston, IL 60201 (SAN 111-3089) Tel 847-864-0664; Fax: 847-864-0804; Toll Free: 800-235-3771
E-mail: info@afb-adlers.com
Web site: http://www.afb-adlers.com.

**Ad-Lib Pubns.,** 51 W. Adams, Box 1102, Fairfield, IA 52556-1102 (SAN 631-7065).

**Advanced Global Distribution Services,** 5880 Oberlin Dr., San Diego, CA 32121 Toll Free Fax: 800-499-3822; Toll Free: 800-284-3580.

**Advanced Marketing Services, Incorporated,** *See* **Advantage Pubs. Group**

**Advantage Pubs. Group,** ( *0-934429; 1-57145; 1-59223* ) 5880 Oberlin Dr., San Diego, CA 92121 (SAN 630-8090) Toll Free: 800-284-3580
E-mail: janetn@advmkt.com
Web site: http://www.advantagebooksonline.com; http://www.laurelglenbooks.com; http://www.thunderbaypress.com; http://www.bathroomreader.com; http://www.silverdolphinbooks.com.

**Adventure Pubns., Inc.,** ( *0-934860; 1-885061; 1-59193* ) 820 Cleveland St., S., Cambridge, MN 55008 (SAN 212-7199) Tel 763-689-9800; Fax: 763-689-9039; Toll Free Fax: 877-725-0088; Toll Free: 800-678-7006
E-mail: orders@adventurepublications.net.

**Advertising Specialties, Inc.,** 4920 River Rd., Pascagoula, MS 39567 (SAN 108-6316) Tel 601-769-7904
Web site: http://www.advmkt.com; http://www.advantagebooksonline.com.

**Affiliated Bk. Distributor,** Div. of North Shore Distributors, Inc., 1200 N. Branch St., Chicago, IL 60622 (SAN 169-2267).

**Africa World Pr.,** ( *0-86543; 1-59221* ) 541 W. Ingham Ave., Trenton, NJ 08638 (SAN 692-3925) Tel 609-695-3200; Fax: 609-695-6466
E-mail: awprsp@africanworld.com
Web site: http://www.africanworld.com.

**Afrikan World Bk. Distributor,** 1356 W. North Ave., Baltimore, MD 21217 (SAN 631-2020).

**Afro-American Bk. Distributor,** 2537 Prospect, Houston, TX 77004 (SAN 169-8257).

**Agencia de Publicaciones de Puerto Rico,** GPO Box 4903, San Juan, PR 00936 (SAN 169-9296).

**Agritech Publishing Group, Inc.,** Div. of Agritech Corp., 825 W. Samalayuca Dr., Tucson, AZ 85704-3912 (SAN 174-612X) Tel 520-544-2542.

**AHA, Inc.,** ( *0-918545* ) P.O. Box 8405, Santa Cruz, CA 95061-8405 (SAN 295-5059) Tel 408-458-9119.

**Aha Punana Leo,** ( *0-9645646; 1-58191; 1-890270* ) 928 Nuuanu Ave., Suite 315, Honolulu, HI 96817-5193
E-mail: haawina@leoki.uhh.hawaii.edu
Web site: http://www.ahapunanaleo.org.

**AIMS International Bks., Inc.,** ( *0-922852* ) 7709 Hamilton Ave., Cincinnati, OH 45231-3103 (SAN 630-270X) Tel 513-521-5590; Fax: 513-521-5592; Toll Free: 800-733-2067
E-mail: aimsbooks@fuse.net
Web site: http://www.aimsbooks.com.

**A-K News Company,** *See* **Aramark Magazine & Bk. Co.**

**AK Pr. Distribution,** ( *1-873176; 1-902593* ) 674-A 23rd St., Oakland, CA 94612-1163 (SAN 298-2234) Tel 510-208-1700; Fax: 510-208-1701
E-mail: akpress@akpress.org
Web site: http://www.akpress.org.

Wholesalers & Distributors

**AKJ Educational Services, Inc.,** 5609-2A Fishers Ln., Rockville, MD 20852 (SAN 170-5431) Tel 301-770-4030; Fax: 301-770-2338; Toll Free: 800-770-2338
E-mail: info@akjedsvcs.com
Web site: http://www.akjedsvcs.com.

**Alabama Bk. Store,** Orders Addr.: P.O. Box 1279, Tuscaloosa, AL 35401-1626 Tel 205-758-4532; Fax: 205-758-5525; Toll Free: 800-382-2665 (orders only); Edit Addr.: 1015 University Blvd., Tuscaloosa, AL 35403-1279 (SAN 100-0063)
E-mail: ABS@AlabamaBook.com
Web site: http://www.AlabamaBook.com.

**Alamo Square Distributors,** P.O. Box 14543, San Francisco, CA 94114 Tel: 415-863-7456
E-mail: alamosqdist@earthlink.net.

**Alba Hse.,** ( *0-8189* ) Div. of Society of St. Paul, 2187 Victory Blvd., Staten Island, NY 10314-6603 (SAN 201-2405) Tel 718-761-0047; Fax: 718-761-0057; 718-698-8390; Toll Free: 800-343-2522
E-mail: albabooks@aol.com
Web site: http://www.albahouse.org.

**Alexander Distributing,** *See* **aBOOKS Distributing**

**Alexander News Company,** *See* **Blue Ridge News Co.**

**Alfonsi Enterprises,** 8621 Gavinton Ct., Dublin, OH 43017-9615 (SAN 169-4227).

**All America Distributors Corp.,** 8431 Melrose Pl., Los Angeles, CA 90069-5382 (SAN 168-972X) Tel 213-651-2650; Fax: 213-655-9452
E-mail: psi@loop.com.

**Allentown News Agency, Inc.,** Orders Addr.: P.O. Box 446, Allentown, PA 18105; Edit Addr.: 719-723 Liberty St., Allentown, PA 18105 (SAN 169-7226) Tel 610-432-4441; Fax: 610-432-2708.

**Alliance Hse., Inc.,** ( *0-9665234* ) 220 Ferris Ave., Suite 201, White Plains, NY 10603 Tel 914-328-5456; Fax: 914-946-1929
E-mail: alliancehs@aol.com.

**Alonso Bk. & Periodical Services, Inc.,** 7670 Richmond Hwy., Alexandria, VA 22306 (SAN 170-7035) Tel 703-765-1211.

**Alpen Bks,** 3616 South Rd., Suite C-1, Mukilteo, WA 98275 Tel 425-290-8587; Fax: 425-290-9461.

**Alpha & Omega Distributor,** P.O. Box 36640, Colorado Springs, CO 80936-3664 (SAN 169-0515).

**Alpha Bks.,** ( *0-02; 0-672; 0-7357; 0-7897; 1-56761; 1-57595; 0-7431; 1-59257* ) Div. of Pearson Technology Group, 201 W. 103rd St., Indianapolis, IN 46290 (SAN 219-6298) Tel 317-581-3500 Toll Free: 800-571-5840 (orders)
Web site: http://www.idiotsguides.com.

**Alpha Publishing, Inc.,** ( *0-9717585* ) P.O. Box 53788, Lafayette, LA 70505 Tel 337-237-7049; Fax: 337-237-7060; Toll Free: 800-749-4009 Do not confuse with companies with the same or similar name in Mamaroneck, NY, Mount Clair, CA, Louisville, KY, Pheonix, AZ, Annapolis, MD
E-mail: joycedwyer@cs.com.

**Alpine News Distributors,** Div. of Mountain States Distributors, 0105 Marand Rd., Glenwood Springs, CO 81601 Tel 970-945-2269; Fax: 970-945-2260.

**AMACOM,** ( *0-7612; 0-8144* ) Orders Addr.: P.O. Box 169, Saranac Lake, NY 12983 (SAN 227-3578) Tel 518-891-5510; Fax: 518-891-2372; Toll Free: 800-250-5308 (orders & customer service); Edit Addr.: 1601 Broadway, New York, NY 10019-7420 (SAN 201-1670) Tel 212-586-8100; Fax: 212-903-8168
E-mail: cust_serv@amanet.org
Web site: http://www.amacombooks.org.

**Amarillo Periodical Distributors,** P.O. Box 3823, Lubbock, TX 70404 (SAN 156-4986) Tel 806-745-6000.

**Amazon.Com,** ( *1-58060* ) 1200 12th Ave. S., Suite 1200, Seattle, WA 98144 (SAN 179-4205) Tel 206-266-6817; Orders Addr.: P.O. Box 80387, Seattle, WA 98108-0387 (SAN 156-143X) Tel 206-622-2335; Fax: 206-622-2405; 1 Centerpoint Blvd., non-carton, New Castle, DE 19720 (SAN 155-3992); 1 Centerpoint Blvd., carton, New Castle, DE 19720 (SAN 156-1405); 520 S. Brandon, non-carton, Seattle, WA 98108 (SAN 152-6642); 520 S. Brandon, carton, Seattle, WA 98108 (SAN 156-1383); 1600 E. Newlands Dr., carton, Fernley, NV 89408 (SAN 156-5982); 1600 E. Newlands Dr., non-carton, Fernley, NV 89408 (SAN 156-6008); Edit Addr.: 520 Pike St., Seattle, WA 98101 (SAN 155-3984); P.O. Box 81226, Seattle, WA 98108-1226
E-mail: catalog-dept@amazon.com
Web site: http://www.amazon.com.

**Ambassador Bks. & Media,** 42 Chasner St., Hempstead, NY 11550 (SAN 120-064X) Tel 516-489-4011; Fax: 516-489-5661; Toll Free: 800-431-8913
E-mail: ambassador@absbook.com
Web site: http://www.absbook.com.

**Ambassador Book Service,** *See* **Ambassador Bks. & Media**

**AMCAL, Inc.,** ( *0-911855; 1-57624; 1-884358; 1-58625; 1-58913; 1-59282* ) 2500 Bisso Ln., Bldg. 500, Concord, CA 94520 (SAN 263-9025)
E-mail: amcal@amcalart.com
Web site: http://www.amcalart.com.

**American Bk. Ctr.,** Brooklyn Navy Yard, Bldg. 3, Brooklyn, NY 11205 (SAN 630-8821) Tel 718-834-0170.

**American Buddhist Shim Gum Do Assn., Inc.,** ( *0-9614427* ) 203 Chestnut Hill Ave., Brighton, MA 02135 (SAN 113-2873) Tel 617-787-1506; Fax: 617-787-2708
E-mail: marystackhouse@shimgumdo.org
Web site: http://www.shimgumdo.org.

**American Business Systems, Inc.,** 315 Littleton Rd., Chelmsford, MA 01824 (SAN 264-8229) Tel 508-250-9600; Fax: 508-250-8027; Toll Free: 800-356-4034.

**American Education Corp., The,** ( *0-87570; 1-58636* ) 7506 N. Broadway, Suite 505, Oklahoma City, OK 73116-9016 (SAN 654-6250) Tel 405-840-6031; Fax: 405-848-3960; Toll Free: 800-222-2811
Web site: http://www.amered.com.

**American Educational Computer, Incorporated,** *See* **American Education Corp., The**

**American International Distribution Corp.,** Orders Addr.: P.O. Box 80, Williston, VT 05495-0020 Tel 802-862-0095 (ext. 115); Fax: 802-864-7749; Toll Free: 800-426-4742; Edit Addr.: 50 Winter Sport Ln., Williston, VT 05495 (SAN 630-2238) Toll Free: 800-488-2665.

**American Kennel Club Museum of the Dog,** ( *0-9615072* ) 1721 S. Mason Rd., Saint Louis, MO 63131 (SAN 110-8751) Tel 314-821-3647; Fax: 314-821-7381.

**American Magazine Service,** *See* **Prebound Periodicals**

**American Map Corp.,** ( *0-8416; 981-234* ) Div. of Langenscheidt Pubs., Inc., 46-35 54th Rd., Maspeth, NY 11378 (SAN 202-4624) Tel 718-784-0055; Fax: 718-784-0640; Toll Free: 800-432-6277
E-mail: customerservice@americanmap.com
Web site: http://www.americanmap.com.

**American Marketing & Publishing Company,** *See* **Christian Publishing Network**

**American Micro Media,** 19 N. Broadway, Box 306, Red Hook, NY 12571 (SAN 653-9920) Tel 914-758-5567.

**American Overseas Bk. Co., Inc.,** 550 Walnut St., Norwood, NJ 07648 (SAN 169-4863) Tel 201-767-7600; Fax: 201-784-0263
E-mail: books@aobc.com
Web site: http://www.aobc.com.

**American Society of Agronomy,** ( *0-89118* ) 677 S. Segoe Rd., Madison, WI 53711-1086 (SAN 107-5683) Tel 608-273-8080; Fax: 608-273-2021
Web site: http://www.agronomy.org.

**American Society of Civil Engineers,** ( *0-7844; 0-87262* ) 1801 Alexander Bell Dr., Reston, VA 20191-4400 (SAN 204-7594) Tel 703-295-6300; Fax: 703-295-6211; Toll Free: 800-548-2723
E-mail: marketing@asce.org
Web site: http://www.pubs.asce.org.

**American West Bks.,** 1831 Industrial Way, No. 101, Sanger, CA 93657-9501 (SAN 630-8570) Toll Free: 800-497-4909 Do not confuse with American West Bks., Albuquerque, NM
E-mail: JBM12@CSUFresno.edu.

**American Wholesale Bk. Co.,** Subs. of Books-A-Million, Orders Addr.: 121 25th St., S., Birmingham, AL 35210 (SAN 631-7391) Tel 205-956-4151; Fax: 205-956-5530.

**Americana Souvenirs & Gifts,** ( *1-890541* ) 206 Hanover St., Gettysburg, PA 17325-1911 (SAN 169-7366) Toll Free: 800-692-7436.

**America's Hobby Ctr.,** 146 W. 22nd St., New York, NY 10011 (SAN 111-0403) Tel 212-675-8922.

**Ames News Agency, Inc.,** 2110 E. 13th St., Ames, IA 50010 (SAN 169-2550).

**Amoskeag News Agency,** 92 Allard Dr., Manchester, NH 03102 (SAN 169-4537) Tel 603-623-5343.

**AMS Pr., Inc.,** ( *0-404* ) Brooklyn Navy Yard Bldg. 292, Suite 417, 63 Flushing Ave., New York, NY 11205 (SAN 106-6706) Tel 718-875-8100; Fax: 212-995-5413 Do not confuse with companies with the same or similar name in Los Angeles, CA, Pittsburgh, PA
E-mail: amserve@earthlink.net.

**Anchor Distributors,** 30 Hunt Valley Cir., New Kensington, PA 15068 (SAN 631-077X) Tel 724-334-7000; Fax: 724-334-1200; Toll Free: 800-444-4484
E-mail: marketing@whitakerhouse.com.

**Anderson News - Tacoma,** 9914 32nd Ave., S., Lakewood, WA 98499 (SAN 108-1322) Tel 253-581-1940; Fax: 253-584-5941; Toll Free: 800-552-2000 (in Washington).

**Anderson News Co.,** P.O. Box 386, Cloverdale, VA 24077-0386 (SAN 168-9223); 6355 N. Palafox St., Pensacola, FL 32503 (SAN 168-9363) Tel 904-477-0920; 2541 Westcott Blvd., Knoxville, TN 37931 Tel 423-966-7575; 3911 Volunteer Dr., Chattanooga, TN 37416 (SAN 169-7862) Tel 423-894-3945; 6301 Forbing Rd., Little Rock, AR 72219 Tel 501-562-7360; 3777 Hartsfield Rd., Tallahassee, FL 32303 Tel 904-575-8070; 1857 W. Grant, P.O. Box 5465, Tucson, AZ 85705 Tel 520-622-2831; 5184 Sullivan Gardens Pkwy., Kingsport, TN 37660-8104 (SAN 241-6131); 390 Exchange St., Box 1624, New Haven, CT 06506 (SAN 241-6158) Tel 203-777-5545; 5000 Moline St., Denver, CO 80239-2622 Tel 303-321-1111; 1709 N. East St., Flagstaff, AZ 86002 (SAN 168-9290) Tel 520-774-6171; Fax: 520-779-1958; 4935 Covington Way, Memphis, TN 38128; P.O. Box 22968, Chattanooga, TN 37422; P.O. Box 36003, Knoxville, TN 37930-6003; P.O. Box 280077, Memphis, TN 38168-0077; P.O. Box 6660, Pensacola, FL 32503 Do not confuse with Anderson News Company, Pinellas Park, FL.

**Anderson News, LLC,** 3840 Vineland Rd., Orlando, FL 32811-6427 (SAN 169-1201) Tel 407-841-8738; Fax: 407-839-4043; Toll Free: 800-338-3988; P.O. Box 616898, Orlando, FL 32811
E-mail: wigginsd@andersonnews.com.

**Anderson-Austin News Co., LLC,** 808 Newtown Cir., No. B, Lexington, KY 40511-1230 (SAN 169-2836) Tel 606-254-2765; Fax: 606-254-3328.

**Andich Brothers News Company,** *See* **Tobias News Co.**

**Andrews McMeel Publishing,** ( *0-8362; 0-7407* ) Orders Addr.: c/o Simon & Schuster, Inc. 100 Front St., Riverside, NJ 08075 Toll Free Fax: 800-943-9831; Toll Free: 800-943-9839 (Customer Service; 800-897-7650 (Credit Dept.); Edit Addr.: 4520 Main St., Kansas City, MO 64111-7701 (SAN 202-540X) Tel 816-932-6600; Fax: 816-932-6749; Toll Free: 800-851-8923
Web site: http://www.AndrewsMcMeel.com.

**Andrzejewski's Marian Church Supply,** *See* **A & M Church Supplies**

**Angler's Bk. Supply,** 1380 W. Second Ave., Eugene, OR 97402 (SAN 631-4546) Tel 541-342-8355; Fax: 541-342-1785; Toll Free: 800-260-3869.

**answers period, inc.,** ( *0-917875* ) Orders Addr.: P.O. Box 427, Goliad, TX 77963 (SAN 112-6431) Tel 361-645-2268; Toll Free: 800-852-4752
Web site: http://www.answersbook.com.

**Anthracite News Company,** *See* **Great Northern Distributors, Inc.**

**Anthroposophic Press, Incorporated,** *See* **SteinerBooks, Inc.**

**Antiquarian Bookstore, The,** 1070 Lafayette Rd., Portsmouth, NH 03801 (SAN 158-9938) Tel 603-436-7250.

**Antique Collectors' Club,** ( *0-902028; 0-907462; 1-85149* ) Orders Addr.: 91 Market St. Industrial Park, Wappingers Falls, NY 12590 (SAN 630-7787) Tel 845-297-0003; Fax: 845-297-0068; Toll Free: 800-252-5231 (orders)
E-mail: info@antiquecc.com
Web site: http://www.antiquecc.com;
http://www.antiquecc.com.

**AOAC International,** ( *0-935584* ) 481 N. Frederick Ave. Suite 500, Gaithersburg, MD 20877-2417 (SAN 260-3411) Tel 301-924-7077; Fax: 301-924-7089; Toll Free: 800-379-2622
E-mail: aoac@aoac.org
Web site: http://www.aoac.org.

**AOL Time Warner Book Group,** *See* **Time Warner Bk. Group**

**A-One Bk. Distributors, Inc.,** 1121 Lincoln Ave., Unit 17, Holbrook, NY 11741-2264 (SAN 630-7981).

**Aperture Foundation, Inc.,** ( *0-89381; 0-912334; 0-900406; 1-931788* ) Orders Addr.: 20 E. 23rd St., New York, NY 10010 (SAN 201-1832) Tel 212-505-5555; Fax: 212-979-7759; Edit Addr.: 16365 James Madison Hwy., Gordonsville, VA 22942 Tel 540-672-7600; Fax: 540-672-7540
E-mail: editorial@aperture.org;
customerservice@aperture.org
Web site: http://www.aperture.org.

**APG Sales and Fulfillment,** Div. of Warehousing and Fulfillment Specialists, LLC (WFS, LLC), 1501 County Hospital Rd., Nashville, TN 37218 (SAN 630-818X) Tel 615-254-2450; Fax: 615-254-2405; Toll Free: 800-327-5113
E-mail: sswift@agpbooks.com.
Web site: http://www.apgbooks.com.

**Apollo Bks.,** ( 0-938290 ) 91 Market St., Wappingers Falls, NY 12590-2333 (SAN 170-0928).

**Apollo Library Bk. Supplier,** 865 Kent Ln., Philadelphia, PA 19115 (SAN 159-8031).

**Appalachian Bible Co.,** ( 1-889049 ) Orders Addr.: 522 Princeton Rd., Johnson City, TN 37605 (SAN 169-7889) Tel 423-282-9475; Fax: 423-282-9110; Toll Free: 800-289-2772; Edit Addr.: P.O. Box 1573, Johnson City, TN 37601
E-mail: appainc@aol.com.

**Appalachian Bk. Distributors,** Orders Addr.: 522 Princeton Rd., Johnson City, TN 37601 (SAN 630-7388) Tel 423-282-9475; Fax: 423-282-9110; Toll Free: 800-759-2779; Edit Addr.: 506 Princeton Rd., Johnson City, TN 37601.

**Appalachian, Incorporated,** *See* **Appalachian Bible Co.**

**Apple Bk. Co.,** Div. of Scholastic Bk. Fairs, Inc., P.O. Box 217156, Charlotte, NC 28221-0156 Tel 704-596-6641; Fax: 704-599-1738; Toll Free: 800-331-1993; 5901 N. Northwoods Business Pkwy., Charlotte, NC 28269 (SAN 108-4569).

**Arabic & Islamic Univ. Pr.,** 4263 Fountain Ave., Los Angeles, CA 90029 (SAN 107-6299) Tel 323-665-1000; Fax: 323-665-3107.

**Aramark Magazine & Bk. Co.,** P.O. Box 25489, Oklahoma City, OK 73125 (SAN 169-6971) Tel 405-843-9383; Fax: 405-843-0379 Do not confuse with Aramark Magazine & Bk. Services, Inc., Norfolk, VA.

**Aramark Magazine & Bk. Services, Inc.,** Box 2240, Norfolk, VA 23501 (SAN 169-8680) Do not confuse with Aramark Magazine & Book Co., Oklahoma City, OK.

**Arbit Bks., Inc.,** ( 0-930038 ) 8050 N. Port Washington Rd., Milwaukee, WI 53217 (SAN 169-913X) Tel 414-352-4404.

**Ardic Bk. Distributors, Inc.,** 331 High St., 2nd Flr., Burlington, NJ 08016-4411 (SAN 170-5415).

**Argus International Corp.,** Subs. of ICS International Group, Skypark Business Pk., P.O. Box 4082, Irvine, CA 92716-4082 (SAN 681-9761) Tel 714-552-8494 (phone/fax).

**Aries Pr.,** ( 0-933646 ) P.O. Box 30081, Chicago, IL 60630 (SAN 111-9168) Tel 312-725-8300.

**Aries Productions, Inc.,** ( 0-910035 ) Orders Addr.: P.O. Box 29396, Sappington, MO 63126 (SAN 669-0009); Edit Addr.: 9633 Cinnabar Dr., Sappington, MO 63126 (SAN 241-2004) Tel 314-849-3722
E-mail: uspsisquad@aol.com
Web site: http://www.ussisquad.com.

**Arizona Periodicals, Inc.,** P.O. Box 5780, Yuma, AZ 85366-5780 Tel 520-782-1822.

**Arkansas Bk. Co.,** 1207 E. Second St., Little Rock, AR 72202-2732 (SAN 168-9460) Tel 501-375-1184.

**Arlington Card Co., Bk. Dept.,** 140 Gansett Ave., Cranston, RI 02910 (SAN 108-5794) Tel 401-942-3188.

**Armstrong, J. B. News Agency,** *See* **News Group, The**

**Arrow, G. H. Co.,** P.O. Box 676, Bala Cynwyd, PA 19004 (SAN 111-3771) Tel 215-227-3211; Fax: 215-221-0631; Toll Free: 800-775-2776.

**Arrowhead Magazine Co., Inc.,** P.O. Box 5947, San Bernardino, CA 92412 (SAN 169-0094) Tel 909-799-8294; Fax: 909-799-3774; 1055 Cooley Ave., San Bernardino, CA 92408 (SAN 249-2717) Tel 909-370-4420.

**Ars Obscura,** ( 0-9623780 ) P.O. Box 4424, Seattle, WA 98104-0424 (SAN 113-5368) Tel 206-324-9792.

**Art Institute of Chicago,** ( 0-86559 ) Orders Addr.: a/o Museum Shop Mail Order Dept., 1224 W. Van Buren, 3rd Flr., Chicago, IL 60607 Tel 312-563-5150; Fax: 312-563-1973 (attn: Museum Shop); Edit Addr.: 111 S. Michigan Ave., Chicago, IL 60603-6110 (SAN 204-479X) Tel 312-443-3540; Fax: 312-443-1334
Web site: http://www.artic.edu.

**Art Media Resources, Ltd.,** ( 1-878529; 1-58886 ) 1507 S. Michigan Ave., Chicago, IL 60605 (SAN 253-8199) Tel 312-663-5351; Fax: 312-663-5177
E-mail: info@artmediaresources.com
Web site: http://www.artmediaresources.com.

**Artisoft, Inc.,** ( 0-927538 ) 1 S. Church Ave., Suite 2200, Tucson, AZ 85745 (SAN 287-458X) Tel 520-670-7100; Fax: 520-670-7101; Toll Free: 800-233-5564.

**Arts End Bks.,** ( 0-933292 ) P.O. Box 703, Spencer, MA 01562 (SAN 213-6082) Tel 508-885-9904
E-mail: artsend@ma.ultranet.com.

**ARVEST,** P.O. Box 200248, Denver, CO 80220 (SAN 159-8694) Tel 303-388-8486; Fax: 303-355-4213; Toll Free: 800-739-0761
E-mail: copy@concentric.net.

**ASM International,** ( 0-87170 ) 9639 Kinsman Rd., Materials Park, OH 44073-0002 (SAN 204-7586) Tel 440-338-5151; Fax: 440-338-4634; Toll Free: 800-336-5152 (ext. 5900) Do not confuse with ASM International, Inc., Fort Lauderdale, FL
E-mail: Cust-Srv@asminternational.org
Web site: http://www.asminternational.org/.

**Aspen Pubs., Inc.,** ( 0-444; 0-7896; 0-8342; 0-87189; 0-87622; 0-89443; 0-912862 ) Subs. of Wolters Kluwer Nv, Orders Addr.: 7210 McKinney Cir., Frederick, MD 21704 Fax: 301-417-7550; Toll Free Fax: 800-901-9075; Toll Free: 800-638-8437; 800-234-1660 (Customer Service); Edit Addr.: 1185 Avenue of the Americas, 37th Flr., New York, NY 10036 (SAN 203-4999) Tel 212-597-0200; Fax: 212-597-0338
E-mail: customer.service@aspenpubl.com
Web site: http://www.aspenpublishers.com.

**Aspen West Publishing,** ( 0-9615390; 1-885348 ) 8535 S. 700 W., Unit C, Sandy, UT 84070 (SAN 112-7993) Tel 801-565-1370; Fax: 801-565-1373; Toll Free: 800-222-9133 (orders only)
E-mail: kent@aspenwest.com
Web site: http://www.aspenwest.com.

**Associated Publishers Group,** *See* **APG Sales and Fulfillment**

**Associated Univ. Presses,** ( 0-8453 ) 2010 Eastpark Blvd., Cranbury, NJ 08512 (SAN 281-2959) Tel 609-655-4770; Fax: 609-655-8366
E-mail: aup440@aol.com
Web site: http://arts.fdu.edu/aup/; http://www.aupresses.com.

**Association of Official Analytical Chemists,** *See* **AOAC International**

**Astran, Inc.,** 591 SW Eighth St., Miami, FL 33130-3413 (SAN 169-1082) Tel 305-858-4300; Fax: 305-858-0405; Toll Free: 800-431-4957
Web site: http://www.astranbooks.com.

**ATEXINC, Corp.,** ( 0-9702332 ) 13104 Canterbury Rd., Leawood, KS 66209 (SAN 631-774X) Tel 913-663-3703; Fax: 913-663-1881 Do not confuse with Atex, Inc., Bedford, MA
E-mail: atexinc@aol.com
Web site: http://www.atexinc.com.

**Athena Productions, Inc.,** 5500 Collins Ave., No. 901, Miami Beach, FL 33140 Tel 305-868-8482; Fax: 305-868-8891.

**Atlas News Co.,** Div. of Hudson News Co., P.O. Box 779, Boylston, MA 01505-0779 (SAN 169-3360).

**Atlas Publishing Co.,** ( 0-930575 ) 1464 36th St., Ogden, UT 84403 (SAN 110-3873) Tel 801-627-1043.

**AtlasBooks.com,** 30 Amberwood Pkwy., Ashland, OH 44805 Fax: 419-281-6883; Toll Free: 800-247-6553.

**Audio Bk. Co.,** ( 0-89926 ) 125 N. Aspen Ave., Suite 2, Azusa, CA 91702 (SAN 158-1414) Fax: 626-969-6099; Toll Free: 800-423-8273
E-mail: sales@audiobookco.com.
Web site: http://www.audiobookco.com.

**Audio Language Studies, Incorporated,** *See* **Durkin Hayes Publishing Ltd.**

**Audubon Prints & Bks.,** 9720 Spring Ridge Ln., Vienna, VA 22182 (SAN 111-820X).

**Augsburg Fortress Publishers, Publishing House of The Evangelical Lutheran Church in America,** *See* **Augsburg Fortress, Pubs.**

**Augsburg Fortress, Pubs.,** ( 0-8006; 0-8066 ) Orders Addr.: P.O. Box 1209, Minneapolis, MN 55440-1209 (SAN 169-4081) Tel 612-330-3300; Fax: 612-330-3455; Toll Free: 800-722-7766; Toll Free: 800-328-4648 (orders only); Edit Addr.: 100 S. Fifth St., Suite 700, Minneapolis, MN 55402
E-mail: info@augsburgfortress.org;
productinfo@augsburgfortress.org;
subscriptions@augsburgfortress.org;
customerservice@augsburgfortress.org
Web site: http://www.augsburgfortress.org.

**Augusta News Co.,** 25 Second St., Apt. 124, Hallowell, ME 04347-1481 (SAN 169-3026).

**Auromere, Inc.,** ( 0-89744 ) 2621 W. US Hwy. 12, Lodi, CA 95242-9200 (SAN 169-0043) Fax: 209-339-3715; Toll Free: 800-735-4691
E-mail: sasp@lodinet.com
Web site: http://www.auromere.com.

**Austin Management Group,** Orders Addr.: P.O. Box 3206, Paducah, KY 42002-3206 (SAN 135-3349); Edit Addr.: 1051 Husbands Rd., Paducah, KY 42003 (SAN 249-6844) Tel 502-442-1052.

**Auto-Bound, Inc.,** 909 Marina Village Pkwy., No. 67B, Alameda, CA 94501-1048 (SAN 170-0782) Tel 510-521-8655; Fax: 510-521-8755; Toll Free: 800-523-5833.

**Autonomedia,** ( 0-936756; 1-57027 ) Orders Addr.: P.O. Box 568, Brooklyn, NY 11211-0568; Edit Addr.: 55 S. 11th St., Brooklyn, NY 11211-0568 (SAN 221-3869) Tel 718-963-2603
E-mail: info@autonomedia.org
Web site: http://www.autonomedia.org.

**Avanti Enterprises, Inc.,** 18901 Springfield, Flossmoor, IL 60422 (SAN 158-3727) Tel 708-799-6464; Fax: 708-799-8713; Toll Free: 800-799-6464.

**Avenue Bks.,** 2270 Porter Way, Stockton, CA 95207-3339 (SAN 122-4158).

**Avery BookStores, Inc.,** 308 Livingston St., Brooklyn, NY 11217 (SAN 169-510X).

**Aviation Bk. Co.,** ( 0-911720; 0-911721; 0-916413 ) 7201 Perimeter Rd., S., No. C, Seattle, WA 98108-3812 (SAN 120-1530) Tel 206-767-5232; Fax: 206-763-3428; Toll Free: 800-423-2708
E-mail: sales@aviationbook.com.

**Avonlea Bks., Inc.,** Orders Addr.: P.O. Box 74, White Plains, NY 10602-0074 (SAN 680-4446) Tel 914-946-5923; Fax: 914-761-3119; Toll Free: 800-423-0622
E-mail: avonlea@bushkin.com
Web site: http://www.bushkin.com.

**B T P Distribution,** 4135 Northgate Blvd., Suite 5, Sacramento, CA 95834-1226 (SAN 631-2489) Tel 916-567-2496; Fax: 916-441-6749.

**Baggins Bks.,** 3560 Meridian St., Bellingham, WA 98225-1731 (SAN 156-501X) Do not confuse with Baggin's Books in Doylestown, PA.

**Baker & Taylor Bks.,** ( 0-8480 ) Orders Addr.: Commerce Service Ctr., 251 Mt. Olive Church Rd., Commerce, GA 30599-9988 (SAN 169-1503) Tel 404-335-5000; Toll Free: 800-775-1800 (orders); 800-775-1200 (customer service); Reno Service Ctr., 1160 Trademark Dr., Reno, NV 89511 (SAN 169-4464) Tel 775-850-3800; Fax: 775-850-3826 (customer service); Toll Free Fax: 800-775-7480 (orders); Edit Addr.: National Sales Hdqtrs., 5 Lakepointe Plaza, Suite 500, 2709 Water Ridge Pkwy., Charlotte, NC 28217 (SAN 169-5606) Fax: 704-329-8989; Toll Free: 800-775-1800 (information) ; 1120 US Hwy. 22, E., Bridgewater, NJ 08807 (SAN 169-4901) Toll Free: 800-775-1500 (customer service) ; Momence Service Ctr., 5012 S. Gladiolus St., Momence, IL 60954-1799 (SAN 169-2100) Tel 815-472-2444 (international customers); Fax: 815-472-9886 (international customers); Toll Free: 800-775-2300 (customer service, academic libraries)
E-mail: btinfo@btol.com
Web site: http://www.btol.com.

**Baker & Taylor International,** 1120 US Hwy. 22 E., Box 6885, Bridgewater, NJ 08807 (SAN 200-6804) Tel 908-541-7000; Fax: 908-729-4037.

**Baker Bk. Hse., Inc.,** ( 0-8007; 0-8010; 1-58558; 1-58743 ) Orders Addr.: P.O. Box 6287, Grand Rapids, MI 49516-6287 Toll Free Fax: 800-398-3111 (orders only); Toll Free: 800-877-2665 (orders only); Edit Addr.: 6030 E. Fulton, Ada, MI 49301 Tel 616-676-9185; Fax: 616-676-9573
Web site: http://www.bakerbooks.com.

**Ballantine Bks.,** ( 0-345; 0-449; 0-8041; 0-87637; 1-4000 ) Div. of Random Hse., Inc., Orders Addr.: 400 Hahn Rd., Westminster, MD 21157 Tel 410-848-1900; Toll Free Fax: 800-767-4465; Toll Free: 800-726-0600 (customer service); 800-733-3000 (orders); Edit Addr.: 1540 Broadway, 11th Flr., New York, NY 10036 (SAN 214-1175) Tel 212-782-9000; Fax: 212-940-7539; Toll Free: 800-733-3000
E-mail: bfi@randomnhouse.com;
thenry@randomhouse.com
Web site: http://www.randomhouse.com.

**Ballantine Publishing Group,** *See* **Ballantine Bks.**

**Balzekas Museum of Lithuanian Culture,** 6500 S. Pulaski Rd., Chicago, IL 60629 (SAN 110-8522) Tel 773-582-6500; Fax: 773-582-5133.

**Banner of Truth, The,** ( 0-85151 ) Orders Addr.: P.O. Box 621, Carlisle, PA 17013 Tel 717-249-5747; Fax: 717-249-0604; Toll Free: 800-263-8085; Edit Addr.: 63 E. Louther St., Carlisle, PA 17013 (SAN 112-1553) E-mail: info@banneroftruth.org
Web site: http://www.banneroftruth.co.uk.

**Bantam Bks.,** ( *0-553; 0-593; 0-7704; 1-4000* ) Div. of Bantam Dell Publishing Group, Orders Addr.: 400 Hahn Rd., Westminster, MD 21157 Tel 410-848-1900 ; Toll Free: 800-726-0600; Edit Addr.: 1540 Broadway, New York, NY 10036-4094 Tel 212-354-6500; Fax: 212-492-8941; Toll Free Fax: 800-233-3294; Toll Free: 800-223-6834 (Bulk orders); 800-726-0600 (Orders/Customer service) E-mail: bantampublicity@randomhouse.com Web site: http://www.bantam.com.

**Bantam Doubleday Dell Publishing Group,** ( *0-553* ) Div. of Random Hse., Inc., Orders Addr.: 2451 S. Wolf Rd., Des Plaines, IL 60018 Toll Free: 800-323-9872 (orders); 800-258-4233 (EDI ordering); Edit Addr.: 1540 Broadway, New York, NY 10036 (SAN 631-3310) Tel 212-782-9591; Fax: 212-782-9646 Web site: http://www.rharlpublishing.com.

**Barnes & Noble Bks.-Imports,** ( *0-389* ) Div. of Rowman & Littlefield Pubs., Inc., 4720 Boston Way, Lanham, MD 20706 (SAN 206-7803) Tel 301-459-3366; Toll Free: 800-462-6420.

**Barnes & Noble, Inc.,** ( *0-7607; 0-88029; 1-4028* ) 122 Fifth Ave., New York, NY 10011 (SAN 141-3651) Tel 212-633-3300 E-mail: staylor@bn.com.

**Barricade Bks., Inc.,** ( *0-934878; 0-942637; 0-9623032; 1-56980* ) 185 Bridge Plaza N., Suite 308A, Fort Lee, NJ 07024 (SAN 299-1780) Tel 201-944-7600; Fax: 201-944-6363; Toll Free: 800-592-6657 E-mail: customerservice@barricadebooks.com Web site: http://www.barricadebooks.com.

**Basic Crafts Co.,** 6001 66th Ave., No. 10, Riverdale, MD 20737-1717 (SAN 169-5622) Toll Free: 800-847-4127 (outside New York).

**Bay News, Inc.,** 3333 NW 35th Ave., Portland, OR 97210 Tel 503-219-3001; Fax: 503-241-1877.

**Bayou Bks.,** 1005 Monroe St., Gretna, LA 70053 (SAN 120-1913) Tel 504-368-1171; Toll Free: 800-843-1724.

**Bayside Distribution,** *See* **Bayside Entertainment Distribution**

**Bayside Entertainment Distribution,** ( *0-7691* ) 885 Riverside Pkwy., West Sacramento, CA 95605 (SAN 631-1261) Tel 916-371-2800; Fax: 916-371-1995; Toll Free: 800-525-5709 E-mail: stecon@baysidedist.com.

**BBC Audiobooks America,** ( *0-563; 0-7540; 0-7927; 0-89340; 1-55504* ) Orders Addr.: P.O. Box 1450, Hampton, NH 03843-1450 (SAN 208-4864) Tel 603-926-8744; Fax: 603-929-3890; Toll Free: 800-621-0182; Edit Addr.: 1 Lafayette Rd., Hampton, NH 03843 E-mail: customerservice@bbcaudiobooksamerica.com Web site: http://www.bbcaudiobooksamerica.com.

**BCM Pubns., Inc.,** ( *0-86508* ) 237 Fairfield Ave., Upper Darby, PA 19082-2206 (SAN 211-7762) Tel 610-352-7177; Fax: 610-352-5561; Toll Free: 800-226-4685 E-mail: info@bcmintl.org; 103046.613@compuserve.com Web site: http://www.bcmintl.org.

**Beaver News Co., Inc.,** 230 W. Washington St., Rensselaer, IN 47978 (SAN 630-8864).

**Beck's Bk. Store,** 4520 N. Broadway, Chicago, IL 60640 (SAN 159-8139) Tel 773-784-7963; Fax: 773-784-0066 E-mail: rsvltrd@aol.com Web site: http://www.aol.members/becks.html.

**Beechwood Pubns., Inc.,** P.O. Box 1158, Kennett Square, PA 19348 (SAN 107-5853) Tel 610-444-5991 ; Fax: 215-566-4178.

**Beekman Pubs., Inc.,** ( *0-8464* ) P.O. Box 888, Woodstock, NY 12498-0888 (SAN 170-1622) Tel 845-679-2300; Fax: 845-679-2301; Toll Free: 888-233-5626 E-mail: beekman@beekmanpublishers.com Web site: http://www.beekmanpublishers.comw; http://www.beekman.net.

**Beeler, Thomas T. Publisher,** ( *1-57490* ) Orders Addr.: P.O. Box 659, Hampton Falls, NH 03844-0659; Edit Addr.: 22 King St., Hampton Falls, NH 03844-2414 Tel 603-772-1175; Fax: 603-778-9025; Toll Free: 800-818-7574 E-mail: tombeeler@hotmail.com Web site: http://www.beelerpub.com.

**Before Columbus Foundation,** 655 13th St., Suite 300, The Raymond Hse., Oakland, CA 94612 (SAN 159-2955) Tel 510-268-9775.

**Behrman Hse., Inc.,** ( *0-87441* ) 11 Edison Pl., Springfield, NJ 07081 (SAN 201-4459) Tel 973-379-7200; Fax: 973-379-7280; Toll Free: 800-221-2755 E-mail: webmaster@behrmanhouse.com Web site: http://www.behrmanhouse.com.

**Beijing Bk. Co., Inc.,** 701 E. Linden Ave., Linden, NJ 07036-2495 (SAN 169-5673) Tel 908-862-0909; Fax: 908-862-4201.

**Bell Magazine,** Orders Addr.: P.O. Box 1957, Monterey, CA 93940 (SAN 159-7221); Edit Addr.: 3 Justin Ct., Monterey, CA 93940 (SAN 169-0353) Tel 408-642-4668.

**Benjamin News Group,** P.O. Box 16147, Missoula, MT 59806 (SAN 631-6476) Tel 406-721-7801; Fax: 406-721-7802 E-mail: nypguy@dreamscape.com.

**Bennett & Curran, Inc.,** ( *1-879607* ) 1545 W. Tufts Ave., Suite M, Englewood, CO 80110-5575 Tel 303-783-2255; Fax: 303-783-2256 E-mail: Jeff@bennettandcurran.com.

**Berkeley Educational Paperbacks,** 2480 Bancroft Way, Berkeley, CA 94704 (SAN 168-9509) Tel 510-848-7907.

**Berkley Publishing Group,** ( *0-425; 0-515* ) Div. of Penguin Putnam, Inc., Orders Addr.: 405 Murray Hill Pkwy., East Rutherford, NJ 07073 Toll Free: 800-788-6262 (individual consumer sales); 800-847-5515 (orders); 800-631-8571 (customer service); Edit Addr.: 375 Hudson St., New York, NY 10014 (SAN 201-3991) Tel 212-366-2000; Fax: 212-366-2385 E-mail: online@penguinputnam.com Web site: http://www.penguinputnam.com.

**Bernan Assocs.,** ( *0-400; 0-527; 0-89059* ) Div. of Kraus Organization, The, Orders Addr.: 4611-F Assembly Dr., Lanham, MD 20706-4391 (SAN 169-3182) Tel 301-459-7666; Fax: 301-459-0056; Toll Free Fax: 800-865-3450; Toll Free: 800-274-4888 E-mail: order@bernan.com; query@bernan.com Web site: http://www.bernan.com.

**Best Bk. Ctr., Inc.,** 1016 Ave. Ponce De Leon, San Juan, PR 00926 (SAN 132-4403) Tel 809-727-7945; Fax: 809-268-5022.

**Best Continental Bk. Co., Inc.,** P.O. Box 615, Merrifield, VA 22116 (SAN 107-3737) Tel 703-280-1400.

**Bethany Hse. Pubs.,** ( *0-7642; 0-87123; 1-55661; 1-56179; 1-57778; 1-880089; 1-59066* ) Div. of Baker Book Hse., Inc., Orders Addr.: P.O. Box 6287, Grand Rapids, MI 49516-6287 Toll Free: 800-877-2665; Edit Addr.: 11400 Hampshire Ave., S., Bloomington, MN 55438-2455 (SAN 201-4416) Tel 952-829-2500; Fax: 952-996-1393; Toll Free: 800-877-2665 E-mail: orders@bakerbooks.com Web site: http://www.bethanyhouse.com.

**Beyda & Assocs., Inc.,** 6943 Valjean Ave., Van Nuys, CA 91406 (SAN 169-0426) Tel 818-988-3102; Fax: 818-994-8724; Toll Free: 800-422-3932 (orders only) E-mail: sales@beydabooks.com.

**BHB International, Inc.,** Orders Addr.: 302 W. North 2nd St., Seneca, SC 29678 (SAN 631-0915) Tel 864-885-9444; Fax: 864-885-1090 E-mail: bhbbooks@aol.com Web site: http://www.bhbinternational.com.

**Biblio Distribution,** Div. of National Book Network, Orders Addr.: 15200 NBN Way, Blue Ridge Summit, PA 17214 Toll Free Fax: 800-338-4550; Toll Free: 800-462-6420; Edit Addr.: 4501 Forbes Blvd., Suite 200, Lanham, MD 20706 (SAN 211-724X) Tel 301-459-3366; Fax: 301-429-5746 E-mail: custserv@nbnbooks.com Web site: http://www.bibliodistribution.com.

**Biblio Distribution Center,** *See* **Biblio Distribution**

**Biddy Bks.,** 1235 168 Model Rd., Manchester, TN 37355 (SAN 157-8561) Tel 931-728-6967.

**Bilingual Educational Services, Inc.,** ( *0-86624; 0-89075* ) 2514 S. Grand Ave., Los Angeles, CA 90007 (SAN 218-4680) Tel 213-749-6213; Fax: 213-749-1820; Toll Free: 800-448-6032 E-mail: bes@besbooks.com; Sales@besbooks.com Web site: http://www.besbooks.com.

**Bilingual Pubns. Co., The,** 270 Lafayette St., New York, NY 10012 (SAN 164-8993) Tel 212-431-3500; Fax: 212-431-3567 Do not confuse with Bilingual Pubns., in Denver, CO E-mail: lindagoodman@juno.com.

**Birdlegs Christian Apparel,** P.O. Box 189, Duluth, GA 30136-0189 (SAN 631-3280) Toll Free: 800-545-0790.

**Black Box Corp.,** 1000 Park Dr., Lawrence, PA 15055 (SAN 277-1985) Tel 412-746-5500; Fax: 412-746-0746.

**Black Magazine Agency,** Box 1018, Logansport, IN 46947 (SAN 107-0819) Tel 219-753-2429; Fax: 219-753-5480; Toll Free: 800-782-9787.

**Blackburn News Agency,** P.O. Box 1039, Kingsport, TN 37662 (SAN 169-7900).

**Blackwell North America,** ( *0-913262; 0-916472; 0-946344* ) Orders Addr.: 6024 SW Jean Rd., Bldg. G, Lake Oswego, OR 97034 (SAN 169-7048) Tel 503-684-1140; Fax: 503-639-2481; Toll Free: 800-547-6426 (in Oregon); Edit Addr.: 100 University Ct., Blackwood, NJ 08012 (SAN 169-4596) Tel 856-228-8900; Toll Free: 800-257-7341.

**Blair, John F. Pub.,** ( *0-89587; 0-910244* ) 1406 Plaza Dr., Winston-Salem, NC 27103 (SAN 201-4319) Tel 336-768-1374; Fax: 336-768-9194; Toll Free: 800-222-9796 E-mail: blairpub@blairpub.com Web site: http://www.blairpub.com.

**Bloch Publishing Co.,** ( *0-8197* ) 118 E. 28th St., Suite 501-503, New York, NY 10016-8413 (SAN 214-204X) Tel 212-532-3977; Fax: 212-779-9169 E-mail: BlochPub@worldnet.att.net Web site: http://www.blochpub.com/.

**Bloomington News Agency,** P.O. Box 3757, Bloomington, IL 61702-3757 (SAN 169-1732).

**Blue Cat,** ( *0-932679; 0-936200* ) 469 Barbados, Walnut, CA 91789 (SAN 214-0322) Tel 909-594-3317.

**Blue Mountain Arts Inc.,** ( *0-88396; 1-58786* ) Orders Addr.: P.O. Box 4549, Boulder, CO 80306 (SAN 299-9609) Tel 303-449-0536; 954-522-0055; Fax: 303-417-6496; 954-522-5330; Toll Free Fax: 800-256-1213; Toll Free: 800-473-2082 E-mail: ordersbma@mindspring.com.

**Blue Mountain Arts (R) by SPS Studios, Incorporated,** *See* **Blue Mountain Arts Inc.**

**Blue Ridge News Co.,** 21 Westside Dr., No. B, Asheville, NC 28806-2846 (SAN 169-6335).

**Blue Ridge News, Inc.,** 101 E. Patrick St., Frederick, MD 21701-5629 (SAN 169-3158) Tel 301-694-8440.

**Boley International Subscription Agency, Inc.,** 1001 Fries Mill Rd., Blackwood, NJ 08012 (SAN 159-6225) Tel 609-629-2500.

**Bollett Library Resources,** 1340 Ridgeview Dr., McHenry, IL 60050 Tel 815-759-1700; Fax: 815-759-9552.

**Bonneville News Co.,** 965 Beardsley Pl., Salt Lake City, UT 84119 Tel 801-972-5454; Fax: 801-972-1075; Toll Free: 800-748-5453.

**Book Box, Inc.,** 3126 Purdue Ave., Los Angeles, CA 90066 (SAN 243-2285) Tel 310-391-2313.

**Book Buy Back,** 5150 Candlewood St., No. 6, Lakewood, CA 90712 (SAN 631-7251) Tel 562-461-9355; Fax: 562-461-9445.

**Book Clearing Hse.,** 46 Purdy St., Harrison, NY 10528 (SAN 125-5169) Tel 914-835-0015; Fax: 914-835-0398; Toll Free: 800-431-1579 E-mail: bookch@aol.com; bchouse@delphi.com.

**Book Co., The,** 145 S. Glencoe St., Denver, CO 80222-1152 (SAN 200-2809).

**Book Distribution Ctr.,** ( *0-941722* ) Div. of Free Islamic Literatures, Inc., Orders Addr.: P.O. Box 35844, Houston, TX 77235 (SAN 241-6395); Edit Addr.: P.O. Box 31669, Houston, TX 77231 (SAN 226-2770).

**Book Distribution Ctr., Inc.,** Orders Addr.: P.O. Box 64631, Virginia Beach, VA 23467 (SAN 134-8019) Tel 757-456-0005; Fax: 757-552-0837; Edit Addr.: 4617 N. Witchduck Rd., Virginia Beach, VA 23455 (SAN 169-8672) E-mail: sales@bookdist.com Web site: http://www.bookdist.com.

**Book Dynamics, Inc.,** ( *0-9612440* ) 18 Kennedy Blvd., East Brunswick, NJ 08816 (SAN 169-5649) Tel 732-545-5151; Fax: 732-545-5959; Toll Free: 800-441-4510.

**Book Fairs of Covina,** 1030 Bonita Ave., La Verne, CA 91750 (SAN 630-6225) Tel 909-593-0697; 1650 W. Orange Grove Ave., Pomona, CA 91768-2153 (SAN 299-2434).

**Book Gallery,** ( *1-878382* ) 632 S. Quincy Ave., Apt. 1, Tulsa, OK 74120-4635 (SAN 630-9321).

**Book Home, The,** 119 E. Dale St., Colorado Springs, CO 80903-4701 (SAN 249-3055) Tel 719-634-5885.

**Book Hse., Inc., The,** 208 W. Chicago St., Jonesville, MI 49250-0125 (SAN 169-3859) Tel 517-849-2117; Fax: 517-849-9716; Toll Free Fax: 800-858-9716; Toll Free: 800-248-1146 E-mail: bhinfo@thebookhouse.com.

*Wholesalers & Distributors*

**Book Margins, Inc.,** 7100 Valley Green Rd., Fort Washington, PA 19034-2206 (SAN 106-7788) Tel 215-223-5300
E-mail: paul.gross@bookmargins.com.
Web site: http://www.bookmargins.com.

**Book Mart, The,** 1153 E. Hyde Pk., Inglewood, CA 90302 (SAN 168-969X).

**Book Masters/El Rancho,** P.O. Box 2039, Mansfield, OH 44905 (SAN 630-8872) Fax: 419-281-6883; Toll Free: 800-247-6553.

**Book Publishing Co., The,** ( *0-913990; 1-57067; 0-9669317; 0-9673108* ) P.O. Box 99, Summertown, TN 38483 (SAN 202-439X) Tel 931-964-3571; Fax: 931-964-3518; Toll Free: 888-260-8458 Do not confuse with Book Publishing Co., Seattle, WA
E-mail: bookpub@bookpubco.com
Web site: http://www.bookpubco.com.

**Book Sales, Inc.,** ( *0-7858; 0-89009; 1-55521* ) Orders Addr.: 114 Northfield Ave., Edison, NJ 08837 (SAN 169-488X) Tel 732-225-0530; Fax: 732-779-6058; 732-225-2257; Toll Free: 800-526-7257; Edit Addr.: 276 Fifth Ave., Suite 206, New York, NY 10001 (SAN 299-4062) Tel 212-779-4972; Fax: 212-779-6058
E-mail: booksales@eclipse.net
Web site: http://www.booksales.com.

**Book Service of Puerto Rico,** 102 De Diego, Santurce, PR 00907 (SAN 169-9326) Tel 809-728-5000; Fax: 809-726-6131
E-mail: bellbook@coqui.net
Web site: http://home.coqui.net/bellbook.

**Book Service Unlimited,** P.O. Box 31108, Seattle, WA 98103-1108 (SAN 169-877X) Toll Free: 800-347-0042.

**Book Services International,** Orders Addr.: P.O. Box 1434-SMS, Fairfield, CT 06430 (SAN 157-9541) Tel 203-374-4939; Fax: 203-384-6099; Toll Free: 800-243-2790.

**Book Shelf, The,** 919 Central Ave., Fort Dodge, IA 50501 (SAN 169-2658) Tel 515-573-3535.

**Book Travelers West,** Orders Addr.: 9551 Landfall Dr., Huntington Beach, CA 92646 Tel 714-968-2301.

**Book Warehouse,** 5154 NW 165th St., Hialeah, FL 33014-6335.

**Book Wholesalers, Inc.,** ( *0-7587; 1-4046; 1-4131; 1-4155; 1-4156* ) 1847 Mercer Rd., Lexington, KY 40511-1001 (SAN 135-5449) Toll Free: 800-888-4478
E-mail: jcarrico@bwibooks.com; nb
Web site: http://www.bwibooks.com.

**Book World,** 311 Sagamore Pkwy., N., Lafayette, IN 47904 (SAN 135-4051) Tel 765-448-1131 Do not confuse with companies with the same or similar name in Sun Lakes, AZ, Roanoke, VA
E-mail: fsjintl@pworld.net.ph.

**Bookazine Co., Inc.,** 75 Hook Rd., Bayonne, NJ 07002 (SAN 169-5665) Tel 201-339-7777; Fax: 201-339-7778; Toll Free: 800-221-8112.

**Booklegger, The,** ( *0-936421* ) Orders Addr.: P.O. Box 2626, Grass Valley, CA 95945 (SAN 697-9548); Edit Addr.: 13100 Grass Valley Ave., Suite D, Grass Valley, CA 95945 (SAN 120-6125) Tel 530-272-1556 ; Fax: 530-272-2133; Toll Free Fax: 800-250-2199; Toll Free: 800-262-1556
E-mail: order@booklegger.com
Web site: http://www.booklegger.com/.

**Bookline,** Div. of Michiana News Service, Inc., 2232 S. 11th St., Niles, MI 49120 (SAN 169-3948) Tel 616-684-3013; Fax: 616-684-8740.

**Booklines Hawaii, Ltd.,** ( *1-929844; 1-58849* ) 269 Pali'i St., Mililani, HI 96789 (SAN 630-6624) Tel 877-828-4852; Fax: 808-676-2031
E-mail: cynthiar@booklines.com
Web site: http://www.booklineshawaii.com.

**Bookmark, Inc., The,** 14643 W. 95th St., Lenexa, KS 66215 (SAN 131-4017) Tel 913-894-1288; Fax: 913-894-1842; Toll Free: 800-642-1288.

**BookMasters,** 6745 FM 2738, Burleson, TX 76028-1167 (SAN 630-8406) Do not confuse with BookMasters Inc., Ashland, OH.

**BookMasters, Inc.,** ( *0-917889* ) Orders Addr.: P.O. Box 388, Mansfield, OH 44903 (SAN 631-3566) Tel 419-281-1802; Fax: 419-281-6883; Toll Free: 800-247-6553; 30 Amberwood Pkwy., Ashland, OH 44805 Fax: 419-281-6886 Do not confuse with BookMasters, Burleson, TX
E-mail: order@bookmaster.com;
info@bookmasters.com.
Web site: http://www.bookmasters.com.

**Bookmen, Inc.,** Orders Addr.: 525 N. Third St., Minneapolis, MN 55401 (SAN 169-409X) Tel 612-359-5757; Fax: 612-341-2903; Toll Free Fax: 800-266-5636; Toll Free: 800-328-8411 (customer service)
Web site: http://www.bookmen.com.

**BookMobile,** ( *0-929636* ) 2402 University Ave. W., No. 701, Saint Paul, MN 55114-1701 (SAN 249-7719) Tel 612-642-9241 Do not confuse with BookMobile in Port Ludlow WA.

**Bookpeople,** ( *0-914728* ) 7900 Edgewater Dr., Oakland, CA 94621 (SAN 168-9517) Tel 510-632-4700; Fax: 510-632-1281; Toll Free Fax: 800-999-4650
E-mail: custserv@bponline.com;
bpeople@bponline.com
Web site: http://www.bponline.com.

**Books & Research, Inc.,** 32 Main St., Hastings On Hudson, NY 10706-1602 (SAN 130-1101) Fax: 914-478-1315
E-mail: brinc@ix.netcom.com
Web site: http://www.books-and-research.com.

**Books International, Incorporated,** ( *1-891078* ) Orders Addr.: P.O. Box 605, Herndon, VA 20172-0605 (SAN 131-761X) Tel 703-661-1500; Fax: 703-661-1501
E-mail: mgreenwald@sorosny.org.

**Books Nippan,** *See* Digital Manga Distribution

**Books to Grow On,** 826 S. Aiken Ave., Pittsburgh, PA 15232 (SAN 128-438X); 210 S. Highland Ave., Pittsburgh, PA 15206 Fax: 412-621-5324.

**Books West,** 5757 Arapahoe Ave., Unit D2, Boulder, CO 80303 (SAN 631-4724) Tel 303-449-5995; Fax: 303-449-5951; Toll Free: 800-378-4188 Do not confuse with Books West, San Diego, CA
E-mail: wnack@rmi.net.

**Booksellers Order Service,** 828 S. Broadway, Tarrytown, NY 10591-5112 (SAN 106-5181) Tel 914-591-2665; Fax: 914-591-2720; Toll Free: 800-637-0037.

**Booksmith Promotional Co.,** 100 Paterson Plank Rd., Jersey City, NJ 07307 (SAN 664-5364) Tel 201-659-2768; Fax: 201-659-3631.

**Booksource, The,** ( *0-7383; 0-911891; 0-9641084; 1-890760* ) 1230 Macklind Ave., Saint Louis, MO 63110-1432 (SAN 169-4324) Tel 314-647-0600; Fax: 314-647-2622; Toll Free: 800-444-0435
E-mail: vstadts@freewwweb.com
Web site: http://www.booksource.com.

**Booksurge, LLC,** ( *1-59109; 1-59457* ) 5341 Dorchester Rd., Suite 16, North Charleston, SC 29418 (SAN 255-2132) Tel 843-579-0000; Fax: 843-577-7506; Toll Free: 866-308-6235
E-mail: editor@booksurge.com;
info@imprintbooks.com
Web site: http://www.booksurge.com;
http://www.imprintbooks.com.

**BookWorksUSA,** 385 Freeport Blvd., Suite 3, Sparks, NV 89431
E-mail: bookworksusa@mac.com.

**BookWorld Distribution Services, Incorporated,** *See* BookWorld Services, Inc.

**BookWorld Services, Inc.,** ( *1-884962* ) 1933 Whitfield Pk. Loop, Sarasota, FL 34241 (SAN 173-0568) Tel 941-758-8094; Fax: 941-753-9396; Toll Free Fax: 800-777-2525; Toll Free: 800-444-2524 (orders only)
E-mail: central@bookworld.com;
sales@bookworld.com
Web site: http://www.bookworld.com.

**Bookworm,** 14 Griffin St., Northport, ME 04849-4446 (SAN 170-8074).

**Bookworm Bookfairs,** 968 Farmington Ave., W., West Hartford, CT 06107 (SAN 156-5621).

**Bookworm, The,** 417 Monmouth Dr., Cherry Hill, NJ 08002 (SAN 120-9531) Tel 609-667-5884.

**Borchardt, G. Inc.,** 136 E. 57th St., New York, NY 10022 (SAN 285-8614) Tel 212-753-5785; Fax: 212-838-6518.

**Borders, Inc.,** 9910 N. By NE Blvd., Bldg. 4, Fishers, IN 46038 (SAN 152-5352); Plaza Las Americas, Space 497, 1st Flr. 525 F D Roosevelt Ave., Hato Rey, PR 00918 (SAN 193-2314); 455 Industrial Blvd., Suite E, La Vergne, TN 37086 (SAN 156-6474); Edit Addr.: 100 Phoenix Dr., Ann Arbor, MI 48108 (SAN 152-3546) Tel 734-477-1100; Fulfillment Addr.: a/o Fulfillment Center, 100 Phoenix Dr., Ann Arbor, MI 48108-2202 (SAN 197-0917).

**Bound to Stay Bound Bks.,** ( *0-9718238* ) 1880 W. Morton Rd., Jacksonville, IL 62650 (SAN 169-1996) Toll Free Fax: 800-747-2872; Toll Free: 800-637-6586
Web site: http://www.btsb.com.

**Bowers & Merena Galleries, Inc.,** ( *0-943161* ) Orders Addr.: P.O. Box 1224, Wolfeboro, NH 03894 (SAN 168-9746) Tel 603-569-5095; Fax: 603-569-5319; Toll Free: 800-222-5993; Edit Addr.: 61 S. Main St., Wolfeboro, NH 03894 (SAN 668-2561).

**Boydell & Brewer, Inc.,** ( *0-85115; 0-85991; 0-86193; 0-907239; 1-870252* ) Div. of Boydell & Brewer, Ltd., 668 Mount Hope Ave., Rochester, NY 14620-2731 Tel 585-275-0419; Fax: 585-271-8778
E-mail: boydell@boydellusa.net
Web site: http://www.boydell.co.uk.

**BPDI,** 1000 S. Lynndale Dr., Appleton, WI 54914 (SAN 631-6859) Tel 920-830-7897; Fax: 920-830-3857.

**Brauninger News Co.,** Orders Addr.: Box 290, Trenton, NJ 08602-0290 (SAN 169-4936) Tel 609-396-1500; Fax: 609-394-2594
E-mail: philfriend@worldnet.att.net.

**Breakfast Poems,** 3424 Preston Ave., NW, Roanoke, VA 24012 Tel 540-366-5886 (phone/fax).

**Bridge Pubns., Inc.,** ( *0-88404; 1-57318; 1-4031* ) 4751 Fountain Ave., Los Angeles, CA 90029 (SAN 208-3884) Tel 323-953-3320; Fax: 323-953-3328; Toll Free: 800-722-1733
E-mail: info@bridgepub.com
Web site: http://www.bridgepub.com;
http://www.clearbodyclearmind.com.

**Bright Horizons Specialty Distributors, Inc.,** 138 Springside Rd., Asheville, NC 28803 (SAN 110-4101) Tel 704-684-8840; Fax: 704-681-1790; Toll Free: 800-437-3959 (orders only).

**Brisco Pubns.,** ( *0-9603576* ) P.O. Box 2161, Palos Verdes Peninsula, CA 90274 (SAN 133-0268) Tel 310-534-4943; Fax: 310-534-8437.

**Broadman & Holman Pubs.,** ( *0-8054; 0-87981; 1-55819; 1-58640; 0-8400* ) Div. of LifeWay Christian Resources of the Southern Baptist Convention, 127 Ninth Ave., N., Nashville, TN 37234 (SAN 201-937X) Tel 615-251-2520; Fax: 615-251-5026 (Books Only); 615-251-2036 (Bibles Only); 615-251-2413 (Gifts/Supplies Only); Toll Free: 800-296-4036 (orders/returns); 800-251-3225; 800-725-5416
E-mail: broadmanholman@lifeway.com
Web site: http://www.broadmanholman.com.

**Brodart Co.,** ( *0-87272* ) Orders Addr.: 500 Arch St., Williamsport, PA 17705 (SAN 169-7684) Tel 717-326-2461; 570-326-2461 (International); Fax: 570-326-1479; 519-759-1144 (Canada); Toll Free Fax: 800-999-6799; Toll Free: 800-233-8467 (US & Canada)
E-mail: bookinfo@brodart.com
Web site: http://www.brodart.com.

**Brookings Institution Pr.,** ( *0-8157* ) 1775 Massachusetts Ave., NW, Washington, DC 20036-2188 (SAN 201-9396) Tel 202-797-6258; Fax: 202-797-6004; Toll Free: 800-275-1447
E-mail: brookinfo@brook.edu; bibooks@brook.edu
Web site: http://www.brookings.edu.

**Brotherhood of Life, Inc.,** ( *0-914732* ) P.O. Box 46306, Las Vegas, NV 89114-6306 (SAN 111-3674) Fax: 702-319-5577
E-mail: brotherhoodoflife@hotmail.com
Web site: http://www.brotherhoodoflife.com.

**Brown, David Bk. Co.,** Orders Addr.: P.O. Box 511, Oakville, CT 06779 (SAN 630-9461) Tel 860-945-9329; Fax: 860-945-9468; Toll Free: 800-791-9354
E-mail: david.brown.bk.co@snet.net
Web site: http://www.oxbowbooks.com.

**Brunner News Agency,** 217 Flanders Ave., P.O. Box 598, Lima, OH 45801 (SAN 169-6777) Tel 419-225-5826; Fax: 419-225-5537; Toll Free: 800-998-1727
E-mail: brunnews@aol.com
Web site: http://www.readmoreshallmark.com.

**Buckeye News Co.,** 6800 W. Central Ave., Suite F, Toledo, OH 43617-1157 (SAN 169-6874).

**Budget Bk. Service, Inc.,** Div. of LDAP, Inc., 386 Park Ave. S., Suite 1913, New York, NY 10016-8804 (SAN 169-5762) Fax: 212-679-2247.

**Budget Marketing, Inc.,** P.O. Box 1805, Des Moines, IA 50306 (SAN 285-8754).

**Budgetext,** Orders Addr.: P.O. Box 1487, Fayetteville, AR 72702 (SAN 111-3321) Tel 501-443-9205; Fax: 501-442-3064; Toll Free: 800-643-3432; Edit Addr.: 1936 N. Shiloh Dr., Fayetteville, AR 72704 (SAN 249-3330)
E-mail: wmorgan@absc.com;
scaldwell@budgetext.com
Web site: http://www.budgetext.com.

**Burlington News Agency,** Hercules Dr., P.O. Box 510, Colchester, VT 05446-0510 (SAN 169-8583) Tel 802-655-7000.

**Burns News Agency,** P.O. Box 1211, Rochester, NY 14603-1211 (SAN 169-5320).

**Byrrd Enterprises, Inc.,** ( *1-886715* ) 1302 Lafayette Dr., Alexandria, VA 22308 (SAN 169-8605) Tel 703-765-5626; Fax: 703-768-4086; Toll Free: 800-628-0901
E-mail: byrrdbooks@aol.com.

**C & B Bk. Hse.,** 21 Oak Ridge Rd., Monroe, CT 06468 (SAN 159-8279).

**C & H News Co.,** P.O. Box 2768, Corpus Christi, TX 78403-2768 (SAN 169-8249).

Full publisher information is available in the Publisher Name Index

**Calico Subscription Co.,** P.O. Box 640337, San Jose, CA 95164-0337 (SAN 285-9173) Tel 408-432-8700; Fax: 408-432-8813; Toll Free: 800-952-2542.

**California Princeton Fulfillment Services,** 1445 Lower Ferry Rd., Ewing, NJ 08618 (SAN 630-639X) Tel 609-883-1759 (ext. 536); Toll Free: 800-777-4726 E-mail: donnaw@cpfs.pupress.princeton.edu.

**Calvary Distribution,** ( 0-9676661; 0-9700218; 1-931667 ) Div. of Calvary Chapel of Costa Mesa, 3232 W. MacArthur Blvd., Santa Ana, CA 92704 (SAN 631-7405) Tel 714-545-6548; Fax: 714-641-8201; Toll Free: 800-444-7664 E-mail: mail@calvaryd.org Web site: http://www.calvaryd.org.

**Cambridge Bk. Co.,** ( 0-8428 ) Div. of Simon & Schuster, Inc., 4350 Equity Dr., Box 249, Columbus, OH 43216 (SAN 169-5703) Toll Free: 800-238-5833 Web site: http://www.simonsays.com/.

**Cambridge Univ. Pr.,** ( 0-521; 0-511 ) Orders Addr.: 100 Brook Hill Dr., West Nyack, NY 10994-2133 (SAN 281-3769) Tel 845-353-7500; Fax: 845-353-4141; Toll Free: 800-872-7423 (orders, returns, credit & accounting); 800-937-9600; Edit Addr.: 40 W. 20th St., New York, NY 10011-4211 (SAN 200-206X) Tel 212-924-3900; Fax: 212-691-3239 E-mail: orders@cup.org; information@cup.org; customer_service@cup.org Web site: http://www.cup.org.

**Canyonlands Pubns.,** ( 0-9702595 ) Orders Addr.: P.O. Box 16175, Bellemont, AZ 86015-6175 (SAN 114-3824) Tel 520-779-3888; Fax: 520-779-3778; Toll Free: 800-283-1983; Edit Addr.: 4860 N. Ken Morey, Bellemont, AZ 86015 E-mail: books@infomagic.com.

**Cape News Co.,** P.O. Box 568680, Rockledge, FL 32955 Tel 407-636-5909.

**Capital Business Systems,** Div. of Capital Business Service, Orders Addr.: P.O. Box 2088, Napa, CA 94558 (SAN 698-3146) Tel 707-252-8844; Fax: 707-252-6368; Edit Addr.: 2033 First St., Napa, CA 94558.

**Capital City,** 2537 Daniels St., Madison, WI 53704-6772 (SAN 200-5328) Tel 608-223-2000; Fax: 608-223-2010.

**Capital News Co.,** 961 Palmyra, Jackson, MS 39203 Tel 601-355-8341; Fax: 601-352-1343.

**Capitol News Agency,** P.O. Box 7886, Richmond, VA 23231 (SAN 249-2768); 5203 Hatcher St., Richmond, VA 23231-0271 Tel 804-222-7252.

**Capitol Preservation Committee,** *See* **Pennsylvania Capitol Preservation Committee**

**Capper Pr.,** 1503 SW 42nd, Topeka, KS 66609 (SAN 285-8886) Tel 913-274-4324; Fax: 913-274-4305; Toll Free: 800-678-5779 (ext. 4324).

**Cards Bks. N Things,** 1446 St., Rd. 2 West, La Porte, IN 46350 (SAN 159-8295).

**Carolina Biological Supply Co., Pubns. Dept.,** ( 0-89278 ) 2700 York Rd., Burlington, NC 27215-3398 (SAN 249-2784) Tel 336-584-0381; Fax: 910-584-3399; Toll Free Fax: 800-222-7112; Toll Free: 800-334-5551 E-mail: carolina@carolina.com. Web site: http://www.carolina.com.

**Carolina Cassette Distributors,** Orders Addr.: P.O. Box 429, New Bern, NC 28560 (SAN 110-8395) Fax: 919-638-1291; Edit Addr.: 2600 Oaks Rd., New Bern, NC 28560 (SAN 659-2155) Tel 919-638-5583.

**Carolina News Co.,** Orders Addr.: P.O. Box 10, Fayetteville, NC 28302; Edit Addr.: 245 Tillinghast St., Fayetteville, NC 28301 Tel 910-483-4135.

**Cascade News, Inc.,** 1055 Commerce Ave., Longview, WA 98632 (SAN 169-8761) Tel 360-425-2450; Fax: 360-425-2451.

**Casemate Pubs. & Bk. Distributors, LLC,** ( 0-9711709; 1-932033 ) Orders Addr.: 2114 Darby Rd., 2nd Flr., Havertown, PA 19083 Tel 610-853-9131; Fax: 610-853-9146 E-mail: casemate@casematepublishing.com Web site: http://www.casematepublishing.com.

**Casino Distributors,** Orders Addr.: P.O. Box 849, Pleasantville, NJ 08232 (SAN 169-457X) Tel 609-646-4165; Fax: 609-645-0152; Edit Addr.: 10 Canale Dr., Pleasantville, NJ 08234 (SAN 249-3276).

**Casper Magazine Agency,** P.O. Box 2340, Casper, WY 82602 (SAN 159-8325).

**Cassette Book Company,** *See* **Audio Bk. Co.**

**Catholic Bookrack Service,** 700 E. Elm St., La Grange, IL 60525 (SAN 169-2178) Tel 708-482-0044; Fax: 708-482-9644.

**Catholic Literary Guild, Inc.,** 200 Hamilton Ave., White Plains, NY 10601 (SAN 285-8908) Tel 914-949-4444.

**Catweasel Productions,** *See* **Ars Obscura**

**Cave of the Winds,** P.O. Box 826, Manitou Springs, CO 80829 Tel 719-685-5444 Web site: http://www.caveofthewinds.com.

**CBLS Pubs.,** ( 1-878907; 1-59529 ) 119 Brentwood St., Marietta, OH 45750 (SAN 169-5517) Tel 740-374-9458; Fax: 740-374-8029 E-mail: cbls@cbls.com Web site: http://www.cbls.com.

**CD Distributing, Inc.,** P.O. Box 4965, Missoula, MT 59806-4965 (SAN 169-4367) Fax: 406-454-0415.

**Cedar Fort, Inc./CFI Distribution,** ( 0-934126; 1-55517 ) 925 N. Main St., Springville, UT 84663-1051 (SAN 170-2858) Tel 801-489-4084; Fax: 801-489-1097; Toll Free Fax: 800-388-3727; Toll Free: 800-759-2665 E-mail: sales@cedarfort.com; cedarfort@cedarfort.com; editorial@cedarfort.com Web site: http://www.cedarfort.com.

**Cedar Graphics,** *See* **Igram Pr.**

**Centennial Pubns.,** 1400 Ash Dr., Fort Collins, CO 80521 (SAN 630-494X) Tel 970-493-2041 Do not confuse with Centennial Pubns., Grand Junction, CO.

**Center for Applied Psychology, Incorporated,** *See* **Childswork/Childsplay**

**Central Arizona Distributing,** 4932 W. Pasadena Ave., Glendale, AZ 85301 (SAN 170-6128) Tel 602-939-6511.

**Central Illinois Periodicals,** P.O. Box 3757, Bloomington, IL 61701 (SAN 630-8945) Tel 309-829-9405.

**Central Kentucky News Distributing Company,** *See* **Anderson-Austin News Co., LLC**

**Central News of Sandusky,** 5716 McCartney Rd., Sandusky, OH 44870-1538 (SAN 169-684X).

**Central Programs,** 802 N. 41st St., Bethany, MO 64424 Tel 660-425-7777.

**Centralia News Co.,** 232 E. Broadway, Centralia, IL 62801 (SAN 159-8341) Tel 618-532-5601.

**CentroLibros de Puerto Rico, Inc.,** Santa Rosa Unit, Bayamon, PR 00960 (SAN 631-1245) Tel 787-275-0460; Fax: 787-275-0360.

**Century Bk. Distribution,** 814 Boon, Traverse City, MI 49686 Tel 231-933-6405 (phone/fax).

**Ceramic Book & Literature Service,** *See* **CBLS Pubs.**

**Chambers Kingfisher Graham Publishers, Incorporated,** *See* **Larousse Kingfisher Chambers, Inc.**

**Champaign-Urbana News Agency,** Orders Addr.: P.O. Box 793, Champaign, IL 61824 (SAN 630-8953) Tel 217-351-7047; Edit Addr.: 503 Kenyon, Champaign, IL 61820.

**Chelsea Green Publishing,** ( 0-930031; 1-890132; 1-931498; 88-86283 ) Orders Addr.: P.O. Box 428, White River Junction, VT 05001 (SAN 669-7631) Tel 802-295-6300; Fax: 802-295-6444; Toll Free: 800-639-4099; Edit Addr.: 205 Gates-Briggs Bldg., Main St., White River Junction, VT 05001 Web site: http://www.chelseagreen.com.

**Cheng & Tsui Co.,** ( 0-646; 0-88727; 0-917056 ) 25 West St., Boston, MA 02111-1213 (SAN 169-3387) Tel 617-988-2401; Fax: 617-426-3669 E-mail: service@cheng-tsui.com. Web site: http://www.cheng-tsui.com.

**Chicago Distribution Ctr.,** 11030 S. Langley Ave., Chicago, IL 60628 (SAN 630-6047) Tel 773-568-1550 ; Fax: 773-660-2235; Toll Free: 800-621-2736; 800-621-8471 (credit & collections).

**Chicago Review Pr., Inc.,** ( 0-914090; 0-914091; 1-55652; 1-56976 ) 814 N. Franklin St., Chicago, IL 60610 (SAN 213-5744) Tel 312-337-0747; Fax: 312-337-5985; Toll Free: 800-888-4741 (orders only) E-mail: orders@ipgbook.com frontdesk@ipgbook.com Web site: http://www.ipgbook.com.

**Chico News Agency,** P.O. Box 690, Chico, CA 95927 (SAN 168-9533) Tel 530-895-1000; Fax: 530-895-0158.

**Children's Bookfair Co., The,** 700 E. Grand Ave., Chicago, IL 60611-3472 (SAN 630-6705) Tel 312-477-7323; 837 W. Altgeld St., Chicago, IL 60614 (SAN 630-6713).

**Children's Library of Poetry,** P.O. Box 831, Dearborn Heights, MI 48127 Tel 313-563-3030; Fax: 313-563-6888 E-mail: poetrylibrary@aol.com.

**Child's World, Inc.,** ( 0-89565; 0-913778; 1-56766; 1-59296 ) Orders Addr.: P.O. Box 326, Chanhassen, MN 55317-0326 (SAN 211-0032) Tel 952-906-3939; Fax: 952-906-3940; Toll Free: 800-599-7323; Edit Addr.: 7081 W. 192nd Ave., Eden Prairie, MN 55346 E-mail: info@childsworld.com Web site: http://www.childsworld.com.

**Childswork/Childsplay,** ( 1-882732; 1-58815 ) Div. of The Guidance Channel, Orders Addr.: P.O. Box 760, Plainview, NY 11803-0760 Tel 516-349-5520; Fax: 516-349-5521; Toll Free: 800-962-1141; 135 Dupont St., Plainview, NY 11803-0760 E-mail: karens@at-risk.com; info@childswork.com Web site: http://www.childswork.com.

**China Bks. & Periodicals, Inc.,** ( 0-8351 ) 2929 24th St., San Francisco, CA 94110-4126 (SAN 145-0557) Tel 415-282-2994; Fax: 415-282-0994 E-mail: info@chinabooks.com. Web site: http://www.chinabooks.com.

**China Cultural Ctr.,** 970 N. Broadway, Suite 103, Los Angeles, CA 90012 (SAN 111-8161) Tel 213-489-3827; Fax: 213-489-3080.

**China House Gallery, China Institute in America,** *See* **China Institute Gallery, China Institute in America**

**China Institute Gallery, China Institute in America,** ( 0-9654270 ) 125 E. 65th St., New York, NY 10021 (SAN 110-8743) Tel 212-744-8181; Fax: 212-628-4159 E-mail: gallery@chinainstitute.org Web site: http://www.chinainstitute.org.

**Chinese American Co.,** 44 Kneeland St., Boston, MA 02111 (SAN 159-7248) Fax: 617-451-2318.

**Chivers North America,** *See* **BBC Audiobooks America**

**Christian Bk. Distributors,** Orders Addr.: P.O. Box 7000, Peabody, MA 01961-7000 (SAN 630-5458) Tel 978-977-5000; Fax: 978-977-5010 Web site: http://www.christianbook.com.

**Christian Distribtuion Services, Inc.,** 1230 Heil Quaker Blvd., Lavergne, TN 37086 Tel 615-793-5955; Fax: 615-793-5973.

**Christian Literature Crusade, Inc.,** ( 0-87508 ) Div. of CLC Publications, Orders Addr.: P.O. Box 1449, Fort Washington, PA 19034-8449 Tel 215-542-1242; Fax: 215-542-7580; Toll Free: 800-659-1240; Edit Addr.: 701 Pennsylvania Ave., Fort Washington, PA 19034 (SAN 169-7358) E-mail: joinclc@juno.com Web site: http://www.clcusa.org.

**Christian Printing Service,** 4861 Chino Ave., Chino, CA 91710-5132 (SAN 108-2647) Tel 714-871-5200.

**Christian Publishing Network,** ( 0-9628406 ) P.O. Box 405, Tulsa, OK 74101 (SAN 631-2756) Tel 918-296-4673 (918-296-HOPE); Toll Free: 888-688-8125 E-mail: vpsales@olp.net.

**Chronicle Bks. LLC,** ( 0-8118; 0-87701; 0-938491 ) 85 Second St., San Francisco, CA 94105 (SAN 202-165X) Tel 415-537-4200; Fax: 415-537-4460; Toll Free Fax: 800-858-7787; Toll Free: 800-722-6657 (orders only) E-mail: orders@chroniclebooks.com Web site: http://www.chroniclebooks.com.

**Church of Scientology Information Service-Pubns.,** ( 0-915598 ) c/o Bridge Pubns., Inc., 1414 N. Catalina, Los Angeles, CA 90029 (SAN 268-9774).

**Church Richards Co.,** 10001 Roosevelt Rd., Westchester, IL 60154 (SAN 285-8975) Toll Free: 800-323-0227.

**Cibolo Nature Ctr.,** P.O. Box 9, Boerne, TX 78006 Tel 830-249-4616.

**Circa Pubns., Inc.,** 415 Fifth Ave., Pelham, NY 10803-0408 (SAN 169-6122) Tel 914-738-5570; Toll Free: 800-582-5952 (orders only).

**Circle Bk. Service, Inc.,** ( 0-87397 ) P.O. Box 626, Tomball, TX 77377 (SAN 158-2526) Tel 281-255-6824; Fax: 281-255-8158; Toll Free: 800-227-1591 E-mail: orders@circlebook.com Web site: http://www.circlebook.com.

**City News Agency,** Orders Addr.: P.O. Box 561129, Charlotte, NC 28256-1129 (SAN 169-782X); Edit Addr.: P.O. Box 2069, Newark, OH 43055 (SAN 169-6947); 220 Cherry Ave., NE, Canton, OH 44702-1198 (SAN 169-6602); 303 E. Lasalle St., South Bend, IN 46617 (SAN 159-9992); 417 S. McKinnley, Harrisburg, IL 62946 (SAN 169-1961).

**Clarks Out of Town News,** 303 S. Andrews Ave., Fort Lauderdale, FL 33301 (SAN 159-8384) Tel 954-467-1543.

**Classroom Reading Service,** 10038 S. Pioneer Blvd., Santa Fe Springs, CA 90670 (SAN 131-3959) Tel 562-942-9501; Fax: 562-942-9370; Toll Free: 800-422-6657 E-mail: crsbooks@aol.com.

**Client Distribution Services,** 425 Madison Ave., New York, NY 10017 (SAN 631-760X) Tel 212-223-2969; Fax: 212-223-1504 Do not confuse with Client Distribution Services, Jackson, TN.
E-mail: skail@cds.aeneas.com;
tflowers@cdsbooks.com;
Web site: http://www.cdsbooks.com/.

**Clover Bk. Service,** 1220 S. Monroe St., Covingtons, LA 70433-3639 (SAN 106-472X) Tel 504-875-0038.

**Cobblestone Publishing Co.,** ( 0-382; 0-942389; 0-9607638 ) Div. of Cricket Magazine Group, 30 Grove St., Suite C, Peterborough, NH 03458 (SAN 237-9937) Tel 603-924-7209; Fax: 603-924-7380; Toll Free: 800-821-0115
E-mail: custsvc@cobblestone.mv.com
Web site: http://www.cobblestonepub.com.

**Cogan Bks.,** ( 0-940688 ) 15020 Desman Rd., La Mirada, CA 90638 (SAN 168-9649) Tel 714-523-0309 ; Fax: 714-523-0796; Toll Free: 800-733-3630.

**Cokesbury,** 201 Eighth Ave., S., Nashville, TN 37203 (SAN 200-6863) Tel 615-749-6409; Toll Free: 800-672-1789.

**Cold Cut Comics Distribution,** 475-D Stockton Ave., San Jose, CA 95126 (SAN 631-6409) Tel 408-293-3844; Fax: 408-293-6645
E-mail: comics@coldcut.com
Web site: http://www.coldcut.com.

**Cole, Bill Enterprises, Inc.,** P.O. Box 60, Randolph, MA 02368-0060 (SAN 685-6373) Tel 617-986-2653.

**Collector Bks.,** ( 0-89145; 1-57432 ) Div. of Schroeder Publishing Co., Inc., Orders Addr.: P.O. Box 3009, Paducah, KY 42003 (SAN 157-5368) Tel 270-898-6211; 270-898-7903; Fax: 270-898-8890; 270-898-1173; Toll Free: 800-626-5420 (orders only); Edit Addr.: 5801 Kentucky Dam Rd., Paducah, KY 42003 (SAN 200-7479)
E-mail: Info@collectorbooks.com;
info@AQSquilt.com
Web site: http://www.AQSquilt.com;
http://www.collectorbooks.com.

**College Bk. Co. of California, Inc.,** 6590 Darrin Way, Cypress, CA 90630 (SAN 269-0802) Tel 714-894-4791.

**Collegedale Distributors,** *See* **Tree of Life Midwest**

**Colonial Williamsburg Foundation,** ( 0-87935; 0-910412 ) P.O. Box 3532, Williamsburg, VA 23187-3532 (SAN 128-4630) Fax: 757-565-8999 (orders only); Toll Free: 800-446-9240 (orders only)
Web site: http://www.colonialwilliamsburg.com.

**Colorado Periodical Distributor, Inc.,** 1227 Pitkin St., Grand Junction, CO 81502 Tel 970-242-3865; Fax: 970-242-3760.

**Columbia County News Agency, Inc.,** 135 Warren St., Hudson, NY 12534 (SAN 169-5339) Tel 518-828-1017.

**Columbia Univ. Pr.,** ( 0-231 ) 61 W. 62nd St., New York, NY 10023 (SAN 212-2472) Tel 212-459-0600; Fax: 212-459-3678
Web site: http://www.columbia.edu/cu/cup.

**Comag Marketing Group,** 1790 Broadway, Suite 401, New York, NY 10019 (SAN 169-5800) Tel 212-841-8365; Fax: 212-977-9401.

**Comics Hawaii Distributors,** *See* **Hobbies Hawaii Distributors**

**Common Ground Distributors, Inc.,** Orders Addr.: P.O. Box 25249, Asheville, NC 28813-1249 Toll Free: 800-654-0626; Edit Addr.: 115 Fairview Rd., Asheville, NC 28803-2307 (SAN 113-8006) Tel 828-274-5575; Fax: 828-274-1955
E-mail: orders@comground.com.

**Communication Service Corporation,** *See* **Gryphon Hse., Inc.**

**Communications Technology, Inc.,** ( 0-918232 ) P.O. Box 209, Rindge, NH 03461 (SAN 159-8198) Tel 603-899-6957.

**Computer & Technical Bks.,** 6338 Ranchview Ln., N., Osseo, MN 55311-3924 (SAN 630-8120).

**Computer Book Service,** *See* **Levy Home Entertainment**

**Conde Nast Pubns., Inc.,** ( 1-878494 ) Four Times Sq., 20th Flr., New York, NY 10036 (SAN 285-905X) Tel 212-880-8800; Fax: 212-880-8289.

**Consortium Bk. Sales & Distribution,** Orders Addr.: 1045 Westgate Dr., Suite 90, Saint Paul, MN 55114-1065 (SAN 200-6049) Tel 651-221-9035; Fax: 651-221-0124; Toll Free: 800-283-3572 (orders)
E-mail: consortium@cbsd.com
Web site: http://www.cbsd.com.

**Contemporary Arts Pr.,** ( 0-931818 ) Div. of La Mamelle, Inc., P.O. Box 3123, San Francisco, CA 94119-3123 (SAN 170-5423) Tel 415-282-0286.

**Continental Bk. Co., Inc.,** ( 0-9626800 ) Eastern Div., 80-00 Cooper Ave., Bldg. No. 29, Glendale, NY 11385 (SAN 169-5436) Tel 718-326-0560; Fax: 718-326-4276; Toll Free: 800-364-0350; Western Div., 625 E. 70th Ave., No. 5, Denver, CO 80229 (SAN 630-2882) Tel 303-289-1761; Fax: 303-289-1764 Do not confuse with Continental Book Company, Denver, CO
E-mail: esl@continentalbook.com;
bonjour@continentalbook.com;
tag@continentalbook.com; hola@continentalbook.com
Web site: http://www.continentalbook.com.

**Continuum International Publishing Group, Inc.,** ( 0-304; 0-7201; 0-8044; 0-8264 ) Orders Addr.: 22883 Quicksilver Dr., Dulles, VA 20166 (SAN 253-3391) Fax: 703-661-1501; Toll Free: 800-561-7704; Edit Addr.: 370 Lexington Ave., New York, NY 10017-6503 (SAN 213-8220) Tel 212-953-5858; Fax: 212-953-5944
E-mail: info@continuum-books.com
Web site: http://www.continuum-books.com.

**Continuum Publishing Company,** *See* **Continuum International Publishing Group, Inc.**

**Cook Communications Ministries,** ( 0-7459; 0-7814; 0-88207; 0-89191; 0-89693; 0-912692; 1-55513; 1-56476; 983-45027; 983-45018; 983-45031 ) 4050 Lee Vance View, Colorado Springs, CO 80918 Tel 719-536-0100; Fax: 719-536-3269; Toll Free: 800-708-5550; 55 Woodslee Ave., Paris, ON N3L 3E5 Toll Free Fax: 888-642-8606; Toll Free: 800-263-2664 Do not confuse with Cook Communications Ministries International, same address
E-mail: bergerj@cookministries.org
Web site: http://www.cookministries.com.

**Cookbooks by Morris Press,** *See* **Morris Publishing**

**Coos Bay Distributors,** 131 N. Schoneman St., Coos Bay, OR 97420 (SAN 169-7064) Tel 541-888-5912.

**Copper Island News,** 1010 Wright St., Marquette, MI 49855-1834 (SAN 169-3824).

**Cornell Univ. Pr.,** ( 0-8014; 0-87546 ) Orders Addr.: P.O. Box 6525, Ithaca, NY 14851 (SAN 281-5680) Tel 607-277-2211; Toll Free Fax: 800-688-2877; Edit Addr.: Sage House, 512 E. State St., Ithaca, NY 14851 (SAN 202-1862) Tel 607-277-2338
E-mail: orders@plymbridge.com;
cupress-sales@cornell.edu; cupressinfo@cornell.edu
Web site: http://www.cornellpress.cornell.edu.

**Cornerstone Publishing & Distribution, Inc.,** ( 1-929281 ) P.O. Box 490, Bountiful, UT 84011-0490 Tel 801-295-9451; Fax: 801-295-0196; Toll Free: 800-453-0812
E-mail: rrhopkins@utah-inter.net.

**Coronet Bks.,** ( 0-89563; 91-7916 ) 311 Bainbridge St., Philadelphia, PA 19147 (SAN 210-6043) Tel 215-925-2762; Fax: 215-925-1912 Do not confuse with Coronet Bks. & Pubns., Eagle Point, OR
E-mail: rsmolin@ix.netcom.com;
order@coronetbooks.com
Web site: http://www.coronetbooks.com.

**Council Oak Bks.,** ( 0-933031; 1-57178 ) Orders Addr.: 2105 E. 15th St., Suite B, Tulsa, OK 74104 (SAN 689-5522) Toll Free: 800-247-8850 (orders only); Edit Addr.: 5806 S. Perkins Rd., Stillwater, OK 74074
E-mail: sdennison@counciloakbooks.com
Web site: http://www.counciloakbooks.com.

**Country News Distributors,** Div. of Bakers, Inc., P.O. Box 1258, Brattleboro, VT 05302-1258 (SAN 169-8575).

**Countryside Bks.,** ( 0-88453 ) 2410 Northside Dr., Clearwater, FL 33761-2216 (SAN 107-4415) Tel 813-796-7337.

**Coutts Library Service, Inc.,** 1823 Maryland Ave., Box 1000, Niagara Falls, NY 14302-1000 (SAN 169-5401) Tel 716-282-8627; Fax: 905-356-5064; Toll Free: 800-772-4304
E-mail: coutts@wizbang.coutts.on.ca.

**Cove Distributors,** 6325 Erdman Ave., Baltimore, MD 21205 (SAN 158-9814) Toll Free: 800-622-5656 (Orders).

**Cowley Distributing, Inc.,** 732 Heisinger Rd., Jefferson City, MO 65109 (SAN 169-426X) Tel 573-636-6511; Fax: 573-636-6262; Toll Free: 800-364-5950 (orders).

**Cox Subscriptions, Inc.,** 411 Marcia Dr., Goldsboro, NC 27530 (SAN 107-0061) Tel 919-735-1001; Fax: 919-734-3332; Toll Free: 800-553-8088.

**CPG Publishing, Inc.,** ( 1-931411 ) Orders Addr.: c/o CPG Distribution, 7253 Grayson Rd., Harrisburg, PA 17111 Toll Free: 800-501-6883 (orders & customer service); Edit Addr.: P.O. Box 6424, New York, NY 10150 Tel 212-573-9180; Fax: 212-573-9181 Do not confuse with C P G Publishing Company in Gold Canyon, AZ
E-mail: cpgdistribution@juno.com.

**Craftsman Bk. Co.,** ( 0-910460; 0-934041; 1-57218 ) 6058 Corte del Cedro, Carlsbad, CA 92009 (SAN 159-7000) Tel 760-438-7828; Fax: 760-438-0398; Toll Free: 800-829-8123
E-mail: jacobs@costbook.com
Web site: http://www.craftsman-book.com.

**CRC Pubns.,** ( 0-930265; 0-933140; 1-56212 ) 2850 Kalamazoo Ave., SE, Grand Rapids, MI 49560 (SAN 212-727X) Tel 616-224-0724; Fax: 616-224-0834; Toll Free 888-642-8606; Toll Free: 800-333-8300 ; P.O. Box 5070, Burlington, ON L7R 3Y8
E-mail: sales@crcpublications.org
Web site: http://www.crcpublications.org.

**Creative Homeowner,** ( 0-932944; 1-58011; 1-880029 ) Div. of Federal Marketing Corp., 24 Park Way, Upper Saddle River, NJ 07458-9960 (SAN 213-6627) Tel 201-934-7100; Fax: 201-934-7593; Toll Free: 800-631-7795
E-mail: info@creativehomeowner.com
Web site: http://www.creativehomeowner.com.

**Creative Homeowner Press,** *See* **Creative Homeowner**

**Crescent Imports & Pubns.,** ( 0-933127 ) P.O. Box 7827, Ann Arbor, MI 48107-7827 (SAN 111-3976) Tel 734-665-3492; Fax: 734-677-1717; Toll Free: 800-521-9744
E-mail: crescentus@aol.com
Web site: http://www.crescentimports.com.

**Crescent International, Inc.,** 2238 Otranto Rd., Charleston, SC 29418 (SAN 110-0777) Tel 803-797-6363; Fax: 803-797-6367.

**Critics' Choice,** *See* **Critics' Choice Video, Inc.**

**Critics' Choice Video, Inc.,** ( 1-932566 ) 900 N Rohlwing Rd., Itasca, IL 60143 Tel 630-775-3300; Fax: 603-775-3340
Web site: http://www.ccvideo.com/.

**Cromland,** 1995 Highland Ave., Suite 200, Bethlehem, PA 18020 (SAN 254-6736) Tel 610-997-3000; Fax: 610-997-8880; Toll Free: 800-944-5554 (U.S. & Canada)
E-mail: info@cromland.com
Web site: http://www.cromland.com.

**CrossLife Expressions,** ( 0-9636049; 1-57838 ) Div. of Exchanged Life Ministries, Inc., 10610 E. Bethany Dr., Suite A, Aurora, CO 80014 (SAN 169-0590) Tel 303-750-0440; Fax: 303-750-1228; Toll Free: 800-750-6818
E-mail: info@crosslifebooks.com
Web site: http://www.crosslifebooks.com.

**Crowley, Inc.,** 16120 U.S. Hwy. 19 N., Suite 220, Clearwater, FL 34624-6862 (SAN 285-9130) Tel 813-531-5889.

**Crown Agents Service, Ltd.,** 3100 Massachusetts Ave., NW, Washington, DC 20008 (SAN 285-919X).

**CSSS,** 7184 Manchester St., Saint Louis, MO 63143 (SAN 631-4392) Tel 314-645-6080; Fax: 314-645-3280; Toll Free: 800-275-4055.

**Culpepper Press,** *See* **BookMobile**

**Cultural Hispana/Ameriketako Liburuak,** Orders Addr.: P.O. Box 7729, Silver Spring, MD 20907 (SAN 159-2823); Edit Addr.: 1413 Crestridge Dr., Silver Spring, MD 20910 (SAN 249-3063) Tel 301-585-0134
E-mail: mokordo@erols.com
Web site: http://www.coloquio.com/libros.html.

**CUP Services,** 750 Cascadilla St., Ithaca, NY 14851 (SAN 630-6519) Tel 607-277-2211; Fax: 607-277-6292; Toll Free: 800-666-2211.

**Cybernetics Technology Corp.,** ( 0-923458 ) 1370 Port Washington Blvd., Port Washington, NY 11050-2628 (SAN 295-933X) Tel 516-883-7676.

**Cypress Bk. Co., Inc.,** ( 0-934643 ) Subs. of China International Bk. Trading Corp., 3450 Third St., Unit 4B, San Francisco, CA 94124 (SAN 112-1162) Tel 415-821-3582; Fax: 415-821-3523; Toll Free: 800-383-1688
E-mail: sales@cypressbook.com;
info@cypressbook.com; cypbook@pacbell.net
Web site: http://www.cypressbook.com.

**D & H News Co., Inc.,** 79 Albany Post Rd., Montrose, NY 10548 (SAN 169-5533) Tel 914-737-3152.

**Daedalus Bks.,** 9645 Gerwig Ln., Columbia, MD 21046-1520 (SAN 158-9202) Tel 410-309-2700
E-mail: tstock@daedalus-books.com;
custserv@daedalus-books.com
Web site: http://www.daedalus-books.com.

**Dakota News,** 221 Petro Ave., Box 1310, Sioux Falls, SD 57101 (SAN 169-7854) Tel 605-336-3000; Fax: 605-336-7279; Toll Free: 800-658-5498.

**Dakota West Bks.,** P.O. Box 9324, Rapid City, SD 57701 (SAN 630-351X) Tel 605-348-1075; Fax: 605-348-0615.

**Darr Subscription Agency,** P.O. Box 575, Louisburg, KS 66053-0575 (SAN 285-9149) Toll Free: 800-850-3741
E-mail: lgriff@midusa.net.

**Dawson Subscription Service,** *See* **Faxon Illinois Service Ctr.**

**Day School Magazine Service,** P.O. Box 262, Brooklyn, NY 11219 (SAN 285-9157) Tel 718-871-1486; Fax: 718-435-2342
E-mail: Elciv@juno.com.

**De Gruyter, Walter Inc.,** ( *0-89925; 1-56445; 3-11* ) Subs. of Walter de Gruyter & Co. (GW), 200 Saw Mill River Rd., Hawthorne, NY 10532 (SAN 201-3088) Tel 914-747-0110; Fax: 914-747-1326
E-mail: customerservice@degruyterny.com
Web site: http://www.degruyter.com

**De Vore Group/Carla Bks. & More,** Orders Addr.: P.O. Box 10276, San Juan, PR 00922 (SAN 159-8309) Tel 809-721-7645; Fax: 809-722-9216; Edit Addr.: 1409 Ave. Ponce De Leon, San Juan, PR 00907-4023 (SAN 249-2776).

**DeHoff Christian Bookstore,** 749 NW Broad St., Murfreesboro, TN 37129 (SAN 184-4202) Tel 615-893-8322; Fax: 615-896-7447; Toll Free: 800-695-5385.

**Dehoff Publications,** *See* **DeHoff Christian Bookstore**

**Delmar Learning,** ( *0-314; 0-7668; 0-7693; 0-8273; 0-87350; 0-916032; 0-944132; 0-9653629; 1-56253; 1-56593; 1-56930; 1-4018* ) Div. of Thomson Learning, Orders Addr.: c/o Thomson Learning Order Fulfilment, P.O. Box 6904, Florence, KY 41022 Toll Free Fax: 800-487-8488; Toll Free: 800-347-7707; c/o Thomson Delmar Learning Clinical Health Care Series Thomson Delmar Learning Clinical Health Care, P.O. Box 3419, Scranton, PA 18505-0419 Fax: 570-347-9072; Toll Free: 888-427-5800; Edit Addr.: P.O. Box 15015, Albany, NY 12212-5015 (SAN 206-7544) Tel 518-348-2300; Fax: 518-373-6345; Toll Free: 800-998-7498; 5 Maxwell Dr., Clifton Park, NY 12065-2919 (SAN 658-0440)
E-mail: cbutler@delmar.com;
clinicalmanuals@thomson.com
Web site: http://www.delmarlearning.com;
http://www.clinicalmanuals.com/.

**Delmar News Agency, Inc.,** P.O. Box 7169, Newark, DE 19714-7169 (SAN 169-0892) Tel 302-455-9922; Toll Free: 800-441-7025.

**Delmar Thomson Learning,** *See* **Delmar Learning**

**DeLong Subscription Agency,** P.O. Box 806, Lafayette, IN 47902 (SAN 285-9246) Toll Free: 800-992-2092.

**Deltiologists of America,** ( *0-913782* ) P.O. Box 8, Norwood, PA 19074 (SAN 170-3072) Tel 610-485-8572.

**Demco Media, Ltd.,** ( *0-606* ) Affil. of Demco, Inc., Orders Addr.: P.O. Box 14260, Madison, WI 53714-0260; Edit Addr.: 2810 Crossroads Dr., Suite 2700, Madison, WI 53718-7942 (SAN 111-1167) Fax: 608-241-0666; Toll Free Fax: 800-828-0401 (orders); Toll Free: 800-448-8939 (Turtleback customer orders/service) Demco Media titles are available only to schools and libraries. Not available to the retail market.
E-mail: mediacustserv@demco.com
Web site: http://www.demcomedia.com.

**Derstine, Roy Bk. Co.,** 14 Birch Rd., Kinnelon, NJ 07405 (SAN 130-822X) Tel 973-838-1109.

**DeRu's Fine Arts,** ( *0-939370* ) 9100 E. Artesia Blvd., Bellflower, CA 90706 (SAN 159-3862) Tel 562-920-1312; Fax: 562-920-3077
E-mail: derusgal@aol.com.

**Deseret Bk. Co.,** ( *0-87579; 0-87747; 1-57345; 1-59038* ) Div. of Deseret Management Corp., Orders Addr.: P.O. Box 30178, Salt Lake City, UT 84130 (SAN 150-763X) Tel 801-534-1515; 801-517-3165 (Wholesale Dept.); Fax: 801-517-3338; Toll Free: 800-453-3876; Edit Addr.: 40 E. South Temple, Salt Lake City, UT 84111
E-mail: dbwhsale@deseretbook.com;
wholesale@deseretbook.com
Web site: http://www.deseretbook.com.

**Desert News,** 3242 S. Richey St., Tucson, AZ 85713 (SAN 114-3875) Tel 520-747-0428.

**Desert News Co.,** 42257 6th St W., Suite 304, Lancaster, CA 93534-7163 (SAN 249-2849) Toll Free: 800-266-4571.

**Devin-Adair Pubs., Inc.,** ( *0-8159* ) P.O. Box A, Old Greenwich, CT 06870 (SAN 112-062X) Tel 203-531-7755; Fax: 718-359-8568.

**DeVorss & Co.,** ( *0-87516* ) Orders Addr.: P.O. Box 1389, Camarillo, CA 93011-1389 (SAN 168-9886) Tel 805-322-9011; Fax: 805-322-9010; Toll Free: 800-843-5743; Edit Addr.: 553 Constitution Ave., Camarillo, CA 93012
E-mail: service@devorss.com
Web site: http://www.devorss.com.

**Diamond Book Distributors, Inc.,** 1966 Greenspring Dr., Suite 300, Timonium, MD 21093 (SAN 110-9502) Tel 410-560-7100; Fax: 410-560-7148; Toll Free: 800-452-6642
E-mail: service@diamondcomics.com;
books@diamondcomics.com
Web site: http://www.diamondcomics.com.

**Diamond Comic Distributors, Inc.,** ( *1-59396* ) Div. of Diamond Comic Distributors, Inc., 1966 Greenspring Dr., Suite 300, Timonium, MD 21093 Tel 410-560-7100; Fax: 410-560-2583; Toll Free: 800-452-6642
E-mail: wjanice@diamondcomics.com
Web site: http://www.diamondbookdistributors.com/.

**Diamond Distributors, Inc.,** 1966 Greenspring Dr., Suite 300, Timonium, MD 21093 Tel 410-560-7100.

**Digital Manga Distribution,** ( *0-945814; 1-56970* ) Div. of Digital Manga, Inc., 1123 Dominguez St., Unit K, Carson, CA 90746-3539 (SAN 111-817X) Tel 310-604-9701; Fax: 310-604-1134; Toll Free: 877-721-9701
E-mail: distribution@emanga.com
Web site: http://www.dmd-sales.com/.

**Dillon Bk.,** Subs. of Harold Dillon, Inc., 460 S. Marion Pkwy., Apt. 851B, Denver, CO 80209-2508 (SAN 169-0493) Tel 303-442-5323; Toll Free: 800-525-0842.

**Discount Bk. Distributors,** 1854 Wallace School Rd., No. E, Charleston, SC 29407-4822 (SAN 107-2250) Tel 843-556-6582.

**Distribooks, Inc.,** Div. of Midwest European Pubns., Inc., 8120 N. Ridgeway, Skokie, IL 60076 (SAN 630-9763) Tel 847-676-1596; Fax: 847-676-1195
E-mail: info@distribooks.com.

**Distribuidora Escolar, Inc.,** 2250 SW 99th Ave., Miami, FL 00165-7569 (SAN 169-1104).

**Distributed Art Pubs./D.A.P.,** ( *1-881616; 1-891024* ) Orders Addr.: a/o D.A.P. Book Distribution Ctr., 575 Prospect St., Lakewood, NJ 08701 Tel 732-363-5679; Toll Free: 800-338-2665; Edit Addr.: 155 Sixth Ave., 2nd Flr., New York, NY 10013-1507 (SAN 630-6446) Tel 212-627-1999; Fax: 212-627-9484
E-mail: dap@dapinc.com
Web site: http://www.artbook.com/.

**Distribution Solutions Group,** 1120 Rte. 22 E., Bridgewater, NJ 08807-0885 Toll Free: 866-374-4748.

**Distributors International,** Div. of Dennis-Landman Pubs., 1150 18th St., Santa Monica, CA 90403 (SAN 129-8089) Tel 310-828-0680
E-mail: info@moviecraft.com
Web site: http://www.moviecraft.com.

**Distributors, The,** ( *0-942520* ) 702 S. Michigan, South Bend, IN 46601 (SAN 169-2488) Tel 219-232-8500; Fax: 312-803-0887; Toll Free: 800-348-5200.

**Divine, Inc.,** ( *0-87305* ) 15 Southwest Park, Westwood, MA 02090-1725 (SAN 159-8619) Tel 781-329-3350; Fax: 781-329-9875; Toll Free: 800-766-0039
E-mail: helpdesk@faxon.com;
pubservices@faxon.com
Web site: http://www.faxon.com.

**Dixie News Co.,** P.O. Box 561129, Charlotte, NC 28256-1129 (SAN 169-636X) Tel 704-376-0140; Fax: 704-335-8604; Toll Free: 800-532-1045.

**D&J Bk. Distributors,** ( *1-883080* ) 229-21B Merrick Blvd., Laurelton, NY 11413 (SAN 630-5091) Tel 718-949-5400; Fax: 718-949-6161; Toll Free: 800-446-4707.

**Dog Museum, The,** *See* **American Kennel Club Museum of the Dog**

**Dogwise,** *See* **Dogwise Publishing**

**Dogwise Publishing,** ( *1-929242* ) P.O. Box 2778, Wentachee, WA 98807 (SAN 631-1415) Tel 509-663-9115; Fax: 509-662-7233; Toll Free: 800-776-2665
E-mail: mail@dogwise.com; charlenew@dogwise.com
Web site: http://www.dogwise.com.

**Doherty, Tom Assocs., LLC,** ( *0-312; 0-7653; 0-8125* ) Div. of Holtzbrinck Publishers, Orders Addr.: 16365 James Madison Hwy., Gordonsville, VA 22942-8501 Toll Free Fax: 800-672-2054; Toll Free: 888-330-8477 ; Edit Addr.: 175 Fifth Ave., New York, NY 10010 Tel 212-674-5151; Fax: 540-672-7540 (customer service).

**Donars Spanish Bks.,** P.O. Box 808, Lafayette, CO 80026 (SAN 108-1586) Tel 303-666-9175; Toll Free: 800-552-3316
E-mail: donars@prolynx.com.

**Doubleday,** *See* **Doubleday Publishing**

**Doubleday Publishing,** ( *0-385; 1-4000* ) Div. of Doubleday Broadway Publishing Group, Orders Addr.: 400 Hahn Rd., Westminster, MD 21157 (SAN 281-6083) Tel 410-848-1900; Toll Free: 800-726-0600 ; Edit Addr.: 1540 Broadway, New York, NY 10036-4094 (SAN 201-0089) Tel 212-782-9000; 212-572-4961 Bulk orders; Toll Free Fax: 800-659-2436 Orders only; Toll Free: 800-726-0600 Customer service; 800-669-1536 Electronic orders
Web site: http://www.doubleday.com

**Downtown Bk. Ctr., Inc.,** ( *0-941010* ) 247 SE First St., Suites 236-237, Miami, FL 33131 (SAN 169-1112) Tel 305-377-9941
E-mail: raxdown@aol.com.

**Dr. Leisure,** ( *0-9638802; 1-887471* ) P.O. Box 1137, Kihei, HI 96753 Tel 808-879-4160
E-mail: drleisure@drleisure.com
Web site: http://www.drleisure.com.

**Dreamhaven Bks.,** ( *0-9630944; 1-892058* ) 912 W. Lake St., Minneapolis, MN 55408 (SAN 630-0154) Tel 612-823-6161; Fax: 612-823-6062; Toll Free: 800-379-0657
E-mail: dreamhvn@visi.com
Web site: http://www.visi.com/~dreamhvn.

**Drown News Agency,** P.O. Box 2080, Folsom, CA 95763-2080 (SAN 169-0450).

**Dufour Editions,** ( *0-8023* ) P.O. Box 7, Chester Springs, PA 19425-0007 (SAN 201-341X) Tel 610-458-5005; Fax: 610-458-7103; Toll Free: 800-869-5677
E-mail: dufour8023@aol.com;
info@dufoureditions.com
Web site: http://go.to/Dufour; http://members.aol.com/Dufour8023/index.html.

**Durkin Hayes Publishing Ltd.,** ( *0-88625; 0-88646; 1-55204* ) 2221 Niagara Falls Blvd., Niagara Falls, NY 14304-1696 (SAN 630-9518) Tel 716-731-9177; Fax: 716-731-9180; Toll Free: 800-962-5200
E-mail: info@dhaudio.com
Web site: http://www.dhaudio.com.

**Duval News Co.,** Orders Addr.: P.O. Box 61297, Jacksonville, FL 32203 (SAN 169-1015); Edit Addr.: 5638 Commonwealth Ave., Jacksonville, FL 32205 (SAN 249-2865) Tel 904-783-2350.

**Duval-Bibb Publishing Co.,** ( *0-937713* ) Div. of Mareeco Enterprises, Inc., Orders Addr.: 1808 B St. NW, Suite 140, Auburn, WA 98001 Toll Free Fax: 800-548-1169; Toll Free: 800-518-3541; P.O. Box 24168, Tampa, FL 33623-4168 (SAN 111-8641) Tel 813-281-0091; Fax: 813-282-0220
E-mail: reese.cop@gte.net
Web site: http://lonepinepublishing.com/ordering.

**DUX Sales & Marketing,** Orders Addr.: 209 A St., Penrose, CO 81240 Tel 719-372-0402.

**Eagle Business Systems,** ( *0-928210* ) P.O. Box 1240, El Toro, CA 92630-1240 (SAN 285-7510) Tel 714-859-9622.

**Eagle Feather Trading Post, Inc.,** 168 W. 12th St., Ogden, UT 84404 (SAN 630-8996) Tel 801-393-3991 ; Fax: 801-745-0903; Toll Free: 800-547-3364 (orders only).

**Eaglecrafts,** Orders Addr.: 168 W. 12th St., Ogden, UT 84404 (SAN 630-6381) Tel 801-393-3991; Fax: 801-745-0903; Toll Free: 800-547-3364 (orders only)
E-mail: porsturbo@aol.com.

**Eakin Pr.,** ( *0-89015; 1-57168* ) P.O. Drawer 90159, Austin, TX 78709-0159 (SAN 207-3633) Tel 512-288-1771; Fax: 512-288-1813; Toll Free: 800-880-8642
E-mail: sales@eakinpress.com; tom@eakinpress.com
Web site: http://www.eakinpress.com.

**EAL Enterprises, Inc.,** Div. of Ambassador Bk. Service, 42 Chasner St., Hempstead, NY 11550 (SAN 169-6645) Toll Free: 800-431-8913.

**East Kentucky News, Inc.,** 416 Teays Rd., Paintsville, KY 41240 (SAN 169-2879) Tel 606-789-8169.

**East Texas Distributing,** 7171 Grand Blvd., Houston, TX 77054 (SAN 169-8265) Tel 713-748-2520; Fax: 713-748-2504.

**Eastern Bk. Co.,** Orders Addr.: P.O. Box 4540, Portland, ME 04112-4540 Fax: 207-774-0331; Toll Free Fax: 800-214-3895; Toll Free: 800-937-0331; Edit Addr.: 131 Middle St., Portland, ME 04112 (SAN 169-3050) Tel 207-774-0331
E-mail: info@ebc.com
Web site: http://www.ebc.com.

**Eastern News Distributors,** Subs. of Hearst Corp., 250 W. 55th St., New York, NY 10019 (SAN 169-5738) Tel 212-649-4484; Fax: 212-265-6239; Toll Free: 800-221-3148; 1 Media Way, 12406 Rte. 250, Milan, OH 44846-9705 (SAN 200-7711); 227 W. Trade St., Charlotte, NC 28202 (SAN 631-600X) Tel 704-348-8427
E-mail: enews@hearst.com.

**Eastern Subscription Agency,** 5413 Wynnefield Ave., Philadelphia, PA 19102 (SAN 285-9467) Tel 215-473-5309.

**Easton News Co.,** 2601 Dearborn St., Easton, PA 18042 (SAN 169-7315).

**Eastview Editions,** *( 0-89860 )* P.O. Box 247, Bernardsville, NJ 07924 (SAN 169-4952) Tel 908-204-0535.

**East-West Export Bks.,** c/o Univ. of Hawaii Pr., 2840 Kolowalu St., Honolulu, HI 96822 Tel 808-956-8830; Fax: 808-988-6052
E-mail: royden@hawaii.edu
Web site: http://www.2.hawaii.edu/uhpress/eweb.

**Eastwind Bks. & Arts, Inc.,** 1435-A Stockton St., San Francisco, CA 94133 (SAN 127-3159) Tel 415-772-5888; Fax: 415-772-5885
E-mail: info@eastwindsf.com
Web site: http://www.eastwindsf.com.

**Eau Claire News Co., Inc.,** 8100 Partridge Rd., Eau Claire, WI 54703-9646 (SAN 169-9059) Tel 715-835-5437.

**ebrary, Inc.,** 360 N. Bernardo Ave., Mountainview, CA 94043 Tel 650-230-0700; Fax: 650-230-0881
Web site: http://www.ebrary.com.

**ebrary.com,** *See* **ebrary, Inc.**

**EBS, Inc. Bk. Service,** 290 Broadway, Lynbrook, NY 11563 (SAN 169-5487) Tel 516-593-1195; Fax: 516-596-2911.

**EBSCO Subscription Services,** 5724 Hwy. 280 E., Birmingham, AL 35242-6818 (SAN 285-9394) Tel 205-991-6000; Fax: 205-991-1479
E-mail: jacomo@ebsco.com

**Econo-Clad Bks.,** *( 0-613; 0-7857; 0-8085; 0-8335; 0-88103 )* Div. of American Cos., Inc., Orders Addr.: P.O. Box 1777, Topeka, KS 66601 (SAN 169-2763) Tel 913-233-4252; Toll Free: 800-255-3502; Edit Addr.: 2101 N. Topeka Blvd., Topeka, KS 66608-1830 (SAN 249-2687)
E-mail: hkopperud@sagebrushcorp.com
Web site: http://www.sagebrushcorp.com.

**Economical Wholesale Co.,** 6 King Philip Rd., Worcester, MA 01606 (SAN 169-3646).

**Ediciones del Norte,** *( 0-910061 )* P.O. Box 5130, Hanover, NH 03755 (SAN 241-2993).

**Ediciones Universal,** *( 0-89729; 1-59388 )* Orders Addr.: P.O. Box 450353, Miami, FL 33245-0353 (SAN 658-0548); Edit Addr.: 3090 SW Eighth St., Miami, FL 33135 (SAN 207-2203) Tel 305-642-3355; Fax: 305-642-7978
E-mail: marta@ediciones.com
Web site: http://www.ediciones.com.

**Editorial Cernuda, Inc.,** 1040 27th Ave., SW, Miami, FL 33135 (SAN 158-8850) Tel 305-264-9400.

**Education Guide, Inc.,** *( 0-914880 )* P.O. Box 421, Randolph, MA 02368 (SAN 201-4580) Tel 617-376-0066; Fax: 617-376-0067.

**Educational Bk. Distributors,** P.O. Box 2510, Novato, CA 94948 (SAN 158-2259) Tel 415-883-3530; Fax: 415-883-4280; Toll Free: 800-761-5501
E-mail: PblshrSvcs@aol.com.

**Educational Record Ctr., Inc.,** 3233 Burnt Mill Dr., Suite 100, Wilmington, NC 28403-2698 (SAN 630-592X) Tel 910-251-1235; Fax: 910-343-0311; Toll Free Fax: 888-438-1637; Toll Free: 800-438-1637
E-mail: info@erc-inc.com
Web site: http://www.erc-inc.com.

**Edu-Tech Corp., The,** 65 Bailey Rd., Fairfield, CT 06432 (SAN 157-5392) Tel 203-374-4212; Fax: 203-374-8050; Toll Free: 800-338-5463
E-mail: edutcorp@aol.com.

**Edward Weston Graphic, Incorporated,** *See* **Weston, Edward Fine Arts**

**El Qui-Jote Bk., Inc.,** 12651 Monarch, Houston, TX 77047 (SAN 107-8666) Tel 713-433-3388.

**Elder's Bk. Store,** 2115 Elliston Pl., Nashville, TN 37203 (SAN 112-6091) Tel 615-327-1867.

**Ellis News Co.,** Affil. of L-S Distributors, 130 E. Grand Ave., South San Francisco, CA 94080 (SAN 169-0183) Tel 415-873-2094; Fax: 415-873-4222; Toll Free: 800-654-7040 (orders only).

**ELS Educational Services,** *( 0-87789; 0-89285; 0-89318 )* Orders Addr.: 200 Old Tappan Rd., Old Tappan, NJ 07675; Edit Addr.: 1357 Second St., Santa Monica, CA 90401-1102 (SAN 281-6326).

**Elsevier,** *( 0-08; 0-444; 0-7204; 0-916086; 1-85617; 1-59278 )* Orders Addr.: P.O. Box 945, New York, NY 10159-0945 (SAN 251-2564) Toll Free: 888-437-4636 ; 11830 Westline Industrial Dr., Saint Louis, MO 63146 (SAN 200-2108) Tel 314-453-7095 (Outside US); Toll Free Fax: 800-535-9935; Toll Free:

800-545-2522; 800-460-3110 (Outside US); Edit Addr.: 655 Ave. of the Americas, New York, NY 10010-5107 (SAN 200-2051) Tel 212-989-5800; Fax: 212-633-3680
E-mail: usinfo-f@elsevier.com; custserv@elsevier.com
Web site: http://www.elsevier.com.

**Elsevier Science,** *See* **Elsevier**

**Emery-Pratt Co.,** Orders Addr.: 1966 W. Main St., Owosso, MI 48867-1397 (SAN 170-1401) Tel 989-723-5291; Fax: 989-723-4677; Toll Free Fax: 800-523-6379; Toll Free: 800-762-5683 (library orders only); 800-248-3887 (customer service only) Distributor to Libraries & Hospitals
E-mail: custserv@emery-pratt.com
Web site: http://www.emery-pratt.com.

**Empire Comics,** 375 Stone Rd., Rochester, NY 14616 (SAN 110-943X) Tel 716-442-0371; Fax: 716-442-7807
E-mail: empires@frontiernet.net.

**Empire News of Jamestown,** Foot Ave. & Extension St., Box 2029, Sta. A, Jamestown, NY 14702 (SAN 169-5371).

**Empire Publishing Service,** *( 1-58690 )* P.O. Box 1344, Studio City, CA 91614-0344 (SAN 630-5687) Tel 818-784-8918
E-mail: empirepubsvc@att.net.

**Empire State News Corp.,** Orders Addr.: P.O. Box 1167, Buffalo, NY 14240-1167 Tel 716-681-1100; Fax: 716-681-1120; Toll Free: 800-414-6247; Edit Addr.: 2800 Walden Ave., Cheektowaga, NY 14225-4772 (SAN 169-5177)
Web site: http://www.esnc.com.

**Enfield Publishing & Distribution Co., Inc.,** *( 0-9656184; 1-893598 )* Orders Addr.: P.O. Box 699, Enfield, NH 03748 Tel 603-632-7377; Fax: 603-632-5611; Edit Addr.: 234 May St., Enfield, NH 03748
E-mail: enfield@connriver.net
Web site: http://www.enfielddistribution.com.

**Entrepreneur Start a Business Store,** 9114 River Look Ln., Fair Oaks, CA 95628-6565 (SAN 133-1485) Fax: 916-863-0361.

**Epic Book Promotions,** 914 Nolan Way, Chula Vista, CA 91911-2408 Tel 619-498-8547; Fax: 619-498-8540
E-mail: gvjack@pacbell.net.

**Epson Mid-Atlantic,** Subs. of Epson America, Inc., 8 Neshaminy Interplex, Suite 319, Trerose, PA 19053 (SAN 285-7243) Tel 215-245-2180.

**Eriksson Enterprises,** 126 Sunset Dr., Farmington, UT 84025-3426 (SAN 110-5892).

**ETD KroMar Temple,** P.O. Box 535695, Grand Prairie, TX 75053-5625 (SAN 169-8435) Tel 254-778-5261; Fax: 254-778-5267.

**European Bk. Co., Inc.,** 925 Larkin St., San Francisco, CA 94109 (SAN 169-0191) Tel 415-474-0626; Fax: 415-474-0630; Toll Free: 877-746-3666
E-mail: info@europeanbook.com.

**European Press Service - PBD America Wholesalers,** 30 Edison Dr., Wayne, NJ 07470-4713 (SAN 630-7825).

**Evans Bk. Distribution & Pubs., Inc.,** *( 0-9654884; 1-56684 )* 895 W. 1700 S., Salt Lake City, UT 84104 Tel 801-975-1315; Fax: 801-975-1343; Toll Free: 877-655-2665.

**Evans Book,** *See* **Evans Bk. Distribution & Pubs., Inc.**

**Excaliber Publishing Co.,** *( 1-881353 )* 7954 W. Bury Ave., San Diego, CA 92126 (SAN 297-6412) Tel 619-695-3091; Fax: 619-695-3095.

**Exciting Times,** 17430C Crenshaw Blvd., Torrance, CA 90504 (SAN 114-4642) Tel 310-515-2676; Fax: 310-515-1382.

**Executive Bks.,** *( 0-937539 )* Div. of Life Management Services, Inc., 206 W. Allen St., Mechanicsburg, PA 17055-6240 (SAN 156-5419) Tel 717-766-9499; Fax: 717-766-6565; Toll Free: 800-233-2665
E-mail: jason@executivebooks.com
Web site: http://www.executivebooks.com.

**Faber & Faber, Inc.,** *( 0-571 )* Affil. of Farrar, Straus & Giroux, LLC, Orders Addr.: c/o Van Holtzbrinck Publishing Services, 16365 James Madison Hwy., Gordonsville, VA 22942 Fax: 540-572-7540; Toll Free: 888-330-8477; Edit Addr.: 19 Union Sq., W, New York, NY 10003-3304 (SAN 218-7256) Tel 212-741-6900; Fax: 212-633-9385.

**Fairfield Bk. Service Co.,** 150 Margherita Lawn, Stratford, CT 06615 (SAN 131-0976) Tel 203-375-7607.

**FaithWorks,** Div. of National Book Network, Orders Addr.: 15200 NBN Way, Blue Ridge Summit, PA 17214 Toll Free: 877-323-4550; Edit Addr.: 9247 Hunterboro Dr., Brentwood, TN 37027 Tel 615-221-6442 (phone/fax) Do not confuse with Faithworks in Bronx NY
E-mail: custserv@faithworksonline.com
Web site: http://www.faithworksonline.com.

**FaithWorks/NBN,** *See* **FaithWorks**

**Falk Bks. Inc., W.E.,** 7491 N. Federal Hwy., PMB 267, Boca Raton, FL 33487.

**Falk, W. E.,** *See* **Falk Bks. Inc., W.E.**

**Fall River News Co., Inc.,** 144 Robeson St., Fall River, MA 02720-4925 (SAN 169-3425) Tel 508-679-5266.

**Family History World,** P.O. Box 129, Tremonton, UT 84337 (SAN 159-673X) Fax: 801-250-6727; Toll Free: 800-377-6058
E-mail: genealogy@utahlinx.com
Web site: http://www.genealogical-institute.com.

**Family Reading Service,** 1601 N. Slappey Blvd., Albany, GA 31701-1431 (SAN 169-1376).

**Far West Bk. Service,** 3515 NE Hassalo, Portland, OR 97232 (SAN 107-6760) Tel 503-234-7664; Fax: 503-231-0573; Toll Free: 800-964-9378.

**Farrar, Straus & Giroux,** *( 0-374 )* Div. of Holtzbrinck Publishers, Orders Addr.: c/o Holtzbrinck Publishers, 16365 James Madison Hwy., Gordonsville, VA 22942 Toll Free Fax: 800-672-2054; Toll Free: 888-330-8477 ; Edit Addr.: 19 Union Sq., W., New York, NY 10003 (SAN 206-782X) Tel 212-741-6900; Fax: 212-463-0641
E-mail: sales@fsgee.com; fsg.editorial@fsgee.com
Web site: http://www.fsbassociates.com/fsg/index.htm.

**Faxon Company, The,** *See* **Divine, Inc.**

**Faxon Illinois Service Ctr.,** Affil. of Dawson Holdings PLC, 1001 W. Pines Rd., Oregon, IL 61061-9570 (SAN 286-0147) Tel 815-732-9001; Toll Free: 800-852-7404
E-mail: postmaster@dawson.com; sandy.nordman@dawson.com
Web site: http://www.faxon.com.

**Fayette County News Agency,** Orders Addr.: P.O. Box 993, Uniontown, PA 15401 Tel 724-437-1181; Edit Addr.: Cherry Tree Square 42 Matthew Dr., Uniontown, PA 15401 (SAN 169-765X).

**FEC News Distributing,** 2201 Fourth Ave., N., Lake Worth, FL 33461-3835 (SAN 169-1341) Tel 407-547-3000; Fax: 407-547-3080.

**Feedback Services,** P.O. Box 220, Brooklin, ME 04616 (SAN 631-6816) Tel 207-359-2781; Fax: 207-359-5532; Toll Free: 800-800-8671
E-mail: feedback@hypernet.com.

**Feldheim, Philipp Inc.,** *( 0-87306; 1-58330 )* 202 Airport Executive Pk., Nanuet, NY 10954 (SAN 106-6307) Tel 845-356-2282; Fax: 845-425-1908; Toll Free: 800-237-7149
E-mail: mike613@netvision.net.il
Web site: http://www.feldheim.com.

**Fell, Frederick Pubs., Inc.,** *( 0-8119; 0-88391 )* 2131 Hollywood Blvd., Suite 305, Hollywood, FL 33020-6750 Tel 954-925-0555; Fax: 954-925-5244
E-mail: info@fellpub.com
Web site: http://www.fellpub.com.

**Fennell, Reginald F. Subscription Service,** 1002 W. Michigan Ave., Jackson, MI 49202 (SAN 159-6071) Tel 517-782-3132; Fax: 517-782-1109.

**FEP, A Booksource Co.,** 1230 Macklind Ave., Saint Louis, MO 63110 (SAN 169-1317) Tel 314-647-0600 ; Fax: 314-647-6850; Toll Free: 800-444-0435
Web site: http://www.booksource.com.

**Fiddlecase Bks.,** HC 63 Box 104, East Alstead, NH 03602 (SAN 200-7495) Tel 603-835-7889.

**Fiesta Bk. Co.,** *( 0-88473 )* P.O. Box 490641, Key Biscayne, FL 33149 (SAN 201-8470) Tel 305-858-4843.

**Fiesta Publishing Corporation,** *See* **Fiesta Bk. Co.**

**Fine Assocs.,** One Farragut Sq., S., Washington, DC 20006 (SAN 169-0914) Tel 202-628-2609.

**Finn News Agency, Inc.,** 4415 State Rd. 327, Auburn, IN 46706-9542 (SAN 169-2356).

**Fire Protection Publications,** *See* **IFSTA**

**Firebird Distributing, LLC,** 1945 P St., Eureka, CA 95501-3007 (SAN 631-1229) Toll Free: 800-353-3575
E-mail: griffins@northcoast.com.;
sales@firebirddistributing.com
Web site: http://www.firebirddistributing.com.

**Firefly Bks., Ltd.,** *( 0-920668; 1-55209; 1-895565; 1-896284; 1-55297 )* 4 Daybreak Ln., Westport, CT 06880-2157
E-mail: service@fireflybooks.com
Web site: http://www.fireflybooks.com/.

**Fischer, Carl LLC,** ( *0-8258* ) Orders Addr.: 2480 Industrial Blvd., Paoli, PA 19301 Fax: 610-644-7110; Toll Free: 800-762-2328; Edit Addr.: 65 Bleeker St., New York, NY 10012-2420 (SAN 107-4245) Tel 212-772-0900; Fax: 212-477-6996; Toll Free: 800-762-2328 E-mail: cf-info@carlfischer.com. Web site: http://www.carlfischer.com.

**Fish, Enrica Medical Bks.,** 814 Washington Ave., SE, Minneapolis, MN 55414 (SAN 157-8588) Tel 612-623-0707; Fax: 612-623-0539; Toll Free: 800-728-8398.

**Flannery Co.,** 13123 Aerospace Dr., Victorville, CA 92394 (SAN 168-9754) Tel 760-246-8995; Fax: 760-246-8595; Toll Free: 800-456-3400.

**Flannery, J. F. Company,** *See* **Flannery Co.**

**Fleming, Robert Hull Museum,** ( *0-934658* ) Univ. of Vermont, 61 Colchester Ave., Burlington, VT 05405 (SAN 110-8824) Tel 802-656-2273; Fax: 802-656-8059 Web site: http://www.uvm.edu/~fleming/store/index.html.

**Flora & Fauna Bks.,** P.O. Box 15718, Gainesville, FL 32604 (SAN 133-1221) Tel 352-373-5630; Fax: 352-373-3249 E-mail: ffbks@aol.com Web site: http://www.ffbooks.com.

**Florida Classics Library,** ( *0-912451* ) P.O. Drawer 1657, Port Salerno, FL 34992-1657 (SAN 265-2404) Tel 561-546-9380 (orders); Fax: 561-546-7545 (orders).

**Florida Schl. Bk. Depository,** 1125 N. Ellis Rd., P.O. Box 6578, Jacksonville, FL 32236 (SAN 161-8423) Tel 904-781-7191; Fax: 904-781-3486; Toll Free: 800-447-7957.

**Flury & Co.,** 322 First Ave S., Seattle, WA 98104 (SAN 107-5748) Tel 206-587-0260.

**FM International,** 913 Stewart St., Madison, WI 53713 Tel 608-271-7922.

**Focus Publishing/R. Pullins Co., Inc.,** ( *0-941051; 1-58510* ) 311 Merrimac St., Newburyport, MA 01950 (SAN 665-2654) Tel 978-462-1378 (orders); 978-462-7288; Fax: 978-462-9035; Toll Free: 800-848-7236 (orders) E-mail: pullins@pullins.com. Web site: http://www.pullins.com.

**Fodor's Travel Guides,** *See* **Fodor's Travel Pubns.**

**Fodor's Travel Pubns.,** ( *0-609; 0-676; 0-679; 0-7615; 1-878867; 1-4000* ) Div. of Random Hse., Information Group, Orders Addr.: 400 Hahn Rd., Westminster, MD 21157 Tel 410-848-1900; Toll Free: 800-726-0600; Edit Addr.: 280 Park Ave., Tenth Flr., New York, NY 10017 Tel 212-572-8784; Fax: 212-572-2248 Web site: http://www.fodors.com.

**Follett Audiovisual Resources,** *See* **Follett Media Distribution**

**Follett Educational Services,** Orders Addr.: 1433 Internationale Pkwy., Woodridge, IL 60517 (SAN 631-7901) Tel 800-621-4272; Fax: 630-972-4673; Edit Addr.: 5563 S. Archer Ave., Chicago, IL 60638 (SAN 169-1899) E-mail: mpetrou@fes.follett.com.

**Follett Library Resources,** ( *0-329* ) Div. of the Follett Corp., 1340 Ridgeview Dr., McHenry, IL 60050 (SAN 169-1902) Tel 815-759-1700; Toll Free: 800-435-6170.

**Follett Media Distribution,** 220 Exchange Dr., Suite A, Crystal Lake, IL 60014 (SAN 631-7316) Tel 815-455-1555; Fax: 815-455-7090; Toll Free: 888-281-1216.

**Fordham Univ. Pr.,** ( *0-8232* ) University Box L, Bronx, NY 10458 (SAN 201-6516) Tel 718-817-4780; Fax: 718-817-4785 E-mail: mnoonan@fordham.edu Web site: http://www.fordhampress.com.

**Forest Sales & Distributing Co.,** ( *0-9712183* ) 4157 Saint Louis St., New Orleans, LA 70119 (SAN 157-5511) Tel 504-486-3331; Fax: 504-486-6223; Toll Free: 800-347-2106 E-mail: tbooks2@juno.com.

**Forsa Editores,** ( *1-881714* ) Orders Addr.: P.O. Box 9020314, San Juan, PR 00902-0314 Tel 787-721-1792 ; Fax: 707-707-1797; Toll Free: 888-225-8984; Edit Addr.: No. 1594 J.T. Pinero Ave., Caparra Heights, PR 00920 E-mail: forsa@forsaeditores.com Web site: http://www.forsaeditores.com.

**Forsyth Travel Library, Inc.,** ( *0-9614539* ) 1750 E. 131st St., P.O. Box 480800, Kansas City, MO 64148-0800 (SAN 169-2755) Tel 816-942-9050; Fax: 816-942-6969; Toll Free: 800-367-7984 (orders only) E-mail: forsyth@gvi.net Web site: http://www.forsyth.com.

**Franklin Bk. Co., Inc.,** 7804 Montgomery Ave., Elkins Park, PA 19027 (SAN 121-4160) Tel 215-635-5252; Fax: 215-635-6155 E-mail: service@franklinbook.com Web site: http://www.franklinbook.com.

**Franklin Readers Service,** P.O. Box 662, Dunn Loring, VA 22027-0662 (SAN 285-9599).

**Franklin Square Overseas,** 17-19 Washington St., Tenafly, NJ 07670-2084 (SAN 285-9637) Tel 201-569-2500; Fax: 201-569-5141 E-mail: esstn@ebsco.com.

**Fraser Publishing Co.,** ( *0-87034; 0-918632* ) Div. of Alvin Q. Garbanzo, Inc., Orders Addr.: P.O. Box 217, Flint Hill, VT 22747 (SAN 213-9537) Toll Free: 877-996-3336 E-mail: info@fraserbooks.com Web site: http://www.fraserbooks.com.

**Freihofer, A. G.,** 175 Fifth Ave., New York, NY 10010 (SAN 285-9602) Tel 272-460-7500; Fax: 272-473-6272.

**French & European Pubns., Inc.,** ( *0-320; 0-7859; 0-8288* ) Rockefeller Ctr. Promenade, 610 Fifth Ave., New York, NY 10020-2497 (SAN 206-8109) Tel 212-581-8810; Fax: 212-265-1094 E-mail: frenchbookstore@aol.com Web site: http://www.frencheuropean.com.

**Fris News Co.,** 194 River Ave., Holland, MI 49423 (SAN 159-8643).

**Frontline Communications,** *See* **YWAM Publishing**

**Fulcrum, Incorporated,** *See* **Fulcrum Publishing**

**Fulcrum Publishing,** ( *0-912347; 1-55591; 1-56373* ) 16100 Table Mountain Pkwy., Suite 300, Golden, CO 80403 (SAN 200-2825) Tel 303-277-1623; Fax: 303-279-7111; Toll Free Fax: 800-726-7112; Toll Free: 800-992-2908 E-mail: dianneh@fulcrum-books.com Web site: http://www.fulcrum-books.com; http://www.fulcrum-gardening.com.

**Fulfillment Services, Inc.,** Orders Addr.: 1955 W. Grant Rd., No. 230, Tucson, AZ 85745 Tel 520-798-1530.

**Fulmont News Co.,** Affil. of Rubin Periodical Group, P.O. Box 1211, Rochester, NY 14603-1211 (SAN 169-5029) Tel 518-843-2421.

**Fultz News Agency,** 2008 Woodbrook, Denton, TX 76205 (SAN 169-8168).

**Futech Educational Products, Inc.,** ( *0-9627001; 1-889192* ) 2999 N. 44th St., Suite 225, Phoenix, AZ 85018-7248 Tel 602-808-8765; Fax: 602-278-5667; Toll Free: 800-597-6278.

**F&W Pubns., Inc.,** ( *0-89134; 0-89879; 0-932620; 1-55870; 1-58180; 1-58297; 1-884910* ) Orders Addr.: 4700 E. Galbraith Rd., Cincinnati, OH 45236 Tel 513-531-2690; Fax: 513-531-4082; Toll Free Fax: 888-590-4082; Toll Free: 800-289-0963; c/o AERO Fulfillment Services, 2800 Henkle Dr., Lebanon, OH 45036 E-mail: marcia.jones@fwpubs.com Web site: http://www.fwpublications.com; http://www.artistsmagazine.com; http://www.artistsnetwork.com; http://www.davidandcharles.co.uk; http://www.krause.com; http://www.familytreemagazine.com; http://www.howdesign.com; http://www.idonline.com; http://www.memorymakersmagazine.com; http://www.popularwoodworking.com; http://www.writersdigest.com; http://www.writersmarket.com; http://www.writersonlineworkshops.com.

**G A M Printers & Grace Christian Bookstore,** *See* **GAM Pubn.**

**Galda Library Services, Inc.,** 33 Richdale Ave., Cambridge, MA 02140 (SAN 630-5806) Tel 617-864-8232.

**Galesburg News Agency, Inc.,** Five E. Simmons St., Galesburg, IL 61401 (SAN 169-1945).

**Galveston News Agency, Inc.,** P.O. Box 7608, San Antonio, TX 78207-0608 (SAN 169-8230).

**GAM Pubn.,** P.O. Box 25, Sterling, VA 20167 (SAN 158-7218) Tel 703-450-4121; Fax: 703-450-5311.

**Gamboge International, Inc.,** 18 Brittany Ave., Trumbull, CT 06611 (SAN 631-046X) Tel 203-261-2130; Fax: 203-452-0180 E-mail: gamboge@pcaet.com.

**Gannon Distributing Co.,** ( *0-88307* ) 100 La Salle Cir., No. A, Santa Fe, NM 87505-6916 (SAN 201-5889).

**Gardner's Bk. Service,** 16461 N. 25th Ave., Phoenix, AZ 85023-3111 (SAN 106-9322) Tel 602-863-6000; Fax: 602-863-2400 (orders only); Toll Free: 800-851-6001 (orders only) E-mail: gbsbooks@bgsbooks.com Web site: http://www.gbsbooks.com.

**Garrett Educational Corp.,** ( *0-944483; 1-56074* ) Orders Addr.: P.O. Box 1588, Ada, OK 74820 (SAN 169-6955) Tel 580-332-6884; Fax: 580-332-1560; Toll Free: 800-654-9366; Edit Addr.: 130 E. 13th St., Ada, OK 74820 (SAN 243-2722) E-mail: mail@garrettbooks.com. Web site: http://www.garrettbooks.com.

**Gasman News Agency,** 2211 Third Ave., S., Escanaba, MI 49829 (SAN 169-3794).

**Gaunt, Inc.,** ( *0-912004; 1-56169* ) 3011 Gulf Dr., Holmes Beach, FL 34217-2199 (SAN 202-9413) Tel 941-778-5211; Fax: 941-778-5252; Toll Free: 800-942-8683 (US & Canada) E-mail: info@gaunt.com; sales@gaunt.com Web site: http://www.gaunt.com.

**Gaunt, William W. & Sons, Incorporated,** *See* **Gaunt, Inc.**

**Gefen Bks.,** ( *0-86343; 965-229* ) 12 New St., Hewlett, NY 11557-2012 Tel 516-295-2805; Fax: 516-295-2739; Toll Free: 800-477-5257 E-mail: gefenny@gefenpublishing.com Web site: http://www.israelbooks.com.

**Gem Guides Bk. Co.,** ( *0-935182; 0-937799; 1-889786* ) 315 Cloverleaf Dr., Suite F, Baldwin Park, CA 91706 (SAN 221-1637) Tel 626-855-1611; Fax: 626-855-1610 E-mail: gembooks@aol.com Web site: http://www.gemguidesbooks.com.

**Gemini Enterprises,** P.O. Box 8251, Stockton, CA 95208 (SAN 128-1402).

**Genealogical Sources, Unlimited,** ( *0-913857* ) 407 Ascot Ct., Knoxville, TN 37923-5807 (SAN 170-8058) Tel 865-690-7831.

**Genealogy Digest,** 960 N. 400 E., North Salt Lake, UT 84054-1920 (SAN 110-389X); 420 S. 425 W., Bountiful, UT 84010 (SAN 243-2439).

**General Medical Pubs.,** ( *0-935236* ) P.O. Box 210, Venice, CA 90294-0210 (SAN 215-689X) Tel 310-392-4911.

**Generic Computer Products, Inc.,** ( *0-918611* ) P.O. Box 790, Marquette, MI 49855 (SAN 284-8856) Tel 906-226-7600; Fax: 906-226-8309.

**Geographia Map Co., Inc.,** ( *0-88433* ) 231 Hackensack Plank Rd., Weehawken, NJ 07087 (SAN 132-5566) Tel 201-863-3866; Fax: 201-863-5977.

**Gerold International Booksellers, Inc.,** 35-23 Utopia Pkwy., Flushing, NY 11358 (SAN 129-959X) Tel 718-358-4741; Fax: 718-358-3688.

**Gibson, Dot Pubns.,** ( *0-941162* ) Orders Addr.: P.O. Box 117, Waycross, GA 31502-0117 (SAN 200-4143) Tel 912-285-2848; Fax: 912-285-0349; Toll Free: 800-336-8095; Edit Addr.: 383 Bonneyman Rd., Blackshear, GA 31516 (SAN 200-9676) E-mail: info@dotgibson.com Web site: http://www.dotgibson.com.

**Gilmore-Howard,** P.O. Box 1268, Arlington, TX 76004-1268 (SAN 157-485X).

**Giron Bks.,** ( *0-9741393* ) 2130 W. 21st. St., Chicago, IL 60608-2608 Tel 773-847-3000; Fax: 773-847-9197; Toll Free: 800-405-4276 E-mail: isbn_san@gironbooks.com Web site: http://www.gironbooks.com.

**G-Jo Institute/Deer Haven Hills, Inc.,** ( *0-916878* ) Orders Addr.: P.O. Box 548, Columbus, NC 28722-0548 Tel 828-863-4660; Edit Addr.: P.O. Box 1460, Columbus, NC 28722-1460 (SAN 111-0004) E-mail: office@g-jo.com Web site: http://www.g-jo.com.

**G-Jo Institute/Falkyn, Incorporated,** *See* **G-Jo Institute/Deer Haven Hills, Inc.**

**GL Services,** 4588 Interstate Dr., Cincinnati, OH 45246 Tel 805-677-6815.

**Global Engineering Documents-Latin America,** 3909 NE 163rd St., Suite 110, North Miami Beach, FL 33160 (SAN 630-7868) Tel 305-944-1099; Fax: 305-944-1028 E-mail: global.csa@ihs.com.

**Global Info Centres,** *See* **Global Engineering Documents-Latin America**

**Globe Pequot Pr., The,** ( *0-7627; 0-87106; 0-88742; 0-914788; 0-933469; 0-934802; 0-941130; 1-56440; 1-57034; 1-58574; 1-59228* ) Div. of Morris Communications Corp., Orders Addr.: P.O. Box 480, Guilford, CT 06437-0480 (SAN 201-9892) Toll Free Fax: 800-820-2329 (in Connecticut); Toll Free: 800-243-0495 (24 hours); Edit Addr.: 246 Goose Ln., Guilford, CT 06437 Tel 203-458-4500; Fax: 203-458-4604 E-mail: info@globe-pequot.com; adessaint@globe-pequot.com Web site: http://www.globe-pequot.com.

Wholesalers & Distributors

**Goldberg, Louis Library Bk. Supplier,** 45 Belvidere St., Nazareth, PA 18064 (SAN 169-7536) Tel 610-759-9458; Fax: 610-759-8134.

**Goldenrod Music, Inc.,** 1310 Turner Rd., Lansing, MI 48906-4342 (SAN 630-5962) Tel 517-484-1777 E-mail: music@goldenrod.com Web site: http://www.goldenrod.com.

**Goldenrod/Horizon Distribution,** *See* **Goldenrod Music, Inc.**

**Goldman, S. Otzar Hasefarim, Inc.,** 125 Ditmas Ave., Brooklyn, NY 11218 (SAN 169-5770) Tel 718-972-6200; Fax: 718-972-6204; Toll Free: 800-972-6201.

**Good News Magazine Distributors,** 85 Crescent Ave., New Rochelle, NY 10801 (SAN 113-7271) Toll Free: 800-624-7257.

**Gopher News Co.,** 420 First Ave., NW, Rochester, MN 55901 (SAN 169-4138) Tel 507-282-8641 (phone/fax).

**Gopher News Company,** *See* **St. Marie's Gopher News Co.**

**Gospel Mission, Inc.,** Orders Addr.: P.O. Box 318, Choteau, MT 59422 (SAN 170-3196) Tel 406-466-2311; Edit Addr.: 316 First St., NW, Choteau, MT 59422 (SAN 234-2455).

**Goyescas Corp. of Florida,** 2155 NW 26th Ave., Miami, FL 33142 (SAN 169-1120).

**Graham Services, Inc.,** 180 James Dr., E., Saint Rose, LA 70087-9481 (SAN 169-2895) Tel 504-467-5863; Fax: 504-464-6196; Toll Free: 800-457-7323 (in Los Angeles only) E-mail: gsi@aol.com.

**Great Lakes Reader's Service, Inc.,** Orders Addr.: P.O. Box 1078, Detroit, MI 48231 (SAN 285-9912) Tel 313-965-4577; Fax: 313-965-2445.

**Great Northern Distributors, Inc.,** 634 South Ave., Rochester, NY 14620-1316 (SAN 169-7676) Tel 717-342-8159.

**Greathall Productions, Inc.,** ( *1-882513* ) Orders Addr.: P.O. Box 5061, Charlottesville, VA 22905-5061 Tel 434-296-4288; Fax: 434-296-4490; Toll Free: 800-477-6234 E-mail: greathall@greathall.com Web site: http://www.greathall.com.

**Green Gate Bks.,** 6700 W. Chicago St., Chandler, AZ 85226 (SAN 169-6785) Tel 480-961-5176; Fax: 480-961-5256; Toll Free: 800-228-3816 E-mail: ggb@wcoil.com Web site: http://www.greengatebooks.com.

**Green Leaves Pr.,** 214 Camden Rd., NE, Atlanta, GA 30309 Tel 404-351-3344; Fax: 404-351-2371.

**Grey Owl Indian Craft Co., Inc.,** 132-05 Merrick Blvd., P.O. Box 468, Jamaica, NY 11434 (SAN 132-9979) Tel 718-341-4000.

**Griffin Skye Co.,** 1945 P St., Eureka, CA 95501 Tel 707-444-8768; Fax: 707-444-6600 E-mail: griffins@northcoast.com.

**GRM Group,** 443 Fifth Ave., Pelham, NY 10803 Tel 914-738-6066; Fax: 914-738-6073 E-mail: richards@grmgroup.com.

**Grolier Americana,** 1111 Crandon Blvd., Apt. C501, Key Biscayne, FL 33149-2734 (SAN 108-1764) Tel 305-551-6711.

**Grove/Atlantic, Inc.,** ( *0-8021; 0-87113; 1-55584* ) 841 Broadway, 4th Flr., New York, NY 10003-4793 (SAN 201-4890) Tel 212-614-7850; Fax: 212-614-7886; Toll Free: 800-521-0178.

**Gryphon Hse., Inc.,** ( *0-87659; 1-58904* ) Orders Addr.: P.O. Box 207, Beltsville, MD 20704-0207 (SAN 169-3190) Tel 301-595-9500; Fax: 301-595-0051; Toll Free: 800-638-0928; Edit Addr.: 10726 Tucker St., Beltsville, MD 20705 E-mail: info@ghbooks.com Web site: http://www.gryphonhouse.com.

**Guardian Bk. Co.,** P.O. Box 202, Ottawa Lake, MI 49267-0202 (SAN 163-7355).

**Gulf States Book Fairs,** *See* **Gulf States Educational Bks.**

**Gulf States Educational Bks.,** Orders Addr.: 368 Laurel Dr., Satsuma, AL 36572 (SAN 158-7870) Toll Free: 800-533-1189.

**Gumdrop Bks.,** Div. of Central Programs, Inc., Orders Addr.: P.O. Box 505, Bethany, MO 64424 (SAN 631-4988) Tel 660-425-3923; Fax: 660-425-3970; Toll Free: 800-821-7199; Edit Addr.: 100 N. 16th St., Bethany, MO 64424 (SAN 131-0860) E-mail: wecare@gumdropbooks.com Web site: http://www.gumdropbooks.com.

**H & M Distribution,** 41 Monroe Tpke., Trumbull, CT 06611 Tel 800-698-7781; Fax: 203-459-5095.

**Hagerstown News Distributors,** *See* **Mid-States Distributors**

**Hale, Robert & Co., Inc.,** 1803 132nd Ave., NE, Suite 4, Bellevue, WA 98005 (SAN 200-6995) Tel 425-881-5212; Fax: 425-881-0731; Toll Free: 800-733-5330.

**Ham Radio's Bookstore,** *See* **Radio Bookstore**

**Hamakor Judaica, Inc.,** 7777 Merrimac Ave., Niles, IL 60714 (SAN 169-1791) Tel 847-966-4040; Fax: 847-966-4033; Toll Free: 800-552-4088.

**Hamel, Bernard H. Spanish Bk. Corp.,** 10977 Santa Monica Blvd., Los Angeles, CA 90025 (SAN 111-8862) Tel 310-475-0453; Fax: 310-473-6132 E-mail: spanish@primenet.com Web site: http://www.BernardHamel.com; http://www.SpanishBooksUSA.com.

**Hamilton News Co., Ltd.,** 41 Hamilton Ln., Glenmont, NY 12077 (SAN 169-5312) Tel 518-463-1135; Fax: 518-463-3154.

**Hammond Castle Museum,** 80 Hesperus Ave., Gloucester, MA 01930 Tel 978-283-7673.

**Hammond Publishing Co., Inc.,** ( *1-883882* ) P.O. Box 279, G7166 N. Saginaw St., Mount Morris, MI 48458 (SAN 185-142X) Tel 810-686-8881; Fax: 810-686-0561; Toll Free: 800-521-3440 (orders only) E-mail: hammondpub@juno.com.

**Hamon, Gerard Incorporated,** *See* **Lafayette Bks.**

**Handleman,** 2050 S. Santa Cruz St., No. 1100, Anaheim, CA 92805-6816 (SAN 106-4886) Tel 626-912-8182.

**Handler News Agency,** P.O. Box 27007, Omaha, NE 68127-0007 (SAN 169-4405).

**Harcourt Brace & Company,** *See* **Harcourt Trade Pubs.**

**Harcourt Trade Pubs.,** ( *0-15* ) Div. of Harcourt, Inc., Orders Addr.: 6277 Sea Harbor Dr., Orlando, FL 32887 (SAN 200-285X) Tel 619-699-6707; Toll Free Fax: 800-235-0256; Toll Free: 800-543-1918 (trade orders, inquiries, claims); Edit Addr.: 525 B St., Suite 1900, San Diego, CA 92101-4495 (SAN 200-2736) Tel 619-231-6616; 15 E. 26th St., 15th Flr., New York, NY 10010 Tel 212-592-1000 E-mail: apbcs@harcourtbrace.com Web site: http://www.harcourtbooks.com.

**Harness, Miller,** 350 Page Rd., Washington, NC 27889-8753 (SAN 169-5789) Toll Free: 800-526-6310.

**Harper Religious Books,** *See* **HarperSanFrancisco**

**HarperCollins Pubs.,** ( *0-00; 0-06; 0-688; 0-690; 0-694; 0-7322* ) Div. of News Corp., Orders Addr.: 1000 Keystone Industrial Pk., Scranton, PA 18512-4621 (SAN 215-3742) Tel 570-941-1500; Toll Free Fax: 800-822-4090; Toll Free: 800-242-7737 (orders only); Edit Addr.: 10 E. 53rd St., New York, NY 10022-5299 (SAN 200-2086) Tel 212-207-7000 Web site: http://www.harpercollins.com.

**HarperSanFrancisco,** ( *0-06; 0-85924; 0-86683* ) Div. of HarperCollins General Bks. Group, Orders Addr.: 1000 Keystone Industrial Pk., Scranton, PA 18512 Toll Free Fax: 800-822-4090; Toll Free: 800-242-7737; Edit Addr.: 353 Sacramento St., Suite 500, San Francisco, CA 94111 Tel 415-477-4400; Fax: 415-477-4444 Web site: http://www.harpercollins.com.

**Harrisburg News Co.,** 980 Briarsdale Rd., Harrisburg, PA 17109 (SAN 169-7420) Tel 717-561-8377; Fax: 717-561-1466 Web site: http://www.harrisburgnewsco.com.

**Harrison Hse., Inc.,** ( *0-89274; 1-57794* ) Orders Addr.: P.O. Box 35035, Tulsa, OK 74153 (SAN 208-676X) Tel 918-494-5944; Fax: 918-494-3665; Toll Free: 800-888-4126; Edit Addr.: 2448 E. 81st St., Suite 4800, Tulsa, OK 74137 E-mail: ioporders@aidcvt.com; hh2@eaglemgmt.com Web site: http://www.harrisonhouse.com.

**Harry-Young Pubn. Services Agency, Inc.,** 6261 Manchester Blvd., Buena Park, CA 90621-2259 (SAN 110-8832).

**Harvard Assocs., Inc.,** ( *0-924346* ) 10 Holworthy St., Cambridge, MA 02138 (SAN 110-2939) Tel 617-492-0660; Fax: 617-492-4610; Toll Free: 800-774-5646 E-mail: info@harvassoc.com Web site: http://www.harvassoc.com.

**Harvard Univ. Art Museums Shop,** 32 Quincy St., Cambridge, MA 02138 (SAN 111-3372) Tel 617-495-8286; Fax: 617-495-9985 E-mail: appleyar@fas.harvard.edu Web site: http://www.artmuseums.harvard.edu.

**Harvest Distributors,** *See* **ARVEST**

**Hastings Bks.,** ( *0-940846* ) 116 N. Wayne Ave., Wayne, PA 19087 (SAN 205-048X).

**Hawaiian Magazine Distributor,** 3375 Koapaka St., No. D180, Honolulu, HI 98619-1865 (SAN 169-1619).

**Health Communications, Inc.,** ( *0-922352; 0-932194; 0-941405; 1-55874; 0-7573* ) 3201 SW 15th St., Deerfield Beach, FL 33442-8157 (SAN 212-100X) Tel 954-360-0909; Fax: 954-360-0034; Toll Free: 800-851-9100 Do not confuse with Health Communications, Inc., Edison, NJ E-mail: hci@hcibooks.com; terryy@hcibooks.com; lorig@hcibooks.com Web site: http://www.hcibooks.com.

**Hearst Distribution Group, Incorporated, Book Division,** *See* **Comag Marketing Group**

**Hearthland Bks.,** 1724 Morningside Dr., Suite B, Shelbyville, IN 46176 Toll Free: 888-346-4286 Web site: http://www.hearthlandbooks.com.

**Heartland Bk. Co.,** 10195 N. Lake Ave., Olathe, KS 66061 (SAN 631-2497) Tel 913-829-1784.

**Heffernan Audio Visual,** Orders Addr.: P.O. Box 5906, San Antonio, TX 78201-0906 Tel 210-732-4333; Fax: 210-732-5906; Edit Addr.: 2111 West Ave., San Antonio, TX 78201-2822 (SAN 166-8722) E-mail: sales@heffernanav.com Web site: http://www.heffernanav.com.

**Heffernan School Supply,** *See* **Heffernan Audio Visual**

**Heimburger Hse. Publishing Co.,** ( *0-911581* ) 7236 W. Madison St., Forest Park, IL 60130 (SAN 264-0929) Tel 708-366-1973 (phone/fax) E-mail: heimburgerhouse@heimburgerhouse.com Web site: http://www.heimburgerhouse.com.

**Heirloom Bible Pubs.,** Orders Addr.: P.O. Box 118, Wichita, KS 67201-0118 (SAN 630-2793) Fax: 316-267-1850; Toll Free: 800-676-2448; Edit Addr.: 9020 E. 35th St N., Wichita, KS 67226-2017.

**Helix,** 310 S. Racine St., Chicago, IL 60607 (SAN 111-915X) Tel 312-421-6000; Fax: 312-421-1586.

**Herald Pr.,** ( *0-8361* ) Div. of Mennonite Publishing Hse., Inc., 616 Walnut Ave., Scottdale, PA 15683-1999 (SAN 202-2915) Tel 412-887-8500; 724-887-8500; Fax: 724-887-3111; Toll Free: 800-245-7894 (orders only) Do not confuse with Herald Pr., Charlotte, NC E-mail: hp@mph.org Web site: http://www.mph.org.

**Herald Publishing Hse.,** ( *0-8309* ) P.O. Box 390, Independence, MO 64051-0390 Tel 816-521-3015; Fax: 816-521-3066; Toll Free: 800-767-8181; 1001 W. Walnut St., Independence, MO 64051-0390 (SAN 111-7556) E-mail: hhmark@heraldhouse.org Web site: http://www.heraldhouse.org.

**Heritage Bookstore,** Orders Addr.: 2101 W. Chesterfield Blvd., Suite A101, Springfield, MO 65807-8672 (SAN 111-7696).

**Hervey's Booklink & Cookbook Warehouse,** P.O. Box 831870, Richardson, TX 75083 (SAN 630-9747).

**Hesteria Records & Publishing Co.,** 124 Hagar Ct., Santa Cruz, CA 95064 Tel 831-459-2575; Fax: 831-457-2917 E-mail: alissa@aainnovators.com Web site: http://www.aainnovators.com.

**Hi Jolly Library Service,** 150 N. Gay St., Susanville, CA 96130-3902 (SAN 133-5944).

**Hibel, Edna Studio,** P.O. Box 9967, Riviera Beach, FL 33419 (SAN 111-1574) Tel 561-848-9640; Toll Free: 800-275-3426.

**Hicks News Agency, Incorporated,** *See* **NEWSouth Distributors**

**High Windy Audio,** ( *0-942303* ) Orders Addr.: P.O. Box 553, Fairview, NC 28730 (SAN 630-382X) Tel 828-628-1728; Fax: 828-628-4435; Toll Free: 800-637-8679; Edit Addr.: 260 Lambeth Walk, Fairview, NC 28730 (SAN 666-9654) Tel 828-628-1728 E-mail: office@highwindy.com; highwindy@aol.com Web site: http://www.highwindy.com.

**Hill City News Agency, Inc.,** 3228 Odd Fellow Rd., Lynchburg, VA 24501 (SAN 169-8656) Tel 804-845-4231; Fax: 804-845-0864.

**Hillsboro News,** Orders Addr.: P.O. Box 25738, Tampa, FL 33622-5738 Tel 813-622-0880; Edit Addr.: 7002 Parke E. Blvd., Tampa, FL 33610.

**Himber Bks.,** Div. of F. C. Himber & Son's, Inc., 1380 W. Second Ave., Eugene, OR 97402 Tel 541-686-8003 ; Toll Free: 800-888-5904.

**Himber, F. C.,** *See* **Himber Bks.**

**Hinrichs, E. Louis,** P.O. Box 1090, Lompoc, CA 93438-1090 (SAN 133-1493) Tel 805-736-7512 E-mail: booklompoc@aol.com.

*Wholesalers & Distributors*

**Hippocrene Bks., Inc.,** *( 0-7818; 0-87052; 0-88254 )* 171 Madison Ave., New York, NY 10016-1002 (SAN 213-2060) Tel 718-454-2366 (sales); 212-685-4371 (editorial); Fax: 718-454-1391 (sales/order inquiry); 212-779-9338 (editorial)
E-mail: hippocrenebooks.com; hippocre@ix.netcom.com; contact@hippocrenebooks.com
Web site: http://www.hippocrenebooks.com.

**Historic Aviation Bks.,** 121 Fifth Ave., Suite 300, New Brighton, MN 55112 (SAN 129-5284) Tel 651-635-0100; Fax: 651-635-0700.

**Historic Cherry Hill,** *( 0-943366 )* 523 1/2 S. Pearl St., Albany, NY 12202 (SAN 110-8859) Tel 518-434-4791 ; Fax: 518-434-4806.

**Hobbies Hawaii Distributors,** 4420 Lawehana St., No. 3, Honolulu, HI 96818 (SAN 630-8619) Tel 808-423-0265; Fax: 808-423-1635.

**Holiday Enterprises, Inc.,** 3328 US Hwy. 123, Rochester Bldg., Greenville, SC 29611 (SAN 169-779X) Tel 864-220-3161; Fax: 864-295-9757.

**Holmes & Meier Pubs., Inc.,** *( 0-8419 )* Orders Addr.: 41 Monroe Tpke., Trumbull, CT 06611 Tel 800-698-7781; Fax: 800-557-5601; Edit Addr.: 160 Broadway E. Bldg, 9th Flr., New York, NY 10038 (SAN 201-9280) Tel 212-374-0100; Fax: 212-374-1313
E-mail: info@holmesandmeier.com
Web site: http://www.holmesandmeier.com.

**Holtzbrinck Pubs.,** *( 0-374 )* Orders Addr.: 16365 James Madison Hwy., Gordonsville, VA 22942 (SAN 631-5011) Tel 540-672-7600; Fax: 540-672-7540 (Customer Service); 540-672-7664; Toll Free Fax: 800-672-2054 (Order Dept.); Toll Free: 888-330-8477 ; Edit Addr.: 175 Fifth Ave., New York, NY 10010 Tel 212-674-5151; Fax: 212-677-6487; Toll Free: 800-488-5233
E-mail: dean.athans.@hbpubny.com
Web site: http://www.vhpsva.com/bookseller/.

**Holyoke News Co., Inc.,** 720 Main St., P.O. Box 990, Holyoke, MA 01041 (SAN 169-3468) Tel 413-534-4537; Fax: 413-538-7161; Toll Free: 800-628-8372
E-mail: sales@holyoke-news.com.

**Homestead Bk., Inc.,** *( 0-930180 )* Orders Addr.: P.O. Box 31608, Seattle, WA 98103 (SAN 662-037X); Edit Addr.: 6101 22nd Ave., NW, Seattle, WA 98107 (SAN 169-8796) Tel 206-782-4532; Fax: 206-784-9328; Toll Free: 800-426-6777 (orders only)
Web site: http://www.homesteadbook.com.

**Honor Bks.,** *( 1-56292 )* 2448 E. 81st St., Suite 4800, Tulsa, OK 74137-4285 (SAN 631-1687) Tel 918-523-5600; Fax: 918-496-3588; Toll Free: 800-678-2126 Do not confuse with Honor Bks., Rapid City, SD
E-mail: info@honorbooks.com
Web site: http://www.honorbooks.com/.

**Hood, Alan C. & Co., Inc.,** *( 0-911469 )* P.O. Box 775, Chambersburg, PA 17201 (SAN 270-8221) Tel 717-267-0867; Fax: 717-267-0572.

**Hotho & Co.,** 916 Norwood St., Fort Worth, TX 76107-2994 (SAN 169-8192) Tel 817-335-1833.

**Houghton Mifflin Co.,** *( 0-395; 0-87466; 0-9631591; 1-57630; 1-881527; 0-618 )* 222 Berkeley St., Boston, MA 02116 (SAN 215-3793) Tel 617-351-5000
Web site: http://www.hmco.com.

**Houghton Mifflin Co. Trade & Reference Div.,** *( 0-395; 0-618 )* Orders Addr.: 181 Ballardvalle St., Wilmington, MA 01887 Tel 978-661-1300; Toll Free: 800-225-3362; Edit Addr.: 222 Berkeley St., Boston, MA 02116 (SAN 200-2388) Tel 617-351-5000; Fax: 617-227-5409; 215 Park Ave., S., New York, NY 10003 Tel 212-420-5800; Fax: 212-420-5855
Web site: http://www.hmco.com/.

**Houghton Mifflin Company (College Division),** *See* **Houghton Mifflin Co. Trade & Reference Div.**

**Houston Paperback Distributor,** 4114 Gairloch Ln., Houston, TX 77025-2912 (SAN 169-8273).

**HPK Educational Resource Ctr.,** *( 0-89895 )* Div. of H. P. Koppelmann, Inc., 140 Van Block Ave., Hartford, CT 06141 (SAN 169-071X) Tel 860-549-6210; Toll Free: 800-243-7724.

**Hubbard,** P.O. Box 100, Defiance, OH 43512 (SAN 169-6726) Tel 419-784-4455; Fax: 419-782-1662; Toll Free: 800-582-0657
E-mail: hubbard@bright.net.

**Hudson County News Co.,** 1305 Paterson Plank Rd., North Bergen, NJ 07047 (SAN 169-4782) Tel 201-867-3600.

**Hudson Hills Pr. LLC,** *( 0-933920; 0-9646042; 1-55595 )* Orders Addr.: P.O. Box 205, Manchester, VT 05254; Edit Addr.: 74-2 Union St., Manchester, VT 05254 (SAN 213-0815) Tel 802-362-6450; Fax: 802-362-6459
E-mail: artbooks@hudsonhills.com.

**Hudson Hills Press, Incorporated,** *See* **Hudson Hills Pr. LLC**

**Hudson Valley News Distributors,** P.O. Box 1236, Newburgh, NY 12550 (SAN 169-6084) Tel 914-562-3399; Fax: 914-562-6010.

**Hyperion Pr.,** *( 0-7868; 1-56282; 1-4013 )* Div. of Disney Bk. Publishing, Inc., A Walt Disney Co., Orders Addr.: 3 Center Plaza, Boston, MA 02108 Toll Free: 800-759-0190; Edit Addr.: 77 W. 66th St., 11th Flr., New York, NY 10023-6298 Tel 212-456-0100; Fax: 212-456-0108
Web site: http://www.hyperionbooks.com.

**Iaconi, Mariuccia Bk. Imports,** *( 0-9628720 )* 970 Tennessee St., San Francisco, CA 94107 (SAN 161-1364) Tel 415-821-1216; Fax: 415-821-1596; Toll Free: 800-955-9577
E-mail: mibibook@ixnetcom.com
Web site: http://www.mibibook.com.

**i.b.d., Ltd.,** *( 0-88431 )* 24 Hudson St., Kinderhook, NY 12106 (SAN 630-7779) Tel 518-758-1755; Fax: 518-758-6702
E-mail: lankhof@ibdltd.com
Web site: http://www.ibdltd.com.

**ibooks.com,** *( 0-7561 )* 804-C Rio Grande St., Austin, TX 78701-2220 Tel 512-478-2700; Fax: 512-478-0500
E-mail: kim@ibooks.com
Web site: http://www.ibooks.com/.

**ICG Muse, Inc.,** 73 Spring St., Suite 206, New York, NY 10012 (SAN 631-7200) Tel 212-343-1119; Fax: 212-343-1116.

**ID International Bk. Service,** 126 Old Ridgefield Rd., Wilton, CT 06897-3017 (SAN 630-8074) Tel 203-834-2272; Fax: 203-762-9725
E-mail: orders@idintl.com.

**Idaho News Agency,** 2710 Julia St., Coeur D'Alene, ID 83814 (SAN 169-1651) Tel 208-664-3444.

**Ideal Foreign Bks., Inc.,** 132-10 Hillside Ave., Richmond Hill, NY 11418 (SAN 169-6173) Tel 718-297-7477; Fax: 718-297-7645; Toll Free: 800-284-2490 (orders only).

**IFSTA,** *( 0-87939 )* Orders Addr.: c/o Oklahoma State Univ., Fire Protection Pubns., 930 N. Willis, Stillwater, OK 74078-8045 Tel 405-744-5723; Fax: 405-744-8204; Toll Free: 800-654-4055 (orders only)
Web site: http://www.ifsta.org/.

**Ignatius Pr.,** *( 0-89870; 1-58617 )* Div. of Guadalupe Assocs., Inc., Orders Addr.: P.O. Box 1339, Fort Collins, CO 80522-1339 Tel 970-221-3920; Fax: 970-221-3964; Toll Free Fax: 800-278-3566; Toll Free: 800-651-1531 (credit card orders, no minimum, individual orders); 877-320-9276 (bookstore orders); Edit Addr.: 2515 McAllister St., San Francisco, CA 94118 (SAN 214-3887) Tel 415-387-2324; Fax: 415-387-0896
E-mail: info@ignatius.com
Web site: http://www.ignatius.com.

**Igram Pr.,** *( 0-911119; 1-930279 )* 311 Parsons Dr., Hiawatha, IA 52233 (SAN 263-1709) Tel 319-393-3600; Fax: 319-393-3934; Toll Free: 800-393-2399
E-mail: clabarr@cedargraphicsinc.com.

**Illinois News Service,** *See* **News Group - Illinois, The**

**Image Processing Software, Inc.,** *( 0-924507 )* 6409 Appalachian Way, Madison, WI 53705 (SAN 265-5977) Tel 608-233-5033; 4414 Regent St., Madison, WI 53705 (SAN 249-3020).

**Imperial News Co., Inc.,** 5131 Post Rd., Dublin, OH 43017-1160 (SAN 169-5509) Fax: 516-752-8515.

**Imported Bks.,** Orders Addr.: St., Dallas, TX 75208 (SAN 169-8095) Tel 214-941-6497.

**In Between Bks.,** *( 0-935430 )* P.O. Box 790, Sausalito, CA 94966 (SAN 213-6236) Tel 415-383-8447; Fax: 415-381-3513; 415-381-1938
E-mail: inbetweenbooks@atthebutterflytree.com
Web site: http://www.atthebutterflytree.com.

**Incor Periodicals,** 32150 Hwy. 34, Tangent, OR 97389-9704 (SAN 169-7072) Tel 541-926-8889; Fax: 541-926-9553.

**Independent Institute,** *( 0-945999 )* 100 Swan Way, Suite 200, Oakland, CA 94621-1428 (SAN 135-2938) Tel 510-632-1366; Fax: 510-568-6040; Toll Free: 800-927-8733
E-mail: info@indenpendent.org; orders@independent.org
Web site: http://www.independent.org.

**Independent Magazine Co.,** 2970 N. Ontario St., Burbank, CA 91504-2016 (SAN 159-8783).

**Independent Pubs. Group,** Subs. of Chicago Review Pr., 814 N. Franklin, Chicago, IL 60610 (SAN 202-0769) Tel 312-337-0747; Fax: 312-337-5985; Toll Free: 800-888-4741
E-mail: lreardon@ipgbook.com; usold@ipgbook.com
Web site: http://www.ipgbook.com.

**Independent Pubs. Marketing,** 6824 Oaklawn Ave., Edina, MN 55435 (SAN 630-5725) Tel 612-920-9044 ; Fax: 612-920-7662; Toll Free: 800-669-9044
Web site: http://www.Stjohns.ipm.worldnet.att.net.

**Indiana Periodicals, Inc.,** 2120 S. Meridian St., Indianapolis, IN 46225 (SAN 169-2380) Tel 317-786-1488; Fax: 317-782-4999.

**Ingham Publishing, Inc.,** *( 0-9611804; 1-891130 )* Orders Addr.: P.O. Box 12642, Saint Petersburg, FL 33733-2642 Tel 813-343-4811; Fax: 813-381-2807; Edit Addr.: 5650 First Ave., N., Saint Petersburg, FL 33710 (SAN 112-8930)
E-mail: ftreflex@concentric.net.

**Ingram Bk. Co.,** Subs. of Ingram Industries, Inc., Orders Addr.: 1 Ingram Blvd., P.O. Box 3006, La Vergne, TN 37086-1986 (SAN 169-7978) Tel 615-213-5000; Fax: 615-213-3976 (Electronic Orders); Toll Free Fax: 800-285-3296 (fax inquiry US & Canada); 800-876-0186 (orders); 877-663-5367 (Canadian orders); Toll Free: 800-937-8000 (orders only); 800-937-8200 (customer service US & Canada); 800-289-0687 (Canadian orders only customer service); 800-234-6737 (electronic orders US & Canada)) Do not confuse with Ingram Pr., Sacramento, CA
E-mail: customerservice@ingrambook.com; flashback@ingrambook.com; ics-sales@ingrambook.com
Web site: http://www.ingrambook.com.

**Ingram Entertainment, Inc.,** Two Ingram Blvd. (Corp. Headquarters), La Vergne, TN 37089-7006 (SAN 630-6780) Tel 615-287-4000; Fax: 615-287-4995; Toll Free: 800-759-5000; 7900 Hickman Rd., Des Moines, IA 50322-4432 (SAN 630-6950) Tel 515-254-7000; Fax: 515-254-7021; 26361 Curtiss Wright Pkwy., Suite D, Richmond Heights, OH 44143 (SAN 630-6896) Tel 216-732-3675; Fax: 216-732-8980; Toll Free: 800-621-1333; 15002 Sommermeyer, Houston, TX 77041-5333 (SAN 630-7000) Tel 713-937-3600; Fax: 713-466-4316; 910 Kimberly Dr., Carol Stream, IL 60188 (SAN 630-690X) Tel 630-871-0222; Fax: 630-871-7804; Toll Free: 800-621-1333; 7911 NE 33rd Dr., Suite 270, Portland, OR 97211-1920 (SAN 630-7116) Tel 503-281-2673; Fax: 503-284-6046; 3401 Investment Blvd., Suite 1, Hayward, CA 94545 (SAN 630-6993) Tel 510-670-1670; Fax: 510-670-4666; Toll Free: 800-621-1333; 2611 S. Roosevelt, Suite 102, Tempe, AZ 85282-2017 (SAN 630-7094) Tel 602-966-6691; Fax: 602-894-0329; 4703 Fulton Industrial Blvd., Atlanta, GA 30336-2017 (SAN 630-6845) Tel 404-691-6280; Fax: 404-696-3944; 400 Airport Executive Pk., Spring Valley, NY 10977-7404 (SAN 630-7078) Tel 914-425-3191; Fax: 914-425-7521; 7949 Woodley Blvd., Van Nuys, CA 91406 (SAN 630-7183) Tel 818-375-5027; Fax: 818-375-5001; 1293 Heil Quaker Blvd., Suite B, P.O. Box 7006, La Vergne, TN 37086-7006 (SAN 630-7051) Fax: 615-793-6196; Toll Free: 800-688-3110; 5500 Oakbrook Pkwy., Suite 220, Norcross, GA 30093 (SAN 630-6853) Tel 404-447-4663; Fax: 404-446-7711; Toll Free: 800-876-0832; 3114 S. 24th St., Kansas City, KS 66106-4709 (SAN 630-7027) Tel 913-362-0391; Fax: 913-362-0605; Toll Free: 800-621-1333; 6635 NE 59th Pl., Portland, OR 97218-2709 (SAN 630-7124) Tel 503-284-3313; Fax: 503-284-3876; Toll Free: 800-876-0834; 7319 Innovation Blvd., Fort Wayne, IN 46818-1371 (SAN 630-6985) Fax: 219-489-8850; Toll Free: 800-759-5588; 8779 Greenwood Pl., Savage, MD 20763 (SAN 630-7019) Tel 301-490-1166; Fax: 301-490-0031; Toll Free: 800-621-1333; 1521 W. Copans Rd., Suite 105, Pompano Beach, FL 33064 (SAN 630-7108) Tel 954-971-5412; Fax: 954-971-3113; Toll Free: 800-888-3876; 20435 E. Business Pkwy., Walnut, CA 91789-2999 (SAN 630-7191) Tel 714-594-6569; Fax: 714-595-0735; Toll Free: 800-759-4422; 7710 King St., Anchorage, AK 99518 (SAN 630-6837) Tel 907-344-9666; Fax: 907-344-9738; Toll Free: 800-621-1333; 1349 Charwood Rd., Hanover, MD 21076-3114 (SAN 630-6861) Tel 410-850-9191; Fax: 410-850-9229; 110 Shawmut Rd., Canton, MA 02021-1412 (SAN 630-687X) Tel 617-575-9585; Fax: 617-575-9586; 100 Dobbs Ln., Suite 206, Cherry Hill, NJ 08034-1435 (SAN 630-6888) Tel 609-428-8668; Fax: 609-428-8536; Toll Free: 800-288-7565; 11235 Knott Ave., Suite C, Cypress, CA 90630-5401 (SAN 630-6918) Tel 714-373-8855; Fax: 714-373-8858; Toll Free: 800-759-4422; 1430 Bradley Ln., No. 102, Carrollton, TX 75007-4855 (SAN 630-6926) Tel 214-245-6088; Fax: 214-323-3890; Toll Free:

800-621-1333; 2259 Merritt Dr., Garland, TX 75041-6138 (SAN 630-6934) Tel 214-840-6621; Fax: 214-840-3357; Toll Free: 800-727-0688; 10990 E. 55th Ave., Denver, CO 80239-2007 (SAN 630-6942) Tel 303-371-8372; Fax: 303-373-4583; 35245 Schoolcraft, Livonia, MI 48150-1209 (SAN 630-6969) Tel 313-422-9955; Fax: 313-422-1171; 3540 NW 56th St., Fort Lauderdale, FL 33309-2260 (SAN 630-6977) Tel 305-733-7440; Fax: 305-735-7752; 6733 S. Sepulveda, Suite 108, Los Angeles, CA 90045-1525 (SAN 630-7035) Tel 213-410-4067; Fax: 213-410-0919; Toll Free: 800-759-4422; 2070 W. 96th St., Bloomington, MN 55431 (SAN 630-7043) Tel 952-881-0032; Fax: 952-881-3430; Toll Free: 800-825-3112; 25 Branca Rd., East Rutherford, NJ 07073-2121 (SAN 630-706X) Tel 201-933-9797; Fax: 201-933-5139; Toll Free: 800-621-1333; 5576 Inland Empire Blvd, Bldg. G, Suite A, Ontario, CA 91764-5117 (SAN 630-7086) Tel 714-948-7998; Fax: 714-948-9778; Freeport Ctr., Bldg. H-12 N., P.O. Box 1387, Clearfield, UT 84016-1387 (SAN 630-7132) Tel 801-775-0555; Fax: 801-773-8172; 2700 Merchantile Dr., Suite 100, Rancho Cordova, CA 95742-6574 (SAN 630-7140) Tel 916-638-8090; Fax: 916-638-8021; Toll Free: 800-866-1568; 4660 Viewridge Ave., Suite B, San Diego, CA 92123-1638 (SAN 630-7159) Tel 619-569-9816; Fax: 619-569-1542; Toll Free: 800-365-5229; 6411 S. 216th, Bldg. F, Kent, WA 98032-1392 (SAN 630-7167) Tel 206-395-3515; Fax: 206-395-0650; 445 W. Freedom Ave., Orange, CA 92865 (SAN 630-7175) Tel 714-282-1232; Fax: 714-282-2245; 201 Ingram Dr., Roseburg, OR 97470; 12600 SE Hwy. 212, Bldg. B, Clackamas, OR 97015-9081 Tel 615-287-4000
Web site: http://www.ingramentertainment.com.

**Ingram Software,** Subs. of Ingram Distribution Group, Inc., 1759 Wehrle, Williamsville, NY 14221 (SAN 285-760X) Toll Free: 800-828-7250; 900 W. Walnut Ave., Compton, CA 90220 (SAN 285-7065).

**Inland Empire Periodicals,** *See* **Incor Periodicals**

**Integral Yoga Pubns.,** ( *0-932040* ) Satchidananda Ashram-Yogaville, Rte. 1, Box 1720, Buckingham, VA 23921 (SAN 285-0338) Tel 804-969-1706; Fax: 804-969-1463; Toll Free: 800-262-1008 (orders)
Web site: http://www.yogaville.org/pubs.html.

**Interactive Knowledge,** *See* **netLibrary, Inc.**

**Interlink Publishing Group, Inc.,** ( *0-940793; 1-56656* ) 46 Crosby St., Northampton, MA 01060-1804 (SAN 664-8908) Tel 413-582-7054; Fax: 413-582-6731; Toll Free: 800-238-5465
E-mail: info@interlinkbooks.com; editor@interlinkbooks.com
Web site: http://www.interlinkbooks.com.

**InterMountain Periodical Distributors,** *See* **Majic Enterprises**

**International Academy of Healing, The,** *See* **Southwood Healing Institute**

**International Brecht Society,** ( *0-9623206* ) c/o Marc Silberman, Univ. of Wisconsin, German Dept., 818 Van Hisc Hall, Madison, WI 53706 Tel 608-262-2192 ; Fax: 608-262-4747 Do not confuse with Pittsburgh, PA, AU.

**International Magazine Service,** Div. of Periodical Pubs. Service Bureau, 1 N. Superior St., Sandusky, OH 44870 (SAN 285-9955) Tel 419-626-0623.

**International Networking Assn.,** 4130 Citrus Ave., Suite 5, Rocklin, CA 95677 (SAN 631-1857).

**International Periodical Distributors,** 674 Via de la Valle, Suite 204, Solana Beach, CA 92075 (SAN 250-5290) Tel 619-481-5928; Toll Free: 800-999-1170; 800-228-5144 (in Canada).

**International Publishers Marketing,** Orders Addr.: 22883 Quicksilver Dr., Dulles, VA 20166 (SAN 253-3375) Toll Free: 800-758-3756; Edit Addr.: P.O. Box 605, Herndon, VA 20172-0605 Fax: 703-661-1501.

**International Pubns. Service,** ( *0-8002* ) Div. of Taylor & Francis, Inc., Orders Addr.: 325 Chestnut St., 8th Flr., Levittown, PA 19057-4700 Fax: 215-785-5515; Toll Free: 800-821-8312
E-mail: bkorders@tandfpa.com.

**International Readers League,** Div. of Periodical Pubs. Service Bureau, 1 N. Superior St., Sandusky, OH 44870 (SAN 285-9971) Tel 419-626-0633.

**International Service Co.,** International Service Bldg., 333 Fourth Ave., Indialantic, FL 32903-4295 (SAN 169-5134) Tel 407-724-1443 (phone/fax).

**International Specialized Bk. Services,** 920 NE 58th Ave., Suite 300, Portland, OR 97213-3786 (SAN 169-7129) Tel 503-287-3093; Fax: 503-280-8832; Toll Free: 800-944-6190
E-mail: info@isbs.com.
Web site: http://www.isbs.com.

**International Thomson Publishing,** *See* **Thomson Learning**

**Internet Systems, Inc.,** Subs. of Internet Systems, Inc., 20250 Century Blvd., Germantown, MD 20874 (SAN 129-9611) Tel 301-540-5100; Fax: 301-540-5522; Toll Free: 800-638-8725
Web site: http://www.pwl.com/Internet.

**Interstate Distributors,** 199 Commander Shea Blvd., Quincy, MA 02171 (SAN 170-4885) Tel 617-328-9500; Toll Free: 800-365-6430.

**Interstate Periodical Distributors,** P.O. Box 2237, Madison, WI 53701 (SAN 169-9105) Tel 608-271-3600; Fax: 608-277-2410; Toll Free: 800-752-3131.

**Intertech Bk. Services, Inc.,** 25971 Sarazen Dr., South Riding, VA 20152-1741 (SAN 630-5253).

**Intrepid Group, Inc., The,** 1331 Red Cedar Cir., Fort Collins, CO 80524 (SAN 631-5429) Tel 970-493-3793 ; Fax: 970-493-8781
E-mail: intrepid@fril.com.

**Iowa & Illinois News,** 8645 Northwest Blvd., Davenport, IA 52806-6418 (SAN 169-2607).

**Iowa State Pr.,** ( *0-8138* ) 2121 S. State Ave., Ames, IA 50014-8300 (SAN 202-7194) Tel 515-292-0140; Fax: 515-292-3348
E-mail: orders@isupress.com
Web site: http://www.iowastatepress.com.

**Iowa State University Press,** *See* **Iowa State Pr.**

**Irish American Bk. Co.,** Subs. of Roberts Rinehart Pubs., Inc., P.O. Box 666, Niwot, CO 80544-0666 Tel 303-652-2710; Fax: 303-652-2689; Toll Free: 800-452-7115
E-mail: irishbooks@aol.com
Web site: http://www.irishvillage.com.

**Irish Bks. & Media, Inc.,** ( *0-937702* ) Orders Addr.: 1433 E. Franklin Ave., Suite 20, Minneapolis, MN 55404-2135 (SAN 111-8870) Tel 612-871-3505; Fax: 612-871-3358; Toll Free: 800-229-3505 Do not confuse with Irish Bks. in New York, NY
E-mail: Irishbook@aol.com
Web site: http://www.irishbook.com.

**Ironside International Pubs., Inc.,** ( *0-935554* ) Orders Addr.: P.O. Box 55, Alexandria, VA 22313 (SAN 206-2380) Tel 703-684-6111; Fax: 703-683-5486; Edit Addr.: 3000 S. Eads St., Arlington, VA 22202 (SAN 663-656X).

**Islamic Bk. Service,** 1209 Cleburne, Hoston, TX 77004 (SAN 169-2453) Tel 713-528-1440; Fax: 713-528-1085.

**Island Heritage Publishing,** ( *0-89610; 0-931548* ) Div. of The Madden Corp., 94-411 Koaki St., Waipahu, HI 96797 (SAN 211-1403) Tel 808-564-8888; Fax: 808-564-8999; Toll Free: 800-468-2800
E-mail: hawaii4u@islandheritage.com
Web site: http://www.islandheritage.com/.

**iUniverse, Inc.,** ( *0-9665514; 1-58348; 0-9668591; 1-893652; 0-595* ) Orders Addr.: 2021 Pine Lake Rd., Suite 100, Lincoln, NE 68512 (SAN 254-9425) Tel 402-323-7800; Fax: 402-323-7824; Toll Free: 877-823-9235
E-mail: pubservices@iuniverse.com; custservice@iuniverse.com
Web site: http://www.iUniverse.com.

**iUniverse.com, Incorporated,** *See* **iUniverse, Inc.**

**James & Law Co.,** Orders Addr.: P.O. Box 2468, Clarksburg, WV 26302-2468 (SAN 169-894X); Edit Addr.: Middletown Mall I-79 & U. S. 250, Fairmont, WV 26554 (SAN 169-8966) Tel 304-624-7401.

**Janway,** 11 Academy Rd., Cogan Station, PA 17728 (SAN 108-3708) Tel 717-494-1239; Fax: 717-494-1350; Toll Free: 800-877-5242.

**Jeanies Classics,** ( *0-9609672* ) Orders Addr.: 2123 Oxford St., Rockford, IL 61103 (SAN 271-7409); Edit Addr.: 2123 Oxford St., Rockford, IL 61103 (SAN 271-7395) Tel 815-968-4544.

**Jean's Dulcimer Shop & Crying Creek Pubs.,** P.O. Box 8, Hwy. 32, Cosby, TN 37722 (SAN 249-9282) Tel 423-487-5543.

**Jech Distributors,** 674 Via De La Valle, No. 204, Solana Beach, CA 92075-2462 (SAN 107-0258) Tel 619-452-7251.

**Jellyroll Productions,** *See* **Osborne Enterprises Publishing**

**Jende-Hagan, Incorporated,** *See* **Renaissance Hse. Pubs.**

**J&J Bk. Sales,** 22661 Lambert St., Suite 205, Lake Forest, CA 92630 (SAN 253-8075) Tel 949-770-1486 ; Fax: 949-770-4826
E-mail: jacki@hydrasystems.com
Web site: http://www.divanet.com/matilda.

**J&L Bk. Co.,** Orders Addr.: P.O. Box 13100, Spokane, WA 99213 (SAN 129-6817) Fax: 509-534-0152; 509-534-7713; Toll Free: 800-288-9756; Edit Addr.: 1710 Trent, Spokane, WA 99220 (SAN 243-2145).

**Johns Hopkins Univ. Pr.,** ( *0-8018* ) Div. of Johns Hopkins Univ., 2715 N. Charles St., Baltimore, MD 21218-4319 (SAN 202-7348) Tel 410-516-6900; Fax: 410-516-6998; Toll Free: 800-537-5487
E-mail: hfscustserv@mail.press.jhu.edu
Web site: http://muse.jhu.edu/; http://www.jhupbooks.com.

**Johnson Bks.,** ( *0-917895; 0-933472; 1-55566* ) Div. of Johnson Publishing Co., 1880 S. 57th Ct., Boulder, CO 80301 (SAN 201-0313) Tel 303-443-9766; Fax: 303-998-7594; Toll Free: 800-258-5830
E-mail: books@jpcolorado.com
Web site: http://www.johnsonbooks.com.

**Johnson News Agency,** P.O. Box 9009, Moscow, ID 83843 (SAN 169-1678).

**Johnson, Walter J. Inc.,** ( *0-8472* ) 1 New York Plaza 28th Flr., New York, NY 10004-1901 (SAN 209-1828).

**Jonathan David Pubs., Inc.,** ( *0-8246* ) 68-22 Eliot Ave., Middle Village, NY 11379 (SAN 169-5274) Tel 718-456-8611; Fax: 718-894-2818
E-mail: jondavpub@aol.com
Web site: http://www.jdbooks.com.

**Jones, Bob Univ. Pr.,** ( *0-89084; 1-57924; 1-59166* ) 1700 Wade Hampton Blvd., Greenville, SC 29614 (SAN 223-7512) Tel 864-242-5731; Fax: 864-298-8398; Toll Free Fax: 800-525-8398; Toll Free: 800-845-5731
E-mail: bjup@bjup.com
Web site: http://www.bjup.com.

**Joseph Ruzicka, Incorporated,** *See* **Southeast Library Bindery, Inc.**

**Joshua Morris Publishing, Incorporated,** *See* **Reader's Digest Children's Publishing, Inc.**

**Joyce Media, Inc.,** ( *0-917002* ) P.O. Box 57, Acton, CA 93510 (SAN 208-7197) Tel 805-269-1169; Fax: 805-269-2139
E-mail: joycemed@pacbell.net
Web site: http://joycemedia.com

**Junior League of Greensboro Pubns.,** ( *0-9605788* ) 220 State St., Greensboro, NC 27408 (SAN 112-9597) Fax: 336-275-0677
E-mail: Jlgso@aol.com.

**K. F. Enterprises,** *See* **Production Assocs., Inc.**

**K. M. R. Enterprises,** ( *0-9656379* ) 5731 Pony Express Trail, Pollock Pines, CA 95726 (SAN 299-237X) Tel 530-644-1410.

**Kable News Co., Inc.,** Subs. of AMREP Corp., 641 Lexington Ave., 6th Flr., New York, NY 10022 (SAN 169-5835) Tel 212-705-4600; Toll Free: 800-223-6640
E-mail: info@kable.com.

**Kalispell News Agency,** P.O. Box 4965, Missoula, MT 59806-4965 (SAN 169-4383) Toll Free: 800-955-1266.

**Kamkin, Victor,** 4956 Boiling Brook Pkwy., Rockville, MD 20852 Tel 301-881-5973; Fax: 301-881-1637; Toll Free: 800-852-6546; 925 Broadway, New York, NY 10010 (SAN 113-7395) Tel 212-673-0776; Fax: 212-673-2473.

**Kane/Miller Bk. Pubs.,** ( *0-916291; 1-929132* ) Orders Addr.: P.O. Box 8515, La Jolla, CA 92038 (SAN 295-8945) Tel 858-456-0540; Fax: 858-456-9641; Toll Free: 800-968-1930
E-mail: kira@kanemiller.com
Web site: http://www.kanemiller.com; http://www.everyonepoops.com.

**Kansas City Periodical Distributing,** Orders Addr.: P.O. Box 14948, Lenexa, KS 66285-4948 (SAN 107-9433) ; Edit Addr.: 9605 Dice Ln., Lenexa, KS 66215 Tel 913-541-8600.

**Kansas State Reading Circle,** 715 W. Tenth St., C-170, Topeka, KS 66601 (SAN 169-2771).

**Karol Video,** Div. of Karol Media, Inc., Orders Addr.: P.O. Box 7600, Wilkes Barre, PA 18773 Tel 717-822-8899; Fax: 717-822-8226; Toll Free: 800-526-4773
E-mail: karolm@epix.net
Web site: http://www.karolmedia.com.

**Kaybee Montessori, Inc.,** 7895-K Cessna Ave., Gaithersburg, MD 20879 (SAN 133-1256) Tel 301-963-2101; Fax: 301-963-2197; Toll Free: 800-732-9304.

**Kazi Pubns., Inc.,** ( *0-933511; 0-935782; 1-56744* ) 3023 W. Belmont Ave., Chicago, IL 60618 (SAN 162-3397) Tel 773-267-7001; Fax: 773-267-7002
E-mail: info@kazi.org
Web site: http://www.kazi.org.

*Wholesalers & Distributors*

**KCS,** P.O. Box 1077, Peoria, AZ 85380 (SAN 631-2160) Tel 602-974-2179; Fax: 602-972-1486; Toll Free: 800-593-3152.

**Keith Distributors,** 1055 S. Ballenger Hwy., Flint, MI 48532 (SAN 112-6377) Tel 801-238-9104; 810-238-9104; Fax: 810-238-9028; Toll Free: 800-373-2366
E-mail: keithsbooks@juno.com.

**Kelley, Augustus M. Pubs.,** ( 0-678 ) Orders Addr.: P.O. Box 1048, Fairfield, NJ 07004-1048 (SAN 206-9768) Tel 212-685-7202 (phone/fax).

**Kendall Whaling Museum,** ( 0-937854 ) 27 Everett St., P.O. Box 297, Sharon, MA 02067 (SAN 204-9783) Tel 781-784-5642; Fax: 781-784-0451; Toll Free: 800-927-1133 (orders)
Web site: http://www.kwm.org.

**Kensington Publishing Corp.,** ( 0-7860; 0-8184; 0-8217; 1-55817; 1-57566; 0-7582 ) 850 Third Ave., New York, NY 10022-6222 Tel 212-407-1500; Fax: 212-935-0699; Toll Free: 800-221-2647
E-mail: jmclean@kensingtonbooks.com
Web site: http://www.kensingtonbooks.com.

**Kent News Agency, Inc.,** P.O. Box 1828, Scottsbluff, NE 69363-1828 (SAN 169-4448) Tel 303-286-9694; 308-635-2225; Fax: 308-635-1563; Toll Free: 877-290-4740
E-mail: kentrob@prairieweb.com.

**Keramos,** P.O. Box 7500, Ann Arbor, MI 48107 (SAN 169-3670) Tel 313-439-1261.

**Kerhulas News Co.,** P.O. Box 751, Union, SC 29379 (SAN 169-7838).

**Ketab Corp.,** ( 1-883819 ) Orders Addr.: 1419 Westwood Blvd., Los Angeles, CA 90024 (SAN 107-7791) Tel 818-908-0808; Fax: 818-908-1457
E-mail: ketab@ketab.com.
Web site: http://www.ketab.com.

**Key Bk. Service, Inc.,** ( 0-934636 ) P.O. Box 1434, Fairfield, CT 06430 (SAN 169-0671) Tel 203-374-4939; Fax: 203-384-6099.

**Kidsbooks, Inc.,** 220 Monroe Tpke., No. 560, Monroe, CT 06468-2247 (SAN 169-0795).

**King Electronics Distributing,** 1711 Southeastern Ave., Indianapolis, IN 46201-3990 (SAN 107-6795) Tel 317-639-1484; Fax: 317-639-4711.

**Kinokuniya Bookstores of America Co., Ltd.,** 1581 Webster St., San Francisco, CA 94115 (SAN 121-8441) Tel 415-567-7625; Fax: 415-567-4109.

**Kinokuniya Pubns. Service of New York,** 10 W. 49th St., New York, NY 10020 (SAN 157-5414) Tel 212-765-1465; Fax: 212-307-5593
E-mail: kinokuniya@kinokuniya.com
Web site: http://www.kinokuniya.com.

**Kirkbride, B.B. Bible Co., Inc.,** ( 0-88707; 0-934854 ) P.O. Box 606, Indianapolis, IN 46206-0606 (SAN 169-2372) Tel 317-633-1900; Fax: 317-633-1444; Toll Free: 800-428-4385
E-mail: hyperbible@aol.com
Web site: http://www.kirkbride.com.

**Kitrick Management Co., Ltd.,** P.O. Box 15523, Cincinnati, OH 45215 (SAN 132-6236) Tel 513-782-2930; Fax: 513-782-2936
E-mail: bachb@aol.com.

**Klein's Booklein,** Orders Addr.: P.O. Box 968, Fowlerville, MI 48836 (SAN 631-3329) Tel 517-223-3964; Fax: 517-223-1314; Toll Free: 800-266-5534; Edit Addr.: One Klein Dr., Fowlerville, MI 48836 (SAN 631-3337).

**Knopf, Alfred A. Inc.,** ( 0-375; 0-394; 0-676; 0-679 ) Div. of The Knopf Publishing Group, Orders Addr.: 400 Hahn Rd., Westminster, MD 21157 Tel 410-848-1900; Toll Free Fax: 800-659-2436; Toll Free: 800-733-3000 (orders); Edit Addr.: 299 Park Ave., New York, NY 10171 (SAN 202-5825) Tel 212-751-2600; Fax: 212-572-2593; Toll Free: 800-726-0600
E-mail: customerservice@randomhouse.com
Web site: http://www.randomhouse.com/knopf.

**Kodansha America, Inc.,** ( 0-87011; 1-56836 ) 575 Lexington Ave., 23rd Flr., New York, NY 10022-6102 (SAN 201-0526) Tel 917-322-6200; Fax: 212-935-6929; Toll Free: 800-451-7556
E-mail: Kabooks@aol.com.

**Koen Bk. Distributors,** Orders Addr.: 10 Twosome Dr., P.O. Box 600, Moorestown, NJ 08057 (SAN 169-4642) Tel 609-235-4444; Fax: 609-727-6914; Toll Free Fax: 800-225-3840; Toll Free: 800-257-8481
E-mail: kbdinfo@koen.com
Web site: http://www.koen.com.

**Koen Pacific,** Orders Addr.: 18249 Olympic Ave., S., Tukwila, WA 98188-4722 (SAN 631-5593) Tel 206-575-7544; Fax: 206-575-7444; Toll Free: 800-995-4840
E-mail: info@koenpacific.com.

**Kraus Reprint,** *See* **Periodicals Service Co.**

**Kumarian Pr., Inc.,** ( 0-931816; 1-56549; 1-887208 ) 1294 Blue Hills Ave., Bloomfield, CT 06002 (SAN 212-5978) Tel 860-243-2098; Fax: 860-243-2867; Toll Free: 800-289-2664
E-mail: Kpbooks@kpbooks.com.
Web site: http://www.kpbooks.com.

**Kurian, George Reference Bks.,** ( 0-914746 ) Orders Addr.: P.O. Box 519, Baldwin Place, NY 10505 (SAN 203-1981); Edit Addr.: 3689 Campbell Ct., Yorktown Heights, NY 10598 (SAN 110-6236) Tel 914-962-3287.

**Kurtzman Bk. Sales Co.,** 17348 W. 12 Mile Rd., Southfield, MI 48076 (SAN 114-0787) Tel 248-557-7230; Fax: 248-557-8705; Toll Free: 800-869-0505.

**Kuykendall's Pr., Bookstore Div.,** P.O. Box 627, Athens, AL 35612-0627 (SAN 168-9185) Tel 256-232-1754; Toll Free: 800-781-1754.

**L L Company,** ( 0-937892 ) 1647 Manning Ave., Los Angeles, CA 90024 (SAN 110-0009) Tel 310-615-0116; Fax: 310-640-6863; Toll Free: 800-473-3699
E-mail: wallacelab@aol.com.

**La Belle News Agency,** 814 University Blvd., Steubenville, OH 43952 (SAN 169-6858) Tel 740-282-9731.

**La Cite French Bks.,** Div. of The La Cite Group, Inc., P.O. Box 64504, Los Angeles, CA 90064-0504 (SAN 168-9789)
E-mail: lacite@aol.com.

**La Moderna Poesia, Inc.,** 5246 SW Eighth St., Miami, FL 33134 (SAN 169-1139) Tel 305-446-9884; Fax: 305-445-1635.

**Lafayette Bks.,** P.O. Box 758, Mamaroneck, NY 10543-0758 (SAN 135-292X) Tel 914-833-0248.

**Lakeport Distributors, Inc.,** 139 W. 18th St., P.O. Box 6195, Erie, PA 16501 (SAN 169-734X).

**Lambert Bk. Hse., Inc.,** ( 0-89315 ) 4139 Parkway Dr., Florence, AL 35630-6347 (SAN 180-5169) Tel 205-764-4098; 256-974-1529 (orders ask Stan Johnson); Fax: 205-766-9200; Toll Free: 800-551-8511
E-mail: Info@lambertbookhouse.com.

**Landmark Audiobooks,** 4865 Sterling Dr., Boulder, CO 80301 Fax: 303-443-3775
Web site: http://www.landmarkaudio.com.

**Landmark Bk. Co.,** ( 0-929194 ) 131 Hicks St., Brooklyn, NY 11201-2318 (SAN 169-5843).

**Langenscheidt Pubs., Inc.,** ( 0-88729; 3-468; 1-58573; 3-324 ) Subs. of Langenscheidt KG, 46-35 54th Rd., Maspeth, NY 11378 (SAN 276-9441) Tel 718-784-0055 (ext. 108); Fax: 718-784-1216; Toll Free: 800-432-6277
E-mail: spohja@langenscheidt.com
Web site: http://www.langenscheidt.com; http://www.hagstrommap.com.

**Larousse Kingfisher Chambers, Inc.,** ( 0-7534; 1-85697; 970-22 ) 215 Park Ave., S., New York, NY 10003 (SAN 297-7540) Tel 212-420-5800; Fax: 212-686-1082; 181 Ballardvale St., Wilmington, MA 01887
Web site: http://www.lkcpub.com.

**Las Vegas News Agency,** 2312 Silver Bluff Ct., Las Vegas, NV 89134-6092.

**Lash Distributors,** 7106 Geoffrey Way, Frederick, MD 21704 (SAN 169-3131).

**Last Gasp Eco-Funnies, Inc.,** ( 0-86719 ) Orders Addr.: P.O. Box 410067, San Francisco, CA 94141-0067 (SAN 216-8308); Edit Addr.: 777 Florida St., San Francisco, CA 94110-2025 (SAN 170-3242) Tel 415-824-6636; Fax: 415-824-1836; Toll Free: 800-366-5121
E-mail: lastgasp@hooked.net.

**Laster, Larry D. Old & Rare Bks., Prints & Maps,** 2416 Maplewood Ave., Winston-Salem, NC 27103 (SAN 112-9600) Tel 336-724-7544; Fax: 336-724-9055.

**Latcorp, Ltd.,** 10 Norden Ln., Huntington Station, NY 11746 (SAN 159-8910) Tel 516-271-0548; Fax: 516-549-8849.

**Latin American Bk. Source, Inc.,** 289 Third Ave., Chula Vista, CA 91910 Tel 619-426-1226; Fax: 619-426-0212
Web site: http://www.latinbooks.com.

**Latta, J. S. Incorporated,** *See* **Latta's**

**Latta's,** 1502 Fourth Ave., P.O. Box 2668, Huntington, WV 25726 (SAN 169-8982) Fax: 304-525-5038; Toll Free: 800-624-3501.

**LEA Bk. Distributors (Libros Espana y America),** ( 1-883110 ) 170-23 83rd Ave., Jamaica Hills, NY 11432 (SAN 170-5407) Tel 718-291-9891; Fax: 718-291-9830
E-mail: leabook@idt.net
Web site: http://www.leabooks.com.

**Learning Collection, The,** 5180 Smith Rd., Suite B, Denver, CO 80216-4431 (SAN 630-8287) Tel 303-722-9843.

**Lectorum Pubns., Inc.,** ( 0-9625162; 1-880507; 1-930332 ) Subs. of Scholastic, Inc., 205 Chubb Ave., Lyndhurst, NJ 07071-3520 Tel 212-965-7322; Fax: 212-727-3035; Toll Free Fax: 877-532-8676; 877-532-8678; Toll Free: 800-345-5946
E-mail: info@lectorum.com
Web site: http://www.lectorum.com.

**Lee Bks.,** ( 0-939818 ) Div. of Lee S. Cole & Assocs., Inc., 524 San Anselmo Ave., No 215, San Anselmo, CA 94960-2614 (SAN 110-649X) Tel 415-456-4388; Fax: 415-456-7532; Toll Free: 800-828-3550 Do not confuse with other companies with the same or similar names in Jacksonville, FL, Columbia, SC
E-mail: lcs@lsc-associates.com
Web site: http://www.lsc-associates.com.

**Left Bank Books Distribution & Publishing,** *See* **Left Bank Distribution**

**Left Bank Distribution,** ( 0-939306 ) 92 Pike St., Seattle, WA 98101-2025 (SAN 216-5368)
E-mail: leftbank@leftbankbooks.com
Web site: http://www.leftbankbooks.com.

**Leman Pubns., Inc.,** ( 0-943721; 0-9602970 ) Div. of Rodale Pr. Co., Box 4100, 741 Corporate Cir., Suite A, Golden, CO 80401-5622 (SAN 213-3415) Fax: 303-277-0370; Toll Free: 800-877-3775.

**Leonard, Hal Corp.,** ( 0-634; 0-7935; 0-88188; 0-9607350; 1-56516 ) Orders Addr.: P.O. Box 13819, Milwaukee, WI 53213-0819 Tel 414-774-3630; Fax: 414-774-3259; Toll Free: 800-524-4425; Edit Addr.: 7777 W. Bluemound Rd., Milwaukee, WI 53213 (SAN 239-250X)
E-mail: halinfo@halleonard.com
Web site: http://www.halleonard.com.

**Lerner Publishing Group,** ( 0-8225; 0-87614; 0-929371; 0-930494; 1-57505; 1-58013 ) Orders Addr.: 1251 Washington Ave., N., Minneapolis, MN 55401 Toll Free Fax: 800-332-1132; Toll Free: 800-328-4929
E-mail: custserve@lernerbook.com
Web site: http://www.lernerbooks.com; http://www.karben.com.

**Lerner Publishing Group, The,** *See* **Lerner Publishing Group**

**Levine, J. Religious Supplies,** Five W. 30th St., New York, NY 10001 (SAN 169-5878) Tel 212-695-6888; Fax: 212-643-1044
E-mail: sales@levine.judica.com.

**Levy, Charles Co.,** 1200 N. North Branch St., Chicago, IL 60622 (SAN 159-835X) Tel 312-440-4400.

**Levy Home Entertainment,** Div. of Charles Levy Co., 4201 Raymond Dr., Hillside, IL 60162 (SAN 176-2478) Tel 708-547-4400; 708-649-4158; Fax: 708-547-4503; Toll Free: 800-947-1967
E-mail: jsemeneck@levybooks.com.

**Lewis International, Inc.,** ( 0-9666771; 1-930983 ) 2201 NW 102nd Pl., No. 1, Miami, FL 33172 Tel 305-436-7984; Fax: 305-436-7985; Toll Free: 800-259-5962
E-mail: sales@lewisinternational.com
Web site: http://www.lewisinternational.com.

**Lewis, John W. Enterprises,** 168 Perez St., P.O. Box 3375, Santurce, PR 00936 (SAN 169-9334) Tel 809-722-0104.

**Liberation Distributors,** ( 0-89928 ) P.O. Box 5341, Chicago, IL 60680 (SAN 169-880X) Tel 773-248-3442.

**LibertyTree Press,** *See* **Independent Institute**

**Libraries Unlimited,** ( 0-313; 0-87287; 1-56308; 1-59158 ) Div. of Greenwood Publishing Group, Orders Addr.: a/o Customer Service Group, Dept. 2229, P.O. Box 5007, Westport, CT 06881 Fax: 603-431-2214; Toll Free: 800-225-5800; Edit Addr.: 6931 S. Yosemite St., Englewood, CO 80112 Tel 303-770-1220; Fax: 303-220-8843
E-mail: lubooks@lu.com.
Web site: http://www.lu.com.

**Library & Educational Services,** P.O. Box 146, Berrien Springs, MI 49103 Tel 616-695-1800; Fax: 616-695-8500
E-mail: libraryanded@juno.com.

**Library Bk. Selection Service,** P.O. Box 277, 2714 McGraw Dr., Bloomington, IL 61704 (SAN 169-1740) Tel 309-663-1411; Fax: 309-664-0059.

**Library Video Co.,** ( *1-4171* ) P.O. Box 580, Wynnewood, PA 19096 (SAN 631-3205) Fax: 610-645-4050; Toll Free: 800-843-3620 E-mail: cs@libraryvideo.com. Web site: http://www.libraryvideo.com.

**Libreria Bereana,** 1825 San Alejandro, Urb San Ignacio, Rio Piedras, PR 00927-6819 (SAN 169-9288) Tel 809-764-6175.

**Libros de Espana y America,** *See* **LEA Bk. Distributors (Libros Espana y America)**

**Libros Sin Fronteras,** P.O. Box 2085, Olympia, WA 98507 Tel 360-357-4332; Fax: 360-357-4964 E-mail: info@librossinfronteras.com Web site: http://www.librossinfronteras.com.

**Light & Life Publishing Co.,** ( *0-937032; 1-880971* ) 4808 Park Glen Rd., Minneapolis, MN 55416 (SAN 213-8565) Tel 952-925-3888; Fax: 952-925-3918 E-mail: info@light-n-life.com Web site: http://www.light-n-life.com.

**Light Impressions Corp.,** ( *0-87992* ) Orders Addr.: P.O. Box 940, Rochester, NY 14603-0940 (SAN 169-619X) Toll Free Fax: 800-826-5539; Toll Free: 800-828-6216; Edit Addr.: P.O. Box 22708, Rochester, NY 14692-2708 Web site: http://www.lightimpresionsdirect.com.

**Lightning Source, Inc.,** 1246 Heil Quaker Blvd., LaVergne, TN 37086 (SAN 179-6976) Tel 615-213-4595; Fax: 615-213-4426.

**Likely Story Bookfairs, A,** 7210 SW 57th Ave., Suite 207-A, South Miami, FL 33143 (SAN 631-1210) Tel 305-668-9183; Fax: 305-667-3323.

**Lilly News Agency,** P.O. Box 280077, Memphis, TN 38168-0077 (SAN 168-9452).

**LIM Productions, LLC,** ( *1-929617* ) 3553 Northdale St., NW, Uniontown, OH 44685-8004 Toll Free: 877-628-4532 E-mail: customerservice@limproductions.com Web site: http://www.limproductions.com.

**Limerock Bks., Inc.,** P.O. Box 57, New Canaan, CT 06840 (SAN 630-8708) Tel 203-322-5352; Fax: 203-322-2182 Do not confuse with Limerock Books, Thomaston, ME E-mail: limerockbk@aol.com Web site: http://www.netpocus.com/limerock.

**Linden Tree Children's Records & Bks.,** 170 State St., Los Altos, CA 94022 (SAN 131-744X) Tel 415-949-3390; Fax: 415-949-0346.

**Ling's International Bks.,** Orders Addr.: P.O. Box 82684, San Diego, CA 92138 (SAN 169-0116) Tel 619-292-8104; Fax: 619-292-8207; Edit Addr.: 3396 Via Cabo Verde., Escondido, CA 92029-7459.

**Linx Educational Publishing, Inc.,** ( *1-891818* ) P.O. Box 50009, Jacksonville Beach, FL 32240 Tel 904-241-1861; Fax: 904-241-3279; Toll Free Fax: 888-546-9338; Toll Free: 800-717-5469 E-mail: Liniangraham@lixedu.com Web site: http://www..linxedu.com.

**Lippincott Williams & Wilkins,** ( *0-316; 0-397; 0-683; 0-7817; 0-8067; 0-8121; 0-88167; 0-89004; 0-89313; 0-89640; 0-911216; 1-881063; 4-260* ) Orders Addr.: P.O. Box 1600, Hagerstown, MD 21741 Fax: 301-223-2400; Toll Free: 800-638-3030; Edit Addr.: 530 Walnut St., Philadelphia, PA 19106-3621 (SAN 201-0933) Tel 215-521-8300; Fax: 215-521-8902; Toll Free: 800-638-3030; 351 W. Camden St., Baltimore, MD 21201 Tel 410-528-4000; 345 Hudson St., 16th Flr., New York, NY 10014 Tel 212-886-1200; 16522 Hunters Green Pkwy., Hagerstown, MD 21740 Tel 301-223-2300; Fax: 301-223-2398; Toll Free: 800-638-3030 E-mail: custserv@lww.com; orders@lww.com Web site: http://www.lww.com.

**Lippincott-Raven Publishers,** *See* **Lippincott Williams & Wilkins**

**Literal Book Distributors: Books in Spanish,** Orders Addr.: P.O. Box 7113, Langley Park, MD 20787; Edit Addr.: 7705 Georgia Ave. NW, Suite 102, Washington, DC 20012 (SAN 113-2784) Tel 202-723-8688; Fax: 202-882-6592; Toll Free: 800-366-8680.

**Little Brown & Co.,** ( *0-316; 0-8212* ) Div. of Time Warner Bk. Group, Orders Addr.: 3 Center Plaza, Boston, MA 02108-2084 (SAN 630-7248) Tel 617-227-0730; Toll Free Fax: 800-286-9471; Toll Free: 800-759-0190; Edit Addr.: Time & Life Bldg., 1271 Avenue of the Americas, New York, NY 10020 (SAN 200-2205) Tel 212-522-8700; Fax: 212-522-2067; Toll Free: 800-343-9204 E-mail: cust.service@littlebrown.com Web site: http://www.littlebrown.com.

**Little Dania's Juvenile Promotions,** Div. of Booksmith Promotional Co., 100 Paterson Plank Rd., Jersey City, NJ 07307 (SAN 169-5681) Tel 201-659-2317; Fax: 201-659-3631 E-mail: hochberga@aol.com

**Little Professor Bk. Ctrs., Inc.,** P.O. Box 3160, Ann Arbor, MI 48106-3160 (SAN 144-2503) Toll Free: 800-899-6232.

**Login Fulfillment Services,** *See* **LPC Group**

**London Bridge,** Div. of General Distribution Services, Orders Addr.: 4500 Witmer Industrial EST, Niagara Falls, NY 14305-1386 Toll Free: 800-805-1083.

**Lone Pine Publishing,** ( *0-919433; 1-55105* ) 1808 B St., NW, Suite 140, Auburn, WA 98001 Tel 425-204-5965; Fax: 425-204-6036; Toll Free Fax: 800-548-1169; Toll Free: 800-518-3541 E-mail: rtruppner@lonepinepublishing.com Web site: http://www.lonepinepublishing.com.

**Lonely Planet Pubns.,** ( *0-86442; 0-908086; 1-55992; 2-84070; 1-86450; 1-74059; 88-7063; 1-74104* ) 150 Linden St., Oakland, CA 94607 (SAN 659-6541) Tel 510-893-8555; Fax: 510-893-8563; Toll Free: 800-275-8555 (orders, 9am - 5pm Pacific Time) E-mail: gary.todoroff@lonelyplanet.com Web site: http://www.lonelyplanet.com.

**Long Beach Bks., Inc.,** P.O. Box 179, Long Beach, NY 11561-0179 (SAN 164-632X) Tel 718-471-5934.

**Looseleaf Law Pubns., Inc.,** ( *0-930137; 1-889031* ) Orders Addr.: P.O. Box 650042, Fresh Meadows, NY 11365-0042 Tel 718-359-5559; Fax: 718-539-0941; Toll Free: 800-647-5547; Edit Addr.: 43-08 162nd St., Flushing, NY 11358 (SAN 135-0099) E-mail: llawpub@erols.com Web site: http://www.looseleaflaw.com.

**Lord's Line,** ( *0-915952* ) 1065 Lomita Blvd., No. 434, Harbor City, CA 90710-1944 (SAN 169-0051).

**Los Angeles Mart, The,** 1933 S. Broadway, Suite 665, Los Angeles, CA 90007 (SAN 168-9797) Tel 213-748-6449; Fax: 714-523-0796.

**Louisville Distributors,** *See* **United Magazine**

**Louisville News Co.,** P.O. Box 36, Columbia, KY 42728 (SAN 169-281X) Tel 502-384-3444; Fax: 502-384-9324.

**LPC Group,** c/o CDS, 193 Edwards Dr., Jackson, TN 38305 (SAN 630-5644) Fax: 731-935-7731; 731-423-1973; Toll Free Fax: 800-351-5073; Toll Free: 800-343-4499 E-mail: lpc-info@lpcgroup.com Web site: http://www.lpcgroup.com.

**Lubrecht & Cramer, Ltd.,** ( *0-934454; 0-945345* ) 18 E. Main St., Port Jervis, NY 12771; Edit Addr.: P.O. Box 3110, Port Jervis, NY 12771 (SAN 214-1256) Toll Free: 800-920-9334; 350 Fifth Ave., Suite 3304, New York, NY 10118-0069 E-mail: lubrecht@frontiernet.net; books@lubrechtcramer.com Web site: http://www.lubrechtcramer.com.

**Ludington News Co.,** 1600 E. Grand Blvd., Detroit, MI 48211-3195 (SAN 169-3751) Tel 313-929-7600.

**Lushena Bks.,** ( *1-930097* ) 607 Country Club Dr., Unit E, Bensenville, IL 60106 (SAN 630-5105) Tel 630-238-8708; Fax: 630-238-8824 E-mail: Lushenabks@yahoo.com Web site: http://lushena.com.

**L-W, Inc.,** ( *0-89538* ) P.O. Box 69, Gas City, IN 46933 (SAN 159-6292) Tel 765-674-6450; Fax: 765-674-3503; Toll Free: 800-777-6450 E-mail: catalogs@lwbooks.com; lwbooks@comteek.com Web site: http://www.lwbooks.com.

**Lynx Hse. Pr.,** ( *0-89924* ) 420 W. 24th Ave., Spokane, WA 99203-1922 (SAN 250-3344) Tel 309-624-4594; Fax: 309-623-4238 E-mail: cnhowell@mail.ewu.edu.

**M & J Bk. Fair Service,** 2307 Sherwood Cir., Minneapolis, MN 55431 (SAN 169-4030).

**M & M News Agency,** Orders Addr.: P.O. Box 1129, La Salle, IL 61301 (SAN 169-2062) Fax: 815-223-2828; Toll Free: 800-245-6247.

**M L E S,** *See* **Pathway Bk. Service**

**Ma'ayan,** *See* **WellSpring Bks.**

**MacGregor News Agency,** 1733 Industrial Park Dr., Mount Pleasant, MI 48858 (SAN 169-3921) Toll Free: 800-626-1982.

**Macmillan USA,** *See* **Alpha Bks.**

**MacRae's Indian Bk. Distributor,** 1605 Cole St., P.O. Box 652, Enumclaw, WA 98022 (SAN 157-5473) Tel 360-825-3737.

**Madison Art Ctr., Inc.,** ( *0-913883* ) 211 State St., Madison, WI 53703 Tel 608-257-0158; Fax: 608-257-5722 E-mail: mac@itis.com Web site: http://www.madisonartcenter.org.

**Magazine Distributors, Inc.,** 15 Sparks St., Plainville, CT 06062 (SAN 169-0817).

**Magazines, Inc.,** 1135 Hammond St., Bangor, ME 04401 (SAN 169-3034) Tel 207-942-8237; Fax: 207-942-9226; Toll Free: 800-649-9224 (in Maine) E-mail: pam@mint.net.

**Mahoning Valley Distributing Agency, Inc.,** 2556 Rush Blvd., Youngstown, OH 44507 Tel 330-788-6162; Fax: 330-788-9046.

**Majic Enterprises,** 313 E. Main St., Niles, MI 49120-2305 (SAN 169-8508).

**Majors, J. A. Co.,** Orders Addr.: 1401 Lakeway Dr., Lewisville, TX 75057 (SAN 169-8117) Tel 972-353-1100; Fax: 972-353-1300; Toll Free: 800-633-1851 E-mail: dallas@majors.com Web site: http://www.majors.com.

**Manchester News Co., Inc.,** P.O. Box 4838, Manchester, NH 03108-4838 (SAN 169-4480).

**Manhattan Publishing Co.,** Div. of U.S. & Europe Bks., Inc., P.O. Box 850, Croton-on-Hudson, NY 10520 (SAN 113-7476) Tel 914-271-5194; Fax: 914-271-5856 Web site: http://www.manhattanpublishing.com.

**Manitowoc News Agency,** 907 S. Eighth St., Manitowoc, WI 54220 (SAN 159-9046).

**Manning's Bks. & Prints,** 580M Crespi Dr., Pacifica, CA 94044 (SAN 157-5384) Fax: 650-355-1851 E-mail: manningsbks@aol.com Web site: http://www.printsoldandrare.com.

**Many Feathers Bks. & Maps,** 2626 W. Indian School Rd., Phoenix, AZ 85017 (SAN 158-8877) Tel 602-266-1043; Toll Free: 800-279-7652.

**Marco Bk. Distributors,** ( *0-88298* ) P.O. Box 30108, Brooklyn, NY 11203-0108 (SAN 169-5142) Tel 718-774-0750; Fax: 718-774-0380; Toll Free: 800-842-4234.

**Marcus Wholesale,** P.O. Box 1618, R49 E. Hwy. 4, Murphys, CA 95247 (SAN 185-0296).

**Mardelva News Co., Inc.,** 8999 Ocean Hwy., Delmar, MD 21875 (SAN 169-3247) Tel 410-742-8613; Fax: 410-742-2616.

**Marshall-Mangold Distribution Co., Inc.,** 4805 Nelson Ave., Baltimore, MD 21215-2507 (SAN 169-3115) Toll Free: 800-972-2665.

**Maruzen International Co., Ltd.,** 1200 Harbor Blvd., 10th Flr., Weehawken, NJ 07087 (SAN 630-6012) Tel 201-865-4400; Fax: 201-865-4845.

**Marvin Law Bk.,** 11020 27th Ave., S., Burnsville, MN 55337 (SAN 163-898X) Tel 612-644-2236.

**Matthews Medical Bk. Co.,** Four Sperry Rd., Fairfield, NJ 07004 (SAN 169-4316) Tel 973-276-7991; Fax: 973-276-7994.

**Maughan, Graham,** *See* **Maughan, Graham Publishing Co.**

**Maughan, Graham Publishing Co.,** 50 E. 500, S., Provo, UT 84601-3203 (SAN 110-3903) Tel 801-377-3335; Toll Free: 800-234-3335.

**Maus Tales,** 77-490 Loma Vista, La Quinta, CA 92253 Fax: 760-564-6669 E-mail: maustales@aol.com.

**Maverick Distributors,** ( *1-884646* ) Orders Addr.: Drawer 7289, Bend, OR 97708 (SAN 298-3222) Tel 541-382-2728; Fax: 541-382-8444; Toll Free: 800-333-8046.

**Maxwell Scientific International, Inc.,** ( *0-8277* ) Div. of Pergamon Pr., Inc., 1345 Ave. of the Americas, No. 1036C, New York, NY 10105-0302 (SAN 169-524X) Tel 914-592-9141.

**MBI Distribution Services,** ( *0-7603; 0-87938; 0-912612; 1-85010* ) Div. of MBI Publishing Co. LLC, Orders Addr.: 729 Prospect Ave., Osceola, WI 54020 (SAN 169-9164) Tel 715-294-3345; Fax: 715-294-4448; Toll Free: 800-458-0454; Edit Addr.: 380 Jackson St., Suite 200, Saint Paul, MN 55101-3885 Tel 651-287-5000; Fax: 651-287-5001 E-mail: mbibks@win.bright.net Web site: http://www.motorbooks.com.

**MBS Textbook Exchange, Inc.,** Orders Addr.: 2711 W. Ash, Columbia, MO 65203-4613 (SAN 140-7015) Tel 573-445-2243; Fax: 573-446-5254; Toll Free: 800-325-0929 (orders); 800-325-0530 (customer service) Web site: http://www.mbsbooks.com.

**McCaslin, Boyce,** 3 Greenbriar Dr., Saint Louis, MO 63124-1819 (SAN 110-8298).

**McCoy Church Goods,** 1010 Howard Ave., San Mateo, CA 94401 (SAN 107-2315) Tel 415-342-0924.

**McCrory's Books,** *See* **McCrory's Wholesale Bks.**

**McCrory's Wholesale Bks.,** Orders Addr.: P.O. Box 2032, Alexandria, LA 71301 (SAN 108-5999); Edit Addr.: 1808 Rapides Ave., Alexandria, LA 71301.

Wholesalers & Distributors

**McGraw-Hill Cos., The,** ( *0-02; 0-07* ) 6480 Jimmy Carter Blvd., Norcross, GA 30071-1701 (SAN 254-881X) Tel 614-755-5637; Fax: 614-755-5611; Orders Addr.: 860 Taylor Station Rd., Blacklick, OH 43004-0545 (SAN 200-254X) Fax 614-755-5645; Toll Free: 800-338-3987 (college); 800-525-5003 (subscriptions); 800-352-3566 (books - US/Canada orders); 800-722-4726 (orders & customer service); P.O. Box 545, Blacklick, OH 43004-0545 Fax: 614-759-3759; Toll Free: 877-833-5524; a/o General Customer Service, P.O. Box 182604, Columbus, OH 43272 Fax: 614-759-3759; Toll Free: 877-833-5524 E-mail: customer.service@mcgraw-hill.com Web site: http://www.ebooks.mcgraw-hill.com/; http://www.mcgraw-hill.com.

**McGraw-Hill Osborne,** ( *0-07; 0-88134; 0-931988* ) Div. of The McGraw-Hill Professional, 2100 Powell St., 10th Flr., Emeryville, CA 94608 (SAN 274-3450) Tel 510-596-6600; Fax: 510-420-7740; Toll Free: 800-227-0900 E-mail: customer.service@mcgraw-hill.com Web site: http://www.osborne.com.

**McGraw-Hill Primis Custom Publishing,** ( *0-390* ) Div. of McGraw-Hill Higher Education, 148 Princeton-Hightstown Rd., Hightstown, NJ 08520-1450 Tel 609-426-5721; Toll Free: 800-962-9342.

**McGraw-Hill/Contemporary,** ( *0-658; 0-8092; 0-8325; 0-8442; 0-88499; 0-89061; 0-913327; 0-940279; 0-941263; 0-9630646; 1-56626; 1-56943; 1-57028* ) Div. of McGraw-Hill Higher Education, 4255 W. Touhy Ave., Lincolnwood, IL 60712 (SAN 169-2208) Tel 847-679-5500; Fax: 847-679-2494; Toll Free Fax: 800-998-3103; Toll Free: 800-323-4900 E-mail: c_patton-vanbuskirk@mcgraw-hill.com; ntcpub@tribune.com Web site: http://www.ntc-cb.com.

**McKay, David Co., Inc.,** ( *0-679; 0-88326; 0-89440* ) Subs. of Random Hse., Inc., Orders Addr.: 400 Hahn Rd., Westminster, MD 21157 Tel 410-848-1900; Toll Free: 800-733-3000 (orders only); Edit Addr.: 201 E. 50th St., MD 4-6, New York, NY 10022 (SAN 200-240X) Tel 212-751-2600; Fax: 212-872-8026.

**McKnight Sales Co.,** P.O. Box 4138, Pittsburgh, PA 15202 (SAN 169-7587) Tel 412-761-4443; Fax: 412-761-0122; Toll Free: 800-208-8078 E-mail: sales@mscmags.com Web site: http://www.mscmags.com.

**McLemore, Hollern & Assocs.,** Orders Addr.: 3538 Maple Park Dr., Kingwood, TX 77339 Tel 281-360-5204.

**McPherson & Co.,** ( *0-914232; 0-929701* ) Orders Addr.: P.O. Box 1126, Kingston, NY 12402 (SAN 203-0624) Tel 845-331-5807; Toll Free: 800-613-8219 E-mail: bmcpher@ulster.net Web site: http://www.mcphersonco.com.

**Medicina Biologica,** 2937 NE Flanders St., Portland, OR 97232 (SAN 113-0226) Tel 503-287-6775; Fax: 503-235-3520 E-mail: med_bio@imagina.com.

**Mel Bay Pubns., Inc.,** ( *0-7866; 0-87166; 1-56222* ) Orders Addr.: Four Industrial Dr., Pacific, MO 63069; Edit Addr.: P.O. Box 66, Pacific, MO 63069-0066 (SAN 657-3630) Tel 636-257-3970; Fax: 636-257-5062; Toll Free: 800-863-5229 E-mail: catalog@melbay.com; email@melbay.com Web site: http://www.melbay.com.

**Melton Book Company, Incorporated,** *See* **Nelson Direct**

**Merced News Co.,** 1324 Coldwell Ave., Modesto, CA 95350-5702 (SAN 168-9894) Tel 209-722-5791.

**Mercedes Book Distributors Corporation,** *See* **Mercedes Distribution Ctr., Inc.**

**Mercedes Distribution Ctr., Inc.,** Brooklyn Navy Yard, Bldg. No. 3, Brooklyn, NY 11205 (SAN 169-5150) Tel 718-522-7111; Fax: 718-935-9647; Toll Free: 800-339-4804 E-mail: contact@.mdist.com.

**Merkos Pubns.,** 291 Kingston Ave., Brooklyn, NY 11213 (SAN 631-1040) Tel 718-778-0226; Fax: 718-778-4148.

**Merry Thoughts,** ( *0-88230* ) 364 Adams St., Bedford Hills, NY 10507 (SAN 169-5061) Tel 914-241-0447; Fax: 914-241-0247.

**Metamorphosis Publishing Company,** *See* **Metamorphous Pr., Inc.**

**Metamorphous Pr., Inc.,** ( *0-943920; 1-55552* ) Orders Addr.: P.O. Box 10616, Portland, OR 97296-0616 (SAN 110-8786) Tel 503-228-4972; Fax: 503-223-9117; Toll Free: 800-937-7771 (orders only); Edit Addr.: 2950 NW 29th Ave., Portland, OR 97210 E-mail: metabooks@metamodels.com Web site: http://www.metamodels.com.

**Metro Systems,** 3381 Stevens Creek Blvd., Suite 209, San Jose, CA 95117 (SAN 113-1016) Tel 408-247-4050; Fax: 408-247-4236.

**Metropolitan News Co.,** 47-25 34th, Long Island City, NY 11101 (SAN 159-9089) Do not confuse with Metropolitan News Co. in Los Angeles, CA.

**Miami Bks., Inc.,** 17842 State Rd. 9, Miami, FL 33162 (SAN 106-8997) Tel 305-652-3231.

**Miami Valley News Agency,** 2127 Old Troy Pike, Dayton, OH 45404 (SAN 169-6718) Fax: 513-233-8544; Toll Free: 800-791-5137.

**Michiana News Service,** 2232 S. 11th St., Niles, MI 49120 (SAN 110-5051) Tel 616-684-3013; Fax: 616-684-8740.

**Michigan Church Supply,** P.O. Box 279, Mount Morris, MI 48458-0279 (SAN 184-413X) Toll Free: 800-521-3440.

**Michigan State Univ. Pr.,** ( *0-87013; 0-937191* ) 1405 S. Harrison Rd. Suite 25, East Lansing, MI 48823 (SAN 202-6295) Tel 517-355-9543; Fax: 517-432-2611 E-mail: msupress@msu.edu Web site: http://www.msupress.msu.edu.

**Mickler's Bks., Inc.,** 61 Alafaya Woods Blvd., No. 197, Oviedo, FL 32765 Tel 407-365-8500; Toll Free Fax: 800-726-0585 E-mail: orders@micklers.com Web site: http://www.micklers.com.

**Micklers Floridiana, Incorporated,** *See* **Mickler's Bks., Inc.**

**Microdistributors International, Inc.,** ( *0-918025* ) Subs. of Medcomp Technologies, Inc., 34 Maple Ave., P.O. Box 8, Armonk, NY 10504 (SAN 296-158X) Tel 914-273-6480.

**Mid Penn Magazine Agency,** 100 Eck Cir., Williamsport, PA 17701 (SAN 169-7692).

**Mid South Manufacturing Agency, Incorporated,** *See* **Mid-South Magazine Agency, Inc.**

**Mid-Cal Periodical Distributors,** P.O. Box 245230, Sacramento, CA 95824-5230 (SAN 169-0078).

**Midpoint National, Inc.,** 1263 Southwest Blvd., Kansas City, MO 66103-1901 (SAN 630-9860) Tel 913-831-2233; Fax: 913-362-7401; Toll Free: 800-228-4321.

**Midpoint Trade Bks., Inc.,** Orders Addr.: 1263 Southwest Blvd., Kansas City, KS 66103 (SAN 631-3736) Tel 913-831-2233; Fax: 913-362-7401; Toll Free: 800-742-6139 (consumer orders); Edit Addr.: 27 W. 20th St., No. 1102, New York, NY 10011 (SAN 631-1075) Tel 212-727-0190; Fax: 212-727-0195; P.O. Box 411037, Kansas City, MO 64141-1037 (SAN 253-8539) Tel 913-362-7400; Fax: 913-362-7401 E-mail: midpointny1@aol.com Web site: http://midpt.com.

**Mid-South Magazine Agency, Inc.,** P.O. Box 4585, Jackson, MS 39296-4585 (SAN 286-0163) Toll Free: 800-748-9444.

**Mid-State Periodicals, Inc.,** P.O. Box 3455, Quincy, IL 62305-3455 Tel 217-222-0833; Fax: 217-222-1256.

**Mid-States Distributors,** 1201 Sheffler Dr., Chambersburg, PA 17201 (SAN 169-3166) Tel 717-263-2413; Fax: 717-263-7289.

**Midtown Auto Bks.,** 212 Burnet Ave., Syracuse, NY 13203 (SAN 169-6289).

**Midwest European Pubns.,** 915 Foster St., Evanston, IL 60201 (SAN 169-1937) Tel 847-866-6289; Fax: 847-866-6290; Toll Free: 800-380-8919 E-mail: info@mep-eli.com Web site: http://www.mep-eli.com.

**Midwest Library Service,** 11443 St. Charles Rock Rd., Bridgeton, MO 63044-2789 (SAN 169-4243) Tel 314-739-3100; Fax: 314-739-1326; Toll Free Fax: 800-962-1009; Toll Free: 800-325-8833 E-mail: hudson@midwestls.com.

**Military History Assocs.,** 407B E. Sixth St., No. 200, Austin, TX 78701-3739 (SAN 111-7866).

**Milligan News Co., Inc.,** 150 N. Autumn St., San Jose, CA 95110 (SAN 169-0272) Tel 408-286-7604; Fax: 408-298-0235; Toll Free: 800-873-2387.

**Minerva Science Bookseller, Inc.,** 175 Fifth Ave., New York, NY 10010 (SAN 286-0171).

**Mississippi Library Media & Supply Co.,** P.O. Box 108, Brandon, MS 39043-0108 (SAN 169-4189) Tel 601-824-1900; Fax: 601-824-1999; Toll Free: 800-257-7566 (in Mississippi).

**MIT Pr.,** ( *0-262* ) Orders Addr.: c/o Triliteral LLC, 100 Maple Ridge Dr., Cumberland, RI 02864 Tel 401-531-2800; Fax: 401-531-2801; Toll Free Fax: 800-406-9145; Toll Free: 800-405-1619; Edit Addr.: 5 Cambridge Ctr., Suite 4, Cambridge, MA 02142-1493 (SAN 202-6414) Tel 617-253-5646; Fax: 617-253-6779 E-mail: mitpress-orders@mit.edu Web site: http://mitpress.mit.edu.

**Mobile News Co.,** 1118 14th St., Tuscaloosa, AL 35401-3318 (SAN 168-924X) Tel 334-479-1435.

**Modesto News Co.,** 1324 Coldwell Ave., Modesto, CA 95350-5702 (SAN 168-9908) Tel 209-577-5551.

**Montfort Pubns.,** ( *0-910984* ) Div. of Montfort Missionaries, 26 S. Saxon Ave., Bay Shore, NY 11706-8993 (SAN 169-5053) Tel 631-665-0726; Fax: 631-665-4349 Web site: http://www.montfortmissionaries.com.

**Mook & Blanchard,** 546 S. Hofgaarden, La Puente, CA 91744 (SAN 168-9703) Tel 626-968-6424; Fax: 626-968-6877; Toll Free: 800-875-9911 E-mail: mookbook@ix.netcom.com Web site: http://www.mookandblanchard.com.

**Moon Over the Mountain Publishing Company,** *See* **Leman Pubns., Inc.**

**More, Thomas Assn.,** 205 W. Monroe St., 5th Flr., Chicago, IL 60606-5097 (SAN 169-1880) Tel 312-609-8880; Toll Free: 800-835-8965.

**Morehouse Publishing,** ( *0-8192* ) Orders Addr.: P.O. Box 1321, Harrisburg, PA 17105-1321 (SAN 202-6511) Tel 717-541-8130; Fax: 717-541-8128; Toll Free: 800-877-0012; Edit Addr.: 4775 Linglestown Rd., Harrisburg, PA 17112 Tel 717-541-8130; 717-236-0366; Fax: 717-541-8136 E-mail: morehouse@morehousegroup.com Web site: http://www.morehousegroup.com.

**Morlock News Co., Inc.,** 496 Duanesburg Rd., Schenectady, NY 12306 (SAN 169-6246).

**Morris Publishing,** ( *0-7392; 0-9631249; 1-57502; 1-885591* ) Subs. of Morris Pr. & Office Supplies, 3212 E. Hwy. 30, P.O. Box 2110, Kearney, NE 68847 Tel 308-236-7888; Fax: 308-237-0263; Toll Free: 800-650-7888 Do not confuse with companies with the same or similar name in Sarveta, PA, Plymouth Meeting, PA, Beecher City, IL, Urbana, IL, San Francisco, CA E-mail: publish@morrispublishing.com; kimmyw414@yahoo.com; snowgers@mcn.org Web site: http://morrispublishing.com.

**Moshy Brothers, Inc.,** 127 W. 25th St., New York, NY 10001 (SAN 169-5886) Tel 212-255-0613.

**Mother Lode Distributing,** 17890 Lime Rock Dr., Sonora, CA 95370-8707 (SAN 169-0361).

**Motorbooks International Wholesalers & Distributors,** *See* **MBI Distribution Services**

**Mountain Pr. Publishing Co., Inc.,** ( *0-87842* ) Orders Addr.: P.O. Box 2399, Missoula, MT 59806-2399 (SAN 202-8832) Tel 406-728-1900; Fax: 406-728-1635; Toll Free: 800-234-5308; Edit Addr.: 1301 S. Third West, Missoula, MT 59801 (SAN 662-0868) E-mail: johnargyle@aol.com; mtnpress@montana.com Web site: http://www.mountainpresspublish.com.

**Mountain States News Distributor,** P.O. Drawer P, Fort Collins, CO 80522 Tel 970-221-2330; Fax: 970-221-1251.

**Mountaineers Bks., The,** ( *0-89886; 0-916890; 0-938567; 1-59485* ) Div. of Mountaineers, Orders Addr.: 1001 SW Klickitat Way, Suite 201, Seattle, WA 98134-1162 (SAN 212-8756) Tel 206-223-6303; Fax: 206-223-6306; Toll Free: 800-568-7604 E-mail: mbooks@mountaineersbooks.org Web site: http://www.mountaineersbooks.org.

**Mouse Works,** ( *0-7364; 1-57082* ) Div. of Disney Bk. Publishing, Inc., A Walt Disney Co., 114 Fifth Ave., New York, NY 10011 (SAN 298-0797) Tel 212-633-4400; Fax: 212-633-4811 Web site: http://www.disneybooks.com.

**Moznaim Publishing Corp.,** ( *0-940118; 1-885220* ) 4304 12th Ave., Brooklyn, NY 11219 (SAN 214-4123) Tel 718-438-7680; Fax: 718-438-1305; Toll Free: 800-364-5118.

**Mr. Paperback/Publishers News Co.,** 6030 Fostoria Ave., Findlay, OH 45840 (SAN 169-393X) Tel 419-424-6774; Fax: 419-420-1805; Toll Free: 800-872-0031.

**M-S News Co., Inc.,** P.O. Box 13278, Wichita, KS 67213-0278 Fax: 316-267-5405.

**Mullare News Agency, Inc.,** P.O. Box 578, Brockton, MA 02401 (SAN 169-3379) Tel 508-580-1000; Fax: 508-586-0968.

**Wholesalers & Distributors**

**Multilingual Bks.,** Orders Addr.: P.O. Box 440632, Miami, FL 33144 (SAN 169-1155) Tel 305-471-9847 Do not confuse with Multilingual Bks., Seattle, WA.

**Mumford Library Bks., Inc.,** 7847 Bayberry Rd., Jacksonville, FL 32256 (SAN 156-7721) Fax: 904-730-8913; Toll Free: 800-367-3927.

**Mumford Library Book Sales,** *See* **Mumford Library Bks., Inc.**

**Murr's Library Service,** 4045 E. Palm Ln., No. 5, Phoenix, AZ 85008-3116 (SAN 107-3222) Fax: 602-273-1217; Toll Free: 888-273-0279.

**Muses, The,** 820 W. Union St., Morganton, NC 28655.

**Music Design, Inc.,** 4650 N. Port Washington Rd., Milwaukee, WI 53212 (SAN 200-7649) Tel 414-961-8380; Fax: 414-961-8381; Toll Free: 800-862-7232
E-mail: order@musicdesign.com
Web site: http://www.musicdesign.com.

**Music Sales Corp.,** ( *0-7119; 0-8256* ) Orders Addr.: 445 Bellvale Rd., P.O. Box 572, Chester, NY 10918 (SAN 662-0876) Tel 845-469-2271; Fax: 845-469-7544; Toll Free Fax: 800-345-6842; Toll Free: 800-431-7187; Edit Addr.: 257 Park Ave., S., 20th Flr., New York, NY 10010 (SAN 282-0277) Tel 212-254-2100; Fax: 212-254-2103
Web site: http://www.musicsales.com.

**Musicart West,** P.O. Box 1900, Orem, UT 84059-1900 (SAN 110-1250) Tel 801-225-0859; Toll Free: 800-950-1900 (orders only).

**MVP Wholesales,** 9301 W. Hwy. 290, No. D, Austin, TX 78736-7817 (SAN 630-9550) Tel 512-416-1452; Toll Free: 800-328-7931 (phone/fax).

**Mystic Seaport Museum, Inc.,** ( *0-913372* ) 75 Greenmanville Ave., Mystic, CT 06355-0990 (SAN 213-7550) Tel 860-572-5347; Fax: 860-572-5348
E-mail: publications@mysticseaport.org.

**NACSCORP, Inc.,** Subs. of National Assn. of College Stores, Orders Addr.: 528 E. Lorain St., Oberlin, OH 44074-1298 (SAN 134-2118) Tel 440-775-7777; Toll Free Fax: 800-344-5059; Toll Free: 800-321-3883 (orders only); 800-458-9303 (backorder status only); 800-334-9882 (support programs/technical support)
E-mail: service@nacscorp.com; orders@nacscorp.com
Web site: http://www.nacscorp.com.

**Najarian Music Co., Inc.,** 269 Lexington St., Waltham, MA 02452 (SAN 169-3344) Tel 781-899-2200; Fax: 781-899-0838.

**Napa Book Company,** *See* **Napa Children's Bk. Co.**

**Napa Children's Bk. Co.,** 1239 First St., Napa, CA 94559 (SAN 122-2732) Tel 707-224-3893; Fax: 707-224-1212.

**National Assn. of the Deaf,** ( *0-913072* ) 814 Thayer Ave., Silver Spring, MD 20910 (SAN 159-4974) Tel 301-587-6282; Fax: 301-587-4873
E-mail: sales@nad.org
Web site: http://www.nad.org.

**National Bk. Co.,** Keystone Industrial Pk., Scranton, PA 18512 Tel 717-346-2020; Toll Free: 800-233-4830 Do not confuse with National Book Company, Portland, OR.

**National Bk. Network,** Div. of Rowman & Littlefield Pubs., Inc., Orders Addr.: 15200 NBN Way, Blue Ridge Summit, PA 17214 (SAN 630-0065) Tel 717-794-3800; Fax: 717-794-3803; Toll Free Fax: 800-338-4550; Toll Free: 800-462-6420; a/o Les Petriw, 67 Mowat Ave., Suite 241, Toronto, ON M6P 3K3 Tel 416-534-1660; Fax: 416-534-3699; Edit Addr.: 4501 Forbes Blvd., Suite 200, Lanham, MD 20706 Tel 301-459-3366; Fax: 301-429-5747
E-mail: lpetriw@nbnbooks.com
Web site: http://www.nbnbooks.com.

**National Catholic Reading Distributor,** 997 Macarthur Blvd., Mahwah, NJ 07430 (SAN 169-4855) Tel 201-825-7300; Fax: 201-825-8345; Toll Free: 800-218-1903
E-mail: paulistp@pipeline.com.

**National Health Federation,** Box 688, Monrovia, CA 91016 (SAN 227-9266) Tel 626-357-2181; Fax: 818-303-0642
E-mail: nhf@earthlink.net
Web site: http://www.healthfreedom.net.

**National Learning Corp.,** ( *0-8293; 0-8373* ) 212 Michael Dr., Syosset, NY 11791 (SAN 206-8869) Tel 516-921-8888; Fax: 516-921-8743; Toll Free: 800-645-6337
E-mail: sales@passbooks.com.

**National Magazine Service,** Orders Addr.: P.O. Box 834, Mars, PA 16046 (SAN 169-7595); Edit Addr.: 535 Linden Way, Pittsburgh, PA 15202 Tel 412-898-0001.

**National Organization Service, Inc.,** 4515 Fleur Dr., Suite 301, Des Moines, IA 50321-2369 (SAN 107-1548) Fax: 515-256-8028; Toll Free: 800-747-3032.

**National Rifle Assn.,** ( *0-935998* ) a/o Office of the General Counsel, 11250 Waples Mill Rd., Fairfax, VA 22030 (SAN 213-859X) Tel 703-267-1269; Fax: 703-267-3985; Toll Free: 800-672-3888.

**National Sales, Inc.,** 1818 W. 2300 South, Salt Lake City, UT 84119 (SAN 159-9127) Tel 801-972-2300; Fax: 801-972-2883.

**National Technical Information Service, U.S. Dept. of Commerce,** ( *0-934213* ) Orders Addr.: 5285 Port Royal Rd., Springfield, VA 22161 (SAN 205-7255) Tel 703-605-6000; Fax: 703-605-6900; Toll Free: 800-553-6847
E-mail: orders@ntis.gov; info@ntis.gov
Web site: http://wnc.fedworld.gov; http://www.ntis.gov.

**Native Bks.,** P.O. Box 37095, Honolulu, HI 96837 (SAN 631-1121) Tel 808-845-8949; Fax: 808-847-6637; Toll Free: 800-887-7751.

**Naval Institute Pr.,** ( *0-87021; 1-55750; 1-59114* ) Orders Addr.: 2062 Generals Hwy., Annapolis, MD 21401 (SAN 662-0930) Tel 410-268-6110; Fax: 410-571-1703; Toll Free: 800-233-8764; Edit Addr.: 291 Wood Rd., Beach Hall, Annapolis, MD 21402-5034 (SAN 202-9006)
E-mail: psappington@usni.org
Web site: http://www.navalinstitute.org.

**Neighborhood Periodical Club, Inc.,** 653 Northland Blvd., Cincinnati, OH 45240-3215 (SAN 285-9262) Tel 513-851-8600; Fax: 513-851-8695.

**Nelson Direct,** P.O. Box 140300, Nashville, TN 37214 (SAN 169-8133) Toll Free: 800-441-0511 (sales); 800-933-9673
E-mail: csalazar@thomasnelson.com
Web site: http://www.nelsondirect.com.

**Nelson News, Inc.,** P.O. Box 27007, Omaha, NE 68127-0007 (SAN 169-443X) Tel 402-734-3333; Fax: 402-731-0516.

**Nelson, Thomas Inc.,** ( *0-7852; 0-8407; 0-8499; 0-86605; 0-89840; 0-918956; 1-4003* ) Orders Addr.: P.O. Box 141000, Nashville, TN 37214-1000 (SAN 209-3820) Fax: 615-902-1866; Toll Free: 800-251-4000; Edit Addr.: 501 Nelson Pl., Nashville, TN 37214
E-mail: thomasnelson.com
Web site: http://www.thomasnelson.com.

**Nelson, Tommy,** ( *0-7852; 0-8407; 0-8499; 1-4003* ) Div. of Thomas Nelson, Inc., Orders Addr.: P.O. Box 141000, Nashville, TN 37214 Fax: 615-902-3330; Edit Addr.: 501 Nelson Pl., Nashville, TN 37214 Tel 615-889-9000; Toll Free: 800-251-4000
E-mail: mduncan@tommynelson.com
Web site: http://www.tommynelson.com.

**Ner Tamid Bk. Distributors,** P.O. Box 10401, Riviera Beach, FL 33419-0401 (SAN 169-135X) Tel 561-686-9095.

**Net Productions,** 210 Elm Cir., Colorado Springs, CO 80906-3348 (SAN 159-9143).

**netLibrary, Inc.,** ( *0-585* ) 4888 Pearl East Cir., Boulder, CO 80301 (SAN 253-9497) Tel 303-415-2548; Fax: 303-381-7000; 303-381-8999; Toll Free: 800-413-4557
E-mail: mgilbert@netlibrary.com
Web site: http://www.netlibrary.com.

**New Alexandrian Bookstore,** 110 N Cayuga St., Ithaca, NY 14850-4331 (SAN 159-4958) Tel 607-272-1163.

**New Century Pr.,** ( *1-890035* ) 1055 Bay Blvd., Suite C, Chula Vista, CA 91911-1628 Tel 619-476-7400; Fax: 619-476-7474; Toll Free: 800-519-2465 (orders) Do not confuse with companies with the same or similar name in Bermuda Dunes CA, New York NY
E-mail: sales@newcenturypress.com
Web site: http://www.newcenturypress.com.

**New Concepts Bks. & Tapes Distributors,** Orders Addr.: P.O. Box 55068, Houston, TX 77255 (SAN 114-2682) Tel 713-465-7736; Fax: 713-465-7106; Toll Free: 800-842-4807; Edit Addr.: 9722 Pine Lake, Houston, TX 77055 (SAN 630-7531).

**New England Bk. Reps.,** Orders Addr.: 35 Dalton Rd., Belmont, MA 02478 Tel 617-484-4659.

**New England Bk. Service, Inc.,** 457 Pond Rd., North Ferrisburg, VT 05493 (SAN 170-0952) Tel 802-453-7637; Fax: 802-453-7642; Toll Free: 800-356-5772
E-mail: nebs@together.net.

**New England Mobile Bk. Fair,** 82 Needham St., P.O. Box 610159, Newton Highlands, MA 02461 (SAN 169-3530) Tel 617-527-5817; Fax: 617-527-0113.

**New Era Pubns., Inc.,** ( *0-939830* ) P.O. Box 130109, Ann Arbor, MI 48113-0109 (SAN 111-8757) Tel 734-663-1929 Do not confuse with New Era Pubns. in Happy Camp, CA.

**New Jersey Bk. Agency,** Orders Addr.: P.O. Box 144, Morris Plains, NJ 07950 (SAN 106-861X) Tel 973-267-7093; Fax: 973-292-3177; Edit Addr.: 59 Leamoor Dr., Morris Plains, NJ 07950 (SAN 243-2307) Tel 973-267-7093; 908-204-9899.

**New Jersey Bks., Inc.,** 59 Market St., Newark, NJ 07102 Tel 973-624-8070; Toll Free: 800-772-3678.

**New Leaf Distributing Co., Inc.,** ( *0-9627209* ) Div. of Al-Wali Corp., 401 Thornton Rd., Lithia Springs, GA 30122-1557 (SAN 169-1449) Tel 770-948-7845; Fax: 770-944-2313; Toll Free Fax: 800-326-1066; Toll Free: 800-326-2665
E-mail: NewLeaf@NewLeaf-dist.com
Web site: http://www.NewLeaf-dist.com.

**New Life Foundation,** ( *0-911203* ) P.O. Box 2230, Pine, AZ 85544-2230 (SAN 170-3986) Tel 928-476-3224; Fax: 928-476-4743; Toll Free: 800-293-3377 (wholesale only)
E-mail: info@anewlife.org
Web site: http://www.anewlife.org.

**New London News Co.,** 25 Westwood Ave., New London, CT 06320-2726 (SAN 169-0752).

**New World Library,** ( *0-931432; 0-945934; 1-57731; 1-880032* ) 14 Pamaron Way, Novato, CA 94949 (SAN 211-8777) Tel 415-884-2100; Fax: 415-884-2199; Toll Free: 800-972-6657 (retail orders only) Do not confuse with New World Library Publishing Co., Los Altos, CA
E-mail: escort@nwlib.com
Web site: http://www.newworldlibrary.com.

**New World Resource Ctr.,** 2600 W. Fullerton Ave., Chicago, IL 60647-3008 (SAN 169-1848).

**New York Periodical Distributors,** P.O. Box 29, Massena, NY 13662-0029 (SAN 169-6149).

**New York Univ. Pr.,** ( *0-8147* ) Div. of New York Univ., 838 Broadway, 3rd Flr., New York, NY 10003-4812 (SAN 658-1293) Tel 212-998-2575; Fax: 212-995-3833; Toll Free: 800-996-6987
E-mail: orders@nyupress.nyu.edu
Web site: http://www.nyupress.nyu.edu.

**Newborn Enterprises, Inc.,** P.O. Box 1713, Altoona, PA 16603 (SAN 169-7242) Tel 814-944-3593; Fax: 814-944-1881; Toll Free: 800-227-0285 (in Pennsylvania).

**News Group - Illinois, The,** 1301 SW Washington St., Peoria, IL 61602 (SAN 169-216X) Tel 309-673-4549; Fax: 309-673-8883.

**News Group, The,** P.O. Box 25367, Winston-Salem, NC 27114 (SAN 169-6513) Fax: 910-765-8842 Do not confuse with companies with the same name in Columbus, SC, Anchorage, AK, Elizabeth, NC.

**News Supply Co.,** 216 S. La Huerta Cir., Carlsbad, NM 88220-9620 (SAN 159-9151).

**Newsdealers Supply Co., Inc.,** P.O. Box 3516, Tallahassee, FL 32315-3516.

**NEWSouth Distributors,** P.O. Box 61297, Jacksonville, FL 32236-1297 (SAN 159-8732).

**Newsstand Distributors,** 155 W. 14th St., Ogden, UT 84404 (SAN 169-8494) Fax: 810-621-7336; Toll Free: 800-283-6247; 800-231-4834 (in Utah).

**Ng Hing Kee,** 648 Jackson St., San Francisco, CA 94133 (SAN 107-1084) Tel 415-781-8330; Fax: 415-397-9766.

**Niagara County News,** 70 Nicholls St., Lockport, NY 14094 (SAN 169-541X) Tel 716-433-6466.

**Noelke, Carl B.,** 529 Main, Box 563, La Crosse, WI 54602 (SAN 111-8315) Tel 608-782-8544.

**Nonagon,** 1556 Douglas Dr., El Cerrito, CA 94530 (SAN 654-0503) Tel 510-237-5290.

**Nor-Cal News Co.,** 2040 Petaluma Blvd., P.O. Box 2508, Petaluma, CA 94953 (SAN 169-0035) Tel 707-763-2606; Fax: 707-763-3905.

**North American Bk. Distributors,** P.O. Box 510, Hamburg, MI 48139 (SAN 630-4680) Tel 810-231-3728.

**North Carolina News Co.,** P.O. Box 1051, Durham, NC 27702-1051 Tel 919-682-5779.

**North Carolina Schl. Bk. Depository, Inc.,** P.O. Box 950, Raleigh, NC 27602-0950 (SAN 169-6467) Tel 919-833-6615.

**North Carolina Wesleyan College Pr.,** ( *0-933598* ) 3400 N. Wesleyan Blvd., Rocky Mount, NC 27804 (SAN 238-6364) Tel 919-985-5153; Fax: 919-977-3701.

**North Central Bk. Distributors,** N57 W13636 Carmen Ave., Menomonee Falls, WI 53051 (SAN 173-5195) Tel 414-781-3299; Fax: 414-781-4432; Toll Free: 800-966-3299.

**North Country Bks., Inc.,** ( *0-925168; 0-932052; 0-9601158; 1-59531* ) 311 Turner St., Utica, NY 13501 (SAN 110-828X) Tel 315-735-4877
E-mail: ncbooks@adelphia.net.

**Wholesalers & Distributors**

**North Shore Distributors,** 1200 N. Branch, Chicago, IL 60622 (SAN 169-2275).

**North Shore News Co., Inc.,** 150 Blossom St., Lynn, MA 01902 (SAN 169-3492).

**North Texas Periodicals, Inc.,** Orders Addr.: P.O. Box 3823, Lubbock, TX 79452 Tel 806-745-6000; Fax: 806-745-7028; Edit Addr.: 118 E. 70th St., Lubbock, TX 79404
E-mail: ntp@hts-online_net.

**Northern News Co.,** P.O. Box 467, Petoskey, MI 49770-0467 (SAN 169-3964) Toll Free: 800-632-7138 (Michigan only).

**Northern Schl. Supply Co.,** P.O. Box 2627, Fargo, ND 58108 (SAN 169-6548) Fax: 800-891-5836.

**Northern Sun,** 2916 E. Lake St., Minneapolis, MN 55406 (SAN 249-9290) Tel 612-729-2001; Fax: 612-729-0149; Toll Free: 800-258-8579.

**Northern Sun Merchandising,** *See* **Northern Sun**

**Northwest News,** 1560 NE First St., No. 13, Bend, OR 97701 (SAN 111-8587) Tel 541-382-6065; 3100 Merriman Rd., Medford, OR 97501 Tel 541-779-5225.

**Northwest News Co., Inc.,** Orders Addr.: P.O. Box 4965, Missoula, MT 59806 (SAN 660-9406); Edit Addr.: 1701 Ranklin St., Missoula, MT 59802-1629 (SAN 169-4391) Tel 406-721-7801.

**Northwestern Univ. Pr.,** ( *0-8101* ) Orders Addr.: 11030 S. Langley Ave., Chicago, IL 60628 Tel 773-568-1550 ; Fax: 773-660-2235; Toll Free Fax: 800-621-8476; Toll Free: 800-621-2736; Edit Addr.: 625 Colfax St., Evanston, IL 60208-4210 (SAN 202-5787) Tel 847-491-5313; Fax: 847-491-8150
E-mail: nupress@northwestern.edu
Web site: http://www.nupress.northwestern.edu.

**Norton News Agency,** 801 Cedar Cross Rd., Dubuque, IA 52003-7735 (SAN 169-2631); 1467 Service Dr., Winona, MN 55987 (SAN 156-4889).

**Norton, W. W. & Co., Inc.,** ( *0-393; 0-920256* ) Orders Addr.: 800 Keystone Industrial Pk., Scranton, PA 18512 (SAN 157-1869) Tel 570-346-2020; Fax: 570-346-1442; Toll Free Fax: 800-548-6515; Toll Free: 800-233-4830 (book orders only); Edit Addr.: 500 Fifth Ave., New York, NY 10110-0017 (SAN 202-5795) Tel 212-354-5500; Fax: 212-869-0856; Toll Free: 800-223-2584
E-mail: webmaster@wwnorton.com;
Tworrell@wwnorton.com
Web site: http://www.wwnorton.com/trade;
http://www.wwnorton.com.

**NTC/Contemporary Publishing Company,** *See* **McGraw-Hill/Contemporary**

**Nueces News Agency,** P.O. Box 2768, 209 N. Padre Island Dr., Corpus Christi, TX 78403 (SAN 169-8079).

**Nueva Vida Distributors,** 4300 Montana Ave., El Paso, TX 79903-4503 (SAN 107-8615) Tel 915-565-6215; Fax: 915-565-1722.

**Nutri-Bks. Corp.,** Div. of Royal Pubns., Inc., 790 W. Tennessee Ave., P.O. Box 5793, Denver, CO 80223 Tel 303-778-8383; Fax: 303-744-9383; Toll Free: 800-279-2048 (orders only).

**NuvoMedia,** ( *0-9673181* ) 900 Island Dr. # 200, Redwood City, CA 94065-5150
E-mail: publish@nuvomedia.com
Web site: http://www.rocket-ebook.com.

**Oak Knoll Pr.,** ( *0-938768; 1-884718; 1-58456* ) 310 Delaware St., New Castle, DE 19720 (SAN 216-2776) Tel 302-328-7232; Fax: 302-328-7274; Toll Free: 800-996-2556 Do not confuse with Oak Knoll Press in Hardy, VA
E-mail: oakknoll@oakknoll.com
Web site: http://www.oakknoll.com.

**Ohio Periodical Distributors,** P.O. Box 145449, Cincinnati, OH 45250-5449 (SAN 169-6904) Fax: 513-853-6245; Toll Free: 800-777-2216.

**Ohio Univ. Pr.,** ( *0-8214* ) Orders Addr.: 11030 S. Langley Ave., Chicago, IL 60628 Tel 773-568-1559; Fax: 773-660-2235; Toll Free Fax: 800-621-8476; Toll Free: 800-621-2736; Edit Addr.: Scott Quadrangle, Athens, OH 45701 (SAN 282-0773) Tel 740-593-1154; Fax: 740-593-4536
E-mail: gilbert@ohiou.edu
Web site: http://www.ohiou.edu/oupress/.

**Oil City News Co.,** 112 Innis St., Oil City, PA 16301-2930 (SAN 169-7501).

**Ollis Bk. Corp.,** Orders Addr.: P.O. Box 258, Steger, IL 60475 (SAN 658-1323); Edit Addr.: 28 E. 35th St., Steger, IL 60475 (SAN 169-2224) Tel 312-755-5151; Fax: 708-755-5153; Toll Free: 800-323-0343.

**Olson News Agency,** P.O. Box 129, Ishpeming, MI 49849 (SAN 169-3832).

**Omnibooks,** 456 Vista Del Mar Dr., Aptos, CA 95003-4832 (SAN 168-9487) Tel 408-688-4098; Toll Free: 800-626-6671.

**Onondaga News Agency,** 474 E. Brighton Ave., Syracuse, NY 13210 (SAN 169-6297) Tel 315-475-3121.

**Options Unlimited,** 550 Swan Creek Ct., Suwanee, GA 30174 (SAN 631-3949) Tel 770-237-3282 Do not confuse with Options Unlimited, Inc., Green Bay, WI.

**Orange News Company,** *See* **Anderson News, LLC**

**Orbit Bks. Corp.,** 43 Timberline Dr., Poughkeepsie, NY 12603 (SAN 169-6157) Tel 914-462-5653; Fax: 914-462-8409.

**Orca Bk. Pubs.,** ( *0-920501; 1-55143* ) Orders Addr.: P.O. Box 468, Custer, WA 98240-0468 (SAN 630-9674) Tel 250-380-1229; Fax: 250-380-1892; Toll Free: 800-210-5277
E-mail: melanie@orcabook.com;
mcolgan@orcabook.com
Web site: http://www.orcabook.com.

**Osborne Enterprises Publishing,** ( *0-932117* ) P.O. Box 255, Port Townsend, WA 98368 (SAN 242-7567) Tel 360-385-1200; Fax: 360-385-6572; Toll Free: 800-246-3255 (orders only)
E-mail: jpo@olympus.net
Web site: http://www.jerryosborne.com.

**Osborne/McGraw-Hill,** *See* **McGraw-Hill Osborne**

**Osiander Bk. Trade,** 7483H Candlewood Rd., Hanover, MD 21076-3102 (SAN 130-0970).

**Otter B Bks.,** ( *0-9617681; 1-890625* ) 1891 16th Ave., Santa Cruz, CA 95062 (SAN 664-9793) Tel 831-476-5334
E-mail: OtterBBooks@WebTV.net.

**Outbooks, Incorporated,** *See* **Vistabooks**

**Outdoorsman, The,** Orders Addr.: P.O. Box 268, Boston, MA 02134 (SAN 169-3352).

**Outlet Book Company, Incorporated,** *See* **Random Hse. Value Publishing**

**Oxford Univ. Pr., Inc.,** ( *0-19; 0-904147; 0-947946; 1-85221* ) Orders Addr.: 2001 Evans Rd., Cary, NC 27513 (SAN 202-5892) Tel 919-677-0977 (general voice); Fax: 919-677-1303 (customer service); Toll Free: 800-445-9714 (customer service - inquiry); 800-451-7556 (customer service - orders); Edit Addr.: 198 Madison Ave., New York, NY 10016-4314 (SAN 202-5884) Tel 212-726-6000 (general voice); Fax: 212-726-6440 (general fax)
E-mail: orders@oup-usa.org; custserv@oup-usa.org
Web site: http://www.oup-usa.org.

**Ozark Magazine Distributing, Incorporated,** *See* **Ozark News Distributor, Inc.**

**Ozark News Agency, Inc.,** P.O. Box 1150, Fayetteville, AR 72702.

**Ozark News Distributor, Inc.,** 1630 N. Eldon, Springfield, MO 65803 (SAN 169-4332) Tel 417-862-9224; Fax: 417-862-6642; Toll Free: 800-743-0380.

**P & G Wholesale,** P.O. Box 1548, Fargo, ND 58102 (SAN 156-4536).

**P. D. Music Headquarters, Inc.,** Orders Addr.: P.O. Box 252, New York, NY 10014 (SAN 282-5880) Tel 212-242-5322.

**Pacific Bks.,** ( *1-885375* ) Orders Addr.: P.O. Box 3562, Santa Barbara, CA 93130 (SAN 630-2548) Tel 805-687-8340; Fax: 805-687-2514; Edit Addr.: 2573 Treasure Dr., Santa Barbara, CA 93105.

**Pacific Magazine-Bk. Wholesaler,** 1515 NW 51st St., Seattle, WA 98107 (SAN 274-3884) Tel 206-789-5333.

**Pacific Periodical Services, LLC,** *See* **Anderson News - Tacoma**

**Pacific Trade Group,** 68-309 Crozier Dr., Waialua, HI 96791 (SAN 169-1635) Tel 808-636-2300; Fax: 808-636-2301.

**Paladin Pr.,** ( *0-87364; 1-58160; 1-891268* ) Orders Addr.: c/o Gunbarrel Tech Ctr., 7077 Winchester Cir., Boulder, CO 80301 (SAN 662-1066) Tel 303-443-7250; Fax: 303-442-8741; Toll Free: 800-392-2400 (Credit Card Orders Only)
E-mail: sales@paladin-press.com;
service@paladin-press.com;
editorial@paladin-press.com
Web site: http://www.flying-machines.com;
http://www.sycamoreisland.com; http://www.paladin-press.com.

**Palgrave,** *See* **Palgrave Macmillan**

**Palgrave Macmillan,** ( *0-312; 0-333; 1-4039* ) Div. of Saint Martin's Press, LLC, Orders Addr.: 16365 James Madison Hwy., Gordonsville, VA 22942-8501 Toll Free Fax: 800-672-2054; Toll Free: 888-330-8477; Edit Addr.: 175 Fifth Ave., New York, NY 10010 Tel 212-982-9300; Fax: 212-777-6359; Toll Free: 800-221-7945
Web site: http://www.palgrave.com.

**Palmer News Co., Inc.,** 1050 Republican, P.O. Box 1400, Topeka, KS 66601 Tel 913-234-6679; Fax: 913-234-6338.

**Palmer News, Inc.,** 9605 Dice Ln., Lenexa, KS 66215 Tel 913-541-8600; Fax: 913-541-9413
E-mail: palmerco@oni.com.

**Palmetto News Co.,** 200 Sunbelt Ct., Greer, SC 29650-9349.

**Palmyra Publishing Co.,** ( *0-9666627* ) P.O. Box 1164, Sioux Falls, SD 57101-1164 Tel 605-330-2707; Fax: 605-330-6009
E-mail: alyajim@sd.cybernex.net.

**Paperback Books, Incorporated,** *See* **Book Distribution Ctr., Inc.**

**Paperbacks for Educators,** ( *0-9702376* ) 426 W. Front St., Washington, MO 63090 (SAN 103-3379) Tel 636-239-1999; Fax: 636-239-4515; Toll Free Fax: 800-514-7323; Toll Free: 800-227-2591
E-mail: paperbacks@mail.usmo.com
Web site: http://www.any-book-in-print.com.

**Parks & History Assn.,** ( *1-887878* ) 126 Raleigh St., SE, Washington, DC 20032 (SAN 122-4670) Tel 202-472-3083; Fax: 202-755-0469.

**Parkwest Pubns., Inc.,** ( *0-88186* ) 451 Communipaw Ave., Jersey City, NJ 07304 (SAN 264-6846) Tel 201-432-3257; Fax: 201-432-3708
E-mail: parkwest@parkwestpubs.com;
info@parkwestpubs.com
Web site: http://www.parkwestpubs.com.

**Parliament News Co., Inc.,** P.O. Box 910, Santa Clarita, CA 91380-9010 (SAN 168-9924).

**Parnassus Bk. Distributors,** 200 Academy Way, Columbia, SC 29206-1445 (SAN 631-0680) Tel 803-782-7748; Toll Free: 800-782-7760.

**Partners Bk. Distributing, Inc.,** Orders Addr.: P.O. Box 580, Holt, MI 48842; Edit Addr.: 2325 Jarco Dr., Holt, MI 48842 (SAN 630-4559) Tel 517-694-3205; Toll Free: 800-336-3137 (orders).

**Partners Book Distributing, Incorporated,** *See* **Partners Pubs. Group, Inc.**

**Partners Pubs. Group, Inc.,** Orders Addr.: P.O. Box 580, Holt, MI 48842 Tel 517-694-3205; Fax: 517-694-0617; Toll Free: 800-336-3137; Edit Addr.: 2325 Jarco Dr., Holt, MI 48842 (SAN 631-3418).

**Partners/West,** 1901 Raymond Ave., SW, Suite C, Renton, WA 98055 (SAN 631-421X) Tel 425-227-8486; Fax: 425-204-1448; Toll Free: 800-563-2385.

**Pathfinder Pr.,** ( *0-87348; 0-913460* ) Orders Addr.: P.O. Box 162767, Atlanta, GA 30321 Tel 404-769-0600; Fax: 707-667-1411; Edit Addr.: 4794 Clark Howell Hwy., Suite B-5, College Park, GA 30349; 545 E. Eighth Ave., New York, NY 10018 (SAN 202-5906) Do not confuse with companies with the same or similar names in Alameda, CA, Battle Ground, WA, Elicott City, MD
E-mail: orders@pathfinderpress.com
Web site: http://www.pathfinderpress.com.

**Pathway Bk. Service,** Div. of MLES, Inc., Orders Addr.: P.O. Box 89, Gilsum, NH 03448 Toll Free: 800-345-6665; Edit Addr.: 4 White Brook Rd., Gilsum, NH 03448 (SAN 170-0545) Tel 603-357-0236; Fax: 603-357-2073
E-mail: pbs@pathwaybook.com
Web site: http://www.pathwaybook.com.

**Paul & Co. Pubs. Consortium, Inc.,** Div. of Independent Publishers Group, Orders Addr.: 814 N. Franklin St., Chicago, IL 60610 Tel 312-337-0747; Fax: 312-337-5985; Toll Free: 800-888-4741; Edit Addr.: P.O. Box 442, Concord, MA 01742 (SAN 630-5318)
E-mail: frontdesk@ipgbook.com
Web site: http://www.ipgbook.com.

**Paulsen, G. Co.,** 27 Sheep Davis Rd., Pembroke, NH 03275 (SAN 169-4499) Tel 603-225-9787.

**PBD, Inc.,** 1650 Bluegrass Lakes Pkwy., Alpharetta, GA 30004 (SAN 126-6039) Tel 770-442-8633; Fax: 770-442-9742
Web site: http://www.pbd.com.

**Pearson Education,** ( *0-582* ) Orders Addr.: 200 Old Tappan Rd., Old Tappan, NJ 07675 (SAN 200-2175) Tel 201-767-5152; Toll Free Fax: 800-922-0579; 800-445-6991; Toll Free: 800-428-5331; Edit Addr.: One Lake St., Upper Saddle River, NJ 07458 Tel 201-236-7000; Fax: 201-236-6549
E-mail: eugene.wang@pearsonptr.com;
carole.wilkins@phschool.com;
emily.mcgee@pearson.ed.com;
joann.kebrdle@pearsoned.com
Web site: http://www.pearsoned.com.

**Pee Dee News Co.,** 2321 Lawrens Cir., Florence, SC 29501-9408.

Full publisher information is available in the Publisher Name Index

**Pegasus Pr.,** ( *1-889818* ) 101 Booter Rd., Fairview, NC 28730 Tel 828-628-3883; Fax: 828-628-3886 Do not confuse with companies with the same name in Vashon Island, WA, San Diego, CA, Kerrville, TX, Lake Forest, IL
E-mail: dicesare1@mindspring.com
Web site: http://www.pegpress.org.

**Pegram, Christine,** 1901 Upper Cove Terr., Sarasota, FL 33581 (SAN 110-0254) Tel 941-921-2467.

**Pekin News Agency,** 1637 Monroe St., Madison, WI 53711-2021 (SAN 169-2151).

**Pelican Publishing Co., Inc.,** ( *0-88289; 0-911116; 1-56554; 1-58980* ) Orders Addr.: P.O. Box 3110, Gretna, LA 70054 (SAN 212-0623) Tel 504-368-1175 ; Fax: 504-368-1195; Toll Free: 800-843-1724; 1000 Burmaster St., Gretna, LA 70053 Do not confuse with companies with the same or similar names in Lowell, MA, Dallas, TX
E-mail: promo@pelicanpub.com;
Sales@pelicanpub.com
Web site: http://www.bedandbreakfastguide.com; http://www.epelican.com; http://www.eirishbooks.com.

**Pen Notes, Inc.,** ( *0-939564* ) 61 Bennington Ave., Freeport, NY 11520 (SAN 107-3621) Tel 516-868-5753; Fax: 516-868-8441
E-mail: pennotes@worldnet.att.net.

**Penguin Group (USA) Inc.,** ( *0-14* ) Orders Addr.: 405 Murray Hill Pkwy., East Rutherford, NJ 07073-2136 (SAN 282-5074) Fax: 201-933-2903 (customer service); Toll Free Fax: 800-227-9604; Toll Free: 800-788-6262 (individual consumer sales); 800-526-0275 (reseller sales); 800-631-8571 (reseller customer service); Edit Addr.: 375 Hudson St., New York, NY 10014 Tel 212-366-2000; Fax: 212-366-2666
E-mail: pmccarthy@penguinputman.com
Web site: http://www.penguinputnam.com.

**Penguin Putnam, Incorporated,** *See* **Penguin Group (USA) Inc.**

**Pen-Mar News Distributors,** *See* **Americana Souvenirs & Gifts**

**Penmarch Publishing,** 3932 S. Willow Ave., Sioux Falls, SD 57105 Toll Free: 800-282-2399.

**Penn News Co.,** 944 Franklin St., Johnstown, PA 15905 (SAN 169-7390).

**Pennsylvania Capitol Preservation Committee,** ( *0-9643048* ) P.O. Box 202231, Harrisburg, PA 17120 Tel 717-783-6484; Fax: 717-772-0742
Web site: http://cpc.leg.state.pa.us.

**Penton Overseas, Inc.,** ( *0-939001; 1-56015; 1-59125* ) 2470 Impala Dr., Carlsbad, CA 92008 (SAN 631-0826) Tel 760-431-0060; Fax: 760-431-8110; Toll Free: 800-748-5804
Web site: http://www.pentonoverseas.com.

**Peoples Publishing Group, Inc., The,** ( *1-56256; 1-58984; 1-4138* ) Orders Addr.: P.O. Box 513, Saddle Brook, NJ 07633 Tel 201-712-0090; Fax: 201-712-1534; Toll Free: 800-822-1080; Edit Addr.: 299 Market St., Saddle Brook, NJ 07663
E-mail: sales@peoplespublishing.com;
customersupport@peoplespublishing.com;
editorial@peoplespublishing.com;
solvier@peoplespublishing.com
Web site: http://www.peoplespublishing.com/.

**Perelandra, Ltd.,** ( *0-927978; 0-9617713* ) Orders Addr.: P.O. Box 3603, Warrenton, VA 20188 (SAN 665-0198) Tel 540-937-2153; Fax: 540-937-3360; Toll Free: 800-960-8806
E-mail: email@perelandra-ltd.com
Web site: http://www.perelandra-ltd.com.

**Periodical Distributors, Incorporated,** *See* **North Texas Periodicals, Inc.**

**Periodical Marketing Services,** 1065 Bloomfield Ave., Clifton, NJ 07012 (SAN 250-5304) Tel 201-342-6334.

**Periodical Pubs. Service Bureau,** One N. Superior St., Sandusky, OH 44870 (SAN 285-9351) Tel 419-626-0623.

**Periodicals Service Co.,** ( *0-527; 0-8115; 3-262; 3-601* ) 11 Main St., Germantown, NY 12526 (SAN 164-8608) Tel 518-537-4700; Fax: 518-537-5899
E-mail: psc@backsets.com
Web site: http://www.backsets.com.

**Perma-Bound Bks.,** ( *0-605; 0-7804; 0-8000; 0-8479* ) Div. of Hertzberg-New Method, Inc., 617 E. Vandalia Rd., Jacksonville, IL 62650 (SAN 169-202X) Tel 217-243-5451; Fax: 217-243-7505; Toll Free Fax: 800-551-1169; Toll Free: 800-637-6581 (customer service)
E-mail: books@permabound.com
Web site: http://www.perma-bound.com.

**Perrone,** Calle 11. # 372-A Urb. Hill Brothers, San Juan, PR 00924 Tel 787-764-6112; Fax: 787-754-2374
E-mail: ecruz@perroneimporters.com
Web site: http://www.perroneimporters.com

**Perry Enterprises,** ( *0-941518* ) 3907 N. Foothill Dr., Provo, UT 84604 (SAN 171-0281) Tel 801-226-1002.

**Petterson Antiques,** 201 King St., Charleston, SC 29401 (SAN 114-2399) Tel 803-723-5714.

**Pictorial Histories Distribution,** 1416 Quarrier St., Charleston, WV 25301 Tel 304-342-1848; Fax: 304-343-0594; Toll Free: 888-982-7472
E-mail: wvbooks@newwave.net.

**Pittsfield News Co., Inc.,** 6 Westview Rd., Pittsfield, MA 01201 (SAN 124-2768) Tel 413-445-5682; Fax: 413-445-5683.

**Plains Distribution Service,** P.O. Box 931, Moorhead, MN 56561 (SAN 169-6556).

**Planeta Publishing Corp.,** ( *0-9715256; 0-9719950* ) 2057 NW 87th Ave., Miami, FL 33172 Tel 305-470-0016; 305-571-8400; Fax: 305-470-6267; Toll Free: 800-407-4770
E-mail: mnormanppc@aol.com
Web site: http://www.planetapublishing.com.

**Players Pr., Inc.,** ( *0-88734* ) P.O. Box 1132, Studio City, CA 91614-0132 (SAN 239-0213) Tel 818-789-4980
E-mail: Playerspress@att.net.

**Plough Publishing Hse., The,** ( *0-87486* ) Rte. 381 N., Farmington, PA 15437 (SAN 202-0092) Tel 724-329-1100; Fax: 724-329-0914; Toll Free: 800-521-8011
E-mail: plough@plough.com
Web site: http://www.plough.com.

**PMG Bks. Ltd.,** 321 Nolan St., San Antonio, TX 78202 (SAN 631-3183) Tel 210-226-0772; Fax: 210-224-5194.

**Pocket Bks.,** ( *0-671; 0-7432; 0-7434; 1-4165* ) Div. of Simon & Schuster, Inc., Orders Addr.: 100 Front St., Riverside, NJ 08075 Toll Free Fax: 800-943-9831; Toll Free: 800-223-2336; Edit Addr.: 1230 Ave. of the Americas, New York, NY 10020 (SAN 202-5922) Tel 212-698-7000
E-mail: ssonline_feedback@simonsays.com
Web site: http://www.simonsays.com.

**Polybook Distributors,** Orders Addr.: P.O. Box 109, Mount Vernon, NY 10550 Tel 914-664-1633; Fax: 904-428-3953; Edit Addr.: 22 S. Sixth Ave., Mount Vernon, NY 10550 (SAN 169-5568).

**Pomona Valley News Agency,** 10736 Fremont Ave., Ontario, CA 91762 (SAN 169-0019) Tel 909-591-3885.

**Pop-M Company,** *See* **Book Margins, Inc.**

**Popular Subscription Service,** P.O. Box 1566, Terre Haute, IN 47808 (SAN 285-9386) Tel 812-466-1258; Fax: 812-466-9443; Toll Free: 800-466-5038
E-mail: info@popularsubscriptionsvc.com
Web site: http://www.popularsubscriptionsvc.com.

**Portland News Co.,** Orders Addr.: P.O. Box 6970, Scarborough, ME 04070-6970 (SAN 169-3093) Toll Free: 800-639-1708 (in Maine); Edit Addr.: 10 Southgate Rd., Scarborough, ME 04074 Tel 207-883-1300.

**Portsmouth News Agency,** 3051 Walnut St., Portsmouth, OH 45662 (SAN 169-6831).

**Powells.com,** Orders Addr.: 40 NW Tenth Ave., Portland, OR 97209 Tel 800-291-2676
Web site: http://www.powells.com/.

**Pratz News Agency,** Orders Addr.: P.O. Box 892, Deming, NM 88030 (SAN 159-9275).

**Prebound Periodicals,** 2101 N. Topeka Blvd., Topeka, KS 66608 (SAN 285-8037) Tel 785-233-4252.

**Premier Pubs., Inc.,** ( *0-915665* ) P.O. Box 330309, Fort Worth, TX 76163 (SAN 292-5966) Tel 817-293-7030 ; Fax: 817-293-3410.

**Presbyterian Publishing Corp.,** ( *0-664* ) 100 Witherspoon St., Louisville, KY 40202-1396 Toll Free: 800-227-2872
E-mail: rpinotti@presbypub.com.

**Princeton Bk. Co. Pubs.,** ( *0-87127; 0-916622* ) Orders Addr.: P.O. Box 831, Hightstown, NJ 08520-0831 (SAN 630-1568) Tel 609-426-0602; Fax: 609-426-1344; Toll Free: 800-220-7149; Edit Addr.: 614 Rte. 130, Hightstown, NJ 08520 (SAN 244-8076)
E-mail: pbc@dancehorizons.com; elysian@aosi.com
Web site: http://www.dancehorizons.com.

**Printed Matter, Inc.,** ( *0-89439* ) 535 W. 22nd St., New York, NY 10011 (SAN 169-5924) Tel 212-925-0325; Fax: 212-925-0464
E-mail: dplatzker@printedmatter.org;
staff@printedmatter.org
Web site: http://www.printedmatter.org.

**Production Assocs., Inc.,** ( *1-887120* ) 1206 W. Collins Ave., Orange, CA 92867 Tel 714-771-6519; Fax: 714-771-2456; Toll Free: 800-535-8368
E-mail: mikec@production-associates.com
Web site: http://www.production-associates.com.

**Proe & Proe,** Orders Addr.: 3522 James St., Suite 212B, Syracuse, NY 13206 Tel 315-432-0474.

**Professional Book Distributors, Incorporated,** *See* **PBD, Inc.**

**Professional Media Service Corp.,** 1160 Trademark Dr., Suite 109, Reno, NV 89511 (SAN 630-5776) Toll Free Fax: 800-253-8853; Toll Free: 800-223-7672.

**Provident Music Distribution,** 1 Maryland Farms, Brentwood, TN 37027 Tel 615-373-3950; Fax: 615-373-0386; Toll Free: 800-333-9000
Web site: http://www.providentmusic.com.

**Public Lands Interpretive Assn.,** ( *1-879343* ) 6501 Fourth St., NW, No. 1, Albuquerque, NM 87107-5800 (SAN 133-3119) Tel 505-345-9498; Fax: 505-344-1543.

**Publication Consultants,** ( *0-9644809; 1-888125; 1-59433* ) 7617 Highlander Dr., Anchorage, AK 99518 Tel 907-349-2424
E-mail: evan@alaskabooks.biz
Web site: http://www.alaskabooks.biz.

**Publications Unlimited,** 7512 Coconut Dr., Lake Worth, FL 33467-6511 (SAN 285-9432) Tel 407-434-4688.

**Publishers Business Service, Inc.,** P.O. Box 25674, Chicago, IL 60625 (SAN 285-9459) Tel 312-561-5552.

**Publishers Clearing Hse.,** 382 Channel Dr., Port Washington, NY 11050 (SAN 285-9440) Tel 516-883-5432.

**Publishers Continental Sales Corp.,** 613 Franklin Sq., Michigan City, IN 46360 (SAN 285-9475) Tel 219-874-4245; Fax: 219-872-8961.

**Publishers Distributing Co.,** Div. of Liberation Pubns., Inc., P.O. Box 4371, Los Angeles, CA 90078 (SAN 630-4249) Tel 323-860-6070; Fax: 323-467-0152; Toll Free: 800-464-4574.

**Publishers Group West,** Subs. of Publishers Group Inc., 1700 Fourth St., Berkeley, CA 94710 (SAN 202-8522) Tel 510-528-1444; Fax: 510-528-3444; Toll Free: 800-788-3123; 800-788-3122 (electronic orders)
Web site: http://www.pgw.com.

**Publishers Media,** ( *0-934064* ) 1447 Valley View Rd., Glendale, CA 91202-1716 (SAN 159-6683) Tel 818-548-1998.

**Publishers News Company,** *See* **Mr. Paperback/ Publishers News Co.**

**Publishers Services,** Orders Addr.: P.O. Box 2510, Novato, CA 94948 (SAN 201-3037) Tel 415-883-3530 ; Fax: 415-883-4280.

**Publishers Wholesale Assocs., Inc.,** Orders Addr.: P.O. Box 2078, Lancaster, PA 17608-2078 (SAN 630-7450) Fax: 717-397-9253; Edit Addr.: 231 N. Shippen St., Lancaster, PA 17608.

**Pulley Learning Assocs.,** 210 Alpine Meadow Rd., Winchester, VA 22602-6701 (SAN 133-1434).

**Purple Unicorn Bks.,** ( *0-931998* ) 1928 W. Kent Rd., Duluth, MN 55812-1154 (SAN 111-0071) Tel 218-525-4781 Do not confuse with Purple Unicorn in Augusta, ME.

**Putnam Publishing Group, The,** ( *0-399; 0-698; 0-89828* ) Div. of Penguin Putnam, Inc., Orders Addr.: 405 Murray Hill Pkwy., East Rutherford, NJ 07073-2136 Toll Free Fax: 800-227-9604; Toll Free: 800-788-6262 (individual consumer sales); 800-631-8571 (reseller customer service); 800-526-0275 (reseller sales); Edit Addr.: 375 Hudson St., New York, NY 10014 (SAN 202-5531) Tel 212-366-2000; Fax: 212-366-2643
E-mail: online@penguinputnam.com
Web site: http://www.penguinputnam.com.

**Quality Bks., Inc.,** ( *0-89196* ) 1003 W. Pines Rd., Oregon, IL 61061-9680 (SAN 169-2127) Tel 815-732-4450; Fax: 815-732-4499; Toll Free: 800-323-4241 (libraries only)
E-mail: quality.books@dawson.com.

**Quality Book Fairs,** 110 W. Liberty St., Medina, OH 44256 (SAN 630-7752) Tel 330-725-6977; Fax: 330-723-5325.

**Quality Schl. Plan, Inc.,** P.O. Box 10203, Des Moines, IA 50381-0001 (SAN 285-953X).

**Quest, The,** ( *1-888861* ) 3 Danforth Dr., No. 650, Northboro, MA 01532 (SAN 299-2884) Tel 508-393-7131; Fax: 419-828-2070; Toll Free: 800-777-9149 (orders)
E-mail: thequest@att.net
Web site: http://www.spiritwells.com.

**QW, Inc.,** ( *1-928547* ) P.O. Box 463180, Mount Clemens, MI 48046-3180 Tel 810-954-2986; Fax: 810-954-1085; Toll Free: 800-838-8854
E-mail: janinerange@ameritech.net
Web site: http://www.qwincorporated.com.

**R & W Distribution, Inc.,** 87 Bright St., Jersey City, NJ 07302 (SAN 169-4723) Tel 201-333-1540; Fax: 201-333-1541
E-mail: rwmag@mail.idt.net.

**R T R Publishing Company,** *See* **Red Toad Road Co.**

**Radio Bookstore,** P.O. Box 209, Rindge, NH 03461-0209 (SAN 111-3496) Tel 603-899-6957 Do not confuse with Radio Bookstore Pr., Bellevue, WA.

**Rainier News, Inc.,** 3400-D Industry Dr., E., Fife, WA 98424-1853 (SAN 169-8745) Toll Free: 800-843-2995 (in Washington).

**Raintree Pubs.,** *( 0-8114; 0-8172; 0-8393; 0-7398 )* Div. of Harcourt, Inc., Orders Addr.: P.O. Box 26015, Austin, TX 78755 Toll Free Fax: 877-578-2638; Toll Free: 888-363-4266; Edit Addr.: 10801 N. Mopac Expressway, Bldg. 3, Austin, TX 78759 (SAN 658-1757) Tel 512-343-8227; Fax: 646-935-3713 Web site: http://www.raintreelibrary.com.

**Raintree Steck-Vaughn Publishers,** *See* **Raintree Pubs.**

**Random Hse., Inc.,** *( 0-307; 0-345; 0-375; 0-394; 0-553; 0-676; 0-679; 0-87665; 1-58836; 1-4000 )* Div. of Bertelsmann AG, Orders Addr.: 400 Hahn Rd., Westminster, MD 21157 (SAN 202-5515) Tel 410-848-1900; Toll Free Fax: 800-659-2436; Toll Free: 800-726-0600 (customer service/orders); Edit Addr.: 1540 Broadway, New York, NY 10036 (SAN 202-5507) Tel 212-782-9000; Fax: 212-302-7985 E-mail: customerservice@randomhouse.com Web site: http://www.randomhouse.com.

**Random Hse. Value Publishing,** *( 0-517; 0-609; 0-87000; 1-4000 )* Div. of Random Hse., Diversified Pub. Group, Orders Addr.: 400 Hahn Rd., Westminster, MD 21157 Toll Free: 800-733-3000 (orders); 800-726-0600 (customer service, credit, electronic ordering dept.); Edit Addr.: 280 Park Ave., 11th Flr., New York, NY 10017 Tel 212-572-2400 Web site: http://www.randomhouse.com.

**Read News Agency,** 2501 Greensboro Ave., Tuscaloosa, AL 35401-6520 Tel 205-752-3515.

**Reader's Digest Children's Publishing, Inc.,** *( 0-276; 0-7621; 0-88705; 0-88850; 0-89577; 1-57584; 1-57619; 0-7944 )* Subs. of Reader's Digest Assn., Inc., Reader's Digest Rd., Pleasantville, NY 10570-7000 (SAN 283-2143) Tel 914-244-4800; Fax: 914-244-4841 Web site: http://www.readersdigestkids.com.

**Readex Bk. Exchange,** Box 1125, Carefree, AZ 85377 (SAN 159-9291).

**Reading Circle, The,** 1456 N. High St., Columbus, OH 43201-0458 (SAN 169-670X) Tel 614-299-9673; Fax: 614-299-1388.

**Reading Peddler Bk. Fairs,** 10580 3/4 W. Pico Blvd., Los Angeles, CA 90064 (SAN 157-9770) Tel 310-559-2665.

**Readmor,** Orders Addr.: P.O. Box 7264, Grand Rapids, MI 49508 (SAN 169-3875); Edit Addr.: 301 S. Rath Ave., Ludington, MI 49431 Tel 231-843-2537.

**Readmore Academic Services,** Orders Addr.: P.O. Box 1459, Blackwood, NJ 08012 (SAN 630-5741) Tel 609-227-1100; Fax: 609-227-8322; Toll Free: 800-645-6595; Edit Addr.: 700 Black Horse Pike, Suite 207, Blackwood, NJ 08012.

**Readmore, Inc.,** 22 Cortlandt St., New York, NY 10007 (SAN 159-9313) Tel 212-349-5540; Fax: 212-233-0746; Toll Free: 800-221-3306.

**Red Sea Pr.,** *( 0-932415; 1-56902 )* 11 Princess Rd., Suites D, E & F, Lawrenceville, NJ 08648 (SAN 630-1983) Tel 609-844-9583; Fax: 609-844-0198 E-mail: africawpress@nyo.com Web site: http://www.africanworld.com/.

**Red Toad Road Co.,** *( 1-889287 )* Orders Addr.: P.O. Box 642, Havre de Grace, MD 21078 Tel 410-939-4092; Fax: 410-939-5614; Edit Addr.: 223 Heather Way, Havre de Grace, MD 21078 E-mail: redtoadroad@aol.com Web site: http://www.amazon.com/shops/redtoadroad.

**Red Wheel/Weiser,** *( 0-87728; 0-943233; 1-57324; 1-57863; 1-59003 )* Div. of Weiser Bks., Orders Addr.: P.O. Box 612, York Beach, ME 03910-0612 Tel 207-363-4393; Fax: 207-363-5799; Toll Free Fax: 877-337-3309; Toll Free: 800-423-7087 (orders only) E-mail: customerservice@redwheelweiser.com Web site: http://www.redwheelweiser.com; http://www.weiserbooks.com.

**Redwing Bk. Co.,** 44 Linden St., Brookline, MA 02445 (SAN 163-3597) Tel 617-738-4664; Fax: 617-738-4620; Toll Free: 800-873-3946 E-mail: bob@redwingbooks.com Web site: http://www.redwingbooks.com.

**Reference Bk. Ctr.,** 175 Fifth Ave., New York, NY 10010 (SAN 159-9356) Tel 212-677-2160; Fax: 212-533-0826.

**Regent Bk. Co., Inc.,** Orders Addr.: P.O. Box 750, Lodi, NJ 07644-0750 Tel 973-574-7600; Fax: 973-574-7605; Toll Free: 800-999-9554; Edit Addr.: 25 Saddle River Ave., South Hackensack, NJ 07606 (SAN 169-4715) E-mail: info@regentbook.com Web site: http://www.regentbook.com.

**Regina Bks.,** *( 0-941690; 1-930053 )* Orders Addr.: P.O. Box 280, Claremont, CA 91711 (SAN 239-2968) Tel 909-624-8466; Fax: 909-626-1345; Edit Addr.: 1905 Bridgeport Ave., Claremont, CA 91711.

**Renaissance Hse. Pubs.,** *( 0-935810; 0-939650; 1-55838 )* Div. of Primer Pubs., 5738 N. Central Ave., Phoenix, AZ 85012 Tel 602-234-1574; Fax: 602-234-3062; Toll Free: 800-521-9221 (orders) E-mail: bfessler@earthlink.net.

**Replica Bks.,** *( 0-7351 )* Div. of Baker & Taylor, Orders Addr.: 1200 US Hwy., 22 E., Bridgewater, NJ 08807 Tel 908-541-7392; Fax: 908-541-7875; Toll Free: 800-775-1800; Edit Addr.: P.O. Box 6885, Bridgewater, NJ 08807-0885 E-mail: btinfo@baker-taylor.com.

**Research Bks., Inc.,** 38 Academy St., P.O. Box 1507, Madison, CT 06443 Tel 203-245-3279; Fax: 203-245-1830 E-mail: info@researchbooks.com.

**Resource Software International, Inc.,** *( 0-87539 )* Affil. of Datamatics Management, 330 New Brunswick Ave., Fords, NJ 08863 (SAN 264-8628) Tel 732-738-8500; Fax: 732-738-9603; Toll Free: 800-673-0366 E-mail: info@datamaticsinc.com Web site: http://www.tc-1.com.

**Rhinelander News Agency,** 314 Courtney, Crescent Lake, WI 54501 (SAN 159-9372) Tel 715-362-6397.

**Rhodes News Agency,** *See* **Treasure Valley News**

**Richardson's Bks., Inc.,** 2014 Lou Ellen Ln., Houston, TX 77018 (SAN 169-829X) Tel 713-688-2244; Fax: 713-688-8420; Toll Free: 800-392-8562.

**Richardson's Educators,** *See* **Richardson's Bks., Inc.**

**Rinehart, Roberts Pubs.,** *( 0-911797; 0-943173; 1-57098; 1-57140; 1-879373; 1-58979 )* Orders Addr.: 4720 Boston Way, Lanhan, MD 20706 Tel 301-459-3366; Toll Free Fax: 800-238-4650; Toll Free: 800-462-6420; Edit Addr.: c/o Rowman & Littlefield Publishing Group, 5360 Manhattan Cir., No. 101, Boulder, CO 80303 (SAN 264-3510) Tel 303-543-7835 E-mail: books@robertsrinehart.com Web site: http://www.robertsrinehart.com.

**Rio Grande Bk. Co.,** P.O. Box 2795, McAllen, TX 78502-2795 (SAN 169-8354).

**Rishor News Co., Inc.,** 109 Mountain Laurel Dr., Butler, PA 16001-3921 (SAN 159-9402).

**Rittenhouse Bk. Distributors,** *( 0-87381 )* Orders Addr.: 511 Feheley Dr., King of Prussia, PA 19406 (SAN 213-4454) Tel 610-277-1414; Fax: 610-227-0390; Toll Free Fax: 800-223-7488; Toll Free: 800-345-6425 E-mail: alan.yockey@rittenhouse.com; joan.townshend@rittenhouse.com Web site: http://www.rittenhouse.com.

**Ritter Bk. Co.,** 7011 Foster Pl., Downers Grove, IL 60516-3446 (SAN 169-1856).

**River Road Recipes Cookbook,** 9523 Fenway Dr., Baton Rouge, LA 70809 (SAN 132-7852) Tel 504-924-0300 ; Fax: 504-927-2547; Toll Free: 800-204-1726.

**Riverside,** *( 0-934298; 1-55518 )* Orders Addr.: P.O. Box 370, Iowa Falls, IA 50126 (SAN 169-2666) Tel 641-648-4271; Toll Free: 800-922-9777 (Telemarketing); Edit Addr.: 636 S. Oak St., Iowa Falls, IA 50126 (SAN 631-2063) Toll Free Fax: 800-822-4271; Toll Free: 800-247-5111 E-mail: orders@riversideworld.com Web site: http://www.riversideworld.com.

**Riverside Bk. & Bible Resource,** 1500 Riverside Dr., Iowa Falls, IA 50126 Tel 515-648-4801; Toll Free Fax: 800-822-4271; Toll Free: 800-247-5111.

**Riverside World,** *See* **Riverside**

**Roadrunner Library Service,** c/o Kerbs, 700 Highview Ave., Glen Ellyn, IL 60137-5504.

**Roberts, F.M. Enterprises,** *( 0-912746 )* P.O. Box 608, Dana Point, CA 92629-0608 (SAN 201-4688) Tel 714-493-1977; Fax: 714-493-7124.

**Rockbottom Bks.,** Pentagon Towers, P.O. Box 398166, Minneapolis, MN 55439 (SAN 108-4402) Tel 612-831-2120.

**Rockland Catskill, Inc.,** 26 Church St., Spring Valley, NY 10977 (SAN 169-6254) Tel 914-356-1222; Fax: 914-356-8415; Toll Free: 800-966-6247.

**Rocky Mount News Agency,** Two Great State Ln., Rocky Mount, NC 27801.

**Rogue Valley News Agency, Inc.,** 550 Airport Rd., Medford, OR 97504-4156 (SAN 169-7137).

**Rohr, Hans E.,** 76 State St., Newburyport, MA 01950-6616 (SAN 113-8804).

**Roig Spanish Bks.,** 146 W. 29th St., No. 3W, New York, NY 10001-5303 (SAN 165-1021) Tel 212-695-6410; Fax: 212-695-6811 E-mail: roig@interport.net.

**Rosenblum's,** *See* **Rosenblum's World of Judaica, Inc.**

**Rosenblum's World of Judaica, Inc.,** 2906 W. Devon Ave., Chicago, IL 60659 (SAN 169-1864) Tel 773-262-1700; Fax: 773-262-1930; Toll Free: 800-626-6536.

**Rounder Kids Music Distribution,** Orders Addr.: P.O. Box 516, Montpelier, VT 05602 (SAN 630-6675) Tel 802-223-5825; Fax: 802-223-5303; Toll Free: 800-223-6357; Edit Addr.: 79 River Rd., Montpelier, VT 05602 E-mail: Pauls@rounder.com.

**Rowman & Littlefield Pubs., Inc.,** *( 0-8476; 0-87471; 0-7425 )* Div. of University Press of America, P.O. Box 191, Blue Ridge Summit, PA 17214-0191 Tel 717-794-3800; Fax: 717-794-3801; Orders Addr.: 15200 NBN Way, Blue Ridge Summit, PA 17214 Tel 717-794-3800; Fax: 717-794-3803; Toll Free Fax: 800-338-4550; Toll Free: 800-462-6420; 67 Mowat Ave., Suite 241, Toronto, ON M6K 3E3 Tel 416-534-1660; Fax: 416-534-3699; Edit Addr.: 4501 Forbes Blvd., Suite 200, Lanham, MD 20706 (SAN 203-3704) Tel 301-459-3366; Fax: 301-429-5747 E-mail: Rogers@univpress.com Web site: http://www.rowmanlittlefield.com.

**Rushmore News, Inc.,** 924 East St. Andrew, Rapid City, SD 57701 (SAN 169-7846) Tel 605-342-2617; Fax: 605-342-9091; Toll Free: 800-423-0501 E-mail: afreese911@aol.com.

**Russell News Agency, Inc.,** P.O. Box 158, Sarasota, FL 33578 (SAN 169-1287).

**Russica Bk. & Art Shop, Inc.,** 799 Broadway, New York, NY 10003 (SAN 165-1072) Tel 212-473-7480; Fax: 212-473-7486.

**S & S News & Greeting,** 5304 15th Ave., S., Minneapolis, MN 55417-1812 (SAN 159-9453) Tel 612-224-8227; Toll Free: 800-346-9892.

**S & W Distributors, Inc.,** 1600-H E. Wendover Ave., Greensboro, NC 27405.

**S. A. V. E. with Victor Hotho,** *See* **S.A.V.E. Suzie & Vic Enterprises**

**S V E & Churchill Media,** *( 0-7932; 0-89290; 1-56357 )* 6677 N. Northwest Hwy., Chicago, IL 60631-1304 (SAN 208-3930) Tel 773-775-9550; Fax: 773-775-5091; Toll Free Fax: 800-624-1678; Toll Free: 800-829-1900 E-mail: custserv@svemedia.com Web site: http://www.svemedia.com.

**SAAN Corp.,** 189-01 Springfield Ave., Suite 201, Flossmoor, IL 60422 (SAN 631-0419) Tel 708-799-5225; Fax: 708-799-8713.

**Safari Museum Pr.,** 111 N. Lincoln Ave., Chanute, KS 66720 Tel 630-431-2730; Fax: 630-431-3848.

**Sagebrush Pr.,** *( 0-930704 )* P.O. Box 87, Morongo Valley, CA 92256 (SAN 113-387X) Tel 760-363-7398 Do not confuse with companies with same name in Cedarville, CA, Salt Lake City, UT.

**Saint Joe Distribution Center,** *See* **American Bk. Ctr.**

**Saks News, Inc.,** P.O. Box 1857, Bismarck, ND 58502 (SAN 169-653X).

**Sams Technical Publishing, LLC,** *( 0-7906 )* 9852 E. 30th St., Indianapolis, IN 46229 Toll Free Fax: 800-552-3910; Toll Free: 800-428-7267 E-mail: samstech@samswebsite.com Web site: http://www.samswebsite.com.

**San Diego Museum of Art,** *( 0-937108 )* Orders Addr.: P.O. Box 122107, San Diego, CA 92112-2107 Tel 619-696-1970; Fax: 619-232-9367 Web site: http://www.sdmart.org.

**San Franciscana,** *( 0-934715 )* P.O. Box 590955, San Francisco, CA 94159 (SAN 161-1607) Tel 415-751-7222.

**San Val, Inc.,** 1230 Macklind Ave., Saint Louis, MO 63110-1432 (SAN 159-947X) Tel 314-644-6100; Fax: 314-647-0979; Toll Free: 800-458-8438 E-mail: sanval@misn.com Web site: http://www.sanval.com.

**Sandlapper Publishing Co., Inc.,** *( 0-87844 )* Orders Addr.: P.O. Box 730, Orangeburg, SC 29115 (SAN 203-2678) Toll Free Fax: 800-337-9420 (orders); Toll Free: 800-849-7263 (orders); Edit Addr.: 1281 Amelia St., NE., Orangeburg, SC 29116 Tel 803-533-1658; Fax: 803-534-5223.

**Santa Barbara Botanic Garden,** *( 0-916436 )* 1212 Mission Canyon Rd., Santa Barbara, CA 93105 (SAN 208-8398) Tel 805-682-4726; Fax: 805-563-0352.

**Santa Barbara News Agency,** 725 S. Kellogg Ave., Goleta, CA 93117-3806 (SAN 168-9665) Tel 805-564-5200.

**Santa Monica Software, Inc.,** 30018 Zenith Point Rd., Malibu, CA 90265-4264 (SAN 630-6764) Tel 310-457-8381; Fax: 310-395-7635.

**Santillana USA Publishing Co., Inc.,** ( *0-88272; 1-56014; 1-58105; 84-294; 1-58986; 1-59437* ) Div. of Grup Santillana De Ediciones, S.A., 2105 NW 86th Ave., Miami, FL 33122 (SAN 205-1133) Tel 305-591-9522; Fax: 305-591-9145; Toll Free Fax: 800-530-8099 (orders); Toll Free: 800-245-8584 E-mail: customerservice@santillanausa.com Web site: http://www.santillanausa.com/.

**Saphrograph Corp.,** ( *0-87557* ) 5409 18th Ave., Brooklyn, NY 11204 (SAN 110-4128) Tel 718-331-1233; Fax: 718-331-8231.

**Sathya Sai Bk. Ctr. of America,** ( *1-57836* ) 305 W. First St., Tustin, CA 92780 (SAN 111-3542) Tel 714-669-0522; Fax: 714-669-9138 Web site: http://www.sathyasai.org/inform/tustin.html.

**S.A.V.E. Suzie & Vic Enterprises,** 303 N. Main, P.O. Box 30, Schulenburg, TX 78956 (SAN 630-6365) Tel 409-743-4145; Fax: 409-743-4147.

**SCB Distributors,** 15608 S. New Century Dr., Gardena, CA 90248-2129 (SAN 630-4818) Tel 310-532-9400; Fax: 310-532-7001; Toll Free: 800-729-6423 (orders only) E-mail: aaron@scbdistributors.com; info@scbdistributors.com Web site: http://www.scbdistributors.com.

**Schiffer Publishing, Ltd.,** ( *0-7643; 0-88740; 0-916838* ) 4880 Lower Valley Rd., Atglen, PA 19310 (SAN 208-8428) Tel 610-593-1777; Fax: 610-593-2002 E-mail: schifferii@aol.com Web site: http://www.schifferbooks.com.

**Schmul Publishing Co., Inc.,** ( *0-88019* ) Orders Addr.: P.O. Box 716, Salem, OH 44460-0716 (SAN 180-2771) Tel 330-222-2249; Fax: 330-222-0001; Toll Free: 800-772-6657; Edit Addr.: 3583 Newgarden Rd., Salem, OH 44460 E-mail: spchale@valunet.com Web site: http://www.wesleyanbooks.com.

**Schoenhof's Foreign Bks., Inc.,** ( *0-87774* ) Subs. of Editions Gallimard, 486 Green St., Cambridge, MA 02139 (SAN 212-0062) Tel 617-547-8855; Fax: 617-547-8551 E-mail: info@schoenhofs.com Web site: http://www.schoenhofs.com.

**Scholar's Bookshelf,** ( *0-945726* ) 110 Melrick Rd., Cranbury, NJ 08512 (SAN 110-8360) Tel 609-395-6933 E-mail: books@scholarsbookshelf.com Web site: http://www.scholarsbookshelf.com.

**Scholastic, Inc.,** ( *0-439; 0-590* ) Orders Addr.: c/o HarperCollins, 1000 Keystone Industrial Pk., Scranton, PA 18512 Toll Free: 800-242-7737; Edit Addr.: 557 Broadway, New York, NY 10012-3999 (SAN 202-5442) Tel 212-343-6100; Fax: 212-343-6802; Toll Free: 800-325-6149 (customer service) Web site: http://www.scholastic.com.

**Scholium International, Inc.,** ( *0-333; 0-87936* ) P.O. Box 1519, Port Washington, NY 11050-0306 (SAN 169-5282) Tel 516-767-7171; Fax: 516-944-9824 E-mail: info@scholium.com Web site: http://www.scholium.com.

**School Aid Co.,** ( *0-87385* ) 911 Colfax Dr., P.O. Box 123, Danville, IL 61832 (SAN 158-3719) Tel 217-442-6855; Toll Free: 800-447-2665.

**School Aids,** 9335 Interline Ave., Baton Rouge, LA 70809-1910 (SAN 169-2909) Tel 504-926-4498.

**School Bk. Service,** 3650 Coral Ridge Dr., Suite 112, Coral Springs, FL 33065-2559 (SAN 158-6963) Tel 954-341-7207; Fax: 954-341-7303; Toll Free: 800-228-7361 E-mail: compedge@ix.netcom.com.

**School of Metaphysics,** 163 Moonvalley Rd., Windyville, MO 65783 (SAN 159-5423) Tel 417-345-8411; Fax: 417-345-6668 E-mail: som@som.org Web site: http://www.som.org.

**Schroeder News Company,** *See* **Merced News Co.**

**Schroeder's Bk. Haven,** 104 Michigan Ave., League City, TX 77573 (SAN 122-7998) Tel 281-332-5226; Fax: 281-332-1695; Toll Free: 800-894-5032 E-mail: schroedr@interloc.com.

**Schulze News Co.,** 2451 Eastman Ave., Suite 13, Oxnard, CA 93030-5193 (SAN 169-0434) Tel 805-642-9759.

**Schuylkill News Service,** 1764 W. Market St., Pottsville, PA 17901 (SAN 159-9518) Tel 717-622-7510.

**Schwartz, Arthur & Co., Inc./Woodstocker Bks.,** ( *1-879504* ) 15 Meads Mountain Rd., Woodstock, NY 12498-1016 (SAN 630-0464) Tel 845-679-4024; Fax: 845-679-4093; Toll Free: 800-669-9080 (orders only) E-mail: aschwartz@aschwartzbooks.com Web site: http://www.aschwartzbooks.com.

**Schwartz Brothers, Inc.,** 822 Montgomery Ave., No. 204, Narberth, PA 19072-1937 (SAN 285-7529) Fax: 301-459-6418; Toll Free: 800-638-0243.

**Schwarz, F. A. O.,** 500 Pierce St., Somerset, NJ 08873-1270 (SAN 170-8554).

**Scientific & Medical Pubns. of France, Inc.,** 100 E. 42nd St., Suite 1510, New York, NY 10017 (SAN 169-5940) Tel 212-983-6278; Fax: 212-687-1407.

**Seaboard Sub Agency,** 44 S. Fulton St., Allentown, PA 18102 (SAN 285-9718) Tel 610-435-8174; Fax: 610-435-0290.

**Selective Bks., Inc.,** ( *0-912584* ) P.O. Box 1140, Clearwater, FL 34617 (SAN 204-577X) Tel 813-447-0100.

**Selective Publishers, Incorporated,** *See* **Selective Bks., Inc.**

**Semler News Agency,** Orders Addr.: P.O. Box 350, New Castle, PA 16101 (SAN 169-7471); Edit Addr.: P.O. Box 526, Morgantown, WV 26505 (SAN 169-8990).

**Seneca News Agency,** Box 631, Geneva, NY 14456 (SAN 169-5304) Tel 315-789-3551; Fax: 315-781-1015.

**Sentai Distributors,** 8839 Shirley Ave., Northridge, CA 91324 (SAN 168-9959) Tel 818-886-3113; Fax: 818-886-0423 Web site: http://www.plasticmodels.com.

**Sepher-Hermon Pr.,** ( *0-87203* ) 1153 45th St., Brooklyn, NY 11219 (SAN 169-5959) Tel 718-972-9010; Fax: 718-972-6935.

**Serendipity Couriers, Inc.,** 470 Du Bois St., San Rafael, CA 94901-3911 (SAN 169-0329) Tel 415-459-4000; Fax: 415-459-0833; Toll Free: 800-459-4005 (Bay area only) E-mail: dipity@14.netcom.com.

**Service News Co.,** 1306 N. 23rd St., Wilmington, NC 28406 (SAN 169-6491) Tel 910-762-0837; Fax: 910-762-9539; Toll Free: 800-552-8238; P.O. Box 5027, Macon, GA 31208; Pope's Island, Box D-629, New Bedford, MA 02742 (SAN 169-3514).

**Shambhala Pubns., Inc.,** ( *0-87773; 1-56957; 1-57062; 1-59030* ) Horticultural Hall, 300 Massachusetts Ave., Boston, MA 02115 (SAN 203-2481) Tel 617-424-0030; Fax: 617-236-1563 E-mail: editors@shambhala.com Web site: http://www.shambhala.com.

**Sharon News Agency Co.,** 527 Silver St., Sharon, PA 16146 (SAN 169-7633).

**Shasta Abbey Buddhist Supplies,** P.O. Box 1163, Mount Shasta, CA 96067 Tel 530-926-4208; Fax: 530-926-0428.

**Shea Bks.,** 1563 Solano Ave., Suite 206, Berkeley, CA 94707 (SAN 159-9720) Tel 510-528-5201; Fax: 510-528-4987.

**Shelter Pubns., Inc.,** ( *0-936070* ) Orders Addr.: P.O. Box 279, Bolinas, CA 94924 (SAN 122-8463) Tel 415-868-0280; Fax: 415-868-9053; Toll Free: 800-307-0131; Edit Addr.: 285 Dogwood Rd., Bolinas, CA 94924 E-mail: shelter@shelterpub.com Web site: http://www.shelterpub.com.

**Shen's Bks.,** ( *1-885008* ) 40951 Fremont Blvd., Fremont, CA 94538 (SAN 138-2926) Tel 510-668-1898; Fax: 510-668-1057; Toll Free: 800-456-6660 E-mail: info@shens.com Web site: http://www.shens.com.

**Sheridan Hse., Inc.,** ( *0-911378; 0-924486; 1-57409* ) 145 Palisade St., Dobbs Ferry, NY 10522 (SAN 204-5915) Tel 914-693-2410; Fax: 914-693-0776; Toll Free: 888-743-7425 (orders only) Do not confuse with Sheridan House, Inc., in Ft. Lauderdale, FL E-mail: Sheribks@aol.com Web site: http://www.sheridanhouse.com.

**Shinder's Book Company,** *See* **Shinders Readmore Bookstore, Inc.**

**Shinders Readmore Bookstore, Inc.,** 733 Hennepin Ave., Minneapolis, MN 55403 (SAN 125-6157) Tel 612-333-3628.

**Shoppers Guide Pr.,** 706 N. Fifth, Alpine, TX 79830 (SAN 159-9550) Tel 915-837-7426.

**Siena Library Co.,** 2101 Pennsylvania Ave., Suite 101, York, PA 17404 (SAN 631-2896) Tel 717-852-8712; Fax: 717-852-8554 E-mail: siena@cyberia.com; siena@blazenet.net.

**Sierra News Co.,** 2136 Pony Express Ct., Stockton, CA 95215-7946 (SAN 169-4472).

**Silky Way, Inc.,** 1227 38th Ave., San Francisco, CA 94122-1334 (SAN 169-3328).

**Silver Bow News Distributing Co., Inc.,** 219 E. Park St., Butte, MT 59701 (SAN 169-4359) Tel 406-782-6995.

**Silver, Burdett & Ginn, Inc.,** ( *0-382; 0-663* ) Orders Addr.: P.O. Box 2500, Lebanon, IN 46052 Toll Free Fax: 800-841-8939; Toll Free: 800-552-2259; Edit Addr.: P.O. Box 480, Parsippany, NJ 07054 (SAN 204-5982); 108 Wilmot Rd., Suite 380, Midwest Div., Deerfield, IL 60015 (SAN 111-6517) Tel 708-945-1240; 1925 Century Blvd. NE, Suite 14, Southeast Div., Atlanta, GA 30345 (SAN 111-6509); 8445 Freeport Pkwy., Suite 400, South Div., Irving, TX 75063 (SAN 108-0458) Tel 214-915-4200; 2001 The Alameda, West Div., San Jose, CA 95126 (SAN 111-6525) Tel 408-248-6854; 160 Gould St., East Div., Needham Heights, MA 02194-2310 E-mail: customerservice@scottforesman.com Web site: http://www.scottforesman.com/.

**Simon & Schuster,** ( *0-671; 0-684; 0-689; 0-914676; 0-7432* ) Div. of Simon & Schuster, Inc., Orders Addr.: 100 Front St., Riverside, NJ 08075 (SAN 200-2442) Toll Free Fax: 800-943-9831; Toll Free: 800-223-2348 (customer service); 800-223-2336 (ordering); Edit Addr.: 1230 Avenue of the Americas, New York, NY 10020 (SAN 200-2450) Tel 212-698-7000; Fax: 212-698-7007; Toll Free: 800-897-7650 (customer financial services) E-mail: ssonline_feedback@simonsays.com; consumer.customerservice@simonandschuster.com Web site: http://www.simonandschuster.com/ebooks; http://www.oasis.simonandschuster.com; http://www.simonsays.com.

**Simon & Schuster Children's Publishing,** ( *0-02; 0-671; 0-684; 0-689; 0-7434* ) Orders Addr.: 100 Front St., Riverside, NJ 08075 Toll Free Fax: 800-943-9831; Toll Free: 800-223-2336; Edit Addr.: 1230 Avenue of the Americas, New York, NY 10020 Tel 212-698-7200 Web site: http://www.simonsays.com.

**Simon & Schuster, Inc.,** ( *0-671* ) Div. of Viacom Co., Orders Addr.: 100 Front St., Riverside, NJ 08075 Toll Free Fax: 800-943-9831; Toll Free: 800-223-2336 (orders); 800-223-2348 (customer service); Edit Addr.: 1230 Ave. of the Americas, New York, NY 10020.

**Simon & Schuster Trade,** *See* **Simon & Schuster**

**Skandisk, Inc.,** ( *0-9615394; 1-57534* ) 6667 W. Old Shakopee Rd., Suite 109, Bloomington, MN 55438-2622 (SAN 695-4405) Tel 952-829-8998; Fax: 952-829-8992; Toll Free: 800-468-2424 (orders) E-mail: lhamnes@skandisk.com; tomten@skandisk.com Web site: http://www.skandisk.com.

**S&L Sales Co., Inc.,** Orders Addr.: P.O. Box 2067, Waycross, GA 31502 (SAN 107-413X) Tel 912-283-0210; Fax: 912-283-0261; Toll Free: 800-243-3699 (orders only).

**Slatner, Thomas & Co., Inc.,** 193 Palisade Ave., 3rd Flr., Jersey City, NJ 07036-1112 (SAN 130-9862) Tel 201-420-6700; Fax: 201-420-6787.

**Slavica Pubs.,** ( *0-89357* ) c/o Indiana University, 2611 E. Tenth St., Bloomington, IN 47408-2618 (SAN 208-8576) Tel 812-856-4186; Fax: 812-856-4187 E-mail: slavica@indiana.edu Web site: http://www.slavica.com.

**Sleuth Pubns., Ltd.,** ( *0-915341* ) 3398 Washington, San Francisco, CA 94118 (SAN 130-9374) Tel 415-771-2689.

**Small Press Distribution,** *See* **SPD-Small Pr. Distribution**

**Smith, Gibbs Pub.,** ( *0-87905; 1-58685* ) Orders Addr.: P.O. Box 667, Layton, UT 84041 (SAN 201-9906) Toll Free Fax: 800-213-3023 (orders); Toll Free: 800-748-5439 (orders); Edit Addr.: 1877 E. Gentile St., Layton, UT 84040 Tel 801-544-9800; Fax: 801-546-8853 E-mail: info@gibbs-smith.com; text@gibbs-smith.com Web site: http://www.gibbs-smith.com.

**Smith News Agency,** 118 S. Mitchell St., Cadillac, MI 49601 (SAN 169-3727).

**Smith, W. H. Publishers, Incorporated,** *See* **Smithmark Pubs., Inc.**

**Smithmark Pubs., Inc.,** ( *0-7651; 0-8317* ) Div. of US Media Holdings, 115 W. 18th St., 5th Flr., New York, NY 10011-4113 (SAN 176-0912) Tel 212-519-1300; Fax: 212-519-1310; Toll Free: 800-932-0070 (customer service); Raritan Plaza 111, Fieldcrest Ave., Edison, NJ 08837 (SAN 658-1625) Tel 732-225-6499 (phone/fax); Toll Free Fax: 800-732-8688.

**Smyrna Pr.,** ( *0-918266* ) Box 1151, Union City, NJ 07087 Tel 201-617-7247; Fax: 201-617-0203 E-mail: smyrnapress@hotmail.com.

**Snow Pocket Distributors,** Orders Addr.: c/o Sowbel, P.O. Box 64, West Topsham, VT 05086 Tel 802-439-6875 E-mail: sotops@sover.net Web site: http://www.dragonflies.com.

**Snyder Magazine Agency,** 3050 S. 9th Terr., Kansas City, KS 66103-2629 (SAN 285-9750).

**Social Studies Schl. Service,** ( 1-56004 ) 10200 Jefferson Blvd., P.O. Box 802, Culver City, CA 90232-0802 (SAN 168-9592) Tel 310-839-2436; Fax: 310-839-2249; Toll Free: 800-421-4246
E-mail: sssservice@aol.com
Web site: http://www.socialstudies.com.

**Society for Visual Education, Incorporated,** See **S V E & Churchill Media**

**Solafide Bk.,** P.O. Box 1981, Oldsmar, FL 34677-6981
E-mail: solabook@gte.net.

**Sonata Publishing,** ( 0-9642529 ) Orders Addr.: 1277 S. Adams St., Glendale, CA 91205 Tel 818-380-7155; Fax: 818-242-5551
E-mail: buttwinick@earthlink.net.

**Sort Card Co., The,** 400 S. Summit View Dr., Fort Collins, CO 80524-1424 (SAN 159-9607).

**Sounds True, Inc.,** ( 1-56455; 1-59179 ) 413 S. Arthur Ave., Boulder, CO 80027 Tel 303-665-3151; Fax: 303-665-5292; Toll Free: 800-333-9185
E-mail: traviss@soundstrue.com
Web site: http://www.soundstrue.com.

**Source Bks.,** ( 0-940147; 0-85650 ) Orders Addr.: 204 E. 4th St., Suite O, Santa Ana, CA 92701 (SAN 248-2231) Tel 714-558-8944 (phone/fax); Toll Free: 800-695-4237 Do not confuse with Source Bks., Nashville, TN
E-mail: studio185@earthlink.net.

**South Asia Bks.,** ( 0-8364; 0-88386 ) P.O. Box 502, Columbia, MO 65205 (SAN 207-4044) Tel 573-474-0116; Fax: 573-474-8124
E-mail: sabooks@juno.com
Web site: http://www.southasiabooks.com.

**South Atlantic News,** Orders Addr.: P.O. Box 61297, Jacksonville, FL 32236-1297; Edit Addr.: 1426 NE Eighth Ave., Ocala, FL 32678.

**South Carolina Bookstore,** Orders Addr.: P.O. Box 4767, West Columbia, SC 29171 (SAN 131-2294) Tel 803-796-8200; Fax: 803-794-6927; Toll Free: 800-845-8200; Edit Addr.: 523 Jasper St., West Columbia, SC 29169 (SAN 243-2390).

**South Central Bks., Inc.,** 1106 S. Strong Blvd., McAlester, OK 74501-6952 (SAN 108-1144) Tel 405-275-4522; Toll Free: 800-548-9858.

**South Eastern Bk. Co., Inc.,** 3333 Hwy. 641 N., P.O. Box 309, Murray, KY 42071 (SAN 630-4869) Tel 270-753-0732; Fax: 270-759-4742; Toll Free Fax: 800-433-6966 (orders); Toll Free: 800-626-3952 (orders)
E-mail: orders@sebook.com
Web site: http://www.sebook.com.

**South Louisiana News Company,** See **Southern Periodicals, Inc.**

**Southeast Library Bindery, Inc.,** P.O. Box 35484, Greensboro, NC 27425-5484 (SAN 159-9445) Tel 336-931-0800
E-mail: 70304.3023@compuserve.com
Web site: http://www.webmasters.net/bookbinding/.

**Southeast Periodical & Bk. Sales, Inc.,** 10100 NW 25th St., Box 520155-Biscayne Annex, Miami, FL 33152.

**Southeastern Educational Toy & Bk. Distributors,** Orders Addr.: P.O. Box 15129, Charlotte, NC 28211 (SAN 630-8104) Tel 704-364-6988; Edit Addr.: 4217 Park Rd., Charlotte, NC 28209 Tel 704-527-1921; Fax: 704-527-1653.

**Southeastern Library Service,** Subs. of Haskins Hse., P.O. Box 44, Gainesville, FL 32602-0044 (SAN 159-9615) Tel 352-372-3823.

**Southern Bk. Service,** ( 0-9663836 ) 5154 NW 165th St., Palmetto Lakes Industrial Pk., Hialeah, FL 33014-6335 (SAN 169-0981) Tel 305-624-4545; Fax: 305-621-0425; Toll Free: 800-766-3254
Web site: http://southernbooks.com.

**Southern Cross Pubns.,** 1734 W. Roseberry Rd., P.O. Box 717, Donnelly, ID 83615 (SAN 110-8549) Tel 208-325-8606; Fax: 208-325-3400
E-mail: scp@cyberhighway.net
Web site: http://www.thoughtlines.com/southerncross/.

**Southern Library Bindery Co.,** 2952 Sidco Dr., Nashville, TN 37204 (SAN 169-7986).

**Southern Michigan News Co.,** 2571 Saradan, P.O. Box 908, Jackson, MI 49204 (SAN 169-3697) Tel 517-784-7163; Toll Free: 800-248-2213 (in Michigan); 800-828-2140.

**Southern Periodicals, Inc.,** P.O. Box 407, Rayne, LA 70578-0407 (SAN 113-2520); 102 Industrial Dr., Rayne, LA 70578.

**Southern Territory Assocs.,** Orders Addr.: 4508 64th St., Lubbock, TX 79414 Toll Free Fax: 800-799-9777; Toll Free: 800-331-7016.

**Southern Tier News Co.,** P.O. Box 2128, Elmira Heights, NY 14903 (SAN 169-5223).

**Southern Wisconsin News,** 4838 N. County Rd. Y, Milton, WI 53563 (SAN 169-9121) Tel 608-756-2376 ; Fax: 608-756-2357.

**Southwest Cookbook Distributors,** Orders Addr.: P.O. Box 707, Bonham, TX 75418 (SAN 200-4925) Tel 903-583-8898; Fax: 903-583-2522; Toll Free: 800-725-8898 (orders); Edit Addr.: 1430 Texas Ave., Bonham, TX 75418 (SAN 630-8325).

**Southwest Natural Cultural Heritage Association,** See **Public Lands Interpretive Assn.**

**Southwest News Co.,** Box 5465, Tucson, AZ 85704 (SAN 159-9631).

**Southwestern Bk. Distributors,** c/o Kerbs, 700 Highview Ave., Glen Ellyn, IL 60137-5504 (SAN 160-2373).

**Southwood Healing Institute,** ( 1-893657 ) R.R. 1, Box 286 C, Machias, ME 04654 Tel 207-255-8856; Fax: 207-255-4506
E-mail: dlight@midmaine.com; malcolmsou@aol.com
Web site: http://www.southwoodhealing.com.

**Sovereign News Company,** See **Trans World News**

**Spama, Inc.,** 78 Lake St., Jersey City, NJ 07306-3407 (SAN 169-5967).

**Spanish & European Bookstore, Inc.,** 3102 Wilshire Blvd., Los Angeles, CA 90010 Tel 213-739-8899; Fax: 213-739-0087.

**Spanish Bookstore-Wholesale, The,** 10977 Santa Monica Blvd., Los Angeles, CA 90025-4538 (SAN 168-9835) Tel 310-475-0453; Fax: 310-473-6132
E-mail: BernardHamel@SpanishbooksUSA.com
Web site: http://www.BernardHamel.com.

**Spanish Hse. Distributors,** 1360 NW 88th Ave., Miami, FL 33172-3093 (SAN 169-1171) Tel 305-592-6136; Fax: 305-592-0087; Toll Free: 800-767-7726.

**Spanishtech, Inc.,** Div. of Editor's Bureau, Ltd., P.O. Box 68, Westport, CT 06881 (SAN 289-9620) Tel 203-452-7655.

**SPD-Small Pr. Distribution,** ( 0-914068 ) 1341 Seventh St., Berkeley, CA 94710-1409 (SAN 204-5826) Tel 510-524-1668; Fax: 510-524-0852; Toll Free: 800-869-7553 (orders)
E-mail: orders@spdbooks.org
Web site: http://www.spdbooks.org.

**Specialized Bk. Service, Inc.,** 307 Autumn Ridge Rd., Fairfield, CT 06432-1003 (SAN 166-9788) Tel 203-377-6510; Fax: 203-377-4792.

**Specialty Bk. Services,** 1150 N. San Francisco, Flagstaff, AZ 86001 (SAN 130-8114) Tel 520-779-7843.

**Specialty Promotions,** 6841 S. Cregier Ave., Chicago, IL 60649 (SAN 110-9987) Tel 773-493-6900.

**Speedimpex U.S.A., Inc.,** 35-02 48th Ave., Long Island City, NY 11101-2421 (SAN 169-5479) Tel 718-392-7477; Fax: 718-361-0815
E-mail: nsalvatore@speedimpex.com
Web site: http://www.speedimpex.com.

**Spencer Museum of Art,** ( 0-913689 ) Affil. of Univ. of Kansas, Univ. of Kansas 1301 Mississippi St., Lawrence, KS 66045-7500 (SAN 111-347X) Tel 785-864-4710; Fax: 785-864-3112
E-mail: spencerart@ku.edu
Web site: http://www.ukans.edu/~sma.

**Spring Arbor Distributors, Inc.,** Subs. of Ingram Industries Inc., 4271 Edison Ave., Chino, CA 91710; 7315 Innovation Blvd., Fort Wayne, IN 46818-1371; 201 Ingram Dr., Roseburg, OR 97470-7148; Newbury Rd., East Windsor, CT 06088; 25420 Weakley Rd., Petersburg, VA 23803; 11333 E. 53rd Ave., Denver, CO 80239-2108; Edit Addr.: 1 Ingram Blvd., La Vergne, TN 37086-1976 Fax: 615-213-5192; Toll Free: 800-395-4340; 800-395-7234 (customer service)
E-mail: orders@springarbor.com.

**Springwater Bks.,** Orders Addr.: P.O. Box 194, Springwater, NY 14560-0194 (SAN 111-8900); Edit Addr.: Main St. & East Ave., Springwater, NY 14560-0194 (SAN 243-2412) Tel 716-669-2450.

**Sprout, Inc.,** Orders Addr.: 430 Tenth Street, NW, Suite 007, Atlanta, GA 30318 Tel 404-892-9600; Fax: 404-881-1383.

**Square Deal Records,** 303 Higuera St., San Luis Obispo, CA 93401-4209 (SAN 170-6799) Tel 805-543-3636; Fax: 805-543-3938; Toll Free: 800-253-4114
E-mail: sdrsslo@aol.com.

**St. Marie's Gopher News Co.,** 9000 Tenth Ave., N., Minneapolis, MN 55427 (SAN 169-4103) Tel 612-546-5300; Fax: 612-546-1487.

**St. Martin's Pr.,** ( 0-312; 0-8050; 0-940687; 0-9603648; 1-55927; 1-58063; 1-58238 ) Div. of Holtzbrinck Publishers, Orders Addr.: 16365 James Madison Hwy., Gordonville, VA 22942 Tel 540-672-7600; Fax: 540-672-7540 (customer service); Toll Free Fax: 800-672-2054; Toll Free: 888-330-8477; Edit Addr.: 175 Fifth Ave., New York, NY 10010 (SAN 200-2132) Tel 212-726-0200 (College Div.);

212-674-5151 (Trade Div.); Fax: 212-686-9491 (College Div.); 212-674-3179 (Trade Div.); Toll Free: 800-470-4767 (College Div.); 800-221-7945 (Trade Div.)
E-mail: webmaster@stmartins.com; enquiries@stmartins.com
Web site: http://www.smpcollege.com; http://www.stmartins.com.

**St. Mary Seminary Bookstore,** 28700 Euclid Ave., Wyckliffe, OH 44092 (SAN 169-667X) Tel 216-943-7600.

**Stackpole Bks.,** ( 0-8117 ) 5067 Ritter Rd., Mechanicsburg, PA 17055 (SAN 202-5396) Tel 717-796-0411; Fax: 717-796-0412
E-mail: sales@stackpolebooks.com
Web site: http://www.stackpolebooks.com.

**Star Bright Bks., Inc.,** ( 1-887734; 1-932065 ) 42-26 28th St., Suite 2C, Long Island City, NY 11101 (SAN 254-5225) Tel 718-784-9112; Fax: 718-784-9012; Toll Free: 800-788-4439
E-mail: info@starbrightbooks.com
Web site: http://www.starbrightbooks.com.

**Starkmann Inc.,** 38 River St., Winchester, MA 01890 (SAN 126-6128) Tel 781-721-1537; Fax: 781-721-2825
E-mail: biggs@starkmann.co.uk.

**Starmaster Co.,** 6911 Haverhill Dr., Knoxville, TN 37909 (SAN 108-1217) Tel 423-588-6661.

**State Mutual Bk. & Periodical Service, Ltd.,** ( 0-7855; 0-89771 ) Orders Addr.: P.O. Box 1199, Bridgehampton, NY 11932-1199.

**State News Agency,** 2750 Griffith Rd., Winston Salem, NC 27103-6418 (SAN 169-6424).

**SteinerBooks, Inc.,** ( 0-8334; 0-88010; 0-89345; 0-910142; 1-58420; 1-85584; 0-9701097 ) Orders Addr.: P.O. Box 960, Herndon, VA 20172-0960 Tel 703-661-1594 (orders); Fax: 702-661-1501; Toll Free Fax: 800-277-7947 (orders); Toll Free: 800-856-8664 (orders); Edit Addr.: P.O. Box 799, Great Barrington, MA 01230 Tel 413-528-8233; Fax: 413-528-8826; Fulfillment Addr.: 22883 Quicksilver Dr., Dulles, VA 20166 (SAN 253-9519) Tel 703-661-1529; Fax: 703-996-1010
E-mail: service@steinerbooks.org
Web site: http://www.lindisfarne.org; http://www.bellpondbooks.com; http://www.steinerbooks.org.

**Sterling Publishing Co., Inc.,** ( 0-8069; 1-4027 ) 387 Park Ave., S., New York, NY 10016-8810 (SAN 211-6324) Tel 212-532-7160; Fax: 212-213-2495; Toll Free Fax: 800-775-8736 (warehouse) Do not confuse with companies with similar names in Falls Church, VA, Fallbrook, CA, Lewisville, TX
E-mail: custservice@sterlingpub.com
Web site: http://www.sterlingpub.com.

**Sterling Publishing Company, Incorporated,** See **Sterling Publishing Co., Inc.**

**Stevens, Mark Industries,** Div. of Christian World, Inc., 1215 N. Portland, Oklahoma City, OK 73107 (SAN 631-127X) Tel 405-948-1077; Fax: 405-948-1110; Toll Free: 800-654-6760.

**Stowe, Daniel J. Foundation,** P.O. Box 1046, Belmont, NC 28012.

**Strauss Consultants,** 48 W. 25th St., 11th Flr., New York, NY 10010-2708 Toll Free Fax: 888-528-8273; Toll Free: 800-236-7918
E-mail: strausscon@aol.com.

**Strelow, James C.,** 9440 El Blanco Ave., Fountain Valley, CA 92708 (SAN 132-4144) Tel 714-962-3697.

**Studio Bks.,** ( 0-14; 0-670 ) Div. of Penguin Putnam, Orders Addr.: c/o Penguin USA, 405 Murray Hill Pkwy., East Rutherford, NJ 07073-2136 Tel 201-387-0600; Fax: 201-385-6521; Toll Free: 800-526-0275 Do not confuse with Studiobooks, McLean, NY
Web site: http://www.penguinputnam.com/.

**Stylus Publishing, LLC,** ( 1-57922 ) Orders Addr.: P.O. Box 605, Herndon, VA 20172-0605; Edit Addr.: 22883 Quicksilver Dr., Sterling, VA 20166-2012 (SAN 299-1853) Tel 703-661-1581; Fax: 703-661-1501 Do not confuse with companies with the same name in Sunnyvale, CA, Quakertown, PA
E-mail: stylusmail@presswarehouse.com
Web site: http://www.styluspub.com.

**Subscription Acct.,** 84 Needham, Newton Highlands, MA 02161 (SAN 285-9424).

**Subscription Hse., Inc.,** 209 Harvard St., Suite 407, Brookline, MA 02146-5005 (SAN 285-9343).

**Subterranean Co.,** Orders Addr.: P.O. Box 160, Monroe, OR 97456 Tel 541-847-5274; Fax: 541-847-6018
E-mail: subco@clipper.net.

**Success Education Assn.,** Box 175, Roanoke, VA 24002 (SAN 159-9690).

**Sun Life,** ( 0-937930 ) 2399 Cool Springs Rd., Thaxton, VA 24174 (SAN 240-8333) Tel 540-586-4898.

**Sun News Company,** *See* **Anderson News Co.**

**Sunbelt Media, Incorporated,** *See* **Eakin Pr.**

**Sunbelt Pubns., Inc.,** ( 0-916251; 0-932653; 0-9606704; 0-9620402 ) 1250 Fayette St., El Cajon, CA 92020-1511 (SAN 630-0790) Tel 619-258-4911; Fax: 619-258-4916; Toll Free: 800-626-6579 E-mail: sunbeltpub@prodigy.net Web site: http://www.sunbeltpub.com.

**Sunburst Communications, Inc.,** ( 0-7805; 0-911831; 1-55636; 1-55826 ) 101 Castleton St., Pleasantville, NY 10570 (SAN 213-5620) Tel 914-747-3310; Toll Free: 800-431-1934 E-mail: webmaster@nysunburst.com Web site: http://www.sunburst.com.

**Sundance Publishing,** ( 0-7608; 0-88741; 0-940146; 1-56801 ) Orders Addr.: P.O. Box 1326, Littleton, MA 01460 (SAN 169-3484) Tel 978-486-9201; Fax: 978-486-1053; Toll Free Fax: 800-456-2419; Toll Free: 800-343-8204 Do not confuse with Sundance Publishing, Inc., Patchogue, NY E-mail: info@sundancepub.com Web site: http://www.sundancepub.com/.

**Sunset Bks./Sunset Publishing Corp.,** ( 0-376 ) 80 Willow Rd., Menlo Park, CA 94025-3691 Tel 650-321-3600; Fax: 650-324-1532; Toll Free: 800-227-7346 (except California); 800-321-0372 (in California) Web site: http://sunsetbooks.com.

**Sunshine Harbor,** 825 Glen Arden Way, Altamonte Springs, FL 32701 (SAN 159-6640) Tel 407-339-0401.

**Suttertown Publishing,** P.O. Box 214, Dunsmuir, CA 96025 Tel 530-235-4034.

**Swedenborg Foundation, Inc.,** ( 0-87785 ) 320 N. Church St., West Chester, PA 19380 (SAN 111-7920) Tel 610-430-3222; Fax: 610-430-7982; Toll Free: 800-355-3222 (customer service) E-mail: info@swedenborg.com Web site: http://www.Swedenborg.com.

**Swenson, Jim,** 2610 Riverside Ln., NE, Rochester, MN 55901 (SAN 285-9505).

**Swift News Agency,** Orders Addr.: P.O. Box 160, Poncha Springs, CO 81242 (SAN 282-3810); Edit Addr.: 338 E. Hwy. 50, Poncha Springs, CO 81242 (SAN 169-0639).

**Symmes Systems,** ( 0-916352 ) 3977 Briarcliff Rd., NE, Atlanta, GA 30345-2647 (SAN 169-1465) Tel 404-876-7260.

**T A Bookstore,** *See* **Shea Bks.**

**Tabby Hse. Bks.,** ( 0-9627974; 1-881539 ) Orders Addr.: 4429 Shady Ln., Charlotte Harbor, FL 33980 Tel 941-629-7646; Fax: 941-629-4270 E-mail: publisher@tabbyhouse.com Web site: http://www.tabbyhouse.com.

**Tallahassee News Co., Inc.,** 3777 Hartsfield Rd., Tallahassee, FL 32303-1120.

**Tapestry Pr., Inc.,** ( 1-930819 ) 3649 Conflans Rd., No. 103, Irving, TX 75061 Tel 972-399-8856; Fax: 972-313-9060 Do not confuse with companies with the same or similar name in Acton, MA, Springville, UT, Biloxi, MS E-mail: info@tapestrypressinc.com Web site: http://www.summitbooks.com.

**Tapeworm Video Distributor, Inc.,** 27833 Avenue Hopkins, Unit 6, Valencia, CA 91355-3407 (SAN 630-8767) Tel 805-257-4904; Fax: 805-257-4820; Toll Free: 800-367-8437 E-mail: sales@tapeworm.com Web site: http://www.tapeworm.com.

**Tatnuck BookSeller, The,** 335 Chandler St., Worcester, MA 01602-3402 (SAN 169-3654) Tel 508-756-7644.

**Taylor & Francis, Inc.,** ( 0-335; 0-415; 0-8448; 0-85066; 0-89116; 0-903796; 0-905273; 1-56032; 1-85000 ) Orders Addr.: 10650 Toebben Dr., Independence, KY 41051 Tel Toll Free Fax: 800-248-4724; Toll Free: 800-634-7064; Edit Addr.: 325 Chestnut St., Philadelphia, PA 19106 (SAN 241-9246) Tel 215-625-8900; Fax: 215-625-2940; 29 W. 35th St., New York, NY 10001 Tel 212-216-7800; Fax: 212-564-7854 E-mail: info@taylorandfrancis.com Web site: http://www.taylorandfrancis.com.

**TBN Enterprises,** *See* **Ironside International Pubs., Inc.**

**Technical Bk. Co.,** P.O. Box 25934, Los Angeles, CA 90025-8994 (SAN 168-9851) Toll Free: 800-233-5150.

**Techno Mecca, Inc.,** 4412 W. Pico Blvd., 2nd Flr., Los Angeles, CA 90019 (SAN 631-7812) Tel 213-353-3900; Fax: 213-353-3910 E-mail: tjtj@tmecca.com Web site: http://www.tmecca.com.

**Temme Haus Pr.,** ( 0-9727036 ) 1784 Palm Ave., Stockton, CA 95205 (SAN 253-1925) Tel 209-463-5527.

**Temple News Agency,** *See* **ETD KroMar Temple**

**Ten Speed Pr.,** ( 0-89815; 0-913668; 1-58008 ) Orders Addr.: P.O. Box 7123, Berkeley, CA 94707 (SAN 202-7674) Fax: 510-559-1629 (orders); Toll Free: 800-841-2665; 555 Richmond St., W. Suite 405, Box 702, Toronto, ON M5V 3B1 Tel 416-703-7775; Fax: 416-703-9992 E-mail: order@tenspeed.com; alan@tenspeed.ca; greg@tenspeed.com Web site: http://www.tenspeed.com.

**Tesla Bk. Co.,** ( 0-914119; 0-9603536 ) P.O. Box 121873, Chula Vista, CA 91912-6573 (SAN 241-8703) Tel 619-585-8487; Toll Free: 800-398-2056 E-mail: bfeuling@teslabook.com.

**Texas A&M Univ. Pr.,** ( 0-89096; 1-58544 ) 4354 TAMU John H. Lindsey Bldg., Lewis St., College Station, TX 77843-4354 (SAN 658-1919) Tel 979-845-1436; Fax: 979-847-8752; Toll Free Fax: 888-617-2421 (orders); Toll Free: 800-826-8911 (orders) E-mail: wjl@tampress.tamu.edu Web site: http://www.tamu.edu/upress/.

**Texas Art Supply,** 2001 Montrose Blvd., Houston, TX 77006 (SAN 169-8303) Tel 713-526-5221; Fax: 713-524-7474; Toll Free: 800-888-9278 E-mail: info@texasart.com Web site: http://www.texasart.com.

**Texas Bk. Co.,** P.O. Box 212, Greenville, TX 75403 Fax: 903-454-2442; Toll Free: 800-527-1016 E-mail: monica@texasbook.com; diana@texasbook.com.

**Texas Bookman, The,** ( 1-931040 ) 2700 Lone Star Dr., Dallas, TX 75212-6209 (SAN 106-875X) Toll Free: 800-566-2665 E-mail: texas.bookman@halfpricebooks.com.

**Texas Hill Country Cookbook,** P.O. Box 126, Round Mountain, TX 78663 (SAN 110-831X) Tel 210-825-3242; Fax: 210-825-3244; Toll Free: 800-231-3553.

**Texas Library Bk. Sales,** 1408 West Koenig Lane, Austin, TX 78756 (SAN 169-8044) Tel 512-452-4140.

**Thames Bk. Co.,** 1 Quarry Rd., Mystic, CT 06355-3200 (SAN 169-0760).

**Thieme Medical Pubs., Inc.,** ( 0-86577; 0-913258; 1-58890 ) Subs. of Georg Thieme Verlag Stuttgart, 333 Seventh Ave., 5th Flr., New York, NY 10001 (SAN 169-5983) Tel 212-760-0888; Fax: 212-947-1112; Toll Free: 800-782-3488 (orders only) E-mail: Info@Thieme.com; custserv@thieme.de Web site: http://www.thieme.com.

**Thieme-Stratton, Inc.,** *See* **Thieme Medical Pubs., Inc.**

**Thinkers' Pr., Inc.,** ( 0-938650; 1-888710 ) Orders Addr.: P.O. Box 8, Davenport, IA 52805-0008 Tel 319-323-1226; Fax: 319-323-0511; Toll Free: 800-397-7117 (orders only); Edit Addr.: 1101 W. Fourth St., Davenport, IA 52802 (SAN 162-7759) E-mail: tpi@chessco.com Web site: http://www.chessco.com.

**Thomas Brothers Maps,** ( 0-88130; 1-58174 ) Div. of Rand McNally & Co., 17731 Cowan, Irvine, CA 92614 (SAN 158-8192) Fax: 949-757-1564; Toll Free: 800-899-6277 Web site: http://www.thomas.com.

**Thompson Schl. Bk. Depository,** Orders Addr.: P.O. Box 60160, Oklahoma City, OK 73146 (SAN 159-9747) Tel 405-525-9458; Fax: 405-524-5443; Edit Addr.: 39 NE 24th St., Oklahoma City, OK 73143.

**Thomson Learning,** 10650 Toebben Dr., Independence, KY 41051 (SAN 631-2144) Tel 859-525-6620; Fax: 859-525-0978; Toll Free: 800-347-7707 (customer service); 800-842-3636 (orders); a/o Customer Service, P.O. Box 6904, Florence, KY 41022-6904 Toll Free Fax: 800 487-8488; Toll Free: 800 354-9706 Web site: http://www.thomsonlearning.com.

**Thomson, Linda,** P.O. Box 1225, Orem, UT 84059-1225 (SAN 110-3881) Tel 801-226-0155; Fax: 801-226-0166; Toll Free: 800-226-0155.

**Thorndike Pr.,** ( 0-7838; 0-7862; 0-8161; 0-89621; 1-56054 ) Div. of Gale Group, 295 Kennedy Memorial Dr., Waterville, ME 04901 Tel 207-859-1053; 207-859-1020; 207-859-1000; Toll Free Fax: 800-558-4676; Toll Free: 800-223-1244 (ext. 15); 800-877-4253 (customer resource ctr.) E-mail: knobloch@galegroup.com; barb.littfield@galegroup.com Web site: http://www.galegroup.com/thorndike.

**Tiffin News Agency,** 1024 S. Bon Aire Ave., Tiffin, OH 44883-2553 (SAN 169-6866).

**Tiger Bk. Distributors, Ltd.,** 328 S. Jefferson, Chicago, IL 60661 (SAN 631-0672) Tel 312-382-1160; Fax: 312-382-0323.

**Time Warner Bk. Group,** ( 0-446 ) Orders Addr.: 3 Center Plaza, Boston, MA 02108 Toll Free Fax: 800-286-9471; Toll Free: 800-759-0190; Edit Addr.: 135 W. 50th St. Sports Illustrated Building, New York, NY 10020-1393 Tel 212-522-7381; Toll Free Fax: 800-477-5925 Web site: http://www.timewarner.com.

**TIS, Inc.,** ( 0-89917; 1-56581; 0-7421 ) Orders Addr.: P.O. Box 669, Bloomington, IN 47402 Tel 812-332-3307; Fax: 812-331-7690; Toll Free: 800-367-4002; Edit Addr.: 5005 N. State Rd. 37 Business, Bloomington, IN 47404.

**Titan Bookstore,** P.O. Box 34080, Fullerton, CA 92634-9480 (SAN 106-4851).

**Title Bks., Inc.,** 3013 Second Ave. S, Birmingham, AL 35233 (SAN 168-9207) Tel 205-324-2596.

**TMW Media Group, Inc.,** 2321 Abbot Kinney Blvd., Venice, CA 90291 Tel 310-577-8581; Fax: 310-574-0886; Toll Free: 800-262-8862 E-mail: vqvideo@tmwmedia.com Web site: http://www.tmwmedia.com.

**Tobias News Co.,** 130 18th St., Rock Island, IL 61201 (SAN 169-2186) Tel 309-788-7517.

**Todd Communications,** ( 1-57833; 1-878100 ) 203 W. 15th Ave., Suite 102, Anchorage, AK 99501 (SAN 298-6280) Tel 907-274-8633; Fax: 907-276-6858 E-mail: info@toddcom.com

**Total Information, Inc.,** 844 Dewey Ave., Rochester, NY 14613 (SAN 123-7373) Tel 716-254-0621.

**Tracor Technology Resources (TTR), Specialized Bk. Distributors,** 1601 Research Blvd., Rockville, MD 20850 (SAN 169-3220) Tel 301-251-4970.

**Trafalgar Square,** ( 0-943955; 1-57076 ) Orders Addr.: P.O. Box 257, North Pomfret, VT 05053 (SAN 213-8859) Tel 802-457-1911; Fax: 802-457-1913; Toll Free: 800-423-4525; Edit Addr.: Howe Hill Rd., North Pomfret, VT 05053 E-mail: tsquare@sover.net Web site: http://www.trafalgarsquarebooks.com.

**Trans World News,** 3700 Kelley Ave., Cleveland, OH 44114-4533 (SAN 169-6688) Tel 216-391-4800; Fax: 216-391-9911; Toll Free: 800-321-9858.

**Transaction Pubs.,** ( 0-7658; 0-87855; 0-88738; 1-56000; 1-4128 ) 390 Campus Dr., Somerset, NJ 08873 (SAN 202-7941) Tel 732-445-2280; Fax: 732-445-3138; Toll Free: 888-999-6778 E-mail: orders@transactionpub.com; agarbie@transactionpub.com Web site: http://www.transactionpub.com.

**Transamerican & Export News Co.,** 591 Camino de la Reina St., Suite 200, San Diego, CA 92108-3192 (SAN 169-0140) Tel 619-297-8065; Fax: 619-297-5353.

**Trans-Atlantic Pubns., Inc.,** 311 Bainbridge St., Philadelphia, PA 19147 (SAN 694-0234) Tel 215-925-5083; Fax: 215-925-1912 Do not confuse with Transatlantic Arts, Inc., Albuquerque, NM E-mail: order@transatlanticpub.com Web site: http://www.transatlanticpub.com.

**Traveler Restaurant,** 741 Buckley Hwy., Union, CT 06076 (SAN 111-8218) Tel 860-684-4920.

**Treasure Chest Bks.,** ( 0-918080; 1-887896; 0-9700750 ) Orders Addr.: P.O. Box 5250, Tucson, AZ 85703-0250 (SAN 209-3251) Tel 520-623-9558; Fax: 520-624-5888; Toll Free Fax: 800-715-5888; Toll Free: 800-969-9558; Edit Addr.: 451 N. Bonita Ave., Tucson, AZ 85745 Tel 602-623-9558 E-mail: info@treasurechestbooks.com; info@rionuevo.com Web site: http://www.rionuevo.com/; http://www.treasurechestbooks.com

**Treasure Chest Publications,** *See* **Treasure Chest Bks.**

**Treasure Valley News,** 4242 S. Eagleson Rd. Ste. 108B, Boise, ID 83705-4985.

**Tree Frog Trucking Co.,** 318 SW Taylor St., Portland, OR 97204 (SAN 169-7188) Tel 503-227-4760; Fax: 503-227-0829.

**Tree of Life Midwest,** P.O. Box 2629, Bloomington, IN 47402-2629 (SAN 169-7994) Toll Free: 800-999-4200.

**Triangle News Co., Inc.,** 3498 Grand Ave., Pittsburgh, PA 15225 (SAN 169-7447).

**Tri-County News Co., Inc.,** 1376 W. Main St., Santa Maria, CA 93458 (SAN 169-0345) Tel 805-925-6541; Fax: 805-925-3565 E-mail: trico2000@aol.com Web site: http://tri-countynews.com.

**Trinity Pr. International,** ( *1-56338* ) Orders Addr.: P.O. Box 1321, Harrisburg, PA 17105-1321 Tel 717-541-8130; Fax: 717-671-5929; Toll Free: 800-877-0012; Edit Addr.: 4775 Linglestown Rd., Harrisburg, PA 17112 (SAN 253-8156) Fax: 717-541-8128 (administrative); 717-541-8136 (editorial) E-mail: trinity@morehousegroup.com Web site: http://www.trinitypressintl.

**Tri-State News Agency,** P.O. Box 778, Johnson City, TN 37601 (SAN 169-7897) Tel 423-926-8159; 604 Rolling Hills Dr., Johnson City, TN 37601 (SAN 282-4744).

**Tri-State Periodicals, Inc.,** Orders Addr.: P.O. Box 1110, Evansville, IN 47706-1110 Tel 812-867-7416; Edit Addr.: 9844 Heddon Rd., Evansville, IN 47711 (SAN 241-7537) Tel 812-867-7419.

**Trucatriche,** Orders Addr.: 3800 Main St., Suite 8, Chula Vista, CA 91911 Tel 619-426-2690; Fax: 619-426-2695 E-mail: info@trucatriche.com.

**Tulare County News,** Box 831, Visalia, CA 93279 (SAN 169-0442) Tel 559-734-9206; Fax: 559-734-5732; Toll Free: 800-479-6006.

**Turner Subscription Agency,** Subs. of Dawson Holdings PLC, 1005 W Pines Rd., Oregon, IL 61061-9681 (SAN 107-7112) Tel 815-732-4476; Fax: 815-732-4489; Toll Free: 800-847-4201 E-mail: postmaster@dawson.com.

**Tuttle Publishing,** ( *0-8048; 4-900737* ) Orders Addr.: 364 Innovation Dr., North Clarendon, VT 05759-9436 Tel 802-773-8930; Fax: 802-773-6993; Toll Free Fax: 800-329-8885; Toll Free: 800-526-2778; Edit Addr.: 153 Milk St., 4th Flr., Boston, MA 02109 (SAN 213-2621) Tel 617-951-4080; Fax: 617-951-4045; Toll Free: 800) 247 1060 E-mail: info@tuttlepublishing.com Web site: http://www.tuttlemartialarts.com; http://www.tuttlepublishing.com.

**Twentieth Century Christian Bks.,** ( *0-89098* ) 2809 Granny White Pike, Nashville, TN 37204 (SAN 206-2550) Tel 615-383-3842.

**Twin City News Agency, Inc.,** P.O. Box 466, Lafayette, IN 47902-0466 Tel 765-742-1051.

**Tyndale Hse. Pubs.,** ( *0-8423; 1-4143* ) Orders Addr.: P.O. Box 80, Wheaton, IL 60189-0080 (SAN 206-7749) Tel 630-668-8310; Fax: 630-668-3245; Toll Free: 800-323-9400; Edit Addr.: 351 Executive Dr., Wheaton, IL 60188 Web site: http://www.tyndale.com.

**Ubiquity Distributors, Inc.,** 607 Degraw St., Brooklyn, NY 11217 (SAN 200-7428) Tel 718-875-5491; Fax: 718-875-8047.

**Ultra Bks.,** P.O. Box 945, Oakland, NJ 07436 (SAN 112-9074) Tel 201-337-8787.

**Ulverscroft Large Print Bks., Ltd.,** ( *0-7089* ) Div. of F. A Thorpe, Orders Addr.: P.O. Box 1230, West Seneca, NY 14224-1230; Edit Addr.: 1881 Ridge Rd., West Seneca, NY 14224-1230 (SAN 208-3035) Tel 716-674-4270; Fax: 716-674-4195; Toll Free: 800-955-9659 E-mail: enquiries@ulverscroft.co.uk Web site: http://www.ulverscroft.co.uk.

**Unarius Academy of Science Pubns.,** ( *0-932642; 0-935097* ) Orders Addr.: 145 S. Magnolia Ave., El Cajon, CA 92020-4522 (SAN 168-9614) Tel 619-444-7062; Fax: 619-444-9637; Toll Free: 800-475-7062 E-mail: uriel@unarius.org Web site: http://www.unarius.org.

**Underground Railroad, The,** 2769 Club House Rd., Mobile, AL 36605-4373 (SAN 630-7892) Tel 334-432-8811.

**UNIPUB,** *See* **Bernan Assocs.**

**Unique Bks., Inc.,** 5010 Kemper Ave., Saint Louis, MO 63139 (SAN 630-0472) Tel 314-776-6695; Fax: 314-776-0841; Toll Free: 800-533-5446.

**United Magazine,** Orders Addr.: P.O. Box 36, Columbia, KY 42728-0036 (SAN 169-2852) Tel 502-384-3444; Fax: 502-384-9324; Edit Addr.: 361 Industrial Park Rd., Louisville, KY 42728-0036 (SAN 250-3336).

**United Nations Pubns.,** ( *0-680; 0-89714; 92-1; 92-808; 952-9520* ) 2 United Nations Plaza, Sales Section, Publishing Div., Rm. DC2-853, New York, NY 10017 (SAN 206-6718) Tel 212-963-7680 UN Bookshop; 212-963-8302; Fax: 212-963-4910 UN Bookshop; 212-963-3489; Toll Free: 800-553-3210 UN Bookshop; 800-253-9646 (bookshop orders) E-mail: publications@un.org Web site: http://www.un.org/pubs.

**United News Co., Inc.,** 111 Lake St., P.O. Box 3426, Bakersfield, CA 93305 (SAN 169-7579) Tel 805-323-7864.

**United Society of Shakers,** ( *0-915836* ) 707 Shaker Rd., New Gloucester, ME 04260 (SAN 158-619X) Tel 207-926-4597; Fax: 207-926-3559 E-mail: sdlshakers@aol.com Web site: http://www.shaker.lib.me.us.

**United Subscription Service,** 527 Third Ave., No. 284, New York, NY 10016-4100 (SAN 286-0104).

**Univ of Arizona Critical Languages Program,** 1230 N. Park Ave., Suite 102, Tucson, AZ 85719.

**Univ. of Arizona Pr.,** ( *0-8165* ) 355 S. Euclid Ave., Suite 103, Tucson, AZ 85719 (SAN 205-468X) Tel 520-621-1441; Fax: 520-621-8899 E-mail: orders@uapress.arizona.edu Web site: http://www.uapress.arizona.edu.

**Univ. of California Pr.,** ( *0-520* ) Orders Addr.: 1445 Lower Ferry Rd., Ewing, NJ 08618 Tel 609-883-1759 (Customer Service); Fax: 609-883-7413; Toll Free Fax: 800-999-1958 ( U.S. & Canada); Toll Free: 800-777-4726 ( U.S. & Canada); Edit Addr.: 2120 Berkeley Way, Berkeley, CA 94720 Tel 510-642-4247; 510-643-7154 (Journals); Fax: 510-643-7127; 510-642-1144 (Marketing); 510-642-9917 (Journals) E-mail: orders@cpfs.pupress.princeton.edu; journals@ucop.edu; askucp@ucpress.edu Web site: http://www.ucpress.edu.

**Univ. of Chicago Pr.,** ( *0-226; 0-89065; 0-943056; 1-892850* ) Orders Addr.: 11030 S. Langley Ave., Chicago, IL 60628 (SAN 202-5280) Tel 773-568-1550 ; Fax: 773-660-2235; Toll Free Fax: 800-621-8476 (US & Canada); Toll Free: 800-621-2736 (US & Canada); Edit Addr.: 1427 E. 60th St., Chicago, IL 60637 (SAN 202-5299) Tel 773-702-7700; Fax: 773-702-9756 E-mail: general@press.uchicago.edu; kh@press.uchicago.edu Web site: http://www.press.uchicago.edu.

**Univ. of Hawaii Pr.,** ( *0-8248; 0-87022* ) Orders Addr.: 2840 Kolowalu St., Honolulu, HI 96822-1888 (SAN 202-5353) Tel 808-956-8255; Fax: 808-988-6052 E-mail: uhpmkt@hawaii.edu; uhpbooks@hawaii.edu Web site: http://www.uhpress.hawaii.edu.

**Univ. of Michigan Pr.,** ( *0-472* ) Orders Addr.: P.O. Box 1104, Ann Arbor, MI 48106-1104 (SAN 282-4884) Tel 734-764-4388; Fax: 734-936-0456; Edit Addr.: 839 Greene St., Ann Arbor, MI 48106 E-mail: um.press@umich.edu Web site: http://www.press.umich.edu/.

**Univ. of Nebraska Pr.,** ( *0-8032* ) P.O. Box 880484, Lincoln, NE 68588-0484 (SAN 202-5337); 233 N. Eighth St., Lincoln, NE 68588-0255 Tel 402-472-3581 E-mail: pressmail@unl.edu Web site: http://www.nebraskapress.unl.edu.

**Univ. of New Mexico Pr.,** ( *0-8263* ) 3721 Spirit Dr., SE, Albuquerque, NM 87106-5631 Tel 505-277-4810 (orders); Fax: 505-277-3350; Toll Free Fax: 800-622-8667; Toll Free: 800-249-7737 (orders only); Edit Addr.: 1720 Lomas Blvd., NE, Albuquerque, NM 87131-1591 (SAN 213-9588) Tel 505-277-2346; Fax: 505-277-9270 E-mail: unmpress@unm.edu Web site: http://www.unmpress.com.

**Univ. of Oklahoma Pr.,** ( *0-8061* ) Orders Addr.: 4100 28th Ave., NW, Norman, OK 73069-8218 (SAN 203-3194) Tel 405-325-2000; Fax: 405-364-5798; Toll Free: 800-627-7377; Edit Addr.: 1005 Asp Ave., Norman, OK 73019-6051 Fax: 405-325-4000 Web site: http://www.oupress.com.

**Univ. of Texas Pr.,** ( *0-292* ) Orders Addr.: P.O. Box 7819, Austin, TX 78713-7819 (SAN 212-9876) Tel 512-471-7233; Fax: 512-320-0668; Toll Free: 800-252-3206; Edit Addr.: University of Texas at Austin, Austin, TX 78713-7819 E-mail: utpress@utpress.ppb.utexas.edu Web site: http://www.utexas.edu/utpress.

**Univ. of Washington Pr.,** ( *0-295; 1-902716* ) Orders Addr.: P.O. Box 50096, Seattle, WA 98145-5096 (SAN 212-2502); Edit Addr.: 1326 Fifth Ave., Suite 555, Seattle, WA 98101 Tel 206-543-8870; Fax: 206-685-3460; Toll Free Fax: 800-669-7993; Toll Free: 800-441-4115; 1126 N. 98th St., Seattle, WA 98103 E-mail: uwpord@u.washington.edu Web site: http://www.washington.edu/uwpress.

**Univ. of Wisconsin Pr.,** ( *0-299* ) Orders Addr.: c/o Chicago Dist Ctr., 11030 S. Langley Ave., Chicago, IL 60628 Tel 773-568-1550; Fax: 773-660-2235; Toll Free Fax: 800-621-8476 (orders only); Toll Free: 800-621-2736 (orders only); Edit Addr.: 1930 Monroe St., 3rd Flr., Madison, WI 53711 Tel 608-263-1110; Fax: 608-263-1132 E-mail: uwiscpress@uwpress.wisc.edu Web site: http://www.wisc.edu/wisconsinpress/.

**Univ. Pr. of America,** ( *0-7618; 0-8191; 1-879691* ) Orders Addr.: 15200 NBN Way, P.O. Box 190, Blue Ridge Summit, PA 17214-0190 (SAN 253-2387) Tel 717-794-3800; Fax: 717-794-3803; Toll Free Fax: 800-338-4550; Toll Free: 800-462-6420; Edit Addr.: 4501 Forbes Blvd., Suite 200, Lanham, MD 20706 (SAN 200-2256) Tel 301-459-3366; Fax: 301-429-5747 E-mail: custserv@rowman.com Web site: http://www.univpress.com.

**Univ. Pr. of New England,** ( *0-87451; 0-915032; 1-58465* ) Orders Addr.: 37 Lafayette St., Lebanon, NH 03766-1405 Tel 603-643-7100 (Sales Director); Toll Free: 800-421-1561; Edit Addr.: 23 S. Main St., Hanover, NH 03755-2048 (SAN 203-3283) Tel 603-448-1533; Fax: 603-643-1540 E-mail: University.Press@Dartmouth.edu Web site: http://www.upne.com.

**Univelt, Inc.,** ( *0-87703; 0-912183* ) Orders Addr.: P.O. Box 28130, San Diego, CA 92198-0130 (SAN 170-3099) Tel 760-746-4005; Fax: 760-746-3139; Edit Addr.: 740 Metcalf St., Suite 13, Escondido, CA 92025-1671 (SAN 658-2095) E-mail: 76121.1532@compuserve.com Web site: http://univelt.staigerland.com.

**Universal Subscription Service,** P.O. Box 35445, Houston, TX 77035 (SAN 287-4768).

**Universe Publishing,** ( *0-7893; 0-87663; 1-55550* ) Div. of Rizzoli International Pubns., Inc., 300 Park Ave. S., 3rd Flr., New York, NY 10010 (SAN 202-537X) Tel 212-387-3400; Fax: 212-387-3444 Do not confuse with similar names in North Hollywood, CA, Englewood, NJ, Mendocino, CA.

**University Bk. Service,** Orders Addr.: P.O. Box 608, Grove City, OH 43123 (SAN 169-6912); Edit Addr.: 2297 Southwest Blvd., Suite A, Grove City, OH 43123 (SAN 282-4841) Toll Free: 800-634-4272.

**University Publishing Assocs., Inc.,** ( *0-8026* ) 4720 Boston Way, Lanham, MD 20706 (SAN 630-1878) Tel 301-459-3366.

**Urban Land Institute,** ( *0-87420* ) 1025 Thomas Jefferson St. NW, Suite 500 W., Washington, DC 20007-5201 (SAN 203-3399) Tel 202-624-7000; Fax: 202-624-7140; Toll Free: 800-321-5011 E-mail: bookstore@uli.org Web site: http://www.ULI.ORG.

**U.S. Games Systems, Inc.,** ( *0-88079; 0-913866; 1-57281* ) 179 Ludlow St., Stamford, CT 06902 (SAN 158-6483) Tel 203-353-8400; Fax: 203-353-8431; Toll Free: 800-544-2637 E-mail: usgames@aol.com Web site: http://www.usgamesinc.com.

**V H P S Holtzbrinck Publishers,** *See* **Holtzbrinck Pubs.**

**Vagabond Bks.,** P.O. Box 492264, Los Angeles, CA 90049-8264 E-mail: vagabondbk@aol.com.

**Val Publishing,** 16 S. Terrace Ave., Mount Vernon, NY 10551 (SAN 107-6876) Tel 914-664-7077.

**Valentine Publishing Group,** Orders Addr.: P.O. Box 902582, Palmdale, CA 93590-2582; Edit Addr.: 18543 Devonshire St., Northridge, CA 91324 Tel 818-831-0649; Fax: 818-831-6659 E-mail: sales@vpg.net.

**Valiant International Multi-Media Corp.,** 55 Ruta Ct., South Hackensack, NJ 07606 (SAN 652-8813) Tel 201-229-9800; Fax: 201-814-0418.

**Valley Distributors, Inc.,** 2947 Felton Rd., Norristown, PA 19401 (SAN 169-7498) Tel 610-279-7650; Fax: 610-279-9093; Toll Free: 800-355-2665 (orders only).

**Valley Media, Inc.,** 1276 Santa Anita Ct., Woodland, CA 95776 Tel 530-661-6600; Fax: 530-661-5472 E-mail: valley@valley-media.com Web site: http://www.valsat.com.

**Valley Record Distributors,** *See* **Valley Media, Inc.**

**Van Dyke News Agency,** 2238 W. Pinedale Ave., Fresno, CA 93711-0453 (SAN 168-9630) Tel 209-291-7768; Fax: 209-291-7770.

**Van Khoa Bks.,** 9200 Bolsa Ave., Suite 123, Westminster, CA 92683 (SAN 110-7534) Tel 714-892-0801 E-mail: vankhoa@vinet.com.

**Verham News Corp.,** 75 Main St., West Lebanon, NH 03784 (SAN 169-4561) Fax: 603-298-8843.

**Vida Life Publishers International,** *See* **Vida Pubs.**

**Vida Pubs.,** ( *0-8297* ) 8325 NW 53rd St., Suite 100, Miami, FL 33166 Tel 305-463-8432; Fax: 305-463-9329; Toll Free: 800-843-2548 E-mail: vidapubsales@harpercollins.com Web site: http://www.editorialvida.com

Full publisher information is available in the Publisher Name Index

**Viking Penguin,** *( 0-14; 0-670 )* Div. of Penguin Group (USA) Inc., Orders Addr.: 405 Murray Hill Pkwy., East Rutherford, NJ 07073 Toll Free: 800-788-6262 (individual consumer sales); 800-631-8571 (reseller customer service); 800-526-0275 (reseller sales); Edit Addr.: 375 Hudson St., New York, NY 10014-3657 (SAN 298-0258) Tel 212-366-2000; Fax: 212-366-2952; Toll Free: 800-331-4624 E-mail: publicity@warnerbooks.com Web site: http://www.penguinputnam.com/.

**Vinabind,** P.O. Box 340, Steelville, MO 65565 (SAN 159-9828).

**Vincennes News Agency,** P.O. Box 1110, Evansville, IN 47706-1110 (SAN 169-2518).

**Virginia Periodical Distributors,** *See* **Aramark Magazine & Bk. Services, Inc.**

**Vision Distributors,** *( 0-9626732 )* Div. of Infinite Creations, Inc., Orders Addr.: P.O. Box 9839, Santa Fe, NM 87504 Tel 505-986-8221.

**Vision Press,** *See* **Vision Distributors**

**Vision Video,** *( 1-56364 )* Orders Addr.: P.O. Box 540, Worcester, PA 19490 Tel 610-584-3500; Fax: 610-584-4610; Toll Free: 800-523-0226; Edit Addr.: 2030 Wentz Church Rd., Worcester, PA 19490 (SAN 298-7392) E-mail: info@gatewayfilms.com; info@visionvideo.com Web site: http://www.gatewayfilms.com.

**Vistabooks,** *( 0-89646 )* 0637 Blue Ridge Rd., Silverthorne, CO 80498-8931 (SAN 211-0849) Tel 970-468-7673 (phone/fax) E-mail: vistabooks@compuserve.com Web site: http://www.vistabooks.com.

**Vitality Distributors,** 940 NW 51st Pl., Fort Lauderdale, FL 33309 (SAN 169-0973) Toll Free: 800-226-8482.

**Vroman's, A. C.,** *( 0-9639197 )* 695 E. Colorado Blvd., Pasadena, CA 91101 (SAN 169-0027) Tel 626-449-5320; Fax: 626-792-7308.

**WA Bk. Service,** 26 Ranick Rd., Hauppauge, NY 11788 (SAN 107-2943) Tel 516-234-2255; Fax: 516-234-2268.

**Wabash Valley News Agency,** 2200 N. Curry Pike, No. 2, Bloomington, IN 47404-1486 (SAN 169-250X).

**Waffle, O. G. Bk. Co. (The Bookhouse),** P.O. Box 586, Marion, IA 52302 (SAN 112-8817) Tel 319-373-1832.

**Waldenbooks Company, Incorporated,** *See* **Waldenbooks, Inc.**

**Waldenbooks, Inc.,** *( 0-681 )* Div. of Borders Group, Inc., a/o Calendar Orders, 455 Industrial Blvd., Ste. C, LaVergne, TN 37086 (SAN 179-3373); Orders Addr.: One Waldenbooks Dr., LaVergne, TN 37096; 11625 Venture, Mira Loma, CA 91752 Tel 909-361-4025; Edit Addr.: 100 Phoenix Dr., Ann Arbor, MI 48108-2202 (SAN 200-8858) Tel 734-477-1100 E-mail: customerservice@waldenbooks.com Web site: http://www.waldenbooks.com; http://www.preferredreader.com.

**Walker Art Ctr.,** *( 0-935640 )* Orders Addr.: 750 Vineland Pl., Minneapolis, MN 55403 (SAN 206-1880) Tel 612-375-7638; Fax: 612-375-7565 E-mail: lisa.middag@walkerart.org; paul.schumacher@walkerart.org.

**Wallace's College Bk. Co.,** P.O. Box 689, Nicholasville, KY 40340-0689 (SAN 169-2844) Tel 606-255-0886; Fax: 606-259-9892; Toll Free Fax: 800-433-9329 (orders only); Toll Free: 800-354-9590 (orders only); 800-354-9500 E-mail: orders@wallaces.com.

**Warner Bks., Inc.,** *( 0-445; 0-446 )* Div. of Time Warner Bk. Group, Orders Addr.: c/o Little Brown & Co., 3 Center Plaza, Boston, MA 02108-2084 Tel 800-286-9471; Toll Free: 800-759-0190; Edit Addr.: 1271 Avenue of the Americas, New York, NY 10020 (SAN 281-8892) Tel 212-522-7200 Web site: http://www.warnerbooks.com.

**Warner Pr. Pubs.,** *( 0-87162; 1-59317 )* Orders Addr.: P.O. Box 2499, Anderson, IN 46018-2499 (SAN 691-4241) Tel 765-642-0256; Fax: 765-642-5652; Toll Free: 800-848-2464; Edit Addr.: 1200 E. Fifth St., Anderson, IN 46012 (SAN 111-8110) Tel 765-644-7721; Fax: 765-622-9511; Toll Free: 800-741-7721 (orders only) Web site: http://www.choa.org.

**Warner Publishing Services,** Orders Addr.: 9210 King Palm Dr., Tampa, FL 33619 Tel 813-664-8000; Edit Addr.: 135 W. 50th St., 7th Flr., New York, NY 10020 (SAN 200-5522) Tel 212-522-8900.

**Washington Bk. Distributors,** 4930A Eisenhower Ave., Alexandria, VA 22304 (SAN 631-0095) Tel 703-212-9113; Fax: 703-212-9114; Toll Free: 800-699-9113 E-mail: zacwbd@prodigy.net Web site: http://www.washingtonbk.com.

**Washington Toy Co.,** 2163 28th Ave., San Francisco, CA 94116-1732 (SAN 107-1718).

**Watson, W. R. & Staff,** 150 Mariner Green Ct., Corte Madera, CA 94925 (SAN 286-0155) Tel 510-524-6156; Fax: 510-526-5023.

**Waverly News Co.,** 17 State St., Newburyport, MA 01950 (SAN 169-3522).

**Waymont Bk. Co.,** 136 Steuben St., Jersey City, NJ 07302 (SAN 630-768X) Tel 201-434-4268; Fax: 201-432-1293 E-mail: waymont@worldnet.att.net.

**Wayne State Univ. Pr.,** *( 0-8143 )* Leonard N. Simons Bldg., 4809 Woodward Ave., Detroit, MI 48201-1309 (SAN 202-5221) Tel 313-577-6120; Fax: 313-577-6131; Toll Free: 800-978-7323 (customer orders) E-mail: j.stephenson@wayne.edu Web site: http://wsupress.wayne.edu.

**Weatherhill, Inc.,** *( 0-8348 )* 41 Monroe Tpke., Trumbull, CT 06611-1315 (SAN 209-9529) Tel 203-459-5090; Fax: 203-459-5095; Toll Free: 800-437-7840 E-mail: weatherhill@weatherhill.com Web site: http://www.weatherhill.com.

**Weatherhill, John Incorporated,** *See* **Weatherhill, Inc.**

**Weiner News Co.,** 1011 N. Frio, P.O. Box 7608, San Antonio, TX 78207 (SAN 169-8427) Tel 210-226-9333; Fax: 210-226-8679.

**Weiser, Samuel Incorporated,** *See* **Red Wheel/Weiser**

**Weiser Wholesale,** 2750-C Peace Portal Dr., Blaine, WA 98230 Tel 604-513-1622.

**WellSpring Bks.,** P.O. Box 2765, Woburn, MA 01888-1465 (SAN 111-3399) Do not confuse with companies with the same or similar names in Albuquerque, NM, Ukiah, CA, Adelphia, NJ, Woburn, MA, Groton, VT.

**Wenatchee News Agency,** 434 Rock Island Rd., East Wenatchee, WA 98802-5360 (SAN 169-8885) Tel 509-662-3511.

**West Pr.,** *( 0-9740164 )* 1663 W. Grant Rd., Tucson, AZ 85745 (SAN 631-6794) Toll Free: 888-637-0337 E-mail: joel@westpress.com Web site: http://www.westpress.com.

**West Texas News Co.,** Orders Addr.: 1214 Barranca, El Paso, TX 79935; Edit Addr.: P.O. Box 26488, El Paso, TX 79926 (SAN 169-8184) Tel 915-594-7586; Fax: 915-594-7589.

**Western Book Distributors/Booksource,** *See* **Western Booksource, Inc.**

**Western Booksource, Inc.,** 4935 Metart Shwayn, Tillamook, OR 97141 (SAN 158-4332) Toll Free: 800-825-0100; 230 Fifth Ave., No. 1104, New York, NY 10001 Tel 212-889-9339; Fax: 212-889-9572.

**Western Library Bks.,** 560 S. San Vicente Blvd., Los Angeles, CA 90048 (SAN 168-9878) Tel 213-653-8880.

**Western Merchandisers,** 2900 Airport Rd., Denton, TX 76207-2102 (SAN 156-4633).

**Western Michigan News,** *See* **Readmor**

**Western Record Sales,** 2991 Saint Andrews Rd., Fairfield, CA 94533-7839 (SAN 630-6667).

**Western Reserve Historical Society,** *( 0-911704 )* 10825 East Blvd., Cleveland, OH 44106 (SAN 110-8387) Tel 216-721-5722; Fax: 216-721-0645.

**Weston, Edward Fine Arts,** P.O. Box 3098, Chatsworth, CA 91313-3098 (SAN 168-9967) Tel 818-885-1044; Fax: 818-885-1021.

**Weston Woods Studios, Inc.,** *( 0-7882; 0-89719; 1-55592; 1-56008 )* Div. of Scholastic, Inc., 12 Oakwood Ave., Norwalk, CT 06850 (SAN 630-3838) Tel 203-226-3355; Fax: 203-845-0498; Toll Free: 800-290-7531; 800-243-5020 (customer service) E-mail: Leighcorra@aol.com Web site: http://www.scholastic.com.

**Westwater Bks.,** *( 0-916370 )* Div. of Belknap Photographic Services, Inc., P.O. Box 2560, Evergreen, CO 80437 (SAN 208-3698) Tel 303-674-5410; Fax: 303-670-0586; Toll Free: 800-628-1326.

**Whatever Publishing, Incorporated,** *See* **New World Library**

**Whitaker Distributors,** *See* **Anchor Distributors**

**Whitehurst & Clark,** 100 Newfield Ave., Edison, NJ 08837 (SAN 630-8716) Tel 732-225-2727; 732-417-9575; Fax: 732-225-1562; 732-417-1562; Toll Free: 800-488-8040.

**Whiting News Co.,** 1417 119th St., Whiting, IN 46394 (SAN 169-2542).

**Whitlock & Co.,** 10001 Roosevelt Rd., Westchester, IL 60153 (SAN 285-9645).

**Whitman Distribution Co.,** Orders Addr.: P.O. Box 513, Lebanon, NH 03766 (SAN 631-0540) Fax: 603-448-2576; Toll Free: 800-353-3730; Edit Addr.: 10 Water St., Lebanon, NH 03766 E-mail: distribution@whitmancommunications.com.

**Whitman Publishing & Distribution Company,** *See* **Whitman Distribution Co.**

**Wholesale Distributors,** P.O. Box 126, Burlington, IA 52601 (SAN 145-8051) Tel 319-753-1683; Fax: 319-753-5988; Toll Free: 800-272-1556.

**Wickel, W. W. Co., Inc.,** 520 N. Exchange Ct., Aurora, IL 60504 (SAN 135-1230) Tel 630-820-0044; Fax: 630-820-0057; Toll Free: 800-728-0708.

**Wieser Educational, Inc.,** 30085 Comercio, Santa Margarita, CA 92688 (SAN 630-7361) Tel 714-858-4920; Fax: 714-858-0209; Toll Free: 800-880-4433 E-mail: info@wieser-ed.com Web site: http://www.wieser-ed.com.

**Wilcor International Bk. Dept.,** 700 Broad St., Utica, NY 13501-1336 (SAN 107-7023) Tel 315-733-3542.

**Wilcox & Follet Company,** *See* **Follett Educational Services**

**Wilderness Adventure Bks.,** *( 0-923568; 0-9611596 )* P.O. Box 856, Manchester, MI 48158 (SAN 110-8883) Tel 734-433-1595; Fax: 734-433-0946; Toll Free: 800-852-8652 E-mail: sales@wildernessbooks.org; ddmpub@aol.com Web site: http://www.wildernessbooks.org.

**William Thomson,** *See* **Thomson, Linda**

**Williamson, Darcy,** *See* **Southern Cross Pubns.**

**Wilshire Bk. Co.,** *( 0-87980 )* 12015 Sherman Rd., North Hollywood, CA 91605-3781 (SAN 168-9932) Tel 818-765-8579; Fax: 818-765-2922 E-mail: mpowers@mpowers.com Web site: http://www.mpowers.com.

**Wilson & Assocs.,** *( 0-9710427 )* P.O. Box 2569, Alvin, TX 77512 Tel 281-388-0196; Fax: 413-683-8503 Do not confuse with Wilson & Associates, Gig Harbor, WA E-mail: john@wilsonpublishing.com; pwilson@wilsonpublishing.com Web site: http://www.orsapress.com; http://www.thebookdistributor.com; http://www.wilsonpublishing.com

**Wilson & Sons,** P.O. Box 996, Bellevue, WA 98009 (SAN 129-0010) Tel 425-392-1965 E-mail: dchief@seanst.com.

**Windham County News Co.,** P.O. Box 8127, Brattleboro, VT 05304 (SAN 159-9917) Tel 802-254-2373.

**Wine Appreciation Guild, Ltd.,** *( 0-932664; 1-891267 )* 360 Swift Ave., Unit 30, South San Francisco, CA 94080-6220 (SAN 169-0264) Tel 650-866-3020; Fax: 650-866-3513; Toll Free: 800-242-9462 (orders only) E-mail: wineappreciation.com Web site: http://www.wineappreciation.com.

**Winebaum News, Inc.,** P.O. Box 1620, Raymond, NH 03077-3620 (SAN 169-4529).

**Wittenborn Art Bks.,** *( 0-8150; 0-89648 )* Orders Addr.: P.O. Box 2210, San Francisco, CA 94126 Toll Free: 800-660-6403; Edit Addr.: 1109 Geary Blvd., San Francisco, CA 94109 Tel 415-292-6500; Fax: 415-292-6594 E-mail: wittenborn@earthlink.net Web site: http://www.art-books.com.

**Wizard Works,** *( 0-9621543; 0-9622... )* Orders Addr.: P.O. Box 1125, Homer, AK 99603-1125 Tel 907-235-8757 (phone/fax); Toll Free: 877-210-2665 E-mail: Wizard@xyz.net Web site: http://www.xyz.net/~wizard.

**Wolper Sales Agency, Inc.,** 6 Centre Sq., Suite 302A, Easton, PA 18042-3606 (SAN 285-9785) Tel 610-559-9550; Fax: 610-559-9898.

**Wolverine Distributing, Inc.,** *( 0-941875 )* P.O. Box 503, Powell, WY 82435 (SAN 666-1211) Tel 307-754-2948; Fax: 307-754-2968; Toll Free: 800-967-1633 E-mail: wolverine@tctwest.net.

**Wolverine Gallery,** *See* **Wolverine Distributing, Inc.**

**Women Ink,** 777 United Nations Plaza, New York, NY 10017 (SAN 630-8309) Tel 212-687-8633; Fax: 212-661-2704 E-mail: wink@womenink.org Web site: http://www.womenink.org.

**Woodbine Publishing Co., The,** 15621 Chemical Ln., No. B, Huntington Beach, CA 92649 (SAN 114-4243) Tel 714-894-9080; Fax: 714-894-4949; Toll Free: 800-451-4788 Web site: http://www.safaripress.com.

**Woodcrafters Lumber Sales, Inc.,** 212 NE Sixth Ave., Portland, OR 97232 (SAN 112-6075) Tel 503-231-0226; Toll Free: 800-777-3709.

**Word for Today, The,** ( *0-936728; 1-931713* ) Orders Addr.: P.O. Box 8000, Costa Mesa, CA 92628 (SAN 110-8379) Toll Free: 800-272-9673; Edit Addr.: 3232 W. MacArthur Blvd., Santa Ana, CA 92704 (SAN 214-2260) Tel 714-825-9673 Toll Free: 800-272-9637 E-mail: info@twft.com Web site: http://www.twft.com.

**Word of Life Distributors,** 2717 W. Olympic Blvd., Suite 103, Los Angeles, CA 90006 (SAN 108-433X) Tel 213-382-4538; Fax: 213-382-1154; Toll Free: 800-347-7057.

**Words Distributing Co.,** ( *0-914728* ) Div. of Bookpeople, 7900 Edgewater Dr., Oakland, CA 94621 (SAN 154-7763) Tel 510-632-4700; Fax: 510-632-1281; Toll Free: 800-999-4650; 800-593-9673 (orders).

**Workman Publishing Co., Inc.,** ( *0-7611; 0-89480; 0-911104; 1-56305* ) 708 Broadway, New York, NY 10003 (SAN 203-2821) Tel 212-254-5900; Fax: 212-254-8098; Toll Free: 800-722-7202 E-mail: mged@workman.com Web site: http://www.workmanweb.com; http://www.workman.com.

**World Pubns., Inc.,** ( *0-7669; 0-9640034; 1-57215; 0-7429; 1-4132* ) Orders Addr.: P.O. Box 622, North Dighton, MA 02764; Edit Addr.: 455 Somerset Ave., Bldg. 2A, North Dighton, MA 02764 (SAN 631-7014) Tel 508-880-5555; Fax: 508-880-0469 Do not confuse with World Publications, Inc., Winter Park, FL E-mail: sales@wrldpub.com Web site: http://www.wrldpub.com/.

**World Univ.,** ( *0-941902* ) P.O. Box 2470, Benson, AZ 85602 (SAN 239-7943) Tel 520-586-2985; Fax: 520-586-4764 E-mail: desertsanctuary@theriver.com Web site: http://worlduniversity.org.

**World Wide Distributors, Limited,** *See* **Island Heritage Publishing**

**World Wide Hunting Books,** *See* **Woodbine Publishing Co., The**

**World Wide Pubns.,** ( *0-89066* ) 1303 Hennepin Ave., Minneapolis, MN 55403-1780 (SAN 159-9941) Tel 612-338-0500; Fax: 612-338-3029; Toll Free: 800-788-0442.

**World Wisdom Books, Incorporated,** *See* **World Wisdom, Inc.**

**World Wisdom, Inc.,** ( *0-941532* ) P.O. Box 2682, Bloomington, IN 47402-2682 (SAN 239-1406) Tel 812-333-4088 (ext. 32); Fax: 812-333-1642 E-mail: mknason@worldwisdom.com Web site: http://www.worldwisdom.com.

**Worldwide Media Service, Inc.,** Affil. of Hudson County News Agency, 30 Montgomery St., Jersey City, NJ 07302-3821 (SAN 630-4826) Tel 201-332-7100; Fax: 201-332-0265; Toll Free: 800-345-6478 Web site: http://www.americanmagazine.com.

**Wright Bk./Educational,** 2195 Owendale Dr., Dayton, OH 45439 (SAN 159-9968).

**Writers & Bks.,** ( *0-9618487* ) 339 East Ave. Ste. 301, Rochester, NY 14604-2615 (SAN 156-9678).

**Wybel Marketing Group,** Orders Addr.: 213 W. Main St., Barrington, IL 60010 Tel 847-382-0384.

**Wyoming Periodical Distributor,** P.O. Box 2340, Casper, WY 82601 (SAN 169-9245).

**X-S Bks., Inc.,** 81 Brookside Ave., Amsterdam, NY 12010-0740 (SAN 169-4634).

**Yankee Bk. Peddler, Inc.,** 999 Maple St., Contoocook, NH 03229 (SAN 169-4510) Tel 603-746-3102; Fax: 603-746-5628; Toll Free: 800-258-3774 E-mail: ybp@office.ybp.com Web site: http://www.ybp.com.

**Yankee Paperback & Textbook Co.,** P.O. Box 18880, Tucson, AZ 85731 (SAN 112-1073) Tel 520-325-7229 (phone/fax); Toll Free: 800-340-2665 (in Arizona, California, Nevada, Colorado, New Mexico and Utah only).

**Yankee Paperback Distributors,** *See* **Yankee Paperback & Textbook Co.**

**Yankee Peddler Bookshop,** ( *0-918426* ) 2006 Ridge Rd., Ontario, NY 14519 (SAN 209-925X) Tel 315-524-4352; Fax: 315-524-3365 E-mail: byankeep@rochester.rr.com Web site: www.shoprochester.com//yankeepeddler-abc.

**Ye Olde Genealogie Shoppe,** ( *0-932924; 1-878311* ) Orders Addr.: P.O. Box 39128, Indianapolis, IN 46239 (SAN 200-7010) Tel 317-862-3330; Toll Free: 800-419-0200 (orders) E-mail: yogs@iquest.net Web site: www.yogs.com.

**Yellow Moon Pr.,** ( *0-938756* ) P.O. Box 381316, Cambridge, MA 02238 (SAN 216-4809) Tel 617-776-2230; Fax: 617-776-8246; Toll Free: 800-497-4385 (orders) E-mail: story@yellowmoon.com Web site: http://www.yellowmoon.com.

**Young News, Inc.,** 1600 E. Grand Blvd., Detroit, MI 48211-3144 (SAN 169-3999) Fax: 517-753-7774.

**Yuma News, Incorporated,** *See* **Arizona Periodicals, Inc.**

**YWAM Publishing,** ( *0-927545; 0-9615534; 1-57658* ) Div. of Youth with a Mission International, Orders Addr.: P.O. Box 55787, Seattle, WA 98155 (SAN 695-8265) Tel 425-771-1153; Fax: 425-775-2383; Toll Free: 800-922-2143; Edit Addr.: 7825 230th St., SW, Edmonds, WA 98026 (SAN 248-4021) E-mail: customerservice@ywampublishing.com Web site: http://www.ywampublishing.com

**Zabel, C. & W. Co.,** Orders Addr.: P.O. Box 953, East Brunswick, NJ 08816-0953 (SAN 169-4731) Tel 732-254-1000; Fax: 732-254-0121; Edit Addr.: 24 Rebel Run Dr., East Brunswick, NJ 08816 (SAN 241-6441) Tel 201-947-3300.

**Zeitlin Periodicals Co., Inc.,** 7917 Lark Meadow Ave., Las Vegas, NV 89131-4710 (SAN 160-8088).

**Zondervan,** ( *0-310; 0-937336* ) Subs. of HarperCollins US, c/o Zondervan, Order Processing-B36, 5300 Patterson Ave., SE, Grand Rapids, MI 49530 (SAN 203-2694) Tel 616-698-6900; Fax: 616-698-3439; Toll Free Fax: 800-934-6381 (fax orders); Toll Free: 800-727-1309 (orders & customer service) E-mail: zprod@zph.com Web site: http://www.zondervan.com.

**Zondervan Publishing House,** *See* **Zondervan**

**Zubal, John T. Inc.,** ( *0-939738* ) 2969 W. 25th St., Cleveland, OH 44113 (SAN 165-5841) Tel 216-241-7640; Fax: 216-241-6966 Web site: http://www.zuba.com.